D1604504

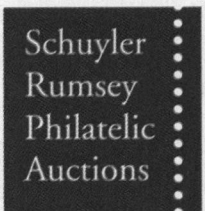

SCOTT®

2018 Classic Specialized Catalogue

TWENTY-FOURTH EDITION

STAMPS AND COVERS OF THE WORLD INCLUDING U.S.

1840–1940

(BRITISH COMMONWEALTH TO 1952)

Published November 2017

AMOS MEDIA

911 Vandemark Road, Sidney, OH 45365-4129

Publishers of *Linn's Stamp News*, *Linn's Stamp News Monthly*, *Coin World* and *Coin World Monthly*.

Table of Contents

See Volumes 1A/1B – 6A/6B of the Scott *Standard Postage Stamp Catalogue* for stamps issued from 1941 to 2017 (British Commonwealth 1953-2017)

Scott Catalogue Mission Statement

The Scott Catalogue Team exists to serve the recreational, educational and commercial hobby needs of stamp collectors and dealers.

We strive to set the industry standard for philatelic information and products by developing and providing goods that help collectors identify, value, organize and present their collections.

Quality customer service is, and will continue to be, our highest priority. We aspire toward achieving total customer satisfaction.

Copyright Notice

Trademark Notice

ISBN 978-89487-530-4

Library of Congress Card No. 2-3301

Acknowledgments

Our appreciation and gratitude go to the following individuals who have assisted us in preparing information included in this year's Scott Catalogues. Some helpers prefer anonymity. These individuals have generously shared their stamp knowledge with others through the medium of the Scott Catalogue.

Those who follow provided information that is in addition to the hundreds of dealer price lists and advertisements and scores of auction catalogues and realizations that were used in producing the catalogue values. It is from those noted here that we have been able to obtain information on items not normally seen in published lists and advertisements. Support from these people goes beyond data leading to catalogue values, for they also are key to editorial changes.

A special acknowledgment to Liane and Sergio Sismondo of The Classic Collector for their assistance and knowledge sharing that has aided in the preparation of this year's Standard and Classic Specialized Catalogues.

Michael E. Aldrich (Michael E. Aldrich, Inc.)
Roland Austin
Robert Ausubel (Great Britain Collectors Club)
John Birkinbine II
Thurston Bland (Bubba Bland Philatelics)
Roger S. Brody
Peter Bylen
Tina & John Carlson (JET Stamps)
Richard A Champagne (Richard A. Champagne, Ltd.)
Henry Chlanda
David & Julia Crawford
Steven D. Crippe (Gradedstamps.com)
Tony L. Crumbley (Carolina Coin & Stamp, Inc.)
Christopher Dahle
Ubaldo Del Toro
Leon Djerahian
Bob & Rita Dumaine (Sam Houston Duck Co.)
Sister Theresa Durand
Mark Eastzer (Markest Stamp Co.)
Paul G. Eckman
George Epstein (Allkor Stamp Co.)
Henry Fisher
Robert A. Fisher
Jeffrey M. Forster
Robert S. Freeman
Richard Friedberg
Michael Fuchs
Bob Genisol (Sultan Stamp Center)
Stan Goldfarb
Allen Grant (Rushstamps (Retail) Ltd.)
Daniel E. Grau
Jan E. Gronwall
Bruce Hecht (Bruce L. Hecht Co.)
Peter Hoffman
Armen Hovsepian (Armenstamp)
Philip J. Hughes
Doug Iams
Chris Jackson (Society for Czechoslovak Philately)
Eric Jackson
John Jamieson (Saskatoon Stamp and Coin)
N. M. Janoowalla
Edward R. Jastrem
Peter Jeannopoulos
Stephen Joe (International Stamp Service)
William A. Jones
Richard Juzwin
Allan Katz (Ventura Stamp Co.)
Stanford M. Katz
Lewis Kaufman (The Philatelic Foundation)
Patricia Kaufmann (Confederate Stamp Alliance)
Jon Kawaguchi (Ryukyu Philatelic Specialist Society)
Roland Kretschmer
William V. Kriebel (Brazil Philatelic Association)
George Krieger
Victor Krievans
Frederick P. Lawrence
Ken Lawrence
John R. Lewis (The William Henry Stamp Co.)
Ulf Lindahl
Ignacio Llach (Filatelia Llach S.L.)
Marilyn R. Mattke
Brian Metz
Gary Morris (Pacific Midwest Co.)
Peter Mosiondz, Jr.
Bruce M. Moyer (Moyer Stamps & Collectibles)
Richard H. Muller
Leonard Nadybal
Dr. Tiong Tak Ngo
Nik & Lisa Oquist
Dr. Everett Parker
Don Peterson (International Philippine Philatelic Society)
Stanley M. Piller (Stanley M. Piller & Associates)
Virgil Pirvulescu
Todor Drumev Popov
Peter W. W. Powell
Bob Prager (Gary Posner, Inc.)
Siddique Mahmudur Rahman
Ghassan D. Riachi
Omar Rodriguez
Mehrdad Sadri (Persiphila)
Theodosios Sampson PhD
Alexander Schauss (Schauss Philatelics)
Jacques C. Schiff, Jr. (Jacques C. Schiff, Jr., Inc.)
Chuck & Joyce Schmidt
Michael Schreiber
Craig Selig
J. Randall Shoemaker (Philatelic Stamp Authentication and Grading, Inc.)
Jeff Siddiqui
Sergio & Liane Sismondo (The Classic Collector)
Jay Smith
Merle Spencer (The Stamp Gallery)
Frank J. Stanley, III
Alfred E. Staubus
Peter Thy
Scott R. Trepel (Siegel Auction Galleries)
Dan Undersander (United Postal Stationery Society)
Herbert R. Volin
Philip T. Wall
Giana Wayman
Gary B. Weiss
Ralph Yorio
Val Zabijaka (Zabijaka Auctions)
Michal Zika
Steven Zirinsky (Zirinsky Stamps)
Alfonso G. Zulueta, Jr.

AMOS MEDIA

SCOTT 911 VANDEMARK ROAD, SIDNEY, OHIO 45365 937-498-0802

More than 17,000 value changes are recorded for the 2018 Scott Classic Specialized Catalogue of Stamps and Covers 1840-1940.

Greetings, Fellow Scott Catalog User:

Welcome to the 2018 Scott *Classic Specialized Catalogue of Stamps and Covers 1840-1940*. Now in its 24th year, the Scott Classic Specialized catalog is widely recognized as the best single-volume catalog for classic-era stamps of the world.

Almost 6,800 value changes were made to the 2018 Scott Classic Specialized catalog. Add to this almost 10,400 value changes brought over from the 12 volumes of the 2018 Scott *Standard Postage Stamp Catalogue*, and the total number of value changes soars to more than 17,000.

Each year special editorial consultant Sergio Sismondo works tirelessly to help the editors expand the editorial content and listed values in the Scott Classic Specialized catalog, and this year was no exception. James E. Kloetzel, editor emeritus, and Bill Jones, a former Scott associate editor, also provided substantial input by updating values and making significant editorial enhancements throughout the catalog.

Special thanks also go to our many advisors who offer improvements each year to make this catalog an invaluable reference work for worldwide classic stamps.

Now we turn to the content of this year's catalog.

The marketplace for Canada and Canadian Provinces overall has been soft during the past year, and the large number of value changes in the 2018 Scott Classic Specialized catalog tend to reflect that weakness. Many exceptions occur among scarce-to-rare stamps that seldom appear in the Scott benchmark grade of very fine. For these scarce stamps in nice quality, demand continues to far exceed supply.

Examples of stamps where demand exceeds supply especially include a number of classic issues in mint never-hinged condition. Early Newfoundland stamps and Canada's Small Queens see higher values for never-hinged stamps.

On the other hand, Newfoundland stamps from the 1897 issue through to about 1931 tend to show slight decreases in value.

In Canada, classic issues are very much holding their own. Values for many 20th-century stamps show the effects of a softening of the market, but not in a major way. Decreases in values are selected and rather modest.

A careful review resulted in more than 100 value changes among the listings for the United States administration of Cuba. Some of the changes are significant.

In 1898 Spain relinquished its claims over Cuba to the United States in the aftermath of the Spanish-American War. In 1898, Puerto Principe, a provincial capital now known as the city of Camaguey, ran low on stamps. Cuban stamps issued in 1896 and 1898 were surcharged for provisional use.

Values for these surcharged stamps, known as the Puerto Principe issues, increase significantly in the 2018 Scott Classic Specialized catalog. On-cover values have been added to these listings for the first time.

The stamps of Hejaz (Saudi Arabia) received a thorough review, with almost 675 value changes. A mix of increases and decreases can be found among the values for this region. The 1922 20-para postage due stamp (Scott LJ8) jumps from $25 unused to $35, and from $27.50 used to $40.

In addition to the more than 130 value changes for Mauritius that were carried over from Vol. 4B of the 2018 Scott Standard catalog, more than 145 value changes were made to listings that appear only in the Scott Classic Specialized catalog.

More than 1,400 value changes were made to Italian States. When combined with the more than 650 value changes made in Vol. 3B of the Scott Standard catalog, approximately 2,050 values were changed for Italian States stamps during the 2018 catalog season. These changes reflect a general softening of the market.

An abundance of editorial enhancements found throughout

Various notes and footnotes have been clarified or expanded throughout the catalog to further explain complicated listings, and other notes have been screened carefully to ensure accuracy.

Canada No. 195d, the 1932 1¢ dark green, is now recognized as being a rotary press, dry printing on gummed paper. Previously, this stamp was thought to be a flat-plate printing and was listed as such, but recent convincing research indicates the listing for this stamp in catalogs has been inaccurate.

Listing clarifications occur throughout for Canada semi-official airmail stamps, and a number of new lettered minors have been added for Scott CL30 and CL49.

Almost 230 minors were added to New Zealand, along with three major numbers. The 1871 2-penny blue is now listed as Scott 38A, and the 2p vermillion has been assigned Scott 38B. Only one of each is known, but they are well-documented. The 1871 2p blue is the newly listed Scott 42A. The new minor listings include perforation varieties; color varieties; and vertical and horizontal pairs, imperforate between.

A new major number, Scott 1A, was added to Fiume. The Hungary 20-filler Harvesters gray-brown stamp overprinted "FIUME" was issued Dec. 2, 1918. The black overprint is in bold sans-serif letters. Fiume Scott 1-23 are overprinted with a serif font. The new listing is valued at $4,000 unused and $2,500 used. Many new minor varieties also are added to Fiume.

Values for never-hinged stamps were added throughout the Iceland listings, many for the first time. Also notable for Iceland are numerous new on-cover and revenue-cancellation listings.

Values for postally used Wurttemberg Official stamps are added for the first time.

Likewise, a few on-cover values are added for the first time to Mexico. New on-cover values also appear among the listings for Mauritius.

Two printings exist for the first stamps of Azerbaijan issued in 1919. The printing on thin white paper is listed as Scott 1-10. In the 2018 Scott Classic Specialized catalog, the set on grayish paper is now listed as major numbers 1A-10A.

In addition to the hundreds of value changes made to the Saudi Arabia listings, almost 100 new minors are added to the listings of Hejaz.

Scott printing and imaging coordinator Stacey Mahan and scanning specialist Lori Billing work tirelessly each year to improve the images in the Scott catalogs, and this edition of the Scott Classic Specialized catalog bears the fruits of their efforts.

As an example of what has been added this year, see Turkey Scott 565-582. New images have been added for this 1919 stamp set overprinted on stamps of 1911-19. The overprint in Turkish reads: "Accession to the Throne of His Majesty, 3rd July 1334-1918." The overprint also features the tughra (or monogram) of Sultan Mohammed VI. Some of the stamps in the set feature ornaments as part of the overprint, and some are surcharged with new denominations.

The 24th edition Scott Classic Specialized catalog brings to a close the 2018 Scott catalog season, during which we celebrated the 150th anniversary of the Scott catalogs.

As always, we encourage you to pay special attention to the Classic Specialized Additions, Deletions & Number Changes found on page 47A in this volume.

While you settle in with your stamp album and Scott catalog, relax and enjoy the world's greatest hobby.

Donna Houseman

Donna Houseman/Catalogue Editor

Addresses, Telephone Numbers, Web Sites, E-Mail Addresses of General & Specialized Philatelic Societies

Collectors can contact the following groups for information about the philately of the areas within the scope of these societies, or inquire about membership in these groups. Aside from the general societies, we limit this list to groups that specialize in particular fields of philately, particular areas covered by the Scott *Standard Postage Stamp Catalogue*, and topical groups. Many more specialized philatelic societies exist than those listed below. These addresses are updated yearly, and are, to the best of our knowledge, correct and current. Groups should inform the editors of address changes whenever they occur. The editors also want to hear from other such specialized groups not listed.

Unless otherwise noted all website addresses begin with http://

American Philatelic Society
100 Match Factory Place
Bellefonte PA 16823-1367
Ph: (814) 933-3803
www.stamps.org
E-mail: apsinfo@stamps.org

American Stamp Dealers Association, Inc.
P.O. Box 692
Leesport PA 19553
Ph: (800) 369-8207
www.americanstampdealer.com
E-mail: asda@americanstampdealer.com

National Stamp Dealers Association
Richard Kostka, President
3643 Private Road 18
Pinckneyville IL 62274-3426
Ph: (800) 875-6633
www.nsdainc.org
E-mail: nsda@nsdainc.org

International Society of Worldwide Stamp Collectors
Joanne Berkowitz, MD
P.O. Box 19006
Sacramento CA 95819
www.iswsc.org
E-mail: executivedirector@iswsc.org

Royal Philatelic Society
41 Devonshire Place
London, W1G 6JY
UNITED KINGDOM
www.rpsl.org.uk
E-mail: secretary@rpsl.org.uk

Royal Philatelic Society of Canada
P.O. Box 929, Station Q
Toronto, ON, M4T 2P1
CANADA
Ph: (888) 285-4143
www.rpsc.org
E-mail: info@rpsc.org

Young Stamp Collectors of America
Janet Houser
100 Match Factory Place
Bellefonte PA 16823-1367
Ph: (814) 933-3820
www.stamps.org/ysca/intro.htm
E-mail: ysca@stamps.org

Philatelic Research Resources

(The Scott editors encourage any additional research organizations to submit data for inclusion in this listing category)

American Philatelic Research Library
Tara Murray
100 Match Factory Place
Bellefonte PA 16823
Ph: (814) 933-3803
www.stamplibrary.org
E-mail: libraryestamps.org

Institute for Analytical Philately, Inc.
P.O. Box 8035
Holland MI 49422-8035
Ph: (616) 399-9299
www.analyticalphilately.org
E-mail: info@analyticalphilately.org

The Western Philatelic Library
P.O. Box 2219
1500 Partridge Ave.
Sunnyvale CA 94087
Ph: (408) 733-0336
www.fwpf.org

Groups focusing on fields or aspects found in worldwide philately (some might cover U.S. area only)

American Air Mail Society
Stephen Reinhard
P.O. Box 110
Mineola NY 11501
www.americanairmailsociety.org
E-mail: sreinhard1@optonline.net

American First Day Cover Society
Douglas Kelsey
P.O. Box 16277
Tucson AZ 85732-6277
Ph: (520) 321-0880
www.afdcs.org
E-mail: afdcs@afdcs.org

American Revenue Association
Eric Jackson
P.O. Box 728
Leesport PA 19533-0728
Ph: (610) 926-6200
www.revenuer.org
E-mail: eric@revenuer.com

American Topical Association
Vera Felts
P.O. Box 8
Carterville IL 62918-0008
Ph: (618) 985-5100
www.americantopicalassn.org
E-mail: americantopical@msn.com

Christmas Seal & Charity Stamp Society
John Denune
234 E. Broadway
Granville OH 43023
Ph: (740) 587-0276
www.seal-society.org
E-mail: john@christmasseals.net

Errors, Freaks and Oddities Collectors Club
Scott Shaulis
P.O. Box 549
Murrysville PA 15668-0549
Ph: (724) 733-4134
www.efocc.org

First Issues Collectors Club
Kurt Streepy, Secretary
3128 E. Mattatha Drive
Bloomington IN 47401
www.firstissues.org
E-mail: secretary@firstissues.org

International Society of Reply Coupon Collectors
Peter Robin
P.O. Box 353
Bala Cynwyd PA 19004
E-mail: peterrobin@verizon.net

The Joint Stamp Issues Society
Richard Zimmermann
29A Rue Des Eviats
Lalaye F-67220
FRANCE
www.philarz.net
E-mail: richard.zimmermann@club-internet.fr

National Duck Stamp Collectors Society
Anthony J. Monico
P.O. Box 43
Harleysville PA 19438-0043
www.ndscs.org
E-mail: ndscs@ndscs.org

No Value Identified Club
Albert Sauvanet
Le Clos Royal B, Boulevard des Pas Enchantes
St. Sebastien-sur Loire, 44230
FRANCE
E-mail: alain.vailly@irin.univ nantes.fr

The Perfins Club
Ken Masters
111 NW 94th Street Apt. 102
Kansas City MO 64155-2993
Ph: (816) 835-5907
www.perfins.org
E-mail: kmasters@aol.com

Postage Due Mail Study Group
John Rawlins
13, Longacre
Chelmsford, CM1 3BJ
UNITED KINGDOM
E-mail: john.rawlins2@ukonline.co.uk.

Post Mark Collectors Club
Bob Milligan
7014 Woodland Oaks
Magnolia TX 77354
Ph: (281) 259-2735
www.postmarks.org
E-mail: bob.milligan@gmail.net

Postal History Society
George McGowan
P.O. Box 482
East Schodack NY 12063-0482
www.postalhistorysociety.org
E-mail: geolotus2003@nycap.rr.com

Precancel Stamp Society
Charles Adrion
P.O. Box 10295
Rochester NY 14610
Ph: (585) 319-0600
www.precancels.com
E-mail: pss.promotion@rochester.rr.com

United Postal Stationery Society
Stuart Leven
1659 Branham Lane Suite F-307
San Jose CA 95118-2291
www.upss.org
E-mail: poststat@gmail.com

United States Possessions Philatelic Society
Daniel F. Ring
P.O. Box 113
Woodstock IL 60098
www.uspps.net
E-mail: danielfring@hotmail.com

Groups focusing on U.S. area philately as covered in the Standard Catalogue

Canal Zone Study Group
Tom Brougham
737 Neilson St.
Berkeley CA 94707
www.CanalZoneStudyGroup.com
E-mail: czsgsecretary@gmail.com

Carriers and Locals Society
Martin Richardson
P.O. Box 74
Grosse Ile MI 48138
www.pennypost.org
E-mail: martinr362@aol.com

Confederate Stamp Alliance
Patricia A. Kaufmann
10194 N. Old State Road
Lincoln DE 19960
Ph. (302) 422-2656
www.csalliance.org
E-mail: trishkauf@comcast.net

Hawaiian Philatelic Society
Kay H. Hoke
P.O. Box 10115
Honolulu HI 96816-0115
Ph: (808) 521-5721

Plate Number Coil Collectors Club
Gene Trinks
16415 W. Desert Wren Court
Surprise AZ 85374
Ph: (623) 322-4619
www.pnc3.org
E-mail: gctrinks@cox.net

Ryukyu Philatelic Specialist Society
Laura Edmonds, Secy.
P.O. Box 240177
Charlotte NC 28224-0177
Ph: (336) 509-3739
www.ryukyustamps.org
E-mail: secretary@ryukyustamps.org

United Nations Philatelists
Blanton Clement, Jr.
P.O. Box 146
Morrisville PA 19067-0146
www.unpi.com
E-mail: bclemjr@yahoo.com

United States Stamp Society
Executive Secretary
P.O. Box 6634
Katy TX 77491-6634
www.usstamps.org

U.S. Cancellation Club
Joe Crosby
E-mail: joecrosby@cox.nat

U.S. Philatelic Classics Society
Rob Lund
2913 Fulton St.
Everett WA 98201-3733
www.uspcs.org
E-mail: membershipchairman@uspcs.org

Groups focusing on philately of foreign countries or regions

Aden & Somaliland Study Group
Gary Brown
P.O. Box 106
Briar Hill, Victoria, 3088
AUSTRALIA
E-mail: garyjohn951@optushome.com.au

American Society of Polar Philatelists (Antarctic areas)
Alan Warren
P.O. Box 39
Exton PA 19341-0039
www.polarphilatelists.org

Andorran Philatelic Study Circle
D. Hope
17 Hawthorn Drive
Stalybridge, Cheshire, SK15 1UE
UNITED KINGDOM
E-mail: andorranpsc@btinternet.com

Australian States Study Circle of The Royal Sydney Philatelic Club
Ben Palmer
GPO 1751
Sydney, N.S.W., 2001
AUSTRALIA
www.philas.org.au/states

Austria Philatelic Society
Ralph Schneider
P.O. Box 23049
Belleville IL 62223
Ph: (618) 277-6152
www.austriaphilatelicsociety.com
E-mail: rschneiderstamps@att.net

American Belgian Philatelic Society
Edward de Bary
11 Wakefield Drive Apt. 2105
Asheville NC 28803
E-mail: emdeb@charter.net

Bechuanalands and Botswana Society
Neville Midwood
69 Porlock Lane
Furzton, Milton Keynes, MK4 1JY
UNITED KINGDOM
www.nevsoft.com
E-mail: bbsoc@nevsoft.com

Bermuda Collectors Society
John Pare
405 Perimeter Road
Mount Horeb WI 53572
www.bermudacollectorssociety.com
E-mail: pare16@mhtc.net

Brazil Philatelic Association
William V. Kriebel
1923 Manning St.
Philadelphia PA 19103-5728
www.brazilphilatelic.org
E-mail: info@brazilphilatelic.org

British Caribbean Philatelic Study Group
Duane Larson
2 Forest Blvd.
Park Forest IL 60466
www.bcpsg.com
E-mail: dlarson283@aol.com

The King George VI Collectors Society (British Commonwealth)
Brian Livingstone
21 York Mansions, Prince of Wales Drive
London, SW11 4DL
UNITED KINGDOM
www.kg6.info
E-mail: livingstone484@btinternet.com

British North America Philatelic Society (Canada & Provinces)
Andy Ellwood
10 Doris Avenue
Gloucester, ON, KIT 3W8
CANADA
www.bnaps.org
E-mail: secretary@bnaps.org

British West Indies Study Circle
John Seidl
4324 Granby Way
Marietta GA 30062
Ph: (770) 642-6424
www.bwisc.org
E-mail: john.seidl@gmail.com

Burma Philatelic Study Circle
Michael Whittaker
1, Ecton Leys, Hillside
Rugby, Warwickshire, CV22 5SL
UNITED KINGDOM
www.burmastamps.homecall.co.uk
E-mail: manningham8@mypostoffice.co.uk

Cape and Natal Study Circle
Dr. Guy Dillaway
P.O. Box 181
Weston MA 02493
www.nzsc.demon.co.uk

Ceylon Study Circle
R. W. P. Frost
42 Lonsdale Road, Cannington
Bridgewater, Somerset, TA5 2JS
UNITED KINGDOM
www.ceylonsc.org
E-mail: rodney.frost@tiscali.co.uk

Channel Islands Specialists Society
Richard Flemming
64, Falconers Green, Burbage
Hinckley, Leicestershire, LE10 2SX
UNITED KINGDOM
www.ciss1950.org.uk
E-mail: secretary@ciss1950.org.uk

China Stamp Society
H. James Maxwell
1050 West Blue Ridge Boulevard
Kansas City MO 64145-1216
www.chinastampsociety.org
E-mail: president@chinastampsociety.org

Colombia/Panama Philatelic Study Group (COPAPHIL)
Thomas P. Myers
P.O. Box 522
Gordonsville VA 22942
www.copaphil.org
E-mail: tpmphil@hotmail.com

Association Filatelic de Costa Rica
Giana Wayman
c/o Interlink 102, P.O. Box 52-6770
Miami FL 33152
E-mail: scotland@racsa.co.cr

Society for Costa Rica Collectors
Dr. Hector R. Mena
P.O. Box 14831
Baton Rouge LA 70808
www.socorico.org
E-mail: hrmena@aol.com

International Cuban Philatelic Society
Ernesto Cuesta
P.O. Box 34434
Bethesda MD 20827
www.cubafil.org
E-mail: ecuesta@philat.com

Cuban Philatelic Society of America ®
P.O. Box 141656
Coral Gables FL 33114-1656
www.cubapsa.com
E-mail: cpsa.usa@gmail.com

Cyprus Study Circle
Colin Dear
10 Marne Close, Wem
Shropshire, SY4 5YE
UNITED KINGDOM
www.cyprusstudycircle.org/index.htm
E-mail: colindear@talktalk.net

Society for Czechoslovak Philately
Tom Cossaboom
P.O. Box 4124
Prescott AZ 86302
Ph: (928) 771-9097
www.csphilately.org
E-mail: klfckl@aol.com

Danish West Indies Study Unit of the Scandinavian Collectors Club
Arnold Sorensen
7666 Edgedale Drive
Newburgh IN 47630
Ph: (812) 480-6532
www.scc-online.org
E-mail: valbydwi@hotmail.com

East Africa Study Circle
Michael Vesey-Fitzgerald
Gambles Cottage, 18 Clarence Road
Lyndhurst, SO43 7AL
UNITED KINGDOM
www.easc.org.uk
E-mail: secretary@easc.org.uk

Egypt Study Circle
Mike Murphy
109 Chadwick Road
London, SE15 4PY
UNITED KINGDOM
Trent Ruebush: North American Agent
E-mail: tkruebrush@gmail.com
www.egyptstudycircle.org.uk
E-mail: egyptstudycircle@hotmail.com

Estonian Philatelic Society
Juri Kirsimagi
29 Clifford Ave.
Pelham NY 10803
Ph: (914) 738-3713

Ethiopian Philatelic Society
Ulf Lindahl
21 Westview Place
Riverside CT 06878
Ph: (203) 722-0769
http://ethiopianphilatelicsociety.weebly.com
E-mail: ulindahl@optonline.net

Falkland Islands Philatelic Study Group
Carl J. Faulkner
615 Taconic Trail
Williamstown MA 01267-2745
Ph: (413) 458-4421
www.fipsg.org.uk
E-mail: cfaulkner@taconicwilliamstown.com

Faroe Islands Study Circle
Norman Hudson
40 Queen's Road, Vicar's Cross
Chester, CH3 5HB
UNITED KINGDOM
www.faroeislandssc.org
E-mail: jntropics@hotmail.com

Former French Colonies Specialist Society
COLFRA
BP 628
75367 Paris, Cedex 08
FRANCE
www.colfra.org
E-mail: secretaire@colfra.org

France & Colonies Philatelic Society
Edward Grabowski
111 Prospect St., 4C
Westfield NJ 07090
www.franceandcolps.org
E-mail: edjjg@alum.mit.edu

Gibraltar Study Circle
Susan Dare
22, Byways Park, Strode Road
Clevedon, North Somerset, BS21 6UR
UNITED KINGDOM
E-mail: smldare@yahoo.co.uk

Germany Philatelic Society
P.O. Box 6547
Chesterfield MO 63006
www.germanyphilatelicusa.org

Plebiscite-Memel-Saar Study Group of the German Philatelic Society
Clayton Wallace
100 Lark Court
Alamo CA 94507
E-mail: claytonwallace@comcast.net

Great Britain Collectors Club
Steve McGill
10309 Brookhollow Circle
Highlands Ranch CO 80129
www.gbstamps.com/gbcc
E-mail: steve.mcgill@comcast.net

International Society of Guatemala Collectors
Jaime Marckwordt
449 St. Francis Blvd.
Daly City CA 94015-2136
www.guatemalastamps.com
E-mail:
membership@guatamalastamps.com

Haiti Philatelic Society
Ubaldo Del Toro
5709 Marble Archway
Alexandria VA 22315
www.haitiphilately.org
E-mail: u007ubi@aol.com

Federacion Filatelica de la Republica de Honduras (Honduran Philatelic Federation, FFRH)
Mauricio Mejia
Apartado postal 1465
Tegucigalpa
HONDURAS

Hong Kong Stamp Society
Ming W. Tsang
P.O. Box 206
Glenside PA 19038
www.hkss.org
E-mail: hkstamps@yahoo.com

Society for Hungarian Philately
Robert Morgan
2201 Roscomare Road
Los Angeles CA 90077-2222
Ph: (978) 682-0242
www.hungarianphilately.org
E-mail: alan@hungarianstamps.com

India Study Circle
John Warren
P.O. Box 7326
Washington DC 20044
Ph: (202) 564-6876
www.indiastudycircle.org
E-mail: warren.john@epa.gov

Indian Ocean Study Circle
E. S. Hutton
29 Patermoster Close
Waltham Abby, Essex, EN9 3JU
UNITED KINGDOM
www.indianoceanstudycircle.com
E-mail: secretary@indianoceanstudy-circle.com

Society of Indo-China Philatelists
Ron Bentley
2600 N. 24th St.
Arlington VA 22207
www.sicp-online.org
E-mail: ron.bentley@verizon.net

Iran Philatelic Study Circle
Mehdi Esmaili
P.O. Box 750096
Forest Hills NY 11375
www.iranphilatelic.org
E-mail: m.esmaili@earthlink.net

Eire Philatelic Association (Ireland)
David J. Brennan
P.O. Box 704
Bernardsville NJ 07924
www.eirephilatelicassoc.org
E-mail: brennan704@aol.com

Society of Israel Philatelists
Becky Dean
100 Match Factory Place
Bellefonte PA 16823-1367
Ph: (814) 933-3802 ext. 212
www.israelstamps.com
E-mail: israelstamps@gmail.com

Italy and Colonies Study Circle
Richard Harlow
7 Duncombe House, 8 Manor Road
Teddington, TW11 8BE
UNITED KINGDOM
www.icsc.pwp.blueyonder.co.uk
E-mail: harlowr@gmail.com

International Society for Japanese Philately
William Eisenhauer
P.O. Box 230462
Tigard OR 97281
www.isjp.org
E-mail: secretary@isjp.org

Latin American Philatelic Society
Jules K. Beck
30½ St. #209
St. Louis Park MN 55426-3551

Liberian Philatelic Society
William Thomas Lockard
P.O. Box 106
Wellston OH 45692
Ph: (740) 384-2020
E-mail: tlockard@zoomnet.net

Liechtenstudy USA (Liechtenstein)
Paul Tremaine
410 SW Ninth St.
Dundee OR 97115
Ph: (503) 538-4500
www.liechtenstudy.org
E-mail: editor@liechtenstudy.org

Lithuania Philatelic Society
John Variakojis
8472 Carlisle Court
Burr Ridge IL 60527
Ph: (630) 974-6525
www.lithuanianphilately.com/lps
E-mail: variakojis@sbcglobal.net

Luxembourg Collectors Club
Gary B. Little
7319 Beau Road
Sechelt, BC, VON 3A8
CANADA
lcc.luxcentral.com
E-mail: gary@luxcentral.com

Malaya Study Group
David Tett
16 Broadway, Gustard Wood
Wheathampstead, Herts, AL4 8LN
UNITED KINGDOM
www.m-s-g.org.uk
E-mail: davidtett@aol.com

Malta Study Circle
Rodger Evans
Ravensbourne, Hook Heath Road
Woking, Surrey, GU22 OLB
UNITED KINGDOM
www.maltastudycircle.org.uk
E-mail: carge@hotmail.co.uk

Mexico-Elmhurst Philatelic Society International
Thurston Bland
50 Regato
Rancho Santa Margarita CA 92688-3003
www.mepsi.org

Asociacion Mexicana de Filatelia AMEXFIL
Jose Maria Rico, 129, Col. Del Valle
Mexico City DF, 03100
MEXICO
www.amexfil.mx
E-mail: amexfil@gmail.com

Society for Moroccan and Tunisian Philately S.P.L.M.
206, bld. Pereire
Paris 75017
FRANCE
splm-philatelie.org
E-mail: splm206@aol.com

Nepal & Tibet Philatelic Study Group
Ken Goss
2643 Wagner Place
EL Dorado Hills CA 95762
Ph: (510) 207-5369
www.fuchs-online.com/ntpsc/
E-mail: kfgoss@comcast.net

American Society for Netherlands Philately
Hans Kremer
50 Rockport Court
Danville CA 94526
Ph: (925) 820-5841
www.asnp1975.com
E-mail: hkremer@usa.net

New Zealand Society of Great Britain
Michael Wilkinson
121 London Road
Sevenoaks, Kent, TN13 1BH
UNITED KINGDOM
www.nzsgb.org.uk
E-mail: mwilkin799@aol.com

Nicaragua Study Group
Erick Rodriguez
11817 SW 11th St.
Miami FL 33184-2501
clubs.yahoo.com/clubs/nicaraguastudygroup
E-mail: nsgsec@yahoo.com

Society of Australasian Specialists/Oceania
David McNamee
P.O. Box 37
Alamo CA 94507
www.sasoceania.org
E-mail: treasurer@sasoceania.com

Orange Free State Study Circle
J. R. Stroud
24 Hooper Close
Burnham-on-sea, Somerset, TA8 1JQ
UNITED KINGDOM
orangefreestatephilately.org.uk
E-mail: richardstroudph@gofast.co.uk

Pacific Islands Study Circle
John Ray
24 Woodvale Ave.
London, SE25 4AE
UNITED KINGDOM
www.pisc.org.uk
E-mail: info@pisc.org.uk

Pakistan Philatelic Study Circle
Jeff Siddiqui
P.O. Box 7002
Lynnwood WA 98046
E-mail: jeffsiddiqui@msn.com

ASOFILPA (Panama)
Vladimir Berrio-Lemm
Entrega Domicilio
Panama 0817
PANAMA
E-mail: panahistoria@wordpress.com

Papuan Philatelic Society
Steven Zirinsky
P.O. Box 49, Ansonia Station
New York NY 10023
Ph: (718) 706-0616
www.communigate.co.uk/york/pps
E-mail: szirinsky@cs.com

International Philippine Philatelic Society
Donald J. Peterson
P.O. Box 122
Brunswick MD 21716
Ph: (301) 834-6419
www.theipps.info
E-mail: dpeterson4526@gmail.com

Pitcairn Islands Study Group
Dr. Everett L. Parker
117 Cedar Breeze South
Glenburn ME 04401-1734
Ph: (386) 688-1358
www.pisg.net
E-mail: eparker@hughes.net

Polonus Philatelic Society (Poland)
Daniel Lubelski
P.O. Box 60438
Rossford OH 43460
Ph: (419) 410-9115
www.polonus.org
E-mail: info@polonus.org

International Society for Portuguese Philately
Clyde Homen
1491 Bonnie View Road
Hollister CA 95023-5117
www.portugalstamps.com
E-mail: ispp1962@sbcglobal.net

Rhodesian Study Circle
William R. Wallace
P.O. Box 16381
San Francisco CA 94116
www.rhodesianstudycircle.org.uk
E-mail: bwall8rscr@earthlink.net

Rossica Society of Russian Philately
Alexander Kolchinsky
1506 Country Lake Drive
Champaign IL 6821-6428
www.rossica.org
E-mail: alexander.kolchinsky@rossica.org

St. Helena, Ascension & Tristan Da Cunha Philatelic Society
Dr. Everett L. Parker
117 Cedar Breeze South
Glenburn ME 04401-1734
Ph: (386) 688-1358
www.shatps.org
E-mail: eparker@hughes.net

St. Pierre & Miquelon Philatelic Society
James R. (Jim) Taylor
2335 Paliswood Road SW
Calgary, AB, T2V 3P6
CANADA
www.stamps.org/spm

Associated Collectors of El Salvador
Joseph D. Hahn
1015 Old Boalsburg Road Apt G-5
State College PA 16801-6149
www.elsalvadorphilately.org
E-mail: jdhahn2@gmail.com

Fellowship of Samoa Specialists
Donald Mee
23 Leo St.
Christchurch, 8051
NEW ZEALAND
www.samoaexpress.org
E-mail: donanm@xtra.co.nz

Sarawak Specialists' Society
Stephen Schumann
2417 Cabrillo Drive-
Hayward CA 94545
Ph: (510) 785-4794
www.britborneostamps.org.uk
E-mail: sdsch@earthlink.net

Scandinavian Collectors Club
Steve Lund
P.O. Box 16213
St. Paul MN 55116
www.scc-online.org
E-mail: steve88h@aol.com

Slovakia Stamp Society
Jack Benchik
P.O. Box 555
Notre Dame IN 46556

Philatelic Society for Greater Southern Africa
Alan Hanks
34 Seaton Drive
Aurora, ON, L4G 2K1
CANADA
www.psgsa.thestampweb.com

South Sudan Philatelic Society
William Barclay
1370 Spring Hill Road
South Londonderry VT 05155
E-mail: barclayphilatelics@gmail.com

Spanish Philatelic Society
Robert H. Penn
1108 Walnut Drive
Danielsville PA 18038
Ph: (610) 844-8963
E-mail: roberthpenn43@gmail.com

Sudan Study Group
Paul Grigg
19 Howmead
Berkeley, GLOS, GL13 9AR
England
UNITED KINGDOM
www.sudanstamps.org

American Helvetia Philatelic Society (Switzerland, Liechtenstein)
Richard T. Hall
P.O. Box 15053
Asheville NC 28813-0053
www.swiss-stamps.org
E-mail: secretary2@swiss-stamps.org

Tannu Tuva Collectors Society
Ken R. Simon
P.O. Box 385
Lake Worth FL 33460-0385
Ph: (561) 588-5954
www.tuva.tk
E-mail: yurttuva@yahoo.com

Society for Thai Philately
H. R. Blakeney
P.O. Box 25644
Oklahoma City OK 73125
E-mail: HRBlakeney@aol.com

Transvaal Study Circle
Chris Board
36 Wakefield Gardens
London, SE19 2NR
UNITED KINGDOM
www.transvaalstamps.org.uk
E-mail: c.board@macace.net

Ottoman and Near East Philatelic Society (Turkey and related areas)
Bob Stuchell
193 Valley Stream Lane
Wayne PA 19087
www.oneps.org
E-mail: rstuchell@msn.com

Ukrainian Philatelic & Numismatic Society
Martin B. Tatuch
5117 8th Road N.
Arlington VA 22205-1201
www.upns.org
E-mail: treasurer@upns.org

Vatican Philatelic Society
Sal Quinonez
1 Aldersgate, Apt. 1002
Riverhead NY 11901-1830
Ph: (516) 727-6426
www.vaticanphilately.org

British Virgin Islands Philatelic Society
Giorgio Migliavacca
P.O. Box 7007
St. Thomas VI 00801-0007
www.islandsun.com/category/collectables/
E-mail: issun@candwbvi.net

West Africa Study Circle
Martin Bratzel
1233 Virginia Ave.
Windsor, ON, N8S 2Z1
CANADA
www.wasc.org.uk
E-mail: marty_bratzel@yahoo.ca

Western Australia Study Group
Brian Pope
P.O. Box 423
Claremont, Western Australia, 6910
AUSTRALIA
www.wastudygroup.com
E-mail: black5swan@yahoo.com.au

Yugoslavia Study Group of the Croatian Philatelic Society
Michael Lenard
1514 N. Third Ave.
Wausau WI 54401
Ph: (715) 675-2833
E-mail: mjlenard@aol.com

Topical Groups

Americana Unit
Dennis Dengel
17 Peckham Road
Poughkeepsie NY 12603-2018
www.americanaunit.org
E-mail: ddengel@americanaunit.org

Astronomy Study Unit
John Budd
728 Sugar Camp Way
Brooksville FL 34604
Ph: (352) 345-4799
E-mail: jwgbudd@gmail.com

Bicycle Stamp Club
Steve Andreasen
2000 Alaskan Way, Unit 157
Seattle WA 98121
E-mail: steven.w.andreasen@gmail.com

Biology Unit
Alan Hanks
34 Seaton Drive
Aurora, ON, L4G 2K1
CANADA
Ph: (905) 727-6993

Bird Stamp Society
S. A. H. (Tony) Statham
Ashlyns Lodge, Chesham Road,
Berkhamsted, Hertfordshire HP4 2ST
UNITED KINGDOM
www.bird-stamps.org/bss
E-mail: tony.statham@sky.com

Captain Cook Society
Jerry Yucht
8427 Leale Ave.
Stockton CA 95212
www.captaincooksociety.com
E-mail: US@captaincooksociety.com

The CartoPhilatelic Society
Marybeth Sulkowski
2885 Sanford Ave, SW, #32361
Grandville MI 49418-1342
www.mapsonstamps.org
E-mail: secretary@mapsonstamps.org

Casey Jones Railroad Unit
Roy W. Menninger MD
P.O. Box 5511
Topeka KS 66605
Ph: (785) 231-8366
www.uqp.de/cjr/index.htm
E-mail: roymenn85@gmail.com

Cats on Stamps Study Unit
Robert D. Jarvis
2731 Teton Lane
Fairfield CA 94533
www.catstamps.info
E-mail: bobmarci@aol.com

Chemistry & Physics on Stamps Study Unit
Dr. Roland Hirsch
20458 Water Point Lane
Germantown MD 20874
www.cpossu.org
E-mail: rfhirsch@cpossu.org

Chess on Stamps Study Unit
Ray C. Alexis
608 Emery St.
Longmont CO 80501
E-mail: chessstuff911459@aol.com

Christmas Philatelic Club
Jim Balog
P.O. Box 774
Geneva OH 44041
www.christmasphilatelicclub.org
E-mail: jpb4stamps@windstream.net

Cricket Philatelic Society
A.Melville-Brown, President
11 Weppons, Ravens Road
Shoreham-by-Sea
West Sussex, BN43 5AW
UNITED KINGDOM
www.cricketstamp.net
E-mail: mel.cricket.100@googlemail.com

Dogs on Stamps Study Unit
Morris Raskin
202A Newport Road
Monroe Township NJ 08831
Ph: (609) 655-7411
www.dossu.org
E-mail: mraskin@cellurian.com

Earth's Physical Features Study Group
Fred Klein
515 Magdalena Ave.
Los Altos CA 94024
epfsu.jeffhayward.com

Ebony Society of Philatelic Events and Reflections, Inc. (African-American topicals)
Manuel Gilyard
800 Riverside Drive, Suite 4H
New York NY 10032-7412
www.esperstamps.org
E-mail: gilyardmani@aol.com

Europa Study Unit
Tonny E. Van Loij
3002 S. Xanthia St.
Denver CO 80231-4237
Ph: (303) 752-0189
www.europastudyunit.org
E-mail: tvanloij@gmail.com

Fine & Performing Arts
Deborah L. Washington
6922 S. Jeffery Blvd., #7 - North
Chicago IL 60649
E-mail: brasslady@comcast.net

Fire Service in Philately
John Zaranek
81 Hillpine Road
Cheektowaga NY 14227-2259
Ph: (716) 668-3352
E-mail: jczaranek@roadrunner.com

Gay & Lesbian History on Stamps Club
Joe Petronie
P.O. Box 190842
Dallas TX 75219-0842
www.facebook.com/glhsc
E-mail: glhsc@aol.com

Gems, Minerals & Jewelry Study Unit
Mrs. Gilberte Proteau
138 Lafontaine
Beloeil QC J3G 2G7
CANADA
Ph: (978) 851-8283
E-mail: gilberte.ferland@sympatico.ca

Graphics Philately Association
Mark H. Winnegrad
P.O. Box 380
Bronx NY 10462-0380
www.graphics-stamps.org
E-mail: indybruce1@yahoo.com

Journalists, Authors & Poets on Stamps
Ms. Lee Straayer
P.O. Box 6808
Champaign IL 61826
E-mail: lstraayer@dcbnet.com

Lighthouse Stamp Society
Dalene Thomas
1805 S Balsam St., #106
Lakewood CO 80232
Ph: (303) 986-6620
www.lighthousestampsociety.org
E-mail: dalene@lighthousestampsociety.org

Lions International Stamp Club
John Bargus
108-2777 Barry Road RR 2
Mill Bay, BC, V0R 2P2
CANADA
Ph: (250) 743-5782

Mahatma Gandhi On Stamps Study Circle
Pramod Shivagunde
Pratik Clinic, Akluj
Solapur, Maharashtra, 413101
INDIA
E-mail: drnanda@bom6.vsnl.net.in

Masonic Study Unit
Stanley R. Longenecker
930 Wood St.
Mount Joy PA 17552-1926
Ph: (717) 669-9094
E-mail: natsco@usa.net

Mathematical Study Unit
Monty Strauss
4209 88th St.
Lubbock TX 79423-2941
www.mathstamps.org

Medical Subjects Unit
Dr. Frederick C. Skvara
P.O. Box 6228
Bridgewater NJ 08807
E-mail: fcskvara@optonline.net

Military Postal History Society
Ed Dubin
1 S. Wacker Drive, Suite 3500
Chicago IL 60606
www.militaryPHS.org
E-mail: dubine@comcast.net

Mourning Stamps and Covers Club
James Camak, Jr.
3801 Acapulco Ct.
Irving TX 75062
www.mscc.ms
E-mail: jamescamak7@gmail.com

Napoleonic Age Philatelists
Ken Berry
4117 NW 146th St.
Oklahoma City OK 73134-1746
Ph: (405) 748-8646
www.nap-stamps.org
E-mail: krb4117@att.net

Old World Archeological Study Unit
Caroline Scannell
11 Dawn Drive
Smithtown NY 11787-1761
www.owasu.org
E-mail: editor@owasu.org

Petroleum Philatelic Society International
Feitze Papa
922 Meander Dr.
Walnut Creek CA 94598-4239
E-mail: oildad@astound.net

Rotary on Stamps Unit
Gerald L. Fitzsimmons
105 Calla Ricardo
Victoria TX 77904
rotaryonstamps.org
E-mail: glfitz@suddenlink.net

Scouts on Stamps Society International
Lawrence Clay
P.O. Box 6228
Kennewick WA 99336
Ph: (509) 735-3731
www.sossi.org
E-mail: rfrank@sossi.org

Ships on Stamps Unit
Les Smith
302 Conklin Ave.
Penticton, BC, V2A 2T4
CANADA
Ph: (250) 493-7486
www.shipsonstamps.org
E-mail: lessmith440@shaw.ca

Space Unit
David Blog
P.O. Box 174
Bergenfield NJ 07621
www.space-unit.com
E-mail: davidblognj@gmail.com

Sports Philatelists International
Mark Maestrone
2824 Curie Place
San Diego CA 92122-4110
www.sportstamps.org
Email: president@sportstamps.org

Stamps on Stamps Collectors Club
Alf Jordan
156 W. Elm St.
Yarmouth ME 04096
www.stampsonstamps.org
E-mail: ajordan1@maine.rr.com

Windmill Study Unit
Orville Tysseling
9740 Washington Church Rd.
Miamisburg OH 45342-4510
www.wsu.world

Wine On Stamps Study Unit
David Wolfersberger
768 Chain Ridge Road
St. Louis MO 63122-3259
Ph: (314) 961-5032
www.wine-on-stamps.org
E-mail: dewolf2@swbell.net

Women on Stamps Study Unit
Hugh Gottfried
2232 26th St.
Santa Monica CA 90405-1902
E-mail: hgottfried@adelphia.net

Expertizing Services

The following organizations will, for a fee, provide expert opinions about stamps submitted to them. Collectors should contact these organizations to find out about their fees and requirements before submitting philatelic material to them. The listing of these groups here is not intended as an endorsement by Amos Media Co.

General Expertizing Services

American Philatelic Expertizing Service (a service of the American Philatelic Society)
100 Match Factory Place
Bellefonte PA 16823-1367
Ph: (814) 237-3803
Fax: (814) 237-6128
www.stamps.org
E-mail: ambristo@stamps.org
Areas of Expertise: Worldwide

B. P. A. Expertising, Ltd.
P.O. Box 1141
Guildford, Surrey, GU5 0WR
UNITED KINGDOM
E-mail: sec@bpaexpertising.org
Areas of Expertise: British Commonwealth, Great Britain, Classics of Europe, South America and the Far East

Philatelic Foundation
341 W. 38th St., 5th Floor
New York NY 10018
Ph: (212) 221-6555
Fax: (212) 221-6208
www.philatelicfoundation.org
E-mail: philatelicfoundation@verizon.net
Areas of Expertise: U.S. & Worldwide

Philatelic Stamp Authentication and Grading, Inc.
P.O. Box 41-0880
Melbourne FL 32941-0880
Customer Service: (305) 345-9864
www.psaginc.com
E-mail: info@psaginc.com
Areas of Expertise: U.S., Canal Zone, Hawaii, Philippines, Canada & Provinces

Professional Stamp Experts
P.O. Box 6170
Newport Beach CA 92658
Ph: (877) STAMP-88
Fax: (949) 833-7955
www.collectors.com/pse
E-mail: pseinfo@collectors.com
Areas of Expertise: Stamps and covers of U.S., U.S. Possessions, British Commonwealth

Royal Philatelic Society Expert Committee
41 Devonshire Place
London, W1N 1PE
UNITED KINGDOM
www.rpsl.org.uk/experts.html
E-mail: experts@rpsl.org.uk
Areas of Expertise: Worldwide

Expertizing Services Covering Specific Fields Or Countries

China Stamp Society Expertizing Service
1050 W. Blue Ridge Blvd.
Kansas City MO 64145
Ph: (816) 942-6300
E-mail: hjmesq@aol.com
Areas of Expertise: China

Confederate Stamp Alliance Authentication Service
Gen. Frank Crown, Jr.
P.O. Box 278
Capshaw AL 35742-0396
Ph: (302) 422-2656
Fax: (302) 424-1990
www.csalliance.org
E-mail: csaas@knology.net
Areas of Expertise: Confederate stamps and postal history

Errors, Freaks and Oddities Collectors Club Expertizing Service
138 East Lakemont Drive
Kingsland GA 31548
Ph: (912) 729-1573
Areas of Expertise: U.S. errors, freaks and oddities

Estonian Philatelic Society Expertizing Service
39 Clafford Lane
Melville NY 11747
Ph: (516) 421-2078
E-mail: esto4@aol.com
Areas of Expertise: Estonia

Hawaiian Philatelic Society Expertizing Service
P.O. Box 10115
Honolulu HI 96816-0115
Areas of Expertise: Hawaii

Hong Kong Stamp Society Expertizing Service
P.O. Box 206
Glenside PA 19038
Fax: (215) 576-6850
Areas of Expertise: Hong Kong

International Association of Philatelic Experts United States Associate members:

Paul Buchsbayew
119 W. 57th St.
New York NY 10019
Ph: (212) 977-7734
Fax: (212) 977-8653
Areas of Expertise: Russia, Soviet Union

William T. Crowe
P.O. Box 2090
Danbury CT 06813-2090
E-mail: wtcrowe@aol.com
Areas of Expertise: United States

John Lievsay
(see American Philatelic Expertizing Service and Philatelic Foundation)
Areas of Expertise: France

Robert W. Lyman
P.O. Box 348
Irvington on Hudson NY 10533
Ph and Fax: (914) 591-6937
Areas of Expertise: British North America, New Zealand

Robert Odenweller
P.O. Box 401
Bernardsville NJ 07924-0401
Ph and Fax: (908) 766-5460
Areas of Expertise: New Zealand, Samoa to 1900

Sergio Sismondo
The Regency Tower, Suite 1109
770 James Street
Syracuse NY 13203
Ph: (315) 422-2331
Fax: (315) 422-2956
Areas of Expertise: British East Africa, Camerouns, Cape of Good Hope, Canada, British North America

International Society for Japanese Philately Expertizing Committee
132 North Pine Terrace
Staten Island NY 10312-4052
Ph: (718) 227-5229
Areas of Expertise: Japan and related areas, except WWII Japanese Occupation issues

International Society for Portuguese Philately Expertizing Service
P.O. Box 43146
Philadelphia PA 19129-3146
Ph and Fax: (215) 843-2106
E-mail: s.s.washburne@worldnet.att.net
Areas of Expertise: Portugal and Colonies

Mexico-Elmhurst Philatelic Society International Expert Committee
P.O. Box 1133
West Covina CA 91793
Areas of Expertise: Mexico

Ukrainian Philatelic & Numismatic Society Expertizing Service
30552 Dell Lane
Warren MI 48092-1862
Areas of Expertise: Ukraine, Western Ukraine

V. G. Greene Philatelic Research Foundation
P.O. Box 204, Station Q
Toronto, ON, M4T 2M1
CANADA
Ph: (416) 921-2073
Fax: (416) 921-1282
www.greenefoundation.ca
E-mail: vggfoundation@on.aibn.com
Areas of Expertise: British North America

Information on Catalogue Values, Grade and Condition

Catalogue Value

The Scott Catalogue value is a retail value; that is, an amount you could expect to pay for a stamp in the grade of Very Fine with no faults. Any exceptions to the grade valued will be noted in the text. The general introduction on the following pages and the individual section introductions further explain the type of material that is valued. The value listed for any given stamp is a reference that reflects recent actual dealer selling prices for that item.

Dealer retail price lists, public auction results, published prices in advertising and individual solicitation of retail prices from dealers, collectors and specialty organizations have been used in establishing the values found in this catalogue. Amos Media Co. values stamps, but Amos Media is not a company engaged in the business of buying and selling stamps as a dealer.

Use this catalogue as a guide for buying and selling. The actual price you pay for a stamp may be higher or lower than the catalogue value because of many different factors, including the amount of personal service a dealer offers, or increased or decreased interest in the country or topic represented by a stamp or set. An item may occasionally be offered at a lower price as a "loss leader," or as part of a special sale. You also may obtain an item inexpensively at public auction because of little interest at that time or as part of a large lot.

Stamps that are of a lesser grade than Very Fine, or those with condition problems, generally trade at lower prices than those given in this catalogue. Stamps of exceptional quality in both grade and condition often command higher prices than those listed.

Values for pre-1900 unused issues are for stamps with approximately half or more of their original gum. Stamps with most or all of their original gum may be expected to sell for somewhat more, and stamps with less than half of their original gum may be expected to sell for somewhat less than the values listed. On rarer stamps, it may be expected that the original gum will be somewhat more disturbed than it will be on more common issues. Unused stamps issued from 1900 to the present are assumed to have full original gum. From breakpoints in most countries' listings, stamps are valued as never hinged, due to the wide availability of stamps in that condition. These notations are prominently placed in the listings and in the country information preceding the listings. Some countries also feature listings with dual values for hinged and never-hinged stamps.

Values for early and valuable stamps are for examples with certificates of authenticity from acknowledged expert committees, or examples sold with the buyer having the right of certification. This applies to examples with original gum as well as examples without gum. Beware of stamps offered "as is," as the gum on some unused stamps offered with"original gum" may be fraudulent, and stamps offered as unused without gum may in some cases be altered used stamps.

Grade

A stamp's grade and condition are crucial to its value. The accompanying illustrations show examples of Very Fine stamps from different time periods, along with examples of stamps in Fine to Very Fine and Extremely Fine grades as points of reference. When a stamp seller offers a stamp in any grade from fine to superb without further qualifying statements, that stamp should not only have the centering grade as defined, but it also should be free of faults or other condition problems.

FINE-VERY FINE stamps may be somewhat off center on one side, or slightly off center on two sides. Imperforate stamps will have two full margins, and the design will not touch any edge. For perforated stamps, the perfs are well clear of the design, but are still noticeably off center. *However, early issues of a country may be printed in such a way that the design naturally is very close to the edges. In these cases, the perforations may cut into the design very slightly.* Used stamps will not have a cancellation that detracts from the design.

VERY FINE stamps may be slightly off center on one or two sides, but the design will be well clear of the edge. The stamp will present a nice, balanced appearance. Imperforate stamps will have four full margins. *However, early issues of many countries may be printed in such a way that the perforations may touch the design on one or more sides. Where this is the case, a boxed note will be found defining the centering and margins of the stamps being valued.* Used stamps will have light or otherwise neat cancellations. This is the grade used to establish Scott Catalogue values.

EXTREMELY FINE stamps are close to being perfectly centered. Imperforate stamps will have even margins that are larger than full margins. *Even the earliest perforated issues will have perforations clear of the design on all sides.*

Amos Media Co. recognizes that there is no formally enforced grading scheme for postage stamps, and that the final price you pay or obtain for a stamp will be determined by individual agreement at the time of transaction.

Full Margins

The spacing of the designs of classic stamps on their plates differ widely between countries and often between issues of a single country or sometimes even between stamps within a single issue. Because margin size is a significant determinant of grade and value, the *Scott Classic Specialized Catalogue* often includes the dimensions of "full margins" in millimeters in the listings. "Full margin" (a term coined by Edwin Mueller in his catalogue of imperforate European stamps) is defined as half the space between two stamps on the plate. It is the margin that would result from a stamp being cut from its neighbor exactly in the center of the margin space between the stamps. Since the spacing of many early classics is somewhat irregular, the average spacing is used. The horizontal and vertical margins may not be equal on the plate, and in such instances both measurements are given, vertical margins first followed by horizontal margins. In instances where different printings of a single issue were made from plates differing in spacing, the smallest existing spacing is given. Scott has adopted the Mueller convention of giving 1/4mm as the smallest "full margin" measurement even in those cases where there was almost no space between the designs on a plate.

Condition

Grade addresses only centering and (for used stamps) cancellation. *Condition* refers to factors other than grade that affect a stamp's desirability.

Factors that can increase the value of a stamp include exceptionally wide margins, particularly fresh color, the presence of selvage, and plate or die varieties. Unusual cancels on used stamps (particularly those of the 19th century) can greatly enhance their value as well.

Factors other than faults that decrease the value of a stamp include loss of original gum, regumming, a hinge remnant or foreign object adhering to the gum, natural inclusions, straight edges, and markings or notations applied by collectors or dealers.

Faults include missing pieces, tears, pin or other holes, surface scuffs, thin spots, creases, toning, short or pulled perforations, clipped perforations, oxidation or other forms of color changelings, soiling, stains, and such man-made changes as reperforations or the chemical removal or lightening of a cancellation.

Grading Illustrations

On the following seven pages are illustrations of various stamps from countries appearing in *The Classic Specialized Catalogue*. These stamps are arranged by country, and they represent early or important issues that are often found in widely different grades in the marketplace. The editors believe the illustrations will prove useful in showing the margin size and centering that will be seen on the various issues.

Use this Illustrated Grading Chart in conjunction with the Illustrated Gum Chart that follows it to better understand the grade and gum condition of stamps valued in the Scott Catalogues.

In addition to the matters of margin size, centering and original gum, collectors are reminded that the very fine stamps valued in the Scott catalogues also will possess fresh color and intact perforations, and they will be free from defects.

The three grades shown for each stamp are computer manipulated using single digitized master illustrations.

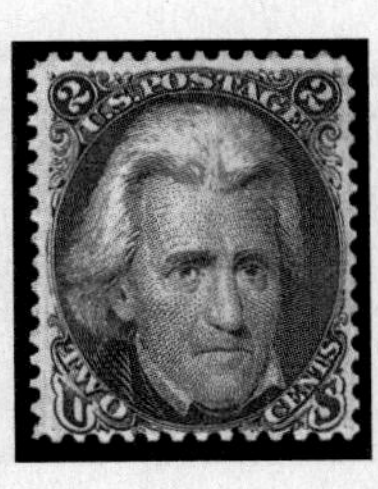

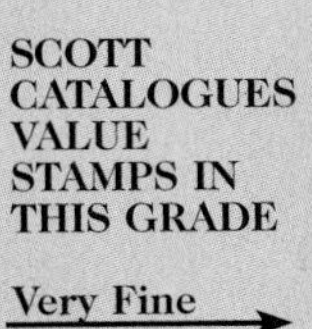

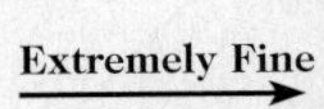

Fine-Very Fine

SCOTT CATALOGUES VALUE STAMPS IN THIS GRADE

Very Fine

Extremely Fine

Fine-Very Fine →

SCOTT CATALOGUES VALUE STAMPS IN THIS GRADE

Very Fine →

Extremely Fine →

Fine-Very Fine →

SCOTT CATALOGUES VALUE STAMPS IN THIS GRADE

Very Fine →

Extremely Fine →

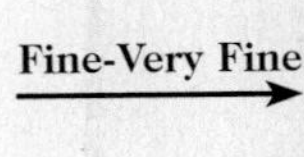

SCOTT CATALOGUES VALUE STAMPS IN THIS GRADE

Very Fine

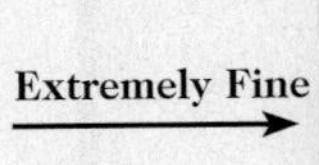

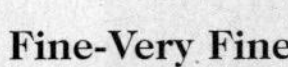

Fine-Very Fine

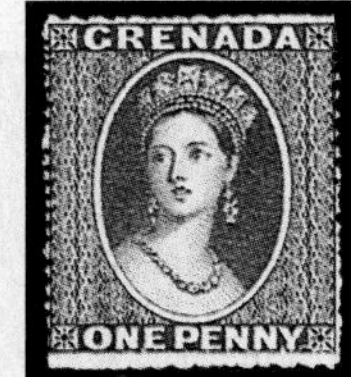

SCOTT CATALOGUES VALUE STAMPS IN THIS GRADE

Very Fine

Extremely Fine

Fine-Very Fine

SCOTT CATALOGUES VALUE STAMPS IN THIS GRADE

Very Fine

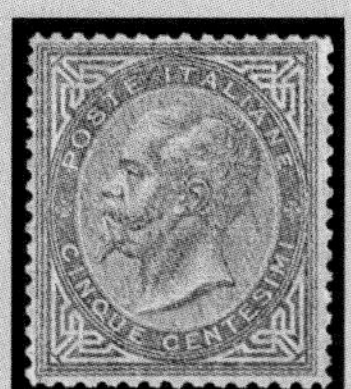

Extremely Fine

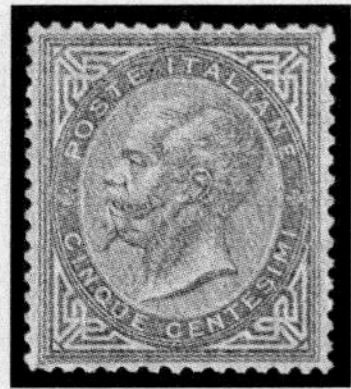

Fine-Very Fine
SCOTT CATALOGUES VALUE STAMPS IN THIS GRADE
Very Fine
Extremely Fine
Fine-Very Fine
SCOTT CATALOGUES VALUE STAMPS IN THIS GRADE
Very Fine
Extremely Fine

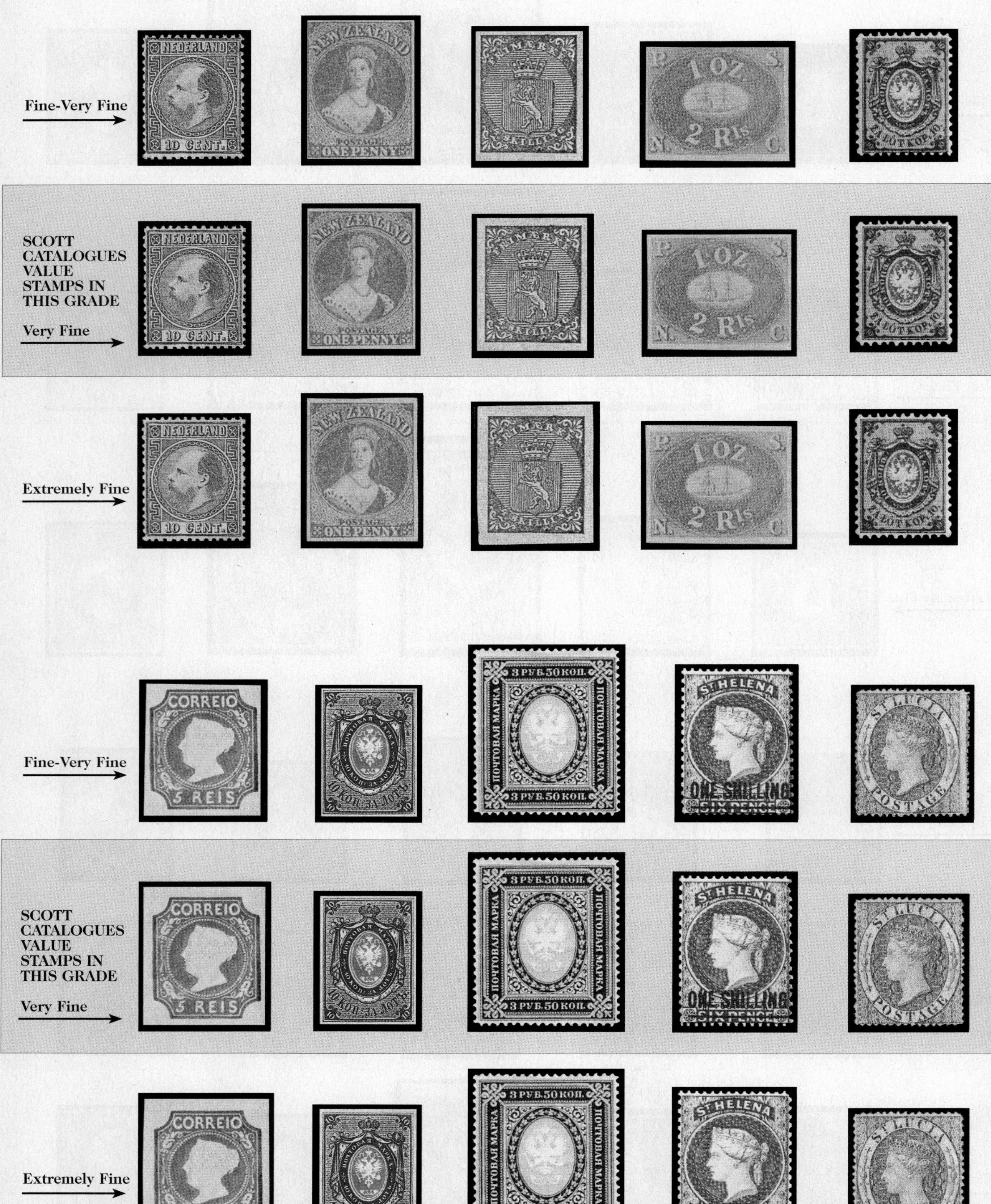
Fine-Very Fine
SCOTT CATALOGUES VALUE STAMPS IN THIS GRADE
Very Fine
Extremely Fine
Fine-Very Fine
SCOTT CATALOGUES VALUE STAMPS IN THIS GRADE
Very Fine
Extremely Fine

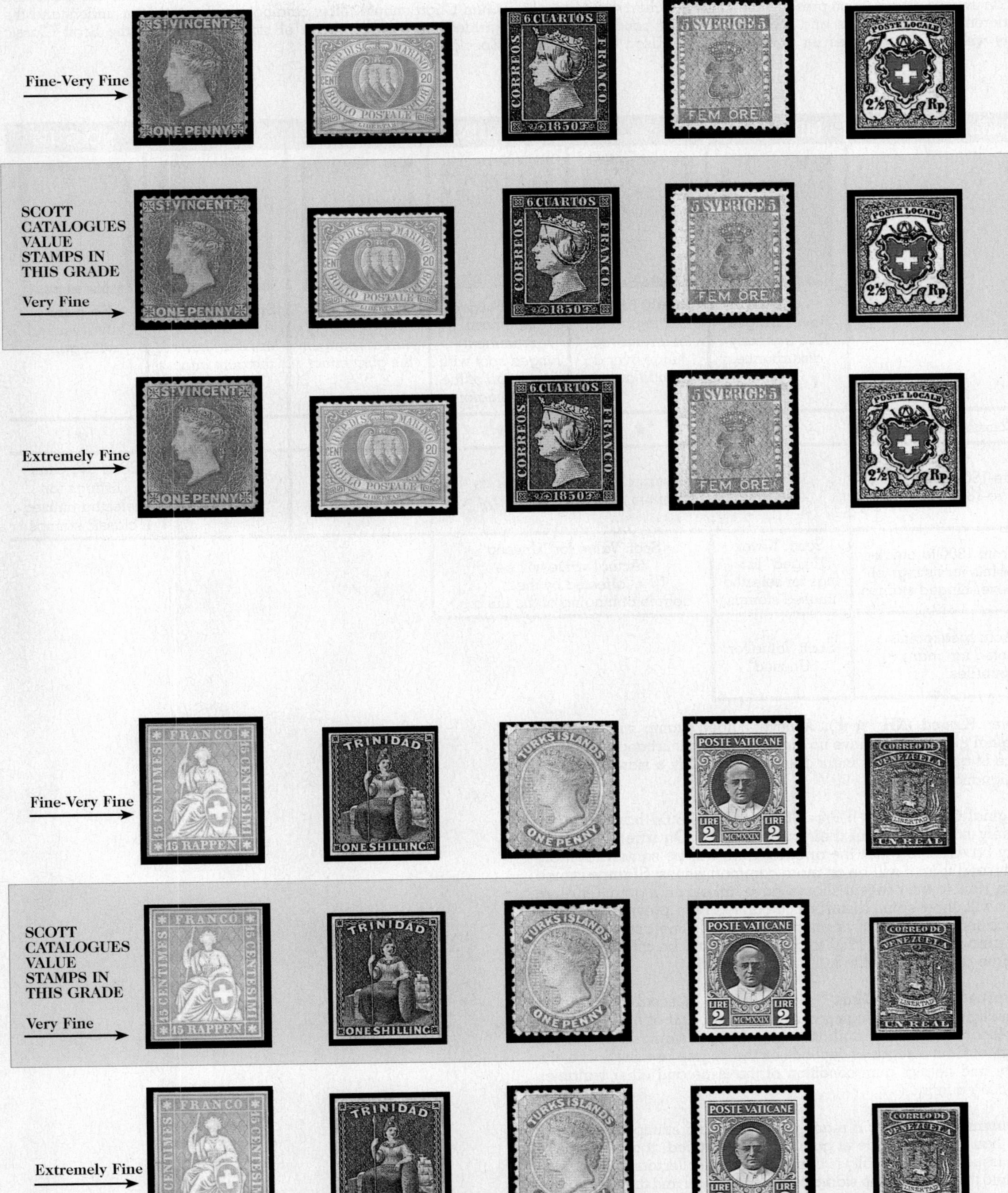
Fine-Very Fine
SCOTT CATALOGUES VALUE STAMPS IN THIS GRADE
Very Fine
Extremely Fine
Fine-Very Fine
SCOTT CATALOGUES VALUE STAMPS IN THIS GRADE
Very Fine
Extremely Fine

For purposes of helping to determine the gum condition and value of an unused stamp, Scott presents the following chart which details different gum conditions and indicates how the conditions correlate with the Scott values for unused stamps. Used together, the Illustrated Grading Chart on the previous pages and this Illustrated Gum Chart should allow catalogue users to better understand the grade and gum condition of stamps valued in the *Scott Classic Specialized Catalogue*.

Gum Categories:	MINT N.H.	ORIGINAL GUM (O.G.)				NO GUM
	 **Mint Never Hinged** *Free from any disturbance*	 **Lightly Hinged** *Faint impression of a removed hinge over a small area*	 **Hinge Mark or Remnant** *Prominent hinged spot with part or all of the hinge remaining*	 **Large part o.g.** *Approximately half or more of the gum intact*	**Small part o.g.** *Approximately less than half of the gum intact*	**No gum** *Only if issued with gum*
Commonly Used Symbol:	★★	★	★	★	★	(★)
Pre-1900 Issues (Pre-1879 for U.S.)	Very fine pre-1900 stamps in these categories trade at a premium over Scott value			Scott Value for "Unused"		Scott "No Gum" listings for selected unused classic stamps
From 1900 to breakpoints for listings of never-hinged stamps	Scott "Never Hinged" listings for selected unused stamps	Scott Value for "Unused" (Actual value will be affected by the degree of hinging of the full o.g.)				
From breakpoints noted for many countries	Scott Value for "Unused"					

Never Hinged (NH; ★★): A never-hinged stamp will have full original gum that will have no hinge mark or disturbance. The presence of an expertizer's mark does not disqualify a stamp from this designation.

Original Gum (OG; ★): Pre-1900 stamps should have approximately half or more of their original gum. On rarer stamps, it may be expected that the original gum will be somewhat more disturbed than it will be on more common issues. Stamps issued from 1900 to the present should have full original gum. Original gum will show some disturbance caused by a previous hinge(s) which may be present or entirely removed. The actual value of a stamp issued from 1900 to the present will be affected by the degree of hinging of the full original gum.

Disturbed Original Gum: Gum showing noticeable effects of humidity, climate or hinging over more than half of the gum. The significance of gum disturbance in valuing a stamp in any of the Original Gum categories depends on the degree of disturbance, the rarity and normal gum condition of the issue and other variables affecting quality.

Regummed (RG; (★)): A regummed stamp is a stamp without gum that has had some type of gum privately applied at a time after it was issued. This normally is done to deceive collectors and/or dealers into thinking that the stamp has original gum and therefore has a higher value. A regummed stamp is considered the same as a stamp with none of its original gum for purposes of grading.

Catalogue Values for Stamps on Covers

Definition of a Cover

Covers are philatelically defined as folded letters, folded covers or envelopes, with or without postage stamps, that have passed through the mail and bear postal or other markings of philatelic interest. Before the introduction of envelopes about 1840, people folded letters and wrote the address on the outside. Many people covered their letters with an extra sheet of paper on the outside for the address, producing the term "cover." Used stamped envelopes and wrappers and other items of postal stationery also are considered covers. Additionally, a newspaper stamp properly used on a newspaper or newspaper wrapper is considered to be an "on cover" usage, as is a postage stamp used on a post card. Occasionally, the term "newsprint" is used; this refers to either a newspaper or a one-page printed leaflet.

Catalogue Value

The Scott Catalogue value for a stamp on cover, as for a stamp off cover, is a retail value; that is, an amount you could expect to pay for that cover in a grade of Very Fine, as defined below. Folded letters, folded covers, envelopes, stationery entires and newspapers are valued as whole and complete, not as fronts of letter sheets or envelopes or as fragments of newspapers or circulars. Values given are for covers bearing stamps that are "tied on" by the cancellation. A stamp is said to be "tied" to a cover when the cancellation or postmark falls on both the stamp and the cover. Exceptions, such as some of the listings for newspaper stamps used on newspapers, always will be noted. Values for bisected, trisected, etc. stamps on cover are for items on which the cancellation ties the stamp across the cut. Values for U.S. patriotic covers of the Civil War period (bearing pictorial designs of a patriotic nature) are for the most common designs.

It should be noted that conventions observed for calculating the catalogue value of a cover with several different stamps vary somewhat between countries and types of covers. In a general way, however, the most common procedure may be summarized as follows: the stamp which has the highest "value on cover" is counted with its on-cover value, while the other stamps are added on to the total with their normal value as used stamps "off cover."

The value generally is given for the stamps as they are most commonly found on a cover. In some cases a stamp is most commonly found alone, paying a specified rate for the envelope, given its weight, destination and method of intended delivery. For instance, a one-half ounce letter sent internally in England by ordinary first class mail during the 19th century needed one penny of postage. Since such letters were very common, it follows that stamps with denominations of one penny are most often found on envelopes or folded letters paying that one-half ounce internal rate. One penny stamps also are found on letters together with other stamps making up different rates. A pair of one penny stamps may pay for a double weight envelope, four one penny stamps for an envelope addressed to France, six one penny stamps for an envelope addressed to Prussia, Italy or Spain, and so forth. Since letters addressed abroad are less common than letters addressed internally, the value of the one penny stamps given refers to the single usage. That is not true across the board, as there are many stamps issued during the 19th century that are more scarce used singly than in combination with other stamps. In all these other cases, the value given is intended to reflect the least scarce of the combinations.

If the value of a single stamp on a cover is of particular philatelic

Countries with listings for stamps on covers in the Scott *Classic Specialized Catalogue of Stamps & Covers*

United States
Confederate States
Guam
Hawaii
Aden
Afghanistan
La Aguera
Aitutaki
Alaouites
Albania
Algeria
Allenstein
Spanish Andorra
French Andorra
Anjouan
Antigua
Argentina
  Buenos Aires
  Cordoba
  Corrientes
Ascension
Australia
Austria
  Lombardy-Venetia
Austrian
  Offices in Crete
  Offices in the Turkish Empire
Barbados
Basutoland
Batum
Bechuanaland Protectorate
Belgian Congo
Belgium
Benin
Bermuda
Bolivia
Bosnia and Herzegovina
Brazil
British Columbia and
  Vancouver Island
British Guiana
British Honduras
Bulgaria
Cameroun
Canada
Cape Juby
Caroline Islands
Castellorizo
Ceylon
Chad
Chile
Cochin-China
Corfu
Cuba
Cyrenaica
Dahomey
Dalmatia
Danish West Indies
Danzig
Diego-Suarez
Denmark
Ecuador
Epirus
Eritrea
Ethiopia
Fiji
Fiume
Finland
France
French Offices Abroad
  China
  Crete
  Egypt-Alexandria
  Egypt-Port Said
French Colonies
French Congo
French Equatorial Africa
French Guiana
French Guinea
French India
French Morocco
French Polynesia
French Sudan
Gabon
German East Africa
German New Guinea
German South West Africa
German States
  Baden
  Bavaria
  Bergedorf
  Bremen
  Brunswick
  Hamburg
  Hanover
  Lubeck
  Mecklenburg-Schwerin
  Mecklenburg-Strelitz
  Oldenburg
  Prussia
  Saxony
  Schleswig-Holstein
  Thurn and Taxis
  Wurttemberg
  North German Confederation
Germany
German Offices Abroad
  China
  Morocco
  Turkish Empire
Grand Comoro
Great Britain
Great Britain Offices Abroad
  Eritrea
  Morocco
  Turkish Empire
Greece
Greenland
Guadeloupe
Guatemala
Heligoland
Hong Kong
Iceland
India
Indo-China
Inini
Iran
Italian Colonies
Italian East Africa
Italian States
  Modena
  Parma
  Romagna
  Roman States
  Sardinia
  Tuscany
  Two Sicilies
Italy
Italian Offices Abroad
  China
  Africa
  Crete
  Turkish Empire
  Aegean Islands
Ivory Coast
Kiauchau
Labuan
Latakia
Libya
Liechtenstein
Luxembourg
Madagascar (French Offices)
Madeira
Malta
Mariana Islands
Marienwerder
Marshall Islands
Martinique
Mauritania
Mauritius
Mayotte
Memel
Mexico
Moheli
Monaco
Morocco
Netherlands
New Brunswick
New Caledonia
Newfoundland
New Hebrides, French
New Zealand
Nicaragua
Niger
Northern Rhodesia
Norway
Nossi Be
Nova Scotia
Nyasaland Protectorate
Obock
Oltre Giuba
Paraguay
Peru
Philippines
Portugal
Prince Edward Island
Puerto Rico
Reunion
Ruanda-Urundi
Russia
Saar
Ste.-Marie de Madagascar
St. Pierre & Miquelon
Samoa
San Marino
Saudi Arabia
Senegal
Senegambia & Niger
Somalia
Somali Coast
South Africa
Southern Rhodesia
South West Africa
Spain
Straits Settlements
Sudan
Swaziland
Sweden
Switzerland
Tahiti
Tannu Tuva
Togo
Transvaal
Tripolitania
Tunisia
Ubangi-Shari
Upper Senegal & Niger
Upper Silesia
Upper Volta (Burkina Faso)
Uruguay
Wallis & Futuna Islands
Vatican City
Venezuela
Zanzibar

importance, as in the case of the stamps that pay for reduced rates for the delivery of newspapers or other printed matter, then their different value for this usage is indicated in footnotes or as a separate listing. It clearly is impossible to add to a catalogue of worldwide stamps the detailed information regarding the relative scarcity and value of all rates and combinations. We have limited ourselves to some of the more noteworthy and important cases.

In the majority of cases, the value of a cover assumes that the stamps on it have been used in the period contemporaneous with their issuance. Late uses are sometimes considered premium items, but in most cases late and very late usages are of no significance in postal history and detract from the value of the cover.

Condition

When evaluating a cover, care must be given to the factors that determine the overall condition of the item. It is generally more difficult to grade and evaluate a cover than a stamp. The condition of the stamps affixed to the cover must be taken into account — always in relation to the criteria for the particular issue. The Scott Catalogue does specify the grade and condition of the stamps for which a value is given, so it is important to consult this information. In addition, the condition of the cover must be taken into account. Values are for covers that are reasonably well preserved given the period of usage and the country of origin. A tiny nick or tear, or slight reduction from opening, are normal for 19th century covers. Folded letters may be expected to have tears on the reverse from opening, and often they will have file folds. Unless these factors affect the stamps or postal markings, they should not detract from the on-cover values given in the catalogue.

Just as with stamps, various factors can lower the value of a cover. Missing pieces, serious tears, holes, creases, toning, stains and alterations of postal markings are examples of factors that lower the value of a cover. The necessity of considering these factors for the cover, as well as having to consider the condition of the stamps on the cover, helps to explain why it is more difficult to determine the value of a cover than a stamp off cover.

Factors Enhancing the Value of a Cover

A further difficulty in the valuation of covers is the necessity of considering factors other than the stamps used on a cover and the condition of the stamps and the cover. As stated previously, catalogue values listed herein generally reflect the most common uses of stamps on covers that are reasonably well preserved given the period of usage. Consideration of factors that may enhance the value of covers for the most part is beyond the scope of the Scott Catalogue. However, it is critical to understand that there are many such factors. Following is a list of many of the factors that often will increase the value of a cover.

- postal markings indicating origin, transit and arrival;
- postal markings indicating rates paid, which include postage, registration, acknowledgment of receipt, express charges, insurance, postage due, forwarding and many others;
- postal markings indicating carriers such as stagecoaches, trains, ships, aircraft, etc.;
- markings applied by censors, other civilian or military authorities, and others;
- scarce or rare destinations and routings;
- interruptions in the delivery system due to accidents, wars, natural calamities, etc.;
- unusual combinations of stamps;
- printed or hand-drawn pictorial, advertising or patriotic cover designs;
- unusual quality of stamps, postal markings or cover;
- and, outside of postal history, particularly noteworthy addressee, sender or contents.

Catalogue Listing Policy

It is the intent of Amos Media Co. to list all postage stamps of the world in the Scott *Standard Postage Stamp Catalogue*. The only strict criteria for listing is that stamps be decreed legal for postage by the issuing country and that the issuing country actually have an operating postal system. Whether the primary intent of issuing a given stamp or set was for sale to postal patrons or to stamp collectors is not part of our listing criteria. Scott's role is to provide basic comprehensive postage stamp information. It is up to each stamp collector to choose which items to include in a collection.

It is Scott's objective to seek reasons why a stamp should be listed, rather than why it should not. Nevertheless, there are certain types of items that will not be listed. These include the following:

1. Unissued items that are not officially distributed or released by the issuing postal authority. If such items are officially issued at a later date by the country, they will be listed. Unissued items consist of those that have been printed and then held from sale for reasons such as change in government, errors found on stamps or something deemed objectionable about a stamp subject or design.

2. Stamps "issued" by non-existent postal entities or fantasy countries, such as Nagaland, Occusi-Ambeno, Staffa, Sedang, Torres Straits and others. Also, stamps "issued" in the name of legitimate stamp-issuing countries that are not authorized by those countries.

3. Semi-official or unofficial items not required for postage. Examples include items issued by private agencies for their own express services. When such items are required for delivery, or are valid as prepayment of postage, they are listed.

4. Local stamps issued for local use only. Postage stamps issued by governments specifically for "domestic" use, such as Haiti Scott 219-228, or the United States non-denominated stamps, are not considered to be locals, since they are valid for postage throughout the country of origin.

5. Items not valid for postal use. For example, a few countries have issued souvenir sheets that are not valid for postage. This area also includes a number of worldwide charity labels (some denominated) that do not pay postage.

6. Egregiously exploitative issues such as stamps sold for far more than face value, stamps purposefully issued in artificially small quantities or only against advance orders, stamps awarded only to a selected audience such as a philatelic bureau's standing order customers, or stamps sold only in conjunction with other products. All of these kinds of items are usually controlled issues and/or are intended for speculation. These items normally will be included in a footnote.

7. Items distributed by the issuing government only to a limited group, such as a stamp club, philatelic exhibition or a single stamp dealer or other private company. These items normally will be included in a footnote.

8. Stamps not available to collectors. These generally are rare items, all of which are held by public institutions such as museums. The existence of such items often will be cited in footnotes.

The fact that a stamp has been used successfully as postage, even on international mail, is not in itself sufficient proof that it was legitimately issued. Numerous examples of so-called stamps from non-existent countries are known to have been used to post letters that have successfully passed through the international mail system.

There are certain items that are subject to interpretation. When a stamp falls outside our specifications, it may be listed along with a cautionary footnote.

A number of factors are considered in our approach to analyzing how a stamp is listed. The following list of factors is presented to share with you, the catalogue user, the complexity of the listing process.

Additional printings — "Additional printings" of a previously issued stamp may range from an item that is totally different to cases where it is impossible to differentiate from the original. At least a minor number (a small-letter suffix) is assigned if there is a distinct change in stamp shade, noticeably redrawn design, or a significantly different perforation measurement. A major number (numeral or numeral and capital-letter combination) is assigned if the editors feel the "additional printing" is sufficiently different from the original that it constitutes a different issue.

Commemoratives — Where practical, commemoratives with the same theme are placed in a set. Occasionally, however, stamp sets that were released over a period of years have been separated. Appropriately placed footnotes will guide you to each set's continuation.

Definitive sets — Blocks of numbers generally have been reserved for definitive sets, based on previous experience with any given country. If a few more stamps were issued in a set than originally expected, they often have been inserted into the original set with a capital-letter suffix, such as U.S. Scott 634A. If many more stamps than the originally allotted block were released before the set was completed, two or more blocks of numbers may have been needed to accomodate the entire set or series. Appropriately placed footnotes will guide you to each set's continuation.

Overprints — The color of an overprint is always noted if it is other than black. Where more than one color of ink has been used on overprints of a single set, the color used is noted. Early overprint and surcharge illustrations were altered to prevent their use by forgers.

Understanding the Listings

On the opposite page is an enlarged "typical" listing from this catalogue. Below are detailed explanations of each of the highlighted parts of the listing.

1 **Scott number** — Scott catalogue numbers are used to identify specific items when buying, selling or trading stamps. Each listed postage stamp from every country has a unique Scott catalogue number. Therefore, Germany Scott 99, for example, can only refer to a single stamp. Although the Scott catalogue usually lists stamps in chronological order by date of issue, there are exceptions. When a country has issued a set of stamps over a period of time, those stamps within the set are kept together without regard to date of issue. This follows the normal collecting approach of keeping stamps in their natural sets.

When a country issues a set of stamps over a period of time, a group of consecutive catalogue numbers is reserved for the stamps in that set, as issued. If that group of numbers proves to be too few, capital-letter suffixes, such as "A" or "B," may be added to existing numbers to create enough catalogue numbers to cover all items in the set. A capital-letter suffix indicates a major Scott catalogue number listing. Scott uses a suffix letter only once. Therefore, a catalogue number listing with a capital-letter suffix will not also be found with the same letter (lower case) used as a minor-letter listing. If there is a Scott 16A in a set, for example, there will not also be a Scott 16a. However, a minor-letter "a" listing may be added to a major number containing an "A" suffix (Scott 16Aa, for example).

Suffix letters are cumulative. A minor "b" variety of Scott 16A would be Scott 16Ab, not Scott 16b.

There are times when a reserved block of Scott catalogue numbers is too large for a set, leaving some numbers unused. Such gaps in the numbering sequence also occur when the catalogue editors move an item's listing elsewhere or have removed it entirely from the catalogue. Scott does not attempt to account for every possible number, but rather attempts to assure that each stamp is assigned its own number.

Scott numbers designating regular postage normally are only numerals. Scott numbers for other types of stamps, such as air post, semi-postal, postal tax, postage due, occupation and others have a prefix consisting of one or more capital letters or a combination of numerals and capital letters.

2 **Illustration number** — Illustration or design-type numbers are used to identify each catalogue illustration. For most sets, the lowest face-value stamp is shown. It then serves as an example of the basic design approach for other stamps not illustrated. Where more than one stamp use the same illustration number, but have differences in design, the design paragraph or the description line clearly indicates the design on each stamp not illustrated. Where there are both vertical and horizontal designs in a set, a single illustration may be used, with the exceptions noted in the design paragraph or description line.

When an illustration is followed by a lower-case letter in parentheses, such as "A2(b)," the trailing letter indicates which overprint or surcharge illustration applies.

Illustrations normally are 70 percent of the original size of the stamp. Oversized stamps, blocks and souvenir sheets are reduced even more. Overprints and surcharges are shown at 100 percent of their original size if shown alone, but are 70 percent of original size if shown on stamps. In some cases, the illustration will be placed above the set, between listings or omitted completely. Overprint and surcharge illustrations are not placed in this catalogue for purposes of expertizing stamps.

3 **Paper color** — The color of a stamp's paper is noted in italic type when the paper used is not white.

4 **Listing styles** — There are two principal types of catalogue listings: major and minor.

Major listings are in a larger type style than minor listings. The catalogue number is a numeral that can be found with or without a capital-letter suffix, and with or without a prefix.

Minor listings are in a smaller type style and have a small-letter suffix or (if the listing immediately follows that of the major number) may show only the letter. These listings identify a variety of the major item. Examples include perforation, color, watermark or printing method differences, multiples (some souvenir sheets, booklet panes and se-tenant combinations), and singles of multiples.

Examples of major number listings include 16, 28A, B97, C13A, 10N5, and 10N6A. Examples of minor numbers are 16a and C13Ab.

5 **Basic information about a stamp or set** — Introducing each stamp issue is a small section (usually a line listing) of basic information about a stamp or set. This section normally includes the date of issue, method of printing, perforation, watermark and, sometimes, some additional information of note. *Printing method, perforation and watermark apply to the following sets until a change is noted.* Stamps created by overprinting or surcharging previous issues are assumed to have the same perforation, watermark, printing method and other production characteristics as the original. Dates of issue are as precise as Scott is able to confirm and often reflect the dates on first-day covers, rather than the actual date of release.

6 **Denomination** — This normally refers to the face value of the stamp; that is, the cost of the unused stamp at the post office at the time of issue. When a denomination is shown in parentheses, it does not appear on the stamp. This includes the non-denominated stamps of the United States, Brazil and Great Britain, for example.

7 **Color or other description** — This area provides information to solidify identification of a stamp. In many recent cases, a description of the stamp design appears in this space, rather than a listing of colors.

8 **Year of issue** — In stamp sets that have been released in a period that spans more than a year, the number shown in parentheses is the year that stamp first appeared. Stamps without a date appeared during the first year of the issue. Dates are not always given for minor varieties.

9 **Value unused and Value used** — The Scott catalogue values are based on stamps that are in a grade of Very Fine unless stated otherwise. Unused values refer to items that have not seen postal, revenue or any other duty for which they were intended. Pre-1900 unused stamps that were issued with gum must have at least most of their original gum. Later issues are assumed to have full original gum. From breakpoints specified in most countries' listings, stamps are valued as never hinged. Stamps issued without gum are noted. Modern issues with PVA or other synthetic adhesives may appear ungummed. Self-adhesive stamps are valued as appearing undisturbed on their original backing paper. For a more detailed explanation of these values, please see the "Catalogue Value," "Condition" and "Understanding Valuing Notations" sections elsewhere in this introduction.

In some cases, where used stamps are more valuable than unused stamps, the value is for an example with a contemporaneous cancel, rather than a modern cancel or a smudge or other unclear marking. For those stamps that were released for postal and fiscal purposes, the used value represents a postally used stamp. Stamps with revenue cancels generally sell for less. Scott values for used self-adhesive stamps are for examples either on piece or off piece.

Stamps separated from a complete se-tenant multiple usually will be worth less than a pro-rated portion of the se-tenant multiple, and stamps lacking the attached labels that are noted in the listings will be worth less than the values shown.

10 **Changes in basic set information** — Bold type is used to show any changes in the basic data given for a set of stamps. These basic categories include perforation gauge measurements, paper type, printing method and watermark.

11 **Total value of a set** — The total value of sets of three or more stamps issued after 1900 are shown. The set line also notes the range of Scott numbers and total number of stamps included in the grouping. The actual value of a set consisting predominantly of stamps having the minimum value of twenty cents may be less than the total value shown. Similary, the actual value or catalogue value of se-tenant pairs or of blocks consisting of stamps having the minimum value of twenty cents may be less than the catalogue values of the component parts.

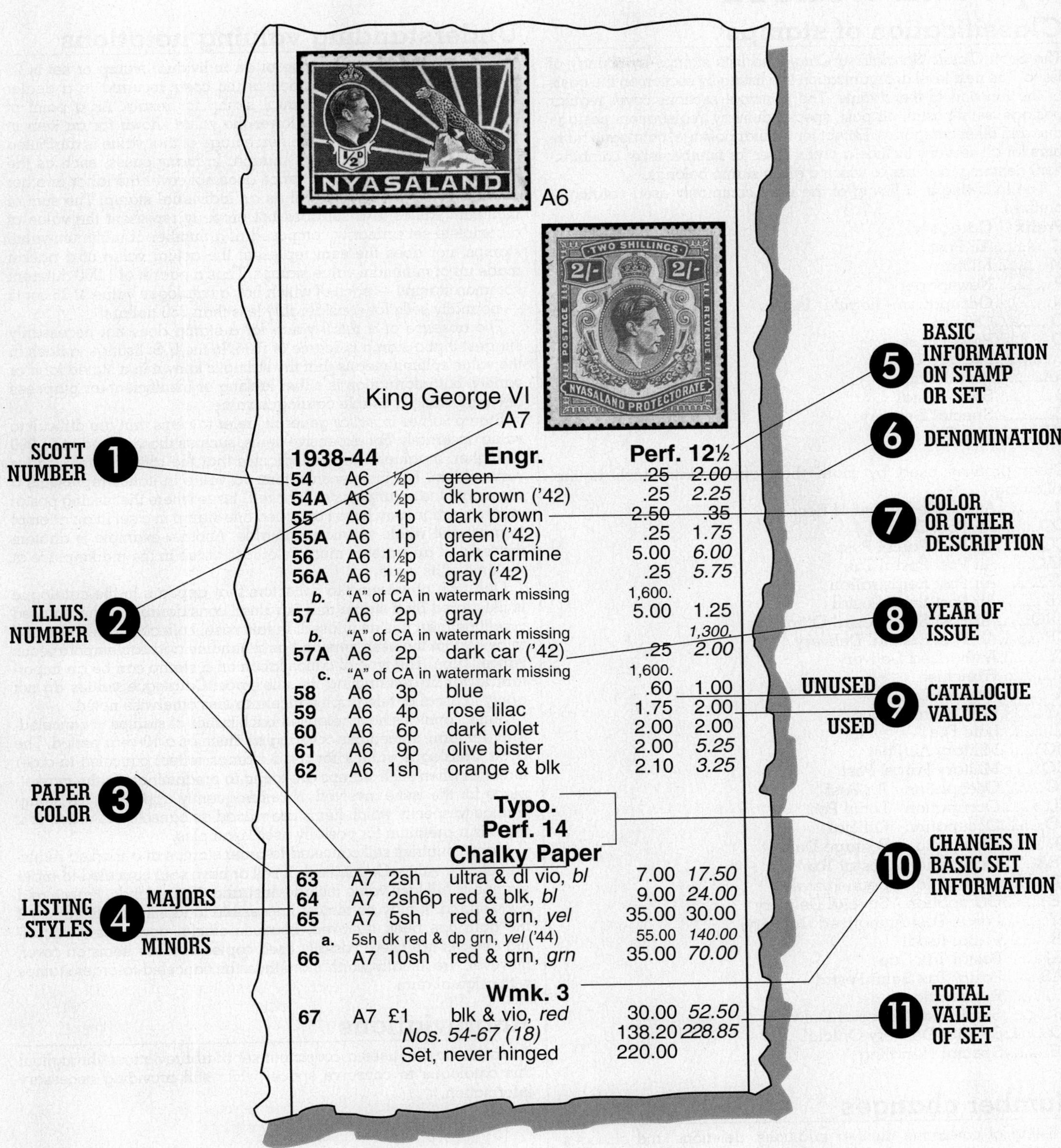
NYASALAND
A6
TWO SHILLINGS
2/- 2/-
POSTAGE
REVENUE
NYASALAND PROTECTORATE
King George VI
A7
1938-44 Engr. Perf. 12½
54 A6 ½p green .25 2.00
54A A6 ½p dk brown ('42) .25 2.25
55 A6 1p dark brown 2.50 .35
55A A6 1p green ('42) .25 1.75
56 A6 1½p dark carmine 5.00 6.00
56A A6 1½p gray ('42) .25 5.75
b. "A" of CA in watermark missing 1,600.
57 A6 2p gray 5.00 1.25
b. "A" of CA in watermark missing 1,300.
57A A6 2p dark car ('42) .25 2.00
c. "A" of CA in watermark missing 1,600.
58 A6 3p blue .60 1.00
59 A6 4p rose lilac 1.75 2.00
60 A6 6p dark violet 2.00 2.00
61 A6 9p olive bister 2.00 5.25
62 A6 1sh orange & blk 2.10 3.25
Typo.
Perf. 14
Chalky Paper
63 A7 2sh ultra & dl vio, bl 7.00 17.50
64 A7 2sh6p red & blk, bl 9.00 24.00
65 A7 5sh red & grn, yel 35.00 30.00
a. 5sh dk red & dp grn, yel ('44) 55.00 140.00
66 A7 10sh red & grn, grn 35.00 70.00
Wmk. 3
67 A7 £1 blk & vio, red 30.00 52.50
Nos. 54-67 (18) 138.20 228.85
Set, never hinged 220.00
1 SCOTT NUMBER
2 ILLUS. NUMBER
3 PAPER COLOR
4 LISTING STYLES
MAJORS
MINORS
5 BASIC INFORMATION ON STAMP OR SET
6 DENOMINATION
7 COLOR OR OTHER DESCRIPTION
8 YEAR OF ISSUE
9 CATALOGUE VALUES
UNUSED
USED
10 CHANGES IN BASIC SET INFORMATION
11 TOTAL VALUE OF SET

Special Notices

Classification of stamps

The Scott *Classic Specialized Catalogue* lists stamps by country of issue. The next level of organization is a listing by section on the basis of the function of the stamps. The principal sections cover regular postage, semi-postal, air post, special delivery, registration, postage due and other categories. Except for regular postage, catalogue numbers for all sections include a prefix letter (or number-letter combination) denoting the class to which a given stamp belongs.

The following is a listing of the most commonly used catalogue prefixes.

Prefix Category
C............Air Post
M...........Military
P............Newspaper
N............Occupation - Regular Issues
O...........Official
Q...........Parcel Post
J............Postage Due
RA.........Postal Tax
B............Semi-Postal
E............Special Delivery
MR.........War Tax

Other prefixes used by more than one country include the following:
H............Acknowledgment of Receipt
CO.........Air Post Official
CQ.........Air Post Parcel Post
RAC.......Air Post Postal Tax
CF..........Air Post Registration
CB.........Air Post Semi-Postal
CBO......Air Post Semi-Postal Official
CE.........Air Post Special Delivery
EY..........Authorized Delivery
S............Franchise
G...........Insured Letter
GY.........Marine Insurance
I.............Late Fee
MC........Military Air Post
MQ........Military Parcel Post
NC.........Occupation - Air Post
NL..........Occupation - Local Post
NO.........Occupation - Official
NJ..........Occupation - Postage Due
NRA.......Occupation - Postal Tax
NB..........Occupation - Semi-Postal
NE.........Occupation - Special Delivery
QY.........Parcel Post Authorized Delivery
AR..........Postal-fiscal
RAJ........Postal Tax Due
RAB.......Postal Tax Semi-Postal
F............Registration
EB..........Semi-Postal Special Delivery
EO.........Special Delivery Official
QE.........Special Handling

Number changes

A listing of catalogue number additions, deletions and changes from the previous edition of the catalogue appears in each volume. Only number changes affecting the *Classic Specialized Catalogue* have been included in this volume. See *Classic Catalogue* Number Additions, Deletions & Changes in the table of contents for the location of this list.

Understanding valuing notations

The *minimum catalogue value* of an individual stamp or set is 25 cents. This represents a portion of the costs incurred to a dealer when he prepares an individual stamp for resale. As a point of philatelic-economic fact, the lower the value shown for an item in this catalogue, the greater the percentage of that value is attributed to dealer mark up and profit margin. In many cases, such as the 25-cent minimum value, that price does not cover the labor or other costs involved with stocking it as an individual stamp. The sum of minimum values in a set does not properly represent the value of a complete set primarily composed of a number of minimum-value stamps, nor does the sum represent the actual value of a packet made up of minimum-value stamps. Thus a packet of 1,000 different common stamps — each of which has a catalogue value of 25 cents — normally sells for considerably less than 250 dollars!

The *absence of a retail value* for a stamp does not necessarily suggest that a stamp is scarce or rare. In the U.S. listings, a dash in the value column means that the stamp is known in a stated form or variety, but information is either lacking or insufficient for purposes of establishing a usable catalogue value.

Stamp values in *italics* generally refer to items that are difficult to value accurately. For expensive items, such as those priced at $1,000 or higher, a value in italics indicates that the affected item trades very seldom. For inexpensive items, a value in italics represents a warning. One example is a "blocked" issue where the issuing postal administration may have controlled one stamp in a set in an attempt to make the whole set more valuable. Another example is an item that sold at an extreme multiple of face value in the marketplace at the time of its issue.

One type of warning to collectors that appears in the catalogue is illustrated by a stamp that is valued considerably higher in used condition than it is as unused. In this case, collectors are cautioned to be certain the used version has a genuine and contemporaneous cancellation. The type of cancellation on a stamp can be an important factor in determining its sale price. Catalogue values do not apply to fiscal or telegraph cancels, unless otherwise noted.

Some countries have released back issues of stamps in canceled-to-order form, sometimes covering as much as a 10-year period. The Scott Catalogue values for used stamps reflect canceled-to-order material when such stamps are found to predominate in the marketplace for the issue involved. Notes frequently appear in the stamp listings to specify which items are valued as canceled-to-order, or if there is a premium for postally used examples.

Many countries sell canceled-to-order stamps at a marked reduction of face value. Countries that sell or have sold canceled-to-order stamps at *full* face value include Australia, Netherlands, France and Switzerland. It may be almost impossible to identify such stamps if the gum has been removed, because official government canceling devices are used. Postally used copies of these items on cover, however, are usually worth more than the canceled-to-order stamps with original gum.

Abbreviations

Amos Media Co. uses a consistent set of abbreviations throughout this catalogue to conserve space, while still providing necessary information.

COLOR ABBREVIATIONS

amb..... amber
anil...... aniline
ap........ apple
aqua ... aquamarine
az .... azure
bis .... bister
bl .... blue
bld....... blood
blk .... black
bril........ brilliant
brn....... brown
brnsh... brownish
brnz..... bronze
brt........ bright
brnt...... burnt
car....... carmine
cer .... cerise
chlky.... chalky
cham... chamois
chnt ..... chestnut
choc..... chocolate
chr .... chrome
cit......... citron
cl.......... claret
cob ...... cobalt
cop ...... copper
crim..... crimson
cr .... cream
dk .... dark
dl .... dull
dp........ deep
db........ drab
emer.... emerald
gldn..... golden
grysh... grayish
grn....... green
grnsh... greenish
hel .... heliotrope
hn .... henna
ind .... indigo
int .... intense
lav .... lavender
lem ...... lemon
lil .... lilac
lt .... light
mag..... magenta
man..... manila
mar..... maroon
mv .... mauve
multi..... multicolored
mlky .... milky
myr...... myrtle
ol .... olive
olvn ..... olivine
org....... orange
pck ...... peacock
pnksh .. pinkish
Prus ..... Prussian
pur....... purple
redsh... reddish
res .... reseda
ros .... rosine
ryl .... royal
sal .... salmon
saph .... sapphire
scar ..... scarlet
sep .... sepia
sien ...... sienna
sil......... silver
sl.......... slate
stl......... steel
turq...... turquoise
ultra..... ultramarine
Ven ...... Venetian
ver .... vermilion
vio........ violet
yel........ yellow
yelsh.... yellowish

When no color is given for an overprint or surcharge, black is the color used. Abbreviations for colors used for overprints and surcharges include: "(B)" or "(Blk)," black; "(Bl)," blue; "(R)," red; and "(G)," green.

Additional abbreviations in this catalogue are shown below:

Adm. ....Administration
AFL...................American Federation of Labor
Anniv. ....Anniversary
APS ....American Philatelic Society
Assoc. ....Association
ASSR.................Autonomous Soviet Socialist Republic
b. ....Born
BEP...................Bureau of Engraving and Printing
Bicent. ....Bicentennial
Bklt. ....Booklet
Brit. ....British
btwn. ....Between
Bur.....................Bureau
c. or ca. ....Circa
Cat. ....Catalogue
Cent. ....Centennial, century, centenary
CIO ....Congress of Industrial Organizations
Conf. ....Conference
Cong. ....Congress
Cpl. ....Corporal
CTO ....Canceled to order
d. ....Died
Dbl. ....Double
EDU..................Earliest documented use
Engr...................Engraved
Exhib.................Exhibition
Expo. ....Exposition
Fed. ....Federation
GB ....Great Britain
Gen. ....General
GPO ....General post office
Horiz. ....Horizontal
Imperf. ....Imperforate
Impt...................Imprint
Intl. ....International
Invtd. ....Inverted
L ....Left
Lieut., lt. ....Lieutenant
Litho. ....Lithographed
LL ....Lower left
LR.....................Lower right
mm ....Millimeter
Ms. ....Manuscript
Natl. ....National
No. ....Number
NY ....New York
NYC..................New York City
Ovpt. ....Overprint
Ovptd. ....Overprinted
P ....Plate number
Perf. ....Perforated, perforation
Phil. ....Philatelic
Photo. ....Photogravure
PO ....Post office
Pr. ....Pair
P.R. ....Puerto Rico
Prec. ....Precancel, precanceled
Pres. ....President
PTT ....Post, Telephone and Telegraph
Rio ....Rio de Janeiro
Sgt. ....Sergeant
Soc. ....Society
Souv. ....Souvenir
SSR ....Soviet Socialist Republic, see ASSR
St. ....Saint, street
Surch. ....Surcharge
Typo. ....Typographed
UL......................Upper left
Unwmkd. ....Unwatermarked
UPU ....Universal Postal Union
UR ....Upper right
US ....United States
USPOD ....United States Post Office Department
USSR ....Union of Soviet Socialist Republics
Vert. ....Vertical
VP ....Vice president
Wmk. ....Watermark
Wmkd. ....Watermarked
WWI ....World War I
WWII ....World War II

Examination

Amos Media Co. will not comment upon the genuineness, grade or condition of stamps, because of the time and responsibility involved. Rather, there are several expertizing groups that undertake this work for both collectors and dealers. Neither will Amos Media Co. appraise or identify philatelic material. The company cannot take responsibility for unsolicited stamps or covers sent by individuals.

How to order from your dealer

When ordering stamps from a dealer, it is not necessary to write the full description of a stamp as listed in this catalogue. All you need is the name of the country, the Scott catalogue number and whether the desired item is unused or used. For example, "Japan Scott 422 unused" is sufficient to identify the unused stamp of Japan listed as "422 A206 5y brown."

Basic Stamp Information

A stamp collector's knowledge of the combined elements that make a given stamp issue unique determines his or her ability to identify stamps. These elements include paper, watermark, method of separation, printing, design and gum. On the following pages each of these important areas is briefly described.

Paper

Paper is an organic material composed of a compacted weave of cellulose fibers and generally formed into sheets. Paper used to print stamps may be manufactured in sheets, or it may have been part of a large roll (called a web) before being cut to size. The fibers most often used to create paper on which stamps are printed include bark, wood, straw and certain grasses. In many cases, linen or cotton rags have been added for greater strength and durability. Grinding, bleaching, cooking and rinsing these raw fibers reduces them to a slushy pulp, referred to by paper makers as "stuff." Sizing and, sometimes, coloring matter is added to the pulp to make different types of finished paper.

After the stuff is prepared, it is poured onto sieve-like frames that allow the water to run off, while retaining the matted pulp. As fibers fall onto the screen and are held by gravity, they form a natural weave that will later hold the paper together. If the screen has metal bits that are formed into letters or images attached, it leaves slightly thinned areas on the paper. These are called watermarks.

When the stuff is almost dry, it is passed under pressure through smooth or engraved rollers - dandy rolls - or placed between cloth in a press to be flattened and dried.

Stamp paper falls broadly into two types: wove and laid. The nature of the surface of the frame onto which the pulp is first deposited causes the differences in appearance between the two. If the surface is smooth and even, the paper will be of fairly uniform texture throughout. This is known as *wove paper*. Early papermaking machines poured the pulp onto a continuously circulating web of felt, but modern machines feed the pulp onto a cloth-like screen made of closely interwoven fine wires. This paper, when held to a light, will show little dots or points very close together. The proper name for this is "wire wove," but the type is still considered wove. Any U.S. or British stamp printed after 1880 will serve as an example of wire wove paper.

Closely spaced parallel wires, with cross wires at wider intervals, make up the frames used for what is known as *laid paper*. A greater thickness of the pulp will settle between the wires. The paper, when held to a light, will show alternate light and dark lines. The spacing and the thickness of the lines may vary, but on any one sheet of paper they are all alike. See Russia Scott 31-38 for examples of laid paper.

Batonne, from the French word meaning "a staff," is a term used if the lines in the paper are spaced quite far apart, like the printed ruling on a writing tablet. Batonne paper may be either wove or laid. If laid, fine laid lines can be seen between the batons. The laid lines, which are a form of watermark, may be geometrical figures such as squares, diamonds, rectangles or wavy lines.

Quadrille is the term used when the lines in the paper form little squares. *Oblong quadrille* is the term used when rectangles, rather than squares, are formed. See Mexico-Guadalajara Scott 35-37 for examples of oblong quadrille paper.

Paper also is classified as thick or thin, hard or soft, and by color if dye is added during manufacture. Such colors may include yellowish, greenish, bluish and reddish.

Brief explanations of other types of paper used for printing stamps, as well as examples, follow.

Pelure — Pelure paper is a very thin, hard and often brittle paper that is sometimes bluish or grayish in appearance. See Serbia Scott 169-170.

Native — This is a term applied to handmade papers used to produce some of the early stamps of the Indian states. Stamps printed on native paper may be expected to display various natural inclusions that are normal and do not negatively affect value. Japanese paper, originally made of mulberry fibers and rice flour, is part of this group. See Japan Scott 1-18.

Manila — This type of paper is often used to make stamped envelopes and wrappers. It is a coarse-textured stock, usually smooth on one side and rough on the other. A variety of colors of manila paper exist, but the most common range is yellowish-brown.

Silk — Introduced by the British in 1847 as a safeguard against counterfeiting, silk paper contains bits of colored silk thread scattered throughout. The density of these fibers varies greatly and can include as few as one fiber per stamp or hundreds. U.S. revenue Scott R152 is a good example of an easy-to-identify silk paper stamp.

Silk-thread paper has uninterrupted threads of colored silk arranged so that one or more threads run through the stamp or postal stationery. See Great Britain Scott 5-6 and Switzerland Scott 14-19.

Granite — Filled with minute cloth or colored paper fibers of various colors and lengths, granite paper should not be confused with either type of silk paper. Austria Scott 172-175 and a number of Swiss stamps are examples of granite paper.

Chalky — A chalk-like substance coats the surface of chalky paper to discourage the cleaning and reuse of canceled stamps, as well as to provide a smoother, more acceptable printing surface. Because the designs of stamps printed on chalky paper are imprinted on what is often a water-soluble coating, any attempt to remove a cancellation will destroy the stamp. *Do not soak these stamps in any fluid.* To remove a stamp printed on chalky paper from an envelope, wet the paper from underneath the stamp until the gum dissolves enough to release the stamp from the paper. See St. Kitts-Nevis Scott 89-90 for examples of stamps printed on this type of chalky paper.

India — Another name for this paper, originally introduced from China about 1750, is "China Paper." It is a thin, opaque paper often used for plate and die proofs by many countries.

Double — In philately, the term double paper has two distinct meanings. The first is a two-ply paper, usually a combination of a thick and a thin sheet, joined during manufacture. This type was used experimentally as a means to discourage the reuse of stamps.

The design is printed on the thin paper. Any attempt to remove a cancellation would destroy the design. U.S. Scott 158 and other Banknote-era stamps exist on this form of double paper.

The second type of double paper occurs on a rotary press, when the end of one paper roll, or web, is affixed to the next roll to save time feeding the paper through the press. Stamp designs are printed over the joined paper and, if overlooked by inspectors, may get into post office stocks.

Goldbeater's Skin — This type of paper was used for the 1866 issue of Prussia, and was a tough, translucent paper. The design was printed in reverse on the back of the stamp, and the gum applied over the printing. It is impossible to remove stamps printed on this type of paper from the paper to which they are affixed without destroying the design.

Ribbed — Ribbed paper has an uneven, corrugated surface made by passing the paper through ridged rollers. This type exists on some copies of U.S. Scott 156-165.

Various other substances, or substrates, have been used for stamp manufacture, including wood, aluminum, copper, silver and gold foil, plastic, and silk and cotton fabrics.

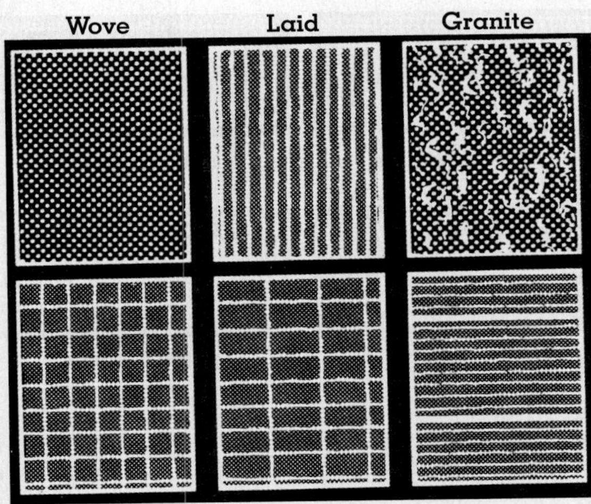

Wove Laid Granite

Quadrille Oblong Quadrille Laid Battone

Watermarks

Watermarks are an integral part of some papers. They are formed in the process of paper manufacture. Watermarks consist of small designs, formed of wire or cut from metal and soldered to the surface of the mold or, sometimes, on the dandy roll. The designs may be in the form of crowns, stars, anchors, letters or other characters or symbols. These pieces of metal - known in the paper-making industry as "bits" - impress a design into the paper. The design sometimes may be seen by holding the stamp to the light. Some are more easily seen with a watermark detector. This important tool is a small black tray into which a stamp is placed face down and dampened with a fast-evaporating watermark detection fluid that brings up the watermark image in the form of dark lines against a lighter background. These dark lines are the thinner areas of the paper known as the watermark. Some watermarks are extremely difficult to locate, due to either a faint impression, watermark location or the color of the stamp. There also are electric watermark detectors that come with plastic filter disks of various colors. The disks neutralize the color of the stamp, permitting the watermark to be seen more easily.

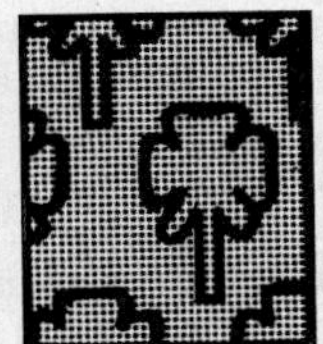

Multiple watermarks of Crown Agents and Burma

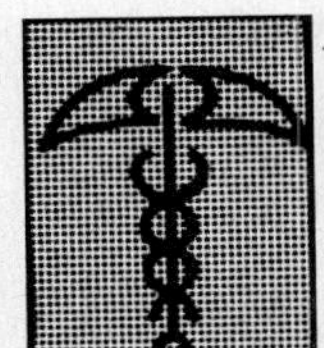

Watermarks of Uruguay, Vatican City and Jamaica

WARNING: Some inks used in the photogravure process dissolve in watermark fluids (Please see the section on Soluble Printing Inks). Also, see "chalky paper."

Watermarks may be found normal, reversed, inverted, reversed and inverted, sideways or diagonal, as seen from the back of the stamp. The relationship of watermark to stamp design depends on the position of the printing plates or how paper is fed through the press. On machine-made paper, watermarks normally are read from right to left. The design is repeated closely throughout the sheet in a "multiple-watermark design." In a "sheet watermark," the design appears only once on the sheet, but extends over many stamps. Individual stamps may carry only a small fraction or none of the watermark.

"Marginal watermarks" occur in the margins of sheets or panes of stamps. They occur on the outside border of paper (ostensibly outside the area where stamps are to be printed). A large row of letters may spell the name of the country or the manufacturer of the paper, or a border of lines may appear. Careless press feeding may cause parts of these letters and/or lines to show on stamps of the outer row of a pane.

Soluble Printing Inks

WARNING: Most stamp colors are permanent; that is, they are not seriously affected by short-term exposure to light or water. Some colors may fade from excessive exposure to light. There are stamps printed with inks that dissolve easily in water or in fluids used to detect watermarks. Use of these inks was intentional to prevent the removal of cancellations. Water affects all aniline inks, those on so-called safety paper and some photogravure printings - all such inks are known as *fugitive colors. Removal from paper of such stamps requires care and alternatives to traditional soaking.*

Separation

"Separation" is the general term used to describe methods used to separate stamps. The three standard forms currently in use are perforating, rouletting and die-cutting. These methods are done during the stamp production process, after printing. Sometimes these methods are done on-press or sometimes as a separate step. The earliest issues, such as the 1840 Penny Black of Great Britain (Scott 1), did not have any means provided for separation. It was expected the stamps would be cut apart with scissors or folded and torn. These are examples of imperforate stamps. Many stamps were first issued in imperforate formats and were later issued with perforations. Therefore, care must be observed in buying single imperforate stamps to be certain they were issued imperforate and are not perforated copies that have been altered by having the perforations trimmed away. Stamps issued imperforate usually are valued as singles. However, imperforate varieties of normally perforated stamps should be collected in pairs or larger pieces as indisputable evidence of their imperforate character.

PERFORATION

The chief style of separation of stamps, and the one that is in almost universal use today, is perforating. By this process, paper between the stamps is cut away in a line of holes, usually round, leaving little bridges of paper between the stamps to hold them together. Some types of perforation, such as hyphen-hole perfs, can be confused with roulettes, but a close visual inspection reveals that paper has been removed. The little perforation bridges, which project from the stamp when it is torn from the pane, are called the teeth of the perforation.

As the size of the perforation is sometimes the only way to differentiate between two otherwise identical stamps, it is necessary to be able to accurately measure and describe them. This is done with a perforation gauge, usually a ruler-like device that has dots or graduated lines to show how many perforations may be counted in the space of two centimeters. Two centimeters is the space universally adopted in which to measure perforations.

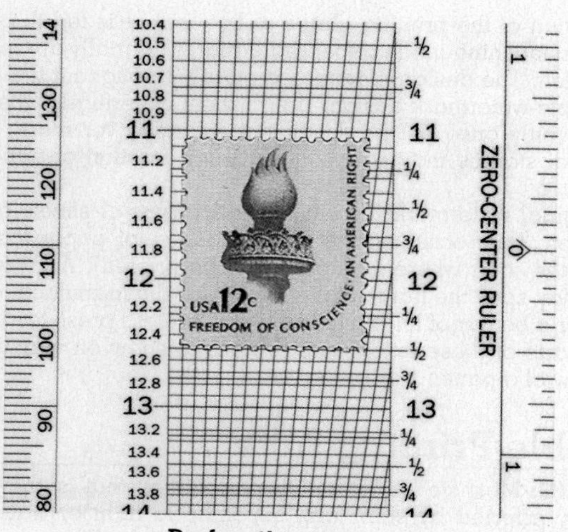

Perforation gauge

To measure a stamp, run it along the gauge until the dots on it fit exactly into the perforations of the stamp. If you are using a graduated-line perforation gauge, simply slide the stamp along the surface until the lines on the gauge perfectly project from the center of the bridges or holes. The number to the side of the line of dots or lines that fit the stamp's perforation is the measurement. For example, an "11" means that 11 perforations fit between two centimeters. The description of the stamp therefore is "perf. 11." If the gauge of the perforations on the top and bottom of a stamp differs from that on the sides, the result is what is known as *compound perforations*. In measuring compound perforations, the gauge at top and bottom is always given first, then the sides. Thus, a stamp that measures 11 at top and bottom and 10 1/2 at the sides is "perf. 11 x 10 1/2." See U.S. Scott 632-642 for examples of compound perforations.

Stamps also are known with perforations different on three or all four sides. Descriptions of such items are clockwise, beginning with the top of the stamp.

A perforation with small holes and teeth close together is a "fine perforation." One with large holes and teeth far apart is a "coarse perforation." Holes that are jagged, rather than clean-cut, are "rough perforations." *Blind perforations* are the slight impressions left by the perforating pins if they fail to puncture the paper. Multiples of stamps showing blind perforations may command a slight premium over normally perforated stamps.

The term *syncopated perfs* describes intentional irregularities in the perforations. The earliest form was used by the Netherlands from 1925-33, where holes were omitted to create distinctive patterns. Beginning in 1992, Great Britain has used an oval perforation to help prevent counterfeiting. Several other countries have started using the oval perfs.

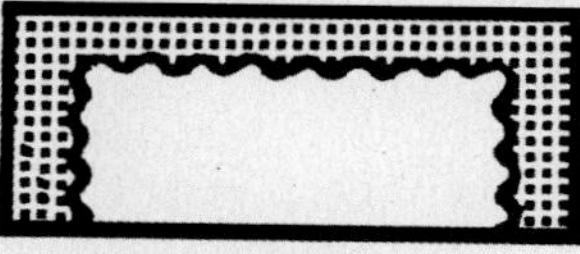

perce en arc

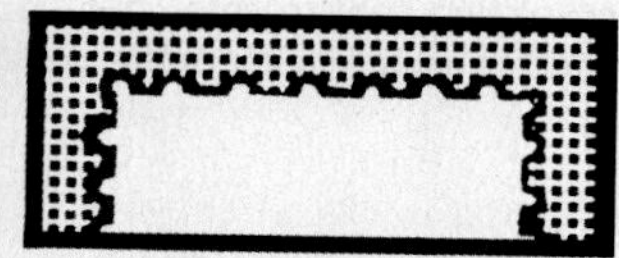

perce en lignes

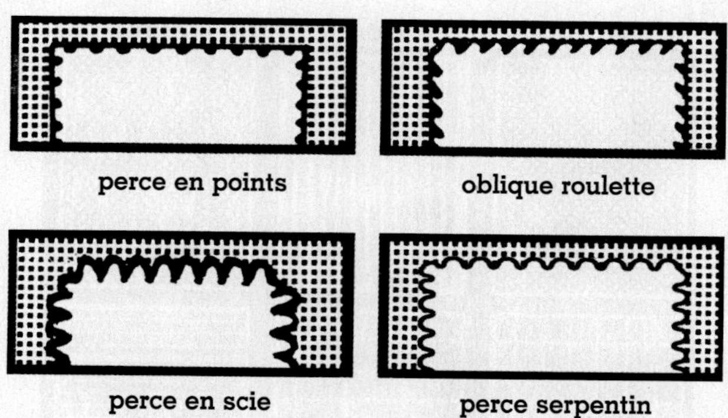

perce en points — oblique roulette — perce en scie — perce serpentin

ROULETTING

In rouletting, the stamp paper is cut partly or wholly through, with no paper removed. In perforating, some paper is removed. Rouletting derives its name from the French roulette, a spur-like wheel. As the wheel is rolled over the paper, each point makes a small cut. The number of cuts made in a two-centimeter space determines the gauge of the roulette, just as the number of perforations in two centimeters determines the gauge of the perforation.

The shape and arrangement of the teeth on the wheels varies. Various roulette types generally carry French names:

Perce en lignes - rouletted in lines. The paper receives short, straight cuts in lines. This is the most common type of rouletting. See Mexico Scott 500.

Perce en points - pin-rouletted. This differs from a small perforation because no paper is removed, although round, equidistant holes are pricked through the paper. See Mexico Scott 242-256.

Perce en arc and perce en scie - pierced in an arc or saw-toothed designs, forming half circles or small triangles. See Hanover (German States) Scott 25-29.

Perce en serpentin - serpentine roulettes. The cuts form a serpentine or wavy line. See Brunswick (German States) Scott 13-18.

Once again, no paper is removed by these processes, leaving the stamps easily separated, but closely attached.

DIE-CUTTING

The third and most recently developed major form of stamp separation is die-cutting. This is a method where a die in the pattern of separation is created that later cuts the stamp paper in a stroke motion. Although some standard stamps bear die-cut perforations, this process is primarily used for modern self-adhesive postage stamps.

Printing Processes

ENGRAVING (Intaglio, Line-engraving, Etching)

Master die - The initial operation in the process of line engraving is making the master die. The die is a small, flat block of softened steel upon which the stamp design is recess engraved in reverse.

Master die

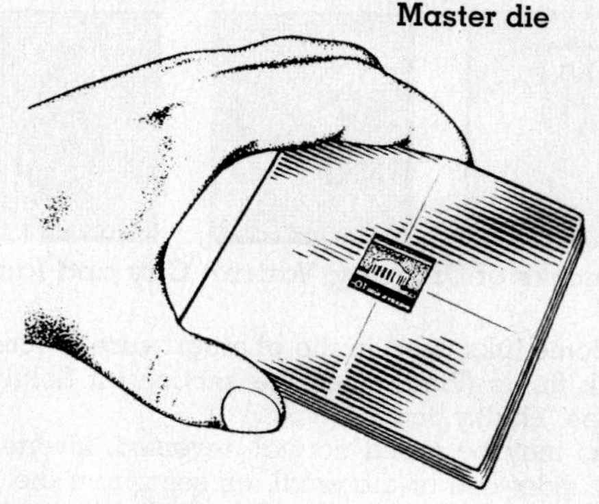

Photographic reduction of the original art is made to the appropriate size. It then serves as a tracing guide for the initial outline of the design. The engraver lightly traces the design on the steel with his graver, then slowly works the design until it is completed. At various points during the engraving process, the engraver hand-inks the die and makes an impression to check his progress. These are known as progressive die proofs. After completion of the engraving, the die is hardened to withstand the stress and pressures of later transfer operations.

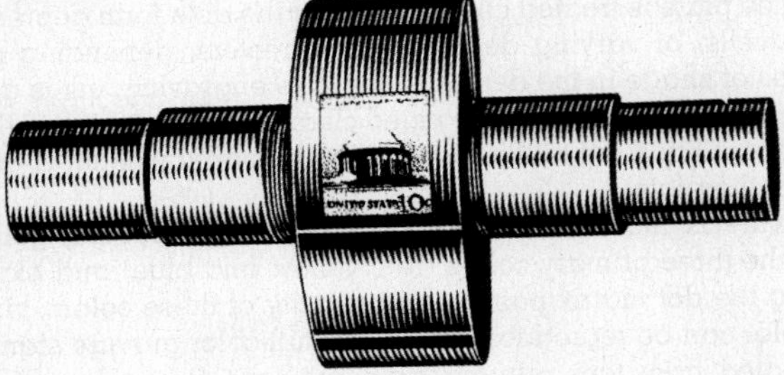
Transfer roll

Transfer roll — Next is production of the transfer roll that, as the name implies, is the medium used to transfer the subject from the master die to the printing plate. A blank roll of soft steel, mounted on a mandrel, is placed under the bearers of the transfer press to allow it to roll freely on its axis. The hardened die is placed on the bed of the press and the face of the transfer roll is applied to the die, under pressure. The bed or the roll is then rocked back and forth under increasing pressure, until the soft steel of the roll is forced into every engraved line of the die. The resulting impression on the roll is known as a "relief" or a "relief transfer." The engraved image is now positive in appearance and stands out from the steel. After the required number of reliefs are "rocked in," the soft steel transfer roll is hardened.

Different flaws may occur during the relief process. A defective relief may occur during the rocking in process because of a minute piece of foreign material lodging on the die, or some other cause. Imperfections in the steel of the transfer roll may result in a breaking away of parts of the design. This is known as a relief break, which will show up on finished stamps as small, unprinted areas. If a damaged relief remains in use, it will transfer a repeating defect to the plate. Deliberate alterations of reliefs sometimes occur. "Altered reliefs" designate these changed conditions.

Plate — The final step in pre-printing production is the making of the printing plate. A flat piece of soft steel replaces the die on the bed of the transfer press. One of the reliefs on the transfer roll is positioned over this soft steel. Position, or layout, dots determine the correct position on the plate. The dots have been lightly marked on the plate in advance. After the correct position of the relief is determined, the design is rocked in by following the same method used in making the transfer roll. The difference is that this time the image is being transferred from the transfer roll, rather than to it. Once the design is entered on the plate, it appears in reverse and is recessed. There are as many transfers entered on the plate as there are subjects printed on the sheet of stamps. It is during this process that double and shifted transfers occur, as well as re-entries. These are the result of improperly entered images that have not been properly burnished out prior to rocking in a new image.

Transferring the design to the plate

Following the entering of the required transfers on the plate, the position dots, layout dots and lines, scratches and other markings generally are burnished out. Added at this time by the siderographer are any required *guide lines, plate numbers* or other *marginal markings*. The plate is then hand-inked and a proof impression is taken. This is known as a plate proof. If the impression is approved, the plate is machined for fitting onto the press, is hardened and sent to the plate vault ready for use.

On press, the plate is inked and the surface is automatically wiped clean, leaving ink only in the recessed lines. Paper is then forced under pressure into the engraved recessed lines, thereby receiving the ink. Thus, the ink lines on engraved stamps are slightly raised, and slight depressions (debossing) occur on the back of the stamp. Prior to the advent of modern high-speed presses and more advanced ink formulations, paper had to be dampened before receiving the ink. This sometimes led to uneven shrinkage by the time the stamps were perforated, resulting in improperly perforated stamps, or misperfs. Newer presses use drier paper, thus both *wet* and *dry printings* exist on some stamps.

Rotary Press — Until 1914, only flat plates were used to print engraved stamps. Rotary press printing was introduced in 1914, and slowly spread. Some countries still use flat-plate printing.

After approval of the plate proof, older *rotary press plates* require additional machining. They are curved to fit the press cylinder. "Gripper slots" are cut into the back of each plate to receive the "grippers," which hold the plate securely on the press. The plate is then hardened. Stamps printed from these bent rotary press plates are longer or wider than the same stamps printed from flat-plate presses. The stretching of the plate during the curving process is what causes this distortion.

Re-entry — To execute a re-entry on a flat plate, the transfer roll is re-applied to the plate, often at some time after its first use on the press. Worn-out designs can be resharpened by carefully burnishing out the original image and re-entering it from the transfer roll. If the original impression has not been sufficiently removed and the transfer roll is not precisely in line with the remaining impression, the resulting double transfer will make the re-entry obvious. If the registration is true, a re-entry may be difficult or impossible to distinguish. Sometimes a stamp printed from a successful re-entry is identified by having a much sharper and clearer impression than its neighbors. With the advent of rotary presses, post-press re-entries were not possible. After a plate was curved for the rotary press, it was impossible to make a re-entry. This is because the plate had already been bent once (with the design distorted).

Double Transfer — This is a description of the condition of a transfer on a plate that shows evidence of a duplication of all, or a portion of the design. It usually is the result of the changing of the registration between the transfer roll and the plate during the rocking in of the original entry. Double transfers also occur when only a portion of the design has been rocked in and improper positioning is noted. If the worker elected not to burnish out the partial or completed design, a strong double transfer will occur for part or all of the design.

It sometimes is necessary to remove the original transfer from a plate and repeat the process a second time. If the finished re-worked image shows traces of the original impression, attributable to incomplete burnishing, the result is a partial double transfer.

Re-engraved — Alterations to a stamp design are sometimes necessary after some stamps have been printed. In some cases, either the original die or the actual printing plate may have its "temper" drawn (softened), and the design will be re-cut. The resulting impressions from such a re-engraved die or plate may differ slightly from the original issue, and are known as "re-engraved." If the alteration was made to the master die, all future printings will be consistently different from the original. If alterations were made to the printing plate, each altered stamp on the plate will be slightly different from each other, allowing specialists to reconstruct a complete printing plate.

Dropped Transfers — If an impression from the transfer roll has not been properly placed, a dropped transfer may occur. The final stamp image will appear obviously out of line with its neighbors.

Short Transfer — Sometimes a transfer roll is not rocked its entire length when entering a transfer onto a plate. As a result, the finished transfer on the plate fails to show the complete design, and the finished stamp will have an incomplete design printed. This is known as a "short transfer." U.S. Scott No. 8 is a good example of a short transfer.

TYPOGRAPHY (Letterpress, Surface Printing, Flexography, Dry Offset, High Etch)

Although the word "Typography" is obsolete as a term describing a printing method, it was the accepted term throughout the first century of postage stamps. Therefore, appropriate Scott listings in this catalogue refer to typographed stamps. The current term for this form of printing, however, is "letterpress."

As it relates to the production of postage stamps, letterpress printing is the reverse of engraving. Rather than having recessed areas trap the ink and deposit it on paper, only the raised areas of the design are inked. This is comparable to the type of printing seen by inking and using an ordinary rubber stamp. Letterpress includes all printing where the design is above the surface area, whether it is wood, metal or, in some instances, hardened rubber or polymer plastic.

For most letterpress-printed stamps, the engraved master is made in much the same manner as for engraved stamps. In this instance, however, an additional step is needed. The design is transferred to another surface before being transferred to the transfer roll. In this way, the transfer roll has a recessed stamp design, rather than one done in relief. This makes the printing areas on the final plate raised, or relief areas.

For less-detailed stamps of the 19th century, the area on the die not used as a printing surface was cut away, leaving the surface area raised. The original die was then reproduced by stereotyping or electrotyping. The resulting electrotypes were assembled in the required number and format of the desired sheet of stamps. The plate used in printing the stamps was an electroplate of these assembled electrotypes.

Once the final letterpress plates are created, ink is applied to the raised surface and the pressure of the press transfers the ink impression to the paper. In contrast to engraving, the fine lines of letterpress are impressed on the surface of the stamp, leaving a debossed surface. When viewed from the back (as on a typewritten page), the corresponding line work on the stamp will be raised slightly (embossed) above the surface.

PHOTOGRAVURE (Gravure, Rotogravure, Heliogravure)

In this process, the basic principles of photography are applied to a chemically sensitized metal plate, rather than photographic paper. The design is transferred photographically to the plate through a halftone, or dot-matrix screen, breaking the reproduction into tiny dots. The plate is treated chemically and the dots form depressions, called cells, of varying depths and diameters, depending on the degrees of shade in the design. Then, like engraving, ink is applied to the plate and the surface is wiped clean. This leaves ink in the tiny cells that is lifted out and deposited on the paper when it is pressed against the plate.

Gravure is most often used for multicolored stamps, generally using the three primary colors (red, yellow and blue) and black. By varying the dot matrix pattern and density of these colors, virtually any color can be reproduced. A typical full-color gravure stamp will be created from four printing cylinders (one for each color). The original multicolored image will have been photographically separated into its component colors.

For examples of the first photogravure stamps printed (1914), see Bavaria Scott 94-114.

LITHOGRAPHY (Offset Lithography, Stone Lithography, Dilitho, Planography, Collotype)

The principle that oil and water do not mix is the basis for lithography. The stamp design is drawn by hand or transferred from engraving to the surface of a lithographic stone or metal plate in a greasy (oily) substance. This oily substance holds the ink, which will later be transferred to the paper. The stone (or plate) is wet with an acid fluid, causing it to repel the printing ink in all areas not covered by the greasy substance.

Transfer paper is used to transfer the design from the original stone or plate. A series of duplicate transfers are grouped and, in turn, transferred to the final printing plate.

Photolithography — The application of photographic processes to lithography. This process allows greater flexibility of design, related to use of halftone screens combined with line work. Unlike photogravure or engraving, this process can allow large, solid areas to be printed.

Offset — A refinement of the lithographic process. A rubber-covered blanket cylinder takes the impression from the inked lithographic plate. From the "blanket" the impression is *offset* or transferred to the paper. Greater flexibility and speed are the principal reasons offset printing has largely displaced lithography. The term "lithography" covers both processes, and results are almost identical.

EMBOSSED (Relief) Printing

Embossing, not considered one of the four main printing types, is a method in which the design first is sunk into the metal of the die. Printing is done against a yielding platen, such as leather or linoleum. The platen is forced into the depression of the die, thus forming the design on the paper in relief. This process is often used for metallic inks.

Embossing may be done without color (see Sardinia Scott 4-6); with color printed around the embossed area (see Great Britain Scott 5 and most U.S. envelopes); and with color in exact registration with the embossed subject.

INK COLORS

Inks or colored papers used in stamp printing often are of mineral origin, although there are numerous examples of organic-based pigments. As a general rule, organic-based pigments are far more subject to varieties and change than those of mineral-based origin.

The appearance of any given color on a stamp may be affected by many aspects, including printing variations, light, color of paper, aging and chemical alterations.

Numerous printing variations may be observed. Heavier pressure or inking will cause a more intense color, while slight interruptions in the ink feed or lighter impressions will cause a lighter appearance. Stamps printed in the same color by water-based and solvent-based inks can differ significantly in appearance. Hand-mixed ink formulas (primarily from the 19th century) produced under different conditions (humidity and temperature) account for notable color variations in early printings of the same stamp (see U.S. Scott 248-250, 279B, for example). Different sources of pigment can also result in significant differences in color.

Light exposure and aging are closely related in the way they affect stamp color. Both eventually break down the ink and fade colors, so that a carefully kept stamp may differ significantly in color from an identical copy that has been exposed to light. If stamps are exposed to light either intentionally or accidentally, their colors can be faded or completely changed in some cases.

Papers of different quality and consistency used for the same stamp printing may affect color appearance. Most pelure papers, for example, show a richer color when compared with wove or laid papers. See Russia Scott 181a, for an example of this effect.

The very nature of the printing processes can cause a variety of differences in shades or hues of the same stamp. Some of these shades are scarcer than others, and are of particular interest to the advanced collector.

Gum

The Illustrated Gum Chart in the first part of this introduction shows and defines various types of gum condition. Because gum condition has an important impact on the value of unused stamps, we recommend studying this chart and the accompanying text carefully.

The gum on the back of a stamp may be shiny, dull, smooth, rough, dark, white, colored or tinted. Most stamp gumming adhesives use gum arabic or dextrine as a base. Certain polymers such as polyvinyl alcohol (PVA) have been used extensively since World War II.

The *Scott Standard Postage Stamp Catalogue* does not list items by types of gum. The *Scott Specialized Catalogue of United States Stamps* does differentiate among some types of gum for certain issues.

Reprints of stamps may have gum differing from the original issues. In addition, some countries have used different gum formulas for different seasons. These adhesives have different properties that may become more apparent over time.

Many stamps have been issued without gum, and the catalogue will note this fact. See, for example, United States Scott 40-47. Sometimes, gum may have been removed to preserve the stamp. Germany Scott B68, for example, has a highly acidic gum that eventually destroys the stamps. This item is valued in the catalogue with gum removed.

Reprints and Reissues

These are impressions of stamps (usually obsolete) made from the original plates or stones. If they are valid for postage and reproduce obsolete issues (such as U.S. Scott 102-111), the stamps are *reissues.* If they are from current issues, they are designated as *second, third,* etc., *printing.* If designated for a particular purpose, they are called *special printings.*

When special printings are not valid for postage, but are made from original dies and plates by authorized persons, they are *official reprints. Private reprints* are made from the original plates and dies by private hands. An example of a private reprint is that of the 1871-1932 reprints made from the original die of the 1845 New Haven, Conn., postmaster's provisional. *Official reproductions* or imitations are made from new dies and plates by government authorization. Scott will list those reissues that are valid for postage if they differ significantly from the original printing.

The U.S. government made special printings of its first postage stamps in 1875. Produced were official imitations of the first two stamps (listed as Scott 3-4), reprints of the demonetized pre-1861 issues (Scott 40-47) and reissues of the 1861 stamps, the 1869 stamps and the then-current 1875 denominations. Even though the official imitations and the reprints were not valid for postage, Scott lists all of these U.S. special printings.

Most reprints or reissues differ slightly from the original stamp in some characteristic, such as gum, paper, perforation, color or watermark. Sometimes the details are followed so meticulously that only a student of that specific stamp is able to distinguish the reprint or reissue from the original.

Remainders and Canceled to Order

Some countries sell their stock of old stamps when a new issue replaces them. To avoid postal use, the *remainders* usually are canceled with a punch hole, a heavy line or bar, or a more-or-less regular-looking cancellation. The most famous merchant of remainders was Nicholas F. Seebeck. In the 1880s and 1890s, he arranged printing contracts between the Hamilton Bank Note Co., of which he was a director, and several Central and South American countries. The contracts provided that the plates and all remainders of the yearly issues became the property of Hamilton. Seebeck saw to it that ample stock remained. The "Seebecks," both remainders and reprints, were standard packet fillers for decades.

Some countries also issue stamps *canceled-to-order (CTO),* either in sheets with original gum or stuck onto pieces of paper or envelopes and canceled. Such CTO items generally are worth less than postally used stamps. In cases where the CTO material is far more prevalent in the marketplace than postally used examples, the catalogue value relates to the CTO examples, with postally used examples noted as premium items. Most CTOs can be detected by the presence of gum. However, as the CTO practice goes back at least to 1885, the gum inevitably has been soaked off some stamps so they could pass as postally used. The normally applied postmarks usually differ slightly from standard postmarks, and specialists are able to tell the difference. When applied individually to envelopes by philatelically minded persons, CTO material is known as *favor canceled* and generally sells at large discounts.

Cinderellas and Facsimiles

Cinderella is a catch-all term used by stamp collectors to describe phantoms, fantasies, bogus items, municipal issues, exhibition seals, local revenues, transportation stamps, labels, poster stamps and many other types of items. Some cinderella collectors include in their collections local postage issues, telegraph stamps, essays and proofs, forgeries and counterfeits.

A *fantasy* is an adhesive created for a nonexistent stamp-issuing authority. Fantasy items range from imaginary countries (Occusi-Ambeno, Kingdom of Sedang, Principality of Trinidad or Torres Straits), to non-existent locals (Winans City Post), or nonexistent transportation lines (McRobish & Co.'s Acapulco-San Francisco Line).

On the other hand, if the entity exists and could have issued stamps (but did not) or was known to have issued other stamps, the items are considered *bogus* stamps. These would include the Mormon postage stamps of Utah, S. Allan Taylor's Guatemala and Paraguay inventions, the propaganda issues for the South Moluccas and the adhesives of the Page & Keyes local post of Boston.

Phantoms is another term for both fantasy and bogus issues.

Facsimiles are copies or imitations made to represent original stamps, but which do not pretend to be originals. A catalogue illustration is such a facsimile. Illustrations from the Moens catalogue of the 19th century were occasionally colored and passed off as stamps. Since the beginning of stamp collecting, facsimiles have been made for collectors as space fillers or for reference. They often carry the word "facsimile," "falsch" (German), "sanko" or "mozo" (Japanese), or "faux" (French) overprinted on the face or stamped on the back. Unfortunately, over the years a number of these items have had fake cancels applied over the facsimile notation and have been passed off as genuine.

Forgeries and Counterfeits

Forgeries and counterfeits have been with philately virtually from the beginning of stamp production. Over time, the terminology for the two has been used interchangeably. Although both forgeries and counterfeits are reproductions of stamps, the purposes behind their creation differ considerably.

Among specialists there is an increasing movement to more specifically define such items. Although there is no universally accepted terminology, we feel the following definitions most closely mirror the items and their purposes as they are currently defined.

Forgeries (also often referred to as *Counterfeits*) are reproductions of genuine stamps that have been created to defraud collectors. Such spurious items first appeared on the market around 1860, and most old-time collections contain one or more. Many are crude and easily spotted, but some can deceive experts.

An important supplier of these early philatelic forgeries was the Hamburg printer Gebruder Spiro. Many others with reputations in this craft included S. Allan Taylor, George Hussey, James Chute, George Forune, Benjamin & Sarpy, Julius Goldner, E. Oneglia and L.H. Mercier. Among the noted 20th-century forgers were Francois Fournier, Jean Sperati and the prolific Raoul DeThuin.

Forgeries may be complete replications, or they may be genuine stamps altered to resemble a scarcer (and more valuable) type. Most forgeries, particularly those of rare stamps, are worth only a small fraction of the value of a genuine example, but a few types, created by some of the most notable forgers, such as Sperati, can be worth as much or more than the genuine. Fraudulently produced copies are known of most classic rarities and many medium-priced stamps.

In addition to rare stamps, large numbers of common 19th- and early 20th-century stamps were forged to supply stamps to the early packet trade. Many can still be easily found. Few new philatelic forgeries have appeared in recent decades. Successful imitation of well-engraved work is virtually impossible. It has proven far easier to produce a fake by altering a genuine stamp than to duplicate a stamp completely.

Counterfeit (also often referred to as *Postal Counterfeit* or *Postal Forgery*) is the term generally applied to reproductions of stamps that have been created to defraud the government of revenue. Such items usually are created at the time a stamp is current and, in some cases, are hard to detect. Because most counterfeits are seized when the perpetrator is captured, postal counterfeits, particularly used on cover, are usually worth much more than a genuine example to specialists. The first postal counterfeit was of Spain's 4-cuarto carmine of 1854 (the real one is Scott 25). Apparently, the counterfeiters were not satisfied with their first version, which is now very scarce, and they soon created an engraved counterfeit, which is common. Postal counterfeits quickly followed in Austria, Naples, Sardinia and the Roman States. They have since been created in many other countries as well, including the United States.

An infamous counterfeit to defraud the government is the 1-shilling Great Britain "Stock Exchange" forgery of 1872, used on telegraph forms at the exchange that year. The stamp escaped detection until a stamp dealer noticed it in 1898.

Fakes

Fakes are genuine stamps altered in some way to make them more desirable. One student of this part of stamp collecting has estimated that by the 1950s more than 30,000 varieties of fakes were known. That number has grown greatly since then. The widespread existence of fakes makes it important for stamp collectors to study their philatelic holdings and use relevant literature. Likewise, collectors should buy from reputable dealers who guarantee their stamps and make full and prompt refunds should a purchased item be declared faked or altered by some mutually agreed-upon authority. Because fakes always have some genuine characteristics, it is not always possible to obtain unanimous agreement among experts regarding specific items. These students may change their opinions as philatelic knowledge increases. More than 80 percent of all fakes on the philatelic market today are regummed, reperforated (or perforated for the first time), or bear forged overprints, surcharges or cancellations.

Stamps can be chemically treated to alter or eliminate colors. For example, a pale rose stamp can be re-colored to resemble a blue shade of high market value. In other cases, treated stamps can be made to resemble missing color varieties. Designs may be changed by painting, or a stroke or a dot added or bleached out to turn an ordinary variety into a seemingly scarcer stamp. Part of a stamp can be bleached and reprinted in a different version, achieving an inverted center or frame. Margins can be added or repairs done so deceptively that the stamps move from the "repaired" into the "fake" category.

Fakers have not left the backs of the stamps untouched either. They may create false watermarks, add fake grills or press out genuine grills. A thin India paper proof may be glued onto a thicker backing to create the appearance an issued stamp, or a proof printed on cardboard may be shaved down and perforated to resemble a stamp. Silk threads are impressed into paper and stamps have been split so that a rare paper variety is added to an otherwise inexpensive stamp. The most common treatment to the back of a stamp, however, is regumming.

Some in the business of faking stamps have openly advertised fool-proof application of "original gum" to stamps that lack it, although most publications now ban such ads from their pages. It is believed that very few early stamps have survived without being hinged. The large number of never-hinged examples of such earlier material offered for sale thus suggests the widespread extent of regumming activity. Regumming also may be used to hide repairs or thin spots. Dipping the stamp into watermark fluid, or examining it under longwave ultraviolet light often will reveal these flaws.

Fakers also tamper with separations. Ingenious ways to add margins are known. Perforated wide-margin stamps may be falsely represented as imperforate when trimmed. Reperforating is commonly done to create scarce coil or perforation varieties, and to eliminate the naturally occurring straight-edge stamps found in sheet margin positions of many earlier issues. Custom has made straight-edged stamps less desirable. Fakers have obliged by perforating straight-edged stamps so that many are now uncommon, if not rare.

Another fertile field for the faker is that of overprints, surcharges and cancellations. The forging of rare surcharges or overprints began in the 1880s or 1890s. These forgeries are sometimes difficult to detect, but experts have identified almost all. Occasionally, overprints or cancellations are removed to create non-overprinted stamps or seemingly unused items. This is most commonly done by removing a manuscript cancel to make a stamp resemble an unused example. "SPECIMEN" overprints may be removed by scraping and repainting to create non-overprinted varieties. Fakers use inexpensive revenues or pen-canceled stamps to generate unused stamps for further faking by adding other markings. The quartz lamp or UV lamp and a high-powered magnifying glass help to easily detect removed cancellations.

The bigger problem, however, is the addition of overprints, surcharges or cancellations - many with such precision that they are very difficult to ascertain. Plating of the stamps or the overprint can be an important method of detection.

Fake postmarks may range from many spurious fancy cancellations to a host of markings applied to transatlantic covers, to adding normally appearing postmarks to definitives of some countries with stamps that are valued far higher used than unused. With the increased popularity of cover collecting, and the widespread interest in postal history, a fertile new field for fakers has come about. Some have tried to create entire covers. Others specialize in adding stamps, tied by fake cancellations, to genuine stampless covers, or replacing less expensive or damaged stamps with more valuable ones. Detailed study of postal rates in effect at the time a cover in question was mailed, including the analysis of each handstamp used during the period, ink analysis and similar techniques, usually will unmask the fraud.

Restoration and Repairs

Scott Publishing Co. bases its catalogue values on stamps that are free of defects and otherwise meet the standards set forth earlier in this introduction. Most stamp collectors desire to have the finest copy of an item possible. Even within given grading categories there are variances. This leads to a controversial practice that is not defined in any universal manner: stamp *restoration*.

There are broad differences of opinion about what is permissible when it comes to restoration. Carefully applying a soft eraser to a stamp or cover to remove light soiling is one form of restoration, as is washing a stamp in mild soap and water to clean it. These are fairly accepted forms of restoration. More severe forms of restoration include pressing out creases or removing stains caused by tape. To what degree each of these is acceptable is dependent upon the individual situation. Further along the spectrum is the freshening of a stamp's color by removing oxide build-up or the effects of wax paper left next to stamps shipped to the tropics.

At some point in this spectrum the concept of *repair* replaces that of restoration. Repairs include filling thin spots, mending tears by reweaving or adding a missing perforation tooth. Regumming stamps may have been acceptable as a restoration or repair technique many decades ago, but today it is considered a form of fakery.

Restored stamps may or may not sell at a discount, and it is possible that the value of individual restored items may be enhanced over that of their pre-restoration state. Specific situations dictate the resultant value of such an item. Repaired stamps sell at substantial discounts from the value of sound stamps.

When the purchaser of an item has any reason to suspect that an item has been repaired, and the detection of such a repair is beyond his own ability, he should seek expert advice. There are services that specialize in giving such advice.

Terminology

Booklets — Many countries have issued stamps in small booklets for the convenience of users. This idea continues to become increasingly popular in many countries. Booklets have been issued in many sizes and forms, often with advertising on the covers, the panes of stamps or on the interleaving.

The panes used in booklets may be printed from special plates or made from regular sheets. All panes from booklets issued by the United States and many from those of other countries contain stamps that are straight edged on the sides, but perforated between. Others are distinguished by orientation of watermark or other identifying features. Any stamp-like unit in the pane, either printed or blank, that is not a postage stamp is considered to be a *label* in the catalogue listings.

Scott lists and values booklet panes only. Complete booklets are listed and valued in only a few cases, such as Grenada Scott 1055 and some forms of British prestige booklets. Individual booklet panes are listed only when they are not fashioned from existing sheet stamps and, therefore, are identifiable from their sheet stamp counterparts.

Panes usually do not have a used value assigned to them because there is little market activity for used booklet panes, even though many exist used and there is some demand for them.

Cancellations — The marks or obliterations put on stamps by postal authorities to show that they have performed service and to prevent their reuse are known as cancellations. If the marking is made with a pen, it is considered a "pen cancel." When the location of the post office appears in the marking, it is a "town cancellation." A "postmark" is technically any postal marking, but in practice the term generally is applied to a town cancellation with a date. When calling attention to a cause or celebration, the marking is known as a "slogan cancellation." Many other types and styles of cancellations exist, such as duplex, numerals, targets, fancy and others. See also "precancels," below.

Coil Stamps — These are stamps that are issued in rolls for use in dispensers, affixing and vending machines. Those coils of the United States, Canada, Sweden and some other countries are perforated horizontally or vertically only, with the outer edges imperforate. Coil stamps of some countries, such as Great Britain and Germany, are perforated on all four sides and may in some cases be distinguished from their sheet stamp counterparts by watermarks, counting numbers on the reverse or other means.

Errors — Stamps that have some major, consistent, unintentional deviation from the normal are considered errors. Errors include, but are not limited to, missing or wrong colors, wrong paper, wrong watermarks, inverted centers or frames on multicolor printing, inverted or missing surcharges or overprints, double impressions, missing perforations and others. Factually wrong or misspelled information, if it appears on all examples of a stamp, are not considered errors in the true sense of the word. They are errors of design. Inconsistent or randomly appearing items, such as misperfs or color shifts, are classified as freaks.

Overprints and Surcharges — Overprinting involves applying wording or design elements over an already existing stamp. Overprints can be used to alter the place of use (such as "Canal Zone" on U.S. stamps), to adapt them for a special purpose ("Porto" on Denmark's 1913-20 regular issues for use as postage due stamps, Scott J1-J7) or to commemorate a special occasion (United States Scott 647-648).

A *surcharge* is a form of overprint that changes or restates the face value of a stamp or piece of postal stationery.

Surcharges and overprints may be handstamped, typeset or, occasionally, lithographed or engraved. A few hand-written overprints and surcharges are known. The world's first surcharge was a handstamped "2" on the United States City Despatch Post stamps of 1846.

Precancels — Stamps that are canceled before they are placed in the mail are known as precancels. Precanceling usually is done to expedite the handling of large mailings and generally allow the affected mail pieces to skip certain phases of mail handling.

In the United States, precancellations generally identified the point of origin; that is, the city and state. This information appeared across the face of the stamp, usually centered between parallel lines. More recently, bureau precancels retained the parallel lines, but the city and state designations were dropped. Recent coils have a service inscription that is present on the original printing plate. These show the mail service paid for by the stamp. Since these stamps are not intended to receive further cancellations when used as intended, they are considered precancels. Such items often do not have parallel lines as part of the precancellation.

In France, the abbreviation *Affranchts* in a semicircle together with the word *Postes* is the general form of precancel in use. Belgian precancellations usually appear in a box in which the name of the city appears. Netherlands precancels have the name of the city enclosed between concentric circles, sometimes called a "lifesaver." Precancellations of other countries usually follow these patterns, but may be any arrangement of bars, boxes and city names.

Precancels are listed in the Scott catalogues only if the precancel changes the denomination (Belgium Scott 477-478); if the precanceled stamp is different from the non-precanceled version (such as untagged U.S. precancels); or if the stamp exists only precanceled (France Scott 1096-1099, U.S. Scott 2265).

Proofs and Essays — Proofs are impressions taken from an approved die, plate or stone in which the design and color are the same as the stamp issued to the public. Trial color proofs are impressions taken from approved dies, plates or stones in colors that vary from the final version. An essay is the impression of a design that differs in some way from the issued stamp. "Progressive die proofs" generally are considered to be essays.

Provisionals — These are stamps that are issued on short notice and intended for temporary use pending the arrival of regular issues. They usually are issued to meet such contingencies as changes in government or currency, shortage of necessary postage values or military occupation.

During the 1840s, postmasters in certain American cities issued stamps that were valid only at specific post offices. In 1861, postmasters of the Confederate States also issued stamps with limited validity. Both of these examples are known as "postmaster's provisionals."

Se-tenant — This term refers to an unsevered pair, strip or block of stamps that differ in design, denomination or overprint.

Unless the se-tenant item has a continuous design (see U.S. Scott 1451a, 1694a) the stamps do not have to be in the same order as shown in the catalogue (see U.S. Scott 2158a).

Specimens — The Universal Postal Union required member nations to send samples of all stamps they released into service to the International Bureau in Switzerland. Member nations of the UPU received these specimens as samples of what stamps were valid for postage. Many are overprinted, handstamped or initial-perforated "Specimen," "Canceled" or "Muestra." Some are marked with bars across the denominations (China-Taiwan), punched holes (Czechoslovakia) or back inscriptions (Mongolia).

Stamps distributed to government officials or for publicity purposes, and stamps submitted by private security printers for official approval, also may receive such defacements.

The previously described defacement markings prevent postal use, and all such items generally are known as "specimens."

Tete Beche — This term describes a pair of stamps in which one is upside down in relation to the other. Some of these are the result of intentional sheet arrangements, such as Morocco Scott B10-B11. Others occurred when one or more electrotypes accidentally were placed upside down on the plate, such as Colombia Scott 57a. Separation of the tete-beche stamps, of course, destroys the tete beche variety.

British Colonial and Crown Agents Watermarks

Watermarks 1 to 4, 314, 373, and 384, common to many British territories, are illustrated here to avoid duplication.

The letters "CC" of Wmk. 1 identify the paper as having been made for the use of the Crown Colonies, while the letters "CA" of the others stand for "Crown Agents." Both Wmks. 1 and 2 were used on stamps printed by De La Rue & Co.

Wmk. 3 was adopted in 1904; Wmk. 4 in 1921; Wmk. 46 in 1879; Wmk. 314 in 1957; Wmk. 373 in 1974; and Wmk. 384 in 1985.

In Wmk. 4a, a non-matching crown of the general St. Edwards type (bulging on both sides at top) was substituted for one of the Wmk. 4 crowns which fell off the dandy roll. The non-matching crown occurs in 1950-52 printings in a horizontal row of crowns on certain regular stamps of Johore and Seychelles, and on various postage due stamps of Barbados, Basutoland, British Guiana, Gold Coast, Grenada, Northern Rhodesia, St. Lucia, Swaziland and Trinidad and Tobago. A variation of Wmk. 4a, with the non-matching crown in a horizontal row of crown-CA-crown, occurs on regular stamps of Bahamas, St. Kitts-Nevis and Singapore.

Wmk. 314 was intentionally used sideways, starting in 1966. When a stamp was issued with Wmk. 314 both upright and sideways, the sideways varieties usually are listed also – with minor numbers. In many of the later issues, Wmk. 314 is slightly visible.

Wmk. 373 is usually only faintly visible.

Wmk. 1
Crown and C C

Wmk. 2
Crown and C A

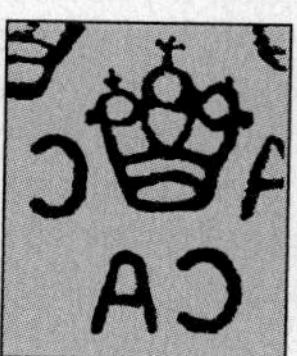

Wmk. 3
Multiple Crown and C A

Wmk. 4
Multiple Crown and Script C A

Wmk. 4a

Wmk. 46

Wmk. 314
St. Edward's Crown and C A Multiple

Wmk. 373

Wmk. 384

Dies of British Colonial Stamps

DIE A:
1. The lines in the groundwork vary in thickness and are not uniformly straight.
2. The seventh and eighth lines from the top, in the groundwork, converge where they meet the head.
3. There is a small dash in the upper part of the second jewel in the band of the crown.
4. The vertical color line in front of the throat stops at the sixth line of shading on the neck.

DIE B:
1. The lines in the groundwork are all thin and straight.
2. All the lines of the background are parallel.
3. There is no dash in the upper part of the second jewel in the band of the crown.
4. The vertical color line in front of the throat stops at the eighth line of shading on the neck.

DIE I:
1. The base of the crown is well below the level of the inner white line around the vignette.
2. The labels inscribed "POSTAGE" and "REVENUE" are cut square at the top.
3. There is a white "bud" on the outer side of the main stem of the curved ornaments in each lower corner.
4. The second (thick) line below the country name has the ends next to the crown cut diagonally.

DIE Ia.
1 as die II.
2 and 3 as die I.

DIE Ib.
1 and 3 as die II.
2 as die I.

DIE II:
1. The base of the crown is aligned with the underside of the white line around the vignette.
2. The labels curve inward at the top inner corners.
3. The "bud" has been removed from the outer curve of the ornaments in each corner.
4. The second line below the country name has the ends next to the crown cut vertically.

Crowned Circle Handstamps and Great Britain Stamps Used Abroad

Crowned Circle Handstamps

Prior to the introduction of postage stamps in a number of British colonies, British postal authorities furnished post offices in these colonies with crowned circle handstamps. Crowned circle handstamps also were issued to a number of British post offices in foreign countries. These handstamps were to be used on mail sent to foreign countries or on mail between two foreign ports. The postage paid by the sender was to be noted in manuscript on the cover.

Crowned circle handstamps from the colonies of British America are listed. Similar handstamps were also furnished to post offices in British possessions outside of British America, such as New Zealand, Lagos and the Ionian Islands; areas where Britain maintained consular offices, such as Cairo, Egypt; and British Postal Agency offices, such as Rio de Janeiro, Brazil and San Juan, Puerto Rico. These items are not listed at this time, but such expansion is planned for future editions.

Some of these handstamps were used for various purposes after the advent of postage stamps. Values are for covers with clearly legible handstamps, produced prior to the advent of the colony's stamps. The color of the handstamp is black unless otherwise noted.

Types of Crowned Circle Handstamps

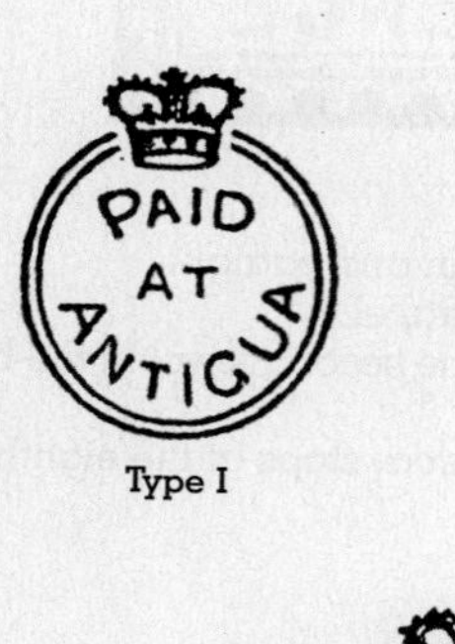

Type I

Type II

Type III

Type IV

Type V

Type VI

Type VII

Type VIII

Type IX

Great Britain Stamps Used Abroad

In some British colonies, postage stamps of Great Britain were used prior to the introduction of the colony's own postage stamps. Special cancels, most of which show an alphanumeric code, were furnished to the postmasters in these colonies to be used on these Great Britain stamps. Cancels and Great Britain stamps were furnished to colonies outside of the British America area as well as to British consular offices and British Postal Agency offices, but only the obliterators of British colonies in British America are listed at this time.

Cancel numbers assigned and used by post offices in the British American colonies were numbered A01-A15, A18, A27-A37, A39-A49, A51-A62 and A64-A78. A typical example of these cancels is shown below. Similar cancels with different alphanumeric codes, not listed in this catalogue, were assigned to the other colonies, consular offices and Postal Agency offices, as were cancels that are not similar in appearance.

The values quoted are for very fine off cover examples of the Great Britain stamps specified in parentheses in the listing with a legible and clearly identifiable alphanumeric combination. Such examples on cover sell for more.

These listings generally are limited to off cover stamps only. Other stamps that may have been sent to these offices may exist on covers that bear these cancels, but the cancel may not be on the stamp. Such items would need to be collected as complete covers.

Any valid Great Britain stamp brought to these colonies prior to the introduction of the colony's own postage stamps would have received these cancels if properly posted, but in virtually all instances the Great Britain stamps specified in these listings are those that were sent to these colonies by British postal officals during the years noted in the listings.

These canceling devices were returned to Great Britain and put to use there, so some of these cancels may be found on other Great Britain stamps from later periods.

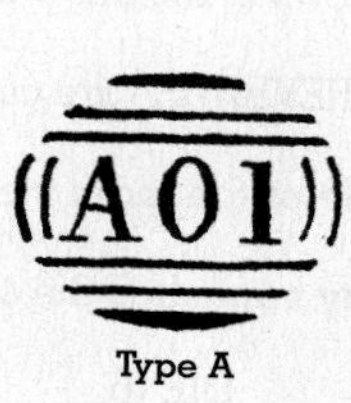

Type A

Type B

For a list of Crowned Circle handstamps and Great Britain stamps used abroad, see end of Index and Identifier.

The British Commonwealth of Nations

Dominions, Colonies, Territories, Offices and Independent Members

Comprising stamps of the British Commonwealth and associated nations.

1. Great Britain

Great Britain: Including England, Scotland, Wales and Northern Ireland.

2. The Dominions, Present and Past

AUSTRALIA

The Commonwealth of Australia was proclaimed on January 1, 1901. It consists of six former colonies as follows:

New South Wales
Queensland
South Australia
Victoria
Tasmania
Western Australia

Territories belonging to, or administered by Australia: Nauru, New Guinea, Papua.

CANADA

The Dominion of Canada was created by the British North America Act in 1867. The following provinces were former sepa- rate colonies and issued postage stamps:

British Columbia and Vancouver Island
New Brunswick
Newfoundland
Nova Scotia
Prince Edward Island

INDIA

The Republic of India was inaugurated on January 26, 1950. It succeeded the Dominion of India which was proclaimed August 15, 1947, when the former Empire of India was divided into Pakistan and the Union of India. The Republic is composed of about 40 predominantly Hindu states of three classes: governor's provinces, chief commissioner's provinces and princely states. India also has various territories, such as the Andaman and Nicobar Islands.

The old Empire of India was a federation of British India and the native states. The more important princely states were autonomous. Of the more than 700 Indian states, these 43 are familiar names to philatelists because of their postage stamps.

CONVENTION STATES

Chamba
Faridkot
Gwalior
Jhind
Nabha
Patiala

NATIVE FEUDATORY STATES

Alwar
Bamra
Barwani
Bhopal
Bhor
Bijawar
Bundi
Bussahir
Charkhari
Cochin
Dhar
Dungarpur
Duttia
Faridkot (1879-86)
Hyderabad
Idar
Indore
Jaipur
Jammu
Jammu and Kashmir
Jasdan
Jhalawar
Jind (1875-76)
Kashmir
Kishangarh
Kotah
Las Bela
Morvi
Nandgaon
Nowanuggur
Orchha
Poonch
Rajasthan
Rajpeepla
Sirmoor
Soruth
Tonk
Travancore
Wadhwan

NEW ZEALAND

Became a dominion on September 26, 1907. The following islands and territories are, or have been, administered by New Zealand:

Aitutaki
Cook Islands (Rarotonga)
Niue
Penrhyn
Samoa (Western Samoa)

SOUTH AFRICA

Under the terms of the South African Act (1909) the self-governing colonies of Cape of Good Hope, Natal, Orange River Colony and Transvaal united on May 31, 1910, to form the Union of South Africa. It became an independent republic May 3, 1961.

Under the terms of the Treaty of Versailles, South-West Africa, formerly German South-West Africa, was mandated to the Union of South Africa.

3. Colonies, Past and Present; ControlledTerritory and Independent Members of the Commonwealth

Aden
Antigua
Ascension
Bahamas
Bahrain
Barbados
Barbuda
Basutoland
Batum
Bechuanaland
Bechuanaland Prot.
Bermuda
British Central Africa
British East Africa
British Guiana
British Honduras
British New Guinea
British Solomon Islands
British Somaliland
Brunei
Bushire
Cameroons
Cape of Good Hope
Cayman Islands
Ceylon
Crete, British Administration
Cyprus
Dominica
East Africa & Uganda Protectorates
Egypt
Falkland Islands
Fiji
Gambia
German East Africa
Gibraltar
Gilbert & Ellice Islands
Gold Coast
Grenada
Griqualand West
Heligoland
Hong Kong
Ionian Islands
Jamaica
Kenya, Uganda & Tanzania
Kuwait
Labuan
Lagos
Leeward Islands
Madagascar
Malaya
Federated Malay States
Johore
Kedah
Kelantan
Negri Sembilan
Pahang
Perak
Selangor
Sungei Ujong
Trengganu
Maldive Islands
Malta
Mauritius
Mesopotamia
Montserrat
Natal
Nevis
New Britain
New Hebrides
Niger Coast Protectorate
Nigeria
North Borneo
Northern Nigeria
Northern Rhodesia
North West Pacific Islands
Nyasaland Protectorate
Orange River Colony
Palestine
Pitcairn Islands
Rhodesia
St. Christopher
St. Helena
St. Kitts-Nevis-Anguilla
St. Lucia
St. Vincent
Samoa
Sarawak
Seychelles
Sierra Leone
Solomon Islands
Somaliland Protectorate
Southern Nigeria
Southern Rhodesia
Straits Settlements
Sudan
Swaziland
Tanganyika
Tasmania
Tobago
Togo
Tonga
Transvaal
Trinidad
Trinidad and Tobago
Turks and Caicos
Turks Islands
Uganda
Virgin Islands
Zanzibar
Zululand

POST OFFICES IN FOREIGN COUNTRIES

Africa
East Africa Forces
Middle East Forces
Bangkok
China
Morocco
Turkish Empire

Colonies, Former Colonies, Offices, Territories Controlled by Parent States

Belgium

Belgian Congo
Ruanda-Urundi

Denmark

Danish West Indies
Faroe Islands
Greenland
Iceland

France

COLONIES PAST AND PRESENT, CONTROLLED TERRITORIES

Alaouites
Alexandretta
Algeria
Alsace & Lorraine
Anjouan
Annam & Tonkin
Benin
Cameroun
Castellorizo
Chad
Cilicia
Cochin China
Dahomey
Diego Suarez
Djibouti (Somali Coast)
French Congo
French Equatorial Africa
French Guiana
French Guinea
French India
French Morocco
French Sudan
Gabon
Grand Comoro
Guadeloupe
Indo-China
Inini
Ivory Coast
Latakia
Lebanon
Madagascar
Martinique
Mauritania
Mayotte
Memel
Middle Congo
Moheli
New Caledonia
New Hebrides
Niger Territory
Nossi-Be
Obock
Oceania (French Polynesia)
Reunion
Rouad, Ile
Ste.-Marie de Madagascar
St. Pierre & Miquelon
Senegal
Senegambia & Niger
Somali Coast
Syria
Tahiti
Togo
Tunisia
Ubangi-Shari
Upper Senegal & Niger
Upper Volta
Wallis & Futuna Islands

POST OFFICES IN FOREIGN COUNTRIES

China
Crete
Egypt
Turkish Empire
Zanzibar

Germany

EARLY STATES

Baden
Bavaria
Bergedorf
Bremen
Brunswick
Hamburg
Hanover
Lubeck
Mecklenburg-Schwerin
Mecklenburg-Strelitz
Oldenburg
Prussia
Saxony
Schleswig-Holstein
Wurttemberg

FORMER COLONIES

Cameroun (Kamerun)
Caroline Islands
German East Africa
German New Guinea
German South-West Africa
Kiauchau
Mariana Islands
Marshall Islands
Samoa
Togo

Italy

EARLY STATES

Modena
Parma
Romagna
Roman States
Sardinia
Tuscany
Two Sicilies
  Naples
  Neapolitan Provinces
  Sicily

FORMER COLONIES, CONTROLLED TERRITORIES, OCCUPATION AREAS

Aegean Islands
  Calimno (Calino)
  Caso
  Cos (Coo)
  Karki (Carchi)
  Leros (Lero)
  Lipso
  Nisiros (Nisiro)
  Patmos (Patmo)
  Piscopi
  Rodi (Rhodes)
  Scarpanto
  Simi
  Stampalia
Castellorizo
Corfu
Cyrenaica
Eritrea
Ethiopia (Abyssinia)
Fiume
Italian East Africa
Libya
Oltre Giuba
Saseno
Somalia (Italian Somaliland)
Tripolitania

POST OFFICES IN FOREIGN COUNTRIES "ESTERO"*

Austria
Bengasi
China
  Peking
  Tientsin
Crete
Tripoli
Turkish Empire
  Constantinople
  Durazzo
  Janina
  Jerusalem
  Salonika
  Scutari
  Smyrna
  Valona

*Stamps overprinted "ESTERO" were used in various parts of the world.

Netherlands

Netherlands Antilles
  (Curacao)
Netherlands Indies
Netherlands New Guinea
Surinam (Dutch Guiana)

Portugal

COLONIES PAST AND PRESENT, CONTROLLED TERRITORIES

Angola
Angra
Azores
Cape Verde
Funchal
Horta
Inhambane
Kionga
Lourenco Marques
Macao
Madeira
Mozambique
Mozambique Co.
Nyassa
Ponta Delgada
Portuguese Africa
Portuguese Congo
Portuguese Guinea
Portuguese India
Quelimane
St. Thomas & Prince Islands
Tete
Timor
Zambezia

Russia

ALLIED TERRITORIES AND REPUBLICS, OCCUPATION AREAS

Armenia
Aunus (Olonets)
Azerbaijan
Batum
Estonia
Far Eastern Republic
Georgia
Karelia
Latvia
Lithuania
North Ingermanland
Ostland
Russian Turkestan
Siberia
South Russia
Tannu Tuva
Transcaucasian Fed.
Republics
Ukraine
Wenden (Livonia)
Western Ukraine

Spain

COLONIES PAST AND PRESENT, CONTROLLED TERRITORIES

Aguera, La
Cape Juby
Cuba
Elobey, Annobon & Corisco
Fernando Po
Mariana Islands
Philippines
Puerto Rico
Rio de Oro
Spanish Guinea
Spanish Morocco
Spanish Sahara

POST OFFICES IN FOREIGN COUNTRIES

Morocco
Tangier
Tetuan

COMMON DESIGN TYPE

PORTUGAL & COLONIES

Pictured in this section are issues where one illustration has been used for a number of countries in the Catalogue. Not included in this section are overprinted stamps or those issues which are illustrated in each country.

Vasco da Gama

Fleet Departing CD20

Fleet Arriving at Calicut — CD21

Embarking at Rastello CD22

Muse of History CD23

San Gabriel, da Gama and Camoens CD24

Archangel Gabriel, the Patron Saint — CD25

Flagship San Gabriel — CD26

Vasco da Gama — CD27

Fourth centenary of Vasco da Gama's discovery of the route to India.

1898

Azores 93-100
Macao.......................................67-74
Madeira.....................................37-44
Portugal 147-154
Port. Africa 1-8
Port. Congo 75-98
Port. India 189-196
St. Thomas & Prince Islands ...170-193
Timor 45-52

Nos. 93-100 (8)	122.00	76.25
Nos. 67-74 (8)	136.00	96.75
Nos. 37-44 (8)	44.55	34.00
Nos. 147-154 (8)	169.30	43.45
Nos. 1-8 (8)	24.75	21.70
Nos. 75-98 (24)	50.50	34.45
Nos. 189-196 (8)	20.25	12.95

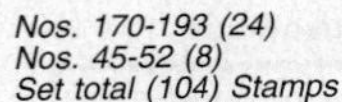

Nos. 170-193 (24)	38.75	34.30
Nos. 45-52 (8)	19.50	8.75
Set total (104) Stamps	625.60	362.60

Pombal
POSTAL TAX
POSTAL TAX DUES

Marquis de Pombal — CD28

Planning Reconstruction of Lisbon, 1755 — CD29

Pombal Monument, Lisbon — CD30

Sebastiao Jose de Carvalho e Mello, Marquis de Pombal (1699-1782), statesman, rebuilt Lisbon after earthquake of 1755. Tax was for the erection of Pombal monument. Obligatory on all mail on certain days throughout the year.

Postal Tax Dues are inscribed 'Multa'

1925

Angola RA1-RA3, RAJ1-RAJ3
Azores RA9-RA11, RAJ2-RAJ4
Cape Verde RA1-RA3, RAJ1-RAJ3
Macao.............. RA1-RA3, RAJ1-RAJ3
Madeira............ RA1-RA3, RAJ1-RAJ3
Mozambique..... RA1-RA3, RAJ1-RAJ3
Portugal RA11-RA13, RAJ2-RAJ4
Port. Guinea RA1-RA3, RAJ1-RAJ3
Port. India....... RA1-RA3, RAJ1-RAJ3
St. Thomas & Prince
Islands RA1-RA3, RAJ1-RAJ3
Timor RA1-RA3, RAJ1-RAJ3

Nos. RA1-RA3,RAJ1-RAJ3 (6)	6.60	6.60
Nos. RA9-RA11,RAJ2-RAJ4 (6)	6.60	9.30
Nos. RA1-RA3,RAJ1-RAJ3 (6)	6.00	5.40
Nos. RA1-RA3,RAJ1-RAJ3 (6)	18.50	10.50
Nos. RA1-RA3,RAJ1-RAJ3 (6)	4.35	12.45
Nos. RA1-RA3,RAJ1-RAJ3 (6)	2.55	2.70
Nos. RA11-RA13,RAJ2-RAJ4 (6)	5.80	5.20
Nos. RA1-RA3,RAJ1-RAJ3 (6)	3.30	2.70
Nos. RA1-RA3,RAJ1-RAJ3 (6)	3.45	3.45
Nos. RA1-RA3,RAJ1-RAJ3 (6)	3.60	3.60
Nos. RA1-RA3,RAJ1-RAJ3 (6)	2.10	3.90
Set total (66) Stamps	62.85	65.80

Vasco da Gama CD34

Mousinho de Albuquerque CD35

Dam CD36

Prince Henry the Navigator CD37

Affonso de Albuquerque CD38

Plane over Globe CD39

1938-39

Angola 274-291, C1-C9
Cape Verde 234-251, C1-C9
Macao.......................289-305, C7-C15
Mozambique...............270-287, C1-C9
Port. Guinea 233-250, C1-C9
Port. India 439-453, C1-C8
St. Thomas & Prince
Islands ... 302-319, 323-340, C1-C18
Timor 223-239, C1-C9

Nos. 274-291,C1-C9 (27)	132.90	22.85
Nos. 234-251,C1-C9 (27)	100.00	31.20
Nos. 289-305,C7-C15 (26)	701.70	135.60
Nos. 270-287,C1-C9 (27)	63.45	11.20
Nos. 233-250,C1-C9 (27)	88.05	30.70
Nos. 439-453,C1-C8 (23)	74.75	25.50
Nos. 302-319,323-340,C1-C18 (54)	319.25	190.35
Nos. 223-239,C1-C9 (26)	149.25	73.15
Set total (237) Stamps	1,629.	520.55

FRENCH COMMUNITY

Colonial Exposition

People of French Empire CD70

Women's Heads CD71

France Showing Way to Civilization CD72

"Colonial Commerce" CD73

International Colonial Exposition, Paris.

1931

Cameroun...............................213-216
Chad 60-63
Dahomey 97-100
Fr. Guiana 152-155
Fr. Guinea 116-119
Fr. India 100-103
Fr. Polynesia.............................76-79
Fr. Sudan.................................102-105
Gabon......................................120-123
Guadeloupe 138-141
Indo-China...............................140-142
Ivory Coast 92-95
Madagascar.............................169-172
Martinique................................129-132
Mauritania...................................65-68
Middle Congo 61-64
New Caledonia 176-179
Niger..73-76
Reunion 122-125
St. Pierre & Miquelon..............132-135
Senegal 138-141
Somali Coast............................135-138
Togo...254-257
Ubangi-Shari 82-85
Upper Volta..................................66-69
Wallis & Futuna Isls. 85-88

Nos. 213-216 (4)	23.00	18.25
Nos. 60-63 (4)	22.00	22.00
Nos. 97-100 (4)	26.00	26.00
Nos. 152-155 (4)	22.00	22.00
Nos. 116-119 (4)	19.75	19.75
Nos. 100-103 (4)	18.00	*18.00*
Nos. 76-79 (4)	30.00	30.00
Nos. 102-105 (4)	19.00	19.00
Nos. 120-123 (4)	17.50	17.50
Nos. 138-141 (4)	19.00	19.00
Nos. 140-142 (3)	11.50	11.50
Nos. 92-95 (4)	22.50	22.50
Nos. 169-172 (4)	7.90	5.00
Nos. 129-132 (4)	21.00	21.00
Nos. 65-68 (4)	22.00	22.00
Nos. 61-64 (4)	20.50	20.50
Nos. 176-179 (4)	24.00	24.00
Nos. 73-76 (4)	21.50	21.50
Nos. 122-125 (4)	22.00	22.00
Nos. 132-135 (4)	24.00	24.00
Nos. 138-141 (4)	20.00	20.00
Nos. 135-138 (4)	22.00	22.00
Nos. 254-257 (4)	22.00	22.00
Nos. 82-85 (4)	21.00	21.00
Nos. 66-69 (4)	19.00	19.00
Nos. 85-88 (4)	35.00	35.00
Set total (103) Stamps	552.15	544.50

Paris International Exposition
Colonial Arts Exposition

"Colonial Resources" CD74 CD77

Overseas Commerce CD75

Exposition Building and Women CD76

"France and the Empire" CD78

Cultural Treasures of the Colonies CD79

Souvenir sheets contain one imperf. stamp.

1937

Cameroun.................................217-222A
Dahomey 101-107
Fr. Equatorial Africa 27-32, 73

Fr. Guiana	162-168
Fr. Guinea	120-126
Fr. India	104-110
Fr. Polynesia	117-123
Fr. Sudan	106-112
Guadeloupe	148-154
Indo-China	193-199
Inini	41
Ivory Coast	152-158
Kwangchowan	132
Madagascar	191-197
Martinique	179-185
Mauritania	69-75
New Caledonia	208-214
Niger	73-83
Reunion	167-173
St. Pierre & Miquelon	165-171
Senegal	172-178
Somali Coast	139-145
Togo	258-264
Wallis & Futuna Isls.	89

Nos. 217-222A (7)	18.80	20.30
Nos. 101-107 (7)	23.60	27.60
Nos. 27-32, 73 (7)	28.10	32.10
Nos. 162-168 (7)	22.50	24.50
Nos. 120-126 (7)	24.00	28.00
Nos. 104-110 (7)	21.15	36.50
Nos. 117-123 (7)	58.50	75.00
Nos. 106-112 (7)	23.60	27.60
Nos. 148-154 (7)	19.55	21.05
Nos. 193-199 (7)	17.70	19.70
No. 41 (1)	19.00	22.50
Nos. 152-158 (7)	22.20	26.20
No. 132 (1)	9.25	11.00
Nos. 191-197 (7)	19.25	21.75
Nos. 179-185 (7)	19.95	21.70
Nos. 69-75 (7)	20.50	24.50
Nos. 208-214 (7)	39.00	50.50
Nos. 73-83 (11)	42.70	46.70
Nos. 167-173 (7)	21.70	23.20
Nos. 165-171 (7)	49.60	64.00
Nos. 172-178 (7)	21.00	23.80
Nos. 139-145 (7)	25.60	32.60
Nos. 258-264 (7)	20.40	20.40
No. 89 (1)	28.50	37.50
Set total (154) Stamps	616.15	738.70

Curie

Pierre and Marie Curie CD80

40th anniversary of the discovery of radium. The surtax was for the benefit of the Intl. Union for the Control of Cancer.

1938

Cameroun	B1
Cuba	B1-B2
Dahomey	B2
France	B76
Fr. Equatorial Africa	B1
Fr. Guiana	B3
Fr. Guinea	B2
Fr. India	B6
Fr. Polynesia	B5
Fr. Sudan	B1
Guadeloupe	B3
Indo-China	B14
Ivory Coast	B2
Madagascar	B2
Martinique	B2
Mauritania	B3
New Caledonia	B4
Niger	B1
Reunion	B4
St. Pierre & Miquelon	B3
Senegal	B3
Somali Coast	B2
Togo	B1

No. B1 (1)	10.00	10.00
Nos. B1-B2 (2)	8.50	2.40
No. B2 (1)	9.50	9.50
No. B76 (1)	21.00	12.50
No. B1 (1)	24.00	24.00
No. B3 (1)	13.50	13.50
No. B2 (1)	8.75	8.75
No. B6 (1)	10.00	10.00
No. B5 (1)	20.00	20.00
No. B1 (1)	12.50	12.50
No. B3 (1)	11.00	10.50
No. B14 (1)	12.00	12.00
No. B2 (1)	11.00	7.50
No. B2 (1)	11.00	11.00
No. B2 (1)	13.00	13.00
No. B3 (1)	7.75	7.75
No. B4 (1)	16.50	17.50
No. B1 (1)	15.00	15.00
No. B4 (1)	14.00	14.00
No. B3 (1)	21.00	22.50
No. B3 (1)	10.50	10.50
No. B2 (1)	7.75	7.75
No. B1 (1)	20.00	20.00
Set total (24) Stamps	308.25	292.15

Caillie

Rene Calle and Map of Northwestern Africa — CD81

Death centenary of Rene Caillie (1799-1838), French explorer.

All three denominations exist with colony name omitted.

1939

Dahomey	108-110
Fr. Guinea	161-163
Fr. Sudan	113-115
Ivory Coast	160-162
Mauritania	109-111
Niger	84-86
Senegal	188-190
Togo	265-267

Nos. 108-110 (3)	1.20	3.60
Nos. 161-163 (3)	1.20	3.20
Nos. 113-115 (3)	1.20	3.20
Nos. 160-162 (3)	1.05	2.55
Nos. 109-111 (3)	1.05	3.80
Nos. 84-86 (3)	1.05	2.35
Nos. 188-190 (3)	1.05	2.90
Nos. 265-267 (3)	1.05	3.30
Set total (24) Stamps	8.85	24.90

New York World's Fair

Natives and New York Skyline CD82

1939

Cameroun	223-224
Dahomey	111-112
Fr. Equatorial Africa	78-79
Fr. Guiana	169-170
Fr. Guinea	164-165
Fr. India	111-112
Fr. Polynesia	124-125
Fr. Sudan	116-117
Guadeloupe	155-156
Indo-China	203-204
Inini	42-43
Ivory Coast	163-164
Kwangchowan	133-134
Madagascar	209-210
Martinique	186-187
Mauritania	112-113
New Caledonia	215-216
Niger	87-88
Reunion	174-175
St. Pierre & Miquelon	205-206
Senegal	191-192
Somali Coast	179-180
Togo	268-269
Wallis & Futuna Isls.	90-91

Nos. 223-224 (2)	2.80	2.40
Nos. 111-112 (2)	1.60	3.20
Nos. 78-79 (2)	1.60	3.20
Nos. 169-170 (2)	2.60	2.60
Nos. 164-165 (2)	1.60	3.20
Nos. 111-112 (2)	3.00	*8.00*
Nos. 124-125 (2)	4.80	4.80
Nos. 116-117 (2)	1.60	3.20
Nos. 155-156 (2)	2.50	2.50
Nos. 203-204 (2)	2.05	2.05
Nos. 42-43 (2)	7.50	9.00
Nos. 163-164 (2)	1.50	3.00
Nos. 133-134 (2)	2.50	2.50
Nos. 209-210 (2)	1.50	2.50
Nos. 186-187 (2)	2.35	2.35
Nos. 112-113 (2)	1.40	2.80
Nos. 215-216 (2)	3.35	3.35
Nos. 87-88 (2)	1.40	2.80
Nos. 174-175 (2)	2.80	2.80
Nos. 205-206 (2)	4.80	6.00
Nos. 191-192 (2)	1.40	2.80
Nos. 179-180 (2)	1.40	2.80
Nos. 268-269 (2)	1.40	2.80
Nos. 90-91 (2)	6.00	6.00
Set total (48) Stamps	63.45	86.65

French Revolution

Storming of the Bastille — CD83

French Revolution, 150th anniv. The surtax was for the defense of the colonies.

1939

Cameroun	B2-B6
Dahomey	B3-B7
Fr. Equatorial Africa	B4-B8, CB1
Fr. Guiana	B4-B8, CB1
Fr. Guinea	B3-B7
Fr. India	B7-B11
Fr. Polynesia	B6-B10, CB1
Fr. Sudan	B2-B6
Guadeloupe	B4-B8
Indo-China	B15-B19, CB1
Inini	B1-B5
Ivory Coast	B3-B7
Kwangchowan	B1-B5
Madagascar	B3-B7, CB1
Martinique	B3-B7
Mauritania	B4-B8
New Caledonia	B5-B9, CB1
Niger	B2-B6
Reunion	B5-B9, CB1
St. Pierre & Miquelon	B4-B8
Senegal	B4-B8, CB1
Somali Coast	B3-B7
Togo	B2-B6
Wallis & Futuna Isls.	B1-B5

Nos. B2-B6 (5)	60.00	60.00
Nos. B3-B7 (5)	47.50	47.50
Nos. B4-B8,CB1 (6)	120.00	120.00
Nos. B4-B8,CB1 (6)	79.50	79.50
Nos. B3-B7 (5)	47.50	47.50
Nos. B7-B11 (5)	28.75	*32.50*
Nos. B6-B10,CB1 (6)	122.50	122.50
Nos. B2-B6 (5)	50.00	50.00
Nos. B4-B8 (5)	50.00	50.00
Nos. B15-B19,CB1 (6)	85.00	85.00
Nos. B1-B5 (5)	75.00	87.50
Nos. B3-B7 (5)	43.75	43.75
Nos. B1-B5 (5)	46.25	46.25
Nos. B3-B7,CB1 (6)	65.50	65.50
Nos. B3-B7 (5)	52.50	52.50
Nos. B4-B8 (5)	42.50	42.50
Nos. B5-B9,CB1 (6)	101.50	101.50
Nos. B2-B6 (5)	60.00	60.00
Nos. B5-B9,CB1 (6)	87.50	87.50
Nos. B4-B8 (5)	67.50	72.50
Nos. B4-B8,CB1 (6)	56.50	56.50
Nos. B3-B7 (5)	45.00	45.00
Nos. B2-B6 (5)	42.50	42.50
Nos. B1-B5 (5)	95.00	95.00
Set total (128) Stamps	1,572.	1,593.

Plane over Coastal Area CD85

All five denominations exist with colony name omitted.

1940

Dahomey	C1-C5
Fr. Guinea	C1-C5
Fr. Sudan	C1-C5
Ivory Coast	C1-C5
Mauritania	C1-C5
Niger	C1-C5
Senegal	C12-C16

Nos. C1-C5 (5)	4.00	4.00
Nos. C1-C5 (5)	4.00	4.00
Nos. C1-C5 (5)	4.00	4.00
Nos. C1-C5 (5)	3.80	3.80
Nos. C1-C5 (5)	3.50	3.50
Nos. C1-C5 (5)	3.50	3.50
Nos. C12-C16 (5)	3.50	3.50
Nos. C1-C5 (5)	3.15	3.15
Set total (40) Stamps	29.45	29.45

BRITISH COMMONWEALTH OF NATIONS

The listings follow established trade practices when these issues are offered as units by dealers. The Peace issue, for example, includes only one stamp from the Indian state of Hyderabad. The U.P.U. issue includes the Egypt set. Pairs are included for those varieties issues with bilingual designs se-tenant.

Silver Jubilee

Windsor Castle and King George V CD301

Reign of King George V, 25th anniv.

1935

Antigua	77-80
Ascension	33-36
Bahamas	92-95
Barbados	186-189
Basutoland	11-14
Bechuanaland Protectorate	117-120
Bermuda	100-103
British Guiana	223-226
British Honduras	108-111
Cayman Islands	81-84
Ceylon	260-263
Cyprus	136-139
Dominica	90-93
Falkland Islands	77-80
Fiji	110-113
Gambia	125-128
Gibraltar	100-103
Gilbert & Ellice Islands	33-36
Gold Coast	108-111
Grenada	124-127
Hong Kong	147-150
Jamaica	109-112
Kenya, Uganda, Tanzania	42-45
Leeward Islands	96-99
Malta	184-187
Mauritius	204-207
Montserrat	85-88
Newfoundland	226-229
Nigeria	34-37
Northern Rhodesia	18-21
Nyasaland Protectorate	47-50
St. Helena	111-114
St. Kitts-Nevis	72-75
St. Lucia	91-94
St. Vincent	134-137
Seychelles	118-121
Sierra Leone	166-169
Solomon Islands	60-63
Somaliland Protectorate	77-80
Straits Settlements	213-216
Swaziland	20-23
Trinidad & Tobago	43-46
Turks & Caicos Islands	71-74
Virgin Islands	69-72

The following have different designs but are included in the omnibus set:

Great Britain	226-229
Offices in Morocco (Sp. Curr.)	67-70
Offices in Morocco	226-229
Offices in Morocco (Fr. Curr.)	422-425
Offices in Morocco (Tangier)	508-510
Australia	152-154
Canada	211-216
Cook Islands	98-100
India	142-148
Nauru	31-34
New Guinea	46-47
New Zealand	199-201
Niue	67-69
Papua	114-117
Samoa	163-165
South Africa	68-71
Southern Rhodesia	33-36
South-West Africa	121-124

Nos. 77-80 (4)	20.25	*20.50*
Nos. 33-36 (4)	58.50	*120.00*
Nos. 92-95 (4)	25.00	*43.00*
Nos. 186-189 (4)	30.15	49.30
Nos. 11-14 (4)	12.10	*23.00*
Nos. 117-120 (4)	17.00	*31.25*
Nos. 100-103 (4)	18.00	*58.25*
Nos. 223-226 (4)	18.35	35.50
Nos. 108-111 (4)	15.25	*15.35*
Nos. 81-84 (4)	19.95	19.50

Nos. 260-263 (4)	10.15	19.10
Nos. 136-139 (4)	39.75	34.40
Nos. 90-93 (4)	18.85	19.85
Nos. 77-80 (4)	51.00	13.75
Nos. 110-113 (4)	15.25	29.00
Nos. 125-128 (4)	12.20	25.25
Nos. 100-103 (4)	28.75	42.75
Nos. 33-36 (4)	31.50	50.00
Nos. 108-111 (4)	26.25	62.85
Nos. 124-127 (4)	16.70	40.60
Nos. 147-150 (4)	59.00	18.75
Nos. 109-112 (4)	17.00	39.00
Nos. 42-45 (4)	8.75	11.00
Nos. 96-99 (4)	35.75	49.60
Nos. 184-187 (4)	22.00	33.70
Nos. 204-207 (4)	47.60	58.25
Nos. 85-88 (4)	10.25	30.25
Nos. 226-229 (4)	17.50	12.05
Nos. 34-37 (4)	13.25	59.75
Nos. 18-21 (4)	16.75	16.25
Nos. 47-50 (4)	39.75	80.25
Nos. 111-114 (4)	31.15	33.25
Nos. 72-75 (4)	11.55	18.50
Nos. 91-94 (4)	16.00	20.80
Nos. 134-137 (4)	9.45	21.25
Nos. 118-121 (4)	17.50	32.50
Nos. 166-169 (4)	24.25	56.00
Nos. 60-63 (4)	27.25	38.00
Nos. 77-80 (4)	17.00	48.25
Nos. 213-216 (4)	15.00	25.10
Nos. 20-23 (4)	6.80	18.25
Nos. 43-46 (4)	14.05	27.75
Nos. 71-74 (4)	8.40	14.50
Nos. 69-72 (4)	25.00	55.25
Nos. 226-229 (4)	7.25	7.45
Nos. 67-70 (4)	14.35	26.10
Nos. 226-229 (4)	8.20	28.90
Nos. 422-425 (4)	3.90	2.00
Nos. 508-510 (3)	18.80	23.85
Nos. 152-154 (3)	45.75	60.35
Nos. 211-216 (6)	24.85	13.35
Nos. 98-100 (3)	9.65	12.00
Nos. 142-148 (7)	23.25	11.80
Nos. 31-34 (4)	9.90	9.90
Nos. 46-47 (2)	4.35	1.70
Nos. 199-201 (3)	21.75	31.75
Nos. 67-69 (3)	11.30	26.50
Nos. 114-117 (4)	9.20	17.00
Nos. 163-165 (3)	4.40	5.50
Nos. 68-71 (4)	57.00	155.00
Nos. 33-36 (4)	27.75	45.25
Nos. 121-124 (4)	13.00	36.10
Set total (245) Stamps	1,311.	2,086.

Coronation

Queen Elizabeth and King George VI
CD302

1937

Aden 13-15
Antigua 81-83
Ascension 37-39
Bahamas 97-99
Barbados 190-192
Basutoland 15-17
Bechuanaland Protectorate 121-123
Bermuda 115-117
British Guiana 227-229
British Honduras 112-114
Cayman Islands 97-99
Ceylon 275-277
Cyprus 140-142
Dominica 94-96
Falkland Islands 81-83
Fiji 114-116
Gambia 129-131
Gibraltar 104-106
Gilbert & Ellice Islands 37-39
Gold Coast 112-114
Grenada 128-130
Hong Kong 151-153
Jamaica 113-115
Kenya, Uganda, Tanzania 60-62
Leeward Islands 100-102
Malta 188-190
Mauritius 208-210
Montserrat 89-91
Newfoundland 230-232
Nigeria 50-52
Northern Rhodesia 22-24
Nyasaland Protectorate 51-53
St. Helena 115-117
St. Kitts-Nevis 76-78
St. Lucia 107-109
St. Vincent 138-140
Seychelles 122-124
Sierra Leone 170-172
Solomon Islands 64-66
Somaliland Protectorate 81-83
Straits Settlements 235-237
Swaziland 24-26
Trinidad & Tobago 47-49
Turks & Caicos Islands 75-77
Virgin Islands 73-75

The following have different designs but are included in the omnibus set:

Great Britain 234
Offices in Morocco (Sp. Curr.) 82
Offices in Morocco (Fr. Curr.) 439
Offices in Morocco (Tangier) 514
Canada 237
Cook Islands 109-111
Nauru 35-38
Newfoundland 233-243
New Guinea 48-51
New Zealand 223-225
Niue 70-72
Papua 118-121
South Africa 74-78
Southern Rhodesia 38-41
South-West Africa 125-132

Nos. 13-15 (3)	3.00	5.75
Nos. 81-83 (3)	1.85	3.75
Nos. 37-39 (3)	2.75	2.75
Nos. 97-99 (3)	1.15	3.05
Nos. 190-192 (3)	1.10	1.95
Nos. 15-17 (3)	1.15	3.00
Nos. 121-123 (3)	.95	3.35
Nos. 115-117 (3)	1.25	5.00
Nos. 227-229 (3)	1.45	3.05
Nos. 112-114 (3)	1.20	2.35
Nos. 97-99 (3)	1.10	2.30
Nos. 275-277 (3)	8.25	10.35
Nos. 140-142 (3)	3.75	6.50
Nos. 94-96 (3)	.85	2.40
Nos. 81-83 (3)	2.90	2.30
Nos. 114-116 (3)	1.35	5.75
Nos. 129-131 (3)	.95	3.95
Nos. 104-106 (3)	2.25	6.45
Nos. 37-39 (3)	.85	2.00
Nos. 112-114 (3)	3.10	10.00
Nos. 128-130 (3)	1.00	.85
Nos. 151-153 (3)	23.00	12.50
Nos. 113-115 (3)	1.25	1.25
Nos. 60-62 (3)	1.00	2.35
Nos. 100-102 (3)	1.55	4.00
Nos. 188-190 (3)	1.25	1.60
Nos. 208-210 (3)	2.05	3.75
Nos. 89-91 (3)	1.00	3.35
Nos. 230-232 (3)	7.00	2.80
Nos. 50-52 (3)	3.25	8.50
Nos. 22-24 (3)	.95	2.25
Nos. 51-53 (3)	1.05	1.30
Nos. 115-117 (3)	1.45	2.05
Nos. 76-78 (3)	.95	2.05
Nos. 107-109 (3)	1.05	2.05
Nos. 138-140 (3)	.80	4.75
Nos. 122-124 (3)	1.20	1.90
Nos. 170-172 (3)	1.95	5.65
Nos. 64-66 (3)	.90	2.00
Nos. 81-83 (3)	1.10	3.40
Nos. 235-237 (3)	3.25	1.60
Nos. 24-26 (3)	1.05	1.75
Nos. 47-49 (3)	1.00	1.00
Nos. 75-77 (3)	1.30	1.15
Nos. 73-75 (3)	2.20	6.90
No. 234 (1)	.25	.25
No. 82 (1)	.80	.80
No. 439 (1)	.35	.25
No. 514 (1)	.55	.55
No. 237 (1)	.35	.25
Nos. 109-111 (3)	.85	.80
Nos. 35-38 (4)	1.10	5.50
Nos. 233-243 (11)	41.90	30.40
Nos. 48-51 (4)	1.40	7.90
Nos. 223-225 (3)	1.40	2.75
Nos. 70-72 (3)	.80	2.05
Nos. 118-121 (4)	1.60	5.25
Nos. 74-78 (5)	9.25	10.80
Nos. 38-41 (4)	3.55	15.50
Nos. 125-132 (8)	5.00	8.40
Set total (189) Stamps	172.90	258.20

Peace

King George VI and Parliament Buildings, London
CD303

Return to peace at the close of World War II.

1945-46

Aden 28-29
Antigua 96-97
Ascension 50-51
Bahamas 130-131
Barbados 207-208
Bermuda 131-132
British Guiana 242-243
British Honduras 127-128
Cayman Islands 112-113
Ceylon 293-294
Cyprus 156-157
Dominica 112-113
Falkland Islands 97-98
Falkland Islands Dep. 1L9-1L10
Fiji 137-138
Gambia 144-145
Gibraltar 119-120
Gilbert & Ellice Island 52-53
Gold Coast 128-129
Grenada 143-144
Jamaica 136-137
Kenya, Uganda, Tanzania 90-91
Leeward Islands 116-117
Malta 206-207
Mauritius 223-224
Montserrat 104-105
Nigeria 71-72
Northern Rhodesia 46-47
Nyasaland Protectorate 82-83
Pitcairn Islands 9-10
St. Helena 128-129
St. Kitts-Nevis 91-92
St. Lucia 127-128
St. Vincent 152-153
Seychelles 149-150
Sierra Leone 186-187
Solomon Islands 80-81
Somaliland Protectorate 108-109
Trinidad & Tobago 62-63
Turks & Caicos Islands 90-91
Virgin Islands 88-89

The following have different designs but are included in the omnibus set:

Great Britain 264-265
Offices in Morocco (Tangier) 523-524
Aden
Kathiri State of Seiyun 12-13
Qu'aiti State of Shihr and Mukalla 12-13
Australia 200-202
Basutoland 29-31
Bechuanaland Protectorate 137-139
Burma 66-69
Cook Islands 127-130
Hong Kong 174-175
India 195-198
Hyderabad 51
New Zealand 247-257
Niue 90-93
Pakistan-Bahawalpur O16
Samoa 191-194
South Africa 100-102
Southern Rhodesia 67-70
South-West Africa 153-155
Swaziland 38-40
Zanzibar 222-223

Nos. 28-29 (2)	.95	2.50
Nos. 96-97 (2)	.50	.80
Nos. 50-51 (2)	.90	1.80
Nos. 130-131 (2)	.50	1.40
Nos. 207-208 (2)	.50	1.10
Nos. 131-132 (2)	.55	.55
Nos. 242-243 (2)	1.05	1.40
Nos. 127-128 (2)	.50	.50
Nos. 112-113 (2)	.60	.80
Nos. 293-294 (2)	.60	2.10
Nos. 156-157 (2)	1.00	.70
Nos. 112-113 (2)	.50	.50
Nos. 97-98 (2)	.90	1.35
Nos. 1L9-1L10 (2)	1.40	1.00
Nos. 137-138 (2)	.50	1.75
Nos. 144-145 (2)	.50	.95
Nos. 119-120 (2)	.75	1.00
Nos. 52-53 (2)	.50	.50
Nos. 128-129 (2)	1.85	3.75
Nos. 143-144 (2)	.50	.95
Nos. 136-137 (2)	.80	12.50
Nos. 90-91 (2)	.65	.65
Nos. 116-117 (2)	.50	1.50
Nos. 206-207 (2)	.65	2.00
Nos. 223-224 (2)	.50	1.05
Nos. 104-105 (2)	.50	.50
Nos. 71-72 (2)	.70	2.75
Nos. 46-47 (2)	1.25	2.00
Nos. 82-83 (2)	.50	.50
Nos. 9-10 (2)	1.40	1.40
Nos. 128-129 (2)	.65	.70
Nos. 91-92 (2)	.50	.50
Nos. 127-128 (2)	.50	.60
Nos. 152-153 (2)	.50	.50
Nos. 149-150 (2)	.55	.50
Nos. 186-187 (2)	.50	.50
Nos. 80-81 (2)	.50	1.50
Nos. 108-109 (2)	.70	.50
Nos. 62-63 (2)	.50	.50
Nos. 90-91 (2)	.50	.50
Nos. 88-89 (2)	.50	.50
Nos. 264-265 (2)	.50	.70
Nos. 523-524 (2)	1.50	3.00
Nos. 12-13 (2)	.50	.90
Nos. 12-13 (2)	.50	1.25
Nos. 200-202 (3)	1.60	3.00
Nos. 29-31 (3)	2.10	2.60
Nos. 137-139 (3)	2.05	4.75
Nos. 66-69 (4)	1.60	1.30
Nos. 127-130 (4)	2.00	1.85
Nos. 174-175 (2)	6.75	3.15
Nos. 195-198 (4)	4.75	3.60
No. 51 (1)	.25	.25
Nos. 247-257 (11)	3.95	3.90
Nos. 90-93 (4)	1.70	2.20
No. O16 (1)	5.50	7.00
Nos. 191-194 (4)	2.05	1.00
Nos. 100-102 (3)	1.20	4.00
Nos. 67-70 (4)	1.40	1.75
Nos. 153-155 (3)	1.85	3.25
Nos. 38-40 (3)	2.40	5.50
Nos. 222-223 (2)	.65	1.00
Set total (149) Stamps	73.20	113.00

Silver Wedding Issue

King George VI and Queen Elizabeth
CD304 CD305

1948-49

Aden 30-31
Kathiri State of Seiyun 14-15
Qu'aiti State of Shihr and Mukalla 14-15
Antigua 98-99
Ascension 52-53
Bahamas 148-149
Barbados 210-211
Basutoland 39-40
Bechuanaland Protectorate 147-148
Bermuda 133-134
British Guiana 244-245
British Honduras 129-130
Cayman Islands 116-117
Cyprus 158-159
Dominica 114-115
Falkland Islands 99-100
Falkland Islands Dep. 1L11-1L12
Fiji 139-140
Gambia 146-147
Gibraltar 121-122
Gilbert & Ellice Islands 54-55
Gold Coast 142-143
Grenada 145-146
Hong Kong 178-179
Jamaica 138-139
Kenya, Uganda, Tanzania 92-93
Leeward Islands 118-119
Malaya
Johore 128-129
Kedah 55-56
Kelantan 44-45
Malacca 1-2
Negri Sembilan 36-37
Pahang 44-45
Penang 1-2
Perak 99-100
Perlis 1-2
Selangor 74-75
Trengganu 47-48
Malta 223-224
Mauritius 229-230
Montserrat 106-107
Nigeria 73-74
North Borneo 238-239
Northern Rhodesia 48-49
Nyasaland Protectorate 85-86
Pitcairn Islands 11-12
St. Helena 130-131
St. Kitts-Nevis 93-94
St. Lucia 129-130
St. Vincent 154-155
Sarawak 174-175
Seychelles 151-152
Sierra Leone 188-189
Singapore 21-22
Solomon Islands 82-83
Somaliland Protectorate 110-111
Swaziland 48-49
Trinidad & Tobago 64-65
Turks & Caicos Islands 92-93
Virgin Islands 90-91
Zanzibar 224-225

The following have different designs but are included in the omnibus set:

Great Britain 267-268
Offices in Morocco (Sp. Curr.) 93-94
Offices in Morocco (Tangier) 525-526
Bahrain 62-63
Kuwait 82-83
Oman 25-26

South Africa....................................106
South-West Africa 159

Nos. 30-31 (2)	37.90	45.00
Nos. 14-15 (2)	18.85	17.50
Nos. 14-15 (2)	18.55	14.75
Nos. 98-99 (2)	12.55	12.75
Nos. 52-53 (2)	60.55	57.95
Nos. 148-149 (2)	45.25	40.30
Nos. 210-211 (2)	18.35	13.05
Nos. 39-40 (2)	52.80	55.25
Nos. 147-148 (2)	45.35	50.25
Nos. 133-134 (2)	47.75	55.25
Nos. 244-245 (2)	24.25	28.45
Nos. 129-130 (2)	22.75	53.20
Nos. 116-117 (2)	22.75	28.50
Nos. 158-159 (2)	58.50	78.05
Nos. 114-115 (2)	25.25	32.75
Nos. 99-100 (2)	112.10	83.60
Nos. 1L11-1L12 (2)	4.25	6.00
Nos. 139-140 (2)	18.20	10.75
Nos. 146-147 (2)	21.25	21.25
Nos. 121-122 (2)	61.00	78.00
Nos. 54-55 (2)	14.25	22.75
Nos. 142-143 (2)	35.25	37.75
Nos. 145-146 (2)	21.75	21.75
Nos. 178-179 (2)	303.50	96.50
Nos. 138-139 (2)	27.85	60.25
Nos. 92-93 (2)	50.25	67.75
Nos. 118-119 (2)	7.00	8.25
Nos. 128-129 (2)	29.25	53.25
Nos. 55-56 (2)	35.25	50.25
Nos. 44-45 (2)	35.75	62.75
Nos. 1-2 (2)	35.40	49.75
Nos. 36-37 (2)	28.10	38.20
Nos. 44-45 (2)	28.00	38.05
Nos. 1-2 (2)	40.50	37.80
Nos. 99-100 (2)	27.80	37.75
Nos. 1-2 (2)	33.50	58.00
Nos. 74-75 (2)	30.25	25.30
Nos. 47-48 (2)	35.25	62.75
Nos. 223-224 (2)	40.55	45.25
Nos. 229-230 (2)	17.75	45.25
Nos. 106-107 (2)	9.25	18.25
Nos. 73-74 (2)	17.85	22.80
Nos. 48-49 (2)	92.80	90.25
Nos. 85-86 (2)	18.25	30.25
Nos. 11-12 (2)	44.75	48.50
Nos. 130-131 (2)	32.80	42.80
Nos. 93-94 (2)	11.25	7.25
Nos. 129-130 (2)	22.25	45.25
Nos. 154-155 (2)	27.75	30.25
Nos. 174-175 (2)	50.40	52.90
Nos. 151-152 (2)	16.25	45.75
Nos. 188-189 (2)	24.75	26.25
Nos. 21-22 (2)	116.00	45.40
Nos. 82-83 (2)	13.40	13.40
Nos. 110-111 (2)	8.40	8.75
Nos. 48-49 (2)	40.30	47.75
Nos. 64-65 (2)	32.75	38.25
Nos. 92-93 (2)	11.25	16.25
Nos. 90-91 (2)	16.25	22.25
Nos. 224-225 (2)	29.60	38.00
Nos. 267-268 (2)	40.40	40.25
Nos. 93-94 (2)	20.10	25.35
Nos. 525-526 (2)	23.10	29.25
Nos. 62-63 (2)	38.45	72.50
Nos. 82-83 (2)	45.50	45.50
Nos. 25-26 (2)	46.00	47.50
No. 106 (1)	.90	1.25
No. 159 (1)	1.10	.35
Set total (134) Stamps	2,457.	2,654.

U.P.U. Issue

Mercury and Symbols of Communications — CD306

Plane, Ship and Hemispheres — CD307

Mercury Scattering Letters over Globe CD308

U.P.U. Monument, Bern CD309

Universal Postal Union, 75th anniversary.

1949

Aden 32-35
Kathiri State of Seiyun..............16-19
Qu'aiti State of Shihr and Mukalla...............................16-19
Antigua 100-103
Ascension.......................................57-60
Bahamas 150-153
Barbados 212-215
Basutoland.......................................41-44
Bechuanaland Protectorate......149-152
Bermuda.....................................138-141
British Guiana...........................246-249
British Honduras.......................137-140
Brunei 79-82
Cayman Islands.......................118-121
Cyprus 160-163
Dominica....................................116-119
Falkland Islands 103-106
Falkland Islands Dep...........1L14-1L17
Fiji 141-144
Gambia......................................148-151
Gibraltar....................................123-126
Gilbert & Ellice Islands................56-59
Gold Coast 144-147
Grenada......................................147-150
Hong Kong 180-183
Jamaica 142-145
Kenya, Uganda, Tanzania 94-97
Leeward Islands 126-129
Malaya
Johore 151-154
Kedah...57-60
Kelantan......................................46-49
Malacca.......................................18-21
Negri Sembilan 59-62
Pahang..46-49
Penang..23-26
Perak.......................................101-104
Perlis 3-6
Selangor......................................76-79
Trengganu 49-52
Malta...225-228
Mauritius...................................231-234
Montserrat 108-111
New Hebrides, British 62-65
New Hebrides, French 79-82
Nigeria...75-78
North Borneo............................240-243
Northern Rhodesia.......................50-53
Nyasaland Protectorate...............87-90
Pitcairn Islands............................13-16
St. Helena 132-135
St. Kitts-Nevis...............................95-98
St. Lucia 131-134
St. Vincent.................................170-173
Sarawak....................................176-179
Seychelles 153-156
Sierra Leone..............................190-193
Singapore 23-26
Solomon Islands..........................84-87
Somaliland Protectorate...........112-115
Southern Rhodesia 71-72
Swaziland 50-53
Tonga...87-90
Trinidad & Tobago 66-69
Turks & Caicos Islands 101-104
Virgin Islands................................92-95
Zanzibar.....................................226-229

The following have different designs but are included in the omnibus set:

Great Britain.............................276-279
Offices in Morocco (Tangier) 546-549
Australia..223
Bahrain 68-71
Burma 116-121
Ceylon 304-306
Egypt 281-283
India 223-226
Kuwait 89-92
Oman 31-34
Pakistan-Bahawalpur 26-29, O25-O28
South Africa.............................109-111
South-West Africa 160-162

Nos. 32-35 (4)	5.50	7.80
Nos. 16-19 (4)	3.10	3.60
Nos. 16-19 (4)	2.95	3.95
Nos. 100-103 (4)	4.15	6.85
Nos. 57-60 (4)	12.40	10.00
Nos. 150-153 (4)	5.60	9.55
Nos. 212-215 (4)	4.40	14.15
Nos. 41-44 (4)	4.75	10.00
Nos. 149-152 (4)	3.35	7.25
Nos. 138-141 (4)	4.75	5.55
Nos. 246-249 (4)	2.75	4.20
Nos. 137-140 (4)	3.35	4.75
Nos. 79-82 (4)	7.75	6.75
Nos. 118-121 (4)	4.00	6.40
Nos. 160-163 (4)	4.60	8.30
Nos. 116-119 (4)	2.30	5.65
Nos. 103-106 (4)	14.90	17.10
Nos. 1L14-1L17 (4)	15.50	14.00
Nos. 141-144 (4)	3.35	14.00
Nos. 148-151 (4)	3.10	7.10
Nos. 123-126 (4)	5.90	8.75
Nos. 56-59 (4)	4.70	7.85
Nos. 144-147 (4)	3.05	6.95
Nos. 147-150 (4)	2.15	3.55
Nos. 180-183 (4)	57.25	18.25
Nos. 142-145 (4)	2.25	2.45
Nos. 94-97 (4)	2.90	3.40
Nos. 126-129 (4)	3.05	9.60
Nos. 151-154 (4)	4.70	8.90
Nos. 57-60 (4)	4.80	12.00
Nos. 46-49 (4)	4.25	12.65
Nos. 18-21 (4)	4.25	17.30
Nos. 59-62 (4)	3.50	10.75
Nos. 46-49 (4)	3.00	7.25
Nos. 23-26 (4)	5.10	11.75
Nos. 101-104 (4)	3.65	10.75
Nos. 3-6 (4)	3.95	14.25
Nos. 76-79 (4)	4.90	12.30
Nos. 49-52 (4)	4.95	9.75
Nos. 225-228 (4)	4.50	4.85
Nos. 231-234 (4)	4.35	6.70
Nos. 108-111 (4)	3.40	3.85
Nos. 62-65 (4)	1.60	4.25
Nos. 79-82 (4)	24.25	24.25
Nos. 75-78 (4)	2.80	9.25
Nos. 50-53 (4)	5.00	6.50
Nos. 87-90 (4)	4.05	4.05
Nos. 13-16 (4)	18.50	16.50
Nos. 132-135 (4)	4.85	7.10
Nos. 95-98 (4)	3.35	4.70
Nos. 131-134 (4)	2.55	3.85
Nos. 170-173 (4)	2.20	5.05
Nos. 176-179 (4)	8.15	10.85
Nos. 153-156 (4)	3.25	4.10
Nos. 190-193 (4)	3.00	5.10
Nos. 23-26 (4)	18.00	13.20
Nos. 84-87 (4)	4.05	4.90
Nos. 112-115 (4)	3.95	8.70
Nos. 71-72 (2)	1.95	2.25
Nos. 50-53 (4)	2.80	4.65
Nos. 87-90 (4)	3.00	5.25
Nos. 66-69 (4)	3.15	3.15
Nos. 101-104 (4)	2.70	4.10
Nos. 92-95 (4)	2.60	5.90
Nos. 226-229 (4)	5.45	13.50
Nos. 276-279 (4)	1.35	2.10
Nos. 546-549 (4)	3.20	10.15
No. 223 (1)	.60	.55
Nos. 68-71 (4)	5.00	16.75
Nos. 116-121 (6)	7.15	5.30
Nos. 304-306 (3)	3.35	4.25
Nos. 281-283 (3)	5.75	2.70
Nos. 223-226 (4)	35.50	10.50
Nos. 89-92 (4)	6.10	10.25
Nos. 31-34 (4)	5.55	15.75
Nos. 26-29,O25-O28 (8)	2.00	42.00
Nos. 109-111 (3)	2.20	3.00
Nos. 160-162 (3)	3.00	5.50
Set total (309) Stamps	465.05	670.75

University Issue

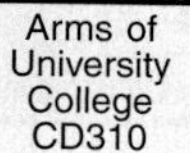

Arms of University College CD310

Alice, Princess of Athlone CD311

1948 opening of University College of the West Indies at Jamaica.

1951

Antigua 104-105
Barbados 228-229
British Guiana...........................250-251
British Honduras.......................141-142
Dominica...................................120-121
Grenada.....................................164-165
Jamaica 146-147
Leeward Islands 130-131
Montserrat 112-113
St. Kitts-Nevis...........................105-106
St. Lucia 149-150
St. Vincent................................174-175
Trinidad & Tobago 70-71
Virgin Islands................................96-97

Nos. 104-105 (2)	1.35	3.25
Nos. 228-229 (2)	1.85	1.55
Nos. 250-251 (2)	1.10	1.25
Nos. 141-142 (2)	1.40	2.15
Nos. 120-121 (2)	1.40	1.75
Nos. 164-165 (2)	1.20	1.60
Nos. 146-147 (2)	.90	.70
Nos. 130-131 (2)	1.35	4.00
Nos. 112-113 (2)	.85	1.50
Nos. 105-106 (2)	.90	1.50
Nos. 149-150 (2)	1.40	1.50
Nos. 174-175 (2)	1.00	2.15
Nos. 70-71 (2)	.75	.75
Nos. 96-97 (2)	1.50	3.75
Set total (28) Stamps	16.95	27.40

Classic Specialized Additions, Deletions & Number Changes

Number in 2017 Catalogue	Number in 2018 Catalogue
United States Carriers' Stamps	
new	1LB8c
new	1LB8d
Revenue Stamps	
new	R112b
R112b	R112c
R112c	R112d
R115a	R115c
R115b	R115a
new	R115b
new	R115d
Confederate States of America	
new	21XU3B
new	43XU1b
18XU2	deleted
Angola	
new	37a
new	37b
new	37c
new	37d
new	180b
new	208a
new	215b
Argentina	
new	4Ae
new	5b
new	5c
new	5d
new	5e
new	6d
new	6e
new	6f
7i	7d
7j	7e
7k	7g
7Cd	7Ci
7Ce	7Cj
new	7Ck
7Fg	7Fq
7Fq	7Fr
7Fr	7Fs
7Fs	7Ft
7Ht	7Hu
7Hu	7Hv
7Hv	7Hw
new	8c
new	8d
new	11a
new	11c
new	11d
new	11e
new	11f
new	11g
new	11h
new	11i
new	12d
new	12e
new	12f
new	12g
new	13a
new	13b
new	13c
new	13d
new	13e
new	13f
new	13g
Argentina	
new	13h
new	13i
new	13j
new	13k
new	13m
new	13n
new	13o
new	13p
new	13q
new	14a
new	38a
new	41k
new	282a
new	282b
Austria	
new	290e
new	290f
new	290g
new	290h
new	290i
new	290j
new	290k
new	291e
new	291f
new	291h
new	291i
new	292c
new	293a
new	295c
new	297a
Azerbaijan	
new	1A-10A
Canada	
new	104d
new	104e
new	104f
new	CL30u
new	CL30v
new	CL30w
new	CL30x
new	CL30y
new	CL30z
new	CL49c
new	CL49d
Ceylon	
new	210a
new	MR2c
Colombia	
new	GO21
new	GO21a
new	GO21b
Cook Islands	
new	66a
Crete	
10a	deleted
10b	deleted
10c	deleted
10d	deleted
Egypt	
new	4f
Epirus	
new	4CA
new	4RR
new	5a
new	6a
new	21a
new	22a
Fernando Po	
new	17A
Fiume	
new	1A
1a	1b
new	86a
new	86b
new	86c
new	87a
new	87b
new	88a
new	88b
new	88c
new	88d
new	89a
new	89b
new	90a
new	90b
new	90c
new	90d
new	90e
new	91a
new	92a
new	92b
new	92c
new	92d
new	92e
new	92f
new	93a
new	93b
new	93c
new	94a
new	95a
new	95b
new	95c
new	96a
new	98a
France	
new	7h
new	7i
new	12b
new	13b
14d	14e
new	14d
new	17b
new	18d
new	19c
new	19d
new	21b
new	21c
new	24a
new	29b
new	30a
new	31b
new	32a
new	33d
new	33e
new	35b
new	36b
new	36c
new	37g
France	
new	37h
new	C4b
Grenada	
8d	deleted
9e	deleted
35a	deleted
37b	deleted
Heligoland	
new	5c
new	6a
new	11a
new	21f
new	21g
Hong Kong	
new	66g
new	91a
new	97a
new	99a
new	101a
new	103a
new	104a
new	108a
new	154a
new	154b
new	157Bd
Hungary	
new	O21a
new	O22a
new	O23a
new	O24a
new	O25a
Iceland	
O21h	deleted
new	O22a
O28b	deleted
Indo-China	
new	3a
new	19b
new	27a
new	27b
new	29a
new	32a
new	34a
new	39a
new	40a
new	72a
Ireland	
new	1b
new	2c
new	3a
new	5a
new	7a
new	12a
new	13a
Italian States - Roman States	
new	19f
new	20b
new	21f
new	22k
new	22m
new	23q
new	23r

Italian States - Roman States

Number in 2017 Catalogue	Number in 2018 Catalogue
new	24f
new	25q
new	25r

Jamaica

Number in 2017 Catalogue	Number in 2018 Catalogue
new	79b
new	79c
new	83b
new	83c
new	84b
new	84c
new	92a
new	93a

Leeward Islands

Number in 2017 Catalogue	Number in 2018 Catalogue
new	17b

Maldive Islands

Number in 2017 Catalogue	Number in 2018 Catalogue
new	7a

Mauritania

Number in 2017 Catalogue	Number in 2018 Catalogue
new	B2c

Mauritius

Number in 2017 Catalogue	Number in 2018 Catalogue
new	4j
new	17c
new	17d

Mexico

Number in 2017 Catalogue	Number in 2018 Catalogue
new	64d

Middle Congo

Number in 2017 Catalogue	Number in 2018 Catalogue
new	7a
new	48b

Moheli

Number in 2017 Catalogue	Number in 2018 Catalogue
new	11a
new	16a

Natal

Number in 2017 Catalogue	Number in 2018 Catalogue
new	72b

New Zealand

Number in 2017 Catalogue	Number in 2018 Catalogue
new	19a
new	28d
new	28e
new	31b
new	31c
new	31d
new	31e
new	32f
new	32g
new	36c
new	37c
new	38A
new	38B
new	39a
new	39b
new	41a
new	42b
new	42c
new	42A
new	43a
new	44a
new	44b
new	44c
new	44d
new	46a
new	51c
new	51i
new	51f
new	51g
new	52b
new	52c
new	52i
new	52f
new	52g
new	53f
new	53g
new	54f
new	54g
new	54i
new	55f
new	55g
new	55i
new	56f
new	56g
new	56h
new	56i
new	61e
new	61f
new	62d
new	63b
new	64b
new	65a
new	65b
new	67d
new	67Ac
new	68b
new	69a
new	72e
new	72f
new	91b
new	99Bc
new	99Bd
new	99Be
new	99Bf
new	99Bg
new	100b
new	100c
new	100d
new	100e
new	100f
new	100g
new	101c
new	101d
new	101e
new	101f
new	101g
new	101h
new	102a
new	102c
new	102d
new	102e
new	102f
new	103b
new	103c
new	103d
new	103e
new	103f
new	104a
new	104b
new	104c
new	104d
new	105b
new	105c
new	105d
new	107e
new	107i
new	107j
new	107k
new	108g
new	108h
new	108i
new	108j
new	108k
new	108l
new	108m
new	108n
new	108o
new	108p
new	108q
new	109i
new	109k
new	110a
110a	110b
110b	110c
new	110i
new	110k
new	111a
new	111e
new	111f
new	112a
new	112e
new	112f
new	112g
new	112i
new	112k
new	113b
new	113e
new	113f
new	113i
new	113k
new	114e
new	114f
new	114g
new	114i
new	114k
115a	deleted
115c	deleted
new	115e
new	115f
new	115g
new	115h
new	115i
new	115k
new	116e
new	116f
new	116g
new	116h
new	116i
new	116k
new	117e
new	117i
new	117k
new	118e
new	118f
new	118g
new	118h
new	119a
new	119e
new	119f
new	119k
new	120a
new	120e
new	120f
new	120i
new	120k
new	121b
new	126a
new	126b
new	127a
new	127b
new	128a
new	133a
new	133b
new	133c
new	134a
new	136a
new	136b
new	136c
new	137a
new	137b
new	137c
new	138a
new	138b
new	138c
new	138d
new	139a
new	145a
new	145b
new	146a
new	146b
new	147a
new	147b
new	148a
new	148b
new	149a
new	149b
new	150a
new	150b
new	151a
new	151b
new	152a
new	152b
new	153b
new	153c
new	154b
new	154c
new	155a
new	155b
new	156a
new	156b
new	158b
new	158c
new	159b
new	159c
new	162a
new	163a
new	164a
new	184c
new	186c
new	187a
new	189a
new	192a
new	197a
new	198a
new	207a
new	207b
new	209b
new	209c
new	210b
new	211b
new	212b
new	215c
new	216b

Niger Coast Protectorate

Number in 2017 Catalogue	Number in 2018 Catalogue
new	55a

Niue

Number in 2017 Catalogue	Number in 2018 Catalogue
new	20b
new	20c
new	26a
new	26b
new	27a
new	27b
new	28a
new	28b
new	29a
new	29b
new	32a
new	32b
new	33a
new	34a

North Borneo

Number in 2017 Catalogue	Number in 2018 Catalogue
new	69b
new	98a

Number in 2017 Catalogue	Number in 2018 Catalogue
North Ingermanland	
new	2b
new	3c
Nyasaland Protectorate	
new	57Ab
new	57b
new	57Ac
Saudi Arabia	
new	L34a
new	L34b
new	L34c
new	L35a
new	L46b
new	L48Ac
new	L48Ad
new	L51d
new	L51e
new	L65c
new	L85b
new	L85c
new	L86d
new	L88c
new	L94b
new	L97b
new	L99d
new	L101c
new	L102b
new	L104b
new	L106d
new	L107d
new	L107e
new	L135c
new	L135d
new	L135e
new	L135f
new	L135g
new	L135h
new	L135i
new	L135j
new	L135k
new	L136d
new	L136e
new	L136f
new	L136g
new	L136h
new	L136i
new	L136j
new	L136k
new	L136l
new	L136m
new	L136n
new	L136o
new	L138f
new	L138g
new	L138h
new	L138i
new	L138j
new	L138k
new	L139b
new	L139c
new	L139d
new	L139e
new	L140c
new	L140d
new	L140e
new	L140f
new	L140g
new	L140h
new	L140i
new	L141c
new	L141d
new	L141e
new	L141f
new	L147d
Saudi Arabia	
new	L153c
new	LJ5a
new	LJ7c
new	LJ26e
new	LJ26f
new	LJ26g
new	LJ27d
new	LJ27e
new	LJ27f
new	LJ27g
new	LJ28d
new	LJ28e
new	LJ29e
new	LJ29f
new	LJ29g
new	LJ29h
new	LJ29i
new	LJ29j
new	LJ30e
new	LJ30f
new	LJ30g
new	LJ30h
new	LJ32e
new	LJ32f
new	LJ32g
new	LJ32h
new	LJ32i
new	LJ33d
new	LJ34e
new	LJ38a
Siberia	
new	53a
Sierra Leone	
new	48d
South Russia	
new	59a
South West Africa	
new	C1b
new	C2b
Spain	
new	287b
new	287c
new	288b
new	289c
new	290a
new	292a
new	501b
new	502b
new	503b
new	504b
new	504c
new	506b
new	506c
new	509b
Straits Settlements	
new	138b
Sweden	
new	31c
new	31d
Thailand	
new	1c
new	1d
new	20e
new	20f
new	20g
Tonga	
new	36e

UNITED STATES

yu-ˌnī-təd ˈstāts

GOVT. — Republic
AREA — 3,615,211 sq. mi.
POP. — 226,545,805 (1980)
CAPITAL — Washington, DC

In addition to the 48 States and the District of Columbia, the Republic includes Alaska, Hawaii, Guam, the Commonwealth of Puerto Rico, the Virgin Islands, American Samoa, Wake, Midway, and a number of small islands in the Pacific Ocean, all of which use stamps of the United States.

100 Cents = 1 Dollar

Catalogue values for unused stamps in this country are for Never Hinged items, beginning with Scott 772 in the regular postage section, Scott C19 in the air post section, Scott RW1 in the hunting permit stamps section.

Watermarks

Wmk. 190 — "USPS" in Single-lined Capitals

Wmk. 191 — Double-lined "USPS" in Capitals

Wmk. 190PI — PIPS, used in the Philippines
Wmk. 191PI — PIPS, used in the Philippines
Wmk. 191C — US-C, used for Cuba
Wmk. 191R — USIR

POSTMASTERS' PROVISIONALS

Values for Envelopes are for entires.

Alexandria, Va.

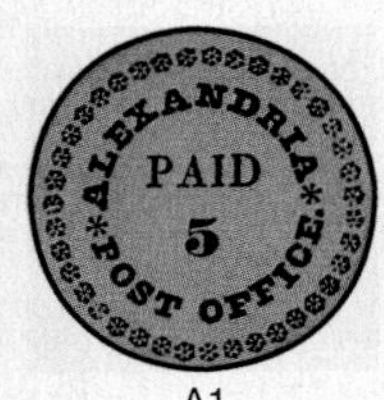

A1

Type I — 40 asterisks in circle.
Type II — 39 asterisks in circle.

1846 Typeset *Imperf.*

		Unused	Used
1X1	A1 5c black, *buff*, type I		*325,000.*
a.	5c black, *buff*, type II	*625,000.*	
	On cover (I or II)		*500,000.*
1X2	A1 5c black, *blue*, type I, on cover		—

All known examples of Nos. 1X1-1X2 are cut to shape.

Annapolis, Md.

ENVELOPE

E1

Printed in upper right corner of envelope

1846

		Unused	Used
2XU1	E1 5c carmine red, *white*		*600,000.*

Handstamped impressions of the circular design with "2" in blue or red exist on envelopes and letter sheets. Values: blue $17,500, red $30,000.

A letter sheet exists with circular design and "5" handstamped in red. Values: blue $10,000, red $12,500.

A similar circular design in blue was used as a postmark.

Baltimore, Md.

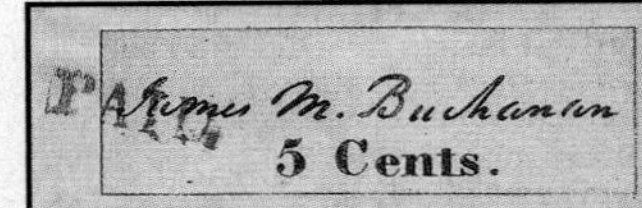

Signature of Postmaster — A1

Printed from a plate of 12 (2x6) containing nine 5c stamps (Pos. 1-6, 8, 10, 12) and three 10c (Pos. 7, 9, 11).

1845 Engr. *Imperf.*

		Unused	Used
3X1	A1 5c black		*6,000.*
	On cover		*15,000.*
	Vertical pair on cover		*150,000.*
3X2	A1 10c black, on cover		*80,000.*
3X3	A1 5c black, *bluish*	*65,000.*	*6,000.*
	On cover		*13,500.*
3X4	A1 10c black, *bluish*		*50,000.*
	On cover		—

Nos. 3X1-3X4 were printed from a plate of 12 (2x6) containing nine 5c and three 10c.

Off cover values are for stamps canceled by either pen or handstamp. Stamps on covers tied by handstamps command premiums.

ENVELOPES

E1

Three Separate Handstamps

The color given is that of the "PAID 5" and oval. "James M. Buchanan" is handstamped in black, blue or red. The paper is manila, buff, white, salmon or grayish.

1845 Handstamped
Various Papers

		Unused	Used
3XU1	E1 5c blue		*6,500.*
3XU2	E1 5c red		*10,000.*
3XU3	E1 10c blue		*20,000.*
3XU4	E1 10c red		*20,000.*

On the formerly listed "5+5" envelopes, the second "5" in oval is believed not to be part of the basic prepaid marking.

Boscawen, N. H.

A1

1846 (?) Typeset *Imperf.*

		Unused	Used
4X1	A1 5c dull blue, *yellowish*, on cover		*300,000.*

Brattleboro, Vt.

Initials of Postmaster (FNP) — A1

Plate of 10 (5x2).

1846 Engr. *Imperf.*
Thick Softwove Paper Colored Through

		Unused	Used
5X1	A1 5c black, *buff*		*7,500.*
	On cover		*27,500.*
	Two singles on cover		—

Lockport, N. Y.

A1

Handstamped, "5" in Black Ms

1846 *Imperf.*

		Unused	Used
6X1	A1 5c red, *buff*, on cover		*300,000.*

Millbury, Mass.

George Washington—A1

Printed from a Woodcut

1846 *Imperf.*

		Unused	Used
7X1	A1 5c black, *bluish*	—	*50,000.*
	On cover		*200,000.*

New Haven, Conn.

ENVELOPES

E1

1845 Handstamped
Signed in Blue, Black, Magenta or Red

		Unused	Used
8XU1	E1 5c red (M)		*100,000.*
8XU2	E1 5c red, *light bluish* (Bk)		*125,000.*
8XU3	E1 5c dull blue, *buff* (Bl)		*75,000.*
8XU4	E1 5c dull blue (Bl)		*60,000.*

Values of Nos. 8XU1-8XU4 are a guide to value. They are based on auction realizations and retail sales and take condition into consideration. All New Haven envelopes are of equal rarity (each is unique), with the exception of No. 8XU2, of which two exist. An entire of No. 8XU2 is the finest example known, and this is reflected in the value shown. The other envelopes are valued according to condition as much as rarity.

Reprints were made at various times between 1871 and 1932. They differ in shade and paper from the originals.

New York, N. Y.

George Washington — A1

Plate of 40 (5x8). Nos. 9X1d, 9X2, 9X2d and 9X3 unused are valued without gum.

Nos. 9X1-9X3 and varieties unused are valued without gum. Examples with original gum are extremely scarce and will command higher prices.

1845-46 Engr. *Imperf.*
Bluish Wove Paper

		Unused	Used
9X1	A1 5c black, signed ACM, connected, *1846*	1,500.	475.
	On cover		600.
	On cover to France or England		*2,250.*
	On cover to other European countries		*5,500.*
	Pair	5,750.	1,450.
	Pair on cover		2,000.
	Pair on cover to England		*4,500.*
	Pair on cover to Canada		*5,500.*
	Vertical pair, 9X1 and 9X1e	*85,000.*	
	Strip of 3 on cover		*9,000.*
	Strip of 4 on cover		*100,000.*
a.	Signed ACM, AC connected	1,750.	550.
	On cover		700.
	On cover to France or England		*2,250.*
	On cover to other European countries		*6,000.*
	Pair, Nos. 9X1 and 9X1a, on cover		*15,000.*
b.	Signed A.C.M.	*4,500.*	*675.*
	On cover		*825.*
	On cover to France or England		*2,750.*
	On cover to other European countries		*6,000.*
	Pair		*2,400.*
	Pair on cover		*3,250.*
c.	Signed MMJr		*10,000.*
	On cover		—
	Pair on cover front		*26,500.*
d.	Signed RHM	*13,000.*	*3,500.*
	On cover		*5,500.*
	On cover from New Hamburgh, N.Y.		*12,500.*
e.	Without signature	*3,750.*	900.
	On cover		1,350.
	On cover to France or England		*2,500.*
	On cover to other European countries		*6,000.*
	On cover, July 15, 1845		*27,500.*
	Pair on cover		*2,900.*

These stamps were usually initialed "ACM" in magenta ink, as a control, before being sold or passed through the mails.

A plate of 9 (3x3) was made from which proofs were printed in black on white and deep blue papers; also in blue, green, brown and red on white bond paper. Stamps from this plate were not issued, and it is possible that it is an essay, as the design differs slightly from the issued stamps from the sheet of 40. No examples from the plate of nine are known used.

1847 Engr. *Imperf.*
Blue Wove Paper

		Unused	Used
9X2	A1 5c black, signed ACM connected	*6,500.*	3,500.
	On cover		*5,750.*
	Pair on cover		—
a.	Signed RHM		—
b.	Signed ACM, AC connected		*8,000.*
d.	Without signature	*11,000.*	*7,500.*

On the listing example of No. 9X2a the "R" is illegible and does not match those of the other "RHM" signatures.

No. 9X2b is unique.

1847 Engr. *Imperf.*
Gray Wove Paper

		Unused	Used
9X3	A1 5c black, signed ACM connected	5,250.	2,250.
	On cover		*5,250.*
	On cover to Europe		*8,500.*
	Pair		*7,750.*
	Pair on cover		*8,750.*
a.	Signed RHM		*7,000.*
b.	Without signature		*13,000.*

Providence, R.I.

A1 & A2

1846 **Engr.** ***Imperf.***

10X1 A1 5c gray black 350. *2,000.*
No gum 225.
On cover, tied by postmark *21,500.*
On cover, tied by pen cancel *11,000.*
On cover, pen canceled *6,500.*
Two on cover —

10X2 A2 10c gray black 1,150. *16,500.*
No gum 725.
On cover, pen canceled *50,000.*
a. Se-tenant with 5c *2,000.*

Plate of 12 (3x4) contains 11-5c and 1-10c.

Reprints were made in 1898. Each stamp bears one of the following letters on the back: B. O. G. E. R. T. D. U. R. B. I. N. Value of 5c, $65; 10c, $160; sheet, $1,000.

Reprint singles or sheets without back print sell for more.

St. Louis, Mo.

A1 A2 A3

Missouri Coat of Arms

Nos. 11X1-11X8 unused are valued without gum.

Wove Paper Colored Through

1845-46 **Engr.** ***Imperf.***

Greenish Wove Paper

11X1 A1 5c black, *greenish* *50,000.* *8,000.*
On cover *17,500.*
Two on cover *25,000.*
Strip of 3 plus single on cover *45,000.*

11X2 A2 10c black, *greenish* *50,000.* *8,000.*
On cover *14,000.*
Pair on cover *22,500.*
Strip of 3 on cover *70,000.*

11X3 A3 20c black, *greenish* *160,000.*
On cover —
On cover, #11X5, two #11X3 *325,000.*

Three varieties of 5c, 3 of 10c, 2 of 20c.

1846 **Gray Lilac Paper**

11X4 A1 5c black, (III), *gray lilac* — *55,000.*
On cover —

11X5 A2 10c black, *gray lilac* *50,000.* *12,500.*
On cover *16,000.*
Strip of 3 on cover *160,000.*

11X6 A3 20c black, *gray lilac* *100,000.* *60,000.*
On cover *70,000.*
Pair on cover *145,000.*

One variety of 5c, 3 of 10c, 2 of 20c.

No. 11X6 unused is unique. It is in the grade of fine and valued thus.

1847 **Pelure Paper**

11X7 A1 5c black, *bluish* — *11,000.*
On cover *16,000.*
Two on cover *37,500.*

11X8 A2 10c black, *bluish* *17,500.* *15,000.*
On cover *20,000.*
a. Impression of 5c on back *77,500.*

Three varieties of 5c, 3 of 10c.

Values of Nos. 11X7-11X8 reflect the usual poor condition of these stamps, which were printed on fragile pelure paper. Attractive examples with minor defects sell for considerably more.

Used values are for pen-canceled stamps.

No. 11X8a is unique.

Please Note:
Stamps are valued in the grade of very fine unless otherwise indicated. Values for early and valuable stamps are for examples with certificates of authenticity from acknowledged expert committees, or examples sold with the buyer having the right of certification. This applies to examples with original gum as well as examples without gum. Beware of stamps offered "as is," as the gum on some unused stamps offered with "original gum" may be fraudulent, and stamps offered as unused without gum may in some cases be altered or faintly canceled used stamps.

Manuscript Cancels on Used Stamps

Manuscript (pen) cancels reduce the value of used stamps by about 50%. See the Scott U.S. Specialized Catalogue for individual valuations.

GENERAL ISSUES

All Issues from 1847 to 1894 are Unwatermarked.

Benjamin Franklin — A1

1847, July 1 **Engr.** ***Imperf.***

Thin Bluish Wove Paper

1 A1 5c red brn, *bluish* 6,500. 375.
No gum 2,300.
Pen Cancel 200.
On cover 450.
a. 5c dark brown 8,750. 800.
No gum 3,250.
On cover 900.
b. 5c orange brown 10,000. 750.
No gum 3,500.
On cover 850.
c. 5c red orange *25,000.* *9,500.*
No gum *9,500.*
On cover *10,500.*
d. 5c brown orange — 1,000.
No gum *4,500.*
On cover 1,150.

George Washington — A2

2 A2 10c black, *bluish* *35,000.* 800.
No gum *15,000.*
Pen Cancel 500.
On cover 1,050.

REPRODUCTIONS of 1847 ISSUE

A3

A4

Actually, official imitations made from new plates of 50 subjects made by the Bureau of Engraving and Printing by order of the Post Office Department. These were not valid for postal use.

5c. On the originals the left side of the white shirt frill touches the oval on a level with the top of the "F" of "Five." On the reproductions it touches the oval about on a level with the top of the figure "5." On the originals, the bottom of the right leg of the "N" in "CENTS" is blunt. On the reproductions, the "N" comes to a point at the bottom.

10c. On the reproductions, line of coat at left points to right tip of "X" and line of coat at right points to center of "S" of CENTS. On the originals, line of coat points to "T" of TEN and between "T" and "S" of CENTS. The bottom of the right leg of the "N" of "CENTS" shows the same difference as on the 5c originals and reproductions. On the reproductions, the gap between the bottom legs of the left "X" is noticeably wider than the gap on the right "X." On the originals, the gaps are of equal width. On the reproductions the eyes have a sleepy look, the line of the mouth is straighter, and in the curl of hair near the left cheek is a strong black dot, while the originals have only a faint one.

1875 ***Imperf.***

Bluish paper, without gum

3 A3 5c red brown 850.
4 A4 10c black 1,050.

Except as noted here and in footnotes for selected issues, values for 1851-57 issues are for examples that clearly show all of the illustrated type characteristics. Stamps that have weakly defined or missing type characteristics sell for less.

In Nos. 5-17, the 1¢, 3¢ and 12¢ have very small margins between the stamps. The 5¢ and 10¢ have moderate size margins. The values of these stamps take the margin size into consideration.

Values for Nos. 5A, 6b and 19b are for the less distinct positions. Best examples sell for more.

Values for No. 16 are for outer line recut at top. Other recuts sell for more.

Franklin — A5

Type I

Type Ib

ONE CENT.

Type I. Has complete curved lines outside the labels with "U. S. Postage" and "One Cent." The scrolls below the lower label are turned under, forming little balls. The ornaments at top are substantially complete.

Values for type I are for stamps showing the marked characteristics plainly. Copies of type I showing the balls indistinctly sell for much lower prices.

Type Ib. As type I, but balls below bottom label are not as clear. Plume-like scrolls at bottom are incomplete.

1851-57 ***Imperf.***

5 A5 1c blue, type I (7R1E) *225,000.* *67,500.*
On cover *87,500.*

Values for No. 5 are for examples with margins touching or cutting slightly into the design.

Value for No. 5 unused is for a stamp with no gum.

5A A5 1c blue, type 1b *32,500.* *7,500.*
No gum *12,000.*
On cover *9,000.*

Values for No. 5A are for sound examples with margins just clear to just touching the design on one or two sides. Examples with margins well clear of the design all around are scarce and will sell for more than the values shown.

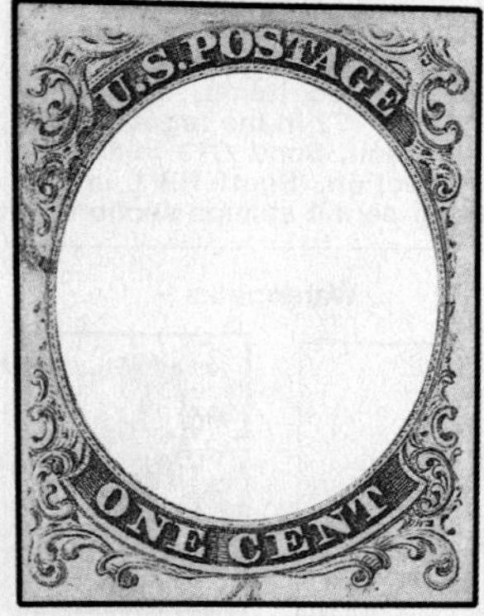

A6

Type Ic

Type Ia. Same as type I at bottom, but top ornaments and outer line at top are partly cut away.

Type Ic. Same as type Ia, but bottom right plume and ball ornament incomplete. Bottom left plume complete or nearly complete.

6 A6 1c blue, type 1a ('57) *45,000.* *10,000.*
No gum *20,000.*
On cover *14,500.*
Strip of 3 on cover *75,000.*
6b A6 1c blue, type 1c *7,000.* *3,250.*
No gum *3,000.*
On cover *4,250.*

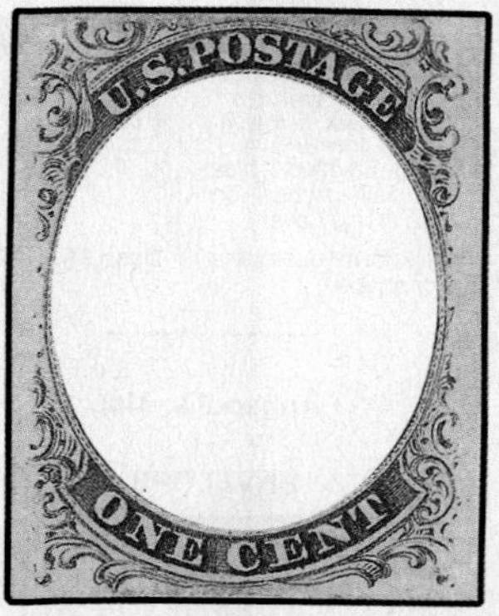

A7

Type II — Same as Type I at top, but the little balls of the bottom scrolls and the bottoms of

the lower plume ornaments are missing. The side ornaments are substantially complete.

7 A7 1c blue, type II 1,000. 125.
No gum 375.
On cover 155.

A8

Type IIIa

Type III. The top and bottom curved lines outside the labels are broken in the middle. The side ornaments are substantially complete.

Type IIIa. Similar to type III with the outer line broken at top or bottom but not both.

8 A8 1c blue, type III *25,000.* 1,800.
No gum *7,500.*
On cover 2,000.

Values for type III are for at least a 2mm break in each outer line. Examples of type III with wider breaks in outer lines command higher prices; those with smaller breaks sell for much less.

8A A8 1c blue, type IIIa 6,000. 800.
No gum 2,250.
On cover 875.

Stamps of type IIIa with bottom line broken command higher prices than those with top line broken. See note after No. 8 on width of break of outer lines.

A9

Type IV. Similar to type II, but with the curved lines outside the labels recut at top or bottom or both.

9 A9 1c blue, type IV ('52) 725.00 80.00
No gum 240.00
On cover 100.00

a. Printed on both sides, reverse inverted *50,000.*
b. Diagonal half used as ½c on cover *60,000.*

No. 9a is unique.

The No. 9b cover, a printed-matter circular mailed in 1853, is unique. The circular likely should have been sent at the 1c rate for printed matter in effect at the time. However, both the sending (New Haven, Conn.) and receiving (Hartford, Conn.) post offices treated it as fully prepaid with c postage applied. Value is based on 2013 auction realization.

Washington — A10

All of the 3c stamps of the 1851 and 1857 issues were recut at least to the extent of the outer frame lines, sometimes the inner lines at the sides (type II stamps), and often other lines in triangles, diamond blocks, label blocks and/or top/bottom frame lines.

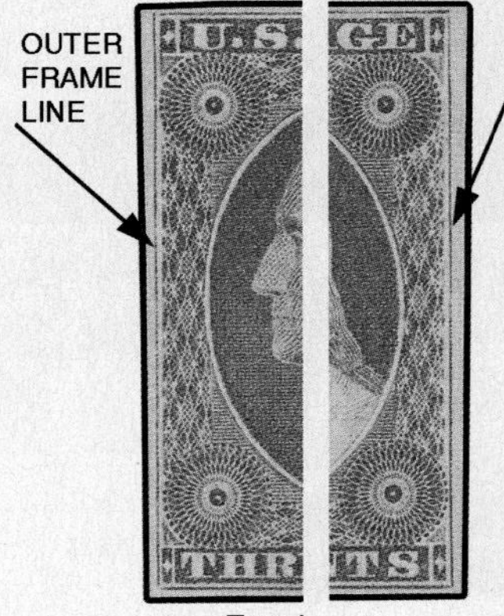

Type I

THREE CENTS.

Type I — There is an outer frame line on all four sides. The outer frame lines at the sides are always recut.

10 A10 3c org brown, type I 4,000. 180.00
No gum 1,500.
On cover 260.00

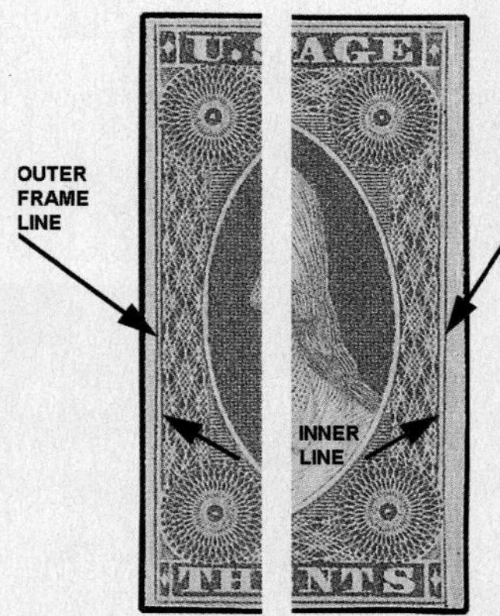

Type II

Type II — As type I, but with the inner lines at the sides added by recutting on the plate.

10A A10 3c org brown, type II 3,250. 140.00
No gum 1,250.
On cover 190.00
b. Printed on both sides *55,000.*

Only one example of No. 10Ab is recorded.

11 A10 3c dull red, type I ('55) 275.00 15.00
No gum 110.00
On cover 17.50

11A A10 3c dull red, type II ('53-'55) 250.00 15.00
No gum 85.00
On cover 17.50
c. Vertical half used as 1c on cover *5,000.*
d. Diagonal half used as 1c on cover *5,000.*
e. Double impression *30,000.*

Thomas Jefferson — A11

FIVE CENTS.

Type I — Projections on all four sides.

12 A11 5c red brown, type I ('56) *30,000.* 675.
No gum *11,000.*
On domestic cover 1,150.

Washington — A12

TEN CENTS

Type I — The "shells" at the lower corners are practically complete. The outer line below the label is very nearly complete. The outer lines are broken above the middle of the top label and the "X" in each upper corner.

13 A12 10c green, type I ('55) *19,000.* 800.
No gum *8,500.*
On domestic cover 900.

A13

Type II — The design is complete at the top. The outer line at the bottom is broken in the middle. The shells are partly cut away, as shown.

14 A13 10c green, type II ('55) 5,000. 140.
No gum 1,800.
On domestic cover 190.

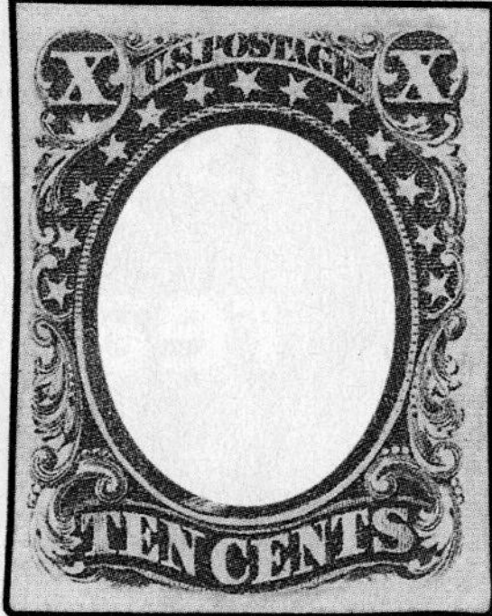
A14

Type III — The outer lines are broken above the top label and the "X" numerals. The outer line at the bottom and the shells are partly cut away, as shown, similar to type II.

15 A14 10c green, type III ('55) 5,000. 140.
No gum 1,800.
On domestic cover 190.

A15

Type IV. The outer lines have been recut at top or bottom or both.

Types I, II, III and IV have complete ornaments at the sides of the stamps and three pearls at each outer edge of the bottom panel.

16 A15 10c green, type IV ('55) *37,500.* 1,600.
No gum *15,000.*
On domestic cover 1,900.

Washington — A16

17 A16 12c gray black 6,250. 250.
No gum 2,100.
Single, on cover 1,500.
a. Diagonal half used as 6c on cover *2,500.*
b. Vertical half used as 6c on cover *8,500.*
c. Printed on both sides *40,000.*

Values for 1857-61 issues are for examples that clearly show all the illustrated type characteristics. Stamps that have weakly defined or missing type characteristics sell for less.

Nos. 18-39 have small or very small margins. The values take into account the margin size. See footnotes for more specific information on selected issues.

SAME DESIGNS AS 1851-57 ISSUES

1857-61 ***Perf. 15½***

18 A5 1c blue, type I ('61) 2,100. 500.
No gum 800.
On cover 650.
Short ornaments at either top or bottom —

19 A6 1c blue, type Ia *42,500.* *9,000.*
No gum *20,000.*
On cover *9,500.*
b. blue, type Ic 4,250. 2,750.
No gum *1,750.*
On cover *3,750.*

20 A7 1c blue, type II 850. 250.
No gum 375.
On cover 325.

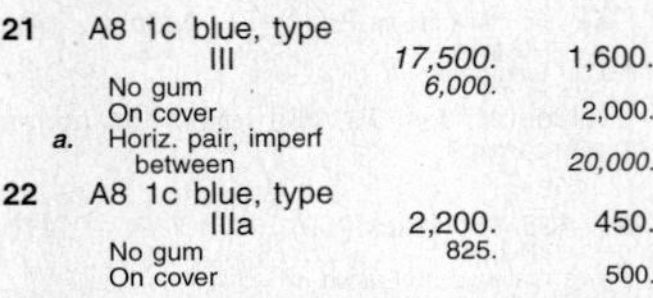

21 A8 1c blue, type III 17,500. 1,600.
No gum 6,000.
On cover 2,000.
a. Horiz. pair, imperf between 20,000.

22 A8 1c blue, type IIIa 2,200. 450.
No gum 825.
On cover 500.

Beware of pairs of No. 22 with faint blind perforations between that sometimes are offered as pairs imperf. between.

23 A9 1c blue, type IV 10,000. 900.
No gum 4,250.
On cover 1,100.

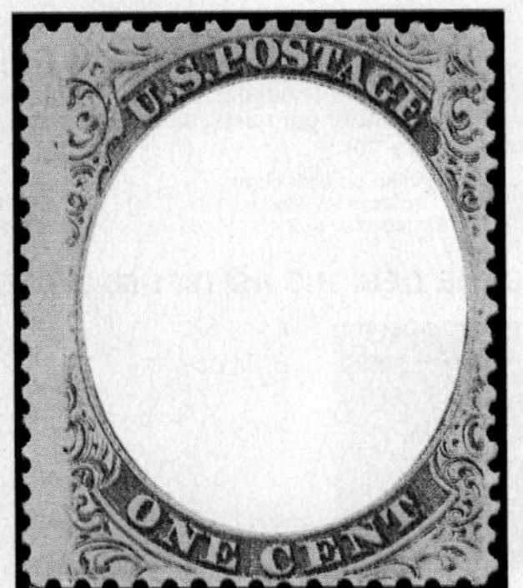

Franklin — A20

ONE CENT
Type V — Similar to type III of 1851-57 but with side ornaments partly cut away. About one-half of all positions have side scratches. Wide breaks in top and bottom framelines.
Type Va — Stamps from Plate 5 with almost complete ornaments at right side and no side scratches. Many, but not all, stamps from Plate 5 are Type Va, the remainder being Type V.

24 A20 1c blue, type V 140.00 37.50
No gum 60.00
On cover 45.00
Long curl in hair and curl over "C" of "Cent" (52, 92R8) 290.00 120.00
On cover 140.00
b. Laid paper 7,500.

25 A10 3c rose, type I 2,750. 175.00
No gum 950.
On cover 190.00
b. Vert. pair, imperf. horizontally 10,000.

25A A10 3c rose, type II 9,000. 850.
No gum 4,000.
On cover 950.

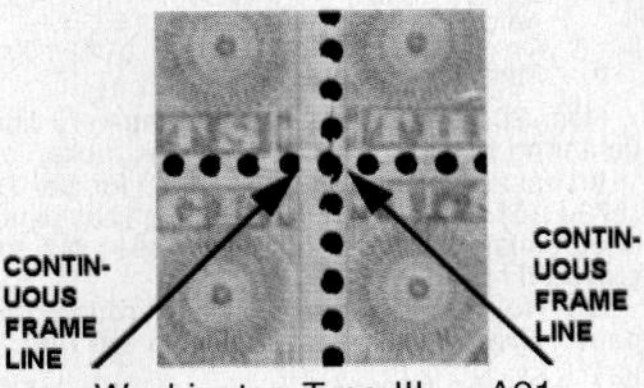

Washington Type III — A21

THREE CENTS
Type III — There are no outer frame lines at top and bottom. The side frame lines were recut so as to be continuous from the top to the bottom of the plate. Stamps from the top or bottom rows show the ends of the side frame lines and may be mistaken for Type IV.

26 A21 3c dull red, type III 65.00 10.00
No gum 27.50
On cover 11.00
b. Horiz. pair, imperf. vertically 14,000.
On cover —
c. Vert. pair, imperf. horizontally 16,000.
d. Horizontal pair, imperf. between
e. Double impression 15,000.
On cover —

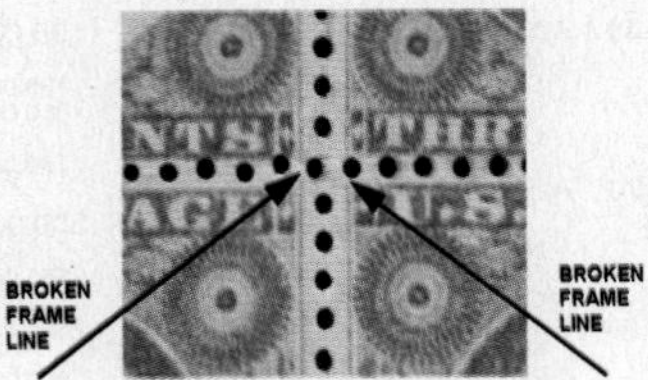

Washington (Type IV) — A21a

Type IV — As type III, but the side frame lines extend only to the top and bottom of the stamp design. All Type IV stamps are from plates 10 and 11 (each of which exists in three states), and these plates produced only Type IV. The side frame lines were recut individually for each stamp, thus being broken between the stamps vertically.
Beware of type III stamps with frame lines that stop at the top of the design (from top row of plate) or bottom of the design (from bottom row of plate). These are often mistakenly offered as No. 26A.

26A A21a 3c dull red, type IV 600.00 140.00
No gum 260.00
On cover 180.00
f. Horiz. strip of 3, imperf. vert., on cover 14,500.

No. 26Af is unique.

27 A11 5c brick red, type I ('58) 80,000. 1,450.
No gum 20,000.
On cover 1,800.
N.Y. Ocean Mail +1,000.

28 A11 5c red brown, type I 60,000. 1,050.
No gum 15,000.
On cover 1,250.
b. Bright red brown 70,000. 2,300.
No gum 20,000.

28A A11 5c Indian red, type I ('58) 175,000. 3,500.
No gum 40,000.
On cover 5,000.

No. 28A unused is valued in the grade of fine. Only four examples are recorded with any amount of gum.

29 A11 5c brown, type I ('59) 5,500. 350.
No gum 1,750.
On cover 500.

Jefferson — A22

FIVE CENTS.
Type II — The projections at top and bottom are partly cut away.

30 A22 5c org brn, type II ('61) 1,200. 1,300.
No gum 500.
On cover 2,250.

30A A22 5c brown, type II ('60) 2,200. 280.
No gum 825.
On cover 325.
b. Printed on both sides 35,000.

31 A12 10c green, type I 35,000. 1,100.
No gum 11,500.
On domestic cover 1,300.

32 A13 10c green, type II 5,750. 180.
No gum 2,000.
On domestic cover 225.

33 A14 10c green, type III 5,750. 180.
No gum 2,000.
On domestic cover 225.

34 A15 10c green, type IV 50,000. 2,100.
No gum 20,000.
On domestic cover 2,500.

Example I Example II
Washington (Two typical examples) — A23

TEN CENTS
Type V — The side ornaments are slightly cut away. Usually only one pearl remains at each end of the lower label, but some copies show two or three pearls at the right side. At the bottom the outer line is complete and the shells nearly so. The outer lines at top are complete except over the right "X."

35 A23 10c green, type V ('59) 210.00 55.00
No gum 95.00
On domestic cover 67.50

No. 36 outer frame lines recut on plate

TWELVE CENTS. Printed from two plates.
Plate 1 (No. 36) — Outer frame lines were recut on the plate and are complete. Very narrow spacing of stamps on the plate.

36 A16 12c black (Plate 1) 1,750. 300.
No gum 550.
Single on cover 700.
a. Diagonal half used as 6c on cover 17,500.
c. Horizontal pair, imperf. between 12,500.

Typical No. 36B, outer frame lines not recut

Plate III (No. 36B) — Weak outer frame lines from the die were not recut and are noticeably uneven or broken, sometimes partly missing. Somewhat wider spacing of stamps on the plate.

36B A16 12c black, plate III ('59) 700. 250.
No gum 325.
Single on cover 1,150.

Washington A17 Franklin A18

37 A17 24c gray lilac ('60) 1,450. 400.
a. 24c gray 1,450. 400.
No gum 525.
On cover to England 1,000.

38 A18 30c orange ('60) 1,900. 425.
No gum 700.
On cover to Germany or France 1,350.

Washington — A19

39 A19 90c blue ('60) 3,000. 10,000.
No gum 1,200.
On cover 225,000.

See Die and Plate proofs in the Scott United States Specialized Catalogue for imperfs. of the 12c, 24c, 30c, 90c.
Genuine cancellations on the 90c are rare. Used examples must be accompanied by certificates of authenticity issued by recognized expertizing committees.

REPRINTS OF 1857-60 ISSUE
White paper, without gum.

1875 ***Perf. 12***

40 A5 1c bright blue 575.
41 A10 3c scarlet 2,750.
42 A22 5c org brown 1,150.
43 A12 10c blue green 2,500. 13,000.
44 A16 12c greenish black 2,750.
45 A17 24c blackish violet 3,000. 10,000.
46 A18 30c yel orange 3,000.
47 A19 90c deep blue 3,500.

Nos. 41-46 are valued in the grade of fine.
Nos. 40-47 exist imperforate. Very infrequent sales preclude establishing a value at this time. One set of imperforate pairs is recorded and it sold for $110,000 in a 2009 auction.

Essays-Trial Color Proofs

The paper of former Nos. 55-62 (Nos. 63E11e, 65-E15h, 67-E9e, 69-E6e, 72-E7h, Essay section, Nos. 70eTC, 71bTC, Trial Color Proof section, Scott U.S. Specialized) is thin and semitransparent. That of the postage issues is thicker and more opaque, except Nos. 62B, 70c and 70d.

Franklin — A24

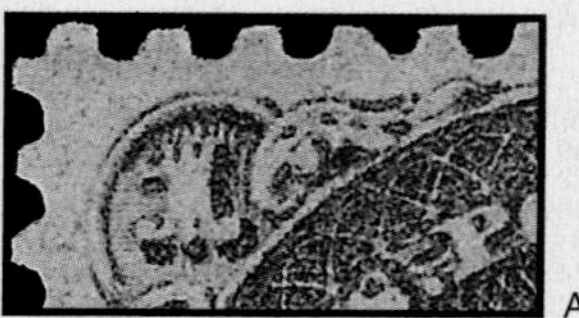
A24

Washington — A25

A25

Jefferson — A26

A26

Washington — A27

A27

A27a

Washington — A28

A28

Washington
A29

Franklin
A30

Washington — A31

A31

1c — There is a dash under the tip of the ornament at right of the numeral in upper left corner.

3c — Ornaments at corners end in a small ball.

5c — There is a leaflet in the foliated ornaments at each corner.

10c (A27) — A heavy curved line has been cut below the stars and an outer line added to the ornaments above them.

12c — There are corner ornaments consisting of ovals and scrolls.

90c — Parallel lines form an angle above the ribbon with "U. S. Postage"; between these lines there is a row of dashes and a point of color at the apex of the lower line.

1861 *Perf. 12*

62B A27a 10c dark green *8,250.* 1,600.
No gum *3,500.*
On cover 2,100.
On patriotic cover 3,000.

1861-62 *Perf. 12*

63 A24 1c blue 275.00 45.00
No gum 100.00
On cover (single) 52.50
On patriotic cover 225.00
a. 1c ultramarine *2,500.* *900.00*
No gum *1,000.*
b. 1c dark blue 800.00 *875.00*
No gum 300.00
c. Laid paper, horiz. or vert. *8,500.* *4,500.*
d. Vertical pair, imperf. horiz. —
e. Printed on both sides, reverse inverted — *35,000.*

The editors would like to see authenticated evidence of the existence of No. 63d.

64 A25 3c pink *14,000.* 600.00
No gum *5,000.*
On cover 775.00
On patriotic cover 1,400.
a. 3c pigeon blood pink *50,000.* *4,500.*
No gum *15,000.*
On cover *5,000.*
On patriotic cover *7,500.*
b. 3c rose pink 600.00 150.00
No gum 225.00
On cover 180.00
On patriotic cover 250.00

65 A25 3c rose 125.00 3.00
No gum 50.00
On cover 3.50
On patriotic cover 90.00
b. Laid paper, horiz. or vert. — *1,100.*
d. Vertical pair, imperf. horiz. *15,000.* *1,500.*
No gum *6,500.*
e. Printed on both sides, reverse inverted *40,000.* *8,000.*
f. Double impression *12,500.*

The 3c lake can be found under No. 66 in the Trial Color Proofs section of the Scott U.S. Specialized Catalogue. The imperf 3c lake under No. 66P in the same section. The imperf 3c rose can be found in the Die and Plate Proofs section of the Specialized.

67 A26 5c buff *27,500.* 750.
No gum *10,500.*
On cover 1,000.
On patriotic cover *3,750.*
a. 5c brown yellow *30,000.* 1,100.
No gum *11,500.*
b. 5c olive yellow — 4,750.

Values of Nos. 67, 67a, 67b reflect the normal small margins.

68 A27 10c green 950. 55.00
No gum 375.
On cover 75.00
On patriotic cover 375.00
On cover to Canada 100.00
a. 10c dark green 1,350. 85.00
No gum 450.
b. Vertical pair, imperf. horiz. *30,000.*

69 A28 12c black 1,700. 95.00
No gum 675.
On domestic cover 135.00
On patriotic cover 850.00
On cover to France or Germany with #65 160.00

70 A29 24c red lilac ('62) 3,000. 300.00
No gum 1,150.
On cover 350.00
On patriotic cover *3,000.*
a. 24c brown lilac 3,250. 325.00
No gum 1,250.
b. 24c steel blue ('61) *16,500.* 850.00
No gum *6,250.*
On cover 1,300.
c. 24c violet, thin paper *35,000.* 2,250.
No gum *13,500.*
d. 24c pale gray violet, thin paper *25,000.* 3,000.
No gum *6,000.*

There are numerous shades of the 24c stamp in this and the following issue.

Nos. 70c and 70d are on a thinner, harder and more transparent paper than Nos. 70, 70a, 70b or the latter Nos. 78, 78a, 78b and 78c.

71 A30 30c orange 2,600. 200.
No gum 950.
On cover to France or Germany 380.
On patriotic cover *3,500.*
a. Printed on both sides —

Values for No. 71 are for examples with small margins, especially at sides. Large-margined examples sell for much more.

72 A31 90c blue 3,000. 575.
No gum 1,200.
On cover *25,000.*
a. 90c pale blue 3,000. 625.
No gum 1,200.
b. 90c dark blue 3,750. 950.
No gum 1,500.

Please Note:
Stamps are valued in the grade of very fine unless otherwise indicated.
Values for early and valuable stamps are for examples with certificates of authenticity from acknowledged expert committees, or examples sold with the buyer having the right of certification.
This applies to examples with original gum as well as examples without gum.
Beware of stamps offered "as is," as the gum on some unused stamps offered with "original gum" may be fraudulent, and stamps offered as unused without gum may in some cases be altered or faintly canceled used stamps.

DESIGNS AS 1861 ISSUE

Andrew Jackson
A32

Abraham Lincoln
A33

1861-66 *Perf. 12*

73 A32 2c black ('63) 325.00 55.00
No gum 140.00
On cover 75.00
On patriotic cover *2,000.*
a. Diagonal half used as 1c as part of 3c rate on cover 1,500.
b. Diagonal half used alone as 1c on cover *3,000.*
c. Horiz. half used as 1c as part of 3c rate on cover *3,500.*
d. Vert. half used as 1c as part of 3c rate on cover 2,000.
e. Vert. half used alone as 1c on cover *4,000.*
f. Printed on both sides, reverse not inverted *27,500.*
g. Laid paper — *11,500.*

No. 73f unused is unique. It has perfs cut off on two sides and is valued thus.

The 3c scarlet can be found under No. 74 in the Scott U.S. Specialized Catalogue Trial Color Proofs section.

75 A26 5c red brown ('62) 5,750. 425.
No gum 2,100.
On cover 700.
On patriotic cover *4,000.*

Values for No. 75 reflect the normal small margins.

76 A26 5c brown ('63) 1,350. 120.
No gum 525.
On cover 180.
On patriotic cover 2,000.
a. 5c black brown 2,250. 400.
No gum 850.
b. Laid paper —

Values of Nos. 76, 76a reflect the normal small margins.

77 A33 15c black ('66) 4,750. 170.
No gum 1,750.
On cover to France or Germany 200.

78 A29 24c lilac ('62) 2,600. 350.
No gum 900.
On cover, #78, 78a or 78b 400.
a. 24c grayish lilac 2,750. 400.
No gum 950.
b. 24c gray 2,750. 425.
No gum 950.
c. 24c blackish violet *100,000.* *19,000.*
No gum *30,000.*
On cover *25,000.*

Only three examples are recorded of No. 78c unused with original gum. No. 78c unused with and without gum are valued in the grade of fine-very fine.

d. Printed on both sides, reverse inverted *22,500.*
On cover *35,000.*

SAME DESIGNS AS 1861-66 ISSUES

Grill

Embossed with grills of various sizes. Some authorities believe that more than one size of grill probably existed on one of the grill rolls.

A peculiarity of the United States issues from 1867 to 1870 is the grill or embossing. The object was to break the fiber of the paper so that the ink of the canceling stamp would soak in and make washing for a second using impossible. The exact date at which grilled stamps came into use is unsettled. Luff's "Postage Stamps of the United States" places the date as probably August 8, 1867.

Horizontal measurements are given first.

GRILL WITH POINTS UP

Grills A and C were made by a roller covered with ridges shaped like an inverted V. Pressing the ridges into the stamp paper forced the paper into the pyramidal pits between the ridges, causing irregular breaks in the paper. Grill B was made by a roller with raised bosses.

A. GRILL COVERING THE ENTIRE STAMP

1867 *Perf. 12*

79 A25 3c rose 8,500. 1,400.
No gum 2,750.
On cover 1,900.
b. Printed on both sides —

Nos. 79, 79b, are valued for fine-very fine centering but with minor perforation faults.

An essay which is often mistaken for No. 79 (#79-E15) shows the points of the grill as small squares faintly impressed in the paper, but not cutting through it.

On No. 79 the grill breaks through the paper. Examples free from defects are rare.

80 A26 5c brown *260,000.*
a. 5c dark brown *260,000.*
81 A30 30c orange *240,000.*

Four examples of Nos. 80 and 80a (two of each shade), and eight examples of No. 81 (one in the New York Public Library Miller collection and not available to collectors) are known. All are more or less faulty and/or off center. Values are for off-center examples with small perforation faults.

B. GRILL ABOUT 18x15mm (22x18 POINTS)

82 A25 3c rose *900,000.*

The four known examples of No. 82 are valued in the grade of fine.

C. GRILL ABOUT 13x16mm (16 TO 17 BY 18 TO 21 POINTS)

The grilled area on each of four C grills in the sheet may total about 18x15mm when a normal C grill adjoins a fainter grill extending to the right or left edge of the stamp.

This is caused by a partial erasure on the grill roller when it was changed to produce C grills instead of the all-over A grill.

The imperf. can be found in the *Scott U.S. Specialized Catalogue* Die and Plate Proofs section.

83 A25 3c rose 5,500. 1,100.
No gum 2,000.
On cover 1,300.

GRILL WITH POINTS DOWN

The grills were produced by rollers with the surface covered, or partly covered, by pyramidal bosses. On the D, E and F grills the tips of the pyramids are vertical ridges. On the Z grill the ridges are horizontal.

D. GRILL ABOUT 12x14mm (15 BY 17 TO 18 POINTS)

84 A32 2c black *16,000.* 4,250.
No gum *6,500.*
On cover 4,750.

No. 84 is valued in the grade of fine.

85 A25 3c rose *8,000.* 1,000.
No gum *2,400.*
On cover 1,150.

Z. GRILL ABOUT 11x14mm (13 TO 14 BY 18 POINTS)

85A A24 1c blue *3,000,000.*

Two examples of No. 85A are known. One is contained in the New York Public Library collection, which is on long-term loan to the Smithsonian National Postal Museum.

85B A32 2c black 17,500. 1,100.
No gum 6,750.
On cover 1,300.
85C A25 3c rose *25,000.* 3,250.
No gum *9,000.*
On cover 3,750.
85D A27 10c green *600,000.*

Six examples of No. 85D are known. One is contained in the New York Public Library collection. Value is for a well-centered example with small faults.

85E A28 12c intense black *17,500.* 2,400.
No gum *6,500.*
On cover 2,900.
85F A33 15c black *2,000,000.*

Two examples of No. 85F are documented, one in the grade of very good, the other extremely fine. Value is for the extremely fine example.

E. GRILL ABOUT 11x13mm (14 BY 15 TO 17 POINTS)

86 A24 1c blue 3,000. 400.
No gum 1,100.
a. 1c dull blue 3,000. 375.
No gum 1,100.
On cover, #86 or 86a 525.
87 A32 2c black 1,700. 180.
No gum 650.
On cover 275.
a. Diagonal half used as 1c on cover *2,000.*
b. Vertical half used as 1c on cover *2,000.*
88 A25 3c rose 950. 27.50
No gum 350.
On cover 32.50
a. 3c lake red 1,250. 75.00
No gum 475.
b. Two diagonal halves from different stamps used as 3c stamp (fraudulent use), one half having grill with points up, on cover —
89 A27 10c green 5,000. 325.
No gum 2,000.
On cover 425.
90 A28 12c black 4,750. 375.
No gum 1,900.
On cover 525.
91 A33 15c black 12,500. 600.
No gum 4,500.
On cover 700.

F. GRILL ABOUT 9x13mm (11 TO 12 BY 15 TO 17 POINTS)

92 A24 1c blue 2,800. 425.
No gum 925.
a. 1c pale blue 2,300. 375.
No gum 700.
On cover 475.
93 A32 2c black 400. 55.00
No gum 140.
On cover 70.00
a. Vertical half used as 1c as part of 3c rate on cover *1,250.*
b. Diagonal half used as 1c as part of 3c rate on cover *1,250.*
c. Horizontal half used alone as 1c on cover *2,500.*
d. Diagonal half used alone as 1c on cover *2,500.*
94 A25 3c red 350. 10.00
a. 3c rose 350. 10.00
No gum 150.
On cover, #94 or 94a 11.00
c. Vertical pair, imperf. horiz. *15,000.*
d. Printed on both sides *9,000.* *42,500.*

The imperf. 3c can be found in the Scott U.S. Specialized Catalogue Die and Plate Proofs section.

95 A26 5c brown 3,250. 850.
No gum 1,200.
On cover 900.
a. 5c black brown 4,500. 2,300.
No gum 1,750.

Values of Nos. 95, 95a reflect the normal small margins.

96 A27 10c yel grn 2,500. 225.
On cover 275.
97 A28 12c black 2,800. 250.
No gum 1,000.
On cover 300.
98 A33 15c black 4,000. 275.
No gum 1,500.
On cover 300.
99 A29 24c gray lilac 8,500. 1,500.
No gum 3,250.
On cover 2,500.
100 A30 30c orange 9,000. 900.
No gum 3,300.
On cover 1,800.

Values for No. 100 are for examples with small margins, especially at sides. Large-margined examples sell for much more.

101 A31 90c blue 14,500. 2,250.
No gum 5,500.
On cover *100,000.*

RE-ISSUE OF 1861-66 ISSUES
Without Grill, Hard White Paper White Crackly Gum

1875 ***Perf. 12***

102 A24 1c blue *750.* *1,600.*
No gum *330.*
On cover —
103 A32 2c black *3,250.* *11,000.*
No gum *1,500.*
104 A25 3c brown red *3,750.* *14,000.*
No gum *1,700.*
105 A26 5c brown *2,400.* *6,500.*
No gum *1,100.*
106 A27 10c green *2,900.* *125,000.*
No gum *1,400.*
107 A28 12c black *3,500.* *13,000.*
No gum *1,600.*
108 A33 15c black *4,250.* *32,500.*
No gum *2,000.*
109 A29 24c deep violet *5,500.* *18,000.*
No gum *2,600.*
110 A30 30c brownish org *5,750.* *18,000.*
No gum *2,700.*
111 A31 90c blue *6,750.* *225,000.*
No gum *3,250.*

These stamps can be distinguished from the 1861-66 issues by the shades and the paper which is hard and very white instead of yellowish. The gum is white and crackly.

Five examples are recorded of No. 111 used, one of which has a non-contemporaneous cancel. Value is for centered and sound example (two are known thus).

Franklin — A34

Post Horse and Rider — A35

G. Grill measuring 9½x9mm (12 by 11 to 11½ points)

1869 **Hard Wove Paper** ***Perf. 12***

112 A34 1c buff 575. 130.
No gum 210.
On cover, single 260.
b. Without grill *32,500.*
113 A35 2c brown 500. 75.
No gum 190.
On cover, single 135.
b. Without grill *14,000.*
c. Half used as 1c on cover, diagonal, vertical or horizontal *6,000.*
d. Printed on both sides *62,500.*

Locomotive A36

Washington A37

114 A36 3c ultramarine 225. 16.00
No gum 90.
On cover 24.00
a. Without grill *13,000.* *18,000.*
Without grill, gray paper 3,750.
b. Vert. one-third used as 1c on cover —
c. Vert. two-thirds used as 2c on cover *10,000.*

d.	Double impression	*15,000.*	
e.	Printed on both sides, reverse inverted	*55,000.*	

Two examples recorded of No. 114a on normal paper: one with pen cancel but with original gum, 1994 Philatelic Foundation certificate; and one lifted from a cover, original gum adhering, examined, and placed back, 2011 Philatelic Foundation certificate. Also, four examples of No. 114a on gray paper: a single lifted from cover, examined, and hinged back in place, 1991 Philatelic Foundation certificate; and a strip of three on piece, mostly detached from piece, with full gum, 1978 and 2006 Philatelic Foundation certificates.

Nos. 114d and 114e each are unique. No. 114d has a pre-printing paper fold.

115 A37 6c ultramarine		2,500.	200.
	No gum	1,000.	
	On cover		475.
b.	Vertical half used as 3c on cover		*50,000.*

Shield and Eagle — A38

S. S. Adriatic — A39

116 A38 10c yellow		1,850.	110.
	No gum	725.	
	On cover		375.
117 A39 12c green		1,850.	120.
	No gum	725.	
	On cover		450.

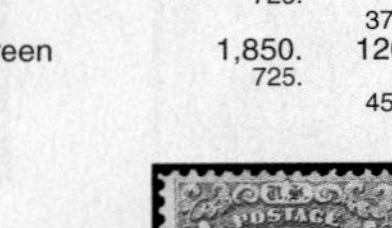

Landing of Columbus — A40

Type I. Picture unframed.

No. 118 has horizontal shading lines at the left and right sides of the vignette.

118 A40 15c brn & bl, type I		9,500.	800.
	No gum	3,250.	
	On cover		1,800.
a.	Without grill	*11,500.*	

A40a

Type II. Picture framed.

No. 119 has diagonal shading lines at the left and right sides of the vignette.

119 A40a 15c brn & bl, type II		3,000.	200.
	No gum	1,050.	
	On cover		800.
b.	Center inverted	*1,000,000.*	*22,500.*
	No gum	*700,000.*	
c.	Center double, one inverted		*80,000.*

"The Declaration of Independence" A41

120 A41 24c green & vio		7,500.	600.
	No gum	2,600.	
	On domestic cover		*12,500.*
a.	Without grill	*14,000.*	
b.	Center inverted	*750,000.*	*37,500.*
	On cover		*130,000.*

Shield, Eagle and Flags — A42

Lincoln — A43

121 A42 30c ultra & carmine		4,000.	400.
	No gum	1,450.	
	On domestic cover		*17,500.*
a.	Without grill	*10,000.*	
b.	Flags inverted	*750,000.*	*90,000.*
	No gum	*300,000.*	

Seven examples of No. 121b unused are recorded. Only one has part of its original gum.

122 A43 90c carmine & black		11,000.	1,700.
	No gum	3,750.	
	On cover		*430,000.*
a.	Without grill	*22,500.*	

Values of varieties of Nos. 112-122 without grill are for examples with original gum.

Most examples of Nos. 119b, 120b are faulty. Values are for stamps with fine centering and only minimal faults. No. 120b unused is valued without gum, as all of the three examples available to collectors are without gum.

RE-ISSUE OF 1869 ISSUE

Produced by the National Bank Note Co.

Without grill, hard white paper, with white crackly gum.

The gum is almost always somewhat yellowed with age, and unused stamps with original gum are valued with such gum.

A new plate of 150 subjects was made for the 1c. The plate for the frame of the 15c was made using the same die as that used to make the type I frame for No. 118. For No. 118, the lines on each side of the vignette area were entered onto the plate itself, one position at a time. Upon close examination, each stamp position will be found to exhibit minute differences in these horizontal fringe lines.

1875 ***Perf. 12***

123 A34 1c buff		525.	425.
	No gum	220.	
	On cover		*3,000.*
124 A35 2c brown		600.	750.
	No gum	250.	
	On cover		*12,500.*
125 A36 3c blue		*5,000.*	*27,500.*
	No gum	2,500.	
	On cover		—

Used value for No. 125 is for an attractive fine to very fine example with minimal faults.

126 A37 6c blue		1,700.	*3,000.*
	No gum	750.	
	On cover		—
127 A38 10c yellow		1,600.	1,800.
	No gum	700.	
	On cover		*22,500.*
128 A39 12c green		2,000.	*3,000.*
	No gum	900.	
	On cover		—
129 A40 15c brn & bl, Type III		1,300.	1,000.
	No gum	575.	
	On cover		*22,500.*
a.	Imperf. horizontally, single	*14,000.*	*30,000.*
	No gum	*5,000.*	

Two used examples of No. 129a are recorded. Both have faults and are valued thus.

130 A41 24c grn & violet		2,000.	1,600.
	No gum	900.	
	On cover		*27,500.*
131 A42 30c ultra & car		2,250.	2,750.
	No gum	1,000.	
132 A43 90c car & blk		3,750.	*6,000.*
	No gum	1,500.	

Soft Porous Paper

1880-82

133 A34 1c buff, issued with gum		325.	*550.*
	No gum	140.	
	On cover		1,900.
a.	1c brown orange, issued without gum ('81 and '82)	325.	

PRODUCED BY THE NATIONAL BANK NOTE COMPANY

Franklin — A44

A44

Jackson — A45

A45

Washington — A46

A46

Lincoln — A47

A47

Edwin M. Stanton — A48

A48

Jefferson — A49

A49

Henry Clay — A50

A50

Daniel Webster — A51

A51

Gen. Winfield Scott A52

Alexander Hamilton A53

Commodore O.H. Perry — A54

H. GRILL ABOUT 10x12mm (11 TO 13 BY 14 TO 16 POINTS)

The "H" grills can be separated into early state and late state, based on the shape of the tip of the grill. Early-state grills show a point or very small vertical line at the tip of the pyramid, while late-state grills show the pyramid tips truncated and flat.

Early-state "H" grills tend to be on vertical-mesh wove paper, while later printings and all late-state grills were printed on horizontal-mesh wove paper, resulting in stamp designs being approximately ¼mm shorter than the designs printed on vertical-mesh wove paper. The late-stage "H" grills virtually all seem to have been used only after Jan. 1873.

Poor printing quality often resulted in grills that show only a few grill points or a very few rows of points. This is especially true of the "H" grills. When there are not enough grill points to clearly identify whether the grill is an "H" or an "I," it must be assumed it is the lower-valued "H" grill variety. Authentication is advised for these stamps with high catalogue values.

White Wove Paper, Thin to Medium Thick.

1870-71 ***Perf. 12***

134 A44 1c ultra		2,000.	200.00
	No gum	700.	
	On cover		240.00
b.	Pair, one without grill		—
135 A45 2c red brown		1,000.	75.00
	No gum	360.	
	On cover		100.00
b.	Diagonal half used as 1c on cover		—
c.	Vertical half used as 1c on cover		—
136 A46 3c green		575.	32.50
	No gum	190.	
	On cover		37.50
b.	Printed on both sides		—

The imperf. 3c can be found in the Scott U.S. Specialized Catalogue Die and Plate Proofs section.

137 A47 6c carmine		5,000.	400.
	No gum	1,750.	
	On cover		500.
b.	Pair, one without grill		—

138 A48 7c vermilion ('71) 4,250. 475.
No gum 1,550.
On cover 650.
b. Pair, one without grill —
139 A49 10c brown 7,000. 800.
No gum 2,550.
On cover 1,000.
b. Pair, one without grill, one with split grill, on cover —
140 A50 12c dull vio *32,500.* 3,500.
No gum *14,000.*
On cover *6,500.*
Double grill —
141 A51 15c orange 7,500. 1,500.
No gum 2,500.
On cover 2,250.
142 A52 24c purple — 6,500.
On cover —
143 A53 30c black 20,000. 3,750.
No gum 7,500.
On cover 4,750.
144 A54 90c carmine 25,000. 2,250.
No gum 10,000.
On cover —

I. GRILL ABOUT 8½x10mm (10 TO 11 BY 10 TO 13 POINTS)

The "I" grills can be separated into early state and late state, based on the shape of the tip of the grill. Early state grills show small tips of the pyramid, while late state grills show the pyramid tips truncated and flat.

Early state "I" grills tend to be on vertical-mesh wove paper, while later printings and all late-state grills were printed on horizontal-mesh wove paper, resulting in stamp designs being approximately ¼mm shorter than the designs printed on vertical-mesh wove paper. The late-stage "I" grills all seem to have been used only after Jan. 1873.

Values are for stamps with grills that are clearly identifiable. Poor printing quality often resulted in grills that show only a few grill points or a very few rows of points. When there are not enough grill points to clearly identify whether the grill is an "H" or an "I," it must be assumed it is the lower-valued "H" grill variety. Authentication is advised for these stamps with high catalogue values.

134A A44 1c ultramarine *2,750.* *375.00*
No gum *800.00*
On cover —
135A A45 2c red brown *2,000.* *325.00*
On cover —
136A A46 3c green *850.00* *100.00*
On cover —
a. Pair, one without grill —
On cover —
137A A47 6c carmine *7,000.* *950.00*
138A A48 7c vermilion ('71) *6,500.* *850.00*
No gum *2,200.*
139A A49 10c brown *17,500.* *8,500.*
Pair, on cover *12,000.*

There are two unused examples of No. 139A recorded. One is fine and the other is very fine plus. The catalogue value is for the latter. The pair on cover is the only example of No. 139A on cover. One stamp in the pair is defective, and the cover is valued thus.

140A A50 12c dull violet *30,000.*

Two examples are recorded of No. 140A unused, and it is valued in the grade of fine.

141A A51 15c orange *16,500.* *7,500.*
On cover —

Three examples are recorded of No. 141A unused, and value is for a fine example.

Earliest documented use: June 15, 1870.

143A A53 30c black *75,000.*

Only one recorded example of No. 143A, which is valued in the grade of fine-very fine.

144A A54 90c carmine — *15,000.*

The unused No. 144A has a vertically split grill and is unique.

White Wove Paper
Without Grill.

1870-71 ***Perf. 12***

145 A44 1c ultra 650. 20.00
No gum 240.
On cover 22.50
146 A45 2c red brown 300. 17.50
No gum 115.
On cover 20.00
a. Diagonal half used as 1c on cover *700.00*
b. Vertical half used as 1c on cover *800.00*
c. Horiz. half used as 1c on cover *800.00*
d. Double impression *9,000.*
147 A46 3c green 200. 1.80
No gum 80.
On cover 2.30
a. Printed on both sides, reverse inverted *17,500.*
b. Double impression *30,000.*

Nos. 147a and 147b are valued in the grade of fine.

The imperf. 3c can be found in the Scott U.S. Specialized Catalogue Die and Plate Proofs section.

148 A47 6c carmine 900. 22.50
No gum 290.
On cover 27.50
a. Vertical half used as 3c on cover *6,500.*
b. Double impression, on cover *20,000.*
c. Double paper — *100.00*

No. 148b is unique.

149 A48 7c ver ('71) 900. 90.00
No gum 290.
On cover 150.00
150 A49 10c brown 2,000. 32.50
No gum 800.
On cover 47.50
151 A50 12c dull violet 2,850. 210.00
No gum 1,050.
On cover 450.00
152 A51 15c brt org 3,500. 210.00
No gum 1,300.
On cover 350.00
a. Double impression *9,000.*

No. 152a is unique. It has fine centering and faults and is valued thus.

153 A52 24c purple 1,700. 220.00
No gum 600.
On cover *1,500.*
a. Double paper — —
154 A53 30c black 7,000. 275.00
No gum 2,600.
On cover 875.00
155 A54 90c carmine 5,000. 325.00
No gum 1,900.
On cover —

PRINTED BY THE CONTINENTAL BANK NOTE COMPANY

Designs of the 1870-71 Issue with secret marks on the values from 1c to 15c, as described and illustrated:

The object of secret marks was to provide a simple and positive proof that these stamps were produced by the Continental Bank Note Company and not by their predecessors.

Almost all of the stamps of the Continental Bank Note Co. printing including the Department stamps and some of the Newspaper stamps may be found upon a paper that shows more or less the characteristics of a ribbed paper. The ribbing may be oriented either vertically or horizontally, with horizontal ribbing being far more common than vertical ribbing. Values are for the most common varieties.

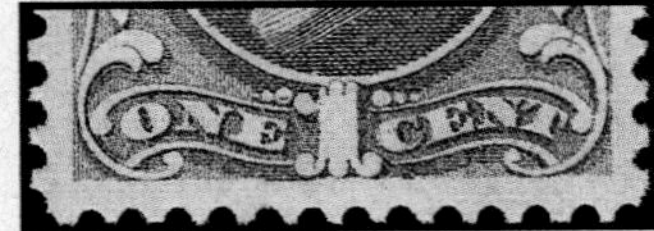

Franklin — A44a

1c. In the pearl at the left of the numeral "1" there is a small crescent.

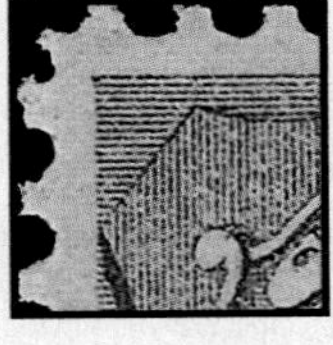

Jackson — A45a

2c. Under the scroll at the left of "U. S." there is a small diagonal line. This mark seldom shows clearly. The stamp, No. 157, can be distinguished by its color.

Washington — A46a

3c. The under part of the upper tail of the left ribbon is heavily shaded.

Lincoln — A47a

6c. The first four vertical lines of the shading in the lower part of the left ribbon have been strengthened.

Stanton — A48a

7c. Two small semi-circles are drawn around the ends of the lines that outline the ball in the lower right hand corner.

Jefferson — A49a

10c. There is a small semi-circle in the scroll at the right end of the upper label.

Clay — A50a

12c. The balls of the figure "2" are crescent shaped.

Webster — A51a

15c. In the lower part of the triangle in the upper left corner two lines have been made heavier forming a "V." This mark can be found on some of the Continental and American (1879) printings, but not all stamps show it.

Secret marks were added to the dies of the 24c, 30c and 90c but new plates were not made from them. The various printings of the 30c and 90c can be distinguished only by the shades and paper.

Experimental J. Grill about 7x9½mm exists on all values except 24c and 90c. Grill was composed of truncated pyramids and was so strongly impressed that some points often broke through the paper.

White Wove Paper, Thin to Thick
Without Grill

1873, July (?) ***Perf. 12***

156 A44a 1c ultra 200. 5.75
No gum 90.
On cover 7.25
a. Double paper *2,000.* *500.00*
e. With grill *2,000.*
f. Imperf., pair — *1,500.*
157 A45a 2c brown 325. 22.50
No gum 125.
On cover 27.50
a. Double paper *1,500.* 200.00
c. With grill *1,850.* *750.00*
d. Double impression *16,500.*
e. Vertical half used as 1c on cover *1,000.*

No. 157d is unique.

158 A46a 3c green 110. 1.00
No gum 40.
On cover 1.20
a. Double paper 600. 100.00
e. With grill *550.*
h. Horizontal pair, imperf. vert. —
i. Horizontal pair, imperf. between *1,300.*
j. Double impression *7,000.*
k. Printed on both sides *20,000.*

Nos. 158j and 158k are valued in the grade of fine.

The imperf 3c, with and without grill, can be found in the Scott U.S. Specialized Catalogue Die and Plate Proofs section.

159 A47a 6c dull pink 375. 18.00
No gum 120.
On cover 27.50
a. Diagonal half used as 3c on cover *7,250.*
b. With grill *1,800.*
c. Double paper — *900.00*
160 A48a 7c org ver 1,000. 85.00
No gum 350.
On cover 160.00
a. With grill *3,500.*
b. Double paper —
161 A49a 10c brown 800. 25.00
No gum 250.
On cover 40.00
a. Double paper *3,500.* *900.00*
c. With grill *3,750.*
d. Horizontal pair, imperf. between *17,500.*
162 A50a 12c blkish vio 2,200. 135.00
No gum 725.
On cover 325.00
a. With grill *5,500.*
163 A51a 15c yel org 2,000. 150.00
No gum 675.
On cover 340.00
a. With grill *5,750.*
b. Double paper *1,250.*
164 A52 24c purple *357,500.*

The Philatelic Foundation has certified as genuine a 24c on vertically ribbed paper, and that is the unique stamp listed as No. 164. Specialists believe that only Continental used ribbed paper. It is not known for sure whether or not Continental also printed the 24c value on regular paper; if it did, specialists currently are not able to distinguish these from No. 153. The catalogue value represents a 2004 auction sale price realized.

165 A53 30c gray blk 3,750. 130.
No gum 1,200.
On cover *700.*
a. Double paper —
c. With grill *22,500.*
166 A54 90c rose car 2,100. 275.00
No gum 700.
On cover *7,500.*

Special Printing of the 1873 Issue

Hard, White Wove Paper
Without Gum

1875 ***Perf. 12***

167 A44a 1c ultramarine *14,000.*
168 A45a 2c dark brown *6,000.*
169 A46a 3c blue green *21,500.* —
170 A47a 6c dull rose *18,000.*
171 A48a 7c reddish ver *4,000.*
172 A49a 10c pale brown *17,000.*

173 A50a 12c dark violet *5,500.*
174 A51a 15c bright org *15,500.*
175 A52 24c dull purple *3,400. 22,500.*
176 A53 30c greenish blk *12,000.*
177 A54 90c vio carmine *18,000.*

Although perforated, these stamps were usually cut apart with scissors. As a result, the perforations are often much mutilated and the design is frequently damaged.

These can be distinguished from the 1873 issue by the shades; also by the paper, which is very white instead of yellowish.

These and the subsequent issues listed under the heading of "Special Printings" are special printings of stamps then in current use which, together with the reprints and re-issues, were made for sale to collectors. They were available for postage except for the Officials, Newspaper and Periodical, and demonetized issues.

Only three examples of No. 175 used have been certified. They all have small faults and are valued thus.

Yellowish Wove Paper

1875 ***Perf. 12***

178 A45a 2c vermilion 325. 15.00
No gum 100.
On cover 17.50
a. Double paper — —
b. Half used as 1c on cover *750.00*
c. With grill 900. *2,750.*

The imperf 2c can be found in the Scott U.S. Specialized Catalogue Die and Plate Proofs section.

Zachary Taylor — A55

179 A55 5c blue 700. 25.00
No gum 225.
On cover 40.00
a. Double paper *950.*
c. With grill 4,500.

SPECIAL PRINTING OF 1875 ISSUE
Hard, White Wove Paper
Without Gum

1875

180 A45a 2c carmine ver *70,000.*
181 A55 5c bright blue *450,000.*

Unlike Nos. 167-177, Nos. 180-181 were not cut apart with scissors.

Please Note:

Stamps are valued in the grade of very fine unless otherwise indicated.

Values for early and valuable stamps are for examples with certificates of authenticity from acknowledged expert committees, or examples sold with the buyer having the right of certification.

This applies to examples with original gum as well as examples without gum.

Beware of stamps offered "as is," as the gum on some unused stamps offered with "original gum" may be fraudulent, and stamps offered as unused without gum may in some cases be altered or faintly canceled used stamps.

IMPORTANT INFORMATION REGARDING VALUES FOR NEVER-HINGED STAMPS

Collectors should be aware that the values given for never-hinged stamps from No. 182 on are for stamps in the grade of very fine, just as the values for all stamps in the catalogue are for very fine stamps unless indicated otherwise. The never-hinged premium as a percentage of value will be larger for stamps in extremely fine or superb grades, and the premium will be smaller for fine-very fine, fine or poor examples. This is particularly true of the issues of the late-19th and early-20th centuries.

VALUES FOR NEVER-HINGED STAMPS PRIOR TO SCOTT 182

This catalogue does not value pre-1879 stamps in never-hinged condition. Premiums for never-hinged condition in the classic era invariably are even larger than those premiums listed for the 1879 and later issues. Generally speaking, the earlier the stamp is listed in the catalogue, the larger will be the never-hinged premium.

For values of the most popular U.S. stamps in various conditions, including never hinged from No. 182 on, and in the grades of very good, fine, fine to very fine, very fine, very fine to extremely fine, extremely fine, extremely fine to superb, and superb, see the *Scott Stamp Values U.S. Specialized by Grade*, updated and issued each year as part of the U.S. specialized catalogue.

PRINTED BY THE AMERICAN BANK NOTE COMPANY

Identification by Paper Type:

Collectors traditionally have identified American Bank Note Co. issues by the soft, porous paper on which they were printed. However, the Continental Bank Note Co. used some intermediate papers as early as 1877 and a soft paper from August 1878 through early 1879, before the consolidation of the companies. When the consolidation occurred in the late afternoon of Feb. 4, 1879, American Bank Note Co. took over the presses, plates, paper, ink, and the employees of Continental. Undoubtedly they also acquired panes of finished stamps and sheets of printed stamps that had not yet been gummed and/or perforated. Since the soft paper that was in use at the time of the consolidation and after is approximately the same texture and thickness as the soft paper that American Bank Note Co. began using regularly in June or July of 1879, all undated soft paper stamps have traditionally been classified as American Bank Note Co. printings.

However, if a stamp bears a dated cancellation or is on a dated cover from Feb. 4, 1879 or earlier, collectors (especially specialist collectors) must consider the stamp to be a Continental Bank Note printing. Undated stamps off cover, and stamps and covers dated Feb. 5 or later, traditionally have been considered to be American Bank Note Co. printings since that company held the contract to print U.S. postage stamps beginning on that date. The most dedicated and serious specialist students sometimes attempt to determine the stamp printer of the issues on soft, porous paper in an absolute manner (by scientifically testing the paper and/or comparing printing records).

SAME AS 1870-75 ISSUES
Soft Porous Paper
Varying from Thin to Thick

1879 ***Perf. 12***

182 A44a 1c dark ultra 200. 6.00
Never hinged 675.
No gum 80.
On cover 6.50
183 A45a 2c vermilion 100. 5.00
Never hinged 370.
No gum 40.
On cover 5.50
a. Double impression — *5,500.*
b. Half used as 1c on cover *750.00*

No. 183a is valued in the grade of fine.

184 A46a 3c green 90. 1.00
Never hinged 330.
No gum 35.
On cover 1.10
b. Double impression *5,000.*

No. 184b is valued in the grade of fine.

The imperf 3c can be found in the Scott U.S. Specialized Catalogue Die and Plate Proofs section.

185 A55 5c blue 425. 16.00
Never hinged *1,400.*
No gum 130.
On cover 27.50
186 A47a 6c pink 900. 22.50
Never hinged *3,100.*
No gum 275.
On cover 27.50
187 A49 10c brn, without secret mark 3,000. 40.00
Never hinged *10,000.*
No gum 1,000.
On cover 57.50
a. Double paper *10,000.* —
188 A49a 10c brn, with secret mark 1,700. 30.00
Never hinged *6,000.*
No gum 600.
On cover 45.00
189 A51a 15c red orange 180. 27.50
Never hinged 600.
No gum 70.
On cover 82.50
190 A53 30c full black 850. 90.00
Never hinged *2,800.*
No gum 300.
On cover 450.00
191 A54 90c carmine 2,000. 350.00
Never hinged *7,000.*
No gum 650.
On cover *5,000.*

The Continental Bank Note Co. was consolidated with the American Bank Note Co. on February 4, 1879. The American Bank Note Company used many plates of the Continental Bank Note Company to print the ordinary postage, Departmental and Newspaper stamps. Therefore, stamps bearing the Continental Company's imprint were not always its product.

The A. B. N. Co. also used the 30c and 90c plates of the N. B. N. Co. Some of No. 190 and all of No. 217 were from A. B. N. Co. plate 405.

Early printings of No. 188 were from Continental plates 302 and 303 which contained the normal secret mark of 1873. After those plates were re-entered by the A. B. N. Co. in 1880, pairs or multiple pieces contained combinations of normal, hairline or missing marks. The pairs or other multiples usually found contain at least one hairline mark which tended to disappear as the plate wore.

A. B. N. Co. plates 377 and 378 were made in 1881 from the National transfer roll of 1870. No. 187 from these plates has no secret mark.

The imperf. 90c can be found in the Scott U.S. Specialized Catalogue Die and Plate Proofs section.

Special Printing of the 1879 Issue
Soft Porous Paper
Without Gum

1880 ***Perf. 12***

192 A44a 1c dark ultra *57,500.*
193 A45a 2c black brown *17,000.*
194 A46a 3c blue green *120,000.*
195 A47a 6c dull rose *67,500.*
196 A48a 7c scarlet ver *6,750.*
197 A49a 10c deep brown *34,500.*
198 A50a 12c blkish pur *9,500.*
199 A51a 15c orange *29,000.*
200 A52 24c dark violet *9,000.*
201 A53 30c grnish blk *20,000.*
202 A54 90c dull carmine *29,000.*
203 A45a 2c scarlet ver *100,000.*
204 A55 5c deep blue *240,000.*

Nos. 192 and 194 are valued in the grade of fine.

No. 197 was printed from Continental plate 302 (or 303) after plate was re-entered. Therefore, the stamp may show normal, hairline or missing secret mark.

Unlike the 1875 hard-paper Special Printings (Nos. 167-177), the 1880 soft-paper Special Printings were never cut apart with scissors.

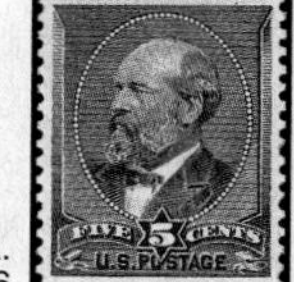

James A. Garfield — A56

1882

205 A56 5c yellow brown 240. 12.00
Never hinged 775.
No gum 90.
On cover 25.00

Special Printing

1882 ***Perf. 12***

Soft porous paper, without gum

205C A56 5c gray brown *55,000.*

DESIGNS OF 1873 RE-ENGRAVED

Franklin — A44b

1c — The vertical lines in the upper part of the stamp have been so deepened that the background often appears to be solid. Lines of shading have been added to the upper arabesques.

1881-82

206 A44b 1c gray blue 70.00 1.00
Never hinged 225.00
No gum 25.00
On cover 1.75
a. Double impression —

No. 206a is a partial double impression, with "ONE 1 CENT," etc. at bottom doubled.

Earliest documented use: Oct. 11, 1881.

Washington — A46b

3c. The shading at the sides of the central oval appears only about one-half the previous width. A short horizontal dash has been cut about 1mm below the "TS" of "CENTS."

207 A46b 3c blue green 70.00 .80
Never hinged 225.00
No gum 25.00
On cover .95
c. Double impression *5,000.*
On cover *5,500.*

Lincoln — A47b

6c. On the original stamps four vertical lines can be counted from the edge of the panel to the outside of the stamp. On the re-engraved stamps there are but three lines in the same place.

208 A47b 6c rose 750. 100.00
Never hinged 2,350.
No gum 225.
On Cover 130.00
a. 6c deep brown red 550. 170.00
Never hinged 1,750.
No gum 150.
On cover *400.00*

Jefferson — A49b

10c. On the original stamps there are five vertical lines between the left side of the oval and the edge of the shield. There are only four lines on the re-engraved stamps. In the lower part of the latter, also, the horizontal lines of the background have been strengthened.

No.	Description	Unused	Used
209	A49b 10c brown ('82)	160.	6.00
	Never hinged	475.	
	No gum	65.	
	On cover		11.00
b.	10c black brown	3,000.	375.00
	Never hinged	6,000.	
	No gum	950.	
	On cover		*550.00*
c.	Double impression		—

Specimen stamps (usually overprinted "Sample") without overprint exist in a brown shade that differs from No. 209. The unoverprinted brown specimen is cheaper than No. 209. Expertization is recommended.

Washington A57

Jackson A58

Nos. 210-211 were issued to meet the reduced first class rate of 2 cents for each half ounce, and the double rate, which Congress approved Mar. 3, 1883, effective Oct. 1, 1883.

1883, Oct. 1 ***Perf. 12***

No.	Description	Unused	Used
210	A57 2c red brown	45.00	.75
	Never hinged	135.00	
	No gum	17.00	
	On cover		.85
211	A58 4c blue green	225.	25.00
	Never hinged	800.	
	No gum	80.	
	On cover		50.00

Imperfs can be found in the Scott U.S. Specialized Catalogue Die and Plate Proofs section.

Special Printing

1883-85 Soft porous paper ***Perf. 12***

No.	Description	Unused	Used
211B	A57 2c pale red brn, with gum ('85)	375.	—
	Never hinged	900.	
	No gum	130.	
c.	Horizontal pair, imperf. between	*2,000.*	
	Never hinged	*3,000.*	
211D	A58 4c deep blue grn	*47,500.*	

No. 211D is without gum.

Franklin — A59

1887 ***Perf. 12***

No.	Description	Unused	Used
212	A59 1c ultramarine	90.00	2.50
	Never hinged	290.00	
	No gum	35.00	
	On cover		3.25
213	A57 2c green	40.00	.60
	Never hinged	120.00	
	No gum	15.00	
	On cover		.75
b.	Printed on both sides		—

Imperf 1c, 2c can be found in the Scott U.S. Specialized Catalogue Die and Plate Proofs section.

No.	Description	Unused	Used
214	A46b 3c vermilion	60.00	50.00
	Never hinged	180.00	
	No gum	25.00	
	On cover (single)		90.00
	Nos. 212-214 (3)	190.00	53.10

1888 ***Perf. 12***

No.	Description	Unused	Used
215	A58 4c carmine	180.	25.00
	Never hinged	525.	
	No gum	60.	
	On cover		47.50
216	A56 5c indigo	200.	17.50
	Never hinged	625.	
	No gum	75.	
	On cover		35.00
217	A53 30c orange brn	250.	90.00
	Never hinged	900.	
	No gum	80.	
	On cover		*1,400.*
218	A54 90c purple	850.	225.00
	Never hinged	2,600.	
	No gum	275.	
	On cover		*10,000.*
	Nos. 215-218 (4)	1,480.	357.50

Imperfs can be found in the Scott U.S. Specialized Catalogue Die and Plate Proofs section.

Franklin A60

Washington A61

Jackson A62

Lincoln A63

Grant A64

Garfield A65

William T. Sherman A66

Daniel Webster A67

Henry Clay A68

Jefferson A69

Perry — A70

1890-93 ***Perf. 12***

No.	Description	Unused	Used
219	A60 1c dull blue	20.	.75
	On cover		.80
219D	A61 2c lake	160.	5.50
	Never hinged	500.	
	On cover		7.50
220	A61 2c carmine	20.00	.70
	Never hinged	60.00	
	On cover		.75
a.	Cap on left "2"	150.00	12.50
	Never hinged	425.00	
c.	Cap on both "2's"	650.00	35.00
	Never hinged	1,800.	
221	A62 3c purple	55.00	9.00
	Never hinged	175.00	
	On cover		17.50
222	A63 4c dark brown	80.00	4.75
	Never hinged	240.00	
	On cover		10.00
223	A64 5c chocolate	60.00	4.75
	Never hinged	185.00	
	On cover		12.50
224	A65 6c brown red	50.00	25.00
	Never hinged	160.00	
	On cover		40.00
225	A66 8c lilac ('93)	45.00	17.00
	On cover		32.50
226	A67 10c green	160.00	5.00
	On cover		10.00
227	A68 15c indigo	180.00	25.00
	Never hinged	550.00	
	On cover		60.00
228	A69 30c black	280.00	30.00
	Never hinged	850.00	
	On cover		*600.00*
229	A70 90c orange	450.00	140.00
	Never hinged	1,350.	
	On cover		—
	Nos. 219-229 (12)	1,560.	267.45

The No. 220 with "cap on right 2" variety is due to imperfect inking, not a plate defect.

Imperfs. can be found in the *Scott U.S. Specialized Catalogue* Die and Plate Proofs section.

COLUMBIAN EXPOSITION ISSUE

Columbus in Sight of Land — A71

Landing of Columbus A72

Flagship of Columbus A73

Fleet of Columbus A74

Columbus Soliciting Aid from Isabella A75

Columbus Welcomed at Barcelona A76

Columbus Restored to Favor — A77

Columbus Presenting Natives A78

Columbus Announcing his Discovery A79

Columbus at La Rábida A80

Recall of Columbus A81

Isabella Pledging her Jewels A82

Columbus in Chains A83

Columbus Describing his Third Voyage A84

Isabella & Columbus A85

Columbus A86

1893 ***Perf. 12***

No.	Description	Unused	Used
230	A71 1c deep blue	14.00	.40
	Never hinged	32.50	
	On cover		.90
231	A72 2c brn vio	12.50	.30
	Never hinged	31.00	
	On cover		.35
232	A73 3c green	35.00	15.00
	dull green	35.00	15.00
	dark green	35.00	15.00
	Never hinged	97.50	
	On cover		30.00
233	A74 4c ultra	50.00	8.00
	Never hinged	140.00	
	On cover		22.50
a.	4c blue (error)	*17,500.*	*16,500.*
	Never hinged	*32,500.*	

No. 233a exists in two shades. No. 233a used is valued with small faults, as almost all examples come thus.

No.	Description	Unused	Used
234	A75 5c chocolate	50.00	8.50
	Never hinged	140.00	
	On cover		22.50
235	A76 6c purple	50.00	22.50
	Never hinged	140.00	
a.	6c red violet	50.00	22.50
	Never hinged	140.00	
	On cover, #235 or 235a		45.00
236	A77 8c magenta	47.50	10.00
	Never hinged	140.00	
	On cover		20.00
237	A78 10c blk brn	90.00	8.00
	Never hinged	250.00	
	On cover		27.50
238	A79 15c dark green	200.00	72.50
	Never hinged	600.00	
	On cover		210.00
239	A80 30c org brn	225.00	90.00
	On cover		375.00
240	A81 50c slate blue	425.	175.
	Never hinged	1,250.	
	No gum	190.	
	On cover		600.
241	A82 $1 salmon	1,000.	525.
	Never hinged	3,400.	
	No gum	500.	
	On cover		*1,800.*
242	A83 $2 brown red	1,050.	525.
	Never hinged	3,500.	
	No gum	500.	
	On cover		*1,900.*
243	A84 $3 yel grn	1,350.	750.
	Never hinged	4,250.	
	No gum	675.	
a.	$3 olive green	1,350.	750.
	Never hinged	4,250.	
	No gum	675.	
	On cover, #243 or 243a		*2,500.*
244	A85 $4 crim lake	2,000.	950.
	Never hinged	7,000.	
	No gum	1,000.	
a.	$4 rose carmine	2,000.	950.
	Never hinged	7,000.	
	No gum	1,000.	
	On cover		*4,000.*
245	A86 $5 black	2,300.	1,150.
	Never hinged	9,500.	
	No gum	1,150.	
	On cover		*4,750.*

World's Columbia Expo., Chicago, May 1-Oct. 30, 1893.

Nos. 230-245 are known imperf., but were not regularly issued.

See Scott U.S. Specialized Catalogue Die and Plate Proofs section for the 2c.

Never-Hinged Stamps

See note before No. 182 regarding premiums for never-hinged stamps.

Bureau Issues

Starting in 1894, the Bureau of Engraving and Printing at Washington produced most U.S. postage stamps.

Until 1965 Bureau-printed stamps were engraved except Nos. 525-536 which were offset.

The combination of lithography and engraving (see #1253) was first used in 1964, and photogravure (see #1426) in 1971.

Franklin
A87

Washington
A88

Jackson
A89

Lincoln
A90

Grant
A91

Garfield
A92

Sherman
A93

Webster
A94

Clay
A95

Jefferson
A96

Perry
A97

James Madison
A98

John Marshall — A99

1894 Unwmk. *Perf. 12*

No.	Description	Unused	Used
246	A87 1c ultramarine	30.00	7.00
	Never hinged	90.00	
	On cover		22.50
247	A87 1c blue	60.00	4.00
	Never hinged	175.00	
	On cover		18.50

TWO CENTS:

Triangle A (Type I)

Type I (Triangle A). The horizontal lines of the ground work run across the triangle and are of the same thickness within it as without.

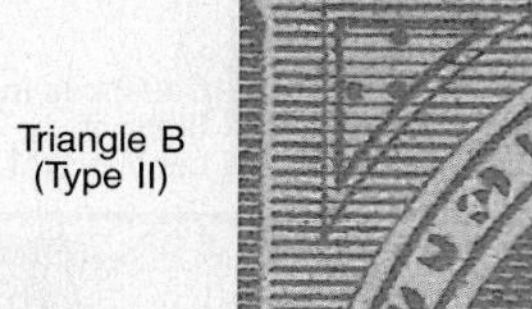
Triangle B (Type II)

Type II (Triangle B). The horizontal lines cross the triangle but are thinner within it than without. Other minor design differences exist, but the change to Triangle B is a sufficient determinant.

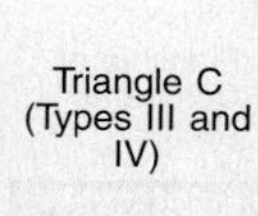
Triangle C (Types III and IV)

Type III (Triangle C). The horizontal lines do not cross the double lines of the triangle. The lines within the triangle are thin, as in Type II. The rest of the design is the same as Type II, except that most of the designs had the dot in the "S" of "CENTS" removed. Stamps with this dot present are listed; some specialists refer to them as "Type IIIa" varieties.

Type IV

Type IV (Triangle C). See No. 279B and its varieties. Type IV is from a new die with many major and minor design variations including, (1) re-cutting and lengthening of hairline, (2) shaded toga button, (3) strengthening of lines on sleeve, (4) additional dots on ear, (5) "T" of "TWO" straight at right, (6) background lines extend into white oval opposite "U" of "UNITED." Many other differences exist.

No.	Description	Unused	Used
248	A88 2c pink, type I	30.00	9.00
	Never hinged	90.00	
	On cover		16.00
a.	Vert. pair, imperf horiz.	*5,500.*	
249	A88 2c car lake, type I	140.00	7.00
	Never hinged	420.00	
	On cover		12.50
a.	Double impression		—
250	A88 2c car, type I	29.00	3.00
	Never hinged	85.00	
	On cover		4.00
a.	2c rose, type I	36.00	6.00
	Never hinged	105.00	
	On cover		7.25
b.	2c scarlet, type I	26.00	3.00
	Never hinged	80.00	
	On cover		6.00
d.	Horizontal pair, imperf. between	*2,000.*	
251	A88 2c car, type II	375.00	14.00
	Never hinged	1,100.	
	On cover		22.50
a.	2c scarlet, type II	350.00	13.00
	Never hinged	1,050.	
	On cover		21.00
252	A88 2c car, type III	125.00	13.00
	Never hinged	375.00	
	On cover		22.50
a.	2c scarlet, type III	110.00	15.00
	Never hinged	325.00	
	On cover		20.00
b.	Horiz. pair, imperf. vert.	*5,000.*	
c.	Horiz. pair, imperf. between	*5,500.*	

Former Nos. 252a, 252b are now Nos. 252b, 252c.

No.	Description	Unused	Used
253	A89 3c purple	110.00	12.00
	Never hinged	325.00	
	On cover		27.50
254	A90 4c dark brn	190.00	11.00
	Never hinged	550.00	
	On cover		22.50
255	A91 5c chocolate	110.00	9.00
	Never hinged	325.00	
	On cover		22.50
c.	Vert. pair, imperf. horiz.	*3,500.*	
256	A92 6c dull brown	160.00	27.50
	Never hinged	475.00	
	On cover		50.00
a.	Vert. pair, imperf. horiz.	*3,000.*	
	P# block of 6, Impt., T I	*30,000.*	
257	A93 8c vio brn ('95)	160.00	20.00
	Never hinged	475.00	
	On cover		50.00
258	A94 10c dark green	275.00	20.00
	Never hinged	850.00	
	On cover		37.50
259	A95 15c dark blue	275.00	65.00
	Never hinged	850.00	
	On cover		125.00
260	A96 50c orange	475.	140.
	Never hinged	1,425.	
	On cover		950.

Type I

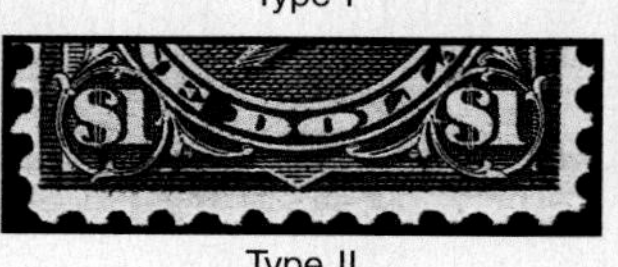
Type II

ONE DOLLAR

Type I. The circles enclosing "$1" are broken where they meet the curved line below "One Dollar."

Type II. The circles are complete.

No.	Description	Unused	Used
261	A97 $1 blk, type I	1,000.	350.
	Never hinged	3,150.	
	No gum	400.	
	On cover		*2,750.*
261A	A97 $1 blk, type II	2,100.	800.
	Never hinged	6,500.	
	No gum	850.	
	On cover		*4,500.*
262	A98 $2 bright blue	2,750.	1,200.
	Never hinged	8,750.	
	No gum	1,100.	
	On cover		*5,000.*
263	A99 $5 dark green	4,000.	2,600.
	Never hinged	14,000.	
	No gum	2,100.	
	On cover		—

For imperfs. and the 2c pink, vert. pair, imperf. hoirz., see Scott U.S. Specialized Catalogue Die and plate Proofs.

Wmk. 191 Horizontally or Vertically

1895 *Perf. 12*

No.	Description	Unused	Used
264	A87 1c blue	6.00	.60
	Never hinged	17.50	
	On cover		1.25
265	A88 2c car, type I	35.00	3.50
	Never hinged	105.00	
	On cover		5.50
266	A88 2c car, type II	40.00	5.50
	Never hinged	120.00	
	On cover		8.50
267	A88 2c car, type III	5.50	.50
	Never hinged	16.00	
	On cover		.65
a.	2c pink, type III	20.00	5.00
	Never hinged	60.00	
	On cover		6.00
b.	2c vermilion, type III ('99)	*50.00*	15.00
c.	2c rose carmine, type III ('99)	—	—

The three left vertical rows from plate 170 are type II, the balance being type III.

No.	Description	Unused	Used
268	A89 3c purple	37.50	2.25
	Never hinged	115.00	
	On cover		8.00
269	A90 4c dark brown	42.50	3.50
	Never hinged	125.00	
	On cover		8.00
270	A91 5c chocolate	35.00	3.50
	Never hinged	105.00	
	On cover		8.00
271	A92 6c dull brown	120.00	8.50
	Never hinged	360.00	
	On cover		27.50
a.	Wmkd. USIR	*15,000.*	*8,500.*
272	A93 8c violet brown	70.00	2.75
	Never hinged	210.00	
	On cover		14.00
a.	Wmkd. USIR	*6,000.*	950.00
273	A94 10c dark green	95.00	2.25
	Never hinged	280.00	
	On cover		15.00
274	A95 15c dark blue	210.00	17.50
	Never hinged	625.00	
	On cover		55.00
275	A96 50c orange	260.	40.00
	Never hinged	775.	
	On cover		400.00
a.	50c red orange	350.	47.50
	Never hinged	1,050.	
	On cover		425.00
276	A97 $1 black, type I	600.	95.
	Never hinged	1,800.	
	No gum	250.	
	On cover		*2,250.*
276A	A97 $1 black, type II	1,250.	200.
	Never hinged	3,750.	
	No gum	500.	
	On cover		*3,750.*
277	A98 $2 bright blue	900.	400.
	Never hinged	2,900.	
	No gum	375.	
a.	$2 dark blue	900.	400.
	Never hinged	2,900.	
	No gum	375.	
	On cover		*3,500.*
278	A99 $5 dark green	2,000.	600.
	Never hinged	6,250.	
	No gum	800.	
	On cover		*10,000.*

For imperfs. and the 1c horiz. pair, imperf. vert., see Scott U.S. Specialized Catalogue Die and Plate Proofs.

For "I.R." overprints see Nos. R155, R156-R158.

No. 271a unused is valued in the grade of fine.

Wmk. 191 Horizontally or Vertically

1897-1903 *Perf. 12*

No.	Description	Unused	Used
279	A87 1c dp grn, horiz. wmk ('98)	9.00	.50
	Never hinged	25.00	
	On cover		.60
a.	Vert. wmk (error)	*50.00*	*7.50*
	Never hinged	*150.00*	
	On cover		*22.50*
279B	A88 2c red, type IV ('99)	9.00	.40
	Never hinged	25.00	
	On cover		.50
c.	2c rose carmine, type IV ('99)	275.00	220.00
	Never hinged	850.00	
d.	2c orange red, type IV, horiz. wmk. ('00)	11.50	2.00
	Never hinged	32.50	
	On cover		2.50
e.	2c orange red, type IV, vert. wmk.	*55.00*	*12.50*
	Never hinged	*170.00*	
	On cover		*22.50*
f.	2c carmine, type IV	10.00	2.00
	reddish carmine, *Dec. 1898*	10.00	2.00
	Never hinged	27.50	
	On cover		2.25
g.	2c pink, type IV	55.00	7.50
	Never hinged	165.00	
	On cover		8.00
h.	2c vermilion, type IV ('99)	12.50	3.00
	Never hinged	35.00	
	On cover		5.00
i.	2c brown org, type IV ('99)	*400.00*	*100.00*
	Never hinged	*950.00*	
j.	Booklet pane of 6, red, type IV, horiz. wmk. ('00)	500.00	*3,000.*
	Never hinged	1,000.	
k.	Booklet pane of 6, red, type IV, vertical watermark ('02)	500.00	—
	Never hinged	1,000.	
l.	As No. 279B, all color missing (FO)	*500.00*	
280	A90 4c rose brn ('98)	30.00	3.25
	Never hinged	80.00	
a.	4c lilac brown	30.00	3.25
	Never hinged	80.00	
b.	4c orange brown	30.00	3.00
	Never hinged	80.00	
	On cover, #280, 280a or 280b		7.50
281	A91 5c dk blue ('98)	32.50	2.25
	Never hinged	100.00	
	On cover		10.00
282	A92 6c lake ('98)	45.00	6.50
	Never hinged	140.00	
	On cover		17.50
a.	6c purple lake	75.00	20.00
	Never hinged	225.00	

Type I. The tips of the foliate ornaments do not impinge on the white curved line below "ten cents."

No.	Description	Unused	Used
282C	A94 10c brn, type I ('98)	175.00	6.50
	Never hinged	525.00	
	On cover		18.00

Type II. The tips of the ornaments break the curved line below the "e" of "ten" and the "t" of "cents."

No.	Description	Unused	Used
283	A94 10c org brn, type II, horiz. wmk.	150.00	6.00
	Never hinged	450.00	
	On cover		17.50
a.	Vert. wmk. ('00)	*250.00*	*15.00*

	Never hinged	*775.00*	
	On cover		*35.00*
284	A95 15c ol grn ('98)	150.00	13.00
	Never hinged	475.00	
	On cover		32.50
	Nos. 279-284 (8)	600.50	38.40

For "I.R." overprints, see Nos. R153-R155A.

TRANS-MISSISSIPPI EXPOSITION ISSUE

Marquette on the Mississippi A100

Farming in the West — A101

Indian Hunting Buffalo A102

Frémont on the Rocky Mountains A103

Troops Guarding Wagon Train — A104

Hardships of Emigration A105

Western Mining Prospector A106

Western Cattle in Storm A107

Mississippi River Bridge A108

1898, June 17 Wmk. 191 *Perf. 12*

285	A100 1c dk yel grn	25.00	7.00
	Never hinged	70.00	
	On cover		10.00
286	A101 2c copper red	22.50	2.75
	Never hinged	60.00	
	On cover		3.75
287	A102 4c orange	100.00	25.00
	Never hinged	275.00	
	On cover		60.00
288	A103 5c dull blue	90.00	25.00
	Never hinged	250.00	
	On cover		50.00
289	A104 8c violet brown	130.00	47.50
	Never hinged	375.00	
	On cover		120.00
a.	Vert. pair, imperf. horiz.	*27,500.*	
290	A105 10c gray vio	135.00	35.00
	Never hinged	380.00	
	On cover		90.00
291	A106 50c sage grn	550.00	175.00
	Never hinged	1,650.	
	On cover		1,750.

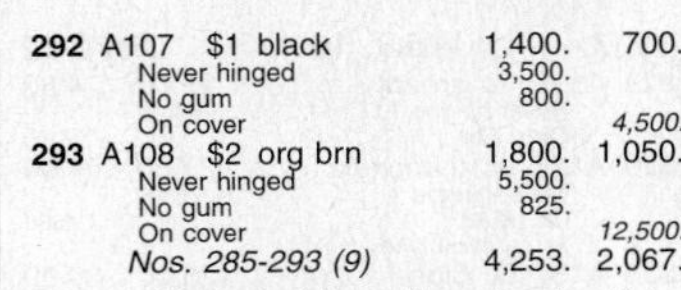

292	A107 $1 black	1,400.	700.
	Never hinged	3,500.	
	No gum	800.	
	On cover		*4,500.*
293	A108 $2 org brn	1,800.	1,050.
	Never hinged	5,500.	
	No gum	825.	
	On cover		*12,500.*
	Nos. 285-293 (9)	4,253.	2,067.

Trans-Mississippi Exposition, Omaha, Neb., June 1 to Nov. 1, 1898.

For "I.R" overprints see #R158A-R158B.

Never-Hinged Stamps
See note before No. 182 regarding premiums for never-hinged stamps.

PAN-AMERICAN EXPOSITION ISSUE

Fast Lake Navigation A109

"Empire State" Express A110

Electric Automobile A111

Bridge at Niagara Falls — A112

Canal Locks at Sault Ste. Marie — A113

Fast Ocean Navigation — A114

1901, May 1 Wmk. 191 *Perf. 12*

294	A109 1c grn & blk	16.00	3.00
	Never hinged	40.00	
	On cover		4.50
a.	Center inverted	*12,500.*	*25,000.*
	Never hinged	*22,500.*	
	On cover		—
295	A110 2c car & blk	15.00	1.00
	Never hinged	37.50	
	On cover		1.50
a.	Center inverted	*55,000.*	*55,000.*
296	A111 4c dp red brn & blk	70.00	18.00
	Never hinged	170.00	
	On cover		42.50
a.	Center inverted	*85,000.*	—
297	A112 5c ultra & black	75.00	17.00
	Never hinged	180.00	
	On cover		45.00
298	A113 8c brn vio & blk	90.00	50.00
	Never hinged	230.00	
	On cover		110.00
299	A114 10c yel brn & blk	115.00	30.00
	Never hinged	300.00	
	On cover		125.00
	Nos. 294-299 (6)	381.00	119.00
	Nos. 294-299, never hinged	957.50	

No. 296a was a special printing.

Almost all unused examples of Nos. 295a and 296a have partial or disturbed gum. Values are for examples with full original gum that is slightly disturbed.

Franklin A115

Washington A116

Jackson A117

Grant A118

Lincoln A119

Garfield A120

Martha Washington A121

Webster A122

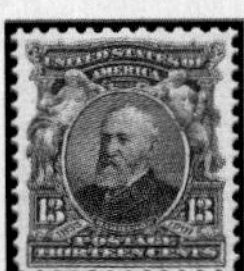

Benjamin Harrison A123

Clay A124

Jefferson A125

David G. Farragut A126

Madison A127

Marshall A128

Many stamps of this issue are known with blurred printing due to having been printed on dry paper.

1902-03 Wmk. 191 *Perf. 12*

300	A115 1c blue grn ('03)	11.00	.25
	Never hinged	27.50	
	On cover		.30
b.	Booklet pane of 6	600.00	*11,500.*
	Never hinged	1,150.	
	Wmk. horiz.	*2,000.*	
301	A116 2c car ('03)	15.00	.50
	Never hinged	37.50	
	On cover		.55
c.	Booklet pane of 6	500.00	*6,000.*
	Never hinged	950.00	
302	A117 3c brt vio ('03)	50.00	3.75
	Never hinged	130.00	
	On cover		11.00
303	A118 4c brn ('03)	55.00	2.25
	Never hinged	140.00	
	On cover		12.00
304	A119 5c blue ('03)	60.00	2.00
	Never hinged	150.00	
	On cover		6.00
305	A120 6c claret ('03)	60.00	5.50
	Never hinged	150.00	
	On cover		16.00
306	A121 8c vio black	45.00	3.25
	Never hinged	110.00	
	On cover		8.00
307	A122 10c pale red brn ('03)	60.00	3.00
	Never hinged	150.00	
	On cover		9.50
308	A123 13c purple blk	40.00	10.00
	Never hinged	100.00	
	On cover		37.50
309	A124 15c ol grn ('03)	175.00	12.50
	Never hinged	450.00	
	On cover		75.00
310	A125 50c org ('03)	375.	35.00
	deep orange	375.	35.00
	Never hinged	1,100.	
	On cover		700.00
311	A126 $1 black ('03)	600.00	90.00
	Never hinged	1,800.	
	No gum	240.00	
	On cover		1,500.
312	A127 $2 dk bl ('03)	800.00	190.00
	Never hinged	2,475.	
	No gum	325.00	
	On cover		2,500.
313	A128 $5 dk grn ('03)	2,000.	675.00
	Never hinged	*6,250.*	
	No gum	750.00	
	On cover		*5,000.*
	Nos. 300-313 (14)	4,346.	1,033.

For listings of designs A127 and A128 with Perf. 10 see Nos. 479 and 480.

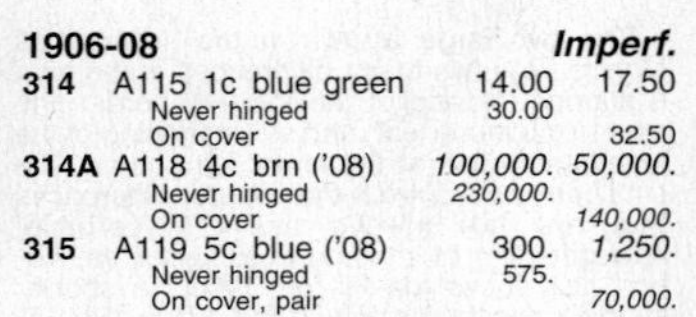

1906-08 *Imperf.*

314	A115 1c blue green	14.00	17.50
	Never hinged	30.00	
	On cover		32.50
314A	A118 4c brn ('08)	*100,000.*	*50,000.*
	Never hinged	*230,000.*	
	On cover		*140,000.*
315	A119 5c blue ('08)	300.	*1,250.*
	Never hinged	575.	
	On cover, pair		*70,000.*

No. 314A was issued imperforate but all examples were privately perforated with large oblong perforations at the sides (Schermack type III).

Beware of examples of No. 303 with trimmed perforations and fake private perfs added.

Used examples of Nos. 314 and 315 must have contemporaneous cancels.

COIL STAMPS

Warning! Imperforate stamps are known fraudulently perforated to resemble coil stamps and part-perforate varieties. Fully perforated stamps and booklet stamps also are known with perforations fraudulently trimmed off to resemble coil stamps.

1908 *Perf. 12 Horizontally*

316	A115 1c blue green	*125,000.*	
	Pair	*335,000.*	
317	A119 5c blue	*5,750.*	—
	Never hinged	*12,000.*	
	Pair	*15,000.*	
	Never hinged	*45,000.*	

Perf. 12 Vertically

318	A115 1c blue green	*4,250.*	
	Never hinged	*9,500.*	
	Pair	*11,000.*	

Coil stamps for use in vending and affixing machines are perforated on two sides only, either horizontally or vertically.

They were first issued in 1908, using perf. 12. This was changed to 8½ in 1910, and to 10 in 1914.

Imperforate sheets of certain denominations were sold to the vending machine companies which applied a variety of private perforations and separations.

Several values of the 1902 and later issues are found on an apparently coarse ribbed paper caused by worn blankets on the printing press and are not true paper varieties.

All examples of Nos. 316-318 must be accompanied by certificates of authenticity issued by recognized expertizing committees.

No. 318 mint never hinged is valued in the grade of fine.

Washington — A129

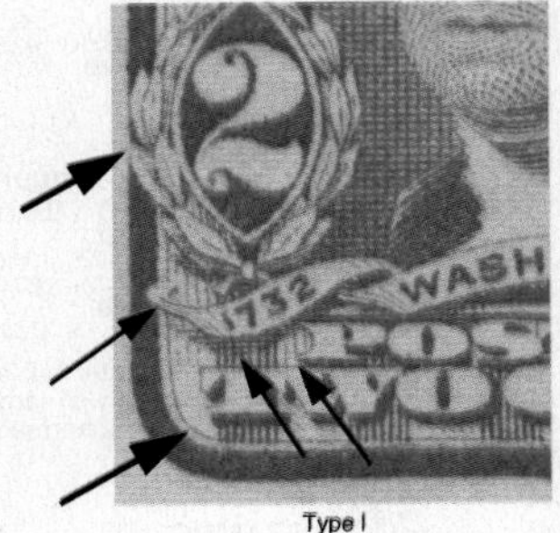

Type I

Type II

The two large arrows in the illustrations highlight the two major differences of the type II stamps: closing of the thin left border line next to the laurel leaf, and strengthening of the inner frame line at the lower left corner. The small arrows point out three minor differences that are not always easily discernible: strengthening of shading lines under the ribbon just above the "T" of "TWO," a shorter shading line to the left of the "P" in "POSTAGE," and shortening of a shading line in the left side ribbon.

Type I

1903, Nov. 12 Wmk. 191 *Perf. 12*

No.	Description	Unused	Used
319	A129 2c car, type I	6.00	.25
	Never hinged	15.00	
	On cover		.30
a.	2c lake	—	
b.	2c carmine rose	15.00	.40
	Never hinged	45.00	
	On cover		.60
c.	2c scarlet	10.00	.30
	Never hinged	25.00	
	On cover		.40
d.	Vert. pair, imperf. horiz., No. 319	7,500.	
	Never hinged	17,500.	
e.	Vert. pair, imperf. between	—	
f.	Vert. pair, rouletted between	4,000.	

During the use of No. 319, the postmaster of San Francisco discovered in his stock panes that had the perforations missing between the top two rows of stamps. To facilitate their separation, the imperf rows were rouletted, and the stamps were sold over the counter. These vertical pairs with regular perfs all around and rouletted between are No. 319r. No 319e is from a different source. One example has been authenticated, and collectors are warned that other pairs exist with faint blind perfs or indentations from the perforating machine.

No.	Description	Unused	Used
g.	Booklet pane of 6, carmine	125.00	450.00
	Never hinged	240.00	
n.	Booklet pane of 6, carmine rose	275.00	700.00
	Never hinged	500.00	
p.	Booklet pane of 6, scarlet	185.00	625.00
	Never hinged	350.00	

Type II

1908 Wmk. 191 *Perf. 12*

No.	Description	Unused	Used
319F	A129 2c lake	10.00	.30
	Never hinged	25.00	
	On cover		.35
i.	2c carmine	65.00	50.00
	Never hinged	150.00	
	On cover		150.00
j.	2c carmine rose	100.00	1.75
	Never hinged	225.00	
k.	2c scarlet	70.00	2.00
	Never hinged	160.00	
h.	Booklet pane of 6, carmine	900.00	—
	Never hinged	1,500.	
l.	Booklet pane of 6, scarlet	—	
q.	Booklet pane of 6, lake	300.00	800.00
	Never hinged	575.00	

Type I

1906, Oct. 2 Wmk. 191 *Imperf.*

No.	Description	Unused	Used
320	A129 2c carmine	15.00	19.00
	Never hinged	32.50	
	On cover		25.00
b.	2c scarlet	17.50	15.00
	Never hinged	37.50	
	On cover		22.50
c.	2c carmine rose	75.00	42.50
	Never hinged	150.00	

Type II

1908 Wmk. 191 *Imperf.*

No.	Description	Unused	Used
320A	A129 2c lake	45.00	50.00
	Never hinged	100.00	
	On cover		100.00
d.	2c carmine	135.00	25.00
	Never hinged	200.00	
	On cover		2,500.

No. 320Ad was issued imperforate, but all examples were privately perforated with large oblong perforations at the sides (Schermack type III).

COIL STAMPS

1908 *Perf. 12 Horizontally*

No.	Description	Unused	Used
321	A129 2c car, type I, pair	450,000.	250,000.
	On cover, single		250,000.

Four authenticated unused pairs of No. 321 are known and available to collectors. A fifth, unauthenticated pair is in the New York Public Library Miller collection, which is on long-term loan to the Smithsonian National Postal Museum. The value for an unused pair is for a fine-very fine example. Two fine pairs are recorded and one very fine pair.

There are no authenticated unused single stamps recorded. The used value is for a single on cover, of which two authenticated examples are known, both used from Indianapolis in 1908.

Numerous counterfeits exist.

Perf. 12 Vertically

No.	Description	Unused	Used
322	A129 2c carmine, type II	7,000.	—
	Never hinged	15,000.	
	Pair	17,500.	

This Government Coil Stamp should not be confused with those of the International Vending Machine Co., which are perforated 12½.

All examples of Nos. 321-322 must be accompanied by certificates of authenticity issued by recognized expertizing committees.

LOUISIANA PURCHASE EXPOSITION ISSUE

St. Louis, Mo., Apr. 30 - Dec. 1, 1904

Robert R. Livingston A130

Thomas Jefferson A131

James Monroe A132

William McKinley A133

Map of Louisiana Purchase A134

1904, Apr. 30 Wmk. 191 *Perf. 12*

No.	Description	Unused	Used
323	A130 1c green	22.50	4.75
	Never hinged	60.00	
	On cover		7.00
324	A131 2c carmine	22.50	2.00
	Never hinged	60.00	
	On cover		3.00
a.	Vertical pair, imperf. horiz.	25,000.	
325	A132 3c violet	65.00	27.50
	Never hinged	170.00	
	On cover		65.00
326	A133 5c dark blue	70.00	22.50
	Never hinged	180.00	
	On cover		50.00
327	A134 10c red brown	125.00	27.50
	Never hinged	300.00	
	On cover		125.00
	Nos. 323-327 (5)	305.00	84.25
	Nos. 323-327, never hinged	770.00	

JAMESTOWN EXPOSITION ISSUE

Hampton Roads, Va., Apr. 26 - Dec. 1, 1907

Captain John Smith — A135

Founding of Jamestown A136

Pocahontas A137

1907 Wmk. 191 *Perf. 12*

No.	Description	Unused	Used
328	A135 1c green	25.00	4.50
	Never hinged	65.00	
	On cover		8.00
329	A136 2c carmine	27.50	4.00
	Never hinged	75.00	
	On cover		6.00
a.	2c carmine lake		—
330	A137 5c blue	125.00	30.00
	Never hinged	300.00	
	On cover		80.00
	Nos. 328-330 (3)	177.50	38.50
	Nos. 328-330, never hinged	440.00	

Franklin A138

Washington A139

There are several types of some of the 2c and 3c stamps of this and succeeding issues. These types are described under the dates at which they first appeared.

Illustrations of Types I-VII of the 2c (A140) and Types I-IV of the 3c (A140) are reproduced by permission of H. L. Lindquist.

1908-09 Wmk. 191 *Perf. 12*

No.	Description	Unused	Used
331	A138 1c green	6.25	.40
	Never hinged	16.00	
	On cover		.55
a.	Booklet pane of 6	150.00	700.00
	Never hinged	300.00	

No. 331 exists in horizontal pair, imperforate between, a variety resulting from booklet experiments. Not regularly issued. Value in the grade of fine, $3,750.

No. 331a used is valued with a contemporaneous cancel. A certificate of authenticity is advised.

No.	Description	Unused	Used
332	A139 2c carmine	5.75	.35
	Never hinged	14.00	
	On cover		.40
a.	Booklet pane of 6	135.00	500.00
	Never hinged	240.00	
b.	2c lake	4,250.	

No. 332a used is valued with a contemporaneous cancel. A certificate of authenticity is advised.

No. 332b is valued in the grade of fine.

Washington — A140

TYPE I

THREE CENTS.

Type I. The top line of the toga rope is weak and the rope shading lines are thin. The 5th line from the left is missing. The line between the lips is thin. (For descriptions of 3c types II, III and IV, see notes and illustrations preceding Nos. 484, 529-530.)

Used on both flat plate and rotary press printings.

No.	Description	Unused	Used
333	A140 3c dp vio, type I	27.50	3.00
	Never hinged	70.00	
	On cover		8.50
334	A140 4c org brn	35.00	1.50
	Never hinged	87.50	
	On cover		7.00
335	A140 5c blue	45.00	2.25
	Never hinged	110.00	
	On cover		8.50
336	A140 6c red orange	60.00	6.00
	Never hinged	140.00	
	On cover		22.50
337	A140 8c olive green	45.00	2.75
	Never hinged	105.00	
	On cover		18.00
338	A140 10c yellow ('09)	67.50	1.80
	Never hinged	160.00	
	On cover		10.00
339	A140 13c bl grn ('09)	37.50	17.50
	Never hinged	90.00	
	On cover		110.00
340	A140 15c pale ultra ('09)	65.00	6.00
	Never hinged	150.00	
	On cover		125.00
341	A140 50c violet ('09)	275.00	20.00
	Never hinged	650.00	
	On cover		5,000.
342	A140 $1 vio brn ('09)	450.00	90.00
	Never hinged	1,050.	
	On cover		6,000.
	Nos. 331-342 (12)	1,120.	151.55

For listings of other perforated sheet stamps of A138, A139 and A140 see:

Nos. 357-366 Bluish paper
Nos. 374-382, 405-407 Single line wmk. Perf. 12
Nos. 423A-423C Single line wmk. Perf 12x10
Nos. 423D-423E Single line wmk. Perf 10x12
Nos. 424-430 Single line wmk. Perf. 10
Nos. 461 Single line wmk. Perf. 11
Nos. 462-469 unwmk. Perf. 10
Nos. 498-507 unwmk. Perf. 11
Nos. 519 Double line wmk. Perf. 11
Nos. 525-530 and 536 Offset printing
Nos. 538-546 Rotary press printing

Imperf

No.	Description	Unused	Used
343	A138 1c green	4.50	5.00
	Never hinged	9.00	
	On cover		12.00
344	A139 2c carmine	4.50	2.75
	Never hinged	9.00	
	On cover		8.00
345	A140 3c dp violet, type I	9.00	20.00
	Never hinged	19.00	
	On cover		65.00
346	A140 4c org brn ('09)	12.50	20.00
	Never hinged	25.00	
	On cover		100.00
347	A140 5c blue ('09)	25.00	32.50
	Never hinged	50.00	
	On cover		140.00
	Nos. 343-347 (5)	55.50	80.25
	Nos. 343-347, never hinged	129.00	

For listings of other imperforate stamps of designs A138, A139 and A140 see Nos. 383, 384, 408, 409 and 459 Single line wmk.

Nos. 481-485 unwmk.
Nos. 531-535 Offset printing

The values for used coil stamps are for examples with contemporaneous cancels that can be authenticated by expertizing committees. Used coils with cancels most commonly from the 1950s exist, and these and stamps with other non-contemporaneous cancels sell for less than the values shown.

COIL STAMPS

1908-10 *Perf. 12 Horizontally*

No.	Description	Unused	Used
348	A138 1c green	40.00	55.00
	Never hinged	80.00	
	On cover		90.00
349	A139 2c carmine ('09)	100.00	150.00
	Never hinged	225.00	
	On cover		180.00
350	A140 4c org brn ('10)	140.00	240.00
	Never hinged	325.00	
	On cover		375.00
351	A140 5c blue ('09)	140.00	300.00
	Never hinged	325.00	
	On cover		625.00
	Nos. 348-351 (4)	420.00	745.00

1909 *Perf. 12 Vertically*

No.	Description	Unused	Used
352	A138 1c green	100.00	225.00
	Never hinged	230.00	
	On cover		350.00
353	A139 2c carmine	90.00	220.00
	Never hinged	200.00	
	On cover		375.00
354	A140 4c org brn	200.00	275.00
	Never hinged	425.00	
	On cover		450.00
355	A140 5c blue	210.00	300.00
	Never hinged	450.00	
	On cover		475.00
356	A140 10c yellow	3,250.	6,000.
	Never hinged	8,000.	
	On cover		10,000.

For listings of other coil stamps of designs A138, A139 and A140, see #385-396, 410-413, 441-458 (single line wmk.), #486-496 (unwatermarked).

Beware of stamps offered as No. 356 which may be examples of No. 338 with perfs. trimmed at top and/or bottom. Beware also of plentiful fakes in the marketplace of Nos. 348-355, made by fraudulently perforating imperforate stamps or by fraudulently trimming perforations off fully perforated stamps. Authentication of all these coils is advised.

BLUISH PAPER

This was made with 35 percent rag stock instead of all wood pulp. The "bluish" color (actually grayish blue) goes through the paper showing clearly on the back as well as on the face.

1909 *Perf. 12*

357 A138 1c green 85.00 *150.00*
Never hinged 180.00
On cover 250.00

358 A139 2c carmine 80.00 *150.00*
Never hinged 170.00
On cover 200.00

359 A140 3c dp vio, type I 1,800. *12,500.*
Never hinged 4,000.
On cover —

360 A140 4c org brn *27,500.*
Never hinged *80,000.*

361 A140 5c blue 5,750. *20,000.*
Never hinged *14,500.*
On cover 27,500.

Only two examples of No. 361 used off cover (three additional on cover) are recorded. Value used is for the better of the two examples, which is well-centered but has two reattached perforations.

362 A140 6c red org 1,250. *12,500.*
Never hinged 3,000.
On cover *22,500.*

363 A140 8c olive green *30,000.*
Never hinged *85,000.*

364 A140 10c yellow 1,600. *10,000.*
Never hinged 4,000.
On cover —

365 A140 13c blue green 2,600. *4,000.*
Never hinged 6,000.
On cover —

366 A140 15c pale ultra 1,250. *12,500.*
Never hinged 3,000.
On cover —

Nos. 360 and 363 were not regularly issued.

Used examples of Nos. 357-366 must bear contemporaneous cancels, and Nos. 359-366 used must be accompanied by certificates of authenticity issued by recognized expertizing committees.

LINCOLN CENTENARY OF BIRTH ISSUE

Lincoln — A141

1909, Feb. 12 **Wmk. 191** *Perf. 12*

367 A141 2c carmine 4.50 1.75
Never hinged 9.50
On cover 4.00

Imperf

368 A141 2c carmine 12.50 19.00
Never hinged 24.00
On cover 37.50

BLUISH PAPER

Perf. 12

369 A141 2c carmine 140.00 *225.00*
Never hinged 300.00
On cover 375.00

Used examples of No. 369 must bear contemporaneous cancels. Expertizing is recommended.

ALASKA-YUKON-PACIFIC EXPOSITION ISSUE

William H. Seward — A142

1909, June 1 **Wmk. 191** *Perf. 12*

370 A142 2c carmine 6.75 2.00
Never hinged 15.00
On cover 5.00
a. Imperf. (error), P#5209 block of 6 —

No. 370a comes from error panes found in perforated stock. Plate 5209 was used only to print the perforated Alaska-Yukon-Pacific Exposition issue. No 370a can only be collected as a plate-number stamp or multiple. Without an attached plate number 5209, the stamps from this pane cannot be differentiated from No. 371.

Imperf

371 A142 2c carmine 14.00 21.00
Never hinged 30.00
On cover 40.00
On cover, Expo. station machine canc. *450.00*

Seattle, Wash., June 1 to Oct. 16.

HUDSON-FULTON CELEBRATION ISSUE

"Half Moon" and Steamship A143

1909, Sept. 25 **Wmk. 191** *Perf. 12*

372 A143 2c carmine 10.00 4.75
Never hinged 21.00
On cover 8.50

Imperf

373 A143 2c carmine 20.00 27.50
Never hinged 40.00
On cover 40.00

Tercentenary of the discovery of the Hudson River and Centenary of Robert Fulton's steamship.

DESIGNS OF 1908-09 ISSUES

1910-11 **Wmk. 190** *Perf. 12*

374 A138 1c green 6.00 .25
Never hinged 14.00
On cover .30
a. Booklet pane of 6 225.00 *400.00*
Never hinged 375.00
b. Double impression *300.00*

375 A139 2c carmine 6.00 .25
Never hinged 14.00
On cover .30
a. Booklet pane of 6 125.00 *300.00*
Never hinged 200.00
b. 2c lake *800.00* —
Never hinged *1,750.*
c. As "b," booklet pane of 6 *10,000.*
d. Double impression *750.00* —
Never hinged *1,500.*

376 A140 3c dp vio, type I ('11) 18.00 2.00
Never hinged 40.00
On cover 8.00

377 A140 4c brown ('11) 27.50 1.00
Never hinged 65.00
On cover 7.50

378 A140 5c blue ('11) 27.50 .75
Never hinged 65.00
On cover 5.25

379 A140 6c red org ('11) 37.50 1.25
Never hinged 85.00
On cover 13.00

380 A140 8c ol grn ('11) 90.00 15.00
Never hinged 200.00
On cover 45.00

381 A140 10c yellow ('11) 80.00 6.00
Never hinged 190.00
On cover 22.50

382 A140 15c pale ultra ('11) 225.00 20.00
Never hinged 500.00
On cover 100.00
Nos. 374-382 (9) 517.50 46.50

1910, Dec. *Imperf.*

383 A138 1c green 2.50 *2.75*
Never hinged 5.00
On cover 6.00

384 A139 2c carmine 4.00 2.75
Never hinged 8.00
On cover 4.00

The values for used coil stamps are for examples with contemporaneous cancels that can be authenticated by expertizing committees. Used coils with cancels most commonly from the 1950s exist, and these and stamps with other non-contemporaneous cancels sell for less than the values shown.

COIL STAMPS

1910, Nov. 1 *Perf. 12 Horizontally*

385 A138 1c green 45.00 *50.00*
Never hinged 100.00
On cover 90.00

386 A139 2c carmine 120.00 90.00
Never hinged 260.00
On cover 175.00

1910-11 *Perf. 12 Vertically*

387 A138 1c green 190.00 140.00
Never hinged 400.00
On cover 250.00

388 A139 2c carmine 1,400. *2,250.*
Never hinged 3,250.
On cover *3,000.*

Stamps offered as No. 388 frequently are privately perforated examples of No. 384, or examples of No. 375 with top and/or bottom perfs trimmed.

389 A140 3c dp vio, type I ('11) *110,000.* *10,000.*
Never hinged *240,000.*
On cover *27,500.*

No. 389 is valued in the grade of fine.

Stamps offered as No. 389 sometimes are examples of No. 376 with top and/or bottom perfs trimmed.

Beware also of plentiful fakes in the marketplace of Nos. 385-387.

Expertization by competent authorities is recommended.

1910 *Perf. 8½ Horizontally*

390 A138 1c green 4.50 *14.00*
Never hinged 10.00
On cover 17.50

391 A139 2c carmine 42.50 *50.00*
Never hinged 90.00
On cover 70.00

1910-13 *Perf. 8½ Vertically*

392 A138 1c green 27.50 *50.00*
Never hinged 65.00
On cover 75.00

393 A139 2c carmine 45.00 45.00
Never hinged 105.00
On cover 80.00

394 A140 3c dp vio, type I ('11) 60.00 65.00
Never hinged 135.00
On cover 125.00

395 A140 4c brown ('12) 60.00 *65.00*
Never hinged 135.00
On cover 125.00

396 A140 5c blue ('13) 60.00 *65.00*
Never hinged 135.00
On cover 120.00
Nos. 392-396 (5) 252.50 290.00

Beware also of plentiful fakes in the marketplace of Nos. 390-393.

PANAMA-PACIFIC EXPOSITION ISSUE

San Francisco, Cal., Feb. 20 - Dec. 4, 1915

Vasco Nunez de Balboa — A144

Pedro Miguel Locks, Panama Canal — A145

Golden Gate — A146

Discovery of San Francisco Bay — A147

1913 **Wmk. 190** *Perf. 12*

397 A144 1c green 15.00 2.00
Never hinged 35.00
On cover 3.50

398 A145 2c carmine 16.00 1.00
Never hinged 35.00
On cover 1.75
a. 2c carmine lake *1,500.*
Never hinged *2,500.*
b. 2c lake *5,250.* 3,000.
Never hinged *8,500.*

399 A146 5c blue 65.00 10.00
Never hinged 150.00
On cover 27.50

400 A147 10c orange yel 110.00 20.00
Never hinged 250.00
On cover 57.50

400A A147 10c orange 160.00 17.50
Never hinged 360.00
On cover 75.00
Nos. 397-400A (5) 366.00 50.50
Nos. 397-400A, never hinged 830.00

1914-15 *Perf. 10*

401 A144 1c green 25.00 7.00
Never hinged 60.00
On cover 16.00

402 A145 2c car ('15) 65.00 2.75
Never hinged 160.00
On cover 6.50

403 A146 5c blue ('15) 150.00 17.50
Never hinged 375.00
On cover 55.00

404 A147 10c org ('15) 650.00 70.00
Never hinged 1,600.
On cover 175.00
Nos. 401-404 (4) 890.00 97.25
Nos. 401-404, never hinged 2,195.

1912-14 **Wmk. 190** *Perf. 12*

405 A140 1c green 6.50 .25
Never hinged 15.00
On cover .30
a. Vert. pair, imperf. horiz. *2,000.* —
b. Booklet pane of 6 65.00 *75.00*
Never hinged 110.00
c. Double impression *5,500.*

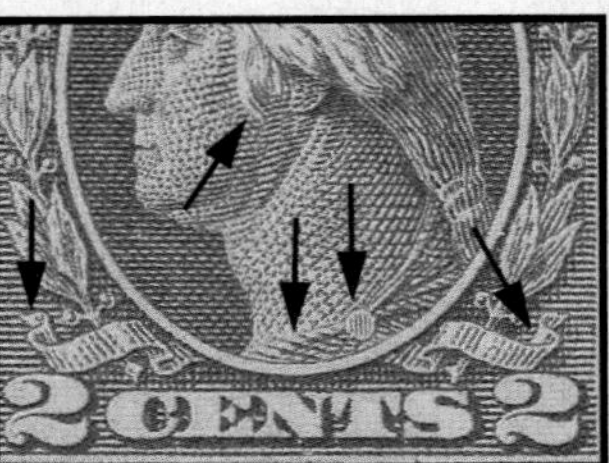

TYPE I

TWO CENTS

Type I. There is one shading line in the first curve of the ribbon above the left "2" and one in the second curve of the ribbon above the right "2."

The button of the toga has only a faint outline.

The top line of the toga rope, from the button to the front of the throat, is also very faint.

The shading lines of the face terminate in front of the ear with little or no joining, to form a lock of hair.

Used on both flat plate and rotary press printings.

406 A140 2c car, type I 6.50 .25
Never hinged 15.00
On cover .30
a. Booklet pane of 6 65.00 *90.00*
Never hinged 110.00
b. Double impression *1,250.* —
c. 2c lake, type I *2,000.* *6,000.*
Never hinged *3,750.*

407 A140 7c black ('14) 70.00 14.00
Never hinged 150.00
On cover 75.00
Nos. 405-407 (3) 83.00 14.50

1912 *Imperf.*

408 A140 1c green 1.00 1.00
Never hinged 2.00
On cover 1.75

409 A140 2c car, type I 1.20 1.20
Never hinged 2.40
On cover 2.00

COIL STAMPS

1912 *Perf. 8½ Horizontally*

410 A140 1c green 6.00 *12.50*
Never hinged 13.00
On cover 17.50

411 A140 2c carmine, type I 10.00 *17.50*
Never hinged 22.50
On cover 22.50

Perf. 8½ Vertically

412 A140 1c green 25.00 *40.00*
Never hinged 55.00
On cover 50.00

413 A140 2c carmine, type I 60.00 50.00
Never hinged 130.00
On cover 60.00
Nos. 410-413 (4) 101.00 120.00

Beware also of plentiful fakes in the marketplace of Nos. 410-413.

Franklin — A148

1912-14 **Wmk. 190** *Perf. 12*

414 A148 8c pale ol grn 37.50 2.00
Never hinged 90.00
On cover 15.00

415 A148 9c sal red ('14) 47.50 14.00
Never hinged 110.00
On cover 50.00

416 A148 10c orange yellow 37.50 .80
Never hinged 90.00
On cover 2.75
a. 10c brown yellow *1,250.*
Never hinged *2,750.*

417 A148 12c cl brn ('14) 37.50 5.00
Never hinged 90.00
On cover 25.00

418 A148 15c gray 77.50 4.00
Never hinged 175.00
On cover 17.50

419 A148 20c ultra ('14) 175.00 17.50
Never hinged 375.00
On cover *150.00*

420 A148 30c org red ('14) 105.00 17.50
Never hinged 230.00
On cover *250.00*

421 A148 50c violet ('14) 325.00 27.50
Never hinged 725.00
On cover 2,000.
Nos. 414-421 (8) 842.50 88.30

No. 421 almost always has an offset of the frame lines on the back under the gum. No. 422 does not have this offset.

VALUES FOR VERY FINE STAMPS

Please note: Stamps are valued in the grade of Very Fine unless otherwise indicated.

1912, Feb. 12 Wmk. 191 *Perf. 12*

422 A148 50c violet 200.00 25.00
Never hinged 450.00
On cover 2,000.
423 A148 $1 violet brown 450.00 80.00
Never hinged 950.00
On cover 7,000.

Perforated sheet stamps of type A148: #431-440 (single line wmk., perf. 10), #460 (double line wmk. perf. 10), #470-478 (unwmkd., perf. 10), #508-518 (unwmkd., perf. 11).

1914 Compound Perforations

As the Bureau of Engraving and Printing made the changeover to perf 10 from perf 12, in the normal course of their stamp production they perforated limited quantities of 1c, 2c and 5c stamps with the old 12-gauge perforations in one direction and the new 10-gauge perforations in the other direction. These were not production errors. These compound-perforation stamps previously were listed as Nos. 424a, 424b, 425c, 425d and 428a.

All examples of Nos. 423A-423E must be accompanied by certificates of authenticity issued by a recognized expertizing committee. Fakes made from perf 12, perf 10 and imperfs exist.

1914 Wmk. 190 *Perf. 12x10*

423A A140 1c green *15,000. 5,500.*
Never hinged —
On cover, pair 17,500.

Formerly No. 424a. Seventeen unused and 52 used examples are recorded. Value for unused is for a sound stamp with perfs touching or just cutting the design. Value for used is for a sound stamp in the grade of fine-very fine. Of the used examples, 23 are precanceled Quincy IL (very scarce) or Chicago (usually inverted). The unused block of four, used block of four and pair on cover are each unique (top stamp of pair on cover with small piece missing and valued thus). The block of 4 has perfs slightly cutting at top and is valued thus.

423B A140 2c rose red, type I *175,000. 12,500.*

Formerly No. 425d. One unused (a plate #7082 single) and 31 used examples are recorded. Value for used is for a sound stamp in the grade of fine-very fine. There are no precancels known on this issue.

423C A140 5c blue *16,000.*

Formerly No. 428a. 25 used examples are recorded. No unused examples are recorded. Three examples are precanceled: Tampa FL (2) and Rahway NJ (1). Value is for a sound stamp in the grade of fine-very fine. The pair is unique (one stamp creased, the other with a small tear).

Earliest documented use: April 14, 1915 (dated cancel on off-cover stamp).

1914 Wmk. 190 *Perf. 10x12*

423D A140 1c green *10,000.*
On postcard 22,500.

Formerly No. 424b. 42 used examples are recorded. No unused examples are recorded. 37 examples are precanceled: Dayton OH (34), Buffalo NY (2) and Elkhart IN (1). Value is for a sound stamp in the grade of fine-very fine. The use on postcard is unique.

Earliest documented use: Dec. 19, 1914.

423E A140 2c rose red, type I —

Formerly No. 425c. Only one used example has been certified (by the Philatelic Foundation). It is well centered, has a machine cancel, and has small thinning and a crease.

1913-15 Wmk. 190 *Perf. 10*

424 A140 1c green 2.25 .25
Never hinged 4.75
On cover .25
c. Vert. pair, imperf. horiz. 3,000. 2,750.
Never hinged 4,500.
d. Booklet pane of 6 ('13) 5.25 *7.50*
Never hinged 8.75
e. As "d," imperf. 1,350.
f. Vert. pair, imperf. between and with straight edge at top 13,000.

For former Nos. 424a and 424b, see Nos. 423A and 423D.

All known examples of No. 424e are without gum.

The unique example of No. 424f is never hinged, and it is valued thus.

425 A140 2c rose red, type I 2.10 .25
Never hinged 4.25
On cover .25
e. Booklet pane of 6, *1913* 17.50 *25.00*
Never hinged 30.00

For former Nos. 425c and 425d, see Nos. 423A and 423D.

426 A140 3c dp vio, type I 14.00 1.25
Never hinged 32.50
On cover 3.50
427 A140 4c brown 32.50 .90
Never hinged 75.00
On cover 5.00
428 A140 5c blue 32.50 .90
Never hinged 75.00
On cover 3.00

For former No. 428a, see No. 423C.

429 A140 6c red orange 45.00 1.75
Never hinged 105.00
On cover 9.00
430 A140 7c black 80.00 4.75
Never hinged 180.00
On cover 37.50
431 A148 8c pale olive grn 30.00 2.75
Never hinged 72.50
On cover 8.00
a. Double impression —
432 A148 9c salmon red 40.00 8.00
Never hinged 95.00
On cover 27.50
433 A148 10c org yellow 40.00 .90
Never hinged 95.00
On cover 7.50
434 A148 11c dk grn ('15) 20.00 8.00
Never hinged 50.00
On cover 25.00
435 A148 12c claret brown 22.50 5.50
Never hinged 60.00
On cover 17.50
Block of 4 100.00 45.00
a. 12c copper red 27.50 6.50
Never hinged 67.50
On cover 20.00
437 A148 15c gray 110.00 7.25
Never hinged 250.00
On cover 52.50
438 A148 20c ultra 175.00 6.00
Never hinged 400.00
On cover 150.00
439 A148 30c orange red 210.00 20.00
Never hinged 475.00
On cover 250.00
440 A148 50c violet ('15) 425.00 20.00
Never hinged 1,000.
On cover 1,750.
Nos. 424-440 (16) 1,281. 88.45

The values for used coil stamps are for examples with contemporaneous cancels that can be authenticated by expertizing committees. Used coils with cancels most commonly from the 1950s exist, and these and stamps with other non-contemporaneous cancels sell for less than the values shown.

COIL STAMPS

1914 *Perf. 10 Horizontally*

441 A140 1c green 1.00 *1.50*
Never hinged 2.00
On cover 2.75
442 A140 2c carmine, type I 10.00 *45.00*
Never hinged 22.50
On cover 60.00

1914 *Perf. 10 Vertically*

443 A140 1c green 30.00 *45.00*
Never hinged 65.00
On cover 60.00
444 A140 2c car, type I 50.00 40.00
Never hinged 120.00
On cover 57.50
a. 2c lake 2,000.
445 A140 3c violet, type I 210.00 *250.00*
Never hinged 500.00
On cover 500.00
446 A140 4c brown 130.00 *150.00*
Never hinged 280.00
On cover 200.00
447 A140 5c blue 45.00 *125.00*
Never hinged 100.00
On cover 140.00
Nos. 443-447 (5) 465.00 610.00

Beware also of plentiful fakes in the marketplace of Nos. 441-447.

ROTARY PRESS STAMPS

The Rotary Press Stamps are printed from plates that are curved to fit around a cylinder. This curvature produces stamps that are slightly larger, either horizontally or vertically, than those printed from flat plates. Designs of stamps from flat plates measure about 18½-19mm wide by 22mm high.

When the impressions are placed sidewise on the curved plates the designs are 19½-20mm wide; when they are placed vertically the designs are 22½ to 23mm high. A line of color (not a guide line) shows where the curved plates meet or join on the press.

ROTARY PRESS COIL STAMPS

Stamp designs: 18½-19x22½mm

1915-16 *Perf. 10 Horizontally*

448 A140 1c green 7.50 *17.50*
Never hinged 16.00
On cover 30.00

Type II

TWO CENTS.

Type II. Shading lines in ribbons as on type I.

The toga button, rope and rope shading lines are heavy.

The shading lines of the face at the lock of hair end in a strong vertical curved line.

Used on rotary press printings only.

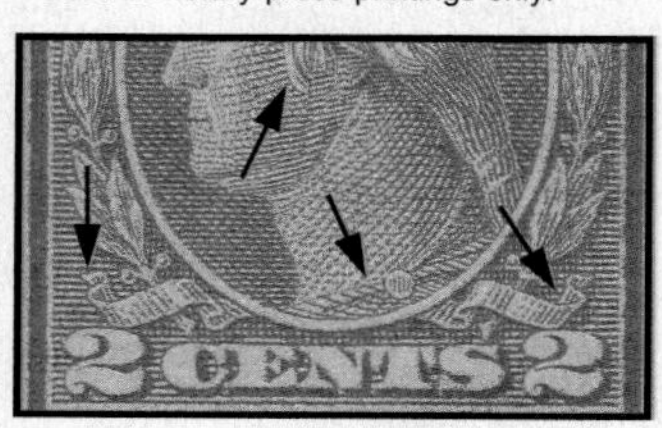

Type III

Type III. Two lines of shading in the curves of the ribbons.

Other characteristics similar to type II.

Used on rotary press printings only.

Fraudulently altered examples of type III (Nos. 455, 488, 492 and 540) have had one line of shading scraped off to make them resemble type II (Nos. 454, 487, 491 and 539).

449 A140 2c red, type I 2,500. 600.00
Never hinged 5,500.
On cover, type I 1,500.
450 A140 2c car, type III ('16) 12.50 *25.00*
Never hinged 27.50
On cover, type III 45.00

1914-16 *Perf. 10 Vertically*

Stamp designs: 19½-20x22mm

452 A140 1c green 10.00 *17.50*
Never hinged 21.00
On cover 30.00
453 A140 2c carmine rose, type I 140.00 40.00
Never hinged 300.00
On cover, type I 50.00
454 A140 2c red, type II 70.00 22.50
Never hinged 160.00
On cover, type II 50.00
455 A140 2c carmine, type III 8.00 3.50
Never hinged 18.00
On cover, type III 8.00
456 A140 3c vio, type I ('16) 225.00 170.00
Never hinged 500.00
On cover 250.00
457 A140 4c brown ('16) 25.00 30.00
Never hinged 55.00
On cover 50.00
458 A140 5c blue ('16) 27.50 30.00
Never hinged 60.00
On cover 50.00
Nos. 452-458 (7) 505.50 313.50

Horizontal Coil

1914, June 30 *Imperf.*

459 A140 2c car, type I 200. *1,300.*
Never hinged 300.

When the value for a used stamp is higher than the unused value, the stamp must have a contemporaneous cancel. Valuable stamps of this type should be accompanied by certificates of authenticity issued by recognized expertizing committees. The used value for No. 459 is for an example with such a certificate.

Beware of examples of No. 453 with perforations fraudulently trimmed to resemble single examples of No. 459.

FLAT PLATE PRINTINGS

1915, Feb. 8 Wmk. 191 *Perf. 10*

460 A148 $1 violet black 650. 140.
Never hinged 1,450.
On cover 12,000.

1915, June 17 Wmk. 190 *Perf. 11*

461 A140 2c pale carmine red, type I 150. *375.*
Never hinged 325.
On cover 1,200.

Beware of fraudulently perforated examples of No. 409 being offered as No. 461.

See note on used stamps following No. 459.

Unwatermarked

From 1916 onward all postage stamps except Nos. 519 and 832b are on unwatermarked paper.

1916-17 Unwmk. *Perf. 10*

462 A140 1c green 7.00 .35
Never hinged 16.00
On cover .50
a. Booklet pane of 6 9.50 *12.50*
Never hinged 16.00
463 A140 2c carmine, type I 4.50 .40
Never hinged 10.00
On cover .45
a. Booklet pane of 6 110.00 *110.00*
Never hinged 180.00
464 A140 3c violet, type I 65.00 17.50
Never hinged 165.00
On cover 40.00

Beware of fraudulently perforated examples of No. 483 being offered as No. 464.

465 A140 4c org brn 35.00 2.25
Never hinged 80.00
On cover 10.00
466 A140 5c blue 65.00 2.25
Never hinged 150.00
On cover 12.00
467 A140 5c car (error in plate of 2c, '17) 425.00 *2,000.*
Never hinged 800.00
On cover 5,000.

No. 467 is an error caused by using a 5c transfer roll in re-entering three subjects: 7942 UL 74, 7942 UL 84, 7942 LR 18; the balance of the subjects on the plate being normal 2c entries. No. 467 imperf. is listed as No. 485. The error perf 11 on unwatermarked paper is No. 505.

468 A140 6c red orange 80.00 8.00
Never hinged 180.00
On cover 35.00
469 A140 7c black 110.00 13.00
Never hinged 250.00
On cover 45.00
470 A148 8c olive green 30.00 7.00
Never hinged 115.00
On cover 25.00
471 A148 9c salmon red 55.00 17.50
Never hinged 125.00
On cover 40.00
472 A148 10c orange yel 100.00 2.50
Never hinged 230.00
On cover 8.50
473 A148 11c dark green 42.50 19.00
Never hinged 90.00
On cover 47.50
474 A148 12c claret brn 47.50 7.25
Never hinged 110.00
On cover 22.50
475 A148 15c gray 170.00 15.00
Never hinged 375.00
On cover 85.00
476 A148 20c lt ultra 200.00 17.50
Never hinged 475.00
On cover 725.00
476A A148 30c orange red *2,000.*
Never hinged 4,250.

No. 476A is valued in the grade of fine.

477 A148 50c lt violet ('17) 850. 80.00
Never hinged 1,900.
On cover 2,250.
478 A148 $1 violet black 600. 27.50
Never hinged 1,400.
On cover 3,000.
Nos. 462-466,468-476,477-478 (16) 2,462. 237.00

TYPES OF 1902-03 ISSUE

1917, Mar. 22 Unwmk. *Perf. 10*

479 A127 $2 dark blue 210.00 40.00
Never hinged 475.00
On cover (other than first flight or Zeppelin) *1,250.*

480 A128 $5 light green 170.00 35.00
Never hinged 375.00
On cover *1,250.*

1916-17 *Imperf.*

481 A140 1c green 1.25 .95
Never hinged 1.90
On cover 1.50

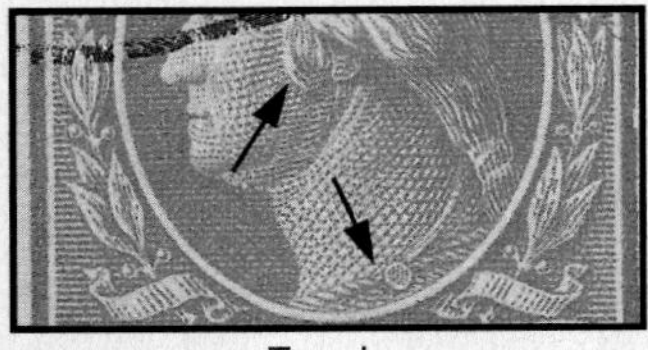

Type Ia

TWO CENTS

Type Ia. The design characteristics are similar to type I except that all of the lines of the design are stronger.

The toga button, toga rope and rope shading lines are heavy.

The latter characteristics are those of type II, which, however, occur only on impressions from rotary plates.

Used only on flat plates 10208 and 10209.

482 A140 2c carmine, type I 1.50 1.30
Never hinged 2.60
On cover 2.50

482A A140 2c deep rose, type Ia — *65,000.*
On cover *70,000.*

No. 482A was issued imperforate but all examples were privately perforated with large oblong perforations at the sides (Schermack type III).

Type II

THREE CENTS

Type II. The top line of the toga rope is strong and the rope shading lines are heavy and complete.

The line between the lips is heavy.

Used on both flat plate and rotary press printings.

483 A140 3c violet, type I ('17) 12.00 10.00
Never hinged 24.00
On cover 25.00

484 A140 3c violet, type II 10.00 8.00
Never hinged 20.00
On cover 14.00

485 A140 5c car (error in plate of 2c) ('17) *9,000.*
Never hinged *14,000.*

Although No. 485 is valued as a single stamp, such examples are seldom seen in the marketplace.

No. 485 usually is seen as the center stamp in a block of 9 with 8 No. 482 (value with #485 never hinged, $22,500) or as two center stamps in a block of 12 (value with both No. 485 never hinged, $42,500).

ROTARY PRESS COIL STAMPS
(See note over No. 448)

1916-18 *Perf. 10 Horizontally*
Stamp designs: 18½-19x22½mm

486 A140 1c green ('18) .85 .85
Never hinged 1.75
On cover 1.15

487 A140 2c carmine, type II 12.50 14.00
Never hinged 27.50
On cover 19.00

488 A140 2c carmine, type III 3.00 *5.00*
Never hinged 6.50
On cover 7.00

489 A140 3c vio, type I ('17) 4.50 2.25
Never hinged 10.00
On cover 3.50

Nos. 486-489 (4) 20.85 22.10

1916-22 *Perf. 10 Vertically*
Stamp designs: 19½-20x22mm

490 A140 1c green .50 *.60*
Never hinged 1.05
On cover .80

491 A140 2c carmine, type II 2,500. 800.00
Never hinged 5,250.
On cover, type II 1,100.

492 A140 2c carmine, type III 9.00 1.00
Never hinged 19.00
On cover, type III 1.40

493 A140 3c vio, type I ('17) 14.00 4.50
Never hinged 30.00
On cover, type I 8.00

494 A140 3c vio, type II ('18) 10.00 2.50
Never hinged 21.50
On cover, type II 4.00

495 A140 4c org brn ('17) 10.00 7.00
Never hinged 21.50
On cover 10.00

496 A140 5c blue ('19) 3.25 2.50
Never hinged 7.00
On cover 3.00

497 A148 10c org yel ('22) 17.50 17.50
Never hinged 35.00
On cover 22.50

Blind Perfs

Listings of imperforate-between varieties are for examples which show no trace of "blind perfs," traces of impressions from the perforating pins which do not cut into the paper.

Some unused stamps have had the gum removed to eliminate the impressions from the perforating pins. These stamps do not qualify as the listed varieties.

TYPES OF 1913-15 ISSUE
FLAT PLATE PRINTINGS

1917-19 Unwmk. *Perf. 11*

498 A140 1c green .35 .25
Never hinged .75
On cover .30
a. Vertical pair, imperf. horiz. 800.00
Never hinged *1,600.*
b. Horizontal pair, imperf. between 600.00
Never hinged *1,350.*
c. Vertical pair, imperf. between *700.00* —
d. Double impression 250.00 *3,750.*
e. Booklet pane of 6 2.50 *2.00*
Never hinged 4.25
f. Booklet pane of 30 *1,050.* *12,500.*
Never hinged *1,700.*
g. Perf. 10 at top or bottom *15,000.* *20,000.*
Never hinged *27,500.*

No. 498g used is valued in the grade of fine.

499 A140 2c rose, type I .35 .25
Never hinged .75
On cover, type I .30
a. Vertical pair, imperf. horiz., type I 1,000.
Never hinged 2,000.
b. Horiz. pair, imperf. vert., type I *550.00* *600.00*
Never hinged *1,100.*
c. Vert. pair, imperf. btwn., type I *900.00* *300.00*
e. Booklet pane of 6, type I 4.00 *2.50*
Never hinged 6.75
f. Booklet pane of 30, type I *21,000.* —
Never hinged *30,000.*
g. Double impression, type I 200.00 *2,000.*
Never hinged *400.00*
On cover —
h. 2c lake, type I 500.00 800.00
Never hinged *1,000.*
On cover —
i. As "e," single stamp, lake —

No. 499b is valued in the grade of fine. No 499g used is valued in the grade of fine.

500 A140 2c deep rose, type Ia 250.00 240.00
Never hinged 550.00
On cover, type Ia *650.00*
Never hinged *2,750.*

No. 500 exists with imperforate top sheet margin. Examples have been altered by trimming perforations. Some also have faked Schermack perfs.

501 A140 3c lt vio, type I 9.00 .40
Never hinged 20.00
On cover, type I .50
b. Booklet pane of 6, type I 75.00 *80.00*
Never hinged 125.00
c. Vert. pair, imper. horiz., type I *2,100.*
Never hinged *3,250.*
d. Double impression *3,500.* *3,500.*
Never hinged *5,000.*

No. 501d is valued in the grade of fine.

502 A140 3c dark violet, type II 12.00 .75
Never hinged 27.50
On cover, type II 1.00
b. Bklt. pane of 6, type II 60.00 *75.00*
Never hinged 100.00
c. Vert. pair, imperf. horiz., type II *1,400.* *850.00*
Never hinged *2,750.*
On cover *1,400.*
d. Double impression 800.00 *1,000.*
Never hinged 1,600.
e. Perf. 10 at top or bottom *15,000.* *30,000.*
Never hinged *21,500.*

503 A140 4c brown 8.50 .40
Never hinged 19.00
On cover 2.10
b. Double impression —

504 A140 5c blue 7.50 .35
Never hinged 17.00
On cover .45
a. Horizontal pair, imperf. between *20,000.* —
b. Double impression *1,750.* *1,600.*

505 A140 5c rose (error in plate of 2c) 325.00 *600.00*
Never hinged 625.00
On cover 2,250.

506 A140 6c red orange 11.00 .40
Never hinged 25.00
On cover 2.50
a. Perf. 10 at top or bottom *30,000.* *8,000.*
b. Double impression, never hinged *2,000.*

No. 506a also exists as a transitional stamp gauging partly perf 10 and partly perf 11 at top. Value thus the same as normal 506a.

No. 506b is a partial double impression. Two authenticated examples are documented.

507 A140 7c black 24.00 1.25
Never hinged 55.00
On cover 7.75

508 A148 8c olive bister 11.00 .65
Never hinged 25.00
On cover 2.75
b. Vertical pair, imperf. between — —
c. Perf. 10 at top or bottom *9,000.*

509 A148 9c salmon red 11.00 1.60
Never hinged 25.00
On cover 13.00
a. Perf. 10 at top or bottom *7,500.*
Never hinged *37,500.*

No. 509a also exists as a transitional stamp gauging partly perf 10 and partly perf 11 at top or bottom. Value thus the same as normal 509a.

510 A148 10c orange yellow 15.00 .25
Never hinged 34.00
On cover 2.00
a. 10c brown yellow *1,400.*
Never hinged *3,250.*

511 A148 11c lt green 7.50 2.25
Never hinged 17.00
On cover 8.50
a. Perf. 10 at top or bottom *4,000.* *3,750.*
Never hinged *7,500.*

No. 511a also exists as a transitional stamp gauging partly perf 10 and partly perf 11 at top or bottom. Value thus the same as normal 511a.

512 A148 12c claret brown 7.50 .40
Never hinged 17.00
On cover 4.00
a. 12c brown carmine 8.50 .50
Never hinged 19.00
On cover 4.50
b. Perf. 10 at top or bottom *27,500.* *15,000.*
On cover —

513 A148 13c apple grn ('19) 9.50 5.50
Never hinged 21.00
On cover 19.00
Block of 4 40.00 45.00

514 A148 15c gray 32.50 1.40
Never hinged 75.00
On cover 25.00
a. Perf. 10 at bottom *10,000.*

515 A148 20c lt ultra 40.00 .45
Never hinged 85.00
On cover 75.00
b. Vertical pair, imperf. between *1,750.* *3,250.*
c. Double impression *1,250.*
Never hinged *2,500.*
d. Perf. 10 at top or bottom — *12,500.*

No. 515b is valued in the grade of fine.

Beware of pairs with blind perforations inside the design of the top stamp that are offered as No. 515b.

No. 515c is a partial double impression.

516 A148 30c orange red 27.50 1.50
Never hinged 65.00
On cover 150.00
a. Perf. 10 at top or bottom *20,000.* *15,000.*
Never hinged *37,500.*
b. Double impression —

No. 516a used is valued in the grade of fine.

517 A148 50c red violet 45.00 .75
Never hinged 110.00
On cover *400.00*
b. Vertical pair, imperf. between & with natural straight edge at bottom *6,000.*
c. Perf. 10 at top or bottom *17,500.*

No. 517b is valued in average condition and may be a unique used pair (precanceled). The editors would like to see authenticated evidence of an unused pair.

518 A148 $1 violet brown 37.50 1.50
Never hinged 95.00
On cover *550.00*
b. $1 deep brown *1,900.* *1,250.*
Never hinged *4,000.*

Nos. 498-504,506-518 (20) 566.70 260.30

No. 518b is valued in the grade of fine to very fine.

TYPE OF 1908-09 ISSUE

1917, Oct. 10 Wmk. 191 *Perf. 11*

519 A139 2c carmine 425.00 *1,800.*
Never hinged 900.00
On cover *3,500.*

Beware of examples of No. 344 fraudulently perforated and offered as No. 519. Obtaining a certificate from a recognized expertizing committee is strongly recommended.

Warning: See note following No. 459 regarding used stamps.

Franklin — A149

1918, Aug. Unwmk. *Perf. 11*

523 A149 $2 org red & blk 500. 240.
Never hinged 1,100.
On cover *2,000.*

524 A149 $5 dp grn & blk 160. 30.00
Never hinged 340.
On cover *2,500.*

See No. 547 for $2 carmine & black.

TYPES OF 1917-19 ISSUE
OFFSET PRINTING

1918-20 Unwmk. *Perf. 11*

525 A140 1c gray green 2.50 .90
Never hinged 6.00
On cover 1.75
a. 1c dark green 10.00 1.75
Never hinged 25.00
c. Horizontal pair, imperf. between *750.00* *650.00*
d. Double impression 40.00 *750.00*
Never hinged 90.00

No. 525c is valued in the grade of fine and with natural straight edge at right, as virtually all recorded examples come thus. No. 525d used is valued in the grade of very good.

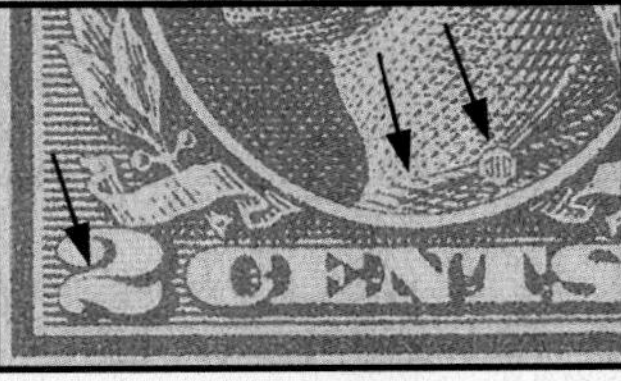

Type IV

TWO CENTS

Type IV — Top line of the toga rope is broken.

The shading lines in the toga button are so arranged that the curving of the first and last form "D (reversed) ID."

The line of color in the left "2" is very thin and usually broken.

Used on offset printings only.

Type V

Type V — Top line of the toga is complete.

There are five vertical shading lines in the toga button.

The line of color in the left "2" is very thin and usually broken.

The shading dots on the nose are as shown on the diagram.

Used on offset printings only.

Type Va

Type Va — Characteristics are the same as type V except in the shading dots of the nose. The third row of dots from the bottom has four dots instead of six. The overall height is ⅓mm shorter than the other types.

Used on offset printings only.

Type VI

Type VI — General characteristics the same as type V except that the line of color in the left "2" is very heavy.

Used on offset printings only.

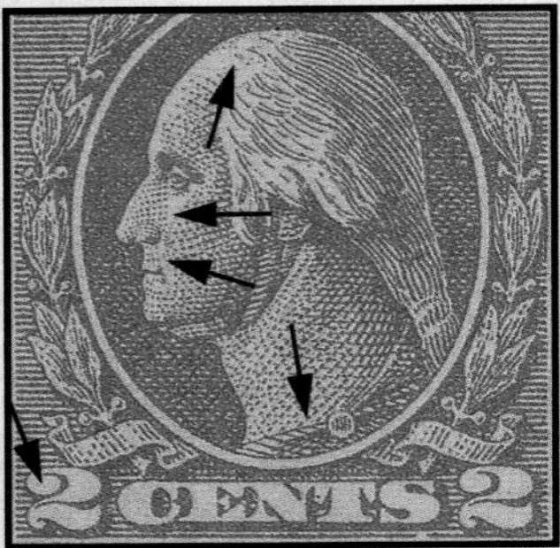

TYPE VII

Type VII — The line of color in the left "2" is invariably continuous, clearly defined and heavier than in type V or Va but not as heavy as type VI.

An additional vertical row of dots has been added to the upper lip.

Numerous additional dots have been added to the hair on top of the head.

Used on offset printings only.

No.	Description	Unused	Used
526	A140 2c car, type IV ('20)	25.00	4.00
	Never hinged	57.50	
	On cover, type IV		11.00
527	A140 2c car, type V ('20)	18.00	1.25
	Never hinged	40.00	
	On cover, Type V		2.75
a.	Double impression	100.00	—
	Never hinged	225.00	
b.	Vert. pair, imperf. horiz.	850.00	
c.	Horiz. pair, imperf. vert.	1,000.	—
528	A140 2c car, type Va ('20)	8.00	.40
	Never hinged	20.00	
	On cover, type Va		.75
c.	Double impression	60.00	
	Never hinged	150.00	
g.	Vert. pair, imperf. between	3,250.	
528A	A140 2c car, type VI ('20)	47.50	2.00
	Never hinged	115.00	
	On cover, type VI		3.75
d.	Double impression	200.00	900.00
	Never hinged	450.00	
f.	Vert. pair, imperf. horiz.		—
h.	Vert. pair, imperf. between	5,000.	
528B	A140 2c car, type VII ('20)	20.00	.75
	Never hinged	50.00	
	On cover, type VII		1.00
e.	Double impression	77.50	400.00

No. 528Be used is valued in the grade of very good to fine.

TYPE III

THREE CENTS

Type III — The top line of the toga rope is strong but the 5th shading line is missing as in type I.

Center shading line of the toga button consists of two dashes with a central dot.

The "P" and "O" of "POSTAGE" are separated by a line of color.

The frame line at the bottom of the vignette is complete.

Used on offset printings only.

TYPE IV

Type IV — The shading lines of the toga rope are complete.

The second and fourth shading lines in the toga button are broken in the middle and the third line is continuous with a dot in the center.

The "P" and "O" of "POSTAGE" are joined.

The frame line at the bottom of the vignette is broken.

Used on offset printings only.

No.	Description	Unused	Used
529	A140 3c vio, type III	3.50	.50
	Never hinged	7.75	
	On cover, type III		.60
a.	Double impression	50.00	800.00
	Never hinged	115.00	
b.	Printed on both sides	2,500.	

No. 529a used is valued in the grade of very good.

No.	Description	Unused	Used
530	A140 3c pur, type IV	2.00	.30
	Never hinged	4.50	
a.	Double impression	40.00	750.00
	Never hinged	90.00	
	On cover		1,500.
b.	Printed on both sides	750.00	
	Never hinged	1,100.	
c.	Triple impression	1,750.	—
	Nos. 525-530 (8)	126.50	10.10

No. 530a used is valued in the grade of fine.

1918-20 ***Imperf.***

No.	Description	Unused	Used
531	A140 1c green ('19)	12.00	12.00
	Never hinged	21.00	
	On cover		17.50
532	A140 2c car rose, type IV ('20)	37.50	42.50
	Never hinged	70.00	
	On cover		75.00
533	A140 2c car, type V ('20)	110.00	125.00
	Never hinged	175.00	
	On cover		210.00
534	A140 2c car, type Va ('20)	15.00	15.00
	Never hinged	26.00	
	On cover		17.50
534A	A140 2c car, type VI ('20)	40.00	40.00
	Never hinged	75.00	
	On cover		45.00
534B	A140 2c car, type VII ('20)	2,000.	1,500.
	Never hinged	3,750.	
	On cover		5,000.
535	A140 3c vio, type IV	10.00	6.00
	Never hinged	18.00	
	On cover		12.50
a.	Double impression	100.00	—
	Never hinged	200.00	
	Nos. 531-534A,535 (6)	224.50	240.50

1919, Aug. 15 ***Perf. 12½***

No.	Description	Unused	Used
536	A140 1c gray green	20.00	35.00
	Never hinged	45.00	
	On postcard, single		225.00
	On cover, pair		300.00
a.	Horiz. pair, imperf. vert.	1,000.	

VICTORY ISSUE

"Victory" and Flags of the Allies — A150

FLAT PLATE PRINTING

Unwmk.

1919, Mar. 3 **Engr.** ***Perf. 11***

No.	Description	Unused	Used
537	A150 3c violet	10.00	3.25
	Never hinged	20.00	
	On cover		11.00
a.	3c deep red violet	1,250.	1,750.
	Never hinged	2,300.	
	On cover		—
b.	3c light reddish violet	150.00	50.00
	Never hinged	300.00	
	On cover		250.00
c.	3c red violet	200.00	60.00
	Never hinged	400.00	
	On cover		275.00

Victory of the Allies in World War I.

No. 537a is valued in the grade of fine.

ROTARY PRESS PRINTINGS

1919 **Unwmk.** ***Perf. 11x10***

Stamp designs: 19½-20x22-22¼mm

No.	Description	Unused	Used
538	A140 1c green	10.00	9.00
	Never hinged	23.00	
	On cover		22.50
a.	Vert. pair, imperf. horiz.	60.00	125.00
	Never hinged	125.00	
539	A140 2c carmine rose, type II	2,700.	17,500.
	Never hinged	4,250.	
	On cover, type II		60,000.
540	A140 2c car rose, type III	12.00	9.50
	Never hinged	27.50	
	On cover, type III		25.00
a.	Vert. pair, imperf horiz.	60.00	140.00
	Never hinged	125.00	
b.	Horiz. pair, imperf. vert.	2,000.	
541	A140 3c vio, type II	40.00	32.50
	Never hinged	100.00	
	On cover		100.00

The part perforate varieties of Nos. 538a and 540a were issued in sheets and may be had in blocks; similar part perforate varieties, Nos. 490 and 492, are from coils and are found only in strips.

See note over No. 448 regarding No. 539.

No. 539 is valued in the grade of fine.

No. 540b is valued in the grade of fine.

1920, May 26 ***Perf. 10x11***

Stamp design: 19x22½-22¾mm

No.	Description	Unused	Used
542	A140 1c green	12.50	1.50
	Never hinged	30.00	
	On cover		5.50

1921 ***Perf. 10***

Stamp design: 19x22½mm

No.	Description	Unused	Used
543	A140 1c green	.70	.40
	Never hinged	1.75	
	On cover		.45
a.	Horizontal pair, imperf. between	4,500.	

1922 ***Perf. 11***

Stamp design: 19x22½mm

No.	Description	Unused	Used
544	A140 1c green	22,500.	3,500.
	Never hinged	35,000.	
	On cover		7,500.

No. 544 is valued in the grade of fine.

1921

Stamp designs: 19½-20x22mm

No.	Description	Unused	Used
545	A140 1c green	170.00	200.00
	Never hinged	450.00	
	On cover		1,800.
546	A140 2c carmine rose, type III	105.00	190.00
	Never hinged	230.00	
	On cover		800.00
a.	Perf. 10 on left side	7,500.	17,500.

No. 546a used is valued in the grade of very good. It is unique used.

FLAT PLATE PRINTING

1920, Nov. 1 ***Perf. 11***

No.	Description	Unused	Used
547	A149 $2 carmine & black	110.	35.
	Never hinged	240.	
	On cover (commercial)		1,000.
a.	$2 lake & black	190.	35.
	Never hinged	400.	

PILGRIM TERCENTENARY ISSUE

"Mayflower" A151

Landing of the Pilgrims — A152

Signing of the Compact — A153

1920, Dec. 21 **Unwmk.** ***Perf. 11***

No.	Description	Unused	Used
548	A151 1c green	3.75	2.00
	Never hinged	9.25	
	On cover		3.50
549	A152 2c carmine rose	5.00	1.60
	Never hinged	12.00	
	On cover		2.50
550	A153 5c deep blue	30.00	12.50
	Never hinged	65.00	
	On cover		22.50
	Nos. 548-550 (3)	38.75	16.10
	Nos. 548-550, never hinged	97.50	

Tercentenary of the landing of the Pilgrims at Plymouth, Mass.

Nathan Hale A154

Franklin A155

Harding A156

Washington A157

Lincoln A158

Martha Washington A159

Theodore Roosevelt A160

Garfield A161

McKinley A162

Grant A163

Jefferson A164

Monroe A165

Rutherford B. Hayes A166

Grover Cleveland A167

American Indian A168

Statue of Liberty A169

Golden Gate — A170

Niagara Falls — A171

American Buffalo A172

Arlington Amphitheater A173

Lincoln Memorial A174

US Capitol A175

Head of Freedom Statue, Capitol Dome — A176

FLAT PLATE PRINTINGS

1922-25 Unwmk. *Perf. 11*

551 A154 ½c ol brn ('25) .25 .25
Never hinged .50
552 A155 1c dp grn ('23) 1.25 .25
Never hinged 2.75
a. Booklet pane of 6 7.50 *4.00*
Never hinged 12.50
553 A156 1½c yel brn ('25) 2.00 .25
Never hinged 4.10
554 A157 2c carmine ('23) 1.10 .25
Never hinged 2.50
On cover .25
a. Horiz. pair, imperf. vert. *250.00*
b. Vert. pair, imperf. horiz. *6,000.*
Never hinged *10,000.*
c. Booklet pane of 6 7.00 *3.00*
Never hinged 12.00
d. Perf. 10 at top or bottom *17,500.* *9,500.*
On cover *20,000.*

No. 554d unused is unique. It is never hinged and has a natural straight edge at left. Value represents the sale price at 2001 auction.

555 A158 3c violet ('23) 13.00 1.20
Never hinged 27.50
556 A159 4c yel brn ('23) 16.00 .50
Never hinged 35.00
On cover 9.00
a. Vert. pair, imperf. horiz. *12,500.*
b. Perf. 10 at top or bottom *3,500.* *22,500.*

No. 556a is unique. It resulted from a sheet that was damaged and patched during production.

No. 556b used also exists as a transitional stamp gauging 10 at left top and 11 at right top. Value the same.

557 A160 5c dark blue 16.00 .30
Never hinged 35.00
a. Imperf., pair *2,000.*
Never hinged *4,000.*
b. Horiz. pair, imperf. vert. —
c. Perf. 10 at top or bottom — *9,500.*
On cover *17,500.*
558 A161 6c red orange 30.00 1.00
Never hinged 65.00
559 A162 7c black ('23) 7.25 .75
Never hinged 15.50
560 A163 8c ol grn ('23) 37.50 1.00
Never hinged 80.00
561 A164 9c rose ('23) 11.00 1.25
Never hinged 25.00
562 A165 10c orange ('23) 13.50 .35
Never hinged 30.00
a. Vert. pair, imperf. horiz. *2,000.*
Never hinged *3,250.*
b. Imperf., pair *1,900.*
c. Perf. 10 at top or bottom *70,000.* *15,000.*

No. 562a is valued in the grade of fine, with gum and without blue defacing lines. No. 562b is valued without gum and without blue pencil defacing lines. No. 562c is valued in the grade of fine.

563 A166 11c greenish blue 1.25 .60
Never hinged 2.75
a. 11c light bluish green 1.25 .60
Never hinged 2.75
d. Imperf., pair *20,000.*

Many other intermediate shades exist for Nos. 563 and 563a, all falling within the blue or green color families.

564 A167 12c brn vio ('23) 4.75 .35
Never hinged 10.50
a. Horiz. pair, imperf. vert. *3,750.*
565 A168 14c blue ('23) 4.25 .90
Never hinged 9.50
566 A169 15c gray 16.00 .30
Never hinged 35.00
567 A170 20c car rose ('23) 16.00 .30
Never hinged 35.00
a. Horiz. pair, imperf. vert. *2,500.*
Never hinged *5,000.*
568 A171 25c yel grn 13.50 .75
Never hinged 30.00
b. Vert. pair, imperf. horiz. *3,250.*
c. Perf. 10 at one side *5,000.* *11,000.*
Never hinged *7,500.*

No. 568b is valued in the grade of fine. No. 568c used is valued in the grade of fine.

569 A172 30c ol brn ('23) 22.50 .60
Never hinged 50.00
570 A173 50c lilac 32.50 .40
Never hinged 70.00
571 A174 $1 vio brn ('23) 35.00 .80
Never hinged 75.00
572 A175 $2 dp blue ('23) 55.00 9.00
Never hinged 120.00
573 A176 $5 car & bl ('23) 90.00 15.00
Never hinged 180.00
a. $5 car lake & dk bl 175.00 30.00
Never hinged 350.00
Nos. 551-573 (23) 439.60 36.35
Nos. 551-573, never hinged 940.60

For other listings of perforated stamps of designs A154 to A173 see:
Nos. 578 & 579, Perf. 11x10
Nos. 581-591, Perf. 10
Nos. 594-596, Perf. 11
Nos. 632-642, 653, 692-696, Perf. 11x10½
Nos. 697-701, Perf. 10½x11
This series also includes #622-623 (perf. 11), 684-687 & 720-723.

1923-25 *Imperf.*
Stamp design 19¼x22¼mm

575 A155 1c green 5.00 5.00
Never hinged 11.00
576 A156 1½c yel brn ('25) 1.25 *1.50*
Never hinged 2.70

The 1½c A156 Rotary press imperforate is listed as No. 631.

577 A157 2c carmine 1.30 1.25
Never hinged 2.90
a. 2c carmine lake —
Nos. 575-577 (3) 7.55 7.75
Nos. 575-577, never hinged 16.60

ROTARY PRESS PRINTINGS
(See note over No. 448)

1923 *Perf. 11x10*

578 A155 1c green 75.00 *160.00*
Never hinged 150.00
On cover *700.00*
579 A157 2c carmine 70.00 *140.00*
Never hinged 140.00
On cover *400.00*

Nos. 578-579 were made from coil waste of Nos. 597, 599 and measure approximately 19¾x22¼mm.

1923-26 *Perf. 10*

581 A155 1c green 10.00 .75
Never hinged 21.00
582 A156 1½c brown ('25) 6.00 .65
Never hinged 13.00
Never hinged *650.00*
Never hinged *650.00*
583 A157 2c car ('24) 3.00 .30
Never hinged 6.25
On cover 2.50
a. Booklet pane of 6 110.00 *150.00*
Never hinged 200.00
584 A158 3c violet ('25) 27.50 3.00
Never hinged 60.00
585 A159 4c yel brn ('25) 17.50 .65
Never hinged 37.50
On cover 15.00
586 A160 5c blue ('25) 17.50 .40
Never hinged 37.50
a. Horizontal pair, imperf. vertically *7,500.*

No. 586a is unique, precanceled, with average centering and small faults, and it is valued as such.

587 A161 6c red org ('25) 9.25 .60
Never hinged 20.00
588 A162 7c black ('26) 12.50 6.25
Never hinged 26.00
589 A163 8c ol grn ('26) 27.50 4.50
Never hinged 57.50
590 A164 9c rose ('26) 6.00 2.50
Never hinged 12.50
591 A165 10c org ('25) 40.00 .50
Never hinged 85.00
Nos. 581-591 (11) 176.75 20.10
Nos. 581-591, never hinged 371.25

1923 *Perf. 11*

594 A155 1c green *35,000.* *10,500.*
With gum *65,000.*
On cover *18,000.*

The main listing for No. 594 unused is for an example without gum; both unused and used are valued with perforations just touching frameline on one side.

595 A157 2c carmine 240.00 *375.00*
Never hinged 450.00
On cover 550.00

Nos. 594-595 were made from coil waste of Nos. 597 and 599, and measure approximately 19¾x22¼mm.

596 A155 1c green *175,000.*
Precanceled *130,000.*

No. 596 was made from rotary press sheet waste and measures approximately 19¼x22½mm. A majority of the examples carry the Bureau precancel "Kansas City, Mo." No. 596 is valued in the grade of fine.

COIL STAMPS
ROTARY PRESS

1923-29 *Perf. 10 Vertically*
Stamp designs approximately 19¾x22¼mm

597 A155 1c green .30 .25
Never hinged .60
Three on cover 2.25
598 A156 1½c brown ('25) .90 .25
Never hinged 1.80

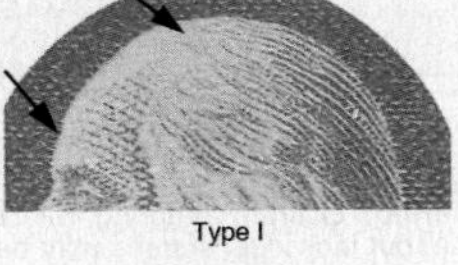
Type I

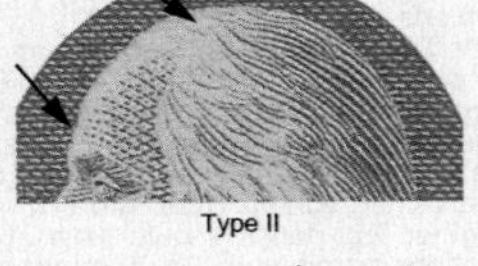
Type II

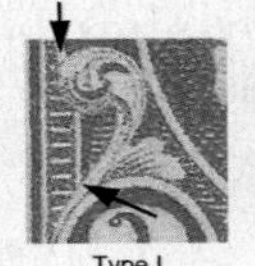
Type I

Type II

TYPE I. No line outlining forehead. No heavy hair lines at top center of head. Outline of left acanthus scroll generally faint at top and toward base at left side.

TYPE II. Thin line outlining forehead. Three heavy hair lines at top center of head; two being outstanding in the white area. Outline of left acanthus scroll very strong and clearly defined at top (under left edge of lettered panel) and at lower curve (above and to left of numeral oval). This type appears only on Nos. 599A and 634A.

599 A157 2c car, type I .35 .25
Never hinged .70
On cover 1.10
b. 2c carmine lake, type I, never hinged *300.00* —
Never hinged *950.00*
599A A157 2c car, type II ('29) 100.00 16.00
Never hinged 200.00
On cover 32.50
600 A158 3c violet ('24) 6.25 .25
Never hinged 12.50
On cover 6.00
601 A159 4c yel brn 3.75 .35
Never hinged 7.50
On cover 14.00
602 A160 5c dk blue ('24) 1.75 .25
Never hinged 3.50
603 A165 10c orange ('24) 3.50 .25
Never hinged 7.00

The 6c design A161 coil stamp is listed as No. 723.

1923-25 *Perf. 10 Horizontally*
Stamp designs: 19¼x22½mm

604 A155 1c green ('24) .40 .25
Never hinged .80
Three on cover 6.00
605 A156 1½c yel brn ('25) .40 .25
Never hinged .80
606 A157 2c carmine .40 .25
Never hinged .80
On cover 3.50
a. 2c carmine lake *75.00* —
Never hinged *150.00*
Nos. 597-599,600-606 (10) 18.00 2.60
Nos. 597-599, 600-606, never hinged 36.00

HARDING MEMORIAL ISSUE

Warren G. Harding — A177

FLAT PLATE PRINTING
Stamp designs: 19¼x22¼mm

1923 *Perf. 11*

610 A177 2c black .50 .25
Never hinged 1.00
On cover .30
a. Horiz. pair, imperf. vert. *2,000.*
b. Imperf. (error), P#14870 block of 6 *25,000.*

No. 610a is valued in the grade of fine.

No. 610b comes from left side error panes found in a normal pad of No. 610 stamps before No. 611 was issued. Two left side plate blocks and one top position plate block are recorded. Plate #14870 was not used to print No. 611. Loose stamps separated from the top and left plate blocks are indistinguishable from No. 611.

Imperf

611 A177 2c black 4.50 4.00
Never hinged 9.00

ROTARY PRESS PRINTING
Stamp designs: 19¼x22½mm

612 A177 2c black 15.00 1.75
Never hinged 32.50
On cover 3.25

Perf. 11

613 A177 2c black *40,000.*

Tribute to President Warren G. Harding, who died August 2, 1923.

No. 613 was produced from rotary press sheet waste. It is valued in the grade of fine.

HUGUENOT-WALLOON TERCENTENARY ISSUE

Tercentary of the settling of the Walloons and in honor of the Huguenots.

"New Netherland" A178

Landing at Fort Orange A179

Monument to Jan Ribault at Duvall County, Fla. — A180

FLAT PLATE PRINTINGS

1924, May 1 *Perf. 11*

614 A178 1c dark green 2.30 *3.00*
Never hinged 4.25
On cover 4.50
615 A179 2c carmine rose 3.75 2.25
Never hinged 7.00
On cover 3.50
616 A180 5c dark blue 15.00 13.00
Never hinged 27.50
Nos. 614-616 (3) 21.05 18.25
Nos. 614-616, never hinged 38.75

LEXINGTON-CONCORD ISSUE

150th anniv. of the Battle of Lexington-Concord.

Washington at Cambridge A181

"Birth of Liberty," by Henry Sandham
A182

The Minute Man, by Daniel Chester French
A183

1925, Apr. 4 *Perf. 11*
617 A181 1c deep green 2.00 2.50
Never hinged 3.75
On cover 3.75
618 A182 2c carmine rose 3.50 4.00
Never hinged 6.50
On cover 5.50
619 A183 5c dark blue 14.00 13.00
Never hinged 26.00
Nos. 617-619 (3) 19.50 19.50
Nos. 617-619, never hinged 36.25

150th anniv. of the Battle of Lexington-Concord.

NORSE-AMERICAN ISSUE

Sloop "Restaurationen"
A184

Viking Ship
A185

1925, May 18 *Perf. 11*
620 A184 2c carmine & black 3.00 2.75
Never hinged 6.00
On cover 4.50
621 A185 5c dark blue & black 9.00 9.00
Never hinged 19.00

100th anniv. of the arrival in NY on Oct. 9, 1825, of the sloop "Restaurationen" with the first group of immigrants from Norway to the U.S.

Benjamin Harrison
A186

Woodrow Wilson
A187

1925-26 *Perf. 11*
622 A186 13c green ('26) 9.00 .75
Never hinged 19.00
623 A187 17c black 9.00 .30
Never hinged 19.00

SESQUICENTENNIAL EXPOSITION ISSUE

Liberty Bell — A188

1926, May 10 *Perf. 11*
627 A188 2c carmine rose 2.25 .50
Never hinged 4.00
On cover 1.00

150th anniv. of the Declaration of Independence, Philadelphia, June 1-Dec. 1.

ERICSSON MEMORIAL ISSUE

Statue of John Ericsson — A189

1926, May 29 *Perf. 11*
628 A189 5c gray lilac 5.00 3.25
Never hinged 8.50

John Ericsson, builder of the "Monitor."

BATTLE OF WHITE PLAINS ISSUE

Alexander Hamilton's Battery — A190

1926, Oct. 18 *Perf. 11*
629 A190 2c carmine rose 1.60 1.70
Never hinged 2.75
On cover 2.25

Battle of White Plains, NY, 150th anniv.

INTERNATIONAL PHILATELIC EXHIBITION ISSUE
Souvenir Sheet

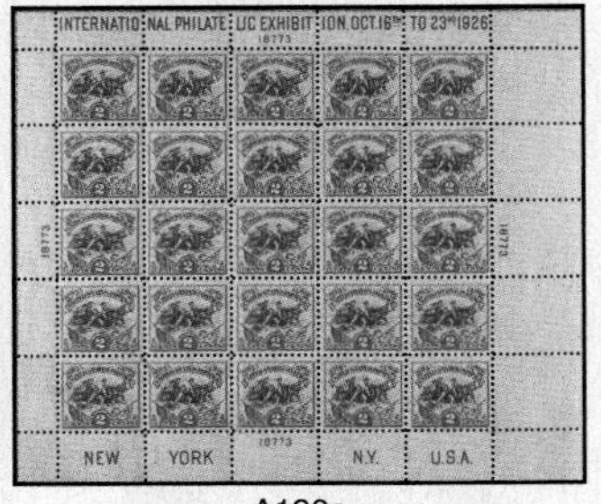
A190a

Condition valued:
Centering: Overall centering will average very fine, but individual stamps may be better or worse.
Perforations: No folds along rows of perforations.
Gum: There may be some light gum bends but no gum creases.
Hinging: There may be hinge marks in the selvage and on up to two or three stamps, but no heavy hinging or hinge remnants (except in the ungummed portion of the wide selvage.
Margins: Top panes should have about ½ inch bottom margin and 1 inch top margin.
Bottom panes should have about ½ inch top margin and just under ¾ inch bottom margin. Both will have one wide side (usually 1 inch plus) and one narrow (½ inch) side margin. The wide margin corner will have a small diagonal notch on top panes.

1926, Oct. 18 *Perf. 11*
630 A190a 2c carmine rose, pane of 25 325.00 *450.00*
Never hinged 575.00
On cover —

Issued in panes measuring 158-160¼x136-146½mm containing 25 stamps with inscription "International Philatelic Exhibition, Oct. 16th to 23rd, 1926" in top margin.

VALUES FOR VERY FINE STAMPS
Please note: Stamps are valued in the grade of Very Fine unless otherwise indicated.

TYPES OF 1922-26 ISSUE
REGULAR ISSUE
ROTARY PRESS PRINTINGS
(See note above No. 448.)

1926, Aug. 27 ***Imperf.***
631 A156 1½c yellow brown 2.00 1.70
Never hinged 3.00

1926-34 *Perf. 11x10½*
632 A155 1c green ('27) .25 .25
Never hinged .35
Three on cover 1.25
a. Booklet pane of 6 5.00 *4.00*
Never hinged 8.00
b. Vertical pair, imperf. between *3,000.* *3,250.*
Never hinged *5,500.*
c. Horiz. pair, imperf. between *5,000.*

No. 632b is valued in the grade of fine. No. 632c is valued in the grade of fine and never hinged. It is possibly unique.

633 A156 1½c yel brn ('27) 1.70 .25
Never hinged 2.60
634 A157 2c car, type I .25 .25
Never hinged .30
On cover .25
b. 2c carmine lake *180.00* *500.00*
Never hinged *425.00*
c. Horiz. pair, imperf. btwn. *6,000.*
d. Booklet pane of 6, carmine 1.50 1.50
Never hinged 2.50
e. As "d," carmine lake *400.00* *1,000.*
Never hinged *750.00*
f. 2c lake, type I, on cover —

Shades of the carmine exist.
No. 634c is valued in the grade of fine.

634A A157 2c car, type II ('28) 300.00 13.50
Never hinged 600.00
On cover 21.00
635 A158 3c violet ('27) .75 .25
Never hinged 1.20
On cover 2.00
a. 3c bright violet ('34) .35 .25
Never hinged .45
On cover .25
636 A159 4c yel brn ('27) 1.90 .25
Never hinged 3.00
On cover 8.00
637 A160 5c dk blue ('27) 1.90 .25
Never hinged 3.00
638 A161 6c red org ('27) 2.00 .25
Never hinged 3.20
639 A162 7c black ('27) 2.00 .25
Never hinged 3.20
a. Vertical pair, imperf. between 550.00 400.00
Never hinged 1,000.
640 A163 8c ol grn ('27) 2.00 .25
Never hinged 3.20
641 A164 9c rose ('27) 1.90 .25
Never hinged 3.00
642 A165 10c org ('27) 3.25 .25
Never hinged 5.50
Nos. 632-634,635-642 (11) 17.90 2.75
Nos. 632-634, 635-642 never hinged 28.00

The 1½c, 2c, 4c, 5c, 6c, 8c imperf. (dry print) are printer's waste.
For ½c, 11c-50c see Nos. 653, 692-701.

VERMONT SESQUICENTENNIAL ISSUE

Battle of Bennington, 150th anniv. and State independence.

Green Mountain Boy — A191

FLAT PLATE PRINTING

1927, Aug. 3 *Perf. 11*
643 A191 2c carmine rose 1.20 .80
Never hinged 2.00
On cover 1.50

BURGOYNE CAMPAIGN ISSUE

Battles of Bennington, Oriskany, Fort Stanwix and Saratoga.

"The Surrender of General Burgoyne at Saratoga," by John Trumbull
A192

1927, Aug. 3 *Perf. 11*
644 A192 2c carmine rose 3.00 2.10
Never hinged 5.25
On cover 3.00

VALLEY FORGE ISSUE

150th anniversary of Washington's encampment at Valley Forge, Pa.

Washington at Prayer — A193

1928, May 26 *Perf. 11*
645 A193 2c carmine rose 1.15 .50
Never hinged 1.80
On cover .75
a. 2c lake —
Never hinged —

BATTLE OF MONMOUTH ISSUE

150th anniv. of the Battle of Monmouth, N.J., and "Molly Pitcher" (Mary Ludwig Hayes), the heroine of the battle.

No. 634 Overprinted

ROTARY PRESS PRINTING

1928, Oct. 20 *Perf. 11x10½*
646 A157 2c carmine 1.00 1.00
Never hinged 1.60
On cover 1.60
a. "Pitcher" only *675.00*
b. 2c carmine lake *2,500.*

No. 646a is valued in the grade of fine.
Normally the overprints were placed 18mm apart vertically, but pairs exist with a space of 28mm between the overprints.

HAWAII SESQUICENTENNIAL ISSUE

Sesquicentennial Celebration of the discovery of the Hawaiian Islands.

Nos. 634 and 637 Overprinted

ROTARY PRESS PRINTING

1928, Aug. 13 *Perf. 11x10½*
647 A157 2c carmine 4.00 4.00
Never hinged 7.25
On cover 5.75
648 A160 5c dark blue 11.00 12.50
Never hinged 21.50
On cover 20.00

Nos. 647-648 were sold at post offices in Hawaii and at the Postal Agency in Washington, D.C. They were valid throughout the nation.
Normally the overprints were placed 18mm apart vertically, but pairs exist with a space of 28mm between the overprints.

AERONAUTICS CONFERENCE ISSUE

Intl. Civil Aeronautics Conf., Washington, D.C., Dec. 12 - 14, 1928, and 25th anniv. of the 1st airplane flight by the Wright Brothers, Dec. 17, 1903.

Wright Airplane
A194

Globe and Airplane
A195

FLAT PLATE PRINTING

1928, Dec. 12 *Perf. 11*
649 A194 2c carmine rose 1.10 .80
Never hinged 1.75
On cover 1.50
650 A195 5c blue 4.50 3.25
Never hinged 7.00

GEORGE ROGERS CLARK ISSUE

150th anniv. of the surrender of Fort Sackville, the present site of Vincennes, Ind., to Clark.

Surrender of Fort Sackville
A196

1929, Feb. 25 *Perf. 11*
651 A196 2c carmine & black .70 .50
Never hinged 1.15
On cover 1.00

TYPE OF 1922-26 ISSUE
ROTARY PRESS PRINTING

1929, May 25 — *Perf. 11x10½*

653 A154 ½c olive brown .25 .25
Never hinged .35

ELECTRIC LIGHT'S GOLDEN JUBILEE ISSUE

Invention of the 1st incandescent electric lamp by Thomas Alva Edison, Oct. 21, 1879, 50th anniv.

Edison's First Lamp — A197

FLAT PLATE PRINTING

1929 — *Perf. 11*

654 A197 2c carmine rose .65 .65
Never hinged 1.10
On cover 1.10
a. 2c lake —

ROTARY PRESS PRINTING
Perf. 11x10½

655 A197 2c carmine rose .65 .25
Never hinged 1.10
On cover .25

ROTARY PRESS COIL STAMP
Perf. 10 Vertically

656 A197 2c carmine rose 10.00 1.75
Never hinged 20.00
On cover 2.75

Issued: #654, June 5; #655-656, June 11.

SULLIVAN EXPEDITION ISSUE

150th anniversary of the Sullivan Expedition in New York State during the Revolutionary War.

Maj. Gen. John Sullivan — A198

FLAT PLATE PRINTING

1929, June 17 — *Perf. 11*

657 A198 2c carmine rose .55 .55
Never hinged .95
On cover 1.00
a. 2c lake 350.00 250.00
Never hinged 625.00
b. Vert. pair, imperf. btwn. *4,000.*

The unique No. 657b resulted from a paper foldover before perfing, and it has angled errant perfs from another row of horiz. perfs through the left side of the stamps.

Nos. 632-634, 635-642 Overprinted

This special issue was authorized as a measure of preventing losses from post office burglaries. Approximately a year's supply was printed and issued to postmasters. The P.O. Dept. found it desirable to discontinue the State overprinted stamps after the initial supply was used.

ROTARY PRESS PRINTING

1929, May 1 — *Perf. 11x10½*

658 A155 1c green 2.50 2.00
Never hinged 5.00
a. Vertical pair, one without ovpt. *300.00*
Never hinged *500.00*
659 A156 1½c brown 3.25 2.90
Never hinged 6.50
a. Vertical pair, one without ovpt. *475.00*
660 A157 2c carmine 4.00 1.00
Never hinged 7.50
661 A158 3c violet 17.50 15.00
Never hinged 35.00
a. Vertical pair, one without ovpt. *600.00*
Never hinged *800.00*
662 A159 4c yellow brown 17.50 9.00
Never hinged 35.00
a. Vertical pair, one without ovpt. *500.00*
663 A160 5c deep blue 12.50 9.75
Never hinged 25.00
664 A161 6c red orange 25.00 18.00
Never hinged 50.00
665 A162 7c black 25.00 27.50
Never hinged 50.00
666 A163 8c olive green 72.50 65.00
Never hinged 145.00
667 A164 9c light rose 14.00 11.50
Never hinged 27.50
668 A165 10c org yel 22.50 12.50
Never hinged 45.00
Nos. 658-668 (11) 216.25 174.15
Nos. 658-668, never hinged 431.50

See notes following No. 679.

Overprinted

Nebr.

1929, May 1

669 A155 1c green 3.25 2.25
Never hinged 6.50
b. No period after "Nebr." (19338, 19339 UR 26, 36) 50.00
670 A156 1½c brown 3.00 2.50
Never hinged 6.00
671 A157 2c carmine 3.00 1.30
Never hinged 6.00
672 A158 3c violet 11.00 12.00
Never hinged 22.00
a. Vertical pair, one without ovpt. *500.00*
673 A159 4c yellow brown 17.50 15.00
Never hinged 35.00
674 A160 5c deep blue 15.00 15.00
Never hinged 30.00
675 A161 6c red orange 35.00 24.00
Never hinged 70.00
676 A162 7c black 22.50 18.00
Never hinged 45.00
677 A163 8c olive green 30.00 25.00
Never hinged 60.00
678 A164 9c light rose 35.00 27.50
Never hinged 70.00
a. Vertical pair, one without ovpt. *750.00*
679 A165 10c org yel 90.00 22.50
Never hinged 180.00
Nos. 669-679 (11) 265.25 165.05
Nos. 669-679, never hinged 530.50

Nos. 658-661, 669-673, 677-678 are known with the overprints on vertical pairs spaced 32mm apart instead of the normal 22mm.

Important: Nos. 658-679 with original gum have either one horizontal gum breaker ridge per stamp or portions of two at the extreme top and bottom of the stamps, 21mm apart. Multiple complete gum breaker ridges indicate a fake overprint. Absence of the gum breaker ridge indicates either regumming or regumming and a fake overprint.

BATTLE OF FALLEN TIMBERS ISSUE

Memorial to Gen. Anthony Wayne and for 135th anniv. of the Battle of Fallen Timbers, Ohio.

Gen. Anthony Wayne Memorial — A199

FLAT PLATE PRINTING

1929, Sept. 14 — *Perf. 11*

680 A199 2c carmine rose .65 .65
Never hinged 1.00
On cover 1.10

OHIO RIVER CANALIZATION ISSUE

Completion of the Ohio River Canalization Project, between Cairo, Ill. and Pittsburgh, Pa.

Lock No. 5, Monongahela River — A200

1929, Oct. 19 — *Perf. 11*

681 A200 2c carmine rose .55 .55
Never hinged .90
On cover 1.10
a. 2c lake *425.00* —
Never hinged *650.00*
b. 2c carmine lake, never hinged —

MASSACHUSETTS BAY COLONY ISSUE

300th anniversary of the founding of the Massachusetts Bay Colony.

Mass. Bay Colony Seal — A201

1930, Apr. 8 — *Perf. 11*

682 A201 2c carmine rose .65 .50
Never hinged .95
On cover 1.00

CAROLINA-CHARLESTON ISSUE

260th anniv. of the founding of the Province of Carolina and the 250th anniv. of the city of Charleston, S.C.

Gov. Joseph West and Chief Shadoo, a Kiowa — A202

1930, Apr. 10 — *Perf. 11*

683 A202 2c carmine rose 1.00 1.00
Never hinged 1.50
On cover 1.40

TYPES OF 1922-26 ISSUE

Warren G. Harding A203

William H. Taft A204

ROTARY PRESS PRINTING

1930 — *Perf. 11x10½*

684 A203 1½c brown .50 .25
Never hinged .70
685 A204 4c brown .80 .25
Never hinged 1.25
On cover 5.00

ROTARY PRESS COIL STAMPS
Perf. 10 Vertically

686 A203 1½c brown 1.75 .25
Never hinged 2.60
687 A204 4c brown 3.00 .45
Never hinged 4.50
On cover 10.00

BRADDOCK'S FIELD ISSUE

175th anniversary of the Battle of Braddock's Field, otherwise the Battle of Monongahela.

Statue of Col. George Washington — A205

FLAT PLATE PRINTING

1930, July 9 — *Perf. 11*

688 A205 2c carmine rose .85 .85
Never hinged 1.30
On cover 1.00

VON STEUBEN ISSUE

Baron Friedrich Wilhelm von Steuben (1730-1794), participant in the American Revolution.

General von Steuben — A206

FLAT PLATE PRINTING

1930, Sept. 17 — *Perf. 11*

689 A206 2c carmine rose .50 .50
Never hinged .75
On cover 1.05
a. Imperf., pair *2,000.*
Never hinged *3,000.*
b. 2c carmine lake *950.00*

PULASKI ISSUE

150th anniversary (in 1929) of the death of Gen. Casimir Pulaski, Polish patriot and hero of the American Revolutionary War.

General Casimir Pulaski — A207

1931, Jan. 16 — *Perf. 11*

690 A207 2c carmine rose .30 .25
Never hinged .40
On cover .50

TYPE OF 1922-26 ISSUES
ROTARY PRESS PRINTING

1931 — *Perf. 11x10½*

692 A166 11c light blue 2.50 .25
Never hinged 3.75
693 A167 12c brown violet 5.00 .25
Never hinged 8.00
694 A186 13c yellow green 2.25 .25
Never hinged 3.50
695 A168 14c dark blue 4.00 .60
Never hinged 6.25
696 A169 15c gray 7.75 .25
Never hinged 12.00

Perf. 10½x11

697 A187 17c black 4.75 .25
Never hinged 7.25
698 A170 20c carmine rose 7.75 .25
Never hinged 12.50
699 A171 25c blue green 8.00 .25
Never hinged 13.00
700 A172 30c brown 12.50 .25
Never hinged 21.00
701 A173 50c lilac 30.00 .25
Never hinged 50.00
Nos. 692-701 (10) 84.50 2.85
Nos. 692-701, never hinged 137.25

RED CROSS ISSUE

50th anniversary of the founding of the American Red Cross Society.

"The Greatest Mother" — A208

FLAT PLATE PRINTING

1931, May 21 — *Perf. 11*

702 A208 2c black & red .25 .25
Never hinged .35
a. Red cross missing (FO) *40,000.*

One example of No. 702a is documented; believed to be unique. Value reflects most recent sale price at auction in 1994.

YORKTOWN ISSUE

Surrender of Cornwallis at Yorktown, 1781.

Count de Rochambeau, Washington, Count de Grasse — A209

1931, Oct. 19 — *Perf. 11*

703 A209 2c carmine rose & black .35 .25
Never hinged .50
a. 2c lake & black 4.50 .75
Never hinged 6.25
b. 2c dark lake & black *400.00*
Never hinged *750.00*
c. Horiz. pair, imperf. vertically *7,000.*
Never hinged *8,500.*

No. 703c is valued in the grade of fine.

WASHINGTON BICENTENNIAL ISSUE

200th anniversary of the birth of George Washington. Various Portraits of George Washington.

A210

A211

A212

A213

A214

A215

A216

A217

A218

A219

A220

A221

ROTARY PRESS PRINTINGS

1932, Jan. 1 ***Perf. 11x10½***

704 A210 ½c olive brown	.25	.25
Never hinged	.35	
705 A211 1c green	.25	.25
Never hinged	.35	
706 A212 1½c brown	.45	.25
Never hinged	.60	
707 A213 2c carmine rose	.30	.25
Never hinged	.45	
708 A214 3c purple	.55	.25
Never hinged	.80	
709 A215 4c light brown	.60	.25
Never hinged	.85	
710 A216 5c blue	1.40	.25
Never hinged	2.25	
711 A217 6c red orange	2.75	.25
Never hinged	4.50	
712 A218 7c black	.60	.25
Never hinged	.85	
713 A219 8c olive bister	2.50	.50
Never hinged	4.00	
714 A220 9c pale red	2.00	.25
Never hinged	3.25	
715 A221 10c orange yellow	9.00	.25
Never hinged	15.00	
Nos. 704-715 (12)	20.65	3.25
Nos. 704-715, never hinged	33.25	

OLYMPIC WINTER GAMES ISSUE

3rd Olympic Winter Games, held at Lake Placid, N.Y., Feb. 4-13, 1932.

Skier — A222

FLAT PLATE PRINTING

1932, Jan. 25 ***Perf. 11***

716 A222 2c carmine rose	.35	.25
Never hinged	.55	
a. 2c lake	*500.00*	
Never hinged	*1,000.*	

ARBOR DAY ISSUE

Boy and Girl Planting Tree — A223

ROTARY PRESS PRINTING

1932, Apr. 22 ***Perf. 11x10½***

717 A223 2c carmine rose	.25	.25
Never hinged	.35	

60th anniv. of the 1st observance of Arbor Day in Nebr., April, 1872.

Birth centenary of Julius Sterling Morton, who conceived the plan and the name "Arbor Day," while a member of the Nebr. State Board of Agriculture.

OLYMPIC GAMES ISSUE

Issued in honor of the 10th Olympic Games, held at Los Angeles, Calif., July 30 to Aug. 14, 1932.

Runner at Starting Mark A224

Myron's Discobolus A225

ROTARY PRESS PRINTING

1932, June 15 ***Perf. 11x10½***

718 A224 3c purple	1.50	.25
Never hinged	2.00	
719 A225 5c blue	2.25	.25
Never hinged	2.90	

Washington — A226

ROTARY PRESS PRINTING

1932, June 16 ***Perf. 11x10½***

720 A226 3c purple	.35	.25
Never hinged	.45	
b. Booklet pane of 6	35.00	*12.50*
Never hinged	60.00	
c. Vertical pair, imperf. between	*700.00*	*1,750.*
Never hinged	*1,400.*	

ROTARY PRESS COIL STAMPS

1932 ***Perf. 10 Vertically***

721 A226 3c purple	2.75	.25
Never hinged	3.50	

Perf. 10 Horizontally

722 A226 3c purple	1.50	.35
Never hinged	2.00	

Issued: #721, 6/24; #722, 10/12.

TYPE OF 1922-26 ISSUES

1932, Aug. 18 ***Perf. 10 Vertically***

723 A161 6c deep orange	11.00	.30
Never hinged	15.00	

WILLIAM PENN ISSUE

250th anniv. of the arrival in America of Penn (1644-1718), English Quaker and founder of Pennsylvania.

William Penn — A227

FLAT PLATE PRINTING

1932, Oct. 24 ***Perf. 11***

724 A227 3c purple	.45	.25
Never hinged	.60	
a. Vert. pair, imperf. horiz.	—	

DANIEL WEBSTER ISSUE

Daniel Webster — A228

FLAT PLATE PRINTING

1932, Oct. 24 ***Perf. 11***

725 A228 3c purple	.45	.25
Never hinged	.60	

Daniel Webster (1782-1852), statesman.

GEORGIA BICENTENNIAL ISSUE

200th anniv. of the founding of the Colony of Georgia, and honoring Oglethorpe, who landed from England, Feb. 12, 1733, and personally supervised the establishing of the colony.

Gen. James Edward Oglethorpe — A229

FLAT PLATE PRINTING

1933, Feb. 12 ***Perf. 11***

726 A229 3c purple	.50	.25
Never hinged	.65	

PEACE OF 1783 ISSUE

150th anniv. of the issuance by George Washington of the official order containing the Proclamation of Peace marking officially the ending of hostilities in the War for Independence.

Washington's Headquarters, Newburgh, NY — A230

ROTARY PRESS PRINTING

1933, Apr. 19 ***Perf. 10½x11***

727 A230 3c violet	.25	.25
Never hinged	.30	

See No. 752.

CENTURY OF PROGRESS ISSUES

"Century of Progress" Intl. Exhibition, Chicago, which opened June 1, 1933, and centenary of the incorporation of Chicago as a city.

Restoration of Fort Dearborn A231

Federal Building at Chicago, 1933 A232

ROTARY PRESS PRINTING

1933, May 25 ***Perf. 10½x11***

728 A231 1c yellow green	.25	.25
Never hinged	.30	
729 A232 3c purple	.25	.25
Never hinged	.35	

AMERICAN PHILATELIC SOCIETY ISSUE

SOUVENIR SHEETS

Restoration of Fort Dearborn — A231a

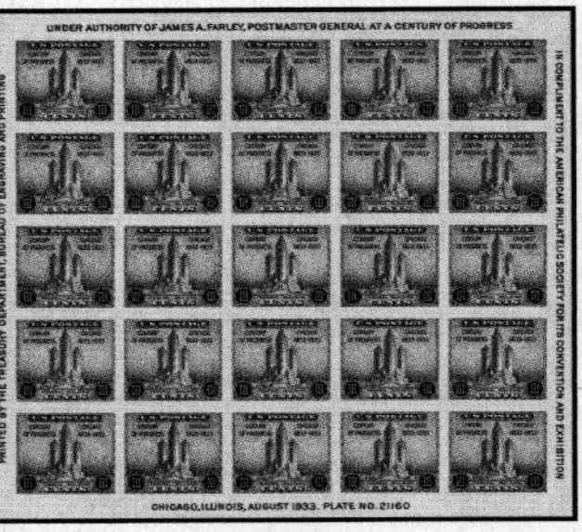
Federal Building at Chicago, 1933 — A232a

Illustrations reduced.

FLAT PLATE PRINTING

1933, Aug. 25 ***Imperf.***

Without Gum

730 A231a 1c deep yellow green, pane of 25	20.00	*25.00*
a. Single stamp	.70	.50
731 A232a 3c purple, pane of 25	20.00	*22.50*
a. Single stamp	.65	.50

Issued in panes measuring 134x120mm. See Nos. 766-767.

NATIONAL RECOVERY ACT ISSUE

Issued to direct attention to and arouse the support of the nation for the National Recovery Act.

Group of Workers — A233

ROTARY PRESS PRINTING

1933, Aug. 15 ***Perf. 10½x11***

732 A233 3c purple	.25	.25
Never hinged	.30	

BYRD ANTARCTIC ISSUE

Issued in connection with the Byrd Antarctic Expedition of 1933 and for use on letters mailed through the Little America Post Office established at the Base Camp of the Expedition in the territory of the South Pole.

World Map on van der Grinten's Projection — A234

FLAT PLATE PRINTING

1933, Oct. 9 ***Perf. 11***

733 A234 3c dark blue	.50	.50
Never hinged	.60	

See Nos. 735, 753.

KOSCIUSZKO ISSUE

Kosciuszko (1746-1817), Polish soldier and statesman served in the American Revolution, on the 150th anniv. of the granting to him of American citizenship.

Statue of Gen. Tadeusz Kosciuszko — A235

FLAT PLATE PRINTING

1933, Oct. 13 ***Perf. 11***

734 A235 5c blue .55 .25
Never hinged .65
a. Horiz. pair, imperf. vert. *1,750.*
Never hinged *2,750.*

NATIONAL STAMP EXHIBITION ISSUE

SOUVENIR SHEET

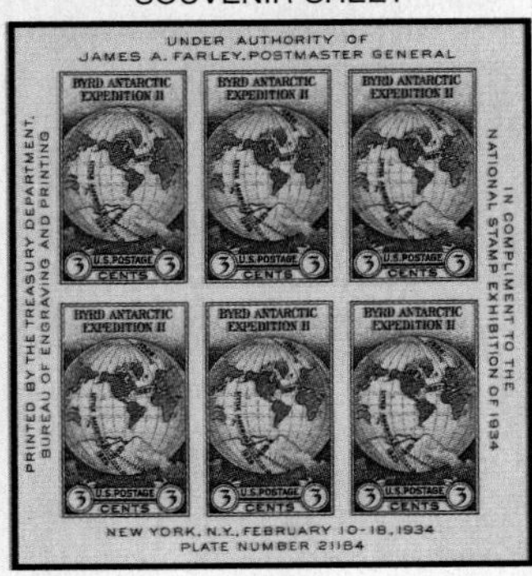

A235a

Illustration reduced.

1934, Feb. 10 ***Imperf.***

Without Gum

735 A235a 3c dark blue, pane of 6 10.00 9.00
a. Single stamp 1.60 1.25

Issued in panes measuring 87x93mm.
See No. 768.

MARYLAND TERCENTENARY ISSUE

300th anniversary of the founding of Maryland.

"The Ark" and "The Dove" — A236

FLAT PLATE PRINTING

1934, Mar. 23 ***Perf. 11***

736 A236 3c carmine rose .30 .25
Never hinged .40
a. Horizontal pair, imperf between *4,000.*
b. 3c lake — —
c. 3c carmine lake, never hinged —

The unique No. 736a resulted from a paper foldover before perfing, and it has angled errant perfs from another column of vert. perfs through the upper-left corner of the left stamp.

MOTHERS OF AMERICA ISSUE

Issued to commemorate Mother's Day.

Adaptation of Whistler's Portrait of his Mother A237

ROTARY PRESS PRINTING

1934, May 2 ***Perf. 11x10½***

737 A237 3c purple .25 .25
Never hinged .30

FLAT PLATE PRINTING

Perf. 11

738 A237 3c purple .25 .25
Never hinged .30

See No. 754.

WISCONSIN TERCENTENARY ISSUE

Arrival of Jean Nicolet, French explorer, on the shores of Green Bay, 300th anniv. According to historical records, Nicolet was the 1st white man to reach the territory now comprising the State of Wisconsin.

Nicolet's Landing A238

FLAT PLATE PRINTING

1934. July 7 ***Perf. 11***

739 A238 3c purple .25 .25
Never hinged .40
a. Vert. pair, imperf. horiz. *575.00*
Never hinged *1,050.*
b. Horiz. pair, imperf. vert. *1,000.*
Never hinged *1,750.*

See No. 755.

NATIONAL PARKS YEAR ISSUE

El Capitan, Yosemite (California) A239

Old Faithful, Yellowstone (Wyoming) A243

Grand Canyon (Arizona) A240

Mt. Rainier and Mirror Lake (Washington) — A241

Mesa Verde (Colorado) A242

Crater Lake (Oregon) A244

Great Head, Acadia Park (Maine) A245

Great White Throne, Zion Park (Utah) A246

Great Smoky Mts. (North Carolina) A248

Mt. Rockwell (Mt. Sinopah) and Two Medicine Lake, Glacier Natl. Park (Montana) A247

FLAT PLATE PRINTING

1934 **Unwmk.** ***Perf. 11***

740 A239 1c green .25 .25
Never hinged .40
a. Vert. pair, imperf. horiz., with gum *1,750.*
Never hinged *3,000.*
741 A240 2c red .30 .25
Never hinged .40
a. Vert. pair, imperf. horiz., with gum *800.00*
Never hinged *1,450.*
b. Horiz. pair, imperf. vert., with gum *900.00*
Never hinged *1,600.*
c. Imperf. P# 21261 block of 20 *7,500.*
742 A241 3c purple .40 .25
Never hinged .50
a. Vert. pair, imperf. horiz., with gum *1,000.*
Never hinged *1,850.*
743 A242 4c brown .50 .40
Never hinged .70
a. Vert. pair, imperf. horiz., with gum *3,500.*
Never hinged *8,000.*
744 A243 5c blue .80 .65
Never hinged 1.10
a. Horiz. pair, imperf. vert., with gum *1,500.*
Never hinged *4,000.*
745 A244 6c dark blue 1.20 .85
Never hinged 1.65
746 A245 7c black .80 .75
Never hinged 1.10
a. Horiz. pair, imperf. vert., with gum *1,250.*
Never hinged *2,000.*
747 A246 8c sage green 1.75 1.50
Never hinged 2.70
748 A247 9c red orange 1.60 .65
Never hinged 2.40
749 A248 10c gray black 3.25 1.25
Never hinged 5.00
Nos. 740-749 (10) 10.85 6.80
Nos. 740-749, never hinged 15.95
Nos. 740-749, P# blks of 6 100.00

Beware of fakes of the part-perforate errors of Nos. 740-749, including those with gum (see "without gum" note before No. 752).
See Nos. 750-751, 756-765, 769-770, 797.

AMERICAN PHILATELIC SOCIETY ISSUE

SOUVENIR SHEET

A248a

Illustration reduced.

1934, Aug. 28 ***Imperf.***

750 A248a 3c purple, pane of 6 20.00 *27.50*
Never hinged 30.00
a. Single stamp 3.25 3.25
Never hinged 4.00

Issued in panes measuring approximately 98x93mm.
See No. 770.

TRANS-MISSISSIPPI PHILATELIC EXPOSITION ISSUE

SOUVENIR SHEET

A248b

Illustration reduced.

1934, Oct. 10 ***Imperf.***

751 A248b 1c green, pane of 6 10.00 12.50
Never hinged 15.00
a. Single stamp 1.65 1.60
Never hinged 2.25

Issued in panes measuring approximately 92x99mm.
See No. 769.

SPECIAL PRINTING

(Nos. 752-771 inclusive)

"Issued for a limited time in full sheets as printed, and in blocks thereof, to meet the requirements of collectors and others who may be interested." — From Postal Bulletin No. 16614.

Issuance of the following 20 stamps in complete sheets resulted from the protest of collectors and others at the practice of presenting, to certain government officials, complete sheets of unsevered panes, imperforate (except Nos. 752 and 753) and generally ungummed.

Designs of Commemorative Issues

Without Gum

NOTE: In 1940 the P.O. Department offered to and did gum full sheets of Nos. 756-765 and 769-770 sent in by owners. No other Special Printings were accepted for gumming.

TYPE OF PEACE ISSUE

Issued in sheets of 400

ROTARY PRESS PRINTING

Perf. 10½x11

1935, Mar. 15 **Unwmk.**

752 A230 3c purple .25 .25

TYPE OF BYRD ISSUE

Issued in sheets of 200

FLAT PLATE PRINTING

Perf. 11

753 A234 3c dark blue .50 .45

No. 753 is similar to No. 733. Positive identification is by blocks or pairs showing guide line between stamps. These lines between stamps are found only on No. 753.

TYPE OF MOTHERS OF AMERICA ISSUE

Issued in sheets of 200

FLAT PLATE PRINTING

Imperf

754 A237 3c deep purple .60 .60

TYPE OF WISCONSIN ISSUE

Issued in sheets of 200

FLAT PLATE PRINTING

Imperf

755 A238 3c deep purple .60 .60

TYPES OF NATIONAL PARKS ISSUE

Issued in sheets of 200

FLAT PLATE PRINTING

Imperf

No.	Type	Description	Unused	Used
756	A239	1c green	.25	.25
757	A240	2c red	.25	.25
758	A241	3c deep purple	.50	.45
759	A242	4c brown	1.00	.95
760	A243	5c blue	1.60	1.40
761	A244	6c dark blue	2.40	2.25
762	A245	7c black	1.60	1.40
763	A246	8c sage green	1.90	1.50
764	A247	9c red orange	2.00	1.75
765	A248	10c gray black	4.00	3.50
		Nos. 756-765 (10)	15.50	13.70
		Nos. 756-765, with original gum, never hinged	114.35	
		Nos. 756-765, P# blocks of 6	254.75	

SOUVENIR SHEETS

Note: Single items from these sheets are identical with other varieties, 766 and 730, 766a and 730a, 767 and 731, 767a and 731a, 768 and 735, 768a and 735a, 769a and 756, 770a and 758.

Positive identification is by blocks or pairs showing wide gutters between stamps. These wide gutters occur only on Nos. 766-770 and measure, horizontally, 13mm on Nos. 766-767; 16mm on No. 768, and 23mm on Nos. 769-770.

TYPE OF CENTURY OF PROGRESS ISSUE

Issued in sheets of 9 panes of 25 stamps each

FLAT PLATE PRINTING

Imperf

No.	Type	Description	Unused	Used
766	A231a	1c yellow green, pane of 25	27.50	30.00
a.		Single stamp	.80	.50
767	A232a	3c deep purple, pane of 25	25.00	25.00
a.		Single stamp	.70	.50

NATIONAL EXHIBITION ISSUE TYPE OF BYRD ISSUE

Issued in sheets of 25 panes of 6 stamps each

FLAT PLATE PRINTING

Imperf

No.	Type	Description	Unused	Used
768	A235a	3c dark blue, pane of six	20.00	15.00
a.		Single stamp	2.80	2.40

TYPES OF NATIONAL PARKS ISSUE

Issued in sheets of 20 panes of 6 stamps each

FLAT PLATE PRINTING

Imperf

No.	Type	Description	Unused	Used
769	A248b	1c green, pane of six	11.00	11.00
a.		Single stamp	1.85	1.80
770	A248a	3c deep purple, pane of six	30.00	24.00
a.		Single stamp	3.25	3.10

TYPE OF AIR POST SPECIAL DELIVERY

Issued in sheets of 200

FLAT PLATE PRINTING

Imperf

No.	Type	Description	Unused	Used
771	APSD1	16c dark blue	2.50	2.60

Catalogue values for unused stamps in this section, from this point to the end, are for Never Hinged items.

VALUES FOR HINGED STAMPS AFTER NO. 771

This catalogue does not value unused stamps after No. 771 in hinged condition. Hinged unused stamps from No. 772 to the present are worth considerably less than the values given for unused stamps, which are for never-hinged examples.

CONNECTICUT TERCENTENARY ISSUE

300th anniv. of the settlement of Connecticut.

Charter Oak A249

ROTARY PRESS PRINTING

Perf. 11x10½

1935, Apr. 26 **Unwmk.**

772 A249 3c rose purple .35 .25

CALIFORNIA PACIFIC EXPOSITION ISSUE

California Pacific Exposition at San Diego.

View of San Diego Exposition A250

Perf. 11x10½

1935, May 29 **Unwmk.**

773 A250 3c purple .35 .25

BOULDER DAM ISSUE

Dedication of Boulder Dam.

Boulder Dam — A251

FLAT PLATE PRINTING

1935, Sept. 30 **Unwmk.** ***Perf. 11***

774 A251 3c purple .35 .25

MICHIGAN CENTENARY ISSUE

Advance celebration of Michigan Statehood centenary.

Michigan State Seal A252

ROTARY PRESS PRINTING

1935, Nov. 1 **Unwmk.** ***Perf. 11x10½***

775 A252 3c purple .35 .25

TEXAS CENTENNIAL ISSUE

Centennial of Texas independence.

Sam Houston, Stephen F. Austin and the Alamo A253

1936, Mar. 2 **Unwmk.** ***Perf. 11x10½***

776 A253 3c purple .35 .25

RHODE ISLAND TERCENTENARY ISSUE

300th anniv. of the settlement of Rhode Island.

Statue of Roger Williams — A254

1936, May 4 **Unwmk.** ***Perf. 10½x11***

777 A254 3c purple .35 .25

THIRD INTERNATIONAL PHILATELIC EXHIBITION ISSUE

SOUVENIR SHEET

A254a

Illustration reduced.

FLAT PLATE PRINTING

1936, May 9 **Unwmk.** ***Imperf.***

No.	Type	Description	Unused	Used
778	A254a	purple, pane of 4	1.75	1.25
a.		3c Type A249	.40	.30
b.		3c Type A250	.40	.30
c.		3c Type A252	.40	.30
d.		3c Type A253	.40	.30

Issued in panes measuring 98x66mm containing four stamps, inscribed in the margins: "Printed by the Treasury Department, Bureau of Engraving and Printing, under authority of James A. Farley, Postmaster General, in compliment to the third International Philatelic Exhibition of 1936. New York, N. Y., May 9-17, 1936. Plate No. 21557 (or 21558)."

ARKANSAS CENTENNIAL ISSUE

100th anniv. of the State of Arkansas.

Arkansas Post, Old and New State Houses A255

ROTARY PRESS PRINTING

Perf. 11x10½

1936, June 15 **Unwmk.**

782 A255 3c purple .35 .25

OREGON TERRITORY ISSUE

Opening of the Oregon Territory, 1836, 100th anniv.

Map of Oregon Territory A256

Perf. 11x10½

1936, July 14 **Unwmk.**

783 A256 3c purple .35 .25

SUSAN B. ANTHONY ISSUE

Susan Brownell Anthony (1820-1906), woman-suffrage advocate, and 16th anniv. of the ratification of the 19th Amendment which grants American women the right to vote.

Susan B. Anthony — A257

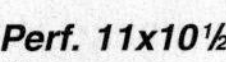

Perf. 11x10½

1936, Aug. 26 **Unwmk.**

784 A257 3c purple .25 .25

ARMY ISSUE

Issued in honor of the United States Army.

George Washington, Nathanael Greene and Mount Vernon — A258

Andrew Jackson, Winfield Scott and the Hermitage A259

Generals Sherman, Grant and Sheridan A260

Generals Robert E. Lee, "Stonewall" Jackson and Stratford Hall A261

US Military Academy, West Point A262

1936-37 **Unwmk.** ***Perf. 11x10½***

No.	Type	Description	Unused	Used
785	A258	1c green	.30	.25
786	A259	2c carmine ('37)	.30	.25
787	A260	3c purple ('37)	.40	.25
788	A261	4c gray ('37)	.60	.25
789	A262	5c ultra ('37)	.75	.25
		Nos. 785-789 (5)	2.35	1.25

NAVY ISSUE

Issued in honor of the United States Navy.

John Paul Jones and John Barry A263

Stephen Decatur and Thomas MacDonough — A264

Admirals David G. Farragut and David D. Porter A265

Admirals William T. Sampson, George Dewey and Winfield S. Schley
A266

Seal of US Naval Academy and Naval Cadets
A267

1936-37 Unwmk. *Perf. 11x10½*

790	A263	1c green	.30	.25
791	A264	2c carmine ('37)	.30	.25
792	A265	3c purple ('37)	.40	.25
793	A266	4c gray ('37)	.60	.25
794	A267	5c ultra ('37)	.75	.25
		Nos. 790-794 (5)	2.35	1.25

ORDINANCE OF 1787 SESQUICENTENNIAL ISSUE

150th anniv. of the adoption of the Ordinance of 1787 and the creation of the Northwest Territory.

Manasseh Cutler, Rufus Putnam and Map of Northwest Territory
A268

Perf. 11x10½

1937, July 13 Unwmk.

795	A268	3c rose purple	.30	.25

VIRGINIA DARE ISSUE

350th anniv. of the birth of Virginia Dare, 1st child born in America of English parents (Aug. 18, 1587), and the settlement at Roanoke Island.

Virginia Dare and Parents — A269

FLAT PLATE PRINTING

1937, Aug. 18 Unwmk. *Perf. 11*

796	A269	5c gray blue	.35	.25

SOCIETY OF PHILATELIC AMERICANS ISSUE

SOUVENIR SHEET

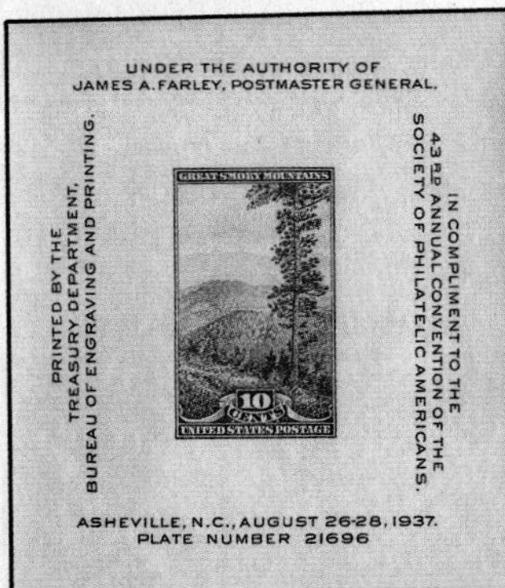

A269a

Illustration reduced.

TYPE OF NATIONAL PARKS ISSUE

1937, Aug. 26 Unwmk. *Imperf.*

797	A269a	10c blue green	.60	.40

Issued in panes measuring 67x78mm.

CONSTITUTION SESQUICENTENNIAL ISSUE

150th anniversary of the signing of the Constitution on September 17, 1787.

Signing of the Constitution
A270

Perf. 11x10½

1937, Sept. 17 Unwmk.

798	A270	3c bright reddish purple	.40	.25

TERRITORIAL ISSUES

Hawaii

Statue of Kamehameha I, Honolulu — A271

Alaska

Landscape with Mt. McKinley
A272

Puerto Rico

La Fortaleza, San Juan
A273

Virgin Islands

Charlotte Amalie
A274

1937 Unwmk. *Perf. 10½x11*

799	A271	3c violet	.35	.25

Perf. 11x10½

800	A272	3c violet	.40	.25
801	A273	3c bright purple	.40	.25
802	A274	3c rose violet	.40	.25
		Nos. 799-802 (4)	1.55	1.00

PRESIDENTIAL ISSUE

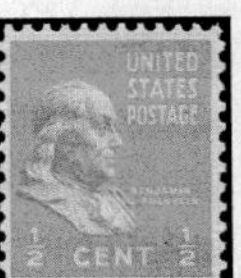

Benjamin Franklin
A275

George Washington
A276

Martha Washington
A277

John Adams
A278

Ulysses S. Grant
A295

Rutherford B. Hayes
A296

Thomas Jefferson
A279

James Madison
A280

James A. Garfield
A297

Chester A. Arthur
A298

White House
A281

James Monroe
A282

Grover Cleveland
A299

Benjamin Harrison
A300

John Q. Adams
A283

Andrew Jackson
A284

William McKinley
A301

Theodore Roosevelt
A302

Martin Van Buren
A285

William H. Harrison
A286

William Howard Taft
A303

Woodrow Wilson
A304

John Tyler — A287

James K. Polk — A288

Warren G. Harding
A305

Calvin Coolidge
A306

Zachary Taylor
A289

Millard Fillmore
A290

Franklin Pierce
A291

James Buchanan
A292

Abraham Lincoln
A293

Andrew Johnson
A294

1938 Unwmk.

803	A275	½c deep orange	.25	.25
804	A276	1c green	.25	.25
b.		Booklet pane of 6	2.00	*.50*
c.		Horiz. pair, imperf between (from booklet pane)		—
805	A277	1½c bister brown	.25	.25
b.		Horiz. pair, imperf. between	100.00	20.00

No. 805b unused is not precanceled. Precanceled examples are considered used and are valued in the used column. They are valued with gum; pairs without gum are worth less.

806	A278	2c rose carmine	.25	.25
b.		Booklet pane of 6	5.50	*1.00*
807	A279	3c light violet	.25	.25
a.		Booklet pane of 6	8.50	*2.00*
b.		Horiz. pair, imperf. between	*2,000.*	—
c.		Imperf., pair	*3,500.*	
d.		As "a," imperf between vert.		—
808	A280	4c bright rose purple	.75	.25
809	A281	4½c dark gray	.40	.25
810	A282	5c bright blue	.35	.25
811	A283	6c red orange	.40	.25
812	A284	7c sepia	.40	.25
813	A285	8c olive green	.40	.25
814	A286	9c rose pink	.45	.25
815	A287	10c brown red	.40	.25
816	A288	11c ultramarine	.75	.25
817	A289	12c bright mauve	1.00	.25
818	A290	13c blue green	1.30	.25
819	A291	14c blue	1.00	.25
820	A292	15c blue gray	.80	.25
821	A293	16c black	1.50	.25
822	A294	17c rose red	1.00	.25

823 A295 18c brn car 2.25 .25
824 A296 19c bright mauve 1.30 .35
825 A297 20c brt bl grn 1.20 .25
826 A298 21c dull blue 1.30 .25
827 A299 22c vermilion 1.20 .40
828 A300 24c gray black 3.25 .25
829 A301 25c deep red lilac 1.20 .25
830 A302 30c dp ultra 3.50 .25
a. 30c blue 20.00 —
b. 30c deep blue *250.00* —
831 A303 50c mauve 5.50 .25

FLAT PLATE PRINTING

1938 ***Perf. 11***

832 A304 $1 purple & black 7.00 .25
a. Vert. pair, imperf. horiz. *1,100.*
b. Watermarked USIR ('51) 200.00 65.00
Hinged 120.00
c. $1 red violet & black ('54) 6.00 .25
d. As "c," vert. pair, imperf. horiz. *900.00*
e. Vert. pair, imperf. btwn. *7,500.*
f. As "c," vert. pair, imperf. btwn. *10,000.*
g. As "c," bright magenta & black *70.00* 50.00
h. As No. 832, red violet & black — —

No. 832c is dry printed from 400-subject flat plates on thick white paper with smooth, colorless gum.

No. 832g is the far end of the color spectrum for the No. 832c stamp, trending toward a more pinkish shade, but the shade is not pink. No. 832g is known in bright magenta and in deep bright magenta; both shades qualify as No. 832g.

No. 832h is a shade variety of the wet printing (No. 832), but the shade essentially matches the red violet normally seen on the dry printing (No. 832c).

833 A305 $2 yel grn & blk 17.50 3.75
834 A306 $5 car & blk 85.00 3.00
a. $5 red brown & black *3,000.* *7,000.*
Hinged *1,850.*
Nos. 803-834 (32) 142.35 14.50
Nos. 803-834, P# blocks of 4 670.95

No. 834 can be chemically altered to resemble Scott 834a. No. 834a should be purchased only with competent expert certification.

Watermarks

All stamps from No. 835 on are unwatermarked.

CONSTITUTION RATIFICATION ISSUE

150th anniversary of the ratification of the United States Constitution.

Old Court House, Williamsburg, Va. — A307

ROTARY PRESS PRINTING

1938, June 21 ***Perf. 11x10½***

835 A307 3c deep violet .45 .25

SWEDISH-FINNISH TERCENTENARY ISSUE

Tercentenary of the founding of the Swedish and Finnish Settlement at Wilmington, Delaware.

Landing of the Swedes and Finns — A308

FLAT PLATE PRINTING

1938, June 27 ***Perf. 11***

836 A308 3c bright reddish purple .35 .25

NORTHWEST TERRITORY SESQUICENTENNIAL

Statue Symbolizing Colonization of the West — A309

ROTARY PRESS PRINTING

1938, July 15 ***Perf. 11x10½***

837 A309 3c bright rose purple .30 .25

IOWA TERRITORY CENTENNIAL ISSUE

Old Capitol, Iowa City A310

1938, Aug. 24 ***Perf. 11x10½***

838 A310 3c violet .40 .25

TYPES OF 1938

ROTARY PRESS COIL STAMPS

1939, Jan. 20 ***Perf. 10 Vertically***

839 A276 1c green .30 .25
840 A277 1½c bister brown .30 .25
841 A278 2c rose carmine .40 .25
842 A279 3c light violet .50 .25
843 A280 4c red violet 7.50 .40
844 A281 4½c dark gray .70 .40
845 A282 5c bright blue 5.00 2.50
846 A283 6c red orange 1.10 .55
847 A287 10c brown red 11.00 1.00

1939, Jan. 27 ***Perf. 10 Horizontally***

848 A276 1c green .85 .25
849 A277 1½c bister brown 1.25 .30
850 A278 2c rose carmine 2.50 .40
851 A279 3c light violet 2.50 .40
Nos. 839-851 (13) 33.90 7.20
Nos. 839-851, joint line pairs (13) 139.90 29.65

GOLDEN GATE INTL. EXPOSITION, SAN FRANCISCO

"Tower of the Sun" — A311

ROTARY PRESS PRINTING

1939, Feb. 18 ***Perf. 10½x11***

852 A311 3c bright purple .30 .25

NEW YORK WORLD'S FAIR ISSUE

Trylon and Perisphere — A312

1939, Apr. 1 ***Perf. 10½x11***

853 A312 3c violet .30 .25

WASHINGTON INAUGURATION ISSUE

Sesquicentennial of the inauguration of George Washington as First President.

George Washington Taking Oath of Office — A313

FLAT PLATE PRINTING

1939, Apr. 30 ***Perf. 11***

854 A313 3c bright purple .60 .25

BASEBALL CENTENNIAL ISSUE

Sand-lot Baseball Game A314

ROTARY PRESS PRINTING

1939, June 12 ***Perf. 11x10½***

855 A314 3c violet 1.75 .25

PANAMA CANAL ISSUE

25th anniv. of the opening of the Panama Canal.

Theodore Roosevelt, Gen. George W. Goethals and Gaillard Cut — A315

FLAT PLATE PRINTING

1939, Aug. 15 ***Perf. 11***

856 A315 3c reddish purple .40 .25

PRINTING TERCENTENARY ISSUE

Issued in commemoration of the 300th anniversary of printing in Colonial America. The Stephen Daye press is in the Harvard University Museum.

Stephen Daye Press — A316

ROTARY PRESS PRINTING

1939, Sept. 25 ***Perf. 10½x11***

857 A316 3c violet .25 .25

50th ANNIVERSARY OF STATEHOOD ISSUE

Map of North and South Dakota, Montana and Washington A317

1939, Nov. 2 ***Perf. 11x10½***

858 A317 3c rose purple .35 .25

FAMOUS AMERICANS ISSUES
AMERICAN AUTHORS

Washington Irving — A318

James Fenimore Cooper — A319

Ralph Waldo Emerson A320

Louisa May Alcott A321

Samuel L. Clemens (Mark Twain) — A322

1940 ***Perf. 10½x11***

859 A318 1c bright blue green .25 .25
860 A319 2c rose carmine .25 .25
861 A320 3c bright purple .25 .25
862 A321 5c ultramarine .35 .25
863 A322 10c dark brown 1.75 1.20
Nos. 859-863 (5) 2.85 2.20

AMERICAN POETS

Henry W. Longfellow A323

John Greenleaf Whittier A324

James Russell Lowell A325

Walt Whitman A326

James Whitcomb Riley — A327

864 A323 1c bright blue green .25 .25
865 A324 2c rose carmine .25 .25
866 A325 3c bright purple .25 .25
867 A326 5c ultramarine .50 .25
868 A327 10c dark brown 1.75 1.25
Nos. 864-868 (5) 3.00 2.25

AMERICAN EDUCATORS

Horace Mann — A328

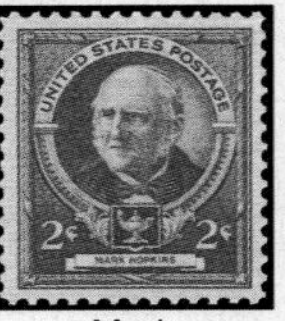

Mark Hopkins — A329

Charles W. Eliot — A330

Frances E. Willard — A331

Booker T. Washington — A332

869 A328	1c bright blue green	.25	.25
870 A329	2c rose carmine	.25	.25
871 A330	3c bright purple	.25	.25
872 A331	5c ultramarine	.50	.25
873 A332	10c dark brown	2.25	1.10
	Nos. 869-873 (5)	3.50	2.10

AMERICAN SCIENTISTS

John James Audubon A333

Dr. Crawford W. Long A334

Luther Burbank — A335

Dr. Walter Reed — A336

Jane Addams — A337

874 A333	1c bright blue green	.25	.25
875 A334	2c rose carmine	.25	.25
876 A335	3c bright purple	.25	.25
877 A336	5c ultramarine	.50	.25
878 A337	10c dark brown	1.50	.85
	Nos. 874-878 (5)	2.75	1.85

AMERICAN COMPOSERS

Stephen Collins Foster — A338

John Philip Sousa — A339

Victor Herbert A340

Edward MacDowell A341

Ethelbert Nevin — A342

879 A338	1c bright blue green	.25	.25
880 A339	2c rose carmine	.25	.25
881 A340	3c bright purple	.25	.25
882 A341	5c ultramarine	.50	.25
883 A342	10c dark brown	3.75	1.35
	Nos. 879-883 (5)	5.00	2.35

AMERICAN ARTISTS

Gilbert Charles Stuart — A343

James A. McNeill Whistler — A344

Augustus Saint-Gaudens A345

Daniel Chester French A346

Frederic Remington — A347

884 A343	1c bright blue green	.25	.25
885 A344	2c rose carmine	.25	.25
886 A345	3c bright purple	.30	.25
887 A346	5c ultramarine	.50	.25
888 A347	10c dark brown	1.75	1.25
	Nos. 884-888 (5)	3.05	2.25

AMERICAN INVENTORS

Eli Whitney — A348

Samuel F. B. Morse — A349

Cyrus Hall McCormick A350

Elias Howe A351

Alexander Graham Bell — A352

889 A348	1c brt blue grn	.25	.25
890 A349	2c rose carmine	.30	.25
891 A350	3c bright purple	.30	.25
892 A351	5c ultramarine	1.10	.30
893 A352	10c dark brown	11.00	2.00
	Nos. 889-893 (5)	12.95	3.05
	Nos. 859-893 (35)	33.10	16.05

PONY EXPRESS, 80th ANNIV. ISSUE

Pony Express Rider A353

1940, Apr. 3 *Perf. 11x10½*

894 A353 3c henna brown .50 .25

PAN AMERICAN UNION ISSUE

Founding of the Pan American Union, 50th anniv.

The Three Graces from Botticelli's "Spring" — A354

1940, Apr. 14 *Perf. 10½x11*

895 A354 3c bright rose purple .30 .25

IDAHO STATEHOOD, 50th ANNIV.

Idaho Capitol, Boise A355

1940, July 3 *Perf. 11x10½*

896 A355 3c bright mauve .35 .25

WYOMING STATEHOOD, 50th ANNIV.

Wyoming State Seal — A356

1940, July 10 *Perf. 10½x11*

897 A356 3c brown violet .35 .25

CORONADO EXPEDITION, 400th ANNIV.

"Coronado and His Captains," painted by Gerald Cassidy A357

1940, Sept. 7 *Perf. 11x10½*

898 A357 3c bright violet .35 .25

NATIONAL DEFENSE ISSUE

Statue of Liberty — A358

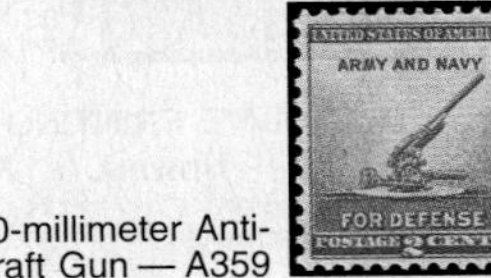
90-millimeter Anti-aircraft Gun — A359

Torch of Enlightenment — A360

1940, Oct. 16 *Perf. 11x10½*

899 A358	1c bright blue green	.25	.25
a.	Vertical pair, imperf. between	600.00	—
b.	Horizontal pair, imperf. between	32.50	—
900 A359	2c rose carmine	.25	.25
a.	Horizontal pair, imperf. between	37.50	—
901 A360	3c bright mauve	.25	.25
a.	Horizontal pair, imperf. between	22.50	—
	Nos. 899-901 (3)	.75	.75

THIRTEENTH AMENDMENT ISSUE

75th anniv. of the 13th Amendment to the Constitution abolishing slavery.

"Emancipation," Statue of Lincoln and Slave, by Thomas Ball — A361

1940, Oct. 20 *Perf. 10½x11*

902 A361 3c violet .50 .25

AIR POST STAMPS

Curtiss Jenny — AP1

FLAT PLATE PRINTINGS
Plates of 100 subjects.

1918 Unwmk. Engr. *Perf. 11*

C1 AP1	6c orange	55.	28.
	Never hinged	110.	
	On cover		50.
C2 AP1	16c green	60.	30.
	Never hinged	120.	
	On cover		55.
C3 AP1	24c car rose & blue	65.	30.
	Never hinged	130.	
	On cover		75.
a.	Center inverted	*450,000.*	
	Never hinged	*850,000.*	
	Nos. C1-C3 (3)	180.00	88.00
	Nos. C1-C3, never hinged	360.00	

Wooden Propeller and Radiator — AP2

Emblem of Air Service — AP3

De Havilland Biplane — AP4

1923 Unwmk. *Perf. 11*

C4 AP2	8c dark green	17.50	12.50
	Never hinged	35.00	
	On cover		22.50
C5 AP3	16c dark blue	60.00	27.50
	Never hinged	120.00	
	On cover		47.50
C6 AP4	24c carmine	65.00	27.50
	Never hinged	130.00	
	On cover		42.50
	Nos. C4-C6 (3)	142.50	67.50
	Nos. C4-C6, never hinged	285.00	

Map of US and Two Mail Planes — AP5

1926-27 Unwmk. *Perf. 11*

C7	AP5 10c dark blue	2.25	.35
	Never hinged	4.00	
C8	AP5 15c olive brown	2.50	2.50
	Never hinged	4.75	
C9	AP5 20c yellow green	6.50	2.00
	Never hinged	12.50	
	Nos. C7-C9 (3)	11.25	4.85
	Nos. C7-C9, never hinged	21.25	

Lindbergh's Airplane "Spirit of St. Louis" — AP6

1927, June 18 Unwmk. *Perf. 11*

C10	AP6 10c dark blue	7.00	2.50
	Never hinged	12.50	
a.	Booklet pane of 3	70.00	*65.00*
	Never hinged	115.00	
b.	Double impression		*16,500.*

Singles from No. C10a are imperf. at sides or imperf. at sides and bottom.

Only one example is recorded of No. C10b.

Nos. C1-C10 were available for ordinary postage.

Beacon on Rocky Mountains AP7

1928, July 25 Unwmk. *Perf. 11*

C11	AP7 5c carmine and blue	5.50	.85
	Never hinged	10.00	
a.	Vert. pair, imperf. between	*7,000.*	

No. C11a is unique. It is torn and valued thus.

Winged Globe — AP8

1930, Feb. 10 Unwmk. *Perf. 11*

Stamp design: 46½x19mm

C12	AP8 5c violet	9.50	.50
	Never hinged	17.50	
a.	Horiz. pair, imperf. between	*4,500.*	

See Nos. C16-C17, C19.

GRAF ZEPPELIN ISSUE

Zeppelin over Atlantic Ocean — AP9

Zeppelin between Continents — AP10

Zeppelin Passing Globe — AP11

1930, Apr. 19 Unwmk. *Perf. 11*

C13	AP9 65c green	180.	150.
	Never hinged	250.	
	On cover or card		160.
C14	AP10 $1.30 brown	375.	350.
	Never hinged	575.	
	On cover		375.
C15	AP11 $2.60 blue	550.	550.
	Never hinged	925.	
	On cover		575.
	Nos. C13-C15 (3)	1,105.	1,050.
	Nos. C13-C15, never hinged	1,750.	

Issued for use on mail carried on the first Europe-Pan-America round trip flight of the Graf Zeppelin in May, 1930. They were withdrawn from sale June 30, 1930.

ROTARY PRESS PRINTING

1931-32 Unwmk. *Perf. 10½x11*

Stamp design: 47½x19mm

C16	AP8 5c violet	4.75	.60
	Never hinged	8.50	
C17	AP8 8c olive bister ('32)	2.25	.40
	Never hinged	3.75	

CENTURY OF PROGRESS ISSUE

Airship "Graf Zeppelin" — AP12

FLAT PLATE PRINTING

1933, Oct. 2 Unwmk. *Perf. 11*

C18	AP12 50c green	45.00	47.50
	Never hinged	75.00	
	On cover		80.00

Issued in connection with the flight of the airship "Graf Zeppelin" in October, 1933, to Miami, Akron and Chicago and from the last city to Europe.

Catalogue values for unused stamps in this section, from this point to the end, are for Never Hinged items.

Type of 1930 Issue

ROTARY PRESS PRINTING

Perf. 10½x11

1934, June 30 Unwmk.

C19	AP8 6c dull orange	3.50	.25

TRANSPACIFIC ISSUES

The "China Clipper" over the Pacific AP13

FLAT PLATE PRINTING

1935, Nov. 22 Unwmk. *Perf. 11*

C20	AP13 25c blue	1.40	1.00

Issued to pay postage on mail transported by the Transpacific air mail service, inaugurated Nov. 22, 1935.

The "China Clipper" over the Pacific AP14

FLAT PLATE PRINTING

1937, Feb. 15 Unwmk. *Perf. 11*

C21	AP14 20c green	11.00	1.75
C22	AP14 50c carmine	11.00	5.00

Eagle Holding Shield, Olive Branch and Arrows AP15

FLAT PLATE PRINTING

1938, May 14 Unwmk. *Perf. 11*

C23	AP15 6c dark blue & carmine	.70	.25
a.	Vert. pair, imperf. horiz.	*300.00*	—
	On cover		1,750.
b.	Horiz. pair, imperf. vert.	*12,500.*	
c.	6¢ ultra & car	200.00	*1,500.*
	On cover		*1,750.*

TRANSATLANTIC ISSUE

Winged Globe — AP16

FLAT PLATE PRINTING

1939, May 16 Unwmk. *Perf. 11*

C24	AP16 30c dull blue	11.00	1.50

AIR POST SPECIAL DELIVERY STAMPS

To provide for the payment of both the postage and the special delivery fee in one stamp.

Great Seal of United States APSD1

FLAT PLATE PRINTING

1934, Aug. 30 Unwmk. *Perf. 11*

CE1	APSD1 16c dark blue	.70	.80
	blue	.70	.80
	Never hinged	.90	

For imperforate variety see No. 771.

Great Seal of United States APSD2

1936, Feb. 10

CE2	APSD2 16c red & blue	.45	.35
	Never hinged	.65	
a.	Horiz. pair, imperf. vert.	*4,250.*	
	Never hinged	*5,250.*	

SPECIAL DELIVERY STAMPS

When affixed to any letter or article of mailable matter, secured immediate delivery, between 7 A. M. and midnight, at any post office.

Messenger Running — SD1

Flat Plate Printing

1885 Unwmk. *Perf. 12*

E1	SD1 10c blue	550.00	80.00
	Never hinged	1,250.	
	On cover		225.00

Messenger Running SD2

1888, Sept. 6

E2	SD2 10c blue	500.00	45.00
	Never hinged	1,150.	
	On cover		135.00

COLUMBIAN EXPOSITION ISSUE

Though not issued expressly for the Exposition, No. E3 is considered to be part of that issue.

1893, Jan. 24

E3	SD2 10c orange	300.00	50.00
	Never hinged	675.00	
	On cover		200.00

Messenger Running SD3

1894, Oct. 10

Line under "TEN CENTS"

E4	SD3 10c blue	850.00	110.00
	Never hinged	2,100.	
	On cover		300.00

No. E5a

1895, Aug. 16 Wmk. 191

E5	SD3 10c blue	210.00	12.50
	Never hinged	500.00	
	On cover		25.00
a.	Dots in curved frame above messenger (Pl. 882)	400.00	50.00
	Never hinged	800.00	
b.	Printed on both sides	—	

Messenger on Bicycle SD4

1902, Dec. 9

E6	SD4 10c ultramarine	230.00	10.00
	Never hinged	525.00	
	On cover		22.50
a.	10c blue	325.00	12.50
	Never hinged	850.00	
	On cover		65.00

Helmet of Mercury and Olive Branch — SD5

1908, Dec. 12

E7	SD5 10c green	65.00	50.00
	Never hinged	140.00	
	On cover		400.00

1911, Jan. Wmk. 190 *Perf. 12*

E8	SD4 10c ultramarine	110.00	10.00
	Never hinged	240.00	
	On cover		30.00
b.	10c violet blue	160.00	14.00
	Never hinged	350.00	
	On cover		25.00

1914, Sept. *Perf. 10*

E9	SD4 10c ultramarine	190.00	12.00
	Never hinged	425.00	
	On cover		65.00
a.	10c blue	260.00	15.00
	Never hinged	575.00	
	On cover		65.00

1916, Oct. 19 Unwmk. *Perf. 10*

E10	SD4 10c pale ultramarine	320.00	50.00
	Never hinged	700.00	
	On cover		200.00

a. 10c blue 375.00 50.00
Never hinged 800.00
On cover 110.00

1917, May 2 ***Perf. 11***
E11 SD4 10c ultramarine 20.00 .75
Never hinged 45.00
On cover 4.00
b. 10c gray violet 35.00 3.00
Never hinged 75.00
On cover 4.00
c. 10c blue 100.00 5.00
Never hinged 210.00
On cover 30.00
d. Perf. 10 at left —

Postman and Motorcycle
SD6

1922, July 12
E12 SD6 10c gray violet 45.00 3.00
Never hinged 95.00
On cover 3.50
a. 10c deep ultramarine 55.00 3.50
Never hinged 130.00
On cover 5.00

Post Office Truck
SD7

FLAT PLATE PRINTING

1925
E13 SD6 15c deep orange 40.00 3.75
Never hinged 75.00
On cover 55.00
E14 SD7 20c black 2.00 1.00
Never hinged 4.00
On cover 25.00
Nos. E12-E14 (3) 87.00 7.75

Motorcycle Type of 1922
ROTARY PRESS PRINTING

1927-31 Unwmk. ***Perf. 11x10½***
E15 SD6 10c gray violet 1.00 .25
Never hinged 1.75
On cover .50
a. 10c red lilac .80 .25
Never hinged 1.40
b. 10c gray lilac .90 .25
Never hinged 1.60
c. Horiz. pair, imperf. btwn., red lilac shade *300.00*
Never hinged *575.00*
E16 SD6 15c orange ('31) .60 .25
Never hinged .90
On cover 1.50

REGISTRATION STAMP

Issued for the prepayment of registry fees; not usable for postage.

Eagle — RS1

ENGRAVED

1911, Dec. 1 Wmk. 190 ***Perf. 12***
F1 RS1 10c ultramarine 80.00 15.00
Never hinged 175.00
On cover 85.00

POSTAGE DUE STAMPS

For affixing, by a postal clerk to any piece of mailable matter, to denote the amount to be collected from the addressee because of insufficient prepayment of postage.

D1

Printed by the American Bank Note Co.

Plates of 200 subjects in two panes of 100 each.

1879 Unwmk. Engr. ***Perf. 12***
J1 D1 1c brown 90.00 14.00
Never hinged 260.00
J2 D1 2c brown 400.00 25.00
Never hinged 1,050.
J3 D1 3c brown 100.00 6.00
Never hinged 280.00
J4 D1 5c brown 775.00 70.00
Never hinged 1,900.
J5 D1 10c brown 900.00 70.00
Never hinged *2,500.*
a. Imperf., pair *2,500.*
J6 D1 30c brown 350.00 65.00
Never hinged 800.00
J7 D1 50c brown 600.00 90.00
Never hinged 1,600.
Nos. J1-J7 (7) 3,215. 340.00

SPECIAL PRINTING

1879
J8 D1 1c deep brown *16,000.*
Never hinged —
J9 D1 2c deep brown *15,000.*
J10 D1 3c deep brown *20,000.*
J11 D1 5c deep brown *13,000.*
J12 D1 10c deep brown *6,500.*
J13 D1 30c deep brown *7,000.*
J14 D1 50c deep brown *7,000.*

1884 Unwmk. ***Perf. 12***
J15 D1 1c red brown 70.00 7.00
Never hinged 190.00
J16 D1 2c red brown 80.00 6.00
Never hinged 225.00
J17 D1 3c red brown 1,050. 350.00
Never hinged 2,500.
J18 D1 5c red brown 600.00 50.00
Never hinged 1,450.
J19 D1 10c red brown 600.00 35.00
Never hinged 1,450.
J20 D1 30c red brown 200.00 70.00
Never hinged 500.00
J21 D1 50c red brown 1,800. 250.00
Never hinged 3,750.
Nos. J15-J21 (7) 4,400. 768.00

1891 Unwmk. ***Perf. 12***
J22 D1 1c bright claret 30.00 2.00
Never hinged 85.00
Never hinged *2,000.*
J23 D1 2c bright claret 32.50 2.00
Never hinged 90.00
J24 D1 3c bright claret 67.50 16.00
Never hinged 180.00
J25 D1 5c bright claret 100.00 16.00
Never hinged 290.00
J26 D1 10c bright claret 165.00 30.00
Never hinged 500.00
J27 D1 30c bright claret 575.00 225.00
Never hinged 1,700.
J28 D1 50c bright claret 600.00 225.00
Never hinged 1,750.
Nos. J22-J28 (7) 1,570. 516.00

See Die and Plate Proofs in the Scott U.S. Specialized catalog for imperfs. on stamp paper.

The color on Nos. J29-J44 will run when immersed in water. Extreme caution is advised.

D2

Printed by the Bureau of Engraving and Printing.

1894 Unwmk. ***Perf. 12***
J29 D2 1c vermilion 2,250. 725.
Never hinged *5,750.*
J30 D2 2c vermilion 775. 350.
Never hinged 1,900.

1894-95
J31 D2 1c deep claret 72.50 12.00
Never hinged 260.00
b. Vertical pair, imperf. horiz. —
J32 D2 2c deep claret 62.50 10.00
Never hinged 240.00
J33 D2 3c deep claret ('95) 200.00 50.00
Never hinged 575.00
J34 D2 5c deep claret ('95) 300.00 55.00
Never hinged 850.00
J35 D2 10c deep claret 350.00 40.00
Never hinged 1,000.
Never hinged *7,500.*
J36 D2 30c deep claret ('95) 550.00 250.00
Never hinged 1,250.
a. 30c carmine 675.00 275.00
Never hinged 1,600.
b. 30c pale rose 450.00 200.00
Never hinged 1,100.
J37 D2 50c deep claret ('95) 1,800. 800.00
Never hinged 4,250.
a. 50c pale rose 1,600. 725.00
Never hinged 3,750.
Nos. J31-J37 (7) 3,335. 1,217.

Shades are numerous in the 1894 and later issues.

See Die and Plate Proofs in the Scott U.S. Specialized for 1c imperf. on stamp paper.

1895-97 Wmk. 191 ***Perf. 12***
J38 D2 1c deep claret 13.50 1.00
Never hinged 40.00
J39 D2 2c deep claret 13.50 1.00
Never hinged 40.00
J40 D2 3c deep claret 100.00 5.00
Never hinged 225.00
J41 D2 5c deep claret 110.00 5.00
Never hinged 280.00
J42 D2 10c deep claret 110.00 7.50
Never hinged 280.00
J43 D2 30c deep claret ('97) 600.00 75.00
Never hinged 1,500.
J44 D2 50c deep claret ('96) 375.00 60.00
Never hinged 925.00
Nos. J38-J44 (7) 1,322. 154.50

1910-12 Wmk. 190 ***Perf. 12***
J45 D2 1c deep claret 40.00 5.00
Never hinged 115.00
a. 1c rose carmine 35.00 5.00
Never hinged 105.00
J46 D2 2c deep claret 40.00 2.00
Never hinged 115.00
a. 2c rose carmine 35.00 2.00
Never hinged 105.00
J47 D2 3c deep claret 625.00 60.00
Never hinged 1,600.
J48 D2 5c deep claret 120.00 12.00
Never hinged 275.00
a. 5c rose carmine 120.00 12.00
Never hinged 275.00
J49 D2 10c deep claret 125.00 20.00
Never hinged 280.00
a. 10c rose carmine 125.00 20.00
Never hinged 280.00
J50 D2 50c deep claret ('12) 1,100. 200.00
Never hinged 2,900.
a. 50c rose carmine 1,150. 190.00
Never hinged *3,000.*
Nos. J45-J50 (6) 2,050. 299.00

1914 ***Perf. 10***
J52 D2 1c carmine lake 80.00 15.00
Never hinged 220.00
a. 1c dull rose 85.00 15.00
Never hinged 230.00
J53 D2 2c carmine lake 62.50 1.00
Never hinged 170.00
a. 2c dull rose 67.50 2.00
Never hinged 180.00
b. 2c vermilion 67.50 2.00
Never hinged 180.00
J54 D2 3c carmine lake 1,050. 75.00
Never hinged 3,000.
a. 3c dull rose 1,000. 75.00
Never hinged 2,900.
J55 D2 5c carmine lake 50.00 6.00
Never hinged 140.00
a. 5c dull rose 45.00 4.00
Never hinged 130.00
J56 D2 10c carmine lake 75.00 4.00
Never hinged 200.00
a. 10c dull rose 80.00 5.00
Never hinged 210.00
J57 D2 30c carmine lake 225.00 55.00
Never hinged 525.00
J58 D2 50c carmine lake *11,500.* 1,700.
Never hinged *21,000.*
Nos. J52-J58 (7) 13,043. 1,856.

No. J58 unused is valued in the grade of fine to very fine.

1916 Unwmk. ***Perf. 10***
J59 D2 1c rose 4,000. 750.00
Never hinged 9,000.
J60 D2 2c rose 250.00 75.00
Never hinged 650.00

1917 Unwmk. ***Perf. 11***
J61 D2 1c carmine rose 2.75 .25
Never hinged 9.00
Never hinged 15.00
a. 1c rose red 2.75 .25
Never hinged 9.00
b. 1c deep claret 2.75 .25
Never hinged 9.00
Never hinged 42.50
J62 D2 2c carmine rose 2.75 .25
Never hinged 9.00
a. 2c rose red 2.75 .25
Never hinged 9.00
b. 2c deep claret 2.75 .25
Never hinged 9.00
J63 D2 3c carmine rose 13.50 .80
Never hinged 35.00
a. 3c rose red 13.50 .80
Never hinged 35.00
b. 3c deep claret 13.50 .80
Never hinged 35.00
J64 D2 5c carmine 11.00 .80
Never hinged 32.50
a. 5c rose red 11.00 .80
Never hinged 32.50
b. 5c deep claret 11.00 .80
Never hinged 32.50
J65 D2 10c carmine rose 22.50 1.00
Never hinged 65.00
a. 10c rose red 22.50 1.00
Never hinged 65.00
b. 10c deep claret 22.50 1.00
Never hinged 65.00
J66 D2 30c carmine rose 80.00 2.00
Never hinged 220.00
a. 30c deep claret 80.00 2.00
Never hinged 220.00
Never hinged *1,500.*
Never hinged *1,650.*
b. As "a," perf 10 at top, precanceled *21,000.*

No. J66b is valued with small faults and fine centering, as the two recorded examples are in this condition and grade. One is precanceled St. Louis, Mo., and the other is precanceled Minneapolis, Minn.

J67 D2 50c carmine rose 140.00 1.00
Never hinged 325.00
a. 50c rose red 140.00 1.00
Never hinged 325.00
b. 50c deep claret 140.00 1.00
Never hinged 325.00
Nos. J61-J67 (7) 272.50 6.10

1925, Apr. 13
J68 D2 ½c dull red 1.00 .25
Never hinged 1.75

D3

D4

1930 Unwmk.
J69 D3 ½c carmine 4.25 1.90
Never hinged 9.50
J70 D3 1c carmine 2.75 .35
Never hinged 6.25
J71 D3 2c carmine 3.75 .35
Never hinged 8.50
J72 D3 3c carmine 20.00 2.75
Never hinged 47.50
J73 D3 5c carmine 18.00 5.00
Never hinged 42.50
J74 D3 10c carmine 42.50 2.00
Never hinged 95.00
J75 D3 30c carmine 125.00 4.00
Never hinged 275.00
J76 D3 50c carmine 175.00 2.00
Never hinged 375.00
J77 D4 $1 carmine 32.50 .35
Never hinged 65.00
a. $1 scarlet 27.50 .35
Never hinged 55.00
J78 D4 $5 scarlet 37.50 .35
Never hinged 85.00
b. carmine 37.50 .35
Never hinged 70.00
Nos. J69-J78 (10) 461.25 19.05

Type of 1930-31 Issue
Rotary Press Printing

1931 Unwmk. ***Perf. 11x10½***
J79 D3 ½c scarlet .90 .25
Never hinged 1.30
a. ½c dull carmine .90 .25
Never hinged 1.30
J80 D3 1c scarlet .25 .25
Never hinged .30
b. dull carmine .25 .25
Never hinged .30
J81 D3 2c scarlet .25 .25
Never hinged .30
b. dull carmine .25 .25
Never hinged .30
J82 D3 3c scarlet .30 .25
Never hinged .45
b. dull carmine .25 .25
Never hinged .40
J83 D3 5c scarlet .50 .25
Never hinged .75
b. dull carmine .40 .25
Never hinged .60
J84 D3 10c scarlet 1.25 .25
Never hinged 1.90
b. dull carmine 1.10 .25
Never hinged 1.80
J85 D3 30c scarlet 7.50 .25
Never hinged 11.50
a. 30c dull carmine 7.50 .25
Never hinged 11.50
J86 D3 50c scarlet 9.00 .25
Never hinged 15.00
a. 50c dull carmine 9.00 .25
Never hinged 15.00

UNITED STATES OFFICES IN CHINA

Issued for sale by the postal agency at Shanghai, at their surcharged value in local currency. Valid to the amount of their original values for the prepayment of postage on mail dispatched from the U.S. postal agency at Shanghai to addresses in the U.S.

Nos. 498-499, 502-504, 506-510, 512, 514-518 Surcharged

1919 Unwmk. *Perf. 11*

K1 A140 2c on 1c green 22.50 *70.00*
Never hinged 67.50
K2 A140 4c on 2c rose, type I 22.50 *70.00*
Never hinged 67.50
K3 A140 6c on 3c vio, type II 55.00 *140.00*
Never hinged 140.00
K4 A140 8c on 4c brown 55.00 *140.00*
Never hinged 140.00
K5 A140 10c on 5c blue 60.00 *140.00*
Never hinged 160.00
K6 A140 12c on 6c red org 80.00 *210.00*
Never hinged 210.00
K7 A140 14c on 7c black 82.50 *210.00*
Never hinged 215.00
K8 A148 16c on 8c ol bis 65.00 *160.00*
Never hinged 170.00
a. 16c on 8c ol grn 55.00 *140.00*
Never hinged 150.00
K9 A148 18c on 9c sal red 60.00 *175.00*
Never hinged 160.00
K10 A148 20c on 10c org yel 55.00 *140.00*
Never hinged 140.00
K11 A148 24c on 12c brn car 75.00 *160.00*
Never hinged 190.00
a. 24c on 12c cl brn 100.00 *225.00*
Never hinged 260.00
K12 A148 30c on 15c gray 82.50 *230.00*
Never hinged 200.00
K13 A148 40c on 20c deep ultra 120.00 *325.00*
Never hinged 275.00
K14 A148 60c on 30c org red 110.00 *275.00*
Never hinged 260.00
K15 A148 $1 on 50c lt vio 550.00 *1,000.*
Never hinged 1,250.
K16 A148 $2 on $1 vio brn 425.00 *750.00*
Never hinged 950.00
a. Double surcharge *10,500.* *12,500.*
Never hinged *17,500.*
Nos. K1-K16 (16) 1,920. *4,195.*

Fake surcharges exist, but most are rather crudely made.

Nos. 498 and 528B Surcharged

1922, July 3

K17 A140 2c on 1c green 100.00 *225.00*
Never hinged 225.00
K18 A140 4c on 2c car, type VII 90.00 *200.00*
Never hinged 210.00
a. "SHANGHAI" omitted *7,500.*
b. "CHINA" only *15,000.*

OFFICIAL STAMPS

The franking privilege having been abolished, as of July 1, 1873, these stamps were provided for each of the departments of Government for the prepayment of postage on official matter.

Penalty franks were first authorized in 1877, and their expanded use after 1879 reduced the need for official stamps, the use of which was finally abolished on July 5, 1884.

Designs, except Post Office, resemble those illustrated but are not identical. Each bears the name of Department. Portraits are as follows: 1c, Franklin; 2c, Jackson; 3c, Washington; 6c, Lincoln; 7c, Stanton; 10c, Jefferson; 12c, Clay; 15c, Webster; 24c, Scott; 30c, Hamilton; 90c, Perry.

Special printings overprinted "SPECIMEN" follow No. O120.

AGRICULTURE

Printed by the Continental Bank Note Co.

O1

Thin Hard Paper

1873 Engr. Unwmk. *Perf. 12*

O1 O1 1c yellow 300.00 *200.00*
Never hinged 650.00
No gum 170.00
On wrapper *2,500.*
O2 O1 2c yellow 275.00 100.00
Never hinged 575.00
No gum 110.00
On cover *4,000.*
O3 O1 3c yellow 225.00 17.50
Never hinged 475.00
No gum 85.00
On cover *900.00*
O4 O1 6c yellow 275.00 60.00
Never hinged 575.00
No gum 110.00
On cover *7,500.*
O5 O1 10c yellow 525.00 200.00
Never hinged 1,150.
No gum 220.00
On cover (parcel label) *6,000.*
O6 O1 12c yellow 450.00 260.00
Never hinged 950.00
No gum 250.00
On cover *12,000.*
O7 O1 15c yellow 425.00 230.00
Never hinged 950.00
No gum 225.00
O8 O1 24c yellow 425.00 250.00
Never hinged 950.00
No gum 225.00
On parcel label —
O9 O1 30c yellow 550.00 280.00
Never hinged 1,200.
No gum 275.00
Nos. O1-O9 (9) 3,450. 1,598.

EXECUTIVE

Franklin—O2

1873

O10 O2 1c carmine 900.00 550.00
Never hinged 2,250.
No gum 450.00
On cover, single franking *3,100.*
O11 O2 2c carmine 575.00 260.00
Never hinged 1,250.
No gum 250.00
On cover, single franking *3,750.*
O12 O2 3c carmine 700.00 225.00
Never hinged 1,600.
No gum 270.00
On cover *1,200.*
a. 3c violet rose 1,000. 275.00
Never hinged 2,250.
No gum 375.00
On cover —
O13 O2 6c carmine 900.00 600.00
Never hinged —
No gum 325.00
On cover *5,000.*
O14 O2 10c carmine 1,200. 1,000.
Never hinged —
No gum 600.00
On cover —
Nos. O10-O14 (5) 4,275. 2,635.

INTERIOR

O3

1873

O15 O3 1c vermilion 75.00 10.00
Never hinged 170.00
No gum 30.00
On cover 160.00
O16 O3 2c vermilion 70.00 12.00
Never hinged 160.00
No gum 30.00
On cover 65.00
O17 O3 3c vermilion 80.00 6.00
Never hinged 175.00
No gum 35.00
On cover 40.00
O18 O3 6c vermilion 70.00 10.00
Never hinged 160.00
No gum 27.50
On cover 95.00
O19 O3 10c vermilion 70.00 20.00
Never hinged 160.00
No gum 27.50
On cover *600.00*
O20 O3 12c vermilion 90.00 12.00
Never hinged 200.00
No gum 35.00
On cover *575.00*
O21 O3 15c vermilion 200.00 25.00
Never hinged 450.00
No gum 80.00
On cover *650.00*
O22 O3 24c vermilion 180.00 20.00
Never hinged 400.00
No gum 60.00
On cover *2,500.*
a. Double impression —
O23 O3 30c vermilion 290.00 20.00
Never hinged 625.00
No gum 110.00
O24 O3 90c vermilion 325.00 50.00
Never hinged 700.00
No gum 120.00
On cover —
Nos. O15-O24 (10) 1,450. 185.00

JUSTICE

O4

1873

O25 O4 1c purple 250.00 100.00
Never hinged 550.00
No gum 100.00
On cover *1,750.*
O26 O4 2c purple 310.00 110.00
Never hinged 700.00
No gum 120.00
On cover *1,500.*
O27 O4 3c purple 320.00 35.00
Never hinged 725.00
No gum 110.00
On cover *575.00*
O28 O4 6c purple 310.00 45.00
Never hinged 700.00
No gum 110.00
On cover *1,200.*
O29 O4 10c purple 310.00 100.00
Never hinged 700.00
No gum 120.00
On cover *4,000.*
O30 O4 12c purple 260.00 75.00
Never hinged 575.00
No gum 95.00
On cover *1,750.*
O31 O4 15c purple 500.00 200.00
Never hinged 1,100.
No gum 220.00
On cover *1,250.*
O32 O4 24c purple 1,250. 425.00
Never hinged —
No gum 550.00
On cover *8,000.*
O33 O4 30c purple 1,300. 350.00
Never hinged —
No gum 550.00
On cover with Nos. O27 & O28 *17,500.*
O34 O4 90c purple 1,900. 900.00
Never hinged —
No gum 800.00
On cover with No. O33 *26,000.*
Nos. O25-O34 (10) 6,710. 2,340.

NAVY

O5

1873

O35 O5 1c ultramarine 160.00 50.00
Never hinged 350.00
No gum 65.00
On cover *750.00*
a. 1c dull blue 175.00 50.00
Never hinged 375.00
No gum 70.00
O36 O5 2c ultramarine 160.00 25.00
Never hinged 350.00
No gum 65.00
On cover *500.00*
a. 2c dull blue 175.00 25.00
Never hinged 385.00
No gum 70.00
O37 O5 3c ultramarine 170.00 15.00
Never hinged 375.00
No gum 60.00
On cover *250.00*
a. 3c dull blue 175.00 15.00
Never hinged 385.00
No gum 62.50
O38 O5 6c ultramarine 150.00 25.00
Never hinged 325.00
No gum 55.00
On cover *750.00*
a. 6c dull blue 175.00 25.00
Never hinged 385.00
No gum 67.50
O39 O5 7c ultramarine 700.00 230.00
Never hinged —
No gum 275.00
On cover *3,000.*
a. 7c dull blue 750.00 230.00
Never hinged —
No gum 275.00
O40 O5 10c ultramarine 210.00 45.00
Never hinged 475.00
No gum 75.00
On cover *6,500.*
a. 10c dull blue 225.00 45.00
Never hinged 500.00
No gum 80.00
O41 O5 12c ultramarine 240.00 45.00
Never hinged 525.00
No gum 100.00
On cover —
O42 O5 15c ultramarine 425.00 75.00
Never hinged —
No gum 160.00
On cover *21,000.*
O43 O5 24c ultramarine 425.00 85.00
Never hinged —
No gum 160.00
On cover *30,000.*
a. 24c dull blue 425.00 80.00
Never hinged —
No gum 160.00
Violet +5.00
O44 O5 30c ultramarine 350.00 50.00
Never hinged —
No gum 140.00
On cover *25,000.*
O45 O5 90c ultramarine 1,050. 375.00
Never hinged —
No gum 450.00
a. Double impression *20,000.*
Nos. O35-O45 (11) 4,040. 1,020.

POST OFFICE

Stamps of the Post Office Department are often on paper with a gray surface. This is essentially a wiping problem, caused by an over-milled carbon black pigment that released acid and etched the plates. There is no premium for stamps on paper with a gray surface.

O6

1873

O47 O6 1c black 25.00 12.00
Never hinged 60.00
No gum 12.00
On cover 75.00
O48 O6 2c black 30.00 10.00
Never hinged 75.00
No gum 13.00
On cover 175.00
a. Double impression *1,000.* 600.00
O49 O6 3c black 10.00 2.00
Never hinged 25.00
No gum 3.00
On cover 25.00
a. Printed on both sides *7,500.*
O50 O6 6c black 30.00 8.00
Never hinged 75.00
No gum 12.00
On cover 85.00
a. Diagonal half used as 3c on cover *5,000.*
b. Double impression *3,000.*
O51 O6 10c black 140.00 55.00
Never hinged 325.00
No gum 60.00
On cover *400.00*
O52 O6 12c black 120.00 12.00
Never hinged 275.00
No gum 40.00
On cover *1,000.*
O53 O6 15c black 140.00 20.00
Never hinged 325.00
No gum 50.00
On cover *5,000.*
O54 O6 24c black 225.00 25.00
Never hinged 500.00
No gum 85.00
O55 O6 30c black 200.00 25.00
Never hinged 450.00
No gum 70.00
On cover —
O56 O6 90c black 220.00 25.00
Never hinged 500.00
No gum 80.00
Nos. O47-O56 (10) 1,140. 194.00

STATE

Franklin — O7

Seward — O8

1873

O57 O7 1c dark green 260.00 75.00
Never hinged 575.00
No gum 110.00
On cover —
O58 O7 2c dark green 310.00 100.00
Never hinged —
No gum 120.00
On cover *1,000.*
O59 O7 3c dark green 220.00 25.00
Never hinged 500.00
No gum 85.00
On cover *600.00*
O60 O7 6c dark green 250.00 30.00
Never hinged 550.00
No gum 110.00
On cover *800.00*
O61 O7 7c dark green 290.00 65.00
Never hinged 650.00
No gum 95.00
On cover *1,000.*
O62 O7 10c dark green 250.00 55.00
Never hinged 575.00
No gum 110.00
On cover *2,000.*
Block of 4 1,150.

O63 O7 12c dark green 310.00 125.00
Never hinged 700.00
No gum 140.00
On cover 1,500.
O64 O7 15c dark green 350.00 90.00
Never hinged 775.00
No gum 150.00
On cover 5,750.
O65 O7 24c dark green 525.00 230.00
Never hinged —
No gum 275.00
On cover 17,500.
O66 O7 30c dark green 500.00 180.00
Never hinged —
No gum 240.00
On cover 12,500.
O67 O7 90c dark green 1,050. 325.00
Never hinged —
No gum 525.00
O68 O8 $2 green & black 1,750. 3,000.
Never hinged 3,750.
No gum 850.00
On cover (parcel label) 175,000.

The No. O68 on parcel label is unique.

O69 O8 $5 green & black 7,500. 13,000.
Never hinged —
No gum 3,500.
O70 O8 $10 green & black 4,500. 7,500.
Never hinged 10,500.
No gum 2,500.
O71 O8 $20 green & black 5,000. 5,500.
Never hinged 11,500.
No gum 2,250.

No. O71 used is valued with a blue or red handstamp favor cancel. Nos. O68-O71 with pen cancels sell for approximately 25-40% of the values shown.

TREASURY

O9

1873
O72 O9 1c brown 120.00 10.00
Never hinged 250.00
No gum 45.00
On cover 100.00
O73 O9 2c brown 125.00 8.00
Never hinged 275.00
No gum 45.00
On cover 75.00
O74 O9 3c brown 110.00 2.00
Never hinged 230.00
No gum 40.00
On cover 100.00
a. Double impression 5,000.
O75 O9 6c brown 120.00 4.00
Never hinged 250.00
No gum 45.00
On cover 75.00
O76 O9 7c brown 250.00 35.00
Never hinged 550.00
No gum 95.00
On cover 750.00
O77 O9 10c brown 240.00 12.00
Never hinged 525.00
No gum 90.00
On cover 450.00
O78 O9 12c brown 350.00 10.00
Never hinged 750.00
No gum 125.00
On cover 600.00
O79 O9 15c brown 300.00 12.00
Never hinged 650.00
No gum 100.00
On cover 850.00
O80 O9 24c brown 725.00 100.00
Never hinged —
No gum 290.00
O81 O9 30c brown 400.00 12.00
Never hinged —
No gum 140.00
On cover 5,000.
O82 O9 90c brown 475.00 15.00
Never hinged —
No gum 160.00
P# strip of 6, Impt. —
Nos. O72-O82 (11) 3,215. 220.00

WAR

O10

1873
O83 O10 1c rose 240.00 15.00
Never hinged 525.00
No gum 90.00
On cover 140.00
O84 O10 2c rose 260.00 15.00
Never hinged 600.00
No gum 110.00
On cover 70.00
O85 O10 3c rose 275.00 5.00
Never hinged 600.00
No gum 120.00
On cover 40.00
O86 O10 6c rose 675.00 10.00
Never hinged 1,450.
No gum 275.00
On cover 60.00

Examples of Nos. O114-O117 which bear Continental Bank Note Co. imprints are often mistaken for/offered as Nos. O83-O86. If there are doubts, expert opinions should be requested.

O87 O10 7c rose 175.00 90.00
Never hinged 375.00
No gum 90.00
On cover 2,000.
O88 O10 10c rose 140.00 25.00
Never hinged 300.00
No gum 45.00
On cover 2,000.
O89 O10 12c rose 275.00 12.00
Never hinged 600.00
No gum 110.00
On cover 450.00
O90 O10 15c rose 85.00 15.00
Never hinged 190.00
No gum 30.00
On cover 3,250.
O91 O10 24c rose 85.00 12.00
Never hinged 190.00
No gum 30.00
On cover 20,000.
O92 O10 30c rose 130.00 12.00
Never hinged 275.00
No gum 45.00
On cover 20,000.
O93 O10 90c rose 225.00 60.00
Never hinged 500.00
No gum 80.00
On parcel label 3,500.
Nos. O83-O93 (11) 2,565. 271.00

AGRICULTURE
Printed by the American Bank Note Co.

1879 **Soft Porous Paper**
O94 O1 1c yel, no gum 5,500.
O95 O1 3c yellow 550.00 150.00
Never hinged 1,250.
No gum 240.00

Two examples of the O95 plate block of 6 with imprint exist, both contained in a unique pane of 100.

INTERIOR
O96 O3 1c vermilion 300.00 400.00
Never hinged 550.00
No gum 160.00
O97 O3 2c vermilion 10.00 3.00
Never hinged 17.50
No gum 3.00
On cover 150.00
O98 O3 3c vermilion 10.00 3.00
Never hinged 22.50
No gum 3.00
On cover 30.00
O99 O3 6c vermilion 10.00 12.50
Never hinged 17.50
No gum 3.00
On cover 200.00
O100 O3 10c vermilion 110.00 75.00
Never hinged 250.00
No gum 60.00
On cover 1,200.
O101 O3 12c vermilion 230.00 115.00
Never hinged 525.00
No gum 130.00
On cover —
O102 O3 15c pale vermilion 400.00 500.00
Never hinged 900.00
No gum 200.00
On cover 6,500.
O103 O3 24c pale vermilion 4,500. 6,250.
Never hinged 10,000.
No gum 2,100.
Nos. O96-O103 (8) 5,570. 7,359.

JUSTICE
O106 O4 3c bluish pur 225.00 125.00
Never hinged 525.00
No gum 110.00
On cover 1,250.
O107 O4 6c bluish pur 475.00 300.00
Never hinged 1,050.
No gum 210.00
On cover 1,000.

No. O107 on cover is unique, but the stamp is damaged. It is valued thus.

POST OFFICE
O108 O6 3c black 30.00 10.00
Never hinged 70.00
No gum 10.00
On cover —

TREASURY
O109 O9 3c brown 80.00 10.00
Never hinged 175.00
No gum 35.00
On cover 110.00
O110 O9 6c brown 200.00 50.00
Never hinged 450.00
No gum 65.00
On cover 300.00
O111 O9 10c brown 275.00 80.00
Never hinged 650.00
No gum 120.00
On cover 750.00
O112 O9 30c brown 2,400. 425.00
Never hinged —
No gum 875.00
O113 O9 90c brown 9,000. 750.00
Never hinged —
No gum 3,000.
Nos. O109-O113 (5) 11,955. 1,315.

WAR
O114 O10 1c rose red 7.50 4.00
Never hinged 15.00
No gum 2.75
On cover 55.00
O115 O10 2c rose red 15.00 4.00
Never hinged 30.00
No gum 5.00
On cover 40.00
Purple +.50
O116 O10 3c rose red 15.00 2.00
Never hinged 30.00
No gum 5.00
On cover 35.00
a. Imperf., pair 5,000.
b. Double impression 7,500.
O117 O10 6c rose red 12.50 3.00
Never hinged 25.00
No gum 4.50
On cover 50.00
Cancellations
O118 O10 10c rose red 75.00 50.00
Never hinged 150.00
No gum 27.50
On cover 1,800.
O119 O10 12c rose red 70.00 14.00
Never hinged 140.00
No gum 25.00
On cover —
O120 O10 30c rose red 225.00 100.00
Never hinged 500.00
No gum 90.00
Nos. O114-O120 (7) 420.00 177.00

SPECIAL PRINTINGS

Special printings of Official stamps were made in 1875 at the time the other Reprints, Re-issues and Special Printings were printed. They are ungummed.

Although perforated, these stamps were sometimes (but not always) cut apart with scissors. As a result the perforations may be mutilated and the design damaged. Values are for very fine stamps with intact perforations.

All values exist imperforate.

Similar to Type D, without period, 11mm long
AGRICULTURE
Printed by the Continental Bank Note Co.

Overprinted in Block Letters

Thin, hard white paper
Carmine Overprint

1875 ***Perf. 12***
O1S D 1c yellow 32.50
a. "Sepcimen" error 2,500.
b. Horiz. ribbed paper 37.50
c. As "b," small dotted "i" in "Specimen" 500.00
O2S D 2c yellow 55.00
a. "Sepcimen" error 3,000.
O3S D 3c yellow 400.00
a. "Sepcimen" error 19,000.
O4S D 6c yellow 400.00
a. "Sepcimen" error 22,500.
O5S D 10c yellow 400.00
a. "Sepcimen" error 19,000.
O6S D 12c yellow 400.00
a. "Sepcimen" error 15,000.
O7S D 15c yellow 400.00
a. "Sepcimen" error 12,500.
O8S D 24c yellow 400.00
a. "Sepcimen" error 12,500.
O9S D 30c yellow 400.00
a. "Sepcimen" error 13,500.
Nos. O1S-O9S (9) 2,888.

EXECUTIVE
Blue Overprint
O10S D 1c carmine 32.50
a. Horiz. ribbed paper 40.00
b. As "a," small dotted "i" in "Specimen" 500.00
O11S D 2c carmine 55.00
O12S D 3c carmine 67.50
O13S D 6c carmine 67.50
O14S D 10c carmine 67.50
Nos. O10S-O14S (5) 290.00

INTERIOR
Blue Overprint
O15S D 1c vermilion 60.00
O16S D 2c vermilion 140.00
a. "Sepcimen" error —

The existence of a genuine example of No. O16Sa has been questioned by specialists. The editors would like to see authenticated evidence of the existence of the single reported example.

O17S D 3c vermilion 2,500.
O18S D 6c vermilion 2,500.
O19S D 10c vermilion 2,500.
O20S D 12c vermilion 2,500.
O21S D 15c vermilion 2,500.
O22S D 24c vermilion 2,500.
O23S D 30c vermilion 2,500.
O24S D 90c vermilion 2,500.
Nos. O15S-O24S (10) 20,200.

JUSTICE
Blue Overprint
O25S D 1c purple 32.50
a. "Specimen" error 1,900.
b. Horiz. ribbed paper 35.00
c. As "b," small dotted "i" in "Specimen" 500.00
O26S D 2c purple 55.00
a. "Sepcimen" error 3,500.
O27S D 3c purple 1,250.
a. "Sepcimen" error 11,000.
O28S D 6c purple 1,250.
O29S D 10c purple 1,250.
O30S D 12c purple 1,250.
a. "Sepcimen" error 19,000.
O31S D 15c purple 1,250.
a. "Sepcimen" error 25,000.
O32S D 24c purple 1,250.
a. "Sepcimen" error 20,000.
O33S D 30c purple 1,250.
a. "Sepcimen" error 15,000.
O34S D 90c purple 1,250.
Nos. O25S-O34S (10) 10,088.

NAVY
Carmine Overprint
O35S D 1c ultramarine 35.00
a. "Sepcimen" error 2,750.
b. Double "Specimen" overprint 1,900.
O36S D 2c ultramarine 75.00
a. "Sepcimen" error 4,500.
O37S D 3c ultramarine 1,750.
O38S D 6c ultramarine 1,750.
O39S D 7c ultramarine 550.00
a. "Sepcimen" error 10,000.
O40S D 10c ultramarine 1,750.
a. "Sepcimen" error 17,500.
O41S D 12c ultramarine 1,750.
a. "Sepcimen" error 21,000.
O42S D 15c ultramarine 1,750.
a. "Sepcimen" error 16,000.
O43S D 24c ultramarine 1,750.
a. "Sepcimen" error 15,000.
O44S D 30c ultramarine 1,750.
a. "Sepcimen" error 17,500.
O45S D 90c ultramarine 1,750.
Nos. O35S-O45S (11) 14,660.

POST OFFICE
Carmine Overprint
O47S D 1c black 45.00
a. "Sepcimen" error 3,250.
b. Inverted overprint 2,500.
O48S D 2c black 325.00
a. "Sepcimen" error 15,000.
O49S D 3c black 1,600.
a. "Sepcimen" error 37,500.
O50S D 6c black 1,600.
O51S D 10c black 1,000.
a. "Sepcimen" error 15,000.
O52S D 12c black 1,600.
O53S D 15c black 1,600.
a. "Sepcimen" error 26,000.
O54S D 24c black 1,600.
a. "Sepcimen" error 22,000.
O55S D 30c black 1,600.
O56S D 90c black 1,600.
a. "Sepcimen" error 25,000.
Nos. O47S-O56S (10) 12,570.

STATE
Carmine Overprint
O57S D 1c bluish green 32.50
a. "Sepcimen" error 1,900.
b. Horiz. ribbed paper 35.00
c. As "b," small dotted "i" in "Specimen" 650.00
d. Double "Specimen" overprint 3,850.
O58S D 2c bluish green 90.00
a. "Sepcimen" error 2,500.
O59S D 3c bluish green 140.00
a. "Sepcimen" error 7,000.
O60S D 6c bluish green 350.00
a. "Sepcimen" error 12,500.
O61S D 7c bluish green 140.00
a. "Sepcimen" error 9,000.
O62S D 10c bluish green 550.00
a. "Sepcimen" error 27,500.
O63S D 12c bluish green 550.00
a. "Sepcimen" error 19,000.
O64S D 15c bluish green 600.00
O65S D 24c bluish green 600.00
a. "Sepcimen" error 25,000.
O66S D 30c bluish green 600.00
a. "Sepcimen" error 27,500.
O67S D 90c bluish green 600.00
a. "Sepcimen" error 27,500.
O68S D $2 green & blk 19,000.
O69S D $5 green & blk 50,000.
O70S D $10 green & blk 110,000.
O71S D $20 green & blk 160,000.
Nos. O57S-O67S (11) 4,253.

TREASURY
Blue Overprint
O72S D 1c dark brown 80.00
O73S D 2c dark brown 450.00

The only two recorded plate blocks of No. O73S are contained in a unique left pane of 100 stamps.

O74S D 3c dark brown 1,600.
O75S D 6c dark brown 1,600.
O76S D 7c dark brown 950.00
O77S D 10c dark brown 1,600.
O78S D 12c dark brown 1,600.
O79S D 15c dark brown 1,600.
O80S D 24c dark brown 1,600.

O81S D 30c dark brown 1,600.
O82S D 90c dark brown 1,650.
Nos. O72S-O82S (11) 14,330.

WAR

Blue Overprint

O83S D 1c deep rose 35.00
a. "Sepcimen" error *3,000.*
O84S D 2c deep rose 125.00
a. "Sepcimen" error *3,500.*
O85S D 3c deep rose 1,400.
a. "Sepcimen" error *30,000.*
O86S D 6c deep rose 1,400.
a. "Sepcimen" error *32,000.*
O87S D 7c deep rose 425.00
a. "Sepcimen" error *17,500.*
O88S D 10c deep rose 1,400.
a. "Sepcimen" error *27,500.*
O89S D 12c deep rose 1,400.
a. "Sepcimen" error *32,000.*
O90S D 15c deep rose 1,400.
a. "Sepcimen" error *30,000.*
O91S D 24c deep rose 1,400.
a. "Sepcimen" error *30,000.*
O92S D 30c deep rose 1,400.
a. "Sepcimen" error *30,000.*
O93S D 90c deep rose 1,400.
a. "Sepcimen" error *30,000.*
Nos. O83S-O93S (11) 11,785.

EXECUTIVE

Printed by the American Bank Note Co.

Soft Porous Paper

1881 **Blue Overprint**

O10xS D 1c violet rose 95.00

NAVY

Carmine Overprint

O35xS D 1c gray blue 100.00
a. Double overprint 1,200.

STATE

O57xS D 1c yellow green 180.00

OFFICIAL POSTAL SAVINGS MAIL

These stamps were used to prepay postage on official correspondence of the Postal Savings Division of the POD. Discontinued Sept. 23, 1914.

O11

Printed by the Bureau of Engraving & Printing

1910-11 **Engr.** **Wmk. 191**

O121 O11 2c black 17.50 2.00
Never hinged 40.00
On cover 12.50
O122 O11 50c dark green 175.00 60.00
Never hinged 425.00
On cover 225.00
O123 O11 $1 ultramarine 200.00 15.00
Never hinged 450.00
On cover 110.00

Wmk. 190

O124 O11 1c dark violet 10.00 2.00
Never hinged 22.50
On cover 15.00
Never hinged 350.00
O125 O11 2c black 65.00 7.00
Never hinged 150.00
On cover 25.00
O126 O11 10c carmine 20.00 2.00
Never hinged 50.00
On cover 20.00
Nos. O121-O126 (6) 487.50 88.00

NEWSPAPER STAMPS

For the prepayment of postage on bulk shipments of newspapers and periodicals. From 1875 on, the stamps were affixed to pages of receipt books, sometimes canceled and retained by the post office. Discontinued on July 1, 1898.

Virtually all used stamps of Nos. PR1-PR4 are canceled by blue brush strokes. All are rare. Most used stamps of Nos. PR9-PR32, PR57-PR79 and PR81-PR89 are pen canceled (or uncanceled), with some of Nos. PR9-PR32 also known canceled by a thick blue brush stroke.

Handstamp cancellations on any of these issues are rare and sell for much more than catalogue values which are for pen-canceled examples.

Used values for Nos. PR90-PR125 are for stamps with handstamp cancellations.

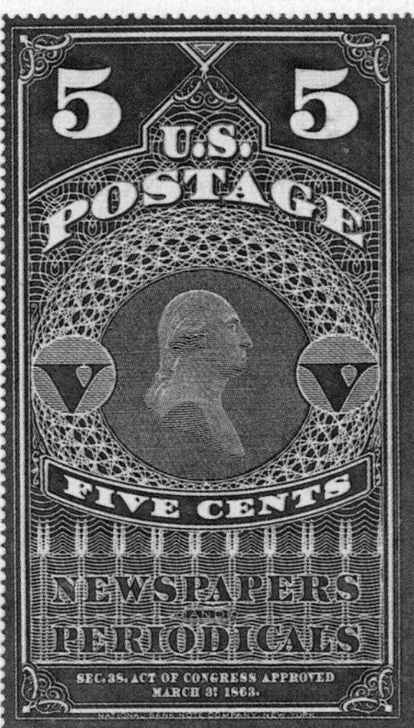

Washington — N1

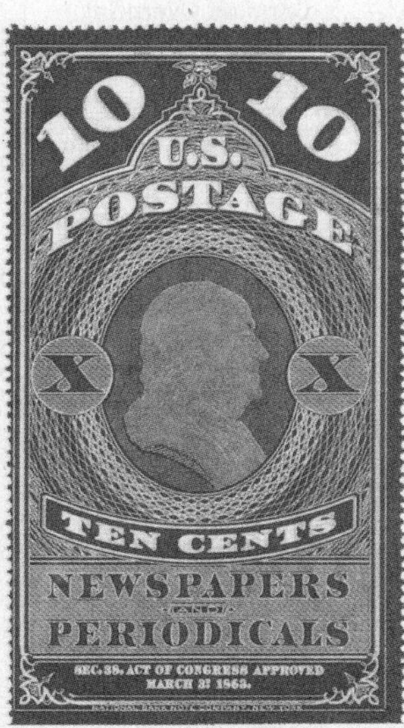

Franklin — N2

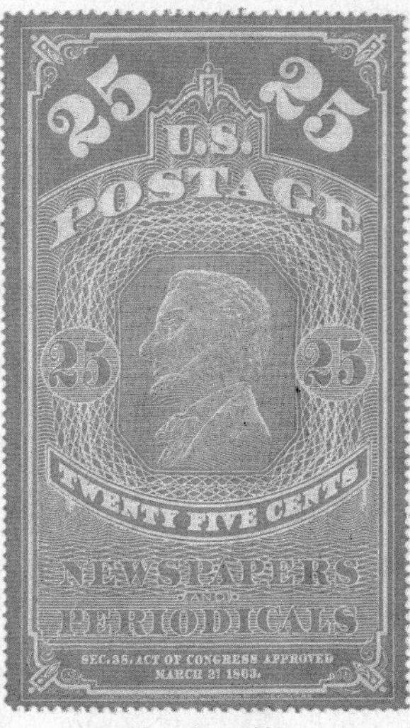

Lincoln — N3

Values for Nos. PR1-PR8 are for examples with perforations on all four sides. Examples with natural straight edges sell for somewhat less. Some panes were fully perforated, while others have natural straight edges either at top or bottom affecting five stamps in the pane of ten.

Printed by the National Bank Note Co.

Thin hard paper, without gum

Size of design: 51x95mm

Typographed and Embossed

1865 **Unwmk.** ***Perf. 12***

Colored Border

PR1 N1 5c dark blue 750.00 *2,000.*
a. 5c light blue 1,350. *4,250.*
PR2 N2 10c blue green 300.00 *2,000.*
a. 10c green 300.00 *2,000.*
b. Pelure paper 400.00 *2,000.*
PR3 N3 25c orange red 400.00 *2,500.*
a. 25c carmine red 425.00 *2,500.*
b. Pelure paper 475.00

Nos. PR1-PR3 used are valued with faults.

White Border

Yellowish paper

PR4 N1 5c light blue 750.00 *5,000.*
a. 5c dark blue 750.00 —
b. Pelure paper 850.00 —
Nos. PR1-PR4 (4) 2,200.

No. PR4 used is valued with faults.

REPRINTS of 1865 ISSUE

Printed by the Continental Bank Note Co. using the original National Bank Note Co. plates

1875 ***Perf. 12***

Hard white paper, without gum

5c White Border, 10c and 25c Colored Border

PR5 N1 5c dull blue 225.00
a. Printed on both sides *5,750.*
PR6 N2 10c dark bluish green 250.00
a. Printed on both sides *4,250.*
PR7 N3 25c dark carmine 300.00
Nos. PR5-PR7 (3) 775.00

The 5c has white border, 10c and 25c have colored borders.

Many fakes exist of Nos. PR1-PR7, some of high quality. Certification is highly recommended.

The Continental Bank Note Co. made another special printing from new plates, which did not have the colored border. These exist imperforate and perforated, but they were not regularly issued. Value, imperf. set $3,250.

Printed by the American Bank Note Co.

Soft porous paper, without gum

1881 **White Border**

PR8 N1 5c dark blue 650.00

Statue of Freedom — N4

"Justice" — N5

Ceres — N6

"Victory" — N7

Clio — N8

Minerva — N9

Vesta — N10

"Peace" N11

"Commerce" N12

Hebe — N13

Indian Maiden — N14

Values for used examples of Nos. PR9-PR113 are for fine-very fine examples for denominations to $3, and fine for denominations of $5 or higher. Used examples of some Scott numbers might not exist without faults.

Printed by the Continental Bank Note Co.

Size of design: 24x35mm

1875, Jan. 1 **Engr.**

PR9 N4 2c black 300.00 40.00
No gum 120.00
PR10 N4 3c black 300.00 45.00
No gum 120.00
PR11 N4 4c black 300.00 40.00
No gum 120.00
PR12 N4 6c black 300.00 45.00
No gum 120.00
PR13 N4 8c black 350.00 65.00
No gum 135.00

No.	Design	Description	Unused	Used
PR14	N4	9c black	600.00	125.00
		No gum	225.00	
PR15	N4	10c black	375.00	60.00
		No gum	135.00	
PR16	N5	12c rose	800.00	100.00
		No gum	325.00	
PR17	N5	24c rose	850.00	125.00
		No gum	350.00	
PR18	N5	36c rose	850.00	150.00
		No gum	350.00	
PR19	N5	48c rose	1,250.	400.00
		No gum	450.00	
PR20	N5	60c rose	1,250.	115.00
		No gum	450.00	
PR21	N5	72c rose	1,500.	375.00
		No gum	550.00	
PR22	N5	84c rose	1,850.	375.00
		No gum	650.00	
PR23	N5	96c rose	2,000.	250.00
		No gum	775.00	
PR24	N6	$1.92 dk brn	1,750.	250.00
		No gum	700.00	
PR25	N7	$3 ver	2,500.	450.00
		No gum	975.00	
PR26	N8	$6 ultra	4,000.	550.00
		No gum	1,600.	
PR27	N9	$9 yel org	4,500.	*2,000.*
		No gum	1,750.	
PR28	N10	$12 bl grn	4,750.	*1,100.*
		No gum	1,850.	
PR29	N11	$24 dk gray vio	4,750.	*1,200.*
		No gum	1,850.	
PR30	N12	$36 brn rose	5,000.	*1,400.*
		No gum	2,000.	
PR31	N13	$48 red brn	7,000.	*1,600.*
		No gum	2,600.	
PR32	N14	$60 violet	6,500.	*1,750.*
		No gum	2,400.	

SPECIAL PRINTING of 1875 ISSUE
Printed by the Continental Bank Note Co.
Hard white paper, without gum

1875

No.	Design	Description	Unused
PR33	N4	2c gray black	700.00
a.		Horiz. ribbed paper	500.00
PR34	N4	3c gray black	700.00
a.		Horiz. ribbed paper	550.00
PR35	N4	4c gray black	700.00
		Horiz. ribbed paper	1,000.
PR36	N4	6c gray black	900.00
PR37	N4	8c gray black	975.00
PR38	N4	9c gray black	1,050.
PR39	N4	10c gray black	1,400.
PR40	N5	12c pale rose	1,500.
PR41	N5	24c pale rose	2,100.
PR42	N5	36c pale rose	2,800.
PR43	N5	48c pale rose	3,750.
PR44	N5	60c pale rose	4,750.
PR45	N5	72c pale rose	4,500.
PR46	N5	84c pale rose	5,250.
PR47	N5	96c pale rose	*8,500.*
PR48	N6	$1.92 dk bn	*20,000.*
PR49	N7	$3 vermilion	*45,000.*
PR50	N8	$6 ultra	*80,000.*
PR51	N9	$9 yellow org	*350,000.*
PR52	N10	$12 blue green	*175,000.*
PR53	N11	$24 dk gray vio	*500,000.*
PR54	N12	$36 brn rose	*250,000.*
PR55	N13	$48 red brown	—
PR56	N14	$60 violet	—

Nos. PR50 and PR52 are valued in the grade of fine.

Although four examples of No. PR51 were sold, only one is currently documented.

No. PR54 is valued in the grade of fine. Although two stamps were sold, only one is currently documented.

All values of this issue, Nos. PR33 to PR56, exist imperforate but were not regularly issued thus. Value, set $60,000.

Printed by the American Bank Note Co.
Soft porous paper

1879 Unwmk. *Perf. 12*

No.	Design	Description	Unused	Used
PR57	N4	2c black	75.00	15.00
		No gum	30.00	
PR58	N4	3c black	85.00	20.00
		No gum	35.00	
PR59	N4	4c black	85.00	20.00
		No gum	35.00	
a.		Double paper	—	
PR60	N4	6c black	125.00	35.00
		No gum	50.00	
PR61	N4	8c black	135.00	35.00
		No gum	55.00	
PR62	N4	10c black	135.00	35.00
		No gum	55.00	
PR63	N5	12c red	500.00	125.00
		No gum	210.00	
PR64	N5	24c red	500.00	125.00
		No gum	210.00	
PR65	N5	36c red	1,000.	325.00
		No gum	475.00	
PR66	N5	48c red	1,000.	300.00
		No gum	450.00	
PR67	N5	60c red	1,250.	275.00
		No gum	550.00	
a.		Imperf., pair	*4,000.*	
PR68	N5	72c red	1,500.	425.00
		No gum	700.00	
PR69	N5	84c red	1,250.	350.00
		No gum	575.00	
PR70	N5	96c red	1,200.	275.00
		No gum	525.00	
PR71	N6	$1.92 pale brn	550.00	175.00
		No gum	225.00	
PR72	N7	$3 red ver	625.00	200.00
		No gum	250.00	

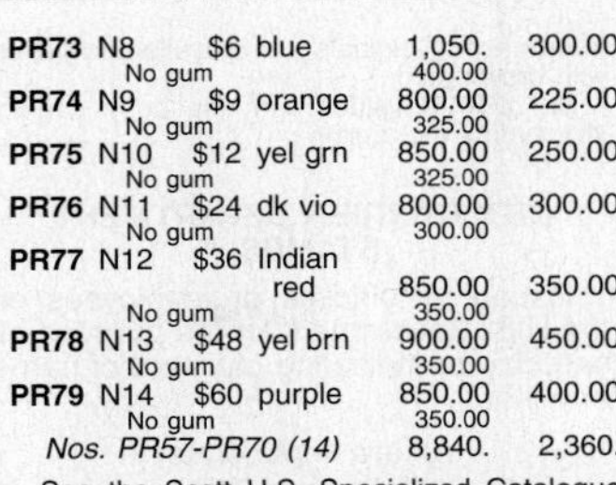

No.	Design	Description	Unused	Used
PR73	N8	$6 blue	1,050.	300.00
		No gum	400.00	
PR74	N9	$9 orange	800.00	225.00
		No gum	325.00	
PR75	N10	$12 yel grn	850.00	250.00
		No gum	325.00	
PR76	N11	$24 dk vio	800.00	300.00
		No gum	300.00	
PR77	N12	$36 Indian red	850.00	350.00
		No gum	350.00	
PR78	N13	$48 yel brn	900.00	450.00
		No gum	350.00	
PR79	N14	$60 purple	850.00	400.00
		No gum	350.00	
		Nos. PR57-PR70 (14)	8,840.	2,360.

See the Scott U.S. Specialized Catalogue Die and Plate Proof section for imperforates.

SPECIAL PRINTING of 1879 ISSUE
Printed by the American Bank Note Co. Without gum

1883

No.	Design	Description	Unused
PR80	N4	2c intense black	1,750.

REGULAR ISSUE
With gum

1885 Unwmk. *Perf. 12*

No.	Design	Description	Unused	Used
PR81	N4	1c black, *July 1, 1885*	95.00	12.50
		Never hinged	225.00	
		No gum	42.50	
PR82	N5	12c carmine	200.00	30.00
		Never hinged	450.00	
		No gum	85.00	
PR83	N5	24c carmine	225.00	32.50
		Never hinged	500.00	
		No gum	95.00	
PR84	N5	36c carmine	350.00	57.50
		Never hinged	800.00	
		No gum	145.00	
PR85	N5	48c carmine	425.00	75.00
		Never hinged	975.00	
		No gum	180.00	
PR86	N5	60c carmine	550.00	100.00
		No gum	240.00	
PR87	N5	72c carmine	550.00	110.00
		No gum	240.00	
PR88	N5	84c carmine	900.00	250.00
		No gum	350.00	
PR89	N5	96c carmine	750.00	190.00
		Never hinged	1,750.	
		No gum	300.00	
		Nos. PR81-PR89 (9)	4,045.	857.50

See the Scott U.S. Specialized Catalogue Die and Plate Proof section for imperforates.

Printed by the Bureau of Engraving and Printing

1894

Soft wove paper, with pale, whitish gum

No.	Design	Description	Unused	Used
PR90	N4	1c intense blk	400.00	*5,000.*
		Never hinged	900.00	
		No gum	160.00	
PR91	N4	2c intense blk	450.00	
		Never hinged	1,075.	
		No gum	190.00	
PR92	N4	4c intense blk	550.00	*13,500.*
		Never hinged	1,275.	
		No gum	210.00	
PR93	N4	6c intense blk	4,500.	
		Never hinged	*11,500.*	
		No gum	1,900.	
PR94	N4	10c intense blk	1,300.	
		Never hinged	*2,400.*	
		No gum	525.00	
PR95	N5	12c pink	2,600.	*4,500.*
		No gum	1,100.	
PR96	N5	24c pink	3,750.	*8,000.*
		No gum	1,850.	
PR97	N5	36c pink	*50,000.*	
PR98	N5	60c pink	*40,000.*	*16,000.*
PR99	N5	96c pink	*50,000.*	—
PR100	N7	$3 scarlet	*50,000.*	
PR101	N8	$6 pale blue	*50,000.*	—
		No gum	*25,000.*	

Nos. PR90, PR95-PR98 used are valued with fine centering and small faults.

No. PR97 unused is valued in the grade of very good to fine. No. PR98 unused is valued in the grade of fine. Nos. PR99-PR100 unused are valued in the grade of fine-very fine.

Statue of Freedom
N15

"Justice"
N16

"Victory" — N17

Clio — N18

Vesta — N19

"Peace" — N20

"Commerce"
N21

Indian Maiden
N22

Size of designs: 1c-50c, 21x34mm; $2-$100, 24x35mm

1895, Feb. 1

No.	Design	Description	Unused	Used
PR102	N15	1c black	230.00	*125.00*
		Never hinged	500.00	
		No gum	90.00	
PR103	N15	2c black	230.00	*125.00*
		Never hinged	500.00	
		No gum	90.00	
PR104	N15	5c black	300.00	*300.00*
		Never hinged	650.00	
		No gum	125.00	
PR105	N15	10c black	600.00	*400.00*
		Never hinged	1,300.	
		No gum	240.00	
PR106	N16	25c car	750.00	*500.00*
		Never hinged	1,650.	
		No gum	300.00	
PR107	N16	50c car	*2,750.*	800.00
		Never hinged	*6,250.*	
		No gum	*875.00*	
PR108	N17	$2 scarlet	2,250.	*1,100.*
		Never hinged	*5,000.*	
		No gum	850.00	
PR109	N18	$5 ultra	2,100.	*1,750.*
		No gum	800.00	
PR110	N19	$10 green	2,500.	*2,000.*
		Never hinged	*5,000.*	
		No gum	900.00	
PR111	N20	$20 slate	3,250.	*2,500.*
		Never hinged	*6,500.*	
		No gum	1,200.	
PR112	N21	$50 dull rose	2,750.	*950.00*
		Never hinged	*6,250.*	
		No gum	1,050.	
PR113	N22	$100 purple	3,500.	*7,000.*
		Never hinged	*7,250.*	
		No gum	1,400.	
		Nos. PR102-PR113 (12)	21,210.	17,550.

1895-97 Wmk. 191

No.	Design	Description	Unused	Used
PR114	N15	1c black	8.00	*25.00*
		Never hinged	20.00	
		No gum	2.75	
PR115	N15	2c black	8.00	*25.00*
		Never hinged	20.00	
		No gum	2.75	
PR116	N15	5c black	13.00	*40.00*
		Never hinged	27.50	
		No gum	4.25	
PR117	N15	10c black	13.00	*25.00*
		Never hinged	27.50	
		No gum	4.25	
PR118	N16	25c carmine	20.00	*65.00*
		Never hinged	45.00	
		No gum	7.00	
PR119	N16	50c carmine	25.00	*75.00*
		Never hinged	55.00	
		No gum	8.50	
PR120	N17	$2 scarlet	30.00	*110.00*
		Never hinged	75.00	
		No gum	10.00	
PR121	N18	$5 dark bl	40.00	*175.00*
		Never hinged	100.00	
		No gum	13.50	
a.		$5 light blue	200.00	*500.00*
		Never hinged	500.00	
		No gum	67.50	
PR122	N19	$10 green	42.50	*175.00*
		Never hinged	105.00	
		No gum	14.00	
PR123	N20	$20 slate	45.00	*200.00*
		Never hinged	110.00	
		No gum	15.00	
PR124	N21	$50 dull rose	75.00	*300.00*
		Never hinged	170.00	
		No gum	27.50	
PR125	N22	$100 purple	65.00	*275.00*
		Never hinged	150.00	
		No gum	22.50	
		Nos. PR114-PR125 (12)	384.50	*1,490.*
		Nos. PR114-PR125, never hinged	905.00	

In 1899 the Government sold 26,989 sets of these stamps, but, as the stock of high values was not sufficient to make up the required number, an additional printing was made of the $5, $10, $20, $50 and $100. These are virtually indistinguishable from earlier printings.

For overprints, see Nos. R159-R160.

PARCEL POST STAMPS

Issued for the prepayment of postage on parcel post packages only.

Post Office Clerk — PP1

City Carrier PP2

Railway Postal Clerk — PP3

Rural Carrier PP4

Mail Train — PP5

Steamship and Mail Tender PP6

Automobile Service PP7

Airplane Carrying Mail — PP8

Manufacturing — PP9

Dairying
PP10

Harvesting
PP11

Fruit Growing
PP12

1913 Wmk. 190 Engr. *Perf. 12*

Q1 PP1 1c carmine rose 4.25 1.60
Never hinged 12.00
On cover, 1913-25 6.00
Q2 PP2 2c carmine rose 5.00 1.25
Never hinged 12.50
On cover, 1913-25 5.75
a. 2c lake *1,750.*
b. 2c carmine lake *350.00*

No. Q2a is valued in the grade of fine to very fine.

Q3 PP3 3c carmine 9.00 6.00
Never hinged 24.00
On cover, 1913-25 19.00
Q4 PP4 4c carmine rose 27.50 3.00
Never hinged 77.50
On cover, 1913-25 65.00
Q5 PP5 5c carmine rose 22.50 2.25
Never hinged 62.50
On cover, 1913-25 42.50
Q6 PP6 10c carmine rose 40.00 3.00
Never hinged 90.00
On cover, 1913-25 55.00
Q7 PP7 15c carmine rose 60.00 13.50
Never hinged 170.00
On cover, 1913-25 400.00
Q8 PP8 20c carmine rose 110.00 25.00
Never hinged 260.00
On cover, 1913-25 850.00
Q9 PP9 25c carmine rose 52.50 8.00
Never hinged 145.00
On cover, 1913-25 300.00
Q10 PP10 50c carmine rose 220.00 45.00
Never hinged 550.00
On cover, 1913-25 —
Q11 PP11 75c carmine rose 80.00 35.00
Never hinged 190.00
On cover, 1913-25 —
Q12 PP12 $1 carmine rose 265.00 40.00
Never hinged 625.00
On cover, 1913-25 1,250.
Nos. Q1-Q12 (12) 895.75 183.60
Nos. Q1-Q12, never hinged 2,218.

PARCEL POST POSTAGE DUE STAMPS

For affixing by a postal clerk to any parcel post package, to denote the amount to be collected from the addressee because of insufficient prepayment of postage.

PPD1

1913 Wmk. 190 Engr. *Perf. 12*

JQ1 PPD1 1c dark green 8.00 4.00
Never hinged 20.00
On cover, 1913-25 160.00
JQ2 PPD1 2c dark green 60.00 16.00
Never hinged 150.00
On cover, 1913-25 225.00
JQ3 PPD1 5c dark green 9.00 4.50
Never hinged 22.50
On cover, 1913-25 200.00
JQ4 PPD1 10c dark green 110.00 40.00
Never hinged 275.00
On cover, 1913-25 650.00
JQ5 PPD1 25c dark green 70.00 4.50
Never hinged 175.00
On cover, 1913-25 —
Never hinged *6,000.*
Nos. JQ1-JQ5 (5) 257.00 69.00
Nos. JQ1-JQ5, never hinged 642.50

SPECIAL HANDLING STAMPS

For use on fourth-class mail to secure the same expeditious handling accorded to first-class mail matter.

PP13

FLAT PLATE PRINTING

1925-28 Engr. Unwmk. *Perf. 11*

QE1 PP13 10c yel grn ('28) 2.00 1.00
Never hinged 4.25
QE2 PP13 15c yel grn ('28) 2.25 .90
Never hinged 4.75
QE3 PP13 20c yel grn ('28) 3.75 1.50
Never hinged 7.75
QE4 PP13 25c dp grn ('25) 20.00 3.75
Never hinged 37.50
a. yel grn ('28) 16.50 *22.50*
Never hinged 32.50
Nos. QE1-QE4 (4) 28.00 7.15
Nos. QE1-QE4, never hinged 54.25

CARRIERS' STAMPS

GENERAL ISSUE CARRIER STAMPS

Issued by the U.S. Government to facilitate payment of fees for delivering and collecting letters.

Franklin — OC1

1851 Engr. Unwmk. *Imperf.*

LO1 OC1 (1c) dull blue, *rose* *7,000.* *8,000.*
On cover from Philadelphia *17,500.*
On cover from New York *30,000.*
On cover from New Orleans with 3c #10 (a 2nd #LO1 removed) *30,000.*

U.S.P.O. Despatch

Eagle — OC2

1851

LO2 OC2 1c blue (shades) 50.00 *80.00*
On cover, used alone 500.00
On cover, precanceled 600.00
On cover, pair or 2 singles *1,500.*
On cover with 1c #9 *8,500.*
On cover with three 1c #9 *4,500.*
On cover with 3c #11 400.
On cover with 3c #25 —
On cover with 3c #26 *600.*
On cover with strip of 3, 3c #26 —
On cover with 5c #30A and 10c #32 *33,000.*
On cover, tied by town handstamp, with 3c #65 (Washington, D.C.) *4,500.*
On 3c envelope #U1, #LO2 pen canceled —
On 3c envelope #U2, #LO2 pen canceled —
Pair on cover (Cincinnati) *1,250.*

1875 *Imperf.*

LO3 OC1 (1c) blue, *rose* 50.

Perf. 12

LO4 OC1 (1c) blue *16,000.*

No. LO4 is valued in the grade of average to fine.

Eagle Reprints

Imperf.

LO5 OC2 1c blue 25.

Perf. 12

LO6 OC2 1c blue 175.

Reprints of the Franklin Carrier are printed in dark blue, instead of the dull blue or deep blue of the originals. Two reprintings of 10,000 each were made in 1875 on the same rose paper as the originals. A third reprinting of 5,000 in 1881 is on soft wove paper.

The first two reprintings of 10,000 each of the Eagle carrier are on hard white paper, ungummed and sometimes perforated. A third reprinting of 10,000 stamps in 1881 is on soft wove paper. Originals are on yellowish paper with brown gum.

No. LO6 is valued with the perfs cutting slightly into the design.

CITY CARRIER DEPARTMENT STAMPS

Issued by officials or employees of the U.S. Government for the purpose of securing or indicating payment of carriers' fees.

All are imperforate.

Baltimore, Md.

C1

1850-55 Typo.

Settings of 10 (2x5) varieties

1LB1 C1 1c red, *bluish* 180. 160.
On cover, tied by handstamp *1,000.*
On cover with 1c #9 —
On cover (tied) with 3c #11 *500.*
On cover (tied) with 3c #11A *500.*
1LB2 C1 1c blue, *bluish* 200. 150.
On cover, tied *1,000.*
On cover (tied) with 3c #11 *500.*
On cover, uncanceled, with 3c #11A *225.*
a. Bluish laid paper — —
1LB3 C1 1c blue 160. 100.
On cover, tied by handstamp *1,500.*
On cover, tied by ms. *250.*
a. Laid paper 200. 150.
On cover, tied by handstamp *1,000.*
b. Block of 14 containing three tete-beche gutter pairs (unique) *6,250.*
1LB4 C1 1c green — 1,000.
On cover, tied by handstamp *5,000.*
On cover, not tied *1,200.*
On cover with 1c #7, tied by handstamp *2,250.*
On cover, not tied, with 3c #10A *2,000.*
On cover with 3c #11, ms. tied —
On 3c envelope #U10 *3,500.*
1LB5 C1 1c red 2,250. 1,750.
On cover, tied by handstamp *4,500.*
On cover, not tied *3,000.*
On cover (tied) with 3c #10 or 10A *5,000.*

C2

1856 Typo.

1LB6 C2 1c blue (shades) 130. 90.
On cover 400.
On cover with 3c #11 or 11A *1,000.*
On cover with 3c #25 (both tied) *1,350.*
On cover with 3c #26 *1,250.*
On cover with 3c #26A —
1LB7 C2 1c red (shades) 130. 90.
On cover *300.*
On cover (tied) with 3c #25 *350.*
On cover (tied) with 3c #26 *350.*

C3

The sheet consisted of at least four panes of 10 placed horizontally, the two center panes tete beche. This makes possible five horizontal tete beche gutter pairs.

Plate of 10 (2x5); 10 Varieties

1857 Typo.

1LB8 C3 1c black (shades) 65. 50.
On cover, tied by handstamp *125.*
On cover (tied) with 3c #26 *225.*
On 3c envelope #U9, tied *225.*
On 3c envelope #U10 *225.*
Strip of 3 (not tied), on cover *4,000.*
a. "SENT" 100. 75.
On cover, tied by handstamp *175.*
On cover (tied) with 3c #26 *250.*
On 3c envelope #U9, tied *250.*
On 3c envelope #U10, tied *250.*
b. Short rays 100. 75.
On cover (tied) with 3c #26 *600.*
c. "ONS," Pos. 5 — —
d. "ONS" and "SENTS," late state Pos. 7, on cover —
1LB9 C3 1c **red** 100. 90.
On cover *175.*
On cover (tied) with 3c #26 *300.*
On 3c envelope #U9 *325.*
On 3c envelope #U10 *325.*
a. "SENT" 140. 110.
On cover (tied) with 3c #26 *500.*
b. Short rays 140. 110.
c. As "b," double impression *800.*

Boston, Mass.

C6

Several Varieties

1849-50 Pelure Paper Typeset

3LB1 C6 1c blue 375. 180.
On cover, tied by handstamp 300.
On cover, uncanceled 150.
On cover with 5c #1 *4,500.*
On cover with two 5c #1 *8,750.*
On cover with 3c #10 *450.*
a. Wrong ornament at left *400.*
On cover, not tied, with certificate —

C7

Several Varieties

1851 Typeset

Wove Paper Colored Through

3LB2 C7 1c blue (shades), *slate* 190. 100.
On cover 220.
On cover with 5c #1 *12,500.*
On cover with 3c #10 500.
On cover with 3c #11A 325.
On 3c envelope #U2, #U5 or #U9 350.

Charleston, S. C.

Honour's City Express

C8

1849 Typo.

Wove Paper Colored Through

4LB1 C8 2c blk, *brn rose* *10,000.*
Cut to shape *4,000.* *4,000.*
On cover, not canceled, with certificate *17,000.*
On cover, cut to shape, tied, with 10c #2 *40,000.*
4LB2 C8 2c blk, *yel,* cut to shape —
On cover, not tied, with certificate *12,500.*
On cover, cut to shape, uncanceled —
On cover, rectangular-cut, tied, with 10c #2 —

No. 4LB1 unused is a unique uncanceled stamp on piece. The used cut-to-shape stamp is also unique. In addition two covers exist bearing No. 4LB1.

No. 4LB2 unused (uncanceled) off cover is unique; three known on cover.

See the Scott U.S. Specialized Catalogue.

4LB2A C8 2c blk, *bl gray,* on cover, cut to shape —

No. 4LB2A is unique.

C10

1854 Wove Paper Typeset

4LB3 C10 2c black *1,500.*
On cover, tied by pen cancel *3,000.*
On cover with 3c #11 or 11A, tied *4,000.*
On cover with 3c #11 or 11A, not tied *3,250.*

C11

Several Varieties

1849-50 **Typeset**

Wove Paper Colored Through

4LB5 C11 2c black, *bluish, pelure* 750. 500.
On cover (not tied) 3,500.
On cover with pair 5c #1b —
On cover with two 5c #1b —
On cover (tied) with 3c #11 or 11A 4,500.
a. "Ceuts" 5,750.
4LB7 C11 2c black, *yellow* 750. 1,000.
On cover, tied by handstamp 9,000.
On cover, not canceled 2,000.
a. "Ccnts," ms. tied on cover 14,500.

No. 4LB5a is unique. It is without gum and is valued thus. No. 4LB7a also is unique.

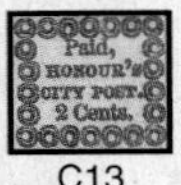

C13

C14

C15

Several varieties of each type

1851-58 **Typeset**

Wove Paper Colored Through

4LB8 C13 2c black, *bluish* 350. 175.
On cover, tied by handstamp 700.
On cover, not tied 300.
On cover with 10c #2 5,500.
On cover, tied, with 3c #10 1,500.
On cover, tied, with 3c #11 or 11A 1,500.
On cover, tied, with 3c #26 1,500.
a. Period after "PAID" 500. 250.
On cover 650.
On cover, ms. tied, with 3c #11 or 11A 750.
b. "Cens" 700. 900.
On cover, ms. tied, with 3c #11 or 11A 3,250.
c. "Conours" and "Bents" —

The No. 4LB8 with No. 2 combination cover is unique. It is a cover front only and is valued thus.

4LB9 C13 2c black, *bluish, pelure* 850. 950.
4LB10 C13 2c black, *pink, pelure,* on cover 7,000.
4LB11 C14 (2c) black, *bluish* — 375.
On cover, tied by handstamp, with 3c #11 or 11A 12,500.
On cover, ms. tied, with 3c #11 or 11A 3,000.
On cover, tied, to foreign destination (Ireland), unique 25,000.
4LB12 C14 (2c) black, *bluish, pelure* — —
4LB13 C15 (2c) black, *bluish* ('58) 750. 400.
On cover with 3c #11A, Aiken, S.C. postmark, tied by handstamp (unique) 6,000.
On cover with 3c #26, tied by pen cancel 4,500.
On cover with 3c #26, tied by handstamp cancel 3,750.
a. Comma after "PAID" 1,100.
b. No period after "Post" 1,400.

Kingman's City Post

C16

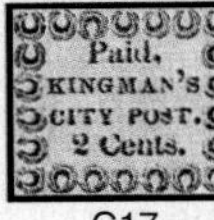

C17

Several varieties of each

Wove Paper Colored Through

1851(?)-58(?) **Typeset**

4LB14 C16 2c black, *bluish* 1,400. 900.
On cover with 3c #11 7,000.
On cover with 3c #26 6,000.
a. "Kingman's" erased 5,000.
4LB15 C17 2c black, *bluish* 800. 800.
On cover —
a. "Kingman's" erased, on cover with 3c #11, tied by pen cancel (unique) 4,500.

Martin's City Post

C18

Several Varieties

1858 **Typeset**

Wove Paper Colored Through

4LB16 C18 2c black, *bluish* 8,000.

Beckman's City Post

Same as C19, but inscribed: "Beckmann's City Post."

1860

4LB17 C19 2c black, on cover —

No. 4LB17 is unique.

Steinmeyer's City Post

C19

C20

Several varieties of Type C19

Type C20 printed from plate of 10 (2x5) varieties

1859 **Typeset**

Wove Paper Colored Through

4LB18 C19 2c black, *bluish* 21,000.
On cover, uncanceled —
4LB19 C20 2c black, *bluish* 4,500. —
4LB20 C20 2c black, *pink* 200. —
4LB21 C20 2c black, *yellow* 200.

Cincinnati, Ohio
Williams' City Post

C20a

1854 **Wove Paper** **Litho.**

9LB1 C20a 2c brown — 4,000.
On cover, tied by handstamp
On cover, tied by pen cancel 4,500.
On cover with 1c #9 7,500.

Cleveland, Ohio
Bishop's City Post

C20b

C20c

1854 **Wove Paper** **Litho.**

10LB1 C20b blue 5,000. 4,000.
On cover, tied by handstamp 15,000.
Pair on cover, canceled by pencil, with 3c #11, with certificate 17,000.

Vertically Laid Paper

10LB2 C20c 2c black, *bluish* 4,000. 6,000.
On cover —
Pair on cover, canceled by pencil, with 3c #11 14,000.

No. 10LB2 unused is unique. It is cut in at bottom and without gum, and is valued thus.

Louisville, Ky.
Wharton's U.S.P.O. Despatch

C21

1857 **Lithographed**

5LB1 C21 (2c) bluish green (shades) 125.

Brown & McGill's U. S. P. O. Despatch

C22

1858, Nov.-1860 **Lithographed**

5LB2 C22 (2c) blue (shades) 250. 750.
On cover, not tied, with 3c #26 750.
On cover with 3c #26, tied by handstamp 6,250.

1858, Feb.-Aug.

5LB3 C22 (2c) black 4,500. 15,000.
On cover, not tied, with 3c #26 17,500.

The value for No. 5LB3 used refers to the finer of the two known used (canceled) examples; it is extremely fine and on a piece with a 3c #26.

New York, N. Y.
United States City Despatch Post

C23

Wove Paper Colored Through

1842 **Engr.**

6LB1 C23 3c black, *grayish* 2,000.
On cover, tied by handstamp 12,000.
On cover, not tied 10,000.

Used examples are Carriers' stamps only when canceled with the regular government cancellation "U.S." in octagonal frame (see illustration), "U.S.CITY DESPATCH POST," or New York circular postmark.

When canceled "FREE" in frame they were used as local stamps. See No. 40L1 in the Scott Specialized Catalogue of United States Stamps.

C24

Wove Paper (unsurfaced) Colored Through

1842-45

6LB2 C24 3c black, *rosy buff* 5,000.
6LB3 C24 3c black, *light blue* 1,500. 750.
On cover, tied by handstamp 2,500.
On cover, not tied 1,000.
6LB4 C24 3c black, *green* 11,500.

Some authorities consider No. 6LB2 to be an essay, and No. 6LB4 a color changeling. No. 6LB2 unused is valued without gum.

Glazed Paper, Surface Colored

6LB5 C24 3c black, *blue green* (shades) 200. 175.
On cover, tied by handstamp 600.
Five on cover 20,000.
a. Double impression 1,500.
b. 3c black, *blue* 650. 300.
On cover 750.
c. As "b," double impression 1,000.
d. 3c black, *green* 1,250. 750.
black, *apple green* 2,000.
Pair 2,750.
On cover 1,250.
e. As "d," double impression —
On cover —
6LB6 C24 3c black, *pink,* on cover front 14,500.

No. 6LB6 is unique.

No. 6LB5 Surcharged in Red

1846

6LB7 C24 2c on 3c black, *bluish grn,* on cover 14,000.

The City Despatch 2c red is listed in the Scott U.S. Specialized Catalogue as a Local stamp.

U.S. MAIL

C27

1849 **Typo.**

Wove Paper, Colored Through

6LB9 C27 1c black, *rose* 100. 100.
On cover, tied by handstamp 350.
On cover with 5c #1 2,000.

1849-50 **Glazed Surface Paper**

6LB10 C27 1c black, *yellow* 100. 100.
On cover, tied by handstamp 350.
On cover with 5c #1 1,500.
6LB11 C27 1c black, *buff* 100. 100.
On cover 250.
On cover, not tied, with 5c #1, with certificate 3,000.
a. Pair, one stamp sideways 2,850.

Philadelphia, Pa.

C28

Several Varieties

Thick Wove Paper Colored Through

1849-50 **Typeset**

7LB1 C28 1c black, *rose* (with "L P") 450.
On cover, tied by handstamp 3,000.
On cover, not canceled 2,000.
On cover with 5c #1 or 1a 6,000.
7LB2 C28 1c black, *rose* (with "S") 3,000.
On cover, not canceled 4,500.
7LB3 C28 1c black, *rose* (with "H") 275.
On cover, tied by handstamp 3,750.
On cover, not canceled 1,000.
On cover with 5c #1 3,500.
7LB4 C28 1c black, *rose* (with "L S") 400. 500.
On cover, not canceled 3,000.
7LB5 C28 1c black, *rose* (with "J J") 7,500.
On cover with 5c #1, uncanceled 70,000.

The unique used No. 7LB5 is an uncanceled stamp on a cover front.

C29

Several Varieties

7LB6 C29 1c black, *rose* 300. 250.
On cover, tied by handstamp 2,500.
On cover, uncanceled 500.
7LB7 C29 1c black, *blue, glazed* 1,000.
On cover, tied by handstamp 6,500.
On cover, uncanceled 1,250.
On cover with 5c #1 3,500.
7LB8 C29 1c blk, *ver,* glazed 700.
On cover, tied by handstamp 1,500.
On cover, uncanceled 900.
On cover with 5c dark brown #1a, uncanceled 12,500.
On cover with 5c orange brown #1b, uncanceled 21,000.
7LB9 C29 1c blk, *yel,* glazed 2,750. 2,250.
On cover, not canceled 4,000.
On cover with 3c #10, uncanceled 2,000.

Cancellations on Nos. 7LB1-7LB9: Normally these stamps were left uncanceled on the letter, but occasionally were accidentally tied by the Philadelphia town postmark which was normally struck in blue ink.

A 1c black on buff (unglazed) of type C29 is believed to be a color changeling.

C30

Settings of 25 (5x5) varieties (Five basic types)

1850-52 **Litho.**

7LB11	C30 1c gold, *black, glazed*	175.	110.
	On cover, tied by handstamp		*600.*
	On cover, uncanceled		*325.*
	On cover (tied) with 5c #1		*3,500.*
	On cover (tied) with 3c #10		*800.*
	On cover (uncanceled) with 3c #10		*250.*
7LB12	C30 1c blue	400.	275.
	On cover, tied by handstamp		*1,250.*
	On cover, not tied		*400.*
	On cover (tied) with 3c #10		*1,750.*
	On cover (tied) with 3c #11		*1,250.*
7LB13	C30 1c black	*750.*	550.
	On cover, tied by handstamp		*2,500.*
	On cover, uncanceled		*1,250.*
	On cover (tied) with 3c #10		—
	On cover (not tied) with 3c #11		*3,250.*

25 varieties of C30.

C31

Handstamped

7LB14	C31 1c blue, *buff*	3,250.

1855(?)

7LB16	C31 1c black	*5,000.*
	On cover with strip of 3, 1c #9	—
	On cover with 3c 1851 stamp removed, tied by handstamp	*7,000.*

C32

1856(?) **Handstamped**

7LB18	C32 1c black	*1,250.*	*2,000.*
	On cover (cut diamond-shaped) with pair 1c #7 and single 1c #9		—
	On cover with strip of 3, 1c #7		*17,000.*
	On cover with 3c #11		*9,500.*
	On 3c envelope #U5		—
	On 3c envelope #U10, not canceled		*9,000.*

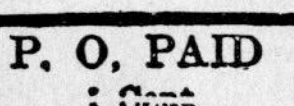

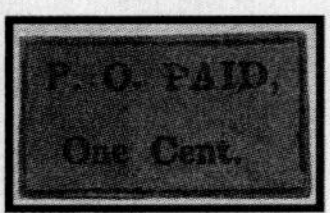

Labels of these designs are believed by most specialists not to be carrier stamps. Those seen are uncanceled, either off cover or affixed to stampless covers of the early 1850s. Some students believe they should be given carrier status.

St. Louis, Mo.

C36

C37

Illustrations enlarged to show details of the two types (note upper corners especially). Sizes of actual designs are 17 1/2x22mm.

1849 **White Wove Paper** **Litho.**
Two Types

8LB1	C36 2c black	*7,000.*	*3,000.*
8LB2	C37 2c black	*6,000.*	—

Cancellation on Nos. 8LB1-8LB2: Black town.

C38

1857 **Litho.**

8LB3	C38 2c blue	*22,500.*
	On cover, tied by handstamp	*55,000.*

The used example off cover is unique. Five covers are recorded.

Cancellations on No. 8LB3: Black boxed "1ct," "Paid" in arc, black pen.

STAMPED ENVELOPES AND WRAPPERS

VALUES

Unless otherwise noted, values are for cut squares in a grade of very fine.

Very fine cut squares will have the design well centered within moderately large margins. Precanceled cut squares must include the entire precancellation.

Values for unused entires are for those without printed or manuscript address. Values for letter sheets are for folded entires. Unfolded examples sell for more. A "full corner" includes back and side flaps and commands a premium.

Wrappers are listed with envelopes of corresponding designs, and indicated by prefix letter "W" instead of "U."

An ALBINO impression is where two or more envelope blanks are fed into the printing press. The one adjacent to the printing die receives the color and the embossing, while the others are embossed only. Albinos are printing errors and are sometimes worth more than normal, inked impressions. Because of the nature of the printing process, many albinos were produced, and most collectors will not pay much, or any, premium for most of them. Albinos of earlier issues, canceled while current, are scarce.

The papers of these issues vary greatly in texture, and in color from yellowish to bluish white and from amber to dark buff.

"+" Some authorities claim that Nos. U37, U48, U49, U110, U124, U125, U130, U133A, U137A, U137B, U137C, W138, U145, U162, U178A, U185, U220, U285, U286, U298, U299, UO3, UO32, UO38, UO45 and UO45A (each with "+" before number) were not regularly issued and are not known to have been used.

U1

"THREE" in short label with curved ends; 13mm wide at top. Twelve varieties.

Washington — U2

"THREE" in short label with straight ends; 15½mm wide at top. Three varieties.

U3

"THREE" in short label with octagonal ends. Two varieties.

U4

"THREE" in wide label with straight ends; 20mm wide at top.

U5

"THREE" in medium wide label with curved ends; 14½mm wide at top. Ten varieties. A sub-variety shows curved lines at either end of label omitted; both T's have longer cross stroke; R is smaller (20 varieties).

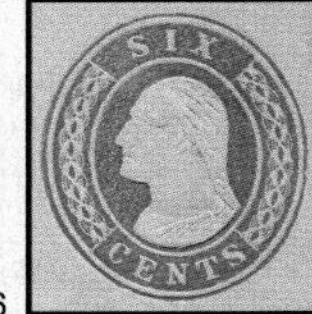

U6

Four varieties.

U7

"TEN" in short label; 15½mm wide at top.

U8

"TEN" in wide label; 20mm wide at top.

1853-55

On Diagonally Laid Paper (Early printings of No. U1 on Horizontally Laid Paper)

U1	U1	3c red	350.00	35.00
		Entire	1,600.	45.00
U2	U1	3c red, *buff*	90.00	30.00
		Entire	850.00	40.00
U3	U2	3c red	950.00	50.00
		Entire	3,500.	100.00
U4	U2	3c red, *buff*	425.00	45.00
		Entire	3,250.	95.00
U5	U3	3c red ('54)	5,750.	500.00
		Entire	*26,000.*	850.00
U6	U3	3c red, *buff* ('54)	3,750.	100.00
		Entire	—	150.00
U7	U4	3c red	5,000.	150.00
		Entire	—	325.00
U8	U4	3c red, *buff*	*8,250.*	175.00
		Entire	—	325.00
U9	U5	3c red ('54)	40.00	4.00
		Entire	140.00	11.00
U10	U5	3c red, *buff* ('54)	20.00	4.00
		Entire	70.00	6.00
U11	U6	6c red	300.00	90.00
		Entire	375.00	175.00
U12	U6	6c red, *buff*	145.00	90.00
		Entire	350.00	200.00

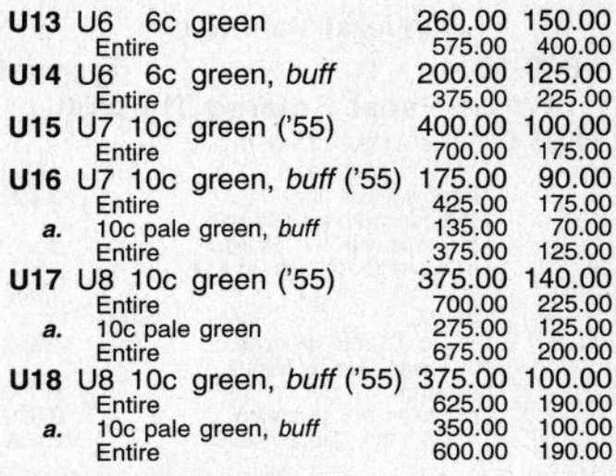

U13	U6	6c green	260.00	150.00
		Entire	575.00	400.00
U14	U6	6c green, *buff*	200.00	125.00
		Entire	375.00	225.00
U15	U7	10c green ('55)	400.00	100.00
		Entire	700.00	175.00
U16	U7	10c green, *buff* ('55)	175.00	90.00
		Entire	425.00	175.00
a.		10c pale green, *buff*	135.00	70.00
		Entire	375.00	125.00
U17	U8	10c green ('55)	375.00	140.00
		Entire	700.00	225.00
a.		10c pale green	275.00	125.00
		Entire	675.00	200.00
U18	U8	10c green, *buff* ('55)	375.00	100.00
		Entire	625.00	190.00
a.		10c pale green, *buff*	350.00	100.00
		Entire	600.00	190.00

Nos. U9, U10, U11, U12, U13, U14, U17, and U18 have been reprinted on white and buff papers, wove or vertically laid, and are not known entire. The originals are on diagonally laid paper. Value, set of 8 reprints on laid, $225. Reprints on wove sell for more.

The first printings of Nos. U1, U2, U3, U4 and U7 have G.F. Nesbitt crests printed on the envelope flaps. Such examples of Nos. U1-U4 with 1853 year-dated cancels sell for a very large premium.

No. U1 with watermark having a space between lines and on horizontally laid paper sells for a substantial premium.

U9

Period after "POSTAGE." (Eleven varieties.)

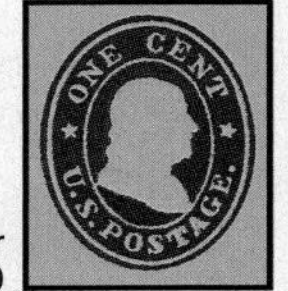

Franklin, Period after "POSTAGE." — U10

Bust touches inner frame-line at front and back.

No period after "POSTAGE" — U11

No period after "POSTAGE." (Two varieties.)

Washington — U12

Nine varieties of type U12.

Envelopes are on diagonally laid paper. Wrappers on vert. or horiz. laid paper, or on unwatermarked white paper (Nos. W22, W25).

1860-61

W18B	U9	1c blue ('61)	*5,500.*	
		Entire	—	
U19	U9	1c blue, *buff*	35.00	12.50
		Entire	85.00	30.00
W20	U9	1c bl, *buff* ('61)	65.00	50.00
		Entire	120.00	75.00
W21	U9	1c bl, *man* ('61)	55.00	45.00
		Entire	125.00	100.00
U21A	U9	1c bl, *org*		*325.00*
		Entire	*1,800.*	
W22	U9	1c bl, *org* ('61)	*3,000.*	
		Entire	*6,000.*	
U23	U10	1c bl, *org*	600.00	350.00
		Entire	825.00	600.00
U24	U11	1c bl, *amb*	350.00	110.00
		Entire	700.00	350.00
W25	U11	1c bl, *man* ('61)	*6,750.*	*1,500.*
		Entire	*17,500.*	*5,500.*
U26	U12	3c red	25.00	17.50
		Entire	55.00	32.50
U27	U12	3c red, *buff*	22.50	12.50
		Entire	45.00	22.50
U28	U12+U9	3c +1c red & bl	250.00	225.00
		Entire	500.00	400.00

U29 U12+U9 3c +1c red & bl, *buff* 250.00 250.00
Entire 500.00 450.00
U30 U12 6c red 1,800. 1,500.
Entire *3,250.*
U31 U12 6c red, *buff* 3,500. 1,450.
Entire *5,000. 15,000.*
U32 U12 10c green 1,250. 450.00
Entire *10,000.* 650.00
U33 U12 10c green, *buff* 1,250. 400.00
Entire *3,250.* 600.00

Nos. U26, U27, U30 to U33 have been reprinted on the same vertically laid paper as the reprints of the 1853-55 issue, and are not known entire. Value, Nos. U26-U27, $75 each; Nos. U30-U33, $75 each.

U13

17 varieties for Nos. U34-U35; 2 varieties for No. U36.

U14

U15

Washington U16

Envelopes are on diagonally laid paper.

U36 and U45 come on vertically or horizontally laid paper.

1861

U34 U13 3c pink 27.50 5.00
Entire 60.00 12.50
U35 U13 3c pink, *buff* 32.50 6.00
Entire 62.50 12.00
U36 U13 3c pink, *blue* (Letter Sheet) 65.00 65.00
Entire 230.00 *500.00*
+U37 U13 3c pink, *orange* *2,750.*
Entire *4,250.*
U38 U14 6c pink 100.00 80.00
Entire 200.00 190.00
U39 U14 6c pink, *buff* 60.00 60.00
Entire 210.00 160.00
U40 U15 10c yellow green 40.00 30.00
Entire 77.50 60.00
a. 10c blue green 40.00 30.00
Entire 77.50 60.00
U41 U15 10c yel grn, *buff* 40.00 30.00
Entire 77.50 52.50
a. 10c blue green, *buff* 40.00 30.00
Entire 77.50 52.50
U42 U16 12c red & brn, *buff* 180.00 180.00
Entire 475.00 *650.00*
a. 12c lake & brown, *buff* *1,250.*
U43 U16 20c red & bl, *buff* 275.00 225.00
Entire 450.00 *1,250.*
U44 U16 24c red & grn, *buff* 225.00 210.00
Entire 625.00 *1,500.*
a. 24c lake & green, *salmon* 275.00 225.00
Entire 750.00 *1,750.*
U45 U16 40c blk & red, *buff* 325.00 400.00
Entire 700.00 *4,500.*

Nos. U38 and U39 have been reprinted on the same papers as the reprints of the 1853-55 issue, and are not known entire. Value, set of 2 reprints, $60.

Jackson — U17

"U.S. POSTAGE" above. Downstroke and tail of "2" unite near the point (seven varieties).

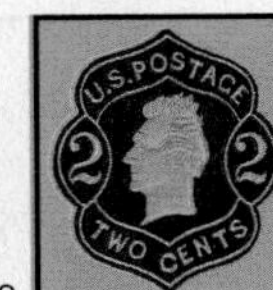
Jackson — U18

"U.S. POSTAGE" above. The downstroke and tail of the "2" touch but do not merge.

Jackson — U19

"U.S. POST" above. Stamp 24-25mm wide (Sixteen varieties).

Jackson — U20

"U.S. POST" above. Stamp 25½-26¼mm wide. (Twenty-five varieties.)
Envelopes are on diagonally laid paper. Wrappers on vertically or horizontally laid paper.

Envelopes are on diagonally laid paper.
Wrappers on vertically or horizontally laid paper.

1863-64

U46 U17 2c black, *buff* 50.00 24.00
Entire 80.00 37.50
W47 U17 2c black, *dark manila* 75.00 65.00
Entire 120.00 90.00
+U48 U18 2c black, *buff* *2,250.*
Entire *4,500.*
+U49 U18 2c black, *orange* 1,750.
Entire 4,000.
U50 U19 2c black, *buff* ('64) 17.50 11.00
Entire 40.00 21.00
W51 U19 2c black, *buff* ('64) 450.00 275.00
Entire 675.00 400.00
U52 U19 2c black, *orange* ('64) 20.00 11.00
Entire 37.50 18.00
W53 U19 2c black, *dark manila* ('64) 42.50 40.00
Entire 175.00 140.00
U54 U20 2c black, *buff* ('64) 17.50 9.50
Entire 37.50 16.00
W55 U20 2c black, *buff* ('64) 95.00 65.00
Entire 160.00 120.00
U56 U20 2c black, *orange* ('64) 20.00 10.00
Entire 34.00 16.00
W57 U20 2c black, *light manila* ('64) 22.50 14.00
Entire 37.50 24.00

Washington — U21

Washington U22

1864-65

U58 U21 3c pink 8.00 1.60
Entire 20.00 3.25
U59 U21 3c pink, *buff* 8.00 1.25
Entire 20.00 3.00
U60 U21 3c brown ('65) 65.00 40.00
Entire 130.00 125.00
U61 U21 3c brown, *buff* ('65) 50.00 30.00
Entire 115.00 80.00
U62 U21 6c pink 80.00 29.00
Entire 180.00 85.00
U63 U21 6c pink, *buff* 40.00 27.50
Entire 100.00 50.00
U64 U21 6c purple ('65) 50.00 26.00
Entire 100.00 55.00
U65 U21 6c purple, *buff* ('65) 40.00 20.00
Entire 70.00 55.00
U66 U22 9c lemon, *buff* ('65) 375.00 250.00
Entire 575.00 *1,000.*
U67 U22 9c orange, *buff* ('65) 125.00 90.00
Entire 210.00 300.00
a. 9c orange yellow, *buff* 125.00 90.00
Entire 210.00 300.00
U68 U22 12c brown, *buff* ('65) 275.00 275.00
Entire 600.00 *1,200.*
U69 U22 12c red brown, *buff* ('65) 125.00 55.00
Entire 180.00 450.00
U70 U22 18c red, *buff* ('65) 70.00 95.00
Entire 180.00 *800.00*
U71 U22 24c blue, *buff* ('65) 70.00 95.00
Entire 225.00 *700.00*
U72 U22 30c green, *buff* ('65) 85.00 80.00
Entire 210.00 *1,500.*
a. 30c yellow green, *buff* 80.00 80.00
Entire 210.00 *1,500.*
U73 U22 40c rose, *buff* ('65) 85.00 *250.00*
Entire 350.00 *2,000.*

Nos. U60 and U61 issued on legal-size covers only.

Printed by George H. Reay, Brooklyn, N. Y.

The engravings in this issue are finely executed.

Franklin — U23

Bust points to the end of the "N" of "ONE."

Jackson — U24

Bust narrow at back. Small, thick figures of value.

Washington — U25

Queue projects below bust.

Lincoln — U26

Neck very long at the back.

Stanton — U27

Bust pointed at the back; figures "7" are normal.

Jefferson — U28

Queue forms straight line with the bust.

Clay — U29

Ear partly concealed by hair, mouth large, chin prominent.

Webster — U30

Has side whiskers.

Scott — U31

Straggling locks of hair at top of head; ornaments around the inner oval end in squares.

Hamilton — U32

Back of bust very narrow, chin almost straight; labels containing figures of value are exactly parallel.

Perry — U33

Front of bust very narrow and pointed; inner lines of shields project very slightly beyond the oval.

1870-71

U74 U23 1c blue 32.50 30.00
Entire 75.00 45.00
a. 1c ultramarine 60.00 35.00
Entire 130.00 60.00
U75 U23 1c blue, *amber* 25.00 27.50
Entire 55.00 40.00
a. 1c ultramarine, *amber* 55.00 30.00
Entire 95.00 55.00
U76 U23 1c blue, *orange* 17.00 15.00
Entire 35.00 22.50
W77 U23 1c blue, *manila* 35.00 35.00
Entire 75.00 70.00
U78 U24 2c brown 35.00 16.00
Entire 57.50 22.50
U79 U24 2c brown, *amber* 14.00 10.00
Entire 40.00 17.50
U80 U24 2c brown, *orange* 8.00 6.50
Entire 15.00 11.00
W81 U24 2c brown, *manila* 25.00 20.00
Entire 60.00 57.50
U82 U25 3c green 7.00 1.00
Entire 16.00 4.00
a. 3c brown (error), entire *8,500.*
U83 U25 3c green, *amber* 6.00 2.00
Entire 17.50 5.00

No.	Design	Description	Unused	Used
U84	U25	3c green, *cream*	8.00	4.50
		Entire	16.00	10.00
U85	U26	6c dark red	17.50	16.00
		Entire	55.00	21.00
a.		6c vermilion	17.50	16.00
		Entire	65.00	20.00
U86	U26	6c dark red, *amber*	30.00	20.00
		Entire	70.00	30.00
a.		6c vermilion, *amber*	30.00	20.00
		Entire	75.00	30.00
U87	U26	6c dark red, *cream*	30.00	25.00
		Entire	70.00	30.00
a.		6c vermilion, *cream*	25.00	20.00
		Entire	70.00	30.00
U88	U27	7c vermilion, *amber* ('71)	55.00	175.00
		Entire	80.00	*900.00*
U89	U28	10c olive black	650.00	900.00
		Entire	900.00	1,200.
U90	U28	10c olive black, *amber*	625.00	800.00
		Entire	1,000.	1,200.
U91	U28	10c brown	82.50	70.00
		Entire	130.00	125.00
U92	U28	10c brown, *amber*	85.00	52.50
		Entire	120.00	125.00
a.		10c dark brown, *amber*	85.00	75.00
		Entire	120.00	125.00
U93	U29	12c plum	100.00	82.50
		Entire	225.00	*450.00*
U94	U29	12c plum, *amber*	110.00	100.00
		Entire	225.00	*650.00*
U95	U29	12c plum, *cream*	225.00	200.00
		Entire	300.00	
U96	U30	15c red orange	75.00	75.00
		Entire	165.00	
a.		15c orange	75.00	
		Entire	200.00	
U97	U30	15c red orange, *amber*	160.00	275.00
		Entire	350.00	
a.		15c orange, *amber*	170.00	
		Entire	350.00	
U98	U30	15c red orange, *cream*	300.00	375.00
		Entire	425.00	
a.		15c orange, *cream*	300.00	
		Entire	425.00	
U99	U31	24c purple	110.00	125.00
		Entire	180.00	
U100	U31	24c purple, *amber*	180.00	300.00
		Entire	375.00	
U101	U31	24c purple, *cream*	225.00	450.00
		Entire	450.00	
U102	U32	30c black	60.00	120.00
		Entire	290.00	*750.00*
U103	U32	30c black, *amber*	180.00	450.00
		Entire	600.00	
U104	U32	30c black, *cream*	150.00	450.00
		Entire	425.00	
U105	U33	90c carmine	125.00	300.00
		Entire	260.00	
U106	U33	90c carmine, *amber*	350.00	900.00
		Entire	800.00	*4,500.*
U107	U33	90c carmine, *cream*	175.00	*2,250.*
		Entire	450.00	*5,000.*

Printed by Plimpton Manufacturing Co.

The profiles in this issue are inferior to the fine engraving of the Reay issue.

U34

Bust forms an angle at the back near the frame. Lettering poorly executed. Distinct circle in "O" of "Postage."

U35

Lower part of bust points to the end of the "E" in "ONE." Head inclined downward.

U36

Bust narrow at back. Thin numerals. Head of "P" narrow. Bust broad at front, ending in sharp corners.

U37

Bust broad. Figures of value in long ovals.

U38

Similar to U37 but the figure "2" at the left touches the oval.

U39

Similar to U37 but the "O" of "TWO" has the center netted instead of plain and the "G" of "POSTAGE" and the "C" of "CENTS" have diagonal crossline.

U40

Bust broad: numerals in ovals short and thick.

U41

Similar to U40 but the ovals containing the numerals are much heavier. A diagonal line runs from the upper part of the "U" to the white frame-line.

U42

Similar to U40 but the middle stroke of "N" in "CENTS" is as thin as the vertical strokes.

U43

Bottom of bust cut almost semi-circularly.

U44

Thin lettering, long thin figures of value.

U45

Thick lettering, well-formed figures of value, queue does not project below bust.

U46

Top of head egg-shaped; knot of queue well marked and projects triangularly.

Taylor — U47

Die 1- Figures of value with thick, curved tops

Die 2- Figures of value with long, thin tops

U48

Neck short at back.

U49

Figures of value turned up at the ends.

U50

Very large head.

U51

Knot of queue stands out prominently.

U52

Ear prominent, chin receding.

U53

No side whiskers, forelock projects above head.

U54

Hair does not project; ornaments around the inner oval end in points.

U55

Back of bust rather broad, chin slopes considerably; labels containing figures of value are not exactly parallel.

U56

Front of bust sloping; inner lines of shields project considerably into the inner oval.

1874-86 **Design U34**

No.		Description	Unused	Used
U108		1c dark blue	175.00	60.00
		Entire	250.00	110.00
	a.	1c light blue	175.00	60.00
		Entire	250.00	125.00
U109		1c dk bl, *amb*	150.00	75.00
		Entire	200.00	140.00
+U110		1c dk blue, *cr*	1,000.	
U111		1c dk blue, *org*	15.00	15.00
		Entire	30.00	25.00
	a.	dk blue, *org*	12.50	12.50
		Entire	30.00	25.00

W112 1c dk blue, *man* 62.50 40.00
Entire 105.00 72.50

Design U35

U113 1c light blue 2.25 1.00
Entire 4.00 2.00
a. 1c dark blue 7.00 7.00
Entire 27.50 20.00
U114 1c lt blue, *amb* 3.25 3.25
Entire 8.25 6.00
a. dk blue, *amb* 17.50 10.00
Entire 30.00 20.00
U115 1c blue, *cr* 4.25 4.25
Entire 10.00 6.50
a. dk blue, *cr* 17.50 8.50
Entire 32.50 20.00
U116 1c lt blue, *org* .75 .40
Entire 1.25 1.00
a. dk blue, *org* 4.00 2.50
Entire 16.00 8.00
U117 1c lt bl, *bl* ('80) 7.50 5.00
Entire 13.50 9.00
U118 1c lt bl, *fawn* ('79) 7.00 5.00
Entire 14.00 10.00
U119 1c lt bl, *man* ('86) 8.00 3.25
Entire 17.00 5.00
W120 1c lt bl, *man* 1.25 1.10
Entire 2.75 1.75
a. dk bl, *man* 8.00 7.00
Entire 16.00 15.00
U121 1c lt bl, *amb man* 17.50 10.00
Entire 29.00 20.00

Design U36

U122 2c brown 140.00 65.00
Entire 190.00 85.00
U123 2c brown, *amb* 67.50 40.00
Entire 125.00 70.00
+U124 2c brn, *crm* 1,000.
+U125 2c brn, *org* 18,000.
Entire *35,000.*
W126 2c brn, *man* 125.00 85.00
Entire 275.00 160.00
W127 2c ver, *man* 2,500. 500.00
Entire 3,250. *5,000.*

Design U37

U128 2c brown 60.00 35.00
Entire 110.00 75.00
U129 2c brn, *amb* 80.00 45.00
Entire 125.00 77.50
+U130 2c brn, *cr* 35,000.
W131 2c brn, *man* 17.50 15.00
Entire 29.00 26.00

Design U38

U132 2c brown 70.00 27.50
Entire 120.00 80.00
U133 2c brn, *amb* 325.00 70.00
Entire 550.00 140.00
+U133A 2c brn, *cr* 70,000.

Design U39

U134 2c brown 800.00 160.00
Entire 1,400. 300.00
U135 2c brn, *amb* 425.00 150.00
Entire 650.00 160.00
U136 2c brn, *org* 50.00 27.50
Entire 80.00 37.50
W137 2c brn, *man* 75.00 40.00
Entire 125.00 55.00
+U137A 2c ver 32,500.
+U137B 2c ver, *amb* 30,000.
Entire —
+U137C 2c ver, *org* 70,000.
+W138 2c ver, *man* 25,000.

Design U40

U139 2c brn ('75) 57.50 37.50
Entire 82.50 47.50
U140 2c brn,*amb* ('75) 85.00 62.50
Entire 130.00 77.50
+U140A 2c reddish brn, *org* ('75) 17,500.
Entire 32,500.
W141 2c brn, *man* ('75) 32.50 25.00
Entire 45.00 32.50
U142 2c ver ('75) 8.00 5.00
Entire 16.00 9.00
a. 2c pink 8.00 5.00
Entire 16.00 9.00
U143 2c ver, *amb* ('75) 9.00 5.00
Entire 16.00 9.00
U144 2c ver, *cr* ('75) 17.50 7.00
Entire 25.00 12.50
+U145 2c ver, *org* ('75) 35,000.
U146 2c ver, *bl* ('80) 110.00 40.00
Entire *200.00* 140.00
U147 2c ver, *fawn* ('75) 7.00 5.00
Entire 15.00 7.00
W148 2c ver, *man* ('75) 4.00 3.50
Entire 9.00 6.50

Design U41

U149 2c ver ('78) 45.00 25.00
Entire 90.00 40.00
a. 2c pink 52.50 27.00
Entire 90.00 42.50
U150 2c ver, *amb* ('78) 35.00 15.00
Entire 60.00 22.50
U151 2c ver, *bl* ('80) 10.00 8.00
Entire 20.00 15.00
a. 2c pink, *blue* 11.00 8.00
Entire 17.50 12.50

U152 2c ver, *fawn* ('78) 10.00 4.00
Entire 17.50 9.00

Design U42

U153 2c ver ('76) 75.00 30.00
Entire 115.00 40.00
U154 2c ver, *amb* ('76) 300.00 90.00
Entire 450.00 175.00
W155 2c ver, *man* ('76) 20.00 10.00
Entire 45.00 20.00

Design U43

U156 2c ver ('81) 1,250. 175.00
Entire 2,000. *500.00*
U157 2c ver, *amb* ('81) *42,500.* *27,500.*
Entire *60,000.*
W158 2c ver, *man* ('81) 90.00 55.00
Entire 200.00 200.00

Design U44

U159 3c green 35.00 10.00
Entire 60.00 17.50
U160 3c grn, *amb* 35.00 10.00
Entire 60.00 20.00
U161 3c grn, *cr* 35.00 12.00
Entire 65.00 30.00
+U162 3c grn, *bl* 75,000.

Design U45

U163 3c green 1.40 .30
Entire 4.25 2.25
U164 3c grn, *amb* 1.50 .70
Entire 4.25 2.00
U165 3c grn, *cr* 8.50 6.50
Entire 19.00 9.00
U166 3c grn, *bl* 7.50 6.00
Entire 17.00 11.00
U167 3c grn, *fawn* ('75) 4.75 3.50
Entire 9.25 5.00

Design U46

U168 3c grn ('81) 1,000. 80.00
Entire 4,250. 275.00
U169 3c grn, *amb* 450.00 140.00
Entire 700.00 300.00
U170 3c grn, *bl* ('81) *11,500.* *2,750.*
Entire *20,000.* *4,250.*
U171 3c grn, *fawn* ('81) *40,000.* *2,750.*
Entire *10,000.*

Design U47

U172 5c bl, die I ('75) 10.00 10.00
Entire 20.00 16.00
U173 5c bl, die I, *amb* ('75) 12.50 11.00
Entire 21.00 17.00
U174 5c bl, die I, *cr* ('75) 95.00 45.00
Entire 175.00 95.00
U175 5c bl, die I, *bl* ('75) 25.00 17.50
Entire 45.00 27.50
U176 5c bl, die I, *fawn* ('75) 150.00 65.00
Entire 250.00
U177 5c bl, die 2 ('75) 11.00 9.00
Entire 18.00 18.00
U178 5c bl, die 2, *amb* ('75) 8.00 8.00
Entire 18.00 19.00
+U178A 5c bl, die 2, *cr* ('76) *10,000.*
Entire *17,500.*
U179 5c bl, die 2, *bl* ('75) 20.00 12.50
Entire 40.00 30.00
U180 5c bl, die 2, *fawn* ('75) 125.00 50.00
Entire 225.00 140.00

Design U48

U181 6c red 8.00 6.50
Entire 15.00 12.50
a. 6c vermilion 8.00 6.50
Entire 15.00 12.50
U182 6c red, *amber* 12.50 6.50
Entire 24.00 15.00
a. 6c ver, *amb* 12.50 6.50
Entire 24.00 15.00
U183 6c red, *cream* 50.00 17.50
Entire 85.00 40.00
a. 6c ver, *cr* 45.00 15.00
Entire 82.50 40.00
U184 6c red, *fawn* ('75) 17.50 12.50
Entire 32.50 29.00

Design U49

+U185 7c vermilion *1,200.*
U186 7c ver, *amb* 125.00 75.00
Entire 225.00

Design U50

U187 10c brown 40.00 20.00
Entire 65.00
U188 10c brn, *amb* 75.00 35.00
Entire 150.00

Design U51

U189 10c choc ('75) 6.00 4.00
Entire 12.00 9.25
a. 10c bister brown 7.00 5.00
Entire 12.50 10.50
b. 10c yellow ocher *3,000.*
Entire *5,250.*
U190 10c choc, *amb* ('75) 7.00 6.00
Entire 13.00 11.50
a. 10c bis brn, *amb* 7.00 6.00
Entire 13.00 11.50
b. 10c yel ocher, *amb* *3,000.*
Entire *5,250.*
U191 10c brn, *oriental buff* ('86) 12.50 8.75
Entire 20.00 11.50
U192 10c brn, *bl* ('86) 12.50 8.00
Entire 20.00 15.00
a. 10c gray blk, *bl* 12.50 7.50
Entire 20.00 15.00
b. 10c red brn, *bl* 12.50 7.50
Entire 20.00 15.00
U193 10c brn, *man* ('86) 12.50 10.00
Entire 22.50 16.00
a. 10c red brn, *man* 12.50 10.00
Entire 22.50 16.00
U194 10c brn, *amb man* ('86) 17.50 9.00
Entire 26.00 17.50
a. 10c red brn, *amb man* 17.50 9.00
Entire 26.00 17.50

Design U52

U195 12c plum 250.00 100.00
Entire 575.00
U196 12c plum, *amb* 200.00 160.00
Entire 350.00
U197 12c plum, *cr* 180.00 130.00
Entire 850.00

Design U53

U198 15c orange 50.00 35.00
Entire 100.00 55.00
U199 15c org, *amb* 140.00 130.00
Entire 300.00
U200 15c org, *cr* 450.00 300.00
Entire 800.00

Design U54

U201 24c purple 175.00 150.00
Entire 260.00
a. Printed on both sides, one inverted and overlapping, cut to shape 450.00
U202 24c pur, *amb* 180.00 100.00
Entire 270.00
U203 24c pur, *cr* 170.00 100.00
Entire 750.00

Design U55

U204 30c black 55.00 25.00
Entire 90.00 65.00
U205 30c blk, *amb* 70.00 60.00
Entire 130.00 *250.00*
U206 30c blk, *cr* ('75) 325.00 325.00
Entire 625.00
U207 30c blk, *oriental buff* ('81) 90.00 80.00
Entire 160.00
U208 30c blk, *blue* ('81) 90.00 80.00
Entire 170.00
U209 30c blk, *man* ('81) 80.00 70.00
Entire 190.00
U210 30c blk, *amb man* ('86) 170.00 100.00
Entire 250.00

Design U56

U211 90c carmine ('75) 85.00 75.00
Entire 140.00 100.00
U212 90c car, *amb* ('75) 175.00 250.00
Entire 250.00
U213 90c car, *cr* ('75) 1,000.
Entire 2,000.
U214 90c car, *oriental buff* ('86) 140.00 250.00
Entire 300.00 300.00
U215 90c car, *bl* ('86) 175.00 250.00
Entire 275.00 325.00
U216 90c car, *man* ('86) 120.00 225.00
Entire 240.00 275.00
U217 90c car, *amb man* ('86) 140.00 *200.00*
Entire 240.00 *300.00*

Note: No. U206 has watermark #2; No. U207 watermark #6 or #7. No U213 has watermark #2; No. U214 watermark #7. These envelopes cannot be positively identified except by the watermark.

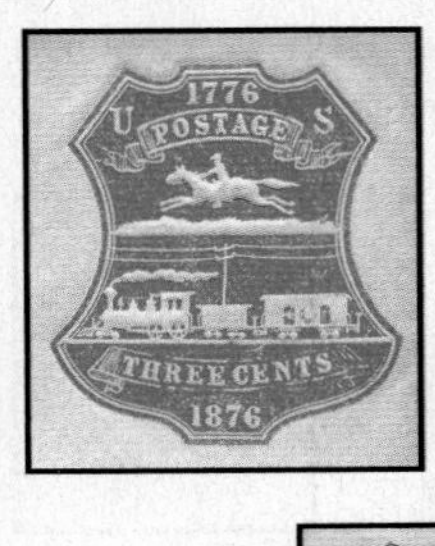

Single line under "POSTAGE" U57

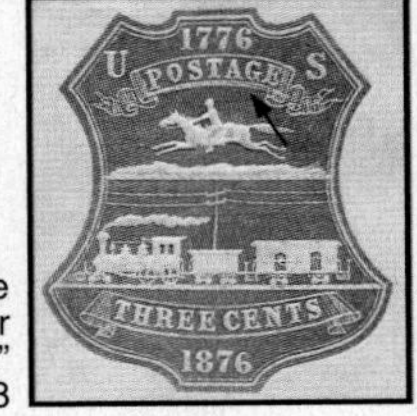

Double line under "POSTAGE" U58

1876

U218 U57 3c red 30.00 25.00
Entire 65.00 50.00
U219 U57 3c green 30.00 17.50
Entire 60.00 40.00
+U220 U58 3c red *27,500.*
Entire *42,500.*
U221 U58 3c green 30.00 25.00
Entire 75.00 50.00

Cent. of the U.S., and the World's Fair at Philadelphia.

Used examples of Nos. U218-U221 with exposition cancels and/or typed addresses sell for a premium.

See No. U582.

Garfield — U59

1882-86

U222 U59 5c brown 5.00 3.00
Entire 10.00 7.50
U223 U59 5c brn, *amb* 5.25 3.50
Entire 11.00 10.00
+U224 U59 5c brn, *oriental buff* ('86) 130.00
Entire 200.00
+U225 U59 5c brn, *bl* 75.00
Entire 120.00
U226 U59 5c brn, *fawn* 300.00
Entire 450.00

Washington — U60

1883, October

U227 U60 2c red 5.50 2.25
Entire 11.00 4.00
a. 2c brown (error), entire *4,000.*
U228 U60 2c red, *amb* 6.50 2.75
Entire 12.00 6.00
U229 U60 2c red, *blue* 8.00 5.00
Entire 12.50 8.00
U230 U60 2c red, *fawn* 9.00 5.25
Entire 14.00 7.00

Wavy lines fine and clear — U61

1883, November

Four Wavy Lines in Oval

U231 U61 2c red 5.00 2.50
Entire 9.50 4.00
U232 U61 2c red, *amb* 6.00 3.75
Entire 11.00 5.75
U233 U61 2c red, *blue* 10.00 7.50
Entire 19.00 10.00

No.	Type	Description	Unused	Used
U234	U61	2c red, *fawn*	7.50	4.75
		Entire	11.00	6.00
W235	U61	2c red, *man*	18.00	6.25
		Entire	30.00	12.50

Wavy lines thick and blurred — U62

Retouched die.

1884, June

No.	Type	Description	Unused	Used
U236	U62	2c red	15.00	4.00
		Entire	20.00	7.75
U237	U62	2c red, *amber*	20.00	10.00
		Entire	30.00	11.00
U238	U62	2c red, *blue*	29.00	12.00
		Entire	40.00	15.00
U239	U62	2c red, *fawn*	20.00	11.00
		Entire	32.50	12.50

See Nos. U260-W269.

3½ links over left "2" — U63

No.	Type	Description	Unused	Used
U240	U63	2c red	90.00	45.00
		Entire	150.00	72.50
U241	U63	2c red, *amb*	550.00	300.00
		Entire	1,500.	750.00
U242	U63	2c red, *fawn*		*25,000.*
		Entire		*47,500.*

2 links below right "2" — U64

No.	Type	Description	Unused	Used
U243	U64	2c red	110.00	75.00
		Entire	155.00	100.00
U244	U64	2c red, *amb*	250.00	100.00
		Entire	400.00	125.00
U245	U64	2c red, *blue*	300.00	210.00
		Entire	500.00	225.00
U246	U64	2c red, *fawn*	300.00	200.00
		Entire	525.00	275.00

Round "O" in "TWO." White lines above "WO" of "TWO" joined to form thick white dash. — U65

No.	Type	Description	Unused	Used
U247	U65	2c red	2,000.	400.00
		Entire	3,000.	*1,100.*
U248	U65	2c red, *amb*	3,750.	750.00
		Entire	5,500.	*1,650.*
U249	U65	2c red, *fawn*	1,100.	500.00
		Entire	1,500.	*750.00*

See Nos. U270-U276.

Jackson — U66

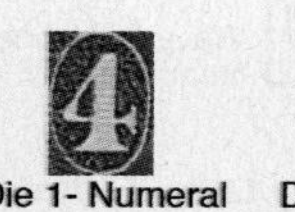

Die 1- Numeral at left is 2¾ mm wide

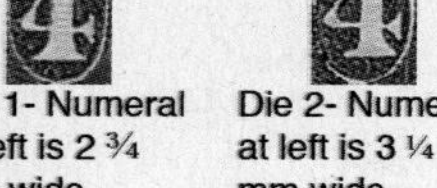

Die 2- Numeral at left is 3¼ mm wide

1883-86

No.	Type	Description	Unused	Used
U250	U66	4c green, die 1	4.00	3.50
		Entire	6.50	6.00
U251	U66	4c grn, die 1, *amb*	5.00	3.50
		Entire	7.50	5.25
U252	U66	4c grn, die 1, *oriental buff* ('86)	13.00	9.00
		Entire	18.00	12.50
U253	U66	4c green, die 1, *blue* ('86)	11.00	6.50
		Entire	18.00	8.00
U254	U66	4c grn, die 1, *man* ('86)	16.00	7.50
		Entire	21.00	15.00
U255	U66	4c grn, die 1, *amb man* ('86)	22.50	10.00
		Entire	32.50	15.00
U256	U66	4c green, die 2	8.00	5.00
		Entire	17.50	6.75
U257	U66	4c grn, die 2, *amb*	12.50	7.00
		Entire	22.50	10.00
U258	U66	4c grn, die 2, *man* ('86)	12.50	7.50
		Entire	22.50	12.50
U259	U66	4c grn, die 2, *amb man* ('86)	12.50	7.50
		Entire	22.50	12.50

1884, May

No.	Type	Description	Unused	Used
U260	U61	2c brown	17.50	5.75
		Entire	20.00	9.00
U261	U61	2c brown, *amber*	17.50	6.50
		Entire	20.00	7.50
U262	U61	2c brown, *blue*	17.50	10.00
		Entire	26.00	14.00
U263	U61	2c brown, *fawn*	15.00	9.25
		Entire	20.00	12.50
W264	U61	2c brown, *manila*	15.00	11.50
		Entire	25.00	19.00

1884, June

Retouched Die

No.	Type	Description	Unused	Used
U265	U62	2c brown	15.00	6.50
		Entire	25.00	12.00
U266	U62	2c brn, *amb*	60.00	40.00
		Entire	70.00	50.00
U267	U62	2c brown, *blue*	22.50	9.00
		Entire	30.00	15.00
U268	U62	2c brown, *fawn*	15.00	11.00
		Entire	21.00	15.00
W269	U62	2c brn, *man*	25.00	15.00
		Entire	32.50	24.00

2 Links Below Right "2"

No.	Type	Description	Unused	Used
U270	U64	2c brown	115.00	50.00
		Entire	150.00	110.00
U271	U64	2c brn, *amb*	425.00	125.00
		Entire	575.00	350.00
U272	U64	2c brown, *fawn*	*7,000.*	*2,000.*
		Entire	*8,500.*	*4,000.*

Round "O" in "Two"

No.	Type	Description	Unused	Used
U273	U65	2c brown	225.00	100.00
		Entire	375.00	190.00
U274	U65	2c brn, *amb*	225.00	100.00
		Entire	375.00	190.00
U275	U65	2c brown, *blue*		*10,000.*
		Entire		*47,500.*
U276	U65	2c brown, *fawn*	700.00	750.00
		Entire	1,000.	*1,200.*

U67

Extremity of bust below the queue forms a point.

Washington — U68

Extremity of bust is rounded.

Similar to U61
Two wavy lines in oval

1884-86

No.	Type	Description	Unused	Used
U277	U67	2c brown	.50	.25
		Entire	1.00	.40
a.		2c brown lake, die 1	22.50	21.00
		Entire	27.50	26.00
U278	U67	2c brn, *amb*	.65	.50
		Entire	1.75	.75
a.		2c brown lake, *amber*	35.00	25.00
		Entire	42.50	32.50
U279	U67	2c brn, *oriental buff* ('86)	6.00	2.10
		Entire	9.50	3.00
U280	U67	2c brown, *blue*	3.00	2.10
		Entire	4.50	3.50
U281	U67	2c brown, *fawn*	3.75	2.40
		Entire	5.50	4.00
U282	U67	2c brn, *man* ('86)	12.00	4.00
		Entire	17.50	6.50
W283	U67	2c brn, *man*	8.00	5.00
		Entire	11.00	6.50
U284	U67	2c brn, *amb man* ('86)	7.00	5.75
		Entire	15.00	7.00
+U285	U67	2c red	600.00	
		Entire	1,200.	
+U286	U67	2c red, *blue*	225.00	
		Entire	350.00	
W287	U67	2c red, *manila*	150.00	
		Entire	210.00	
U288	U68	2c brown	275.00	50.00
		Entire	700.00	150.00
U289	U68	2c brn, *amb*	20.00	13.00
		Entire	25.00	17.00
U290	U68	2c brown, *blue*	850.00	325.00
		Entire	1,600.	450.00
U291	U68	2c brown, *fawn*	25.00	25.00
		Entire	45.00	32.50
W292	U68	2c brn, *man*	30.00	19.00
		Entire	45.00	22.50

Gen. U.S. Grant — US1

Letter Sheet, 160x271mm

1886 Creamy White Paper

No.	Type	Description	Unused	Used
U293	US1	2c green, entire	30.00	20.00

See the Scott U.S. Specialized Catalogue for perforation and inscription varieties.

Franklin — U69

Washington U70

Bust points between third and fourth notches of inner oval "G" of "POSTAGE" has no bar.

U71

Bust points between second and third notches of inner oval; "G" of "POSTAGE" has a bar; ear is indicated by one heavy line; one vertical line at corner of mouth.

U72

Frame same as U71; upper part of head more rounded; ear indicated by two curved lines with two locks of hair in front; two vertical lines at corner of mouth.

Jackson — U73

Grant — U74

There is a space between the beard and the collar of the coat. A button is on the collar.

U75

The collar touches the beard and there is no button.

1887-94 Design U69

No.	Description	Unused	Used
U294	1c blue	.55	.25
	Entire	1.00	.50
U295	1c dk bl ('94)	6.50	2.50
	Entire	10.00	6.50
U296	1c bl, *amb*	3.25	1.25
	Entire	5.50	3.50
U297	1c dk bl, *amb* ('94)	40.00	22.50
	Entire	60.00	27.50
+U298	1c bl, *oriental buff*	*10,000.*	—
	Entire	*16,000.*	
+U299	1c bl, *bl*	*12,500.*	
	Entire	*21,000.*	
U300	1c bl, *man*	.65	.35
	Entire	1.25	.75
W301	1c bl, *man*	.45	.30
	Entire	1.25	.60
U302	1c dk bl, *man* ('94)	27.50	12.50
	Entire	35.00	20.00
W303	1c DK bl, *man* ('94)	12.50	10.00
	Entire	20.00	15.00
U304	1C bl, *amb man*	12.50	5.00
	Entire	17.50	7.50

Design U70

No.	Description	Unused	Used
U305	2c green	15.00	10.00
	Entire	32.50	15.00
U306	2c grn, *amb*	40.00	17.50
	Entire	55.00	22.50
U307	2c grn, *oriental buff*	80.00	40.00
	Entire	120.00	50.00
U308	2c grn, *bl*	*12,500.*	4,250.
	Entire		*22,000.*
U309	2c grn, *man*	*12,500.*	1,000.
	Entire	*25,000.*	1,200.
U310	2c grn, *amb man*	*27,500.*	*2,250.*
	Entire	—	*3,250.*

Design U71

No.	Description	Unused	Used
U311	2c green	.30	.25
	Entire	.70	.25
a.	2c dark green ('94)	.45	.30
	Entire	1.00	.85
b.	Double impression, entire	375.00	
U312	2c grn, *amb*	.40	.25
	Entire	.75	.30
a.	Double impression		
b.	2c dk grn, *amb* ('94)	.55	.35
	Entire	1.00	.85
U313	2c grn, *oriental buff*	.55	.25
	Entire	1.10	.40
a.	2c dk grn, *oriental buff* ('94)	2.00	1.00
	Entire	4.00	4.00
b.	Double impression	150.00	
U314	2c grn, *bl*	.60	.30
	Entire	1.20	.40
a.	2c dk grn, *bl* ('94)	.80	.40
	Entire	1.60	1.50
U315	2c grn, *man*	2.00	.50
	Entire	3.00	1.00
a.	2c dk grn, *man* ('94)	2.75	.75
	Entire	4.00	1.50
W316	2c grn, *man*	3.50	2.50
	Entire	10.00	7.00
U317	2c grn, *amb man*	2.50	1.90
	Entire	5.50	3.00
a.	2c dk grn, *amb man* ('94)	3.50	3.00
	Entire	7.00	4.00

Design U72

No.	Description	Unused	Used
U318	2c green	110.00	12.50
	Entire	190.00	50.00
U319	2c grn, *amb*	160.00	27.50
	Entire	260.00	50.00
U320	2c grn, *oriental buff*	125.00	40.00
	Entire	260.00	70.00
U321	2c grn, *bl*	150.00	70.00
	Entire	280.00	90.00
U322	2c grn, *man*	240.00	70.00
	Entire	300.00	110.00
U323	2c grn, *amb man*	400.00	100.00
	Entire	700.00	175.00

Design U73

No.	Description	Unused	Used
U324	4c carmine	3.25	2.00
	Entire	6.00	2.10
a.	4c lake	3.50	2.00
	Entire	7.00	3.75
b.	4c scarlet ('94)	3.50	2.00
	Entire	7.00	3.75
U325	4c car, *amb*	3.50	3.50
	Entire	7.00	4.00
a.	4c lake, *amber*	3.50	3.50
	Entire	7.25	4.00
b.	4c scarlet, *amber* ('94)	4.00	3.75
	Entire	8.00	4.25
U326	4c car, *oriental buff*	6.00	3.50
	Entire	14.00	6.25
a.	4c lake, *oriental buff*	7.00	3.50
	Entire	15.00	6.25
U327	4c car, *bl*	5.50	4.00
	Entire	12.00	7.00
a.	4c lake, *blue*	6.00	4.00
	Entire	13.00	6.00
U328	4c car, *man*	8.00	7.00
	Entire	13.00	7.50
a.	4c lake, *manila*	8.00	6.00
	Entire	13.00	7.50

b. 4c pink, *manila* 15.00 10.00
Entire 21.00 12.50
U329 4c car, *amb man* 6.00 3.25
Entire 12.50 5.00
a. 4c lake, *amb man* 6.00 3.25
Entire 12.50 5.00
b. 4c pink, *amb man* 15.00 10.00
Entire 21.00 12.50

Design U74

U330 5c blue 3.75 4.00
Entire 7.50 11.00
U331 5c bl, *amb* 5.00 2.50
Entire 11.00 14.00
a. Double impression, entire —
U332 5c bl, *oriental buff* 5.50 4.00
Entire 16.00 18.00
U333 5c blue, *blue* 7.00 6.00
Entire 17.00 15.00

Design U75

U334 5c blue ('94) 17.50 12.50
Entire 35.00 22.50
U335 5c bl, *amb* ('94) 9.00 7.50
Entire 18.00 40.00

Design U55

U336 30c red brn 35.00 45.00
Entire 60.00 *475.00*
a. 30c yellow brown 35.00 45.00
Entire 60.00 *475.00*
b. 30c chocolate 35.00 45.00
Entire 60.00 *475.00*
U337 30c red brn, *amb* 35.00 45.00
Entire 60.00 *475.00*
a. 30c yel brn, *amb* 35.00 45.00
Entire 60.00 *475.00*
b. 30c choc, *amb* 35.00 45.00
Entire 60.00 *475.00*
U338 30c red brn, *oriental buff* 35.00 45.00
Entire 60.00 *475.00*
a. 30c yel brn, *oriental buff* 35.00 45.00
Entire 60.00 *475.00*
U339 30c red brn, *bl* 35.00 45.00
Entire 60.00 *475.00*
a. 30c yel brn, *bl* 35.00 45.00
Entire 60.00 *475.00*
U340 30c red brn, *man* 35.00 45.00
Entire 60.00 *475.00*
a. 30c brown, *manila* 35.00 45.00
Entire 60.00 *475.00*
U341 30c red brn, *amb man* 35.00 45.00
Entire 75.00 *475.00*
a. 30c yel brn, *amb man* 35.00 45.00
Entire 75.00 *475.00*

Design U56

U342 90c purple 55.00 85.00
Entire 100.00 *1,050.*
U343 90c pur, *amb* 65.00 85.00
Entire 120.00 *1,050.*
U344 90c pur, *oriental buff* 75.00 85.00
Entire 140.00 *1,050.*
U345 90c pur, *bl* 75.00 85.00
Entire 140.00 *1,050.*
U346 90c pur, *man* 80.00 85.00
Entire 150.00 *1,050.*
U347 90c pur, *amb man* 80.00 85.00
Entire 150.00 *1,050.*

Columbus and Liberty — U76

1893

U348 U76 1c deep blue 2.00 1.25
Entire 3.00 2.00
U349 U76 2c violet 1.50 .50
Entire 3.50 .60
a. 2c dark slate (error) *2,250.*
Entire *4,500.*
U350 U76 5c chocolate 6.50 7.00
Entire 12.00 10.00
a. 5c slate brown (error) *750.00* *950.00*
Entire *1,100.* *1,500.*
U351 U76 10c slate brown 25.00 27.50
Entire 65.00 57.50
Nos. U348-U351 (4) 35.00 36.25

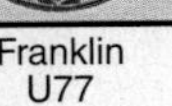
Franklin U77

Washington U78

Bust points to first notch of inner oval and is only slightly concave below.

U79

Bust points to middle of second notch of inner oval and is quite hollow below. Queue has ribbon around it.

U80

Same as die 2, but hair flowing. No ribbon on queue.

Lincoln — U81

Bust pointed but not draped.

U82

Bust broad and draped.

U83

Head larger, inner oval has no notches.

Grant — U84

Similar to design of 1887-95 but smaller.

1899

U352 U77 1c green 2.00 .25
Entire 4.75 .50
U353 U77 1c green, *amber* 5.00 1.50
Entire 8.50 2.75
U354 U77 1c green, *oriental buff* 7.50 2.75
Entire 16.00 3.75
U355 U77 1c green, *blue* 10.00 7.50
Entire 19.00 12.50
U356 U77 1c green, *manila* 2.50 .95
Entire 6.50 2.00
W357 U77 1c green, *manila* 2.75 1.10
Entire 9.00 4.00
U358 U78 2c carmine 3.00 1.75
Entire 8.00 3.25
U359 U78 2c car, *amb* 15.00 12.50
Entire 27.50 21.00
U360 U78 2c carmine, *oriental buff* 17.50 11.00
Entire 30.00 15.00
U361 U78 2c carmine, *blue* 55.00 35.00
Entire 75.00 52.50
U362 U79 2c carmine .35 .25
Entire .65 .30
a. 2c dark lake 30.00 30.00
Entire 37.50 35.00
U363 U79 2c car, *amb* 1.75 .25
Entire 2.75 .60
U364 U79 2c carmine, *oriental buff* 1.20 .25
Entire 3.00 .60
U365 U79 2c carmine, *blue* 1.50 .55
Entire 3.50 2.00
W366 U79 2c car, *man* 9.00 3.25
Entire 15.00 7.50
U367 U80 2c carmine 5.00 2.75
Entire 10.00 6.75
U368 U80 2c car, *amb* 8.00 6.50
Entire 14.00 12.00
U369 U80 2c carmine, *oriental buff* 17.50 12.50
Entire 27.50 20.00
U370 U80 2c carmine, *blue* 11.00 10.00
Entire 25.00 15.00
U371 U81 4c brown 15.00 12.50
Entire 27.50 18.00
U372 U81 4c brown, *amber* 15.00 12.50
Entire 30.00 24.00
U373 U82 4c brown *6,500.* 1,100.
Entire *9,000.*
U374 U83 4c brown 10.00 8.00
Entire 26.00 12.50
U375 U83 4c brown, *amber* 60.00 25.00
Entire 80.00 40.00
W376 U83 4c brown, *manila* 12.50 12.50
Entire 35.00 37.50
U377 U84 5c blue 9.00 9.00
Entire 16.00 16.00
U378 U84 5c blue, *amber* 10.00 10.00
Entire 20.00 17.00

Franklin — U85

Washington — U86

"D" of "UNITED" contains vertical line at right that parallels the left vertical line. One short and two long vertical lines at the right of "CENTS."

Grant — U87

Lincoln — U88

1903

U379 U85 1c green .75 .25
Entire 1.20 .35
U380 U85 1c green, *amber* 10.00 2.00
Entire 20.00 7.00
U381 U85 1c green, *oriental buff* 12.50 2.50
Entire 22.50 3.00
U382 U85 1c green, *blue* 15.00 2.50
Entire 30.00 3.00
U383 U85 1c green, *manila* 3.50 .90
Entire 5.00 1.25
W384 U85 1c green, *manila* 2.50 .40
Entire 4.50 .80
U385 U86 2c carmine .40 .25
Entire .85 .35
a. 2c pink 2.00 1.50
Entire 3.00 2.00
b. 2c red 2.00 1.50
Entire 3.00 2.00
U386 U86 2c carmine, *amber* 2.00 .50
Entire 3.50 .80
a. 2c pink, *amber* 5.50 3.00
Entire 7.50 4.00
b. 2c red, *amber* 12.50 7.00
Entire 20.00 10.00
U387 U86 2c carmine, *oriental buff* 2.00 .30
Entire 3.25 .35
a. 2c pink, *oriental buff* 3.50 2.00
Entire 5.00 3.00
b. 2c red, *oriental buff* 4.00 2.25
Entire 5.50 3.25
U388 U86 2c carmine, *blue* 1.75 .50
Entire 2.75 .60
a. 2c pink, *blue* 17.50 14.00
Entire 30.00 18.00
b. 2c red, *blue* 17.50 14.00
Entire 30.00 18.00
W389 U86 2c carmine, *manila* 15.00 9.00
Entire 25.00 14.00
U390 U87 4c choc 17.50 11.00
Entire 30.00 14.00
U391 U87 4c choc, *amber* 17.50 11.00
Entire 32.50 14.00
W392 U87 4c choc, *manila* 20.00 12.50
Entire 45.00 35.00
U393 U88 5c blue 15.00 11.00
Entire 30.00 16.00
U394 U88 5c blue, *amber* 15.00 11.00
Entire 30.00 18.00

U89

Re-cut die — "D" of "UNITED" is well rounded at right. The three lines at the right of "CENTS" and at the left of "TWO" are usually all short; the lettering is heavier and the ends of the ribbons slightly changed.

1904 Re-cut Die

U395 U89 2c carmine .75 .25
Entire 1.75 .45
a. 2c pink 5.00 2.50
U396 U89 2c carmine, *amber* 7.50 1.00
Entire 12.50 2.00
a. 2c pink, *amber* 8.50 3.00
U397 U89 2c carmine, *oriental buff* 5.00 1.10
Entire 8.00 1.50
a. 2c pink, *oriental buff* 6.50 2.75
U398 U89 2c carmine, *blue* 3.75 .90
Entire 5.50 1.40
a. 2c pink, *blue* 5.00 2.50
W399 U89 2c carmine, *manila* 12.50 8.00
Entire 30.00 24.00
a. 2c pink, *manila* 25.00 17.50
Entire 70.00 85.00
b. Double impression, entire *375.00*

Franklin — U90

Die 1

Die 2

Die 3

Die 4

Die 1 — Wide "D" in "UNITED."
Die 2 — Narrow "D" in "UNITED."
Die 3 — Wide "S-S" in "STATES" (1910).
Die 4 — Sharp angle at back of bust, "N" and "E" of "ONE" are parallel (1912).

1907-16 Die 1

U400 U90 1c green .35 .25
Entire 1.00 .75
Wove paper .35 .25
Entire 2.00 2.00
a. Die 2, laid paper .85 .25
Entire 1.50 .75
Wove paper .85 .25
Entire 1.50 .75
b. Die 3, laid paper .85 .55
Entire 1.50 1.50
Wove paper 2.00 2.00
Entire 6.50 8.00
c. Die 4, laid paper .85 .25
Entire 1.50 1.00
Wove paper .85 .25
Entire 1.50 1.00
U401 U90 1c green, *amber* 2.00 .40
Entire 3.00 2.50
Wove paper 2.00 .40
Entire 3.50 1.50
a. Die 2, laid paper 2.50 1.00
Entire 4.00 3.00
Wove paper 3.00 2.50

Entire 5.00 5.00
b. Die 3, laid paper 3.25 3.00
Entire 4.00 5.00
Wove paper 75.00 50.00
Entire 100.00 75.00
c. Die 4, laid paper 2.00 1.00
Entire 4.00 3.00
Wove paper 2.00 .65
Entire 3.00 2.50

U402 U90 1c green, *oriental buff* .75 .75
Entire 1.00 2.50
Wove paper .75 .75
Entire 1.50 2.50
a. Die 2 12.00 1.50
Entire 18.50 1.75
b. Die 3, laid paper 14.00 1.50
Entire 20.00 2.50
Wove paper 1.00 .75
Entire 2.50 3.00
c. Die 4 1.00 .75
Entire 1.50 2.50

U403 U90 1c green, *blue* .75 .75
Entire 1.50 2.25
Wove paper 1.00 1.00
Entire 2.50 4.00
a. Die 2 12.00 3.00
Entire 16.50 4.00
b. Die 3 11.50 3.00
Entire 16.00 7.00
c. Die 4, laid paper .75 .65
Entire 1.00 1.50
Wove paper 1.00 .75
Entire 2.50 3.50

U404 U90 1c green, *manila* 2.00 1.90
Entire 3.75 4.50
Wove paper .75 1.00
Entire 2.00 5.25
a. Die 3 4.50 3.00
Entire 7.00 4.50

W405 U90 1c green, *manila* .65 .25
Entire 1.00 2.00
Wove paper 1.00 1.00
Entire 3.25 10.00
a. Die 2 60.00 25.00
Entire 90.00 30.00
b. Die 3 11.00 4.00
Entire 36.00 25.00
c. Die 4 *1,000.* —
Entire — —
d. Double impression, entire *175.00*

Washington — U91

U91 Die 1 — carmine

U91 Die 2

U91 Die 3

U91 Die 4

U91 Die 5

U91 Die 6

U91 Die 7

U91 Die 8

Die 1 — Oval "O" in "TWO" and "C" in "CENTS." Front of bust broad.

Die 2 — Similar to 1 but hair re-cut in two distinct locks at top of head.

Die 3 — Round "O" in "TWO" and "C" in "CENTS," coarse lettering.

Die 4 — Similar to 3 but lettering fine and clear, hair lines clearly embossed. Inner oval thin and clear.

Die 5 — All "S's" wide (1910).

Die 6 — Similar to 1 but front of bust narrow (1913).

Die 7 — Similar to 6 but upper corner of front of bust cut away (1916).

Die 8 — Similar to 7 but lower stroke of "S" in "CENTS" is a straight line. Hair as in Die 2 (1916).

Die 1

U406 U91 2c brown red .90 .25
Entire 2.60 .30
a. Die 2 40.00 7.00
Entire 95.00 50.00
b. Die 3 .80 .25
Entire 2.50 1.00

U407 U91 2c brown red, *amber* 6.50 2.00
Entire 9.00 6.00
a. Die 2 350.00 65.00
Entire 700.00 200.00
b. Die 3 4.50 1.25
Entire 7.00 6.00

U408 U91 2c brown red, *oriental buff* 8.75 1.50
Entire 12.00 3.75
a. Die 2 275.00 125.00
Entire 500.00 300.00
b. Die 3 7.50 2.50
Entire 11.00 5.00

U409 U91 2c brn red, *blue* 5.75 2.00
Entire 8.00 3.75
a. Die 2 375.00 200.00
Entire 550.00 500.00
b. Die 3 5.75 1.75
Entire 8.00 3.50

W410 U91 2c brn red, *man* 35.00 35.00
Entire 52.50 45.00

U411 U91 2c carmine .35 .25
Entire 1.00 .75
Wove paper .55 .45
Entire 1.50 1.00
a. Die 2, laid paper .75 .25
Entire 2.00 1.50
Wove paper 1.00 .55
Entire 2.00 .50
b. Die 3, laid paper .75 .25
Entire 2.00 1.00
Wove paper 1.20 1.50
Entire 4.00 7.00
c. Die 4, laid paper .65 .25
Entire 1.00 .75
Wove paper .75 .25
Entire 1.50 1.00
d. Die 5, laid paper .65 .30
Entire 1.50 1.00
Wove paper 1.00 1.00
Entire 2.00 5.00
e. Die 6, laid paper .60 .25
Entire 1.50 .75
Wove paper .60 .25
Entire 1.00 .75
f. Die 7, wove paper 3.00 3.00
Entire 12.00 10.00
Laid paper 75.00 25.00
Entire 125.00 100.00
g. Die 8 37.50 25.00
Entire 52.50 30.00
h. #U411 with added impression of #U400, entire 475.00
i. #U411 with added impression of #U416a, entire 475.00
k. As No. U411, double impression, entire 175.00

U412 U91 2c carmine, *amb* .50 .25
Entire 1.50 .75
Wove paper .50 .25
Entire 1.50 .75
a. Die 2, laid paper 1.00 .25
Entire 3.50 4.00
Wove paper 1.00 1.00
Entire 2.50 15.00
b. Die 3, laid paper 2.25 2.00
Entire 3.00 5.00
Wove paper 45.00 25.00
Entire 75.00 60.00
c. Die 4, laid paper .55 .25
Entire 1.50 .75
Wove paper 1.00 1.00
Entire 5.00 7.50
d. Die 5 .90 .35
Entire 1.50 .55
e. Die 6, laid paper .70 .25
Entire 1.50 .75
Wove paper .60 .25
Entire 1.00 .75
f. Die 7, wove paper 35.00 25.00
Entire 50.00 32.50
Laid paper 125.00 100.00
Entire 250.00 250.00

U413 U91 2c car, *oriental buff* .55 .25
Entire 1.00 .75
Wove paper 1.00 .25
Entire 2.00 .75
a. Die 2, laid paper 2.00 .45
Entire 5.00 3.00
Wove paper 7.00 10.00
Entire 15.00 50.00
b. Die 3 9.00 3.00
Entire 15.00 5.50
c. Die 4, laid paper .55 1.00
Entire 1.25 4.00
Wove paper 1.00 1.00
Entire 2.50 5.00
d. Die 5 3.50 1.25
Entire 5.00 3.25
e. Die 6, laid paper 1.00 .70
Entire 2.00 1.25
Wove paper 1.20 1.00
Entire 3.00 2.00
f. Die 7 100.00 45.00
Entire 135.00 62.50
g. Die 8 25.00 17.50
Entire 40.00 22.50

U414 U91 2c carmine, *blue* .55 .25
Entire 1.30 .75
Wove paper .60 .25
Entire 1.50 .75
a. Die 2, laid paper 1.00 1.00
Entire 5.00 2.50
Wove paper 1.50 8.00
Entire 6.50 30.00
b. Die 3, laid paper 2.75 2.00
Entire 4.00 6.50
Wove paper 50.00 30.00
Entire 75.00 50.00
c. Die 4, laid paper .50 .50
Entire 1.00 3.50
Wove paper 1.00 1.00
Entire 2.50 10.00
d. Die 5, laid paper 1.00 .45
Entire 3.00 1.00
Wove paper 70.00 40.00
Entire 100.00 75.00
e. Die 6, laid paper .65 .30
Entire 1.10 .75
Wove paper .55 .30
Entire 1.50 .75
f. Die 7 37.50 25.00
Entire 50.00 35.00
g. Die 8 37.50 25.00
Entire 50.00 35.00

W415 U91 2c car, *manila* 5.00 2.00
Entire 8.00 *12.00*
Wove paper 50.00 15.00
Entire 70.00 75.00
a. Die 2 5.50 1.25
Entire 8.00 *20.00*
b. Die 5 5.50 2.50
Entire 8.00 *18.00*
c. Die 7 120.00 97.50
Entire 175.00 125.00

U90 4c Die 1

U90 4c Die 2

Die 1 — "F" close to (1mm) left "4."
Die 2 — "F" far from (1¾mm) left "4."

U416 U90 4c black, die 2, laid paper 2.00 1.50
Entire 4.00 6.50
Wove paper 30.00 20.00
Entire 50.00 65.00
a. Die 1, wove paper 1.50 2.00
Entire 5.00 10.00
Laid paper 7.50 4.00
Entire 15.00 10.00

U417 U90 4c black, *amb*, die 2 7.50 2.50
Entire 12.00 4.00
a. Die 1, laid paper .75 2.00
Entire 1.50 20.00
Wove paper 1.00 2.00
Entire 2.50 10.00

Die 1 — Tall "F" in "FIVE"

Die 2 — Short "F" in "FIVE"

Die 1 — Tall "F" in "FIVE."
Die 2 — Short "F" in "FIVE."

U418 U91 5c blue, die 2, laid paper 1.50 1.50
Entire 5.00 6.00
Wove paper .75 1.00
Entire 2.00 5.00
a. Die 1 7.00 2.25
Entire 13.50 6.50
b. 5c blue, *buff*, die 2 (error) *3,250.*
c. 5c blue, *blue*, die 2 (error) *3,000.*
d. As "c," die 1 (error), entire *6,250.*

U419 U91 5c blue, *amber*, die 2, laid paper 1.00 .75
Entire 5.00 5.00
Wove paper 3.00 1.50
Entire 10.00 10.00
a. Die 1 15.00 12.00
Entire 25.00 14.00

Franklin — U92

Die 1

Die 2

Die 3

Die 4

Die 5

(The 1c and 4c dies are the same except for figures of value.)

Die 1 — UNITED nearer inner circle than outer circle.

Die 2 — Large U; large NT closely spaced.

Die 3 — Knob of hair at back of neck. Large NT widely spaced.

Die 4 — UNITED nearer outer circle than inner circle.

Die 5 — Narrow oval C, (also O and G).

Printed by Middle West Supply Co. and International Envelope Corp., Dayton, Ohio.

1915-32 **Die 1**

U420 U92 1c green ('17) .25 .25
Entire .40 .25
a. Die 2 100.00 55.00
Entire, size 8 200.00 70.00
b. Die 3 .35 .25
Entire .50 .25
c. Die 4 .55 .40
Entire .80 .50
d. Die 5 .45 .35
Entire .75 .45

U421 U92 1c grn, *amber* ('17) .55 .30
Entire .80 .45
a. Die 2 400.00 175.00
Entire, size 8 675.00 300.00
b. Die 3 1.40 .65
Entire 2.00 .95
c. Die 4 1.90 .85
Entire 2.50 1.25
d. Die 5 1.10 .55
Entire 1.75 .80

U422 U92 1c grn, *oriental buff* ('17) 2.40 .90
Entire 3.25 1.40
a. Die 4 5.50 1.25
Entire 8.00 2.75

U423 U92 1c grn, *bl* ('17) .50 .35
Entire 1.00 .50
a. Die 3 .80 .45
Entire 1.25 .70
b. Die 4 1.40 .65
Entire 2.50 .95
c. Die 5 .85 .35
Entire 1.60 .65

U424 U92 1c grn, *manila* (unglazed) ('16) 6.50 4.00
Entire 8.00 5.00

W425 U92 1c grn, *manila* (unglazed) ('16) .30 .25
Entire 1.00 .25
a. Die 3 175.00 125.00
Entire 250.00 200.00

U426 U92 1c grn, *brown* (glazed) ('20) 45.00 16.00
Entire 57.50 27.50

W427 U92 1c grn, *brown* (glazed) ('20) 65.00 35.00
Entire 80.00 *60.00*
a. Printed on unglazed side *400.00*
Entire *750.00*

b. Unglazed on both sides — 150.00

U428 U92 1c grn, *brown* (unglazed) ('20) 12.50 7.50
Entire 22.50 24.00

W428A U92 1c grn, *brn* (unglazed) ('20), entire 3,000.

Washington — U93

Die 1

Die 2

Die 3

Die 4

Die 5

Die 6

Die 7

Die 8

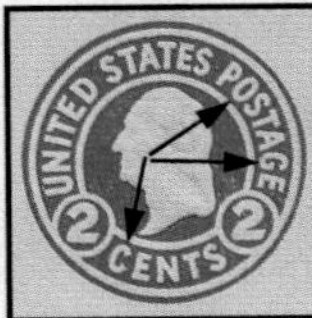

Die 9

(The 1½c, 2c, 3c, 5c, and 6c dies are the same except for figures of value.)

Die 1 — Letters broad. Numerals vertical. Large head (9¼mm). from tip of nose to back of neck. E closer to inner circle than N of cents.

Die 2 — Similar to 1; but U far from left circle.

Die 3 — Similar to 2; but all inner circles very thin (Rejected die).

Die 4 — Large head as in Die 1. C of CENTS close to circle. Baseline of right numeral "2" slants downward to right. Left numeral "2" is larger.

Die 5 — Small head (8¾mm) from tip of nose to back of neck. T and S of CENTS close at bottom.

Die 6 — Similar to 5; but T and S of CENTS far apart at bottom. Left numeral slopes to right.

Die 7 — Large head. Both numerals slope to right. Clean cut lettering. All letters T have short top strokes.

Die 8 — Similar to 7; but all letters T have long top strokes.

Die 9 — Narrow oval C (also O and G).

1915-32 **Die 1**

U429 U93 2c carmine .25 .25
Entire .40 .25
a. Die 2 15.00 7.00
Entire 25.00 10.00
b. Die 3 40.00 50.00
Entire 80.00 *200.00*
c. Die 4 25.00 15.00
Entire 40.00 20.00
d. Die 5 .55 .35
Entire 1.00 .45
e. Die 6 .65 .30
Entire 1.25 .60
f. Die 7 .70 .25
Entire 1.25 .75
g. Die 8 .50 .25
Entire 1.00 .50
h. Die 9 .50 .25
Entire 1.00 .45
i. 2c green (error), die 1, entire *12,500.*
j. #U429 with added impression of #U420 600.00
Entire 1,000.
k. #U429 with added impression of #U416a, entire *3,500.*
l. #U429 with added impression of #U400, entire 950.00
m. #U429, double impression, entire 1,500.
n. As "f," double impression, entire *750.00*
o. As "e," triple impression —
p. As "m," second impression on side flap, entire *250.00*

U430 U93 2c car, *amber* ('16) .30 .25
Entire .50 .25
a. Die 2 20.00 12.50
Entire 30.00 15.00
b. Die 4 50.00 25.00
Entire 70.00 30.00
c. Die 5 1.60 .35
Entire 2.25 .60
d. Die 6 1.25 .40
Entire 2.25 .75
e. Die 7 .75 .35
Entire 1.75 .95
f. Die 8 .70 .30
Entire 1.10 .45
g. Die 9 .65 .25
Entire 1.10 .35
h. As No. U430, with added impression of 4c black (#U416a), entire *600.00*
i. As "g," with added impression of 2c car. die 1 on side flap, entire —

U431 U93 2c car, *oriental buff* ('16) 2.25 .65
Entire 4.75 1.40
a. Die 2 180.00 75.00
Entire 260.00 *250.00*
b. Die 4 75.00 60.00
Entire 100.00 75.00
c. Die 5 3.50 2.00
Entire 6.00 2.75
d. Die 6 3.50 2.00
Entire 7.00 2.75
e. Die 7 3.50 2.00
Entire 6.00 3.25

U432 U93 2c car, *blue* ('16) .30 .25
Entire .60 .25
b. Die 2 40.00 25.00
Entire 55.00 35.00
c. Die 3 140.00 90.00
Entire 190.00 *400.00*
d. Die 4 65.00 50.00
Entire 95.00 55.00
e. Die 5 1.10 .30
Entire 2.00 .75
f. Die 6 1.10 .40
Entire 2.00 .60
g. Die 7 .85 .35
Entire 1.75 .65
h. Die 8 .65 .25
Entire 1.50 .50
i. Die 9 1.00 .30
Entire 2.75 .55
j. 2c purple (error), die 9 —
k. Double impression 650.00

U432A U93 2c car, *manila*, die 7, entire *50,000.*

W433 U93 2c car, *manila*, ('16) .25 .25
Entire .50 .30

W434 U93 2c car, brn (glazed) ('20) 70.00 45.00
Entire 95.00 55.00

W435 U93 2c car, *brn* (unglazed) ('20) 90.00 60.00
Entire 115.00 *150.00*

U436 U93 3c purple ('32) .30 .25
Entire .55 .25
a. 3c dark violet, die 1 ('17) .60 .25
Entire 1.00 .25
b. 3c dark violet, die 5 ('17) 1.75 .75
Entire 3.25 .90
c. 3c dark violet, die 6 ('17) 2.10 1.40
Entire 3.25 1.50
d. 3c dark violet, die 7 ('17) 1.50 .95
Entire 3.00 1.00
e. 3c purple, die 7 ('32) .70 .30
Entire 1.75 .75
f. 3c purple, die 9 ('32) .45 .25
Entire .60 .30
g. 3c carmine (error), die 1 35.00 35.00
Entire 60.00 *70.00*
h. 3c carmine (error), die 5 27.50 —
Entire 50.00 —
i. #U436 with added impression of #U420, entire 900.00
j. #U436 with added impression of #U429, entire 900.00 950.00
k. As "f," double impression, preprinted, entire *600.00*

U437 U93 3c purple, *amb* ('32) .35 .25
Entire .60 .35
a. 3c dk vio, die 1 ('17) 5.50 1.25
Entire 9.00 2.25
b. 3c dk vio, die 5 ('17) 8.50 2.50
Entire 12.00 3.00
c. 3c dk vio, die 6 ('17) 8.50 2.50
Entire 12.00 3.00
d. 3c dk vio, die 7 ('17) 8.50 2.25
Entire 12.00 2.50
e. 3c pur, die 7 ('32) .75 .25
Entire 1.25 .50
f. 3c pur, die 9 ('32) .55 .25
Entire 1.00 .30
g. 3c carmine (error), die 5 375.00 400.00
Entire 475.00 *750.00*
h. 3c black (error), die 1 190.00 —
Entire 300.00 *375.00*

U438 U93 3c dk vio, *oriental buff* ('17) 22.50 5.50
Entire 32.50 21.00
a. Die 5 22.50 5.50
Entire 32.50 27.50
b. Die 6 30.00 8.00
Entire 45.00 35.00
c. Die 7 30.00 10.00
Entire 45.00 45.00

U439 U93 3c purple, *bl* ('32) .35 .25
Entire .75 .25
a. 3c dark violet, die 1 ('17) 7.00 2.00
Entire 14.00 6.00
b. 3c dark violet, die 5 ('17) 7.50 6.00
Entire 15.00 7.50
c. 3c dark violet, die 6 ('17) 7.50 6.00
Entire 15.00 7.50
d. 3c dark violet, die 7 ('17) 10.00 6.00
Entire 17.50 7.50
e. 3c purple, die 7 ('32) .75 .25
Entire 1.50 .50
f. 3c purple, die 9 ('32) .60 .25
Entire 1.50 .45
g. 3c carmine (error), die 5 225.00 300.00
Entire 400.00 *725.00*

U440 U92 4c black ('18) 1.75 .60
Entire 3.25 2.00
a. With added impression of 2c carmine (#U429), die 1, entire 450.00

U441 U92 4c black, *amb* ('18) 3.00 .85
Entire 5.00 2.00
a. 4c black, *amb*, with added impression of 2c car (#U429), die 1 175.00

U442 U92 4c blk, *bl* ('21) 3.25 .85
Entire 5.75 1.75

U443 U93 5c blue ('18) 3.25 2.75
Entire 5.75 3.25

U444 U93 5c blue, *amber* ('18) 4.00 1.60
Entire 6.50 3.50

U445 U93 5c bl, *blue* ('21) 3.25 3.25
Entire 7.50 4.25

For 1½c and 6c see Nos. U481-W485, U529-U531.

Double or triple surcharge listings of 1920-25 are for examples with surcharge directly or partly upon the stamp.

Surcharged on 1874-1920 Envelopes indicated by Numbers in Parentheses

Type 1

1920-21 **Surcharged in Black**

U446 U93 2c on 3c dark vio (U436a, die 1) 11.00 10.00
Entire 22.50 12.50
a. On No. U436b (die 5) 11.00 10.00
Entire 22.50 12.50
b. As "a," double surcharge 140.00
Entire 425.00

Surcharged

Type 2

Rose Surcharge

U447 U93 2c on 3c dark vio (U436a, die 1) 8.00 7.50
Entire 16.00 10.00
b. On No. U436c (die 6) 10.00 8.50
Entire 25.00 10.00

Black Surcharge

U447A U92 2c on 1c green (U420, die 1) Entire 3,000.

U447C U93 2c on 2c carmine (U429, die 1) —

U447D U93 2c on 2c car, *amb* (U430, die 1) 12,000.

U448 U93 2c on 3c dark vio (U436a, die 1) 2.75 2.00
Entire 4.00 2.50
a. On No. U436b (die 5) 2.75 2.00
Entire 4.00 2.50
b. On No. U436c (die 6) 3.50 2.00
Entire 5.00 2.50
c. On No. U436d (die 7) 2.75 2.00
Entire 4.00 2.50

U449 U93 2c on 3c dk vio, *amb* (U437a, die 1) 6.50 6.00
Entire 9.00 7.50
a. On No. U437b (die 5) 13.00 7.50
Entire 17.50 10.00
b. On No. U437c (die 6) 9.50 6.00
Entire 13.50 7.50
c. On No. U437d (die 7) 8.50 6.50
Entire 12.00 8.00

U450 U93 2c on 3c dk vio, *oriental buff* (U438, die 1) 12.50 15.00
Entire 20.00 18.00
a. On No. U438a (die 5) 15.00 15.00
Entire 22.50 18.00
b. On No. U438b (die 6) 15.00 15.00
Entire 22.50 18.00
c. On No. U438c (die 7) 130.00 90.00
Entire 160.00 125.00

U451 U93 2c on 3c dk vio, *blue* (U439a, die 1) 11.00 10.50
Entire 18.00 11.50
b. On No. U439b (die 5) 11.00 10.50
Entire 18.00 11.50
c. On No. U439c (die 6) 11.00 10.50
Entire 18.00 11.50
d. On No. U439d (die 7) 22.50 22.50
Entire 37.50 27.50

Type 2 exists in three city sub-types.

Surcharged

Type 3

Bars 2mm apart, 25 to 26mm in length from outer edges of end bars

U451A U90 2c on 1c green (U400, die 1) *25,000.*
Entire —

U452 U92 2c on 1c green (U420, die 1) 1,750.
Entire 3,250.
a. On No. U420b (die 3) 3,000.
Entire 4,000.
b. As No. U452, double surcharge 3,750.
Entire 4,500.

U453 U91 2c on 2c car (U411b, die 3) 3,500.
Entire 6,000.
a. On No. U411 (die 1) 3,250.
Entire 5,500.

U453B U91 2c on 2c car, *bl* (U414e, die 6) 1,250. 750.00
Entire 2,250.

U453C U91 2c on 2c car, *oriental buff* (U413e, die 6) 1,400. *750.00*
Entire 2,000.
d. On No. U413 (die 1) 1,400.
Entire 2,000.

U454 U93 2c on 2c car (U429e, die 6) 125.00
Entire 225.00
a. On No. U429 (die 1) 300.00
Entire 375.00
b. On No. U429d (die 5) 500.00
Entire 650.00
c. On No. U429f (die 7) 125.00
Entire 200.00

U455 U93 2c on 2c car, *amb* (U430, die 1) 1,250.
Entire 3,000.
a. On No. U430d (die 6) 1,500.
Entire 3,000.
b. On No. U430e (die 7) 1,500.
Entire 3,000.

U456 U93 2c on 2c car, *oriental buff* (U431a, die 2) 225.00
Entire 375.00
a. On No. U431c (die 5) 225.00
Entire 550.00
b. On No. U431e (die 7) 800.00
Entire 950.00
c. As No. U456, double surcharge 700.00

U457 U93 2c on 2c car, *bl* (U432f, die 6) 325.00
Entire 400.00
a. On No. U432e (die 5) 275.00
Entire 475.00
b. On No. U432g (die 7) 650.00
Entire 800.00

U458 U93 2c on 3c dark vio (U436a, die 1) .50 .35
Entire .75 .45
a. On No. U436b (die 5) .50 .40
Entire .75 .50
b. On No. U436c (die 6) .50 .35
Entire .75 .45
c. On No. U436d (die 7) .50 .35
Entire .75 .45
d. As #U458, double surcharge 25.00 7.50
Entire 35.00 10.00
e. As #U458, triple surcharge 90.00
Entire 150.00
f. As #U458, dbl. surch., 1 in magenta 90.00
Entire 150.00
g. As #U458, dbl. surch., types 2 & 3 140.00
Entire 190.00
h. As "a," double surcharge 27.50 15.00
Entire 37.50 20.00
i. As "a," triple surcharge 110.00
Entire 160.00
j. As "a," double surch., both magenta 110.00
Entire 150.00
k. As "b," double surcharge 25.00 8.00
Entire 35.00 11.00
l. As "c," double surcharge 25.00 8.00
Entire 35.00 11.00
m. As "c," triple surcharge 110.00
Entire 150.00
n. Double impression of indicia, single surcharge, entire 450.00

U459 U93 2c on 3c dk vio, *amb* (U437c, die 6) 3.00 1.00
Entire 4.50 1.75
a. On No. U437a (die 1) 4.00 1.00
Entire 5.50 1.75
b. On No. U437b (die 5) 4.00 1.00
Entire 5.50 1.75
c. On No. U437d (die 7) 3.00 1.00
Entire 5.50 1.75
d. As #U459, double surcharge 35.00
Entire 50.00
e. As "a," double surcharge 35.00
Entire 50.00
f. As "b," double surcharge 35.00
Entire 50.00
g. As "b," double surcharge, types 2 & 3 125.00
Entire 175.00
h. As "c," double surcharge 35.00
Entire 50.00

U460 U93 2c on 3c dk vio, *oriental buff* (U438a, die 5) 3.50 2.00
Entire 4.50 2.50
a. On No. U438 (die 1) 3.50 2.00
Entire 4.50 2.50
b. On No. U438b (die 6) 4.00 2.00
Entire 5.50 2.50
c. As #U460, double surcharge 20.00
Entire 30.00
d. As "a," double surcharge 20.00
Entire 30.00
e. As "b," double surcharge 20.00
Entire 30.00
f. As "b," triple surcharge 150.00
Entire 250.00

U461 U93 2c on 3c dk vio, *bl* (U439a, die 1) 6.00 1.00
Entire 8.25 1.50
a. On No. U439b (die 5) 6.00 1.00
Entire 8.25 1.50
b. On No. U439c (die 6) 6.00 2.50
Entire 8.25 3.50
c. On No. U439d (die 7) 12.50 7.50
Entire 17.50 15.00
d. As #U461, double surcharge 17.50
Entire 40.00 30.00
e. As "a," double surcharge 17.50
Entire 40.00 30.00
f. As "b," double surcharge 17.50
Entire 40.00 30.00
g. As "c," double surcharge 17.50
Entire 50.00 40.00

U462 U87 2c on 4c choc (U390) 475.00 260.00
Entire 800.00 500.00

U463 U87 2c on 4c choc, *amb* (U391) 750.00 350.00
Entire 1,200. 500.00

U463A U90 2c on 4c black (U416, die 2) 800.00 400.00
Entire 1,500.

U464 U93 2c on 5c blue (U443) 850.00
Entire 1,600.

Surcharged

Type 4

Bars 1 mm apart, 21 to 23 mm in length from outer edges of end bars

U465 U92 2c on 1c green (U420, die 1) 900.00
Entire 1,900.
a. On No. U420b (die 3) 1,100.
Entire 2,400.

U466 U91 2c on 2c car (U411e, die 6), entire 22,500.

U466A U93 2c on 2c carmine (U429, die 1) 700.00
Entire 1,150.
c. On No. U429d (die 5) 900.00
Entire 1,350.
d. On No. U429e (die 6) 900.00
Entire 1,350.
e. On No. U429f (die 7) 750.00
Entire 1,200.

U466B U93 2c on 2c car, *amb* (U430) *15,000.*
Entire *22,500.*

U466C U93 2c on 2c car, *oriental buff* (U431), entire *15,000.*

U466D U25 2c on 3c green, die 2 (U82) *7,500.*

U467 U45 2c on 3c green, die 2 (U163) 325.00
Entire 525.00

U468 U93 2c on 3c dark vio (U436a, die 1) .70 .45
Entire 1.00 .75
a. On No. U436b (die 5) .70 .50
Entire 1.00 .75
b. On No. U436c (die 6) .70 .50
Entire 1.00 .75
c. On No. U436d (die 7) .70 .50
Entire 1.00 .75
d. As #U468, double surcharge 20.00
Entire 30.00
e. As #U468, triple surcharge 100.00
Entire 150.00
f. As #U468, dbl. surch., types 2 & 4 125.00
Entire 175.00
g. As "a," double surcharge 20.00
Entire 30.00
h. As "b," double surcharge 20.00
Entire 30.00
i. As "c," double surcharge 20.00
Entire 30.00
j. As "c," triple surcharge 100.00
Entire 150.00
k. As "c," inverted surcharge 75.00
Entire 125.00
l. 2c on 3c carmine (error), (U436h) 600.00
Entire 1,400.
m. As #U468, triple surcharge, one inverted, entire *700.00*

U469 U93 2c on 3c dk vio, *amb* (U437a, die 1) 3.75 2.25
Entire 5.00 2.75
a. On No. U437b (die 5) 3.75 2.25
Entire 5.00 2.75
b. On No. U437c (die 6) 3.75 2.25
Entire 5.00 2.75
c. On No. U437d (die 7) 3.75 2.25
Entire 5.00 2.75
d. As #U469, double surcharge 30.00
Entire 40.00
e. As "a," double surcharge 30.00
Entire 40.00
f. As "a," double surcharge, types 2 & 4 100.00
Entire 150.00
g. As "b," double surcharge 30.00
Entire 40.00
h. As "c," double surcharge 30.00
Entire 40.00

U470 U93 2c on 3c dk vio, *oriental buff* (U438, die 1) 6.00 2.50
Entire 10.00 5.00
a. On No. U438a (die 5) 6.00 2.50
Entire 10.00 6.00
b. On No. U438b (die 6) 6.00 2.50
Entire 10.00 6.00
c. On No. U438c (die 7) 42.50 32.50
Entire 70.00 70.00
d. As #U470, double surcharge 25.00
Entire 35.00
e. As #U470, double surch., types 2 & 4 80.00
Entire 130.00
f. As "a," double surcharge 25.00
Entire 35.00
g. As "b," double surcharge 25.00
Entire 35.00

U471 U93 2c on 3c dk vio, *bl* (U439a, die 1) 6.00 1.75
Entire 12.50 3.50
a. On No. U439b (die 5) 7.00 1.75
Entire 13.00 6.00
b. On No. U439c (die 6) 7.00 1.75
Entire 13.00 3.50
c. On No. U439d (die 7) 10.00 10.00
Entire 35.00 30.00
d. As #U471, double surcharge 25.00
Entire 40.00
e. As #U471, double surch., types 2 & 4 160.00
Entire 275.00
f. As "a," double surcharge 25.00
Entire 40.00
g. As "b," double surcharge 25.00
Entire 40.00

U471A U83 2c on 4c brown, (U374), entire 625.00

U472 U87 2c on 4c choc (U390) 11.00 11.00
Entire 25.00 16.00
a. Double surcharge 150.00

U473 U87 2c on 4c choc, *amb* (U391) 17.00 10.00
Entire 27.50 13.50

Surcharged

Double Surcharge, Type 4 and 1c as above

U474 U93 2c on 1c on 3c dark violet (U436a, die 1) 175. *500.*
Entire 325.
a. On No. U436b (die 5) 200.
Entire 500.
b. On No. U436d (die 7) 850.
Entire 1,050.

U475 U93 2c on 1c on 3c dk vio, *amb* (U437a, die 1) 150.
Entire 350.

Surcharged

Type 5

U476 U93 2c on 3c dk vio, *amb* (U437a, die 1) 200.
Entire 475. 450.
a. On No. U437c (die 6) 700.
Entire 1,000.
b. As #U476, double surcharge —

Surcharged

Type 6

U477 U93 2c on 3c dark vio (U436a, die 1) 120.
Entire 175.
a. On No. U436b (die 5) 250.
Entire 300.
b. On No. U436c (die 6) 250.
Entire 300.
c. On No. U436d (die 7) 250.
Entire 300.

U478 U93 2c on 3c dk vio, *amb* (U437a, die 1) 250.
Entire 375.

Handstamped Surcharge in Black or Violet — Type 7

U479 U93 2c on 3c dark violet (Bk) (U436a, die 1) 240. —
Entire 525.
a. On No. U436b (die 5) 625.
Entire 950.
b. On No. U436d (die 7) 425.
Entire 525.

U480 U93 2c on 3c dark violet (V) (U436d, die 7) *4,500.*
Entire *6,500.*
a. Double overprint —

Expertization by competent authorities is required for Nos. U476-U480.

Type of 1916-32 Issue

1925-34 **Die 1**

U481 U93 1½c brown .25 .25
Entire .60 .25
Entire, 1st day cancel 60.00
a. Die 8 .70 .25
Entire 1.00 .50
b. 1½c purple, die 1 (error) ('34) 55.00
Entire 100.00 —
U482 U93 1½c brown, *amber* .90 .40
Entire 1.50 .60
a. Die 8 1.75 .75
Entire 2.25 .80
U483 U93 1½c brown, *bl* 1.60 .95
Entire 2.50 1.25
a. Die 8 2.40 1.25
Entire 3.25 1.40
U484 U93 1½c brown, *manila* 5.00 3.00
Entire 12.00 6.00
W485 U93 1½c brown, *manila* .85 .25
Entire 2.00 .45
a. With added impression of #W433 120.00 —

Surcharged Type 8

1925 **On Envelopes of 1887**

U486 U71 1½c on 2c grn (U311) 500.00
Entire 1,150.
U487 U71 1½c on 2c green, *amb* (U312) 900.00
Entire 1,500.

On Envelopes of 1899

U488 U77 1½c on 1c green (U352) 400.00
Entire 800.00
U489 U77 1½c on 1c grn, *amb* (U353) 110.00 60.
Entire 200.00 90.

On Envelopes of 1907-16

U490 U90 1½c on 1c green (U400, die 1) 6.25 3.50
Entire 10.00 5.50
a. On No. U400a (die 2) 15.00 9.00
Entire 20.00 12.00
b. On No. U400b (die 3) 35.00 17.50
Entire 50.00 22.50
c. On No. U400c (die 4) 9.00 2.50
Entire 13.00 4.00
U491 U90 1½c on 1c grn, *amb* (U401c, die 4) 7.00 3.00
Entire 12.00 8.50
a. On No. U401 (die 1) 12.50 3.50
Entire 17.50 8.50
b. On No. U401a (die 2) 110.00 70.00
Entire 140.00 140.00
c. On No. U401b (die 3) 60.00 50.00
Entire 100.00 100.00
U492 U90 1½c on 1c grn, *oriental buff* (U402a, die 2) 500.00 150.00
Entire 800.00 175.00
a. On No. U402c (die 4) 750.00 250.00
Entire 1,500. 300.00
U493 U90 1½c on 1c grn, *bl* (U403c, die 4) 100.00 65.00
Entire 140.00 70.00
a. On No. U403a (die 2) 100.00 67.50
Entire 140.00 90.00
U494 U90 1½c on 1c grn, *man* (U404, die 1) 300.00 100.00
Entire 550.00 150.00
a. On No. U404a (die 3) 950.00
Entire 1,250.

On Envelopes of 1916-20

U495 U92 1½c on 1c green (U420, die 1) .80 .25
Entire 1.10 .45
a. On No. U420a (die 2) 80.00 52.50
Entire 120.00 90.00
b. On No. U420b (die 3) 2.10 .70
Entire 3.00 .85
c. On No. U420c (die 4) 2.10 .85
Entire 3.00 1.15
d. As #U495, double surcharge 10.00 3.00
Entire 15.00 5.00
e. As "b," double surcharge 10.00 3.00
Entire 15.00 5.00
f. As "c," double surcharge 10.00 3.00
Entire 15.00 5.00
U496 U92 1½c on 1c grn, *amb* (U421, die 1) 15.00 12.50
Entire 27.50 15.00
a. On No. U421b (die 3) 725.00
Entire 1,500.
b. On No. U421c (die 4) 15.00 12.50
Entire 27.50 15.00
U497 U92 1½c on 1c grn, *oriental buff* (U422, die 1) 3.75 1.90
Entire 7.00 2.25
a. On No. U422b (die 4) 67.50
Entire 100.00
U498 U92 1½c on 1c grn, *bl* (U423c, die 4) 1.40 .75
Entire 2.25 1.00
a. On No. U423 (die 1) 2.40 1.50
Entire 4.25 2.00
b. On No. U423b (die 3) 1.75 1.50
Entire 3.25 2.00
U499 U92 1½c on 1c grn, *man* (U424) 8.00 6.00
Entire 16.00 7.00
U500 U92 1½c on 1c grn, *brn* (unglazed) (U428) 60.00 30.00
Entire 85.00 35.00
U501 U92 1½c on 1c grn, *brn* (glazed) (U426) 65.00 30.00
Entire 90.00 35.00
U502 U93 1½c on 2c car (U429, die 1) 200.00 —
Entire 450.00 —
a. On No. U429d (die 5) 250.00
Entire 500.00
b. On No. U429f (die 7) 250.00
Entire 500.00
c. On No. U429e (die 6) 325.00
Entire —
d. On No. U429g (die 8) 450.00
U503 U93 1½c on 2c car, *oriental buff* (U431c, die 5) 200.00 —
Entire 500.00 —
a. Double surcharge —
b. Double surcharge, one inverted *700.00*
U504 U93 1½c on 2c car, *bl* (U432, die 1) 300.00 —
Entire 450.00 —
a. On No. U432g (die 7) 300.00
Entire 450.00
b. As "a," double surcharge, entire *350.00*
c. On No. U432f (die 6), entire *400.00*

On Envelopes of 1925

U505 U93 1½c on 1½c brn (U481, die 1) 300.00
Entire 550.00
a. On No. U481a (die 8) 300.00
Entire 500.00
b. As No. U505, double surcharge, entire *2,000.*
U506 U93 1½c on 1½c brn, *bl* (U483a, die 8) 200.00
Entire 550.00
a. On No. U483 (die 1) 300.00

The paper of No. U500 is not glazed and appears to be the same as that used for the wrappers of 1920.

Surcharged Type 9

Black Surcharge

U507 U69 1½c on 1c blue (U294) 1,750.
Entire 2,400.
U507B U69 1½c on 1c blue, *manila* (U300) 4,750.
Entire 5,750.
U508 U77 1½c on 1c grn, *amb* (U353) 55.00
Entire 90.00
U508A U85 1½c on 1c grn (U379) 2,750.
Entire 5,000.
U509 U85 1½c on 1c grn, *amb* (U380) 12.50 10.00
Entire 27.50 *35.00*
a. Double surcharge 75.00
Entire 100.00
U509B U85 1½c on 1c green, *oriental buff* (U381) 40.00 40.00
Entire 60.00 50.00
U510 U90 1½c on 1c green (U400, die 1) 2.75 1.25
Entire 4.75 1.50
b. On No. U400a (die 2) 9.00 4.00
Entire 13.50 6.00
c. On No. U400b (die 3) 37.50 8.00
Entire 50.00 11.00
d. On No. U400c (die 4) 3.50 1.25
Entire 7.50 2.00
e. As No. U510, double surcharge 25.00
Entire 50.00
U511 U90 1½c on 1c grn, *amb* (U401, die 1) 200.00 100.00
Entire 325.00 150.00
U512 U90 1½c on 1c grn, *oriental buff* (U402, die 1) 8.00 4.00
Entire 15.00 6.50
a. On No. U402c (die 4) 21.00 14.00
Entire 30.00 17.00
U513 U90 1½c on 1c grn, *bl* (U403, die 1) 6.00 4.00
Entire 9.50 5.00
a. On No. U403c (die 4) 6.00 4.00
Entire 9.50 5.00
U514 U90 1½c on 1c grn, *man* (U404, die 1) 30.00 9.00
Entire 45.00 22.50
a. On No. U404a (die 3) 77.50 40.00
Entire 100.00 95.00
U515 U92 1½c on 1c green (U420, die 1) .40 .25
Entire .75 .30
a. On No. U420a (die 2) 15.00 15.00
Entire 30.00 20.00
b. On No. U420b (die 3) .40 .25
Entire .75 .30
c. On No. U420c (die 4) .40 .25
Entire .75 .30
d. As #U515, double surcharge 10.00
Entire 15.00
e. As #U515, inverted surcharge 15.00
Entire 30.00
f. As #U515, triple surcharge 15.00
Entire 30.00
g. As #U515, dbl. surch., one invtd., entire —
h. As "b," double surcharge 10.00
Entire 15.00
i. As "b," inverted surcharge 15.00
Entire 30.00
j. As "b," triple surcharge 25.00
Entire 40.00
k. As "c," double surcharge 10.00
Entire 15.00
l. As "c," inverted surcharge 15.00
Entire 30.00
U516 U92 1½c on 1c grn, *amb* (U421c, die 4) 50.00 27.50
Entire 65.00 37.50
a. On No. U421 (die 1) 55.00 32.50
Entire 70.00 42.50
U517 U92 1½c on 1c grn, *oriental buff* (U422, die 1) 6.25 1.25
Entire 9.00 1.50
a. On No. U422a (die 4) 7.25 1.50
Entire 10.00 2.00
U518 U92 1½c on 1c grn, *bl* (U423b, die 4) 5.00 1.50
Entire 7.50 5.00
a. On No. U423 (die 1) 8.25 4.50
Entire 27.50 18.00
b. On No. U423a (die 3) 27.50 7.50
Entire 40.00 9.00
c. As "a," double surcharge 30.00
Entire 42.50
U519 U92 1½c on 1c grn, *man* (U424, die 1) 25.00 12.00
Entire 42.50 15.00
a. Double surcharge 100.00
U520 U93 1½c on 2c car (U429, die 1) 300.00 —
Entire 475.00 —
a. On No. U429d (die 5) 275.00
Entire 450.00
b. On No. U429e (die 6) 275.00
Entire 475.00
c. On No. U429f (die 7) 275.00
Entire 600.00
U520D U93 1½c on 2c car, *amber* (U430c, die 5), entire —
U520E U92 1½c on 4c black (U440, die 1), entire —

Magenta Surcharge

U521 U92 1½c on 1c grn (U420b, die 3) 4.25 3.50
Entire 6.50 5.50
Entire, 1st day cancel, Washington, D.C. 100.00
a. Double surcharge 75.00
Entire 125.00

Sesquicentennial Exposition Issue

150th anniversary of the Declaration of Independence.

Liberty Bell — U94

Die 1. The center bar of "E" of "postage" is shorter than top bar.
Die 2. The center bar of "E" of "postage" is of same length as top bar.

1926, July 27

U522 U94 2c carmine, die 1 1.00 .50
Entire 1.50 .95
a. Die 2 5.50 3.75
Entire 10.00 5.50

Washington Bicentennial Issue

200th anniversary of the birth of George Washington.

Mount Vernon — U95

2c Die 1 — "S" of "Postage" normal.
2c Die 2 — "S" of "Postage" raised.

1932

U523 U95 1c olive green 1.00 .80
Entire 1.50 1.75
U524 U95 1½c chocolate 2.00 1.50
Entire 2.75 2.50
U525 U95 2c car, die 1 .40 .25
Entire .50 .25
a. 2c carmine, die 2 60.00 20.00
Entire 80.00 27.50
b. 2c carmine, *blue*, die 1 (error) entire *30,000.*
U526 U95 3c violet 1.75 .35
Entire 2.25 .40
U527 U95 4c black 15.00 17.50
Entire 20.00 *35.00*
U528 U95 5c dark blue 3.50 3.50
Entire 4.25 *20.00*
Nos. U523-U528 (6) 23.65 23.90

Type of 1916-32 Issue

1932, Aug. 18

U529 U93 6c orange, die 7 6.00 4.00
Entire 9.50 7.50
U530 U93 6c orange, *amber*, die 7 10.00 10.00
Entire 15.00 12.50
U531 U93 6c orange, *blue*, die 7 10.00 10.00
Entire 15.00 12.50

AIR POST STAMPED ENVELOPES AND AIR LETTER SHEETS

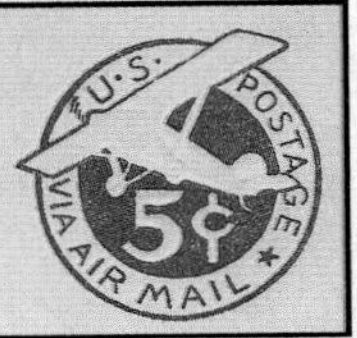

UC1

5c — Vertical rudder is not semi-circular but slopes down to the left. The tail of the plane projects into the G of POSTAGE.

UC2

Die 2 (5c and 8c): Vertical rudder is semi-circular. The tail of the plane touches but does not project into the G of POSTAGE.

Die 2 (6c) — Same as UC2 except three types of numeral.

2a — The numeral "6" is 6½mm wide.
2b — The numeral "6" is 6mm wide.
2c — The numeral "6" is 5½mm wide.

Die 3 (6c): Vertical rudder leans forward. S closer to O than to T of POSTAGE. E of POSTAGE has short center bar. Border types b and d, also without border.

1929-44

UC1	UC1	5c blue	3.00	2.00
a.		Orange and blue border, type b	375.00	*450.00*
UC2	UC2	5c blue, die 2	9.00	5.00
UC3	UC2	6c orange, die 2a ('34)	1.25	.40
a.		With added impression of 3c purple (#U436a), entire without border	*4,000.*	
b.		Double impression of indicium, entire, with bicolored border		—
UC4	UC2	6c orange, die 2b ('42)	3.00	2.00
		Entire, without border	4.50	2.50
UC5	UC2	6c orange, die 2c ('44)	.70	.30
UC6	UC2	6c orange, die 3 ('42)	1.00	.35
a.		6c orange, *blue*, die 3 (error) Entire, without border	*15,000.*	*10,000.*
b.		Double impression, entire	*400.00*	
UC7	UC2	8c olive green, die 2 ('32)	10.00	3.50

OFFICIAL STAMPED ENVELOPES

By the Act of Congress, January 31, 1873, the franking privilege of officials was abolished as of July 1, 1873 and the Postmaster General was authorized to prepare official envelopes. At the same time official stamps were prepared for all Departments. Department envelopes became obsolete July 5, 1884. After that, government offices began to use franked envelopes of varied design. These indicate no denomination and lie beyond the scope of this Catalogue.

Post Office Department

"2" 9mm high — UO1

"3" 9mm high — UO2

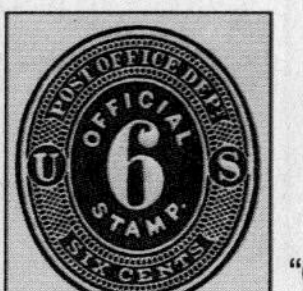
"6" 9½mm high — UO3

1873

UO1	UO1	2c black, *lemon*	22.50	10.00
		Entire	40.00	15.00
UO2	UO2	3c black, *lemon*	15.00	6.50
		Entire	37.50	11.00
+UO3	UO2	3c black	*20,000.*	
		Entire	*45,000.*	
UO4	UO3	6c black, *lemon*	25.00	17.50
		Entire	40.00	25.00

The No. UO3 entire is unique. It has a tear through the stamp that has been professionally repaired. Value based on auction sale in 1999.

"2" 9¼mm high — UO4

"3" 9¼mm high — UO5

"6" 10½mm high — UO6

1874-79

UO5	UO4	2c black, *lemon*	8.00	4.25
		Entire	17.50	7.00
UO6	UO4	2c black	130.00	37.50
		Entire	180.00	57.50
UO7	UO5	3c black, *lemon*	2.75	.85
		Entire	4.25	1.50
UO8	UO5	3c black	1,750.	1,200.
		Entire	4,250.	
UO9	UO5	3c black, *amber*	140.00	40.00
		Entire	175.00	60.00
UO10	UO5	3c black, *blue*	*32,500.*	
		Entire	*42,500.*	
UO11	UO5	3c blue, *blue* ('75)	*22,500.*	
		Entire	*32,500.*	
UO12	UO6	6c black, *lemon*	12.50	6.50
		Entire	26.00	12.50
UO13	UO6	6c black	1,500.	2,100.
		Entire	4,000.	

Fakes exist of Nos. UO3, UO8 and UO13.

Postal Service

UO7

1877

UO14	UO7	black	6.00	4.50
		Entire	11.00	6.00
UO15	UO7	black, *amber*	160.00	50.00
		Entire	625.00	65.00
UO16	UO7	blue, *amber*	180.00	40.00
		Entire	650.00	65.00
UO17	UO7	blue, *blue*	7.50	6.75
		Entire	12.00	10.50

War Department

Franklin — UO8

Bust points to the end of "N" of "ONE".

Jackson — UO9

Bust narrow at the back.

Washington — UO10

Queue projects below the bust.

Lincoln — UO11

Neck very long at the back.

Jefferson — UO12

Queue forms straight line with bust.

Clay — UO13

Ear partly concealed by hair, mouth large, chin prominent.

Webster — UO14

Has side whiskers.

Scott UO15

Hamilton UO16

Back of bust very narrow; chin almost straight; the labels containing the letters "U S" are exactly parallel.

Printed by George H. Reay.

Reay Issue

1873

UO18	UO8	1c dk red	500.00	300.00
		Entire	1,000.	325.00
WO18A	UO8	1c dk red, *man*, entire		—
UO19	UO9	2c dk red	1,500.	400.00
		Entire	2,500.	
UO20	UO10	3c dk red	25.00	42.50
		Entire	40.00	70.00
UO21	UO10	3c dk red, *amb*	*32,500.*	
		Entire	*42,500.*	
UO22	UO10	3c dk red, *cr*	600.00	300.00
		Entire	850.00	350.00
UO23	UO11	6c dk red	250.00	100.00
		Entire	475.00	250.00
UO24	UO11	6c dk red, *cr*	5,000.	425.00
		Entire	7,000.	*3,500.*
UO25	UO12	10c dk red	*9,000.*	2,250.
		Entire	*25,000.*	*4,000.*
UO26	UO13	12c dk red	140.00	60.00
		Entire	240.00	—
UO27	UO14	15c dk red	125.00	55.00
		Entire	210.00	*375.00*
UO28	UO15	24c dk red	150.00	50.00
		Entire	225.00	*1,500.*
UO29	UO16	30c dk red	250.00	150.00
		Entire	500.00	725.00
UO30	UO8	1c ver	200.00	
		Entire	375.00	
WO31	UO8	1c ver, *man*	17.50	14.00
		Entire	35.00	25.00
+UO32	UO9	2c ver	325.00	
		Entire	*22,500.*	
WO33	UO9	2c ver, *man*	250.00	
		Entire	700.00	
UO34	UO10	3c ver	80.00	40.00
		Entire	160.00	125.00
UO35	UO10	3c ver, *amb*	90.00	
		Entire	350.00	
UO36	UO10	3c ver, *cr*	12.50	12.50
		Entire	37.50	26.00
UO37	UO11	6c ver	80.00	
		Entire	170.00	
+UO38	UO11	6c ver, *cr*	450.00	
		Entire	*22,500.*	
UO39	UO12	10c ver	300.00	
		Entire	650.00	
UO40	UO13	12c ver	130.00	
		Entire	200.00	
UO41	UO14	15c ver	200.00	
		Entire	4,000.	
UO42	UO15	24c ver	325.00	
		Entire	600.00	
UO43	UO16	30c ver	275.00	
		Entire	450.00	

UO17

Bottom serif on "S" is thick and short; bust at bottom below hair forms a sharp point.

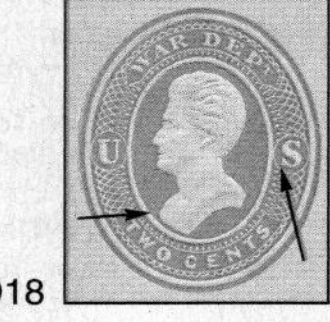
UO18

Bottom serif on "S" is thick and short; front part of bust is rounded.

UO19

Bottom serif on "S" is short; queue does not project below bust.

UO20

Neck very short at the back.

UO21

Knot of queue stands out prominently.

UO22

Ear prominent, chin receding.

UO23

Has no side whiskers; forelock projects above head.

UO24

Back of bust rather broad; chin slopes considerably; the label containing letters "U S" are not exactly parallel.

Plimpton Issue

1875

UO44 UO17 1c red 175.00 85.00
Entire 240.00 175.00
+UO45 UO17 1c red, *amb* 800.00
+UO45A UO17 1c red, *org* *37,500.*
WO46 UO17 1c red, *man* 4.50 2.75
Entire 9.50 6.50
UO47 UO18 2c red 100.00 —
Entire 160.00
UO48 UO18 2c red, *amber* 15.00 17.50
Entire 22.50 27.50
UO49 UO18 2c red, *orange* 12.50 17.50
Entire 27.50 30.00
WO50 UO18 2c red, *manila* 120.00 50.00
Entire 225.00 —
UO51 UO19 3c red 12.50 10.00
Entire 22.50 17.50
UO52 UO19 3c red, *amber* 15.00 10.00
Entire 25.00 16.00
UO53 UO19 3c red, *cream* 5.00 3.75
Entire 9.00 6.50
UO54 UO19 3c red, *blue* 3.75 2.75
Entire 6.00 4.50
UO55 UO19 3c red, *fawn* 6.00 2.75
Entire 11.00 4.00
UO56 UO20 6c red 50.00 30.00
Entire 90.00 —
UO57 UO20 6c red, *amber* 65.00 40.00
Entire 110.00 —
UO58 UO20 6c red, *cream* 175.00 85.00
Entire 450.00
UO59 UO21 10c red 180.00 80.00
Entire 225.00 —
UO60 UO21 10c red, *amber* 750.00
Entire 1,250.
UO61 UO22 12c red 40.00 40.00
Entire 160.00 *250.00*
UO62 UO22 12c red, *amber* 425.00
Entire 700.00
UO63 UO22 12c red, *cream* 450.00
Entire 700.00
UO64 UO23 15c red 225.00 140.00
Entire 300.00 —
UO65 UO23 15c red, *amber* 825.00
Entire 1,050.
UO66 UO23 15c red, *cream* 525.00
Entire 850.00
UO67 UO24 30c red 150.00 140.00
Entire 210.00 —
UO68 UO24 30c red, *amber* 550.00
Entire 1,700.
UO69 UO24 30c red, *cream* 675.00
Entire 1,100.

POSTAL SAVINGS ENVELOPES

Issued under the Act of Congress, approved June 25, 1910, in lieu of penalty or franked envelopes. Unused remainders, after mid-October 1914, were overprinted with the Penalty Clause. Regular stamped envelopes, redeemed by the Government, were also overprinted for official use.

UO25

1911

UO70 UO25 1c green 75.00 25.00
Entire 110.00 42.50
UO71 UO25 1c green, *oriental buff* 190.00 85.00
Entire 300.00 100.00
UO72 UO25 2c carmine 13.00 4.00
Entire 21.00 12.00
a. 2c carmine, *manila* (error) *1,200.* *1,000.*
Entire *1,800.* *1,400.*

REVENUE STAMPS

Nos. R1-R102 were used to pay taxes on documents and proprietary articles including playing cards. Until Dec. 25, 1862, the law stated that a revenue stamp could be used only for payment of the tax upon the particular instrument or article specified on its face. After that date stamps, except the Proprietary, could be used indiscriminately.

Values quoted are for pen-canceled stamps. Stamps with handstamped cancellations sell at higher prices. Stamps canceled with cuts, punches or holes sell for less. See the Scott U.S. Specialized Catalogue.

General Issue
First Issue

Head of Washington in Oval. Various Frames as Illustrated.

Nos. R1b to R42b, part perforate, occur perforated sometimes at sides only and sometimes at top and bottom only. The higher values, part perforate, are perforated at sides only. Imperforate and part perforate revenues often bring much more in pairs or blocks than as single stamps. Part perforate revenues with an asterisk (*) after the value exist imperforate horizontally or vertically.

The experimental silk paper is a variety of the old paper and has only a very few minute fragments of fiber.

Some of the stamps were in use eight years and were printed several times. Many color variations occurred, particularly when unstable pigments were used and the color was intended to be purple or violet, such as the 4c Proprietary, 30c and $2.50 stamps. Before 1868 dull colors predominate on these and the early red stamps. In later printings of the 4c Proprietary, 30c and $2.50 stamps, red predominates in the mixture, and on the dollar values the red is brighter. The early $1.90 stamp is dull purple, imperf. or perforated. In a later printing, perforated only, the purple is darker.

R1

George Washington — R2

Old Paper

1862-71 **Engr.** ***Perf. 12***

R1 R1 1c Express, red
a. Imperf. 75.00
b. Part perf. 55.00*
c. Perf. 1.50
d. As No. R1c, silk paper *350.00*
e. As No. R1c, vertical pair, imperf. between *200.00*
f. As "c," foreign entry of 2c, pos. 210 —
R2 R1 1c Playing Cards, red
a. Imperf. 3,500.
b. Part perf. 2,250.
c. Perf. 210.00
R3 R1 1c Proprietary, red
a. Imperf. 1,250.
b. Part perf. 275.00*
c. Perf. .50
d. As No. R3c, silk paper 60.00
R4 R1 1c Telegraph, red
a. Imperf. 800.00
c. Perf. 20.00
Scratched plate 35.00
R5 R2 2c Bank Check, blue
a. Imperf. 1.50
Privately rouletted —
b. Part perf. 5.50*
c. Perf. .50
e. As No. R5c, Double impression 800.00
f. As No. R5c, pair imperf between 400.00
R6 R2 2c Bank Check, orange
b. Part perf. 60.00*
c. Perf. .45
d. As No. R6c, silk paper 275.00
e. As No. R6c, orange, *green* 700.00
f. As No. R6c, vert. half used as 1c on document 250.00
R7 R2 2c Certificate, blue
a. Imperf. 17.50
Scratched plate 30.00
Foreign entry, top numerals (1¢) —
c. Perf. 32.50
Foreign entry, top numerals (1¢) 100.00
R8 R2 2c Certificate, orange
c. Perf. 45.00
R9 R2 2c Express, blue
a. Imperf. 15.00
b. Part perf. 35.00*
c. Perf. .40
R10 R2 2c Express, orange
b. Part perf. *2,750.*
c. Perf. 14.00
Cracked plate —
d. As No. R10c, silk paper 200.00
R11 R2 2c Playing Cards, blue
a. Imperf. *1,500.*
b. Part perf. 325.00
c. Perf. 4.50
R12 R2 2c Playing Cards, org
c. Perf. 55.00
R13 R2 2c Proprietary, blue
a. Imperf. 1,200.
b. Part perf. 350.
c. Perf. .40
Double transfer covering entire stamp 750.00
d. As No. R13c, silk paper 250.00
Double transfer (T13a) 350.00
e. ultramarine 300.00
f. As No. R13c, horiz. half used as 1c on document —
R14 R2 2c Proprietary, orange
c. Perf. 65.00
R15 R2 2c U.S. Internal Revenue, orange ('64)
a. Imperf —
b. Part perf. —
c. Perf. .25
d. As No. R15c, silk paper 1.00
e. As No. R15c, orange, *green* *2,000.*
f. As No. R15c, half used as 1c on document *250.00*

R3

R16 R3 3c Foreign Exchange, green
b. Part perf. 1,000.
c. Perf. 5.00
Gouged plate ("bruised chin"), positions 18, 19, 20, 21 —
d. As No. R16c, silk paper 200.00
R17 R3 3c Playing Cards, green ('63)
a. Imperf. *40,000.*
c. Perf. 175.00
R18 R3 3c Proprietary, green
b. Part perf. 1,250.
c. Perf. 9.00
d. As No. R18c, silk paper 150.00
e. As No. R18c, double impression *1,250.*
f. As No. R18c, printed on both sides *3,500.*
R19 R3 3c Telegraph, green
a. Imperf. 100.00
b. Part perf. 30.00
c. Perf. 3.00
R20 R3 4c Inland Exchange, brown ('63)
c. Perf. 2.25
d. As No. R20c, silk paper 190.00
R21 R3 4c Playing Cards, slate ('63)
c. Perf. 700.00
R22 R3 4c Proprietary, purple
a. Imperf. —
b. Part perf. 600.00
c. Perf. 8.50
d. As No. R22c, silk paper 250.00

There are shade and color variations of Nos. R21-R22.

R23 R3 5c Agreement, red
c. Perf. .50
d. As No. R23c, silk paper 4.50
e. As No. R23c, diag. half used as 2c on document *2,500.*
R24 R3 5c Certificate, red
a. Imperf. 4.00
b. Part perf. 15.00
c. Perf. .50
Scratched plate, position 170 —
d. As No. R24c, silk paper 1.10
Complete double transfer —
f. As No. R24d, impression of No. R3 on back *2,750.*
R25 R3 5c Express, red
a. Imperf. 8.00
b. Part perf. 8.00*
c. Perf. .40
R26 R3 5c Foreign Exchange, red
b. Part perf. —
c. Perf. .50
d. As No. R26c, silk paper 650.00
R27 R3 5c Inland Exchange, red
a. Imperf. 10.00
b. Part perf. 6.75
c. Perf. .60
Double transfer at left and right 60.00
d. As No. R27c, silk paper 17.50
e. As No. R27c, double impression —
R28 R3 5c Playing Cards, red ('63)
c. Perf. 40.00
d. As No. R28c, silk paper *800.00*
e. Double impression *1,400.*
R29 R3 5c Proprietary, red ('64)
c. Perf. 30.00
Scratched plate 45.00
d. As No. R29c, silk paper 325.00
R30 R3 6c Inland Exchange, orange ('63)
c. Perf. 2.25
d. As No. R30c, silk paper 290.00
R31 R3 6c Proprietary, orange ('71)
c. Perf. *1,600.*

Nearly all examples of No. R31 are faulty or repaired and poorly centered. The catalogue value is for a fine centered stamp with minor faults which do not detract from its appearance.

R32 R3 10c Bill of Lading, blue
a. Imperf. 55.00
b. Part perf. 500.00
c. Perf. 1.75
Tool gouge, position 151 —
e. As No. R32c, half used as 5c on document *300.00*
R33 R3 10c Certificate, blue
a. Imperf. 400.00
Cracked plate —
b. Part perf. 950.00*
c. Perf. .35
Scratched plate —
d. As No. R33c, silk paper 6.00
e. As No. R33c, half used as 5c on document *300.00*
R34 R3 10c Contract, blue
b. Part perf. 575.00
be. As No. R34b, ultramarine 900.00
c. Perf. .50
ce. As No. R34c, ultramarine 1.00
d. As No. R34c, silk paper 4.25
f. As No. R34c, vertical half used as 5c on document *300.00*
R35 R3 10c Foreign Exchange, blue
c. Perf. 14.00
d. As No. R35c, silk paper —
e. As No. R35c, ultramarine 20.00
R36 R3 10c Inland Exchange, blue
a. Imperf. 500.00
b. Part perf. 4.50*
c. Perf. .30
Double transfer at right —
Scratched plate —
d. As No. R36c, silk paper 125.00
e. As No. R36c, half used as 5c on document *300.00*
R37 R3 10c Power of Attorney, blue
a. Imperf. 1,100.
b. Part perf. 30.00
c. Perf. 1.00
e. As No. R37c, half used as 5c on document *300.00*
R38 R3 10c Proprietary, blue ('64)
c. Perf. 19.00
R39 R3 15c Foreign Exchange, brown ('63)
c. Perf. 17.00
e. Double impression *1,250.*
R40 R3 15c Inland Exchange, brown
a. Imperf. 45.00
b. Part perf. 14.00
c. Perf. 2.00
e. As No. R40b, double impression *2,100.*
f. As No. R40c, double impression *850.00*
R41 R3 20c Foreign Exchange, red
a. Imperf. 95.00
c. Perf. 80.00
d. As No. R41c, silk paper 425.00
R42 R3 20c Inland Exchange, red
a. Imperf. 17.00
b. Part perf. 22.50

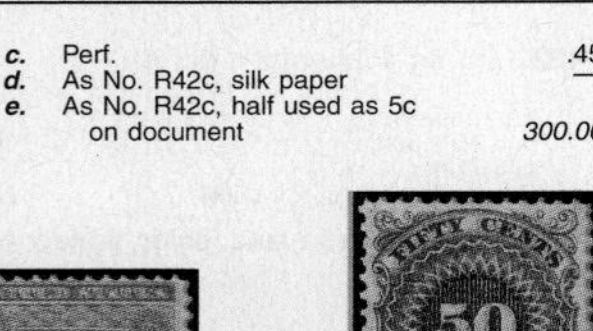

- *c.* Perf. .45
- *d.* As No. R42c, silk paper —
- *e.* As No. R42c, half used as 5c on document 300.00

R4

R5

R43 R4 25c Bond, red
- *a.* Imperf. 300.00
- *b.* Part perf. 6.75
- Pair 60.00
- *c.* Perf. 3.75

R44 R4 25c Certificate, red
- *a.* Imperf. 11.00
- *b.* Part perf. 6.75*
- *c.* Perf. .50
- Scratched plate, position 57 —
- *d.* As No. R44c, silk paper 2.75
- *e.* As No. R44c, printed on both sides 3,500.
- *f.* As No. R44c, impression of No. R48 on back 6,000.

R45 R4 25c Entry of Goods, red
- *a.* Imperf. 22.50
- *b.* Part perf. 325.00
- *c.* Perf. 1.50
- *d.* As No. R45c, silk paper 125.00

R46 R4 25c Insurance, red
- *a.* Imperf. 12.50
- *b.* Part perf. 19.00
- *c.* Perf. .30
- *d.* As No. R46c, silk paper 7.00
- *e.* As No. R46c, double impression 600.00

R47 R4 25c Life Insurance, red
- *a.* Imperf. 50.00
- *b.* Part perf. 1,000.
- *c.* Perf. 11.00

R48 R4 25c Power of Attorney, red
- *a.* Imperf. 10.00
- *b.* Part perf. 45.00
- *c.* Perf. 1.00
- *d.* As No. R48c, silk paper 1,750.

R49 R4 25c Protest, red
- *a.* Imperf. 35.00
- *b.* Part perf. 1,100.
- *c.* Perf. 10.00

R50 R4 25c Warehouse Receipt, red
- *a.* Imperf. 55.00
- *b.* Part perf. 1,200.
- *c.* Perf. 45.00

R51 R4 30c Foreign Exchange, lilac
- *a.* Imperf. 200.00
- *b.* Part perf. 10,000.
- *c.* Perf. 60.00
- *d.* As No. R51c, silk paper 600.00

R52 R4 30c Inland Exchange, lilac
- *a.* Imperf. 72.50
- *b.* Part perf. 90.00
- *c.* Perf. 8.50
- *d.* As No. R52c, silk paper —

There are shade and color variations of Nos. R51-R52.

R53 R4 40c Inland Exchange, brown
- *a.* Imperf. 2,500.
- *b.* Part perf. 9.00
- *c.* Perf. 8.00
- *d.* As No. R53c, silk paper 350.00
- *f.* As No. R53c, double impression —

R54 R5 50c Conveyance, blue
- *a.* Imperf. 20.00
- *b.* Part perf. 3.50
- *c.* Perf. .35
- *ce.* As No. R54c, ultramarine .50
- *d.* As No. R54c, silk paper, blue 3.00
- *de.* As No. R54d, ultramarine —

R55 R5 50c Entry of Goods, blue
- *b.* Part perf. 17.50
- *c.* Perf. .60
- *d.* As No. R55c, silk paper 150.00

R56 R5 50c Foreign Exchange, blue
- *a.* Imperf. 75.00
- *b.* Part perf. 125.00
- *c.* Perf. 7.50
- *e.* As No. R56c, double impression 600.00

R57 R5 50c Lease, blue
- *a.* Imperf. 35.00
- *b.* Part perf. 250.00
- *c.* Perf. 10.00

R58 R5 50c Life Insurance, blue
- *a.* Imperf. 45.00
- *b.* Part perf. 200.00
- *c.* Perf. 1.75
- *e.* As No. R58c, double impression 900.00

R59 R5 50c Mortgage, blue
- *a.* Imperf. 22.50
- *b.* Part perf. 5.00
- *c.* Perf. .70
- Tool gouge, position 63 40.00
- *d.* As No. R59c, silk paper —
- *e.* As No. R59a, double impression —
- *f.* As No. R59c, double impression —

R60 R5 50c Original Process, blue
- *a.* Imperf. 5.50
- *b.* Part perf. 4,000.
- *c.* Perf. 1.00
- *d.* As No. R60c, silk paper 7.50
- *e.* As No. R60c, half used as 25c on document —

R61 R5 50c Passage Ticket, blue
- *a.* Imperf. 140.00
- *b.* Part perf. 500.00
- *c.* Perf. 2.25

R62 R5 50c Probate of Will, blue
- *a.* Imperf. 55.00
- *b.* Part perf. 250.00
- *c.* Perf. 22.50

R63 R5 50c Surety Bond, blue
- *a.* Imperf. 400.00
- *b.* Part perf. 2.75
- *c.* Perf. .30
- *e.* As No. R63c, ultramarine .75

R64 R5 60c Inland Exchange, orange
- *a.* Imperf. 110.00
- *b.* Part perf. 82.50
- *c.* Perf. 9.00
- *d.* As No. R64c, silk paper 85.00

R65 R5 70c Foreign Exchange, green
- *a.* Imperf. 725.00
- *b.* Part perf. 200.00
- *c.* Perf. 14.00
- Double transfer at top —
- *d.* As No. R65c, silk paper 75.00

R6

R7

R66 R6 $1 Conveyance, red
- *a.* Imperf. 27.50
- *b.* Part perf. 5,500.
- *c.* Perf. 27.50
- *d.* As No. R66c, silk paper 200.00

R67 R6 $1 Entry of Goods, red
- *a.* Imperf. 50.00
- *c.* Perf. 2.75
- Scratched plate, position 43 15.00
- *d.* As No. R67c, silk paper 180.00

R68 R6 $1 Foreign Exchange, red
- *a.* Imperf. 90.00
- *c.* Perf. .75
- Recut frame lines at upper left 6.00
- *d.* As No. R68c, silk paper 150.00
- *e.* As No. R68d, half used as 50c on document 300.00

R69 R6 $1 Inland Exchange, red
- *a.* Imperf. 17.00
- *b.* Part perf. 6,000.*
- *c.* Perf. .70
- Pair 2.00
- *d.* As No. R69c, silk paper 6.00
- *e.* As No. R69c, horiz. pair, imperf. vert. —
- *f.* As No. R69c, half used as 50c on document 300.00

No. R69e is an error from a pane of stamps that was intended to be issued fully perforated. It can be differentiated from No. R69b by the color, paper and date of cancel. Expertization is strongly recommended.

R70 R6 $1 Lease, red
- *a.* Imperf. 50.00
- *c.* Perf. 4.50
- *e.* As No. R70c, half used as 50c on document 500.00

R71 R6 $1 Life Insurance, red
- *a.* Imperf. 300.00
- *c.* Perf. 10.00
- *d.* As No. R71c, silk paper 600.00
- *e.* As No. R71c, half used as 50c on document 1,000.

R72 R6 $1 Manifest, red
- *a.* Imperf. 47.50
- *c.* Perf. 40.00
- *e.* As No. R72c, half used as 50c on document 300.00

R73 R6 $1 Mortgage, red
- *a.* Imperf. 27.50
- *c.* Perf. 300.00

R74 R6 $1 Passage Ticket, red
- *a.* Imperf. 350.00
- *c.* Perf. 350.00

R75 R6 $1 Power of Attorney, red
- *a.* Imperf. 100.00
- *c.* Perf. 2.75
- *e.* As No. R75c, half used as 50c on document —

R76 R6 $1 Probate of Will, red
- *a.* Imperf. 100.00
- Pair 300.00
- *c.* Perf. 55.00

R77 R7 $1.30 Foreign Exchange, orange ('63)
- *a.* Imperf. 10,000.
- *c.* Perf. 85.00

R78 R7 $1.50 Inland Exchange, blue
- *a.* Imperf. 32.50
- *c.* Perf. 7.00
- Top and bottom frame lines doubled —

R79 R7 $1.60 Foreign Exchange, green ('63)
- *a.* Imperf. 1,500.
- *c.* Perf. 180.00

R80 R7 $1.90 Foreign Exchange, purple ('63)
- *a.* Imperf. 12,500.
- *c.* Perf. 200.00
- *d.* As No. R80c, silk paper 350.00

There are many shade and color variations of No. R80.

R8

R81 R8 $2 Conveyance, red
- *a.* Imperf. 250.00
- *b.* Part perf. 2,750.
- *c.* Perf. 4.00
- Scratched plate, position 9 —
- *d.* As No. R81c, silk paper 40.00
- *e.* As No. R81c, half used as $1 on document 600.00

R82 R8 $2 Mortgage, red
- *a.* Imperf. 150.00
- *c.* Perf. 7.00
- *d.* As No. R82c, silk paper 60.00
- *e.* As No. R82c, half used as $1 on document 900.00

R83 R8 $2 Probate of Will, red ('63)
- *a.* Imperf. 7,750.
- *c.* Perf. 90.00
- *e.* As No. R83c, half used as $1 on document 750.00

R84 R8 $2.50 Inland Exchange, purple ('63)
- *a.* Imperf. 10,000.
- *c.* Perf. 22.50
- *d.* As No. R84c, silk paper 40.00
- *e.* As No. R84c, double impression 1,650.

There are many shade and color variations of Nos. R84c and R84d.

R85 R8 $3 Charter Party, green
- *a.* Imperf. 200.00
- *c.* Perf. 11.00
- Scratched plate, position 44 —
- *d.* As No. R85c, silk paper 175.00
- *e.* As No. R85c, printed on both sides 7,000.
- *f.* As No. R85c, half used as $1.50 on document —
- *g.* As No. R85c, impression of No. RS208 on back 17,000.

R86 R8 $3 Manifest, green
- *a.* Imperf. 200.00
- *c.* Perf. 55.00

R87 R8 $3.50 Inland Exchange, blue ('63)
- *a.* Imperf. 9,000.
- *c.* Perf. 70.00
- *e.* As No. R87c, printed on both sides 4,000.

The $3.50 has stars in upper corners.

R9

R10

R88 R9 $5 Charter Party, red
- *a.* Imperf. 300.00
- *c.* Perf. 10.00
- *d.* As No. R88c, silk paper 170.00

R89 R9 $5 Conveyance, red
- *a.* Imperf. 50.00
- *c.* Perf. 11.00
- *d.* As No. R89c, silk paper 160.00

R90 R9 $5 Manifest, red
- *a.* Imperf. 250.00
- *c.* Perf. 120.00

R91 R9 $5 Mortgage, red
- *a.* Imperf. 200.00
- *c.* Perf. 25.00

R92 R9 $5 Probate of Will, red
- *a.* Imperf. 750.00
- *c.* Perf. 27.50

R93 R9 $10 Charter Party, green
- *a.* Imperf. 900.00
- *c.* Perf. 37.50

R94 R9 $10 Conveyance, green
- *a.* Imperf. 175.00
- *c.* Perf. 77.50

R95 R9 $10 Mortgage, green
- *a.* Imperf. 900.00
- *c.* Perf. 40.00

R96 R9 $10 Probate of Will, green
- *a.* Imperf. 3,500.
- *c.* Perf. 45.00

R97 R10 $15 Mortgage, blue
- *a.* Imperf. 3,750.
- *c.* Perf. 300.00
- *e.* As No. R97c, ultramarine 400.00
- *f.* As No. R97c, milky blue 450.00

R98 R10 $20 Conveyance, orange
- *a.* Imperf. 175.00
- *c.* Perf. 125.00
- *d.* As No. R98c, silk paper 175.00

R99 R10 $20 Probate of Will, orange
- *a.* Imperf. 3,500.
- *c.* Perf. 3,000.

R100 R10 $25 Mortgage, red ('63)
- *a.* Imperf. 2,700.
- *c.* Perf. 250.00
- *d.* As No. R100c, silk paper 300.00
- *e.* As No. R100c, horiz. pair, imperf. between 2,750.

R101 R10 $50 U.S. Internal Revenue, green ('63)
- *a.* Imperf. 325.00
- *c.* Perf. 210.00

R11

Illustration R11 reduced.

R102 R11 $200 U.S. Int. Rev., green & red ('64)
- *a.* Imperf. 2,500.
- *c.* Perf. 850.00

DOCUMENTARY STAMPS
Second Issue

After release of the First Issue revenue stamps, the Bureau of Internal Revenue received many reports of fraudulent cleaning and re-use. The Bureau ordered a Second Issue with new designs and colors, using a patented "chameleon" paper which is usually violet or pinkish, with silk fibers.

While designs are different from those of the first issue, stamp sizes and make up of the plates are the same as for corresponding denominations.

R12

R12a

George Washington
Various Frames and Numeral Arrangements

1871 *Perf. 12*

R103 R12 1c blue & black 100.00
Cut cancel 40.00
a. Inverted center 1,600.

R104 R12 2c blue & black 2.75
Cut cancel .30
a. Inverted center 5,000.

R105 R12a 3c blue & black 60.00
Cut cancel 25.00

R106 R12a 4c blue & black 150.00
Cut cancel 60.00
a. Horiz. half used as 2c on document 500.00
b. Vert. half used as 2c on document 1,000.

R107 R12a 5c blue & black 2.00
Cut cancel .50
a. Inverted center 4,000.
b. Half used as 2c on document 1,000.

R108 R12a 6c blue & black 275.00
Cut cancel 90.00

R109 R12a 10c blue & black 1.50
Cut cancel .30
a. Inverted center 2,000.
b. Double impression of center —
c. Half used as 5c on document 300.00

No. R109a is valued in the grade of fine.

R110 R12a 15c blue & black 100.00
Cut cancel 35.00

R111 R12a 20c blue & black 10.00
Cut cancel 4.00
a. Inverted center 7,000.

No. R111a is valued in the grade of fine and with small faults, as almost all examples have faults.

R13

R13a

R112 R13 25c blue & black 1.50
Cut cancel .30
a. Inverted center 13,000.
b. Imperf. —
c. Privately rouletted, sewing machine perfs 160.00
Cut cancel 80.00
d. Privately perforated 8 525.00

R113 R13 30c blue & black 175.00
Cut cancel 70.00

R114 R13 40c blue & black 150.00
Cut cancel 50.00

R115 R13a 50c blue & black 1.40
Cut cancel .35
a. Inverted center 1,150.
Punch cancel 325.00
b. Imperf. —
c. Privately perforated, sewing machine perfs 450.00
d. Privately perforated 8-9 —

R116 R13a 60c blue & black 250.00
Cut cancel 80.00

R117 R13a 70c blue & black 100.00
Cut cancel 35.00
a. Inverted center 4,000.
Cut cancel 1,250.

R13b

R118 R13b $1 blue & black 10.00
Cut cancel 2.25
a. Inverted center 6,000.
Punch cancel 1,000.
b. Half used as 50c on document 1,000.

R119 R13b $1.30 blue & black 750.00
Cut cancel 175.00

R120 R13b $1.50 blue & black 22.50
Cut cancel 9.00
a. Privately perforated sewing machine perfs 2,500.

R121 R13b $1.60 blue & black 750.00
Cut cancel 325.00

R122 R13b $1.90 blue & black 500.00
Cut cancel 150.00

R13c

R123 R13c $2 blue & black 25.00
Cut cancel 10.00

R124 R13c $2.50 blue & black 60.00
Cut cancel 30.00

R125 R13c $3 blue & black 75.00
Cut cancel 35.00

R126 R13c $3.50 blue & black 500.00
Cut cancel 130.00

R13d

R127 R13d $5 blue & black 40.00
Cut cancel 15.00
a. Inverted center 3,000.
Punch cancel 1,100.

R128 R13d $10 blue & black 260.00
Cut cancel 90.00

R13e

R129 R13e $20 blue & black 1,000.
Cut cancel 300.00

R130 R13e $25 blue & black 950.00
Cut cancel 300.00

R131 R13e $50 blue & black 1,200.
Cut cancel 350.00

R13f

R132 R13f $200 red, blue & black 9,000.
Cut cancel 3,500.

Printed in sheets of one.

R13g

R133 R13g $500 red org, grn & blk 17,500.

Printed in sheets of one.

Value for No. R133 is for a very fine appearing example with a light circular cut cancel or with minor flaws.

Inverted Centers: Fraudulently produced inverted centers exist, some excellently made.

Confusion resulting from the fact that all 1c through $50 denominations of the Second Issue were uniform in color, caused the ordering of a new printing with values in distinctive colors.

Plates used were those of the preceding issue.

Third Issue
Various Frames and Numeral Arrangements.
Violet "Chameleon" Paper with Silk Fibers.

1871-72 *Perf. 12*

R134 R12 1c claret & black ('72) 65.00
Cut cancel 30.00

R135 R12 2c orange & black .40
Cut cancel .25
a. 2c vermilion & black (error) 900.00
b. Inverted center 475.00
c. Imperf., pair —
d. As No. R135, double impression of frame 1,750.
e. As No. R135, frame printed on both sides 1,800.
f. As No. R135, double impression of center 150.00

R136 R12a 4c brown & black ('72) 110.00
Cut cancel 45.00

R137 R12a 5c orange & black .35
Cut cancel .25
a. Inverted center 5,000.
b. Half used as 2c on document 1,000.

No. R137a is valued in the grade of fine.

R138 R12a 6c orange & black ('72) 125.00
Cut cancel 50.00

R139 R12a 15c brown & black ('72) 27.50
Cut cancel 10.00
a. Inverted center 16,000.
Cut cancel 9,000.

R140 R13 30c orange & black ('72) 50.00
Cut cancel 15.00
a. Inverted center 3,500.
Cut cancel 1,750.

R141 R13 40c brown & black ('72) 110.00
Cut cancel 35.00

R142 R13a 60c orange & black ('72) 140.00
Cut cancel 55.00

R143 R13a 70c green & black ('72) 90.00
Cut cancel 30.00

R144 R13b $1 green & black ('72) 3.00
Cut cancel .80
a. Inverted center 15,000.

No. R144a is valued in the grade of fine.

R145 R13c $2 vermilion & black ('72) 55.00
Cut cancel 25.00

R146 R13c $2.50 claret & black ('72) 110.00
Cut cancel 35.00
a. Inverted center 22,500.

R147 R13c $3 green & black ('72) 110.00
Cut cancel 35.00

R148 R13d $5 vermilion & black ('72) 50.00
Cut cancel 20.00

R149 R13d $10 green & black ('72) 400.00
Cut cancel 85.00

R150 R13e $20 orange & black ('72) 900.00
Cut cancel 350.00
a. $20 vermilion & black (error) 1,250.

See note on Inverted Centers after No. R133.

1874 *Perf. 12*

R151 R12 2c orange & black, *green* .25
Cut cancel .25
a. Inverted center 800.00
Cut cancel 375.00

Liberty — R14

1875-78 *Perf. 12*

R152 R14 2c blue, *blue*
a. silk paper 3.00 .45
b. Wmk. 191R ('78) 2.00 .35
c. Wmk. 191R, rouletted 6 75.00 32.50
d. As "a," vert. pair, imperf. horiz. 525.00
e. As "b," imperf., pair 350.00
f. As "b," vert. pair, imperf. horiz. 350.00

The watermarked paper came into use in 1878. The rouletted stamps probably were introduced in 1881.

Nos. 279, 267a, 267, 279Bg, 279B, 272-274 Overprinted in Red or Blue

a

b

1898 **Wmk. 191** *Perf. 12*

For Nos. R153-R160, values in the first column are for unused examples, values in the second column are for used.

R153 A87 (a) 1c green (R) 5.00 2.75

R154 A87 (b) 1c green (R) .35 .35
a. Overprint inverted 35.00 22.50
b. Overprint on back instead of face, inverted 4,000.
c. Pair, one without overprint 10,000.
d. Half used as ½c on document 750.00

R155 A88 (b) 2c pink, III (Bl) .30 .25
b. 2c **carmine,** type III (Bl) .35 .25
c. As No. R155, overprint inverted 6.50 4.50
d. Vertical pair, one without overprint 1,750.

e. Horiz. pair, one without overprint —
f. As No. R155, overprint on back instead of face, inverted 350.00
i. Double ovt., one split *750.00*
R155A A88 (b) 2c pink, IV (Bl) .25 .25
g. 2c **carmine,** type IV (Bl) .25 .25
h. As No. R155A, overprint inverted 2.75 2.00

Handstamped Type "b" in Magenta

R156 A93 8c violet brown *5,250.*
R157 A94 10c dark green *4,000.*
R158 A95 15c dark blue *6,250.*

Nos. R156-R158 were emergency provisionals, privately prepared, not officially issued.

Privately Prepared Provisionals

No. 285 Overprinted in Red

1898 **Wmk. 191** ***Perf. 12***
R158A A100 1c dark yellow green *12,500. 10,000.*

No. 285 Ovptd. "I.R./P.I.D. & Son" in Red

R158B A100 1c dark yellow green *25,000. 30,000.*

No. R158B is valued with small faults as each of the four recorded examples have faults.

Nos. R158A-R158B were overprinted with federal government permission by the Purvis Printing Co. upon order of Capt. L. H. Chapman of the Chapman Steamboat Line. Both the Chapman Line and P. I. Daprix & Son operated freight-carrying steamboats on the Erie Canal. The Chapman Line touched at Syracuse, Utica, Little Falls and Fort Plain; the Daprix boat ran between Utica and Rome. Overprintings of 250 of each stamp were made.

Dr. Kilmer & Co. provisional overprints and St. Louis provisional proprietary stamps are listed under "Private Die Medicine Stamps" in the Scott U.S. Specialized Catalogue.

Newspaper Stamp No. PR121 Srchd. Vertically in Red

1898 ***Perf. 12***
R159 N18 $5 dark blue, surcharge reading down 550.00 325.00
R160 N18 $5 dark blue, surcharge reading up 150.00 140.00

Battleship — R15

Inscribed: "Series of 1898" and "Documentary."

There are 2 styles of rouletting for the 1898 proprietary and documentary stamps, an ordinary roulette 5½ and one where small rectangles of the paper are cut out, called hyphen hole perf. 7.

1898 **Wmk. 191R** ***Rouletted 5½***
R161 R15 ½c orange 5.00 *25.00*
R162 R15 ½c dark gray .30 .25
a. Vert. pair, imperf. horiz. 125.00
R163 R15 1c pale blue .25 .25
a. Vert. pair, imperf. horiz. 8.00
b. Imperf., pair *600.00*
R164 R15 2c car rose .30 .30
a. Vert. pair, imperf. horiz. 125.00
b. Imperf., pair 400.00
c. Horiz. pair, imperf. vert. 375.00
R165 R15 3c dark blue 3.50 .35
R166 R15 4c pale rose 2.50 .35
a. Vert. pair, imperf. horiz. 250.00
R167 R15 5c lilac .65 .35
a. Pair, imperf. horiz. or vert. 350.00 175.00
b. Horiz. pair, imperf. btwn. *650.00*
R168 R15 10c dark brown 2.00 .25
a. Vert. pair, imperf. horiz. 40.00 35.00
b. Horiz. pair, imperf. vert. —
R169 R15 25c pur brown 7.50 .50
R170 R15 40c blue lilac 125.00 1.50
Cut cancel .35
R171 R15 50c slate violet 35.00 .25
a. Imperf., pair *400.00*
b. Horiz. pair, imperf. btwn. *450.00*
R172 R15 80c bister 125.00 .50
Cut cancel .25

No. R167b may not be genuine.

Hyphen Hole Perf. 7

R163p 1c .30 .25
R164p 2c .35 .25
R165p 3c 40.00 1.40
R166p 4c 17.50 1.60
R167p 5c 17.50 .35
R168p 10c 10.00 .25
R169p 25c 20.00 .50
R170p 40c 210.00 35.00
Cut cancel 12.50
R171p 50c 75.00 1.00
b. Horiz. pair, imperf. btwn. — *250.00*
R172p 80c 250.00 60.00
Cut cancellation 20.00

Commerce — R16

1898 ***Rouletted 5½***
R173 R16 $1 dark green 30.00 .25
a. Vert. pair, imperf. horiz. 800.00
b. Horiz. pair, imperf. vert. — 325.00
p. Hyphen hole perf. 7 37.50 2.00
Cut cancel .75
R174 R16 $3 dark brown 55.00 1.25
Cut cancel .30
a. Horiz. pair, imperf. vert. 500.00
p. Hyphen hole perf. 7 100.00 3.50
Cut cancel .40
R175 R16 $5 orange red 90.00 2.00
Cut cancel .30
R176 R16 $10 black 175.00 3.50
Cut cancel .65
a. Horiz. pair, imperf. vert. —
R177 R16 $30 red 600.00 175.00
Cut cancel 47.50
R178 R16 $50 gray brown 350.00 7.00
Cut cancel 2.50

See Nos. R182-R183.

John Marshall — R17

Alexander Hamilton — R18

James Madison — R19

1899 ***Imperf.***

Without Gum

R179 R17 $100 yel brn & blk 350.00 40.00
Cut cancel 22.50
R180 R18 $500 car lake & blk 2,500. 800.00
Cut cancel 350.00
R181 R19 $1000 grn & blk 1,750. 350.00
Cut cancel 150.00

1900 ***Hyphen-hole perf. 7***

Allegorical Figure of Commerce

R182 R16 $1 carmine 55.00 .55
Cut cancel .30
R183 R16 $3 lake (fugitive ink) 350.00 60.00
Cut cancel 10.00

Warning: The ink on No. R183 will run in water.

a

Surcharged type "a"

1900
R184 R16 $1 gray 45.00 .40
Cut cancel .30
a. Horiz. pair, imperf. vert —
b. Surcharge omitted 140.00
As "b," cut cancel 82.50
R185 R16 $2 gray 45.00 .40
Cut cancel .25
R186 R16 $3 gray 190.00 15.00
Cut cancel 6.00
R187 R16 $5 gray 100.00 11.00
Cut cancel 1.60
R188 R16 $10 gray 250.00 25.00
Cut cancel 4.50
R189 R16 $50 gray 2,250. 575.00
Cut cancel 140.00

b

Surcharged type "b"

Warning: If Nos. R190-R194 are soaked, the center part of the surcharged numeral may wash off. Before the surcharging, a square of soluble varnish was applied to the middle of some stamps.

1902
R190 R16 $1 green 60.00 3.50
Cut cancel .30
a. Inverted surcharge *190.00*
R191 R16 $2 green 60.00 2.50
Cut cancel .45
a. Surcharged as No. R185 150.00 90.00
b. Surcharged as No. R185, in violet *2,000.* —
c. As "a," double surcharge *150.00*
d. As "a," triple surcharge *850.00*
e. Pair, Nos. R191c and R191d *1,650.*
R192 R16 $5 green 275.00 42.50
Cut cancel 5.00
a. Surcharge omitted 450.00
b. Pair, one without surcharge *600.00*
R193 R16 $10 green 525.00 225.00
Cut cancel 80.00
R194 R16 $50 green 3,000. 1,250.
Cut cancel 350.00

R20

Inscribed "Series of 1914"

Offset Printing

1914 **Wmk. 190** ***Perf. 10***
R195 R20 ½c rose 16.00 5.00
R196 R20 1c rose 3.50 .30
R197 R20 2c rose 5.00 .30
R198 R20 3c rose 125.00 40.00
R199 R20 4c rose 35.00 2.50
R200 R20 5c rose 12.00 .40
R201 R20 10c rose 10.00 .25
R202 R20 25c rose 60.00 .60
R203 R20 40c rose 40.00 3.00
R204 R20 50c rose 15.00 .35
R205 R20 80c rose 250.00 17.00
Nos. R195-R205 (11) 571.50 69.70

Wmk. 191R

R206 R20 ½c rose 1.60 .50
R207 R20 1c rose .25 .25
R208 R20 2c rose .30 .25
R209 R20 3c rose 1.50 .25
R210 R20 4c rose 4.50 .50
R211 R20 5c rose 2.00 .35
R212 R20 10c rose .80 .25
R213 R20 25c rose 10.00 1.50
R214 R20 40c rose 150.00 15.00
Cut cancel .50
R215 R20 50c rose 35.00 .40
Cut cancel .25
R216 R20 80c rose 225.00 35.00
Cut cancel 1.25
Nos. R206-R216 (11) 430.95 54.25

Liberty — R21

Inscribed "Series 1914"

Engr.

R217 R21 $1 green 85.00 .55
Cut cancel .25
a. $1 yellow green 85.00 .25
R218 R21 $2 carmine 150.00 1.00
Cut cancel .25
R219 R21 $3 purple 175.00 5.00
Cut cancel .80
R220 R21 $5 blue 120.00 4.50
Cut cancel .65
R221 R21 $10 yel org 375.00 7.50
Cut cancel 1.10
R222 R21 $30 vermilion 900.00 21.00
Cut cancel 2.25
R223 R21 $50 violet 2,000. 1,000.
Cut cancel 450.00

See Nos. R240-R245, R257-R259, R276-R281.

Portrait Types of 1899 Inscribed "Series of 1915" (#R224), or "Series of 1914"

1914-15 **Without Gum** ***Perf. 12***
R224 R19 $60 brown *(Lincoln)* 250.00 150.00
Cut cancel 70.00
R225 R17 $100 green *(Washington)* 77.50 45.00
Cut cancel 16.00
R226 R18 $500 blue *(Hamilton)* — 650.00
Cut cancel 275.00
R227 R19 $1000 orange *(Madison)* — 750.00
Cut cancel 325.00

The stamps of types R17, R18 and R19 in this and subsequent issues were issued in vertical strips of 4 which are imperforate at the top, bottom and right side; therefore, single stamps are always imperforate on one or two sides.

R22

Offset Printing

1917 **Wmk. 191R** ***Perf. 11***
R228 R22 1c carmine rose .35 .25
R229 R22 2c carmine rose .25 .25
R230 R22 3c carmine rose 1.75 .40
R231 R22 4c carmine rose .75 .25
R232 R22 5c carmine rose .30 .25
R233 R22 8c carmine rose 3.00 .35
R234 R22 10c carmine rose .40 .25
R235 R22 20c carmine rose .75 .25
R236 R22 25c carmine rose 1.75 .25
R237 R22 40c carmine rose 2.25 .50
R238 R22 50c carmine rose 2.50 .25
R239 R22 80c carmine rose 9.00 .35
Nos. R228-R239 (12) 23.05 3.60

Liberty Type of 1914 without "Series 1914"

1917-33 ***Engr.***
R240 R21 $1 yellow green 12.50 .30
a. $1 green 9.50 .25

R241 R21 $2 rose 20.00 .25
R242 R21 $3 violet 75.00 1.50
Cut cancel .30
R243 R21 $4 yellow brown ('33) 50.00 2.00
Cut cancel .30
R244 R21 $5 dark blue 35.00 .35
Cut cancel .25
R245 R21 $10 orange 75.00 1.40
Cut cancel .30

Portrait Types of 1899 without "Series of" and Date

Portraits: $30, Grant. $60, Lincoln. $100, Washington. $500, Hamilton. $1,000, Madison.

1917 Without Gum *Perf. 12*

R246 R17 $30 dp org, green numerals 55.00 13.00
Cut cancel 2.25
a. As "b," imperf. pair *900.00*
b. Numerals in blue 125.00 3.50
Cut cancel 1.50
R247 R19 $60 brown 65.00 8.00
Cut cancel .85
R248 R17 $100 green 45.00 2.00
Cut cancel .50
R249 R18 $500 blue, red numerals 350.00 50.00
Cut cancel 15.00
a. Numerals in orange 425.00 65.00
R250 R19 $1000 orange 175.00 20.00
Cut cancel 7.50
a. Imperf., pair *2,000.*

See note after No. R227.

1928-29 Offset Printing *Perf. 10*

R251 R22 1c carmine rose 2.10 1.60
R252 R22 2c carmine rose .60 .30
R253 R22 4c carmine rose 7.00 4.00
R254 R22 5c carmine rose 1.75 .55
R255 R22 10c carmine rose 2.75 1.25
R256 R22 20c carmine rose 6.00 4.50

Engr.

R257 R21 $1 green 200.00 45.00
Cut cancel 5.00
R258 R21 $2 rose 90.00 5.00
R259 R21 $10 orange 325.00 75.00
Cut cancel 30.00

1929 Offset Printing *Perf. 11x10*

R260 R22 2c carmine rose ('30) 3.00 2.75
R261 R22 5c carmine rose ('30) 2.00 1.90
R262 R22 10c carmine rose 9.25 6.75
R263 R22 20c carmine rose 15.00 8.25

Used values for Nos. R264-R310 are for stamps which are neither cut nor perforated with initials. Examples with cut cancellations or perforated initials are valued in the Scott U. S. Specialized Catalogue.

Types of 1917-33 Overprinted in Black

SERIES 1940

Offset Printing

1940 Wmk. 191R *Perf. 11*

R264 R22 1c rose pink 3.75 2.40
R265 R22 2c rose pink 5.00 2.25
R266 R22 3c rose pink 11.00 5.00
R267 R22 4c rose pink 5.00 .80
R268 R22 5c rose pink 5.00 1.25
R269 R22 8c rose pink 22.50 17.00
R270 R22 10c rose pink 2.50 .65
R271 R22 20c rose pink 3.25 .80
R272 R22 25c rose pink 8.00 1.50
R273 R22 40c rose pink 6.75 .90
R274 R22 50c rose pink 11.00 .55
R275 R22 80c rose pink 14.00 1.75

Engr.

R276 R21 $1 green 80.00 1.25
R277 R21 $2 rose 80.00 2.00
R278 R21 $3 violet 115.00 37.50
R279 R21 $4 yellow brown 210.00 35.00
R280 R21 $5 dark blue 100.00 20.00
R281 R21 $10 orange 275.00 50.00

Types of 1917 Handstamped "Series 1940" like R264-R281 in Blue (Nos. R282, R284), Green (Nos. R283, R286) or Violet (No. R285)

1940 Wmk. 191R *Perf. 12*
Without Gum

R282 R17 $30 vermilion 1,250.
a. With black 2-line handstamp in larger type *25,000.*
R283 R19 $60 brown 2,400.
a. As #R282a, cut cancel *12,500.*
R284 R17 $100 green 4,500.
R285 R18 $500 blue 3,000.
a. As #R282a *3,250.* *4,000.*

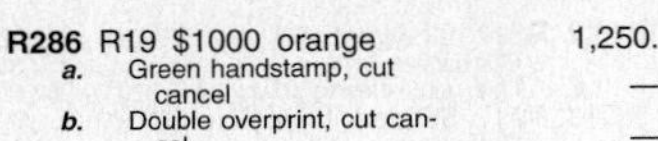

R286 R19 $1000 orange 1,250.
a. Green handstamp, cut cancel —
b. Double overprint, cut cancel —

Alexander Hamilton
R23

Levi Woodbury
R24

Overprinted in Black SERIES 1940

Various Portraits: 2c, Oliver Wolcott, Jr. 3c, Samuel Dexter. 4c, Albert Gallatin. 5c. G. W. Campbell. 8c, Alexander Dallas. 10c, William H. Crawford. 20c, Richard Rush. 25c, S. D. Ingham. 40c. Louis McLane. 50c, William J. Duane. 80c, Roger B. Taney. $2, Thomas Ewing. $3, Walter Forward. $4, J. C. Spencer. $5, G. M. Bibb. $10, R. J. Walker. $20, William M. Meredith.

1940 Engr. Wmk. 191R *Perf. 11*

R288 R23 1c carmine 5.75 4.50
a. Imperf, pair, without gum *250.00*
R289 R23 2c carmine 8.50 4.00
a. Imperf, pair, without gum *250.00*
R290 R23 3c carmine 30.00 12.00
a. Imperf, pair, without gum *250.00*
R291 R23 4c carmine 62.50 27.50
a. Imperf, pair, without gum *250.00*
R292 R23 5c carmine 4.75 .80
a. Imperf, pair, without gum *250.00*
R293 R23 8c carmine 85.00 60.00
a. Imperf, pair, without gum *250.00*
R294 R23 10c carmine 4.25 .60
a. Imperf, pair, without gum *250.00*
R295 R23 20c carmine 5.50 4.25
a. Imperf, pair, without gum *250.00*
R296 R23 25c carmine 5.00 .75
a. Imperf, pair, without gum *250.00*
R297 R23 40c carmine 75.00 30.00
a. Imperf, pair, without gum *250.00*
R298 R23 50c carmine 8.00 .60
a. Imperf, pair, without gum *250.00*
R299 R23 80c carmine 200.00 110.00
a. Imperf, pair, without gum *475.00*

R300 R24 $1 carmine 50.00 .60
a. Imperf, pair, without gum *250.00*
R301 R24 $2 carmine 100.00 .90
R302 R24 $3 carmine 190.00 95.00
a. Imperf, pair, without gum *1,400.*
R303 R24 $4 carmine 150.00 50.00
R304 R24 $5 carmine 85.00 3.00
R305 R24 $10 carmine 150.00 10.00
R305A R24 $20 carmine *3,000.* 1,100.
b. Imperf, pair, without gum *700.00*

Thomas Corwin — R25

Various Frames and Portraits: $50, James Guthrie. $60, Howell Cobb. $100, P. F. Thomas. $500, J. A. Dix, $1,000, S. P. Chase.

Perf. 12
Without Gum

R306 R25 $30 car 230.00 75.00
R306A R25 $50 car — *8,500.*
R307 R25 $60 car 450.00 80.00
a. Vert. pair, imperf. btwn. *2,750.* *1,450.*
R308 R25 $100 car 375.00 100.00
R309 R25 $500 car — 5,000.
R310 R25 $1000 car — 550.00

The $30 to $1,000 denominations in this and following similar issues, and the $2,500, $5,000 and $10,000 stamps of 1952-58 have straight edges on one or two sides. They were issued without gum through No. R723.

PROPRIETARY STAMPS

Stamps for use on proprietary articles were included in the first general issue of 1862-71. They are Nos. R3, R13-R14, R18, R22, R29, R31, R38.

Washington — RB1

RB1a

Various Frame Designs

1871-74 Engr. *Perf. 12*

RB1 RB1 1c grn & blk
a. Violet paper ('71) 8.00
b. Green paper ('74) 14.00
c. As "a," Imperf. 80.00
d. As "a." Inverted center *5,250.*
RB2 RB1 2c grn & blk
a. Violet paper ('71) 8.75
b. Green paper ('74) 30.00
c. As "a," Invtd. center *40,000.*
d. As "b," Invtd. center *8,000.*
e. As "b," vert. half used as 1c on document —

Only three examples recorded of the inverted center on violet paper, No. RB2c. Value is for example with very good to fine centering and very small faults.

RB2d is valued with fine centering and small faults.

RB3 RB1a 3c grn & blk
a. Violet paper ('71) 32.50
b. Green paper ('74) 67.50
c. As "a," privately perforated, sewing machine perfs 650.00
d. As "a," inverted center *14,000.*

No. RB3d is valued with small faults because all of the 8 recorded examples have faults.

RB4 RB1a 4c grn & blk
a. Violet paper ('71) 16.00
b. Green paper ('74) 25.00
c. As "a," inverted center *15,000.*
d. As "b," vert. half used as 2c on document —

No. RB4c is valued with small faults as all seven of the recorded examples have faults.

RB5 RB1a 5c grn & blk
a. Violet paper ('71) 175.00
b. Green paper ('74) 250.00
c. As "a," inverted center *155,000.*

No. RB5c is unique. Value represents price realized in 2000 auction sale.

RB6 RB1a 6c grn & blk
a. Violet paper ('71) 57.50
b. Green paper ('74) 140.00
RB7 RB1a 10c grn & blk ('73)
a. Violet paper ('71) 300.00
b. Green paper ('74) 65.00

See note on Inverted Centers after No. R133.

RB1b

RB8 RB1b 50c grn & blk ('73)
a. Violet paper ('71) 1,000.
b. Green paper ('74) 850.00
RB9 RB1b $1 grn & blk ('73)
a. Violet paper ('71) *3,500.*
b. Green paper ('74) *12,500.*

RB1c

RB10 RB1c $5 grn & blk ('73)
a. Violet paper ('71) *11,000.*
b. Green paper ('74) *75,000.*

No. RB10b is valued with small faults.

Washington — RB2

RB2a

Various Frame Designs
Green Paper

1875-81 *Perf.*
Unmwkd. (Silk Paper), Wmk. 191R

RB11 RB2 1c green
a. Silk paper 2.25
b. Wmk 191R .50
c. Rouletted 6 175.00
d. As No. RB11b, vert. pair, imperf btwn. 400.00
RB12 RB2 2c brown
a. Silk paper 3.25
b. Wmk 191R 2.00
c. Rouletted 6 190.00
RB13 RB2a 3c orange
a. Silk paper 14.00
b. Wmk 191R 4.00
c. Rouletted 6 160.00
d. As No. RB13c, horiz. pair, imperf. between *2,500.*
e. As No. RB13c, vert. pair, imperf. between *2,500.*
f. Privately perforated, sewing machine perfs —
RB14 RB2a 4c red brown
a. Silk paper 10.00
b. Wmk 191R 9.00
c. Rouletted 6 *22,000.*

RB15 RB2a 4c red
b. Wmk 191R 6.00
c. Rouletted 6 450.00
RB16 RB2a 5c black
a. Silk paper 200.00
b. Wmk 191R 125.00
c. Rouletted 6 *1,850.*
RB17 RB2a 6c violet blue
a. Silk paper 35.00
b. Wmk 191R 25.00
c. Rouletted 6 *1,100.*
RB18 RB2a 6c violet
b. Wmk 191R 35.00
c. Rouletted 6 *2,500.*
RB19 RB2a 10c blue ('81)
b. Wmk 191R 400.00

Many fraudulent roulettes exist.

Battleship — RB3

Inscribed "Series of 1898." and "Proprietary."

See note on rouletting preceding No. R161.

Rouletted 5½

1898 Wmk. 191R Engr.

RB20 RB3 ⅛c yel grn .25 .25
a. Vert. pair, imperf. horiz. —
b. Vert. pair, imperf. btwn. *1,100.*
RB21 RB3 ¼c brown .25 .25
a. ¼c red brown .25 .25
b. ¼c yellow brown .25 .25
c. ¼c orange brown .25 .25
d. ¼c bister .25 .25
e. Vert. pair, imperf. horiz. — —
f. Printed on both sides —
RB22 RB3 ⅜c dp org .30 .30
a. Horiz. pair, imperf. vert. 12.50
b. Vert. pair, imperf. horiz. —
RB23 RB3 ⅝c deep ultra .25 .25
Double transfer 1.50
a. Vert. pair, imperf. horiz. 85.00 —
b. Horiz. pair, imperf. btwn. *450.00* *400.00*
RB24 RB3 1c dark green 2.25 .50
a. Vert. pair, imperf. horiz. *450.00*
RB25 RB3 1¼c violet .35 .25
a. 1¼c brown violet .25 .25
b. Vert. pair, imperf. btwn. —
RB26 RB3 1⅞c dull blue 15.00 2.00
RB27 RB3 2c violet brown 1.40 .35
a. Horiz. pair, imperf. vert. 60.00
RB28 RB3 2½c lake 5.00 .35
a. Vert. pair, imperf. horiz. 400.00
RB29 RB3 3¾c olive gray 42.50 15.00
RB30 RB3 4c purple 16.00 1.50
RB31 RB3 5c brn org 15.00 1.50
a. Vert. pair, imperf. horiz. — *400.00*
b. Horiz. pair, imperf. vert. — *750.00*
Nos. RB20-RB31 (12) 98.55 22.50

Hyphen Hole Perf. 7

RB20p ⅛c .30 .25
RB21p ¼c .25 .25
b. ¼c yellow brown .25 .25
c. ¼c orange brown .25 .25
d. ¼c bister .25 .25
RB22p ⅜c .50 .35
RB23p ⅝c .30 .25
RB24p 1c 30.00 15.00
RB25p 1¼c .30 .30
a. 1¼c brown violet .25 .25
RB26p 1⅞c 40.00 9.00
RB27p 2c 10.00 1.00
RB28p 2½c 7.50 .40
RB29p 3¾c 100.00 27.50
RB30p 4c 70.00 22.50
RB31p 5c 85.00 25.00

See note before No. R161.

RB4

Inscribed "Series of 1914"

Offset Printing

1914 Wmk. 190 *Perf. 10*

RB32 RB4 ⅛c black .25 .35
Block of 4 1.25 1.60
RB33 RB4 ¼c black 4.00 1.50
RB34 RB4 ⅜c black .35 .35
RB35 RB4 ⅝c black 10.00 3.00
RB36 RB4 1¼c black 7.50 1.75
RB37 RB4 1⅞c black 80.00 22.50
RB38 RB4 2½c black 19.00 3.50
RB39 RB4 3⅛c black 230.00 67.50
RB40 RB4 3¾c black 75.00 27.50
RB41 RB4 4c black 110.00 45.00
RB42 RB4 4⅜c black *3,000.* —
RB43 RB4 5c black 200.00 110.00
Nos. RB32-RB41,RB43 (11) 736.10 282.95

Wmk. 191R

RB44 RB4 ⅛c black .35 .30
RB45 RB4 ¼c black .25 .25
RB46 RB4 ⅜c black .75 .45
RB47 RB4 ½c black 4.25 3.75
RB48 RB4 ⅝c black .30 .25
RB49 RB4 1c black 5.50 5.50
RB50 RB4 1¼c black .65 .40
RB51 RB4 1½c black 4.25 3.00
RB52 RB4 1⅞c black 1.35 .90
RB53 RB4 2c black 7.50 6.00
RB54 RB4 2½c black 2.00 1.40
RB55 RB4 3c black 6.00 4.00
RB56 RB4 3⅛c black 10.00 5.00
RB57 RB4 3¾c black 22.50 11.00
RB58 RB4 4c black .50 .30
RB59 RB4 4⅜c black 22.50 11.00
RB60 RB4 5c black 6.00 3.75
RB61 RB4 6c black 90.00 52.50
RB62 RB4 8c black 30.00 16.00
RB63 RB4 10c black 20.00 11.00
RB64 RB4 20c black 40.00 24.00
Nos. RB44-RB64 (21) 274.65 160.75

RB5

1919 Offset Printing *Perf. 11*

RB65 RB5 1c dark blue .25 .25
RB66 RB5 2c dark blue .35 .25
RB67 RB5 3c dark blue 1.50 .75
RB68 RB5 4c dark blue 2.25 .75
RB69 RB5 5c dark blue 3.00 1.25
RB70 RB5 8c dark blue 27.50 20.00
RB71 RB5 10c dark blue 12.50 5.00
RB72 RB5 20c dark blue 20.00 7.50
RB73 RB5 40c dark blue 75.00 25.00
Nos. RB65-RB73 (9) 142.35 60.75

FUTURE DELIVERY STAMPS

Issued to facilitate the collection of a tax upon each sale, agreement of sale or agreement to sell any products or merchandise at any exchange or board of trade, or other similar place for future delivery.

Documentary Stamps of 1917 Overprinted in Black or Red

Type I

Offset Printing

1918-34 Wmk. 191R *Perf. 11*

Overprint Horizontal (Lines 8mm apart)

Left Value — Unused With Gum

Right Value — Used

RC1 R22 2c carmine rose 8.75 .25
RC2 R22 3c carmine rose ('34) 47.50 37.50
Cut cancel 20.00
RC3 R22 4c carmine rose 17.50 .25
Cut cancel .25
b. Double impression of stamp 10.00
RC3A R22 5c carmine rose ('33) 100.00 7.50
RC4 R22 10c carmine rose 24.00 .35
a. Double overprint — 5.25
b. "FUTURE" omitted — *325.00*
c. "DELIVERY FUTURE" 37.50
RC5 R22 20c carmine rose 40.00 .25
Cut cancel .25
a. Double overprint 21.00
RC6 R22 25c carmine rose 85.00 .60
Cut cancel .30
RC7 R22 40c carmine rose 110.00 1.25
Cut cancel .35
RC8 R22 50c carmine rose 27.50 .35
Cut cancel .25
a. "DELIVERY" omitted — *110.00*
RC9 R22 80c carmine rose 190.00 15.00
Cut cancel 4.00
a. Double overprint 37.50

Engr.

Overprint Vertical, Reading Up (Lines 2mm apart)

RC10 R21 $1 green (R) 75.00 .35
Cut cancel .25
a. Overprint reading down *450.00*
b. Black overprint —
Cut cancel 125.00
RC11 R21 $2 rose 85.00 .45
Cut cancel .25
RC12 R21 $3 violet (R) 270.00 3.50
Cut cancel .30
a. Overprint reading down — 52.50
RC13 R21 $5 dark blue (R) 150.00 .60
Cut cancel .25
RC14 R21 $10 orange 180.00 1.35
Cut cancel .30
a. "DELIVERY FUTURE" *110.00*
RC15 R21 $20 olive bister 450.00 9.00
Cut cancel .80

Overprint Horizontal (Lines 11½mm apart)

Perf. 12

Without Gum

RC16 R17 $30 vermilion, green numerals 150.00 5.50
Cut cancel 1.75
a. Numerals in blue 160.00 4.75
Cut cancel 2.00
b. Imperf., blue numerals *150.00*
RC17 R19 $50 olive green (*Cleveland*) 125.00 3.00
Cut cancel .90
a. $50 olive bister 125.00 2.75
Cut cancel .25
RC18 R19 $60 brown 160.00 9.00
Cut cancel 1.20
a. Vert. pair, imperf. horiz. *950.00*
RC19 R17 $100 yellow green ('34) 260.00 37.50
Cut cancel 9.00
RC20 R18 $500 blue, red numerals (R) 325.00 25.00
Cut cancel 9.00
a. Numerals in orange — 70.00
Cut cancel 15.00
RC21 R19 $1000 orange 230.00 7.50
Cut cancel 2.00
a. Vert. pair, imperf. horiz. *1,350.*

See note after No. R227.

1923-24 Offset Printing *Perf. 11*

Overprint Horizontal (Lines 2mm apart)

RC22 R22 1c carmine rose 1.25 .25
RC23 R22 80c carmine rose 200.00 3.50
Cut cancel .70

Type II

1925-34 Engr.

RC25 R21 $1 green (R) 100.00 2.00
Cut cancel .45
RC26 R21 $10 orange (Bk) ('34) 260.00 29.00
Cut cancel 18.00

Overprint Type I

1928-29 Offset Printing *Perf. 10*

RC27 R22 10c carmine rose *5,000.*
RC28 R22 20c carmine rose *5,000.*

Some specialists have questioned the status of No. RC28, believing known examples to be either fraudulently reperforated examples of No. RC5, or examples of No. R256 with fake overprints applied. The editors would like to see authenticated evidence of the existence of No. RC28.

STOCK TRANSFER STAMPS

Issued to facilitate the collection of a tax on all sales or agreements to sell, or memoranda of sales or delivery of, or transfers of legal title to shares or certificates of stock.

Documentary Stamps Nos. R228 to R259 Overprinted in Black or Red

Offset Printing

1918-22 Wmk. 191R *Perf. 11*

Overprint Horizontal (Lines 8mm apart)

RD1 R22 1c carmine rose 1.00 .25
a. Double overprint — —
RD2 R22 2c carmine rose .25 .25
a. Double overprint — 15.00
Double overprint, cut cancel 7.50
RD3 R22 4c carmine rose .25 .25
a. Double overprint — 4.25
Double overprint, cut cancel 2.10
b. "STOCK" omitted 10.50
d. Ovpt. lines 10mm apart —
RD4 R22 5c carmine rose .30 .25
a. Ovpt. lines 7mm apart —
RD5 R22 10c carmine rose .30 .25
a. Double overprint — 5.25
Double overprint, cut cancel 2.75
b. "STOCK" omitted —
RD6 R22 20c carmine rose .55 .25
a. Double overprint 6.25
b. "STOCK" double —
RD7 R22 25c carmine rose 2.25 .30
Cut cancel .25
RD8 R22 40c carmine rose ('22) 2.25 .25
RD9 R22 50c carmine rose .80 .25
a. Double overprint —
RD10 R22 80c carmine rose 10.00 .45
Cut cancel .25

Engr.

Overprint Vertical, Reading Up (Lines 2mm apart)

RD11 R21 $1 green (R) 225.00 40.00
Cut cancel 10.00
a. Overprint reading down 300.00 60.00
Overprint reading down, cut cancel 20.00
RD12 R21 $1 green (Bk) 3.00 .30
a. Pair, one without overprint — *180.00*
b. Overprinted on back instead of face, inverted — *150.00*
c. Overprint reading down — 7.50
d. $1 yellow green 3.00 .25
RD13 R21 $2 rose 3.00 .25
a. Overprint reading down 11.50
Overprint reading down, cut cancel 1.50
b. Vert. pair, imperf. horiz. *800.00*
RD14 R21 $3 violet (R) 35.00 6.00
Cut cancel .30
RD15 R21 $4 yellow brown 15.00 .30
Cut cancel .25
RD16 R21 $5 dark blue (R) 10.00 .30
Cut cancel .25
a. Overprint reading down 42.50 1.35
Overprint reading down, cut cancel .25
RD17 R21 $10 orange 37.50 .45
Cut cancel .25
RD18 R21 $20 olive bister ('21) 150.00 18.00
Cut cancel 4.50
a. Overprint reading down —

Overprint Horizontal (Lines 11½mm apart)

1918 Without Gum *Perf. 12*

RD19 R17 $30 ver, grn numerals 55.00 6.50
Cut cancel 2.25
a. Numerals in blue 200.00 75.00
RD20 R19 $50 ol grn, *Cleveland* 160.00 70.00
Cut cancel 27.50
RD21 R19 $60 brown 350.00 30.00
Cut cancel 12.00
RD22 R17 $100 green 50.00 7.50
Cut cancel 3.00
RD23 R18 $500 blue (R) 550.00 160.00
Cut cancel 75.00
a. Numerals in orange 175.00
RD24 R19 $1,000 orange 425.00 110.00
Cut cancel 35.00

See note after No. R227.

1928 Offset Printing *Perf. 10*

Overprint Horizontal (Lines 8mm apart)

RD25 R22 2c carmine rose 5.50 .30
RD26 R22 4c carmine rose 5.50 .30
RD27 R22 10c carmine rose 5.50 .30
a. Inverted overprint *1,400.*
b. Ovpt. lines 9½mm apart —
RD28 R22 20c carmine rose 6.50 .35
RD29 R22 50c carmine rose 10.00 .50

Engr.

Overprint Vertical, Reading Up (Lines 2mm apart)

RD30 R21 $1 green 60.00 .35
Cut cancel .25
a. $1 yellow green 60.00 .50
RD31 R21 $2 carmine rose 55.00 .35
a. Pair, one without overprint 225.00 190.00
RD32 R21 $10 orange 60.00 .50
Cut cancel .25

Overprinted Horiz. in Black

1920 Offset Printing *Perf. 11*

RD33	R22	2c carmine rose	12.50	1.00
RD34	R22	10c carmine rose	3.00	.35
b.		Inverted overprint	*2,250.*	*1,250.*
RD35	R22	20c carmine rose	5.75	.25
a.		Horiz. pair, one without overprint	210.00	
d.		Inverted overprint (perf. initials)		—
RD36	R22	50c carmine rose	5.00	.30

Engr.

RD37	R21	$1 green	85.00	17.50
		Cut cancel		3.25
RD38	R21	$2 rose	100.00	17.50
		Cut cancel		3.25

Offset Printing

Perf. 10

RD39	R22	2c carmine rose	13.00	1.10
RD40	R22	10c carmine rose	5.25	.55
RD41	R22	20c carmine rose	6.00	.25
		Cut cancel		.25

Used values for Nos. RD42-RD372 are for stamps which are neither cut nor perforated with initials. Stamps with cut cancellations or perforated initials are valued in the Scott U.S. Specialized Catalogue.

Documentary Stamps of 1917-33 Overprinted in Black

Offset Printing

1940 Wmk. 191R *Perf. 11*

RD42	R22	1c rose pink	4.50	.65
a.		"Series 1940" inverted (pos. 31LR)	*950.00*	*600.00*

No. RD42a always comes with a natural straight edge at left.

RD43	R22	2c rose pink	6.00	.65
RD45	R22	4c rose pink	7.50	.35
RD46	R22	5c rose pink	8.00	.25
RD48	R22	10c rose pink	14.00	.35
RD49	R22	20c rose pink	17.00	.35
RD50	R22	25c rose pink	17.00	1.10
RD51	R22	40c rose pink	11.00	1.00
RD52	R22	50c rose pink	12.50	.35
RD53	R22	80c rose pink	280.00	110.00

Engr.

RD54	R21	$1 green	50.00	.60
RD55	R21	$2 rose	55.00	1.00
RD56	R21	$3 violet	350.00	18.00
RD57	R21	$4 yellow brown	125.00	1.60
RD58	R21	$5 dark blue	100.00	2.00
RD59	R21	$10 orange	275.00	10.00
RD60	R21	$20 olive bister	500.00	150.00

Nos. RD19-RD24 Handstamped in Blue "Series 1940"

1940 Wmk. 191R *Perf. 12*

Without Gum

RD61	R17	$30 ver	*2,000.*	1,500.
RD62	R19	$50 ol grn	*2,500.*	*2,500.*
		Cut cancel		1,250.
a.		Double ovpt., perf. initial		*1,400.*
RD63	R19	$60 brown	*5,500.*	*3,000.*
RD64	R17	$100 green	*5,000.*	850.00
RD65	R18	$500 blue		4,250.
RD66	R19	$1,000 orange		
		Cut cancel		*5,000.*

Alexander Hamilton ST1

Levi Woodbury ST2

Overprinted in Black **SERIES 1940**

Same Portraits as Nos. R288-R310.

1940 Engr. Wmk. 191R *Perf. 11*

RD67	ST1	1c brt grn	17.50	3.25
a.		Imperf, pair, without gum	*250.00*	
RD68	ST1	2c brt grn	10.00	1.75
a.		Imperf, pair, without gum	*250.00*	
RD70	ST1	4c brt grn	19.00	4.50
a.		Imperf, pair, without gum	*250.00*	
RD71	ST1	5c brt grn	12.00	1.75
a.		Imperf, pair, without gum	*250.00*	
b.		Without overprint, cut cancel		*850.00*
RD73	ST1	10c brt grn	16.00	2.10
a.		Imperf, pair, without gum	*250.00*	
RD74	ST1	20c brt grn	19.00	2.40
a.		Imperf, pair, without gum	*250.00*	
RD75	ST1	25c brt grn	60.00	10.50
a.		Imperf, pair, without gum	*250.00*	
RD76	ST1	40c brt grn	125.00	50.00
a.		Imperf, pair, without gum	*250.00*	
RD77	ST1	50c brt grn	16.00	2.10
a.		Imperf, pair, without gum	*250.00*	
RD78	ST1	80c brt grn	180.00	75.00
a.		Imperf, pair, without gum	*250.00*	
RD79	ST2	$1 brt grn	75.00	4.25
a.		Without overprint, perf. initial		*750.00*
RD80	ST2	$2 brt grn	75.00	12.00
a.		Imperf, pair, without gum	*250.00*	
RD81	ST2	$3 brt grn	110.00	15.00
a.		Imperf, pair, without gum	*250.00*	
RD82	ST2	$4 brt grn	800.00	300.00
a.		Imperf, pair, without gum	*250.00*	
RD83	ST2	$5 brt grn	110.00	16.00
a.		Imperf, pair, without gum	*250.00*	
RD84	ST2	$10 brt grn	250.00	60.00
a.		Imperf, pair, without gum	*250.00*	
RD85	ST2	$20 brt grn	1,250.	125.00
a.		Imperf, pair, without gum	*250.00*	

Nos. RD67-RD85 exist imperforate, without overprint. Value, set of pairs, $750.

Thomas Corwin — ST3

Overprinted "SERIES 1940"

Various frames and portraits as Nos. R306-R310.

Perf. 12

Without Gum

RD86	ST3	$30 brt grn	*6,000.*	200.00
RD87	ST3	$50 brt grn	3,000.	900.00
RD88	ST3	$60 brt grn	*5,000.*	1,900.
RD89	ST3	$100 brt grn	*2,500.*	450.00
RD90	ST3	$500 brt grn		*4,500.*
RD91	ST3	$1,000 brt grn		*4,000.*

Nos. RD86-RD91 exist as unfinished imperforates with complete receipt tabs, without overprints or serial numbers. Known in singles, pairs (Nos. RD86-RD88 and Nos. RD90-RD91, value $300 per pair; No. RD89, value $150 per pair), panes of four with plate number, uncut sheets of four panes (with two plate numbers), cross gutter blocks of eight, and blocks of four with vertical gutter between and plate number.

HUNTING PERMIT STAMPS

Catalogue values for all unused stamps in this section are for stamps with never-hinged original gum. Minor natural gum skips and bends are normal on Nos. RW1-RW20. No-gum stamps are without signature or other cancel.

Nos. RW1-RW12 were issued in panes of 28, of which 10 stamps have a straight edge on one or two sides. Such examples sell for 20%-30% less than the values shown.

Department of Agriculture

Various Designs Inscribed "U. S. Department of Agriculture"

Mallards Alighting — HP1

Engraved: Flat Plate Printing

1934 Unwmk. *Perf. 11*

Inscribed "Void after June 30, 1935"

RW1	HP1	$1 blue	750.	175.
		Hinged	300.	
		No gum	175.	
a.		Imperf., vertical pair	—	
b.		Vert. pair, imperf. horiz.	—	

Used value is for stamp with handstamp or manuscript cancel.

It is almost certain that No. RW1a is No. RW1b with vertical perfs trimmed off. No horizontal pairs of No. RW1a are known. All recorded pairs are vertical, with narrow side margins. Both varieties probably are printer's waste since examples exist with gum on front or without gum.

1935

Inscribed "Void after June 30, 1936"

RW2	HP2	$1 rose lake	725.	160.
		deep rose lake	—	
		Hinged	350.	
		No gum	165.	

1936

Inscribed "Void after June 30, 1937"

RW3	HP3	$1 brown black	325.	1000.00
		Hinged	150.	
		No gum	90.	

1937

Inscribed "Void after June 30, 1938"

RW4	HP4	$1 light green	275.	65.00
		Hinged	125.	
		No gum	75.	

1938

Inscribed "Void after June 30, 1939"

RW5	HP5	$1 light violet	375.	75.00
		Hinged	175.	
		No gum	75.	

Department of the Interior

Various Designs Inscribed "U. S. Department of the Interior"

Green-Winged Teal — HP6

1939

Inscribed "Void after June 30, 1940"

RW6	HP6	$1 chocolate	225.	45.00
		Hinged	100.	
		No gum	55.	

1940

Inscribed "Void after June 30, 1941"

RW7	HP7	$1 sepia	225.	35.00
		Hinged	95.	
		No gum	45.	

CONFEDERATE STATES OF AMERICA

3¢ 1861 POSTMASTERS' PROVISIONALS

With the secession of South Carolina from the Union on Dec. 20, 1860, a new era began in U.S. history as well as its postal history. Other Southern states quickly followed South Carolina's lead, which in turn led to the formation of the provisional government of the Confederate States of America on Feb. 4, 1861.

President Jefferson Davis' cabinet was completed Mar. 6, 1861, with the acceptance of the position of Postmaster General by John H. Reagan of Texas. The provisional government had already passed regulations that required payment for postage in cash and that effectively carried over the U.S. 3c rate until the new Confederate Post Office Department took over control of the system.

Soon after entering on his duties, Reagan directed the postmasters in the Confederate States and in the newly seceded states to "continue the performance of their duties as such, and render all accounts and pay all moneys (sic) to the order of the Government of the U.S. as they have heretofore done, until the Government of the Confederate States shall be prepared to assume control of its postal affairs."

As coinage was becoming scarce, postal patrons began having problems buying individual stamps or paying for letters individually, especially as stamp stocks started to run short in certain areas. Even though the U.S. Post Office Department was technically in control of the postal system and southern postmasters were operating under Federal authority, the U.S.P.O. was hesitant in re-supplying seceded states with additional stamps and stamped envelopes.

The U.S. government had made the issuance of postmasters' provisionals illegal many years before, but the southern postmasters had to do what they felt was necessary to allow patrons to pay for postage and make the system work. Therefore, a few postmasters took it upon themselves to issue provisional stamps in the 3c rate then in effect.

Interestingly, these were stamps and envelopes that the U.S. government did not recognize as legal, but they did do postal duty unchallenged in the Confederate States. Yet the proceeds were to be remitted to the U.S. government in Washington! Six authenticated postmasters' provisionals in the 3c rate have been recorded.

On May 13, 1861, Postmaster General Reagan issued his proclamation "assuming control and direction of postal service within the limits of the Confederate States of America on and after the first day of June," with new postage rates and regulations.

The Federal government suspended operations in the Confederate States (except for western Virginia and the seceding state of Tennessee) by a proclamation issued by Postmaster General Montgomery Blair on May 27, 1861, effective from May 31, 1861, and June 10 for western and middle Tennessee.

As Tennessee did not join the Confederacy until July 2, 1861, the unissued 3c Nashville provisional was produced in a state that was in the process of seceding, while the other provisionals were used in the Confederacy before the June 1 assumption of control of postal service by the Confederate States of America.

Illustrations are reduced in size.

XU numbers are envelope entires.

FORT VALLEY, GA.

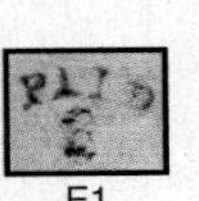

E1

E2

Handstamped Envelope

7AXU1	E1	3c black	—

HILLSBORO, N.C.

A1

Handstamped Adhesive

1AX1 A1 3c bluish black, on cover —

No. 1AX1 is unique. This is the same handstamp as used for No. 39X1. 3c usage is determined from the May 27, 1861 circular date stamp.

JACKSON, MISS.

E1

Handstamped Envelope

2AXU1 E1 3c black *3,500.*

See Nos. 43XU1-43XU4.

MADISON COURT HOUSE, FLA.

A1

"CNETS"

Typeset Adhesive

3AX1 A1 3c gold — *20,000.*
On cover *120,000.*
a. "CNETS" *22,500.*

No. 3AX1a is unique.

See No. 137XU1.

NASHVILLE, TENN.

A1

Typeset Adhesive (5 varieties)

4AX1 A1 3c carmine 400.

No. 4AX1 was prepared by Postmaster McNish with the U.S. rate, but the stamp was never issued.
See Nos. 61X2-61XU2.

SELMA, ALA.

E1

Handstamped Envelope

5AXU1 E1 3c black *1,950.*

See Nos. 77XU1-77XU3.

TUSCUMBIA, ALA.

E1

Handstamped Envelope, impression at upper right

6AXU1 E1 3c dull red, *buff* *17,500.*

Dangerous forgeries exist of No. 6AXU1.
See Nos. 84XU1-84XU3.

For later additions, listed out of numerical sequence, see:
***#7AXU1*, Fort Valley, Ga.**

PROVISIONAL ISSUES

These stamps and envelopes were issued by individual postmasters generally between June 1, 1861, when the use of U.S. stamps stopped in the Confederacy, and Oct. 16, 1861, when the 1st Confederate Government stamps were issued.

They were occasionally issued at later periods, especially in Texas, when regular issues of Government stamps were unavailable.

Canceling stamps of the post offices were often used to produce envelopes, some of which were supplied in advance by private citizens.

These envelopes and other stationery therefore may be found in a wide variety of papers, colors, sizes & shapes, including patriotic and semi-official types.

It is often difficult to determine whether the impression made by the canceling stamp indicates provisional usage or merely postage paid at the time the letter was deposited in the post office. Occasionally the same mark was used for both purposes.

The *press-printed* provisional envelopes are in a different category. They were produced in quantity, using envelopes procured in advance by the postmaster, such as those of Charleston, Lynchburg, Memphis, etc.

The press-printed envelopes are listed and valued on all known papers.

The handstamped provisional envelopes are listed and valued according to type and variety of handstamp, but not according to paper. Many exist on such a variety of papers that they defy accurate, complete listing.

The value of a handstamped provisional envelope is determined *primarily* by the clarity of the markings and its overall condition and attractiveness, rather than type of paper.

All handstamped provisional envelopes, when used, should also show the postmark of the town of issue.

Most handstamps are impressed at top right, although they exist from some towns in other positions.

Illustrations in this section are reduced in size.

XU numbers are envelope entires.

ABERDEEN, MISS.

E1

Handstamped Envelopes

1XU1 E1 5c black *7,000.*
a. 10c (ms.) on 5c black *9,000.*

No. 1XU1a is unique.

ABINGDON, VA.

E1

Handstamped Envelopes

2XU1 E1 2c black *12,500.*
a. 5c (ms.) on 2c black *15,000.*
2XU2 E1 5c black 1,750.
On patriotic cover *3,000.*
2XU3 E1 10c black *2,200.* *3,500.*

No. 2XU1 is unique. No. 2XU3 unused and used are each unique.

ALBANY, GA.

E1

E2

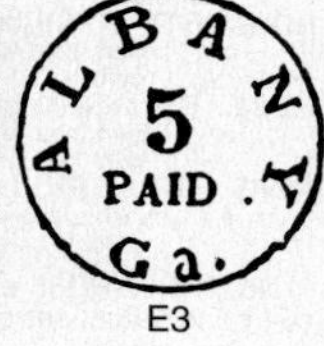

E3

E4

Handstamped Envelopes

3XU1 E1 5c greenish blue 1,000.
On patriotic cover —
3XU2 E2 10c greenish blue *1,750.*
a. 10c on 5c greenish blue *3,500.*
3XU5 E3 5c greenish blue —
3XU6 E4 10c greenish blue *3,500.*

Only one example each recorded of Nos. 3XU2, 3XU2a and 3XU6. No. 3XU2 is a cover front only and is valued as such. No. 3XU2a is the unique Confederate example of one provisional marking revaluing another.

The existence of No. 3XU5 is in question. The editors would like to see an authenticated example of this marking.

ANDERSON COURT HOUSE, S.C.

E1

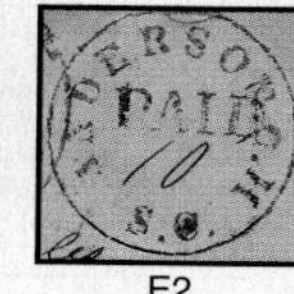

E2

E3

Handstamped Envelopes

4XU1 E1 5c black 1,000. *2,750.*
4XU2 E2 10c (ms.) black *2,500.*
4XU3 E3 (2c) black, denomination omitted (circular rate) *2,250.*

ATHENS, GA

A1 — Type I

A1 — Type II

E1

Typographed Adhesives (from woodcuts of two types)

Pairs, both horizontal and vertical, always show one of each type.

5X1 A1 5c purple (shades) 1,000. 1,400.
Pair — 3,500.
On cover 2,250.
Pair on cover 7,000.
Strip of 4 on cover (horiz.) *10,000.*
a. Tete beche pair (vertical) *7,500.*
Tete beche pair on cover *20,000.*
5X2 A1 5c red 5,750. 5,750.
On cover *17,500.*
Pair on cover —

The colorless ornaments in the four corners of No. 5X2 were recut making them wider than those in No. 5X1.

Dangerous fakes exist of Nos. 5X1 and 5X2. Certificates of authenticity from recognized committees are strongly recommended.

Handstamped Envelopes

5XU1 E1 10c black, on patriotic cover *2,500.*

The markings on No. 5XU1 are the same as those used on stampless envelopes. On the unique listed example of No. 5XU1, there is a handwritten note on the inside of the flap: 'Andrew had these envelopes stamped & I am obliged to use them or loose the postage.' Two or more similar covers from the same correspondence are known, but without the note under the flap. While these also may be provisional use, it cannot be proven, and these covers are considered handstamp paid covers.

ATLANTA, GA.

E1

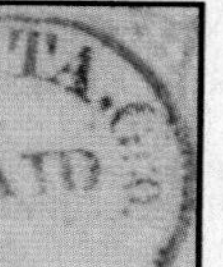

E2

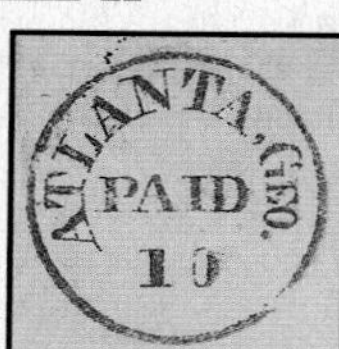

E2

Handstamped Envelopes

6XU1 E1 5c red *5,000.*
6XU2 E1 5c black 160. 1,000.
On patriotic cover *3,500.*
a. 10c on 5c black *2,500.*
On patriotic cover —
6XU3 E2 PAID, black *1,000.*

No. 6UX3 was probably used for drop letters and circulars.

6XU4 E3 2c black *3,000.*

6XU5 E3 5c black 1,500.
On patriotic cover 3,500.
a. 10c on 5c black *2,500.*
6XU6 E3 10c black 550. —
On patriotic cover

Only one example recorded of No. 6XU1.

E3

Handstamped Envelopes

6XU8 E3 5c black 3,500.
6XU9 E3 10c black ("10" upright) 3,250.

Only one example recorded of No. 6XU8.

AUSTIN, MISS.

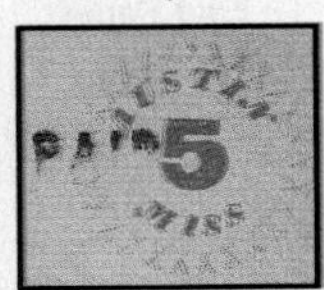
E1

Press-printed Envelope (typeset)

8XU1 E1 5c red, *amber* *75,000.*

One example recorded.

AUSTIN, TEX.

E1a

Handstamped Adhesive

9X1 E1a 10c black, *white* or *buff* —
On cover, uncanceled *18,000.*
On cover, tied —

Only one example of No. 9X1 tied on cover is recorded.

Handstamped Envelope

9XU1 E1a 10c black 2,500.

AUTAUGAVILLE, ALA.

E1

E2

Handstamped Envelopes

10XU1 E1 5c black *20,000.*
10XU2 E2 5c black *20,000.*

No. 10XU2 is unique.

BALCONY FALLS, VA.

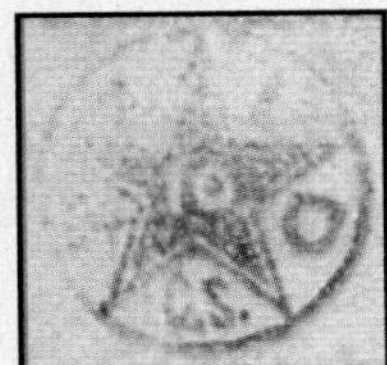
E1

Handstamped Envelope

122XU1 E1 10c blue *2,000.*

The use of No. 122XU1 as a provisional marking is in question. The editors would like to see authenticated evidence of its use as a provisional.

BARNWELL COURT HOUSE, S. C.

E1

Handstamped Envelope

123XU1 E1 5c black *3,000.*

These are two separate handstamps.
All recorded uses are on addressed covers without postmarks.

BATON ROUGE, LA.

A1

A2

Typeset Adhesives

Ten varieties of each

11X1 A1 2c green *8,250.* *5,000.*
On cover *50,000.*
a. "McCcrmick" *35,000.* *35,000.*
On cover *55,000.*
11X2 A2 5c **green & carmine** 1,500. 1,400.
On cover *5,000.*
a. "McCcrmick" *10,000.* *3,500.*
On cover *15,000.*

Only one example each is recorded of No. 11X1a unused, used and on cover.

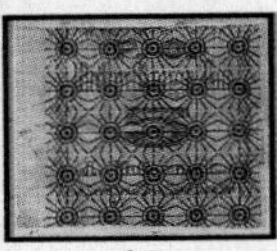
A3

A4

Ten varieties of each

11X3 A3 5c green & carmine *10,000.* *4,000.*
On cover *10,000.*
a. "McCcrmick" *32,500.*
11X4 A4 10c blue *50,000.*
On cover *75,000.*

Nos. 11X3a and 11X4 on cover are unique.

BEAUMONT, TEX.

A1

A2

Typeset Adhesives

Several varieties of each

12X1 A1 10c black, *yellow* —
On cover *55,000.*
12X2 A1 10c black, *pink* *20,000.*

No. 12X1 is smaller than No. 12X2.

On cover *27,500.*
12X3 A2 10c black, *yellow*, on cover *90,000.*

One example recorded of No. 12X3.

BLUFFTON, S. C.

E1

Handstamped Envelope

124XU1 E1 5c black *4,750.*

Only one example recorded of No. 124XU1.

BRIDGEVILLE, ALA.

A1

Handstamped Adhesive in black within red pen-ruled squares

13X1 A1 5c black & red, pair on cover *20,000.*

CAMDEN, S. C.

E1

E2

Handstamped Envelopes

125XU1 E1 5c black *2,500.*
125XU2 E2 10c black *750.*

No. 125XU2 unused was privately carried and is addressed but has no postal markings. No. 125XU2 is indistinguishable from a handstamp paid cover when used.

CANTON, MISS.

E1

"P" in star is initial of Postmaster William Priestly.

Handstamped Envelopes

14XU1 E1 5c black 4,000.
a. 10c (ms.) on 5c black 5,000.

CAROLINA CITY, N. C.

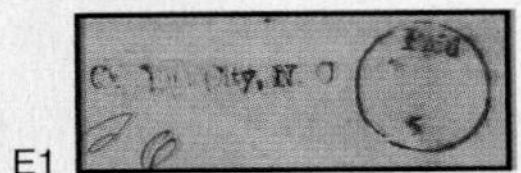
E1

Handstamped Envelope

118XU1 E1 5c black *5,000.*

CARTERSVILLE, GA.

E1

Handstamped Envelope

126XU1 E1 (5c) red *1,500.*

CHAPEL HILL, N. C.

E1

Handstamped Envelope

15XU1 E1 5c black *4,500.*

CHARLESTON, S. C.

A1

E1

E2

Lithographed Adhesive

16X1 A1 5c blue 1,400. 800.
On cover *2,500.*
Pair, on cover *5,000.*

Values are for stamps showing parts of the outer frame lines on at least 3 sides. The vast majority of this stamp small faults and are valued thus. Completely sound examples are scarce and sell for more.

Press-printed Envelopes (typographed from woodcut)

16XU1 E1 5c blue 1,250. *1,750.*
16XU2 E1 5c blue, *amber* 1,250. *2,250.*
16XU3 E1 5c blue, *orange* 1,250. *2,250.*
16XU4 E1 5c blue, *buff* 1,250. *1,500.*
16XU5 E1 5c blue, *blue* 1,250. *2,250.*
16XU6 E2 10c blue, *orange* *80,000.*

The No. 16XU6 used entire is unique; value based on 1997 auction sale.
Beware of fakes of the E1 design.

Handstamped Cut Square

16XU7 E2 10c black *2,000.*

There is only one example of No. 16XU7. It is a cutout, not an entire. It may not have been mailed from Charleston, and it may not have paid postage.

CHARLOTTE, N. C.

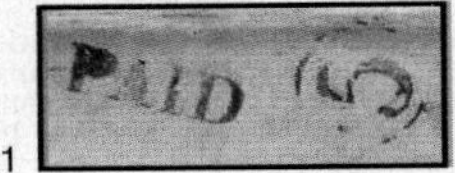
E1

146XU1 E1 5c blue, "5" in circle and straight line "PAID" *3,500.*

CHARLOTTESVILLE, VA.

E1

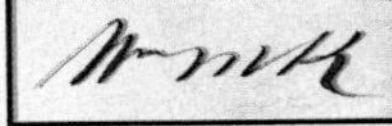
Control

Handstamped Envelopes, Manuscript Initials

127XU1 E1 5c blue —
127XU2 E1 10c blue —

The control initials appear at the upper right on the front of the envelope.

CHATTANOOGA, TENN.

E1

E2

Handstamped Envelopes

17XU2 E1 5c black 1,750.
17XU3 E2 5c on 2c black *5,000.*

No. 17XU3 is unique.

CHRISTIANSBURG, VA.

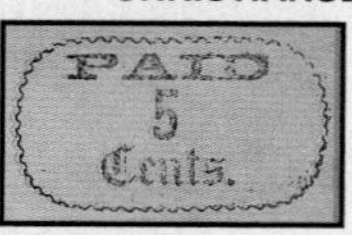

E1

Handstamped Envelopes

Impressed at top right

99XU1 E1 5c black *2,250.*
99XU2 E1 5c blue *2,000.*
99XU4 E1 5c green on U.S. envelope No. U27 *4,500.*
99XU5 E1 10c blue *3,500.*

The absence of 5c and 10c handstamped paid markings from this town suggests that Nos. 99XU1-99XU5 were used as both provisional and handstamped paid markings.

COLAPARCHEE, GA.

E1

Control

Handstamped Envelope

119XU1 E1 5c black *3,500.*

There are only two recorded examples of No. 119XU1, and both are used from Savannah with a general issue stamp.

The control appears on the front of the envelope.

COLUMBIA, S. C.

Oval Control

Circular Control

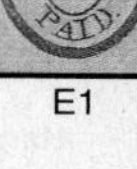

E1

E2

E3

E4

E5

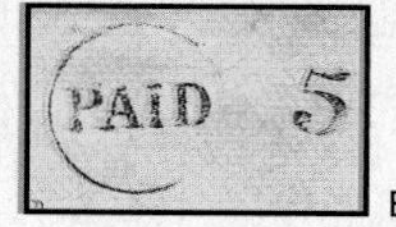

E6

E7

E8

Handstamped Envelopes

18XU1 E1 5c blue 550. 900.
a. 10c on 5c blue *3,500.*
18XU4 E2 5c blue, oval control on front *7,500.*
a. Oval control on back *1,250.*
18XU7 E3 5c blue, oval control on back 1,000.
18XU8 E4 5c blue oval control on back 1,000.
a. Circular control on back 2,000.
18XU9 E4 10c blue oval control on back 1,250.
18XU10 E5 10c blue oval control on back 1,250.
18XU11 E6 5c blue oval control on front *2,500.*
18XU12 E6 10c blue oval control on back 1,250.
18XU13 E7 5c blue oval control on back 1,000.
a. Circular control on back 1,500.
18XU14 E8 5c blue oval control on back 1,000.
a. No control (unused) —

COLUMBIA, TENN.

E1

Handstamped Envelope

113XU1 E1 5c red *6,000.*

One example recorded.

COLUMBUS, GA.

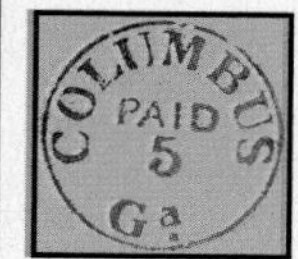

E1

Handstamped Envelopes

19XU1 E1 5c blue *900.*
19XU2 E1 10c red *3,250.*

COURTLAND, ALA.

E1

Handstamped Envelopes (from woodcut)

103XU1 E1 5c red *37,500.*

CUTHBERT, GA

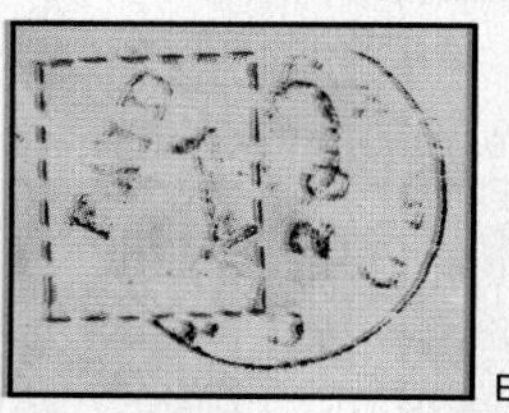
E1

Handstamped Envelope

95XU1 E1 10c black *750.*

The unique example of No. 95XU1 was used by having a C.S.A. 10c #12c placed over it.

DALTON, GA

E1

Handstamped Envelopes

20XU1 E1 5c black *750.*
a. Denomination omitted (5c rate) *875.*
b. 10c (ms.) on 5c black *1,500.*
c. 20c (ms.) on 5c black —
20XU2 E1 10c black 1,250.

DANVILLE, VA.

A1

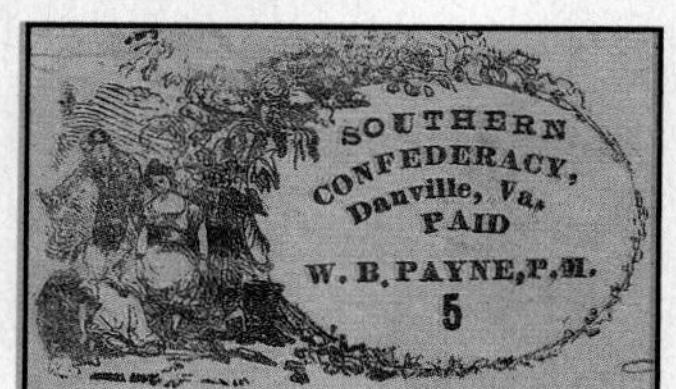

Design measures 60x37mm — E1

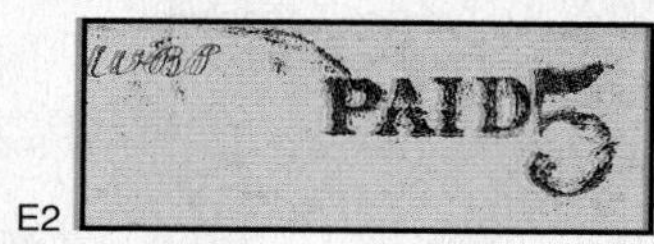

E2

E3

E4

E5

E6

Typeset Adhesive
Wove Paper

21X1 A1 5c red *7,500.*
On cover *32,500.*
Cut to shape *6,250.*
On cover, cut to shape *27,500.*

Two varieties known.

Cancellation: blue town.

Laid Paper

21X2 A1 5c red *10,000.*

Press-printed Envelopes (typographed)

Two types: "SOUTHERN" in straight or curved line

Impressed (usually) at top left

21XU1 E1 5c black *7,000.*
21XU2 E1 5c black, *amber* *7,000.*
21XU3 E1 5c black, *dark buff* *7,000.*

The existence of No. 21XU2 is in question. The editors would like to see authenticated evidence of its existence.

Unissued 10c envelopes (type E1, in red) are known. All recorded examples are envelopes that show evidence of added stamps being torn off.

Dangerous forgeries exist of No. 21XU1.

Handstamped Envelopes

21XU3A E2 5c black (ms "WBP" initials) *1,000.*
21XU3B E3 5c black (ms "WPB" initials) *8,500.*
21XU4 E4 10c black *2,500.*
21XU6 E5 10c black *2,750.*
21XU7 E6 10c black (ms "WBP" initials) —

Types E4 and E5 both exist on one cover.

On No. 21XU3B, the "PAID 5 Cents" handstamp is to the left, and the "PAID" and ms. "5" are toward the right. It is unique.

DEMOPOLIS, ALA.

E1

Handstamped Envelopes, Signature in ms.

22XU1 E1 5c black ("Jno. Y. Hall") *3,500.*
22XU2 E1 5c black ("J. Y. Hall") *3,500.*
22XU3 E1 5c (ms.) black ("J. Y. Hall") *4,000.*

EATONTON, GA.

E1

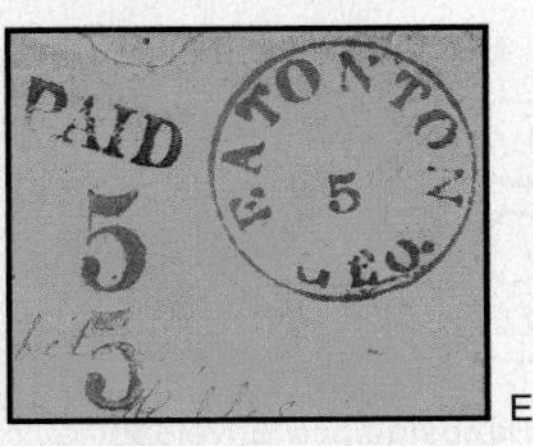
E2

Handstamped Envelopes

23XU1 E1 5c black *3,000.*
a. 10 (ms) on 5c black —
23XU2 E2 5c + 5c black *5,000.*

EMORY, VA.

A1

Handstamped Adhesives ("PAID" and "5" in circle on selvage of U.S. 1c 1857 issue)

Perf. 15 on three sides

24X1 A1 5c blue, on cover, tied *27,500.*

Also known with "5" above "PAID."

E1

E2

Handstamped Envelopes

24XU1 E1 5c blue *4,000.*
24XU2 E2 10c blue *5,000.*

One example each recorded of Nos. 24XU1 and 24XU2.

FINCASTLE, VA.

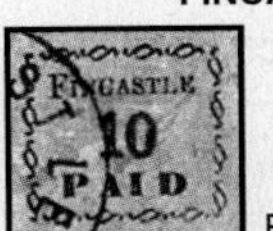
E1

Press-printed Envelope (typeset)

Impressed at top right

104XU1 E1 10c black *20,000.*

One example recorded of No. 104XU1.

FORSYTH, GA.

E1

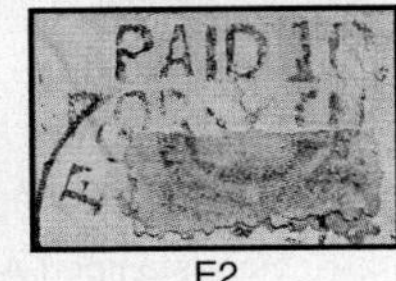
E2

Handstamped Envelope

120XU1 E1 10c black *2,000.*
120XU2 E2 10c black *1,250.*

Only one example each recorded of Nos. 120XU1 and 120XU2.

FORT VALLEY, GA.

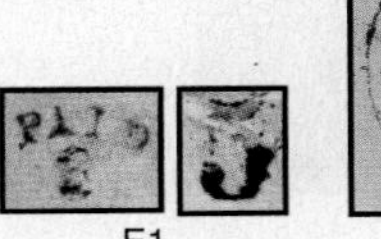
E1

E2

Handstamped Envelope

148XU1 E1 5c on 3c black *3,250.*

Black circle control on front of envelope. Unique.

FRANKLIN, N. C.

E1

E2

Press-printed Envelope (typeset) (No. 25XU1)

Impressed at top right

25XU1 E1 5c blue, *buff* *30,000.*
25XU2 E2 5c black, large "5" woodcut in 31mm circular town mark *2,500.*

The one known No. 25XU1 envelope shows black circular Franklin postmark with manuscript date.

FRAZIERSVILLE, S. C.

E1

Handstamped Envelope, "5" manuscript

128XU1 E1 5c black *5,000.*

Only one example recorded of No. 128XU1.

FREDERICKSBURG, VA.

A1

Sheets of 20, two panes of 10 varieties each

Typeset Adhesives

Thin bluish paper

26X1 A1 5c blue, *bluish* 900. 1,250.
On cover *5,500.*
Pair on cover *12,000.*
26X2 A1 10c red (shades), *bluish* 2,250.

GAINESVILLE, ALA.

E1

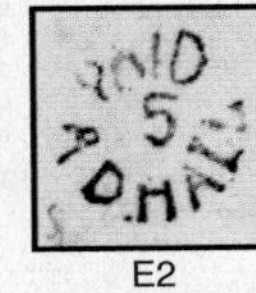
E2

E3

Handstamped Envelopes

27XU1 E1 5c black *4,500.*
27XU2 E2 5c black *5,000.*
27XU3 E3 10c ("01") black *12,000.*

GALVESTON, TEX.

E1

Handstamped Envelopes

98XU1 E1 5c black 500. *1,500.*
98XU2 E1 10c black *2,000.*

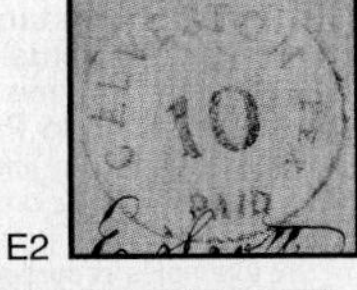
E2

E3

Handstamped Envelopes

98XU3 E2 10c black 550. *2,750.*
98XU4 E2 20c black *3,500.*
98XU5 E3 5c black *4,500.*

GASTON, N. C.

E1

Handstamped Envelope

129XU1 E1 5c black *6,000.*

Only one example recorded of No. 129XU1.

GEORGETOWN, S. C.

E1

Control

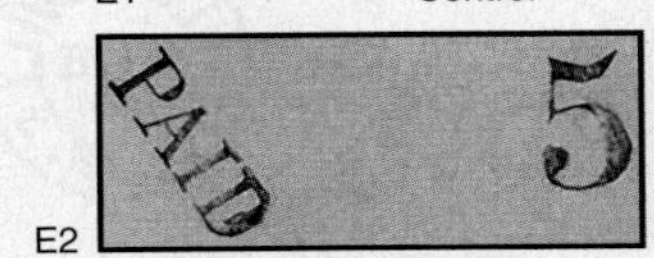
E2

Handstamped Envelopes

28XU1 E1 5c black *1,000.*
28XU2 E2 5c black, separate "5" and straightline "PAID" handstamps, control on reverse — *1,750.*

GOLIAD, TEX.

A1

A2

Typeset Adhesives

29X1 A1 5c black *16,500.*
29X2 A1 5c black, *gray* *11,500.*
29X3 A1 5c black, *rose* *12,000.*
On cover front *47,500.*
29X4 A1 10c black — *25,000.*
29X5 A1 10c black, *rose* *12,000.*

Type A1 stamps are signed "Clarke-P.M." vertically in black or red.

29X6 A2 5c black, *gray* *22,500.*
a. "GOILAD" *12,000.*
Pair, left stamp the error —
29X7 A2 10c black, *buff* *12,000.*
On cover *40,000.*
a. "GOILAD" *15,000.*
On cover *30,000.*
29X8 A2 5c black, *dark blue,* on cover *18,000.*
29X9 A2 10c black, *dark blue* *27,500.*

GONZALES, TEX.

Colman & Law were booksellers when John B. Law (of the firm) was appointed Postmaster. The firm used a small lithographed label on drugs and on the front or inside of books they sold.

A1

Lithographed Adhesives on colored glazed paper

30X1 A1 (5c) gold, *dark blue,* pair on cover, *1861* *15,000.*
30X2 A1 (10c) gold, *garnet,* on cover, *1864* *25,000.*
30X3 A1 (10c) gold, *black,* on cover, *1865* *50,000.*

No. 30X1 must bear double-circle town cancel as validating control. The control was applied to the labels in the sheet before their sale as stamps. When used, the stamps bear an additional Gonzales double-circle postmark.

GREENSBORO, ALA.

E1

E2

E3

Handstamped Envelopes

31XU1 E1 5c black *3,000.*
31XU2 E1 10c black *2,750.*
31XU3 E2 10c black *6,000.*
31XU4 E3 10c on 5c black, on cover *3,000.*

GREENSBORO, N. C.

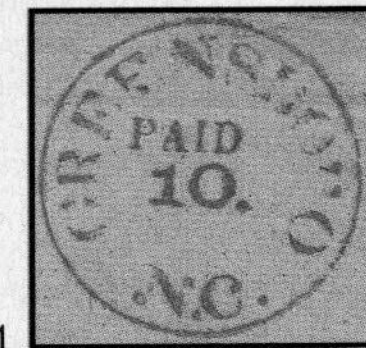

E1

Handstamped Envelope

32XU1 E1 10c red 1,250.

GREENVILLE, ALA.

A1

A2

Typeset Adhesives
On pinkish surface-colored glazed paper.

33X1 A1 5c blue & red *25,000.*
On cover *47,500.*
33X2 A2 10c red & blue, on cover *47,500.*

Two used examples each are known of Nos. 33X1-33X2, and all are on covers. Covers bear a postmark but it was not used to cancel the stamps.

The former No. 33X1a has been identified as a fake.

GREENVILLE, TENN.

E1

144XU1 E1 5c black *5,000.*

Only one example of No. 144XU1 is recorded.

GREENVILLE COURT HOUSE, S. C.

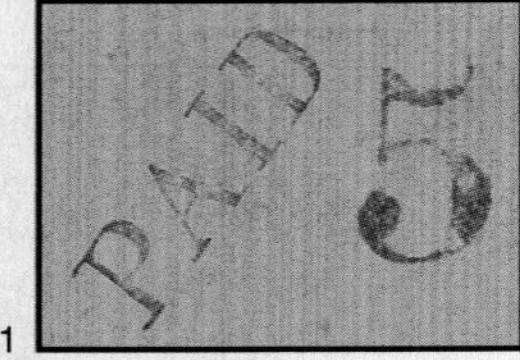

E1

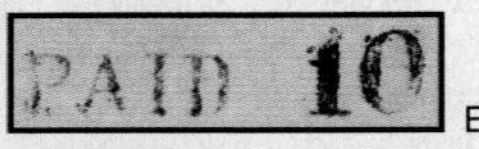

E2

Control A

Control B

Control C

Handstamped Envelopes (Several types)

34XU1 E1 5c black *2,000.*
34XU2 E2 10c black *2,000.*
a. 20c (ms.) on 10c black *3,000.*

Envelopes must bear one of three different postmark controls on the back. When the control postmark is dated, the date must be the same or prior to the date of the postmark on the front of the envelope.

GREENWOOD DEPOT, VA.

A1

"PAID" Handstamped Adhesive ("PAID" with value and signature in ms.)
Laid Paper

35X1 A1 10c black, *gray blue,* on cover 22,500.
On cover, tied —

Six examples recorded of No. 35X1, all on covers. One of these is in the British Library collection. Of the remaining five, only one has the stamp tied to the cover.

GRIFFIN, GA.

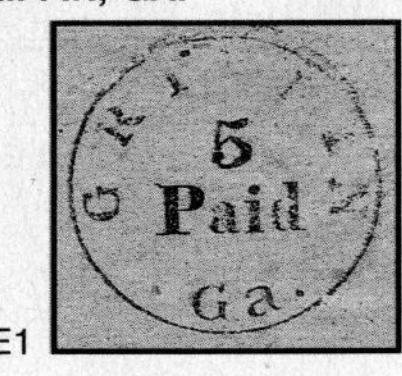

E1

Handstamped Envelopes

102XU1 E1 5c black 2,000.
102XU2 E1 10c black *5,000.*

No. 102XU2 is on a large piece of an envelope with July 25 postmark at left. It is unique.

GROVE HILL, ALA.

A1

Handstamped Adhesive (from woodcut)

36X1 A1 5c black —
On cover, tied *75,000.*

Two examples are recorded. One is on cover tied by the postmark. The other is canceled by magenta pen on a cover front.

HALLETTSVILLE, TEX.

A1

Handstamped Adhesive
Ruled Letter Paper

37X1 A1 10c black, *gray blue,* on cover *15,000.*

One example known.

HAMBURGH, S. C.

E1

Handstamped Envelope

112XU1 E1 5c black *8,000.*

HARRISBURGH (Harrisburg), TEX.

E1

E2

Handstamped Envelope

130XU1 E1 5c black *5,500.* —
130XU2 E2 10c black

The unused 5c entire is the only example recorded of No. 130XU1

HELENA, TEX.

A1

Typeset Adhesives
Several varieties

38X1 A1 5c black, *buff* *22,500.* *20,000.*
38X2 A1 10c black, *gray* *40,000.*

On 10c "Helena" is in upper and lower case italics.

Used examples are valued with small faults or repairs, as all recorded have faults.

HILLSBORO, N. C.

A1

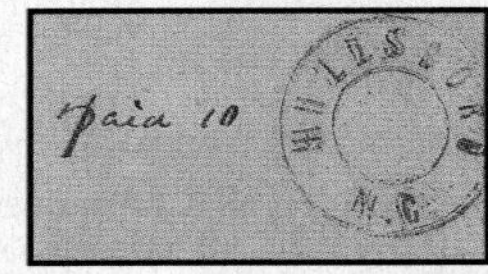

Handstamped Adhesive

39X1 A1 5c black, on cover *15,000.*

See 3c 1861 Postmaster's Provisional No. 1AX1.

Ms./Handstamped Envelope

39XU1 E1 10c "paid 10" in manuscript with undated blue town cancel as control on face *2,250.*

No. 39XU1 is unique.

HOLLANDALE, TEX.

E1

Handstamped Envelope

132XU1 E1 5c black —

HOUSTON, TEX.

E1

No. 40XU1a

Handstamped Envelopes

40XU1 E1 5c red — 800.
On patriotic cover —
a. 10c (ms.) on 5c red *11,000.*
40XU2 E1 10c red — *2,000.*
40XU3 E1 10c black *6,750.*
40XU4 E1 5c +10c red *2,500.*
40XU5 E1 10c +10c red *2,500.*

Nos. 40XU2-40XU5 show "TEX" instead of "TXS."

HUNTSVILLE, TEX.

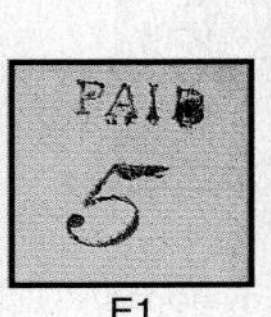

E1

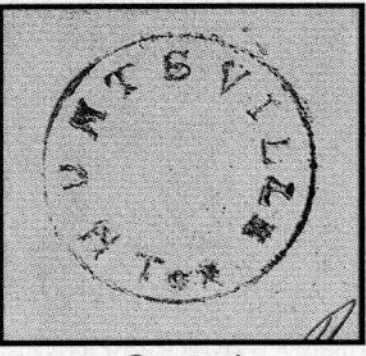
Control

Handstamped Envelope

92XU1 E1 5c black *5,000.*

No. 92XU1 exists with "5" outside or within control circle.

INDEPENDENCE, TEX.

A1

A2

Handstamped Adhesives

41X1 A1 10c black, *buff,* on cover, uncanceled, cut to shape *20,000.*
41X2 A1 10c black, *dull rose,* on cover —

With small "10" and "Pd" in manuscript

41X3 A2 10c black, *buff,* on cover, uncanceled, cut to shape *32,500.*

No. 41X1 is unique.

All known examples of Nos. 41X1-41X3 are uncanceled on covers with black "INDEPENDANCE TEX." (sic) postmark.
The existence of No. 41X2 has been questioned by specialists. The editors would like to see authenticated evidence of the existence of this item.

ISABELLA, GA.

E1

Handstamped Envelope, Manuscript "5"

133XU1 E1 5c black *5,000.*

Only one example recorded of No. 133XU1.

IUKA, MISS.

E1

Handstamped Envelope

42XU1 E1 5c black *1,750.*

JACKSON, MISS.

E1

Handstamped Envelopes

Two types of numeral

43XU1 E1 5c black 750.
a. 10c on 5c black *2,750.*
b. 5c on 3c black *1,500.*
43XU2 E1 10c black *2,000.*
a. 5c on 10c black *3,750.*
43XU4 E1 10c on 5c blue *2,750.*

The 5c also exists on a lettersheet.
See 3c 1861 Postmaster's Provisional No. 2AXU1.

JACKSONVILLE, ALA.

E1

Handstamped Envelope

110XU1 E1 5c black — *3,000.*

JACKSONVILLE, FLA.

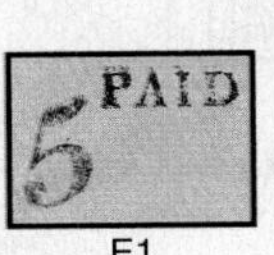

E1

Control

Handstamped Envelope

134XU1 E1 5c black *4,000.*

Undated double circle postmark control on reverse. No. 134XU1 is unique.

JETERSVILLE, VA.

A1

Handstamped Adhesive ("5" with ms. "AHA." initials)

Laid Paper

44X1 A1 5c black, vertical pair on cover, uncanceled *16,000.*

JONESBORO, TENN.

E1

Handstamped Envelopes

45XU1 E1 5c black *6,000.*
45XU2 E1 5c dark blue *5,000.*

KINGSTON, GA.

E1

E2

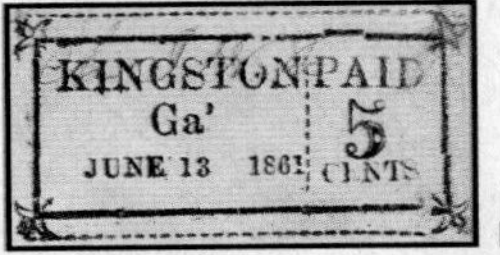

E3

E4

Typeset Envelopes (design types E1-E2, E4 are handstamps; typeset design E3 probably impressed by hand but possibly press printed)

46XU1 E1 5c black 3,000.
46XU2 E2 5c black 3,250.
46XU4 E3 5c black *12,500.*
46XU5 E4 5c black *2,000.*

There is only one recorded example of No. 46XU4.

KNOXVILLE, TENN.

A1

Typographed Adhesives (stereotype from woodcut)

Grayish Laid Paper

47X1 A1 5c brick red *1,750.* 1,400.
On cover, tied by handstamp *8,000.*
Pair on cover *7,500.*
47X2 A1 5c carmine *2,750.* 2,250.
On cover, tied by handstamp *7,500.*
47X3 A1 10c green, on cover *57,750.*

The #47X3 cover is unique. Value is based on 1997 auction sale.

E1

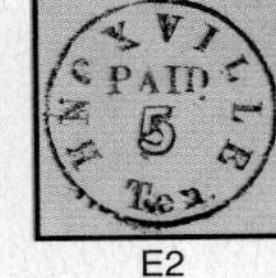

E2

Press-printed Envelopes (typographed)

47XU1 E1 5c blue *2,500.*
47XU2 E1 5c blue, *orange* *5,000.*
47XU3 E1 10c red (cut to shape) *7,500.*
47XU4 E1 10c red, *orange* (cut to shape) *7,500.*

Only one example each recorded of Nos. 47XU3 and 47XU4.
Dangerous fakes exist of Nos. 47XU1 and 47XU2.

Handstamped Envelopes

47XU5 E2 5c black *1,400.*
a. 10c on 5c black *3,500.*

Type E2 exists with "5" above or below "PAID."

LA GRANGE, TEX.

E1

Handstamped Envelopes

48XU1 E1 5c black — 3,250.
48XU2 E1 10c black 3,250.

LAKE CITY, FLA.

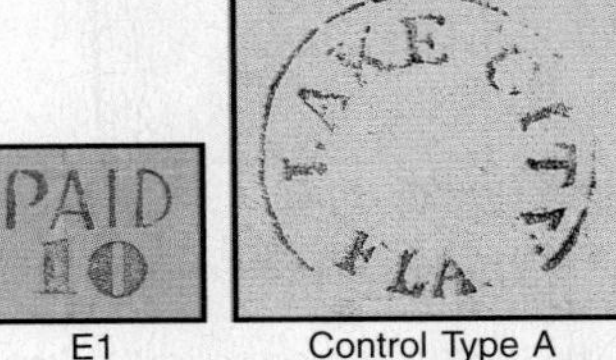

E1 Control Type A

E. R. Ives.

Control Type B

Handstamped Envelope

96XU1 E1 10c black *3,500.*

Envelopes have black circle control mark, or printed name of E. R. Ives, postmaster, on back.

LAURENS COURT HOUSE, S. C.

E1

E2

Control

Handstamped Envelopes

116XU1 E1 5c black *2,000.*
116XU2 E2 5c black *2,000.*

Envelopes have a 25mm undated control mark on reverse. No. 116XU1 is unique.

LENOIR, N. C.

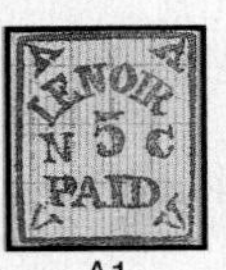

A1

E1

Handstamped Adhesive (from woodcut)

White wove paper with cross-ruled orange lines

49X1 A1 5c blue & orange *7,250.* *6,750.*
On cover, pen canceled *15,000.*
On cover, tied by handstamp *22,500.*

Cancellations: blue town, blue "Paid" in circle, black pen.

Handstamped Envelopes

49XU1 A1 5c blue *4,000.*
49XU2 A1 10c (5c+5c) blue *25,000.*
49XU3 E1 5c blue *4,500.*
49XU4 E1 5c black *4,500.*

No. 49XU2 is unique.

LEXINGTON, MISS.

E1

Handstamped Envelopes

50XU1 E1 5c black *4,500.*
50XU2 E1 10c black *6,000.*

Only one example is recorded of No. 50XU2.

LEXINGTON, VA.

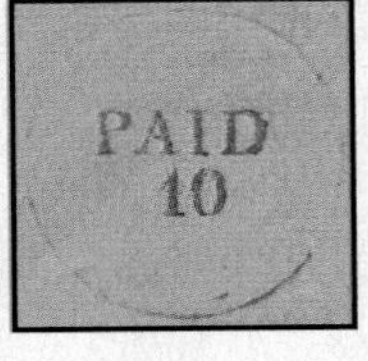

E1

Handstamped Envelopes

135XU1 E1 5c blue *350.*
135XU2 E1 10c blue *350.*

Nos. 135XU1-135XU2 by themselves are indistinguishable from stampless covers when used.

LIBERTY, VA. (and Salem, Va.)

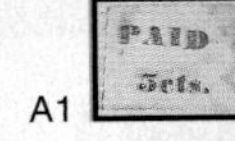

A1

Typeset Adhesive (probably impressed by hand)

Laid Paper

74X1 A1 5c black, on cover, uncanceled *35,000.*
On cover, uncanceled, with Salem postmark *40,000.*

Two known on covers with Liberty, Va. postmark; one cover known with the nearby Salem, Va. office postmark.

LIMESTONE SPRINGS, S. C.

A1

Handstamped Adhesive

121X1 A1 5c black, *light blue*, on cover 10,000.
Two on cover 15,000.
121X2 A1 5c black, *white*, two on cover 32,500.

Stamps are cut round or rectangular. Covers are not postmarked. The No. 121X2 cover bears the only two recorded examples of this stamp.

LIVINGSTON, ALA.

A1

Lithographed Adhesive

51X1 A1 5c blue 15,000.
On cover 75,000.
Pair on cover 120,000.

The pair on cover is unique.

LYNCHBURG, VA.

A1

E1

Typographed Adhesive (stereotype from woodcut)

52X1 A1 5c blue (shades) 1,800. 1,500.
On cover 6,500.
Pair on cover 20,000.

Press-printed Envelopes (typographed)

Impressed at top right or left

52XU1 E1 5c black 700.00 4,000.
52XU2 E1 5c black, *amber* 4,000.
52XU3 E1 5c black, *buff* 4,000.
52XU4 E1 5c black, *brown* 4,000.
On patriotic cover —

MACON, GA.

A1

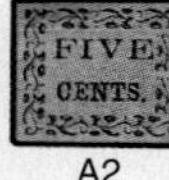
A2

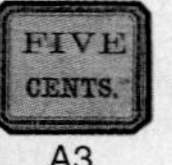
A3

A4

Typeset Adhesives
Several varieties of type A1, 10 of A2, 5 of A3

Wove Paper

53X1 A1 5c black, *light blue green* (shades) 1,250. 1,000.
On cover 6,000.
Pair on cover 14,000.

Warning: Dangerous forgeries exist of the normal variety and the Comma after "OFFICE" variety. Certificates of authenticity from recognized committees are strongly recommended.

53X3 A2 5c black, *yellow* 2,500. 1,250.
On cover 6,000.
Pair on cover 11,000.
Pair on patriotic cover 25,000.
53X4 A3 5c black, *yellow* (shades) 3,000. 2,250.
On cover 7,500.
Pair on cover 11,000.
a. Vertical tête bêche pair —
53X5 A4 2c black, *gray green*
On cover 50,000.

Laid Paper

53X6 A2 5c black, *yellow* 6,000. 6,000.
On cover 8,000.
53X7 A3 5c black, *yellow* 6,000.
On cover 9,000.
53X8 A1 5c black, *light blue green* 1,750. 2,250.
On cover 4,500.

No. 53X4a is unique.

E1

Handstamped Envelope

Two types: "PAID" over "5," "5" over "PAID"

53XU1 E1 5c black 250. 650.
On patriotic cover 1,900.

Values are for "PAID" over "5" variety. "5" over "PAID" is much scarcer.

MADISON, GA.

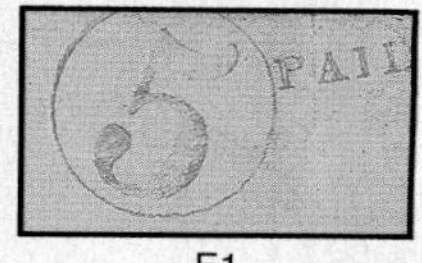
E1

Handstamped Envelope

136XU1 E1 5c red 600.

No. 136XU1 is indistinguishable from a handstamp paid cover when used.

MADISON COURT HOUSE, FLA.

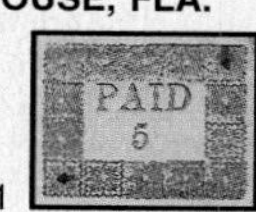
E1

Typeset Envelope

137XU1 E1 5c black, *yellow* 35,000.

No. 137XU1 is unique.
See 3c 1861 Postmaster's Provisional No. 3AX1.

MARIETTA, GA.

E1

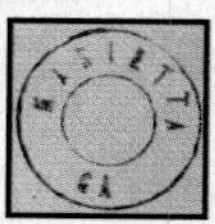
Control

E2

Handstamped Envelopes

54XU1 E1 5c black 500.
a. 10c on 5c black 1,750.

With Double Circle Control

54XU3 E1 10c black
54XU4 E2 5c black 2,000.

The existence of No. 54XU3 has been questioned by specialists. The editors would like to see authenticated evidence that verifies this listing.

MARION, VA.

A1

Adhesives with Typeset frame and Handstamped numeral in center

55X1 A1 5c black 7,500.
On cover 20,000.
55X2 A1 10c black 16,500. 10,000.
On cover 35,000.
55X3 A1 5c black, *bluish, laid paper* — —

The 2c, 3c, 15c and 20c are believed to be bogus items printed later using the original typeset frame.

MARS BLUFF, S. C.

E1

145XU1 E1 5c black 2,000.

The No. 145XU1 marking is a provisional only when unused, used from another town or used under a general issue.

MEMPHIS, TENN.

A1

56X1a Partial Print

A2

Typographed Adhesives (stereotyped from woodcut)

56X1 A1 2c blue (shades) 100. 1,250.
On cover 12,500.
a. Partial print 250. —

On No. 56X1a, a breaking off of the plate at the right edge caused incomplete printing (approximately 2/3 of the stamp) on stamps in positions 5, 10, 15, 20 and 50.

56X2 A2 5c red (shades) 150. 250.
On cover 2,000.
Pair on cover 4,000.
Strip of 4 on cover 9,000.
On patriotic cover 9,000.
Pair on patriotic cover 12,500.
a. Tête bêche pair 1,500.
Pair on cover 9,500.
b. Pair, one sideways 2,500.
c. Pelure paper — —

Press-printed Envelopes (typographed)

56XU1 A2 5c red (shades) 3,000.
56XU2 A2 5c red, *amber* 3,000.
56XU3 A2 5c red, *orange* 2,500.
56XU4 A2 5c red, *cream* 5,750.

Only one example of No. 56XU4 is recorded. It is on a cover on which a C.S.A. No. 11 is affixed over the provisional to pay the postage.

MICANOPY, FLA.

E1

Handstamped Envelope

105XU1 E1 5c black 11,500.

One example recorded.

MILLEDGEVILLE, GA.

E1

E2

E3

Handstamped Envelopes

Two types of No. 57XU5: Type I, tall, thin "1" and "0" of "10"; Type II, short, fat "1" and "0" of "10."

57XU1 E1 5c black 500.
a. Wide spacing between "I" and "D" of "PAID" 600.
b. 10c on 5c black 1,000.
57XU2 E1 5c blue 800.
57XU4 E2 10c black 375. 1,200.
a. Wide spacing between "I" and "D" of "PAID" 1,200.
57XU5 E3 10c black, type I 450. 800.
a. Type II 1,500.

On No. 57XU4, the "PAID/10" virtually always falls outside the Milledgeville control marking (as in illustration E1).

The existence of No. 57XU2 as a provisional has been questioned by specialists. The editors would like to see authenticated evidence of provisional use of this marking.

MILTON, N. C.

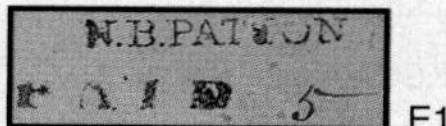
E1

Handstamped Envelope, "5" Manuscript

138XU1 E1 5c black 3,000.

MOBILE, ALA.

A1

Lithographed Adhesives

58X1 A1 2c black 2,250. 1,200.
On cover 6,000.
Pair on cover 20,000.
Three singles on one cover 20,000.
Five stamps on one cover 24,000.
58X2 A1 5c blue 350. 450.
On cover 2,000.
Pair on cover 2,750.
Strip of 3 on cover 10,000.
Strip of 4 on cover 25,000.

The existence of a strip of 5 of No. 58X2 has been questioned by specialists. The editors would like to see authenticated evidence of the existence of this strip either on or off cover.

MONTGOMERY, ALA.

E1

E1a

Handstamped Envelopes

59XU1 E1 5c red — *1,100.*
a. 10c on 5c red — *2,750.*
59XU2 E1 5c blue — 400. *1,000.*
59XU3 E1a 10c red — *900.*
59XU4 E1a 10c blue — *1,250.*
59XU5 E1a 10c black — 850.

E2

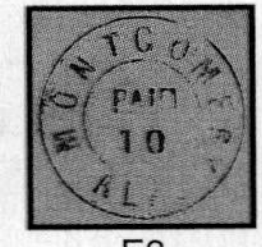

E3

59XU7 E2 2c red — *2,500.*
59XU7A E2 2c blue — *3,500.*
59XU8 E2 5c black — *2,000.*
59XU9 E3 10c black — *2,000.*
59XU10 E3 10c red — *1,750.*

The existence of No. 59XU10 is in question. The editors would like to see an authenticated example of this marking.

MT. LEBANON, LA.

A1

Woodcut Adhesive (mirror image of design)

60X1 A1 5c red brown, on cover — *255,000.*

One example known. Value represents sale price at 2009 auction.

NASHVILLE, TENN.

A2

E1

Typographed Adhesives (stereotyped from woodcut)
Gray Blue Ribbed Paper

61X2 A2 5c carmine (shades) — 1,000. 650.
On cover — 3,500.
Pair on cover — *6,000.*
a. Vertical tête bêche pair — *4,000.*
On cover — *25,000.*
61X3 A2 5c brick red (shades) — 1,000. 900.
On cover — 3,500.
Pair on cover — *7,500.*
61X4 A2 5c gray (shades) — 1,250. 1,500.
On cover — *7,500.*
Pair on cover — *7,500.*
61X5 A2 5c violet brown (shades) — 1,250. 750.
On cover — 4,250.
Pair on cover — *6,000.*
a. Vertical tete beche pair — *5,000.* *7,500.*
Pair on cover — —
61X6 A2 10c green — — *7,500.*
On cover — *22,500.*
On cover with No. 61X2 — *27,500.*

E1

Handstamped Envelopes

61XU1 E1 5c blue — 900.
61XU2 E1 10c on 5c blue — *2,750.*

See 3c Postmaster's Provisional No. 4AX1.

NEW ORLEANS, LA.

A1

A2

Typographed Adhesives (stereotyped from woodcut)
Plate of 40

62X1 A1 2c blue — 225. *800.*
On cover — *5,000.*
Pair on cover — *10,000.*
Three singles on one cover — *20,000.*
Three singles + #62X4, on cover — —
Five singles on one cover — *12,500.*
Strip of 5 on cover — *30,000.*
a. Printed on both sides, on cover — *10,500.*
62X2 A1 2c red (shades) — 190. *1,000.*
On cover — *25,000.*
62X3 A2 5c brown, *white* — 300. 200.
On cover — 450.
Pair on cover — 850.
Strip of 5 on cover — *5,000.*
a. Printed on both sides — *3,750.*
On cover — *7,500.*
b. 5c ocher — 700. 625.
On cover — 2,750.
Pair on cover — 3,500.
c. 5c chocolate brown — *1,500.*
62X4 A2 5c red brn, *bluish* — 325. 200.
On cover — 425.
Pair on cover — 700.
Block of 4 on cover — *5,000.*
a. Printed on both sides — *3,250.*
On cover — *9,000.*
62X5 A2 5c yel brn, *off-white* — 160. *250.*
On cover — 850.
Pair on cover — 1,200.
Strip of 5 on cover — —
62X6 A2 5c red (shades) — — *14,000.*
62X7 A2 5c red (shades), *bluish* — *15,000.*

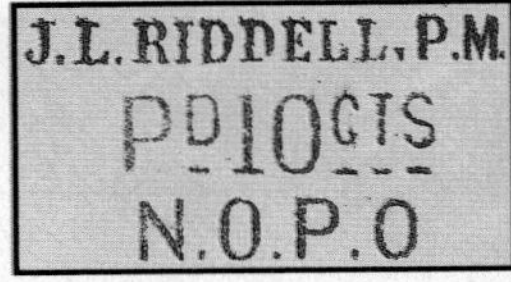

E1

Handstamped Envelopes

62XU1 E1 5c black — 4,500.
62XU2 E1 10c black — *11,500.*

"J. L. RIDDELL, P. M." omitted

62XU3 E1 2c black — *9,500.*

Some authorities question the use of No. 62XU3 as a provisional.

NEW SMYRNA, FLA.

A1

Handstamped Adhesive
On white paper with blue ruled lines

63X1 A1 10c ("O1") on 5c black — *50,000.*

One example known. It is uncanceled on a postmarked patriotic cover.

NORFOLK, VA.

E1

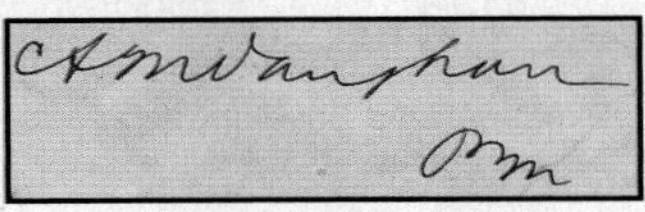
Manuscript Signature

Handstamped Envelopes
Ms Signature on Back

139XU1 E1 5c blue — 1,000. *1,750.*
139XU2 E1 10c blue — *1,750.*

OAKWAY, S. C.

A1

Handstamped Adhesive (from woodcut)

115X1 A1 5c black, on cover — *60,000.*

Two used examples of No. 115X1 are recorded, both on cover. Value represents 2012 auction realization for the cover on which the stamp is tied by manuscript "Paid."

PENSACOLA, FLA.

E1

Handstamped Envelopes

106XU1 E1 5c black — *5,000.*
a. 10c (ms.) on 5c black — *5,250.*

PETERSBURG, VA.

A1

Typeset Adhesive
Ten varieties
Thick white paper

65X1 A1 5c red (shades) — *2,250.* 600.
On cover — 2,500.
Pair on cover — *12,500.*

PITTSYLVANIA COURT HOUSE, VA.

A1

Typeset Adhesives

66X1 A1 5c dull red, wove paper — *7,500.* *9,000.*
Octagonally cut — *7,000.*
On cover — *40,000.*
On cover, octagonally cut — *20,000.*
66X2 A1 5c dull red, laid paper — *5,500.*
On cover — —
Octagonally cut — *4,500.*
On cover, octagonally cut — *50,000.*

PLAINS OF DURA, GA.

E1

Handstamped Envelopes, Ms. Initials

140XU1 E1 5c black — —
140XU2 E1 10c black — *5,000.*

No. 140XU2 is unique.

PLEASANT SHADE, VA.

A1

Typeset Adhesive
Five varieties

67X1 A1 5c blue — *8,000.* *20,000.*
On cover — *40,000.*
Pair on cover — *55,000.*

PLUM CREEK, TEX.

E1

Manuscript Adhesive

141X1 E1 10c black, *blue,* on cover — —

The stamps have ruled lines with the value "10" in manuscript. Size and shape vary.

PORT GIBSON, MISS.

E1

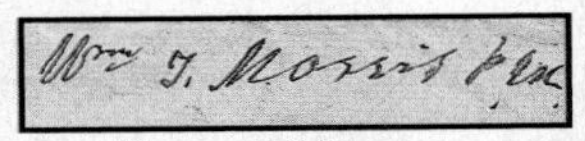
Manuscript Signature

Handstamped Envelope, Ms Signature

142XU1 E1 5c black — —

PORT LAVACA, TEX.

A1

Typeset Adhesive

107X1 A1 10c black, on cover — *25,000.*

One example known. It is uncanceled on a postmarked cover.

RALEIGH, N. C.

E1

Handstamped Envelopes

68XU1 E1 5c red 400.
68XU2 E1 5c blue *3,000.*

RHEATOWN, TENN.

A1

Typeset Adhesive

Three varieties

69X1 A1 5c red *6,000.* *6,500.*
On cover, ms. cancel *20,000.*
On cover, tied by handstamp *37,500.*
Pair *15,000.*

RICHMOND, TEX.

E1

Handstamped Envelopes or Letter Sheets

70XU1 E1 5c red 2,500.
a. 10c on 5c red *5,000.*
70XU2 E1 10c red 2,000.
a. 15c (ms.) on 10c red *5,000.*

RINGGOLD, GA.

E1

Handstamped Envelope

71XU1 E1 5c blue black *8,500.*

RUTHERFORDTON, N. C.

A1

Handstamped Adhesive, Ms. "Paid 5cts"

72X1 A1 5c black, cut round, on cover (uncanceled) *60,000.*

No. 72X1 is unique.

SALEM, N. C.

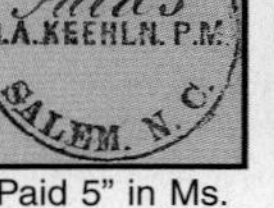

"Paid 5" in Ms. — E1 "Paid 5" Handstamped — E2

Handstamped Envelopes

73XU1 E1 5c black 1,400.
73XU2 E1 10c black *3,500.*
73XU3 E2 5c black *2,250.*
a. 10c on 5c black *2,800.*

Reprints exist on various papers. They either lack the "Paid" and value or have them counterfeited.

SALISBURY, N. C.

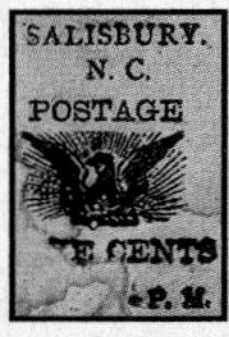

E1

Press-printed Envelope (typeset)

Impressed at top left

75XU1 E1 5c black, *greenish* *15,000.*

One example known. Part of the envelope was torn away (now repaired), leaving part of design missing.

SAN ANTONIO, TEX.

E1

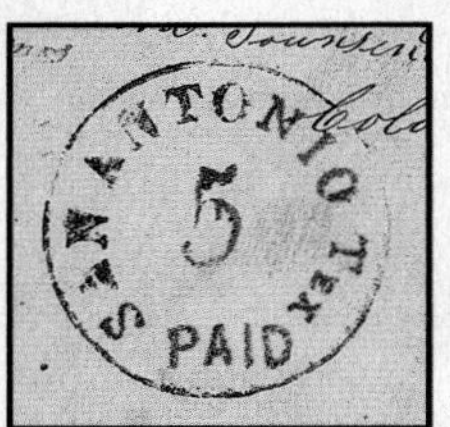

E2

Control

Handstamped Envelopes

76XU1 E1 10c black 500. *2,000.*
76XU1A E2 5c black *13,000.*
76XU2 E2 10c black *2,500.*

Black circle control mark is on front or back. One example of No. 76XU1A is recorded.

SAVANNAH, GA.

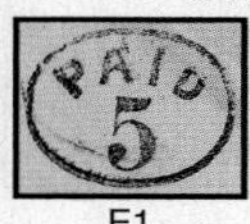

E1

Control

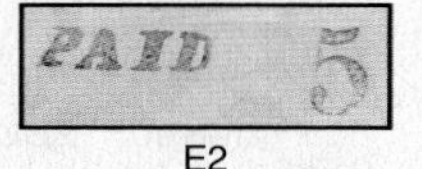

E2

Handstamped Envelopes

101XU1 E1 5c black 400.
a. 10c on 5c black 1,500.
101XU2 E2 5c black 600.
a. 20c on 5c black *2,000.*
101XU3 E1 10c black 750.
101XU4 E2 10c black 750.

Envelopes must have octagonal control mark. One example is known of No.101XU2a.

SELMA, ALA.

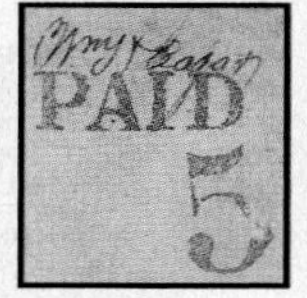

E1

Handstamped Envelopes; Signature in Ms.

77XU1 E1 5c black *1,250.*
a. 10c on 5c black *3,000.*
77XU2 E1 10c black *2,500.*

Signature is that of Postmaster William H. Eagar.

See 3c 1861 Postmaster's Provisional No. 5AX1.

SPARTA, GA.

E1

Handstamped Envelopes

93XU1 E1 5c red — 2,250.
93XU2 E1 10c red *5,000.*

Only one example recorded of No. 93XU2.

SPARTANBURG, S. C.

A1

A2

Handstamped Adhesives

(on ruled or plain wove paper)

78X1 A1 5c black, cut to shape
Cut square *27,500.*
On cover, cut to shape *20,000.*
Pair on cover *30,000.*
a. "Paid" instead of denomination, revalued to 5c with "PAID" and "5" in small circle handstamps —
78X2 A2 5c black, *bluish* *4,000.*
On cover *15,000.*
78X3 A2 5c black, *brown* *4,000.*
On cover *18,000.*

Most examples of Nos. 78X1-78X3 are cut round. Cut square examples in sound condition are worth much more.

E1

Control

Handstamped Envelopes

78XU1 E1 10c black (control on reverse) *5,000.*

STATESVILLE, N. C.

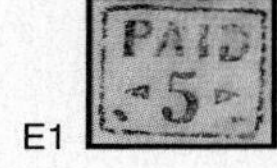

E1

Handstamped Envelopes

79XU1 E1 5c black *1,500.*
a. 10c on 5c black *3,000.*

Unused examples of No. 79XU1 are reprints.

SUMTER, S. C.

E1

Handstamped Envelopes

80XU1 E1 5c black 500.
a. 10c on 5c black *900.*
80XU2 E1 10c black 600.
a. 2c (ms.) on 10c black *1,100.*

Used examples of Nos. 80XU1-80XU2 are indistinguishable from handstamped "Paid" covers.

TALBOTTON, GA.

E1

Handstamped Envelopes

94XU1 E1 5c black 900.
a. 10c on 5c black *2,000.*
94XU2 E1 10c black 1,000.

TALLADEGA, ALA.

E1

Handstamped Envelopes

143XU1 E1 5c black *1,500.* —
143XU2 E1 10c black *1,500.* —

These same markings were used on handstamped "Paid" covers.

TELLICO PLAINS, TENN.

A1

Typeset Adhesives

Settings of two 5c and one 10c

Laid Paper

81X1 A1 5c red 2,500. —
On cover *40,000.*
81X2 A1 10c red 4,000.

THOMASVILLE, GA.

E1

Control

Handstamped Envelopes

82XU1 E1 5c black 750.
On patriotic cover *2,750.*

On No. 82XU1, the control is on the reverse of the cover. The dated control is known with five different dates, including June 1, June 13,

June 21, and August 23. The patriotic envelope is unique.

E2

82XU2 E2 5c black 1,000.

TULLAHOMA, TENN.

E1

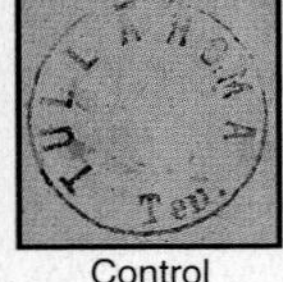

Control

Handstamped Envelope

111XU1 E1 10c black *6,000.*

The control appears either on the front or the back of the envelope.

TUSCALOOSA, ALA.

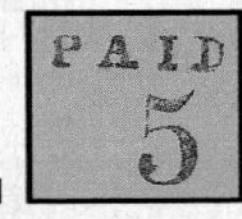

E1

Handstamped Envelopes

83XU1 E1 5c black 250.
83XU2 E1 10c black 250.

Used examples of Nos. 83XU1-83XU2 are indistinguishable from handstamped "Paid" covers.

TUSCUMBIA, ALA.

E1

Handstamped Envelopes

84XU1 E1 5c black 4,000.
84XU2 E1 5c red *5,000.*
84XU3 E1 10c black *5,250.*

See 3c 1861 Postmaster's Provisional No. 6AXU1.

UNIONTOWN, ALA.

A1

Typeset Adhesives
(settings of 4 (2x2), 4 varieties of each value)
Laid Paper

86X1 A1 2c dark blue, *gray blue,* on cover —
86X2 A1 2c dark blue, sheet of 4 *40,000.*
86X3 A1 5c green, *gray blue* *4,000.* *3,250.*
On cover *15,000.*
86X4 A1 5c green *4,000.* *3,250.*
On cover *15,000.*
Pair on cover *22,500.*
86X5 A1 10c red, *gray blue* —
On cover *40,000.*

Two examples known of No. 86X1, both on cover (drop letters), one uncanceled and one pen canceled.

The only recorded examples of No. 86X2 are in a unique sheet of 4.

The item listed as No. 86X5 used is an uncanceled stamp on a large piece with part of addressee's name in manuscript.

UNIONVILLE, S. C.

A1

Handstamped Adhesive "PAID" and "5" applied separately
Paper with Blue Ruled Lines

87X1 A1 5c black, *grayish* —
On cover, uncanceled *17,500.*
On cover, tied —
Pair on patriotic cover *32,500.*

The pair on patriotic cover is the only pair recorded.

VALDOSTA, GA.

E1

Control

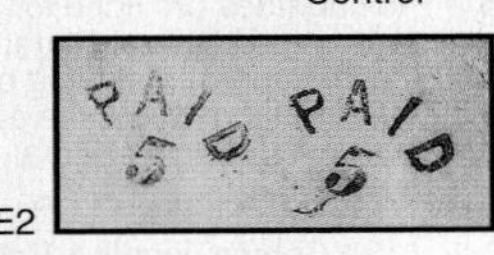

E2

Handstamped Envelopes

100XU1 E1 10c black *9,000.*
100XU2 E2 5c +5c black —

The black circle control must appear on front of the No. 100XU2 envelope and on the back of the No. 100XU1 envelope.

There is one recorded cover each of Nos. 100XU1-100XU2.

VICTORIA, TEX.

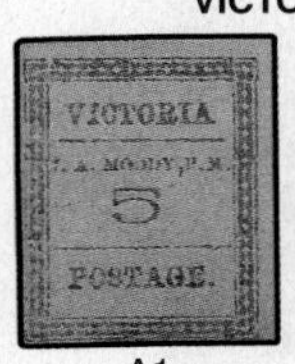

A1

A2

Typeset Adhesives
Surface colored paper

88X1 A1 5c red brown, *green* *20,000.*
88X2 A1 10c red brown, *green* *22,500.*
On cover *115,000.*
88X3 A2 10c red brown, *green,* pelure paper *32,500.* *30,000.*

WALTERBOROUGH, S. C.

E1

Handstamped Envelopes

108XU1 E1 10c black, *buff* —
108XU2 E1 10c carmine *4,000.*

The existence of No. 108XU1 is in question. The editors would like to see authenticated evidence of its existence.

WARRENTON, GA.

E1

Handstamped Envelopes

89XU1 E1 5c black 2,100.
a. 10c (ms.) on 5c black 1,000.

Fakes of the Warrenton provisional marking based on the illustration shown are known on addressed but postally unused covers.

WASHINGTON, GA.

E1

Handstamped Envelope

117XU1 E1 10c black *2,000.*

Envelopes must have black circle postmark control on the back. Examples with the undated control on the front are not considered provisional unless a dated postmark is also present.

WEATHERFORD, TEX.

E1

Handstamped Envelopes (woodcut with "PAID" inserted in type)

109XU1 E1 5c black *2,000.*
109XU2 E1 5c +5c black *11,000.*

One example is known of No. 109XU2.

WILKESBORO, N. C.

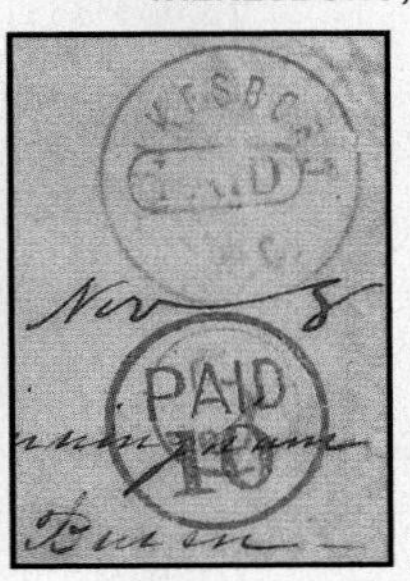

E1

Handstamped Envelope

147XU1 E1 5c black, revalued to 10c —

No. 147XU1 is unique.

WINNSBOROUGH, S. C.

E1 Control

Handstamped Envelopes

97XU1 E1 5c black *2,000.*
On patriotic cover *3,750.*
97XU2 E1 10c black *3,500.*

Envelopes must have black circle control on front or back.

WYTHEVILLE, VA.

E1

Control

Handstamped Envelope

114XU1 E1 5c black 900.

For later additions, listed out of numerical sequence, see:

- **#*74X1*, Liberty, Va.**
- **#*92XU1*, Huntsville, Tex.**
- **#*93XU1*, Sparta, Ga.**
- **#*94XU1*, Talbotton, Ga.**
- **#*95XU1*, Cuthbert, GA**
- **#*96XU1*, Lake City, Fla.**
- **#*97XU1*, Winnsborough, S.C.**
- **#*98XU1*, Galveston, Tex.**
- **#*99XU1*, Christiansburg, Va.**
- **#*100XU1*, Valdosta, Ga.**
- **#*101XU1*, Savannah, Ga.**
- **#*102XU1*, Griffin, Ga.**
- **#*103XU1*, Courtland, Ala.**
- **#*104XU1*, Fincastle, Va.**
- **#*105XU1*, Micanopy, Fla.**
- **#*106XU1*, Pensacola, Fla.**
- **#*107X1*, Port Lavaca, Tex.**
- **#*108XU1*, Walterborough, S.C.**
- **#*109XU1*, Weatherford, Tex.**
- **#*110XU1*, Jacksonville, Ala.**
- **#*111XU1*, Tullahoma, Tenn.**
- **#*112XU1*, Hamburgh, S.C.**
- **#*113XU1*, Columbia, Tenn.**
- **#*114XU1*, Wytheville, Va.**
- **#*115X1*, Oakway, S.C.**
- **#*116XU1*, Laurens Court House, S.C.**
- **#*117XU1*, Washington, Ga.**
- **#*118XU1*, Carolina City, N.C.**
- **#*119XU1*, Colaparchee, Ga.**
- **#*120XU1*, Forsyth, Ga.**
- **#*121XU1*, Limestone Springs, S.C.**
- **#*122XU1*, Balcony Falls, Va.**
- **#*123XU1*, Barnwell Court House, S.C.**
- **#*124XU1*, Bluffton, S.C.**
- **#*125XU1*, Camden, S.C.**
- **#*126XU1*, Cartersville, Ga.**
- **#*127XU1*, Charlottesville, Va.**
- **#*128XU1*, Fraziersville, S.C.**
- **#*129XU1*, Gaston, N.C.**
- **#*130XU1*, Harrisburgh, Tex.**
- **#*132XU1*, Hollandale, Tex.**
- **#*133XU1*, Isabella, Ga.**
- **#*134XU1*, Jacksonville, Fla.**
- **#*135XU1*, Lexington, Va.**
- **#*136XU1*, Madison, Ga.**
- **#*137XU1*, Madison Court House, Fla.**
- **#*138XU1*, Milton, N.C.**
- **#*139XU1*, Norfolk, Va.**
- **#*140XU1*, Plains of Dura, Ga.**
- **#*141X1*, Plum Creek, Tex.**
- **#*142XU1*, Port Gibson, Miss.**
- **#*143XU1*, Talladega, Ala.**
- **#*144XU1*, Greenville, Tenn.**
- **#*145XU1*, Mars Bluff, S.C.**
- **#*146XU1*, Charlotte, N.C.**
- **#*147XU1*, Wilkesboro, N.C.**
- **#*148XU1*, Fort Valley, Ga.**

GENERAL ISSUES

Jefferson Davis — A1

1861 Unwmk. Litho. *Imperf.*

1 A1 5c green (shades) 300. 175.
No gum 175.
On cover 300.
a. 5c light green 275. 175.
No gum 160.
b. 5c dark green 375. 250.
No gum 225.
c. 5c olive green 400. 250.
No gum 240.
On cover 300.

Thomas Jefferson — A2

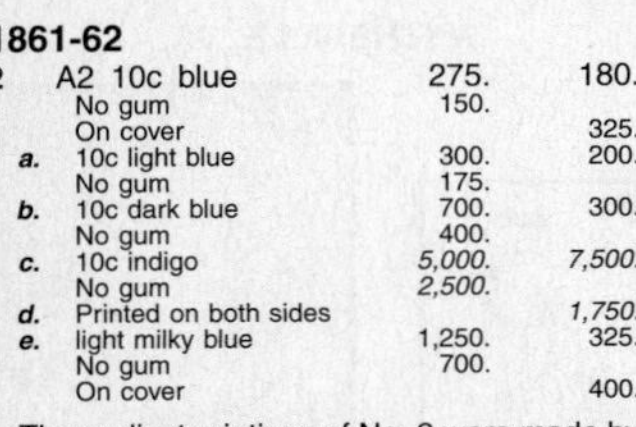

1861-62

2 A2 10c blue 275. 180.
No gum 150.
On cover 325.
a. 10c light blue 300. 200.
No gum 175.
b. 10c dark blue 700. 300.
No gum 400.
c. 10c indigo *5,000.* *7,500.*
No gum *2,500.*
d. Printed on both sides *1,750.*
e. light milky blue 1,250. 325.
No gum 700.
On cover 400.

The earliest printings of No. 2 were made by Hoyer & Ludwig, the later ones by J. T. Paterson & Co.

Stamps of the later printings usually have a small colored dash below the lowest point of the upper left spandrel.

Andrew Jackson — A3

1862

3 A3 2c green 1,000. 750.
No gum 575.
On cover *3,500.*
a. 2c bright yellow green *2,000.* —
No gum *1,300.*
On cover *4,000.*

4 A1 5c blue 225. 125.
No gum 125.
On cover 275.
a. 5c dark blue 275. 175.
No gum 150.
b. 5c light milky blue 350. 200.
No gum 190.

5 A2 10c rose (shades) 2,400. 450.
No gum 1,250.
On cover 750.
a. 10c carmine *3,750.* *1,900.*
No gum *2,200.*
On cover *5,000.*
On patriotic cover —

Jefferson Davis — A4

Typo.

6 A4 5c light blue 18. 28.
No gum 9.
Pair on cover 100.

7 A4 5c blue (De La Rue thin paper) 22. 22.
No gum 12.
Pair on cover 95.
a. 5c deep blue 28. 35.
No gum 14.
b. Printed on both sides *2,500.* *1,400.*
Pair on cover *4,000.*

No. 6 has fine, clear impression. No. 7 has coarser impression and the color is duller and often blurred.

Both 2c and 10c stamps, types A4 and A10, were privately printed in various colors.

Andrew Jackson — A5

1863 **Engr.**

8 A5 2c brown red 75. *350.*
No gum 40.
a. 2c pale red 90. *450.*
No gum 45.
Single on cover, #8 or 8a *1,500.*

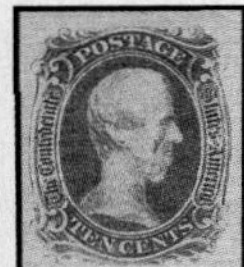

A6

Thick or Thin Paper

9 A6 10c blue 950. 500.
No gum 600.
a. 10c milky blue (first printing) 1,000. 550.
No gum 600.
b. 10c gray blue 1,050. 600.
No gum 650.
On cover 1,500.

Jefferson Davis — A6a

10 A6a 10c blue (with frame line) 5,750. 2,100.
No gum 3,750.
a. 10c milky blue 5,750. 2,100.
No gum 3,750.
b. 10c greenish blue 6,250. 2,100.
No gum 4,250.
c. 10c dark blue 6,250. 2,100.
No gum 4,250.
On cover *3,250.*

Values of Nos. 10, 10a, 10b and 10c are for examples showing parts of lines on at least three sides. Used stamps showing 4 complete lines sell for approximately 3 to 4 times the values given. Unused stamps showing 4 complete lines are exceedingly rare (only two recorded), and the one sound example is valued at $35,000.

A7

There are many slight differences between A7 and A8, the most noticeable being the additional line outside the ornaments at the four corners of A8.

1863-64

11 A7 10c blue 18. *20.*
No gum 10.
On cover 125.
a. 10c milky blue 55. 60.
No gum 30.
b. 10c dark blue 25. 30.
No gum 12.
c. 10c greenish blue 30. 50.
No gum 17.
d. 10c green 85. *80.*
No gum 55.
e. Officially perforated 12½ (Archer & Daly printing) 400. 350.
On cover *900.*

A8

12 A8 10c blue 22. 25.
No gum 11.
On cover 135.
a. 10c milky blue 55. 60.
No gum 30.
b. 10c light blue 21. 22.
No gum 11.
c. 10c greenish blue 40. *50.*
No gum 20.
d. 10c dark blue 24. 25.
No gum 12.
e. 10c green 150. 140.
No gum 85.
f. Officially perforated 12½ (Archer & Daly printing) 400. 375.
On cover *900.*

The paper of Nos. 11 and 12 varies from thin hard to thick soft. The stamp that sometimes is offered as "laid paper" is actually normal paper with thick, streaky gum.

George Washington — A9

1863

13 A9 20c green 45. *400.*
No gum 28.
On cover *1,250.*
a. 20c yellow green 80. *450.*
No gum 50.
b. 20c dark green 65. *500.*
No gum 40.
Short transfer at right 130.
c. 20c bluish green 100. —
No gum 65.
d. Diagonal half used as 10c on cover *2,000.*
e. Horizontal half used as 10c on cover *3,500.*

John C. Calhoun — A10

1862 **Typo.**

14 A10 1c orange 100.
No gum 60.
a. 1c deep orange 140.
No gum 85.

No. 14 was never put in use.

CANAL ZONE

kə-'nal 'zōn

LOCATION — A strip of land 10 miles wide, extending through the Republic of Panama, between the Atlantic and Pacific Oceans.

GOVT. — From 1904-79 a U.S. Government Reservation; from 1979-99 under joint control of the Republic of Panama and the U.S.

AREA — 552.8 sq. mi.

POP. — 41,800 (est. 1976)

The Canal Zone, site of the Panama Canal, was leased in perpetuity to the U.S. for a cash payment of $10,000,000 and a yearly rental. Treaties between the two countries provided for joint jurisdiction by the U.S. and Panama, 1979-1999, with Panama handling postal service. At the end of 1999, the canal, in its entirety, reverted to Panama.

100 Centavos = 1 Peso
100 Centesimos = 1 Balboa
100 Cents = 1 Dollar

Catalogue values for unused stamps in this country are for Never Hinged items, beginning with Scott 118 in the regular postage section and Scott C6 in the air post section.

Watermarks

Wmk. 190 — "USPS" in Single-lined Capitals

Wmk. 191 — Double-lined "USPS" in Capitals

Map of Panama — A1

Violet to Violet-Blue Handstamp on Panama Nos. 72, 72a-72c, 78, 79.

On the 2c "PANAMA" is normally 13mm long. On the 5c and 10c it measures about 15mm.

On the 2c, "PANAMA" reads up on the upper half of the sheet and down on the lower half. On the 5c and 10c, "PANAMA" reads up at left and down at right on each stamp.

On the 2c only, varieties exist with inverted "V" for "A," accent on "A," inverted "N," etc., in "PANAMA."

Unwmk.

1904, June 24 **Engr.** ***Perf. 12***

1 A1 2c rose, both "PANAMA" reading up or down 650. 400.
a. "CANAL ZONE" inverted *1,000.* 850.
b. "CANAL ZONE" double *4,250.* 2,000.
c. "CANAL ZONE" double, both inverted *20,000.*
d. "PANAMA" reading down and up 750. 650.
e. As "d," "CANAL ZONE" invtd. *9,000.* *9,000.*
f. Vert. pair, "PANAMA" reading up on top 2c, down on other *2,100.* *2,100.*
g. As "f," "CANAL ZONE" inverted *20,000.*

2 A1 5c blue 300. 190.
a. "CANAL ZONE" inverted 775. 600.
b. "CANAL ZONE" double 2,250. 1,500.
c. Pair, one without "CANAL ZONE" overprint *5,000.* *5,000.*
d. "CANAL ZONE" overprint diagonal, reading down to right 800. 700.

3 A1 10c yellow 400. 230.
a. "CANAL ZONE" inverted 775. 600.
b. "CANAL ZONE" double *14,000.*
c. Pair, one without "CANAL ZONE" overprint *6,000.* *5,000.*
Nos. 1-3 (3) 1,350. 820.00

Cancellations consist of town and/or bars in magenta or black, or a mixture of both colors.

Nos. 1-3 were withdrawn July 17, 1904.

Forgeries of the "Canal Zone" overprint and cancellations are numerous.

United States Nos. 300, 319, 304, 306 & 307 Ovptd. in Black

1904, July 18 **Wmk. 191**

4 A115 1c blue green 37.50 22.50
5 A129 2c carmine 32.50 25.00
a. 2c scarlet 32.50 30.00
6 A119 5c blue 95.00 65.00
7 A121 8c violet black 140.00 85.00
8 A122 10c pale red brown 130.00 90.00
Nos. 4-8 (5) 435.00 287.50

Beware of fake overprints.

A2

A3

CANAL ZONE — Regular Type

CANAL ZONE — Antique Type

1904-06 **Unwmk.**

Black Overprint on Stamps of Panama

9 A2 1c green 2.50 2.00
a. "CANAL" in antique type 90.00 90.00
b. "ZONE" in antique type 60.00 60.00
c. Inverted overprint *7,500.* *6,000.*
d. Double overprint *2,750.* *2,000.*

10 A2 2c rose 4.00 2.50
a. Inverted overprint 225.00 275.00
b. "L" of "CANAL" sideways *2,000.* *2,250.*

"PANAMA" (15mm long) reading up at left, down at right

Overprint "CANAL ZONE" in Black, "PANAMA" and Bar in Red

11 A3 2c rose 6.50 4.50
a. "ZONE" in antique type 175.00 175.00
b. "PANAMA" overprint inverted, bar at bottom 600.00 *675.00*

12 A3 5c blue 7.50 2.75
a. "CANAL" in antique type 75.00 65.00
b. "ZONE" in antique type 75.00 65.00
c. "CANAL ZONE" double 800.00 800.00
d. "PANAMA" double 1,100. 1,000.
e. "PANAMA" inverted, bar at bottom 1,000. 1,250.
f. "PANAAM" at right *950.00* *750.00*

13 A3 10c yellow 17.00 12.00
a. "CANAL" in antique type 180.00 180.00
b. "ZONE" in antique type 175.00 160.00
c. "PANAMA" ovpt. double 650.00 650.00
d. "PANAMA" overprint in red brown 27.50 22.50
Nos. 11-13 (3) 31.00 19.25

With Added Surcharge in Red

a

14	A3 8c on 50c bister brn	27.50	25.00
a.	"ZONE" in antique type	1,150.	1,150.
b.	"CANAL ZONE" inverted	450.00	425.00
c.	"PANAMA" overprint in rose brown	35.00	35.00
d.	As "c," "CANAL" in antique type	*1,750.*	*850.00*
e.	As "c," "ZONE" in antique type	*1,750.*	
f.	As "c," "8 cts" double	*1,100.*	
g.	As "c," "8" omitted	*4,500.*	
h.	As "c," "cts 8"	—	

Nos. 11-14 are overprinted or surcharged on Panama Nos. 77, 77e, 78, 78c, 78d, 78f, 78g, 78h, 79 79c, 79e, 79g and 81 respectively.

On No. 14 with original gum, the gum is almost always disturbed. Unused stamps are valued thus.

Panama No. 74a, 74b Overprinted "CANAL ZONE" in Regular Type in Black and Surcharged Type "a" in Red Both "PANAMA" (13mm long) Reading Up

15	A3(a) 8c on 50c bister brown	2,000.	*4,750.*
a.	"PANAMA" reading down and up	*6,000.*	—

On No. 15 with original gum, the gum is almost always disturbed. Unused stamps are valued thus.

Map of Panama — A4

Panama Nos. 19 and 21 Surcharged in Black

a: PANAMA CANAL ZONE 1 ct. PANAMA

b: PANAMA CANAL ZONE 1 ct. PANAMA

c: PANAMA CANAL ZONE 1 ct. PANAMA

d: PANAMA CANAL ZONE 2 cts. PANAMA

e: PANAMA CANAL ZONE 2 cts. PANAMA

f: PANAMA CANAL ZONE 2 cts. PANAMA

There were three printings of each denomination, differing principally in the relative position of the various parts of the surcharges. Varieties occur with inverted "V" for the final "A" in "PANAMA," "CA" spaced, "ZO" spaced, "2c" spaced, accents in various positions, and with bars shifted so that two bars appear on top or bottom of the stamp (either with or without the corresponding bar on top or bottom) and sometimes with only one bar at top or bottom.

1906

16	A4 1c on 20c violet, type a	1.90	1.60
a.	Type b	1.90	1.60
b.	Type c	1.90	1.50
c.	As No. 16, double surcharge		*2,000.*
17	A4 2c on 1p lake, type d	2.50	2.50
a.	Type e	2.50	2.50
b.	Type f	20.00	20.00

Panama Nos. 74, 74a and 74b Overprinted "CANAL ZONE" in Regular Type in Black and Surcharged in Red

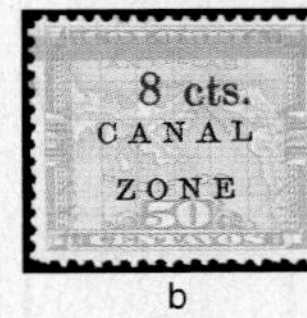
b

c

1905-06

Both "PANAMA" Reading Up

18	A3(b) 8c on 50c bister brown	50.00	50.00
a.	"ZONE" in antique type	200.00	180.00
b.	"PANAMA" reading down and up	160.00	150.00
19	A3(c) 8c on 50c bister brown	50.00	37.50
a.	"CANAL" in antique type	210.00	180.00
b.	"ZONE" in antique type	210.00	180.00
c.	"8 cts" double	*1,100.*	*1,100.*
d.	"PANAMA" reading down and up	110.00	90.00

On Nos. 18-19 with original gum, the gum is usually disturbed. Unused stamps are valued thus.

Panama No. 81 Overprinted "CANAL ZONE" in Regular Type in Black and Surcharged in Red Type "c" plus Period

"PANAMA" reading up and down

20	A3(c) 8c on 50c bister brown	35.00	37.50
a.	"CANAL" antique type	200.00	180.00
b.	"ZONE" in antique type	200.00	180.00
c.	"8 cts" omitted	800.00	800.00
d.	"8 cts" double	*1,500.*	
e.	"cts 8"	—	

Nos. 14 and 18-20 exist without CANAL ZONE overprint but were not regularly issued and are considered printer's waste. Forgeries of the overprint varieties of Nos. 9-15 and 18-20 are known.

On No. 20 with original gum, the gum is usually disturbed. Unused stamps are valued thus.

Francisco Hernandez de Cordoba — A5

Vasco Nunez de Balboa — A6

Fernández de Córdoba A7

Justo Arosemena A8

Manuel J. Hurtado — A9

Jose de Obaldia — A10

Stamps of Panama Overprinted in Black

1906-07 *Perf. 12*

Overprint Reading Up

21	A5 2c red & black	25.00	25.00
a.	"CANAL" only	*4,000.*	

Overprint Reading Down

22	A6 1c green & black	2.00	.90
a.	Horiz. pair, imperf. btwn.	1,100.	1,100.
b.	Vert. pair, imperf. btwn.	*2,000.*	*2,000.*
c.	Vert. pair, imperf. horiz.	*2,250.*	*1,750.*
d.	Inverted overprint reading up	550.00	550.00
e.	Double overprint	275.00	275.00
f.	Double overprint, one inverted	1,750.	1,600.
g.	Invtd. center, ovpt. reading up	*3,500.*	*4,750.*
h.	Horiz. pair, imperf vert.	*5,000.*	
23	A7 2c red & black	3.00	1.00
a.	Horizontal pair, imperf. between	2,000.	2,000.
b.	Vertical pair, one without overprint	2,500.	2,500.
c.	Double overprint	600.00	650.00
d.	Double overprint, one diagonal	800.00	800.00
e.	Double overprint, one diagonal, in pair with normal	2,500.	
f.	2c carmine red & black	5.00	2.75
g.	As "f," inverted center and overprint reading up		*14,000.*
h.	As "d," one "ZONE CANAL"	*4,000.*	
i.	"CANAL" double	*6,250.*	
24	A8 5c ultramarine & black	5.75	2.00
c.	Double overprint	500.00	400.00
d.	"CANAL" only	*7,000.*	
e.	"ZONE CANAL"	*5,000.*	
25	A9 8c purple & black	20.00	8.00
a.	Horizontal pair, imperf. between and at left margin	*1,750.*	*4,000.*
26	A10 10c violet & black	20.00	7.00
a.	Dbl. ovpt., one reading up	*5,000.*	
b.	Overprint reading up	*5,500.*	
	Nos. 22-26 (5)	50.75	18.90

Nos. 22-25 occur with "CA" of "CANAL" spaced ½mm further apart on position No. 50 of the setting.

The used pair of No. 25a is unique.

Cordoba A11

Arosemena A12

Hurtado — A13

Jose de Obaldia — A14

1909

Overprint Reading Down

27	A11 2c vermilion & black	12.00	5.00
a.	Horizontal pair, one without overprint	*2,600.*	
b.	Vert. pair, one without ovpt.	*3,500.*	
28	A12 5c deep blue & black	40.00	12.50
29	A13 8c violet & black	37.50	14.00

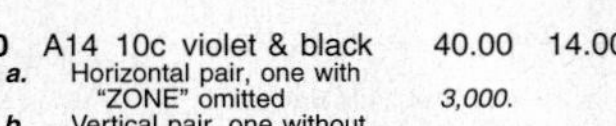

30	A14 10c violet & black	40.00	14.00
a.	Horizontal pair, one with "ZONE" omitted	*3,000.*	
b.	Vertical pair, one without overprint	*4,000.*	
	Nos. 27-30 (4)	129.50	45.50

Nos. 27-30 occur with "CA" spaced (position 50).

Do not confuse No. 27 with Nos. 39d or 53a.

On No. 30a, the stamp with "ZONE" omitted is also missing most of "CANAL."

For designs A11-A14 with overprints reading up, see Nos. 32-35, 39-41, 47-48, 53-54, 56-57.

Black Overprint Reading Up

Vasco Nunez de Balboa — A15

Type I

Type I Overprint: "C" with serifs both top and bottom. "L," "Z" and "E" with slanting serifs.

Compare Type I overprint with Types II to V illustrated before Nos. 38, 46, 52 and 55.

1909-10

31	A15 1c dark green & black	4.25	1.25
a.	Inverted center and overprint reading down		*22,500.*
c.	Bklt. pane of 6, handmade, perf. margins	*500.00*	
32	A11 2c vermilion & black	4.50	1.25
a.	Vert. pair, imperf. horiz.	1,000.	1,000.
c.	Bklt. pane of 6, handmade, perf. margins	*800.00*	
d.	Double overprint (I)		*6,000.*
33	A12 5c deep blue & black	17.00	3.50
a.	Double overprint	375.00	375.00
34	A13 8c violet & black	11.00	5.00
a.	Vertical pair, one without overprint	*1,750.*	
35	A14 10c violet & black	47.50	20.00
	Nos. 31-35 (5)	84.25	31.00

No. 32d is unique and has small faults.

See Nos. 38, 46, 52, 55.

A16

A17

Black Surcharge

1911, Jan. 14

36	A16 10c on 13c gray	6.00	2.00
a.	"10 cts" inverted	300.00	300.00
b.	"10 cts" omitted	300.00	

Many used stamps offered as No. 36b are merely No. 36 from which the surcharge has been chemically removed.

1914, Jan. 6

37	A17 10c gray	47.50	11.00

Black Overprint Reading Up

Type II: "C" with serif at top only. "L" and "E" with vertical serifs. "O" tilts to left

1912-16

38	A15 1c green & black	10.00	3.00
a.	Vertical pair, one without overprint	1,750.	1,750.
b.	Booklet pane of 6, imperf. margins	575.00	
c.	Booklet pane of 6, handmade, perf. margins	*1,000.*	

39 A11 2c vermilion & black 8.00 1.10
- *a.* Horiz. pair, right stamp without overprint *1,250.*
- *b.* Horiz. pair, left stamp without overprint *1,500.*
- *c.* Booklet pane of 6, imperf. margins 550.00
- *d.* Overprint reading down 200.00
- *e.* As "d," inverted center 600.00 *750.00*
- *f.* As "e," booklet pane of 6, handmade, perf. margins *8,000.*
- *g.* As "c," handmade, perf. margins 900.00 800.00
- *h.* As No. 39, "CANAL" only 1,100.

40 A12 5c deep blue & black 20.00 2.50
- *a.* With Cordoba portrait of 2c *12,500.*

41 A14 10c violet & black 60.00 7.50
Nos. 38-41 (4) 98.00 14.10

Map of Panama Canal A18

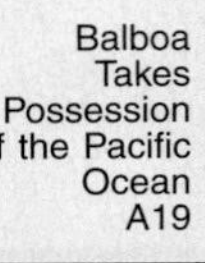

Balboa Takes Possession of the Pacific Ocean A19

Gatun Locks — A20

Culebra Cut — A21

1915, Mar. 1
Blue Overprint, Type II

42 A18 1c dark green & black 8.75 6.50
43 A19 2c carmine & black 12.00 4.25
44 A20 5c blue & black 10.00 5.75
45 A21 10c orange & black 19.00 11.00
Nos. 42-45 (4) 49.75 27.50

Black Overprint Reading Up

Type III Overprint: Similar to Type I but letters appear thinner, particularly the lower bar of "L," "Z" and "E." Impressions are often light, rough and irregular, and not centered.

1915-20

46 A15 1c green & black 175.00 125.00
- *a.* Overprint reading down 375.00
- *b.* Double overprint 225.00
- *c.* "ZONE" double *6,500.*
- *d.* Double overprint, one reads "ZONE CANAL" 2,000.

47 A11 2c orange vermilion & black 2,750. 60.00
48 A12 5c deep blue & black 450.00 130.00
Nos. 46-48 (3) 3,375. 315.00

Spacing between words of overprint on Nos. 46-48 is 9¼mm; spacing varieties are not known. This should not be confused with a fairly common 9¼mm spacing of the 2c value of type I, nor with an uncommon 9¼mm spacing variety of the 5c of type I.

S.S. "Panama" in Culebra Cut — A22

S.S. "Panama" in Culebra Cut — A23

S.S. "Cristobal" in Gatun Locks — A24

1917, Jan. 23
Blue Overprint, Type II

49 A22 12c purple & black 17.50 5.25
50 A23 15c bright blue & black 50.00 17.50
51 A24 24c yellow brown & black 35.00 13.00
Nos. 49-51 (3) 102.50 35.75

Black Overprint Reading Up

Type IV: "C" thick at bottom, "E" with center bar same length as top and bottom bars

1918-20

52 A15 1c green & black 32.50 10.00
- *a.* Overprint reading down 175.00 —
- *b.* Booklet pane of 6 600.00
- *c.* Booklet pane of 6, left vertical row of 3 without overprint *7,500.*
- *d.* Booklet pane of 6, right vertical row of 3 with double overprint *7,500.*
- *e.* Horiz. bklt. pair, left stamp without overprint *3,000.*
- *f.* Horiz. bklt. pair, right stamp with double overprint *3,000.*
- *g.* Double overprint, booklet single 3,000.

53 A11 2c vermilion & black 110.00 6.00
- *a.* Overprint reading down 150.00 150.00
- *b.* Horiz. pair, right stamp without ovpt. (from misregistered overprints) 2,000.
- *c.* Booklet pane of 6 1,050.
- *d.* Booklet pane of 6, left vertical row of 3 without overprint *15,000.*
- *e.* Horiz. bklt. pair, left stamp without overprint *3,000.*
- *f.* Horiz. sheet pair, one without overprint (from foldover) *1,750.*

54 A12 5c deep blue & black 150.00 32.50
Nos. 52-54 (3) 292.50 48.50

No. 53e used is unique and is on cover.

Black Overprint Reading Up

Type V: Smaller block type 1¾mm high. "A" with flat top

1920-21

55 A15 1c light green & black 22.50 3.25
- *a.* Overprint reading down 300.00 225.00
- *b.* Horiz. pair, right stamp without ovpt. *1,750.*
- *c.* Horiz. pair, left stamp without ovpt. 1,000.
- *d.* "ZONE" only *4,000.* —
- *e.* Booklet pane of 6 *2,250.*
- *f.* As No. 55, "CANAL" double *2,000.*

56 A11 2c orange vermilion & black 8.50 1.75
- *a.* Double overprint 500.00
- *b.* Double overprint, one reading down 600.00
- *c.* Horiz. pair, right stamp without overprint 1,400.
- *d.* Horiz. pair, left stamp without overprint 1,000.
- *e.* Vertical pair, one without overprint 1,500.
- *f.* "ZONE" double 900.00
- *g.* Booklet pane of 6 900.00
- *h.* As No. 56, "CANAL" double 800.

57 A12 5c deep blue & black 300.00 45.00
- *a.* Horiz. pair, right stamp without overprint *2,250.*
- *b.* Horiz. pair, left stamp without overprint *2,250.*

Nos. 55-57 (3) 331.00 50.00

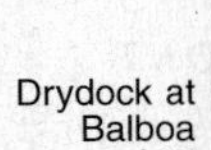
Drydock at Balboa A25

Ship in Pedro Miguel Locks — A26

1920, Sept.
Black Overprint Type V

58 A25 50c orange & black 250.00 160.00
59 A26 1b dark violet & black 175.00 50.00

Jose Vallarino — A27

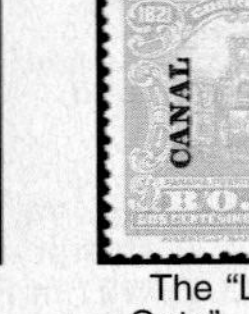
The "Land Gate" — A28

Bolivar's Tribute — A29

Municipal Building in 1821 and 1921 — A30

Statue of Balboa — A31

Tomas Herrera — A32

Jose de Fabrega — A33

Type V overprint in black, reading up, on all values except the 5c which is overprinted with larger type in red

1921, Nov. 13

60 A27 1c green 3.75 1.50
- *a.* "CANAL" double *1,900.*
- *b.* Booklet pane of 6 *900.00*

61 A28 2c carmine 2.75 1.00
- *a.* Overprint reading down 200.00 *225.00*
- *b.* Double overprint 900.00
- *c.* Vertical pair, one without overprint *3,500.*
- *d.* "CANAL" double *1,900.*
- *f.* Booklet pane of 6 *2,000.*

62 A29 5c blue (R) 10.00 3.00
- *a.* Overprint reading down (R) 60.00

63 A30 10c violet 18.00 7.50
- *a.* Overprint, reading down 90.00

64 A31 15c light blue 47.50 17.50
65 A32 24c black brown 67.50 22.50
66 A33 50c black 145.00 85.00
Nos. 60-66 (7) 294.50 138.00

Experts question the status of the 5c with a small type V overprint in red or black.

Type III overprint in black, reading up

1924, Jan. 28

67 A27 1c green 500. 200.
- *a.* "ZONE CANAL" reading down 800.
- *b.* "ZONE" only, reading down *1,900.*
- *c.* Se-tenant pair, #67a and 67b *2,750.*

Coat of Arms — A34

1924, Feb.

68 A34 1c dark green 10.00 4.50
69 A34 2c carmine 7.00 2.75

The 5c to lb values were prepared but never issued. See listing in the Scott U.S. specialized catalogue.

United States Nos. 551-554, 557, 562, 564-566, 569, 570 and 571 Overprinted in Red (No. 70) or Black (all others)

Type A: Letters "A" with Flat Tops

Type A
Letters "A" with Flat Tops

1924-25 Unwmk. *Perf. 11*

70 A154 ½c olive brown .25 .70
- Never hinged .40

71 A155 1c deep green 1.40 1.00
- Never hinged 2.50
- *a.* Inverted overprint 500.00 500.00
- *b.* "ZONE" inverted 350.00 325.00
- *c.* "CANAL" only 1,150.
- *d.* "ZONE CANAL" 400.00
- *e.* Booklet pane of 6 80.00 —

72 A156 1½c yellow brown 2.00 1.70
- Never hinged 3.25

73 A157 2c carmine 6.75 1.70
- Never hinged 10.50
- *a.* Booklet pane of 6 175.00

74 A160 5c dark blue 16.00 7.00
- Never hinged 25.00

75 A165 10c orange 40.00 20.00
- Never hinged 65.00

76 A167 12c brown violet 32.50 30.00
- Never hinged 62.50
- *a.* "ZONE" inverted *3,750.* *3,000.*

77 A168 14c dark blue 27.50 22.50
- Never hinged 45.00

78 A169 15c gray 45.00 37.50
- Never hinged 70.00

79 A172 30c olive brown 32.50 20.00
- Never hinged 52.50

80 A173 50c lilac 75.00 45.00
- Never hinged 150.00

81 A174 $1 violet brown 225.00 95.00
- Never hinged 400.00

Nos. 70-81 (12) 503.90 282.10

Normal spacing between words of the overprint is 9¼mm. Minor spacing variations are known.

All examples of Nos. 71b and 76a have a natural straight edge at right.

Type B: Letters "A" with Sharp Pointed Tops

Type B

1925-28

84 A157 2c carmine 27.50 8.00
- Never hinged 45.00
- *a.* "CANAL" only *2,250.*
- *b.* "ZONE CANAL" 425.00
- *c.* Horizontal pair, one without overprint *3,500.*
- *d.* Booklet pane of 6 175.00
- *e.* Vertical pair, "a" and "b" se-tenant *3,500.*

85 A158 3c violet 3.75 3.00
- Never hinged 6.00
- *a.* "ZONE ZONE" 550.00 550.00

86 A160 5c dark blue 3.50 2.75
- Never hinged 6.00
- *a.* "ZONE ZONE" (LR18) 1,000.
- *b.* "CANAL" inverted (LR7) 950.00
- *c.* Inverted overprint 500.00
- *d.* Horizontal pair, one without overprint *3,250.*
- *e.* Overprinted "ZONE CANAL" 350.00
- *f.* "ZONE" only *2,000.*
- *g.* Vertical pair, one without overprint, other overprint inverted *2,250.*
- *h.* "CANAL" only *2,250.*

87 A165 10c orange 35.00 12.00
- Never hinged 52.50
- *a.* "ZONE ZONE" (LR18) *3,000.*

88 A167 12c brown violet 20.00 12.50
- Never hinged 34.00
- *a.* "ZONE ZONE" (LR18) *5,000.*

89 A168 14c dark blue 27.50 15.00
- Never hinged 45.00

90 A169 15c gray 7.50 4.50
- Never hinged 12.00
- *a.* "ZONE ZONE" (LR18) *5,500.*

91 A187 17c black 4.50 2.75
Never hinged 7.50
a. "ZONE" only 1,000.
b. "CANAL" only 2,000.
c. "ZONE CANAL" 275.00
92 A170 20c carmine rose 7.25 3.25
Never hinged 12.00
a. "CANAL" inverted (UR48) *6,500.*
b. "ZONE" inverted (LL76) *4,750.*
c. "ZONE CANAL" (LL91) *4,750.*
93 A172 30c olive brown 5.75 3.75
Never hinged 9.00
94 A173 50c lilac 230.00 165.00
Never hinged 400.00
95 A174 $1 violet brown 120.00 55.00
Never hinged 250.00
Nos. 84-95 (12) 492.25 287.50

Overprint Type B on U.S. Sesquicentennial Stamp No. 627

1926
96 A188 2c carmine rose 4.50 3.75
Never hinged 7.00

On this stamp there is a space of 5mm instead of 9mm between the two words of the overprint.

Overprint Type B in Black on U.S. Nos. 583, 584, 591

1926-27 ***Perf. 10***
97 A157 2c carmine 45.00 11.00
Never hinged 75.00
a. Pair, one without overprint *2,500.*
b. Booklet pane of 6 500.00
c. "CANAL" only *2,000.*
d. "ZONE" only *2,750.*
98 A158 3c violet 7.50 4.25
Never hinged 11.00
99 A165 10c orange 18.00 7.50
Never hinged 27.50
Nos. 97-99 (3) 70.50 22.75

No. 97d is valued in the grade of fine. Very fine examples are not known.

Overprint Type B in Black on U.S. Nos. 632, 634 (Type I), 635, 637, 642

1927-31 ***Perf. 11x10½***
100 A155 1c green 1.75 1.40
Never hinged 2.60
a. Vertical pair, one without overprint *3,500.*
101 A157 2c carmine 1.75 1.00
Never hinged 2.50
a. Booklet pane of 6 200.00
102 A158 3c violet 4.25 2.75
Never hinged 6.25
a. Booklet pane of 6, handmade, perf. margins *6,500.*
103 A160 5c dark blue 25.00 10.00
Never hinged 45.00
104 A165 10c orange 17.50 10.00
Never hinged 26.00
Nos. 100-104 (5) 50.25 25.15

Wet and Dry Printings
Canal Zone stamps printed by both the "wet" and "dry" process are Nos. 105, 108-109, 111-114, 117, J25, J27.

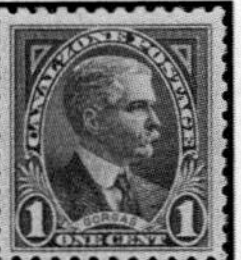
Maj. Gen. William Crawford Gorgas A35

Maj. Gen. George Washington Goethals A36

Gaillard Cut — A37

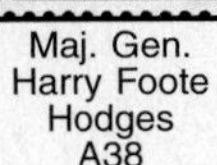
Maj. Gen. Harry Foote Hodges A38

Lt. Col. David DuB. Gaillard A39

Maj. Gen. William L. Sibert — A40

Jackson Smith — A41

Rear Adm. Harry H. Rousseau A42

Col. Sydney B. Williamson A43

J.C.S. Blackburn — A44

1928-40 ***Perf. 11***
105 A35 1c green (22,392,147) .25 .25
Never hinged .25
106 A36 2c carmine .25 .25
Never hinged .30
a. Booklet pane of 6 15.00 *20.00*
Never hinged 22.50
107 A37 5c blue 1.00 .40
Never hinged 1.30
108 A38 10c orange .25 .25
Never hinged .25
109 A39 12c brown violet .75 .60
Never hinged 1.00
110 A40 14c blue .85 .85
Never hinged 1.20
111 A41 15c gray black .40 .35
Never hinged .55
112 A42 20c dark brown .60 .25
Never hinged .80
113 A43 30c black .80 .70
Never hinged 1.10
114 A44 50c rose lilac 1.50 .65
Never hinged 2.00
Nos. 105-114 (10) 6.65 4.55

For surcharges and overprints, see Nos. J21-J24, O1-O8.
Coils are listed as Nos. 160-161.

United States Nos. 720 and 695 Overprinted type B

1933, Jan. 14 ***Perf. 11x10½***
115 A226 3c deep violet 2.75 .25
Never hinged 4.00
b. "CANAL" only *2,600.*
c. Booklet pane of 6, handmade, perf. margins 80.00 —
116 A168 14c dark blue 4.50 3.50
Never hinged 7.00
a. "ZONE CANAL" *1,500.*

Gen. George Washington Goethals — A45

20th anniversary of the opening of the Panama Canal.

1934 ***Perf. 11***
117 A45 3c red violet .25 .25
Never hinged .30
a. Booklet pane of 6 *12.50* *32.50*
b. As "a," handmade, perf. margins 160.00 —

Coil is listed as No. 153.

Catalogue values for unused stamps in this section, from this point to the end, are for Never Hinged items.

United States Nos. 803 and 805 Overprinted in Black

1939, Sept. 1 ***Perf. 11x10½***
118 A275 ½c red orange .25 .25
119 A277 1½c bister brown .25 .25

Panama Canal Anniversary Issue

Balboa-Before — A46

Balboa-After — A47

Gaillard Cut-Before A48

Gaillard Cut-After A49

Bas Obispo-Before — A50

Bas Obispo-After A51

Gatun Locks-Before — A52

Gatun Locks-After A53

Canal Channel-Before A54

Canal Channel-After — A55

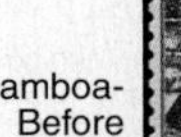

Gamboa-Before A56

Gamboa-After — A57

Pedro Miguel Locks-Before — A58

Pedro Miguel Locks-After A59

Gatun Spillway-Before A60

Gatun Spillway-After — A61

25th anniversary of the opening of the Panama Canal.

1939, Aug. 15
120 A46 1c yellow green .60 .30
121 A47 2c rose carmine .70 .35
122 A48 3c purple .70 .25
123 A49 5c dark blue 2.00 1.25
124 A50 6c red orange 4.50 3.00
125 A51 7c black 4.75 3.00
126 A52 8c green 7.00 3.25
127 A53 10c ultramarine 5.50 5.00
128 A54 11c blue green 11.00 8.00
129 A55 12c brown carmine 11.00 7.50
130 A56 14c dark violet 11.00 7.00
131 A57 15c olive green 14.00 5.75
132 A58 18c rose pink 15.00 8.50
133 A59 20c brown 17.50 7.00
134 A60 25c orange 27.50 17.50
135 A61 50c violet brown 30.00 6.00
Nos. 120-135 (16) 162.75 83.65

AIR POST STAMPS

Nos. 105-106 Surcharged in Dark Blue

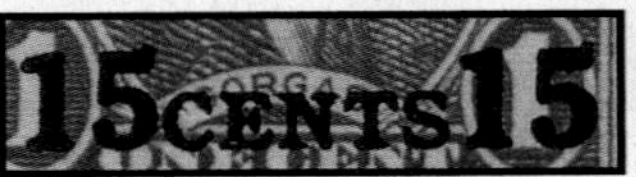
Type I - Flag of "Five" pointing up

Type II - Flag of "5" curved

1929-31 Engr. Unwmk. *Perf. 11*

C1	A35	15c on 1c green, type I	7.50	4.75
C2	A35	15c on 1c yellow green, type II	60.00	47.50
C3	A36	25c on 2c carmine	3.50	2.00
		Nos. C1-C3 (3)	71.00	54.25

Nos. 114 and 106 Surcharged

1929, Dec. 31

C4	A44	10c on 50c lilac	8.00	5.75
C5	A36	20c on 2c carmine	4.50	1.25
a.		Dropped "2" in surcharge	85.00	60.00

Catalogue values for unused stamps in this section, from this point to the end, are for Never Hinged items.

Gaillard Cut — AP1

1931-49

C6	AP1	4c red violet	.75	.65
C7	AP1	5c yellow green	.60	.30
C8	AP1	6c yellow brown	.75	.35
C9	AP1	10c orange	1.00	.35
C10	AP1	15c blue	1.25	.30
C11	AP1	20c red violet	2.00	.25
C12	AP1	30c rose lake	7.50	1.50
C13	AP1	40c yellow	3.50	1.10
C14	AP1	$1 black	10.00	1.60
		Nos. C6-C14 (9)	27.35	6.40

For overprints, see Nos. CO1-CO14.

Douglas Plane over Sosa Hill — AP2

Planes and Map of Central America AP3

Pan American Clipper and Scene near Fort Amador AP4

Pan American Clipper at Cristobal Harbor AP5

Pan American Clipper over Gaillard Cut — AP6

Pan American Clipper Landing AP7

10th anniversary of Air Mail service and the 25th anniversary of the opening of the Panama Canal.

1939, July 15

C15	AP2	5c greenish black	3.75	2.25
C16	AP3	10c dull violet	3.50	3.00
C17	AP4	15c light brown	5.00	1.00
C18	AP5	25c blue	17.50	8.00
C19	AP6	30c rose carmine	17.50	6.00
C20	AP7	$1 green	45.00	27.50
		Nos. C15-C20 (6)	92.25	47.75

POSTAGE DUE STAMPS

Prior to 1914, many of the postal issues were handstamped "Postage Due" and used as postage due stamps.

Postage Due Stamps of the U.S. Nos. J45a, J46a and J49a Overprinted in Black

1914, Mar. Wmk. 190 *Perf. 12*

J1	D2	1c rose carmine	85.00	15.00
J2	D2	2c rose carmine	250.00	42.50
J3	D2	10c rose carmine	1,000.	40.00
		Nos. J1-J3 (3)	1,335.	97.50

Castle Gate (See footnote) — D1

Statue of Columbus D2

Pedro J. Sosa D3

1915, Mar. Unwmk.

Blue Overprint, Type II, on Postage Due Stamps of Panama

J4	D1	1c olive brown	11.00	5.00
J5	D2	2c olive brown	225.00	17.50
J6	D3	10c olive brown	50.00	10.00
		Nos. J4-J6 (3)	286.00	32.50

Type D1 was intended to show a gate of San Lorenzo Castle, Chagres, and is so labeled. By error the stamp actually shows the main gate of San Geronimo Castle, Portobelo.

Surcharged in Red

1915, Nov.

J7	D1	1c on 1c olive brown	110.00	14.00
J8	D2	2c on 2c olive brown	22.50	7.50
J9	D3	10c on 10c olive brown	22.50	5.00
		Nos. J7-J9 (3)	155.00	26.50

Columbus Statue — D4

Capitol, Panama City — D5

1919, Dec.

Surcharged in Carmine by Panama Canal Press, Mount Hope, C. Z.

"Canal Zone" Type III

J10	D4	2c on 2c olive brown	30.00	11.00
J11	D5	4c on 4c olive brown	35.00	12.50
a.		"ZONE" omitted	*9,250.*	
b.		"4" omitted	*8,500.*	

Blue Overprint, Type V, on Postage Due Stamp of Panama

1922

J11C	D1	1c dark olive brown	—	5.00
d.		"CANAL ZONE" reading down	200.00	

United States Postage Due Stamps Nos. J61, J62b and J65b Overprinted

Type A

Letters "A" with Flat Tops

1924, July 1 *Perf. 11*

J12	D2	1c carmine rose	110.00	27.50
J13	D2	2c deep claret	55.00	15.00
J14	D2	10c deep claret	250.00	50.00
		Nos. J12-J14 (3)	415.00	92.50

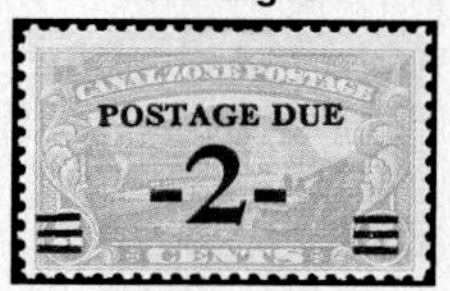

U.S. Postage Stamps Nos. 552, 554 and 562 Overprinted Type A and additional Overprint in Red or Blue

1925, Feb.

J15	A155	1c deep green (R)	90.00	15.00
J16	A157	2c carmine (Bl)	22.50	7.00
J17	A165	10c orange (R)	55.00	11.00
a.		"POSTAGE DUE" double	800.00	
b.		"E" of "POSTAGE" omitted	750.00	
c.		As "b," "POSTAGE DUE" double	*3,250.*	
		Nos. J15-J17 (3)	167.50	33.00

Overprinted Type B

Letters "A" with Sharp Pointed Tops On U.S. Postage Due Stamps Nos. J61, J62, J65, J65a

1925, June 24

J18	D2	1c carmine rose	8.00	2.75
a.		"ZONE ZONE" (LR18)	1,500.	
J19	D2	2c carmine rose	15.00	2.75
a.		"ZONE ZONE" (LR18)	1,500.	
J20	D2	10c carmine rose	150.00	20.00
a.		Vert. pair, one without ovpt.	*3,000.*	
b.		10c rose red	*250.00*	150.00
c.		As "b," double overprint	*450.00*	—
		Nos. J18-J20 (3)	173.00	25.50

Regular Issue of 1928-29 Surcharged

Canal Zone Seal — D6

1929-30

J21	A37	1c on 5c blue	3.75	1.75
		Never hinged	7.50	
a.		"POSTAGE DUE" missing	*5,500.*	
J22	A37	2c on 5c blue	6.50	2.50
		Never hinged	13.00	
J23	A37	5c on 5c blue	6.50	2.75
		Never hinged	13.00	
J24	A37	10c on 5c blue	6.50	2.75
		Never hinged	13.00	
		Nos. J21-J24 (4)	23.25	9.75

On No. J23 the three short horizontal bars in the lower corners of the surcharge are omitted.

1932-41

J25	D6	1c claret	.25	.25
		Never hinged	.30	
J26	D6	2c claret	.25	.25
		Never hinged	.30	
J27	D6	5c claret	.35	.25
		Never hinged	.50	
J28	D6	10c claret	1.75	1.50
		Never hinged	2.25	
J29	D6	15c claret	1.25	1.00
		Never hinged	1.60	
		Nos. J25-J29 (5)	3.85	3.25

GUAM

'gwäm

LOCATION — One of the Mariana Islands in the Pacific Ocean, about 1450 miles east of the Philippines
GOVT. — United States Possession
AREA — 206 sq. mi.
POP. — 9,000 (est. 1899)
CAPITAL — Agaña

Formerly a Spanish possession, Guam was ceded to the United States in 1898 following the Spanish-American War. Stamps overprinted "Guam" were superseded by the regular postage stamps of the United States in 1901.

100 Cents = 1 Dollar

United States Nos. 279, 279B, 279Bc, 268, 280a, 281, 282, 272, 282C, 283, 284, 275, 275a, 276 and 276A Overprinted

1899 Wmk. 191 *Perf. 12*

Black Overprint

1	A87	1c deep green	20.00	*25.00*
		Never hinged	40.00	
		On cover		*200.00*

A bogus inverted overprint exists.

2	A88	2c red, type IV	17.50	*25.00*
		On cover		*200.00*
		Never hinged	35.00	
a.		rose carmine, type IV	30.00	30.00
		Never hinged	60.00	
		On cover		*225.00*
3	A89	3c purple	140.00	*175.00*
		Never hinged	275.00	
		On cover		*400.00*
4	A90	4c lilac brown	125.00	*175.00*
		Never hinged	250.00	
		On cover		*450.00*
5	A91	5c blue	32.50	*45.00*
		Never hinged	65.00	
		On cover		*200.00*
6	A92	6c lake	125.00	*190.00*
		Never hinged	250.00	
		On cover		*450.00*
7	A93	8c violet brown	125.00	*160.00*
		Never hinged	275.00	
		On cover		*450.00*
8	A94	10c brown, type I	45.00	*55.00*
		Never hinged	90.00	
		On cover		*275.00*
9	A94	10c brown, type II	*2,750.*	—
		Never hinged	*5,500.*	
10	A95	15c olive green	150.00	140.00
		Never hinged	300.00	
		On cover		*900.00*
11	A96	50c orange	350.00	*400.00*
		Never hinged	700.00	
		On cover		*1,500.*
a.		50c red orange	550.00	—
		Never hinged	1,100.	

Red Overprint

12	A97	$1 black, type I	350.00	*400.00*
		Never hinged	700.00	
		On cover		*3,500.*
13	A97	$1 black, type II	*3,750.*	
		Never hinged	—	
		Nos. 1-8,10-12 (11)	1,480.	*1,790.*

Counterfeits of the overprint exist.
No. 13 exists only in the special printing.

SPECIAL DELIVERY STAMP

United States No. E5 Overprinted in Red

1899 **Wmk. 191** ***Perf. 12***

E1 SD3 10c blue 150. *200.00*
Never hinged 275.
On cover *1,500.*
a. Dots in curved frame above messenger (Plate 882) 200.
Never hinged 400.

Counterfeits of the overprint exist.

The special stamps for Guam were replaced by the regular issues of the United States.

Guam Guard Mail stamps of 1930 are listed in the Scott U.S. specialized catalogue.

HAWAII

hə-ˈwä-yē

LOCATION — Group of 20 islands in the Pacific Ocean, about 2,000 miles southwest of San Francisco.
GOVT. — Former Kingdom and Republic
AREA — 6,435 sq. mi.
POP. — 150,000 (est. 1899)
CAPITAL — Honolulu

Until 1893 an independent kingdom, from 1893 to 1898 a republic, the Hawaiian Islands were annexed to the US in 1898.

100 Cents = 1 Dollar

Values for Nos. 1-4 are for examples with minor damage that has been skillfully repaired.

Values of Hawaii stamps vary considerably according to condition. For Nos. 1-4, values are for examples with minor damage that has been skillfully repaired.

A1

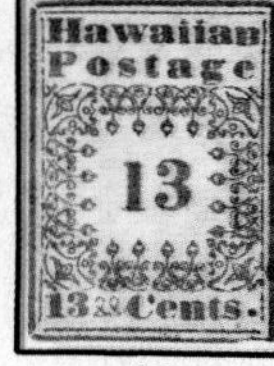
A2

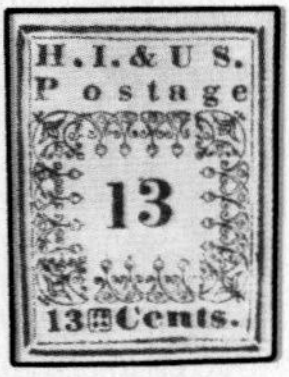
A3

1851-52 **Unwmk.** **Typeset** ***Imperf.***
Pelure Paper

1 A1 2c blue *660,000.* *250,000.*
On cover *2,250,000.*
2 A1 5c blue *55,000.* *35,000.*
On cover *90,000.*
3 A2 13c blue *37,000.* *29,000.*
On cover *75,000.*
4 A3 13c blue *52,500.* *35,000.*
On cover *80,000.*

Nos. 1-4 are known as the "Missionaries."

Two varieties of each. Nos. 1-4, off cover, are almost invariably damaged.

No. 1 unused and on cover are each unique; the on-cover value is based on a 2013 auction sale.

King Kamehameha III

A4

A5

Printed in Sheets of 20 (4x5)

1853 **Engr.**
Thick White Wove Paper

5 A4 5c blue 1,900. 1,900.
On cover *5,000.*
On cover with U.S. #17 *12,000.*
a. Line through "Honolulu" (Pos. 2) *3,000.* *3,000.*
6 A5 13c dark red 875. *1,700.*
On cover *25,000.*
On cover with #5 *12,500.*
On cover with U.S. #11 (pair) *25,000.*
On cover with U.S. #17 *32,500.*
On cover with #5 and U.S. #17 *32,500.*
On cover with #8 and U.S. #36b *38,500.*

See Nos. 8-11.

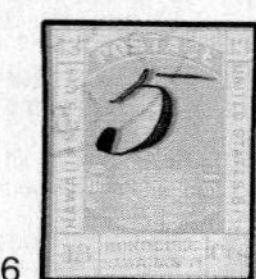
A6

1857

7 A6 5c on 13c dark red *7,000.* *10,000.*
On cover with pair U.S. #7 and 14 *57,500.*
On cover with pair U.S. #11, 14 *55,000.*
On cover with U.S. #14 *50,000.*
On cover with U.S. #17 *45,000.*

Beware of fake manuscript surcharges. Expertization is strongly recommended.

1857 **Thin White Wove Paper**

8 A4 5c blue 700. *750.*
On cover with U.S. #11 —
On cover with U.S. #7, 15 *6,000.*
On cover with U.S. #17 *10,000.*
On cover with U.S. #26 —
On cover with U.S. #35 *11,000.*
On cover with U.S. #36 *10,000.*
On cover with U.S. #69 *12,500.*
On cover with U.S. #76 —
a. Line through "Honolulu" (Pos. 2) *1,350.* *1,350.*
On cover with U.S. #17 *7,500.*
b. Double impression *3,500.* *4,750.*

1861 **Thin Bluish Wove Paper**

9 A4 5c blue 400. 400.
On cover *5,000.*
On cover with U.S. #36b *3,250.*
On cover with U.S. #65 *3,000.*
On cover with U.S. #65, 73 *6,500.*
On cover with U.S. #68 *4,250.*
On cover with U.S. #76 *7,000.*
a. Line through "Honolulu" (Pos. 2) *950.* *1,000.*

RE-ISSUE

1868 **Ordinary White Wove Paper**

10 A4 5c blue 27.50
a. Line through "Honolulu" (Pos. 2) 80.
11 A5 13c dull rose 325.

Remainders of Nos. 10 and 11 were overprinted "SPECIMEN." See Nos. 10S-11Sb in the Scott U.S. Specialized catalogue.

Nos. 10 and 11 were never placed in use but stamps (both with and without overprint) were sold at face value at the Honolulu post office.

REPRINTS (Official Imitations)

Original

Reprint

Original

Reprint

5c — *Originals have two small dots near the left side of the square in the upper right corner. These dots are missing in the reprints.*

13c — *The bottom of the 3 of 13 in the upper left corner is flattened in the originals and rounded in the reprints. The "t" of "Cts" on the left side is as tall as the "C" in the reprints, but shorter in the originals.*

1889

10R A4 5c blue 65.
Block of 4 280.
11R A5 13c orange red 300.
Block of 4 1,450.

On August 19, 1892, the remaining supply of reprints was overprinted in black "REPRINT." The reprints (both with and without overprint) were sold at face value. See the Scott U.S. Specialized Catalogue.

Values for the Numeral stamps, Nos. 12-26, are for examples with four reasonably large margins. Unused values are for stamps without gum.

A7

A8

A9

1859-62 **Typeset**

12 A7 1c light blue, *bluish white* *15,000.* *15,000.*
a. "1 Ce" omitted *22,500.*
b. "nt" omitted — —

No. 12a is unique.

13 A7 2c light blue, *bluish white* *6,250.* *5,000.*
On cover *12,500.*
a. 2c dark blue, *grayish white* *6,750.* *5,000.*
b. Comma after "Cents" — *6,750.*
On cover *12,500.*
c. No period after "LETA" — —
14 A7 2c black, *greenish blue* ('62) *8,000.* *6,000.*
On cover *10,000.*
a. "2-Cents." —

1859-63

15 A7 1c black, *grayish* ('63) 650. *2,750.*
On cover —
a. Tête bêche pair *9,000.*
b. "NTER" —
c. Period omitted after "Postage" 850.
16 A7 2c black, *grayish* 1,000. 850.
On cover *5,000.*
a. "2" at top of rectangle *3,750.* *3,750.*
b. Printed on both sides — *21,000.*
c. "NTER" *3,250.* *6,500.*
d. 2c black, *grayish white* 1,000. 850.
e. Period omitted after "Cents" —
f. Overlapping impressions — —
g. "TAGE" — —
17 A7 2c dark blue, *bluish* ('63) *12,000.* *8,750.*
a. "ISL" — —
18 A7 2c black, *blue gray* ('63) *3,250.* *6,000.*
On cover *18,000.*

1864-65

19 A7 1c black 600. *10,000.*
20 A7 2c black 775. *1,500.*
On cover *19,000.*
21 A8 5c blue, *blue* ('65) 900. 700.
On cover with U.S. #65 —
On cover with U.S. #68 —
On cover with U.S. #76 *8,250.*
a. Tête bêche pair *10,500.*
b. 5c bluish black, *grayish white* *14,000.* *3,750.*

No. 21b unused is unique. No. 21b used is also unique but defective.

22 A9 5c blue, *blue* ('65) 575. *900.*
On cover *13,000.*
On cover with U.S. #76 *9,250.*
On cover with U.S. #63 and 76 —
a. Tête bêche pair *18,000.*
b. 5c blue, *grayish white* —
c. Overlapping impressions —

1864 — **Laid Paper**

No.	Description	Unused	Used
23	A7 1c black	300.	*2,500.*
	On cover with U.S. #76		*12,000.*
a.	"HA" instead of "HAWAIIAN"	*3,500.*	
b.	Tête bêche pair	*6,000.*	
c.	Tête bêche pair, Nos. 23, 23a	*18,000.*	
24	A7 2c black	350.	*1,050.*
a.	"NTER"	*3,250.*	
b.	"S" of "POSTAGE" omitted	*1,500.*	
c.	Tête bêche pair	*7,000.*	

A10

1865 — **Wove Paper**

No.	Description	Unused	Used
25	A10 1c dark blue	350.	
a.	Double impression	—	
b.	With inverted impression of No. 21 on face	*18,500.*	
26	A10 2c dark blue	350.	

Nos. 12 to 26 were typeset and were printed in settings of ten, each stamp differing from the others.

King Kamehameha IV — A11

1861-63 — **Litho.**

Horizontally Laid Paper

No.	Description	Unused	Used
27	A11 2c pale rose	350.	350.
	On cover		*1,000.*
a.	2c carmine rose ('63)	3,000.	2,850.

Vertically Laid Paper

No.	Description	Unused	Used
28	A11 2c pale rose	325.	325.
	On cover		*1,500.*
a.	2c carmine rose ('63)	400.	*450.*
	On cover		*2,000.*

RE-ISSUE

1869 — **Engr.** — **Thin Wove Paper**

No.	Description	Unused	Used
29	A11 2c red	45.00	—

No. 29 was not issued for postal purposes although canceled examples are known. It was sold only at the Honolulu post office, at first without overprint and later with overprint "CANCELLED." See No. 29S in the Scott U.S. Specialized Catalogue.

See Nos. 50-51 and note following No. 51.

Princess Victoria Kamamalu — A12

King Kamehameha IV — A13

King Kamehameha V — A14

King Kamehameha V — A15

Mataio Kekuanaoa — A16

1864-86 — **Engr.** — ***Perf. 12***

Wove Paper

No.	Description	Unused	Used
30	A12 1c purple ('86)	11.00	8.00
	Never hinged	25.00	
	On cover		150.00
a.	1c mauve ('71)	60.00	20.00
	Never hinged	95.00	
b.	1c violet ('78)	20.00	10.00
	Never hinged	45.00	
31	A13 2c rose vermilion	65.00	12.50
	Never hinged	150.00	
a.	2c vermilion ('86)	55.00	17.50
	Never hinged	130.00	
	On cover		500.00
b.	Half used as 1c on cover with #32		*8,500.*
32	A14 5c blue ('66)	175.00	30.00
	Never hinged	375.00	
	On cover		250.00
	On cover with any U.S. issues of 1861-67		*5,000.*
	On cover with U.S. #116		*15,000.*
	On cover with U.S. #116 and 69		*25,000.*
33	A15 6c yellow green ('71)	45.00	10.00
	Never hinged	100.00	
	On cover		300.00
a.	6c bluish green ('78)	35.00	10.00
	Never hinged	85.00	
	On cover		300.00
	On cover with U.S. #179		*1,500.*
	On cover with U.S. #185		*1,000.*
b.	As "a," horiz. pair, imperf.	*2,250.*	
34	A16 18c dull rose ('71)	100.00	42.50
	Never hinged	220.00	
	On cover		350.00
	Nos. 30-34 (5)	396.00	103.00
	Set, never hinged	860.00	

No. 32 has traces of rectangular frame lines surrounding the design. Nos. 39 and 52C have no such frame lines.

For overprints see Nos. 53, 58-60, 65, 66C, 71.

King David Kalakaua A17

Prince William Pitt Leleiohoku A18

1875

No.	Description	Unused	Used
35	A17 2c brown	9.00	3.00
	Never hinged	22.00	
	On cover		200.00
36	A18 12c black	75.00	32.50
	Never hinged	165.00	
	On cover		400.00

See Nos. 38, 43, 46. For overprints see Nos. 56, 62-63, 66, 69.

Princess Likelike A19

King David Kalakaua A20

Queen Kapiolani — A21

Statue of King Kamehameha I — A22

King William Lunalilo — A23

Queen Emma Kaleleonalani — A24

1882

No.	Description	Unused	Used
37	A19 1c blue	11.00	6.00
	Never hinged	27.50	
	On cover		60.00
38	A17 2c lilac rose	125.00	47.50
	Never hinged	275.00	
	On cover		150.00
39	A14 5c ultramarine	15.00	3.00
	Never hinged	35.00	
	On cover		27.50
a.	Vert. pair, imperf. horiz.	*5,000.*	*6,000.*
40	A20 10c black	50.00	25.00
	Never hinged	115.00	
	On cover		160.00
41	A21 15c red brown	70.00	27.50
	Never hinged	150.00	
	On cover		200.00
	Nos. 37-41 (5)	271.00	109.00
	Set, never hinged	602.50	

1883-86

No.	Description	Unused	Used
42	A19 1c green	3.00	2.00
	Never hinged	7.00	
	On cover		25.00
43	A17 2c rose ('86)	5.00	1.00
	Never hinged	11.00	
	On cover		25.00
a.	2c dull red	65.00	22.50
	Never hinged	140.00	
44	A20 10c red brown ('84)	40.00	11.00
	Never hinged	90.00	
	On cover		125.00
45	A20 10c vermilion	45.00	14.00
	Never hinged	100.00	
	On cover		125.00
46	A18 12c red lilac	90.00	40.00
	Never hinged	225.00	
	On cover		425.00
47	A22 25c dark violet	160.00	65.00
	Never hinged	350.00	
	On cover		375.00
48	A23 50c red	200.00	90.00
	Never hinged	425.00	
	On cover		525.00
49	A24 $1 rose red	325.00	275.00
	Never hinged	675.00	
	On cover		*8,000.*
	Maltese cross cancellation		150.00
	Nos. 42-49 (8)	868.00	498.00
	Set, never hinged	1,833.	

Other fiscal cancellations exist on No. 49.

Nos. 48-49 are valued used with postal cancels. Canceled-to-order cancels exist and are worth less.

REPRODUCTION and REPRINT

Yellowish Wove Paper

1886-89 — **Engr.** — ***Imperf.***

No.	Description	Unused	Used
50	A11 2c orange vermilion	170.00	
	Never hinged	275.00	
51	A11 2c carmine ('89)	35.00	
	Never hinged	50.00	

In 1885, the Postmaster General wished to have on sale complete sets of Hawaii's portrait stamps, but was unable to find either the stone from which Nos. 27 and 28 were printed, or the plate from which No. 29 was printed. He therefore sent an example of No. 29 to the American Bank Note Company, with an order to engrave a new plate like it and print 10,000 stamps therefrom, of which 5000 were overprinted "SPECIMEN" in blue.

The original No. 29 was printed in sheets of fifteen (5x3), but the plate of these "Official Imitations" was made up of fifty stamps (10x5). Later, in 1887, the original die for No. 29 was discovered, and, after retouching, a new plate was made and 37,500 stamps were printed (No. 51). These, like the originals, were printed in sheets of fifteen. They were delivered during 1889 and 1890. In 1892, all remaining unsold in the Post Office were overprinted "Reprint".

No. 29 is red in color, and printed on very thin white wove paper. No. 50 is orange vermilion in color, on medium, white to buff paper. In No. 50 the vertical line on the left side of the portrait touches the horizontal line over the label "Elua Keneta", while in the other two varieties, Nos. 29 and 51, it does not touch the horizontal line by half a millimeter. In No. 51 there are three parallel lines on the left side of the King's nose, while in No. 29 and No. 50 there are no such lines. No. 51 is carmine in color and printed on thick, yellowish to buff, wove paper.

It is claimed that both Nos. 50 and 51 were available for postage, although not made to fill a postal requirement. They exist with favor cancellation. No. 51 also is known postally used. See Nos. 50S-51S in the Scott U.S. specialized catalogue.

Queen Liliuokalani — A25

1890-91 — ***Perf. 12***

No.	Description	Unused	Used
52	A25 2c dull violet ('91)	15.00	1.50
	Never hinged	25.00	
	On cover		25.00
a.	Vert. pair, imperf. horiz.	*3,750.*	
52C	A14 5c deep indigo	125.00	150.00
	Never hinged	280.00	
	On cover		500.00

Stamps of 1864-91 Overprinted in Red

Three categories of double overprints:
I. Both overprints heavy.
II. One overprint heavy, one of moderate strength.
III. One overprint heavy, one of light or weak strength.

1893 — **Overprinted in Red**

No.	Description	Unused	Used
53	A12 1c purple	9.00	13.00
	Never hinged	20.00	
	On cover		35.00
a.	"189" instead of "1893"	600.00	—
b.	No period after "GOVT"	*275.00*	*275.00*
f.	Double overprint (III)	*600.00*	
54	A19 1c blue	9.00	*15.00*
	Never hinged	21.00	
	On cover		40.00
b.	No period after "GOVT"	*140.00*	*150.00*
e.	Double overprint (II)	*1,500.*	
f.	Double overprint (III)	*400.00*	
55	A19 1c green	2.00	*3.00*
	Never hinged	4.00	
	On cover		25.00
d.	Double overprint (I)	*650.00*	*650.00*
f.	Double overprint (III)	*250.00*	*250.00*
g.	Pair, one without ovpt.	*10,000.*	
56	A17 2c brown	12.50	*20.00*
	Never hinged	27.50	
	On cover		60.00
b.	No period after "GOVT"	*325.00*	—
57	A25 2c dull violet	2.00	1.50
	Never hinged	3.00	
	On cover		25.00
a.	"18 3" instead of "1893"	*900.00*	*900.00*
d.	Double overprint (I)	*1,300.*	*1,000.*
f.	Double overprint (III)	*190.00*	*190.00*
g.	Inverted overprint	*4,000.*	*4,750.*
58	A14 5c deep indigo	15.00	*30.00*
	Never hinged	32.00	
	On cover		100.00
b.	No period after "GOVT"	*275.00*	*250.00*
f.	Double overprint (III)	*1,250.*	*675.00*
59	A14 5c ultramarine	7.00	3.00
	Never hinged	15.00	
	On cover		40.00
d.	Double overprint (I)	*6,500.*	
e.	Double overprint (II)	*3,750.*	*3,750.*
f.	Double overprint (III)		*600.00*
g.	Inverted overprint	*1,500.*	*1,500.*
60	A15 6c green	17.50	*25.00*
	Never hinged	40.00	
	On cover		140.00
e.	Double overprint (II)	*1,100.*	
61	A20 10c black	14.00	*20.00*
	Never hinged	30.00	
	On cover		125.00
e.	Double overprint (II)	*1,000.*	*900.00*
f.	Double overprint (III)	*225.00*	
61B	A20 10c red brown	*15,000.*	*29,000.*
	Never hinged	*25,000.*	
62	A18 12c black	14.00	*20.00*
	Never hinged	30.00	
	On cover		150.00
d.	Double overprint (I)	*2,000.*	
e.	Double overprint (II)	*1,750.*	
63	A18 12c red lilac	175.00	*250.00*
	Never hinged	400.00	
	On cover		550.00
64	A22 25c dark violet	35.00	*45.00*
	Never hinged	70.00	
	On cover		225.00
b.	No period after "GOVT"	*350.00*	*350.00*
	Never hinged	*600.00*	

f. Double overprint (III) 1,250.
Nos. 53-61,62-64 (12) 312.00 *445.50*
Nos. 53-61, 62-64 never hinged 692.75

Virtually all known examples of No. 61B are cut in at the top.

Overprinted in Black

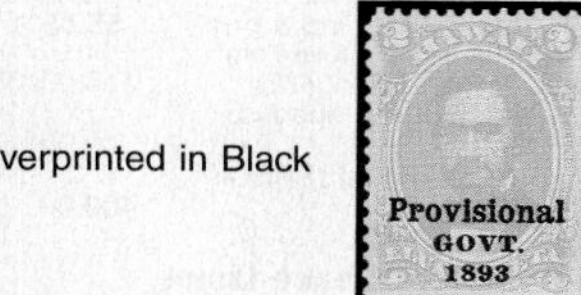

65 A13 2c vermilion 85.00 *90.00*
Never hinged 200.00
On cover *450.00*
b. No period after "GOVT" *300.00* *300.00*
66 A17 2c rose 2.50 *2.50*
Never hinged 3.75
On cover 25.00
b. No period after "GOVT" 70.00 70.00
d. Double overprint (I) *4,000.*
e. Double overprint (II) *2,750.*
f. Double overprint (III) *300.00*
66C A15 6c green *15,000.* *29,000.*
On cover —
67 A20 10c vermilion 22.50 *30.00*
Never hinged 45.00
On cover 125.00
f. Double overprint (III) *1,250.*
68 A20 10c red brown 12.00 *13.00*
Never hinged 24.00
On cover 100.00
f. Double overprint (III) *4,000.*
69 A18 12c red lilac 350.00 *500.00*
Never hinged 575.00
On cover 950.00
70 A21 15c red brown 27.50 *35.00*
Never hinged 55.00
On cover 300.00
e. Double overprint (II) *2,000.*
71 A16 18c dull rose 40.00 40.00
Never hinged 80.00
On cover 225.00
a. "18 3" instead of "1893" *525.00* *525.00*
b. No period after "GOVT" *350.00* *350.00*
d. Double overprint (I) *650.00*
f. Double overprint (III) *275.00* —
g. Pair, one without ovpt. *3,500.*
h. As "b," double overprint (II) *1,750.*
72 A23 50c red 90.00 *120.00*
Never hinged 180.00
On cover 600.00
b. No period after "GOVT" *500.00* *500.00*
Never hinged *775.00*
f. Double overprint (III) *1,000.*
73 A24 $1 rose red 160.00 *190.00*
Never hinged 325.00
On cover 775.00
b. No period after "GOVT" *525.00* 500.00
Nos. 65-66,67-73 (9) 789.50 *1,021.*
Nos. 65-66, 67-73 never hinged 1,485.

Coat of Arms — A26

View of Honolulu — A27

Statue of Kamehameha I — A28

Stars and Palms — A29

S. S. "Arawa" — A30

Pres. Sanford Ballard Dole — A31

1894

74 A26 1c yellow 2.00 1.50
Never hinged 4.00
On cover 25.00
75 A27 2c brown 2.00 .60
Never hinged 4.00
On cover 25.00
76 A28 5c rose lake 5.00 2.00
Never hinged 11.00
On cover 25.00
77 A29 10c yellow green 8.00 5.00
Never hinged 18.00
On cover 45.00
78 A30 12c blue 17.50 *20.00*
Never hinged 37.50
On cover 150.00
79 A31 25c deep blue 22.50 17.50
Never hinged 47.50
On cover 100.00
Nos. 74-79 (6) 57.00 *46.60*
Set, never hinged 122.50

Numerous double transfers exist on Nos. 75 and 81.

"CENTS" Added — A32

1899

80 A26 1c dark green 2.00 1.50
Never hinged 4.50
On cover 25.00
81 A27 2c rose 1.50 1.00
Never hinged 3.50
On cover 20.00
a. 2c salmon 1.50 1.50
Never hinged 3.50
b. Vert. pair, imperf. horiz. *4,250.*
82 A32 5c blue 8.00 4.00
Never hinged 20.00
On cover 25.00
Nos. 80-82 (3) 11.50 6.50
Set, never hinged 28.00

OFFICIAL STAMPS

Lorrin Andrews Thurston — O1

1896 Engr. Unwmk. *Perf. 12*

O1 O1 2c green 45.00 20.00
Never hinged 110.00
On cover 400.00
O2 O1 5c black brown 45.00 20.00
Never hinged 110.00
On cover 425.00
O3 O1 6c deep ultramarine 45.00 20.00
Never hinged 110.00
On cover —
O4 O1 10c bright rose 45.00 20.00
Never hinged 110.00
On cover 475.00
O5 O1 12c orange 55.00 22.50
Never hinged 135.00
On cover —
O6 O1 25c gray violet 65.00 22.50
Never hinged 160.00
On cover —
Nos. O1-O6 (6) 300.00 125.00
Set, never hinged 735.00

Used values for Nos. O1-O6 are for stamps canceled-to-order "FOREIGN OFFICE/HONOLULU H.I." in double circle without date. Values of postally used stamps: Nos. O1-O2, O4, $50 each; No. O3, $125; No. O5, $160; No. O6, $200.

The stamps of Hawaii were replaced by those of the United States.

ADEN

'ä-dᵊn

LOCATION — Southern Arabia
GOVT. — British colony and protectorate
AREA — 112,075 sq. mi.
POP. — 48,338
CAPITAL — Aden

Aden used India stamps before 1937.

12 Pies = 1 Anna
16 Annas = 1 Rupee

Catalogue values for unused stamps in this country are for Never Hinged items.

STAMPS OF INDIA USED IN ADEN

Type A

Type B

Stamps of India with Types A or B cancellations associated with circular datestamps of "ADEN," "ADEN CAMP," "ADEN STEAMER POINT" OR "ADEN CANTONMENT". Many other cancellations exist. Values shown are for the most common cancellation.

1854

A1 ½a blue, Die I (#2) *250.00*
Pair (#2) *900.00*
Strip or block of 4 (#2) *5,500.*
A4 1a red (#4) *350.00*
1a Pair (#4), #132 cancel *2,250.*
A7 2a green (#5) *500.00*
Pair (#5) *2,250.*
A11 4a bl & car (#6, 6a) *425.00*
Pair (#6, 6a) *1,650.*
Strip of 3 (#6, 6a) —

Values for #A11 are for stamps and covers bearing stamps that are cut to shape. Examples with complete margins sell for much more. Multiples will have a cancellation on each stamp.

Virtually all stamps of British India, including officials from 1854 to 1937, may be found used in Aden. The listings below include issues from 1855 to 1936. Values are for clear strikes of the more common postmarks.

1855-64 Unwmk.
Blue Glazed Paper

A13 4a black (#9) *90.00*
A14 8a rose (#10) *90.00*

1855-64 Unwmk. White Paper

A15 ½p blue (#11) *15.00*
A16 1a brown (#12) *17.50*
A17 2a dull rose (#13) *65.00*
A18 2a buff (#15) *65.00*
a. 2a orange (#15a) *75.00*
A19 4a black (#16) *25.00*
A20 4a green (#17) *25.00*
A21 8a rose (#18) *75.00*

1860-64 Unwmk.

A22 8p lilac (#19) *25.00*
A23 8p lilac, *bluish* (#19C) —

1865-67 Wmk. 38

A24 ½a blue (#20) *10.00*
A25 8p lilac (#21) *35.00*
A26 1a brown (#22) *10.00*
A27 2a orange (#23) *12.50*
a. 2a yellow (#23a) *17.50*
A28 4a green (#24) *75.00*
A29 8a rose (#25) —

1866-68 Wmk. 38

A30 4a green (#26) *15.00*
A31 4a blue green (#26B) *12.00*
A32 6a8p slate (#27) *75.00*
A33 8a rose ('68)(#28) *25.00*

1866 Wmk. 36

A34 6a violet (#29) —
A35 6a violet (#30) —

1873-76 Wmk. 38

A36 ½a blue (#31) *10.00*
A37 9p lilac (#32) —
A38 6a bister (#33) *12.00*
A39 12a red brown (#34) *50.00*
A40 1r slate (#35) *75.00*

1882-87 Wmk. 39

A41 ½a green (#36) *8.00*
A42 9p rose (#37) *12.00*
A43 1a maroon (#38) *7.00*
A44 1a6p bister brown (#39) *12.00*
A45 2a ultra (#40) *7.00*
A46 3a brown orange (#41) *10.00*
A47 4a olive green (#42) *10.00*
A48 4a6p green (#43) *20.00*
A49 8a red violet (#44) *14.00*
A50 12a violet, *red* (#45) *15.00*
A51 1r gray (#46) *25.00*

1891

A52 2½a on 4a6p green (#47) *12.50*

1892

A53 2a6p green (#48) *10.00*
A54 1r aniline car & grn (#49) *25.00*
A55 1r car rose & green (#49a) *15.00*

1895

A56 2r brown & rose (#50) —
A57 3r green & brown (#51) —
A58 5r vio & ultra (#52) —

1898

A59 ¼a on ½a green (#53) *10.00*

1899-1900

A60 3p car rose (#54) *7.00*
A61 3p gray (#55) *10.00*
A62 ½a light green (#56) *7.00*
A63 1a carmine rose (#57) *7.00*
A64 2a violet (#58) *8.00*
A65 2a6p ultramarine (#59) *10.00*

1902-09

A68 3p gray (#60) *7.00*
A69 ½a green (#61) *8.00*
A70 1a carmine rose (#62) *7.00*
A71 2a violet (#63) *7.00*
A72 2a6p ultramarine (#64) *9.00*
A73 3a brown orange (#65) *9.00*
A74 4a olive green (#66) *9.00*
A75 6a bister (#67) *25.00*
A76 8a red violet (#68) *10.00*
A77 12a red (#69) *20.00*
A78 1r car rose & grn (#70) *15.00*
A79 2r brown & rose (#71) *20.00*
A80 3r green & brown ('04) (#72) *75.00*
A81 5r vio & ultra ('04) (#73) *100.00*
A82 10r car rose & grn ('09) (#74) —
A83 15r ol gray & ultra ('09) (#75) —
A84 25r ultra & org brn (#76) —

1905

A85 ¼p on ½a green (#77) *8.00*

1906

A86 ½a green (#78) *7.50*
A87 1a carmine rose (#79) *7.50*

1911-23

A88 3p gray (#80) *7.50*
A89 ½a green (#81) *7.50*
A90 1a carmine rose (#82) *7.50*
A91 1a dk brown (#83) *7.50*
A92 2a dull violet (#84) *7.50*
A93 2a6p ultramarine (#85) *17.50*
A94 3a brown orange (#86) *7.50*
A95 3a ultramarine (#87) *7.50*
A96 4a olive green (#88) *7.50*
A97 6a yel bister (#89) *7.50*
A98 6a bister (#90) *7.50*
A99 8a red violet (#91) *12.50*
A100 12a claret (#92) *12.50*
A101 1r grn & red brn (#93) *12.50*
A102 2r brn & car rose (#94) *15.00*
A103 5r vio & ultra (#95) *25.00*
A104 10r car rose & grn (#96) —
A105 15r ol grn & ultra (#97) —
A106 25r ultra & brn org (#98) —

1913-26

A107 2a6p ultramarine (#99) *7.50*
A108 2a6p orange ('26) (#100) *17.50*

1919

A109 1½a chocolate (#101) *8.00*

1921-26
A110 1½a chocolate (#102) 20.00
A111 1½a rose ('26) (#103) 8.00

1921
A112 9p on 1a rose (#104) 7.50

1922
A113 ¼p on ½a green (#105) 7.50

1926-36
A114 3p slate (#106) 7.50
A115 ½a green (#107) 7.50
A116 1a dark brown (#108) 7.50
A117 1½a car rose ('29) (#109) 7.50
A118 2a dull violet (#110) 7.50
A119 2a vermilion ('34) (#111) 17.50
A120 2a6p buff (#112) 7.50
A121 3a ultramarine (#113) 7.50
A122 3a blue ('30) (#114) 7.50
A123 3a car rose ('32) (#115) 7.50
A124 4a olive green (#116) 7.50
A125 6a bister ('35) (#117) 10.00
A126 8a red violet (#118) 7.50
A127 12a claret (#119) 7.50
A128 1r grn & brn (#120) 7.50
A129 2r brn org & car rose (#121) 9.00
A130 5r dk vio & ultra (#122) 20.00
A131 10r carmine & green (#123) —
A132 15r ol grn & ultra (#124) —
A133 25r ultra & brn (#125) —

1926-32
A134 2a dull violet (#126) 7.50
A135 2a vermilion ('32) (#127) —
A136 4a olive green (#128) 7.50

1931, Feb. 9
A137 ¼a brn & olive grn (#129) 12.50
A138 ½a grn & vio (#130) 10.00
A139 1a choc & red vio (#131) 10.00
A140 2a blue green (#132) 30.00
A141 3a car & choc (#133) 40.00
A142 1r deep blue (#134) 75.00

1932
A143 9p dark green (#135) 7.50
A144 1a3p violet (#136) 7.50
A145 3a6p dark green (#137) 7.50

1934
A146 ½a green (#138) 7.50
A147 1a dark brown (#139) 7.50

1935
A148 ½a lt grn & blk (#142) 10.00
A149 9p dull grn & blk (#143) 10.00
A150 1a brn & blk (#144) 10.00
A151 1½a vio & blk (#145) 10.00
A152 2½a brn org & blk (#146) 10.00
A153 3½a blue & blk (#147) 15.00
A154 8a rose lil & blk (#148) 30.00

A cancellation reading "Support the Jubilee Fund / Aden" exists and is very scarce. Values on postcards or covers from $250.

OFFICIAL STAMPS OF INDIA USED IN ADEN

1866 **Unwmk.**
AO1 ½a blue (#O1) —
AO2 1a brown (#O3) —
AO3 8a rose (#O4) —

Wmk. 38
AO4 ½a blue (#O5) 55.00
AO5 8p lilac (#O6) —
AO6 1a brown (#O7) 55.00
AO7 2a yellow (#O8) —
AO8 4a green (#O9) —
AO9 4a green (#O10) —

1866-73 **Wmk. 38**
AO10 ½a blue (#O16) 10.00
AO11 ½a blue, re-engraved (#O17) —
AO12 1a brown (#O18) 10.00
AO13 2a orange (#O19) 17.50
AO14 4a green (#O20) 15.00
AO15 8a rose (#O21) 15.00

1874-82
AO16 ½a blue, re-engraved (#O22) 10.00
AO17 1a brown (#O23) 8.00
AO18 2a orange (#O24) 50.00
AO19 4a green (#O25) 22.50
AO20 8a rose (#O26) 25.00

1883-87 **Wmk. 39**
AO21 ½a green (#O27) 10.00
AO22 1a maroon (#O28) 10.00
AO23 2a ultra (#O29) 15.00
AO24 4a ol green (#O30) 10.00
AO25 8a red violet (#O31) 10.00
AO26 1r car rose & green (#O32) 10.00

1899-1900
AO28 3p car rose (#O33) 10.00
AO29 ½a light green (#O34) 12.50
AO30 1a car rose (#O35) 10.00
AO31 2a violet (#O36) 12.50

1902-05
AO32 3p gray (#O37) 10.00
AO33 ½a green (#O38) 10.00
AO34 1a carmine rose (#O39) 10.00
AO35 2a violet (#O40) 10.00
AO36 4a olive green (#O41) 10.00
AO37 6a bister (#O42) 10.00
AO38 8a red lilac (#O43) 12.50
AO39 1r car rose & grn ('05) (#O44) 15.00

1906-07
AO40 ½a green (#O45) 10.00
AO41 1a carmine rose (#O46) 10.00

1909
AO42 2r brn & rose (#O47) —
AO43 5r vio & ultra (#O48) —
AO44 10r car rose & grn (#O49) —
AO44a 10r red & grn (#O49a) —
AO45 15r ol gray & ultra (#O50) —
AO46 25r ultra & org brn (#O51) —

1911-23
AO47 3p gray (#O52) 7.50
AO48 ½a green (#O53) 7.50
AO49 1a carmine rose (#O54) 7.50
AO50 1a dk brown (#O55) 7.50
AO51 2a dull violet (#O56) 7.50
AO52 4a olive green (#O57) 7.50
AO53 6a bister (#O58) 10.00
AO54 8a red violet (#O59) 7.50
AO55 1r grn & brn (#O60) 12.50
AO56 2r brn & car rose (#O61) 25.00
AO57 5r vio & ultra (#O62) —
AO58 10r car rose & grn (#O63) —
AO59 15r ol grn & ultra (#O64) —
AO60 25r ultra & brn org (#O65) —

While only stamps of India were sold in Aden, stamps from other countries were canceled there. Aden was a major transfer point for mail from the Far East, Indian Ocean and East Africa and it was not uncommon for ships to arrive with uncanceled mail aboard. This included mail not canceled in the country of origin and letters posted at sea prior to the 1894 use of Paquebot markings. Such mail appropriately received Aden postmarks as it transited the country.

STAMPS OF CEYLON USED IN ADEN

Type A cancellation with associated circular datestamp.

1857-66
A167 6p plum (#2) —
A168 1p blue (#3) —
A169 2p deep green (#4) 350.00
a. 2p yellow green (#4a) 425.00
A170 5p org brn (#6) —
A171 6p bis brn (#28) —
A172 9p deep brn (#32) —
A173 10p vermilion (#33) —
A174 1sh violet (#34) —
A175 1p blue (#46) —
A176 6p chocolate brn (#53) —
A177 9p brown (#55) —

STAMPS OF GREAT BRITAIN USED IN ADEN

Type A cancellation with associated circular datestamp.

1856-62
A190 1p rose red (#20) —
A191 4p rose (#26) —
A192 6p lilac (#39) —
A193 1sh green (#42) —

STAMPS OF MAURITIUS USED IN ADEN

Type A cancellation with associated circular datestamp.

1848-63
A200 1p org red (#5b) 1,000.
A201 9p magenta (#11) —
A202 2p blue (#14c) —
A203 2p blue (#15) —
A204 6p blue (#18) —
A205 1sh vermilion (#19) —
A206 2p blue (#25) —
A207 4p rose (#26) —

ISSUES UNDER BRITISH ADMINISTRATION

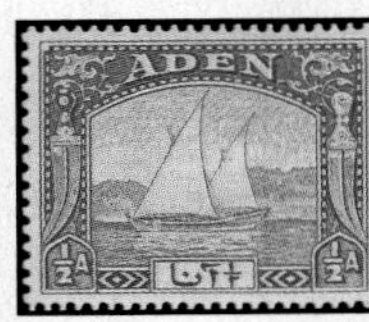

Dhow — A1

Perf. 13x11½

1937, Apr. 1 **Engr.** **Wmk. 4**
1 A1 ½a lt green 4.50 2.75
On cover 19.00
2 A1 9p dark green 4.25 3.50
On cover 20.00
3 A1 1a black brown 4.25 2.00
On cover 12.00
4 A1 2a red 4.75 3.00
On cover 20.00
5 A1 2½a blue 6.75 2.25
On cover 14.00
6 A1 3a carmine rose 11.00 9.00
On cover 55.00
7 A1 3½a gray blue 10.00 6.00
On cover 35.00
8 A1 8a rose lilac 30.00 12.00
On cover 55.00
9 A1 1r brown 60.00 13.00
On cover 65.00
10 A1 2r orange yellow 120.00 40.00
On cover 140.00
11 A1 5r rose violet 300.00 125.00
On cover .478
a. 5r reddish purple, aniline 400.00 175.00
On cover 475.00
12 A1 10r olive green 850.00 650.00
On cover 800.00
Nos. 1-12 (12) 1,406. 868.50
Set, hinged 675.00
Set, perforated "SPECIMEN" 800.00

Covers: Values for Nos. 10-12 are for overfranked covers, usually philatelic.

Common Design Types pictured following the introduction.

Coronation Issue
Common Design Type

1937, May 12 ***Perf. 13½x14***
13 CD302 1a black brown .80 1.25
On cover 4.00
14 CD302 2½a blue .95 1.50
On cover 6.00
15 CD302 3½a gray blue 1.25 3.00
On cover 12.50
Nos. 13-15 (3) 3.00 5.75
Set, hinged 2.00
Set, perforated "SPECIMEN" 165.00

Values are for covers with correct frankings. Philatelic covers sell for less.

Aidrus Mosque — A2

¾a, 5r, Camel Corpsman. 1a, 2r, Aden Harbor. 1½a, 1r, Adenese dhow. 2½a, 8a, Mukalla. 3a, 14a, 10r, Capture of Aden, 1839.

1939-48 **Engr.** **Wmk. 4** ***Perf. 12½***
16 A2 ½a green (7/42) 1.75 .50
a. ½a yellow green .90 .65
b. ½a blue green (9/48) 4.50 5.50
17 A2 ¾a red brn 2.50 1.40
a. ¾a brn vio 3.50 3.50
18 A2 1a brt lt blue 1.25 .40
a. 1a light blue 2.25 .35
19 A2 1½a red 2.25 .65
20 A2 2a dark brown 1.50 .25
a. 2a sepia 4.25 2.25
21 A2 2½a brt ultra 1.50 .30
22 A2 3a rose car & dk brn 1.50 .25
23 A2 8a orange 1.75 .40
b. 8a red orange 2.50 .55
23A A2 14a lt bl & brn blk ('45) 3.50 1.00
24 A2 1r bright green 4.50 2.00
a. 1r emerald green 4.00 2.25
25 A2 2r dp mag & bl blk ('44) 11.00 2.75
a. 2r rose vio & indigo 12.50 3.75
26 A2 5r dp ol & lake brn (1/44) 30.00 11.00
a. 5r olive grn & red brn 30.00 12.00
27 A2 10r brt vio & brn 55.00 14.50
a. 10r dark pur & lake brn 40.00 16.00
Nos. 16-27 (13) 118.00 35.40
Set, cheapest shades, hinged 40.00
Set, perforated "SPECIMEN" 400.00

Peace Issue
Common Design Type
Perf. 13½x14

1946, Oct. 15 **Engr.** **Wmk. 4**
28 CD303 1½a carmine .25 1.50
29 CD303 2½a deep blue .70 1.00
a. Wmk. inverted 1,750.
Hinged 975.00
Set, perforated "SPECIMEN" 145.00

Return to peace at end of World War II.

Silver Wedding Issue
Common Design Types

1949, Jan. 17 **Photo.** ***Perf. 14x14½***
30 CD304 1½a scarlet .40 2.50

Engraved; Name Typographed
Perf. 11½x11
31 CD305 10r purple 37.50 42.50

25th anniv. of the marriage of King George VI and Queen Elizabeth.

UPU Issue
Common Design Types

Srchd. in Annas and Rupees

Engr.; Name typo. on Nos. 33-34
1949, Oct. 10 ***Perf. 13½, 11x11½***
32 CD306 2½a on 20c dp ultra .60 1.60
33 CD307 3a on 30c dp car 1.90 1.60
34 CD308 8a on 50c org 1.25 1.60
35 CD309 1r on 1sh blue 1.75 3.00
Nos. 32-35 (4) 5.50 7.80

75th anniv. of the formation of the UPU.

Nos. 18 and 20-27 Surcharged in Black or Carmine

1951, Oct. 1 **Wmk. 4** ***Perf. 12½***
36 A2 5c on 1a #18a .25 .40
a. On #18 .65 .55
37 A2 10c on 2a #20a .25 .45
a. On #20 .65 .50
b. On 2a sepia brown .65 .45
38 A2 15c on 2½a .40 1.30
a. Double surcharge 1,600.
Hinged 1,000.
39 A2 20c on 3a .50 .40
a. On 3a dp sepia & car rose 2.25 2.25
40 A2 30c on 8a #23b (C) .60 .70
41 A2 50c on 8a #23b 1.25 .50
a. Double surcharge, one albino 3,250.
42 A2 70c on 14a (#23A) 2.25 1.60
a. On 14a dk sepia & br lt blue 4.00 2.75
43 A2 1sh on 1r #24a 2.75 .30
44 A2 2sh on 2r #25 15.00 3.50
a. On #25a 10.00 7.00
b. On #25, albino surcharge 1,400.
Hinged 750.00
45 A2 5sh on 5r #26 27.50 12.00
a. On 5r lake brown & sage green 25.00 12.50
46 A2 10sh on 10r #27 37.50 14.00
Nos. 36-46 (11) 88.25 35.15

Surcharge on No. 40 includes 2 bars.

Number 38a occured when one sheet was fed through the printing press twice, one time at a slight angle. Values for No. 38a are for examples with the surcharges clearly separated. Some positions have the 2nd overprint almost directly over the 1st, and, while rare, are in less demand and sell for less.

Nos. 37b, 39a, 42a and 45a are surcharged on stamps especially produced for this purpose and were not issued in these shades without surcharge.

KATHIRI

LOCATION — In Eastern Aden Protectorate
GOVT. — Sultanate
CAPITAL — Seiyun

The stamps of the Kathiri State of Seiyun were valid for use throughout Aden. Used stamps generally bear Aden GPO or Aden Camp cancels. Examples with cancels from offices in the Eastern Protectorate command a premium.

Sultan Ja'far bin Mansur al Kathiri — A1

Seiyun — A2

Minaret at Tarim — A3

Designs: 2½a, Mosque at Seiyun. 3a, Palace at Tarim. 8a, Mosque at Seiyun, horiz. 1r, South Gate, Tarim. 2r, Kathiri House. 5r, Mosque at Tarim.

1942 Engr. Wmk. 4 ***Perf. 13¾x14***

1 A1 ½a dark green .25 *.75*
 a. Perf. 14 line .50 *1.00*
2 A1 ¾a copper brown .40 *1.60*
 a. Perf. 14 line .55 *1.00*
3 A1 1a deep blue .75 *.75*
 a. Perf. 14 line .75 *1.00*

Perf. 13x11½, 11½x13

4 A2 1½a dark car rose .75 *1.00*
 a. 1½a dp car rose, aniline 2.25 *2.25*
5 A3 2a sepia brown .40 *.95*
 a. 2a sepia 1.50 *2.25*
6 A3 2½a deep blue 1.30 1.00
7 A2 3a dk car rose & dull brn 1.85 *3.50*
 a. 3a car & sepia brn 2.00 *3.00*
8 A2 8a orange red 1.50 .90
9 A3 1r green 6.00 4.00
10 A2 2r rose vio & dk blue 14.00 *22.50*
 a. 2r dp pur & dk bl 15.00 *24.00*
11 A3 5r gray green & fawn 35.00 30.00
 Nos. 1-11 (11) 62.20 *66.95*
Set, perforated "SPECIMEN" 340.00

For surcharges see Nos. 20-27.

Nos. 4, 6 Ovptd. in Black or Red

a

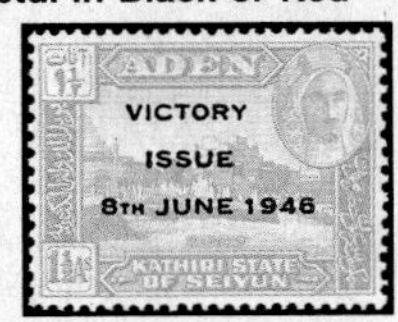

b

Perf. 13x11½, 11½x13

1946, Oct. 15 Wmk. 4

12 A2 (a) 1½a dark car rose .25 *.65*
13 A3 (b) 2½a deep blue (R) .25 .25
 a. Inverted overprint 1,200.
  Hinged 700.00

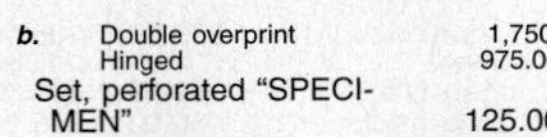
 b. Double overprint 1,750.
  Hinged 975.00
Set, perforated "SPECIMEN" 125.00

Victory of the Allied Nations in WWII.
All examples of No. 13b have the 2nd overprint almost directly over the 1st.

Silver Wedding Issue
Common Design Types

1949, Jan. 17 Photo. ***Perf. 14x14½***

14 CD304 1½a scarlet .35 *2.50*

Engraved; Name Typo.
Perf. 11½x11

15 CD305 5r green 18.50 *15.00*

25th anniv. of the marriage of King George VI and Queen Elizabeth.

UPU Issue
Common Design Types

Srchd. in Annas and Rupees

Engr.; Name Typo. on Nos. 17-18

1949, Oct. 10 ***Perf. 13½, 11x11½***

16 CD306 2½a on 20c dp ultra .25 *.50*
17 CD307 3a on 30c dp car 1.30 1.00
18 CD308 8a on 50c orange .55 *1.00*
19 CD309 1r on 1sh blue 1.00 *1.10*
 Nos. 16-19 (4) 3.10 *3.60*

75th anniv. of the formation of the UPU.

Nos. 3 and 5-11 Srchd. in Carmine or Black

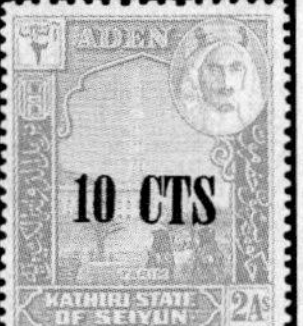

Perf. 14, 13x11½, 11½x13

1951, Oct. 1 Engr. Wmk. 4

20 A1 5c on 1a (C) .25 *1.75*
21 A3 10c on 2a #5a .30 *1.50*
 a. On #5 .45 *.95*
22 A3 15c on 2½a .30 *2.00*
23 A2 20c on 3a #7 .35 *2.25*
 a. On #7a .90 *1.50*
24 A2 50c on 8a .60 *1.25*
25 A3 1sh on 1r 2.00 *3.50*
26 A2 2sh on 2r #10 12.50 *32.50*
 a. On #10a 30.00 *55.00*
27 A3 5sh on 5r 35.00 *50.00*
 Nos. 20-27 (8) 51.30 94.75

QUAITI

LOCATION — In Eastern Aden Protectorate
GOVT. — Sultanate
CAPITAL — Mukalla

The stamps of the Quaiti State of Shihr and Mukalla were valid for use throughout Aden. Used stamps generally bear Aden GPO or Aden Camp cancels. Examples with cancels from offices in the Eastern Protectorate command a premium.

Sultan Sir Saleh bin Ghalib al Qu'aiti — A1

Mukalla Harbor — A2

Buildings at Shibam — A3

Designs: 2a, Gateway of Shihr. 3a, Outpost of Mukalla. 8a, View of 'Einat. 1r, Governor's Castle, Du'an. 2r, Mosque in Hureidha. 5r, Meshhed.

1942 Engr. Wmk. 4 ***Perf. 13¾x14***

1 A1 ½a dark green 1.50 .55
 a. ½a olive green 29.00 *40.00*
 b. Perf. 14 line .75 .50
2 A1 ¾a copper brown 2.25 .30
 a. Perf. 14 line 1.40 1.00
3 A1 1a deep blue 1.00 1.00
 a. Perf. 14 line 1.00 1.00
 b. 1a blue 2.00 2.00

Perf. 13x11½, 11½x13

4 A2 1½a dk car rose 1.75 .55
 a. 1½a car rose, aniline 2.00 *1.40*
5 A2 2a black brown 1.75 *1.90*
 a. 2a yellowish brown 27.50 *37.50*
 b. 2a sepia 2.25 2.25
6 A3 2½a deep blue .50 .30
7 A2 3a dk car rose & dl brn 1.10 1.00
 a. 3a dp car & sepia 2.00 1.50
8 A3 8a orange red 1.10 .40
9 A2 1r green 6.75 4.50
 a. Missing "A" in "CA" of watermark 1,300. *1,200.*
10 A3 2r rose vio & dk blue 17.50 13.00
 a. 2r dp pur & dp bl 19.00 14.00
11 A3 5r gray grn & fawn 35.00 19.00
 Nos. 1-11 (11) 70.20 42.50
Set, perforated "SPECIMEN" 340.00

For surcharges see Nos. 20-27.

Nos. 4, 6 Ovptd. in Black or Carmine like Kathiri Nos. 12-13

1946, Oct. 15 ***Perf. 11½x13, 13x11½***

12 A2 (b) 1½a dk car rose .25 *1.00*
13 A3 (a) 2½a deep blue (C) .25 .25
Set, perforated "SPECIMEN" 125.00

Victory of the Allied Nations in WWII.

Silver Wedding Issue
Common Design Types

1949, Jan. 17 Photo. ***Perf. 14x14½***

14 CD304 1½a scarlet .55 *3.75*

Engraved; Name Typo.
Perf. 11½x11

15 CD305 5r green 18.00 11.00

25th anniv. of the marriage of King George VI and Queen Elizabeth.

UPU Issue
Common Design Types
Surcharged with New Values in Annas and Rupees

Engr.; Name Typo. on Nos. 17 and 18

1949, Oct. 10 ***Perf. 13½, 11x11½***

16 CD306 2½a on 20c dp ultra .25 *.50*
17 CD307 3a on 30c dp car 1.40 *1.45*
18 CD308 8a on 50c org .40 *1.10*
19 CD309 1r on 1sh blue .90 .90
 a. Surcharge omitted *4,250.*
  Hinged *2,750.*
 Nos. 16-19 (4) 2.95 3.95

Nos. 3, 5-11 & Types Srchd. in Carmine or Black

Perf. 14, 13x11½, 11½x13

1951, Oct. 1 Engr. Wmk. 4

20 A1 5c on 1a (C) .25 .25
21 A2 10c on 2a .25 .25
 a. On #5a (12/18/46) 28.00 *40.00*
 b. On #5b 1.00 *1.50*
22 A3 15c on 2½a .25 .25
23 A2 20c on 3a #7 .30 *.65*
 a. 20c on 3a #7a .40 .25
 b. Double surcharge, one albino 575.00
24 A3 50c on 8a org red .55 *2.50*
 a. 50c on 8a scarlet .25 *.50*
25 A2 1sh on 1r 2.25 .55
26 A3 2sh on 2r 9.50 *25.00*
27 A3 5sh on 5r 17.50 *37.50*
 Nos. 20-27 (8) 30.85 *66.95*

AFGHANISTAN

af-'ga-nə-,stan

LOCATION — Central Asia, bounded by Iran, Russian Turkestan, India, Baluchistan and China
GOVT. — Constitutional Monarchy
AREA — 251,773 sq. mi.
POP. — 10,000,000
CAPITAL — Kabul

12 Shahi = 6 Sanar = 3 Abasi =
2 Krans = 1 Rupee Kabuli
60 Paisas = 1 Rupee (1921)
100 Pouls = 1 Rupee Afghani (1927)

CHARACTERS OF VALUE.

Shahi.
1871-78 A7 1876 A8

Sanar. Abasi. 6 Shahi.
1871-78 1871 1872

1 Rupee. ½ Rupee.
1874 1876(A8) 1876 (A7)

1 Rupee. Rupee.
1872 1874 1876 (A8) 1877-78

From 1871 to 1892 and 1898, the Moslem year date appears on the stamp. Numerals as follows:

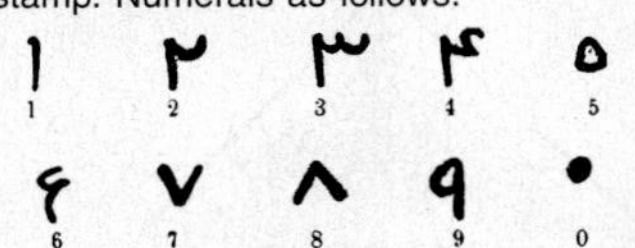

Until 1891, cancellation consisted of cutting or tearing a piece from the stamps. Such examples should not be considered as damaged.

Values are for cut square examples of good color. Cut to shape or faded examples sell for much less, particularly Nos. 2-10.

Nos. 2-108 are on laid paper of varying thickness except where wove is noted.

Until 1907, all stamps were issued ungummed.

The tiger's head on types A1 to A11 symbolizes the name of the contemporary amir, Sher (Tiger) Ali.

Kingdom of Kabul

A1

Tiger's Head, Type I — A2

Tiger's Head, Type II — A2a

Both circles dotted. Outer circle measures 28mm in diameter. Type I: has well-defined inner and outer circles with evenly spaced dots.

Type II: has no well-defined inner and outer circles, and the dots are randomly spaced.

1871 Unwmk. Litho. *Imperf.*

Dated "1288"

No.	Type	Stamp	Unused	Used
1	A1	1sh black (30mm diameter)	1,350.	60.00
		On cover		—
2	A2	1sh black	925.00	50.00
		On cover		*800.00*
2A	A2a	1sh black	525.00	35.00
		On cover		*550.00*
3	A2	1sa black	650.00	32.50
		On cover		*800.00*
3A	A2a	1sa black	210.00	55.00
		On cover		*550.00*
4	A2	1ab black	250.00	60.00
		On cover		*900.00*
4A	A2a	1ab black	100.00	60.00
		On cover		*600.00*
		Nos. 1-4A (7)	4,010.	352.50

Thirty varieties of the shahi, 10 of the sanar and 5 of the abasi.

Similar designs without the tiger's head in the center are revenues.

A3

Outer circle dotted

Dated "1288"

No.	Type	Stamp	Unused	Used
5	A3	1sh black	525.00	35.00
		On cover		500.00
6	A3	1sa black	300.00	50.00
		On cover		*600.00*
7	A3	1ab black	200.00	32.50
		On cover		*550.00*
		Nos. 5-7 (3)	1,025.	117.50

Five varieties of each.

A4

Toned Wove Paper

1872 Dated "1289"

No.	Type	Stamp	Unused	Used
8	A4	6sh violet	*1,500.*	*900.*
		On cover		12,500.
9	A4	1rup violet	*1,750.*	*1,350.*
		On cover		—

Two varieties of each. Date varies in location. Printed in sheets of 4 (2x2) containing two of each denomination.

Most used examples are smeared with a greasy ink cancel.

A4a

White Laid Paper

1873 Dated "1290"

No.	Type	Stamp	Unused	Used
10	A4a	1sh black	25.00	12.00
		On cover		325.00
a.		Corner ornament missing	*550.00*	*500.00*
b.		Corner ornament retouched	*75.00*	*45.00*

15 varieties. Nos. 10a, 10b are the sixth stamp on the sheet.

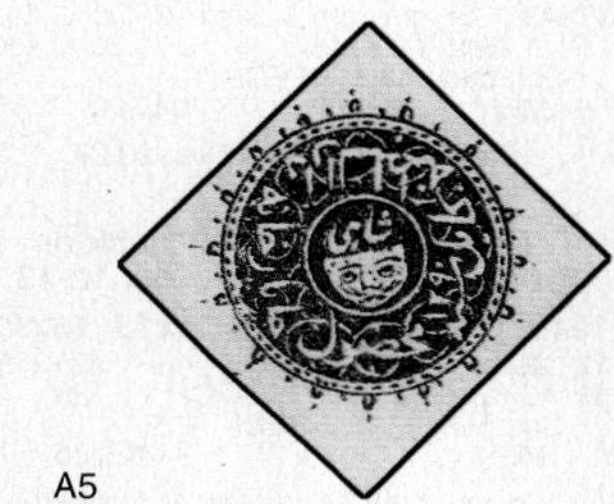

A5

1873

No.	Type	Stamp	Unused	Used
11	A5	1sh black	22.50	11.00
		On cover		300.00
11A	A5	1sh violet	*750.00*	

Sixty varieties of each.

1874 Dated "1291"

No.	Type	Stamp	Unused	Used
12	A5	1ab black	90.00	55.00
		On cover		—
13	A5	½rup black	37.50	20.00
		On cover		—
14	A5	1rup black	40.00	24.00
		On cover		250.00
		Nos. 12-14 (3)	167.50	99.00

Five varieties of each.

Nos. 12-14 were printed on the same sheet. Se-tenant varieties exist.

A6

1875 Dated "1292"

No.	Type	Stamp	Unused	Used
15	A6	1sa black	*375.00*	*350.00*
		On cover		1,100.
a.		Wide outer circle	*1,200.*	*750.00*
16	A6	1ab black	425.00	400.00
17	A6	1sa brown violet	75.00	30.00
a.		Wide outer circle	300.00	*190.00*
18	A6	1ab brown violet	80.00	60.00

Ten varieties of the sanar, five of the abasi.

Nos. 15-16 and 17-18 were printed in the same sheets. Se-tenant pairs exist.

A7

1876 Dated "1293"

No.	Type	Stamp	Unused	Used
19	A7	1sh black	325.00	200.00
		On cover		2,500.
20	A7	1sa black	375.00	200.00
		On cover		1,000.
21	A7	1ab black	750.00	425.00
22	A7	½rup black	450.00	275.00
23	A7	1rup black	875.00	275.00
24	A7	1sh violet	450.00	275.00
25	A7	1sa violet	425.00	300.00
		On cover		2,000.
26	A7	1ab violet	525.00	275.00
27	A7	½rup violet	225.00	60.00
28	A7	1rup violet	225.00	75.00

12 varieties of the shahi and 3 each of the other values.

A8

1876 Dated "1293"

No.	Type	Stamp	Unused	Used
29	A8	1sh gray	16.00	10.00
		On cover		300.00
29A	A8a	1sh gray	65.00	30.00
30	A8	1sa gray	20.00	8.00
31	A8	1ab gray	42.50	20.00
32	A8	½rup gray	50.00	25.00
33	A8	1rup gray	50.00	17.50
34	A8	1sh olive blk	140.00	80.00
35	A8	1sa olive blk	190.00	100.00
36	A8	1ab olive blk	400.00	250.00
37	A8	½rup olive blk	275.00	275.00
38	A8	1rup olive blk	375.00	400.00
39	A8	1sh green	30.00	8.00
40	A8	1sa green	40.00	25.00
41	A8	1ab green	85.00	60.00
42	A8	½rup green	125.00	80.00
43	A8	1rup green	110.00	125.00
44	A8	1sh ocher	32.50	15.00
45	A8	1sa ocher	40.00	24.00
		On cover		400.00
46	A8	1ab ocher	80.00	50.00
47	A8	½rup ocher	100.00	65.00
48	A8	1rup ocher	140.00	125.00
49	A8	1sh violet	37.50	15.00
50	A8	1sa violet	37.50	15.00
51	A8	1ab violet	50.00	15.00
52	A8	½rup violet	70.00	27.50
53	A8	1rup violet	100.00	40.00

24 varieties of the shahi, 4 of which show denomination written:

A8a

12 varieties of the sanar, 6 of the abasi and 3 each of the ½ rupee and rupee.

A9

1877 Dated "1294"

No.	Type	Stamp	Unused	Used
54	A8a	1sh gray	10.00	*15.00*
55	A9	1sa gray	10.00	9.00
56	A9	1ab gray	11.00	9.00
57	A9	½rup gray	14.50	*20.00*
58	A9	1rup gray	16.00	*20.00*
59	A9	1sh black	14.50	*20.00*
60	A9	1sa black	25.00	*10.00*
61	A9	1ab black	42.50	*15.00*
62	A9	½rup black	45.00	*30.00*
63	A9	1rup black	45.00	*30.00*
64	A9	1sh green	32.50	32.50
		On cover		300.00
a.		Wove paper	40.00	40.00
65	A9	1sa green	15.00	*12.00*
a.		Wove paper	20.00	20.00
66	A9	1ab green	17.50	*16.00*
a.		Wove paper	30.00	30.00
67	A9	½rup green	30.00	*30.00*
a.		Wove paper	32.50	*42.50*
68	A9	1rup green	27.50	*32.50*
a.		Wove paper	32.50	*42.50*
69	A9	1sh ocher	12.50	5.25
70	A9	1sa ocher	12.50	7.25
71	A9	1ab ocher	32.50	24.50
72	A9	½rup ocher	40.00	35.00
73	A9	1rup ocher	50.00	35.00
74	A9	1sh violet	15.00	8.00
75	A9	1sa violet	12.50	5.00
76	A9	1ab violet	19.00	12.00
77	A9	½rup violet	27.50	30.00
78	A9	1rup violet	27.50	30.00

25 varieties of the shahi, 8 of the sanar, 3 of the abasi and 2 each of the ½ rupee and rupee.

Some examples of Nos. 54-78 show a "94" year date. These are valued less.

A10

A11

1878 Dated "1295"

No.	Type	Stamp	Unused	Used
79	A10	1sh gray	5.00	10.00
		On cover		300.00
80	A10	1sa gray	8.00	10.00
81	A10	1ab gray	12.50	10.00
82	A10	½rup gray	15.00	15.00
83	A10	1rup gray	15.00	15.00
84	A10	1sh black	10.00	
85	A10	1sa black	10.00	
86	A10	1ab black	37.50	
87	A10	½rup black	35.00	
88	A10	1rup black	35.00	
89	A10	1sh green	32.50	*55.00*
90	A10	1sa green	10.00	9.00
91	A10	1ab green	35.00	30.00
92	A10	½rup green	32.50	30.00
93	A10	1rup green	60.00	40.00
		On cover		200.00
94	A10	1sh ocher	27.50	10.00
95	A10	1sa ocher	12.00	*15.00*
		On cover		50.00
96	A10	1ab ocher	45.00	35.00
97	A10	½rup ocher	65.00	45.00
98	A10	1rup ocher	27.50	*30.00*
99	A10	1sh violet	10.00	*15.00*
100	A10	1sa violet	30.00	25.00
101	A10	1ab violet	17.50	15.00
102	A10	½rup violet	55.00	35.00
103	A10	1rup violet	45.00	30.00
104	A11	1sh gray	7.00	7.00
105	A11	1sh black	*100.00*	50.00
106	A11	1sh green	10.00	5.00
107	A11	1sh ocher	10.00	9.00
		On cover		300.00
108	A11	1sh violet	8.00	8.00
		On cover		300.00

40 varieties of the shahi, 30 of the sanar, 6 of the abasi and 2 each of the ½ rupee and 1 rupee.

Some examples of Nos. 79-108 show a "95" year date. These are valued less.

The 1876, 1877 and 1878 issues were printed in separate colors for each main post office on the Peshawar-Kabul-Khulm (Tashkurghan) postal route. Some specialists consider the black printings to be proofs or trial colors.

There are many shades of these colors.

1ab, Type I (26mm) — A12

1ab, Type II (28mm) — A13

A14

A15

Dated "1298", numerals scattered through design

Handstamped, in watercolor

1881-90

Thin White Laid Batonne Paper

No.	Type	Stamp	Unused	Used
109	A12	1ab violet	5.00	3.00
		On cover		100.00
109A	A13	1ab violet	8.00	3.00
		On cover		150.00

110 A12 1ab black brn 8.00 3.00
On cover — 100.00
a. Ordinary thin wove paper — 20.00
111 A12 1ab rose 12.00 3.00
On cover 50.00
b. Se-tenant with No. 111A 16.00 —
111A A13 1ab rose 9.00 3.00
On cover 100.00
112 A14 2ab violet 10.00 3.00
On cover 50.00
113 A14 2ab black brn 12.00 6.00
On cover 50.00
114 A14 2ab rose 20.00 10.00
On cover 75.00
115 A15 1rup violet 12.00 12.00
a. 1rup deep violet 15.00 10.00
b. Pair, tête-bêche 55.00 —
116 A15 1rup black brn 14.00 10.00
117 A15 1rup rose 12.50 7.50

Thin White Wove Batonne Paper

118 A12 1ab violet 15.00 5.00
On cover 200.00
119 A12 1ab vermilion 30.00 10.00
a. 1ab reddish claret 30.00
120 A12 1ab rose 30.00 25.00
121 A14 2ab violet 30.00 25.00
On cover 600.00
a. Ordinary thin wove paper 32,50 32.50
122 A14 2ab vermilion 30.00 16.00
122A A14 2ab black brn
On cover 200.00
123 A15 1rup violet 15.00 8.00
a. 1rub blackish violet 17.50 —
124 A15 1rup vermilion 14.00 7.50
125 A15 1rup black brn 19.00 8.00

Thin White Laid Batonne Paper

126 A12 1ab brown org 20.00 8.00
On cover 300.00
126A A13 1ab brn org (II) 22.50 9.00
On cover 50.00
b. 1ab orange vermilion 22.50 9.00
127 A12 1ab carmine lake 20.00 8.00
On cover 100.00
a. Laid paper 22.50 10.00
128 A14 2ab brown org 22.50 8.00
a. 2ab claret brown, laid paper 20.00
129 A14 2ab carmine lake 20.00 8.00
On cover 70.00
130 A15 1rup brown org 35.00 15.00
a. 1rub red orange 30.00
131 A15 1rup car lake 37.50 15.00

Yellowish Laid Batonne Paper

132 A12 1ab purple 10.00 10.00
a. 1ab purple, wove paper 30.00
133 A12 1ab red 12.50 10.00

1884 Colored Wove Paper

133A A13 1ab purple, *yel* (II) 17.50 17.50
134 A12 1ab purple, *grn* 20.00
135 A12 1ab purple, *blue* 32.50 21.00
136 A12 1ab red, *grn* 37.50
137 A12 1ab red, *yel* 30.00
139 A12 1ab red, *rose* 50.00
140 A14 2ab red, *yel* 30.00
142 A14 2ab red, *rose* 30.00
143 A15 1rup red, *yel* 55.00 20.00
145 A15 1rup red, *rose* 65.00 25.00

Thin Colored Ribbed Paper

146 A14 2ab red, *yellow* 40.00
147 A15 1rup red, *yellow* 80.00
148 A12 1ab lake, *lilac* 40.00
149 A14 2ab lake, *lilac* 40.00
150 A15 1rup lake, *lilac* 40.00
151 A12 1ab lake, *green* 40.00
152 A14 2ab lake, *green* 40.00
153 A15 1rup lake, *green* 40.00

1886-88 Colored Wove Paper

155 A12 1ab black, *magenta* 60.00
156 A12 1ab claret brn, *org* 50.00
156A A12 1ab red, *org* 40.00
156B A14 2ab red, *org* 40.00
156C A15 1rup red, *org* 40.00

Laid Batonné Paper

157 A12 1ab black, *lavender* 40.00
158 A12 1ab cl brn, *grn* 40.00
159 A12 1ab black, *pink* 60.00
160 A14 2ab black, *pink* 100.00
161 A15 1rup black, *pink* 70.00

Laid Paper

162 A12 1ab black, *pink* 80.00
163 A14 2ab black, *pink* 80.00
164 A15 1rup black, *pink* 80.00
165 A12 1ab brown, *yel* 80.00
166 A14 2ab brown, *yel* 80.00
167 A15 1rup brown, *yel* 80.00
168 A12 1ab blue, *grn* 80.00
169 A14 2ab blue, *grn* 80.00
170 A15 1rup blue, *grn* 80.00

1891 Colored Wove Paper

175 A12 1ab green, *rose* 100.00
176 A15 1rup pur, *grn batonne* 100.00

Nos. 109-176 fall into three categories:

1. Those regularly issued and in normal postal use from 1881 on, handstamped on thin white laid or wove paper in strip sheets containing 12 or more impressions of the same denomination arranged in two irregular rows, with the impressions often touching or overlappng.

2. The 1884 postal issues provisionally printed on smooth or ribbed colored wove paper as needed to supplement low stocks of the normal white paper stamps.

3. The "special" printings made in a range of colors on several types of laid or wove colored papers, most of which were never used for normal printings. These were produced periodically from 1886 to 1891 to meet philatelic demands. Although nominally valid for postage, most of the special printings were exported directly to fill dealers' orders, and few were ever postally used. Many of the sheets contained all three denominations with impressions separated by ruled lines. Sometimes different colors were used, so se-tenant multiples of denomination or color exist. Many combinations of stamp and paper colors exist besides those listed.

Various shades of each color exist.

Type A12 is known dated "1297."

Counterfeits, lithographed or typographed, are plentiful.

Kingdom of Afghanistan

A16

A17

A18

Dated "1309"

1891 Pelure Paper Litho.

177 A16 1ab slate blue 2.00 2.00
a. Tete beche pair 19.00
178 A17 2ab slate blue 12.00 12.00
179 A18 1rup slate blue 27.50 27.50
Nos. 177-179 (3) 41.50 41.50

Revenue stamps of similar design exist in various colors.

Nos. 177-179 were printed in panes on the same sheet, so se-tenant gutter pairs exist. Examples in black or red are proofs.

A Mosque Gate and Crossed Cannons (National Seal) A19

Dated "1310" in Upper Right Corner

1892 Flimsy Wove Paper

180 A19 1ab black, *green* 3.50 3.00
181 A19 1ab black, *orange* 4.50 4.50
182 A19 1ab black, *yellow* 3.50 3.00
183 A19 1ab black, *pink* 4.00 3.25
184 A19 1ab black, *lil rose* 4.00 4.00
185 A19 1ab black, *blue* 6.00 5.50
186 A19 1ab black, *salmon* 4.50 3.75
187 A19 1ab black, *magenta* 4.00 4.00
188 A19 1ab black, *violet* 4.00 4.00
188A A19 1ab black, *scarlet* 4.00 3.00

Many shades exist.

A20

A21

Undated

1894 Flimsy Wove Paper

189 A20 2ab black, *green* 12.00 8.00
190 A21 1rup black, *green* 14.50 13.00

24 varieties of the 2 abasi and 12 varieties of the rupee.

Nos. 189-190 and F3 were printed se-tenant in the same sheet. Pairs exist.

A21a

Dated "1316"

1898 Flimsy Wove Paper

191 A21a 2ab black, *pink* 3.00
192 A21a 2ab black, *magenta* 3.00
193 A21a 2ab black, *yellow* 1.40
193A A21a 2ab black, *salmon* 3.50
194 A21a 2ab black, *green* 1.75
195 A21a 2ab black, *purple* 2.40
195A A21a 2ab black, *blue* 22.50
Nos. 191-195A (7) 37.55

Nos. 191-195A were not regularly issued. Genuinely used examples are scarce. No. 195A was found in remainder stocks and probably was never released.

A22

A23

A24

1907 Engr. *Imperf.*

Medium Wove Paper

196 A22 1ab blue green 50.00 30.00
a. 1ab emerald 75.00 30.00
b. Double impression *500.00*
c. Printed on both sides 450.00
197 A22 1ab brt blue 45.00 25.00
198 A23 2ab deep blue 45.00 25.00
a. Double impression *550.00*
199 A24 1rup green 100.00 50.00
a. 1rup blue green 100.00 75.00

Zigzag Roulette 10

200 A22 1ab green *2,750.* 350.00
a. Double impression *1,500.*
b. Printed on both sides *1,750.*
c. Double impression and printed on both sides *2,500.*
d. 1ab blue green *2,750.* 350.00
201 A23 2ab blue *2,500.* —

1908 *Serrate Roulette 13*

201A A22 1ab green — —
b. 1ab emerald green, on cover *1,250.*
On cover *1,250.*
201B A23 2ab blue *3,500.*

Nos. 201A and 201Ab are only known used on cover.

No. 201B is known only unused.

Perf. 12 on 2, 3 or 4 Sides

202 A22 1ab green — 65.00
a. 1ab yellow-green — 65.00
203 A23 2ab deep blue 35.00 20.00
a. Horiz. pair, imperf between 450.00
204 A24 1rup blue green 125.00 65.00
a. 1rub turquoise blue 125.00 65.00
b. 1rub dull yellowish green 125.00 65.00
c. Pair, imperf. between 400.00
Nos. 202-204 (3) 160.00 150.00

Twelve varieties of the 1 abasi, 6 of the 2 abasi, 4 of the 1 rupee.

Nos. 196-204 were issued in small sheets containing 3 or 4 panes. Gutter pairs, normal and tete beche, exist.

Two plates were used for the 1 abasi: plate I, inner vert. lines extend into lower left panel; plate II, inner vert. lines do not extend into lower left panel.

A25

A26

A27

1909-19 Typo. *Perf. 12*

205 A25 1ab ultra 5.00 2.00
a. Imperf., pair 48.00
206 A25 1ab red ('16) 1.60 1.25
a. Imperf. 30.00
207 A25 1ab rose ('18) 1.60 1.00
208 A26 2ab green 2.75 2.25
a. Imperf., pair 48.00
b. Horiz. pair, imperf. btwn.
208C A26 2ab yellow ('16) 3.25 2.75
209 A26 2ab bis ('18-'19) 3.25 *3.25*
210 A27 1rup lilac brn 7.50 6.50
a. 1rup red brown 7.50 7.50
211 A27 1rup ol bis ('16) 10.00 8.00
Nos. 205-211 (8) 34.95 27.00

A28

1913

212 A28 2pa drab brown 20.00 6.00
a. 2pa red brown 20.00 6.00

No. 212 is inscribed "Tiket waraq dak" (Postal card stamps). It was usable only on postcards and not accepted for postage on letters.

Nos. 196-212 sometimes show letters of a papermaker's watermark, "Howard & Jones, London."

Royal Star — A29

1920, Aug. 24 *Perf. 12*

Size: 39x46mm

214 A29 10pa rose 175.00 100.00
On cover 450.00
215 A29 20pa red brown 275.00 175.00
On cover 700.00
216 A29 30pa green 375.00 250.00
On cover 1,200.
Nos. 214-216 (3) 825.00 525.00

2nd Independence Day. Issued to commemorate the first anniversary of the signing of the armistice that ended the war of independence (Third Afghan War).

Issued in sheets of two.

No. 214 exists in two sizes: 38.5mmx45mm, position 1 in sheet; 38.5mmx46mm, position 2.

1921, Mar. **Size: 22½x28¼mm**

217 A29 10pa rose	2.50	1.25
a. Perf. 11 ('27)	22.50	13.00
218 A29 20pa red brown	4.50	2.50
219 A29 30pa yel green	6.50	3.00
a. Tete beche pair	55.00	32.50
b. 30pa green	6.50	3.50
c. As "b," Tete beche pair	55.00	32.50
Nos. 217-219 (3)	13.50	6.75

3rd Independence Day.
Two types of the 10pa, three of the 20pa.

Hstmpd. in black on Nos. 217-219

1923, Feb. 26

219D A29a 10pa rose	—	125.00
219E A29a 20pa red brown	—	125.00
219F A29a 30pa yel green	400.00	—

5th Independence Day.
Two types of handstamp exist.
Forgeries exist.
See No. Q13B-Q13E.

These handstamps were used by the Kabul post office on incoming foreign mail from 1921 until Afghanistan joined the Universal Postal Union April 1, 1928. Afghan stamps were applied to foreign mail arriving in the country and were canceled with these postage-due handstamps to indicate that postage was to be collected from the addressee. The handstamps were applied primarily to Nos. 217-219, 227-235, 236, and 237-246. Values are the same as for stamps with postal cancellations. A third type of handstamp exists with no distinctive outer border.

A30

1924, Feb. 26 ***Perf. 12***

220 A30 10pa chocolate	45.00	30.00
a. Tete beche pair	150.00	100.00

6th Independence Day.
Printed in sheets of four consisting of two tete beche pairs, and in sheets of two. Two types exist.

Some authorities believe that Nos. Q15-Q16 were issued as regular postage stamps.

Crest of King Amanullah
A32

Size: 29x37mm

1925, Feb. 26 ***Perf. 12***

222 A32 10pa light brown	75.00	35.00

7th Independence Day.
Printed in sheets of 8 (two panes of 4).

Wove Paper

1926, Feb. 28 **Size: 26x33mm**

224 A32 10pa dark blue	8.00	8.00
a. Imperf., pair	32.50	
b. Horiz. pair, imperf. btwn.	75.00	
c. Vert. pair, imperf. btwn.		
d. Laid paper	40.00	13.00

7th anniv. of Independence. Printed in sheets of 4, and in sheets of 8 (two panes of 4). Tete beche gutter pairs exist.

Tughra and Crest of Amanullah
A33

1927, Feb.

225 A33 10pa magenta	14.00	12.00
a. Vertical pair, imperf. between	75.00	

Dotted Background

226 A33 10pa magenta	20.00	13.00
a. Horiz. pair, imperf. between	75.00	

The surface of No. 226 is covered by a net of fine dots.
8th anniv. of Independence. Printed in sheets of 8 (two panes of 4).
Tete-beche gutter pairs exist. Value, pair $85.

National Seal — A34

A35

A36

1927, Oct. ***Imperf.***

227 A34 15p pink	1.40	1.40
228 A35 30p Prus green	2.75	1.25
229 A36 60p light blue	3.75	3.25
Nos. 227-229 (3)	7.90	5.90

1927, Nov. ***Perf. 11, 11¾***

230 A34 15p pink	1.75	1.40
231 A35 30p Prus green	3.25	1.40
232 A36 60p bright blue	3.50	2.00
a. Tete beche pair	17.50	17.50
Nos. 230-232 (3)	8.50	4.80

A37

A38

A39

A40

1928, Feb. ***Perf. 11, 11¾***

233 A37 10p gray green	1.25	.40
a. Tete beche pair	14.00	6.50
b. Vert. pair, imperf. horiz.	11.00	11.00
c. Vertical pair, imperf. between		
234 A38 25p car rose	1.50	.40
235 A39 40p ultra	2.00	.75
a. Tete beche pair	15.00	*16.00*
236 A40 50p red	2.50	1.00
Nos. 233-236 (4)	7.25	2.55

Nos. 230-232 are usually imperforate on one or two sides. The sheets of these stamps are oten imperforate at the outer margin.

Tughra and Crest of Amanullah — A41

1928, Feb. 27

236D A41 15p pink	5.00	5.00
a. Tete beche pair	12.00	10.00
b. Horiz. pair, imperf. vert.	22.50	19.00
c. As "a," imperf. vert., block of 4	75.00	

9th anniv. of Independence. This stamp is always imperforate on one or two sides.
A 15p blue of somewhat similar design was prepared for the 10th anniv., but was not issued due to Amanullah's dethronement. Value, $15.

Types of 1927 in New Colors

A42

1929-30

236E A34 15p ultra	1.75	1.40
236F A42 30p dp green ('30)	1.75	1.25
236G A36 60p black ('29)	4.00	2.25
Nos. 236E-236G (3)	7.50	4.90

No. 236F has been redrawn. A narrow border of pearls has been added and "30," in European and Arabic numerals, inserted in the upper spandrels.

A43

1928-30 ***Perf. 11, 12***

237 A43 2p dull blue	7.75	4.50
a. Vertical pair, imperf. between	20.00	
238 A43 2p lt rose ('30)	.65	.55
240 A37 10p choc ('30)	3.00	1.25
a. 10p brown purple ('29)	8.50	4.00
242 A38 25p Prus green ('29)	4.00	1.25
244 A39 40p rose ('29)	3.50	1.25
a. Tete beche pair	14.50	
b. Vert. pair, imperf. horiz.	11.00	
246 A40 50p dk blue ('29)	5.00	1.50
Nos. 237-246 (10)	31.15	12.85

The sheets of these stamps are often imperforate at the outer margins.
Nos. 237-238 are newspaper stamps.

This handstamp was used for ten months by the Revolutionary Gov't in Kabul as a control mark on outgoing mail. It occasionally fell on the stamps but there is no evidence that it was officially used as an overprint. Unused examples were privately made.

Independence Monument
A46

Laid Paper
Without Gum

Wmk. Large Seal in the Sheet

1931, Aug. **Litho.** ***Perf. 12***

262 A46 20p red	2.50	1.25

13th Independence Day.

National Assembly Chamber
A47

A48

National Assembly Building
A49

A50

National Assembly Chamber
A51

National Assembly Building A52

Wove Paper

1932 Unwmk. Typo. *Perf. 12*

263	A47	40p olive	1.15	.40
264	A48	60p violet	1.50	.80
265	A49	80p dark red	2.00	1.25
266	A50	1af black	16.00	7.50
267	A51	2af ultra	7.00	4.00
268	A52	3af gray green	7.50	3.50
		Nos. 263-268 (6)	35.15	17.45

Formation of the Natl. Council. Imperforate or perforated examples on ungummed chalky paper are proofs.

See Nos. 304-305.

Mosque at Balkh — A53

Kabul Fortress A54

Parliament House, Darul Funun — A55

Parliament House, Darul Funun — A56

Arch of Qalai Bist — A57

Memorial Pillar of Knowledge and Ignorance A58

Independence Monument A59

Minaret at Herat — A60

Arch of Paghman A61

Ruins at Balkh — A62

Minarets of Herat — A63

Great Buddha at Bamian — A64

1932 Typo. *Perf. 12*

269	A53	10p brown	.80	.25
270	A54	15p dk brown	.60	.30
271	A55	20p red	.95	.25
272	A56	25p dk green	1.35	.25
273	A57	30p red	1.35	.25
274	A58	40p orange	1.75	.50
275	A59	50p blue	2.40	1.40
a.		Tete beche pair	12.00	
276	A60	60p blue	2.25	.90
277	A61	80p violet	4.00	2.00
278	A62	1af dark blue	7.00	.80
279	A63	2af dk red violet	7.75	2.25
280	A64	3af claret	9.50	3.00
		Nos. 269-280 (12)	39.70	12.15

Counterfeits of types A53-A65 exist.

See Nos. 290-295, 298-299, 302-303.

Entwined 2's — A65

Type I

Type II

Two types:

Type I — Numerals shaded. Size about 21x29mm.

Type II — Numerals unshaded. Size about 21¾x30mm.

1931-38 *Perf. 12, 11x12*

281	A65	2p red brn (I)	.40	.50
282	A65	2p olive blk (I) ('34)	.30	.80
283	A65	2p grnsh gray (I) ('34)	.40	.75
283A	A65	2p black (I) ('36)	.25	.75
284	A65	2p salmon (II) ('38)	.50	.75
284A	A65	2p rose (I) ('38)	.50	.90
b.		Imperf., pair	10.00	

Imperf

285	A65	2p black (II) ('37)	.75	.75
286	A65	2p salmon (II) ('38)	.75	.75
		Nos. 281-286 (8)	3.85	5.95

The newspaper rate was 2 pouls.

Independence Monument — A66

1932, Aug. *Perf. 12*

287	A66	1af carmine	5.50	3.25

14th Independence Day.

A67

1929 Liberation Monument, Kabul.

1932, Oct. Typo.

288	A67	80p red brown	2.00	1.50

Arch of Paghman — A68

1933, Aug.

289	A68	50p light ultra	3.00	1.50

15th Independence Day.
No. 289 exists imperf. Value, $5.

Types of 1932 and

Royal Palace, Kabul A69

Darrah- Shikari Pass, Hindu Kush — A70

1934-38 Typo. *Perf. 12*

290	A53	10p deep violet	.30	.25
291	A54	15p turq green	.50	.25
292	A55	20p magenta	.50	.25
293	A56	25p deep rose	.60	.25
294	A57	30p orange	.65	.30
295	A58	40p blue black	.75	.30
296	A69	45p dark blue	2.75	1.50
297	A69	45p red ('38)	.50	.25
298	A59	50p orange	.80	.25
299	A60	60p purple	1.00	.45
300	A70	75p red	4.00	2.00
301	A70	75p dk blue ('38)	1.00	.65
302	A61	80p brown vio	1.60	.80
303	A62	1af red violet	3.25	1.60
304	A51	2af gray black	5.25	2.40
305	A52	3af ultra	6.00	3.00
		Nos. 290-305 (16)	29.45	14.50

Nos. 290, 292, 300, 304, 305 exist imperf.

Independence Monument — A71

1934, Aug. Litho. Without Gum

306	A71	50p pale green	3.25	2.75
a.		Tete beche pair	11.50	11.50

16th year of Independence. Each sheet of 40 (4x10) included 4 tete beche pairs as lower half of sheet was inverted.

Independence Monument — A74

1935, Aug. 15 Laid Paper

309	A74	50p dark blue	3.50	2.40

17th year of Independence.

Fireworks Display A75

Wove Paper

1936, Aug. 15 *Perf. 12*

310	A75	50p red violet	3.25	2.50

18th year of Independence.

Independence Monument and Nadir Shah — A76

1937

311	A76	50p vio & bis brn	2.75	2.10
a.		Imperf., pair	9.50	9.50

19th year of Independence.

Mohammed Nadir Shah — A77

1938 Without Gum *Perf. 11x12*

315	A77	50p brt blue & sepia	2.75	2.40
a.		Imperf. pair	24.00	19.00

20th year of Independence.

Mohammed Nadir Shah — A78

1939 ***Perf. 11, 12x11***

317	A78 50p deep salmon	2.40	1.50

21st year of Independence.

National Arms A79

Parliament House, Darul Funun — A80

Royal Palace, Kabul A81

Independence Monument — A82

Independence Monument and Nadir Shah — A83

Mohammed Zahir Shah — A84

Mohammed Zahir Shah A85

Perf. 11, 11x12, 12x11, 12

1939-61 **Typo.**

318	A79	2p intense blk	.30	*.70*
318A	A79	2p brt pink ('61)	.30	*.70*
		Size: 36.5x24mm		
319	A80	10p brt purple	.30	.25
		Size: 31.5x21mm		
320	A80	15p brt green	.35	.25
		Size: 34x22.5mm		
321	A80	20p red lilac	.50	.25
322	A81	25p rose red	.60	.30
322A	A81	25p green ('41)	.35	.25
323	A81	30p orange	.50	.25
a.		Vert. pair, imperf between		—
324	A81	40p dk gray	1.00	.50
325	A82	45p brt carmine	1.00	.40

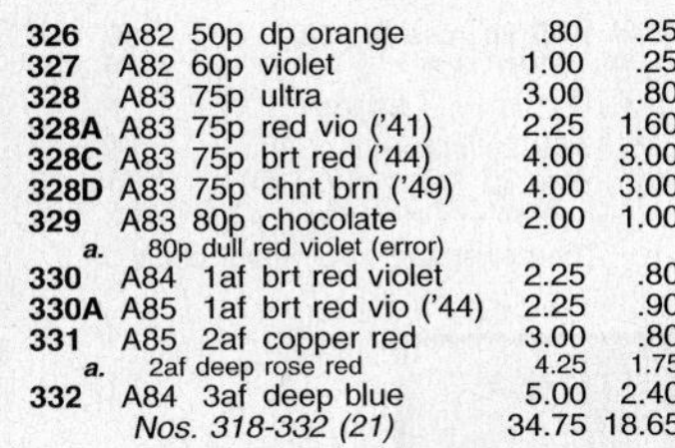

326	A82	50p dp orange	.80	.25
327	A82	60p violet	1.00	.25
328	A83	75p ultra	3.00	.80
328A	A83	75p red vio ('41)	2.25	1.60
328C	A83	75p brt red ('44)	4.00	3.00
328D	A83	75p chnt brn ('49)	4.00	3.00
329	A83	80p chocolate	2.00	1.00
a.		80p dull red violet (error)		
330	A84	1af brt red violet	2.25	.80
330A	A85	1af brt red vio ('44)	2.25	.90
331	A85	2af copper red	3.00	.80
a.		2af deep rose red	4.25	1.75
332	A84	3af deep blue	5.00	2.40
		Nos. 318-332 (21)	34.75	18.65

Many shades exist in this issue.
On No. 332 the King faces slightly left.
No. 318A issued with and without gum.
See #795A-795B in *Scott Standard Postage Stamp Catalogue*, Vol. 1. For similar design see #907A in Scott Standard catalogue, Vol. 1.

Mohammed Nadir Shah — A86

1940, Aug. 23 ***Perf. 11***

333	A86 50p gray green	2.00	1.50

22nd year of Independence.

AIR POST STAMPS

Plane over Kabul AP1

Perf. 12, 12x11, 11

1939, Oct. 1 **Typo.** **Unwmk.**

C1	AP1	5af orange	6.00	4.50
a.		Imperf., pair ('47)	29.00	29.00
b.		Horiz. pair, imperf. vert.	32.50	32.50
C2	AP1	10af blue	6.50	4.50
a.		10af lt bl	8.00	6.00
b.		Imperf., pair ('47)	29.00	
c.		Horiz. pair, imperf. vert.	32.50	
C3	AP1	20af emerald	12.00	7.50
a.		Imperf., pair ('47)	29.00	
b.		Horiz. pair, imperf. vert.	32.50	
c.		Vert. pair, imperf. horiz.	35.00	
		Nos. C1-C3 (3)	24.50	16.50

These stamps come with clean-cut or rough perforations. Counterfeits exist.

REGISTRATION STAMPS

R1

Dated "1309"
Pelure Paper

1891 **Unwmk.** **Litho.** ***Imperf.***

F1	R1 1r slate blue	2.40	
a.	Tete beche pair	13.50	

Genuinely used examples of No. F1 are rare. Counterfeit cancellations exist.

R2

Dated "1311"

1893 **Thin Wove Paper**

F2	R2 1r black, *green*	2.00	

Genuinely used examples of No. F2 are rare. Counterfeit cancellations exist.

R3

1894 **Undated**

F3	R3 2ab black, *green*	9.50	*11.00*

12 varieties. See note below Nos. 189-190.

R4

1898-1900 **Undated**

F4	R4 2ab black, *deep rose*	4.50	4.50
F5	R4 2ab black, *lilac rose*	6.50	5.00
F6	R4 2ab black, *magenta*	8.00	5.00
F7	R4 2ab black, *salmon*	4.50	4.50
F8	R4 2ab black, *orange*	4.50	4.50
F9	R4 2ab black, *yellow*	4.50	3.50
F10	R4 2ab black, *green*	4.50	3.50
	Nos. F4-F10 (7)	37.00	30.50

Many shades of paper.

Nos. F4-F10 come in two sizes, measured between outer frame lines: 52x36mm, 1st printing; 46x33mm, 2nd printing. The outer frame line (not pictured) is 3-6mm from inner frame line.

Used on P.O. receipts.

OFFICIAL STAMPS

(Used only on interior mail.)

Coat of Arms O1

1909 **Unwmk.** **Typo.** ***Perf. 12***
Wove Paper

O1	O1 red	1.25	1.25
a.	Carmine ('19?)	2.50	6.50

Later printings of No. O1 in scarlet, vermilion, claret, etc., on various types of paper, were issued until 1927.

Coat of Arms — O2

1939-68? **Typo.** ***Perf. 11, 12***

O3	O2	15p emerald	1.10	.80
O4	O2	30p ocher ('40)	1.50	1.50
O5	O2	45p dark carmine	1.25	1.25
O6	O2	50p brt car ('68)	.70	.70
a.		50p carmine rose ('55)	1.25	.70
O7	O2	1af brt red violet	2.00	1.75
		Nos. O3-O7 (5)	6.55	6.00

Size of 50p, 24x31mm, others 22½x28mm.

PARCEL POST STAMPS

Coat of Arms — PP1

PP2

PP3

PP4

1909 **Unwmk.** **Typo.** ***Perf. 12***

Q1	PP1	3sh bister	1.25	*2.25*
a.		Imperf., pair	—	
Q2	PP2	1kr olive gray	3.50	*3.50*
a.		Imperf., pair	—	
Q3	PP3	1r orange	3.25	3.25
Q4	PP3	1r olive green	24.00	4.50
Q5	PP4	2r red	4.00	4.00
		Nos. Q1-Q5 (5)	36.00	17.50

Type I

Type II

A 1909 undenominated dull olive green Official parcel post stamp exists with two types. Type I has thinner and more rays below the crest; Type II has fewer and wider rays. Values: *$400* each. A pair, imperf between, exists. Value, $1,250. A complete sheet is known perforated on all sides.

1916-18

Q6	PP1	3sh green	1.75	*3.50*
Q7	PP2	1kr pale red	3.00	1.50
a.		1kr rose red ('18)	4.00	4.00
Q8	PP3	1r brown org	3.50	1.75
a.		1r deep brown ('18)	12.00	3.00
Q9	PP4	2r blue	6.25	*6.50*
		Nos. Q6-Q9 (4)	14.50	*13.25*

Nos. Q1-Q9 sometimes show letters of the papermaker's watermark "HOWARD & JONES LONDON."

Ungummed stamps are remainders. They sell for one-third the price of mint stamps.

Old Habibia College, Near Kabul — PP5

1921 **Wove Paper**

Q10	PP5 10pa chocolate		5.00	5.75
a.	Tete beche pair		22.50	22.50
Q11	PP5 15pa light brn		7.00	7.50
a.	Tete beche pair		27.50	27.50
Q12	PP5 30pa red violet		12.50	7.50
a.	Tete beche pair		40.00	40.00
b.	Laid paper		*15.00*	*15.00*
Q13	PP5 1r brt blue		14.00	14.00
a.	Tete beche pair		65.00	65.00
	Nos. Q10-Q13 (4)		38.50	34.75

Stamps of this issue are usually perforated on one or two sides only.

The laid paper of No. Q12b has a papermaker's watermark in the sheet.

Handstamped in black on Nos. Q10-Q13

PP5a

1923, Feb. 26

Q13B	PP5a 10pa chocolate	—	—
Q13C	PP5a 15pa light brn	—	—
Q13D	PP5a 30pa red violet	—	—
Q13E	PP5a 1r brt blue	—	—

5th Independence Day.

Two types of handstamp exist.

Forgeries exist.

PP6

1924-26 **Wove Paper**

Q15	PP6 5kr ultra ('26)	50.00	50.00
Q16	PP6 5r lilac	20.00	25.00

A 15r rose exists, but is not known to have been placed in use. Value, unused $350.

PP7

PP8

1928-29 ***Perf. 11, 11xImperf.***

Q17	PP7 2r yellow orange	8.00	7.00
Q18	PP7 2r green ('29)	7.50	7.50
Q19	PP8 3r deep green	10.50	10.50
Q20	PP8 3r brown ('29)	9.50	10.50
	Nos. Q17-Q20 (4)	35.50	35.50

POSTAL TAX STAMPS

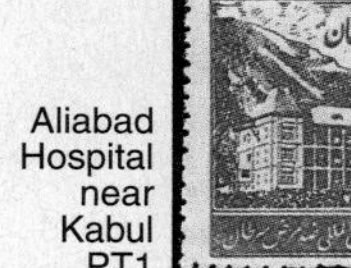

Aliabad Hospital near Kabul PT1

Pierre and Marie Curie PT2

Perf. 12x11½, 12

1938, Dec. 22 **Typo.** **Unwmk.**

RA1	PT1 10p peacock grn	3.25	*5.00*
RA2	PT2 15p dull blue	3.25	*5.00*

Obligatory on all mail Dec. 22-28, 1938. The money was used for the Aliabad Hospital. See note with CD80.

AGÜERA, LA

ä-gwä'rä

LOCATION — An administrative district in southern Rio de Oro on the north-west coast of Africa.

GOVT. — Spanish possession

AREA — Because of indefinite political boundaries, figures for area and population are not available.

100 Centimos = 1 Peseta

Type of 1920 Issue of Rio de Oro Overprinted

1920, June Typo. Unwmk. ***Perf. 13***

1	A8 1c blue green	2.60	*3.25*
	Never hinged	5.75	
	On cover		*65.00*
2	A8 2c olive brown	2.60	*3.25*
	Never hinged	5.75	
	On cover		*65.00*
3	A8 5c deep green	2.60	*3.25*
	Never hinged	5.75	
	On cover		*65.00*
4	A8 10c light red	2.60	*3.25*
	Never hinged	5.75	
	On cover		*65.00*
5	A8 15c yellow	2.60	*3.25*
	Never hinged	5.75	
	On cover		*65.00*
6	A8 20c lilac	2.60	*3.25*
	Never hinged	5.75	
	On cover		*65.00*
7	A8 25c deep blue	2.60	*3.25*
	Never hinged	5.75	
	On cover		*75.00*
8	A8 30c dark brown	2.60	*3.25*
	Never hinged	5.75	
	On cover		*75.00*
9	A8 40c pink	2.60	*3.25*
	Never hinged	5.75	
	On cover		*75.00*
10	A8 50c bright blue	8.50	*10.00*
	Never hinged	17.50	
	On cover		*125.00*
11	A8 1p red brown	13.50	*20.00*
	Never hinged	25.00	
	On cover		*250.00*
12	A8 4p dark violet	40.00	*60.00*
	Never hinged	80.00	
	On cover		*650.00*
13	A8 10p orange	85.00	*125.00*
	Never hinged	170.00	
	On cover		*1,300.*
	Nos. 1-13 (13)	170.40	244.25
	Set, never hinged	400.00	

Values for Nos. 1-13 are for stamps with fine centering. Exceptional examples with very fine centering are scarce and command at least 50% premium.

Commercial covers are scarce. Philatelic covers sell for less.

Values for stamps in blocks of 4

1	A8	1c blue green	14.00	*15.00*
2	A8	2c olive brown	14.00	*15.00*
3	A8	5c deep green	14.00	*15.00*
4	A8	10c light red	14.00	*15.00*
5	A8	15c yellow	14.00	*15.00*
6	A8	20c lilac	14.00	*15.00*
7	A8	25c deep blue	14.00	*15.00*
8	A8	30c dark brown	14.00	*15.00*
9	A8	40c pink	14.00	*15.00*
10	A8	50c bright blue	32.50	*60.00*
11	A8	1p red brown	77.50	*82.50*
12	A8	4p dark violet	260.00	*275.00*
13	A8	10p orange	490.00	*525.00*

Values for Specimen Stamps (numbered A.000.000 on reverse)

1S	A8	1c blue green	8.25
2S	A8	2c olive brown	8.25
3S	A8	5c deep green	8.25
4S	A8	10c light red	8.25
5S	A8	15c yellow	8.25
6S	A8	20c lilac	8.25
7S	A8	25c deep blue	8.25
8S	A8	30c dark brown	8.25
9S	A8	40c pink	8.25
10S	A8	50c bright blue	21.00
11S	A8	1p red brown	21.00
12S	A8	4p dark violet	77.50
13S	A8	10p orange	150.00

King Alfonso XIII — A2

Two Types of 1c:

Type I: Two dots above "U" of "AGUERA," large letters.

Type II: No dots above "U" of "AGUERA," smaller letters.

1922, June

14	A2 1c turquoise bl (I)	1.25	*1.50*
	Never hinged	2.50	
	On cover		*45.00*
a.	Type II	95.00	
15	A2 2c dark green	1.40	*1.50*
	Never hinged	2.50	
	On cover		*45.00*
16	A2 5c blue green	1.40	*1.50*
	Never hinged	2.50	
	On cover		*45.00*
17	A2 10c red	1.40	*1.50*
	Never hinged	2.50	
	On cover		*45.00*
18	A2 15c red brown	1.40	*1.50*
	Never hinged	2.50	
	On cover		*45.00*
19	A2 20c yellow	1.40	*1.50*
	Never hinged	2.50	
	On cover		*45.00*
20	A2 25c deep blue	1.40	*1.50*
	Never hinged	2.50	
	On cover		*45.00*
21	A2 30c dark brown	1.40	*1.50*
	Never hinged	2.50	
	On cover		*52.50*
22	A2 40c rose red	1.60	*2.00*
	Never hinged	3.50	
	On cover		*57.50*
23	A2 50c red violet	5.50	*5.75*
	Never hinged	12.00	
	On cover		*77.50*
24	A2 1p rose	13.00	*15.00*
	Never hinged	24.00	
	On cover		*140.00*
25	A2 4p violet	35.00	*37.50*
	Never hinged	57.50	
	On cover		*350.00*
26	A2 10p orange	50.00	*55.00*
	Never hinged	90.00	
	On cover		*575.00*
	Nos. 14-26 (13)	116.15	127.25
	Set, never hinged	200.00	

Values for stamps in blocks of 4

14	A2	1c turquoise bl (I)	8.00
15	A2	2c dark green	8.00
16	A2	5c blue green	8.00
17	A2	10c red	8.00
18	A2	15c red brown	8.00
19	A2	20c yellow	8.00
20	A2	25c deep blue	8.00
21	A2	30c dark brown	9.25
22	A2	40c rose red	9.25
23	A2	50c red violet	29.00
24	A2	1p rose	60.00
25	A2	4p violet	165.00
26	A2	10p orange	250.00

Values for Specimen Stamps (numbered A.000.000 on reverse)

14S	A2	1c turquoise bl (I)	6.25
15S	A2	2c dark green	6.25
16S	A2	5c blue green	6.25
17S	A2	10c red	6.25
18S	A2	15c red brown	6.25
19S	A2	20c yellow	6.25
20S	A2	25c deep blue	6.25
21S	A2	30c dark brown	9.25
22S	A2	40c rose red	9.25
23S	A2	50c red violet	12.00
24S	A2	1p rose	12.00
25S	A2	4p violet	37.50
26S	A2	10p orange	62.50

For later issues, see Spanish Sahara.

AITUTAKI

ˌit-ə-ˈtäk-ē

LOCATION — One of the larger Cook Islands, in the South Pacific Ocean northeast of New Zealand
GOVT. — A dependency of the British dominion of New Zealand
AREA — 7 sq. mi.
POP. — 1,719

The Cook Islands were attached to New Zealand in 1901. Stamps of Cook Islands were used in 1932-72.

12 Pence = 1 Shilling

Watermark

Wmk. 61- Single-lined NZ and Star Close Together

Stamps of New Zealand Surcharged in Red or Blue

a

b

1903 Engr. Wmk. 61 *Perf. 14*

1 A18(a) ½p green (R) 4.75 *7.00*
On cover *140.00*
2 A35(b) 1p rose (Bl) 5.00 *6.25*
On cover *140.00*

c

d

e

f

Perf. 11

3 A22(c) 2½p blue (R) 19.50 15.00
On cover 140.00
4 A23(d) 3p yel brn (Bl) 19.00 *16.50*
On cover 160.00
5 A26(e) 6p red (Bl) 32.50 27.50
On cover 190.00
6 A29(f) 1sh scar (Bl) 60.00 *95.00*
On cover *375.00*
a. 1sh orange red (Bl) 72.50 *105.00*
On cover *400.00*
b. 1sh orange brown (Bl) 145.00 *150.00*
On cover *825.00*
c. As #6, no period after "Tiringi" 675.00 *975.00*
d. As #6a, no period after "Tiringi" 850.00 *1,150.*
e. As #6b, no period after "Tiringi" 1,350. *1,500.*

Values for covers are for commercially used and properly franked items. Philatelic usages also exist and sell for less.

1911, Sept. Typo. *Perf. 14x15*

7 A41(a) ½p yel grn (R) 1.00 *8.75*

Engr.
Perf. 14

9 A22(c) 2½p dp blue (R) 8.50 *19.00*
a. No period after "Ava" 175.00 *275.00*

g

h

1913-16 Typo.

10 A42(b) 1p rose (Bl) 3.25 *13.50*

Engr.

12 A41(g) 6p car rose (Bl) ('16) 50.00 *145.00*
13 A41(h) 1sh ver (Bl) ('14) 60.00 *150.00*

1916-17 *Perf. 14x14½*

17 A45(g) 6p car rose (Bl) 9.00 *29.00*
a. Perf 14x13½ 13.50 *52.50*
b. Vert. pair, #17, 17a 52.50 *175.00*
18 A45(h) 1sh ver (Bl) ('17) 14.00 *95.00*
a. Perf 14x13½ 27.00 *95.00*
b. Vert. pair, #18, 18a 140.00 *450.00*
c. No dot on"i" of "Tai" 250.00 *750.00*
d. No dot on second "i" of "Tiringi" 350.00 *850.00*
e. No dot on third "i" of "Tiringi" 475.00 *1,150.*
Nos. 1-18 (13) 286.50 *627.50*

New Zealand Stamps of 1909-19 Overprinted in Red or Dark Blue

1917-20 Typo. *Perf. 14x15*

19 A43 ½p yellow grn ('20) 1.00 *6.25*
20 A42 1p car (Bl) ('20) 5.00 *35.00*
21 A47 1½p gray black 4.50 *32.50*
22 A47 1½p brown org ('19) .90 *7.50*
23 A43 3p choc (Bl) ('19) 3.75 *22.00*

Engr. *Perf. 14x14½*

24 A44 2½p dull blue ('18) 1.90 *16.00*
a. Perf 14x13½ 2.10 *25.00*
b. Vert. pair, #24, 24a 40.00 *150.00*
25 A45 3p vio brn (Bl) ('18) 1.75 *32.50*
a. Perf 14x13½ 1.90 *40.00*
b. Vert. pair, #25, 25a 35.00 *175.00*
26 A45 6p car rose (Bl) 5.00 *22.50*
a. Perf 14x13½ 7.25 *22.50*
b. Vert. pair, #26, 26a 47.50 *150.00*
27 A45 1sh vermilion (Bl) 13.00 *35.00*
a. Perf 14x13½ 16.00 *50.00*
b. Vert. pair, #26, 26a 75.00 *190.00*
Nos. 19-27 (9) 36.80 209.25

Landing of Capt. Cook A15

Avarua Waterfront A16

Capt. James Cook — A17

Palm — A18

Houses at Arorangi — A19

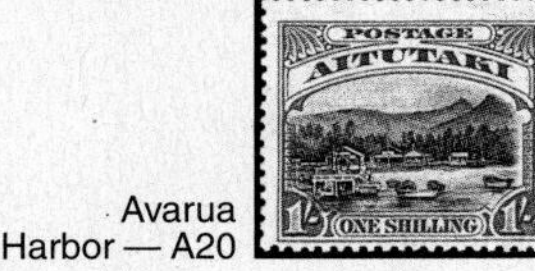

Avarua Harbor — A20

1920 Engr. Unwmk. *Perf. 14*

28 A15 ½p green & black 3.75 26.00
29 A16 1p car & blk 3.75 18.00
Double derrick flaw 12.50
30 A17 1½p brown & blk 6.25 *13.00*
31 A18 3p dp blue & blk 2.75 *15.00*
32 A19 6p slate & red brn 6.25 15.00
33 A20 1sh claret & blk 10.00 *22.50*
Nos. 28-33 (6) 32.75 *109.50*

Inverted centers, double frames, etc. are from printers waste.

Rarotongan Chief (Te Po) — A21

1924-27 Wmk. 61 *Perf. 14*

34 A15 ½p green & blk ('27) 2.10 *25.00*
35 A16 1p carmine & blk 6.25 *12.50*
Double derrick flaw 16.00
36 A21 2½p blue & blk ('27) 8.00 *80.00*
Nos. 34-36 (3) 16.35 *117.50*

ALAOUITES

ˈal-au-ˌwītz

LOCATION — A division of Syria, in Western Asia.
GOVT. — Under French Mandate
AREA — 2,500 sq. mi.
POP. — 278,000 (approx. 1930)
CAPITAL — Latakia

This territory became an independent state in 1924, although still administered under the French Mandate. In 1930 it was renamed Latakia and Syrian stamps overprinted "Lattaquie" superseded the stamps of Alaouites. For these and subsequent issues see Latakia and Syria.

100 Centimes = 1 Piaster

Issued under French Mandate

Stamps of France Surcharged

Nos. 1-6, 16-18

Nos. 7-15, 19-21

Two types of surcharge , 4p on 85c: type 1, 1¼-1½mm between "4" and "P"; type 2, 2mm between "4" and "P."

Two types of surcharge, 5p, 10p, 25p: type 1, 1-1¾mm between value and "Piastres"; type 2, 3mm between value and "Piastres."

1925 Unwmk. *Perf. 14x13½*

1 A16 10c on 2c vio brn 4.00 4.00
Never hinged 5.25
On cover *32.50*
b. Grayish (GC) paper (#110b) 5.00 4.50
Never hinged 7.25
On cover *35.00*
c. "0" before "P" omitted 40.00 40.00
Never hinged 70.00
2 A22 25c on 5c orange 4.00 4.00
Never hinged 5.25
On cover *32.50*
3 A20 75c on 15c gray grn 7.25 7.25
Never hinged 9.50
On cover *60.00*
b. Wide spacing between "7" and "5" 25.00 25.00
Never hinged 40.00
4 A22 1p on 20c red brn 4.00 4.00
Never hinged 5.25
On cover *32.50*
5 A22 1.25p on 25c blue 4.50 4.50
Never hinged 6.00
On cover *32.50*
6 A22 1.50p on 30c red 14.50 14.50
Never hinged 19.00
On cover *90.00*
7 A22 2p on 35c violet 4.75 *4.75*
Never hinged 6.25
On cover *32.50*
On cover, single franking *50.00*
b. Arabic surcharge inverted 40.00 40.00
Never hinged 60.00
8 A18 2p on 40c red & pale bl 5.50 5.50
Never hinged 7.25
On cover *42.50*
On cover, single franking *65.00*
b. Grayish (GC) paper (#121b) 6.00 6.00
Never hinged 9.00
On cover *32.50*
On cover, single franking *57.50*
9 A18 2p on 45c grn & bl 19.00 19.00
Never hinged 27.00
On cover *125.00*
On cover, single franking *250.00*
10 A18 3p on 60c vio & ultra 8.75 8.75
Never hinged 11.50
On cover *70.00*
On cover, single franking *95.00*
11 A20 3p on 60c lt vio 14.00 14.00
Never hinged 18.50
On cover *95.00*
On cover, single franking *150.00*
b. Double surcharge 165.00 165.00
Never hinged 235.00
c. Small and raised figure "3" 175.00 175.00
Never hinged 270.00
12 A20 4p on 85c ver, type 1 surcharge 3.50 3.50
Never hinged 4.75
On cover *65.00*
On cover, single franking *70.00*
b. Type 2 surcharge 4.00 4.00
Never hinged 5.25
On cover *35.00*
On cover, single franking *45.00*
c. As "b," inverted surcharge 50.00 50.00
Never hinged 75.00
13 A18 5p on 1fr cl & ol grn, type 1 surcharge 8.50 8.50
Never hinged 11.00
On cover *70.00*
On cover, single franking *130.00*
b. Type 2 surcharge 12.00 11.00
Never hinged 17.50
c. As "b," Arabic value omitted 62.50 62.50
Never hinged 95.00
14 A18 10p on 2fr org & pale bl, type 1 surcharge 13.00 13.00
Never hinged 17.00
On cover *85.00*
On cover, single franking *145.00*
b. Surcharge type 2 70.00 70.00
Never hinged 105.00
On cover *100.00*
On cover, single franking *175.00*
15 A18 25p on 5fr bl & buff, type 1 16.00 16.00
Never hinged 21.00
On cover *80.00*
On cover, single franking *160.00*
b. Surcharged Type 2 25.00 20.00
Never hinged 37.50
On cover *110.00*
On cover, single franking *225.00*
Nos. 1-15 (15) 131.25 131.25

For overprints, see Nos. C1-C4.

Same Surcharges on Pasteur Stamps of France

16 A23 50c on 10c green 3.00 3.00
Never hinged 4.50
On cover *30.00*
17 A23 75c on 15c green 3.75 3.75
Never hinged 5.50
On cover *37.50*
18 A23 1.50p on 30c red 3.00 3.00
Never hinged 4.50
On cover *25.00*
19 A23 2p on 45c red 3.75 3.75
Never hinged 5.50
On cover *37.50*
On cover, single franking *50.00*
b. Arabic inscription in surcharge inverted 47.50 47.50
Never hinged 72.50
20 A23 2.50p on 50c blue 5.25 5.25
Never hinged 7.00
On cover *37.50*
On cover, single franking *62.50*
21 A23 4p on 75c blue, type 1 9.00 9.00
Never hinged 13.00
On cover *50.00*
On cover, single franking *80.00*
b. Surcharge type 2 7.00 *7.00*
Never hinged 10.50
On cover *55.00*
On cover, single franking *100.00*
Nos. 16-21 (6) 27.75 *27.75*

Inverted Surcharges

1a A16 10c on 2c vio brn 50.00
Never hinged 50.00
2a A22 25c on 5c orange 50.00
Never hinged 50.00
3a A20 75c on 15c gray grn 50.00
Never hinged 60.00
4a A22 1p on 20c red brn 50.00
Never hinged 50.00
5a A22 1.25p on 25c blue 50.00
Never hinged 50.00
6a A22 1.50p on 30c red 60.00
Never hinged 75.00
7a A22 2p on 35c violet 50.00
Never hinged 75.00
8a A18 2p on 40c red & pale bl 50.00
Never hinged 75.00
9a A18 2p on 45c grn & bl 60.00
Never hinged 75.00

10a A18 3p on 60c vio & ultra 50.00
Never hinged 75.00
11a A20 3p on 60c lt vio 60.00
Never hinged 75.00
12a A20 4p on 85c vermilion 50.00
Never hinged 57.50
13a A18 5p on 1fr cl & ol grn 60.00
Never hinged 57.50
14a A18 10p on 2fr org & pale bl 70.00
Never hinged 75.00
15a A18 25p on 5fr bl & buff 70.00
Never hinged 75.00
16a A23 50c on 10c green 40.00
Never hinged 45.00
17a A23 75c on 15c green 40.00
Never hinged 75.00
18a A23 1.50p on 30c red 45.00
Never hinged 77.50
19a A23 2p on 45c red 40.00
Never hinged 52.50
20a A23 2.50p on 50c blue 40.00
Never hinged 45.00
21a A23 4p on 75c blue 40.00
Never hinged 52.50

Stamps of Syria, 1925, Overprinted in Red, Black or Blue

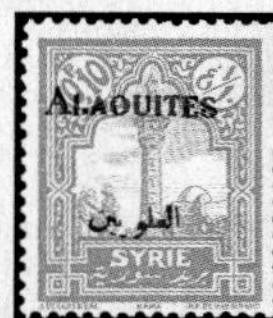

On A3, A5

On A4

1925, Mar. 1 *Perf. 12½, 13½*
25 A3 10c dk violet (R) 1.50 2.25
Never hinged 2.25
On cover 20.00
a. Double overprint 42.50 42.50
Never hinged 65.00
b. Inverted overprint 35.00
Never hinged 57.50
c. Black overprint 37.50 37.50
Never hinged 57.50
d. On Lebanon #50 (error) 125.00
Never hinged 150.00
e. "ALAOUITE," instead of "ALAOUITES" 30.00 30.00
Never hinged 45.00
f. Surcharge on front and back 45.00
Never hinged 90.00
g. Pair, one without overprint 175.00
26 A4 25c olive black (R) 2.25 3.00
Never hinged 3.00
On cover 19.00
a. Inverted overprint 40.00
Never hinged 60.00
b. Blue overprint 50.00 50.00
Never hinged 75.00
27 A4 50c yellow green 1.75 1.75
Never hinged 3.00
On cover 15.00
a. Inverted overprint 40.00 40.00
Never hinged 60.00
b. Blue overprint 50.00 50.00
Never hinged 75.00
c. Red overprint 50.00 50.00
Never hinged 75.00
d. "ALAOUITE," instead of "ALAOUITES" 50.00 50.00
Never hinged 75.00
e. Double overprint 50.00 50.00
Never hinged 75.00
f. Pair, one without overprint 275.00
g. Pair, #27 and #27d 60.00
Never hinged 95.00
28 A4 75c brown orange 2.00 2.25
Never hinged 3.00
On cover 15.00
a. Inverted overprint 45.00 60.00
Never hinged 67.50
b. Double overprint 47.50 65.00
Never hinged 72.50
29 A5 1p magenta 2.75 2.75
Never hinged 4.25
On cover 19.00
a. Inverted overprint 40.00 47.50
Never hinged 60.00
b. "ALACUITES," instead of "ALAOUITES" 30.00 30.00
Never hinged 45.00
c. "ALAOCITES," instead of "ALAOUITES" 35.00 45.00
Never hinged 52.50
d. "ALAO ITES," instead of "ALAOUITES" 40.00 40.00
Never hinged 45.00
e. "ALAOU ES," instead of "ALAOUITES" 60.00 45.00
Never hinged 45.00
f. Double overprint, one inverted 70.00
g. Overprint vertical 120.00
30 A4 1.25p deep green 3.25 3.50
Never hinged 4.50
On cover 15.00
a. Red overprint 50.00 50.00
Never hinged 75.00
b. Double overprint 75.00
31 A4 1.50p rose red (Bl) 2.75 3.00
Never hinged 4.25
On cover 15.00
a. Inverted overprint 45.00 45.00
Never hinged 67.50
b. Black overprint 40.00 40.00
Never hinged 60.00
c. As "b", inverted 80.00
Never hinged 120.00
32 A4 2p dk brown (R) 2.75 3.50
Never hinged 4.25
On cover 19.00
On cover, single franking 25.00
a. Blue overprint 65.00 65.00
Never hinged 100.00
b. Inverted overprint 40.00 40.00
Never hinged 60.00
33 A4 2.50p pck blue (R) 4.25 4.50
Never hinged 6.00
On cover 22.50
On cover, single franking 32.50
a. Black overprint 65.00 65.00
Never hinged 100.00
34 A4 3p orange brown 2.50 2.75
Never hinged 3.50
On cover 22.50
On cover, single franking 37.50
a. Inverted overprint 40.00 40.00
Never hinged 60.00
b. Blue overprint 70.00 70.00
Never hinged 105.00
c. Double overprint 90.00
35 A4 5p violet 3.75 4.00
Never hinged 7.00
On cover 25.00
On cover, single franking 45.00
a. Red overprint 70.00 70.00
Never hinged 105.00
b. Inverted overprint 42.50
Never hinged 65.00
c. On Lebanon #60 (error) 175.00
Never hinged 200.00
d. Surcharge on front and back 40.00
Never hinged 60.00
36 A4 10p violet brown 5.50 6.00
Never hinged 7.25
On cover 32.50
On cover, single franking 50.00
37 A4 25p ultra (R) 9.00 10.00
Never hinged 12.50
On cover 37.50
On cover, single franking 95.00
Nos. 25-37 (13) 44.00 49.25

For overprints see Nos. C5-C19.

Stamps of Syria, 1925, Surcharged in Black or Red

Nos. 38-42

Nos. 43-45

1926
38 A4 3.50p on 75c brn org 2.50 2.75
Never hinged 3.50
On cover 19.00
a. Surcharged on face and back 22.50 22.50
Never hinged 35.00
39 A4 4p on 25c ol blk, type 1 (R) 2.50 2.50
Never hinged 3.75
On cover 19.00
a. Type 2 surcharge 70.00 70.00
Never hinged 105.00
On cover 175.00
b. As "a," inverted surcharge 105.00 105.00
Never hinged 160.00
40 A4 6p on 2.50p pck bl (R) 3.00 3.25
Never hinged 3.75
On cover 25.00
41 A4 12p on 1.25p dp grn 3.25 3.50
Never hinged 4.00
On cover 32.50
a. Inverted surcharge 35.00 35.00
Never hinged 55.00
42 A4 20p on 1.25p dp grn 5.25 5.25
Never hinged 7.25
On cover 62.50
43 A4 4.50p on 75c brn org 5.25 3.25
Never hinged 7.25
On cover 25.00
a. Inverted surcharge 60.00 60.00
Never hinged 90.00
b. Double surcharge 55.00 55.00
Never hinged 87.50
44 A4 7.50p on 2.50p pck bl 4.75 3.25
Never hinged 6.75
On cover 25.00
45 A4 15p on 25p ultra 8.75 5.50
Never hinged 16.00
On cover 45.00
a. Inverted surcharge 50.00
Nos. 38-45 (8) 35.25 29.25

For overprint see No. C21.

Syria No. 199 Ovptd. in Red like No. 25

1928
46 A3 5c on 10c dk violet 2.00 1.75
Never hinged 5.00
On cover 19.00
a. Double surcharge 40.00
Never hinged 60.00

Syria Nos. 178 and 174 Surcharged like Nos. 43-45 in Red

47 A4 2p on 1.25p dp green 16.00 8.00
Never hinged 32.50
On cover 62.50
a. Double surcharge 60.00
Never hinged 90.00
b. Inverted surcharge 50.00 50.00
Never hinged 90.00
48 A4 4p on 25c olive black 11.00 6.50
Never hinged 27.50
On cover 50.00
a. Double surcharge 50.00 50.00
Never hinged 75.00
b. Inverted surcharge 50.00 50.00
Never hinged 75.00

For overprint see No. C20.

49 A4 4p on 25c olive black 82.50 50.00
Never hinged 150.00
On cover —
a. Double impression 150.00
Never hinged 225.00
Nos. 46-49 (4) 111.50 66.25

AIR POST STAMPS

Nos. 8, 10, 13 & 14 with Additional Ovpt. in Black

1925, Jan. 1 **Unwmk.** *Perf. 14x13½*
C1 A18 2p on 40c, type 1 30.00 30.00
Never hinged 47.50
On cover 100.00
On cover, single franking 110.00
a. Inverted overprint 110.00 110.00
Never hinged 165.00
b. on 40c, type 2 17.00 15.00
Never hinged 25.00
On cover 75.00
On cover, single franking 95.00
C2 A18 3p on 60c, type 1 22.50 20.00
Never hinged 34.00
On cover 67.50
On cover, single franking 80.00
a. Inverted overprint 125.00 125.00
Never hinged 190.00
b. on 60c, type 2 15.00 15.00
Never hinged 26.00
On cover 77.50
On cover, single franking 90.00
C3 A18 5p on 1fr, type 1 17.00 14.00
Never hinged 25.00
On cover 75.00
On cover, single franking 110.00
a. Inverted overprint 37.50 37.50
Never hinged 57.50
b. on 2fr, type 2 12.50 12.50
Never hinged 26.00
On cover 100.00
On cover, single franking 150.00
C4 A18 10p on 2fr, type 1 22.00 15.00
Never hinged 35.00
On cover 60.00
On cover, single franking 100.00
a. Inverted overprint 35.00 35.00
Never hinged 52.50
b. on 1fr, type 2 15.00 15.00
Never hinged 26.00
On cover 115.00
On cover, single franking 150.00
Nos. C1-C4 (4) 91.50 79.00

Nos. 32, 34, 35 & 36 With Additional Ovpt. in Green

1925, Mar. 1 *Perf. 13½*
C5 A4 2p dark brown 7.50 6.00
Never hinged 15.00
On cover 37.50
On cover, single franking 50.00
a. Inverted overprint 75.00 75.00
Never hinged 115.00
b. Red overprint 125.00
Never hinged 190.00
C6 A4 3p orange brown 7.50 6.00
Never hinged 15.00
On cover 37.50
On cover, single franking 55.00
a. Inverted overprint 75.00 75.00
Never hinged 110.00
b. Red overprint 100.00
Never hinged 150.00
c. On Lebanon #59 (error) 325.00
Never hinged 450.00
C7 A4 5p violet 7.50 6.00
Never hinged 15.00
On cover 42.50
On cover, single franking 65.00
a. Inverted overprint 75.00 75.00
Never hinged 110.00
b. Red overprint 100.00
Never hinged 150.00
C8 A4 10p violet brown 7.50 6.00
Never hinged 15.00
On cover 50.00
On cover, single franking 95.00
a. Inverted overprint 75.00 75.00
Never hinged 110.00
b. Red overprint 100.00
Never hinged 150.00
Nos. C5-C8 (4) 30.00 24.00

Nos. 32, 34, 35 & 36 With Additional Ovpt. in Red

1926, May 1
C9 A4 2p dark brown 7.50 6.50
Never hinged 16.00
On cover 37.50
On cover, single franking 50.00
a. Red overprint double 175.00 175.00
Never hinged 265.00
b. Black overprint double 175.00 175.00
Never hinged 265.00
c. Black overprint inverted 70.00 70.00
Never hinged 105.00
C10 A4 3p orange brown 7.50 6.50
Never hinged 16.00
On cover 37.50
On cover, single franking 55.00
a. Black overprint inverted 70.00 70.00
Never hinged 105.00
C11 A4 5p violet 8.50 7.50
Never hinged 16.00
On cover 50.00
On cover, single franking 75.00
a. Black overprint inverted 70.00 70.00
Never hinged 105.00
C12 A4 10p violet brown 8.50 7.50
Never hinged 16.00
On cover 55.00
On cover, single franking 100.00
a. Black overprint inverted 70.00 70.00
Never hinged 105.00
Nos. C9-C12 (4) 32.00 28.00

No. C9 has the original overprint in black. Value for examples of Nos. C9-C12 with both original and plane overprint inverted, each $150.

The red plane overprint was also applied to Nos. C5-C8. These are believed to have been essays, and were not regularly issued.

Nos. 27c, 37 and Syria No. 177 With Addtl. Ovpt. of Airplane in Red or Black

1929, June-July
C17 A4 50c yel grn (R) 5.00 5.00
Never hinged 11.50
On cover 17.50
a. Plane overprint double 250.00
Never hinged 375.00
b. Plane ovpt. on face and back 60.00
Never hinged 95.00
c. Pair with plane overprint Tête-bêche 325.00
Never hinged 490.00
d. Double overprint 225.00 225.00
Never hinged 340.00
e. Overprint inverted 125.00
Never hinged 190.00
f. Plane only inverted 250.00
Never hinged 375.00
g. Red surcharge on Lebanon #52 (error) 200.00
Never hinged 250.00
C18 A5 1p magenta (Bk) 9.00 9.00
Never hinged 15.00
On cover 40.00
a. Red overprint 50.00
Never hinged 75.00
C19 A4 25p ultra (R) 52.50 40.00
Never hinged 80.00
On cover 125.00
a. Plane overprint inverted 125.00 125.00
Never hinged 190.00
b. Surcharge double 150.00 150.00
Never hinged 225.00
Nos. C17-C19 (3) 66.50 54.00

Nos. 28 and 30 exist with additional overprint of airplane in red. These stamps were never issued. Value, each $100.

Nos. 47 and 45 With Additional Ovpt. of Airplane in Red

1929-30

C20	A4 2p on 1.25p ('30)	7.25	7.25
	Never hinged	12.00	
	On cover		*45.00*
a.	Surcharge inverted	50.00	50.00
	Never hinged	75.00	
b.	Double surcharge	75.00	75.00
	Never hinged	110.00	
c.	Triple surcharge	175.00	
	Never hinged	265.00	
C21	A4 15p on 25p (Bk + R)	55.00	47.50
	Never hinged	90.00	
	On cover		*110.00*
a.	Plane overprint inverted	225.00	225.00
	Never hinged	275.00	

POSTAGE DUE STAMPS

Postage Due Stamps of France, 1893-1920, Surcharged Like No. 1 (Nos. J1-J2) or No. 7 (Nos. J3-J5)

1925 Unwmk. *Perf. 14x13½*

J1	D2 50c on 10c choc	9.00	9.00
	Never hinged	14.00	
	On cover		*70.00*
J2	D2 1p on 20c ol grn	9.00	9.00
	Never hinged	14.00	
	On cover		*70.00*
J3	D2 2p on 30c red	9.50	9.50
	Never hinged	14.50	
	On cover		*80.00*
J4	D2 3p on 50c vio brn	9.50	9.50
	Never hinged	14.50	
	On cover		*95.00*
J5	D2 5p on 1fr red brn, *straw*	10.00	10.00
	Never hinged	15.00	
	On cover		*95.00*
	Nos. J1-J5 (5)	47.00	*47.00*

1925 Syria Postage Due Stamps Overprinted in Black, Blue or Red

1925 *Perf. 13½*

J6	D5 50c brown, *yel*	5.50	*5.50*
	Never hinged	8.00	
	On cover		*32.50*
a.	Blue overprint	42.50	
	Never hinged	65.00	
b.	Red overprint	42.50	
	Never hinged	65.00	
c.	Overprint inverted	30.00	30.00
	Never hinged	45.00	
J7	D6 1p vio, *rose* (Bl)	5.00	*5.00*
	Never hinged	7.25	
	On cover		*32.50*
a.	Black overprint	150.00	150.00
	Never hinged	200.00	
b.	Double overprint (Bk + Bl)	175.00	175.00
	Never hinged	225.00	
c.	Overprint inverted	40.00	40.00
	Never hinged	60.00	
J8	D5 2p blk, *blue* (R)	6.75	6.75
	Never hinged	9.50	
	On cover		*25.00*
a.	Blue overprint	45.00	
	Never hinged	55.00	
J9	D5 3p blk, *red org* (Bl)	9.00	9.00
	Never hinged	12.00	
	On cover		*37.50*
a.	Overprint inverted	30.00	
J10	D5 5p blk, *bl grn* (R)	11.00	11.00
	Never hinged	16.00	
	On cover		*50.00*
a.	Overprint inverted	30.00	30.00
	Never hinged	45.00	
b.	Black overprint	45.00	
	Never hinged	70.00	
	Nos. J6-J10 (5)	37.25	37.25

The stamps of Alaouites were superseded in 1930 by those of Latakia.

ALBANIA

al-ˈbā-nē-ə

LOCATION — Southeastern Europe
GOVT. — Monarchy
AREA — 11,101 sq. mi.
POP. — 1,003,124
CAPITAL — Tirana

After the outbreak of World War I, the country fell into a state of anarchy when the Prince and all members of the International Commission left Albania. Subsequently, General Ferrero, in command of Italian troops, declared Albania an independent country. A constitution was adopted and a republican form of government was instituted, which continued until 1928 when, by constitutional amendment, Albania was declared to be a monarchy. The President of the republic, Ahmed Zogu, became king of the new state. Many unlisted varieties or surcharges and lithographed labels are said to have done postal duty in Albania and Epirus during this unsettled period.

On April 7, 1939, Italy invaded Albania. King Zog fled but did not abdicate. The king of Italy acquired the crown.

40 Paras = 1 Piaster = 1 Grossion
100 Centimes = 1 Franc (1917)
100 Qintar = 1 Franc

AUSTRIAN POST IN ALBANIA

The Austrian Empire maintained post offices in various coastal towns in Albania beginning in 1854, in conjunction with the operations of the Austrian Lloyd shipping line. The nine offices, with opening and closing dates, are listed in the table below. Since Italian was the official operational language, the names are shown in Italian with the modern equivalent in parentheses.

Post Office	Open	Close
Antivari (Bar)	1854	1878
Durazzo (Durres)	1854	1915
Janina (Ioannina)	1857	1914
Prevesa (Preveza)	1854	1914
Santi Quaranta (Sarande)	1870	1915
Sajada (Sayiadha)	1858	1912
San Giovanni Di Medua (Shengjin)	1879	1915
Scutari (Shkoder)	1901	1915
Valona (Vlore)	1854	1915

Values in the first column for Nos. 2A1-2A353 are for stamps without defects tied to piece with legible partial strikes of town cancellations; values in the second column are for stamps without defects tied to cover by complete strikes of town cancellations. Stamps with legible town cancellations off cover sell for 25-50% of the on-piece value.

Issue dates refer to dates of stamps' issue, not necessarily to their usage with specific Albanian postal markings.

ANTIVARI

Stamps of Lombardy-Venetia Canceled in black with single circle date stamp with post office name, month and date, without year

1863 *Perf. 14*

2A1	2s yellow (#15)	575.00	2,000.
2A2	3s green (#16)	525.00	2,200.
2A3	5s rose (#17)	525.00	2,000.
2A4	10s blue (#18)	500.00	1,750.
2A5	15s yel brn (#19)	575.00	1,850.

1864-65 *Perf. 9½*

2A6	2s yellow (#20)	450.00	1,500.
2A7	3s green (#21)	200.00	850.00
2A8	5s rose (#22)	150.00	700.00
2A9	10s blue (#23)	125.00	500.00
2A10	15s yel brn (#24)	160.00	600.00

Stamps of Austrian Offices in the Turkish Empire Canceled in black or red brown with single circle date stamp with post office name, month and date, without year

1867-83 *Coarse Print*

2A11	2s yellow (#1)	87.50	650.00
2A12	3s green (#2)	110.00	600.00
2A13	5s red (#3)	75.00	350.00
2A14	10s blue (#4)	70.00	300.00
2A15	15s brown (#5)	75.00	300.00
2A16	25s gray lilac (#6)	100.00	900.00
2A17	50s brown (#7)	110.00	*4,000.*

Fine Print

2A18	2s yellow (#7C)	1,200.	—
2A19	3s green (#7D)	85.00	475.00
2A20	5s red (#7E)	82.50	350.00
2A21	10s blue (#7F)	70.00	290.00
2A22	15s org brown (#7I)	175.00	975.00
2A23	25s gray lilac (#7J)	300.00	*5,250.*

Stamps of Lombardy-Venetia Canceled in blue with single circle date stamp with post office name, month and date, without year

1863 *Perf. 14*

2A24	2s yellow (#15)	800.00	2,750.
2A25	3s green (#16)	750.00	2,850.
2A26	5s rose (#17)	750.00	1,650.
2A27	10s blue (#18)	700.00	2,400.
2A28	15s yel brn (#19)	800.00	2,500.

1864-65 *Perf. 9½*

2A29	2s yellow (#20)	525.00	1,650.
2A30	3s green (#21)	275.00	1,050.
2A31	5s rose (#22)	150.00	700.00
2A32	10s blue (#23)	190.00	675.00
2A33	15s yel brn (#24)	225.00	800.00

Stamps of Austrian Offices in the Turkish Empire Canceled in blue with single circle date stamp with post office name, month and date, without year

1867-83 *Coarse Print*

2A34	2s yellow (#1)	125.00	825.00
2A35	3s green (#2)	150.00	750.00
2A36	5s red (#3)	120.00	500.00
2A37	10s blue (#4)	115.00	450.00
2A38	15s brown (#5)	120.00	475.00
2A39	25s gray lilac (#6)	145.00	1,100.
2A40	50s brown (#7)	150.00	*4,250.*

Fine Print

2A41	2s yellow (#7C)	1,250.	—
2A42	3s green (#7D)	125.00	625.00
2A43	5s red (#7E)	125.00	525.00
2A44	10s blue (#7F)	115.00	450.00
2A45	15s org brown (#7I)	225.00	1,125.
2A46	25s gray lilac (#7J)	350.00	*5,500.*

Stamps of Austria Canceled in blue with single circle date stamp with post office name, month and date, without year

1863-64

2A47	2kr yellow (#22)	*1,150.*	—
2A48	3kr green (#23)	*1,150.*	—
2A49	5kr red (#24)	*1,150.*	—
2A50	10kr blue (#25)	*1,150.*	—
2A51	15kr yel brown (#26)	*1,150.*	—

DURAZZO

Stamps of Lombardy-Venetia Canceled in black with single circle date stamp with post office name, month and date, without year

1863 *Perf. 14*

2A52	2s yellow (#15)	350.00	1,250.
2A53	3s green (#16)	300.00	1,350.
2A54	5s rose (#17)	300.00	1,100.
2A55	10s blue (#18)	250.00	850.00
2A56	15s yel brn (#19)	325.00	1,000.

1864-65 *Perf. 9½*

2A57	2s yellow (#20)	425.00	1,275.
2A58	3s green (#21)	160.00	675.00
2A59	5s rose (#22)	110.00	525.00
2A60	10s blue (#23)	85.00	325.00
2A61	15s yel brn (#24)	115.00	450.00

Stamps of Austrian Offices in the Turkish Empire Canceled in black or red brown with single circle date stamp with post office name, month and date, without year

1867-83 *Coarse Print*

2A62	2s yellow (#1)	87.50	650.00
2A63	3s green (#2)	110.00	600.00
2A64	5s red (#3)	75.00	350.00
2A65	10s blue (#4)	70.00	300.00
2A66	15s brown (#5)	75.00	300.00
2A67	25s gray lilac (#6)	100.00	900.00
2A68	50s brown (#7)	110.00	*4,000.*

Fine Print

2A69	2s yellow (#7C)	1,200.	—
2A70	3s green (#7D)	85.00	475.00
2A71	5s red (#7E)	82.50	350.00
2A72	10s blue (#7F)	70.00	290.00
2A73	15s org brown (#7I)	175.00	975.00
2A74	25s gray lilac (#7J)	300.00	*5,250.*

Stamps of Lombardy-Venetia Canceled in blue with single circle date stamp with post office name, month and date, without year

1863 *Perf. 14*

2A75	2s yellow (#15)	*1,300.*	*4,500.*
2A76	3s green (#16)	*1,250.*	*4,500.*
2A77	5s rose (#17)	*1,250.*	*4,250.*
2A78	10s blue (#18)	*1,200.*	*4,000.*
2A79	15s yel brn (#19)	*1,300.*	*4,100.*

1864-65 *Perf. 9½*

2A80	2s yellow (#20)	625.00	1,950.
2A81	3s green (#21)	375.00	1,350.
2A82	5s rose (#22)	325.00	1,200.
2A83	10s blue (#23)	300.00	1,000.
2A84	15s yel brn (#24)	325.00	1,100.

Stamps of Austrian Offices in the Turkish Empire Canceled in blue with single circle date stamp with post office name, month and date, without year

1867-83 *Coarse Print*

2A85	2s yellow (#1)	125.00	825.00
2A86	3s green (#2)	150.00	750.00
2A87	5s red (#3)	120.00	500.00
2A88	10s blue (#4)	115.00	450.00
2A89	15s brown (#5)	120.00	475.00
2A90	25s gray lilac (#6)	145.00	1,100.
2A91	50s brown (#7)	150.00	*4,250.*

Fine Print

2A92	2s yellow (#7C)	1,250.	—
2A93	3s green (#7D)	125.00	625.00
2A94	5s red (#7E)	125.00	525.00
2A95	10s blue (#7F)	115.00	450.00
2A96	15s org brown (#7I)	225.00	1,125.
2A97	25s gray lilac (#7J)	350.00	*5,500.*

Stamps of Austrian Offices in the Turkish Empire Canceled in black with "thimble" (diameter 20mm or less) circular date stamp with post office name and date

1867-83 *Coarse Print*

2A99	2s yellow (#1)	200.00	1,000.
2A100	3s green (#2)	215.00	950.00
2A101	5s red (#3)	185.00	700.00
2A102	10s blue (#4)	175.00	650.00
2A103	15s brown (#5)	175.00	650.00
2A104	25s gray lilac (#6)	200.00	1,250.
2A105	50s brown (#7)	215.00	*4,400.*

Fine Print

2A106	2s yellow (#7C)	1,300.	—
2A107	3s green (#7D)	200.00	825.00
2A108	5s red (#7E)	190.00	700.00
2A109	10s blue (#7F)	175.00	650.00
2A110	15s org brown (#7I)	290.00	1,325.
2A111	25s gray lilac (#7J)	400.00	*5,750.*

Use of this cancellation is known beginning in 1877.

Stamps of Austrian Offices in the Turkish Empire Canceled in blue with "thimble" (diameter 20mm or less) circular date stamp with post office name and date

1867-83 *Coarse Print*

2A112	2s yellow (#1)	300.00	1,325.
2A113	3s green (#2)	325.00	1,250.
2A114	5s red (#3)	285.00	1,000.
2A115	10s blue (#4)	275.00	950.00
2A116	15s brown (#5)	280.00	975.00
2A117	25s gray lilac (#6)	300.00	1,575.
2A118	50s brown (#7)	325.00	*4,750.*

Fine Print

2A119	2s yellow (#7C)	1,400.	—
2A120	3s green (#7D)	300.00	1,125.
2A121	5s red (#7E)	285.00	1,000.
2A122	10s blue (#7F)	275.00	950.00
2A123	15s org brown (#7I)	385.00	1,625.
2A124	25s gray lilac (#7J)	500.00	*6,000.*

Use of this cancellation is known beginning in 1872.

Austrian Offices in Turkish Empire issues canceled in black with circular Durazzo date stamp with post office name, month, date and year date exist but are very rare.

JANINA

Stamps of Lombardy-Venetia Canceled in black with single circle date stamp with post office name, month and date, without year

1863 *Perf. 14*

2A126	2s yellow (#15)	240.00	1,000.
2A127	3s green (#16)	200.00	1,200.
2A128	5s rose (#17)	200.00	900.00
2A129	10s blue (#18)	160.00	625.00
2A130	15s yel brn (#19)	225.00	725.00

1864-65 *Perf. 9½*

2A131	2s yellow (#20)	375.00	1,150.
2A132	3s green (#21)	125.00	550.00
2A133	5s rose (#22)	80.00	400.00
2A134	10s blue (#23)	50.00	200.00
2A135	15s yel brn (#24)	85.00	325.00

Stamps of Austrian Offices in the Turkish Empire

Canceled in black or red brown with single circle date stamp with post office name, month and date, without year

1867-83		*Coarse Print*	
2A136	2s yellow (#1)	57.50	525.00
2A137	3s green (#2)	75.00	475.00
2A138	5s red (#3)	47.50	215.00
2A139	10s blue (#4)	40.00	165.00
2A140	15s brown (#5)	42.50	175.00
2A141	25s gray lilac (#6)	67.50	775.00
2A142	50s brown (#7)	75.00	*4,000.*

Fine Print

2A143	2s yellow (#7C)	1,175.	—
2A144	3s green (#7D)	55.00	350.00
2A145	5s red (#7E)	50.00	225.00
2A146	10s blue (#7F)	40.00	165.00
2A147	15s org brown (#7I)	150.00	850.00
2A148	25s gray lilac (#7J)	275.00	*5,250.*

Stamps of Austria

Canceled in black or red brown with single circle date stamp with post office name, month and date, without year

1867-83		*Coarse Print*	
2A149	2kr yellow (#27)	625.00	—
2A150	3kr green (#28)	625.00	—
2A151	5kr red (#29)	625.00	—
2A152	10kr blue (#30)	625.00	*2,250.*
2A153	15kr brown (#31)	625.00	2,250.
2A154	25kr gray lilac (#32)	625.00	—
2A155	50kr brown (#33)	700.00	—

Fine Print

2A156	2kr yellow (#34)	625.00	—
2A157	3kr green (#35)	625.00	—
2A158	5kr red (#36)	625.00	—
2A159	10kr blue (#37)	625.00	*2,250.*
2A160	15kr org brown (#38)	625.00	2,250.
2A161	25kr gray (#39)	725.00	
2A162	50kr brown (#40)	750.00	—

Stamps of Austrian Offices in the Turkish Empire

Canceled in black with circular date stamp with post office name, month and date, with year date

1867-83		*Coarse Print*	
2A163	2s yellow (#1)	57.50	525.00
2A164	3s green (#2)	75.00	475.00
2A165	5s red (#3)	47.50	215.00
2A166	10s blue (#4)	40.00	165.00
2A167	15s brown (#5)	42.50	175.00
2A168	25s gray lilac (#6)	67.50	775.00
2A169	50s brown (#7)	75.00	*4,000.*

Fine Print

2A170	2s yellow (#7C)	1,175.	—
2A171	3s green (#7D)	55.00	350.00
2A172	5s red (#7E)	50.00	225.00
2A173	10s blue (#7F)	40.00	165.00
2A174	15s org brown (#7I)	150.00	850.00
2A175	25s gray lilac (#7J)	275.00	*5,250.*

Use of this cancellation is known beginning in 1880.

PREVESA

Stamps of Lombardy-Venetia

Canceled in black with single circle date stamp with post office name, month and date, without year

1863		*Perf. 14*	
2A176	2s yellow (#15)	275.00	1,000.
2A177	3s green (#16)	225.00	1,150.
2A178	5s rose (#17)	225.00	900.00
2A179	10s blue (#18)	200.00	675.00
2A180	15s yel brn (#19)	275.00	800.00

1864-65		*Perf. 9½*	
2A181	2s yellow (#20)	375.00	1,150.
2A182	3s green (#21)	125.00	550.00
2A183	5s rose (#22)	80.00	400.00
2A184	10s blue (#23)	50.00	200.00
2A185	15s yel brn (#24)	85.00	325.00

Stamps of Austrian Offices in the Turkish Empire

Canceled in black with single circle date stamp with post office name, month and date, without year

1867-83		*Coarse Print*	
2A186	2s yellow (#1)	37.50	450.00
2A187	3s green (#2)	57.50	400.00
2A188	5s red (#3)	27.50	140.00
2A189	10s blue (#4)	20.00	92.50
2A190	15s brown (#5)	24.00	100.00
2A191	25s gray lilac (#6)	50.00	700.00
2A192	50s brown (#7)	57.50	*3,850.*

Fine Print

2A193	2s yellow (#7C)	1,150.	—
2A194	3s green (#7D)	35.00	275.00
2A195	5s red (#7E)	32.50	150.00
2A196	10s blue (#7F)	20.00	87.50
2A197	15s org brown (#7I)	135.00	775.00
2A198	25s gray lilac (#7J)	250.00	*5,000.*

Stamps of Lombardy-Venetia

Canceled in blue with single circle date stamp with post office name, month and date, without year

1863		*Perf. 14*	
2A199	2s yellow (#15)	575.00	2,000.
2A200	3s green (#16)	525.00	2,200.
2A201	5s rose (#17)	525.00	2,000.
2A202	10s blue (#18)	500.00	1,750.
2A203	15s yel brn (#19)	575.00	1,850.

1864-65		*Perf. 9½*	
2A204	2s yellow (#20)	525.00	1,650.
2A205	3s green (#21)	275.00	1,050.
2A206	5s rose (#22)	220.00	875.00
2A207	10s blue (#23)	190.00	675.00
2A208	15s yel brn (#24)	225.00	800.00

Stamps of Austrian Offices in the Turkish Empire

Canceled in black with circular date stamp with post office name, month and date, with year date

1867-83		*Coarse Print*	
2A209	2s yellow (#1)	57.50	525.00
2A210	3s green (#2)	75.00	475.00
2A211	5s red (#3)	47.50	215.00
2A212	10s blue (#4)	40.00	165.00
2A213	15s brown (#5)	42.50	175.00
2A214	25s gray lilac (#6)	67.50	775.00
2A215	50s brown (#7)	75.00	*4,000.*

Fine Print

2A216	2s yellow (#7C)	1,175.	—
2A217	3s green (#7D)	55.00	340.00
2A218	5s red (#7E)	50.00	225.00
2A219	10s blue (#7F)	40.00	165.00
2A220	15s org brown (#7I)	150.00	850.00
2A221	25s gray lilac (#7J)	275.00	*5,250.*

Use of this cancellation is known beginning in 1874.

DULCIGNO / S. GIOVANNI DI MEDUA

Stamps of Austrian Offices in the Turkish Empire

Canceled in black with circular date stamp with post office name, month and date, with year date

1867-83		*Coarse Print*	
2A222	2s yellow (#1)	650.00	2,500.
2A223	3s green (#2)	675.00	2,450.
2A224	5s red (#3)	640.00	2,200.
2A225	10s blue (#4)	40.00	165.00
2A226	15s brown (#5)	625.00	2,150.
2A227	25s gray lilac (#6)	650.00	2,750.
2A228	50s brown (#7)	675.00	*5,750.*

Fine Print

2A229	2s yellow (#7C)	1,750.	—
2A230	3s green (#7D)	650.00	2,350.
2A231	5s red (#7E)	640.00	2,200.
2A232	10s blue (#7F)	625.00	2,150.
2A233	15s org brown (#7I)	725.00	2,800.
2A234	25s gray lilac (#7J)	850.00	*7,250.*

Stamps of Austrian Offices in the Turkish Empire

Canceled in blue with circular date stamp with post office name, month and date, with year date

1867-83		*Coarse Print*	
2A235	2s yellow (#1)	1,150.	*4,250.*
2A236	3s green (#2)	1,150.	*4,000.*
2A237	5s red (#3)	1,150.	*3,900.*
2A238	10s blue (#4)	1,150.	*3,800.*
2A239	15s brown (#5)	1,150.	*3,750.*
2A240	25s gray lilac (#6)	1,150.	*4,375.*
2A241	50s brown (#7)	1,200.	*7,500.*

Fine Print

2A242	2s yellow (#7C)	*2,250.*	—
2A243	3s green (#7D)	1,100.	*4,000.*
2A244	5s red (#7E)	1,150.	*3,900.*
2A245	10s blue (#7F)	1,150.	*3,800.*
2A246	15s org brown (#7I)	1,250.	*4,400.*
2A247	25s gray lilac (#7J)	1,350.	*8,750.*

SAN GIOVANNI DI MEDUA

Stamps of Austrian Offices in the Turkish Empire

Canceled in black with circular date stamp with post office name, month and date, with year date

1867-83		*Coarse Print*	
2A248	2s yellow (#1)	440.00	*1,825.*
2A249	3s green (#2)	450.00	1,750.
2A250	5s red (#3)	425.00	1,500.
2A251	10s blue (#4)	415.00	1,450.
2A252	15s brown (#5)	420.00	1,475.
2A253	25s gray lilac (#6)	450.00	2,100.
2A254	50s brown (#7)	450.00	*5,250.*

Fine Print

2A255	2s yellow (#7C)	1,400.	—
2A256	3s green (#7D)	300.00	1,625.
2A257	5s red (#7E)	285.00	1,500.
2A258	10s blue (#7F)	275.00	1,450.
2A259	15s org brown (#7I)	385.00	2,150.
2A260	25s gray lilac (#7J)	500.00	*6,500.*

Use of this cancellation is known beginning in March, 1881.

SANTI QUARANTA

Stamps of Austrian Offices in the Turkish Empire

Canceled in black with circular date stamp with post office name, month and date, with year date

1867-83		*Coarse Print*	
2A261	2s yellow (#1)	200.00	1,000.
2A262	3s green (#2)	215.00	950.00
2A263	5s red (#3)	185.00	700.00
2A264	10s blue (#4)	175.00	650.00
2A265	15s brown (#5)	180.00	650.00
2A266	25s gray lilac (#6)	200.00	1,250.
2A267	50s brown (#7)	215.00	—

Fine Print

2A268	2s yellow (#7C)	1,300.	—
2A269	3s green (#7D)	200.00	825.00
2A270	5s red (#7E)	190.00	700.00
2A271	10s blue (#7F)	175.00	650.00
2A272	15s org brown (#7I)	290.00	1,325.
2A273	25s gray lilac (#7J)	400.00	*5,750.*

Use of this cancellation is known beginning in March 28, 1870.

Stamps of Austrian Offices in the Turkish Empire

Canceled in black with 23mm circular date stamp with post office name, month and date, with year date

1867-83		*Coarse Print*	
2A274	2s yellow (#1)	300.00	1,325.
2A275	3s green (#2)	325.00	1,250.
2A276	5s red (#3)	285.00	1,000.
2A277	10s blue (#4)	275.00	950.00
2A278	15s brown (#5)	280.00	975.00
2A279	25s gray lilac (#6)	300.00	1,575.
2A280	50s brown (#7)	325.00	—

Fine Print

2A281	2s yellow (#7C)	1,400.	—
2A282	3s green (#7D)	300.00	1,125.
2A283	5s red (#7E)	285.00	1,000.
2A284	10s blue (#7F)	275.00	950.00
2A285	15s org brown (#7I)	385.00	1,625.
2A286	25s gray lilac (#7J)	500.00	*6,000.*

Use of this cancellation is known beginning in November, 1878.

SCUTARI D'ALBANIA

Stamps of Lombardy-Venetia

Canceled in black with "thimble" (diameter 20mm or less) circular date stamp with post office name and date

1864-65		*Perf. 9½*	
2A287	2s yellow (#20)	—	—
2A288	3s green (#21)	—	—
2A289	5s rose (#22)	*3,000.*	—
2A290	10s blue (#23)	*3,000.*	*11,500.*
2A291	15s yel brn (#24)	*3,000.*	—

Stamps of Austrian Offices in the Turkish Empire

Canceled in black with "thimble" circular date stamp with post office name and date

1867-83		*Coarse Print*	
2A292	2s yellow (#1)	1,700.	—
2A293	3s green (#2)	1,750.	—
2A294	5s red (#3)	1,700.	—
2A295	10s blue (#4)	1,700.	*6,250.*
2A296	15s brown (#5)	1,700.	—
2A297	25s gray lilac (#6)	1,700.	—
2A298	50s brown (#7)	1,750.	—

Fine Print

2A299	2s yellow (#7C)	*2,800.*	—
2A300	3s green (#7D)	1,700.	—
2A301	5s red (#7E)	1,700.	—
2A302	10s blue (#7F)	1,700.	*6,250.*
2A303	15s org brown (#7I)	1,800.	—
2A304	25s gray lilac (#7J)	1,950.	—

Also known on Ottoman stamps, and on covers franked with Ottoman stamps.

VALONA

Stamps of Lombardy-Venetia

Canceled in black with single circle date stamp with post office name, month and date, without year

1863		*Perf. 14*	
2A305	2s yellow (#15)	800.00	2,750.
2A306	3s green (#16)	750.00	2,850.
2A307	5s rose (#17)	750.00	1,650.
2A308	10s blue (#18)	700.00	2,400.
2A309	15s yel brn (#19)	800.00	2,500.

1864-65		*Perf. 9½*	
2A310	2s yellow (#20)	625.00	1,950.
2A311	3s green (#21)	375.00	1,350.
2A312	5s rose (#22)	325.00	1,200.
2A313	10s blue (#23)	300.00	1,000.
2A314	15s yel brn (#24)	325.00	1,100.

Stamps of Austrian Offices in the Turkish Empire

Canceled in black or red brown with single circle date stamp with post office name, month and date, without year

1867-83		*Coarse Print*	
2A315	2s yellow (#1)	87.50	650.00
2A316	3s green (#2)	110.00	600.00
2A317	5s red (#3)	77.50	340.00
2A318	10s blue (#4)	70.00	300.00
2A319	15s brown (#5)	75.00	300.00
2A320	25s gray lilac (#6)	100.00	900.00
2A321	50s brown (#7)	110.00	*4,000.*

Fine Print

2A322	2s yellow (#7C)	1,200.	—
2A323	3s green (#7D)	85.00	475.00
2A324	5s red (#7E)	82.50	350.00
2A325	10s blue (#7F)	70.00	290.00
2A326	15s org brown (#7I)	180.00	975.00
2A327	25s gray lilac (#7J)	300.00	*5,250.*

Stamps of Austrian Offices in the Turkish Empire

Canceled in blue with single circle date stamp with post office name, month and date, without year

1867-83		*Coarse Print*	
2A328	2s yellow (#1)	125.00	825.00
2A329	3s green (#2)	150.00	750.00
2A330	5s red (#3)	120.00	500.00
2A331	10s blue (#4)	115.00	450.00
2A332	15s brown (#5)	120.00	475.00
2A333	25s gray lilac (#6)	145.00	1,100.
2A334	50s brown (#7)	150.00	*4,250.*

Fine Print

2A335	2s yellow (#7C)	1,250.	—
2A336	3s green (#7D)	125.00	625.00
2A337	5s red (#7E)	125.00	525.00
2A338	10s blue (#7F)	115.00	450.00
2A339	15s org brown (#7I)	225.00	1,125.
2A340	25s gray lilac (#7J)	350.00	*5,500.*

Stamps of Austrian Offices in the Turkish Empire

Canceled in black with circular date stamp with post office name, month and date, with year date

1867-83		*Coarse Print*	
2A341	2s yellow (#1)	57.50	525.00
2A342	3s green (#2)	75.00	475.00
2A343	5s red (#3)	47.50	215.00
2A344	10s blue (#4)	40.00	165.00
2A345	15s brown (#5)	42.50	175.00
2A346	25s gray lilac (#6)	67.50	775.00
2A347	50s brown (#7)	75.00	*4,000.*

Fine Print

2A348	2s yellow (#7C)	1,175.	—
2A349	3s green (#7D)	55.00	340.00
2A350	5s red (#7E)	50.00	225.00
2A351	10s blue (#7F)	40.00	165.00
2A352	15s org brown (#7I)	150.00	850.00
2A353	25s gray lilac (#7J)	275.00	*5,250.*

GREEK CONSULAR POST IN EPIRUS

The Greek Postal Administration maintained facilities within the consular office at Ioannina, and in the postal agencies at Arta and Preveza.

Post Office	Open	Close
Arta (105)	1852	1881
Ioannina (99)	1852	1881
Preveza (104)	1853	1881

The post office of Arta became a regular Greek post office after annexation of that city on June 24, 1881.

Additional premiums for stamps of Greece with postmarks of the consular office in Epirus. The first column contains values for single stamps or for single stamps on piece; the second, for stamps on cover.

Rhombus of Dots with Numeral

Numeral 99	+25.	+150.
Numeral 104	+650.	*+2,000.*
Numeral 105	+275.	—

Circular Datestamps

Ioannina	+80.	*+375.*
Preveza	+800.	—
Arta (105) (until 6/23/81)	+80.	*+375.*
Arta (105) (after 6/24/81)	+20.	+150.

Greece annexed Arta on June 24, 1881. Greek stamps used from that date on are not "Used in Albania."

Watermarks

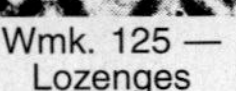

Wmk. 125 — Lozenges

Wmk. 220 — Double Headed Eagle

Issues of 1908 Turkey Stamps Handstamped

Perf. 12, 13½ and Compound

1913, June **Unwmk.**

1	A19	2½pi violet brown	750.00	900.00

With Additional Overprint in Carmine

2	A19	10pa blue green	675.00	650.00

Handstamped on Issue of 1909

4	A21	5pa ocher	450.00	450.00
5	A21	10pa blue green	350.00	225.00
6	A21	20pa car rose	350.00	250.00
7	A21	1pi ultra	325.00	250.00
		On newspaper or wrapper		*450.00*
8	A21	2pi blue black	500.00	450.00
10	A21	5pi dark violet	1,400.	1,500.
11	A21	10pi dull red	*5,000.*	*4,750.*

For surcharge see No. 19.

Additional values of 25pi dark green and 50pi red brown were overprinted and sold only to dealers. Values, 25pi $8,000, 50pi $16,000.

With Additional Overprint in Blue or Carmine

13A	A21	10pa blue green	900.00	850.00
14	A21	20pa car rose (Bl)	800.00	850.00
15	A21	1pi brt blue (C)	1,900.	1,750.

Handstamped on Newspaper Stamp of 1911

17	A21	2pa olive green	425.00	425.00

Handstamped on Postage Due Stamp of 1908

18	A19	1pi black, *dp rose*	3,000.	2,500.

No. 18 was used for regular postage.

No. 6 Surcharged With New Value

19	A21	10pa on 20pa car rose	1,250.	1,250.

The overprint on Nos. 1-19 was handstamped and is found inverted, double, etc.

Nos. 6, 7 and 8 exist with the handstamp in red, blue or violet, but these varieties are not known to have been regularly issued.

A 2pi black was overprinted and sold only to dealers. Values, $3,750 unused, $3,250 used.

A 2pa on 5pa newspaper stamp and a 2pi postage due stamp exist with the handstamp, but these are not known to have been regularly issued. Values, $1,800 and $725, respectively.

Covers: Commercial covers of Nos. 1-19 are very scarce.

Excellent counterfeits exist of Nos. 1 to 19.

A1

Handstamped on White Laid Paper Without Eagle and Value Issued Without Gum

1913, July ***Imperf.***

20	A1	(1pi) black	325.00	*525.00*
		Cut to shape	190.00	*275.00*
	a.	Sewing machine perf.	575.00	*725.00*

Value Typewritten in Violet Issued Without Gum

1913, Aug. **With Eagle**

21	A1	10pa violet	12.00	12.00
	a.	Double impression	—	—
22	A1	20pa red & black	16.00	13.50
	a.	"2p para"	—	—
23	A1	1gr black	16.00	16.00
24	A1	2gr blue & violet	20.00	16.00
25	A1	5gr violet & blue	24.00	21.00
26	A1	10gr blue	24.00	21.00
		Nos. 21-26 (6)	112.00	99.50

Nos. 21-26 exist with the eagle inverted or omitted and with numerous errors in the figures of value and the spelling of the word "grosh."

A2

Handstamped on White Laid Paper Eagle and Value in Black Issued Without Gum

1913, Nov. ***Perf. 11½***

27	A2	10pa green	4.00	3.25
	b.	Eagle and value in green	1,750.	1,750.
	c.	10pa red (error)	32.50	32.50
	d.	10pa violet (error)	32.50	32.50
29	A2	20pa red	6.00	4.75
	b.	20pa green (error)	42.50	32.50
30	A2	30pa violet	6.00	4.75
	a.	30pa ultramarine (error)	32.50	32.50
	b.	30pa red (error)	32.50	32.50
31	A2	1gr ultramarine	8.00	7.25
	a.	1gr green (error)	32.50	32.50
	b.	1gr black (error)	32.50	32.50
	c.	1gr violet (error)	32.50	32.50
33	A2	2gr black	12.00	8.00
	a.	2gr violet (error)	40.00	40.00
	b.	2gr blue (error)	40.00	40.00
		Nos. 27-33 (5)	36.00	28.00

The stamps of this issue are known with eagle or value inverted or omitted.

1st anniv. of Albanian independence.

Counterfeits exist.

Skanderbeg (George Castriota) — A3

1913, Dec. **Typo.** ***Perf. 14***

35	A3	2q orange brn & buff	3.50	1.75
36	A3	5q green & blue grn	3.50	1.75
37	A3	10q rose red	3.50	1.75
38	A3	25q dark blue	3.50	1.75
39	A3	50q violet & red	8.50	3.50
40	A3	1fr deep brown	20.00	10.50
		Nos. 35-40 (6)	42.50	*21.00*

For overprints and surcharges see Nos. 41-52, 105, J1-J9.

Nos. 35-40 Handstamped in Black or Violet

1914, Mar. 7

41	A3	2q orange brn & buff	50.00	*65.00*
42	A3	5q grn & bl grn (V)	50.00	*65.00*
43	A3	10q rose red	50.00	*65.00*
44	A3	25q dark blue (V)	50.00	*65.00*
45	A3	50q violet & red	50.00	*65.00*
46	A3	1fr deep brown	50.00	*65.00*
		Nos. 41-46 (6)	300.00	390.00

Issued to celebrate the arrival of Prince Wilhelm zu Wied on Mar. 7, 1914.

Nos. 35-40 Surcharged in Black

a

b

1914, Apr. 2

47	A3 (a)	5pa on 2q	2.10	2.10
48	A3 (a)	10pa on 5q	2.10	2.10
49	A3 (a)	20pa on 10q	3.50	2.75
50	A3 (b)	1gr on 25q	3.50	3.50
51	A3 (b)	2gr on 50q	3.50	3.50
52	A3 (b)	5gr on 1fr	14.00	10.50
		Nos. 47-52 (6)	28.70	24.45

For overprints see Nos. 105, J6-J9.

Inverted Surcharge

47a	A3 (a)	5pa on 2q	24.00	24.00
48a	A3 (a)	10pa on 5q	22.50	22.50
49a	A3 (a)	20pa on 10q	24.00	24.00
50a	A3 (b)	1gr on 25q	24.00	24.00
51a	A3 (b)	2gr on 50q	28.00	28.00
52b	A3 (b)	5gr on 1fr	90.00	90.00
		Nos. 47a-52b (6)	212.50	212.50

Korce (Korytsa) Issues

A4

1914 **Handstamped** ***Imperf.***

52A	A4	10pa violet & red	200.00	200.00
	c.	10pa black & red	325.00	325.00
53	A4	25pa violet & red	200.00	200.00
	a.	25pa black & red	425.00	425.00

Nos. 52A-53a were handstamped directly on the cover, so the paper varies. They were also produced in sheets; these are rarely found. Nos. 52A-53a were issued by Albanian military authorities.

Counterfeits exists of Nos. 52A and 53.

A5

1917 **Typo. & Litho.** ***Perf. 11½***

54	A5	1c dk brown & grn	17.50	12.00
55	A5	2c red & green	17.50	12.00
56	A5	3c gray grn & grn	17.50	12.00
57	A5	5c green & black	16.00	8.00
58	A5	10c rose red & black	16.00	8.00
59	A5	25c blue & black	16.00	8.00
60	A5	50c violet & black	16.00	10.00
61	A5	1fr brown & black	16.00	10.00
		Nos. 54-61 (8)	132.50	80.00

A6

1917-18

62	A6	1c dk brown & grn	2.75	2.40
63	A6	2c red brown & grn	2.75	2.40
	a.	"CTM" for "CTS"	72.50	120.00
64	A6	3c black & green	2.75	2.40
	a.	"CTM" for "CTS"	80.00	135.00
65	A6	5c green & black	4.00	4.00
66	A6	10c dull red & black	4.00	4.00
67	A6	50c violet & black	7.25	6.50
68	A6	1fr red brn & black	20.00	17.50
		Nos. 62-68 (7)	43.50	39.20

Counterfeits abound of Nos. 54-68, 80-81.

No. 65 Surcharged in Red

1918

80	A6	25c on 5c green & blk	275.00	*325.00*

A7

1918

81	A7	25c blue & black	72.50	95.00

General Issue

A8

A9

Handstamped in Rose or Blue

XV I MCMXIX

1919 ***Perf. 12½***

84	A8	(2)q on 2h brown	7.50	7.50
85	A8	5q on 16h green	7.50	7.50
86	A8	10q on 8h rose (Bl)	7.50	7.50
87	A8	25q on 64h blue	8.50	8.50
88	A9	25q on 64h blue	*300.00*	*300.00*
89	A8	50q on 32h violet	7.50	7.50
90	A8	1fr on 1.28k org, *bl*	9.00	9.00
		Nos. 84-90 (7)	*347.50*	*347.50*

See Nos. J10-J13. Compare with types A10-A14. For overprints see Nos 91-104.

Handstamped in Rose or Blue

1919, Jan. 16

No.	Type	Description	Unused	Used
91	A8	(2)q on 2h brown	14.00	14.00
92	A8	5q on 16h green	10.50	10.50
93	A8	10q on 8h rose (Bl)	10.50	10.50
94	A8	25q on 64h blue	140.00	140.00
95	A9	25q on 64h blue	45.00	60.00
96	A8	50q on 32h violet	14.00	14.00
97	A8	1fr on 1.28k org, *bl*	14.00	14.00
		Nos. 91-97 (7)	248.00	263.00

Handstamped in Violet

1919

No.	Type	Description	Unused	Used
98	A8	(2)q on 2h brown	17.50	17.50
99	A8	5q on 16h green	17.50	17.50
100	A8	10q on 8h rose	17.50	17.50
101	A8	25q on 64h blue	17.50	17.50
102	A9	25q on 64h blue	140.00	140.00
103	A8	50q on 32h violet	17.50	17.50
104	A8	1fr on 1.28k org, *bl*	17.50	17.50
		Nos. 98-104 (7)	245.00	245.00

No. 50 Overprinted in Violet

1919 ***Perf. 14***

No.	Type	Description	Unused	Used
105	A3	1gr on 25q blue	32.50	25.00

A10

A11

1919, June 5 ***Perf. 11½, 12½***

No.	Type	Description	Unused	Used
106	A10	10q on 2h brown	7.00	7.00
107	A11	15q on 8h rose	7.00	7.00
108	A11	20q on 16h green	7.00	7.00
109	A10	25q on 64h blue	7.00	7.00
110	A11	50q on 32h violet	7.00	7.00
111	A11	1fr on 96h orange	7.00	7.00
112	A10	2fr on 1.60k vio, *buff*	25.00	21.00
		Nos. 106-112 (7)	67.00	63.00

Nos. 106-108, 110 exist with inverted surcharge.

A12 A13

Surcharged in Black or Violet

1919

No.	Type	Description	Unused	Used
113	A12	10q on 8h car	7.00	7.00
114	A12	15q on 8h car (V)	7.00	7.00
115	A13	20q on 16h green	7.00	7.00
116	A13	25q on 32h violet	7.00	7.00
117	A13	50q on 64h blue	20.00	14.00
118	A13	1fr on 96h orange	8.50	7.00
119	A12	2fr on 1.60k vio, *buff*	14.00	10.50
		Nos. 113-119 (7)	70.50	59.50

A14

Overprinted in Blue or Black Without New Value

1920 ***Perf. 12½***

No.	Type	Description	Unused	Used
120	A14	1q gray (Bl)	100.00	95.00
121	A14	10q rose (Bk)	14.00	*32.50*
a.		Double overprint	150.00	*150.00*
122	A14	20q brown (Bl)	45.00	40.00
123	A14	25q blue (Bk)	525.00	*600.00*
124	A14	50q brown vio (Bk)	60.00	*80.00*
		Nos. 120-124 (5)	744.00	*847.50*

Counterfeit overprints exist of Nos. 120-128.

Surcharged in Black with New Value

No.	Type	Description	Unused	Used
125	A14	2q on 10q rose (R)	14.00	*21.00*
126	A14	5q on 10q rose (G)	14.00	*17.50*
127	A14	25q on 10q rose (Bl)	14.00	*21.00*
128	A14	50q on 10q rose (Br)	14.00	*35.00*
		Nos. 125-128 (4)	56.00	94.50

Stamps of type A14 (Portrait of the Prince zu Wied) were not placed in use without overprint or surcharge.

A15

Post Horn Overprinted in Black

1920 ***Perf. 14x13***

No.	Type	Description	Unused	Used
129	A15	2q orange	10.50	8.50
130	A15	5q deep green	17.50	15.00
131	A15	10q red	32.50	32.50
132	A15	25q light blue	55.00	30.00
133	A15	50q gray green	12.50	10.50
134	A15	1fr claret	12.50	10.50
		Nos. 129-134 (6)	140.50	107.00

Type A15 was never placed in use without post horn or "Besa" overprint.

Stamps of Type A15 (No Post Horn) Overprinted

1921

No.	Type	Description	Unused	Used
135	A15	2q orange	7.00	7.00
136	A15	5q deep green	7.00	7.00
137	A15	10q red	14.00	12.00
138	A15	25q light blue	25.00	21.00
139	A15	50q gray green	14.00	12.00
140	A15	1fr claret	14.00	12.00
		Nos. 135-140 (6)	81.00	71.00

For surcharge & overprints see Nos. 154, 156-157.

Stamps of these types, and with "TAKSE" overprint, were unauthorized and never placed in use. They are common.

Gjirokaster
A18

Korcha
A19

Designs: 5q, Kanina. 10q, Berati. 25q, Bridge at Vezirit. 50q, Rozafat. 2fr, Dursit.

1923 **Typo.** ***Perf. 12½, 11½***

No.	Type	Description	Unused	Used
147	A18	2q orange	.70	*1.40*
148	A18	5q yellow green	.70	*1.10*
149	A18	10q carmine	.70	*1.10*
150	A18	25q dark blue	.70	*1.10*
151	A18	50q dark green	.70	*1.10*
152	A19	1fr dark violet	.70	*2.75*
153	A19	2fr olive green	4.25	*7.00*
		Nos. 147-153 (7)	8.45	*15.55*

For overprints & surcharges see Nos. 158-185, B1-B8.

No. 135 Surcharged

1922 ***Perf. 14x13***

No.	Type	Description	Unused	Used
154	A15	1q on 2q orange	3.25	*8.50*

Stamps of Type A15 (No Post Horn) Overprinted

1922

No.	Type	Description	Unused	Used
156	A15	5q deep green	5.00	*8.00*
157	A15	10q red	5.00	*8.00*

Nos. 147-151 Ovptd. in Black and Violet

1924, Jan. ***Perf. 12½***

No.	Type	Description	Unused	Used
158	A18	2q red orange	10.00	*20.00*
159	A18	5q yellow green	10.00	*20.00*
160	A18	10q carmine	7.50	*14.50*
161	A18	25q dark blue	7.50	*14.50*
162	A18	50q dark green	11.50	*20.00*
		Nos. 158-162 (5)	46.50	89.00

The words "Mbledhje Kushtetuese" are in taller letters on the 25q than on the other values. Opening of the Constituent Assembly.

Counterfeits of Nos. 158 and 161 are plentiful.

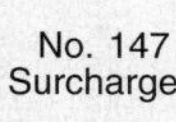

No. 147 Surcharged

1924

No.	Type	Description	Unused	Used
163	A18	1q on 2q red orange	3.00	*8.00*

Nos. 163, 147-152 Overprinted

1924

No.	Type	Description	Unused	Used
164	A18	1q on 2q orange	2.75	*7.25*
165	A18	2q orange	2.75	*7.25*
166	A18	5q yellow green	2.75	*7.25*
167	A18	10q carmine	2.75	*7.25*
168	A18	25q dark blue	2.75	*7.25*
169	A18	50q dark green	6.25	*14.00*
170	A19	1fr dark violet	6.25	*17.50*
		Nos. 164-170 (7)	26.25	*67.75*

Issued to celebrate the return of the Government to the Capital after a revolution.

Nos. 163, 147-152 Overprinted

1925

No.	Type	Description	Unused	Used
171	A18	1q on 2q orange	3.25	*8.00*
172	A18	2q orange	3.25	*8.00*
173	A18	5q yellow green	3.25	*8.00*
174	A18	10q carmine	3.25	*8.00*
175	A18	25q dark blue	3.25	*8.00*
176	A18	50q dark green	3.25	*12.00*
177	A19	1fr dark violet	6.25	*16.00*
		Nos. 171-177 (7)	25.75	*68.00*

Proclamation of the Republic, Jan. 21, 1925. The date "1921" instead of "1925" occurs once in each sheet of 50.

Counterfeits exist.

Nos. 163, 147-153 Overprinted

1925

No.	Type	Description	Unused	Used
178	A18	1q on 2q orange	1.10	*1.60*
a.		Inverted overprint	12.50	12.50
179	A18	2q orange	1.10	*1.60*
180	A18	5q yellow green	1.10	*1.60*
a.		Inverted overprint	12.50	12.50
181	A18	10q carmine	1.10	*1.60*
182	A18	25q dark blue	1.10	*1.60*
183	A18	50q dark green	1.10	*1.60*
184	A19	1fr dark violet	5.00	*4.00*
185	A19	2fr olive green	7.50	*4.00*
		Nos. 178-185 (8)	19.10	17.60

Counterfeits exist.

President Ahmed Zogu
A25 A26

1925 ***Perf. 13½, 13½x13***

No.	Type	Description	Unused	Used
186	A25	1q orange	.25	.25
187	A25	2q red brown	.25	2.00
188	A25	5q green	.25	.25
189	A25	10q rose red	.25	.25
190	A25	15q gray brown	.75	*2.00*
191	A25	25q dark blue	.25	.25
192	A25	50q blue green	.85	*1.50*
193	A26	1fr red & ultra	1.75	2.00
194	A26	2fr green & orange	1.90	*2.00*
195	A26	3fr brown & violet	4.00	*5.00*
196	A26	5fr violet & black	4.50	6.75
		Nos. 186-196 (11)	15.00	22.25

No. 193 in ultramarine and brown, and No. 194 in green and brown were not regularly issued. Value, set $15.

For overprints & surcharges see Nos. 197-209, 238-248.

Nos. 186-196 Overprinted in Various Colors

1927

No.	Type	Description	Unused	Used
197	A25	1q orange (V)	.60	1.00
198	A25	2q red brn (G)	.25	.30
199	A25	5q green (R)	1.25	.50
200	A25	10q rose red (Bl)	.25	.30
201	A25	15q gray brn (G)	7.00	*14.00*
202	A25	25q dk blue (R)	.50	.40
203	A25	50q blue grn (Bl)	.50	.40
204	A26	1fr red & ultra (Bk)	1.40	*.55*
205	A26	2fr green & org (Bk)	1.50	*.80*
206	A26	3fr brown & vio (Bk)	2.40	*1.60*
207	A26	5fr violet & blk (Bk)	3.50	*2.75*
		Nos. 197-207 (11)	19.15	22.60

No. 200 exists perf. 11.

For surcharges see Nos. 208-209, 238-240.

Nos. 200, 202 Surcharged in Black or Red

1928

No.	Type	Description	Unused	Used
208	A25	1q on 10q rose red	.50	.55
a.		Inverted surcharge	4.00	4.00
209	A25	5q on 25q dk blue (R)	.50	.55
a.		Inverted surcharge	4.00	4.00

A27

King Zog I — A28

Black Overprint

1928 *Perf. 14x13½*

No.	Type	Description	Unused	Used
210	A27	1q orange brown	5.00	*9.50*
211	A27	2q slate	5.00	*9.50*
212	A27	5q blue green	5.00	*12.00*
213	A27	10q rose red	4.00	*12.00*
214	A27	15q bister	15.00	*47.50*
215	A27	25q deep blue	6.00	*12.00*
216	A27	50q lilac rose	10.00	*15.00*

Red Overprint

Perf. 13½x14

No.	Type	Description	Unused	Used
217	A28	1fr blue & slate	10.00	12.00
		Nos. 210-217 (8)	60.00	*129.50*

Compare with types A29-A32.

A29

A30

Black or Red Overprint

1928 *Perf. 14x13½*

No.	Type	Description	Unused	Used
218	A29	1q orange brown	12.50	*25.00*
219	A29	2q slate (R)	12.50	*25.00*
220	A29	5q blue green	10.00	*20.00*
221	A29	10q rose red	10.00	*16.00*
222	A29	15q bister	15.00	*27.50*
223	A29	25q deep blue (R)	10.00	*16.00*
224	A29	50q lilac rose	10.00	*16.00*

Perf. 13½x14

No.	Type	Description	Unused	Used
225	A30	1fr blue & slate (R)	12.50	*20.00*
226	A30	2fr green & slate (R)	12.50	*20.00*
		Nos. 218-226 (9)	105.00	185.50

Proclamation of Ahmed Zogu as King of Albania.

A31

A32

Black Overprint

1928 *Perf. 14x13½*

No.	Type	Description	Unused	Used
227	A31	1q orange brown	.40	*1.25*
228	A31	2q slate	.40	*1.25*
229	A31	5q blue green	2.75	*3.50*
230	A31	10q rose red	.40	*1.25*
231	A31	15q bister	15.00	*24.00*
232	A31	25q deep blue	.40	*1.25*
233	A31	50q lilac rose	.75	*2.00*

Perf. 13½x14

No.	Type	Description	Unused	Used
234	A32	1fr blue & slate	1.50	*2.50*
235	A32	2fr green & slate	1.50	*4.00*
236	A32	3fr dk red & ol bis	7.50	*12.00*
237	A32	5fr dull vio & gray	7.50	*16.00*
		Nos. 227-237 (11)	38.10	69.00

The overprint reads "Kingdom of Albania."

Nos. 203, 202, 200 Surcharged in Black

1929 *Perf. 13½x13, 11½*

No.	Type	Description	Unused	Used
238	A25	1q on 50q blue green	.40	*.55*
239	A25	5q on 25q dark blue	.40	*.55*
240	A25	15q on 10q rose red	.60	*1.00*
		Nos. 238-240 (3)	1.40	2.10

Nos. 186-189, 191-194 Overprinted in Black or Red

1929 *Perf. 11½, 13½*

No.	Type	Description	Unused	Used
241	A25	1q orange	7.50	*20.00*
242	A25	2q red brown	7.50	*20.00*
243	A25	5q green	7.50	*20.00*
244	A25	10q rose red	7.50	*20.00*
245	A25	25q dark blue	7.50	*20.00*
246	A25	50q blue green (R)	10.00	*24.00*
247	A26	1fr red & ultra	14.00	*35.00*
248	A26	2fr green & orange	14.00	*35.00*
		Nos. 241-248 (8)	75.50	194.00

34th birthday of King Zog. The overprint reads "Long live the King."

Lake Butrinto — A33

King Zog I — A34

Zog Bridge — A35

Ruin at Zog Manor A36

Perf. 14, 14½

1930, Sept. 1 **Photo.** **Wmk. 220**

No.	Type	Description	Unused	Used
250	A33	1q slate	.25	.25
251	A33	2q orange red	.25	.25
252	A34	5q yellow green	.25	.25
253	A34	10q carmine	.25	.25
254	A34	15q dark brown	.25	.25
255	A34	25q dark ultra	.25	.25
256	A33	50q slate green	.70	.55
257	A35	1fr violet	1.10	1.00
258	A35	2fr indigo	1.50	1.10
259	A36	3fr gray green	3.50	2.25
260	A36	5fr orange brown	4.50	3.50
		Nos. 250-260 (11)	12.80	9.90

2nd anniversary of accession of King Zog I.

For overprints see Nos. 261-270, 299-309, J39. For surcharges see Nos. 354-360 in *Scott Standard Postage Stamp Catalogue*, Vol. 1.

Nos. 250-259 Overprinted in Black

1934, Dec. 24

No.	Type	Description	Unused	Used
261	A33	1q slate	8.50	*12.00*
262	A33	2q orange red	8.50	*12.00*
263	A34	5q yellow green	8.50	9.50
264	A34	10q carmine	9.25	*12.00*
265	A34	15q dark brown	9.25	*12.00*
266	A34	25q dark ultra	9.25	*12.00*
267	A33	50q slate green	10.00	*16.00*
268	A35	1fr violet	11.00	*20.00*
269	A35	2fr indigo	12.00	*25.00*
270	A36	3fr gray green	15.00	*35.00*
		Nos. 261-270 (10)	101.25	165.50

Tenth anniversary of the Constitution.

Allegory of Death of Skanderbeg A37

Albanian Eagle in Turkish Shackles A38

5q, 25q, 40q, 2fr, Eagle with wings spread.

1937 **Unwmk.** **Perf. 14**

No.	Type	Description	Unused	Used
271	A37	1q brown violet	.25	.25
272	A38	2q brown	.50	.35
273	A38	5q lt green	.50	.50
274	A37	10q olive brown	.50	*.80*
275	A38	15q rose red	.80	*1.00*
276	A38	25q blue	1.50	*2.00*
277	A37	50q deep green	3.75	3.25
278	A38	1fr violet	9.00	6.00
279	A38	2fr orange brown	12.00	9.00
		Nos. 271-279 (9)	28.80	23.15

Souvenir Sheet

No.	Type	Description	Unused	Used
280		Sheet of 3	17.50	*150.00*
a.		A37 20q red violet	3.50	*6.25*
b.		A38 30q olive brown	3.50	*6.25*
c.		A38 40q red	3.50	*6.25*

25th anniv. of independence from Turkey, proclaimed Nov. 26, 1912.

Queen Geraldine and King Zog — A40

1938 **Perf. 14**

No.	Type	Description	Unused	Used
281	A40	1q slate violet	.30	.40
282	A40	2q red brown	.30	.40
283	A40	5q green	.30	.40
284	A40	10q olive brown	1.10	.80
285	A40	15q rose red	1.10	.80
286	A40	25q blue	2.75	2.00
287	A40	50q Prus green	5.75	4.00
288	A40	1fr purple	11.50	8.00
		Nos. 281-288 (8)	23.10	16.80

Souvenir Sheet

No.	Type	Description	Unused	Used
289		Sheet of 4	32.50	*125.00*
a.		A40 20q dark red violet	7.75	*9.75*
b.		A40 30q brown olive	7.75	*9.75*

Wedding of King Zog and Countess Geraldine Apponyi, Apr. 27, 1938.

No. 289 contains 2 each of Nos. 289a, 289b.

Queen Geraldine — A42

National Emblems — A43

Designs: 10q, 25q, 30q, 1fr, King Zog.

1938

No.	Type	Description	Unused	Used
290	A42	1q dp red violet	.25	*.55*
291	A43	2q red orange	.25	*.55*
292	A42	5q deep green	.50	.50
293	A42	10q red brown	.50	*1.00*
294	A42	15q deep rose	1.00	*1.25*
295	A42	25q deep blue	1.40	1.40
296	A43	50q gray black	8.50	6.00
297	A42	1fr slate green	12.50	9.00
		Nos. 290-297 (8)	24.90	20.25

Souvenir Sheet

No.	Type	Description	Unused	Used
298		Sheet of 3	22.50	*75.00*
b.		A43 20q Prussian green	7.00	*12.00*
c.		A42 30q deep violet	7.00	*12.00*

10th anniv. of royal rule. They were on sale for 3 days (Aug. 30-31, Sept. 1) only, during which their use was required on all mail.

No. 298 contains Nos. 294, 298b, 298c.

Issued under Italian Dominion

Nos. 250-260 Overprinted in Black

1939 **Wmk. 220** **Perf. 14**

No.	Type	Description	Unused	Used
299	A33	1q slate	1.25	*1.25*
		Never hinged	3.25	
300	A33	2q orange red	1.25	*1.25*
		Never hinged	3.25	
301	A34	5q yellow green	1.25	*1.25*
		Never hinged	3.25	
302	A34	10q carmine	1.25	*1.25*
		Never hinged	3.25	
303	A34	15q dark brown	2.00	*3.75*
		Never hinged	4.75	
304	A34	25q dark ultra	2.00	*3.75*
		Never hinged	4.75	
305	A33	50q slate green	2.50	*5.00*
		Never hinged	6.50	
306	A35	1fr violet	2.50	*5.00*
		Never hinged	6.50	
307	A35	2fr indigo	3.25	*9.50*
		Never hinged	8.00	
308	A36	3fr gray green	7.75	*22.50*
		Never hinged	19.00	
309	A36	5fr orange brown	10.00	*25.00*
		Never hinged	24.00	
		Nos. 299-309 (11)	35.00	79.50
		Set, on overfranked philatelic cover		160.00

Resolution adopted by the Natl. Assembly, Apr. 12, 1939, offering the Albanian Crown to Italy.

A46

A47

Native Costumes — A48

King Victor Emmanuel III A49 A50

Native Costume — A51

Monastery A52

Designs: 2fr, Bridge at Vezirit. 3fr, Ancient Columns. 5fr, Amphitheater.

1939 **Unwmk.** **Photo.** **Perf. 14**

No.	Type	Description	Unused	Used
310	A46	1q blue gray	1.25	.50
		Never hinged	3.25	
311	A47	2q olive green	1.25	.50
		Never hinged	3.25	
312	A48	3q golden brown	1.25	.50
		Never hinged	3.25	
313	A49	5q green	1.25	.25
		Never hinged	3.25	
314	A50	10q brown	1.25	.25
		Never hinged	3.25	
315	A50	15q crimson	1.25	.25
		Never hinged	3.25	
316	A50	25q sapphire	2.00	.80
		Never hinged	4.75	
317	A50	30q brt violet	2.50	1.40
		Never hinged	6.50	
318	A51	50q dull purple	3.25	3.25
		Never hinged	8.00	
319	A49	65q red brown	5.00	11.50
		Never hinged	13.00	
320	A52	1fr myrtle green	7.50	9.50
		Never hinged	19.00	
321	A52	2fr brown lake	11.50	19.00
		Never hinged	29.00	

322 A52 3fr brown black 19.00 35.00
Never hinged 47.50
323 A52 5fr gray violet 25.00 *50.00*
Never hinged 65.00
Nos. 310-323 (14) 83.25 132.70
Set, on overfranked philatelic cover 275.00

For overprints and surcharges see Nos. 331-353 in *Scott Standard Postage Stamp Catalogue*, Vol. 1.

SEMI-POSTAL STAMPS

Nos. 148-151 Surcharged in Red and Black

1924, Nov. 1
B1 A18 5q + 5q yel grn 11.00 *30.00*
B2 A18 10q + 5q carmine 11.00 *30.00*
B3 A18 25q + 5q dark blue 11.00 *30.00*
B4 A18 50q + 5q dark grn 11.00 *30.00*
Nos. B1-B4 (4) 44.00 *120.00*

Nos. B1 to B4 with Additional Surcharge in Red and Black

1924
B5 A18 5q + 5q + 5q yel grn 11.00 26.00
B6 A18 10q + 5q + 5q car 11.00 26.00
B7 A18 25q + 5q + 5q dk bl 11.00 26.00
B8 A18 50q + 5q + 5q dk grn 11.00 26.00
Nos. B5-B8 (4) 44.00 *104.00*

AIR POST STAMPS

Airplane Crossing Mountains AP1

Wmk. 125

1925, May 30 **Typo.** ***Perf. 14***
C1 AP1 5q green 2.25 *3.50*
C2 AP1 10q rose red 2.25 *3.50*
C3 AP1 25q deep blue 2.25 *3.50*
C4 AP1 50q dark green 3.50 *6.00*
C5 AP1 1fr dk vio & blk 6.25 *10.50*
C6 AP1 2fr ol grn & vio 10.50 *17.50*
C7 AP1 3fr brn org & dk grn 12.50 *17.50*
Nos. C1-C7 (7) 39.50 *62.00*

Nos. C1-C7 exist imperf. Value $3,000.
For overprint see Nos. C8-C28.

Nos. C1-C7 Overprinted

1927, Jan. 18
C8 AP1 5q green 5.25 *10.50*
a. Dbl. overprint, one invtd. 50.00
C9 AP1 10q rose red 5.25 *10.50*
a. Inverted overprint 45.00
b. Dbl. overprint, one invtd. 50.00
C10 AP1 25q deep blue 4.75 *9.50*
C11 AP1 50q dark grn 3.25 *6.50*
a. Inverted overprint 45.00
C12 AP1 1fr dk vio & blk 3.25 *6.50*
a. Inverted overprint 45.00
b. Double overprint 45.00
C13 AP1 2fr ol grn & vio 7.50 *10.50*
C14 AP1 3fr brn org & dk grn 10.50 *15.00*
Nos. C8-C14 (7) 39.75 *69.00*

Nos. C1-C7 Overprinted

1928, Apr. 21
C15 AP1 5q green 5.25 *10.50*
a. Inverted overprint 70.00
C16 AP1 10q rose red 5.25 *10.50*
C17 AP1 25q deep blue 5.25 *10.50*
C18 AP1 50q dark green 10.00 *21.00*
C19 AP1 1fr dk vio & blk 55.00 *110.00*
C20 AP1 2fr ol grn & vio 55.00 *110.00*
C21 AP1 3fr brn org & dk grn 55.00 *110.00*
Nos. C15-C21 (7) 190.75 *382.50*

First flight across the Adriatic, Valona to Brindisi, Apr. 21, 1928.

The variety "SHQYRTARE" occurs once in the sheet for each value. Value 3 times normal.

Nos. C1-C7 Overprinted in Red Brown

1929, Dec. 1
C22 AP1 5q green 6.00 *8.75*
C23 AP1 10q rose red 6.00 *8.75*
C24 AP1 25q deep blue 6.00 *8.75*
C25 AP1 50q dk grn 125.00 *175.00*
C26 AP1 1fr dk vio & blk 225.00 *350.00*
C27 AP1 2fr ol grn 225.00 *350.00*
C28 AP1 3fr brn org & dk grn 225.00 *350.00*
Nos. C22-C28 (7) 818.00 *1,251.*

Excellent counterfeits exist.

King Zog and Airplane over Tirana AP2

AP3

1930, Oct. 8 **Photo.** **Unwmk.**
C29 AP2 5q yellow green 1.00 *1.75*
C30 AP2 15q rose red 1.00 *1.75*
C31 AP2 20q slate blue 1.00 *1.75*
C32 AP2 50q olive green 2.00 *2.75*
C33 AP3 1fr dark blue 3.00 *5.25*
C34 AP3 2fr olive brown 10.00 *17.50*
C35 AP3 3fr purple 22.50 *17.50*
Nos. C29-C35 (7) 40.50 *48.25*

For overprints and surcharges see Nos. C36-C45.

Nos. C29-C35 Overprinted

1931, July 6
C36 AP2 5q yellow grn 5.25 *10.50*
a. Double overprint 140.00
C37 AP2 15q rose red 5.25 *10.50*
C38 AP2 20q slate blue 5.25 *10.50*
C39 AP2 50q olive grn 5.25 *10.50*
C40 AP3 1fr dark blue 30.00 *60.00*
C41 AP3 2fr olive brn 30.00 *60.00*
C42 AP3 3fr purple 30.00 *60.00*
a. Inverted overprint 275.00
Nos. C36-C42 (7) 111.00 *222.00*

1st air post flight from Tirana to Rome.

Only a very small part of this issue was sold to the public. Most of the stamps were given to the Aviation Company to help provide funds for conducting the service.

Issued under Italian Dominion

Nos. C29-C30 Overprinted in Black

1939, Apr. 19 **Unwmk.** ***Perf. 14***
C43 AP2 5q yel green 2.50 *7.00*
Never hinged 6.50
C44 AP2 15q rose red 2.50 *7.00*
Never hinged 6.50

No. C32 With Additional Surcharge

C45 AP2 20q on 50q ol grn 5.00 *11.50*
Never hinged 13.00
a. Inverted overprint — —
Nos. C43-C45 (3) 10.00 *25.50*
Set on flown cover 95.00

See note after No. 309.

King Victor Emmanuel III and Plane over Mountains AP4

1939, Aug. 4 **Photo.**
C46 AP4 20q brown 32.50 15.00
Never hinged 80.00
On commercial cover 40.00

Shepherds AP5

Map of Albania Showing Air Routes — AP6

Designs: 20q, Victor Emmanuel III and harbor view. 50q, Woman and river valley. 1fr, Bridge at Vezirit. 2fr, Ruins. 3fr, Women waving to plane.

1940, Mar. 20 **Unwmk.**
C47 AP5 5q green 1.25 *1.25*
Never hinged 3.25
C48 AP6 15q rose red 1.25 *1.90*
Never hinged 3.25
C49 AP5 20q deep blue 2.50 *3.25*
Never hinged 3.25
C50 AP6 50q brown 3.25 *9.50*
Never hinged 8.00
C51 AP5 1fr myrtle green 6.50 *12.50*
Never hinged 8.00
C52 AP6 2fr brown black 9.50 *19.00*
Never hinged 24.00
C53 AP6 3fr rose violet 16.00 *25.00*
Never hinged 40.00
Nos. C47-C53 (7) 40.25 *72.40*
Set on overfranked philatelic cover 175.00

SPECIAL DELIVERY STAMPS

Issued under Italian Dominion

King Victor Emmanuel III — SD1

1940 **Unwmk.** **Photo.** ***Perf. 14***
E1 SD1 25q bright violet 4.50 *7.50*
Never hinged 11.00
E2 SD1 50q red orange 11.50 *18.00*
Never hinged 29.00
Set on overfranked philatelic cover 55.00

POSTAGE DUE STAMPS

Nos. 35-39 Handstamped in Various Colors

1914, Feb. 23 **Unwmk.** ***Perf. 14***
J1 A3 2q org brn & buff (Bl) 10.50 4.50
J2 A3 5q green (R) 10.50 4.50
J3 A3 10q rose red (Bl) 15.00 4.50
J4 A3 25q dark blue (R) 17.50 4.50
J5 A3 50q vio & red (Bk) 26.00 14.00
Nos. J1-J5 (5) 79.50 32.00

The two parts of the overprint are handstamped separately. Stamps exist with one or both handstamps inverted, double, omitted or in wrong color.

Nos. 48-51 Overprinted in Black

1914, Apr. 16
J6 A3 (a) 10pa on 5q green 5.25 4.50
J7 A3 (a) 20pa on 10q rose red 5.25 4.50
J8 A3 (b) 1gr on 25q blue 5.25 4.50
J9 A3 (b) 2gr on 50q vio & red 5.25 4.50
Nos. J6-J9 (4) 21.00 18.00

Same Design as Regular Issue of 1919, Overprinted

1919, Feb. 10 ***Perf. 11½, 12½***
J10 A8 (4)q on 4h rose 13.00 10.50
J11 A8 (10)q on 10k red, *grn* 13.00 10.50
J12 A8 20q on 2k org, *gray* 13.00 10.50
J13 A8 50q on 5k brn, *yel* 13.00 10.50
Nos. J10-J13 (4) 52.00 42.00

Fortress at Scutari — D3

Post Horn Overprinted in Black

1920, Apr. 1 ***Perf. 14x13***
J14 D3 4q olive green .75 *4.50*
J15 D3 10q rose red 1.50 *6.50*
J16 D3 20q bister brn 1.50 *6.50*
J17 D3 50q black 4.00 *17.50*
Nos. J14-J17 (4) 7.75 *35.00*

D5

Background of Red Wavy Lines

1922 ***Perf. 12½, 11½***

J23 D5 4q black, *red* 1.10 *4.50*
J24 D5 10q black, *red* 1.10 *4.50*
J25 D5 20q black, *red* 1.10 *4.50*
J26 D5 50q black, *red* 1.10 *4.50*
Nos. J23-J26 (4) 4.40 *18.00*

Nos. J23-J26 Overprinted in White

1925

J27 D5 4q black, *red* 1.90 *4.50*
J28 D5 10q black, *red* 1.90 *4.50*
J29 D5 20q black, *red* 1.90 *4.50*
J30 D5 50q black, *red* 1.90 *4.50*
Nos. J27-J30 (4) 7.60 *18.00*

The 10q with overprint in gold was a trial printing. It was not put in use.

D7

Overprinted "QIND. AR" in Red

1926, Dec. 24 ***Perf. 13½x13***

J31 D7 10q dark blue .75 3.50
J32 D7 20q green .75 3.50
J33 D7 30q red brown 1.50 *7.00*
J34 D7 50q dark brown 2.75 *13.00*
Nos. J31-J34 (4) 5.75 *27.00*

Coat of Arms — D8

Wmk. Double Headed Eagle (220)

1930, Sept. 1 Photo. ***Perf. 14, 14½***

J35 D8 10q dark blue 6.75 *21.00*
J36 D8 20q rose red 2.75 *13.00*
J37 D8 30q violet 2.75 *13.00*
J38 D8 50q dark green 2.75 *13.00*
Nos. J35-J38 (4) 15.00 *60.00*

Nos. J36-J38 exist with overprint "14 Shtator 1943" (see Nos. 332-344 in *Scott Standard Postage Stamp Catalogue*, Vol. 1) which is private and fraudulent on these stamps.

No. 253 Overprinted

1936 ***Perf. 14***

J39 A34 10q carmine 15.00 *45.00*
a. Hyphens on each side of "Takse" ('39) 100.00 *200.00*

Issued under Italian Dominion

Coat of Arms — D9

1940 Unwmk. Photo. ***Perf. 14***

J40 D9 4q red orange *37.50* *75.00*
Never hinged 95.00
J41 D9 10q bright violet *37.50* *75.00*
Never hinged 95.00
J42 D9 20q brown *37.50* *75.00*
Never hinged 95.00
J43 D9 30q dark blue *37.50* *75.00*
Never hinged 95.00
J44 D9 50q carmine rose *37.50* *75.00*
Never hinged 95.00
Nos. J40-J44 (5) *187.50* *375.00*

ALEXANDRETTA

ˌa-lig-ˌzan-ˈdre-tə

LOCATION — A political territory in northern Syria, bordering on Turkey
GOVT. — French mandate
AREA — 10,000 sq. mi. (approx.)
POP. — 220,000 (approx.)

Included in the Syrian territory mandated to France under the Versailles Treaty, the name was changed to Hatay in 1938. The following year France returned the territory to Turkey in exchange for certain concessions. See Hatay.

100 Centimes = 1 Piaster

Stamps of Syria, 1930-36, Overprinted or Surcharged in Black or Red

a

b

c

d

e

1938 Unwmk. ***Perf. 12x12½***

1 A6 (a) 10c vio brn 3.50 3.50
2 A6 (a) 20c brn org 3.50 3.00

Perf. 13½

3 A9 (b) 50c vio (R) 4.50 3.50
4 A10 (b) 1p bis brn 4.50 3.00
5 A9 (b) 2p dk vio (R) 5.75 3.50
6 A13 (b) 3p yel grn (R) 9.00 7.00
7 A10 (b) 4p yel org 10.00 7.00
8 A16 (b) 6p grnsh blk (R) 12.00 8.00
9 A18 (b) 25p vio brn 25.00 25.00
10 A15 (c) 75c org red 9.00 9.00
11 A10 (d) 2.50p on 4p yel org 7.50 4.00
12 AP2 (e) 12.50p on 15p org red 20.00 15.00
Nos. 1-12 (12) 114.25 91.50
Set, never hinged 275.00

Issue dates: Nos. 1-9, Apr. 14, Nos. 10-12, Sept. 2.

Covers: Values for commercial covers begin at about $75.

Nos. 4, 7, 10-12 Ovptd. in Black

1938, Nov. 10

13 A15 75c 60.00 60.00
a. Overprint inverted 500.00
14 A10 1p 37.50 37.50
a. "Sandjah d'Alexandrette" omitted 300.00
15 A10 2.50p on 4p 32.50 32.50
16 A10 4p 37.50 37.50
a. "Sandjah d'Alexandrette" omitted 300.00
17 AP2 12.50p on 15p 90.00 90.00
a. "Sandjah d'Alexandrette" omitted 1,500.
Nos. 13-17 (5) 257.50 257.50
Set, never hinged 450.00

Death of Kemal Ataturk, pres. of Turkey.

AIR POST STAMPS

Air Post Stamps of Syria, 1937, Overprinted Type "b" in Red or Black

1938, Apr. 14 Unwmk. ***Perf. 13***

C1 AP14 ½p dark vio (R) 4.00 *4.75*
C2 AP15 1p black (R) 4.00 *5.00*
C3 AP14 2p blue grn (R) 5.50 *7.00*
C4 AP15 3p deep ultra 6.00 *7.50*
C5 AP14 5p rose lake 11.00 *17.50*
C6 AP15 10p red brown 11.50 *19.00*
C7 AP14 15p lake brown 14.50 *22.50*
C8 AP15 25p dk blue (R) 20.00 *30.00*
Nos. C1-C8 (8) 76.50 *113.25*
Set, never hinged 225.00

POSTAGE DUE STAMPS

Postage Due Stamps of Syria, 1925-31, Ovptd. Type "b" in Black or Red

1938, Apr. 14 Unwmk. ***Perf. 13½***

J1 D5 50c brown, *yel* 6.00 5.50
J2 D6 1p violet, *rose* 7.00 6.00
J3 D5 2p blk, *blue* (R) 8.00 7.50
J4 D5 3p blk, *red org* 10.00 9.00
J5 D5 5p blk, *bl grn* (R) 16.00 14.50
J6 D7 8p blk, *gray bl* (R) 22.50 20.00
Nos. J1-J6 (6) 69.50 62.50
Set, never hinged 225.00

On No. J2, the overprint is vertical, reading up, other denominations, horizontal.

Stamps of Alexandretta were discontinued in 1938 and replaced by those of Hatay.

ALGERIA

al-ˈjir-ē-ə

LOCATION — North Africa
GOVT. — French Colony
AREA — 847,552 sq. mi.
POP. — 7,234,684
CAPITAL — Algiers

100 Centimes = 1 Franc

Catalogue values for unused stamps in this country are for Never Hinged items, beginning with Scott 109 in the regular postage section, and Scott B27 in the semi-postal section.

STAMPS OF FRANCE USED IN ALGERIA

Stamps of France used in Algeria

From 1849 to 1924, stamps of France were used at post offices in Algeria. From 1849 to 1862, stamps were canceled by a lozenge-shaped canceler with small numeral identifiers between 3710 and 4448, each of 83 post offices being identified by its number. From 1862 to 1876, similar cancelers, with larger numerals ranging from 5000 to 5177, were used by 156 post offices. After 1876, each post office used its own circular date stamp.

Grill and Town Cancels

Canceled with grill, on large piece with Algerian town name (first column) or on cover with town name on envelope (second column).

1849 **On France No. 6**

A6G A1 25c lt blue, *bluish*

Alger	70.00	340.00
Arzew	600.00	3,400.
Bouffarich	600.00	3,400.
Constantine	87.50	440.00
Cherchell	87.50	460.00
Dellys	87.50	460.00
Djidjeli	110.00	460.00
Douera	87.50	460.00
Douera + Coleah	600.00	3,400.
Mostaganem	80.00	400.00
Orleans-ville	240.00	1,200.
Philippeville	80.00	400.00
Tenez	87.50	440.00

The 25c value is the least expensive of the French stamps used in Algeria. Other values of the first issue exist used in Algeria and are worth more than the values shown.

Small Figures in Dotted Lozenge

Single (first column) or on cover (second column).

1849 **On France No. 6**

A6S A1 25c lt blue, *bluish*

3710 — Alger, *from*	52.50	180.00
3711 — L'Arba, *from*	400.00	3,400.
3712 — Arzew, *from*	260.00	2,400.
3713 — Aumale, *from*	130.00	1,250.
3714 — Batna, *from*	120.00	1,100.
3715 — Blidah, *from*	67.50	300.00
3716 — Bone, *from*	60.00	240.00
3717 — Bouffarich, *from*	240.00	2,250.
3718 — Bougie, *from*	110.00	1,000.
3719 — Cherchell, *from*	120.00	1,100.
3720 — Coleah, *from*	300.00	2,800.
3721 — Constantine, *from*	60.00	240.00
3722 — Dellys, *from*	220.00	2,000.
3723 — Dely-Ibrahim, *from*	440.00	4,200.
3724 — Djidjeli, *from*	225.00	2,000.
3725 — Douera, *from*	225.00	2,000.
3726 — Mascara, *from*	100.00	1,000.
3727 — Medeah, *from*	80.00	400.00
3728 — Mers-el-Kebir, *from*	225.00	2,400.
3729 — Milianah, *from*	100.00	1,000.
3730 — Mostaganem, *from*	67.50	320.00
3731 — Nemours, *from*	130.00	1,400.
3732 — Oran, *from*	65.00	240.00
3733 — Orleansville, *from*	87.50	750.00
3734 — Philippeville, *from*	75.00	320.00
3735 — Setif, *from*	87.50	525.00
3736 — Sidi-Bel-Abbes, *from*	75.00	350.00
3737 — Stora, *from*	650.00	
3738 — Tenez, *from*	87.50	525.00
3739 — Tlemcen, *from*	80.00	450.00

All other values of the set exist used in Algeria. They are worth more than the values shown above, which are for cancellations on the 25c value.

1849 **On France No. 15**

A15S A3 20c blue, *bluish* (I)

3710 — Alger, *from*	2.40	9.50
3711 — L'Arba, *from*	60.00	540.00
3712 — Arzew, *from*	40.00	340.00
3713 — Aumale, *from*	22.50	150.00
3714 — Batna, *from*	20.00	100.00
3715 — Blidah, *from*	4.00	32.50
3716 — Bone, *from*	4.00	20.00
3717 — Bouffarik, *from*	40.00	275.00
3718 — Bougie, *from*	20.00	110.00
3719 — Cherchell, *from*	24.00	125.00
3720 — Coleah, *from*	47.50	400.00
3721 — Constantine, *from*	3.25	14.00
3722 — Dellys, *from*	35.00	260.00
3723 — Dely-Ibrahim, *from*	55.00	550.00
3724 — Djidjeli, *from*	40.00	275.00
3725 — Douera, *from*	40.00	275.00
3726 — Mascara, *from*	12.50	100.00
3727 — Medeah, *from*	12.50	100.00

3728 — Mers-el-Kebir, *from* 45.00 350.00
3729 — Milianah, *from* 16.00 100.00
3730 — Mostaganem, *from* 4.75 27.50
3731 — Nemours, *from* 24.00 150.00
3732 — Oran, *from* 3.25 14.00
3733 — Orleansville, *from* 16.00 120.00
3734 — Philippeville, *from* 4.75 24.00
3735 — Setif, *from* 12.00 67.50
3736 — Sidi-Bel-Abbes, *from* 4.75 27.50
3737 — Stora, *from* 170.00 3,200.
3738 — Tenez, *from* 16.00 240.00
3739 — Tlemcen, *from* 5.50 40.00
3751 — El Arrouch, *from* 72.50 875.00
3752 — Biskra, *from* 40.00 340.00
3753 — Boghar, *from* 55.00 675.00
3754 — La Calle, *from* 40.00 400.00
3755 — Gudiel, *from* 225.00 *5,400.*
3756 — Guelma, *from* 16.00 140.00
3757 — Lambese, *from* 140.00 1,600.
3758 — Milah, *from* — —
3759 — Saida, *from* 65.00 750.00
3760 — Smendou, *from* 80.00 800.00
3761 — St. Denis-du-Sig, *from* 20.00 150.00
3762 — Tebessa, *from* 52.50 500.00
3763 — Teniet-el-Haad, *from* 52.50 675.00
3764 — Tiaret, *from* 50.00 450.00
3774 — El Affroun, *from* 120.00 *4,600.*
3774 — Mouzaiaville, *from* 110.00 875.00
3775 — Ain Benian, *from* — —
3776 — Bou-Medfa, *from* 87.50 875.00
3777 — Marengo, *from* 35.00 340.00
3793 — Miserghin, *from* 62.50 800.00
3795 — Valmy d'Algerie, *from* 80.00 750.00
3846 — Penthievre, *from* 105.00 1,200.
3912 — La Maison Carree, *from* 55.00 1,000.
4005 — Soukaras, *from* 55.00 650.00
4007 — Laghouat, *from* 80.00 750.00
4104 — Jemmapes, *from* 40.00 400.00
4106 — La Reghaia, *from* 200.00 2,600.
4116 — Ain-Benida, *from* 35.00 400.00
4120 — Pont-l'Oued Djer, *from* 72.50 1,000.
4122 — Staoueli, *from* 80.00 1,100.
4187 — Gastonville, *from* 80.00 950.00
4189 — Lalla Maghrnia, *from* 80.00 950.00
4190 — Tizi-Ouzou, *from* 62.50 725.00
4361 — Bou Tkelis, *from* 80.00 950.00
4362 — Le tlelat, *from* 100.00 1,200.
4363 — Ain-Temouchent *from* 55.00 600.00
4364 — Relizane *from* 80.00 800.00
4365 — Assi-Ameur, *from* 100.00 1,500.
4366 — Aboukir, *from* 300.00 4,200.
4367 — Ain Tedeles, *from* 80.00 800.00
4368 — La Stidia, *from* 225.00 4,000.
4369 — Fondouk, *from* 100.00 1,200.
4370 — Kouba, *from* 200.00 3,000.
4371 — Fort Napoleon, *from* 80.00 950.00
4372 — Dra-el-Mizan, *from* 120.00 1,500.
4373 — Rouiba, *from* 190.00 3,000.
4374 — Cheragas, *from* 190.00 *5,200.*
4446 — Geryville, *from* 260.00 *4,600.*
4447 — Oued-el-Hamman, *from* 240.00 *4,600.*
4448 — Sebdou, *from* — —

All other values of the set exist used in Algeria. They are worth more than the values shown above, which are for cancellations on the 25c value.

Large Figures in Dotted Lozenge

Single (first column) or on cover (second column).

1870-76 **On France No. 58**

A58L A13 25c blue, *bluish*
5000 — Aboukir, *from* 60.00 750.00
5001 — Ain Beida, *from* 80.00 950.00
5002 — Ain Beniam, *from* — —
5002 — Saint-Charles, *from* 80.00 1,100.
5003 — Ain Tedeles, *from* 40.00 475.00
5004 — Ain Temouchena, *from* 20.00 140.00
5005 — Alger, *from* 2.40 5.50
5006 — L'Arba, *from* 20.00 160.00
5007 — El Arrouch *from* 24.00 175.00
5008 — Arzew, *from* 20.00 150.00
5009 — Assi-Ameur, *from* 80.00 460.00
5010 — Aumale, *from* 14.00 65.00
5011 — Batna, *from* 4.75 24.00
5012 — Biskra, *from* 12.50 55.00
5013 — Blidah, *from* 3.25 20.00
5014 — Boghar, *from* 35.00 275.00
5015 — Bone, *from* 4.75 16.00
5016 — Bou-Tletis, *from* 52.50 650.00
5017 — Bouffarik, *from* 12.50 55.00
5018 — Bougie, *from* 4.75 20.00
5019 — La Calle, *from* 27.50 240.00
5020 — Cheragas, *from* 65.00 1,200.
5020 — Palestro, *from* 65.00 725.00
5021 — Cherchell, *from* 16.00 75.00
5022 — Coleah, *from* 24.00 150.00
5023 — Constantine, *from* 3.25 12.00
5024 — Dellys, *from* 16.00 100.00
5025 — Dely-Ibrahim, *from* 40.00 340.00
5026 — Djidjeli, *from* 20.00 120.00
5027 — Douera, *from* 24.00 160.00
5028 — Dra-el-Mizan, *from* 55.00 650.00
5029 — Fondouk, *from* 45.00 600.00
5030 — Fort Napoleon, *from* 40.00 400.00
5030 — Fort National, *from* 40.00 275.00
5031 — Gastonville, *from* 47.50 600.00
5031 — Robertville, *from* 47.50 650.00
5032 — Geryville, *from* 62.50 750.00
5033 — Gudiel, *from* — —
5033 — Guyotville, *from* 62.50 1,000.
5034 — Guelma, *from* 10.50 40.00
5035 — Jemmapes, *from* 12.00 65.00
5036 — Kouba, *from* 40.00 400.00
5037 — Laghouat *from* 35.00 275.00
5038 — Lalla Maghrnia, *from* 35.00 340.00
5039 — Lambese, *from* 40.00 400.00
5040 — La Maison Carree, *from* 35.00 325.00
5041 — Marengo, *from* 32.50 260.00
5042 — Mascara, *from* 4.75 20.00
5043 — Medeah, *from* 4.75 20.00
5044 — Mers-el-Kebir, *from* 35.00 275.00
5045 — Milah, *from* — —
5045 — Col des Beni Aicha, *from* 77.50 1,050.
5046 — Milianah, *from* 5.50 24.00
5047 — Miserghin *from* 40.00 400.00
5048 — Mostaganem, *from* 4.50 20.00
5049 — Mouzaiaville, *from* 47.50 675.00
5050 — Nemours, *from* 10.50 55.00
5051 — Oran, *from* 2.25 6.50
5052 — Orleansville, *from* 4.50 20.00
5053 — Oued-el-Hammam, *from* 70.00 800.00
5054 — Penthievre, *from* 67.50 750.00
5055 — Philippeville, *from* 2.40 10.00
5056 — Pont de la Oued Djer, *from* 55.00 800.00
5056 — Bou Medfa, *from* 55.00 800.00
5057 — La Reghaia *from* 62.50 800.00
5057 — L'Alma, *from* 62.50 1,000.
5058 — Relizane, *from* 14.00 100.00
5059 — Rouiba, *from* 45.00 875.00
5060 — Saida, *from* 16.00 140.00
5061 — Sebdou, *from* 62.50 725.00
5062 — Setif, *from* 4.50 20.00
5063 — Sidi-bel Abbes, *from* 4.00 16.00
5064 — Smendou, *from* 52.50 750.00
5065 — Soukaras, *from* 22.50 150.00
5066 — Staoueli, *from* 65.00 700.00
5067 — La Stidia, *from* 65.00 1,000.
5068 — Stora, *from* 275.00 —
5069 — St-Cloud-d'Algerie, *from* 35.00 500.00
5070 — St. Denis-du-Sig, *from* 16.00 87.50
5071 — Tebessa, *from* 35.00 400.00
5072 — Tenez, *from* 16.00 80.00
5073 — Teniet-el-Haad, *from* 27.50 200.00
5074 — Le Tlelat, *from* 40.00 450.00
5075 — Tlemcen, *from* 4.50 20.00
5076 — Tiaret, *from* 10.50 80.00
5077 — Tizzi Ouzou, *from* 25.00 160.00
5078 — Valmy, *from* 62.50 650.00
5081 — Beni Mancour, *from* 80.00 1,100.
5093 — Ain el Arba, *from* 80.00 1,000.
5108 — Sidi-Moussa, *from* 100.00 1,200.
5109 — Djelfa, *from* 20.00 275.00
5110 — Bou Kanifis, *from* 62.50 700.00
5111 — Collo, *from* 50.00 500.00
5112 — Duzerville, *from* 50.00 700.00
5113 — Mondovi, *from* 80.00 750.00
5114 — Barral, *from* 80.00 1,200.
5115 — Hussein Dey, *from* 60.00 750.00
5116 — Birtouta, *from* 60.00 1,000.
5117 — Berrouaghia, *from* 80.00 1,000.
5117 — Gue de Constantine, *from* 80.00 2,750.
5120 — El Kantours, *from* 80.00 950.00
5120 — Bou Sfer, *from* 80.00 1,000.
5122 — Les Trembles, *from* 80.00 875.00
5123 — Perregaux, *from* 80.00 950.00
5124 — Bizot, *from* 45.00 550.00
5125 — Bordj Bou-Arreridj, *from* 45.00 475.00
5126 — Ouled Mimoun, *from* 80.00 725.00
5126 — Lamoriciere, *from* 80.00 1,200.
5127 — Gar Rouban, *from* 80.00 1,200.
5128 — Daya, *from* 57.50 875.00
5130 — Oued-el-Halleg, *from* 57.50 700.00
5131 — Le Affroun, *from* 90.00 4,000.
5131 — Bou Saada, *from* 80.00 1,000.
5133 — Kroubs, *from* 80.00 750.00
5134 — Bouguirat, *from* 80.00 750.00
5135 — L'Hillil *from* 57.50 725.00
5136 — Ammi-Moussa, *from* 80.00 750.00
5137 — Sidi-Ali-ben-Youd, *from* 75.00 950.00
5138 — Oued-Zenati, *from* 60.00 950.00
5140 — Affreville, *from* 62.50 875.00
5141 — Duperre, *from* 62.50 875.00
5142 — Boghari, *from* 80.00 950.00
5143 — Akbou, *from* 100.00 1,050.
5144 — Khenchela, *from* 80.00 1,000.
5145 — Zemmorah, *from* 87.50 1,050.
5146 — Bordj Menaiel, *from* 80.00 1,000.
5147 — La Chiffa, *from* 80.00 1,050.
5148 — Rebeval, *from* 87.50 1,400.
5149 — La Senia, *from* — —
5150 — Oued-Athmenia, *from* 80.00 1,000.
5151 — Birkadem, *from* 87.50 1,100.
5152 — Ponteba, *from* 87.50 1,100.
5157 — Oued-Slyt, *from* 100.00 1,300.
5158 — Oued-Fodda, *from* 100.00 1,300.
5159 — Akib-Zamoun, *from* 175.00 1,750.
5160 — Attatba, *from* 120.00 1,700.
5161 — Ain-Arnat, *from* 1,750. —
5162 — Sidi-Brahim, *from* 100.00 1,450.
5163 — Oued-Riou, *from* 120.00 2,250.
5164 — Henneya, *from* 275.00 4,500.
5165 — Ain Fekarin, *from* 175.00 3,500.
5166 — Bourkika, *from* 120.00 2,000.
5167 — Sidi-Ali, *from* — —
— Sidi-Ali straight-line cancellation, *from* *3,600.*
5168 — Blad-el-Hadjadj, *from* 140.00 2,600.
5169 — Bordj-Bouira, *from* 300.00 *5,750.*
5171— Beni Saf, *from* 400.00 *6,500.*
5172 — Bir Rabalou, *from* 400.00 *6,500.*

ISSUES OF FRENCH ALGERIA

Stamps of France Overprinted in Red, Blue or Black

a

b

c

d

1924-26 **Unwmk.** ***Perf. 14x13½***

No.	Type	Description	Unused	Used
1	A16(a)	1c dk gray (R)	.40	.40
		Never hinged	.80	
		On cover		10.00
a.		1c pale gray	.80	.80
		Never hinged	1.60	
		On cover		10.00
2	A16(a)	2c violet brn	.40	.40
		Never hinged	.80	
		On cover		10.00
3	A16(a)	3c orange	.40	.40
		Never hinged	.80	
		On cover		10.00
a.		Grayish paper	.65	.65
		Never hinged	1.20	
		On cover		10.00
4	A16(a)	4c yel brn (Bl)	.40	.40
		Never hinged	.80	
		On cover		8.00
5	A22(a)	5c orange (Bl)	.40	.40
		Never hinged	.80	
		On cover		1.75
6	A16(a)	5c green ('25)	.80	.80
		Never hinged	1.20	
		On cover		1.75
7	A23(a)	10c green	.80	.40
		Never hinged	1.25	
		On cover		2.25
b.		Booklet pane of 10	—	
		Complete booklet, 2 #7b	300.00	
8	A22(a)	10c green ('25)	.80	.40
		Never hinged	1.20	
		On cover		2.00
a.		Pair, one without overprint	1,600.	
		Never hinged	2,250.	
9	A20(a)	15c slate grn	.40	.40
		Never hinged	.80	
		On cover		1.20
10	A23(a)	15c green ('25)	1.20	.40
		Never hinged	1.60	
		On cover		2.00
11	A22(a)	15c red brn (Bl) ('26)	.40	.40
		Never hinged	.80	
		On cover		1.20
12	A22(a)	20c red brn (Bl)	.40	.40
		Never hinged	.80	
		On cover		1.20
a.		Pair, one without overprint	1,600.	
		Never hinged	2,250.	
13	A22(a)	25c blue (R)	.80	.40
		Never hinged	1.20	
		On cover		1.20
a.		Booklet pane of 10	—	
		Complete booklet, 2 #13a	1,450.	
b.		Pair, one without overprint	1,900.	
		Never hinged	2,400.	
14	A23(a)	30c red (Bl)	2.40	.80
		Never hinged	3.25	
		On cover		2.40
15	A22(a)	30c cerise ('25)	.80	.80
		Never hinged	1.20	
a.		"ALGERIE" double	225.00	150.00
		Never hinged	275.00	
16	A22(a)	30c lt bl (R) ('25)	.80	.80
		Never hinged	1.20	
		On cover		4.00
a.		Booklet pane of 10	—	
		Complete booklet, 2 #16a	550.00	
17	A22(a)	35c violet	.80	.80
		Never hinged	1.20	
		On cover		4.75
18	A18(b)	40c red & pale bl	1.20	.80
		Never hinged	1.60	
		On cover		3.25
19	A22(a)	40c ol brn (R) ('25)	1.20	.80
		Never hinged	1.60	
		On cover		4.00
20	A18(b)	45c grn & bl (R)	1.20	.80
		Never hinged	1.25	
		On cover		8.00
a.		Double overprint	325.00	
		Never hinged	450.00	
21	A23(a)	45c red (Bl) ('25)	1.25	.80
		Never hinged	1.75	
		On cover		6.50
22	A23(a)	50c blue (R)	1.20	.80
		Never hinged	1.60	
		On cover		5.50
23	A20(a)	60c lt violet	1.20	.80
		Never hinged	1.60	
		On cover		8.75
a.		Inverted overprint		*3,250.*
24	A20(a)	65c rose (Bl)	1.20	.80
		Never hinged	1.60	
		On cover		5.00
25	A23(a)	75c blue (R)	1.25	.75
		Never hinged	1.60	
		On cover		9.00
a.		Double overprint	325.00	325.00
		Never hinged	475.00	
26	A20(a)	80c ver ('26)	2.00	1.20
		Never hinged	2.40	
		On cover		17.50
27	A20(a)	85c ver (Bl)	1.20	1.20
		Never hinged	1.60	
		On cover		8.00
		On cover, single franking		15.00
28	A18(b)	1fr cl & ol grn	2.00	1.20
		Never hinged	2.40	
		On cover		4.00
		On cover, single franking		9.50
a.		Olive green omitted	325.00	325.00
		Never hinged	475.00	
29	A22(a)	1.05fr ver ('26)	1.60	1.60
		Never hinged	2.40	
		On cover		20.00
		On cover, single franking		67.50
30	A18(c)	2fr org & pale bl	2.40	1.60
		Never hinged	3.25	
		On cover		16.00
		On cover, single franking		67.50
31	A18(b)	3fr vio & bl ('26)	5.50	2.40
		Never hinged	8.00	
		On cover		35.00
		On cover, single franking		100.00
a.		Blue omitted	325.00	
		Never hinged	475.00	
32	A18(d)	5fr bl & buff (R)	16.00	12.00
		Never hinged	20.00	
		On cover		45.00
		On cover, single franking		165.00
		Nos. 1-32 (32)	52.80	36.35

No. 15 was issued precanceled only. Values for precanceled stamps in first column are for those which have not been through the post and have original gum. Values in second column are for postally used, gumless stamps.

For surcharges see Nos. 75, P1.

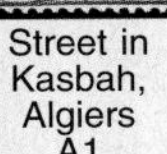

Street in Kasbah, Algiers
A1

Mosque of Sidi Abd-er-Rahman
A2

La Pêcherie Mosque — A3

Marabout of Sidi Yacoub
A4

1926-39 Typo. *Perf. 14x13½*

33 A1 1c olive .25 .25
Never hinged .40
On cover 6.50
a. Imperforate 110.00
Never hinged 150.00
34 A1 2c red brown .25 .25
Never hinged .40
On cover 6.50
35 A1 3c orange .25 .25
Never hinged .40
On cover 5.50
36 A1 5c blue green .25 .25
Never hinged .40
On cover 2.00
37 A1 10c brt violet .40 .25
Never hinged .80
On cover 2.00
a. Booklet pane of 10 —
Complete booklet, 2 #37a 400.00
38 A2 15c orange brn .40 .25
Never hinged .80
On cover 1.60
a. Imperforate 110.00
Never hinged 150.00
b. Booklet pane of 10 —
Complete booklet, 2 #38b 350.00
39 A2 20c green .40 .25
Never hinged .80
On cover 4.00
a. yel grn, precanceled ('38) 2.00 1.20
Never hinged 2.40
40 A2 20c deep rose .25 .25
Never hinged .40
On cover 6.50
a. Imperforate 120.00
Never hinged 175.00
41 A2 25c blue grn .40 .25
Never hinged .80
On cover 2.40
42 A2 25c blue ('27) .80 .40
Never hinged 1.60
On cover 2.40
a. Imperforate 120.00
Never hinged 175.00
43 A2 25c vio bl ('39) .25 .25
Never hinged .40
On cover 2.40
44 A2 30c blue .40 .40
Never hinged .80
On cover 8.75
a. Imperforate 120.00
Never hinged 175.00
45 A2 30c bl grn ('27) 1.25 .80
Never hinged 1.75
On cover 4.75
46 A2 35c dp violet 1.60 1.20
Never hinged 2.40
On cover 12.50
47 A2 40c olive green .40 .25
Never hinged .80
On cover 2.75
a. Booklet pane of 10 —
Complete booklet, 2 #47a 325.00
b. Imperforate 120.00
Never hinged 175.00
48 A3 45c violet brn .80 .40
Never hinged 1.20
On cover 3.25
49 A3 50c blue .40 .40
Never hinged .80
On cover 1.60
a. Booklet pane of 10 —
Complete booklet, 2 #49a 400.00
b. Imperforate 125.00
Never hinged 180.00
c. Vert. pair, #49 and 49b 225.00
Never hinged 320.00
50 A3 50c dk red ('30) .40 .25
Never hinged .55
On cover 1.60
a. Booklet pane of 10 —
Complete booklet, 2 #50a 450.00
b. Imperforate 120.00
Never hinged 175.00
51 A3 60c yellow grn .40 .40
Never hinged .80
On cover 4.50
52 A3 65c blk brn ('27) 3.25 2.40
Never hinged 4.00
On cover 8.75
53 A1 65c ultra ('38) .40 .40
Never hinged .80
On cover 4.00
a. Booklet pane of 10 —
Complete booklet, 2 #53a 160.00
54 A3 75c carmine 1.20 .80
Never hinged 1.60
On cover 3.50
a. Imperforate 125.00
Never hinged 180.00
b. Vert. pair, #54 and 54a 225.00
Never hinged 320.00
55 A3 75c blue ('29) 4.75 .80
Never hinged 8.00
On cover 2.00
56 A3 80c orange red 1.20 .80
Never hinged 1.60
On cover 8.75
57 A3 90c red ('27) 8.00 4.00
Never hinged 12.00
On cover 6.75
On cover, single franking 16.00
a. Imperforate 120.00
Never hinged 175.00
58 A4 1fr gray grn & red brn 1.20 .80
Never hinged 1.60
On cover 8.00
On cover, single franking 12.00
a. Imperforate 175.00
Never hinged 240.00
59 A3 1.05fr lt brown 1.20 .80
Never hinged 1.60
On cover 8.75
On cover, single franking 20.00
60 A3 1.10fr mag ('27) 8.00 4.00
Never hinged 12.00
On cover 20.00
On cover, single franking 80.00
61 A4 1.25fr dk bl & ultra 1.60 1.20
Never hinged 2.40
On cover 16.00
On cover, single franking 24.00
62 A4 1.50fr dk bl & ultra ('27) 5.50 .80
Never hinged 8.00
On cover 9.50
On cover, single franking 17.50
a. Imperforate 400.00
Never hinged 550.00
63 A4 2fr prus bl & blk brn 4.75 1.20
Never hinged 6.50
On cover 8.00
On cover, single franking 12.00
a. Imperforate 125.00
Never hinged 180.00
b. 2fr Prus blue & black 7.25 2.60
Never hinged 10.50
64 A4 3fr violet & org 8.00 1.60
Never hinged 12.00
On cover 16.00
On cover, single franking 24.00
65 A4 5fr red & violet 16.00 4.75
Never hinged 20.00
On cover 27.50
On cover, single franking 45.00
a. "ALCERIE," instead of "ALGERIE" 100.00 67.50
Never hinged 145.00
66 A4 10fr ol brn & rose ('27) 80.00 47.50
Never hinged 120.00
On cover 92.50
On cover, single franking 145.00
a. Imperforate 800.00
Never hinged 1,200.
b. 10fr sepia brn & dark red 87.50 52.50
Never hinged 125.00
On cover 87.50
On cover, single franking 145.00
67 A4 20fr vio & grn ('27) 8.00 8.00
Never hinged 12.00
On cover 16.00
On cover, single franking 32.50
Nos. 33-67 (35) 162.60 86.85

A 90c red, design A1, was prepared but not issued. Values: unused $950, never hinged $1,350.

Type A4, 50c blue and rose red, inscribed "CENTENAIRE-ALGERIE" is France No. 255.

See design A24 in *Scott Standard Postage Stamp Catalogue*, Vol. 1. For stamps and types surcharged see Nos. 68-74, 131, 136, 187, B1-B13, J27, P2 in this catalogue and Scott Standard catalogue, Vol. 1.

Five Trees Instead of Four (Position 53)

58d A4 1fr gray grn & red brn 27.50 16.00
Never hinged 40.00
61d A4 1.25fr dk blue & ultra 32.50 24.00
Never hinged 52.50
62d A4 1.50fr dk blue & ultra ('27) 32.50 16.00
Never hinged 47.50
63d A4 2fr prus blue & blk brn 32.50 24.00
Never hinged 52.50
64d A4 3fr violet & orange 45.00 27.50
Never hinged 65.00
65d A4 5fr red & violet 130.00 120.00
Never hinged 200.00
66d A4 10fr olive brn & rose ('27) 650.00 550.00
Never hinged 925.00
67d A4 20fr violet & green ('27) 650.00 550.00
Never hinged 925.00

Stamps of 1926 Surcharged

1927

68 A2 10c on 35c dp violet .25 .25
Never hinged .40
On cover 5.50
69 A2 25c on 30c blue .25 .25
Never hinged .40
On cover 2.40
70 A2 30c on 25c blue grn .40 .25
Never hinged .55
On cover 4.75
71 A3 65c on 60c yel grn 1.60 1.20
Never hinged 2.40
On cover 2.75
72 A3 90c on 80c org red 1.40 .95
Never hinged 1.90
On cover 6.75
73 A3 1.10fr on 1.05fr lt brn 1.00 .50
Never hinged 1.40
On cover 20.00
74 A4 1.50fr on 1.25fr dk bl & ultra 3.25 1.50
Never hinged 4.00
On cover 9.50
Nos. 68-74 (7) 8.15 4.90

Bars cancel the old value on Nos. 68, 69, 73, 74.

No. 4 Surcharged

1927

75 A16 5c on 4c yellow brown .40 .40
Never hinged .80
On cover 6.50
a. Blue surcharge 1,250. *1,400.*
Never hinged 1,750.

Bay of Algiers
A5

1930, May 4 Engr. *Perf. 12½*

78 A5 10fr red brown 21.00 21.00
Never hinged 32.50
On cover 47.50
a. Imperf., pair 150.00
b. Perf 11 24.00 24.00
Never hinged 40.00
On cover 120.00

Cent. of Algeria and for Intl. Phil. Exhib. of North Africa, May, 1930.

One example of No. 78 was sold with each 10fr admission.

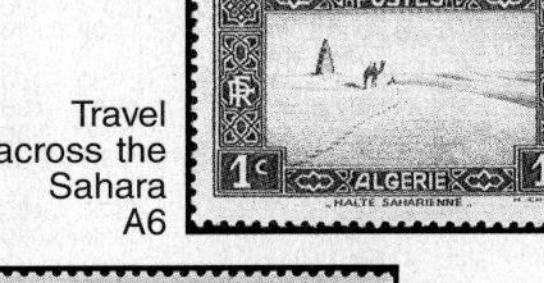

Travel across the Sahara
A6

Arch of Triumph, Lambese
A7

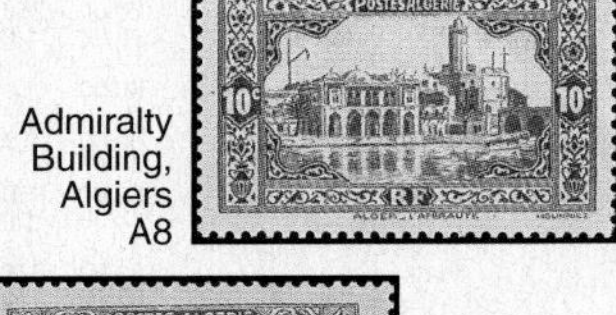

Admiralty Building, Algiers
A8

Kings' Tombs near Touggourt
A9

El-Kebir Mosque, Algiers
A10

Oued River at Colomb-Bechar
A11

Sidi Bon Medine Cemetery at Tlemcen
A13

View of Ghardaia
A12

1936-41 Engr. *Perf. 13*

79 A6 1c ultra .25 .40
Never hinged .40
On cover 4.75
80 A11 2c dk violet .25 .40
Never hinged .40
On cover 4.75
81 A7 3c dk blue grn .25 .40
Never hinged .40
On cover 4.75
82 A12 5c red violet .40 .25
Never hinged .40
On cover 4.00
83 A8 10c emerald .25 .40
Never hinged .40
On cover 4.00
84 A9 15c red .25 .40
Never hinged .40
On cover 2.40
85 A13 20c dk blue grn .40 .40
Never hinged .80
On cover 2.40
86 A10 25c rose vio 1.20 .80
Never hinged 1.60
On cover 1.60
87 A12 30c yellow grn .80 .40
Never hinged 1.20
On cover 4.00
88 A9 40c brown vio .40 .40
Never hinged .80
On cover 1.60
89 A13 45c deep ultra 2.00 1.20
Never hinged 2.40
On cover 4.50
90 A8 50c red 1.20 .40
Never hinged 1.60
On cover 1.60
91 A6 65c red brn 8.00 4.00
Never hinged 12.00
On cover 12.00
92 A6 65c rose car ('37) .80 .80
Never hinged 1.20
On cover 2.40
93 A6 70c red brn ('39) .40 .40
Never hinged .80
On cover 2.40
94 A11 75c slate bl .80 .40
Never hinged 1.20
On cover 2.40
95 A7 90c henna brn 2.40 1.60
Never hinged 4.00
On cover 2.40
On cover, single franking 4.00
96 A10 1fr brown .80 .40
Never hinged 1.20
On cover 2.40
On cover, single franking 4.00
97 A8 1.25fr lt violet 1.20 .80
Never hinged 1.60
On cover 4.00
On cover, single franking 12.00
98 A8 1.25fr car rose ('39) .80 .40
Never hinged 1.20
On cover 6.50
On cover, single franking 11.00
99 A11 1.50fr turq blue 2.40 .80
Never hinged 4.00
On cover 4.00
On cover, single franking 5.50
99A A11 1.50fr rose ('40) .80 .80
Never hinged 1.20
On cover 5.50
On cover, single franking 20.00
100 A12 1.75fr henna brn .40 .40
Never hinged .80
On cover 4.00
On cover, single franking 6.50
101 A7 2fr dk brown .80 .40
Never hinged 1.20
On cover 4.00
On cover, single franking 5.50
102 A6 2.25fr yellow grn 20.00 13.50
Never hinged 27.50
On cover 27.50
On cover, single franking 40.00
103 A12 2.50fr dk ultra ('41) .80 .80
Never hinged 1.20
On cover 5.50
On cover, single franking 20.00
104 A13 3fr magenta 1.20 .80
Never hinged 1.60
On cover 6.50
On cover, single franking 12.00
105 A10 3.50fr pck blue 6.50 4.00
Never hinged 8.00
On cover 16.00
On cover, single franking 24.00

106 A8 5fr slate blue 1.60 .80
Never hinged 2.40
On cover 4.00
On cover, single franking 9.50
107 A11 10fr henna brn 1.20 .80
Never hinged 1.60
On cover 6.50
On cover, single franking 14.00
108 A9 20fr turq blue 1.60 1.20
Never hinged 2.40
On cover 8.00
On cover, single franking 17.50
Nos. 79-108 (31) 60.15 38.95

See Nos. 124-125, 162 in *Scott Standard Postage Stamp Catalogue*, Vol. 1.

Nos. 82 and 100 with surcharge "E. F. M. 30frs" (Emergency Field Message) were used in 1943 to pay cable tolls for US and Canadian servicemen.

For other surcharges see Nos. 122, B27.

Catalogue values for unused stamps in this section, from this point to the end of the section, are for Never Hinged items.

Algerian Pavilion — A14

1937 *Perf. 13*
109 A14 40c brt green 2.00 1.20
On cover 4.00
110 A14 50c rose carmine 2.00 .80
On cover 2.40
111 A14 1.50fr blue 2.75 1.20
On cover 4.00
On cover, single franking 6.50
112 A14 1.75fr brown black 2.75 1.60
On cover 5.50
On cover, single franking 12.00
Nos. 109-112 (4) 9.50 4.80

Paris International Exposition.

Constantine in 1837 — A15

1937
113 A15 65c deep rose 1.20 .80
On cover 2.40
114 A15 1fr brown 12.00 1.60
On cover 4.00
On cover, single franking 7.25
115 A15 1.75fr blue green 1.60 .80
On cover 4.00
On cover, single franking 5.50
116 A15 2.15fr red violet 1.60 .80
On cover 4.00
On cover, single franking 4.00
Nos. 113-116 (4) 16.40 4.00

Taking of Constantine by the French, cent.

Ruins of a Roman Villa — A16

1938
117 A16 30c green 2.00 .80
On cover 4.00
118 A16 65c ultra .80 .80
On cover 6.50
119 A16 75c rose violet 2.00 .80
On cover 12.50
120 A16 3fr carmine rose 5.50 4.00
On cover 20.00
On cover, single franking 32.50
121 A16 5fr yellow brown 8.00 5.50
On cover 24.00
On cover, single franking 35.00
Nos. 117-121 (5) 18.30 11.90

Centenary of Philippeville.

No. 90 Surcharged in Black

1938
122 A8 25c on 50c red .80 .40
On cover 3.50
a. Double surcharge 100.00 60.00
b. Inverted surcharge 72.50 47.50
c. Pair, one without surcharge 400.00

Types of 1936 Numerals of Value on Colorless Background

1939
124 A7 90c henna brown 1.20 .40
On cover 1.60
125 A10 2.25fr blue green 1.20 .80
On cover 5.50
On cover, single franking 9.50

For surcharge see No. B38 in *Scott Standard Postage Stamp Catalogue*, Vol. 1.

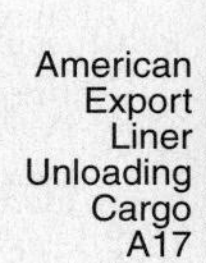

American Export Liner Unloading Cargo A17

1939
126 A17 20c green 4.00 1.60
On cover 4.00
127 A17 40c red violet 4.00 1.60
On cover 4.00
128 A17 90c brown black 2.40 .80
On cover 2.40
129 A17 1.25fr rose 9.50 4.00
On cover 8.00
On cover, single franking 12.00
130 A17 2.25fr ultra 4.00 2.40
On cover 8.00
On cover, single franking 12.00
Nos. 126-130 (5) 23.90 10.40

New York World's Fair.

Type of 1926, Surcharged in Black

Two types of surcharge:
I — Bars 6mm
II — Bars 7mm

1939-40 *Perf. 14x13½*
131 A1 1fr on 90c crimson (I) .80 .40
On cover 1.60
a. Booklet pane of 10 —
Complete booklet, 2 #131a 625.00
b. Double surcharge (I) 175.00
c. Inverted surcharge (I) 87.50
d. Pair, one without surch. (I) *2,000.*
e. Type II ('40) 8.00 1.60
On cover 4.00
f. Inverted surcharge (II) 95.00
g. Pair, one without surch. (II) *2,000.*

SEMI-POSTAL STAMPS

Regular Issue of 1926 Surcharged in Black or Red

1927 **Unwmk.** *Perf. 14x13½*
B1 A1 5c +5c bl grn 1.60 1.60
Never hinged 2.40
On cover 35.00
B2 A1 10c +10c lilac 1.60 1.60
Never hinged 2.40
On cover 35.00
B3 A2 15c +15c org brn 1.60 1.60
Never hinged 2.40
On cover 32.50
B4 A2 20c +20c car rose 1.60 1.60
Never hinged 2.40
On cover 47.50
B5 A2 25c +25c bl grn 1.60 1.60
Never hinged 2.40
On cover 21.00
B6 A2 30c +30c lt bl 1.60 1.60
Never hinged 2.40
On cover 32.50
B7 A2 35c +35c dp vio 1.60 1.60
Never hinged 2.40
On cover 47.50
B8 A2 40c +40c ol grn 1.60 1.60
Never hinged 2.40
On cover 20.00
B9 A3 50c +50c dp bl (R) 1.60 1.60
Never hinged 2.40
On cover 20.00
a. Double surcharge 460.00 *475.00*
Never hinged 675.00
B10 A3 80c +80c red org 1.60 1.60
Never hinged 2.40
On cover 47.50
B11 A4 1fr +1fr gray grn & red brn 1.60 1.60
Never hinged 2.40
On cover 32.50
B12 A4 2fr +2fr Prus bl & blk brn 32.50 32.50
Never hinged 47.50
On cover 65.00
B13 A4 5fr +5fr red & vio 40.00 40.00
Never hinged 55.00
On cover 87.50
Nos. B1-B13 (13) 90.10 90.10

The surtax was for the benefit of wounded soldiers. Government officials speculated in this issue.

Railroad Terminal, Oran SP1

Ruins at Djemila SP2

Mosque of Sidi Abd-er-Rahman SP3

Designs: 10c+10c, Rummel Gorge, Constantine. 15c+15c, Admiralty Buildings, Algiers. 25c+25c, View of Algiers. 30c+30c, Trajan's Arch, Timgad. 40c+40c, Temple of the North, Djemila. 75c+75c Mansourah Minaret, Tlemcen. 1f+1f, View of Ghardaia. 1.50f+1.50f, View of Tolga. 2f+2f, Tuareg warriors. 3f+3f, Kasbah, Algiers.

1930 **Engr.** *Perf. 12½*
B14 SP1 5c +5c orange 12.00 12.00
Never hinged 16.00
On cover 24.00
B15 SP1 10c +10c ol grn 12.00 12.00
Never hinged 16.00
On cover 24.00
B16 SP1 15c +15c dk brn 12.00 12.00
Never hinged 16.00
On cover 24.00
B17 SP1 25c +25c black 12.00 12.00
Never hinged 16.00
On cover 24.00
B18 SP1 30c +30c dk red 12.00 12.00
Never hinged 16.00
On cover 27.50
B19 SP1 40c +40c ap grn 12.00 12.00
Never hinged 16.00
On cover 16.00
B20 SP2 50c +50c ultra 9.50 9.50
Never hinged 16.00
On cover 16.00
B21 SP2 75c +75c red pur 9.50 9.50
Never hinged 16.00
On cover 17.50
B22 SP2 1fr +1fr org red 9.50 9.50
Never hinged 16.00
On cover 21.00
B23 SP2 1.50fr +1.50fr deep ultra 9.50 9.50
Never hinged 16.00
On cover 32.50
B24 SP2 2fr +2fr dk car 9.50 9.50
Never hinged 16.00
On cover 21.00
B25 SP2 3fr +3fr dk grn 9.50 9.50
Never hinged 16.00
On cover 45.00
B26 SP3 5fr +5fr grn & car 24.00 24.00
Never hinged 32.50
On cover 47.50
a. Center inverted 750.00
Never hinged 1,200.
b. Center brown 450.00
Never hinged 625.00
Nos. B14-B26 (13) 153.00 153.00

Centenary of the French occupation of Algeria. The surtax on the stamps was given to the funds for the celebration.

Nos. B14-B26 exist imperf. Value, set in pairs, $800.

Catalogue values for unused stamps in this section, from this point to the end of the section, are for Never Hinged items.

No. 102 Surcharged in Red

1938 *Perf. 13*
B27 A6 65c +35c on 2.25fr yel grn 1.60 1.20
On cover 45.00
a. Inverted surcharge 350.00
b. Pair, one without surcharge 1,875.

20th anniversary of Armistice.

No. 79 with surcharge is considered an essay. Values: unused $260, never hinged $350.

René Caillié, Charles Lavigerie and Henri Duveyrier SP14

1939 **Engr.**
B28 SP14 30c +20c dk bl grn 2.40 2.40
On cover 8.00
B29 SP14 90c +60c car rose 2.40 2.40
On cover 4.00
B30 SP14 2.25fr +75c ultra 20.00 16.00
On cover 32.50
On cover, single franking 75.00
B31 SP14 5fr +5fr brn blk 40.00 32.50
On cover 52.50
On cover, single franking 87.50
Nos. B28-B31 (4) 64.80 53.30

Pioneers of the Sahara.

French and Algerian Soldiers SP15

1940 **Photo.** *Perf. 12*
B32 SP15 1fr +1fr bl & car 1.60 1.20
On cover 4.50
a. Double surcharge 260.00
B33 SP15 1fr +2fr brn rose & blk 1.60 1.20
On cover 4.50
B34 SP15 1fr +4fr dp grn & red 2.40 2.00
On cover 6.50
B35 SP15 1fr +9fr brn & car 4.00 2.75
On cover 9.50
Nos. B32-B35 (4) 9.60 7.15

The surtax was used to assist the families of mobilized men.

Nos. B32-B35 exist without surcharge. Value set, $325.

POSTAGE DUE STAMPS

D1

Perf. 14x13½
1926-27 **Typo.** **Unwmk.**
J1 D1 5c light blue .40 .30
Never hinged .80
On cover 4.75
J2 D1 10c dk brn .40 .30
Never hinged .80
On cover 4.75
J3 D1 20c olive grn .80 .30
Never hinged 1.20
On cover 4.75
J4 D1 25c car rose .80 .65
Never hinged 2.00
On cover 5.50

J5 D1 30c rose red 1.20 .50
Never hinged 1.75
On cover 5.50
J6 D1 45c blue grn 1.60 .65
Never hinged 2.40
On cover 5.50
J7 D1 50c brn vio .80 .25
Never hinged 1.20
On cover 4.75
J8 D1 60c green ('27) 3.25 .90
Never hinged 4.00
On cover 6.50
J9 D1 1fr red brn, *straw* .40 .30
Never hinged .80
On cover 4.75
J10 D1 2fr lil rose ('27) .80 .30
Never hinged 1.20
On cover 4.75
J11 D1 3fr deep blue ('27) .80 .30
Never hinged 1.20
On cover 4.75
Nos. J1-J11 (11) 11.25 4.75

See Nos. J25-J26, J28-J32 in *Scott Standard Postage Stamp Catalogue*, Vol 1. For surcharges, see Nos. J18-J20.

D2

1926-27
J12 D2 1c olive grn .40 .40
Never hinged .80
On cover 4.75
J13 D2 10c violet 1.60 .80
Never hinged 2.40
On cover 5.50
J14 D2 30c bister 1.60 .80
Never hinged 2.40
On cover 5.50
J15 D2 60c dull red 1.20 .80
Never hinged 1.60
On cover 5.50
J16 D2 1fr brt vio ('27) 20.00 4.00
Never hinged 32.50
On cover 13.50
J17 D2 2fr lt bl ('27) 16.00 1.60
Never hinged 24.00
On cover 10.50
Nos. J12-J17 (6) 40.80 8.40

See note below France No. J51.
For surcharges, see Nos. J21-J24.

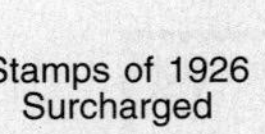
Stamps of 1926 Surcharged

1927
J18 D1 60c on 20c olive grn 2.00 .80
Never hinged 2.75
On cover 8.00
J19 D1 2fr on 45c blue grn 2.75 1.60
Never hinged 4.00
On cover 9.50
J20 D1 3fr on 25c car rose 1.60 .80
Never hinged 2.40
On cover 8.00
Nos. J18-J20 (3) 6.35 3.20

Recouvrement Stamps of 1926 Surcharged

1927-32
J21 D2 10c on 30c bis ('32) 5.50 4.00
Never hinged 8.00
On cover 13.50
J22 D2 1fr on 1c olive grn 4.00 1.60
Never hinged 8.00
On cover 9.50
J23 D2 1fr on 60c dl red ('32) 24.00 .80
Never hinged 35.00
On cover 7.25
J24 D2 2fr on 10c violet 16.00 12.00
Never hinged 24.00
On cover 35.00
Nos. J21-J24 (4) 49.50 18.40

NEWSPAPER STAMPS

Nos. 1 and 33 Surcharged in Red

1924-26 Unwmk. *Perf. 14x13½*
P1 A16 ½c on 1c dk gray .40 .40
Never hinged .80
On cover 47.50
a. Triple surcharge 300.00
Never hinged 400.00
P2 A1 ½c on 1c olive ('26) .40 .40
Never hinged .80
On cover 40.00

ALLENSTEIN

'a-lən-ˌshtin

LOCATION — In East Prussia
AREA — 4,457 sq. mi.
POP. — 540,000 (estimated 1920)
CAPITAL — Allenstein

Allenstein, a district of East Prussia, held a plebiscite in 1920 under the Versailles Treaty, voting to join Germany rather than Poland. Later that year, Allenstein became part of the German Republic.

100 Pfennig = 1 Mark

Stamps of Germany, 1906-20, Overprinted

Perf. 14, 14½, 14x14½, 14½x14
1920 Wmk. 125
1 A16 5pf green .40 1.15
Never hinged 1.10
On cover 13.00
On cover, single franking 150.00
2 A16 10pf carmine .40 1.15
Never hinged 1.10
On cover 13.00
On cover, single franking 22.50
3 A22 15pf dk vio .40 1.15
Never hinged 1.10
On cover 13.00
On cover, single franking 14.00
4 A22 15pf vio brn 5.50 11.50
Never hinged 16.00
On cover 42.50
a. 15pf red brown 65.00 350.00
Never hinged 150.00
On cover 440.00
5 A16 20pf bl vio .40 1.50
Never hinged 1.40
On cover 13.00
On cover, single franking 16.00
a. 20pf ultramarine 26.00 105.00
Never hinged 105.00
On cover 450.00
On cover, single franking 150.00
6 A16 30pf org & blk, *buff* .40 1.50
Never hinged 1.40
On cover 13.00
7 A16 40pf lake & blk .40 1.15
Never hinged 1.10
On cover 13.00
On cover, single franking 15.00
8 A16 50pf pur & blk, *buff* .40 1.15
Never hinged 1.10
On cover 13.00
On cover, single franking 32.50
9 A16 75pf grn & blk .40 1.15
Never hinged 1.10
On cover 17.50
On cover, single franking 85.00
10 A17 1m car rose 1.60 5.00
Never hinged 4.00
On cover 35.00
On cover, single franking —
a. Double overprint 275.00 1,100.
11 A17 1.25m green 1.60 5.25
Never hinged 4.50
On cover 40.00
On cover, single franking 65.00
a. Double overprint — —
b. 1.25m bluish green 12.00 35.00
Never hinged 24.00
On cover 85.00
On cover, single franking 210.00
12 A17 1.50m yel brn .95 4.00
Never hinged 3.50
On cover 42.50
On cover, single franking 85.00
a. 1.50m red brown 26.00 60.00
Never hinged 60.00
On cover 105.00
On cover, single franking 160.00
b. 1.50m dark brown 40.00 120.00
Never hinged 110.00
On cover 150.00
On cover, single franking 225.00
13 A21 2.50m lilac rose (shades) 2.40 10.50
Never hinged 6.25
On cover 35.00
On cover, single franking 140.00
14 A19 3m blk vio 2.40 5.25
Never hinged 6.25
On cover 52.50
a. Double overprint 325.00 1,150.
Never hinged 650.00
b. Inverted overprint — —
Nos. 1-14 (14) 17.65 51.40
Set, never hinged 50.00

The 5pf brown (Germany No. 118), 10pf orange (No. 119), 20pf green (No. 121), 30pf blue (No. 123) and 40pf (No. 124) exist with this overprint but were not regularly issued. Value, each: $75 hinged, $145 never hinged.Nos. 4 and 4a exist with Allenstein overprint not covering DEUTSCHE REICH. No. 4 value, $32.50 hinged; $82.50 never hinged; $300 used. No. 4a is rare.

Overprinted

15 A16 5pf green .40 1.00
Never hinged .85
On cover 13.00
16 A16 10pf carmine .40 1.00
Never hinged .85
On cover 13.00
On cover, single franking 15.00
17 A22 15pf dark vio .40 1.00
Never hinged .85
On cover 13.00
a. 15pf blackish violet 14.00 95.00
Never hinged 35.00
On cover 175.00
18 A22 15pf vio brn 20.00 40.00
Never hinged 52.50
On cover 85.00
a. 15pf red brown 70.00 350.00
Never hinged 140.00
19 A16 20pf blue vio .65 1.50
Never hinged 1.40
On cover 13.00
On cover, single franking 30.00
a. 20pf ultramarine 100.00 150.00
Never hinged 260.00
On cover 220.00
20 A16 30pf org & blk, *buff* .40 1.00
Never hinged .85
On cover 13.00
On cover, single franking 20.00
21 A16 40pf lake & blk .40 1.00
Never hinged .85
On cover 13.00
On cover, single franking 19.00
22 A16 50pf pur & blk, *buff* .40 1.00
Never hinged .85
On cover 17.00
On cover, single franking 32.50
23 A16 75pf grn & blk .65 1.50
Never hinged 1.40
On cover 17.00
a. 75pf blue green & brownish black 13.00 25.00
Never hinged 26.00
On cover 85.00
24 A17 1m car rose 1.60 3.00
Never hinged 3.00
On cover 35.00
On cover, single franking 125.00
a. Inverted overprint 600.00 800.00
Never hinged 800.00
25 A17 1.25m green 1.60 3.00
Never hinged 3.00
On cover 35.00
On cover, single franking 55.00
a. 1.25m bluish green 10.00 17.50
Never hinged 22.50
On cover 65.00
On cover, single franking 100.00
26 A17 1.50m yel brn 1.25 3.00
Never hinged 2.25
On cover 35.00
On cover, single franking 75.00
a. 1.50m red brown 13.00 60.00
Never hinged 30.00
On cover 100.00
On cover, single franking 150.00
b. 1.50m dark brown 15.00 80.00
Never hinged 35.00
On cover 130.00
On cover, single franking 175.00
27 A21 2.50m lilac rose (shades) 2.75 7.50
Never hinged 5.25
On cover 35.00
On cover, single franking 125.00
28 A19 3m blk vio 1.75 3.00
Never hinged 3.00
On cover 42.50
On cover, single franking 160.00
a. Inverted overprint 400.00 975.00
Never hinged 725.00
b. Double overprint 200.00 600.00
Never hinged 600.00
Nos. 15-28 (14) 32.65 68.50
Set, never hinged 75.00

The 40pf carmine rose (Germany No. 124) exists with this oval overprint, but it is doubtful whether it was regularly issued. Value $105 hinged, $210 never hinged.

ANDORRA, SPANISH ADMINISTRATION

an-'dor-ə

LOCATION — On the southern slope of the Pyrenees Mountains between France and Spain.
GOVT. — Co-principality
AREA — 179 sq. mi.
POP. — 5,231
CAPITAL — Andorre

Andorra is subject to the joint control of France and the Spanish Bishop of Urgel and pays annual tribute to both. The country has no monetary unit of its own, the peseta and franc both being in general use.

100 Centimos = 1 Peseta
100 Centimes = 1 Franc

A majority of the Spanish Andorra stamps issued to about 1950 are poorly centered. The fine examples that are valued will be somewhat off center. Very poorly centered examples (perfs cutting design) sell for less. Well centered very fine stamps are scarce and sell for approximately twice the values shown (Nos. 1-24, E1-E3), or 50% more (Nos. 25-49, E4-E5).

Stamps of Spain, 1922-26, Overprinted in Red or Black

Perf. 13½x12½, 12½x11½, 14
1928 Unwmk.
1 A49 2c olive green .55 .55
Never hinged 2.10
On cover 27.50
a. 2c bronze green 2.75 2.75
Never hinged 8.50

Control Numbers on Back

2 A49 5c car rose (Bk) .80 .80
Never hinged 2.60
On cover 27.50
a. 5c rose 5.50 5.25
Never hinged 17.50
3 A49 10c green .80 .80
Never hinged 3.50
On cover 27.50
a. 10c bluish green 22.50 —
Never hinged 42.50
4 A49 15c slate blue 3.25 3.25
Never hinged 7.00
On cover 37.50
a. 15c dk slate green 10.00 10.00
Never hinged 16.50
5 A49 20c violet 3.25 3.50
Never hinged 7.00
On cover 37.50
a. 20c violet 16.50 —
Never hinged 35.00
6 A49 25c rose red (Bk) 3.25 3.50
Never hinged 8.00
On cover 37.50
7 A49 30c black brown 18.00 16.50
Never hinged 45.00
On cover 82.50
a. 30c grayish brown 21.00 21.00
Never hinged 55.00
b. As "a," inverted overprint 160.00 50.00
8 A49 40c deep blue 18.00 11.00
Never hinged 52.50
On cover 70.00
a. 40c grayish blue 37.50 32.50
Never hinged 100.00
9 A49 50c orange (Bk) 18.00 14.50
Never hinged 52.50
On cover 72.50
a. 50c yellow orange 37.50 32.50
Never hinged 100.00
c. Inverted ovpt., perf 14 160.00 —
10 A49a 1p blue blk 23.00 23.50
Never hinged 60.00
On cover 87.50
11 A49a 4p lake (Bk) 150.00 175.00
Never hinged 350.00
On cover 650.00
12 A49a 10p brown (Bk) 275.00 275.00
Never hinged 600.00
On cover —
a. Double overprint 1,000.
Never hinged 2,000.
Nos. 1-12 (12) 513.90 527.90
Set, never hinged 1,200.

Counterfeit overprints exist.

Covers: Values for covers are for commercial items with proper frankings. Overfranked items and other philatelic covers sell for much less.

Values for blocks of 4

1	A49	2c olive green	3.00	3.00
a.		2c bronze green	14.50	15.50

2 A49 5c carmine rose (Bk) 3.50 3.50
a. 5c rose 32.50 32.50
3 A49 10c green 3.50 3.50
a. 10c bluish green 120.00 —
4 A49 15c slate blue 16.50 *17.50*
a. 15c dk slate green 55.00 *57.50*
5 A49 20c lilac 14.50 *19.00*
a. 20c violet 87.50 —
6 A49 25c rose red (Bk) 16.50 *19.00*
7 A49 30c brown 110.00 *120.00*
a. 30c grayish brown 105.00 —
8 A49 40c deep blue 110.00 77.50
a. 40c grayish blue 165.00 165.00
9 A49 50c orange (Bk) 105.00 100.00
a. 50c yellow orange 190.00 190.00
10 A49 1p blue black 275.00 140.00
11 A49 4p lake (Bk) 850.00 *1,000.*
12 A49 10p brown (Bk) 1,750. *1,900.*

Specimen Stamps, Numbered A.000.000 on Reverse

2S A49 5c rose (Bk) 180.00
Never hinged 250.00
3S A49 10c dark green 180.00
Never hinged 250.00
4S A49 15c dk slate blue 180.00
Never hinged 250.00
5S A49 20c grayish lilac (R) 180.00
Never hinged 250.00
6S A49 25c rose red (Bk) 180.00
Never hinged 250.00
7S A49 30c brown 240.00
Never hinged 325.00
8S A49 40c dark blue 240.00
Never hinged 325.00
9S A49 50c orange (Bk) 240.00
Never hinged 325.00
10S A49 1p blue black 275.00
Never hinged 400.00
10aS A49 1p blue black, perf 14 350.00
11aS A49 4p lake (Bk) 350.00
Never hinged 450.00
12bS A49 10p brown (Bk) 375.00
Never hinged 525.00

1928 ***Perf. 14***

1b A49 2c olive green 12.50 12.50
Never hinged 18.00
On cover 75.00
On cover, single franking 250.00
2b A49 5c rose (Bk) 575.00 *700.00*
Never hinged 800.00
3b A49 10c green 4.00 *4.50*
Never hinged 8.00
On cover 65.00
On cover, single franking 200.00
3c A49 10c dark green 4.50 4.50
Never hinged 9.00
On cover 75.00
On cover, single franking 200.00
4b A49 15c dk slate blue 12.50 12.50
Never hinged 17.50
On cover 75.00
On cover, single franking 250.00
5b A49 20c grayish lilac (R) 250.00 *300.00*
Never hinged 350.00
5c A49 20c lilac (C) 180.00 225.00
Never hinged 275.00
6a A49 25c rose red (Bk) — —
b. As "a," inverted overprint 125.00 65.00
7c A49 30c brown 27.50 27.50
Never hinged 40.00
On cover 125.00
On cover, single franking 300.00
8b A49 40c deep blue 32.50 32.50
Never hinged 50.00
On cover 125.00
On cover, single franking 300.00
8c A49 40c dark blue — —
9b A49 50c orange (Bk) 600.00 *700.00*
c. As "b," inverted overprint 150.00 80.00
10a A49 1p blue black 600.00 *700.00*
Never hinged 775.00
11a A49 4p carmine lake (Bk) 375.00 *400.00*
Never hinged 500.00
11b A49 4p reddish violet (Bk) — —
12b A49 10p brown (Bk) 450.00 *550.00*
Never hinged 650.00

La Vall
A1

St. Juan de Caselles
A2

St. Julia de Loria — A3

St. Coloma — A4

General Council — A5

1929, Nov. 25 **Engr.** ***Perf. 14***

13 A1 2c olive green 1.10 .60
Never hinged 2.25

Control Numbers on Back

14 A2 5c carmine lake 3.50 1.25
Never hinged 8.00
15 A3 10c yellow green 3.50 *4.50*
Never hinged 8.50
16 A4 15c slate green 3.50 *4.50*
Never hinged 9.00
17 A3 20c violet 3.50 *4.50*
Never hinged 8.50
18 A4 25c carmine rose 7.75 6.25
Never hinged 16.00
19 A1 30c olive brown 115.00 *175.00*
Never hinged 290.00
20 A2 40c dark blue 4.50 3.00
Never hinged 16.00
21 A3 50c deep orange 5.50 4.50
Never hinged 15.00
22 A5 1p slate 12.50 14.50
Never hinged 40.00
23 A5 4p deep rose 90.00 *110.00*
Never hinged 190.00
24 A5 10p bister brown 100.00 *140.00*
Never hinged 200.00
Nos. 13-24 (12) 350.35 *468.60*
Set, never hinged 800.00

Nos. 13-24 exist imperforate. Value, $950.

1931-38 ***Perf. 11½***

13a A1 2c 6.25 .80
Never hinged 11.00

Control Numbers on Back

14a A2 5c 10.00 2.25
Never hinged 17.50
15a A3 10c 10.00 2.00
Never hinged 17.50
16a A4 15c 30.00 25.00
Never hinged 41.00
17a A3 20c 10.00 6.00
Never hinged 17.50
18a A4 25c 10.00 6.00
Never hinged 17.50
19a A1 30c ('33) 175.00 65.00
Never hinged 225.00
20a A2 40c ('35) 17.00 13.00
Never hinged 25.00
22a A5 1p ('38) 40.00 25.00
Never hinged 65.00
Nos. 13a-22a (9) 308.25 145.05
Set, never hinged 500.00

Without Control Numbers

1936-43 ***Perf. 11½x11***

25 A1 2c red brown ('37) 2.00 1.60
Never hinged 3.75
26 A2 5c dark brown 2.00 1.60
Never hinged 3.75
27 A3 10c blue green 13.00 3.25
Never hinged 35.00
a. 10c yellow green 120.00 62.50
Never hinged 165.00
28 A4 15c blue green ('37) 7.50 3.50
Never hinged 14.50
a. 15c yellow green 8.00 5.75
Never hinged 8.50
29 A3 20c violet 7.00 3.50
Never hinged 10.00
30 A4 25c deep rose ('37) 3.25 *3.25*
Never hinged 4.25
31 A1 30c carmine 5.50 3.25
Never hinged 6.25
31A A2 40c dark blue *700.00* —
Never hinged 1,200.
b. Perf 14 250.00
Never hinged 350.00
32 A1 45c rose red ('37) 2.00 1.60
Never hinged 2.90
33 A3 50c deep orange 10.00 5.75
Never hinged 14.00
34 A1 60c deep blue ('37) 7.00 3.50
Never hinged 10.00
34A A5 1p slate 800.00 —
Never hinged 1,500.
35 A5 4p deep rose ('43) 40.00 *47.50*
Never hinged 100.00
36 A5 10p bister brn ('43) 52.50 *57.50*
Never hinged 120.00
Nos. 25-31,32-34,35-36 (12) 151.75 135.80
Set, never hinged 325.00

Nos. 26, 28, 32 exist imperforate. Value hinged, $290.

Beware of counterfeits of Nos. 31A and 34A. Purchase of stamps with certificates is strongly advised.

AIR POST STAMPS

A set of 12 stamps, inscribed "CORREU AER / SOBRETAXA" was authorized in 1932 for a proposed private air service between Andorra and Barcelona. These stamps were prepared but not issued. Value, set $40. The stamps were also overprinted "FRANQUICIA DEL CONSELL" for official use. Value, set $140.

SPECIAL DELIVERY STAMPS

Special Delivery Stamp of Spain, 1905 Overprinted

1928 **Unwmk.** ***Perf. 14***

Without Control Number on Back

E1 SD1 20c red 80.00 *95.00*
Never hinged 150.00
On cover *800.00*

With Control Number on Back

E2 SD1 20c pale red 50.00 *50.00*
Never hinged 90.00
On cover 120.00

Eagle over Mountain Pass — SD2

1929 ***Perf. 14***

With Control Number on Back

E3 SD2 20c scarlet 25.00 20.00
Never hinged 35.00

Perf 11 ½ examples are numbered A000.000 and are specimens. Value, $400.

1937 ***Perf. 11½x11***

Without Control Number on Back

E4 SD2 20c red 7.75 *9.50*
Never hinged 8.75

ANDORRA, FRENCH ADMINISTRATION

Stamps and Types of France, 1900-1929, Overprinted

Perf. 14x13½

1931, June 16 **Unwmk.**

1 A16 1c gray 1.25 *1.25*
Never hinged 1.40
On cover 21.00
On cover, single franking 250.00
a. Double overprint *2,000.* *2,000.*
Never hinged *2,750.*
2 A16 2c red brown 1.60 *1.60*
Never hinged 1.75
On cover 21.00
On cover, single franking 160.00
3 A16 3c orange 1.60 *1.60*
Never hinged 1.75
On cover 21.00
On cover, single franking 160.00
4 A16 5c green 2.40 *2.40*
Never hinged 3.25
On cover 21.00
On cover, single franking 160.00
5 A16 10c lilac 4.00 *4.75*
Never hinged 6.00
On cover 21.00
On cover, single franking 160.00
6 A22 15c red brown 5.50 5.50
Never hinged 9.25
On cover 27.50
On cover, single franking 87.50
7 A22 20c red violet 8.75 *9.50*
Never hinged 14.00
On cover 37.50
On cover, single franking 160.00
8 A22 25c yellow brn 9.50 *10.00*
Never hinged 17.50
On cover 50.00
On cover, single franking 160.00
9 A22 30c green 9.50 *10.00*
Never hinged 16.00
On cover 50.00
On cover, single franking 160.00
10 A22 40c ultra 10.00 *12.00*
Never hinged 17.50
On cover 42.50
On cover, single franking 70.00
11 A20 45c lt violet 20.00 *21.50*
Never hinged 32.50
On cover 55.00
On cover, single franking 140.00
12 A20 50c vermilion 13.50 *15.00*
Never hinged 19.00
On cover 55.00
a. Pair, one without overprint 525.00
Never hinged 800.00
On cover, single franking 140.00
13 A20 65c gray green 28.00 28.00
Never hinged 42.50
On cover 100.00
On cover, single franking 250.00
14 A20 75c rose lilac 32.50 28.00
Never hinged 46.00
On cover 100.00
On cover, single franking 325.00
15 A22 90c red 40.00 *45.00*
Never hinged 56.00
On cover 125.00
On cover, single franking 350.00
16 A20 1fr dull blue 40.00 *45.00*
Never hinged 62.50
On cover 125.00
On cover, single franking 350.00
17 A22 1.50fr light blue 45.00 *47.50*
Never hinged 80.00
On cover 140.00
On cover, single franking 350.00

Overprinted

18 A18 2fr org & pale bl 87.50 *95.00*
Never hinged 100.00
On cover 140.00
On cover, single franking 325.00
19 A18 3fr brt vio & rose 115.00 *125.00*
Never hinged 225.00
On cover 250.00
On cover, single franking 350.00
20 A18 5fr dk bl & buff 140.00 *145.00*
Never hinged 220.00
On cover 290.00
On cover, single franking 500.00
21 A18 10fr grn & red 300.00 *350.00*
Never hinged 435.00
On cover 1,250.
On cover, single franking —
22 A18 20fr mag & grn 400.00 *575.00*
Never hinged 800.00
On cover 2,150.
On cover, single franking —
Nos. 1-22 (22) 1,316. *1,579.*

See No. P1 for ½c on 1c gray.

Nos. 9, 15 and 17 were not issued in France without overprint.

Chapel of Meritxell
A50

Bridge of St. Anthony
A51

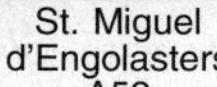

St. Miguel d'Engolasters
A52

Gorge of St. Julia
A53

Old Andorra
A54

1932-43 **Engr.** ***Perf. 13***

23 A50 1c gray blk .55 *.65*
Never hinged .70
On cover 5.00
On cover, single franking 35.00
24 A50 2c violet .90 .90
Never hinged .70
On cover 5.00
On cover, single franking 35.00
25 A50 3c brown .90 *.95*
Never hinged .70
On cover 5.00
On cover, single franking 35.00

No.	Type	Description	Unused	Used
26	A50	5c blue green	.90	*.95*
		Never hinged	1.00	
		On cover		5.00
		On cover, single franking		35.00
27	A51	10c dull lilac	1.40	1.40
		Never hinged	1.50	
		On cover		5.00
		On cover, single franking		35.00
28	A50	15c deep red	2.00	2.00
		Never hinged	3.00	
		On cover		8.50
		On cover, single franking		35.00
29	A51	20c lt rose	13.50	11.00
		Never hinged	21.00	
		On cover		50.00
		On cover, single franking		100.00
30	A52	25c brown	6.50	5.50
		Never hinged	7.75	
		On cover		60.00
		On cover, single franking		175.00
31	A51	25c brn car ('37)	11.00	*14.00*
		Never hinged	16.00	
		On cover		27.50
		On cover, single franking		55.00
32	A51	30c emerald	4.75	4.75
		Never hinged	5.75	
		On cover		30.00
		On cover, single franking		77.50
33	A51	40c ultra	13.50	11.00
		Never hinged	21.00	
		On cover		35.00
		On cover, single franking		70.00
34	A51	40c brn blk ('39)	1.25	1.25
		Never hinged	1.75	
		On cover		7.00
		On cover, single franking		55.00
35	A51	45c lt red	13.50	11.00
		Never hinged	21.00	
		On cover		55.00
		On cover, single franking		100.00
36	A51	45c bl grn ('39)	6.00	5.25
		Never hinged	9.00	
		On cover		35.00
		On cover, single franking		70.00
37	A52	50c lilac rose	14.50	13.00
		Never hinged	21.00	
		On cover		42.50
		On cover, single franking		85.00
38	A51	50c lt vio ('39)	6.00	5.50
		Never hinged	8.75	
		On cover		35.00
		On cover, single franking		70.00
38A	A51	50c grn ('40)	2.40	2.40
		Never hinged	3.00	
		On cover		37.50
		On cover, single franking		100.00
39	A51	55c lt vio ('38)	24.00	16.00
		Never hinged	37.50	
		On cover		70.00
		On cover, single franking		110.00
40	A51	60c yel brn ('38)	1.60	1.60
		Never hinged	1.75	
		On cover		7.00
		On cover, single franking		70.00
41	A52	65c yel grn	65.00	52.50
		Never hinged	87.50	
		On cover		110.00
		On cover, single franking		160.00
42	A51	65c blue ('38)	18.50	14.50
		Never hinged	25.00	
		On cover		70.00
		On cover, single franking		140.00
43	A51	70c red ('39)	2.40	2.40
		Never hinged	3.50	
		On cover		14.00
		On cover, single franking		70.00
44	A52	75c violet	11.00	8.75
		Never hinged	17.50	
		On cover		42.50
		On cover, single franking		140.00
45	A51	75c ultra ('39)	4.50	*4.75*
		Never hinged	6.50	
		On cover		35.00
		On cover, single franking		70.00
46	A51	80c green ('38)	27.50	23.00
		Never hinged	45.00	
		On cover		110.00
		On cover, single franking		210.00
46A	A53	80c bl grn ('40)	.40	.40
		Never hinged	.50	
		On cover		27.50
		On cover, single franking		90.00
47	A53	90c deep rose	6.50	6.50
		Never hinged	10.50	
		On cover		52.50
		On cover, single franking		140.00
48	A53	90c dk grn ('39)	3.50	3.50
		Never hinged	5.25	
		On cover		27.50
		On cover, single franking		110.00
49	A53	1fr blue grn	20.00	14.50
		Never hinged	32.50	
		On cover		55.00
		On cover, single franking		90.00
50	A53	1fr scarlet ('38)	32.50	24.00
		Never hinged	47.50	
		On cover		140.00
		On cover, single franking		350.00
51	A53	1fr dp ultra ('39)	.40	.40
		Never hinged	.40	
		On cover		7.00
		On cover, single franking		70.00
51A	A53	1.20fr brt vio ('42)	.40	.40
		Never hinged	.50	
		On cover		5.00
		On cover, single franking		42.50
52	A50	1.25fr rose car ('33)	60.00	45.00
		Never hinged	95.00	
		On cover		55.00
		On cover, single franking		110.00
52A	A50	1.25fr rose ('38)	5.50	4.00
		Never hinged	7.00	
		On cover		27.50
		On cover, single franking		110.00
52B	A53	1.30fr sepia ('40)	.40	.40
		Never hinged	.50	
		On cover		60.00
		On cover, single franking		160.00
53	A54	1.50fr ultra	24.00	19.50
		Never hinged	35.00	
		On cover		60.00
		On cover, single franking		110.00
53A	A53	1.50fr crim ('40)	.40	.40
		Never hinged	.50	
		On cover		55.00
		On cover, single franking		140.00
54	A53	1.75fr violet ('33)	120.00	*120.00*
		Never hinged	190.00	
		On cover		135.00
		On cover, single franking		165.00
55	A53	1.75fr dk bl ('38)	47.50	40.00
		Never hinged	70.00	
		On cover		150.00
		On cover, single franking		350.00
56	A53	2fr red violet	13.00	11.50
		Never hinged	17.50	
		On cover		27.50
		On cover, single franking		90.00
56A	A50	2fr rose red ('40)	1.60	1.60
		Never hinged	2.40	
		On cover		32.50
		On cover, single franking		70.00
56B	A50	2fr dk bl grn ('42)	.40	.40
		Never hinged	.50	
		On cover		3.50
		On cover, single franking		40.00
57	A50	2.15fr dk vio ('38)	65.00	52.50
		Never hinged	100.00	
		On cover		175.00
		On cover, single franking		375.00
58	A50	2.25fr ultra ('39)	8.75	8.75
		Never hinged	14.00	
		On cover		35.00
		On cover, single franking		110.00
58A	A50	2.40fr red ('42)	.80	.40
		Never hinged	.80	
		On cover		9.00
		On cover, single franking		140.00
59	A50	2.50fr gray blk ('39)	8.00	8.00
		Never hinged	14.00	
		On cover		42.50
		On cover, single franking		115.00
59A	A50	2.50fr dp ultra ('40)	2.75	2.75
		Never hinged	4.00	
		On cover		35.00
		On cover, single franking		70.00
60	A53	3fr orange brn	13.50	10.50
		Never hinged	21.00	
		On cover		32.50
		On cover, single franking		90.00
60A	A50	3fr red brn ('40)	.40	.40
		Never hinged	.50	
		On cover		35.00
		On cover, single franking		70.00
60B	A50	4fr sl bl ('42)	.40	.40
		Never hinged	.50	
		On cover		10.00
		On cover, single franking		70.00
60C	A50	4.50fr dp vio ('42)	2.00	2.00
		Never hinged	2.25	
		On cover		7.75
		On cover, single franking		60.00
61	A54	5fr brown	.90	.80
		Never hinged	1.00	
		On cover		8.50
		On cover, single franking		705.00
62	A54	10fr violet	1.00	.80
		Never hinged	1.25	
		On cover		8.50
		On cover, single franking		70.00
62B	A54	15fr dp ultra ('42)	1.20	1.20
		Never hinged	1.40	
		On cover		12.00
		On cover, single franking		70.00
63	A54	20fr rose lake	1.20	.80
		Never hinged	1.40	
		On cover		8.50
		On cover, single franking		62.50
63A	A51	50fr turq bl ('43)	1.60	1.20
		Never hinged	2.25	
		On cover		13.00
		On cover, single franking		70.00
		Nos. 23-63A (56)	698.05	598.00

A 20c ultra exists but was not issued. Value: unused, $27,500; never hinged $42,500.

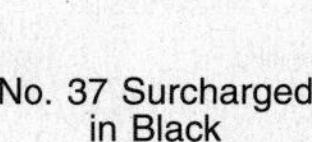

No. 37 Surcharged in Black

1935, Sept. 18

No.	Type	Description	Unused	Used
64	A52	20c on 50c lil rose	18.50	17.00
a.		Double surcharge	*7,000.*	
		Never hinged	*10,000.*	

Coat of Arms — A55

1936-42 *Perf. 14x13*

No.	Type	Description	Unused	Used
65	A55	1c black ('37)	.25	.25
66	A55	2c blue	.25	*.25*
67	A55	3c brown	.25	*.25*
68	A55	5c rose lilac	.25	*.25*
69	A55	10c ultra ('37)	.25	*.25*
70	A55	15c red violet	2.75	2.25
71	A55	20c emerald ('37)	.25	*.25*
72	A55	30c cop red ('38)	.80	*.80*
72A	A55	30c blk brn ('42)	.40	.40
73	A55	35c Prus grn ('38)	70.00	70.00
74	A55	40c cop red ('42)	.80	.80
75	A55	50c Prus grn ('42)	.80	.80
76	A55	60c turq bl ('42)	.80	.80
77	A55	70c vio ('42)	.80	.80
		Nos. 65-77 (14)	78.65	78.15
		Set, never hinged	135.00	

POSTAGE DUE STAMPS

Postage Due Stamps of France, 1893-1931, Overprinted

On Stamps of 1893-1926

1931-33 Unwmk. *Perf. 14x13½*

No.	Type	Description	Unused	Used
J1	D2	5c blue	2.40	2.40
J2	D2	10c brown	2.40	2.40
J3	D2	30c rose red	1.60	1.60
J4	D2	50c violet brn	2.40	2.40
J5	D2	60c green	34.00	34.00
J6	D2	1fr red brn, *straw*	2.40	2.40
J7	D2	2fr brt violet	16.00	16.00
J8	D2	3fr magenta	3.25	3.25
		Nos. J1-J8 (8)	64.45	64.45

On Stamps of 1927-31

No.	Type	Description	Unused	Used
J9	D4	1c olive grn	3.25	3.25
J10	D4	10c rose	5.50	*6.50*
J11	D4	60c red	27.50	26.50
J12	D4	1fr Prus grn ('32)	110.00	*120.00*
J13	D4	1.20fr on 2fr bl	80.00	80.00
J14	D4	2fr ol brn ('33)	200.00	*225.00*
J15	D4	5fr on 1fr vio	120.00	120.00
		Nos. J9-J15 (7)	546.25	581.25

D5

D6

1935-41 **Typo.**

No.	Type	Description	Unused	Used
J16	D5	1c gray green	3.25	3.25
J17	D6	5c light blue ('37)	6.75	6.75
J18	D6	10c brown ('41)	4.00	*5.50*
J19	D6	2fr violet ('41)	11.00	8.75
J20	D6	5fr red orange ('41)	19.00	11.00
		Nos. J16-J20 (5)	44.00	35.25

NEWSPAPER STAMP

France No. P7 Overprinted

1931 Unwmk. *Perf. 14x13½*

No.	Type	Description	Unused	Used
P1	A16	½c on 1c gray	1.25	1.25
		On cover		*40.00*
		On cover, single franking		*60.00*
a.		Double overprint	*3,000.*	
		Never Hinged	*4,000.*	

ANGOLA

aŋ'gō-lə

LOCATION — Southwestern Africa between Belgian Congo and South West Africa.

GOVT. — Portuguese colony

AREA — 481,351 sq. mi.

POP. — 3,484,300

CAPITAL — Luanda

1000 Reis = 1 Milreis

100 Centavos = 1 Escudo (1913)

100 Centavos = 1 Angolar (1932)

Watermark

Wmk. 232 — Maltese Cross

Portuguese Crown — A1

1870-77 Typo. Unwmk. *Perf. 12½*

Thin to Medium Paper

No.	Type	Description	Unused	Used
1	A1	5r gray black	3.25	2.00
b.		5r black	3.25	2.00
2	A1	10r yellow	30.00	20.00
a.		10r orange	30.00	20.00
3	A1	20r bister	3.00	2.25
b.		20r pale bister	3.00	2.25
4	A1	25r red	15.00	10.00
a.		25r rose	250.00	175.00
5	A1	40r blue ('77)	275.00	175.00
6	A1	50r green	70.00	15.00
a.		50r page green	70.00	15.00
7a	A1	100r lilac	15.00	5.00
b.		100r pale lilac	15.00	5.00
8a	A1	200r orange ('77)	7.00	4.00
9a	A1	300r choc ('77)	20.00	12.00

Perf. 13½

No.	Type	Description	Unused	Used
1a	A1	5r gray black	10.00	4.50
1c	A1	5r black	10.00	4.50
2b	A1	10r yellow	27.50	13.00
2c	A1	10r orange yellow	25.00	20.00
3a	A1	20r bister	750.00	475.00
4b	A1	25r red	27.50	20.00
4c	A1	25r rose	42.50	30.00
5a	A1	40r blue ('77)	250.00	150.00
6b	A1	50r green	750.00	425.00
7	A1	100r lilac	6.50	3.50
7c	A1	100r pale lilac	6.50	3.50
8	A1	200r orange ('77)	4.50	2.00
9	A1	300r choc ('77)	6.00	3.50

Perf. 14

No.	Type	Description	Unused	Used
4d	A1	25r rose	800.00	460.00

Thick Paper

Perf. 12½

No.	Type	Description	Unused	Used
1d	A1	5r black	80.00	67.50
2d	A1	10r orange yellow	140.00	85.00
3c	A1	20r bister	110.00	85.00
4e	A1	25r red	70.00	50.00
6c	A1	50r green	100.00	67.50
7d	A1	100r lilac	140.00	65.00

1881-85 ***Perf. 12½, 13½***

No.	Type	Description	Unused	Used
10	A1	10r green ('83)	8.50	4.75
a.		Perf. 12½	37.50	22.50
11	A1	20r carmine rose ('85)	21.00	14.00
12	A1	25r violet ('85)	12.50	5.00
a.		Perf. 13½	12.50	7.25
13	A1	40r buff ('82)	13.00	4.75
a.		Perf. 13½	45.00	4.75
15	A1	50r blue	45.00	10.00
a.		Perf. 13½	82.50	12.50
		Nos. 10-15 (5)	100.00	38.50

Two types of numerals are found on Nos. 2, 11, 13, 15.

The cliche of 40r in plate of 20r error, was discovered before the stamps were issued. All examples were defaced by a blue pencil mark. Values, $2,100 unused; in pair with 20r, $2,400.

In perf. 12½, Nos. 1-4, 4a and 6, as well as 7a, were printed in 1870 on thicker paper and 1875 on normal paper. Stamps of the earlier printing sell for 2 to 5 times more than those of the 1875 printing.

Some reprints of the 1870-85 issues are on a smooth white chalky paper, ungummed and perf. 13½. Value, each $17.50.

Other reprints of these issues are on thin ivory paper with shiny white gum and clear-cut perf. 13½. Value, each $24.

Covers: covers bearing Nos. 1-15 are rare; values start at about $1,800.

King Luiz — A2

1886 Embossed Perf. 12½

16 A2 5r black 14.00 6.50
  a. Perf. 13½ 22.50 16.00
17 A2 10r green 14.00 6.50
  a. Perf. 13½ 27.50 12.50
  b. 10r deep green, perf 12½ 14.00 6.50
18 A2 20r rose 19.00 12.50
  a. Perf. 13½ 22.50 12.50
  b. 20r carmine rose, Perf. 13½ 22.50 12.50
  c. As "a," printed on reverse side *125.00 115.00*
19 A2 25r red violet 15.00 4.00
  a. Double impression *175.00 125.00*
  b. Triple impression *240.00 240.00*
20 A2 40r chocolate 17.50 7.50
21 A2 50r blue 21.00 4.00
  a. Double impression *175.00 125.00*
22 A2 100r yellow brn 30.00 10.00
23 A2 200r gray violet 40.00 13.00
24 A2 300r orange 40.00 14.00
  Nos. 16-24 (9) 210.50 78.00

For surcharges see Nos. 61-69, 172-174, 208-210.

Reprints of 5r, 20r & 100r have cleancut perf. 13½.

King Carlos — A3

1893-94 Typo. Perf. 11½, 12½, 13½
Chalk-Surfaced Paper
Perf. 12½

25 A3 5r yellow 3.75 1.50
26 A3 10r redsh violet 5.00 3.00
27 A3 15r chocolate 5.25 2.25
30 A3 50r light blue 5.25 2.25
31 A3 75r carmine 20.00 12.00
32 A3 80r lt green 20.00 9.00
33 A3 100r brown, *buff* 20.00 9.00
34 A3 150r car, *rose* 30.00 17.50
35 A3 200r dk blue, *lt bl* 30.00 17.50
36 A3 300r dk blue, *sal* 35.00 17.50

Perf. 11½

25a A3 5r yellow 3.00 1.25
27a A3 15r chocolate 7.00 3.00
28 A3 20r lavender 7.00 3.00
29 A3 25r green 3.25 1.60
30a A3 50r light blue 3.75 2.00
31a A3 75r carmine 13.25 9.50
33a A3 100r brown, *buff* 55.00 47.50
34a A3 150r car, *rose* 16.00 10.00

Perf. 13½

35a A3 200r dk blue, *lt bl* 14.00 12.00
36a A3 300r dk blue, *sal* 14.00 12.00

Enamel Paper
Perf. 12½

29a A3 25r green 3.00 1.50
30b A3 50r light blue 10.00 4.00

Perf. 11½

25b A3 5r yellow 2.25 1.60
26a A3 10r redsh violet 2.50 1.80
29b A3 25r green 3.25 3.00
31b A3 75r carmine 9.25 7.75

Perf. 13½

25c A3 5r yellow 1.80 1.50
29c A3 25r green 7.00 3.75
30c A3 50r light blue 7.75 6.25
31c A3 75r carmine 7.75 6.25

For surcharges see Nos. 70-81, 175-179, 213-216, 234.

No. P1 Surcharged in Blue

1894, Aug. Perf. 13½

37 N1 25r on 2½r brown 75.00 60.00
  a. Double surcharge, one inverted 175.00
  b. Perf. 11½ 110.00 85..00
  c. Perf. 12½ 90.00 67.50
  d. As 'c,' double surcharge, one inverted 140.00 125.00

King Carlos — A5

1898-1903 Perf. 11½
Name and Value in Black except 500r

38 A5 2½r gray .65 .50
39 A5 5r orange .65 .50
40 A5 10r yellow grn .65 .50
41 A5 15r violet brn 3.25 1.60
42 A5 15r gray green ('03) 1.60 1.40
43 A5 20r gray violet .70 .50
44 A5 25r sea green 1.60 .75
45 A5 25r car ('03) .85 .45
46 A5 50r blue 2.75 1.00
47 A5 50r brown ('03) 8.00 3.75
48 A5 65r dull blue ('03) 8.50 5.75
49 A5 75r rose 11.00 6.00
50 A5 75r red violet ('03) 3.00 2.00
51 A5 80r violet 10.00 3.00
52 A5 100r dk blue, *blue* 2.00 1.40
53 A5 115r org brn, *pink* ('03) 11.00 7.50
54 A5 130r brn, *straw* ('03) 11.00 7.50
55 A5 150r brn, *straw* 11.00 6.00
56 A5 200r red vio, *pink* 7.50 1.75
57 A5 300r dk blue, *rose* 6.50 5.00
58 A5 400r dull bl, *straw* ('03) 12.50 3.50
59 A5 500r blk & red, *bl* ('01) 16.00 5.00
60 A5 700r vio, *yelsh* ('01) 35.00 17.00
  Nos. 38-60 (23) 165.70 82.35

For surcharges and overprints see Nos. 83-102, 113-117, 159-171, 181-183, 217-218, 221-225.

Stamps of 1886-94 Surcharged in Black or Red

Two types of surcharge:
I — 3mm between numeral and REIS.
II — 4½mm spacing.

1902 Perf. 12½

61 A2 65r on 40r choc 12.00 6.50
62 A2 65r on 300r org, I 12.00 6.50
  a. Type II 12.00 6.50
63 A2 115r on 10r green 10.00 5.00
  a. Inverted surcharge 90.00 50.00
  b. Perf. 13½ 75.00 45.00
64 A2 115r on 200r gray vio 10.00 5.00
65 A2 130r on 50r blue 13.00 5.00
66 A2 130r on 100r brown 8.50 5.00
67 A2 400r on 20r rose 110.00 65.00
  a. Perf. 13½ 175.00 92.50
68 A2 400r on 25r violet 22.50 12.00
69 A2 400r on 5r black (R) 20.00 13.00
  a. Double surcharge 75.00 50.00
  Nos. 61-69 (9) 218.00 123.00

For surcharges see Nos. 172-174, 208-210.

Chalk-Surfaced Paper
Perf. 11½

70 A3 65r on 5r yel, I 11.00 6.50
72 A3 65r on 20r lav 11.00 6.50
75a A3 115r on 100r brn, *buff* 325.00 225.00
76 A3 115r on 150r car, *rose* 17.50 13.00
77a A3 130r on 15r choc, I 8.00 4.50
77b A3 130r on 15r choc, II 8.00 4.50
78 A3 130r on 75r carmine 60.00 50.00
80a A3 400r on 50r lt bl, I 32.50 15.00

Perf. 12½

71 A3 65r on 10r red vio, I 7.25 5.50
71a A3 65r on 10r red vio, II 7.25 5.50
73 A3 65r on 25r green 15.00 9.00
74 A3 115r on 80r lt grn 15.00 9.00
75 A3 115r on 100r brn, *buff* 15.00 7.25
76b A3 115r on 150r car, *rose* 24.00 15.00
77 A3 130r on 15r choc 6.50 5.50
78b A3 130r on 75r carmine 15.00 11.00
79 A3 130r on 300r dk bl, *sal* 20.00 15.00
80 A3 400r on 50r lt bl, I 11.00 5.50
81 A3 400r on 200r bl, *bl* 11.00 8.00

Perf. 13½

75b A3 115r on 100r brn, *buff* 80.00 40.00
76a A3 115r on 150r car, *rose* 25.00 15.00
79a A3 130r on 300r dk bl, *sal* 35.00 12.50
81a A3 400r on 200r bl, *bl* 375.00 225.00

Enamel Paper
Perf. 11½

70a A3 65r on 5r yel, II 11.00 7.00
70b A3 65r on 5r yel, I 11.00 7.00
71b A3 65r on 10r red vio, I 12.00 7.00
71c A3 65r on 10r red vio, II 12.00 7.00
72a A3 65r on 20r lav 12.00 7.00
78c A3 130r on 75r carmine 9.00 8.00

Enamel Paper
Perf. 12½

73a A3 65r on 25r green 7.00 5.00
80b A3 400r on 50r lt bl, I 9.00 6.00
80c A3 400r on 50r lt bl, II 9.00 6.00

Perf. 13½

73b A3 65r on 25r green 7.00 5.00
78a A3 130r on 75r carmine 70.00 55.00
80d A3 400r on 50r lt bl, I 275.00 —

Wove Paper
Perf. 11½

82b N1 400r on 2½r brn, II 5.25 3.75

Perf. 12½

82 N1 400r on 2½r brn, I 1.75 1.60
82a N1 400r on 2½r brn, II 1.75 1.60

Perf. 13½

82c N1 400r on 2½r brn, II 2.25 2.00
  Nos. 70-82 (13) 202.00 142.35

For surcharges see Nos. 175-180, 211-216, 234-235.

Reprints of Nos. 65, 67, 68 and 69 have clean-cut perforation 13½.

Stamps of 1898 Overprinted — a

1902 Perf. 11½

83 A5 15r brown 2.50 1.75
84 A5 25r sea green 2.00 1.00
85 A5 50r blue 4.50 2.00
86 A5 75r rose 7.00 5.25
  Nos. 83-86 (4) 16.00 10.00

For surcharge see No. 116.

No. 48 Surcharged in Black

1905

87 A5 50r on 65r dull blue 6.00 3.00

For surcharge see No. 183.

Stamps of 1898-1903 Overprinted in Carmine or Green — b

1911

88 A5 2½r gray .60 .50
89 A5 5r orange yel .60 .50
90 A5 10r light green .60 .50
91 A5 15r gray green .85 .70
92 A5 20r gray violet .90 .75
93 A5 25r car (G) .90 .75
94 A5 50r brown 3.25 1.75
95 A5 75r lilac 6.75 3.25
96 A5 100r dk blue, *bl* 6.75 3.50
97 A5 115r org brn, *pink* 3.75 1.75
98 A5 130r brn, *straw* 3.75 1.75
99 A5 200r red lil, *pnksh* 4.50 2.40
100 A5 400r dull bl, *straw* 4.50 1.75
101 A5 500r blk & red, *bl* 4.50 2.25
102 A5 700r violet, *yelsh* 4.50 2.50
  Nos. 88-102 (15) 46.70 24.60

Inverted and double overprints of Nos. 88-102 were made intentionally.

For surcharges see Nos. 217-218, 221-222, 224.

King Manuel II — A6

Overprinted in Carmine or Green

1912 Perf. 11½x12

103 A6 2½r violet .75 *.50*
104 A6 5r black .75 *.50*
105 A6 10r gray green .75 .50
106 A6 20r carmine (G) .75 .50
107 A6 25r violet brown .75 .50
108 A6 50r dk blue 1.75 1.40
109 A6 75r bister brown 2.00 1.75
110 A6 100r brown, *lt green* 3.75 2.25
111 A6 200r dk green, *salmon* 3.75 2.40
112 A6 300r black, *azure* 3.75 2.40
  Nos. 103-112 (10) 18.75 12.70

For surcharges see Nos. 219-220, 226-227.

No. 91 Surcharged in Black

1912, June Perf. 11½

113 A5 2½r on 15r gray green 6.00 3.75
114 A5 5r on 15r gray green 6.75 3.75
115 A5 10r on 15r gray green 5.25 3.75
  Nos. 113-115 (3) 18.00 11.25

Inverted and double surcharges of Nos. 113-115 were made intentionally.

Nos. 86 and 50 Surcharged in Black and Overprinted in Violet — c

1912

116 A5 25r on 75r rose 110.00 60.00
117 A5 25r on 75r red violet 7.50 6.00
  a. "REUPBLICA" 135.00 70.00
  b. "25" omitted 135.00 70.00
  c. "REPUBLICA" omitted 135.00 70.00

Ceres — A7

With Imprint

1914 Chalky Paper Perf. 15x14
Name and Value in Black

118 A7 ¼c olive brown 2.00 .90
  Never hinged 3.25
119 A7 ½c black 2.00 .90
  Never hinged 3.25
120 A7 1c blue green 2.00 .90
  Never hinged 3.25
121 A7 1½c lilac brown 4.00 2.25
  Never hinged 6.50
122 A7 2c carmine 7.00 3.25
  Never hinged 11.00
123 A7 2½c violet 1.40 .60
  Never hinged 2.25
124 A7 5c blue 3.00 1.60
  Never hinged 4.75
125 A7 7½c yellow brn 4.00 2.40
  Never hinged 6.50
126 A7 8c slate 4.00 2.40
  Never hinged 6.50
127 A7 10c orange brn 4.00 2.40
  Never hinged 6.50
128 A7 15c brown rose 6.00 2.50
  Never hinged 9.50
129 A7 20c yel green 3.00 1.60
  Never hinged 4.75
130 A7 30c brown, *green* 3.00 2.40
  Never hinged 4.75
131 A7 40c brown, *pink* 3.00 2.40
  Never hinged 4.75
132 A7 50c orange, *sal* 11.00 8.25
  Never hinged 17.50
133 A7 1e green, *blue* 8.00 4.75
  Never hinged 13.00
  Nos. 118-133 (16) 67.40 39.50

1915-22 **Ordinary Paper**

134 A7 ¼c olive brown .45 .45
Never hinged .75
a. Thick carton paper 1.10 1.00
Never hinged 1.75
135 A7 ½c black .45 .45
Never hinged .75
a. Thick carton paper 1.10 1.00
Never hinged 1.75
136 A7 1c blue green .45 .45
Never hinged .75
a. 1c dark green .45 .45
Never hinged .75
137 A7 1c yellow green ('18) .45 .45
Never hinged .75
138 A7 1½c lilac brown .45 .45
Never hinged .75
a. Thick carton paper 1.25 1.10
Never hinged 1.75
139 A7 2c carmine .55 .45
Never hinged .85
140 A7 2½c dark violet .55 .45
Never hinged .85
a. 2½ pale violet ('18) .55 .45
Never hinged .85
141 A7 3c orange 27.50 24.00
Never hinged 45.00
142 A7 4c dull rose ('21) .45 .45
Never hinged .70
143 A7 5c blue 1.75 1.40
Never hinged 2.60
a. 5c pale blue ('18) .45 .45
Never hinged .70
144 A7 6c lilac ('21) .45 .45
Never hinged .70
145 A7 7c ultra ('21) .45 .45
Never hinged .70
146 A7 7½c yellow brn ('20) .55 .45
Never hinged .85
147 A7 8c slate .60 .55
Never hinged 1.00
148 A7 10c orange brn ('18) .55 .45
Never hinged .90
149 A7 12c olive brown ('21) 1.50 1.00
Never hinged 2.40
150 A7 15c plum ('20) .55 .45
Never hinged .90
151 A7 15c brown rose ('21) .55 .45
Never hinged .90
152 A7 20c yel green ('18) 6.75 5.00
Never hinged 10.50
153 A7 30c gray green ('21) 1.00 .65
Never hinged 1.40
154 A7 80c pink ('21) 1.75 1.00
Never hinged 2.75
a. 80c bright rose 1.75 1.00
Never hinged 2.75
155 A7 2e dark violet ('22) 3.50 3.00
Never hinged 5.50
Nos. 134-155 (22) 51.25 42.90

1921-26 ***Perf. 12x11½***

156 A7 ¼c olive brown ('24) .45 .45
Never hinged .75
157 A7 ½c black .45 .45
Never hinged .75
158 A7 1c blue green ('24) .45 .45
Never hinged .75
a. 1c dark green .45 .45
Never hinged .75
b. 1c pale yellow green ('21) .45 .45
Never hinged .75
158C A7 1½c lilac brown ('24) .45 .45
Never hinged .75
158D A7 2c carmine ('24) .45 .45
Never hinged .75
a. 2c carmine-red .45 .45
Never hinged .75
158E A7 2c gray ('25) .75 .55
Never hinged 1.10
158F A7 2½c lt violet ('24) .45 .45
Never hinged .75
158G A7 3c orange .45 .45
Never hinged .70
158H A7 4c dull rose .45 .45
Never hinged .70
a. 4c pink .45 .45
Never hinged .70
158I A7 4½c gray .45 .45
Never hinged .70
158J A7 5c blue ('24) .45 .45
Never hinged .75
a. 5c pale blue .45 .45
Never hinged .75
158K A7 6c lilac .45 .45
Never hinged .70
158L A7 7c ultra .45 .45
Never hinged .70
158M A7 7½c yellow brown ('24) .55 .45
Never hinged .85
158N A7 8c slate ('24) .55 .45
Never hinged .85
158O A7 10c orange brn ('24) .45 .40
Never hinged .75
158P A7 12c olive brn .75 .60
Never hinged 1.20
158Q A7 12c dp green ('25) .75 .50
Never hinged 1.20
158R A7 15c plum ('24) .45 .35
Never hinged .75
158S A7 20c yel green 1.75 1.60
Never hinged 2.75
158T A7 24c ultra ('25) 1.60 1.20
Never hinged 2.50
158U A7 25c choc ('25) 1.60 1.20
Never hinged 2.50
158V A7 30c gray grn .75 .60
Never hinged 1.10
a. 30c deep green .75 .60
Never hinged 1.10
158W A7 40c turq blue 1.20 .70
Never hinged 1.90
158X A7 50c lt violet ('25) 1.40 .70
Never hinged 2.10
158Y A7 60c dk blue ('22) 1.50 1.00
Never hinged 2.40
158Z A7 60c dp rose ('26) 75.00 47.50
Never hinged 125.00
159A A7 80c pink ('22) 1.75 1.00
Never hinged 2.75
159B A7 1e rose ('22) 1.75 1.00
Never hinged 2.75
Nos. 156-159B (29) 97.95 65.20

Glazed Paper

1921-25 ***Perf. 12x11½***

159C A7 1e rose 1.75 1.75
Never hinged 2.75
159D A7 1e deep blue ('25) 3.25 1.60
Never hinged 5.00
159E A7 2e dark violet ('22) 2.25 1.25
Never hinged 3.75
159F A7 5e buff ('25) 14.00 11.50
Never hinged 25.00
159G A7 10e pink ('25) 30.00 25.00
Never hinged 50.00
159H A7 20e pale turq ('25) 100.00 70.00
Never hinged 175.00
Nos. 159C-159H (6) 151.25 111.10

For surcharges see Nos. 228-229, 236-239.

Stamps of 1898-1903 Overprinted type "c" in Red or Green

1914 ***Perf. 11½, 12***

159 A5 10r yel green (R) 7.50 5.50
160 A5 15r gray green (R) 6.75 5.50
161 A5 20r gray violet (G) 2.75 2.00
163 A5 75r red violet (G) 2.00 1.40
164 A5 100r blue, *blue* (R) 4.50 3.75
165 A5 115r org brn, *pink* (R) *150.00*
167 A5 200r red vio, *pnksh* (G) 2.75 1.75
169 A5 400r dl bl, *straw* (R) 50.00 50.00
170 A5 500r blk & red, *bl* (R) 6.75 6.25
171 A5 700r vio, *yelsh* (G) 35.00 27.00

Inverted and double overprints were made intentionally. No. 165 was not regularly issued. Red overprints on the 20r, 75r, 200r were not regularly issued. The 130r was not regularly issued without surcharge (No. 225).

On Nos. 63-65, 74-76, 78-79, 82
Perf. 11½, 12½, 13½

172 A2 115r on 10r (R) 17.00 17.00
a. Perf. 13½ 17.00 17.00
173 A2 115r on 200r (R) 22.50 22.50
174 A2 130r on 50r (R) 110.00 110.00
175 A3 115r on 80r (R) 210.00 200.00
176 A3 115r on 100r (R) 250.00 200.00
a. Perf. 11½ 300.00 300.00
b. Perf. 13½ 900.00 850.00
177 A3 115r on 150r (G) 250.00 200.00
a. Perf. 12½ 250.00 200.00
b. Perf. 13½ 750.00 700.00
178 A3 130r on 75r (G) 8.25 7.50
a. Perf. 12½ 9.00 7.50
179 A3 130r on 300r (R) 10.50 8.25
a. Perf. 12½ 17.50 16.00
180 N1 400r on 2½r (R) 1.10 4.00
a. Perf. 11½ 5.25
b. Perf. 13½ 1.10 .85
Nos. 172-180 (9) 879.35 766.10

Nos. 85-87 Overprinted in Red or Green

On Stamps of 1902
Perf. 11½, 12

181 A5 50r blue (R) 2.50 2.25
182 A5 75r rose (G) 6.00 4.50

On No. 87

183 A5 50r on 65r dull blue (R) 5.50 1.75
Nos. 181-183 (3) 14.00 10.75

Inverted and double surcharges of Nos. 181-183 were made intentionally.

Common Design Types pictured following the introduction.

Vasco da Gama Issue of Various Portuguese Colonies

Common Design Types CD20-CD27 Srchd.

On Stamps of Macao

1913 ***Perf. 12½ to 16***

184 ¼c on ½a blue grn 2.25
Never hinged 3.75
185 ½c on 1a red 2.25 1.75
Never hinged 3.75
186 1c on 2a red violet 2.40 1.75
Never hinged 3.75
187 2½c on 4a yel green 1.75 1.25
Never hinged 3.00
188 5c on 8a dk blue 1.75 1.25
Never hinged 3.00
189 7½c on 12a vio brn 8.00 5.50
Never hinged 13.50
190 10c on 16a bister brn 2.75 2.00
Never hinged 4.75
191 15c on 24a bister 3.75 2.00
Never hinged 5.50
Nos. 184-191 (8) 24.90 15.50

On Stamps of Portuguese Africa
Perf. 14 to 15

192 ¼c on 2½r blue grn 1.25 .85
Never hinged 2.25
193 ½c on 5r red 1.25 .85
Never hinged 2.25
194 1c on 10r red violet 1.25 .85
Never hinged 2.25
195 2½c on 25r yel grn 1.25 .85
Never hinged 2.25
196 5c on 50r dk blue 1.25 .85
Never hinged 2.25
197 7½c on 75r vio brn 7.50 6.75
Never hinged 12.00
198 10c on 100r bister brn 3.00 2.00
Never hinged 4.75
199 15c on 150r bister 3.50 2.25
Never hinged 5.75
Nos. 192-199 (8) 20.25 15.25

On Stamps of Timor

200 ¼c on ½a blue grn 2.25 1.75
Never hinged 3.75
201 ½c on 1a red 2.25 1.75
Never hinged 3.75
202 1c on 2a red vio 2.40 1.75
Never hinged 3.75
203 2½c on 4a yel grn 1.75 1.25
Never hinged 3.00
204 5c on 8a dk blue 1.75 1.25
Never hinged 3.00
205 7½c on 12a vio brn 8.00 5.50
Never hinged 13.50
206 10c on 16a bis brn 2.75 2.00
Never hinged 4.75
207 15c on 24a bister 3.75 2.00
Never hinged 5.50
Nos. 200-207 (8) 24.90 17.25
Nos. 184-207 (24) 70.05 48.00

Provisional Issue of 1902 Overprinted in Carmine

1915 ***Perf. 11½, 12½, 13½***

208 A2 115r on 10r green 2.00 2.00
a. Perf. 12½ *2.50* *2.25*
209 A2 115r on 200r gray vio 2.25 1.90
210 A2 130r on 100r brown 1.90 1.60
211 A3 115r on 80r lt green 2.50 2.25
212 A3 115r on 100r brn, *buff* 2.25 2.00
a. Perf. 11½ 100.00 90.00
b. Perf. 13½ 16.00 13.50
213 A3 115r on 150r car, *rose* 1.60 1.60
a. Perf. 12½ 3.75 3.25
b. Perf. 13½ 2.60 2.25
214 A3 130r on 15r choc 1.60 1.60
a. Perf. 12½ 8.25 6.75
215 A3 130r on 75r carmine 3.25 2.00
a. Perf. 13½ 5.00 4.25
b. Perf. 12½ 3.25 2.00
216 A3 130r on 300r dk bl, *sal* 2.00 2.00
a. Perf. 13½ 3.75 2.50
Nos. 208-216 (9) 19.35 16.95

Stamps of 1911-14 Surcharged in Black

d

e

On Stamps of 1911

1919 ***Perf. 11½***

217 A5 (d) ½c on 75r red lilac 3.25 2.60
218 A5 (d) 2½c on 100r blue, *grysh* 3.50 2.60

On Stamps of 1912
Perf. 11½x12

219 A6 (e) ½c on 75r bis brn 2.00 1.50
220 A6 (e) 2½c on 100r brn, *lt grn* 3.50 2.60

On Stamps of 1914

221 A5 (d) ½c on 75r red lil 2.25 1.90
222 A5 (d) 2½c on 100r bl, *grysh* 2.60 2.25
Nos. 217-222 (6) 17.10 13.45

Inverted and double surcharges were made for sale to collectors.

Nos. 163, 98 and Type of 1914 Surcharged in Black

1921

223 A5 (c) 00.5c on 75r *400.00* *350.00*
224 A5 (b) 4c on 130r (#98) 3.00 3.00
225 A5 (c) 4c on 130r brn, *straw* 7.50 7.50
a. Without surcharge *240.00*

Nos. 109 and 108 Surcharged with New Values and Bars in Black

226 A6 00.5c on 75r 2.25 1.90
227 A6 1c on 50r 2.50 2.50

Nos. 133 and 138 Surcharged with New Values and Bars in Black

228 A7 00.5c on 7½c 2.50 2.25
Never hinged 4.00
229 A7 04c on 15c 3.00 3.00
Never hinged 4.50
Nos. 224-229 (6) 20.75 20.15
Nos. 223-229 (7) *420.75* *370.15*

The 04c surcharge exists on the 15c brown rose, perf 12x11½, No. 139.

Some authorities question the status of No. 223.

Nos. 81-82 Surcharged

1925 ***Perf. 12½***

234 A3 40c on 400r on 200r bl, *bl* 1.50 1.10
a. Perf. 13½ 11.00 7.50
235 N1 40c on 400r on 2½r brn 1.10 1.10
a. Perf. 13½ 1.10 1.10

Nos. 150-151, 154-155 Surcharged

1931 ***Perf. 12x 11½***

236 A7 50c on 60c deep rose 2.25 2.00
Never hinged 4.25
237 A7 70c on 80c pink 4.50 3.00
Never hinged 7.50
238 A7 70c on 1e deep blue 4.00 3.00
Never hinged 6.75
239 A7 1.40e on 2e dark violet 2.50 2.00
Never hinged 4.25
Nos. 236-239 (4) 13.25 10.00

Ceres — A14

Perf. 12x11½

1932-46 **Typo.** **Wmk. 232**

243 A14 1c bister brn .30 .25
244 A14 5c dk brown .35 .30
245 A14 10c dp violet .35 .30
246 A14 15c black .35 .30
247 A14 20c gray .40 .30
248 A14 30c myrtle grn .40 .30
249 A14 35c yel grn ('46) 7.50 4.50
250 A14 40c dp orange .40 .30
251 A14 45c lt blue 1.75 1.25
252 A14 50c lt brown .30 .25
253 A14 60c olive grn 1.00 .30
254 A14 70c orange brn 1.10 .30
255 A14 80c emerald .75 .25

No.	Type	Description	Unused	Used
256	A14	85c rose	5.50	2.00
257	A14	1a claret	1.10	.30
258	A14	1.40a dk blue	11.50	1.75
258A	A14	1.75a dk blue ('46)	16.00	5.25
259	A14	2a dull vio	5.25	.55
260	A14	5a pale yel grn	10.50	1.75
261	A14	10a olive bis	20.00	5.25
262	A14	20a orange	52.50	5.25
		Nos. 243-262 (21)	137.30	31.00
		Set, never hinged	175.00	

For surcharges see Nos. 263-267, 271-273; see 294A-300, J31-J36 in *Scott Standard Postage Stamp Catalogue*, Vol. 1.

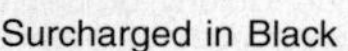

Surcharged in Black

5 ½mm between bars and new value.

1934

No.	Type	Description	Unused	Used
263	A14	10c on 45c lt bl	3.50	2.50
264	A14	20c on 85c rose	3.50	2.50
265	A14	30c on 1.40a dk bl	3.50	2.50
266	A14	70c on 2a dl vio	4.50	3.25
267	A14	80c on 5a pale yel grn	7.00	2.75
		Nos. 263-267 (5)	22.00	13.50
		Set, never hinged	37.50	

See Nos. 294A-300 in *Scott Standard Postage Stamp Catalogue*, Vol. 1.

Nos. J26, J30 Surcharged in Black

1935 Unwmk. *Perf. 11½*

No.	Type	Description	Unused	Used
268	D2	5c on 6c lt brown	2.50	1.60
269	D2	30c on 50c gray	2.50	1.60
270	D2	40c on 50c gray	2.50	1.60
		Nos. 268-270 (3)	7.50	4.80
		Set, never hinged	14.00	

No. 255 Surcharged in Black

1938 Wmk. 232 *Perf. 12x11½*

No.	Type	Description	Unused	Used
271	A14	5c on 80c emerald	1.10	.55
272	A14	10c on 80c emerald	1.60	.75
273	A14	15c on 80c emerald	2.25	.75
		Nos. 271-273 (3)	4.95	2.05
		Set, never hinged	8.25	

Vasco da Gama Issue
Common Design Types
Engr.; Name & Value Typo. in Black
Perf. 13½x13

1938, July 26 Unwmk.

No.	Type	Description	Unused	Used
274	CD34	1c gray green	.25	.25
275	CD34	5c orange brn	.30	.30
276	CD34	10c dk carmine	.40	.30
277	CD34	15c dk violet brn	.40	.30
278	CD34	20c slate	.40	.30
279	CD35	30c rose violet	.55	.40
280	CD35	35c brt green	1.00	.75
281	CD35	40c brown	.40	.25
282	CD35	50c brt red vio	.55	.25
283	CD36	60c gray black	1.10	.30
284	CD36	70c brown vio	1.10	.30
285	CD36	80c orange	1.10	.30
286	CD36	1a red	1.10	.30
287	CD37	1.75a blue	2.10	1.00
288	CD37	2a brown car	3.25	1.50
289	CD37	5a olive grn	13.50	1.50
290	CD38	10a blue vio	29.00	1.90
291	CD38	20a red brown	42.50	4.25
		Nos. 274-291 (18)	99.00	14.45
		Set, never hinged	150.00	

For surcharges see Nos. 301-304 in *Scott Standard Postage Stamp Catalogue*, Vol. 1.

Marble Column and Portuguese Arms with Cross — A20

1938, July 29 *Perf. 12½*

No.	Type	Description	Unused	Used
292	A20	80c blue green	3.75	2.25
293	A20	1.75a deep blue	20.00	6.00
294	A20	20a dk red brown	60.00	27.00
		Nos. 292-294 (3)	83.75	35.25
		Set, never hinged	140.00	

Visit of the President of Portugal to this colony in 1938.

AIR POST STAMPS

Plane Over Globe
Common Design Type
Perf. 13½x13

1938, July 26 Engr. Unwmk.
Name and Value in Black

No.	Type	Description	Unused	Used
C1	CD39	10c red orange	.60	.40
C2	CD39	20c purple	.60	.40
C3	CD39	50c orange	.60	.40
C4	CD39	1a ultra	.60	.40
C5	CD39	2a lilac brn	1.25	.40
C6	CD39	3a dk green	2.50	.60
C7	CD39	5a red brown	6.00	.90
C8	CD39	9a rose carmine	9.25	1.90
C9	CD39	10a magenta	12.50	3.00
		Nos. C1-C9 (9)	33.90	8.40
		Set, Never Hinged	47.50	

No. C7 exists with overprint "Exposicao Internacional de Nova York, 1939-1940" and Trylon and Perisphere. Value; used & unused $110., never hinged, $160.

POSTAGE DUE STAMPS

D1

1904 Unwmk. Typo. *Perf. 11½x12*

No.	Type	Description	Unused	Used
J1	D1	5r yellow grn	.55	.45
J2	D1	10r slate	.55	.45
J3	D1	20r yellow brn	1.00	.55
J4	D1	30r orange	1.00	.55
J5	D1	50r gray brown	1.25	.90
J6	D1	60r red brown	11.50	5.50
J7	D1	100r lilac	4.75	3.00
J8	D1	130r dull blue	4.75	3.00
J9	D1	200r carmine	14.00	7.50
J10	D1	500r gray violet	12.00	6.00
		Nos. J1-J10 (10)	51.35	27.90
		Set, never hinged	77.50	

Postage Due Stamps of 1904 Overprinted in Carmine or Green

1911

No.	Type	Description	Unused	Used
J11	D1	5r yellow grn	.40	.30
J12	D1	10r slate	.40	.30
J13	D1	20r yellow brn	.40	.30
J14	D1	30r orange	.55	.30
J15	D1	50r gray brown	.55	.30
J16	D1	60r red brown	1.50	1.00
J17	D1	100r lilac	1.50	1.00
J18	D1	130r dull blue	1.75	1.25
J19	D1	200r carmine (G)	2.25	1.25
J20	D1	500r gray violet	2.50	2.50
		Nos. J11-J20 (10)	11.80	8.50
		Set, Never Hinged	19.00	

D2

1921 *Perf. 11½*

No.	Type	Description	Unused	Used
J21	D2	½c yellow green	.40	.30
J22	D2	1c slate	.40	.30
J23	D2	2c orange brown	.40	.30
J24	D2	3c orange	.40	.30
J25	D2	5c gray brown	.40	.30
J26	D2	6c lt brown	.40	.30
J27	D2	10c red violet	.60	.45
J28	D2	13c dull blue	1.10	.85
J29	D2	20c carmine	1.10	.85
J30	D2	50c gray	1.10	.85
		Nos. J21-J30 (10)	6.30	4.80

For surcharges see Nos. 268-270.

NEWSPAPER STAMP

N1

1893 Typo. Unwmk. *Perf. 11½*

No.	Type	Description	Unused	Used
P1	N1	2½r brown	4.00	1.60
a.		Perf. 12½	4.00	1.40
b.		Perf. 13½	3.50	1.40

No. P1 was also used for ordinary postage. For surcharges see Nos. 37, 82, 180, 235.

POSTAL TAX STAMPS

Pombal Issue
Common Design Types

1925, May 8 Unwmk. *Perf. 12½*

No.	Type	Description	Unused	Used
RA1	CD28	15c lilac & black	1.10	1.10
		Never hinged	1.50	
RA2	CD29	15c lilac & black	1.10	1.10
		Never hinged	1.50	
RA3	CD30	15c lilac & black	1.10	1.10
		Never hinged	1.50	
		Nos. RA1-RA3 (3)	3.30	3.30

"Charity" — PT1

1929 Litho. *Perf. 11*
Without Gum

No.	Type	Description	Unused	Used
RA4	PT1	50c dark blue	8.25	2.25

Coat of Arms — PT2

1939 Without Gum *Perf. 10½*

No.	Type	Description	Unused	Used
RA5	PT2	50c turq green	3.50	.35
RA6	PT2	1a red	5.50	2.25

A 1.50a, type PT2, was issued for fiscal use. Value, $7.50.

POSTAL TAX DUE STAMPS

Pombal Issue
Common Design Types

1925, May 8 Unwmk. *Perf. 12½*

No.	Type	Description	Unused	Used
RAJ1	CD28	30c lilac & black	1.10	1.10
		Never hinged	1.50	
RAJ2	CD29	30c lilac & black	1.10	1.10
		Never hinged	1.50	
RAJ3	CD30	30c lilac & black	1.10	1.10
		Never hinged	1.50	
		Nos. RAJ1-RAJ3 (3)	3.30	3.30

See note after Portugal No. RAJ4.

ANGRA

'aŋ-grə

LOCATION — An administrative district of the Azores, consisting of the islands of Terceira, Sao Jorge and Graciosa.
GOVT. — A district of Portugal
AREA — 275 sq. mi.
POP. — 70,000 (approx.)
CAPITAL — Angra do Heroismo

1000 Reis = 1 Milreis

STAMPS OF PORTUGAL USED IN ANGRA

Barred Numeral "48"

1853 Queen Maria II

No.	Description	Value
A1	5r org brn (#1)	1,350.
A2	25r blue (#2)	75.00
A3	50r dp yel grn (#3)	1,400.
a.	50r blue grn (#3a)	2,000.
A4	100r lilac (#4)	3,750.

1855 King Pedro V (Straight Hair)

No.	Description	Value
A5	5r red brn (#5)	1,450.
A6	25r blue, type II (#6)	67.50
a.	Type I (#6a)	75.00
A7	50r green (#7)	110.00
A8	100r lilac (#8)	140.00

1856-58
King Pedro V (Curled Hair)

No.	Description	Value
A9	5r red brn (#9)	175.00
A10	25r blue, type II (#10)	120.00
a.	Type I (#10a)	85.00
A11	25r rose, type II (#11; '58)	27.50

1862-64 King Luiz

No.	Description	Value
A12	5r brown (#12)	85.00
A13	10r orange (#13)	95.00
A14	25r rose (#14)	20.00
A15	50r yel green (#15)	125.00
A16	100r lilac (#16; '64)	140.00

1866-67 King Luiz *Imperf.*

No.	Description	Value
A17	5r black (#17)	120.00
A18	10r yellow (#18)	200.00
A19	20r bister (#19)	200.00
A20	25r rose (#20)	52.50
A21	50r green (#21)	160.00
A22	80r orange (#22)	160.00
A23	100r dk lilac (#23; '67)	210.00
A24	120r blue (#24)	150.00

Perf. 12½

No.	Description	Value
A28	25r rose (#28)	120.00

King Carlos — A1

Enamel surfaced paper

1892-93 Typo. Unwmk. *Perf. 12½*

No.	Type	Description	Unused	Used
1	A1	5r yellow	5.00	2.75
		Never hinged	6.75	
2	A1	10r redsh violet	5.00	2.75
		Never hinged	6.75	
3	A1	15r chocolate	7.00	4.00
		Never hinged	9.50	
4	A1	20r lavender	9.00	3.00
		Never hinged	12.00	
5	A1	25r green	5.00	.80
		Never hinged	6.75	
7	A1	50r blue	12.00	4.50
		Never hinged	16.00	
8	A1	75r carmine	12.00	6.00
		Never hinged	16.00	
9	A1	80r yellow green	15.00	11.50
		Never hinged	20.00	
10a	A1	100r brown, *yellow*	175.00	150.00
		Never hinged	235.00	
11	A1	150r car, *rose* ('93)	80.00	45.00
		Never hinged	105.00	
12	A1	200r dk blue, *bl* ('93)	80.00	45.00
		Never hinged	105.00	
13	A1	300r dk blue, *sal* ('93)	90.00	45.00
		Never hinged	120.00	
		Nos. 1-13 (11)	320.00	170.30

Enamel surfaced paper, Perf 13½

No.	Type	Description	Unused	Used
1b	A1	5r yellow	4.00	2.75
		Never hinged	5.50	
2a	A1	10r reddish violet	5.75	4.00
		Never hinged	8.00	

3a A1 15r chocolate 7.00 4.00
Never hinged 10.00
4a A1 20r lavender 9.00 3.25
Never hinged 12.50
7a A1 50r blue 14.00 7.00
Never hinged 20.00
10 A1 100r brown, *yellow* 60.00 16.00
Never hinged 85.00
11a A1 150r carmine, *rose* 75.00 60.00
Never hinged 105.00
12a A1 200r dark blue, *blue* ('93) 75.00 60.00
Never hinged 105.00
13a A1 300r dark blue, *salmon* 80.00 60.00
Never hinged 110.00

Enamel surfaced paper, perf 11½

1a A1 5r yellow 14.00 7.00
Never hinged 20.00
5b A1 25r green 6.00 1.25
Never hinged 8.50

Chalky surfaced paper with lozenges, Perf 12½

1c A1 5r yellow 4.25 1.40
Never hinged 6.00

Chalky surfaced paper with lozenges, Perf 13½

1d A1 5r yellow 4.50 1.60
Never hinged 6.50
5a A1 25r green 10.00 6.00
Never hinged 14.00
7b A1 50r blue — 30.00
Never hinged —

Reprints of 50r, 150r, 200r and 300r, made in 1900, are perf. 11½ and ungummed. Value, each $50. Reprints of all values, made in 1905, have shiny white gum and clean-cut perf. Value, each $22.50.

King Carlos — A2

Name and Value in Black except Nos. 26 and 35

1897-1905 ***Perf. 11½***

14 A2 2½r gray .75 .50
Never hinged 1.00
15 A2 5r orange .75 .50
Never hinged 1.00
a. Diagonal half used as 2½r on newspaper or circular *32.50*
16 A2 10r yellow grn .75 .50
Never hinged 1.00
17 A2 15r brown 10.00 7.00
Never hinged 13.50
18 A2 15r gray grn ('99) 1.00 .70
Never hinged 1.35
19 A2 20r gray violet 2.00 1.50
Never hinged 2.75
20 A2 25r sea green 3.25 1.40
Never hinged 4.50
21 A2 25r car rose ('99) .75 .70
Never hinged 1.00
22 A2 50r dark blue 6.00 2.00
Never hinged 8.00
23 A2 50r ultra ('05) 25.00 12.50
Never hinged 35.00
24 A2 65r slate bl ('98) 1.40 .70
Never hinged 1.90
25 A2 75r rose 4.00 1.90
Never hinged 5.50
26 A2 75r gray brn & car, *straw* ('05) 30.00 12.50
Never hinged 40.00
27 A2 80r violet 1.60 1.40
Never hinged 2.10
28 A2 100r dk blue, *bl* 3.50 2.00
Never hinged 4.75
29 A2 115r org brn, *pink* ('98) 4.00 2.25
Never hinged 5.50
30 A2 130r gray brn, *straw* ('98) 4.00 2.25
Never hinged 5.50
31 A2 150r lt brn, *straw* 3.50 2.00
Never hinged 4.75
32 A2 180r sl, *pnksh* ('98) 5.00 3.25
Never hinged 6.75
33 A2 200r red vio, *pnksh* 6.00 5.50
Never hinged 8.00
34 A2 300r blue, *rose* 18.00 8.00
Never hinged 24.00
35 A2 500r blk & red, *bl* 24.00 16.00
Never hinged 32.50
a. Perf. 12½ 40.00 20.00
Never hinged 60.00
Nos. 14-35 (22) 155.25 85.05

Yellowish paper

15b A2 5r orange .65 .45
Never hinged .85
21b A2 25r carmine rose ('99) 1.00 .50
Never hinged 1.35
24b A2 65r slate blue ('98) 1.10 .55
Never hinged 1.50
29a A2 115r orange, *yellowish* *6.75* *3.75*
Never hinged *9.00*

Azores stamps were used in Angra from 1906 to 1931, when they were superseded by those of Portugal.

ANJOUAN

'an-jü-wän

LOCATION — One of the Comoro Islands in the Mozambique Channel between Madagascar and Mozambique.
GOVT. — French Colony.
AREA — 89 sq. mi.
POP. — 20,000 (approx. 1912)
CAPITAL — Mossamondu
See Comoro Islands.

100 Centimes = 1 Franc

PRE-STAMP POSTAL MARKINGS

Three-line handstamp:
Perçu (*Manuscript denomination*)
pour affranchissement
Le Receveur de la Poste

1892, Feb.-Mar.

A1 0f25 on cover *9,500.*
A2 0f50 on cover *9,500.*

This handstamp was used provisionally, when stocks of French Colonies General Issue stamps had run out, and supplies of the first Anjouan issue had not yet arrived.

Navigation and Commerce — A1

Perf. 14x13½

1892-1907 Typo. Unwmk.

Name of Colony in Blue or Carmine

1 A1 1c black, *blue* 1.75 1.75
Never hinged 2.50
On cover 250.00
2 A1 2c brown, *buff* 2.75 1.75
Never hinged 4.25
On cover 250.00
3 A1 4c claret, *lav* 5.50 4.00
Never hinged 7.00
On cover 275.00
4 A1 5c green, *grnsh* 9.50 6.25
Never hinged 16.50
On cover 150.00
On newspaper or wrapper, single franking 550.00
5 A1 10c blk, *lavender* 11.50 6.75
Never hinged 21.00
On cover 150.00
6 A1 10c red ('00) 37.50 30.00
Never hinged 65.00
On cover 300.00
7 A1 15c blue, quadrille paper 17.00 11.50
Never hinged 27.50
On cover 125.00
8 A1 15c gray, *lt gray*('00) 27.50 22.50
Never hinged 52.50
On cover 250.00
9 A1 20c red, *green* 17.50 11.00
Never hinged 30.00
On cover 225.00
On cover, single franking 300.00
10 A1 25c black, *rose* 17.50 14.00
Never hinged 30.00
On cover 250.00
On cover, single franking 375.00
11 A1 25c blue ('00) 30.00 22.50
Never hinged 56.00
On cover 275.00
On cover, single franking 440.00
12 A1 30c brn, *bister* 35.00 22.50
Never hinged 60.00
On cover 190.00
On cover, single franking 250.00
13 A1 35c blk, *yel* ('06) 18.00 10.00
Never hinged 30.00
On cover 150.00
On cover, single franking 250.00
14 A1 40c red, *straw* 37.50 32.50
Never hinged 75.00
On cover 300.00
On cover, single franking 440.00
15 A1 45c blk, *gray grn* ('07) 140.00 115.00
Never hinged 280.00
On cover 650.00
On cover, single franking 800.00
a. Perf 11 425.00
Never hinged 575.00
16 A1 50c car, *rose* 42.50 32.50
Never hinged 82.50
On cover 375.00
On cover, single franking 550.00
17 A1 50c brn, *az* ('00) 32.50 32.50
Never hinged 62.50
On cover 375.00
On cover, single franking 500.00
18 A1 75c vio, *orange* 37.50 27.50
Never hinged 77.50
On cover 350.00
On cover, single franking 525.00
19 A1 1fr brnz grn, *straw* 85.00 77.50
Never hinged 180.00
On cover 550.00
On cover, single franking 700.00
Nos. 1-19 (19) 606.00 482.00

Perf. 13½x14 stamps are counterfeits.
Covers: Values are for commercial covers used at Anjouan.

Issues of 1892-1907 Surcharged in Black or Carmine

1912

Spacing between figures of surcharge 1.5mm (5c), 2mm (10c)

20 A1 5c on 2c brn, *buff* 1.25 1.25
Never hinged 1.90
On cover 110.00
21 A1 5c on 4c cl, *lav* (C) 1.40 *1.50*
Never hinged 2.40
On cover 105.00
a. Pair, one without surcharge *1,000.* *1,100.*
22 A1 5c on 15c blue (C) 1.40 1.40
Never hinged 2.25
On cover 110.00
a. Pair, one without surcharge *1,100.* *1,000.*
23 A1 5c on 20c red, *green* 1.40 1.40
Never hinged 2.25
On cover 110.00
a. Pair, one without surcharge *1,100.* *1,100.*
24 A1 5c on 25c blk, *rose* (C) 1.50 *1.75*
Never hinged 2.75
On cover 100.00
25 A1 5c on 30c brn, *bis* (C) 2.00 *2.10*
Never hinged 3.25
On cover 110.00
26 A1 10c on 40c red, *straw* 2.00 *2.25*
Never hinged 3.25
On cover 150.00
27 A1 10c on 45c black, *gray green* (C) 2.40 2.40
Never hinged 3.75
On cover 150.00
28 A1 10c on 50c car, *rose* 5.75 *6.50*
Never hinged 8.00
On cover 210.00
29 A1 10c on 75c vio, *org* 4.00 *4.50*
Never hinged 6.25
On cover 190.00
30 A1 10c on 1fr brnz grn, *straw* 5.25 *5.75*
Never hinged 7.25
On cover 210.00
a. Pair, one without surcharge *1,250.* *1,200.*
Nos. 20-30 (11) 28.35 30.80

Spacing between figures of surcharge 2.25mm (5c), 2.75mm (10c)

20a A1 5c on 2c brn, *buff* 12.50 12.50
Never hinged 24.00
21b A1 5c on 4c cl, *lav* (C) 12.50 12.50
Never hinged 24.00
22b A1 5c on 15c blue (C) 14.00 14.00
Never hinged 21.00
23b A1 5c on 20c red, *green* 14.00 14.00
Never hinged 30.00
24a A1 5c on 25c blk, *rose* (C) 14.00 14.00
Never hinged 30.00
25a A1 5c on 30c brn, *bis* (C) 14.00 14.00
Never hinged 30.00
26a A1 10c on 40c red, *straw* 45.00 45.00
Never hinged 97.50
27a A1 10c on 45c black, *gray green* (C) 57.50 57.50
Never hinged 110.00
28a A1 10c on 50c car, *rose* 95.00 95.00
Never hinged 160.00
29a A1 10c on 75c vio, *org* 87.50 87.50
Never hinged 150.00
30b A1 10c on 1fr brnz grn, *straw* 95.00 95.00
Never hinged 160.00
Nos. 20a-30b (11) 461.00 461.00

Nos. 20-30 were available for use in Madagascar and the Comoro archipelago.

The stamps of Anjouan were superseded by those of Madagascar, and in 1950 by those of Comoro Islands.

ANNAM & TONKIN

a-'nam and 'tän-'kin

LOCATION — In French Indo-China bordering on the China Sea on the east and Siam on the west.
GOVT. — French Protectorate
AREA — 97,503 sq. mi.
POP. — 14,124,000 (approx. 1890)
CAPITAL — Annam: Hue; Tonkin: Hanoi

For administrative purposes, the Protectorates of Annam, Tonkin, Cambodia, Laos and the Colony of Cochin-China were grouped together and were known as French Indo-China.

100 Centimes = 1 Franc

Catalogue values for unused stamps are for examples without gum as most stamps were issued in that condition.

Stamps of French Colonies, 1881-86 Handstamped Surcharged in Black

Perf. 14x13½

1888, Jan. 21 Unwmk.

1 A9 1c on 2c brn, *buff* 47.50 *50.00*
On cover *150.00*
a. Inverted surcharge 200.00 *200.00*
b. Sideways surcharge 200.00 *210.00*
c. Pair, one surcharge inverted 250.00
2 A9 1c on 4c claret, *lav* 37.50 35.00
On cover *125.00*
a. Inverted surcharge 200.00 *210.00*
b. Double surcharge 275.00 225.00
c. Sideways surcharge 200.00 *210.00*
3 A9 5c on 10c blk, *lav* 47.50 37.50
On cover *125.00*
a. Inverted surcharge 200.00 200.00
b. Double surcharge 225.00 225.00

Hyphen between "A" and "T"

7 A9 1c on 2c brn, *buff* 350.00 *400.00*
On cover *1,000.*
a. Inverted surcharge 750.00 *775.00*
b. Sideways surcharge 750.00 *775.00*
c. Pair, Nos. 1, 7 9,000.
8 A9 1c on 4c claret, *lav* 525.00 *625.00*
On cover *1,000.*
9 A9 5c on 10c blk, *lav* 220.00 *240.00*
On cover *600.00*

A 5c on 2c was prepared but not issued. Value $8,500.
In these surcharges there are different types of numerals and letters.
There are numerous other errors in the placing of the surcharges, including double one inverted, double both inverted, double one sideways, and pair one without surcharge. Such varieties command substantial premiums.
These stamps were superseded in 1892 by those of Indo-China.

ANTIGUA

an-ˈtēg-(w)ə

LOCATION — In the West Indies, southeast of Puerto Rico
GOVT. — Presidency of the Leeward Islands Colony
AREA — 171 sq. mi.
POP. — 34,523
CAPITAL — St. John's

Antigua stamps were discontinued in 1890 and resumed in 1903. In the interim, stamps of Leeward Islands were used. Between 1903-1956, stamps of Antigua and Leeward Islands were used concurrently.

12 Pence = 1 Shilling
20 Shillings = 1 Pound

Catalogue values for unused stamps in this country are for Never Hinged items, beginning with Scott 96.

Watermark

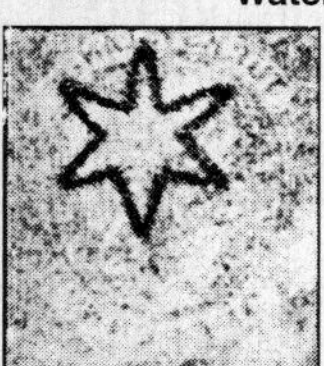

Wmk. 5 — Star

PRE-STAMP POSTAL MARKINGS

Crowned Circle handstamp types I and IV are pictured in the Crowned Circle Handstamps and Great Britain Used Abroad section.

St. John's

1850

A1 I "Antigua" crowned circle handstamp in red, on cover 800.

Covers used from 1860-1869 are valued at $650.

English Harbor

1857

A2 IV "English Harbor" crowned circle handstamp, on cover 10,000.

STAMPS OF GREAT BRITAIN USED IN ANTIGUA

Numeral cancellation type A is pictured in the Crowned Circle Handstamps and Great Britain Used Abroad section.

1858-60

A02 (St. John's)

A3 A 1p rose red (#20) 775.
A4 A 2p blue (#17) 1,850.
A5 A 2p blue (#29, P8, 9) 1,100.
Plate 7 1,350.
A6 A 4p rose (#26) 675.
A7 A 6p lilac (#27) 210.
A8 A 1sh green (#28) 3,500.

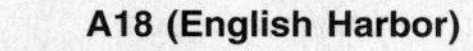

A18 (English Harbor)

A9 A 2p blue (#29, P7) 11,500.
A10 A 4p rose (#26) 11,500.
A11 A 6p lilac (#27) 2,500.
A12 A 1sh green (#28) —

Forged cancellations exist.

Values for unused stamps are for examples with original gum as defined in the catalogue introduction. Any exceptions will be noted. Very fine examples of Nos. 1-8, 11, 18-20 will have perforations touching the design on at least one frameline due to the narrow spacing of the stamps on the plates. Stamps with perfs clear of the framelines on all four sides are extremely scarce and will command higher prices.

Queen Victoria — A1

Rough Perf. 14-16

1862 Engr. Unwmk.

1 A1 6p blue green 950.00 600.00
On cover 5,500.
a. Perf. 11-13 *8,500.*
b. Perf. 11-13x14-16 *3,750.*
c. Perf. 11-13 compound with 14-16 *3,750.*

There is a question whether Nos. 1a-1c ever did postal duty.

Values for No. 1 are for stamps with perfs. cutting into the design. Values for No. 1b are for examples without gum.

1863-67 Wmk. 5

2 A1 1p dull rose 135.00 60.00
On cover *575.00*
a. Vert. pair, imperf. btwn. *37,500.*
b. Imperf., pair 2,750.
c. 1p lilac rose 150.00 82.50
On cover *650.00*
3 A1 1p vermilion ('67) 275.00 32.50
On cover *450.00*
a. Horiz. pair, imperf. btwn. *37,500.*
4 A1 6p green 775.00 30.00
On cover *800.00*
a. 6p yellow green *4,750.* 120.00
On cover *2,350.*
b. Pair, imperf. btwn. —
c. 6p dark green 850.00 30.00
On cover *900.00*

1872 Wmk. 1 *Perf. 12½*

5 A1 1p lake 220.00 22.50
On cover *800.00*
6 A1 1p vermilion 225.00 26.50
On cover *800.00*
7 A1 6p blue green 600.00 12.50
On cover *800.00*

Queen Victoria — A2

1873-79 *Perf. 14*

8 A1 1p lake 250.00 12.50
On cover *625.00*
a. Half used as ½p on cover *9,500.*
b. 1p lake rose 250.00 12.50
On cover *625.00*

Typo.

9 A2 2½p red brown ('79) 700.00 210.00
On cover *2,250.*
a. Large "2" with slanting bottom line *12,500.* *3,100.*
10 A2 4p blue ('79) 290.00 18.00

Engr.

11 A1 6p blue green ('76) 450.00 22.50
On cover *1,000.*

No. 9a is the result of damage to the plate.

1882-86 Typo. Wmk. 2

12 A2 ½p green 5.00 *20.00*
On cover *250.00*
13 A2 2½p red brown 225.00 67.50
On cover *750.00*
a. Large "2" with slanting bottom line *4,000.* *1,450.*
14 A2 2½p ultra ('86) 8.50 *17.00*
On cover *200.00*
a. Large "2" with slanting bottom line 475.00 *300.00*
15 A2 4p blue 350.00 19.00
On cover *200.00*
16 A2 4p brown org ('86) 2.50 *3.75*
On cover *50.00*
17 A2 1sh violet ('86) 190.00 175.00
On cover *2,000.*

Engr.

18 A1 1p carmine ('84) 2.60 *4.50*
On cover *50.00*
a. 1p rose 67.50 20.00
On cover *150.00*
19 A1 6p deep green 77.50 *150.00*
On cover *1,600.*

No. 13a is the result of damage to the plate.

Nos. 18 and 18a were used for a time in St. Christopher and are identified by the "A12" cancellation.

1884 *Perf. 12*

20 A1 1p rose red 65.00 20.00
On cover *1,000.*

Seal of the Colony — A3

King Edward VII — A4

1903 Typo. Wmk. 1 *Perf. 14*

21 A3 ½p blue grn & blk 4.00 *7.50*
a. Bluish paper ('09) 100.00 100.00
22 A3 1p car & black 13.50 1.50
a. Bluish paper ('09) 92.50 92.50
23 A3 2p org brn & vio 8.25 *27.50*
24 A3 2½p ultra & black 17.50 *25.00*
25 A3 3p ocher & gray green 12.00 *24.00*
26 A3 6p black & red vio 35.00 *60.00*
27 A3 1sh violet & ultra 57.50 *70.00*
28 A3 2sh pur & gray green 95.00 *125.00*
29 A3 2sh6p red vio & blk 30.00 *75.00*
30 A4 5sh pur & gray green 115.00 *165.00*
Nos. 21-30 (10) 387.75 *580.50*
Set, overprinted "SPECIMEN" 225.00

The 2½p, 1sh and 5sh exist on both ordinary and chalky paper.

1907 Chalky Paper

21b A3 ½p 4.00 *5.00*
24a A3 2½p 50.00 *75.00*
27a A3 1sh 80.00 *145.00*
30a A4 5sh 200.00 *260.00*

1908-20 Wmk. 3

31 A3 ½p green 5.25 *5.25*
a. ½p blue green ('17) 8.00 7.50
b. ½p dk grn, thick paper ('20) 3.00 *5.00*
32 A3 1p carmine 12.50 2.75
a. 1p scarlet ('15) 8.00 3.75
33 A3 2p org brn & dull vio ('12) 5.25 *35.00*
34 A3 2½p ultra 24.00 *19.00*
a. 2½p bright blue 35.00 25.00
35 A3 3p ocher & grn ('12) 7.00 *21.00*
a. 3p orange & dp grn ('18) 8.00 *24.00*
36 A3 6p blk & red vio ('11) 8.25 *47.50*
a. 6p grnsh black & magenta ('15) 8.50 *50.00*
37 A3 1sh vio & ultra 27.50 *80.00*
a. 1sh dk violet & dk blue ('15) 20.00 *75.00*
38 A3 2sh vio & green ('12) 110.00 *130.00*
Nos. 31-38 (8) 199.75 *340.50*

Nos. 33, 35 to 38 are on chalky paper.
For overprints see Nos. MR1-MR3.

George V — A6

1913

41 A6 5sh violet & green, chalky paper 100.00 *160.00*
a. 5sh dull violet & bright green, ordinary paper 95.00 *150.00*
Overprinted "SPECIMEN" 95.00

St. John's Harbor — A7

1921-29 Wmk. 4

42 A7 ½p green 3.25 .60
43 A7 1p rose red 4.50 .60
a. 1p bright scarlet ('29) 42.50 4.50
44 A7 1p dp violet ('23) 8.75 1.75
a. 1p mauve ('21) 20.00 8.00
45 A7 1½p orange ('22) 6.50 *8.00*
46 A7 1½p rose red ('26) 10.00 2.00
47 A7 1½p fawn ('29) 3.25 .75
48 A7 2p gray 4.50 .90
49 A7 2½p ultra 17.00 5.00
a. 2½ bright blue ('22) 10.00 *20.00*
50 A7 2½p orange ('23) 2.75 *20.00*

Chalky Paper

51 A7 3p violet, *yel* ('25) 16.00 10.00
52 A7 6p vio & red vio 8.50 7.50
53 A7 1sh black, *emer* ('29) 6.50 9.00
54 A7 2sh vio & ultra, *blue* ('27) 12.00 *65.00*
55 A7 2sh6p blk & red, *blue* ('27) 52.50 *47.50*
56 A7 3sh grn & vio ('22) 52.50 *105.00*
57 A7 4sh blk & red ('22) 52.50 *77.50*
Nos. 42-57 (16) 261.00 *361.10*
Set, overprinted or perforated "SPECIMEN" 450.00

Wmk. 3

Chalky Paper

58 A7 3p violet, *yel* 5.00 *15.00*
59 A7 4p black & red, *yel* ('22) 2.50 *6.50*
60 A7 1sh black, *emerald* 4.75 *10.50*
61 A7 2sh vio & ultra, *bl* 14.50 *35.00*
62 A7 2sh6p blk & red, *bl* 19.00 *70.00*
63 A7 5sh grn & red, *yel* ('22) 9.25 *60.00*
64 A7 £1 vio & black, *red* ('22) 300.00 *425.00*
Nos. 58-64 (7) 355.00 *622.00*
Set, overprinted "SPECIMEN" 200.00

Old Dockyard, English Harbour — A8

Govt. House, St. John's — A9

Nelson's "Victory," 1805 — A10

Sir Thomas Warner's Ship, 1632 — A11

Perf. 12½

1932, Jan. 27 Engr. Wmk. 4

67	A8	½p green	4.75	*8.75*
68	A8	1p scarlet	6.50	*9.00*
69	A8	1½p lt brown	4.75	*5.50*
70	A9	2p gray	9.00	*27.50*
71	A9	2½p ultra	8.75	*9.75*
72	A9	3p orange	8.75	*14.00*
73	A10	6p violet	16.00	14.00
74	A10	1sh olive green	21.00	*32.50*
75	A10	2sh6p claret	57.50	*82.50*
76	A11	5sh red brown & black	125.00	*150.00*
		Nos. 67-76 (10)	262.00	*353.50*
		Set, never hinged	650.00	
		Set, perforated "SPECIMEN"	250.00	

Tercentenary of the colony.

Forged cancellations abound, especially dated "MY 18 1932."

Common Design Types pictured following the introduction.

Silver Jubilee Issue

Common Design Type

1935, May 6 ***Perf. 13½x14***

77	CD301	1p car & blue	2.25	*3.75*
78	CD301	1½p gray blk & ultra	2.50	1.00
79	CD301	2½p blue & brn	6.50	1.75
80	CD301	1sh brt vio & ind	9.00	*14.00*
a.		Double frame, one albino	2,000.	
		Nos. 77-80 (4)	20.25	*20.50*
		Set, never hinged	32.50	
		Set, perforated "SPECIMEN"	110.00	

Coronation Issue

Common Design Type

1937, May 12 ***Perf. 11x11½***

81	CD302	1p carmine	.50	*1.00*
82	CD302	1½p brown	.35	*1.00*
83	CD302	2½p deep ultra	1.00	*1.75*
		Nos. 81-83 (3)	1.85	*3.75*
		Set, never hinged	2.75	
		Set, perforated "SPECIMEN"	100.00	

English Harbour — A14

Nelson's Dockyard — A15

Fort James — A16

St. John's Harbor — A17

1938-51 Engr. ***Perf. 12½***

84	A14	½p yel green	.30	*1.50*
		Never hinged	.45	
a.		½p green ('42)	.30	*1.50*
		Never hinged	.45	
85	A15	1p scarlet	2.25	2.50
		Never hinged	3.25	
a.		1p red ('42)	2.00	3.25
		Never hinged	4.25	
86	A15	1½p red brown ('43)	1.80	*2.75*
		Never hinged	3.00	
a.		1½p chocolate brown	4.25	2.00
		Never hinged	6.75	
b.		1½p lake brown ('49)	18.00	15.00
		Never hinged	34.00	
87	A14	2p gray	.70	*1.00*
		Never hinged	1.10	
a.		2p slate ('51)	4.50	*5.75*
		Never hinged	9.00	
88	A15	2½p ultra ('43)	.75	*.90*
		Never hinged	1.10	
a.		2½p deep ultramarine	.60	*1.00*
		Never hinged	1.10	
89	A16	3p pale orange ('44)	.75	*1.10*
		Never hinged	1.10	
a.		3p orange	.50	*1.00*
		Never hinged	1.10	
90	A17	6p purple	2.75	1.25
		Never hinged	3.25	
91	A17	1sh brown & blk	3.50	2.00
		Never hinged	6.00	
a.		1sh red brown & black ('49)	22.50	12.50
		Never hinged	34.00	
b.		As "a," double frame, one albino	*4,500.*	
		Never hinged	*6,250.*	
92	A16	2sh6p dp claret ('42)	16.00	18.00
		Never hinged	26.00	
a.		2sh6p brown purple	30.00	17.50
		Never hinged	50.00	
93	A17	5sh grayish olive green ('44)	9.00	10.00
		Never hinged	15.00	
a.		5sh olive green	15.00	12.50
		Never hinged	25.00	
94	A15	10sh red vio ('48)	11.00	*35.00*
		Never hinged	17.00	
95	A16	£1 Prussian blue ('48)	22.50	*55.00*
		Never hinged	27.50	
		Nos. 84-95 (12)	71.30	*131.00*
		Set, never hinged	105.00	
		Set, overprinted "SPECIMEN"	300.00	

See Nos. 107-113, 115-116, 118-121, 136-142, 144-145 in *Scott Standard Postage Stamp Catalogue*, Vol. 1.

For overprint see Nos. 125-126 in Scott Standard catalogue, Vol. 1.

Catalogue values for unused stamps in this section, from this point to the end of the section, are for Never Hinged items.

Peace Issue

Common Design Type

1946, Nov. 1 Wmk. 4 ***Perf. 13½x14***

96	CD303	1½p brown	.25	*.25*
97	CD303	3p dp orange	.25	*.55*
		Set, overprinted "SPECIMEN"	65.00	

Silver Wedding Issue

Common Design Types

1949, Jan. 3 Photo. ***Perf. 14x14½***

98 CD304 2½p bright ultra .55 *2.75*

Engraved; Name Typographed

Perf. 11½x11

99 CD305 5sh dk brown olive 12.00 10.00

UPU Issue

Common Design Types

Perf. 13½, 11x11½

1949, Oct. 10 Wmk. 4

Engr.; Name Typo. on 3p and 6p

100	CD306	2½p deep ultra	.45	*.60*
101	CD307	3p orange	1.90	*2.75*
102	CD308	6p purple	.90	*2.00*
103	CD309	1sh red brown	.90	*1.50*
		Nos. 100-103 (4)	4.15	*6.85*

University Issue

Common Design Types

Perf. 14x14½

1951, Feb. 16 Engr. Wmk. 4

104	CD310	3c chocolate & blk	.45	*1.50*
105	CD311	12c purple & blk	.90	*1.75*

WAR TAX STAMPS

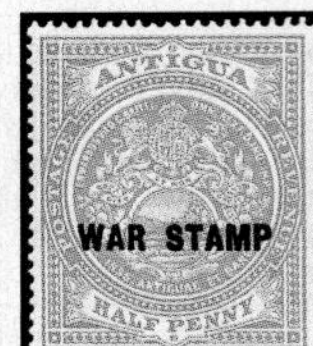

No. 31 and Type A3 Overprinted in Black or Red

1916-18 Wmk. 3 ***Perf. 14***

MR1	A3	½p green	2.40	2.90
a.		Thick paper	4.00	
MR2	A3	½p green (R) ('17)	1.60	*2.90*
a.		Thick paper	7.50	
MR3	A3	1½p orange ('18)	1.10	*1.45*
a.		½p orange & yellow ('19)	1.10	*2.00*
b.		½p deep orange & yellow ('20)	1.10	*2.00*
		Nos. MR1-MR3 (3)	5.10	*7.25*
		Set, overprinted "SPECIMEN"	75.00	

ARGENTINA

ˌär-jən-ˈtē-nə

LOCATION — In South America
GOVT. — Republic
AREA — 1,084,120 sq. mi.
POP. — 12,760,880
CAPITAL — Buenos Aires

100 Centavos = 1 Peso

Watermarks

Wmk. 84 — Italic RA

Wmk. 85 — Small Sun, 4½mm

Wmk. 86 — Large Sun, 6mm

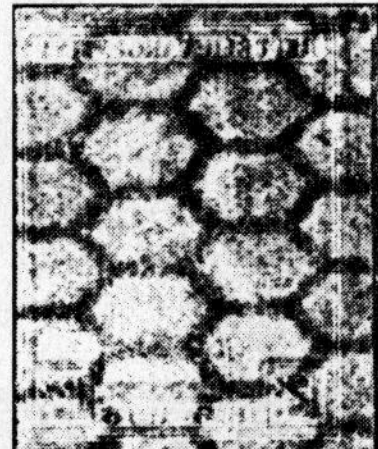

Wmk. 87 — Honeycomb

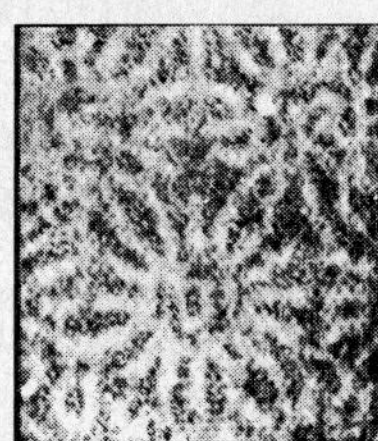

Wmk. 88 — Multiple Suns

Wmk. 89 — Large Sun

In this watermark the face of the sun is 7mm in diameter, the rays are heavier than in the large sun watermark of 1896-1911 and the watermarks are placed close together, so that parts of several frequently appear on one stamp. This paper was intended to be used for fiscal stamps and is usually referred to as "fiscal sun paper."

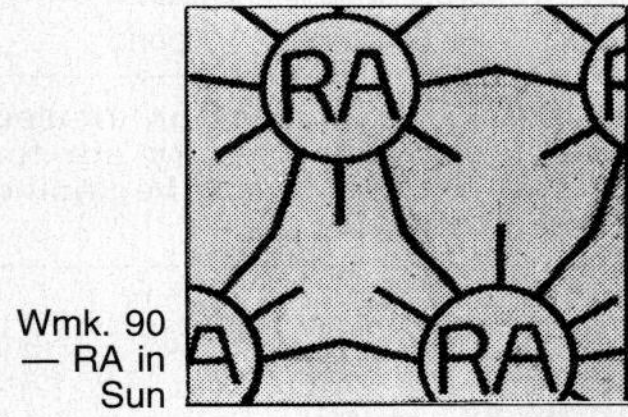

Wmk. 90 — RA in Sun

In 1928 watermark 90 was slightly modified, making the diameter of the Sun 9mm instead of 10mm. Several types of this watermark exist.

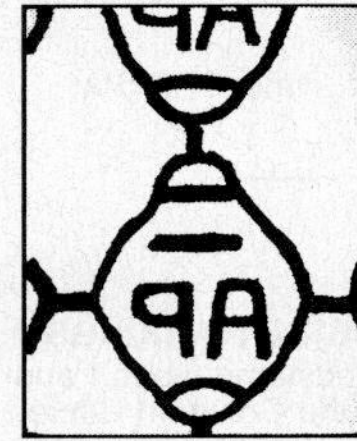

Wmk. 205 — AP in Oval

The letters "AP" are the initials of "AHORRO POSTAL." This paper was formerly used exclusively for Postal Savings stamps.

Wmk. 287 — Double Circle and Letters in Sheet

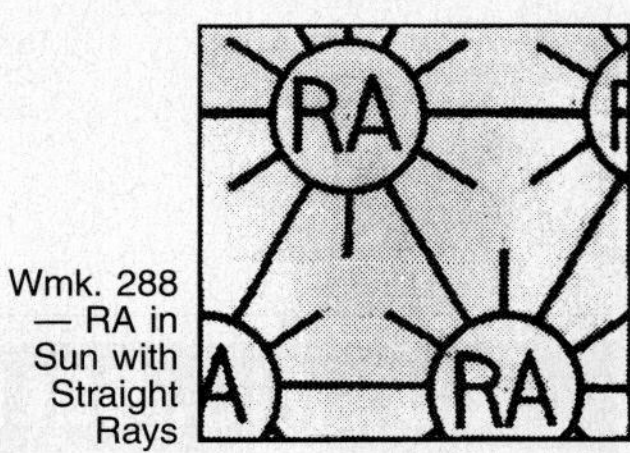

Wmk. 288 — RA in Sun with Straight Rays

PRE-STAMP POSTAL MARKINGS

Crowned Circle handstamp types I and VII are pictured in the Crowned Circle Handstamps and Great Britain Used Abroad section.

Buenos Aires

Crowned Circle Handstamps Types I or VII

1851, Jan. 5

A1 In red, on cover 900.00
A2 In black, on cover 900.00

> Values are for clear cancellations on sound, fault-free stamps, with average to fine centering. In many cases, very fine examples are rare or non-existent.

STAMPS OF GREAT BRITAIN USED IN ARGENTINA

Canceled with barred oval "B32" obliterator

Black B32 Cancel — No. A29

Blue B32 Cancel — No. A29

1860-73

A3 1p rose red (#20) 55.00
A4 1p rose red (#33, see footnote), *value from* 45.00

#A4 plate numbers P71-74, 76, 78-81, 85, 87, 89-97, 99, 101, 103-104, 107-108, 110, 112-114, 117-121, 123, 125, 127, 129-131, 135-136, 138-140, 142-143, 145, 147, 149-151, 155, 159, 163-164, 166, 169, 172.

A5 2p blue (#29, P8-9) *value from* 55.00
A6 2p blue, (#30, P12-14) *value from* 55.00
A7 3p rose (#37) 325.00
A8 3p rose (#44) 125.00
A9 3p rose (#49, P4-10) *value from* 55.00
A10 4p rose (#26) 125.00
A11 4p vermilion (#34, P3) 120.00
a. vermilion (#34a, P4) 125.00
A12 4p vermilion, plates 10-12 (#43), *value from* 60.00
a. 4p dull vermilion, plates 7-9, 13 (#43a), *value from* 60.00
A13 6p lilac (#27) 120.00
A14 6p lilac (#39, P3) —
a. 6p lilac (#39b, P4) —
A15 6p lilac (#45, P5) 95.00
Plate 6 175.00
A16 6p dull violet (#50, P6) 105.00
A17 6p violet (#51, P8-9) 85.00
A18 6p brown, (#59, P11) 55.00
a. 6p pale buff, #59b, P11) 100.00
A19 9p straw (#40) 350.00
a. 9p bister (#40a) 400.00
A20 9p straw (#46) 575.00
A21 9p bister (#52) 350.00
A22 10p red brown (#53) 400.00
A23 1sh green (#28) 325.00
A24 1sh green (#42) 200.00
A25 1sh green (#48, P4) 190.00
A26 1sh green (#54, P4-6) *value from* 55.00
Plate 7 90.00
A27 1sh green (#64, P8) —
A28 2sh blue (#55) 250.00
A29 5sh rose (#57) 600.00

STAMPS OF ITALIAN OFFICES ABROAD USED IN ARGENTINA

Between 1874 and 1878, the Italian Consulate in Buenos Aires operated postal facilities for handling mail addressed to Italy. Stamps of the Italian Offices Abroad general issue were sold locally for franking this mail. These stamps were canceled on arrival at Genoa with a two-line italic postmark.

2A1 *"Da Buenos-Aires coi Postali Italiani"* on Italian stamps overprinted "ESTERO," from 300.00
On cover, with stamps optd. "ESTERO", from *9,000.*
2A2 *"Da Buenos-Aires coi Postali Italiani"* on cover, unpaid and with Italian Postage Due, from 1,500.

Mail could also be consigned to the Consular Agencies without prepayment of postage, in which case it was taxed upon arrival in Italy.

Mail could also be sent through the Consular Agencies to Europe by the English or French Paquet systems. Generally, these countries did not recognize the prepayment of postage by italian stamps, and such letters were assessed postage due charges and penalties upon arrival. Such covers are very rare.

> Values for Unused
> Unused values for Nos. 5-17 are for examples without gum. Examples with original gum command higher prices. Unused values of Nos. 1-4B and stamps after No. 17 are for examples with original gum as defined in the catalogue introduction.

Argentine Confederation

Symbolical of the Argentine Confederation — A1

Unwmk.

1858, May 1 Litho. *Imperf.*

1 A1 5c red 1.50 *40.00*
On cover *200.00*
a. Colon after "5" 1.75 *32.50*
On cover 200.00
b. Colon after "V" 1.75 *32.50*
On cover 200.00
c. Horiz. strip with all 9 types 25.00
2 A1 10c green 2.50 *90.00*
On cover 700.00
a. With period after "10" (55R1) 20.00 *225.00*
On cover *750.00*
b. 10c dark green 3.25 *75.00*
On cover *600.00*
c. As "a," dark green 30.00 *225.00*
On cover *750.00*
d. 10c pale green on thick paper 5.00 *110.00*
On cover *600.00*
e. Horiz. strip with all 9 types 40.00 —
f. Diagonal half used as 5c on cover *725.00*
g. Horiz. half used as 5c on cover *3,000.*
3 A1 15c blue 18.00 *250.00*
On cover *3,000.*
a. 15c dark blue 200.00 *500.00*
On cover *4,500.*
b. Horiz. strip with all 9 types 300.00
c. Horiz. third used as 5c on cover *10,000.*
d. Vert. third used as 5c on cover *10,000.*
e. Diagonal third used as 5c on cover *10,000.*
f. Diagonal two-thirds used as 10c on cover —
g. As "a," dark blue, horiz. strip with all 9 types 3,000. —
Nos. 1-3 (3) 22.00 *380.00*

There are nine varieties of Nos. 1, 2 and 3. Counterfeits and forged cancellations of Nos. 1-3 are plentiful.

Symbolical of the Argentine Confederation — A2

1860, Jan.

4 A2 5c red 3.25 *100.00*
On cover 900.00
c. Strip with all 8 types 30.00 —
f. 5c blood red 450.00 —
g. As "f," strip with all 8 types 4,500. —
4A A2 10c green 7.00 —
d. Strip with all 8 types 80.00 —
e. "APGENTINA" 12.00
h. 10c dark green 8.00 —
4B A2 15c blue 30.00 —
e. Strip with all 8 types 300.00 —
i. 15c dark blue 35.00 —
Nos. 4-4B (3) 40.25

Nos. 4A and 4B were never placed in use. Some compostitions of Nos. 4-4B contain 8 different types across the sheet. Other settings exist with minor variations. Counterfeits and forged cancellations of Nos. 4-4B are plentiful.

Argentine Republic

Seal of the Republic — A3

Broad "C" in "CENTAVOS," Accent on "U" of "REPUBLICA"

1862, Jan. 11

5 A3 5c rose 49.00 37.50
On cover 200.00
a. 5c rose lilac 150.00 35.00
On cover 200.00
b. 5c brick red 150.00 37.50
c. 5c orange red 150.00 37.50
d. 5c salmon 150.00 37.50
e. 5c vermilion 150.00 37.50
6 A3 10c green 175.00 80.00
On cover 500.00
b. Diagonal half used as 5c on cover *7,000.*
c. 10c dark green on ribbed paper — 400.00
On cover —
d. 10c olive green 275.00 160.00
On cover, *from* *800.00*
e. 10c grass green 275.00 160.00
On cover, *from* *800.00*
f. 10c apple green 275.00 160.00
On cover, *from* 800.00
7 A3 15c blue 350.00 225.00
On cover 3,000.
a. Without accent on "U" *8,000.* *5,000.*
b. Tete beche pair *150,000.* *120,000.*
d. 15c ultramarine 500.00 350.00
On cover, *from* 3,500.
e. Diagonal third used as 5c on cover *12,000.*
g. 15c dark blue 600.00 350.00
On cover 3,500.

Only one used example of No. 7b is known. It has faults. Two unused examples are known. One is sound with origional gum, the other is in a block, without gum, and has tiny faults.

Broad "C" in "CENTAVOS," No Accent on "U"

1863

7C A3 5c rose 20.00 *21.00*
On cover 150.00
i. 5c rose lilac 200.00 250.00
On cover 1,300.
j. 5c carmine rose 175.00 25.00
On cover 180.00
k. Double impression — *800.00*
m. Worn plate (rose) 500.00 52.50
On cover 250.00
n. Worn plate (red) 250.00 60.00
On cover 200.00
o. Worn plate (lilac rose) 250.00 200.00
On cover 1,000.
p. Accent between "P" and "U" 250.00 90.00
On cover 500.00
7F A3 10c yellow green 1,000. 250.00
On cover 1,500.
q. 10c olive green *1,500.* 400.00
On cover 2,000.
r. 10c green, ribbed paper 1,200. 350.00
On cover 2,000.
s. Worn plate (green) 1,200. 375.00
On cover 2,000.
t. Worn plate (olive green) 650.00 500.00
On cover 2,500.

Narrow "C" in "CENTAVOS," No Accent on "U"

1864

7H A3 5c rose red 225.00 32.50
On cover 300.00
u. 5c carmine rose 325.00 50.00
On cover 450.00
v. 5c lilac rose 250.00 200.00
On cover 1,000.
w. 5c brick red — 300.00
On cover —

The so-called reprints of 10c and 15c are counterfeits. They have narrow "C" and straight lines in shield. Nos. 7C and 7H have been extensively counterfeited.

Rivadavia Issue

Bernardino Rivadavia
A4 A5

Rivadavia — A6

1864-67 Engr. Wmk. 84 *Imperf.*

Clear Impressions

8 A4 5c brown rose *2,500.* *250.*
On cover 3,000.
a. 5c brick red ('67) *2,500.* *250.*
On cover 2,000.
b. Partial double impression — 500.
c. Ribbed paper 2,750. 300.00
On cover 600.00
d. Very thin paper — 300.00
9 A5 10c green *3,000.* *1,750.*
On cover *16,000.*
10 A6 15c blue *13,500.* *6,500.*
On cover *80,000.*

Perf. 11½

Dull to Worn Impressions

11 A4 5c brown rose ('65) 40.00 15.00
On cover 100.00
a. 5c red, fine impression ('64) 40.00 15.00
On cover 100.00
c. 5c rose, fine impression ('64) 42.50 15.00
On cover 100.00
d. 5c brick red, fine impression ('64) 45.00 20.00
On cover 125.00
e. 5c rose red, fine impression ('64) 40.00 15.00
On cover 100.00
f. 5c lilac red, fine impression ('64) 45.00 18.00
On cover 125.00
g. 5c brick red, worn impression ('64) 40.00 15.00
On cover 100.00
h. 5c lilac red, worn impression ('64) 40.00 15.00
On cover 100.00
i. Horizontal pair, imperf. vert. *3000.*

11B A4 5c lake 100.00 22.00
On cover 150.00
12 A5 10c green 150.00 70.00
On cover 350.00
a. Diagonal half used as 5c on cover 2,000.
b. Vert. half used as 5c on cover 3,000.
c. Horiz. pair, imperf vert. 5,000.
d. Thick (carton) paper, worn impress. 150.00 80.00
On cover —
e. Ribbed paper, worn impression 250.00 150.00
On cover —
f. Diagonal half used as 5c on cover 2,000.
g. Vertical half used as 5c on cover 3,000.
13 A6 15c blue 450.00 150.00
On cover 1,500.
a. Thin paper, fine impression 500.00 180.00
On cover —
b. Blued paper, fine impression 600.00 270.00
On cover —
c. One third used as 5c on cover —
d. 15c blue, worn impression 14.00 60.00
On cover 600.00
e. 15c sky blue, worn impression 150.00 65.00
On cover 600.00
f. 15c dark blue, worn impression 150.00 75.00
On cover 600.00
g. 15c slate blue, worn impression 175.00 75.00
On cover 700.00
h. 15c greenish blue, worn impression 175.00 75.00
On cover 700.00
i. 15c indigo, worn impression 175.00 75.00
On cover 700.00
j. 15c violet blue, worn impression — 200.00
On cover —
k. 15c cobalt, worn impression — 225.00
On cover —
m. Complete double impression 1000.00 600.00
On cover —
n. 15c Ribbed paper, worn impression 275.00 150.00
On cover —
o. Thin paper, worn impression 200.00 100.00
p. Thick paper, worn impression 200.00 100.00
On cover —
q. Horizontal pair, imperf. vert. 5000.

1867-72 Unwmk. *Imperf.*
14 A4 5c carmine ('72) 350. 100.
On cover 600.
a. Double impression 400. 110.
On cover 750.
15 A4 5c rose, thin white paper 350. 100.
On cover 600.
15A A5 10c green, medium white paper *3,000.* *3,200.*
On cover 40,000.
16 A6 15c blue, medium white paper *3,000.* *2,700.*
On cover —

Nos. 15A-16 issued without gum.

1867 *Perf. 11½*
17 A4 5c carmine 1,000. 200.00
On cover 1,200.
a. 5c dark carmine rose 1,000. 200.00
On cover 1,200.
b. Double impression — 500.00
On cover —

Rivadavia A7

Manuel Belgrano A8

Jose de San Martin — A9

Groundwork of Horizontal Lines

1867-68 *Perf. 12*
18 A7 5c vermilion 225.00 17.50
On cover 75.00
c. Double impression 75.00
On cover —
18A A8 10c green 50.00 7.50
On cover 50.00
b. Diag. half used as 5c on cover 2,500.

19 A9 15c blue 100.00 22.50
On cover 250.00

Groundwork of Crossed Lines
20 A7 5c vermilion 15.00 1.25
On cover 15.00
a. Double impression 25.00
On cover —
21 A9 15c blue 120.00 15.00
On cover 250.00

See Nos. 27, 33-34, 39 and types A19, A33, A34, A37. For surcharges and overprints see Nos. 30-32, 41-42, 47-51, O6-O7, O26.

Gen. Antonio G. Balcarce A10

Mariano Moreno A11

Carlos Maria de Alvear A12

Gervasio Antonio Posadas A13

Cornelio Saavedra — A14

1873
22 A10 1c purple 6.00 2.25
On cover 20.00
On cover, single franking 100.00
a. 1c gray violet 10.00 2.25
On cover 20.00
On cover, single franking 100.00
23 A11 4c brown 6.00 .75
On cover 6.00
a. 4c red brown 15.00 2.00
On cover 20.00
24 A12 30c orange 140.00 25.00
On cover 400.00
a. Vert. pair, imperf horiz. *4,000.*
25 A13 60c black 160.00 5.00
On cover 1,400.
26 A14 90c blue 60.00 3.00
On cover *5,000.*
Nos. 22-26 (5) 372.00 36.00

For overprints see Nos. O5, O12-O14, O19-O21, O25, O29.

Four examples of No. 24a are known. Three examples of No. 26 are known on cover.

1873 Laid Paper
27 A8 10c green 325.00 32.50
On cover 250.00

Nos.18, 18A Surcharged in Black

Nos. 30-31

No. 32

1877, Feb. Wove Paper
30 A7 1c on 5c vermilion 75.00 25.00
On cover *600.00*
a. Inverted surcharge 1,000. 300.00
31 A7 2c on 5c vermilion 125.00 75.00
On cover *1,500.*
a. Inverted surcharge 1,200. 750.00
32 A8 8c on 10c green 160.00 40.00
On cover *250.00*
b. Inverted surcharge 2,500. 1,000.
Nos. 30-32 (3) 360.00 140.00

Varieties also exist with double and triple surcharges, surcharge on reverse, 8c on No. 27, all made clandestinely from the original cliches of the surcharges.

Forgeries of these surcharges include the inverted and double varieties.

1876-77 *Rouletted*
33 A7 5c vermilion 200.00 85.00
On cover *600.00*
34 A7 8c lake ('77) 35.00 .65
On cover 75.00

Belgrano A17

Dalmacio Vélez Sarsfield A18

San Martín — A19

1878 *Rouletted*
35 A17 16c green 12.00 1.10
On cover 22.50
a. Vert. pair without horiz. roulettes 1,500.
36 A18 20c blue 20.00 2.25
On cover 150.00
37 A19 24c blue 30.00 3.50
On cover 75.00
Nos. 35-37 (3) 62.00 6.85

See No. 56. For overprints see Nos. O9-O10, O15-O17, O22, O28.

Vicente Lopez — A20

Alvear — A21

1877-80 *Perf. 12*
38 A20 2c yellow green 5.00 .75
On cover 15.00
a. 2c green 8.00 .75
On cover 15.00
39 A7 8c lake ('80) 4.50 .75
On cover 3.00
a. 8c brown lake *52.50* .75
On cover 30.00
40 A21 25c lake ('78) 30.00 6.00
On cover 1,500.
Nos. 38-40 (3) 39.50 7.50

For overprints see Nos. O4, O11, O18, O24.

No. 18 Surcharged in Black

Large "P"

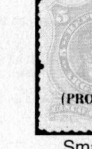

Small "P"

Large "P" and Wide "V" in "PROVISORIO"

1882
41 A7 ½c on 5c ver 2.75 2.75
On cover 100.00
a. Double surcharge 100.00 100.00
On cover *500.00*
b. Inverted surcharge 50.00 50.00
On cover *500.00*
c. "PROVISORIO" omitted 110.00 110.00
On cover *750.00*
d. Fraction omitted 100.00
e. "PROVISOBIO" 50.00 50.00
On cover *500.00*
f. Pair, one without surcharge 250.00

Perforated across Middle of Stamp
42b A7 ½c on 5c ver 40.00 30.00
On cover *900.00*

Small "P" and Narrow "V" in "PROVISORIO"
41g A7 ½c on 5c ver 2.75 2.75
On cover 100.00
41h Double surcharge 50.00 50.00
On cover *700.00*
41i Inverted surcharge 75.00 75.00
On cover *700.00*
41j Fraction omitted 30.00 30.00
On cover *300.00*
41k "PROVISORIQ" 60.00 60.00

Perforated across Middle of Stamp
42 A7 ½c on 5c ver 6.00 6.00
On cover 400.00
a. "PROVISORIO" 50.00 50.00

A23

1882 Typo. *Perf. 12½*
43 A23 ½c brown 2.25 1.50
On cover 10.00
a. Imperf., pair 100.00 80.00
b. ½c chestnut 100.00 50.00
44 A23 1c red 15.00 6.00
On cover 15.00
45 A23 12c ultra 90.00 14.00
On cover 50.00

Perf. 14¼
44A A23 1c red 3.50 1.50
On cover 5.00
45A A23 12c ultra 65.00 12.00
On cover 50.00

Engr.
46 A23 12c grnsh blue 225.00 16.00
On cover 250.00
Nos. 43-46 (6) 400.75 51.00

See type A29. For overprints see Nos. O2, O8, O23, O27.

No. 21 Surcharged in Red

a

b

c

1884 Engr. *Perf. 12*
47 A9 (a) ½c on 15c blue 3.00 2.00
On cover 50.00
a. Groundwork of horiz. lines 150.00 90.00
On cover 700.00
b. Inverted surcharge 35.00 25.00
On cover *300.00*
48 A9 (b) 1c on 15c blue 22.50 16.50
On cover 250.00
a. Groundwork of horiz. lines 13.00 11.50
On cover *250.00*
b. Inverted surcharge 100.00 62.50
c. Double surcharge 50.00 40.00
On cover 500.00
d. Triple surcharge 400.00

Nos. 20-21 Surcharged in Black
49 A7 (a) ½c on 5c ver 5.00 4.50
On cover 100.00
a. Inverted surcharge 200.00 150.00
On cover *1,000.*
b. Date omitted 200.00 —
c. Pair, one without surcharge 500.00
d. Double surcharge 550.00
50 A9 (a) ½c on 15c blue 15.00 12.00
On cover 250.00
a. Groundwork of horiz. lines 50.00 35.00
On cover *500.00*
b. Inverted surcharge 90.00 70.00
c. Pair, one without surcharge 400.00
51 A7 (c) 4c on 5c ver 12.00 9.00
On cover 100.00
a. Inverted surcharge 35.00 28.00
On cover *300.00*
b. Double surcharge 700.00 350.00
On cover *1,250.*
c. Pair, one without surcharge but with "4" in manuscript 750.00 650.00
d. Pair, one without surcharge 400.00
Nos. 47-51 (5) 57.50 44.00

A29

1884-85 Engr. Perf. 12
52 A29 ½c red brown 1.50 .65
On wrapper or newsprint 15.00
a. Horiz. pair, imperf vert. 1,200.
53 A29 1c rose red 7.00 .65
On cover 5.00
a. Horiz. pair, imperf vert. 300.00 250.00
54 A29 12c deep blue 35.00 1.50
On cover 10.00
a. 12c grnsh blue ('85) 50.00 1.50
On cover 10.00
b. Horiz. pair, imperf vert. 300.00 250.00
Nos. 52-54 (3) 43.50 2.80

For overprints see Nos. O1, O3, O9.

San Martin Type of 1878

1887 Engr.
56 A19 24c blue 20.00 1.40
On cover 75.00

Justo Jose de Urquiza — A30

Lopez — A31

Miguel Juarez Celman — A32

Rivadavia (Large head) — A33

Rivadavia (Small head) A34

Domingo F. Sarmiento A35

Nicolas Avellaneda — A36

San Martin — A37

Julio A. Roca — A37a

Belgrano — A37b

Manuel Dorrego — A38

Moreno — A39

Bartolome Mitre — A40

CINCO CENTAVOS.
A33 — Shows collar on left side only.

A34 — Shows collar on both sides. Lozenges in background larger and clearer than in A33.

1888-90 Litho. Perf. 11½
57 A30 ½c blue 1.75 .75
On cover 75.00
b. Vert. pair, imperf. horiz. 200.00 200.00
c. Horiz. pair, imperf. vert. 200.00 200.00
58 A31 2c yel grn 20.00 10.00
On cover 150.00
b. Vert. pair, imperf. horiz. 130.00
c. Horiz. pair, imperf. vert. 250.00
59 A32 3c blue green 3.50 1.50
On cover 15.00
b. Horiz. pair, imperf. vert. 60.00
c. Horiz. pair, imperf. btwn. 130.00
d. Vert. pair, imperf. btwn. 25.00 25.00
60 A33 5c carmine 18.00 .75
On cover 30.00
b. Vert. pair, imperf. horiz. 175.00
61 A34 5c carmine 26.00 2.25
On cover 50.00
b. Vert. pair, imperf. btwn. 200.00
c. Vert. pair, imperf. horiz. 400.00
62 A35 6c red 50.00 20.00
On cover 250.00
b. Vert. pair, imperf. btwn. 150.00
c. Perf. 12 100.00 50.00
On cover 350.00
63 A36 10c brown 26.00 1.50
On cover 50.00
64 A37 15c orange 27.50 2.25
On cover 150.00
d. Vert. pair, imperf. btwn. 600.00
64A A37a 20c green 25.00 1.50
On cover 150.00
64B A37b 25c purple 45.00 4.00
On cover 2,500.
65 A38 30c brown 40.00 4.00
On cover 2,000.
b. 30c reddish chocolate brown 400.00 80.00
On cover 1,000.
c. Horiz. pair, imperf. btwn. 700.00 500.00
66 A39 40c slate, perf. 12 150.00 3.00
On cover 2,500.
a. Perf. 11½ 300.00 4.00
On cover 2,500.
b. Horiz. pair, imperf. btwn. (#66) 800.00
67 A40 50c blue 350.00 20.00
On cover 3,500.
Nos. 57-67 (13) 782.75 71.50

In this issue there are several varieties of each value, the difference between them being in the relative position of the head to the frame.

Imperf., Pairs

57a	A30	½c	85.00	67.50
58a	A31	2c	100.00	
59a	A32	3c	45.00	27.50
61a	A34	5c		100.00
62a	A35	6c	150.00	150.00
63a	A36	10c	55.00	
64c	A37	15c		200.00
65a	A38	30c	325.00	225.00

Values for Stamps with "MUESTRA" Overprint

59S	3c	blue green	30.00
63S	10c	brown	30.00
64S	15c	orange	30.00
64AS	20c	green	30.00
64BS	25c	purple	30.00
65S	30c	brown	30.00
66S	40c	slate	30.00

Urquiza A41

Velez Sarsfield A42

Miguel Juarez Celman A43

Rivadavia (Large head) A44

Sarmiento A45

Juan Bautista Alberdi A46

1888-89 Engr. Perf. 11½, 11½x12
68 A41 ½c ultra .75 .45
On newspaper, single franking 50.00
a. Vert. pair, imperf. horiz. — —
b. Imperf., pair 30.00 —
69 A42 1c brown 1.50 .75
On cover 3.00
a. Vert. pair, imperf. horiz. 65.00
b. Vert. pair, imperf. btwn. —
c. Imperf., pair 30.00
d. Horiz. pair, imperf. btwn. 100.00
70 A43 3c blue green 6.00 1.75
On cover 6.00
71 A44 5c rose 4.50 .75
On cover 2.50
a. Imperf., pair 50.00 —
72 A45 6c blue black 3.00 .90
On cover 8.00
b. Perf. 11½x12 15.00 4.50
On cover 15.00
73 A46 12c blue 8.75 3.75
On cover 12.00
a. Imperf., pair 45.00
b. bluish paper 9.50 3.75
On cover 12.00
c. Perf. 11½ 14.00 3.00
On cover 15.00
Nos. 68-73 (6) 24.50 8.35

Nos. 69-70 exist with papermakers' watermarks.

See No. 77, types A50, A61. For surcharges see Nos. 83-84.

Jose Maria Paz — A48

Santiago Derqui — A49

Rivadavia (Small head) A50

Avellaneda A51

Moreno A53

Mitre A54

Posadas — A55

1890 Engr. Perf. 11½
75 A48 ¼c green .65 .45
On wrapper or newspaper, single franking 50.00
76 A49 2c violet 1.50 .75
On cover 2.00
a. 2c purple 2.00 .75
On cover 2.00
b. 2c slate 2.00 .75
On cover 2.50
c. Horiz. pair, imperf. btwn. 30.00 25.00
d. Imperf., pair 37.50
e. Perf. 11½x12 9.00 .75
On cover 3.00
77 A50 5c carmine 3.50 .45
On cover 2.50
a. Imperf., pair 70.00 32.50
b. Perf. 11½x12 10.00 1.25
On cover 2.50
c. Vert. pair, imperf. btwn. 75.00 60.00
d. Horiz. pair, imperf. btwn. 75.00 60.00
78 A51 10c brown 4.50 .75
On cover 6.00
b. Imperf., pair 150.00
c. Vert. pair, imperf. btwn. 225.00
80 A53 40c olive green 8.00 1.50
On cover 450.00
a. Imperf., pair 55.00
b. Horiz. pair, imperf. btwn. 250.00
81 A54 50c orange 9.00 1.50
On cover 450.00
a. Imperf., pair 80.00
b. Perf. 11½x12 40.00 3.00
c. 50c lemon yellow 50.00
82 A55 60c black 20.00 4.50
a. Imperf., pair —
b. Vert. pair, imperf. btwn. 125.00 100.00
c. 60c blue black 25.00 2.50
Nos. 75-82 (7) 47.15 9.90

Type A50 differs from type A44 in having the head smaller, the letters of "Cinco Centavos" not as tall, and the curved ornaments at sides close to the first and last letters of "Republica Argentina."

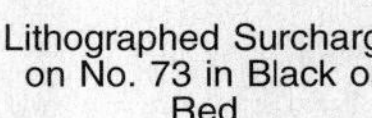
Lithographed Surcharge on No. 73 in Black or Red

1890 Perf. 11½x12
83 A46 ¼c on 12c blue .75 .75
On wrapper, single franking 15.00
a. Perf. 11½ 50.00 40.00
b. Double surcharge 75.00 47.50
c. Inverted surcharge 100.00
84 A46 ¼c on 12c blue (R) .75 .75
On wrapper, single franking 15.00
a. Double surcharge 55.00 50.00
b. Perf. 11½ 8.00 6.00
On wrapper, single franking 45.00

Surcharge is different on Nos. 83 and 84.

Nos. 83-84 exist as pairs, one without surcharge. These were privately produced.

Rivadavia A57

Jose de San Martin A58

Gregorio Araoz de Lamadrid A59

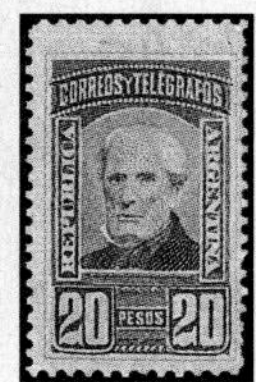
Admiral Guillermo Brown A60

1891 Engr. Perf. 11½
85 A57 8c carmine rose 1.50 .65
On cover 2.00
a. Imperf., pair 130.00
86 A58 1p deep blue 50.00 12.00
On cover —
87 A59 5p ultra 325.00 45.00
On cover —
88 A60 20p green 500.00 100.00
Nos. 85-88 (4) 876.50 157.65

Nos. 86-88 with violet oval or black boxed cancellations were used on parcels. Stamps so used are worth about 25% less than the values shown.

A 10p brown and a 50p red were prepared but not issued. Values: 10p $2,250 for fine, 50p $1,000 with rough or somewhat damaged perfs.

Velez Sarsfield — A61

1890 Perf. 11½
89 A61 1c brown 1.25 .65
On cover 2.50
b. Horiz. pair, imperf. btwn. 550.00

Type A61 is a re-engraving of A42. The figure "1" in each upper corner has a short horizontal serif instead of a long one pointing downward. In type A61 the first and last letters of "Correos y Telegrafos" are closer to the curved ornaments below than in type A42. Background is of horizontal lines (cross-hatching on No. 69).

"Santa Maria," "Nina" and "Pinta" — A62

1892, Oct. 12 Wmk. 85 *Perf. 11½*

90 A62 2c light blue 8.50 3.00
On cover 30.00
a. Double impression 225.00
91 A62 5c dark blue 9.50 4.00
On cover, #90, 91 50.00

Discovery of America, 400th anniv. Counterfeits of Nos. 90-91 are litho.

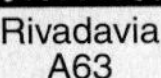

Rivadavia
A63

Belgrano
A64

San Martin — A65

1892-95 Wmk. 85 *Perf. 11½*

92 A63 ½c dull blue 1.00 .35
Never hinged 1.50
On wrapper 10.00
a. ½c bright ultra 80.00 40.00
Never hinged 120.00
On wrapper *100.00*
93 A63 1c brown .65 .50
Never hinged .95
On cover 1.00
94 A63 2c green 1.00 .35
Never hinged 1.50
On cover 1.00
95 A63 3c org ('95) 1.75 .35
Never hinged 2.50
On cover 1.50
96 A63 5c carmine 1.75 .35
Never hinged 2.50
On cover 1.00
b. 5c green (error) 700.00 700.00
On cover *3,500.*
98 A64 10c car rose 13.50 .60
Never hinged 20.00
On cover 1.50
99 A64 12c dp bl ('93) 10.00 .60
Never hinged 15.00
On cover 1.50
100 A64 16c gray 16.50 .65
Never hinged 25.00
On cover 2.00
101 A64 24c gray brown 16.50 .65
Never hinged 25.00
On cover 3.00
102 A64 50c blue green 27.50 .75
Never hinged 42.50
On cover 10.00
103 A65 1p lake ('93) 12.00 1.00
Never hinged 18.00
On cover 100.00
a. 1p red brown 20.00 5.00
Never hinged 30.00
On cover *175.00*
104 A65 2p dark green 27.50 3.50
Never hinged 42.50
On cover 150.00
105 A65 5p dark blue 37.50 3.50
Never hinged 55.00
On cover 250.00
Nos. 92-105 (13) 167.15 13.15

Perf. 12

92E A63 ½c dull blue 6.00 1.00
Never hinged 9.00
On wrapper 10.00
93E A63 1c brown 10.00 2.00
Never hinged 15.00
On cover 1.00
94E A63 2c green 10.00 3.00
Never hinged 15.00
On cover 1.00
95E A63 3c org ('95) 30.00 5.00
Never hinged 45.00
On cover 1.50
96E A63 5c carmine 35.00 1.00
Never hinged 52.50
On cover 1.00
98E A64 10c car rose 21.00 3.50
Never hinged 32.50
On cover 1.50
99E A64 12c dp bl ('93) 40.00 4.00
Never hinged 60.00
On cover 1.50
100E A64 16c gray 40.00 4.00
Never hinged 60.00
On cover 2.00
101E A64 24c gray brown 30.00 17.00
Never hinged 45.00
On cover 50.00
102E A64 50c blue green 30.00 6.00
Never hinged 45.00
On cover 50.00
104E A65 2p dark green 125.00 40.00
Never hinged 190.00
On cover 150.00
Nos. 92E-104E (11) 377.00 86.50

Perf. 11½x12

92F A63 ½c dull blue 18.00 10.00
Never hinged 27.50
On wrapper 10.00
93F A63 1c brown 15.00 8.00
Never hinged 22.50
On cover 1.00
94F A63 2c green 40.00 15.00
Never hinged 60.00
On cover 1.00
95F A63 3c org ('95) 55.00 22.50
Never hinged 82.50
On cover 1.50
96F A63 5c carmine 20.00 4.00
Never hinged 30.00
On cover 1.00
98F A64 10c car rose 30.00 7.50
Never hinged 45.00
On cover 1.50
99F A64 12c dp bl ('93) 60.00 27.50
Never hinged 90.00
On cover 1.50
100F A64 16c gray 60.00 27.50
Never hinged 90.00
On cover 2.00
102F A64 50c blue green 60.00 10.00
Never hinged 90.00
On cover 50.00
103F A64 1p red brown 60.00 10.00
Never hinged 90.00
On cover 50.00
104F A65 2p dark green 175.00 75.00
Never hinged 260.00
On cover 150.00
Nos. 92F-104F (11) 593.00 217.00

Part-perforate varieties of Nos. 92-99 include vert. and/or horiz. pairs, imperf. between. Valued from $45.

The high values of this and succeeding issues are frequently punched with the word "INUTILIZADO," parts of the letters showing on each stamp. These punched stamps sell for only a small fraction of the catalogue values.

Examples of No. 95 in yellow shades are changelings.

Reprints of No. 96b have white gum. The original stamp has yellowish gum. Value $125.

Imperf., Pairs

92b A63 ½c 60.00
Never hinged 90.00
93a A63 1c 60.00
Never hinged 90.00
94a A63 2c 30.00
Never hinged 45.00
96a A63 5c 30.00
Never hinged 45.00
98a A64 10c 60.00
Never hinged 90.00
99a A64 12c 60.00
Never hinged 90.00
100a A64 16c 60.00
Never hinged 90.00
101a A64 24c 60.00
Never hinged 90.00
102a A64 50c 60.00
Never hinged 90.00
103b A65 1p 60.00
Never hinged 90.00
105a A65 5p 150.00
Never hinged 225.00

Nos. 102a, 103b and 105a exist only without gum; the other imperfs are found with or without gum, and values are the same for either condition.

Vertical Pairs, Imperf. Between

92c A63 ½c 125.00
Never hinged 190.00
93b A63 1c 100.00
Never hinged 150.00
94b A63 2c 50.00
Never hinged 75.00
95a A63 3c 250.00
Never hinged 375.00
96c A63 5c 45.00 —
Never hinged 67.50
98b A64 10c 100.00
Never hinged 150.00
99b A64 12c 100.00
Never hinged 150.00

Horizontal Pairs, Imperf. Between

93c A63 1c 110.00
Never hinged 170.00
94c A63 2c 55.00
Never hinged 82.50
96d A63 5c 55.00 45.00
Never hinged 82.50
98c A64 10c 110.00
Never hinged 170.00

1896-97 Wmk. 86 *Perf. 11½*

106 A63 ½c slate .65 .30
Never hinged .95
On wrapper 10.00
a. ½c gray blue .65 .30
Never hinged .95
On wrapper 10.00
b. ½c indigo .65 .30
Never hinged .95
On wrapper 10.00
107 A63 1c brown .65 .30
Never hinged .95
On cover 1.00
108 A63 2c yellow green .65 .30
Never hinged .95
On cover 1.00
109 A63 3c orange .65 .30
Never hinged .95
On cover 1.50
110 A63 5c carmine .65 .30
Never hinged .95
On cover 1.00
a. Imperf., pair 100.00
111 A64 10c carmine rose 10.00 .30
Never hinged 15.00
On cover 1.50
112 A64 12c deep blue 5.00 .30
Never hinged 7.50
On cover 1.50
a. Imperf., pair —
113 A64 16c gray 13.50 .90
Never hinged 20.00
On cover 5.00
114 A64 24c gray brown 13.50 1.25
Never hinged 20.00
On cover 6.00
a. Imperf., pair 100.00 —
Never hinged 150.00
115 A64 30c orange ('97) 13.50 .70
Never hinged 20.00
On cover 5.00
116 A64 50c blue green 13.50 .70
Never hinged 20.00
On cover 10.00
117 A64 80c dull violet 20.00 .90
Never hinged 30.00
On cover 20.00
118 A65 1p lake 30.00 1.60
Never hinged 45.00
On cover *40.00*
119 A65 1p20c black ('97) 13.50 3.50
Never hinged 20.00
On cover 125.00
120 A65 2p dark green 20.00 10.00
Never hinged 30.00
On cover 150.00
121 A65 5p dark blue 135.00 13.50
Never hinged 200.00
On cover 250.00
Nos. 106-121 (16) 290.75 35.15

Perf. 12

106E A63 ½c slate 2.00 1.00
Never hinged 3.00
On wrapper 10.00
a. ½c gray blue 10.00 4.00
Never hinged 15.00
On wrapper 10.00
b. ½c indigo 10.00 4.00
Never hinged 15.00
On wrapper 10.00
107E A63 1c brown 1.75 1.00
Never hinged 2.50
On cover 1.00
108E A63 2c yellow green 2.50 1.00
Never hinged 3.75
On cover 1.00
109E A63 3c orange 45.00 2.00
Never hinged 67.50
On cover 1.50
110E A63 5c carmine 3.50 1.00
Never hinged 5.25
On cover 1.00
111E A64 10c car rose 15.00 1.00
Never hinged 22.50
On cover 1.50
112E A64 12c deep blue 11.00 2.00
Never hinged 16.50
On cover 1.50
113E A64 16c gray 35.00 5.50
Never hinged 52.50
On cover 5.00
114E A64 24c gray brown 52.50 11.00
Never hinged 77.50
On cover 6.00
115E A64 30c orange ('97) 52.50 2.50
Never hinged 77.50
On cover 5.00
116E A64 50c blue green 65.00 .80
Never hinged 97.50
On cover 10.00
117E A64 80c dull violet 65.00 22.50
Never hinged 97.50
On cover 20.00
118E A65 1p lake 65.00 3.50
Never hinged 97.50
On cover *40.00*
119E A65 1p20c black ('97) 65.00 22.50
Never hinged 97.50
On cover 125.00
121E A65 5p dark blue 800.00 20.00
Never hinged 1,200.
On cover 250.00
Nos. 106E-121E (15) 1,281. 97.30

Perf. 11½x12

106F A63 ½c slate 20.00 11.00
Never hinged 30.00
On wrapper 10.00
107F A63 1c brown 30.00 25.00
Never hinged 45.00
On cover 1.00
108F A63 2c yellow green 20.00 11.00
Never hinged 30.00
On cover 1.00
109F A63 3c orange 13.00 8.00
Never hinged 19.50
On cover 1.50
110F A63 5c carmine 26.00 4.50
Never hinged 40.00
On cover 1.00
111F A64 10c car rose 45.00 18.00
Never hinged 67.50
On cover 1.50
112F A64 12c deep blue 47.50 15.00
Never hinged 72.50
On cover 1.50
113F A64 16c gray 60.00 20.00
Never hinged 90.00
On cover 5.00
115F A64 30c org ('97) — 75.00
Never hinged —
On cover 5.00
116F A64 50c blue green — 75.00
Never hinged —
On cover 10.00
117F A64 80c dull violet — 75.00
Never hinged —
On cover 20.00
119F A65 1p20c black ('97) 100.00 60.00
Never hinged 150.00
On cover 125.00
Nos. 106F-119F (12) 361.50 397.50

Vertical Pairs, Imperf. Between

106c A63 ½c 200.00
Never hinged 300.00
107a A63 1c 125.00
Never hinged 190.00
108a A63 2c 125.00
Never hinged 190.00
109a A63 3c 200.00
Never hinged 300.00
110b A63 5c 125.00 125.00
Never hinged 190.00
112b A64 12c 125.00 100.00
Never hinged 190.00

Horizontal Pairs, Imperf. Between

107b A63 1c 125.00
Never hinged 190.00
108b A63 2c 125.00
Never hinged 190.00
110c A63 5c 125.00 80.00
Never hinged 190.00
111a A64 10c 125.00
Never hinged 190.00
112c A64 12c 125.00
Never hinged 190.00

Allegory, Liberty Seated
A66 A67

1899-1903 *Perf. 11½*

122 A66 ½c yel brn .40 .30
Never hinged .60
On cover, single franking 20.00
123 A66 1c green .60 .30
Never hinged .90
On cover 1.00
124 A66 2c slate .60 .30
Never hinged .90
On cover 1.00
125 A66 3c org ('01) .80 .50
Never hinged 120.00
On cover 1.50
126 A66 4c yel ('03) 1.40 .60
Never hinged 2.10
On cover 2.00
127 A66 5c car rose .60 .30
Never hinged .90
On cover 1.00
128 A66 6c blk ('03) .90 .60
Never hinged 135.00
On cover 2.00
129 A66 10c dk grn 1.40 .40
Never hinged 2.10
On cover 1.50
130 A66 12c dull blue .95 .60
Never hinged 1.40
On cover 2.00
131 A66 12c ol grn ('01) .95 .60
Never hinged 1.40
On cover 2.00
132 A66 15c sea grn ('01) 2.50 .60
Never hinged 3.75
On cover 2.50
132B A66 15c dl blue ('01) 2.50 .60
Never hinged 3.75
On cover 2.50
133 A66 16c orange 8.00 8.00
Never hinged 12.00
On cover 25.00
134 A66 20c claret 1.90 .30
Never hinged 2.75
On cover 1.00
135 A66 24c violet 4.00 1.00
Never hinged 6.00
On cover 5.00
136 A66 30c rose 7.25 .60
Never hinged 11.00
On cover 5.00
137 A66 30c ver ('01) 4.00 .50
Never hinged 6.00
On cover 5.00
a. 30c scarlet 47.50 3.00
Never hinged 72.50
On cover 12.50
138 A66 50c brt blue 4.50 .50
Never hinged 6.75
On cover 10.00
139 A67 1p bl & blk 15.00 1.25
Never hinged 22.50
On cover *225.00*
a. Center inverted *2,000.* *1,000.*
b. Perf. 12 500.00 160.00
140 A67 5p org & blk 57.50 11.00
Never hinged 22.50
Punch cancellation 3.00
a. Center inverted *2,750.* *2,500.*
141 A67 10p grn & blk 70.00 18.00
Punch cancellation 3.00
a. Center inverted *5,000.*
Punch cancellation 675.00
142 A67 20p red & blk 200.00 35.00
Never hinged 300.00
Punch cancellation 3.00
a. Center invtd. (punch cancel) *4,000.*
Nos. 122-142 (22) 385.75 81.85

Nos. 139-142 used are valued with violet oval or black boxed parcel cancels. Examples with letter cancels are worth ⅓rd more.

Part-perforate varieties of Nos. 122-129, 132, 138 include vert. and/or horiz. pairs, imperf. between. Valued from $3.

Perf. 12

122E A66 ½c yellow brown 1.50 1.20
Never hinged 2.25
On cover, single franking 20.00
123E A66 1c green 2.00 .60
Never hinged 3.00
On cover 1.00
124E A66 2c slate 1.50 .60
Never hinged 2.25
On cover 1.00

125E A66 3c orange ('01) 3.50 1.75
Never hinged 5.25
On cover 1.50
126E A66 4c yellow ('03) 10.00 3.50
Never hinged 15.00
On cover 2.00
127E A66 5c carmine rose 5.25 .60
Never hinged 7.75
On cover 1.00
128E A66 6c black ('03) 8.50 2.00
Never hinged 13.00
On cover 2.00
129E A66 10c dark green 8.50 1.75
Never hinged 13.00
On cover 1.50
130E A66 12c dull blue 8.50 2.00
Never hinged 13.00
On cover 2.00
131E A66 12c ol grn ('01) 8.50 2.00
Never hinged 13.00
On cover 2.00
132E A66 15c sea grn ('01) 17.00 1.75
Never hinged 26.00
On cover 2.50
133E A66 16c orange 10.00 9.50
Never hinged 15.00
On cover 25.00
134E A66 20c claret 12.00 9.50
Never hinged 18.00
On cover 1.00
135E A66 24c violet 11.00 8.50
Never hinged 16.50
On cover 5.00
136E A66 30c rose 28.00 3.50
Never hinged 42.50
On cover 5.00
137E A66 30c ver ('01) 60.00 4.00
Never hinged 90.00
On cover 5.00
a. 30c scarlet 47.50 3.00
Never hinged 72.50
On cover 12.50
138E A66 50c brt blue 27.50 3.50
Never hinged 42.50
On cover 10.00
139E A67 1p bl & blk 500.00 160.00
Never hinged 750.00
On cover *225.00*
Nos. 122E-139E (18) 723.25 216.25

Perf. 11½x12

122F A66 ½c yellow brown 25.00 15.00
Never hinged 37.50
On cover, single franking 20.00
123F A66 1c green 25.00 15.00
Never hinged 37.50
On cover 1.00
124F A66 2c slate 12.00 3.00
Never hinged 18.00
On cover 1.00
125F A66 3c orange ('01) 47.50 18.00
Never hinged 72.50
On cover 1.50
127F A66 5c carmine rose 12.00 6.00
Never hinged 18.00
On cover 1.00
128F A66 6c black ('03) 32.50 20.00
Never hinged 13.00
On cover 2.00
129F A66 10c dark green 30.00 6.50
Never hinged 45.00
On cover 1.50
130F A66 12c dull blue 50.00 15.00
Never hinged 75.00
On cover 2.00
131F A66 12c ol grn ('01) 50.00 10.00
Never hinged 75.00
On cover 2.00
132F A66 15c sea grn ('01) 50.00 8.00
Never hinged 75.00
On cover 2.50
134F A66 20c claret 60.00 12.00
Never hinged 90.00
On cover 1.00
135F A66 24c violet 50.00 10.00
Never hinged 75.00
On cover 5.00
136F A66 30c rose 120.00 20.00
Never hinged 175.00
On cover 5.00
137F A66 30c ver ('01) 140.00 25.00
Never hinged 210.00
On cover 5.00
138F A66 50c brt blue 120.00 20.00
Never hinged 175.00
On cover 10.00
Nos. 122F-138F (15) 824.00 203.50

Imperf., Pairs

122a A66 ½c 35.00
Never hinged 52.50
123a A66 1c 50.00
Never hinged 75.00
124a A66 2c 17.50
Never hinged 26.00
125a A66 3c 325.00
Never hinged 490.00
127a A66 5c 17.50
Never hinged 26.00
128a A66 6c 60.00
Never hinged 90.00
129a A66 10c 50.00
Never hinged 75.00
132a A66 15c 50.00
Never hinged 75.00

Vertical Pairs, Imperf. Between

122b A66 ½c 10.00 9.50
Never hinged 15.00
123b A66 1c 10.00 9.50
Never hinged 15.00
124b A66 2c 5.00 4.50
Never hinged 7.50
125b A66 3c 325.00 200.00
Never hinged 490.00
126a A66 4c 400.00 275.00
Never hinged 600.00
127b A66 5c 4.50 2.50
Never hinged 6.75
128b A66 6c 13.50 10.00
Never hinged 20.00
129b A66 10c 85.00
Never hinged 130.00

132c A66 15c 15.00 10.00
Never hinged 22.50

Horizontal Pairs, Imperf. Between

122c A66 ½c 30.00 19.00
Never hinged 45.00
123c A66 1c 47.50 27.50
Never hinged 72.50
124c A66 2c 10.00 5.00
Never hinged 15.00
125c A66 3c 325.00 200.00
Never hinged 490.00
126b A66 4c 400.00
Never hinged 600.00
127c A66 5c 10.00 5.00
Never hinged 15.00
128c A66 6c 17.00 10.00
Never hinged 26.00
129c A66 10c 17.00 10.00
Never hinged 26.00
132d A66 15c 40.00 23.00
Never hinged 60.00
138a A66 50c 165.00
Never hinged 250.00

River Port of Rosario A68

1902, Oct. 26 *Perf. 11½, 11½x12*
143 A68 5c deep blue 4.75 2.00
Never hinged 7.00
On cover 20.00
a. Imperf., pair 95.00
Never hinged 140.00
b. Vert. pair, imperf. btwn. 60.00
Never hinged 90.00
c. Horiz. pair, imperf. btwn. 90.00
Never hinged 135.00

Completion of port facilities at Rosario.

San Martin
A69 A70

1908-09 **Typo.** *Perf. 13½x12½*
144 A69 ½c violet .50 .30
Never hinged .75
145 A69 1c brnsh buff .50 .30
Never hinged .75
146 A69 2c chocolate .60 .30
Never hinged .75
147 A69 3c green .65 .40
Never hinged .95
148 A69 4c redsh violet 1.25 .40
Never hinged 1.90
149 A69 5c carmine .60 .30
Never hinged .90
150 A69 6c olive bister .75 .40
Never hinged 1.10
151 A69 10c gray green 1.75 .30
Never hinged 2.50
152 A69 12c yellow buff 1.00 .60
Never hinged 1.50
153 A69 12c dk blue ('09) 1.75 .30
Never hinged 2.50
155 A69 20c ultra 1.25 .30
Never hinged 1.90
156 A69 24c red brown 3.50 .60
Never hinged 5.25
157 A69 30c dull rose 6.00 .60
Never hinged 9.00
158 A69 50c black 6.00 .50
Never hinged 9.00
159 A70 1p sl bl & pink 18.00 2.50
Never hinged 27.50
Nos. 144-159 (15) 44.10 8.10

The 1c blue was not issued. Value $500.

Wmk. 86 appears on ½, 1, 6, 20, 24 and 50c. Other values have similar wmk. with wavy rays.

Stamps lacking wmk. are from outer rows printed on sheet margin.

Perf. 13½

146A A69 2c chocolate 1.20 .25
Never hinged 1.75
147A A69 3c green 2.00 1.00
Never hinged 3.00
148A A69 4c redsh violet 1.30 .50
Never hinged 2.00
149A A69 5c carmine 1.00 .30
Never hinged 1.50
c. rose carmine 1.00 .30
Never hinged 1.50
151A A69 10c gray green 6.25 2.25
Never hinged 9.50
152A A69 12c yellow buff 1.20 .70
Never hinged 1.75
153A A69 12c dk blue ('09) 4.25 1.00
Never hinged 6.50
154A A69 15c apple green .60 .50
Never hinged .90
156A A69 24c red brown 4.75 1.30
Never hinged 7.00
157A A69 30c dull rose 9.50 1.30
Never hinged 14.00

159A A70 1p sl bl & pink 20.00 3.00
Never hinged 30.00
b. 1p rose & indigo 300.00 100.00
Never hinged 450.00

Pyramid of May — A71

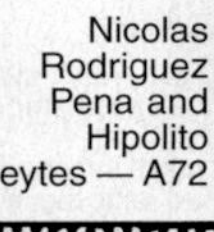

Nicolas Rodriguez Pena and Hipolito Vieytes — A72

Meeting at Pena's Home — A73

Designs: 3c, Miguel de Azcuenaga (1754-1833) and Father Manuel M. Alberti (1763-1811). 4c, Viceroy's house and Fort Buenos Aires. 5c, Cornelio Saavedra (1759-1829). 10c, Antonio Luis Beruti (1772-1842) and French distributing badges. 12c, Congress building. 20c, Juan Jose Castelli (1764-1812) and Domingo Matheu (1765-1831). 24c, First council. 30c, Manuel Belgrano (1770-1820) and Juan Larrea (1782-1847). 50c, First meeting of republican government, May 25, 1810. 1p, Mariano Moreno (1778-1811) and Juan Jose Paso (1758-1833). 5p, Oath of the Junta. 10p, Centenary Monument. 20p, Jose Francisco de San Martin (1778-1850).

Inscribed "1810 1910"

Various Frames

1910, May 1 **Engr.** *Perf. 11½*
160 A71 ½c bl & gray bl .30 .25
161 A72 1c bl grn & blk .30 .30
b. Horiz. pair, imperf. btwn. *65.00*
162 A73 2c olive & gray .25 .30
163 A72 3c green .70 .40
164 A73 4c dk blue & grn .70 .40
165 A71 5c carmine .40 .25
166 A73 10c yel brn & blk 1.10 .50
167 A73 12c brt blue 1.10 .50
168 A72 20c gray brn & blk 3.25 .60
169 A73 24c org brn & bl 1.75 1.25
170 A72 30c lilac & blk 1.75 1.00
171 A71 50c car & blk 4.50 1.25
172 A72 1p brt blue 9.50 3.25
173 A73 5p orange & vio 72.50 35.00
Punch cancel 5.00
174 A71 10p orange & blk 90.00 62.50
Punch cancel 10.00
175 A71 20p dp blue & ind 150.00 100.00
Punch cancel 15.00
Nos. 160-175 (16) 338.10 207.75

Centenary of the republic.

Center Inverted

160a A71 ½c *1,000.*
161a A72 1c *1,000.*
162a A73 2c *800.00*
164a A73 4c *650.00*
167a A73 12c *1,000.*
171a A71 50c *1,000.*
173a A73 5p *750.00*

Domingo F. Sarmiento — A87

1911, May 15 **Typo.** *Perf. 13½*
176 A87 5c gray brn & blk .80 .40

Domingo Faustino Sarmiento (1811-88), pres. of Argentina, 1868-74.

Agriculture — A88

Size: 19x25mm

Wmk. 86, without Face

1911 **Engr.** *Perf. 12*
177 A88 5c vermilion .40 .25
178 A88 12c deep blue 5.00 .50

Size: 18x23mm

Wmk. 86, with Face

1911 **Typo.** *Perf. 13½x12½*
179 A88 ½c violet .50 .30
180 A88 1c brown ocher .30 .30
181 A88 2c chocolate .30 .25
a. Perf. 13½ 15.00 4.00
b. Imperf., pair *40.00*
182 A88 3c green .50 .50
183 A88 4c brown violet .50 .30
184 A88 10c gray green .50 .30
185 A88 20c ultra 4.00 .95
186 A88 24c red brown 6.00 3.75
187 A88 30c claret 3.00 .50
188 A88 50c black 6.00 .80
Nos. 179-188 (10) 21.60 7.95

The 5c dull red is a proof. In this issue Wmk. 86 comes: straight rays (4c, 20c, 24c) and wavy rays (2c). All other values exist with both forms.

Wmk. 87 (Horiz. or Vert.)

1912-14 *Perf. 13½x12½*
189 A88 ½c violet .30 .30
190 A88 1c ocher .30 .30
191 A88 2c chocolate .50 .30
192 A88 3c green .50 .50
193 A88 4c brown violet .50 .60
194 A88 5c red .40 .30
195 A88 10c deep green 1.75 .30
196 A88 12c deep blue .60 .30
197 A88 20c ultra 3.00 .50
198 A88 24c red brown 6.00 2.00
199 A88 30c claret 5.00 7.00
200 A88 50c black 9.00 .90
Nos. 189-200 (12) 27.85 13.30

See Nos. 208-212. For overprints see Nos. OD1-OD8, OD47-OD54, OD102-OD108, OD146-OD152, OD183-OD190, OD235-OD241, OD281-OD284, OD318-OD323.

Perf. 13½

189a A88 ½c 1.00 .30
190a A88 1c 1.00 .30
191a A88 2c 1.00 .30
192a A88 3c 150.00 30.00
193a A88 4c 2.50 1.25
194a A88 5c .90 .30
196a A88 12c 3.50 1.50
197a A88 20c 9.00 .90
Nos. 189a-197a (8) 168.90 34.85

A89

1912-13 *Perf. 13½*
201 A89 1p dull bl & rose 10.00 1.10
Punch cancel .30
202 A89 5p slate & ol grn 19.00 7.00
Punch cancel 1.00
203 A89 10p violet & blue 75.00 17.50
Punch cancel 1.40
204 A89 20p blue & claret 210.00 80.00
Punch cancel 2.00
Nos. 201-204 (4) 314.00 105.60

1915 **Unwmk.** *Perf. 13½x12½*
208 A88 1c ocher .50 .30
209 A88 2c chocolate .90 .30
212 A88 5c red .50 .30
Nos. 208-212 (3) 1.90 .90

Only these denominations were printed on paper without watermark.

Other stamps of the series are known unwatermarked but they are from the outer rows of sheets the other parts of which are watermarked.

Francisco Narciso de Laprida A90

Declaration of Independence A91

A92 A92a
Jose de San Martin

Perf. 13½, 13½x12½

1916, July 9 Litho. Wmk. 87

215 A90 ½c violet .60 .30
216 A90 1c buff .50 .30

Perf. 13½x12½

217 A90 2c chocolate .60 .30
218 A90 3c green .60 .60
219 A90 4c red violet .60 .60

Perf. 13½

220 A91 5c red .50 .30
a. Imperf., pair *40.00*
221 A91 10c gray green 1.50 .30
222 A92 12c blue .90 .35
223 A92 20c ultra .70 .70
224 A92 24c red brown 2.75 1.40
225 A92 30c claret 2.75 1.60
226 A92 50c gray black 6.75 1.60
227 A92a 1p slate bl & red 10.00 10.00
Punch cancel .50
a. Imperf., pair *325.00*
228 A92a 5p black & gray grn 100.00 80.00
Punch cancel 15.00
229 A92a 10p violet & blue 150.00 135.00
Punch cancel 9.00
230 A92a 20p dull blue & cl 150.00 100.00
Punch cancel 7.00
a. Imperf., pair 650.00
Nos. 215-230 (16) 428.75 333.35

Cent. of Argentina's declaration of independence of Spain, July 9, 1816.

The watermark is either vert. or horiz. on Nos. 215-220, 222; only vert. on No. 221, and only horiz. on Nos. 223-230.

For overprints see Nos. OD9, OD55-OD56, OD109, OD153, OD191-OD192, OD285, OD324.

A93

A94

A94a

1917 *Perf. 13½*

231 A93 ½c violet .30 .30
Never hinged .45
a. Imperf. pair 70.00
Never hinged 105.00
232 A93 1c buff .30 .30
Never hinged .45
a. Imperf. pair 70.00
Never hinged 105.00
233 A93 2c brown .30 .30
Never hinged .45
a. Imperf. pair 70.00
Never hinged 105.00
234 A93 3c lt green .70 .30
Never hinged 1.05
a. imperf. pair 70.00
Never hinged 105.00
235 A93 4c red violet .70 .30
Never hinged 1.05
a. Imperf, pair 70.00
Never hinged 105.00
236 A93 5c red .30 .30
Never hinged .45
a. Imperf, pair *15.00*
Never hinged 22.50
237 A93 10c gray green .30 .30
Never hinged .45
a. Imperf, pair 70.00
Never hinged 105.00
Nos. 231-237 (7) 2.90 2.10

Perf. 13½x12½

231B A93 ½c violet .30 .30
Never hinged .45
232B A93 1c buff .40 .40
Never hinged .60
233B A93 2c brown .40 .40
Never hinged .60
234B A93 3c lt green .70 .30
Never hinged 1.05
235B A93 4c red violet .70 .30
Never hinged 1.05
236B A93 5c red .30 .30
Never hinged .45
237B A93 10c gray green .30 .30
Never hinged .45
Nos. 231B-237B (7) 3.10 2.30

Perf. 13½

238 A94 12c blue 1.00 .25
Never hinged 1.50
239 A94 20c ultra 2.50 .30
Never hinged 3.75
240 A94 24c red brown 6.00 3.00
Never hinged 9.00
241 A94 30c claret 6.00 1.50
Never hinged 9.00
242 A94 50c gray black 6.00 .60
Never hinged 9.00
243 A94a 1p slate bl & red 6.00 .60
Never hinged 9.00
244 A94a 5p blk & gray grn 19.00 3.00
Never hinged 29.00
Punch cancel 1.50
245 A94a 10p violet & blue 47.50 12.00
Never hinged 72.50
Punch cancel 1.50
246 A94a 20p dull blue & cl 90.00 50.00
Never hinged 135.00
Punch cancel 1.00
a. Center inverted 1,500. 1,500.
Nos. 231-246 (16) 186.90 73.35

The watermark is either vert. or horiz. on Nos. 231-236, 238 and 231B-236B, 238B; only vert. on No. 237 and 237B, and only horiz. on Nos. 239-246.

All known examples of No. 246a are off-center to the right.

Juan Gregorio Pujol — A95

1918, June 15 Litho. *Perf. 13½*

247 A95 5c bister & gray .60 .30
Never hinged .90

Cent. of the birth of Juan G. Pujol (1817-61), lawyer and legislator.

1918-19 Unwmk. *Perf. 13½*

248 A93 ½c violet .30 .25
249 A93 1c buff .30 .25
Never hinged .45
a. Imperf., pair 14.00
Never hinged 21.00
250 A93 2c brown .30 .25
Never hinged .45
251 A93 3c lt green .50 .25
Never hinged .75
252 A93 4c red violet .50 .25
Never hinged .75
253 A93 5c red .30 .25
Never hinged .75
254 A93 10c gray green .80 .25
Never hinged 1.20
255 A94 12c blue 1.25 .25
Never hinged 1.90
256 A94 20c ultra 1.40 .25
Never hinged 2.10
257 A94 24c red brown 2.40 .25
Never hinged 3.50
258 A94 30c claret 3.00 .30
Never hinged 4.50
259 A94 50c gray black 6.00 .50
Never hinged 9.00
Nos. 248-259 (12) 17.05 3.30

Perf. 13½x12½

248B A93 ½c violet .30 .25
Never hinged .45
249B A93 1c buff .30 .25
Never hinged .45
250B A93 2c brown .30 .25
Never hinged .45
251B A93 3c lt green .50 .25
Never hinged .75
252B A93 4c red violet .50 .25
Never hinged .75
253B A93 5c red .30 .25
Never hinged .75
254B A93 10c gray green 1.10 .25
Never hinged 1.60
Nos. 248B-254B (7) 3.30 1.75

The stamps of this issue sometimes show letters of papermakers' watermarks.

There were two printings, in 1918 and 1923, using different ink and paper.

1920 Wmk. 88

264 A93 ½c violet .50 .25
Never hinged .75
265 A93 1c buff .50 .25
Never hinged .75
266 A93 2c brown .50 .25
Never hinged .75
267 A93 3c green 1.50 1.00
Never hinged 2.25
268 A93 4c red violet 2.00 1.50
Never hinged 3.00
269 A93 5c red .50 .25
Never hinged .75
270 A93 10c gray green 4.50 .25
Never hinged 6.75

Perf. 13½

264A A93 ½c violet .80 .30
Never hinged 1.20
265A A93 1c buff .80 .30
Never hinged 1.20
266A A93 2c brown 1.00 .30
Never hinged 1.50
267A A93 3c green 2.00 1.00
Never hinged 3.00
269A A93 5c red 4.00 .30
Never hinged 6.00
270A A93 10c gray green 55.00 15.00
Never hinged 82.50
271 A94 12c blue 3.00 .30
Never hinged 4.50
272 A94 20c ultra 4.25 .40
Never hinged 6.50
274 A94 30c claret 15.00 3.00
Never hinged 22.50
275 A94 50c gray black 10.00 3.00
Never hinged 15.00
Nos. 264-275 (17) 105.85 27.65

See Nos. 292-300, 304-307A, 310-314, 318, 322.

For overprints see Nos. OD10-OD20, OD57-OD71, OD74, OD110-OD121, OD154-OD159, OD161-OD162, OD193-OD207, OD209-OD211, OD242-OD252, OD254-OD255, OD286-OD290, OD325-OD328, OD330.

Belgrano's Mausoleum A96

Creation of Argentine Flag A97

Gen. Manuel Belgrano — A98

1920, June 18

280 A96 2c red 1.00 .30
a. Perf. 13½x12½ 2.00 .50
281 A97 5c rose & blue 1.00 .30
282 A98 12c green & blue 2.00 1.00
a. "1320" instead of "1820" 12.00 5.00
b. "AROENTINA" 12.00 5.00
Nos. 280-282 (3) 4.00 1.60

Belgrano (1770-1820), Argentine general, patriot and diplomat.

Gen. Justo Jose de Urquiza — A99

1920, Nov. 11

283 A99 5c gray blue .60 .30

Gen. Justo Jose de Urquiza (1801-70), pres. of Argentina, 1854-60. See No. 303.

Bartolome Mitre — A100

1921, June 26 Unwmk.

284 A100 2c violet brown .50 .30
285 A100 5c light blue .50 .30

Bartolome Mitre (1821-1906), pres. of Argentina, 1862-65.

Allegory, Pan-America — A101

1921, Aug. 25 *Perf. 13½*

286 A101 3c violet .55 .30
287 A101 5c blue 2.00 .30
288 A101 10c vio brown 2.50 .50
289 A101 12c rose 3.00 1.00
Nos. 286-289 (4) 8.05 2.10

Inscribed "Buenos Aires-Agosto de 1921" A102

Inscribed "Republica Argentina" A103

1921, Oct. *Perf. 13½x12½*

290 A102 5c rose .60 .30
Never hinged .90
291 A103 5c rose 2.50 .30
Never hinged 3.75

Perf. 13½

290A A102 5c rose 6.00 .50
Never hinged 9.00
291A A103 5c rose 2.50 .30
Never hinged 3.75

1st Pan-American Postal Cong., Buenos Aires, Aug., 1921.

See Nos. 308-309, 319. For overprints see Nos. OD72, OD160, OD208, OD253, OD329.

1920 Wmk. 89 *Perf. 13½x12½*

292 A93 ½c violet 1.60 .80
Never hinged 2.50
293 A93 1c buff 4.50 1.50
Never hinged 6.75
294 A93 2c brown 3.50 .50
Never hinged 5.25
297 A93 5c red 4.50 .35
Never hinged 6.75
298 A93 10c gray green 4.50 .35
Never hinged 6.75
Nos. 292-298,300 (6) 30.60 4.50

Perf. 13½

294A A93 2c brown 7.00 1.50
Never hinged 11.00
297A A93 5c red 52.50 9.00
Never hinged 75.00
298A A93 10c gray green 40.00 2.00
Never hinged 60.00
299 A94 12c blue *3,000.* 200.00
Never hinged 4,500.
300 A94 20c ultra 12.00 1.00
Never hinged 18.00

1920

303 A99 5c gray blue 450.00 300.00
Never hinged 675.00

1922-23 Wmk. 90 *Perf. 13½*

304 A93 ½c violet .60 .25
Never hinged 675.00
305 A93 1c buff 1.00 .30
Never hinged 1.50
306 A93 2c brown 1.00 .30
Never hinged 1.50
307 A93 3c green .60 .40
Never hinged .90
307A A93 4c red violet 1.50 1.00
Never hinged 2.25
308 A102 5c rose 10.00 3.00
Never hinged 15.00
309 A103 5c red 5.00 .80
Never hinged 7.50
310 A93 10c gray green 9.00 1.00
Never hinged 13.50
311 A94 12c blue 1.00 .40
Never hinged 1.50
312 A94 20c ultra 2.00 .50
Never hinged 3.00
313 A94 24c red brown 20.00 10.00
Never hinged 30.00
314 A94 30c claret 10.00 1.00
Never hinged 15.00

Perf. 13½x12½

304B A93 ½c violet .50 .30
Never hinged .75
305B A93 1c buff .50 .30
Never hinged .75
306B A93 2c brown .50 .30
Never hinged .75
307B A93 3c green 1.00 .80
Never hinged 1.50
307C A93 4c red violet 22.50 10.00
Never hinged 35.00
308B A102 5c rose 3.00 .60
Never hinged 4.50
309B A103 5c red .50 .25
Never hinged .75
310B A93 10c gray green 2.25 .25
Never hinged 3.50
Nos. 304-310B (20) 92.45 31.75

Paper with Gray Overprint RA in Sun

1922-23 Unwmk. *Perf. 13½*

318 A93 2c brown 3.00 1.00
Never hinged 4.50
319 A103 5c red 10.00 1.00
Never hinged 15.00
322 A94 20c ultra 30.00 1.50
Never hinged 45.00
Nos. 318-322 (3) 43.00 3.50

Perf. 13½x12½

318A A93 2c brown 3.00 1.00
Never hinged 4.50
319A A103 5c red 3.00 .30
Never hinged 4.50

A104

San Martín — A105

With Period after Value

Perf. 13½x12½

1923, May Litho. Wmk. 90

323 A104 ½c red violet .50 .30
Never hinged .75
324 A104 1c buff .50 .30
Never hinged .75
325 A104 2c dark brown .50 .30
Never hinged .75
326 A104 3c lt green .50 .40
Never hinged .75
327 A104 4c red brown .50 .40
Never hinged .75
328 A104 5c red .50 .30
Never hinged .75
329 A104 10c dull green 3.50 .30
Never hinged 5.25
330 A104 12c deep blue .50 .30
Never hinged .75
331 A104 20c ultra 1.50 .30
Never hinged 2.25
332 A104 24c lt brown 3.50 3.00
Never hinged 5.25
333 A104 30c claret 15.00 .50
Never hinged 22.50
334 A104 50c black 7.50 .50
Never hinged 11.00

Perf. 13½

323A A104 ½c red violet .50 .30
Never hinged .75
324A A104 1c buff .50 .30
Never hinged .75
325A A104 2c dark brown .50 .30
Never hinged .75
326A A104 3c lt green .50 .40
Never hinged .75
327A A104 4c red brown .50 .40
Never hinged .75
328A A104 5c red .50 .30
Never hinged .75
329A A104 10c dull green 3.50 .30
Never hinged 5.25
330A A104 12c deep blue .50 .30
Never hinged .75
331A A104 20c ultra 1.50 .30
Never hinged 2.25
332A A104 24c lt brown 3.50 3.00
Never hinged 5.25
333A A104 30c claret 15.00 .50
Never hinged 22.50
334A A104 50c black 7.50 .50
Never hinged 11.00

Without Period after Value

Perf. 13½

Wmk. 87

335 A105 1p blue & red 10.00 .50
Never hinged 15.00
336 A105 5p gray lil & grn 30.00 6.00
Never hinged 45.00
Punch cancel 1.00
337 A105 10p clar & blue 90.00 15.00
Never hinged 135.00
Punch cancel 2.00
338 A105 20p sl & brn lake 120.00 45.00
Never hinged 175.00
Punch cancel 1.25
a. Center inverted
Nos. 323-338 (28) 319.00 80.30

Nos. 335-338 and 353-356 canceled with round or oval killers in purple (revenue cancellations) sell for one-fifth to one-half as much as postally used copies.

For overprints see Nos. 399-404.

Design of 1923 Without Period after Value

Perf. 13½x12½

1923-24 Litho. Wmk. 90

340 A104 ½c red violet .50 .30
Never hinged .75
341 A104 1c buff .50 .30
Never hinged .75
342 A104 2c dk brown .50 .30
Never hinged .75
343 A104 3c green .60 .30
Never hinged .90
a. Imperf., pair 8.00
Never hinged 12.00
344 A104 4c red brown .60 .30
Never hinged .90
345 A104 5c red .50 .30
Never hinged .75
346 A104 10c dull green .50 .30
Never hinged .75
347 A104 12c deep blue .60 .30
Never hinged .90
348 A104 20c ultra .90 .30
Never hinged 1.35
349 A104 24c lt brown 2.50 1.25
Never hinged 3.75
350 A104 25c purple 1.25 .30
Never hinged 1.90
351 A104 30c claret 2.50 .30
Never hinged 3.75
352 A104 50c black 6.00 .30
Never hinged 9.00

Perf. 13½

340B A104 ½c red violet 125.00 40.00
Never hinged 190.00
345B A104 5c red 55.00 22.50
Never hinged 82.50
346B A104 10c dull green 55.00 22.50
Never hinged 82.50
349B A104 24c lt brown 92.50 30.00
Never hinged 135.00
353 A105 1p blue & red 6.00 .30
Never hinged 9.00
354 A105 5p dk vio & grn 30.00 1.50
Never hinged 45.00
Punch cancel 1.00
355 A105 10p claret & blue 75.00 6.00
Never hinged 110.00
Punch cancel 2.00
356 A105 20p slate & lake 105.00 15.00
Never hinged 160.00
Punch cancel 1.25
Nos. 340-356 (21) 560.95 142.65

1931-33 Typo.

343b A104 3c 3.00 .50
345a A104 5c 4.50 .50
346a A104 10c 7.50 .50
347a A104 12c 15.00 3.00
348a A104 20c 50.00 2.50
350a A104 25c 40.00 1.75
351a A104 30c 21.00 1.25
Nos. 343b-351a (7) 141.00 10.00

The typographed stamps were issued only in coils and have a rough impression with heavy shading about the eyes and nose. Nos. 343 and 346 are known without watermark.

Nos. 341-345, 347-349, 351a may be found in pairs, one with period.

See note after No. 338. See Nos. 362-368. For overprints see Nos. OD21-OD33, OD75-OD87, OD122-OD133, OD163-OD175, OD212-OD226, OD256-OD268, OD291-OD304, OD331-OD345.

Rivadavia — A106

1926, Feb. 8 *Perf. 13½*

357 A106 5c rose .60 .30

Presidency of Bernardino Rivadavia, cent.

Rivadavia A108

San Martin A109

General Post Office, 1926 — A110

General Post Office, 1826 — A111

1926, July 1 *Perf. 13½x12½*

358 A108 3c gray green .40 .30
359 A109 5c red .40 .30

Perf. 13½

360 A110 12c deep blue 1.25 .40
361 A111 25c chocolate 1.60 .25
a. "1326" for "1826" 15.00 5.00
Nos. 358-361 (4) 3.65 1.25

Centenary of the Post Office.

For overprints see Nos. OD34, OD88, OD134, OD227-OD228, OD269, OD305, OD346.

Type of 1923-31 Issue Without Period after Value

1927 Wmk. 205 *Perf. 13½x12½*

362 A104 ½c red violet .50 .50
a. Pelure paper 2.50 2.50
363 A104 1c buff .50 .50
364 A104 2c dark brown .50 .30
a. Pelure paper .70 .70
365 A104 5c red .50 .30
a. Period after value 9.00 6.00
b. Pelure paper .70 .70
366 A104 10c dull green 5.00 3.00
367 A104 20c ultra 47.50 4.75

Perf. 13½

368 A105 1p blue & red 36.00 6.00
Nos. 362-368 (7) 90.50 15.35

Arms of Argentina and Brazil A112

Wmk. RA in Sun (90)

1928, Aug. 27 *Perf. 12½x13*

369 A112 5c rose red 1.50 .40
370 A112 12c deep blue 2.50 .70

Cent. of peace between the Empire of Brazil and the United Provinces of the Rio de la Plata.

Allegory, Discovery of the New World — A113

"Spain" and "Argentina" — A114

"America" Offering Laurels to Columbus A115

1929, Oct. 12 Litho. *Perf. 13½*

371 A113 2c lilac brown 2.00 .40
372 A114 5c light red 2.00 .40
373 A115 12c dull blue 6.00 1.00
Nos. 371-373 (3) 10.00 1.80

Discovery of America by Columbus, 437th anniv.

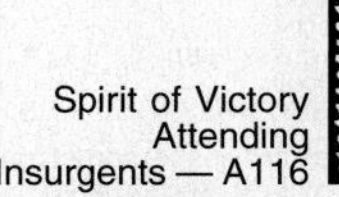

Spirit of Victory Attending Insurgents — A116

March of the Victorious Insurgents A117

Perf. 13½x12½ (A116), 12½x13 (A117)

1930

374 A116 ½c violet gray 1.00 .50
375 A116 1c myrtle green 1.00 .50
376 A117 2c dull violet 1.00 .50
377 A116 3c green .50 .50
378 A116 4c violet .80 .70
379 A116 5c rose red .70 .30
380 A116 10c gray black 1.00 .70
381 A117 12c dull blue 1.50 .70
382 A117 20c ocher 1.50 .80
383 A117 24c red brown 5.00 2.00
384 A117 25c green 6.00 2.00
385 A117 30c deep violet 8.00 3.00
386 A117 50c black 10.00 4.00
387 A117 1p sl bl & red 24.00 8.00
388 A117 2p black & org 30.00 12.00
389 A117 5p dull grn & blk 92.50 35.00
390 A117 10p dp red brn & dull blue 120.00 40.00
391 A117 20p yel grn & dl bl 210.00 90.00
392 A117 50p dk grn & vio 750.00 650.00
Nos. 374-390 (17) 304.50 111.20

Revolution of 1930.

Nos. 387-392 with oval (parcel post) cancellation sell for less.

For overprint see No. 405.

1931 *Perf. 12½x13*

393 A117 ½c red violet .50 .50
394 A117 1c gray black 1.50 1.00
395 A117 3c green 1.50 .70
396 A117 4c red brown .80 .50
397 A117 5c red .70 .50
a. Plane omitted, top left corner 3.00 1.50
398 A117 10c dull green 1.50 .70
Nos. 393-398 (6) 6.50 3.90

Revolution of 1930.

Stamps of 1924-25 Overprinted in Red or Green

1931, Sept. 6 *Perf. 13½, 13½x12½*

399 A104 3c green .40 .40
400 A104 10c dull green .60 .60
401 A104 30c claret (G) 4.50 2.50
402 A104 50c black 4.50 3.00

Overprinted in Blue

403 A105 1p blue & red 5.50 3.00
404 A105 5p dk violet & grn 60.00 20.00

No. 388 Overprinted in Blue

Perf. 12½x13

405 A117 2p black & orange 10.00 7.50
Nos. 399-405 (7) 85.50 37.00

1st anniv. of the Revolution of 1930.

See Nos. C30-C34.

Refrigeration Compressor — A118

Perf. 13½x12½

1932, Aug. 29 Litho.

406 A118 3c green 1.00 .50
407 A118 10c scarlet 2.00 .40
408 A118 12c gray blue 7.00 1.10
Nos. 406-408 (3) 10.00 2.00

6th Intl. Refrigeration Congress.

Port of La Plata A119

Pres. Julio A. Roca — A120

Municipal Palace A121

Cathedral of La Plata — A122

Dardo Rocha A123

Perf. 13½x13, 13x13½ (10c)

1933, Jan.

409	A119	3c green & dk brn	.40	.30
410	A120	10c orange & dk vio	.60	.30
411	A121	15c dk bl & dp bl	2.50	1.50
412	A122	20c violet & yel brn	1.75	.90
413	A123	30c dk grn & vio brn	13.00	6.00
		Nos. 409-413 (5)	18.25	9.00

50th anniv. of the founding of the city of La Plata, Nov. 19th, 1882.

Christ of the Andes — A124

Buenos Aires Cathedral A125

1934, Oct. 1 ***Perf. 13x13½, 13½x13***

414	A124	10c rose & brown	1.00	.30
415	A125	15c dark blue	3.00	.60

32nd Intl. Eucharistic Cong., Oct. 10-14.

"Liberty" with Arms of Brazil and Argentina A126

Symbolical of "Peace" and "Friendship" A127

1935, May 15 ***Perf. 13x13½***

416	A126	10c red	1.00	.30
417	A127	15c blue	2.00	.60

Visit of Pres. Getulio Vargas of Brazil.

Belgrano A128

Sarmiento A129

Urquiza — A130

Louis Braille — A131

San Martin — A132

Brown — A133

Moreno A134

Alberdi A135

Nicolas Avellaneda A136

Rivadavia A137

Mitre A138

Bull (Cattle Breeding) A139

Martin Güemes A140

Agriculture A141

Merino Sheep (Wool) A142

Sugar Cane A143

Oil Well (Petroleum) — A144

Map of South America A145 A146

Fruit — A147

Iguacu Falls (Scenic Wonders) A148

Grapes (Vineyards) A149

Cotton — A150

Two types of A140:
Type I — Inscribed Juan Martin Guemes.
Type II — Inscribed Martin Güemes.

Perf. 13, 13½x13, 13x13½

1935-51 Litho. Wmk. 90

418	A128	½c red violet	.30	.25
419	A129	1c buff	.30	.25
a.		Typo.	.80	.25
420	A130	2c dark brown	.50	.25
421	A131	2½c black ('39)	.30	.25
422	A132	3c green	.50	.25
423	A132	3c lt gray ('39)	.50	.25
424	A134	3c lt gray ('46)	.50	.25
425	A133	4c lt gray	.50	.25
426	A133	4c sage grn ('39)	.40	.25
427	A134	5c yel brn, typo.	.25	.25
a.		Tete beche pair, typo.	20.00	10.00
b.		Booklet pane of 8, typo.		
c.		Booklet pane of 4, typo.		
d.		Litho.	5.00	.50
428	A135	6c olive green	.40	.25
429	A136	8c orange ('39)	.40	.25
430	A137	10c car, perf. 13½ (typo.)	.25	.25
a.		Perf. 13½x13	2.00	.25
431	A137	10c brown ('42)	.25	.25
432	A138	12c brown	1.00	.25
433	A138	12c red ('39)	.25	.25
434	A139	15c slate bl ('36)	1.50	.25
435	A139	15c pale ultra ('39)	1.00	.25
436	A140	15c lt gray bl (II) ('42)	45.00	2.00
437	A140	20c lt ultra (I)	1.00	.25
438	A140	20c lt ultra (II) ('36)	1.00	.25
439	A140	20c bl gray (II) ('39)	.35	.25
439A	A139	20c dk bl & pale bl, ('42) 22x33mm	1.00	.25
440	A139	20c blue ('51)	.25	.25
a.		Typo.	.25	.25
441	A141	25c car & pink ('36)	.50	.25
442	A142	30c org brn & yel brown ('36)	.80	.25
443	A143	40c dk vio ('36)	.70	.25
444	A144	50c red & org ('36)	.70	.25
445	A145	1p brn blk & lt bl ('36)	25.00	1.00
446	A146	1p brn blk & lt bl ('37)	15.00	.30
a.		Chalky paper	100.00	2.00
447	A147	2p brn lake & dk ultra ('36)	1.00	.25
448	A148	5p ind & ol grn ('36)	3.00	.25
449	A149	10p brn lake & blk	15.00	1.00
450	A150	20p bl grn & brn ('36)	25.00	3.00
		Nos. 418-450 (34)	144.40	14.55

See Nos. 485-500, 523-540, 659, 668 in *Scott Standard Postage Stamp Catalogue*, Vol. 1. For overprints see Nos. O37-O41, O43-O51, O53-O56, O58-O78, O108, O112, OD35-OD46, OD89-OD101, OD135-OD145, OD176-OD182C, OD229-OD234F, OD270-OD280, OD306-OD317, OD347-OD357 in this catalogue or Scott Standard catalogue, Vol. 1.

No. 439A exists with attached label showing medallion. Value $42.50 unused, $22.50 used.

Souvenir Sheet

A151

Without Period after Value

1935, Oct. 17 Litho. *Imperf.*

452	A151	Sheet of 4	75.00	35.00
a.		10c dull green	16.50	7.50

Phil. Exhib. at Buenos Aires, Oct. 17-24, 1935. The stamps were on sale during the 8 days of the exhibition only. Sheets measure 83x101mm.

Plaque — A152

1936, Dec. 1 ***Perf. 13x13½***

453	A152	10c rose	.80	.40

Inter-American Conference for Peace.

Domingo Faustino Sarmiento — A153

1938, Sept. 5

454	A153	3c sage green	.50	.50
455	A153	5c red	.50	.50
456	A153	15c deep blue	1.00	.50
457	A153	50c orange	4.00	1.00
		Nos. 454-457 (4)	6.00	2.50

50th anniv. of the death of Domingo Faustino Sarmiento, pres., educator and author.

"Presidente Sarmiento" — A154

1939, Mar. 16

458	A154	5c greenish blue	.50	.30

Final voyage of the training ship "Presidente Sarmiento."

Allegory of the UPU — A155

Coat of Arms — A157

Post Office, Buenos Aires — A156

Iguacu Falls — A158

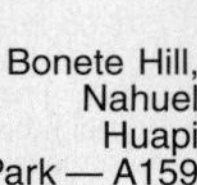

Bonete Hill, Nahuel Huapi Park — A159

Allegory of Modern Communications A160

Argentina, Land of Promise A161

Lake Frias, Nahuel Huapi Park — A162

Perf. 13x13½, 13½x13

1939, Apr. 1 **Photo.**

459	A155	5c rose carmine	.70	.25
460	A156	15c grnsh black	.70	.40
461	A157	20c brt blue	.70	.25
462	A158	25c dp blue grn	1.10	.40
463	A159	50c brown	1.60	.90
464	A160	1p brown violet	4.25	2.40
465	A161	2p magenta	18.50	15.00
466	A162	5p purple	42.50	30.00
		Nos. 459-466 (8)	70.05	49.60

Universal Postal Union, 11th Congress.

Souvenir Sheets

A163

A164

1939, May 12 **Wmk. 90** ***Imperf.***

467	A163	Sheet of 4	6.50	5.00
a.		5c rose carmine (A155)	1.40	1.00
b.		20c bright blue (A157)	1.40	1.00
c.		25c deep blue green (A158)	1.40	1.00
d.		50c brown (A159)	1.40	1.00
468	A164	Sheet of 4	6.50	5.00

Issued in four forms:

a.	Unsevered horizontal pair of sheets, type A163 at left, A164 at right	27.50	16.00
b.	Unsevered vertical pair of sheets, type A163 at top, A164 at bottom	27.50	16.00
c.	Unsevered block of 4 sheets, type A163 at left, A164 at right	55.00	55.00
d.	Unsevered block of 4 sheets, type A163 at top, A164 at bottom	55.00	55.00

11th Cong. of the UPU and the Argentina Intl. Phil. Exposition (C.Y.T.R.A.).
No. 468 contains Nos. 467a-467d.

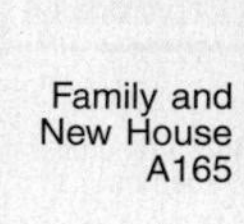

Family and New House A165

Perf. 13½x13

1939, Oct. 2 **Litho.** **Wmk. 90**

469	A165	5c bluish green	.50	.25

1st Pan-American Housing Congress.

Bird Carrying Record A166

Head of Liberty and Arms of Argentina A167

Record and Winged Letter A168

Perf. 13x13½, 13½x13 (#472)

1939, Dec. 11 **Photo.**

470	A166	1.18p indigo	14.00	10.00
471	A167	1.32p bright blue	14.00	10.00
472	A168	1.50p dark brown	52.50	35.00
		Nos. 470-472 (3)	80.50	55.00

These stamps were issued for the recording and mailing of flexible phonograph records.

Map of the Americas — A169

1940, Apr. 14 ***Perf. 13x13½***

473	A169	15c ultramarine	.50	.25

50th anniv. of the Pan American Union.

Souvenir Sheet

Reproductions of Early Argentine Stamps — A170

Wmk. RA in Sun (90)

1940, May 25 **Litho.** ***Imperf.***

474	A170	Sheet of 5	11.00	8.00
a.		5c dark blue (Corrientes A2)	1.75	1.50
b.		5c red (Argentina A1)	1.75	1.50
c.		5c dark blue (Cordoba #1)	1.75	1.50
d.		5c red (Argentina A3)	1.75	1.50
e.		10c dark blue (Buenos Aires A1)	1.75	1.50

100th anniv. of the first postage stamp.

AIR POST STAMPS

Airplane Circles the Globe — AP1

Eagle — AP2

Wings Cross the Sea — AP3

Condor on Mountain Crag — AP4

Perforations of Nos. C1-C37 vary from clean-cut to rough and uneven, with many skipped perfs.

Perf. 13x13½, 13½x13

1928, Mar. 1 **Litho.** **Wmk. 90**

C1	AP1	5c lt red	1.50	.60
C2	AP1	10c Prus blue	2.50	1.10
C3	AP2	15c lt brown	2.50	1.00
C4	AP1	18c lilac gray	4.00	3.00
a.		18c brown lilac	4.50	3.00
b.		Double impression	375.00	
C5	AP2	20c ultra	3.00	1.00
C6	AP2	24c deep blue	5.00	3.00
C7	AP3	25c brt violet	5.00	1.60
C8	AP3	30c rose red	6.00	1.25
C9	AP4	35c rose	5.00	1.10
C10	AP1	36c bister brn	3.00	1.60
C11	AP4	50c gray black	5.00	.75
C12	AP2	54c chocolate	5.00	2.25
C13	AP2	72c yellow grn	6.00	2.25
a.		Double impression	350.00	
C14	AP3	90c dk brown	11.00	2.00
C15	AP3	1p slate bl & red	13.00	.90
C16	AP3	1.08p rose & dk bl	18.00	5.00
C17	AP4	1.26p dull vio & grn	25.00	10.00
C18	AP4	1.80p blue & lil rose	25.00	10.00
C19	AP4	3.60p gray & blue	50.00	22.00
		Nos. C1-C19 (19)	195.50	70.40

The watermark on No. C4a is larger than on the other stamps of this set, measuring 10mm across Sun.

Zeppelin First Flight

Air Post Stamps of 1928 Overprinted in Blue

1930, May

C20	AP2	20c ultra	10.00	5.00
C21	AP4	50c gray black	20.00	10.00
a.		Inverted overprint	475.00	
C22	AP3	1p slate bl & red	25.00	12.50
a.		Inverted overprint	650.00	
C23	AP4	1.80p blue & lil rose	70.00	30.00
C24	AP4	3.60p gray & blue	200.00	90.00
		Nos. C20-C24 (5)	325.00	147.50

Overprinted in Green

C25	AP2	20c ultra	13.00	8.00
C26	AP4	50c gray black	15.00	10.00
C27	AP3	90c dark brown	13.00	8.00
C28	AP3	1p slate bl & red	25.00	15.00
C29	AP4	1.80p blue & lil rose	700.00	500.00
a.		Thick paper	850.00	
		Nos. C25-C29 (5)	766.00	541.00

Air Post Stamps of 1928 Overprinted in Red or Blue

On AP1-AP2

On AP3-AP4

1931

C30	AP1	18c lilac gray	2.00	1.50
C31	AP2	72c yellow green	14.00	10.50
C32	AP3	90c dark brown	14.00	10.50

C33 AP4 1.80p bl & lil rose (Bl) 30.00 22.50
C34 AP4 3.60p gray & blue 57.50 40.00
Nos. C30-C34 (5) 117.50 85.00

1st anniv. of the Revolution of 1930.

Zeppelin Issue

Nos. C1, C4, C4a, C14 Overprinted in Blue or Red

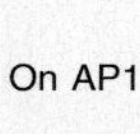

On AP1

On AP3

1932, Aug. 4

C35 AP1 5c lt red (Bl) 3.00 2.00
C36 AP1 18c lilac gray (R) 12.50 9.00
a. 18c brown lilac (R) 100.00 60.00
C37 AP3 90c dark brown (R) 32.50 26.00
Nos. C35-C37 (3) 48.00 37.00

Plane and Letter — AP5

Mercury — AP6

Plane in Flight — AP7

Perf. 13½x13, 13x13½

1940, Oct. 23 **Photo.** **Wmk. 90**

C38 AP5 30c deep orange 5.00 .25
C39 AP6 50c dark brown 7.50 .25
C40 AP5 1p carmine 1.75 .25
C41 AP7 1.25p deep green .50 .25
C42 AP5 2.50p bright blue 1.25 .25
Nos. C38-C42 (5) 16.00 1.25

OFFICIAL STAMPS

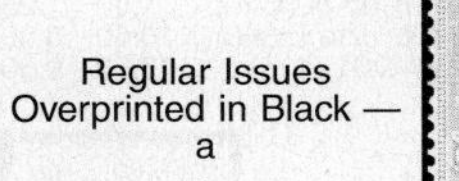

Regular Issues Overprinted in Black — a

1884-87 **Unwmk.** ***Perf. 12, 14***

O1 A29 ½c brown *40.00* *25.00*
O2 A23 1c red 12.00 8.00
b. Perf. 12 100.00 80.00
O3 A29 1c red 1.00 .50
On cover —
b. Double overprint 100.00 100.00
O4 A20 2c green 1.00 .50
On cover —
b. Double overprint 120.00 120.00
O5 A11 4c brown 1.00 .50
On cover —
O6 A7 8c lake 1.00 1.00
On cover —
O7 A8 10c green 100.00 50.00
O8 A23 12c ultra (#45) 1.50 1.00
a. Perf. 14 1,000. 250.00
O9 A29 12c grnsh blue 1.50 1.00
On cover —
O10 A19 24c blue 2.00 1.50
On cover —
O11 A21 25c lake 30.00 25.00
O12 A12 30c orange 80.00 70.00
O13 A13 60c black 50.00 40.00
O14 A14 90c blue 30.00 25.00
b. Double overprint 120.00 120.00
Nos. O1-O14 (14) 351.00 249.00

Inverted Overprint

O1a A29 ½c 30.00 20.00
O2a A23 1c Perf. 14 100.00 80.00
c. Perf. 12 75.00 —
O3a A29 1c 2.50 1.25
O4a A20 2c 120.00 120.00
O5a A11 4c 60.00 50.00
O6a A7 8c (Inverted overprint on reverse) *500.00* —
O8b A23 12c Perf. 12 — —
O9a A29 12c 300.00 250.00
O10a A19 24c 6.00 5.00
O13a A13 60c 150.00 120.00
O14a A14 90c 120.00 120.00

1884 ***Rouletted***

O15 A17 16c green 3.00 2.00
a. Double overprint 25.00 —
b. Inverted overprint 300.00
O16 A18 20c blue 15.00 12.00
a. Inverted overprint 120.00 80.00
O17 A19 24c blue 2.00 1.50
a. Inverted overprint 6.00 5.00
b. Double ovpt., one inverted 250.00 —
Nos. O15-O17 (3) 20.00 15.50

Overprinted Diagonally in Red

1885 ***Perf. 12***

O18 A20 2c green 3.00 2.00
a. Inverted overprint 100.00 100.00
O19 A11 4c brown 3.00 2.00
a. Inverted overprint 100.00 —
b. Double overprint 100.00 100.00
O20 A13 60c black 50.00 40.00
O21 A14 90c blue 450.00 275.00

1885 ***Rouletted***

O22 A19 24c blue 27.50 20.00

On all of these stamps, the overprint is found reading both upwards and downwards.

Counterfeits exist of No. O21 overprint and others.

Regular Issues Handstamped Horizontally in Black — b

1884 ***Perf. 12, 14***

O23 A23 1c red 100.00 50.00
a. Perf. 12 400.00 300.00
O24 A20 2c green, diagonal overprint 60.00 40.00
a. Horizontal overprint 450.00 300.00
O25 A11 4c brown 25.00 20.00
O26 A7 8c lake 25.00 10.00
O27 A23 12c ultra 60.00 50.00

Overprinted Diagonally

O28 A19 24c bl, rouletted 50.00 35.00
O29 A13 60c black 30.00 15.00

Counterfeit overprints exist.

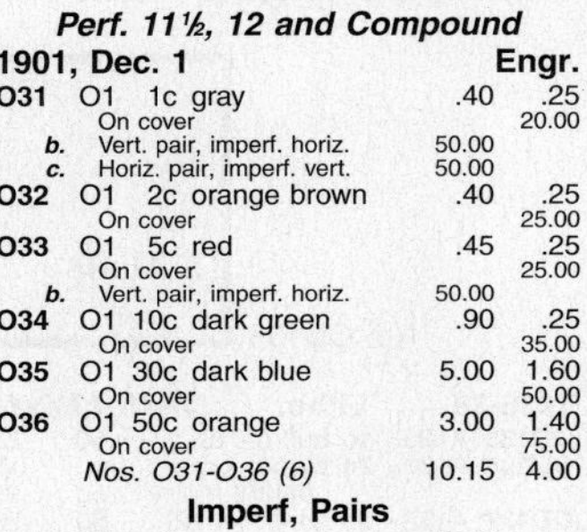

Liberty Head — O1

Perf. 11½, 12 and Compound

1901, Dec. 1 **Engr.**

O31 O1 1c gray .40 .25
On cover 20.00
b. Vert. pair, imperf. horiz. 50.00
c. Horiz. pair, imperf. vert. 50.00
O32 O1 2c orange brown .40 .25
On cover 25.00
O33 O1 5c red .45 .25
On cover 25.00
b. Vert. pair, imperf. horiz. 50.00
O34 O1 10c dark green .90 .25
On cover 35.00
O35 O1 30c dark blue 5.00 1.60
On cover 50.00
O36 O1 50c orange 3.00 1.40
On cover 75.00
Nos. O31-O36 (6) 10.15 4.00

Imperf, Pairs

O31a O1 1c 80.00
O32a O1 2c 80.00
O33a O1 5c 100.00
O34a O1 10c 80.00
O35a O1 30c 100.00
O36a O1 50c 150.00

Regular Stamps of 1935-51 Overprinted in Black — c

Perf. 13x13½, 13½x13, 13

1938-54 **Wmk. RA in Sun (90)**

O37 A129 1c buff ('40) .40 .25
O38 A130 2c dk brn ('40) .40 .25
O39 A132 3c grn ('39) 1.00 .25
O40 A132 3c lt gray ('39) .40 .25
O41 A134 5c yel brn .40 .25
O42 A195 5c car ('53) .40 .25
O43 A137 10c carmine .55 .25
O44 A137 10c brn ('39) .45 .25
O45 A140 15c lt gray bl, type II ('47) .40 .25
O46 A139 15c slate blue .75 .25
O47 A139 15c pale ultra ('39) .45 .25
O48 A139 20c blue ('53) 1.10 .40
O49 A141 25c carmine .40 .25
a. Overprint 11mm .55 .25
O49B A143 40c dk violet 1.50 .35
O50 A144 50c red & org .40 .25
a. Overprint 11mm .40 .25
O51 A146 1p brn blk & lt bl ('40) .45 .25
a. Overprint 11mm .45 .40
O52 A224 1p choc & lt bl ('51) 1.50 .25
a. Overprint 11mm .40 .25
O53 A147 2p brn lake & dk ultra (ovpt. 11mm) ('54) 1.50 .25
Nos. O37-O53 (18) 12.45 4.75

OFFICIAL DEPARTMENT STAMPS

Regular Issues of 1911-38 Overprinted in Black Ministry of Agriculture

No. OD1

1913 **Type I** ***Perf. 13½x12½***

OD1 A88 2c choc (#181) .50 .25
OD2 A88 1c ocher (#190) .50 .25
OD3 A88 2c choc (#191) 1.00 .50
OD4 A88 5c red (#194) 1.00 .50
a. Perf. 13½ (#194a) 3.00 1.00
OD5 A88 12c dp bl (#196) 1.00 .50
a. Perf. 13½ (#196a) 3.00 .50
Nos. OD2-OD5 (4) 3.50 1.75

1915

OD6 A88 1c ocher (#208) 1.50 .50
OD7 A88 2c chocolate (#209) 1.00 .50
OD8 A88 5c red (#212) 1.00 .50
Nos. OD6-OD8 (3) 3.50 1.50

No. OD9

1916 ***Perf. 13½***

OD9 A91 5c red (#220) .50 .25

No. OD11

No. OD15

1918

OD10 A94 12c blue (#238) 1.50 .50
OD11 A93 1c buff (#249) .50 .25
OD12 A93 2c brown (#250) .50 .25
OD13 A93 5c red (#253) .50 .25
OD14 A94 12c blue (#255) .50 .25
OD15 A94 20c ultra (#256) .50 .25
Nos. OD10-OD15 (6) 4.00 1.75

1920 ***Perf. 13½, 13½x12½ (OD16)***

OD16 A93 1c buff (#265) 1.00 .50
OD17 A93 2c brown (#266A) 4.00 1.00
OD18 A93 5c red (#269A) .70 .30
a. Perf. 13½x12½ (#269) .70 .30
Nos. OD16-OD18 (3) 5.70 1.80

1922 ***Perf. 13½***

OD19 A94 12c blue (#311) 2.00 .75
OD20 A94 20c ultra (#312) 75.00

No. OD23

1923 ***Perf. 13½x12½***

OD21 A104 1c buff (#324) 1.00 .50
a. Perf. 13½ (#324A) 5.00 2.00
OD22 A104 2c dk brn (#325) .50 .25
OD23 A104 5c red (#328) .50 .25
a. Perf. 13½ (#328A) 1.00 .50
OD24 A104 12c deep blue (#330) .80 .25
OD25 A104 20c ultra (#331) .80 .25
a. Perf. 13½ (#331A) 6.00 2.00
Nos. OD21-OD25 (5) 3.60 1.50

1924

OD26 A104 1c buff (#341) .50 .25
a. Inverted ovpt. 20.00 15.00
OD27 A104 2c dk brn (#342) .50 .25
a. Pair, one with period 16.00 16.00
OD29 A104 5c red (#345) .50 .25
a. Pair, one with period 20.00 20.00
OD30 A104 10c dl grn (#346) .50 .25
OD31 A104 12c dp bl (#347) .50 .25
OD32 A104 20c dp bl (#348) .50 .25
a. Inverted ovpt. 80.00 60.00
Nos. OD26-OD32 (6) 3.00 1.50

No. OD34

1926

OD34 A110 12c deep blue (#360) .50 .25

No. OD28B

Type II

1931-36 ***Perf. 13x13½, 13½x13***

OD27B A104 2c dk brn (#342) 5.00 2.00
OD28B A104 3c green (#343) .50 .25
OD29B A104 5c red (#345) .50 .25
OD30B A104 10c dl grn (#346) .50 .25
c. Typo (coil) (#346a) .50 .25
OD32B A104 20c ultra (#348) 1.00 .50
c. Typo (coil) (#348a) .50 .25
OD33B A104 30c claret (#351) .50 .25
c. Typo (coil) (#351a) .50 .25

No. OD36

1936-38 **Litho.**

OD35 A129 1c buff (#419) .50 .25
OD36 A130 2c dk brn (#420) .50 .25
OD37 A132 3c green (#422) .50 .25
OD38 A134 5c yel brn (#427) .50 .25
OD40 A139 15c lt gray bl (#436) 2.50 .30
OD41 A140 20c lt ultra (#437) 3.00 .30
OD42 A140 20c lt ultra (#438) .80 .25
OD43 A141 25c car & pink (#441), perf. 13x13½ .50 .25
OD44 A142 30c org brn & yel brown (#442) .50 .25
OD45 A145 1p brn blk & Lt bl (#445) 3.50 1.50
OD46 A146 1p brn blk & lt bl (#446) .60 .30
Nos. OD35-OD46 (11) 13.40 4.15

Typo. *Perf. 13½*

OD38A A134 5c yel brn (#427) .50 .25
OD39A A137 10c carmine (#430) .50 .25
b. Perf. 13½x13 (#430a) 1.00 .50

Ministry of War

No. OD47

1913 **Type I** *Perf. 13½x12½*

OD47 A88 2c choc (#181) .80 .30
OD48 A88 1c ocher (#190) .30 .25
OD49 A88 2c choc (#191) 4.00 .50
a. Perf. 13½ (#191a) 15.00 5.00
OD50 A88 5c red (#194) 1.00 .50
a. Inverted ovpt. 50.00 —
OD51 A88 12c dp bl (#196) .50 .25
a. Perf. 13½ (#196a) 5.00 1.00
Nos. OD48-OD51 (4) 5.80 1.50

1915

OD52 A88 1c ocher (#208) 30.00 6.00
OD53 A88 2c chocolate (#209) 4.00 .80
OD54 A88 5c red (#212) 4.00 .80
Nos. OD52-OD54 (3) 38.00 7.60

1916 *Perf. 13½*

OD55 A91 5c red (#220) 3.00 .50
OD56 A92 12c blue (#222) 3.00 .50

1918

OD57 A93 1c buff (#232) 1.00 .50
a. Perf. 13½x12½ (#232B) 8.00 3.00
OD58 A93 2c brown (#233) 5.00 .80
a. Perf. 13½x12½ (#233B) 1.50 .50
OD59 A93 5c red (#236B) (Perf. 13½x12½) 1.50 .50
OD60 A94 12c blue (#238) 2.00 .80
Nos. OD57-OD60 (4) 9.50 2.60

1918

OD61 A93 1c buff (#249) 1.50 .50
a. Perf. 13½x12½ (#249B) 6.00 5.00
OD62 A93 2c brown (#250) .50 .25
a. Perf. 13½x12½ (#250B) 1.00 .50
OD63 A93 5c red (#253) 1.00 .50
a. Perf. 13½x12½ (#253B) .50 .25
OD64 A94 12c blue (#255) 1.50 .50
OD65 A94 20c ultra (#256) 4.00 .60
Nos. OD61-OD65 (5) 8.50 2.35

1920

OD66 A93 2c brown (#266A) 2.50 .50
a. Perf. 13½x12½ (#266) .50 .25
OD67 A93 5c red (#269A) 1.50 .50
a. Perf. 13½x12½ (#269) 1.00 .25
OD68 A94 12c blue (#271) 1.00 .50
Nos. OD66-OD68 (3) 5.00 1.50

1921

OD69 A94 12c blue (#299) 5.00 1.00

No. OD72

1922

OD70 A93 1c buff (#305) 3.00 .30
OD71 A93 2c brown (13½x12½) (#306B) 5.00 1.00
OD72 A103 5c red (#309) 2.00 .50
OD73 A94 20c ultra (#312) 1.00 .50
Nos. OD70-OD73 (4) 11.00 2.30

Perf. 13½x12½

OD74 A93 2c brown (#318A) 5.00 1.00

1923 *Perf. 13½x12½*

OD75 A104 1c buff (#324) 1.00 .50
a. Inverted ovpt. 20.00 18.00
b. Perf. 13½ (#324A) 5.00 1.50
OD76 A104 2c dk brn (#325) .50 .25
a. Perf. 13½ (#325A) 2.00 .50
OD77 A104 5c red (#328) .50 .25
a. Inverted ovpt. 20.00 18.00
b. Perf. 13½ (#328A) 1.50 .50
OD78 A104 12c dp bl (#330) 1.00 .50
OD79 A104 20c ultra (#331) 2.00 .50
a. Perf. 13½ (#331A) 3.00 .25
b. As "a.," inverted ovpt. 20.00 18.00
Nos. OD75-OD79 (5) 5.00 2.00

1924

OD80 A104 1c buff (#341) 5.00 1.00
OD81 A104 2c dk brn (#342) .50 .25
a. Pair, one with period 15.00 —
OD82 A104 3c green (#343) .80 .25
OD83 A104 5c red (#345) .50 .25
a. Pair, one with period 15.00 —
OD84 A104 10c dl grn (#346) 2.00 .25
OD85 A104 20c ultra (#348) .50 .25
a. Pair, one with period 15.00 —
OD86 A104 30c claret (#351) 5.00 .50
OD87 A105 1p blue & red (#353) 5.00 .30
Nos. OD80-OD87 (8) 19.30 3.05

No. OD88

1926

OD88 A109 5c red (#359) 1.50 .25

No. OD82B

Type II

1931-36 *Perf. 13½x12½, 13 (OD87B)*

OD82B A104 3c green (#343) 1.50 .50
OD83B A104 5c red (#345) .60 .25
c. Inverted ovpt. — 60.00
OD84B A104 10c dl grn (#346) .50 .25
c. Typo (coil) (346a) 1.50 .50
OD85B A104 20c ultra (#348) 1.00 .30
c. Typo (coil) (#348a) 5.00 .50
OD86B A104 30c claret (#351) .80 .25
c. Typo (coil) (#351a) 2.00 .50
OD87B A105 1p blue & red (#353) 5.00 .30
Nos. OD82B-OD87B (6) 9.40 1.85

No. OD90

1936-38 **Litho.**

OD89 A129 1c buff (#419) .50 .25
OD90 A130 2c dk brn (#420) .50 .25
OD91 A132 3c green (#422) .50 .25
OD92 A134 5c yel brn (#427) .50 .25
OD93 A137 10c car (#430) .50 .25
OD94 A139 15c slate bl (#434) .80 .25
OD95 A140 20c lt ultra (#437) 7.00 .50
OD96 A140 20c lt ultra (#438) .50 .25
OD97 A141 25c car & pink (#441) .50 .25
OD98 A142 30c org brn & yel brown (#442) .50 .25
OD99 A144 50c red & org (#444) .70 .25
OD100 A145 1p brn blk & lt bl (#445) 2.00 .60
OD101 A146 1p brn blk & lt bl (#446) 1.00 .50
Nos. OD89-OD101 (13) 15.50 4.10

Typo. *Perf. 13½*

OD92B A134 5c yel brn (#427) .50 .25
c. Inverted ovpt. 20.00 15.00
OD93B A137 10c car (#430) .50 .25
c. Inverted ovpt. 50.00 35.00
d. Perf. 13½x13 (#430a) 1.00 .50

Ministry of Finance

No. OD102

1913 **Type I** *Perf. 13½x12½*

OD102 A88 2c choc (#181) .50 .25
OD103 A88 1c ocher (#190) .50 .25
OD104 A88 2c choc (#191) .50 .25
OD105 A88 5c red (#194) .50 .25
OD106 A88 12c dp bl (#196) .50 .25
a. Perf. 13½ (#196a) 90.00 35.00
Nos. OD103-OD106 (4) 2.00 1.00

1915

OD107 A88 2c choc (#209) .50 .25
OD108 A88 5c red (#212) .50 .25

1916 *Perf. 13½*

OD109 A91 5c red (#220) .70 .30

1917

OD110 A93 2c brown (#233) .50 .25
OD111 A93 5c red (#236) 4.00 .50
OD112 A94 12c blue (#238) .50 .25
Nos. OD110-OD112 (3) 5.00 1.00

1918

OD113 A93 2c brown (#250) 100.00
OD114 A93 5c red (#253) .50 .25
a. Perf. 13½x12½ (#253B) .70 .25
OD115 A94 12c blue (#255) .70 .25
OD116 A94 20c ultra (#256) 1.00 .50
Nos. OD113-OD116 (4) 2.20 101.00

1920

OD117 A93 1c buff (#265) 3.00 1.00
OD118 A93 2c brown (#266) 4.50 1.50
OD119 A93 5c #269 6.00 1.50
a. Perf. 13½ (#269A) 1.50 .30
OD120 A94 12c blue (#271) (perf. 13½) 1.50 .30
Nos. OD117-OD120 (4) 15.00 4.30

1922

OD121 A94 20c ultra (#312) 40.00 7.00

1923 *Perf. 13½x12½, 13½*

OD122 A104 1c buff (#324) 20.00 10.00
a. Perf. 13½ (#324A) 2.00 1.00
OD123 A104 2c dk brn (#325) .50 .25
a. Perf. 13½ (#325A) 10.00 1.00
OD124 A104 5c red (#328) .50 .25
a. Inverted ovpt. — 35.00
b. Perf. 13½ (#328A) 1.00 .50
OD125 A104 12c dp bl (#330) .70 .25
a. Perf. 13½ (#330A) 3.00 .30
OD126 A104 20c ultra (#331) .50 .25
a. Perf. 13½ (#331A) 2.50 .30
Nos. OD122-OD126 (5) 22.20 11.00

1924 *Perf. 13½x12½*

OD127 A104 2c dk brn (#342) 250.00 250.00
OD128 A104 5c red (#345) 1.00 .25
OD130 A104 12c dp bl (#347) 40.00 17.50
OD131 A104 20c ultra (#348) .50 .25
Nos. OD127-OD131 (4) 291.50 268.00

1926

OD134 A110 12c dp bl (#360) 30.00 12.50

No. OD129B

No. OD133B

1931-36 **Type II**

OD127B A104 3c green (#343) 25.00 10.00
OD129B A104 10c dl grn (#346) .50 .25
c. Typo (coil) (#346a) .60 .25
OD131B A104 20c ultra (#348) 1.00 .50
c. Typo (coil) (#348a) .50 .25
OD132B A104 30c claret (#351) .50 .25
c. Typo (coil) (#351a) 1.50 .25

Perf. 13

OD133B A105 1p blue & red (#353) 1.00 .50
Nos. OD127B-OD133B (5) 28.00 11.50

No. OD135

1936-38 **Litho.** *Perf. 13½x13*

OD135 A129 1c buff (#419) .50 .25
OD136 A130 2c dk brn (#420) .50 .25
OD137 A132 3c green (#422) .50 .25
OD138 A134 5c yel brn (Perf. 13½) (#427d) .50 .25
OD139 A137 10c car (#430) .50 .30
OD140 A139 15c slate blue (#434) ('36) 2.00 .80
a. Inverted ovpt. — 80.00
OD141 A140 20c lt ultra (#437) 2.50 .25
OD142 A140 20c lt ultra (#438) .50 .25
OD143 A142 30c org brn & yel brown (#442) .50 .25
OD144 A145 1p brn blk & lt bl (#445) 5.00 1.50
OD145 A146 1p brn blk & lt bl (#446) .60 .30
Nos. OD135-OD145 (11) 13.60 4.65

Typo. *Perf. 13½*

OD138A A134 5c yel brn (#427) .50 .25
b. Inverted ovpt. 50.00 50.00
OD139A A137 10c car (#430) .50 .25
b. Perf. 13½x13 (#430a) 18.00 1.50

Ministry of the Interior

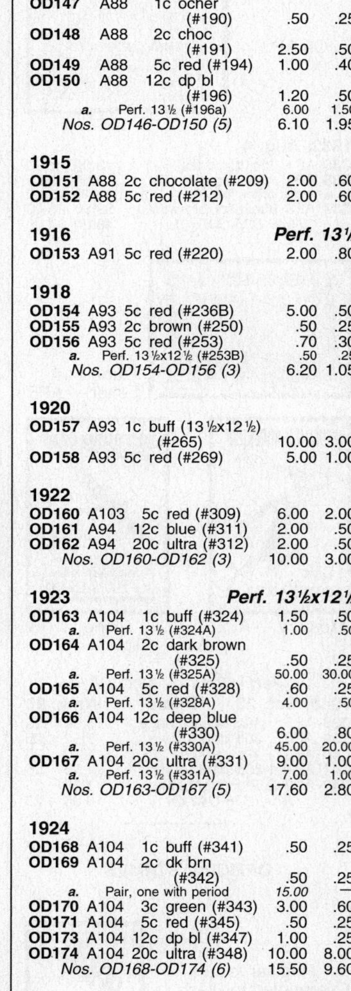
No. OD147

1913 **Type I** *Perf. 13½x12½*

OD146 A88 2c choc (#181) .90 .30
OD147 A88 1c ocher (#190) .50 .25
OD148 A88 2c choc (#191) 2.50 .50
OD149 A88 5c red (#194) 1.00 .40
OD150 A88 12c dp bl (#196) 1.20 .50
a. Perf. 13½ (#196a) 6.00 1.50
Nos. OD146-OD150 (5) 6.10 1.95

1915

OD151 A88 2c chocolate (#209) 2.00 .60
OD152 A88 5c red (#212) 2.00 .60

1916 *Perf. 13½*

OD153 A91 5c red (#220) 2.00 .80

1918

OD154 A93 5c red (#236B) 5.00 .50
OD155 A93 2c brown (#250) .50 .25
OD156 A93 5c red (#253) .70 .30
a. Perf. 13½x12½ (#253B) .50 .25
Nos. OD154-OD156 (3) 6.20 1.05

1920

OD157 A93 1c buff (13½x12½) (#265) 10.00 3.00
OD158 A93 5c red (#269) 5.00 1.00

1922

OD160 A103 5c red (#309) 6.00 2.00
OD161 A94 12c blue (#311) 2.00 .50
OD162 A94 20c ultra (#312) 2.00 .50
Nos. OD160-OD162 (3) 10.00 3.00

1923 *Perf. 13½x12½*

OD163 A104 1c buff (#324) 1.50 .50
a. Perf. 13½ (#324A) 1.00 .50
OD164 A104 2c dark brown (#325) .50 .25
a. Perf. 13½ (#325A) 50.00 30.00
OD165 A104 5c red (#328) .60 .25
a. Perf. 13½ (#328A) 4.00 .50
OD166 A104 12c deep blue (#330) 6.00 .80
a. Perf. 13½ (#330A) 45.00 20.00
OD167 A104 20c ultra (#331) 9.00 1.00
a. Perf. 13½ (#331A) 7.00 1.00
Nos. OD163-OD167 (5) 17.60 2.80

1924

OD168 A104 1c buff (#341) .50 .25
OD169 A104 2c dk brn (#342) .50 .25
a. Pair, one with period 15.00 —
OD170 A104 3c green (#343) 3.00 .60
OD171 A104 5c red (#345) .50 .25
OD173 A104 12c dp bl (#347) 1.00 .25
OD174 A104 20c ultra (#348) 10.00 8.00
Nos. OD168-OD174 (6) 15.50 9.60

No. OD172B

Type II

1931-36 *Perf. 13½x12½*

OD170B A104 3c green (#343) .70 .25
OD171B A104 5c red (#345) .70 .25
OD172B A104 10c dull green (#346) .50 .25
c. Typo (coil) (#346a) .50 .25
OD174B A104 20c ultra (#348) .50 .25
c. Typo (coil) (#348a) 1.00 .50
OD175B A104 30c claret (#351) 3.00 .50
c. Typo (coil) (#351a) 6.00 2.00
Nos. OD170B-OD175B (5) 5.40 1.50

No. OD182A

1936-38 Litho. *Perf. 13½x13*

OD176 A129 1c buff (#419) .50 .25
OD177 A130 2c dk brn (#420) .50 .25
OD178 A132 3c green (#422) .50 .25
OD178A A134 5c yel brn (#427d) .50 .25
OD180 A139 15c slate bl (#434) ('36) .70 .30
OD181 A140 20c lt ultra (#437) 3.00 .50
OD182 A140 20c lt ultra (#438) .50 .25
OD182A A142 30c org brn & yel brown (#442) .50 .25
OD182B A145 1p brn blk & lt blue (#445) 5.00 2.00
OD182C A146 1p brn blk & lt bl (#446) ('37) .60 .30
Nos. OD176-OD182C (10) 12.30 4.60

Typo. *Perf. 13½*

OD178D A134 5c yel brn (#427) .60 .25
e. Inverted ovpt. 75.00
OD179D A137 10c car (#430) .80 .30
e. Perf. 13½x13 (#430a) .50 .25

Ministry of Justice and Instruction

No. OD184

1913 Type I *Perf. 13½x12½*

OD183 A88 2c choc (#181) 3.00 .50
OD184 A88 1c ocher (#190) 4.00 .50
OD185 A88 2c choc (#191) 2.50 .50
a. Perf. 13½ (#191a) 30.00 10.00
OD186 A88 5c red (#194) 1.00 .50
OD187 A88 12c dp bl (#196) 1.50 .50
Nos. OD184-OD187 (4) 9.00 2.00

1915

OD188 A88 1c ocher (#208) 1.00 .50
OD189 A88 2c chocolate (#209) 1.00 .50
OD190 A88 5c red (#212) 2.00 .80
Nos. OD188-OD190 (3) 4.00 1.80

1916 *Perf. 13½*

OD191 A91 5c red (#220) 1.00 .50
OD192 A92 12c blue (#222) 2.00 .80

1918

OD193 A93 1c buff (#232) 1.00 .50
a. Perf. 13½x12½ (#232B) 1.00 .50
OD194 A93 2c brown (#233) 4.00 .50
a. Perf. 13½x12½ (#233B) 2.00 .50
OD195 A93 5c red (#236) 9.00 1.00
a. Perf. 13½x12½ (#236B) 1.00 .50
OD196 A94 12c blue (#238) 45.00 10.00
Nos. OD193-OD196 (4) 59.00 12.00

OD197 A93 1c buff (#249) .60 .30
a. Perf. 13½x12½ (#249B) 20.00 7.00
OD198 A93 2c brown (#250) .30 .25
a. Perf. 13½x12½ (#250B) .50 .25
OD199 A93 5c red (#253) .50 .25
a. Perf. 13½x12½ (#253B) .60 .30
OD200 A94 12c blue (#255) .50 .25
OD201 A94 20c ultra (#256) .70 .30
Nos. OD197-OD201 (5) 2.60 1.35

1920 *Perf. 13½x12½*

OD202 A93 1c buff (#265) .70 .25
OD203 A93 2c brown (#266) .50 .25
OD204 A93 5c red (#269) .50 .25
a. Perf. 13½ (#269A) 8.00 2.50
OD205 A94 12c blue (perf. 13½) (#271) 1.00 .50
Nos. OD202-OD205 (4) 2.70 1.25

1922 *Perf. 13½*

OD206 A93 1c buff (#305) 3.00 1.00
a. Perf. 13½x12½ (#305B) .70 .25
OD207 A93 2c brown, (perf. 13½x12½) (#306B) 4.00 1.00
OD208 A103 5c red (#309) .70 .25
a. Perf. 13½x12½ (#309B) .50 .25
OD209 A94 12c blue (#311) 20.00 4.00
OD210 A94 20c ultra (#312) 4.00 .60
Nos. OD206-OD210 (5) 31.70 6.85

1922 *Perf. 13½x12½*

OD211 A93 2c brown (#318A) 3.50 .70

1923

OD212 A104 1c buff (#324) .60 .25
a. Perf. 13½ (#324A) 1.20 .50
OD213 A104 2c dk brn (#325) .50 .25
a. Perf. 13½ (#325A) 1.00 .50
b. As "a," inverted ovpt. 25.00 20.00
OD214 A104 5c red (#328) .50 .25
a. Perf. 13½ (#328A) .50 .25
OD215 A104 12c dp bl (#330) .50 .25
OD216 A104 20c ultra (#331) .50 .25
a. Perf. 13½ (#331A) 1.20 .30
Nos. OD212-OD216 (5) 2.60 1.25

1924

OD218 A104 1c buff (#341) .50 .25
OD219 A104 2c dk brn (#342) .50 .25
a. Pair, one with period 15.00 —
OD220 A104 3c green (#343) .60 .25
OD221 A104 5c red (#345) .50 .25
a. Pair, one with period 15.00 —
OD222 A104 10c dl grn (#346) 1.00 .50
OD223 A104 12c dp bl (#347) .50 .25
OD224 A104 20c ultra (#348) .50 .25
Nos. OD218-OD224 (7) 4.10 2.00

1926

OD227 A109 5c red (#359) .50 .25
a. Inverted ovpt. 35.00 30.00
OD228 A110 12c dp bl (#360) .50 .25

No. OD217B

Type II

1931-36 *Perf. 13½x12½, 13*

OD217B A104 ½c red vio (#340) 5.00 2.00
OD218B A104 1c buff (#341) .50 .25
OD220B A104 3c green (#343) .50 .25
c. Typo (coil) (#343b) .50 .25
OD221B A104 5c red (#345) .50 .25
OD222B A104 10c dl grn (#346) .50 .25
c. Typo (coil) (#346a) .50 .25
OD223B A104 12c dp bl (#347) 1.20 .30
OD224B A104 20c ultra (#348) .50 .25
c. Typo (coil) (#348a) .50 .25
OD225B A104 30c claret (#351) .50 .25
c. Typo (coil) (#351a) 1.30 .50
OD226B A105 1p blue & red (Perf. 13½) (#353) 1.00 .50
Nos. OD217B-OD226B (9) 10.20 4.30

No. OD229

1936-38 *Perf. 13½x13*

OD229 A129 1c buff (#419) .50 .25
OD230 A130 2c dk brn (#420) .50 .25
OD231 A132 3c green (#422) .50 .25
OD232 A134 5c yel brn (#427d) .50 .25
OD234 A139 15c slate bl (#434) 1.00 .25
OD234A A140 20c lt ultra (#437) .50 .25
OD234B A140 20c lt ultra (#438) .60 .25
OD234C A141 25c car & pink (#441) .50 .25
OD234D A142 30c org brn & yel brn (#442) .50 .25
OD234E A145 1p brn blk &l lt bl (#445) 2.00 .60
OD234F A146 1p brn blk &l lt bl (#446) 3.00 .30
Nos. OD229-OD234F (11) 10.10 3.15

Typo. *Perf. 13½*

OD232A A134 5c yel brn (#427) .50 .25
OD233 A137 10c car (#430) .50 .25
a. Perf. 13½x13 (#430a) .50 .25

Ministry of Marine

No. OD236

1913 Type I *Perf. 13½x12½*

OD235 A88 2c choc (#181) .60 .25
a. Perf. 13½ (#181a) 150.00 75.00
OD236 A88 1c ocher (#190) .50 .25
OD237 A88 2c choc (#191) 8.00 .50
OD238 A88 5c red (#194) .50 .25
a. Perf. 13½ (#194a) 40.00 8.00
OD239 A88 12c dp bl (#196) .60 .30
Nos. OD236-OD239 (4) 9.60 1.30

1915

OD240 A88 2c chocolate (#209) 3.00 .50
OD241 A88 5c red (#212) 2.00 .25

1918

OD242 A93 1c buff (#232) .70 .30
OD243 A93 2c brown (#233) .70 .25
OD244 A93 5c red (#236) .70 .25
a. Perf. 13½ (#236B) 1.00 .50
Nos. OD242-OD244 (3) 2.10 .80

1920 *Perf. 13½*

OD245 A93 1c buff (#249) .50 .25
OD246 A93 2c brown (#250) .70 .25
a. Perf. 13½x12½ (#250) 1.00 .50
OD247 A93 5c red (#253) 3.50 .25
a. Perf. 13½x12½ (#253B) .60 .25
OD248 A94 12c blue (#255) 2.50 .30
OD249 A94 20c ultra (#256) 8.00 1.50
Nos. OD245-OD249 (5) 15.20 2.55

1920

OD250 A93 1c buff (#265A) (perf. 13½x12½) .50 .25
OD251 A93 2c brown (#266A) .70 .30
a. Perf. 13½x12½ (#266) .80 .30
OD252 A93 5c red (#269A) .80 .25
Nos. OD250-OD252 (3) 2.00 .80

1922

OD253 A103 5c red (#309) 3.00 .50
a. Perf. 13½x12½ (#309B) 1.50 .30
OD254 A94 12c blue (#311) 30.00 10.00
OD255 A94 20c ultra (#312) 45.00 8.00
Nos. OD253-OD255 (3) 78.00 18.50

1923 *Perf. 13½x12½*

OD256 A104 1c buff (#324) .50 .25
a. Perf. 13½ (#324A) 87.50 50.00
OD257 A104 2c dk brn (#325) 1.00 .50
a. Inverted overprint — 75.00
b. Perf. 13½ (#325A) 1.00 .50
OD258 A104 5c red (#328) 2.50 .25
a. Inverted overprint — 75.00
b. Perf. 13½ (#328A) 15.00 2.00
c. As "b," inverted overprint — 75.00
OD259 A104 12c deep blue (#330) 1.20 .40
a. Perf. 13½ (#330A) 10.00 1.50
OD260 A104 20c ultra (#331) 2.00 .40
a. Perf. 13½ (#331A) 3.50 1.00
Nos. OD256-OD260 (5) 7.20 1.80

1924

OD261 A104 1c buff (#341) 3.00 1.00
OD262 A104 2c dk brn (#342) .50 .25
a. Pair, one with period 15.00 —
OD264 A104 5c red (#345) .50 .25
a. Pair, one with period — 40.00
OD266 A104 20c ultra (#348) 3.50 .25
Nos. OD261-OD266 (4) 7.50 1.75

1926

OD269 A109 5c red (#359) .50 .25

No. OD264B

Type II

1931-36 *Perf. 13½x12½, 13*

OD263B A104 3c grn (#343) 1.50 .40
OD264B A104 5c red (#345) 1.50 .25
OD265B A104 10c dl grn (#346) 2.00 .50
c. Typo (coil) (#346a) .60 .25
OD266B A104 20c ultra (#348) 7.00 1.00
c. Typo (coil) (#348a) 5.00 .50
OD267B A104 30c claret (#351) 3.00 .50
OD268B A105 1p blue & red (Perf. 13½) (#353) 40.00 20.00

No. OD270

1936-38 *Perf. 13½x13*

OD270 A129 1c buff (#419) .50 .25
OD271 A130 2c dk brn (#420) .50 .25
OD272 A132 3c green (#422) .50 .25
OD273 A134 5c yel brn (#427d) .50 .25
OD275 A139 15c slate bl (#434) ('36) 1.00 .30
OD276 A140 20c lt ultra (#437) 1.20 .30
OD277 A140 20c lt ultra (#438) 1.00 .30
OD278 A142 30c org brn & yel brn (#442) ('36) .60 .25
OD279 A145 1p brn blk & lt bl (#445) ('36) 8.00 2.00
OD280 A146 1p brn blk & lt bl (#446) ('37) 2.00 .50
Nos. OD270-OD280 (10) 15.80 4.65

Typo. *Perf. 13½*

OD273A A134 5c yel brn (#427) .50 .25
b. Inverted overprint 25.00 25.00
OD274A A137 10c car (#430) 2.00 .25
b. Perf. 13½x13 (#430a) .60 .25

Ministry of Public Works

No. OD281

1913 Type I *Perf. 13½x12½*

OD281 A88 2c choc (#181) 1.00 .25
a. Perf. 13½ (#181a) 4.00 1.00
OD282 A88 1c ocher (#190) 1.00 .25
OD283 A88 5c red (#194) .80 .25
OD284 A88 12c dp bl (#196) 5.00 1.00
a. Perf. 13½ (#196a) 15.00 6.00
Nos. OD282-OD284 (3) 6.80 1.50

1916 *Perf. 13½*

OD285 A91 5c red (#220) 35.00 10.00

1918 *Perf. 13½x12½*

OD286 A93 2c brown (#233) 30.00 20.00
OD287 A93 5c red (#236) 18.00 9.00

1920 *Perf. 13½*

OD288 A93 2c brown (#266) 35.00 8.00
OD289 A93 5c red (#269) 5.00 1.00
OD290 A94 12c blue (#271) 50.00 20.00
Nos. OD288-OD290 (3) 90.00 29.00

1923 *Perf. 13½x12½*

OD291 A104 1c buff (#324) .60 .25
a. Perf. 13½ (#324A) 40.00 15.00
OD292 A104 2c dk brn (#325) .50 .25
a. Perf. 13½ (#325A) .80 .25
OD293 A104 5c red (#328) .60 .30
a. Perf. 13½ (#328A) .80 .25
OD294 A104 12c dp bl (#330) .80 .30
a. Perf. 13½ (#330A) 2.00 .50
OD295 A104 20c ultra #331 2.00 .50
a. Perf. 13½ (#331A) 2.50 .50
Nos. OD291-OD295 (5) 4.50 1.60

1924

OD296 A104 1c buff (#341) .50 .25
OD297 A104 2c dk brn (#342) .50 .25
a. Pair, one with period 15.00 —
OD299 A104 5c red (#345) .50 .25
OD301 A104 12c dp bl (#347) 30.00 8.00
OD302 A104 20c ultra (#348) .50 .25
Nos. OD296-OD302 (5) 32.00 9.00

1926

OD305 A109 5c red (#359) .60 .25

No. OD299B

Type II

1931-36 *Perf. 13½x12½, 13*

OD298B A104 3c grn (#343) .50 .25
c. Typo (coil) (#343b) 25.00 5.00

OD299B A109 5c red (#345) .60 .25
OD300B A104 10c dl grn (#346) .60 .25
c. Typo (coil) (#346a) 2.00 .25
OD301B A104 20c ultra typo (coil) (#348b) 50.00 10.00
OD303B A104 30c claret (#351) 1.00 .25
OD304B A105 1p blue & red (13½) (#353) 70.00 20.00
Nos. OD298B-OD304B (6) 122.70 31.00

No. OD307

1936-38 ***Perf. 13½x13***
OD306 A129 1c buff (#419) .50 .25
OD307 A130 2c dk brn (#420) .50 .25
OD308 A132 3c green (#422) .50 .25
OD309 A134 5c yel brn (#427d) .50 .25
OD311 A139 15c slate bl (#434) 1.50 .25
OD312 A140 20c lt ultra (#437) 2.00 .30
OD313 A140 20c lt ultra (#438) .50 .25
OD314 A142 30c org brn & yel brn (#442) ('36) .60 .25
OD315 A144 50c red & org (#444) ('36) .60 .30
OD316 A145 1p brn blk & lt bl (#445) ('36) 4.00 1.00
OD317 A146 1p brn blk & lt bl (#446) ('37) 1.20 .40
Nos. OD306-OD317 (11) 12.40 3.75

Typo. ***Perf. 13½***
OD309A A134 5c yel brn (#427) .60 .25
b. Inverted overprint — *75.00*
OD310 A137 10c car (#430) 1.00 .30
a. Perf. 13½x13 (#430a) 1.00 .30

Ministry of Foreign Affairs and Religion

No. OD318

1913 **Type I** ***Perf. 13½x12½***
OD318 A88 2c choc (#181) 45.00 9.00
OD319 A88 1c ocher (#190) .50 .25
OD320 A88 2c choc (#191) .50 .25
OD321 A88 5c red (#194) 1.20 .30
OD322 A88 12c dp bl (#196) .60 .25
a. Perf. 13½ (#196a) 50.00 20.00
Nos. OD319-OD322 (4) 2.80 1.05

1915
OD323 A88 5c red (#212) 1.00 .50

1916 ***Perf. 13½***
OD324 A91 5c red (#220) 1.20 .50

1918
OD325 A94 20c ultra (#256) 5.00 2.00

1922
OD326 A93 1c buff, perf. 13½x12½ (#265) 1.00 .40
OD327 A93 5c red (#269) .50 .30

1922-23 ***Perf. 13½x12½***
OD328 A93 2c brn (#306) 40.00 15.00
OD329 A103 5c red (#309B) 100.00

Perf. 13½
OD330 A93 12c blue (#311) 100.00
OD330A A94 20c ultra (#312) 100.00

1923 ***Perf. 13½x12½***
OD331 A104 1c buff (#324) .60 .30
a. Perf. 13½ (#324A) 25.00 10.00
OD332 A104 2c dk brn (#325) .50 .25
a. Perf. 13½ (#325A) 5.00 2.00
OD333 A104 5c red (#328) .50 .25
a. Perf. 13½ (#328A) 2.00 .30
OD334 A104 12c dp bl (#330) .50 .25
a. Perf. 13½ (#330A) 1.50 .50
OD335 A104 20c ultra (#331) .50 .25
Nos. OD331-OD335 (5) 2.60 1.30

No. OD344

1924
OD337 A104 1c buff (#341) .60 .25
OD338 A104 2c dk brn (#342) .50 .25
a. Pair, one with period 15.00 —
OD339 A104 3c green (#343) .50 .25
OD340 A104 5c red (#345) .50 .25
a. Pair, one with period 15.00 —
OD341 A104 10c dl grn (#346) 4.00 .50
OD342 A104 12c dp bl (#347) .60 .30
OD343 A104 20c ultra (#348) .60 .30
OD344 A104 30c claret (#351) .70 .30
Nos. OD337-OD344 (8) 8.00 2.40

1926
OD346 A110 12c dp bl (#360) .50 .25

Type II
1931-36 ***Perf. 13½x12½, 13½***
OD336B A104 ½c red vio (#340) 2.50 1.00
OD341B A104 10c dl grn (#346) .60 .30
OD343B A104 20c ultra (typo, coil) (#348a) .60 .30
OD344B A104 30c claret (typo, coil) (#351a) .60 .30
OD345B A105 1p blue & red, perf. 13½ (#353) .60 .30
Nos. OD336B-OD345B (5) 4.90 2.20

No. OD347

1935-37 **Typo.** ***Perf. 13x13½***
OD347 A129 1c buff (#419) .50 .25
OD348 A130 2c dk brn (#420) .50 .25
OD349 A132 3c green (#422) .50 .25
OD350 A134 5c yel brn (#427d) .50 .25
OD352 A139 15c slate bl (#434) .70 .30
OD353 A140 20c lt ultra (#437) 1.00 .50
OD354 A140 20c lt ultra (#438) .50 .25
OD355 A142 30c org brn & yel brn (#442) .50 .25
OD356 A145 1p brn blk & lt bl (#445) 6.00 2.50
OD357 A146 1p brn blk & lt bl (#446) .70 .50
Nos. OD347-OD357 (10) 11.40 5.30

Typo. ***Perf. 13½***
OD350B A134 5c yel brn (#427) .60 .25
OD351B A137 10c car (#430) .50 .25
c. Perf. 13½x13 (#430a) 2.00 .25

BUENOS AIRES

The central point of the Argentine struggle for independence. At intervals Buenos Aires maintained an independent government but after 1862 became a province of the Argentine Republic.

8 Reales = 1 Peso

Values of Buenos Aires Nos. 1-8 vary according to condition. Quotations are for fine examples. Very fine to superb specimens sell at much higher prices, and inferior or poor stamps sell at reduced values, depending on the condition of the individual specimen.

Nos. 1-8 are normally found without gum, and the values below are for such items. Examples with original gum sell for higher prices.

Steamship — A1

1858 **Unwmk.** **Typo.** ***Imperf.***
1 A1 1 (in) pesos lt brn 500.00 300.
On cover *1,800.*
a. Double impression *700.*
2 A1 2 (dos) pesos blue 300.00 150.
On cover *1,000.*
a. 2p indigo 450.00 *220.*
On cover *1,500.*
b. Diag. half used as 1p on cover *7,500.*
3 A1 3 (tres) pesos grn 1,500. *950.*
On cover *6,500.*
a. 3p dark green 2,000. *1,500.*
On cover *8,000.*
b. 3p emerald green 2,000. 1,500.
On cover —
4 A1 4 (cuatro) pesos ver 5,000. *4,500.*
On cover *20,000.*
a. Half used as 2p on cover *25,000.*
b. 4p chestnut brown (error) *30,000.* *40,000.*
5 A1 5 (cinco) pesos org 5,000. *3,000.*
On cover *29,000.*
a. 5p ocher 5,000. *3,000.*
On cover *29,000.*
b. 5p olive yellow 5,000. *3,000.*
On cover *29,000.*

Issued: Nos. 2-5, Apr. 29; No. 1, Oct. 26.

1858, Oct. 26
6 A1 4 (cuatro) reales brown 350.00 300.
On cover *1,500.*
a. 4r gray brown 400.00 300.
On cover *1,500.*
b. 4r chestnut 350.00 300.
On cover *1,500.*

1859, Jan. 1
7 A1 1 (in) pesos blue 200. *100.*
On cover *1,500.*
a. 1p indigo 300. *150.*
On cover *2,000.*
b. Impression on reverse of stamp in blue *28,500.*
c. Double impression 2,800. *700.*
d. Vert. tête-bêche pair *675,000.*
e. Horiz. tête-bêche pair —
f. Half used as 4r on cover *7,500.*

A canceled vertical tête-bêche pair, No. 7d, sold at a New York City auction in 2008 for $661,250.

8 A1 1 (to) pesos blue 600. 325.
On cover *2,500.*
a. 1 (to) deep blue 650.00 *300.*
On cover *2,750.*
b. Partial double impression 800.00 500.
On cover *2,750.*

No. 7e is valued with faults.

Nos. 1, 2, 3 and 7 have been reprinted on very thick, hand-made paper. The same four stamps and No. 8 have been reprinted on thin, hard, white wove paper.

Counterfeits of Nos. 1-8 are plentiful.

Liberty Head — A2

1859, Sept. 3
9 A2 4r green, *bluish* 400.00 275.00
On cover, pair *1,000.*
On cover, single franking *2,000.*
a. 4r green, blurred impression 200.00 100.00
On cover *2,000.*
b. 4r olive green, blurred impression 400.00 250.00
On cover *3,000.*
10 A2 1p blue, fine impression 40.00 30.00
On cover *200.00*
a. 1p milky blue, blurred impression 250.00 125.00
On cover *750.00*
b. 1p indigo 250.00 125.00
On cover *750.00*
c. 1p greenish blue, blurred impression 250.00 125.00
On cover *750.00*
d. Double impression 600.00 400.00
On cover —
e. Partial double impression 325.00 175.00
On cover —
11 A2 2p vermilion, fine impression 500.00 300.00
On cover *2,000.*
a. 2p red, blurred impression 375.00 125.00
On cover *1,200.*
b. Vert. half used as 1p on cover *4,000.*

Both fine and blurred impressions of these stamps may be found. They have generally been called Paris and Local prints, respectively, but the opinion now obtains that the differences are due to the impression and that they do not represent separate issues. Values are for fine impressions. Rough or blurred impressions sell for less.

Many shades exist of Nos. 1-11.

1862, Oct. 4
12 A2 1p rose 350.00 150.00
On cover *1,500.*
a. 1p carmine 425.00 200.00
On cover *2,000.*
b. 1p rose, blurred impression 100.00 40.00
On cover *500.00*
c. As "a," blurred impression 200.00 80.00
On cover *1,000.*
13 A2 2p blue 350.00 90.00
On cover *900.00*
a. 2p blue, blurred impression 220.00 50.00
On cover *700.00*
b. 2p indigo, blurred impression — 500.00

All three values have been reprinted in black, brownish black, blue and red brown on thin hard white paper. The 4r has also been reprinted in green on bluish paper.

Values are for fine impressions. Rough or blurred impressions sell for less.

No. 13 exists with papermaker's wmk.

CORDOBA

A province in the central part of the Argentine Republic.

100 Centavos = 1 Peso

Arms of Cordoba — A1

Unwmk.
1858, Oct. 28 **Litho.** ***Imperf.***
Laid Paper
1 A1 5c blue 150.
On cover, pen canceled *1,250.*
2 A1 10c black *3,000.*

Cordoba stamps were printed on laid paper, but stamps from edges of the sheets sometimes do not show any laid lines and appear to be on wove paper. Counterfeits are plentiful.

CORRIENTES

The northeast province of the Argentine Republic.

1 Real M(oneda) C(orriente) = 12½ Centavos M.C. = 50 Centavos
100 Centavos Fuertes = 1 Peso Fuerte

Nos. 1-2 were issued without gum. Nos. 3-8 were issued both with and without gum (values the same).

Ceres — A1

Unwmk.
1856, Aug. 21 **Typo.** ***Imperf.***
1 A1 1r black, *blue* 100.00 *40.00*
On cover *450.00*

No. 1 used is valued with pen cancellation.

Pen Stroke Through "Un Real"

1860, Feb. 8
2 A1 (3c) black, *blue* 600.00 *120.00*
On cover *1,250.*

No. 2 used is valued with pen cancellation.

Ceres — A2

1860-80
3 A2 (3c) black, *blue* 9.50 *30.00*
On cover *150.00*

4 A2 (2c) blk, *yel grn* ('64) 50.00 *100.00*
On cover 250.00
a. (2c) black, *blue green* 92.50 *150.00*
On cover 750.00
5 A2 (2c) blk, *yel* ('67) 7.50 *19.00*
On cover 100.00
6 A2 (3c) blk, *dk bl* ('71) 3.00 *19.00*
On cover 100.00
7 A2 (3c) blk, *rose red* ('76) 150.00 70.00
On cover 275.00
a. (3c) black, *lil rose* ('75) 200.00 100.00
On cover 400.00
8 A2 (3c) blk, *dk rose* ('79) 8.00 *35.00*
On cover 200.00
a. (3c) black, *red vio* ('77) 75.00 50.00
On cover 200.00
Nos. 3-8 (6) 228.00 273.00

Pen canceled examples of Nos. 3-8 that do not indicate the town of origin sell for much less.

Printed from settings of 8 varieties, 3 or 4 impressions constituting a sheet. Some impressions were printed inverted and tete beche pairs may be cut from adjacent impressions.

From Jan. 1 to Feb. 24, 1864, No. 4 was used as a 5 centavos stamp but examples so used can only be distinguished when they bear dated cancellations.

The reprints show numerous spots and small defects which are not found on the originals. They are printed on gray blue, dull blue, gray green, dull orange and light magenta papers.

ARMENIA

är-ˈmē-nē-ə

LOCATION — South of Russia bounded by Georgia, Azerbaijan, Iran and Turkey
GOVT. — Republic
AREA — 11,306 sq. mi.
POP. — 1,109,200
CAPITAL — Yerevan

With Azerbaijan and Georgia, Armenia made up the Transcaucasian Federation of Soviet Republics.

Stamps of Armenia were replaced in 1923 by those of Transcaucasian Federated Republics.

100 Kopecks = 1 Ruble

Counterfeits abound of all overprinted and surcharged stamps.

Watermark

Diamonds — Wmk. 171

Perforations
Perforations are the same as the basic Russian stamps.

National Republic

Russian Stamps of 1902-19 Handstamped

At least thirteen types exist of both framed and unframed overprints ("a" and "c"). The device is the Armenian "H," initial of Hayasdan (Armenia). Inverted and double overprints are found.

Surcharged

Type I — Without periods (two types).
Type II — Periods after 1st "K" and "60."

Black Surcharge

1919 Unwmk. *Perf. 14x14½*
1 A14 60k on 1k orange (II) 2.75 2.75
a. Imperf. (I) 5.00 5.00
b. Imperf. (II) 1.25 1.25

Violet Surcharge

2 A14 60k on 1k orange (II) 1.00 1.00

Handstamped in Violet
a

6 A15 4k carmine 3.50 3.50
7 A14 5k claret, imperf. 9.00 9.00
a. Perf. 8.00 6.00
9 A14 10k on 7k lt blue 6.00 6.00
10 A11 15k red brn & bl 3.50 3.50
11 A8 20k blue & car 2.50 2.50
13 A11 35k red brn & grn 4.75 4.75
14 A8 50k violet & green 4.25 4.25
15 A14 60k on 1k orange (II) 3.50 3.50
a. Imperf. (I) 6.00 6.00
b. Imperf. (II) 10.00 10.00
18 A13 5r dk bl, grn & pale bl 18.00 18.00
a. Imperf. 9.00 9.00
19 A12 7r dk green & pink 35.00 15.00
20 A13 10r scar, yel & gray 40.00 15.00

Handstamped in Black

31 A14 2k green, imperf. 3.00 3.00
a. Perf. 6.00 6.00
32 A14 3k red, imperf. 3.00 3.00
a. Perf. 10.00 10.00
33 A15 4k carmine 5.00 5.00
a. Imperf. 10.00 10.00
34 A14 5k claret 1.25 1.25
a. Imperf. 10.00 10.00
36 A15 10k dark blue 2.50 2.50
37 A14 10k on 7k lt blue 2.00 *5.00*
38 A11 15k red brn & bl 1.00 *5.00*
a. Imperf. 5.00 *15.00*
39 A8 20k blue & car 2.00 *5.00*
40 A11 25k green & gray vio 2.00 *5.00*
41 A11 35k red brn & grn 2.00 *4.00*
42 A8 50k violet & green 3.00 *5.00*
43 A14 60k on 1k orange (II) 5.00 5.00
43A A11 70k brown & org 3.00 3.00
b. Imperf. 2.00 *4.00*
44 A9 1r pale brn, dk brn & org 3.00 *5.00*
a. Imperf. 8.00 8.00
45 A12 3½r mar & lt grn, imperf. 3.00 *6.00*
a. Perf. 6.00 6.00
46 A13 5r dk bl, grn & pale bl 6.00 6.00
a. Imperf. 10.00 10.00
47 A12 7r dk green & pink 7.25 7.25
48 A13 10r scar, yel & gray 35.00 *50.00*

Handstamped in Violet
c

Wove Paper

Unwmk. *Perf.*
62 A14 2k green, imperf. 12.00 12.00
a. Perf. 18.00 18.00
63 A14 3k red, imperf. 2.50 2.50
a. Perf. 15.00 15.00
64 A15 4k carmine 10.00 10.00
65 A14 5k claret 3.50 3.50
a. Imperf. 3.50 3.50
67 A15 10k dark blue 5.00 *10.00*
68 A14 10k on 7k lt bl 3.50 3.50
69 A11 15k red brn & bl 3.00 *5.00*
70 A8 20k blue & car 3.00 *5.00*
71 A11 25k grn & gray vio 7.50 *15.00*
72 A11 35k red brn & grn 15.00 14.00
73 A8 50k violet & grn 5.00 *10.00*
74 A14 60k on 1k org (II) 6.00 *8.00*
a. Imperf. (I) 6.00 *8.00*
b. Imperf. (II) 6.00 *8.00*
75 A9 1r pale brn, dk brn & org 12.50 12.50
a. Imperf. 10.00 10.00
76 A12 3½r mar & lt grn, imperf. 5.00 5.00
a. Perf. 6.00 6.00
77 A13 5r dk bl, grn & pale bl, imperf. 12.50 12.50
a. Perf. 8.00 8.00
78 A12 7r dk green & pink 20.00 20.00
79 A13 10r scar, yel & gray 20.00 20.00

Imperf

85 A11 70k brown & org 6.00 6.00

Handstamped in Black

Perf.

90 A14 1k orange 8.00 8.00
a. Imperf. 10.00 10.00
91 A14 2k green, imperf. 1.25 1.25
a. Perf. 8.00 8.00
92 A14 3k red, imperf. 5.00 *10.00*
a. Perf. 2.00 2.00
93 A15 4k carmine 3.00 3.00
94 A14 5k claret 1.25 1.25
a. Imperf. 3.50 *5.00*
95 A14 7k light blue 10.00 *15.00*
96 A15 10k dark blue 10.00 *15.00*
97 A14 10k on 7k lt bl 1.00 *2.00*
98 A11 15k red brn & bl 2.00 *4.00*
99 A8 20k blue & car 1.75 *3.00*
100 A11 25k grn & gray vio 2.00 *5.00*
101 A11 35k red brn & grn 2.00 *4.00*
102 A8 50k violet & grn 2.00 *5.00*
102A A14 60k on 1k org, imperf. (I) 5.00 *5.00*
b. Imperf. (II) 5.00 *10.00*
c. Perf. (II) 5.00 5.00
103 A9 1r pale brn, dk brn & org 2.00 *5.00*
a. Imperf. 2.00 *5.00*
104 A12 3½r maroon & lt grn 4.75 8.00
a. Imperf. 15.00 15.00
105 A13 5r dk bl, grn & pale bl 15.00 15.00
a. Imperf. 6.00 6.00
106 A12 7r dk green & pink 5.00 *10.00*
107 A13 10r scar, yel & gray 20.00 *45.00*

Imperf

113 A11 70k brown & org 2.50 *4.00*

Handstamped in Violet or Black

Violet Surcharge, Type f

1920 *Perf.*
120 A14 3r on 3k red, imperf. 10.00 15.00
a. Perf. 10.00 15.00
121 A14 5r on 3k red 10.00 10.00
122 A15 5r on 4k car 10.00 *12.00*
123 A14 5r on 5k claret, imperf. 5.00 *12.00*
a. Perf. 12.00 *20.00*
124 A15 5r on 10k dk blue 20.00 *30.00*
125 A14 5r on 10k on 7k lt bl 20.00 *30.00*
126 A8 5r on 20k bl & car 10.00 *15.00*

Imperf

127 A14 5r on 2k green 12.00 12.00
128 A11 5r on 35k red brn & grn 12.00 12.00

Black Surcharge, Type f or Type g (#130)

Perf.

130 A14 1r on 1k orange 10.00 12.00
a. Imperf. 15.00 15.00
131 A14 3r on 3k red 10.00 10.00
a. Imperf. 5.00 5.00
132 A15 3r on 4k carmine 25.00 25.00
133 A14 5r on 2k grn, imperf. 2.50 2.50
a. Perf. 5.00 5.00
134 A14 5r on 3k red 10.00 10.00
a. Imperf. 5.00 5.00
135 A15 5r on 4k carmine 4.00 4.00
a. Imperf. 10.00 10.00
136 A14 5r on 5k claret 4.00 4.00
a. Imperf. 2.00 2.00
137 A14 5r on 7k lt blue 3.00 3.00
138 A15 5r on 10k dk blue 2.00 2.00
139 A14 5r on 10k on 7k lt bl 2.00 2.00
140 A11 5r on 14k bl & rose 2.50 2.50
141 A11 5r on 15k red brn & blue 1.00 1.00
a. Imperf. 2.50 2.50
142 A8 5r on 20k bl & car 1.00 *5.00*
a. Imperf. 30.00 30.00
143 A11 5r on 20k on 14k bl & rose 75.00 *100.00*
144 A11 5r on 25k grn & gray vio 10.00 *15.00*

Black Surcharge, Type g or Type f (#148A, 151)

145 A14 10r on 1k org, imperf. 1.10 1.10
a. Perf. *125.00 125.00*
146 A14 10r on 3k red *175.00 175.00*
147 A14 10r on 5k claret 18.00 18.00
a. Imperf. 15.00
148 A8 10r on 20k bl & car 15.00 15.00
148A A11 10r on 25k grn & gray vio 10.00 10.00
149 A11 10r on 25k grn & gray vio 5.00 *6.00*
a. Imperf. 10.00 *20.00*
150 A11 10r on 35k red brn & grn 2.00 2.00
151 A8 10r on 50k brn vio & grn 50.00 50.00
152 A8 10r on 50k brn vio & grn 3.00 *4.00*
152A A11 10r on 70k brn & org, imperf. 5.00 5.00
b. Perf. *240.00 240.00*
152C A8 25r on 20k bl & car 4.75 4.75
153 A11 25r on 25k grn & gray vio 5.00 5.00
154 A11 25r on 35k red brn & grn 20.00 20.00
a. Imperf. 4.00 4.00
155 A8 25r on 50k vio & grn 5.00 5.00
a. Imperf. 6.00 6.00
156 A11 25r on 70k brn & org 8.00 8.00
a. Imperf. 5.00 5.00
157 A9 50r on 1r pale brn, dk brn & org, imperf. 2.00 2.00
a. Perf. 10.00 *15.00*
158 A13 50r on 5r dk bl, grn & lt bl 25.00 25.00
a. Imperf. 45.00 45.00
159 A12 100r on 3½r mar & lt grn 10.00 *15.00*
a. Imperf. 10.00 10.00
160 A13 100r on 5r dk bl, grn & pale bl 12.00 12.00
a. Imperf. 25.00 25.00
161 A12 100r on 7r dk grn & pink 12.00 15.00
a. Imperf. 42.00 42.00
162 A13 100r on 10r scar, yel & gray 15.00 20.00

Wmk. Wavy Lines (168)
Perf. 11½
Vertically Laid Paper

163 A12 100r on 3½r blk & gray *120.00 120.00*
164 A12 100r on 7r blk & yel *120.00 120.00*

No. 168

1920 Unwmk. *Imperf.*
Wove Paper

166 A14 (g) 1r on 60k on 1k org (I) 12.00 14.50
168 A14 (f) 5r on 1k orange 12.00 12.00
173 A11 (f) 5r on 35k red brn & grn 12.00 12.00
177 A11 (g) 50r on 70k brn & org 6.00 10.00
179 A12 (g) 50r on 3½r mar & lt grn 20.00 20.00
181 A9 (g) 100r on 1r pale brn, dk brn & org 20.00 20.00

Romanov Issues

No. 187

No. 187C

Surcharged Types g or f (#185-187, 190) on Stamps of 1913

1920 *Perf. 13½*
184 A16 1r on 1k brn org 175.00 175.00
185 A18 3r on 3k rose red 24.00 24.00
186 A19 5r on 4k dull red 12.00 12.00
187 A22 5r on 14k blue grn 50.00 50.00
187A A19 10r on 4k dull red 40.00
187B A26 10r on 35k gray vio & dk grn
187C A19 25r on 4k dull red 20.00 20.00
188 A26 25r on 35k gray vio & dk grn 3.25 3.25

189 A28 25r on 70k yel grn & brn 3.25 3.25
190 A31 50r on 3r dk vio 2.50 2.50
190A A16 100r on 1k brn org 125.00 125.00
190B A17 100r on 2k green 125.00 125.00
191 A30 100r on 2r brown 12.50 12.50
192 A31 100r on 3r dk vio 12.50 12.50

On Stamps of 1915, Type g

Thin Cardboard
Inscriptions on Back
Perf. 12

193 A21 100r on 10k blue 20.00
194 A23 100r on 15k brn 20.00
195 A24 100r on 20k ol grn 18.00

On Stamps of 1916, Type f

Perf. 13½

196 A20 5r on 10k on 7k brown 8.00 8.00
197 A22 5r on 20k on 14k bl grn 15.00 25.00

Surcharged Types f or g (#204-205A, 207-207C, 210-211) over Type c

Type c in Violet
Perf.

200 A15 5r on 4k car 6.00 *8.00*
201 A15 5r on 10k dk bl 25.00 25.00
202 A11 5r on 15k red brn & bl 5.00 5.00
203 A8 5r on 20k blue & car 10.00 10.00
204 A11 10r on 25k grn & gray vio 12.00 12.00
205 A11 10r on 35k red brn & grn 3.50 3.50
205A A8 10r on 50k brn vio & grn 12.00 12.00
206 A8 25r on 50k brn vio & grn 150.00 150.00
207 A9 50r on 1r pale brn, dk brn & org, imperf. 30.00 30.00
a. Perf. 30.00 30.00
207B A12 100r on 3½r mar & lt grn 50.00 50.00
207C A12 100r on 7r dk grn & pink 60.00 60.00

Imperf

208 A14 5r on 2k green 30.00 30.00
209 A14 5r on 5k claret 30.00 30.00
210 A11 25r on 70k brn & org 40.00 *50.00*
211 A13 100r on 5r dk bl, grn & pale bl 100.00 *110.00*

Surcharged Types g or f (212-213, 215, 219-219A, 221-222) over Type c

Type c in Black
Perf.

212 A14 5r on 7k lt bl 150.00 150.00
213 A14 5r on 10k on 7k lt bl 6.00 6.00
214 A11 5r on 15k red brn & bl 5.00 *7.00*
215 A8 5r on 20k blue & car 3.50 3.50
215A A11 10r on 5r on 25k grn & gray vio 50.00 50.00
216 A11 10r on 35k red brn & grn 50.00 *60.00*
217 A8 10r on 50k brn vio & grn 12.00 *15.00*
217A A9 50r on 1r pale brn, dk brn & org 35.00 *50.00*
b. Imperf. 40.00 *50.00*
217C A12 100r on 3½r mar & lt grn 30.00 30.00
218 A13 100r on 5r dk bl, grn & pale bl 35.00 *40.00*
a. Imperf. 45.00 *55.00*
219 A12 100r on 7r dk grn & pink 35.00 *50.00*
219A A13 100r on 10r scar, yel & gray 45.00 *55.00*

Imperf

220 A14 1r on 60k on 1k org (I) 35.00 35.00
221 A14 5r on 2k green 6.00 6.00
222 A14 5r on 5k claret 10.00 *12.00*
223 A11 10r on 70k brn & org 30.00 *40.00*
224 A11 25r on 70k brn & org 25.00 *30.00*

Surcharged Types g or f (#233) over Type a

Type a in Violet
Imperf

231 A9 50r on 1r pale brn, dk brn & org 170.00 170.00
232 A13 100r on 5r dk bl, grn & pale bl 100.00 *110.00*

Type a in Black

Perf.

233 A8 5r on 20k blue & car 6.00 6.00
233A A11 10r on 25k grn & gray vio 20.00 20.00
234 A11 10r on 35k red brn & grn 175.00 175.00
235 A12 100r on 3½r mar & lt grn 10.00 10.00
a. Imperf. 10.00 10.00

Imperf

237 A14 5r on 2k green 150.00 150.00
237A A11 10r on 70k brn & org

Surcharged Type a and New Value

Type a in Violet
Perf.

238 A11 10r on 15k red brn & blue 30.00 30.00

Type a in Black

239 A8 5r on 20k blue & car 4.00 5.00
239A A8 10r on 20k blue & car *20.00* *20.00*
239B A8 10r on 50k brn red & grn *30.00* *40.00*

Imperf

240 A12 100r on 3½r mar & lt grn 50.00 *60.00*

Surcharged Type c and New Value

Type c in Black

1920 ***Perf.***

241 A15 5r on 4k red 6.00 *8.00*
242 A11 5r on 15k red brn & bl 4.00 *6.00*
243 A8 10r on 20k blue & car *20.00* *20.00*
243A A11 10r on 25k grn & gray vio 12.00 *15.00*
244 A11 10r on 35k red brn & grn 45.00 *50.00*
a. With additional srch. "5r" — —
245 A12 100r on 3½r mar & lt grn 10.00 *15.00*

No. 248

Imperf

247 A14 3r on 3k red 10.00 *15.00*
248 A14 5r on 2k green 3.00 *7.00*
249 A9 50r on 1r pale brn, dk brn & org 20.00 20.00

Type c in Violet

249A A14 5r on 2k green 8.00 12.00

Russia AR1-AR3 Surcharged

A1 A2 A3

Perf. 14½x15
Wmk. 171

250 A1 60k on 1k red & buff 60.00 60.00
251 A2 1r on 1k red & buff 60.00 60.00
252 A3 5r on 5k green & buff 60.00 60.00
253 A3 5r on 10k brn & buff 60.00 60.00

Russian Semi-Postal Stamps of 1914-18 Srchd. with Armenian Monogram & New Values

On Stamps of 1914

Unwmk. ***Perf.***

255 SP5 25r on 1k red brn & dk grn, *straw* 72.50 72.50
256 SP5 25r on 3k mar & gray grn, *pink* 72.50 72.50
257 SP5 50r on 7 dk brn & dk grn, *buff* 90.00 90.00
258 SP5 100r on 1k red brn & dk grn, *straw* 90.00 90.00
259 SP5 100r on 3k mar & gray grn, *pink* 90.00 90.00
260 SP5 100r on 7k dk brn & dk grn, *buff* 90.00 90.00

No. 261

On Stamps of 1915-19

261 SP5 25r on 1k org brn & gray 100.00 100.00
262 SP5 25r on 3k car & gray 90.00 90.00
263 SP5 50r on 10k dk bl & brn 50.00 50.00
264 SP5 100r on 1k org brn & gray 90.00 90.00
265 SP5 100r on 10k dk bl & brn 90.00 90.00

These surcharged semi-postal stamps were used for ordinary postage.

A set of 10 stamps in the above designs was prepared in 1920, but not issued for postal use, though some were used fiscally. Value of set, $10. Exist imperf with "SPECIMEN" overprint. Value of set, $40. Reprints exist.

Soviet Socialist Republic

Hammer and Sickle — A7

Mythological Monster — A8

Symbols of Soviet Republics on Designs from old Armenian Manuscripts A9

Ruined City of Ani — A10

Mythological Monster — A11

Armenian Soldier — A12

Mythological Monster A13

Soviet Symbols, Armenian Designs — A14

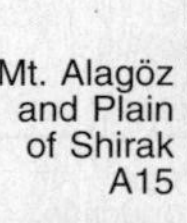

Mt. Alagöz and Plain of Shirak A15

Fisherman on River Aras — A16

Post Office in Erevan and Mt. Ararat A17

Ruin in City of Ani — A18

Street in Erevan — A19

Lake Sevan and Sevan Monastery — A20

Mythological Subject from old Armenian Monument — A21

Mt. Ararat — A22

1921 Unwmk. *Perf. 11½, Imperf.*

278	A7	1r gray green	.50	
279	A8	2r slate gray	.50	
280	A9	3r carmine	.50	
281	A10	5r dark brown	.50	
282	A11	25r gray	.50	.50
283	A12	50r red	.30	
284	A13	100r orange	.30	
285	A14	250r dark blue	.30	
286	A15	500r brown vio	.30	
287	A16	1000r sea green	.40	
288	A17	2000r bister	1.75	
289	A18	5000r dark brown	1.00	
290	A19	10,000r dull red	1.00	
291	A20	15,000r slate blue	1.25	
292	A21	20,000r lake	1.50	
293	A22	25,000r gray blue	2.00	
294	A22	25,000r brown olive	8.00	
		Nos. 278-294 (17)	20.60	

Except the 25r, Nos. 278-294 were not regularly issued and used. Counterfeits exist.
For surcharges see Nos. 347-390.

Russian Stamps of 1909-17 Surcharged

Lozenges of Varnish on Face

1921, Aug. Wove Paper *Perf. 13½*

295	A9	5000r on 1r	25.00
296	A12	5000r on 3½r	25.00
297	A13	5000r on 5r	25.00
298	A12	5000r on 7r	25.00
299	A13	5000r on 10r	25.00
		Nos. 295-299 (5)	125.00

Nos. 295-299 were not officially issued. Counterfeits abound.

A23

Mt. Ararat & Soviet Star — A24

Soviet Symbols — A25

Crane — A26

Peasant — A27

Harpy — A28

Peasant Sowing — A29

Soviet Symbols — A30

Forging — A31

Plowing A32

1922 *Perf. 11½*

300	A23	50r green & red	.85
301	A24	300r slate bl & buff	1.00
302	A25	400r blue & pink	1.00
303	A26	500r vio & pale lil	1.00
304	A27	1000r dull bl & pale bl	1.00
305	A28	2000r black & gray	1.25
306	A29	3000r black & grn	1.25
307	A30	4000r black & lt brn	1.25
308	A31	5000r blk & dull red	1.25
309	A32	10,000r black & pale rose	1.25
a.		Tête-bêche pair	42.50
		Nos. 300-309 (10)	11.10

Nos. 300-309 were not issued without surcharge.
Stamps of types A23 to A32, printed in other colors than Nos. 300 to 309, are essays.

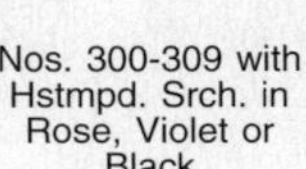

Nos. 300-309 with Hstmpd. Srch. in Rose, Violet or Black

1922

310	10,000 on 50r (R)	90.00	90.00
311	10,000 on 50r (V)	60.00	60.00
312	10,000 on 50r	30.00	30.00
313	15,000 on 300r (R)	120.00	120.00
314	15,000 on 300r (V)	90.00	90.00
315	15,000 on 300r	30.00	30.00
316	25,000 on 400r (V)	60.00	60.00
317	25,000 on 400r	30.00	30.00
318	30,000 on 500r (R)	120.00	120.00
319	30,000 on 500r (V)	60.00	60.00
320	30,000 on 500r	30.00	30.00
321	50,000 on 1000r (R)	120.00	120.00
322	50,000 on 1000r (V)	60.00	60.00
323	50,000 on 1000r	25.00	25.00
324	75,000 on 3000r	30.00	30.00
325	100,000 on 2000r (R)	120.00	275.00
326	100,000 on 2000r (V)	60.00	60.00
327	100,000 on 2000r	25.00	25.00
328	200,000 on 4000r (V)	12.00	12.00
329	200,000 on 4000r	12.00	12.00
330	300,000 on 5000r (V)	60.00	60.00
331	300,000 on 5000r	25.00	25.00
332	500,000 on 10,000r (V)	60.00	60.00
333	500,000 on 10,000r	12.00	12.00
	Nos. 310-333 (24)	1,341.	1,496.

Forgeries exist.

Goose — A33

Armenian Woman at Well — A35

Armenian Village Scene A34

Mt. Ararat A36

Mt. Ararat A37

New Values in Gold Kopecks, Handstamped Surcharge in Black

1922 *Imperf.*

334	A33	1(k) on 250r rose	18.00	18.00
335	A33	1(k) on 250r gray	24.00	24.00
336	A34	2(k) on 500r rose	10.00	10.00
337	A34	3(k) on 500r gray	10.00	10.00
338	A35	4(k) on 1000r rose	10.00	10.00
339	A35	4(k) on 1000r gray	18.00	18.00
340	A36	5(k) on 2000r gray	10.00	10.00
341	A36	10(k) on 2000r rose	10.00	10.00
342	A37	15(k) on 5000r rose	62.50	62.50
343	A37	20(k) on 5000r gray	10.00	10.00
		Nos. 334-343 (10)	182.50	182.50

Nos. 334-343 were issued for postal tax purposes.
Nos. 334-343 exist without surcharge but are not known to have been issued in that condition. Counterfeits exist of both sets.

Regular Issue of 1921 Handstamped with New Values in Black or Red Short, Thick Numerals

1922 *Imperf.*

347	A8	2(k) on 2r (R)	60.00	60.00
350	A11	4(k) on 25r (R)	100.00	100.00
353	A13	10(k) on 100r (R)	24.00	24.00

354 A14 15(k) on 250r 3.50 3.50
355 A15 20(k) on 500r 18.00 18.00
a. With "k" written in red 12.00 12.00
357 A22 50(k) on 25,000r bl (R) 300.00 300.00
358 A22 50(k) on 25,000r brn ol (R) 150.00 150.00
359 A22 50(k) on 25,000r brn ol
Nos. 347-358 (7) 655.50 655.50

Perf. 11½

360 A7 1(k) on 1r, imperf. *75.00 75.00*
a. Perf. *50.00 50.00*
361 A7 1(k) on 1r (R) *45.00 45.00*
a. Imperf. *50.00 70.00*
362 A8 2(k) on 2r, imperf. *47.50* 47.50
a. Perf. *50.00 50.00*
363 A15 2(k) on 500r *100.00 125.00*
a. Imperf. *100.00 100.00*
364 A15 2(k) on 500r (R) 150.00 150.00
365 A11 4(k) on 25r, imperf. *30.00 30.00*
a. Perf. *50.00 50.00*
366 A12 5(k) on 50r, imperf. 24.00 *36.00*
a. Perf. *100.00 100.00*
367 A13 10(k) on 100r *24.00 24.00*
a. Imperf. *50.00 50.00*
368 A21 35(k) on 20,000r, imperf. *90.00 100.00*
a. With "k" written in violet *90.00 90.00*
b. Perf. *90.00 90.00*
c. As "a," perf. *90.00 90.00*
d. With "kop" written in violet, imperf.
Nos. 360-368 (9) *585.50 632.50*

Manuscript Surcharge in Red

Perf. 11½

371 A14 1k on 250r dk bl *50.00 50.00*

Handstamped in Black or Red

Tall, Thin Numerals

No. 381

Imperf

377 A11 4(k) on 25r (R) 5.00 5.00
379 A13 10(k) on 100r 90.00 *100.00*
380 A15 20(k) on 500r 7.25 7.25
381 A22 50k on 25,000r bl *20.00 90.00*
a. Surcharged "50" only 60.00 60.00
382 A22 50k on 25,000r bl (R) 14.50 14.50
382A A22 50k on 25,000r brn ol 29.00 29.00
Nos. 377-382A (6) *165.75 245.75*

On Nos. 381, 382 and 382A the letter "k" forms part of the surcharge.

Perf. 11½

383 A7 1(k) on 1r (R) *40.00 40.00*
a. Imperf. 100.00
384 A14 1(k) on 250r 60.00 60.00
385 A15 2(k) on 500r 10.00 10.00
a. Imperf. 24.00 24.00
386 A15 2(k) on 500r (R) 24.00 24.00
387 A9 3(k) on 3r 35.00 35.00
a. Imperf. 40.00 40.00
388 A21 3(k) on 20,000r, imperf. 12.00 12.00
a. Perf. 60.00 60.00
389 A11 4(k) on 25r 30.00 30.00
a. Imperf. 120.00 120.00
390 A12 5(k) on 50r, imperf. *12.00 12.00*
a. Perf. *18.00 75.00*
Nos. 383-390 (8) *223.00 223.00*

ASCENSION

ə-'sen_t-shən

LOCATION — An island in the South Atlantic Ocean, 900 miles from Liberia

GOVT. — A part of the British Crown Colony of St. Helena

AREA — 34 sq. mi.

POP. — 188 (1931 census)

In 1922 Ascension was placed under the administration of the Colonial Office and annexed to the British Crown Colony of St. Helena. The only post office is at Georgetown.

12 Pence = 1 Shilling
20 Shillings = 1 Pound

STAMPS OF GREAT BRITAIN USED IN ASCENSION

Stamps of Great Britain with clearly legible circular or oval datestamps of Ascension.

1855-86

A1 1p red brown (#16), *from* *9,000.*
A2 6p lilac, (#27) —
A3 1p rose red (#33), *from* *3,500.*
A4 6p lilac (#45, P5), *from* *9,000.*
A5 1sh green (#48) —
A6 1sh green (#54, P7) —
A7 6p gray (#62, P15, 16), *from* *7,250.*
A8 1p lilac (#89), *from* 100.00
A9 6p on 6p violet (#95) —

Values for Nos. A1-A7 are for complete covers with the Great Britain stamps canceled on arrival in England and with an Ascension postmark struck elsewhere on the cover.

No. A3 exists with plate numbers 71, 74, 76, 78, 83, 85, 96, 100, 102-104, 122, 134, 154, 155, 157, 160, 168, 178. Value is for the most common plate numbers.

1887-92 Victoria Jubilee

A10 ½p ver (#111) 130.00
A11 1½p vio & grn (#112) 875.00
A12 2p grn & car rose (#113) 375.00
A13 2½p vio, *blue* (#114) 190.00
A14 3p vio, *yel* (#115) 750.00
A15 4p brn & grn (#116) 475.00
A16 4½p car rose & grn (#117) 1,350.
A17 5p lil & bl (#118) 525.00
A18 6p vio, *rose* (#119) 425.00
A19 9p bl & lil (#120) 1,100.
A20 10p car rose & lil (#121) 1,325.
A21 1sh green (#122) 1,250.

1900

A22 ½p blue grn (#125) 160.00
A23 1sh car rose & green (#126) 1,350.

1902-11 King Edward VII

A24 ½p gray grn (#127) 100.00
A25 1p carmine (#128) 35.00
On cover 300.00
A26 1½p vio & grn (#129) 425.00
A27 2p grn & car (#130) 225.00
A28 2½p ultra (#131) 250.00
A29 3p vio, *yel* (#132) 425.00
A30 4p brn & grn (#133) 1,050.
A31 4p orange (#144) 425.00
A32 5p lil & ultra (#134) 425.00
A33 6p dull vio (#135) 375.00
A34 7p gray (#145) 500.00
A35 9p ultra & vio (#136) 625.00
A36 10p car rose & vio (#137) 825.00
A37 1sh car rose & green (#138) 200.00
A38 2sh 6p dull vio (#139) 1,850.
A39 5sh car rose (#140) 2,600.
A40 10sh ultra (#141) *4,250.*
A41 £1 green (#142) *11,500.*

Only one example is known of No. A41.

1911-12 King George V

A42 ½p green (#151) 250.00
A43 ½p yel grn (#153) 100.00
A44 1p scarlet (#154) 100.00

1912

A45 ½p green (#157) 100.00
A46 1p scarlet (#158) 100.00

1912-22

A47 ½p green (#159) 85.00
A48 1p scarlet (#160) 40.00
On cover 275.00
A49 1½p red brn (#161) 100.00
A50 2p org, die 1 (#162) 100.00
a. Die II (#162a) 900.00
A51 2½p ultra (#163) 135.00
A52 3p bluish vio (#164) 175.00
A53 4p slate grn (#165) 240.00
A54 5p yel brn (#166) 325.00
A55 6p rose lil (#167) 175.00
A56 7p olive grn (#168) 775.00
A57 8p black, *yel* (#169) 825.00
A58 9p blk brn (#170) 725.00
A59 9p olive grn (#183) 1,850.
A60 10p lt blue (#171) 775.00
A61 1sh bister (#172) 225.00
A62 2sh 6p gray brn (#179) 2,350.
A63 5sh car rose (#180) *4,000.*

Catalogue values for unused stamps in this country are for Never Hinged items, beginning with Scott 50.

Stamps and Types of St. Helena, 1912-22 Overprinted in Black or Red

1922 Wmk. 4 *Perf. 14*

1 A9 ½p green & blk 8.00 *27.50*
On cover *110.00*
2 A10 1p green 8.00 *27.50*
On cover *110.00*
3 A101 ½p rose red 21.00 *60.00*
On cover *325.00*
4 A9 2p gray & blk 21.00 16.00
On cover *110.00*
5 A9 3p ultra 16.00 *28.00*
On cover *110.00*
6 A10 8p dl vio & blk 34.00 *62.50*
On cover *200.00*
7 A10 2sh ultra & blk, *blue* 120.00 *150.00*
On cover *225.00*
8 A10 3sh vio & blk 175.00 *200.00*
On cover *300.00*

Wmk. 3

9 A9 1sh blk, *gray grn* (R) 35.00 *60.00*
On cover *275.00*
Nos. 1-9 (9) 438.00 *631.50*
Set, never hinged 675.00
Set, overprinted "SPECIMEN" 825.00

Covers: Values for Nos. 7-8 on covers are for overfranked covers, usually philatelic.

All values are known with forged cancellations, many of them dated "MY 24 23."

Nos. 1, 4, 6 and 8 are from special printings, made expressly to be overprinted, and do not exist without overprint.

Seal of Colony — A3

1924-33 Typo. Wmk. 4 *Perf. 14*

Chalky Paper

10 A3 ½p black & gray 6.75 *19.00*
11 A3 1p green & blk 7.00 *17.00*
a. 1p br bl grn & gray blk ('33) 135.00 *625.00*
12 A3 1½p rose red 10.00 *50.00*
13 A3 2p bluish gray & gray 25.00 13.00
14 A3 3p ultra 10.00 *19.00*
15 A3 4p blk & gray, *yel* 60.00 *100.00*
16 A3 5p ol & lil ('27) 24.00 *29.00*
17 A3 6p rose lil & gray 62.50 *125.00*
18 A3 8p violet & gray 21.00 *52.50*
19 A3 1sh brown & gray 25.00 *62.50*
20 A3 2sh ultra & gray, *blue* 72.50 *115.00*
21 A3 3sh blk & gray, *blue* 110.00 *110.00*
Nos. 10-21 (12) 433.75 *712.00*
Set, never hinged 675.00
Set, overprinted "SPECIMEN" 1,000.

View of Georgetown — A4

Map of Ascension — A5

Sooty Tern Breeding Colony A9

Designs: 1½p, Pier at Georgetown. 3p, Long Beach. 5p, Three Sisters. 5sh, Green Mountain.

1934, July 2 Engr.

23 A4 ½p violet & blk 1.10 1.00
24 A5 1p lt grn & blk 2.25 1.60
25 A4 1½p red & black 2.25 *2.75*
26 A5 2p org & black 2.25 *3.00*
27 A4 3p ultra & blk 2.75 1.90
28 A4 5p blue & black 2.75 *4.00*
29 A5 8p dk brn & blk 5.25 *6.75*
30 A9 1sh car & blk 22.50 12.00
31 A5 2sh6p violet & blk 57.50 50.00
32 A4 5sh brown & blk 62.50 *70.00*
Nos. 23-32 (10) 161.10 *153.00*
Set, never hinged 240.00
Set, perforated "SPECIMEN" 500.00

Common Design Types pictured following the introduction.

Silver Jubilee Issue

Common Design Type

1935, May 6 *Perf. 11x12*

33 CD301 1½p car & dk blue 3.50 *12.50*
34 CD301 2p blk & ultra 10.00 *37.50*
35 CD301 5p ind & grn 22.50 *30.00*
36 CD301 1sh brn vio & indigo 22.50 *40.00*
Nos. 33-36 (4) 58.50 *120.00*
Set, never hinged 100.00
Set, perforated "SPECIMEN" 450.00

25th anniv. of the reign of King George V.

Coronation Issue

Common Design Type

1937, May 19 *Perf. 13½x14*

37 CD302 1p deep green .75 1.50
38 CD302 2p deep orange 1.00 .65
39 CD302 3p bright ultra 1.00 .60
Nos. 37-39 (3) 2.75 *2.75*
Set, never hinged 3.50
Set, perforated "SPECIMEN" 475.00

Georgetown — A11

Designs: No. 41, 41A, 2p, 4p, Green Mountain. No. 41D, 6p, 10sh, Three Sisters. 1½p, 2sh6p, Pier at Georgetown. 3p, 5sh, Long Beach.

Perf. 13, 13½ (#41, 44, 45), 14 (#43C)

1938-53 Center in Black

40 A11 ½p violet ('44) .80 *4.00*
Never hinged 1.50
a. Perf. 13½ 4.00 *4.00*
Never hinged 7.75
41 A11 1p green 30.00 13.50
Never hinged 45.00
41A A11 1p org yel ('42) .25 *.60*
Never hinged .45
b. Perf. 14 ('49) .40 *16.00*
Never hinged .70
c. Perf. 13½ 8.00 *9.00*
Never hinged 14.50
41D A11 1p green ('49) .35 *1.50*
Never hinged .60
42 A11 1½p red ('44) .65 *.80*
Never hinged 1.00
a. Perf. 14 ('49) 1.90 *13.50*
Never hinged 3.50
b. Perf. 13½ 5.75 1.40
Never hinged 8.00
42C A11 1½p lilac rose ('53) .30 *6.50*
Never hinged .55
d. Perf. 14 ('49) 1.35 *1.10*
Never hinged 2.00

e.		1½p carmine, perf 14	6.50	6.50
		Never hinged	12.00	
43	A11	2p orange ('44)	.50	.40
		Never hinged	.80	
a.		Perf. 14 ('49)	2.25	*37.50*
		Never hinged	3.50	
b.		Perf. 13½	5.75	1.00
		Never hinged	8.75	
43C	A11	2p red ('49)	.90	*1.90*
		Never hinged	1.35	
44	A11	3p ultra	65.00	30.00
		Never hinged	110.00	
44A	A11	3p black ('44)	.35	*.80*
		Never hinged	.70	
c.		Perf. 13½ ('40)	13.50	4.00
		Never hinged	21.00	
44B	A11	4p ultra ('44)	3.00	3.00
		Never hinged	5.25	
d.		Perf. 13½	10.00	3.75
		Never hinged	17.50	
45	A11	6p gray blue	7.25	2.50
		Never hinged	11.50	
a.		Perf. 13 ('44)	7.50	7.50
		Never hinged	12.50	
46	A11	1sh dk brn ('44)	3.50	2.00
		Never hinged	5.00	
a.		Perf. 13½	13.00	3.00
		Never hinged	22.50	
47	A11	2sh6p car ('44)	20.00	*37.50*
		Never hinged	30.00	
a.		Perf. 13½	30.00	11.50
		Never hinged	47.50	
b.		Frame printed doubly, one albino	*3,750.*	
		Never hinged	*5,250.*	
48	A11	5sh yel brn ('44)	25.00	42.50
		Never hinged	40.00	
a.		Perf. 13½	62.50	11.00
		Never hinged	100.00	
49	A11	10sh red vio ('44)	45.00	*62.50*
		Never hinged	62.50	
a.		Perf. 13½	65.00	50.00
		Never hinged	120.00	
b.		10sh brt aniline red pur, perf 13	65.00	50.00
		Never hinged	125.00	
		Nos. 40-49 (16)	202.85	*210.00*
		Set, never hinged	320.00	

Catalogue values for unused stamps in this section, from this point to the end of the section, are for Never Hinged items.

Peace Issue

Common Design Type

Perf. 13½x14

1946, Oct. 21 Engr. Wmk. 4

50	CD303	2p deep orange	.45	1.15
51	CD303	4p deep blue	.45	.65
		Set, perforated "SPECIMEN"	400.00	

Silver Wedding Issue

Common Design Types

1948, Oct. 20 Photo. *Perf. 14x14½*

52	CD304	3p black	.55	.45

Engraved; Name Typographed

Perf. 11½x11

53	CD305	10sh red violet	60.00	*57.50*

The stamps formerly listed as Nos. 54-56 have been merged into the rest of the George VI definitive series as Nos. 41//43C.

UPU Issue

Common Design Types

Engr.; Name Typo. on Nos. 58, 59

1949, Oct. 10 *Perf. 13½, 11x11½*

57	CD306	3p rose carmine	1.40	*2.00*
58	CD307	4p indigo	4.75	1.50
59	CD308	6p olive	1.75	3.50
60	CD309	1sh slate	4.50	3.00
		Nos. 57-60 (4)	12.40	10.00

AUSTRALIAN STATES

NEW SOUTH WALES

'nü sauth 'wā,ə,lz

LOCATION — Southeast coast of Australia in the South Pacific Ocean
GOVT. — British Crown Colony
AREA — 309,432 sq. mi.
POP. — 1,500,000 (estimated, 1900)
CAPITAL — Sydney

In 1901 New South Wales united with five other British colonies to form the Commonwealth of Australia. Stamps of Australia are now used.

12 Pence = 1 Shilling
20 Shillings = 1 Pound

Watermarks

Wmk. 12 — Crown and Single-lined A

Wmk. 13 — Large Crown and Double-lined A

Wmk. 49 — Double-lined Numerals Corresponding with the Value

Wmk. 50 — Single-lined Numeral

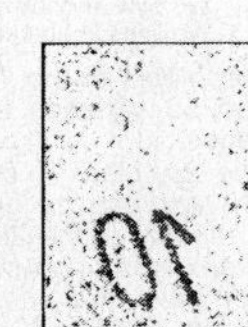

Wmk. 51 — Single-lined Numeral

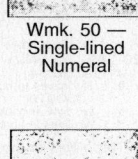

Wmk. 52 — Single-lined Numeral

Wmk. 53 — 5/-

Wmk. 54 — Small Crown and NSW

Wmk. 55 — Large Crown and NSW

Wmk. 56 — NSW

Wmk. 57 — 5/- NSW in Diamond

Wmk. 58 — 20/- NSW in Circle

Wmk. 70 — V and Crown

Wmk. 199 — Crown and A in Circle

Values for unused stamps are for examples with original gum as defined in the catalogue introduction except for Nos. 1-20 which are rarely found with gum and are valued without gum. Very fine examples of Nos. 35-100, F3-F5, J1-J10 and O1-O40 will have perforations touching the framelines or design on one or more sides due to the narrow spacing of the stamps on the plates and imperfect perforation methods. Stamps with perfs clear of the design on all four sides are scarce and will command higher prices.

Seal of the Colony — A1

A1 has no clouds. A2 has clouds added to the design, except in pos. 15.

Unwmk.

1850, Jan. 1 Engr. *Imperf.*

Yellowish Wove Paper

1	A1	1p red	11,000.	725.00
a.		1p brownish red	12,000.	725.00
c.		1p carmine	12,000.	725.00
d.		1p crimson lake	12,000.	725.00

Bluish Wove Paper

1b	A1	1p red	11,000.	725.00
1e	A1	1p lake	12,000.	725.00

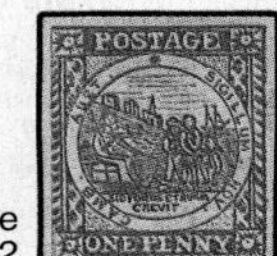

Seal of the Colony — A2

Re-engraved, with Clouds

1850, Aug. Yellowish Wove Paper

2	A2	1p red carmine	9,000.	600.00
f.		Hill unshaded (Pos. 2/3)	13,500.	925.00
g.		No clouds (Pos. 3/5	13,500.	925.00
h.		No trees (Pos. 2/2)	13,500.	925.00
2i	A2	1p vermilion	9,000.	750.00

Bluish Wove Paper

2c	A2	1p carmine red	9,000.	850.00
j.		Hill unshaded	13,500.	850.00
k.		No clouds	13,500.	850.00
l.		No trees	13,500.	850.00
2m	A2	1p brownish lake	9,000.	750.00
2n	A2	1p crimson lake	9,000.	750.00
2o	A2	1p gooseberry red	11,000.	750.00

Laid Paper

2b	A2	1p carmine red, *yellowish*	14,500.	800.00
p.		Hill unshaded	—	1,350.
q.		No clouds	—	1,350.
r.		No trees	—	1,350.
2e	A2	1p carmine red, *bluish*		
2s	A2	1p vermilion, *bluish*	15,500.	675.00

Printed in panes of 25 (5x5). Twenty-five varieties.

Stamps from early impressions of the plate sell at considerably higher prices.

No. 1 was reproduced by the collotype process in a souvenir sheet distributed at the London International Stamp Exhibition 1950. The paper is white.

Plate I — A3

Plate II — A4

Plate I: Vertically lined background.

Plate I re-touched: Lines above and below "POSTAGE" and "TWO PENCE" deepened. Outlines of circular band around picture also deepened.

Plate II (First re-engraving of Plate I): Horizontally lined background; the bale on the left side is dated and there is a dot in the star in each corner.

Plate II retouched: Dots and dashes added in lower spandrels.

Plate I

1850, Jan. 1 — Early Impressions

3a A3 2p gray blue, *yelsh wove* 18,000. 625.00
b. Double line on bale (Pos. 2/7) 1,250.
3c A3 2p deep blue, *yelsh wove* 18,000. 725.00

Intermediate Impressions

3d A3 2p gray blue, *yelsh wove* 9,500. 450.00
3e A3 2p deep blue, *yelsh wove* 10,000. 500.00

Late (worn plate) Impressions

3 A3 2p blue, *yelsh wove* 6,750. 225.00
3f A3 2p deep blue, *yelsh wove* 7,250. 250.00

Printed in panes of 24 (12x2). Twenty-four varieties.

Plate I, Retouched

4 A3 2p blue, *yelsh wove* 9,500. 400.00
4a A3 2p gray blue, *yelsh wove* 9,000. 500.00

Twelve varieties.

Plate II

1850, Apr. — Early Impressions

5h A3 2p gray blue, *yelsh wove* 12,500. 375.00
j. "CREVIT" omitted (Pos. 2/1) — 1,000.
k. Pick & shovel omitted (Pos. 1/10) — 625.00
l. No whip (Pos. 1/4, 1/8, 2/8) — 525.00
5m A3 2p bright blue, *bluish wove* 12,500. 375.00
5n A3 2p indigo blue, *yelsh wove* 12,500. 400.00
5o A3 2p lilac blue, *yelsh wove* *2,000.*

Late (worn plate) Impressions

5 A4 2p blue, *yelsh wove* 7,250. 180.00
5a A4 2p blue, *bluish wove* 7,250. 180.00
5b A4 2p blue, *grayish wove* 7,250. 180.00
5p A4 2p prussian blue, *bluish wove* 7,250. 225.00
c. "CREVIT" omitted — 675.00
d. Pick and shovel omitted — 450.00
e. No whip *10,000.* 325.00

Plate II, Retouched

5F A4 2p blue, *bluish wove* 9,500. 300.00
g. No whip — 475.00
i. "CREVIT" omitted 650.00
5q A4 2p prussian blue, *bluish wove* 9,500. 400.00

Eleven varieties.

Plate III
A5

Plate IV
A6

Plate III (Second re-engraving of Plate I): The bale is not dated and, with the exception of Nos. 7, 10 and 12, it is single-lined. There are no dots in the stars.

Plate IV (Third re-engraving of Plate I): The bale is double-lined and there is a circle in the center of each star.

1850-51 — Wove Paper

6 A5 2p bl, *grayish wove* 8,500. 300.00
a. Fan with 6 segments — 650.00
b. Double-lined bale — 425.00
c. No whip — 475.00
6d A5 2p ultramarine 9,500. 300.00
7 A6 2p blue, *bluish wove* ('51) 8,000. 250.00
7b A6 2p blue, *grayish wove* 8,000. 275.00
c. Fan with 6 segments (Pos. 2/8) — 425.00
d. No clouds (Pos. 2/10) — 425.00
e. Hill not shaded (Pos. 1/12) 450.00
f. No waves (Pos. 1/9, 2/5) 325.00
7g A6 2p 2p ultramarine 9,000. 300.00
7h A6 2p 2p prussian blue 9,000. 250.00

Laid Paper

7a A6 2p ultramarine 9,000. 275.00
7i A6 2p prussian blue 10,000. 375.00
j. Fan with 6 segments (Pos. 2/8) — 450.00
k. No clouds (Pos. 2/10) — 450.00
l. Hill not shaded (Pos. 1/12) 450.00
m. No waves (Pos. 1/9, 2/5) 400.00
n. "PENOE" (Pos. 1/10, 2/12) 475.00

Twenty-four varieties.

Plate V — A7

A8

Plate V (Fourth re-engraving of Plate I): There is a pearl in the fan-shaped ornament below the central design.

1850-51 — Wove Paper

8 A7 2p blue, *grayish wove* ('51) 8,000. 300.00
b. Fan with 6 segments (Pos. 2/8) — 500.00
c. Pick and shovel omitted (Pos. 2/5) — 525.00
8d A7 2p ultramarine 8,000. 300.00

Laid Paper

8a A7 2p ultramarine 9,500. 425.00
e. Fan with 6 segments (Pos. 2/8) — 600.00
f. Pick and shovel omitted (Pos. 2/5) — 575.00

Yellowish Wove Paper

9a A8 3p green 9,500. 375.00
9h A8 3p emerald green 10,000. 375.00
e. No whip (Pos. 4/3, 4/4) — 600.00
f. "SIGIIIUM" for "SIGILLUM" (Pos. 5/3) — 725.00
9g A8 3p myrtle green *22,500.* *1,600.*

Bluish Wove Paper

9 A8 3p yellow green 9,500. 325.00
9d A8 3p emerald green 10,000. 325.00
i. No whip (Pos. 4/3, 4/4) — 500.00
j. "SIGIIIUM" for "SIGILLUM" (Pos. 5/3) — 650.00

Laid Paper

9b A8 3p green, *yellowish laid* 12,500. 925.00
k. No whip (Pos. 4/3, 4/4) — 1,100.
l. "SIGIIIUM" for "SIGILLUM" (Pos. 5/3) — 1,250.
9c A8 3p green, *bluish laid* 12,500. 925.00
9m A8 3p bright green, *yellowish laid* 15,000. 1,000.

Twenty-four varieties of No. 8, twenty-five of No. 9.

Queen Victoria — A9

TWO PENCE
Plate I — Background of wavy lines.
Plate II — Stars in corners.
Plate III (Plate I re-engraved) — Background of crossed lines.

1851 — Yellowish Wove Paper

10 A9 1p carmine 4,500. 400.00
b. No leaves to right of "SOUTH" *6,000.* 1,000.
c. Two leaves to right of "SOUTH" *6,000.* 1,100.
d. "WALE" *6,000.* 1,100.
11 A9 2p ultra, Plate I 1,900. 135.00

1852 — Bluish Laid Paper

12 A9 1p orange brown 6,750. 600.00
a. 1p claret 6,750. 575.00
b. As "a," no leaves to right of "SOUTH" 1,250.
c. As "a," two leaves to right of "SOUTH" 1,300.
d. As "a," "WALE" 1,300.

Queen Victoria — A10

SIX PENCE
Plate I — Background of fine lines.
Plate II (Plate I re-engraved) — Background of coarse lines.

1852-55

Bluish or Grayish Wove Paper

13 A9 1p red 1,900. 200.00
a. 1p carmine 2,000. 200.00
b. 1p scarlet 2,000. 250.00
c. 1p brick red 1,900. 200.00
d. As "c," no leaves to right of "SOUTH" 4,250. 400.00
e. As "c," two leaves to right of "SOUTH" 475.00
f. As "c," "WALE" 550.00
14 A9 2p blue, Plate I 1,350. 45.00
a. 2p ultramarine 1,700. 45.00
b. 2p slate 1,350. 45.00
c. 2p chalky blue 1,350. 45.00
d. 2p prussian blue 1,000. 45.00
15 A10 2p blue, Plate II ('53) 2,250. 125.00
a. "WAEES" *3,000.* 550.00
b. 2p deep ultramarine 2,150. 160.00
c. 2p prussian blue 2,150. 135.00
d. As "c," "WAEES" — 550.00
16 A9 2p blue, Plate III ('55) 1,000. 90.00
a. "WALES" partly covered with wavy lines — 325.00
b. 2p blue, *white paper* ('55) 1,000. 95.00
c. As "b," "WALES" partly covered with wavy lines — 300.00
17 A9 3p green 3,500. 210.00
a. 3p emerald 4,000. 300.00
b. As "a," "WACES" 800.00
c. 3p deep green 4,000. 300.00
d. 3p yellow green 4,000. 275.00
e. As "d," "WACES" — 625.00
f. 3p blue green, *thick paper* 4,000. 325.00
g. As "f," "WACES" 900.00
18 A9 6p brown, Plate I 3,750. 450.00
a. "WALLS" *4,500.* 1,350.
b. 6p black brown 4,500. 1,250.
c. 6p yellow brown 4,250. 350.00
d. 6p chocolate brown 4,000. 350.00
e. 6p yellow brown, *white paper* *1,350.*
f. As "e," ""WALLS" *2,400.*
19 A9 6p brown, Plate II 4,500. 425.00
a. 6p bister brown 4,250. 425.00
20 A9 8p yellow ('53) 12,500. 1,100.
a. 8p orange 13,500. 1,100.
b. No leaves to right of "SOUTH" — 2,250.
c. No bow at back of head — 2,250.
d. No lines in spandrel — 1,350.

The plates of the 1, 2, 3 and 8p each contained 50 varieties and those of the 6p 25 varieties.

The 2p, plate II, 6p, plate II, and 8p have been reprinted on grayish blue wove paper. The reprints of the 2p have the spandrels and background much worn. Most of the reprints of the 6p have no floreate ornaments to the right and left of "South." On all the values the wreath has been retouched.

Type of 1851 and

A11

A12

A13

A14

1854-55 — Wmk. 49 — *Imperf.*

23 A9 1p orange 450.00 57.50
a. No leaves to right of "SOUTH" 975.00 200.00
b. Two leaves to right of "SOUTH" 1,250. 225.00
c. "WALE" 1,250. 225.00
d. 1d orange vermilion 450.00 57.50
24 A9 2p blue 400.00 27.50
a. 2p ultramarine 400.00 27.50
b. 2p Prussian blue 400.00 27.50
25 A9 3p green 575.00 57.50
a. "WACES" *1,700.* 225.00
b. Watermarked "2" 7,250. 2,250.

Value for No. 25b is for copy with the design cut into.

26 A11 5p green 1,600. 800.00
27 A12 6p sage green 1,600. 110.00
28 A12 6p brown 1,600. 45.00
a. Watermarked "8" 4,600. 175.00
29 A12 6p gray 1,600. 110.00
a. 6p greenish gray 1,600. 110.00
b. 6p bluish gray 1,600. 110.00
c. 6p deep slate 1,800. 110.00
d. As "c," wmk sideways 1,350.
e. 6p fawn 1,700. 175.00
f. As "e," watermarked "8" *4,500.* 160.00
g. As "f," wmk sideways *600.00*
30 A13 8p orange ('55) *17,000.* 1,900.
a. 8p yellow *18,000.* 1,600.
31 A14 1sh pale red brown 4,250. 140.00
a. 1sh red 3,750. 110.00
b. 1sh rose vermilion 4,000. 110.00
c. As "b," watermarked "8" *10,000.* 250.00

See Nos. 38-42, 56, 58, 65, 67.

Nos. 38-42 exist with wide margins. Stamps with perforations trimmed are often offered as Nos. 26, 30, and 30a.

A15

1856 — *Imperf.*

32 A15 1p red 350.00 27.50
a. 1p orange red 325.00 27.50
b. As "a," printed on both sides *4,200.* *2,750.*
c. Watermarked "2" *9,500.*
d. 1p carmine vermilion 350.00 27.50
33 A15 2p blue 300.00 16.00
a. Watermarked "1" *9,500.*
b. Watermarked "5" 1,000. 110.00
c. Watermarked "8" *8,250.*
d. 2p dp turquoise blue 325.00 16.00
e. 2p ultramarine 300.00 16.00
f. 2p pale blue 300.00 16.00
34 A15 3p green 1,600. 125.00
a. 3p yellow green 1,450. 125.00
b. Watermarked "2" *5,000.*
c. 3p bluish green ('56) 1,600. 125.00
Nos. 32-34 (3) 2,250. 168.50

The two known examples of No. 33c are in museums. Both are used.

The 1p has been reprinted in orange on paper watermarked Small Crown and NSW, and the 2p in deep blue on paper watermarked single lined "2." These reprints are usually overprinted "SPECIMEN."

See Nos. 34C-37, 54, 63, 90.

1859 — Litho.

34C A15 2p light blue — 1,250.
On cover *4,500.*

1860-63 — Engr. — Wmk. 49 — *Perf. 13*

35 A15 1p red 160.00 25.00
a. 1p orange 160.00 25.00
b. Perf. 12x13 *2,100.*
c. Perf. 12 250.00 25.00
36 A15 2p blue, perf. 12 225.00 15.00
a. Watermarked "1" *4,000.*
c. Perf. 12x13 *3,400.* 250.00
37 A15 3p blue green 90.00 13.50
a. 3p yellow green 110.00 10.50
b. 3p deep green 110.00 10.00
c. Watermarked "6" 225.00 16.00
d. Perf. 12 900.00 55.00
38 A11 5p dark green 110.00 29.00
a. 5p yellow green 250.00 87.50
b. Perf. 12 450.00 125.00
39 A12 6p brown, perf. 12 725.00 85.00
a. 6p gray, perf. 12 725.00 75.00
40 A12 6p violet 160.00 8.00
a. 6p aniline lilac 1,600. 170.00
b. Watermarked "5" 850.00 32.50
c. Watermarked "12" 800.00 27.50
e. Perf. 12 625.00 22.50
f. As "b," wmk sideways *800.00*
41 A13 8p yellow 450.00 50.00
a. 8p orange 475.00 50.00
b. As "a," perf. 12 *6,250.* 1,450.
c. 8p red orange 450.00 65.00
d. As "c," perf 12 *6,250.* 1,450.
42 A14 1sh rose 300.00 9.00
a. 1sh carmine 250.00 10.00
b. As "a," perf. 12 1,350. 75.00
c. 1sh crimson lake 250.00 10.00
d. 1sh brownish red, perf 12 1,350. 45.00
e. As "a," pair, imperf. between —
Nos. 35-42 (8) 2,220. 234.50

1864 — Wmk. 50 — *Perf. 13*

43 A15 1p red 80.00 27.50

A16

1861-80 Wmk. 53 *Perf. 13*

44 A16 5sh dull violet 350.00 77.50
- *a.* 5sh purple 450.00 105.00
- *b.* 5sh dull violet, perf. 12 2,250. 400.00
- *c.* 5sh purple, perf. 12 — 110.00
- *d.* 5sh purple, perf. 10 325.00 110.00
- *e.* 5sh purple, perf. 12x10 475.00 110.00
- *f.* 5sh royal purple, perf 13 ('72) 900.00 97.50
- *g.* 5sh deep rose lilac, perf 13 ('75) 225.00 57.50
- *h.* 5sh rose lilac, perf 10 ('83) 300.00 75.00
- *i.* 5sh purple, perf 10x12 ('85) — 260.00
- *j.* 5sh reddish purple, perf 10 ('86) 280.00 75.00
- *k.* 5sh rose lilac, perf 11 ('88) 350.00 225.00

See No. 101. For overprint see No. O11.

Reprints are perf. 10 and overprinted "REPRINT" in black.

A17

A18

1862-65 Typo. Unwmk. *Perf. 13*

45 A17 1p red ('65) 225.00 47.50
- *a.* Perf. 14 200.00 90.00
- *b.* 1p brick red ('65) 225.00 47.50

46 A18 2p blue 150.00 10.00
- *a.* Perf. 14 200.00 105.00

1863-64 Wmk. 50 *Perf. 13*

47 A17 1p red 77.50 9.00
- *a.* Watermarked "2" 225.00 35.00
- *b.* 1p dark red brown 310.00 45.00
- *c.* 1p brick red 77.50 9.00
- *d.* 1p brick red, shiny surfaced paper ('65) 335.00 200.00
- *e.* Horiz. pair, imperf between 2,800.

48 A18 2p blue 55.00 3.00
- *a.* Watermarked "1" 145.00 6.00
- *b.* 2p cobalt blue 55.00 3.00
- *c.* 2p Prussian blue 60.00 4.25

1862 Wmk. 49 *Perf. 13*

49 A18 2p blue 125.00 32.50
- *a.* Watermarked "5" 125.00 32.50
- *b.* Perf. 12x13 *875.00* 450.00
- *c.* Perf. 12 225.00 75.00

See Nos. 52-53, 61-62, 70-71.

A19

A20

1867, Sept. Wmk. 51, 52 *Perf. 13*

50 A19 4p red brown 125.00 9.50
- *a.* Imperf.
- *b.* 4p pale red brown 125.00 9.50

51 A20 10p lilac 55.00 9.50
- Ovptd. "SPECIMEN" 45.00
- *b.* Horiz. pair, imperf between *3,500.*

See Nos. 55, 64, 91, 97, 117, 129.

A21

A22

A23

Typo.; Engr. (3p, 5p, 8p)

1871-84 Wmk. 54 *Perf. 13*

52 A17 1p red 35.00 3.50
- *a.* Perf. 10 325.00 45.00
- *b.* Perf. 13x10 35.00 2.50
- *c.* Horiz. pair, imperf between *3,250.*
- *d.* 1p scarlet, perf. 10 — 200.00

53 A18 2p blue 42.50 2.00
- *a.* Imperf.
- *b.* Horiz. pair, imperf vert. *3,750.*
- *c.* Perf. 10 *400.00* 27.50
- *d.* Perf. 13x10 35.00 1.50
- *e.* Perf. 12x13
- *f.* 2p Prussian blue, perf. 11x12 *400.00 60.00*
- *g.* As "f," perf. 10 145.00 22.50

54 A15 3p green ('74) 85.00 8.00
- *a.* Perf. 11 225.00 130.00
- *b.* Perf. 12 — *225.00*
- *c.* Perf. 10x12 225.00 50.00
- *d.* Perf. 11x12 175.00 45.00
- *e.* Perf. 10 160.00 17.50
- *f.* 3p bright green, perf. 13x10 175.00 25.00
- *g.* As "f," perf. 10 145.00 22.50

55 A19 4p red brown ('77) 125.00 20.00
- *a.* Perf. 10 275.00 95.00
- *b.* Perf. 13x10 85.00 5.00
- *c.* Perf. 10x13 175.00 27.50

56 A11 5p dk grn, perf. 10 ('84) 45.00 42.50
- *a.* Horiz. pair, imperf between 2,250.
- *b.* Perf. 12 325.00 125.00
- *c.* Perf. 10x12 140.00 72.50
- *d.* Perf. 10x13
- *e.* 12x10 67.50 42.50

57 A21 6p lilac ('72) 105.00 3.00
- *a.* Horiz. pair, imperf. between — *3,500.*
- *b.* Perf. 13x10 125.00 3.00
- *c.* Perf. 10 300.00 21.00

58 A13 8p yellow ('77) 225.00 30.00
- *a.* Imperf.
- *b.* Perf. 10 550.00 45.00
- *c.* Perf. 13x10 250.00 42.50

59 A22 9p on 10p red brown, perf. 12 (Bk) 25.00 18.00
- *a.* Double surcharge, blk & bl *400.00*
- *b.* Perf. 12x10 *475.00 350.00*
- *c.* Perf. 10 15.00 11.50
- *d.* Perf. 12x11 17.00 10.00
- *e.* Perf. 11x12 — —
- *f.* Perf. 13 77.50 15.00
- *g.* Perf. 11 67.50 13.50
- *h.* Perf. 10x11 77.50 25.00

60 A23 1sh black ('76) 175.00 12.50
- *b.* Perf. 13x10 275.00 14.50
- *c.* Perf. 10 250.00 35.00
- *d.* Perf. 11 — —
- *e.* Vert. pair, imperf between *3,500.*
- *f.* Pair, imperf *2,800.*
- *Nos. 52-60 (9)* 862.50 139.50

The surcharge on No. 59 measures 15mm.

See Nos. 66, 68. For overprints see Nos. O1-O10.

Typo.; Engr. (3p, 5p, 8p)

1882-91 Wmk. 55 *Perf. 11x12*

61 A17 1p red 10.00 1.40
- *a.* Perf. 10 22.50 2.50
- *b.* Perf. 10x13 140.00 11.00
- *c.* Perf. 10x12 310.00 75.00
- *d.* Perf. 12x11 135.00
- *e.* Perf. 10x11 *550.00* 135.00
- *f.* Perf. 11 175.00
- *g.* Perf. 13 1,100. 500.00
- *h.* Perf. 13x10 72.50 3.00
- *i.* Perf. 12x10 — 225.00
- *j.* Perf. 11x10 — —
- *k.* Horiz. pair, imperf between *2,100.*

62 A18 2p blue 14.50 1.10
- *a.* Perf. 10 67.50 1.25
- *b.* Perf. 13x10 170.00 8.50
- *c.* Perf. 13 550.00 125.00
- *d.* Perf. 12x10 500.00 125.00
- *e.* Perf. 11 125.00
- *f.* Perf. 12x11 500.00 125.00
- *g.* Perf. 11x10 550.00 190.00
- *h.* Perf. 12 2275.00
- *i.* Double impression — 800.00

63 A15 3p green 11.00 11.00
- *a.* Imperf., pair 500.00
- *b.* Vert. pair, imperf. btwn. —
- *c.* Horiz. pair, imperf. vert. 675.00 675.00
- *d.* Double impression — —
- *e.* Perf. 10 32.50 2.50
- *f.* Perf. 11 11.00 2.50
- *g.* Perf. 12 17.50 2.75
- *h.* Perf. 12x11 12.50 3.25
- *i.* Perf. 10x12 55.00 4.75
- *m.* Perf. 10x11 35.00 3.75
- *n.* Perf. 12x10 55.00 4.75
- *o.* Wmk sideways 67.50 12.50

64 A19 4p red brown 85.00 3.00
- *a.* Perf. 10 — 17.00
- *b.* Perf. 10x12 250.00 75.00
- *c.* Perf. 12 300.00 225.00

65 A11 5p dk blue green 12.50 1.50
- *a.* Imperf., pair 550.00
- *b.* Perf. 11 12.50 1.50
- *c.* Perf. 10 27.50 2.00
- *d.* Perf. 12 28.00 2.00
- *e.* Perf. 10x12 175.00 47.50
- *f.* 5p green, perf. 12x11 12.50 1.50
- *g.* 5p green, perf. 11x10 90.00 90.00
- *h.* 5p green, perf. 12x10 110.00 14.00
- *i.* 5p green, perf. 10x11 90.00 90.00
- *j.* 5p green, perf. 11 16.00 2.50
- *k.* Wmk sideways 25.00 8.00

66 A21 6p lilac, perf. 10 105.00 2.75
- *a.* Horiz. pair, imperf. between *3,000.*
- *b.* Perf. 10x12 110.00 2.00
- *c.* Perf. 11x12 145.00 16.50
- *d.* Perf. 12 145.00 11.50
- *e.* Perf. 11x10 125.00 125.00
- *f.* Perf. 11 145.00 9.00
- *g.* Perf. 10x13 400.00

67 A13 8p yellow, perf. 10 220.00 25.00
- *a.* Perf. 11 220.00 30.00
- *b.* Perf. 12 325.00 35.00
- *c.* Perf. 10x12 250.00 67.50

68 A23 1sh black 135.00 9.00
- *a.* Perf. 10x13 — —
- *b.* Perf. 10 145.00 8.00
- *c.* Perf. 11 275.00 20.00
- *d.* Perf. 10x12 — 325.00
- *Nos. 61-68 (8)* 593.00 54.75

Nos. 63 and 65 exist with two types of watermark 55 — spacings of 1mm or 2mm between crown and NSW.

See No. 90. For surcharges and overprints see Nos. 92-94, O12-O19.

The 1, 2, 4, 6, 8p and 1sh have been reprinted on paper watermarked Large Crown and NSW. The 1, 2, 4p and 1sh are perforated 11x12, the 6p is perforated 10 and the 8p 11. All are overprinted "REPRINT," the 1sh in red and the others in black.

Perf. 11x12

1886-87 Typo. Wmk. 56

Bluish Revenue Stamp Paper

70 A17 1p scarlet 13.00 6.00
- *a.* Perf. 10 35.00 13.00

71 A18 2p dark blue 32.50 6.00
- *a.* Perf. 10 105.00 15.00

For overprint, see No. O20.

A24

Perf. 12 (#73-75), 12x10 (#72, 75A) and Compound

1885-86 "POSTAGE" in Black

72 A24 5sh green & vio 850.00 125.00
- *a.* Perf. 10 — —
- *b.* Perf. 13 — —

73 A24 10sh rose & vio 1,750. 275.00
- *a.* Perf. 13 — —

74 A24 £1 rose & vio 9,000. —
- *a.* Perf. 13 — 5,250.

"POSTAGE" in Blue

Bluish Paper

75 A24 10sh rose & vio 325.00 80.00
- *b.* Perf. 10 1,350. 300.00
- *c.* Perf. 12x11 — —

White Paper

75A A24 £1 rose & vio 6,750. *4,250.*

For overprints, see Nos. O21-O23.

The 5sh with black overprint and the £1 with blue overprint have been reprinted on paper watermarked NSW. They are perforated 12x10 and are overprinted "REPRINT" in black.

"POSTAGE" in Blue

1894 White Paper

76 A24 10sh rose & violet, perf 12 450.00 105.00
- *a.* Double overprint
- *b.* 10sh mauve & claret, perf 10 850.00 275.00
- *c.* 10sh mauve & violet, perf 11 750.00 190.00
- *d.* 10sh mauve & violet, perf 12x11 425.00 125.00

See No. 108B.

View of Sydney A25

Emu A26

Captain Cook — A27

Victoria and Coat of Arms — A28

Lyrebird A29

Kangaroo A30

1888-89 Wmk. 55 *Perf. 11x12*

77 A25 1p violet 10.00 1.40
- *a.* Perf. 12 14.00 1.10
- *b.* Perf. 12x11½ 42.50 2.40

78 A26 2p blue 16.00 1.40
- *a.* Imperf., pair 400.00
- *b.* Perf. 12 25.00 .95
- *c.* Perf. 12x11½ 29.00 .95

79 A27 4p brown 25.00 8.75
- *a.* Perf. 12x11½ 87.50 20.00
- *b.* Perf. 12 72.50 10.00
- *c.* Perf. 11 700.00 200.00
- *d.* Imperf.

80 A28 6p carmine rose 57.50 8.75
- *a.* Perf. 12 47.50 15.00
- *b.* Perf. 12x11½ 57.50 8.75

81 A29 8p red violet 42.50 9.50
- *a.* Perf. 12 42.50 9.50
- *b.* Perf. 12x11½ 75.00 20.00

82 A30 1sh maroon ('89) 57.50 8.75
- *a.* Imperf., pair 1,000.
- *b.* Perf. 12x11½ 57.50 4.25
- *c.* Perf. 12 72.50 4.25
- *d.* 1sh violet brown, perf 11x12 40.00 9.25
- *e.* 1sh violet brown, perf 12x11½ 75.00 11.50
- *f.* 1sh violet brown, perf 12 75.00 11.50
- *Nos. 77-82 (6)* 208.50 38.55
- Set, ovptd. "SPECIMEN" 290.00

First British settlement in Australia, cent.
For overprints see Nos. O24-O29.

1888 Wmk. 56 *Perf. 11x12*

83 A25 1p violet 35.00 4.00

84 A26 2p blue 115.00 6.00

See Nos. 104B-106C, 113-115, 118, 125-127, 130.

Map of Australia — A31

Governors Capt. Arthur Phillip (above) and Lord Carrington — A32

1888-89 Wmk. 53 *Perf. 10*

85 A31 5sh violet ('89) 475.00 105.00
- *a.* 5sh deep purple 450.00 105.00

86 A32 20sh ultra 600.00 225.00

See Nos. 88, 120. For overprints see Nos. O30-O31.

1890 Wmk. 57 *Perf. 10*

87 A31 5sh violet 400.00 77.50
- *a.* Perf. 11 450.00 100.00
- *b.* Perf. 10x11 550.00 77.50
- *c.* Perf. 12 700.00 115.00
- *d.* 5sh mauve, perf 10 425.00 77.50
- *e.* 5sh mauve, perf 11 425.00 92.50
- *f.* Horiz. pair, imperf btwn. —

Perf. 11x12, 12x11

Wmk. 58

88 A32 20sh ultra 225.00 90.00
- *a.* Perf. 11 275.00 90.00
- *b.* Perf. 12 700.00 275.00
- *c.* 20sh cobalt blue, perf 10 525.00 275.00
- *d.* As "c," perf 11 350.00 90.00
- Nos. 87-88, ovptd. "SPECIMEN" 260.00

For overprints see Nos. O32-O33.

"Australia" — A33

1890, Dec. 22 Wmk. 55 *Perf. 11x12*

89 A33 2½p ultra 14.00 5.75
- *a.* Perf. 12 29.00 5.75
- *b.* Perf. 12x11½ 87.50 —
- Overprinted "SPECIMEN" 27.50

For overprint see No. O35.

Type of 1856

1891 Engr. Wmk. 52 *Perf. 10*

90 A15 3p green 15.00 *100.00*
- *a.* Double impression —
- *b.* 3p light green 22.50 *125.00*

Type of 1867

1893 Typo. *Perf. 11*

91 A20 10p lilac 35.00 11.50
- *a.* Perf. 10 42.50 14.00
- *b.* Perf. 11x10 or 10x11 47.50 18.00
- *c.* Perf. 12x11 250.00 35.00

Types of 1862-84 Surcharged in Black

a

b

1891, Jan. 5 Wmk. 55 *Perf. 11x12*

92 A17(a) ½p on 1p gray 21.00 *14.00*
a. Imperf. —
b. Surcharge omitted
c. Double surcharge *550.00*
93 A21(b) 7½p on 6p brown 21.00 14.00
a. Perf. 10 21.00 14.00
b. Perf. 11 20.00 11.50
c. Perf. 12 24.00 14.00
d. Perf. 10x12 24.00 14.00

Perf. 12x11½

94 A23(b) 12½p on 1sh red 14.00 12.00
a. Perf. 11x12 22.50 22.50
b. Perf. 10 29.00 25.00
c. Perf. 11 30.00 25.00
d. Perf. 12 35.00 25.00
Nos. 92-94 (3) 56.00 40.00
Nos. 92-94 overprinted "SPECIMEN" 80.00

For overprints see Nos. O34, O36-O37.

Victoria — A37

1892-97 *Perf. 11x12*

95 A37 ½p slate ('97) 5.75 .85
a. Perf. 12x11½ 5.75 .85
b. Perf. 12 5.50 .85
c. As #95, horiz. pair, imperf between *1,350.*
d. ½p gray, perf. 10 80.00 7.25
e. As "d," perf. 10x12 140.00 18.00
f. As "d," perf. 11 160.00 14.00
g. As "d," perf. 11x12 2.25 .50
As "g," overprinted "SPECIMEN" 22.50

See Nos. 102, 109, 121. For overprint see No. O38.

Types of 1867-71

1897 *Perf. 11x12*

96 A22 9p on 10p red brn (Bk) 20.00 17.50
a. 9p on 10p org brn (Bk) 20.00 17.50
b. Surcharge omitted —
c. Double surcharge 375.00 375.00
d. Perf. 11 25.00 24.00
e. Perf. 12 25.00 22.50
97 A20 10p violet 25.00 16.00
a. Perf. 12x11½ 25.00 16.00
b. Perf. 11 47.50 22.50
c. Perf. 12 35.00 17.50
Nos. 96-97, overprinted "SPECIMEN" 75.00

The surcharge on No. 96 measures 13½mm.
For overprints see Nos. O39-O40.

Seal
A38

Victoria
A39

A40

ONE PENNY:
Die I — The first pearl in the crown at the left is merged into the arch, the shading under the fleur-de-lis is indistinct, and the "s" of "WALES" is open.
Die II — The first pearl is circular, the vertical shading under the fleur-de-lis is clear, and the "s" of "WALES" not so open.

2½ PENCE:
Die I — There are 12 radiating lines in the star on the Queen's breast.
Die II — There are 16 radiating lines in the star. The eye is nearly full of color.

1897 *Perf. 12*

98 A38 1p rose red, II 4.75 .50
a. Die I, perf. 11x12 5.75 .50
b. Imperf., pair —
c. Imperf. horiz., pair 700.00
d. Die I, perf. 12x11½ 5.50 .50
e. Die I, perf. 12 11.50 1.75
f. Die II, perf. 12x11½ 4.75 .50
g. Die II, perf. 11x12 4.75 .50
99 A39 2p deep blue 13.50 .65
a. Perf. 11x12 9.00 .65
b. Perf. 12x11½ 7.75 .65
100 A40 2½p dp purple, II 20.00 4.25
a. Die I, perf. 12x11 22.50 4.75
b. Die I, perf. 11 25.00 7.75
c. Die I, perf. 11½x12 25.00 4.25
d. Die II, perf. 11x12 21.00 4.25
e. Die II, perf. 11½x12 25.00 4.25
Nos. 98-100 (3) 38.25 5.40
Nos. 98-100 overprinted "SPECIMEN" 70.00

Sixtieth year of Queen Victoria's reign.
See Nos. 103-104, 110-112, 122-124.

Type of 1861

1897 Engr. Wmk. 53 *Perf. 11*

101 A16 5sh red violet 105.00 29.00
a. Horiz. pair, imperf. btwn. *11,000.*
b. Perf. 11x12 or 12x11 130.00 42.50
c. Perf. 12 140.00 52.50

Perf. 12x11½, 11½x12

1899, Oct. Typo. Wmk. 55

HALF PENNY:
Die I — Narrow "H" in "HALF."

102 A37 ½p blue green, I 3.50 .95
a. Imperf., pair 190.00 *325.00*
103 A39 2p ultra 5.75 .95
a. Imperf., pair 325.00
104 A40 2½p dk blue, II 8.00 3.25
a. Imperf., pair 325.00
104B A27 4p org brown 22.50 13.50
c. 4p red brown 24.00 12.00
d. As "c," imperf. pair 750.00
105 A28 6p emerald 135.00 52.50
a. Imperf., pair 600.00
106 A28 6p orange 29.00 6.75
a. 6p yellow 26.00 10.75
b. Imperf., pair 475.00
106C A29 8p magenta 42.50 8.00
Nos. 102-106C (7) 246.25 85.90

Lyrebird — A41

1903 *Perf. 12x11½*

107 A41 2sh6p blue green 87.50 42.50
Overprinted "SPECIMEN" 85.00

See Nos. 119, 131.

"Australia" — A42

1903 Wmk. 70 *Perf. 12½*

108 A42 9p org brn & ultra 29.00 7.25
Overprinted "SPECIMEN" 52.50
a. Perf. 11 5,250. 1,850.

See No. 128.

Type of 1885-86

1904 Wmk. 56 *Perf. 12x11*

"POSTAGE" in Blue

108B A24 10sh brt rose & vio 325.00 125.00
c. Perf. 11 525.00 200.00
d. Perf. 14 400.00 135.00
e. 10sh aniline crimson & violet, perf 12 650.00 200.00
f. As "e," perf 12x11 475.00 130.00
g. 10sh claret & violet, chalky paper, perf 12x11 475.00 175.00

The watermark (NSW) of No. 108B is 20x7mm, with rounded angles in "N" and "W." On No. 75, the watermark is 21x7mm, with sharp angles in the "N" and "W."

HALF PENNY:
Die II — Wide "H" in "HALF."

Perf. 11, 11x12½, 12x11½ and Compound

1905-06 Wmk. 12

109 A37 ½p blue grn, II 6.00 1.10
a. ½p blue green, I 6.25 1.10
b. Booklet pane of 12 —
110 A38 1p car rose, II 4.75 .50
a. Booklet pane of 6 —
b. Booklet pane of 12 —
111 A39 2p deep ultra 4.75 .50
112 A40 2½p dk blue, II 9.00 5.25
113 A27 4p org brown 21.00 8.75
a. 4p red brown 27.50 7.00
114 A28 6p orange 29.00 6.00
a. 6p yellow 35.00 6.00
b. Perf. 11 525.00
115 A29 8p magenta 52.50 11.00
117 A20 10p violet 32.50 10.00
118 A30 1sh vio brown 57.50 5.75
119 A41 2sh6p blue green 77.50 40.00

Wmk. 199

Perf. 12x11 or 11x12

120 A32 20sh ultra 225.00 87.50
a. Perf 12 300.00 97.50
b. Perf 11 225.00 80.50
Nos. 109-115,117-120 (11) 519.50 176.35

1906-07 Wmk. 13

121 A37 ½p green, I 8.75 3.25
122 A38 1p rose, II 17.00 2.25
123 A39 2p ultra 17.00 2.25
124 A40 2½p blue, II 110.00 *200.00*
125 A27 4p org brown 29.00 25.00
126 A28 6p orange 67.50 37.50
127 A29 8p red violet 42.50 37.50
128 A42 9p org brn & ultra, perf. 12x12½ ('06) 22.50 4.50
a. Perf. 11 175.00 140.00
b. 9p org brn & ultra, perf. 12x12½ 27.50 4.00
129 A20 10p violet 62.50 *87.50*
130 A30 1sh vio brown 92.50 18.00
a. Perf. 11 —
131 A41 2sh6p blue green 125.00 105.00
Nos. 121-131 (11) 594.25 522.75

Portions of some of the sheets on which the above are printed show the watermark "COMMONWEALTH OF AUSTRALIA." Stamps may also be found from portions of the sheet without watermark.

SEMI-POSTAL STAMPS

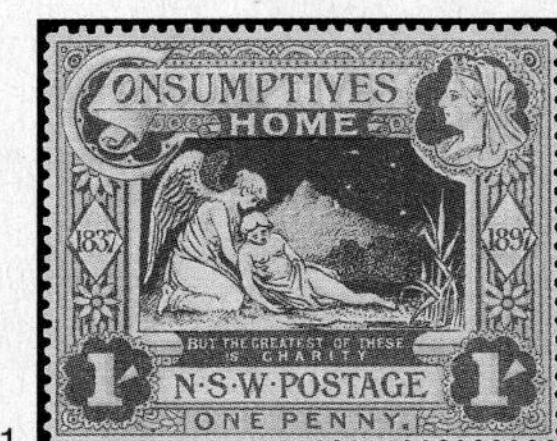

SP1

Allegory of Charity
SP2

1897, June Wmk. 55 *Perf. 11*

B1 SP1 1p (1sh) grn & brn 72.50 72.50
B2 SP2 2½p (2sh6p) rose, bl & gold 350.00 350.00
Nos. B1-B2 overprinted "SPECIMEN" 275.00

Diamond Jubilee of Queen Victoria.
The difference between the postal and face values of these stamps was donated to a fund for a home for consumptives.

REGISTRATION STAMPS

Queen Victoria — R1

Unwmk.

1856, Jan. 1 Engr. *Imperf.*

F1 R1 (6p) orange & blue 1,700. 250.00
F2 R1 (6p) red & blue 1,800. 210.00
a. Frame printed on back *13,500.* *5,750.*

1860 *Perf. 12, 13*

F3 R1 (6p) orange & blue 950.00 75.00
F4 R1 (6p) red & blue 950.00 80.00

Nos. F1 to F4 exist also on paper with papermaker's watermark in sheet.

1863 Wmk. 49

F5 R1 (6p) red & blue 225.00 25.00
a. (6p) red & Prussian blue 250.00 27.50
b. (6p) red & indigo 375.00 35.00
c. Double impression of frame — *800.00*

Fifty varieties.
Nos. F1-F2 were reprinted on thin white wove unwatermarked paper and on thick yellowish wove unwatermarked paper; the former are usually overprinted "SPECIMEN."
No. F4 was reprinted on thin white wove unwatermarked paper; perf. 10 and overprinted "REPRINT" in black.

POSTAGE DUE STAMPS

D1

Perf. 10, 11, 11½, 12 and Compound

1891-92 Typo. Wmk. 55

J1 D1 ½p grn, perf 10 10.00 10.00
a. Chalky paper —
J2 D1 1p green 21.00 3.75
a. Perf 12 45.00 9.00
b. Chalky paper 19.00 6.25
J3 D1 2p green 29.00 5.75
a. Perf 12x10 47.50 7.00
b. Chalky paper 22.50 9.25
J4 D1 3p green 47.50 21.00
b. Chalky paper 55.00 37.50
J5 D1 4p green 42.50 11.50
a. Chalky paper 45.00 20.00
J6 D1 6p grn, perf 10 27.50 17.50
J7 D1 8p grn, perf 10 160.00 42.50
J8 D1 5sh grn, perf 10 325.00 105.00
a. Perf 11 575.00 175.00
b. Perf 11x12 — 300.00

Perf. 12x10

J9 D1 10sh green 600.00 —
a. Perf. 10 750.00 80.00
J10 D1 20sh green 700.00 —
a. Perf. 10 1,000. 125.00
b. Perf. 12 1,350.
Nos. J1-J10 (10) 1,963. 217.00

Used values for Nos. J8-J10 are for c-t-o stamps.

Nos. J1-J5 exist on both ordinary and chalky paper.
Used values for Nos. J8-J10 are for c-t-o stamps.

OFFICIAL STAMPS

Regular Issues Overprinted in Black or Red

Perf. 10, 11, 12, 13 and Compound

1879-80 Wmk. 54

O1 A17 1p red 30.00 5.75
a. Perf. 10 350.00 65.00
b. Perf. 10x13 72.50 9.50
O2 A18 2p blue 47.50 5.25
a. Perf. 11x12 525.00
b. Perf. 10 525.00 77.50
O3 A15 3p green (R) 1,100. 550.00
O4 A15 3p green 350.00 60.00
a. Watermarked "6" — 925.00
b. Double overprint — *925.00*
c. 3p yel grn, perf 10 350.00 60.00
d. 3p yel grn, perf 12 425.00 175.00
O5 A19 4p red brown 400.00 21.00
a. Perf. 10x13 450.00 190.00
O6 A11 5p dark green 42.50 27.50
O7 A21 6p lilac 600.00 20.00
a. Perf. 10 800.00 75.00
b. Perf. 13x10 450.00 90.00
O8 A13 8p yellow (R) *1,750.* 500.00
O9 A13 8p yellow — 52.50
a. Perf. 10 625.00 175.00

O10 A23 1sh black (R) 600.00 17.50
a. Perf. 10 — 35.00
b. Perf. 10x13 — 77.50
c. Perf. 13x10 — 29.00

1880 **Wmk. 53**
O11 A16 5sh lilac, perf. 11 400.00 135.00
a. Double overprint 4,500. *2,400.*
b. Perf. 10 1,000. 225.00
c. Perf. 12x10 900.00 225.00
d. Perf. 13 1,250. 200.00
e. Perf. 10x12 —

Two No. O14 overprint types: Type I, "O" and "S" 7mm apart. Type II, "O" and "S" 5.5mm apart.

1881 **Wmk. 55**
O12 A17 1p red 35.00 6.00
a. Perf. 10x13 200.00
O13 A18 2p blue 21.00 2.40
a. Perf. 10x13 400.00 200.00
O14 A15 3p green (I) 17.50 8.50
a. Double overprint (I) 1,200.
b. Perf. 12 325.00 200.00
c. Perf. 11
d. Type II ovpt 25.00 15.00
e. As "b," type II ovpt 350.00 250.00
f. Wmk sideways 25.00 8.00
O15 A19 4p red brown 35.00 7.50
a. Perf. 10x12 350.00 200.00
b. Perf. 12 350.00 350.00
O16 A11 5p dark green 32.50 *35.00*
a. Perf. 12 250.00
b. Perf. 12x10 — —
c. Perf. 12x11 ('85) 65.00 16.00
O17 A21 6p lilac 50.00 11.50
a. Perf. 12 105.00
b. Perf. 11x12 — —
c. Perf. 12x11 ('85) 100.00 27.50
O18 A13 8p yellow 57.50 25.00
a. Double overprint — —
b. Perf. 12 350.00 525.00
c. Perf. 11 ('85) 52.50 32.50
d. Perf. 10x12 or 12x10 ('85) 52.50 25.00
e. Triple overprint — —
O19 A23 1sh black (R) 72.50 *21.00*
a. Double overprint 525.00
b. Perf. 10x13 140.00
c. Perf. 11x12, comb. 57.50 21.00
Nos. O12-O19 (8) 321.00 116.90

Beware of other red overprints on watermark 55 stamps.

1881 **Wmk. 56**
O20 A17 1p red 105.00 17.50

1887-90
O21 A24 10sh on #75 — *3,200.*
O22 A24 £1 on #75A *19,500.* *9,250.*

No. 75 Overprinted

1889
O23 A24 10sh rose & vio *5,750.* *1,450.*
Overprinted "SPECIMEN" 125.00
a. Perf. 10 *7,500.* *3,500.*

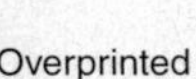

Overprinted

1888-89 **Wmk. 55**
O24 A25 1p violet 6.25 2.00
a. Overprinted "O" only
O25 A26 2p blue 9.50 1.40
O26 A27 4p red brown 25.00 9.50
O27 A28 6p carmine 18.00 12.00
O28 A29 8p red lilac 47.50 32.50
a. Perf 12 60.00 40.00
O29 A30 1sh vio brown 45.00 9.50
a. Double overprint
b. 1sh purple brown, perf 12 45.00 9.50
c. 1sh maroon, perf 11x12 ('90) 45.00 9.50
d. 1sh maroon, perf 12 45.00 9.50
Nos. O24-O29 (6) 151.25 66.90

Wmk. 53
O30 A31 5sh violet (R) *2,000.* *800.00*
O31 A32 20sh ultra *17,500.* 1,150.

1890 **Wmk. 57**
O32 A31 5sh violet *400.00* 150.00
a. 5sh, dull lilac, perf. 12 1,100. 250.00
b. 5sh lilac, perf 10 675.00 200.00

Wmk. 58
O33 A32 20sh ultra *18,000.* *1,750.*
O32b, O33 ovptd. "SPECIMEN" 325.00

Centenary of the founding of the Colony (Nos. O24-O33).

1891 **Wmk. 55**
O34 A17(a) ½p on 1p gray & black 125.00 125.00
a. Double overprint
O35 A33 2½p ultra 24.00 14.00
O36 A21(b) 7½p on 6p brn & black 72.50 85.00
O37 A23(b) 12½p on 1sh red & black 125.00 *140.00*

1892
O38 A37 ½p gray, perf 11x12 12.50 *24.00*
a. Perf 10 16.00 *27.50*
b. Perf 12 15.00 *20.00*
c. Perf 12x11½ 27.50 22.50
Overprinted "SPECIMEN" 45.00

1894 **Wmk. 54**
O39 A22 9p on 10p red brn 1,100. 1,100.
Overprinted "SPECIMEN" 85.00

Wmk. 52
O40 A20 10p lilac, perf. 13 325.00 *175.00*
a. Perf. 11x10 or 10x11 475.00 *450.00*
b. Perf 10 400.00
c. Double overprint, one albino —
Overprinted "SPECIMEN" 75.00

The official stamps became obsolete on Dec. 31, 1894. In Aug., 1895, sets of 32 varieties of "O.S." stamps, together with some envelopes and postal cards, were placed on sale at the Sydney post office at £2 per set.

These sets contained most of the varieties listed above and a few which are not known in the original issues. An obliteration consisting of the letters G.P.O. or N.S.W. in three concentric ovals was lightly applied to the center of each block of four stamps.

It is understood that the earlier stamps and many of the overprints were reprinted to make up these sets.

QUEENSLAND

'kwēnz-ˌland

LOCATION — Northeastern part of Australia
GOVT. — British Crown Colony
AREA — 670,500 sq. mi.
POP. — 498,129 (1901)
CAPITAL — Brisbane

Originally a part of New South Wales, Queensland was constituted a separate colony in 1859. It was one of the six British Colonies that united in 1901 to form the Commonwealth of Australia.

12 Pence = 1 Shilling
20 Shillings = 1 Pound

MORETON BAY

Until 1860, Queensland, then known as Moreton Bay, utilized the postal service of New South Wales, and stamps of New South Wales were used until November 1, 1860. The New South Wales post offices in Queensland, with their opening dates and assigned canceler numbers, were:

Post Office	Opened
Brisbane	1834 (#95)
Burnett's Inn (became Goodes Inn)	1850 (#108)
Callandoon	1850 (#74)
Condamine	1856 (#151)
Dalby	1854 (#133)
Drayton	1846 (#85)
Gayndah	1850 (#86)
Gladstone	1854 (#131)
Goodes Inn	1858 (#108)
Ipswich	1846 (#87)
Maryborough	1849 (#96)
Rockhampton	1858 (#201)
Surat	1852 (#110)
Taroom	1856 (#152)
Toowoombs	1858 (#214)
Warwick	1848 (#81)

Values for unused stamps are for examples with original gum as defined in the catalogue introduction. Very fine examples of Nos. 4-73, 84-125, 128-140, and F1-F3b will have perforations touching the design on at least one or more sides due to the narrow spacing of the stamps on the plates. Stamps with perfs clear of the design on all four sides are scarce and will command higher prices.

Watermarks

Wmk. 5 — Small Star

Wmk. 6 — Large Star

Wmk. 12 — Crown and Single-lined A

Wmk. 13 — Crown and Double-lined A

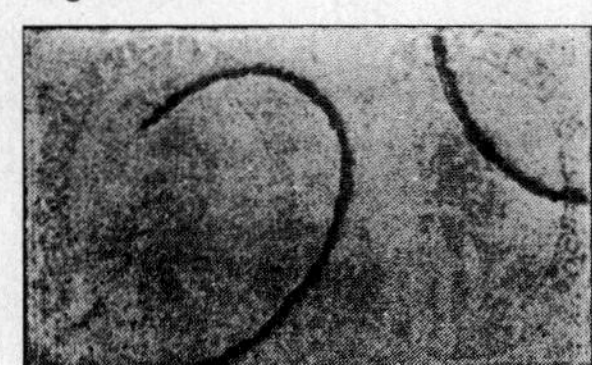

Wmk. 65 — "Queensland Postage Stamps" in Sheet in Script Capitals

Wmk. 66

Wmks. 66 & 67 — "Queensland" in Large Single-lined Roman Capitals in the Sheet and Short-pointed Star to Each Stamp (Stars Vary Slightly in Size and Shape)

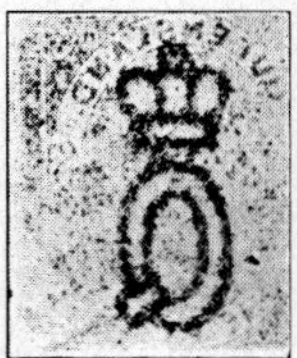

Wmk. 68 — Crown and Q

Wmk. 69 — Large Crown and Q

There are two varieties of the watermark 68, differing slightly in the position and shape of the crown and the tongue of the "Q."

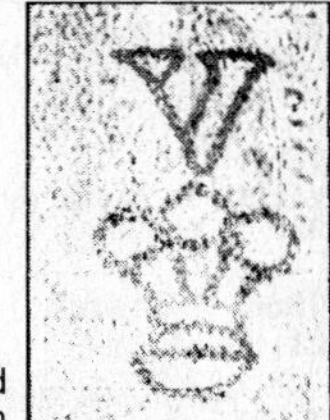

Wmk. 70 — V and Crown

Queen Victoria — A1

Wmk. 6
1860, Nov. 1 **Engr.** ***Imperf.***
1 A1 1p deep rose 6,600. 1,050.
2 A1 2p deep blue 16,250. 2,250.
3 A1 6p deep green 10,250. 1,050.

Clean-Cut Perf. 14 to 16
4 A1 1p deep rose 2,750. 375.
5 A1 2p deep blue 1,450. 140.
a. Horiz. pair, imperf between — *4,250.*
6 A1 6p deep green 1,450. 110.

Clean-Cut Perf. 14 to 16
1860-61 **Wmk. 5**
6A A1 2p blue 975.00 135.00
b. Horiz. pair, imperf. between 11,500.
6D A1 3p brown ('61) 775.00 110.00
6E A1 6p deep green 1,350. 95.00
6F A1 1sh gray violet 1,450. 120.00

Regular Perf. 14
6H A1 1p rose 225.00 62.50
6I A1 2p deep blue 625.00 105.00

Rough Perf. 14 to 16

7 A1 1p deep rose 115.00 57.50
8 A1 2p blue 300.00 52.50
a. Horiz. pair, imperf between 10,250. —
9 A1 3p brown ('61) 105.00 60.00
a. Horiz. pair, imperf. vert. 10,250. —
10 A1 6p deep green 575.00 52.50
a. 6p yellow green 675.00 42.50
11 A1 1sh dull violet 1,150. 140.00

Thick Yellowish Paper

Square Perf. 12½ to 13

1862-67 Unwmk.

12 A1 1p Indian red 575.00 115.00
13 A1 1p orange ('63) 140.00 22.50
a. Perf. 13, round holes ('67) 160.00 42.50
b. Horiz. pair, imperf. between —
c. Imperf., pair — 3,000.
14 A1 2p deep blue 100.00 15.00
a. 2p pale blue 200.00 60.00
b. Perf. 13, round holes ('67) 100.00 27.50
c. Imperf., pair — 2,750.
e. Horiz. pair, imperf. between *16,000.*
f. Vert. pair, imperf. between *5,250.*
15 A1 3p brown ('63) 125.00 62.50
a. Imperf. —
b. Perf. 13, round holes ('67) 130.00 60.00
16 A1 6p yellow grn ('63) 195.00 32.50
a. 6p green 300.00 100.00
b. Perf. 13, round holes ('67) 200.00 32.50
c. Imperf., pair — 2,850.
d. Horiz. pair, imperf. between — 17,500.
e. 6p apple green ('63) 225.00 37.50
17 A1 1sh gray ('63) 500.00 47.50
b. Imperf. horizontally
c. Horiz. pair, imperf. between — 18,000.
d. Perf. 13, round holes ('67) 500.00 47.50
e. Vert. pair, imperf between —

White Wove Paper

1865 Wmk. 5 *Rough Perf. 13*

18 A1 1p orange 125.00 60.00
a. Horiz. pair, imperf. between *5,750.*
19 A1 2p light blue 130.00 30.00
a. Vert. pair, imperf. between *9,000.*
b. Half used as 1p on cover *4,500.*
d. 2p deep blue 180.00 45.00
20 A1 6p yellow green 240.00 45.00
a. 6p deep green 300.00 22.50
Nos. 18-20 (3) 495.00 135.00

1865 *Perf. 12½x13*

18B A1 1p orange vermilion 175.00 85.00
19C A1 2p blue 300.00 85.00

Perf. 13, Round Holes

1866 Wmk. 65

21 A1 1p orange vermilion 210.00 52.50
22 A1 2p blue 110.00 32.50
b. Diagonal half used as 1p on cover —

1865 *Perf. 12½x13*

21A A1 1p orange vermilion 300.00 80.00
22C A1 2p blue 300.00 80.00

1866 Unwmk. Litho. *Perf. 13*

23 A1 4p lilac 425.00 22.50
a. 4p slate 425.00 30.00
Handstamped "SPECIMEN" 47.50
24 A1 5sh pink 1,150. 150.00
a. 5sh bright rose 1,250. 180.00
Handstamped "SPECIMEN" 75.00
b. Vert. pair, imperf between *9,000.*

Wmk. 66, 67

1868-74 Engr. *Perf. 13*

25 A1 1p orange ('71) 100.00 9.25
26 A1 2p blue 77.50 6.00
a. 2p pale blue 82.50 6.50
b. 2p bright blue 87.50 4.75
c. 2p greenish blue 175.00 4.25
d. 2p dark blue 90.00 4.25
27 A1 3p grnsh brn ('71) 200.00 12.50
a. 3p brown 125.00 11.50
b. 3p olive brown 200.00 11.50
28 A1 6p yel grn ('71) 250.00 14.00
a. 6p deep green 325.00 35.00
b. 6p green 240.00 18.00
30 A1 1sh grnsh gray ('72) 825.00 100.00
31 A1 1sh violet ('74) 425.00 37.50
a. 1sh brownish gray 850.00 110.00

Perf. 12

32 A1 1p orange 600.00 47.50
33 A1 2p blue 975.00 80.00
34 A1 3p brown 775.00 325.00
a. 3p greenish gray — 325.00
35 A1 6p deep green 1,900. 52.50
36 A1 1sh violet 900.00 87.50

Perf. 13x12

36A A1 1p orange 250.00
37 A1 2p blue *1,650.* 50.00
37A A1 3p brown *1,000.*

The reprints are perforated 13 and the colors differ slightly from those of the originals.

1868-75 Wmk. 68 *Perf. 13*

38 A1 1p orange 115.00 8.75
a. Imperf pair 825.00
39 A1 1p rose ('74) 105.00 17.00
a. 1p deep rose red 175.00 16.00
40 A1 2p blue 90.00 5.00
a. Vert. pair, imperf between —
b. Imperf., pair 725.00
c. 2p pale blue ('74) 92.50 6.50
41 A1 3p brown ('75) 140.00 21.00
42 A1 6p yel green ('69) 200.00 14.00
a. 6p apple green 240.00 17.50
b. 6p deep green 225.00 17.50
c. As "a," imperf pair 725.00
43 A1 1sh violet ('75) 400.00 87.50
Nos. 38-43 (6) *1,050.* 153.25

1876-78 *Perf. 12*

44 A1 1p orange 77.50 9.50
a. Imperf. *775.00*
b. 1p pale org vermilion 85.00 9.75
c. Vert. pair, imperf between —
45 A1 1p rose 90.00 20.00
a. 1p salmon 125.00 20.00
46 A1 2p blue 75.00 2.40
a. 2p pale blue 160.00 29.00
b. 2p deep blue 75.00 3.50
47 A1 3p brown 125.00 17.50
48 A1 6p yellow green 275.00 9.50
a. 6p apple green 300.00 15.50
b. 6p deep green 265.00 16.00
c. 6p green 290.00 9.25
49 A1 1sh violet 100.00 17.50
m. Vert. pair, imperf between —
n. 1sh purple 275.00 9.75
Nos. 44-49 (6) 742.50 76.40

Nos. 44, 49 exist in vertical pairs, imperf. between.

Perf. 13x12

49B A1 1p orange 250.00
49C A1 2p blue *1,500.* 325.00
49D A1 4p yellow 575.00
49E A1 6p deep green 575.00

Perf. 12½x13

49G A1 1p org ver 600.00
49H A1 2p deep blue 600.00

The reprints are perforated 12 and are in paler colors than the originals.

1879 Unwmk. *Perf. 12*

50 A1 6p pale emerald 450.00 40.00
a. Horiz. pair, imperf. vert. 2,250.

A2

1875-81 Litho. Wmk. 68 *Perf. 13*

50B A1 4p yellow ('75) *2,000.* 110.00
a. Handstamped "SPECIMEN" 110.00

Perf. 12

51 A1 4p buff ('76) 1,675. 45.00
a. 4p yellow 1,675. 45.00
52 A1 2sh pale blue ('81) 170.00 62.50
Fiscal cancellation 5.75
a. 2sh deep blue 200.00 62.50
b. Imperf. —
c. 2sh blue 175.00 62.50
d. As "c" horiz. pair, imperf. vert. *9,000.* —
53 A2 2sh6p lt red ('81) 340.00 100.00
Fiscal cancellation 5.75
a. 2sh6p bright scarlet 340.00 100.00
54 A1 5sh org brn ('81) 475.00 150.00
Fiscal cancellation 7.00
a. 5sh fawn 475.00 150.00
55 A1 10sh brown ('81) 875.00 250.00
Fiscal cancellation 7.00
a. Imperf., pair *1,750.*
b. 10sh bister brown 825.00 250.00
56 A1 20sh rose ('81) *2,000.* *400.00*
Fiscal cancellation 9.25
Nos. 50B-56 (7) 7,535. 1,118.

Nos. 53-56, 62-64, 74-83 with pen (revenue) cancellations removed are often offered as unused.

A3

1879-81 Typo. Wmk. 68 *Perf. 12*

57 A3 1p rose red 62.50 10.00
a. 1p red orange 87.50 11.00
b. 1p brown orange 115.00 10.00
c. "QOEENSLAND" *675.00* *125.00*
d. Imperf. —
e. Vert. pair, imperf. horiz. *1,100.*
f. As "a" "QOGENSLAND" 275.00 47.50
g. As "b" "QOGENSLAND" 550.00 65.00
58 A3 2p gray blue 90.00 5.00
a. 2p deep ultra 95.00 5.00
b. Imperf. —
c. "PENGE" 400.00 60.00
d. "TW" joined 87.50 1.75
e. Vert. pair, imperf. horiz. 1,750.
59 A3 4p orange yellow 375.00 60.00
a. Imperf. —
b. Horiz. pair, imperf. vert. *12,750.* —
60 A3 6p yellow green 200.00 8.00
a. Imperf. —
b. Horiz. pair, imperf. vert. —
c. 6p deep green 190.00 8.00
61 A3 1sh pale violet ('81) 175.00 15.00
a. 1sh deep violet 190.00 14.00
Nos. 57-61 (5) 902.50 98.00

The stamps of type A3 were electrotyped from plates made up of groups of four types, differing in minor details. Two dies were used for the 1p and 2p, giving eight varieties for each of those values.

Nos. 59-60 exist imperf. vertically.

For surcharge see No. 65.

Moiré on Back

1878-79 Unwmk.

62 A3 1p brown org ('79) 800.00 125.00
a. "QOEENSLAND" 2,000.
63 A3 2p deep ultra ('79) 800.00 62.50
a. "PENGE" *4,750.* 800.00
64 A1 1sh red violet 250.00 115.00
Nos. 62-64 (3) 1,850. 302.50

No. 57b Surcharged Vertically in Black

1880 Wmk. 68

65 A3 ½p on 1p brn org 450.00 250.00
a. "QOEENSLAND" 2,000. 1,400.

On No. 65, the surcharge reads from bottom to top. Stamps with surcharges reading downward are fakes.

A4

1882-83 Typo. *Perf. 12*

66 A4 1p pale red 12.00 1.10
a. 1p rose 12.00 1.10
b. Imperf. pair —
c. 1p deep vermilion 12.00 1.15
67 A4 2p gray blue 25.00 1.10
a. 2p deep ultra 25.00 1.10
b. Horiz. pair, imperf between —
68 A4 4p yellow ('83) 42.50 4.75
a. "PENGE" 325.00 70.00
b. Imperf., single —
69 A4 6p yellow green 30.00 35.00
70 A4 1sh violet ('83) 60.00 11.00
a. 1sh lilac 27.50 7.00
b. 1sh deep purple 25.00 7.00
c. 1sh pale mauve 20.00 7.00
Nos. 66-70 (5) 169.50 52.95

There are eight minor varieties of the 1p, twelve of the 2p and four each of the other values. On the 1p there is a period after "PENNY." On all values the lines of shading on the neck extend from side to side.

Compare design A4 with A6, A10, A11, A15, A16.

1883 *Perf. 9½x12*

71 A4 1p rose 200.00 77.50
72 A4 2p gray blue 650.00 92.50
73 A4 1sh pale violet 350.00 95.00
Nos. 71-73 (3) 1,200. 265.00

Beware of faked perfs.

See Nos. 94, 95, 100.

A5

Wmk. 68 Twice Sideways

1882-85 Engr. *Perf. 12*

Thin Paper

74 A5 2sh ultra 275.00 70.00
75 A5 2sh6p vermilion 160.00 32.50
76 A5 5sh car rose ('85) 125.00 35.00
77 A5 10sh brown 275.00 60.00
78 A5 £1 dk grn ('83) 650.00 175.00
Nos. 74-78 (5) 1,485. 372.50

The 2sh, 5sh and £1 exist imperf.

There are two varieties of the watermark on Nos. 74-78, as in the 1879-81 issue.

Stamps with revenue cancels sell for $3.25-6.50.

1886 Wmk. 69 *Perf. 12*

Thick Paper

79 A5 2sh ultra 300.00 67.50
80 A5 2sh6p vermilion 60.00 30.00
81 A5 5sh car rose 55.00 50.00
82 A5 10sh dark brown 140.00 55.00
83 A5 £1 dark green 350.00 90.00
Nos. 79-83 (5) 905.00 292.50

High value stamps with cancellations removed are offered as unused.

Stamps with revenue cancels sell for $3.25-6.50.

See Nos. 126-127, 141-144.

A6

Redrawn

1887-89 Typo. Wmk. 68 *Perf. 12*

84 A6 1p orange 17.50 1.00
85 A6 2p gray blue 17.50 1.00
a. 2p deep ultra 17.50 1.00
b. Half used as 1c on cover —
86 A6 2sh red brown ('89) 90.00 75.00
a. 2sh pale brown 75.00 65.00

Perf. 9½x12

88 A6 2p deep ultra *450.00* 90.00
Nos. 84-88 (4) *575.00* 167.00

The 1p has no period after the value.

In the redrawn stamps the shading lines on the neck are not completed at the left, leaving an irregular white line along that side.

Variety "LA" joined exists on Nos. 84-86, 88, 90, 91, 93, 97, 98, 102.

On No. 88 beware of faked perfs.

A7

A8

1890-92 *Perf. 12½, 13*

89 A7 ½p green 14.00 2.00
a. ½p pale green 18.50 2.00
b. ½p deep blue green 8.00 2.00
90 A6 1p orange red 8.75 .50
a. Imperf, pair 325.00 350.00
b. Double impression 750.00
91 A6 2p gray blue 9.50 .50
a. 2p pale blue 11.50 1.00
92 A8 2½p rose carmine 17.00 2.75
93 A6 3p brown ('92) 9.50 4.25
94 A4 4p orange 27.50 4.75
a. "PENGE" for "PENCE" 150.00 30.00
b. 4p orange yellow 30.00 5.50
c. As "b," "PENGE" for "PENCE" 160.00 42.50
d. 4p yellow 17.50 4.75
e. As "d," "PENGE" for "PENCE" 110.00 32.50
95 A4 6p green 11.50 2.50
96 A6 2sh red brown 45.00 57.50
a. 2sh pale brown 55.00 62.50
Nos. 89-96 (8) 142.75 74.75

The ½p and 3p exist imperf.

1895 Wmk. 69 *Perf. 12½, 13*

Thick Paper

98 A6 1p orange 5.00 .75
a. 1p reddish vermilion 5.00 .75
99 A6 2p gray blue 6.75 .75

Perf. 12

100 A4 1sh pale violet 42.50 25.00
Nos. 98-100 (3) 54.25 26.50

A9

A10

Moiré on Back

1895 Unwmk. *Perf. 12½, 13*
101 A9 ½p green 11.00 7.00
a. Without moire 80.00
b. ½p deep green 10.50 6.00
102 A6 1p orange 3.00 2.75
a. "PE" missing 325.00 350.00
b. 1p reddish vermilion 2.75 2.75

Wmk. 68
103 A9 ½p green 3.50 2.00
a. ½p deep green 3.50 2.00
b. Printed on both sides 300.00
c. Double impression —
104 A10 1p orange 4.00 .50
a. 1p pale red 8.00 .75
105 A10 2p gray blue 37.50 .50

Wmk. 69
Thick Paper
106 A9 ½p green, perf 12½ 3.00 6.00
a. Perf 13 3.00 6.00
b. Perf 12 45.00
c. 1p deep green, perf 12 45.00

1895-96 Unwmk. Thin Paper
Crown and Q Faintly Impressed
107 A9 ½p green 2.50 6.00
108 A10 1p orange 3.50 2.25
108A A6 2p gray blue 13.00 *175.00*

A11

A12

A13

1895-96 Wmk. 68
109 A11 1p red 8.00 .75
110 A12 2½p rose 25.00 6.00
a. 2½p carmine 25.00 6.00
111 A13 5p violet brown 30.00 6.00
111A A11 6p yellow green *22,500.*

Only a few used examples of No. 111A are known, and readable cancels are from 1902. It is suggested that this otherwise unissued design was accidentally included in the plate of No. 120.

A14

A15

A16

A17

A18

A19

TWO PENCE:
Type I — Point of bust does not touch frame.
Type II — First redrawing. The top of the crown, the chignon and the point of the bust touch the frame. The forehead is completely shaded.
Type III — Second redrawing. The top of crown does not touch the frame, though the chignon and the point of the bust do. The forehead and the bridge of the nose are not shaded.

1897-1900 *Perf. 12½, 13*
112 A14 ½p deep green 5.50 8.50
a. Perf. 12 175.00
113 A15 1p red 3.00 .60
a. Perf. 12 8.50 4.00
114 A16 2p gray blue (I) 8.00 7.50
a. Perf. 12 1,100. 7.50
115 A17 2½p rose 18.00 30.00
116 A17 2½p violet, *blue* 10.00 3.50
117 A15 3p brown 8.50 3.25
118 A15 4p bright yellow 12.50 3.50
119 A18 5p violet brown 9.00 3.25
120 A15 6p yellow green 8.00 3.75
121 A19 1sh lilac 15.00 4.00
a. 1sh light violet 15.00 4.00
122 A19 2sh turq blue 35.00 50.00
Nos. 112-122 (11) 132.50 117.85

See Nos. 130-140.

1898 *Serrated Roulette 13*
123 A15 1p scarlet 19.00 8.00
a. Serrated and perf. 13 10.00 7.00
b. Serrated in black 18.00 14.00
c. Serrated without color and in black 20.00 *27.50*
d. Same as "b," and perf. 13 80.00 *100.00*
e. Same as "c," and perf. 13 100.00 110.00

Victoria — A20

1899 Typo. *Perf. 12, 12½, 13*
124 A20 ½p blue green 3.50 2.75
a. ½p green, perf 12 120.00 65.00
b. ½p pale green 9.50 4.25

Unwatermarked stamps are proofs.

"Australia" — A21

NINE PENCE:
Type I — "QUEENSLAND" 18x1 ½mm.
Type II — "QUEENSLAND" 17½x1 ¼mm.

1903 Wmk. 70 *Perf. 12½*
125 A21 9p org brn & ultra, II 55.00 8.00
a. Type I 42.50 8.00

See No. 128.

Type of 1882
1903-06 Wmk. 68 *Perf. 12, 12½-13*
Typographed, Perf. 12½-13 Irreg. ('03)
125B A5 5sh rose 200.00 92.50
125C A5 £1 dark green 2,250. 750.00

Lithographed, Perf. 12 ('05-'06)
126 A5 5sh rose 165.00 110.00
127 A5 £1 dark green 575.00 140.00
c. Perf. 12½-13 Irreg. 1,100. 180.00

1907 Typo. Wmk. 13 *Perf. 12½*
128 A21 9p yel brn & ultra, I 25.00 5.00
a. Type II 80.00 6.50
b. Perf. 11, type II 5,500. 825.00

1907 Wmk. 68 *Perf. 12½, 13*
129 A16 2p ultra, type II 11.00 6.00
129A A18 5p dark brown 16.00 6.50
b. 5p olive brown 12.50 4.75

1907-09 Wmk. 12
130 A20 ½p deep green 2.25 *4.75*
131 A15 1p red 3.25 .30
a. Imperf., pair 425.00
132 A16 2p ultra, II 32.50 3.75
133 A16 2p ultra, III 4.00 .30
134 A15 3p pale brown 22.00 3.00
135 A15 4p bright yellow 11.50 4.75
136 A15 4p gray black ('09) 25.00 6.75
137 A18 5p brown 35.00 19.00
a. 5p olive brown 20.00 22.50
138 A15 6p yellow green 21.00 4.50
139 A19 1sh violet 21.00 3.75
140 A19 2sh turquoise bl 55.00 37.50

Wmk. 12 Sideways
Litho.
141 A5 2sh6p dp org 45.00 52.50
a. 2sh6p dull orange ('10) 80.00 95.00
b. 2sh6p reddish orange ('12) 200.00 *240.00*
142 A5 5sh rose 85.00 70.00
a. 5sh deep rose ('10) 110.00 110.00
b. 5sh carmine red ('12) 275.00 *300.00*
143 A5 10sh dark brown 150.00 80.00
a. 10sh sepia ('12) 450.00 325.00
144 A5 £1 blue green 425.00 140.00
a. £1 dp blue green ('10) 600.00 375.00
b. £1 yellow green ('12) 1,900. 1,500.
Nos. 130-144 (15) 937.50 430.85

POSTAL FISCAL STAMPS

Authorized for postal use from Jan. 1, 1880. Authorization withdrawn July 1, 1892.

Used values are for examples with postal cancellations used from Jan. 1, 1880 through June 30, 1892.

Beware of stamps with a pen cancellation removed and a fake postmark added.

Queen Victoria — PF1

1866-74 Engr. Unwmk. *Perf. 13*
AR1 PF1 1p blue 105.00 47.50
AR2 PF1 6p violet 250.00 175.00
AR3 PF1 1sh green 240.00 140.00
AR4 PF1 2sh brown 260.00 140.00
AR5 PF1 2sh 6p red 475.00 275.00
AR6 PF1 5sh yellow 925.00 375.00
AR7 PF1 6sh yellow *1,250.*
AR8 PF1 10sh yel grn 925.00 325.00
AR9 PF1 20sh rose 1,250. *500.00*

Wmk. 68
AR10 PF1 1p blue 52.50 *47.50*
AR11 PF1 6p violet 115.00 *115.00*
AR12 PF1 6p blue 425.00 325.00
AR13 PF1 1sh green 125.00 92.50
AR14 PF1 2sh brown 200.00 110.00
AR15 PF1 5sh yellow 650.00 225.00
AR16 PF1 10sh yel grn 925.00 *325.00*
AR17 PF1 20sh rose 1,250. *500.00*

Queen Victoria — PF2

1872-73 Wmk. 69 *Perf. 13*
AR18 PF2 1p lilac 35.00 29.00
AR19 PF2 6p brown 175.00 87.50
AR20 PF2 1sh green 200.00 105.00
AR21 PF2 2sh blue 325.00 140.00
AR22 PF2 2sh 6p ver 400.00 200.00
AR23 PF2 5sh org brn 275.00 120.00
AR24 PF2 10sh brown 600.00 *225.00*
AR25 PF2 20sh rose 1,100. *325.00*

Perf. 12
AR26 PF2 1p lilac 35.00 29.00
AR27 PF2 6p brown 175.00 87.50
AR28 PF2 2sh blue 325.00 140.00
AR29 PF2 2sh 6p ver 200.00 100.00
AR30 PF2 5sh org brn 275.00 125.00
AR31 PF2 10sh brown 600.00 *225.00*
AR32 PF2 20sh rose 1,100. *325.00*

Unwmk.
Perf. 13
AR33 PF2 1p lilac 40.00 20.00
AR34 PF2 6p lilac 200.00 100.00
AR35 PF2 6p brown 175.00 77.50
AR36 PF2 1sh green 115.00 47.50
AR37 PF2 2sh blue 140.00 *115.00*
AR38 PF2 2sh 6p ver 250.00 125.00
AR39 PF2 5sh org brn 400.00 140.00
AR40 PF2 10sh brown 650.00 225.00
AR41 PF2 20sh rose 1,100. 325.00

Perf. 12
AR42 PF2 1p lilac 40.00 20.00
AR43 PF2 6p lilac 200.00 100.00
AR44 PF2 6p brown 175.00 77.50
AR45 PF2 1sh green 115.00 47.50
AR46 PF2 2sh blue 140.00 115.00
AR47 PF2 2sh 6p ver 250.00 125.00
AR48 PF2 5sh org brn 400.00 140.00
AR49 PF2 10sh brown 650.00 225.00
AR50 PF2 20sh rose 1,100. 325.00

Queen Victoria — PF3

1878-79 Engr. Unwmk. *Perf. 12*
AR51 PF3 1p violet 275.00 140.00

Wmk. 68
AR52 PF3 1p violet 175.00 105.00

SEMI-POSTAL STAMPS

Queen Victoria, Colors and Bearers — SP1

SP2

Perf. 12, 12½
1900, June 19 Wmk. 68
B1 SP1 1p red lilac 150.00 135.00
On cover 250.00
B2 SP2 2p deep violet 400.00 300.00
On cover 500.00
Nos. B1-B2 on one cover *900.00*

These stamps were sold at 1sh and 2sh respectively. The difference was applied to a patriotic fund in connection with the Boer War.

REGISTRATION STAMPS

R1

Clean-Cut Perf. 14 to 16
1861 Wmk. 5 Engr.
F1 R1 (6p) olive yellow 675.00 125.00
a. Horiz. pair, imperf. vert. *8,000.*

Rough Perf. 14 to 16
F2 R1 (6p) dull yellow 110.00 72.50

1864 *Perf. 12½ to 13*
F3 R1 (6p) golden yellow 125.00 50.00
a. Imperf.
b. Double impression 2,750. 2,750.

The reprints are watermarked with a small truncated star and perforated 12.

SOUTH AUSTRALIA

ˈsauth o-ˈstrāl-yə

LOCATION — Central part of southern Australia
GOVT. — British Colony
AREA — 380,070 sq. mi.
POP. — 358,346 (1901)
CAPITAL — Adelaide

South Australia was one of the six British colonies that united in 1901 to form the Commonwealth of Australia.

12 Pence = 1 Shilling
20 Shillings = 1 Pound

Values for unused stamps are for examples with original gum as defined in the catalogue introduction.

Very fine examples of Nos. 10-60 and O1-O60 will have perforations slightly cutting into the framelines or design on one or more sides due to the narrow spacing of the stamps on the plates.

Stamps with perfs clear on all sides are scarce to rare and will command higher to substantially higher prices.

Watermarks

Wmk. 6 — Star with Long Narrow Points

Wmk. 7 — Star with Short Broad Points

Wmk. 70 — Crown and V

Wmk. 72 — Crown and SA

Wmk. 73 — Crown and SA, Letters Close

Wmk. 74 — Crown and Single-lined A

Queen Victoria — A1

1855-56 Engr. Wmk. 6 *Imperf.*
London Print

1 A1 1p dark green 9,750. 525.
2 A1 2p dull carmine 825. 100.
3 A1 6p deep blue 4,250. 200.
4 A1 1sh violet ('56) *26,500.*

No. 4 was never put in use. Nos. 1 and 3 without watermark are proofs.

Six examples each of Nos. 1-4 were hand-stamped "CANCELLED" in oval in 1855-56 by the printers, Perkins Bacon, for presentation to members of Sir Rowland Hill's family. Values, *from* $12,500.

1856-59 Local Print

5 A1 1p dp yel grn ('58) *9,750.* 625.00
 a. 1p yellow green ('58) *8,750.* 750.00
6 A1 2p blood red 3,250. 90.00
 a. Printed on both sides *1,400.*
 b. 2p orange red ('56) 2,400. 92.50
7 A1 2p pale red ('57) 775. 55.00
 a. Printed on both sides *900.00*
8 A1 6p slate blue ('57) 4,400. 200.00
9 A1 1sh orange ('57) 11,250. 500.00
 a. Printed on both sides — —
 b. 1sh red orange — 775.00

1858-59 *Rouletted*

10 A1 1p yel grn ('59) 1,050. 70.00
 a. Horiz. pair, imperf. between — —
 b. 1p pale yellow green ('59) 1,050. 75.00
11 A1 2p pale red ('59) 375.00 22.50
 a. Printed on both sides *875.00*
12 A1 6p slate blue 850.00 70.00
13 A1 1sh orange ('59) 1,900. 55.00
 c. Printed on both sides *2,000.*

See Nos. 14-16, 19-20, 25-26, 28-29, 32, 35-36, 41-43, 47, 51-52, 69-70, 73, 113, 118. For overprints see Nos. O1-O2, O5, O7, O9, O11-O13, O17, O20, O27, O30, O32, O39-O40, O42, O52, O76, O85.

A2

A3

Surcharge on #22-24, 34, 49-50

1860-69 *Rouletted*

14 A1 1p dl bl grn 150.00 55.00
 a. 1p deep green 575.00 90.00
 b. 1p bright green 145.00 55.00
15 A1 1p sage green 165.00 55.00
 a. 1p deep yellow green ('69) 300.00
 b. 1p pale sage green ('65) 145.00
16 A1 2p ver ('62) 165.00 5.50
 a. Horiz. pair, imperf. btwn. 4,000. 775.00
 b. Rouletted and perf. all around *2,750.* *700.00*
 c. 2p pale red 275.00 4.25
 d. As "c," printed on both sides — 575.00
 e. 2p bright vermilion ('64) 165.00 5.25
18 A2 4p dull vio ('67) 175.00 45.00
19 A1 6p grnsh bl ('63) 275.00 4.75
20 A1 6p dull blue 350.00 7.50
 a. 6p sky blue 275.00 7.75
 b. 6p Prussian blue 1,050. 57.50
 c. Horiz. pair, imperf btwn. *3,250.*
 d. 6p ultramarine 275.00 4.95
 e. Horiz. pair, imperf. btwn. (#20f) — *2,500.*
 f. 6p indigo blue — 75.00
 g. Rouletted and perf. all around (#20f) *575.00*
 h. 6p violet blue 450.00 8.00
 i. 6p violet ultramarine ('68) 425.00 7.00
21 A3 9p gray lilac ('69) 165.00 10.50
 a. Double impression — —
 b. Horiz. pair, imperf between 4,500.
 c. Rouletted and perf. all around *2,900.* *275.00*
22 A3 10p on 9p red org (Bl) ('66) 500.00 50.00
23 A3 10p on 9p yel (Bl) ('67) 750.00 35.00
24 A3 10p on 9p yel (Blk) ('69) 3,750. 90.00
 a. Inverted surcharge — *7,500.*
 c. Printed on both sides — *1,250.*
 d. Rouletted x perf. 10 —
24E A1 1sh yellow ('61) 1,375. 35.00
 f. Vert. pair, imperf. btwn. — 6,000.
25 A1 1sh lake brn ('65) 350.00 14.00
 a. Horiz. pair, imperf. btwn. — *2,500.*
26 A1 1sh brown ('63) 425.00 35.00
 a. 1sh chestnut ('64) 375.00 12.50
 b. 1sh gray brown ('63) 450.00 35.00
27 A2 2sh car ('67) 550.00 37.50
 a. Vert. pair, imperf. btwn. *2,750.*

There are six varieties of the surcharge "TEN PENCE" in this and subsequent issues.

Nos. 16b, 20g, 21c, 28a, 32c, 33a are rouletted remainders that were later perforated.

See Nos. 31, 33, 46, 48, 53, 63, 68, 72, 74, 112, 113B, 119-120. For surcharges & overprints see Nos. 34, 44-45, 49-50, 59, 67, 71, O4, O6, O8, O10, O16-O19, O18, O21, O26, O28-O29, O31, O33, O36-O38, O41, O41B, O43, O53. Compare with design A6a.

1867-72 *Perf. 11½ to 12½xRoulette*

28 A1 1p blue green 575.00 72.50
 a. Rouletted and perf. all around 775.00
29 A1 1p grayish green ('70) 425.00 32.50
 a. 1p bright green ('68) 375.00 27.50
 b. 1p pale bright green ('67) 400.00 32.50
31 A2 4p dull violet ('68) 3,250. 175.00
 a. 4p purple ('69) — 145.00
32 A1 6p Prus blue 900.00 22.00
 a. 6p sky blue 950.00 22.00
 b. Printed on both sides — —
 c. Rouletted and perf. all around — *425.00*
 d. 6p indigo blue ('69) 1,000. 29.00
 e. As "d," rouletted and perf. all around — *550.00*
33 A3 9p gray lilac ('72) — *300.00*
34 A3 10p on 9p yel (Bl) ('68) 1,500. 40.00
 a. Printed on both sides — *1,250.*
35 A1 1sh chestnut ('68) 475.00 27.50
36 A1 1sh lake brown ('69) 475.00 25.00
 a. Rouletted and perf. all around — —

Nos. 44-45 Surcharged

1867-74 *Perf. 11½-12½*

41 A1 1p yel grn 185.00 25.00
42 A1 1p blue green 190.00 25.00
 a. Printed on both sides
 b. Horiz. pair, imperf between 1,150.
 c. 1p pale bright green ('68) 400.00 75.00
 d. 1p gray green ('68) 350.00 75.00
43 A1 2p vermilion 1,500.
44 A2 3p on 4p sky blue (Blk) ('70) 625.00 20.00
 a. 3p on 4p ultra, black surcharge 165.00 10.50
 b. Surcharge omitted *45,000.* *22,500.*
 c. Double surcharge 4,000.
 d. Surcharged on both sides 3,250.
 e. Rouletted — *1,500.*
 f. 3p on 4p Prussian blue ('71) *925.00*
46 A2 4p dull violet 110.00 9.25
 a. 4p dull purple ('68) 120.00 17.50
47 A1 6p Prussian blue 325.00 8.00
 a. 6p sky blue 650.00 12.50
 b. Imperf. vert., pair —
 c. Horiz. pair, imperf x perf 11½ *2,500.*
 d. 6p indigo ('69) 350.00 20.00
48 A3 9p red lilac ('72) 120.00 9.00
 a. 9p violet 220.00 9.00
 b. 9p red violet 220.00 9.50
 c. Printed on both sides *925.00*
49 A3 10p on 9p yel (Bl) ('68) *2,200.* 55.00
50 A3 10p on 9p yel (Blk) ('69) 450.00 75.00
51 A1 1sh dp brn 185.00 12.50
52 A1 1sh red brown 200.00 12.50
 a. 1sh chestnut 220.00 21.00
 b. 1sh lake brown ('68) 240.00 20.00
53 A2 2sh carmine 175.00 14.00
 a. Printed on both sides 800.00
 b. Horiz. pair, imperf. vert. —
 c. 2sh pale rose pink ('69) 2,200. 190.00
 d. 2sh deep rose pink ('69) — 125.00
 e. 2sh carmine red ('69) 190.00 22.50

Perf. 10

42e A1 1p brt grn ('71) 300.00 22.50
42f A1 1p pale br grn ('70) 350.00 22.50
42g A1 1p gray green ('70) 350.00 25.00
44g A2 3p on 4p pale ultra (Blk) ('71) 625.00 19.00
44h A2 3p on 4p ultra (Blk) ('71) 170.00 10.00
44i A2 3p on 4p Pruss bl (Blk) ('71) *1,100.*
45 A2 3p on 4p sl bl (Red) ('70) 1,400. 115.00
46b A2 4p dull lilac ('70) 190.00 12.50
46c A2 4p dull pur ('71) 190.00 12.50
47e A1 6p br blue ('70) 375.00 20.00
47f A1 6p indigo ('71) 525.00 18.50
52c A1 1sh chest ('71) 350.00 45.00

Perf. 10x11½-12½, 11½-12½x10, or Compound

42h A1 1p pale br grn 350.00 24.00
 i Printed on both sides —
42j A1 1p deep green 200.00 12.50
42k A1 1p gray green 325.00 19.00
44j A2 3p on 4p ultra (Blk) 575.00 90.00
46d A2 4p dull lilac — 23.00
46e A2 4p slate lilac 200.00 21.00
47g A1 6p Prus blue 275.00 9.50
47h A1 6p br Pruss blue 300.00 12.00
50a A3 10p on 9p yel (Blk) 300.00 57.50
52d A1 1sh chestnut 400.00 90.00
53f A2 2sh carmine 350.00 70.00
53g A2 2sh rose pink — 250.00

See Nos. 67, O14, O28, O36.

A6

A6a

1868 Typo. Wmk. 72 *Rouletted*

54 A6a 2p orange red 160.00 3.50
 a. Imperf.
 b. Printed on both sides 775.00
 c. Horiz. pair, imperf. btwn. 1,400.
 d. 2p deep brick red 170.00 7.50

1869 *Perf. 11½ to 12½xRoulette*

55 A6a 2p orange red *200.00*

1870 *Perf. 10xRoulette*

56 A6a 2p orange red 550.00 42.50

Perf. 10, 11½, 12½ and Compound

1868-75

57 A6 1p bl grn ('75) 110.00 8.50
58 A6a 2p orange red 25.00 1.25
 a. Printed on both sides 450.00
 b. Horiz. pair, imperf. vert.

Engr.

59 A3 10p on 9p yel (Bl) *1,800.*

1869 Typo. Wmk. 6 *Rouletted*

60 A6a 2p orange red 190.00 25.00
 a. Imperf.
 b. Printed on both sides

Perf. 11½ to 12½xRoulette

61 A6a 2p orange red *2,250.* 135.00

Perf. 11½ to 12½

61B A6a 2p orange red — *1,250.*

See Nos. 62, 64-66, 97-98, 105-106, 115-116, 133-134, 145-146. For surcharges & overprints see Nos. 75, O3, O22-O25, O34-O35, O44-O47, O49, O55-O56, O62-O63, O68-O69, O74, O78-O79.

1871 Wmk. 70 *Perf. 10*

62 A6a 2p orange red 200.00 55.00

Engr.

63 A2 4p dull violet 5,750. 325.00
 a. Printed on both sides *4,750.*

Examples of the 4p from edge of sheet sometimes lack watermark.

Perf. 10, 11½, 12½ and Compound

1876-80 Typo. Wmk. 73

64 A6 1p green 40.00 1.75
65 A6a 2p orange 50.00 .60
66 A6a 2p blood red ('80) 325.00 6.75
 Nos. 64-66 (3) 415.00 9.10

See Nos. 97-98, 105-106, 115-116, 133-134, 145-146.

No. 71

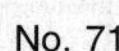

1876-84 Engr. Wmk. 7

67 A2 3p on 4p ultra (Blk) 175.00 32.50
 a. 3p on 4p deep blue 140.00 22.50
 b. Double surcharge *1,900.*
68 A2 4p reddish violet 100.00 6.50
 a. 4p dull violet 100.00 8.00
 b. 4p slate violet ('79) 175.00 17.50
69 A1 6p deep blue 150.00 5.00
 a. Horiz. pair, imperf. between —
 b. Imperf.

c. 6p bright blue, perf 10 225.00 19.00
d. 6p Prussian blue, perf 10 200.00 25.00
70 A1 6p pale ultra ('84) 110.00 3.00
71 A3 8p on 9p bister brn 225.00 11.00
a. 8p on 9p yellow brown 200.00 10.50
b. 8p on 9p gray brown ('80) 190.00 10.00
d. Double surcharge 2,750.
e. Vert. pair, imperf between 3,250.
72 A3 9p rose lilac 16.00 5.00
a. Printed on both sides 675.00
73 A1 1sh red brown 85.00 4.00
a. 1sh brown 90.00 4.00
b. 1sh chocolate 40.00 4.00
c. As "b," horiz. pair, imperf. btwn. 475.00
d. 1sh sepia 29.00 5.00
e. As "d," vert. pair, imperf. btwn. 650.00
f. 1sh reddish lake brown, perf 10 525.00
74 A2 2sh carmine 50.00 8.00
a. Horiz. pair, imperf. vert. *1,950.*
b. Imperf., pair

For overprint see No. O41.

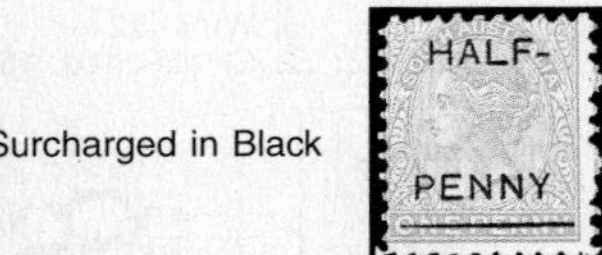

Surcharged in Black

1882 Wmk. 73 *Perf. 10*
75 A6 ½p on 1p green 15.00 12.50

A9

A10

A11

A12

Perf. 10, 11½, 12½ and Compound
1883-93 Typo.
76 A9 ½p chocolate brown 17.50 2.50
a. ½p red brown ('89) 9.50 2.40
b. ½p bister brown 6.00 4.00
78 A10 3p deep green ('93) 24.00 5.50
a. 3p olive green ('90) 26.00 5.50
b. 3p sage green ('86) 26.00 3.25
79 A11 4p violet ('90) 60.00 3.25
a. 4p aniline violet ('93) 52.50 7.50
80 A12 6p pale blue ('87) 65.00 4.00
a. 6p blue ('87) 52.50 1.40
Nos. 76-80 (4) 166.50 15.25

See Nos. 96, 100-101, 104, 108-109, 111. For surcharges & overprints see Nos. 94-95, 99, O48, O50-O51, O54, O57-O61, O64, O66-O67, O71, O73, O75, O81-O82.

A13

1886-96 *Perf. 11½ to 12½*
81 A13 2sh6p violet 90.00 10.00
a. 2sh6p bright aniline violet 100.00 10.00
82 A13 5sh rose 110.00 20.00
83 A13 10sh green 275.00 75.00
84 A13 15sh buff 875.00 275.00
85 A13 £1 blue 550.00 190.00
86 A13 £2 red brn 3,750. 550.00
87 A13 50sh rose red 4,500. 700.00
88 A13 £3 ol grn 5,500. 650.00
89 A13 £4 lemon 9,000. 1,450.
90 A13 £5 gray *8,750.*
90A A13 £5 brn ('96) *5,500.* 1,100.
91 A13 £10 bronze *8,500.* *1,500.*
92 A13 £15 silver *32,500.* 2,400.
93 A13 £20 lilac *37,500.* 2,750.

Perf. 10
81b A13 2sh6p violet 135.00 17.50
82a A13 5sh rose 155.00 20.00
83a A13 10sh green 300.00 90.00
84a A13 15sh buff 800.00 400.00
85a A13 £1 blue 575.00 200.00
86a A13 £2 red brown 4,000. 575.00
87a A13 50sh rose red 4,750. 800.00
88a A13 £3 olive green 6,000. 750.00
89a A13 £4 lemon 11,500. 525.00
90b A13 £5 gray *9,000.*
91a A13 £10 bronze *9,000.* *2,000.*
92a A13 £15 silver *32,500.*
93a A13 £20 lilac *40,000.*

For overprints see Nos. O83-O84.

#94, 99

#95

Perf. 10, 11½x12½ and Compound
1891 Brown Surcharge
94 A11 2½p on 4p green 8.00 3.00
a. "½" nearer the "2" 27.50 20.00
b. Pair, imperf. between *3,750.*
c. Fraction bar omitted 125.00 90.00

Carmine Surcharge
95 A12 5p on 6p red brn 20.00 7.00
a. No period after "D" 190.00

See No. 99. For overprints see Nos. O48, O57, O59.

Many stamps of the issues of 1855-91 have been reprinted; they are all on paper watermarked Crown and SA, letters wide apart, and are overprinted "REPRINT."

1893 Typo. *Perf. 15*
96 A9 ½p brown 12.50 1.60
a. Horiz. pair, imperf. btwn 400.00
b. Pair, perf. 12 btwn; perf. 15 around 350.00 75.00
97 A6 1p green 42.50 1.00
98 A6a 2p orange 25.00 1.00
a. Vert. pair, imperf. between 1,000.
99 A11 2½p on 4p green 55.00 3.00
a. "½" nearer the "2" 135.00 35.00
b. Fraction bar omitted
100 A11 4p gray violet 42.50 4.25
101 A12 6p blue 70.00 4.50
Nos. 96-101 (6) 247.50 15.35

Kangaroo, Palm — A16

Coat of Arms — A17

1894, Mar. 1
102 A16 2½p blue violet 45.00 6.50
103 A17 5p dull violet 45.00 4.00

See Nos. 107, 110, 117, 135-136, 147, 151. For overprints see Nos. O65, O70, O72, O80.

1895-97 *Perf. 13*
104 A9 ½p pale brown 5.50 .50
105 A6 1p green 12.50 .45
a. Vert. pair, imperf. between
106 A6a 2p orange 16.00 .25
107 A16 2½p blue violet 10.00 2.25
108 A10 3p olive green ('97) 6.00 3.50
109 A11 4p bright violet 6.50 1.00
110 A17 5p dull violet 11.00 1.75
111 A12 6p blue 11.00 1.60
a. 6p pale blue ('96) 11.00 1.60
Nos. 104-111 (8) 78.50 11.30

Some authorities regard the so-called redrawn 1p stamps with thicker lettering (said to have been issued in 1897) as impressions from a new or cleaned plate.

Perf. 11½, 12½, Clean-Cut, Compound
1896 Engr. Wmk. 7
112 A3 9p lilac rose 16.00 5.75
113 A1 1sh dark brown 27.50 5.00
a. Horiz. pair, imperf. vert. 475.00
c. Vert. pair, imperf. btwn. 650.00
113B A2 2sh carmine 42.50 7.25
Nos. 112-113B (3) 86.00 18.00

Adelaide Post Office — A18

1899 Typo. Wmk. 73 *Perf. 13*
114 A18 ½p yellow green 8.00 1.50
115 A6 1p carmine 10.00 1.50
a. 1p scarlet 9.00 1.50
116 A6a 2p purple 6.50 .25
117 A16 2½p dark blue 10.00 2.50
Nos. 114-117 (4) 34.50 5.75

See Nos. 132, 144. For overprint see No. O77.

Perf. 11½, 12½
1901 Engr. Wmk. 72
118 A1 1sh dark brown 24.00 17.50
a. 1sh red brown 27.50 37.50
b. Horiz. pair, imperf. vert.
119 A2 2sh carmine 27.50 12.50

1902
120 A3 9p magenta 21.00 25.00

A19

The measurements given in parentheses are the length of the value inscription in the bottom panel.

Perf. 11½, 12½ and Compound
1902-03 Typo. Wmk. 73
121 A19 3p ol grn (18.5mm) 17.50 3.00
a. 3p olive grn (20mm), perf 12 35.00 32.75
b. Wmk sideways *1,850.*
122 A19 4p red org (17mm) 30.00 4.50
a. 4p red org (17.5-18mm), perf 12 25.00 2.75
123 A19 6p blue grn (16-16.5mm) 12.50 3.00
a. 6p blue grn (15mm), perf 12 27.50 15.00
124 A19 8p ultra (value 19mm long) 9.00 17.50
124A A19 8p ultra (value 16½mm long) ('03) 12.50 17.50
b. "EIGNT" 2,400. *3,250.*
125 A19 9p claret 15.00 11.00
a. Vert. pair, imperf. between 2,750.
b. Horiz. pair, imperf. between
c. 9p claret, perf 12 125.00 27.50
126 A19 10p org buff 18.50 19.00
127 A19 1sh brn ('03) 27.50 9.00
a. Horiz. pair, imperf. btwn.
b. Vert. pair, imperf. btwn. 2,750.
c. "Postage" and denomination in red brown *1,100.* *1,000.*
128 A19 2sh6p purple 40.00 15.00
a. 2sh6p pale violet 90.00 50.00
129 A19 5sh rose 135.00 80.00
130 A19 10sh grn ('03) 225.00 100.00
131 A19 £1 blue 500.00 275.00
Nos. 121-131 (12) 1,043. 554.50

1904 *Perf. 12x11½*
132 A18 ½p yellow green 8.50 2.75
133 A6 1p rose 8.75 1.00
134 A6a 2p purple 15.00 1.00
135 A16 2½p dark blue 15.00 4.25
136 A17 5p dull violet 21.00 2.25
Nos. 132-136 (5) 68.25 11.25

A20

1904-08 *Perf. 12 and 12x11½*
137 A20 6p blue grn 42.50 3.25
a. Vert. pair, imperf. between *5,000.*
138 A20 8p ultra ('06) 17.50 9.00
139 A20 9p claret 24.00 7.00
139A A20 10p org buff ('07) 18.00 25.00
b. Vert. pair, imperf. between 4,250.
c. Horiz. pair, imperf. between 3,000. 3,250.
140 A20 1sh brown 32.50 4.25
a. Vert. pair, imperf between 2,750.
b. Horiz. pair, imperf between 3,000.
141 A20 2sh6p pur ('05) 85.00 42.50
142 A20 5sh scarlet 85.00 52.50
a. 5sh pale rose, Perf 12½, small holes ('10) 125.00 70.00
142B A20 10sh grn ('08) 225.00 *160.00*
143 A20 £1 dp blue 240.00 175.00
a. Perf 12½, small holes ('10) 350.00 200.00
Nos. 137-143 (9) 769.50 478.50

See Nos. 148-150, 152-157.

1906-12 Wmk. 74
144 A18 ½p green 16.00 1.40
145 A6 1p carmine 7.00 .25
146 A6a 2p purple 8.00 .30
a. Horiz. pair, imperf. between 2,500.
147 A16 2½p dk blue ('11) 11.00 13.50
148 A20 3p ol grn (value 19mm long) 15.50 6.25
a. Horiz. pair, imperf. between *6,000.*
149 A20 3p ol grn (value 17mm long) ('09) 17.00 11.00
150 A20 4p red org 25.00 9.00
151 A17 5p dl vio ('08) 30.00 6.75
152 A20 6p bl grn ('07) 8.50 9.50
a. Vert. pair, imperf. between 2,000. 2,750.
153 A20 8p ultra ('09) 13.50 *22.50*
154 A20 9p claret 22.50 6.00
a. Vert. pair, imperf. between 2,100.
b. Horiz. pair, imperf. between *5,000.*
155 A20 1sh brown 13.00 5.50
a. Horiz. pair, imperf. between *3,100.*
b. Vert. pair, imperf. between 3,750.
156 A20 2sh6p pur ('09) 80.00 32.50
a. 2sh6p pale violet, perf 12 ('10) 80.00 37.50
b. 2sh6p pale violet, perf 12½ ('12) 130.00 120.00
157 A20 5sh lt red ('12) 145.00 145.00
Nos. 144-157 (14) 412.00 269.45

OFFICIAL STAMPS

For Departments
Regular Issues Overprinted in Red, Black or Blue:

A. (Architect), A. G. (Attorney General), A. O. (Audit Office), B. D. (Barracks Department), B. G. (Botanical Gardens), B. M. (Bench of Magistrates), C. (Customs), C. D. (Convict Department), C. L. (Crown Lands), C. O. (Commissariat Officer), C. S. (Chief Secretary), C. Sgn. (Colonial Surgeon), C. P. (Commissioner of Police), C. T. (Commissioner of Titles), D. B. (Destitute Board), D. R. (Deed Registry), E. (Engineer), E. B. (Education Board),

G. P. (Government Printer), G. S. (Government Storekeeper), G. T. (Goolwa Tramway), G. F. (Gold Fields), H. (Hospital), H. A. (House of Assembly), I. A. (Immigration Agent), I. E. (Intestate Estates), I. S. (Inspector of Sheep), L. A. (Lunatic Asylum), L. C. (Legislative Council), L. L. (Legislative Library), L. T. (Land Titles), M. (Military), M. B. (Marine Board), M. R. (Manager of Railways), M. R. G. (Main Roads Gambierton), N. T. (Northern Territory), O. A. (Official Assignee), P. (Police), P. A. (Protector of Aborigines), P. O. (Post Office),

P. S. (Private Secretary), P. W. (Public Works), R. B. (Road Board), R. G. (Registrar General of Births, &c.), S. (Sheriff), S. C. (Supreme Court), S.G. (Surveyor General), S. M. (Stipendiary Magistrate), S. T. (Superintendent of Telegraph), T. (Treasurer), T. R. (Titles Registry), V. (Volunteers), V. A. (Valuator), V. N. (Vaccination), W. (Waterworks).

1868-74 Wmk. 6 *Rouletted*

O1 A1 1p green *350.00*
O2 A1 2p pale red *275.00*
O3 A6a 2p vermilion *120.00*
O4 A2 4p dull violet *275.00*
O5 A1 6p slate blue *275.00*
O6 A3 9p gray lilac *500.00*
O7 A1 1sh brown *275.00*
O8 A2 2sh carmine *275.00*

Perf. 11½ to 12½ x Roulette

O9 A1 1p green *275.00*
O10 A2 4p dull violet *850.00*
O11 A1 6p blue *210.00*
O12 A1 1sh brown *200.00*

Perf. 10, 11½, 12½ and Compound

O13 A1 1p green *160.00*
O14 A2 3p on 4p sl bl (Red) *750.00*
O15 A2 3p on 4p sl bl (Blk) *275.00*
O16 A2 4p dull violet *200.00*
O17 A1 6p deep blue *275.00*
O18 A3 9p violet *500.00*
O19 A3 10p on 9p yel (Blk) *500.00*
O20 A1 1sh brown *140.00* *160.00*
O21 A2 2sh carmine *100.00*

Rouletted
Wmk. 72

O22 A6a 2p orange *120.00*

Perf. 11 ½ x Roulette

O23 A6a 2p orange *160.00*
 a. Perf 10 x Roulette *275.00*

Perf. 10, 11½, 12½ and Compound

O24 A6a 2p orange *22.50*

Wmk. 70
Perf. 10

O25 A6a 2p orange *110.00*
O26 A2 4p dull violet *275.00*

For General Use

Overprinted in Black

Perf. 10, 11½, 12½ and Compound

1874 Wmk. 6

O27 A1 1p green — *500.00*
 a. 1p dp yel green, perf 11½-12½x10 3,500. *400.00*
 b. As "a," printed on both sides 1,275.
O28 A2 3p on 4p ultra 8,750. *3,000.*
 a. No period after "S" *4,000.*
O29 A2 4p dull violet 95.00 9.50
 a. Inverted overprint
 b. No period after "S" 85.00
 c. Perf. 11½-12½x10 3,000. 600.00
O30 A1 6p deep blue 240.00 10.00
 a. No period after "S" 110.00
 b. 6p Prussian blue, perf 11½-12½x10 175.00 12.00
O31 A3 9p violet *4,250.* *1,700.*
 a. No period after "S" *4,750.* *2,400.*
O32 A1 1sh red brown 125.00 10.00
 a. Double overprint 225.00
 b. No period after "S" 400.00 90.00
O33 A2 2sh carmine 275.00 30.00
 a. Double overprint
 b. No period after "S" 165.00
 c. 2sh carmine, perf 11½-12½x10 160.00

1874-75 Wmk. 72

O34 A6 1p blue green 240.00 37.50
 a. Inverted overprint
O35 A6a 2p orange 60.00 7.50

1876-86 Wmk. 7

O37 A2 4p dull violet 75.00 6.00
O38 A2 4p reddish vio 75.00 3.00
 a. Double overprint
 b. Inverted overprint 300.00
 c. Dbl. ovpt., one inverted
O39 A1 6p dark blue 150. 5.50
 a. Double overprint 190.00
 b. Inverted overprint
O40 A1 6p ultramarine 150.00 5.50
 a. Double overprint
 b. Inverted overprint
O41B A3 9p violet *9,000.*
O42 A1 1sh red brown 52.50 9.00
 a. Inverted overprint 750.00 275.00
 b. Double overprint
O43 A2 2sh carmine 300.00 9.00
 a. Double overprint 275.00
 b. Inverted overprint 325.00
 c. No period after "S" 90.00

1880-91 Wmk. 73

O44 A6 1p blue green 12.00 1.00
 a. Inverted overprint 40.00
 b. Double overprint 52.50 35.00
 c. Dbl. ovpt., one inverted *750.00*
O45 A6 1p yellow green 14.50 1.00
O46 A6a 2p orange 10.00 .80
 a. Inverted overprint 17.50
 b. Double overprint 70.00 32.50
 c. Overprinted sideways
 d. Dbl. ovpt., one inverted
 e. Dbl. ovpt., both inverted 95.00
O47 A6a 2p blood red 52.50 8.75
O48 A11 2½p on 4p green 57.50 8.75
 a. "½" nearer the "2" - 67.50
 b. Double overprint
 c. Pair, one without ovpt.
 Nos. O44-O48 (5) 146.50 20.30

1882-90 *Perf. 10*

O49 A6 ½p on 1p green 57.50 13.50
 a. Inverted overprint
O50 A11 4p violet 57.50 5.00
O51 A12 6p blue 20.00 1.25
 a. Double overprint
 b. No period after "S"
 Nos. O49-O51 (3) 135.00 19.75

Overprinted in Black

Perf. 10, 11½, 12½ and Compound

1891 Wmk. 7

O52 A1 1sh red brown 37.50 5.25
 a. No period after "S" 55.00
 b. 1sh lake brown, perf 11½-12½ 45.00 10.00
O53 A2 2sh carmine 90.00 10.00
 a. Double overprint
 b. No period after "S" 115.00

1891-95 Wmk. 73

O54 A9 ½p brown 12.50 6.25
 a. No period after "S" 87.50 52.50
O55 A6 1p blue green 17.50 2.00
 a. Double overprint 72.50 30.00
 b. No period after "S" 75.00 17.50
O56 A6a 2p orange 12.00 .50
 a. No period after "S" 45.00
O57 A11 2½p on 4p green 40.00 10.00
 a. "½" nearer the "2" 82.50 30.00
 b. Inverted overprint 145.00
O58 A11 4p violet 47.50 3.50
 a. Double overprint
O59 A12 5p on 6p red brn 50.00 14.50
O60 A12 6p blue 18.50 2.50
 a. Double overprint
 b. No period after "S"
 Nos. O54-O60 (7) 198.00 39.25

1893 *Perf. 15*

O61 A9 ½p brown 24.00 7.75
O62 A6 1p green 10.00 1.25
O63 A6a 2p orange 10.00 .50
 a. Inverted overprint 16.50
 b. Double overprint 22.50
O64 A11 4p gray violet 57.50 4.50
 a. Double overprint 160.00 32.50
O65 A17 5p dull violet 72.50 10.00
O66 A12 6p blue 24.00 3.00
 Nos. O61-O66 (6) 198.00 27.00

1896 *Perf. 13*

O67 A9 ½p brown 14.50 5.75
 a. Triple overprint 160.00
O68 A6 1p green 17.50 .60
 a. No period after "S" 52.50 10.00
O69 A6a 2p orange 17.50 .50
 a. No period after "S" 50.00 10.00
O70 A16 2½p blue violet 60.00 6.75
 a. No period after "S" 30.00
O71 A11 4p brt violet 60.00 3.00
 a. Double overprint 125.00 32.50
 b. No period after "S" 125.00 24.00
O72 A17 5p dull violet 62.50 12.00
 a. No period after "S"
O73 A12 6p blue 27.50 2.00
 a. No period after "S" 90.00 60.00
 Nos. O67-O73 (7) 259.50 30.60

On No. O67a, one overprint is upright, two sideways.

Same Overprint in Dark Blue

1891-95 *Perf. 10*

O74 A6 1p green 200.00 7.50
O75 A12 6p blue

Black Overprint

Perf. 11½, 12½, Clean-Cut

1897 Wmk. 7

O76 A1 1sh brown 35.00 5.50
 a. Double overprint
 b. No period after "S" 375.00

Overprinted in Black

1900 Wmk. 73 *Perf. 13*

O77 A18 ½p yellow green 12.50 5.75
 a. Inverted overprint 110.00
 b. No period after "S" 62.50
 c. As "b," inverted overprint —
O78 A6 1p carmine rose 11.50 1.60
 a. Inverted overprint 45.00 32.50
 b. Double overprint 475.00
 c. No period after "S" 82.50 22.50
O79 A6a 2p purple 12.50 .80
 a. Inverted ovpt. 40.00 22.00
 b. No period after "S" 77.50 21.00
O80 A16 2½p dark blue 75.00 18.50
 a. Inverted overprint 57.50
 b. No period after "S" 225.00
O81 A11 4p violet 60.00 4.50
 a. Inverted overprint 165.00
 b. No period after "S" 200.00
O82 A12 6p blue 20.00 4.50
 a. No period after "S" 110.00
 Nos. O77-O82 (6) 191.50 35.65

1901 *Perf. 10*

O83 A13 2sh6p violet *3,500.* *2,500.*
O84 A13 5sh rose *3,500.* *2,500.*

On Nos. O77-O82 the letters "O.S." are 11½mm apart; on Nos. O83-O84, 14½mm apart.

Overprinted in Black

1903 Wmk. 72 *Perf. 11½, 12½*

O85 A1 1sh red brown 47.50 11.00

TASMANIA

taz-ˈmā-nē-ə

LOCATION — An island off the south-eastern coast of Australia
GOVT. — British Colony
AREA — 26,215 sq. mi.
POP. — 172,475 (1901)
CAPITAL — Hobart

Tasmania was one of the six British colonies that united in 1901 to form the Commonwealth of Australia. The island was originally named Van Diemen's Land by its discoverer, Abel Tasman, the present name having been adopted in 1853. Stamps of Australia are now used.

12 Pence = 1 Shilling
20 Shillings = 1 Pound

Watermarks

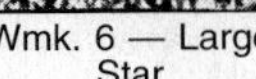

Wmk. 6 — Large Star

Wmk. 139 Double-lined Numeral

Wmk. 49 Double-lined Numeral

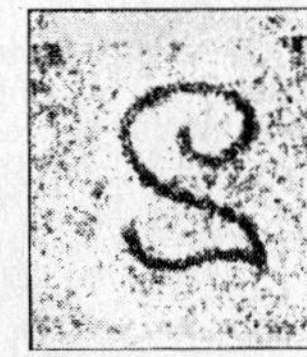

Wmk. 50 Single-lined "2"

Wmk. 75 Double-lined Numeral

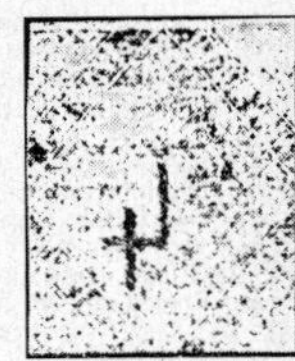

Wmk. 51 Single-lined "4"

Wmk. 52 — Single-lined "10"

Wmk. 70 — V and Crown

Wmk. 13 — Crown & Double-lined A

Wmk. 76 — TAS

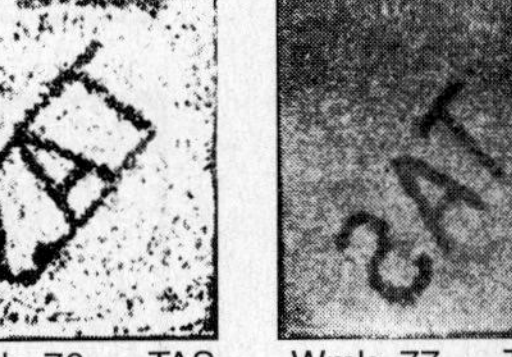

Wmk. 77 — TAS

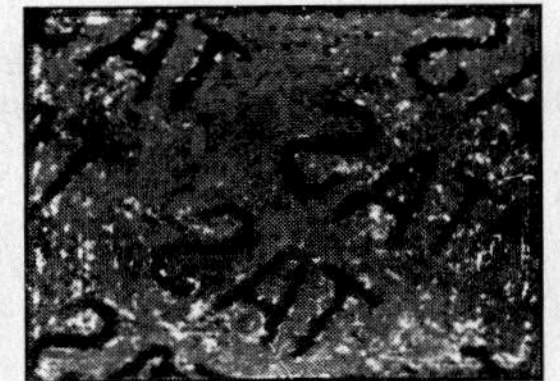

Wmk. 78 — Multiple TAS

Values for unused stamps are for examples with original gum as defined in the catalogue introduction except for Nos. 1-2b and 10 which are valued without gum as few examples exist with any remaining original gum. Very fine examples of Nos. 17-75a will have perforations touching the design on one or more sides due to the narrow spacing of the stamps on the plates. Stamps with perfs clear of the design on all four sides are scarce and command higher prices.

Queen Victoria
A1 A2

Unwmk.

1853, Nov. 1 Engr. *Imperf.*

1 A1 1p blue, fine impression, soft paper 11,500. 1,600.
 a. 1p blue, blurred impression, hard paper 11,000. 1,350.
2 A2 4p red orange 6,250. 550.00
 a. 4p yellow orange 5,750. 425.00
 Cut to shape 25.00

b. 4p orange, blurred impression ('55) 5,750. 425.00
Cut to shape 25.00

Twenty-four varieties of each.

No. 1 is the first printing, which was printed on a soft yellowish paper. Background lines are clear and distinct. The second printing, No. 1a, was made on thin hard white paper and demonstrates a wearing of the plate, with blurred background lines.

Two plates were made for No. 2. Plate I (Nos. 2, 2a) is finely engraved, with all lines clear and sharp. Plate II (No. 2b) is more coarsely done, with blurred impressions and thicker background lines.

The 4p on vertically laid paper is believed to be a proof. Value, unused, $7,500.

The reprints are made from defaced plates and show marks across the face of each stamp. They are on thin and thick, unwatermarked paper and thin cardboard; only the first are perforated. Nearly all the reprints of Tasmania may be found with and without the overprint "REPRINT."

Nos. 1-47A with pen or revenue cancellations sell for a small fraction of the price of postally used examples. Stamps are found with pen cancellation removed.

Queen Victoria — A3

1855 Wmk. 6 Wove Paper
4 A3 1p dark carmine 10,500. 1,000.
5 A3 2p green 5,750. 500.00
a. 2p deep green 5,750. 600.00
6 A3 4p deep blue 5,000. 145.00
a. 4p blue 5,000. 145.00

1856-57 Unwmk.
7 A3 1p pale red 13,500. 700.00
8 A3 2p emerald ('57) 16,500. 1,000.
9 A3 4p blue ('57) 2,650. 140.00
a. 4p deep blue ('57) 2,650. 140.00
b. 4p pale blue ('57) — 180.00

1856 Pelure Paper
10 A3 1p brown red 8,250. 800.00

1857-69 Wmk. 49, 75
11 A3 1p carmine ('67) 375.00 32.50
a. 1p orange red ('65) 375.00 37.50
b. 1p brown red 625.00 42.50
c. Double impression 650.00 300.00
d. 1p brick red ('63) 450.00 42.50
e. Wmk. 50 (error) ('69) —
12 A3 2p sage green ('60) 400.00 95.00
a. 2p yellow green 950.00 125.00
b. 2p green — 67.50
c. 2p dull emerald green 150.00
d. As "b," double impression 325.00
13 A3 4p pale blue 425.00 30.00
a. 4p blue 425.00 32.50
b. Printed on both sides —
c. 4p deep blue — 95.00
d. As "a," double impression 275.00
e. As "c," double impression 315.00
g. 4p cobalt blue — 95.00
Nos. 11-13 (3) 1,200. 157.50

See Nos. 17-19, 23-25, 29-31, 35-37, 39-41, 45-47A.

A4

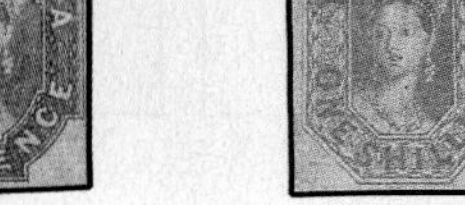
A4a

1858-67
14 A4 6p gray lilac ('63) 750.00 95.00
a. 6p red violet ('67) 1,150. 190.00
b. Double impression ('63) 450.00
c. 6p dull lilac 1,250. 100.00
15 A4 6p blue gray ('65) 1,150. 150.00
16 A4a 1sh vermilion *825.00* 90.00
Nos. 14-16 (3) 2,725. 335.00

No. 15 watermarked large star was not regularly issued.

Issued: No. 14c, 16, 1/58; No. 14, 4/63; No. 15, 2/65; No. 14a, 4/67.

1864 *Rouletted*
17 A3 1p carmine *950.00* 325.00
a. 1p brick red — 500.00
18 A3 2p yellow grn — 1,250.
19 A3 4p blue — 475.00
21 A4 6p gray lilac — 525.00
22 A4a 1sh vermilion — 1,350.

Values for Nos. 17-22 are for stamps showing rouletting on two or three sides. Examples with full roulettes on all four sides are rare.

1864-69 *Perf. 10*
23 A3 1p brick red 175.00 65.00
a. 1p carmine 145.00 55.00
b. 1p orange red 175.00 55.00
c. As "b," double impression —
24 A3 2p yellow green 825.00 160.00
a. 2p sage green 850.00 240.00
25 A3 4p blue 400.00 22.50
a. Double impression 240.00
26 A4 6p lilac 575.00 42.50
a. 6p red lilac 850.00 105.00
27 A4 6p slate blue 775.00 105.00
28 A4a 1sh vermilion 575.00 52.50
a. Horiz. pair, imperf. vert.
Nos. 23-28 (6) 3,325. 447.50

1864-91 *Perf. 12*
29 A3 1p carmine 120.00 25.00
a. 1p orange red 160.00 *40.00*
b. 1p brick red 140.00 62.50
c. Double impression —
d. Wmkd. "2" *3,000.*
As "d," pen cancel 325.00
30 A3 2p yellow green 625.00 100.00
a. 2p dark green 475.00 240.00
b. 2p sage green 475.00 240.00
31 A3 4p blue 325.00 26.00
a. 4p deep blue 325.00 25.00
b. 4p cobalt blue — 67.50
32 A4 6p red lilac 170.00 47.50
a. Horiz. pair, imperf between —
b. Vert. pair, imperf between —
c. 6p violet 400.00 32.50
d. As "c," Vert. pair, imperf between —
e. 6p purple ('84) 175.00 22.50
f. Horiz. pair, imperf between *2,200.* —
g. 6p dull claret ('91) 52.50 15.00
34 A4a 1sh vermilion 450.00 75.00
a. Double impression — 200.00
b. Horiz. pair, imperf. between *3,500.*

Perf. 10x12
29e A3 1p carmine *3,250.*
31c A3 4p blue *2,750.*

Perf. 12½
29f A3 1p carmine 100.00 25.00
29g A3 1p orange red 160.00 52.50
29h A3 1p brick red 160.00 52.50
30a A3 2p yellow green 775.00 180.00
30b A3 2p sage green 675.00 190.00
31d A3 4p blue 425.00 57.50
31e A3 4p bright blue 425.00 60.00
32h A4 6p purple 850.00 145.00
32i A4 6p slate violet 575.00 67.50
33 A4 6p slate blue 775.00 110.00
34c A4a 1sh vermilion 675.00 140.00

Perf. 11½
32j A4 6p dull lilac 240.00 25.00
32k A4 6p lilac 225.00 25.00
l. Pair, imperf between 1,750.
32m A4 6p dp slate lil ('75) 220.00 25.00
n. Imperf, pair — 1,400.
32o A4 6p brt vio ('78) 240.00 37.50
p. Double impression 160.00
q. Horiz. pair, imperf between *3,750.*
32r A4 6p dl reddish lil ('79) 200.00 45.00
34d A4a 1sh dl ver ('73) 325.00 70.00
e. Horiz. pair, imperf between
34f A4a 1sh brnsh ver ('73) 300.00 70.00

The reprints are on unwatermarked paper, perforated 11½, and on thin cardboard, imperforate and perforated.

1867 *Pin-perf. 5½ to 9½*
35 A3 1p carmine 1,250. 400.00
36 A3 2p yel grn 975.00
37 A3 4p blue 625.00
38 A4 6p gray 650.00
38A A4 6p red lilac 1,350.
38B A4a 1sh vermilion —

Pin-perf. 13½ to 14½
35a A3 1p brick red 800.00
35b A3 1p dull vermilion 800.00
35c A3 1p carmine
36a A3 2p yel grn 1,350.
37a A3 4p pale blue 700.00
38Ac A4 6p gray violet 1,375.
38Bd A4a 1sh vermilion

Oblique Roulette 14-15
39 A3 1p carmine 1,200.
a. 1p brick red 1,200.
b. 1p dull vermilion 1,250.
40 A3 2p yel grn 1,600.
41 A3 4p blue 1,250.
42 A4 6p gray 2,000.
43 A4 6p red lilac —
44 A4a 1sh vermilion 2,500.

Oblique Roulette 10-10½
39c A3 1p carmine *3,000.* 750.00
39d A3 1p brick red 850.00
40a A3 2p yellow green 1,250.
41a A3 4p blue 950.00
43a A4 6p gray lilac 1,750.

Oblique Roulette Imperf 10-10½
41b A3 4p blue 950.00

1868 *Serrate Perf. 19*
45 A3 1p carmine 850.00 250.00
46 A3 2p yellow green 850.00
47 A3 4p blue *1,900.* 250.00
47A A3 6p purple — 1,200.
47B A3 1sh vermilion —

Queen Victoria — A5

1870-71 Typo. Wmk. 50 *Perf. 11½*
48 A5 2p blue green 200.00 10.00
a. Double impression 5,500. 2,000.
b. Perf. 12 210.00 11.00
c. 2p green 325.00 20.00
d. As "c," perf. 12 200.00 11.00
e. As "d," imperf, pair —

See Nos. 49-75, 98, 108-109.

Wmk. 51 *Perf. 12*
49 A5 1p rose ('71) 150.00 60.00
a. Imperf., pair 1,300. 1,200.
50 A5 4p blue 1,350. 525.00

Wmk. 52
51 A5 1p rose 130.00 21.00
a. Imperf. pair 1,350. 1,350.
c. Perf. 11½ 1,350.
52 A5 10p black 27.50 52.50
a. Imperf. pair 750.00
b. Perf. 11½ 52.50 52.50

The reprints are on unwatermarked paper. The 4p has also been reprinted on thin cardboard, imperf and perf.

1871-76 Wmk. 76 *Perf. 11½*
53 A5 1p rose 17.00 2.50
a. Imperf.
c. Perf. 12 155.00 29.00
d. 1p carmine 22.50 3.50
e. 1p pink 22.50 3.50
f. As "d," perf. 12 170.00 30.00
g. As "e," perf. 12 170.00 14.00
53B A5 1p ver ('73) 325.00 80.00
54 A5 2p dp grn ('72) 80.00 2.75
a. 2p yellow green 375.00 5.00
b. 2p blue green 57.50 2.75
c. Imperf. pair 1,750.
d. 2p green, perf. 12 700.00 150.00
e. Double impression
55 A5 3p brown 80.00 6.00
a. 3p purple brown 80.00 5.00
b. As "a," imperf. pair 1,150.
c. 3p brownish purple 70.00 5.00
56 A5 3p red brn ('71) 90.00 5.00
a. 3p indian red 75.00 5.00
b. Imperf. pair 140.00
c. Vert. pair, imperf. horiz.
d. Perf. 12 145.00 24.00
e. 3p deep red brown, perf. 12 145.00 24.00
f. As "e," pair, imperf. between
57 A5 4p dull yel ('76) 150.00 45.00
a. Perf. 12 375.00 25.00
b. 4p ocher 90.00 10.00
c. 4p buff 75.00 12.00
58 A5 9p blue 32.50 9.00
a. Imperf. pair 575.00
b. Perf. 12 60.00 52.50
c. Double impression *3,500.*
59 A5 5sh bright violet 325.00 85.00
a. Imperf.
b. Horiz. pair, imperf. vert.
c. Perf. 12 500.00 475.00
d. 5sh purple 350.00 85.00
e. 5sh purple, perf. 12 575.00
Pen cancel 11.00
Nos. 53-59 (8) 1,100. 235.25

The reprints are on unwatermarked paper, the 5sh has also been reprinted on thin cardboard; all are perforated.

1878 Wmk. 77 *Perf. 14*
60 A5 1p rose 11.00 1.25
61 A5 2p deep green 12.00 1.25
62 A5 8p violet brown 15.00 10.00
Nos. 60-62 (3) 38.00 12.50

The 8p has been reprinted on thin unwatermarked paper, perforated 11½.

1880-83 *Perf. 12, 11½*
63 A5 3p indian red, perf. 12 10.00 9.00
a. Imperf. pair 475.00
b. Horiz. pair, imperf. between *2,500.*
c. Perf. 11½ 25.00 5.50
64 A5 4p lem, perf. 11½ ('83) 80.00 20.00
a. 4p olive yellow, perf. 11½ 160.00 30.00
b. Printed on both sides *1,600.*
c. Imperf.
d. 4p deep yellow, perf. 12 140.00 32.50

Type of 1871 Surcharged in Black

1889 *Perf. 14*
65 A5 ½p on 1p carmine 11.00 *25.00*
a. "al" sideways in surcharge *2,000.* *1,675.*

No. 65 has been reprinted on thin cardboard, perforated 12, with the surcharge "Halfpenny" 19mm long.

1889-96 *Perf. 11½*
66 A5 ½p red orange 3.25 3.50
a. ½p yellow orange 3.25 3.50
b. Perf. 12 5.50 *7.00*
67 A5 1p dull red 15.00 3.50
a. 1p vermilion 11.00 3.00
68 A5 1p car, perf. 12 8.25 3.25
a. 1p pink, perf. 12 42.50 15.00
b. 1p salmon rose, perf. 12 35.00 12.50
c. Imperf. pair 400.00 *375.00*

Perf. 12
69 A5 4p bister ('96) 16.00 7.50
70 A5 9p chalky bl ('96) 10.00 3.50
Nos. 66-70 (5) 52.50 21.25

1891 Wmk. 76 *Perf. 11½*
71 A5 ½p orange 80.00 50.00
a. ½p brown orange 52.50 45.00
b. Imperf. pair 325.00
c. Perf. 12 70.00 45.00
72 A5 1p salmon rose 25.00 11.00
a. 1p carmine, perf. 12 45.00 42.50
73 A5 4p ol bis, perf. 12 25.00 32.50
Nos. 71-73 (3) 130.00 93.50

See Nos. 98, 108-109.

Surcharged in Black

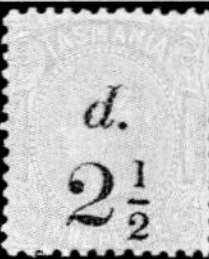

1891 Wmk. 77 *Perf. 11½*
Surcharge 14mm High
74 A5 2½p on 9p lt blue 17.50 9.25
a. Dbl. surcharge, one invtd. 850.00 *950.00*
b. Imperf. pair —

Perf. 12
Surcharge 15mm High
75 A5 2½p on 9p lt blue 8.50 7.75
a. Surcharged in blue 10.00 6.50

No. 74 has been reprinted on thin unwatermarked paper, imperforate. There is also a reprint on thin cardboard, in deep ultramarine, with surcharge 16½mm high, and perforated 12.

A8

A9

1892-99 Typo. *Perf. 14*
76 A8 ½p orange & vio 4.25 4.25
77 A9 2½p magenta 7.25 7.25
78 A8 5p pale bl & brn 11.50 7.25
79 A8 6p blue vio & blk 15.00 7.25
80 A8 10p red brn & grn ('99) 29.00 21.00
81 A8 1sh rose & green 15.00 7.25
82 A8 2sh6p brown & blue 47.50 35.00
83 A8 5sh brn vio & red 92.50 42.50
84 A8 10sh brt vio & brn 160.00 115.00
85 A8 £1 green & yel 700.00 450.00
Nos. 76-85 (10) 1,082. 696.75

No. 80 shows the numeral on white tablet. See Nos. 99, 110-111.

Lake Marion — A10

Mt. Wellington — A11

View of Hobart — A12

Tasman's Arch — A13

Spring River, Port Davey — A14

Russell Falls — A15

Mt. Gould and Lake St. Clair — A16

Dilston Falls — A17

1899-1900 Engr. Wmk. 78 *Perf. 14*

86	A10	½p dark green	16.00	12.00
87	A11	1p carmine	10.50	3.00
88	A12	2p violet	25.00	3.50
89	A13	2½p dark blue	35.00	17.50
90	A14	3p dark brown	18.00	9.00
91	A15	4p ocher	42.50	12.00
92	A16	5p ultramarine	47.50	29.00
93	A17	6p lake	45.00	37.50
		Nos. 86-93 (8)	239.50	123.50

See Nos. 94-97, 102-107, 114-117.

Perf. 11, 12½, 11x12½

1902-03 Litho., Typo. Wmk. 70

94	A10	½p green	8.00	2.75
95	A11	1p carmine	15.00	2.40
96	A11	1p dull red	22.50	3.00
97	A12	2p violet	14.00	1.40
98	A5	9p blue	15.00	7.25
a.		9p ultramarine	750.00	
b.		9p indigo	240.00	
c.		Perf. 11	15.00	15.00
d.		Perf 12½, wmkd. sideways	40.00	17.00
99	A8	1sh rose & green	32.50	10.50
a.		Perf. 11	75.00	75.00
		Nos. 94-99 (6)	107.00	27.30

Nos. 94, 97 are litho., Nos. 96, 98-99 typo. No. 95 was printed both ways.

No. 78 Surcharged in Black

1904 Wmk. 77 *Perf. 14*

100	A8	1½p on 5p blue & brn	2.75	2.75

Perf. 11, 12, 12½ and Compound

1905-08 Typo. Wmk. 13

102	A10	½p dull green	4.25	.95
a.		Booklet pane of 12		
103	A11	1p carmine	3.50	.60
a.		Booklet pane of 18		
104	A12	2p violet	18.00	.80
105	A14	3p dark brown	15.00	9.00
106	A15	4p ocher	25.00	7.25
107	A17	6p lake	70.00	12.50
108	A5	8p violet brown	35.00	16.00
109	A5	9p blue	130.00	8.00
110	A8	1sh rose & green	24.00	9.25
111	A8	10sh brt vio & brn	325.00	*350.00*
a.		Perf. 11	475.00	475.00
		Nos. 102-111 (10)	649.75	414.35

Nos. 104-107 also printed litho.

1911 Redrawn

114	A12	2p bright violet	15.00	7.50
a.		Perf. 11	17.00	8.50
b.		Compound perf. 11, 12½	85.00	27.50
c.		Compound perf. 12, 12½	575.00	
115	A15	4p dull yellow	72.50	72.50
a.		Perf. 11	82.50	
116	A17	6p lake	35.00	*55.00*
a.		Perf. 11	52.50	
b.		Compound perf. 11, 12½	525.00	
		Nos. 114-116 (3)	122.50	135.00

The redrawn 2p measures 33½x25mm instead of 32½x24½mm. There are many slight changes in the clouds and other parts of the design.

The 4p is much lighter, especially the waterfall and trees above it. This appears to be a new or cleaned plate rather than a redrawn one.

In the redrawn 6p there are more colored lines in the waterfall and the river and more white dots in the trees.

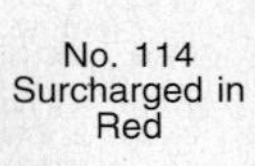
No. 114 Surcharged in Red

1912

117	A12	1p on 2p brt vio	2.75	2.75
a.		Perf. 11	3.50	3.50
b.		Compound perf. 12½ 11	240.00	*260.00*

POSTAL FISCAL STAMPS

Authorized for postal use by Act of November 1, 1882. Authorization withdrawn Nov. 30, 1900.

Used values are for examples with postal cancellations used from Nov. 1, 1882 through Nov. 30, 1900.

Beware of stamps with a pen cancellation removed, often regummed or with a fake postmark added.

PF1

PF2

St. George and the Dragon
PF3 PF4

1863-80 Engr. Wmk. 139 *Imperf.*

AR1	PF1	3p green	*450.00*	*200.00*
AR2	PF2	2sh 6p car	*450.00*	*180.00*
AR3	PF3	5sh green	*525.00*	*250.00*
AR4	PF3	5sh brown	*900.00*	*550.00*
AR5	PF4	10sh sal ('80)	*900.00*	*575.00*
a.		10sh orange	*1,200.*	*550.00*

For overprint see No. AR32.

Perf. 10

AR6	PF1	3p green	*475.00*	*300.00*
AR7	PF2	2sh 6p car	*450.00*	
AR8	PF3	5sh brown	*650.00*	*475.00*
AR9	PF4	10sh orange	*525.00*	

Perf. 12

AR10	PF1	3p green	*500.00*	*375.00*
AR11	PF2	2sh 6p car	*500.00*	*425.00*
AR12	PF3	5sh green	*500.00*	*350.00*
AR13	PF3	5sh brown	*950.00*	
AR14	PF4	10sh orange	*600.00*	*375.00*

Perf. 12½

AR15	PF1	3p green	*800.00*	
AR16	PF2	2sh 6p car	*375.00*	
AR17	PF3	5sh brown	*650.00*	
AR18	PF4	10sh orange	*575.00*	

Perf. 11½

AR19	PF1	3p green		
AR20	PF2	2sh 6p car	*750.00*	*425.00*
AR21	PF3	5sh green	*300.00*	*200.00*
AR22	PF4	10sh salmon	*350.00*	*300.00*
a.		10sh orange	*300.00*	*140.00*

Wmk. 77

Perf. 12

AR23	PF2	2sh 6p car	72.50	52.50

For overprint see No. AR33.

Duck-billed Platypus — PF5

1880 Engr. Wmk. 77 *Perf. 14*

AR24	PF5	1p slate	42.50	12.00
AR25	PF5	3p brown	29.00	7.75
AR26	PF5	6p lilac	140.00	21.00
AR27	PF5	1sh rose	200.00	35.00

For overprints see Nos. AR28-AR31.

Nos. AR24-AR27, AR2, AR23, 85 Overprinted "REVENUE"

1900, Nov. 15

AR28	PF5	1p slate	42.50	42.50
AR29	PF5	3p brown	42.50	*45.00*
AR30	PF5	6p lilac	*300.00*	140.00
AR31	PF5	1sh rose	*500.00*	240.00
AR32	PF2	2sh 6p car (#AR2)	*675.00*	525.00
AR33	PF2	2sh 6p car (#AR23)	*450.00*	
AR34	PF4	10sh orange	950.00	950.00
AR35	A8	£1 grn & yel (#85)	375.00	*350.00*

Nos. AR28-AR35 were not supposed to be postally used. Because of imprecise terminology, postal use was tolerated until all postal use of revenues ceased on Nov. 30, 1900.

Other denominations and watermarks were overprinted after postal use was no longer allowed.

VICTORIA

vik-'tōr-ē-ə

LOCATION — In the extreme southeastern part of Australia
GOVT. — British Colony
AREA — 87,884 sq. mi.
POP. — 1,201,341 (1901)
CAPITAL — Melbourne

Victoria was one of the six former British colonies which united on Jan. 1, 1901, to form the Commonwealth of Australia.

12 Pence = 1 Shilling
20 Shillings = 1 Pound

Unused values for Nos. 1-16 are for stamps without gum as these stamps are seldom found with original gum. Otherwise, unused values are for stamps with original gum as defined in the catalogue introduction.

Very fine examples of all rouletted, perforated and serrate perforated stamps from Nos. 9-109 and F2 will have roulettes, perforations or serrate perforations touching the design. Examples clear on four sides range from scarce to rare and will command higher prices.

Watermarks

Wmk. 6 — Large Star

Wmk. 80

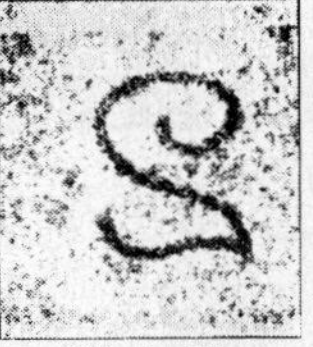
Wmk. 50

Wmk. 80a

Wmk. 81

Wmk. 139

Wmk. 49

Wmk. 75

Wmk. 70 — V and Crown

Wmk. 13 — Crown & Double-lined A

Queen Victoria — A1

A1 TYPES

1p:

Type I — "VICTORIA" very close to top of design, with very thin line of color between "VICTORIA" and frameline.

Type II — Thicker line of color between "VICTORIA" and frameline at top.

2p:

Type I — Border, two sets of nine wavy lines crisscrossing. Background, 22 groups of wavy triple lines below "VICTORIA."

Type II — Border, same. Background, 15 groups of wavy triple lines below "VICTORIA."

Type III — Border, two sets of five wavy lines crisscrossing. Background, same as type II.

3p:

Type I — Orb poorly defined, with white area at right and thicker at left. Central band of orb does not protrude at left.

Type II — Orb clearly defined, with white outlines at left and right. Central band of orb protrudes at left.

1850 Litho. Unwmk. *Imperf.*

1 A1 1p dull red, II 4,000. 225.00
a. 1p dull org ver, II 5,500. 750.00
b. 1p brownish red, II ('51) 1,500. 210.00
c. 1p dull brown, I *19,000.* 2,500.
d. 1p orange vermilion, I *30,000.* 5,500.
e. 1p orange brown, I 2,100.
2 A1 1p rose, II *3,500.* 200.00
a. 1p pink, II *1,750.* 190.00
b. 1p reddish brown, II ('51) *5,500.* 190.00
3 A1 3p blue, I *6,500.* 450.00
a. 3p light blue, II ('52) *2,250.* 110.00
b. 3p bright blue, I 7,500. 625.00
4 A1 3p indigo, II *3,000.* 100.00
a. 3p pale grnsh blue, II ('52) *3,500.* 210.00
Nos. 1-4 (4) 17,000. 975.00

Nos. 1-4 exist with and without frame line.

5 A1 2p lilac, I *7,500.* 550.00
a. 2p brn lilac, I *7,000.* 550.00
b. 2p orange brown, I *2,500.*
6 A1 2p brn lilac, II 2,500. 250.00
a. 2p gray lilac, II *6,000.* 200.00
7 A1 2p brn lilac, III *7,250.* 200.00
a. 2p gray lilac, III *11,000.* 500.00
b. Value omitted, III *17,500.*
8 A1 2p yel brn, III 3,000. 200.00

A used pair of No. 5b, the 2 pence, type I, orange brown shade, issued in January 1850, realized the equivalent of U.S. $10,400 at an Australian auction in 2004.

A used example of No. 7b, with "butterfly" cancellation, realized the equivalent of U.S. $12,910 at an Australian auction in 2004.

Rouletted 7

9 A1 1p vermilion *3,350.*
10 A1 3p blue 2,500. 250.00
a. 3p deep blue *2,500.* 300.00

Perf. 12

12 A1 3p blue *2,000.* 175.00
a. 3p deep blue *2,000.* 175.00

Victoria on Throne — A2

1852 Engr. *Imperf.*

14 A2 2p reddish brn 400.00 45.00
a. 2p chestnut 175.00
b. 2p purple brown 575.00 30.00

No. 14 was reprinted on paper with watermark 70, imperf. & perf. 12½, overprinted "REPRINT."

1854 Litho.

15 A2 2p gray brown 450.00 45.00
a. 2p purple black 37.50
16 A2 2p brown lilac 300.00 40.00
a. 2p red lilac — 37.50
b. As "a," "TVO" for "TWO" *10,000.* 1,500.

Fifty varieties.

A3

A4

1854-58 Typo.

17 A3 6p yellow orange 375.00 32.50
a. 6p dull orange 375.00 32.50
b. 6p reddish brown 725.00 72.50

See Nos. 19-20, 22-24A, 26-28.

Lithographed

18 A4 1sh blue 1,100. 35.00
a. 1sh greenish blue 1,250. 35.00
b. 1sh indigo blue — 180.00

See Nos. 21, 25.

Typographed

19 A3 2sh green 3,000. 250.00

1857-58 *Rouletted 7, 9½*

20 A3 6p orange — 87.50
a. 6p yellow orange — 100.00
b. 6p reddish brown — 115.00

Lithographed

21 A4 1sh blue — 160.00
a. 1sh greenish blue — 160.00

Typographed

22 A3 2sh green ('58) *7,000.* 675.00

Small Serrate Perf. 19

23 A3 6p orange — 125.00

Large Serpentine Perf. 10½

24 A3 6p orange — 125.00

Serrate x Serpentine Perf.

24A A3 6p orange — 200.00

1859 Litho. *Perf. 12*

25 A4 1sh blue 250.00 25.00
a. 1sh greenish blue 275.00 27.50
b. 1sh indigo blue — 52.50

Typographed

26 A3 2sh green 525.00 70.00

1861 Wmk. "SIX PENCE" (80)

27 A3 6p black 300.00 80.00

Wmk. Single-lined "2" (50)

1864 *Perf. 12, 13*

28 A3 2sh blue, *green* 350.00 13.00

A5

Wmk. Large Star (6)

1856, Oct. Engr. *Imperf.*

29 A5 1p green 250.00 42.50

1858 *Rouletted 5½-6½*

30 A5 6p blue 350.00 28.00
a. 6p light blue 450.00 45.00

Nos. 29 and 30 have been reprinted on paper watermarked V and Crown. They are imperforate and overprinted "REPRINT."

A6

1857-61 Typo. *Imperf.*

Wove Paper

31 A6 1p yellow green 175.00 25.00
a. Printed on both sides *2,750.*
b. 1p deep green 230.00 47.50
32 A6 4p vermilion 450.00 15.00
a. Printed on both sides *2,750.*
b. 4p brownish vermilion 425.00 15.00
33 A6 4p rose 375.00 15.00
a. 4p dull red 260.00 12.00

Rouletted 7 to 9½

34 A6 1p yellow green 625.00 140.00
35 A6 4p rose — 57.50
a. 4p vermilion 160.00
b. 4p dull red 60.00
35A A6 4p vermilion 575.00

Perf. 12

36 A6 1p yellow green — 500.00

Unwmk. *Imperf.*

37 A6 1p blue green 425.00 22.50
a. 1p emerald green 22.50
38 A6 2p lilac 400.00 21.00
a. 2p gray lilac 400.00 20.00
39 A6 4p rose *575.00* 47.50
a. 4p rose pink 575.00 42.50
b. 4p reddish pink 47.50

Examples of No. 39 printed in dull carmine on thin paper are regarded as printer's waste and of little value. They are also found printed on both sides.

Rouletted 7 to 9½

40 A6 1p emerald green 575.00 37.50
a. 1p pale emerald 525.00 35.00
41 A6 2p lilac 1,150. 725.00
42 A6 4p rose pink 400.00 11.50
a. Vert. pair, imperf. btwn. *750.00*
b. 4p reddish pink 20.00
c. 4p bright rose 400.00 11.50

Perf. 12

43 A6 1p blue green 225.00 20.00
a. 1p yellow green 325.00 24.00
b. Horiz. pair, imperf. btwn. —
c. As "a," on thin, glazed "Bordeaux" paper 240.00
44 A6 2p lilac 450.00
a. 2p gray lilac 400.00
45 A6 4p rose 300.00 8.00
b. Vert. pair, imperf. btwn. —

Rouletted 5½-6½

45C A6 4p dull rose 1,250.

Serrate Rouletted 19

45A A6 2p lilac 1,100. 600.00

Laid Paper

Imperf

46 A6 4p rose 825.00 35.00

Rouletted 5 to 7

47 A6 2p violet 275.00 10.50
a. 2p brown lilac 225.00 15.00
b. 2p dark lilac 300.00 25.00
48 A6 4p rose 250.00 7.25
a. 4p pale dull red, vertically laid paper 260.00 7.25
b. 4p pale dull red, horizontally laid paper *1,250.*
c. 4p dull rose red 225.00 6.25

Serrate Rouletted 19

48D A6 4p rose red *825.00*

Perf. 12

49 A6 1p green 300.00 25.00
a. Laid lines close together 35.00
50 A6 4p rose 200.00 15.00
a. Laid lines close together 13.00

Wove Paper

1860 Wmk. Value in Words (80)

51 A6 1p pale yellowish green 130.00 10.50
a. Wmk. "FOUR PENCE" (error) *9,750.*
b. 1p yellow green 125.00 7.25
52 A6 2p gray lilac 200.00 10.00
a. 2p brown lilac ('61) — 52.50
b. 2p bluish slate ('61) 200.00 9.50
c. 2p slate gray ('62) 9.50
d. 2p bluish gray ('63) 230.00 35.00

Wmk. "THREE PENCE" (80)

53 A6 2p bluish gray ('63) 225.00 25.00
a. 2p gray lilac ('62) 325.00 22.50

Single-lined "2" (50)

54 A6 2p lilac 300.00 18.00
a. 2p gray lilac 275.00 22.50
b. 2p brown lilac 225.00 21.00
c. As "a," wmkd. single-lined "6" *7,750.*
d. 2p gray violet ('63) 220.00 20.00
e. 2p slate ('63) 290.00 35.00

A7

1860 Unwmk. Laid Paper

56 A7 3p deep blue 625.00 77.50

Wmk. Value in Words (80)

Perf. 11½ to 12

1860-64 Wove Paper

57 A7 3p blue ('63) 240.00 12.50
a. "TRREE" instead of "THREE" in watermark 800.00
b. 3p pale blue ('61) 240.00 45.00
c. 3p bright blue ('61) 225.00 12.50
d. 3p deep blue ('64) 230.00 10.00
58 A7 3p claret 180.00 37.50
a. Perf. 13 240.00 47.50
59 A7 4p rose 200.00 7.75
a. 4p rose pink 12.50
b. 4p rose red 170.00 7.00
c. 4p rose carmine 12.50
60 A7 6p orange *5,750.* 350.00
61 A7 6p black 250.00 10.50
a. 6p gray black 275.00 9.25

Wmk. "FIVE SHILLINGS" (80)

62 A7 4p rose *3,000.* 30.00

Wmk. Single-lined "4" (80a)

1863 *Imperf.*

63 A7 4p rose — *175.00*

Rouletted

64 A7 4p rose *3,250.* 350.00

Perf. 11½ to 12

65 A7 4p rose 180.00 10.50

1863 Unwmk. *Perf. 12*

66 A7 4p rose 625.00 30.00
a. 4p rose pink, thin glazed "Bordeaux" paper 22.50
b. 4p rose, thick coarse paper 600.00 22.50

A8

A9

1861-63 Wmk. 80 *Perf. 11½ to 12*

67 A8 1p green 140.00 17.00
a. 1p olive green 16.00
68 A9 6p black 140.00 15.00
a. 6p gray black 145.00 17.00
b. 6p jet black 160.00 18.00

Wmk. Double-lined "1" (139)

69 A8 1p green 250.00 18.00
a. 1p dull green — 15.00
b. Horiz. pair, imperf between —

Wmk. Single-lined Figures (50)

70 A8 1p green 115.00 11.50
a. 1p apple green 115.00 11.50
b. 1p olive green 100.00 17.00
71 A9 6p gray black 140.00 10.00
a. 6p jet black — 11.50
b. 6p jet black, perf 13 170.00 11.50
c. 6p gray black, perf 13 170.00 11.50

The 1p and 6p of 1861-63 are known on paper without watermark but were probably impressions on the margins of watermarked sheets.

A10

A11

A12

A13

Wmk. Single-lined Figures (50, 80a, 81)

1863-67 *Perf. 11½ to 13*

74 A10 1p green 120.00 8.50
a. Double impression 1,500.
75 A10 2p gray lilac 120.00 15.00
a. 2p violet 115.00 11.50
76 A10 4p rose 140.00 5.00
a. Double impression 1,500.
77 A11 6p blue 115.00 4.25
78 A10 8p orange 700.00 115.00
79 A12 10p brn, *rose* 200.00 10.50
80 A13 1sh blue, *blue* 200.00 6.50
Nos. 74-80 (7) 1,595. 164.75

See Nos. 81-82, 84-96, 99-101, 108-112, 115-119, 124-126, 144, 188. Compare type A11 with type A54.

A14

Wmk. Double-lined "1" (139)

81 A10 1p green 125.00 7.00
82 A10 2p gray lilac 325.00 10.50
83 A14 3p lilac 325.00 100.00
84 A11 6p blue 115.00 9.50
Nos. 81-84 (4) 890.00 127.00

See Nos. 97, 113, 114, 155, 186. Compare type A14 with type A51.

Wmk. Double-lined "2" (49)

85 A11 6p blue *4,250.*

Wmk. Single-lined "4" (80a)

86 A10 1p green 200.00 30.00
87 A10 2p gray lilac 250.00 10.50
88 A11 6p blue *2,750.*

Wmk. Double-lined "4" (75)

89 A10 1p green 2,500. 160.00
90 A10 2p gray lilac 250.00 8.00
91 A10 4p rose 300.00 9.50
92 A11 6p blue 325.00 35.00

Wmk. Single-lined "6" (50)

93 A10 1p green 325.00 42.50
94 A10 2p gray lilac 350.00 11.50

Wmk. Single-lined "8" (50)

95 A10 1p green 300.00 27.50
96 A10 2p gray lilac 325.00 10.50
97 A14 3p lilac 250.00 57.50
99 A12 10p slate 1,000. 200.00

Wmk. "SIX PENCE" (80)

100 A10 1p green 1,150. 57.50
100A A10 2p slate gray *16,000.*
101 A11 6p blue 800.00 42.50
a. 6p indigo blue — 42.50

All values of the 1864-67 series except the 3p and 8p are known on unwatermarked paper. They are probably varieties from watermarked sheets which have been so placed on the printing press that some of the stamps escaped the watermark.

One example of the 2p gray lilac, type A10, is reported to exist with only "PENCE" of watermark 80 showing. Some believe this is part of the "SIX PENCE" watermark.

1870 Wmk. "THREE PENCE" (80)

108 A11 6p blue 475.00 17.50

Wmk. "FOUR PENCE" (80)

109 A11 6p blue 800.00 52.50

A15

1867-78 Wmk. (70) *Perf. 11½ to 13*

110 A10 1p green 115.00 5.75
a. 1p bright olive green 125.00 5.75
111 A10 2p lilac 110.00 5.25
a. 2p gray lilac 125.00 9.50
112 A10 2p lilac, *lilac* 130.00 14.00
113 A14 3p red lilac 400.00 65.00
a. 3p lilac 475.00 72.50
114 A14 3p orange 47.50 6.50
a. 3p yellow 77.50 7.75
b. 3p org brn, glazed paper ('78) 52.50 17.00
115 A10 4p rose 130.00 11.50
a. 4p dl rose, glazed paper ('79) 125.00 6.00
b. Wmk sideways 200.00
116 A11 6p blue 60.00 4.75
117 A11 6p ultra 72.50 5.00
a. 6p lilac blue 130.00 17.50
b. 6p light Prussian blue ('75) 145.00 4.75
118 A10 8p brn, *rose* 140.00 10.50
a. 8p choc, *pink* ('78) 160.00 11.50
b. Perf. 13x12 *460.00*
119 A13 1sh bl, *blue* 325.00 17.50
120 A15 5sh bl, *yel* 3,250. 500.00
121 A15 5sh bl & rose 400.00 32.50
a. Without blue line under crown 375.00 30.00
b. 5sh ind bl & car 425.00 42.50
122 A15 5sh ultra & rose 325.00 42.50

See Nos. 126, 144, 188. For surcharge see No. 124.

For additional stamps of type A15, see No. 191. Compare type A15 with type A58.

A16

1870 *Perf. 13*

123 A16 2p lilac 115.00 2.60
a. Perf. 12 125.00 3.50

No. 110 Surcharged in Red

1873, July 19 *Perf. 13, 12*

124 A10 ½p on 1p green 100.00 24.00
a. Perf. 12 125.00 24.00

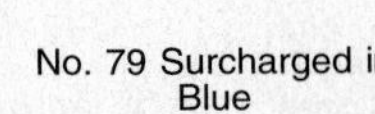

No. 79 Surcharged in Blue

1871 Wmk. Single-lined "10" (81)

125 A12 9p on 10p brn, *rose* 650.00 25.00
a. Double surcharge *2,500.*

A19

1873-78 Typo.

126 A10 8p brown, *rose* ('78) 175.00 10.50
127 A19 9p brown, *rose* 175.00 27.50

For additional stamps of type A19, see Nos. 128-129, 174-175. Compare type A19 with type A55.

1875 Wmk. V and Crown (70)

128 A19 9p brown, *rose* 200.00 27.50

No. 128 Surcharged in Blue

1876

129 A19 8p on 9p brn, *rose* 350.00 32.50

A21

A22

A23

A24

A25

1873-81 *Perf. 13, 12*

130 A21 ½p rose ('74) 24.00 2.00
a. ½p pink, glazed paper ('80) 24.00 2.00
b. ½p lil rose ('74) 27.50 2.90
131 A21 ½p rose, *rose* ('78) 70.00 42.50
132 A22 1p grn ('75) 52.50 3.25
a. 1p yel grn, glazed paper 52.50 3.50
133 A22 1p grn, *gray* ('78) 240.00 110.00
134 A22 1p grn, *yel* ('78) 160.00 30.00
135 A23 2p violet 77.50 1.30
a. 2p pale mv ('80) 77.50 1.25
b. 2p pale mv, glazed paper ('79) 77.50 1.60
136 A23 2p vio, *grnsh* ('78) 325.00 40.00
137 A23 2p vio, *buff* ('78) 300.00 40.00
137A A23 2p vio, *lil* ('78) — *1,200.*
138 A24 1sh bl, *bl* ('76) 130.00 6.75
a. 1sh brt bl, *bl*, glazed paper ('83) 145.00 12.00
139 A25 2sh bl, *grn* ('81) 240.00 35.00
a. 2sh ultra, *grnsh*, glazed paper ('84) 45.00
b. Wmk sideways 50.00

See Nos. 140, 156A-158, 184, 189-190. Compare design A21 with design A46, A24 with A56, A25 with A57.

1878 Double-lined Outer Oval

140 A23 2p violet 77.50 3.75
b. Vert. pair, lower stamp imperf horiz. *3,000.*

A26

A27

A28

1880-84 *Perf. 12½*

141 A26 1p green ('84) 140.00 22.50
142 A27 2p brown 50.00 1.40
143 A27 2p lilac 37.50 2.25
144 A10 4p car rose 260.00 15.00
a. 4p lilac rose 125.00 11.50
145 A28 4p car rose ('81) 115.00 10.00
a. 4p pink ('82) 115.00 9.50
Nos. 141-145 (5) 602.50 51.15

See Nos. 156, 185, 187. Compare design A26 with design A47, A27 with A49, A28 with A52.

A29

A30

A31

A32

A33

A34

1884-86

146 A29 ½p rose 22.50 2.25
a. ½p salmon ('85) 26.00 2.40
147 A30 1p green 29.00 2.40
a. 1p pea green 35.00 3.25
148 A31 2p violet 32.50 1.25
a. 2p lilac rose 32.50 1.25
149 A30 3p bister 20.00 2.40
a. 3p ocher 20.00 2.40
150 A32 4p magenta 110.00 6.25
a. 4p violet (error) *6,000.* *1,250.*
151 A30 6p bright blue ('85) 125.00 5.00
a. 6p ultramarine ('85) 85.00 4.75
b. 6p gray blue ('85) 82.50 4.75
152 A33 8p rose, *rose* 52.50 14.00
153 A34 1sh blue, *yel* 175.00 24.00
154 A33 2sh olive, *grn* 115.00 6.25
Nos. 146-154 (9) 681.50 63.80

See Nos. 177-178, 192A. Compare designs A31-A32 with designs A37-A38.

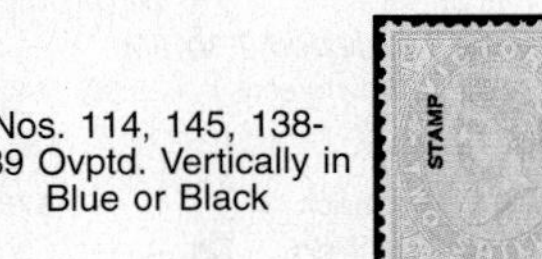

Nos. 114, 145, 138-139 Ovptd. Vertically in Blue or Black

1885

155 A14 3p orange (Bl) 115.00 47.50
156 A28 4p car rose (Bl) 105.00 72.50
156A A24 1sh bl, *bl* (Bl) *3,500.*
Revenue cancel *1,250.*
157 A24 1sh bl, *bl* (Bk) 175.00 37.50
158 A25 2sh bl, *grn* (Bk) 175.00 35.00
a. Wmk sideways 100.00 25.00
Nos. 155-156,157-158 (4) 570.00 192.50

Reprints of 4p and 1sh have brighter colors than originals. They lack the overprint "REPRINT."

A35

A36

A37

A38

A39

A40

1886-87 *Perf. 12½*

159 A35 ½p lilac 37.50 9.50
160 A35 ½p rose 17.50 1.40
160A A35 ½p scarlet 7.75 1.40
161 A36 1p green 16.00 2.25
162 A37 2p violet 20.00 .55
a. 2p red lilac 11.50 .70
b. Imperf. *1,100.*
163 A38 4p red 22.50 2.40
164 A39 6p blue 37.50 3.25
165 A39 6p ultra 32.50 1.10
166 A40 1sh lilac brown 37.50 3.75
Nos. 159-166 (9) 228.75 25.60

See No. 180.

A41

1889

167 A41 1sh6p blue 260.00 140.00
168 A41 1sh6p orange 35.00 15.00

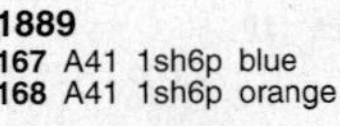

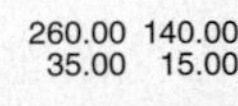

A42

Southern Cross — A43

Queen Victoria — A44

1890-95 *Perf. 12½*

169 A42 1p org brn 10.00 .75
a. 1p chocolate brown 12.50 1.10
170 A42 1p yel brn 12.50 .55
171 A42 1p brn org, *pink* ('91) 10.50 4.50
172 A43 2½p brn red, *yel* 19.00 1.75
173 A44 5p choc ('91) 15.00 3.75
174 A19 9p green ('92) 45.00 16.00
175 A19 9p rose red 32.50 6.00
a. 9p rose ('95) 37.50 11.50
176 A40 1sh deep claret 37.50 2.40
a. 1sh red brown 32.50 1.40
b. 1sh maroon 87.50 5.25
177 A33 2sh yel grn 37.50 17.50
178 A33 2sh emerald 35.00 19.00
Nos. 169-178 (10) 254.50 72.20

In 1891 many stamps of the early issues were reprinted. They are on paper watermarked V and Crown, perforated 12, 12½, and overprinted "REPRINT."

See Nos. 181, 183, 192. Compare type A43 with type A50, A44 with A53.

A45

1897

179 A45 1½p yellow green 6.00 *6.50*

See No. 182. Compare type A45 with type A48.

1899

180 A35 ½p emerald 25.00 5.75
181 A42 1p brt rose 11.50 .55
182 A45 1½p red, *yel* 5.75 3.50
183 A43 2½p dark blue 15.00 15.00
Nos. 180-183 (4) 57.25 24.80

1901

184 A21 ½p blue green 3.75 3.25
a. "VICTCRIA" 110.00 62.50
185 A27 2p violet 14.00 3.00
186 A14 3p brown org 22.50 50.00
187 A28 4p bister 42.50 25.00
188 A11 6p emerald 17.50 13.00
189 A24 1sh orange yel 87.50 65.00
190 A25 2sh blue, *rose* 72.50 55.00
191 A15 5sh rose red & bl 90.00 72.50
Nos. 184-191 (8) 350.25 286.75

1901

192 A42 1p olive green 11.50 7.50
192A A30 3p sage green 40.00 19.00

Nos. 192-192A were available for postal use until June 30, 1901, and thereafter restricted to revenue use.

A46 A47

A48 A49

A50 A51

A52 A53

A54 A55

A56

A57

A58

1901 ***Perf. 11, 12½ and Compound***

193 A46 ½p blue green 5.75 1.40
194 A47 1p rose red 4.50 .65
a. 1p rose 14.00 1.00
b. Wmk sideways 10.00 5.00
195 A48 1½p red, *yellow* 3.75 1.25
a. Perf. 11 110.00 110.00
196 A49 2p violet 21.00 1.10
197 A50 2½p blue 15.00 1.10
198 A51 3p brown org 15.00 2.50
a. Wmk sideways 20.00 8.00
199 A52 4p bister 10.50 1.25
200 A53 5p chocolate 17.50 1.10
201 A54 6p emerald 21.00 2.40
202 A55 9p rose 26.00 4.00
a. Wmk sideways 30.00 10.00
203 A56 1sh org yel 29.00 5.00
204 A57 2sh blue, *rose* 40.00 5.00
205 A58 5sh rose red & bl 110.00 35.00
a. 5sh carmine & blue 110.00 26.00
Nos. 193-205 (13) 319.00 61.75

See Nos. 209-229, 232.

King Edward VII
A59 A60

1901-05

206 A59 £1 deep rose 350.00 150.00
a. Perf. 11 ('05) 475.00 225.00
208 A60 £2 dk blue ('02) 700.00 450.00
a. Perf. 11 ('05) 2,250. 1,400.

See Nos. 230-231.

1903 **Redrawn**

209 A56 1sh yellow 35.00 5.75
a. 1sh orange 32.50 4.75

No. 209 has the network lighter than No. 203. In the latter the "P" and "E" of "POSTAGE" are in a position more nearly horizontal than on No. 209.

Perf. 11, 12x12½, 12½, 12½x11

1905-10 **Wmk. 13**

218 A46 ½p blue green 4.75 .75
219 A47 1p rose red 2.40 .35
a. 1p carmine rose 15.00 3.00
b. Wmk sideways 10.00 5.00
220 A49 2p violet 9.25 .75
a. 2p purple 10.00 .90
221 A50 2½p blue 5.75 1.00
222 A51 3p brown org 15.00 3.00
a. 3p dull yellow 17.50 3.00
223 A52 4p bister 12.50 1.75
224 A53 5p chocolate 12.50 4.75
225 A54 6p emerald 24.00 2.00
226 A55 9p orange brown 24.00 5.00
a. 9p brown rose 26.00 5.25
227 A55 9p car rose 17.50 3.00
228 A56 1sh yellow ('08) 24.00 4.50
229 A58 5sh orange red & ultra 130.00 26.00
a. 5sh rose red & ultra 140.00 32.50
230 A59 £1 pale red ('07) 450.00 240.00
a. £1 rose ('10) 350.00 240.00
231 A60 £2 dull blue 1,150. 725.00
Nos. 218-229 (12) 281.65 52.85

No. 220 Surcharged in Red

1912, July 1

232 A49 1p on 2p violet 1.75 1.25

POSTAL-FISCAL STAMPS

On Jan. 1, 1884, all postage and fiscal stamps were made available for either purpose. Fiscal stamps became invalid after June 30, 1901.

Used values are for examples with postal cancellations used from Jan. 1, 1884 through June 30, 1901.

Beware of stamps with a pen cancellation removed, often regummed or with a fake postmark added.

Stamps inscribed "Stamp Duty" that were issued primarily in postal rates in the normal postage stamp size are listed in the postage section (Nos. 146-178, 180-183, 192-192A). The stamps meeting primarily fiscal rates and in the larger fiscal stamp size, are listed here in the Postal-Fiscal section.

Stamps Inscribed "Stamp Statute"

Victoria — PF1

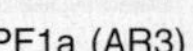
PF1a (AR3)

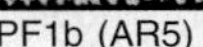
PF1b (AR5)

PF1c (AR6)

Coat of Arms — PF2

PF3

Wmk. V and Crown (70)

1870-83 **Typo.** ***Perf. 13***

AR1 PF1a 1p green 90.00 75.00
Revenue cancel 7.25
a. Perf. 12½ 140.00 120.00
AR2 PF1 3p lilac 1,150. 600.00
Revenue cancel 140.00
AR3 PF1a 4p red 1,000. 500.00
Revenue cancel 125.00
AR4 PF1a 6p blue 125.00 45.00
Revenue cancel 14.00
a. Perf. 12 140.00 35.00
Revenue cancel 10.50
AR5 PF1b 1sh blue, *blue* 140.00 45.00
Revenue cancel 14.00
a. Perf. 12 140.00 50.00
Revenue cancel 17.50
b. Perf. 12½ 140.00 45.00
Revenue cancel 14.00
c. Wmk. 50, perf. 13 140.00 32.50
Revenue cancel 11.50
d. Wmk. 50, perf. 12 160.00 37.50
Revenue cancel 13.00
AR6 PF1c 2sh blue, *grn* 225.00 130.00
Revenue cancel 30.00
a. Perf. 12 225.00 —
Revenue cancel 35.00
b. Wmk. 50, perf. 13 300.00 125.00
Revenue cancel 17.50
c. Wmk. 50, perf. 12 325.00 125.00
Revenue cancel 21.00
AR7 PF2 2sh6p org, *yel* 650.00 260.00
Revenue cancel 72.50
a. Perf. 12 650.00 260.00
Revenue cancel 72.50
b. Perf. 12½ — 300.00
Revenue cancel 87.50
AR8 PF1a 5sh blue, *yel* 600.00 140.00
Revenue cancel 72.50
a. Perf. 12 650.00 —
b. Perf. 12½ 650.00 140.00
Revenue cancel 72.50
AR9 PF1a 10sh brn, *rose* 1,600. 375.00
Revenue cancel 90.00
a. Perf. 12 —
b. Wmk. 50, perf. 13 1,600. 350.00
Revenue cancel 75.00
c. Wmk. 50, perf. 12
AR10 PF1a £1 lil, *yel* 1,250. 350.00
Revenue cancel 90.00
a. Perf. 12 1,150. 325.00
Revenue cancel 90.00
b. Perf. 12½ 1,150. 325.00
Revenue cancel 90.00
AR11 PF3 £5 blk, *grn* 10,000. 1,900.
Revenue cancel 135.00
a. Perf. 12 —
b. Perf. 12½ 10,000. 1,900.
Revenue cancel 150.00

Nos. AR1-AR12 distributed for postal use from Jan. 1, 1884 through Apr. 23, 1884.

No. AR1 Surcharged "½d/HALF"

1879-96

AR12 PF1 ½p on 1p grn 120.00 105.00
Revenue cancel 42.50

Stamps Inscribed "Stamp Duty"

PF4 PF5

PF6

PF7

PF8

PF9

PF10

PF11

PF12 PF13 PF14 PF15 PF16 PF17 PF18 PF19 PF20 PF21 PF22 PF23 PF24

PF25

PF26

PF27

PF28

Wmk. V and Crown (70)

1879-96 **Litho.** ***Perf. 13***

AR13	PF4	1p green	140.00	45.00
		Revenue cancel		14.00
a.		Perf. 12	140.00	45.00
		Revenue cancel		14.00
b.		Perf. 12½	—	—
AR14	PF8	1sh 6p pink	375.00	50.00
		Revenue cancel		21.00
a.		Perf. 12	—	65.00
		Revenue cancel		26.00
b.		Perf. 12½	—	—
AR15	PF11	3sh vio, *blue*	875.00	85.00
		Revenue cancel		21.00
a.		Perf. 12	1,000.	100.00
		Revenue cancel		21.00
b.		Perf. 12½	—	—
AR16	PF12	4sh orange	175.00	35.00
		Revenue cancel		11.00
a.		Perf. 12	175.00	35.00
		Revenue cancel		11.00
b.		Perf. 12½	—	—
AR17	PF14	6sh green	575.00	70.00
		Revenue cancel		12.50
a.		Perf. 12½	—	—
AR18	PF15	10sh brn, *pink*	925.00	175.00
		Revenue cancel		62.50
a.		Perf. 12	—	—
b.		Perf. 12½	—	—
AR19	PF16	15sh lilac	1,750.	325.00
		Revenue cancel		125.00
AR20	PF17	£1 orange	800.00	110.00
		Revenue cancel		25.00
a.		Perf. 12½	800.00	110.00
AR21	PF18	£1 5sh pink	2,400.	450.00
		Revenue cancel		125.00
AR22	PF19	£1 10sh olive	2,750.	275.00
		Revenue cancel		75.00
AR23	PF20	35sh lilac	*10,000.*	
		Revenue cancel		350.00
AR24	PF21	£2 blue	—	240.00
		Revenue cancel		37.50
AR25	PF22	45sh violet	5,000.	425.00
		Revenue cancel		92.50
AR26	PF23	£5 rose	9,000.	1,000.
		Revenue cancel		125.00
AR27	PF24	£6 blue, *pink*	—	1,500.
		Revenue cancel		175.00
AR28	PF25	£7 vio, *blue*	—	1,500.
		Revenue cancel		175.00
AR29	PF26	£8 scarlet, *yel*	—	1,700.
		Revenue cancel		200.00
AR30	PF27	£9 green, *grn*	—	1,700.
		Revenue cancel		200.00

Typo.

AR31	PF4	1p green	105.00	45.00
		Revenue cancel		8.75
a.		Perf. 12	105.00	45.00
		Revenue cancel		8.75
b.		Perf. 12½	—	—
AR32	PF5	1p brown	40.00	7.75
		Revenue cancel		1.40
a.		Perf. 12	40.00	9.25
		Revenue cancel		1.40
b.		Perf. 12½	—	—
AR33	PF6	6p blue	140.00	22.50
		Revenue cancel		5.75
a.		Perf. 12	140.00	37.50
		Revenue cancel		5.75
b.		Perf. 12½	—	—
AR34	PF7	1sh blue, *blue*	140.00	11.50
		Revenue cancel		5.75
a.		Perf. 12	140.00	14.00
		Revenue cancel		5.75
b.		Perf. 12½	140.00	13.00
		Revenue cancel		5.75
AR35	PF7	1sh blue, *yel,* perf 12½	200.00	45.00
		Revenue cancel		17.50
AR36	PF8	1sh 6p pink	260.00	50.00
		Revenue cancel		17.50
AR37	PF9	2sh blue, *grn*	325.00	45.00
		Revenue cancel		13.00
a.		Perf. 12	—	50.00
		Revenue cancel		13.00
b.		Perf. 12½	350.00	52.50
		Revenue cancel		13.00
AR38	PF10	2sh 6p org, perf 12½	175.00	37.50
a.		2sh6p yellow ('85)	115.00	17.50
b.		2sh6p lemon yellow ('92)	115.00	18.00
		Revenue cancel		5.75
AR39	PF11	3sh violet, *bl,* perf 12½	700.00	65.00
		Revenue cancel		14.00
AR40	PF11	3sh bister	125.00	29.00
		Revenue cancel		21.00
AR41	PF12	4sh org, perf 12½	140.00	26.00
		Revenue cancel		7.25
AR42	PF13	5sh claret, *yel*	110.00	11.50
		Revenue cancel		5.75
a.		Perf. 12	125.00	22.50
		Revenue cancel		5.75
b.		Perf. 12½	100.00	22.50
		Revenue cancel		5.75
AR43	PF13	5sh car rose	140.00	35.00
		Revenue cancel		7.25
AR44	PF14	6sh green	200.00	85.00
		Revenue cancel		16.00
AR45	PF15	10sh brn, *pink*	—	175.00
		Revenue cancel		57.50
a.		Perf. 12	—	—
b.		Perf. 12½	—	—
AR46	PF15	10sh green	325.00	65.00
		Revenue cancel		20.00
AR47	PF16	15sh brown	1,200.	145.00
		Revenue cancel		42.50
AR48	PF17	£1 org, *yel,* perf 12½	875.00	80.00
		Revenue cancel		25.00
a.		Perf. 12	1,100.	95.00
		Revenue cancel		30.00
AR49	PF18	£1 5sh pink	2,250.	160.00
		Revenue cancel		75.00
AR50	PF19	£1 10sh olive	1,750.	135.00
		Revenue cancel		50.00
AR51	PF21	£2 blue	1,350.	125.00
		Revenue cancel		27.50
a.		Perf. 12	—	200.00
		Revenue cancel		27.50
AR52	PF22	45sh gray lilac	5,000.	180.00
		Revenue cancel		62.50
AR53	PF23	£5 rose, perf. 12	—	900.00
		Revenue cancel		105.00
a.		perf. 12½	—	1,100.
		Revenue cancel		150.00
AR54	PF28	£10 lilac	5,500.	210.00
		Revenue cancel		62.50
a.		Perf. 12	5,500.	325.00
		Revenue cancel		62.50

Nos. AR49-AR52, AR54, used, are valued cto.

PF29

PF30

PF31

Wmk. V and Crown (70)

1879-1900 **Engr.** ***Perf. 12½***

AR55	PF29	£25 green	—	900.00
		Revenue cancel		110.00
a.		Perf. 13		—
b.		Perf. 12		—
AR56	PF30	£50 violet	—	975.00
		Revenue cancel		125.00
a.		Perf. 13		—
AR57	PF31	£100 red	—	1,000.
		Revenue cancel		225.00
a.		Perf. 13		—
b.		Perf. 12		—
		Revenue cancel		225.00

Typo.

AR58	PF29	£25 green	—	325.00
a.		Lithographed		—
		Revenue cancel		100.00
AR59	PF30	£50 violet	—	500.00
a.		Lithographed		—
		Revenue cancel		140.00
AR60	PF31	£100 red	—	650.00
a.		Lithographed		—
		Revenue cancel		225.00

Nos. AR55-AR60, used, are valued cto.

PF32

1887-90 **Typo.**

AR61	PF32	£5 cl & ultra	*4,000.*	175.00
		Revenue cancel		82.50
AR62	PF32	£6 blue & yel	*5,000.*	200.00
		Revenue cancel		90.00
AR63	PF32	£7 blk & red	*5,500.*	225.00
		Revenue cancel		110.00
AR64	PF32	£8 org & lil	*6,000.*	250.00
		Revenue cancel		110.00
AR65	PF32	£9 red & green	*6,500.*	275.00
		Revenue cancel		135.00

Nos. AR61-AR65, used, are valued cto.

SEMI-POSTAL STAMPS

SP1

Queen Victoria and Figure of Charity
SP2

Wmk. V and Crown (70)

1897, Oct. **Typo.** ***Perf. 12½***

B1 SP1 1p deep blue 27.50 27.50
B2 SP2 2½p red brown 140.00 110.00

These stamps were sold at 1sh and 2sh6p respectively. The premium was given to a charitable institution.

Victoria Cross — SP3

Scout Reporting
SP4

1900

B3 SP3 1p brown olive 125.00 75.00
B4 SP4 2p emerald 225.00 225.00

These stamps were sold at 1sh and 2sh respectively. The premium was given to a patriotic fund in connection with the South African War.

REGISTRATION STAMPS

R1

Unwmk.

1854, Dec. 1 **Typo.** ***Imperf.***

F1 R1 1sh rose & blue 2,500. 225.00

1857 ***Rouletted 7***

F2 R1 1sh rose & blue 8,750. 425.00

LATE FEE STAMP

LF1

Unwmk.

1855, Jan. 1 **Typo.** ***Imperf.***

I1 LF1 6p lilac & green 1,900. 275.00

POSTAGE DUE STAMPS

D1

Wmk. V and Crown (70)

1890 **Typo.** ***Perf. 12½***

J1 D1 ½p claret & blue 8.00 7.00
J2 D1 1p claret & blue 11.50 2.60
J3 D1 2p claret & blue 18.00 3.25
J4 D1 4p claret & blue 27.50 4.75
J5 D1 5p claret & blue 26.00 3.50
J6 D1 6p claret & blue 27.50 6.50
J7 D1 10p claret & blue 140.00 90.00
J8 D1 1sh claret & blue 90.00 14.00
J9 D1 2sh claret & blue 200.00 92.50
J10 D1 5sh claret & blue 300.00 140.00
Nos. J1-J10 (10) 848.50 364.10

1891-94

J11 D1 ½p lake & blue 5.50 *7.75*
J12 D1 1p brn red & blue ('93) 15.00 2.75
J13 D1 2p brn red & blue ('93) 26.00 2.00
J14 D1 4p lake & blue ('94) 22.50 11.50
Nos. J11-J14 (4) 69.00 24.00

1894-96

J15 D1 ½p bl grn & rose 9.50 3.00
J16 D1 1p bl grn & rose 9.00 3.00
J17 D1 2p bl grn & rose 18.00 3.50
J18 D1 4p bl grn & rose 18.00 3.00
J19 D1 5p bl grn & rose 22.50 22.50
J20 D1 6p bl grn & rose 20.00 14.00
J21 D1 10p bl grn & rose 45.00 20.00
J22 D1 1sh bl grn & rose 32.50 6.00
J23 D1 2sh yel grn & rose 115.00 37.50
J24 D1 5sh yel grn & rose 200.00 75.00
Nos. J15-J24 (10) 489.50 187.50

1897-99

J15a D1 ½p yel grn & pale scar 9.00 1.75
J16a D1 1p yel grn & pale scar 10.00 1.25
J17a D1 2p yel grn & pale scar 13.50 1.25
J18a D1 4p yel grn & pale scar 27.50 2.25
J19a D1 5p yel grn & pale scar 27.50 7.00
J20a D1 6p yel grn & pale scar 12.00 4.50
Nos. J15a-J20a (6) 99.50 18.00

1905-09 **Wmk. 13**

J25 D1 ½p yel grn & rose 10.00 *13.00*
a. ½p pale green & pink 24.00 22.50
J26 D1 1p yel grn & rose 12.00 4.50
a. 1p pale green & pink 92.50 11.50
J27 D1 2p yel grn & rose 29.00 5.25
J28 D1 4p yel grn & rose 35.00 21.00
Nos. J25-J28 (4) 86.00 43.75

A 5p with wmk. 13 exists but was not issued.

WESTERN AUSTRALIA

ˈwes-tərn o-ˈstrāl-yə

LOCATION — Western part of Australia, occupying about a third of that continent
GOVT. — British Colony
AREA — 975,920 sq. mi.
POP. — 184,124 (1901)
CAPITAL — Perth

Western Australia was one of the six British colonies that united on January 1, 1901, to form the Commonwealth of Australia.

12 Pence = 1 Shilling
20 Shillings = 1 Pound

Unused values for Nos. 1-10 are for stamps without gum as these stamps are seldom found with original gum. Otherwise, unused values are for stamps with original gum as defined in the catalogue introduction.

Very fine examples of all rouletted and perforated stamps from Nos. 6-34 have roulettes or perforations touching the design. Examples clear on all four sides range from scarce to rare and will command higher prices.

Watermarks

Wmk. 82 — Swan

Wmk. 83 — Crown and W A

Wmk. 70 — V and Crown

Wmk. 13 — Crown & Double-lined A

Wmk. 74 — Crown and Single-lined A

Swan
A1 A2

1854-57 **Engr.** **Wmk. 82** ***Imperf.***

1 A1 1p black 1,350. 275.

Litho.

2 A2 2p brown, *red* ('57) 4,000. 800.
a. 2p brown, *deep red* ('57) 4,250. 1,100.
b. Printed on both sides 4,250. 950.

See Nos. 4, 6-7, 9, 14-39, 44-52, 54, 59-61. For surcharges see Nos. 41, 55-56.

A3

A4

3 A3 4p blue 450. 275.
a. Frame inverted *95,000.*
As "a," cut to shape *27,500.*
b. 4p slate blue 3,750. 1,350.
4 A2 6p bronze ('57) *6,000.* *900.*
5 A4 1sh pale brown 550. 400.
a. 1sh dark brown 700. 450.
b. 1sh dark red brown 2,250. 1,000.
c. 1sh pale red brown 26,500. 4,000.

Engraved

Rouletted

6 A1 1p black 3,200. 750.

Lithographed

7 A2 2p brn, *red* ('57) *9,500.* 1,900.
a. Printed on both sides 2,300.
8 A3 4p blue — 675.
9 A2 6p bronze ('57) *12,500.* 2,000.
10 A4 1sh brown 5,000. 1,000.

The 1p, 2p, 4p and 6p are known with pin-perforation but this is believed to be unofficial.

No. 7a is only recorded used and with pin perforations.

1860 **Engr.** ***Imperf.***

14 A1 2p vermilion 140.00 130.00
a. 2p pale orange 140.00 130.00
15 A1 4p blue 325. *2,000.*
16 A1 6p dull green 2,100. 875.00

Rouletted

17 A1 2p vermilion 800.00 250.00
a. 2p pale orange 650.00 250.00
18 A1 4p deep blue 5,000. —
19 A1 6p dull green 4,500. 750.00

1861 ***Clean-Cut Perf. 14 to 16***

20 A1 1p rose 700.00 200.00
a. Imperf.
21 A1 2p blue 140.00 45.00
a. Imperf., pair
b. Horiz. pair, imperf. vert.
22 A1 4p vermilion 1,550. *2,400.*
a. Imperf.
23 A1 6p purple brn 525.00 92.50
a. Imperf.
24 A1 1sh green 875.00 140.00
a. Imperf.

Rough Perf. 14 to 16

24B A1 1p rose 300.00 65.00
24C A1 6p pur brn, *bluish* 3,500. 525.00
24D A1 1sh deep green 2,500. 425.00

Perf. 14

25 A1 1p rose 400.00 110.00
25A A1 2p blue 180.00 72.50
25B A1 4p vermilion 450.00 300.00

Unwmk. ***Perf. 13***

26 A1 1p lake 115.00 7.75
28 A1 6p violet 240.00 77.50

1865-79 **Wmk. 1** ***Perf. 12½***

29 A1 1p bister 110.00 10.00
30 A1 1p yel ocher 130.00 15.00
31 A1 2p yellow 125.00 4.75
a. 2p lilac (error) ('79) *20,000.* *17,500.*
b. 2p chrome yellow 160.00 11.00
32 A1 4p carmine 120.00 8.75
a. Double impression *42,500.*
33 A1 6p violet 160.00 11.50
a. 6p lilac 300.00 11.50
b. 6p red lilac 300.00 11.50
c. Double impression *27,500.*
34 A1 1sh brt grn 200.00 21.00
Handstamped "SPECIMEN" 175.00
a. 1sh sage green 525.00 45.00
Nos. 29-34 (6) 845.00 71.00

An unused example of No. 31a realized the equivalent of U.S. $12,330 at an Australian auction in 2005.

A used example of No. 31a realized the equivalent of U.S. $16,180 at an Australian auction in 2005.

An unused example of No. 32a, with short perforations, realized the equivalent of U.S. $38,530 at an Australian auction in 2005.

A used example of No. 33c realized the equivalent of U.S. $27,740 at an Australian auction in 2005.

1872-78 ***Perf. 14***

35 A1 1p bister 180.00 7.25
36 A1 1p yellow ocher 115.00 5.00
37 A1 2p yellow 115.00 2.40
38 A1 4p carmine 750.00 140.00
39 A1 6p lilac 200.00 6.50
Nos. 35-39 (5) 1,360. 161.15

A5

1872 **Typo.**

40 A5 3p red brown 72.50 7.25
a. 3p brown 72.50 8.50
Handstamped "SPECIMEN" 140.00

See Nos. 53, 92. For surcharges see Nos. 57, 69-72A.

No. 31 Surcharged in Green

1875 Engr. *Perf. 12½*

41 A1 1p on 2p yellow 625.00 80.00
  a. Pair, one without surcharge
  b. "O" of "ONE" omitted
  c. Triple surcharge *5,500.*

Forged surcharges exist.

1882 Wmk. 2 *Perf. 12*

44 A1 1p ocher yellow 125.00 8.00
46 A1 2p yellow 160.00 7.75
47 A1 4p carmine 300.00 60.00
48 A1 6p pale violet 575.00 60.00
  Nos. 44-48 (4) 1,160. 135.75

1882 *Perf. 14*

49 A1 1p ocher yellow 45.00 3.00
50 A1 2p yellow 50.00 3.00
51 A1 4p carmine 180.00 17.50
52 A1 6p pale violet 140.00 5.25
  a. 6p violet 140.00 6.50
  Handstamped "SPECIMEN" 160.00

Typographed

53 A5 3p red brown 14.00 4.50
  a. 3p brown 29.00 4.50
  Nos. 49-53 (5) 429.00 33.25

1883 Engr. *Perf. 12x14*

54 A1 1p ocher yellow 4,000. 300.00

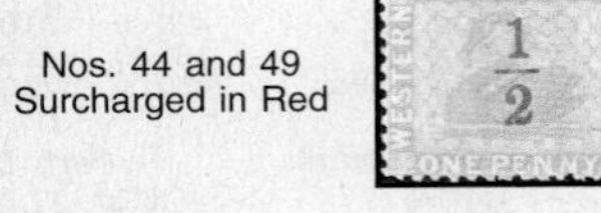

Nos. 44 and 49 Surcharged in Red

1884 *Perf. 12*

55 A1 ½p on 1p ocher yel 18.00 *32.50*

Perf. 14

56 A1 ½p on 1p ocher yel 30.00 *40.00*
  a. Thin fraction bar 97.50 *115.00*

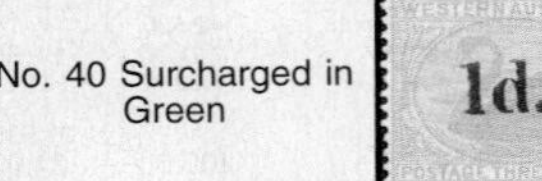

No. 40 Surcharged in Green

1885 Typo. Wmk. 1

57 A5 1p on 3p red brown 87.50 26.00
  a. 1p on 3p brown 115.00 27.50
  b. "1" with straight top 240.00 75.00
  c. As "a," "1" with straight top 275.00 75.00

A8

Wmk. Crown and C A (2)

1885 Typo. *Perf. 14*

58 A8 ½p green 7.25 1.25

See No. 89.

1888 Engr.

59 A1 1p rose 35.00 5.75
60 A1 2p slate 90.00 2.75
61 A1 4p red brown 130.00 37.50
  Nos. 59-61 (3) 255.00 46.00

A9

A10

A11 A12

1890-93 Typo.

62 A9 1p carmine rose 35.00 2.00
63 A10 2p slate 37.50 3.00
64 A11 2½p blue 20.00 3.25
65 A12 4p orange brown 14.00 2.75
66 A12 5p bister 15.00 5.00
67 A12 6p violet 21.00 6.50
68 A12 1sh olive green 26.00 7.50
  Nos. 62-68 (7) 168.50 30.00

See Nos. 73-74, 76, 80, 90, 94.

Nos. 40 and 53a Surcharged in Green

1893 Wmk. Crown and C C (1)

69 A5 1p on 3p red brown 16.00 7.75
  a. 1p on 3p brown 16.00 7.50
  b. Double surcharge *1,600.*

Wmkd. Crown and C A (2)

70 A5 1p on 3p brown 77.50 10.50

Nos. 40a and 53a Surcharged in Green

1895 Wmk. Crown and C C (1)

71 A5 ½p on 3p brown 13.00 *35.00*
  a. Double surcharge *1,250.*

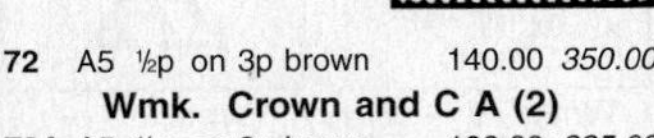

No. 72 Surcharged in Green and Red

72 A5 ½p on 3p brown 140.00 *350.00*

Wmk. Crown and C A (2)

72A A5 ½p on 3p brown 100.00 *225.00*

After the supply of paper watermarked Crown and C C was exhausted, No. 72A was printed. Ostensibly this was to provide samples for Postal Union distribution, but a supply for philatelic demands was also made.

Types of 1890-93 and

A15

1899-1901 Typo. Wmk. 83

73 A9 1p carmine rose 7.75 1.75
74 A10 2p yellow 29.00 3.50
75 A15 2½p blue ('01) 14.00 4.75
  Nos. 73-75 (3) 50.75 10.00

A16

A17

A18

A19

A20

A21

A22

Southern Cross — A23

Queen Victoria

A24 A25

Perf. 12½, 12x12½

1902-05 Wmk. 70

76 A9 1p car rose 22.00 1.00
  a. 1p salmon — —
  b. Perf. 11 400.00 35.00
  c. Perf. 12½x11 1,200. 675.00
77 A16 2p yellow 22.50 4.75
  a. Perf. 11 400.00 57.50
  b. Perf. 12½x11 *1,750.* *1,100.*
79 A17 4p org brn 29.00 4.00
  a. Perf. 11 1,400. 450.00
80 A12 5p ol bis, perf 12½ ('05) 175.00 115.00
  a. Perf. 11 90.00 *100.00*
81 A18 8p pale yel grn 30.00 4.75
82 A19 9p orange 50.00 17.50
  b. Perf. 11 175.00 *185.00*
83 A20 10p red 57.50 13.00
84 A21 2sh org red, *yel* ('06) 115.00 32.50
  a. Perf. 11 500.00 225.00
  b. 2sh orange brown, *yel* ('11) 77.50 19.00
  c. 2sh bright red, *yel* 130.00 19.00
  d. As "c," perf. 11 350.00 200.00
85 A22 2sh6p dk bl, *rose* 77.50 14.00
86 A23 5sh blue green 125.00 45.00
87 A24 10sh violet 300.00 130.00
  a. 10sh bright purple 725.00 400.00
88 A25 £1 brown org 450.00 225.00
  a. £1 orange 750.00 425.00
  Nos. 76-88 (12) 1,454. 606.50

Perf. 12½, 12x12½

1905-12 Wmk. 13

89 A8 ½p dp grn ('10) 8.00 *9.25*
  a. Perf 11 *2,750.*
90 A9 1p rose 18.00 1.75
  e. Perf. 11 55.00 21.00
  f. Perf. 12½x11 *1,100.* 475.00
91 A16 2p yellow 11.50 3.25
  a. Perf. 11 65.00 32.50
  b. Perf. 12½x11 *925.00* 525.00
92 A5 3p brown 37.50 4.75
  a. Perf. 11 29.00 9.50
  b. Perf. 12½x11 — 1,200.
93 A17 4p orange brn 35.00 12.00
  a. 4p bister brown 37.50 13.00
  b. Perf. 11 1,100. 290.00
94 A12 5p olive bis 29.00 15.00
  a. Perf. 11, pale olive bister 52.50 18.00
  b. Perf. 11, olive green 32.50 24.00
95 A18 8p pale yel grn ('12) 32.50 *82.50*
96 A19 9p orange 45.00 8.75
  b. Perf. 11 200.00 *240.00*
97 A20 10p red orange 37.50 35.00
98 A23 5s blue green 240.00 180.00
  Nos. 89-98 (10) 494.00 352.25

For surcharge see No. 103.

A26

A27

1906-07 Wmk. 83 *Perf. 14*

99 A26 6p bright violet 40.00 3.25
100 A27 1sh olive green 50.00 6.50

1912 Wmk. 74 *Perf. 11½x12*

101 A26 6p bright violet 21.00 19.00
102 A27 1sh gray green 45.00 29.00
  a. Perf. 12½ *2,750.*

No. 91 Surcharged

1912 Wmk. 13 *Perf. 12½*

103 A16 1p on 2p yellow 2.00 *2.50*
  a. Perf compound 12½x11 *750.00* *500.00*

Stamps of Western Australia were replaced by those of Australia.

POSTAL-FISCAL STAMPS

Postal use of the 1p telegraph stamp was authorized beginning Oct. 25, 1886.

Used values are for examples with postal cancellations.

Beware of stamps with a pen cancellation removed and a fake postmark added.

PF1

1886 Wmk. 1 *Perf. 14*

AR1 PF1 1p bister 65.00 9.25

Perf. 12½

AR2 PF1 1p bister 65.00 7.75

Authorized for postal use by the Post and Telegraph Act of Sept. 5, 1893 were the current revenue stamps through the 1sh value.

Beware of stamps with a pen cancellation removed and a fake postmark added.

Because the Act specified current stamps, postally used examples from the provisional issue of of 1881 are not included here.

PF2

1882 Wmk. 2 *Perf. 14*

AR3 PF2 1p purple 26.00 4.00
AR4 PF2 2p purple 260.00 100.00
AR5 PF2 3p purple 90.00 5.75
AR6 PF2 6p purple 105.00 7.75
AR7 PF2 1sh purple 180.00 15.00

The 6p is known postally used but was not authorized.

Wmk. 83

AR8 PF2 1p purple 22.50 4.50
AR9 PF2 3p purple 85.00 5.75
AR10 PF2 6p purple 85.00 6.00
AR11 PF2 1sh purple 180.00 22.50

Nos. AR7, AR11 have a rectangular outer frame and a circular frame around the swan.

Higher values are known with postal cancels, some postally used, but these were not authorized.

AUSTRALIA

o-'strāl-yə

LOCATION — Oceania, south of Indonesia, bounded on the west by the Indian Ocean

GOVT. — Self-governing dominion of the British Commonwealth

AREA — 2,967,909 sq. mi.

POP. — 6,866,590

CAPITAL — Canberra

Australia includes the former British colonies of New South Wales, Victoria, Queensland, South Australia, Western Australia and Tasmania.

12 Pence = 1 Shilling
20 Shillings = 1 Pound

Catalogue values for unused stamps in this country are for Never Hinged items, beginning with Scott 197 in the regular postage section, Scott C6 in the air post section, and Scott J71 in the postage due section.

Watermarks

Wmk. 8 — Wide Crown and Wide A

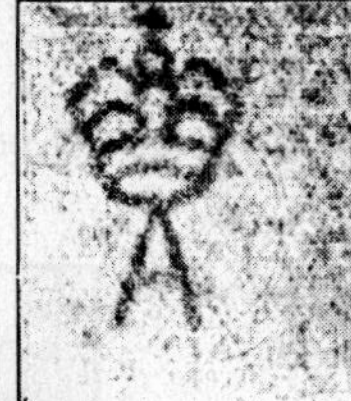

Wmk. 9 — Wide Crown and Narrow A

Wmk. 10 — Narrow Crown and Narrow A

Wmk. 11 — Multiple Crown and A

Wmk. 12 — Crown and Single-lined A

Wmk. 13 — Large Crown and Double-lined A

Wmk. 55 — Large Crown and NSW

Wmk. 203 — Small Crown and A Multiple

Wmk. 228 — Small Crown and C of A Multiple

Kangaroo and Map — A1

Die I — The inside frameline has a break at left, even with the top of the letters of the denomination.

Die II — The frameline does not show a break (repaired die).

Die III — The left inside frameline shows a break opposite the face of the kangaroo.

Die IV — As Die III, with a break in the top outside frameline above the "ST" of "AUSTRALIA." The upper right inside frameline has an incomplete corner.

Dies are only indicated when there are more than one for any denomination.

1913 Typo. Wmk. 8 *Perf. 11½, 12*

No.	Type	Description	Unused	Used
1	A1	½p green	11.50	7.50
		Never hinged	17.00	
		On cover		30.00
a.		½p yellow green	10.00	6.50
b.		½p deep green	10.00	6.50
c.		Wmk. sideways, crown pointing to left		*18,000.*
d.		Wmk. sideways, crown pointing to right		*30,000.*
e.		Wmk. inverted	52.50	17.50
f.		Printed on gummed side	*2,250.*	
2	A1	1p car (I)	17.50	1.75
		Never hinged	24.00	
		On cover		7.00
a.		1p red (I)	12.50	1.75
b.		1p pale red (I)	12.50	1.75
		Never hinged	22.50	
c.		1p rose red (I)	12.50	1.75
d.		1p carmine (II)	12.50	1.75
		Never hinged	22.50	
		On cover		8.00
e.		1p red (II)	14.00	1.75
f.		1p pale red (II)	14.00	1.75
g.		1p rose red (II)	14.00	1.75
h.		1p carmine (III)	24.00	2.25
		Never hinged	40.00	
		On cover		9.75
i.		1p red (III)	22.50	1.75
j.		1p pale red (III)	22.50	1.75
k.		1p rose red (III)	22.50	1.75
l.		As #2, wmk. sideways	*1,200.*	*300.00*
m.		As "d," wmk. sideways	*1,300.*	*325.00*
n.		As #2, wmk. inverted	47.50	16.00
o.		As "d," wmk. inverted	47.50	16.00
p.		As "h," wmk. inverted	70.00	12.00
3	A1	2p gray	70.00	10.00
		Never hinged	175.00	
		On cover		37.50
a.		2p deep gray	62.50	10.00
b.		2p slate	62.50	10.00
c.		As #3, wmk. inverted	110.00	29.00
4	A1	2½p dark blue	70.00	22.50
		Never hinged	190.00	
		On cover		62.50
a.		2½p indigo	62.50	22.50
5	A1	3p ol bis, die I	140.00	17.50
		Never hinged	310.00	
		On cover		90.00
a.		Die II	450.00	85.00
		Never hinged	*850.00*	
		On cover		170.00
b.		Pair, #5-5a	725.00	325.00
c.		3p pale olive green (I)	125.00	17.50
		Never hinged	300.00	
d.		As "c," (II)	275.00	90.00
		Never hinged	*625.00*	
e.		Pair, #5c-5d	725.00	350.00
f.		3p green (I)	115.00	13.50
		Never hinged	290.00	
g.		As "f," (II)	275.00	85.00
		Never hinged	*625.00*	
h.		As #5, wmk. inverted	180.00	55.00
i.		As "a," wmk. inverted	630.00	220.00
j.		Pair, #5f-5g	800.00	400.00
6	A1	4p orange	150.00	40.00
		Never hinged	700.00	
		On cover		115.00
a.		4p deep orange	130.00	40.00
		Never hinged	630.00	
b.		4p yellow orange	460.00	97.50
		Never hinged	1,035.	
		On cover		275.00

Many examples offered as No. 6b are either Nos. 6 or 6a with faded color.

No.	Type	Description	Unused	Used
7	A1	5p org brn	150.00	50.00
		Never hinged	375.00	
		On cover		160.00
8	A1	6p ultra (II)	140.00	30.00
		Never hinged	450.00	
		On cover		160.00
a.		6p blue (II)	125.00	32.50
		Never hinged	430.00	
		On cover		195.00
b.		As #8, (III)	*4,000.*	*1,300.*
c.		As #8, wmk. inverted	150.00	65.00
d.		As "a," wmk. inverted	150.00	65.00
e.		As "b," wmk. inverted	*2,250.*	*750.00*
9	A1	9p purple	160.00	37.50
		Never hinged	575.00	
		On cover		170.00
a.		9p violet	140.00	37.50
b.		9p deep violet	140.00	37.50
10	A1	1sh blue green	130.00	29.00
		Never hinged	700.00	
		On cover		220.00
a.		1sh emerald	115.00	22.50
b.		As "a," aniline ink	140.00	29.00
c.		As "a," wmk. inverted	1,150.	97.50
11	A1	2sh brown	300.00	140.00
		Never hinged	1,250.	
		On telegram form or parcel		300.00
a.		2sh dark brown	315.00	145.00
12	A1	5sh yel & gray	550.00	260.00
		Never hinged	2,000.	
		On cover		—
a.		5sh chrome yel & gray	550.00	260.00
13	A1	10sh pink & gray	1,600.	800.00
		Never hinged	4,250.	
		On cover		—
a.		10sh pink & slate	1,150.	800.00
14	A1	£1 ultra & brn	4,000.	2,500.
		Never hinged	9,250.	
		On cover		—
a.		£1 ultra & red brn	3,300.	2,100.
15	A1	£2 dp rose & blk	8,500.	4,000.
		Never hinged	16,000.	
		On cover		—
a.		£2 rose & gray	5,750.	3,250.
		Never hinged	12,500.	
b.		£2 rose & jet black	5,750.	3,250.
		Never hinged	12,500.	
		Nos. 1-12 (12)	1,889.	645.75

On No. 4, "2½d" is colorless in solid blue background.

See Nos. 38-59, 96-102, 121-129, 206.

King George V A2

Kookaburra (Kingfisher) A3

1913-14 Unwmk. Engr. *Perf. 11*

No.	Type	Description	Unused	Used
17	A2	1p carmine	5.25	*7.00*
		Never hinged	8.00	
a.		Vert. pair, imperf. between	*3,250.*	
18	A3	6p lake brown ('14)	115.00	70.00
		Never hinged	260.00	

See No. 95.

A4

ONE PENNY

Die I — Normal die, having outside the oval band with "AUSTRALIA" a white line and a heavy colored line.

Die Ia — As die I with a small white spur below the right serif at foot of the "1" in left tablet.

Die II — A heavy colored line between two white lines back of the emu's neck. A white scratch crossing the vertical shading lines at the lowest point of the bust.

TWO PENCE

Die I — The numeral "2" is thin. The upper curve is 1mm. across and a very thin line connects it with the foot of the figure.

Die II — The "2" is thicker than in die I. The top curve is 1½mm across and a strong white line connects it with the foot of the figure. There are thin vertical lines across the ends of the groups of short horizontal lines at each side of "TWO PENCE."

THREE PENCE

Die I — The ends of the thin horizontal lines in the background run into the solid color of the various parts of the design. The numerals are thin and the letters of "THREE PENCE" are thin and irregular.

Die II — The oval about the portrait, the shields with the numerals, etc., are outlined by thin white lines which separate them from the horizontal background lines. The numerals are thick and the letters of "THREE PENCE" are heavy and regular.

FIVE PENCE

Die I — The top of the flag of the "5" is slightly curved.

Die II — The top of the flag of the "5" is flat. There are thin white vertical lines across the ends of the short horizontal lines at each side of "FIVE PENCE."

1914-24 Typo. Wmk. 9 *Perf. 14*

19 A4 ½p emer ('15) 3.75 1.75
Never hinged 8.50
a. Thin "½" at right *20,000. 5,750.*
20 A4 ½p org ('23) 4.00 4.00
Never hinged 7.00
21 A4 1p red (I) 11.00 1.75
Never hinged 15.00
a. 1p carmine rose (I) 22.50 4.00
Never hinged 40.00
b. 1p red (Ia) 550.00 9.75
Never hinged 1,150.
c. 1p carmine (II) ('18) 85.00 35.00
Never hinged 175.00
d. 1p scar (I), rough paper 22.50 9.75
e. 1p rose red (Ia), rough paper 800.00 29.00
f. 1p brt rose (Ia), rough paper 750.00 115.00
22 A4 1p vio (I) ('22) 7.00 1.75
Never hinged 11.50
a. 1p red violet 10.50 5.25
Never hinged 14.00
23 A4 1p grn (I) ('24) 5.75 2.50
Never hinged 10.50
24 A4 1½p choc ('18) 7.50 2.25
Never hinged 12.50
a. 1½p red brown 8.00 2.50
Never hinged 18.00
b. 1½p black brown 7.00 2.50
Never hinged 11.50
25 A4 1½p emer ('23) 7.50 2.75
Never hinged 12.50
a. Rough paper 260.00 160.00
26 A4 1½p scar ('24) 4.25 1.10
Never hinged 7.00
27 A4 2p brn org (I) ('20) 17.50 3.25
Never hinged 32.50
a. 2p orange (I) ('20) 17.50 2.50
Never hinged 32.50
b. Booklet pane of 6
28 A4 2p red (I) ('22) 17.50 3.25
Never hinged 30.00
29 A4 2p red brn (I) ('24) 22.50 12.50
Never hinged 37.50
30 A4 3p ultra (I) ('24) 32.50 7.75
Never hinged 70.00
31 A4 4p org ('15) 45.00 4.00
Never hinged 92.50
a. 4p yellow 140.00 32.50
Never hinged 600.00
32 A4 4p violet ('21) 22.50 21.00
Never hinged 37.50
33 A4 4p lt ultra ('22) 67.50 13.00
Never hinged 140.00
34 A4 4p ol bis ('24) 35.00 13.00
Never hinged 70.00
35 A4 4½p violet ('24) 27.50 6.75
Never hinged 60.00
36 A4 5p org brn (I) ('15) 37.50 7.25
Never hinged 110.00
37 A4 1sh4p lt blue ('20) 140.00 35.00
Never hinged 475.00
Nos. 19-37 (19) 515.75 144.60

See Nos. 60-76, 113-120, 124.

1915 *Perf. 11½, 12*

38 A1 2p gray 160.00 17.00
Never hinged 325.00
a. Wmk. inverted 1,250.
39 A1 2½p dark blue 140.00 37.50
Never hinged 300.00
40 A1 6p ultra (II) 325.00 29.00
Never hinged 875.00
a. Die III *4,250.* 1,450.
b. 6p bright blue (II) 350.00 85.00
c. As "b," Die III *4,000.* 1,500.
d. As #40, wmk. inverted *2,500.*
41 A1 9p violet 325.00 60.00
Never hinged 1,400.
a. Wmk. inverted *3,500.* 2,000.
42 A1 1sh blue green 275.00 35.00
Never hinged 1,250.
43 A1 2sh brown 1,050. 125.00
Never hinged 4,750.
44 A1 5sh yellow & gray 1,500. 475.00
Never hinged 3,250.
a. Wmk. inverted 1,250. 425.00
b. Yellow double 15,000. 4,000.
Nos. 38-44 (7) 3,775. 778.50

1915-24 Wmk. 10

45 A1 2p gray (I) 37.50 10.50
Never hinged 62.50
a. Die II, shiny paper 45.00 17.50
Never hinged 62.50
46 A1 2½p dark blue 30.00 17.50
Never hinged 47.50
a. "1" of fraction omitted *45,000. 50,000.*
47 A1 3p ol bis (I) 37.50 9.50
Never hinged 72.50
a. Die II 175.00 57.50
Never hinged 325.00
b. 3p lt olive (IV) 52.50 14.00
Never hinged 92.50
48 A1 6p ultra (II) 120.00 17.50
Never hinged 275.00
a. 6p chalky blue (III) 125.00 22.50
Never hinged 250.00
b. 6p ultra (III) 1,600. 500.00
c. 6p ultra (IV) 120.00 20.00
Never hinged 250.00
49 A1 6p yel brn (IV, '23) 32.50 7.25
Never hinged 62.50
50 A1 9p violet (IV) 80.00 22.50
Never hinged 190.00
a. 9p lilac (II) 82.50 22.50
Never hinged 200.00
51 A1 1sh blue grn (II, '16) 72.50 14.00
Never hinged 190.00
b. Die IV 75.00 14.00
Never hinged 195.00
52 A1 2sh brn ('16) 325.00 27.50
Never hinged 975.00
53 A1 2sh vio brn (II, '24) 140.00 37.50
Never hinged 325.00
54 A1 5sh yel & gray ('18) 325.00 125.00
Never hinged 850.00
55 A1 10sh brt pink & gray ('17) 1,050. 400.00
Never hinged 1,750.
56 A1 £1 ultra & brn org ('16) 3,450. 2,100.
Never hinged 9,250.
a. £1 ultra & brn ('16) 3,250. 2,100.
Never hinged 10,500.
57 A1 £1 gray (IV, '24) 900.00 425.00
Never hinged 2,250.
58 A1 £2 dp rose & blk ('19) 7,000. 3,250.
Never hinged 14,000.
59 A1 £2 rose & vio brn ('24) 5,250. 3,250.
Never hinged 12,500.
Nos. 45-54 (10) 1,200. 288.75

Perf. 14, 14½, 14½x14

1918-23 Wmk. 11

60 A4 ½p emerald 3.50 3.25
Never hinged 8.00
a. Thin "½" at right 140.00 160.00
61 A4 1p rose (I) 27.50 19.00
Never hinged 45.00
62 A4 1p dl grn (I) ('24) 9.25 9.25
Never hinged 17.50
63 A4 1½p choc ('19) 8.00 4.25
Never hinged 17.50
a. 1½p red brown ('19) 12.50 4.50
Never hinged 26.00
Nos. 60-63 (4) 48.25 35.75

1924 Unwmk. *Perf. 14*

64 A4 1p green (I) 5.75 6.25
Never hinged 12.50
65 A4 1½p carmine 9.25 7.50
Never hinged 17.50

Perf. 14, 13½x12½

1926-30 Wmk. 203

66 A4 ½p orange 3.75 2.25
Never hinged 7.00
a. Perf. 14 ('27) 7.50 8.25
Never hinged 11.50
67 A4 1p green (I) 3.75 1.10
Never hinged 8.00
a. 1p green (Ia) 55.00 *70.00*
Never hinged 75.00
b. Perf. 14 4.50 1.75
Never hinged 9.25
68 A4 1½p rose red ('27) 4.50 2.00
Never hinged 9.25
c. Perf. 14 ('26) 11.50 2.00
Never hinged 22.50
69 A4 1½p red brn ('30) 6.25 4.50
Never hinged 9.75
70 A4 2p red brn (II, '28) 9.25 5.75
Never hinged 20.00
a. Perf. 14 (I, '27) 45.00 29.00
Never hinged 85.00
71 A4 2p red (II) ('30) 11.50 3.25
Never hinged 22.50
a. Tête bêche pair 175,000.
b. 2p red (I) ('30) 7.00 3.50
Never hinged 12.00
c. Unwmkd. (II) ('31) *2,000. 2,500.*
72 A4 3p ultra (II) ('29) 35.00 5.50
Never hinged 57.50
a. 3p ultra (I) 70.00 22.50
Never hinged 150.00
b. Perf. 14 45.00 11.50
Never hinged 80.00
73 A4 4p ol bis ('29) 29.00 6.75
Never hinged 52.50
a. Perf. 14 ('28) 125.00 50.00
Never hinged 300.00
74 A4 4½p dk vio ('27) 26.00 10.50
Never hinged 45.00
a. Perf. 13½x12½ ('28) 85.00 32.50
Never hinged 150.00
75 A4 5p brn buff (II) ('30) 45.00 14.00
Never hinged 85.00
76 A4 1sh4p pale turq bl ('28) 200.00 37.50
Never hinged 500.00
a. Perf. 14 ('27) 260.00 140.00
Never hinged 775.00
Nos. 66-76 (11) 374.00 93.10

For surcharges & overprints see Nos. 106-107, O3-O4.

Parliament House, Canberra A5

1927, May 9 Unwmk. Engr. *Perf. 11*

94 A5 1½p brown red 1.10 1.10
Never hinged 2.00
a. Vert. pair, imperf. btwn. *5,000. 4,250.*
b. Horiz. pair, imperf. btwn. *11,000. 11,000.*

Opening of Parliament House at Canberra.

Melbourne Exhibition Issue

Kookaburra Type of 1914

1928, Oct. 29

95 A3 3p deep blue 5.50 8.00
Never hinged 8.25
a. Pane of 4 200.00 *260.00*
Never hinged 300.00

No. 95a was issued at the Melbourne Intl. Phil. Exhib. No marginal inscription. Printed in sheets of 60 stamps (15 panes). No. 95a exists imperf. Value, $300,000.

No. 95 was printed in sheets of 120 and issued Nov. 2 throughout Australia.

Kangaroo-Map Type of 1913

Perf. 11½, 12

1929-30 Wmk. 203 Typo.

96 A1 6p brown 35.00 22.50
Never hinged 57.50
97 A1 9p violet 75.00 26.00
Never hinged 160.00
98 A1 1sh blue green 70.00 14.50
Never hinged 165.00
99 A1 2sh red brown 150.00 29.00
Never hinged 425.00
100 A1 5sh yel & gray 475.00 150.00
Never hinged 1,000.
101 A1 10sh pink & gray 1,000. 725.00
Never hinged 2,000.
102 A1 £2 dl red & blk ('30) 5,250. 925.00
Never hinged 11,500.
Nos. 96-102 (7) 7,055. 1,892.

For overprint see No. O5.

Black Swan — A6

1929, Sept. 28 Unwmk. Engr. *Perf. 11*

103 A6 1½p dull red 2.00 2.00
Never hinged 3.25

Centenary of Western Australia.

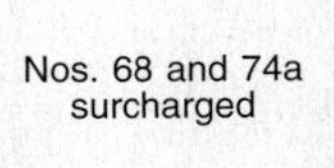

Capt. Charles Sturt — A7

1930, June 2

104 A7 1½p dark red 1.25 1.25
Never hinged 2.50
105 A7 3p dark blue 7.50 *10.00*
Never hinged 11.00

Capt. Charles Sturt's exploration of the Murray River, cent.

Nos. 68 and 74a surcharged

FIVE
PENCE

1930 Wmk. 203 *Perf. 13½x12½*

106 A4 2p on 1½p rose red 2.50 1.25
Never hinged 4.00
107 A4 5p on 4½p dark violet 14.00 *15.00*
Never hinged 21.00

"Southern Cross" over Hemispheres A8

Perf. 11, 11½

1931, Mar. 19 Unwmk.

111 A8 2p dull red 1.25 1.25
Never hinged 2.50
112 A8 3p blue 6.25 6.25
Never hinged 10.00
Nos. 111-112,C2 (3) 15.50 15.50

Trans-oceanic flights (1928-1930) of Sir Charles Edward Kingsford-Smith (1897-1935).

See No. C3 for similar design. For overprints see Nos. CO1, O1-O2.

Types of 1913-23 Issues

Perf. 13½x12½

1931-36 Typo. Wmk. 228

113 A4 ½p org ('32) 7.50 7.50
Never hinged 11.50
114 A4 1p green (I) 2.50 .40
Never hinged 4.50
115 A4 1½p red brn ('36) 8.00 15.00
Never hinged 12.50
116 A4 2p red (II) 2.50 .30
Never hinged 4.50
117 A4 3p ultra (II) ('32) 32.50 2.25
Never hinged 75.00
118 A4 4p ol bis ('33) 29.00 2.25
Never hinged 55.00
120 A4 5p brn buff (II) ('32) 22.50 2.25
Never hinged 35.00

Perf. 11½, 12; 13½x12½ (1sh4p)

121 A1 6p yel brn ('36) 30.00 *37.50*
Never hinged 52.50
122 A1 9p violet ('32) 42.50 9.00
Never hinged 115.00
124 A4 1sh4p lt blue ('32) 115.00 11.00
Never hinged 160.00
125 A1 2sh red brn ('35) 7.50 5.25
Never hinged 12.50
126 A1 5sh yel & gray ('32) 350.00 27.50
Never hinged 925.00
127 A1 10sh pink & gray ('32) 600.00 225.00
Never hinged 2,000.
128 A1 £1 gray ('35) 1,400. 375.00
Never hinged 2,500.
129 A1 £2 dl rose & blk ('34) 4,500. 800.00
Never hinged 9,250.
Nos. 113-129 (15) 7,150. 1,520.

For redrawn 2sh see No. 206. For overprints see Nos. O6-O11.

Sydney Harbor Bridge — A9

1932, Mar. 14 Unwmk. Engr. *Perf. 11*

130 A9 2p red 4.50 *5.25*
Never hinged 7.00
131 A9 3p blue 7.50 *9.50*
Never hinged 11.50
132 A9 5sh gray green 575.00 350.00
Never hinged 1,600.

Wmk. 228
Perf. 10½
Typo.

133 A9 2p red 4.00 2.25
Never hinged 5.75

Opening of the Sydney Harbor Bridge on Mar. 19, 1932.

Value for 5sh, used, is for CTO examples.

For overprints see Nos. O12-O13.

Kookaburra — A14

1932, June 1 *Perf. 13½x12½*

139 A14 6p light brown 17.00 1.10
Never hinged 27.50

Male Lyrebird — A16

1932, Feb. 15 Unwmk. *Perf. 11*
Size: 21½x25mm

141 A16 1sh dark green 42.50 4.50
Never hinged 110.00

See No. 175. See No. 300 in *Scott Standard Postage Stamp Catalogue*, Vol. 1. For overprint see No. O14.

Yarra Yarra Tribesman, Yarra River and View of Melbourne
A17

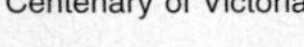

Wmk. 228
1934, July 2 Engr. *Perf. 10½*

142 A17 2p vermilion 3.00 1.75
Never hinged 4.50
a. Perf. 11½ 10.50 4.50
Never hinged 20.00
143 A17 3p blue 4.00 *6.50*
Never hinged 10.00
a. Perf. 11½ 5.00 *9.00*
Never hinged 9.00
144 A17 1sh black 55.00 27.50
Never hinged 110.00
a. Perf. 11½ 65.00 32.50
Never hinged 120.00
Nos. 142-144 (3) 62.00 35.75

Centenary of Victoria.

Merino Sheep — A18

1934, Nov. 1 *Perf. 11½*

147 A18 2p copper red 8.00 2.00
Never hinged 11.50
a. Die II 15.00 5.75
Never hinged 29.00
148 A18 3p dark blue 15.00 *19.00*
Never hinged 20.00
149 A18 9p dark violet 35.00 *50.00*
Never hinged 75.00
Nos. 147-149 (3) 58.00 71.00

Capt. John Macarthur (1767-1834), "father of the New South Wales woolen industry."

Two dies of 2p: I, shading on hill in background uneven from light to dark. II, shading is uniformly dark.

Cenotaph in Whitehall, London — A19

1935, Mar. 18 *Perf. 13½x12½*

150 A19 2p red 2.50 .50
Never hinged 5.25

Perf. 11

151 A19 1sh black 50.00 45.00
Never hinged 100.00

Anzacs' landing at Gallipoli, 20th anniv.

The 1sh perf 13½x12½ is a plate proof. Value, unused $2,250, mint never hinged $3,500.

George V on His Charger "Anzac" — A20

1935, May 2 *Perf. 11½*

152 A20 2p red 2.75 .35
Never hinged 5.00
153 A20 3p blue 8.00 *12.50*
Never hinged 17.50
154 A20 2sh violet 35.00 *47.50*
Never hinged 85.00
Nos. 152-154 (3) 45.75 60.35

25th anniv. of the reign of King George V.

Amphitrite Joining Cables between Australia and Tasmania
A21

1936, Apr. 1

157 A21 2p red 1.25 .60
Never hinged 2.75
158 A21 3p dark blue 3.75 3.50
Never hinged 5.50

Australia/Tasmania telephone link.

Edward VIII

A unique block of six unissued 2-penny King Edward VIII stamps realized the equivalent of U.S. $387,000 when it was sold at a London auction in 2014. A single stamp was separated from the block and sold at a Melbourne auction in 2015 for the equivalent of U.S. $123,600.

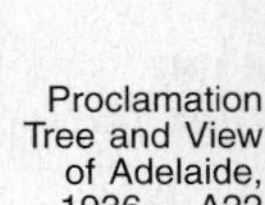

Proclamation Tree and View of Adelaide, 1936 — A22

1936, Aug. 3

159 A22 2p red 1.00 .60
Never hinged 2.25
160 A22 3p dark blue 3.75 3.75
Never hinged 5.75
161 A22 1sh green 14.00 10.00
Never hinged 27.50
Nos. 159-161 (3) 18.75 14.35

Centenary of South Australia.

Gov. Arthur Phillip at Sydney Cove — A23

1937, Oct. 1 *Perf. 13x13½*

163 A23 2p red 1.00 .45
Never hinged 3.25
164 A23 3p ultra 3.75 3.25
Never hinged 6.50
165 A23 9p violet 15.00 13.00
Never hinged 25.00
Nos. 163-165 (3) 19.75 16.70

150th anniversary of New South Wales.

Kangaroo
A24

Queen Elizabeth
A25

King George VI
A26 A27

Koala — A28

Merino Sheep — A29

Kookaburra (Kingfisher)
A30

Platypus
A31

Queen Elizabeth and King George VI in Coronation Robes
A32 A33

King George VI and Queen Elizabeth
A34

Type I

Type II

Two Types of A25 and A26:

Type I — Highlighted background. Lines around letters of Australia Postage and numerals of value.

Type II — Background of heavy diagonal lines without the highlighted effect. No lines around letters and numerals.

Perf. 13½x14, 14x13½
1937-46 Engr. Wmk. 228

166 A24 ½p org, perf. 15x14 ('42) .85 .70
Never hinged 2.25
a. Perf. 13½x14 ('38) 1.40 .60
Never hinged 3.50
167 A25 1p emerald (I) 1.10 1.00
Never hinged 2.25
168 A26 1½p dull red brn (II) 6.25 5.75
Never hinged 11.50
a. Perf. 15x14 ('41) 4.75 14.00
Never hinged 8.00
169 A26 2p scarlet (I) 1.10 .60
Never hinged 2.25
170 A27 3p ultramarine 40.00 24.00
Never hinged 75.00
a. 3p dp ultra, thin paper ('38) 40.00 4.50
Never hinged 75.00
171 A28 4p grn, perf. 15x14 ('42) 1.10 .30
Never hinged 2.25
a. Perf. 13½x14 ('38) 3.25 3.00
Never hinged 9.00
172 A29 5p pale rose vio, perf. 14x15 ('46) 1.40 1.10
Never hinged 2.25
a. Perf. 14x13½ ('38) 3.00 .90
Never hinged 4.50
173 A30 6p vio brn, perf. 15x14 ('42) 1.25 .30
Never hinged 3.00
a. Perf. 13½x14 12.50 2.25
Never hinged 26.00
b. 6p chocolate, perf. 15x14 1.40 .55
Never hinged 2.25
174 A31 9p sep, perf. 14x15 ('43) 2.00 .45
Never hinged 3.00
a. Perf. 14x13½ ('38) 4.50 2.25
Never hinged 9.75
175 A16 1sh gray grn, perf. 15x14 ('41) 1.40 .40
Never hinged 2.00
a. Perf. 13½x14 27.50 3.50
Never hinged 72.50
176 A27 1sh4p mag ('38) 1.60 *3.25*
Never hinged 3.50

Perf. 13½

177 A32 5sh dl red brn ('38) 9.75 4.50
Never hinged 26.00
a. Thin paper ('48) 4.00 3.50
Never hinged 5.25
178 A33 10sh dl gray vio ('38) 35.00 20.00
Never hinged 57.50
a. Thin paper ('48) 35.00 29.00
Never hinged 45.00
179 A34 £1 bl gray ('38) 70.00 42.50
Never hinged 115.00
a. Thin paper ('48) 70.00 62.50
Never hinged 100.00
Nos. 166-179 (14) 172.80 104.85

No. 175 measures 17½x21½mm.

Nos. 177-179 were issued on chalk-surfaced paper. Nos. 177a-179a were printed on a thin, rough ordinary paper. The watermark is more distinct on Nos. 177a-179a, while impressions are not as sharp as on Nos. 177-179.

See Nos. 223A, 293, 295, 298, 300 in this catalogue or *Scott Standard Postage Stamp Catalogue*, Vol. 1. For surch. & overprints see Nos. 190, M1, M4-M5, M7.

1938-42 *Perf. 15x14*

180 A25 1p emerald (II) 1.00 .70
181 A25 1p dl red brn (II) ('41) .70 .60
181B A26 1½p bl grn (II) ('41) .70 *2.25*
182 A26 2p scarlet (II) 1.00 .30
182B A26 2p red vio (II) ('41) .40 .30
183 A27 3p dk ultra ('40) 29.00 4.50
Never hinged 57.50
183A A27 3p dk vio brn ('42) .40 .30
Nos. 180-183A (7) 33.20 8.95
Set, never hinged 72.50

No. 183 differs from Nos. 170-170a in the shading lines on the king's left eyebrow which go downward, left to right, instead of the reverse. Also, more of the left epaulette shows.

For surcharges & ovpt. see Nos. 188-189, M3.

Coil Perforation

A special perforation was applied to stamps intended for use in coils to make separation easier. It consists of small and large holes (2 small, 10 large, 2 small) on the stamps' narrow side. Some of the stamps so perforated were sold in sheets.

This coil perforation may be found on Nos. 166, 181, 182, 182B, 193, 215, 223A, 231. See *Scott Standard Postage Stamp Catalogue Vol. 1* for Nos. 257, 315-316, 319, 319a and others.

Nurse, Sailor, Soldier and Aviator — A35

Perf. 13½x13
1940, July 15 Engr. Wmk. 228

184 A35 1p green 1.10 *3.25*
Never hinged 2.50
185 A35 2p red 1.10 *1.90*
Never hinged 2.50
186 A35 3p ultra 8.00 *12.50*
Never hinged 16.00
187 A35 6p chocolate 17.00 *27.50*
Never hinged 32.50
Nos. 184-187 (4) 27.20 45.15

Australia's participation in WWII.

No. 182 Surcharged in Blue

1941, Dec. 10 *Perf. 15x14*

188 A26 2½p on 2p red .75 *1.00*
Never hinged 1.50

No. 183 Surcharged in Black and Yellow

189 A27 3½p on 3p dk ultra .90 *2.25*
Never hinged 1.75

No. 172a Surcharged in Purple

Perf. 14x13½

190 A29 5½p on 5p pale rose vio 3.25 *6.50*
Never hinged 5.00
Nos. 188-190 (3) 4.90 9.75

Queen Elizabeth
A36 A37

King George VI
A38 A39

George VI and Blue Wrens
A40

Emu
A41

1942-44 Engr. *Perf. 15x14*

191 A36 1p brown vio ('43) .45 .25
192 A37 1½p green .70 .25
193 A38 2p lt rose vio ('44) .70 .25
194 A39 2½p red .70 .30
195 A40 3½p ultramarine .95 .70
196 A41 5½p indigo 1.75 .35
Nos. 191-196 (6) 5.25 2.10
Set, never hinged 9.00

See Nos. 224-225. For overprint see No. M2.

Catalogue values for unused stamps in this section, from this point to the end of the section, are for Never Hinged items.

Duke and Duchess of Gloucester
A42

1945, Feb. 19 Engr. *Perf. 14½*

197 A42 2½p brown red .30 .25
198 A42 3½p bright ultra .45 *1.25*
199 A42 5½p indigo .55 *1.25*
Nos. 197-199 (3) 1.30 *2.75*

Inauguration of the Duke of Gloucester as Governor General.

Official Crest and Inscriptions
A43

Dove and Australian Flag
A44

Angel of Peace; "Motherhood" and "Industry"
A45

1946, Feb. 18 Wmk. 228 *Perf. 14½*

200 A43 2½p carmine .25 .25
201 A44 3½p deep ultra .65 *1.75*
202 A45 5½p deep yellow green .70 *1.00*
Nos. 200-202 (3) 1.60 *3.00*

End of WWII. See Nos. 1456-1458 in *Scott Standard Postage Stamp Catalogue*, Vol. 1.

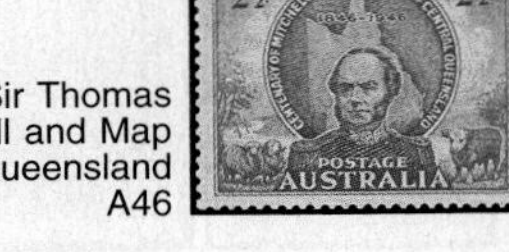

Sir Thomas Mitchell and Map of Queensland
A46

1946, Oct. 14

203 A46 2½p dark carmine .25 .25
204 A46 3½p deep ultra .75 1.60
205 A46 1sh olive green .75 .60
Nos. 203-205 (3) 1.75 2.45

Sir Thomas Mitchell's exploration of central Queensland, cent.

Kangaroo-Map Type of 1913 Redrawn

1945, Dec. Typo. *Perf. 11½*

206 A1 2sh dk red brown 5.50 5.50

The R and A of AUSTRALIA are separated at the base and there is a single line between the value tablet and "Two Shillings." On No. 125 the tail of the R touches the A, while two lines appear between value tablet and "Two Shillings." There are many other minor differences in the design.

For overprint see No. M6.

John Shortland
A47

Pouring Steel
A48

Loading Coal — A49

1947, Sept. Engr. *Perf. 14½x14*

207 A47 2½p brown red .35 .25

Perf. 14½

208 A48 3½p deep blue .65 *1.50*
209 A49 5½p deep green .65 *.75*
Nos. 207-209 (3) 1.65 2.50

150th anniv. of the discovery of the Hunter River estuary, site of Newcastle by Lieut. John Shortland. By error the 2½p shows his father, Capt. John Shortland.

Princess Elizabeth — A50

Perf. 14x14½

1947, Nov. 20 Wmk. 228

210 A50 1p brown violet .40 .45

See No. 215.

Hereford Bull
A51

Crocodile
A52

1948, Feb. 16 *Perf. 14½*

211 A51 1sh3p violet brown 2.25 1.40
212 A52 2sh chocolate 2.25 .35

See No. 302 in *Scott Standard Postage Stamp Catalogue*, Vol. 1.

William J. Farrer — A53

Design: No. 214, Ferdinand von Mueller.

1948 *Perf. 14½x14*

213 A53 2½p red .50 .25
214 A53 2½p dark red .45 .25

William J. Farrer (1845-1906), wheat researcher, and Ferdinand von Mueller (1825-1896), German-born botanist.

Issue dates: No. 213, July 12. No. 214, Sept. 13.

Elizabeth Type of 1947

1948, Aug. Unwmk. *Perf. 14x14½*

215 A50 1p brown violet .40 .25

Scout in Uniform — A55

1948, Nov. 15 Engr. Wmk. 228

216 A55 2½p brown red .45 .25

Pan-Pacific Scout Jamboree, Victoria, Dec. 29, 1948 to Jan. 9, 1949. See No. 249.

Arms of Australia — A56

1949-50 Wmk. 228 *Perf. 14x13½*

218 A56 5sh dark red 4.50 .85
219 A56 10sh red violet 29.00 2.00
220 A56 £1 deep blue 45.00 8.50
221 A56 £2 green ('50) 200.00 26.00
Nos. 218-221 (4) 278.50 37.35

Henry Hertzberg Lawson (1867-1922), Author and Poet — A57

Perf. 14½x14

1949, June 17 Unwmk.

222 A57 2½p rose brown .50 .25

Outback Mail Carrier and Plane — A58

1949, Oct. 10

223 A58 3½p violet blue .60 .55

UPU, 75th anniv.

Types of 1938, 1942-44 and

Aborigine — A59

1948-50 Unwmk. *Perf. 14½x14*

223A A24 ½p orange ('49) .45 .25
224 A37 1½p green ('49) .35 .45
225 A38 2p lt rose violet 1.00 .55

Wmk. 228

226 A59 8½p dark brown ('50) .55 .45
Nos. 223A-226 (4) 2.35 1.70

Issued: 2p, Dec.; ½p, Sept.; 1½p, 8/29; 8½p, 8/14.

See No. 248; No. 303 in *Scott Standard Postage Stamp Catalogue*, Vol. 1.

John Forrest — A60

1949, Nov. 28 Wmk. 228

227 A60 2½p brown red .50 .25

Forrest (1847-1918), explorer & statesman.

New South Wales
A61

Victoria
A62

First stamp designs.

Perf. 14½x14

1950, Sept. 27 Unwmk.

228 A61 2½p rose brown .45 .25
229 A62 2½p rose brown .45 .25
a. Pair, #228-229 1.40 1.10

Cent. of Australian adhesive postage stamps. Issued in sheets of 160 stamps containing alternate copies of Nos. 228 and 229.

Elizabeth
A63

George VI
A64

1950-51 Engr. Unwmk.

230 A63 1½p deep green .85 .75
231 A63 2p yellow grn ('51) .30 .25
232 A64 2½p violet brn ('51) .30 *.45*
233 A64 3p dull green ('51) .35 .25
Nos. 230-233 (4) 1.80 1.70

Issued: 1½p, 6/19; 2p, 3/28; 2½p, 5/23; 3p, 11/14.

A65

A66

1950-52 Wmk. 228

234 A64 2½p red .25 .25
235 A64 3p red ('51) .35 *.45*
236 A65 3½p red brown ('51) .35 .25
237 A65 4½p scarlet ('52) .45 *.90*
238 A65 6½p choc ('52) .35 .55
238A A65 6½p blue green ('52) .45 .25
239 A66 7½p deep blue ('51) .50 .55
Nos. 234-239 (7) 2.70 3.20

Issued: 2½p, 4/12; 3p, 2/28; 7½p, 10/31; 3½p, 11/28; 4½p, No. 238, 2/20; No. 238A, 4/9.

A67

Founding of the Commonwealth of Australia, 50th Anniv. — A68

Designs: No. 240, Sir Edmund Barton. No. 241, Sir Henry Parkes. 5½p, Duke of York opening first Federal Parliament. 1sh6p, Parliament House, Canberra.

Perf. 14½x14

1951, May 1 Engr. Unwmk.

240 3p carmine 1.60 .25
241 3p carmine 1.60 .25
a. A67 Pair, #240, 241 3.50 3.50
242 A68 5½p deep blue .90 *3.00*
243 A68 1sh6p red brown 1.40 1.40
Nos. 240-243 (4) 5.50 4.90

Edward Hammond Hargraves — A69

Design: No. 245, Charles Joseph Latrobe (1801-1875), first governor of Victoria.

1951, July 2

244 A69 3p rose brown 1.00 .25
245 A69 3p rose brown 1.00 .25
a. Pair, #244, 245 2.50 2.50

Discovery of gold in Australia, cent. (No. 244); Establishment of representative government in Victoria, cent. (No. 245). Sheets contain alternate rows of Nos. 244 and 245.

King George VI — A70

1952, Mar. 19 Wmk. 228 *Perf. 14½*

247 A70 1sh½p slate blue 2.50 .85

Aborigine Type of 1950 Redrawn
Size: 20½x25mm

248 A59 2sh6p dark brown 5.75 1.10

Portrait as on A59; lettering altered and value repeated at lower left. See No. 303 in *Scott Standard Postage Stamp Catalogue*, Vol. 1.

Scout Type of 1948
Dated "1952-53"
Perf. 14x14½

1952, Nov. 19 Wmk. 228

249 A55 3½p red brown .45 .25

Pan-Pacific Scout Jamboree, Greystanes, Dec. 30, 1952, to Jan. 9, 1953.

AIR POST STAMPS

Airplane over Bush Lands — AP1

Unwmk.

1929, May 20 Engr. *Perf. 11*

C1 AP1 3p deep green 9.25 8.50
Never hinged 14.50
a. Booklet pane of 4 ('30) 450.00

Kingsford-Smith Type of 1931

1931, Mar. 19

C2 A8 6p gray violet 8.00 8.00
Never hinged 11.50

AP3

1931, Nov. 4

C3 AP3 6p olive brown 17.00 14.00
Never hinged 35.00

For overprint see No. CO1.

Mercury and Hemispheres AP4

1934, Dec. 1 *Perf. 11*

C4 AP4 1sh6p violet brown 40.00 8.00
Never hinged 97.50

Perf. 13½x14

1937, Oct. 22 Wmk. 228

C5 AP4 1sh6p violet brown 8.50 1.40
Never hinged 14.50

Catalogue values for unused stamps in this section, from this point to the end of the section, are for Never Hinged items.

Mercury and Globe — AP5

1949, Sept. 1 *Perf. 14½*

C6 AP5 1sh6p sepia 2.25 .60

AIR POST OFFICIAL STAMP

No. C3 Overprinted

Perf. 11, 11½

1931, Nov. 17 Unwmk.

CO1 AP3 6p olive brown 35.00 *35.00*
Never hinged 57.50

Issued primarily for official use, but to prevent speculation, a quantity was issued for public distribution.

POSTAGE DUE STAMPS

Very fine examples of Nos. J1-J38 will have perforations touching the design on one or more sides due to the narrow spacing of the stamps on the plates. Stamps with perfs clear of the design on all four sides are scarce and will command higher prices.

D1

1902 Typo. Wmk. 55 *Perf. 11½, 12*

J1 D1 ½p emerald 11.50 11.50
J2 D1 1p emerald 17.50 11.50
a. Perf. 11 *2,800.* *1,400.*
b. Perf. 11x11½ 450.00 250.00
J3 D1 2p emerald 32.00 11.50
a. Perf. 11x11½ 600.00 200.00
J4 D1 3p emerald 32.00 21.00
J5 D1 4p emerald 45.00 25.00
J6 D1 6p emerald 70.00 17.00
J7 D1 8p emerald 180.00 140.00
J8 D1 5sh emerald 400.00 125.00
Nos. J1-J8 (8) 788.00 362.50

D2

Perf. 11½, 12, Compound with 11

1902-04

J9 D2 ½p emerald 17.50 *11.50*
a. Perf. 11 775.00 400.00
J10 D2 1p emerald, Perf 12x11 17.00 5.75
a. Perf. 11 200.00 42.50
b. Perf 11½ 400.00 200.00
c. Perf 11x11½ 37.50 11.50
J11 D2 2p emerald 23.00 5.75
a. Perf. 11 260.00 57.50
b. Perf 12 — 225.00
c. Perf 11x11½ 120.00 37.50
d. Perf 11x12 140.00 45.00
J12 D2 3p emerald 160.00 26.00
a. Perf. 11 225.00 63.00
b. Perf 12 450.00 170.00
J13 D2 4p emerald 140.00 32.00
a. Perf. 11 400.00 115.00
J14 D2 5p emerald 140.00 35.00
a. Perf. 11 500.00 86.00
b. Perf 12 100.00 23.00
J15 D2 6p emerald 160.00 29.00
a. Perf. 11 260.00 32.00
J16 D2 8p emerald 325.00 120.00
J17 D2 10p emerald 175.00 29.00
a. Perf 12x11½ 150.00 29.00
J18 D2 1sh emerald 160.00 29.00
a. Perf. 11 500.00 90.00
b. Perf 12x11½ 125.00 32.00
J19 D2 2sh emerald 200.00 32.00
a. Perf 11½, 12 200.00 40.00
J20 D2 5sh emerald 500.00 57.50
a. Perf. 11 1,700. 600.00

Perf. 11

J21 D2 10sh emerald *4,000.* *3,200.*
J22 D2 20sh emerald *8,500.* *5,500.*
Nos. J9-J20 (12) 2,018. 412.50

Perf. 11½, 12 Compound with 11

1906 Wmk. 12

J23 D2 ½p emerald 16.00 16.00
J24 D2 1p emerald 35.00 5.75
a. Perf. 11 *3,500.* *1,450.*
J25 D2 2p emerald 62.50 11.50
J26 D2 3p emerald 1,150. 450.00
J27 D2 4p emerald 140.00 27.50
a. Perf. 11 *4,600.* *2,900.*
J28 D2 6p emerald 490.00 35.00
Nos. J23-J28 (6) 1,894. 545.75

1907 Wmk. 13 *Perf. 11½x11*

J29 D2 ½p emerald 42.50 *85.00*
J30 D2 1p emerald 260.00 140.00
J31 D2 2p emerald 375.00 290.00
J32 D2 4p emerald 500.00 290.00
J33 D2 6p emerald 550.00 400.00
Nos. J29-J33 (5) 1,728. 1,205.

D3

Perf. 11 (2sh, 10sh, 20sh), 11½x11 (1sh, 5sh)

1908-09 Wmk. 12

J34 D3 1sh emer ('09) 225.00 29.00
J35 D3 2sh emerald *1,800.* —
J36 D3 5sh emerald 775.00 75.00
J37 D3 10sh emerald *5,200.* —
J38 D3 20sh emerald *29,000.* —

D4

1909-23 Wmk. 13 *Perf. 12x12½*

J39 D4 ½p green & car 32.00 *45.00*
a. Perf 11, green & rose ('14) 20.00 17.00
b. Perf 12½, green & scarlet ('13) 37.50 29.00
c. Perf 14 ('19) 20.00 17.00
J40 D4 1p green & car 23.00 9.75
a. Perf 11, yel grn & rose, thicker paper, thick yellowish gum 4,600. 1,725.
b. Perf 11, bright apple green & rose, thin paper, thin white gum ('14) 20.00 8.50
c. Perf 14 ('14) 70.00 17.00
J41 D4 2p green & car 32.00 5.75
a. Perf 11 — —
b. Perf 14 ('18) 29.00 7.50
J42 D4 3p green & car 35.00 14.50
a. Perf 14, green & rose ('16) 150.00 52.00
J43 D4 4p green & car 24.00 11.50
a. Perf 14 ('21) 200.00 70.00
J44 D4 6p green & car 35.00 14.00
a. Perf 11 — —
J45 D4 1sh green & car 33.00 9.25
a. Perf 14, yel grn & scarlet ('23) 45.00 23.00
J46 D4 2sh green & car 115.00 16.00
J47 D4 5sh green & car 175.00 17.00
J48 D4 10sh green & car 450.00 325.00
a. Perf 14, yel grn & scarlet ('21) 2,600.
J49 D4 £1 green & car 1,100. 575.00
a. Perf 14, yel grn & scarlet ('21) 1,600.
Nos. J39-J49 (11) 2,054. 1,043.

Nos. J39-J48 and J40a, J41a, J44a are from the 1909 printings and have thicker paper and thick yellowish gum. The other listings are from the 1912-23 printings on thinner paper with thin white gum.

1922-30 Wmk. 10 *Perf. 14, 11 (4p)*

J50 D4 ½p grn & car ('23) 9.25 7.50
J51 D4 1p green & car 7.50 2.25
J52 D4 1½p green & rose ('25) 4.25 7.50
J53 D4 2p green & car 9.25 4.25
J54 D4 3p green & car 17.00 3.25
J55 D4 4p green & car ('30) 17.00 8.00
a. Perf 14 52.00 23.00
J56 D4 6p green & car 37.50 18.50
Nos. J50-J56 (7) 101.75 51.25
Set, never hinged 200.00

1931-36 Wmk. 228 *Perf. 11*

J57 D4 ½p yel grn & rose ('34) 23.00 23.00
J58 D4 1p yel grn & rose ('32) 9.00 2.25
a. Perf 14 14.00 11.50
J59 D4 2p yel grn & rose ('33) 10.50 2.25
a. Perf 14 11.50 11.50
J60 D4 3p yel grn & rose ('36) 140.00 115.00
J61 D4 4p yel grn & rose ('34) 29.00 4.50
J62 D4 6p yel grn & rose ('36) 550.00 500.00
J63 D4 1sh yel grn & rose ('34) 70.00 30.00
Nos. J57-J63 (7) 831.50 677.00
Set, never hinged 1,400.

D5

Engraved; Value Typo.

1938 *Perf. 14½x14*

J64 D5 ½p green & car 3.50 *3.50*
J65 D5 1p green & car 12.50 1.10
J66 D5 2p green & car 12.50 2.25
J67 D5 3p green & car 55.00 23.00
J68 D5 4p green & car 16.00 1.10
J69 D5 6p green & car 100.00 45.00
J70 D5 1sh green & car 57.50 20.00
Nos. J64-J70 (7) 257.00 95.95
Set, never hinged 400.00

Catalogue values for unused stamps in this section, from this point to the end of the section, are for Never Hinged items.

Type of 1938
Value Tablet Redrawn

Original

Redrawn

Pence denominations: "D" has melon-shaped center in redrawn tablet. The redrawn 3p differs slightly, having semi-melon-shaped "D" center, with vertical white stroke half filling it.

1sh. 1938: Numeral "1" narrow, with six background lines above.

1sh. 1947: Numeral broader, showing more white space around dotted central ornament. Three lines above.

1946-57 **Wmk. 228**

J71	D5	½p grn & car ('56)	7.00	5.75
J72	D5	1p grn & car ('47)	4.50	1.10
J73	D5	2p green & car	8.00	1.10
J74	D5	3p green & car	10.00	1.10
J75	D5	4p grn & car ('52)	14.00	1.40
J76	D5	5p grn & car ('48)	18.50	2.25
J77	D5	6p grn & car ('47)	18.50	2.90
J78	D5	7p grn & car ('53)	8.00	7.00
J79	D5	8p grn & car ('57)	26.00	23.00
J80	D5	1sh grn & car ('47)	29.00	4.50
		Nos. J71-J80 (10)	143.50	50.10

MILITARY STAMPS

Nos. 166, 191, 183A, 173, 175, 206 and 177 Overprinted in Black

a

b

c

1946

Wrong font "6"

AN AN

Normal & Narrow "N"

Perf. 14½x14, 15x14, 11½, 13½x13

1946-47 **Wmk. 228**

M1	A24(a)	½p orange	3.50	3.50
		Never hinged	5.75	
a.		Wrong font "6" in ovpt.	90.00	*170.00*
b.		Narrow "N"	97.50	*185.00*
M2	A36(b)	1p brown vio	3.50	3.50
		Never hinged	5.75	
a.		Blue overprint	115.00	77.50
		Never hinged	140.00	
M3	A27(b)	3p dk vio brn	3.50	*3.50*
		Never hinged	5.75	
a.		Double overprint	850.00	
M4	A30(a)	6p brn violet	12.00	11.50
		Never hinged	18.00	
a.		Wrong font "6" in ovpt.	160.00	*240.00*
b.		Narrow "N"	160.00	*240.00*
M5	A16(a)	1sh gray green	12.00	11.50
		Never hinged	18.00	
a.		Wrong font "6" in ovpt.	200.00	*290.00*
b.		Narrow "N"	200.00	*290.00*
M6	A1(c)	2sh dk red brn	35.00	45.00
		Never hinged	70.00	
M7	A32(c)	5sh dl red brn	140.00	*200.00*
		Never hinged	250.00	
a.		Thin paper (#177a) ('48)	115.00	*200.00*
		Never hinged	160.00	
		Nos. M1-M7 (7)	209.50	278.50

"B.C.O.F." stands for "British Commonwealth Occupation Force."

Issue dates: Nos. M1-M3, Oct. 11, 1946; Nos. M4-M7, May 8, 1947.

OFFICIAL STAMPS

OVERPRINTED AND PERFORATED OFFICIAL STAMPS

Overprinted and perforated Official stamps are comparatively more difficult to find well centered than the basic issues on which they are printed. This is because poorly centered sheets that had been discarded were purposely chosen to be overprinted to save money.

Perforated Initials

In 1913-31, postage stamps were perforated "OS" for official Australian Federal and State government use. The first of such issues were punched with large initials 14mm high and containing 18 and 17 holes in the O and S, respectively. When stamps with this size initial fell apart, a smaller size was used. This was 8.5mm high and had 12 or 11 holes in the O and S. A third size OS, 9mm high was also used for a short time. Stamps exist with double or triple perforatioins. The system of perforated initials was replaced in 1931 by printed initials.

PERFORATED LARGE OS

OA Plus Scott Number

1913 **Wmk. 8**

OA1	A1	½p green	20.00	11.00
		Never hinged	35.00	
		On newspaper, postal card		75.00
e.		Wmk. inverted		92.50
OA2	A1	1p car (I)	18.00	4.00
		Never hinged	37.50	
		On circular, cover		35.00
d.		Die II	24.00	6.50
		Never hinged	40.00	
		On circular, cover		37.50
n.		As #OA2, wmk. inverted	92.50	9.00
o.		As "d," wmk. inverted	92.50	9.00
OA3	A1	2p gray	35.00	14.50
		Never hinged	55.00	
		On cover		97.50
OA4	A1	2½p dark blue	335.00	145.00
		Never hinged	600.00	
		On cover		400.00
OA5	A1	3p ol bis (I)	185.00	82.50
		Never hinged	315.00	
		On cover		200.00
a.		Die II	345.00	92.50
		Never hinged	*690.00*	
		On cover	290.00	
b.		Pair, #OA5-OA5a	*850.00*	
h.		As #OA5, wmk. inverted	125.00	57.50
i.		As "a," wmk. inverted	460.00	110.00
OA6	A1	4p orange	185.00	25.00
		Never hinged	345.00	
		On cover		97.50
b.		4p yellow orange	260.00	110.00
OA7	A1	5p org brn	160.00	37.50
		Never hinged	315.00	
		On cover		185.00
OA8	A1	6p ultra (I)	160.00	30.00
		Never hinged	375.00	
		On cover		185.00
c.		Wmk. inverted	260.00	92.50
OA9	A1	9p purple	145.00	55.00
		Never hinged	345.00	
		On cover		230.00
c.		Wmk. inverted		3,100.

All examples of the 9p purple with inverted watermark were released as #OA9c, of which 6 used specimens are known.

OA10	A1	1sh blue green	185.00	33.00
		Never hinged	350.00	
		On cover		290.00
c.		Wmk. inverted	690.00	220.00
OA11	A1	2sh brown	400.00	185.00
		Never hinged	1,380.	
		On cover		—
OA12	A1	5sh yel & gray	1,000.	575.00
		Never hinged	1,750.	
		On cover		—
OA13	A1	10sh pink & gray	2,300.	1,450.
		Never hinged	3,800.	
		On cover		—
OA14	A1	£1 ultra & brn	3,600.	2,650.
		Never hinged	5,500.	
		On cover		—
OA15	A1	£2 dp rose & blk	6,600.	3,500.
		Never hinged	9,700.	
		On cover		—

PERFORATED SMALL OS

OB Plus Scott Number

1914 **Wmk. 8**

OB1	A1	½p green	16.00	11.00
		Never hinged	35.00	
		On newspaper, postcard		115.00
e.		Wmk. inverted		55.00
OB2	A1	1p car (I)	18.50	7.25
		Never hinged	35.00	
		On circular, cover		52.50
d.		Die II	25.00	4.00
		Never hinged	45.00	
		On circular, cover		29.00
h.		Die III	20.00	2.75
		Never hinged	40.00	
		On circular, cover		29.00
OB3	A1	2p gray	65.00	6.00
		Never hinged	105.00	
		On cover		75.00
c.		Wmk. inverted	105.00	16.00
OB4	A1	2½p dark blue	335.00	125.00
		Never hinged	690.00	
		On cover		350.00
OB5	A1	3p ol bis (I)	90.00	8.00
		Never hinged	185.00	
		On cover		115.00
a.		Die II	240.00	57.50
		Never hinged	*460.00*	
		On cover		170.00
b.		Pair, #OB5-OB5a		—
h.		As # OB5, wmk. inverted		
i.		As "a," wmk. inverted	*360.00*	*92.50*
OB6	A1	4p orange	200.00	92.50
		Never hinged	400.00	
		On cover		275.00
b.		4p yellow orange	260.00	115.00
OB7	A1	5p org brn	160.00	55.00
		Never hinged	315.00	
		On cover		230.00
OB8	A1	6p ultra (II)	97.50	16.00
		Never hinged	230.00	
		On cover		145.00
c.		Wmk. inverted	240.00	87.50
OB9	A1	9p purple	97.50	30.00
		Never hinged	230.00	
		On cover		170.00
OB10	A1	1sh blue green	115.00	30.00
		Never hinged	290.00	
		On cover		315.00
OB11	A1	2sh brown	260.00	125.00
		Never hinged	860.00	
		On cover		—
OB12	A1	5sh yel & gray	1,250.	660.00
		Never hinged	2,200.	
		On cover		—
OB13	A1	10sh pink & gray	2,600.	1,600.
		Never hinged	4,900.	
		On cover		—
OB14	A1	£1 ultra & brn	4,300.	2,650.
		Never hinged	6,000.	
		On cover		—
OB15	A1	£2 dp rose & black	7,200.	4,300.
		Never hinged	12,000.	
		On cover		—

1914-24 **Wmk. 9**

OB19	A4	½p emerald	13.00	3.50
OB20	A4	½p orange	21.00	13.00
OB21	A4	1p red (I)	14.50	1.00
c.		1p carmine (II)	400.00	18.00
d.		1p scarlet (I), rough paper	27.50	8.00
e.		1p rose red (Ia), rough paper	290.00	18.00
f.		1p brt rose (Ia), rough paper	550.00	52.50
OB22	A4	1p violet (I)	30.00	17.50
OB23	A4	1p green (I)	10.00	2.75
OB24	A4	1½p choc	35.00	3.50
a.		1½p red brown	27.50	2.50
OB25	A4	1½p emerald	18.00	1.60
OB26	A4	1½p scarlet	8.50	.80
OB27	A4	2p brn org (I)	17.50	1.60
OB28	A4	2p red (I)	22.50	5.25
OB29	A4	2p red brn (I)	25.00	20.00
OB30	A4	3p ultra (I)	40.00	8.00
OB31	A4	4p orange	52.50	4.50
a.		4p yellow	290.00	65.00
OB32	A4	4p violet	55.00	17.50
OB33	A4	4p ultra	80.00	14.50
OB34	A4	4p ol bis	52.50	8.00
OB35	A4	4½p violet	140.00	16.00
OB36	A4	5p org brn (I)	65.00	11.50
a.		5p chestnut (I), rough paper	*1,700.*	160.00

All examples of the 5p chestnut on rough paper were released as #OB36a.

OB37	A4	1sh4p light blue	70.00	22.50

1915 **Wmk. 9**

OB38	A1	2p gray	105.00	14.50
OB40	A1	6p ultra (II)	170.00	20.00
a.		Die III	1,800.	500.00
OB41	A1	9p violet	240.00	87.50
OB42	A1	1sh blue green	240.00	52.50
OB43	A1	2sh brown	720.00	125.00
OB44	A1	5sh yellow & gray	920.00	170.00

1915-24 **Wmk. 10**

OB45	A1	2p gray (I)	25.00	6.50
a.		Die II	40.00	20.00
OB46	A1	2½p dark blue	62.50	16.00
OB47	A1	3p ol bis (I)	32.50	5.75
a.		Die II	115.00	55.00
b.		Die IV	32.50	18.50
OB48	A1	6p ultra (II)	45.00	8.00
b.		Die III	1,450.	450.00
c.		Die IV	62.50	18.50
OB49	A1	6p yel brn (IV)	29.00	3.50
OB50	A1	9p violet (II)	35.00	16.00
a.		9p lilac (III)	35.00	16.00
OB51	A1	1sh blue grn (I)	30.00	3.50
a.		Die IV	30.00	4.50
OB52	A1	2sh brown	145.00	20.00
OB53	A1	2sh vio brn (II)	72.50	16.00
OB54	A1	5sh yel & gray	230.00	60.00
OB55	A1	10sh brt pink & gray	525.00	80.00
OB56	A1	£1 ultra & brn	2,650.	1,600.
OB57	A1	£1 gray (IV)	920.00	460.00
OB58	A1	£2 rose & blk	2,650.	1,150.

1918-20 **Wmk. 11**

OB60	A4	½p emerald	20.00	8.00
OB61	A4	1p rose (I)	140.00	52.50
OB62	A4	1p green (I)	20.00	20.00
OB63	A4	1½p chocolate	24.00	3.50
a.		1½p red brown	29.00	3.00

1924 **Unwmk.**

OB64	A4	1p green	92.50	87.50
OB65	A4	1½p carmine	97.50	87.50

1926-30 **Wmk. 203** ***Perf. 13½x12½***

OB66	A4	½p orange	5.25	1.60
a.		Perf. 14	230.00	97.50
OB67	A4	1p green (I)	5.25	1.60
a.		Die Ia	125.00	160.00
b.		Perf. 14	13.00	1.60
OB68	A4	1½p rose red	9.75	2.50
c.		Perf. 14	27.50	2.50
OB69	A4	1½p red brn	21.00	5.00
OB70	A4	2p red brn (II)	35.00	18.00
a.		Die I, perf. 14	160.00	52.50
OB71	A4	2p red (II)	21.00	5.00
OB72	A4	3p ultra (I)	37.50	6.50
a.		Die II	29.00	5.00
b.		Perf. 14	80.00	17.00
OB73	A4	4p ol bis	29.00	5.00
a.		Perf. 14	170.00	52.50
OB74	A4	4½p violet	170.00	45.00
a.		Perf. 13½x12½	125.00	125.00
OB75	A4	5p brn buff (II)	65.00	9.25
OB76	A4	1sh4p pale turq bl	300.00	32.50
a.		Perf. 14	400.00	160.00

1928

OB95	A3	3p deep blue	17.50	11.50

1928-30 **Wmk. 203**

OB96	A1	6p brown	30.00	5.25
OB97	A1	9p violet	57.50	7.25
OB98	A1	1sh blue green	30.00	5.25
OB99	A1	2sh red brown	87.50	11.50
OB100	A1	5sh yel & gray	260.00	97.50
OB101	A1	10sh pink & gray	2,300.	
OB102	A1	£2 dl red & blk	4,300.	

1930

OB104	A7	1½p dark red	13.00	9.25
OB105	A7	3p dark blue	18.00	11.00

PERFORATED MEDIUM OS

OC Plus Scott Number

1927

OC94	A5	1½p brown red	20.00	10.00

1929

OC103	A6	1½p dull red	20.00	13.00

1929

OCC1	AP1	3p deep green	30.00	16.00

OVERPRINTED OFFICIAL STAMPS

See note at beginning of section.

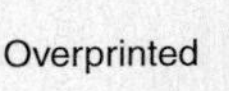

On Regular Issue of 1931

1931, May 4 **Unwmk.** ***Perf. 11, 11½***

O1	A8	2p dull red	160.00	45.00
O2	A8	3p blue	450.00	80.00

These stamps were issued primarily for official use but to prevent speculation a quantity was issued for public distribution.

Used values are for CTO examples.

Counterfeit overprints exist.

On Regular Issues of 1928-32

1932 **Wmk. 203** ***Perf. 13½x12½***

O3	A4	2p red (II)	25.00	13.00
O4	A4	4p olive bister	40.00	26.00

Perf. 11½, 12

O5	A1	6p brown	97.50	90.00

1932-33 **Wmk. 228** ***Perf. 13½x12½***

O6	A4	½p orange	9.25	6.00
a.		Inverted overprint	—	—
O7	A4	1p green (I)	6.00	2.00
O8	A4	2p red (II)	13.00	6.50
a.		Inverted overprint		—
O9	A4	3p ultra (II) ('33)	18.00	9.25
O10	A4	5p brown buff	57.50	52.50

Perf. 11½, 12

O11	A1	6p yellow brown	45.00	35.00
a.		Inverted overprint		—
		Nos. O6-O11 (6)	148.75	111.25
		Set, never hinged	275.00	

1932 **Unwmk.** ***Perf. 11, 11½***

O12	A9	2p red	7.25	6.00
O13	A9	3p blue	24.00	24.00
O14	A16	1sh gray green	72.50	52.50
		Nos. O12-O14 (3)	103.75	82.50
		Set, never hinged	160.00	

AUSTRIA

'os-trē-ə

LOCATION — Central Europe
AREA — 32,378 sq. mi.
POP. — 6,760,233
CAPITAL — Vienna

Before 1867 Austria was an absolute monarchy, which included Hungary and Lombardy-Venetia. In 1867 the Austro-Hungarian Monarchy was established, with Austria and Hungary as equal partners. After World War I, in 1918, the different nationalities established their own states and only the German-speaking parts remained, forming a republic under the name "Deutschosterreich" (German Austria), which name was shortly again changed to "Austria." In 1938 German forces occupied Austria, which became part of the German Reich.

60 Kreuzer = 1 Gulden
100 Neu-Kreuzer = 1 Gulden (1858)
100 Heller = 1 Krone (1899)
100 Groschen = 1 Schilling (1925)

Unused stamps without gum sell for about one-third or less of the values quoted.

Watermarks

Wmk. 91 — "BRIEF-MARKEN" In Double-lined Capitals Across the Middle of the Sheet

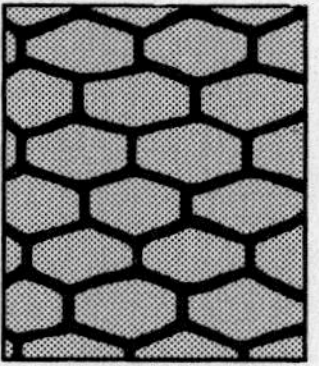

Wmk. 109 — Webbing

Wmk. 125 — Lozenges

Wmk. 140 — Crown

Wmk. 237 — Swastikas

Issues of the Austrian Monarchy (including Hungary)

Coat of Arms — A1

NINE KREUZER

Type I. One heavy line around coat of arms center. On the 9kr the top of "9" is about on a level with "Kreuzer" and not near the top of the label. Each cliche has the "9" in a different position.

Type IA. As type I, but with 1 ¼mm between "9" and "K."

Type II. One heavy line around coat of arms center. On the 9kr the top of "9" is much higher than the top of the word "Kreuzer" and nearly touches the top of the label.

Type III. As type II, but with two, thinner, lines around the center.

Wmk. K.K.H.M. in Sheet or Unwmk.

1850 Typo. *Imperf.*

The stamps of this issue were at first printed on a rough hand-made paper, varying in thickness and having a watermark in script letters K.K.H.M., the initials of Kaiserlich Königliches Handels-Ministerium (Imperial and Royal Ministry of Commerce), vertically in the gutter between the panes. Parts of these letters show on margin stamps in the sheet. From 1854 a thick, smooth machine-made paper without watermark was used.

Thin to Thick Paper

No.	Description	Unused	Used
1	A1 1kr yellow	1,650.	115.00
	No gum	425.00	
	On cover		425.00
a.	Printed on both sides	*2,000.*	150.00
b.	1kr orange	2,350.	150.00
	No gum	590.00	
	On cover		475.00
c.	1kr brown orange	3,475.	625.00
	No gum	875.00	
	On cover		2,300.
e.	1kr cadmium yellow	2,250.	130.00
	No gum	650.00	
	On cover		500.00
2	A1 2kr black	1,375.	82.50
	No gum	350.00	
	On cover		290.00
a.	Ribbed paper	—	4,550.
	On cover		*13,500.*
b.	2kr gray black	2,350.	120.00
	No gum	600.00	
	On cover		375.00
d.	Half used as 1kr on cover		*52,500.*
	Half used as 1kr on cover, single franking		—

A cover bearing one example of the 2 kreuzer and a diagonally bisected example of the same stamp realized the equivalent of U.S. $50,950 at a Zurich auction in 2003.

A faulty cover bearing one example of the 2 kreuzer diagonally bisected, paying a 1 kreuzer rate, realized the equivalent of U.S. $41,520 at a Zurich auction in 2004.

No.	Description	Unused	Used
e.	2kr silver gray ('50, 1st printing)	3,600.	650.00
	No gum	900.00	
	On cover		1,550.
3	A1 3kr red	825.00	4.00
	No gum	210.00	
	On cover		25.00
a.	Ribbed paper	*4,000.*	160.00
	No gum	1,000.	
	On cover		500.00
b.	Laid paper	—	*19,000.*
	On cover		*23,500.*
c.	Printed on both sides		*10,000.*
d.	3kr dark carmine	1,750.	25.00
	No gum	450.00	
	On cover		100.00
4	A1 6kr brown	1,000.	6.00
	No gum	250.00	
	On cover		30.00
a.	Ribbed paper		*2,450.*
	On cover		*6,750.*
c.	Diagonal half used as 3kr on cover		*20,000.*
d.	6kr black brown	—	210.00
	On cover		400.00
e.	6kr pale reddish brown	1,500.	11.00
	No gum	375.00	
	On cover		42.50
5	A1 9kr blue, type II	2,350.	9.00
	No gum	590.00	
	On cover		50.00
a.	9kr blue, type I	*2,250.*	19.00
	No gum	550.00	
	On cover		100.00
b.	9kr blue, type IA	*15,000.*	*1,250.*
	On cover		*2,500.*
c.	Laid paper, type III		*15,000.*
d.	Printed on both sides, type II		*9,250.*
f.	9kr pale blue, type I	2,000.	13.00
	No gum	500.00	
	On cover		90.00
g.	9kr very dark blue, type III	2,700.	57.50
	No gum	675.00	
	On cover		160.00

1854

Machine-made Paper, Type III

No.	Description	Unused	Used
1d	A1 1kr yellow	1,450.	100.00
	No gum	360.00	
	On cover		300.00
1f	A1 1kr cadmium yellow	*2,000.*	140.00
	No gum	525.00	
	On cover		375.00
1g	A1 1kr yellow ocher	*2,300.*	140.00
	No gum	590.00	
	On cover		425.00
1h	A1 1kr golden yellow	*3,850.*	250.00
	No gum	1,000.	
	On cover		575.00
1i	A1 1kr mustard yellow		475.00
1j	A1 1kr lemon yellow	*1,500.*	110.00
	No gum	375.00	
	On cover		325.00
2c	A1 2kr black	1,750.	80.00
	No gum	450.00	
	On cover		275.00
3e	A1 3kr red	475.00	4.25
	No gum	115.00	
	On cover		16.50
f.	3kr red, type I	4,650.	52.50
	No gum	1,150.	
	On cover		200.00
4b	A1 6kr brown	975.00	8.25
	No gum	240.00	
	On cover		32.50
4f	A1 6kr reddish brown	*1,050.*	7.75
	No gum	260.00	
	On cover		40.00
5e	A1 9kr blue	1,025.	4.25
	No gum	260.00	
	On cover		21.00
5h	A1 9kr dark slate blue	*1,450.*	13.50
	No gum	360.00	
	On cover		82.50

Full margins = 1 ½mm.

In 1852-54, Nos. 1-5, rouletted 14, were used in Tokay and Homonna. A 12kr blue exists, but was not issued. Value, $100,000.

The reprints are type III in brighter colors, some on paper watermarked "Briefmarken" in the sheet.

For similar design see Lombardy-Venetia A1.

Values for used pairs

Hand-made Paper

No.	Description	Value
1	A1 1kr yellow	375.00
	On cover	1,000.
1b	A1 1kr orange	390.00
	On cover	1,100.
1c	A1 1kr brown orange	1,300.
	On cover	2,900.
1e	A1 1kr cadmium yellow	425.00
	On cover	1,100.
2	A1 2kr black	310.00
	On cover	3,200.
2b	A1 2kr gray black	315.00
	On cover	2,900.
2e	A1 2kr silver gray	1,800.
	On cover	—
3	A1 3kr red	21.00
	On cover	82.50
3d	A1 3kr dark carmine	57.50
	On cover	190.00
4	A1 6kr brown	90.00
	On cover	310.00
5	A1 9kr blue, type II	32.50
	On cover	525.00
5a	A1 9kr blue, type I	140.00
	On cover	400.00
5f	A1 9kr pale blue, type I	140.00
	On cover	400.00

Machine-made Paper, Type III

No.	Description	Value
1d	A1 1kr yellow	300.00
	On cover	875.00
1f	A1 1kr cadmium yellow	540.00
	On cover	1,500.
1g	A1 1kr yellow ocher	435.00
	On cover	1,250.
1h	A1 1kr golden yellow	540.00
	On cover	1,500.
1j	A1 1kr lemon yellow	325.00
	On cover	875.00
2c	A1 2kr black	275.00
	On cover	2,700.
3e	A1 3kr red	16.50
	On cover	110.00
3f	A1 3kr red, type I	130.00
	On cover	300.00
4b	A1 6kr brown	75.00
	On cover	200.00
5e	A1 9kr blue	32.50
	On cover	105.00

Values for used strips of 3

Hand-made Paper

No.	Description	Value
1	A1 1kr yellow	900.00
	On cover	1,900.
1b	A1 1kr orange	1,000.
	On cover	2,100.
1c	A1 1kr brown orange	2,300.
	On cover	4,800.
1e	A1 1kr cadmium yellow	1,050.
	On cover	2,100.
2	A1 2kr black	950.00
	On cover	2,150.
2b	A1 2kr gray black	1,000.
	On cover	1,900.
2e	A1 2kr silver gray	3,500.
3	A1 3kr red	70.00
	On cover	275.00
3d	A1 3kr dark carmine	200.00
	On cover	540.00
4	A1 6kr brown	440.00
	On cover	900.00
5	A1 9kr blue, type II	175.00
	On cover	825.00
5a	A1 9kr blue, type I	400.00
	On cover	950.00
5f	A1 9kr pale blue, type I	375.00

Machine-made Paper, Type III

No.	Description	Value
1d	A1 1kr yellow	800.00
	On cover	1,750.
1f	A1 1kr cadmium yellow	1,300.
	On cover	*2,750.*
1g	A1 1kr yellow ocher	1,050.
	On cover	2,750.
1h	A1 1kr golden yellow	1,300.
	On cover	2,650.
1j	A1 1kr lemon yellow	800.00
	On cover	1,700.
2c	A1 2kr black	875.00
	On cover	1,850.
3e	A1 3kr red	45.00
	On cover	400.00
3f	A1 3kr red, type I	350.00
	On cover	750.00
4b	A1 6kr brown	325.00
	On cover	800.00
5e	A1 9kr blue	140.00
	On cover	450.00

Values for used blocks of 4

Hand-made Paper

1	A1	1kr yellow		*8,000.*
1b	A1	1kr orange		*8,750.*
1c	A1	1kr brown orange		
1e	A1	1kr cadmium yellow		*8,750.*
2	A1	2kr black		*13,750.*
2b	A1	2kr gray black		*15,000.*
2e	A1	2kr silver gray		
3	A1	3kr red	*14,500.*	*3,500.*
3d	A1	3kr dark carmine	*16,500.*	*5,750.*
4	A1	6kr brown	*16,500.*	*7,000.*
4d	A1	6kr black brown		
5	A1	9kr blue, type II	*45,000.*	*6,750.*
5a	A1	9kr blue, type I	*55,000.*	*7,000.*
5f	A1	9kr pale blue, type I		*7,000.*

Machine-made Paper, Type III

1d	A1	1kr yellow		*7,500.*
1f	A1	1kr cadmium yellow		
1g	A1	1kr yellow ocher		*9,000.*
1h	A1	1kr golden yellow		*6,500.*
1j	A1	1kr lemon yellow		*6,500.*
2c	A1	2kr black	*50,000.*	*13,750.*
3e	A1	3kr red	*10,000.*	*1,650.*
3f	A1	3kr red, type I		*5,750.*
4b	A1	6kr brown	*10,000.*	*5,750.*
5e	A1	9kr blue	*13,000.*	*2,750.*

Values for stamps used in Lombardy-Venetia

Hand-made Paper

1 A1 1kr yellow, *from* 365.00
On cover, *from* *5,800.*
1b A1 1kr orange, *from* 425.00
On cover, *from* *7,000.*
2 A1 2kr black, *from* 325.00
On cover, *from* *4,000.*
3 A1 3kr red, *from* 57.50
On cover, *from* 375.00
3a A1 3kr red (ribbed paper), *from* 250.00
On cover, *from* *1,600.*
4 A1 6kr brown, *from* 62.50
On cover, *from* 475.00
5 A1 9kr blue (II)(from) 250.00
On cover, *from* *2,100.*
5a A1 9kr blue (I)(from) 100.00
On cover, *from* *1,100.*

Machine-made Paper, Type III

1d A1 1kr yellow, *from* *650.00*
On cover, *from* *16,500.*
2c A1 2kr black, *from* *575.00*
On cover, *from* *11,250.*
3e A1 3kr red, *from* 325.00
On cover, *from* 2,100.
4b A1 6kr brown, *from* 375.00
On cover, *from* *3,750.*
5e A1 9kr blue, *from* 500.00
On cover, *from* *4,100.*

Values for Stamps Cancelled First Day of Issue (June 1, 1850)

1 A1 1kr yellow —
On cover —
2 A1 2kr black —
On cover *67,500.*
3 A1 3kr red *1,300.*
On cover *25,000.*
4 A1 6kr brown *1,450.*
On cover *30,000.*
5a A1 9kr blue, type I 1,450.
On cover *25,000.*

Values for Stamps with Red Cancellations

Hand-Made Paper

1 A1 1kr yellow 3,500.
2 A1 2kr black 1,300.
3 A1 3kr red 675.00
4 A1 6kr brown 625.00
5 A1 9kr blue, type II 875.00

Machine-Made Paper

1a A1 1kr yellow 1,250.
2c A1 2kr black 475.00
3e A1 3kr red 240.00
4b A1 6kr brown 90.00
5e A1 9kr blue 60.00

Values for Stamps with Blue Cancellations

Hand-Made Paper

1 A1 1kr yellow 1,075.
2 A1 2kr black 1,000.
3 A1 3kr red 250.00
4 A1 6kr brown 275.00
5 A1 9kr blue, type II 300.00

Machine-Made Paper

1a A1 1kr yellow 800.00
2c A1 2kr black 825.00
3e A1 3kr red 120.00
4b A1 6kr brown 120.00
5e A1 9kr blue 160.00

Rouletted 14

1 A1 1kr yellow —
On cover, Tokay cancellation —
2 A1 2kr black —
On cover, Tokay cancellation —
3 A1 3kr red *1,575.*
On cover, Tokay cancellation *11,500.*
4 A1 6kr brown *2,150.*
On cover, Tokay cancellation *30,000.*
5a A1 9kr blue, type I *1,850.*
On cover, Tokay cancellation *21,000.*

This roulette was applied to stamps by the postmasters of the Tokay and Hommona post offices (now in Hungary) post offices during 1852-54.

A2

A3

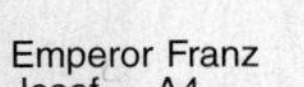
Emperor Franz Josef — A4

A5

A6

Two Types of Each Value.

Type I. Loops of the bow at the back of the head broken, except the 2kr. In the 2kr, the "2" has a flat foot, thinning to the right. The frame line in the UR corner is thicker than the line below. In the 5kr the top frame line is unbroken.

Type II. Loops complete. Wreath projects further at top of head. In the 2kr, the "2" has a more curved foot of uniform thickness, with a shading line in the upper and lower curves. The frame line UR is thicker than the line below. In the 5kr the top frame line is broken.

1858-59 Embossed *Perf. 14½*

6 A2 2kr yellow, type II 1,225. 55.00
No gum 200.00
On cover 125.00
a. 2kr yellow, type I 3,000. 400.00
No gum 400.00
On cover 725.00
b. 2kr orange, type II 3,750. 450.00
No gum 600.00
On cover 900.00
c. Half used as 1kr on cover *41,500.*
d. 2kr dark orange, type II 7,250. *725.00*
No gum 1,450.
On cover *1,350.*

7 A3 3kr black, type II *2,500.* 175.00
No gum 400.00
On cover 400.00
a. 3kr black, type I 2,000. 240.00
No gum 275.00
On cover 475.00
b. 3kr gray black, type I 600.00
No gum
On cover *1,350.*

8 A3 3kr green, type II ('59) 1,350. 140.00
No gum 240.00
On cover 325.00
a. 3k bluish green, type II ('59) 2,000. 175.00
No gum 275.00
On cover 350.00

9 A4 5kr red, type II 475.00 2.40
No gum 80.00
On cover 6.50
a. 5kr red, type I 2,000. 20.00
No gum 350.00
On cover 55.00
b. 5kr red, type II with type I frame 950.00 32.50
No gum 175.00
On cover 72.50

10 A5 10kr brown, type II 875.00 4.75
No gum 140.00
On cover 12.00
a. 10kr brown, type I 2,400. 24.00
No gum 400.00
On cover 95.00
b. Half used as 5kr on cover, single franking *16,000.*
c. Half used as 5kr on 15kr rate cover *20,000.*

11 A6 15kr blue, type II 800.00 2.00
No gum 140.00
On cover 14.50
a. Type I 2,400. 24.00
No gum 400.00
On cover 47.50
b. Half used as 7kr on cover —
c. 15k deep blue, Type I 2,750. 65.00
No gum 475.00
On cover 65.00

The reprints are of type II and are perforated 10½, 11, 12, 12½ and 13. There are also imperforate reprints of Nos. 6 to 8.

For similar designs see Lombardy-Venetia A2-A6.

Values for used pairs

6 A2 2kr yellow, type II 125.00
On cover 1,300.
6a A2 2kr yellow, type I 875.00
On cover 3,250.
6b A2 2kr orange, type II 675.00
On cover —
7 A3 3kr black, type II 525.00
On cover 2,350.
7a A3 3kr black, type I 600.00
On cover 2,500.
7b A3 3kr gray black, type I 1,325.
On cover —
8 A3 3kr green, type II ('59) 400.00
On cover 2,200.
9 A4 5kr red, type II 5.50
On cover 20.00
9a A4 5kr red, type I 47.50
On cover 95.00
9b A4 5kr red, type II with type I frame 75.00
On cover —
10 A5 10kr brown, type II 16.00
On cover 40.000
10a A5 10kr brown, type I 95.00
On cover 160.00
11 A6 15kr blue, type II 14.00
On cover 30.00
11a A6 15kr blue, type I 50.00
On cover 145.00

Values for used strips of 3

6 A2 2kr yellow, type II 200.00
On cover *2,500.*
6a A2 2kr yellow, type I 1,450.
On cover *4,750.*
7 A3 3kr black, type II 800.00
On cover —
7a A3 3kr black, type I 950.00
On cover —
7b A3 3kr gray black, type I 3,000.
On cover —
8 A3 3kr green, type II ('59) 650.00
On cover —
9 A4 5kr red, type II 20.00
On cover 125.00
9a A4 5kr red, type I 80.00
On cover 240.00
9b A4 5kr red, type II with type 1 frame 125.00
On cover —
10 A5 10kr brown, type II 45.00
On cover 275.00
10a A5 10kr brown, type I 160.00
On cover 375.00
11 A6 15kr blue, type II 32.50
On cover 140.00
11a A6 15kr blue, type I 110.00
On cover 250.00

Values for used strips of 4

6 A2 2kr yellow, type II 535.00
6a A2 2kr yellow, type I 2,350.
7 A3 3kr black, type II 1,325.
7a A3 3kr black, type I 1,650.
7b A3 3kr gray black, type II *3,250.*
8 A3 3kr green, type II 1,250.
9 A4 5kr red, type II 65.00
9a A4 5kr red, type II 215.00
9b A4 5kr red, type II with type I frame —
10 A5 10kr brown, type II 175.00
10a A5 10kr brown, type I 375.00
11 A6 15kr blue, type II 110.00
11a A6 15kr blue, type I 325.00

Values for blocks of 4

6 A2 2kr yellow, type II *2,750.*
6a A2 2kr yellow, type I *7,250.*
7 A3 3kr black, type II *4,000.*
7a A3 3kr black, type I *15,000.* *4,750.*
7b A3 3kr gray black, type I —
8 A3 3kr green, type II ('59) *4,000.*
9 A4 5kr red, type II *3,900.* 400.00
On cover 950.00
9a A4 5kr red, type I 725.00
On cover 1,800.
9b A4 5kr red, type II with type 1 frame
10 A5 10kr brown, type II 825.00
On cover 1,850.
10a A5 10kr brown, type I 1,500.
On cover 3,300.
11 A6 15kr blue, type II 575.00
On cover 1,500.
11a A6 15kr blue, type I 1,200.
On cover 2,700.

Values for stamps, covers used in Lombardy-Venetia

6 A2 2kr yellow, type II, *from* *900.00*
On cover, *from* *14,500.*
6a A2 2kr yellow, type I, *from* *1,750.*
On cover, *from* —
6b A2 2kr orange, type II, *from* 2,750.
On cover —
7 A3 3kr black, type II, *from* 350.00
On cover, *from* *3,750.*
7a A3 3kr black, type I, *from* 450.00
On cover, *from* *5,000.*
7b A3 3kr gray black, type I, *from* —
On cover, *from* —
8 A3 3kr green, type II ('59)(from) *450.00*
On cover, *from* *6,250.*
9 A4 5kr red, type II, *from* 200.00
On cover, *from* *1,550.*
9a A4 5kr red, type I, *from* 200.00
On cover, *from* *1,800.*
9b A4 5kr red, type II with type I frame, *from* —
On cover, *from* —
10 A5 10kr brown, type II, *from* 200.00
On cover, *from* *2,500.*
10a A5 10kr brown, type I, *from* 250.00
On cover, *from* *3,500.*
11 A6 15kr blue, type II, *from* 275.00
On cover, *from* *5,000.*
11a A6 15kr blue, type I, *from* 400.00
On cover, *from* *5,500.*

Values for Stamps with Red Cancellations

6 A2 2kr yellow, type II *160.00*
6a A2 2kr yellow, type I *750.00*
6b A2 2kr orange, type II 4,750.
7 A3 3kr black, type II 240.00
7a A3 3kr black, type I 290.00
8 A3 3kr green, type II ('59) 250.00
9 A4 5kr red, type II 30.00
9a A4 5kr red, type I 200.00
10 A5 10kr brown, type II 25.00
10a A5 10kr brown, type I 115.00
11 A6 15kr blue, type II 12.50
11a A6 15kr blue, type I 110.00

Values for Stamps with Blue Cancellations

6 A2 2kr yellow, type II 1,250.
6a A2 2kr yellow, type I 1,950.
6b A2 2kr orange, type II 2,300.
7 A3 3kr black, type II 1,150.
7a A3 3kr black, type I 1,325.
8 A3 3kr green, type II ('59) 675.00
9 A4 5kr red, type II 100.00
9a A4 5kr red, type I 115.00
10 A5 10kr brown, type II 110.00
10a A5 10kr brown, type I 210.00
11 A6 15kr blue, type II 115.00
11a A6 15kr blue, type I 200.00

Values for Stamps on Cover Cancelled First Day of Issue (Nov. 1, 1858)

6a A2 2kr yellow, type I *25,000.*
7a A3 3kr black, type I *14,000.*
9a A4 5kr red, type I *10,000.*
10a A5 10kr brown, type I *11,000.*
11a A6 15kr blue, type I *12,500.*

Franz Josef — A7

1860-61 Embossed *Perf. 14*

12 A7 2kr yellow 450.00 35.00
No gum 90.00
On cover 65.00
a. Half used as 1kr on cover *25,000.*

13 A7 3kr green 375.00 30.00
No gum 90.00
On cover 75.00
a. 3kr yellow green 500.00 35.00
No gum 125.00
On cover 72.50

14 A7 5kr red 290.00 1.00
No gum 72.50
On cover 4.00
a. 5kr deep red 375.00 3.00
No gum 90.00
On cover 11.00

15 A7 10kr brown 325.00 3.00
No gum 80.00
On cover 7.25
a. Half used as 5kr on cover *9,000.*
b. 10kr deep brown 500.00 8.50
No gum 125.00
On cover 20.00

16 A7 15kr blue 475.00 3.00
No gum 115.00
On cover 5.50
a. 15k deep blue 650.00 4.75
No gum 160.00
On cover 11.00

Values for Pairs

12 A7 2kr yellow 1,300. 70.00
On cover 700.00
13 A7 3kr green 1,250. 72.50
On cover 975.00
14 A7 5kr red 800.00 4.00
On cover 18.00
15 A7 10kr brown 900.00 7.50
On cover 32.50
16 A7 15kr blue 1,050. 5.00
On cover 25.00

Values for Strips of 3

12 A7 2kr yellow 140.00
On cover 2,400.
13 A7 3kr green 130.00
On cover 2,250.
14 A7 5kr red 18.00
On cover 70.00
15 A7 10kr brown 35.00
On cover 190.00
16 A7 15kr blue 30.00
On cover 130.00

Values for Strips of 4

12 A7 2kr yellow 250.00
13 A7 3kr green 240.00
14 A7 5kr red 42.50
15 A7 10kr brown 105.00
16 A7 15kr blue 75.00

Values for Blocks of 4

12 A7 2kr yellow 4,800. 1,750.
On cover 5,000.
13 A7 3kr green 4,700. 1,750.
On cover 4,700.
14 A7 5kr red 2,650. 250.00
On cover 775.00
15 A7 10kr brown 3,500. 500.00
On cover 1,400.
16 A7 15kr blue 4,400. 375.00
On cover 1,100.

Values for stamps, covers used in Lombardy-Venetia

12 A7 2kr yellow, *from* 550.00
On cover, *from* *13,750.*
13 A7 3kr green, *from* 460.00
On cover, *from* *12,500.*
14 A7 5kr red, *from* 165.00
On cover, *from* 1,850.
15 A7 10kr brown, *from* 220.00
On cover, *from* *2,100.*
16 A7 15kr blue, *from* 375.00
On cover, *from* *5,750.*

The reprints are perforated 9, 9½, 10, 10½, 11, 11½, 12, 12½, 13 and 13½.

There are also imperforate reprints of the 2 and 3kr.

For similar design see Lombardy-Venetia A7.

Coat of Arms — A8

1863

17 A8 2kr yellow 675.00 110.00
No gum 140.00
On cover 225.00
a. Half used as 1kr on cover —

18 A8 3kr green 525.00 100.00
No gum 125.00
On cover 225.00
a. 3kr yellow green 800.00 120.00
No gum 200.00
On cover 300.00
19 A8 5kr rose 625.00 15.00
No gum 115.00
On cover 40.00
a. 5kr carmine rose 650.00 22.00
No gum 160.00
On cover 60.00
20 A8 10kr blue 1,650. 18.50
No gum 350.00
On cover 47.50
a. 10kr deep blue 1,600. 22.00
No gum 400.00
On cover 60.00
21 A8 15kr yellow brown 1,650. 18.00
No gum 300.00
On cover 54.00
a. 15kr deep brown 1,700. 24.00
No gum 425.00
On cover 72.50

Values for used pairs

17 A8 2kr yellow 290.00
18 A8 3kr green 250.00
19 A8 5kr rose 30.00
20 A8 10kr blue 40.00
21 A8 15kr yellow brown 47.50

Values for Stamps with Red Cancellations

17 A8 2kr yellow 2,000.
18 A8 3kr green 200.00
19 A8 5kr rose 54.00
20 A8 10kr blue 47.50
21 A8 15kr yellow brown 47.50

Values for Stamps with Blue Cancellations

17 A8 2kr yellow 550.00
18 A8 3kr green 325.00
19 A8 5kr rose 57.50
20 A8 10kr blue 115.00
21 A8 15kr yellow brown 105.00

For similar design see Lombardy-Venetia A1.

Wmk. 91, or, before July 1864, Unwmkd.

1863-64 *Perf. 9½*

22 A8 2kr yellow ('64) 190.00 15.00
No gum 35.00
On cover 45.00
a. Ribbed paper 550.00
On cover 1,500.
b. Half used as 1kr on cover 27,500.
c. 2kr deep yellow 235.00 22.00
No gum 57.50
On cover 60.00
23 A8 3kr green ('64) 190.00 15.00
No gum 45.00
On cover 54.00
a. 3kr deep green ('64) 275.00 22.00
No gum 55.00
On cover 72.50
24 A8 5kr rose 55.00 .75
No gum 12.50
On cover 5.40
a. Ribbed paper 775.00
On cover 2,100.
b. 5kr carmine rose 175.00 3.75
No gum 45.00
On cover 8.00
25 A8 10kr blue 250.00 3.50
No gum 55.00
On cover 12.00
a. Half used as 5kr on cover 22,500.
b. 10kr greenish blue 290.00 8.50
No gum 72.50
On cover 14.00
26 A8 15kr yellow brown 225.00 2.25
No gum 50.00
On cover 8.75
a. 15kr deep brown 275.00 3.50
No gum 65.00
On cover 12.00
Nos. 22-26 (5) 910.00 36.50

Values for Pairs

22 A8 2kr yellow ('64) 40.00
23 A8 3kr green ('64) 40.00
24 A8 5kr rose 1.75
25 A8 10kr blue 9.50
26 A8 15kr yellow brown 9.00

Values for Stamps with Red Cancellations

22 A8 2kr yellow ('64) 525.00
23 A8 3kr green ('64) 42.50
24 A8 5kr rose 22.00
25 A8 10kr blue 14.00
26 A8 15kr yellow brown 9.00

Values for Stamps with Blue Cancellations

22 A8 2kr yellow ('64) 130.00
23 A8 3kr green ('64) 35.00
24 A8 5kr rose 7.25
25 A8 10kr blue 15.00
26 A8 15kr yellow brown 11.00

Values for Stamps with Green Cancellations

22 A8 2kr yellow ('64) 1,100.
23 A8 3kr green ('64) 1,100.
24 A8 5kr rose 375.00

The reprints are perforated 10½, 11½, 13 and 13½. There are also imperforate reprints of the 2 and 3kr.

Issues of Austro-Hungarian Monarchy

From 1867 to 1871 the independent postal administrations of Austria and Hungary used the same stamps.

A9

A10

5 kr:

Type I. In arabesques in lower left corner, the small ornament at left of the curve nearest the figure "5" is short and has three points at bottom.

Type II. The ornament is prolonged within the curve and has two points at bottom. The corresponding ornament at top of the lower left corner does not touch the curve (1872).

Type III. Similar to type II but the top ornament is joined to the curve (1881). Two different printing methods were used for the 1867-74 issues. The first produced stamps on which the hair and whiskers were coarse and thick, from the second they were fine and clear.

1867-72 Wmk. 91 Typo. *Perf. 9½*
Coarse Print

27 A9 2kr yellow 120.00 3.00
Never hinged 240.00
On cover 13.00
a. Half used as 1kr on cover —
b. 2kr lemon yellow 190.00 6.00
Never hinged 350.00
On cover 21.00
c. 2kr ochre yellow 190.00 8.75
Never hinged 350.00
On cover 45.00
d. 2kr yellowish orange 120.00 2.75
Never hinged 225.00
On cover 15.00
e. 2kr deep orange 190.00 6.00
Never hinged 390.00
On cover 30.00
f. 2kr brown orange 290.00 17.50
Never hinged 575.00
On cover 77.50
28 A9 3kr green 140.00 2.90
Never hinged 240.00
On cover 16.50
a. 3kr pale yellow green 140.00 3.00
Never hinged 275.00
On cover 18.00
b. 3kr blue green 190.00 4.00
Never hinged 350.00
On cover 30.00
c. 3kr deep green 250.00 6.00
Never hinged 475.00
On cover 42.50
d. 3kr emerald green 300.00 15.00
Never hinged 600.00
On cover 90.00
29 A9 5kr rose, type II 87.50 .25
Never hinged 165.00
On cover 3.00
a. 5kr rose, type I 95.00 .25
Never hinged 175.00
On cover 3.00
b. Perf. 10½, type II 190.00
Never hinged 300.00
c. Cliché of 3kr in plate of 5kr 37,500.
d. 5kr lilac rose, type I 95.00 1.20
Never hinged 175.00
No gum 20.00
On cover 4.25
e. 5kr brick red, type II 150.00 1.75
Never hinged 275.00
No gum 22.00
On cover 8.00
f. 5kr violet red, type I 260.00 2.75
Never hinged 450.00
On cover 14.50
30 A9 10kr blue 290.00 2.40
Never hinged 500.00
On cover 42.50
On cover, single franking 54.00
a. Half used as 5kr on cover —
b. 10kr pale milky blue 325.00 6.00
Never hinged 600.00
On cover 42.50
c. 10kr deep blue 325.00 3.00
Never hinged 540.00
On cover 45.00
31 A9 15kr brown 290.00 6.50
Never hinged 550.00
On cover 20.00
a. 15kr deep brown 440.00 29.00
Never hinged 800.00
On cover 60.00
b. 15kr yellowish brown 325.00 7.75
Never hinged 600.00
On cover 29.00
c. 15kr gray brown 300.00 8.75
Never hinged 600.00
On cover 40.00
d. 15kr reddish brown 350.00 13.00
Never hinged 650.00
On cover 54.00
32 A9 25kr lilac 87.50 21.00
Never hinged 165.00
On cover 165.00
a. 25kr gray lilac 47.50 17.50
Never hinged 95.00
On cover 165.00
b. 25kr brown violet 325.00 65.00
Never hinged 650.00
On cover 350.00
c. 25kr violet 52.50 19.00
Never hinged 105.00
On cover 160.00
d. 25kr brownish lilac 87.50 40.00
Never hinged 165.00
On cover 240.00
e. 25kr dull gray 900.00 350.00
Never hinged 1,500.
On cover 1,200.

Perf. 12

33 A10 50kr light brown 40.00 130.00
Never hinged 70.00
On cover 3,000.
a. 50kr pale red brown 500.00 210.00
Never hinged 850.00
On cover 3,400.
b. 50kr brownish rose 500.00 325.00
Never hinged 850.00
On cover 3,750.
c. Pair, imperf. btwn., vert. or horizontal 725.00 1,700.

There are 3 known examples of No. 29c. Each has small defects. The value for No. 29c is for a defective example. An undamaged example believed to be unique was sold at a German auction in 2013 for the equivalent of US $275,000.00.

Issues for Austria only

1874-80 Fine Print *Perf. 9½*

34 A9 2kr yellow ('76) 14.50 .90
Never hinged 30.00
On cover 13.00
f. 2kr lemon yellow 19.00 12.00
Never hinged 45.00
On cover 21.00
35 A9 3kr green ('76) 65.00 .90
Never hinged 130.00
On cover 17.50
f. 3kr yellow green 95.00 .90
Never hinged 165.00
On cover 18.50
36 A9 5kr rose, type III 4.50 .25
Never hinged 9.50
On cover 3.50
f. 5kr carmine rose 4.75 .25
Never hinged 16.50
On cover 4.75
37 A9 10kr blue ('75) 160.00 .60
Never hinged 350.00
On cover 29.00
f. 10kr pale blue 210.00 .90
Never hinged 450.00
On cover 24.00
38 A9 15kr brown ('77) 8.75 7.75
Never hinged 21.00
On cover 60.00
f. 15kr deep chestnut brown 20.00 13.00
Never hinged 42.50
On cover 47.50
39 A9 25kr gray lil ('78) 1.10 190.00
Never hinged 3.00
On cover 10,000.
f. 25kr gray violet 22.50 225.00
Never hinged 47.50
On cover 10,000.
40 A10 50kr red brown 14.50 190.00
Never hinged 40.00
On cover 12,500.

Perf. 9

34a A9 2kr 250.00 65.00
On cover 600.00
35a A9 3kr 225.00 30.00
On cover 600.00
36a A9 5kr 87.50 3.50
On cover 150.00
37a A9 10kr 440.00 35.00
On cover 775.00
38a A9 15kr 625.00 130.00
On cover 1,100.

Perf. 10½

34b A9 2kr 60.00 4.50
On cover 57.50
35b A9 3kr 100.00 2.75
On cover 57.50
36b A9 5kr 14.50 .90
On cover 30.00
37b A9 10kr 225.00 2.75
On cover 65.00
38b A9 15kr 250.00 27.50
On cover 210.00

Perf. 12

34c A9 2kr 275.00 160.00
On cover 525.00
35c A9 3kr 250.00 27.50
On cover 425.00
36c A9 5kr 60.00 5.00
On cover 130.00
37c A9 10kr 525.00 130.00
On cover 725.00
38c A9 15kr 825.00 190.00
On cover 1,150.
40b A10 50kr brown ('80) 19.00 190.00
On cover 13,750.
c. Perf. 10½x12 325.00 —

Perf. 13

34d A9 2kr 325.00 360.00
On cover 950.00
35d A9 3kr 225.00 36.00
On cover 425.00
36d A9 5kr 130.00 21.00
On cover 115.00
37d A9 10kr 275.00 100.00
On cover 600.00
38d A9 15kr 625.00 475.00
On cover —
40a A10 50kr 30.00 250.00
On cover —

Perf. 9x10½

34e A9 2kr 440.00 87.50
On cover —
35e A9 3kr 360.00 77.50
On cover —
36e A9 5kr 140.00 18.00
On cover —
37e A9 10kr 410.00 105.00
On cover —

Various compound perforations exist.

Values are for stamps that do not show the watermark. Stamps showing the watermark often sell for more.

For similar designs see Offices in the Turkish Empire A1-A2.

A11

Perf. 9, 9½, 10, 10½, 11½, 12, 12½

1883 Inscriptions in Black

41 A11 2kr brown 6.00 .45
Never hinged 16.00
On cover 12.00
42 A11 3kr green 6.00 .35
Never hinged 24.00
On cover 12.00
43 A11 5kr rose 75.00 .30
Never hinged 190.00
On cover 3.00
a. Vert. pair, imperf. btwn. 190.00 425.00
Never hinged 325.00
44 A11 10kr blue 4.50 .35
Never hinged 16.00
On cover 15.00
45 A11 20kr gray 55.00 4.25
Never hinged 165.00
On cover 240.00
c. Perf 9 1,650.
46 A11 50kr red lilac, perf 9½ 375.00 80.00
Never hinged 1,200.
On cover 3,400.
On parcel post receipt card 390.00
a. 50kr brown lilac & black, perf 10 350.00 120.00
On cover 4,000.
On parcel post receipt card 425.00

The last printings of Nos. 41-46 are watermarked "ZEITUNGS-MARKEN" instead of "BRIEF-MARKEN." Values are for stamps that do not show watermark.

The 5kr has been reprinted in a dull red rose, perforated 10½.

For similar design see Offices in the Turkish Empire A3.

For surcharges see Offices in the Turkish Empire Nos. 15-19.

Values for stamps with "BRIEF-MARKEN" watermark

41a	A11	2kr brown	8.75	.70
42a	A11	3kr green	8.75	.70
43b	A11	5kr rose	110.00	.55
44a	A11	10kr blue	6.50	.60
45a	A11	20kr gray	82.50	6.50
46b	A11	50kr red lilac	465.00	120.00

Values for stamps with "ZEITUNGS-MARKEN" watermark

41b	A11	2kr brown	30.00	13.00
42b	A11	3kr green	30.00	13.00
43c	A11	5kr rose	120.00	10.50
44b	A11	10kr blue	30.00	10.50
45b	A11	20kr gray	92.50	40.00
46c	A11	50kr red lilac	500.00	190.00

A12

A13

Perf. 9 to 13½, also Compound

1890-96 Unwmk. Granite Paper

Numerals in black, Nos. 51-61

51 A12 1kr dark gray 1.50 .30
Never hinged 4.25
On cover 6.50
a. Pair, imperf. between 225.00 540.00
Never hinged 400.00
b. Half used as ½kr on cover 150.00
As "b," on postcard 120.00
52 A12 2kr light brown .35 .30
Never hinged 2.90
On cover 2.40
53 A12 3kr gray green .45 .30
Never hinged 3.25
On cover 3.00
a. Pair, imperf. between 325.00 650.00
Never hinged 475.00
54 A12 5kr rose .45 .30
Never hinged 3.25
On cover 1.50
a. Pair, imperf. between 260.00 450.00
Never hinged 390.00

55 A12 10kr ultramarine 1.10 .30
Never hinged 6.00
On cover 6.50
a. Pair, imperf. between 360.00 650.00
Never hinged 575.00
56 A12 12kr claret 2.60 .40
Never hinged 12.00
On cover 47.50
On parcel post receipt card 11.00
a. Pair, imperf. between — 800.00
57 A12 15kr lilac 2.60 .40
Never hinged 12.00
On cover 15.00
On parcel post receipt card 13.00
a. Pair, imperf. between 475.00 900.00
Never hinged 700.00
58 A12 20kr olive green 37.50 2.40
Never hinged 115.00
On cover 350.00
On parcel post receipt card 16.00
59 A12 24kr gray blue 2.25 1.50
Never hinged 11.50
On cover 600.00
On parcel post receipt card 16.00
a. Pair, imperf. between 475.00 700.00
Never hinged 900.00
60 A12 30kr dark brown 2.75 .80
Never hinged 11.50
On cover 210.00
On parcel post receipt card 16.00
61 A12 50kr violet, perf 10 6.00 11.00
Never hinged 15.00
On cover 3,750.
On parcel post receipt card 36.00
a. Perf 9½ 26.00 15.00
Never hinged 65.00
On cover 4,700.
On parcel post receipt card 36.00

Engr.

62 A13 1gld dark blue 3.00 3.00
Never hinged 9.50
On cover 1,400.
On parcel post receipt card 37.50
63 A13 1gld pale lilac ('96) 45.00 4.50
Never hinged 120.00
On cover 1,250.
On parcel post receipt card 80.00
64 A13 2gld carmine 3.25 24.00
Never hinged 12.00
On cover 2,500.
On parcel post receipt card 130.00
65 A13 2gld gray green ('96) 15.00 47.50
Never hinged 47.50
On cover 2,600.
On parcel post receipt card 200.00
Nos. 51-65 (15) 123.80 97.00

Nearly all values of the 1890-1907 issues are found with numerals missing in one or more corners, some with numerals printed on the back.

For surcharges see Offices in the Turkish Empire Nos. 20-25, 28-31.

A14

Perf. 9 to 13½, also Compound

1891 Typo. Numerals in black

66 A14 20kr olive green 1.90 .30
Never hinged 11.00
On cover 18.00
On parcel post receipt card 9.50
67 A14 24kr gray blue 3.25 .95
Never hinged 12.00
On cover 240.00
On parcel post receipt card 9.50
68 A14 30kr brown 1.90 .30
Never hinged 12.00
On cover 37.50
On parcel post receipt card 9.50
a. Pair, imperf. between 275.00 700.00
Never hinged 600.00
b. Perf. 9 110.00 55.00
Never hinged 240.00
On cover —
69 A14 50kr violet 1.90 .40
Never hinged 15.00
On cover 475.00
On parcel post receipt card 12.00
Nos. 66-69 (4) 8.95 1.95

For surcharges see Offices in the Turkish Empire Nos. 26-27.

A15

A16

A17

A18

Perf. 10½ to 13½ and Compound

1899 Without Varnish Bars

Numerals in black, Nos. 70-82

70 A15 1h lilac .75 .25
Never hinged 2.40
On cover 4.75
On parcel post receipt card 9.50
b. Imperf. 60.00 150.00
Never hinged 130.00
Imperf. pair 150.00 325.00
Never hinged 290.00
c. Perf. 10½ 32.50 8.00
On cover 150.00
d. Numerals inverted 2,250. 3,400.
71 A15 2h dark gray 2.75 .65
Never hinged 19.00
On cover 6.00
On parcel post receipt card 9.50
72 A15 3h bister brown 6.50 .25
Never hinged 21.00
On cover 1.75
On parcel post receipt card 9.50
b. "3" in lower right corner sideways 3,000.
73 A15 5h blue green 7.25 .25
Never hinged 21.00
On cover 1.20
On parcel post receipt card 9.50
c. Perf. 10½ 22.50 4.75
Never hinged 42.50
On cover 47.50
74 A15 6h orange .75 .25
Never hinged 2.40
On cover 3.25
On parcel post receipt card 9.50
75 A16 10h rose 16.00 .25
Never hinged 57.50
On cover 1.20
On parcel post receipt card 9.50
b. Perf. 10½ 875.00 210.00
Never hinged 1,450.
On cover —
76 A16 20h brown 5.25 .25
Never hinged 20.00
On cover 4.50
On parcel post receipt card 9.50
77 A16 25h ultramarine 60.00 .35
Never hinged 190.00
On cover 5.40
On parcel post receipt card 9.50
78 A16 30h red violet 19.00 2.75
Never hinged 72.50
On cover 22.50
On parcel post receipt card 15.00
b. Horiz. pair, imperf. btwn. 600.00 —
Never hinged 925.00
80 A17 40h green 32.50 3.50
Never hinged 100.00
On cover 30.00
On parcel post receipt card 15.00
81 A17 50h gray blue 17.50 4.25
Never hinged 60.00
On cover 45.00
On parcel post receipt card 15.00
b. All four "50's" parallel 3,100.
82 A17 60h brown 50.00 1.25
Never hinged 150.00
On cover 35.00
On parcel post receipt card 15.00
b. Horiz. pair, imperf. btwn. 550.00 —
Never hinged 1,050.
c. Perf. 10½ 105.00 5.40
Never hinged 175.00
On cover 32.50

Engr.

83 A18 1k carmine rose 6.00 .45
Never hinged 21.00
On cover 175.00
On parcel post receipt card 15.00
a. 1k carmine 6.00 .25
Never hinged 21.00
On cover 240.00
On parcel post receipt card 18.00
b. Vert. pair, imperf. btwn. 250.00 350.00
Never hinged 425.00
84 A18 2k gray lilac 52.50 .45
Never hinged 165.00
On cover 1,350.
On parcel post receipt card 24.00
a. Vert. pair, imperf. btwn. 440.00 725.00
Never hinged 800.00
85 A18 4k gray green 10.50 18.00
Never hinged 40.00
On cover 1,100.
On parcel post receipt card 90.00
Nos. 70-85 (15) 287.25 33.15

For surcharges see Offices in Crete Nos. 1-7, Offices in the Turkish Empire Nos. 32-45.

1901 With Varnish Bars

70a A15 1h lilac 1.60 .45
Never hinged 7.50
On cover 4.75
71a A15 2h dark gray 6.50 .40
Never hinged 37.50
On cover 5.75
72a A15 3h bister brown .80 .25
Never hinged 2.60
On cover 2.40
73a A15 5h blue green .80 .25
Never hinged 2.60
On cover 1.20
74a A15 6h orange .80 .25
Never hinged 2.60
On cover 3.25
75a A16 10h rose .80 .25
Never hinged 3.50
On cover 1.20
76a A16 20h brown .80 .25
Never hinged 5.00
On cover 4.75
77a A16 25h ultra .80 .25
Never hinged 5.00
On cover 4.75
78a A16 30h red violet 3.25 .80
Never hinged 11.00
On cover 13.00
79 A17 35h green .80 .25
Never hinged 2.50
On cover 11.00
80a A17 40h green 3.25 4.75
Never hinged 12.00
On cover 22.50
81a A17 50h gray blue 4.75 11.00
Never hinged 12.50
On cover 45.00
82a A17 60h brown 3.25 1.60
Never hinged 9.50
On cover 27.00
Nos. 70a-78a,79,80a-82a (13) 28.20 20.75

The diagonal yellow bars of varnish were printed across the face to prevent cleaning.

A19

A20

A21

Perf. 12½ to 13½ and Compound

1905-07 Typo.

Without Varnish Bars

Colored Numerals

86 A19 1h lilac .25 .35
Never hinged .40
On cover 4.00
87 A19 2h dark gray .25 .25
Never hinged .40
On cover 4.75
88 A19 3h bister brown .25 .25
Never hinged 1.60
On cover 2.00
89 A19 5h dk blue green 12.00 .25
Never hinged 26.00
On cover 1.20
90 A19 5h yellow grn ('06) .25 .25
Never hinged .80
On cover .70
91 A19 6h deep orange .25 .25
Never hinged 2.40
On cover 2.40
92 A20 10h carmine ('06) .50 .25
Never hinged 1.60
On cover .70
93 A20 12h violet ('07) 1.20 .80
Never hinged 4.25
On cover 130.00
On parcel post receipt card 9.50
94 A20 20h brown ('06) 4.00 .25
Never hinged 11.50
On cover 7.50
95 A20 25h ultra ('06) 4.00 .40
Never hinged 10.50
On cover 9.25
96 A20 30h red violet ('06) 8.00 .40
Never hinged 22.00
On cover 22.50

Black Numerals

97 A20 10h carmine 16.00 .25
Never hinged 80.00
On cover .90
98 A20 20h brown 40.00 1.60
Never hinged 130.00
On cover 9.00
99 A20 25h ultra 40.00 2.40
Never hinged 120.00
On cover 16.50
100 A20 30h red violet 55.00 4.75
Never hinged 175.00
On cover 30.00

White Numerals

101 A21 35h green 2.00 .25
Never hinged 12.00
On cover 9.50
102 A21 40h deep violet 2.00 .80
Never hinged 12.00
On cover 18.00

103 A21 50h dull blue 2.00 *3.50*
Never hinged 12.00
On cover 25.00
104 A21 60h yellow brown 2.00 .80
Never hinged 12.00
On cover 18.00
105 A21 72h rose 2.00 1.75
Never hinged 16.00
On cover 350.00
Nos. 86-105 (20) 191.95 19.80
Set, never hinged 650.00

For surcharges see Offices in Crete Nos. 8-14.

1904 ***Perf. 13x13½***

With Varnish Bars

86a A19 1h lilac .35 *.95*
Never hinged 1.60
On cover 4.75
87a A19 2h dark gray 1.40 .95
Never hinged 6.50
On cover 13.00
88a A19 3h bister brown 2.00 .25
Never hinged 6.50
On cover 1.75
89a A19 5h dk blue green 3.25 .25
Never hinged 9.50
On cover 1.20
91a A19 6h deep orange 8.00 .30
Never hinged 30.00
On cover 2.75
97a A20 10h carmine 1.75 .25
Never hinged 14.50
On cover 1.20
98a A20 20h brown 29.00 1.20
Never hinged 100.00
On cover 8.00
99a A20 25h ultra 29.00 .80
Never hinged 92.50
On cover 8.00
100a A20 30h red violet 45.00 1.60
Never hinged 145.00
On cover 16.00
101a A21 35h green 29.00 .55
Never hinged 97.50
On cover 80.00
102a A21 40h deep violet 27.50 4.00
Never hinged 97.50
On cover 80.00
103a A21 50h dull blue 29.00 9.50
Never hinged 97.50
On cover 80.00
104a A21 60h yellow brown 40.00 1.60
Never hinged 160.00
On cover 30.00
105a A21 72h rose 2.00 2.25
Never hinged 16.00
On cover 325.00
Nos. 86a-105a (14) 247.25 24.45
Set, never hinged 875.00

Stamps of the 1901, 1904 and 1905 issues perf. 9 or 10½, also compound with 12½, were not sold at any post office, but were supplied only to some high-ranking officials. This applies also to the contemporaneous issues of Austrian Offices Abroad.

1904 ***Perf. 13x12½***

With Varnish Bars

86b A19 1h lilac .80 *.95*
Never hinged 3.00
On cover 4.75
87b A19 2h dark gray 2.00 .55
Never hinged 7.00
On cover 13.00
88b A19 3h bister brown 2.00 .25
Never hinged 8.00
On cover 1.75
89b A19 5h dk blue green 4.50 .25
Never hinged 12.00
On cover 1.20
91b A19 6h deep orange 9.50 .30
Never hinged 35.00
On cover 3.00
97b A20 10h carmine 2.40 .25
Never hinged 20.00
On cover 1.20
98b A20 20h brown 29.00 .80
Never hinged 110.00
On cover 8.00
99b A20 25h ultra 29.00 .80
Never hinged 95.00
On cover 8.00
100b A20 30h red violet 45.00 1.60
Never hinged 145.00
On cover 16.00
101b A21 35h green 29.00 2.00
Never hinged 100.00
On cover 80.00
102b A21 40h deep violet 28.00 9.50
Never hinged 100.00
On cover 80.00
103b A21 50h dull blue 30.00 10.00
Never hinged 100.00
On cover 105.00
104b A21 60h yellow brown 40.00 1.20
Never hinged 165.00
On cover 30.00
Nos. 86b-104b (13) 251.20 28.45
Set, never hinged 900.00

Stamps of the 1901, 1904 and 1905 issues perf. 9 or 10½, also compound with 12½, were not sold at any post office, but were supplied only to some high-ranking officials. This applies also to the contemporaneous issues of Austrian Offices Abroad.

Karl VI — A22

Franz Josef — A23

Schönbrunn Palace — A24

Franz Josef — A25

Designs: 2h, Maria Theresa. 3h, Joseph II. 5h, 10h, 25h, Franz Josef. 6h, Leopold II. 12h, Franz I. 20h, Ferdinand I. 30h, Franz Josef as youth. 35h, Franz Josef in middle age. 60h, Franz Josef on horseback. 1k, Franz Josef in royal robes. 5k, Hofburg, Vienna.

1908-16 **Typo.** ***Perf. 12½***

Ordinary paper ('08-'13)

110 A22 1h gray black .35 *.95*
Never hinged .75
On cover 4.75
111 A22 2h blue violet .25 *.70*
Never hinged .75
On cover 4.75
112 A22 3h magenta .25 .25
Never hinged .75
On cover 4.50
113 A22 5h yellow green .25 .25
Never hinged .50
On cover .90
a. Booklet pane of 6 *27.50*
114 A22 6h orange brown 1.50 *2.10*
Never hinged 7.00
On cover 16.00
115 A22 10h rose .25 .25
Never hinged .50
On cover .90
a. Booklet pane of 6 *82.50*
116 A22 12h scarlet 1.50 *2.10*
Never hinged 8.00
On cover 20.00
117 A22 20h choc. 1.90 .25
Never hinged 10.00
On cover 11.50
118 A22 25h ultramarine 2.75 .45
Never hinged 12.00
On cover 3.25
119 A22 30h olive green 11.00 .65
Never hinged 24.00
On cover 12.00
120 A22 35h slate 2.40 .25
Never hinged 26.00
On cover 9.50

Engr.

121 A23 50h dark green .55 .25
Never hinged 11.00
On cover 32.50
a. Vert. pair, imperf. btwn. 200.00 *400.00*
Never hinged 475.00
b. Horiz. pair, imperf. btwn. 200.00 *400.00*
Never hinged 475.00
122 A23 60h deep carmine .25 .25
Never hinged 1.75
On cover 20.50
a. Vert. pair, imperf. btwn. 160.00 *400.00*
Never hinged 475.00
b. Horiz. pair, imperf. btwn. 160.00 *400.00*
Never hinged 475.00
123 A23 72h dk brown 1.60 .40
Never hinged 14.50
On cover 100.00
124 A23 1k purple 12.00 .25
Never hinged 37.50
On cover 54.00
On cover, value declared 240.00
a. Vert. pair, imperf. btwn. 200.00 *350.00*
Never hinged 470.00
b. Horiz. pair, imperf. btwn. 200.00 *350.00*
Never hinged 410.00
125 A24 2k lake & olive grn 20.00 .40
Never hinged 80.00
On cover 95.00
On cover, value declared 475.00
126 A24 5k bister & dk vio 40.00 6.00
Never hinged 140.00
On cover (value declared) *925.00*
127 A25 10k blue, bis & dp brn 190.00 65.00
Never hinged 500.00
On cover (value declared) *1,550.*
Nos. 110-127 (18) 286.80 80.75
Set, never hinged 875.00

Chalky Paper ('08-'13)

110a A22 1h gray black .25 .25
Never hinged 4.00
On cover 4.25
111a A22 2h violet .25 .25
Never hinged 6.50
On cover 4.50
112a A22 3h magenta .50 .25
Never hinged 4.00
On cover 3.50
113b A22 5h yellow green .25 .25
Never hinged 2.00
On cover .90
c. Booklet pane of 6 *25.00*
114a A22 6h buff ('13) .55 *.80*
Never hinged 8.00
On cover 16.00
115b A22 10h rose .25 .25
Never hinged 4.00
On cover .90
c. Booklet pane of 6 *75.00*
116a A22 12h scarlet .80 1.20
Never hinged 12.00
On cover 18.50
117a A22 20h chocolate 4.75 .45
Never hinged 35.00
On cover 10.50
118a A22 25h deep blue 2.00 .45
Never hinged 24.00
On cover 3.00
119a A22 30h olive green 9.50 .65
Never hinged 47.50
On cover 32.50
120a A22 35h slate 2.40 .25
Never hinged 24.00
On cover 12.00

Wartime Printings on Grayish Paper ('16)

122c A23 60h deep carmine 1.40 *1.90*
Never hinged 6.50
On cover *80.00*
123a A23 72h dk brown 3.50 2.75
Never hinged 24.00
On cover —
124c A23 1k purple 20.00 1.75
Never hinged 72.50
On cover —
125a A24 2k lake & olive grn 28.00 4.50
Never hinged 100.00
On cover (value declared) —
126a A24 5k bister & dk vio 55.00 11.00
Never hinged 320.00
On cover (value declared) —

Definitive set issued for the 60th year of the reign of Emperor Franz Josef.

Nos. 110a-120a, 121, and 123-127 were issued in 1908. Nos. 110-20 and 122 were issued in 1913.

All values exist imperforate. They were not sold at any post office, but presented to a number of high government officials. This applies also to all imperforate stamps of later issues, including semi-postals, etc., and those of the Austrian Offices Abroad.

Litho. forgeries of No. 127 exist.

For overprint and surcharge see #J47-J48. For similar designs see Offices in Crete A5-A6, Offices in the Turkish Empire A16-A17.

Birthday Jubilee Issue

No. 144

Similar to 1908 Issue, but designs enlarged by labels at top and bottom bearing dates "1830" and "1910"

1910 **Typo.**

128 A22 1h gray black 4.00 *8.00*
Never hinged 12.50
On cover 40.00
129 A22 2h violet 4.75 *16.00*
Never hinged 20.00
On cover 65.00
130 A22 3h magenta 4.00 *12.00*
Never hinged 15.00
On cover 40.00
131 A22 5h yellow green .25 .35
Never hinged 2.25
On cover 9.00
132 A22 6h buff 3.25 *12.00*
Never hinged 12.50
On cover 60.00
133 A22 10h rose .25 .35
Never hinged 2.25
On cover 9.00
134 A22 12h scarlet 3.25 *12.00*
Never hinged 15.00
On cover 65.00
135 A22 20h chocolate 3.25 *12.00*
Never hinged 30.00
On cover 92.50
136 A22 25h deep blue 1.60 *2.40*
Never hinged 10.00
On cover 16.00
137 A22 30h olive green 3.25 *12.00*
Never hinged 18.00
On cover 92.50
138 A22 35h slate 3.25 *12.00*
Never hinged 18.00
On cover 120.00

Engr.

139 A23 50h dark green 5.50 *12.00*
Never hinged 18.00
On cover 180.00
140 A23 60h deep car 5.50 *12.00*
Never hinged 18.00
On cover 165.00
141 A23 1k purple 5.50 *16.00*
Never hinged 18.00
On cover 375.00
142 A24 2k lake & ol grn 140.00 *225.00*
Never hinged 280.00
On cover (value declared) *1,250.*
143 A24 5k bister & dk vio 110.00 *225.00*
Never hinged 200.00
On cover (value declared) *2,000.*
144 A25 10k blue, bis & dp brn 175.00 *325.00*
Never hinged 360.00
On cover (value declared) *2,750.*
Nos. 128-144 (17) 472.60 *914.10*
Set, never hinged 1,050.

80th birthday of Emperor Franz Josef.
All values exist imperforate.
Litho. forgeries of Nos. 142-144 exist.

Austrian Crown — A37

Franz Josef — A38

Coat of Arms
A39 A40

Two sizes of Type A40:
Type I: 25x30mm
Type II: 26x29mm

1916-18 **Typo.**

145 A37 3h brt violet .25 .25
Never hinged .25
On cover 4.25
146 A37 5h lt green .25 .25
Never hinged .30
On cover 1.20
a. Booklet pane of 6 *15.50*
b. Booklet pane of 4 + 2 labels *30.00*
147 A37 6h deep orange .25 *.80*
Never hinged .85
On cover 24.00
148 A37 10h magenta .25 .25
Never hinged .30
On cover 1.20
a. Booklet pane of 6 *30.00*
149 A37 12h light blue .25 *.90*
Never hinged 1.30
On cover 40.00
150 A38 15h rose red .40 .25
Never hinged 2.25
On cover 2.10
a. Booklet pane of 6 *16.50*
151 A38 20h chocolate 4.00 .25
Never hinged 14.00
On cover 12.00
152 A38 25h blue 4.00 .80
Never hinged 21.00
On cover 13.00
153 A38 30h slate 6.50 .65
Never hinged 21.00
On cover 16.00
154 A39 40h olive green .25 .25
Never hinged 1.60
On cover 6.00
155 A39 50h blue green .25 .25
Never hinged 1.60
On cover 18.00
156 A39 60h deep blue .25 .25
Never hinged 1.60
On cover 25.00
157 A39 80h orange brown .25 .25
Never hinged 1.60
On cover 32.50
158 A39 90h red violet .25 .25
Never hinged 1.60
On cover 80.00
159 A39 1k car, *yel* ('18) .25 .25
Never hinged 1.60
On cover 100.00

Engr.

160 A40 2k dark blue (I) 4.00 .40
Never hinged 6.50
On cover 130.00

a. Type II 11.00 1.20
Never hinged 32.50
161 A40 3k claret (I) 24.00 1.20
Never hinged 57.50
On cover 200.00
a. Type II 92.50 18.00
Never hinged 290.00
162 A40 4k deep green (I) 8.00 2.40
Never hinged 13.50
a. Type II 4.40 3.50
Never hinged 24.00
163 A40 10k deep violet (I) 27.50 *52.50*
Never hinged 92.50
a. Type II 120.00 *240.00*
Never hinged 290.00
On cover 400.00
Nos. 145-163 (19) 81.15 62.40
Set, never hinged 240.00

Stamps of type A38 have two varieties of the frame. Stamps of type A40 have various decorations about the shield.

Nos. 145-163 exist imperf. Value set, $475 hinged, $875 never hinged.

1917 Ordinary Paper

164 A40 2k lt bl (I) 2.00 .80
Never hinged 5.50
On cover 140.00
a. Type II 2.60 .55
Never hinged 5.75
165 A40 3k car rose (I) 47.50 .80
Never hinged 125.00
On cover 210.00
a. Type II 250.00 165.00
Never hinged 2,000.
166 A40 4k yel grn (I) 3.25 1.25
Never hinged 9.00
a. Type II 22.50 22.50
Never hinged 80.00
167 A40 10k violet (I) 140.00 110.00
Never hinged 335.00
a. Type II 5,500. —
Never hinged *8,100.*
Nos. 164-167 (4) 192.75 112.85
Set, never hinged 475.00

Nos. 164-167 exist imperf. Value set, $325 unused, $650 never hinged.

See Nos. 172-175 (granite paper). For overprints and surcharges see Nos. 181-199, C1-C3, J60-J63, N1-N5, N10-N19, N33-N37, N42-N51. Western Ukraine 2-7, 11-15, 19-28, 57-58, 85-89, 94-103, N3-N14, NJ13.

Emperor Karl I — A42

1917-18 Typo.

168 A42 15h dull red .40 .40
Never hinged 2.00
On cover 3.25
a. Booklet pane of 6 *16.50*
169 A42 20h dk green ('18) .40 .40
Never hinged 2.00
On cover 5.40
a. 20h green ('17) .80 .65
Never hinged 7.50
On cover 16.50
170 A42 25h blue .40 .40
Never hinged 5.50
On cover 14.00
171 A42 30h dull violet 2.00 .40
Never hinged 4.00
On cover 18.00
Nos. 168-171 (4) 3.20 1.60
Set, never hinged 13.50

Nos. 168-171 exist imperf. Value set, $160 unused, $400 never hinged.

For overprints and surcharges see Nos. N6-N9, N20, N38-N41, N52, N64. Western Ukraine 1, 8, 16-18, 90-93, N15-N18.

1918-19 Engr. Granite Paper

172 A40 2k light blue (II) 1.20 *.45*
Never hinged 2.00
On cover 150.00
a. Perf. 11½ 725.00 *1,200.*
Never hinged 1,600.
b. Type I 1.75 *2.90*
Never hinged 3.50
On cover 180.00
173 A40 3k car rose (II) .40 *.80*
Never hinged .75
On cover 300.00
a. Type I 1.90 *2.90*
Never hinged 3.50
On cover 425.00
174 A40 4k yel grn (II) ('19) 4.00 *20.00*
Never hinged 11.00
On cover 350.00
a. Type I 14.00 *29.00*
Never hinged 47.50
On cover 475.00
175 A40 10k lt vio (II) ('19) 8.00 *32.50*
Never hinged 26.00
On cover 690.00
a. Type I ('19) 44.00 —
Never hinged 140.00
Nos. 172-175 (4) 13.60 *53.75*
Set, never hinged 40.00

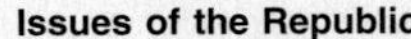

Issues of the Republic

Austrian Stamps of 1916-18 Overprinted

1918-19 Unwmk. *Perf. 12½*

181 A37 3h bright violet .25 .25
Never hinged .70
On cover 4.25
182 A37 5h light green .25 .25
Never hinged .70
On cover 1.20
183 A37 6h deep orange .80 *3.25*
Never hinged 3.75
On cover 24.00
184 A37 10h magenta .25 .25
Never hinged .70
On cover .90
185 A37 12h light blue .40 *2.40*
Never hinged 3.75
On cover 40.00
a. 12h deep greenish blue 30.00
Never hinged 105.00
186 A42 15h dull red .80 *2.00*
Never hinged 3.00
On cover 3.50
187 A42 20h deep green .40 .25
Never hinged 1.40
On cover 1.20
188 A42 25h blue .80 .25
Never hinged 3.00
On cover 5.40
189 A42 30h dull violet .80 .25
Never hinged 3.00
On cover 2.40
190 A39 40h olive green .80 .25
Never hinged 3.00
On cover 8.00
191 A39 50h deep green .80 *2.00*
Never hinged 3.00
On cover 12.00
192 A39 60h deep blue 1.20 *2.00*
Never hinged 3.75
On cover 16.00
193 A39 80h orange brown .40 .80
Never hinged 1.40
On cover 16.00
a. Inverted overprint 275.00 *325.00*
Never hinged 650.00
194 A39 90h red violet 1.20 .80
Never hinged 3.75
On cover 24.00
195 A39 1k carmine, *yel* 1.40 .80
Never hinged 4.50
On cover 24.00

Granite Paper

196 A40 2k light blue (II) .25 .25
Never hinged .35
On cover 40.00
a. Horiz. pair, imperf. between 240.00
Never hinged 400.00
b. Vert. pair, imperf. between 400.00
Never hinged 1,200.
c. Perf. 11½ 95.00 *110.00*
Never hinged 175.00
On cover 350.00
197 A40 3k car rose (II) .35 *.80*
Never hinged .75
On cover 165.00
198 A40 4k yel grn (II) 1.60 *3.25*
Never hinged 3.00
On cover 290.00
a. Perf. 11½ 16.00 35.00
Never hinged 32.50
On cover —
199 A40 10k deep violet (II) 9.50 *20.00*
Never hinged 19.00
On cover 575.00
a. Type I 100.00 *190.00*
Never hinged 225.00
Nos. 181-199 (19) 22.25 *40.10*
Set, never hinged 62.50

Nos. 181, 182, 184, 187-191, 194, 197 and 199 exist imperforate. Value: 181//194, each $18; 197, $150; 199, $225.

Post Horn — A43

Coat of Arms — A44

Allegory of New Republic — A45

1919-20 Typo. *Perf. 12½*
Ordinary Paper

200 A43 3h gray .25 .25
Never hinged .30
On cover 4.25
a. 3h deep gray 2.25 *4.75*
Never hinged 4.75
On cover 16.00
b. 3h gray black 150.00 *225.00*
Never hinged 325.00
On cover 400.00
201 A44 5h yellow green .25 .25
Never hinged .30
On cover 4.25
202 A44 5h gray ('20) .25 .25
Never hinged .30
On cover 4.25
a. 5h deep gray 9.00 *18.50*
Never hinged 18.50
On cover 40.00
b. 5h gray black 290.00 *400.00*
Never hinged 475.00
On cover —
203 A43 6h orange .25 *.50*
Never hinged .45
On cover 24.00
204 A44 10h deep rose .25 .25
Never hinged .30
On cover 1.20
205 A44 10h red ('20) .25 .25
Never hinged .30
On cover 1.20
a. Thick grayish paper ('20) .25 .40
Never hinged .30
On cover 1.80
206 A43 12h grnsh blue .25 *4.00*
Never hinged .40
On cover 40.00
a. 12h deep greenish blue 52.50 *210.00*
Never hinged 210.00
On cover —
207 A43 15h bister ('20) .35 *.80*
Never hinged .65
On cover 4.25
a. Thick grayish paper ('20) .25 .40
Never hinged .30
On cover 1.60
208 A45 20h dark green .25 .25
Never hinged .30
On cover 1.00
a. 20h yellow green .25 .25
Never hinged .30
On cover 1.50
b. As "a," thick grysh paper ('20) 1.60 *4.00*
Never hinged 2.10
On cover 9.00
209 A44 25h blue .25 .25
Never hinged .30
On cover 4.75
a. 25h pale blue 16.50 *27.50*
Never hinged 40.00
On cover 45.00
b. 25h deep blue 210.00 *290.00*
Never hinged 390.00
On cover —
210 A43 25h violet ('20) .25 .25
Never hinged .30
On cover 2.40
211 A45 30h dark brown .25 .25
Never hinged .30
On cover 3.00
212 A45 40h violet .25 .25
Never hinged .30
On cover 4.50
213 A45 40h lake ('20) .25 .25
Never hinged .35
On cover 3.25
214 A44 45h olive green .30 *.80*
Never hinged .40
On cover 24.00
215 A45 50h dark blue .25 .25
Never hinged .30
On cover 2.40
a. Thick grayish paper ('20) .40 *.95*
Never hinged .85
On cover 3.25
216 A43 60h ol grn ('20) .25 .25
Never hinged .30
On cover 5.75
217 A44 1k carmine, *yel* .25 .25
Never hinged .30
On cover 16.00
218 A44 1k light blue ('20) .25 .25
Never hinged .35
On cover 10.50
a. 1k deep blue 155.00 *290.00*
Never hinged 350.00
On cover —
Nos. 200-218 (19) 4.90 9.85

All values exist imperf. (For regularly issued imperfs, see Nos. 227-235.)

For overprints and surcharge see Nos. B11-B19, B30-B38, J102, N21, N27, N53, N58, N65, N71.

Parliament Building A46

1919-20 Engr. *Perf. 12½, 11½*
Granite Paper

219 A46 2k ver & blk .25 *.80*
Never hinged 1.25
On cover 80.00
a. Center inverted *2,750.*
Never hinged *6,500.*
b. Perf. 11½ 1.60 *3.25*
Never hinged 1.80
On cover 47.50
220 A46 2½k ol bis ('20) .30 *.25*
Never hinged .60
On cover 8.00
221 A46 3k bl & blk brn .25 .25
Never hinged .60
On cover 12.00
a. Perf. 11½ 5.75 *20.00*
Never hinged 10.50
On cover 29.00
222 A46 4k car & blk .25 .25
Never hinged .60
On cover 16.00
a. Center inverted *950.00* *3,250.*
Never hinged *2,400.*
b. Perf. 11½ 2.00 *6.50*
Never hinged 4.50
On cover 20.00
223 A46 5k black ('20) .25 .25
Never hinged .60
On cover 8.00
a. Perf. 11½x12½ 55.00 *87.50*
Never hinged 160.00
b. Perf. 11½ 2.75 *7.25*
Never hinged 6.00
On cover 21.00
224 A46 7½k plum .30 *.40*
Never hinged 1.25
On cover 8.00
a. Perf. 11½ 120.00 *240.00*
Never hinged 290.00
On cover —
b. Perf. 11½x12½ 80.00 *240.00*
Never hinged 240.00
225 A46 10k olive grn & blk brn .30 *.40*
Never hinged 1.25
On cover 16.00
a. Perf. 11½x12½ 160.00 *300.00*
Never hinged 475.00
b. Perf. 11½ 13.50 *30.00*
Never hinged 32.50
On cover 72.50
226 A46 20k lil & red ('20) .25 *.40*
Never hinged .60
On cover 24.00
a. Center inverted *60,000.* *40,000.*
b. Perf. 11½ 72.50 175.00
Never hinged 175.00
On cover 325.00
Nos. 219-226 (8) 2.15 *3.00*
Set, never hinged 6.75

Nos. 220-222, 225-226 exist imperforate between. Values, per pair: unused $200-$350; never hinged $400-$725.

See No. 248. For overprints and surcharge see Nos. B23-B29, B43-B49.

1920 Typo. *Imperf.*
Ordinary Paper

227 A44 5h yellow green .35 *.95*
Never hinged .65
On cover 12.00
228 A44 5h gray .25 .25
Never hinged .30
On cover 4.25
229 A44 10h deep rose .25 .25
Never hinged .30
On cover 1.80
230 A44 10h red .25 .25
Never hinged .30
On cover 1.80
231 A43 15h bister .25 .25
Never hinged .30
On cover 4.75
232 A43 25h violet .25 .25
Never hinged .30
On cover 3.50
233 A45 30h dark brown .25 .25
Never hinged .30
On cover 4.25
234 A45 40h violet .25 *.25*
Never hinged .35
On cover 3.50
235 A43 60h olive green .25 *.25*
Never hinged .35
On cover 4.75
Nos. 227-235 (9) 2.35 2.95

Arms
A47 A48

1920-21 Typo. *Perf. 12½*
White Paper

238 A47 80h rose .25 .25
Never hinged .35
On cover .90
a. Thick grayish paper .25 .25
Never hinged .35
On cover .90
239 A47 1k black brown .25 .25
Never hinged .35
On cover .90
a. Thick grayish paper .25 .25
Never hinged .35
On cover .90
241 A47 1½k green ('21) .30 .25
Never hinged 1.15
On cover 2.10
a. Thick grayish paper .45 .25
Never hinged .90
On cover 1.50
242 A47 2k blue .25 .30
Never hinged .35
On cover 1.20
a. Thick grayish paper .25 .25
Never hinged .35
On cover 1.50
243 A48 3k yel grn & dk grn ('21) .25 *.30*
Never hinged .50
On cover 1.20

a. Thick grayish paper .25 .35
Never hinged .35
On cover 1.20
b. 3k pale green & blue green, white paper 8.75 *35.00*
Never hinged 21.00
On cover 70.00
c. 3k pale green & blue green, thick grayish paper 12.00 *32.50*
Never hinged 34.00
On cover 70.00
d. 3k dark green & blackish green, thick grayish paper 325.00 *575.00*
Never hinged 650.00
On cover —

244 A48 4k red & clar ('21) .25 .25
Never hinged .50
On cover 2.40
a. Thick grayish paper .45 .35
Never hinged .65
On cover 2.40

245 A48 5k vio & clar ('21) .25 .25
Never hinged .50
On cover 2.10
a. Thick grayish paper .45 .35
Never hinged .85
On cover 2.10

246 A48 7½k yel & brn ('21) .25 *.30*
Never hinged .50
On cover 2.75

247 A48 10k ultra & bl ('21) .25 *.25*
Never hinged .50
On cover 2.75
a. Thick grayish paper .45 .40
Never hinged .85
On cover 3.00
Nos. 238-247 (9) 2.30 2.40
Set, never hinged 4.75

For overprints and surcharges see Nos. B20-B22, B39-B42.

1921 **Engr.**

248 A46 50k dk violet, *yel* .95 *1.60*
Never hinged 1.60
On cover 80.00
a. Perf. 11½ 14.50 *77.50*
Never hinged 23.00
On cover 240.00

Symbols of Agriculture A49

Symbols of Labor and Industry A50

1922-24 **Typo.** ***Perf. 12½***

250 A49 ½k olive bister .25 *.65*
Never hinged .30
On cover 24.00

251 A50 1k brown .25 .25
Never hinged .30
On cover 8.00

252 A50 2k cobalt blue .25 .25
Never hinged .30
On cover 7.25

253 A49 2½k orange brown .25 .25
Never hinged .30
On cover 8.00

254 A50 4k dull violet .25 *1.00*
Never hinged .25
On cover 40.00

255 A50 5k gray green .25 .25
Never hinged .30
On cover 1.20

256 A49 7½k gray violet .25 .25
Never hinged .30
On cover 1.40

257 A50 10k claret .25 .25
Never hinged .30
On cover 1.20

258 A49 12½k gray green .25 .25
Never hinged .30
On cover 1.20

259 A49 15k bluish green .25 .25
Never hinged .30
On cover 9.50

260 A49 20k dark blue .25 .25
Never hinged .30
On cover 1.20

261 A49 25k claret .25 .25
Never hinged .30
On cover 1.20

262 A50 30k pale gray .25 .25
Never hinged .30
On cover 8.00

263 A50 45k pale red .25 .25
Never hinged .30
On cover 7.25

264 A50 50k orange brown .25 .25
Never hinged .30
On cover 1.80

265 A50 60k yellow green .25 .25
Never hinged .30
On cover 8.00

266 A50 75k ultramarine .25 .25
Never hinged .30
On cover 6.00

267 A50 80k yellow .25 .25
Never hinged .30
On cover 1.40

268 A49 100k gray .25 .25
Never hinged .30
On cover 1.20

269 A49 120k brown .25 .25
Never hinged .30
On cover 9.00

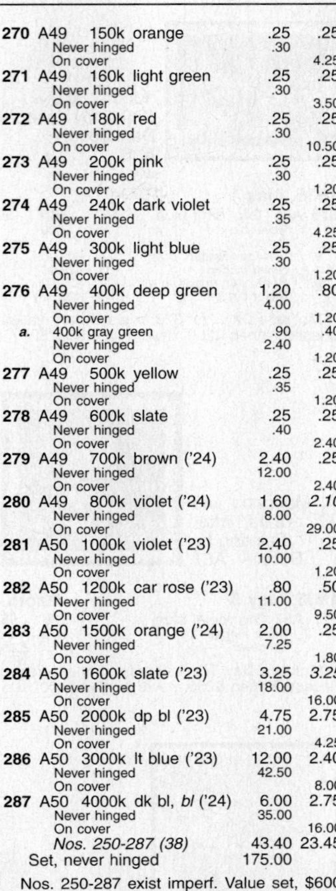

270 A49 150k orange .25 .25
Never hinged .30
On cover 4.25

271 A49 160k light green .25 .25
Never hinged .30
On cover 3.50

272 A49 180k red .25 .25
Never hinged .30
On cover 10.50

273 A49 200k pink .25 .25
Never hinged .30
On cover 1.20

274 A49 240k dark violet .25 .25
Never hinged .35
On cover 4.25

275 A49 300k light blue .25 .25
Never hinged .30
On cover 1.20

276 A49 400k deep green 1.20 .80
Never hinged 4.00
On cover 1.20
a. 400k gray green .90 .40
Never hinged 2.40
On cover 1.20

277 A49 500k yellow .25 .25
Never hinged .35
On cover 1.20

278 A49 600k slate .25 .25
Never hinged .40
On cover 2.40

279 A49 700k brown ('24) 2.40 .25
Never hinged 12.00
On cover 2.40

280 A49 800k violet ('24) 1.60 *2.10*
Never hinged 8.00
On cover 29.00

281 A50 1000k violet ('23) 2.40 .25
Never hinged 10.00
On cover 1.20

282 A50 1200k car rose ('23) .80 .50
Never hinged 11.00
On cover 9.50

283 A50 1500k orange ('24) 2.00 .25
Never hinged 7.25
On cover 1.80

284 A50 1600k slate ('23) 3.25 *3.25*
Never hinged 18.00
On cover 16.00

285 A50 2000k dp bl ('23) 4.75 2.75
Never hinged 21.00
On cover 4.25

286 A50 3000k lt blue ('23) 12.00 2.40
Never hinged 42.50
On cover 8.00

287 A50 4000k dk bl, *bl* ('24) 6.00 2.75
Never hinged 35.00
On cover 16.00
Nos. 250-287 (38) 43.40 23.45
Set, never hinged 175.00

Nos. 250-287 exist imperf. Value set, $600 unused, $1,200 never hinged.

Symbols of Art and Science — A51

1922-24 **Engr.** ***Perf. 12½***

288 A51 20k dark brn, 26x29mm .25 .25
Never hinged .30
On cover 8.00

289 A51 25k blue, 26x29mm .25 .25
Never hinged .30
On cover 3.50
b. dp blue, 26x29mm .45 .25
Never hinged .95
On cover 4.75

290 A51 50k brown red, 26x29mm .25 .25
Never hinged .30
On cover 4.25
b. Vert. pair, imperf. btwn. 250.00 *350.00*
Never hinged 475.00
d. deep brownish red, 26x29mm 4.50 4.50
Never hinged 10.00
On cover 50.00
e. brownish red, 26x29mm .50 .50
Never hinged 1.50
On cover 10.00
f. brown red, 25x29½mm .25 .25
Never hinged .30
On cover 5.00
j. brownish red, 25x29½mm .50 .50
Never hinged 1.50
On cover 10.00
k. dp brownish red, 25x29½mm 4.50 4.50
Never hinged 10.00
On cover 50.00

291 A51 100k green, 26x29mm 2.50 .25
Never hinged 4.00
On cover 12.00
b. Vert. pair, imperf. btwn. — *475.00*
Never hinged
c. pale olive green, 26x29mm 3.00 *3.00*
Never hinged 6.50
On cover 12.00
d. dp green, 25x29½mm 50.00 *50.00*
Never hinged 100.00
On cover —
e. green, 25x29½mm .25 *.25*
Never hinged .30
On cover 4.25
f. pale olive green, 25x29½mm 2.50 *1.50*
Never hinged 4.00
On cover 8.00

292 A51 200k dk violet, 26x29mm 1.50 .25
Never hinged 3.00
On cover 12.00
b. Vert. pair, imperf. btwn. 250.00
Never hinged 475.00
c. dk violet, 25x29½mm .50 .25
Never hinged 1.50
On cover 8.00

293 A51 500k dp orange, 25x29½mm .25 *.25*
Never hinged 1.20
On cover 20.00
a. dp orange, 26x29mm 15.00 15.00
Never hinged 35.00
On cover 40.00

294 A51 1000k blk vio, *yel*, 25x29½mm .25 .25
Never hinged .30
On cover 8.00
b. Vert. pair, imperf. btwn. 360.00
Never hinged 500.00
c. Horiz. pair, imperf. btwn. 360.00
Never hinged 500.00

295 A51 2000k ol grn, *yel*, 25x29½mm .25 .25
Never hinged .35
On cover 12.00
a. Vert. pair, imperf. btwn. 360.00
Never hinged 475.00
b. yellow green, *yel*, 25x29½mm 8.00
Never hinged 16.00
c. dk green, *yel*, 25x29½mm 125.00 125.00
Never hinged 250.00

296 A51 3000k clar brn, 25x29½mm ('23) 10.00 .40
Never hinged 40.00
On cover 20.00

297 A51 5000k gray blk, 25x29½mm ('23) 6.50 .80
Never hinged 12.00
On cover 65.00
a. dp gray blk, 25x29½mm 10.00 8.00
Never hinged 20.00
On cover 65.00

Granite Paper

298 A51 10,000k red brn, 26x29mm ('24) 4.50 *4.50*
Never hinged 14.00
On cover *575.00*
Nos. 288-298 (11) 26.50 7.70
Set, never hinged 72.50

1922-24 ***Perf. 11½***

288a A51 20k dk brown, 26x29mm 1.60 1.60
Never hinged 5.50
On cover 24.00

289a A51 25k blue, 26x29mm 1.25 1.25
Never hinged 4.00
On cover 30.00
c. dp blue, 26x29mm .75 *1.40*
Never hinged 3.25
On cover 32.50

290a A51 50k brown red, 26x29mm 1.60 1.60
Never hinged 6.25
On cover 42.50
g. brownish red, 26x29mm 5.00 5.00
Never hinged 11.00
On cover —
h. dp brownish red, 26x29mm 8.00 8.00
Never hinged 20.00
On cover —
i. dp brownish red, 25x29½mm 8.00 8.00
Never hinged 20.00
On cover —

291a A51 100k green, 26x29mm 4.75 4.75
Never hinged 16.00
On cover 54.00
h. dp green, 26x29mm 6.50 6.50
Never hinged 20.00
On cover —
i. green, 25x29½mm 15.00 15.00
Never hinged 40.00
On cover —

292a A51 200k dk violet, 26x29mm 5.50 5.50
Never hinged 20.00
On cover 80.00

294a A51 1000k bk violet, 25x29½mm 240.00 240.00
Never hinged 475.00
On cover *1,200.*

Perf. 12½x11½

290c A51 50k dk brown red, 26x29mm — *1,400.*

Nos. 288-298 come in two design sizes: 25x29½mm and 26x29mm.

On Nos. 281-287, 291-298 "kronen" is abbreviated to "k" and transposed with the numerals.

Nos. 288-298 exist imperf. Value set, $410 hinged, $750 never hinged.

Numeral A52

Fields Crossed by Telegraph Wires A53

Golden Eagle — A54

Church of Minorite Friars — A55

1925-32 **Typo.** ***Perf. 12***

303 A52 1g dark gray .40 .25
Never hinged 1.05
On cover 2.10

304 A52 2g claret .40 .25
Never hinged 1.45
On cover 1.80
a. 2g red lilac ('32) .55 .25
Never hinged 3.25
On cover 1.80

305 A52 3g scarlet .40 .25
Never hinged 1.45
On cover 1.50

306 A52 4g grnsh blue ('27) 1.20 .25
Never hinged 4.25
On cover 2.40

307 A52 5g brown orange 1.60 .25
Never hinged 5.00
On cover 2.10

308 A52 6g ultramarine 1.60 .25
Never hinged 5.75
On cover 3.25
a. 6g violet blue 1.90 .25
Never hinged 8.00
On cover 4.25

309 A52 7g chocolate 1.60 .25
Never hinged 6.50
On cover 2.10

310 A52 8g yellow green 4.00 .25
Never hinged 17.00
On cover 1.80

311 A53 10g orange .80 .25
Never hinged 1.05
On cover 1.80

313 A53 15g red lilac .80 .25
Never hinged 1.05
On cover 1.50

314 A53 16g dark blue .80 .25
Never hinged 1.05
On cover 1.80

315 A53 18g olive green 1.20 *.80*
Never hinged 3.75
On cover 2.40

316 A54 20g dark violet 1.20 .25
Never hinged 5.75
On cover 1.20

317 A54 24g carmine 1.20 .40
Never hinged 5.75
On cover 2.10

318 A54 30g dark brown 1.20 .25
Never hinged 5.75
On cover 3.00

319 A54 40g ultramarine 1.20 .25
Never hinged 5.75
On cover 3.00

320 A54 45g yellow brown 1.60 .25
Never hinged 6.50
On cover 5.00

321 A54 50g gray 1.60 .30
Never hinged 11.00
On cover 5.40

322 A54 80g turquoise blue 3.50 *4.50*
Never hinged 27.50
On cover 36.00

Perf. 12½

Engr.

323 A55 1s deep green 20.00 1.60
Never hinged 80.00
On cover 15.00
a. 1s light green 375.00 24.00
Never hinged 1,750.
On cover 100.00
b. As "a," pair, imperf between 925.00
Never hinged 675.00

324 A55 2s brown rose 8.00 *10.50*
Never hinged 27.00
On cover 47.50
Nos. 303-324 (21) 54.30 *21.85*
Set, never hinged 225.00

Nos. 303-324 exist imperf. Value, set unused $475; never hinged $2,000.

For type A52 surcharged see No. B118.

Güssing — A56

National Library, Vienna — A57

15g, Hochosterwitz. 16g, 20g, Durnstein. 18g, Traunsee. 24g, Salzburg. 30g, Seewiesen. 40g, Innsbruck. 50g, Worthersee. 60g, Hohenems. 2s, St. Stephen's Cathedral, Vienna.

1929-30 Typo. *Perf. 12½*

Size: 25½x21½mm

326 A56 10g brown orange .65 .25
Never hinged 6.50
On cover 1.80
327 A56 10g bister ('30) .65 .25
Never hinged 9.00
On cover 1.80
328 A56 15g violet brown .65 *1.40*
Never hinged 4.00
On cover 11.00
329 A56 16g dark gray .25 .25
Never hinged 1.00
On cover 5.00
330 A56 18g blue green .40 .50
Never hinged 9.00
On cover 11.00
331 A56 20g dark gray ('30) .80 .25
Never hinged 22.50
On cover 7.25
332 A56 24g maroon 6.50 *8.00*
Never hinged 35.00
On cover 11.50
333 A56 24g lake ('30) 6.50 .50
Never hinged 45.00
On cover 3.00
334 A56 30g dark violet 6.50 .25
Never hinged 47.50
On cover 3.25
335 A56 40g dark blue 8.00 .25
Never hinged 80.00
On cover 3.00
336 A56 50g gray violet ('30) 27.50 .25
Never hinged 160.00
On cover 5.75
337 A56 60g olive green 17.50 .25
Never hinged 145.00
On cover 4.75

Engr.

Size: 21x26mm

338 A57 1s black brown 8.00 .25
Never hinged 45.00
On cover 15.00
a. Horiz. pair, imperf. btwn. 260.00
Never hinged 450.00
b. Vert. pair, imperf. btwn. 260.00
Never hinged 450.00
339 A57 2s dark green 16.00 12.00
Never hinged 65.00
On cover
a. Horiz. pair, imperf. btwn. 325.00
Never hinged 575.00
Nos. 326-339 (14) 99.90 24.65
Set, never hinged 675.00

Nos. 326, 328-330 and 332-339 exist imperf. Values, set of 12 unused hinged $1,450, never hinged $2,000.

Type of 1929-30 Issue

Designs: 12g, Traunsee. 64g, Hohenems.

1932 *Perf. 12*

Size: 21x16½mm

340 A56 10g olive brown .80 .25
Never hinged 3.00
On cover 2.40
341 A56 12g blue green 1.60 .25
Never hinged 5.50
On cover 2.50
342 A56 18g blue green 1.60 *3.25*
Never hinged 4.50
On cover 6.00
343 A56 20g dark gray .80 .25
Never hinged 6.50
On cover 2.40
344 A56 24g carmine rose 8.00 .25
Never hinged 24.00
On cover 2.10
345 A56 24g dull violet 4.75 .25
Never hinged 16.00
On cover 2.10
346 A56 30g dark violet 20.00 .25
Never hinged 60.00
On cover 3.00
347 A56 30g carmine rose 8.00 .25
Never hinged 24.00
On cover 3.00
a. Vert. pair, imperf. btwn. 45.00
Never hinged, #347a 60.00
348 A56 40g dark blue 24.00 1.60
Never hinged 95.00
On cover 4.25
349 A56 40g dark violet 8.00 .40
Never hinged 35.00
On cover 4.25
350 A56 50g gray violet 24.00 .40
Never hinged 95.00
On cover 15.00
351 A56 50g dull blue 8.00 .40
Never hinged 32.50
On cover 4.75
352 A56 60g gray green 65.00 4.00
Never hinged 250.00
On cover 8.00
353 A56 64g gray green 24.00 .40
Never hinged 100.00
On cover 12.00
Nos. 340-353 (14) 198.55 12.20
Set, never hinged 750.00

For overprints and surcharges see Nos. B87-B92, B119-B121.

Nos. 340-353 exist imperf. Values, set unused hinged, $575, never hinged $1,200.

Used values for Nos. 354-389 are for stamps with philatelic favor cancels. Values for postally used examples are 50%-100% more.

Burgenland A67

Tyrol A68

Costumes of various districts: 3g, Burgenland. 4g, 5g, Carinthia. 6g, 8g, Lower Austria. 12g, 20g, Upper Austria. 24g, 25g, Salzburg. 30g, 35g, Styria. 45g, Tyrol. 60g, Vorarlberg bridal couple. 64g, Vorarlberg. 1s, Viennese family. 2s, Military.

1934-35 Typo. *Perf. 12*

354 A67 1g dark violet .25 .25
Never hinged .30
On cover —
355 A67 3g scarlet .25 .25
Never hinged .30
On cover 1.50
356 A67 4g olive green .25 .25
Never hinged .30
On cover 4.25
357 A67 5g red violet .25 .25
Never hinged .30
On cover 2.40
358 A67 6g ultramarine .25 .25
Never hinged .75
On cover 3.00
359 A67 8g green .25 .25
Never hinged .35
On cover 2.40
360 A67 12g dark brown .25 .25
Never hinged .35
On cover 1.50
361 A67 20g yellow brown .25 .25
Never hinged .35
On cover 4.25
362 A67 24g grnsh blue .25 .25
Never hinged .35
On cover 1.50
363 A67 25g violet .25 .25
Never hinged .80
On cover 3.25
364 A67 30g maroon .25 .25
Never hinged .75
On cover 1.80
365 A67 35g rose carmine .35 *.35*
Never hinged 1.75
On cover 4.25

Perf. 12½

366 A68 40g slate gray .30 .25
Never hinged 2.50
On cover 1.80
367 A68 45g brown red .30 .25
Never hinged 2.50
On cover 4.25
368 A68 60g ultramarine .55 .40
Never hinged 4.00
On cover 3.25
369 A68 64g brown .80 .25
Never hinged 4.75
On cover 6.50
370 A68 1s deep violet 1.20 .65
Never hinged 10.50
On cover 9.25
371 A68 2s dull green 45.00 *45.00*
Never hinged 160.00
On cover 150.00

Designs Redrawn

Perf. 12 (6g), 12½ (2s)

372 A67 6g ultra ('35) .25 .25
Never hinged .50
On cover 2.40
373 A68 2s emerald ('35) 3.50 *3.50*
Never hinged 8.50
On cover 30.00
Nos. 354-373 (20) 55.00 53.65
Set, never hinged 200.00

The design of No. 358 looks as though the man's ears were on backwards, while No. 372 appears correctly.

On No. 373 there are seven feathers on each side of the eagle instead of five.

Nos. 354-373 exist imperf. Values, set unused hinged $410, never hinged $700.

For surcharges see Nos. B128-B131.

Dollfuss Mourning Issue

Engelbert Dollfuss — A85

1934-35 Engr. *Perf. 12½*

374 A85 24g greenish black .35 *.35*
Never hinged 1.60
On overfranked cover 4.25
375 A85 24g indigo ('35) .80 *.80*
Never hinged 3.25
On cover 6.00

Nos. 374-375 exist imperf. Value, each unused hinged $200, never hinged $400.

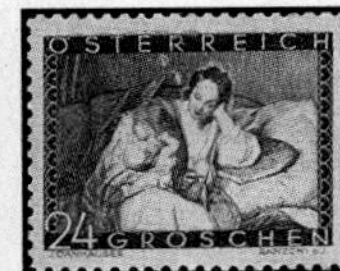

"Mother and Child," by Joseph Danhauser A86

1935, May 1

376 A86 24g dark blue .80 .35
Never hinged 2.00
On cover 3.25
a. Vert. pair, imperf. btwn. 300.00
Never hinged 425.00
b. Horiz. pair, imperf. btwn. 275.00
Never hinged 400.00

Mother's Day. No. 376 exists imperf. Value, unused hinged $200, never hinged $475.

"Madonna and Child," after Painting by Dürer — A87

1936, May 5 Photo.

377 A87 24g violet blue .65 *.55*
Never hinged 1.75
On cover 5.00

Mother's Day. No. 377 exists imperf. Value, unused hinged $250, never hinged $400.

Farm Workers — A88

Design: 5s, Construction workers.

1936, June Engr. *Perf. 12½*

378 A88 3s red orange 13.50 13.50
Never hinged 32.50
On cover 47.50
379 A88 5s brown black 32.50 *32.50*
Never hinged 52.50
On cover 120.00

Nos. 378-379 exist imperf. Values, set unused hinged $350, never hinged $800.

Engelbert Dollfuss — A90

1936, July 25

380 A90 10s dark blue 725.00 *725.00*
Never hinged 1,100.
On cover 1,750.

Second anniv. of death of Engelbert Dollfuss, chancellor.

Value, used, is for CTO examples.

Exists imperf. Value, $1,900, never hinged $3,250.

Mother and Child — A91

1937, May 5 Photo. *Perf. 12*

381 A91 24g henna brown .65 *.80*
Never hinged 1.60
On cover 5.40

Mother's Day. Exists imperf. Values, unused hinged $200, never hinged $325.

S.S. Maria Anna A92

Steamships: 24g, Uranus, 64g, Oesterreich.

1937, June 9

382 A92 12g red brown 1.10 .55
Never hinged 5.50
On cover 5.40
383 A92 24g deep blue 1.10 .55
Never hinged 5.50
On cover 4.25
384 A92 64g dark green 1.10 *.55*
Never hinged 3.50
On cover 13.00
Nos. 382-384 (3) 3.30 *1.65*
Set, never hinged 14.50

Centenary of steamship service on Danube River. Exist imperf. Value, set never hinged $3,500.

First Locomotive, "Austria" A95

Designs: 25g, Modern steam locomotive. 35g, Modern electric train.

1937, Nov. 22

385 A95 12g black brown .25 .25
Never hinged 3.00
On cover 3.00
386 A95 25g dark violet .65 *.65*
Never hinged 4.00
On cover 7.00
387 A95 35g brown red 2.00 *2.00*
Never hinged 8.00
On cover 11.00
Nos. 385-387 (3) 2.90 *2.90*
Set, never hinged 15.00

Centenary of Austrian railways. Exist imperf. Value, set never hinged $325.

Rose and Zodiac Signs — A98

1937 Engr. *Perf. 13x12½*

388 A98 12g dark green .25 *.25*
Never hinged .80
On cover 2.10
389 A98 24g dark carmine .25 .25
Never hinged .80
On cover 2.10
Set, never hinged 1.60

Nos. 388-389 exist imperf. Value, set never hinged $275.

Austria was incorporated into Germany on March 13, 1938, and German stamps were introduced on April 4. Austrian stamps remained valid for use until Sept. 30, 1938, at the rate of 1 mark = 1.50 schilling.

The listings below are for German stamps used in Austria after annexation, bearing clear Austrian cancellations. The catalogue numbers assigned are those of the basic German stamp, preceded by the letter "A." The numbers of one German set, listed under Danzig, are prefixed "AD."

German and Austrian Carrying Nazi Flag — A95

Wmk. Swastikas (237)
1938, Apr. 8 Photo. *Perf. 14x13½*
Size: 23x28mm

A484 A95 6pf dark green 1.20
On cover 2.50

Unwmk. *Perf. 12½*
Size: 21½x26mm

A485 A95 6pf deep green .85
On cover 2.25
On propaganda cover 2.50

Union of Austria and Germany.

Cathedral Island — A96

Hermann Goering Stadium — A97

Town Hall, Breslau — A98

Centennial Hall, Breslau — A99

1938, June 21 Engr. *Perf. 14*

A486 A96 3pf dark brown 1.00
On cover 4.25
A487 A97 6pf deep green .85
On cover 2.50
A488 A98 12pf copper red .85
On cover 2.50
A489 A99 15pf violet brown 1.40
On cover 8.25
Set, on philatelic cover 10.00

16th German Gymnastic and Sports Festival held at Breslau, July 23-31, 1938.

Nazi Emblem — A100

1939, Apr. 4 Photo. Wmk. 237

A490 A100 6pf dark green 5.00
On cover 16.50
A491 A100 12pf deep carmine 5.00
On cover 16.50
Set, on philatelic cover 16.50

Young Workers' Professional Competitions.

St. Mary's Church — A101

The Krantor, Danzig — A102

1939, Sept. 18

A492 A101 6pf dark green 1.00
On cover 3.25
A493 A102 12pf orange red 1.00
On cover 3.25
Set on philatelic cover 3.25

Unification of Danzig with the Reich.

Stamps of Danzig, 1925-39, Surcharged in Black

a

b

c

1939 Wmk. 109 *Perf. 14*

AD241 A19(b) 4rpf on 35pf ultra 9.00
On cover 35.00
AD242 A19(b) 12rpf on 7pf yel grn 5.75
On cover 16.50
AD243 A19(a) 20rpf gray —
On cover —

Wmk. 237

AD244 A19(a) 3rpf brown 8.25
On cover 50.00
AD245 A19(a) 5rpf orange 9.00
On cover 22.50
AD246 A19(a) 8rpf yellow grn 10.00
On cover 25.00
AD247 A19(a) 10rpf blue grn 11.00
On cover 27.50
AD248 A19(a) 15rpf scarlet —
On cover —
AD249 A19(a) 25rpf carmine —
On cover —
AD250 A19(a) 30rpf dk violet —
On cover —
AD251 A19(a) 40rpf dk blue —
On cover —
AD252 A19(a) 50rpf brt bl & red —
On cover —

Thick Paper

AD253 A20(c) 1rm on 1g red org & blk —
On cover —

Wmk. 125
Thin White Paper

AD254 A20(c) 2rm on 2g rose & blk —
On cover —

Johannes Gutenberg and Library at Leipzig — A103

6pf, "High House," Leipzig. 12pf, Old Town Hall, Leipzig. 25pf, View of Leipzig Fair.

Inscribed "Leipziger Messe"

Perf. 10½
1940, Mar. 3 Photo. Unwmk.

A494 A103 3pf dark brown .85
On cover 3.75
A495 A103 6pf dk gray green .85
On cover 2.50
A496 A103 12pf henna brown .85
On cover 2.50
A497 A103 25pf ultra 2.50
On cover 8.25
Set, on philatelic cover 8.25

Leipzig Fair.

SEMI-POSTAL STAMPS

Adolf Hitler — SP101

1938, Apr. 13 Engr. Unwmk.

AB118 SP101 12 + 38pf copper red 3.25
On cover 8.25
On commemorative cover, *from* 12.50

Hitler's 49th birthday.

Horsewoman — SP102

1938, July 20

AB119 SP102 42 + 108pf dp brn 67.50
On cover 120.00

5th "Brown Ribbon" at Munich.

Adolf Hitler — SP103

1938, Sept. 1

AB120 SP103 6 + 19pf deep grn 5.00
On cover 12.50

1938 Nazi Congress at Nuremberg. The surtax was for Hitler's National Culture Fund.

Theater at Saarbrücken — SP104

1938, Oct. 9 Photo. Wmk. 237

AB121 SP104 6 + 4pf blue grn 3.00
On cover 10.00
AB122 SP104 12 + 8pf dk car 4.25
On cover 14.00

Inauguration of the theater of the District of Saarpfalz at Saarbrücken. The surtax was for Hitler's National Culture Fund.

Castle of Forchtenstein — SP105

Designs (scenes in Austria and various flowers): 4pf+3pf, Flexenstrasse in Vorarlberg. 5pf+3pf, Zell am See, Salzburg. 6pf+4pf, Grossglockner. 8pf+4pf, Ruins of Aggstein. 12pf+6pf, Prince Eugene Monument, Vienna. 15pf+10pf, Erzberg. 25pf+15pf, Hall, Tyrol. 40pf+35pf, Braunau.

Unwmk.
1938, Nov. 18 Engr. *Perf. 14*

AB123 SP105 3 + 2pf olive brn .50
On cover 2.50
AB124 SP105 4 + 3pf indigo 2.50
On cover 5.75
AB125 SP105 5 + 3pf emerald .85
On cover 3.25
AB126 SP105 6 + 4pf dk grn .40
On cover 2.10
AB127 SP105 8 + 4pf red org 2.50
On cover 7.50
AB128 SP105 12 + 6pf dk car .65
On cover 2.50
AB129 SP105 15 + 10pf dp cl 7.50
On cover 21.00
AB130 SP105 25 + 15pf dk blue 7.50
On cover 16.50
AB131 SP105 40 + 35pf plum 12.50
On cover 42.50
Set, on philatelic cover 50.00

The surtax was for "Winter Help."

Sudeten Couple — SP114

1938, Dec. 2 Photo. Wmk. 237

AB132 SP114 6 + 4pf blue grn 5.00
On cover 15.00
AB133 SP114 12 + 8pf dk car 4.50
On cover 16.50
Set, on philatelic cover 18.50

Annexation of the Sudeten Territory. The surtax was for Hitler's National Culture Fund.

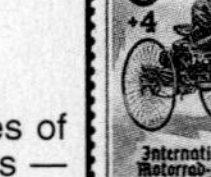
Early Types of Automobiles — SP115

Designs: 12pf+8pf, Racing cars. 25pf+10pf, Modern automobile.

1939

AB134 SP115 6 + 4pf dk grn 12.50
On cover 25.00
AB135 SP115 12 + 8pf brt car 12.50
On cover 25.00
AB136 SP115 25 + 10pf dp blue 21.00
On cover 37.50
Set, on philatelic cover 57.50

Berlin Automobile and Motorcycle Exhibition. The surtax was for Hitler's National Culture Fund. For overprints see Nos. B141-B143.

Adolf Hitler — SP118

Unwmk.
1939, Apr. 13 Engr. *Perf. 14*

AB137 SP118 12 + 38pf carmine 6.75
On cover 16.50
On philatelic cover 14.00

Hitler's 50th birthday. The surtax was for Hitler's National Culture Fund.

Exhibition Building — SP119

1939, Apr. 22 Photo. *Perf. 12½*

AB138 SP119 6 + 4pf dk green 4.25
On cover 14.00
AB139 SP119 15 + 5pf dp plum 4.25
On cover
Set, on philatelic cover 16.50

Horticultural Exhib. held at Stuttgart. Surtax for Hitler's National Culture Fund.

Adolf Hitler — SP120

Perf. 14x13½
1939, Apr. 28 Wmk. 237

AB140 SP120 6 + 19pf blk brn 6.75
On cover 16.50

Day of National Labor. The surtax was for Hitler's National Culture Fund.
See No. AB147.

Nos. B134-B136 Overprinted in Black

1939, May 18 *Perf. 14*

AB141 SP115 6 + 4pf dk green 57.50
On cover 150.00
AB142 SP115 12 + 8pf brt car 57.50
On cover 150.00
AB143 SP115 25 + 10pf dp blue 57.50
On cover 150.00
Set, on philatelic cover 225.00

Nurburgring Auto Races, 5/21, 7/23/39.

Racehorse "Investment" and Jockey — SP121

1939, June 18 Engr. Unwmk.
AB144 SP121 25 + 50pf ultra 30.00
On cover 82.50

70th anniv. of the German Derby. The surtax was divided between Hitler's National Culture Fund and the race promoters.

Man Holding Rearing Horse — SP122

1939, July 12
AB145 SP122 42 + 108pf dp brn 35.00
On cover 90.00

6th "Brown Ribbon" at Munich.

"Venetian Woman" by Albrecht Dürer — SP123

1939, July 12 Photo. Wmk. 237
AB146 SP123 6 + 19pf dk grn 15.00
On cover 35.00

Day of German Art. The surtax was used for Hitler's National Culture Fund.

Hitler Type of 1939
Inscribed "Reichsparteitag 1939"

1939, Aug. 25 ***Perf. 14x13½***
AB147 SP120 6 + 19pf black brn 13.00
On cover 30.00

1939 Nazi Congress at Nuremberg.

Meeting in German Hall, Berlin — SP124

Designs: 4pf+3pf, Meeting of postal and telegraph employees. 5pf+3pf, Professional competitions. 6pf+4pf, 6pf+9pf, Professional camp. 8pf+4pf, 8pf+12pf, Gold flag competitions. 10pf+5pf, Awarding prizes. 12&f+6pf, 12pf+18pf, Automobile race. 15pf+10pf, Sports. 16pf+10pf, 16pf+24pf, Postal police. 20pf+10pf, 20pf+30pf, Glider workshops. 24pf+10pf, 24pf+36pf, Mail coach. 25pf+15pf, Convalescent home, Konigstein.

Perf. 13½x14
1939-41 Unwmk. Photo.
AB148 SP124 3 + 2pf bis brn 7.50
On cover 25.00
AB149 SP124 4 + 3pf sl blue 7.50
On cover 25.00
AB150 SP124 5 + 3pf brt bl grn 3.00
On cover 9.00
AB151 SP124 6 + 4pf myr grn 1.75
On cover 6.75
AB151A SP124 6 + 9pf dk grn ('41) 2.10
On cover 5.75
AB152 SP124 8 + 4pf dp org 2.10
On cover 8.25
AB152A SP124 8 + 12pf hn brn ('41) 2.10
On cover 8.25
AB153 SP124 10 + 5pf dk brn 2.50
On cover 8.25
AB154 SP124 12 + 6pf rose brn 1.60
On cover 6.75
AB154A SP124 12 + 18pf dk car rose ('41) 1.60
On cover 5.75
AB155 SP124 15 + 10pf dp red lilac 4.25
On cover 16.50

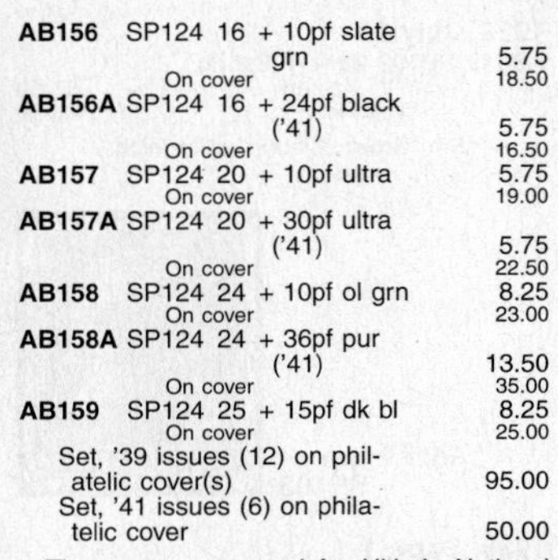

AB156 SP124 16 + 10pf slate grn 5.75
On cover 18.50
AB156A SP124 16 + 24pf black ('41) 5.75
On cover 16.50
AB157 SP124 20 + 10pf ultra 5.75
On cover 19.00
AB157A SP124 20 + 30pf ultra ('41) 5.75
On cover 22.50
AB158 SP124 24 + 10pf ol grn 8.25
On cover 23.00
AB158A SP124 24 + 36pf pur ('41) 13.50
On cover 35.00
AB159 SP124 25 + 15pf dk bl 8.25
On cover 25.00
Set, '39 issues (12) on philatelic cover(s) 95.00
Set, '41 issues (6) on philatelic cover 50.00

The surtax was used for Hitler's National Culture Fund and the Postal Employees' Fund.

Elbogen Castle — SP136

Buildings: 4pf+3pf, Drachenfels on the Rhine. 5pf+3pf, Kaiserpfalz at Goslar. 6pf+4pf, Clocktower at Graz. 8pf+4pf, Town Hall, Frankfurt. 12pf+6pf, Guild House, Klagenfurt. 15pf+10pf, Ruins of Schreckenstein Castle. 25pf+15pf, Fortress of Salzburg. 40pf+35pf, Castle of Hohentwiel.

1939 Unwmk. Engr. ***Perf. 14***
AB160 SP136 3 + 2pf dk brn .40
On cover 3.00
AB161 SP136 4 + 3pf gray blk 3.25
On cover 8.25
AB162 SP136 5 + 3pf emerald .85
On cover 3.00
AB163 SP136 6 + 4pf slate grn .60
On cover 1.75
AB164 SP136 8 + 4pf red org 2.10
On cover 4.50
AB165 SP136 12 + 6pf dk car .65
On cover 1.75
AB166 SP136 15 + 10pf brn vio 7.50
On cover 16.50
AB167 SP136 25 + 15pf ultra 7.50
On cover 16.50
AB168 SP136 40 + 35pf rose vio 9.00
On cover 25.00
Set, on philatelic cover 42.50

Hall of Honor at Chancellery, Berlin — SP145

1940, Mar. 28
AB169 SP145 24 + 76pf dk grn 25.00
On cover 37.50

2nd National Stamp Exposition, Berlin.

Child Greeting Hitler — SP146

Perf. 14x13½
1940, Apr. 10 Photo. Wmk. 237
AB170 SP146 12 + 38pf cop red 7.50
On cover 18.50

51st birthday of Adolf Hitler.

Armed Warrior — SP147

1940, Apr. 30 Unwmk. ***Perf. 14***
AB171 SP147 6 + 4pf sl grn & lt grn 1.75
On cover 5.50

Issued to commemorate May Day.

Horseman — SP148

Perf. 14x13½
1940, June 22 Wmk. 237
AB172 SP148 25 + 100pf dp ultra 15.00
On cover 30.00

Blue Ribbon race, Hamburg, June 30, 1940. Surtax for Hitler's National Culture Fund.

Chariot — SP149

Unwmk.
1940, July 20 Engr. ***Perf. 14***
AB173 SP149 42 + 108pf brown 45.00
On cover 82.50

7th "Brown Ribbon" at Munich.
The surtax was for Hitler's National Culture Fund and the promoters of the race.

View of Malmedy — SP150

Design: 12pf+8pf, View of Eupen.

Perf. 14x13½
1940, July 25 Photo. Wmk. 237
AB174 SP150 6 + 4pf dk green 4.25
On cover 8.25
AB175 SP150 12 + 8pf org red 4.25
On cover 8.25
Set, on philatelic cover 8.50

Issued on the occasion of the reunion of Eupen-Malmedy with the Reich.

Rocky Cliffs of Heligoland — SP152

1940, Aug. 9 Unwmk.
AB176 SP152 6 + 94pf brt bl grn & red org 15.00
On cover 24.00

Heligoland's 50th year as part of Germany.

Artushof in Danzig — SP153

Buildings: 4pf+3pf, Town Hall, Thorn. 5pf+3pf, Castle at Kaub. 6pf+4pf, City Theater, Poznan. 8pf+4pf, Castle at Heidelberg. 12pf+6pf, Porta Nigra Trier. 15pf+10pf, New German Theater, Prague. 25pf+15pf, Town Hall, Bremen. 40pf+35pf, Town Hall, Munster.

1940, Nov. 5 Engr. ***Perf. 14***
AB177 SP153 3 + 2pf dk brn .85
On cover 4.25
AB178 SP153 4 + 3pf bluish blk 1.25
On cover 6.75
AB179 SP153 5 + 3pf yel grn .85
On cover 2.50
AB180 SP153 6 + 4pf dk grn .85
On cover 1.75
AB181 SP153 8 + 4pf dp org 2.50
On cover 6.75
AB182 SP153 12 + 6pf carmine .85
On cover 1.75
AB183 SP153 15 + 10pf dk vio brn 5.00
On cover 11.00
AB184 SP153 25 + 15pf dp ultra 5.00
On cover 11.50
AB185 SP153 40 + 35pf red lil 8.25
On cover 18.50
Set, on philatelic cover 30.00

von Behring — SP162

1940, Nov. 26 Photo.
AB186 SP162 6 + 4pf dp green 3.00
On cover 7.50
AB187 SP162 25 + 10pf brt ultra 3.75
On cover 10.00
Set, on philatelic cover 10.00

Dr. Emil von Behring (1854-1917), bacteriologist.

AIR POST STAMPS

Count Zeppelin

Airship Gondola

1938, July 5 Unwmk. ***Perf. 13½***
AC59 AP11 25pf dull blue 3.00
On cover 10.00
AC60 AP12 50pf green 3.00
On cover 10.00
Set, on philatelic cover 13.50

Count Ferdinand von Zeppelin (1838-1917), airship inventor and builder.

SEMI-POSTAL STAMPS

Issues of the Monarchy

Emperor Franz Josef — SP1

Perf. 12½
1914, Oct. 4 Typo. Unwmk.
B1 SP1 5h green .40 *.80*
Never hinged 1.00
B2 SP1 10h rose .80 *1.60*
Never hinged 1.75
Set, never hinged 2.75

Nos. B1-B2 were sold at an advance of 2h each over face value. Exist imperf.; value, set $120.

The Firing Step — SP2

Designs: 5h+2h, Cavalry. 10h+2h, Siege gun. 20h+3h, Battleship. 35h+3h, Airplane.

1915, May 1

B3 SP2 3h + 1h violet brn 1.20 *.40*
Never hinged 1.50
B4 SP2 5h + 2h green .25 .25
Never hinged .50
B5 SP2 10h + 2h deep rose .25 .25
Never hinged .50
B6 SP2 20h + 3h Prus blue 4.00 *2.40*
Never hinged 10.00
B7 SP2 35h + 3h ultra 6.50 *5.50*
Never hinged 22.50
Nos. B3-B7 (5) 12.20 *8.80*
Set, never hinged 35.00

Exist imperf. Value, set $325 hinged and $525 never hinged.

Issues of the Republic

Types of Austria, 1919-20, Overprinted in Black

1920, Sept. 16 ***Perf. 12½***

B11 A44 5h gray, *yellow* .55 *1.60*
Never hinged 1.20
B12 A44 10h red, *pink* .55 *1.25*
Never hinged 1.20
B13 A43 15h bister, *yel* .25 *.80*
Never hinged .95
B14 A45 20h dark grn, *bl* .25 *.65*
Never hinged .80
B15 A43 25h violet, *pink* .25 *.75*
Never hinged .80
B16 A45 30h brown, *buff* 1.40 *2.90*
Never hinged 3.50
B17 A45 40h carmine, *yel* .25 *.80*
Never hinged .95
B18 A45 50h dark bl, *blue* .25 *.65*
Never hinged .80
B19 A43 60h ol grn, *azure* 1.40 *2.75*
Never hinged 3.25
B20 A47 80h red .35 *.75*
Never hinged .80
B21 A47 1k orange brown .35 *.80*
Never hinged .80
B22 A47 2k pale blue .35 *.80*
Never hinged .80

Granite Paper

Imperf

B23 A46 2½k brown red .40 *1.00*
Never hinged 1.20
B24 A46 3k dk blue & green .50 *1.25*
Never hinged 1.20
B25 A46 4k carmine & violet .65 *1.50*
Never hinged 1.60
B26 A46 5k blue .55 *1.25*
Never hinged 1.20
B27 A46 7½k yellow green .55 *1.25*
Never hinged 1.20
B28 A46 10k gray grn & red .55 *1.40*
Never hinged 1.60
B29 A46 20k lilac & orange .75 *1.75*
Never hinged 2.00
Nos. B11-B29 (19) 10.15 *23.90*
Set, never hinged 26.00

Carinthia Plebiscite. Sold at three times face value for the benefit of the Plebiscite Propaganda Fund.

Nos. B11-B19 exist imperf. Values, set unused hinged $290, never hinged $400.

Types of Regular Issues of 1919-21 Overprinted

1921, Mar. 1 ***Perf. 12½***

B30 A44 5h gray, *yellow* .25 *.80*
Never hinged .55
B31 A44 10h orange brown .25 *.80*
Never hinged .55
B32 A43 15h gray .25 *.80*
Never hinged .55
B33 A45 20h green, *yellow* .25 *.80*
Never hinged .55
B34 A43 25h blue, *yellow* .25 *.80*
Never hinged .55
B35 A45 30h violet, *bl* .50 *1.60*
Never hinged 1.10
B36 A45 40h org brn, *pink* .55 *2.00*
Never hinged 1.40
B37 A45 50h green, *blue* 1.25 *3.25*
Never hinged 2.25
B38 A43 60h lilac, *yellow* .50 *1.60*
Never hinged 1.05
B39 A47 80h pale blue .50 *1.60*
Never hinged 1.20
B40 A47 1k red org, *blue* .40 *1.60*
Never hinged .80
B41 A47 1½k green, *yellow* .25 *.80*
Never hinged .50
B42 A47 2k lilac brown .25 *.80*
Never hinged .50

Overprinted

B43 A46 2½k light blue .25 *.80*
Never hinged .55
B44 A46 3k ol grn & brn red .25 *.80*
Never hinged .55
B45 A46 4k lilac & orange .80 *2.75*
Never hinged 1.65
B46 A46 5k olive green .25 *1.60*
Never hinged .55
B47 A46 7½k brown red .30 *1.60*
Never hinged .70
B48 A46 10k blue & olive grn .30 *1.60*
Never hinged .65
B49 A46 20k car rose & vio .50 *2.40*
Never hinged 1.20
Nos. B30-B49 (20) 8.10 *28.80*
Set, never hinged 18.00

Nos. B30-B49 were sold at three times face value, the excess going to help flood victims. Exists imperf. Values, set unused hinged $300, never hinged $525.

Nos. B50-B76, B93-B98, B112-B117, B122-B127, B132-B137 and B146-B164 exist imperf, on handmade paper, printed in black or in colors other than those of the issued stamps. These are proofs.

Franz Joseph Haydn — SP9

Musicians: 5k, Mozart. 7½k, Beethoven. 10k, Schubert. 25k, Anton Bruckner. 50k, Johann Strauss (son). 100k, Hugo Wolf.

1922, Apr. 24 **Engr.** ***Perf. 12½***

B50 SP9 2½k brn, perf. 11½ 7.25 7.25
Never hinged 22.50
a. Perf. 12½ 11.00 *12.00*
Never hinged 30.00
B51 SP9 5k dark blue 1.25 1.25
Never hinged 2.40
B52 SP9 7½k black 2.00 2.00
Never hinged 4.00
a. Perf. 11½ 110.00 110.00
Never hinged 240.00
B53 SP9 10k dark violet 2.75 2.40
Never hinged 9.50
a. Perf. 11½ 3.25 3.25
Never hinged 16.00
B54 SP9 25k dark green 4.75 *4.75*
Never hinged 12.50
a. Perf. 11½ 4.75 4.75
Never hinged 16.00
B55 SP9 50k claret 2.40 2.40
Never hinged 5.50
B56 SP9 100k brown olive 8.00 *8.00*
Never hinged 16.00
a. Perf. 11½ 10.50 10.50
Never hinged 47.50
Nos. B50-B56 (7) 28.40 *28.05*
Set, never hinged 72.50

These stamps were sold at 10 times face value, the excess being given to needy musicians.

Used values are for examples with philatelic favor cancels. Postally used stamps are worth 50%-100% more.

All values exist imperf. Values, set unused hinged $900, never hinged $1,750.

A 1969 souvenir sheet without postal validity contains reprints of the 5k in black, 7½k in claret and 50k in dark blue, each overprinted "NEUDRUCK" in black at top. It was issued for the Vienna State Opera Centenary Exhibition.

View of Bregenz — SP16

Designs: 120k, Mirabelle Gardens, Salzburg. 160k, Church at Eisenstadt. 180k, Assembly House, Klagenfurt. 200k, "Golden Roof," Innsbruck. 240k, Main Square, Linz. 400k, Castle Hill, Graz. 600k, Abbey at Melk. 1000k, Upper Belvedere, Vienna.

Various Frames

1923, May 22 ***Perf. 12½***

B57 SP16 100k dk green 4.00 *4.00*
Never hinged 9.00
B58 SP16 120k deep blue 4.00 *4.00*
Never hinged 9.00
B59 SP16 160k dk violet 4.00 *4.00*
Never hinged 9.00
B60 SP16 180k red violet 4.00 *4.00*
Never hinged 9.00
B61 SP16 200k lake 4.00 *4.00*
Never hinged 9.00
B62 SP16 240k red brown 4.00 *4.00*
Never hinged 9.00
B63 SP16 400k dark brown 4.00 *4.00*
Never hinged 9.00
B64 SP16 600k olive brn 4.00 *4.00*
Never hinged 14.00
B65 SP16 1000k black 4.00 *4.00*
Never hinged 24.00
Nos. B57-B65 (9) 36.00 *36.00*
Set, never hinged 100.00

Nos. B57-B65 were sold at five times face value, the excess going to needy artists.

Used values are for examples with philatelic favor cancels. Values for postally used: Nos. B57-B64, each $8; No. B65 $14.

All values exist imperf. on both regular and handmade papers. Values, set hinged $700, never hinged $1,000.

Feebleness — SP25

Designs: 300k+900k, Aid to industry. 500k+1500k, Orphans and widow. 600k+1800k, Indigent old man. 1000k+3000k, Alleviation of hunger.

1924, Sept. 6 **Photo.**

B66 SP25 100k + 300k yel grn 4.00 *4.00*
Never hinged 9.00
B67 SP25 300k + 900k red brn 4.00 *4.00*
Never hinged 9.00
B68 SP25 500k + 1500k brn vio 4.00 *4.00*
Never hinged 9.00
B69 SP25 600k + 1800k pck bl 8.00 *6.50*
Never hinged 17.50
B70 SP25 1000k + 3000k brn org 9.50 *8.00*
Never hinged 23.00
Nos. B66-B70 (5) 29.50 *26.50*
Set, never hinged 67.50

The surtax was for child welfare and anti-tuberculosis work.

Used values are for examples with philatelic favor cancels. Values for postally used are 2-2.5 times values shown.

Set exists imperf. Values, set unused hinged $350, never hinged $525.

Siegfried Slays the Dragon — SP30

Designs: 8g+2g, Gunther's voyage to Iceland. 15g+5g, Brunhild accusing Kriemhild. 20g+5g, Nymphs telling Hagen the future. 24g+6g, Rudiger von Bechelaren welcomes the Nibelungen. 40g+10g, Dietrich von Bern vanquishes Hagen.

1926, Mar. 8 **Engr.**

Design size 27½x28½mm

B71 SP30 3g + 2g olive blk .95 .80
Never hinged 1.75
On cover 8.00
B72 SP30 8g + 2g indigo .40 .40
Never hinged .45
On cover 8.00
B73 SP30 15g + 5g dk claret .35 .35
Never hinged .45
On cover 8.00
B74 SP30 20g + 5g olive grn .50 .50
Never hinged .70
On cover 12.00
B75 SP30 24g + 6g dk violet .50 .50
Never hinged .75
On cover 12.00
B76 SP30 40g + 10g red brn 2.40 2.40
Never hinged 11.00
On cover 16.00
Nos. B71-B76 (6) 5.10 4.95
Set, never hinged 15.00

Design size 28½x27½mm

B72a SP30 8g + 2g indigo 2.25 2.00
Never hinged 7.00
On cover 8.00
B73a SP30 15g + 5g dk claret 2.00 4.00
Never hinged 4.75
On cover 12.00
B74a SP30 20g + 5g olive grn 40.00 40.00
Never hinged 95.00
On cover 200.00
B75a SP30 24g + 6g dk violet 2.75 7.25
Never hinged 6.50
On cover 18.00
B76a SP30 40g + 10g red brn 7.25 12.00
Never hinged 17.50
On cover 24.00
Nos. B72a-B76a (5) 54.25 *65.25*
Set, never hinged 130.00

Nibelungen issue. The surtax was for child welfare.

Used values are for examples with philatelic favor cancels. Values for postally used are 1.5 times values shown.

Nos. B71-B76 exist imperf. Values, set unused hinged $350, never hinged $500.

Pres. Michael Hainisch — SP36

1928, Nov. 5

B77 SP36 10g dark brown 5.50 4.75
Never hinged 9.50
B78 SP36 15g red brown 5.50 4.75
Never hinged 9.50
B79 SP36 30g black 5.50 4.75
Never hinged 9.50
B80 SP36 40g indigo 5.50 4.75
Never hinged 9.50
Nos. B77-B80 (4) 22.00 *19.00*
Set, never hinged 37.50

Tenth anniversary of Austrian Republic. Sold at double face value, the premium aiding war orphans and children of war invalids.

Used values are for examples with philatelic favor cancels. Values for postally used are 2.5 times values shown.

Set exists imperf, without gum. Value, set $625.

Pres. Wilhelm Miklas — SP37

1930, Oct. 4

B81 SP37 10g light brown 7.25 *7.25*
Never hinged 21.00
B82 SP37 20g red 7.25 *7.25*
Never hinged 21.00
B83 SP37 30g brown violet 7.25 *7.25*
Never hinged 21.00
B84 SP37 40g indigo 7.25 *7.25*
Never hinged 21.00
B85 SP37 50g dark green 7.25 *7.25*
Never hinged 21.00
B86 SP37 1s black brown 7.25 *7.25*
Never hinged 21.00
Nos. B81-B86 (6) 43.50 *43.50*
Set, never hinged 125.00

Nos. B81-B86 were sold at double face value. The excess aided the anti-tuberculosis campaign and the building of sanatoria in Carinthia.

Used values are for examples with philatelic favor cancels. Values for postally used are 3 times values shown.

Set exists imperf, without gum. Value, set $950.

Regular Issue of 1929-30 Overprinted in Various Colors

1931, June 20

B87 A56 10g bister (Bl) 27.50 *27.50*
Never hinged 95.00
B88 A56 20g dk gray (R) 27.50 *27.50*
Never hinged 95.00
B89 A56 30g dk violet (Gl) 27.50 *27.50*
Never hinged 95.00
B90 A56 40g dk blue (Gl) 27.50 *27.50*
Never hinged 95.00
B91 A56 50g gray vio (O) 27.50 *27.50*
Never hinged 95.00

B92 A57 1s black brn (Bk) 27.50 *27.50*
Never hinged 95.00
Nos. B87-B92 (6) 165.00 *165.00*
Set, never hinged 550.00

Rotary convention, Vienna.

Nos. B87 to B92 were sold at double their face values. The excess was added to the beneficent funds of Rotary International.

Used values are for examples with philatelic favor cancels. Values for postally used are 2 times values shown.

Exists imperf.

Ferdinand Raimund — SP38

Poets: 20g, Franz Grillparzer. 30g, Johann Nestroy. 40g, Adalbert Stifter. 50g, Ludwig Anzengruber. 1s, Peter Rosegger.

1931, Sept. 12

B93 SP38 10g dark violet 13.50 *11.00*
Never hinged 27.50
B94 SP38 20g gray black 13.50 *11.00*
Never hinged 27.50
B95 SP38 30g orange red 13.50 *11.00*
Never hinged 27.50
B96 SP38 40g dull blue 13.50 *11.00*
Never hinged 27.50
B97 SP38 50g gray green 13.50 *11.00*
Never hinged 27.50
B98 SP38 1s yellow brown 13.50 *11.00*
Never hinged 27.50
Nos. B93-B98 (6) 81.00 *66.00*
Set, never hinged 160.00

Nos. B93-B98 were sold at double face value. The surtax aided unemployed young people.

Used values are for examples with philatelic favor cancels. Values for postally used are 3 times values shown.

Set exists imperf, without gum. Value, set $950.

Chancellor Ignaz Seipel — SP44

1932, Oct. 12 ***Perf. 13***

B99 SP44 50g ultra 12.00 *9.50*
Never hinged 27.50

Msgr. Ignaz Seipel, Chancellor of Austria, 1922-29. Sold at double face value, the excess aiding wounded veterans of World War I.

Used value is for a cancelled-to-order example. Value for postally used $27.50.

Exists imperf, without gum. Value $800.

Ferdinand Georg Waldmüller SP45

Artists: 24g, Moritz von Schwind. 30g, Rudolf von Alt. 40g, Hans Makart. 64g, Gustav Klimt. 1s, Albin Egger-Lienz.

1932, Nov. 21

B100 SP45 12g slate green 20.00 *16.00*
Never hinged 45.00
B101 SP45 24g dp violet 20.00 *16.00*
Never hinged 45.00
B102 SP45 30g dark red 20.00 *16.00*
Never hinged 45.00
B103 SP45 40g dark gray 20.00 *16.00*
Never hinged 45.00
B104 SP45 64g dark brown 20.00 *16.00*
Never hinged 45.00
B105 SP45 1s claret 20.00 *16.00*
Never hinged 45.00
Nos. B100-B105 (6) 120.00 *96.00*
Set, never hinged 260.00

Nos. B100 to B105 were sold at double their face values. The surtax was for the assistance of charitable institutions.

Used values are for examples with philatelic favor cancels. Values for postally used, each $60.

Set exists imperf, without gum. Value, set $1,200.

Mountain Climbing SP51

Designs: 24g, Ski gliding. 30g, Walking on skis. 50g, Ski jumping.

1933, Jan. 9 **Photo.** ***Perf. 12½***

B106 SP51 12g dark green 6.50 *6.50*
Never hinged 20.00
B107 SP51 24g dark violet 95.00 *75.00*
Never hinged 245.00
B108 SP51 30g brown red 12.00 *12.00*
Never hinged 32.50
B109 SP51 50g dark blue 95.00 *75.00*
Never hinged 230.00
Nos. B106-B109 (4) 208.50 *168.50*
Set, never hinged 525.00

Meeting of the Intl. Ski Federation, Innsbruck, Feb. 8-13.

These stamps were sold at double their face value. The surtax was for the benefit of "Youth in Distress."

Used values are for examples with philatelic favor cancels. Values for postally used, 25%-80% higher.

Set exists imperf, without gum. Value, set $4,000.

Stagecoach, after Painting by Moritz von Schwind — SP55

1933, June 23 **Engr.** ***Perf. 12½***

Ordinary Paper

B110 SP55 50g dp ultra 150.00 150.00
Never hinged 260.00
On cover 260.00
a. Granite paper 325.00 325.00
Never hinged 600.00
On cover 725.00

Sheets of 25.

Used values are for examples with philatelic favor cancels. Values for postally used, 50% higher.

Nos. B110 and B110a exist imperf. Value, No. B110 unused hinged, $2,400.

Souvenir Sheet

Perf. 12

Granite Paper

B111 Sheet of 4 2,500. 2,400.
Never hinged 3,050.
On cover (overfranked) *4,000.*
a. SP55 50g deep ultra 475.00 475.00
Never hinged 650.00
On cover *950.00*

Intl. Phil. Exhib., Vienna, 1933. In addition to the postal value of 50g the stamp was sold at a premium of 50g for charity and of 1.60s for the admission fee to the exhibition.

Size of No. B111: 126x103mm.

Used values are for examples with philatelic favor cancels. Values for postally used, 35% higher.

A 50g dark red in souvenir sheet, with dark blue overprint ("NEUDRUCK WIPA 1965"), had no postal validity.

Sheet margins of No. B111 are uniformly gummed. When sold at the WIPA exhibition, each example of No. B111 was affixed to a heavy dark bluish gray folder with 3 dabs of water soluable glue. When removed these glue spots appear similar to hinge marks. Some consider No. B111 to be never hinged if no additional hinge marks appear beyond the three dissolved glue spots.

No. B111 exists imperf.

St. Stephen's Cathedral in 1683 — SP56

Marco d'Aviano, Papal Legate — SP57

Designs: 30g, Count Ernst Rudiger von Starhemberg. 40g, John III Sobieski, King of Poland. 50g, Karl V, Duke of Lorraine. 64g, Burgomaster Johann Andreas von Liebenberg.

1933, Sept. 6 **Photo.** ***Perf. 12½***

B112 SP56 12g dark green 24.00 *20.00*
Never hinged 55.00
B113 SP57 24g dark violet 20.00 *16.00*
Never hinged 52.50
B114 SP57 30g brown red 20.00 *16.00*
Never hinged 52.50
B115 SP57 40g blue black 32.50 *20.00*
Never hinged 75.00
B116 SP57 50g dark blue 20.00 *16.00*
Never hinged 52.50
B117 SP57 64g olive brown 27.50 *16.00*
Never hinged 67.50
Nos. B112-B117 (6) 144.00 *104.00*
Set, never hinged 350.00

Deliverance of Vienna from the Turks, 250th anniv., and Pan-German Catholic Congress, Sept. 6, 1933.

The stamps were sold at double their face value, the excess being for the aid of Catholic works of charity.

Used values are for examples with philatelic favor cancels. Values for postally used, 2-3 times values shown.

Types of Regular Issue of 1925-30 Surcharged

a

b

c

1933, Dec. 15

B118 A52(a) 5g + 2g ol grn .25 *.25*
Never hinged .80
B119 A56(b) 12g + 3g lt blue .25 *.25*
Never hinged .95
B120 A56(b) 24g + 6g brn org .25 *.25*
Never hinged .80
B121 A57(c) 1s + 50g org red 35.00 *32.50*
Never hinged 77.50
Nos. B118-B121 (4) 35.75 *33.25*
Set, never hinged 75.00

Winterhelp.

Used values are for examples with philatelic favor cancels. Values for postally used, 2-3 times values shown.

Anton Pilgram — SP62

Architects: 24g, J. B. Fischer von Erlach. 30g, Jakob Prandtauer. 40g, A. von Siccardsburg & E. van der Null. 60g, Heinrich von Ferstel. 64g, Otto Wagner.

1934, Dec. 2 **Engr.** ***Perf. 12½***

Thick Yellowish Paper

B122 SP62 12g black 9.50 8.00
Never hinged 20.00
B123 SP62 24g dull violet 9.50 8.00
Never hinged 20.00
B124 SP62 30g carmine 9.50 8.00
Never hinged 20.00
B125 SP62 40g brown 9.50 8.00
Never hinged 20.00
B126 SP62 60g blue 9.50 8.00
Never hinged 20.00
B127 SP62 64g dull green 9.50 8.00
Never hinged 20.00
Nos. B122-B127 (6) 57.00 *48.00*
Set, never hinged 120.00

Used values are for examples with philatelic favor cancels. Values for postally used, each $20.

Exist imperf. Values, set unused hinged $650, never hinged $850.

Nos. B124-B127 exist in horiz. pairs imperf. between. Value, each $250-$325.

These stamps were sold at double their face value. The surtax on this and the following issues was devoted to general charity.

Types of Regular Issue of 1934 Surcharged in Black

c

d

1935, Nov. 11 ***Perf. 12, 12½***

B128 A67(d) 5g + 2g emerald .50 *.80*
Never hinged 1.60
B129 A67(d) 12g + 3g blue .95 .95
Never hinged 2.40
B130 A67(d) 24g + 6g lt brown .50 *.80*
Never hinged 1.60
B131 A68(c) 1s + 50g ver 32.50 32.50
Never hinged 80.00
Nos. B128-B131 (4) 34.45 35.05
Set, never hinged 80.00

Winterhelp. Set exists imperf. Values, set unused hinged $175, never hinged $260.

Set without surcharge unused hinged $250, never hinged $325.

Prince Eugene of Savoy — SP68

Military Leaders: 24g, Field Marshal Laudon. 30g, Archduke Karl. 40g, Field Marshal Josef Radetzky. 60g, Admiral Wilhelm Tegetthoff. 64g, Field Marshal Franz Conrad Hotzendorff.

1935, Dec. 1 ***Perf. 12½***

B132 SP68 12g brown 10.50 9.50
Never hinged 21.00
B133 SP68 24g dark green 10.50 9.50
Never hinged 21.00
B134 SP68 30g claret 10.50 9.50
Never hinged 21.00
B135 SP68 40g slate 10.50 9.50
Never hinged 21.00
B136 SP68 60g deep ultra 10.50 9.50
Never hinged 21.00
B137 SP68 64g dark violet 10.50 9.50
Never hinged 21.00
Nos. B132-B137 (6) 63.00 57.00
Set, never hinged 125.00

These stamps were sold at double their face value.

Used values are for examples with philatelic favor cancels. Values for postally used, each $20.

Set exists imperf. Values, set unused hinged $650, never hinged $850.

Slalom Turn — SP74

Designs: 24g, Jumper taking off. 35g, Slalom turn. 60g, Innsbruck view.

1936, Feb. 20 **Photo.**

B138 SP74 12g Prus green 1.60 1.60
Never hinged 4.75
B139 SP74 24g dp violet 2.40 2.40
Never hinged 6.50

B140 SP74 35g rose car 24.00 24.00
Never hinged 60.00
B141 SP74 60g sapphire 24.00 24.00
Never hinged 60.00
Nos. B138-B141 (4) 52.00 52.00
Set, never hinged 130.00

Ski concourse issue. These stamps were sold at twice face value.

Used values are for examples with philatelic favor cancels. Value for postally used set, $110.

Set exists imperf. Values, set unused hinged $600, never hinged $750.

St. Martin of Tours — SP78

Designs: 12g+3g, Medical clinic. 24g+6g, St. Elizabeth of Hungary. 1s+1s, "Flame of Charity."

1936, Nov. 2 **Unwmk.**
B142 SP78 5g + 2g dp green .25 .25
Never hinged .40
B143 SP78 12g + 3g dp violet .25 .25
Never hinged .40
B144 SP78 24g + 6g dp blue .35 .35
Never hinged .40
B145 SP78 1s + 1s dk car 7.50 7.50
Never hinged 13.00
Nos. B142-B145 (4) 8.35 8.35
Set, never hinged 14.00

Winterhelp.

Used values are for examples with philatelic favor cancels. Values for postally used: Nos. B142-B144, each 80¢; No. B145, $19.

Set exists imperf. Values, set unused hinged $400, never hinged $500.

Josef Ressel — SP82

Inventors: 24g, Karl von Ghega. 30g, Josef Werndl. 40g, Carl Auer von Welsbach. 60g, Robert von Lieben. 64g, Viktor Kaplan.

1936, Dec. 6 **Engr.**
B146 SP82 12g dk brown 2.75 2.75
Never hinged 8.00
B147 SP82 24g dk violet 2.75 2.75
Never hinged 8.00
B148 SP82 30g dp claret 2.75 2.75
Never hinged 8.00
B149 SP82 40g gray violet 2.75 2.75
Never hinged 8.00
B150 SP82 60g vio blue 2.75 2.75
Never hinged 8.00
B151 SP82 64g dk slate green 2.75 2.75
Never hinged 8.00
Nos. B146-B151 (6) 16.50 16.50
Set, never hinged 47.50

These stamps were sold at double their face value.

Used values are for examples with philatelic favor cancels. Values for postally used: each $6.75.

Exists imperf, without gum. Value, set unused hinged $800, never hinged $1,000.

Nurse and Infant — SP88

12g+3g, Mother and child. 24g+6g, Nursing the aged. 1s+1s, Sister of Mercy with patient.

1937, Oct. 18 **Photo.**
B152 SP88 5g + 2g dk green .30 .25
Never hinged .80
B153 SP88 12g + 3g dk brown .30 .25
Never hinged .80
B154 SP88 24g + 6g dk blue .30 .25
Never hinged .80
B155 SP88 1s + 1s dk carmine 4.00 3.50
Never hinged 8.75
Nos. B152-B155 (4) 4.90 4.25
Set, never hinged 11.00

Winterhelp.

Used values are for examples with philatelic favor cancels. Values for postally used: Nos. B152-B154, each 40c; No. B155, $13.50.

Set exists imperf. Values, set unused hinged $125, never hinged $160.

Gerhard van Swieten — SP92

Physicians: 8g, Leopold Auenbrugger von Auenbrugg. 12g, Karl von Rokitansky. 20g, Joseph Skoda. 24g, Ferdinand von Hebra. 30g, Ferdinand von Arlt. 40g, Joseph Hyrtl. 60g, Theodor Billroth. 64g, Theodor Meynert.

1937, Dec. 5 **Engr.** ***Perf. 12½***
B156 SP92 5g choc 2.40 2.00
Never hinged 5.50
B157 SP92 8g dk red 2.40 2.00
Never hinged 5.50
B158 SP92 12g brown blk 2.40 2.00
Never hinged 5.50
B159 SP92 20g dk green 2.40 2.00
Never hinged 5.50
B160 SP92 24g dk violet 2.40 2.00
Never hinged 5.50
B161 SP92 30g brown car 2.40 2.00
Never hinged 5.50
B162 SP92 40g dp olive grn 2.40 2.00
Never hinged 5.50
B163 SP92 60g indigo 2.40 2.00
Never hinged 5.50
B164 SP92 64g brown vio 2.40 2.00
Never hinged 5.50
Nos. B156-B164 (9) 21.60 18.00
Set, never hinged 52.50

These stamps were sold at double their face value.

Used values are for examples with philatelic favor cancels. Values for postally used: each $5.25.

Set exists imperf, without gum. Value, set $2,250.

AIR POST STAMPS

Issues of the Monarchy

Types of Regular Issue of 1916 Surcharged

1918, Mar. 30 **Unwmk.** ***Perf. 12½***
Grayish paper
C1 A40 1.50k on 2k lilac 1.60 *7.50*
Never hinged 4.00
On cover 95.00
C2 A40 2.50k on 3k ocher 10.50 *32.50*
Never hinged 25.00
On cover 110.00
a. Inverted surcharge *1,200.*
Never hinged 2,400.
b. Perf. 11½ 725.00 *1,100.*
Never hinged 1,600.
On cover 1,350.
c. Perf. 12½x11½ 65.00 *140.00*
Never hinged 160.00
On cover 160.00

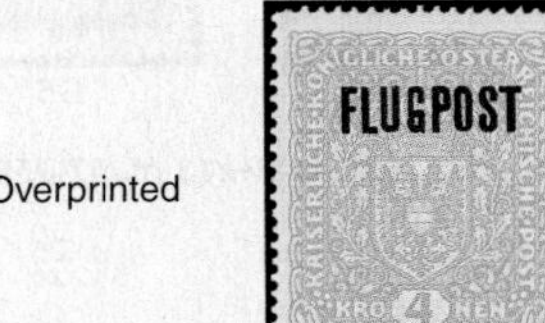

Overprinted

C3 A40 4k gray 4.75 *20.00*
Never hinged 8.00
On cover —
Nos. C1-C3 (3) 16.85 *60.00*
Set, never hinged 40.00

Exist imperf, without gum. Value, set $450.

White paper
C1a A40 1.50k on 2k lilac 2.40 *8.50*
Never hinged 5.75
On cover 160.00
C2d A40 2.50k on 3k ocher 8.00 *24.00*
Never hinged 16.00
On cover 175.00
C3a A40 4k gray 8.00 *24.00*
Never hinged 16.00
On cover —
On cover, overfranked 120.00
Nos. C1a-C3a (3) 18.40 *56.50*
Set, never hinged 37.75

Set exists imperf. Values, set unused hinged $325, never hinged $525.

Nos. C1-C3 also exist without surcharge or overprint. Values, set perf unused hinged $475, never hinged $1,050. Values, set imperf, unused hinged $425, never hinged $850.

A 7k on 10k red brown was prepared but not regularly issued. Values: perf, $550 unused hinged, $1,600 never hinged; imperf, without gum, $1,050.

Issues of the Republic

Hawk — AP1

Wilhelm Kress — AP2

1922-24 **Typo.** ***Perf. 12½***
C4 AP1 300k claret .35 .35
Never hinged .70
On cover 77.50
C5 AP1 400k green ('24) 5.00 4.75
Never hinged 12.00
On cover 160.00
C6 AP1 600k bister .25 .25
Never hinged .40
On cover 77.50
C7 AP1 900k brn orange .25 .25
Never hinged .40
On cover 77.50

Engr.
C8 AP2 1200k brn violet .25 .25
Never hinged .40
On cover 77.50
C9 AP2 2400k slate .25 .25
Never hinged .40
On cover 77.50
C10 AP2 3000k dp brn ('23) 3.25 2.75
Never hinged 8.00
On cover 120.00
C11 AP2 4800k dark bl ('23) 2.75 2.75
Never hinged 6.50
On cover 120.00
Nos. C4-C11 (8) 12.35 11.60
Set, never hinged 29.00

Values for used are for stamps with philatelic favor cancels. Postally used value, set $45.

Set exists imperf. Values, set unused hinged $350, never hinged $500.

Plane and Pilot's Head — AP3

Airplane Passing Crane — AP4

1925-30 **Typo.** ***Perf. 12½***
C12 AP3 2g gray brown .40 .40
Never hinged .80
On cover 12.00
C13 AP3 5g red .40 .40
Never hinged .80
On cover 8.00
a. Horiz. pair, imperf. btwn. 800.00
Never hinged 1,250.
C14 AP3 6g dark blue .80 .80
Never hinged 2.75
On cover 12.00
C15 AP3 8g yel green .80 .80
Never hinged 2.75
On cover 12.00
C16 AP3 10g dp org ('26) .80 .80
Never hinged 4.00
On cover 16.00
a. Horiz. pair, imperf. btwn. 800.00
Never hinged 1,250.
C17 AP3 15g red vio ('26) .40 .40
Never hinged .80
On cover 12.00
a. Horiz. pair, imperf. btwn. 800.00
Never hinged 1,250.
C18 AP3 20g org brn ('30) 11.00 11.00
Never hinged 32.50
On cover 16.00
C19 AP3 25g blk vio ('30) 4.75 4.75
Never hinged 9.50
On cover 55.00
C20 AP3 30g bister ('26) 8.00 8.00
Never hinged 27.50
On cover 47.50
C21 AP3 50g bl gray ('26) 13.50 13.50
Never hinged 40.00
On cover 47.50
C22 AP3 80g dk grn ('30) 2.40 2.40
Never hinged 8.00
On cover 32.50

Photo.
C23 AP4 10g orange red .80 .80
Never hinged 2.00
On cover 12.00
a. Horiz. pair, imperf. btwn. 800.00
Never hinged 1,250.
C24 AP4 15g claret .80 .80
Never hinged 1.60
On cover 9.50
C25 AP4 30g brn violet .80 .80
Never hinged 1.60
On cover 12.00
C26 AP4 50g gray black .80 .80
Never hinged 1.60
On cover 12.00
C27 AP4 1s deep blue 8.00 8.00
Never hinged 40.00
On cover 16.00
C28 AP4 2s dark green 1.60 1.60
Never hinged 6.50
On cover 20.00
a. Vertical pair, imperf. btwn. 800.00
Never hinged 1,250.
C29 AP4 3s red brn ('26) 52.50 52.50
Never hinged 105.00
On cover 90.00
C30 AP4 5s indigo ('26) 13.50 13.50
Never hinged 27.50
On cover 60.00

Size: 25½x32mm
C31 AP4 10s blk brown, *gray* ('26) 8.00 8.00
Never hinged 16.00
On cover 400.00
Nos. C12-C31 (20) 130.05 130.05
Set, never hinged 325.00

Values for used are for stamps with philatelic favor cancels. Postally used value, set $200.

Exists imperf. Values, set unused hinged $850, never hinged $1,100.

Airplane over Güssing Castle — AP5

Airplane over the Danube — AP6

Designs (each includes plane): 10g, Maria-Worth. 15g, Durnstein. 20g, Hallstatt. 25g, Salzburg. 30g, Upper Dachstein and Schladminger Glacier. 40g, Lake Wetter. 50g, Arlberg. 60g, St. Stephen's Cathedral. 80g, Church of the Minorites. 2s, Railroad viaduct, Carinthia. 3s, Gross Glockner mountain. 5s, Aerial railway. 10s, Seaplane and yachts.

1935, Aug. 16 **Engr.** ***Perf. 12½***
C32 AP5 5g rose violet .25 .25
Never hinged .80
On cover 4.00
C33 AP5 10g red orange .25 .25
Never hinged .80
On cover 4.00
C34 AP5 15g yel green .80 .80
Never hinged 1.60
On cover 8.00
C35 AP5 20g gray blue .25 .25
Never hinged .80
On cover 6.50
C36 AP5 25g violet brn .25 .25
Never hinged .80
On cover 6.50
C37 AP5 30g brn orange .25 .25
Never hinged .80
On cover 6.50
C38 AP5 40g gray green .25 .25
Never hinged .80
On cover 8.00
C39 AP5 50g light sl bl .25 .25
Never hinged .80
On cover 12.00
C40 AP5 60g black brn .35 .35
Never hinged .80
On cover 12.00
C41 AP5 80g light brown .40 .40
Never hinged .80
On cover 12.00

C42 AP6 1s rose red .35 .35
Never hinged .80
On cover 12.00
C43 AP6 2s olive green 2.40 2.00
Never hinged 6.50
On cover 40.00
C44 AP6 3s yellow brn 12.00 8.00
Never hinged 27.50
On cover 55.00
C45 AP6 5s dark green 4.00 2.75
Never hinged 16.00
On cover 160.00
C46 AP6 10s slate blue 52.50 52.50
Never hinged 95.00
On cover 325.00
Nos. C32-C46 (15) 74.55 68.90
Set, never hinged 150.00

Values for used are for stamps with philatelic favor cancels. Postally used value, set $175.

Set exists imperf. Values, set unused hinged $375, never hinged $475.

POSTAGE DUE STAMPS

Issues of the Monarchy

D1

Perf. 10 to 13½

1894-95 Typo. Wmk. 91

J1 D1 1kr brown 2.00 1.25
Never hinged 8.75
On cover 20.00
Single franking on postcard 90.00
Single franking on printed matter 95.00
a. Perf. 13½ 45.00 62.50
Never hinged 95.00
On cover *75.00*
b. Half used as ½kr on cover 80.00
J2 D1 2kr brown ('95) 2.75 2.40
Never hinged 10.50
On cover 24.00
a. Pair, imperf. btwn. 200.00 300.00
Never hinged 350.00
b. Half used as 1kr on cover 200.00
J3 D1 3kr brown 3.25 1.25
Never hinged 11.00
On cover 11.00
On cover, single franking 13.00
a. Half used as 1½kr on cover 160.00
J4 D1 5kr brown 3.25 .80
Never hinged 12.00
On cover 8.00
On cover, single franking 9.50
a. Perf. 13½ 25.00 25.00
Never hinged 60.00
On cover 65.00
b. Pair, imperf. btwn. 160.00 *250.00*
Never hinged 275.00
J5 D1 6kr brown ('95) 2.75 *6.50*
Never hinged 8.75
On cover 72.50
a. Half used as 3kr on cover 200.00
J6 D1 7kr brown ('95) .80 *6.00*
Never hinged 4.75
On cover 110.00
a. Vert. pair, imperf. btwn. 275.00 *550.00*
Never hinged 475.00
b. Horiz. pair, imperf. btwn. 275.00 *550.00*
Never hinged 475.00
J7 D1 10kr brown 4.75 .95
Never hinged 20.00
On cover 16.00
a. Half used as 5kr on cover 140.00
J8 D1 20kr brown .80 *6.00*
Never hinged 4.75
On cover 240.00
J9 D1 50kr brown 35.00 72.50
Never hinged 80.00
On cover *2,400.*
Nos. J1-J9 (9) 55.35 97.65

Values for Nos. J1-J9 are for stamps that do not show the watermark. Stamps showing the watermark often sell for more.

See Nos. J204-J231 in *Scott Standard Postage Stamp Catalogue*, Vol. 1.

D2

1899-1900 ***Imperf.***

J10 D2 1h brown .25 *.40*
Never hinged 2.40
On cover 11.00
J11 D2 2h brown .25 *.55*
Never hinged 2.40
On cover 12.00
J12 D2 3h brown ('00) .25 *.40*
Never hinged 2.40
On cover 11.00
J13 D2 4h brown 2.00 2.00
Never hinged 9.00
On cover 14.50
J14 D2 5h brown ('00) 1.60 *1.25*
Never hinged 12.00
On cover 9.50
J15 D2 6h brown .25 *.50*
Never hinged 3.25
On cover 35.00
J16 D2 10h brown .25 *.50*
Never hinged 3.25
On cover 6.50
J17 D2 12h brown .35 *2.40*
Never hinged 4.00
On cover 65.00
J18 D2 15h brown .35 *1.60*
Never hinged 3.25
On cover 40.00
J19 D2 20h brown 24.00 4.75
Never hinged 77.50
On cover 16.00
J20 D2 40h brown 2.40 *2.60*
Never hinged 16.00
On cover *275.00*
J21 D2 100h brown 4.75 3.25
Never hinged 24.00
On cover *1,300.*
Nos. J10-J21 (12) 36.70 20.20

Perf. 10½, 12½, 13½ and Compound

J22 D2 1h brown .55 .25
Never hinged 2.40
On cover 5.50
J23 D2 2h brown .40 .25
Never hinged 2.40
On cover 4.75
J24 D2 3h brown ('00) .40 .25
Never hinged 2.40
On cover 12.00
J25 D2 4h brown .65 .25
Never hinged 2.40
On cover 13.00
J26 D2 5h brown ('00) .55 .25
Never hinged 3.25
On cover 4.75
J27 D2 6h brown .40 .25
Never hinged 3.25
On cover 6.50
J28 D2 10h brown .55 .25
Never hinged 4.00
On cover 4.00
J29 D2 12h brown .55 .75
Never hinged 5.50
On cover 47.50
J30 D2 15h brown .80 .80
Never hinged 5.50
On cover 24.00
J31 D2 20h brown .95 .25
Never hinged 8.00
On cover 12.00
J32 D2 40h brown 1.25 .75
Never hinged 12.00
On cover *240.00*
J33 D2 100h brown 24.00 2.00
Never hinged 87.50
On cover *1,050.*
Nos. J22-J33 (12) 31.05 6.30

Nos. J10-J33 exist on unwmkd. paper.

For surcharges see Offices in the Turkish Empire Nos. J1-J5.

D3

Ordinary Thin Paper

1910-13 Unwmk. ***Perf. 12½***

J34b D3 1h carmine 3.25 2.00
Never hinged 12.00
On cover 55.00
J35 D3 2h carmine .50 .35
Never hinged 1.60
On cover 8.00
d. Half used as 1h on cover 95.00
J36 D3 4h carmine .50 .25
Never hinged 1.60
On cover 8.00
c. Half used as 2h on cover 95.00
d. Used as 5h with manuscript "5" on cover 175.00
J37 D3 6h carmine .50 .25
Never hinged 1.60
On cover 8.00
c. Used as 5h with manuscript "5" on cover 175.00
J38 D3 10h carmine .50 .25
Never hinged 1.60
On cover 1.60
c. Half used as 5h on cover 47.50
J39 D3 14h carmine ('13) 4.00 2.75
Never hinged 16.00
On cover 325.00
J40b D3 20h carmine 5.50 .25
Never hinged 32.50
On cover 8.00
c. Half used as 10h on cover 95.00
J41 D3 25h carmine ('10) 8.00 6.50
Never hinged 40.00
On cover *1,100.*
J42 D3 30h carmine 8.00 .35
Never hinged 24.00
On cover 55.00
J43 D3 50h carmine 12.00 .40
Never hinged 87.50
On cover 80.00
J44 D3 100h carmine 16.00 .80
Never hinged 65.00
On cover *1,100.*
Nos. J34-J44 (9) 50.00 11.90
Nos. J34b-J44 (11) 58.75 14.15

All values exist on ordinary paper, Nos. J34-J38, J40, J42-J44 on chalky paper and Nos. J34-J38, J40, J44 on thin ordinary paper. In most cases, values are for the least expensive stamp of the types. Some of the expensive types sell for considerably more.

All values exist imperf.
See Offices in the Turkish Empire type D3.

1908-13 Chalky Paper

J34a D3 1h carmine 1.60 *4.75*
Never hinged 4.00
On cover 24.00
J35a D3 2h carmine 4.00 *9.50*
Never hinged 12.00
On cover 35.00
J36a D3 4h carmine 2.40 *2.40*
Never hinged 8.00
On cover 8.00
J37a D3 6h carmine 1.20 *2.75*
Never hinged 4.00
On cover 12.00
J38a D3 10h carmine 8.00 .55
Never hinged 24.00
On cover 4.00
J40 D3 20h carmine 8.00 .25
Never hinged 35.00
On cover 35.00
J42a D3 30h carmine 8.00 3.25
Never hinged 40.00
On cover 72.50
J43a D3 50h carmine 12.00 9.50
Never hinged 52.50
On cover 120.00
J44a D3 100h carmine 16.00 16.00
Never hinged 65.00
On cover 1,100.

1909 Thin Translucent Paper

J34 D3 1h carmine .80 *1.60*
Never hinged 2.40
On cover 24.00
J35b D3 2h carmine 2.00 1.20
Never hinged 8.00
On cover 9.50
J36b D3 4h carmine 9.50 1.20
Never hinged 20.00
On cover 12.00
J37b D3 6h carmine .50 *.80*
Never hinged 1.60
On cover 12.00
J38b D3 10h carmine .50 .55
Never hinged 3.25
On cover 4.00
J40a D3 20h carmine 42.50 7.50
Never hinged 1.20
On cover 95.00
J44b D3 100h carmine 85.00 50.00
Never hinged 220.00
On cover —

See Offices in the Turkish Empire type D3.

1911, July 16

J45 D3 5k violet 80.00 12.50
Never hinged 250.00
On cover —
J46 D3 10k violet 240.00 4.00
Never hinged 750.00
On cover —

Nos. J45-J46 exist imperf. Value set: unused hinged $900; never hinged $1,200.

Regular Issue of 1908 Overprinted or Surcharged in Carmine or Black

No. J47

No. J48

1916, Oct. 21

J47 A22 1h gray (C) .25 .25
Never hinged .40
On cover 14.50
a. Pair, one without overprint 210.00
Never hinged 300.00
J48 A22 15h on 2h vio (Bk) .25 *.55*
Never hinged 1.20
On cover 25.00
a. Inverted surcharge 400.00
Never hinged 750.00
Set, never hinged 1.60

D4

D5

Perf. 12½, 12½x13 (#J57-J59)

1916, Oct. 1

J49 D4 5h rose red .25 .25
Never hinged .40
On cover 8.00
J50 D4 10h rose red .25 .25
Never hinged .40
On cover 5.50
a. Half used as 5h on cover 65.00
J51 D4 15h rose red .25 .25
Never hinged .40
On cover 16.00
J52 D4 20h rose red .25 .25
Never hinged .40
On cover 6.50
J53 D4 25h rose red .25 *.95*
Never hinged .80
On cover 325.00
J54 D4 30h rose red .25 *.40*
Never hinged .40
On cover 22.50
a. Half used as 15h on cover 160.00
J55 D4 40h rose red .25 *.40*
Never hinged .40
On cover 16.00
a. Half used as 20h on cover 140.00
J56 D4 50h rose red .95 *3.25*
Never hinged 2.40
On cover 160.00
J57 D5 1k ultramarine .25 *.40*
Never hinged 4.00
On cover 550.00
a. Horiz. pair, imperf. btwn. 250.00 *550.00*
Never hinged 550.00
b. Perf 12½ 30.00 7.50
Never hinged 80.00
On cover *850.00*
J58 D5 5k ultramarine 2.75 *3.25*
Never hinged 8.00
a. Perf 12½ 75.00 57.50
Never hinged 200.00
J59 D5 10k ultramarine 3.50 1.60
Never hinged 14.50
a. Perf 12½ 150.00 80.00
Never hinged 375.00
Nos. J49-J59 (11) 9.20 *11.25*
Set, never hinged 32.50

Exists imperf. Value set: unused hinged $150, never hinged $400.

For overprints see J64-J74, Western Ukraine Nos. 54-55, NJ1-NJ6, Poland Nos. J1-J10.

Type of Regular Issue of 1916 Surcharged

1917

J60 A38 10h on 24h blue 1.60 .55
Never hinged 8.00
J61 A38 15h on 36h violet .50 .25
Never hinged 2.00
J62 A38 20h on 54h orange .25 *.40*
Never hinged 2.00
J63 A38 50h on 42h chocolate .35 .35
Never hinged 2.00
Nos. J60-J63 (4) 2.70 1.55
Set, never hinged 14.00

All values of this issue are known imperforate, also without surcharge, perforated and imperforate. Values, set imperf unused hinged $160, never hinged $250. Value of set without surcharge imperf unused hinged $200, never hinged $350. Same values for set without surcharge, perf 12½.

For surcharges see Poland Nos. J11-J12

Issues of the Republic

Postage Due Stamps of 1916 Overprinted

1919

J64 D4 5h rose red .25 .25
Never hinged .40
a. Inverted overprint 250.00 325.00
Never hinged 325.00
J65 D4 10h rose red .25 .25
Never hinged .40
J66 D4 15h rose red .25 *.40*
Never hinged .80
J67 D4 20h rose red .25 *.40*
Never hinged .80
J68 D4 25h rose red 8.00 *27.50*
Never hinged 21.00
J69 D4 30h rose red .25 *.40*
Never hinged .40
J70 D4 40h rose red .25 *.80*
Never hinged .80
J71 D4 50h rose red .30 *1.25*
Never hinged 1.20
J72 D5 1k ultramarine 4.50 *16.00*
Never hinged 14.50
J73 D5 5k ultramarine 8.75 *16.00*
Never hinged 24.00
J74 D5 10k ultramarine 10.50 4.00
Never hinged 32.50
Nos. J64-J74 (11) 33.55 *67.25*
Set, never hinged 100.00

Nos. J64, J65, J67, J70 exist imperf. Value, 4 values hinged $325.

D6

D7

1920-21 ***Perf. 12½***

No.	Type	Description	Unused	Used
J75	D6	5h bright red	.25	.35
J76	D6	10h bright red	.25	.25
J77	D6	15h bright red	.25	1.60
J78	D6	20h bright red	.25	.25
J79	D6	25h bright red	.25	1.60
J80	D6	30h bright red	.25	.35
J81	D6	40h bright red	.25	.35
J82	D6	50h bright red	.25	.35
J83	D6	80h bright red	.25	.45
J84	D7	1k ultramarine	.25	.35
a.		Thick grayish paper	.25	.40
J85	D7	1½k ultra ('21)	.25	.35
a.		Thick grayish paper	.25	.40
J86	D7	2k ultra ('21)	.25	.35
a.		Thick grayish paper	.25	.40
J87	D7	3k ultra ('21)	.25	.95
a.		Thick grayish paper	.25	.40
J88	D7	4k ultra ('21)	.25	.95
a.		Thick grayish paper	.25	.65
J89	D7	5k ultramarine	.25	.35
a.		Thick grayish paper	.80	4.00
J90	D7	8k ultra ('21)	.25	.95
a.		Thick grayish paper	.25	1.20
J91	D7	10k ultramarine	.25	.45
a.		Thick grayish paper	.30	2.00
J92	D7	20k ultra ('21)	.30	2.00
a.		Thick grayish paper	.40	2.40
		Nos. J75-J92 (18)		12.25
		Set, never hinged	4.75	

Nos. J84 to J92 exist imperf. Values, set unused hinged $150, never hinged $250.

Imperf

No.	Type	Description	Unused	Used
J93	D6	5h bright red	.25	.65
J94	D6	10h bright red	.25	.40
J95	D6	15h bright red	.25	1.60
J96	D6	20h bright red	.25	.40
J97	D6	25h bright red	.25	1.60
J98	D6	30h bright red	.25	1.25
J99	D6	40h bright red	.25	.65
J100	D6	50h bright red	.25	1.10
J101	D6	80h bright red	.25	.85
		Nos. J93-J101 (9)		8.50
		Set, never hinged	3.25	

No. 207a Surcharged in Dark Blue

1921, Dec. ***Perf. 12½***

No.	Type	Description	Unused	Used
J102	A43	7½k on 15h bister	.25	.25
		Never hinged	.25	
		On cover		8.00
a.		Inverted surcharge	450.00	500.00
		Never hinged	575.00	

D8

1922

No.	Type	Description	Unused	Used
J103	D8	1k reddish buff	.25	.35
J104	D8	2k reddish buff	.25	.40
J105	D8	4k reddish buff	.25	.65
J106	D8	5k reddish buff	.25	.35
J107	D8	7½k reddish buff	.25	1.20
J108	D8	10k blue green	.25	.50
J109	D8	15k blue green	.25	.75
J110	D8	20k blue green	.25	.55
J111	D8	25k blue green	.25	1.25
J112	D8	40k blue green	.25	.40
J113	D8	50k blue green	.25	1.25
		Nos. J103-J113 (11)		7.65
		Set, never hinged	5.25	

Issue date: Nos. J108-J113, June 2.

D9

D10

1922-24

No.	Type	Description	Unused	Used
J114	D9	10k cobalt blue	.25	.40
		Never hinged	.25	
J115	D9	15k cobalt blue	.25	.55
		Never hinged	.25	
J116	D9	20k cobalt blue	.25	.55
		Never hinged	.25	
J117	D9	50k cobalt blue	.25	.55
		Never hinged	.25	
J118	D10	100k plum	.25	.25
		Never hinged	.50	
J119	D10	150k plum	.25	.25
		Never hinged	.50	
J120	D10	200k plum	.25	.25
		Never hinged	.50	
J121	D10	400k plum	.25	.25
		Never hinged	.50	
J122	D10	600k plum ('23)	.25	.40
		Never hinged	1.60	
J123	D10	800k plum	.25	.25
		Never hinged	.50	
J124	D10	1,000k plum ('23)	.25	.25
		Never hinged	1.60	
J125	D10	1,200k plum ('23)	1.00	4.75
		Never hinged	3.25	
J126	D10	1,500k plum ('24)	.25	.80
		Never hinged	1.60	
J127	D10	1,800k plum ('24)	3.25	12.00
		Never hinged	9.50	
J128	D10	2,000k plum ('23)	.40	1.60
		Never hinged	3.25	
J129	D10	3,000k plum ('24)	5.50	24.00
		Never hinged	16.00	
J130	D10	4,000k plum ('24)	3.25	20.00
		Never hinged	9.50	
J131	D10	6,000k plum ('24)	3.25	27.50
		Never hinged	22.50	
		Nos. J114-J131 (18)	19.65	94.60
		Set, never hinged	70.00	

J103-J131 sets exist imperf. Values, both sets unused hinged $450, never hinged $650.

D11

D12

1925-34 ***Perf. 12½***

No.	Type	Description	Unused	Used
J132	D11	1g red	.25	.25
		Never hinged	.25	
J133	D11	2g red	.25	.25
		Never hinged	.25	
J134	D11	3g red	.25	.25
		Never hinged	.30	
J135	D11	4g red	.25	.25
		Never hinged	.30	
J136	D11	5g red ('27)	.25	.25
		Never hinged	.30	
J137	D11	6g red	.25	.25
		Never hinged	.55	
J138	D11	8g red	.25	.25
		Never hinged	.55	
J139	D11	10g dark blue	.25	.25
		Never hinged	3.25	
J140	D11	12g dark blue	.25	.25
		Never hinged	.40	
J141	D11	14g dark blue ('27)	.25	.25
		Never hinged	.55	
J142	D11	15g dark blue	.25	.25
		Never hinged	.40	
J143	D11	16g dark blue ('29)	.25	.25
		Never hinged	1.20	
J144	D11	18g dark blue ('34)	1.25	2.75
		Never hinged	2.00	
J145	D11	20g dark blue	.25	.25
		Never hinged	1.20	
J146	D11	23g dark blue	.40	.25
		Never hinged	2.00	
J147	D11	24g dark blue ('32)	1.60	.25
		Never hinged	9.50	
J148	D11	28g dark blue ('27)	1.60	.25
		Never hinged	9.50	
J149	D11	30g dark blue	.25	.25
		Never hinged	3.25	
J150	D11	31g dark blue ('29)	1.25	.25
		Never hinged	9.50	
J151	D11	35g dark blue ('30)	1.25	.25
		Never hinged	9.50	
J152	D11	39g dark blue ('32)	1.60	.25
		Never hinged	12.00	
J153	D11	40g dark blue	2.00	2.50
		Never hinged	5.50	
J154	D11	60g dark blue	2.00	2.00
		Never hinged	5.50	
J155	D12	1s dark green	2.75	1.25
		Never hinged	24.00	
J156	D12	2s dark green	25.00	4.00
		Never hinged	105.00	
J157	D12	5s dark green	87.50	45.00
		Never hinged	240.00	
J158	D12	10s dark green	35.00	8.00
		Never hinged	120.00	
		Nos. J132-J158 (27)	166.70	70.50
		Set, never hinged	575.00	

Issues of 1925-27 exist imperf. Values, set of 18 unused hinged $600, never hinged $800.

Issued: 3g, 2s-10s, Dec; 5g, 28g, 1/1; 14g, June; 31g, 2/1; 35g, Jan; 24g, 39g, Sept; 16g, May; 18g, 6/25; others, 6/1.

Coat of Arms
D13 D14

1935, June 1

No.	Type	Description	Unused	Used
J159	D13	1g red	.25	.25
		Never hinged	.30	
J160	D13	2g red	.25	.25
		Never hinged	.30	
J161	D13	3g red	.25	.25
		Never hinged	.30	
J162	D13	5g red	.25	.25
		Never hinged	.30	
J163	D13	10g blue	.25	.25
		Never hinged	.30	
J164	D13	12g blue	.25	.25
		Never hinged	.30	
J165	D13	15g blue	.25	.50
		Never hinged	.55	
J166	D13	20g blue	.25	.25
		Never hinged	.55	
J167	D13	24g blue	.25	.25
		Never hinged	1.20	
J168	D13	30g blue	.25	.25
		Never hinged	1.20	
J169	D13	39g blue	.35	.25
		Never hinged	1.60	
J170	D13	60g blue	.50	1.25
		Never hinged	1.60	
J171	D14	1s green	.80	.35
		Never hinged	3.50	
J172	D14	2s green	1.50	1.00
		Never hinged	8.00	
J173	D14	5s green	3.00	4.00
		Never hinged	16.00	
J174	D14	10s green	4.75	.65
		Never hinged	20.00	
		Nos. J159-J174 (16)	13.40	10.25
		Set, never hinged	55.00	

On Nos. J163-J170, background lines are horiz.

Nos. J159-J174 exist imperf. Values, set unused hinged $160, never hinged $350.

MILITARY STAMPS

Issues of the Austro-Hungarian Military Authorities for the Occupied Territories in World War I

See Bosnia and Herzegovina for similar designs inscribed "MILITARPOST" instead of "FELDPOST."

Stamps of Bosnia of 1912-14 Overprinted

1915 **Unwmk.** ***Perf. 12½***

No.	Type	Description	Unused	Used
M1	A23	1h olive green	.25	.40
		Never hinged	.40	
		On cover		35.00
M2	A23	2h bright blue	.25	.40
		Never hinged	.40	
		On cover		32.50
M3	A23	3h claret	.25	.40
		Never hinged	.40	
		On cover		35.00
M4	A23	5h green	.25	.25
		Never hinged	.25	
		On cover		20.00
M5	A23	6h dark gray	.25	.40
		Never hinged	.45	
		On cover		47.50
M6	A23	10h rose carmine	.25	.25
		Never hinged	.25	
		On cover		20.00
M7	A23	12h deep ol grn	.25	.80
		Never hinged	.80	
		On cover		35.00
M8	A23	20h orange brn	.35	.80
		Never hinged	.80	
		On cover		55.00
M9	A23	25h ultramarine	.25	.80
		Never hinged	.80	
		On cover		55.00
M10	A23	30h orange red	3.25	6.50
		Never hinged	6.50	
		On cover		65.00
M11	A24	35h myrtle grn	2.50	4.75
		Never hinged	5.00	
		On cover		150.00
M12	A24	40h dark violet	2.50	4.75
		Never hinged	5.00	
		On cover		175.00
M13	A24	45h olive brown	2.50	4.75
		Never hinged	5.00	
		On cover		200.00
M14	A24	50h slate blue	2.50	4.75
		Never hinged	5.00	
		On cover		225.00
M15	A24	60h brn violet	.40	.80
		Never hinged	.80	
		On cover		160.00
M16	A24	72h dark blue	2.50	4.75
		Never hinged	5.00	
		On cover		—
M17	A25	1k brn vio, *straw*	2.50	4.75
		Never hinged	5.00	
		On cover		—
M18	A25	2k dk gray, *blue*	2.50	4.75
		Never hinged	5.00	
		On cover		—
		On postal money order or receipt		100.00
M19	A26	3k car, *green*	20.00	47.50
		Never hinged	50.00	
		On cover		—
		On postal money order or receipt		—
		On overfranked philatelic cover		—
M20	A26	5k dk vio, *gray*	20.00	40.00
		Never hinged	40.00	
		On cover		—
		On postal money order or receipt		—
		On overfranked philatelic cover		—
M21	A25	10k dk ultra, *gray*	150.00	300.00
		Never hinged	310.00	
		On cover		—
		On postal money order or receipt		—
		On overfranked philatelic cover		—
		Nos. M1-M21 (21)	213.50	432.55
		Set, never hinged	420.00	

Exists imperf. Values, set unused hinged $450, never hinged $875.

Nos. M1-M21 also exist with overprint double, inverted and in red. These varieties were made by order of an official but were not regularly issued. Values, each set: unused $325; never hinged $650.

Covers: On cover values are for stamps on postal money order receipts.

M1

M2

Emperor Franz Josef

Perf. 11½, 12½ and Compound

1915-17 **Engr.**

No.	Type	Description	Unused	Used
M22	M1	1h olive green	.25	.25
		Never hinged	.30	
		On cover		9.50
M23	M1	2h dull blue	.25	.35
		Never hinged	.40	
		On cover		9.50
		Single franking on printed matter		25.00
M24	M1	3h claret	.25	.25
		Never hinged	.25	
		On cover		9.50
M25	M1	5h green	.25	.25
		Never hinged	.25	
		On cover		4.00
a.		Perf. 11½	100.00	150.00
		Never hinged	200.00	
b.		Perf. 11½x12½	150.00	240.00
		Never hinged	325.00	
c.		Perf. 12½x11½	200.00	325.00
		Never hinged	400.00	
M26	M1	6h dark gray	.25	.35
		Never hinged	.25	
		On cover		14.50
M27	M1	10h rose carmine	.25	.25
		Never hinged	.80	
		On cover		4.00
M28	M1	10h gray bl ('17)	.25	.35
		Never hinged	1.20	
		On cover		12.00
M29	M1	12h deep olive grn	.25	.40
		Never hinged	.65	
		On cover		20.00
M30	M1	15h car rose ('17)	.25	.40
		Never hinged	.25	
		On cover		8.00
a.		Perf. 11½	8.00	27.50
		Never hinged	27.50	
M31	M1	20h orange brn	.35	.40
		Never hinged	3.00	
		On cover		10.00
M32	M1	20h ol green ('17)	.25	.50
		Never hinged	2.00	
		On cover		15.00
M33	M1	25h ultramarine	.25	.35
		Never hinged	1.60	
		On cover		12.50
M34	M1	30h vermilion	.35	.50
		Never hinged	1.60	
		On cover		21.00
M35	M1	35h dark green	.35	.65
		Never hinged	3.00	
		On cover		35.00
M36	M1	40h dark violet	.35	.65
		Never hinged	3.00	
		On cover		35.00
M37	M1	45h olive brown	.35	.65
		Never hinged	3.00	
		On cover		50.00
M38	M1	50h myrtle green	.35	.65
		Never hinged	3.00	
		On cover		32.50

M39 M1 60h brown violet .35 *.65*
Never hinged 3.00
On cover 85.00
M40 M1 72h dark blue .35 *.65*
Never hinged 3.00
On cover 100.00
M41 M1 80h org brn ('17) .35 .35
Never hinged 3.00
On cover 67.50
M42 M1 90h magenta ('17) .80 *1.25*
Never hinged 5.00
On cover 125.00
M43 M2 1k brn vio, *straw* 1.60 *2.50*
Never hinged 10.00
On cover 85.00
M44 M2 2k dk gray, *blue* .80 1.60
Never hinged 8.50
On cover 85.00
M45 M2 3k car, *green* .80 *6.50*
Never hinged 6.75
On cover 250.00
M46 M2 4k dk vio, *gray* ('17) .80 *8.00*
Never hinged 5.00
On cover 500.00
M47 M2 5k dk vio, *gray* 20.00 *37.50*
Never hinged 50.00
On cover 675.00
M48 M2 10k dk ultra, *gray* 4.00 *16.00*
Never hinged 10.00
On cover 1,000.
Nos. M22-M48 (27) 34.70 *82.20*
Set, never hinged 125.00

Nos. M22-M48 exist imperf. Values, set unused hinged $250, never hinged $475.

For overprints see Montenegro Nos. 1N1-1N4.

Emperor Karl I
M3 M4

1917-18 ***Perf. 12½***

M49 M3 1h grnsh blue ('18) .25 .25
Never hinged .40
On cover 6.50
a. Perf. 11½ 5.50 *16.00*
Never hinged 16.00
M50 M3 2h red org ('18) .25 *.25*
Never hinged .40
On cover 6.50
M51 M3 3h olive gray .25 *.25*
Never hinged .40
On cover 6.50
a. Perf. 11½ 20.00 *47.50*
Never hinged 47.50
b. Perf. 11½x12½ 32.50 *80.00*
Never hinged 80.00
M52 M3 5h olive green .25 *.25*
Never hinged .75
On cover 4.25
M53 M3 6h violet .25 *.25*
Never hinged .40
On cover 12.50
M54 M3 10h orange brn .25 *.25*
Never hinged .65
On cover 4.25
M55 M3 12h blue .25 *.25*
Never hinged .40
On cover 17.00
a. Perf. 11½ 4.00 *12.00*
Never hinged 12.00
M56 M3 15h bright rose .25 *.25*
Never hinged .40
On cover 5.00
M57 M3 20h red brown .25 *.25*
Never hinged .40
On cover 6.75
M58 M3 25h ultramarine .25 *.55*
Never hinged 1.75
On cover 8.50
M59 M3 30h slate .25 .25
Never hinged .85
On cover 12.50
M60 M3 40h olive bister .25 *.25*
Never hinged .40
On cover 10.00
a. Perf. 11½ 2.50 *6.50*
Never hinged 6.50
M61 M3 50h deep green .25 *.25*
Never hinged .85
On cover 21.00
a. Perf. 11½ 8.00 *32.50*
Never hinged 32.50
M62 M3 60h car rose .25 *.40*
Never hinged .85
On cover 17.00
M63 M3 80h dull blue .25 *.25*
Never hinged .40
On cover 25.00
M64 M3 90h dk violet .35 *.80*
Never hinged 2.50
On cover 85.00
M65 M4 2k rose, *straw* .25 *.25*
Never hinged .85
On cover 42.50
a. Perf. 11½ 4.00 *12.00*
Never hinged 12.00
M66 M4 3k green, *blue* 1.25 *2.75*
Never hinged 5.00
On cover 210.00
M67 M4 4k rose, *green* 16.00 *24.00*
Never hinged 85.00
On cover —
a. Perf. 11½ 40.00 *80.00*
Never hinged 80.00
M68 M4 10k dl vio, *gray* 1.25 *8.00*
Never hinged 8.50
On cover 850.00
a. Perf. 11½ 16.00 *47.50*
Never hinged 47.50
Nos. M49-M68 (20) 22.85 *40.00*
Set, never hinged 87.50

Nos. M49-M68 exist imperf. Values, set unused hinged $160, never hinged $325. Also exist in pairs, imperf between. Values, each: unused $60, never hinged $120.

See No. M82. For surcharges and overprints see Italy Nos. N1-N19, N33, Western Ukraine Nos. 44-63, 75, 95-101, Poland Nos. 30-40, Romania Nos. 1N1-1N17.

Emperor Karl I — M5

1918 **Typo.** ***Perf. 12½***

M69 M5 1h grnsh blue 24.00
Never hinged 60.00
M70 M5 2h orange 9.50
Never hinged 25.00
M71 M5 3h olive gray 9.50
Never hinged 25.00
M72 M5 5h yellow green .40
Never hinged .85
M73 M5 10h dark brown .40
Never hinged .85
M74 M5 20h red .80
Never hinged 2.50
M75 M5 25h blue .80
Never hinged 2.50
M76 M5 30h bister 95.00
Never hinged 210.00
M77 M5 45h dark slate 95.00
Never hinged 210.00
M78 M5 50h deep green 47.50
Never hinged 125.00
M79 M5 60h violet 95.00
Never hinged 250.00
M80 M5 80h rose 65.00
Never hinged 170.00
M81 M5 90h brown violet 1.60
Never hinged 4.25

Engr.

M82 M4 1k ol bister, *blue* .40
Never hinged .85
Nos. M69-M82 (14) 444.90
Set, never hinged 1,050.

Nos. M69-M82 were on sale at the Vienna post office for a few days before the Armistice signing. They were never issued at the Army Post Offices. They exist imperf. Values, set unused hinged $800, never hinged $1,600.

For surcharges see Italy Nos. N20-N33, Romania 1N35-1N47.

MILITARY SEMI-POSTAL STAMPS

Emperor Karl I — MSP7

Empress Zita — MSP8

Perf. 12½x13

1918, July 20 **Unwmk.** **Typo.**

MB1 MSP7 10h gray green .40 *.80*
Never hinged 1.00
MB2 MSP8 20h magenta .40 *.80*
Never hinged 1.00
MB3 MSP7 45h blue .40 *.80*
Never hinged 1.00
Nos. MB1-MB3 (3) 1.20 *2.40*
Set, never hinged 3.00

These stamps were sold at a premium of 10h each over face value. The surtax was for "Karl's Fund."

For overprints see Western Ukraine Nos. 31-33.

Exist imperf. Values, set hinged unused $95, never hinged $240.

MILITARY NEWSPAPER STAMPS

Mercury — MN1

1916 **Unwmk.** **Typo.** ***Perf. 12½***

MP1 MN1 2h blue .25 *.35*
Never hinged .40
On newspaper 30.00
a. Perf. 11½ 1.25 *2.00*
Never hinged 3.25
On newspaper —
b. Perf. 12½x11½ 240.00 240.00
Never hinged 450.00
On newspaper —
MP2 MN1 6h orange .50 *1.50*
Never hinged 2.00
On newspaper 250.00
MP3 MN1 10h carmine .55 *1.50*
Never hinged 2.50
On newspaper 250.00
MP4 MN1 20h brown 1.25 *1.50*
Never hinged 3.00
On newspaper 425.00
a. Perf. 11½ 4.00 *8.00*
Never hinged 8.00
On newspaper —
Nos. MP1-MP4 (4) 2.55 *4.85*
Set, never hinged 8.00

Exist imperf. Values, Nos. MP2-MP3, unused hinged each $1.60, never hinged $6.50; Nos. MP1, MP4, unused hinged each $40, never hinged $120.

For surcharges see Italy Nos. NP1-NP4.

NEWSPAPER STAMPS

From 1851 to 1866, the Austrian Newspaper Stamps were also used in Lombardy-Venetia.

Values for unused stamps 1851-67 are for fine examples with original gum. Examples without gum sell for about a third or less of the figures quoted.

Issues of the Monarchy

Mercury — N1

Three Types
Type I — The "G" has no crossbar.
Type II — The "G" has a crossbar.
Type IIa — as type II but the rosette is deformed. Two spots of color in the "G."

1851-56 **Unwmk.** **Typo.** ***Imperf.***
Machine-made Paper

P1 N1 (0.6kr) bl, type IIa 175.00 110.00
No gum 30.00
On newspaper 340.00
On wrapper 250.00
a. Blue, type I 250.00 130.00
No gum 50.00
On newspaper 425.00
On wrapper 325.00
b. Ribbed paper 625.00 240.00
No gum 110.00
On newspaper 500.00
On wrapper 375.00
c. Blue, type II 600.00 250.00
No gum 125.00
On newspaper 750.00
On wrapper 750.00
P2 N1 (6kr) yel, type I *31,000.* *10,000.*
No gum *22,500.*
On newspaper *19,500.*
On wrapper *18,500.*
a. (6kr) brown orange, type I — *12,000.*
P3 N1 (30kr) rose, type I — *13,000.*
No gum *34,000.*
On newspaper *24,500.*
On wrapper *23,500.*
P4 N1 (6kr) scar, type II ('56) *85,000.* *13,500.*
No gum *32,500.*

Full margins = 1½mm at top and bottom, ½mm at sides.

Values for pairs

P1 N1 (0.6kr) blue, type IIa 375.00 500.00
On newspaper 600.00
P1a N1 (0.6kr) blue, type I 525.00 400.00
On newspaper 650.00
P1b N1 (0.6kr) blue, type I, ribbed paper 1,300. 475.00
On newspaper *800.00*
P1c N1 (0.6kr) blue, type II 1,250. 750.00
On newspaper —

Values for strips of 3

P1 N1 (0.6kr) blue, type IIa 600.00 725.00
On newspaper 900.00
P1a N1 (0.6kr) blue, type I 825.00 750.00
On newspaper 1,350.
P1b N1 (0.6kr) blue, type I, ribbed paper *2,100.* 900.00
On newspaper 1,350.
P1c N1 (0.6kr) blue, type II — 1,450.
On newspaper —

Values for blocks of 4

P1 N1 (0.6kr) blue, type IIa *2,000.* *1,700.*
P1a N1 (0.6kr) blue, type I *2,250.* *3,000.*
P1b N1 (0.6kr) blue, type I, ribbed paper *4,500.* *3,250.*
P1c N1 (0.6kr) blue, type II — —

From 1852 No. P3 and from 1856 No. P2 were used as 0.6 kreuzer values.

Values for Nos. P2-P3 unused are for stamps without gum. Pale shades sell at considerably lower values.

Originals of Nos. P2 and P3 are usually in pale colors and poorly printed. Values are for stamps clearly printed and in bright colors. Numerous reprints of Nos. P1 to P4 were made between 1866 and 1904. Those of Nos. P2 and P3 are always well printed and in much deeper colors. All reprints are in type I, but occasionally show faint traces of a crossbar on "G" of "ZEITUNGS."

N2

Two Types of the 1858-59 Issue
Type I — Loops of the bow at the back of the head broken.
Type II — Loops complete. Wreath projects further at top of head.

1858-59 **Embossed**

P5 N2 (1kr) blue, type I 650.00 625.00
No gum 75.00
On newspaper 1,100.
On wrapper 1,100.
a. (1kr) deep blue, type I 800.00 700.00
No gum 150.00
On newspaper 1,100.
On wrapper 875.00
P6 N2 (1kr) lilac, type II ('59) 875.00 300.00
No gum 100.00
On newspaper 600.00
On wrapper 575.00
a. (1kr) dark lilac, type II 1,650. 450.00
No gum 250.00
On newspaper 575.00
On wrapper 550.00
b. (1kr) dark slate lilac, type II — 650.00
On wrapper 1,300.
c. (1kr) gray, type II 2,400. 725.00
No gum 375.00
On newspaper 1,000.
On wrapper 950.00

Values for pairs

P5 N2 (1kr) blue, type I 1,400. *1,750.*
P6 N2 (1kr) lilac, type II 1,900. 1,200.
P6a N2 (1kr) dark lilac, type II — 900.00

Values for strips of 3

P5 N2 (1kr) blue, type I *2,100.* *2,250.*
P6 N2 (1kr) lilac, type II *3,000.* *1,400.*
P6a N2 (1kr) dark lilac, type II —

Values for blocks of 4

P5 N2 (1kr) blue, type I *3,250.* *4,750.*
P6 N2 (1kr) lilac, type II *5,500.* *3,500.*
P6a N2 (1kr) dark lilac, type II — *5,500.*

N3

1861

P7 N3 (1kr) gray 175.00 175.00
No gum 25.00
On newspaper 375.00
On wrapper 350.00
a. (1kr) gray lilac 625.00 240.00
No gum 120.00
On newspaper 525.00
On wrapper 475.00
b. (1kr) deep lilac 2,500. 800.00
No gum 475.00
On newspaper 1,500.
On wrapper 1,450.
c. (1kr) brownish lilac 550.00 275.00
No gum 140.00
On newspaper 600.00
On wrapper 575.00

Values for pairs

P7 N3 (1kr) gray 350.00 *425.00*
On newspaper 800.00
On wrapper 750.00
P7a N3 (1kr) gray lilac — 525.00
P7b N3 (1kr) deep lilac —

The embossing on the reprints of the 1858-59 and 1861 issues is not as sharp as on the originals.

N4

Wmk. 91, or, before July 1864, Unwmkd.

1863

P8 N4 (1.05kr) gray 45.00 16.50
No gum 8.00
On newspaper 125.00
On wrapper 110.00
a. Tete beche pair *125,000.*
b. (1.05kr) gray lilac 100.00 20.00
No gum 25.00
On newspaper 100.00
On wrapper 90.00
c. (1.05kr) brownish lilac 57.50 21.00
On newspaper 100.00
On wrapper 85.00

Values for pairs

P8 N4 (1.05kr) gray 125.00 42.50
P8b N4 (1.05kr) gray lilac 175.00 75.00

Values are for stamps that do not show the watermark. Stamps showing the watermark often sell for more.

The embossing of the reprints is not as sharp as on the originals.

Mercury — N5

Three Types

Type I — Helmet not defined at back, more or less blurred. Two thick short lines in front of wing of helmet. Shadow on front of face not separated from hair.

Type II — Helmet distinctly defined. Four thin short lines in front of wing. Shadow on front of face clearly defined from hair.

Type III — Outer white circle around head is open at top (closed on types I and II). Greek border at top and bottom is wider than on types I and II.

Coarse Print

1867-73 Typo. Wmk. 91

P9 N5 (1kr) vio, type I 75.00 8.50
On newspaper 50.00
On wrapper 25.00
a. (1kr) violet, type II ('73) 225.00 25.00
On newspaper 190.00
On wrapper 95.00

1874-76 Fine Print

P9B N5 (1kr) vio, type III ('76) .55 .40
On newspaper 7.00
On wrapper 4.50
c. (1kr) gray lilac, type I ('76) 225.00 32.50
On newspaper 145.00
On wrapper 90.00
d. (1kr) violet, type II 65.00 8.50
On newspaper 80.00
On wrapper 50.00
e. Double impression, type III 175.00

Stamps of this issue, except No. P9Bc, exist in many shades, from gray to lilac brown and deep violet. Stamps in type III exist also privately perforated or rouletted.

Mercury — N6

1880

P10 N6 ½kr blue green 8.50 1.25
On newspaper 30.00
On wrapper 16.00
a. ½kr yellow green 5.00 .95
On newspaper 32.50
On wrapper 17.50

Nos. P9B and P10 also exist on thicker paper without sheet watermark and No. P10 exists with unofficial perforation.

N7

Without Varnish Bars

1899 Unwmk. *Imperf.*

P11 N7 2h dark blue .25 .25
Never hinged .85
On newspaper 4.25
On wrapper 4.50
P12 N7 6h orange 1.60 *2.00*
Never hinged 5.00
On newspaper 85.00
On wrapper 80.00
P13 N7 10h brown 1.60 .95
Never hinged 8.00
On newspaper 42.50
On wrapper 40.00
P14 N7 20h rose 1.60 2.00
Never hinged 8.00
On newspaper 175.00
On wrapper 165.00
Nos. P11-P14 (4) 5.05 5.20

1901 With Varnish Bars

P11a N7 2h dark blue 2.40 .25
Never hinged 12.00
On newspaper 8.50
On wrapper 8.50
P12a N7 6h orange 16.00 24.00
Never hinged 50.00
On newspaper 250.00
On wrapper 250.00
P13a N7 10h brown 16.00 8.00
Never hinged 50.00
On newspaper 210.00
On wrapper 200.00
P14a N7 20h rose 20.00 *65.00*
Never hinged 60.00
On newspaper 425.00
On wrapper 400.00
Nos. P11a-P14a (4) 54.40 97.25

Nos. P11-P14 were re-issued in 1905. They exist privately perforated.

Mercury — N8

1908 *Imperf.*

P15 N8 2h dark blue .80 .25
Never hinged 4.00
On newspaper 8.50
On wrapper 8.00
a. Tete beche pair 200.00 *325.00*
Never hinged 425.00
P16 N8 6h orange 3.25 .50
Never hinged 11.00
On newspaper 65.00
On wrapper 60.00
P17 N8 10h carmine 3.25 .40
Never hinged 14.00
On newspaper 65.00
On wrapper 60.00
P18 N8 20h brown 3.25 .40
Never hinged 14.00
On newspaper 100.00
On wrapper 90.00
Nos. P15-P18 (4) 10.55 1.55

All values are found on chalky, regular and thin ordinary paper. They exist privately perforated.

Mercury — N9

1916 *Imperf.*

P19 N9 2h brown .25 *.40*
Never hinged 1.00
On newspaper 9.00
On wrapper 8.50
P20 N9 4h green .35 *1.25*
Never hinged 2.00
On newspaper 130.00
On wrapper 125.00
P21 N9 6h dark blue .55 *1.25*
Never hinged 2.00
On newspaper 130.00
On wrapper 125.00
P22 N9 10h orange .60 *1.25*
Never hinged 2.50
On newspaper 130.00
On wrapper 125.00
P23 N9 30h claret .55 *1.60*
Never hinged 2.00
On newspaper 210.00
On wrapper 200.00
Nos. P19-P23 (5) 2.30 5.75
Set, never hinged 9.50

Nos. P19-P23 exist privately perforated.

Issues of the Republic

Newspaper Stamps of 1916 Overprinted

1919

P24 N9 2h brown .25 *.80*
Never hinged .35
On newspaper 5.00
On wrapper 4.25
P25 N9 4h green .40 *6.50*
Never hinged .95
On newspaper 32.50
On wrapper 30.00
P26 N9 6h dark blue .25 *8.00*
Never hinged .50
On newspaper 45.00
On wrapper 42.50
P27 N9 10h orange .40 *9.50*
Never hinged .95
On newspaper 62.50
On wrapper 60.00
P28 N9 30h claret .25 *16.00*
Never hinged .50
On newspaper 77.50
On wrapper 75.00
Nos. P24-P28 (5) 1.55 *40.80*
Set, never hinged 3.25

Nos. P24-P28 exist privately perforated.

Mercury — N10

1920-21 *Imperf.*

P29 N10 2h violet .25 .25
Never hinged .25
P30 N10 4h brown .25 *.25*
Never hinged .25
P31 N10 5h slate .25 .25
Never hinged .25
P32 N10 6h turq blue .25 .25
Never hinged .25
P33 N10 8h green .25 *.40*
Never hinged .25
P34 N10 9h yellow ('21) .25 .25
Never hinged .25
P35 N10 10h red .25 .25
Never hinged .25
P36 N10 12h blue .25 *.40*
Never hinged .25
P37 N10 15h lilac ('21) .25 .25
Never hinged .25
a. Thick grayish paper .35 2.50
Never hinged 3.25
P38 N10 18h blue grn ('21) .25 *.25*
Never hinged .25
a. Thick grayish paper .25 *.40*
Never hinged .25
P39 N10 20h orange .25 *.25*
Never hinged .25
a. Thick grayish paper .25 *.45*
Never hinged .25
P40 N10 30h yellow brn ('21) .25 .25
Never hinged .25
a. Thick grayish paper .25 *.45*
Never hinged .25
P41 N10 45h green ('21) .25 *.40*
Never hinged .35
P42 N10 60h claret .25 .25
Never hinged .25
a. Thick grayish paper .25 *1.30*
Never hinged .25
P43 N10 72h chocolate ('21) .25 *.40*
Never hinged .35
P44 N10 90h violet ('21) .25 *.80*
Never hinged .35
a. Thick grayish paper .25 *1.25*
Never hinged .40
P45 N10 1.20k red ('21) .25 *.80*
Never hinged .40
P46 N10 2.40k yellow grn ('21) .25 *.80*
Never hinged .40
P47 N10 3k gray ('21) .25 *.80*
Never hinged .35
a. Thick grayish paper .25 *.80*
Never hinged .25
Nos. P29-P47 (19) 7.55
Set, never hinged 4.00

Nos. P29-P47 exist privately perforated.

Mercury — N11

1921-22

P48 N11 45h gray .25 .25
P49 N11 75h brown org ('22) .25 .25
P50 N11 1.50k ol bister ('22) .25 .25
P51 N11 1.80k gray blue ('22) .25 .25
P52 N11 2.25k light brown .25 .25
P53 N11 3k dull green ('22) .25 .25
P54 N11 6k claret ('22) .25 *.25*
P55 N11 7.50k bister .25 *.40*
Nos. P48-P55 (8) *2.15*
Set, never hinged 4.75

Used values are for cancelled-to-order stamps. Postally used examples are worth much more.

Nos. P48-P55 exist privately perforated.

NEWSPAPER TAX STAMPS

Values for unused stamps 1853-59 are for examples in fine condition with gum. Examples without gum sell for about one-third or less of the figures quoted.

Issues of the Monarchy

NT1

Unwmk.

1853, Mar. 1 Typo. *Imperf.*

PR1 NT1 2kr green 1,800. 57.50
No gum 350.00
On newspaper 300.00
a. 2kr deep green 2,000. 72.50
No gum 400.00
On newspaper 325.00
b. 2kr yellow green 2,150. 100.00
No gum 450.00
On newspaper 350.00
c. 2kr blue green 2,100. 65.00
No gum 450.00
On newspaper 325.00

Full margins = 1¼mm at top and bottom, ¾mm at sides.

The reprints are in finer print than the more coarsely printed originals, and on a smooth toned paper.

Values for Nos. PR2-PR9 are for stamps that do not show the watermark. Stamps showing the watermark often sell for more.

NT2

Two Types.

Type I — The banderol on the Crown of the left eagle touches the beak of the eagle.

Type II — The banderol does not touch the beak.

Wmk. 91, or, before July 1864, Unwmkd.

1858-59

PR2 NT2 1kr blue, type II ('59) 50.00 5.50
No gum 10.00
On newspaper 17.50
a. 1kr blue, type I 1,225. 190.00
No gum 250.00
On newspaper 425.00
b. Printed on both sides, type II —
PR3 NT2 2kr brn, type II ('59) 47.50 6.75
No gum 10.00
On newspaper 16.00
a. 2kr red brown, type II 600.00 240.00
No gum 125.00
On newspaper 475.00
PR4 NT2 4kr brn, type I 425.00 *1,100.*
No gum 115.00
On newspaper 3,000.
a. 4kr deep brown, type I 650.00 1,250.
No gum 145.00
On newspaper 3,250.

Nos. PR2a, PR3a, and PR4 were printed only on unwatermarked paper. Nos. PR2 and PR3 exist on unwatermarked and watermarked paper.

Nos. PR2 and PR3 exist in coarse and (after 1874) in fine print, like the contemporary postage stamps.

The reprints of the 4kr brown are of type II and on a smooth toned paper.

Issue date: 4kr, Nov. 1.

See Lombardy-Venetia for the 1kr in black and the 2kr, 4fk in red.

NT3

1877 Redrawn

PR5 NT3 1kr blue 12.50 1.40
No gum 1.50
On newspaper 5.50

a. 1kr pale ultramarine 2,900.
On newspaper 11,500.

PR6 NT3 2kr brown 14.00 6.75
No gum 1.75
On newspaper 10.00

In the redrawn stamps the shield is larger and the vertical bar has eight lines above the white square and nine below, instead of five.

Nos. PR5 and PR6 exist also watermarked "WECHSEL" instead of "ZEITUNGS-MARKEN."

NT4

1890, June 1

PR7 NT4 1kr brown 9.00 1.00
No gum 1.35
On newspaper 6.00

PR8 NT4 2kr green 10.00 1.50
No gum 1.75
On newspaper 8.00

#PR5-PR8 exist with private perforation.

NT5

1890, June 1 Wmk. 91 *Perf. 12½*

PR9 NT5 25kr carmine 95.00 *200.00*
Never hinged 160.00
No gum 22.50
On newspaper *47.50*
Fiscal cancellation 425.00
a. Perf 13 125.00 *240.00*
Never hinged 220.00

Nos. PR1-PR9 did not pay postage, but were a fiscal tax, collected by the postal authorities on newspapers.

Values for stamps in pairs

PR1	NT1	2kr green	5,000.	—
PR2	NT2	1kr blue, type II	125.00	35.00
PR2a	NT2	1kr blue, type I	3,000.	700.00
PR2b	NT2	1kr blue, printed on both sides		—
PR3	NT2	2kr brown, type II	125.00	—
PR3a	NT2	2kr red brown, type II	1,500.	—
PR4	NT2	4kr brown, type I	1,000.	—
PR5	NT3	1kr blue	60.00	5.00
PR6	NT3	2kr brown	50.00	*50.00*
PR7	NT4	1kr brown	40.00	5.00
PR8	NT4	2kr green	40.00	6.00
PR9	NT5	25kr carmine	225.00	*500.00*

SPECIAL HANDLING STAMPS

(For Printed Matter Only)
Issues of the Monarchy

Mercury
SH1

1916 Unwmk. *Perf. 12½*

QE1 SH1 2h claret, *yellow* 1.20 *4.00*
Never hinged 3.25
On cover 50.00

QE2 SH1 5h dp green, *yellow* 1.20 *4.00*
Never hinged 3.25
On cover 50.00

Set, never hinged 6.50

SH2

1917 *Perf. 12½*

QE3 SH2 2h claret, *yellow* .25 *.40*
Never hinged .80
On cover 35.00
a. Pair, imperf. between 325.00 *650.00*
Never hinged 650.00
b. Perf. 11½x12½ 150.00 *260.00*
Never hinged 800.00
On cover 250.00
c. Perf. 12½x11½ 225.00 *325.00*
Never hinged 950.00
On cover 340.00
d. Perf. 11½ 1.60 *4.00*
Never hinged 4.00
On cover 42.50

QE4 SH2 5h dp grn, *yel* .25 *.40*
Never hinged .80
On cover 42.50
a. Pair, imperf. between 325.00 *650.00*
Never hinged 650.00
b. Perf. 11½x12½ 120.00 *150.00*
Never hinged 800.00
On cover 250.00
c. Perf. 12½x11½ 190.00 *260.00*
Never hinged 950.00
On cover 340.00
d. Perf. 11½ 1.60 *4.00*
Never hinged 4.00
On cover 42.50

Set, never hinged 1.60

Nos. QE1-QE4 exist imperforate.

Issues of the Republic

Nos. QE3 and QE4 Overprinted

1919

QE5 SH2 2h claret, *yellow* .35 .25
Never hinged .80
On cover 17.00
a. Inverted overprint 325.00
Never hinged 650.00
b. Perf. 11½x12½ 6.00 *12.00*
Never hinged 10.50
On cover 125.00
c. Perf. 12½x11½ 110.00 *290.00*
Never hinged 325.00
On cover 375.00
d. Perf. 11½ .40 *1.25*
Never hinged 1.25
On cover 30.00

QE6 SH2 5h dp grn, *yel* .35 *.25*
Never hinged .80
On cover 21.00
a. Perf. 11½x12½ 1.60 *4.50*
Never hinged 4.00
On cover 125.00
b. Perf. 12½x11½ 40.00 *95.00*
Never hinged 87.50
On cover 375.00
c. Perf. 11½ .35 *.80*
Never hinged .80
On cover 35.00

Set, never hinged 1.60

Nos. QE5 and QE6 exist imperforate. Value, set unused hinged $175; never hinged $360.

No. QE3 Surcharged in Dark Blue

1921

QE7 SH2 50h on 2h claret, *yel* .25 *.80*
Never hinged .80
On cover 75.00

SH4

1922 *Perf. 12½*

QE8 SH4 50h lilac, *yellow* .25 *.25*
Never hinged .40
On cover 210.00

Nos. QE5-QE8 exist in vertical pairs, imperf between. No. QE8 exists imperf. Value: unused hinged $125; never hinged $250.

OCCUPATION STAMPS

Issued under Italian Occupation

Issued in Trieste

Austrian Stamps of 1916-18 Overprinted

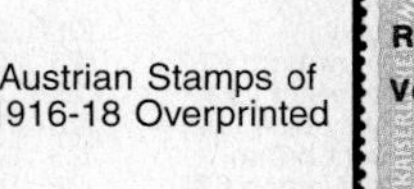

1918 Unwmk. *Perf. 12½*

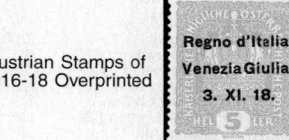

N1 A37 3h bright vio 1.60 1.60
Never hinged 3.25
a. Double overprint 57.50 57.50
b. Inverted overprint 57.50 57.50

N2 A37 5h light grn 1.60 1.60
Never hinged 3.25
a. Inverted overprint 57.50 57.50
c. Double overprint — 57.50

N3 A37 6h dp orange 2.50 2.50
Never hinged 5.00

N4 A37 10h magenta 25.00 4.00
Never hinged 50.00
a. Inverted overprint 57.50 57.50

N5 A37 12h light bl 3.25 3.25
Never hinged 6.50
a. Double overprint 57.50 57.50

N6 A42 15h dull red 1.60 1.60
Never hinged 3.25
a. Inverted overprint 57.50 57.50
b. Double overprint 57.50 57.50

N7 A42 20h dark green 1.60 1.60
Never hinged 3.25
a. Inverted overprint 57.50 57.50
c. Double overprint 140.00

N8 A42 25h deep blue 12.50 12.50
Never hinged 25.00
a. Inverted overprint 225.00 225.00

N9 A42 30h dl violet 3.25 3.25
Never hinged 6.50

N10 A39 40h olive grn 275.00 *290.00*
Never hinged 550.00

N11 A39 50h dark green 12.50 12.50
Never hinged 25.00

N12 A39 60h deep blue 29.00 29.00
Never hinged 57.50

N13 A39 80h orange brn 20.00 20.00
Never hinged 40.00
a. Inverted overprint —

N14 A39 1k car, *yel* 20.00 20.00
Never hinged 40.00
a. Double overprint 130.00

N15 A40 2k light bl 450.00 *500.00*
Never hinged 900.00

N16 A40 4k yellow grn 1,050. *1,250.*
Never hinged 2,600.

Handstamped

N17 A40 10k dp violet *30,000.* *52,000.*
Never hinged *45,000.*

Granite Paper

N18 A40 2k light blue 675.00
Never hinged 1,350.

N19 A40 3k car rose 650.00 *700.00*
Never hinged 1,300.

Nos. N1-N14 (14) 409.40 403.40
Set, never hinged 975.00

Some authorities question the authenticity of No. N18.

Counterfeits of Nos. N10, N15-N19 are plentiful.

A variety of N19 exists on ordinary paper. Only 50 examples are known. Values, $8,250 unused, $12,250 never hinged.

A 90h stamp was printed but not issued because the Austrian stamps were replaced by Italian stamps. Only 50 90h were printed. Values, $4,100 unused, $8,000 never hinged.

Italian Stamps of 1901-18 Overprinted

Wmk. 140 *Perf. 14*

N20 A42 1c brown 3.25 *8.25*
Never hinged 8.00
a. Inverted overprint 32.50 32.50

N21 A43 2c orange brn 3.25 *8.25*
Never hinged 8.00
a. Inverted overprint 29.00 29.00

N22 A48 5c green 2.50 2.50
Never hinged 6.25
a. Inverted overprint 57.50 57.50
b. Double overprint 140.00

N23 A48 10c claret 2.50 2.50
Never hinged 6.25
a. Inverted overprint 85.00 *85.00*
b. Double overprint 140.00

N24 A50 20c brn orange 2.50 *3.25*
Never hinged 6.25
a. Inverted overprint 110.00 110.00
b. Double overprint 130.00 130.00

N25 A49 25c blue 2.50 *4.00*
Never hinged 6.25
a. Double overprint —
b. Inverted overprint 130.00 130.00

N26 A49 40c brown 16.00 *29.00*
Never hinged 40.00
a. Inverted overprint —

N27 A45 45c olive grn 6.50 *10.00*
Never hinged 16.00
a. Inverted overprint 160.00 160.00

N28 A49 50c violet 12.50 12.50
Never hinged 30.00

N29 A49 60c brown car 85.00 *160.00*
Never hinged 210.00
a. Inverted overprint —
b. Double overprint 375.00

N30 A46 1 l brn & green 40.00 *57.50*
Never hinged 100.00
a. Inverted overprint —

Nos. N20-N30 (11) 176.50 *297.75*
Set, never hinged 525.00

Italian Stamps of 1901-18 Surcharged

N31 A48 5h on 5c green 1.60 *3.25*
Never hinged 4.00
a. "5" omitted 125.00 125.00
b. Inverted surcharge 125.00 125.00

N32 A50 20h on 20c brn org 1.60 3.25
Never hinged 4.00
a. Double surcharge 125.00 125.00

Issued in the Trentino

Austrian Stamps of 1916-18 Overprinted

1918 Unwmk. *Perf. 12½*

N33 A37 3h bright vio 12.50 12.50
Never hinged 19.00
a. Double overprint 130.00 130.00
b. Inverted overprint 125.00 125.00

N34 A37 5h light grn 10.00 5.00
Never hinged 15.00
a. "8 nov. 1918" *3,400.*
b. Inverted overprint 125.00 125.00

N35 A37 6h dp orange 125.00 110.00
Never hinged 190.00

N36 A37 10h magenta 10.00 8.25
Never hinged 15.00
a. "8 nov. 1918" 250.00 250.00

N37 A37 12h light blue 325.00 290.00
Never hinged 490.00

N38 A42 15h dull red 12.50 10.00
Never hinged 19.00

N39 A42 20h dk grn 8.25 8.25
Never hinged 12.50
a. "8 nov. 1918" 325.00 325.00
b. Double overprint 130.00 130.00
c. Inverted overprint 57.50 57.50
d. 20h pale green *1,250.* 3,000.
Never hinged *1,900.*

N40 A42 25h deep blue 75.00 65.00
Never hinged 110.00

N41 A42 30h dl violet 29.00 25.00
Never hinged 42.50

N42 A39 40h olive grn 100.00 90.00
Never hinged 150.00

N43 A39 50h dk grn 65.00 50.00
Never hinged 97.50
a. Inverted overprint 325.00 325.00

N44 A39 60h deep blue 110.00 90.00
Never hinged 165.00
a. Double overprint 325.00 325.00

N45 A39 80h org brn 160.00 130.00
Never hinged 240.00

N46 A39 90h red violet 2,250. 3,100.
Never hinged 4,500.

N47 A39 1k car, *yel* 150.00 125.00
Never hinged 225.00

N48 A40 2k light blue 750.00 *900.00*
Never hinged 1,500.

N49 A40 4k yel green *3,400.* *4,100.*
Never hinged 6,750.

N50 A40 10k dp vio, blk ovpt. *235,000.*
Never hinged
a. dp vio, gray ovpt. *25,000.* *25,000.*
Never hinged 37,500.
On cover 42,500.
b. 10k pale violet, gray ovpt. *27,500.* 25,000.
Never hinged 37,500.
On cover 42,500.

Granite Paper

N51 A40 2k light blue *1,650.* *2,250.*
Never hinged *3,300.*

Counterfeits of Nos. N33-N51 are plentiful.

Italian Stamps of 1901-18 Overprinted

Wmk. 140 *Perf. 14*

N52 A42 1c brown 4.00 *11.50*
Never hinged 10.00
a. Inverted overprint 110.00 110.00
b. Double overprint 125.00

N53 A43 2c orange brn 4.00 *11.50*
Never hinged 10.00
a. Inverted overprint 110.00 110.00

N54 A48 5c green 4.00 *11.50*
Never hinged 10.00
a. Inverted overprint 110.00 110.00
b. Double overprint 125.00 125.00

N55 A48 10c claret 4.00 *11.50*
Never hinged 10.00
a. Inverted overprint 160.00 160.00
b. Double overprint 125.00 125.00

N56 A50 20c brn orange 4.00 *11.50*
Never hinged 10.00
a. Inverted overprint 160.00 160.00

N57 A49 40c brown 130.00 85.00
Never hinged 325.00

N58 A45 45c olive grn 65.00 85.00
Never hinged 160.00
a. Double overprint 375.00 *375.00*

N59 A49 50c violet 65.00 *85.00*
Never hinged 160.00

N60 A46 1 l brn & green 65.00 *85.00*
Never hinged 160.00
a. Double overprint 375.00 *375.00*

Nos. N52-N60 (9) 345.00 397.50

Italian Stamps of 1906-18 Surcharged

N61 A48 5h on 5c green 2.50 *4.00*
Never hinged 6.25
N62 A48 10h on 10c claret 2.50 *4.00*
Never hinged 6.25
a. Inverted overprint 110.00 *110.00*
N63 A50 20h on 20c brn org 2.50 *4.00*
Never hinged 6.25
a. Double surcharge 110.00 *110.00*
Nos. N61-N63 (3) 7.50 *12.00*

General Issue

Italian Stamps of 1901-18 Surcharged

1919
N64 A42 1c on 1c brown 1.60 *4.00*
Never hinged 4.00
a. Inverted surcharge 25.00 25.00
N65 A43 2c on 2c org brn 1.60 *4.00*
Never hinged 4.00
a. Double surcharge 375.00
b. Inverted surcharge 20.00 20.00
c. Ovpted. "corona" 67.50 67.50
N66 A48 5c on 5c green 1.60 1.60
Never hinged 4.00
a. Inverted surcharge 65.00 65.00
b. Double surcharge 125.00
N67 A48 10c on 10c claret 1.60 1.60
Never hinged 4.00
a. Inverted surcharge 65.00 65.00
b. Double surcharge 125.00 125.00
c. Ovpted. "oorona" 120.00
Never hinged 300.00
d. Ovpted. "corena" 120.00 120.00
N68 A50 20c on 20c brn org 1.60 1.60
Never hinged 4.00
a. Double surcharge 160.00 *160.00*
b. Half used as 10c on cover 400.00
N69 A49 25c on 25c blue 1.60 *2.50*
Never hinged 4.00
a. Double surcharge 160.00
N70 A49 40c on 40c brown 1.60 *4.00*
Never hinged 4.00
a. "ccrona" 150.00 150.00
N71 A45 45c on 45c ol grn 1.60 *4.00*
Never hinged 4.00
a. Inverted surcharge 180.00 180.00
N72 A49 50c on 50c violet 1.60 *4.00*
Never hinged 4.00
N73 A49 60c on 60c brn car 1.60 *4.00*
Never hinged 4.00
a. "00" for "60" 180.00 *180.00*

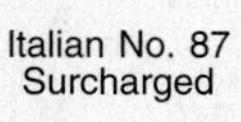

Italian No. 87 Surcharged

N74 A46 1cor on 1 l brn & green 5.00 *10.00*
Never hinged 12.50
Nos. N64-N74 (11) 21.00 41.30

Surcharges similar to these but differing in style or arrangement of type were used in Dalmatia.

OCCUPATION SPECIAL DELIVERY STAMPS

Issued in Trieste

Special Delivery Stamp of Italy of 1903 Overprinted

1918 Wmk. 140 *Perf. 14*
NE1 SD1 25c rose red 75.00 130.00
Never hinged 190.00
a. Inverted overprint 400.00 400.00

General Issue

Special Delivery Stamps of Italy of 1903-09 Surcharged

1919
NE2 SD1 25c on 25c rose 2.50 *3.25*
Never hinged 6.25
a. Double surcharge 130.00 130.00
NE3 SD2 30c on 30c bl & rose 4.00 *6.50*
Never hinged 10.00
a. Pair, on stamp without surcharge *1,500.*

OCCUPATION POSTAGE DUE STAMPS

Issued in Trieste

Postage Due Stamps of Italy, 1870-94, Overprinted

1918 Wmk. 140 *Perf. 14*
NJ1 D3 5c buff & mag 1.60 1.60
Never hinged 4.00
a. Inverted overprint 29.00 29.00
b. Double overprint 260.00
NJ2 D3 10c buff & mag 1.60 1.60
Never hinged 4.00
a. Inverted overprint 110.00 110.00
NJ3 D3 20c buff & mag 3.25 3.25
Never hinged 8.00
a. Double overprint 260.00
b. Inverted overprint 110.00 *110.00*
NJ4 D3 30c buff & mag 6.50 6.50
Never hinged 16.00
NJ5 D3 40c buff & mag 50.00 *60.00*
Never hinged 125.00
a. Inverted overprint 375.00 375.00
NJ6 D3 50c buff & mag 110.00 *160.00*
Never hinged 275.00
a. Inverted overprint 450.00 450.00
NJ7 D3 1 l bl & mag 250.00 *500.00*
Never hinged 625.00
Nos. NJ1-NJ7 (7) 422.95 732.95

General Issue

Postage Due Stamps of Italy, 1870-1903 Surcharged

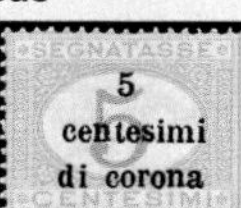

1919 Buff & Magenta
NJ8 D3 5c on 5c 2.50 2.50
Never hinged 6.25
a. Inverted overprint 37.50 37.50
NJ9 D3 10c on 10c 2.50 2.50
Never hinged 6.25
a. Center and surcharge invtd. 260.00 260.00
NJ10 D3 20c on 20c 4.00 2.50
Never hinged 10.00
a. Double overprint 260.00 260.00
NJ11 D3 30c on 30c 4.00 *5.00*
Never hinged 10.00
NJ12 D3 40c on 40c 4.00 *5.00*
Never hinged 10.00
NJ13 D3 50c on 50c 6.50 *8.25*
Never hinged 16.00

Surcharged

NJ14 D3 1cor on 1 l bl & mag 6.50 *12.50*
Never hinged 16.00
NJ15 D3 2cor on 2 l bl & mag 75.00 *160.00*
Never hinged 190.00
NJ16 D3 5cor on 5 l bl & mag 75.00 *160.00*
Never hinged 190.00
Nos. NJ8-NJ16 (9) 180.00 358.25

AUSTRIAN OFFICES ABROAD

These stamps were on sale and usable at all Austrian post-offices in Crete and in the Turkish Empire.

100 Centimes = 1 Franc

OFFICES IN CRETE

Used values are italicized for stamps often found with false cancellations.

Stamps of Austria of 1899-1901 Issue, Surcharged in Black

a

b

c

d

On Nos. 73a, 75a, 77a, 81a Granite Paper With Varnish Bars

1903-04 Unwmk. *Perf. 12½, 13½*
1 A15(a) 5c on 5h blue green 1.00 *3.00*
Never hinged 3.00
On cover *37.50*
a. Perf 13x12½ 45.00 *125.00*
Never hinged 160.00
On cover *160.00*
2 A16(b) 10c on 10h rose .45 *4.00*
Never hinged 2.10
On cover *50.00*
3 A16(b) 25c on 25h ultra 40.00 25.00
Never hinged 110.00
On cover *425.00*
a. Perf 13x12½ 100.00 *120.00*
Never hinged 160.00
On cover —
4 A17(c) 50c on 50h gray blue 8.00 *110.00*
Never hinged 26.00
On cover *1,250.*
a. Perf 13x12½ 25.00
Never hinged 65.00
On cover —

On Nos. 83, 83a, 84, 85 Without Varnish Bars

5 A18(d) 1fr on 1k car rose 1.25 *85.00*
Never hinged 2.00
On cover *1,800.*
a. 1fr on 1k carmine 8.00 *85.00*
Never hinged 26.00
b. Horiz. pair, imperf. btwn. *225.00* —
Never hinged *375.00*
c. Vert. pair, imperf. btwn. — —
6 A18(d) 2fr on 2k ('04) 7.75 *325.00*
Never hinged 24.00
7 A18(d) 4fr on 4k ('04) 11.00 *600.00*
Never hinged 34.00
On cover —
Nos. 1-7 (7) 69.45 1,152.

Surcharged on Austrian Stamps of 1904-05 On Nos. 89, 97

1905 Without Varnish Bars
8a A19(a) 5c on 5h blue green 50.00 45.00
Never hinged 110.00
On cover *190.00*
9 A20(b) 10c on 10h car 1.00 *11.50*
Never hinged 6.00
On cover *60.00*

On Nos. 89a, 97a, 99a, 103a With Varnish Bars

8 A19(a) 5c on 5h bl grn 3.00 6.00
Never hinged 5.75
On cover *42.50*
b. Perf 13x12½ 17.00 *85.00*
Never hinged 30.00
On cover 170.00
9a A20(b) 10c on 10h carmine 32.50 32.50
Never hinged 80.00
On cover *170.00*
10 A20(b) 25c on 25h ultra 1.00 *110.00*
Never hinged 3.00
On cover *850.00*
b. Perf 13x12½ 1.30 *150.00*
Never hinged 1.50
On cover 850.00
11 A21(b) 50c on 50h dl bl 2.50 *475.00*
Never hinged 6.50
On cover —
b. Perf 13x12½ 17.50 *1,250.*
Never hinged 30.00
On cover —

Surcharged on Austrian Stamps and Type of 1906-07 Without Varnish Bars

1907 *Perf. 12½, 13½*
12 A19(a) 5c on 5h yel green (#90) 1.00 *3.00*
Never hinged 2.50
On cover *32.50*
13 A20(b) 10c on 10h car (#92) 1.40 *20.00*
Never hinged 4.00
On cover *150.00*
14 A20(b) 15c on 15h vio 1.75 *22.00*
Never hinged 4.50
On cover *240.00*
Nos. 12-14 (3) 4.15 *45.00*

A5

A6

1908 Typo. *Perf. 12½*
15 A5 5c green, *yellow* .35 *1.00*
Never hinged .75
On cover *12.50*
16 A5 10c scarlet, *rose* .40 *1.00*
Never hinged 1.00
On cover *13.50*
17 A5 15c brown, *buff* .45 *4.75*
Never hinged 1.50
On cover *210.00*
18 A5 25c dp blue, *blue* 15.00 3.75
Never hinged 37.50
On cover *110.00*
a. 25c deep blue, greenish blue paper 25.00 *42.50*
Never hinged 50.00
On cover *100.00*

Engr.

19 A6 50c lake, *yellow* 2.75 *30.00*
Never hinged 8.50
On cover *425.00*
20 A6 1fr brown, *gray* 6.75 *57.50*
Never hinged 17.00
On cover *1,350.*
a. Vert pair, imperf. btwn. *225.00*
Never hinged *325.00*
Nos. 15-20 (6) 25.70 *98.00*

Nos. 15-18 are on paper colored on the surface only. All values exist imperforate.

60th year of the reign of Emperor Franz Josef, for permanent use.

Paper Colored Through

1914 Typo.
21 A5 10c rose, *rose* 1.15 *2,000.*
Never hinged 2.75
On cover *4,250.*
22 A5 25c ultra, *blue* 2.00 *150.00*
Never hinged 1.60
On cover *1,250.*
On parcel post receipt card *650.00*

Nos. 21 and 22 exist imperforate.

STAMPS OF LOMBARDY-VENETIA USED IN AUSTRIAN OFFICES IN THE TURKISH EMPIRE

From 1863 to 1867 the stamps of Lombardy-Venetia (Nos. 15 to 24) were used at the Austrian Offices in the Turkish Empire. Values for stamps are for examples with neat and legible town cancellations of the most common types from the larger post offices. Values for scarcer cancellation types and for cancellations from smaller post offices are much higher. Values for covers are also for the most common frankings. Covers bearing unusual frankings and unusual combinations of stamps are also worth much more.

Aegean Islands:	Leros
	Meteline
	Rhodes
	Scio
	Scio-Cesme
Albania:	Dulcigno San Giovanni di Medusa
	Durazzo
	Santi Quaranta
	San Giovanni
	Scutari
	Valona
Bulgaria:	Burgas
	Kustendje
	Philippoli
	Rustschuk
	Sofia
	Varna
	Widdin
Crete:	Candia
	La Canea
	Rettimo
Cyprus:	Larnaca
Egypt:	Alexandria
	Port Said
Greece:	Cavalla
	Corfu
	Janina
	Lagos
	Prevesa
	Salonica
	Sayada
	Serres
	Volo
Moldavia-Walachia:	Bakau
	Berlad
	Bottuschan
	Bukarest
	Czernawoda
	Fokschan
	Galatz
	giurgevo
	Ibralia
	Jassy
	Piatra
	Ploeschti
	Roman
	Sulina
	Tekutsch
	Tultscha
Montenegro:	Antivari
Serbia:	Belgrade
Turkey (Ottoman Empire):	Adrianopoli
	Alexandrette
	Beyrut
	Haifa (Caifa)
	Cesme
	Constantinople
	Dardanelles
	Gallipoli
	Ineboli
	Jaffa
	Jerusalem
	Kerassunda
	Latakia
	Mersina
	Rodosto
	Samsun
	Sinope
	Smyrna
	Tenedos
	Trebizonde
	Tripoli in Syria

1863 ***Perf. 14***

A15 A8 2s yellow, *value from* 220.00
On cover, *value from* 875.00
Single franking, on cover, *value from* *5,200.*
A16 A8 3s green, *value from* 130.00
On cover, *value from* 1,000.
Single franking, on cover, *value from* *4,500.*
A17 A8 5s rose, *value from* 130.00
On cover, *value from* 675.00
Single franking, on cover, *value from* *2,800.*
A18 A8 10s blue, *value from* 82.50
On cover, *value from* 330.00
A19 A8 15s yellow brown, *value from* 175.00
On cover, *value from* 550.00

Values for Pairs, with legible cancellations

A15 A8 2s yellow, *value from* 450.00
On cover, *value from* 1,575.
A16 A8 3s green, *value from* 675.00
On cover, *value from* 2,850.
A17 A8 5s rose, *value from* 300.00
On cover, *value from* 1,250.
A18 A8 10s blue, *value from* 165.00
On cover, *value from* 675.00
A19 A8 15s yellow brown, *value from* 350.00
On cover, *value from* 1,175.

1864-65 **Wmk. 91** ***Perf. 9½***

A20 A8 2s yellow ('65), *value from* 400.00
On cover, *value from* 1,475.
Single franking, on cover —
A21 A8 3s green, *value from* 100.00
On cover, *value from* 600.00
Single franking, on cover, *value from* *2,750.*
A22 A8 5s rose, *value from* 47.50
On cover, *value from* 375.00
Single franking, on cover, *value from* *1,850.*
A23 A8 10s blue, *value from* 16.00
On cover, *value from* 67.50
A24 A8 15s yellow brown, *value from* 55.00
On cover, *value from* 240.00

Only one example is known of No. A20 on single franking cover.

Values for Pairs, with legible cancellations

A20 A8 2s yellow ('65), *value from* 800.00
On cover, *value from* 2,750.
A21 A8 3s green, *value from* 340.00
On cover, *value from* 2,750.
A22 A8 5s rose, *value from* 165.00
On cover, *value from* 825.00
A23 A8 10s blue, *value from* 50.00
On cover, *value from* 235.00
A24 A8 15s yellow brown, *value from* 110.00
On cover, *value from* 475.00

OFFICES IN THE TURKISH EMPIRE

100 Soldi = 1 Florin
40 Paras = 1 Piaster

Values for unused stamps are for examples with gum. Examples without gum sell for about one-third or less of the figures quoted. Used values are italicized for stamps often found with false cancellations.

For similar designs in Kreuzers, see early Austria.

A1

A2

Two different printing methods were used, as in the 1867-74 issues of Austria. They may be distinguished by the coarse or fine lines of the hair and whiskers and by the paper, which is more transparent on the later issue.

1867 **Typo.** **Wmk. 91** ***Perf. 9½***

Coarse Print

1	A1 2sld orange	2.40	*27.50*
	Never hinged	4.00	
	On cover		*3,000.*
a.	2sld yellow	65.00	80.00
	Never hinged	115.00	
	On cover		*1,000.*
2	A1 3sld green	150.00	67.50
	Never hinged	275.00	
	On cover		*775.00*
a.	3sld dark green	325.00	200.00
	Never hinged	550.00	
	On cover		*425.00*
3	A1 5sld red	240.00	14.00
	Never hinged	575.00	
	On cover		*1,000.*
a.	5sld carmine	325.00	40.00
	Never hinged	975.00	
	On cover		*900.00*
b.	5sld red lilac	275.00	24.00
	Never hinged	675.00	
	On cover		—
4	A1 10sld blue	200.00	2.40
	Never hinged	300.00	
	On cover		27.50
a.	10sld light blue	275.00	3.25
	Never hinged	400.00	
	On cover		35.00
b.	10sld dark blue	240.00	3.25
	Never hinged	375.00	
	On cover		37.50
5	A1 15sld brown	24.00	8.00
	Never hinged	37.50	
	On cover		50.00
a.	15sld dark brown	95.00	65.00
	Never hinged	250.00	
	On cover		125.00
b.	15sld reddish brown	40.00	16.00
	Never hinged	60.00	
	On cover		60.00
c.	15sld gray brown	80.00	16.00
	Never hinged	150.00	
	On cover		55.00
6	A1 25sld violet	24.00	*40.00*
	Never hinged	40.00	
	On cover		*1,500.*
a.	25sld brown violet	40.00	*60.00*
	Never hinged	72.50	
	On cover		*1,500.*
b.	25sld gray lilac	120.00	47.50
	Never hinged	250.00	
	On cover		*1,650.*
7	A2 50sld brn, perf. 10½	1.25	*65.00*
	Never hinged	1.75	
	On cover		*8,750.*
a.	Perf. 12	100.00	*110.00*
	Never hinged	160.00	
b.	Perf. 13	325.00	—
	Never hinged	650.00	
k.	Perf. 9	27.50	*140.00*
	Never hinged	65.00	
l.	50sld pale red brn, perf. 12	160.00	160.00
	Never hinged	275.00	
	On cover		*8,500.*
m.	Vert. pair, imperf. btwn.	300.00	*550.00*
	Never hinged	425.00	
n.	Horiz. pair, imperf. btwn.	300.00	*550.00*
	Never hinged	425.00	
o.	Perf. 10½x9	85.00	*160.00*
	Never hinged	120.00	

Perf. 9, 9½, 10½ and Compound

1876-83 **Fine Print**

7C	A1 2sld yellow ('83)	.40	*3,000.*
	Never hinged	.75	
7D	A1 3sld green ('78)	1.20	27.50
	Never hinged	2.75	
	On cover, single franking		275.00
p.	Perf. 10½x9	—	450.00
	Never hinged	—	
7E	A1 5sld red ('78)	.40	*24.00*
	Never hinged	1.35	
	On cover		—
q.	Perf. 9		350.00
	On cover		—
7F	A1 10sld blue	100.00	1.25
	Never hinged	210.00	
	On cover, single franking		*21.00*
r.	Perf. 10½	190.00	15.50
	Never hinged	350.00	
	On cover, single franking		*77.50*
s.	Perf. 9	150.00	*250.00*
	Never hinged	280.00	
	On cover, single franking		*750.00*
t.	Perf. 10½x9	—	165.00
	On cover, single franking		*575.00*
7I	A1 15sld org brn ('81)	12.00	*160.00*
	Never hinged	27.50	
	On cover, single franking		*1,900.*
u.	Perf. 10½		425.00
	On cover		—
7J	A1 25sld gray lil ('83)	.80	*360.00*
	Never hinged	1.60	
	On cover, single franking		*15,000.*
	Nos. 7C-7J (6)	114.80	3,573.

The 10 soldi was reprinted in deep dull blue, perforated 10½. Value, $6.50.

A3

1883 ***Perf. 9½***

8	A3 2sld brown	.25	*190.00*
	Never hinged	.45	
	On cover		—
9	A3 3sld green	1.20	*35.00*
	Never hinged	6.00	
	On cover, single franking		*300.00*
10	A3 5sld rose	.25	*20.00*
	Never hinged	.45	
	On cover, single franking		*225.00*
a.	Perf. 10	5.50	*135.00*
	Never hinged	17.00	
	On cover		—
11	A3 10sld blue	.80	.80
	Never hinged	2.40	
	On cover, single franking		22.50
a.	Perf. 10½		200.00
	On cover		—
12	A3 20sld gray, perf. 10	6.50	*600.00*
	Never hinged	18.00	
	On cover		—
a.	Perf. 9½	1.60	*9.50*
	Never hinged	3.75	
	On cover, single franking		*750.00*
13	A3 50sld red lilac	1.25	*20.00*
	Never hinged	3.75	
	On cover, single franking		*2,250.*
	Nos. 8-13 (6)	10.25	865.80

No. 9 Surcharged

10 PARAS ON 3 SOLDI:

Type I — Surcharge 16½mm across. "PARA" about ½mm above bottom of "10." 2mm space between "10" and "P"; 1½mm between "A" and "10." Perf. 9½ only.

Type II — Surcharge 15¼ to 16mm across. "PARA" on same line with figures or slightly higher or lower. 1½mm space between "10" and "P"; 1mm between "A" and "10." Perf. 9½ and 10.

1886 ***Perf. 9½, 10***

14	A4 10pa on 3sld grn, type II, perf. 10	.35	*8.00*
	Never hinged	.60	
	On cover		150.00
a.	10pa on 3sld green, type I	200.00	500.00
	Never hinged	350.00	
b.	Inverted surcharge, type I		*2,000.*
c.	As #14, perf. 9½	.95	20.00
	Never hinged	2.50	
	On cover		150.00

Nos. 14 and 14c were overprinted in Vienna. Nos. 14a and 14b were overprinted in Constantinople.

Surcharged on Austria Nos. 42-46

1888

15	A11 10pa on 3kr grn	4.00	12.00
	Never hinged	12.00	
	On cover		*77.50*
a.	"01 PARA 10"		*1,200.*
16	A11 20pa on 5kr rose	.40	*12.00*
	Never hinged	1.75	
	On cover		*90.00*
a.	Double surcharge	400.00	
	Never hinged	1,200.	
17	A11 1pi on 10kr blue	65.00	1.60
	Never hinged	135.00	
	On cover		17.00
a.	Perf. 13½		800.00
b.	Double surcharge		—
18	A11 2pi on 20kr gray	1.60	*6.50*
	Never hinged	4.75	
	On cover		*340.00*
19	A11 5pi on 50kr vio	2.00	*20.00*
	Never hinged	4.00	
	On cover		*1,350.*
	Nos. 15-19 (5)	73.00	52.10

Austria Nos. 52-55, 58, 61 Surcharged

1890-92 **Unwmk.** ***Perf. 9 to 13½***

Granite Paper

20	A12 8pa on 2kr brn ('92)	.25	*.65*
	Never hinged	.50	
	On cover		17.50
a.	Perf. 9½	12.00	16.00
	Never hinged	32.50	
	On cover		95.00
21	A12 10pa on 3kr green	.55	.65
	Never hinged	1.25	
	On cover		13.00
a.	Pair, imperf. between		*550.00*
22	A12 20pa on 5kr rose	.35	*.65*
	Never hinged	.65	
	On cover		6.00
a.	Perf 13½x11½	110.00	110.00
	Never hinged	225.00	
23	A12 1pi on 10kr ultra	.40	.25
	Never hinged	.95	
	On cover		8.50
a.	Pair, imperf. between		*550.00*
24	A12 2pi on 20kr ol grn	8.00	*32.50*
	Never hinged	16.00	
	On cover		*700.00*
a.	Perf. 9½	185.00	
	Never hinged	300.00	
25	A12 5pi on 50kr vio	12.00	*72.50*
	Never hinged	24.00	
	On cover		*1,850.*
a.	Perf. 9½	185.00	
	Never hinged	300.00	
	Nos. 20-25 (6)	21.55	*107.20*

Values on cover for Nos. 20-25 are for covers paying the correct rate. Overfranked covers are usually philatelic and are valued at 25 percent more than the combined values of the used stamps attached.

See note after Austria No. 65 on missing numerals, etc.

Austria Nos. 66, 69 Surcharged

1891 ***Perf. 10 to 13½***

26	A14 2pi on 20kr green	6.50	1.60
	Never hinged	16.00	
	On cover		42.50
a.	Perf. 9¼	200.00	160.00
	Never hinged	400.00	
	On cover		*2,250.*

27 A14 5pi on 50kr violet 3.25 3.25
Never hinged 8.00
On cover 450.00

Two types of the surcharge on No. 26 exist.

Austria Nos. 62-65 Surcharged

1892 *Perf. 10½, 11½*

28 A13 10pi on 1gld blue 12.00 *32.50*
Never hinged 37.50
On cover 125.00
29 A13 20pi on 2gld car 16.00 *60.00*
Never hinged 50.00
On cover 125.00
a. Double surcharge —

Values on cover for Nos. 28-29 are for over-franked complete covers, usually philatelic.

1896 *Perf. 10½, 11½, 12½*

30 A13 10pi on 1gld pale lil 18.50 *22.50*
Never hinged 52.50
On cover *1,700.*
On overfranked cover 95.00
a. Perf. 12½ 45.00 375.00
Never hinged 120.00
31 A13 20pi on 2gld gray grn 37.50 *75.00*
Never hinged 110.00
On overfranked cover 130.00
a. Perf. 12½ 45.00 375.00
Never hinged 120.00

Austria Nos. 73, 75, 77, 81, 83-85 Surcharged

#32-35

#36-38

Perf. 12½, 13½ and Compound

1900 **Without Varnish Bars**

32 A15 10pa on 5h bl grn 4.75 .80
Never hinged 21.00
On cover 15.00
33 A16 20pa on 10h rose 5.50 .80
Never hinged 28.00
On cover 15.00
b. Perf. 12½x10½ 400.00 350.00
Never hinged 1,200.
On cover —
34 A16 1pi on 25h ultra 3.25 .40
Never hinged 16.00
On cover 8.00
b. Perf. 10½ 24.00 16.00
Never hinged 80.00
On cover 100.00
35 A17 2pi on 50h gray bl 8.00 4.00
Never hinged 40.00
On cover 37.50
a. Perf. 10½ 50.00 42.50
Never hinged 160.00
On cover 200.00
36 A18 5pi on 1k car rose .55 .40
Never hinged 4.50
On cover *425.00*
a. 5pi on 1k carmine .80 *1.20*
Never hinged 8.00
On cover *500.00*
b. Horiz. or vert. pair, imperf. btwn. 160.00
Never hinged 300.00
37 A18 10pi on 2k gray lil 2.00 *3.50*
Never hinged 13.00
On cover *1,000.*
On parcel post receipt card *200.00*
a. Horiz. pair, imperf. btwn. —
38 A18 20pi on 4k gray grn 1.60 *8.00*
Never hinged 12.00
On cover *2,100.*
On parcel post receipt card *500.00*
Nos. 32-38 (7) 25.65 *17.90*

In the surcharge on Nos. 37 and 38 "piaster" is printed "PIAST."

1901 **With Varnish Bars**

32a A15 10pa on 5h blue green 1.60 2.75
Never hinged 12.50
On cover 16.50
33a A16 20pa on 10h rose 2.40 *400.00*
Never hinged 12.00
On cover 600.00
34a A16 1pi on 25h ultra 1.20 .80
Never hinged 8.00
On cover 21.00
35b A17 2pi on 50h gray blue 2.75 8.00
Never hinged 17.50
On cover 42.50
Nos. 32a-35b (4) 7.95 411.55

A4

A5

A6

1906 *Perf. 12½ to 13½*

Without Varnish Bars

39 A4 10pa dark green 12.00 4.00
Never hinged 32.50
On cover 17.00
40 A5 20pa rose .80 *1.20*
Never hinged 4.75
On cover 15.00
41 A5 1pi ultra .80 .40
Never hinged 4.00
On cover 15.00
42 A6 2pi gray blue .80 *1.20*
Never hinged 4.00
On cover 32.50
Nos. 39-42 (4) 14.40 6.80

1903 **With Varnish Bars**

39a A4 10pa dark green 4.75 2.00
Never hinged 12.00
On cover 15.00
40a A5 20pa rose 3.25 .80
Never hinged 10.50
On cover 15.00
41a A5 1pi ultra 2.40 .40
Never hinged 8.00
On cover 15.00
42a A6 2pi gray blue 160.00 3.25
Never hinged 325.00
On cover 37.50
Nos. 39a-42a (4) 170.40 6.45

1907 **Without Varnish Bars**

43 A4 10pa yellow green .55 *2.00*
Never hinged 1.60
On cover 32.50
45 A5 30pa violet .55 *4.00*
Never hinged 1.60
On cover 97.50

A7

A8

1908 **Typo.** *Perf. 12½*

46 A7 10pa green, *yellow* .25 *.40*
Never hinged .75
On cover 15.00
47 A7 20pa scarlet, *rose* .25 *.40*
Never hinged .75
On cover 15.00
48 A7 30pa brown, *buff* .40 *2.00*
Never hinged 1.25
On cover 65.00
49 A7 1pi deep bl, *blue* 14.50 .25
Never hinged 65.00
On cover 12.50
a. 1pi greenish blue, *blue* 15.00 1.50
Never hinged 67.50
On cover 13.50
50 A7 60pa vio, *bluish* .65 *5.50*
Never hinged 1.60
On cover 250.00

Engr.

51 A8 2pi lake, *yellow* .65 .25
Never hinged 3.25
On cover 110.00
52 A8 5pi brown, *gray* .65 *.95*
Never hinged 4.00
On cover 625.00
53 A8 10pi green, *yellow* .95 *2.40*
Never hinged 5.00
On cover *1,250.*
54 A8 20pi blue, *gray* 2.40 *4.75*
Never hinged 9.50
On cover *1,750.*
Nos. 46-54 (9) 20.70 *16.90*

Nos. 46-50 are on paper colored on the surface only. 60th year of the reign of Emperor Franz Josef I, for permanent use.

Nos. 46-50 exist imperforate. Values, set: unused $275, never hinged $650.

Paper Colored Through

1913-14 **Typo.**

57 A7 20pa rose, *rose* ('14) .55 *650.00*
Never hinged 2.00
On cover 2,750.
58 A7 1pi ultra, *blue* .35 *.55*
Never hinged .90
On cover 12.50

Nos. 57 and 58 exist imperforate.

POSTAGE DUE STAMPS

Type of Austria D2 Surcharged in Black

1902 **Unwmk.** *Perf. 12½, 13½*

J1 D2 10pa on 5h gray green 1.60 *8.00*
Never hinged 8.00
On cover 575.00
a. 10pa on 5h yellow green 6.50
Never hinged 16.00
J2 D2 20pa on 10h gray green 1.60 *12.00*
Never hinged 11.00
On cover 425.00
a. 20pa on 10h yellow green 4.00
Never hinged 10.00
J3 D2 1pi on 20h gray green 1.60 *12.00*
Never hinged 10.00
On cover 425.00
a. 1pi on 20h yellow green 4.00
Never hinged 10.00
J4 D2 2pi on 40h gray green 1.60 *12.00*
Never hinged 13.00
On cover 700.00
a. 2pi on 40h yellow green 16.00
Never hinged 42.50
J5 D2 5pi on 100h gray green 1.60 *8.00*
Never hinged 8.00
On cover 1,000.
a. 5pi on 100h yellow green 8.00
Never hinged 35.00
Nos. J1-J5 (5) 8.00 *52.00*

Shades of Nos. J1-J5 exist, varying from yellowish to dark green.

D3

1908 **Typo.** *Perf. 12½*

Chalky Paper

J6 D3 ¼pi pale green 3.25 *13.50*
Never hinged 12.00
On cover 750.00
J7 D3 ½pi pale green 2.00 *11.00*
Never hinged 8.00
On cover 325.00
J8 D3 1pi pale green 2.40 *8.00*
Never hinged 8.00
On cover 325.00
J9 D3 1½pi pale green 1.20 *24.00*
Never hinged 8.00
On cover 425.00
J10 D3 2pi pale green 1.60 *20.00*
Never hinged 12.00
On cover 675.00
J11 D3 5pi pale green 2.40 *14.50*
Never hinged 9.50
On cover *1,250.*
J12 D3 10pi pale green 16.00 *150.00*
Never hinged 65.00
On cover —
J13 D3 20pi pale green 11.00 *160.00*
Never hinged 35.00
On cover —
J14 D3 30pi pale green 16.00 14.50
Never hinged 72.50
On cover —
Nos. J6-J14 (9) 55.85 *415.50*

Chalky paper

J6a D3 ¼pi dark green 2.50 *21.00*
Never hinged 7.25
On cover 825.00
J7a D3 ½pi dark green 1.75 *21.00*
Never hinged 7.25
On cover 825.00
J8a D3 1pi dark green 1.75 *21.00*
Never hinged 7.25
On cover 825.00
J9a D3 1½pi dark green 1.75 *21.00*
Never hinged 6.50
On cover 825.00
J10a D3 2pi dark green 6.00 *30.00*
Never hinged 13.00
On cover —
J12a D3 10pi dark green 60.00 *625.00*
Never hinged 160.00
On cover —
J13a D3 20pi dark green 55.00 *650.00*
Never hinged 135.00
On cover —
J14a D3 30pi dark green 100.00 40.00
Never hinged 275.00
On cover —
Nos. J6a-J14a (8) 228.75 *1,429.*

Thin ordinary paper

J6b D3 ¼pi dark green 4.00 *37.50*
Never hinged 12.00
On cover 1,000.
J7b D3 ½pi dark green 1.60 *37.50*
Never hinged 8.00
On cover 1,000.
J8b D3 1pi dark green 1.60 *32.50*
Never hinged 8.00
On cover 1,000.
J9b D3 1½pi dark green 2.50 *85.00*
Never hinged 8.00
On cover —
J10b D3 2pi dark green 3.25 *90.00*
Never hinged 12.00
On cover —
J11a D3 5pi dark green 6.50 *50.00*
Never hinged 16.00
On cover —
J12b D3 10pi dark green 60.00 *625.00*
Never hinged 145.00
On cover —
J13b D3 20pi dark green 47.50 *625.00*
Never hinged 120.00
On cover —
J14b D3 30pi dark green 32.50 *170.00*
Never hinged 87.50
On cover —
Nos. J6b-J14b (9) 159.45 *1,753.*

Thick ordinary paper

J6c D3 ¼pi dark green 4.00 *37.50*
Never hinged 16.00
On cover 750.00
J7c D3 ½pi dark green 1.60 *19.00*
Never hinged 8.00
On cover 750.00
J8c D3 1pi dark green 1.60 *19.00*
Never hinged 8.00
On cover 750.00
J9c D3 1½pi dark green 1.60 *75.00*
Never hinged 8.00
On cover 950.00
J10c D3 2pi dark green 2.50 *100.00*
Never hinged 12.00
On cover —
J11b D3 5pi dark green 4.00 *27.50*
Never hinged 16.00
On cover —
J12c D3 10pi dark green 47.50 *625.00*
Never hinged 145.00
On cover —
J13c D3 20pi dark green 47.50 *625.00*
Never hinged 180.00
On cover —
J14c D3 30pi dark green 8.00 *27.50*
Never hinged 27.50
On cover —
Nos. J6c-J14c (9) 118.30 *1,556.*

No. J6-J14 exist imperforate.

Forgeries exist.

LOMBARDY-VENETIA

Formerly a kingdom in the north of Italy forming part of the Austrian Empire. Milan and Venice were the two principal cities. Lombardy was annexed to Sardinia in 1859, and Venetia to the kingdom of Italy in 1866.

100 Centesimi = 1 Lira
100 Soldi = 1 Florin (1858)

Unused examples without gum of Nos. 1-24 are worth approximately 20% of the values given, which are for stamps with original gum as defined in the catalogue introduction.

For similar designs in Kreuzers, see early Austria.

Coat of Arms — A1

15 CENTESIMI:

Type I — "5" is on a level with the "1." One heavy line around coat of arms center.

Type II — As type I, but "5" is a trifle sideways and is higher than the "1."

Type III — As type II, but two, thinner, lines around center.

45 CENTESIMI:

Type I — Lower part of "45" is lower than "Centes." One heavy line around coat of arms center. "45" varies in height and distance from "Centes."

Type II — One heavy line around coat of arms center. Lower part of "45" is on a level with lower part of "Centes."

Type III — As type II, but two, thinner, lines around center.

Wmk. K.K.H.M. in Sheet or Unwmkd.

1850 Typo. *Imperf.*

Thick to Thin Paper

1 A1 5c buff 6,000. 200.00
No gum 1,500.
On cover 575.00
On cover, single franking 625.00
On cover, single franking, printed matter 1,900.
a. Printed on both sides 21,500. 675.00
No gum 5,350.
On cover 1,700.
b. 5c yellow 11,250. 650.00
No gum 3,000.
On cover 3,350.
On cover, single franking 3,400.
c. 5c orange 6,500. 225.00
No gum 1,775.
On cover 675.00
On cover, single franking 700.00
d. 5c lemon yellow — 2,500.
On cover 10,000.
On cover, single franking 10,000.
e. 5c greenish lemon yellow — 7,500.
On cover, single franking 22,500.
3 A1 10c black 6,000. 200.00
No gum 1,500.
On cover 575.00
On cover, single franking 625.00
a. 10c gray black 6,000. 175.00
No gum 1,500.
On cover 575.00
On cover, single franking 625.00
b. 10c silver gray 16,500. 1,800.
No gum 4,100.
On cover 5,250.
On cover, single franking 5,250.
e. 10c charcoal black 7,500. 350.00
No gum 1,900.
On cover 1,000.
On cover, single franking 1,000.
4 A1 15c red, type III 1,900. 7.50
No gum 650.00
On cover 30.00
a. 15c carmine, type III 3,000. 11.50
No gum 750.00
On cover 45.00
b. 15c red, type I 4,500. 29.00
No gum 1,125.
On cover 125.00
c. Ribbed paper, type II — 900.00
No gum —
On cover 2,250.
d. Ribbed paper, type I 27,500. 275.00
No gum 7,000.
On cover 675.00
f. 15c red, type II 2,400. 30.00
No gum 600.00
On cover 120.00
h. Laid paper, type III 19,000.
On cover 75,000.
i. 15c carmine, type I 4,500. 57.50
No gum 1,125.
On cover 225.00
5 A1 30c brown 6,750. 26.50
No gum 1,600.
On cover 110.00
a. Ribbed paper 13,500. 175.00
No gum 3,400.
On cover 425.00
c. 30c pale brown 7,500. 57.50
No gum 1,900.
On cover 225.00
d. 30c reddish brown 8,250. 30.00
No gum 2,100.
On cover 125.00
6 A1 45c blue, type III 20,000. 60.00
No gum 5,000.
On cover 250.00
a. 45c blue, type I 21,250. 60.00
No gum 5,500.
On cover 250.00
b. Ribbed paper, type I — 750.00
No gum —
On cover 1,900.
c. 45c blue, type II 190,000. 75.00
No gum 50,000.
On cover 300.00
e. 45c ultramarine, type III 20,000. 650.00
No gum 5,250.
On cover 2,650.
f. 45c pale grayish blue, type III 34,000. 375.00
No gum 9,000.
On cover 1,500.
g. 45c pale grayish ultramarine, type III — 1,050.
On cover 4,250.
h. 45c sky blue, type I 24,500. 100.00
No gum 6,500.
On cover 425.00

1854

Machine-made Paper, Type III

3c A1 10c black 12,250. 500.00
No gum 3,100.
On cover 1,500.
3d A1 10c gray black 15,000. 1,400.
No gum 3,750.
On cover 4,250.
4g A1 15c pale red 2,100. 6.00
No gum 525.00
On cover 25.00
4j A1 15c salmon 2,100. 6.00
No gum 525.00
On cover 25.00
5b A1 30c brown ('55) 7,500. 26.50
No gum 1,900.
On cover 110.00
5e A1 30c grayish brown, rough impression 15,000. 75.00
No gum 3,750.
On cover 300.00
6d A1 45c blue 18,000. 75.00
No gum 4,500.
On cover 300.00
6i A1 45c cobalt 18,000. 75.00
No gum 4,500.
On cover 300.00

Full margins = 1 ½mm.

See note about the paper of the 1850 issue of Austria. *The reprints are type III, in brighter colors.*

Values for pairs

Thick to Thin Hand-made Paper

1 A1 5c buff 13,500. 400.00
On cover 1,200.
1a A1 5c buff, printed on both sides 1,500.
On cover 3,750.
3 A1 10c black 13,500. 400.00
On cover 1,200.
4 A1 15c red, type III 4,200. 27.50
On cover 100.00
4b A1 15c red, type I 10,000. 90.00
On cover 325.00
4c A1 15c Ribbed paper, type II 6,000.
On cover —
4d A1 15c Ribbed paper, type I 600.00
On cover 1,700.
4f A1 15c red, type II 5,250. 90.00
On cover 275.00
4h A1 15c red, type III, laid paper —
5 A1 30c brown 14,750. 125.00
On cover 350.00
5a A1 30c Ribbed paper 550.00
On cover 1,500.
6 A1 45c blue, type III 200.00
On cover 725.00
6a A1 45c blue, type I 200.00
On cover 725.00
6b A1 45c Ribbed paper, type I 1,650.
On cover 4,500.
6c A1 45c blue, type II 250.00
On cover 1,000.

Machine-made Paper

3c A1 10c black 1,050.
On cover 3,250.
4g A1 15c pale red 4,500. 15.00
On cover 67.50
5b A1 30c brown 16,500. 75.00
On cover 300.00
6d A1 45c blue 39,500. 250.00
On cover 1,000.

Values for strips of 3

Thick to Thin Hand-made Paper

1 A1 5c buff 20,000. 675.00
On cover 2,250.
1a A1 5c buff, printed on both sides 1,500.
On cover 7,250.
3 A1 10c black 20,000. 675.00
On cover 2,250.
4 A1 15c red, type III 6,250. 210.00
On cover 650.00
4b A1 15c red, type I 15,000. 425.00
On cover 1,500.
4d A1 15c Ribbed paper, type I 2,650.
On cover 7,500.
4f A1 15c red, type II 8,000. 425.00
On cover 1,500.
5 A1 30c brown 575.00
On cover 2,000.
5a A1 30c Ribbed paper 3,000.
On cover 9,000.
6 A1 45c blue, type III 1,000.
On cover 3,250.
6a A1 45c blue, type I 1,000.
On cover 3,250.
6b A1 45c Ribbed paper, type I 3,750.
On cover 12,000.
6c A1 45c blue, type II 1,200.
On cover 4,400.

Machine-made Paper

3c A1 10c black — 2,000.
On cover 6,000.
4g A1 15c pale red 6,900. 140.00
On cover 425.00
5b A1 30c brown 625.00
On cover 2,100.
6d A1 45c blue 1,150.
On cover 3,600.

Values for strips of 4

1 A1 5c buff 26,500. 3,400.
On cover 11,500.
3 A1 10c black 20,000. 4,250.
On cover 13,500.
4 A1 15c red, type III
On cover
4b A1 15c red, type I 20,000. 1,000.
On cover 2,850.
4f A1 15c red, type II 10,500. 1,000.
On cover 2,850.
5 A1 30c brown 1,150.
On cover 3,250.
5a A1 30c ribbed paper 5,000.
On cover 14,000.
6 A1 45c blue, type III 1,800.
On cover 5,500.
6a A1 45c blue, type I 1,800.
On cover 5,500.
6b A1 45c blue, type I, ribbed paper 5,750.
On cover 17,000.
6c A1 45c blue, type II 2,250.
On cover 6,750.

Machine-made Paper

3c A1 10c black 10,500.
On cover —
4g A1 15c pale red 575.00
On cover 1,750.
5b A1 30c grown 1,250.
On cover 3,750.
6d A1 45c blue 2,200.
On cover 6,500.

Values for blocks of 4

Thick to Thin Hand-made Paper

1 A1 5c buff 100,000. 32,500.
On cover 112,500.
1a A1 5c 5c buff, printed on both sides, on cover 82,500.
3 A1 10c black 50,000. 95,000.
4 A1 15c red, type III 16,500. 8,000.
On cover 29,000.
4b A1 15c red, type I 25,000.
On cover 82,500.
4f A1 15c red, type II 22,500. 21,000.
On cover 52,500.
5 A1 30c brown 90,000. 30,000.
On cover 82,500.
6 A1 45c blue, type III 26,500.
On cover 82,500.
6a A1 45c blue, type I 52,500.
On cover 180,000.
6c A1 45c blue, type II 100,000.

Machine-made Paper

3c A1 10c black —
On cover —
4g A1 15c pale red 10,000. 4,750.
On cover 11,500.
5b A1 30c brown 37,500. 14,000.
On cover 42,500.
6d A1 45c blue 82,500. 22,500.
On cover 67,500.

Values for stamps used in Austria

Thick to Thin Hand-made Paper

1 A1 5c buff (from) 575.
On cover (from) 13,250.
3 A1 10c black (from) 275.
On cover (from) 2,100.
4 A1 15c red, type III (from) 225.
On cover (from) 2,250.
4b A1 15c red, type I (from) 155.
On cover (from) 1,250.
4c A1 15c Ribbed paper, type II (from) 1,450.
On cover (from) 7,000.
4d A1 15c Ribbed paper, type I (from) 450.
On cover (from) 2,650.
4f A1 15c red, type II (from) 200.
On cover (from) 210.
5 A1 30c brown (from) 155.
On cover (from) 1,250.
5a A1 30c Ribbed paper (from) 310.
On cover (from) 2,300.
6 A1 45c blue, type III (from) 425.
On cover (from) 3,750.
6a A1 45c blue, type I (from) 275.
On cover (from) 2,350.
6b A1 45c Ribbed paper, type I (from) 1,250.
On cover (from)
6c A1 45c blue, type II (from) 375.
On cover (from) 2,900.

Machine-made Paper

3c A1 10c black (from) 675.
On cover (from) 6,500.
4g A1 15c pale red (from) 210.
On cover (from) 2,000.
5b A1 30c brown (from) 300.
On cover (from) 2,500.
6d A1 45c blue (from) 500.
On cover (from) 4,750.

A2 A3

A4 A5

A6

Two Types of Each Value.

Type I — Loops of the bow at the back of the head broken.

Type II — Loops complete. Wreath projects further at top of head.

1858-62 Embossed *Perf. 14½*

7 A2 2s yel, type II 2,400. 150.00
No gum 600.00
On cover 375.00
On cover, single franking 425.00
a. 2s yellow, type I 12,000. 900.00
No gum 3,000.
On cover 2,250.
On cover, single franking 2,500.
b. 2s bright yellow, type I 13,000. 1,000.
No gum 3,500.
On cover 2,600.
8 A3 3s black, type II 18,000. 190.00
No gum 4,500.
On cover 475.00
On cover, single franking 525.00
a. 3s black, type I 6,750. 375.00
No gum 1,700.
On cover 950.00
On cover, single franking 1,050.
b. Perf. 16, type I — 2,250.
On cover 5,750.
c. Perf. 15x16 or 16x15, type I 12,500. 750.00
No gum 3,100.
On cover 1,900.
d. 3s gray black, type I 13,000. 1,000.
No gum 3,500.
On cover 2,500.
9 A3 3s grn, type II ('62) 1,325. 140.00
No gum 350.00
On cover 285.00
On cover, single franking 650.00
a. 3s bluish green 1,800. 190.00
No gum 450.00
On cover 375.00
10 A4 5s red, type II 750.00 12.00
No gum 190.00
On cover 32.50
a. 5s red, type I 2,400. 45.00
No gum 600.00
On cover 120.00
b. Printed on both sides, type II 6,750.
c. 5s bright red, type I 2,400. 45.00
No gum 600.00
On cover 115.00
11 A5 10s brn, type II 5,250. 24.00
No gum 1,350.
On cover 60.00
a. 10s brown, type I 1,500. 140.00
No gum 375.00
On cover 350.00
b. 10s dark brown, type I 2,250. 210.00
No gum 575.00
On cover 525.00
12 A6 15s blue, type II 6,000. 125.00
No gum 1,500.
On cover 300.00
a. 15s blue, type I 12,000. 225.00
No gum 4,000.
On cover 575.00
b. Printed on both sides, type II 18,750.
c. 15s bright blue, type I 13,250. 275.00
No gum 3,400.
On cover 650.00
d. 15s bright blue, type II 6,750. 150.00
No gum 1,700.
On cover 375.00

The reprints are of type II and are perforated 10½, 11, 11½, 12, 12½ and 13. There are also imperforate reprints of Nos. 7-9.

Values for pairs

7 A2 2s yellow, type II 5,250. 325.00
On cover 950.00
On cover, pair only (4 soldi rate) —
7a A2 2s yellow, type I 26,000. 1,900.
On cover 4,750.
On cover, pair only (4 soldi rate) —
8 A3 3s black, type II 40,000. 400.00
On cover 1,000.
On cover, pair only (6 soldi rate) —
8a A3 3s black, type I 15,000. 800.00
On cover 1,900.
8b A3 3s Perf. 16, type I 3,100.
9 A3 3s green, type II 2,900. 300.00
On cover 600.00
10 A4 5s red, type II 1,650. 27.50
On cover 82.50
10a A4 5s red, type I 5,250. 95.00
On cover 275.00
11 A5 10s brown, type II 11,500. 52.50
On cover 175.00
11a A5 10s brown, type I 3,250. 290.00
On cover 750.00
12 A6 15s blue, type II 13,000. 275.00
On cover 750.00
12a A6 15s blue, type I 26,500. 500.00
On cover 1,500.

Values for used strips of 3

7 A2 2s yellow, type II 575.
On cover 2,100.
7a A2 2s yellow, type I 2,800.
On cover 8,250.
8 A3 3s black, type II 750.
On cover 2,800.
8a A3 3s black, type I 1,500.
On cover 4,500.
9 A3 3s green, type II 750.
On cover 3,750.
10 A4 5s red, type II 82.50
On cover 375.
10a A4 5s red, type I 375.
On cover 1,400.
11 A5 10s brown, type II 250.
On cover 1,000.
11a A5 10s brown, type I 950.
On cover 3,000.
12 A6 15s blue, type II 600.
On cover 2,750.
12a A6 15s blue, type I 1,300.
On cover 5,250.

Values for strips of 4

7 A2 2s yellow, type II 1,500.
On cover 5,100.
7a A2 2s yellow, type I 4,500.
On cover 12,000.
8 A3 3s black, type II 1,750.
On cover 5,750.
8a A3 3s black, type I 3,000.
On cover 9,500.
9 A3 3s green, type II 2,750.
On cover 6,750.
10 A4 5s red, type II 375.
On cover 1,500.
10a A4 5s red, type I 1,250.
On cover 3,600.
11 A5 10s brown, type II 675.
On cover 2,100.
11a A5 10s brown, type I 1,750.
On cover 5,100.
12 A6 15s blue, type II 1,300.
On cover 5,250.

12a A6 15s blue, type I 2,650.
On cover 12,000.

Values for blocks of 4

7 A2 2s yellow, type II *11,000.* *13,250.*
On cover —
7a A2 2s yellow, type I —
8a A3 3s black, type I —
9 A3 3s green, type II *4,500.* *26,000.*
On cover —
10 A4 5s red, type II *4,000.* *2,500.*
On cover *12,500.*
10a A4 5s red, type I *11,500.* *9,500.*
On cover *26,500.*
11 A5 10s brown, type II *30,000.* *10,000.*
On cover —
11a A5 10s brown, type I *6,750.* *19,500.*
On cover
12 A6 15s blue, type II *33,750.* *9,500.*
On cover *45,000.*
12a A6 15s blue, type I *25,000.*
On cover —

Values for stamps used in Austria

7 A2 2s yellow, type II (from) 1,000.
On cover (from) *16,500.*
7a A2 2s yellow, type I (from) *2,100.*
8 A3 3s black, type II (from) 250.
On cover (from) 1,450.
8a A3 3s black, type I (from) 525.
On cover (from) 2,250.
9 A3 3s green, type II (from) 500.
On cover (from) 2,900.
10 A4 5s red, type II (from) 200.
On cover (from) 2,100.
10a A4 5s red, type I (from) 225.
On cover (from) 2,700.
11 A5 10s brown, type II (from) 225.
On cover (from) 2,700.
11a A5 10s brown, type I (from) 325.
On cover (from) 3,700.
12 A6 15s blue, type II (from) 350.
On cover (from) *5,600.*
12a A6 15s blue, type I (from) 575.
On cover (from) *8,250.*

A7

1861-62 ***Perf. 14***

13 A7 5s red 7,125. 7.00
No gum 1,800.
On cover 26.00
14 A7 10s brown ('62) 13,000. 75.00
No gum 3,250.
On cover 190.00

The reprints are perforated 9, 9 ½, 10½, 11, 12, 12½ and 13. There are also imperforate reprints of the 2 and 3s.

The 2, 3 and 15s of this type exist only as reprints.

Values for pairs

13 A7 5s red *15,000.* 22.50
On cover 72.50
14 A7 10s brown 28,500. 265.00
On cover 1,300.

Values for strips of 3

13 A7 5s red 75.00
On cover 325.00
14 A7 10s brown 1,050.
On cover 3,400.

Values for strips of 4

13 A7 5s red 265.00
On cover 1,200.
14 A7 10s brown 2,650.
On cover *8,250.*

Values for blocks of 4

13 A7 5s red *30,000.* 2,250.
On cover 8,250.
14 A7 10s brown *26,500.*
On cover *90,000.*

Values for stamps used in Austria

13 A7 5s red 250.00
On cover 2,500.
14 A7 10s brown 1,125.
On cover —

A8

1863

15 A8 2s yellow 425.00 225.00
No gum 165.00
On cover 675.00
On cover, single franking 750.00
16 A8 3s green 5,250. 125.00
No gum 1,325.
On cover 375.00
On cover, single franking 1,500.
17 A8 5s rose 6,750. 37.50
No gum 1,700.
On cover 95.00
18 A8 10s blue 14,000. 90.00
No gum 3.500.
On cover 225.00
On cover, single franking 250.00
19 A8 15s yellow brown 12,000. 340.00
No gum 3,000.
On cover 1,000.

Values for pairs

15 A8 2s yellow *925.00* 475.00
On cover 1,500.
On cover, alone (4 soldi rate)
16 A8 3s green *11,500.* 265.00
On cover 850.00
On cover, alone (6 soldi rate)
17 A8 5s rose *15,000.* 82.50
On cover 225.00
18 A8 10s blue *31,000.* 215.00
On cover 700.00
19 A8 15s yellow brown *26,500.* 725.00
On cover 2,250.

Values for strips of 3

15 A8 2s yellow 825.
On cover *3,000.*
16 A8 3s green 1,300.
On cover *4,750.*
17 A8 5s rose 300.00
On cover 1,250.
18 A8 10s blue 650.00
On cover 2,500.
19 A8 15s yellow brown 1,600.
On cover *6,000.*

Values for strips of 4

15 A8 2s yellow 1,900.
On cover *6,750.*
16 A8 3s green 2,750.
On cover *10,000.*
17 A8 5s rose 675.00
On cover 1,800.
18 A8 10s blue 2,500.
On cover 6,500.
19 A8 15s yellow brown 3,750.
On cover *10,500.*

Values for blocks of 4

15 A8 2s yellow *1,950.* *18,000.*
On cover *40,000.*
16 A8 3s green *26,500.*
On cover
17 A8 5s rose *4,100.*
On cover *12,000.*
18 A8 10s blue
19 A8 15s yellow brown *60,000.* *22,500.*
On cover *64,000.*

Values for stamps used in Austria

15 A8 2s yellow 750.00
On cover *19,000.*
16 A8 3s green 200.00
On cover 2,400.
17 A8 5s rose 250.00
On cover 2,700.
18 A8 10s blue 500.00
On cover 6,500.
19 A8 15s yellow brown 650.00
On cover *10,000.*

1864-65 **Wmk. 91** ***Perf. 9½***

20 A8 2s yellow ('65) 640.00 *900.00*
No gum 160.00
On cover 2,650.
On cover, single franking 2,900.
21 A8 3s green 55.00 52.50
No gum 14.00
On cover 105.00
On cover, single franking 375.00
22 A8 5s rose 9.00 11.50
No gum 2.25
On cover 27.50
23 A8 10s blue 110.00 22.50
No gum 27.50
On cover 45.00
On cover, single franking 60.00
24 A8 15s yellow brown 1,250. 210.00
No gum 310.00
On cover 625.00

Nos. 15-24 reprints are perforated 10½ and 13. There are also imperforate reprints of the 2s and 3s.

Values for pairs

20 A8 2s yellow 1,400. *1,900.*
On cover *8,250.*
21 A8 3s green 120.00 115.00
On cover 260.00
On cover alone (6 soldi rate)
22 A8 5s rose 20.00 24.50
On cover 67.50
23 A8 10s blue 240.00 47.50
On cover 125.00
24 A8 15s yellow brown 2,750. 450.00
On cover 1,400.

Values for strips of 3

20 A8 2s yellow 5,300.
On cover *10,250.*
21 A8 3s green 300.00
On cover *2,300.*
22 A8 5s rose 60.00
On cover 240.00
23 A8 10s blue 160.00
On cover 800.00
24 A8 15s yellow brown 725.00
On cover 2,300.

Values for strips of 4

20 A8 2s yellow 12,500.
21 A8 3s green 1,300.
On cover *6,000.*
22 A8 5s rose 325.00
On cover 1,100.
23 A8 10s blue *1,200.*
On cover 4,000.
24 A8 15s yellow brown 2,500.
On cover 7,500.

Values for blocks of 4

20 A8 2s yellow 2,850. *17,000.*
21 A8 3s green 250.00
22 A8 5s rose 40.00 *1,500.*
On cover *4,850.*
23 A8 10s blue 500.00 *11,250.*
On cover *36,000.*
24 A8 15s yellow brown 5,500. *9,500.*
On cover *32,500.*

Value for No. 20 in used block of four is for an example with faults.

Values for stamps used in Austria

20 A8 2s yellow 1,500.
21 A8 3s green 145.00
On cover 1,650.
22 A8 5s rose 160.00
On cover 2,500.
23 A8 10s blue 330.00
On cover *4,500.*
24 A8 15s yellow brown 500.00
On cover *6,750.*

NEWSPAPER TAX STAMPS

From 1853 to 1858 the Austrian Newspaper Tax Stamp 2kr green (No. PR1) was also used in Lombardy-Venetia, at the value of 10 centesimi.

NT1

Type I — The banderol of the left eagle touches the beak of the eagle.

Type II — The banderol does not touch the beak.

1858-59 **Unwmk.** **Typo.** ***Imperf.***

PR1 NT1 1kr black, type I ('59) 3,750. *4,750.*
No gum 1,400.
On newspaper *17,500.*
PR2 NT1 2kr red, type II ('59) 500.00 75.00
No gum 200.00
On newspaper 425.00
a. Watermark 91 1,650. 115.00
On newspaper —
PR3 NT1 4kr red, type I *150,000.* *5,500.*
No gum *23,000.*
On newspaper *26,000.*

The reprints are on a smooth toned paper and are all of type II.

Values for blocks of 4

PR1 NT1 1kr black, type I 50,000.
PR2 NT1 2kr red, type II 3,750.

Values for stamps used in Austria

PR1 NT1 1kr black, type I *5,500.*
PR2 NT1 2kr red, type II *1,250.*

AZERBAIJAN

ˌa-zæer-ˌbī-ˈjän

(Azerbaidjan)

LOCATION — Southernmost part of Russia in Eastern Europe, bounded by Georgia, Dagestan, Caspian Sea, Persia and Armenia
GOVT. — A Soviet Socialist Republic
AREA — 32,686 sq. mi.
POP. — 2,096,973 (1923)
CAPITAL — Baku

100 Kopecks = 1 Ruble

National Republic

Standard Bearer — A1

Farmer at Sunset — A2

Baku — A3

Temple of Eternal Fires — A4

1919 **Unwmk.** **Litho.** ***Imperf.***

On White Paper

1	A1	10k multicolored	.40	*.40*
2	A1	20k multicolored	.40	*.40*
3	A2	40k green, yellow & blk	.40	*.40*
4	A2	60k red, yellow & blk	.55	*.55*
5	A2	1r blue, yellow & blk	.90	*.90*
6	A3	2r red, bister & blk	.90	*.90*
7	A3	5r blue, bister & blk	1.90	*2.00*
8	A3	10r olive grn, bis & blk	1.90	*1.90*
9	A4	25r blue, red & black	3.25	*50.00*
10	A4	50r ol grn, red & black	4.50	*4.75*
		Nos. 1-10 (10)	15.10	*62.20*

For surcharges see Nos. 57-64, 75-80.

1920

On Grayish Paper

1A	A1	10k multicolored	.25	*20.00*
2A	A1	20k multicolored	.25	*20.00*
3A	A2	40k green, yellow & blk	.25	*30.00*
4A	A2	60k red, yellow & blk	.25	*30.00*
5A	A2	1r blue, yellow & blk	.40	*30.00*
6A	A3	2r red, bister & blk	.40	*40.00*
7A	A3	5r blue, bister & blk	.45	*40.00*
8A	A3	10r olive grn, bis & blk	.65	*40.00*
9A	A4	25r blue, red & black	1.10	*225.00*
10A	A4	50r ol grn, red & black	1.40	*175.00*
		Nos. 1A-10A (10)	5.40	*650.00*

Soviet Socialist Republic

Symbols of Labor — A5

Oil Well — A6

Bibi Eibatt Oil Field — A7

Khan's Palace, Baku — A8

Globe and Workers — A9

Maiden's Tower, Baku — A10

Goukasoff House A11

Blacksmiths — A12

Hall of Judgment, Baku — A13

1922

No.	Type	Description	Unused	Used
15	A5	1r gray green	.25	.35
16	A6	2r olive black	.60	.60
17	A7	5r gray brown	.25	.35
18	A8	10r gray	.60	.70
19	A9	25r orange brown	.25	.40
20	A10	50r violet	.25	.40
21	A11	100r dull red	.35	.50
22	A12	150r blue	.35	.50
23	A9	250r violet & buff	.35	.50
24	A13	400r dark blue	.40	.50
25	A12	500r gray vio & blk	.40	.50
26	A13	1000r dk blue & rose	.40	.60
27	A8	2000r blue & black	.40	.50
28	A7	3000r brown & blue	.45	.50
a.		Tete beche pair	18.00	18.00
29	A11	5000r black, *ol grn*	.75	.90
		Nos. 15-29 (15)	6.05	7.80

Counterfeits exist of Nos. 1-29. They generally sell for more than genuine examples.

For overprints and surcharges see Nos. 32-41, 43, 45-55, 65-72, 300-304, 307-333.

Nos. 15, 17, 23, 28, 27 Handstamped from Metal Dies in a Numbering Machine

1922

No.	Type	Description	Unused	Used
32	A5	10,000r on 1r	19.50	17.50
33	A7	15,000r on 5r	19.50	27.50
34	A9	33,000r on 250r	6.25	6.25
35	A7	50,000r on 3000r	32.50	10.00
36	A8	66,000r on 2000r	19.50	12.00
		Nos. 32-36 (5)	97.25	73.25

Same Surcharges on Regular Issue and Semi-Postal Stamps of 1922

1922-23

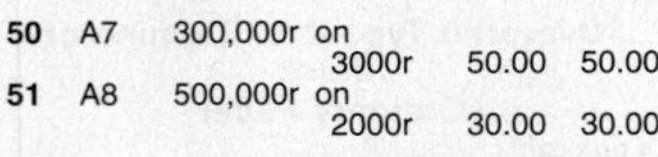

No.	Type	Description	Unused	Used
36A	A7	500r on 5r	180.00	190.00
37	A6	1000r on 2r	30.00	36.00
38	A8	2000r on 10r	18.00	9.00
39	A8	5000r on 2000r	9.00	3.75
40	A11	15,000r on 5000r	15.00	12.00
41	A5	20,000r on 1r	24.00	14.50
42	SP1	25,000r on 500r	60.00	—
43	A7	50,000r on 5r	60.00	60.00
44	SP2	50,000r on 1000r	60.00	—
45	A11	50,000r on 5000r	18.00	18.00
45A	A8	60,000r on 2000r	120.00	225.00
46	A11	70,000r on 5000r	150.00	47.50
47	A6	100,000r on 2r	18.00	18.00
48	A8	200,000r on 10r	12.00	12.00
49	A9	200,000r on 25r	18.00	19.00
50	A7	300,000r on 3000r	50.00	50.00
51	A8	500,000r on 2000r	30.00	30.00

Regular Issue Stamps of 1922-23 Surcharged

No.	Type	Description	Unused	Used
52	A7	500r on #33	650.00	700.00
53	A11	15,000r on #46	650.00	700.00
54	A7	300,000r on #35	750.00	800.00
55	A8	500,000r on #36	650.00	700.00

The surcharged semi-postal stamps were used for regular postage.

Same Surcharges on Stamps of 1919

No.	Type	Description	Unused	Used
57	A1	25,000r on 10k	.85	1.50
58	A1	50,000r on 20k	.85	1.50
59	A2	75,000r on 40k	2.00	4.00
60	A2	100,000r on 60k	.85	1.50
61	A2	200,000r on 1r	.85	1.50
62	A3	300,000r on 2r	1.10	1.50
63	A3	500,000r on 5r	1.10	1.50
64	A2	750,000r on 40k	4.25	5.50
		Nos. 57-64 (8)	11.85	18.50

Handstamped from Settings of Rubber Type in Black or Violet

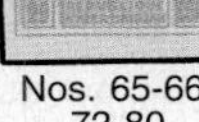

Nos. 65-66, 72-80

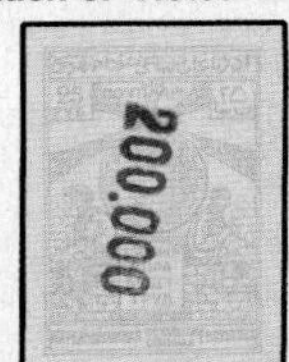

Nos. 67-70

On Stamps of 1922

No.	Type	Description	Unused	Used
65	A6	100,000r on 2r	27.50	27.50
66	A8	200,000r on 10r	80.00	80.00
67	A8	200,000r on 10r (V)	80.00	80.00
68	A9	200,000r on 25r (V)	80.00	80.00
a.		Black surcharge	80.00	80.00
69	A7	300,000r on 3000r (V)	40.00	40.00
70	A8	500,000r on 2000r (V)	72.50	72.50
a.		Black surcharge	90.00	90.00
72	A11	1,500,000r on 5000r (V)	140.00	140.00
a.		Black surcharge	120.00	120.00

On Stamps of 1919

No.	Type	Description	Unused	Used
75	A1	50,000r on 20k	4.00	
76	A2	75,000r on 40k	4.00	
77	A2	100,000r on 60k	4.00	
78	A2	200,000r on 1r	4.00	
79	A3	300,000r on 2r	4.00	
80	A3	500,000r on 5r	4.00	

Inverted and double surcharges of Nos. 32-80 sell for twice the normal price.

Counterfeits exist of Nos. 32-80.

Baku Province

Regular and Semi-Postal Stamps of 1922 Handstamped in Violet or Black

The overprint reads "Bakinskoi P(ochtovoy) K(ontory)," meaning Baku Post Office.

1922 Unwmk. *Imperf.*

No.	Type	Description	Unused	Used
300	A5	1r gray green	100.00	
301	A7	5r gray brown	100.00	200.00
302	A12	150r blue	100.00	100.00
303	A9	250r violet & buff	100.00	200.00
304	A13	400r dark blue	75.00	75.00
305	SP1	500r bl & pale bl	100.00	150.00
306	SP2	1000r brown & bis	100.00	
307	A8	2000r blue & black	120.00	150.00
308	A7	3000r brown & blue	100.00	
309	A11	5000r black, *ol grn*	120.00	
		Nos. 300-309 (10)	1,015.	

Stamps of 1922 Handstamped in Violet

БАКИНСКАГО Г-П-Т.О. №1

Ovpt. reads: Baku Post, Telegraph Office No. 1.

1924 Overprint 24x2mm

No.	Type	Description	Unused	Used
312	A12	150r blue	65.00	
313	A9	250r violet & buff	65.00	
314	A13	400r dark blue	65.00	
317	A8	2000r blue & black	65.00	
318	A7	3000r brn & blue	65.00	
319	A11	5000r black, *ol grn*	200.00	

Overprint 30x3½mm

No.	Type	Description	Unused	Used
323	A12	150r blue	100.00	125.00
324	A9	250r violet & buff	100.00	
325	A13	400r dark blue	100.00	100.00
328	A8	2000r blue & black	100.00	100.00
329	A7	3000r brn & blue	100.00	150.00
330	A11	5000r black, *ol grn*	100.00	

Overprinted on Nos. 32-33, 35

No.	Type	Description	Unused	Used
331	A5	10,000r on 1r	500.00	
332	A7	15,000r on 5r	500.00	
333	A7	50,000r on 3000r	500.00	
		Nos. 312-333 (15)	2,625.	

The overprinted semipostal stamps were used for regular postage.

A 24x2mm handstamp on #17, B1-B2, and 30x3½mm on Nos. 15, 17, B1-B2, was of private origin.

SEMI-POSTAL STAMPS

Carrying Food to Sufferers SP1

1922 Unwmk. *Imperf.*

No.	Type	Description	Unused	Used
B1	SP1	500r blue & pale blue	.40	190.00

For overprint and surcharge see Nos. 42, 305.

Widow and Orphans — SP2

1922

No.	Type	Description	Unused	Used
B2	SP2	1000r brown & bister	.75	190.00

Counterfeits exist.

For overprint and surcharge see Nos. 44, 306.

AZORES

'ā-ˌzōrz

LOCATION — Group of islands in the North Atlantic Ocean, due west of Portugal
GOVT. — Integral part of Portugal, former colony
AREA — 922 sq. mi.
POP. — 253,935 (1930)
CAPITAL — Ponta Delgada

Azores stamps were supplanted by those of Portugal in 1931.

1000 Reis = 1 Milreis
100 Centavos = 1 Escudo (1912)

Stamps of Portugal Overprinted in Black or Carmine

A

B

C

There are three types of surcharge. Type A: "C" and "O" rounded; "C" and "O" thinner; "C" and "O" raised. Type B: "C" and "O" rounded; "C" and "O" close together. Type C: "C" and "O" almost rectangular.

Type A

1868 Unwmk. *Imperf.*

1 A14 5r black 3,500. 2,400.
2 A14 10r yellow 13,750. 10,000.
3 A14 20r bister 200.00 140.00
4 A14 50r green 200.00 140.00
5 A14 80r orange 200.00 150.00
6 A14 100r lilac 200.00 150.00

The reprints are on thick chalky white wove paper, ungummed, and on thin ivory paper with shiny white gum. Value $35-42.50 each.

1868-70 *Perf. 12½*

5 REIS:
Type I — The "5" at the right is 1mm from end of label.
Type II — The "5" is 1½mm from end of label.

7 A14 5r black, type I (C) 60.00 30.00
a. Type II 70.00 70.00
b. As "a," double impression of stamp 125.00 110.00
8 A14 10r yellow 120.00 40.00
a. Inverted overprint *250.00 150.00*
b. 10r orange yellow 92.50 70.00
9 A14 20r bister 50.00 65.00
10 A14 25r rose 50.00 11.00
a. Inverted overprint — —
b. 25r deep rose 70.00 11.00
11 A14 50r green 160.00 150.00
a. 50r pale green 200.00 190.00
12 A14 80r orange 160.00 150.00
13 A14 100r lilac ('69) 160.00 150.00
a. 100r pale mauve 200.00 200.00
14 A14 120r blue 150.00 130.00
a. 120r deep blue 175.00 150.00
15 A14 240r violet 800.00 400.00

The reprints are on thick chalky white paper ungummed, perf 13½, and on thin ivory paper with shiny white gum, perf 13½. Value $30 each.

Overprint Type B

1871-75 *Perf. 12½*

21 A15 5r black (C) 13.50 8.75
a. Inverted overprint *47.50 42.50*
23 A15 10r yellow 40.00 25.00
a. Inverted overprint — —
b. Double overprint 60.00 47.50
24 A15 20r bister 30.00 26.00
a. Ribbed paper 52.50 35.00
25 A15 25r rose 17.00 4.25
a. Inverted overprint — —
b. Double overprint *40.00*
c. Perf. 14 190.00 85.00
d. Dbl. impression of stamp — —
26 A15 50r green 85.00 42.50
e. Ribbed paper 85.00 42.50
27 A15 80r orange 90.00 50.00
28 A15 100r lilac 100.00 60.00
a. Perf. 14 195.00 150.00
29 A15 120r blue 200.00 125.00
a. Inverted overprint — —
b. Ribbed paper 325.00 260.00

Nos. 21-29 exist with overprint "b."

Perf. 13½

21b A15 5r black (C) 12.50 6.50
23c A15 10r yellow 40.00 25.00
24b A15 20r bister 60.00 30.00
25e A15 25r rose 25.00 3.75
26a A15 50r green 100.00 57.50
27a A15 80r orange 125.00 62.50

Perf. 14

25c A15 25r rose 165.00 57.50

Overprint Type A

Perf. 12½

21c A15 5r black (C) 20.00 9.50
23d A15 10r yellow 27.50 20.00
24c A15 20r yellow 55.00 30.00
24d A15 20r olive bister 32.50 21.00
24e A15 20r yellow bister 32.50 21.00
24f A15 20r bister, ribbed paper 37.50 24.00
25f A15 25r rose 18.00 4.50
b. Double overprint 37.50 27.50
25g A15 25r rose, ribbed paper 30.00 7.75
26b A15 50r green 100.00 27.50
27b A15 80r orange 110.00 60.00
28b A15 100r lilac 110.00 70.00
29c A15 120r blue 150.00 95.00
30 A15 240r violet 1,000. 675.00
30a A15 240r violet, ribbed paper 1,000. 725.00

Overprint Type C

Perf. 12½

21d A15 5r black (C) 13.00 6.75
23e A15 10r yellow 27.50 12.50
24g A15 20r bister 27.50 12.50
25h A15 25r rose 16.00 3.25
26c A15 50r green 80.00 25.00
27c A15 80r orange 100.00 50.00
28c A15 100r lilac 80.00 37.50
29d A15 120r blue 160.00 80.00

Perf. 13½

21e A15 5r black (C) 13.00 6.75
21f A15 5r double impression of stamp 125.00 80.00
23f A15 10r yellow 50.00 25.00
24h A15 20r bister 50.00 25.00
25i A15 25r rose 17.00 3.25
26d A15 50r green 92.50 52.50
27d A15 80r orange 140.00 62.50
28d A15 100r lilac 110.00 45.00
29e A15 120r blue 160.00 80.00

Perf. 14

28e A15 100r lilac 175.00 100.00

The reprints are of type "b." All values exist are on thick chalky white paper ungummed, perf 13½ (value, each $29) and also on thin white paper with shiny white gum and perforated 13½ (value, each $30). The 5r, 10r, 15r, 50r and 120r also exist on thick chalky white paper ungummed, perf 12½. Value, each $80.

Overprint Type C in Black

15 REIS:
Type I — The figures of value, 1 and 5, at the right in upper label are close together.
Type II — The figures of value at the right in upper label are spaced.

1875-80 *Perf. 13½*

32 A15 10r yellow green 150.00 125.00
33c A15 15r lilac brown 70.00 47.50
a. Inverted overprint *150.00*
34 A15 50r blue 140.00 60.00
a. 50r pale blue 175.00 95.00
35 A15 150r blue 200.00 175.00
36 A15 150r yellow 300.00 175.00
37 A15 300r violet 95.00 65.00

Perf. 12½

31 A15 10r blue green 150.00 125.00
32a A15 10r yellow green 130.00 95.00
33b A15 15r lilac brown 20.00 18.00
34b A15 50r pale blue 175.00 95.00
35a A15 150r blue 200.00 150.00

Overprint Type B

Perf. 13½

37a A15 300r violet 100.00 67.50

Perf. 12½

33 A15 15r lilac brown 30.00 21.00
35b A15 150r blue 210.00 150.00

The reprints have the same papers, gum and perforations as those of the preceding issue.

Overprint Type C in Black

1880 *Perf. 12½*

38 A17 25r bluish gray 150.00 95.00
a. Perf 13½ 150.00 42.50
39 A18 25r red lilac 60.00 9.50
a. Perf 13½ 60.00 9.50
b. 25r gray — —
c. As "b," perf 13½ 50.00 9.50
d. As "c," double overprint

Overprint Type C in Carmine or Black

Ordinary Paper

1881-82

40 A16 5r black (C) 29.00 12.00
a. perf 13½ 29.00 12.00
41 A23 25r brown ('82) 55.00 8.00
a. Double overprint — —
b. perf 13½ 55.00 8.00
42 A19 50r blue 190.00 47.50
a. perf 13½ 190.00 47.50
Nos. 40-42 (3) 274.00 67.50

Enamel Surfaced Paper

40b A16 5r black (C) 160.00 95.00
41c A16 25r brown ('82) 55.00 8.00
d. perf 13½ 55.00 8.00

Reprints of Nos. 38, 39, 39a, 40 and 42 have the same papers, gum and perforations as those of preceding issues.

Overprinted in Red or Black — d

15, 20 REIS

Type I — The figures of value are some distance apart and close to the end of the label.
Type II — The figures are closer together and farther from the end of the label. On the 15 reis this is particularly apparent in the upper right figures.

1882-85 Ordinary Paper *Perf. 12½*

43 A16 5r black (R) 20.00 10.00
45 A15 10r green 90.00 50.00
a. Inverted overprint — —
47 A15 15r lilac brn 35.00 20.00
b. Inverted overprint — —
48 A15 20r bister 70.00 40.00
a. Inverted overprint — —
50 A23 25r brown 30.00 4.50
51 A15 50r blue *2,500. 1,250.*
52 A24 50r blue 24.00 3.50
a. Double overprint — —
53a A15 80r orange 125.00 110.00
b. Double overprint — —
54 A15 100r lilac 125.00 95.00
55 A15 150r blue *2,500. 900.00*
56 A15 150r yellow 125.00 110.00
57 A15 300r violet 125.00 110.00
58 A21 5r slate (R) 25.00 6.00
60 A15 1000r black (R) 225.00 125.00

Perf. 13½

43a A16 5r black (R) 29.00 14.00
45b A15 10r green 97.50 62.50
47c A15 15r lilac brown 75.00 85.00
48b A15 20r bister 150.00 85.00
50a A23 25r brown 26.00 4.50
51a A15 50r blue 1,100. 925.00
52b A24 50r blue 42.50 4.50
53c A15 80r orange 175.00 110.00
54a A15 100r lilac 150.00 110.00
55a A15 150r blue 900.00 800.00
56a A15 150r yellow 110.00 85.00
57a A15 300r violet 110.00 85.00
60a A15 1000r black ('85) (R) 140.00 125.00

Perf. 11½

50b A23 25r brown 26.00 4.50

Enamel Surfaced Paper

Perf. 12½

43b A16 5r black (R) 70.00 47.50
44 A21 5r slate 19.00 4.50
a. Double overprint —
c. Inverted overprint —
45d A15 10r green 125.00 110.00
46 A22 10r green ('84) 32.50 14.00
a. Double overprint —
47d A15 15r lilac brown 87.50 75.00
48c A15 20r bister 87.50 75.00
49 A15 20r car ('85) 150.00 125.00
a. Double overprint 190.00 —
50c A23 25r brown 27.50 4.50
52c A24 50r blue 27.50 4.50
53 A15 80r yellow 80.00 62.50
53b A15 80r orange 80.00 62.50
54b A15 100r lilac 62.50 55.00
56b A15 150r yellow 65.00 57.50
57b A15 300r violet 87.50 77.50
59 A24a 500r black (R) 300.00 175.00

Perf. 13½

44b A21 5r slate 32.50 11.00
45e A15 10r green 125.00 100.00
46b A22 10r green ('84) 32.50 14.00
47e A15 15r lilac brown 95.00 75.00
48e A15 20r bister 900.00 55.00
49b A15 20r car ('85) 150.00 125.00
50d A23 25r brown 30.00 4.50
52d A24 50r blue 37.50 14.00
53d A15 80r orange 95.00 75.00
56c A15 150r yellow 110.00 92.50
57c A15 300r violet 110.00 92.50

Perf. 11½

44d A21 5r slate 37.50 22.50
46c A22 10r green ('84) 32.50 14.00
50e A23 25r brown 27.50 4.50
52e A24 50r blue 27.50 4.50
58a A21 5r slate (R) 15.00 3.00

Reprints of the 1882-85 issues have the same papers, gum and perforations as those of preceding issues.

1887 Black Overprint

61 A25 20r pink 50.00 19.00
a. Inverted overprint — —
b. Double overprint — —
62 A26 25r lilac rose 60.00 3.00
a. Inverted overprint — —
b. Double ovpt., one invtd. — —
63 A26 25r red violet 60.00 3.00
a. Double overprint — —
64 A24a 500r red violet 250.00 110.00
a. Perf. 13½ 400.00 240.00
Nos. 61-64 (4) 420.00 135.00

Nos. 58-64 inclusive have been reprinted on thin white paper with shiny white gum and perforated 13½. Value: Nos. 58, 61-64, each $22.50; No. 59, $85; No. 60, $50.

Prince Henry the Navigator Issue

Portugal Nos. 97-109 Overprinted

1894, Mar. 4 *Perf. 14*

65 A46 5r orange yel 3.50 3.00
Never hinged 7.00
a. Inverted overprint *60.00 60.00*
66 A46 10r violet rose 3.50 3.00
Never hinged 7.00
a. Double overprint — —
b. Inverted overprint — —
67 A46 15r brown 4.25 4.00
Never hinged 8.25
68 A46 20r violet 4.50 4.25
Never hinged 8.50
a. Double overprint — —
69 A47 25r green 5.00 4.50
Never hinged 9.50
a. Double overprint *75.00 75.00*
b. Inverted overprint *75.00 75.00*
70 A47 50r blue 12.50 6.75
Never hinged 24.00
71 A47 75r dp carmine 22.50 9.50
Never hinged 47.50
72 A47 80r yellow grn 30.00 10.00
Never hinged 52.50
73 A47 100r lt brn, *pale buff* 30.00 8.00
Never hinged 52.50
a. Double overprint — —
74 A48 150r lt car, *pale rose* 60.00 19.00
Never hinged 77.50
75 A48 300r dk bl, *sal buff* 100.00 30.00
Never hinged 150.00
76 A48 500r brn vio, *pale lil* 140.00 45.00
Never hinged 150.00
77 A48 1000r gray blk, *yelsh* 200.00 70.00
Never hinged 325.00
a. Double overprint 700.00 500.00
Nos. 65-77 (13) 615.75 217.00

St. Anthony of Padua Issue

Portugal Nos. 132-146 Overprinted in Red or Black

No. 78

No. 79

1895, June 13 *Perf. 12*

78 A50 2½r black (R) 3.00 1.25
79 A51 5r brown yel 9.50 3.00
80 A51 10r red lilac 9.50 4.50
81 A51 15r red brown 14.50 7.00
82 A51 20r gray lilac 16.00 9.50
83 A51 25r grn & vio 10.00 3.00
84 A52 50r blue & brn 32.50 15.00
85 A52 75r rose & brn 47.50 40.00
86 A52 80r lt grn & brn 75.00 47.50
87 A52 100r choc & blk 75.00 42.50
88 A53 150r vio rose & bis 200.00 100.00
89 A53 200r blue & bis 200.00 100.00
90 A53 300r slate & bis 250.00 110.00
91 A53 500r vio brn & grn 500.00 150.00
92 A53 1000r vio & grn 800.00 225.00
Nos. 78-92 (15) 2,243. 858.25

7th cent. of the birth of Saint Anthony of Padua.

Common Design Types pictured following the introduction.

Vasco da Gama Issue
Common Design Types

1898, Apr. 1 *Perf. 14, 15*

93 CD20 2½r blue green 3.50 1.25
Never hinged 5.00
94 CD21 5r red 3.50 1.50
Never hinged 5.00
95 CD22 10r gray lilac 7.00 3.00
Never hinged 10.00
96 CD23 25r yel grn 7.00 3.00
Never hinged 10.00
97 CD24 50r dark blue 10.00 9.50
Never hinged 15.00
98 CD25 75r vio brn 21.00 14.00
Never hinged 32.50
99 CD26 100r bis brn 27.50 14.00
Never hinged 40.00
100 CD27 150r bister 42.50 30.00
Never hinged 62.50
Nos. 93-100 (8) 122.00 76.25

For overprints and surcharges see Nos. 141-148.

King Carlos — A28

1906 **Typo.** *Perf. 11½x12*

101 A28 2½r gray .45 .40
Never hinged .50
a. Inverted overprint *35.00 35.00*
102 A28 5r orange yel .45 .40
Never hinged .50
a. Inverted overprint *35.00 35.00*
103 A28 10r yellow grn .45 .40
Never hinged .50
104 A28 20r gray vio .70 .50
Never hinged .80
105 A28 25r carmine .70 .40
Never hinged .80
106 A28 50r ultra 6.00 4.75
Never hinged 6.75
107 A28 75r brown, *straw* 2.10 *1.25*
Never hinged 2.40
108 A28 100r dk blue, *bl* 2.10 *1.40*
Never hinged 2.40
109 A28 200r red lilac, *pnksh* 2.25 *1.40*
Never hinged 2.60
110 A28 300r dk blue, *rose* 6.75 *5.75*
Never hinged 8.00
111 A28 500r black, *blue* 16.00 14.00
Never hinged 19.00
Nos. 101-111 (11) 37.95 30.65

"Acores" and letters and figures in the corners are in red on the 2½, 10, 20, 75 and 500r and in black on the other values.

King Manuel II — A29

1910, Apr. 1 *Perf. 14x15*

112 A29 2½r violet .50 .40
113 A29 5r black .50 .40
114 A29 10r dk green .50 .40
115 A29 15r lilac brn .90 .65
116 A29 20r carmine 1.25 1.00
117 A29 25r violet brn .50 .50
a. Perf. 11½ 3.00 1.60
118 A29 50r blue 3.00 1.60
119 A29 75r bister brn 3.00 1.60
120 A29 80r slate 3.00 1.60
121 A29 100r brown, *lt grn* 5.00 3.75
122 A29 200r green, *sal* 5.00 3.75
123 A29 300r black, *blue* 3.00 2.75
124 A29 500r olive & brown 9.50 10.00
125 A29 1000r blue & black 21.00 19.00
Nos. 112-125 (14) 56.65 47.40

The errors of color 10r black, 15r dark green, 25r black and 50r carmine are considered to be proofs.

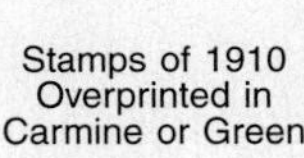
Stamps of 1910 Overprinted in Carmine or Green

1910

126 A29 2½r violet .40 .35
a. Inverted overprint 12.50 12.50
127 A29 5r black .40 .35
a. Inverted overprint 12.50 12.50
128 A29 10r dk green .40 .35
a. Inverted overprint 12.50 12.50
129 A29 15r lilac brn 1.90 1.40
a. Inverted overprint 12.50 12.50
130 A29 20r carmine (G) 1.90 1.40
a. Inverted overprint 22.50 22.50
b. Double overprint 22.50 22.50
131 A29 25r violet brn .40 .30
a. Perf. 11½ 65.00 57.50
132 A29 50r blue 1.40 1.25
133 A29 75r bister brn 1.40 .95
a. Double overprint 12.50 12.50
134 A29 80r slate 1.40 .95
135 A29 100r brown, *grn* 1.10 .90
136 A29 200r green, *sal* 1.10 *.95*
137 A29 300r black, *blue* 3.50 2.25
138 A29 500r olive & brn 4.50 *3.25*
139 A29 1000r blue & blk 11.00 *7.00*
Nos. 126-139 (14) 30.80 *21.65*

Vasco da Gama Issue Overprinted or Surcharged in Black

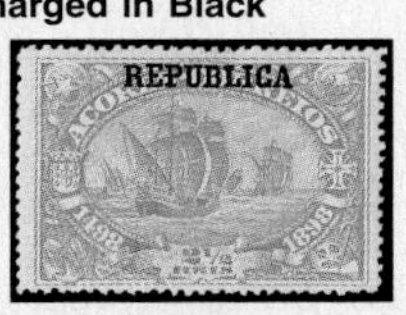

e

f

g

1911 *Perf. 14, 15*

141 CD20(e) 2½r blue green .65 .50
142 CD21(f) 15r on 5r red .65 .50
143 CD23(e) 25r yellow grn .65 .50
144 CD24(e) 50r dk blue 2.25 1.40
145 CD25(e) 75r violet brn 1.90 1.75
146 CD27(f) 80r on 150r bister 2.00 1.90
147 CD26(e) 100r yellow brn 2.10 1.90
a. Double surcharge 40.00 40.00
148 CD22(g) 1000r on 10r lil 20.00 15.00
Nos. 141-148 (8) 30.20 23.45

Postage Due Stamps of Portugal Overprinted or Surcharged in Black

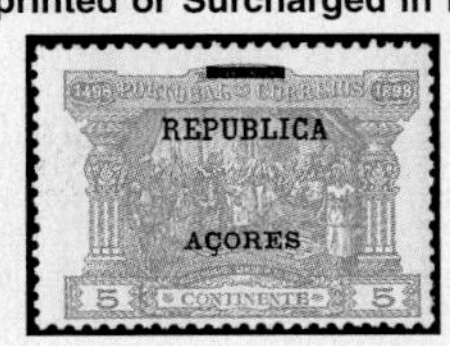

1911 *Perf. 12*

149 D1 5r black 1.25 1.10
150 D1 10r magenta 2.75 1.10
a. "Acores" double 30.00 15.00
151 D1 20r orange 5.25 3.75
152 D1 200r brn, *buff* 30.00 20.00
a. "Acores" inverted 100.00
153 D1 300r on 50r slate 30.00 19.00
154 D1 500r on 100r car, *pink* 30.00 18.00
Nos. 149-154 (6) 99.25 62.95

Ceres Issue of Portugal Overprinted in Black or Carmine

With Imprint
Chalky Paper

1912-21 *Perf. 15x14*

155 A64 ¼c olive brown 3.00 1.25
Never hinged 4.50
156 A64 ½c black (C) 3.00 1.25
Never hinged 4.50
157 A64 1c dp grn ('13) 3.00 1.25
Never hinged 4.50
158 A64 1½c choc ('13) 4.00 3.00
Never hinged 6.00
159 A64 2c car ('13) 6.00 3.00
Never hinged 9.00
160 A64 2½c violet 5.00 1.10
Never hinged 7.00
161 A64 5c dp blue ('13) 5.00 1.10
Never hinged 7.00
162 A64 7½c yel brn ('13) 12.00 7.00
Never hinged 18.00
163 A64 8c slate ('13) 12.00 7.00
Never hinged 18.00
164 A64 10c org brn ('13) 13.00 7.50
Never hinged 20.00
165 A64 15c plum ('13) 17.00 7.50
Never hinged 26.00
166 A64 20c vio brn, *grn* ('13) 15.00 7.00
Never hinged 22.50
a. 20c pale brown, *green* 15.00 7.00
Never hinged 22.50
167 A64 30c brn, *pink* ('13) 80.00 60.00
Never hinged 120.00
168 A64 30c brn, *yel* ('19) 2.25 1.90
Never hinged 3.50
169 A64 50c org, *sal* ('13) 6.50 2.75
Never hinged 10.00
170 A64 50c org, *yel* ('13) 6.50 2.75
Never hinged 10.00
171 A64 1e dp grn, *bl* ('13) 7.00 6.00
Never hinged 11.00

Nos. 155 and 160 also exist on glazed non-chalky paper.

Perf. 12x11½

172 A64 14c dk bl, *yel* ('21) 3.00 *1.90*
Never hinged 4.50
Nos. 155-172 (18) 203.25 123.25

Nos. 155 and 160 exist on glazed paper.

Ordinary Paper

1917-21 *Perf. 15x14*

173 A64 ¼c olive brown .55 .40
Never hinged .85
a. Inverted overprint 12.50 9.50
Never hinged 19.00
b. Thick carton paper 3.50 3.25
Never hinged 5.25
174 A64 ½c black (C) .55 .40
Never hinged .85
a. Thick carton paper 2.25 1.75
Never hinged 3.50
175 A64 1c deep green 1.10 .80
Never hinged 1.60
a. Inverted overprint 12.50
Never hinged 19.00
176 A64 1c dp brn ('18) .55 .40
Never hinged .85
a. Inverted overprint 17.50
Never hinged 27.00
177 A64 1½c choc 1.10 .80
Never hinged 1.50
a. Inverted overprint 13.00
Never hinged 19.00
178 A64 1½c dp grn ('18) .55 .50
Never hinged .85
a. Inverted overprint 17.50
Never hinged 26.00
179 A64 2c carmine .80 .65
Never hinged 1.20
a. Inverted overprint 20.00
Never hinged 30.00
180 A64 2c orange ('19) .55 .50
Never hinged .85
a. Inverted overprint 25.00
Never hinged 37.50
181 A64 2½c violet .80 .65
Never hinged 1.20
182 A64 3c rose ('18) .80 .65
Never hinged 1.20
183 A64 3½c lt grn ('18) .55 .50
Never hinged .85
184 A64 4c lt grn ('19) .55 .50
Never hinged .85
185 A64 5c deep blue .80 .65
Never hinged 1.20
186 A64 5c yel brn ('21) .75 .65
Never hinged 1.15
187 A64 6c dull rose ('20) .55 .50
Never hinged .85
188 A64 7½c yellow brown 6.75 3.75
Never hinged 10.00
189 A64 7½c dp bl ('19) 1.90 1.75
Never hinged 2.75
190 A64 8c slate .80 .70
Never hinged 1.20
191 A64 10c orange brown 8.00 4.00
Never hinged 12.00
192 A64 15c plum .85 .65
Never hinged 1.25
193 A64 30c gray brn ('21) 1.90 1.60
Never hinged 2.75
194 A64 60c blue ('21) 1.90 1.50
Never hinged 2.75
Nos. 173-194 (22) 32.65 22.50

1918-26 *Perf. 12x11½*

195 A64 ¼c olive brown .55 .55
Never hinged .75
a. Thick carton paper 2.25 1.75
Never hinged 3.25
196 A64 ½c black (R) .55 .40
Never hinged .75
197 A64 1c deep brown .55 .40
Never hinged .75
198 A64 1½c deep green .90 .70
Never hinged 1.25
199 A64 2c org ('19) .55 .50
Never hinged .75
a. Inverted overprint 24.00
Never hinged 35.00
b. Thick carton paper 13.00 12.00
Never hinged 18.00
200 A64 3c rose .90 .65
Never hinged 1.25
201 A64 3c dull ultra ('25) .40 .30
Never hinged .55
202 A64 4c lt grn ('19) .55 .50
Never hinged .55
a. Inverted overprint 21.00
Never hinged 30.00
203 A64 5c ol brn ('21) .55 .50
Never hinged .75
204A A64 6c dull rose ('20) .55 .50
Never hinged .75
b. Thick carton paper 1.25 1.00
Never hinged 1.90
204 A64 6c choc ('25) .55 .50
Never hinged .75
205 A64 7½c dp bl ('19) 75.00 50.00
Never hinged 105.00
206 A64 8c bl grn ('24) .80 .55
Never hinged 1.10
207 A64 8c org ('25) 1.00 .95
Never hinged 1.40
208 A64 10c org brn .55 .50
Never hinged .75
209 A64 12c bl gray ('20) 2.75 1.75
Never hinged 3.75
210 A64 12c dp grn ('22) .90 .75
Never hinged 1.25
a. Inverted overprint 20.00
Never hinged 28.00
211 A64 13½c chlky bl ('20) 2.75 1.90
Never hinged 3.75
212 A64 15c blk (R) ('24) .55 .50
Never hinged .75
213 A64 16c brt ultra ('26) .95 .90
Never hinged 1.35
214 A64 20c choc ('21) .90 .75
Never hinged 1.25
a. Thick carton paper 7.00 6.00
Never hinged 10.00
215 A64 20c dp grn ('24) 1.25 .95
Never hinged 1.75
a. Double overprint 22.50 22.50
Never hinged 30.00
216 A64 20c gray ('24) .80 .60
Never hinged 1.10
217 A64 24c grnsh bl ('21) .90 .55
Never hinged 1.25
218 A64 25c sal ('23) .70 .50
Never hinged 1.00
219 A64 30c gray brn ('21) 1.90 1.60
Never hinged 2.75
220 A64 32c dp grn ('26) 2.75 2.40
Never hinged 3.75
221 A64 36c red ('21) .85 .65
Never hinged 1.20
222 A64 40c dp bl ('23) 1.00 .70
Never hinged 1.40
a. "CORREIC" for "CORREIO" 67.50 67.50
Never hinged 95.00
223 A64 40c blk brn ('24) 1.90 1.00
Never hinged 2.75
a. "CORREIC" for "CORREIO" 67.50 67.50
Never hinged 95.00
224 A64 48c brt rose ('26) 5.00 3.00
Never hinged 7.00
225 A64 50c yellow ('23) 1.90 1.50
Never hinged 2.75
226 A64 60c blue ('21) 1.90 1.50
Never hinged 2.75
227 A64 64c pale ultra ('26) 5.00 2.25
Never hinged 7.00
228 A64 75c dull rose ('24) 5.00 4.00
Never hinged 7.00
229 A64 80c dull rose ('21) 2.50 2.10
Never hinged 3.50
230 A64 80c violet ('24) 2.50 1.90
Never hinged 3.50
231 A64 90c chlky bl ('21) 2.50 2.10
Never hinged 3.50
232 A64 96c dp rose ('26) 7.50 3.50
Never hinged 11.00
233 A64 1e violet ('21) 2.50 2.10
Never hinged 3.50
234 A64 1.10e yel brn ('21) 2.75 2.10
Never hinged 3.75
235 A64 1.20e yel grn ('22) 3.25 2.10
Never hinged 4.50
236 A64 2e slate grn ('22) 10.00 6.50
Never hinged 14.00
Nos. 195-236 (42) 156.55 107.15

1924-30 *Perf. 12x11½*

Glazed Paper

237 A64 1e gray vio 3.75 3.25
Never hinged 5.75
237A A64 1.20e buff 8.25 6.00
Never hinged 12.50
237B A64 1.50e blk vio 9.75 6.75
Never hinged 14.50
237C A64 1.50e lilac ('25) 8.50 6.75
Never hinged 13.00
237D A64 1.60e dp bl ('25) 8.50 7.00
Never hinged 13.00
237E A64 2.40e apple grn ('30) 125.00 60.00
Never hinged 190.00
237F A64 3e lil pink ('28) 150.00 60.00
Never hinged 225.00

237G A64 3.20e gray grn ('26) 9.75 9.50
Never hinged 14.50
237H A64 5e emer ('25) 19.00 10.00
Never hinged 29.00
237I A64 10e pink ('25) 125.00 27.50
Never hinged 150.00
237J A64 20e pale turq ('25) 300.00 82.50
Never hinged 300.00
Nos. 237-237J (11) 767.50 279.25

For same overprint on surcharged stamps, see Nos. 300-306. For same design without imprint see Nos. 307-313.

Castello-Branco Issue

Stamps of Portugal, 1925, Overprinted in Black or Red

1925, Mar. 29 *Perf. 12½*
238 A73 2c orange .25 .25
239 A73 3c green .25 .25
240 A73 4c ultra (R) .25 .25
241 A73 5c scarlet .25 .25
242 A74 10c pale blue .25 .25
243 A74 16c red orange .40 .30
244 A75 25c car rose .40 .30
245 A74 32c green .50 .50
246 A75 40c grn & blk (R) .50 .50
247 A74 48c red brn 1.10 1.10
248 A76 50c blue green 1.10 1.00
249 A76 64c orange brn 1.10 1.00
250 A76 75c gray blk (R) 1.10 1.00
251 A75 80c brown 1.10 1.00
252 A76 96c car rose 1.40 1.10
253 A77 1.50e dk bl, *bl* (R) 1.40 1.10
254 A75 1.60e indigo (R) 1.50 1.40
255 A77 2e dk grn, *grn* (R) 2.50 2.10
256 A77 2.40e red, *org* 3.25 2.40
257 A77 3.20e blk, *grn* (R) 6.00 5.25
Nos. 238-257 (20) 24.60 21.30

First Independence Issue

Stamps of Portugal, 1926, Overprinted in Red

1926, Aug. 13 *Perf. 14, 14½*
Center in Black
258 A79 2c orange .35 .35
259 A80 3c ultra .35 .35
260 A79 4c yellow grn .35 .35
261 A80 5c black brn .35 .35
262 A79 6c ocher .35 .35
263 A80 15c dk green .75 .70
264 A81 20c dull violet .75 .70
265 A82 25c scarlet .75 .70
266 A81 32c deep green .75 .70
267 A82 40c yellow brn .75 .70
268 A82 50c olive bis 3.00 2.00
269 A82 75c red brown 3.00 2.10
270 A83 1e black violet 4.00 3.00
271 A84 4.50e olive green 15.00 10.00
Nos. 258-271 (14) 30.50 22.35

The use of these stamps instead of those of the regular issue was obligatory on Aug. 13 and 14, Nov. 30 and Dec. 1, 1926.

Centering is vital to the value of Nos. 258-299. Stamps in grades of less than VF sell at significant discounts from the values here.

Second Independence Issue

Same Overprint on Stamps of Portugal, 1927, in Red

1927, Nov. 29 **Center in Black**
272 A86 2c lt brown .30 .30
273 A87 3c ultra .30 .30
274 A86 4c orange .30 .30
275 A88 5c dk brown .30 .30
276 A89 6c orange brn .30 .30
277 A87 15c black brn .30 .30
278 A86 25c gray 1.25 1.25
279 A89 32c blue grn 1.25 1.25
280 A90 40c yellow grn 1.00 .75
281 A90 96c red 5.00 3.25
282 A88 1.60e myrtle grn 5.00 3.25
283 A91 4.50e bister 15.00 8.75
Nos. 272-283 (12) 30.30 20.30

Third Independence Issue

Same Overprint on Stamps of Portugal, 1928, in Red

1928, Nov. 27 **Center in Black**
284 A93 2c lt blue .30 .30
285 A94 3c lt green .30 .30
286 A95 4c lake .30 .30
287 A96 5c olive grn .30 .30
288 A97 6c orange brn .30 .30
289 A94 15c slate .65 .60
290 A95 16c dk violet .75 .75
291 A93 25c ultra .75 .75
292 A97 32c dk green .80 .80
293 A96 40c olive brn .80 .80
294 A95 50c red orange 2.00 1.75
295 A94 80c lt gray 2.00 1.75
296 A97 96c carmine 4.00 3.00
297 A96 1e claret 4.00 3.00
298 A93 1.60e dk blue 4.00 3.00
299 A98 4.50e yellow 9.00 8.50
Nos. 284-299 (16) 30.25 26.20

Types of Portugal Nos. 285, 296 & 298F Overprinted & Surcharged in Black

1929-30 *Perf. 12x11½, 15x14*
300 A64 4c on 25c pink ('30) .75 .75
Never hinged 1.15
301 A64 4c on 60c dp blue 1.40 1.40
Never hinged 2.10
a. Perf. 15x14 4.75 4.75
Never hinged 7.25
302 A64 10c on 25c pink 1.50 1.50
Never hinged 2.25
303 A64 12c on 25c pink 1.40 1.40
Never hinged 2.10
304 A64 15c on 25c pink 1.40 1.40
Never hinged 2.10
305 A64 20c on 25c pink 2.50 2.40
Never hinged 3.75
306 A64 40c on 1.10e yel brn 5.00 4.75
Never hinged 7.50
Nos. 300-306 (7) 13.95 13.60

Portugal Nos. 400-401, 403-404, 408, 412, 416 Overprinted in Black or Red

1930 *Perf. 14*
Without Imprint at Foot
307 A85 4c orange .90 .70
Never hinged 1.35
308 A85 5c dp brown 3.00 2.75
Never hinged 4.50
309 A85 10c orange red 1.50 1.10
Never hinged 2.25
310 A85 15c black (R) 1.50 1.10
Never hinged 2.25
311 A85 40c brt green 1.40 .90
Never hinged 2.10
312 A85 80c violet 15.00 12.00
Never hinged 22.50
313 A85 1.60e dk blue 4.00 1.75
Never hinged 6.00
Nos. 307-313 (7) 27.30 20.30

Black or Red Overprint

1930-31 *Perf. 12x11½*
With Imprint at Foot
313A A64 4c orange .55 .50
Never hinged .85
313B A64 5c blk brn ('31) 4.00 3.25
Never hinged 6.00
313C A64 6c red brn ('31) .40 .30
Never hinged .60
313D A64 15c black (R) .95 .70
Never hinged 1.45
313E A64 16c dp blue ('31) 2.75 1.90
Never hinged 4.25
313F A64 32c deep green 3.25 2.25
Never hinged 5.00
313G A64 40c brt grn ('31) 1.50 .75
Never hinged 2.25
313H A64 48c dull pink ('31) 3.50 3.00
Never hinged 5.25
313I A64 50c bister ('31) 4.75 3.50
Never hinged 7.25
313J A64 50c red brn ('31) 4.75 3.50
Never hinged 7.25
313K A64 64c brn rose ('31) 9.00 5.00
Never hinged 13.50
313L A64 75c car rose ('31) 4.75 3.50
Never hinged 7.25
313M A64 80c dk grn ('31) 4.75 3.00
Never hinged 7.25
313N A64 1e brn lake 40.00 27.50
Never hinged 60.00
313O A64 1.25e dk blue 2.75 2.25
Never hinged 4.25
Nos. 313A=313O (15) 87.65 60.90

The original stamps (Portugal Nos. 496A-496R) were printed at the Lisbon Mint from new plates produced from the original dies. The paper is whiter than the paper used for earlier Ceres stamps. The gum is white.

POSTAGE DUE STAMPS

Portugal Nos. J7-J13 Overprinted in Black

1904 **Unwmk.** *Perf. 12*
J1 D2 5r brown 1.25 1.10
J2 D2 10r orange 1.40 1.10
J3 D2 20r lilac 2.25 1.10
J4 D2 30r gray green 2.25 1.75
a. Double overprint
J5 D2 40r gray violet 4.00 2.40
J6 D2 50r carmine 6.75 4.50
J7 D2 100r dull blue 8.50 8.25
Nos. J1-J7 (7) 26.40 20.20

Same Overprinted in Carmine or Green (Portugal Nos. J14-J20)

1911
J8 D2 5r brown .75 .65
J9 D2 10r orange .75 .65
J10 D2 20r lilac .95 .85
J11 D2 30r gray green .95 .85
J12 D2 40r gray violet 1.50 1.10
J13 D2 50r carmine (G) 7.75 7.50
J14 D2 100r dull blue 2.75 2.75
Nos. J8-J14 (7) 15.40 14.35

Portugal Nos. J21-J27 Overprinted in Black

1918
J15 D3 ½c brown .75 .75
a. Inverted overprint 6.00
b. Double overprint 6.00
J16 D3 1c orange .75 .75
a. Inverted overprint 6.00
b. Double overprint 6.00
J17 D3 2c red lilac .95 .85
a. Inverted overprint 4.00
b. Double overprint 6.00
J18 D3 3c green .75 .75
a. Inverted overprint 6.00
b. Double overprint 6.00
J19 D3 4c gray .75 .75
a. Inverted overprint 6.00
b. Double overprint 6.00
J20 D3 5c rose .75 .75
b. Double overprint 6.00
J21 D3 10c dark blue .75 .75
Nos. J15-J21 (7) 5.45 5.35

Stamps and Type of Portugal Postage Dues, 1921-27, Overprinted in Black

1922-24 *Perf. 11½x12*
J30 D3 ½c gray green ('23) .35 .35
J31 D3 1c gray green ('23) .55 .45
J32 D3 2c gray green ('23) .55 .45
J33 D3 3c gray green ('24) .90 .45
J34 D3 8c gray green ('24) .90 .45
J35 D3 10c gray green ('24) .90 .45
J36 D3 12c gray green ('24) .90 .45
J37 D3 16c gray green ('24) .95 .45
J38 D3 20c gray green .95 .45
J39 D3 24c gray green .95 .45
J40 D3 32c gray green ('24) .95 .45
J41 D3 36c gray green .95 .60
J42 D3 40c gray green ('24) .95 .60
J43 D3 48c gray green ('24) .95 .60
J44 D3 50c gray green .95 .60
J45 D3 60c gray green 1.50 .70
J46 D3 72c gray green 1.50 .70
J47 D3 80c gray green ('24) 5.00 4.25
J48 D3 1.20e gray green 5.75 4.75
Nos. J30-J48 (19) 26.40 17.65

NEWSPAPER STAMPS

Newspaper Stamps of Portugal, Nos. P1, P1a, Overprinted Types c & d in Black or Red and

N3

Perf. 12½, 13½ (#P4)
1876-88 **Unwmk.**
P1 N1 (c) 2½r olive 13.00 5.50
a. Inverted overprint
b. Perf 13½ 8.00 3.50
P2 N1 (d) 2½r olive ('82) 5.75 1.90
a. Inverted overprint — —
b. Double overprint — —
c. Perf 13½ 3.00 1.00
d. 2½r emerald green 3.00 1.00
e. As "d," perf 13½ 3.00 1.00
f. As "d," perf 11½ 20.00 3.00
g. As "d," ribbed paper 3.00 1.00
P3 N3 2r black ('85) 6.00 3.00
a. Inverted overprint —
b. Double overprint, one inverted —
c. Perf 13½ 3.00 1.50
P4 N1 (d) 2½r bister ('82) 5.75 1.90
a. Double overprint 9.00
b. Perf 11½ 20.00 3.00
c. Perf 13½, ribbed paper 3.00 1.00
d. Perf 11½, enamel paper 3.00 1.00
P5 N3 2r black (R) ('88) 19.00 16.00
a. Perf 13½ 10.00 6.00
Nos. P1-P5 (5) 49.50 28.30

Reprints of the newspaper stamps have the same papers, gum and perforations as reprints of the regular issues. Value $2 each.

PARCEL POST STAMPS

Portugal Nos. Q1-Q17 Ovptd. in Black or Red

1921-22 **Unwmk.** *Perf. 12*
Q1 PP1 1c lilac brown .50 .45
a. Inverted overprint 6.00
Q2 PP1 2c orange .50 .45
a. Inverted overprint 6.00
Q3 PP1 5c light brown .50 .45
a. Inverted overprint 6.00
b. Double overprint 6.00
Q4 PP1 10c red brown .75 .45
a. Inverted overprint 6.00
b. Double overprint 6.00
Q5 PP1 20c gray blue .75 .45
a. Inverted overprint 6.00
b. Double overprint 6.00
Q6 PP1 40c carmine .75 .45
a. Double overprint 8.00
Q7 PP1 50c black (R) 1.00 *1.90*
Q8 PP1 60c dark blue (R) 1.00 *1.90*
Q9 PP1 70c gray brown 2.50 1.25
a. Double overprint 6.00
Q10 PP1 80c ultra 2.50 1.25
Q11 PP1 90c light violet 2.50 1.25
Q12 PP1 1e light green 2.50 1.25
Q13 PP1 2e pale lilac 7.00 3.50
Q14 PP1 3e olive 12.00 3.75
Q15 PP1 4e ultra 15.00 3.75
Q16 PP1 5e gray 15.00 7.25
Q17 PP1 10e chocolate 50.00 25.00
Nos. Q1-Q17 (17) 114.75 54.75

POSTAL TAX STAMPS

These stamps represent a special fee for the delivery of postal matter on certain days in the year. The money derived from their sale is applied to works of public charity.

Nos. 128 and 157 Overprinted in Carmine

1911-13 Unwmk. *Perf. 14x15*

RA1 A29 10r dark green 1.50 1.10

The 20r of this type was for use on telegrams. Value $2.25 unused, $1.90 used.

Perf. 15x14

RA2 A64 1c deep green 5.00 3.75

The 2c of this type was for use on telegrams. Value $7.00 unused, $5.00 used.

Portugal No. RA4 Overprinted in Black

1915 *Perf. 12*

RA3 PT2 1c carmine .65 .35

The 2c of this type was for use on telegrams. Value $1.10 unused, 85c used.

Postal Tax Stamp of 1915 Surcharged

1924

RA4 PT2 15c on 1c rose 1.10 *.90*

The 30c on 2c of this type was for use on telegrams. Value $3.00 unused, $1.90 used.

Comrades of the Great War Issue

Postal Tax Stamps of Portugal, 1925, Overprinted

1925, Apr. 8 *Perf. 11*

RA5	PT3	10c brown	1.10	1.10
RA6	PT3	10c green	1.10	1.10
RA7	PT3	10c rose	1.10	1.10
RA8	PT3	10c ultra	1.10	1.10
		Nos. RA5-RA8 (4)	4.40	4.40

The use of Nos. RA5-RA11 in addition to the regular postage was compulsory on certain days. If the tax represented by these stamps was not prepaid, it was collected by means of Postal Tax Due Stamps.

Pombal Issue

Common Design Types

1925 *Perf. 12½*

RA9	CD28	20c dp grn & blk	1.10	1.10
RA10	CD29	20c dp grn & blk	1.10	1.10
RA11	CD30	20c dp grn & blk	1.10	1.10
		Nos. RA9-RA11 (3)	3.30	3.30

POSTAL TAX DUE STAMPS

Portugal No. RAJ1 Ovptd. in Black

1925, Apr. 8 Unwmk. *Perf. 11x11½*

RAJ1 PTD1 20c brown orange 1.10 .95

See note after No. RA8.

Pombal Issue

Common Design Types

1925, May 8 *Perf. 12½*

RAJ2	CD28	40c dp grn & blk	1.10	*2.00*
RAJ3	CD29	40c dp grn & blk	1.10	*2.00*
RAJ4	CD30	40c dp grn & blk	1.10	*2.00*
		Nos. RAJ2-RAJ4 (3)	3.30	*6.00*

See note after No. RA8.

BAHAMAS

bə-ˈhä-mə

LOCATION — A group of about 700 islands and 2,000 rocks in the West Indies, off the coast of Florida. Only 30 islands are inhabited.
GOVT. — British Colony
AREA — 5,353 sq. mi.
POP. — 209,505 (1980)
CAPITAL — Nassau

The principal island, on which the capital is located, is New Providence.

12 Pence = 1 Shilling
20 Shillings = 1 Pound

Catalogue values for unused stamps in this country are for Never Hinged items, beginning with Scott 130.

PRE-STAMP POSTAL MARKINGS

Crowned Circle handstamp type III is pictured in the Crowned Circle Handstamps and Great Britain Used Abroad section.

Nassau

1846-58

A1 III "Bahamas" crowned circle handstamp in red, on cover 2,250.

This handstamp, in black, was used from 1899-1935 denoting payment of postage for official mail.

STAMPS OF GREAT BRITAIN USED IN BAHAMAS

Numeral cancellation type A is pictured in the Crowned Circle Handstamps and Great Britain Used Abroad section.

1858-60

A05 (Nassau)

A2	A	1p rose red (#20)	2,500.
A3	A	2p blue (#29, P8)	1,600.
a.		Plate 7	1,600.
A4	A	4p rose (#26)	475.
A5	A	6p lilac (#27)	375.
A6	A	1sh green (#28)	2,750.

Values for unused stamps are for examples with original gum as defined in the catalogue introduction. Very fine examples of Nos. 2-26 will have perforations touching the design or frameline on at least one side due to the narrow spacing of the stamps on the plates. Stamps with perfs clear of the design or framelines on all four sides are extremely scarce and will command higher prices.

Pen cancellations usually indicate revenue use. Such stamps sell for much less than postally canceled examples. Beware of stamps with revenue or pen cancellations removed and forged postal cancellations added.

Queen Victoria — A1

1859-60 Unwmk. Engr. *Imperf.*

1 A1 1p dull lake, thin paper ('60)	75.00	*1,900.*
a. 1p reddish lake, thick paper	*6,000.*	*2,850.*
b. 1p brownish lake, thick paper	*6,000.*	*2,850.*
On cover		*17,500.*
c. As "b," thin paper	*325.*	—

Most unused examples of No. 1 are remainders, and false cancellations are plentiful.

Stamps with pen cancellations may be postally used on inter-island mail. Certificates of authenticity are recommended.

Queen Victoria — A2

1861 *Rough Perf. 14 to 16*

2 A1 1p lake	925.	425.
a. Clean-cut perf. ('60)	7,250.	950.
3 A2 4p dull rose	1,800.	500.
a. Imperf. between, pair	*40,000.*	
4 A2 6p gray lilac	5,500.	750.
a. Pale lilac	4,250.	650.

No. 2 exists perf 11 to 12½. This is a trial perforation by Perkins, Bacon and was not sent to the colony. Value, $2,850.

1862 *Perf. 11½, 12*

5 A1 1p lake	1,250.	225.
a. Pair, imperf. between	*6,250.*	
b. 1p carmine lake	1,900.	325.
c. Perf. 11½x11 or 12x11	2,850.	1,200.
d. As "b," perf. 11½x11 or 12x11	2,600.	1,100.
6 A2 4p dull rose	4,500.	500.
a. Perf. 11½x11 or 12x11	24,500.	1,400.
7 A2 6p gray violet	13,500.	625.
a. Perf. 11½x11 or 12x11	24,500.	2,500.

No. 5a was not issued in the Bahamas. It is unique and faulty.

Perf. 13

8 A1 1p brown lake	950.	160.
a. 1p carmine lake	1,150.	200.
9 A2 4p rose	3,500.	475.
10 A2 6p gray violet	4,250.	600.
a. 6p dull violet	3,500.	575.

Queen Victoria — A3

Engr., Typo. (A3)

1863-65 Wmk. 1 *Perf. 12½*

11 A1 1p lake	140.00	90.00
a. 1p brown lake	120.00	85.00
b. 1p rose lake	160.00	95.00
c. 1p rose red	70.00	55.00
d. 1p red	75.00	55.00
12 A1 1p vermilion	90.00	57.50
13 A2 4p rose	375.00	75.00
a. 4p rose lake	575.00	100.00
b. 4p bright rose	375.00	75.00
14 A2 6p dk violet	200.00	85.00
a. 6p violet	325.00	115.00
b. 6p rose lilac	*8,500.*	*3,500.*
c. 6p lilac	475.00	90.00
15 A3 1sh green ('65)	3,250.	375.00

For surcharge see No. 26.

1863-81 Engr., Typo. (A3) *Perf. 14*

16 A1 1p vermilion	70.00	20.00
17 A1 1p car lake (anil.)	1,500.	
18 A2 4p rose	475.00	50.00
a. 4p deep rose ('76)	550.00	50.00
b. 4p dull rose	1,900.	50.00
19 A3 1sh green ('80)	10.00	10.00
a. 1sh dark green	350.00	50.00

Some examples of No. 16 show a light aniline appearance and care should be taken not to confuse these with No. 17. All known used examples of No. 17 bear fiscal cancels.

Engr., Typo. (A3)

1882-98 Wmk. 2

20 A1 1p vermilion	575.00	75.00
21 A2 4p rose	1,500.	75.00
22 A3 1sh green	50.00	18.00
23 A3 1sh blue grn ('98)	45.00	37.50

Perf. 12

24 A1 1p vermilion	60.00	22.50
25 A2 4p rose	700.00	60.00

No. 14a Surcharged in Black

1883 Engr. Wmk. 1 *Perf. 12½*

26 A2 4p on 6p violet	725.	500.
a. Inverted surcharge	*25,000.*	*12,000.*

The surcharge, being handstamped, is found in various positions. Counterfeit surcharges exist.

Queen Victoria — A5

1884-90 Typo. Wmk. 2 *Perf. 14*

27 A5 1p carmine rose	9.00	3.25
a. 1p pale rose	95.00	16.00
b. 1p car (aniline)	4.00	*8.50*
28 A5 2½p ultra	13.50	3.00
a. 2½p dull blue	95.00	22.50
b. 2½p bright blue	55.00	9.50
29 A5 4p yellow	12.50	5.00
30 A5 6p violet	7.50	*40.00*
31 A5 5sh olive green	90.00	*100.00*
32 A5 £1 brown	350.00	*275.00*
Revenue cancellation		*55.00*
Nos. 27-32 (6)	482.50	*426.25*

Cleaned fiscally used examples of No. 32 are often found with forged postmarks of small post offices added, especially dated "AU 29 94."

Queen's Staircase — A6

1901-03 Engr. Wmk. 1

33 A6 1p carmine & blk	15.00	*4.00*
34 A6 5p org & blk ('03)	11.00	*66.00*
35 A6 2sh ultra & blk ('03)	35.00	*65.00*
36 A6 3sh green & blk ('03)	50.00	*75.00*
Nos. 33-36 (4)	111.00	*210.00*
Set, overprinted "SPECIMEN"	165.00	

See Nos. 48, 58-62, 71, 78, 81-82.

Edward VII — A7

1902 Wmk. 2 Typo.

37 A7 1p carmine rose	2.00	3.25
38 A7 2½p ultra	8.50	1.75
39 A7 4p orange	20.00	*77.50*
a. 4p yellow ('10)	30.00	*90.00*
40 A7 6p bister brn	5.00	*30.00*
41 A7 1sh gray blk & car	26.00	*65.00*
a. 1sh brownish gray & carmine ('07)	28.00	*65.00*

42 A7 5sh violet & ultra 85.00 *110.00*
43 A7 £1 green & blk 325.00 *425.00*
Nos. 37-43 (7) 471.50 *712.50*
Set, overprinted "SPECIMEN" 350.00

Beware of forged postmarks, especially dated "2 MAR 10."

1906-11 **Wmk. 3**
44 A7 ½p green 6.25 4.00
Overprinted "SPECIMEN" 70.00
45 A7 1p car rose 32.50 1.75
46 A7 2½p ultra ('07) 32.50 32.50
47 A7 6p bister brn ('11) 30.00 *60.00*
Nos. 44-47 (4) 101.25 *98.25*

1911-19 **Engr.**
48 A6 1p red & gray blk ('16) 6.00 3.25
a. 1p carmine & black ('11) 23.00 3.50
b. 1p carmine & gray black ('19) 10.00 7.50

For overprints see Nos. B1-B2.

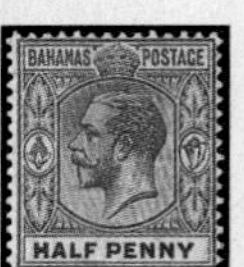
George V — A8

1912-19 **Typo.**
49 A8 ½p green 1.00 *12.50*
a. ½p yellow green 3.25 *19.00*
50 A8 1p car rose (aniline) 4.50 .45
b. 1p deep rose 10.00 3.00
c. 1p rose 14.00 3.75
d. Inverted watermark 250.00 115.00
50A A8 2p gray ('19) 3.00 *3.75*
51 A8 2½p ultra 6.00 *35.00*
a. 2½p deep blue 20.00 *50.00*
52 A8 4p orange 3.25 *22.50*
a. 4p orange yellow 7.00 *25.00*
53 A8 6p bister brown 2.25 *8.50*

Chalky Paper

54 A8 1sh black & car 2.25 *11.50*
a. 1sh jet black & carmine 17.50 *27.50*
55 A8 5sh violet & ultra 50.00 *90.00*
a. 5sh pale violet & deep blue 65.00 *95.00*
56 A8 £1 dull grn & blk 250.00 *425.00*
a. £1 bright green & black 225.00 *375.00*
Nos. 49-56 (9) 322.25 *609.20*
Set, overprinted "SPECIMEN" 375.00

1917-19 **Engr.**
58 A6 3p reddish pur, *buff* 7.00 6.25
a. 3p purple, *yellow* 6.00 *37.50*
59 A6 3p brown & blk ('19) 2.75 *5.00*
60 A6 5p violet & blk 3.50 *9.00*
61 A6 2sh ultra & black 37.50 *70.00*
62 A6 3sh green & black 82.50 70.00
Nos. 58-62 (5) 133.25 *160.25*

Peace Commemorative Issue

King George V and Seal of Bahamas — A9

1920, Mar. 1 **Engr.** ***Perf. 14***
65 A9 ½p gray green 1.25 *7.00*
66 A9 1p deep red 3.50 1.25
67 A9 2p gray 3.50 *9.50*
68 A9 3p brown 3.50 *11.50*
69 A9 1sh dark green 22.50 *45.00*
Nos. 65-69 (5) 34.25 *74.25*
Set, overprinted "SPECIMEN" 225.00

Types of 1901-12
Typo., Engr. (A6)

1921-34 **Wmk. 4**
70 A8 ½p green ('24) .65 .50
71 A6 1p car & black 3.50 *2.75*
72 A8 1p car rose 1.25 .25
73 A8 1½p fawn ('34) 13.00 1.25
74 A8 2p gray ('27) 1.90 *3.00*
75 A8 2½p ultra ('22) 1.25 *3.00*
76 A8 3p violet, *yel* ('31) 8.25 *20.00*
77 A8 4p yellow ('24) 1.90 *5.25*
78 A6 5p red vio & gray blk ('29) 5.50 *57.50*
79 A8 6p bister brn ('22) 1.25 *3.00*
80 A8 1sh blk & red ('26) 8.50 *7.25*
81 A6 2sh ultra & blk ('22) 30.00 27.50
82 A6 3sh grn & blk ('24) 60.00 *82.50*
83 A8 5sh vio & ultra ('24) 45.00 *85.00*
84 A8 £1 grn & blk ('26) 215.00 *425.00*
Nos. 70-84 (15) 396.95 *723.75*
Set, ovptd/perf "SPECIMEN" 500.00

The 3p, 1sh, 5sh and £1 are on chalky paper.

Seal of Bahamas — A10

1930, Jan. 2 **Engr.** ***Perf. 12***
85 A10 1p red & black 3.50 *3.50*
86 A10 3p dp brown & blk 5.50 *19.00*
87 A10 5p dk vio & blk 5.50 *19.00*
88 A10 2sh ultra & black 22.50 *62.50*
89 A10 3sh dp green & blk 52.50 *110.00*
Nos. 85-89 (5) 89.50 *214.00*
Set, perforated "SPECIMEN" 190.00

The dates on the stamps commemorate important events in the history of the colony. The 1st British occupation was in 1629. The Bahamas were ceded to Great Britain in 1729 and a treaty of peace was signed by that country, France and Spain.

Type of 1930 Issue
Without Dates at Top

1931-46
90 A10 2sh ultra & black 15.00 9.00
a. 2sh ultra & slate purple 30.00 *37.50*
b. 2sh ind bl & slate purple 115.00 *50.00*
c. 2sh steel bl & slate pur 18.00 *3.25*
91 A10 3sh dp green & blk 10.00 7.00
a. 3sh deep grn & slate purple 37.50 35.00
b. 3sh deep grn & brownish blk 10.00 6.25
Nos. 90a, 91a perf "SPECIMEN" 92.50

Nos. 90a-91a are on thicker paper with yellowish gum, Later printings are on thinner white paper with colorless gum.

Issued: No. 90a, 91a, 7/14/31; No. 90b, 9/42; nos. 90, 91b, 4/13/43; No. 90c 6/44; No. 91, 1946.

For overprints see Nos. 126-127.

Common Design Types pictured following the introduction.

Silver Jubilee Issue
Common Design Type

1935, May 6 ***Perf. 13½x14***
92 CD301 1½p car & blue 1.25 *4.00*
93 CD301 2½p blue & brn 6.25 *10.00*
94 CD301 6p ol grn & lt bl 8.75 *15.00*
95 CD301 1sh brt vio & ind 8.75 *14.00*
Nos. 92-95 (4) 25.00 *43.00*
Set, never hinged 35.00
Set, perforated "SPECIMEN" 150.00

Flamingos in Flight A11

1935, May 22 ***Perf. 12½***
96 A11 8p car & ultra 7.25 4.25
Never hinged 10.00
Perforated "SPECIMEN" 62.50

Coronation Issue
Common Design Type

1937, May 12 ***Perf. 13½x14***
97 CD302 ½p dp green .25 .25
98 CD302 1½p brown .35 1.40
99 CD302 2½p brt ultra .55 1.40
Nos. 97-99 (3) 1.15 3.05
Set, never hinged 1.75
Set, perforated "SPECIMEN" 110.00

George VI — A12

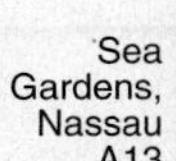

Sea Gardens, Nassau A13

Fort Charlotte A14

Flamingos in Flight A15

1938-46 **Typo.** **Wmk. 4** ***Perf. 14***
100 A12 ½p green 1.00 *1.60*
Never hinged 1.60
a. ½p bluish grn 1.50 *2.75*
Never hinged 2.25
b. ½p myrtle grn 5.50 *8.75*
Never hinged 8.75
101 A12 1p carmine 7.00 4.50
Never hinged 10.00
Complete booklet, 12 #101 in blocks of 6 and 8 #102 in folded block —
101A A12 1p pale gray ('41) .50 *.90*
Never hinged .75
b. 1p olive gray 2.75 *4.00*
Never hinged 4.00
102 A12 1½p red brown 1.25 1.60
Never hinged 1.90
a. 1½p pale red brn 5.75 *3.25*
Never hinged 8.00
103 A12 2p gray 14.00 5.75
Never hinged 21.00
103B A12 2p carmine ('41) .85 .85
Never hinged 1.25
c. "TWO PENCE" double *15,000.*
d. 2p pale rose red 2.75 *4.00*
Never hinged 4.00
104 A12 2½p ultra 2.75 *1.90*
Never hinged 4.00
104A A12 2½p lt violet ('43) 1.10 1.60
Never hinged 1.60
b. "2½ PENNY" double *3,250.* —
Never hinged *4,750.*
105 A12 3p lt violet 13.00 5.00
Never hinged 19.00
105A A12 3p ultra ('43) .50 *1.60*
Never hinged .75
b. 3p bright ultra 3.75 *6.00*
Never hinged 5.50

Engr.
Perf. 12½

106 A13 4p red org & blue .80 *1.25*
Never hinged 1.25
107 A14 6p blue & ol grn .65 *1.25*
Never hinged 1.00
108 A15 8p car & ultra 7.25 3.25
Never hinged 10.50

Typo.
Perf. 14

109 A12 10p yel org ('46) 2.25 .55
Never hinged 3.25

Ordinary Paper

110 A12 1sh blk & brt red 11.50 1.00
Never hinged 16.00
a. 1sh gray blk & car, thick chalky paper 18.00 7.50
Never hinged 30.00
c. 1sh black & car 16.00 8.75
Never hinged 27.50
d. 1sh brownish gray & scar, thin chalky paper 375.00 100.00
Never hinged 575.00
e. 1sh pale brownish gray & crim 12.50 1.90
Never hinged 17.50
112 A12 5sh pur & ultra 17.50 17.50
Never hinged 26.00
a. 5sh lilac & blue 22.00 *27.50*
Never hinged 35.00
b. 5sh lilac & blue, thick chalky paper 150.00 125.00
Never hinged 215.00
c. 5sh reddish lil & bl, thin chalky paper 1,750. 750.00
Never hinged *2,850.*
d. 5sh dull mauve & dp bl 80.00 75.00
Never hinged 125.00
e. 5sh brn pur & dp brt bl 30.00 15.00
Never hinged 45.00
113 A12 £1 bl grn & blk 45.00 *60.00*
Never hinged 67.50
a. £1 dp gray grn & blk, thick chalky paper 225.00 175.00
Never hinged 325.00
b. £1 gray grn & blk 135.00 *120.00*
Never hinged 200.00
Nos. 100-113 (17) 126.90 *110.10*
Set, never hinged 190.00

See Nos. 154-156. For overprints see Nos. 116-125, 128-129.

No. 104 Surcharged in Black

1940, Nov. 28 ***Perf. 14***
115 A12 3p on 2½p ultra 1.25 *2.75*
Never hinged 1.90

Stamps of 1931-42 Overprinted in Black

1942, Oct. 12 ***Perf. 14, 12½, 12***
116 A12 ½p green .25 .75
Never hinged .40
a. Double overprint 1,400.
Never hinged 2,000.
117 A12 1p gray .25 .75
Never hinged .40
118 A12 1½p red brn .35 .75
Never hinged .50
119 A12 2p carmine .40 .80
Never hinged .65
120 A12 2½p ultra .40 .80
Never hinged .65
121 A12 3p ultra .25 .80
Never hinged .35
122 A13 4p red org & blue .35 1.10
Never hinged .50
123 A14 6p blue & ol grn .35 2.10
Never hinged .70
124 A15 8p car & ultra 1.10 .85
Never hinged 1.90
125 A12 1sh blk & car (#110c) 6.50 11.00
Never hinged 9.50
a. On No. 110d 6.50 *5.00*
Never hinged 9.50
b. On No. 110 12.00 *11.00*
Never hinged 19.00
126 A10 2sh dk ultra & blk 6.75 *11.50*
Never hinged 10.00
a. On No. 90b 13.50 *27.50*
Never hinged 20.00
b. On No. 90c 25.00 *32.50*
Never hinged 37.50
127 A10 3sh dp grn & sl pur (#91a) 6.50 *8.00*
Never hinged 10.00
a. On No. 91b 35.00 *45.00*
Never hinged 52.50
128 A12 5sh lilac & ultra (#112a) 17.50 *16.00*
Never hinged 30.00
a. On No. 112c 40.00 *21.00*
Never hinged 60.00
129 A12 £1 grn & blk 22.50 *27.50*
Never hinged 37.50
a. On No. 113a 67.50 *110.00*
Never hinged 100.00
Nos. 116-129 (14) 63.45 *82.70*
Set, never hinged 95.00
Set, perforated "SPECIMEN" 600.00

450th anniv. of the discovery of America by Columbus.

Nos. 125, 128-129 printed on chalky and ordinary paper.

Two printings of the basic stamps were overprinted, the first with dark gum, the second with white gum.

Catalogue values for unused stamps in this section, from this point to the end of the section, are for Never Hinged items.

Peace Issue
Common Design Type
Perf. 13½x14

1946, Nov. 11 **Engr.** **Wmk. 4**
130 CD303 1½p brown .25 .70
131 CD303 3p deep blue .25 .70
Set, perforated "SPECIMEN" 95.00

Infant Welfare Clinic A16

Designs: 1p, Modern agriculture. 1½p, Sisal. 2p, Native straw work. 2½p, Modern dairying. 3p, Fishing fleet. 4p, Out island settlement. 6p, Tuna fishing. 8p, Paradise Beach. 10p, Modern hotel. 1sh, Yacht racing. 2sh, Water skiing. 3sh, Shipbuilding. 5sh, Modern transportation. 10sh, Modern salt production. £1, Parliament Building.

1948, Oct. 11 Unwmk. *Perf. 12*

132	A16	½p orange	.40	*1.60*
133	A16	1p olive green	.40	.45
134	A16	1½p olive bister	.40	*1.00*
135	A16	2p vermilion	.40	.50
136	A16	2½p red brown	.85	*1.00*
137	A16	3p brt ultra	3.25	1.10
138	A16	4p gray black	.75	.90
139	A16	6p emerald	2.75	1.00
140	A16	8p violet	1.25	.90
141	A16	10p rose car	1.25	.75
142	A16	1sh olive brn	3.00	1.25
143	A16	2sh claret	6.25	*11.00*
144	A16	3sh brt blue	12.50	*11.00*
145	A16	5sh purple	20.00	6.50
146	A16	10sh dk gray	15.00	13.00
147	A16	£1 red orange	16.50	*18.00*
		Nos. 132-147 (16)	84.95	*69.95*

300th anniv., in 1947, of the settlement of the colony.

Silver Wedding Issue
Common Design Type
Perf. 14x14½

1948, Dec. 1 Wmk. 4 Photo.
148 CD304 1½p red brown .25 .30

Engr.; Name Typo.
Perf. 11½x11
149 CD305 £1 gray green 45.00 40.00

UPU Issue
Common Design Types
Engr.; Name Typo. on #151 & 152

1949, Oct. 10 *Perf. 13½, 11x11½*

150	CD306	2½p violet	.45	*.80*
151	CD307	3p indigo	2.75	*3.75*
152	CD308	6p blue gray	.90	*3.50*
153	CD309	1sh rose car	1.50	1.50
		Nos. 150-153 (4)	5.60	9.55

George VI Type of 1938
Perf. 13½x14

1951-52 Wmk. 4 Typo.

154	A12	½p claret ('52)	1.25	*3.25*
a.		Wmk. 4a (error)	*4,750.*	
		Lightly hinged	*3,250.*	
b.		Crown missing in wmk.	*11,500.*	
		Lightly hinged	*8,250.*	
155	A12	2p green	1.60	1.00
156	A12	3p rose red ('52)	.75	*4.00*
		Nos. 154-156 (3)	3.60	*8.25*

SEMI-POSTAL STAMPS

No. 48 Overprinted in Red

1917, May 18 Wmk. 3 *Perf. 14*
B1 A6 1p car & black .50 *2.50*
Overprinted "SPECIMEN" 85.00

Type of 1911 Overprinted in Red

1919, Jan. 1
B2 A6 1p red & black .40 *3.25*
a. Double overprint *2,750.*
Overprinted "SPECIMEN" 70.00

This stamp was originally scheduled for release in 1918.

SPECIAL DELIVERY STAMPS

No. 34 Overprinted

1916 Wmk. 1 *Perf. 14*

E1	A6 5p orange & black	7.50	*47.50*
a.	Double overprint	*1,000.*	*1,500.*
b.	Inverted overprint	*1,750.*	*1,800.*
c.	Double ovpt., one invtd.	*1,550.*	*1,750.*
d.	Pair, one without overprint	*35,000.*	*50,000.*

The No. E1 overprint exists in two types. Type I (illustrated) is much scarcer. Type II shows "SPECIAL" farther right, so that the letter "I" is slightly right of the vertical line of the "E" below it.

The first printing of 600 of no. E1 was sold in Canada from May 1, 1916, and under an agreement with the Canadian Post Office were used in combination with Canadian stamps and postmarked in Canada. Values for covers showing such use (canceled before December 13, 1916): from Toronto, $750; from Montreal, $800; from Ottawa, $1,200; from Winnipeg, $2,000.

Type of Regular Issue of 1903 Overprinted

1917, July 2 Wmk. 3
E2 A6 5p orange & black .80 *11.00*
Overprinted "SPECIMEN" 82.50

No. 60 Overprinted in Red

1918
E3 A6 5p violet & black .60 *4.00*
Overprinted "SPECIMEN" 82.50

WAR TAX STAMPS

Stamps of 1912-18 Overprinted

1918, Feb. 21 Wmk. 3 *Perf. 14*

MR1	A8 ½p green	11.50	*55.00*
a.	Double overprint	—	—
b.	Inverted overprint	—	—
MR2	A8 1p car rose	1.25	*1.00*
a.	Double overprint	—	—
b.	Inverted overprint	—	—
MR3	A6 3p brown, *yel*	3.75	*3.50*
a.	Inverted overprint	*1,400.*	*1,500.*
b.	Double overprint	2,000.	*2,150.*
MR4	A8 1sh black & red	125.00	*175.00*
a.	Double overprint	—	
	Nos. MR1-MR4 (4)	141.50	*234.50*

Same Overprint on No. 48a

1918, July 10

MR5	A6 1p car & black	4.50	*6.50*
a.	Double overprint	2,150.	*2,400.*
b.	Double ovpt., one invtd.	1,100.	—
c.	Inverted overprint	*1,900.*	*2,000.*

Nos. 49-50, 54 Overprinted in Black or Red

MR6	A8 ½p green	2.25	2.25
MR7	A8 1p car rose	2.25	.45
a.	Watermarked sideways	600.00	
MR8	A8 1sh black & red (R)	11.50	3.50
	Nos. MR6-MR8 (3)	16.00	6.20
	Set, overprinted "SPECIMEN"	175.00	

Nos. 58-59 Overprinted

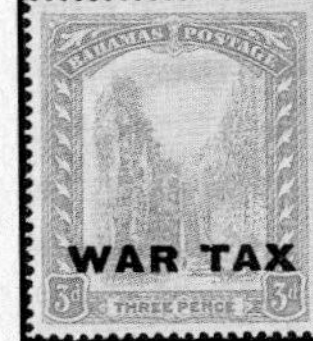

1918-19

MR9	A6 3p brown, *yel*	.90	*3.25*
MR10	A6 3p brown & blk ('19)	.90	*3.75*
	Set, overprinted "SPECIMEN"	95.00	

Nos. 49-50, 54 Overprinted in Red or Black

1919, July 14

MR11	A8 ½p green (R)	.40	*1.60*
MR12	A8 1p car rose	1.90	*1.90*
MR13	A8 1sh blk & red (R)	27.50	*55.00*
	Nos. MR11-MR13 (3)	29.80	*58.50*

No. 59 Overprinted

MR14 A6 3p brn & blk 1.00 *10.00*
Nos. MR11-MR14, overprinted "SPECIMEN" 175.00

BAHRAIN

bä-'rān

LOCATION — An archipelago in the Persian Gulf, including the islands of Bahrain, Muharraq, Sitra, Nebi Saleh, Kasasifeh and Arad.
GOVT. — British-protected territory
AREA — 255 sq. mi.
POP. — 350,798 (1981)
CAPITAL — Manama

12 Pies = 1 Anna
16 Annas = 1 Rupee

Catalogue values for unused stamps in this country are for Never Hinged items, beginning with Scott 62 in the regular postage section.

Indian Postal Administration

Stamps of India, 1926-32, Overprinted in Black — a

Wmk. Multiple Stars (196)

1933, Aug. 10 *Perf. 14*

1	A46	3p gray	4.50	.90
		Never hinged	13.00	
2	A47	½a green	12.00	5.25
		Never hinged	21.00	
3	A68	9p dark green	5.00	5.50
		Never hinged	14.00	
4	A48	1a dark brown	11.00	3.75
		Never hinged	19.00	
5	A69	1a3p violet	18.00	5.00
		Never hinged	21.00	
6	A60	2a vermilion	12.00	22.50
		Never hinged	26.00	
7	A51	3a blue	22.50	*80.00*
		Never hinged	50.00	
8	A70	3a6p deep blue	7.00	.75
		Never hinged	12.00	
9	A61	4a olive green	20.00	*82.50*
		Never hinged	47.50	
10	A54	8a red violet	10.00	.55
		Never hinged	18.00	
11	A55	12a claret	9.00	3.25
		Never hinged	22.00	

Overprinted in Black — b

12	A56	1r green & brown	20.00	17.00
		Never hinged	45.00	
13	A56	2r brn org & car rose	37.50	50.00
		Never hinged	70.00	
14	A56	5r dk violet & ultra	300.00	210.00
		Never hinged	450.00	
		Nos. 1-14 (14)	488.50	486.95

Stamps of India, 1926-32, Overprinted Type "a" in Black

1934

15	A72	1a dark brown	15.00	.65
		Never hinged	26.00	
a.		Complete booklet, containing 16 #15, wmk inverted, in four blocks of 4	*1,500.*	
16	A51	3a carmine rose	8.50	.80
		Never hinged	15.00	
17	A52	4a olive green	9.75	.75
		Never hinged	18.00	
		Nos. 15-17 (3)	33.25	2.20

The cover of No. 15a is red and black on tan, with Mysore Sandal Soup advertisement on front.

India Nos. 138, 111, 111a Overprinted Type "a" in Black

1935-37 *Perf. 13½x14, 14*

18	A71	½a green	10.00	2.25
19	A49	2a vermilion	65.00	10.00
a.		Small die ('37)	100.00	.30

India Stamps of 1937 Overprinted Type "a" in Black

1938-41 Wmk. 196 *Perf. 13½x14*

20	A80	3p slate	12.00	9.00
		Never hinged	19.00	
21	A80	½a brown	7.00	.35
		Never hinged	9.25	
22	A80	9p green	9.00	*15.00*
		Never hinged	11.50	
23	A80	1a carmine	8.00	.35
		Never hinged	11.00	
24	A81	2a scarlet	4.00	6.50
		Never hinged	5.00	
26	A81	3a yel grn ('41)	8.00	13.00
		Never hinged	10.00	
27	A81	3a6p ultra	4.00	*11.00*
		Never hinged	6.00	
28	A81	4a dk brn ('41)	125.00	95.00
		Never hinged	190.00	
30	A81	8a bl vio ('40)	180.00	45.00
		Never hinged	200.00	
31	A81	12a car lake ('40)	105.00	60.00
		Never hinged	140.00	

Overprinted Type "b" in Black

32	A82	1r brn & slate	4.75	3.00
		Never hinged	5.75	
33	A82	2r dk brn & dk vio	12.00	12.00
		Never hinged	16.50	
34	A82	5r dp ultra & dk grn	10.00	*17.50*
		Never hinged	19.00	
35	A82	10r rose car & dk vio ('41)	60.00	65.00
		Never hinged	80.00	
36	A82	15r dk grn & dk brn ('41)	60.00	97.50
		Never hinged	175.00	
37	A82	25r dk vio & bl vio ('41)	95.00	*120.00*
		Never hinged	125.00	
		Nos. 20-37 (16)	703.75	570.20
		Set, never hinged	1,000.	

India Stamps of 1941-43 Overprinted Type "a" in Black

1942-44 Wmk. 196 *Perf. 13½x14*

38 A83 3p slate 2.00 2.50
Never hinged 3.50
39 A83 ½a rose vio ('44) 3.00 *4.50*
Never hinged 6.00
40 A83 9p lt green ('43) 11.00 *24.00*
Never hinged 17.50
41 A83 1a car rose ('44) 5.00 1.00
Never hinged 8.50
42 A84 1a3p bister ('43) 6.50 *22.50*
Never hinged 11.00
43 A84 1½a dk pur ('43) 4.25 *8.50*
Never hinged 8.50
45 A84 2a scarlet ('43) 4.25 2.00
Never hinged 8.25
46 A84 3a violet ('43) 14.00 8.00
Never hinged 24.00
47 A84 3½a ultra 4.50 *27.50*
Never hinged 6.75
48 A85 4a chocolate 3.00 2.50
Never hinged 5.00
49 A85 6a peacock blue 14.00 *13.00*
Never hinged 21.00
50 A85 8a blue vio ('43) 7.00 4.50
Never hinged 7.50
51 A85 12a car lake 10.00 6.50
Never hinged 12.00
Nos. 38-51 (13) 88.50 *127.00*
Set, never hinged 135.00

British Postal Administration

See Oman (Muscat) for similar stamps with surcharge of new value only.

Great Britain Nos. 258 to 263, 243 and 248 Surcharged in Black — c

1948-49 Wmk. 251 *Perf. 14½x14*

52 A101 ½a on ½p green .50 *1.75*
Never hinged .75
53 A101 1a on 1p vermilion .50 *3.50*
Never hinged .75
54 A101 1½a on 1½p lt red brn .50 *4.75*
Never hinged .75
55 A101 2a on 2p lt orange .50 .30
Never hinged .75
56 A101 2½a on 2½p ultra .75 *7.00*
Never hinged 1.10
57 A101 3a on 3p violet .50 .30
Never hinged .75
58 A102 6a on 6p rose lilac .50 .30
Never hinged .75
59 A103 1r on 1sh brown 1.25 .35
Never hinged 1.75

Great Britain Nos. 249A, 250 and 251A Surcharged in Black

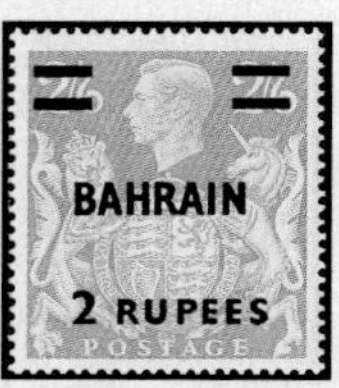

Wmk. 259 *Perf. 14*

60 A104 2r on 2sh6p yel grn 4.50 *8.00*
Never hinged 7.50
61 A104 5r on 5sh dull red 4.75 *8.50*
Never hinged 7.50
61A A105 10r on 10sh ultra 65.00 *70.00*
Never hinged 95.00
Nos. 52-61A (11) 79.25 *104.75*
Set, never hinged 115.00

Surcharge bars at bottom on No. 61A.
Issued: 10r, 7/4/49; others, 4/1/48.

Catalogue values for unused stamps in this section, from this point to the end of the section, are for Never Hinged items.

Silver Wedding Issue

Great Britain Nos. 267 and 268 Surcharged in Black

Perf. 14½x14, 14x14½

1948, Apr. 26 Wmk. 251

62 A109 2½a on 2½p .95 *2.50*
Never hinged 1.45
63 A110 15r on £1 37.50 *70.00*
Never hinged 60.00

Three bars obliterate the original denomination on No. 63.

Olympic Issue

1948, July 29 *Perf. 14½x14*

64 A113 2½a on 2½p brt ultra 1.40 *4.75*
Never hinged 2.25
a. Double surcharge 3,250. *4,000.*
65 A114 3a on 3p dp vio 1.10 *4.25*
Never hinged 1.75
66 A115 6a on 6p red vio 1.75 *4.25*
Never hinged 2.75
67 A116 1r on 1sh dk brn 2.75 *4.25*
Never hinged 4.25
Nos. 64-67 (4) 7.00 *17.50*

A square of dots obliterates the original denomination on No. 67.

UPU Issue

Great Britain No. 276 Srchd. in Black

Great Britain Nos. 277-279 Srchd. in Black

1949, Oct. 10 Photo. *Perf. 14½x14*

68 A117 2½a on 2½p brt ultra .90 *3.50*
Never hinged 1.35
69 A118 3a on 3p brt vio 1.10 *5.25*
Never hinged 1.60
70 A119 6a on 6p red vio 1.00 *4.25*
Never hinged 1.50
71 A120 1r on 1sh brown 2.00 *3.75*
Never hinged 3.00
Nos. 68-71 (4) 5.00 *16.75*

Great Britain Nos. 280-285 Surcharged Type "c" in Black

1950-51 Wmk. 251

72 A101 ½a on ½p lt org 3.00 3.00
Never hinged 4.50
73 A101 1a on 1p ultra 3.50 .35
Never hinged 5.25
74 A101 1½a on 1½p green 3.50 *17.50*
Never hinged 5.25
75 A101 2a on 2p lt red brn 2.00 .35
Never hinged 3.00
76 A101 2½a on 2½p ver 3.75 *16.00*
Never hinged 5.75
77 A102 4a on 4p ultra 3.75 1.90
Never hinged 5.75

Great Britain Nos. 286-288 Surcharged in Black

Type I

Three types of surcharge on No. 78: Type I, "2" level with "RUPEES;" Type II, "2" raised higher than "RUPEES," 15mm between "BAHRAIN" and "2 RUPEES;" Type III, as type II, but 16mm between "BAHRAIN" and "2 RUPEES."

Perf. 11x12
Wmk. 259

78 A121 2r on 2sh6p green, type I ('51) 40.00 15.00
Never hinged 52.50
a. 2r on 2sh6p, type II ('53) 140.00 55.00
b. 2r on 2sh6p, type III ('55) 1,350. 140.00
79 A121 5r on 5sh dl red 17.50 6.50
Never hinged 27.00
80 A122 10r on 10sh ultra 40.00 10.50
Never hinged 60.00
Nos. 72-80 (9) 117.00 *71.10*

Longer bars, at lower right, on No. 80.
Issued: 4a, Nov. 2, 1950; others, May 3, 1951.

Great Britain 1952-54 Stamps Surcharged in Black or Dark Blue

1952-54 Wmk. 298 *Perf. 14½x14*

81 A126 ½a on ½p red org ('53) .45 .25
Never hinged .65
a. "½" omitted 400.00 *375.00*
Never hinged 600.00
82 A126 1a on 1p ultra .45 .25
Never hinged .65
83 A126 1½a on 1½p grn .45 .25
Never hinged .65
84 A126 2a on 2p red brn .45 .25
Never hinged .65
85 A127 2½a on 2½p scar .90 *1.75*
Never hinged 1.35
86 A127 3a on 3p dk pur (Dk Bl) 1.60 .25
Never hinged 2.40
87 A128 4a on 4p ultra 8.25 .50
Never hinged 12.50
88 A129 6a on 6p lil rose 6.00 .45
Never hinged 9.00
89 A132 12a on 1sh3p dk grn 6.00 .75
Never hinged 9.00
90 A131 1r on 1sh6p dk bl 6.00 1.00
Never hinged 9.00
Nos. 81-90 (10) 30.55 5.70

Issued: Nos. 83, 85, 12/5; Nos. 81-82, 84, 8/31/53; Nos. 87, 89-90, 11/2/53; Nos. 86, 88, 1/18/54.

BANGKOK

'baŋ¸käk

LOCATION — Capital of Siam (Thailand).

Stamps were issued by Great Britain under rights obtained in the treaty of 1855. These were in use until July 1, 1885, when the stamps of Siam were designated as the only official postage stamps to be used in the kingdom.

100 Cents = 1 Dollar

STAMPS OF STRAITS SETTLEMENTS USED IN BANGKOK

Oval postmark: "BRITISH CONSULATE BANGKOK" with Royal Arms in center

1877-82

A1 2c bister brown (#10) 475.00
A2 4c rose (#11) 500.00
A3 6c violet (#12) 525.00
A4 8c orange yellow (#13) 475.00
A5 10c on 30c claret (#22) 1,300.
A6 10c on 30c claret (#23) 1,300.
A8 12c blue (#14) 725.00

Excellent counterfeits of Nos. 1-22 are plentiful.

Stamps of Straits Settlements Overprinted in Black

1882 Wmk. 1 *Perf. 14*

1 A2 2c brown *4,500.* 1,950.
2 A2 4c rose *4,250.* 1,650.
b. Double overprint *9,750.*
3 A6 5c brown violet *475.* 550.
4 A2 6c violet *325.* 150.
5 A3 8c yel orange *3,750.* 290.
6 A7 10c slate *700.* 200.
7 A3 12c blue *1,500.* 600.
8 A3 24c green *900.* 190.
9 A4 30c claret *57,500.* 39,000.
10 A5 96c olive gray *9,750.* 4,000.

See note after No. 20.

1882-83 Wmk. 2

11 A2 2c brown *750.00* *450.00*
12 A2 2c rose ('83) *75.00* *57.50*
a. Inverted overprint *19,000.* *14,000.*
b. Double overprint *3,500.* *3,500.*
c. Triple overprint *13,000.*
13 A2 4c rose *900.00* *400.00*
14 A2 4c brown ('83) *100.00* *90.00*
a. Double overprint *4,500.*
15 A6 5c ultra ('83) *375.00* *210.00*
16 A2 6c violet ('83) *325.00* *140.00*
a. Double overprint *9,000.*
17 A3 8c yel orange *250.00* *82.50*
a. Inverted overprint *30,000.* *16,000.*
18 A7 10c slate *225.00* *110.00*
19 A3 12c violet brn ('83) *400.00* *190.00*
20 A3 24c green *8,000.* *3,750.*

Double overprints must have two clear impressions. Partial double overprints exist on a number of values of these issues. They sell for a modest premium over catalogue value depending on how much of the impression is present.

1883 Wmk. 1

21 A5 2c on 32c pale red *3,500.* *3,500.*

On Straits Settlements No. 9

1885 Wmk. 38

22 A7 32c on 2a yel (B+B) *45,000.* —

BARBADOS

bär-ˈbā-ˌdōs

LOCATION — A West Indies island east of the Windwards
GOVT. — British Colony
AREA — 166 sq. mi.
POP. — 270,500 (1981)
CAPITAL — Bridgetown

4 Farthings = 1 Penny
12 Pence = 1 Shilling
20 Shillings = 1 Pound
100 Cents = 1 Dollar (1950)

Catalogue values for unused stamps in this country are for Never Hinged items, beginning with Scott 207 in the regular postage section, and Scott J1 in the postage due section.

Watermarks

Wmk. 5 — Small Star

Wmk. 6 — Large Star

PRE-STAMP POSTAL MARKINGS

Crowned Circle handstamp type I is pictured in the Crowned Circle Handstamps and Great Britain Used Abroad section.

1849

A1	I	"Barbados" crowned circle handstamp in red, on cover	525.00
a.		Used with 1p stamp paying local postage, #A1 the overseas postage	*4,000.*

This handstamp was used 2/17/93 to 3/15/93 as a ½p stamp, 1/23/96 to 5/4/96 as a ¼p stamp. Value $105.

Values for unused stamps are for examples with original gum as defined in the catalogue introduction. Very fine examples of Nos. 10-42a, 44-59a will have perforations touching the design on at least one side due to the narrow spacing of the stamps on the plates and imperfect perforation methods. Stamps with perfs clear of the design on all four sides are extremely scarce and will command higher prices.

Britannia — A1

1852-55 Unwmk. Engr. *Imperf.*
Blued Paper

No.	Type	Description	Unused	Used
1	A1	(½p) deep green	165.00	*375.00*
a.		(½p) yellow green	*9,000.*	800.00
2	A1	(1p) dark blue	45.00	*80.00*
		On cover		300.00
		Pair, on cover		500.00
a.		(1p) blue	65.00	*225.00*
		On cover		400.00
3	A1	(2p) slate blue	30.00	
a.		(2p) grayish slate	325.00	*1,400.*
b.		As "a," vert. half used as 1p on cover		*9,350.*
c.		(2p) deep slate	275.00	
4	A1	(4p) brn red ('55)	130.00	*325.00*
		Nos. 1-4 (4)	370.00	

No. 3, 3c were not placed in use. No. 3c differs from No. 3a in the thickness and color of the gum which is yellowish and blotchy, as well as in shade. Beware of color changelings of Nos. 2-3 that may resemble No. 3a. Certificates of authenticity are required for Nos. 3a and 3b.

Use of No. 3b was authorized from 8/4-9/21/1854.

1855-58 White Paper

No.	Type	Description	Unused	Used
5	A1	(½p) dp grn ('58)	210.00	*230.00*
a.		(½p) yellow green ('57)	600.00	125.00
6	A1	(1p) blue	100.00	70.00
a.		(1p) pale blue	185.00	*80.00*

It is believed that the (4p) brownish red on white paper exists only as No. 17b.

Britannia — A2

1859

No.	Type	Description	Unused	Used
8	A2	6p rose red	850.00	140.00
a.		6p deep rose red	850.00	210.00
9	A2	1sh black	260.00	85.00
a.		1sh brownish black	290.00	125.00
		Pin-perf. 14		
10	A1	(½p) pale yel grn	3,000.	500.00
11	A1	(1p) blue	2,500.	175.00
a.		1p deep blue	2,650.	195.00
		Pin-perf. 12½		
12	A1	(½p) pale yel grn	*10,000.*	800.00
12A	A1	(1p) blue	—	1,750.
		Pin-perf. 14x12½		
12B	A1	(½p) pale yel grn	—	*8,500.*

1861 *Clean-Cut Perf. 14 to 16*

No.	Type	Description	Unused	Used
13	A1	(½p) dark blue grn	200.00	23.00
14	A1	(1p) pale blue	825.00	92.50
a.		(1p) blue	925.00	100.00
b.		Half used as ½p on cover		—
		Rough Perf. 14 to 16		
15	A1	(½p) green	35.00	47.50
a.		(½p) blue green	62.50	*85.00*
b.		Imperf., pair	825.00	
c.		(½p) deep green	37.50	*47.50*
16	A1	(1p) blue	87.50	4.25
a.		Diagonal half used as ½p on cover		—
b.		Imperf., pair	875.00	*650.00*
c.		(1p) deep blue	82.50	4.50
17	A1	(4p) rose red	175.00	77.50
a.		(4p) brown red	210.00	87.50
b.		As "a," imperf., pair	1,750.	
c.		(4p) rose red, imperf., pair	1,200.	
d.		(4p) lake rose	190.00	100.00
e.		As "d," imperf pair	1,800.	
18	A1	(4p) vermilion	350.00	120.00
a.		Imperf., pair	1,650.	
19	A2	6p rose red	400.00	26.00
a.		6p orange red ('64)	180.00	32.50
20	A2	6p orange ver	175.00	37.50
a.		6p vermilion	200.00	32.00
b.		Imperf., pair	825.00	*1,100.*
c.		6p orange ('70)	200.00	52.50
21	A2	1sh brnsh blk	82.50	12.00
a.		1sh black	75.00	10.50
b.		Horiz. pair, imperf. btwn.	10,000.	
c.		1sh blue (error)	*20,000.*	

No. 21c was never placed in use. All examples are pen-marked (some have been removed) and have clipped perfs on one or more sides.

Use of No. 14b, 16a was authorized from 4/63-11/66. Only two full covers are known with bisected 1p stamps. The bisected stamps (Nos. 14b, 16a, 33a, 51b) are typically found on fragments or partial covers.

Perf. 11 to 13

No.	Type	Description	Unused	Used
22	A1	(½p) deep green	*16,500.*	
23	A1	(1p) blue	*2,500.*	

Nos. 22 and 23 were never placed in use.

1870 Wmk. 6 *Rough Perf. 14 to 16*

No.	Type	Description	Unused	Used
24	A1	(½p) green	180.00	11.00
a.		Imperf., pair (#24)	1,400.	
b.		(½p) yellow green	240.00	55.00
25	A1	(1p) blue	2,750.	77.50
a.		Imperf., pair	*3,000.*	
b.		1p blue, *blue*	*4,250.*	135.00
26	A1	(4p) dull red	1,750.	130.00
27	A2	6p vermilion	1,100.	100.00
28	A2	1sh black	500.00	21.00

1871 Wmk. 5

No.	Type	Description	Unused	Used
29	A1	(1p) blue	200.00	4.50
30	A1	(4p) rose red	1,425.	77.50
31	A2	6p vermilion	775.00	28.00
32	A2	1sh black	275.00	18.00

1872 *Clean-Cut Perf. 14½ to 16*

No.	Type	Description	Unused	Used
33	A1	(1p) blue	350.00	3.25
a.		Diagonal half used as ½p on cover		—
34	A2	6p vermilion	1,050.	92.50
35	A2	1sh black	210.00	19.00
		Perf. 11 to 13x14½ to 16		
36	A1	(½p) blue green	400.00	70.00
37	A1	(4p) vermilion	875.00	125.00

1873 *Perf. 14*

No.	Type	Description	Unused	Used
38	A2	3p claret	375.00	140.00
		Wmk. 6		
		Clean-Cut Perf. 14½ to 16		
39	A1	(½p) blue green	500.00	30.00
40	A1	(4p) rose red	1,550.	275.00
41	A2	6p vermilion	1,000.	105.00
a.		Imperf., pair	110.00	*1,750.*
b.		Horiz. pair, imperf. btwn.	11,000.	
42	A2	1sh black	170.00	24.00
a.		Horiz. pair, imperf. btwn.	10,000.	

No. 41 perf 11 to 12 was prepared, but not issued. Value, $10,000.

Britannia — A3

1873 Wmk. 5 *Perf. 15½x15*

No.	Type	Description	Unused	Used
43	A3	5sh dull rose	1,200.	375.00
		Handstamped "SPECIMEN"	375.00	

For surcharged bisects see Nos. 57-59.

1874 Wmk. 6 *Perf. 14*

No.	Type	Description	Unused	Used
44	A2	½p blue green	65.00	17.50
45	A2	1p blue	150.00	5.50
		Clean-Cut Perf. 14½ to 16		
45A	A2	1p blue		*22,000.*

1875 Wmk. 1 *Perf. 12½*

No.	Type	Description	Unused	Used
46	A2	½p yellow green	100.00	9.25
47	A2	4p scarlet	375.00	29.00
48	A2	6p orange	750.00	80.00
a.		6p bright yellow	1,150.	105.00
49	A2	1sh purple	575.00	5.00
		Nos. 46-49 (4)	1,800.	123.25

1875-78 *Perf. 14*

No.	Type	Description	Unused	Used
50	A2	½p yel grn ('76)	26.00	1.00
51	A2	1p ultramarine	150.00	2.25
a.		Half used as ½p on cover		*1,350.*
b.		1p gray blue	150.00	1.60
c.		Watermarked sideways		*1,000.*
52	A2	3p violet ('78)	185.00	16.50
53	A2	4p rose red	160.00	15.00
a.		4p scarlet	250.00	5.00
b.		As "a," perf. 14x12½	*9,000.*	—
54	A2	4p lake	575.00	4.50
55	A2	6p chrome yel	160.00	2.40
a.		6p yellow, wmkd. sideways	400.00	15.00
56	A2	1sh purple ('76)	185.00	9.25
a.		1sh violet	*7,750.*	45.00
b.		1sh dull mauve	575.00	6.00
c.		Half used as 6p on cover		—

Nos. 48, 49, 55, 56 have the watermark sideways.

No. 53b was never placed in use.

A mint example of the one shilling aniline violet (Scott No. 56a) sold for the equivalent of U.S. $15,340 in a Singapore auction in 2003.

A4

A5

Large Surcharge, ("1" 7mm High, "D" 2¾mm High)

1878 Wmk. 5 *Perf. 15½x15*
Slanting Serif

No.	Type	Description	Unused	Used
57	A4	1p on half of 5sh	*6,250.*	850.00
a.		Unsevered pair	*28,500.*	*2,750.*
b.		Unsevered horiz. pair, #57 + 58		*5,500.*
d.		Unsevered horiz. pair, #57 + 58, imperf. between		*44,000.*
e.		Unsevered horiz. pair, #57 + 59	46,000.	9,350.
f.		Comma instead of period after "D"	18,750.	*2,250.*
g.		No period after "D"	—	*1,250.*
		Straight Serif		
58	A4	1p on half of 5sh	8,250.	1,050.
a.		Unsevered pair		4,750.

Small Surcharge, ("1" 6mm, "D" 2½mm High)

No.	Type	Description	Unused	Used
59	A5	1p on half of 5sh	*10,000.*	*1,175.*
a.		Unsevered pair	*42,000.*	*5,500.*

On Nos. 57, 58 and 59 the surcharge is found reading upwards or downwards.

The perforation, which divides the stamp into halves, measures 11½ to 13.

The old denomination has been cut off the bottom of the stamps.

Queen Victoria — A6

1882-85 Typo. Wmk. 2 *Perf. 14*

No.	Type	Description	Unused	Used
60	A6	½p green	35.00	2.25
a.		½p dull green	30.00	2.25
61	A6	1p carmine rose	60.00	1.35
a.		1p rose	90.00	2.75
b.		Half used as ½p on cover		1,800.
62	A6	2½p dull blue	145.00	1.70
a.		2½p ultramarine	125.00	1.70
63	A6	3p magenta	8.50	*30.00*
a.		3p lilac	125.00	50.00
64	A6	4p slate	375.00	4.75
65	A6	4p brown ('85)	16.00	2.25
a.		4p pale brown ('85)	31.50	5.25
66	A6	6p olive gray	85.00	52.50
67	A6	1sh orange brown	32.50	24.00
68	A6	5sh bister	180.00	*215.00*
		Nos. 60-68 (9)	937.00	*333.80*

No. 65 Surcharged in Black

1892

69 A6 ½p on 4p brown 2.75 *6.50*
a. Without hyphen 21.00 *40.00*
b. Double surcharge, one albino —
c. Double surch., red & black 950.00 *1,275.*
d. As "c," without hyphen 3,750. *4,250.*
e. Surcharged "PENNY HALF" 400.00 240.00

A8

1892-1903 Wmk. 2

70 A8 1f sl & car ('96) 2.75 .25
71 A8 ½p green 2.75 .25
72 A8 1p carmine rose 5.50 .25
73 A8 2p sl & org ('99) 12.00 1.25
74 A8 2½p ultramarine 20.00 .25
75 A8 5p olive brn 8.00 5.25
76 A8 6p vio & car 18.50 3.00
77 A8 8p org & ultra 4.50 *32.50*
78 A8 10p bl grn & car 11.00 10.00
79 A8 2sh6p slate & org 55.00 70.00
80 A8 2sh6p pur & grn ('03) 160.00 *325.00*
Nos. 70-80 (11) 300.00 *448.00*
Set, ovptd. "SPECIMEN" 300.00

See Nos. 90-101. For surcharge see No B1.

Victoria Jubilee Issue

Badge of Colony — A9

1897 Wmk. 1

81 A9 1f gray & car 10.00 .75
82 A9 ½p gray green 10.00 .75
83 A9 1p carmine rose 12.00 .75
84 A9 2½p ultra 16.00 1.00
85 A9 5p dk olive brn 37.50 21.50
86 A9 6p vio & car 47.50 27.50
87 A9 8p org & ultra 24.00 *28.50*
88 A9 10p bl grn & car 75.00 *62.50*
89 A9 2sh6p slate & org 110.00 65.00
Nos. 81-89 (9) 342.00 *208.25*
Set, ovptd. "SPECIMEN" 240.00

Bluish Paper

81a A9 1f gray & car 32.50 *35.00*
82a A9 ½p gray green 32.50 *35.00*
83a A9 1p carmine rose 44.00 *47.50*
84a A9 2½p ultra 45.00 *52.50*
85a A9 5p dk olive brn 260.00 *300.00*
86a A9 6p vio & car 150.00 165.00
87a A9 8p org & ultra 160.00 *175.00*
88a A9 10p bl grn & car 215.00 *275.00*
89a A9 2sh6p slate & org 150.00 *150.00*
Nos. 81a-89a (9) 1,089. *1,235.*

Badge Type of 1892-1903

1904-10 Wmk. 3

90 A8 1f gray & car 14.00 3.25
91 A8 1f brown ('09) 11.00 .35
92 A8 ½p green 27.50 .25
a. ½p blue green ('09) 27.50 1.75
93 A8 1p carmine rose 27.50 .25
94 A8 1p carmine ('09) 27.50 .25
95 A8 2p gray ('09) 11.00 *22.50*
96 A8 2½p ultramarine 28.50 .35
a. 2½p bright blue ('10) 60.00 11.00
97 A8 6p vio & car 32.50 *32.50*
98 A8 6p dl vio & vio ('10) 22.50 *35.00*
99 A8 8p org & ultra 70.00 *135.00*
100 A8 1sh blk, *grn* ('10) 18.00 *20.00*
101 A8 2sh6p pur & green 70.00 *160.00*
Nos. 90-101 (12) 360.00 *409.70*

Nelson Centenary Issue

Lord Nelson Monument — A10

1906 Engr. Wmk. 1

102 A10 1f gray & black 18.00 2.50
103 A10 ½p green & black 12.00 .40
104 A10 1p car & black 15.00 .25
105 A10 2p org & black 3.00 *5.50*
106 A10 2½p ultra & black 4.50 1.50
107 A10 6p lilac & black 22.50 *30.00*
108 A10 1sh rose & black 26.00 *62.50*
Nos. 102-108 (7) 101.00 *102.65*

See Nos. 110-112.

The "Olive Blossom" A11

1906, Aug. 15 Wmk. 3

109 A11 1p blk, green & blue 18.00 .30

Tercentenary of the 1st British landing.

Nelson Type of 1906

1907, July 6 Wmk. 3

110 A10 1f gray & black 6.25 *10.00*
111 A10 2p org & black 32.50 *47.50*
112 A10 2½p ultra & black 10.00 *50.00*
a. 2½p indigo & black 825.00 *1,000.*
Nos. 110-112 (3) 48.75 *107.50*

A12

A13

King George V — A14

1912 Typo.

116 A12 ¼p brown 2.00 1.90
117 A12 ½p green 4.75 .25
a. Booklet pane of 6
118 A12 1p carmine 12.00 .25
a. 1p scarlet 45.00 4.25
b. Booklet pane of 6
119 A12 2p gray 7.00 *22.50*
120 A12 2½p ultramarine 1.90 .75
121 A13 3p violet, *yel* 2.25 *17.50*
122 A13 4p blk & scar, *yel* 4.50 *25.00*
123 A13 6p vio & red vio 15.00 15.00
124 A14 1sh black, *green* 14.00 *25.00*
125 A14 2sh vio & ultra, *bl* 65.00 *70.00*
126 A14 3sh grn & violet 115.00 *130.00*
Nos. 116-126 (11) 243.40 *308.15*

Seal of the Colony — A15

1916-18 Engr.

127 A15 ¼p brown .90 .50
128 A15 ½p green 3.50 .25
129 A15 1p red 3.00 .25
130 A15 2p gray 13.00 *37.50*
131 A15 2½p ultramarine 6.50 3.75
132 A15 3p violet, *yel* 10.00 *15.00*
a. 3p deep purple, *yel*, thick paper 45.00 65.00
133 A15 4p red, *yel* 1.50 *17.50*
134 A15 4p red & black ('18) 1.75 *4.50*
135 A15 6p claret 11.00 8.00
136 A15 1sh black, *green* 13.00 *13.50*
137 A15 2sh violet, *blue* 20.00 9.25
138 A15 3sh dark violet 75.00 *180.00*
139 A15 3sh dk vio & grn ('18) 30.00 *115.00*
a. 3sh bright violet & green ('18) 300.00 *450.00*
Nos. 127-139 (13) 189.15 *405.00*

Nos. 134 and 139 are from a re-engraved die. The central medallion is not surrounded by a line and there are various other small alterations.

Victory Issue

Victory

A16 A17

1920, Sept. 9 Wmk. 3

140 A16 ¼p bister & black .35 .85
141 A16 ½p yel green & blk 2.25 .25
a. Booklet pane of 2
142 A16 1p org red & blk 5.00 .25
a. Booklet pane of 2
143 A16 2p gray & black 3.25 *17.00*
144 A16 2½p ultra & dk bl 3.50 *28.50*
145 A16 3p red lilac & blk 3.75 *8.00*
146 A16 4p gray grn & blk 4.00 *8.75*
147 A16 6p orange & blk 5.50 *24.00*
148 A17 1sh yel green & blk 20.00 *55.00*
149 A17 2sh brown & blk 52.50 *80.00*
150 A17 3sh orange & blk 57.50 *100.00*
Set, ovptd. "SPECIMEN" 300.00

1921, Aug. 22 Wmk. 4

151 A16 1p orange red & blk 21.00 .35
Nos. 140-151 (12) 178.60 *322.95*

A18

1921-24 Wmk. 4

152 A18 ¼p brown .30 .25
Never hinged .50
153 A18 ½p green 1.90 1.00
Never hinged 3.00
154 A18 1p carmine 1.00 .25
Never hinged 1.75
155 A18 2p gray 2.00 .25
Never hinged 3.50
156 A18 2½p ultramarine 1.90 *10.00*
Never hinged 3.00
158 A18 6p claret 4.25 *7.50*
Never hinged 7.00
159 A18 1sh blk, *emer* ('24) 60.00 *160.00*
Never hinged 100.00
160 A18 2sh dk vio, *blue* 12.50 *24.00*
Never hinged 20.00
161 A18 3sh dark violet 25.00 *90.00*
Never hinged 37.50

Wmk. 3

162 A18 3p violet, *yel* 2.50 *10.00*
Never hinged 4.00
163 A18 4p red, *yel* 2.25 *25.00*
Never hinged 3.50
164 A18 1sh black, *green* 7.00 *24.00*
Never hinged 11.00
Nos. 152-164 (12) 120.60 *352.25*
Set, ovptd. "SPECIMEN" 215.00

A19

1925-35 Wmk. 4 *Perf. 14*

165 A19 ¼p brown .30 .25
Never hinged .50
166 A19 ½p green .65 .25
Never hinged 1.00
a. Perf. 13½x12½ ('32) 9.50 .25
Never hinged 18.00
b. Booklet pane of 10
167 A19 1p carmine .65 .25
Never hinged 1.00
a. Perf. 13½x12½ ('32) 11.00 .60
Never hinged 19.00
b. Booklet pane of 10
168 A19 1½p org, perf. 13½x12½ ('32) 7.00 1.25
Never hinged 10.00
a. Booklet pane of 6
b. Perf. 14 17.50 4.00
Never hinged 27.50
169 A19 2p gray .80 *4.00*
Never hinged 1.20
170 A19 2½p ultramarine .60 *1.00*
Never hinged 1.00
a. Perf. 13½x12½ ('32) 19.00 8.50
Never hinged 30.00
171 A19 3p vio brn, *yel* 1.25 .55
Never hinged 2.00
172 A19 3p red brn, *yel* ('35) 7.50 7.50
Never hinged 12.00
173 A19 4p red, *yel* .95 *1.25*
Never hinged 1.50
174 A19 6p claret 1.25 1.10
Never hinged 2.00
175 A19 1sh blk, *emerald* 2.50 *8.50*
Never hinged 4.00
a. Perf. 13½x12½ ('32) 75.00 50.00
Never hinged 130.00
176 A19 1sh brn blk, *yel grn* ('32) 6.00 *12.50*
Never hinged 9.00
177 A19 2sh violet, *bl* 8.75 9.00
Never hinged 14.00
178 A19 2sh6p car, *blue* ('32) 32.50 *45.00*
Never hinged 52.50
179 A19 3sh dark violet 14.00 *21.00*
Never hinged 22.50
Nos. 165-179 (15) 84.70 *113.40*

Charles I and George V — A20

1927, Feb. 17 *Perf. 12½*

180 A20 1p carmine lake 1.25 .90
Never hinged 2.25
Overprinted "SPECIMEN" 5.00

Tercentenary of the settlement of Barbados.

Common Design Types pictured following the introduction.

Silver Jubilee Issue

Common Design Type

1935, May 6 *Perf. 11x12*

186 CD301 1p car & dk bl 1.90 .30
a. Damaged turret 600.00 350.00
187 CD301 1½p blk & ultra 4.75 *8.75*
a. Damaged turret 700.00
188 CD301 2½p ultra & brn 2.50 *6.25*
a. Bird by turret 325.00 400.00
189 CD301 1sh brn vio & ind 21.00 *34.00*
a. Kite and horizontal log 750.00 800.00
Nos. 186-189 (4) 30.15 49.30
Set, never hinged 45.00

Coronation Issue

Common Design Type

1937, May 14 *Perf. 13½x14*

190 CD302 1p carmine .25 .25
191 CD302 1½p brown .40 *.80*
192 CD302 2½p bright ultra .45 *.90*
Nos. 190-192 (3) 1.10 1.95
Set, never hinged 2.50
Set, perf "SPECIMEN" 95.00

A21

1938-47 *Perf. 13-14 & Compound*

193 A21 ½p green 5.00 .25
Never hinged 7.00
b. Perf. 14 55.00 1.50
Never hinged 75.00
c. Booklet pane of 10
193A A21 ½p bister ('42) .25 *.45*
Never hinged .25
194 A21 1p carmine 14.00 .25
Never hinged 20.00
b. Perf. 13½x13 195.00 5.00
Never hinged 300.00
c. Booklet pane of 10
194A A21 1p green ('42) .25 .25
Never hinged .25
d. Perf. 13½x13 3.50 1.00
Never hinged 5.25
195 A21 1½p red orange .25 *.65*
Never hinged .25
c. Perf. 14 4.75 .80
Never hinged 7.00
d. Booklet pane of 6
195A A21 2p rose lake ('41) .90 *3.75*
Never hinged 1.35

195B A21 2p brt rose red ('43) .50 *1.00*
Never hinged .85
e. Perf. 14 .50 *2.10*
Never hinged .85
196 A21 2½p ultramarine .65 *.95*
Never hinged 1.05
197 A21 3p brown .65 *3.50*
Never hinged 1.10
b. Perf. 14 .25 .75
Never hinged .35
197A A21 3p deep bl ('47) .65 *2.50*
Never hinged 1.05
198 A21 4p black .25 .25
Never hinged .35
a. Perf. 14 .65 *6.50*
Never hinged 1.05
199 A21 6p violet .65 .65
Never hinged 1.00
199A A21 8p red vio ('46) .45 *3.25*
Never hinged .60
200 A21 1sh brn olive 1.40 .25
Never hinged 2.25
a. 1sh olive green 12.50 3.00
Never hinged 17.00
201 A21 2sh6p brown vio 7.00 2.25
Never hinged 9.50
201A A21 5sh indigo ('41) 6.50 *11.00*
Never hinged 9.50
Nos. 193-201A (16) 39.35 31.20
Set, never hinged 57.50
Set, perf "SPECIMEN" 450.00

For surcharge see No. 209.

Kings Charles I, George VI Assembly Chamber and Mace A22

Perf. 13½x14

1939, June 27 Engr. Wmk. 4

202 A22 ½p deep green 2.15 2.00
Never hinged 3.25
203 A22 1p scarlet 2.15 1.35
Never hinged 3.25
204 A22 1½p deep orange 2.25 .65
Never hinged 3.50
205 A22 2½p ultramarine 3.25 *9.00*
Never hinged 5.25
206 A22 3p yellow brown 3.25 *6.00*
Never hinged 5.25
Nos. 202-206 (5) 13.05 *19.00*
Set, never hinged 21.00
Set, perf "SPECIMEN" 190.00

Tercentenary of the General Assembly.

Catalogue values for unused stamps in this section, from this point to the end of the section, are for Never Hinged items.

Peace Issue
Common Design Type

1946, Sept. 18

207 CD303 1½p deep orange .25 .55
208 CD303 3p brown .25 .55

Nos. 195e, 195B, Surcharged in Black

1947, Apr. 21 *Perf. 14*

209 A21 1p on 2p brt rose red 2.40 5.25
b. Perf. 13½x13 3.25 *6.50*
c. As "b," double surcharge 3,250.

Silver Wedding Issue
Common Design Types
Perf. 14x14½

1948, Nov. 24 Photo. Wmk. 4

210 CD304 1½p orange .35 .55

Engraved; Name Typographed
Perf. 11½x11

211 CD305 5sh dark blue 18.00 12.50

UPU Issue
Common Design Types

1949, Oct. 10 *Perf. 13½, 11x11½*

212 CD306 1½p red orange .55 2.15
213 CD307 3p indigo 2.75 7.50
214 CD308 4p gray .55 3.50
215 CD309 1sh olive .55 1.00
Nos. 212-215 (4) 4.40 14.15

Dover Fort — A23

Admiral Nelson Statue — A24

Designs: 2c, Sugar cane breeding. 3c, Public buildings. 6c, Casting net. 8c, Intercolonial schooner. 12c, Flying Fish. 24c, Old Main Guard Garrison. 48c, Cathedral, vert. 60c, Careenage. $1.20, Map, vert. $2.40, Great Seal, 1660.

Perf. 11x11½ (A23), 13x13½ (A24)

1950, May 1 Engr. Wmk. 4

216 A23 1c slate .35 *4.75*
217 A23 2c emerald .25 *3.25*
218 A23 3c slate & brown 1.25 *4.25*
219 A24 4c carmine .30 .40
220 A23 6c blue .35 *2.50*
221 A23 8c choc & blue 1.60 *4.00*
222 A23 12c olive & aqua 1.25 1.85
223 A23 24c gray & red 1.25 .55
224 A24 48c violet 11.00 9.00
225 A23 60c brn car & bl grn 14.00 13.75
226 A24 $1.20 olive & car 14.00 5.50
227 A23 $2.40 gray 27.50 45.00
Nos. 216-227 (12) 73.10 94.80

University Issue
Common Design Types

1951, Feb. 16 *Perf. 14x14½*

228 CD310 3c turq bl & choc .60 .30
229 CD311 12c ol brn & turq bl 1.25 1.25

Stamp of 1852 A25

Perf. 13½

1952, Apr. 15 Wmk. 4 Engr.

230 A25 3c slate bl & dp grn .40 .30
231 A25 4c rose pink & bl .50 *1.00*
232 A25 12c emer & slate bl .50 *1.00*
233 A25 24c gray blk & red brn 1.00 .80
Nos. 230-233 (4) 2.40 *3.10*

Centenary of Barbados postage stamps.

SEMI-POSTAL STAMP

No. 73 Surcharged in Red

Perf. 14

1907, Jan. 25 Typo. Wmk. 2

B1 A8 1p on 2p sl & org 7.00 *13.00*
a. No period after 1d 70.00 *110.00*
b. Inverted surcharge 2.00 *7.50*
c. Inverted surcharge, no period after 1d 47.50 *105.00*
d. Double surcharge 925.00 *1,000.*
e. Dbl. surch., both invtd. 925.00
f. Dbl. surch., one invtd. *1,200.*
g. Vert. pair, one normal, one surcharge double *1,200.*
h. Pair with surcharges tête-bêche 1,800.

POSTAGE DUE STAMPS

Catalogue values for unused stamps in this section are for Never Hinged items.

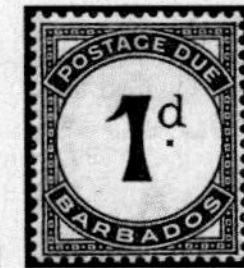

D1

1934-47 Typo. Wmk. 4 *Perf. 14*

J1 D1 ½p green ('35) 1.60 8.50
On cover *75.00*
J2 D1 1p black 2.25 1.75
On cover *75.00*
a. Half used as ½p on cover *2,500.*
J3 D1 3p dk car rose ('47) 26.00 23.00
On cover *200.00*
Nos. J1-J3 (3) 29.85 33.25
Set, perf. "SPECIMEN" 100.00

A 2nd die of the 1p was introduced in 1947.

Use of #J2a was authorized from Mar. 1934 through Feb. 1935. Some examples have "½d" written on the bisect in black or red ink.

On cover values are for properly franked commercial covers. Philatelic usages also exist and sell for less.

1950

J4 D1 1c green .30 *3.00*
On cover 75.00
J5 D1 2c black 1.00 *6.50*
On cover 75.00
J6 D1 6c carmine rose 1.00 *8.50*
On cover 150.00
Nos. J4-J6 (3) 2.30 *18.00*

Values are for 1953 chalky paper printing. Values on ordinary paper, unused $32, used $85.

Wmk. 4a (error)

J4a D1 1c green 450.00 *650.00*
J5a D1 2c black 800.00
J6a D1 6c carmine rose 180.00
Nos. J4a-J6a (3) 1,430.

WAR TAX STAMP

No. 118 Overprinted

1917 Wmk. 3 *Perf. 14*

MR1 A12 1p carmine .55 .25
a. Imperf., pair *2,500.*

BARBUDA

bär-'büd-ə

LOCATION — Northernmost of the Leeward Islands, West Indies
GOVT. — Dependency of Antigua
AREA — 63 sq. mi.
POP. — 1,000 (estimated)
See Antigua.

12 Pence = 1 Shilling

Leeward Islands Stamps of 1912-22 Ovptd. in Black or Red

Die II

For description of dies I and II, see Dies of British Colonial Stamps in the catalogue introduction.

1922, July 13 Wmk. 4 *Perf. 14*

1 A5 ½p green 1.60 *12.00*
2 A5 1p rose red 1.60 *12.00*
3 A5 2p gray 1.60 *7.50*
4 A5 2½p ultramarine 1.60 *10.00*
5 A5 6p vio & red vio 2.10 *21.00*
6 A5 2sh vio & ultra, *bl* 12.50 *55.00*
7 A5 3sh green & violet 30.00 *75.00*
8 A5 4sh blk & scar (R) 37.50 *75.00*

Wmk. 3

9 A5 3p violet, *yel* 1.90 *15.00*
10 A5 1sh blk, *emer* (R) 1.75 *11.00*
11 A5 5sh grn & red, *yel* 62.50 *125.00*
Nos. 1-11 (11) 154.65 *418.50*

Set, never hinged 300.00
Set, overprinted "SPECIMEN" 260.00

Beware of forgeries, especially used examples dated June 1, 1923.

Covers: Values for commercial covers with the 1p, 2p or 3p stamps begin at about $50. Other stamps are very scarce to rare on cover.

BASUTOLAND

bə-ˈsü-tə-ˌland

LOCATION — An enclave in the state of South Africa
GOVT. — British Crown Colony
AREA — 11,716 sq. mi.
POP. — 733,000 (est. 1964)
CAPITAL — Maseru

The Colony, a former independent native state, was annexed to the Cape Colony in 1871. In 1883 control was transferred directly to the British Crown. Stamps of the Cape of Good Hope were used from 1871 to 1910 and those of the Union of South Africa from 1910 to 1933.

12 Pence = 1 Shilling

Catalogue values for unused stamps in this country are for Never Hinged items, beginning with Scott 29 in the regular postage section and Scott J1 in the postage due section.

George V — A1

Crocodile and River Scene

Perf. 12½

1933, Dec. 1 Engr. Wmk. 4

1 A1 ½p emerald 1.50 *2.40*
On cover *8.00*
2 A1 1p carmine 1.25 *1.75*
On cover *6.00*
3 A1 2p red violet 1.50 *1.10*
On cover *6.00*
4 A1 3p ultra 1.25 *1.40*
On cover *8.00*
5 A1 4p slate 2.75 *9.50*
On cover *30.00*
6 A1 6p yellow 3.00 *2.40*
On cover *9.00*
7 A1 1sh red orange 4.25 *5.00*
On cover *24.00*
8 A1 2sh6p dk brown 40.00 *57.50*
On cover *200.00*
9 A1 5sh violet 72.50 *92.50*
On cover *275.00*
10 A1 10sh olive green 225.00 *225.00*
On cover *500.00*
Nos. 1-10 (10) 353.00 *398.55*
Set, never hinged 750.00

Common Design Types pictured following the introduction.

Silver Jubilee Issue

Common Design Type

1935, May 4 ***Perf. 13½x14***

11 CD301 1p car & blue .85 *3.25*
12 CD301 2p gray blk & ultra 1.25 *3.25*
13 CD301 3p blue & brown 4.75 *8.25*
14 CD301 6p brt vio & indigo 5.25 *8.25*
Nos. 11-14 (4) 12.10 *23.00*
Set, never hinged 20.00

Coronation Issue

Common Design Type

1937, May 12 ***Perf. 13½x14***

15 CD302 1p carmine .25 *1.00*
16 CD302 2p rose violet .40 *1.00*
17 CD302 3p bright ultra .50 *1.00*
Nos. 15-17 (3) 1.15 *3.00*
Set, never hinged 1.75

George VI — A2

1938, Apr. 1 ***Perf. 12½***

18 A2 ½p emerald .25 *1.25*
19 A2 1p rose car .90 *.85*
20 A2 1½p light blue .45 *.65*
21 A2 2p rose lilac .45 *.80*
22 A2 3p ultra .50 *1.50*
23 A2 4p gray 1.60 *4.25*
24 A2 6p yel ocher 2.00 *1.75*
25 A2 1sh red orange 2.00 *1.40*
26 A2 2sh6p black brown 11.50 *9.00*
27 A2 5sh violet 27.50 *10.00*
28 A2 10sh olive green 29.00 *24.00*
Nos. 18-28 (11) 76.15 *55.45*
Set, never hinged 130.00

Catalogue values for unused stamps in this section, from this point to the end of the section, are for Never Hinged items.

Peace Issue

South Africa Nos. 100-102 Overprinted

Basic stamps inscribed alternately in English and Afrikaans.

1945, Dec. 3 Wmk. 201 ***Perf. 14***

29 A42 1p rose pink & choc, pair .70 .90
a. Single, English .25 .25
b. Single, Afrikaans .25 .25
30 A43 2p vio & slate blue, pair .70 .75
a. Single, English .25 .25
b. Single, Afrikaans .25 .25
31 A43 3p ultra & dp ultra, pair .70 .95
a. Single, English .25 .25
b. Single, Afrikaans .25 .25
Nos. 29-31 (3) 2.10 2.60

King George VI — A3

King George VI and Queen Elizabeth A4

Princess Margaret Rose and Princess Elizabeth A5

Royal British Family A6

Perf. 12½

1947, Feb. 17 Wmk. 4 Engr.

35 A3 1p red .25 .25
36 A4 2p green .25 .25
37 A5 3p ultra .25 .25
38 A6 1sh dark violet .25 .25
Nos. 35-38 (4) 1.00 1.00

Visit of the British Royal Family, Mar. 11-12, 1947.

Silver Wedding Issue

Common Design Types

1948, Dec. 1 Photo. ***Perf. 14x14½***

39 CD304 1½p brt ultra .30 .25

Engr.; Name Typo.

Perf. 11½

40 CD305 10sh dk brn ol 52.50 *55.00*

UPU Issue

Common Design Types

Engr.; Name Typo. on 3p, 6p

Perf. 13½, 11x11½

1949, Oct. 10 Wmk. 4

41 CD306 1½p blue .50 *1.50*
42 CD307 3p indigo 2.25 *2.00*
43 CD308 6p orange yel 1.25 *5.00*
44 CD309 1sh red brown .75 *1.50*
Nos. 41-44 (4) 4.75 *10.00*

POSTAGE DUE STAMPS

Catalogue values for all unused stamps in this section are for Never Hinged items.

D1

1933-52 Wmk. 4 Typo. ***Perf. 14***

Chalky Paper

J1 D1 1p dark red ('51) 2.00 *8.50*
On cover *80.00*
a. 1p carmine, ordinary paper 3.50 *14.50*
On cover *80.00*
b. 1p dk car, ordinary paper ('38) 50.00 *60.00*
On cover *150.00*
c. Wmk. 4a (error) 160.00
d. Wmk. 4, crown missing (error) 400.00
J2 D1 2p lt violet ('52) .40 *25.00*
On cover *80.00*
a. 2p lt violet, ordinary paper 10.00 *24.00*
On cover *80.00*
b. Wmk. 4a (error) 160.00
c. Wmk. 4, crown missing (error) 400.00

For surcharge see No. J7 in *Scott Standard Postage Stamp Catalogue*, Vol. 1.

On cover values are for properly franked commercial covers. Philatelic usages also exist and sell for less.

OFFICIAL STAMPS

Nos. 1-3 and 6 Overprinted "OFFICIAL"

1934 Wmk. 4 Engr. ***Perf. 12½***

O1 A1 ½p emerald *15,000. 7,500.*
O2 A1 1p carmine *5,500. 3,750.*
O3 A1 2p red violet *6,000. 1,250.*
O4 A1 6p yellow *15,000. 5,000.*

Counterfeits exist.

BATUM

bä-ˈtüm

LOCATION — A seaport on the Black Sea.

Batum is the capital of Adzhar, a territory which, in 1921, became an autonomous republic of the Georgian Soviet Socialist Republic.

Stamps of Batum were issued under the administration of British forces which occupied Batum and environs between December, 1918, and July, 1920, following the Treaty of Versailles.

100 Kopecks = 1 Ruble

Counterfeits of Nos. 1-65 abound.

A1

1919 Unwmk. Litho. ***Imperf.***

1 A1 5k green 7.50 *27.50*
On cover *500.00*
2 A1 10k ultramarine 5.50 *17.50*
On cover *500.00*
3 A1 50k yellow 8.00 *14.00*
On cover *350.00*
4 A1 1r red brown 12.00 *9.50*
On cover *375.00*
a. Printed on both sides *75.00*
5 A1 3r violet 11.50 *20.00*
On cover *625.00*
6 A1 5r brown 11.00 *42.50*
On cover *675.00*
Nos. 1-6 (6) 55.50 *131.00*

For overprints and surcharges see Nos. 13-20, 51-65.

Nos. 7-12, 21-50: numbers in parentheses are those of the basic Russian stamps.

Russian Stamps of 1909-17 Surcharged

1919 On Stamps of 1917

7 10r on 1k orange (#119) 80.00 *80.00*
On cover *750.00*
8 10r on 3k red (#121) 26.50 *32.50*
On cover *700.00*

On Stamp of 1909-12

Perf. 14x14½

9 10r on 5k claret (#77) 950.00 950.00
On cover —

On Stamp of 1917

10 10r on 10k on 7k light blue (#117) 975.00 900.00
On cover —
Nos. 7-10 (4) 2,032. 1,963.

Russian Stamps of 1909-13 Surcharged

1919

11 35k on 4k carmine (#76) *4,000. 6,000.*
Unused on complete postcard *5,000.*
On complete postcard —
12 35k on 4k dull red (#91) *10,000. 13,000.*
Unused on complete postcard *11,500.*
On complete postcard —

This surcharge was intended for postal cards. A few cards which bore adhesive stamps were also surcharged.

Values are for stamps off card and without gum.

Type of 1919 Issue Overprinted

1919 Unwmk. ***Imperf.***

13 A1 5k green 24.00 *15.00*
On cover *400.00*
14 A1 10k dark blue 13.00 *18.00*
On cover *400.00*
15 A1 25k orange 23.00 *18.00*
On cover *350.00*
16 A1 1r pale blue 6.00 *18.00*
On cover *325.00*
17 A1 2r salmon pink 1.75 *9.00*
On cover *325.00*
18 A1 3r violet 1.75 *10.00*
On cover *325.00*
19 A1 5r brown 2.00 *10.00*
On cover *325.00*
a. "CCUPATION" *475.00 475.00*
20 A1 7r dull red 6.00 *11.00*
On cover *350.00*
Nos. 13-20 (8) 77.50 *109.00*

Russian Stamps of 1909-17 Surcharged in Various Colors

10r & 50r

15r

On Stamps of 1917

1919-20 *Imperf.*

No.	Description	Unused	Used
21	10r on 3k red (#121)	25.00	*27.50*
a.	Inverted overprint	500.00	
22	15r on 1k org (R) (#119)	55.00	*100.00*
23	15r on 1k org (Bk) (#119)	100.00	*150.00*
a.	Inverted overprint	750.00	750.00
24	15r on 1k org (V) (#119)	75.00	*110.00*
25	50r on 1k org (#119)	975.00	*800.00*
26	50r on 2k green (#120)	975.00	*1,100.*

On Stamps of 1909-17

Perf. 14x14½

No.	Description	Unused	Used
27	50r on 2k green (#74)	1,000.	850.00
28	50r on 3k red (#75)	1,700.	*2,500.*
29	50r on 4k car (#76)	1,500.	*1,500.*
30	50r on 5k claret (#77)	975.00	*975.00*
31	50r on 10k dk blue (R) (#79)	3,000.	*3,500.*
32	50r on 15k red brn & blue (#81)	700.00	*850.00*

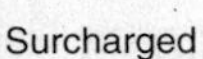

Surcharged

On Stamps of 1909-17

No.	Description	Unused	Used
33	25r on 5k cl (Bk) (#77)	100.00	*150.00*
34	25r on 5k cl (Bl) (#77)	100.00	*150.00*
a.	Inverted overprint	300.00	
35	25r on 10k on 7k lt blue (Bk) (#117)	150.00	*175.00*
36	25r on 10k on 7k lt blue (Bl) (#117)	100.00	*110.00*
37	25r on 20k on 14k bl & rose (Bk) (#118)	100.00	*150.00*
38	25r on 20k on 14k bl & rose (Bl) (#118)	200.00	*200.00*
39	25r on 25k grn & gray vio (Bk) (#83)	160.00	*175.00*
a.	Inverted overprint	250.00	
40	25r on 25k grn & gray vio (Bl) (#83)	100.00	135.00
41	25r on 50k vio & green (Bk) (#85a)	100.00	*110.00*
a.	Inverted overprint		250.00
b.	Tête-bêche, pair (#41, #41a)		350.00
42	25r on 50k vio & green (Bl) (#85a)	100.00	*150.00*
43	50r on 2k green (#74)	250.00	175.00
44	50r on 3k red (#75)	200.00	175.00
45	50r on 4k car (#76)	200.00	*250.00*
46	50r on 5k claret (#77)	200.00	100.00

On Stamps of 1917

Imperf

No.	Description	Unused	Used
47	50r on 2k green (#120)	975.00	*650.00*
48	50r on 3k red (#121)	975.00	*675.00*
49	50r on 5k claret (#123)	*1,600.*	*1,700.*

On Stamp of 1913

Perf. 13½

No.	Description	Unused	Used
50	50r on 4k dull red (Bl) (#91)	100.00	*120.00*

Nos. 3, 13 and 15 Surcharged in Black or Blue

No. 51

No. 55

1920 *Imperf.*

No.	Type	Description	Unused	Used
51	A1	25r on 5k green	75.00	*100.00*
52	A1	25r on 5k grn (Bl)	250.00	100.00
53	A1	25r on 25k orange	35.00	*45.00*
54	A1	25r on 25k org (Bl)	*125.00*	*140.00*
55	A1	50r on 50k yellow	30.00	*40.00*
a.		"50" cut in pieces	18.00	*19.00*
56	A1	50r on 50k yel (Bl)	100.00	125.00
a.		"50" cut in pieces	200.00	200.00
		Nos. 51-56 (6)	*615.00*	*550.00*

The figures of value in the surcharge on Nos. 55a and 56a were file-cut as a counter-forgery measure. Typically, the "5" is cut at bottom and on the right side of the loop. The zero is shorn at top and bottom, leaving the side bars intact. Nos. 55 and 56 are from early printings, before the handstamps were cut.

The surcharges on Nos. 21-56 inclusive are handstamped and are known double, inverted, etc.

Tree Type of 1919 Overprinted Like Nos. 13-20

1920

No.	Type	Description	Unused	Used
57	A1	1r orange brown	2.25	*12.00*
58	A1	2r gray blue	2.25	*12.00*
59	A1	3r rose	2.25	*12.00*
60	A1	5r black brown	2.25	*12.00*
61	A1	7r yellow	2.25	*12.00*
62	A1	10r dark green	2.25	*12.00*
63	A1	15r violet	2.75	*17.50*
64	A1	25r vermilion	2.50	*16.00*
65	A1	50r dark blue	2.75	*20.00*
		Nos. 57-65 (9)	21.50	*125.50*

The variety "BPITISH" occurs on Nos. 57-65. The "P" is actually a broken "R" and appears in Row 1, Pos. 19, in each sheet. Value, about $150 each. No. 65 with this variety, value, $400. Some exist gummed on printed side or both sides.

Nos. 57-65 exist without overprint.

BECHUANALAND

ˌbech-ˈwä-nə-ˌland

(British Bechuanaland)

LOCATION — Southern Africa

GOVT. — A British Crown Colony, which included the area of the former Stellaland, annexed in 1895 to the Cape of Good Hope Colony.

AREA — 51,424 sq. mi.

POP. — 72,700 (1891)

CAPITAL — Vryburg

British Bechuanaland stamps were also used in Bechuanaland Protectorate until 1897.

12 Pence = 1 Shilling

20 Shillings = 1 Pound

Except for the first issue of British Bechuanaland, which was canceled in manuscript, many of the pen cancellations are fiscal cancellations.

Watermarks

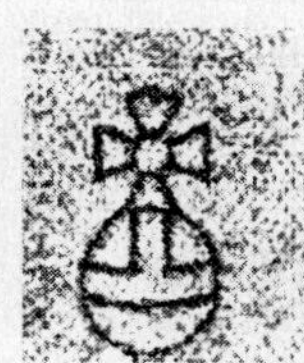

Wmk. 29 — Orb

Wmk. 14 — VR in Italics

Stellaland was annexed by Great Britain in 1885 and became part of British Bechuanaland. Stamps issued by the short-lived republic from 1884-1885 are listed in Volume 6 under Stellaland.

Cape of Good Hope Stamps of 1871-85 Overprinted

1885-87 **Wmk. 1** *Perf. 14*

Black Overprint

No.	Type	Description	Unused	Used
1	A6	4p blue ('86)	95.00	*85.00*

Wmk. 2

Black Overprint

No.	Type	Description	Unused	Used
3	A6	3p claret	60.00	*70.00*

Red Overprint

No.	Type	Description	Unused	Used
4	A6	½p black	35.00	40.00
a.		Overprint in lake	5,500.	*10,000.*
b.		Double overprint in lake & blk	900.00	*1,100.*

Wmk. Anchor (16)

Black Overprint

No.	Type	Description	Unused	Used
5	A6	½p black ('87)	14.00	*27.50*
a.		"ritish"	2,750.	*2,600.*
b.		Double overprint	4,250.	
6	A6	1p rose	27.50	11.00
a.		"ritish"	*7,500.*	*4,250.*
b.		Double overprint		*2,300.*
c.		Missing dot in first "i" of "British"	175.00	*175.00*
7	A6	2p bister	55.00	11.00
a.		"ritish"	9,000.	*5,500.*
b.		Double overprint		2,500.
c.		Missing dot in first "i" of "British"	425.00	175.00
8	A3	6p violet	220.00	47.50
a.		Missing dot in first "i" of "British"	1,250.	*575.00*
9	A3	1sh green ('86)	375.00	190.00
a.		"ritish"	*24,000.*	*18,000.*

There is no period after Bechuanaland on the genuine stamps.

Covers: Values for commercial covers begin at $400.

Great Britain No. 111 Overprinted in Black

1887 **Wmk. 30**

No.	Type	Description	Unused	Used
10	A54	½p vermilion	2.00	*1.50*
		Handstamped "SPECIMEN"	100.00	
a.		Double overprint	2,700.	

For overprints see Bechuanaland Protectorate Nos. 51-53.

A1

A2

A3

1887 **Typo.** **Wmk. 29**

Country Name in Black

No.	Type	Description	Unused	Used
11	A1	1p lilac	25.00	4.25
12	A1	2p lilac	125.00	2.75
a.		2p pale dull lilac	50.00	27.50
13	A1	3p lilac	8.50	*8.75*
a.		3p pale reddish lilac	72.50	22.50
14	A1	4p lilac	65.00	2.75
15	A1	6p lilac	80.00	3.00

Wmk. 14

No.	Type	Description	Unused	Used
16	A2	1sh green	37.50	12.00
17	A2	2sh green	70.00	60.00
18	A2	2sh6p green	80.00	80.00
19	A2	5sh green	125.00	*180.00*
		Pen cancellation		15.00
20	A2	10sh green	275.00	*400.00*
		Pen cancellation		45.00

Wmk. 29

No.	Type	Description	Unused	Used
21	A3	£1 lilac	1,100.	*900.00*
		Pen cancellation		65.00
22	A3	£5 lilac	4,000.	*1,900.*
		Pen cancellation		200.00
		Nos. 11-22 handstamped "SPECIMEN"	1,050.	

The corner designs and central oval differs on No. 22.

For overprints see Bechuanaland Protectorate Nos. 54-58, 60-66. For surcharges see Nos. 23-28, 30, AR2, Cape of Good Hope No. 171.

Fiscal cancels can be pen cancellations or ink stampings.

Beware of cleaned pen (fiscal) cancellations and forged postmarks on Nos. 21-22.

Nos. 11-12, 14-16 Surcharged

Black Surcharge

1888 **Country Name in Black**

No.	Type	Description	Unused	Used
23	A1	1p on 1p lilac	9.25	8.00
a.		Double surcharge		
24	A1	6p on 6p lilac	165.00	20.00

Red Surcharge

No.	Type	Description	Unused	Used
25	A1	2p on 2p lilac	65.00	4.00
a.		"2" with curved tail	350.00	180.00
b.		On 2p pale dull lilac (#12a)	100.00	60.00
26	A1	4p on 4p lilac	450.00	*600.00*

Green Surcharge

No.	Type	Description	Unused	Used
27	A1	2p on 2p lilac		*4,000.*
a.		"2" with curved tail		*20,000.*

Blue Surcharge

No.	Type	Description	Unused	Used
27A	A1	6p on 6p lilac		*25,000.*

Wmk. 14

Black Surcharge

No.	Type	Description	Unused	Used
28	A2	1sh on 1sh green	300.00	100.00

Cape of Good Hope No.41 Overprinted in Green

1889 **Wmk. 16**

No.	Type	Description	Unused	Used
29	A4	½p black	5.00	*40.00*
a.		Double ovpt., one inverted	3,500.	
b.		Double ovpt., one vertical	1,200.	
c.		Pair, one stamp without ovpt.	10,000.	

Exists with "British" missing from shifted overprint.

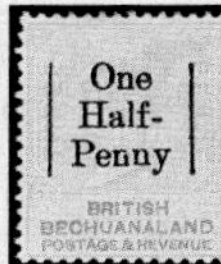

No. 13 Surcharged in Black

1888 **Wmk. 29**

30 A1 ½p on 3p lilac & blk 275.00 *325.00*

Stamps with errors of spelling in the surcharge are fakes.

Cape of Good Hope Nos. 43-44 Overprinted in Black, Reading Up

1891 **Wmk. 16**

31 A4 1p rose 14.00 *18.50*
- *a.* Horiz. pair, one without overprint 26,000.
- *b.* "British" omitted 4,250. —
- *c.* "Bechuanaland" omitted 3,500.

32 A4 2p bister 8.00 2.75
- *a.* Without period 325.00 *390.00*

Nos. 31-32 handstamped "SPECIMEN" 150.00

See Nos. 38-39. Only one example of No. 31b exists. It is in the Royal Collection in London.

Stamps of Great Britain Overprinted in Black

1891-94 **Wmk. 30**

33 A40 1p lilac 7.25 2.00
34 A56 2p green & car 24.00 5.00
35 A59 4p brown & green 4.50 .80
- *a.* Half used as 2p on cover 3,000.

36 A62 6p violet, *rose* 9.00 2.50
37 A65 1sh green ('94) 16.00 *19.50*
- *a.* Half used as 6p on cover —

Nos. 33-37 (5) 60.75 *29.80*

Nos. 33-36 handstamped "SPECIMEN" 200.00

No. 35a was used at the Palapye Post Office in Nov. 1899. No. 37a was used at the Kanye Post Office in Dec. 1904.

For surcharges see Cape of Good Hope Nos. 172, 176-177.

Cape of Good Hope Nos. 43-44 Overprinted, Reading Down

1893-95 **Wmk. 16**

38 A6 1p rose 4.25 3.00
- *a.* No dots over both "i" of "British" 160.00 *160.00*
- *c.* As "a," reading up 4,500.
- *d.* Pair, one without overprint

39 A6 2p bister ('95) 14.00 3.50
- *a.* Double overprint 1,700. 850.00
- *b.* No dots over both "i" of "British" 275.00 175.00
- *d.* As "b," reading up 4,750.

The missing dot-over-i variety exists only on this issue. Nos. 38c and 39d resulted from the sheets being fed into the press upside down.

Nos. 38-39 exist with "British" missing (from shifted overprint).

Cape of Good Hope No. 42 Overprinted

"BECHUANALAND" 16mm Long Overprint Lines 13mm Apart

1897

40 A6 ½p light green 3.25 *20.00*

"BECHUANALAND" 15mm Long Overprint Lines 10½mm Apart

41 A6 ½p light green 22.50 *75.00*

"BECHUANALAND" 15mm Long Overprint Lines 13½mm Apart

42 A6 ½p light green 47.50 *150.00*

Nos. 40-42 (3) 73.25 *245.00*

Nos. 40-42 actually are issues of Bechuanaland Protectorate.

BECHUANALAND PROTECTORATE

ˌbech-ˈwä-nə-ˌland prə-ˈtek-tˌə-ˌrət

LOCATION — In central South Africa, north of the Republic of South Africa, east of South West Africa and bounded on the north by the Caprivi Strip of South West Africa and on the east by Southern Rhodesia
GOVT. — British Protectorate
AREA — 222,000 sq. mi.
POP. — 540,400 (1964)
CAPITAL — Vryburg (to 1895), Mafeking

12 Pence = 1 Shilling
20 Shillings = 1 Pound

Catalogue values for unused stamps in this country are for Never Hinged items, beginning with Scott 137 in the regular postage section.

Additional Overprint in Black on Bechuanaland No. 10

a

b

c

1888-90 **Wmk. 30** ***Perf. 14***

51 A54(a) ½p ver ('90) 275.00 *450.00*
- *a.* Double overprint 1,800. *2,200.*
- *b.* "Protectorrte"
- *c.* As "b," double overprint 20,000.

52 A54(b) ½p ver ('88) 13.00 *55.00*
- Handstamped "SPECIMEN" 100.00
- *a.* Double overprint 375.00

53 A54(c) ½p ver ('90) 225.00 *250.00*
- *a.* Inverted overprint 100.00 *130.00*
- *b.* Double overprint 150.00 *200.00*
- *c.* As "a," double 750.00 *850.00*
- *d.* "Portectorate" — —
- *e.* As "a," "Portectorate" 20,000. —

For surcharge see No. 68.

Bechuanaland Nos. 16-20 Overprinted Type "b" in Black

Wmk. 14

Country Name in Black

54 A2 1sh green 150.00 65.00
- Handstamped "SPECIMEN" 125.00
- *a.* First "o" omitted 6,750. 3,750.

55 A2 2sh green 800.00 *1,200.*
- *a.* First "o" omitted 20,000. —

56 A2 2sh6p green 650.00 *1,100.*
- *a.* First "o" omitted 20,000. —

57 A2 5sh green 1,400. *2,750.*
- *a.* First "o" omitted 25,000. —

58 A2 10sh green 5,250. *7,500.*
- *a.* First "o" omitted 25,000. —

Bechuanaland Nos. 11-15 Ovptd. Type "b" and Srchd. in Black

1888 **Wmk. 29**

Country Name in Black

60 A1 1p on 1p lilac 20.00 *16.00*
- *a.* Short "1" 475.00 *550.00*

61 A1 2p on 2p lilac 45.00 20.00
- *a.* "2" with curved tail 950.00 550.00

63 A1 3p on 3p reddish lil 225.00 *290.00*
64 A1 4p on 4p lilac 475.00 500.00
- *a.* Small "4" 6,000. *6,000.*

65 A1 6p on 6p lilac 125.00 55.00

In #60 the "1" is 2½mm high; in #60a, 2mm.

Value Surcharged in Red

66 A1 4p on 4p lilac 160.00 60.00
- *a.* Double overprint *2,750.*

Cape of Good Hope Type of 1886 Overprinted in Green

1889 **Wmk. 16**

67 A6 ½p black 6.50 *55.00*
- *a.* Double overprint 600.00 *800.00*

No. 67 exists with "Bechuanaland" missing and with ovpt. words reversed (from shifted overprint).

Bechuanaland Protectorate No. 52 Surcharged in Black

Wmk. 30

68 A54 4p on ½p ver 47.50 6.00
- Handstamped "SPECIMEN" 150.00
- *a.* Inverted surcharge *4,500.*
- *b.* "rpence" omitted *7,000.*
- *c.* "ourpence" omitted *12,500.*
- *d.* As "c," inverted surcharge *17,500.*

Stamps of Great Britain 1881-87, Overprinted in Black

1897, Oct.

69 A54 ½p vermilion 2.25 *2.50*
70 A40 1p lilac 4.50 .85
71 A56 2p green & car 14.00 *4.50*
72 A58 3p violet, *yel* 6.25 *12.00*
73 A59 4p brown & green 26.00 25.00
74 A62 6p violet, *rose* 25.00 14.00

Nos. 69-74 (6) 78.00 58.85

Set, handstamped "SPECIMEN" 250.00

For surcharges see Cape of Good Hope Nos. 167-170, 173-175.

Same on Great Britain No. 125

1902, Feb. 25

75 A54 ½p blue green 1.75 *4.00*
- Handstamped "SPECIMEN" 37.50

Stamps of Great Britain, 1902, Overprinted in Black

1904-12

76 A66 ½p gray grn ('06) 2.75 *3.50*
77 A66 1p car ('05) 12.00 .65
78 A66 2½p ultra 12.50 9.00
- *a.* Period after "P" of "Protectorate" 1,100. *1,400.*

79 A74 1sh scar & grn ('12) 60.00 *170.00*
- *a.* 1sh carmine & green 50.00 *125.00*

Nos. 76-79 (4) 87.25 *183.15*

Same on Great Britain No. 143

1908

80 A66 ½p pale yel green 4.25 4.00

Transvaal No. 274 overprinted "Bechuanaland Protectorate," formerly listed as No. 81, now appears as No. AR1 in the Postal-Fiscal Stamps section.

Great Britain No. 154 Overprinted Like Nos. 76-79

1912, Sept. **Wmk. 30** ***Perf. 15x14***

82 A81 1p scarlet 4.00 .90
- *a.* No cross on crown 175.00 87.50
- *b.* 1p aniline scarlet ('14) 190.00 92.50

Great Britain Stamps of 1912-13 Overprinted Like Nos. 76-79

Wmk. Crown and GvR (33)

1913-24

83 A82 ½p green 1.40 *2.00*
84 A83 1p scarlet ('15) 3.25 .85
- *a.* 1p carmine ('22) 30.00 3.00

85 A84 1½p red brn ('20) 7.00 *3.50*
86 A85 2p redsh org (I) 13.00 *4.25*
- *a.* 2p orange (I) ('21) 22.50 4.50
- *b.* 2p orange (II) ('24) 47.50 4.00

87 A86 2½p ultra 4.00 *27.50*
- *a.* 2½p blue ('15) 16.00 *27.50*

88 A87 3p bluish violet 6.75 *16.00*
89 A88 4p slate green 7.25 *40.00*
90 A89 6p dull violet 10.00 *27.50*
- *a.* Double overprint, one albino 22.50

91 A90 1sh bister 22.50 *45.00*
- *a.* 1sh bister brown ('23) 30.00 *35.00*
- Overprinted "SPECIMEN" 85.00

Nos. 83-91 (9) 75.15 *166.60*

The dies of No. 86 are the same as in Great Britain 1912-13 issue.

Wmk. 34 ***Perf. 11x12***

92 A91 2sh6p dk brn ('15) 150.00 *300.00*
- *a.* 2sh6p light brown ('16) 125.00 *300.00*
- *b.* 2sh6p sepia brown ('17) 150.00 *260.00*
- *c.* Double overprint, one albino, on #92 350.00
- *d.* Triple overprint, one albino, on #92b —

93 A91 5sh rose car ('14) 180.00 *450.00*
- *a.* 5sh carmine ('19) 350.00 *500.00*
- *b.* Double overprint, one albino, on #93 450.00
- *c.* Double overprint, one albino, on #93a 525.00

Nos. 92, 93 were printed by Waterlow Bros. & Layton; Nos. 92a, 93a were printed by Thomas De La Rue & Co.

Same Overprint On Retouched Seahorses Stamps of 1919 (Great Britain Nos. 179, 180)

1920-23

94 A91 2sh6p gray brown 100.00 *200.00*
95 A91 5sh car rose 140.00 *325.00*

Nos. 94-95 measure 22.5-23mm vertically. Most examples have a small dot of color at top center, outside of frameline. Perforation holes are larger and usually are evenly spaced.

Great Britain Stamps of 1924 Overprinted like Nos. 76-79

Wmk. Crown and Block GvR Multiple (35)

1925-27 ***Perf. 15x14***

96 A82 ½p green ('27) 1.65 *2.00*
97 A83 1p scarlet 2.25 1.00
99 A85 2p deep org (II) 2.50 1.25
101 A87 3p violet ('26) 5.50 *30.00*
102 A88 4p sl grn ('26) 8.00 *55.00*
103 A89 6p dl vio, chalky paper 75.00 *110.00*
- *a.* 6p purple, ordinary paper 55.00 *57.50*

104 A90 1sh bister ('26) 11.00 *30.00*

Nos. 96-104 (7) 105.90 *229.25*

George V — A11

Perf. 12½

1932, Dec. 12 Engr. Wmk. 4

105 A11 ½p green 2.75 .35
a. Horiz. pair, imperf between 32,500.
106 A11 1p carmine 2.00 .40
107 A11 2p red brown 2.00 .45
108 A11 3p ultra 4.25 *5.00*
109 A11 4p orange 4.50 *12.00*
110 A11 6p red violet 6.75 *8.75*
111 A11 1sh blk & ol grn 5.75 *8.75*
112 A11 2sh blk & org 27.50 *75.00*
113 A11 2sh6p blk & car 26.00 *55.00*
114 A11 3sh blk & red vio 50.00 *65.00*
115 A11 5sh blk & ultra 125.00 *130.00*
116 A11 10sh blk & red brown 300.00 *350.00*
Nos. 105-116 (12) 556.50 *710.70*

Common Design Types pictured following the introduction.

Silver Jubilee Issue
Common Design Type

1935, May 4 ***Perf. 11x12***

117 CD301 1p car & blue 1.75 *6.50*
118 CD301 2p black & ultra 2.25 *5.75*
119 CD301 3p ultra & brown 4.00 *9.00*
120 CD301 6p brown vio & ind 9.00 *10.00*
Nos. 117-120 (4) 17.00 *31.25*
Set, never hinged 24.00

Coronation Issue
Common Design Type

1937, May 12 ***Perf. 13½x14***

121 CD302 1p carmine .25 *.50*
122 CD302 2p brown .30 *1.25*
123 CD302 3p bright ultra .40 *1.60*
Nos. 121-123 (3) .95 3.35
Set, never hinged 1.75

George VI, Cattle and Baobab Tree — A12

1938, Apr. 1 ***Perf. 12½***

124 A12 ½p green 3.00 *3.75*
125 A12 1p rose car .60 .65
126 A12 1½p light blue .75 *1.25*
127 A12 2p brown .60 *.75*
128 A12 3p ultra .75 *3.00*
129 A12 4p orange 1.50 *4.25*
130 A12 6p rose violet 3.25 3.00
131 A12 1sh blk & ol grn 3.50 *9.50*
133 A12 2sh6p black & car 9.00 *20.00*
135 A12 5sh black & ultra 27.50 *32.50*
136 A12 10sh black & brn 19.00 *37.50*
Nos. 124-136 (11) 69.45 *116.15*
Set, never hinged 110.00

Catalogue values for unused stamps in this section, from this point to the end of the section, are for Never Hinged items.

Peace Issue

South Africa Nos. 100-102 Overprinted

Basic stamps inscribed alternately in English and Afrikaans.

1945, Dec. 3 Wmk. 201 ***Perf. 14***

137 A42 1p rose pink & choc, pair .75 *1.50*
a. Single, English .25 .25
b. Single, Afrikaans .25 .25
138 A43 2p vio & slate blue, pair .55 *1.50*
a. Single, English .25 .25
b. Single, Afrikaans .25 .25
139 A43 3p ultra & dp ultra, pair .75 *1.75*
a. Single, English .25 .25
b. Single, Afrikaans .25 .25
c. Vert. pair, one with overprint omitted 17,000.
Nos. 137-139 (3) 2.05 *4.75*

World War II victory of the Allies.

Royal Visit Issue
Types of Basutoland, 1947

Perf. 12½

1947, Feb. 17 Wmk. 4 Engr.

143 A3 1p red .25 .25
144 A4 2p green .25 .25
145 A5 3p ultra .25 .25
146 A6 1sh dark violet .25 .25
Nos. 143-146 (4) 1.00 1.00

Visit of the British Royal Family, 4/17/47.

Silver Wedding Issue
Common Design Types

1948, Dec. 1 Photo. ***Perf. 14x14½***

147 CD304 1½p brt ultra .35 .25

Engr.; Name Typo.

Perf. 11½x11

148 CD305 10sh gray black 45.00 *50.00*

UPU Issue
Common Design Types

Engr.; Name Typo. on 3p and 6p

1949, Oct. 10 ***Perf. 13½, 11x11½***

149 CD306 1½p blue .30 *1.00*
150 CD307 3p indigo 1.50 1.50
151 CD308 6p red lilac .80 *2.75*
152 CD309 1sh olive .75 *2.00*
Nos. 149-152 (4) 3.35 *7.25*

POSTAL-FISCAL STAMPS

Transvaal No. 274 Overprinted

1910, July Wmk. 3

AR1 A27 12sh6p brn org & blk 190.00 *375.00*

This stamp was issued for fiscal use in January 1907, but the "POSTAGE" inscription was not obliterated, and examples were accepted for postal use during 1910-11.

Bechuanaland No. 16 surcharged "£5"

1918 Wmk. 29

AR2 A2 £5 on 1sh green *92,000.* —

Examples without full gum or with no gum sell for much less than the values for examples with full gum.

The known used examples of AR2 are all fiscally used. Value, $1,400.

South Africa No. 3 Overprinted in two lines

1922 Wmk. 177

AR3 A2 1p rose red 50.00 *155.00*
a. Double ovpt, one albino 160.00

POSTAGE DUE STAMPS

Postage Due Stamps of Great Britain Overprinted

On Stamp of 1914-22

1926 Wmk. 33 ***Perf. 14x14½***

J1 D1 1p carmine 11.00 *125.00*

On Stamps of 1924-30
Wmk. 35

J2 D1 ½p emerald 11.00 *75.00*

Overprinted

J3 D1 2p black brown 11.00 *100.00*
Nos. J1-J3 (3) 33.00 *300.00*
Set, never hinged 52.50

D2

1932 Wmk. 4 Typo. ***Perf. 14½***

J4 D2 ½p olive green 6.75 *60.00*
On cover *300.00*
J5 D2 1p carmine rose 8.00 *10.00*
On cover *275.00*
J6 D2 2p dull violet 10.00 *57.50*
On cover *300.00*
b. Thick "d" 120.00
Nos. J4-J6 (3) 24.75 *127.50*
Set, never hinged 40.00
Set, perforated "SPECIMEN" 80.00

Chalky Paper

1958, Nov. 27

J5a D2 1p carmine 1.50 *27.50*
On cover *275.00*
J6a D2 2p violet 1.75 *22.00*
On cover *300.00*
c. Thick "d" 47.50

On cover values are for properly franked commercial covers. Philatelic usages also exist and sell for less.

BELGIAN CONGO

'bel-jən 'käŋ-ˌgō

LOCATION — Central Africa
GOVT. — Belgian colony
AREA — 902,082 sq. mi. (estimated)
POP. — 12,660,000 (1956)
CAPITAL — Léopoldville

Congo was an independent state, founded by Leopold II of Belgium, until 1908 when it was annexed to Belgium as a colony.

100 Centimes = 1 Franc

Independent State

A1

A2

King Leopold II — A3

1886 Unwmk. Typo. ***Perf. 15***

1 A1 5c green 15.00 *26.00*
Never hinged 31.00
On cover —
2 A1 10c rose 5.50 *6.00*
Never hinged 9.25
On cover *550.00*
3 A2 25c blue 60.00 47.50
Never hinged 140.00
On cover *450.00*
a. 25c greenish blue 55.00 45.00
Never hinged 130.00
On cover *450.00*
b. 25c ultramarine 80.00 —
Never hinged 150.00
4 A3 50c olive green 9.00 9.00
Never hinged 13.50
On cover *750.00*
a. 50c dark olive 27.50 25.00
Never hinged 55.00
5 A1 5fr lilac 400.00 350.00
Never hinged 925.00
On cover —
a. Perf. 14 1,100. 650.00
Never hinged —
b. 5fr deep lilac 850.00 525.00
Never hinged —
c. Imperforate 875.00
Nos. 1-5 (5) 489.50 438.50
Set, never hinged 1,100.

Numerous counterfeit stamps and postmarks exist of No. 5.

Postal stationery with stamps added sell for considerably less.

For surcharge see No. Q1.

King Leopold II — A4

1887-94

6 A4 5c grn ('89) 1.00 *1.25*
Never hinged 4.00
On cover *125.00*
7 A4 10c rose ('89) 1.75 1.75
Never hinged 6.50
On cover *125.00*
8 A4 25c blue ('89) 1.75 1.75
Never hinged 6.00
On cover *300.00*
9 A4 50c reddish brn 67.50 32.50
Never hinged 325.00
On cover *500.00*
a. 50c deep brown 105.00 47.50
Never hinged 190.00
On cover *500.00*
10 A4 50c gray ('94) 4.00 *22.50*
Never hinged 13.00
On cover *2,000.*
11 A4 5fr violet 1,350. 550.00
Never hinged —
On cover *6,750.*
12 A4 5fr gray ('92) 165.00 130.00
Never hinged 650.00
On cover, overfranked *1,000.*
On portion of parcel wrapper *1,250.*
13 A4 10fr buff ('91) 625.00 400.00
Never hinged 2,475.
On cover, overfranked *2,000.*
Nos. 6-13 (8) 2,216. 1,140.
Set, never hinged 3,500.

The 25fr and 50fr in gray were not issued. Values, each $30., never hinged $40.

Counterfeits exist of Nos. 10-13, 25fr and 50fr, unused, used, genuine stamps with faked cancels and counterfeit stamps with genuine cancels.

Covers: Postal stationery with stamps added sell for considerably less. Values for Nos. 12-13 are for overfranked covers, usually philatelic.

For surcharges see Nos. Q3-Q6.

Port Matadi — A5

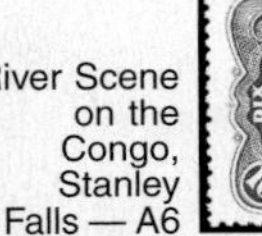
River Scene on the Congo, Stanley Falls — A6

Inkissi Falls — A7

Railroad Bridge on M'pozo River — A8

Hunting Elephants A9

Bangala Chief and Wife — A10

1894-1901 Engr. *Perf. 12½ to 15*

No.	Type	Description	Unused	Used
14	A5	5c pale bl & blk	19.00	19.00
		Never hinged	37.50	
		On cover		*50.00*
15	A5	5c red brn & blk ('95)	4.50	1.75
		Never hinged	8.00	
		On cover		*25.00*
16	A5	5c grn & blk ('00)	2.25	.60
		Never hinged	5.00	
		On cover		*27.50*
a.		Retouched	4.50	1.50
		Never hinged	13.50	
		On cover		50.00
17	A6	10c red brn & blk	19.00	*19.00*
		Never hinged	42.50	
		On cover		*50.00*
18	A6	10c grnsh bl & blk ('95)	4.50	2.00
		Never hinged	9.50	
		On cover		*25.00*
a.		Center inverted	*3,000.*	*3,000.*
		On cover		*10,000.*
19	A6	10c car & blk ('00)	4.75	1.10
		Never hinged	7.50	
		On cover		*60.00*
20	A7	25c yel org & blk	5.25	3.75
		Never hinged	9.25	
		On cover		*25.00*
21	A7	25c lt bl & blk ('00)	5.50	2.50
		Never hinged	9.25	
		On cover		*12.50*
a.		Redrawn frame	1,350.	775.00
22	A8	50c grn & blk	2.00	2.00
		Never hinged	3.50	
		On cover		*80.00*
23	A8	50c ol & blk ('00)	5.50	1.25
		Never hinged	9.25	
		On cover		*60.00*
24	A9	1fr lilac & blk	32.50	17.50
		Never hinged	55.00	
		On cover		*375.00*
a.		1fr rose lilac & black	475.00	37.50
		Never hinged	850.00	
		On cover		*375.00*
25	A9	1fr car & blk ('01)	425.00	9.50
		Never hinged	800.00	
		On cover		*300.00*
26	A10	5fr lake & blk	57.50	40.00
		Never hinged	165.00	
		On cover		*200.00*
a.		5fr carmine rose & black	130.00	62.50
		Never hinged	235.00	
		On cover		*300.00*
		Nos. 14-26 (13)	587.25	119.95
		Set, never hinged	1,100.	

No. 16a has a small circle touching the the frameline, about 2mm from the lower right corner

The frameline has been strenghtened at the top and bottom of No. 21a. It is thicker and more regular than on No. 21.

Covers: Postal stationery with stamps added sell for considerably less. Values for Nos. 26, 26a are for overfranked covers, usually philatelic.

For overprints see Nos. 31-32, 34, 36-37, 39.

Climbing Oil Palms — A11

Congo Canoe A12

1896

No.	Type	Description	Unused	Used
27	A11	15c ocher & blk	5.25	1.25
		Never hinged	9.25	
		On cover		25.00
28	A12	40c bluish grn & blk	5.25	4.00
		Never hinged	9.25	
		On cover		30.00
		Set, never hinged	18.50	

For overprints see Nos. 33, 35.

Congo Village A13

River Steamer on the Congo A14

1898

No.	Type	Description	Unused	Used
29	A13	3.50fr red & blk	200.00	145.00
		Never hinged	325.00	
		On cover		—
a.		Perf. 14x12	575.00	350.00
		Never hinged	—	
30	A14	10fr yel grn & blk	160.00	50.00
		Never hinged	225.00	
		On cover		—
a.		Center inverted	*25,000.*	
b.		Perf. 12	800.00	52.50
		Never hinged	—	
c.		Perf. 12x14	500.00	—
		Never hinged	—	
		As "c," pen canceled		21.00
		Set, never hinged	550.00	

Nos. 29-30 exist imperf. Value, set $850.
For overprints see Nos. 38, 40.

Belgian Congo

Overprinted

1908

No.	Type	Description	Unused	Used
31	A5	5c green & blk	8.75	8.00
		Never hinged	30.00	
		On cover		*45.00*
a.		Handstamped	5.50	3.00
		Never hinged	10.00	
		As "a," on cover		*45.00*
32	A6	10c car & blk	16.00	14.00
		Never hinged	47.50	
		On cover		*45.00*
a.		Handstamped	5.50	3.00
		Never hinged	10.00	
		As "a," on cover		*30.00*
33	A11	15c ocher & blk	9.25	8.00
		Never hinged	32.50	
		On cover		*35.00*
a.		Handstamped	8.50	5.00
		Never hinged	20.00	
		As "a," on cover		*35.00*
34	A7	25c lt blue & blk	5.75	3.00
		Never hinged	13.50	
		On cover		*35.00*
a.		Handstamped	15.00	5.00
		Never hinged	40.00	
		As "a," on cover		*37.50*
b.		As "a," redrawn frame (#21a)	30.00	17.50
		Never hinged	62.50	
c.		Double overprint (#34)	300.00	
35	A12	40c bluish grn & blk	3.25	3.00
		Never hinged	10.50	
		On cover		*45.00*
a.		Handstamped	16.00	8.75
		Never hinged	32.50	
		As "a," on cover		*50.00*
36	A8	50c olive & blk	6.25	3.00
		Never hinged	13.50	
		On cover		*25.00*
a.		Handstamped	8.00	5.50
		Never hinged	20.00	
		As "a," on cover		*25.00*
b.		As #36, inverted overprint	775.00	
37	A9	1fr car & blk	27.50	8.50
		Never hinged	75.00	
		On cover		*100.00*
a.		Handstamped	75.00	17.50
		Never hinged	120.00	
		As "a," on cover		*85.00*
38	A13	3.50fr red & blk	42.50	30.00
		Never hinged	110.00	
		On cover		*125.00*
a.		Handstamped	450.00	200.00
		Never hinged	825.00	
		As "a," on cover		250.00
b.		As #38, inverted overprint	750.00	—
c.		As #38, double overprint	—	—
39	A10	5fr car & blk	75.00	37.50
		Never hinged	165.00	
		On cover		*125.00*
a.		Handstamped	150.00	77.50
		Never hinged	325.00	
		As "a," on cover		*150.00*
40	A14	10fr yel grn & blk	140.00	35.00
		Never hinged	310.00	
		On cover		*150.00*
a.		Perf. 14½	375.00	—
		Never hinged	750.00	
b.		Handstamped	275.00	90.00
		Never hinged	550.00	
		As "a," on cover		*150.00*
c.		Handstamped, perf. 14½	575.00	325.00
		Never hinged	1,050.	
d.		As #40a, double overprint	*600.00*	
		Nos. 31-40 (10)	334.25	150.00
		Set, never hinged	800.00	

Most of the above handstamps are also found inverted and double.

There are two types of handstamped overprints, those applied in Brussels and those applied locally. There are eight types of each overprint. Values listed are the lowest for each stamp.

Covers: Values for Nos. 39, 39a, 40, 40b are for overfranked covers, usually philatelic.

Counterfeits of the handstamped overprints exist.

Imperf examples of No. 37 are proofs.

Port Matadi A15

River Scene on the Congo, Stanley Falls — A16

Climbing Oil Palms — A17

Railroad Bridge on M'pozo River — A18

1909 *Perf. 14*

No.	Type	Description	Unused	Used
41	A15	5c green & blk	1.00	1.00
		Never hinged	3.75	
		On cover		*22.50*
42	A16	10c carmine & blk	1.00	.65
		Never hinged	3.75	
		On cover		*35.00*
43	A17	15c ocher & blk	37.50	20.00
		Never hinged	175.00	
		On cover		*37.50*
44	A18	50c olive & blk	4.25	2.75
		Never hinged	17.50	
		On cover		*92.50*
		Nos. 41-44 (4)	43.75	24.40
		Set, never hinged	200.00	

Port Matadi A19

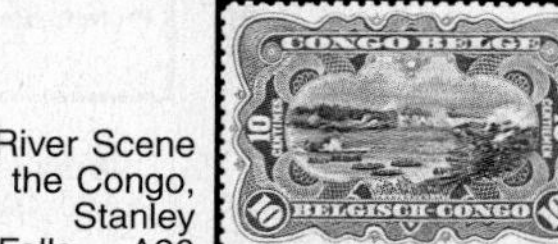

River Scene on the Congo, Stanley Falls — A20

Climbing Oil Palms — A21

Inkissi Falls — A22

Congo Canoe A23

Railroad Bridge on M'pozo River — A24

Hunting Elephants A25

Congo Village A26

Bangala Chief and Wife — A27

River Steamer on the Congo A28

1910-15 Engr. *Perf. 14, 15*

No.	Type	Description	Unused	Used
45	A19	5c green & blk	.75	.30
		Never hinged	1.75	
		On cover		*10.00*
46	A20	10c carmine & blk	.75	.30
		Never hinged	1.75	
		On cover		*10.00*
a.		10c lake & black	62.50	62.50
		Never hinged	125.00	
		On cover		—
47	A21	15c ocher & blk	.70	.30
		Never hinged	1.50	
		On cover		*20.00*
48	A21	15c grn & blk ('15)	.60	.25
		Never hinged	.95	
		On cover		*10.00*
a.		Booklet pane of 10	25.00	
49	A22	25c blue & blk	2.25	.60
		Never hinged	5.00	
		On cover		*11.00*
50	A23	40c bluish grn & blk	3.25	2.50
		Never hinged	5.00	
		On cover		*20.00*
51	A23	40c brn red & blk ('15)	5.50	3.00
		Never hinged	17.50	
		On cover		*110.00*
52	A24	50c olive & blk	5.00	2.50
		Never hinged	11.00	
		On cover		*35.00*
53	A24	50c brn lake & blk ('15)	9.50	3.00
		Never hinged	26.00	
		On cover		*25.00*

54 A25 1fr carmine & blk 4.50 3.75
Never hinged 9.75
On cover 105.00
55 A25 1fr ol bis & blk ('15) 3.50 1.10
Never hinged 11.00
On cover 80.00
56 A26 3fr red & blk 23.00 14.50
Never hinged 50.00
On cover 100.00
57 A27 5fr carmine & blk 35.00 32.50
Never hinged 140.00
On cover 100.00
58 A27 5fr ocher & blk ('15) 2.50 1.25
Never hinged 6.25
On cover 75.00
59 A28 10fr green & blk 29.00 26.00
Never hinged 95.00
On cover 100.00
Nos. 45-59 (15) 125.80 91.85
Set, never hinged 370.00

Nos. 48, 51, 53, 55 and 58 exist imperforate. Value, set $150.

Covers: Value for No. 59 is for overfranked cover, usually philatelic.

For overprints and surcharges see Nos. 64-76, 81-86, B5-B9.

For stamps of Belgian Congo overprinted "RUANDA", "URUNDI" or "EST AFRICAIN ALLEMAND OCCUPATION BELGE", see German East Africa.

Port Matadi A29

Stanley Falls, Congo River — A30

Inkissi Falls — A31

TEN CENTIMES.
Type I — Large white space at top of picture and two small white spots at lower edge. Vignette does not fill frame.
Type II — Vignette completely fills frame.

1915
60 A29 5c green & blk .30 .25
Never hinged 1.00
On cover 6.25
a. Booklet pane of 10 19.00
61 A30 10c car & blk (II) .30 .25
Never hinged 2.00
On cover 6.25
a. 10c carmine & black (I) .30 .25
Never hinged .95
On cover 6.25
d. Booklet pane of 10 (II) 25.00
62 A31 25c blue & blk 1.50 .50
Never hinged 5.00
On cover 12.50
a. Booklet pane of 10 125.00
Nos. 60-62 (3) 2.10 1.00
Set, never hinged 8.00

Nos. 60-62 exist imperforate. Value, set $15.
For surcharges see Nos. 77-80, 87, B1-B4.
For stamps of Belgian Congo overprinted "RUANDA", "URUNDI" or "EST AFRICAIN ALLEMAND OCCUPATION BELGE", see German East Africa.

Stamps of 1910 Issue Surcharged in Red or Black

1921
64 A23 5c on 40c bluish grn & blk (R) .40 .40
Never hinged .70
On cover 7.50
65 A19 10c on 5c grn & blk (R) .40 .40
Never hinged .70
On cover 6.25
66 A24 15c on 50c ol & blk (R) .40 .40
Never hinged .70
On cover 7.50
a. Inverted surcharge 275.00
67 A21 25c on 15c ocher & blk (R) 2.75 1.40
Never hinged 4.25
On cover 25.00
68 A20 30c on 10c car & blk .75 .70
Never hinged 1.40
On cover 9.50
69 A22 50c on 25c bl & blk (R) 2.75 1.50
Never hinged 5.25
On cover 15.00
Nos. 64-69 (6) 7.45 4.80
Set, never hinged 13.00

The position of the new value and the bars varies on Nos. 64 to 69.

No. 54 Overprinted

1921
70 A25 1fr carmine & blk 1.60 1.60
Never hinged 4.00
On cover 110.00
a. Double overprint 125.00
71 A26 3fr red & blk 4.00 3.50
Never hinged 10.00
72 A27 5fr carmine & blk 12.00 11.00
Never hinged 30.00
73 A28 10fr green & blk (R) 8.50 5.75
Never hinged 26.00
Nos. 70-73 (4) 26.10 21.85
Set, never hinged 67.50

Belgian Surcharges

Nos. 51, 53, 60-62 Surcharged in Black or Red

1922
74 A24 5c on 50c .65 .55
Never hinged 1.25
On cover 11.00
a. Inverted surcharge 120.00 120.00
75 A29 10c on 5c (R) .65 .50
Never hinged 1.25
On cover 11.00
76 A23 25c on 40c (R) 3.75 .60
Never hinged 9.50
On cover 30.00
77 A30 30c on 10c (II) .40 .40
Never hinged .75
On cover 7.50
a. 30c on 10c (I) .65 .35
Never hinged 1.25
b. Double surcharge 7.50 7.50
c. Inverted surcharge 190.00 190.00
78 A31 50c on 25c (R) 1.25 .45
Never hinged 3.25
On cover 25.00
a. Inverted surcharge 190.00 190.00
Nos. 74-78 (5) 6.70 2.50
Set, never hinged 16.00

No. 74 has the surcharge at each side.

Congo Surcharges
Nos. 60, 51 Surcharged in Red or Black

a

b

1922
80 A29 10c on 5c (R) .70 .70
Never hinged 2.25
On cover 15.00
a. Inverted surcharge 47.50 37.50
b. Double surcharge 6.00
c. Double surch., one invtd. 50.00
d. Pair, one without surcharge 52.50
e. On No. 45 325.00 325.00
81 A23 25c on 40c 1.25 .65
Never hinged 4.00
On cover 45.00
a. Inverted surcharge 47.50 37.50
b. Double surcharge 6.75
c. "25c" double
d. 25c on 5c, No. 60 225.00 225.00

Nos. 55, 58 Surcharged in Red

1922
84 A25 10c on 1fr (R) .75 .60
Never hinged 2.25
On cover 45.00
a. Double surcharge 17.50
b. Inverted surcharge 47.50 37.50
85 A27 25c on 5fr 2.50 2.50
Never hinged 7.00
On cover 100.00

Nos. 68, 77 Handstamped

86 A20 25c on 30c on 10c 25.00 22.50
Never hinged 45.00
On cover 90.00
87 A30 25c on 30c on 10c (II) 22.50 22.50
Never hinged 42.50
On cover 90.00

Nos. 86-87 exist with handstamp surcharge inverted.
Counterfeit handstamped surcharges exist.

Ubangi Woman — A32

Watusi Cattle — A44

Designs: 10c, Baluba woman. 15c, Babuende woman. No. 91, 40c, 1.25fr, 1.50fr, 1.75fr, Ubangi man. 25c, Basketmaking. 30c, 35c, No. 101, Weaving. No. 102, Carving wood. 50c, Archer. Nos. 92, 100, Weaving. 1fr, Making pottery. 3fr, Working rubber. 5fr, Making palm oil. 10fr, African elephant.

1923-27 Engr. *Perf. 12*
88 A32 5c yellow .35 .25
Never hinged .60
89 A32 10c green .25 .25
Never hinged .60
On cover 15.00
90 A32 15c olive brown .25 .25
Never hinged .60
On cover 6.25
91 A32 20c olive grn ('24) .25 .25
Never hinged .60
On cover 15.00
92 A44 20c green ('26) .50 .25
Never hinged .60
On cover 7.50
93 A44 25c red brown .30 .25
Never hinged .60
On cover 6.25
94 A44 30c rose red ('24) .65 .65
Never hinged 1.90
On cover 21.00
95 A44 30c olive grn ('25) .30 .25
Never hinged .60
On cover 3.00
96 A44 35c green ('27) .75 .45
Never hinged 1.10
On cover 12.50
97 A32 40c violet ('25) .30 .25
Never hinged 1.10
On cover 12.50
98 A44 50c gray blue .30 .25
Never hinged .60
On cover 6.25
99 A44 50c buff ('25) .65 .25
Never hinged .95
On cover 4.00
100 A44 75c red orange .30 .25
Never hinged 1.90
On cover 21.00
101 A44 75c gray bl ('25) .65 .35
Never hinged 1.10
On cover 7.50
102 A44 75c salmon red ('26) .30 .25
Never hinged .60
On cover 6.25
103 A44 1fr bister brown .85 .40
Never hinged 1.50
On cover 27.50
104 A44 1fr dl blue ('25) .65 .25
Never hinged 1.10
On cover 6.25
105 A44 1fr rose red ('27) 1.25 .25
Never hinged 4.25
On cover 6.25
106 A32 1.25fr dl blue ('26) .95 .40
Never hinged 1.90
On cover 12.50
107 A32 1.50fr dl blue ('26) .95 .30
Never hinged 1.90
On cover 19.00
108 A32 1.75fr dl blue ('27) 7.50 5.50
Never hinged 19.00
On cover 25.00
109 A44 3fr gray brn ('24) 6.00 3.25
Never hinged 18.00
On cover 105.00
110 A44 5fr gray ('24) 15.00 8.00
Never hinged 60.00
111 A44 10fr gray blk ('24) 27.50 15.00
Never hinged 115.00

1925-26
112 A44 45c dk vio ('26) .70 .40
Never hinged 1.10
On cover 9.25
113 A44 60c carmine rose .70 .30
Never hinged 1.10
On cover 3.00
Nos. 88-113 (26) 68.15 38.50
Set, never hinged 250.00

For surcharges see Nos. 114, 136-138, 157.

No. 107 Surcharged

1927, June 14
114 A32 1.75fr on 1.50fr dl bl 1.00 1.00
Never hinged 2.00
On cover 19.00

Sir Henry Morton Stanley — A45

1928, June 30 *Perf. 14*
115 A45 5c gray blk .25 .25
Never hinged .35
116 A45 10c dp violet .25 .25
Never hinged .35
On cover 25.00
117 A45 20c orange red .50 .30
Never hinged .75
On cover 25.00
118 A45 35c green 1.25 .75
Never hinged 2.50
On cover 15.00
119 A45 40c red brown .60 .25
Never hinged 1.10
On cover 15.00
120 A45 60c black brn 1.00 .50
Never hinged 1.50
On cover 11.00
121 A45 1fr carmine .40 .25
Never hinged 1.50
On cover 6.25
122 A45 1.60fr dk gray 9.00 8.00
Never hinged 30.00
On cover 50.00
123 A45 1.75fr dp blue 2.00 1.00
Never hinged 4.50
On cover 9.25
124 A45 2fr dk brown 1.60 .95
Never hinged 5.00
On cover 11.00
125 A45 2.75fr red violet 9.00 .45
Never hinged 30.00
On cover 37.50
126 A45 3.50fr rose lake 1.60 1.10
Never hinged 3.75
On cover 40.00
127 A45 5fr slate grn 1.50 1.10
Never hinged 4.25
On cover 30.00
128 A45 10fr violet blue 2.00 1.10
Never hinged 4.50
129 A45 20fr claret 9.00 7.00
Never hinged 30.00
Nos. 115-129 (15) 39.95 23.25
Set, never hinged 130.00

Sir Henry M. Stanley (1841-1904), explorer.
Nos. 115-129 exist in two sizes: 36mm and 37mm high.

Nos. 118, 121-123, 125-126 Surcharged in Red, Blue or Black

1931, Jan. 15

130 A45 40c on 35c 1.50 .65
Never hinged 4.00
On cover 19.00
131 A45 1.25fr on 1fr (Bl) 1.00 .25
Never hinged 2.50
On cover 9.25
132 A45 2fr on 1.60fr 1.50 .50
Never hinged 4.00
On cover 30.00
133 A45 2fr on 1.75fr 1.50 .40
Never hinged 4.00
On cover 35.00
134 A45 3.25fr on 2.75fr (Bk) 4.00 3.00
Never hinged 13.00
On cover 27.50
135 A45 3.25fr on 3.50fr (Bk) 8.75 7.50
Never hinged 25.00
On cover 37.50

Nos. 96, 108, 112 Surcharged in Red

Perf. 12½, 12

136 A44 40c on 35c grn 6.00 5.00
Never hinged 13.50
On cover 42.50
137 A44 50c on 45c dk vio 3.75 2.00
Never hinged 12.50
On cover 37.50

No. 108 Surcharged

138 A32 2(fr) on 1.75fr dl bl 18.50 16.00
Never hinged 62.50
On cover 62.50
Nos. 130-138 (9) 46.50 35.30
Set, never hinged 160.00

View of Sankuru River — A46

Flute Players — A50

Designs: 15c, Kivu Kraal. 20c, Sankuru River rapids. 25c, Uele hut. 50c, Musicians of Lake Leopold II. 60c, Batetelas drummers. 75c, Mangbetu woman. 1fr, Domesticated elephant of Api. 1.25fr, Mangbetu chief. 1.50fr, 2fr, Village of Mondimbi. 2.50fr, 3.25fr, Okapi. 4fr, Canoes at Stanleyville. 5fr, Woman preparing cassava. 10fr, Baluba chief. 20fr, Young woman of Irumu.

1931-37 Engr. *Perf. 11½*

139 A46 10c gray brn ('32) .25 .25
Never hinged .70
On cover 19.00
140 A46 15c gray ('32) .25 .25
Never hinged .70
On cover 19.00
141 A46 20c brn lil ('32) .25 .25
Never hinged .70
On cover 19.00
142 A46 25c dp blue ('32) .25 .25
Never hinged .75
On cover 11.00
143 A50 40c dp grn ('32) .30 .30
Never hinged .75
On cover 11.00
144 A46 50c violet ('32) .25 .25
Never hinged .70
On cover 11.00
b. Booklet pane of 8 7.00
Never hinged 13.00
145 A50 60c vio brn ('32) .30 .30
Never hinged .70
On cover 5.00
146 A50 75c rose ('32) .30 .30
Never hinged .70
On cover 3.00
b. Booklet pane of 8 5.50
Never hinged 9.25
147 A50 1fr rose red ('32) .30 .30
Never hinged .70
On cover 3.00
148 A50 1.25fr red brown .30 .30
Never hinged .70
b. Booklet pane of 8 5.50
Never hinged 9.25
149 A46 1.50fr dk ol gray ('37) .30 .30
Never hinged .80
On cover 3.75
b. Booklet pane of 8 9.00
Never hinged 11.00
150 A46 2fr ultra ('32) .35 .30
Never hinged .80
On cover 7.50
151 A46 2.50fr dp blue ('37) .50 .30
Never hinged 1.40
On cover 7.50
b. Booklet pane of 8 15.00
Never hinged 15.00
152 A46 3.25fr gray blk ('32) .80 .50
Never hinged 2.00
On cover 12.50
153 A46 4fr dl vio ('32) .50 .30
Never hinged .95
On cover 12.50
154 A50 5fr dp vio ('32) 1.00 .40
Never hinged 2.75
On cover 15.00
155 A50 10fr red ('32) 1.25 1.00
Never hinged 4.00
156 A50 20fr blk brn ('32) 2.50 1.50
Never hinged 7.50
Nos. 139-156 (18) 9.95 7.35
Set, never hinged 27.50

No. 109 Surcharged in Red

1932, Mar. 15 *Perf. 12*

157 A44 3.25fr on 3fr gray brn 9.00 6.00
Never hinged 27.00
On cover 75.00

King Albert Memorial Issue

King Albert — A62

1934, May 7 Photo. *Perf. 11½*

158 A62 1.50fr black 1.25 .90
Never hinged 3.00
On cover 7.50

No. 158 exists imperf. Value, $67.50.

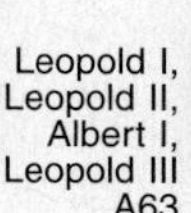

Leopold I, Leopold II, Albert I, Leopold III A63

1935, Aug. 15 Engr. *Perf. 12½x12*

159 A63 50c green 1.75 1.00
Never hinged 4.50
On cover 19.00
160 A63 1.25fr dk carmine 1.75 .35
Never hinged 5.50
On cover 9.25
161 A63 1.50fr brown vio 1.75 .35
Never hinged 5.50
On cover 9.25
162 A63 2.40fr brown org 5.75 5.75
Never hinged 16.00
163 A63 2.50fr lt blue 5.75 2.00
Never hinged 16.00
On cover 9.25
164 A63 4fr brt violet 5.75 2.75
Never hinged 16.00
On cover 15.00
165 A63 5fr black brn 5.75 3.00
Never hinged 16.00
On cover 20.00
Nos. 159-165 (7) 28.25 15.20
Set, never hinged 80.00

Founding of Congo Free State, 50th anniv.

Nos. 159-165 exist imperf. Value set, $3,500.

For surcharges see Nos. B21-B22.

Molindi River — A64

Suza River — A66

Bamboos — A65

Rutshuru River — A67

Karisimbi A68

Mitumba Forest A69

1937-38 Photo. *Perf. 11½*

166 A64 5c purple & blk .30 .25
Never hinged .50
On cover 15.00
167 A65 90c car & brn .50 .35
Never hinged .80
168 A66 1.50fr dp red brn & blk .40 .35
Never hinged .90
On cover 7.50
169 A67 2.40fr ol blk & brn .35 .30
Never hinged .95
170 A68 2.50fr dp ultra & blk .50 .30
Never hinged .85
On cover 11.00
171 A69 4.50fr dk grn & brn .55 .45
Never hinged .80
On cover 11.00
172 A69 4.50fr car & sep .50 .50
Never hinged 1.20
On cover 15.00
Nos. 166-172 (7) 3.10 2.50
Set, never hinged 7.50

National Parks.

Nos. 166-171 were issued Mar. 1, 1938. Exist imperf. Value, set $100.

No. 172 was issued in sheets of four measuring 140x111mm. It was sold by subscription, the subscription closing Dec. 31, 1938. Value: unused $3.75; never hinged $8. Exists imperf. Value, $1,250.

See No. B26. For surcharges see Nos. 184, 186 in *Scott Standard Postage Stamp Catalogue*, Vol. 1.

SEMI-POSTAL STAMPS

Types of 1910-15 Issues Surcharged in Red

1918, May 15 Unwmk. *Perf. 14, 15*

B1 A29 5c + 10c grn & bl .50 .50
Never hinged 1.25
B2 A30 10c + 15c car & bl (I) .50 .50
Never hinged 1.25
B3 A21 15c + 20c bl grn & bl .50 .50
Never hinged 1.25
B4 A31 25c + 25c dp bl & pale bl .50 .50
Never hinged 1.25
B5 A23 40c + 40c brn red & bl .75 .75
Never hinged 1.90
B6 A24 50c + 50c brn lake & bl .75 .75
Never hinged 1.90
B7 A25 1fr + 1fr ol bis & bl 3.00 3.00
Never hinged 6.25
B8 A27 5fr + 5fr ocher & bl 15.00 15.00
Never hinged 40.00
B9 A28 10fr + 10fr grn & bl 160.00 160.00
Never hinged 475.00
Nos. B1-B9 (9) 181.50 *181.50*
Set, never hinged 525.00

The position of the cross and the added value varies on the different stamps.

Nos. B1-B9 exist imperforate without gum. Value, set $600.

Perf 15 examples of Nos. B1-B6 are worth approximately twice the values shown.

For overprints, see German East Africa Nos. NB1-NB9.

SP1

Design: No. B11, Inscribed "Belgisch Congo."

1925, July 8 *Perf. 12½*

B10 SP1 25c + 25c car & blk .40 .40
Never hinged .60
B11 SP1 25c + 25c car & blk .40 .40
Never hinged .60
a. Pair, Nos. B10-B11 1.00 1.00
Never hinged 1.60

Colonial campaigns in 1914-1918.

The surtax helped erect at Kinshasa a monument to those who died in World War I.

Nurse Weighing Child — SP3

First Aid Station SP5

Designs: 20c+10c, Missionary & Child. 60c+30c, Congo hospital. 1fr+50c, Dispensary service. 1.75fr+75c, Convalescent area. 3.50fr+1.50fr, Instruction on bathing infant. 5fr+2.50fr, Operating room. 10fr+5fr, Students.

1930, Jan. 16 Engr. *Perf. 11½*

B12 SP3 10c + 5c ver 1.00 1.00
Never hinged 1.25
B13 SP3 20c + 10c dp brn 1.25 1.25
Never hinged 1.60
B14 SP5 35c + 15c dp grn 1.90 1.90
Never hinged 4.00
B15 SP5 60c + 30c dl vio 2.25 2.25
Never hinged 4.50
B16 SP3 1fr + 50c dk car 3.75 3.75
Never hinged 7.50
B17 SP5 1.75fr + 75c dp bl 8.75 8.75
Never hinged 22.50
B18 SP5 3.50fr + 1.50fr rose lake 11.00 11.00
Never hinged 22.50
B19 SP5 5fr + 2.50fr red brn 15.00 15.00
Never hinged 40.00
B20 SP5 10fr + 5fr gray blk 17.50 17.50
Never hinged 52.50
Nos. B12-B20 (9) 62.40 62.40
Set, never hinged 160.00

The surtax was intended to aid welfare work among the natives, especially the children.

Nos. 161, 163 Surcharged "+50c" in Blue or Red

1936, May 15 *Perf. 12½x12*

B21 A63 1.50fr + 50c (Bl) 8.75 5.75
Never hinged 18.00
On cover 37.50
B22 A63 2.50fr + 50c (R) 4.50 3.00
Never hinged 7.00
On cover 37.50
Set, never hinged 25.00

Surtax was for the King Albert Memorial Fund.

Queen Astrid with Congolese Children — SP12

1936, Aug. 29 **Photo.** *Perf. 12½*

B23 SP12 1.25fr + 5c dk brn .65 .65
Never hinged 1.60
On cover 19.00
B24 SP12 1.50fr + 10c dull rose .65 .65
Never hinged 1.60
On cover 19.00
B25 SP12 2.50fr + 25c dk blue 1.25 1.25
Never hinged 3.75
On cover 20.00
Nos. B23-B25 (3) 2.55 2.55
Set, never hinged 7.00

Issued in memory of Queen Astrid. The surtax was for the aid of the National League for Protection of Native Children.

Souvenir Sheet

National Parks — SP13

1938, Oct. 3 *Perf. 11½*

Star in Yellow

B26 SP13 Sheet of 6 67.50 67.50
Never hinged 130.00
On first day cover 80.00
a. 5c ultra & light brown 6.00 6.00
b. 90c ultra & light brown 6.00 6.00
c. 1.50fr ultra & light brown 6.00 6.00
d. 2.40fr ultra & light brown 6.00 6.00
e. 2.50fr ultra & light brown 6.00 6.00
f. 4.50fr ultra & light brown 6.00 6.00

Intl. Tourist Cong. A surtax of 3.15fr was for the benefit of the Congo Tourist Service. Exists imperf. Value $1,350.

Marabou Storks and Vultures — SP14

Buffon's Kob — SP15

Designs: 1.50fr+1.50fr, Pygmy chimpanzees. 4.50fr+4.50fr, Dwarf crocodiles. 5fr+5fr, Lioness.

1939, June 6 **Photo.** *Perf. 14*

B27 SP14 1fr + 1fr dp claret 10.00 *12.00*
Never hinged 19.00
B28 SP15 1.25fr + 1.25fr car 10.00 *12.00*
Never hinged 19.00
B29 SP15 1.50fr + 1.50fr brt pur 10.00 *12.00*
Never hinged 19.00
B30 SP14 4.50fr + 4.50fr sl grn 10.00 *12.00*
Never hinged 19.00
B31 SP15 5fr + 5fr brown 10.00 *12.00*
Never hinged 19.00
Nos. B27-B31 (5) 50.00 *60.00*
Set, never hinged 95.00

Surtax for the Leopoldville Zoological Gardens. Exists imperf. Value, set $225.
Sold in full sets by subscription.

AIR POST STAMPS

Wharf on Congo River AP1

Congo "Country Store" AP2

View of Congo River AP3

Stronghold in the Interior — AP4

Unwmk.

1920, July 1 **Engr.** *Perf. 12*

C1 AP1 50c orange & blk .70 .25
Never hinged 1.90
C2 AP2 1fr dull vio & blk .75 .25
Never hinged 2.25
C3 AP3 2fr blue & blk 1.10 .50
Never hinged 3.50
C4 AP4 5fr green & blk 2.00 .90
Never hinged 6.25
On cover 22.50
Nos. C1-C4 (4) 4.55 1.90
Set, never hinged 14.00

Kraal AP5

Porters on Safari AP6

1930, Apr. 2

C5 AP5 15fr dk brn & blk 3.25 1.10
Never hinged 10.00
C6 AP6 30fr brn vio & blk 3.50 1.75
Never hinged 12.50
Set, never hinged 22.50

Fokker F VII over Congo AP7

1934, Jan. 22 *Perf. 13½x14*

C7 AP7 50c gray black .30 .25
Never hinged .50
C8 AP7 1fr dk carmine .50 .25
Never hinged .80
a. Booklet pane of 8 8.00
Never hinged 12.50
C9 AP7 1.50fr green .50 .25
Never hinged 1.40
C10 AP7 3fr brown .35 .25
Never hinged .80
On cover 19.00
C11 AP7 4.50fr brt ultra .60 .25
Never hinged 1.40
On cover 4.75
a. Booklet pane of 8 14.00
Never hinged 25.00
C12 AP7 5fr red brown .45 .35
Never hinged 1.10
On cover 9.25
C13 AP7 15fr brown vio 1.00 .50
Never hinged 2.10
C14 AP7 30fr red orange 2.00 1.75
Never hinged 5.25
C15 AP7 50fr violet 5.50 3.00
Never hinged 13.50
Nos. C7-C15 (9) 11.20 6.85
Set, never hinged 27.50

The 1fr, 3fr, 4.50fr, 5fr, 15fr exist imperf. Values: 3fr, $37.50; 5fr, $60; 15fr, $32.50.

No. C10 Surcharged in Blue with New Value and Bars

1936, Mar. 25

C16 AP7 3.50fr on 3fr brown .60 .25
Never hinged 1.25
On cover 9.25

POSTAGE DUE STAMPS

In 1908-23 regular postage stamps handstamped "TAXES" or "TAXE," usually boxed, were used in lieu of postage due stamps.

D1

1923 **Typo.** **Unwmk.** *Perf. 14*

J1 D1 5c black brown .25 .25
Never hinged .35
J2 D1 10c rose red .25 .25
Never hinged .35
J3 D1 15c violet .25 .25
Never hinged .60
J4 D1 30c green .30 .25
Never hinged .75
J5 D1 50c ultramarine .40 .35
Never hinged 1.00
J6 D1 50c blue ('29) .45 .35
Never hinged 1.00
J7 D1 1fr gray .55 .40
Never hinged 1.40
Nos. J1-J7 (7) 2.45 2.10
Set, never hinged 6.00

Nos. J1-J7 exist imperf. Value, set $37.50.

PARCEL POST STAMPS

Nos. 5, 11-12 Handstamped Surcharges in Black or Blue

No. Q1

No. Q3

No. Q4

1887-93 **Unwmk.** *Perf. 15*

Q1 A1 3.50fr on 5fr lil 1,400. 1,000.
Q3 A4 3.50fr on 5fr vio 1,200. 675.00
Q4 A4 3.50fr on 5fr vio ('88) 950.00 550.00
Q6 A4 3.50fr on 5fr gray ('93) 190.00 190.00
Never hinged 300.00

Nos. Q1, Q3-Q4, and Q6 are known with inverted surcharge and double surcharge, and No. Q6 in pair with unsurcharged stamp. These varieties sell for somewhat more than the normal surcharges.

Genuine stamps with counterfeit surcharges, counterfeit stamps with counterfeit surcharges, and both with counterfeit cancels exist.

BELGIUM

'bel-jəm

LOCATION — Western Europe, bordering the North Sea
GOVT. — Constitutional Monarchy
AREA — 11,778 sq. mi.
POP. — 9,853,000 (est. 1983)
CAPITAL — Brussels

100 Centimes = 1 Franc

Watermarks

Wmk. 96 (With Frame)

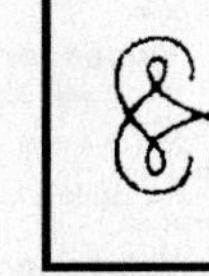
Wmk. 96a (No Frame)

King Leopold I — A1

Wmk. Two "L's" Framed (96)

1849 **Engr.** *Imperf.*

1 A1 10c brown *2,600.* 100.00
No gum 1,700.
On cover 175.00
a. 10c red brown *4,300.* 425.00
No gum 2,500.
On cover 750.00
b. 10c bister brown *2,900.* 140.00
No gum 1,800.
On cover 260.00
c. 10c dark brown *2,650.* 85.00
No gum 1,800.
On cover 210.00
2 A1 20c blue *2,650.* 57.50
No gum 1,900.
On cover 145.00
a. 20c milky blue *3,700.* 160.00
No gum 2,300.
On cover 400.00
b. 20c greenish blue *3,900.* 290.00
No gum 2,500.
On cover 500.00
c. 20c dark blue *3,100.* 62.50
No gum 2,000.
On cover 150.00

Full margins = ½mm.

The reprints are on thick and thin wove and thick laid paper unwatermarked.

A souvenir sheet containing reproductions of the 10c, 20c and 40c of 1849-51 with black burelage on back was issued Oct. 17, 1949, for the cent. of the 1st Belgian stamps. It was sold at BEPITEC 1949, an intl. stamp exhib. at Brussels, and was not valid. Value, $15.

Values for pairs

1 A1 10c brown 200.
On cover 450.
2 A1 20c blue 175.
On cover 425.

Values for strips of 3

1 A1 10c brown 900.
On cover 2,250.
2 A1 20c blue 675.
On cover 2,250.

Values for strips of 4

1 A1 10c brown 1,900.
On cover *10,000.*
2 A1 20c blue 1,600.
On cover *10,000.*

Values for blocks of 4

1 A1 10c brown 3,500.
On cover 10,000.
2 A1 20c blue 3,750.
On cover 10,000.

King Leopold I — A2

1849-50 — Thin Paper

No.	Description	Unused	Used
3	A2 10c brown ('50)	*2,500.*	100.00
	No gum	2,000.	
	On cover		175.00
4	A2 20c blue ('50)	*2,200.*	62.50
	No gum	1,500.	
	On cover		145.00
5	A2 40c carmine rose	*2,000.*	525.00
	No gum	1,500.	
	On cover		1,000.

Full margins = ½mm.

Thick Paper

No.	Description	Unused	Used
3a	A2 10c brown ('50)	*2,500.*	100.00
	No gum	2,100.	
	On cover		175.00
4a	A2 20c blue ('50)	*2,200.*	62.50
	No gum	1,550.	
	On cover		145.00
5a	A2 40c carmine rose	*2,000.*	525.00
	No gum	1,550.	
	On cover		1,000.

Values for pairs

No.	Description	Value
3	A2 10c brown ('50)	250.
	On cover	400.
4	A2 20c blue ('50)	175.
	On cover	290.
5	A2 40c carmine rose	1,150.
	On cover	1,425.

Values for strips of 3

No.	Description	Value
3	A2 10c brown ('50)	675.
	On cover	1,000.
4	A2 20c blue ('50)	425.
	On cover	675.
5	A2 40c carmine rose	1,775.
	On cover	2,250.

Values for strips of 4

No.	Description	Value
3	A2 10c brown ('50)	1,400.
	On cover	2,250.
4	A2 20c blue ('50)	900.
	On cover	1,350.
5	A2 40c carmine rose	2,250.
	On cover	2,900.

Values for blocks of 4

No.	Description	Value
3	A2 10c brown ('50)	2,500.
	On cover	3,500.
4	A2 20c blue ('50)	1,600.
	On cover	2,250.
5	A2 40c carmine rose	4,750.
	On cover	5,500.

Wmk. Two "L's" Without Frame (96a)

1851-54

Thick Wove Paper

No.	Description	Unused	Used
6	A2 10c brown	625.00	8.50
	No gum	375.00	
	On cover		17.50
a.	Ribbed paper ('54)	1,000.	62.50
7	A2 20c blue	800.00	8.00
	No gum	475.00	
	On cover		17.50
a.	Ribbed paper ('54)	1,000.	62.50
8	A2 40c car rose	*4,250.*	110.00
	No gum	2,300.	
	On cover		160.00
a.	Ribbed paper ('54)	*5,000.*	260.00

Full margins = ½mm.

Nos. 6a, 7a, 8a must have regular and parallel ribs covering the whole stamp.

Thin to Medium Wove Paper

No.	Description	Unused	Used
6b	A2 10c brown	675.00	9.00
	No gum	400.00	
	On cover		17.50
7b	A2 20c blue	875.00	8.50
	No gum	500.00	
	On cover		17.50
8b	A2 40c car rose	*4,200.*	110.00
	No gum	2,400.	
	On cover		170.00

Values for used pairs

No.	Description	Value
6	A2 10c brown	22.50
	On cover	65.00
7	A2 20c blue	22.50
	On cover	67.50
8	A2 40c car rose	265.00
	On cover	475.00

Values for strips of 3

No.	Description	Value
6	A2 10c brown	80.00
	On cover	140.00
7	A2 20c blue	85.00
	On cover	145.00
8	A2 40c car rose	575.00
	On cover	900.00

Values for strips of 4

No.	Description	Value
6	A2 10c brown	140.00
	On cover	275.00
7	A2 20c blue	140.00
	On cover	275.00
8	A2 40c car rose	1,350.
	On cover	2,000.

Values for blocks of 4

No.	Description	Value
6	A2 10c brown	300.00
	On cover	800.00
7	A2 20c blue	300.00
	On cover	800.00
8	A2 40c car rose	2,750.
	On cover	3,750.

1861 — Unwmk.

Stamps 17½x22mm; Oval 17¼high

No.	Description	Unused	Used
9	A2 1c green ('61)	*225.00*	125.00
	No gum	140.00	
	On wrapper		900.00
a.	1c pale green	225.00	140.00
	No gum	150.00	
	On wrapper		925.00
b.	1c dark green	225.00	150.00
	No gum	175.00	
	On wrapper		975.00
c.	1c deep bottle green	575.00	375.00
	No gum	425.00	
	On wrapper		1,100.
10	A2 10c brown	475.00	9.00
	No gum	325.00	
	On cover		15.00
a.	10c dark brown	500.00	11.00
	No gum	325.00	
	On cover		15.00
11	A2 20c blue	500.00	9.00
	No gum	325.00	
	On cover		15.00
a.	20c dark blue	525.00	10.50
	No gum	340.00	
	On cover		15.00
12	A2 40c vermilion	*3,750.*	150.00
	No gum	2,100.	
	On cover		160.00
a.	40c carmine rose	4,000.	150.00
	No gum	2,250.	
	On cover		160.00

Full margins = ½mm.

Nos. 9 and 13 were valid for postage on newspapers and printed matter only.

Reprints of Nos. 9-12 are on thin wove paper. The colors are brighter than those of the originals. They were made from the dies and show lines outside the stamps.

Values for pairs

No.	Description	Value
9	A2 1c green	290.00
	On cover	975.00
10	A2 10c brown	22.50
	On cover	40.00
11	A2 20c blue	22.50
	On cover	35.00
12	A2 40c vermilion	175.00
	On cover	310.00

Values for strips of 3

No.	Description	Value
9	A2 1c green	450.00
	On cover	1,100.
10	A2 10c brown	57.50
	On cover	90.00
11	A2 20c blue	57.50
	On cover	90.00
12	A2 40c vermilion	575.00
	On cover	1,000.

Values for strips of 4

No.	Description	Value
9	A2 1c green	775.00
	On cover	1,400.
10	A2 10c brown	110.00
	On cover	180.00
11	A2 20c blue	125.00
	On cover	190.00
12	A2 40c vermilion	1,500.
	On cover	1,800.

Values for blocks of 4

No.	Description	Value
9	A2 1c green	1,000.
	On cover	2,250.
10	A2 10c brown	350.00
	On cover	675.00
11	A2 20c blue	350.00
	On cover	725.00
12	A2 40c vermilion	2,300.
	On cover	3,600.

1858 — Unwmk.

Stamps 18x21mm; Oval 16½high

No.	Description	Unused	Used
10b	A2 10c brown	675.00	10.75
	No gum	375.00	
	On cover		18.00
11b	A2 20c blue	675.00	10.75
	No gum	375.00	
	On cover		18.00
12b	A2 40c vermilion	4,600.	110.00
	No gum	3,000.	
	On cover		200.00

Values for pairs

No.	Description	Value
10b	A2 10c brown	35.00
	On cover	150.00
11b	A2 20c blue	35.00
	On cover	150.00
12b	A2 40c vermilion	260.00
	On cover	775.00

Values for strips of 3

No.	Description	Value
10	A2 10c brown	90.00
	On cover	225.00
11	A2 20c blue	90.00
	On cover	225.00
12	A2 40c vermilion	725.00
	On cover	1,350.

Values for strips of 4

No.	Description	Value
10	A2 10c brown	175.00
	On cover	360.00
11	A2 20c blue	175.00
	On cover	375.00
12	A2 40c vermilion	1,750.
	On cover	2,500.

Values for blocks of 4

No.	Description	Value
10	A2 10c brown	350.00
	On cover	725.00
11	A2 20c blue	350.00
	On cover	725.00
12	A2 40c vermilion	*5,000.*
	On cover	*6,750.*

> Values for Nos. 13-16 are for stamps with perfs cutting into the design. Values for perforated stamps from Nos. 17 through 107 are for examples with perforations touching the design on one or two sides. Stamps with all perforations clear are exceptional and command substantial premiums.

1865, Sept. — *Perf. 14½*

No.	Description	Unused	Used
13	A2 1c green	62.50	26.00
	Never hinged	140.00	
	No gum	30.00	
	On wrapper		450.00
14	A2 10c brown	80.00	3.75
	Never hinged	180.00	
	No gum	35.00	
	On cover		9.00
a.	10c reddish brown	100.00	4.50
	Never hinged	250.00	
	No gum	52.50	
	On cover		9.50
15	A2 20c blue	80.00	3.50
	Never hinged	180.00	
	No gum	40.00	
	On cover		9.00
a.	20c turquoise blue	—	50.00
	On cover		75.00
16	A2 40c carmine rose	450.00	25.00
	Never hinged	975.00	
	No gum	210.00	
	On cover		60.00
a.	40c bright vermilion	525.00	67.50
	Never hinged	1,200.	
	No gum	310.00	
	On cover		90.00
b.	40c pomegranate red	1,100.	110.00
	Never hinged	2,400.	
	No gum	625.00	
	On cover		210.00
	Nos. 13-16 (4)	672.50	58.25

1863 — *Perf. 12½*

No.	Description	Unused	Used
13a	A2 1c green	200.00	80.00
	Never hinged	475.00	
	No gum	92.50	
	On wrapper		600.00
14b	A2 10c brown	225.00	5.00
	Never hinged	500.00	
	No gum	92.50	
	On cover		11.00
15b	A2 20c blue	225.00	5.00
	Never hinged	500.00	
	No gum	92.50	
	On cover		12.00
16c	A2 40c carmine rose	1,200.	35.00
	Never hinged	2,800.	
	No gum	600.00	
	On cover		75.00
16d	A2 40c vermilion	1,300.	45.00
	Never hinged	3,000.	
	No gum	600.00	
	On cover		90.00

1863, August — *Perf. 12½x13½*

No.	Description	Unused	Used
13b	A2 1c green	80.00	45.00
	Never hinged	180.00	
	No gum	37.50	
	On wrapper		475.00
13c	A2 1c emerald green	85.00	42.50
	Never hinged	200.00	
	No gum	40.00	
	On wrapper		525.00
14c	A2 10c brown	115.00	4.00
	Never hinged	260.00	
	No gum	47.50	
	On cover		10.00
15c	A2 20c blue	120.00	4.00
	Never hinged	275.00	
	No gum	47.50	
	On cover		10.00
16e	A2 40c carmine rose	650.00	35.00
	Never hinged	1,400.	
	No gum	315.00	
	On cover		67.50
16f	A2 40c bright vermilion	700.00	45.00
	Never hinged	1,600.	
	No gum	375.00	
	On cover		90.00

Values for Nos. 13-16f are for stamps with perfs cutting into design.

King Leopold I — A3a
A3

A4

A4a

A5

London Print

1865 — Typo. — *Perf. 14*

No.	Description	Unused	Used
17	A5 1fr pale violet	1,750.	110.00
	Never hinged	3,600.	
	No gum	1,000.	
	On cover		900.00

Brussels Print
Thick (Perf 15) or Thin (Perf 14½x14) Paper

1867 — *Perf. 15*

No.	Description	Unused	Used
18	A3 10c slate	185.00	2.25
	Never hinged	400.00	
	No gum	80.00	
	On cover		5.00
19	A3a 20c blue	290.00	2.00
	Never hinged	650.00	
	No gum	125.00	
	On cover		5.00
a.	20c lilac blue	460.00	2.75
	Never hinged	1,100.	
	No gum	140.00	
	On cover		6.50
20	A4 30c brown	625.00	11.00
	Never hinged	1,400.	
	No gum	300.00	
	On cover		24.00
21	A4a 40c rose	775.00	20.00
	Never hinged	1,700.	
	No gum	350.00	
	On cover		110.00
22	A5 1fr violet	2,000.	97.50
	Never hinged	*4,500.*	
	No gum	850.00	
	On cover		750.00
a.	1fr lilac	2,100.	110.00
	Never hinged	*4,750.*	
	No gum	850.00	
	On cover		850.00

1865-66 — *Perf. 14½x14*

No.	Description	Unused	Used
18a	A3 10c slate	230.00	2.75
	Never hinged	500.00	
	No gum	100.00	
	On cover		5.50
b.	Pair, imperf. between		—
19b	A3a 20c blue	375.00	4.00
	Never hinged	850.00	
	No gum	170.00	
	On cover		5.50
19c	A3a 20c prussian blue	475.00	7.00
	Never hinged	1,100.	
	No gum	200.00	
	On cover		18.00
20a	A4 30c brown	700.00	11.50
	Never hinged	1,650.	
	No gum	350.00	
	On cover		24.00
b.	Pair, imperf. between	*2,000.*	
21a	A4a 40c rose	1,050.	20.00
	Never hinged	2,350.	
	No gum	425.00	
	On cover		90.00
22b	A5 1f violet	1,900.	125.00
	Never hinged	*4,300.*	
	No gum	925.00	
	On cover		700.00
22c	A5 1f dark violet	2,450.	475.00
	Never hinged	*5,600.*	
	No gum	1,300.	
	On cover		1,250.

The reprints are on thin paper, imperforate and ungummed.

Coat of Arms — A6

1866-67 — *Imperf.*

No.	Description	Unused	Used
23	A6 1c gray	250.00	150.00
	Never hinged	600.00	
	No gum	170.00	
	On wrapper		750.00

Perf. 14½x14

No.	Description	Unused	Used
24	A6 1c gray	57.50	16.00
	Never hinged	140.00	
	No gum	40.00	
	On wrapper		67.50
25	A6 2c blue ('67)	190.00	90.00
	Never hinged	475.00	
	No gum	125.00	
	On wrapper		775.00
a.	2c dark blue	200.00	100.00
	Never hinged	500.00	
	No gum	200.00	
	On wrapper		850.00
26	A6 5c brown	240.00	90.00
	Never hinged	550.00	
	No gum	160.00	
	On wrapper		450.00
a.	5c yellowish brown	250.00	92.50
	Never hinged	600.00	
	No gum	170.00	
	On wrapper		525.00

1867 — *Perf. 15*

No.	Description	Unused	Used
24a	A6 1c gray	45.00	16.00
	Never hinged	100.00	
	No gum	30.00	
	On wrapper		55.00
b.	1c bluish gray	300.00	100.00
	Never hinged	650.00	
	No gum	200.00	
	On wrapper		140.00
25b	A6 2c blue	140.00	90.00
	Never hinged	375.00	
	No gum	190.00	
	On wrapper		700.00
c.	2c ultramarine	150.00	110.00
	Never hinged	400.00	
	No gum	100.00	
	On wrapper		825.00
26b	A6 5c brown	175.00	90.00
	Never hinged	440.00	
	No gum	115.00	
	On wrapper		525.00
c.	5c yellowish brown	200.00	92.50
	Never hinged	500.00	
	No gum	130.00	
	On wrapper		625.00
d.	5c bister brown	190.00	95.00
	Never hinged	475.00	
	No gum	125.00	
	On wrapper		625.00
	Nos. 23-26b (2)	390.00	240.00

Nos. 23-26d were valid for postage on newspapers and printed matter only.

Counterfeits exist.

Reprints of Nos. 24-26 are on thin paper, imperforate and without gum.

Imperf. varieties of 1869-1912 (between Nos. 28-105) are without gum.

A7

A8

A9

A10

A11

King Leopold II — A12

1869-70 ***Perf. 15***

28	A7	1c green	8.25	.40
		Never hinged	37.50	
		On cover, single franking		29.00
29	A7	2c ultra ('70)	25.00	1.65
		Never hinged	70.00	
		On cover, single franking		100.00
30	A7	5c buff ('70)	62.50	.75
		Never hinged	210.00	
		On cover, single franking		20.00
31	A7	8c lilac ('70)	67.50	50.00
		Never hinged	170.00	
		On cover, single franking		*725.00*
32	A8	10c green	27.50	.40
		Never hinged	75.00	
		On cover		3.75
33	A9	20c lt ultra ('70)	125.00	.90
		Never hinged	325.00	
		On cover		15.00
34	A10	30c buff ('70)	80.00	4.00
		Never hinged	160.00	
		On cover		10.00
a.		30c reddish ocher ('73)	82.50	4.00
		Never hinged	160.00	
		On cover		10.00
35	A11	40c brt rose ('70)	135.00	6.50
		Never hinged	400.00	
		On cover		120.00
a.		40c rose lilac	230.00	10.00
		Never hinged	500.00	
		On cover		120.00
36	A12	1fr dull lilac ('70)	400.00	17.00
		Never hinged	825.00	
		No gum	250.00	
		On cover		*700.00*
a.		1fr rose lilac	500.00	20.00
		Never hinged	850.00	
		No gum	300.00	
		On cover		*775.00*
		Nos. 28-36 (9)	930.75	81.60

The frames and inscriptions of Nos. 30, 31 and 42 differ slightly from the illustration.

Minor "broken letter" varieties exist on several values.

Nos. 28-30, 32-33, 35-38 also were printed in aniline colors. These are not valued separately.

Nos. 28-36 exist imperforate, without gum. The 1c and 2c are valued from $55 to $85. The 40c and 1fr stamps are scarcer, valued from $500 to $675. Some denominations exist with gum. Pairs command premiums. Large multiples are scarce.

See Nos. 40-43, 49-51, 55.

A13

A14

King Leopold II — A15

1875-78

37	A13	25c olive bister	165.00	1.45
		Never hinged	400.00	
		On cover		8.00
a.		25c ocher	185.00	1.55
		Never hinged	425.00	
		On cover		8.00
38	A14	50c gray	275.00	11.00
		Never hinged	675.00	
		On cover		150.00
		Roller cancel		12.50
a.		50c gray black	325.00	50.00
		Never hinged	700.00	
		On cover		200.00
b.		50c deep black	1,750.	250.00
		Never hinged	—	
		No gum	1,000.	
		On cover		800.00
39	A15	5fr dp red brown	*1,700.*	1,450.
		Never hinged	3,100.	
		No gum	1,000.	
		On cover		*11,000.*
		Roller cancel		700.00
a.		5fr pale brown ('78)	*3,750.*	1,450.
		Never hinged	—	
		No gum	2,250.	
		On cover		*11,000.*
		Roller cancel		700.00

No. 37 exists imperforate, without gum. Value, $250.

Dangerous counterfeits of No. 39 exist.

Printed in Aniline Colors

1881 ***Perf. 14***

40	A7	1c gray green	18.00	.85
		Never hinged	35.00	
		On cover, single franking		32.50
41	A7	2c lt ultra	19.00	3.00
		Never hinged	57.50	
		On cover, single franking		100.00
42	A7	5c orange buff	55.00	1.25
		Never hinged	165.00	
		On cover		30.00
a.		5c red orange	55.00	1.25
		Never hinged	165.00	
		On cover		30.00
43	A8	10c gray green	27.50	1.10
		Never hinged	70.00	
		On cover		5.00
44	A13	25c olive bister	95.00	3.00
		Never hinged	160.00	
		On cover		11.00
		Nos. 40-44 (5)	214.50	9.20

See note following No. 36.

A16

A17

A18

A19

1883

45	A16	10c carmine	27.50	2.50
		Never hinged	62.50	
		On cover		22.00
a.		10c carmine rose	30.00	2.90
		Never hinged	67.50	
		On cover		25.00
46	A17	20c gray	175.00	10.00
		Never hinged	575.00	
		On cover		125.00
a.		20c slate gray	200.00	11.00
		Never hinged	575.00	
		On cover		135.00
47	A18	25c blue	360.00	35.00
		Never hinged	1,200.	
		On cover		190.00
		Roller cancel		15.00
a.		25c dark blue	380.00	35.00
		Never hinged	1,200.	
		On cover		290.00
48	A19	50c violet	325.00	35.00
		Never hinged	800.00	
		On cover		300.00
		Roller cancel		15.00
a.		50c deep violet	350.00	45.00
		Never hinged	1,000.	
		On cover		310.00
		Nos. 45-48 (4)	887.50	82.50

A20

A21

A22

1884-85 ***Perf. 14***

49	A7	1c olive green	16.00	.75
		Never hinged	47.50	
		On cover, single franking		60.00
50	A7	1c gray	4.25	.40
		Never hinged	11.00	
		On cover, single franking		15.00
51	A7	5c green	37.50	.40
		Never hinged	110.00	
		On cover		8.00
52	A20	10c rose, *bluish*	12.50	.40
		Never hinged	37.50	
		On cover		3.50
a.		Grayish paper	13.50	.50
		Never hinged	40.00	
		On cover		5.00
c.		Yellowish paper	*225.00*	22.50
		Never hinged	*500.00*	
		On cover		*100.00*
53	A21	25c blue, *pink* ('85)	15.00	.75
		Never hinged	37.50	
		On cover		7.25
a.		25c blue, *dark rose*	16.50	1.00
		Never hinged	37.50	
		On cover		7.00
54	A22	1fr brown, *grnsh*	*750.00*	17.50
		Never hinged	2,150.	
		No gum	450.00	
		On cover		*550.00*
a.		1fr deep brown, *dk grn*	900.00	20.00
		Never hinged	2,400.	
		No gum	550.00	
		On cover		575.00

The frame and inscription of No. 51 differ slightly from the illustration.

See note after No. 36.

Nos. 50-54 exist imperforate, without gum. The 1c and 10c stamps are valued from $32.50 to $55. The 5c, 25c and 1fr stamps are valued from $160 to $375.

A23

A24

A25

A26

1886-91

55	A7	2c purple brn ('88)	13.50	1.65
		Never hinged	45.00	
		On cover, single franking		*70.00*
56	A23	20c olive, *grnsh*	200.00	1.65
		Never hinged	575.00	
		On cover		21.00
b.		20c deep olive, *grnsh*	210.00	1.90
		Never hinged	590.00	
		On cover		22.50
57	A24	35c vio brn, *brnsh* ('91)	18.00	3.00
		Never hinged	45.00	
		On cover		20.00
58	A25	50c bister, *yelsh*	12.50	2.25
		Never hinged	30.00	
		On cover		50.00
59	A26	2fr violet, *pale lil*	72.50	35.00
		Never hinged	125.00	
		On cover		*625.00*
		Roller cancel		7.50
a.		2fr vio, *brt lilac*	67.50	40.00
		Never hinged	140.00	
		On cover		*675.00*
		Nos. 55-59 (5)	316.50	43.55

Nos. 56 and 57 exist imperforate, without gum. No. 56 is valued at $275. No. 57 is valued at $55.

Values quoted for Nos. 60-107 are for unused and used stamps with label attached. Stamps without label sell for much less.

Coat of Arms A27

King Leopold A28

Type A27 has two 1mm high ornamental bands across the top and bottom of the label. These bands do not appear on Type A32.

1893-1900

60	A27	1c gray	1.00	.25
		Never hinged	1.65	
		On cover, single franking, without label		2.75
61	A27	2c yellow	1.00	1.10
		Never hinged	1.65	
		On cover, single franking, without label		*160.00*
a.		Wmkd. coat of arms in sheet ('95)	—	—
62	A27	2c violet brn ('94)	1.65	.40
		Never hinged	7.50	
		On cover, single franking, without label		*23.00*
63	A27	2c red brown ('98)	3.00	.90
		Never hinged	9.00	
		On cover, single franking, without label		*30.00*
64	A27	5c yellow grn	9.00	.30
		Never hinged	29.00	
		On cover, without label		2.00
65	A28	10c orange brn	4.00	.30
		Never hinged	20.00	
		On cover, without label		*4.00*
66	A28	10c brt rose ('00)	3.25	.40
		Never hinged	11.50	
		On cover, without label		*5.50*
67	A28	20c olive green	15.00	.60
		Never hinged	37.50	
		On cover, without label		*18.00*
68	A28	25c ultra	10.00	.50
		Never hinged	27.50	
		On cover, without label		4.00
a.		No ball to "5" in upper left corner	32.50	12.50
		Never hinged	92.50	
69	A28	35c violet brn	22.50	1.50
		Never hinged	65.00	
		On cover, without label		*15.00*
a.		35c red brown	35.00	2.40
		Never hinged	80.00	
		On cover, without label		*17.50*
70	A28	50c bister	57.50	20.00
		Never hinged	160.00	
		On cover, without label		85.00
71	A28	50c gray ('97)	62.50	2.50
		Never hinged	175.00	
		On cover, without label		*72.50*
72	A28	1fr car, *lt grn*	80.00	20.00
		Never hinged	225.00	
		On cover, without label		175.00
73	A28	1fr orange ('00)	100.00	5.00
		Never hinged	260.00	
		On cover, without label		*185.00*
a.		1fr yellow orange	105.00	6.00
		Never hinged	275.00	
		On cover, without label		*200.00*
74	A28	2fr lilac, *rose*	80.00	70.00
		Never hinged	160.00	
		On cover, without label		450.00
75	A28	2fr lilac ('00)	160.00	13.50
		Never hinged	350.00	
		On cover, without label		*425.00*
		Nos. 60-75 (16)	610.40	137.25
		Set, never hinged	1,700.	

Covers: Values for covers are for commercial items with proper frankings and stamps without labels. Stamps on postcards and printed envelopes sell for less than the values quoted.

Values for stamps with labels attached and perforations clear of the design, and for covers bearing these stamps.

60	A27	1c gray	2.00	.35
		Never hinged	3.25	
		On cover		7.00
61	A27	2c yellow	2.25	2.00
		Never hinged	3.25	
		On cover		400.00
62	A27	2c violet brn	3.25	.75
		Never hinged	15.00	
		On cover		55.00
63	A27	2c red brown	6.00	1.75
		Never hinged	17.50	
		On cover		70.00
64	A27	5c yellow grn	18.00	.55
		Never hinged	57.50	
		On cover		5.00
65	A28	10c orange brn	8.00	.55
		Never hinged	40.00	
		On cover		10.00
66	A28	10c brt rose	6.25	.75
		Never hinged	22.00	
		On cover		15.00
67	A28	20c olive green	30.00	1.10
		Never hinged	75.00	
		On cover		40.00
68	A28	25c ultra	20.00	.90
		Never hinged	55.00	
		On cover		10.00
a.		No ball to "5" in upper left corner	65.00	24.00
		Never hinged	190.00	
69	A28	35c violet brn	45.00	4.00
		Never hinged	130.00	
		On cover		37.50
a.		35c red brown	70.00	4.50
		Never hinged	160.00	
		On cover		47.50
70	A28	50c bister	115.00	37.50
		Never hinged	310.00	
		On cover		190.00
71	A28	50c gray)	125.00	4.50
		Never hinged	350.00	
		On cover		150.00
72	A28	1fr car, *lt grn*	160.00	37.50
		Never hinged	450.00	
		On cover		425.00
73	A28	1fr orange	200.00	9.00
		Never hinged	520.00	
		On cover		450.00
a.		1fr yellow orange	210.00	11.50
		Never hinged	550.00	
		On cover		450.00
74	A28	2fr lilac, *rose*	160.00	135.00
		Never hinged	310.00	
		On cover		950.00
75	A28	2fr lilac	320.00	25.00
		Never hinged	700.00	
		On cover		1,000.

Very thin transparent paper (1904-05)

60a	A27	1c gray	3.75	2.50
		Never hinged	6.00	
62a	A27	2c violet brown	6.00	4.25
		Never hinged	12.00	
64a	A27	5c yellow green	11.50	10.00
		Never hinged	35.00	
66a	A28	10c bright rose	26.00	18.00
		Never hinged	52.50	

68b	A28	25c ultramarine	45.00	30.00
		Never hinged	80.00	
69b	A28	35c violet brown	50.00	32.50
		Never hinged	92.50	
71a	A28	50c gray	100.00	55.00
		Never hinged	200.00	
73b	A28	1fr orange	240.00	145.00
		Never hinged	450.00	

Antwerp Exhibition Issue

Arms of Antwerp — A29

1894

76	A29	5c green, *rose*	4.75	3.25
		Never hinged	12.50	
		On cover, with label		*36.00*
77	A29	10c carmine, *bluish*	3.75	2.50
		Never hinged	7.50	
		On cover, with label		*32.50*
78	A29	25c blue, *rose*	1.00	1.00
		Never hinged	1.00	
		On cover, with label		*55.00*
		Nos. 76-78 (3)	9.50	6.75
		Set, never hinged	22.00	

Brussels Exhibition Issue

St. Michael and Satan
A30 A31

1896-97 ***Perf. 14x14***

79	A30	5c dp violet	1.00	.60
		Never hinged	1.40	
		On cover, with label		*27.50*
		Sheet of 25	25.00	17.50
		Never hinged	40.00	
80	A31	10c orange brown	8.50	3.50
		Never hinged	20.00	
		On cover, with label		*32.50*
		Sheet of 25	425.00	300.00
		Never hinged	550.00	
81	A31	10c lilac brown	.50	.35
		Never hinged	.65	
		On cover, with label		*22.50*
		Sheet of 25	12.50	12.50
		Never hinged	16.00	
		Nos. 79-81 (3)	10.00	4.45
		Set, never hinged	25.00	

A32

A33

A34

A35

A36

A37

A38

A39

Two types of 1c:
I — Periods after "Dimanche" and "Zondag" in label.
II — No period after "Dimanche." Period often missing after "Zondag."

1905-11 ***Perf. 14***

82	A32	1c gray (I) ('07)	1.50	.25
		Never hinged	3.60	
		On cover, single franking, without label		*3.00*
a.		Type II ('08)	2.00	.60
		Never hinged	4.50	
		On cover, single franking, without label		*5.00*
83	A32	2c red brown ('07)	14.50	5.75
		Never hinged	45.00	
		On cover, single franking, without label		*20.00*
84	A32	5c green ('07)	11.50	.60
		Never hinged	32.50	
		On cover, without label		*3.00*
85	A33	10c dull rose	1.75	.60
		Never hinged	4.00	
		On cover, without label		*5.00*
86	A34	20c olive grn	26.00	1.00
		Never hinged	70.00	
		On cover, without label		*20.00*
87	A35	25c ultra	12.00	.85
		Never hinged	32.50	
		On cover, without label		*5.00*
a.		25c deep blue ('11)	13.50	2.00
		Never hinged	40.00	
		On cover, without label		*7.25*
88	A36	35c red brn	27.50	2.40
		Never hinged	75.00	
		On cover, without label		*30.00*
a.		35c purple brown ('05)	27.50	2.40
		Never hinged	72.50	
		On cover, without label		*30.00*
89	A37	50c bluish gray	95.00	4.00
		Never hinged	235.00	
		On cover, without label		*85.00*
90	A38	1fr yellow orange	110.00	8.00
		Never hinged	340.00	
		On cover, without label		*175.00*
a.		1fr orange ('09)	130.00	9.00
		Never hinged	360.00	
		On cover, without label		*190.00*
91	A39	2fr violet	75.00	22.50
		Never hinged	240.00	
		On cover, without label		—
		Bar cancellation		5.00
		Nos. 82-91 (10)	374.75	45.95
		Set, never hinged	800.00	

Values for covers bearing stamps with labels attached, and perforations clear of the design

82	A32	1c gray (I)	7.00
a.		Type II	12.00
83	A32	2c red brown	45.00
84	A32	5c green	7.00
85	A33	10c dull rose	12.00
86	A34	20c olive grn	40.00
87	A35	25c ultra	10.00
a.		25c deep blue	16.50
88	A36	35c red brn	65.00
a.		35c purple brown	70.00
89	A37	50c bluish gray	185.00
90	A38	1fr yellow orange	425.00
a.		1fr orange	450.00
91	A39	2fr violet	—

A40

A41

Lion of Belgium — A42

A43

King Albert I — A44

1912

92	A40	1c orange	.25	.25
		Never hinged	.30	
		On cover, single franking		2.00
93	A41	2c orange brn	.25	.45
		Never hinged	.40	
		On cover, single franking		20.00
94	A42	5c green	.25	.25
		Never hinged	.30	
		On cover		1.00
95	A43	10c red	.75	.40
		Never hinged	2.40	
		On cover		4.00
96	A43	20c olive grn	16.00	4.00
		Never hinged	35.00	
		On cover		22.50
a.		20c bronze green	90.00	27.50
		Never hinged	200.00	
		On cover		125.00
97	A43	35c bister brn	1.00	.70
		Never hinged	2.00	
		On cover		17.50
98	A43	40c green	16.00	14.50
		Never hinged	40.00	
		On cover		65.00
99	A43	50c gray	1.00	.80
		Never hinged	2.10	
		On cover		30.00
100	A43	1fr orange	4.00	3.00
		Never hinged	8.75	
		On cover		110.00
101	A43	2fr violet	17.50	17.50
		Never hinged	29.00	
		On cover		135.00
102	A44	5fr plum	80.00	25.00
		Never hinged	175.00	
		On cover		150.00
		Set, never hinged	800.00	
		Nos. 92-102 (11)	137.00	66.85

Counterfeits exist of Nos. 97-102. Those of No. 102 are common.

Covers: Values for stamps on cover are for stamps with labels attached. Covers bearing stamps without labels are worth about half of the values given.

For overprints see Nos. Q49-Q50, Q52, Q55-Q55A, Q57-Q60.

A45

With Engraver's Name

1912-13 **Larger Head**

103	A45	10c red	.40	.25
		Never hinged	1.25	
		On cover		3.00
a.		Without engraver's name	.25	*.25*
		Never hinged	.30	
		On cover		3.00
104	A45	20c olive green ('13)	.40	.40
		Never hinged	.50	
		On cover		13.50
a.		Without engraver's name	2.00	2.00
		Never hinged	2.40	
		On cover		32.50
105	A45	25c ultramarine	4.25	*.30*
		Never hinged	7.00	
		On cover		7.00
a.		Without engraver's name	.25	*.40*
		Never hinged	.30	
		On cover		6.00
107	A45	40c green ('13)	.50	*.60*
		Never hinged	.70	
		On cover		42.50
		Nos. 103-107 (4)	5.55	1.55
		Set, never hinged	9.50	

For overprints see Nos. Q51, Q53-Q54, Q56.

Albert I
A46

Cloth Hall of Ypres
A47

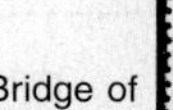

Bridge of Dinant — A48

Library of Louvain — A49

Scheldt River at Antwerp
A50

Anti-slavery Campaign in the Congo
A51

King Albert I at Furnes
A52

Kings of Belgium Leopold I, Albert I, Leopold II
A53

1915-20 **Typo.** ***Perf. 14***

108	A46	1c orange	.25	.25
		Never hinged	.30	
		On cover, single franking		4.00
109	A46	2c chocolate	.25	.25
		Never hinged	.30	
		On cover, single franking		6.00
110	A46	3c gray blk ('20)	.30	.25
		Never hinged	.80	
		On cover		2.00
111	A46	5c green	1.00	.25
		Never hinged	3.25	
		On cover		1.00
112	A46	10c carmine	.90	.25
		Never hinged	3.00	
		On cover		1.00
a.		10c bright carmine	3.00	.30
		Never hinged	6.75	
		On cover		2.00
113	A46	15c purple	1.50	.25
		Never hinged	4.25	
		On cover		2.00
114	A46	20c red violet	3.00	.25
		Never hinged	10.00	
		On cover		4.00
115	A46	25c blue	.50	.40
		Never hinged	1.10	
		On cover		6.75
a.		25c bright blue	1.10	.50
		Never hinged	3.00	
		On cover		7.75

Engr.

116	A47	35c brown org & blk	.50	.30
		Never hinged	2.40	
		On cover		8.00
117	A48	40c green & black	1.00	.30
		Never hinged	1.40	
		On cover		11.50
a.		Vert. pair, imperf. btwn.		
118	A49	50c car rose & blk	4.50	.30
		Never hinged	12.50	
		On cover		11.00
119	A50	1fr violet	32.50	1.00
		Never hinged	90.00	
		On cover		32.50
120	A51	2fr slate	21.00	2.00
		Never hinged	57.50	
		On cover		55.00
a.		2fr gray black	25.00	2.40
		Never hinged	67.50	
		On cover		57.50
b.		2fr pale gray	42.50	7.75
		Never hinged	97.50	
		On cover		115.00
121	A52	5fr dp blue	275.00	125.00
		Never hinged	775.00	
		On cover		325.00
		Telegraph or railroad cancel		55.00
122	A53	10fr brown	20.00	20.00
		Never hinged	35.00	
		On cover		175.00
		Nos. 108-122 (15)	362.20	151.05

Set, never hinged 1,250.

Perf 15

116a A47 35c brown orange & black 1.60 .80
Never hinged 5.00
On cover 8.00
117b A48 40c green & black 1.60 .80
Never hinged 5.00
On cover 11.50
118a A49 50c carmine rose & black 6.00 1.00
Never hinged 17.50
On cover 11.50
119a A50 1f violet 37.50 4.00
Never hinged 110.00
On cover 35.00
120c A51 2f slate 27.50 5.75
Never hinged 77.50
On cover 57.50
121a A52 5f deep blue 350.00 145.00
Never hinged 1,050.
On cover 500.00
122a A53 10f brown 25.00 25.00
Never hinged 50.00
On cover 175.00

Two types each of the 1c, 10c and 20c; three of the 2c and 15c; four of the 5c, differing in the top left corner.

See No. 138. For surcharges see Nos. B34-B47.

Nos. 111-119 were handstamped "T" for local provisional use. See Nos. J16C-J16K.

Perron of Liege (Fountain) — A54

Size: 18¼x28½mm

1919, July 25 *Perf. 11½*
123 A54 25c blue 2.40 .35
Never hinged 8.50
On cover 9.00
a. 25c deep blue 3.00 .45
Never hinged 9.00

Size: 18½x28mm

1919, July 19
123B A54 25c blue 400.00 400.00
c. Sheet of 10 6,000. *6,000.*
Never hinged 7,000.

No. 123B is the first printing, which was issued in sheets of 10. Nos. 123 and 123a were later printings, issued in sheets of 100.

King Albert in Trench Helmet — A55

Perf. 11, 11½, 11½x11, 11x11½

1919 **Size: 18½x22mm**
124 A55 1c lilac brn .25 .25
Never hinged .30
125 A55 2c olive .25 .25
Never hinged .30
On cover, single franking 11.00

Size: 22x26

126 A55 5c green .25 .25
Never hinged .45
On cover 2.50
127 A55 10c carmine, 22x26¾mm .25 .25
Never hinged .50
On cover 2.00
a. Size: 22½x26mm 1.00 .60
Never hinged 2.00
On cover 6.00
128 A55 15c gray vio, 22x26¾mm .30 .30
Never hinged .60
On cover 3.50
a. Size: 22½x26mm 2.40 .60
Never hinged 5.50
On cover 6.75
129 A55 20c olive blk 1.10 1.10
Never hinged 2.00
On cover 23.50
130 A55 25c deep blue 1.60 1.60
Never hinged 2.75
On cover 14.00
131 A55 35c bister brn 3.00 3.00
Never hinged 3.50
132 A55 40c red 5.00 5.00
Never hinged 11.50
On cover 75.00
133 A55 50c red brn 9.50 10.00
Never hinged 19.00
On cover 135.00
134 A55 1fr lt orange 40.00 40.00
Never hinged 77.50
On cover 300.00
135 A55 2fr violet 375.00 375.00
Never hinged 575.00

Size: 28x33½mm

136 A55 5fr car lake 100.00 100.00
Never hinged 175.00
137 A55 10fr claret 110.00 110.00
Never hinged 275.00
Nos. 124-137 (14) 646.50 647.00
Set, never hinged 1,150.

Type of 1915 Inscribed: "FRANK" instead of "FRANKEN"

1919, Dec. *Perf. 14, 15*
138 A52 5fr deep blue 1.75 1.25
Never hinged 3.00
On cover 40.00

Town Hall at Termonde — A56

1920 *Perf. 11½*
139 A56 65c claret & black, 27x22mm .75 .25
Never hinged 1.50
On cover 12.00
a. Center inverted *67,500.*
b. Size: 26¼x22½mm 5.75 2.40
Never hinged 13.50
On cover 16.50

For surcharge see No. 143.

Nos. B48-B50 Surcharged in Red or Black

1921 *Perf. 12*
140 SP6 20c on 5c + 5c (R) .60 .25
Never hinged 1.90
On cover 10.00
a. Inverted surcharge 625.00 625.00
Never hinged 1,100.
On cover 2,200.
141 SP7 20c on 10c + 5c .40 .25
Never hinged 1.10
On cover 7.75
142 SP8 20c on 15c + 15c (R) .60 .25
Never hinged 1.90
On cover 10.00
a. Inverted surcharge 625.00 625.00
Never hinged 1,100.
On cover 2,200.

No. 139 Surcharged in Red

143 A56 55c on 65c claret & blk 1.50 .35
Never hinged 3.50
a. Pair, one without surcharge 2.25 .85
Never hinged 5.00
Nos. 140-143 (4) 3.10 1.10
Set, never hinged 8.50

A58

1922-27 **Typo.** *Perf. 14*
144 A58 1c orange .25 .25
Never hinged .35
On cover, single franking 10.00
145 A58 2c olive ('26) .25 .25
Never hinged .35
On cover, single franking 13.50
146 A58 3c fawn .25 .25
Never hinged .35
On cover 2.50
147 A58 5c gray .25 .25
Never hinged .35
On cover 1.00
148 A58 10c blue grn .25 .25
Never hinged .35
On cover 1.00
149 A58 15c plum ('23) .25 .25
Never hinged .35
On cover 1.25
150 A58 20c black brn .25 .25
Never hinged .45
On cover 2.00
151 A58 25c magenta .25 .25
Never hinged .45
On cover 1.00
a. 25c dull violet ('23) .50 .25
Never hinged 1.25
On cover 1.25
152 A58 30c vermilion .40 .25
Never hinged .60
On cover 4.00
153 A58 30c rose ('25) .35 .25
Never hinged .85
On cover 5.00
154 A58 35c red brown .35 .30
Never hinged .60
On cover 11.50
155 A58 35c blue grn ('27) .80 .35
Never hinged 1.50
On cover 6.75
156 A58 40c rose .50 .25
Never hinged .75
On cover 6.75
157 A58 50c bister ('25) .50 .25
Never hinged .90
On cover 3.00
158 A58 60c olive brn ('27) 3.75 .25
Never hinged 11.00
On cover 1.00
159 A58 1.25fr dp blue ('26) 1.50 1.25
Never hinged 2.25
On cover 50.00
160 A58 1.50fr brt blue ('26) 2.50 .50
Never hinged 4.25
On cover 9.00
a. 1.50fr bright sky blue ('27) 9.00 2.25
Never hinged 21.00
On cover 10.00
b. 1.50fr intense bright blue ('30) 15.00 4.00
Never hinged 62.50
On cover 40.00
161 A58 1.75fr ultra ('27) 1.75 .25
Never hinged 5.50
On cover 1.25
a. Tete beche pair 11.00 5.00
Never hinged 22.00
c. Bklt. pane of 4 + 2 labels 40.00
Nos. 144-161 (18) 14.40 5.90
Set, never hinged 32.50

See Nos. 185-190. For overprints and surcharges see Nos. 191-195, 197, B56, O1-O6.

A59

1921-25 **Engr.**
Perf. 11, 11x11½, 11½, 11½x11, 11½x12, 11½x12½, 12½
162 A59 50c dull blue .30 .25
Never hinged 1.60
On cover 3.00
163 A59 75c scarlet ('22) .25 .25
Never hinged .30
On cover 10.00
164 A59 75c ultra ('24) .45 .25
Never hinged .60
On cover 5.00
165 A59 1fr black brn ('22) .80 .25
Never hinged 2.00
On cover 6.50
166 A59 1fr dk blue ('25) .60 .25
Never hinged .80
On cover 7.00
167 A59 2fr dk green ('22) .90 .25
Never hinged 2.00
On cover 15.00
168 A59 5fr brown vio ('23) 13.50 *15.00*
Never hinged 18.00
On cover 40.00
169 A59 10fr magenta ('22) 9.00 6.50
Never hinged 25.00
On cover 165.00
Nos. 162-169 (8) 25.80 *23.00*
Set, never hinged 52.50

No. 162 measures 18x20¾mm and was printed in sheets of 100.

Philatelic Exhibition Issues

1921, May 26 *Perf. 11½*
170 A59 50c dark blue 3.50 3.50
Never hinged 4.75
a. Sheet of 25 200.00 175.00
Never hinged 225.00

No. 170 measures 17½x21¼mm, was printed in sheets of 25 and sold at the Philatelic Exhibition at Brussels.

The sheet normally has pin holes and a cancellation-like marking in the margin. These are considered unused and the condition valued here.

Souvenir Sheet

1924, May 24 *Perf. 11½*
171 Sheet of 4 225.00 200.00
Never hinged 400.00
a. A59 5fr red brown 10.00 10.00
Never hinged 14.00
On cover 35.00

Sold only at the Intl. Phil. Exhib., Brussels. Sheet size: 130x145mm.

The sheet normally has pin holes and a cancellation-like marking in the margin. These are considered unused and the condition valued here. Sheets with wrinkles, toning or significant gum skips sell for much less.

Kings Leopold I and Albert I — A60

1925 *Perf. 14*
172 A60 10c dp green 8.25 8.25
Never hinged 17.50
173 A60 15c dull vio 3.75 4.50
Never hinged 7.75
On cover 20.00
174 A60 20c red brown 3.75 4.50
Never hinged 7.75
175 A60 25c grnsh black 3.75 4.50
Never hinged 7.75
On cover 40.00
176 A60 30c vermilion 3.75 4.50
Never hinged 7.75
On cover 17.50
177 A60 35c lt blue 3.75 4.50
Never hinged 7.75
178 A60 40c brnsh blk 3.75 4.50
Never hinged 7.75
On cover 40.00
179 A60 50c yellow brn 3.75 4.50
Never hinged 7.75
On cover 30.00
180 A60 75c dk blue 3.75 4.50
Never hinged 7.75
181 A60 1fr dk violet 7.00 7.50
Never hinged 13.50
182 A60 2fr ultra 4.00 4.00
Never hinged 7.75
183 A60 5fr blue blk 3.75 4.50
Never hinged 7.75
184 A60 10fr dp rose 6.75 8.00
Never hinged 17.50
Nos. 172-184 (13) 59.75 68.25
Set, never hinged 126.00

75th anniv. of Belgian postage stamps.

Nos. 172-184 were sold only in sets and only by The Administration of Posts, not at post offices.

A61

1926-27 **Typo.**
185 A61 75c dk violet .75 .70
Never hinged 1.60
On cover 20.00
186 A61 1fr pale yellow .60 .35
Never hinged .75
On cover 15.00
187 A61 1fr rose red ('27) 1.50 .25
Never hinged 2.40
On cover 5.00
a. Tete beche pair 7.50 4.50
c. Bklt. pane 4 + 2 labels 25.00
188 A61 2fr Prus blue 3.25 .45
Never hinged 5.75
On cover 17.50
189 A61 5fr emerald ('27) 32.50 1.60
Never hinged 77.50
On cover 67.50
190 A61 10fr dk brown ('27) 70.00 7.75
Never hinged 160.00
On cover 175.00
Nos. 185-190 (6) 108.60 11.10
Set, never hinged 249.00

For overprints and surcharge see Nos. 196, Q174-Q175.

Stamps of 1921-27 Surcharged in Carmine, Red or Blue

1927
191 A58 3c on 2c olive (C) .25 .25
Never hinged .30
On cover, single franking 18.50
192 A58 10c on 15c plum (R) .25 .25
Never hinged .30
On cover 3.00
193 A58 35c on 40c rose (Bl) .40 .25
Never hinged .60
On cover 2.50
194 A58 1.75fr on 1.50fr brt bl (C) 1.75 .80
Never hinged 3.00
Nos. 191-194 (4) 2.65 1.55
Set, never hinged 3.75

Nos. 153, 185 and 159 Surcharged in Black

1929, Jan. 1

195 A58 5c on 30c rose .25 .25
Never hinged .30
On cover 4.50
196 A61 5c on 75c dk violet .25 .25
Never hinged .30
On cover 4.50
197 A58 5c on 1.25fr dp blue .25 .25
Never hinged .30
On cover 4.50
Nos. 195-197 (3) .75 .75
Set, never hinged .85

The surcharge on Nos. 195-197 is a precancelation which alters the value of the stamp to which it is applied.

Values for precanceled stamps in unused column are for those which have not been through the post and have original gum. Values in second column are for postally used, gumless stamps.

A63

1929-32 Typo. *Perf. 14*

198 A63 1c orange .25 .25
Never hinged .30
199 A63 2c emerald ('31) .45 .45
Never hinged .50
200 A63 3c red brown .25 .25
Never hinged .30
201 A63 5c slate .25 .25
Never hinged .30
c. Bklt. pane of 4 + 2 labels 8.25
202 A63 10c olive grn .25 .25
Never hinged .30
On cover 1.00
c. Bklt. pane of 4 + 2 labels 4.50
203 A63 20c brt violet 1.00 .25
Never hinged 4.00
On cover 15.00
204 A63 25c rose red .45 .25
Never hinged 1.00
On cover 1.00
c. Bklt. pane of 4 + 2 labels 8.25
205 A63 35c green .50 .25
Never hinged 1.10
On cover 2.00
c. Bklt. pane of 4 + 2 labels 9.75
206 A63 40c red vio ('30) .35 .25
Never hinged 1.25
On cover 1.00
c. Bklt. pane of 4 + 2 labels 9.75
207 A63 50c dp blue .45 .25
Never hinged .80
On cover 1.00
c. Bklt. pane of 4 + 2 labels 8.25
208 A63 60c rose ('30) 2.25 .25
Never hinged 7.00
On cover 6.75
c. Bklt. pane of 4 + 2 labels 30.00
209 A63 70c org brn ('30) 1.10 .25
Never hinged 5.00
On cover 4.00
c. Bklt. pane of 4 + 2 labels 22.50
210 A63 75c dk blue ('30) 2.25 .25
Never hinged 9.00
On cover 2.40
b. 75c blue violet 2.40 .25
Never hinged 8.75
On cover 2.40
211 A63 75c dp brown ('32) 6.50 .25
Never hinged 27.50
On cover 2.00
b. Bklt. pane of 4 + 2 labels 100.00
Nos. 198-211 (14) 16.30 3.70
Set, never hinged 62.50

For overprints and surcharges see Nos. 225-226, 240-241, 254-256, 309, O7-O15.

Tete Beche Pairs

201a A63 5c .60 .60
Never hinged 1.50
202a A63 10c .30 .30
Never hinged .75
204a A63 25c 1.75 1.75
Never hinged 4.25
205a A63 35c 2.75 2.75
Never hinged 6.75
206a A63 40c 2.75 2.75
Never hinged 6.75
207a A63 50c 2.25 2.25
Never hinged 5.50
208a A63 60c 8.00 7.50
Never hinged 20.00
209a A63 70c 6.00 5.00
Never hinged 15.00
210a A63 75c 9.00 8.50
Never hinged 22.50
211a A63 75c 30.00 30.00
Never hinged 75.00
Nos. 201a-211a (10) 63.40 61.40
Set, never hinged 160.00

Tete-beche gutter pairs also exist.

A64

1929, Jan. 25 Engr. *Perf. 14½, 14*

212 A64 10fr dk brown 17.50 4.50
Never hinged 37.50
On cover 75.00
213 A64 20fr dk green 100.00 25.00
Never hinged 190.00
On cover 175.00
214 A64 50fr red violet 17.50 17.50
Never hinged 24.00
a. Perf. 14½ 55.00 45.00
Never hinged 87.50
215 A64 100fr brownish lake 17.50 17.50
Never hinged 25.00
a. Perf. 14½ 50.00 40.00
Never hinged 87.50
Nos. 212-215 (4) 152.50 64.50
Set, never hinged 276.50

Peter Paul Rubens — A65

Zenobe Gramme — A66

1930, Apr. 26 Photo. *Perf. 12½x12*

216 A65 35c blue green .40 .25
Never hinged 1.00
On cover 1.00
217 A66 35c blue green .40 .25
Never hinged 1.10
On cover 1.00
Set, never hinged 2.10

No. 216 issued for the Antwerp Exhibition, No. 217 the Liege Exhibition.

Leopold I, by Lievin de Winne — A67

Leopold II, by Joseph Leempoels — A68

Design: 1.75fr, Albert I.

1930, July 1 Engr. *Perf. 11½*

218 A67 60c brown violet .25 .25
Never hinged .35
On cover 1.25
219 A68 1fr carmine .90 .80
Never hinged 2.50
On cover 3.50
220 A68 1.75fr dk blue 2.25 1.25
Never hinged 6.75
On cover 4.50
Nos. 218-220 (3) 3.40 2.30
Set, never hinged 9.60

Centenary of Belgian independence.
For overprints see Nos. 222-224.

Antwerp Exhibition Issue
Souvenir Sheet

Arms of Antwerp A70

1930, Aug. 9 *Perf. 11½*

221 A70 4fr Sheet of 1 300.00 250.00
Never hinged 600.00
On cover 140.00
a. Single stamp 100.00 85.00

Size: 142x141mm. Inscription in lower margin "ATELIER DU TIMBRE-1930-ZEGELFABRIEK." Each purchaser of a ticket to the Antwerp Phil. Exhib., Aug. 9-15, was allowed to purchase one stamp. The ticket cost 6 francs.

The sheet normally has pin holes and a cancellation-like marking in the margin. These are considered unused and the condition valued here. Sheets with wrinkles or toning sell for much less.

Nos. 218-220 Overprinted in Blue or Red

1930, Oct.

222 A67 60c brown vio (Bl) 2.00 2.00
Never hinged 4.00
On cover 6.75
223 A68 1fr carmine (Bl) 8.25 7.75
Never hinged 15.00
On cover 24.00
224 A68 1.75fr dk blue (R) 14.50 14.50
Never hinged 35.00
On cover 42.50
Nos. 222-224 (3) 24.75 24.25
Set, never hinged 55.00

50th meeting of the administrative council of the Intl. Labor Bureau at Brussels.

The names of the painters and the initials of the engraver have been added at the foot of these stamps.

Stamps of 1929-30 Surcharged in Blue or Black

1931, Feb. 20 *Perf. 14*

225 A63 2c on 3c red brown (Bl) .25 .25
Never hinged 2.00
226 A63 10c on 60c rose (Bk) .50 .25
Never hinged 1.75
On cover 8.50
Set, never hinged 3.75

The surcharge on No. 226 is a precancelation which alters the denomination. See note after No. 197.

King Albert — A71

1931, June 15 Photo.

227 A71 1fr brown carmine .50 .25
Never hinged 1.00
On cover 3.00

King Albert — A71a

1932, June 1

228 A71a 75c bister brown 1.25 .25
Never hinged 5.00
On cover 1.00
a. Tete beche pair 6.75 6.75
Never hinged 17.50
c. Bklt. pane 4 + 2 labels 18.00

See No. 257. For overprint see No. O18.

A72

1931-32 Engr.

229 A72 1.25fr gray black .75 .50
Never hinged 2.50
On cover 6.75
230 A72 1.50fr brown vio 1.50 .50
Never hinged 5.25
On cover 5.50
231 A72 1.75fr dp blue .80 .25
Never hinged 1.75
On cover 1.00
232 A72 2fr red brown 1.10 .25
Never hinged 2.60
On cover 5.50
233 A72 2.45fr dp violet 3.00 .40
Never hinged 8.75
On cover 11.50
234 A72 2.50fr black brn ('32) 12.00 .50
Never hinged 25.00
On cover 23.50
235 A72 5fr dp green 25.00 1.10
Never hinged 75.00
On cover 30.00
236 A72 10fr claret 55.00 12.50
Never hinged 155.00
On cover 77.50
Nos. 229-236 (8) 99.15 16.00
Set, never hinged 275.00

Nos. 206 and 209 Surcharged as No. 226, but dated "1932"

1932, Jan. 1

240 A63 10c on 40c red vio 2.75 .35
Never hinged 7.25
On cover 5.00
241 A63 10c on 70c org brn 2.50 .25
Never hinged 6.25
On cover 5.00
Set, never hinged 22.50

See note after No. 197.

Gleaner A73

Mercury A74

1932, June 1 Typo. *Perf. 13½x14*

245 A73 2c pale green .35 .35
Never hinged .50
246 A74 5c dp orange .25 .25
Never hinged .40
On cover, single franking 5.00
247 A73 10c olive grn .25 .25
Never hinged .40
On cover 1.00
a. Tete beche pair 4.00 4.00
Never hinged 7.50
c. Bklt. pane 4 + 2 labels 15.00
248 A74 20c brt violet 1.10 .25
Never hinged 3.25
On cover 37.50
249 A73 25c deep red .70 .25
Never hinged 2.00
On cover 1.60
a. Tete beche pair 3.50 3.50
Never hinged 6.50
c. Bklt. pane 4 + 2 labels 15.00
250 A74 35c dp green 2.75 .25
Never hinged 7.75
On cover 1.00
Nos. 245-250 (6) 5.40 1.60
Set, never hinged 14.50

For overprints see Nos. O16-O17.

Auguste Piccard's Balloon — A75

1932, Nov. 26 Engr. *Perf. 11½*

251 A75 75c red brown 3.50 .30
Never hinged 9.50
On cover 3.00
252 A75 1.75fr dk blue 17.50 2.50
Never hinged 42.50
On cover 7.25
253 A75 2.50fr dk violet 20.00 13.50
Never hinged 60.00
On cover 27.50
Nos. 251-253 (3) 41.00 16.30
Set, never hinged 112.50

Issued in commemoration of Prof. Auguste Piccard's two ascents to the stratosphere.

Nos. 206 and 209 Surcharged as No. 226, but dated "1933"

1933, Nov. *Perf. 14*

254 A63 10c on 40c red vio 17.50 3.50
Never hinged 32.50
On cover 55.00

255 A63 10c on 70c org brn 16.00 1.50
Never hinged 32.50
On cover 7.00
Set, never hinged 100.00

No. 206 Surcharged as No. 226, but dated "1934"

1934, Feb.

256 A63 10c on 40c red vio 16.00 1.50
Never hinged 52.50
On cover 8.00

For Nos. 254 to 256 see note after No. 197.

Regummed examples of Nos. 254-256 are plentiful.

King Albert Memorial Issue

Type of 1932 with Black Margins

1934, Mar. 10 **Photo.**

257 A71a 75c black .30 .25
Never hinged 1.00
On cover 3.50

Congo Pavilion — A76

Designs: 1fr, Brussels pavilion. 1.50fr, "Old Brussels." 1.75fr, Belgian pavilion.

1934, July 1 ***Perf. 14x13½***

258 A76 35c green .75 .40
Never hinged 2.90
On cover 3.00
259 A76 1fr dk carmine 1.25 .40
Never hinged 4.75
On cover 2.00
260 A76 1.50fr brown 5.50 .90
Never hinged 20.00
On cover 10.00
261 A76 1.75fr blue 5.50 .40
Never hinged 22.00
On cover 5.00
Nos. 258-261 (4) 13.00 2.10
Set, never hinged 50.00

Brussels Intl. Exhib. of 1935.

King Leopold III
A80 A81

1934-35 ***Perf. 13½x14***

262 A80 70c olive blk ('35) .35 .25
Never hinged 1.00
On cover 1.00
a. Tete beche pair 1.50 1.00
Never hinged 2.25
c. Bklt. pane 4 + 2 labels 6.25
263 A80 75c brown .65 .25
Never hinged 1.75
On cover 3.00

Perf. 14x13½

264 A81 1fr rose car ('35) 3.00 .35
Never hinged 8.25
On cover 6.00
Nos. 262-264 (3) 4.00 .85
Set, never hinged 11.00

For overprint see No. O19.

Coat of Arms — A82

1935-48 **Typo.** ***Perf. 14***

265 A82 2c green ('37) .25 .25
Never hinged .30
a. 2c yellow green ('44) .25 .25
Never hinged .30
266 A82 5c orange .25 .25
Never hinged .30
On cover .75
267 A82 10c olive bister .25 .25
Never hinged .30
On cover .60
a. Tete beche pair .30 .25
Never hinged .50
b. Bklt. pane 4 + 2 labels 4.50
268 A82 15c dk violet .25 .25
Never hinged .30
On cover 4.00

269 A82 20c lilac .25 .25
Never hinged .30
On cover 4.00
270 A82 25c carmine rose .25 .25
Never hinged .30
On cover 1.25
a. Tete beche pair .30 .40
Never hinged .55
c. Bklt. pane 4 + 2 labels 4.50
271 A82 25c yel org ('46) .25 .25
Never hinged .30
272 A82 30c brown .25 .25
Never hinged .30
On cover 4.50
273 A82 35c green .25 .25
Never hinged .30
On cover 1.00
a. Tete beche pair .30 .30
Never hinged .50
c. Bklt. pane 4 + 2 labels 3.00
274 A82 40c red vio ('38) .25 .25
Never hinged .90
On cover 1.25
275 A82 50c blue .40 .25
Never hinged .80
On cover 1.00
276 A82 60c slate ('41) .25 .25
Never hinged .30
On cover 1.00
277 A82 65c red lilac ('46) .25 .25
Never hinged .75
278 A82 70c lt blue grn ('45) .25 .25
Never hinged .30
On cover 7.75
279 A82 75c lilac rose ('45) .25 .25
Never hinged .70
On cover 3.00
280 A82 80c green ('48) 4.00 .40
Never hinged 8.75
On cover 8.75
281 A82 90c dull vio ('46) .25 .25
Never hinged .50
On cover 2.00
282 A82 1fr red brown ('45) .25 .25
Never hinged .50
On cover 2.00
Nos. 265-282 (18) 8.40 4.65
Set, never hinged 17.00

Several stamps of type A82 exist in various shades.

Nos. 265, 361 were privately overprinted and surcharged "+10FR." by the Association Belgo-Americaine for the dedication of the Bastogne Memorial, July 16, 1950. The overprint is in six types. Value $1.50 per set.

See design O1. For overprints and surcharges see Nos. 312-313, 361-364, 390-394, O20-O22, O24, O26-O28, O33 in this catalogue or *Scott Standard Postage Stamp Catalogue*, Vol. 1.

A83

A83a

Perf. 14, 14x13½, 11½

1936-56 **Photo.**

Size: 17½x21¾mm

283 A83 70c brown .30 .25
Never hinged .50
On cover .75
a. Tete beche pair .80 .80
Never hinged 1.40
c. Bklt. pane 4 + 2 labels 7.50

Size: 20¾x24mm

284 A83a 1fr rose car .30 .25
Never hinged 1.00
On cover 1.50
285 A83a 1.20fr dk brown ('51) .80 .25
Never hinged 1.50
On cover 1.00
a. Perf. 11½ ('56) 1.20 .25
Never hinged 2.75
On cover 1.00
286 A83a 1.50fr brt red vio ('43) .40 .30
Never hinged 1.00
On cover 6.75
287 A83a 1.75fr dp ultra ('43) .25 .25
Never hinged .40
On cover 16.00
288 A83a 1.75fr dk car ('50) .25 .25
Never hinged .30
On cover .75
289 A83a 2fr dk pur ('43) 1.50 1.50
Never hinged 2.00
On cover 29.00
290 A83a 2.25fr grnsh blk ('43) .25 .25
Never hinged .40
On cover 16.00
291 A83a 2.50fr org red ('51) 1.75 .30
Never hinged 6.50
On cover 2.00
a. Perf. 11½ ('56) 20.00 .25
Never hinged 60.00
On cover 6.00
292 A83a 3.25fr chestnut ('43) .25 .25
Never hinged .30
On cover 7.25
293 A83a 5fr dp green ('43) 1.50 .50
Never hinged 3.75
On cover 24.00
Nos. 283-293 (11) 7.55 4.35
Set, never hinged 18.00

Nos. 287-288, 290-291, 293 inscribed "Belgie-Belgique."

See designs A85, A91. For overprints and surcharges see Nos. 314, O23, O25; Nos. O29, O31, O34 in *Scott Standard Postage Stamp Catalogue*, Vol. 1.

A84

1936-51 **Engr.** ***Perf. 14x13½***

294 A84 1.50fr rose lilac ('41) .60 .35
Never hinged 2.00
On cover 8.75
a. 1.50fr magenta ('36) 4.00 2.00
Never hinged 9.75
On cover 14.00
b. 1.50fr rose ('39) 1.00 .40
Never hinged 3.00
On cover 10.00
295 A84 1.75fr dull blue .25 .25
Never hinged .70
On cover 5.00
a. 1.75fr ultramarine ('36) 2.00 .40
Never hinged 4.75
On cover 5.00
b. 1.75fr blue black ('37) 2.75 .40
Never hinged 6.75
On cover 5.75
296 A84 2fr dull vio .40 .30
Never hinged 1.50
On cover 6.75
a. 2fr lilac ('36) 1.50 .60
Never hinged 4.75
On cover 9.00
b. 2fr red violet ('38) 1.00 .35
Never hinged 6.75
On cover 7.75
297 A84 2.25fr gray vio ('41) .25 .25
Never hinged .60
On cover 17.50
298 A84 2.45fr black 45.00 .70
Never hinged 100.00
On cover 3.25
299 A84 2.50fr ol blk ('40) 2.00 .25
Never hinged 8.75
On cover 13.50
300 A84 3.25fr org brn ('41) .30 .25
Never hinged .50
On cover 5.75
301 A84 5fr dull green 2.40 .50
Never hinged 7.00
On cover 16.50
a. 5fr yellow green ('37) 57.50 11.50
Never hinged 165.00
On cover 16.50
b. 5fr olive green ('38) 2.40 .50
Never hinged 7.25
On cover 1.75
302 A84 10fr vio brn .60 .25
Never hinged .90
On cover 10.00
a. 10fr light brown 10.00 .25
Never hinged 35.00
On cover 11.50
303 A84 20fr vermilion 1.00 .30
Never hinged 2.40
On cover 30.00
a. 20fr rose orange ('36) 1.15 .40
Never hinged 4.00
On cover 35.00

Perf. 11½

304 A84 3fr yel brn ('51) .55 .25
Never hinged 1.50
On cover 4.75
305 A84 4fr bl, *bluish* ('50) 4.75 .25
Never hinged 5.00
On cover 2.00
a. White paper 9.00 .25
Never hinged 14.50
306 A84 6fr brt rose car ('51) 2.75 .25
Never hinged 10.00
On cover 9.00
307 A84 10fr brn vio ('51) .55 .25
Never hinged 1.25
On cover 3.00
308 A84 20fr red ('51) 1.10 .25
Never hinged 2.50
On cover 6.75
Nos. 294-308 (15) 62.50 4.65
Set, never hinged 150.00

See No. 1159 in *Scott Standard Postage Stamp Catalogue*, Vol. 1. For overprint and surcharges see Nos. 316-317; No. O32 in Scott Standard catalogue, Vol. 1.

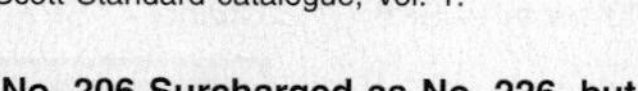

No. 206 Surcharged as No. 226, but dated "1937"

1937 **Unwmk.** ***Perf. 14***

309 A63 10c on 40c red vio .25 .25
Never hinged .30
On cover 5.75

See note after No. 197.

A85

1938-41 **Photo.** ***Perf. 13½x14***

310 A85 75c olive gray .25 .25
Never hinged .60
On cover 1.00
a. Tete beche pair .75 .80
Never hinged 1.50
c. Bklt. pane 4 + 2 labels 6.75
311 A85 1fr rose pink ('41) .25 .25
Never hinged .30
On cover 1.00
a. Tete beche pair .25 .25
Never hinged .40
b. Booklet pane of 6 2.25
c. Bklt. pane 4 + 2 labels 2.25
Set, never hinged .80

For overprints and surcharges see Nos. 315, O25; Nos. O30, O35 in *Scott Standard Postage Stamp Catalogue*, Vol. 1.

Nos. 272, 274, 283, 310, 299, 298 Srchd. in Blue, Black, Carmine or Red

a

b

c

1938-42

312 A82 (a) 10c on 30c (Bl) .25 .25
Never hinged .30
On cover 3.50
313 A82 (a) 10c on 40c (Bl) .25 .25
Never hinged .30
On cover 4.00
314 A83 (b) 10c on 70c (Bk) .25 .25
Never hinged .30
On cover 3.50
315 A85 (b) 50c on 75c (C) .25 .25
Never hinged .40
On cover 4.00
316 A84 (c) 2.25fr on 2.50fr (C) .45 .45
Never hinged .70
On cover 57.50
317 A84 (c) 2.50fr on 2.45fr (R) 11.00 .25
Never hinged 25.00
On cover 15.00
Nos. 312-317 (6) 12.45 1.70
Set, never hinged 26.00

Issue date: No. 317, Oct. 31, 1938.

Basilica and Bell Tower — A86

Water Exhibition Buildings — A87

Designs: 1.50fr, Albert Canal and Park. 1.75fr, Eygenbilsen Cut in Albert Canal.

1938, Oct. 31 ***Perf. 14x13½, 13½x14***

318 A86 35c dk blue grn .25 .25
Never hinged .30
On cover 3.00
319 A87 1fr rose red .45 .30
Never hinged 1.50
On cover 2.00
320 A87 1.50fr vio brn 1.10 .60
Never hinged 4.75
On cover 5.50
321 A87 1.75fr ultra 1.25 .25
Never hinged 4.25
On cover 4.00
Nos. 318-321 (4) 3.05 1.40
Set, never hinged 11.00

Intl. Water Exhibition, Liège, 1939.

SEMI-POSTAL STAMPS

Values quoted for Nos. B1-B24 are for stamps with label attached. Stamps without label sell for one-tenth or less.

St. Martin of Tours Dividing His Cloak with a Beggar
SP1 SP2

Unwmk.

1910, June 1 Typo. *Perf. 14*

B1	SP1	1c gray	.75	.75
B2	SP1	2c purple brn	8.00	8.00
B3	SP1	5c peacock blue	1.90	1.90
B4	SP1	10c brown red	1.90	1.90
B5	SP2	1c gray green	1.90	1.90
B6	SP2	2c violet brn	5.00	5.00
B7	SP2	5c peacock blue	2.25	2.25
B8	SP2	10c carmine	2.25	2.25
		Nos. B1-B8 (8)	23.95	23.95
		Set, never hinged	65.00	

Overprinted "1911" in Black

1911, Apr. 1

B9	SP1	1c gray	27.50	16.00
a.		Inverted overprint		
B10	SP1	2c purple brn	125.00	72.50
B11	SP1	5c peacock blue	8.00	5.25
B12	SP1	10c brown red	8.00	5.25
B13	SP2	1c gray green	42.50	27.50
B14	SP2	2c violet brn	60.00	32.50
B15	SP2	5c peacock blue	8.00	5.25
B16	SP2	10c carmine	8.00	5.25
		Nos. B9-B16 (8)	287.00	169.50
		Set, never hinged	600.00	

Overprinted "CHARLEROI-1911"

1911, June

B17	SP1	1c gray	4.00	2.50
B18	SP1	2c purple brn	16.00	10.00
B19	SP1	5c peacock blue	9.00	6.50
B20	SP1	10c brown red	9.00	6.50
B21	SP2	1c gray green	4.00	2.50
B22	SP2	2c violet brn	11.00	9.00
B23	SP2	5c peacock blue	9.00	6.50
B24	SP2	10c carmine	9.00	6.50
		Nos. B17-B24 (8)	71.00	50.00
		Set, never hinged	175.00	

Nos. B1-B24 were sold at double face value, except the 10c denominations which were sold for 15c. The surtax benefited the national anti-tuberculosis organization.

King Albert I — SP3

1914, Oct. 3 Litho.

B25	SP3	5c green & red	*5.00*	*5.00*
B26	SP3	10c red	*1.00*	*1.00*
B27	SP3	20c violet & red	*15.00*	*15.00*
		Nos. B25-B27 (3)	*21.00*	*21.00*
		Set, never hinged	*90.00*	

Counterfeits of Nos. B25-B27 abound. Probably as many as 90% of the stamps on the market are counterfeits. Values are for genuine examples.

Merode Monument — SP4

1914, Oct. 3

B28	SP4	5c green & red	*4.50*	*3.00*
B29	SP4	10c red	*7.50*	*7.50*
B30	SP4	20c violet & red	*75.00*	*75.00*
		Nos. B28-B30 (3)	*87.00*	*85.50*
		Set, never hinged	*175.00*	

Counterfeits of Nos. B28-B30 abound. Probably as many as 90% of the stamps on the market are counterfeits. Genuine stamps have a tail on the "Q" of "BELGIQUE" at the top of the stamp, counterfeits don't have a tail. Values are for genuine examples.

King Albert I — SP5

1915, Jan. 1 *Perf. 12, 14*

B31	SP5	5c green & red	5.00	3.00
a.		Perf. 12x14	16.00	12.00
B32	SP5	10c rose & red	20.00	6.00
B33	SP5	20c violet & red	25.00	14.00
a.		Perf. 14x12	500.00	250.00
b.		Perf. 12	50.00	32.50
		Nos. B31-B33 (3)	50.00	23.00
		Set, never hinged	150.00	

Nos. B25-B33 were sold at double face value. The surtax benefited the Red Cross.

Types of Regular Issue of 1915 Surcharged in Red

Nos. B34-B40

Nos. B41-B43

Nos. B44-B47

1918, Jan. 15 Typo. *Perf. 14*

B34	A46	1c + 1c dp orange	.50	.50
B35	A46	2c + 2c brown	.60	.60
B36	A46	5c + 5c blue grn	1.40	1.40
B37	A46	10c + 10c red	2.25	2.25
B38	A46	15c + 15c brt violet	3.25	3.25
B39	A46	20c + 20c plum	7.50	7.50
B40	A46	25c + 25c ultra	7.50	7.50

Engr.

B41	A47	35c + 35c lt vio & blk	10.00	10.00
B42	A48	40c + 40c dull red & blk	10.00	10.00
B43	A49	50c + 50c turq blue & blk	12.00	12.00
B44	A50	1fr + 1fr bluish slate	35.00	35.00
B45	A51	2fr + 2fr dp gray grn	100.00	100.00
B46	A52	5fr + 5fr brown	250.00	250.00
B47	A53	10fr + 10fr dp blue	550.00	500.00
		Nos. B34-B47 (14)	990.00	940.00
		Set, never hinged	2,000.	

Discus Thrower — SP6

Racing Chariot — SP7

Runner — SP8

1920, May 20 Engr. *Perf. 12*

B48	SP6	5c + 5c dp green	1.40	1.40
B49	SP7	10c + 5c carmine	1.40	1.40
B50	SP8	15c + 15c dk brown	3.00	3.00
		Nos. B48-B50 (3)	5.80	5.80
		Set, never hinged	17.00	

7th Olympic Games, 1920. Surtax benefited wounded soldiers. Exists imperf.

For surcharges see Nos. 140-142.

Allegory: Asking Alms from the Crown — SP9

1922, May 20

B51	SP9	20c + 20c brown	1.40	1.40
		Never hinged	2.75	

Wounded Veteran — SP10

1923, July 5

B52	SP10	20c + 20c slate gray	2.50	2.50
		Never hinged	7.50	

Surtax on Nos. B51-B52 was to aid wounded veterans.

SP11

1925, Dec. 15 Typo. *Perf. 14*

B53	SP11	15c + 5c dull vio & red	.50	.25
B54	SP11	30c + 5c gray & red	.25	.25
B55	SP11	1fr + 10c chalky blue & red	1.25	1.40
		Nos. B53-B55 (3)	2.00	1.90
		Set, never hinged	3.00	

Surtax for the Natl. Anti-Tuberculosis League.

SP12

St. Martin, by Van Dyck
SP13 SP14

1926, Feb. 10

B56	SP12	30c + 30c bluish grn (red surch.)	.50	.50
B57	SP13	1fr + 1fr lt blue	7.25	7.25
B58	SP14	1fr + 1fr lt blue	1.10	1.25
		Nos. B56-B58 (3)	8.85	9.00
		Set, never hinged	20.00	

The surtax aided victims of the Meuse flood.

Lion and Cross of Lorraine — SP15

Queen Elisabeth and King Albert SP16

1926, Dec. 6 Typo. *Perf. 14*

B59	SP15	5c + 5c dk brown	.25	.25
B60	SP15	20c + 5c red brown	.45	.40
B61	SP15	50c + 5c dull violet	.30	.25

Perf. 11½

Engr.

B62	SP16	1.50fr + 25c dk blue	.75	.70
B63	SP16	5fr + 1fr rose red	6.50	6.00
		Nos. B59-B63 (5)	8.25	7.60
		Set, never hinged	16.00	

Surtax was used to benefit tubercular war veterans.

Boat Adrift SP17

1927, Dec. 15 Engr. *Perf. 11½, 14*

B64	SP17	25c + 10c dk brn	.70	.70
B65	SP17	35c + 10c yel grn	.70	.70
B66	SP17	60c + 10c dp vio	.60	.40
B67	SP17	1.75fr + 25c dk blue	1.50	*2.00*
B68	SP17	5fr + 1fr plum	4.50	*4.75*
		Nos. B64-B68 (5)	8.00	*8.55*
		Set, never hinged	16.00	

The surtax on these stamps was divided among several charitable associations.

Ogives of Orval Abbey — SP18

Monk Carving Capital of Column — SP19

Ruins of Orval Abbey SP20

Design: 60c+15c, 1.75fr+25c, 3fr+1fr, Countess Matilda recovering her ring.

1928, Sept. 15 Photo. *Perf. 11½*

B69	SP18	5c + 5c red & gold	.25	.25
B70	SP18	25c + 5c dk vio & gold	.45	.45

Engr.

B71	SP19	35c + 10c dp grn	1.25	1.25
B72	SP19	60c + 15c red brn	.75	.25
B73	SP19	1.75fr + 25c dk blue	3.25	2.10
B74	SP19	2fr + 40c dp vio	25.00	21.00
B75	SP19	3fr + 1fr red	22.50	20.00

Perf. 14

B76	SP20	5fr + 5fr rose lake	15.50	15.50
B77	SP20	10fr + 10fr ol green	15.50	15.50
		Nos. B69-B77 (9)	84.45	76.30
		Set, never hinged	150.00	

Surtax for the restoration of the ruined Orval Abbey.

St. Waudru, Mons — SP22

St. Rombaut, Malines — SP23

Designs: 25c + 15c, Cathedral of Tournai. 60c + 15c, St. Bavon, Ghent. 1.75fr + 25c, St. Gudule, Brussels. 5fr + 5fr, Louvain Library.

1928, Dec. 1 Photo. *Perf. 14, 11½*

B78 SP22 5c + 5c carmine .25 .25
B79 SP22 25c + 15c ol brn .25 .25

Engr.

B80 SP23 35c + 10c dp grn 1.50 1.50
B81 SP23 60c + 15c red brn .45 .45
B82 SP23 1.75fr + 25c vio bl 10.50 10.50
B83 SP23 5fr + 5fr red vio 21.00 21.00
Nos. B78-B83 (6) 33.95 33.95
Set, never hinged 65.00

The surtax was for anti-tuberculosis work.

Nos. B69-B77 with this overprint in blue or red were privately produced. They were for the laying of the 1st stone toward the restoration of the ruined Abbey of Orval. Value, set, $650.

Forgeries of the overprint exist.

Waterfall at Coo — SP28

Bayard Rock, Dinant — SP29

Designs: 35c+10c, Menin Gate, Ypres. 60c+15c, Promenade d'Orleans, Spa. 1.75fr+25c, Antwerp Harbor. 5fr+5fr, Quai Vert, Bruges.

1929, Dec. 2 Engr. *Perf. 11½*

B93 SP28 5c + 5c red brn .25 .25
B94 SP29 25c + 15c gray blk .95 .90
B95 SP28 35c + 10c green 1.25 1.40
B96 SP28 60c + 15c rose lake .85 .75
B97 SP28 1.75fr + 25c dp blue 6.75 6.75

Perf. 14

B98 SP29 5fr + 5fr dl vio 40.00 40.00
Nos. B93-B98 (6) 50.05 50.05
Set, never hinged 70.00

Bornhem — SP34

Beloeil — SP35

Gaesbeek SP36

25c + 15c, Wynendaele. 70c + 15c, Oydonck. 1fr + 25c, Ghent. 1.75fr + 25c, Bouillon.

1930, Dec. 1 Photo. *Perf. 14*

B99 SP34 10c + 5c violet .25 *.30*
B100 SP34 25c + 15c olive brn .60 .60

Engr.

B101 SP35 40c + 10c brn vio .80 *1.00*
B102 SP35 70c + 15c gray blk .55 .55
B103 SP35 1fr + 25c rose lake 5.50 5.50
B104 SP35 1.75fr + 25c dp bl 7.25 4.50
B105 SP36 5fr + 5fr gray grn 45.00 *52.50*
Nos. B99-B105 (7) 59.95 *64.95*
Set, never hinged 80.00

Philatelic Exhibition Issue

Souvenir Sheet

Prince Leopold — SP41

1931, July 18 Photo. *Perf. 14*

B106 SP41 2.45fr + 55c car brn 225.00 225.00
Never hinged 650.00
a. Single stamp 100.00

Sold exclusively at the Brussels Phil. Exhib., July 18-21, 1931. Size: 122x159mm. Surtax for the Veterans' Relief Fund.

The sheet normally has pin holes and a cancellation-like marking in the margin. These are considered unused and the condition valued here.

Queen Elisabeth — SP42

1931, Dec. 1 Engr.

B107 SP42 10c + 5c red brn .30 *.50*
B108 SP42 25c + 15c dk vio 1.40 *1.50*
B109 SP42 50c + 10c dk grn 1.10 *1.25*
B110 SP42 75c + 15c blk brn .95 .85
B111 SP42 1fr + 25c rose lake 8.00 7.25
B112 SP42 1.75fr + 25c ultra 5.75 4.75
B113 SP42 5fr + 5fr brn vio 65.00 65.00
Nos. B107-B113 (7) 82.50 81.10
Set, never hinged 150.00

The surtax was for the National Anti-Tuberculosis League.

Désiré Cardinal Mercier — SP43

Mercier Protecting Children and Aged at Malines — SP44

Mercier as Professor at Louvain University — SP45

Mercier in Full Canonicals, Giving His Blessing SP46

1932, June 10 Photo. *Perf. 14½x14*

B114 SP43 10c + 10c dk violet 1.10 *.70*
B115 SP43 50c + 30c brt violet 2.75 *3.00*
B116 SP43 75c + 25c olive brn 2.75 2.75
B117 SP43 1fr + 2fr brown red 7.25 7.25

Engr. *Perf. 11½*

B118 SP44 1.75fr + 75c dp blue 85.00 *100.00*
B119 SP45 2.50fr + 2.50fr dk brn 85.00 85.00
B120 SP44 3fr + 4.50fr dull grn 85.00 85.00
B121 SP45 5fr + 20fr vio brn 95.00 *100.00*
B122 SP46 10fr + 40fr brn lake 210.00 *250.00*
Nos. B114-B122 (9) 573.85 *633.70*
Set, never hinged 950.00

Honoring Cardinal Mercier and to obtain funds to erect a monument to his memory.

Belgian Infantryman — SP47

1932, Aug. 4 *Perf. 14½x14*

B123 SP47 75c + 3.25fr red brn 80.00 80.00
Never hinged 125.00
B124 SP47 1.75fr + 4.25fr dk blue 80.00 80.00
Never hinged 125.00

Honoring Belgian soldiers who fought in WWI and to obtain funds to erect a natl. monument to their glory.

Sanatorium at Waterloo SP48

1932, Dec. 1 Photo. *Perf. 13½x14*

B125 SP48 10c + 5c dk vio .30 *.90*
B126 SP48 25c + 15c red vio 1.00 *1.25*
B127 SP48 50c + 10c red brn 1.00 *1.25*
B128 SP48 75c + 15c ol brn 1.00 .80
B129 SP48 1fr + 25c dp red 15.00 12.50
B130 SP48 1.75fr + 25c dp blue 12.00 11.00
B131 SP48 5fr + 5fr gray grn 100.00 *110.00*
Nos. B125-B131 (7) 130.30 *137.70*
Set, never hinged 250.00

Surtax for the assistance of the Natl. Anti-Tuberculosis Society at Waterloo.

View of Old Abbey SP49

Ruins of Old Abbey — SP50

Count de Chiny Presenting First Abbey to Countess Matilda SP56

Restoration of Abbey in XVI and XVII Centuries SP57

Abbey in XVIII Century, Maria Theresa and Charles V — SP58

Madonna and Arms of Seven Abbeys SP60

Designs: 25c+15c, Guests, courtyard, 50c+25c, Transept. 75c+50c, Bell Tower. 1fr+1.25fr, Fountain. 1.25fr+1.75fr, Cloisters. 5fr+20fr, Duke of Brabant placing 1st stone of new abbey.

1933, Oct. 15 *Perf. 14*

B132 SP49 5c + 5c dull grn 57.50 *65.00*
B133 SP50 10c + 15c ol grn 52.50 *57.50*
B134 SP49 25c + 15c dk brn 52.50 *57.50*
B135 SP50 50c + 25c red brn 52.50 *57.50*
B136 SP50 75c + 50c dp grn 52.50 *57.50*
B137 SP50 1fr + 1.25fr cop red 52.50 *57.50*
B138 SP49 1.25fr + 1.75fr gray blk 52.50 *57.50*
B139 SP56 1.75fr + 2.75fr blue 60.00 *65.00*
B140 SP57 2fr + 3fr mag 60.00 *65.00*
B141 SP58 2.50fr + 5fr dull brn 60.00 *65.00*
B142 SP56 5fr + 20fr vio 65.00 *65.00*

Perf. 11½

B143 SP60 10fr + 40fr bl 375.00 *375.00*
Nos. B132-B143 (12) 992.50 *1,045.*
Set, never hinged 1,500.

The surtax was for a fund to aid in the restoration of Orval Abbey. Counterfeits exist.

"Tuberculosis Society" — SP61

1933, Dec. 1 Engr. *Perf. 14x13½*

B144 SP61 10c + 5c blk 1.50 1.50
B145 SP61 25c + 15c vio 5.00 5.00
B146 SP61 50c + 10c red brn 3.75 3.75
B147 SP61 75c + 15c blk brn 16.00 15.00
B148 SP61 1fr + 25c cl 18.00 18.00
B149 SP61 1.75fr + 25c vio bl 21.00 21.00
B150 SP61 5fr + 5fr lilac 175.00 140.00
Nos. B144-B150 (7) 240.25 204.25
Set, never hinged 350.00

The surtax was for anti-tuberculosis work.

Peter Benoit — SP62

1934, June 1 Photo.

B151 SP62 75c + 25c olive brn 6.00 6.00
Never hinged 12.50

The surtax was to raise funds for the Peter Benoit Memorial.

SP63

King Leopold III — SP64

1934, Sept. 15

B152 SP63 75c + 25c ol blk 18.00 17.00
Never hinged 37.50
a. Sheet of 20 925.00 925.00
Never hinged 1,100.
B153 SP64 1fr + 25c red vio 17.00 16.00
Never hinged 37.50
a. Sheet of 20 925.00 925.00
Never hinged 1,100.

The surtax aided the National War Veterans' Fund. Sold for 4.50fr a set at the Exhibition of War Postmarks 1914-18, held at Brussels by the Royal Philatelic Club of Veterans. The price included an exhibition ticket. Sold at Brussels post office Sept. 18-22. No. B152 printed in sheets of 20 (4x5) and 100 (10x10). No. B153 printed in sheets of 20 (4x5) and 150 (10x15).

1934, Sept. 24

B154 SP63 75c + 25c violet 1.50 1.50
Never hinged 2.50
B155 SP64 1fr + 25c red brn 10.50 10.50
Never hinged 20.00

The surtax aided the National War Veterans' Fund. No. B154 printed in sheets of 100 (10x10); No. B155 in sheets of 150 (10x15). These stamps remained in use one year.

Crusader SP65

1934, Nov. 17 Engr. *Perf. 13½x14*

Cross in Red

B156 SP65 10c + 5c blk 1.50 1.50
B157 SP65 25c + 15c brn 2.10 2.00
B158 SP65 50c + 10c dull grn 2.10 2.10
B159 SP65 75c + 15c vio brn 1.00 1.00
B160 SP65 1fr + 25c rose 10.50 10.50
B161 SP65 1.75fr + 25c ultra 9.00 9.00
B162 SP65 5fr + 5fr brn vio 125.00 125.00
Nos. B156-B162 (7) 151.20 151.10
Set, never hinged 550.00

The surtax was for anti-tuberculosis work.

Prince Baudouin, Princess Josephine and Prince Albert SP66

1935, Apr. 10 Photo.

B163 SP66 35c + 15c dk grn 1.25 1.10
B164 SP66 70c + 30c red brn 1.25 .90
B165 SP66 1.75fr + 50c dk blue 4.50 *5.25*
Nos. B163-B165 (3) 7.00 *7.25*
Set, never hinged 20.00

Surtax was for Child Welfare Society.

Stagecoach — SP67

1935, Apr. 27

B166 SP67 10c + 10c ol blk .75 .80
B167 SP67 25c + 25c bis brn 2.25 2.10
B168 SP67 35c + 25c dk green 3.00 2.75
Nos. B166-B168 (3) 6.00 5.65
Set, never hinged 15.00

Printed in sheets of 10. Value, set of 3, $175.

Souvenir Sheet

Franz von Taxis — SP68

1935, May 25 Engr. *Perf. 14*

B169 SP68 5fr + 5fr grnsh blk 150.00 150.00
Never hinged 450.00
a. Single stamp 115.00
Never hinged 140.00

Sheets measure 91½x117mm.
Nos. B166-B169 were issued for the Brussels Philatelic Exhibition (SITEB).
The sheet normally has pin holes and a cancellation-like marking in the margin. These are considered unused and the condition valued here.

Queen Astrid — SP69

1935 Photo. *Perf. 11½*

Borders in Black

B170 SP69 10c + 5c ol blk .25 .25
B171 SP69 25c + 15c brown .25 *.30*
B172 SP69 35c + 5c dk green .25 *.25*
B173 SP69 50c + 10c rose lil .80 .65
B174 SP69 70c + 5c gray blk .25 .25
B175 SP69 1fr + 25c red 1.00 .85
B176 SP69 1.75fr + 25c blue 2.40 1.75
B177 SP69 2.45fr + 55c dk vio 3.00 *3.25*
Nos. B170-B177 (8) 8.20 7.55
Set, never hinged 25.00

Queen Astrid Memorial issue. The surtax was divided among several charitable organizations.
Issued: No. B174, 10/31; others, 12/1.

Borgerhout Philatelic Exhibition Issue

Souvenir Sheet

Town Hall, Borgerhout SP70

1936, Oct. 3

B178 SP70 70c + 30c pur brn 90.00 62.50
Never hinged 275.00
a. Single stamp 45.00
Never hinged 60.00

Sheet measures 115x126mm.
The sheet normally has pin holes and a cancellation-like marking in the margin. These are considered unused and the condition valued here.

Town Hall and Belfry of Charleroi SP71

Charleroi Youth Exhibition

Souvenir Sheet

1936, Oct. 18 Engr.

B179 SP71 2.45fr + 55c gray blue 65.00 60.00
Never hinged 150.00
a. Single stamp 45.00
Never hinged 60.00

Sheet measures 95x120mm.
The sheet normally has pin holes and a cancellation-like marking in the margin. These are considered unused and the condition valued here.

Prince Baudouin — SP72

1936, Dec. 1 Photo. *Perf. 14x13½*

B180 SP72 10c + 5c dk brn .25 .25
B181 SP72 25c + 5c violet .25 *.25*
B182 SP72 35c + 5c dk green .25 *.25*
B183 SP72 50c + 5c vio brn .50 *.60*
B184 SP72 70c + 5c ol grn .25 .25
B185 SP72 1fr + 25c cerise 1.10 .45
B186 SP72 1.75fr + 25c ultra 1.90 1.10
B187 SP72 2.45fr + 2.55fr vio rose 5.25 *6.75*
Nos. B180-B187 (8) 9.75 *9.90*
Set, never hinged 30.00

The surtax was for the assistance of the National Anti-Tuberculosis Society.

1937, Jan. 10

B188 SP72 2.45fr + 2.55fr slate 2.50 2.50
Never hinged 6.50

Intl. Stamp Day. Surtax for the benefit of the Brussels Postal Museum, the Royal Belgian Phil. Fed. and the Anti-Tuberculosis Soc.

Queen Astrid and Prince Baudouin — SP73

1937, Apr. 15 *Perf. 11½*

B189 SP73 10c + 5c mag .25 .25
B190 SP73 25c + 5c ol blk .25 *.25*
B191 SP73 35c + 5c dk grn .25 *.25*
B192 SP73 50c + 5c violet 1.25 *1.25*
B193 SP73 70c + 5c slate .25 *.30*
B194 SP73 1fr + 25c dk car 1.60 1.40
B195 SP73 1.75fr + 25c dp ultra 2.75 2.75
B196 SP73 2.45fr + 1.55fr dk brn 6.75 6.50
Nos. B189-B196 (8) 13.35 12.95
Set, never hinged 45.00

The surtax was to raise funds for Public Utility Works.

Queen Mother Elisabeth — SP74

1937, Sept. 15 *Perf. 14x13½*

B197 SP74 70c + 5c int black .30 .30
B198 SP74 1.75fr + 25c brt ultra .70 .70
Set, never hinged 2.00

Souvenir Sheet

Perf. 11½

B199 Sheet of 4 45.00 25.00
Never hinged 125.00
a. SP74 1.50fr+2.50fr red brn 4.25 3.75
b. SP74 2.45fr+3.55fr red vio 3.75 2.25

Issued for the benefit of the Queen Elisabeth Music Foundation in connection with the Eugene Ysaye intl. competition.
No. B199 contains two se-tenant pairs of Nos. B199a and B199b. Size: 111x145mm. On sale one day, Sept. 15, at Brussels.
The sheet normally has pin holes and a cancellation-like marking in the margin. These are considered unused and the condition valued here.

Princess Josephine-Charlotte SP75

1937, Dec. 1 *Perf. 14x13½*

B200 SP75 10c + 5c sl grn .25 .25
B201 SP75 25c + 5c lt brn .25 .25
B202 SP75 35c + 5c yel grn .25 .25
B203 SP75 50c + 5c ol gray .70 .60
B204 SP75 70c + 5c brn red .25 .25
B205 SP75 1fr + 25c red 1.25 .90
B206 SP75 1.75fr + 25c vio bl 1.50 1.25
B207 SP75 2.45fr + 2.55fr mag 5.75 *6.00*
Nos. B200-B207 (8) 10.20 *9.75*
Set, never hinged 30.00

King Albert Memorial Issue

Souvenir Sheet

King Albert Memorial — SP76

1938, Feb. 17 ***Perf. 11½***

B208 SP76 2.45fr + 7.55fr brn vio 20.00 16.50
Never hinged 62.50
a. Single stamp 15.00
Never hinged 20.00

Dedication of the monument to King Albert.

The sheet normally has pin holes and a cancellation-like marking in the margin. These are considered unused and the condition valued here. Sheets without the "cancellation" are extremely scarce. Values: unused, $525; never hinged, $1,000.

King Leopold III in Military Plane SP77

1938, Mar. 15

B209 SP77 10c + 5c car brn .25 *.30*
B210 SP77 35c + 5c dp grn .35 *.90*
B211 SP77 70c + 5c gray blk .95 .75
B212 SP77 1.75fr + 25c ultra 2.25 2.10
B213 SP77 2.45fr + 2.55fr pur 5.25 4.50
Nos. B209-B213 (5) 9.05 8.55
Set, never hinged 22.50

The surtax was for the benefit of the National Fund for Aeronautical Propaganda.

Basilica of Koekelberg SP78

Interior View of the Basilica of Koekelberg SP79

1938, June 1 **Photo.**

B214 SP78 10c + 5c lt brn .25 .25
B215 SP78 35c + 5c grn .25 .25
B216 SP78 70c + 5c gray grn .25 .25
B217 SP78 1fr + 25c car .70 .60
B218 SP78 1.75fr + 25c ultra .70 .70
B219 SP78 2.45fr + 2.55fr brn vio 3.25 *3.75*

Engr.

B220 SP79 5fr + 5fr dl grn 12.25 11.50
Nos. B214-B220 (7) 17.65 17.30
Set, never hinged 35.00

Souvenir Sheet

1938, July 21 **Engr.** ***Perf. 14***

B221 SP79 5fr + 5fr lt vio 16.00 16.00
Never hinged 25.00
a. Single stamp 14.00
Never hinged 16.00

The surtax was for a fund to aid in completing the National Basilica of the Sacred Heart at Koekelberg.

Nos. B214, B216 and B218 are different views of the exterior of the Basilica.

The sheet normally has pin holes and a cancellation-like marking in the margin. These are considered unused and the condition valued here.

Stamps of 1938 Surcharged in Black

Nos. B222-B223

No. B224

1938, Nov. 10 ***Perf. 11½***

B222 SP78 40c on 35c+5c grn .50 *.60*
B223 SP78 75c on 70c+5c gray grn .75 *.90*
B224 SP78 2.50 +2.50fr on 2.45+2.55fr 6.75 *7.50*
Nos. B222-B224 (3) 8.00 *9.00*
Set, never hinged 19.00

Prince Albert of Liege — SP81

1938, Dec. 10 **Photo.** ***Perf. 14x13½***

B225 SP81 10c + 5c brown .25 .25
B226 SP81 30c + 5c mag .25 *.30*
B227 SP81 40c + 5c olive gray .25 *.30*
B228 SP81 75c + 5c slate grn .25 .25
B229 SP81 1fr + 25c dk car .75 *1.10*
B230 SP81 1.75fr + 25c ultra .75 *1.10*
B231 SP81 2.50fr + 2.50fr dp grn 5.25 *8.25*
B232 SP81 5fr + 5fr brn lake 16.00 12.50
Nos. B225-B232 (8) 23.75 24.05
Set, never hinged 70.00

Henri Dunant SP82

Florence Nightingale SP83

Queen Mother Elisabeth and Royal Children — SP84

Queen Astrid — SP86

King Leopold and Royal Children SP85

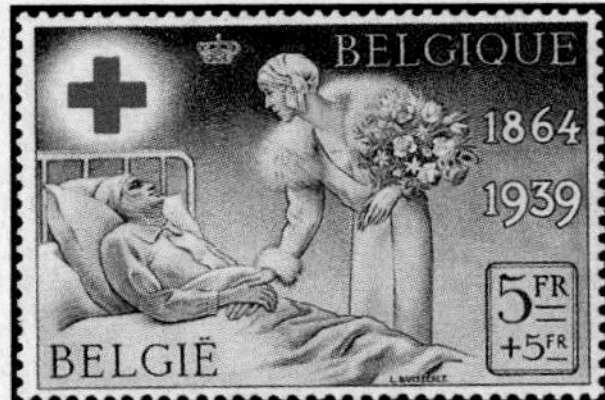

Queen Mother Elisabeth and Wounded Soldier — SP87

1939, Apr. 1 **Photo.** ***Perf. 11½***

Cross in Carmine

B233 SP82 10c + 5c brn .25 .25
B234 SP83 30c + 5c brn car .45 .45
B235 SP84 40c + 5c ol gray .25 *.30*
B236 SP85 75c + 5c slate blk .60 .25
B237 SP84 1fr + 25c brt rose 3.00 1.60
B238 SP85 1.75fr + 25c brt ultra .90 *1.25*
B239 SP86 2.50fr + 2.50fr dl vio 1.90 *2.40*
B240 SP87 5fr + 5fr gray grn 6.50 *8.25*
Nos. B233-B240 (8) 13.85 *14.75*
Set, never hinged 42.50

75th anniversary of the founding of the International Red Cross Society.

Rubens' House, Antwerp SP88

"Albert and Nicolas Rubens" — SP89

Arcade, Rubens' House SP90

"Helena Fourment and Her Children" — SP91

Rubens and Isabelle Brandt — SP92

Peter Paul Rubens — SP93

"The Velvet Hat" — SP94

"Descent from the Cross" SP95

1939, July 1

B241 SP88 10c + 5c brn .25 .25
B242 SP89 40c + 5c brn car .25 .25
B243 SP90 75c + 5c ol blk .65 .65
B244 SP91 1fr + 25c rose 2.50 2.50
B245 SP92 1.50fr + 25c sep 2.75 2.75
B246 SP93 1.75fr + 25c dp ultra 4.50 4.50
B247 SP94 2.50fr + 2.50fr brt red vio 15.00 *15.00*
B248 SP95 5fr + 5fr slate gray 19.00 19.00
Nos. B241-B248 (8) 44.90 44.90
Set, never hinged 140.00

Issued to honor Peter Paul Rubens. The surtax was used to restore Rubens' home in Antwerp.

"Martin van Nieuwenhove" by Hans Memling (1430?-1495), Flemish Painter — SP96

1939, July 1

B249 SP96 75c + 75c olive blk 2.75 2.75
Never hinged 4.50

Twelfth Century Monks at Work — SP97

Reconstructed Tower Seen through Cloister — SP98

Monks Laboring in the Fields SP99

Orval Abbey, Aerial View SP100

Bishop Heylen of Namur, Madonna and Abbot General Smets of the Trappists — SP101

King Albert I and King Leopold III and Shrine — SP102

1939, July 20

B250 SP97 75c + 75c ol blk 3.50 3.75
B251 SP98 1fr + 1fr rose red 2.25 2.25
B252 SP99 1.50fr + 1.50fr dl brn 2.25 2.25
B253 SP100 1.75fr + 1.75fr saph 2.25 2.25
B254 SP101 2.50fr + 2.50fr brt red vio 10.00 9.00

B255 SP102 5fr + 5fr brn car 10.00 10.00
Nos. B250-B255 (6) 30.25 29.50
Set, never hinged 82.50

The surtax was used for the restoration of the Abbey of Orval.

Bruges
SP103

Furnes
SP104

Belfries: 30c+5c, Thuin. 40c+5c, Lierre. 75c+5c, Mons. 1.75fr+25c, Namur. 2.50fr+2.50fr, Alost. 5fr+5fr, Tournai.

1939, Dec. 1 Photo. *Perf. 14x13½*

B256 SP103 10c + 5c ol gray .25 *.25*
B257 SP103 30c + 5c brn org .30 *.40*
B258 SP103 40c + 5c brt red vio .50 *.50*
B259 SP103 75c + 5c olive blk .25 *.25*

Engr.

B260 SP104 1fr + 25c rose car 1.25 *1.50*
B261 SP104 1.75fr + 25c dk blue 1.25 *1.50*
B262 SP104 2.50fr + 2.50fr dp red brn 8.75 *9.50*
B263 SP104 5fr + 5fr pur 12.00 *13.25*
Nos. B256-B263 (8) 24.55 *27.15*
Set, never hinged 65.00

Mons
SP111

Ghent
SP112

Coats of Arms: 40c+10c, Arel. 50c+10c, Bruges. 75c+15c, Namur. 1fr+25c, Hasselt. 1.75fr+50c, Brussels. 2.50fr+2.50fr, Antwerp. 5fr+5fr, Liege.

1940-41 Typo. *Perf. 14x13½*

B264 SP111 10c + 5c multi .25 .25
B265 SP112 30c + 5c multi .25 .25
B266 SP111 40c + 10c multi .25 .25
B267 SP112 50c + 10c multi .25 .25
B268 SP111 75c + 15c multi .25 .25
B269 SP112 1fr + 25c multi .30 .30
B270 SP111 1.75fr + 50c multi .45 .40
B271 SP112 2.50fr + 2.50fr multi 1.25 1.25
B272 SP111 5fr + 5fr multi 1.50 1.50
Nos. B264-B272 (9) 4.75 4.70
Set, never hinged 8.50

Nos. B264, B269-B272 issued in 1941. Surtax for winter relief. See No. B279 in *Scott Standard Postage Stamp Catalogue*, Vol. 1.

Queen Elisabeth Music Chapel
SP120

Bust of Prince Albert of Liege — SP121

1940, Nov. Photo. *Perf. 11½*

B273 SP120 75c + 75c slate 3.50 3.50
B274 SP120 1fr + 1fr rose red 1.25 1.25
B275 SP121 1.50fr + 1.50fr Prus grn 1.25 1.25
B276 SP121 1.75fr + 1.75fr ultra 1.25 1.25
B277 SP120 2.50fr + 2.50fr brn org 3.50 3.50
B278 SP121 5fr + 5fr red vio 3.50 3.50
Nos. B273-B278 (6) 14.25 14.25
Set, never hinged 55.00

The surtax was for the Queen Elisabeth Music Foundation. Nos. B273-B278 were not authorized for postal use, but were sold to advance subscribers either mint or canceled to order. See Nos. B317-B318 in *Scott Standard Postage Stamp Catalogue*, Vol. 1.

AIR POST STAMPS

Fokker FVII/3m over Ostend
AP1

Designs: 1.50fr, Plane over St. Hubert. 2fr, over Namur. 5fr, over Brussels.

Perf. 11½

1930, Apr. 30 Unwmk. Photo.

C1 AP1 50c blue .45 .45
C2 AP1 1.50fr black brn 2.50 2.50
C3 AP1 2fr deep green 2.00 .90
C4 AP1 5fr brown lake 2.00 1.10
Nos. C1-C4 (4) 6.95 4.95
Set, never hinged 22.50

Nos. C1-C4 exist imperf.

1930, Dec. 5

C5 AP1 5fr dark violet 30.00 30.00
Never hinged 65.00

Issued for use on a mail carrying flight from Brussels to Leopoldville, Belgian Congo, starting Dec. 7.
Exists imperf.

Nos. C2 and C4 Surcharged in Carmine or Blue

1935, May 23

C6 AP1 1fr on 1.50fr (C) .55 .40
C7 AP1 4fr on 5fr (Bl) 8.75 8.00
Set, never hinged 42.50

SPECIAL DELIVERY STAMPS

From 1874 to 1903 certain hexagonal telegraph stamps were used as special delivery stamps.

Town Hall, Brussels — SD1

Eupen — SD2

2.35fr, Street in Ghent. 3.50fr, Bishop's Palace, Liege. 5.25fr, Notre Dame Cathedral, Antwerp.

1929 Unwmk. Photo. *Perf. 11½*

E1 SD1 1.75fr dark blue .80 .30
E2 SD1 2.35fr carmine 1.75 .45
E3 SD1 3.50fr dark violet 11.00 10.00
E4 SD1 5.25fr olive green 10.50 10.00

1931

E5 SD2 2.45fr dark green 17.00 2.50
Nos. E1-E5 (5) 41.05 23.25
Set, never hinged 110.00

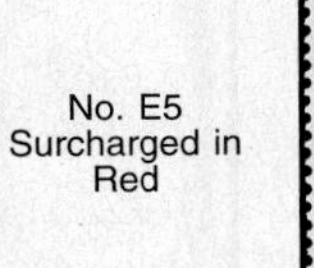

No. E5 Surcharged in Red

1932

E6 SD2 2.50fr on 2.45fr dk grn 18.00 2.00
Never hinged 60.00

POSTAGE DUE STAMPS

D1

1870 Unwmk. Typo. *Perf. 15*

J1 D1 10c green 3.75 2.00
Never hinged 10.00
On cover *110.00*
a. 10c deep green 4.50 3.00
Never hinged 12.50
On cover *120.00*
J2 D1 20c ultra, thin paper 30.00 3.75
Never hinged 140.00
On cover *225.00*
Set, never hinged 140.00

In 1909 many bisects of Nos. J1-J2 were created. The 10c bisect used as 5c on piece sells for $3.50.

No. J2 was also printed in aniline ink on thin paper. Value about the same.

D2

1895-09 *Perf. 14*

J3 D2 5c yellow grn .25 .25
Never hinged .40
On cover 3.50
a. 5c green .85 .25
Never hinged 3.00
On cover 3.50
J4 D2 10c orange brn 17.50 1.75
Never hinged 57.50
On cover 15.00
J5 D2 10c carmine ('00) .25 .25
Never hinged .40
On cover 2.00
a. 10c rose 1.50 .40
Never hinged 3.00
On cover 2.00
J6 D2 20c olive green .25 .25
Never hinged .40
On cover 3.50
J7 D2 30c pale blue ('09) .30 .25
Never hinged .80
On cover 17.50
J8 D2 50c yellow brn 17.50 5.00
Never hinged 57.50
On cover 85.00
J9 D2 50c gray ('00) .75 .45
Never hinged 1.60
On cover 30.00
a. 50c blackish gray 3.75 1.25
Never hinged 10.00
On cover 37.50
J10 D2 1fr carmine 20.00 11.50
Never hinged 50.00
On cover *850.00*
J11 D2 1fr ocher ('00) 6.50 5.00
Never hinged 10.00
On cover *1,000.*
Nos. J3-J11 (9) 63.30 24.70
Set, never hinged 175.00

1916 Redrawn

J12 D2 5c blue grn 25.00 7.00
Never hinged 72.50
On cover 22.50
J13 D2 10c carmine 42.50 11.00
Never hinged 140.00
On cover 15.00
J14 D2 20c dp gray grn 42.50 15.00
Never hinged 140.00
On cover 40.00
J15 D2 30c brt blue 6.00 5.00
Never hinged 14.00
On cover 50.00
J16 D2 50c gray 125.00 60.00
Never hinged 425.00
On cover 150.00
Nos. J12-J16 (5) 241.00 98.00
Set, never hinged 790.00

In the redrawn stamps the lions have a heavy, colored outline. There is a thick vertical line at the outer edge of the design on each side.

Stamps handstamped "T" on Nos. 111-119

1919, Oct.-Nov.

J16C A46 5c green (#111) 1.20 .25
Never hinged 4.25
On cover 17.50
J16D A46 10c carmine (#112) 1.20 .25
Never hinged 4.25
On cover 9.00
J16E A46 15c purple (#113) 2.10 .25
Never hinged 7.50
On cover 17.50
J16F A46 20c red violet (#114) 3.00 .25
Never hinged 11.00
On cover 40.00
J16G A46 25c blue (#115) 1.00 .50
Never hinged 3.75
On cover 60.00
J16H A47 35c brown org & blk (#116) 1.00 .50
Never hinged 3,00
On cover 37.50
J16I A48 40c green & blk (#117) 1.00 .50
Never hinged 3,00
On cover 75.00
J16J A49 50c carmine rose & blk (#118) 5.75 .50
Never hinged 22.50
On cover 90.00
J16K A50 1fr violet (#119) 40.00 3.00
Never hinged 130.00
On cover 225.00
Nos. J16C-J16K (9) 56.25 6.00
Set, never hinged 190.00

Nos. J16C-J16K were handstamped locally for use as provisionals during a shortage of postage due stamps.

D3

1919 *Perf. 14*

J17 D3 5c green .40 .50
J18 D3 10c carmine .95 .35
J19 D3 20c gray green 7.25 1.25
J20 D3 30c bright blue 1.40 .40
J21 D3 50c gray 2.75 .50
Nos. J17-J21 (5) 12.75 3.00
Set, never hinged 40.00

The 5c, 10c, 20c and 50c values also exist perf 14x15.

D4

1922-32

J22 D4 5c dk gray .25 .25
J23 D4 10c green .25 .25
J24 D4 20c deep brown .25 .25
J25 D4 30c ver ('24) .65 .25
a. 30c rose red 1.00 .45
J26 D4 40c red brn ('25) .25 .25
J27 D4 50c ultra 1.90 .25
J28 D4 70c red brn ('29) .30 .25
J29 D4 1fr violet ('25) .45 .25
J30 D4 1fr rose lilac ('32) .55 .25
J31 D4 1.20fr ol grn ('29) .65 .45
J32 D4 1.50fr ol grn ('32) .65 .45
J33 D4 2fr violet ('29) .75 .25
J34 D4 3.50fr dp blue ('29) 1.00 .25
Nos. J22-J34 (13) 7.90 3.65
Set, never hinged 15.00

1934-46 *Perf. 14x13½*

J35 D4 35c green ('35) .40 *.45*
J36 D4 50c slate .25 .25
J37 D4 60c carmine ('38) .40 .30
J38 D4 80c slate ('38) .30 .25
J39 D4 1.40fr gray ('35) .65 .45
J39A D4 3fr org brn ('46) 1.50 .60
J39B D4 7fr brt red vio ('46) 2.25 *3.25*
Nos. J35-J39B (7) 5.75 *5.55*
Set, never hinged 12.00

See Nos. J54-J61 in *Scott Standard Postage Stamp Catalogue*, Vol. 1.

MILITARY PARCEL POST STAMP

Type of Parcel Post Stamp of 1938 Srchd. in Blue

1939 **Unwmk.** *Perf. 13½*

MQ1 PP19 3fr on 5.50fr copper red .30 .25
Never hinged .60

OFFICIAL STAMPS

For franking the official correspondence of the Administration of the Belgian National Railways.

Most examples of Nos. O1-O25 in the marketplace are counterfeits. Values are for genuine examples.

Regular Issue of 1921-27 Overprinted in Black

1929-30 **Unwmk.** *Perf. 14*

O1 A58 5c gray .25 .25
O2 A58 10c blue green .30 .40
O3 A58 35c blue green .40 .30
O4 A58 60c olive green .45 .30
O5 A58 1.50fr brt blue 8.00 6.25
O6 A58 1.75fr ultra ('30) 1.75 2.00
Nos. O1-O6 (6) 11.15 9.50

Same Overprint, in Red or Black, on Regular Issues of 1929-30

1929-31

O7 A63 5c slate (R) .25 .35
O8 A63 10c olive grn (R) .50 .40
O9 A63 25c rose red (Bk) 1.50 .85
O10 A63 35c dp green (R) 1.75 .50
O11 A63 40c red vio (Bk) 1.25 .45
O12 A63 50c dp blue (R) ('31) .80 .35
O13 A63 60c rose (Bk) 10.00 6.00
O14 A63 70c orange brn (Bk) 4.25 1.25
O15 A63 75c black vio (R) ('31) 4.00 .85
Nos. O7-O15 (9) 24.30 11.00

Overprinted on Regular Issue of 1932

1932

O16 A73 10c olive grn (R) .50 .60
O17 A74 35c dp green 9.00 .75
O18 A71a 75c bister brn (R) 1.50 .30
Nos. O16-O18 (3) 11.00 1.65

Overprinted on No. 262 in Red

1935 *Perf. 13½x14*

O19 A80 70c olive black 2.75 .25

Regular Stamps of 1935-36 Overprinted in Red

1936-38 *Perf. 13½, 13½x14, 14*

O20 A82 10c olive bister .25 *.35*
O21 A82 35c green .25 *.40*
O22 A82 50c dark blue .45 .35
O23 A83 70c brown 1.50 .65

Overprinted in Black or Red on Regular Issue of 1938
Perf. 13½x14

O24 A82 40c red violet (Bk) .30 *.35*
O25 A85 75c olive gray (R) .65 .30
Nos. O20-O25 (6) 3.40 2.40

NEWSPAPER STAMPS

Most examples of Nos. P1-P40 in the marketplace are counterfeits. Values are for genuine examples.

Parcel Post Stamps of 1923-27 Overprinted

Perf. 14½x14, 14x14½

1928 **Unwmk.**

P1 PP12 10c vermilion .25 *.40*
P2 PP12 20c turq blue .25 *.40*
P3 PP12 40c olive grn .25 *.40*
P4 PP12 60c orange .70 *.90*
P5 PP12 70c dk brown .45 .40
P6 PP12 80c violet .60 *.70*
P7 PP12 90c slate 2.25 2.00
P8 PP13 1fr brt blue .90 .60
a. 1fr ultramarine 12.00 5.00
P10 PP13 2fr olive grn 1.50 .60
P11 PP13 3fr orange red 1.60 .90
P12 PP13 4fr rose 2.25 1.10
P13 PP13 5fr violet 2.25 1.00
P14 PP13 6fr bister brn 4.50 1.75
P15 PP13 7fr orange 5.00 2.25
P16 PP13 8fr dk brown 6.00 2.75
P17 PP13 9fr red violet 10.00 3.00
P18 PP13 10fr blue green 9.00 2.75
P19 PP13 20fr magenta 15.00 7.00
Nos. P1-P8,P10-P19 (18) 62.75 28.90

Parcel Post Stamps of 1923-28 Overprinted

1929-31

P20 PP12 10c vermilion .25 .25
P21 PP12 20c turq blue .25 .25
P22 PP12 40c olive green .30 .25
a. Inverted overprint
P23 PP12 60c orange .55 .35
P24 PP12 70c dk brown .55 .25
P25 PP12 80c violet .60 .25
P26 PP12 90c gray 2.00 1.00
P27 PP13 1fr ultra .60 .25
a. 1fr bright blue 4.00 2.50
P28 PP13 1.10fr org brn ('31) 6.25 1.40
P29 PP13 1.50fr gray vio ('31) 6.25 1.90
P30 PP13 2fr olive green 2.00 .25
P31 PP13 2.10fr sl gray ('31) 17.00 12.00
P32 PP13 3fr orange red 2.25 .45
P33 PP13 4fr rose 2.25 .70
P34 PP13 5fr violet 3.00 .55
P35 PP13 6fr bister brn 3.75 1.00
P36 PP13 7fr orange 3.75 1.00
P37 PP13 8fr dk brown 3.75 1.00
P38 PP13 9fr red violet 5.25 1.50
P39 PP13 10fr blue green 3.75 1.10
P40 PP13 20fr magenta 13.00 4.50
Nos. P20-P40 (21) 77.35 30.20

PARCEL POST AND RAILWAY STAMPS

Values for used Railway Stamps (Chemins de Fer) stamps are for copies with railway cancellations. Railway Stamps with postal cancellations sell for twice as much.

Coat of Arms — PP1

1879-82 **Unwmk.** **Typo.** *Perf. 14*

Q1 PP1 10c violet brown 110.00 5.75
No gum 50.00
Q2 PP1 20c blue 275.00 17.50
No gum 140.00
Q3 PP1 25c green ('81) 375.00 10.00
No gum 175.00
Q4 PP1 50c carmine 1,750. 10.00
No gum 1,100.
Q5 PP1 80c yellow 2,000. 57.50
No gum 1,150.
Q6 PP1 1fr gray ('82) 275.00 16.00
No gum 140.00

Used examples of Nos. Q1-Q6 with pinholes, a normal state, sell for approximately 40-60 percent of the values given.

Most of the stamps of 1882-1902 (Nos. Q7 to Q28) are without watermark. Twice in each sheet of 100 stamps they have one of three watermarks: (1) A winged wheel and "Chemins de Fer de l'Etat Belge," (2) Coat of Arms of Belgium and "Royaume de Belgique," (3) Larger Coat of Arms, without inscription.

PP2

1882-94 *Perf. 15½x14¼*

Q7 PP2 10c brown ('86) 20.00 1.50
a. 10c rose brown 21.50 1.60
b. 10c chestnut brown 23.50 3.00
Q8 PP2 15c gray ('94) 8.75 7.25
Q9 PP2 20c blue ('86) 65.00 7.00
a. 20c ultramarine ('90) 75.00 4.00
b. 20c greenish blue ('90) 72.50 3.75
Q10 PP2 25c yel grn ('91) 72.50 4.25
a. 25c blue green ('87) 67.50 4.00
Q11 PP2 50c carmine 72.50 2.50
a. 50c rose ('82) 67.50 .75
b. 50c pomegranate 75.00 5.00
Q12 PP2 80c brnsh buff 72.50 .90
a. 80c bister ('83) 67.50 .80
Q13 PP2 80c lemon 75.00 1.60
Q14 PP2 1fr lavender 350.00 3.00
a. 1fr gray 385.00 3.50
b. 1fr bronze 425.00 4.50
Q15 PP2 2fr yel buff ('94) 210.00 67.50

Counterfeits exist.

PP3

Name of engraver below frame

1895-97

Numerals in Black, except 1fr, 2fr

Q16 PP3 10c red brown ('96) 11.00 .60
Never hinged 20.00
Q17 PP3 15c gray 11.00 7.00
Never hinged 18.00
Q18 PP3 20c blue 17.50 1.00
Never hinged 32.50
Q19 PP3 25c green 17.50 1.25
Never hinged 32.50
Q20 PP3 50c carmine 25.00 .80
Never hinged 50.00
Q21 PP3 60c violet ('96) 50.00 1.00
Never hinged 100.00
Q22 PP3 80c ol yel ('96) 50.00 1.40
Never hinged 100.00
Q23 PP3 1fr lilac brown 175.00 3.00
Never hinged 350.00
Q24 PP3 2fr yel buff ('97) 200.00 15.00
Never hinged 400.00

Counterfeits exist.

1901-02 **Numerals in Black**

Q25 PP3 30c orange 21.00 2.00
Never hinged 37.50
Q26 PP3 40c green 26.00 1.75
Never hinged 50.00
Q27 PP3 70c blue 50.00 1.40
Never hinged 100.00
a. Numerals omitted *750.00*
b. Numerals printed on reverse *750.00*
Q28 PP3 90c red 65.00 2.00
Never hinged 140.00
Nos. Q25-Q28 (4) 162.00 7.15

Winged Wheel PP4

Without engraver's name

1902-14 *Perf. 15*

Q29 PP3 10c yel brn & slate .25 .25
Q30 PP3 15c slate & vio .25 .25
Q31 PP3 20c ultra & yel brn .25 .25
Q32 PP3 25c yel grn & red .25 .25
Q33 PP3 30c orange & bl grn .25 .25
Q34 PP3 35c bister & bl grn ('12) .35 .25
Q35 PP3 40c blue grn & vio .25 .25
Q36 PP3 50c pale rose & vio .25 .25
Q37 PP3 55c lilac brn & ultra ('14) .35 .25
Q38 PP3 60c violet & red .25 .25
Q39 PP3 70c blue & red .25 .25
Q40 PP3 80c lemon & vio brn .25 .25
Q41 PP3 90c red & yel grn .25 .25
Q42 PP4 1fr vio brn & org .25 .25
Q43 PP4 1.10fr rose & blk ('06) .25 .25
Q44 PP4 2fr ocher & bl grn .25 .25
Q45 PP4 3fr black & ultra .35 .25
Q46 PP4 4fr yel grn & red ('13) 1.25 .70
Q47 PP4 5fr org & bl grn ('13) .55 .55
Q48 PP4 10fr ol yel & brn vio ('13) .90 .55
Nos. Q29-Q48 (20) 7.25 6.05

Regular Issues of 1912-13 Handstamped in Violet

1915 *Perf. 14*

Q49 A42 5c green 190.00 160.00
Never hinged 230.00
Q50 A43 10c red 1,400. 1,400.
Never hinged 1,850
Q51 A45 10c red 230.00 200.00
Never hinged 300.00
a. With engraver's name 775.00 775.00
Never hinged 925.00
Q52 A43 20c olive grn *1,600.* *1,600.*
Never hinged 2,100
Q53 A45 20c olive grn 260.00 225.00
Never hinged 350.00
a. With engraver's name 775.00 775.00
Never hinged 925.00
Q54 A45 25c ultra 260.00 225.00
Never hinged 350.00
a. With engraver's name 775.00 775.00
Never hinged 925.00
Q55 A43 35c bister brn 350.00 300.00
Never hinged 425.00
Q55A A43 40c green *2,500.* *2,500.*
Never hinged 3,750
Q56 A45 40c green 325.00 275.00
Never hinged 425.00
Q57 A43 50c gray 325.00 275.00
Never hinged 400.00
Q58 A43 1fr orange 325.00 275.00
Never hinged 375.00
Q59 A43 2fr violet *1,900.* *1,650.*
Never hinged 2,200
Q60 A44 5fr plum *4,000.* *3,500.*
Never hinged 4,500.

Excellent forgeries of this overprint exist.

PP5

PP6

1916 **Litho.** *Perf. 13½*

Q61 PP5 10c pale blue 1.10 .25
Q62 PP5 15c olive grn 1.40 .50
Q63 PP5 20c red 2.25 .50
Q64 PP5 25c lt brown 2.25 .50
Q65 PP5 30c lilac 1.40 .50
Q66 PP5 35c gray 1.40 .45
Q67 PP5 40c orange yel 3.00 1.50
Q68 PP5 50c bister 2.25 .45
Q69 PP5 55c brown 3.00 2.25
Q70 PP5 60c gray vio 2.25 .45

Q71 PP5 70c green 2.25 .45
Q72 PP5 80c red brown 2.25 .45
Q73 PP5 90c blue 2.25 .45
Q74 PP6 1fr gray 2.25 .45
Q75 PP6 1.10fr ultra *(Franken)* 27.50 21.00
Q76 PP6 2fr red 25.00 .45
Q77 PP6 3fr violet 25.00 .45
Q78 PP6 4fr emerald 45.00 1.50
Q79 PP6 5fr brown 45.00 3.00
Q80 PP6 10fr orange 45.00 1.50
Nos. Q61-Q80 (20) 241.80 37.05

Type of 1916 Inscribed "FRANK" instead of "FRANKEN"

1920
Q81 PP6 1.10fr ultra 2.00 .45

PP7

PP8

1920 ***Perf. 14***
Q82 PP7 10c blue grn 1.75 .75
Q83 PP7 15c olive grn 1.75 1.10
Q84 PP7 20c red 1.75 .75
Q85 PP7 25c gray brn 2.50 .75
Q86 PP7 30c red vio 27.00 22.50
Q87 PP7 40c pale org 11.00 .75
Q88 PP7 50c bister 9.00 .75
Q89 PP7 55c pale brown 5.50 4.50
Q90 PP7 60c dk violet 10.00 .75
Q91 PP7 70c green 18.00 1.10
Q92 PP7 80c red brown 40.00 1.50
Q93 PP7 90c dull blue 10.00 .75
Q94 PP8 1fr gray 85.00 1.50
Q95 PP8 1.10fr ultra 26.00 2.00
Q96 PP8 1.20fr dk green 11.00 .75
Q97 PP8 1.40fr black brn 11.00 .75
Q98 PP8 2fr vermilion 110.00 1.25
Q99 PP8 3fr red vio 125.00 .85
Q100 PP8 4fr yel grn 125.00 .75
Q101 PP8 5fr bister brn 125.00 .75
Q102 PP8 10fr brown org 125.00 .75
Nos. Q82-Q102 (21) 881.25 45.30

PP9

PP10

Types PP7 and PP9 differ in the position of the wheel and the tablet above it.

Types PP8 and PP10 differ in the bars below "FR".

There are many other variations in the designs.

1920-21 **Typo.**
Q103 PP9 10c carmine .30 .25
Q104 PP9 15c yel grn .30 .25
Q105 PP9 20c blue grn .70 .25
Q106 PP9 25c ultra .65 .25
Q107 PP9 30c chocolate .85 .25
Q108 PP9 35c orange brn .90 .30
Q109 PP9 40c orange 1.10 .25
Q110 PP9 50c rose 1.10 .25
Q111 PP9 55c yel ('21) 4.50 3.25
Q112 PP9 60c dull rose 1.10 .25
Q113 PP9 70c emerald 3.00 .40
Q114 PP9 80c violet 2.25 .25
Q115 PP9 90c lemon 37.50 21.00
Q116 PP9 90c claret 4.50 .40
Q117 PP10 1fr buff 4.50 .35
Q118 PP10 1fr red brown 4.00 .30
Q119 PP10 1.10fr ultra 1.60 .45
Q120 PP10 1.20fr orange 6.25 .30
Q121 PP10 1.40fr yellow 10.00 1.75
Q122 PP10 1.60fr turq blue 18.00 .70
Q123 PP10 1.60fr emerald 40.00 .70
Q124 PP10 2fr pale rose 26.00 .30
Q125 PP10 3fr dp rose 24.00 .30
Q126 PP10 4fr emerald 24.00 .30

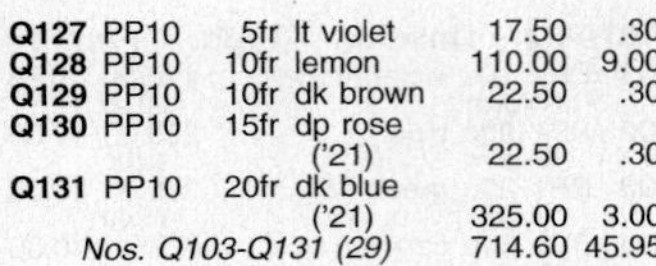

Q127 PP10 5fr lt violet 17.50 .30
Q128 PP10 10fr lemon 110.00 9.00
Q129 PP10 10fr dk brown 22.50 .30
Q130 PP10 15fr dp rose ('21) 22.50 .30
Q131 PP10 20fr dk blue ('21) 325.00 3.00
Nos. Q103-Q131 (29) 714.60 45.95

PP11

1922 **Engr.** ***Perf. 11½***
Q132 PP11 2fr black 4.00 .25
Q133 PP11 3fr brown 37.50 .25
Q134 PP11 4fr green 9.00 .25
Q135 PP11 5r claret 9.00 .25
Q136 PP11 10fr yel brown 10.00 .25
Q137 PP11 15fr rose red 10.00 .25
Q138 PP11 20fr blue 67.50 .25
Nos. Q132-Q138 (7) 147.00 1.75

PP12

PP13

Perf. 14x13½, 13½x14

1923-40 **Typo.**
Q139 PP12 5c red brn .25 .25
Q140 PP12 10c vermilion .25 .25
Q141 PP12 15c ultra .25 .30
Q142 PP12 20c turq blue .25 .25
Q143 PP12 30c brn vio ('27) .25 .25
Q144 PP12 40c olive grn .25 .25
Q145 PP12 50c mag ('27) .25 .25
Q146 PP12 60c orange .25 .25
Q147 PP12 70c dk brn ('24) .25 .25
Q148 PP12 80c violet .25 .25
Q149 PP12 90c sl ('27) 1.25 .25
Q150 PP13 1fr ultra .35 .25
Q151 PP13 1fr brt blue ('28) .55 .25
Q152 PP13 1.10fr orange 3.00 .30
Q153 PP13 1.50fr turq blue 3.25 .30
Q154 PP13 1.70fr dp brn ('31) .75 .60
Q155 PP13 1.80fr claret 4.25 .60
Q156 PP13 2fr ol grn ('24) .35 .25
Q157 PP13 2.10fr gray grn 7.50 .85
Q158 PP13 2.40fr dp violet 4.00 .85
Q159 PP13 2.70fr gray ('24) 35.00 1.40
Q160 PP13 3fr org red .45 .25
Q161 PP13 3.30fr brn ('24) 55.00 1.40
Q162 PP13 4fr rose ('24) .55 .25
Q163 PP13 5fr vio ('24) .90 .25
Q163A PP13 5fr brn vio ('40) .45 .30
Q164 PP13 6fr bis brn ('27) .50 .25
Q165 PP13 7fr org ('27) .90 .25
Q166 PP13 8fr dp brn ('27) .75 .25
Q167 PP13 9fr red vio ('27) 2.50 .25
Q168 PP13 10fr blue grn ('27) 1.10 .25
Q168A PP13 10fr blk ('40) 5.75 5.00
Q169 PP13 20fr mag ('27) 1.90 .25
Q170 PP13 30fr turq grn ('31) 6.00 .40
Q171 PP13 40fr gray ('31) 55.00 .75
Q172 PP13 50fr bis ('27) 9.00 .30
Nos. Q139-Q172 (36) 203.50 18.85

See Nos. Q239-Q262 in *Scott Standard Postage Stamp Catalogue*, Vol. 1. For overprints see Nos. Q216-Q238. Stamps overprinted "Bagages Reisgoed" are revenues.

No. Q158 Srchd.

1924 **Green Surcharge**
Q173 PP13 2.30fr on 2.40fr vio 5.00 .85
Never hinged 30.00
a. Inverted surcharge 57.50

Type of Regular Issue of 1926-27 Overprinted

1928 ***Perf. 14***
Q174 A61 4fr buff 7.50 1.10
Q175 A61 5fr bister 7.50 1.25
Set, never hinged 55.00

Central P.O., Brussels PP15

1929-30 **Engr.** ***Perf. 11½***
Q176 PP15 3fr black brn 2.00 .25
Q177 PP15 4fr gray 2.00 .25
Q178 PP15 5fr carmine 2.00 .25
Q179 PP15 6fr vio brn ('30) 29.00 32.50
Nos. Q176-Q179 (4) 35.00 33.25
Set, never hinged 115.00

No. Q179 Surcharged in Blue

1933
Q180 PP15 4(fr) on 6fr vio brn 25.00 .25
Never hinged 105.00

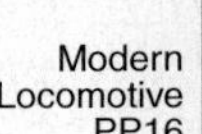

Modern Locomotive PP16

1934 **Photo.** ***Perf. 13½x14***
Q181 PP16 3fr dk green 40.00 9.00
Q182 PP16 4fr red violet 9.50 .25
Q183 PP16 5fr dp rose 37.50 .25
Nos. Q181-Q183 (3) 87.00 9.50
Set, never hinged 275.00

Modern Railroad Train — PP17

Old Railroad Train — PP18

1935 **Engr.** ***Perf. 14x13½, 13½x14***
Q184 PP17 10c rose car .45 .25
Q185 PP17 20c violet .50 .25
Q186 PP17 30c black brn .65 .45
Q187 PP17 40c dk blue .80 .25
Q188 PP17 50c orange red .80 .25
Q189 PP17 60c green .90 .25
Q190 PP17 70c ultra 1.00 .25
Q191 PP17 80c olive blk .90 .25
Q192 PP17 90c rose lake 1.25 .65
Q193 PP18 1fr brown vio 1.25 .25
Q194 PP18 2fr gray blk 2.75 .25
Q195 PP18 3fr red org 3.50 .25
Q196 PP18 4fr violet brn 4.25 .25
Q197 PP18 5fr plum 4.50 .25
Q198 PP18 6fr dp green 5.00 .25
Q199 PP18 7fr dp violet 24.00 .25
Q200 PP18 8fr olive blk 24.00 .25
Q201 PP18 9fr dk blue 24.00 .25
Q202 PP18 10fr car lake 24.00 .25
Q203 PP18 20fr green 125.00 .25
Q204 PP18 30fr violet 125.00 2.75
Q205 PP18 40fr black brn 125.00 3.50
Q206 PP18 50fr rose car 140.00 2.75
Q207 PP18 100fr ultra 350.00 62.50
Nos. Q184-Q207 (24) 989.50 77.10
Set, never hinged 3,375.

Centenary of Belgian State Railway.

Winged Wheel PP19

Surcharged in Red or Blue

1938 **Photo.** ***Perf. 13½***
Q208 PP19 5fr on 3.50fr dk grn 22.50 1.50
Q209 PP19 5fr on 4.50fr rose vio (Bl) .25 .25
Q210 PP19 6fr on 5.50fr cop red (Bl) .50 .25
a. Half used as 3fr on piece 8.00
Nos. Q208-Q210 (3) 23.25 2.00
Set, never hinged 75.00

Nos. Q208-Q210 exist without surcharge. Value, set, $750.

See No. MQ1; Nos. Q297-Q299 in *Scott Standard Postage Stamp Catalogue*, Vol. 1.

Symbolizing Unity Achieved Through Railroads PP20

1939 **Engr.** ***Perf. 13½x14***
Q211 PP20 20c redsh brn 5.00 *5.25*
Q212 PP20 50c vio bl 5.00 *5.25*
Q213 PP20 2fr rose red 5.00 *5.25*
Q214 PP20 9fr slate grn 5.00 *5.25*
Q215 PP20 10fr dk vio 5.00 *5.25*
Nos. Q211-Q215 (5) 25.00 *26.25*
Set, never hinged 30.00

Railroad Exposition and Cong. held at Brussels.

Parcel Post Stamps of 1925-27 Overprinted in Blue or Carmine

Perf. 14½x14, 14x14½

1940 **Unwmk.**
Q216 PP12 10c vermilion .25 .25
Q217 PP12 20c turq bl (C) .25 .25
Q218 PP12 30c brn vio .25 .25
Q219 PP12 40c ol grn (C) .25 .25
Q220 PP12 50c magenta .25 .25
Q221 PP12 60c orange .60 *.55*
Q222 PP12 70c dk brn .25 .25
Q223 PP12 80c vio (C) .25 .25
Q224 PP12 90c slate (C) .25 .25
Q225 PP13 1fr ultra (C) .25 .25
Q226 PP13 2fr ol grn (C) .25 .25
a. Ovpt. inverted 140.00 75.00
Q227 PP13 3fr org red .25 .25
Q228 PP13 4fr rose .25 .25
Q229 PP13 5fr vio (C) .25 .25
Q230 PP13 6fr bis brn .35 .25
Q231 PP13 7fr orange .35 .25
Q232 PP13 8fr dp brn .35 .25
Q233 PP13 9fr red vio .35 .25
Q234 PP13 10fr bl grn (C) .35 .25
Q235 PP13 20fr magenta .60 .25
Q236 PP13 30fr turq grn (C) 1.10 .75
Q237 PP13 40fr gray (C) 2.25 *2.10*
Q238 PP13 50fr bister 1.60 1.10
Nos. Q216-Q238 (23) 11.15 9.25
Set, never hinged 18.00

ISSUED UNDER GERMAN OCCUPATION

German Stamps of 1906-11 Surcharged

Nos. N1-N6

Nos. N7-N9

Wmk. Lozenges (125)

1914-15 ***Perf. 14, 14½***

N1 A16 3c on 3pf brn .45 .25
On cover 5.50
N2 A16 5c on 5pf grn .40 .25
On cover 2.75
N3 A16 10c on 10pf car .50 .25
On cover 2.75
N4 A16 25c on 20pf ultra .50 .25
On cover 2.75
On cover, single franking 4.50
N5 A16 50c on 40pf lake & blk 2.50 1.25
On cover 4.50
On cover, single franking 8.50
N6 A16 75c on 60pf mag .90 *1.25*
On cover 8.50
On cover, single franking 22.50
N7 A16 1fr on 80pf lake & blk, *rose* 2.50 1.75
On cover 12.00
On cover, single franking 27.50
N8 A17 1fr25c on 1m car 20.00 12.50
On cover 42.50
On cover, single franking 85.00
N9 A21 2fr50c on 2m gray bl 18.00 15.00
On cover 125.00
Nos. N1-N9 (9) 45.75 32.75
Set, never hinged 160.00

German Stamps of 1906-18 Surcharged

Nos. N10-N21

No. N22

Nos. N23-N25

1916-18

N10 A22 2c on 2pf drab .25 .25
On cover 8.50
N11 A16 3c on 3pf brn .35 .25
On cover 3.00
N12 A16 5c on 5pf grn .35 .25
On cover 2.00
On cover, single franking 3.00
N13 A22 8c on 7½pf org .65 .35
On cover 4.50
N14 A16 10c on 10pf car .25 .25
On cover 2.50
N15 A22 15c on 15pf yel brn .65 .25
On cover 3.00
N16 A22 15c on 15pf dk vio .65 .45
On cover 3.00
N17 A16 20c on 25pf org & blk, *yel* .35 .35
On cover 8.50
On cover, single franking 27.50
N18 A16 25c on 20pf ultra .35 .25
On cover 5.50
On cover, single franking 5.00
a. 25c on 20pf blue .40 .25
On cover 8.50
On cover, single franking 17.50
N19 A16 40c on 30pf org & blk, *buff* .40 .30
On cover 5.50
On cover, single franking 7.00
N20 A16 50c on 40pf lake & blk .35 .30
On cover 6.00
On cover, single franking 9.00
N21 A16 75c on 60pf mag 1.00 *12.50*
On cover 175.00
N22 A16 1fr on 80pf lake & blk, *rose* 2.00 *2.50*
On cover 70.00
On cover, single franking 115.00
N23 A17 1fr25c on 1m car 2.00 2.00
On cover 85.00
On cover, single franking 150.00
N24 A21 2fr50c on 2m gray bl 27.50 25.00
a. 2fr50c on 1m car (error) *3,500.*
N25 A20 6fr25c on 5m sl & car 40.00 37.50
On overfranked cover 450.00
Nos. N10-N25 (16) 77.10 82.75
Set, never hinged 145.00

A similar series of stamps without "Belgien" was used in parts of Belgium and France while occupied by German forces. See France Nos. N15-N26.

BENIN

bə-'nin

LOCATION — West Coast of Africa
GOVT. — French Possession
AREA — 8,627 sq. mi.
POP. — 493,000 (approx.)
CAPITAL — Benin

In 1895 the French possessions known as Benin were incorporated into the colony of Dahomey.

100 Centimes = 1 Franc

Handstamped on Stamps of French Colonies

1892 **Unwmk.** ***Perf. 14x13½***

Black Overprint

1 A9 1c blk, *bluish* 200.00 170.00
On cover 625.00
2 A9 2c brn, *buff* 180.00 150.00
On cover 600.00
3 A9 4c claret, *lav* 120.00 80.00
Never hinged 200.00
On cover 300.00
4 A9 5c grn, *grnsh* 40.00 32.50
Never hinged 67.50
On cover 140.00
On cover, single franking 500.00
a. Pair, one without overprint 600.00 640.00
5 A9 10c blk, *lavender* 100.00 80.00
On cover 250.00
On cover, single franking 500.00
6 A9 15c blue 40.00 32.50
Never hinged 80.00
On cover 150.00
On cover, single franking 550.00
a. Pair, one without overprint 1,000.
7 A9 20c red, *grn* 250.00 220.00
On cover 925.00
8 A9 25c blk, *rose* 125.00 80.00
On cover 400.00
On cover, single franking 600.00
9 A9 30c brn, *yelsh* 225.00 200.00
On cover *840.00*
10 A9 35c blk, *orange* 225.00 200.00
On cover *1,000.*
11 A9 40c red, *straw* 200.00 180.00
On cover *750.00*
12 A9 75c car, *rose* 500.00 350.00
On cover *1,250.*
13 A9 1fr brnz grn, *straw* 475.00 400.00
On cover *1,350.*

Red Overprint

14 A9 15c blue 120.00 100.00
On cover *325.00*

Blue Overprint

15 A9 5c grn, *grnsh* 2,600. 1,200.
On cover *3,000.*
15A A9 15c blue 2,600. 1,200.
On cover *3,000.*

The overprints of Nos. 1-15A are of four types, three without accent mark on "E." They exist diagonal.

Counterfeits exist of Nos. 1-19.

Inverted Overprint

2a A9 2c brn, *buff* 225.00 225.00
4b A9 5c grn, *grnsh* 190.00 160.00
5b A9 10c blk, *lavender* 190.00 160.00
8b A9 25c blk, *rose* 250.00 225.00
9b A9 30c brn, *yelsh* 400.00 375.00
10b A9 35c blk, *orange* 425.00 375.00
11b A9 40c red, *straw* 375.00 290.00
12b A9 75c car, *rose* 800.00 675.00
13b A9 1fr brnz grn, *straw* 800.00 675.00
15b A9 5c grn, *grnsh* 3,000. 1,400.
15Ac A9 15c grn, *grnsh* 3,000. 1,400.

Red Overprint

14b A9 15c blue *110.00* *95.00*

Double Overprint

4c A9 5c grn, *grnsh* 160.00 120.00
5c A9 10c blk, *lavender* 200.00 175.00
8c A9 25c blk, *rose* 250.00 225.00
10c A9 35c blk, *orange* 500.00 425.00
11c A9 40c red, *straw* 425.00 400.00

Red Overprint

14c A9 15c blue *120.00* *110.00*

Additional Surcharge in Red or Black

1892

16 A9 01c on 5c grn, *grnsh* 360.00 275.00
On cover *950.00*
a. Double surcharge 1,000. 1,000.
17 A9 40c on 15c blue 225.00 120.00
On cover 500.00
a. Double surcharge *3,800.*
18 A9 75c on 15c blue 1,000. 600.00
On cover 2,000.
19 A9 75c on 15c bl (Bk) 3,500. 2,800.
On cover 9,750.

Counterfeits exist.

Navigation and Commerce — A3

1893 **Typo.** ***Perf. 14x13½***

Name of Colony in Blue or Carmine

20 A3 1c blk, *bluish* 5.25 3.25
Never hinged 8.00
On cover 200.00
21 A3 2c brn, *buff* 6.75 4.75
Never hinged 10.00
On cover 200.00
22 A3 4c claret, *lav* 6.75 4.75
Never hinged 9.50
On cover 200.00
23 A3 5c grn, *grnsh* 8.00 5.50
Never hinged 14.00
On cover 87.50
24 A3 10c blk, *lavender* 10.00 6.50
Never hinged 16.00
On cover 92.50
a. Name of country omitted *6,500.*
25 A3 15c blue, quadrille paper 40.00 27.50
Never hinged 80.00
On cover 140.00
26 A3 20c red, *grn* 20.00 16.00
Never hinged 40.00
On cover 190.00
On cover, single franking 300.00
27 A3 25c blk, *rose* 52.50 32.50
Never hinged 105.00
On cover 125.00
On cover, single franking 200.00
28 A3 30c brn, *bis* 27.50 21.00
Never hinged 55.00
On cover 275.00
On cover, single franking 375.00
29 A3 40c red, *straw* 8.00 5.50
Never hinged 9.50
On cover 190.00
On cover, single franking 275.00
30 A3 50c car, *rose* 8.00 7.25
Never hinged 11.00
On cover 190.00
On cover, single franking 250.00
31 A3 75c vio, *org* 12.50 12.50
Never hinged 20.00
On cover 350.00
On cover, single franking 500.00
32 A3 1fr brnz grn, *straw* 72.50 72.50
Never hinged 140.00
On cover 500.00
On cover, single franking *750.00*
Nos. 20-32 (13) 277.75 219.50

Perf. 13½x14 stamps are counterfeits.

Navigation and Commerce — A4

1894 ***Perf. 14x13½***

33 A4 1c blk, *bluish* 2.50 3.25
Never hinged 4.00
On cover 140.00
34 A4 2c brn, *buff* 4.00 3.25
Never hinged 7.25
On cover 140.00
35 A4 4c claret, *lav* 4.00 3.25
Never hinged 7.25
On cover 140.00
36 A4 5c grn, *grnsh* 6.50 4.00
Never hinged 12.00
On cover 55.00
37 A4 10c blk, *lavender* 7.25 5.50
Never hinged 12.00
On cover 50.00
38 A4 15c bl, quadrille paper 16.00 4.75
Never hinged 24.00
On cover 50.00
39 A4 20c red, *grn* 12.00 9.50
Never hinged 21.00
On cover 100.00
On cover, single franking 225.00
40 A4 25c blk, *rose* 16.00 7.25
Never hinged 24.00
On cover 60.00
On cover, single franking 100.00
41 A4 30c brn, *bis* 12.00 10.50
Never hinged 20.00
On cover 92.50
On cover, single franking 125.00
42 A4 40c red, *straw* 24.00 16.00
Never hinged 45.00
On cover 100.00
On cover, single franking 140.00
43 A4 50c car, *rose* 32.50 16.00
Never hinged 52.50
On cover 225.00
On cover, single franking 300.00
44 A4 75c vio, *org* 32.50 14.50
Never hinged 47.50
On cover 350.00
On cover, single franking 500.00
45 A4 1fr brnz grn, *straw* 8.00 6.50
Never hinged 12.00
On cover 375.00
On cover, single franking 625.00
Nos. 33-45 (13) 177.25 104.25

Perf. 13½x14 stamps are counterfeits.

POSTAGE DUE STAMPS

French Colony

Handstamped in Black on Postage Due Stamps of French Colonies

1894 **Unwmk.** ***Imperf.***

J1 D1 5c black 175.00 70.00
On cover 550.00
J2 D1 10c black 175.00 70.00
On cover 550.00
J3 D1 20c black 175.00 70.00
On cover 550.00
J4 D1 30c black 175.00 70.00
On cover 550.00
Nos. J1-J4 (4) 700.00 280.00

Nos. J1-J4 exist with overprint in various positions.

BERMUDA

ˌbər-ˈmyü-də

LOCATION — A group of about 150 small islands of which only 20 are inhabited, lying in the Atlantic Ocean about 580 miles southeast of Cape Hatteras.
GOVT. — British Crown Colony
AREA — 20.5 sq. mi.
POP. — 54,893 (1980)
CAPITAL — Hamilton

4 Farthings = 1 Penny
12 Pence = 1 Shilling
20 Shillings = 1 Pound

Catalogue values for unused stamps in this country are for Never Hinged items, beginning with Scott 131.

PRE-STAMP POSTAL MARKINGS

Crowned Circle handstamp type I is pictured in the Crowned Circle Handstamps and Great Britain Used Abroad section.

1845
A1 I "Hamilton" crowned circle handstamp in red, on cover *4,250.*
A2 I "St. Georges" crowned circle handstamp in red, on cover *9,000.*
A3 I "Ireland Isle" crowned circle handstamp in red, on cover *8,000.*

Earliest known uses: #A1, 11/13/46. #A2, 8/1/45. #A3, 8/1/45.
See Nos. X4-X5 for use as adhesives.

POSTMASTER STAMPS

PM1

1848-56 Unwmk. *Imperf.*
X1 PM1 1p blk, *bluish* (1848) *180,000.*
On cover *160,000.*
a. Dated 1849 *200,000.*
X2 PM1 1p red, *bluish* (1856) *225,000.*
a. Dated 1854 *400,000.*
X3 PM1 1p red (1853) *180,000.*

PM2

Same inscribed "ST GEORGES"

1860
X4 PM2 (1p) red, *yellowish* *100,000.*

Same inscribed "HAMILTON"

1861
X5 PM2 (1p) red, *bluish* 140,000. *130,000.*
X6 PM2 (1p) red *38,500.*

Nos. X1-X3 were produced and used by Postmaster William B. Perot of Hamilton. No. X4 is attributed to Postmaster James H. Thies of St. George's.

Only a few of each stamp exist. Values reflect actual sales figures for stamps in the condition in which they are found.

Values for unused stamps are for examples with original gum as defined in the catalogue introduction. Very fine examples of Nos. 1-1a, 2-15b will have perforations touching the design (or framelines where applicable) on at least one side due to the narrow spacing of the stamps on the plates. Stamps with perfs clear of the design on all four sides are scarce and will command higher prices.

Queen Victoria
A1 A2

A3

A4

A5

1865-74 Typo. Wmk. 1 *Perf. 14*
1 A1 1p rose red 110.00 1.75
a. 1p dull rose 140.00 8.00
b. Imperf. *85,000.* *27,000.*
2 A2 2p blue ('66) 525.00 37.50
a. 2p bright blue 525.00 22.50
3 A3 3p buff ('73) 600.00 80.00
On cover 400.00
a. 3p orange 2,050. 175.00
On cover 550.00
4 A4 6p brown lilac 2,300. 90.00
5 A4 6p lilac ('74) 30.00 17.00
On cover 600.00
6 A5 1sh green 450.00 70.00
On cover 600.00
Nos. 1-6 (6) 4,015. 296.25

See Nos. 7-9, 19-21, 23, 25. For surcharges see Nos. 10-15.
No. 1b is a proof.

1882-1903 *Perf. 14x12½*
7 A3 3p buff 210.00 75.00
8 A4 6p violet ('03) 17.00 *27.50*
9 A5 1sh green ('94) 20.00 *150.00*
On cover 325.00
a. Vert. strip of 3, perf. all around & imperf. btwn. *13,750.*
Nos. 7-9 (3) 247.00 *252.50*

Handstamped Diagonally

1874 *Perf. 14*
10 A5 3p on 1sh green 1,700. 950.

Handstamped Diagonally

11 A1 3p on 1p rose *19,000.* *20,000.*
12 A5 3p on 1sh green 2,850. 975.
a. "P" with top like "R" 2,300. 1,100.
On cover 5,500.

No. 11 is stated to be an essay, but a few examples are known used. Nos. 10-12 are found with double or partly double surcharges.

Surcharged in Black

1875
13 A2 1p on 2p blue 875.00 475.00
On cover 3,250.
a. Without period *27,500.* *13,250.*
b. Round "O" in "One" 1,650. 600.
14 A3 1p on 3p buff 550.00 425.00
a. Round "O" in "One" 800.00 500.00
15 A5 1p on 1sh green 675.00 310.00
On cover 1,750.
a. Inverted surcharge — *50,000.*
b. Without period *40,000.* *20,000.*
c. Round "O" in "One" — 450.00

A6

A7

1880 Wmk. 1
16 A6 ½p brown 8.75 *5.25*
17 A7 4p orange 21.00 2.50
On cover 225.00

See Nos. 18, 24.

A8

1883-1904 Wmk. 2
18 A6 ½p deep gray grn ('93) 4.50 1.00
a. ½p green ('92) 8.75 4.50
19 A1 1p aniline car ('89) 17.00 .30
a. 1p dull rose 200.00 5.25
b. 1p rose red 100.00 4.00
c. 1p carmine rose ('86) 75.00 1.00
20 A2 2p blue ('86) 70.00 8.25
21 A2 2p brn pur ('98) 5.50 2.75
a. 2p aniline pur ('93) 17.50 6.00
22 A8 2½p ultra ('84) 21.00 .50
a. 2½p deep ultra 30.00 3.75
23 A3 3p gray ('86) 27.50 11.00
24 A7 4p brown org ('04) 37.50 *62.50*
25 A5 1sh ol bis ('93) 19.00 24.00
a. 1sh yellow brown 25.00 24.00
Nos. 18-25 (8) 202.00 *110.30*

A9

1901 Black Surcharge
26 A9 1f on 1sh gray 6.00 1.25
Overprinted "SPECIMEN" 92.50
a. 1f on 1sh bluish gray 6.00 1.75
b. As "a," "F" in "FARTHING" doubled *8,500.* *11,000.*

The second "F" is inserted by hand.

Dry Dock — A10

1902-03
28 A10 ½p gray grn & blk ('03) 15.00 3.75
29 A10 1p car rose & brown 10.00 .35
30 A10 3p ol grn & violet 6.50 *3.50*
Nos. 28-30 (3) 31.50 7.60
Set, overprinted "SPECIMEN" 160.00

1906-10 Wmk. 3
31 A10 ¼p pur & brn ('08) 2.10 1.90
32 A10 ½p gray grn & blk 24.00 1.25
33 A10 ½p green ('09) 25.00 4.50
34 A10 1p car rose & brn 40.00 .25
35 A10 1p carmine ('08) 23.00 .50
36 A10 2p orange & gray 9.25 *13.50*
37 A10 2½p blue & brown 29.00 9.50
38 A10 2½p ultra ('10) 26.00 9.50
39 A10 4p vio brn & blue ('09) 3.75 *20.00*
Nos. 31-39 (9) 182.10 *60.90*

Caravel
A11

King George V
A12

1910-24 Engr. *Perf. 14*
40 A11 ¼p brown ('12) 2.10 *3.00*
a. ¼p pale brown 2.50 *1.75*
41 A11 ½p yel green 3.75 .30
a. ½p dark green ('18) 15.00 1.50
42 A11 1p red (I) 20.00 .35
a. 1p carmine (I) ('19) 67.50 10.00
b. 1p rose red (I) ('16) 27.50 .35
43 A11 2p gray ('13) 6.00 *20.00*
44 A11 2½p ultra (I) ('12) 4.25 .75
45 A11 3p violet, *yel* ('13) 3.00 *7.50*
46 A11 4p red, *yellow* ('19) 14.00 *16.00*
47 A11 6p claret ('24) 12.50 *9.00*
a. 6p purple ('12) 20.00 *23.00*
48 A11 1sh blk, *green* ('12) 6.00 *5.00*
a. 1sh black, *olive* ('25) 6.00 *22.50*
Nos. 40-48, optd "SPECIMEN" 500.00

Typographed
Chalky Paper

49 A12 2sh ultra & dl vio, *bl* ('20) 22.50 *62.50*
50 A12 2sh6p red & blk, *bl* 37.50 *100.00*
51 A12 4sh car & black ('20) 75.00 *200.00*
52 A12 5sh red & grn, *yellow* 75.00 *150.00*
a. 5sh dp green & dp red, *yellow* 75.00 *150.00*
53 A12 10sh red & grn, *green* 225.00 *425.00*
a. 10sh red & green, *pale bluish green* ('22) 310.00 *490.00*
54 A12 £1 black & vio, *red* 400.00 *700.00*
Nos. 40-54 (15) 906.60 *1,699.*
Nos. 49-54, optd "SPECIMEN" 1,000.

Types I of 1p and 2½p are illustrated above Nos. 81-97.

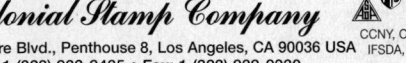

The 1p was printed from two plates, the 2nd of which, No. 42a, exists only in carmine on opaque paper with a bluish tinge. Compare No. MR1 (as No. 42) and MR2 (as No. 42a).

Revenue cancellations are found on Nos. 52-54.

See Nos. 81-97.

Seal of the Colony and King George V
A13

1920-21 Wmk. 3 Ordinary Paper

55 A13 ¼p brown 4.00 *27.00*
56 A13 ½p green 9.50 *19.00*
57 A13 2p gray 18.00 *55.00*

Chalky Paper

58 A13 3p vio & dl vio, *yel* 15.00 *55.00*
59 A13 4p red & blk, *yellow* 15.00 *42.50*
60 A13 1sh blk, *gray grn* 20.00 *60.00*

Ordinary Paper

Wmk. 4

67 A13 1p rose red 4.50 .35
68 A13 2½p ultra 19.00 20.00

Chalky Paper

69 A13 6p red vio & dl vio 32.50 *95.00*
Nos. 55-60,67-69 (9) 137.50 *373.85*

Issued: 6p, 1/19/21; others, 11/11/20.

King George V
A14

1921, May 12 Engr.

71 A14 ¼p brown 4.25 *4.50*
72 A14 ½p green 3.50 *8.50*
73 A14 1p carmine 11.00 .45

Wmk. 3

74 A14 2p gray 12.00 *55.00*
75 A14 2½p ultra 15.00 7.00
76 A14 3p vio, *orange* 7.00 *20.00*
77 A14 4p scarlet, *org* 20.00 *37.50*
78 A14 6p claret 19.00 *65.00*
79 A14 1sh blk, *green* 29.00 *65.00*
Nos. 71-79 (9) 120.75 *262.95*

Tercentenary of "Local Representative Institutions" (Nos. 55-79).

Types of 1910-20 Issue

Types of 1p

Type I

Type II

Type III

Type I, figure "1" has pointed serifs, scroll at top left very weak.

Type II, thick "1" with square serifs, scroll weak.

Type III, thinner "1" with long square serifs, scroll complete with strong line.

Types of 2½p

Type I

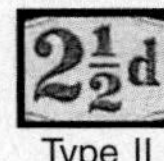

Type II

Type I, small "d," short, thick figures of value.

Type II, larger "d," taller, thinner figures of value.

1922-34 Wmk. 4

81 A11 ¼p brown ('28) 1.90 *3.75*
82 A11 ½p green 1.90 .25
83 A11 1p car, III ('28) 15.00 .35
a. 1p carmine, II ('26) 55.00 7.50
b. 1p carmine, I 21.00 .75
84 A11 1½p red brown ('34) 11.00 .45
85 A11 2p gray ('23) 1.90 1.90
86 A11 2½p ap grn ('23) 3.50 1.90
87 A11 2½p ultra, II ('32) 2.10 .90
a. 2½p ultra, I ('26) 5.00 .60
88 A11 3p ultra ('24) 20.00 *32.50*
89 A11 3p vio, *yellow* ('26) 5.00 1.25
90 A11 4p red, *yellow* ('24) 2.50 1.25
91 A11 6p claret ('24) 1.50 1.00
92 A11 1sh blk, *emer* ('27) 9.00 *11.00*
93 A11 1sh brn blk, *yel grn* ('34) 42.50 *62.50*

Chalky Paper

94 A12 2sh ultra & vio, *bl* ('27) 55.00 *87.50*
a. 2sh bl & dp vio, *dp bl* ('31) 67.50 *100.00*
95 A12 2sh 6p red & blk, *bl* ('27) 75.00 125.00
a. 2sh6p pale org ver & blk, *gray bl* ('30) 3,500. 3,250.
b. 2sh6p dp ver & blk, *deep blue* ('31) 100.00 *150.00*
96 A12 10sh red & grn, *emer* ('24) 160.00 *300.00*
a. 10sh dp red & pale grn, *dp emer* ('31) 175.00 *350.00*
97 A12 12sh 6p ocher & gray blk ('32) 300.00 *425.00*
On cover 3,000.
Nos. 81-97 (17) 707.80 *1,057.*

Revenue cancellations are found on Nos. 94-97.

For the 12sh6p with "Revenue" on both sides, see No. AR1.

Common Design Types pictured following the introduction.

Silver Jubilee Issue

Common Design Type

1935, May 6 *Perf. 11x12*

100 CD301 1p car & dk bl .60 *2.25*
101 CD301 1½p blk & ultra .90 *3.50*
102 CD301 2½p ultra & brn 1.50 2.50
103 CD301 1sh brn vio & ind 15.00 *50.00*
Nos. 100-103 (4) 18.00 *58.25*
Set, never hinged 35.00
Set, perf "SPECIMEN" 250.00

Hamilton Harbor — A15

South Shore — A16

Yacht "Lucie" — A17

Grape Bay — A18

Typical Cottage — A19

Scene at Par-la-Ville — A20

1936-40 *Perf. 12*

105 A15 ½p blue green .25 .25
106 A16 1p car & black .55 .35
107 A16 1½p choc & black 1.25 .60
108 A17 2p lt bl & blk 6.00 2.00
109 A17 2p brn blk & turq bl ('38) 55.00 16.00
109A A17 2p red & ultra ('40) 1.25 1.25
110 A18 2½p dk bl & lt bl 1.25 .30
111 A19 3p car & black 3.25 2.75
112 A20 6p vio & rose lake 1.00 .25
113 A18 1sh deep green 4.00 *19.00*
114 A15 1sh6p brown .60 .25
Nos. 105-114 (11) 74.40 43.00
Set, never hinged 100.00

No. 108, blue border and black center.
No. 109, black border, blue center.

Coronation Issue

Common Design Type

1937, May 14 *Perf. 13½x14*

115 CD302 1p carmine .25 *1.50*
116 CD302 1½p brown .35 *1.75*
117 CD302 2½p bright ultra .65 *1.75*
Nos. 115-117 (3) 1.25 5.00
Set, never hinged 1.75
Set, perf "SPECIMEN" 250.00

Hamilton Harbor — A21

Grape Bay — A22

St. David's Lighthouse
A23

King George VI
A25

Bermudian Water Scene and Yellow-billed Tropic Bird — A24

1938-51 Wmk. 4 *Perf. 12*

118 A21 1p red & blk .60 .25
a. 1p rose red & black 16.00 1.40
119 A21 1½p vio brn & blue 4.75 1.40
a. 1½p dl vio brn & bl ('43) 4.00 .25
120 A22 2½p blue & lt bl 8.50 1.00
120A A22 2½p ol brn & lt bl ('41) 2.50 1.25
b. 2½p dk ol blk & pale blue ('43) 2.50 1.40
121 A23 3p car & blk 16.00 2.25
121A A23 3p dp ultra & blk ('42) 1.40 .25
c. 3p brt ultra & blk ('41) 1.40 .25
Complete booklet, 6 each #118, 119, 109A, 120Ab, 121Ac 160.00
Complete booklet, 6 #121Ac and 18 #112, in blocks of 6, and 12 air mail labels 180.00
121D A24 7½p yel grn, bl & blk ('41) 5.00 2.00
122 A22 1sh green 1.60 .55

Typo.

Perf. 13

123 A25 2sh ultra & red vio, *bl* ('50) 13.50 12.00
a. 2sh ultra & vio, *bl*, perf. 14 9.25 3.50
b. 2sh ultra & dl vio, *bl* (mottled paper), perf. 14 ('42) 9.25 3.50
124 A25 2sh 6p red & blk, *bl* 14.50 8.75
a. Perf. 14 26.00 8.75
125 A25 5sh red & grn, *yel* 17.00 15.00
a. Perf. 14 60.00 20.00
126 A25 10sh red & grn, *grn* ('51) 40.00 *32.50*
a. 10sh brn lake & grn, *grn*, perf. 14 140.00 100.00
b. 10sh red & grn, *grn*, perf. 14 ('39) 225.00 200.00
127 A25 12sh 6p org & gray blk 87.50 72.50
a. 12sh 6p org & gray, perf. 14 110.00 60.00
b. 12sh 6p yel & gray, perf. 14 ('47) 725.00 600.00
c. 12sh 6p brn org & gray, perf. 14 275.00 100.00

Wmk. 3

128 A25 £1 blk & vio, *red* ('51) 52.50 *62.50*
a. £1 blk & pur, *red*, perf. 14 300.00 140.00
b. £1 blk & dk vio, *salmon*, perf. 14 ('42) 87.50 67.50
Nos. 118-128 (14) 265.35 212.20
Set, never hinged 450.00

No. 127b is the so-called "lemon yellow" shade.

Revenue cancellations are found on Nos. 123-128. Stamps with removed revenue cancellations and forged postmarks are abundant.

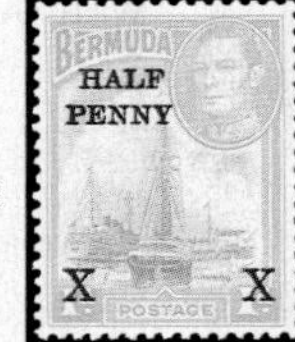

No. 118a Surcharged in Black

1940, Dec. 20 Wmk. 4 *Perf. 12*

129 A21 ½p on 1p rose red & blk .30 2.40
Never hinged 1.00

Catalogue values for unused stamps in this section, from this point to the end of the section, are for Never Hinged items.

Peace Issue

Common Design Type

Perf. 13½x14

1946, Nov. 6 Engr. Wmk. 4

131 CD303 1½p brown .25 .25
132 CD303 3p deep blue .30 .30
Set, perf "SPECIMEN" 190.00

Silver Wedding Issue

Common Design Types

1948, Dec. 1 Photo. *Perf. 14x14½*

133 CD304 1½p red brown .25 .25

Engr.; Name Typo.

Perf. 11½x11

134 CD305 £1 rose carmine 47.50 *55.00*

Postmaster Stamp of 1848 — A26

1949, Apr. 11 Engr. *Perf. 13x13½*

135 A26 2½p dk brown & dp bl .25 .25
136 A26 3p dp blue & black .25 .25
137 A26 6p green & rose vio .45 .45
Nos. 135-137 (3) .95 .95

No. 137 shows a different floral arrangement. Bermuda's first postage stamp, cent.

UPU Issue

Common Design Types

Engr.; Name Typo.

1949, Oct. 10 *Perf. 13½, 11x11½*

138 CD306 2½p slate .50 *1.75*
139 CD307 3p indigo 1.25 1.00
140 CD308 6p rose violet 1.00 .80
141 CD309 1sh blue green 2.00 2.00
Nos. 138-141 (4) 4.75 5.55

POSTAL-FISCAL STAMP

"Revenue Revenue" — PF1

1936 Typo. Wmk. 4 *Perf. 14*
Chalky Paper

AR1 PF1 12sh6p org & grayish blk 1,250. *1,750.*
Revenue cancel 75.00
On cover 3,250.

No. AR1 was authorized for postal use from Feb. 1 through May, 1937 and during Nov. and Dec. 1937. Used values are for examples with dated postal cancels indicating usage during the authorized periods. Beware of bogus and improperly dated favor cancels.

Six covers are known properly used during those time periods.

WAR TAX STAMPS

No. 42 Overprinted

1918 Wmk. 3 *Perf. 14*
MR1 A11 1p rose red 1.25 *2.00*

No. 42a Overprinted

1920
MR2 A11 1p carmine 2.40 *3.00*

BOLIVIA

bə-ˈli-vē-ə

LOCATION — Central South America, separated from the Pacific Ocean by Chile and Peru.
GOVT. — Republic
AREA — 424,165 sq. mi.
POP. — 6,252,250 (est. 1984)
CAPITAL — Sucre (La Paz is the actual seat of government).

100 Centavos = 1 Boliviano

PRE-STAMP POSTAL MARKINGS

BRITISH CONSULAR OFFICES IN BOLIVIA

Crowned Circle handstamp type V is pictured in the Crowned Circle Handstamps and Great Britain Used Abroad section.

Cobija

1862, Mar. 29
A1 V Crowned circle handstamp, in red, on cover

STAMPS OF GREAT BRITAIN USED IN BOLIVIA

Numeral cancellation type A is pictured in the Crowned Circle Handstamps and Great Britain Used Abroad section.

1865-78

C39 (Cobija)

A2 A 1p rose red (#33, P93, 95) —
A3 A 2p blue (#30, P14) —
A4 A 3p rose (#49, P6) —
A5 A 3p rose (#61, P16, 19) —
A6 A 4p pale ol grn (#70, P15) 850.00
A7 A 6p red violet (#51, P9) 850.00
A8 A 6p pale buff (#59b, P11) —
A9 A 6p gray (#62, P13-16) (from) 725.00
A10 A 1sh green (#54, P4-5) 800.00
A11 A 1sh pale green (#64, P10-13) 800.00
A12 A 2sh blue (#55) 1,100.
A13 A 5sh rose (#57, P2) 2,000.

On Feb. 21, 1863, the Bolivian Government decreed contracts for carrying the mails should be let to the highest bidder, the service to commence on the day the bid was accepted, and stamps used for the payment of postage. The winner of the contract would be responsible for expenses and would keep the profits. On Mar. 18, the contract was awarded to Sr. Justiniano Garcia and was in effect until Apr. 29, 1863, when it was rescinded. Stamps in the form illustrated above were prepared in denominations of ½, 1, 2 and 4 reales. All values exist in black and in blue. The blue are twice as scarce as the black. Value, black, $75 each.

It is said that used examples exist on covers, but the authenticity of these covers remains to be established.

Condor — A1

A2

A3

72 varieties of each of the 5c, 78 varieties of the 10c, 30 varieties of each of the 50c and 100c.

The plate of the 5c stamps was entirely reengraved 4 times and retouched at least 6 times. Various states of the plate have distinguishing characteristics, each of which is typical of most, though not all the stamps in a sheet. These characteristics (usually termed types) are found in the shading lines at the right side of the globe. a, vertical and diagonal lines. b, diagonal lines only. c, diagonal and horizontal with traces of vertical lines. d, diagonal and horizontal lines. e, horizontal lines only. f, no lines except the curved ones forming the outlines of the globe.

1867-68 Unwmk. Engr. *Imperf.*

1 A1 5c yel grn, thin paper (a, b) 11.00 *25.00*
Pair, on cover 3,250.
a. 5c blue green (a) 11.00 *30.00*
b. 5c deep green (a) 11.00 *30.00*
c. 5c ol grn, thick paper (a) 450.00 450.00
d. 5c yel grn, thick paper (a) 300.00 300.00
e. 5c yel grn, thick paper (b) 300.00 300.00
f. 5c blue green (b) 11.00 *30.00*
2 A1 5c green (d) 10.00 *25.00*
a. 5c green (c) 15.00 *30.00*
b. 5c green (e) 15.00 *30.00*
c. 5c green (f) 15.00 *30.00*
3 A1 5c vio ('68) 375.00 375.00
a. 5c rose lilac ('68) 375.00 375.00
Revenue cancel 150.00

4 A3 10c brown 400.00 350.00
On cover 10,000.
Revenue cancel 175.00
5 A2 50c orange 35.00
Revenue cancel 15.00
6 A2 50c blue ('68) *500.00*
a. 50c dark blue ('68) *500.00*
Revenue cancel 250.00
7 A3 100c blue 80.00
Revenue cancel 45.00
8 A3 100c green ('68) 250.00
a. 100c pale blue grn ('68) 250.00
Revenue cancel 175.00

Used values are for postally canceled stamps. Pen cancellations usually indicate that the stamps have been used fiscally.

The 500c is an essay.

Reprints of Nos. 3,4, 6 and 8 are common. Value, $10 each. Reprints of Nos. 2 and 5 are scarcer. Value, $25 each.

Coat of Arms
A4 A5

1868-69 *Perf. 12*

Nine Stars

10	A4	5c green	27.50	18.00
11	A4	10c vermilion	45.00	25.00
12	A4	50c blue	70.00	45.00
13	A4	100c orange	80.00	55.00
14	A4	500c black	1,000.	1,000.

Eleven Stars

15	A5	5c green	18.00	12.00
16	A5	10c vermilion	25.00	20.00
a.		Half used as 5c on cover		600.00
17	A5	50c blue	50.00	40.00
18	A5	100c dp orange	60.00	50.00
19	A5	500c black	*3,500.*	*3,500.*

See Nos. 26-27, 31-34.

Arms and "The Law" — A6

1878 Various Frames *Perf. 12*

20	A6	5c ultra	15.00	7.00
21	A6	10c orange	12.00	6.00
a.		Half used as 5c on cover		250.00
22	A6	20c green	45.00	10.00
a.		Half used as 10c on cover		200.00
23	A6	50c dull carmine	120.00	30.00
		Nos. 20-23 (4)	192.00	53.00

(11 Stars) — A7

Numerals Upright

1887 *Rouletted*

24	A7	1c rose	4.00	3.00
25	A7	2c violet	4.00	3.00
26	A5	5c blue	14.50	8.00
27	A5	10c orange	14.50	8.00
		Nos. 24-27 (4)	37.00	22.00

See No. 37.

(9 Stars) — A8

1890 *Perf. 12*

28	A8	1c rose	3.00	2.00
29	A8	2c violet	8.00	4.00
30	A4	5c blue	6.00	2.00
31	A4	10c orange	12.00	3.00
32	A4	20c dk green	25.00	6.00
33	A4	50c red	12.00	8.00
34	A4	100c yellow	25.00	*30.00*
		Nos. 28-34 (7)	91.00	55.00

See Nos. 35-36, 38-39.

1893 Litho. *Perf. 11*

35	A8	1c rose	6.00	5.00
a.		Imperf. pair	100.00	
b.		Horiz. pair, imperf. vert.	100.00	
c.		Horiz. pair, imperf. btwn.	100.00	
36	A8	2c violet	6.00	5.00
a.		Block of 4 imperf. vert. and horiz. through center	200.00	
b.		Horiz. pair, imperf. btwn.	100.00	
c.		Vert. pair, imperf betwn.	100.00	
37	A7	5c blue	8.00	4.00
a.		Vert. pair, imperf. horiz.	100.00	
b.		Horiz. pair, imperf. btwn.	100.00	
38	A8	10c orange	25.00	8.00
a.		Horiz. pair, imperf. btwn.	100.00	
39	A8	20c dark green	100.00	45.00
a.		Imperf. pair, vert. or horiz.	200.00	
b.		Pair, imperf. btwn., vert. or horiz.	175.00	
		Nos. 35-39 (5)	145.00	67.00

Coat of Arms — A9

1894 Unwmk. Engr. *Perf. 14, 14½*
Thin Paper

40	A9	1c bister	1.50	1.25
41	A9	2c red orange	3.00	2.25
42	A9	5c green	1.50	1.25
43	A9	10c yellow brn	1.50	1.25
44	A9	20c dark blue	8.00	8.00
45	A9	50c claret	20.00	20.00
46	A9	100c brown rose	40.00	40.00
		Nos. 40-46 (7)	75.50	74.00

Stamps of type A9 on thick paper were surreptitiously printed in Paris on the order of an official and without government authorization. Some of these stamps were substituted for part of a shipment of stamps on thin paper, which had been printed in London on government order.

When the thick paper stamps reached Bolivia they were at first repudiated but afterwards were allowed to do postal duty. A large quantity of the thick paper stamps were fraudulently canceled in Paris with a cancellation of heavy bars forming an oval. Value of unused set: $5.

To be legitimate, stamps of the thick paper stamps must have genuine cancellations of Bolivia. Value, on cover, each $150.

The 10c blue on thick paper is not known to have been issued.

Some examples of Nos. 40-46 show part of a papermakers' watermark "1011."

For overprints see Nos. 55-59.

President Tomas Frias — A10

President Jose M. Linares — A11

Pedro Domingo Murillo A12

Bernardo Monteagudo A13

Gen. Jose Ballivian — A14

Gen. Antonio Jose de Sucre — A15

Simon Bolivar — A16 Coat of Arms — A17

1897 Litho. *Perf. 12*

47	A10	1c pale yellow grn	2.00	2.00
a.		Vert. pair, imperf. horiz.	100.00	
b.		Vert. pair, imperf. btwn.	100.00	
48	A11	2c red	3.00	2.00
49	A12	5c dk green	2.00	2.00
a.		Horiz. pair, imperf. btwn.	100.00	
50	A13	10c brown vio	2.00	2.00
a.		Vert. pair, imperf. btwn.	100.00	
51	A14	20c lake & blk	10.00	5.00
a.		Imperf., pair	100.00	
52	A15	50c orange	10.00	10.00
53	A16	1b Prus blue	20.00	20.00
54	A17	2b red, yel, grn & blk	60.00	*90.00*
		Nos. 47-54 (8)	109.00	*133.00*

Excellent forgeries of No. 54, perf and imperf, exist, some postally used.

Reprint of No. 53 has dot in numeral. Same value.

Nos. 40-44 Handstamped in Violet or Blue

1899 *Perf. 14½*

55	A9	1c yellow bis	30.00	30.00
56	A9	2c red orange	40.00	*50.00*
57	A9	5c green	17.00	17.00
58	A9	10c yellow brn	30.00	30.00
59	A9	20c dark blue	50.00	*75.00*
		Nos. 55-59 (5)	167.00	202.00

The handstamp is found inverted, double, etc. Values twice the listed amounts. Forgeries of this handstamp are plentiful. "E.F." stands for Estado Federal.

The 50c and 100c (Nos. 45-46) were overprinted at a later date in Brazil. Value, $500.

Antonio José de Sucre — A18

Perf. 11½, 12

1899 Engr. Thin Paper

62	A18	1c gray blue	5.00	2.00
63	A18	2c brnsh red	5.00	2.00
64	A18	5c dk green	5.00	2.00
65	A18	10c yellow org	4.00	2.00
66	A18	20c rose pink	5.00	2.00
67	A18	50c bister brn	10.00	5.00
68	A18	1b gray violet	8.00	4.00
		Nos. 62-68 (7)	42.00	19.00

1901

69	A18	5c dark red	3.00	2.00

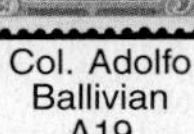
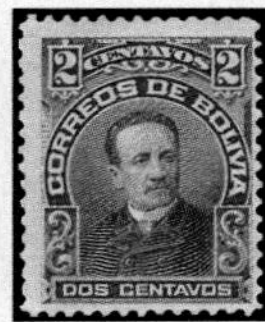

Col. Adolfo Ballivian A19 Eliodoro Camacho A20

President Narciso Campero A21 Jose Ballivian A22

Gen. Andres Santa Cruz — A23 Coat of Arms — A24

1901-04 Engr.

70	A19	1c claret	.85	.30
71	A20	2c green	1.00	.50
73	A21	5c scarlet	1.00	.30
74	A22	10c blue	3.00	.50
75	A23	20c violet & blk	2.00	1.00
76	A24	2b brown	7.00	5.00

Litho.

77	A19	1c claret ('04)	3.00	1.00
		Nos. 70-77 (7)	17.85	8.60

In No. 70 the panel above "CENTAVO" is shaded with continuous lines. In No. 77 the shading is of dots.

Nos. 73-74 exist imperf. Value, pairs, each $50.

See Nos. 103-105, 107, 110.

For surcharges see Nos. 95-96, 193.

Coat of Arms of Dept. of La Paz — A25 Murillo — A26

Jose Miguel Lanza — A27 Ismael Montes — A28

1909 Litho. *Perf. 11*

78	A25	5c blue & blk	15.00	11.00
79	A26	10c green & blk	15.00	11.00
80	A27	20c orange & blk	15.00	11.00
81	A28	2b red & black	15.00	11.00
		Nos. 78-81 (4)	60.00	44.00

Centenary of Revolution of July, 1809.

Nos. 78-81 exist imperf. and tête bêche. Values: imperf. pairs, each $80; tête bêche pairs, each $95. Nos. 79-81 exist with center inverted. Value, each $95.

Miguel Betanzos A29 Col. Ignacio Warnes A30

Murillo A31 Monteagudo A32

Esteban Arce — A33 Antonio Jose de Sucre — A34

Simon Bolivar — A35 Manuel Belgrano — A36

1909 Dated 1809-1825 *Perf. 11½*

82	A29	1c lt brown & blk	1.00	.40
83	A30	2c green & blk	1.50	.60
84	A31	5c red & blk	1.50	.50
85	A32	10c dull bl & blk	2.00	.50
86	A33	20c violet & blk	1.75	.70
87	A34	50c olive bister & blk	2.00	.80
88	A35	1b gray brn & blk	2.50	1.50
89	A36	2b chocolate & blk	2.50	2.00
		Nos. 82-89 (8)	14.75	7.00

War of Independence, 1809-1825.

Nos. 82-89 exist imperf. Value, set of pairs $400.

For surcharge see No. 97.

Warnes A37 Betanzos A38

Arce — A39

Dated 1910-1825

1910 *Perf. 13x13½*

92	A37	5c green & black	.50	.30
a.		Imperf., pair	15.00	
93	A38	10c claret & indigo	.60	.50
a.		Imperf., pair	50.00	
94	A39	20c dull blue & indigo	1.00	.80
a.		Imperf., pair	20.00	
		Nos. 92-94 (3)	2.10	1.60

War of Independence.

Nos. 92-94 may be found with parts of a papermaker's watermark: "A I & Co/EXTRA STRONG/9303."

Both perf and imperf exist with inverted centers.

Nos. 71 and 75 Surcharged in Black

1911 *Perf. 11½, 12*

95	A20	5c on 2c green	.75	.30
a.		Inverted surcharge	10.00	10.00
b.		Double surcharge	12.00	10.00
c.		Period after "1911"	4.50	1.50
d.		Blue surcharge	100.00	80.00
e.		Double dsurch., one invtd.	20.00	20.00
96	A23	5c on 20c vio & blk	30.00	30.00
a.		Inverted surcharge	60.00	60.00
b.		Double surch., one invtd.	80.00	
c.		Period after "1911"	40.00	40.00

No. 83 Handstamp Surcharged in Green

97	A30	20c on 2c grn & blk	*2,500.*	

This provisional was issued by local authorities at Villa Bella, a town on the Brazilian border. The 20c surcharge was applied after the stamp had been affixed to the cover. Excellent forgeries of No. 96-97 exist.

"Justice"

A40 A41

1912

Black or Dark Blue Overprint On Revenue Stamps

98	A40	2c green (Bk)	.75	.30
a.		Inverted overprint	15.00	
99	A41	10c ver (Bl)	6.00	1.00
a.		Inverted overprint	20.00	

A42 A43

Red or Black Overprint

Engr.

100	A42	5c orange (R)	.75	.65
a.		Inverted overprint	20.00	
b.		Pair, one without overprint	50.00	
c.		Black overprint	35.00	

Red or Black Surcharge

101	A43	10c on 1c bl (R)	1.00	.60
a.		Inverted surcharge	25.00	
b.		Double surcharge	25.00	
c.		Dbl. surcharge, one invtd.	40.00	
d.		Black surcharge	200.00	150.00
e.		As "d," inverted	250.00	
f.		As "d," double surcharge	225.00	
g.		Pair, one without black surch.	800.00	

Fakes of No. 101d are plentiful.

Revenue Stamp Surcharged

Type 1 —Serifed "1"s in date

Type 2 — Sans-serif "1"s in date

1917 Litho.

102	10c on 1c blue, Type 1	*5,000.*	*1,750.*
a.	10c on 1c, Type 2	—	*2,000.*

Design similar to type A43.

1,000 examples of Nos. 102 and 102a were reportedly produced, with 90 percent of the issue being type 1 and the balance type 2. No.

102a also exists with overprint in black. Value, used, $2,500.
Excellent forgeries exist.

Types of 1901 and

Frias — A45

Sucre — A46

Bolivar — A47

1913	Engr.		*Perf. 12*	
103 A19	1c car rose		.75	.30
104 A20	2c vermilion		.75	.30
105 A21	5c green		1.00	.25
106 A45	8c yellow		1.50	1.00
107 A22	10c gray		1.50	.25
108 A46	50c dull violet		3.00	1.50
109 A47	1b slate blue		6.00	2.00
110 A24	2b black		10.00	5.00
	Nos. 103-110 (8)		24.50	10.60

No. 107, litho., was not regularly issued.

Nine values commemorating the Guaqui-La Paz railroad were printed in 1915 but never issued. Value, set $25.
The original set is engraved. Crude, typographed forgeries exist.

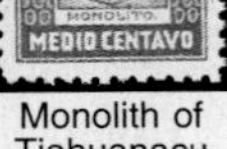

Monolith of Tiahuanacu A48

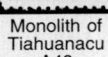

Mt. Potosí A49

Lake Titicaca — A50

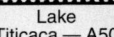

Mt. Illimani — A51

Legislature Building — A53

FIVE CENTAVOS.
Type I — Numerals have background of vertical lines. Clouds formed of dots.
Type II — Numerals on white background. Clouds near the mountain formed of wavy lines.

1916-17	Litho.	*Perf. 11½*	
111 A48	½c brown	.40	.30
a.	Horiz. pair, imperf. vert.	50.00	40.00
112 A49	1c gray green	.50	.30
a.	Imperf., pair	40.00	30.00
113 A50	2c car & blk	.50	.30
a.	Imperf., pair	40.00	30.00
b.	Vert. pair, imperf. horiz.	40.00	30.00
c.	Center inverted	*150.00*	*100.00*
d.	Imperf., center inverted	*250.00*	*150.00*
114 A51	5c dk blue (I)	1.25	.30
a.	Imperf., pair	40.00	30.00
b.	Vert. pair, imperf. horiz.	40.00	30.00
c.	Horiz. pair, imperf. vert.	40.00	30.00
115 A51	5c dk blue (II)	1.00	.50
a.	Imperf., pair	40.00	30.00
116 A53	10c org & bl	1.00	.30
a.	Imperf., pair	60.00	40.00
b.	No period after "Legislativo"	1.00	.30
c.	Center inverted	*200.00*	*125.00*
d.	Vertical pair, imperf. between	60.00	50.00
	Nos. 111-116 (6)	4.65	2.00

For surcharges see Nos. 194-196.

Coat of Arms
A54 A55

Printed by the American Bank Note Co.

1919-20	Engr.	*Perf. 12*	
118 A54	1c carmine	.40	.30
119 A54	2c dk violet	8.00	4.00
120 A54	5c dk green	.75	.30
121 A54	10c vermilion	.75	.30
122 A54	20c dk blue	2.25	.40
123 A54	22c lt blue	1.40	.90
124 A54	24c purple	.90	.60
125 A54	50c orange	7.00	.70
126 A55	1b red brown	9.00	2.50
127 A55	2b black brn	13.50	6.75
	Nos. 118-127 (10)	43.95	16.75

Printed by Perkins, Bacon & Co., Ltd.

1923-27	Re-engraved	*Perf. 13½*	
128 A54	1c carmine ('27)	.40	.30
129 A54	2c dk violet	.40	.30
130 A54	5c dp green	1.00	.30
131 A54	10c vermilion	25.00	18.00
132 A54	20c slate blue	2.50	.50
135 A54	50c orange	5.50	1.50
136 A55	1b red brown	1.50	1.00
137 A55	2b black brown	2.00	.60
	Nos. 128-137 (8)	38.30	22.50

There are many differences in the designs of the two issues but they are too minute to be illustrated or described.
Nos. 128-137 exist imperf. Value, $50 each pair.
See Nos. 144-146, 173-177. For surcharges see Nos. 138-143, 160, 162, 181-186, 236-237.

Stamps of 1919-20 Surcharged in Blue, Black or Red

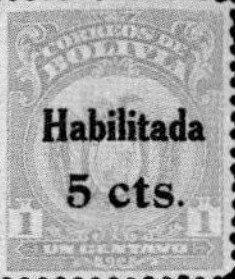

1924		*Perf. 12*	
138 A54	5c on 1c car (Bl)	.40	.30
a.	Inverted surcharge	10.00	6.00
b.	Double surcharge	10.00	6.00
139 A54	15c on 10c ver (Bk)	1.00	.70
a.	Inverted surcharge	12.00	6.00
140 A54	15c on 22c lt bl (Bk)	1.00	.75
a.	Inverted surcharge	12.00	6.00
b.	Double surcharge, one inverted	*16.00*	*6.00*

No. 140 surcharged in red or blue probably are trial impressions. They appear jointly, and with black in blocks.

Same Surcharge on No. 131
Perf. 13½

142 A54	15c on 10c ver (Bk)	1.00	.30
a.	Inverted surcharge	12.00	6.00

No. 121 Surcharged

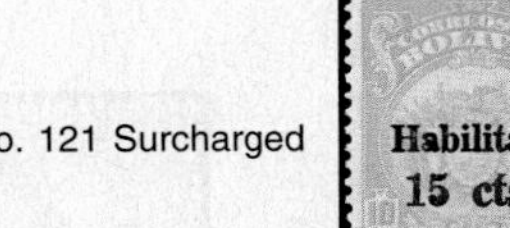

Perf. 12

143 A54	15c on 10c ver (Bk)	1.00	.50
a.	Inverted surcharge	12.00	6.00
b.	Double surcharge	12.00	6.00
	Nos. 138-143 (5)	4.40	2.55

Type of 1919-20 Issue
Printed by Waterlow & Sons
Second Re-engraving

1925	Unwmk.	*Perf. 12½*	
144 A54	5c deep green	1.00	.50
145 A54	15c ultra	1.00	.50
146 A54	20c dark blue	1.00	.50
	Nos. 144-146 (3)	3.00	1.50

These stamps may be identified by the perforation.

Miner — A56

Condor Looking Toward the Sea A57

Designs: 2c, Sower. 5c, Torch of Eternal Freedom. 10c, National flower (kantuta). 15c, Pres. Bautista Saavedra. 50c, Liberty head. 1b, Archer on horse. 2b, Mercury. 5b, Gen. A. J. de Sucre.

1925	Engr.	*Perf. 14*	
150 A56	1c dark green	1.50	
151 A56	2c rose	1.50	
152 A56	5c red, *grn*	1.50	.50
153 A56	10c car, *yel*	2.50	1.00
154 A56	15c red brown	.80	.50
155 A57	25c ultra	2.50	1.00
156 A56	50c dp violet	3.00	1.00
157 A56	1b red	5.00	2.50
158 A57	2b orange	6.00	3.00
159 A56	5b black brn	6.00	3.00
	Nos. 150-159 (10)	30.30	

Cent. of the Republic. The 1c and 2c were not released for general use.
Nos. 150-159 exist imperf. Value, $60 each pair.
For surcharges see Nos. C59-C62.

Stamps of 1919-27 Surcharged in Blue, Black or Red

1927			
160 A54	5c on 1c car (Bl)	4.50	3.25
a.	Inverted surcharge	15.00	15.00
b.	Black surcharge	40.00	40.00

Perf. 12

162 A54	10c on 24c pur (Bk)	4.50	3.25
a.	Inverted surcharge	50.00	50.00
b.	Red surcharge	70.00	70.00

Coat of Arms — A66

Printed by Waterlow & Sons

1927	Litho.	*Perf. 13½*	
165 A66	2c yellow	.50	.35
166 A66	3c pink	.90	.90
167 A66	4c red brown	.75	.75
168 A66	20c lt ol grn	1.00	.35
169 A66	25c deep blue	1.00	.50
170 A66	30c violet	1.50	1.50
171 A66	40c orange	2.00	2.00
172 A66	50c dp brown	2.00	1.00
173 A55	1b red	2.50	2.00
174 A55	2b plum	4.00	3.50
175 A55	3b olive grn	4.50	4.50
176 A55	4b claret	7.50	6.00
177 A55	5b bister brn	8.00	6.50
	Nos. 165-177 (13)	36.15	29.85

For overprints and surcharges see Nos. 178-180, 208, 211-212.

Type of 1927 Issue Overprinted

1927			
178 A66	5c dark green	.50	.30
179 A66	10c slate	.75	.30
180 A66	15c carmine	.75	.35
	Nos. 178-180 (3)	2.00	.95

Exist with inverted overprint. Value $30 each.

Stamps of 1919-27 Surcharged

1928		*Perf. 12, 12½, 13½*	
	Red Surcharge		
181 A54	15c on 20c #122	15.00	15.00
a.	Inverted surcharge	22.50	22.50
182 A54	15c on 20c #132	15.00	15.00
a.	Inverted surcharge	25.00	25.00
b.	Black surcharge	45.00	
183 A54	15c on 20c #146	250.00	160.00
	Black Surcharge		
184 A54	15c on 24c #124	2.25	1.25
a.	Inverted surcharge	8.00	8.00
b.	Blue surcharge	75.00	
185 A54	15c on 50c #125	90.00	*400.00*
a.	Inverted surcharge	120.00	
186 A54	15c on 50c #135	1.75	1.25
a.	Inverted surcharge	10.00	10.00
	Nos. 181-186 (6)	374.00	592.50

Condor — A67

Hernando Siles — A68

Map of Bolivia — A69

Printed by Perkins, Bacon & Co., Ltd.

1928	Engr.	*Perf. 13½*	
189 A67	5c green	1.50	.25
190 A68	10c slate	.50	.25
191 A69	15c carmine lake	3.00	.25
	Nos. 189-191 (3)	5.00	.75

Nos. 104, 111, 113, Surcharged in Various Colors

1930		*Perf. 12, 11½*	
193 A20	1c on 2c (Bl)	2.00	2.00
a.	"0.10" for "0.01"	35.00	35.00
194 A50	3c on 2c (Br)	2.00	2.00
195 A48	25c on ½c (Bk)	2.00	2.00
196 A50	25c on 2c (V)	2.00	2.00
	Nos. 193-196 (4)	8.00	8.00

The lines of the surcharges were spaced to fit the various shapes of the stamps. The surcharges exist inverted, double, etc.
Trial printings were made of the surcharges on Nos. 193 and 194 in black and on No. 196 in brown.

Mt. Potosi — A70

Mt. Illimani — A71

Eduardo Abaroa — A72

Map of Bolivia — A73

Sucre — A74

Bolivar — A75

1931 **Engr.** ***Perf. 14***

No.	Type	Value	Color	Unused	Used
197	A70	2c	green	2.00	1.00
198	A71	5c	light blue	2.00	.30
199	A72	10c	red orange	2.00	.30
200	A73	15c	violet	4.50	.40
201	A73	35c	carmine	3.00	1.25
202	A73	45c	orange	3.00	1.25
203	A74	50c	gray	1.50	1.00
204	A75	1b	brown	2.50	1.40
			Nos. 197-204 (8)	20.50	6.90

No. 198 exists imperf.

See Nos. 207, 241. For surcharges see Nos. 209-210.

Symbols of 1930 Revolution — A76

1931 **Litho.** ***Perf. 11***

No.	Type	Value	Color	Unused	Used
205	A76	15c	scarlet	6.00	1.00
a.			Pair, imperf. between	25.00	
206	A76	50c	brt violet	1.50	1.25
a.			Pair, imperf. between	30.00	

Revolution of June 25, 1930.

For surcharges see Nos. 239-240.

Map Type of 1931 Without Imprint

1932 **Litho.**

No.	Type	Value	Color	Unused	Used
207	A73	15c	violet	4.00	.35

Stamps of 1927-31 Surcharged

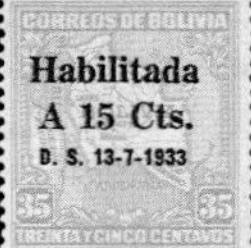

1933 ***Perf. 13½, 14***

No.	Type	Value	Color	Unused	Used
208	A66	5c on 1b	red	1.00	.50
a.			Without period after "Cts"	3.00	3.00
209	A73	15c on 35c	car	.50	.50
a.			Inverted surcharge	30.00	20.00
210	A73	15c on 45c	orange	.60	.60
a.			Inverted surcharge	30.00	20.00
211	A66	15c on 50c	dp brn	2.00	.50
212	A66	25c on 40c	orange	1.00	.50
			Nos. 208-212 (5)	5.10	2.60

The hyphens in "13-7-33" occur in three positions: type 1, both hypens in middle (shown); type 2, both hypens on base line of numbers; type 3, left hypen in middle, right hyphen on base line. Values are the same for all types.

Coat of Arms — A77

1933 **Engr.** ***Perf. 12***

No.	Type	Value	Color	Unused	Used
213	A77	2c	blue green	.50	.30
214	A77	5c	blue	.50	.30
215	A77	10c	red	1.00	.75
216	A77	15c	deep violet	.50	.30
217	A77	25c	dark blue	1.50	.75
			Nos. 213-217 (5)	4.00	2.40

For surcharges see Nos. 233-235, 238.

Mariano Baptista — A78

1935

No.	Type	Value	Color	Unused	Used
218	A78	15c	dull violet	.75	.50

Map of Bolivia — A79

1935

No.	Type	Value	Color	Unused	Used
219	A79	2c	dark blue	.50	.30
220	A79	3c	yellow	.50	.30
221	A79	5c	vermilion	.50	.30
222	A79	5c	blue grn	.50	.30
223	A79	10c	black brn	.50	.30
224	A79	15c	deep rose	.50	.30
225	A79	15c	ultra	.50	.30
226	A79	20c	yellow grn	1.00	.60
227	A79	25c	lt blue	1.50	.30
228	A79	30c	deep rose	1.00	.60
229	A79	40c	orange	2.25	1.00
230	A79	50c	gray violet	2.25	1.00
231	A79	1b	yellow	1.25	.60
232	A79	2b	olive brown	3.00	1.50
			Nos. 219-232 (14)	15.75	7.70

Regular Stamps of 1925-33 Surcharged in Black

1937 ***Perf. 11, 12, 13½***

No.	Type	Value	Color	Unused	Used
233	A77	5c on 2c	bl grn	.30	.30
234	A77	15c on 25c	dk bl	.50	.50
235	A77	30c on 25c	dk bl	.80	.80
236	A55	45c on 1b	red brn	1.00	1.00
237	A55	1b on 2b	plum	1.00	1.00
a.			"1" missing	15.00	15.00
238	A77	2b on 25c	dk bl	1.00	1.00

"Comunicaciones" on one line

No.	Type	Value	Color	Unused	Used
239	A76	3b on 50c	brt vio	2.00	2.00
a.			"3" of value missing	20.00	20.00
240	A76	5b on 50c	brt vio	3.00	3.00
			Nos. 233-240 (8)	9.60	9.60

Exist inverted, double, etc.

President Siles — A80

1937 **Unwmk.** ***Perf. 14***

No.	Type	Value	Color	Unused	Used
241	A80	1c	yellow brown	.50	.50

Native School — A81

Oil Wells — A82

Modern Factories A83

Torch of Knowledge A84

Map of the Sucre-Camiri R. R. — A85

Allegory of Free Education — A86

Allegorical Figure of Learning — A87

Symbols of Industry — A88

Modern Agriculture — A89

1938 **Litho.** ***Perf. 10½, 11***

No.	Type	Value	Color	Unused	Used
242	A81	2c	dull red	.80	.60
243	A82	10c	pink	.90	.50
244	A83	15c	yellow grn	1.40	.40
245	A84	30c	yellow	1.75	.60
246	A85	45c	rose red	3.00	1.25
247	A86	60c	dk violet	2.50	1.25
248	A87	75c	dull blue	2.00	1.75
249	A88	1b	lt brown	4.50	1.00
250	A89	2b	bister	4.00	1.50
			Nos. 242-250 (9)	20.85	8.85

For surcharge see No. 314 in *Scott Standard Postage Stamp Catalogue*, Vol. 1.

Llamas — A90

Vicuna — A91

Coat of Arms — A92

Cocoi Herons — A93

Chinchilla — A94

Toco Toucan — A95

Condor — A96

Jaguar — A97

1939, Jan. 21 ***Perf. 10½, 11½x10½***

No.	Type	Value	Color	Unused	Used
251	A90	2c	green	1.50	.75
252	A90	4c	fawn	1.50	.75
253	A90	5c	red violet	1.50	.75
254	A91	10c	black	1.50	.75
255	A91	15c	emerald	3.00	1.25
256	A91	20c	dk slate grn	3.00	1.25
257	A92	25c	lemon	1.50	.75
258	A92	30c	dark blue	1.50	.75
259	A93	40c	vermilion	2.50	1.00
260	A93	45c	gray	2.50	1.00
261	A94	60c	rose red	2.50	1.00
262	A94	75c	slate blue	2.50	1.00
263	A95	90c	orange	5.00	1.25
264	A95	1b	blue	5.00	1.25
265	A96	2b	rose lake	7.00	1.25
266	A96	3b	dark violet	10.00	1.75
267	A97	4b	brown org	10.00	1.75
268	A97	5b	gray brown	11.50	2.00
			Nos. 251-268 (18)	73.50	20.25

All but 20c exist imperf. Value, each pair $40.

Imperf. counterfeits with altered designs exist of some values.

For surcharges see Nos. 315-317 in *Scott Standard Postage Stamp Catalogue*, Vol. 1.

Flags of 21 American Republics — A98

1940, Apr. **Litho.** ***Perf. 10½***

No.	Type	Value	Color	Unused	Used
269	A98	9b	multicolored	4.50	2.25

Pan American Union, 50th anniversary.

AIR POST STAMPS

Aviation School

AP1 AP2

1924, Dec. **Unwmk.** **Engr.** ***Perf. 14***

No.	Type	Value	Color	Unused	Used
C1	AP1	10c	ver & blk	1.00	.50
a.			Inverted center	*2,500.*	
			Never hinged	4,250.	
C2	AP1	15c	carmine & blk	2.00	2.00
C3	AP1	25c	dk bl & blk	1.50	1.00
C4	AP1	50c	orange & blk	10.00	5.00
C5	AP2	1b	red brn & blk	3.00	3.00

C6 AP2 2b blk brn & blk 20.00 10.00
C7 AP2 5b dk vio & blk 25.00 20.00
Nos. C1-C7 (7) 62.50 41.50

Natl. Aviation School establishment.

These stamps were available for ordinary postage. Nos. C1, C3, C5 and C6 exist imperforate. Value, $400. each pair.

Proofs of the 2b with inverted center exist imperforate and privately perforated. Value, *$2,750.*

For overprints and surcharges see Nos. C11-C23, C56-C58.

Emblem of Lloyd Aéreo Boliviano AP3

1928 **Litho.** ***Perf. 11***
C8 AP3 15c green 2.50 1.50
a. Imperf., pair 70.00 60.00
C9 AP3 20c dark blue 4.00 3.25
C10 AP3 35c red brown 3.25 2.50
Nos. C8-C10 (3) 9.75 7.25

No. C8 exists imperf. between. Value, $60 pair.

For surcharges see Nos. C24-C26, C53-C55.

Graf Zeppelin Issues

Nos. C1-C5 Surcharged or Overprinted in Various Colors

Nos. C11, C19

Nos. C12-C18, C20-C23

1930, May 6 ***Perf. 14***
C11 AP1 5c on 10c ver & blk (G) 20.00 20.00
C12 AP1 10c ver & blk (Bl) 20.00 20.00
C13 AP1 10c ver & blk (Brn) *2,500.* *2,500.*
C14 AP1 15c car & blk (V) 20.00 20.00
C15 AP1 25c dk bl & blk (R) 20.00 20.00
C16 AP1 50c org & blk (Brn) 20.00 20.00
C17 AP1 50c org & blk (R) *1,000.* *1,000.*
C18 AP2 1b red brn & blk (gold) 350.00 350.00

Experts consider the 50c with gold or silver overprint and 5c with black to be trial color proofs.

See notes following No. C23.

Inverted Overprint

C11a AP1 5c on 10c ver & blk (G) 50.00 *50.00*
C12a AP1 10c ver & black (Bl) 150.00 *150.00*
C14a AP1 15c car & blk (V) 100.00 *100.00*
C15a AP1 25c dk blue & blk (R) 150.00 *150.00*
C16a AP1 50c org & blk (Brn) 225.00 *225.00*
C18a AP1 1b red brn & blk(G) 1,750.

Double Overprint

C11b AP1 5c on 10c ver & blk (G) 175.00 *175.00*
C12b AP1 10c ver & black (Bl) 175.00 *175.00*
C14b AP1 15c car & blk (V) 75.00 *75.00*
C15b AP1 25c dk blue & blk (R) 550.00
C16b AP1 50c org & blk (Brn) 225.00 *225.00*

Double Overprint, One Inverted

C11c AP1 5c on 10c ver & blk (G) 200.00 *200.00*
C11d AP1 5c Double surcharge, one sideways 300.00
C12c AP1 10c ver & black (Bl) 200.00 *200.00*
C14c AP1 15c car & blk (V) 450.00
C15c AP1 25c dk blue & blk (R) 150.00 *150.00*
C16c AP1 50c org & blk (Brn) 250.00 *250.00*
C16d AP1 50c Double overprint, both inverted 450.00

Surcharged or Overprinted in Bronze Inks of Various Colors

C19 AP1 5c on 10c ver & blk (G) 120.00 *150.00*
a. Inverted surcharge 200.00 —
C20 AP1 10c ver & blk (Bl) 100.00 *150.00*
a. Inverted surcharge — —
C21 AP1 15c car & blk (V) 100.00 *150.00*
a. Inverted surcharge 150.00 —
C22 AP1 25c dk bl & blk (cop) 100.00 *150.00*
a. Inverted surcharge 150.00 —
C23 AP2 1b red brn & blk (gold) *700.00* *900.00*
a. Inverted surcharge — —
Nos. C19-C23 (5) 1,120. *1,500.*

Flight of the airship Graf Zeppelin from Europe to Brazil and return via Lakehurst, NJ.

Nos. C19 to C23 were intended for use on postal matter forwarded by the Graf Zeppelin.

No. C18 was overprinted with light gold or gilt bronze ink. No. C23 was overprinted with deep gold bronze ink. Nos. C13 and C17 were overprinted with trial colors but were sold with the regular printings. The 5c on 10c is known surcharged in black and in blue.

No. C8-C10 Surcharged

1930, May 6 ***Perf. 11***
C24 AP3 1.50b on 15c 80.00 80.00
a. Inverted surcharge 300.00 300.00
b. Comma instead of period after "1" 100.00 100.00
C25 AP3 3b on 20c 80.00 80.00
a. Inverted surcharge 350.00 350.00
b. Comma instead of period after "3" 125.00 125.00
C26 AP3 6b on 35c *80.00* *80.00*
a. Inverted surcharge 375.00 375.00
b. Comma instead of period after "6" 125.00 125.00
Nos. C24-C26 (3) 240.00 240.00

Airplane and Bullock Cart — AP6

Airplane and River Boat — AP7

1930, July 24 **Litho.** ***Perf. 14***
C27 AP6 5c dp violet 1.50 1.10
C28 AP7 15c red 1.50 1.10
C29 AP7 20c yellow 1.10 .90
C30 AP6 35c yellow grn 1.00 .75
C31 AP7 50c deep blue 2.50 1.50
C32 AP6 1b lt brown 3.50 1.75
C33 AP7 2b deep rose 4.50 2.50
C34 AP6 3b slate 8.00 6.00
Nos. C27-C34 (8) 23.60 15.60

Nos. C27 to C34 exist imperforate. Value, $60 each pair.

For surcharge see No. C52.

Air Service Emblem AP8

1932, Sept. 16 ***Perf. 11***
C35 AP8 5c ultra 3.25 2.40
C36 AP8 10c gray 2.00 1.50
C37 AP8 15c dark rose 2.00 1.50
C38 AP8 25c orange 2.00 1.50
C39 AP8 30c green 1.25 .80
C40 AP8 50c violet 3.25 2.50
C41 AP8 1b dk brown 3.25 2.50
Nos. C35-C41 (7) 17.00 12.70

Map of Bolivia — AP9

1935, Feb. 1 **Engr.** ***Perf. 12***
C42 AP9 5c brown red .30 .30
C43 AP9 10c dk green .30 .30
C44 AP9 20c dk violet .30 .30
C45 AP9 30c ultra .30 .30
C46 AP9 50c orange .50 .50
C47 AP9 1b bister brn .50 .50
C48 AP9 1½b yellow 1.25 .75
C49 AP9 2b carmine 1.25 1.00
C50 AP9 5b green 1.50 1.25
C51 AP9 10b dk brown 5.00 1.75
Nos. C42-C51 (10) 11.20 6.95

Nos. C1, C4, C10, C30 Srchd. in Red (#C52-C56) or Green (#C57-C58) — c

1937, Oct. 6 ***Perf. 11, 14***
C52 AP6 5c on 35c yel grn .50 .40
a. "Carreo" 30.00 30.00
b. Inverted surcharge 20.00
C53 AP3 20c on 35c red brn .75 .60
a. Inverted surcharge 20.00 20.00
C54 AP3 50c on 35c red brn 1.50 1.00
a. Inverted surcharge 50.00 50.00
C55 AP3 1b on 35c red brn 2.00 1.50
a. Inverted surcharge 25.00 20.00
C56 AP1 2b on 50c org & blk 2.50 2.00
a. Inverted surcharge 20.00 15.00
C57 AP1 12b on 10c ver & blk 15.00 10.00
a. Inverted surcharge 75.00 50.00
C58 AP1 15b on 10c ver & blk 15.00 10.00
a. Inverted surcharge 75.00 30.00

Regular Postage Stamps of 1925 Surcharged in Green or Red — d

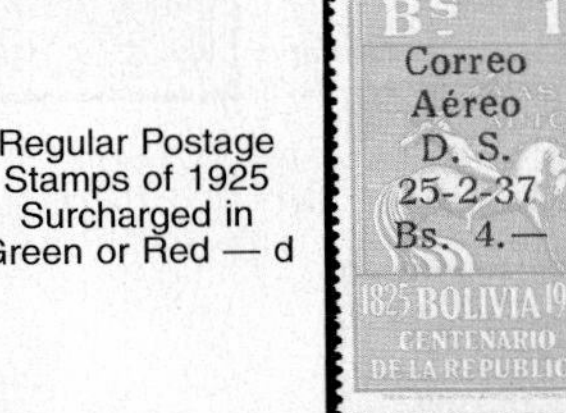

Perf. 14
C59 A56 (d) 3b on 50c dp vio (G) 5.00 5.00
C60 A56 (d) 4b on 1b red (G) 5.00 5.00
C61 A57 (c) 5b on 2b org (G) 6.00 6.00
a. Double surcharge 175.00
C62 A56 (d) 10b on 5b blk brn 8.50 7.00
a. Double surcharge 50.00
Nos. C52-C62 (11) 61.75 48.50

No. C59-C62 exist with inverted surcharge, No. C62a with black and black and red surcharges.

Courtyard of Potosi Mint — AP10

Miner — AP11

Emancipated Woman AP12

Pincers, Torch and Good Will Principles AP15

Airplane over Field AP13

Airplanes and Liberty Monument AP14

Airplane over River AP16

Emblem of New Government AP17

Transport Planes over Map of Bolivia AP18

1938, May **Litho.** ***Perf. 10½***
C63 AP10 20c deep rose .60 .30
C64 AP11 30c gray .60 .30
C65 AP12 40c yellow .70 .40
C66 AP13 50c yellow grn .60 .30
C67 AP14 60c dull blue .75 .40
C68 AP15 1b dull red .75 .40
C69 AP16 2b bister 1.50 .50
C70 AP17 3b lt brown 2.25 1.00
C71 AP18 5b dk violet 3.00 1.00
Nos. C63-C71 (9) 10.75 4.60

40c, 1b, 2b exist imperf.

Chalice — AP19

Virgin of Copacabana AP20

Jesus Christ — AP21

Church of San Francisco, La Paz AP22

St. Anthony of Padua — AP23

1939, July 19 **Litho.** ***Perf. 13½, 10½***
C72 AP19 5c dull violet .75 .50
a. Pair, imperf. between 80.00
C73 AP20 30c lt bl grn 1.00 .50
C74 AP21 45c violet bl 1.00 .50
a. Vertical pair, imperf. between 90.00

C75	AP22	60c carmine	1.50	.75
C76	AP23	75c vermilion	1.50	1.25
C77	AP23	90c deep blue	1.50	.60
C78	AP22	2b dull brown	2.50	.50
C79	AP21	4b deep plum	3.00	1.00
C80	AP20	5b lt blue	7.00	.80
C81	AP19	10b yellow	12.00	1.25
		Nos. C72-C81 (10)	31.75	7.65

2nd National Eucharistic Congress.
For surcharge see No. C112 in *Scott Standard Postage Stamp Catalogue*, Vol. 1.

POSTAGE DUE STAMPS

D1

1931	**Unwmk.**	**Engr.**	***Perf. 14, 14½***	
J1	D1	5c ultra	1.75	*3.50*
J2	D1	10c red	2.50	*3.50*
J3	D1	15c yellow	2.50	*5.00*
J4	D1	30c deep green	2.50	*6.00*
J5	D1	40c deep violet	6.00	*8.00*
J6	D1	50c black brown	12.00	*15.00*
		Nos. J1-J6 (6)	27.25	*41.00*

Symbol of Youth — D2

Torch of Knowledge D3

Symbol of the Revolution of May 17, 1936 — D4

1938		**Litho.**	***Perf. 11***	
J7	D2	5c deep rose	1.75	1.50
a.		Pair, imperf. between	10.00	
J8	D3	10c green	2.00	1.50
J9	D4	30c gray blue	2.00	1.60
		Nos. J7-J9 (3)	5.75	4.60

POSTAL TAX STAMPS

Worker — PT1

Imprint: "LITO. UNIDAS LA PAZ."

Perf. 13½x10½, 10½, 13½

1939		**Litho.**	**Unwmk.**	
RA1	PT1	5c dull violet	1.00	.50
a.		Double impression	15.00	15.00

Redrawn

Imprint: "TALL. OFFSET LA PAZ."

1940			***Perf. 12x11, 11***	
RA2	PT1	5c violet	.75	.30
a.		Horizontal pair, imperf. between	3.00	2.00
b.		Imperf. horiz., pair	10.00	
c.		Double impression	15.00	10.00

Tax of Nos. RA1-RA2 was for the Workers' Home Building Fund.

BOSNIA & HERZEGOVINA

ˈbäz-nē-ə and ˌhert-sə-gō-ˈvē-nə

LOCATION — Dalmatia and Serbia
GOVT. — Provinces of Turkey under Austro-Hungarian occupation, 1879-1908; provinces of Austria-Hungary 1908-1918
AREA — 19,768 sq. mi.
POP. — 2,000,000 (approx. 1918)
CAPITAL — Sarajevo

Following World War I Bosnia and Herzegovina united with the kingdoms of Montenegro and Serbia, and Croatia, Dalmatia and Slovenia, to form the Kingdom of Yugoslavia (See Yugoslavia.)

100 Novcica (Neukreuzer) = 1 Florin (Gulden)
100 Heller = 1 Krone (1900)

Watermark

Wmk. 91 — BRIEF-MARKEN or (from 1890) ZEITUNGS-MARKEN in Double-lined Capitals, Across the Sheet

Coat of Arms — A1

Type I — The heraldic eaglets on the right side of the escutcheon are entirely blank. The eye of the lion is indicated by a very small dot, which sometimes fails to print.

Type II — There is a colored line across the lowest eaglet. A similar line sometimes appears on the middle eaglet. The eye of the lion is formed by a large dot which touches the outline of the head above it.

Type III — The eaglets and eye of the lion are similar to type I. Each tail feather of the large eagle has two lines of shading and the lowest feather does not touch the curved line below it. In types I and II there are several shading lines in these feathers, and the lowest feather touches the curved line.

Varieties of the Numerals

2 NOVCICA:
A — The "2" has curved tail. All are type I.
B — The "2" has straight tail. All are type II.

15 NOVCICA:
C — The serif of the "1" is short and forms a wide angle with the vertical stroke.
D — The serif of the "1" forms an acute angle with the vertical stroke.
The numerals of the 5n were retouched several times and show minor differences, especially in the flag.

Other Varieties

½ NOVCICA:
There is a black dot between the curved ends of the ornaments near the lower spandrels.
G — This dot touches the curve at its right. Stamps of this (1st) printing are litho.
H — This dot stands clear of the curved lines. Stamps of this (2nd) printing are typo.

10 NOVCICA:
Ten stamps in each sheet of type II show a small cross in the upper section of the right side of the escutcheon.

Perf. 9 to 13½ and Compound

1879-94 **Litho.** **Wmk. 91**

Type I

1	A1	½n blk (type II) ('94)	26.00	*37.50*
		Never hinged	37.50	
		On wrapper or address label from printed matter		600.00
2	A1	1n gray	15.00	2.25
		Never hinged	22.50	
		On wrapper or address label from printed matter		275.00
c.		1n gray lilac		3.00
4	A1	2n yellow	22.50	1.50
		Never hinged	35.00	
		On postcard		26.00
		On printed matter		210.00
5	A1	3n green	26.00	3.00
		Never hinged	37.50	
		Single franking on local cover		400.00
6	A1	5n rose red	37.50	.40
		Never hinged	60.00	
		On cover		22.50
7	A1	10n blue	150.00	1.50
		Never hinged	300.00	
		On cover		160.00
8	A1	15n brown (D)	150.00	9.75
		Never hinged	225.00	
		On cover		525.00
a.		15n brown (C)	360.00	50.00
		Never hinged	650.00	
		On cover		1,100.
9	A1	20n gray green ('93)	500.00	13.50
		Never hinged	900.00	
		On cover		1,900.
10	A1	25n violet	130.00	11.00
		Never hinged	190.00	
		On cover		*5,100.*
		On other postal document		750.00
		Nos. 1-10 (9)	1,057.	80.40

No. 2c was never issued. It is usually canceled by blue pencil marks and "mint" examples generally have been cleaned.

Perf. 10½ to 13 and Compound

1894-98 **Typo.**

Type II

1a	A1	½n black	16.50	*22.50*
		Never hinged	26.00	
		On wrapper or address label from printed matter		625.00
2a	A1	1n gray	5.25	1.50
		Never hinged	9.75	
		On wrapper or address label from printed matter		260.00
4a	A1	2n yellow	3.25	.75
		Never hinged	6.00	
		On postcard		11.00
5a	A1	3n green	5.25	1.50
		Never hinged	9.75	
		Single franking on local cover		250.00
6a	A1	5n rose red	125.00	.75
		Never hinged	210.00	
		On cover		15.00
7a	A1	10n blue	7.50	1.10
		Never hinged	13.50	
		On cover		110.00
b.		Pair, imperf btw, perf 10½ all around		*12,500.*
8b	A1	15n brown	6.75	4.50
		Never hinged	12.00	
		On cover		190.00
9a	A1	20n gray green	7.50	6.00
		Never hinged	15.00	
		On cover		1,650.
10a	A1	25n violet	9.00	13.50
		Never hinged	15.00	
		On cover		—
		On other postal document		500.00
		Nos. 1a-10a (9)	186.00	52.10

Type III

6b	A1	5n rose red ('98)	3.75	.75
		Never hinged	11.00	
c.		Perf 10½	12.50	1.50
		Never hinged	19.00	
d.		Perf 11½	75.00	3.00
		Never hinged	110.00	

All the preceding stamps exist in various shades.

Nos. 1a to 10a were reprinted in 1911 in lighter colors, on very white paper and perf. 12½. Value, set $32.50.

A2

A3

Perf. 10½, 12½ and Compound

1900 **Typo.**

11	A2	1h gray black	.25	.25
		Never hinged	.55	
		On cover, postcard, newsprint or wrapper		45.00
12	A2	2h gray	.25	.25
		Never hinged	.55	
		On cover, postcard, newsprint or wrapper		26.00
13	A2	3h yellow	.25	.25
		Never hinged	.55	
		On cover		26.00
14	A2	5h green	.25	.25
		Never hinged	.55	
		On cover		3.00
15	A2	6h brown	.40	.25
		Never hinged	.75	
		On cover		40.00
16	A2	10h red	.25	.25
		Never hinged	.55	
		On cover		5.25
17	A2	20h rose	130.00	12.00
		Never hinged	300.00	
		On cover		340.00
18	A2	25h blue	1.10	1.10
		Never hinged	2.25	
		On cover		52.50
19	A2	30h bister brown	130.00	13.00
		Never hinged	300.00	
		On cover		375.00
20	A2	40h orange	190.00	15.00
		Never hinged	450.00	
		On cover		550.00
21	A2	50h red lilac	.75	.75
		Never hinged	1.90	
		On cover		1,100.
22	A3	1k dark rose	1.00	.60
		Never hinged	2.25	
		On cover		—
23	A3	2k ultra	1.50	*1.90*
		Never hinged	3.25	
		On cover		—
24	A3	5k dull blue grn	3.25	*6.00*
		Never hinged	7.50	
		On cover		—
		Nos. 11-24 (14)	459.25	51.85

All values of this issue except the 3h exist on ribbed paper.

Nos. 17, 19 and 20 were reprinted in 1911. The reprints are in lighter colors and on whiter paper than the originals. Reprints of Nos. 17 and 19 are perf. 10½ and those of No. 20 are perf. 12½. Value each $5. Reprints also exist imperf.

Numerals in Black

1901-04 ***Perf. 12½***

25	A2	20h pink ('02)	.90	.60
		Never hinged	2.25	
		On cover		75.00
26	A2	30h bister brn ('03)	.90	.60
		Never hinged	2.25	
		On cover		75.00
27	A2	35h blue	1.40	.90
		Never hinged	3.00	
		On cover		75.00
a.		35h ultramarine	*175.00*	9.00
		Never hinged	375.00	
		On cover		150.00
28	A2	40h orange ('03)	1.10	.90
		Never hinged	2.60	
		On cover		375.00
29	A2	45h grnsh blue ('04)	1.10	.90
		Never hinged	2.60	
		On cover		560.00
		Nos. 25-29 (5)	5.40	3.90

Nos. 11-16, 18, 21-29 exist imperf. Most of Nos. 11-29 exist perf. 6½; compound with 12½; part perf.; in pairs imperf. between. These were supplied only to some high-ranking officials and never sold at any P.O.

For surcharges, see Yugoslavia Nos. 1LJ14-1LJ22.

View of Deboj A4

The Carsija at Sarajevo — A5

Designs: 2h, View of Mostar. 3h, Pliva Gate, Jajce. 5h, Narenta Pass and Prenj River. 6h, Rama Valley. 10h, Vrbas Valley. 20h, Old Bridge, Mostar. 25h, Bey's Mosque, Sarajevo. 30h, Donkey post. 35h, Jezero and tourists' pavilion. 40h, Mail wagon. 45h, Bazaar at Sarajevo. 50h, Postal car. 2k, St. Luke's Campanile, Jajce. 5k, Emperor Franz Josef.

Perf. Perf 12½

1906 **Engr.** **Unwmk.**

30	A4	1h black	.25	.25
		Never hinged	1.50	
		On cover		7.50
31	A4	2h violet	.25	.25
		Never hinged	1.50	
		On cover		3.75
32	A4	3h olive	.25	.25
		Never hinged	1.50	
		On cover		3.75
33	A4	5h dark green	.35	.35
		Never hinged	4.50	
		On cover		2.25
34	A4	6h brown	.25	*.35*
		Never hinged	1.50	
		On cover		9.75
35	A4	10h carmine	.45	.35
		Never hinged	3.75	
		On cover		2.25
36	A4	20h dark brown	.75	.75
		Never hinged	7.50	
		On cover		15.00
37	A4	25h deep blue	1.50	2.25
		Never hinged	12.00	
		On cover		22.50

38 A4 30h green 1.50 1.10
Never hinged 11.00
On cover 37.50
39 A4 35h myrtle green 1.50 1.10
Never hinged 11.00
On cover 32.50
40 A4 40h orange red 1.50 1.10
Never hinged 15.00
On cover 40.00
41 A4 45h brown red 1.50 2.60
Never hinged 11.00
On cover 75.00
42 A4 50h dull violet 2.25 2.60
Never hinged 15.00
On cover 150.00
43 A5 1k maroon 6.00 3.75
Never hinged 30.00
On cover 300.00
44 A5 2k gray green 7.50 13.00
Never hinged 26.00
On cover —
45 A5 5k dull blue 4.50 9.00
Never hinged 22.50
On cover —
Nos. 30-45 (16) 30.30 39.05

Perf. 9¼

30a A4 1h black .75 1.10
Never hinged 2.50
31a A4 2h violet .75 1.10
Never hinged 2.50
32a A4 3h olive .75 1.10
Never hinged 2.50
33a A4 5h dark green .80 1.10
Never hinged 2.60
34a A4 6h brown .75 1.50
Never hinged 5.75
35a A4 10h carmine .80 1.10
Never hinged 2.60
36a A4 20h dark brown 2.10 4.00
Never hinged 16.00
37a A4 25h deep blue 6.00 11.50
Never hinged 23.00
38a A4 30h green 6.00 8.50
Never hinged 23.00
39a A4 35h myrtle green 6.00 8.50
Never hinged 23.00
40a A4 40h orange red 6.00 8.50
Never hinged 23.00
41a A4 45h brown red 6.00 8.50
Never hinged 23.00
42a A4 50h dull violet 6.00 11.50
Never hinged 23.00
43a A5 1k maroon 12.50 40.00
Never hinged 40.00
44a A5 2k gray green 19.00 60.00
Never hinged 62.50
45a A5 5k dull blue 18.00 57.50
Never hinged 60.00
Nos. 30a-45a (14) 89.35 220.00

Imperf

30b A4 1h black .45 .45
Never hinged 1.10
31b A4 2h violet .50 .45
Never hinged 1.20
32b A4 3h olive .50 .45
Never hinged 1.20
33b A4 5h dark green .60 .45
Never hinged 1.40
34b A4 6h brown .95 .75
Never hinged 2.25
35b A4 10h carmine .60 .45
Never hinged 1.40
36b A4 20h dark brown 2.50 1.25
Never hinged 6.00
37b A4 25h deep blue 5.50 5.25
Never hinged 13.00
38b A4 30h green 6.25 6.00
Never hinged 15.00
39b A4 35h myrtle green 6.25 6.00
Never hinged 15.00
40b A4 40h orange red 6.25 6.00
Never hinged 15.00
41b A4 45h brown red 7.00 6.75
Never hinged 16.00
42b A4 50h dull violet 7.00 6.75
Never hinged 16.00
43b A5 1k maroon 12.50 14.50
Never hinged 30.00
44b A5 2k gray green 19.00 24.00
Never hinged 45.00
45b A5 5k dull blue 15.50 27.50
Never hinged 37.50
Nos. 30b-45b (16) 91.35 107.00

Perf. 12½ and 9¼ Compound

30c A4 1h black 4.50 5.50
Never hinged 8.50
31c A4 2h violet 4.50 5.50
Never hinged 8.50
32c A4 3h olive 4.50 5.50
Never hinged 8.50
33c A4 5h dark green 4.50 5.50
Never hinged 8.50
34c A4 6h brown 4.00 6.00
Never hinged 7.50
35c A4 10h carmine 12.00 10.00
Never hinged 22.50
36c A4 20h dark brown 40.00 12.00
Never hinged 75.00
37c A4 25h deep blue 17.50 32.50
Never hinged 32.50
38c A4 30h green 40.00 32.50
Never hinged 75.00
39c A4 35h myrtle green 40.00 32.50
Never hinged 75.00
40c A4 40h orange red 42.50 42.50
Never hinged 80.00
41c A4 45h brown red 42.50 42.50
Never hinged 80.00
42c A4 50h dull violet 42.50 42.50
Never hinged 80.00
43c A5 1k maroon 87.50 65.00
Never hinged 160.00
44c A5 2k gray green 140.00 140.00
Never hinged 275.00
45c A5 5k dull blue 140.00 140.00
Never hinged 275.00
Nos. 30c-45c (16) 666.50 620.00

Perf. 12½, 9¼ and 6½ Compound

30d A4 1h black 2.25 2.25
Never hinged 5.00
31d A4 2h violet 3.25 2.25
Never hinged 7.00
32d A4 3h olive 3.25 2.25
Never hinged 7.00
33d A4 5h dark green 4.50 2.25
Never hinged 10.00
34d A4 6h brown 3.25 3.25
Never hinged 7.00
35d A4 10h carmine 4.50 4.50
Never hinged 9.50
36d A4 20h dark brown 13.00 13.00
Never hinged 27.50
37d A4 25h deep blue 50.00 50.00
Never hinged 110.00
38d A4 30h green 45.00 45.00
Never hinged 92.50
39d A4 35h myrtle green 47.50 47.50
Never hinged 100.00
40d A4 40h orange red 47.50 47.50
Never hinged 100.00
41d A4 45h brown red 47.50 47.50
Never hinged 100.00
42d A4 50h dull violet 50.00 50.00
Never hinged 110.00
43d A5 1k maroon 87.50 87.50
Never hinged 175.00
44d A5 2k gray green 225.00 225.00
Never hinged 475.00
45d A5 5k dull blue 140.00 140.00
Never hinged 290.00
Nos. 30d-45d (16) 774.00 769.75

Perf. 12½ and 6½ Compound

30e A4 1h black 3.50 3.50
Never hinged 7.50
31e A4 2h violet 3.50 3.50
Never hinged 7.50
32e A4 3h olive 3.50 3.50
Never hinged 7.50
33e A4 5h dark green 3.50 3.50
Never hinged 7.50
34e A4 6h brown 5.50 5.50
Never hinged 12.00
35e A4 10h carmine 6.00 6.00
Never hinged 13.00
36e A4 20h dark brown 14.50 14.50
Never hinged 30.00
37e A4 25h deep blue 20.00 20.00
Never hinged 45.00
38e A4 30h green 21.00 21.00
Never hinged 45.00
39e A4 35h myrtle green 25.00 25.00
Never hinged 55.00
40e A4 40h orange red 19.00 19.00
Never hinged 40.00
41e A4 45h brown red 27.50 27.50
Never hinged 60.00
42e A4 50h dull violet 27.50 27.50
Never hinged 60.00
43e A5 1k maroon 55.00 55.00
Never hinged 120.00
44e A5 2k gray green 95.00 95.00
Never hinged 200.00
45e A5 5k dull blue 87.50 87.50
Never hinged 190.00
Nos. 30e-45e (16) 417.50 417.50

Perf. 9¼ and 6½ Compound

30f A4 1h black 3.50 3.50
Never hinged 7.50
31f A4 2h violet 3.50 3.50
Never hinged 7.50
32f A4 3h olive 3.50 3.50
Never hinged 7.50
33f A4 5h dark green 3.50 3.50
Never hinged 7.50
34f A4 6h brown 5.50 5.50
Never hinged 12.00
35f A4 10h carmine 6.00 6.00
Never hinged 13.00
36f A4 20h dark brown 14.50 14.50
Never hinged 30.00
37f A4 25h deep blue 20.00 20.00
Never hinged 45.00
38f A4 30h green 21.00 21.00
Never hinged 45.00
39f A4 35h myrtle green 25.00 25.00
Never hinged 55.00
40f A4 40h orange red 19.00 19.00
Never hinged 40.00
41f A4 45h brown red 27.50 27.50
Never hinged 60.00
42f A4 50h dull violet 27.50 27.50
Never hinged 60.00
43f A5 1k maroon 55.00 55.00
Never hinged 120.00
44f A5 2k gray green 95.00 95.00
Never hinged 200.00
45f A5 5k dull blue 87.50 87.50
Never hinged 190.00
Nos. 30f-45f (16) 417.50 417.50

Perf. 13½

34g A4 6h brown 21.00 35.00
Never hinged 45.00
36g A4 20h dark brown 82.50 150.00
Never hinged 180.00

Perf. 6½

30h A4 1h black 1.75 5.50
Never hinged 4.00
31h A4 2h violet 1.75 5.50
Never hinged 4.00
32h A4 3h olive 1.75 5.50
Never hinged 4.00
33h A4 5h dark green 1.75 5.50
Never hinged 4.00
34h A4 6h brown 10.50 7.00
Never hinged 22.50
35h A4 10h carmine 14.00 5.50
Never hinged 30.00
36h A4 20h dark brown 16.50 10.50
Never hinged 35.00
37h A4 25h deep blue 32.50 32.50
Never hinged 70.00
38h A4 30h green 37.50 16.50
Never hinged 80.00
39h A4 35h myrtle green 40.00 16.50
Never hinged 85.00
40h A4 40h orange red 47.50 16.50
Never hinged 100.00
41h A4 45h brown red 47.50 32.50
Never hinged 100.00
42h A4 50h dull violet 47.50 25.00
Never hinged 100.00
43h A5 1k maroon 87.50 250.00
Never hinged 180.00
44h A5 2k gray green 140.00 375.00
Never hinged 300.00
45h A5 5k dull blue 130.00 440.00
Never hinged 275.00
Nos. 30h-45h (16) 658.00 1,250.

Perf. 10½

30i A4 1h black 4.50 6.00
Never hinged 9.00
31i A4 2h violet 4.50 7.50
Never hinged 9.00
32i A4 3h olive 4.50 10.00
Never hinged 9.00
33i A4 5h dark green 4.50 10.00
Never hinged 9.00
34i A4 6h brown 10.50 11.00
Never hinged 21.00
35i A4 10h carmine 5.50 7.50
Never hinged 11.00
36i A4 20h dark brown 21.00 32.50
Never hinged 42.50
37i A4 25h deep blue 55.00 87.50
Never hinged 110.00
38i A4 30h green 55.00 120.00
Never hinged 110.00
39i A4 35h myrtle green 55.00 120.00
Never hinged 110.00
40i A4 40h orange red 77.50 130.00
Never hinged 160.00
41i A4 45h brown red 77.50 130.00
Never hinged 160.00
42i A4 50h dull violet 77.50 130.00
Never hinged 160.00
43i A5 1k maroon 160.00 375.00
Never hinged 325.00
44i A5 2k gray green 250.00 450.00
Never hinged 500.00
45i A5 5k dull blue 225.00 440.00
Never hinged 450.00
Nos. 30i-45i (16) 1,088. 2,067.

Perf. 10½ and 9¼ Compound

30j A4 1h black 6.00 6.00
Never hinged 12.00
31j A4 2h violet 10.50 10.50
Never hinged 21.00
32j A4 3h olive 9.50 9.50
Never hinged 19.00
33j A4 5h dark green 9.50 9.50
Never hinged 19.00
34j A4 6h brown 10.50 10.50
Never hinged 21.00
35j A4 10h carmine 12.00 12.00
Never hinged 24.00
36j A4 20h dark brown 16.50 16.50
Never hinged 35.00
37j A4 25h deep blue 24.00 24.00
Never hinged 47.50
38j A4 30h green 32.50 32.50
Never hinged 65.00
39j A4 35h myrtle green 32.50 32.50
Never hinged 65.00
40j A4 40h orange red 22.50 22.50
Never hinged 45.00
41j A4 45h brown red 35.00 35.00
Never hinged 70.00
42j A4 50h dull violet 50.00 50.00
Never hinged 100.00
43j A5 1k maroon 55.00 55.00
Never hinged 110.00
44j A5 2k gray green 275.00 275.00
Never hinged 550.00
45j A5 5k dull blue 120.00 120.00
Never hinged 240.00
Nos. 30j-45j (16) 721.00 721.00

Perf. 10½ and 12½ Compound

30k A4 1h black 6.50 6.50
Never hinged 13.00
31k A4 2h violet 9.00 9.00
Never hinged 18.00
32k A4 3h olive 6.50 6.50
Never hinged 13.00
33k A4 5h dark green 6.50 6.50
Never hinged 13.00
34k A4 6h brown 10.50 10.50
Never hinged 21.00
35k A4 10h carmine 12.00 12.00
Never hinged 24.00
36k A4 20h dark brown 14.50 14.50
Never hinged 29.00
37k A4 25h deep blue 29.00 29.00
Never hinged 57.50
38k A4 30h green 32.50 32.50
Never hinged 65.00
39k A4 35h myrtle green 23.00 .2300
Never hinged 45.00
40k A4 40h orange red 22.50 22.50
Never hinged 45.00
41k A4 45h brown red 30.00 30.00
Never hinged 60.00
42k A4 50h dull violet 24.00 24.00
Never hinged 47.50
43k A5 1k maroon 55.00 55.00
Never hinged 110.00
44k A5 2k gray green 140.00 140.00
Never hinged 275.00
45k A5 5k dull blue 140.00 140.00
Never hinged 275.00
Nos. 30k-45k (16) 561.50 538.73

Perf. 10½, 12½ and 9¼ Compound

30l A4 1h black 4.50 4.50
Never hinged 9.00
31l A4 2h violet 6.50 6.50
Never hinged 13.00
32l A4 3h olive 5.25 5.25
Never hinged 10.50
33l A4 5h dark green 6.50 6.50
Never hinged 13.00
34l A4 6h brown 10.50 10.50
Never hinged 21.00
35l A4 10h carmine 12.00 12.00
Never hinged 24.00
36l A4 20h dark brown 14.50 14.50
Never hinged 29.00
37l A4 25h deep blue 27.50 27.50
Never hinged 55.00
38l A4 30h green 32.50 32.50
Never hinged 65.00
39l A4 35h myrtle green 32.50 32.50
Never hinged 65.00
40l A4 40h orange red 32.50 32.50
Never hinged 65.00
41l A4 45h brown red 35.00 35.00
Never hinged 70.00
42l A4 50h dull violet 35.00 35.00
Never hinged 70.00
43l A5 1k maroon 52.50 52.50
Never hinged 105.00
44l A5 2k gray green 130.00 130.00
Never hinged 140.00
45l A5 5k dull blue 625.00 625.00
Never hinged 1,250.
Nos. 30l-45l (16) 1,062. 1,062.

For overprint and surcharges see Nos. 126, B1-B4, Yugoslavia Nos. 1L38, 1LB5-1LB7.

Birthday Jubilee Issue

Designs of 1906 Issue, with "1830-1910" in Label at Bottom

1910 *Perf. 12½*

46 A4 1h black .40 .40
Never hinged 1.50
On cover 57.50
47 A4 2h violet .40 .40
Never hinged 1.50
On cover 37.50
48 A4 3h olive .40 .40
Never hinged 1.50
On cover 37.50
49 A4 5h dark green .40 .40
Never hinged 1.50
On cover 11.00
50 A4 6h orange brn .40 .40
Never hinged 2.25
On cover 67.50
51 A4 10h carmine .75 .25
Never hinged 2.25
On cover 11.00
52 A4 20h dark brown 1.50 2.25
Never hinged 4.50
On cover 110.00
53 A4 25h deep blue 2.25 3.75
Never hinged 7.50
On cover 130.00
54 A4 30h green 2.25 3.75
Never hinged 7.50
On cover 190.00
55 A4 35h myrtle grn 2.25 3.75
Never hinged 7.50
On cover 190.00
56 A4 40h orange red 2.25 3.75
Never hinged 7.50
On cover 210.00
57 A4 45h brown red 3.00 7.50
Never hinged 11.00
On cover 260.00
58 A4 50h dull violet 3.75 7.50
Never hinged 15.00
On cover 375.00
59 A5 1k maroon 4.50 7.50
Never hinged 15.00
On cover 750.00
60 A5 2k gray green 15.00 52.50
Never hinged 52.50
On cover —
61 A5 5k dull blue 1.50 9.00
Never hinged 4.50
On cover —
Nos. 46-61 (16) 41.00 103.50

80th birthday of Emperor Franz Josef. For overprints, see Yugoslavia Nos. 1L1-1L16.

Scenic Type of 1906

Views: 12h, Jaice. 60h, Konjica. 72h, Vishegrad.

1912

62 A4 12h ultra 5.25 6.75
Never hinged 13.50
On cover 110.00
63 A4 60h dull blue 3.00 4.50
Never hinged 7.50
On cover 190.00
64 A4 72h carmine 11.00 22.50
Never hinged 32.50
On cover 410.00
Nos. 62-64 (3) 19.25 33.75

Value, imperf set: hinged $110; never hinged $210.

See Austria for similar designs inscribed "FELDPOST" instead of "MILITARPOST."

Emperor Franz Josef
A23 A24

A25

A26

1912-14 Various Frames

No.	Design	Description	Unused	Used
65	A23	1h olive green	.40	.25
		Never hinged	1.50	
		On cover		5.25
66	A23	2h brt blue	.40	.25
		Never hinged	1.50	
		On cover		5.25
67	A23	3h claret	.40	.25
		Never hinged	1.50	
		On cover		5.25
68	A23	5h green	.40	.25
		Never hinged	1.50	
		On cover		1.90
69	A23	6h dark gray	.40	.25
		Never hinged	1.50	
		On cover		11.00
70	A23	10h rose car	.40	.25
		Never hinged	1.50	
		On cover		1.90
71	A23	12h dp olive grn	.55	.40
		Never hinged	2.25	
		On cover		19.00
72	A23	20h orange brn	2.75	.25
		Never hinged	10.00	
		On cover		11.00
73	A23	25h ultra	1.50	.25
		Never hinged	6.00	
		On cover		11.00
74	A23	30h orange red	1.50	.25
		Never hinged	6.00	
		On cover		26.00
75	A24	35h myrtle grn	1.50	.25
		Never hinged	7.50	
		On cover		22.50
76	A24	40h dk violet	4.50	.25
		Never hinged	22.50	
		On cover		19.00
77	A24	45h olive brn	2.25	.40
		Never hinged	12.50	
		On cover		37.50
78	A24	50h slate blue	2.25	.25
		Never hinged	15.00	
		On cover		30.00
79	A24	60h brown vio	1.50	.25
		Never hinged	7.50	
		On cover		30.00
80	A24	72h dark blue	3.25	*5.25*
		Never hinged	9.00	
		On cover		190.00
81	A25	1k brn vio, *straw*	8.25	.75
		Never hinged	32.50	
		On cover		225.00
82	A25	2k dk gray, *bl*	7.50	.75
		Never hinged	22.50	
		On cover		—
83	A26	3k carmine, *grn*	8.25	*11.00*
		Never hinged	52.50	
		On cover		—
84	A26	5k dk vio, *gray*	15.00	*30.00*
		Never hinged	67.50	
		On cover		—
85	A25	10k dk ultra, *gray* ('14)	90.00	*125.00*
		Never hinged	210.00	
		On cover		—
		Nos. 65-85 (21)	152.95	176.80

Value, imperf set: hinged $325; never hinged $675.

For overprints and surcharges see Nos. 127, B5-B8, Austria M1-M21.

A27

A28

1916-17 *Perf. 12½*

No.	Design	Description	Unused	Used
86	A27	3h dark gray	.25	*.40*
		Never hinged	.75	
		On cover		19.00
87	A27	5h olive green	.30	*.60*
		Never hinged	1.10	
		On cover		7.50
88	A27	6h violet	.60	*.75*
		Never hinged	1.50	
		On cover		22.50
89	A27	10h olive brown	2.25	*3.00*
		Never hinged	6.00	
		On cover		15.00
a.		10h bister	2.25	3.75
		Never hinged	6.00	
		On cover		19.00
90	A27	12h blue gray	.75	*1.10*
		Never hinged	2.25	
		On cover		22.50
91	A27	15h car rose	.25	.25
		Never hinged	.40	
		On cover		5.25
92	A27	20h brown	.75	*1.10*
		Never hinged	2.25	
		On cover		30.00
93	A27	25h blue	.75	*1.10*
		Never hinged	2.25	
		On cover		30.00
94	A27	30h dark green	.75	*1.10*
		Never hinged	2.25	
		On cover		37.50
95	A27	40h vermilion	.75	*1.10*
		Never hinged	2.25	
		On cover		45.00
96	A27	50h green	.75	*1.10*
		Never hinged	3.00	
		On cover		45.00
97	A27	60h lake	.75	*1.10*
		Never hinged	3.00	
		On cover		75.00
98	A27	80h orange brn	3.75	1.50
		Never hinged	11.00	
		On cover		150.00
a.		Perf. 11½	3.75	*7.50*
		Never hinged	11.00	
		On cover		300.00
99	A27	90h dark violet	3.00	*1.90*
		Never hinged	9.00	
		On cover		300.00
a.		Perf. 11½	1,050.	—
		Never hinged	1,850.	
101	A28	2k claret, *straw*	1.90	*3.00*
		Never hinged	6.00	
		On cover		—
102	A28	3k green, *bl*	2.25	*3.75*
		Never hinged	7.50	
		On cover		—
103	A28	4k carmine, *grn*	7.50	*13.50*
		Never hinged	22.50	
		On cover		—
104	A28	10k dp vio, *gray*	19.00	*37.50*
		Never hinged	37.50	
		On cover		—
		Nos. 86-104 (18)	46.30	73.85

Value, imperf set: hinged $260; never hinged $525.

For overprints see Nos. B11-B12.

Emperor Karl I

A29 A30

1917 *Perf. 12½*

No.	Design	Description	Unused	Used
105	A29	3h olive gray	.25	*.30*
		Never hinged	.60	
		On cover		12.50
a.		Perf. 11½	110.00	*240.00*
		Never hinged	260.00	
		On cover		—
b.		Perf. 12½x11½	22.50	*52.50*
		Never hinged	45.00	
		On cover		—
106	A29	5h olive green	.25	*.30*
		Never hinged	.40	
		On cover		4.50
107	A29	6h violet	.40	*.90*
		Never hinged	2.25	
		On cover		27.50
108	A29	10h orange brn	.25	.25
		Never hinged	.40	
		On cover		3.00
a.		Perf. 11½x12½	190.00	*260.00*
		Never hinged	325.00	
		On cover		—
b.		Perf. 11½	260.00	*560.00*
		Never hinged	525.00	
		On cover		—
109	A29	12h blue	.40	*.90*
		Never hinged	3.00	
		On cover		29.00
110	A29	15h brt rose	.25	.25
		Never hinged	.75	
		On cover		4.50
111	A29	20h red brown	.25	.25
		Never hinged	.75	
		On cover		11.00
112	A29	25h ultra	.75	*.75*
		Never hinged	3.75	
		On cover		22.50
113	A29	30h gray green	.40	*.40*
		Never hinged	3.00	
		On cover		47.50
114	A29	40h olive bis	.40	*.40*
		Never hinged	2.25	
		On cover		15.00
115	A29	50h dp green	.75	*.75*
		Never hinged	3.75	
		On cover		40.00
116	A29	60h car rose	.55	*.75*
		Never hinged	3.75	
		On cover		45.00
a.		Perf. 11½	26.00	*60.00*
		Never hinged	40.00	
		On cover		—
117	A29	80h steel blue	.40	*.65*
		Never hinged	1.50	
		On cover		135.00
118	A29	90h dull violet	1.10	*1.90*
		Never hinged	7.50	
		On cover		190.00
119	A30	2k carmine, *straw*	1.50	.75
		Never hinged	11.00	
		On cover		300.00
120	A30	3k green, *bl*	21.00	*24.00*
		Never hinged	75.00	
		On cover		—
121	A30	4k carmine, *grn*	7.50	*15.00*
		Never hinged	30.00	
		On cover		—
122	A30	10k dp violet, *gray*	3.75	*13.50*
		Never hinged	15.00	
		On cover		—
		Nos. 105-122 (18)	40.15	*62.00*

Value, imperf set: hinged $190; never hinged $375.

Nos. 47 and 66 Overprinted in Red

1918

No.	Design	Description	Unused	Used
126	A4	2h violet	.50	*1.50*
		Never hinged	1.50	
		On cover		45.00
b.		Inverted overprint	37.50	
		Never hinged	60.00	
d.		Double overprint	19.00	
		Never hinged	30.00	
f.		Double overprint, one inverted	30.00	
		Never hinged	60.00	
127	A23	2h bright blue	.50	*1.50*
		Never hinged	1.50	
		On cover		45.00
a.		Pair, one without overprint	—	
b.		Inverted overprint	15.00	
		Never hinged	30.00	
c.		Double overprint	11.00	
		Never hinged	26.00	
d.		Double overprint, one inverted	22.50	
		Never hinged	45.00	

Emperor Karl I — A31

1918 Typo. *Perf. 12½, Imperf.*

No.	Design	Description	Unused	Used
128	A31	2h orange	11.00	
		Never hinged	26.00	
129	A31	3h dark green	11.00	
		Never hinged	26.00	
130	A31	5h lt green	11.00	
		Never hinged	26.00	
131	A31	6h blue green	11.00	
		Never hinged	26.00	
132	A31	10h brown	11.00	
		Never hinged	26.00	
133	A31	20h brick red	11.00	
		Never hinged	26.00	
134	A31	25h ultra	11.00	
		Never hinged	26.00	
135	A31	45h dk slate	11.00	
		Never hinged	26.00	
136	A31	50h lt bluish grn	11.00	
		Never hinged	26.00	
137	A31	60h blue violet	11.00	
		Never hinged	26.00	
138	A31	70h ocher	11.00	
		Never hinged	26.00	
139	A31	80h rose	11.00	
		Never hinged	26.00	
140	A31	90h violet brn	11.00	
		Never hinged	26.00	

Engr.

No.	Design	Description	Unused	Used
141	A30	1k ol grn, *grnsh*	*1,900.*	
		Never hinged	*3,000.*	
		Nos. 128-140 (13)	143.00	

Nos. 128-141 were prepared for use in Bosnia and Herzegovina, but were not issued there. They were sold after the Armistice at the Vienna post office for a few days.

Nos. 128-141 exist imperf. Values: Nos. 128-140, hinged $190, never hinged $325; No. 141, hinged $1,900, never hinged $3,000.

SEMI-POSTAL STAMPS

Nos. 33 and 35 Surcharged in Red

Type 1

Type 2

Type 3

1914, Nov. 1 Unwmk. *Perf. 12½*

No.	Design	Description	Unused	Used
B1	A4	7h on 5h dk grn (1)	.40	*.75*
		Never hinged	.75	
		On cover		22.50
a.		Type 2	1.50	*3.75*
		Never hinged	4.50	
		On cover		67.50
b.		Type 3	11.00	*30.00*
		Never hinged	32.50	
		On cover		135.00
B2	A4	12h on 10h car (1)	.40	*.75*
		Never hinged	.75	
		On cover		22.50
a.		Type 2	1.50	*3.75*
		Never hinged	4.50	
		On cover		67.50
b.		Type 3	11.00	*30.00*
		Never hinged	32.50	
		On cover		135.00

Nos. B1-B2 exist with double and inverted surcharges. Values, double surcharge, each: unused $22.50, never hinged $37.50. Values, inverted surcharge, each: unused $26, never hinged $45.

Nos. 33, 35 Surcharged in Red or Blue

1915, July 10 *Perf. 12½*

No.	Design	Description	Unused	Used
B3	A4	7h on 5h (R)	12.00	*19.00*
		Never hinged	26.00	
		On cover		92.50
a.		Perf. 9¼	240.00	*275.00*
		Never hinged	500.00	
		On cover		—
B4	A4	12h on 10h (Bl)	.40	*.55*
		Never hinged	2.25	
		On cover		45.00

Nos. B3-B4 exist with double and inverted surcharges. Value about $30 each.

Nos. 68, 70 Surcharged in Red or Blue

The overprint on Nos. B5-B6 is found in four types, differing in length of surcharge lines:

I — date 18mm, denomination 14mm.
II — date 16mm, denomination 14mm.
III — date 18mm, denomination 16mm.
IV — date 16mm, denomination 16mm.

1915, Dec. 1

No.	Design	Description	Unused	Used
B5	A23	7h on 5h (R) (I)	.75	*2.10*
		Never hinged	2.25	
		On cover		45.00
a.		"1915" at top and bottom	37.50	*67.50*
		Never hinged	67.50	
b.		Type II	.75	2.25
		Never hinged	2.25	
		On cover		45.00
B6	A23	12h on 10h (Bl) (II)	1.50	*5.25*
		Never hinged	4.50	
		On cover		45.00
a.		Surcharged "7 Heller."	37.50	*75.00*
		Never hinged	67.50	
b.		Type I	22.50	*37.50*
		Never hinged	45.00	
		On cover		110.00
c.		Type III	1.40	*4.25*
		Never hinged	3.75	
		On cover		52.50

d.	Type IV	37.50	*100.00*
	Never hinged	75.00	
	On cover		150.00

Nos. B5-B6 exist with double and inverted surcharges. Values, each: unused $22.50, never hinged $37.50.

Nos. B5a and B6a exist double and inverted. Value: each, $750.

Nos. 68, 70 Surcharged in Red or Blue

The overprint on Nos. B7-B8 is found in two types, differing in length of surcharge lines:
I — date 18mm, denomination 14mm.
II — date 16mm, denomination 14mm.

1916, Feb. 1

B7	A23 7h on 5h (R) (I)	.75	*.75*
	Never hinged	1.50	
	On cover		45.00
a.	Type II	.75	*1.10*
	Never hinged	1.50	
	On cover		45.00
B8	A23 12h on 10h (Bl) (I)	.75	*.75*
	Never hinged	1.50	
	On cover		45.00
a.	Type II	.75	*.75*
	Never hinged	1.40	
	On cover		45.00

Nos. B7-B8 exist with double and inverted surcharges. Values: double surcharge, each $19 unused, $37.50 never hinged; inverted surcharge, each $15 unused, $30 never hinged.

Wounded Soldier — SP1

Blind Soldier — SP2

1916, July 10 **Engr.**

B9	SP1 5h (+ 2h) green	.85	*1.90*
	Never hinged	2.25	
	On cover		67.50
B10	SP2 10h (+ 2h) magenta	1.50	*2.60*
	Never hinged	3.75	
	On cover		67.50

Nos. B9-B10 exist imperf. Value, set: hinged $110, never hinged $225. For overprints, see Yugoslavia Nos. 1LB3-1LB4.

Nos. 89, 89a, 91 Overprinted

1917, May 9

B11	A27 10h bister (#89a)	.25	*.25*
	Never hinged	.30	
	On cover		55.00
a.	On 10h olive brown (#89)	3.75	*13.50*
	Never hinged	15.00	
	On cover		110.00
B12	A27 15h carmine rose	.25	*.50*
	Never hinged	.30	
	On cover		7.50

Nos. B11-B12 exist imperf. Value, set: hinged $150, never hinged $225.

Nos. B11-B12 exist with double and inverted overprint. Values: double surcharge, each $15 unused, $30 never hinged; inverted surcharge, each $22.50 unused, $45 never hinged.

Design for Memorial Church at Sarajevo SP3

Archduke Francis Ferdinand — SP4

Duchess Sophia and Archduke Francis Ferdinand SP5

1917, June 20 **Typo.** ***Perf. 12½***

B13	SP3 10h violet black	.35	*.40*
	Never hinged	.55	
	On cover		82.50
a.	Perf 11½	1.90	11.00
	Never hinged	13.50	
	On cover		150.00
B14	SP4 15h claret	.35	*.40*
	Never hinged	.55	
	On cover		65.00
a.	Perf 11½	1.90	11.00
	Never hinged	13.50	
	On cover		110.00
B15	SP5 40h deep blue	.25	*.40*
	Never hinged	.35	
	On cover		50.00
a.	Perf 11½	1.90	11.00
	Never hinged	13.50	
	On cover		110.00
	Nos. B13-B15 (3)	.95	1.20

Assassination of Archduke Ferdinand and Archduchess Sophia. Sold at a premium of 2h each, which helped build a memorial church at Sarajevo.

Exist imperf. Value, set: hinged $35; never hinged $90.

Blind Soldier — SP6

Design: 15h, Wounded soldier.

1918, Mar. 1 **Engr.** ***Perf. 12½***

B16	SP6 10h (+ 10h) grnsh bl	.65	*1.50*
	Never hinged	1.90	
	On cover		65.00
B17	SP6 15h (+ 10h) red brn	.65	*1.50*
	Never hinged	1.90	
	On cover		65.00

Nos. B16-B17 exist imperf. Value, set: hinged $67.50; never hinged $125. For overprints, see Yugoslavia Nos. 1LB1-1LB2.

Emperor Karl I — SP8

Design: 15h, Empress Zita.

1918, July 20 **Typo.** ***Perf. 12½x13***

B18	SP8 10h gray green	.50	*1.25*
	Never hinged	1.50	
	On cover		95.00
B19	SP8 15h brown red	.50	*1.25*
	Never hinged	1.50	
	On cover		95.00
B20	SP8 40h violet	.50	*1.25*
	Never hinged	1.50	
	On cover		95.00
	Nos. B18-B20 (3)	1.50	*3.75*

Sold at a premium of 10h each which went to the "Karl's Fund."

Nos. B18-B20 exist imperf. Value, set: hinged $75; never hinged $150.

POSTAGE DUE STAMPS

D1

1904 **Unwmk.** ***Perf. 12½***

J1	D1 1h black, red & yel	.75	.30
	Never hinged	1.40	
	On cover		130.00
J2	D1 2h black, red & yel	.75	.30
	Never hinged	1.40	
	On cover		130.00
J3	D1 3h black, red & yel	.75	.30
	Never hinged	1.40	
	On cover		130.00
J4	D1 4h black, red & yel	.75	.30
	Never hinged	1.40	
	On cover		225.00
J5	D1 5h black, red & yel	3.75	.30
	Never hinged	7.50	
	On cover		95.00
J6	D1 6h black, red & yel	.75	.30
	Never hinged	1.40	
	On cover		150.00
J7	D1 7h black, red & yel	5.25	*3.75*
	Never hinged	11.00	
	On cover		225.00
J8	D1 8h black, red & yel	5.25	2.25
	Never hinged	11.00	
	On cover		190.00
J9	D1 10h black, red & yel	.75	.30
	Never hinged	2.25	
	On cover		75.00
J10	D1 15h black, red & yel	.75	.30
	Never hinged	2.25	
	On cover		130.00
J11	D1 20h black, red & yel	6.00	.30
	Never hinged	11.00	
	On cover		95.00
J12	D1 50h black, red & yel	3.00	.40
	Never hinged	6.00	
	On cover		550.00
J13	D1 200h black, red & grn	26.00	3.00
	Never hinged	47.50	
	On cover		—
	Nos. J1-J13 (13)	54.50	12.10
	Set, never hinged	105.00	

For overprints and surcharges see Western Ukraine Nos. 61-72, Yugoslavia Nos. 1LJ23-1LJ26.

Perf. 12½x13

J1a	D1 1h black, red & yel	1.20	.80
	Never hinged	2.40	
J2a	D1 2h black, red & yel	.80	.80
	Never hinged	1.60	
J3a	D1 3h black, red & yel	.80	.80
	Never hinged	1.60	
J4a	D1 4h black, red & yel	.80	.80
	Never hinged	1.60	
J5a	D1 5h black, red & yel	3.50	.55
	Never hinged	7.25	
J6a	D1 6h black, red & yel	.80	.40
	Never hinged	1.60	
J7a	D1 7h black, red & yel	4.75	*4.75*
	Never hinged	9.50	
J8a	D1 8h black, red & yel	4.75	2.00
	Never hinged	9.50	
J9a	D1 10h black, red & yel	1.20	.40
	Never hinged	2.40	
J10a	D1 15h black, red & yel	1.20	.40
	Never hinged	2.40	
J11a	D1 20h black, red & yel	7.25	.80
	Never hinged	14.50	
J12a	D1 50h black, red & yel	3.25	.80
	Never hinged	6.50	
J13a	D1 200h black, red & grn	27.50	3.25
	Never hinged	55.00	
	Nos. J1a-J13a (13)	57.80	16.55
	Set, never hinged	115.00	

Perf. 13¼x13

J1b	D1 1h black, red & yel	2.40	2.75
	Never hinged	5.00	
J2b	D1 2h black, red & yel	.80	.55
	Never hinged	1.60	
J3b	D1 3h black, red & yel	.80	.80
	Never hinged	1.60	
J4b	D1 4h black, red & yel	.80	.55
	Never hinged	1.60	
J6b	D1 6h black, red & yel	.80	.55
	Never hinged	1.60	
J7b	D1 7h black, red & yel	4.75	*4.75*
	Never hinged	10.00	
J8b	D1 8h black, red & yel	4.75	2.00
	Never hinged	10.00	
J10b	D1 15h black, red & yel	1.20	.80
	Never hinged	2.50	
J11b	D1 20h black, red & yel	6.50	1.60
	Never hinged	13.50	
J12b	D1 50h black, red & yel	4.00	1.20
	Never hinged	8.50	
	Nos. J1b-J12b (10)	26.80	15.55
	Set, never hinged	55.00	

Perf. 10½

J1c	D1 1h black, red & yel	11.00	11.00
	Never hinged	20.00	
J2c	D1 2h black, red & yel	11.00	11.00
	Never hinged	20.00	
J4c	D1 4h black, red & yel	11.00	11.00
	Never hinged	20.00	
J5c	D1 5h black, red & yel	16.00	16.00
	Never hinged	30.00	
J6c	D1 6h black, red & yel	20.00	20.00
	Never hinged	37.50	
J7c	D1 7h black, red & yel	15.00	*15.00*
	Never hinged	27.50	
J8c	D1 8h black, red & yel	45.00	45.00
	Never hinged	85.00	
J9c	D1 10h black, red & yel	17.50	17.50
	Never hinged	32.50	
J10c	D1 15h black, red & yel	47.50	47.50
	Never hinged	90.00	
J11c	D1 20h black, red & yel	47.50	47.50
	Never hinged	90.00	
J12c	D1 50h black, red & yel	47.50	47.50
	Never hinged	90.00	
	Nos. J1c-J12c (11)	289.00	289.00
	Set, never hinged	540.00	

Perf. 9¼

J1d	D1 1h black, red & yel	4.75
	Never hinged	9.00
J2d	D1 2h black, red & yel	4.75
	Never hinged	9.00
J3d	D1 3h black, red & yel	22.50
	Never hinged	40.00
J4d	D1 4h black, red & yel	22.50
	Never hinged	40.00
J5d	D1 5h black, red & yel	22.50
	Never hinged	40.00
J6d	D1 6h black, red & yel	20.00
	Never hinged	35.00
J7d	D1 7h black, red & yel	16.00
	Never hinged	30.00
J8d	D1 8h black, red & yel	6.00
	Never hinged	10.00
J9d	D1 10h black, red & yel	13.50
	Never hinged	25.00
J10d	D1 15h black, red & yel	6.00
	Never hinged	11.00
J11d	D1 20h black, red & yel	24.00
	Never hinged	42.50
J12d	D1 50h black, red & yel	21.00
	Never hinged	40.00
J13d	D1 200h black, red & grn	25.00
	Never hinged	45.00
	Nos. J1d-J13d (13)	208.50
	Set, never hinged	335.00

Perf. 12½, 13 and 10½ Compound

J1e	D1 1h black, red & yel	12.00
	Never hinged	22.50
J2e	D1 2h black, red & yel	12.00
	Never hinged	22.50
J4e	D1 4h black, red & yel	21.00
	Never hinged	37.50
J5e	D1 5h black, red & yel	21.00
	Never hinged	37.50
J6e	D1 6h black, red & yel	21.00
	Never hinged	37.50
J7e	D1 7h black, red & yel	21.00
	Never hinged	37.50
J9e	D1 10h black, red & yel	27.50
	Never hinged	50.00
J10e	D1 15h black, red & yel	7.50
	Never hinged	13.50
J11e	D1 20h black, red & yel	65.00
	Never hinged	120.00
J12e	D1 50h black, red & yel	25.00
	Never hinged	45.00
	Nos. J1e-J12e (10)	233.00
	Set, never hinged	420.00

Perf. 12½, 13 and 9¼ Compound

J1f	D1 1h black, red & yel	22.50
	Never hinged	40.00
J2f	D1 2h black, red & yel	42.50
	Never hinged	75.00
J3f	D1 3h black, red & yel	6.00
	Never hinged	11.00
J4f	D1 4h black, red & yel	14.50
	Never hinged	25.00
J6f	D1 6h black, red & yel	11.00
	Never hinged	20.00
J8f	D1 8h black, red & yel	13.00
	Never hinged	22.50
J9f	D1 10h black, red & yel	24.00
	Never hinged	45.00
J10f	D1 15h black, red & yel	17.50
	Never hinged	32.50
J11f	D1 20h black, red & yel	21.00
	Never hinged	37.50
J12f	D1 50h black, red & yel	27.50
	Never hinged	50.00
J13f	D1 200h black, red & grn	55.00
	Never hinged	100.00
	Nos. J1f-J13f (11)	254.50
	Set, never hinged	455.00

Imperf

J1g	D1 1h black, red & yel	4.50
	Never hinged	8.00
J2g	D1 2h black, red & yel	4.50
	Never hinged	8.00
J3g	D1 3h black, red & yel	4.50
	Never hinged	8.00
J4g	D1 4h black, red & yel	4.50
	Never hinged	8.00
J5g	D1 5h black, red & yel	4.50
	Never hinged	8.00
J6g	D1 6h black, red & yel	4.50
	Never hinged	8.00
J7g	D1 7h black, red & yel	14.50
	Never hinged	25.00
J8g	D1 8h black, red & yel	16.00
	Never hinged	27.50
J9g	D1 10h black, red & yel	4.50
	Never hinged	8.00
J10g	D1 15h black, red & yel	4.50
	Never hinged	8.00
J11g	D1 20h black, red & yel	35.00
	Never hinged	62.50
J12g	D1 50h black, red & yel	15.00
	Never hinged	27.50
J13g	D1 200h black, red & grn	50.00
	Never hinged	90.00
	Nos. J1g-J13g (13)	166.50
	Set, never hinged	295.00

D2

1916-18 *Perf. 12½*

J14	D2	2h red ('18)	.40	*1.50*
		Never hinged	.60	
J15	D2	4h red ('18)	.25	*1.50*
		Never hinged	.60	
J16	D2	5h red	.40	*1.50*
		Never hinged	1.10	
J17	D2	6h red ('18)	.25	*1.50*
		Never hinged	.60	
J18	D2	10h red	.40	*1.50*
		Never hinged	.60	
		On cover		260.00
J19	D2	15h red	3.00	*9.00*
		Never hinged	6.00	
J20	D2	20h red	.40	*1.50*
		Never hinged	1.10	
		On cover		300.00
J21	D2	25h red	1.10	*3.75*
		Never hinged	3.00	
J22	D2	30h red	.90	*3.75*
		Never hinged	3.00	
		On cover		375.00
J23	D2	40h red	8.25	*21.00*
		Never hinged	26.00	
J24	D2	50h red	26.00	*62.50*
		Never hinged	62.50	
J25	D2	1k dark blue	3.75	*11.00*
		Never hinged	22.50	
J26	D2	3k dark blue	15.00	*40.00*
		Never hinged	60.00	
		Nos. J14-J26 (13)	60.10	*160.00*
		Set, never hinged	185.00	

Nos. J25-J26 have colored numerals on a white tablet.

Value, imperf. set: unused $135, never hinged $300.

For surcharges see Italy Nos. NJ1-NJ7, Yugoslavia 1LJ1-1LJ13.

NEWSPAPER STAMPS

Bosnian Girl — N1

1913 **Unwmk.** *Imperf.*

P1	N1	2h ultra	.75	*.75*
		Never hinged	1.90	
P2	N1	6h violet	2.25	*3.50*
		Never hinged	6.75	
P3	N1	10h rose	2.60	*3.50*
		Never hinged	9.00	
P4	N1	20h green	3.00	*3.75*
		Never hinged	11.00	
		Nos. P1-P4 (4)	8.60	11.50

Used values are for postally used examples. Favor-canceled stamps are valued the same as unused.

After Bosnia and Herzegovina became part of Yugoslavia, stamps of type N1 perf., and imperf. copies surcharged with new values, were used as regular postage stamps. See Yugoslavia Nos. 1L17-1L22, 1L43-1L45.

SPECIAL DELIVERY STAMPS

"Lightning" — SH1

1916 **Unwmk.** **Engr.** *Perf. 12½*

QE1	SH1	2h vermilion	.25	.75
		Never hinged	.55	
a.		Perf. 11½x12½	375.00	
		Never hinged	600.00	
QE2	SH1	5h deep green	.40	1.10
		Never hinged	1.10	
a.		Perf. 11½	15.00	37.50
		Never hinged	37.50	

Nos. QE1-QE2 exist imperf. Values, set: unused $130, never hinged $260.

For surcharges see Italy Nos. NE1-NE2, Yugoslavia Nos. 1LE1-1LE2.

BRAZIL

brə-'zil

Brasil (after 1918)

LOCATION — On the north and east coasts of South America, bordering on the Atlantic Ocean.
GOVT. — Republic
AREA — 3,286,000 sq. mi.
POP. — 132,580,000 (est. 1984)
CAPITAL — Brasilia

Brazil was an independent empire from 1822 to 1889, when a constitution was adopted and the country became officially known as The United States of Brazil.

1000 Reis = 1 Milreis

> Values for unused stamps are for examples with original gum as defined in the catalogue introduction except for Nos. 1-98, which are valued without gum. Nos. 1-52 with original gum command a substantial premium (up to 100%). Nos. 53-78 with original gum command a premium of up to 50%. Nos. 79-98 with original gum command a premium of 10%-25%.

Watermarks

Wmk. 97 "CORREIO FEDERAL REPUBLICA DOS ESTADOS UNIDOS DO BRAZIL" in Sheet

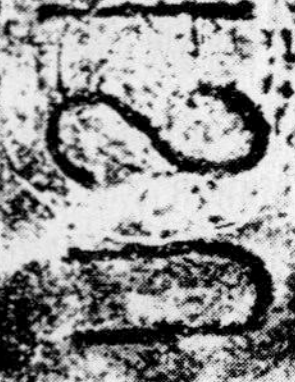

Wmk. 98 "IMPOSTO DE CONSUMO REPUBLICA DOS ESTADOS UNIDOS DO BRAZIL" in Sheet

Wmk. 99 — "CORREIO"

Wmk. 100 — "CASA DA MOEDA" in Sheet

Because of the spacing of this watermark, a few stamps in each sheet may show no watermark.

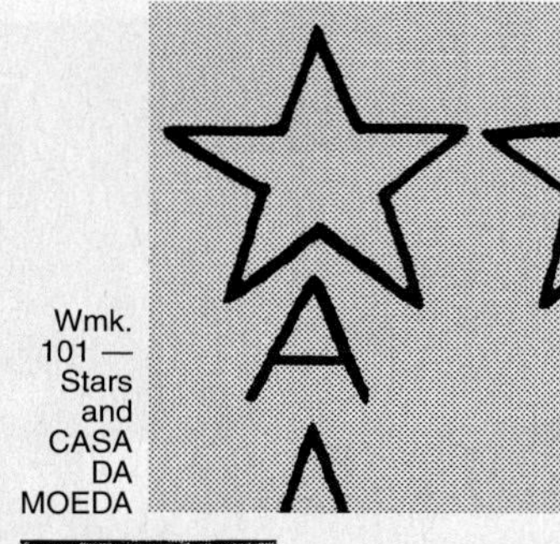

Wmk. 101 — Stars and CASA DA MOEDA

Wmk. 116 — Crosses and Circles

Wmk. 127 — Quatrefoils

Wmk. 193 — ESTADOS UNIDOS DO BRASIL

Wmk. 206 — Star-framed CM, Multiple

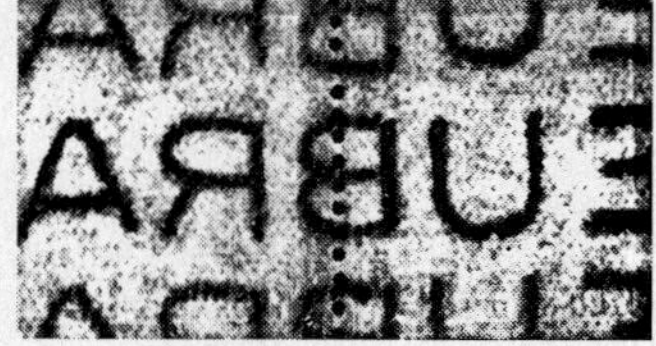

Wmk. 218 — E U BRASIL Multiple, Letters 8mm High

Wmk. 221 ESTADOS UNIDOS DO BRASIL, Multiple, Letters 6mm High

Wmk. 222 — CORREIO BRASIL and 5 Stars in Squared Circle

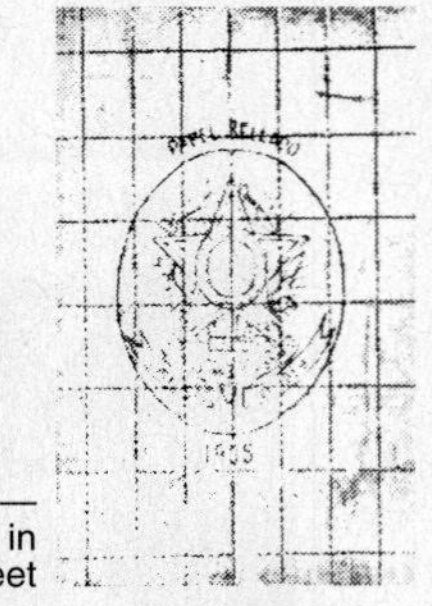

Wmk. 236 — Coat of Arms in Sheet

Watermark (reduced illustration) covers 22 stamps in sheet.

Wmk. 245 — Multiple "CASA DA MOEDA DO BRASIL" and Small Formee Cross

Wmk. 249 — "CORREIO BRASIL" multiple

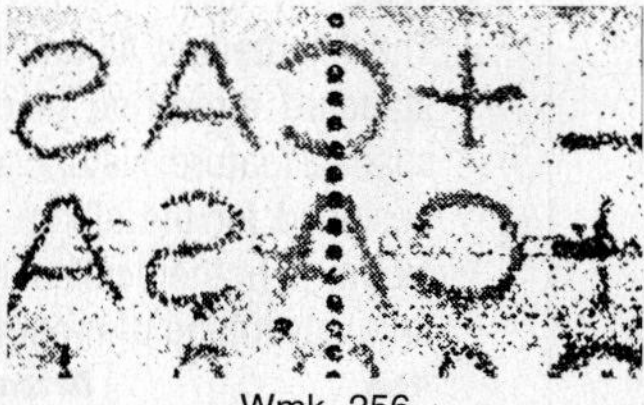

Wmk. 256 "CASA+DA+MOEDA+DO+BRAZIL" in 8mm Letters

Wmk. 264 — "*CORREIO*BRASIL*" Multiple, Letters 7mm High

GREAT BRITAIN POST OFFICES IN BRAZIL

PRE-STAMP POSTAL MARKINGS

Crowned Circle handstamp type IX is pictured in the Crowned Circle Handstamps and Great Britain Used Abroad section.

Bahia

1851, Jan. 6

A1	IX	Crowned circle handstamp, on cover	*3,000.*
A2	IX	Crowned circle handstamp, in red, on cover	*5,500.*
A3	IX	Crowned circle handstamp, in green, on cover	—

Pernambuco

A4	IX	Crowned circle handstamp, on cover	*6,250.*
A5	IX	Crowned circle handstamp, in red, on cover	3,000.

Rio de Janeiro

A6	IX	Crowned circle handstamp, on cover	*2,900.*
A7	IX	Crowned circle handstamp, in red, on cover	800.
A8	IX	Crowned circle handstamp, in green, on cover	—

STAMPS OF GREAT BRITAIN USED IN BRAZIL

> Values are for clear cancellations on sound, fault-free stamps, with average to fine centering. In many cases, very fine examples are rare or non-existent.

1860-73

Numeral Cancellation Type B, C81 (Bahia)

A9	A	1p	rose red (#33, P90, 93, 96, 108, 113, 117, 135, 140, 147, 155) (from)	50.00
A10	A	1½p	lake red (#32, P3)	125.00
A11	A	2p	blue (#29, P9, 12)	85.00
A12	A	2p	bl (#30, P13-14) (from)	75.00
A13	A	3p	rose (#44)	—
A14	A	3p	rose (#49, P4, 6, 8-10) (from)	60.00
A15	A	3p	rose (#61, P11)	—
A16	A	4p	ver (#43, P8-13) (from)	55.00
A17	A	6p	lilac (#45, P5)	—
A18	A	6p	dull violet (#50, P6)	160.00
A19	A	6p	red vio (#51, P8-9) (from)	80.00
A20	A	6p	pale buff (#59b, P11-12) (from)	110.00
	a.		6p brown (#59, P11)	110.00
A21	A	6p	gray (#60, P12)	—
A22	A	6p	gray (#62, P13)	—
A23	A	9p	straw (#46)	475.00
A24	A	9p	bister (#52)	275.00
A25	A	1sh	green (#48)	190.00
A26	A	1sh	green (#54, P4-6) (from)	55.00
			Plate 7	55.00
A27	A	1sh	deep green (#64a, P8-9) (from)	95.00
A28	A	2sh	blue (#55)	300.00
A29	A	5sh	rose (#57, P1)	550.00

Numeral Cancellation Type B, C82 (Pernambuco)

No. A48

A30	A	1p	rose red (#33, P85, 108, 111, 130-132, 149, 157, 159, 160, 187(from)	50.00
A31	A	2p	blue (#29, P9, 12)	60.00
A32	A	2p	blue (#30, P13-14) (from)	60.00
A33	A	3p	rose (#44)	125.00
A34	A	3p	rose (#49, P4-7, 10) (from)	60.00
A35	A	3p	rose (#61, P11)	—
A36	A	4p	vermilion (#43, P9-14) (from)	55.00
A37	A	6p	lilac (#45, P5-6)	—
A38	A	6p	dull violet (#50, P6)	90.00
A39	A	6p	red violet (#51, P8-9) (from)	80.00
A40	A	6p	brown (#59, P11)	90.00
	a.		6p pale buff (#59b, P11-12)	60.00
A41	A	6p	gray (#60, P12)	—
A42	A	9p	straw (#46)	475.00
A43	A	9p	bister (#52)	250.00
A44	A	10p	red brown (#53)	325.00
A45	A	1sh	green (#48)	190.00
A46	A	1sh	green (#54, P4-6) (from)	55.00
			Plate 7	55.00
A47	A	2sh	blue (#55)	275.00
A48	A	5sh	rose (#57, P1)	550.00

Numeral Cancellation Type B, C83 (Rio de Janeiro)

A49	A	1p	rose red (#20)	50.00
A50	A	1p	rose red (#33, P71, 76, 80, 82, 86, 94, 103, 113, 117, 119, 123, 130, 132, 134-135, 146, 148, 159, 161, 166, 185, 200, 204 (from)	42.50
A51	A	2p	blue (#29, P9, 12)	42.50

A52 A 2p blue (#30, P13-14) (from) 42.50
A53 A 3p rose (#49, P4-8) (from) 50.00
A54 A 3p rose (#61, P11) —
A55 A 4p vermilion (#43, P8-13) (from) 55.00
A56 A 6p lilac (#45, P5) 110.00
A57 A 6p dull violet (#50, P6) 82.50
A58 A 6p red violet (#51, P8-9) 77.50
A59 A 6p brown (#59, P11) 82.50
a. 6p pale buff (#59b, P11) 50.00
A60 A 6p gray (#60, P12) —
A61 A 9p straw (#46) 450.00
A62 A 9p bister (#52) 225.00
A63 A 10p red brown (#53) 300.00
A64 A 1sh green (#48) 150.00
A65 A 1sh green (#54, P4-6) (from) 50.00
Plate 7 90.00
A66 A 1sh green (#64, P8-9) (from) 80.00
A67 A 2sh blue (#55) 150.00
A68 A 5sh rose (#57, P1) 550.00
Plate 2 700.00

ISSUES OF THE EMPIRE

A1

Fine Impressions
Grayish or Yellowish Paper
Unwmk.

1843, Aug. 1 **Engr.** ***Imperf.***
1 A1 30r black 4,500. 550.
On cover 11,000.
On cover, single franking 16,500.
c. Pair, #1-2 950,000.
d. Strip of 3, 2 #1, 1 #2 850,000.
2 A1 60r black 600. 275.
On cover 9,000.
3 A1 90r black 4,000. 1,300.
On cover 14,000.
On cover, single franking 30,000.

Nos. 1-3b were issued with gum, but very few unused examples retain even a trace of their original gum. Stamps with original gum command substantial premiums.

Fine impressions are true black and have background lathework complete.

Most examples of Nos. 1-3b are printed on yellowish or grayish paper. They also exist on white paper, usually thin and somewhat translucent. Such examples are scarce and command premiums.

Nos. 1c and 1d are each unique.

Intermediate Impressions

1a A1 30r 4,250. 525.
On cover 10,500.
On cover, single franking 16,500.
2a A1 60r 1,100. 275.
On cover 8,500.
3a A1 90r 3,750. 1,300.
On cover 13,000.
On cover, single franking 30,000.

Intermediate impressions are grayish black and have weaker lathework in the background.

Worn Impressions

1b A1 30r 4,000. 500.
On cover, pair 10,000.
On cover, single franking 16,500.
2b A1 60r 1,000. 250.
On cover 8,000.
3b A1 90r 3,500. 1,250.
On cover 12,000.
On cover, single franking 30,000.

Worn impressions have white areas in the background surrounding the numerals due to plate wear affecting especially the lathework.

A2

Grayish or Yellowish Paper

1844-46
7 A2 10r black 125.00 25.00
On cover 275.00
On cover, single franking —
8 A2 30r black 145.00 35.00
On cover 300.00
9 A2 60r black 125.00 25.00
On cover 250.00
10 A2 90r black 1,000. 120.00
On cover 750.00
11 A2 180r black 4,500. 1,800.
On cover 11,000.
12 A2 300r black 6,500. 2,000.
On cover 16,000.
13 A2 600r black 6,000. 2,200.
On cover —

Nos. 8, 9 and 10 exist on thick paper and are considerably scarcer.

A3

Grayish or Yellowish Paper

1850, Jan. 1
21 A3 10r black 30.00 35.00
On cover 300.00
On cover, single franking —
22 A3 20r black 92.50 120.00
On cover 575.00
23 A3 30r black 12.00 3.50
On cover 60.00
24 A3 60r black 12.00 3.00
On cover 30.00
25 A3 90r black 110.00 14.50
On cover 120.00
26 A3 180r black 115.00 65.00
On cover 650.00
27 A3 300r black 400.00 72.50
On cover 550.00
28 A3 600r black 500.00 110.00
On cover 1,500.

No. 22 used is generally found precanceled with a single horizontal line in pen or blue crayon or with two diagonal pen lines. Value precanceled without gum, $75.

All values except the 90r were reprinted in 1910 on very thick paper.

1854
37 A3 10r blue 14.50 12.00
On cover 400.00
On cover, single franking 450.00
a. 10r pale blue 17.50 17.50
On cover 450.00
b. 10r steel blue 85.00 50.00
On cover 750.00
38 A3 30r blue 40.00 65.00
On cover 500.00
a. 30r dark blue 70.00 50.00
On cover 500.00
b. 30r steel blue 400.00 100.00
On cover 750.00

A4

1861
39 A4 280r red 160.00 110.00
No gum 100.00
On cover 750.00
40 A4 430r yellow 200.00 160.00
No gum 160.00
On cover 1,500.

Nos. 39-40 have been reprinted on thick white paper with white gum. They are printed in aniline inks and the colors are brighter than those of the originals.

1866 ***Perf. 13½***
42 A3 10r blue 125.00 150.00
On cover —
43 A3 20r black 1,100. 500.00
On cover —
44 A3 30r black 350.00 190.00
On cover 600.00
45 A3 30r blue 800.00 925.00
On cover —

46 A3 60r black 140.00 30.00
On cover 600.00
47 A3 90r black 725.00 350.00
On cover 675.00
48 A3 180r black 925.00 350.00
On cover —
49 A4 280r red 800.00 850.00
On cover 2,500.
50 A3 300r black 750.00 400.00
On cover —
51 A4 430r yellow 725.00 425.00
On cover 4,000.
52 A3 600r black 725.00 300.00
On cover 3,250.

Fraudulent perforations abound. Purchases should be accompanied by certificates of authenticity.

A 10r black is questioned.

A5

A6

A7

A8

A8a

A9

Emperor Dom Pedro — A9a

100 reis

Type I — Left frameline weak and incomplete and composed of a single line which never touches the upper ornaments.

Type II — Left frameline incomplete and composed of a double outer line which does not touch the upper ornaments.

Type III — Left frameline complete and composed of two continuous outer lines which meet the upper ornaments.

Thick or Thin White Wove Paper

1866, July 1 ***Perf. 12***
53 A5 10r vermilion 14.50 5.00
On cover 375.00
On cover, single franking 500.00
b. 10r carmine vermilion 35.00 15.00
On cover 375.00
On cover, single franking 500.00
54 A6 20r red lilac 25.00 3.50
On cover 325.00
On cover, single franking 375.00
a. 20r dull violet 80.00 30.00
On cover 400.00
On cover, single franking 500.00
56 A7 50r blue 35.00 2.50
On cover 60.00
On cover, single franking 275.00
57 A8 80r slate violet 92.50 6.00
On cover 160.00
On cover, single franking 550.00
b. 80r rose lilac 100.00 10.00
On cover 175.00
On cover, single franking 600.00

58 A8a 100r blue green, type III 35.00 1.90
On cover 25.00
a. 100r green (shades), type I 35.00 1.90
On cover 35.00
c. 100r green (shades), type II 75.00 5.00
On cover 67.50
59 A9 200r black 120.00 12.00
On cover 80.00
a. Half used as 100r on cover 1,750.
60 A9a 500r orange 250.00 35.00
On cover 425.00
Nos. 53-60 (7) 572.00 65.90

The 10r and 20r exist imperf. on both white and bluish paper. Some authorities consider them proofs.

Nos. 58 and 65 are found in three types.

Bluish Paper

53a A5 10r 600.00 500.00
On cover —
54b A6 20r 190.00 35.00
On cover —
56a A7 50r 225.00 30.00
On cover 350.00
57a A8 80r 300.00 35.00
On cover —
58b A8a 100r Type II 960.00 140.00
On cover 275.00
d. A8a 100r Type I 9,000. —
On cover —

1876-77 ***Rouletted***
61 A5 10r vermilion ('77) 72.50 35.00
On cover 275.00
On cover, single franking —
62 A6 20r red lilac ('77) 85.00 30.00
On cover 250.00
On cover, single franking 425.00
63 A7 50r blue ('77) 85.00 8.50
On cover 275.00
On cover, single franking —
64 A8 80r violet ('77) 210.00 20.00
On cover 375.00
65 A8a 100r green 50.00 1.50
On cover 50.00
66 A9 200r black ('77) 100.00 9.25
On cover 140.00
a. Half used as 100r on cover 1,000.
67 A9a 500r orange 225.00 42.50
On cover 700.00
Nos. 61-67 (7) 827.50 146.75

A10

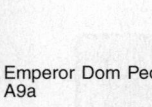

A11

A12

A13

A14

A15

A16

A17

A18

A19

A20

1878-79 *Rouletted*

68 A10 10r vermilion 14.50 3.50
On cover *275.00*
On cover, single franking 500.00
69 A11 20r violet 19.00 3.00
On cover 100.00
On cover, single franking 500.00
a. 20r dark violet 24.00 6.00
On cover 125.00
On cover, single franking 600.00
b. 20r rose lilac 17.50 5.50
On cover 125.00
On cover, single franking 600.00
70 A12 50r blue 30.00 2.00
On cover 100.00
On cover, single franking 175.00
71 A13 80r lake 35.00 10.00
On cover *375.00*
On cover, single franking *1,375.*
72 A14 100r green 35.00 1.50
On cover 35.00
73 A15 200r black 175.00 17.50
On cover 200.00
a. Half used as 100r on cover *1,000.*
74 A16 260r dk brown 100.00 27.50
On cover 550.00
75 A18 300r bister 100.00 7.25
On cover 550.00
a. One-third used as 100r on cover *10,000.*
76 A19 700r red brown 190.00 100.00
On cover *3,500.*
77 A20 1000r gray lilac 225.00 47.50
On cover 600.00
On cover, single franking *2,500.*
Nos. 68-77 (10) 923.50 219.75

1878, Aug. 21 *Perf. 12*

78 A17 300r orange & grn 100.00 25.00
On cover 600.00

Nos. 68-78 exist imperforate.

A21

A22

A23

Small Heads
Laid Paper

Perf. 13, 13½ and Compound

1881, July 15

79 A21 50r blue 140.00 23.00
On cover 165.00
On cover, single franking 375.00
80 A22 100r olive green 600.00 40.00
On cover 165.00
81 A23 200r pale red brn 600.00 140.00
On cover 250.00
a. Half used as 100r on cover *2,100.*

On Nos. 79 and 80 the hair above the ear curves forward. On Nos. 83 and 88 it is drawn backward. On the stamps of the 1881 issue the beard is smaller than in the 1882-85 issues and fills less of the space between the neck and the frame at the left.

See No. 88.

A24

A25

A26

A27

Two types each of the 100 and 200 reis.

100 REIS:

Type I — Groundwork formed of diagonal crossed lines and horizontal lines.

Type II — Groundwork formed of diagonal crossed lines and vertical lines.

200 REIS:

Type I — Groundwork formed of diagonal and horizontal lines.

Type II — Groundwork formed of diagonal crossed lines.

Larger Heads
Laid Paper

Perf. 12½ to 14 and Compound

1882-84

82 A24 10r black 12.00 *25.00*
On cover 275.00
83 A25 100r ol grn, type I 42.50 4.50
On cover 45.00
b. 100r dark green, type II 250.00 14.50
On cover 125.00
84 A26 200r pale red brn, type I 100.00 30.00
On cover 100.00
a. Half used as 100r on cover *1,300.*
85 A27 200r pale rose, type II 55.00 5.50
On cover 55.00
a. Diag. half used as 100r on cover 950.00
Nos. 82-85 (4) 209.50 65.00

See No. 86.

A28

A29

A30

Three types of A29

Type I — Groundwork of horizontal lines.

Type II — Groundwork of diagonal crossed lines.

Type III — Groundwork solid.

Perf. 13, 13½, 14 and Compound

1884-85

86 A24 10r orange 3.00 2.75
On cover 225.00
On cover, single franking 250.00
87 A28 20r slate green 35.00 3.50
On cover 275.00
a. 20r olive green 35.00 3.50
On cover 275.00
b. Half used as 10r on newspaper *3,500.*
88 A21 50r bl, head larger 35.00 3.50
On cover 60.00
On cover, single franking 115.00
90 A29 100r lilac, type I 150.00 3.00
On cover 65.00
a. 100r lilac, type II 450.00 75.00
On cover 275.00
b. 100r lilac, type III 325.00 55.00
On cover 250.00
91 A30 100r lilac 200.00 5.00
On cover 85.00
Nos. 86-91 (5) 423.00 17.75

A31

Perf. 13, 13½, 14 and Compound

1885

92 A31 100r lilac 125.00 3.00
On cover 22.50

Compare design A31 with A35.

A32

Southern Cross — A33

Crown — A34

1887

93 A32 50r chalky blue 35.00 5.00
On cover 30.00
On cover, single franking 125.00
94 A33 300r gray blue 230.00 30.00
On cover 400.00
On cover, single franking 600.00
95 A34 500r olive 140.00 14.00
On cover 275.00
On cover, single franking 450.00
Nos. 93-95 (3) 405.00 49.00

A35

A36

Entrance to Bay of Rio de Janeiro — A37

1888

96 A35 100r lilac 72.50 1.90
On cover 16.75
a. Imperf., pair 150.00 *175.00*
97 A36 700r violet 80.00 *110.00*
On cover *750.00*
98 A37 1000r dull blue 275.00 110.00
On cover *1,500.*
Nos. 96-98 (3) 427.50 221.90

Issues of the Republic

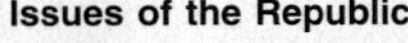

Southern Cross — A38

Wove Paper, Thin to Thick

Perf. 12½ to 14, 11 to 11½, and 12½ to 14x11 to 11½, Rough or Clean-Cut

Engraved; Typographed (#102)

1890-91

99 A38 20r gray green 2.50 1.90
On postcard 35.00
On cover, single franking 175.00
a. 20r blue green 2.50 1.90
On postcard 35.00
On cover, single franking 175.00
b. 20r emerald 19.00 7.00
On postcard 40.00
On cover, single franking 190.00
100 A38 50r gray green 6.25 1.90
On postcard 35.00
On cover, single franking 150.00
a. 50r olive green 14.00 7.00
On postcard 40.00
On cover, single franking 165.00
b. 50r yellow green 14.00 7.00
On postcard 40.00
On cover, single franking 165.00
c. 50r dark slate green 8.25 4.00
On postcard 40.00
On cover, single franking 165.00
d. Horiz. pair, imperf. btwn. —
101 A38 100r lilac rose 475.00 6.00
On cover *100.00*
102 A38 100r red lil, redrawn 30.00 1.90
On cover 20.00
a. Tete beche pair *25,000.* *19,000.*
On cover *35,000.*
103 A38 200r purple 10.00 1.90
On cover 30.00
a. 200r violet 12.00 2.50
On cover 32.50
b. 200r violet blue 27.50 3.50
On cover 35.00
c. Half used as 100r on cover 875.00
104 A38 300r dark violet 90.00 6.00
On cover 175.00
a. 300r gray 90.00 10.00
On cover 150.00
b. 300r gray blue 100.00 10.00
On cover 150.00
c. 300r slate violet 175.00 30.00
On cover 150.00
105 A38 500r olive bister 21.00 9.50
On cover 150.00
a. 500r olive gray 21.00 11.50
On cover 165.00
106 A38 500r slate 21.00 13.50
On cover 175.00
107 A38 700r fawn 19.00 *19.00*
On cover 180.00
a. 700r chocolate 24.00 26.00
On cover 180.00
108 A38 1000r bister 17.50 3.50
On cover 225.00
a. 1000r yellow buff 35.00 8.50
On cover 240.00
Nos. 99-108 (10) 692.25 65.10

The redrawn 100r may be distinguished by the absence of the curved lines of shading in the left side of the central oval. The pearls in the oval are not well aligned and there is less shading at right and left of "CORREIO" and "100 REIS."

A 100 reis stamp of type A38 but inscribed "BRAZIL" instead of "E. U. DO BRAZIL" was not placed in issue but postmarked copies are known. A reprint on thick paper was made in 1910.

No. 101 exists imperf., not regularly issued.

For surcharges see Nos. 151-158.

Liberty Head — A39

Perf. 12½ to 14, 11 to 11½ and 12½ to 14x11 to 11½

1891, May 1 **Typo.**

109 A39 100r blue & red 42.50 1.75
On cover 15.00
a. Frame inverted 175.00 110.00
On cover 500.00
b. Tete beche pair 850.00 *925.00*
On cover *2,500.*
c. 100r ultra & red 42.50 1.90
On cover 15.00

Liberty Head — A40

Perf. 11, 11½, 13, 13½, 14 and Compound

1893, Jan. 18 **Litho.**

111 A40 100r rose 75.00 1.75
On cover, single franking 37.50
a. 100r rose, perf 13 150.00 3.50
On cover, single franking 40.00

A41

A41a

Sugarloaf Mountain

A42

A42a

Liberty Head

Hermes — A43

Perf. 11 to 11½, 12½ to 14 and 12½ to 14x11 to 11½

1894-97 **Unwmk.**

112 A41 10r rose & blue 2.50 .90
On postcard, with other stamps 15.00
On cover, with other stamps 10.00
Single franking, on newspaper *150.00*
113 A41a 10r rose & blue 2.50 .90
On postcard, with other stamps 15.00
On cover, with other stamps 10.00
Single franking, on newspaper *150.00*
114 A41a 20r orange & bl ('97) 1.40 .40
On postcard, with other stamps 15.00
On cover, with other stamps 10.00
Single franking, on newspaper 50.00
a. 20r reddish orange & blue ('94) 1.75 .75
115 A41a 50r dk blue & blue 13.00 1.60
On postcard 3.00
Pair, on cover 10.00
a. 20r blue ('97) 6.00 4.00
116 A42 100r carmine & blk 5.00 .50
On cover 10.00
a. Vert. pair, imperf. btwn. *100.00*
b. 100r rose & black ('96) 9.00 .70
118 A42a 200r orange & blk 1.25 .50
a. Imperf. horiz., pair 80.00
b. Vert. pair, imperf. btwn. 80.00
c. 200r reddish orange & black ('94) 6.00 .60
d. Half used as 100r on cover 850.00
119 A42a 300r green & blk 19.00 .70
On cover, single franking 25.00
a. 300r pale green & black ('94) 18.00 1.25
On cover, single franking 30.00
120 A42a 500r blue & blk 30.00 2.00
On cover 60.00
a. 500r indigo & black ('94) 190.00 6.00
121 A42a 700r light lilac & blk 20.00 2.00
On cover 80.00
a. 700r lilac & black ('97) 18.00 1.75
On cover 80.00
122 A43 1000r green & vio 72.50 2.00
On cover 100.00
a. 1000r pale green & mauve ('94) 75.00 4.00
On cover 110.00
124 A43 2000r blk & gray lil 85.00 20.00
On cover 375.00
a. 2000r black & gray lilac, *chalky paper* ('94) 60.00 15.00
On cover 350.00
Nos. 112-124 (11) 252.15 31.50

Values for Nos. 112-124 are for the most common perforation variety of each stamp. Some perforations and combinations command premiums.

Values for this set are for stamps cut into the design on one or two sides due to the narrow spacing of the stamps in the setting of the plates and imperfect perforation methods. Between 1902 and 1905 these stamps were reissued with wider spacing between subjects and perforated 11½. These are listed as Nos. 113a-122b below.

The head of No. 116 exists in five types. See Nos. 140-150A, 159-161, 166-171d.

Wider Spacing Between Stamps

1902-05 ***Perf. 11½***

113a A41a 10r rose & bl 8.50 12.00
114b A41a 20r orange & bl 8.00 .50
119b A42a 300r green & blk 35.00 1.20
120b A42a 500r blue & blk 35.00 1.20
122b A43 1000r green & vio 275.00 10.00

1889 Issue of Newspaper Stamps Surcharged (Type N1)

a

b

c

1898 **Green Surcharge** ***Rouletted***

125 (b) 700r on 500r yel 8.50 *12.00*
126 (c) 1000r on 700r yel 42.50 35.00
a. Surcharged "700r" 850.00 1,000.
127 (c) 2000r on 1000r yel 35.00 18.00
128 (c) 2000r on 1000r brn 25.00 7.25

Violet Surcharge

129 (a) 100r on 50r brn yel 2.50 *55.00*
130 (c) 100r on 50r brn yel 90.00 75.00
131 (c) 300r on 200r blk 4.00 1.40
a. Double surcharge 190.00 325.00

The surcharge on No. 130 is handstamped. The impression is blurred and lighter in color than on No. 129. The two surcharges differ most in the shapes and serifs of the figures "1."

Counterfeits exist of No. 126a.

Black Surcharge

132 (b) 200r on 100r violet 4.00 1.40
a. Double surcharge 95.00 *200.00*
b. Inverted surcharge 95.00 *200.00*
132C (b) 500r on 300r car 6.50 3.50
133 (b) 700r on 500r green 9.50 2.40

Blue Surcharge

134 (b) 500r on 300r car 7.50 6.25

Red Surcharge

135 (c) 1000r on 700r ultra 27.50 17.00
a. Inverted surcharge 240.00 —

Surcharged on 1890-94 Issues

d

e

Perf. 11 to 14 and Compound

Black Surcharge

136 N3(e) 20r on 10r blue 3.75 7.00
137 N2(d) 200r on 100r red lilac 25.00 17.00
a. Double surcharge 275.00 300.00
b. 200r on 100r pink 175.00 120.00

Surcharge on No. 137 comes blue to deep black.

Blue Surcharge

138 N3(e) 50r on 20r green 9.50 11.50

Red Surcharge

139 N3(e) 100r on 50r green 21.00 24.00
a. Blue surcharge 15.00

The surcharge on 139a exists inverted, and in pair, one without surcharge.

Types of 1894-97

1899 ***Perf. 5½-7 and 11-11½x5½-7***

140 A41a 10r rose & bl 6.00 *14.00*
141 A41a 20r orange & bl 9.25 9.25
142 A41a 50r dk bl & lt bl 12.00 *37.50*
143 A42 100r carmine & blk 20.00 5.50
144 A42a 200r orange & blk 12.00 3.50
145 A42a 300r green & blk 75.00 8.75
Nos. 140-145 (6) 134.25 78.50

Perf. 8½-9½, 8½-9½x11-11½

146 A41a 10r rose & bl 6.00 3.50
147 A41a 20r orange & bl 19.00 3.50
147A A41a 50r dk bl & bl 160.00 35.00
148 A42 100r carmine & blk 37.50 1.75
149 A42a 200r orange & blk 19.00 1.25
150 A42a 300r green & blk 75.00 6.00
150A A43 1000r green & vio 160.00 15.00
Nos. 146-150A (7) 476.50 66.00

Nos. 140-150A are valued with perfs just cut into the design on one or two sides. Expect some irregularity of the perforations.

Issue of 1890-93 Surcharged in Violet or Magenta

Perf. 11 to 11½, 12½ to 14 and Compound

1899, June 25

151 A38 50r on 20r gray grn 2.50 *3.50*
a. Double surcharge 150.00 150.00
152 A38 100r on 50r gray grn 2.50 *3.50*
b. Double surcharge 125.00 125.00
153 A38 300r on 200r pur 9.25 *14.50*
a. Double surcharge 300.00 —
b. Pair, one without surcharge 500.00 —
154 A38 500r on 300r ultra, perf. 13 22.50 8.75
a. 500r on 300r gray lilac 35.00 10.00
b. Pair, one without surcharge 500.00 *575.00*
c. 500r on 300r slate violet 45.00 17.00
155 A38 700r on 500r ol bis 30.00 7.00
a. Pair, one without surcharge 500.00 —
156 A38 1000r on 700r choc 22.50 7.00
157 A38 1000r on 700r fawn 22.50 7.00
a. Pair, one without surcharge 500.00 *575.00*
158 A38 2000r on 1000r bister (perf 11-11½) 37.50 5.25
a. 2000r on 1000r yel buff (perf 13) 60.00 5.25
b. Pair, one without surcharge 500.00 *575.00*
Nos. 151-158 (8) 149.25 56.50

Types of 1894-97

Perf. 11, 11½, 13 and Compound

1900

159 A41a 50r green 13.00 .70
160 A42 100r rose 25.00 .35
a. Frame around inner oval 125.00 4.75
161 A42a 200r blue 14.50 .40
Nos. 159-161 (3) 52.50 1.45

Three types exist of No. 161, all of which have the frame around inner oval.

Cabral Arrives at Brazil — A44

Independence Proclaimed — A45

"Emancipation of Slaves" — A46

Allegory, Republic of Brazil — A47

1900, Jan. 1 **Litho.** ***Perf. 12½***

162 A44 100r red 7.25 5.75
a. Imperf., pair 400.00 500.00
163 A45 200r green & yel 7.25 5.75
164 A46 500r blue 7.25 5.75
165 A47 700r emerald 7.25 5.75
Nos. 162-165 (4) 29.00 23.00

Discovery of Brazil, 400th anniversary.

Types of 1894-97
Wmk. (97? or 98?)

1905 ***Perf. 11, 11½***

166 A41a 10r rose & bl 7.00 4.75
167 A41a 20r orange & bl 12.50 2.40
168 A41a 50r green 25.00 3.50
169 A42 100r rose 32.50 1.25
170 A42a 200r dark blue 19.00 1.25
171 A42a 300r green & blk 65.00 2.40
Nos. 166-171 (6) 161.00 15.55

Positive identification of Wmk. 97 or 98 places stamp in specific watermark groups below.

Wmk. 97

166b A41a 10r rose & blue 37.50 19.00
167b A41a 20r orange & blue 37.50 9.50
168b A41a 50r green 72.50 9.50
169b A42 100r rose 250.00 35.00
170b A42a 200r dark blue 150.00 4.75
171b A42a 300r green & blk 450.00 35.00
171A A43 1000r green & vio 350.00 35.00
Nos. 166b-171A (7) 1,348. 147.75

Wmk. 98

166c A41a 10r rose & blue 50.00 50.00
167c A41a 20r orange & blue 100.00 24.00
168c A41a 50r green 200.00 35.00
169c A42 100r rose 100.00 4.75
170c A42a 200r dark blue 150.00 4.75
171d A42a 300r green & blk 350.00 35.00
Nos. 166c-171d (6) 950.00 153.50

Allegory, Pan-American Congress A48

1906, July 23 **Litho.** **Unwmk.**

172 A48 100r carmine rose 30.00 30.00
173 A48 200r blue 80.00 10.00

Third Pan-American Congress.

Aristides Lobo A48a

Benjamin Constant A49

Pedro Alvares Cabral A50

Eduardo Wandenkolk A51

Manuel Deodoro da Fonseca A52

Floriano Peixoto A53

Prudente de Moraes A54

Manuel Ferraz de Campos Salles A55

Francisco de Paula Rodrigues Alves — A56

Liberty Head — A57

A58

A59

1906-16 Engr. *Perf. 12*

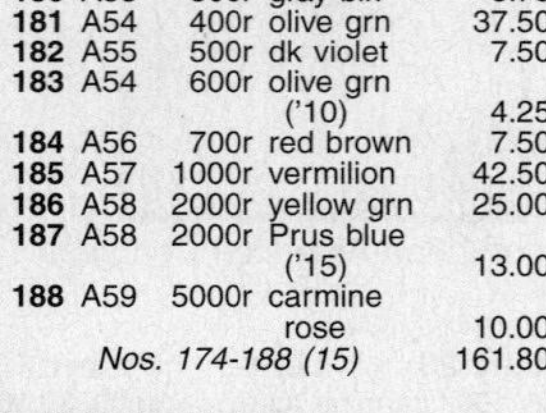

174	A48a	10r bluish slate	1.10	.25
175	A49	20r aniline vio	1.10	.25
176	A50	50r green	1.10	.25
a.		Booklet pane of 6 ('08)	47.50	*150.00*
177	A51	100r anil rose	2.50	.25
a.		Imperf. vert., coil ('16)	4.75	.40
b.		Booklet pane of 6 ('08)	95.00	*150.00*
178	A52	200r blue	2.50	.25
a.		Booklet pane of 6 ('08)	72.50	*150.00*
179	A52	200r ultra ('15)	2.50	.40
a.		Imperf. vert., coil ('16)	2.50	.40
180	A53	300r gray blk	3.75	.80
181	A54	400r olive grn	37.50	2.40
182	A55	500r dk violet	7.50	.80
183	A54	600r olive grn ('10)	4.25	1.60
184	A56	700r red brown	7.50	3.50
185	A57	1000r vermilion	42.50	1.25
186	A58	2000r yellow grn	25.00	.80
187	A58	2000r Prus blue ('15)	13.00	1.25
188	A59	5000r carmine rose	10.00	2.40
		Nos. 174-188 (15)	161.80	16.45

Allegorical Emblems: Liberty, Peace, Industry, etc. — A60

1908, July 14

189	A60	100r carmine	24.00	1.75

National Exhibition, Rio de Janeiro.

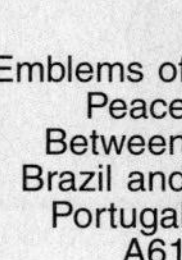

Emblems of Peace Between Brazil and Portugal A61

1908, July 14

190	A61	100r red	11.00	1.25

Opening of Brazilian ports to foreign commerce, cent. Medallions picture King Carlos I of Portugal and Pres. Affonso Penna of Brazil.

Bonifacio, Bolivar, Hidalgo, O'Higgins, San Martin, Washington — A62

1909

191	A62	200r deep blue	13.50	1.50

For surcharge see No. E1.

Nilo Peçanha — A63

1910, Nov. 15

192	A63	10,000r brown	11.00	3.00

Baron of Rio Branco — A64

1913-16

193	A64	1000r deep green	5.00	.50
194	A64	1000r slate ('16)	29.00	.80

Cabo Frio — A65

Perf. 11½

1915, Nov. 13 Litho. Wmk. 99

195	A65	100r dk grn, *yelsh*	5.00	4.00

Founding of the town of Cabo Frio, 300th anniversary.

Bay of Guajara A66

1916, Jan. 5

196	A66	100r carmine	11.00	6.00

City of Belem, 300th anniversary.

Revolutionary Flag — A67

1917, Mar. 6

197	A67	100r deep blue	18.00	8.50

Revolution of Pernambuco, Mar. 6, 1817.

Rodrigues Alves — A68

Unwmk.

1917, Aug. 31 Engr. *Perf. 12*

198	A68	5000r red brown	80.00	12.50

Liberty Head

A69 A70

Perf. 12½, 13, 13x13½.

1918-20 Typo. Unwmk.

200	A69	10r orange brn	.70	.30
201	A69	20r slate	.70	.30
202	A69	25r ol gray ('20)	.70	.30
203	A69	50r green	40.00	4.00
204	A70	100r rose	2.25	.30
a.		Imperf., pair	—	
205	A70	300r red orange	25.00	4.00
206	A70	500r dull violet	25.00	4.00
		Nos. 200-206 (7)	94.35	13.20

1918-20 Wmk. 100

207	A69	10r red brown	8.00	2.00
a.		Imperf., pair	—	
207B	A69	20r slate	1.90	1.90
c.		Imperf., pair	—	
208	A69	25r ol gray ('20)	1.00	.65
209	A69	50r green	1.90	.65
210	A70	100r rose	62.50	.65
a.		Imperf., pair	—	
211	A70	200r dull blue	8.00	.65
212	A70	300r orange	62.50	5.00
213	A70	500r dull violet	62.50	9.50
214	A70	600r orange	3.50	*9.50*
		Nos. 207-214 (9)	211.80	30.50

Because of the spacing of this watermark, a few stamps in each sheet may show no watermark.

"Education" — A72

1918 Engr. *Perf. 11½*

215	A72	1000r blue	8.00	.30
216	A72	2000r red brown	35.00	10.00
217	A72	5000r dark violet	10.00	10.00
		Nos. 215-217 (3)	53.00	20.30

Watermark note below No. 257 also applies to Nos. 215-217.

See Nos. 233-234, 283-285, 404, 406, 458, 460. For surcharge see No. C30.

Railroad A73

"Industry" A74

"Aviation" A75

Mercury A76

"Navigation" — A77

Perf. 13½x13, 13x13½

1920-22 Typo. Unwmk.

218	A73	10r red violet	1.00	.50
219	A73	20r olive green	1.00	.50
220	A74	25r brown violet	.90	.50
221	A74	50r blue green	1.10	.50
222	A74	50r org brn ('22)	1.90	.50
223	A75	100r rose red	3.75	.50
224	A75	100r orange ('22)	10.00	.50
225	A75	150r violet ('21)	1.90	.50
226	A75	200r blue	6.00	.50
227	A75	200r rose red ('22)	10.50	.50
228	A76	300r olive gray	17.00	.65
229	A76	400r dull blue ('22)	30.00	4.25
230	A76	500r red brown	24.00	.65
		Nos. 218-230 (13)	109.05	10.55

See Nos. 236-257, 265-266, 268-271, 273-274, 276-281, 302-311, 316-322, 326-340, 357-358, 431-434, 436-441, 461-463B, 467-470, 472-474, 488-490, 492-494. For surcharges see Nos. 356-358, 376-377.

Perf. 11, 11½

Engr. Wmk. 100

231	A77	600r red orange	2.75	.50
232	A77	1000r claret	7.00	.30
a.		Perf. 8½	50.00	9.50
233	A72	2000r dull violet	27.50	.95
234	A72	5000r brown	21.00	11.00
		Nos. 231-234 (4)	58.25	12.75

Nos. 233 and 234 are inscribed "BRASIL CORREIO." Watermark note below No. 257 also applies to Nos. 231-234.

See No. 282.

King Albert of Belgium and President Epitacio Pessoa A78

1920, Sept. 19 Engr. *Perf. 11½x11*

235	A78	100r dull red	1.00	1.00

Visit of the King and Queen of Belgium.

Types of 1920-22 Issue

Perf. 13x13½, 13x12½

1922-29 Typo. Wmk. 100

236	A73	10r red violet	.30	.25
237	A73	20r olive green	.30	.25
238	A75	20r gray vio ('29)	.30	.25
239	A74	25r brown violet	.35	.25
240	A74	50r blue grn	4.25	*45.00*
241	A74	50r org brn ('23)	.50	.40
242	A75	100r rose red	30.00	.50
243	A75	100r orange ('26)	.65	.25
244	A75	100r turq grn ('28)	.65	.25
245	A75	150r violet	2.50	.50
246	A75	200r blue	400.00	15.00
247	A75	200r rose red	.50	.25
248	A75	200r ol grn ('28)	3.50	3.75
249	A76	300r olive gray	2.50	.30
250	A76	300r rose red ('29)	.40	.30
251	A76	400r blue	2.50	.25
252	A76	400r orange ('29)	1.00	3.25
253	A76	500r red brown	10.00	.65
254	A76	500r ultra ('29)	14.50	.25
255	A76	600r brn org ('29)	12.00	4.50
256	A76	700r dull vio ('29)	12.00	2.50
257	A76	1000r turq bl ('29)	14.50	1.00
		Nos. 236-257 (22)	513.20	*79.90*

Because of the spacing of the watermark, a few stamps in each sheet show no watermark.

A booklet exists with panes of 6 (2x3), created from the left margin blocks of sheet stamps of Nos. 241, 243, 247, 249 and 253. Once removed from the booklet, they cannot be separately identified.

"Agriculture" — A79

1922 Unwmk. *Perf. 13x13½*

258	A79	40r orange brown	.70	.50
259	A79	80r grnsh blue	.50	*3.25*

See Nos. 263, 267, 275.

Declaration of Ypiranga — A80

Dom Pedro I and Jose Bonifacio — A81

National Exposition and President Pessoa — A82

Unwmk.

1922, Sept. 7 Engr. *Perf. 14*

No.	Type	Description	Unused	Used
260	A80	100r ultra	5.00	.75
261	A81	200r red	7.00	.50
262	A82	300r green	7.00	.50
		Nos. 260-262 (3)	19.00	1.75

Cent. of independence and Natl. Exposition of 1922.

Agriculture Type of 1922

Perf. 13½x12

1923 Wmk. 100 Typo.

No.	Type	Description	Unused	Used
263	A79	40r orange brown	.75	*7.50*

Brazilian Army Entering Bahia — A83

Unwmk.

1923, July 12 Litho. *Perf. 13*

No.	Type	Description	Unused	Used
264	A83	200r rose	11.00	6.50

Centenary of the taking of Bahia from the Portuguese.

Types of 1920-22 Issue

Perf. 13x13½

1924 Typo. Wmk. 193

No.	Type	Description	Unused	Used
265	A73	10r red violet	9.00	7.50
266	A73	20r olive green	10.50	7.50
267	A79	40r orange brown	7.50	2.75
268	A74	50r orange brown	10.00	*30.00*
269	A75	100r orange	7.50	.75
270	A75	200r rose	10.50	.75
271	A76	400r blue	8.00	4.75
		Nos. 265-271 (7)	63.00	*54.00*

Arms of Equatorial Confederation, 1824 — A84

Unwmk.

1924, July 2 Litho. *Perf. 11*

No.	Type	Description	Unused	Used
272	A84	200r bl, blk, yel, & red	4.00	2.75
a.		Red omitted	350.00	350.00

Centenary of the Equatorial Confederation.

Chemically bleached fakes of No. 272a are more common than the genuine error. Expertization is advised.

Types of 1920-22 Issue

Perf. 9½ to 13½ and Compound

1924-28 Typo. Wmk. 101

No.	Type	Description	Unused	Used
273	A73	10r red violet	.75	.35
274	A73	20r olive gray	.75	.35
275	A79	40r orange brn	.75	.35
276	A74	50r orange brn	.75	.35
277	A75	100r red orange	2.25	.35
278	A75	200r rose	1.00	.35
279	A76	300r ol gray ('25)	10.00	1.25
280	A76	400r blue	6.00	.50
281	A76	500r red brown	15.00	.50

Engr.

No.	Type	Description	Unused	Used
282	A77	600r red org ('26)	2.50	.35
283	A72	2000r dull vio ('26)	7.50	.75
284	A72	5000r brown ('26)	22.50	.85
285	A72	10,000r rose ('28)	30.00	2.00
		Nos. 273-285 (13)	99.75	8.30

Nos. 283-285 are inscribed "BRASIL CORREIO."

Ruy Barbosa — A85

1925 Wmk. 100 *Perf. 11½*

No.	Type	Description	Unused	Used
286	A85	1000r claret	6.25	1.75

1926 Wmk. 101

No.	Type	Description	Unused	Used
287	A85	1000r claret	2.10	.40

"Justice" — A86

Scales of Justice and Map of Brazil — A87

Perf. 13½x13

1927, Aug. 11 Typo. Wmk. 206

No.	Type	Description	Unused	Used
288	A86	100r deep blue	1.10	.65
289	A87	200r rose	.95	.40

Founding of the law courses, cent.

Liberty Holding Coffee Leaves — A88

1928, Feb. 5

No.	Type	Description	Unused	Used
290	A88	100r blue green	1.75	.80
291	A88	200r carmine	1.10	.50
292	A88	300r olive black	9.00	.40
		Nos. 290-292 (3)	11.85	1.70

Introduction of the coffee tree in Brazil, bicent.

Official Stamps of 1919 Surcharged in Red or Black

Perf. 11, 11½

1928 Wmk. 100 Engr.

No.	Type	Description	Unused	Used
293	O3	700r on 500r org	8.00	8.00
a.		Inverted surcharge	210.00	210.00
294	O3	1000r on 100r rose red (Bk)	4.75	.60
295	O3	2000r on 200r dull bl	6.50	1.00
296	O3	5000r on 50r grn	6.50	1.60
297	O3	10,000r on 10r ol grn	30.00	2.50
		Nos. 293-297 (5)	55.75	13.70

Nos. 293-297 were used for ordinary postage.

Stamps in the outer rows of the sheets are often without watermark.

Ruy Barbosa — A89

Perf. 9, 9½x11, 11, and Compound

1929 Wmk. 101

No.	Type	Description	Unused	Used
300	A89	5000r blue violet	20.00	.95

See Nos. 405, 459. For surcharge see No. C29.

Types of 1920-22 Issue

Perf. 13½x12½

1929 Typo. Wmk. 218

No.	Type	Description	Unused	Used
302	A75	20r gray violet	.40	.25
303	A75	50r red brown	.40	.25
304	A75	100r turq green	.55	.25
305	A75	200r olive green	22.50	5.00
306	A76	300r rose red	1.10	.25
307	A76	400r orange	1.25	*2.00*
308	A76	500r ultra	14.00	.65
309	A76	600r brown org	16.00	1.25
310	A76	700r dp violet	4.25	.25
311	A76	1000r turq blue	7.50	.25
		Nos. 302-311 (10)	67.95	10.40

Wmk. 218 exists both in vertical alignment and in echelon.

Wmk. in echelon

No.	Type	Description	Unused	Used
302a	A75	20r	.50	.40
303a	A75	50r	140.00	75.00
306a	A76	300r	1.25	1.25
308a	A76	500r	200.00	47.50
311a	A76	1000r	10.00	11.00

Architectural Fantasies A90 A91

Architectural Fantasy — A92

Perf. 13x13½

1930, June 20 Wmk. 206

No.	Type	Description	Unused	Used
312	A90	100r turq blue	2.00	1.25
313	A91	200r olive gray	3.25	.80
314	A92	300r rose red	5.50	1.25
		Nos. 312-314 (3)	10.75	3.30

Fourth Pan-American Congress of Architects and Exposition of Architecture.

Types of 1920-22 Issue

1930 Wmk. 221 *Perf. 13x12½*

No.	Type	Description	Unused	Used
316	A75	20r gray violet	.40	.35
317	A75	50r red brown	.40	.35
318	A75	100r turq blue	.80	.35
319	A75	200r olive green	4.75	1.25
320	A76	300r rose red	.95	.35
321	A76	500r ultra	2.40	.35
322	A76	1000r turq blue	40.00	1.50
		Nos. 316-322 (7)	49.70	4.50

Imperforates

From 1930 to 1947, imperforate or partly perforated sheets of nearly all commemorative and some definitive issues were obtainable.

Types of 1920-22 Issue

Perf. 11, 13½x13, 13x12½

1931-34 Typo. Wmk. 222

No.	Type	Description	Unused	Used
326	A75	10r deep brown	.25	.25
327	A75	20r gray violet	.25	.25
328	A74	25r brn vio ('34)	.25	1.25
330	A75	50r blue green	.25	.25
331	A75	50r red brown	.25	.25
332	A75	100r orange	.50	.25
334	A75	200r dp carmine	1.00	.40
335	A76	300r olive green	1.40	.25
336	A76	400r ultra	3.00	.25
337	A76	500r red brown	6.00	.25
338	A76	600r brown org	6.50	.25
339	A76	700r deep violet	6.50	.25
340	A76	1000r turq blue	21.00	.25
		Nos. 326-340 (13)	47.15	4.40

Getulio Vargas and Joao Pessoa A93

Vargas and Pessoa A94

Oswaldo Aranha A95 A96

Antonio Carlos A97

Pessoa A98

Vargas — A99

Unwmk.

1931, Apr. 29 Litho. *Perf. 14*

No.	Type	Description	Unused	Used
342	A93	10r + 10r lt bl	.25	*13.00*
343	A93	20r + 20r yel brn	.25	*9.50*
344	A95	50r + 50r bl grn, red & yel	.25	*.40*
a.		Red missing at left	.90	*1.60*
345	A93	100r + 50r orange	.55	.45
346	A93	200r + 100r green	.55	.45
347	A94	300r + 150r multi	.55	.45
348	A93	400r + 200r dp rose	1.90	1.00
349	A93	500r + 250r dk bl	1.40	1.10
350	A93	600r + 300r brn vio	.95	*13.00*
351	A94	700r + 350r multi	1.75	.90
352	A96	1000r + 500r brt grn, red & yel	3.75	.55
353	A97	2000r + 1000r gray blk & red	15.00	.80
354	A98	5000r + 2500r blk & red	32.50	13.50
355	A99	10000r + 5000r brt grn & yel	80.00	24.00
		Nos. 342-355 (14)	139.65	79.10

Revolution of Oct. 3, 1930. Prepared as semi-postal stamps, Nos. 342-355 were sold as ordinary postage stamps with stated surtax ignored.

Nos. 306, 320 and 250 Surcharged

Perf. 13½x12½

1931, July 20 Wmk. 218

No.	Type	Description	Unused	Used
356	A76	200r on 300r rose red	1.75	1.25
a.		Wmk. in echelon	30.00	30.00
b.		Inverted surcharge	47.50	

Perf. 13x12½

Wmk. 221

No.	Type	Description	Unused	Used
357	A76	200r on 300r rose red	.50	.25
a.		Inverted surcharge	55.00	55.00

Perf. 13½x12½

Wmk. 100

No.	Type	Description	Unused	Used
358	A76	200r on 300r rose red	92.50	92.50

Map of South America Showing Meridian of Tordesillas — A100

Joao Ramalho and Tibiriça A101

Martim Affonso de Souza A102

King John III of Portugal A103

Disembarkation of M. A. de Souza at Sao Vicente — A104

Wmk. 222

1932, June 3 Typo. *Perf. 13*

359	A100	20r dk violet	.40	.50
360	A101	100r black	.60	.50
361	A102	200r purple	1.25	.40
362	A103	600r red brown	2.10	2.25

Engr.

Wmk. 101

Perf. 9½, 11, 9½x11

363	A104	700r ultra	3.50	2.75
		Nos. 359-363 (5)	7.85	6.40

1st colonization of Brazil at Sao Vicente, in 1532, under the hereditary captaincy of Martim Affonso de Souza.

Revolutionary Issue

Map of Brazil — A105

Soldier and Flag — A106

Allegory: Freedom, Justice, Equality A107

Soldier's Head A108

"LEX" and Sword A109

Symbolical of Law and Order — A110

Symbolical of Justice — A111

Perf. 11½

1932, Sept. Litho. Unwmk.

364	A105	100r brown org	.55	2.40
365	A106	200r dk car	.45	.85
366	A107	300r gray green	2.40	4.25
367	A108	400r dark blue	8.75	8.75
368	A105	500r blk brn	8.75	8.75
369	A107	600r red	8.75	8.75
370	A106	700r violet	4.25	*8.75*
371	A108	1000r orange	2.10	*8.75*
372	A109	2000r dark brn	17.00	*24.00*
373	A110	5000r yellow grn	21.00	*40.00*
374	A111	10000r plum	24.00	*45.00*
		Nos. 364-374 (11)	98.00	160.25

Issued by the revolutionary forces in the state of Sao Paulo during the revolt of September, 1932. Subsequently the stamps were recognized by the Federal Government and placed in general use.

Excellent counterfeits of Nos. 373 and 374 exist. Favor cancels, applied at a later date, abound.

City of Vassouras and Illuminated Memorial — A112

Wmk. 222

1933, Jan. 15 Typo. *Perf. 12*

375	A112	200r rose red	1.40	1.10

City of Vassouras founding, cent.

Nos. 306, 320 Surcharged

Perf. 13½x12½

1933, July 28 Wmk. 218

376	A76	200r on 300r rose red	1.00	1.00
a.		Wmk. 218 in echelon (No. 306a)	19.00	19.00
b.		Wmk. 100 (No. 250)	140.00	140.00

Perf. 13x12½

Wmk. 221

377	A76	200r on 300r rose red	.65	.65
a.		Inverted surcharge	42.50	
b.		Double surcharge	42.50	

Religious Symbols and Inscriptions — A113

Wmk. 222

1933, Sept. 3 Typo. *Perf. 13*

378	A113	200r dark red	1.00	.85

1st Natl. Eucharistic Congress in Brazil.

"Flag of the Race" A114

1933, Aug. 18

379	A114	200r deep red	2.00	.85

The raising of the "Flag of the Race" and the 441st anniv. of the sailing of Columbus from Palos, Spain, Aug. 3, 1492.

Republic Figure, Flags of Brazil and Argentina — A115

Wmk. 101

1933, Oct. 7 Engr. *Perf. 11½*

380	A115	200r blue	.45	.35

Thick Laid Paper

1933, Dec. Wmk. 236 *Perf. 11, 11½*

381	A115	400r green	1.50	1.25
382	A115	600r brt rose	5.00	6.75
383	A115	1000r lt violet	7.25	4.75
		Nos. 380-383 (4)	14.20	13.10

Visit of President Justo of the Argentina to Brazil, Oct. 2-7, 1933.

Allegory: "Faith and Energy" — A116

1933 Typo. Wmk. 222

384	A116	200r dark red	.30	.25
385	A116	200r dark violet	.85	.25

See Nos. 435, 471, 491.

Allegory of Flight — A117

Wmk. 236

1934, Apr. 15 Engr. *Perf. 12*

386	A117	200r blue	.80	.65

1st Natl. Aviation Congress at Sao Paulo.

A118

Wmk. 222

1934, May 12 Typo. *Perf. 11*

387	A118	200r dark olive	.40	.40
388	A118	400r carmine	2.25	2.25
389	A118	700r ultra	2.40	2.25
390	A118	1000r orange	6.00	1.00
		Nos. 387-390 (4)	11.05	5.90

7th Intl. Fair at Rio de Janeiro.

Christ of Corcovado A119

1934, Oct. 20

392	A119	300r dark red	4.25	4.25
a.		Tete beche pair	17.00	17.00
393	A119	700r ultra	17.00	17.00
a.		Tete beche pair	72.50	72.50

Visit of Eugenio Cardinal Pacelli, later Pope Pius XII, to Brazil.

The three printings of Nos. 392-393, distinguishable by shades, sell for different prices.

José de Anchieta A120

Thick Laid Paper

1934, Nov. 8 Wmk. 236 *Perf. 11, 12*

394	A120	200r yellow brown	.90	.60
395	A120	300r violet	.75	.40
396	A120	700r blue	3.00	3.00
397	A120	1000r lt green	6.00	1.75
		Nos. 394-397 (4)	10.65	5.75

Jose de Anchieta, S.J. (1534-1597), Portuguese missionary and "father of Brazilian literature."

A121

"Brazil" and "Uruguay" — A122

Wmk. 222

1935, Jan. 8 Typo. *Perf. 11*

398	A121	200r orange	1.10	.55
399	A122	300r yellow	1.40	1.25
400	A122	700r ultra	5.00	5.00
401	A121	1000r dk violet	13.00	8.00
		Nos. 398-401 (4)	20.50	14.80

Visit of President Terra of Uruguay.

View of Town of Igarassu A123

1935, July 1

402	A123	200r maroon & brn	1.60	.55
403	A123	300r vio & olive brn	1.60	.45

Captaincy of Pernambuco founding, 400th anniv.

Types of 1918-29

Thick Laid Paper

Perf. 9½, 11, 12, 12x11

1934-36 Engr. Wmk. 236

404	A72	2000r violet	12.50	.60
405	A89	5000r blue vio ('36)	17.00	1.25
406	A72	10000r claret ('36)	15.00	1.75
		Nos. 404-406 (3)	44.50	3.60

No. 404 is inscribed "BRASIL CORREIO."

Revolutionist A124

Bento Gonçalves da Silva — A125

Duke of Caxias A126

Perf. 11, 12

1935, Sept. 20-1936, Jan.

407	A124	200r black	1.40	1.40
408	A124	300r rose lake	1.40	.80
409	A125	700r dull blue	4.50	6.50
410	A126	1000r light violet	5.00	4.00
		Nos. 407-410 (4)	12.30	12.70

Centenary of the "Ragged" Revolution.

Federal District Coat of Arms A127

Wmk. 222

1935, Oct. 19 Typo. *Perf. 11*

411	A127	200r blue	4.00	4.00

8th Intl. Sample Fair held at Rio de Janeiro.

Coutinho's Ship — A128

Arms of Fernandes Coutinho — A129

1935, Oct. 25

412	A128	300r maroon	3.00	1.25
413	A129	700r turq blue	5.50	3.75

400th anniversary of the establishment of the first Portuguese colony at Espirito Santo by Vasco Fernandes Coutinho.

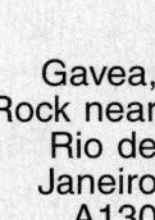

Gavea, Rock near Rio de Janeiro A130

1935, Oct. 12 Wmk. 245 *Perf. 11*

414	A130	300r brown & vio	2.75	2.00
415	A130	300r blk & turq bl	2.75	2.00
416	A130	300r Prus bl & ultra	2.75	2.00
417	A130	300r crimson & blk	2.75	2.00
		Nos. 414-417 (4)	11.00	8.00

"Child's Day," Oct. 12.

Viscount of Cairu — A131

Perf. 11, 12x11

1936, Jan. 20 Engr. Wmk. 236

418	A131	1200r violet	10.00	6.00

Jose da Silva Lisboa, Viscount of Cairu (1756-1835).

View of Cametá A132

1936, Feb. 26 *Perf. 11, 12*

419	A132	200r brown orange	1.75	1.40
420	A132	300r green	1.75	1.00

300th anniversary of the founding of the city of Cameta, Dec. 24, 1635.

Coining Press A133

Thick Laid Paper

1936, Mar. 24 *Perf. 11*

421	A133	300r pur brn, *cr*	1.25	1.25

1st Numismatic Cong. at Sao Paulo, Mar., 1936.

Carlos Gomes — A134

"Il Guarany" — A135

Thick Laid Paper

1936, July 11 *Perf. 11, 11x12*

422	A134	300r dull rose	1.00	.70
423	A134	300r black brown	1.00	.70
424	A135	700r ocher	3.25	2.00
425	A135	700r blue	3.75	2.75
		Nos. 422-425 (4)	9.00	6.15

Birth cent. of Antonio Carlos Gomes, who composed the opera "Il Guarany."

Scales of Justice — A136

Wmk. 222

1936, July 4 Typo. *Perf. 11*

426	A136	300r rose	2.00	.65

First National Judicial Congress.

Federal District Coat of Arms A137

1936, Nov. 13 Typo. Wmk. 249

427	A137	200r rose red	1.25	.65

Ninth International Sample Fair held at Rio de Janeiro.

Eucharistic Congress Seal — A138

1936, Dec. 17 Wmk. 245 *Perf. 11½*

428	A138	300r grn, yel, bl & blk	1.25	.60

2nd Natl. Eucharistic Congress in Brazil.

Botafogo Bay A139

Thick Laid Paper

Wmk. 236

1937, Jan. 2 Engr. *Perf. 11*

429	A139	700r blue	1.60	.80
430	A139	700r black	1.60	.80

Birth cent. of Francisco Pereira Passos, engineer who planned the modern city of Rio de Janeiro.

Types of 1920-22, 1933

Perf. 11, 11½ and Compound

1936-37 Typo. Wmk. 249

431	A75	10r deep brown	.25	.25
432	A75	20r dull violet	.25	.25
433	A75	50r blue green	.25	.25
434	A75	100r orange	.50	.25
435	A116	200r dk violet	1.50	.25
436	A76	300r olive green	.50	.25
437	A76	400r ultra	1.25	.25
438	A76	500r lt brown	1.75	.25
439	A76	600r brn org ('37)	9.00	.25
440	A76	700r deep violet	7.00	.25
441	A76	1000r turq blue	7.75	.25
		Nos. 431-441 (11)	30.00	2.75

Massed Flags and Star of Esperanto A140

1937, Jan. 19

442	A140	300r green	1.75	.90

Ninth Brazilian Esperanto Congress.

Bay of Rio de Janeiro A141

1937, June 9 Unwmk. *Perf. 12½*

443	A141	300r orange red & blk	1.00	.75
444	A141	700r blue & dk brn	2.50	.75

2nd South American Radio Communication Conf. held in Rio, June 7-19.

Globe — A142

Perf. 11, 12

1937, Sept. 4 Wmk. 249

445	A142	300r green	1.50	.65

50th anniversary of Esperanto.

Monroe Palace, Rio de Janeiro A143

Botanical Garden, Rio de Janeiro — A144

1937, Sept. 30 Unwmk. *Perf. 12½*

446	A143	200r lt brn & bl	1.00	.50
447	A144	300r org & ol grn	1.00	.50
448	A143	2000r grn & cerise	13.00	13.00
449	A144	10000r lake & indigo	70.00	60.00
		Nos. 446-449 (4)	85.00	74.00

Brig. Gen. Jose da Silva Paes — A145

1937, Oct. 11 Wmk. 249 *Perf. 11½*

450	A145	300r blue	1.00	.50

Bicentenary of Rio Grande do Sul.

Eagle and Shield — A146

1937, Dec. 2 Typo. *Perf. 11*

451	A146	400r dark blue	2.75	.60

150th anniversary of the US Constitution.

Bags of Brazilian Coffee A147

Frame Engraved, Center Typographed

1938, Jan. 17 Unwmk. *Perf. 12½*

452	A147	1200r multicolored	6.25	.50

Arms of Olinda A148

Perf. 11, 11x11½

1938, Jan. 24 Engr. Wmk. 249

453	A148	400r violet	.80	.35

4th cent. of the founding of the city of Olinda.

Independence Memorial, Ypiranga A149

1938, Jan. 24 Typo. *Perf. 11*

454	A149	400r brown olive	1.00	.50

Proclamation of Brazil's independence by Dom Pedro, Sept. 7, 1822.

Iguaçu Falls — A150

Perf. 12½

1938, Jan. 10 Unwmk. Engr.

455	A150	1000r sepia & yel brn	3.00	1.75
456	A150	5000r ol blk & grn	27.50	22.50

Couto de Magalhaes A151

Perf. 11, 11x11½

1938, Mar. 17 Wmk. 249

457	A151	400r dull green	.80	.40

General Couto de Magalhaes (1837-1898), statesman, soldier, explorer, writer, developer.

Types of 1918-38

Perf. 11, 12x11, 12x11½, 12

1938 Engr. Wmk. 249

458	A72	2000r blue violet	12.00	.30
459	A89	5000r violet blue	45.00	.50
a.		5000r deep blue	37.50	.50
460	A72	10000r rose lake	55.00	1.50
		Nos. 458-460 (3)	112.00	2.30

No. 458 is inscribed "BRASIL CORREIO."

Types of 1920-22

1938 Wmk. 245 Typo. *Perf. 11*

461	A75	50r blue green	1.40	1.10
462	A75	100r orange	3.25	1.10
463	A76	300r olive green	1.40	3.00
463A	A76	400r ultra	225.00	150.00
463B	A76	500r red brown	1.40	*60.00*
		Nos. 461-463B (5)	232.45	215.20

National Archives Building A152

1938, May 20 Wmk. 249

464	A152	400r brown	.75	.40

Centenary of National Archives.

Souvenir Sheets

Sir Rowland Hill — A153

1938, Oct. 22 *Imperf.*

465	A153	Sheet of 10	20.00	20.00
a.		400r dull green, single stamp	1.25	1.25

Brazilian Intl. Philatelic Exposition (Brapex).

Issued in sheets measuring 106x118mm. A few perforated sheets exist.

President Vargas — A154

1938, Nov. 10 *Perf. 11*

Without Gum

466	A154	Sheet of 10	35.00	25.00
a.		400r slate blue, single stamp	1.75	1.75

Constitution of Brazil, set up by President Vargas, Nov. 10, 1937. Size: 113x135½mm.

Types of 1920-33

1939 Typo. Wmk. 256 *Perf. 11*

467	A75	10r red brown	1.00	1.00
468	A75	20r dull violet	2.00	.30
469	A75	50r blue green	1.50	.30
470	A75	100r yellow org	1.50	.30
471	A116	200r dk violet	3.00	.30
472	A76	400r ultra	3.00	.30
473	A76	600r dull orange	4.50	.30
474	A76	1000r turq blue	20.00	.30
		Nos. 467-474 (8)	36.50	3.10

View of Rio de Janeiro — A155

1939, June 14 Engr. Wmk. 249

475	A155	1200r dull violet	2.25	.25

View of Santos — A156

1939, Aug. 23

476	A156	400r dull blue	.50	.40

Centenary of founding of Santos.

Chalice Vine and Blossoms — A157

1939, Aug. 23

477	A157	400r green	1.60	.35

1st South American Botanical Congress held in January, 1938.

Eucharistic Congress Seal — A158

1939, Sept. 3

478	A158	400r rose red	.60	.45

Third National Eucharistic Congress.

Duke of Caxias, Army Patron — A159

1939, Sept. 12 Photo. *Rouletted*

479	A159	400r deep ultra	.60	.45

Issued for Soldiers' Day.

A159a

A159b

A159c

A159d

Designs: 400r, George Washington. 800r, Emperor Pedro II. 1200r, Grover Cleveland. 1600r, Statue of Friendship, given by US.

Unwmk.

1939, Oct. 7 Engr. *Perf. 12*

480	A159a	400r yellow orange	.70	.30
481	A159b	800r dark green	.35	.25
482	A159c	1200r rose car	.70	.25
483	A159d	1600r dark blue	.70	.30
		Nos. 480-483 (4)	2.45	1.10

New York World's Fair.

Benjamin Constant A160

Fonseca on Horseback A162

Manuel Deodoro da Fonseca and President Vargas A161

Wmk. 249

1939, Nov. 15 Photo. *Rouletted*

484	A160	400r deep green	.85	.50
485	A161	1200r chocolate	1.10	.50

Engr. *Perf. 11*

486	A162	800r gray black	.65	.50
		Nos. 484-486 (3)	2.60	1.50

Proclamation of the Republic, 50th anniv.

President Roosevelt, President Vargas and Map of the Americas A163

1940, Apr. 14

487	A163	400r slate blue	1.00	.55

Pan American Union, 50th anniversary.

Types of 1920-33

1940-41 Typo. Wmk. 264 *Perf. 11*

488	A75	10r red brown	.80	.80
489	A75	20r dull violet	.80	.80
489A	A75	50r blue grn ('41)	1.50	*1.75*
490	A75	100r yellow org	2.50	.50
491	A116	200r violet	7.50	.50
492	A76	400r ultra	7.50	.25
493	A76	600r dull orange	10.00	.50
494	A76	1000r turq blue	22.50	.50
		Nos. 488-494 (8)	53.10	*5.60*

Map of Brazil — A164

1940, Sept. 7 Engr.

495	A164	400r carmine	.50	.50
a.		Unwmkd.	50.00	30.00

9th Brazilian Congress of Geography held at Florianopolis.

Victoria Regia Water Lily — A165

President Vargas — A166

Relief Map of Brazil — A167

1940, Oct. 30 Wmk. 249 *Perf. 11*
Without Gum

496 A165 1000r dull violet	1.40	1.75
a. Sheet of 10	14.50	*35.00*
497 A166 5000r red	10.00	10.00
a. Sheet of 10	125.00	*175.00*
498 A167 10,000r slate blue	15.00	7.50
a. Sheet of 10	160.00	*175.00*
Nos. 496-498 (3)	26.40	19.25

New York World's Fair.

All three sheets exist unwatermarked and also with papermaker's watermark of large globe and "AMERICA BANK" in sheet. A few imperforate sheets also exist.

Joaquim Machado de Assis — A168

1940, Nov. 1

499 A168 400r black .65 .25

Birth centenary of Joaquim Maria Machado de Assis, poet and novelist.

Pioneers and Buildings of Porto Alegre — A169

1940, Nov. 2 Wmk. 264

500 A169 400r green .60 .30

Colonization of Porto Alegre, bicent.

Proclamation of King John IV of Portugal — A173

1940, Dec. 1 Wmk. 249

501 A173 1200r blue black 2.50 .50

800th anniv. of Portuguese independence and 300th anniv. of the restoration of the monarchy.

No. 501 was also printed on paper with papermaker's watermark of large globe and "AMERICA BANK." Unwatermarked copies are from these sheets. Value of unwatermarked stamps, $150.

Brazilian Flags and Head of Liberty — A175

Wmk. 256

1940, Dec. 18 Engr. *Perf. 11*

502 A175 400r dull violet	.70	.25
b. Unwmkd.	22.50	22.50

Wmk. 245

502A A175 400r dull violet 75.00 50.00

10th anniv. of the inauguration of President Vargas.

SEMI-POSTAL STAMPS

National Philatelic Exhibition Issue

SP1

Thick Paper

Wmk. Coat of Arms in Sheet (236)

1934, Sept. 16 Engr. *Imperf.*

B1 SP1 200r + 100r dp claret	1.25	*3.00*
B2 SP1 300r + 100r ver	1.25	*3.00*
B3 SP1 700r + 100r brt bl	8.00	*27.50*
B4 SP1 1000r + 100r blk	8.00	*27.50*
Nos. B1-B4 (4)	18.50	*61.00*

The surtax was to help defray the expenses of the exhibition. Issued in sheets of 60, inscribed "EXPOSICAO FILATELICA NACIONAL."

Red Cross Nurse and Soldier SP2

Wmk. 222

1935, Sept. 19 Typo. *Perf. 11*

B5 SP2 200r + 100r pur & red	1.75	1.25
B6 SP2 300r + 100r ol brn & red	2.00	.90
B7 SP2 700r + 100r turq bl & red	12.50	7.00
Nos. B5-B7 (3)	16.25	9.15

3rd Pan-American Red Cross Conf. Exist imperf.

Three Wise Men and Star of Bethlehem — SP3

Angel and Child — SP4

Southern Cross and Child — SP5

Mother and Child — SP6

Wmk. 249

1939-40 Litho. *Perf. 10½*

B8 SP3 100r + 100r chlky bl & bl blk	1.60	1.60
a. Horiz. or vert. pair, imperf. between	40.00	
B9 SP4 200r + 100r brt grnsh bl	2.25	2.10
a. Horizontal pair, imperf. between	40.00	
B10 SP5 400r + 200r ol grn & ol	1.75	1.10
B11 SP6 1200r + 400r crim & brn red	7.00	3.25
a. Vertical pair, imperf. between	40.00	
Nos. B8-B11 (4)	12.60	8.05

Dates of issue: No. B8, 12/20/39; Nos. B9-B11, 2/26/40.

Surtax for charitable institutions.

For surcharges see Nos. C55-C59 in *Scott Standard Postage Stamp Catalogue*, Vol. 1.

AIR POST STAMPS

Nos. O14-O29 Surcharged

1927, Dec. 28 Unwmk. *Perf. 12*

C1 O2 50r on 10r	.45	.35
a. Inverted surcharge	325.00	
b. Top ornaments missing	75.00	
C2 O2 200r on 1000r	2.25	*4.50*
a. Double surcharge	325.00	
C3 O2 200r on 2000r	1.40	*10.00*
a. Double surcharge	750.00	
b. Double surcharge, one inverted	750.00	
C4 O2 200r on 5000r	1.75	1.40
a. Double surcharge	325.00	—
b. Double surcharge, one inverted	350.00	
c. Triple surcharge	450.00	
C5 O2 300r on 500r	1.75	2.25
C6 O2 300r on 600r	.85	.90
b. Pair, one without surch.	—	
C6A O2 500r on 10r	400.00	425.00
C7 O2 500r on 50r	1.75	.70
a. Double surcharge	300.00	—
C8 O2 1000r on 20r	1.40	.45
a. Double surcharge	300.00	—
C9 O2 2000r on 100r	3.00	1.75
a. Pair, one without surcharge	—	
b. Double surcharge	300.00	
C10 O2 2000r on 200r	4.00	1.75
C11 O2 2000r on 10,000r	3.50	.70
C12 O2 5000r on 20,000r	10.00	4.00
C13 O2 5000r on 50,000r	10.00	4.00
C14 O2 5000r on 100,000r	32.50	30.00
C15 O2 10,000r on 500,000r	35.00	20.00
C16 O2 10,000r on 1,000,000r	45.00	37.50
Nos. C1-C6,C7-C16 (16)	154.60	120.25

Nos. C1, C1b, C6A, C7, C8 and C9 have small diamonds printed over the numerals in the upper corners.

Monument to de Gusmao — AP1

Santos-Dumont's Airship — AP2

Augusto Severo's Airship "Pax" — AP3

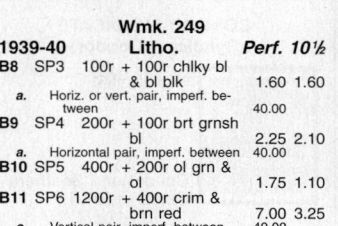

Santos-Dumont's Biplane "14 Bis" — AP4

Ribeiro de Barros's Seaplane "Jahu" — AP5

Perf. 11, 12½x13, 13x13½

1929 Typo. Wmk. 206

C17 AP1 50r blue grn	.35	.25
C18 AP2 200r red	1.40	.25
C19 AP3 300r brt blue	2.25	.25
C20 AP4 500r red violet	2.50	.25
C21 AP5 1000r orange brn	9.00	.40
Nos. C17-C21 (5)	15.50	1.40

See Nos. C32-C36. For surcharges see Nos. C26-C27.

Bartholomeu de Gusmao — AP6

Augusto Severo — AP7

Alberto Santos-Dumont AP8

Perf. 9, 11 and Compound

1929-30 Engr. Wmk. 101

C22 AP6 2000r lt green ('30)	14.00	.50
C23 AP7 5000r carmine	16.00	1.25
C24 AP8 10,000r olive grn	16.00	1.75
Nos. C22-C24 (3)	46.00	3.50

Nos. C23-C24 exist imperf.

See Nos. C37, C40.

Allegory: Airmail Service between Brazil and the US — AP9

1929 Typo. Wmk. 206

C25 AP9 3000r violet 14.00 1.75

Exists imperf. See Nos. C38, C41. For surcharge see No. C28.

Nos. C18-C19 Surcharged in Blue or Red

1931, Aug. 16 *Perf. 12½x13½*

C26 AP2 2500r on 200r (Bl)	30.00	25.00
C27 AP3 5000r on 300r (R)	35.00	30.00

No. C25 Surcharged

1931, Sept. 2 *Perf. 11*

C28 AP9 2500r on 3000r vio 27.50 *27.50*

a. Inverted surcharge 160.00 —

b. Surch. on front and back 160.00

Regular Issues of 1928-29 Surcharged

1932, May Wmk. 101 *Perf. 11, 11½*

C29 A89 3500r on 5000r gray lil 27.50 27.50

C30 A72 7000r on 10,000r rose 27.50 27.50

b. Horiz. pair, imperf. between *750.00*

Imperforates

Since 1933, imperforate or partly perforated sheets of nearly all of the airmail issues have become available.

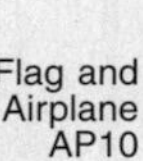

Flag and Airplane AP10

Wmk. 222

1933, June 7 Typo. *Perf. 11*

C31 AP10 3500r grn, yel & dk bl 6.50 2.00

See Nos. C39, C42.

1934 **Wmk. 222**

C32 AP1 50r blue grn 2.75 2.75

C33 AP2 200r red 3.25 .85

C34 AP3 300r brt blue 8.00 2.40

C35 AP4 500r red violet 3.25 .85

C36 AP5 1000r orange brn 11.00 .85

Nos. C32-C36 (5) 28.25 7.70

1934 Wmk. 236 Engr. *Perf. 12x11*

Thick Laid Paper

C37 AP6 2000r lt green 6.75 1.75

Types of 1929, 1933

Perf. 11, 11½, 12

1937-40 Typo. Wmk. 249

C38 AP9 3000r violet 25.00 2.25

C39 AP10 3500r grn, yel & dk bl 4.50 2.00

Engr.

C40 AP7 5000r ver ('40) 9.00 2.00

Nos. C38-C40 (3) 38.50 6.25

Watermark note after No. 501 also applies to No. C40.

Types of 1929-33

Perf. 11, 11½x12

1939-40 Typo. Wmk. 256

C41 AP9 3000r violet 2.40 .90

C42 AP10 3500r bl, dl grn & yel ('40) 2.40 .80

AIR POST SEMI-OFFICIAL STAMPS

Beginning in 1927, the Brazil government contracted with private companies to establish airmail service within Brazil, and from Brazil to cities in Europe and the United States. From 1927 to 1931, four major commercial airlines, Condor, Varig, Empresa de Transportes Aereos Ltda. (better known as E.T.A.) and Luftschiffbau Zeppelin G.m.b.H., carried mail under contract with the Brazil Post Office. Each company issued semi-official airmail stamps to be used on mail carried on these flights. These stamps paid the airmail fee, but postal regulations required that Brazil stamps also be affixed to the envelopes to pay regular Brazilian postage.

CONDOR SYNDICATE (Syndicato Condor)

Condor and Southern Cross — APL1

Wmk. 116

1927, Nov. 8 Litho. *Perf. 14*

1CL1 APL1 500r olive 5.50 4.00

Never hinged 8.25

1CL2 APL1 700r orange 5.50 2.00

Never hinged 8.25

1CL3 APL1 1000r red 5.50 2.00

Never hinged 8.25

1CL4 APL1 1300r green 5.50 2.00

Never hinged 8.25

1CL5 APL1 2000r dp Prus bl 11.00 2.00

Never hinged 16.50

1CL6 APL1 3000r violet 11.00 2.00

Never hinged 16.50

1CL7 APL1 10000r org ver 27.50 45.00

Never hinged 42.50

Nos. 1CL1-1CL7 (7) 71.50 59.00

Nos. 1CL1-1CL7 were printed by the Government Printing Office in Berlin. A second printing was never issued to the public. The stamps from the second printing have paler colors than the stamps from the original printing. Values of second-printing set, unused, $32.50; never hinged, $65.00.

Without "Syndicato Condor"

APL1a

1927

1CL8 APL1a 1300r green 135.00 —

Never hinged 210.00

a. 1300r pale green ('37) 72.50 —

Never hinged 110.00

No. 1CL8 is known with overprints: See Nos. 1CL13, 3CL1-3CL12, 3CLE1-3CLE2, 3CLF1-3CLF2, 4CL6-4CL7.

APL2

1930, Jan. 9 Unwmk. *Perf. 13*

1CL9 APL2 2000r black 180.00 27.50

Never hinged 275.00

On cover 70.00

No. 1CL9 was issued in commemoration of the Rio de Janeiro-Santos-San Francisco-Florianapolis-Itajai flight made January 4, 1927, which included in its list of passengers Dr. Victor Konder, Brazil's minister of transportation and public works. The stamp was printed by Casa da Moneda, Rio de Janeiro.

Nos. 1CL2, 1CL6, 1CL7,1CL8 Surcharged

No. 1CL10

No. 1CL11

No. 1CL12

No. 1CL13

1930, Sept. 10 *Perf. 13*

1CL10 APL1 50r on 700r 9.00 45.00

Never hinged 14.00

a. Inverted surcharge (*150*) 275.00 *450.00*

Never hinged 425.00

b. Double surcharge (*50*) 550.00 *700.00*

Never hinged 825.00

c. Triple surcharge 550.00

Never hinged 825.00

1CL11 APL1 200r on 3000r 9.00 37.50

Never hinged 14.00

1CL12 APL1 350r on 10000r 9.00 37.50

Never hinged 14.00

1CL13 APL1a 750r on 1300r 19.00 35.00

Never hinged 27.50

a. Inverted surcharge (*100*) 375.00 *550.00*

Never hinged 575.00

Nos. 1CL10-1CL13 (4) 46.00 155.00

Nos. CL10-CL13 were issued to pay the rate for letters weighing 5 grams or less.

REGISTRATION STAMPS

No. 1CLF1 — Block letter

No. 1CLF2 — Italic letter

No. 1CLF3 — Italic letter

1930, Sept. 10 *Perf. 13*

1CLF1 APL1 400r on 10000r, (*15,050*) 37.50 55.00

Never hinged 55.00

1CLF2 APL1 400r on 10000r, (*10,100*) 55.00 72.50

Never hinged 82.50

1CLF3 APL1 400r on 1300r, (*5,000*) 110.00 600.00

Never hinged 175.00

a. Inverted surcharge (*100*) 475.00

Never hinged 700.00

Nos. 1CLF1-1CLF3 (3) 202.50 727.50

E.T.A. Empresa de Transportes Aereos Ltda.

Plane — APL3

Perf. 11½

1929, June 17 Litho. Unwmk.

2CL1 APL3 200r brown & carmine (*2,600*) 275.00 300.00

2CL2 APL3 300r violet & red, perf 10¾ (*2,000*) 135.00 190.00

a. Plane inverted 2,250.

b. Block of 4 140.00

2CL3 APL3 1000r blue & red (*2,600*) 135.00 225.00

2CL4 APL3 2000r green & red (*2,600*) 135.00 225.00

2CL5 APL3 5,000r yellow & red (*2,600*) 135.00 225.00

a. Sheet of 16 stamps 3,250.

Nos. 2CL1-2CL5 (5) 815.00 1,165.

The first E.T.A. printing was in sheets of 16 stamps (Nos. 2CL1, 2CL3-2CL5) in four horizontal rows of four stamps each. The stamps were printed on thick paper with thick, streaky yellowish to brownish gum. No. 2CL2 was printed in blocks of four. All 300r stamps have two straight edges.

Plane — APL4

1929

2CL6 APL4 200r brown & carmine 90.00

2CL7 APL4 300r violet & red, perf 11¼ 90.00

a. Sheet of 16 stamps 1,650.

b. Block of 4 375.00

2CL8 APL4 1000r blue & red 90.00

2CL9 APL4 2000r green & red 90.00

2CL10 APL4 5,000r yellow & red 90.00

Nos. 2CL6-2CL10 (5) 450.00

The second E.T.A. printing was in sheets of 16 stamps (Nos. 2CL6, 2CL8-2CL10) in four horizontal rows of four stamps each. The stamps are printed on thinner paper with whitish gum.

No. 2CL7 was printed in blocks of four. All 300r stamps have two straight edges.

A printing also exists in which the five stamps were in one setting of 20 subjects. Sheets thus printed were separated. Examples of the 300r stamp that can be attributed to this printing are rare. A few vertical strips with all five stamps have survived. Value single stamp, $1,600.

VARIG (Viacao Aerea Riograndense)

Overprint in Red on No. 1CL8

No. 3CL1

Large "VARIG"

Small "VARIG"

Wmk. 116

1927, Nov. 9 Litho. *Perf. 14*

3CL1 APL1a 700r on 1300r green (*3,950*) 70.00 55.00

3CL2 APL1a 1300r green, "VARIG" 12.5mm (*15,000*) 14.00 5.00

3CL3 APL1a 1300r green, "VARIG" 9.5mm (*3,950*) 275.00 45.00

Nos. 3CL1-3CL3 (3) 359.00 105.00

Surcharge in Black on No. 1CL8

No. 3CL4

No. 3CL5

No. 3CL6

No. 3CL7

No. 3CL8

1928, Nov. 5

3CL4 APL1a 50r on 1300r green (*4,950*) 14.00 55.00

3CL5 APL1a 350r on 1300r green (*15,000*) 10.00 5.00

a. Inverted overprint 2,250. *550.00*

3CL6 APL1a 700r on 1300r green (*10,000*) 14.00 9.00
a. Inverted overprint 525.00 *900.00*

3CL7 APL1a 1050r on 1300r green (*3,000*) 110.00 110.00

3CL8 APL1a 1400r on 1300r green (*7,000*) 27.50 14.00

Surcharge in Red on No. 1CL8

No. 3CL9

No. 3CL10

No. 3CL11

No. 3CL12

3CL9 APL1a 500r on 1300r green (*2,500*) 27.50 110.00

3CL10 APL1a 1000r on 1300r green (*2,500*) 65.00 165.00

3CL11 APL1a 1500r on 1300r green (*2,500*) 27.50 110.00
a. Se-tenant pair (#3CL10 with #3CL11) (*50*) *3,750.* *3,750.*

3CL12 APL1a 2000r on 1300r green (*2,500*) 27.50 110.00

Nos. 3CL4-3CL12 (9) 323.00 688.00

Varig Logo (Icarus) — APL5

Perf. 13½

1931, Apr. 22 Typo. Unwmk.

3CL13 APL5 50r brn, *buff* (*30,000*) 2.75 7.25

3CL14 APL5 350r red (*60,000*) 5.50 1.00

3CL15 APL5 500r vio, *bluish* (*20,000*) 4.50 4.50

3CL16 APL5 700r red, *yel* (*40,000*) 14.00 2.00

3CL17 APL5 1000r claret, *rose* (*16,000*) 9.00 5.00

3CL18 APL5 1050r grn, *buff* (*15,000*) 9.00 5.50

3CL19 APL5 1400r red brn, *yel* (*15,000*) 25.00 5.50

3CL20 APL5 1500r dk grn, *lt grn* (*16,000*) 5.50 7.50

3CL21 APL5 2000r vio, *rose* (*10,000*) 40.00 11.00

3CL22 APL5 10000r black (*8,000*) 22.50 70.00

Nos. 3CL13-3CL22 (10) 137.75 119.25

Nos. 3CL13-3CL22 are occasionally found with part of a sheet watermark.

APL6

1932

3CL23 APL6 50r olive grn, *rose* (*40,000*) 7.50 27.50

3CL24 APL6 500r stl blue, *straw* (*30,000*) 9.00 9.00

APL7

1933, June 27

3CL25 APL7 50r dp grn, *pale grn* 2.00 4.50

3CL26 APL7 350r chestnut 14.00 2.00

3CL27 APL7 500r blue, *grn* 7.50 6.00

3CL28 APL7 1000r chnt, *rose* 35.00 22.50

3CL29 APL7 2000r dk blue, *rose* 27.50 22.50

Nos. 3CL25-3CL29 (5) 86.00 57.50

APL8

1934, Jan. 18

3CL30 APL8 50r red, *rose* 4.50 1.50

3CL31 APL8 350r yelsh grn 4.50 1.00

3CL32 APL8 500r lilac, *rose* 4.50 2.75

3CL33 APL8 700r grn, *pale grn* 4.50 1.50

3CL34 APL8 1050r org, *pale rose* 2.00 6.00

3CL35 APL8 1400r grnsh blue, *blue* (*30,000*) 2.00 6.00

3CL36 APL8 1500r brn car, *blue* (*25,000*) 4.00 15.00

Nos. 3CL30-3CL36 (7) 26.00 33.75

APL9

1934, June

3CL37 APL9 50r blue (*15,000*) 2.75 35.00

3CL38 APL9 1000r olive brown (*10,000*) 3.75 45.00

3CL39 APL9 1000r bluish grn (*15,000*) 2.75 82.50

3CL40 APL9 1050r pale chnt (*10,000*) 3.75 115.00

3CL41 APL9 1400r pale lil rose (*10,000*) 2.75 70.00

3CL42 APL9 1500r org ver (*15,000*) 2.75 70.00

3CL43 APL9 2000r red brown (*5,880*) 37.50 150.00

Nos. 3CL37-3CL43 (7) 56.00 567.50

SPECIAL DELIVERY

"E" and New Value in Black or Red

No. 3CLE1

No. 3CLE2

1928, Mar. 8

3CLE1 APL1a 700r on 1300r (#3CL1) (R) (*9,600*) 70.00 70.00

1931, Nov. 23

3CLE2 APL1a 700r on 1300r (#3CL2) (B) (*2,000*) 135.00 450.00

1933, Aug. 1

3CLE3 APL5 1000r on 1400r (#3CL19) (R) (*10,000*) 14.00 18.00

1934, Jan. 31

3CLE4 APL5 1000r on 1050r (#3CL34) (R) (*17,860*) 4.50 15.00

1934, June 16

3CLE5 APL5 1000r on 350r (#3CL31) (R) (*9,988*) 4.50 60.00

Nos. 3CLE1-3CLE5 (5) 228.00 613.00

REGISTRATION STAMPS

"R" and New Value in Black or Red

No. 3CLF1

No. 3CLF2

1928, Mar. 8

3CLF1 APL1a 400r on 1300r (#3CL2) (R) (*10,800*) 70.00 70.00

1931, Nov. 23

3CLF2 APL1a 400r on 1300r (#3CL2) (B) (*1,920*) 135.00 450.00

1933, Aug. 1

3CLF3 APL5 400r on 1050r (#3CL18) (B) (*10,000*) 14.00 18.00

1934, Jan. 18

3CLF4 APL5 400r on 700r (#3CL33) (B) (*18,354*) 5.00 15.00

1934, June 16

3CLF5 APL5 400r on 350r (#3CL31) (R) (*9,860*) 5.00 60.00

Nos. 3CLF1-3CLF5 (5) 229.00 613.00

LUFTSCHIFFBAU ZEPPELIN G.M.B.H.

Stamps for Graf Zeppelin Flights

Semi-official airmail stamps of Luftschiffbau Zeppelin G.m.b.H. paid the airmail fee for mail carried on Graf Zeppelin flights from Brazil to North America and Europe. The basic stamps were printed by the Government Printing Office, Berlin.

Graf Zeppelin APL10

Wmk. 127

1930, May 17 Typo. *Perf. 14*

4CL1 APL10 5000r green (*11,950*) 140.00 45.00
Never hinged 375.00
On cover 100.00

4CL2 APL10 10000r red (*11,880*) 27.50 45.00
Never hinged 45.00
On cover 100.00

4CL3 APL10 20000r blue (*5,865*) 90.00 175.00
Never hinged 175.00
On cover 275.00

Nos. 4CL1-4CL3 (3) 257.50 265.00

No. 4CL3 exists with a surcharge "5" known as the Paraiba (or Parahyba) Provisional . The surcharged stamp was used in Paraiba, Brazil. Experiencing a shortage of 5,000r stamps, the local post office was authorized to surcharge a few of the 20,000r stamps it had on hand. The provisional also was used in Recife, Brazil. Expertization of this stamp is essential.

No. 4CL4

No. 4CL5

1930, May 17

4CL4 APL6 5000r on 20000r blue (*4,013*) 225.00 300.00
Never hinged 450.00
On cover 400.00

4CL5 APL6 10000r on 20000r blue (*4,975*) 175.00 300.00
Never hinged 375.00
On cover 400.00

No. 1CL8 Surcharged in Black

No. 4CL6

No. 4CL7

1930, May 25

4CL6 APL1a 5000r on 1300r green (*4,985*) 45.00 90.00
Never hinged 90.00
On cover 1,000.

4CL7 APL1a 10000r on 1300r green 55.00
Never hinged 110.00

No. 4CL8

1930, May 25

4CL8 APL6 5000r green (*7,950*) 135.00 100.00
Never hinged 275.00
On cover 150.00

4CL9 APL6 10000r red (*8,100*) 90.00 100.00
Never hinged 175.00
On cover 150.00

4CL10 APL6 20000r blue (*3,390*) 140.00 400.00
Never hinged 275.00
On cover 450.00

Nos. 4CL8-4CL10 (3) 365.00 600.00

The Brazil Post Office issued stamps for use on mail carried on Zeppelin flights. See Nos. C26-C30.

SPECIAL DELIVERY STAMPS

No. 191 Surcharged

1930 Unwmk. *Perf. 12*

E1 A62 1000r on 200r dp blue 6.50 2.00
a. Inverted surcharge 500.00

POSTAGE DUE STAMPS

D1

1889 Unwmk. Typo. *Rouletted*
J1 D1 10r carmine 2.10 1.40
J2 D1 20r carmine 3.25 2.00
J3 D1 50r carmine 5.50 4.00
J4 D1 100r carmine 2.10 1.40
J5 D1 200r carmine 65.00 15.00
J6 D1 300r carmine 6.75 *8.00*
J7 D1 500r carmine 6.75 *8.00*
J8 D1 700r carmine 11.00 *14.00*
J9 D1 1000r carmine 11.00 10.00
Nos. J1-J9 (9) 113.45 63.80

Counterfeits are common.

1890
J10 D1 10r orange .65 .30
J11 D1 20r ultra .65 .30
J12 D1 50r olive 1.40 .30
J13 D1 200r magenta 6.75 .60
J14 D1 300r blue green 3.25 1.50
J15 D1 500r slate 4.50 3.00
J16 D1 700r purple 5.25 *7.75*
J17 D1 1000r dk violet 6.50 5.00
Nos. J10-J17 (8) 28.95 18.75

Counterfeits are common.

D2

Perf. 11 to 11½, 12½ to 14 and Compound

1895-1901
J18 D2 10r dk blue ('01) 2.10 1.25
J19 D2 20r yellow grn 8.75 3.00
J20 D2 50r yellow grn ('01) 11.00 5.50
J21 D2 100r brick red 7.25 1.25
J22 D2 200r violet 6.75 .60
a. 200r gray lilac ('98) 13.00 2.00
J23 D2 300r dull blue 4.00 2.25
J24 D2 2000r brown 13.00 13.00
Nos. J18-J24 (7) 52.85 26.85

1906 Wmk. 97
J25 D2 100r brick red 8.75 3.00

Wmk. (97? or 98?)
J26 D2 200r violet 8.75 1.25
a. Wmk. 97 350.00 85.00
b. Wmk. 98 14.50 50.00

D3

1906-10 Unwmk. Engr. *Perf. 12*
J28 D3 10r slate .25 .25
J29 D3 20r brt violet .25 .25
J30 D3 50r dk green .30 .25
J31 D3 100r carmine 2.00 .60
J32 D3 200r dp blue 1.10 .30
J33 D3 300r gray blk .40 .60
J34 D3 400r olive grn 1.40 .90
J35 D3 500r dk violet 40.00 40.00
J36 D3 600r violet ('10) 1.40 *3.00*
J37 D3 700r red brown 35.00 30.00
J38 D3 1000r red 1.60 *3.25*
J39 D3 2000r green 5.25 5.50
J40 D3 5000r choc ('10) 1.60 *24.00*
Nos. J28-J40 (13) 90.55 108.90

D4

Perf. 12½, 11, 11x10½

1919-23 Typo.
J41 D4 5r red brown .30 .25
J42 D4 10r violet .60 .25
J43 D4 20r olive gray .30 .25
J44 D4 50r green ('23) .30 .25
J45 D4 100r red 1.75 1.10
J46 D4 200r blue 8.75 2.10
J47 D4 400r brown ('23) 1.75 1.60
Nos. J41-J47 (7) 13.75 5.80

Perf. 12½, 12½x13½

1924-35 Wmk. 100
J48 D4 5r red brown .25 .25
J49 D4 100r red .85 .70
J50 D4 200r slate bl ('29) 1.25 .50
J51 D4 400r dp brn ('29) 1.50 1.00
J52 D4 600r dk vio ('29) 1.75 1.10
J53 D4 600r orange ('35) .75 .50
Nos. J48-J53 (6) 6.35 4.05

1924 Wmk. 193 *Perf. 11x10½*
J54 D4 100r red 55.00 55.00
J55 D4 200r slate blue 6.00 6.00

Perf. 11x10½, 13x13½

1925-27 Wmk. 101
J56 D4 20r olive gray .25 .25
J57 D4 100r red 1.25 .35
J58 D4 200r slate blue 4.50 .50
J59 D4 400r brown 3.25 2.00
J60 D4 600r dk violet 5.50 3.25
Nos. J56-J60 (5) 14.75 6.35

Wmk. E U BRASIL Multiple (218)

1929-30 *Perf. 12½x13½*
J61 D4 100r light red .50 .25
J62 D4 200r blue black 1.75 .50
J63 D4 400r brown 1.75 .50
J64 D4 1000r myrtle green 1.75 .75
Nos. J61-J64 (4) 5.75 2.00

Perf. 11, 12½x13, 13

1931-36 Wmk. 222
J65 D4 10r lt violet ('35) .25 .25
J66 D4 20r black ('33) .25 .25
J67 D4 50r blue grn ('35) .50 .25
J68 D4 100r rose red ('35) .50 .25
J69 D4 200r sl blue ('35) 2.00 .50
J70 D4 400r blk brn ('35) 3.25 2.00
J71 D4 600r dk violet .50 .25
J72 D4 1000r myrtle grn .65 .50
J73 D4 2000r brown ('36) 1.10 1.10
J74 D4 5000r indigo ('36) 1.25 1.00
Nos. J65-J74 (10) 10.25 6.35

1938 Wmk. 249 *Perf. 11*
J75 D4 200r slate blue 2.75 1.00

1940 Typo. Wmk. 256
J76 D4 10r light violet 1.10 1.10
J77 D4 20r black 1.10 1.10
J79 D4 100r rose red 1.10 1.10
J80 D4 200r myrtle green 2.40 1.10
Nos. J76-J80 (4) 5.70 4.40

OFFICIAL STAMPS

Pres. Affonso Penna — O1

Unwmk.

1906, Nov. 15 Engr. *Perf. 12*
O1 O1 10r org & grn 1.00 .30
O2 O1 20r org & grn 1.25 .30
O3 O1 50r org & grn 1.90 .30
O4 O1 100r org & grn 1.00 .30
O5 O1 200r org & grn 1.25 .30
O6 O1 300r org & grn 4.00 .60
O7 O1 400r org & grn 8.25 2.75
O8 O1 500r org & grn 4.00 1.60
O9 O1 700r org & grn 5.25 3.75
O10 O1 1000r org & grn 5.25 1.25
O11 O1 2000r org & grn 7.50 2.25
O12 O1 5000r org & grn 13.50 1.60
O13 O1 10,000r org & grn 13.50 1.40
Nos. O1-O13 (13) 67.65 16.70

The portrait is the same but the frame differs for each denomination of this issue.

Pres. Hermes da Fonseca — O2

1913, Nov. 15 Center in Black
O14 O2 10r gray .40 .55
O15 O2 20r ol grn .40 .55
O16 O2 50r gray .40 .55
O17 O2 100r ver 1.10 .40
O18 O2 200r blue 2.00 .40
O19 O2 500r orange 3.50 .65
O20 O2 600r violet 4.00 2.50
O21 O2 1000r blk brn 5.00 1.75
O22 O2 2000r red brn 7.50 1.75
O23 O2 5000r brown 8.75 3.50
O24 O2 10,000r black 16.00 7.75
O25 O2 20,000r blue 30.00 30.00
O26 O2 50,000r green 55.00 55.00
O27 O2 100,000r org red 200.00 200.00
O28 O2 500,000r brown 325.00 325.00
O29 O2 1,000,000r dk brn 350.00 350.00
Nos. O14-O29 (16) 1,009. 980.35

The portrait is the same on all denominations of this series but there are eight types of the frame.

Pres. Wenceslau Braz — O3

Perf. 11, 11½

1919, Apr. 11 Wmk. 100
O30 O3 10r olive green .50 *9.00*
O31 O3 50r green 1.25 1.25
O32 O3 100r rose red 2.00 .85
O33 O3 200r dull blue 3.50 .85
O34 O3 500r orange 9.25 *40.00*
Nos. O30-O34 (5) 16.50 51.95

The official decree called for eleven stamps in this series but only five were issued.
For surcharges see Nos. 293-297.

NEWSPAPER STAMPS

N1

Rouletted

1889, Feb. 1 Unwmk. Litho.
P1 N1 10r yellow 3.25 7.25
a. Pair, imperf. between 125.00 140.00
P2 N1 20r yellow 9.00 9.00
P3 N1 50r yellow 15.00 12.50
P4 N1 100r yellow 7.50 3.00
P5 N1 200r yellow 3.00 2.50
P6 N1 300r yellow 3.00 2.50
P7 N1 500r yellow 30.00 15.00
P8 N1 700r yellow 3.00 *20.00*
P9 N1 1000r yellow 3.00 *20.00*
Nos. P1-P9 (9) 76.75 91.75

For surcharges see Nos. 125-127.

1889, May 1
P10 N1 10r olive 3.00 1.25
P11 N1 20r green 3.00 1.25
P12 N1 50r brn yel 3.00 1.25
P13 N1 100r violet 4.50 3.00
a. 100r deep violet 7.50 *20.00*
b. 100r lilac 14.00 3.00
P14 N1 200r black 4.50 3.00
P15 N1 300r carmine 17.50 17.50
P16 N1 500r green 75.00 *90.00*
P17 N1 700r pale blue 50.00 *55.00*
a. 700r ultramarine 90.00 *100.00*
b. 700r cobalt 425.00 *450.00*
P18 N1 1000r brown 17.50 *75.00*
Nos. P10-P18 (9) 178.00 247.25

For surcharges see Nos. 128-135.

N2

White Wove Paper Thin to Thick

Perf. 11 to 11½, 12½ to 14 and 12½ to 14x11 to 11½

1890 Typo.
P19 N2 10r blue 22.50 10.00
a. 10r ultramarine 22.50 10.00
P20 N2 20r emerald 70.00 20.00
P21 N2 100r violet 22.50 14.00
Nos. P19-P21 (3) 115.00 44.00

For surcharge see No. 137.

N3

1890-93
P22 N3 10r ultramarine 5.00 3.00
a. 10r blue 9.00 4.00
P23 N3 10r ultra, *buff* 3.00 3.00
P24 N3 20r green 10.00 3.00
a. 20r emerald 10.00 3.00
P25 N3 50r yel grn ('93) 25.00 15.00
Nos. P22-P25 (4) 43.00 24.00

For surcharges see Nos. 136, 138-139.

POSTAL TAX STAMPS

Icarus from the Santos-Dumont Monument at St. Cloud, France — PT1

Perf. 13½x12½, 11

1933, Oct. 1 Typo. Wmk. 222
RA1 PT1 100r deep brown .75 .25

Honoring the Brazilian aviator, Santos-Dumont. Its use was obligatory as a tax on all correspondence sent to countries in South America, the US and Spain. Its use on correspondence to other countries was optional. The funds obtained were used for the construction of airports throughout Brazil.

BRITISH CENTRAL AFRICA

'bri-tish 'sen-trəl 'a-fri-kə

LOCATION — Central Africa, on the west shore of Lake Nyassa
GOVT. — British territory, under charter to the British South Africa Company
AREA — 37,800 sq. mi.
POP. — 1,639,329
CAPITAL — Zomba

In 1907 the name was changed to Nyasaland Protectorate, and stamps so inscribed replaced those of British Central Africa.

12 Pence = 1 Shilling
20 Shillings = 1 Pound

Rhodesia Nos. 2, 4-19 Overprinted in Black

1891-95 Unwmk. *Perf. 14*

No.	Type	Description	Unused	Used
1	A1	1p black	12.00	*11.00*
2	A2	2p gray green & ver	13.00	*5.00*
a.		Half used as 1p on cover ('95)		*7,000.*
3	A2	4p red brn & blk	14.00	*7.50*
4	A1	6p ultramarine	60.00	24.00
5	A1	6p dark blue	19.00	*10.00*
6	A2	8p rose & blue	20.00	*35.00*
a.		8p red & ultra	42.50	*55.00*
7	A1	1sh bis brown	27.50	19.00
8	A1	2sh vermilion	50.00	*60.00*
9	A1	2sh6p gray lilac	90.00	*105.00*
a.		2sh6p gray purple	90.00	*105.00*
10	A2	3sh brn & grn ('95)	90.00	*90.00*
11	A2	4sh gray & ver ('93)	100.00	*110.00*
12	A1	5sh yellow	110.00	*120.00*
13	A1	10sh green	200.00	*230.00*
14	A3	£1 blue	1,300.	*800.00*
15	A3	£2 rose red	1,400.	*1,600.*
16	A3	£5 yel green	2,250.	—
17	A3	£10 red brown	*4,500.*	*5,500.*
		Nos. 1-13 (13)	805.50	*826.50*

High values with fiscal cancellation are fairly common and can be purchased at a small fraction of the above values. This applies to subsequent issues also. The most common fiscal marking consists of an undated double-circle cancel with the words "BRITISH CENTRAL AFRICA" between the circles, and a town name in the center. This cancel exists in various sizes and is usually applied in black.

For surcharge see No. 20.

Rhodesia Nos. 13-14 Surcharged in Black

1892-93

No.	Type	Description	Unused	Used
18	A2	3sh on 4sh gray & ver ('93)	400.00	400.00
19	A1	4sh on 5sh yellow	100.00	*110.00*

No. 2 Surcharged in Black, with Bar

1895

No.	Type	Description	Unused	Used
20	A2	1p on 2p	37.50	*65.00*
a.		Double surcharge	*11,000.*	*8,000.*

A double surcharge, without period after "Penny," and measuring 16mm instead of 18mm, is from a trial printing made at Blantyre. Value, $650.

A4

Coat of Arms of the Protectorate — A5

1895 Unwmk. Typo. *Perf. 14*

No.	Type	Description	Unused	Used
21	A4	1p black	20.00	16.00
22	A4	2p grn & blk	55.00	14.50
23	A4	4p org & blk	90.00	52.50
24	A4	6p ultra & blk	95.00	10.00
25	A4	1sh rose & blk	120.00	42.50
26	A5	2sh6p vio & blk	375.00	375.00
27	A5	3sh yel & blk	225.00	65.00
28	A5	5sh ol & blk	300.00	275.00
29	A5	£1 org & blk	1,200.	800.00
30	A5	£10 ver & blk	*8,000.*	*5,500.*
31	A5	£25 bl grn & blk	*16,000.*	*16,000.*
		Nos. 21-28 (8)	1,280.	850.50
		Nos. 21-29, overprinted "SPECIMEN"	450.00	

1896 Wmk. 2

No.	Type	Description	Unused	Used
32	A4	1p black	4.25	*10.00*
33	A4	2p green & black	22.00	6.00
34	A4	4p org brown & blk	37.50	*21.00*
35	A4	6p ultra & black	50.00	17.50
36	A4	1sh rose & black	50.00	25.00

Wmk. 1 Sideways

No.	Type	Description	Unused	Used
37	A5	2sh6p vio rose & blk	200.00	*160.00*
38	A5	3sh yel & black	180.00	75.00
39	A5	5sh olive & blk	275.00	*275.00*
40	A5	£1 blue & blk	1,200.	650.00
41	A5	£10 ver & blk	*11,000.*	*6,000.*
		Overprinted "SPECIMEN"	275.00	
42	A5	£25 bl grn & blk	*26,000.*	—
		Overprinted "SPECIMEN"	425.00	
		Nos. 32-39 (8)	818.75	*589.50*
		Nos. 32-40, overprinted "SPECIMEN"	450.00	

A6

A7

1897-1901 Wmk. 2

No.	Type	Description	Unused	Used
43	A6	1p ultra & blk	4.00	1.50
44	A6	1p rose & vio ('01)	3.50	.80
45	A6	2p yel & black	3.25	2.50
46	A6	4p car rose & blk	8.00	2.25
47	A6	4p ol grn & vio ('01)	12.00	*13.50*
48	A6	6p grn & blk	60.00	5.25
49	A6	6p red brn & vio ('01)	11.00	4.50
50	A6	1sh gray lil & blk	13.50	8.50

Wmk. 1

No.	Type	Description	Unused	Used
51	A7	2sh6p ultra & blk	100.00	*50.00*
52	A7	3sh gray grn & blk	350.00	*375.00*
53	A7	4sh car rose & blk	130.00	*100.00*
54	A7	10sh ol & blk	325.00	*325.00*
55	A7	£1 dp vio & blk	500.00	275.00
56	A7	£10 org & black	*8,500.*	*2,750.*
		Overprinted "SPECIMEN"	300.00	
		Nos. 43-54 (12)	1,020.	*888.80*
		Nos. 43-55, overprinted "SPECIMEN"	400.00	

No. 52 Surcharged in Red

1897

No.	Type	Description	Unused	Used
57	A7	1p on 3sh	11.00	*20.00*
a.		"PNNEY"	9,500.	7,000.
b.		"PENN"	4,500.	3,750.
c.		Double surcharge	800.00	1,300.

A8

Type I — The vertical framelines are not continuous between stamps.

Type II — The vertical framelines are continuous between stamps.

1898, Mar. 11 Unwmk. *Imperf.*

Type I

Control on Reverse

No.	Type	Description	Unused	Used
58	A8	1p ver & ultra	—	145.00
a.		1p ver & deep ultra	5,500.	150.00
b.		No control on reverse	6,500.	220.00
c.		Control double		525.00
d.		Control on front		*3,900.*
e.		Pair, one without oval	*32,500.*	

Type II

Control on Reverse

No.	Type	Description	Unused	Used
f.		1p ver & ultra	—	800.00

No Control on Reverse

No.	Type	Description	Unused	Used
g.		1p grayish blue & ver, initials on back	16,000.	1,100.
h.		No initials	7,500.	
i.		Oval inverted	32,500.	
j.		Oval double	—	
k.		Pair, with 3 ovals	—	

Perf. 12

Type I

Control on Reverse

No.	Type	Description	Unused	Used
59	A8	1p ver & ultra	6,000.	35.00
a.		1p ver & deep ultra	—	47.50
b.		Two diff. controls on reverse	—	850.00

No Control on Reverse

No.	Type	Description	Unused	Used
d.		1p ver & ultra	5,500.	115.00

There are 30 types of each setting of Nos. 58-59.

No. 58 issued without gum.

Control consists of figures or letters.

Initials are of Postmaster General (J.G. or J.T.G.).

A9

King Edward VII — A10

1903-04 Wmk. 2

No.	Type	Description	Unused	Used
60	A9	1p car & black	9.50	2.25
61	A9	2p vio & dull vio	4.50	2.25
62	A9	4p blk & gray green	3.25	*11.00*
63	A9	6p org brn & blk	4.00	*4.00*
64	A9	1sh pale blue & blk ('04)	5.00	*16.00*

Wmk. 1

No.	Type	Description	Unused	Used
65	A10	2sh6p gray green	70.00	*110.00*
66	A10	4sh vio & dl vio	90.00	*105.00*
67	A10	10sh blk & gray green	200.00	*300.00*
68	A10	£1 scar & blk	360.00	250.00
69	A10	£10 ultra & blk	*8,000.*	*4,750.*
		Overprinted "SPECIMEN"	500.00	
		Nos. 60-68 (9)	746.25	*800.50*
		Nos. 60-68, overprinted "SPECIMEN"	425.00	

1907 Wmk. 3

No.	Type	Description	Unused	Used
70	A9	1p car & black	9.00	3.50
71	A9	2p vio & dull vio	*19,000.*	
72	A9	4p blk & gray grn	*19,000.*	
73	A9	6p org brn & blk	47.50	*60.00*

Nos. 71-72 were not issued.

British Central Africa stamps were replaced by those of Nyasaland Protectorate in 1908.

BRITISH EAST AFRICA

'bri-tish 'ēst 'a-fri-kə

LOCATION — East coast of Africa; modern Kenya. Included all of the territory in East Africa under British control.

Postage stamps were issued by the Imperial British East Africa Company (IBEAC) in May 1900. Transferred to the Crown as a Protectorate July 1, 1895. Postal administration amalgamated with Uganda in 1901 with new stamps issued in July 1903 inscribed 'East Africa and Uganda Protectorates.'

16 Annas = 1 Rupee

STAMPS OF INDIA USED IN BRITISH EAST AFRICA

1890, July-Oct.

A1	½a green (#36)	*600.*
A2	1a maroon (#38)	*540.*
A3	1a6p bister brown (#39)	*900.*
A4	2a ultramarine (#40)	*1,000.*
A5	3a brown orange (#41)	*1,000.*
A6	4a6p green (#43)	*325.*
A7	8a red violet (#44)	*540.*
A8	1r gray (#46)	*1,000.*

As Nos. 1-3 ran out, the Mombasa Post Office utilized unoverprinted Indian stamps for mail. Stamps so used were cancelled with the 21mm Mombasa circular datestamp with indicia C. Indian stamps were also used at Lamu during this period, and stamps with Lamu cancellations are worth much more than the values above.

Stamps of India with British East Africa cancellations at later dates originate on ship mail.

A1

A2

Queen Victoria — A3

1890 Wmk. 30 *Perf. 14*

1	A1	½a on 1p lilac	350.00	240.00

Beware of forgeries.

2	A2	1a on 2p grn & car rose	575.00	350.00
3	A3	4a on 5p lilac & bl	600.00	375.00

Covers: Commercial covers of this issue are rare. Values start at about $2,000.

Fournier and other forgeries exist.

A4

Sun and Crown Symbolical of "Light and Liberty" — A5

1890-94 Unwmk. Litho. *Perf. 14*

14	A4	½a bister brown	1.25	*15.00*
b.		½a deep brown	1.00	*10.00*
c.		As "b," horiz. pair, imperf. btwn.	*1,925.*	775.00
d.		As "b," vert. pair, imperf. btwn.	1,400.	600.00
f.		½a dull brown	6.50	*9.00*
15	A4	1a blue green	9.50	*15.00*
b.		1a deep blue green ('95)	1.00	
c.		"ANL" (broken "D" in "AND")	850.00	850.00
d.		As "c," imperf. pair	18,000.	
16	A4	2a vermilion	5.00	*6.50*
17	A4	2½a black, *yel* ('91)	5.50	*8.50*
a.		Horiz. pair, imperf. btwn.	8,000.	
b.		2½a black, *pale buff* ('92)	110.00	10.50
c.		2½a black, *bright yellow* ('93)	110.00	30.00
e.		As "c," horiz. pair, imperf. btwn.	1,700.	550.00
f.		As "c," vert. pair, imperf. btwn.	1,700.	725.00
18	A4	3a black, *red* ('91)	5.50	*12.00*
b.		Horiz. pair, imperf. btwn.	1,400.	525.00
c.		Vert. pair, imperf. btwn.	1,400.	600.00
d.		3a black, *dull red* ('91)	16.50	*17.50*
19	A4	4a yellow brown	3.00	*14.00*
20	A4	4½a brn vio ('91)	3.00	*21.00*
b.		4½a gray violet ('91)	42.50	19.00
c.		Horiz. pair, imperf. btwn.	2,100.	1,200.
d.		Vert. pair, imperf. btwn.	1,200.	600.00
21	A4	5a blk, *blue* ('94)	1.50	*13.00*
		Handstamped "SPECIMEN"	52.50	
22	A4	7½a black ('94)	1.50	*19.00*
		Handstamped "SPECIMEN"	52.50	
23	A4	8a blue	6.75	*11.50*
24	A4	8a gray	350.00	*350.00*
25	A4	1r rose	7.50	*11.00*
26	A4	1r gray	275.00	275.00
27	A5	2r brick red	17.00	*50.00*
28	A5	3r gray violet	12.00	*60.00*
29	A5	4r ultra	15.00	*60.00*
30	A5	5r gray green	37.50	*85.00*
		Nos. 14-30 (17)	756.50	*1,027.*

Some of the paper used for this issue had a papermaker's watermark and parts of it often can be seen on the stamps.

Values for Nos. 14c, 14d, 17b, 17c, 18b, 18c, 20c, 20d, unused, are for examples with little or no original gum. Stamps with natural straight edges are almost as common as fully perforated stamps from the early printings of Nos. 14-30, and for all printings of the rupee values. Values about the same.

For surcharges and overprints see Nos. 31-53.

1890-93 *Imperf.*

Values for Pairs except No. 19b.

14a	A4	½a bister brown	1,200.	450.
14e	A4	½a deep brown	1,700.	725.
15a	A4	1a blue green	4,750.	1,200.
d.		"ANL" (broken "D")	18,000.	
16a	A4	2a vermilion	4,500.	1,300.
17d	A4	2½a blk, *brt yel*	1,200.	550.
18a	A4	3a black, *red*	1,200.	500.
19a	A4	4a yel brown	4,750.	1,600.
19b	A4	4a gray	1,500.	1,700.
20a	A4	4½a dull violet	2,000.	550.
23a	A4	8a blue	10,000.	1,400.
25a	A4	1r rose	15,000.	1,600.

A6

Handstamped Surcharges

1891 *Perf. 14*

31	A6	½a on 2a ver ("A.D.")	14,000.	1,100.
a.		Double surcharge		*13,000.*
b.		Original denomination not obliterated		*3,000.*
32	A6	1a on 4a yel brn ("A.B.")	21,000.	2,300.

Validation initials are shown in parentheses. See note below No. 35.

Manuscript Surcharges

1891-95

33	A6	½a on 2a ver ("A.B.")	17,000.	1,100.
a.		"½ Annas" ("A.B.")		1,200.
b.		Initialed "A.D."		6,500.
34	A6	½a on 3a blk, *red* ("T.E.C.R.")	700.	60.
b.		Initialed "A.B."	18,000.	2,750.
34A	A6	1a on 3a blk, *red* ("V.H.M.")	16,000.	2,250.
c.		Initialed "T.E.C.R."	23,000.	3,250.
35	A6	1a on 4a yel brn ("A.B.")	12,000.	2,200.

The manuscript initials on Nos. 31-35, given in parentheses, stand for Andrew Dick, Archibald Brown, Victor H. Mackenzie (1891) and T.E.C. Remington (1895).

Three persons applied the surcharge to No. 33, and two persons applied the surcharge to No. 35, resulting in different types.

A7

1894 Printed Surcharges

36	A7	5a on 8a blue	85.00	*110.00*
37	A7	7½a on 1r rose	85.00	*110.00*
		Set, handstamped "SPECIMEN"	100.00	

Stamps of 1890-94 Handstamped in Black

1895

38	A4	½a deep brown	90.00	35.00
b.		Inverted overprint		*6,000.*
c.		½a bister brown		*2,700.*
d.		½a pale brown	120.00	*50.00*
39	A4	1a blue green	200.00	135.00
a.		1a deep blue-green	—	3,250.
b.		"ANL" (broken "D")	3,000.	
40	A4	2a vermilion	220.00	115.00
41	A4	2½a black, *yel*	220.00	67.50
a.		2½a black, *pale buff*	—	2,250.
42	A4	3a black, *dull red*	105.00	60.00
43	A4	4a yel brown	65.00	42.50
44	A4	4½a gray violet	250.00	120.00
a.		4½a brown violet	1,450.	1,150.
45	A4	5a black, *blue*	300.00	170.00
b.		Inverted overprint		*5,000.*
46	A4	7½a black	150.00	100.00
47	A4	8a blue	115.00	90.00
b.		Inverted overprint	*8,000.*	
48	A4	1r rose	67.50	60.00
49	A5	2r brick red	550.00	325.00
50	A5	3r gray violet	275.00	160.00
b.		Inverted overprint		
51	A5	4r ultra	250.00	200.00
52	A5	5r gray green	525.00	*325.00*
		Nos. 38-52 (15)	3,383.	2,005.

Forgeries exist.

Double Overprints

38a	A4	½a	550.	525.
39a	A4	1a	750.	550.
40a	A4	2a	850.	575.
41a	A4	2½a	850.	525.
43a	A4	4a	600.	550.
44b	A4	4½a gray violet	900.	675.
44c	A4	4½a brown violet	3,300.	2,400.
45a	A4	5a	1,100.	1,000.
46a	A4	7½a	850.	675.
47a	A4	8a	750.	725.
48a	A4	1r	700.	675.
50a	A5	3r	1,200.	1,100.
51a	A5	4r	1,100.	1,000.
52a	A5	5r	1,600.	1,600.

Surcharged in Red

1895

53	A4	2½a on 4½a gray vio	225.00	90.00
a.		Double overprint (#44b)	1,200.	1,050.

Stamps of India 1874-95 Overprinted or Surcharged

a

b

c

1895 Wmk. Star (39)

54	A17	½a green	8.50	*6.75*
55	A19	1a maroon	8.00	*7.25*
56	A20	1a6p bister brn	5.25	*5.00*
57	A21	2a ultra	9.00	3.75
58	A28	2a6p green	14.00	3.25
59	A20(a)	2½a on 1a6p bis brn	120.00	57.50
a.		"½" without fraction line	135.00	
d.		As "a," "1" of "½" invtd.	1,200.	725.00
62	A22	3a orange	24.00	*13.50*
63	A23	4a ol grn	50.00	42.50
a.		4a slate green	32.00	26.00
64	A25	8a red violet	35.00	*60.00*
a.		8a red lilac	110.00	85.00
65	A26	12a vio, *red*	27.50	*40.00*
66	A27	1r gray	115.00	80.00
67	A29	1r car & grn	55.00	*160.00*
a.		Dbl. ovpt., one sideways	525.00	1,100.
68	A30	2r bis & rose	120.00	*180.00*
69	A30	3r grn & brn	140.00	*200.00*
70	A30	5r vio & ultra	160.00	*200.00*
a.		Double overprint	2,750.	

Wmk. Elephant's Head (38)

71	A14	6a bister	50.00	*60.00*
		Nos. 54-59,62-71 (16)	941.25	*1,120.*

"Brit1sh" for "British"

54a	A17	½a	*7,250.*	*6,600.*
55a	A19	1a	*8,750.*	*4,750.*
57a	A21	2a	*7,750.*	*7,750.*
58a	A28	2a6p		*5,000.*

"Br1tish" for "British"

54b	A17	½a	450.00	
55b	A19	1a	525.00	
56a	A19	1a6p	550.00	
57b	A21	2a	475.00	*300.00*
58b	A28	2a6p	600.00	325.00
59b	A20(a)	2½a on 1a6p	*1,600.*	
62a	A22	3a	600.00	600.00
63b	A23	4a	800.00	600.00
64b	A25	8a red vio	900.00	775.00
64c	A25	8a red lilac	1,600.	
65a	A26	12a	825.00	825.00
66a	A27	1r gray	1,900.	
67b	A29	1r carmine & grn	1,600.	
71a	A14	6a	1,450.	

"Afr1ca" for "Africa"

54c	A17	½a	525.00	
55c	A19	1a	600.00	
56b	A19	1a6p	650.00	
57c	A21	2a	550.00	*400.00*
58c	A28	2a6p	725.00	425.00
59c	A20(a)	2½a on 1a6p	1,600.	
62b	A22	3a	800.00	
63c	A23	4a	900.00	725.00
64d	A25	8a red vio	925.00	800.00
64e	A25	8a red lilac	1,600.	
65b	A26	12a	950.00	
66b	A27	1r gray	1,900.	
67c	A29	1r carmine & grn	1,600.	
71b	A14	6a	1,600.	

Inverted "a" for "t"

64f	A25	8a red lilac		*17,000.*
67d	A29	1r carmine & grn	*11,000.*	

"Briti" for "British"

54d	A17	½a		*2,000.*
55d	A19	1a		*2,000.*
58d	A28	2a6p		*2,000.*

"Eas" for "East"

58f	A28	2a6p	1,200.	*1,600.*

"E st" for "East"

71c	A14	6a		—

Letter "B" handstamped

68a	A30	2r	*7,250.*	*7,250.*
69a	A30	3r	*7,250.*	*7,250.*
70b	A30	5r	*6,500.*	*6,000.*

No. 59 is surcharged in bright red; surcharges in brown red were prepared for the UPU, but not regularly issued as stamps. See note following No. 93.

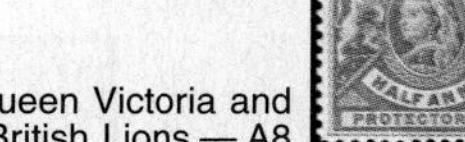

Queen Victoria and British Lions — A8

1896-1901 Engr. Wmk. 2 *Perf. 14*

72	A8	½a yel green	6.50	1.00
73	A8	1a carmine	16.00	.50
a.		1a red	15.00	.50
74	A8	1a dp rose ('01)	32.50	5.00
75	A8	2a chocolate	13.00	8.50
76	A8	2½a dark blue	18.00	2.50
a.		Inverted "S" in "ANNAS"	190.00	75.00
b.		2½a violet blue	20.00	2.50
77	A8	3a gray	10.00	*15.00*
78	A8	4a deep green	8.50	5.00
79	A8	4½a orange	17.50	*20.00*
80	A8	5a dk ocher	9.25	8.00
81	A8	7½a lilac	11.00	*27.00*
82	A8	8a olive gray	11.00	7.00
83	A8	1r ultra	140.00	80.00
a.		1r pale blue	80.00	30.00
84	A8	2r red orange	80.00	35.00
85	A8	3r deep violet	80.00	40.00
86	A8	4r lake	72.50	85.00
87	A8	5r dark brown	70.00	50.00
a.		Thin "U" in "RUPEES"	1,650.	1,350.
		Nos. 72-87 (16)	595.75	389.50
		Set, ovptd. "SPECIMEN"	325.00	

For Overprints see Uganda No. 77-78.

Zanzibar Nos. 38-40, 44-46 Overprinted in Black

1897 Wmk. Rosette (71)

88 A2 ½a yel grn & red 67.50 55.00
89 A2 1a indigo & red 115.00 110.00
90 A2 2a red brn & red 50.00 26.00
91 A2 4½a org & red 60.00 37.50
a. Right serif of left-hand "4" omitted 950.00
b. Fraction bar at right omitted 950.00 600.00
92 A2 5a bister & red 67.50 50.00
a. "tish" omitted 1,900. 1,900.
93 A2 7½a lilac & red 70.00 50.00
a. Ovptd. on front and back —
b. "tish" omitted 2,000.
Nos. 88-93 (6) 430.00 328.50

Nos. 92a and 93b were apparently caused by the presence of foreign matter on the plate during overprinting.

The 1a with red overprint, which includes a period after "Africa", was sent to the UPU, but never placed in use. Nos. 88, 90-93 and 95-100 also exist with period (in black) in sets sent to the UPU. Some experts consider these essays.

Black Ovpt. on Zanzibar #39, 42 New Value Surcharged in Red

1897

95 A2(a) 2½a on 1a 135.00 80.00
a. Black overprint double 7,800.
96 A2(b) 2½a on 1a 325.00 130.00
97 A2(c) 2½a on 1a 160.00 90.00
a. Black overprint double 7,800.
98 A2(a) 2½a on 3a 135.00 67.50
99 A2(b) 2½a on 3a 325.00 120.00
100 A2(c) 2½a on 3a 160.00 75.00
Nos. 95-100 (6) 1,240. 562.50

A special printing of the 2½a surcharge on the 1a and 3a stamps was made for submission to the U.P.U. Stamps have a period after "Africa" in the overprint, and the surcharges included a "2" over "1" error in the fraction of the surcharge. These stamps were never placed in use. The fraction error appears on both the 1a and 3a stamps. Value, each, $1,500.

A10

1898 Wmk. 1 Engr.

102 A10 1r gray blue 95.00 42.50
a. 1r dull blue ('01) 120.00 50.00
b. 1r ultramarine ('03) 425.00 300.00
103 A10 2r orange 140.00 150.00
104 A10 3r dk violet 180.00 *190.00*
105 A10 4r carmine 500.00 *550.00*
106 A10 5r black brown 450.00 *550.00*
107 A10 10r bister 450.00 *600.00*
Overprinted "SPECIMEN" 75.00
108 A10 20r yel green 1,200. *2,500.*
Overprinted "SPECIMEN" 150.00
109 A10 50r lilac 2,500. *9,000.*
Overprinted "SPECIMEN" 300.00
Nos. 102a-107 (6) 1,815. *2,083.*
Nos. 102-107 (6) 1,815. *2,083.*
Nos. 102-106 ovptd. "SPECIMEN" 210.00

Nos. 102-109 are often found with fiscal or Court Fee cancels. Stamps with these cancels can be purchased at a fraction of these values.

The stamps of this country were superseded by the stamps of East Africa and Uganda Protectorate.

BRITISH GUIANA

'bri-tish gē-'a-nə, -'ä-nə

LOCATION — On the northeast coast of South America
GOVT. — British Crown Colony
AREA — 83,000 sq. mi.
POP. — 628,000 (estimated 1964)
CAPITAL — Georgetown

100 Cents = 1 Dollar

Catalogue values for unused stamps in this country are for Never Hinged items, beginning with Scott 242 in the regular postage section and Scott J1 in the postage due section.

STAMPS OF GREAT BRITAIN USED IN BRITISH GUIANA

Numeral cancellation type A is pictured in the Crowned Circle Handstamps and Great Britain Used Abroad section.

1858-60

A03 (Georgetown/Demerara)

A1 A 1p rose red (#20) 400.
A2 A 4p rose (#26) 210.
A3 A 6p lilac (#27) 140.
a. 6p lilac, blued paper (#27c) —
A4 A 1sh green (#28) 2,000.

A04 (New Amsterdam/Berbice)

A5 A 1p rose red (#20) 1,000.
A6 A 2p blue (#29, P8) 1,400.
Plate 7 1,400.
A7 A 4p rose (#26) 450.
A8 A 6p lilac (#27) 350.
A9 A 1sh green (#28) 2,250.

Values for unused stamps are for examples with original gum except for Nos. 6-12 and 35-53, which are valued without gum. Very fine examples of all stamps from No. 6 on will have four clear margins. Inferior examples sell at much reduced prices, depending on the condition of the individual stamp.

A1

1850-51 Typeset Unwmk. *Imperf.*

1 A1 2c blk, *pale rose,* cut to shape ('51) *325,000.*
2 A1 4c black, *orange* *100,000.*
Cut to shape *16,000.*
a. 4c black, *yellow* *130,000.*
Cut to shape *22,500.*
3 A1 4c blk, *yellow* (pelure) *135,000.*
Cut to shape *26,000.*
4 A1 8c black, *green* *70,000.*
Cut to shape *16,000.*
5 A1 12c black, *blue* *35,000.*
Cut to shape *11,000.*
a. 12c black, *pale blue* *40,000.*
Cut to shape *14,000.*
b. 12c black, *indigo* *45,000.*
Cut to shape *13,000.*
c. "1" of "12" omitted, cut to shape *250,000.*
On cover *950,000.*
d. "2" of "12" with straight bottom *25,000.*

These stamps were initialed before use by the Deputy Postmaster General or by one of the clerks of the Colonial Postoffice at Georgetown. The following initials are found: — E. T. E. D(alton); E. D. W(ight); G. B. S(mith); H. A. K(illikelley); W. H. L(ortimer). As these stamps are type-set there are several types of each value.

Ship and Motto of Colony — A2

1852 Litho.

6 A2 1c black, *magenta* *15,000.* *7,000.*
On cover *15,000.*
7 A2 4c black, *blue* *25,000.* *13,000.*
On cover *16,000.*

Both 1c and 4c are found in two types. Examples with paper cracked or rubbed sell for much less.

Some examples are initialed E. D. W(ight).

The reprints are on thicker paper and the colors are brighter. They are perforated 12½ and imperforate. Value $20 each.

Seal of the Colony — A3

Without Line above Value

1853-59 *Imperf.*

8 A3 1c vermilion 8,000. 1,750.

A proof of No. 8 exists in reddish brown, value about $1,600.

Full or Partial White Line Above Value

Types of One Cent:

I: Larger "O" in "ONE," 1mm from end of value tablet.

II: Smaller "O" in "ONE," ¾mm from end of tablet.

III: "O" like Type II, "N" and "T" of "CENTS" widely spaced.

IV: Smaller "O" in "ONE," 1¼mm from end of tablet, letters in "ONE" are closely spaced.

9 A3 1c red (I) 7,750. 2,250.
a. Type II 9,000. 2,500.
b. Type III 11,000. 2,750.
c. Type IV 25,000.
d. 1c brownish red (I) *15,000.* 2,500.
e. 1c brownish red (II) *17,500.* 2,750.
f. 1c brownish red (III) 11,000. 2,750.
g. 1c brownish red (IV) — —
10 A3 4c blue 3,250. 850.
a. 4c dark blue 6,000. 1,200.
b. 4c pale blue 2,250. 750.

On No. 9, "ONE CENT" varies from 11 to 13mm in width.

No. 10 Retouched; White Line above Value Removed

11 A3 4c blue 4,750. 1,100.
a. 4c dark blue 8,500. 1,750.
b. 4c pale blue 3,500. 1,100.

Reprints of Nos. 8 and 10 are on thin paper, perf. 12½ or imperf. The 1c is orange red, the 4c sky blue.

1860

Numerals in Corners Framed

12 A3 4c blue 7,500. 850.00

A4

1856 Typeset *Imperf.*

13 A4 1c black, *mag* *9,500,000.*
14 A4 4c black, *mag* *100,000.* *25,000.*
With initials "C.A.W." (C.E. Watson) *16,000.*
a. 4c black, *rose carmine* *50,000.* *40,000.*
15 A4 4c black, *blue* *150,000.*
16 A4 4c black, *blue, paper colored through* *225,000.*

These stamps were initialed before being issued and the following initials are found: — E. T. E. D.; E. D. W.; W. H. L.; C. A. W. No. 13 is unique.

Scott 13 sold for the equivalent of U.S. $9,500,000 in a New York City auction in 2014.

A5

Wide space between value and "Cents"

1860-61 Litho. *Perf. 12*

Thick Paper

17 A5 1c brown red ('61) 500.00 125.00
18 A5 1c pink 3,500. 300.00
19 A5 2c orange 350.00 65.00
a. 2c deep orange 325.00 60.00
20 A5 8c rose 825.00 130.00
a. 8c brownish rose 1,000. 160.00
21 A5 12c gray 750.00 55.00
a. 12c lilac 850.00 55.00
22 A5 24c green 1,700. 85.00
a. 24c deep green 2,500. 150.00

All denominations of type A5 above four cents are expressed in Roman numerals.

Bisects and trisects are found on covers. These were not officially authorized.

Nos. 21 and 21a are often found with a large red "5d" overprint about the same size as the stamp. This was an accounting marking to indicate postage payable by the Colonial Post Office to Great Britain for the overseas portion of postage collected.

The reprints of the 1c pink are perforated 12½; the other values have not been reprinted.

1862-65 Thin Paper

23 A5 1c brown 925.00 275.00
24 A5 1c black ('63) 160.00 65.00
25 A5 2c orange 150.00 65.00
26 A5 8c rose ('63) 300.00 85.00
27 A5 12c lilac 400.00 55.00
a. 12c purple 400.00 42.50
b. 12c grayish purple ('63) 375.00 37.50
28 A5 24c green 1,700. 110.00

Perf. 12½ and 13

29 A5 1c black 80.00 25.00
30 A5 2c orange 95.00 27.50
31 A5 8c rose 350.00 97.50
32 A5 12c lilac 1,200. 150.00
33 A5 24c green 875.00 80.00

Medium Paper

33A A5 1c black ('64) 70.00 55.00
33B A5 2c dp org ('64) 90.00 32.50
a. 2c orange ('62) 92.50 30.00
33C A5 8c pink ('64) 300.00 80.00
33D A5 12c lilac ('65) 1,250. 130.00
33E A5 24c green ('64) 375.00 65.00
f. 24c deep green 450.00 90.00

Perf. 10

34 A5 12c gray lilac 800.00 97.50

Imperfs. are proofs. See Nos. 44-62.

A6

A7

A8

A9

A10

A11

1862 Typeset *Rouletted*

35 A6 1c black, *rose* *5,750.* *850.*
Unsigned 650.
36 A7 1c black, *rose* *7,500.* *1,400.*
Unsigned 750.
37 A8 1c black, *rose* *9,750.* *1,500.*
Unsigned 1,300.
38 A6 2c black, *yellow* *5,750.* *450.*
Unsigned 2,600.
39 A7 2c black, *yellow* *7,500.* *575.*
Unsigned 3,000.
40 A8 2c black, *yellow* *9,750.* *925.*
Unsigned 3,750.
41 A9 4c black, *blue* *8,000.* *1,400.*
Unsigned 1,400.
42 A10 4c black, *blue* *11,000.* *2,000.*
Unsigned —
a. Without inner lines *8,000.* *1,400.*
As "a," unsigned 1,300.
43 A11 4c black, *blue* *6,500.* *1,100.*
Unsigned 1,300.

Nos. 35-43 were typeset, in sheets of 24 each. They were initialed before use "R. M. Ac. R. G.," being the initials of Robert Mather, Acting Receiver General.

The initials are in black on the 1c and in red on the 2c. An alkali was used on the 4c stamps, which, destroying the color of the paper, caused the initials to appear to be written in white.

Uninitialed stamps are remainders, few sheets having been found.

Stamps with roulette on all sides are valued higher.

Narrow space between value and "Cents"

1860 Thick Paper Litho. *Perf. 12*

44 A5 4c blue 450.00 80.00
c. 4c deep blue 800.00 120.00

Thin Paper

44A A5 4c pale blue 150.00 42.50
d. 4c blue 175.00 55.00

Perf. 12½ and 13

44B A5 4c blue 115.00 32.50

Medium Paper

1863-68 ***Perf. 12½ and 13***

45 A5 1c black ('66) 80.00 40.00
46 A5 2c orange 85.00 10.00
a. 2c orange red ('65) 85.00 10.00
47 A5 4c gray blue ('64) 100.00 25.00
a. 4c blue 130.00 32.50
48 A5 8c rose ('68) 425.00 27.50
a. 8c carmine 500.00 60.00
49 A5 12c lilac ('67) 650.00 50.00
a. 12c brownish lilac 750.00 55.00
Nos. 45-49 (5) 1,340. 152.50

1866-71 ***Perf. 10***

50 A5 1c black 25.00 8.50
a. 1c gray black 26.00 17.25
51 A5 2c orange 65.00 5.00
a. 2c red orange 75.00 7.25
52 A5 4c blue 130.00 11.00
a. Half used as 2c on cover *7,500.*
b. 4c slate blue 150.00 15.00
c. 4c pale blue 120.00 11.00
53 A5 8c rose 300.00 37.50
a. Diagonal half used as 4c on cover —
b. 8c brownish pink 350.00 42.50
c. 8c carmine 425.00 60.00
54 A5 12c lilac 300.00 27.50
a. Third used as 4c on cover —
b. 12c pale lilac ('67) 325.00 27.50
c. 12c gray lilac 300.00 26.00
d. 12c brownish gray 300.00 27.50
Nos. 50-54 (5) 820.00 89.50

1875-76 ***Perf. 15***

58 A5 1c black 65.00 9.00
59 A5 2c orange 185.00 17.00
a. 2c red orange 185.00 17.00
60 A5 4c blue 300.00 120.00
61 A5 8c rose 325.00 110.00
62 A5 12c lilac 925.00 100.00
Nos. 58-62 (5) 1,800. 356.00

Seal of Colony — A12

1863 ***Perf. 12***

63 A12 24c yellow green 275.00 15.50
a. 24c green 350.00 25.00

Perf. 12½ to 13

64 A12 6c blue 200.00 72.50
a. 6c milky blue 200.00 40.00
b. 6c greenish blue 200.00 77.50
c. 6c deep blue 300.00 100.00
65 A12 24c green 275.00 16.00
a. 24c yellow green 300.00 9.00
b. 24c blue green 375.00 9.00
66 A12 48c deep red 425.00 80.00
a. 48c rose 450.00 80.00
b. 48c pale red 400.00 80.00
Nos. 63-66 (4) 1,175. 184.00

1866 ***Perf. 10***

67 A12 6c blue 200.00 40.00
a. 6c ultramarine 215.00 67.50
b. 6c milky blue ('67) 200.00 37.50
68 A12 24c yellow green 275.00 9.00
a. 24c green 375.00 11.00
b. 24c blue green 350.00 9.50
69 A12 48c rose red 425.00 37.50
a. 48c crimson 425.00 45.00
Perforated "SPECIMEN" 300.00
Handstamped "SPECIMEN" 350.00
Nos. 67-69 (3) 900.00 86.50

For surcharges see Nos. 83-92.

1875 ***Perf. 15***

70 A12 6c ultra 1,150. 150.00
71 A12 24c yellow green 850.00 42.50
a. 24c deep green 1,600. 120.00

Seal of Colony — A13

1876 **Typo.** **Wmk. 1** ***Perf. 14***

72 A13 1c slate 3.25 1.75
a. Perf. 14x12½ 225.00
73 A13 2c orange 92.50 4.00
74 A13 4c ultra 150.00 15.00
a. Perf. 12½ 1,450. 250.00
75 A13 6c chocolate 110.00 14.00
76 A13 8c rose 160.00 1.00
77 A13 12c lilac 80.00 2.50
78 A13 24c green 90.00 4.00
79 A13 48c red brown 160.00 50.00
80 A13 96c bister 575.00 325.00
Nos. 72-80 (9) 1,421. 417.25

See Nos. 107-111. For surcharges see Nos. 93-95, 98-101.

Stamps Surcharged by Brush-like Pen Lines

Type a

Type b

Type c

Type d

Surcharge Types:
Type a — Two horiz. lines.
Type b — Two lines, one horiz., one vert.
Type c — Three lines, two horiz., one vert.
Type d — One horiz. line.

On Nos. 75 and 67

1878 ***Perf. 10, 14***

82 A13(a) (1c) on 6c choc 52.50 *150.00*
83 A12(b) (1c) on 6c blue 250.00 90.00
84 A13(b) (1c) on 6c choc 450.00 135.00

On Nos. O3, O8-O10

85 A13(c) (1c) on 4c ultra 425.00 120.00
a. Type b *50,000.* *6,000.*
86 A13(c) (1c) on 6c choc 725.00 135.00
87 A5(c) (2c) on 8c rose *5,250.* 400.00
88A A13(b) (2c) on 8c rose 600.00 240.00

On Nos. O1, O3, O6-O7

89 A5(d) (1c) on 1c blk 325.00 90.00
89A A5(d) (2c) on 8c rose
90 A13(d) (1c) on 1c sl 220.00 80.00
91 A13(d) (2c) on 2c org 450.00 80.00

The provisional values of Nos. 82 to 91 were established by various official decrees. The horizontal lines crossed out the old value, "OFFICIAL," or both.

The existence of No. 89A has been questioned by specialists. The editors would like to see authenticated evidence of its existence.

Nos. 69 and 80 Surcharged with New Values in Black

No. 92

No. 93

No. 94

No. 95

1881

92 A12 1c on 48c red 55.00 7.00
a. Without bar — 725.00
93 A13 1c on 96c bister 6.00 *11.00*
a. Without bar —
b. Bar in red —
94 A13 2c on 96c bister 20.00 *24.00*
a. Without bar —
b. Bar in red —
95 A13 2c on 96c bister 85.00 *160.00*
a. Bar in red —
Nos. 92-95 (4) 166.00 *202.00*

Nos. O4, O5 and Unissued Official Stamps Surcharged with New Values

No. 96

No. 97

Nos. 98, 100

Nos. 99, 101

No. 102

1881

96 A5 1c on 12c lilac (#O4) 155.00 85.00
97 A13 1c on 48c red brn 225.00 140.00
98 A13 2c on 12c lilac 750.00 500.00
99 A13 2c on 12c lilac 110.00 70.00
a. "2" inverted
b. "2" double *950.00* 550.00
c. Pair, #98-99 1,600. 1,850.
d. As "c," "2" doubled 6,000.
e. "OFFICIAL" obliterated by bar —
100 A13 2c on 24c green 1,000. *950.00*
101 A13 2c on 24c green 110.00 70.00
a. "2" inverted
d. Double surcharge 1,325.
102 A12 2c on 24c green (#O5) 400.00 200.00

A27

Typeset

ONE AND TWO CENTS.
Type I — Ship with three masts.
Type II — Brig with two masts.

"SPECIMEN"
Perforated Diagonally across Stamp

1882 **Unwmk.** ***Perf. 12***

103 A27 1c black, *lil rose,* I 80.00 35.00
a. Horiz. pair, imperf between *10,000.*
b. Without "Specimen" 1,500. 600.00
104 A27 1c black, *lil rose,* II 80.00 35.00
a. Without "Specimen" 1,500. 600.00
105 A27 2c black, *yel,* I 115.00 60.00
a. Without "Specimen" 1,300. 700.00
b. Diagonal half used as 1c on cover —
106 A27 2c black, *yel,* II 110.00 65.00
a. Without "Specimen" 1,300. 700.00
Nos. 103-106 (4) 385.00 195.00

Nos. 103-106 were typeset, 12 to a sheet, and, to prevent fraud on the government, the word *"Specimen"* was perforated across them before they were issued. There were 2 settings of the 1c and 3 settings of the 2c, thus there are 24 types of the former and 36 of the latter.

Type of 1876

1882 **Typo.** **Wmk. 2** ***Perf. 14***

107 A13 1c slate 18.00 .50
108 A13 2c orange 57.50 .35
a. "2 CENTS" double *11,500.*
109 A13 4c ultra 110.00 6.50
110 A13 6c brown 6.00 8.00
111 A13 8c rose 140.00 1.00
Nos. 107-111 (5) 331.50 16.35

"INLAND REVENUE" Overprint and Surcharged in Black

A28

Type I Type II

4 CENTS and $4
Type I — Figure "4" is 3mm high.
Type II — Figure "4" is 3½mm high.

6 CENTS
Type I — Top of "6" is flat.
Type II — Top of "6" turns downward.

1889

112 A28 1c lilac 3.00 .55
113 A28 2c lilac 3.00 3.00
114 A28 3c lilac 2.25 .40
115 A28 4c lilac, I 13.00 .45
116 A28 4c lilac, II 24.00 7.50
117 A28 6c lilac, I 23.00 8.50
118 A28 6c lilac, II 15.00 6.50
119 A28 8c lilac 2.25 .65
120 A28 10c lilac 7.50 3.25
121 A28 20c lilac 27.50 22.50
122 A28 40c lilac 47.50 35.00
123 A28 72c lilac 85.00 *72.50*
124 A28 $1 green 575.00 *650.00*
125 A28 $2 green 275.00 *300.00*
126 A28 $3 green 275.00 *300.00*
127 A28 $4 green, I 650.00 *775.00*
127A A28 $4 green, II 2,400. *3,000.*
128 A28 $5 green 400.00 *450.00*
Nos. 112-128 (18) 4,828. 5,636.

For surcharges see Nos.129, 148-151B.

No. 113 Surcharged in Red

1889

129 A29 2c on 2c lilac 6.50 .55

Inverted and double surcharges of "2" were privately made.

A30

1889-1903 **Typo.**

130 A30 1c lilac & gray 8.25 3.50
131 A30 1c green ('90) 1.10 .25
131A A30 1c gray grn ('00) 2.10 *6.00*
132 A30 2c lilac & org 6.25 .25
133 A30 2c lil & rose ('00) 4.00 .40
134 A30 2c vio & blk, *red* ('01) 2.00 .25
135 A30 4c lilac & ultra 5.50 4.00
a. 4c lilac & blue 25.00 4.00
136 A30 5c ultra ('91) 4.50 .25
137 A30 6c lilac & mar 8.50 *25.00*
a. 6c lilac & brown 42.50 27.50
138 A30 6c gray blk & ultra ('02) 8.00 *13.50*
139 A30 8c lilac & rose 18.50 4.00
140 A30 8c lil & blk ('90) 8.75 2.50
141 A30 12c lilac & vio 10.00 4.00
142 A30 24c lilac & grn 7.50 4.00
143 A30 48c lilac & ver 35.00 13.00
144 A30 48c dk gray & lil brn ('01) 35.00 35.00
a. 48c gray & purple brown 60.00 50.00
145 A30 60c gray grn & car ('03) 75.00 *250.00*
146 A30 72c lil & org brn 34.00 *55.00*
a. 72c lilac & yellow brown 77.50 *90.00*
147 A30 96c lilac & carmine 80.00 *85.00*
a. 96c lilac & rose 90.00 *100.00*
Nos. 130-147 (19) 353.95 *505.90*

Stamps of the 1889-1903 issue with pen or revenue cancellation sell for a small fraction of the above quotations.

See Nos. 160-177.

A31

1890 **Red Surcharge**

148 A31 1c on $1 grn & blk 3.50 .50
a. Double surcharge *300.00* *170.00*
149 A31 1c on $2 grn & blk 2.50 1.40
a. Double surcharge *120.00* —
150 A31 1c on $3 grn & blk 3.50 1.40
a. Double surcharge *160.00* —
151 A31 1c on $4 grn & blk, type I 6.50 *13.00*
a. Double surcharge *150.00*
151B A31 1c on $4 grn & blk, type II 15.00 *42.50*
c. Double surcharge
Nos. 148-151B (5) 31.00 *58.80*

Mt. Roraima A32

Kaieteur (Old Man's) Falls — A33

1898 Wmk. 1 Engr.

No.	Type	Description	Unused	Used
152	A32	1c car & gray blk	10.00	2.50
153	A33	2c indigo & brn	40.00	4.75
a.		Horiz. pair, imperf. between	*16,500.*	
b.		2c blue & brown	45.00	4.75
154	A32	5c brown & grn	57.50	6.50
155	A33	10c red & blue blk	30.00	32.50
156	A32	15c blue & red brn	37.50	26.00
		Nos. 152-156 (5)	175.00	72.25

60th anniv. of Queen Victoria's accession to the throne.

Nos. 154-156 Surcharged in Black

1899

No.	Type	Description	Unused	Used
157	A32	2c on 5c brn & grn	4.00	3.25
a.		Without period	185.00	140.00
158	A33	2c on 10c red & bl black	4.50	2.75
a.		"GENTS"	70.00	*92.50*
b.		Inverted surcharge	*750.00*	*875.00*
c.		Without period	25.00	*65.00*
d.		Inverted surcharge	*1,000.*	*1,000.*
159	A32	2c on 15c bl & red brown	4.50	1.50
a.		Without period	80.00	*80.00*
b.		Double surcharge	*1,100.*	*1,500.*
c.		Inverted surcharge	*875.00*	*1,100.*
d.		As "a," inverted surcharge	—	
e.		As "b," one without period	*10,000.*	
		Nos. 157-159 (3)	13.00	7.50

There are many slight errors in the setting of this surcharge, such as: small "E" in "CENTS"; no period and narrow "C"; comma between "T" and "S"; dash between "TWO" and "CENTS"; comma between "N" and "T."

Ship Type of 1889-1903

1905-10 Wmk. 3

Chalky Paper

No.	Type	Description	Unused	Used
160	A30	1c gray green	12.00	1.35
a.		Booklet pane of 6		
161	A30	2c vio & blk, *red*	6.50	.25
162	A30	4c lilac & ultra	9.00	*15.00*
163	A30	5c lil & blue, *bl*	4.25	*8.00*
164	A30	6c gray black & ultra	18.00	*50.00*
165	A30	12c lilac & vio	27.50	*55.00*
166	A30	24c lil & grn ('06)	4.50	*5.50*
167	A30	48c gray & vio brn	17.00	*27.50*
168	A30	60c gray grn & car rose	17.00	*110.00*
169	A30	72c lil & org brn ('07)	42.50	*85.00*
170	A30	96c blk & red, *yel*('06)	42.50	*55.00*
		Overprinted "SPECIMEN"	42.50	
		Nos. 160-170 (11)	200.75	*412.60*

Ordinary Paper

No.	Type	Description	Unused	Used
160b	A30	1c gray green	8.50	.35
161a	A30	2c vio & blk, *red*	17.50	.25
162a	A39	4c lilac & ultra	16.00	22.50
163a	A30	5c lil & blue, *bl*	20.00	22.50
164a	A30	6c gray black & ultra	22.50	50.00
165a	A30	12c lilac & vio	29.00	50.00
166a	A30	24c lil & grn ('06)	14.00	20.00
167a	A30	48c gray & vio brn	32.50	*52.50*
168a	A30	60c gray grn & car rose	27.50	110.00

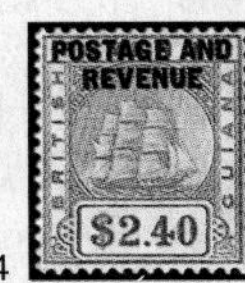

A34

Black Overprint

No.	Type	Description	Unused	Used
171	A34	$2.40 grn & vio	*210.00*	*500.00*
		Overprinted "SPECIMEN"	95.00	

Ship Type of 1889-1903

Type I

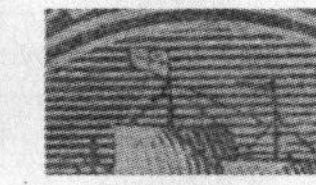
Type II

TWO CENTS

Type I — Only the upper right corner of the flag touches the mast.

Type II — The entire right side of the flag touches the mast.

1907-10 Ordinary Paper

No.	Type	Description	Unused	Used
171A	A30	1c blue green ('10)	16.00	3.00
172	A30	2c red, type I	21.00	1.10
b.		2c red, type II	10.50	.25
174	A30	4c brown & vio	3.50	1.35
175	A30	5c blue	18.50	6.00
176	A30	6c gray & black	16.00	8.50
177	A30	12c orange & vio	5.00	6.50
		Nos. 171A177 (6)	80.00	26.45

George V — A35

1913-17 Perf. 14

No.	Type	Description	Unused	Used
178	A35	1c green	5.00	1.00
a.		bl grn ('17)	2.25	.30
179	A35	2c scarlet	3.75	.25
a.		2c carmine	1.60	.25
180	A35	4c brn & red vio	7.50	.40
181	A35	5c ultra	2.25	1.25
182	A35	6c gray & black	3.75	2.75
183	A35	12c org & vio	1.75	1.25

Chalky Paper

No.	Type	Description	Unused	Used
184	A35	24c dl vio & grn	4.25	*5.00*
185	A35	48c blk & vio brn	30.00	21.00
186	A35	60c grn & car	20.00	*60.00*
187	A35	72c dl vio & org brn	60.00	*100.00*

Surface Colored Paper

No.	Type	Description	Unused	Used
188	A35	96c blk & red, *yel*	32.50	*65.00*

Paper Colored Through

No.	Type	Description	Unused	Used
189	A35	96c blk & red, *yel* ('16)	22.50	*65.00*
		Nos. 178-189 (12)	193.25	*322.90*

The 72c and late printings of the 2c and 5c are from redrawn dies. The ruled lines behind the value are thin and faint, making the tablet appear lighter than before. The shading lines in other parts of the stamps are also lighter. Several paper shades of No. 189 exist.

1921-27 Wmk. 4

No.	Type	Description	Unused	Used
191	A35	1c green	5.75	.40
192	A35	2c rose red	7.75	.30
193	A35	2c dp vio ('23)	3.00	.25
194	A35	4c brn & vio	5.75	.25
195	A35	6c ultra	3.75	.40
196	A35	12c org & vio	3.50	2.00

Chalky Paper

No.	Type	Description	Unused	Used
197	A35	24c dl vio & grn	2.75	*5.50*
198	A35	48c blk & vio brn ('26)	12.00	4.50
199	A35	60c grn & car ('26)	12.50	*57.50*
200	A35	72c dl vio & brn org	37.50	*80.00*
201	A35	96c blk & red, *yel* ('27)	27.50	*55.00*
		Nos. 191-201 (11)	121.75	*206.10*

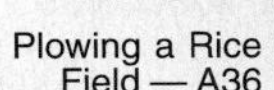
Plowing a Rice Field — A36

Indian Shooting Fish — A37

Kaieteur Falls — A38

Georgetown, Public Buildings A39

1931, July 21 Engr. *Perf. 12½*

No.	Type	Description	Unused	Used
205	A36	1c blue green	3.00	1.75
206	A37	2c dk brown	2.75	.25
207	A38	4c car rose	2.50	.60
208	A39	6c ultra	3.00	*1.50*
209	A38	$1 violet	60.00	*70.00*
		Nos. 205-209 (5)	71.25	*74.10*
		Set, never hinged	100.00	
		Set, Perf "SPECIMEN"	130.00	

Cent. of the union of Berbice, Demerara and Essequibo to form the Colony of British Guiana.

A40

A41

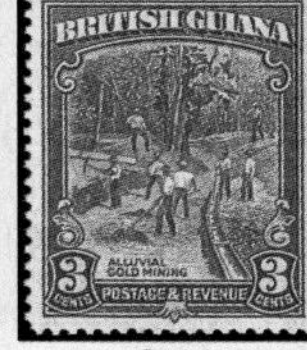
Gold Mining — A42

Kaieteur Falls — A43

Shooting Logs over Falls — A44

Stabroek Market — A45

Sugar Cane in Punts — A46

Forest Road — A47

Victoria Regia Lilies — A48

Mt. Roraima — A49

Sir Walter Raleigh and Son — A50

Botanical Gardens A51

1934, Oct. 1 *Perf. 12½*

No.	Type	Description	Unused	Used
210	A40	1c green	.75	*2.25*
211	A41	2c brown	1.75	1.90
212	A42	3c carmine	.50	.25
b.		Perf. 12½x13½ ('43)	1.10	*1.10*
c.		Perf. 13x13½ ('49)	.75	.25
213	A43	4c vio black	2.50	3.75
a.		Vert. pair, imperf. horiz.	*20,000.*	*20,000.*
214	A44	6c dp ultra	5.50	*7.50*
215	A45	12c orange	.25	*.35*
a.		Perf. 13½x13 ('51)	.70	*1.25*
216	A46	24c rose violet	4.50	*12.00*
217	A47	48c black	10.00	*10.00*
218	A43	50c green	15.00	*22.50*
219	A48	60c brown	32.50	*32.00*
220	A49	72c rose violet	1.60	*2.75*
221	A50	96c black	37.50	*37.50*
222	A51	$1 violet	52.50	50.00
		Nos. 210-222 (13)	164.85	*182.75*
		Set, never hinged	290.00	
		Set, Perf "SPECIMEN"	250.00	

See Nos. 236, 238, 240.

Common Design Types pictured following the introduction.

Silver Jubilee Issue

Common Design Type

1935, May 6 *Perf. 13½x14*

No.	Type	Description	Unused	Used
223	CD301	2c gray blk & ultra	.35	.25
224	CD301	6c blue & brown	1.50	*5.50*
225	CD301	12c indigo & grn	6.50	*9.75*
226	CD301	24c brt vio & ind	10.00	*20.00*
		Nos. 223-226 (4)	18.35	35.50
		Set, never hinged	27.50	
		Set, Perf "SPECIMEN"	140.00	

Coronation Issue

Common Design Type

1937, May 12 *Perf. 13½x14*

No.	Type	Description	Unused	Used
227	CD302	2c brown	.25	.25
228	CD302	4c gray black	.65	.65
229	CD302	6c bright ultra	.55	*2.15*
		Nos. 227-229 (3)	1.45	3.05
		Set, never hinged	1.60	
		Set, Perf "SPECIMEN"	130.00	

A52

A53

A54

A55

A56

A57

A58

Victoria Regia Lilies and Jacanas — A59

1938-52 Engr. Wmk. 4 Perf. 12½

230 A52 1c green .25 .25
Never hinged .35
b. Perf. 14x13 ('49) .65 *1.00*
Never hinged 1.10
231 A53 2c violet blk, perf. 13x14 ('49) .40 .25
Never hinged .60
b. Perf. 12½ .50 .25
Never hinged .65
232 A54 4c black & rose, perf. 13x14 ('52) .65 .25
Never hinged 1.10
a. Perf. 12½ .90 .40
Never hinged 1.50
c. Vert. pair, imperf. between *35,000.* *35,000.*
Never hinged 37,500.
233 A55 6c deep ultra, perf. 13x14 ('49) 1.50 .40
Never hinged 2.15
a. Perf. 12½ 1.00 .25
Never hinged 1.35
234 A56 24c deep green 2.75 .25
Never hinged 3.75
a. Wmk. upright 20.00 12.50
Never hinged 27.50
235 A53 36c purple 3.50 .25
Never hinged 5.00
a. Perf. 13x14 ('51) 3.00 .40
Never hinged 4.50
236 A47 48c orange yel .90 .60
Never hinged 1.35
a. Perf. 14x13 ('51) 1.25 2.25
Never hinged 1.75
237 A57 60c brown 13.50 10.00
Never hinged 20.00
238 A50 96c brown vio 8.00 *3.25*
Never hinged 12.00
a. Perf. 12½x13½ ('44) 8.75 *13.00*
Never hinged 13.00
239 A58 $1 deep violet 17.50 .55
Never hinged 27.50
a. Perf. 14x13 ('51) 300.00 *700.00*
Never hinged 550.00
240 A49 $2 rose vio ('45) 12.50 *27.50*
Never hinged 18.50
a. Perf. 14x13 ('50) 16.00 *37.50*
Never hinged 24.00
241 A59 $3 org brn ('45) 27.50 *40.00*
Never hinged 40.00
a. Perf. 14x13 ('52) 29.50 *55.00*
Never hinged 42.50
Nos. 230-241 (12) 88.95 *83.55*
Set, never hinged 135.00
Set, Perf "SPECIMEN" 375.00

The watermark on No. 234 is sideways.

Catalogue values for unused stamps in this section, from this point to the end of the section, are for Never Hinged items.

Peace Issue
Common Design Type

1946, Oct. 21 Perf. 13½x14

242 CD303 3c carmine .25 *.45*
243 CD303 6c deep blue .80 *.95*
Set, Perf "SPECIMEN" 110.00

Silver Wedding Issue
Common Design Types

1948, Dec. 20 Photo. Perf. 14x14½

244 CD304 3c scarlet .25 *.45*

Engr.
Perf. 11½x11

245 CD305 $3 orange brown 24.00 *28.00*

UPU Issue
Common Design Types
Engr.; Name Typo. on 6c and 12c
Perf. 13½, 11x11½

1949, Oct. 10 Wmk. 4

246 CD306 4c rose carmine .25 *.55*
247 CD307 6c indigo 2.00 2.00
248 CD308 12c orange .25 *.75*
249 CD309 24c blue green .25 *.90*
Nos. 246-249 (4) 2.75 4.20

University Issue
Common Design Types

1951, Feb. 16 Engr. Perf. 14x14½

250 CD310 3c carmine & black .55 *.55*
251 CD311 6c dp ultra & black .55 *.70*

POSTAGE DUE STAMPS

Catalogue values for unused stamps in this section are for Never Hinged items.

D1

Perf. 13½x14

1940-55 Typo. Wmk. 4

J1 D1 1c green, *chalky paper* ('52) 1.50 *22.50*
Never hinged 2.25
On cover 100.00
a. Wmk. 4a (error) 150.00
Never hinged 175.00
b. 1c green, *ordinary paper* ('40) 5.00 12.00
Never hinged 7.00
J2 D1 2c black, *chalky paper* ('52) 4.00 *10.00*
Never hinged 5.00
On cover 100.00
a. Wmk. 4a (error) 145.00
Never hinged 175.00
b. 2c black, *ordinary paper* ('40) 20.00 2.25
Never hinged 30.00
J3 D1 4c ultra ('52) .35 *14.00*
Never hinged .45
On cover 200.00
a. Wmk. 4a (error) 145.00
Never hinged 175.00
J4 D1 12c carmine, *chalky paper* ('55) 17.50 *45.00*
Never hinged 22.50
a. 12c scarlet, *ordinary paper* ('40) 27.50 7.00
Never hinged 40.00
On cover 175.00
Nos. J1-J4 (4) 23.35 *91.50*

Cover values are for properly franked commercial items. Philatelic usages exist and sell for less.

WAR TAX STAMP

Regular Issue No. 179 Overprinted

1918, Jan. 4 Wmk. 3 Perf. 14

MR1 A35 2c scarlet 1.90 .25

The relative positions of "War" and "Tax" vary throughout the sheet.

OFFICIAL STAMPS

Counterfeit overprints exist.

No. 50 Overprinted in Red

1875 Unwmk. Perf. 10

O1 A5 1c black 75.00 26.00
a. Horiz. pair, imperf btwn. 22,500.

Nos. 51, 53-54, 68 Overprinted in Black

O2 A5 2c orange 300.00 17.50
O3 A5 8c rose 375.00 150.00
O4 A5 12c lilac 3,500. 600.00
O5 A12 24c green 2,750. 325.00

For surcharges see Nos. 87, 89, 89A, 96, 102.

Nos. 72-76 Overprinted "OFFICIAL" Similar to #O2-O5

1877 Wmk. 1 Perf. 14

O6 A13 1c slate 350.00 70.00
a. Vert. pair, imperf btwn. *27,500.*
O7 A13 2c orange 160.00 18.00
O8 A13 4c ultramarine 140.00 35.00
O9 A13 6c chocolate 6,600. 725.00
O10 A13 8c rose 2,400. 550.00

The type A13 12c lilac, 24c green and 48c red brown overprinted "OFFICIAL" were never placed in use. A few examples of the 12c and 24c have been seen but the 48c is only known surcharged with new value for provisional use in 1881. See Nos. 97-101.

For surcharges see #85-86, 88A, 90-91.

BRITISH HONDURAS

'bri-tish hän-'dur-əs

LOCATION — Central America bordering on Caribbean on east, Mexico on north and Guatemala on west.
GOVT. — British Crown Colony
AREA — 8,867 sq. mi.
POP. — 130,000 (est. 1972)
CAPITAL — Belmopan

Before British Honduras became a colony (subordinate to Jamaica) in 1862, it was a settlement under British influence. In 1884 it became an independent colony.

12 Pence = 1 Shilling
100 Cents = 1 Dollar (1888)

Catalogue values for unused stamps in this country are for Never Hinged items, beginning with Scott 127 in the regular postage section, Scott J1 in the postage due section.

PRESTAMP POSTAL MARKINGS

Crowned Circle handstamp type II is pictured in the Crowned Circle Handstamps and Great Britain Used Abroad section.

1841

A1 II "Belize" crowned circle handstamp in red, on cover *4,750.*

STAMPS OF GREAT BRITAIN USED IN BRITISH HONDURAS

Numeral cancellation type A is pictured in the Crowned Circle Handstamps and Great Britain Used Abroad section.

1858-60

A06 (Belize)

A2 A 1p rose red (#20) 1,200.
A3 A 4p rose (#26) 475.
A4 A 6p lilac (#27) 450.
A5 A 1sh green (#28) 2,500.

Values for unused stamps are for examples with original gum as defined in the catalogue introduction. Very fine examples of Nos. 1-37 will have perforations touching the design on at least one side due to the narrow spacing of the stamps on the plates. Stamps with perfs clear of the design on all four sides are extremely scarce and will command higher prices.

Queen Victoria — A1

1866 Unwmk. Typo. Perf. 14

1 A1 1p pale blue 72.50 72.50
a. Horiz. pair, imperf. btwn.
b. 1p blue 100.00 82.50
2 A1 6p rose 425.00 195.00
3 A1 1sh green 400.00 145.00
a. Vert. pair, Nos. 1, 3 with gutter btwn. *65,000.*
b. Horiz. pair, Nos. 2, 3 with gutter btwn. *50,000.*

The 6p and 1sh were printed only in a sheet with the 1p. The 1p was later printed in sheets without the 6p and 1sh.

1872 Wmk. 1 Perf. 12½

4 A1 1p pale blue 100.00 30.00
a. 1p deep blue ('74) 110.00 28.00
5 A1 3p reddish brn 180.00 90.00
a. 3p chocolate brn ('74) 200.00 110.00
6 A1 6p rose 450.00 55.00
a. 6p carmine rose ('74) 600.00 72.50
7 A1 1sh green 700.00 42.50
a. Horiz. pair, imperf. btwn. *27,500.*
b. 1sh deep green ('74) 550.00 29.00

For surcharges see Nos. 18-19.
No. 7a is unique and has faults.

1877-79 Perf. 14

8 A1 1p blue 87.50 22.50
a. Horiz. strip of 3, imperf. btwn. *28,000.*
b. 1p pale blue ('78) 95.00 21.00
9 A1 3p brown 170.00 27.50
10 A1 4p violet ('79) 300.00 10.00
11 A1 6p rose ('78) 500.00 225.00
12 A1 1sh green 325.00 14.50

For surcharges see Nos. 20-21, 29.

1882-87 Wmk. 2

13 A1 1p blue ('84) 75.00 25.00
14 A1 1p rose ('84) 27.50 16.00
Overprinted "SPECIMEN" 275.00
a. Diagonal half used as ½p on cover —
b. 1p carmine 60.00 28.00
15 A1 4p violet 100.00 5.75
16 A1 6p yellow ('85) 325.00 240.00
17 A1 1sh gray ('87) 300.00 200.00
Overprinted "SPECIMEN" 75.00

For surcharges see Nos. 22-26, 28-35.

Stamps of 1872-87 Surcharged in Black

1888 Wmk. 1 Perf. 12½

18 A1 2c on 6p rose 350.00 275.00
19 A1 3c on 3p brown *20,000.* *6,500.*

Perf. 14

20 A1 2c on 6p rose 190.00 180.00
a. Diagonal half used as 1c on cover *300.00*
b. Double surcharge 2,700. —
c. "2" with curved tail 3,500. —
21 A1 3c on 3p brown 110.00 *120.00*

Wmk. 2

22 A1	2c on 1p rose	13.00	*45.00*
a.	Diagonal half used as 1c on cover		220.00
b.	Double surcharge	1,100.	1,100.
c.	Inverted surcharge	7,000.	5,500.
23 A1	10c on 4p violet	70.00	20.00
a.	Inverted surcharge		
24 A1	20c on 6p yellow	35.00	*50.00*
25 A1	50c on 1sh gray	475.00	*725.00*
a.	"5" for "50"	*17,500.*	

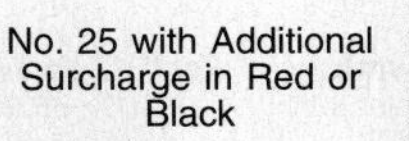
No. 25 with Additional Surcharge in Red or Black

26 A1	2c (R) on 50c on 1sh gray	60.00	*115.00*
a.	"TWO" in black	*18,750.*	*15,000.*
b.	"TWO" double (Blk + R)	*18,750.*	*16,000.*
c.	Diagonal half used as 1c on cover		350.00

Stamps of 1872-87 Srchd. in Black — c

1888-89

28 A1	2c on 1p rose	.80	*2.75*
a.	Diagonal half used as 1c on cover		110.00
29 A1	3c on 3p brown	4.75	1.75
30 A1	10c on 4p violet	27.50	1.00
a.	Double surcharge	*3,500.*	
31 A1	20c on 6p yel ('89)	19.00	15.00
32 A1	50c on 1sh gray	40.00	*105.00*
	Nos. 28-32 (5)	92.05	*125.50*

For other examples of this surcharge see Nos. 36, 47. For overprint see No. 51.

No. 30 with Additional Surcharge in Black or Red

1891

33 A1	6c (Blk) on 10c on 4p	3.00	2.25
a.	"6" and bar inverted	*4,500.*	*1,200.*
b.	"6" only inverted		*6,500.*
34 A1	6c (R) on 10c on 4p	1.90	*2.50*
a.	"6" and bar inverted	*725.00*	*725.00*
b.	"6" only inverted		*6,500.*

Stamps similar to No. 33 but with "SIX" instead of "6," both with and without bar, were prepared but not regularly issued.

See No. 37.

No. 29 with Additional Surcharge in Black

35 A1	5c on 3c on 3p brown	1.60	*2.00*
a.	Double surcharge of "Five" and bar	450.00	*850.00*
b.	Wide space between "I" and "V" of "FIVE"	72.50	*90.00*

Black Surcharge, Type "c"

36 A1	6c on 3p blue	6.00	*25.00*

No. 36 with Additional Surcharge like Nos. 33-34 in Red

1891

37 A1	15c (R) on 6c on 3p blue	16.00	*35.00*
a.	Double surcharge	—	

A8

1891-98 Wmk. 2 *Perf. 14*

38 A8	1c green	3.00	1.50
39 A8	2c carmine rose	4.50	.30
40 A8	3c brown	10.00	5.00
41 A8	5c ultra ('95)	14.50	1.25
42 A8	6c ultramarine	15.00	2.50
43 A8	10c vio & grn ('95)	14.00	*17.50*
a.	10c dull purple & green ('01)	13.00	9.00
44 A8	12c vio & green	3.25	*3.50*
a.	12c pale mauve & green	24.50	7.50
45 A8	24c yellow & blue	7.00	*23.00*
a.	24c orange & blue	35.00	*70.00*
46 A8	25c red brn & grn ('98)	95.00	*160.00*
	Nos. 38-46 (9)	166.25	*214.55*

Numeral tablet on Nos. 43-46 has lined background with colorless value and "c."

For overprints see Nos. 48-50.

Type of 1866 Surcharged Type "c"

1892

47 A1	1c on 1p green	1.00	*1.90*

Regular Issue Overprinted in Black

1899 Overprint 12mm Long

48 A8	5c ultramarine	28.00	3.00
a.	"BEVENUE"	180.00	*175.00*
49 A8	10c lilac & green	19.00	*21.00*
a.	"BEVENUE"	350.00	*425.00*
c.	"REVENU"	725.00	
50 A8	25c red brn & grn	4.25	*42.50*
a.	"BEVENUE"	200.00	*425.00*
c.	"REVE UE"	2,700.	
51 A1	50c on 1sh gray (No. 32)	275.00	450.00
a.	"BEVENUE"	5,500.	6,500.
	Nos. 48-51 (4)	326.25	*516.50*

Two lengths of the overprint are found on the same pane: 12mm (43 to the pane) and 11mm (17 to the pane). The "U" is found in both a tall, narrow type and the more common small type. The tall variety is found in row 1, position 5. The BEVENUE vaiety is found in row 6, position 4.

Overprint 11mm Long

48b	A8	5c	30.00	12.00
49b	A8	10c	22.50	*52.50*
49d	A8	10c "REVENU"	850.00	*950.00*
50b	A8	25c	6.00	*65.00*
51b	A1	50c	425.00	*650.00*

A9

1899-1901

52 A9	5c gray blk & ultra, *bl* ('00)	22.50	3.50
53 A9	10c vio & grn ('01)	13.50	*9.00*
54 A9	50c grn & car rose	30.00	*72.50*
55 A9	$1 grn & car rose	100.00	*155.00*
56 A9	$2 green & ultra	150.00	*200.00*
57 A9	$5 green & black	400.00	*500.00*
	Nos. 52-57 (6)	716.00	*940.00*

Numeral tablet on Nos. 53-54 has lined background with colorless value and "c."

King Edward VII — A10

1902-04 Typo. Wmk. 2

58 A10	1c gray grn & grn ('04)	2.25	*27.50*
59 A10	2c vio & blk, *red*	2.25	.40
60 A10	5c gray blk & ultra, *blue*	19.00	.70
61 A10	20c dl vio & vio ('04)	14.00	*20.00*
	Nos. 58-61 (4)	37.50	*48.60*
	Set, overprinted "SPECIMEN"	80.00	

1904-06 Chalky Paper Wmk. 3

62 A10	1c green	4.00	*2.75*
a.	1c green, ordinary paper	12.00	*16.00*
63 A10	2c vio & blk, *red*	2.75	*.40*
a.	2c vio & blk, *red*, ordinary paper	3.25	.35
64 A10	5c blk & ultra, *bl* ('05)	2.25	.25
65 A10	10c vio & grn ('06)	5.25	*18.00*
67 A10	25c vio & org ('06)	12.00	*60.00*
68 A10	50c grn & car rose ('06)	30.00	*100.00*
69 A10	$1 grn & car rose ('06)	75.00	*120.00*
70 A10	$2 grn & ultra ('06)	160.00	*275.00*
71 A10	$5 grn & blk ('06)	375.00	*450.00*
	Nos. 62-71 (9)	666.25	*1,026.*

1909 Ordinary Paper

72 A10	2c carmine	16.00	.25
73 A10	5c ultramarine	2.75	.25

1911

74 A10	25c black, *green*	7.50	*55.00*

Numeral tablet on Nos. 61, 65-68, 74 has lined background with colorless value and "c."

King George V

A11 A12

1913-17 Wmk. 3 *Perf. 14*

75 A11	1c green	5.00	1.75
a.	1c yellow green	14.00	3.00
76 A11	2c scarlet	6.50	1.75
	Complete booklet of 100 #76, in blocks of 10 (5x2)	4,500.	
a.	2c carmine	6.50	1.25
b.	2c bright scarlet ('15)	9.50	1.20
c.	2c red, *bluish*	15.00	9.50
77 A11	3c orange ('17)	2.00	.25
	Complete booklet of 100 #77, in blocks of 10 (5x2)	—	
78 A11	5c ultra	3.50	1.10

Chalky Paper

79 A12	10c dl vio & ol grn	6.50	*8.00*
a.	10c purple & br green ('17)	25.00	*30.00*
80 A12	25c blk, *gray grn*	1.50	*14.50*
a.	25c black, *emerald*	2.10	*35.00*
b.	25c blk, *bl grn*, olive back	6.00	*13.50*
81 A12	50c vio & ultra, *bl*	30.00	*17.50*
82 A11	$1 black & scar	32.50	*70.00*
83 A11	$2 grn & dull vio	90.00	*120.00*
84 A11	$5 vio & blk, *red*	290.00	*350.00*
	Nos. 75-84 (10)	467.50	*584.85*

See No. 91. For overprints see Nos. MR2-MR5.

With Moire Overprint in Violet

1915

85 A11	1c green	4.75	*25.00*
a.	1c yellow green	.65	*21.00*
86 A11	2c carmine	4.25	.60
87 A11	5c ultramarine	.40	*7.25*
	Nos. 85-87 (3)	9.40	*32.85*

For 'War' overprint see No. MR1.

Peace Commemorative Issue

Seal of Colony and George V

A13

1921, Apr. 28 Engr.

89 A13	2c carmine	6.00	1.00
	Never hinged	10.00	

Similar to A13 but without "Peace Peace"

1922 Wmk. 4

90 A13	4c dark gray	14.00	1.25
	Never hinged	18.50	

Type of 1913-17

1921 Typo. Wmk. 4

91 A11	1c green	9.00	*14.00*

A14

1922-33 Typo. Wmk. 4

92 A14	1c green ('29)	19.00	6.50
93 A14	2c dark brown	2.00	2.00
	Complete booklet of 100 #93, in blocks of 10 (5x2)	—	
94 A14	2c rose red ('27)	12.00	2.00
	Complete booklet of 100 #94, in blocks of 10 (5x2)	—	
95 A14	3c orange ('33)	37.50	5.00
96 A14	4c gray ('29)	22.50	1.00
97 A14	5c ultramarine	2.00	.70

Chalky Paper

98 A14	10c olive grn & lil	4.00	.40
99 A14	25c black, *emerald*	3.25	*9.00*
100 A14	50c ultra & vio, *bl*	8.00	*16.00*
101 A14	$1 scarlet & blk	22.50	*30.00*
102 A14	$2 red vio & grn	50.00	*130.00*

Wmk. 3

103 A14	25c black, *emerald*	8.50	*55.00*
104 A14	$5 blk & vio, *red*	275.00	*300.00*
	Nos. 92-104 (13)	466.25	*557.60*

For surcharges see Nos. B1-B5.

Common Design Types pictured following the introduction.

Silver Jubilee Issue

Common Design Type

Perf. 11x12

1935, May 6 Engr. Wmk. 4

108 CD301	3c black & ultra	2.00	.60
109 CD301	4c indigo & grn	4.50	*4.25*
110 CD301	5c ultra & brn	2.25	*2.50*
111 CD301	25c brn vio & ind	6.50	*8.00*
	Nos. 108-111 (4)	15.25	*15.35*
	Set, never hinged	24.00	

Coronation Issue

Common Design Type

1937, May 12 *Perf. 13½x14*

112 CD302	3c deep orange	.25	.25
113 CD302	4c gray black	.35	.35
114 CD302	5c bright ultra	.60	*1.75*
	Nos. 112-114 (3)	1.20	2.35
	Set, never hinged	2.00	

Mayan Figures A15

Chicle Tapping — A16

Cohune Palm — A17

Local Products A18

Grapefruit Industry A19

Mahogany Logs in River — A20

Sergeant's Cay — A21

Dory — A22

Chicle Industry A23

Court House, Belize — A24

Mahogany Cutting — A25

Seal of Colony — A26

1938 *Perf. 11x11½, 11½x11*
115 A15 1c green & violet .25 1.75
116 A16 2c car & black .25 1.25
a. Perf. 12 ('47) 2.75 1.25
117 A17 3c brown & dk vio .50 1.00
118 A18 4c green & black .50 .90
119 A19 5c slate bl & red vio 1.10 1.00
120 A20 10c brown & yel grn 1.25 .80
121 A21 15c blue & brown 2.25 .90
122 A22 25c green & ultra 1.75 1.50
123 A23 50c dk vio & blk 9.00 4.25
124 A24 $1 ol green & car 17.50 10.00
125 A25 $2 rose lake & ind 21.00 25.00
126 A26 $5 brn & carmine 22.50 37.50
Nos. 115-126 (12) 77.85 85.85
Set, never hinged 175.00

Issued: 3c-5c, 1/10; 1c, 2c, 10c-50c, 2/14; $1-$5, 2/28.

Catalogue values for unused stamps in this section, from this point to the end of the section, are for Never Hinged items.

Peace Issue
Common Design Type
Perf. 13½x14
1946, Sept. 9 **Engr.** **Wmk. 4**
127 CD303 3c brown .25 .25
128 CD303 5c deep blue .25 .25

Silver Wedding Issue
Common Design Types
1948, Oct. 1 **Photo.** *Perf. 14x14½*
129 CD304 4c dark green .25 .70

Engraved; Name Typographed
Perf. 11½x11
130 CD305 $5 light brown 22.50 52.50

St. George's Cay — A27

H.M.S. Merlin — A28

1949, Jan. 10 **Engr.** *Perf. 12½*
131 A27 1c green & ultra .25 1.25
132 A27 3c yel brn & dp blue .25 1.50
133 A27 4c purple & brn ol .25 1.75
134 A28 5c dk blue & brown 1.75 .75
135 A28 10c vio brn & blue grn 1.75 .45
136 A28 15c ultra & emerald 1.75 .45
Nos. 131-136 (6) 6.00 6.15

Battle of St. George's Cay, 150th anniv.

UPU Issue
Common Design Types
Perf. 13½, 11x11½
1949, Oct. 10 **Engr.** **Wmk. 4**
137 CD306 4c blue green .40 .40
138 CD307 5c indigo 1.50 .60
139 CD308 10c chocolate .55 3.00
140 CD309 25c blue .90 .75
Nos. 137-140 (4) 3.35 4.75

University Issue
Common Design Types
1951, Feb. 16 **Engr.** *Perf. 14x14½*
141 CD310 3c choc & purple .55 1.50
142 CD311 10c choc & green .85 .65

SEMI-POSTAL STAMPS

Regular Issue of 1921-29 Surcharged in Black or Red

1932 **Wmk. 4** *Perf. 14*
B1 A14 1c + 1c green 3.00 15.00
B2 A14 2c + 2c rose red 3.00 15.00
B3 A14 3c + 3c orange 3.25 32.50
B4 A14 4c + 4c gray (R) 8.00 35.00
B5 A14 5c + 5c ultra 8.00 15.00
Nos. B1-B5 (5) 25.25 112.50

The surtax was for a fund to aid sufferers from the destruction of the city of Belize by a hurricane in Sept. 1931.

POSTAGE DUE STAMPS

Catalogue values for unused stamps in this section are for Never Hinged items.

D1

1923-64 **Typo.** **Wmk. 4** *Perf. 14*
J1 D1 1c black, *chalky paper* ('56) 1.25 26.00
On cover 165.00
a. 1c black, *white ordinary paper* ('64) 37.50 45.00
b. 1c black, *yellowish thin paper* ('23) 2.75 21.00
J2 D1 2c black, *chalky paper* ('56) 1.25 22.50
On cover 165.00
a. 2c black, *yellowish thin paper* ('23) 2.75 12.00
J3 D1 4c black, *chalky paper* ('56) 2.50 19.00
On cover 275.00
a. 4c black, *yellowish thin paper* ('23) 1.75 9.50
Nos. J1-J3 (3) 5.00 67.50
Nos. J1b, J2a, J3a, overprinted "SPECIMEN" 80.00

On cover values are for properly franked commercial covers. Philatelic usages also exist and sell for less.

WAR TAX STAMPS

Nos. 85, 75 and 77 Overprinted

1916-17 **Wmk. 3** *Perf. 14*
With Moire Overprint
MR1 A11 1c green .80 2.50
a. "WAR" inverted 300.00 350.00

Without Moire Overprint
MR2 A11 1c green ('17) 1.75 5.50
MR3 A11 3c orange ('17) 5.50 9.50
a. Double overprint 425.00 425.00
Nos. MR1-MR3 (3) 8.05 17.50

Nos. 75 and 77 Overprinted

1918
MR4 A11 1c green .25 .40
MR5 A11 3c orange 1.00 3.00

BRUNEI

'brü-ˌnī

LOCATION — On the northwest coast of Borneo
GOVT. — British Protectorate
AREA — 2,226 sq. mi.
POP. — 191,770 (1981)
CAPITAL — Bandar Seri Begawan

Although Brunei became a British protectorate in 1888, postage stamps were not issued until 1906, when the administration was transferred from the Sultan to the British Resident.

100 Cents (Sen) = 1 Dollar

Catalogue values for unused stamps in this country are for Never Hinged items, beginning with Scott 62.

Star and Local Scene — A1a

Perf. 13 to 13½
1895, July 22 **Litho.** **Unwmk.**
A1 A1a ½c brown (shades) 6.50 24.00
Never hinged 9.00
A2 A1a 1c brown lake (shades) 6.00 17.50
Never hinged 7.50
A3 A1a 2c black 4.75 19.00
Never hinged 7.00
A4 A1a 3c deep blue 6.00 16.50
Never hinged 8.50
A5 A1a 5c deep blue green 7.50 20.00
Never hinged 10.50
A6 A1a 8c plum 8.00 50.00
Never hinged 11.00
A7 A1a 10c orange red 9.50 50.00
Never hinged 13.50
a. Imperf pair 3,000.
A8 A1a 25c turquoise 90.00 105.00
Never hinged 125.00
A9 A1a 50c yellow green 26.00 120.00
Never hinged 37.50
A10 A1a $1 yellow olive 27.50 130.00
Never hinged 40.00
Nos. A1-A10 (10) 191.75 552.00

These stamps were valid within Brunei and to Labuan. Prior to Brunei's admission to the UPU in 1906, all overseas mail was sent through Labuan, where Labuan stamps were required for despatch abroad.

Covers bearing examples of Nos. A1-A10, mostly in combination with stamps of Labuan, are usually philatelic. Values start at about $425. Commercial uses of these stamps exist.

Labuan Stamps of 1902-03 Overprinted or Surcharged in Red

1906 **Unwmk.** *Perf. 12 to 16*
1 A38 1c violet & blk 50.00 65.00
a. Black overprint 2,500. 3,000.
2 A38 2c on 3c brn & blk 7.00 21.00
a. "BRUNEI." double 4,500. 3,000.
b. "TWO CENTS." double 6,500.
3 A38 2c on 8c org & blk 32.50 80.00
a. "TWO CENTS." double 14,000.
b. "TWO CENTS." omitted, in pair with normal 15,000.
4 A38 3c brown & blk 38.50 100.00
5 A38 4c on 12c yel & black 8.50 6.00
6 A38 5c on 16c org brn & green 55.00 90.00
7 A38 8c orange & blk 15.00 37.50
8 A38 10c on 16c org brn & green 7.75 26.00
9 A38 25c on 16c org brn & green 125.00 150.00
10 A38 30c on 16c org brn & green 125.00 150.00
11 A38 50c on 16c org brn & green 125.00 150.00
12 A38 $1 on 8c org & blk 125.00 150.00
Nos. 1-12 (12) 714.25 1,026.

The 25c surcharge reads: "25 CENTS."
Covers: Covers bearing this issue are rare.

Scene on Brunei River — A1

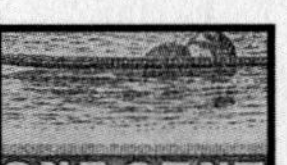
Type I

Type II

Two Types of 1908 1c, 3c:
Type I — Dots form bottom line of water shading. (Double plate.)
Type II — Dots removed. (Single plate.)

1907-21 **Engr.** **Wmk. 3** *Perf. 14*
13 A1 1c yel green & blk 2.75 13.00
14 A1 1c green (II) ('11) .70 2.50
a. Type I ('19) 1.00 2.75
c. Type II, "A" missing from wmk. 260.00
d. Type II, "C" missing from wmk. 260.00
15 A1 2c red & black 3.75 5.25
16 A1 2c brn & blk ('11) 4.75 1.50
17 A1 3c red brn & blk 12.50 26.00
18 A1 3c car (I) ('08) 8.00 1.75
a. Type II ('17) 130.00 45.00
19 A1 4c lilac & blk 9.00 12.00
a. 4c reddish purple & gray black ('10) 80.00 70.00
20 A1 4c claret ('12) 8.00 .90
21 A1 5c ultra & blk 60.00 110.00
22 A1 5c org & blk ('08) 8.50 8.50
23 A1 5c orange ('16) 26.00 25.00
24 A1 8c orange & blk 9.00 27.50
25 A1 8c blue & indigo blue ('08) 8.50 13.00
26 A1 8c ultra ('16) 8.00 32.50
27 A1 10c dk green & blk 5.25 9.00
28 A1 10c violet, *yel* ('12) 8.00 2.10
b. 10c violet, *pale yellow* ('22) 2.00 4.50
29 A1 25c yel brn & blue 37.50 57.50
30 A1 25c violet ('12) 11.00 27.50
b. 25c deep dull purple ('20) 14.00 20.00
31 A1 30c black & pur 30.00 26.00
32 A1 30c org & red vio ('12) 16.00 18.00
33 A1 50c brown & grn 18.00 27.50
34 A1 50c blk, *grn* ('12) 37.50 77.50
35 A1 50c blk, *grnsh bl* ('21) 11.00 42.50
36 A1 $1 slate & red 72.50 110.00
37 A1 $1 red & blk, *bl* ('12) 27.50 57.50
38 A1 $5 lake, *grn* ('08) 200.00 350.00
39 A1 $25 blk, *red* ('08) 650.00 1,200.
Nos. 13-38 (26) 643.70 1,085.

Used value for No. 39 is for a canceled-to-order example dated before December 1941. CTOs dated later are worth about half the value given.

Some stamps in this set exist with watermark reversed or inverted; values are two to five times those shown.

Stamps of 1908-21 Overprinted in Four Lines in Black

1922

14b A1 1c green 12.00 *50.00*
16a A1 2c brown & black 12.00 *50.00*
18b A1 3c carmine 13.00 *55.00*
20a A1 4c claret 20.00 *60.00*
23a A1 5c orange 22.50 *65.00*
28a A1 10c violet, *yellow* 10.00 *65.00*
30a A1 25c violet 16.00 *85.00*
35a A1 50c greenish blue 47.50 *160.00*
37a A1 $1 red & black, *blue* 80.00 *200.00*
Nos. 14b-37a (9) 233.00 *790.00*

Industrial fair, Singapore, Mar. 31-Apr. 15

Type of 1907 Issue

1924-37 **Wmk. 4**

43 A1 1c black ('26) 1.25 .90
44 A1 2c deep brown 1.25 *9.00*
45 A1 2c green ('33) 2.40 1.25
46 A1 3c green 1.75 *7.75*
47 A1 4c claret brown 2.75 1.50
48 A1 4c orange ('29) 2.40 1.25
49 A1 5c orange 16.00 2.00
50 A1 5c lt gray ('31) 24.00 14.00
51 A1 5c brown ('33) 25.00 1.20
52 A1 8c ultra ('27) 7.25 6.00
53 A1 8c gray ('33) 19.00 .90
54 A1 10c violet, *yel* ('37) 40.00 32.50
55 A1 25c dk violet ('31) 24.00 15.00
56 A1 30c org & red vio ('31) 25.00 19.00
57 A1 50c black, *grn* ('31) 20.00 17.50
58 A1 $1 red & blk, *bl* ('31) 29.00 *90.00*
Nos. 43-58 (16) 241.05 *219.75*

For overprints see Nos. N1-N20.

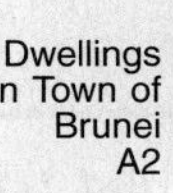

Dwellings in Town of Brunei A2

1924-31

59 A2 6c black 17.00 12.00
60 A2 6c red ('31) 12.00 *13.00*
61 A2 12c blue 5.50 *11.00*
Nos. 59-61 (3) 34.50 *36.00*

See note after Nos. N1-N19.

Catalogue values for unused stamps in this section, from this point to the end of the section, are for Never Hinged items.

Types of 1907-24

1947-51 **Engr.** ***Perf. 14***

62 A1 1c brown .65 *2.50*
63 A1 2c gray .75 *6.00*
a. Perf. 14½x13½ ('50) 2.40 *5.25*
64 A2 3c dark green 1.50 *8.00*
65 A1 5c deep orange 1.00 *1.75*
a. Perf. 14½x13½ ('50) 4.75 *22.00*
66 A2 6c gray black 1.25 *6.75*
67 A1 8c scarlet .60 *1.50*
a. Perf. 13 ('51) .65 *13.00*
68 A1 10c violet 2.25 .40
a. Perf. 14½x13½ ('50) 3.75 6.50
69 A1 15c brt ultra 2.10 *.90*
70 A1 25c red violet 3.25 1.25
a. Perf. 14½x13½ ('51) 4.50 *16.00*
71 A1 30c dp org & gray blk 3.00 1.25
a. Perf. 14½x13½ ('51) 3.50 *22.00*
72 A1 50c black 6.50 1.00
a. Perf. 13 ('50) 2.10 *22.00*
73 A1 $1 scar & gray blk 16.00 2.50
74 A1 $5 red org & grn ('48) 22.50 *25.00*
75 A1 $10 dp claret & gray blk ('48) 110.00 35.00
Nos. 62-75 (14) 171.35 *93.80*
Set, perforated "SPECIMEN" 275.00

Sultan Ahmed and Pile Dwellings A3

1949, Sept. 22 **Wmk. 4** ***Perf. 13***

76 A3 8c car & black 1.50 1.50
77 A3 25c red orange & pur 1.50 *1.90*
78 A3 50c blue & black 1.50 *1.90*
Nos. 76-78 (3) 4.50 5.30

25th anniv. of the reign of Sultan Ahmed Tajudin Akhazul Khair Wad-din.

Common Design Types pictured following the introduction.

UPU Issue

Common Design Types

Engr.; Name Typo. on 15c and 25c

1949, Oct. 10 ***Perf. 13½, 11x11½***

79 CD306 8c rose car 1.25 *1.75*
80 CD307 15c indigo 4.00 2.00
81 CD308 25c red lilac 1.25 *1.50*
82 CD309 50c slate 1.25 *1.50*
Nos. 79-82 (4) 7.75 6.75

Sultan Omar Ali Saifuddin — A4

River Kampong A5

Perf. 13½x13

1952, Mar. 1 **Engr.** **Wmk. 4**

Center in Black

83 A4 1c black .25 .60
84 A4 2c red orange .25 .60
85 A4 3c red brown .25 .35
86 A4 4c green .25 .25
87 A4 6c gray .60 .25
88 A4 8c carmine .60 .60
a. 8c carmine lake & black ('56) 10.00 .25
89 A4 10c olive brown .25 .25
90 A4 12c violet 6.00 .25
91 A4 15c blue 4.00 .25
92 A4 25c purple 3.00 .25
a. 25c reddish purple & black ('53) 5.50 1.10
93 A4 50c ultramarine 3.00 .35
a. 50c blue & black 7.75 .25

Perf. 13

94 A5 $1 dull green 1.75 1.75
a. $1 bronze green & black ('58) 6.00 3.50
95 A5 $2 red 5.50 3.00
96 A5 $5 deep plum 22.50 8.50
a. $5 brnish purple & black ('56) 26.00 8.50
Nos. 83-96 (14) 48.20 17.25

See Nos. 101-114 in *Scott Standard Postage Stamp Catalogue*, Vol. 1.

OCCUPATION STAMPS

Issued under Japanese Occupation

Stamps and Types of 1908-37 Hstmpd. in Violet, Red Violet, Blue or Red

Perf. 14, 14x11½ (#N7)

1942-44 **Wmk. 4**

N1 A1 1c black 11.00 *28.00*
N2 A1 2c green 75.00 *150.00*
N3 A1 2c dull orange 10.00 *15.00*
N4 A1 3c green 45.00 *100.00*
N5 A1 4c orange 12.00 *20.00*
N6 A1 5c brown 9.00 *16.00*
N7 A2 6c slate gray 90.00 *275.00*
N8 A2 6c red 900.00 775.00
N9 A1 8c gray (RV) 1,200. *1,050.*
N10 A2 8c carmine 15.00 *15.00*
N11 A1 10c violet, *yel* 10.00 *32.50*
N12 A2 12c blue 42.50 *32.50*
N13 A2 15c ultra 32.50 *32.50*
N14 A1 25c dk violet 25.00 *70.00*
N15 A1 30c org & red vio 150.00 *225.00*
N16 A1 50c blk, *green* 50.00 *85.00*
N17 A1 $1 red & blk, *bl* 100.00 *75.00*

Wmk. 3

N18 A1 $5 lake, *green* 1,400. *2,750.*
N19 A1 $25 black, *red* 1,500. *2,750.*

Overprints vary in shade. Nos. N3, N7, N10 and N13 without overprint are not believed to have been regularly issued.

No. N1 Surcharged in Red

1944 **Wmk. 4** ***Perf. 14***

N20 A1 $3 on 1c black *15,000.* 7,500.
a. On No. 43 10,000. —

BULGARIA

ˌbəl-ˈgar-ē-ə

LOCATION — Southeastern Europe bordering on the Black Sea on the east and the Danube River on the north
GOVT. — Monarchy
AREA — 42,823 sq. mi.
POP. — 8,929,332 (1983)
CAPITAL — Sofia

In 1885 Bulgaria, then a principality under the suzerainty of the Sultan of Turkey, was joined by Eastern Rumelia. Independence from Turkey was obtained in 1908.

100 Centimes = 1 Franc
100 Stotinki = 1 Lev (1881)

Catalogue values for unused stamps in this country are for Never Hinged items, beginning with Scott 293 in the regular postage section, Scott B1 in the semi-postal section, Scott C15 in the airpost section, Scott E1 in the special delivery section.

Watermarks

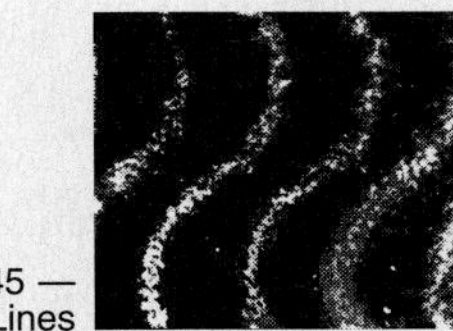

Wmk. 145 — Wavy Lines

Wmk. 168 — Wavy Lines and EZGV in Cyrillic

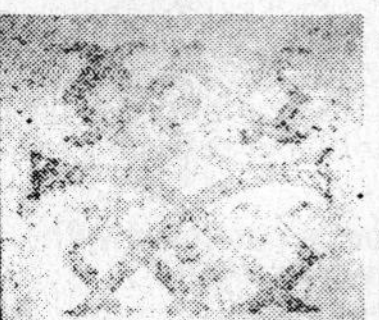

Wmk. 275 — Entwined Curved Lines

AUSTRIAN POST IN BULGARIA

The Austrian Empire maintained post offices in various cities in Bulgaria. The six offices established are listed below. The Austrian Lloyd Agency operated its own office. Filipopoli was open during two periods, the first while under Austrian occupation during the military campaign of 1854-57.

Burgas (Eastern Rumelia)
Filipopoli
Rustschuck
Sofia
Varna
Varna Lloyd Agency
Widdin

Values for Nos. 2A1-2A23 are for stamps without defects tied to cover by complete strikes of town cancellations. Stamps tied to piece with legible full strikes of town cancellations sell for 5-30% of the on-cover value. Stamps with partial strikes of town cancellations sell for 25-50% of the on-piece value.

Stamps of Lombardy-Venetia canceled with Austrian-Levant postmark of Rustschuck in black

2A1 2s yellow (#15) 1,250.
2A2 3s green (#16) 1,400.
2A3 5s rose (#17) 1,100.
2A4 10s blue (#18) 825.
2A5 15s yel brn (#19) 925.

Other Town Cancellations

Burgas (blk) +2,100.
Burgas (bl) +2,100.
Filipopoli +625.
Rustschuck (bl) +225.
Sofia +1,250.

2A6 2s yellow (#20) 1,600.
2A7 3s green (#21) 825.
2A8 5s rose (#22) 650.
2A9 10s blue (#23) 400.
2A10 15s yel brn (#24) 525.

Other Town Cancellations

Burgas (blk) +800.
Burgas (bl) +825.
Filipopoli +10.
Rustschuck (bl) +800.
Sofia +825.
Widdin (blk) +1,450.
Widdin (bl) +4,250.

Stamps of Austrian Levant canceled with Austrian-Levant blue circular date stamp of Varna

Course Print

2A11 2s yellow (#1a) 500.
2A12 3s green (#2) 425.
2A13 5s rose (#3) 100.
2A14 10s blue (#4) 45.
2A15 15s yel brn (#5) 55.
2A16 25s gray lilac (#6b) 800.
2A17 50s brown (#7 4,750.

Fine Print

2A18 2s yellow (#7C) —
2A19 3s green (#7D) 250.
2A20 5s rose (#7E) 110.
2A21 10s blue (#7F) 40.
2A22 15s yel brn (#7I) 875.
2A23 25s gray lilac (#7J) 6,250.

Other Town Cancellations

Burgas +525.
Filipopoli +165.
Rustschuck +70.
Sofia (blk) +1,525.
Sofia (bl) +2,500.
Varna, straight-line (blk) +750.
Varna, straight-line (bl) +1,150.
Varna, thimble (blk) +325.
Varna, thimble (bl) +525.
Varna, Bulgaria cancel +750.
Varna Lloyd Agency +525.
Widdin, thimble (blk) +750.
Widdin, thimble (bl) +1,150.

FRENCH IMPERIAL POST IN BULGARIA

Values for Nos. 3A1-3A8 are for stamps without defects tied to cover by complete strikes of the indicated cancels assigned to the French Post Office in Varna. Stamps off cover sell for 10-20% of the on-cover value.

Stamps of France canceled with small numerals "4018"

3A1 1c ol grn, *pale bl* (#12) —
3A2 5c grn, *grnsh* (#13) —
3A3 10c bister, *yelsh* (#14) 475.00
3A4 20c bl, *bluish* (#15) 500.00
3A5 40c org, *yelsh* (#18) 475.00
3A6 80c lake, *yelsh* (#19) 800.00
3A7 80c rose, *pnksh* (#20) 750.00

Stamp canceled with large numerals "5103"

3A8 40c pale org, *yelsh* (#35) 375.00

Lion of Bulgaria
A1 A2 A3

Perf. 14½x15

1879, May 1 Wmk. 168 Typo.

Laid Paper

1 A1 5c black & orange 160.00 57.50
On cover 2,500.
a. 5c black & yellow 90.00 20.00
On cover 2,500.
2 A1 10c black & green 900.00 200.00
On cover 800.00
b. Vertical half used as 5c on cover 3,750.
3 A1 25c black & violet 440.00 40.00
On cover 300.00
On cover, single franking 600.00
a. Imperf.
b. 25c black & purple 225.00 17.00
On cover 300.00
4 A1 50c black & blue 800.00 160.00
On cover 1,250.
5 A2 1fr black & red 95.00 40.00
On cover 1,500.

1881, Apr. 10

6 A3 3s red & silver 32.50 6.50
On cover 200.00
a. 3s deep carmine & gray 15.00 3.25
On cover 200.00
7 A3 5s black & orange 32.50 6.50
On cover 200.00
a. Background inverted 2,500.
b. 5s black & yellow 15.00 2.50
On cover 200.00
8 A3 10s black & green 175.00 20.00
On cover 500.00
a. 10s black & deep green 85.00 10.00
On cover 500.00
9 A3 15s dp car red & green 175.00 20.00
On cover 250.00
a. 15s car & pale green 85.00 10.00
On cover 250.00
10 A3 25s black & violet 900.00 100.00
On cover 250.00
a. 25s black & purple 350.00 35.00
On cover 250.00
11 A3 30s blue & fawn 32.50 16.00
On cover 300.00
a. 30s deep blue & brown 17.50 10.00
On cover 300.00

1882, Dec. 4

12 A3 3s orange & yel 1.60 .80
On cover 20.00
a. Background inverted 4,000. 4,000.
13 A3 5s green & pale green 12.50 1.20
On cover 20.00
a. 5s rose & pale rose (error) 3,000. 3,000.
On cover 4,000.
14 A3 10s rose & pale rose 16.00 1.20
On cover 20.00
15 A3 15s red vio & pale lil 16.00 1.20
On cover 25.00
16 A3 25s blue & pale blue 14.50 1.60
On cover 20.00
17 A3 30s violet & grn 14.50 1.20
On cover 30.00
18 A3 50s blue & pink 14.50 1.20
On cover 30.00
Nos. 12-18 (7) 89.60 8.40

See Nos. 207-210, 286.

Surcharged in Black, Carmine or Vermilion

A4

A5

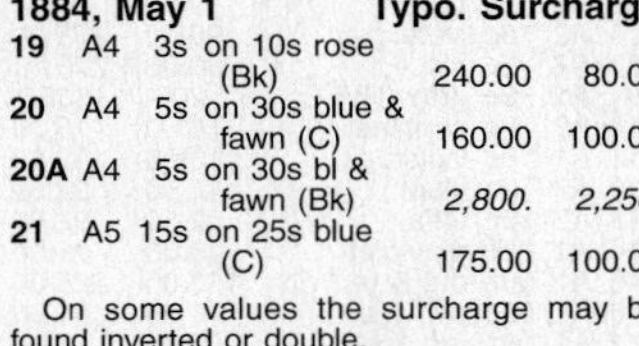

1884, May 1 Typo. Surcharge

19 A4 3s on 10s rose (Bk) 240.00 80.00
20 A4 5s on 30s blue & fawn (C) 160.00 100.00
20A A4 5s on 30s bl & fawn (Bk) *2,800.* *2,250.*
21 A5 15s on 25s blue (C) 175.00 100.00

On some values the surcharge may be found inverted or double.

1885, Apr. 5 Litho. Surcharge

21B A4 3s on 10s rose (Bk) 80.00 80.00
21C A4 5s on 30s bl & fawn (V) 80.00 80.00
21D A5 15s on 25s blue (V) 145.00 100.00
22 A5 50s on 1fr blk & red (Bk) 550.00 360.00
On cover 800.00

Forgeries of Nos. 19-22 are plentiful.

Word below left star in oval has 5 letters
A6

Third letter below left star is "A"
A7

1885, May 25

23 A6 1s gray vio & pale gray 28.00 9.50
On wrapper or newsprint 110.00
24 A7 2s sl grn & pale gray 28.00 6.75
On cover 75.00

Word below left star has 4 letters
A8

Third letter below left star is "b" with cross-bar in upper half
A9

A10

1886-87

25 A8 1s gray vio & pale gray 2.00 .40
26 A9 2s sl grn & pale gray 2.00 .40
27 A10 1 l black & red ('87) 57.50 7.25
Nos. 25-27 (3) 61.50 8.05

For surcharge see No. 40.

A11

Perf. 10½, 11, 11½, 13, 13½

1889 Wove Paper Unwmk.

28 A11 1s lilac 1.60 .40
On wrapper or newspaper 75.00
29 A11 2s gray 2.50 1.25
30 A11 3s bister brown 1.60 .40
31 A11 5s yellow green 12.00 .30
a. Vert. pair, imperf. btwn.
32 A11 10s rose 12.00 .80
33 A11 15s orange 80.00 .80
34 A11 25s blue 12.00 .80
35 A11 30s dk brown 13.50 .80
36 A11 50s green .80 .40
37 A11 1 l orange red .80 .80
Nos. 28-37 (10) 136.80 6.75

The 10s orange is a proof.

Nos. 28-34 exist imperforate. Value, set $225.

See Nos. 39, 41-42. For overprints and surcharges see Nos. 38, 55-56, 77-81, 113.

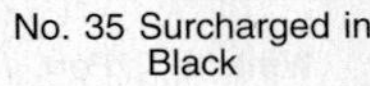

No. 35 Surcharged in Black

1892, Jan. 26

38 A11 15s on 30s brn 40.00 1.60
a. Inverted surcharge *70.00* *52.50*

1894 *Perf. 10½, 11, 11½*

Pelure Paper

39 A11 10s red 7.00 2.00
a. Imperf. *57.50*

No. 26 Surcharged in Red

Wmk. Wavy Lines (168)

1895, Oct. 25 *Perf. 14½x15*

Laid Paper

40 A9 1s on 2s 1.20 .40
a. Inverted surcharge 8.00 6.50
b. Double surcharge *62.50* *62.50*
c. Pair, one without surcharge *125.00* *125.00*

This surcharge on No. 24 is a proof.

Wmk. Coat of Arms in the Sheet

1896, Apr. 30 *Perf. 11½, 13*

Wove Paper

41 A11 2 l rose & pale rose 3.25 2.40
42 A11 3 l black & buff 4.75 5.50

Coat of Arms — A14

1896, Feb. 2 *Perf. 13*

43 A14 1s blue green .35 .25
On wrapper or newspaper 75.00
44 A14 5s dark blue .35 .25
45 A14 15s purple .60 .30
46 A14 25s red 5.75 1.00
Nos. 43-46 (4) 7.05 1.80

Baptism of Prince Boris.

Examples of Nos. 41-46 from sheet edges show no watermark.

Nos. 43, 45-46 were also printed on rough unwatermarked paper.

Cherry Wood Cannon — A15

1901, Apr. 20 Litho. Unwmk.

53 A15 5s carmine 1.50 1.25
54 A15 15s yellow green 1.50 1.25

Insurrection of Independence in April, 1876, 25th anniversary.

Exist imperf. Forgeries exist.

Nos. 30 and 36 Surcharged in Black

1901, Mar. 24 Typo.

55 A11 5s on 3s bister brn 2.50 1.60
a. Inverted surcharge 45.00 45.00
b. Pair, one without surcharge *70.00* *70.00*
56 A11 10s on 50s green 2.50 1.60
a. Inverted surcharge 50.00 50.00
b. Pair, one without surcharge *72.50* *72.50*

Tsar Ferdinand — A17

Type I

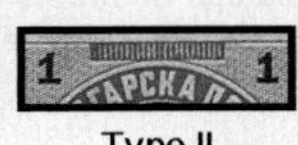

Type II

ONE LEV:

Type I — The numerals in the upper corners have, at the top, a sloping serif on the left side and a short straight serif on the right.

Type II — The numerals in the upper corners are of ordinary shape without the serif at the right.

1901, Oct. 1-1905 Typo. *Perf. 12½*

57 A17 1s vio & gray blk .25 .25
58 A17 2s brnz grn & ind .25 .25
a. Imperf.
59 A17 3s orange & ind .25 .25
60 A17 5s emerald & brn 2.25 .25
61 A17 10s rose & blk 1.50 .25
62 A17 15s claret & gray blk .80 .25
63 A17 25s blue & blk .80 .25
64 A17 30s bis & gray blk 22.50 .30
65 A17 50s dk blue & brn 1.00 .25
66 A17 1 l red org & brnz grn, type I 2.50 1.25
67 A17 1 l brn red & brnz grn, II ('05) 75.00 4.00
68 A17 2 l carmine & blk 7.50 .85
69 A17 3 l slate & red brn 7.50 5.00
Nos. 57-69 (13) 122.10 13.40

For surcharges see Nos. 73, 83-85, 87-88.

Fighting at Shipka Pass — A18

1902, Aug. 29 Litho. *Perf. 11½*

70 A18 5s lake 3.00 1.00
71 A18 10s blue green 3.00 1.00
72 A18 15s blue 12.00 5.00
Nos. 70-72 (3) 18.00 7.00

Battle of Shipka Pass, 1877.

Imperf. copies are proofs.

Excellent forgeries of Nos. 70 to 72 exist.

No. 62 Surcharged in Black

1903, Oct. 1 *Perf. 12½*

73 A17 10s on 15s 6.00 .40
a. Inverted surcharge *57.50* *50.00*
b. Double surcharge *57.50* *50.00*
c. Pair, one without surcharge *100.00* *100.00*
d. 10s on 10s rose & black *325.00* *325.00*

Ferdinand in 1887 and 1907 — A19

1907, Aug. 12 Litho. *Perf. 11½*

74 A19 5s deep green 17.50 1.75
75 A19 10s red brown 25.00 1.75
76 A19 25s deep blue 60.00 3.50
Nos. 74-76 (3) 102.50 7.00

Accession to the throne of Ferdinand I, 20th anniversary.

Nos. 74-76 imperf. are proofs. Nos. 74-76 exist in pairs imperforate between. Values: 5s, $75; 10s, $110; 25s, $160.

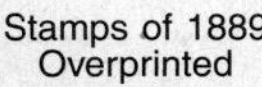
Stamps of 1889 Overprinted

1909

77	A11 1s lilac		1.60	.70
a.	Inverted overprint		21.00	17.50
b.	Double overprint, one inverted		24.00	24.00
78	A11 5s yellow green		1.60	.70
a.	Inverted overprint		25.00	25.00
b.	Double overprint		25.00	25.00

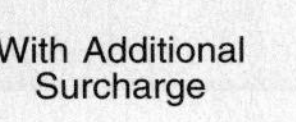
With Additional Surcharge

79	A11 5s on 30s brown (Bk)	2.75	.70
a.	"5" double		
b.	"1990" for "1909"	*700.00*	*550.00*
80	A11 10s on 15s org (Bk)	2.75	.95
a.	Inverted surcharge	17.50	17.50
b.	"1909" omitted	*27.50*	*27.50*
81	A11 10s on 50s dk grn (R)	2.75	.95
a.	"1990" for "1909"	100.00	100.00
b.	Black surcharge	52.50	52.50

Nos. 62 & 64 Surcharged with Value Only

83	A17 5s on 15s (Bl)	2.40	.80
a.	Inverted surcharge	21.00	21.00
84	A17 10s on 15s (Bl)	6.25	.55
a.	Inverted surcharge	21.00	21.00
85	A17 25s on 30s (R)	8.00	1.25
a.	Double surcharge	75.00	75.00
b.	"2" of "25" omitted	87.50	87.50
c.	Blue surcharge	*650.00*	*450.00*

Nos. 59 and 62 Surcharged in Blue

1910, Oct.

87	A17 1s on 3s	4.25	1.60
a.	"1910" omitted	21.00	
88	A17 5s on 15s	4.25	1.60

Tsar Assen's Tower (Crown over lion) A20

Tsar Ferdinand A21

City of Trnovo A22

Tsar Ferdinand A23

Ferdinand A24

Isker River A25

Ferdinand A26

Rila Monastery (Crown at UR) A27

Tsar and Princes — A28

Ferdinand in Robes of Ancient Tsars — A29

Monastery of Holy Trinity — A30

View of Varna — A31

1911, Feb. 14 Engr. *Perf. 12*

89	A20	1s myrtle green	.25	.25
90	A21	2s car & blk	.25	.25
91	A22	3s lake & blk	.45	.25
92	A23	5s green & blk	1.60	.25
93	A24	10s dp red & blk	2.50	.25
94	A25	15s brown bister	5.75	.25
95	A26	25s ultra & blk	.55	.25
96	A27	30s blue & blk	5.75	.25
97	A28	50s ocher & blk	30.00	.25
a.		Center inverted		*4,250.*
98	A29	1 l chocolate	13.50	.25
99	A30	2 l dull pur & blk	3.25	.50
100	A31	3 l blue vio & blk	15.00	5.50
		Nos. 89-100 (12)	78.85	8.50

See Nos. 114-120, 161-162. For overprints and surcharges see Nos. 104-112, 188, B8, Greece N167-N178, N182-N187, Thrace 16-21, Romania 2N1-2N4.

Tsar Ferdinand — A32

1912, Aug. 2 Typo. *Perf. 12½*

101	A32 5s olive green	15.00	2.00
a.	5s pale green	*975.00*	*225.00*
102	A32 10s claret	7.00	3.50
103	A32 25s slate	10.00	5.50
	Nos. 101-103 (3)	32.00	11.00

25th year of reign of Tsar Ferdinand.

Nos. 89-95 Overprinted in Various Colors

1913, Aug. 6 Engr.

104	A20	1s myrtle grn (C)	.50	.25
105	A21	2s car & blk (Bl)	2.00	.25
107	A22	3s lake & blk (Bl Bk)	2.00	.25
108	A23	5s grn & blk (R)	.50	.25
109	A24	10s dp red & blk (Bk)	.50	.25
110	A25	15s brown bis (G)	2.50	1.50
111	A26	25s ultra & blk (R)	8.00	2.50
		Nos. 104-111 (7)	16.00	5.25

Victory over the Turks in Balkan War of 1912-1913.

No. 95 Surcharged in Red

1915, July 6

112	A26 10s on 25s	.95	.25
a.	Pair, one without surcharge	160.00	160.00

No. 28 Surcharged in Green

113	A11 3s on 1s lilac	9.50	4.50

Types of 1911 Re-engraved

1915, Nov. 7 *Perf. 11½, 14*

114	A20	1s dk bl grn	.25	.25
115	A23	5s grn & brn vio	3.25	.25
116	A24	10s red brn & brnsh blk	.25	.25
117	A25	15s olive green	.25	.25
118	A26	25s indigo & blk	.25	.25
119	A27	30s ol grn & red brn	.25	.25
120	A29	1 l dark brown	.40	.30
		Nos. 114-120 (7)	4.90	1.80

Widths: No. 114 is 19½mm; No. 89, 18½mm. No. 118 is 19¼mm; No. 95, 18¼mm. No. 120 is 20mm; No. 98, 19mm. The re-engraved stamps also differ from the 1911 issue in many details of design. Nos. 114-120 exist imperforate. Values, each $11-$22.50.

The 5s exists in two types: I, 20x29.3mm, green and brown violet; II, 19.5x29mm, dark green and brown. There are a number of minor design differences between the two types. The editors would welcome any information that Bulgarian specialists can provide on this and similar varieties on stamps of this period.

The 5s and 10s exist perf. 14x11½.

For Nos. 114-116 and 118 overprinted with Cyrillic characters and "1916-1917," see Romania Nos. 2N1-2N4.

Coat of Arms — A33

Peasant and Bullock — A34

Soldier and Mt. Sonichka — A35

View of Nish — A36

Town and Lake Okhrida — A37

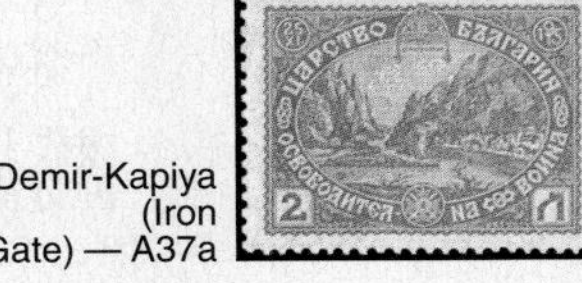
Demir-Kapiya (Iron Gate) — A37a

View of Gevgeli — A38

Perf. 11½, 12½x13, 13x12½

1917-19 Typo.

122	A33	5s green	.40	.25
123	A34	15s slate	.25	.25
124	A35	25s blue	.25	.25
125	A36	30s orange	.25	.25
126	A37	50s violet	.75	.60
126A	A37a	2 l brn org ('19)	.75	.50
127	A38	3 l claret	1.75	1.75
		Nos. 122-127 (7)	4.40	3.85

Liberation of Macedonia. A 1 l dark green was prepared but not issued. Value $1.65.

For surcharges see Nos. B9-B10, B12.

View of Veles — A39

Monastery of St. Clement at Okhrida — A40

1918 *Perf. 13x14*

128	A39 1s gray	.40	.25
129	A40 5s green	.40	.25

Tsar Ferdinand — A41

1918, July 1 *Perf. 12½x13*

130	A41	1s dark green	.80	.25
131	A41	2s dark brown	.80	.25
132	A41	3s indigo	1.60	.40
133	A41	10s brown red	.80	.40
		Nos. 130-133 (4)	4.00	1.30

Ferdinand's accession to the throne, 30th anniv.

Plowing with Oxen — A42

1919 *Perf. 13½x13*

134	A42 1s gray	.25	.25

Sobranye Palace — A43

1919 *Perf. 11½x12, 12x11½*

135	A43 1s black	.25	.25
137	A43 2s olive green	.25	.25

For surcharges see Nos. 186, B1.

Tsar Boris III — A44

1919, Oct. 3

138	A44	3s orange brn	.30	.25
139	A44	5s green	.30	.25
140	A44	10s rose red	.30	.25
141	A44	15s violet	.30	.25
142	A44	25s deep blue	.30	.25

143	A44	30s chocolate	.30	.25
144	A44	50s yellow brn	.30	.25
		Nos. 138-144 (7)	2.10	1.75

1st anniv. of enthronement of Tsar Boris III.
Nos. 135-144 exist imperforate.
For surcharges see Nos. 187, B2-B7.

Birthplace of Vazov at Sopot and Cherrywood Cannon — A47

"The Bear Fighter"-a Character from "Under the Yoke" — A48

Ivan Vazov in 1870 and 1920 A49

Vazov — A50

Homes of Vazov at Plovdiv and Sofia A51

The Monk Paisii — A52

1920, Oct. 20 Photo. *Perf. 11½*

147	A47	30s brown red	.25	.25
148	A48	50s dark green	.35	.25
149	A49	1 l drab	.75	.35
150	A50	2 l light brown	1.75	.90
151	A51	3 l black violet	3.00	1.25
152	A52	5 l deep blue	3.50	1.50
		Nos. 147-152 (6)	9.60	4.50

70th birthday of Ivan Vazov (1850-1921), Bulgarian poet and novelist.

Several values of this series exist imperforate and in pairs imperforate between.

Tsar Ferdinand
A53 A54

Mt. Shar — A55

Bridge over Vardar River — A56

View of Ohrid — A57

Perf. 13x14, 14x13

1921, June 11 Typo.

153	A53	10s claret	.25	.25
154	A54	10s claret	.25	.25
155	A55	10s claret	.25	.25
156	A56	10s rose lilac	.25	.25
157	A57	20s blue	.70	.25
		Nos. 153-157 (5)	1.70	1.25

Nos. 153-157 were intended to be issued in 1915 to commemorate the liberation of Macedonia. They were not put in use until 1921. A 50s violet was prepared but never placed in use. Value $1.75.

View of Sofia — A58

"The Liberator," Monument to Alexander II A59

Monastery at Shipka Pass — A62

Tsar Boris III — A63

Harvesting Grain — A64

Tsar Assen's Tower (No crown over lion) — A65

Rila Monastery (Rosette at upper right) — A66

1921-23 Engr. *Perf. 12*

158	A58	10s blue gray	.25	.25
159	A59	20s deep green	.25	.25
160	A63	25s blue grn ('22)	.25	.25
161	A22	50s orange	.25	.25
162	A22	50s dk blue ('23)	4.00	2.50
163	A62	75s dull vio	.25	.25
164	A62	75s dp blue ('23)	.30	.25
165	A63	1 l carmine	.30	.25
166	A63	1 l dp blue ('22)	.30	.25
167	A64	2 l brown	.30	1.00
168	A65	3 l brown vio	1.40	1.10
169	A66	5 l lt blue	3.75	1.25
170	A63	10 l violet brn	9.50	2.10
		Nos. 158-170 (13)	21.10	9.95

For surcharge see No. 189.

Bourchier in Bulgarian Costume A67

James David Bourchier A68

View of Rila Monastery A69

1921, Dec. 31

171	A67	10s red orange	.25	.25
172	A67	20s orange	.25	.25
173	A68	30s dp gray	.25	.25
174	A68	50s bluish gray	.25	.25
175	A68	1 l dull vio	.25	.25
176	A69	1½ l olive grn	.25	.25
177	A69	2 l deep green	.25	.25
178	A69	3 l Prus blue	.60	.25
179	A69	5 l red brown	1.00	.50
		Nos. 171-179 (9)	3.35	2.50

Death of James D. Bourchier, Balkan correspondent of the London Times.
For surcharges see Nos. B13-B16.

Postage Due Stamps of 1919-22 Surcharged — a

1924

182	D6	10s on 20s yellow	.25	.25
183	D6	20s on 5s gray grn	.25	.25
a.		20s on 5s emerald	*30.00*	*30.00*
184	D6	20s on 10s violet	.25	.25
185	D6	20s on 30s orange	.25	.25
		Nos. 182-185 (4)	1.00	1.00

Nos. 182 to 185 were used for ordinary postage.

Regular Issues of 1919-23 Surcharged in Blue or Red

b

c

186	A43 (a)	10s on 1s black (R)	.25	.25
187	A44 (b)	1 l on 5s emer (Bl)	.25	.25
188	A22 (c)	3 l on 50s dk bl (R)	.25	.25
189	A63 (b)	6 l on 1 l car (Bl)	.60	.25
		Nos. 186-189 (4)	1.35	1.00

The surcharge of No. 188 comes in three types: normal, thick and thin.

Nos. 182, 184-189 exist with inverted surcharge.

Lion of Bulgaria
A70 A71

Tsar Boris III — A72

New Sofia Cathedral — A73

Harvesting A74

1925 Typo. *Perf. 13, 11½*

191	A70	10s red & bl, *pink*	.40	.25
192	A70	15s car & org, *blue*	.40	.25
193	A70	30s blk & buff	.40	.25
a.		Cliche of 15s in plate of 30s		
194	A71	50s choc, *green*	.40	.25
195	A72	1 l dull green	.95	.25
196	A73	2 l dk grn & buff	1.90	.25
197	A74	4 l lake & yellow	1.90	.25
		Nos. 191-197 (7)	6.35	1.75

Several values of this series exist imperforate and in pairs imperforate between.

See Nos. 199, 201. For overprint see No. C2.

Cathedral of Sveta Nedelya, Sofia, Ruined by Bomb — A75

1926 *Perf. 11½*

198	A75	50s gray black	.25	.25

A76 A77

Type A72 Re-engraved. (Shoulder at left does not touch frame)

1926

199	A76	1 l gray	.45	.25
a.		1 l green	.45	.25
201	A76	2 l olive brown	.70	.25

Center Embossed

202	A77	6 l dp bl & pale lemon	1.90	.25
203	A77	10 l brn blk & brn org	4.75	1.75
		Nos. 199-203 (4)	7.80	2.50

For overprints see Nos. C1, C3-C4.

Christo Botev — A78

1926, June 2

204	A78	1 l olive green	.55	.25
205	A78	2 l slate violet	1.20	.25
206	A78	4 l red brown	1.20	1.50
		Nos. 204-206 (3)	2.95	2.00

Botev (1847-76), Bulgarian revolutionary, poet.

Lion Type of 1881 Redrawn

1927-29 *Perf. 13*

No.	Type	Description	Unused	Used
207	A3	10s dk red & drab	.25	.25
208	A3	15s blk & org ('29)	.25	.25
209	A3	30s dk bl & bis brn ('28)	.25	.25
a.		30s indigo & buff	.25	.25
210	A3	50s blk & rose red ('28)	.25	.25
		Nos. 207-210 (4)	1.00	1.00

Scott 207-210 have less detailed scrollwork surrounding the central lion, which is also less detailed than Scott 1-18.

Tsar Boris III — A79

1928, Oct. 3 *Perf. 11½*

No.	Type	Description	Unused	Used
211	A79	1 l olive green	.90	.25
212	A79	2 l deep brown	1.00	.25

St. Clement A80

Konstantin Miladinov A81

George S. Rakovski A82

Drenovo Monastery A83

Paisii — A84

Tsar Simeon — A85

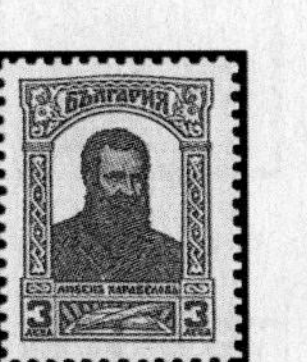

Lyuben Karavelov A86

Vassil Levski A87

Georgi Benkovski A88

Tsar Alexander II A89

1929, May 12

No.	Type	Description	Unused	Used
213	A80	10s dk violet	.25	.25
214	A81	15s violet brn	.25	.40
215	A82	30s red	.30	.25
216	A83	50s olive grn	.50	.25
217	A84	1 l orange brn	1.25	.25
218	A85	2 l dk blue	1.50	.25
219	A86	3 l dull green	3.75	.75
220	A87	4 l olive brown	6.75	.25
221	A88	5 l brown	5.50	.90
222	A89	6 l Prus green	6.75	2.25
		Nos. 213-222 (10)	26.80	5.80

Millenary of Tsar Simeon and 50th anniv. of the liberation of Bulgaria from the Turks.

Royal Wedding Issue

Tsar Boris and Fiancee, Princess Giovanna A90

Queen Ioanna and Tsar Boris — A91

1930, Nov. 12 *Perf. 11½*

No.	Type	Description	Unused	Used
223	A90	1 l green	.35	.40
224	A91	2 l dull violet	.35	.40
225	A90	4 l rose red	.35	.40
226	A91	6 l dark blue	.35	.40
		Nos. 223-226 (4)	1.40	1.60

Fifty-five copies of a miniature sheet incorporating one each of Nos. 223-226 were printed and given to royal, governmental and diplomatic personages.

Tsar Boris III
A92 A93

Perf. 11½, 12x11½, 13

1931-37 **Unwmk.**

No.	Type	Description	Unused	Used
227	A92	1 l blue green	.25	.25
228	A92	2 l carmine	.40	.25
229	A92	4 l red org ('34)	.75	.25
230	A92	4 l yel org ('37)	.25	.25
231	A92	6 l deep blue	.70	.25
232	A92	7 l dp bl ('37)	.25	.25
233	A92	10 l slate blk	8.75	.70
234	A92	12 l lt brown	.40	.25
235	A92	14 l lt brn ('37)	.30	.25
236	A93	20 l claret & org brn	1.00	.45
		Nos. 227-236 (10)	13.05	3.15

Nos. 230-233 and 235 have outer bars at top and bottom as shown on cut A92; Nos. 227-229 and 234 are without outer bars.

See Nos. 251, 279-280, 287. For surcharge see No. 252.

Balkan Games Issues

Gymnast A95

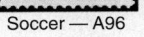

Soccer — A96

Riding — A97

Swimmer A100

"Victory" A101

Designs: 6 l, Fencing. 10 l, Bicycle race.

1931, Sept. 18 *Perf. 11½*

No.	Type	Description	Unused	Used
237	A95	1 l lt green	1.25	1.20
238	A96	2 l garnet	1.75	1.60
239	A97	4 l carmine	3.25	2.00
240	A95	6 l Prus blue	7.50	4.75
241	A95	10 l red org	20.00	12.00
242	A100	12 l dk blue	70.00	32.50
243	A101	50 l olive brn	65.00	67.50
		Nos. 237-243 (7)	168.75	121.55

1933, Jan. 5

No.	Type	Description	Unused	Used
244	A95	1 l blue grn	2.50	3.25
245	A96	2 l blue	4.00	3.50
246	A97	4 l brn vio	6.00	4.50
247	A95	6 l brt rose	12.50	8.00
248	A95	10 l olive brn	90.00	50.00
249	A100	12 l orange	150.00	80.00
250	A101	50 l red brown	425.00	450.00
		Nos. 244-250 (7)	690.00	599.25

Nos. 244-250 were sold only at the philatelic agency.

Boris Type of 1931 Outer Bars at Top and Bottom Removed

1933 *Perf. 13*

No.	Type	Description	Unused	Used
251	A92	6 l deep blue	.80	.25

Type of 1931 Surcharged in Blue

1934

No.	Type	Description	Unused	Used
252	A92	2 (l) on 3 l ol brn	7.25	.60

Soldier Defending Shipka Pass A102

Shipka Battle Memorial A103

Color-Bearer A104

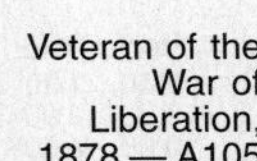

Veteran of the War of Liberation, 1878 — A105

Widow and Orphans — A106

Perf. 10½, 11½

1934, Aug. 26 **Wmk. 145**

No.	Type	Description	Unused	Used
253	A102	1 l green	.70	.75
254	A103	2 l pale red	.70	.40
255	A104	3 l bister brn	2.40	2.25
256	A105	4 l dk carmine	2.00	.75
257	A104	7 l dk blue	2.75	2.75
258	A106	14 l plum	17.00	14.00
		Nos. 253-258 (6)	25.55	20.90

Shipka Pass Battle memorial unveiling.

An unwatermarked miniature sheet incorporating one each of Nos. 253-258 was put on sale in 1938 in five cities at a price of 8,000 leva. Printing: 100 sheets. Value: $1,500.

1934, Sept. 21

No.	Type	Description	Unused	Used
259	A102	1 l bright green	.70	.75
260	A103	2 l dull orange	.70	.40
261	A104	3 l yellow	2.40	2.25
262	A105	4 l rose	2.00	.75
263	A104	7 l blue	2.75	2.75
264	A106	14 l olive bister	17.00	14.00
		Nos. 259-264 (6)	25.55	20.90

An unwatermarked miniature sheet incorporating one each of Nos. 259-263 was issued. Value: $1,500.

Velcho A. Djamjiyata A108

Capt. G. S. Mamarchev A109

1935, May 5 *Perf. 11½*

No.	Type	Description	Unused	Used
265	A108	1 l deep blue	2.00	.60
266	A109	2 l maroon	2.00	.90

Bulgarian uprising against the Turks, cent.

Soccer Game — A110

Cathedral of Alexander Nevski — A111

Soccer Team — A112

Symbolical of Victory — A113

Player and Trophy — A114

The Trophy — A115

1935, June 14

No.	Type	Description	Unused	Used
267	A110	1 l green	12.00	7.50
268	A111	2 l blue gray	12.00	7.50
269	A112	4 l crimson	12.00	7.50
270	A113	7 l brt blue	20.00	7.50
271	A114	14 l orange	20.00	7.50
272	A115	50 l lilac brn	300.00	225.00
		Nos. 267-272 (6)	376.00	262.50

5th Balkan Soccer Tournament.

Gymnast on Parallel Bars A116

Youth in "Yunak" Costume A117

Girl in "Yunak" Costume A118

Pole Vaulting A119

Stadium, Sofia — A120

Yunak Emblem — A121

1935, July 10

No.	Type	Denom.	Color	Unused	Used
273	A116	1 l	green	6.00	7.50
274	A117	2 l	lt blue	6.00	7.50
275	A118	4 l	carmine	8.00	7.50
276	A119	7 l	dk blue	8.00	7.50
277	A120	14 l	dk brown	10.00	7.50
278	A121	50 l	red	170.00	200.00
			Nos. 273-278 (6)	208.00	237.50

8th tournament of the Yunak Gymnastic Organization at Sofia, July 12-14.

Boris Type of 1931

1935 Wmk. 145 ***Perf. 12½, 13***

No.	Type	Denom.	Color	Unused	Used
279	A92	1 l	green	.55	.25
280	A92	2 l	carmine	35.00	.25

Janos Hunyadi A122

King Ladislas Varnenchik A123

Varna Memorial A124

King Ladislas III — A125

Battle of Varna, 1444 — A126

1935, Aug. 4 ***Perf. 10½, 11½***

No.	Type	Denom.	Color	Unused	Used
281	A122	1 l	brown org	3.75	1.50
282	A123	2 l	maroon	3.75	1.75
283	A124	4 l	vermilion	22.50	6.75
284	A125	7 l	dull blue	3.75	2.25
285	A126	14 l	green	4.00	2.00
			Nos. 281-285 (5)	37.75	14.25

Battle of Varna, and the death of the Polish King, Ladislas Varnenchik (1424-44). Nos. 281-285 exist imperf. Value, set $50.

Lion Type of 1881

1935 Wmk. 145 ***Perf. 13***

No.	Type	Denom.	Color	Unused	Used
286	A3	10s	dk red & drab	.70	.25

Boris Type of 1933 Outer Bars at Top and Bottom Removed

1935

No.	Type	Denom.	Color	Unused	Used
287	A92	6 l	gray blue	1.25	.25

Dimitr Monument A127

Haji Dimitr — A128

Haji Dimitr and Stefan Karaja A129

Taking the Oath — A130

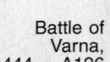

Birthplace of Dimitr A131

1935, Oct. 1 Unwmk. ***Perf. 11½***

No.	Type	Denom.	Color	Unused	Used
288	A127	1 l	green	2.50	1.20
289	A128	2 l	brown	3.50	2.00
290	A129	4 l	car rose	10.00	4.50
291	A130	7 l	blue	12.00	7.50
292	A131	14 l	orange	15.00	7.50
			Nos. 288-292 (5)	43.00	22.70

67th anniv. of the death of the Bulgarian patriots, Haji Dimitr and Stefan Karaja. Nos. 288-292 exist imperf.

Catalogue values for unused stamps in this section, from this point to the end of the section, are for Never Hinged items.

A132

A133

1936-39 ***Perf. 13x12½, 13***

No.	Type	Denom.	Color	Unused	Used
293	A132	10s	red org ('37)	.40	.25
294	A132	15s	emerald	.40	.25
295	A133	30s	maroon	.40	.25
296	A133	30s	yel brn ('37)	.40	.25
297	A133	30s	Prus bl ('37)	.40	.25
298	A133	50s	ultra	.40	.25
299	A133	50s	dk car ('37)	.40	.25
300	A133	50s	slate grn ('39)	.40	.25
			Nos. 293-300 (8)	3.20	2.00

Meteorological Station, Mt. Moussalla A134

Peasant Girl A135

Town of Nessebr A136

1936, Aug. 16 Photo. ***Perf. 11½***

No.	Type	Denom.	Color	Unused	Used
301	A134	1 l	purple	4.00	1.50
302	A135	2 l	ultra	4.00	1.50
303	A136	7 l	dark blue	8.00	3.50
			Nos. 301-303 (3)	16.00	6.50

4th Geographical & Ethnographical Cong., Sofia, Aug. 1936.

Sts. Cyril and Methodius A137

Displaying the Bible to the People A138

1937, June 2

No.	Type	Denom.	Color	Unused	Used
304	A137	1 l	dk green	.60	.30
305	A137	2 l	dk plum	.65	.30
306	A138	4 l	vermilion	.80	.30
307	A137	7 l	dk blue	4.25	1.60
308	A138	14 l	rose red	4.75	1.90
			Nos. 304-308 (5)	11.05	4.40

Millennium of Cyrillic alphabet.

Princess Marie Louise — A139

1937, Oct. 3

No.	Type	Denom.	Color	Unused	Used
310	A139	1 l	yellow green	.70	.25
311	A139	2 l	brown red	.70	.25
312	A139	4 l	scarlet	.70	.40
			Nos. 310-312 (3)	2.10	.90

Issued in honor of Princess Marie Louise.

Tsar Boris III — A140

1937, Oct. 3

No.	Type	Denom.	Color	Unused	Used
313	A140	2 l	brown red	1.00	.45

19th anniv. of the accession of Tsar Boris III to the throne. See No. B11.

National Products Issue

Peasants Bundling Wheat A141

Sunflower A142

Wheat — A143

Chickens and Eggs — A144

Cluster of Grapes — A145

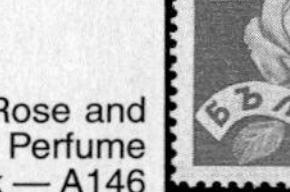

Rose and Perfume Flask — A146

Strawberries A147

Girl Carrying Grape Clusters A148

Rose — A149

Tobacco Leaves — A150

1938 ***Perf. 13***

No.	Type	Denom.	Color	Unused	Used
316	A141	10s	orange	.25	.25
317	A141	10s	red org	.25	.25
318	A142	15s	brt rose	.50	.25
319	A142	15s	deep plum	.50	.25
320	A143	30s	golden brn	.40	.25
321	A143	30s	copper brn	.40	.25
322	A144	50s	black	1.00	.25
323	A144	50s	indigo	1.00	.25
324	A145	1 l	yel grn	1.00	.25
325	A145	1 l	green	1.00	.25
326	A146	2 l	rose pink	1.00	.25

327	A146	2 l rose brn		1.00	.25
328	A147	3 l dp red lil		2.00	.25
329	A147	3 l brn lake		2.00	.25
330	A148	4 l plum		1.50	.25
331	A148	4 l golden brn		1.50	.25
332	A149	7 l vio blue		3.00	1.50
333	A149	7 l dp blue		3.00	1.50
334	A150	14 l dk brown		5.00	1.90
335	A150	14 l red brn		5.00	1.90
		Nos. 316-335 (20)		31.30	10.80

Several values of this series exist imperforate.

Crown Prince Simeon
A151 A153

Designs: 2 l, Same portrait as 1 l, value at lower left. 14 l, similar to 4 l, but no wreath.

1938, June 16

336	A151	1 l brt green	.30	.25
337	A151	2 l rose pink	.30	.25
338	A153	4 l dp orange	.40	.25
339	A151	7 l ultra	1.25	.40
340	A153	14 l dp brown	1.50	.50
		Nos. 336-340 (5)	3.75	1.65

First birthday of Prince Simeon.
Nos. 336-340 exist imperf. Value, set $15.

Tsar Boris III
A155 A156

Various Portraits of Tsar.

1938, Oct. 3

341	A155	1 l lt green	.25	.25
342	A156	2 l rose brown	.95	.25
343	A156	4 l golden brn	.30	.25
344	A156	7 l brt ultra	.50	.50
345	A156	14 l deep red lilac	.55	.50
		Nos. 341-345 (5)	2.55	1.75

Reign of Tsar Boris III, 20th anniv.
Nos. 341-345 exist imperf. Value, set $40.

Early Locomotive
A160

Designs: 2 l, Modern locomotive. 4 l, Train crossing bridge. 7 l, Tsar Boris in cab.

1939, Apr. 26

346	A160	1 l yel green	.50	.30
347	A160	2 l copper brn	.50	.30
348	A160	4 l red orange	3.00	1.50
349	A160	7 l dark blue	9.00	4.00
		Nos. 346-349 (4)	13.00	6.10

50th anniv. of Bulgarian State Railways.

Post Horns and Arrows — A164

Central Post Office, Sofia — A165

1939, May 14 **Typo.**

350	A164	1 l yellow grn	.40	.25
351	A165	2 l brt carmine	.40	.25

Establishment of the postal system, 60th anniv.

Gymnast on Bar — A166

Yunak Emblem — A167

Discus Thrower — A168

Athletic Dancer — A169

Weight Lifter — A170

1939, July 7 **Photo.**

352	A166	1 l yel grn & pale grn	.45	.35
353	A167	2 l brt rose	.50	.35
354	A168	4 l brn & gldn brn	.90	.45
355	A169	7 l dk bl & bl	3.00	1.50
356	A170	14 l plum & rose vio	14.00	10.00
		Nos. 352-356 (5)	18.85	12.65

9th tournament of the Yunak Gymnastic Organization at Sofia, July 4-8.

Tsar Boris III — A171

1940-41 **Typo.**

356A	A171	1 l dl grn ('41)	.80	.25
357	A171	2 l brt crimson	.80	.25

Bulgaria's First Stamp — A172

20 l, Similar design, scroll dated "1840-1940."

1940, May 19 **Photo.** ***Perf. 13***

358	A172	10 l olive black	2.50	2.00
359	A172	20 l indigo	2.50	2.00

Cent. of 1st postage stamp.
Nos. 358-359 exist imperf. Value, set $100.

Peasant Couple and Tsar Boris — A174

Flags over Wheat Field and Tsar Boris — A175

Tsar Boris and Map of Dobrudja
A176

1940, Sept. 20

360	A174	1 l slate green	.25	.25
361	A175	2 l rose red	.25	.25
362	A176	4 l dark brown	.40	.25
363	A176	7 l dark blue	1.00	.65
		Nos. 360-363 (4)	1.90	1.40

Return of Dobrudja from Romania.

Fruit
A177

Bees and Flowers
A178

Plowing
A179

Shepherd and Sheep
A180

Tsar Boris III — A181

Perf. 10 (#364-367), Perf 13 (#368-373)

1940-44 **Typo.** **Unwmk.**

364	A177	10s red orange	.25	.25
365	A178	15s blue	.25	.25
366	A179	30s olive brn ('41)	.25	.25
367	A180	50s violet	.25	.25
368	A181	1 l brt green	.25	.25
a.		Perf 10¼ ('44)	1.75	.50
b.		Perf 10¼x11½ ('44)	.25	.25
c.		Perf 11½x10¼	35.00	35.00
d.		Perf 11½ ('44)	.25	.25
369	A181	2 l rose car	.25	.25
a.		Perf 10¼ ('44)	1.10	.25
b.		Perf 10¼x11½ ('44)	.25	.25
c.		Perf 11½x10¼	25.00	25.00
d.		Perf 11½ ('44)	.25	.25
370	A181	4 l red orange	.25	.25
a.		Perf. 11½ ('41)	3.50	3.00
371	A181	6 l red vio ('44)	.40	.25
372	A181	7 l blue	.30	.25
373	A181	10 l blue grn ('41)	.40	.25
		Nos. 364-373 (10)	2.85	2.50

See Nos. 373A-377; No. 440 in *Scott Standard Postage Stamp Catalogue*, Vol. 1. For overprints see Nos. 455-463, C31-C32 in Scott Standard catalogue, Vol. 1.

1940-41 **Wmk. 145** ***Perf. 13***

373A	A180	50s violet ('41)	.25	.25
374	A181	1 l brt grn	1.20	.25
375	A181	2 l rose car	.40	.25
376	A181	7 l dull blue	.40	.25
377	A181	10 l blue green	.40	.25
		Nos. 373A-377 (5)	2.65	1.25

Watermarked vertically or horizontally.
Nos. 374-375 exist imperf. Value, each $15.

P. R. Slaveikov
A182

Sofronii, Bishop of Vratza
A183

Saint Ivan Rilski — A184

Martin S. Drinov — A185

Hrabar The Monk — A186

Kolio Ficheto — A187

1940, Sept. 23 **Photo.** **Unwmk.**

378	A182	1 l brt bl grn	.25	.25
379	A183	2 l brt carmine	.25	.25
380	A184	3 l dp red brn	.25	.25
381	A185	4 l red orange	.25	.25
382	A186	7 l deep blue	1.00	.60
383	A187	10 l red brn	1.00	.85
		Nos. 378-383 (6)	3.00	2.45

Liberation of Bulgaria from the Turks in 1878.

Johannes Gutenberg
A188

N. Karastoyanov, 1st Bulgarian Printer
A189

1940, Dec. 16

384	A188	1 l slate green	.40	.25
385	A189	2 l orange brown	.40	.25

500th anniv. of the invention of the printing press and 100th anniv. of the 1st Bulgarian printing press.

SEMI-POSTAL STAMPS

Catalogue values for unused stamps in this section are for Never Hinged items.

Regular Issues of 1911-20 Surcharged

a

b

c

Perf. 11½x12, 12x11½

1920, June 20 **Unwmk.**

B1	A43 (a)	2s + 1s ol grn	.25	.25
B2	A44 (b)	5s + 2½s grn	.25	.25
B3	A44 (b)	10s + 5s rose	.25	.25
B4	A44 (b)	15s + 7½s vio	.25	.25
B5	A44 (b)	25s + 12½s dp bl	.25	.25
B6	A44 (b)	30s + 15s choc	.25	.25
B7	A44 (b)	50s + 25s yel brn	.25	.25
B8	A29 (c)	1 l + 50s dk brn	.45	.25
B9	A37a (a)	2 l + 1 l brn org	.45	.40
B10	A38 (a)	3 l + 1½ l claret	1.20	.80
		Nos. B1-B10 (10)	3.85	3.20

Surtax aided ex-prisoners of war. Value, Nos. B1-B7 imperf., $7.75.

Tsar Boris Type of 1937
Souvenir Sheet

1937, Nov. 22 **Photo.** ***Imperf.***

B11	A140	2 l + 18 l ultra	10.00	*20.00*

19th anniv. of the accession of Tsar Boris III to the throne.

Stamps of 1917-21 Surcharged in Black

1939, Oct. 22 ***Perf. 12½, 12***

B12	A34	1 l + 1 l on 15s slate	.25	.25
B13	A69	2 l + 1 l on 1½ l ol grn	.35	.35
B14	A69	4 l + 2 l on 2 l dp grn	.40	.40
B15	A69	7 l + 4 l on 3 l Prus bl	1.25	*1.50*
B16	A69	14 l + 7 l on 5 l red brn	1.75	*2.00*
		Nos. B12-B16 (5)	4.00	*4.50*

Surtax aided victims of the Sevlievo flood. The surcharge on #B13-B16 omits "leva."

AIR POST STAMPS

Regular Issues of 1925-26 Overprinted in Various Colors

1927-28 **Unwmk.** ***Perf. 11½***

C1	A76	2 l ol (R) ('28)	1.75	1.75
C2	A74	4 l lake & yel (Bl)	3.25	3.25
C3	A77	10 l brn blk & brn org (G) ('28)	65.00	15.00

Overprinted Vertically and Surcharged with New Value

C4	A77	1 l on 6 l dp bl & pale lem (C)	1.75	1.75
a.		Inverted surcharge	*340.00*	*275.00*
b.		Pair, one without surcharge	*440.00*	
		Nos. C1-C4 (4)	71.75	21.75

Nos. C2-C4 overprinted in changed colors were not issued, value set $14.

Dove Delivering Message — AP1

1931, Oct. 28 **Typo.**

C5	AP1	1 l dk green	.45	.25
C6	AP1	2 l maroon	.45	.25
C7	AP1	6 l dp blue	.60	.40
C8	AP1	12 l carmine	1.25	.40
C9	AP1	20 l dk violet	1.25	.80
C10	AP1	30 l dp orange	2.40	1.60
C11	AP1	50 l orange brn	3.50	2.75
		Nos. C5-C11 (7)	9.90	6.45

Counterfeits exist. See Nos. C15-C18.

Junkers Plane, Rila Monastery — AP2

1932, May 9

C12	AP2	18 l blue grn	72.50	40.00
C13	AP2	24 l dp red	50.00	30.00
C14	AP2	28 l ultra	30.00	25.00
		Nos. C12-C14 (3)	152.50	95.00

Catalogue values for unused stamps in this section, from this point to the end of the section, are for Never Hinged items.

Types of 1931

1938, Dec. 27

C15	AP1	1 l violet brown	.35	.25
C16	AP1	2 l green	.40	.25
C17	AP1	6 l deep rose	1.25	.50
C18	AP1	12 l peacock blue	1.40	.55
		Nos. C15-C18 (4)	3.40	1.55

Counterfeits exist.

Mail Plane — AP3

Plane over Tsar Assen's Tower — AP4

Designs: 4 l, Plane over Bachkovski Monastery. 6 l, Bojurishte Airport, Sofia. 10 l, Plane, train and motorcycle. 12 l, Planes over Sofia Palace. 16 l, Plane over Pirin Valley. 19 l, Plane over Rila Monastery. 30 l, Plane and Swallow. 45 l, Plane over Sofia Cathedral. 70 l, Plane over Shipka Monument. 100 l, Plane and Royal Cipher.

1940, Jan. 15 **Photo.** ***Perf. 13***

C19	AP3	1 l dk green	.25	.25
C20	AP4	2 l crimson	2.25	.25
C21	AP4	4 l red orange	.25	.25
C22	AP3	6 l dp blue	.50	.25
C23	AP4	10 l dk brown	.50	.25
C24	AP3	12 l dull brown	1.00	.25
C25	AP3	16 l brt bl vio	1.10	.50
C26	AP3	19 l sapphire	1.50	.75
C27	AP4	30 l rose lake	2.25	1.00
C28	AP4	45 l gray violet	5.50	1.25
C29	AP4	70 l rose pink	5.50	1.75
C30	AP4	100 l dp slate bl	18.50	5.00
		Nos. C19-C30 (12)	39.10	11.75

SPECIAL DELIVERY STAMPS

Catalogue values for unused stamps in this section are for Never Hinged items.

Postman on Bicycle SD1

Postman on Motorcycle SD3

Mail Car — SD2

1939 **Unwmk.** **Photo.** ***Perf. 13***

E1	SD1	5 l deep blue	1.20	.25
E2	SD2	6 l copper brn	.25	.25
E3	SD3	7 l copper brn	.35	.25
E4	SD2	8 l red orange	1.20	.25
E5	SD1	20 l bright rose	2.50	.40
		Nos. E1-E5 (5)	5.50	1.40

POSTAGE DUE STAMPS

D1

Large Lozenge Perf. 5½ to 6½

1884 **Typo.** **Unwmk.**

J1	D1	5s orange	875.00	110.00
J2	D1	25s lake	340.00	52.50
J3	D1	50s blue	47.50	32.50
		Nos. J1-J3 (3)	1,263.	195.00

1886 ***Imperf.***

J4	D1	5s orange	440.00	20.00
J5	D1	25s lake	640.00	20.00
J6	D1	50s blue	20.00	17.50
		Nos. J4-J6 (3)	1,100.	57.50

1887 ***Perf. 11½***

J7	D1	5s orange	60.00	9.50
J8	D1	25s lake	20.00	6.00
J9	D1	50s blue	24.00	16.00
		Nos. J7-J9 (3)	104.00	31.50

Same, Redrawn
24 horizontal lines of shading in upper part instead of 30 lines

1892 ***Perf. 10½, 11½***

J10	D1	5s orange	40.00	6.00
J11	D1	25s lake	20.00	6.00

D2

1893 **Pelure Paper**

J12	D2	5s orange	47.50	20.00

D3

1895 ***Imperf.***

J13	D3	30s on 50s blue	35.00	9.50

Perf. 10½, 11½

J14	D3	30s on 50s blue	40.00	9.50

D4

Wmk. Coat of Arms in the Sheet

1896 ***Perf. 13***

J15	D4	5s orange	20.00	3.25
J16	D4	10s purple	12.00	2.75
J17	D4	30s green	9.50	2.40
		Nos. J15-J17 (3)	41.50	8.40

Nos. J15-J17 are also known on unwatermarked paper from the edges of sheets.

In 1901 a cancellation, "T" in circle, was applied to Nos. 60-65 and used provisionally as postage dues.

D5

1901-04 **Unwmk.** ***Perf. 11½***

J19	D5	5s dl rose	.80	.50
J20	D5	10s yel grn	1.60	.50
J21	D5	20s dl bl ('04)	12.00	.50
J22	D5	30s vio brn	4.00	.50
J23	D5	50s org ('02)	9.50	9.50
		Nos. J19-J23 (5)	27.90	11.50

Nos. J19-J23 exist imperf. and in pairs imperf. between. Value, imperf., $250.

D6

Thin Semi-Transparent Paper

1915 **Unwmk.** ***Perf. 11½***

J24	D6	5s green	.50	.25
J25	D6	10s purple	.50	.25
J26	D6	20s dl rose	.50	.25
J27	D6	30s dp org	2.75	.25
J28	D6	50s dp bl	.95	.25
		Nos. J24-J28 (5)	5.20	1.25

1919-21 ***Perf. 11½, 12x11½***

J29	D6	5s emerald	.25	.25
a.		5s gray green ('21)	.30	.25
J30	D6	10s violet	.25	.25
a.		10s light violet ('21)	.25	.25
J31	D6	20s salmon	.25	.25
a.		20s yellow	.25	.25
J32	D6	30s orange	.25	.25
a.		30s red orange ('21)	.65	.65
J33	D6	50s blue	.25	.25
J34	D6	1 l emerald ('21)	.25	.25
J35	D6	2 l rose ('21)	.25	.25
J36	D6	3 l brown org ('21)	.35	.25
		Nos. J29-J36 (8)	2.10	2.00

Stotinki values of the above series surcharged 10s or 20s were used as ordinary postage stamps. See Nos. 182-185.

The 1919 printings are on thicker white paper with clean-cut perforations, the 1921 printings on thicker grayish paper with rough perforations.

Most of this series exist imperforate and in pairs imperforate between.

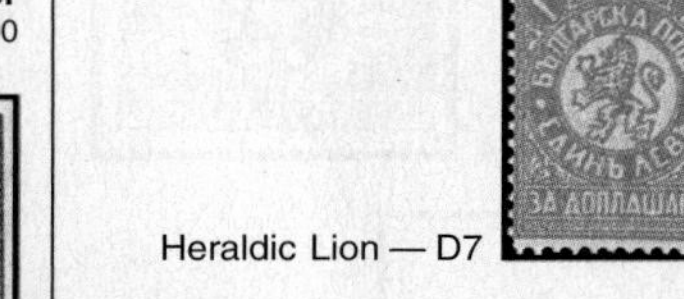

Heraldic Lion — D7

1932, Aug. 15 **Thin Paper**

J37	D7	1 l olive bister	1.60	1.00
J38	D7	2 l rose brown	1.60	1.00
J39	D7	6 l brown violet	3.50	1.20
		Nos. J37-J39 (3)	6.70	3.20

Lion of Trnovo — D8

National Arms — D9

1933, Apr. 10

J40	D8	20s dk brn	.25	.25
J41	D8	40s dp bl	.25	.25
J42	D8	80s car rose	.25	.25
J43	D9	1 l org brn	1.60	.50
J44	D9	2 l olive	1.60	.75
J45	D9	6 l dl vio	.80	.30
J46	D9	14 l ultra	1.20	.50
		Nos. J40-J46 (7)	5.95	2.80

POSTAL TAX STAMPS

The use of stamps Nos. RA1 to RA18 was compulsory on letters, etc., to be delivered on Sundays and holidays. The money received from their sale was used toward maintaining a sanatorium for employees of the post, telegraph and telephone services.

View of Sanatorium PT1

Sanatorium, Peshtera PT2

1925-29 Unwmk. Typo. *Perf. 11½*

RA1	PT1	1 l blk, *grnsh bl*	2.75	.25
RA2	PT1	1 l chocolate ('26)	2.75	.25
RA3	PT1	1 l orange ('27)	3.00	.30
RA4	PT1	1 l pink ('28)	4.50	.30
RA5	PT1	1 l vio, *pnksh* ('29)	4.75	.30
RA6	PT2	2 l blue green	.35	.25
RA7	PT2	2 l violet ('27)	.35	.25
RA8	PT2	5 l deep blue	3.00	.80
RA9	PT2	5 l rose ('27)	3.75	.40
		Nos. RA1-RA9 (9)	25.20	3.10

St. Constantine Sanatorium PT3

1930-33

RA10	PT3	1 l red brn & ol grn	4.00	.25
RA11	PT3	1 l ol grn & yel ('31)	.50	.25
RA12	PT3	1 l red vio & ol brn ('33)	.50	.25
		Nos. RA10-RA12 (3)	5.00	.75

Trojan Rest Home PT4

Sanatorium PT5

1935 Wmk. 145 *Perf. 11, 11½*

RA13	PT4	1 l choc & red org	.30	.25
RA14	PT4	1 l emer & indigo	.30	.25
RA15	PT5	5 l red brn & indigo	1.40	.35
		Nos. RA13-RA15 (3)	2.00	.85

BURMA

ˈbər-mə

LOCATION — Bounded on the north by China; east by China, Laos and Thailand; south and west by the Bay of Bengal, and India.
GOVT. — Self-governing unit of the British Commonwealth
AREA — 261,789 sq. mi.
POP. — 35,313,905 (1983)
CAPITAL — Rangoon

Burma was part of India from 1826 until April 1, 1937, when it became a self-governing unit of the British Commonwealth and received a constitution.

12 Pies = 1 Anna
16 Annas = 1 Rupee

Catalogue values for unused stamps in this country are for Never Hinged items, beginning with Scott 35 in the regular postage section and Scott O28 in the official section.

Watermarks

Wmk. 196 — Multiple Stars

Wmk. 254 — Elephant Heads

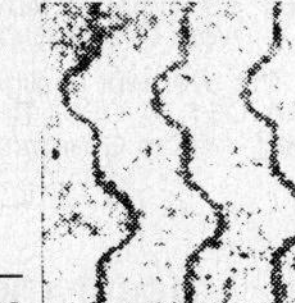
Wmk. 257 — Curved Wavy Lines

George V Stamps of India 1926-36 Overprinted in Black

Wmk. 196

1937, Apr. 1 Typo. *Perf. 14*

1	A46	3p slate	1.25	.25
		Never hinged	2.50	
2	A71	½a green	.65	.25
		Never hinged	1.15	
3	A68	9p dark green	.65	.25
		Never hinged	1.25	
4	A72	1a dark brown	2.75	.25
		Never hinged	5.25	
5	A49	2a ver	.65	.25
		Never hinged	1.15	
6	A57	2a6p buff	.55	.25
		Never hinged	1.10	
7	A51	3a carmine rose	2.75	.50
		Never hinged	5.25	
8	A70	3a6p deep blue	4.25	.25
		Never hinged	8.00	
a.		3a6p dull blue	14.50	*12.00*
		Never hinged	25.00	
9	A52	4a olive green	.75	.25
		Never hinged	1.30	
10	A53	6a bister	.75	.60
		Never hinged	1.50	
11	A54	8a red violet	2.25	.25
		Never hinged	4.25	
12	A55	12a claret	8.50	3.50
		Never hinged	16.00	

Overprint is at the bottom on No. 7.

Overprinted in Black

13	A56	1r green & brown	35.00	5.50
		Never hinged	65.00	
14	A56	2r brn org & car rose	29.00	*40.00*
		Never hinged	47.50	
15	A56	5r dk violet & ultra	32.50	*45.00*
		Never hinged	60.00	
16	A56	10r car & green	135.00	125.00
		Never hinged	250.00	
17	A56	15r ol grn & ultra	450.00	250.00
		Never hinged	750.00	
18	A56	25r blue & ocher	750.00	550.00
		Never hinged	1,400.	
		Nos. 1-18 (18)	1,457.	1,022.
		Set, never hinged	2,600.	

For overprints see Nos. O1-O14, 1N1-1N3, 1N25-1N26, 1N47.

King George VI
A1 A2

Royal Barge — A3

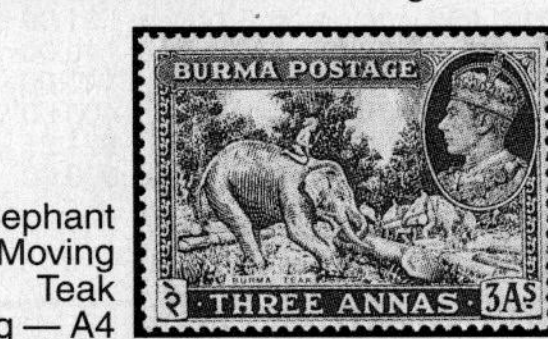
Elephant Moving Teak Log — A4

Farmer Plowing Rice Field — A5

Sailboat on Irrawaddy River — A6

Peacock — A7

George VI — A8

Perf. 13½x14

1938-40 Litho. Wmk. 254

18A	A1	1p red org ('40)	2.25	2.00
		Never hinged	3.50	
19	A1	3p violet	.25	*3.00*
		Never hinged	.35	
20	A1	6p ultramarine	.65	.25
		Never hinged	1.00	
21	A1	9p yel green	1.50	*2.00*
		Never hinged	2.50	
22	A2	1a brown violet	.25	.25
		Never hinged	.30	
23	A2	1½a turq grn	1.20	*3.75*
		Never hinged	2.00	
24	A2	2a carmine	2.25	1.00
		Never hinged	3.75	
		Perf. 13		
25	A3	2a6p rose lake	10.00	3.75
		Never hinged	15.00	
26	A4	3a dk violet	10.00	4.00
		Never hinged	18.00	
27	A5	3a6p dp bl & brt bl	2.50	*9.50*
		Never hinged	4.25	
28	A2	4a slate blue, perf. 13½x14	2.40	.25
		Never hinged	4.00	
29	A6	8a slate green	2.75	.60
		Never hinged	4.25	
		Perf. 13½		
30	A7	1r brt ultra & dk violet	3.00	1.00
		Never hinged	4.25	
31	A7	2r dk vio & red brown	16.00	6.00
		Never hinged	25.00	
32	A8	5r car & dull vio	45.00	*65.00*
		Never hinged	75.00	
33	A8	10r gray grn & brn	50.00	*95.00*
		Never hinged	80.00	
		Nos. 18A-33 (16)	150.00	197.35
		Set, never hinged	240.00	

See Nos. 51-65. For overprints and surcharges see Nos. 34-50, O15-O27, 1N4-1N11, 1N28-1N30, 1N37-1N46, 1N48-1N49.

No. 25 Surcharged in Black

1940, May 6 *Perf. 13*

34	A3	1a on 2a6p rose lake	3.00	2.75
		Never hinged	4.50	

Centenary of first postage stamp.

Catalogue values for unused stamps in this section, from this point to the end of the section, are for Never Hinged items.

Nos. 18A to 33 Overprinted in Black

a

b

1945

35	A1(a)	1p red orange	.25	.25
a.		Pair, one without overprint	1,850.	
		Hinged	1,275.	
36	A1(a)	3p violet	.25	*1.60*
37	A1(a)	6p ultramarine	.25	*.35*
38	A1(a)	9p yel green	.35	*1.40*
39	A2(a)	1a brown violet	.25	.25
40	A2(a)	1½a turq green	.25	.25
41	A2(a)	2a carmine	.25	.25
42	A3(b)	2a6p rose lake	2.25	2.50
43	A4(b)	3a dk violet	1.75	.25
44	A5(b)	3a6p dp bl & brt bl	.25	*.85*
45	A2(a)	4a slate blue	.25	*.85*
46	A6(b)	8a slate green	.25	*1.60*
47	A7(b)	1r brt ultra & dk vio	.50	*.60*
48	A7(b)	2r dk vio & red brown	.50	*1.50*
49	A8(b)	5r car & dull vio	.60	*1.50*
50	A8(b)	10r gray grn & brn	.60	*1.50*
		Nos. 35-50 (16)	8.80	*15.50*

Types of 1938

Perf. 13½x14

1946, Jan. 1 Litho. Wmk. 254

No.	Type	Denom.	Color	Unused	Used
51	A1	3p	brown	.25	*3.75*
52	A1	6p	violet	.25	*.40*
53	A1	9p	dull green	.25	*5.75*
54	A2	1a	deep blue	.25	.25
55	A2	1½a	salmon	.25	.25
56	A2	2a	rose lake	.25	*.60*

Perf. 13

No.	Type	Denom.	Color	Unused	Used
57	A3	2a6p	greenish blue	3.25	*6.75*
58	A4	3a	blue violet	7.00	*9.50*
59	A5	3a6p	ultra & gray blk	2.25	*4.50*
60	A2	4a	rose lil, perf. 13½x14	.60	*1.00*
61	A6	8a	deep magenta	2.00	*6.25*

Perf. 13½

No.	Type	Denom.	Color	Unused	Used
62	A7	1r	dp mag & dk vio	2.10	*3.25*
63	A7	2r	sal & red brn	9.00	6.25
64	A8	5r	red brn & dk grn	10.00	*25.00*
65	A8	10r	dk vio & car	25.00	*37.50*
			Nos. 51-65 (15)	62.70	*111.00*

For overprints see Nos. 70-84, O28-O42.

Burmese Man — A9

Burmese Woman — A10

Mythological Chinze — A11

Elephant Hauling Teak — A12

1946, May 2 *Perf. 13*

No.	Type	Denom.	Color	Unused	Used
66	A9	9p	peacock green	.30	.25
67	A10	1½a	brt violet	.30	.25
68	A11	2a	carmine	.30	.25
69	A12	3a6p	ultramarine	.70	.55
			Nos. 66-69 (4)	1.60	1.30

Victory of the Allied Nations in WWII.

Nos. 51-65 Overprinted in Black

1947, Oct. 1 *Perf. 13½x14, 13, 13½*

No.	Type	Denom.	Color	Unused	Used
70	A1	3p	brown	1.75	.85
71	A1	6p	violet	.25	*.40*
72	A1	9p	dull green	.25	*.40*
a.			Inverted overprint	26.00	*37.50*
73	A2	1a	deep blue	.25	*.40*
74	A2	1½a	salmon	2.40	.25
75	A2	2a	rose lake	.40	.30
76	A3	2a6p	greenish bl	2.40	1.75
77	A4	3a	blue violet	4.50	2.00
78	A5	3a6p	ultra & gray blk	1.75	*3.50*
79	A2	4a	rose lilac	2.50	.50
80	A6	8a	dp magenta	2.50	3.50
81	A7	1r	dp mag & dk vio	8.25	3.75
82	A7	2r	sal & red brn	8.25	*9.75*
83	A8	5r	red brn & dk grn	8.25	*8.00*
84	A8	10r	dk vio & car	5.50	*8.00*
			Nos. 70-84 (15)	49.20	*43.35*

The overprint is slightly larger on Nos. 76 to 78 and 80 to 84. The Burmese characters read "Interim Government."

Other denominations are known with the overprint inverted or double.

OFFICIAL STAMPS

Stamps of India, 1926-34, Overprinted in Black

1937 Wmk. 196 *Perf. 14*

No.	Type	Denom.	Color	Unused	Used
O1	A46	3p	gray	3.75	.25
O2	A71	½a	green	13.00	.25
O3	A68	9p	dark green	4.50	1.90
O4	A72	1a	dark brown	7.25	.35
O5	A49	2a	vermilion	15.50	.85
O6	A57	2a6p	buff	7.25	3.75
O7	A52	4a	olive grn	7.25	.35
O8	A53	6a	bister	7.25	*17.00*
O9	A54	8a	red violet	7.25	3.75
O10	A55	12a	claret	7.25	*14.00*

Overprinted

No.	Type	Denom.	Color	Unused	Used
O11	A56	1r	green & brown	21.00	11.00
O12	A56	2r	buff & car rose	40.00	*80.00*
O13	A56	5r	dk vio & ultra	140.00	82.50
O14	A56	10r	car & green	400.00	*300.00*
			Nos. O1-O14 (14)	681.25	*515.95*
			Set, never hinged	900.00	

For overprint see No. 1N27.

Regular Issue of 1938 Overprinted in Black

Perf. 13½x14, 13, 13½

1939 Wmk. 254

No.	Type	Denom.	Color	Unused	Used
O15	A1	3p	violet	.30	*.45*
O16	A1	6p	ultramarine	.30	*.45*
O17	A1	9p	yel green	4.00	*6.25*
O18	A2	1a	brown violet	.35	*.50*
O19	A2	1½a	turquoise green	3.75	2.75
O20	A2	2a	carmine	1.20	.50
O21	A2	4a	slate blue	4.50	4.75

Overprinted

No.	Type	Denom.	Color	Unused	Used
O22	A3	2a6p	rose lake	19.00	20.00
O23	A6	8a	slate green	15.00	5.00
O24	A7	1r	brt ultra & dk vio	16.00	7.00
O25	A7	2r	dk vio & red brn	30.00	18.00
O26	A8	5r	car & dull vio	25.00	*40.00*
O27	A8	10r	gray grn & brn	130.00	50.00
			Nos. O15-O27 (13)	249.40	155.65
			Set, never hinged	420.00	

For overprints see Nos. 1N12-1N16, 1N31-1N36, 1NO1.

Catalogue values for unused stamps in this section, from this point to the end of the section, are for Never Hinged items.

Nos. 51-56, 60 Overprinted Like Nos. O15-O21

1946 *Perf. 13½x14*

No.	Type	Denom.	Color	Unused	Used
O28	A1	3p	brown	3.75	*5.50*
O29	A1	6p	violet	2.75	2.75
O30	A1	9p	dull green	.70	*5.75*
O31	A2	1a	deep blue	.30	*2.50*
O32	A2	1½a	salmon	.30	.40
O33	A2	2a	rose lake	.35	*2.25*
O34	A2	4a	rose lilac	.35	.90

Nos. 57, 61-65 Ovptd. Like Nos. O22-O27

Perf. 13, 13½

No.	Type	Denom.	Color	Unused	Used
O35	A3	2a6p	greenish blue	2.50	*10.50*
O38	A6	8a	deep magenta	4.50	*6.25*
O39	A7	1r	dp mag & dk vio	1.90	*9.50*
O40	A7	2r	salmon & red brn	10.00	*55.00*
O41	A8	5r	red brn & dk grn	19.00	*67.50*
O42	A8	10r	dk violet & car	20.00	*75.00*
			Nos. O28-O42 (13)	66.40	*243.80*

Nos. O28 to O42 Overprinted in Black

1947

No.	Type	Denom.	Color	Unused	Used
O43	A1	3p	brown	3.00	.50
O44	A1	6p	violet	6.00	.25
O45	A1	9p	dull green	7.75	1.25
O46	A2	1a	deep blue	7.75	1.10
O47	A2	1½a	salmon	13.00	.60
O48	A2	2a	rose lake	7.75	.30
O49	A3	2a6p	greenish bl	42.50	18.00
O50	A2	4a	rose lilac	30.00	.80
O51	A6	8a	dp magenta	30.00	5.00
O52	A7	1r	dp mag & dk vio	*22.00*	3.00
O53	A7	2r	sal & red brn	22.00	*25.00*
O54	A8	5r	red brn & dk grn	22.50	*25.00*
O55	A8	10r	dk vio & car	22.50	*37.50*
			Nos. O43-O55 (13)	236.75	*118.30*

The overprint is slightly larger on Nos. O49 and O51 to O55. The Burmese characters read "Interim Government."

OCCUPATION STAMPS

Issued by Burma Independence Army (in conjunction with Japanese occupation officials)

Henzada Issue

Stamps of Burma, 1937-40, Overprinted in Black Blue, or Red; Nos. 1, 3, 5 Overprinted in Blue or Black

Henzada Type I

1942, May Wmk. 196 *Perf. 14*

No.	Type	Denom.	Color	Unused	Used
1N1	A46	3p	slate	5.00	*25.00*
1N2	A68	9p	dark green	30.00	*80.00*
1N3	A49	2a	vermilion	130.00	*225.00*

On 1938-40 George VI Issue

Perf. 13½x14

Wmk. 254

No.	Type	Denom.	Color	Unused	Used
1N4	A1	1p	red orange	275.00	*400.00*
1N5	A1	3p	violet	47.50	*95.00*
1N6	A1	6p	ultra	30.00	*65.00*
1N7	A1	9p	yel green	1,100.	
1N8	A2	1a	brown violet	11.00	*50.00*
1N9	A2	1½a	turq green	25.00	*85.00*
1N10	A2	2a	carmine	25.00	*85.00*
1N11	A2	4a	slate blue	50.00	*120.00*

On Official Stamps of 1939

No.	Type	Denom.	Color	Unused	Used
1N12	A1	3p	violet	150.00	*300.00*
1N13	A1	6p	ultra	175.00	*300.00*
1N14	A2	1½a	turq green	200.00	*350.00*
1N15	A2	2a	carmine	425.00	550.00
1N16	A2	4a	slate blue	1,350.	

Authorities believe this overprint was officially applied only to postal stationery and that the adhesive stamps existing with it were not regularly issued. It has been called "Henzada Type II."

Myaungmya Issue

1937 George V Issue Overprinted in Black

Myaungmya Type I

1942, May Wmk. 196 *Perf. 14*

No.	Type	Denom.	Color	Unused	Used
1N25	A68	9p	dk green	130.00	
1N26	A70	3a6p	deep blue	85.00	

On Official Stamp of 1937, No. O8

No.	Type	Denom.	Color	Unused	Used
1N27	A53	6a	bister	95.00	

On 1938-40 George VI Issue

Perf. 13½x14

Wmk. 254

No.	Type	Denom.	Color	Unused	Used
1N28	A1	9p	yel green	175.00	
1N29	A2	1a	brown vio	650.00	
1N30	A2	4a	sl blue (blk ovpt. over red)	190.00	

On Official Stamps of 1939

No.	Type	Denom.	Color	Unused	Used
1N31	A1	3p	violet	42.50	*110.00*
1N32	A1	6p	ultra	27.00	*80.00*
1N33	A2	1a	brown vio	28.00	*65.00*
1N34	A2	1½a	turq green	900.00	*1,350.*
1N35	A2	2a	carmine	40.00	*120.00*
1N36	A2	4a	slate blue	40.00	*95.00*

1938-40 George VI Issue Overprinted

Myaungmya Type II

1942, May

No.	Type	Denom.	Color	Unused	Used
1N37	A1	3p	violet	22.00	*90.00*
1N38	A1	6p	ultra	60.00	*130.00*
1N39	A1	9p	yel green	27.00	*85.00*
1N40	A2	1a	brown vio	17.50	*80.00*
1N41	A2	2a	carmine	32.50	*100.00*
1N42	A2	4a	slate blue	60.00	*130.00*

Nos. 30-31 Overprinted

Myaungmya Type III

No.	Type	Denom.	Color	Unused	Used
1N43	A7	1r	brt ultra & dk vio	450.00	*750.00*
1N44	A7	2r	dk vio & red brn	275.00	*550.00*

Pyapon Issue

No. 5 and 1938-40 George VI Issue Overprinted

1942, May

No.	Type	Denom.	Color	Unused	Used
1N45	A1	6p	ultra	100.00	
1N46	A2	1a	brown vio	120.00	*300.00*
1N47	A49	2a	vermilion	100.00	

1N48	A2	2a carmine	160.00	*350.00*
1N49	A2	4a slate blue	850.00	850.00
		Nos. 1N45-1N49 (5)	1,330.	

Nos. 1N47-1N49 are valued in faulty condition.

Counterfeits of the peacock overprints exist.

OCCUPATION OFFICIAL STAMP

Myaungmya Issue

Burma No. O23 Overprinted in Black

1942, May Wmk. 254 *Perf. 13*

1NO1	A6	8a slate green	110.00	*300.00*

Overprint characters translate: "Office use." Two types of overprint differ mainly in base of peacock which is either 5mm or 8mm.

ISSUED UNDER JAPANESE OCCUPATION

Yano Seal — OS1

Wmk. ABSORBO DUPLICATOR and Outline of Elephant in Center of Sheet

Handstamped

1942, June 1 *Perf. 12x11*

Without Gum

2N1	OS1	1(a) vermilion	75.00	*120.00*

This stamp is the handstamped impression of the personal chop or seal of Shizuo Yano, chairman of the committee appointed to re-establish the Burmese postal system. It was prepared in Rangoon on paper captured from the Burma Government Offices. Not every stamp shows a portion of the watermark.

Farmer Plowing — OS2

Vertically Laid Paper

Without Gum

Wmk. ELEPHANT BRAND and Outline of Trumpeting Elephant Covering Several Stamps

1942, June 15 Litho. *Perf. 11x12*

2N2	OS2	1a scarlet	30.00	*35.00*

See illustration OS4.

Same, Surcharged with New Value

1942, Oct. 15

2N3	OS2	5c on 1a scarlet	26.00	*30.00*

Stamps of Japan, 1937-42, as shown, Handstamp Surcharged with New Value in Black

½A. **1R.**

Rice Harvest A83

General Nogi A84

Power Plant A85

Admiral Togo A86

Diamond Mountains, Korea — A89

Meiji Shrine, Tokyo — A90

Yomei Gate, Nikko — A91

Mount Fuji and Cherry Blossoms A94

Torii of Miyajima Shrine — A96

1942, Sept. Wmk. 257 *Perf. 13*

2N4	A83	¼a on 1s fawn	50.00	*52.50*
2N5	A84	½a on 2s crim	55.00	*55.00*
2N6	A85	¾a on 3s green	85.00	*90.00*
2N7	A86	1a on 5s brn lake	82.50	72.50
2N8	A89	3a on 7s dp green	130.00	*150.00*
2N9	A86	4a on 4s dk green	65.00	*72.50*
a.		4a on 4s + 2s dk green (#B5)	190.00	*200.00*
2N10	A90	8a on 8s dk pur & pale vio	180.00	180.00
a.		Red surcharge	300.00	*325.00*
2N11	A91	1r on 10s lake	29.00	*37.50*
2N12	A94	2r on 20s ultra	60.00	60.00
a.		Red surcharge	60.00	60.00
2N13	A96	5r on 30s pck bl	19.00	*32.50*
a.		Red surcharge	30.00	*37.50*
		Nos. 2N4-2N13 (10)	755.50	*802.50*

Numerous double, inverted, etc., surcharges exist.

Re-surcharged in Black

15C.

1942, Oct. 15

2N14	A83	1c on ¼a on 1s	65.00	65.00
2N15	A84	2c on ½a on 2s	65.00	65.00
2N16	A85	3c on ¾a on 3s	65.00	65.00
a.		"3C." in blue	225.00	
2N17	A86	5c on 1a on 5s	90.00	77.50
2N18	A89	10c on 3a on 7s	170.00	150.00
2N19	A86	15c on 4a on 4s	55.00	*60.00*
2N20	A90	20c on 8a on 8s (#2N10)	900.00	750.00
a.		On #2N10a	400.00	200.00
		Nos. 2N14-2N20 (7)	1,410.	1,233.

No. 2N16a was issued in the Shan States.

Done locally, numerous different handstamps of each denomination can exist.

Stamps of Japan, 1937-42, Handstamp Surcharged with New Value in Black

15C.

1942, Oct. 15

2N21	A83	1c on 1s fawn	40.00	24.00
2N22	A84	2c on 2s crim	65.00	45.00
2N23	A85	3c on 3s green	100.00	65.00
a.		"3C." in blue	110.00	*120.00*
2N24	A86	5c on 5s brn lake	100.00	60.00
a.		"5C." in violet	180.00	*200.00*
2N25	A89	10c on 7s dp grn	140.00	82.50
2N26	A86	15c on 4s dk grn	30.00	*30.00*
2N27	A90	20c on 8s dk pur & pale vio	210.00	110.00
		Nos. 2N21-2N27 (7)	685.00	*416.50*

Nos. 2N23a and 2N24a were issued in the Shan States.

Burma State Government Crest — OS3

Unwmk.

1943, Feb. 15 Litho. *Perf. 12*

Without Gum

2N29	OS3	5c carmine	29.00	*35.00*
a.		Imperf.	29.00	*35.00*

This stamp was intended to be used to cover the embossed George VI envelope stamp and generally was sold affixed to such envelopes. It is also known used on private envelopes.

Farmer Plowing — OS4

1943, Mar. Typo. Without Gum

2N30	OS4	1c deep orange	6.00	10.00
2N31	OS4	2c yel green	1.50	*1.20*
2N32	OS4	3c blue	5.00	1.20
a.		Laid paper	24.00	40.00
2N33	OS4	5c carmine	4.00	*8.00*
a.		Small "5c"	32.00	*21.00*
b.		Imperf, pair	130.00	
2N34	OS4	10c violet brown	9.50	*9.50*
2N35	OS4	15c red violet	.75	*4.50*
a.		Laid paper	7.25	*25.00*
2N36	OS4	20c dull purple	.75	*1.20*
2N37	OS4	30c blue green	1.25	*3.00*
		Nos. 2N30-2N37 (8)	28.75	*38.60*

Small "c" in Nos. 2N34 to 2N37.

Burmese Soldier Carving "Independence" OS5

Farmer Rejoicing OS6

Boy with Burmese Flag — OS7

Hyphen-hole Perf., Pin-Perf. x Hyphen-hole Perf.

1943, Aug. 1 Typo.

2N38	OS5	1c orange	1.50	*2.10*
a.		Perf. 11	15.00	*20.00*
2N39	OS6	3c blue	3.00	*4.00*
a.		Perf. 11	15.00	*20.00*
2N40	OS7	5c rose	3.50	*4.25*
a.		Perf. 11	23.00	11.00
		Nos. 2N38-2N40 (3)	8.00	*10.35*

Declaration of the independence of Burma by the Ba Maw government, Aug. 1, 1943.

Burmese Girl Carrying Water Jar — OS8

Elephant Carrying Teak Log — OS9

Watch Tower of Mandalay Palace — OS10

1943, Oct. 1 Litho. *Perf. 12½*

2N41	OS8	1c dp salmon	24.00	18.00
2N42	OS8	2c yel green	1.00	*2.40*
2N43	OS8	3c violet	1.00	*2.75*
2N44	OS9	5c rose	1.00	*1.00*
2N45	OS9	10c blue	2.25	1.25
2N46	OS9	15c vermilion	1.20	*3.50*
2N47	OS9	20c yel green	1.20	*2.10*
2N48	OS9	30c brown	1.20	*2.40*
2N49	OS10	1r vermilion	.75	*2.40*
2N50	OS10	2r violet	.75	*2.75*
		Nos. 2N41-2N50 (10)	34.35	*38.55*

No. 2N49 exists imperforate. Canceled to order examples of Nos. 2N42-2N50 same values as unused.

Bullock Cart OS11

Shan Woman OS12

1943, Oct. 1 *Perf. 12½*

2N51	OS11	1c brown	45.00	*47.50*
2N52	OS11	2c yel green	50.00	*47.50*
2N53	OS11	3c violet	8.00	*14.00*
2N54	OS11	5c ultra	3.50	*8.50*
2N55	OS12	10c blue	18.00	*22.50*
2N56	OS12	20c rose	47.50	22.50
2N57	OS12	30c brown	27.50	*75.00*
		Nos. 2N51-2N57 (7)	199.50	*237.50*

For use only in the Shan States. Perak No. N34 also used in Shan States. Canceled-to-order stamps are valued at ½ used value.

Surcharged in Black

1944, Nov. 1

2N58	OS11	1c brown	5.00	*10.00*
2N59	OS11	2c yel green	1.00	*6.50*
a.		Inverted surcharge	500.00	*850.00*
2N60	OS11	3c violet	2.75	*8.50*
2N61	OS11	5c ultra	3.00	*4.00*
2N62	OS12	10c blue	4.00	3.00
2N63	OS12	20c rose	.85	*2.00*
2N64	OS12	30c brown	1.50	*2.25*
		Nos. 2N58-2N64 (7)	18.10	*36.25*

Top line of surcharge reads: "Bama naing ngan daw" (Burma State). Bottom line repeats denomination in Burmese. Surcharge applied when the Shan States came under Burmese government administration, Dec. 24, 1943. Canceled-to-order stamps same value as unused.

BUSHIRE

bü-'shir

LOCATION — On Persian Gulf

Bushire is an Iranian port that British troops occupied Aug. 8, 1915.

20 Chahis (or Shahis) = 1 Kran
10 Krans = 1 Toman

Watermark

Wmk. 161 — Lion

ISSUED UNDER BRITISH OCCUPATION

Basic Iranian Designs

Iranian Stamps of 1911-13 Overprinted in Black

Perf. 11½, 11½x11
Typo. & Engr.

1915, Aug. 15				**Unwmk.**
N1	A32	1c green & org	175.00	*120.00*
N2	A32	2c red & sepia	175.00	120.00
N3	A32	3c gray brn & grn	200.00	*150.00*
N4	A32	5c brown & car	1,250.	*1,100.*
N5	A32	6c green & red brn	165.00	100.00
N6	A32	9c yel brn & vio	200.00	*150.00*
a.		Double overprint		
N7	A32	10c red & org brn	250.00	*200.00*
N8	A32	12c grn & ultra	250.00	*200.00*
N9	A32	1k ultra & car	265.00	240.00
a.		Double overprint	7,500.	
N10	A32	24c vio & grn	275.00	225.00
N11	A32	2k grn & red vio	700.00	600.00
N12	A32	3k vio & blk	750.00	*650.00*
N13	A32	5k red & ultra	650.00	550.00
N14	A32	10k ol bis & cl	700.00	600.00
		Nos. N1-N14 (14)	6,005.	5,005.

Forged overprints exist of Nos. N1-N29.

The Bushire overprint exists on Iran No. 537 but is considered a forgery.

Covers: Covers of this issue are scarce. Values start at $450.

No Period after "OCCUPATION"

N1b	A32	1c green & org	260.00	275.00
N2b	A32	2c red & sepia	260.00	260.00
N3b	A32	3c gray brn & grn	375.00	425.00
N5b	A32	6c green & red brn	260.00	200.00
N6b	A32	9c yel brn & vio	325.00	400.00
N7b	A32	10c red & org brn	325.00	375.00
N8b	A32	12c grn & ultra	375.00	400.00
N9b	A32	1k ultra & car	625.00	225.00
N10b	A32	24c vio & grn	675.00	425.00
N11b	A32	2k grn & red vio	1,600.	875.00
N12b	A32	3k vio & blk	1,300.	1,250.
N13b	A32	5k red & ultra	1,000.	875.00
N14b	A32	10k ol bis & cl	975.00	775.00

On Iranian Stamps of 1915

No. N15

No. N26

No. N29

Perf. 11, 11½

1915, Sept.				**Wmk. 161**
N15	A33	1c car & indigo	1,000.	1,000.
N16	A33	2c blue & car	15,000.	*15,000.*
N17	A33	3c dk grn	1,100.	*1,100.*
N18	A33	5c red	12,500.	*12,500.*
N19	A33	6c ol grn & car	10,000.	*10,000.*
N20	A33	9c yel brn & vio	1,600.	*1,600.*
N21	A33	10c bl grn & yel brn	2,500.	*2,500.*
N22	A33	12c ultra	4,700.	*4,700.*
N23	A34	1k sil, yel brn & gray	1,700.	1,700.
N24	A33	24c yel brn & dk brn	1,400.	1,400.
N25	A34	2k sil, bl & rose	1,400.	1,400.
N26	A34	3k sil, vio & brn	1,400.	1,400.
N27	A34	5k sil, brn & grn	2,100.	2,100.
a.		Inverted overprint	—	*25,000.*
N28	A35	1t gold, pur & blk	2,500.	*2,500.*
N29	A35	3t gold, cl & red brn	7,800.	*7,800.*

Persia resumed administration of Bushire post office Oct. 16, 1915.

Covers: Commercial covers of this issue are scarce. Values start at about $1,750.

CAMEROUN

ˌka-mə-'rün

(Kamerun)

LOCATION — On the west coast of Africa, north of the equator
AREA — 456,054 sq. mi.
POP. — 9,060,000 (est. 1983)
CAPITAL — Yaounde

Before World War I, Cameroun (Kamerun) was a German Protectorate. It was occupied during the war by Great Britain and France and in 1922 was mandated to these countries by the League of Nations.

100 Pfennig = 1 Mark
12 Pence = 1 Shilling
100 Centimes = 1 Franc

Watermark

Wmk. 125 — Lozenges

STAMPS OF GERMANY USED IN CAMEROUN

Type A

KAMERUN
Post Office opened 2/1/1887, was redesignated Duala 6/1/1901, and closed 9/27/1914.

1A1 A 3pf green (#37) *1,750.*
On cover *2,550.*
1A2 A 5pf violet (#38) 225.00
On cover 550.00
1A3 A 10pf red (#39) 140.00
On cover 280.00
a. 10pf rose (#39b) 1,100.
On cover 4,500.
1A4 A 20pf ultra (#40) 60.00
On cover 150.00
a. 20pf blue (#40b) 60.00
On cover 150.00
1A5 A 25pf red brn (#41a) 1,900.
On cover 3,000.
1A6 A 50pf deep grayish ol grn (#42) 140.00
On cover 375.00
a. 50pf gray (#42a) 165.00
On cover 450.00
b. 50pf brt olive (#42b) *1,100.*
On cover *2,250.*
c. 50pf dk ol grn (#42c) 225.00
On cover 600.00
1A7 A 2m dull vio pur (#36b) 750.00
On cover *3,750.*
a. 2m e lilac (#36d) 1,100.
On cover *4,500.*

1A8 A 3pf gray brn (#46) 47.50
On cover 90.00
a. 3pf brown (#46) 90.00
On cover 110.00
b. 3pf yel brn (#46a) 50.00
On cover 80.00
c. 3pf red brn (#46c) 65.00
On cover 110.00
d. 3pf brown ocher (#46f) 60.00
On cover 110.00
e. 3pf ol brn (#46e) 60.00
On cover 110.00
1A9 A 5pf blue green (#47) 25.00
On cover 45.00
a. 5pf yellow green (#47a) 47.50
On cover 87.50
b. 5pf deep green (#47b) 62.50
On cover 110.00
c. 5pf gray green (#47b) 62.50
On cover 110.00
1A10 A 10pf red (#48) 22.50
On cover 45.00
a. 10pf dark carmine (#48c) 325.00
On cover 600.00
b. 10pf brownish red (#48d) *1,050.*
On cover *2,600.*
c. 10pf rose carmine (#48e) 42.50
On cover 67.50
1A11 A 20pf pale ultra (#49) 30.00
On cover 57.50
a. 20pf Prussian blue (#49a) 360.00
On cover 875.00
b. 20pf grayish ultra (#49b) 85.00
On cover 150.00
c. 20pf blue (#49c) 57.50
On cover 75.00
1A12 A 25pf red orange (#50) 105.00
On cover 375.00
a. 25pf org yel (#50b) 180.00
On cover 300.00
1A13 A 50pf lilac brn (#51) 50.00
On cover 125.00
a. 50pf brown red (#51c) *3,250.*
b. 50pf red brown (#51d) 275.00
On cover 675.00
c. 50pf red lilac brn (#51d) —
d. 50pf dull rose brn (#51e) 72.50
On cover 190.00
1A14 A 2m brown purple (#36) 140.00
On cover 1,500.
a. 2m carmine lilac (#36e) 850.00

BIBUNDI
Post Office in operation 7/5/1891-1/8/1897, 5/22/1906-10/8/1914.
Type A Cancel with 2 Stars Below Year Date

2A1 A 3pf gray brn (#46) 250.00
a. 3pf brown (#46) 300.00
2A2 A 5pf blue grn (#47) 135.00
a. 5pf yel grn (#47a) 200.00
2A3 A 10pf red (#48) 125.00
a. 10pf brownish rose (#48e) 175.00
2A4 A 20pf blue (#49c) 160.00
a. 20pf pale ultra (#49) —
2A5 A 25pf reddish org (#50) 600.00
a. 25pf org yel (#50b) —
2A6 A 50pf lilac brn (#51) 275.00

Type B

BUEA
Post Office in operation 2/15/00-11/15/14.

3A1 B 3pf yel brn (#46a) 150.00
a. 3pf reddish brn (#46c) 150.00
b. 3pf brown ocher (#46f) 150.00
3A2 B 5pf blue green (#47) 175.00
3A3 B 10pf red (#48) 120.00
3A4 B 20pf pale ultra (#49) —
3A5 B 50pf lilac brn (#51) —
3A6 B 2m car lilac (#36e) 1,750.

DUALA/KAMERUN
Post Office in operation 6/1/01-9/27/14.

4A1 B 3pf yel brn (#46a) 55.00
a. 3pf red brn (#46c) 55.00
b. 3pf brn ocher (#46f) 60.00
4A2 B 5pf blue grn (#47) 27.50

GROS-BRATANGA
Post Office in operation 3/1/1893-12/31/1893.

5A1 A 3pf gray brn (#46) 250.00
5A2 A 5pf blue grn (#47) 200.00
a. 5pf yel grn (#47a) 250.00
5A3 A 10pf brownish rose (#48e) 225.00
a. 10pf car rose (#48d) —
5A4 A 20pf blue (#49c) 200.00
a. 20pf Prussian blue (#49e) 1,750.
5A5 A 25pf reddish org (#50) 600.00
a. 25pf org yel (#50b) 950.00
5A6 A 50pf lilac brn (#51) —

KRIBI
Post Office in operation 8/10/1894-10/13/1914.
Type A Cancel with 2 Stars Below Date

6A1 A 3pf yel brn (#46a) 75.00
a. 3pf red brn (#46c) 75.00
b. 3pf brn ocher (#46f) 75.00
c. 3pf gray brn (#46) 250.00
6A2 A 5pf blue grn (#47) 50.00
6A3 A 10pf red (#48) 95.00
a. 10pf brn rose (#48e) 120.00
b. 10pf brn red (#48f) 1,050.
6A4 A 20pf pale ultra (#49) 37.50
c. 20pf blue (#49c) 200.00
6A5 A 25pf red org (#50) 300.00
6A6 A 50pf lilac brn (#51) 95.00
a. 50pf dull rose brn (#51e) 225.00
6A7 A 2m brn purple (#36) 200.00
a. 2m car lilac (#36e) 475.00

RIO DEL REY
Post Office in operation 1/9/1897-8/1914.
Type A Cancel with 3 Stars Centered Below Date

7A1 A 3pf gray brown (#46) 250.00
a. 3pf yel brown (#46a) 200.00
b. 3pf red brown (#46c) 200.00
c. 3pf brown ocher (#46f) 200.00
7A2 A 5pf blue green (#47) 150.00
7A3 A 10pf red (#48) 95.00
7A4 A 20pf pale ultra (#49) 80.00
7A5 A 25pf red orange (#50) 600.00
7A6 A 50pf lilac brown (#51) 425.00

Several cancellation types exist. Values are for most common variety.

Type C

VIKTORIA
Post Office in operation 12/12/1888-9/1914, spelling changed to Victoria 12/1900.

8A1 C 3pf green (#37) —
8A2 C 5pf violet 1,350.
8A3 C 10pf red (#48) 400.00
8A4 C 20pf ultra (#40) 240.00
8A5 C 20pf blue (#49c) 240.00
8A6 C 50pf deep grayish ol grn (#42) 525.00
a. 50pf dk ol grn (#42c) 675.00
8A7 C 2m rose lilac (#36d) 2,950.
8A8 C 3pf yel brn (#46a) 55.00
a. 3pf red brn (#46c) 55.00
b. 3pf brn ocher (#46f) 60.00
c. 3pf ol brn (#46e) 60.00
d. 3pf brown (#46) 145.00
e. 3pf gray brn (#46) 150.00
8A9 C 5pf bl grn (#47) 45.00
a. 5pf yel grn (#47a) 75.00
b. 5pf deep grn (#47b) 260.00
c. 5pf gray grn (#47b) 275.00
8A10 C 10pf red (#48) 37.50
a. 10pf brnish red (#48c) 1,050.
b. 10pf car rose (#48d) 3,150.
c. 10pf brnish rose (#48e) 120.00
8A11 C 20pf pale ultra (#49) 30.00
a. 20pf grayish ultra (#49b) 450.00
b. 20pf blue (#49c) 125.00
8A12 C 25pf red org (#50) 300.00
a. 25pf org yel (#50b) 575.00
8A13 C 50pf lilac brn (#51) 55.00
a. 50pf dull rose brn (#51e) 240.00
8A14 C 2m brn pur (#36) 265.00

VICTORIA/KAMERUN

8A15 B 3pf yel brn (#46a) 150.00
a. 3pf red brn (#46c) 150.00
b. 3pf brn ocher (#46f) 150.00
8A16 B 2m brn pur (#36) 1,300.

Issued under German Dominion

Stamps of Germany Overprinted in Black

1897 Unwmk. Perf. 13½x14½

1 A9 3pf yel brn 11.00 *16.00*
Never hinged 22.50
On cover 95.00
On cover, single franking 225.00
a. 3pf red brown 45.00 *130.00*
Never hinged 160.00
On cover 325.00
On cover, single franking 400.00
b. 3pf dark brown 16.00 *37.50*
Never hinged 52.50
On cover 130.00
On cover, single franking 140.00
c. 3pf olive brown 8.75 *37.50*
Never hinged 26.00
On cover 72.50
On cover, single franking 160.00
2 A9 5pf green 5.25 *8.00*
Never hinged 12.50
On cover 22.50
On cover, single franking 35.00
3 A10 10pf carmine 3.75 *4.50*
Never hinged 11.00
On cover 19.00
On cover, single franking 35.00
4 A10 20pf ultra 4.00 *8.00*
Never hinged 12.00
On cover 22.50
On cover, single franking 50.00
a. Diagonal half used as 10pf on cover 18,750.
5 A10 25pf orange 20.00 *37.50*
Never hinged 52.50
On cover 105.00
On cover, single franking 475.00
6 A10 50pf red brn 16.00 *29.00*
Never hinged 45.00
On cover 60.00
Nos. 1-6 (6) 60.00 *103.00*

Covers: Values for Nos. 1-5 are for covers paying the correct rates. No. 6 is for over-franked complete cover, usually philatelic.

A3

Kaiser's Yacht "Hohenzollern" — A4

1900 Unwmk. Typo. Perf. 14

7 A3 3pf brown 1.25 *1.60*
Never hinged 3.00
On cover 52.50
On cover, single franking 35.00
8 A3 5pf green 13.50 1.20
Never hinged 35.00
On cover 19.00
On cover, single franking 14.50
9 A3 10pf carmine 40.00 1.25
Never hinged 80.00
On cover 19.00
10 A3 20pf ultra 25.00 2.25
Never hinged 52.50
On cover 22.50
a. Vertical half used as 10pf on cover (Longii, '11) 6,750.
11 A3 25pf org & blk, *yel* 1.50 *5.00*
Never hinged 4.00
On cover 45.00
12 A3 30pf org & blk, *sal* 2.00 *4.00*
Never hinged 4.25
On cover 45.00
13 A3 40pf lake & blk 2.00 *4.00*
Never hinged 4.25
On cover 45.00
14 A3 50pf pur & blk, *sal* 2.00 *6.00*
Never hinged 4.25
On cover 37.50
15 A3 80pf lake & blk, *rose* 2.75 *11.00*
Never hinged 6.25
On cover 37.50

Engr. Perf. 14½x14

16 A4 1m carmine 67.50 *67.50*
Never hinged 140.00
On cover 115.00
17 A4 2m blue 5.25 *65.00*
Never hinged 16.00
On cover 115.00
18 A4 3m blk vio 5.25 *105.00*
Never hinged 20.00
On cover 180.00
19 A4 5m slate & car 140.00 *450.00*
Never hinged 340.00
On cover 875.00
Nos. 7-19 (13) 308.00 *723.80*

Covers: Values for Nos. 14-19 are for over-franked complete covers, usually philatelic.

1905-18 Wmk. 125 Typo.

20 A3 3pf brown ('18) .70
Never hinged 1.90
21 A3 5pf green .70 *1.60*
Never hinged 2.00
On cover 32.50
a. Bklt. pane of 6 15.00
b. Bklt. pane of 6, 2 #21 + 4 #22 62.50
c. Booklet pane of 5 + label 375.00
22 A3 10pf carmine ('06) 2.25 *1.50*
Never hinged 6.00
On cover 35.00
a. Bklt pane of 6 17.50
b. Booklet pane of 5 + label *500.00*
23 A3 20pf ultra ('14) 3.00 *125.00*
Never hinged 7.50
On cover 440.00
On cover, single franking 850.00
a. 20pf dull blue ('17) 13.50
Never hinged 30.00
24 A4 1m carmine (26x17 perf holes) ('15) 12.00
Never hinged 45.00
a. 25x17 perf holes ('19) 12.00
Never hinged 45.00
25 A4 5m slate & carmine (26x17 perf holes) ('13) 40.00 *4,250.*
Never hinged 115.00
On cover *7,750.*
a. 5m slate & rose red (26x17 perf holes) 26.00
Never hinged 67.50
b. 5m slate & rose red (25x17 perf holes) ('19) 26.00
Never hinged 67.50
Nos. 20-25 (6) 68.35

The 3pf and 1m were not placed in use.
Nos. 21a, 22a were made from sheet stamps.

Covers: Value for No. 25 is for overfranked complete cover, usually philatelic.

Issued under British Occupation

Stamps of German Cameroun Surcharged

No. 53

No. 62

Wmk. Lozenges (125) (#54-56, 65); Unwmk. (Other Values)

1915 Perf. 14, 14½

Blue Surcharge

53 A3 ½p on 3pf brn 15.00 *60.00*
54 A3 ½p on 5pf grn 7.75 *11.00*
a. Double surcharge *1,100.*
b. Black surcharge
55 A3 1p on 10pf car 1.45 *11.00*
a. "1" with thin serifs 15.00 *75.00*
b. Double surcharge 475.00
c. Black surcharge 18.00 *65.00*
d. As "c," "1" with thin serifs 300.00
e. "C.E.F." omitted 3,100.
f. "1d" double 2,250.

Black Surcharge

56 A3 2p on 20pf ultra 4.00 *24.00*
57 A3 2½p on 25pf org & blk, *yel* 18.50 *60.00*
a. Double surcharge *15,000.*
58 A3 3p on 30pf org & blk, *sal* 15.00 *65.00*
a. Large "3" in "3d" 1,625.
b. Triple surcharge, two albino 525.00
59 A3 4p on 40pf lake & blk 15.00 *65.00*
a. Short "4" in "4d" 1,100. *1,950.*
60 A3 6p on 50pf pur & blk, *sal* 15.00 *65.00*
61 A3 8p on 80pf lake & blk, *rose* 15.00 *65.00*
62 A4 1sh on 1m car 220.00 *1,000.*
a. "S" inverted 1,100. *4,000.*
63 A4 2sh on 2m bl 250.00 *1,050.*
a. "S" inverted 1,100. *4,000.*
64 A4 3sh on 3m blk vio 250.00 *1,050.*
a. "S" inverted 1,100. *4,400.*
b. Double surcharge *16,500.*
65 A4 5sh on 5m sl & car 300.00 *1,100.*
a. "S" inverted 1,425. *4,750.*
Nos. 53-65 (13) 1,127. *4,626.*

The letters "C. E. F." are the initials of "Cameroons Expeditionary Force."
Numerous overprint varieties exist for Nos. 53-65.
Counterfeits exist of Nos. 54a, 54b.

Values for stamp with albino impressions of the surcharge

54c ½p on 5pf, double surcharge, one albino 400.
55g 1p on 10pf, double surcharge, one albino 1,600.
55h 1p on 10pf, triple surcharge, two albino 400.
56a 2p on 20pf, double surcharge, one albino 400.
57b 2½p on 25pf, double surcharge, one albino —
58b 3p on 30pf, triple surcharge, two albino 475.
59b 4p on 40pf, triple surcharge, two albino 375.
59c 4p on 40pf, quadruple surcharge, three albino 2,500.
60a 6p on 50pf, double surcharge, one albino 350.
61a 8p on 80pf, triple surcharge, two albino 1,600.
63b 2sh on 2m, double surcharge, one albino 2,750.
64c 3s on 3m, triple surcharge, two albino 2,750.

See Cameroons for Nos. 66-77.

Issued under French Occupation

Gabon Nos. 37, 49-52, 54, 57-58, 60, 62-64, 66, 69-70 Overprinted

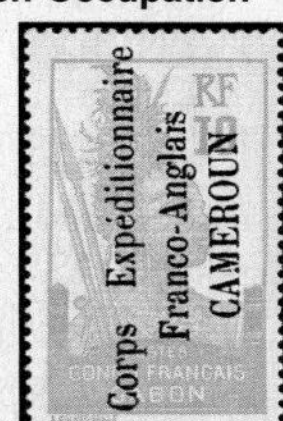

1915 Unwmk. Perf. 13½x14

Inscribed "Congo Français"

101 A10 10c red & car 32.50 24.00
Never hinged 60.00
On cover 275.00
a. "s" of "Corps" inverted 60.00 47.50

Inscribed "Afrique Equatoriale"

102 A10 1c choc & org 110.00 47.50
Never hinged 240.00
On cover 875.00
a. "s" of "Corps" inverted 160.00 75.00
103 A10 2c blk & choc 200.00 150.00
On cover 1,100.
a. "s" of "Corps" inverted 260.00 200.00
104 A10 4c vio & dp bl 200.00 150.00
On cover 1,100.
a. "s" of "Corps" inverted 260.00 200.00
105 A10 5c ol gray & grn 40.00 24.00
Never hinged 80.00
On cover 525.00
b. "s" of "Corps" inverted 60.00 45.00
105A A10 10c red & car *21,500.* *24,000.*
106 A10 20c ol brn & dk vio 210.00 210.00
On cover 1,000.
a. "s" of "Corps" inverted 275.00 275.00
107 A11 25c dp bl & choc 60.00 47.50
Never hinged 130.00
On cover 675.00
a. "s" of "Corps" inverted 260.00 260.00
108 A11 30c gray blk & red 200.00 200.00
On cover 1,100.
a. "s" of "Corps" inverted 260.00 260.00
109 A11 35c dk vio & grn 67.50 45.00
Never hinged 140.00
On cover 550.00
a. Double overprint 1,900.
b. "s" of "Corps" inverted 110.00 65.00
110 A11 40c choc & ultra 200.00 200.00
Never hinged 225.00
On cover 1,000.
a. "s" of "Corps" inverted 260.00 260.00
111 A11 45c car & vio 225.00 225.00
On cover 1,100.
a. "s" of "Corps" inverted 275.00 275.00
112 A11 50c bl grn & gray 225.00 225.00
On cover 1,350.
a. "s" of "Corps" inverted 275.00 275.00
113 A11 75c org & choc 275.00 225.00
On cover 1,350.
a. "s" of "Corps" inverted 375.00 290.00
114 A12 1fr dk brn & bis 260.00 225.00
On cover 1,500.
a. "s" of "Corps" inverted 375.00 290.00
115 A12 2fr car & brn 300.00 260.00
On cover 1,700.
a. "s" of "Corps" inverted 400.00 350.00
Nos. 101-105,106-115 (15) 2,605. 2,258.

The overprint is vertical, reading up, on Nos. 101-106, 114-115, and horizontal on Nos. 107-113.

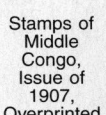

Stamps of Middle Congo, Issue of 1907, Overprinted

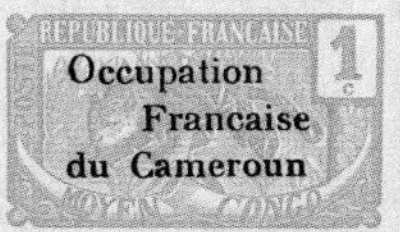

1916 Unwmk.

116 A1 1c ol gray & brn 110.00 110.00
Never hinged 260.00
On cover 675.00
117 A1 2c violet & brn 110.00 110.00
Never hinged 260.00
On cover 675.00
118 A1 4c blue & brown 120.00 120.00
Never hinged 275.00
On cover 750.00
119 A1 5c dk green & blue 32.50 32.50
Never hinged 65.00
On cover 325.00
120 A2 35c violet brn & bl 110.00 75.00
Never hinged 240.00
On cover 450.00
121 A2 45c violet & red 87.50 75.00
Never hinged 175.00
On cover 600.00

The overprint is vert., reading down, on Nos. 120-121.

Same Overprint On Stamps of French Congo, 1900

Wmk. Branch of Thistle (122)

Overprint Horizontal

122 A4 15c dull vio & ol grn 120.00 120.00
On cover 525.00
a. Inverted overprint 200.00 180.00

Wmk. Branch of Rose Tree (123)

Overprint Reading Up

123 A5 20c yellow grn & org 140.00 92.50
On cover 600.00
124 A5 30c car rose & org 110.00 87.50
On cover 750.00
125 A5 40c org brn & brt grn 105.00 80.00
On cover 550.00
126 A5 50c gray vio & lil 110.00 87.50
On cover 675.00
127 A5 75c red vio & org 110.00 85.00
On cover 675.00

Wmk. Branch of Olive (124)

128 A6 1fr gray lilac & ol 125.00 120.00
On cover 800.00
129 A6 2fr carmine & brn 160.00 120.00
On cover 875.00
Nos. 116-129 (14) 1,550. 1,315.

Values are for stamps centered in the grade of fine.
Counterfeits exist of Nos. 101-129.

Overprint Reading Down

123a A5 20c yellow grn & org 140.00 90.00
124a A5 30c car rose & org 110.00 87.50
125a A5 40c org brn & brt grn 105.00 80.00
126a A5 50c gray vio & lil 110.00 80.00
127a A5 75c red vio & org 110.00 85.00
128a A6 1fr gray lilac & ol 125.00 120.00
129a A6 2fr carmine & brn 160.00 120.00

Pairs, One Up, One Down

123b A5 20c yellow grn & org 2,100. 2,100.
124b A5 30c car rose & org 2,100. 2,100.
125b A5 40c org brn & brt grn 2,000. 2,000.
126b A5 50c gray vio & lil 2,000. 2,000.
127b A5 75c red vio & org 2,000. 2,000.
128b A6 1fr gray lilac & ol 2,000. 2,000.
129b A6 2fr carmine & brn 2,200. 2,200.

Stamps of Middle Congo, Issue of 1907 Overprinted

1916-17 Unwmk.

130 A1 1c ol gray & brn .40 .40
Never hinged .65
On cover 67.50
a. Chalky paper .40 .40
Never hinged .65
On cover 67.50
131 A1 2c violet & brn .50 .50
Never hinged .80
On cover 67.50
a. Chalky paper .45 .45
Never hinged .80
On cover 67.50
132 A1 4c blue & brn .75 .75
Never hinged 1.20
On cover 67.50
a. Chalky paper .75 .75
Never hinged 1.20
On cover 67.50
133 A1 5c dk green & bl .50 .40
Never hinged .80
On cover 27.50
a. Chalky paper .50 .40
Never hinged .80
On cover 27.50
134 A1 10c carmine & bl 1.10 .80
Never hinged 1.60
On cover 16.00
a. Chalky paper 1.10 .80
Never hinged 1.60
On cover 16.00
135 A1 15c brn vio & rose ('17) 2.00 .80
Never hinged 3.25
On cover 19.00
a. Chalky paper 2.25 .75
Never hinged 3.00
On cover 19.00
136 A1 20c brown & bl .80 .80
Never hinged 1.40
On cover 22.00
a. Chalky paper .80 .70

Never hinged 1.40
On cover 22.00
137 A2 25c blue & grn .80 .80
Never hinged 1.40
On cover 32.50
On cover, single franking 87.50
a. Triple overprint 550.00 *700.00*
d. Chalky paper .80 .60
Never hinged 1.40
On cover 32.50
138 A2 30c scarlet & grn 1.25 .80
Never hinged 2.00
On cover 40.00
On cover, single franking 75.00
a. Double overprint 400.00 *575.00*
b. Chalky paper 1.25 .80
Never hinged 2.00
On cover 40.00
139 A2 35c vio brn & bl .80 .80
Never hinged 1.40
On cover 40.00
On cover, single franking 75.00
a. Chalky paper .80 .80
Never hinged 1.40
On cover 75.00
140 A2 40c dull grn & brn 2.40 1.60
Never hinged 4.00
On cover 45.00
On cover, single franking 87.50
a. Chalky paper 2.40 1.60
Never hinged 4.00
On cover 45.00
141 A2 45c violet & red 2.40 1.60
Never hinged 4.00
On cover 55.00
On cover, single franking 87.50
a. Chalky paper .240 1.60
Never hinged 4.00
On cover 55.00
142 A2 50c blue grn & red 2.40 1.60
Never hinged 4.00
On cover 62.50
On cover, single franking 125.00
a. Chalky paper 2.40 1.60
Never hinged 4.00
On cover 62.50
143 A2 75c brown & blue 2.40 1.60
Never hinged 4.00
On cover 55.00
On cover, single franking 125.00
a. Chalky paper 2.40 1.60
Never hinged 4.00
On cover 55.00
144 A3 1fr dp grn & vio 2.00 1.60
Never hinged 3.25
On cover 67.50
On cover, single franking 150.00
a. Chalky paper 2.00 1.60
Never hinged 3.25
On cover 67.50
145 A3 2fr vio & gray grn 8.00 6.75
Never hinged 13.50
On cover 80.00
On cover, single franking 160.00
a. Chalky paper 8.00 6.75
Never hinged 13.50
On cover 80.00
146 A3 5fr blue & rose 13.50 11.00
Never hinged 20.00
On cover 100.00
On cover, single franking 200.00
a. Chalky paper 13.50 11.00
Never hinged 20.00
On cover 100.00
Nos. 130-146 (17) 42.00 32.60

No period after "Francaise"

130b A1 1c ol gray & brn 4.75 4.75
Never hinged 8.00
131b A1 2c violet & brn 4.75 4.75
Never hinged 8.00
137b A2 25c blue & grn 6.50 6.50
Never hinged 11.00
138b A2 30c scarlet & grn 6.50 6.50
Never hinged 11.00
139b A2 35c vio brn & bl 6.50 6.50
Never hinged 11.00
140b A2 40c dull grn & brn 8.75 8.75
Never hinged 15.00
141b A2 45c violet & red 8.75 8.75
Never hinged 15.00
142b A2 50c blue grn & red 8.75 8.75
Never hinged 15.00
144b A3 1fr dp grn & vio 14.50 14.50
Never hinged 24.00
Nos. 130b-144b (9) 69.75 69.75

Letter "s" of "Francaise" inverted

137c A2 25c blue & grn 6.50 6.50
Never hinged 11.00
138d A2 30c scarlet & grn 6.50 6.50
Never hinged 11.00
139c A2 35c vio brn & bl 6.50 6.50
Never hinged 11.00
140c A2 40c dull grn & brn 8.00 8.00
Never hinged 13.50
141c A2 45c violet & red 8.00 8.00
Never hinged 13.50
142c A2 50c blue grn & red 8.00 8.00
Never hinged 13.50
143c A2 75c brown & blue 8.00 8.00
Never hinged 13.50
144c A3 1fr dp grn & vio 8.00 8.00
Never hinged 13.50
145c A3 2fr vio & gray grn 32.50 32.50
Never hinged 52.50
146c A3 5fr blue & rose 45.00 45.00
Never hinged 67.50
Nos. 137c-146c (10) 137.00 137.00

On Nos. 137-146 there is 7mm between "Cameroun" and "Occupation."

Provisional French Mandate

Types of Middle Congo, 1907, Overprinted

1921

147 A1 1c ol grn & org .35 .30
Never hinged .50
On cover 55.00
148 A1 2c brown & rose .35 .30
Never hinged .50
On cover 55.00
149 A1 4c gray & lt grn .55 .55
Never hinged .80
On cover 55.00
150 A1 5c dl red & org .55 .55
Never hinged .80
On cover 21.00
a. Double overprint 1,200.
Never hinged 2,000.
151 A1 10c bl grn & lt grn 1.25 .90
Never hinged 2.00
On cover 42.50
152 A1 15c blue & org .55 .55
Never hinged .80
On cover 25.00
153 A1 20c red brn & ol .80 .80
Never hinged 1.25
On cover 16.00
154 A2 25c slate & org 1.20 .80
Never hinged 2.00
On cover 13.50
155 A2 30c rose & ver 1.25 .80
Never hinged 2.00
On cover 22.50
On cover, single franking 50.00
156 A2 35c gray & ultra .80 .80
Never hinged 1.25
On cover 20.00
On cover, single franking 32.50
157 A2 40c ol grn & org 1.25 .80
Never hinged 2.00
On cover 16.00
On cover, single franking 22.50
158 A2 45c brown & rose .80 .80
Never hinged 1.25
On cover 32.50
On cover, single franking 75.00
159 A2 50c blue & ultra 1.25 .80
Never hinged 2.00
On cover 32.50
On cover, single franking 67.50
160 A2 75c red brn & lt grn 1.25 .80
Never hinged 2.00
On cover 40.00
On cover, single franking 62.50
161 A3 1fr slate & org 2.40 2.40
Never hinged 4.00
On cover 55.00
On cover, single franking 65.00
162 A3 2fr ol grn & rose 6.50 5.50
Never hinged 10.50
On cover 62.50
On cover, single franking 120.00
163 A3 5fr dull red & gray 9.50 8.00
Never hinged 14.50
On cover 67.50
On cover, single franking 120.00
Nos. 147-163 (17) 30.60 25.45

The 1c, 2c, 4c, 15c, 20c, 25c and 50c exist with overprint omitted. For listings, see the *Scott Specialized Catalogue of Stamps & Covers.*

Without Overprint

148b A1 2c brown & rose 225.00
Never hinged 325.00
149b A1 4c gray & lt grn 260.00
Never hinged 425.00
152b A1 15c blue & org 1,200.
154b A2 25c slate & org 1,200.
159b A2 50c blue & ultra 260.00
Never hinged 425.00

Nos. 152, 162, 163, 158, 160 Surcharged with New Value and Bars

1924-25

164 A1 25c on 15c bl & org ('25) 1.25 1.25
Never hinged 2.40
On cover 16.00
165 A3 25c on 2fr ol grn & rose 1.25 1.60
Never hinged 2.00
On cover 16.00
166 A3 25c on 5fr red & gray 1.25 1.60
Never hinged 2.00
On cover 16.00
a. Pair, one without new value and bars
167 A2 65c on 45c brn & rose ('25) 2.00 2.00
Never hinged 2.40
On cover 75.00
On cover, single franking 160.00
168 A2 85c on 75c red brn & lt grn ('25) 2.40 2.40
Never hinged 4.00
On cover 62.50
On cover, single franking 110.00
Nos. 164-168 (5) 8.15 8.85

French Mandate

Herder and Cattle Crossing Sanaga River — A5

Tapping Rubber Tree — A6

Rope Suspension Bridge A7

1925-38 Typo. *Perf. 14x13½*

170 A5 1c ol grn & brn vio, *lav* .25 .25
Never hinged .40
On cover 42.50
171 A5 2c rose & grn, *grnsh* .25 .25
Never hinged .40
On cover 42.50
172 A5 4c blue & blk .25 .25
Never hinged .40
On cover 42.50
173 A5 5c org & red vio, *lav* .25 .25
Never hinged .40
On cover 35.00
174 A5 10c red brn & org, *yel* .45 .40
Never hinged .65
On cover 25.00
175 A5 15c sl grn & grn .45 .40
Never hinged .65
On cover 19.00
176 A5 15c lilac & red ('27) 1.00 .80
Never hinged 1.50
On cover 22.50

Perf. 13½x14

177 A6 20c ol brn & red brn .70 .40
Never hinged 1.00
On cover 15.00
178 A6 20c green ('26) .65 .50
Never hinged 1.00
On cover 19.00
179 A6 20c brn red & ol brn ('27) .65 .65
Never hinged .95
On cover 32.50
180 A6 25c lt green & blk .95 .50
Never hinged 1.25
On cover 15.00
181 A6 30c bluish grn & ver .50 .30
Never hinged .65
On cover 12.50
182 A6 30c dk grn & grn ('27) .90 .65
Never hinged 1.30
On cover 32.50
183 A6 35c brown & black 1.10 .50
Never hinged 1.40
On cover 32.50
On cover, single franking 50.00
184 A6 35c dl grn & grn ('38) 1.90 1.20
Never hinged 2.40
On cover 40.00
185 A6 40c orange & vio 2.00 1.20
Never hinged 3.25
On cover 40.00
On cover, single franking 47.50
186 A6 45c dp rose & cer .80 .50
Never hinged 1.25
On cover 22.50
On cover, single franking 32.50
187 A6 45c vio & org brn ('27) 2.25 1.60
Never hinged 3.00
On cover 40.00
On cover, single franking 62.50
188 A6 50c lt green & cer .80 .30
Never hinged 1.25
On cover 12.50
189 A6 55c ultra & car ('38) 1.60 1.60
Never hinged 2.40
On cover 12.50
190 A6 60c red vio & blk .80 .55
Never hinged 1.25
On cover 40.00
On cover, single franking 67.50
191 A6 60c brown red ('26) .95 .55
Never hinged 1.60
On cover 37.50
On cover, single franking 75.00
192 A6 65c indigo & brn 1.20 1.20
Never hinged 1.60
On cover 67.50
On cover, single franking 125.00
193 A6 75c indigo & dp bl .80 .80
Never hinged 1.25
On cover 27.50
On cover, single franking 37.50
194 A6 75c org brn & red vio ('27) 1.40 1.10
Never hinged 1.90
On cover 22.50
On cover, single franking 30.00
195 A6 80c carmine & brn ('38) 1.40 1.20
Never hinged 1.90
On cover 62.50
On cover, single franking 110.00
196 A6 85c dp rose & bl 1.60 1.20
Never hinged 2.40
On cover 55.00
On cover, single franking 120.00
197 A6 90c brn red & cer ('27) 2.75 1.20
Never hinged 4.00
On cover 32.50
On cover, single franking 87.50

Perf. 14x13½

198 A7 1fr indigo & brn 1.20 1.20
Never hinged 1.60
On cover 32.50
On cover, single franking 67.50
199 A7 1fr dull bl ('26) .80 .55
Never hinged 1.40
On cover 42.50
On cover, single franking 80.00
200 A7 1fr ol brn & red vio ('27) 1.10 .80
Never hinged 1.60
On cover 27.50
On cover, single franking 37.50
201 A7 1fr grn & dk brn ('29) 2.40 1.20
Never hinged 4.00
On cover 27.50
On cover, single franking 40.00
202 A7 1.10fr rose red & dk brn ('28) 4.75 *6.50*
Never hinged 8.00
On cover 190.00
On cover, single franking 350.00
203 A7 1.25fr gray & dp bl ('33) 4.75 3.50
Never hinged 7.25
On cover 32.50
On cover, single franking 87.50
204 A7 1.50fr dull bl ('27) 1.20 .80
Never hinged 1.60
On cover 32.50
On cover, single franking 75.00
205 A7 1.75fr brn & org ('33) 1.60 1.20
Never hinged 2.40
On cover 20.00
On cover, single franking 27.50
206 A7 1.75fr dk bl & lt bl ('38) 2.40 1.60
Never hinged 3.25
On cover 37.50
On cover, single franking 67.50
207 A7 2fr dl grn & brn org 2.00 1.20
Never hinged 3.25
On cover 40.00
On cover, single franking 75.00
208 A7 3fr ol brn & red vio ('27) 8.00 2.75
Never hinged 12.00
On cover 40.00
On cover, single franking 92.50
209 A7 5fr brn & blk, *bluish* 3.50 2.00
Never hinged 5.50
On cover 50.00
On cover, single franking 87.50
a. Cliché of 2fr in plate of 5fr 1,450.
Never hinged 1,800.
b. As "a," in pair with #209 1,700.
Never hinged 2,250.
210 A7 10fr org & vio ('27) 14.50 7.25
Never hinged 20.00
On cover 55.00
On cover, single franking 100.00
211 A7 20fr rose & ol grn ('27) 21.00 15.00
Never hinged 32.50
On cover 67.50
On cover, single franking 125.00
Nos. 170-211 (42) 97.80 65.85

Shades exist for several values.

For overprints and surcharge see Nos. 212, 264, 276, 278, 279, B7-B9; No. B21 in *Scott Standard Postage Stamp Catalogue*, Vol. 2.

No. 199 Surcharged with New Value and Bars in Red

1926

212 A7 1.25fr on 1fr dull blue 1.20 .80
Never hinged 1.90
On cover 62.50
On cover, single franking 110.00

Common Design Types pictured following the introduction.

Colonial Exposition Issue
Common Design Types
Name of Country in Black

1931 Engr. *Perf. 12½*

213 CD70 40c deep green 5.50 4.00
Never hinged 8.75
On cover 105.00
214 CD71 50c violet 5.50 4.75
Never hinged 8.75
On cover 87.50
215 CD72 90c red orange 5.50 4.75
Never hinged 8.75
On cover 150.00
On cover, single franking 200.00
216 CD73 1.50fr dull blue 6.50 4.75
Never hinged 10.00
On cover 140.00
On cover, single franking 200.00
Nos. 213-216 (4) 23.00 18.25

Paris International Exposition Issue
Common Design Types

1937 *Perf. 13*

217 CD74 20c deep violet 1.75 1.75
Never hinged 2.75
On cover 105.00
218 CD75 30c dark green 1.75 1.75
Never hinged 2.75
On cover 87.50
219 CD76 40c car rose 1.75 1.75
Never hinged 2.75
On cover 80.00
220 CD77 50c dark brown 1.75 1.75
Never hinged 2.75
On cover 75.00
221 CD78 90c red 1.90 1.90
Never hinged 3.25
On cover 105.00
On cover, single franking 190.00
222 CD79 1.50fr ultramarine 1.90 1.90
Never hinged 3.25
On cover 90.00
On cover, single franking 150.00
Nos. 217-222 (6) 10.80 10.80

French Colonial Art Exhibition
Common Design Type
Souvenir Sheet

1937 *Imperf.*

222A CD77 3fr org red & blk 8.00 *9.50*
Never hinged 12.00
On cover 110.00
On cover, single franking 175.00

New York World's Fair Issue
Common Design Type

1939 *Perf. 12½x12*

223 CD82 1.25fr carmine lake 1.40 1.20
Never hinged 2.00
On cover 80.00
On cover, single franking 150.00
224 CD82 2.25fr ultra 1.40 1.20
Never hinged 2.00
On cover 80.00
On cover, single franking 140.00

For overprints and surcharges see Nos. 280-281, B14-B17; Nos. B23, B25 in *Scott Standard Postage Stamp Catalogue*, Vol. 2.

Mandara Woman — A19

Falls on M'bam River near Banyo — A20

Elephants A21

Man in Yaré — A22

1939-40 **Engr.** *Perf. 13*

225 A19 2c black brn .25 .25
Never hinged .40
226 A19 3c magenta ('40) .25 .25
Never hinged .40
On cover 37.50
227 A19 4c deep ultra .25 .25
Never hinged .40
228 A19 5c red brown .25 .25
Never hinged .40
229 A19 10c dp bl grn .25 .25
Never hinged .40
230 A19 15c rose red .30 .30
Never hinged .50
231 A19 20c plum .30 .30
Never hinged .50
232 A20 25c black brn .65 .65
Never hinged .90
233 A20 30c dk red .80 .70
Never hinged 1.10
234 A20 40c ultra ('40) .80 .80
Never hinged 1.10
On cover 17.50
235 A20 45c sl grn ('40) 2.60 2.25
Never hinged 3.50
On cover 30.00
236 A20 50c brown car .90 .70
Never hinged 1.20
237 A20 60c pck blue ('40) .75 .65
Never hinged .95
On cover 22.50
238 A20 70c plum ('40) 3.25 2.90
Never hinged 4.50
On cover 30.00
239 A21 80c Prus blue 2.60 2.10
Never hinged 3.25
240 A21 90c Prus blue .95 .75
Never hinged 1.40
On cover 42.50
On cover, single franking 92.50
241 A21 1fr car rose 1.90 .95
Never hinged 2.40
242 A21 1fr choc ('40) 1.40 .80
Never hinged 2.00
On cover 6.75
243 A21 1.25fr car rose 4.00 3.25
Never hinged 6.00
On cover 62.50
On cover, single franking 110.00
244 A21 1.40fr org red ('40) 1.25 .95
Never hinged 1.75
On cover 40.00
On cover, single franking 87.50
245 A21 1.50fr chocolate 1.20 .95
Never hinged 1.60
246 A21 1.60fr black brn ('40) 2.50 2.25
Never hinged 3.25
On cover 42.50
On cover, single franking 100.00
247 A21 1.75fr dk blue 1.40 .95
Never hinged 2.10
248 A21 2fr dk green .90 .90
Never hinged 1.20
249 A21 2.25fr dk blue 1.40 .90
Never hinged 2.25
On cover 55.00
On cover, single franking 100.00
250 A21 2.50fr brt red vio ('40) 1.20 1.00
Never hinged 1.60
On cover 32.50
On cover, single franking 55.00
251 A21 3fr dk violet 1.40 .80
Never hinged 2.00
252 A22 5fr black brn 1.40 .95
Never hinged 2.00
253 A22 10fr brt red vio 2.00 1.60
Never hinged 2.75
254 A22 20fr dk green 4.00 3.25
Never hinged 5.50
Nos. 225-254 (30) 41.10 32.85

For overprints and surcharges see Nos. 255-263, 265-275, 277, 278A, 279A, B10-B13; Nos. B22, B24 in *Scott Standard Postage Stamp Catalogue*, Vol. 2.

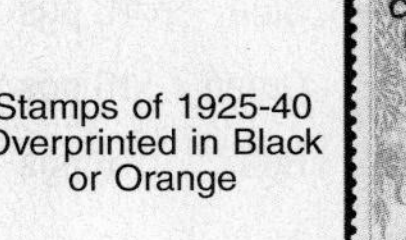
Stamps of 1925-40 Overprinted in Black or Orange

1940 *Perf. 14x13½, 13½x14, 13*

255 A19 2c blk brn (O) 1.60 1.60
Never hinged 2.40
On cover 67.50
256 A19 3c magenta 2.40 2.40
Never hinged 3.25
On cover 120.00
257 A19 4c dp ultra (O) 1.60 1.60
Never hinged 2.40
On cover 67.50
258 A19 5c red brn 5.50 5.50
Never hinged 10.50
On cover 165.00
259 A19 10c dp bl grn (O) 1.60 1.60
Never hinged 2.40
On cover 67.50
260 A19 15c rose red 2.40 2.40
Never hinged 3.25
On cover 120.00
260A A19 20c plum (O) 13.50 13.50
Never hinged 26.00
On cover 230.00
261 A20 25c blk brn 1.60 1.60
Never hinged 2.40
On cover 67.50
b. Inverted overprint 260.00 260.00
Never hinged 375.00
261A A20 30c dk red 14.50 14.50
Never hinged 28.00
On cover 230.00
262 A20 40c ultra 5.50 5.50
Never hinged 10.00
On cover 140.00
263 A20 45c slate green 4.00 4.00
Never hinged 6.50
On cover 125.00
264 A6 50c lt grn & cer 2.40 1.60
Never hinged 4.00
On cover 8.75
a. Inverted overprint 225.00
Never hinged 350.00
265 A20 60c pck bl 6.50 6.50
Never hinged 11.00
On cover 165.00
266 A20 70c plum 3.25 3.25
Never hinged 4.75
On cover 125.00
267 A21 80c Prus bl (O) 5.50 5.50
Never hinged 10.50
On cover 165.00
268 A21 90c Prus bl (O) 1.60 1.60
Never hinged 2.40
On cover 50.00
269 A21 1.25fr car rose 1.60 1.60
Never hinged 2.40
On cover 105.00
270 A21 1.40fr org red 4.75 4.75
Never hinged 7.25
On cover 140.00
271 A21 1.50fr chocolate 1.60 1.60
Never hinged 2.40
On cover 100.00
272 A21 1.60fr blk brn (O) 3.25 3.25
Never hinged 4.75
On cover 110.00
273 A21 1.75fr dk bl (O) 2.40 2.40
Never hinged 4.00
On cover 100.00
274 A21 2.25fr dk bl (O) 1.60 1.60
Never hinged 2.40
On cover 100.00
275 A21 2.50fr brt red vio 1.60 1.60
Never hinged 2.40
On cover 100.00
276 A7 5fr brn & blk, *bluish* 24.00 24.00
Never hinged 40.00
On cover 200.00
277 A22 5fr black brn 24.00 16.00
Never hinged 45.00
On cover 230.00
278 A7 10fr org & vio 32.50 32.50
Never hinged 65.00
On cover 250.00
278A A22 10fr brt red vio 65.00 45.00
Never hinged 140.00
On cover 375.00
279 A7 20fr rose & ol grn 55.00 55.00
Never hinged 110.00
On cover 275.00
279A A22 20fr dk green 190.00 190.00
Never hinged 300.00
On cover 600.00

Same Overprint on Stamps of 1939
Perf. 12½x12

280 CD82 1.25fr car lake 12.00 12.00
Never hinged 20.00
On cover 190.00
281 CD82 2.25fr ultra 12.00 12.00
Never hinged 20.00
On cover 190.00
Nos. 255-281 (31) 504.75 475.95

Issued to note Cameroun's affiliation with General de Gaulle's "Free France" movement. Numerous overprint varieties exist.

SEMI-POSTAL STAMPS

Curie Issue
Common Design Type

1938 **Unwmk.** *Perf. 13*

B1 CD80 1.75fr + 50c brt ultra 10.00 10.00
Never hinged 15.00
On cover 105.00
On cover, single franking 165.00

French Revolution Issue
Common Design Type

Photogravure; Name and Value Typographed in Black

1939

B2 CD83 45c + 25c green 11.50 11.50
Never hinged 17.50
On cover 150.00
B3 CD83 70c + 30c brown 11.50 11.50
Never hinged 17.50
On cover 110.00
B4 CD83 90c + 35c red org 11.50 11.50
Never hinged 17.50
On cover 100.00
B5 CD83 1.25fr + 1fr rose pink 11.50 11.50
Never hinged 17.50
On cover 160.00
On cover, single franking 250.00
B6 CD83 2.25fr + 2fr blue 14.00 14.00
Never hinged 22.50
On cover 150.00
On cover, single franking 220.00
Nos. B2-B6 (5) 60.00 60.00

Stamps of 1925-33 Srchd. in Black

1940 *Perf. 14x13½*

B7 A7 1.25fr + 2fr gray & dp bl 32.50 24.00
Never hinged 65.00
On cover 300.00
B8 A7 1.75fr + 3fr brn & org 32.50 24.00
Never hinged 65.00
On cover 300.00
B9 A7 2fr + 5fr dl grn & brn org 32.50 24.00
Never hinged 65.00
On cover 300.00
Nos. B7-B9 (3) 97.50 72.00

The surtax was used for war relief work.

Regular Stamps of 1939 Surcharged in Black

1940 *Perf. 13*

B10 A20 25c + 5fr blk brn 130.00 110.00
Never hinged 225.00
On cover 450.00
B11 A20 45c + 5fr slate grn 130.00 110.00
Never hinged 225.00
On cover 450.00
B12 A20 60c + 5fr peacock bl 130.00 120.00
Never hinged 225.00
On cover 450.00
B13 A20 70c + 5fr plum 130.00 120.00
Never hinged 225.00
On cover 450.00
Nos. B10-B13 (4) 520.00 460.00

The surtax was used to purchase Spitfire planes for the Free French army.

POSTAGE DUE STAMPS

Man Felling Tree — D1

Perf. 14x13½

1925-27 **Unwmk.** **Typo.**

J1 D1 2c lt bl & blk .30 .50
Never hinged .50
On cover 67.50
J2 D1 4c ol bis & red vio .30 .50
Never hinged .50
On cover 67.50
J3 D1 5c vio & blk .65 .80
Never hinged .80
On cover 67.50
J4 D1 10c red & blk .65 .80
Never hinged .80
On cover 75.00
J5 D1 15c gray & blk .75 .95
Never hinged .95
On cover 75.00
J6 D1 20c olive grn & blk .75 .95
Never hinged .95
On cover 80.00
J7 D1 25c yel & blk 1.40 1.60
Never hinged 2.10
On cover 87.50
J8 D1 30c blue & org 1.60 1.90
Never hinged 2.40
On cover 87.50
J9 D1 50c brn & blk 2.00 2.40
Never hinged 3.50
On cover 92.50
J10 D1 60c bl grn & rose red 2.00 2.40
Never hinged 3.50
On cover 92.50
J11 D1 1fr dl red & grn, *grnsh* 2.40 3.25
Never hinged 4.00
On cover 92.50
J12 D1 2fr red & vio ('27) 4.75 5.50
Never hinged 7.25
On cover 105.00
J13 D1 3fr org brn & ultra ('27) 7.25 8.00
Never hinged 12.00
On cover 120.00
Nos. J1-J13 (13) 24.80 29.55

Shades occur for several values.

Carved Figures — D2

1939 **Engr.** *Perf. 14x13*

J14 D2 5c brt red vio .25 .80
Never hinged .40
On cover 27.50
J15 D2 10c Prus blue .75 .90
Never hinged .90
On cover 27.50

J16	D2 15c car rose	.25	.40
	Never hinged	.40	
	On cover		27.50
J17	D2 20c blk brn	.25	.40
	Never hinged	.40	
	On cover		27.50
J18	D2 30c ultra	.50	.65
	Never hinged	.65	
	On cover		27.50
J19	D2 50c dk grn	.50	.65
	Never hinged	.70	
	On cover		32.50
J20	D2 60c brn vio	.85	1.00
	Never hinged	1.10	
	On cover		32.50
J21	D2 1fr dk vio	1.10	1.20
	Never hinged	1.25	
	On cover		40.00
J22	D2 2fr org red	1.60	1.60
	Never hinged	2.00	
	On cover		40.00
J23	D2 3fr dark blue	2.25	2.40
	Never hinged	2.50	
	On cover		55.00
	Nos. J14-J23 (10)	8.30	10.00

CANADIAN PROVINCES

BRITISH COLUMBIA & VANCOUVER ISLAND

'bri-tish kə-'ləm-bē-ə

and van-'kü-vər 'ī-lənd

LOCATION — On the northwest coast of North America
GOVT. — British Colony
AREA — 355,900 sq. mi.
POP. — 694,300

In 1871 the colony became a part of the Canadian Confederation and the postage stamps of Canada have since been used.

12 Pence = 1 Shilling
20 Shillings = 1 Pound
100 Cents = 1 Dollar (1865)

Values for unused stamps are for examples with original gum as defined in the catalogue introduction. Very fine examples of Nos. 2 and 5-18 will have perforations touching the design on at least one side due to the narrow spacing of the stamps on the plates. Stamps with perfs clear of the design on all four sides are extremely scarce and will command much higher prices.

Queen Victoria — A1

1860 Unwmk. Typo. *Imperf.*

1	A1 2½p dull rose	*25,000.*	

No. 1 was not placed in use and may be a proof or reprint. Most examples are without gum. Value without gum, $18,000.

Perf. 14

2	A1 2½p dull rose	*1,000.*	240.
	Never hinged	*1,150.*	
	On cover		*1,250.*
a.	2½p pale dull rose	*450.*	*250.*
	Never hinged	*675.*	
	On cover		*1,250.*

Two singles of the 2½ pence (Scott No. 2) on a very fine cover sent to Canada via San Francisco was sold for $10,000 at an American auction in 2003.

Two singles of the 2½ pence (Scott No. 2) on a very fine cover sent to Bergamo, Italy, via San Francisco was sold for $17,250 at an American auction in 2004.

VANCOUVER ISLAND

A2

A3

1865 Wmk. 1 *Imperf.*

3	A2 5c rose	*70,000.*	*10,000.*
	Never hinged	*85,000.*	
	No gum	*40,000.*	
	On cover		*37,500.*
4	A3 10c blue	5,000.	1,100.
	Never hinged	*7,000.*	
	On cover		—

Perf. 14

5	A2 5c rose	500.	300.
	Never hinged	750.	
	On cover, *from*		800.
6	A3 10c blue	475.	300.
	Never hinged	850.	
	On cover		—

BRITISH COLUMBIA

Seal of British Columbia — A4

1865, Nov. 1

7	A4 3p blue	160.00	110.00
	Never hinged	350.00	
	On cover, *from*		325.00
a.	3p pale blue	175.00	135.00
	Never hinged	375.00	
	On cover, *from*		325.00

Type A4 of 1865 Surcharged in Various Colors

1867-69 *Perf. 14*

8	2c on 3p brown (Bk)	160.00	150.00
	Never hinged	350.00	
	On cover, *from*		1,150.
9	5c on 3p brt red (Bk) ('69)	300.00	250.00
	Never hinged	625.00	
	On cover, *from*		575.00
10	10c on 3p lilac rose (Bl)	1,900.	
	Never hinged	5,000.	
11	25c on 3p orange (V) ('69)	400.00	325.00
	Never hinged	800.00	
	On cover, *from*		850.00
12	50c on 3p violet (R)	900.00	*1,050.*
	Never hinged	2,000.	
13	$1 on 3p green (G)	2,000.	
	Never hinged	*4,000.*	

Nos. 10 and 13 were not placed in use.

1869 *Perf. 12½*

14	5c on 3p brt red (Bk)	2,250.	1,300.
	Never hinged	*4,750.*	
	On cover		—
15	10c on 3p lilac rose (Bl)	1,300.	1,000.
	Never hinged	*2,750.*	
	On cover		—
16	25c on 3p orange (V)	1,100.	800.00
	Never hinged	*2,400.*	
	On cover, *from*		*1,500.*
17	50c on 3p violet (R)	1,600.	1,000.
	Never hinged	*3,500.*	
	On cover		*2,400.*
18	$1 on 3p green (G)	2,500.	1,750.
	Never hinged	*5,000.*	
	On cover, *from*		—

NEW BRUNSWICK

'nü 'brənz-ˌwik

LOCATION — Eastern Canada, bordering on the Bay of Fundy and the Gulf of St. Lawrence.
GOVT. — British Province
AREA — 27,985 sq. mi.
POP. — 285,594 (1871)
CAPITAL — Fredericton

At one time a part of Nova Scotia, New Brunswick became a separate province in 1784. Upon joining the Canadian Confederation in 1867 its postage stamps were superseded by those of Canada.

12 Pence = 1 Shilling
100 Cents = 1 Dollar (1860)

Crown of Great Britain and Heraldic Flowers of the United Kingdom
A1

1851 Unwmk. Engr. *Imperf.*
Blue Paper

1 A1 3p red 5,500. 550.
On cover 950.
a. 3p dark red 5,750. 600.
On cover 1,100.
b. Half used as 1½p on cover *4,750.*
2 A1 6p olive yellow 7,000. 1,200.
On cover 1,750.
a. 6p orange yellow 7,000. 1,200.
On cover 1,750.
b. Half used as 3p on cover *3,500.*
c. Quarter used as 1½p on cover *30,000.*
d. 6p mustard yellow 10,000. 1,400.
On cover, single franking *2,100.*
3 A1 1sh brt red violet *30,000.* *6,500.*
On cover *11,500.*
a. Half used as 6p on cover *22,500.*
b. Quarter used as 3p on cover *22,500.*
4 A1 1sh dull violet *40,000.* *7,500.*
On cover *18,000.*
a. Half used as 6p on cover *22,500.*
b. Quarter used as 3p on cover *22,500.*

The reprints are on stout white paper. The 3p is printed in orange and the 6p and 1sh in violet black. Value about $275 per set of 3.

Charles Connell — A2

1860 *Perf. 12*

5 A2 5c brown *14,000.*
Pair, no gum *31,500.*

No. 5 was prepared for use but not issued.

The listed pair is the unique multiple of this issue.

Most examples of No. 5 have creases or other faults. Value of an average example is about half that shown here.

Locomotive
A3

Victoria
A4

A5

A6

Steam and Sailing Ship — A7

Edward VII as Prince of Wales — A8

1860-63 White Paper *Perf. 12*

6 A3 1c red lilac 42.50 37.50
Never hinged 90.00
On cover 250.00
On circular, single franking 350.00
a. 1c brown violet 100.00 70.00
Never hinged 200.00
On cover 300.00
On circular, single franking 425.00
b. Horiz. pair, imperf. vert. 700.00
Never hinged 850.00
7 A4 2c orange ('63) 20.00 15.00
Never hinged 50.00
On cover 725.00
a. Vertical pair, imperf. horiz. 750.00
Never hinged —
b. 2c deep orange 25.00 19.00
Never hinged 60.00
c. 2c yellow orange 25.00 19.00
Never hinged 60.00
8 A5 5c yellow green 30.00 22.50
Never hinged 65.00
On cover 47.50
a. 5c blue green 35.00 22.50
Never hinged 65.00
On cover 47.50
As "a," "elongated earring" plate flaw (Pos. 60) 150.00 150.00
Never hinged —
On cover 250.00
b. 5c olive green 175.00 37.50
Never hinged 375.00
On cover 47.50
9 A6 10c vermilion 55.00 47.50
Never hinged 120.00
On cover 100.00
a. Half used as 5c on cover 750.00
b. Double impression 400.00 200.00
On cover —
10 A7 12½c blue 100.00 75.00
Never hinged 200.00
On cover 250.00
11 A8 17c black 55.00 *65.00*
Never hinged 120.00
On cover *5,500.*
Nos. 6-11 (6) 302.50 262.50
Set, never hinged 645.00

NEWFOUNDLAND

'nü-fən̩d̩-lənd

LOCATION — Island in the Atlantic Ocean off the coast of Canada, and Labrador, a part of the mainland
GOVT. — British Dominion
AREA — 42,734 sq. mi.
POP. — 321,177 (1945)
CAPITAL — St. John's

Newfoundland was a self-governing Dominion of the British Empire from 1855 to 1933, when it became a Crown Colony. In 1949 it united with Canada.

12 Pence = 1 Shilling
100 Cents = 1 Dollar (1866)

PRE-STAMP POSTAL MARKINGS

Crowned Circle handstamp type VIII is pictured in the Crowned Circle Handstamps and Great Britain Used Abroad section.

St. John's

1846-57
A1 VIII "St. John's" crowned circle handstamp in red, on cover 1,050.

Issued under British Administration

Values for unused stamps are for examples with original gum as defined in the catalogue introduction. However, very fine examples of Nos. 2-7, 9, 11, 12, 13 and 15 without gum are often traded at values very close to those for examples with original gum.

Watermark

Wmk. 224 Coat of Arms

As the watermark 224 does not show on every stamp in the sheet, pairs are found one with and one without watermark. This applies to all stamps with watermark 224.

Crown of Great Britain and Heraldic Flowers of the United Kingdom — A1

Rose, Thistle and Shamrock — A3

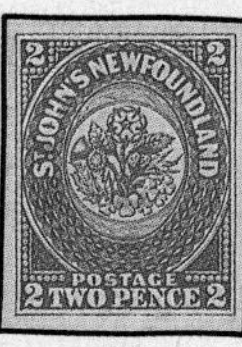
A2

A4

A5

A6

A7

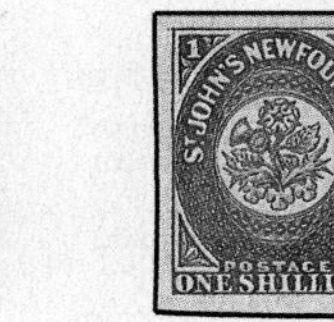
A8

1857 Unwmk. Engr. *Imperf.*
Thick Porous Wove Paper with Mesh

1 A1 1p brn vio 125.00 *200.00*
Never hinged 300.00
On cover 6,500.
a. Half used as ½p on cover *20,000.*
2 A2 2p scar ver *17,500.* 7,000.
On cover *15,000.*
a. Vert. half used as 1p on cover *27,500.*
3 A3 3p green 575.00 500.00
On cover 6,000.
4 A4 4p scar ver *12,500.* 4,250.
On cover 6,000.
a. Half used as 2p on cover *27,500.*
5 A1 5p brn vio 325.00 *425.00*
Never hinged 750.00
On cover 12,000.
6 A5 6p scar ver *27,500.* 5,000.
On cover *30,000.*
7 A6 6½p scar ver 5,000. *4,000.*
On cover *11,000.*
8 A7 8p scar ver 400.00 *475.00*
Never hinged 900.00
On cover *20,000.*
a. Half used as 4p on cover 4,500.
9 A8 1sh scar ver *42,500.* 10,000.
On cover *30,000.*
a. Half used as 6p on cover *20,000.*

1860
Thin to Thick Wove Paper, No Mesh

11 A2 2p orange 475.00 475.00
On cover —
11A A3 3p green 85.00 *110.00*
Never hinged 200.00
On cover 2,000.
12 A4 4p orange 3,750. 1,350.
On cover 11,000.
b. Half used as 2p on cover *27,500.*
12A A1 5p vio brown 85.00 *150.00*
Never hinged 175.00
On cover 8,500.
13 A5 6p orange 5,250. 1,100.
On cover *24,000.*
15 A8 1sh orange *37,500.* 12,000.
On cover —
b. Half used as 6p on cover *20,000.*

A 6½p orange exists as a souvenir item.

A 1sh exists in orange on horizontally or vertically laid paper. Most authorities consider these to be proofs. Value, $20,000.

1861-62

No.	Type	Description	Unused	Used
15A	A1	1p vio brown	175.00	*250.00*
		Never hinged	500.00	
		On cover		—
c.		1p chocolate brown	220.00	*325.00*
		Never hinged	600.00	
		On cover		—
16	A1	1p reddish brown	*12,500.*	
17	A2	2p rose	175.00	*175.00*
		Never hinged	500.00	
		On cover		—
18	A4	4p rose	37.50	*70.00*
		Never hinged	75.00	
		On cover		6,500.
a.		Half used as 2p on cover		—
19	A1	5p reddish brown	75.00	*77.50*
		Never hinged	150.00	
		On cover		*7,500.*
a.		5p orange brown	85.00	*100.00*
		Never hinged	170.00	
		On cover		*7,500.*
b.		5p chocolate brown	110.00	*125.00*
		Never hinged	220.00	
		On cover		*7,500.*
20	A5	6p rose	22.50	*62.50*
		Never hinged	45.00	
		On cover		*8,500.*
a.		Half used as 3p on cover		*18,000.*
21	A6	6½p rose	85.00	*275.00*
		Never hinged	170.00	
		On cover		*9,500.*
22	A7	8p rose	85.00	*300.00*
		Never hinged	170.00	
		On cover		—
23	A8	1sh rose	42.50	*250.00*
		Never hinged	85.00	
		On cover		—
a.		Half used as 6p on cover		*18,000.*

Some sheets of Nos. 11-23 are known with the papermaker's watermark "STACEY WISE 1858" in large capitals. Values unused and used about 25% more than values shown, except about 50% more for unused Nos. 12 and 13, and 75% more for unused No. 16.

No. 16 was prepared but not issued.

False cancellations are found on Nos. 1, 3, 5, 8, 11, 11A, 12A and 17-23.

Forgeries exist of most or all of Nos. 1-23.

Codfish — A9

Harp Seal — A10

Prince Albert — A11

Victoria — A12

Fishing Ship — A13

Victoria — A14

1865-94 *Perf. 12*

White Paper(#24, 27, 28)

Thin Yellowish Paper (#25-26, 29-31)

No.	Type	Description	Unused	Used
24	A9	2c green	110.00	35.00
		Never hinged	350.00	
		On cover		550.00
a.		Thin yellowish paper	140.00	70.00
		Never hinged	400.00	
		On cover		450.00
b.		Half used as 1c on cover		*8,000.*
25	A10	5c brown	600.00	375.00
		Never hinged	—	
		On cover		650.00
a.		Half used as 2c on cover		*10,000.*
26	A10	5c black ('68)	350.00	200.00
		Never hinged	1,200.	
		On cover		425.00
27	A11	10c black	375.00	60.00
		Never hinged	1,000.	
		On cover		475.00
a.		Thin yellowish paper	425.00	115.00
		Never hinged	1,200.	
		On cover		575.00
b.		Half used as 5c on cover		*9,000.*
28	A12	12c pale red brn	85.00	47.50
		Never hinged	200.00	
		On cover		150.00
a.		Thin yellowish paper	600.00	190.00
		Never hinged	—	
		On cover		300.00
b.		Half used as 6c on cover		*4,000.*
29	A12	12c brn, *white* ('94)	70.00	55.00
		Never hinged	190.00	
		On cover		160.00
30	A13	13c orange	250.00	115.00
		Never hinged	650.00	
		On cover		550.00
31	A14	24c blue, thin transluscent paper	75.00	35.00
		Never hinged	200.00	
		On cover		600.00
a.		Thicker white paper ('70)	375.00	300.00
		Never hinged	—	
		On cover		—

See Nos. 38, 40.

Edward VII as Prince of Wales — A15

Queen Victoria — A16

1868-94

No.	Type	Description	Unused	Used
32	A15	1c violet	75.00	60.00
		Never hinged	200.00	
		On cover		550.00
32A	A15	1c brn lil (re-engr. '71)	115.00	75.00
		Never hinged	400.00	
		On cover		475.00
33	A16	3c ver ('70)	400.00	190.00
		Never hinged	*1,200.*	
		On cover		450.00
34	A16	3c blue ('73)	375.00	75.00
		Never hinged	*1,000.*	
		On cover		200.00
35	A16	6c dull rose ('70)	35.00	17.50
		Never hinged	90.00	
		On cover		70.00
a.		6c bright rose	47.50	22.50
		Never hinged	110.00	
		On cover		70.00
36	A16	6c car lake ('94)	50.00	22.50
		Never hinged	120.00	
		On cover		55.00
		Nos. 32-36 (6)	1,050.	440.00

In the re-engraved 1c the top of the letters "N" and "F" are about ½mm from the ribbon with "ONE CENT." In No. 32 they are fully 1mm away. There are many small differences in the engraving.

1876-79 ***Rouletted***

No.	Type	Description	Unused	Used
37	A15	1c brn lilac ('77)	160.00	52.50
		Never hinged	425.00	
		On cover		600.00
38	A9	2c green ('79)	200.00	52.50
		Never hinged	700.00	
		On cover		600.00
39	A16	3c blue ('77)	425.00	15.00
		Never hinged	*1,200.*	
		On cover		100.00
40	A10	5c blue	275.00	15.00
		Never hinged	700.00	
		On cover		150.00
		Nos. 37-40 (4)	1,060.	135.00

A17

A19

A18

A20

1880-96 ***Perf. 12***

No.	Type	Description	Unused	Used
41	A17	1c violet brown	55.00	11.50
		Never hinged	160.00	
		On cover		70.00
42	A17	1c gray brown	55.00	11.50
		Never hinged	160.00	
		On cover		70.00
43	A17	1c brown ('96)	130.00	70.00
		Never hinged	300.00	
		On cover		175.00
44	A17	1c deep green ('87)	25.00	4.25
		Never hinged	60.00	
		On cover		25.00
a.		1c gray green	32.50	5.00
		Never hinged	75.00	
		On cover		25.00
45	A17	1c green ('97)	25.00	4.25
		Never hinged	60.00	
		On cover		30.00
a.		1c yellow green	32.50	*6.00*
		Never hinged	75.00	
		On cover		30.00
46	A19	2c yellow green	70.00	14.00
		Never hinged	150.00	
		On cover		50.00
47	A19	2c green ('96)	110.00	27.50
		Never hinged	275.00	
		On cover		60.00
48	A19	2c red org ('87)	37.50	9.50
		Never hinged	90.00	
		On cover		60.00
a.		Imperf., pair	325.00	
		Never hinged	650.00	
b.		2c orange	37.50	9.50
		Never hinged	90.00	
		On cover		60.00
49	A18	3c blue ('96)	70.00	7.00
		Never hinged	150.00	
		On cover		20.00
a.		3c pale blue	90.00	6.50
		Never hinged	225.00	
		On cover		20.00
b.		3c deep blue	70.00	6.50
		Never hinged	200.00	
		On cover		20.00
51	A18	3c umber brn ('87)	60.00	4.75
		Never hinged	175.00	
		On cover		20.00
a.		3c brown	75.00	4.75
		Never hinged	200.00	
		On cover		28.00
52	A18	3c vio brown ('96)	120.00	90.00
		Never hinged	275.00	
		On cover		150.00
53	A20	5c pale blue	350.00	14.00
		Never hinged	1,000.	
		On cover		40.00
54	A20	5c dark blue ('87)	180.00	10.00
		Never hinged	450.00	
		On cover		35.00
55	A20	5c bright bl ('94)	65.00	6.50
		Never hinged	150.00	
		On cover		25.00
		Nos. 41-55 (14)	1,353.	284.75

No. 48 bisected on cover was not authorized, but it was accepted by the post office for use on Oct. 2, 1897 only. Value, $400.

Newfoundland Dog — A21

Schooner — A22

1887-96

No.	Type	Description	Unused	Used
56	A21	½c rose red	12.50	7.50
		Never hinged	20.00	
		On cover		70.00
		On cover, single franking		*1,500.*
a.		½c deep rose red	15.00	9.00
		Never hinged	22.50	
		On cover		75.00
		On cover, single franking		*1,500.*
57	A21	½c org red ('96)	80.00	45.00
		Never hinged	180.00	
		On cover		125.00
		On cover, single franking		*1,500.*
58	A21	½c black ('94)	14.00	7.25
		Never hinged	30.00	
		On cover		65.00
		On cover, single franking		*1,500.*
59	A22	10c black	130.00	67.50
		Never hinged	275.00	
		On cover		200.00
		Nos. 56-59 (4)	236.50	127.25
		Set, never hinged	505.00	

Queen Victoria — A23

1890

No.	Type	Description	Unused	Used
60	A23	3c slate	30.00	1.60
		Never hinged	90.00	
		On cover		10.00
a.		3c gray lilac	30.00	1.60
		Never hinged	90.00	
		On cover		10.00
b.		3c brown lilac	50.00	1.60
		Never hinged	135.00	
		On cover		10.00
c.		3c lilac	35.00	1.60
		Never hinged	100.00	
		On cover		10.00
d.		3c slate violet	70.00	3.00
		Never hinged	175.00	
		On cover		15.00
e.		Vert. pair, imperf. horiz.	750.00	
		Never hinged	1,650.	

Examples of No. 60 on red tinted paper are from a recovered consignment that fell into the sea. Value, used $4.

For surcharges see Nos. 75-77.

Victoria — A24

Cabot (John?) — A25

Cape Bonavista A26

Caribou Hunting A27

Mining — A28

Logging — A29

Fishing — A30

Cabot's Ship "Matthew" A31

Willow Ptarmigan A32

Seals — A33

Salmon Fishing — A34

Colony Seal — A35

Iceberg off St. John's — A36

Henry VII — A37

1897, June 24

No.	Type	Description	Unused	Used
61	A24	1c deep green	1.60	1.75
		Never hinged	3.25	
		On cover, single franking		125.00
62	A25	2c carmine lake	2.10	1.40
		Never hinged	4.25	
		On cover		200.00
63	A26	3c ultramarine	4.00	1.40
		Never hinged	8.00	
		On cover		12.50
64	A27	4c olive green	6.00	2.75
		Never hinged	12.00	
		On cover		24.00
65	A28	5c violet	11.00	2.75
		Never hinged	22.00	
		On cover		24.00
66	A29	6c red brown	5.50	3.25
		Never hinged	11.00	
		On cover		24.00
67	A30	8c red orange	22.50	15.00
		Never hinged	45.00	
		On cover		80.00
68	A31	10c black brown	22.50	7.50
		Never hinged	45.00	
		On cover		50.00

No.	Type	Description	Unused	Used
69	A32	12c dark blue	25.00	15.00
		Never hinged	50.00	
		On cover		80.00
70	A33	15c scarlet	20.00	13.00
		Never hinged	40.00	
		On cover		80.00
71	A34	24c gray violet	25.00	12.00
		Never hinged	50.00	
		On cover		60.00
72	A35	30c slate	60.00	55.00
		Never hinged	120.00	
		On cover		100.00
73	A36	35c red	110.00	60.00
		Never hinged	220.00	
		On cover		225.00
74	A37	60c black	16.00	11.50
		Never hinged	32.00	
		On cover		60.00
		Nos. 61-74 (14)	331.20	202.30
		Set, never hinged	662.50	

400th anniv. of John Cabot's discovery of Newfoundland; 60th year of Victoria's reign. The ship on the 10c was previously used by the American Bank Note Co. as the "Flagship of Columbus" on US No. 232. The portrait on the 2c, intended to be of John Cabot, is said to be a Holbein painting of his son, Sebastian.

Bisects are known of the 2c, 3c and 6c values but were not authorized; however, the 2c was accepted for use by the post office on Oct. 2, 1897, only. Values, on cover, 2c (1c) $400, 3c (1½c) $400, 6c (3c) $500.

As noted in the catalogue introduction, the value of a stamp on cover generally assumes that the stamp is being used in the period contemporaneous with its issuance. This is particularly true for provisional surcharges when the beginning and ending dates for provisional use are clear. When known, these dates are given, and values are for stamps used within these periods.

No. 60a Surcharged

No. 75

No. 76

No. 77

Available Oct. 19 through Dec. 3, 1897

No.	Type	Description	Unused	Used
75	A23	1c on 3c gray lil	85.00	50.00
		Never hinged	190.00	
		On cover		75.00
a.		Dbl. surch., one diagonal	*2,000.*	
b.		Vert. pair, "ONE CENT" and lower bar omitted on bottom stamp	*4,250.*	
76	A23	1c on 3c gray lil	275.00	225.00
		Never hinged	625.00	
		On cover		275.00
77	A23	1c on 3c gray lil	825.00	700.00
		Never hinged	2,250.	
		On cover		1,600.
a.		Block of 4, #76-77, 2 #75	1,750.	
		Never hinged	*4,500.*	
		Nos. 75-77 (3)	1,185.	975.00
		Set, never hinged	3,065.	

Most examples of Nos. 75-77 are poorly centered. Fine examples sell for about 60% of the values given. No. 75b is valued in the grade of fine.

Trial surcharges of Nos. 75-77 exist with red surcharge and with double surcharge, one in red and one in black, but these were not issued.

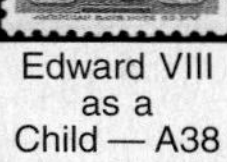

Edward VIII as a Child — A38

Victoria — A39

Edward VII as Prince of Wales — A40

Queen Alexandra as Princess of Wales — A41

Queen Mary as Duchess of York — A42

George V as Duke of York — A43

1897-1901 **Engr.**

No.	Type	Description	Unused	Used
78	A38	½c olive green ('98)	4.25	2.75
		Never hinged	8.50	
		On cover		14.00
79	A39	1c carmine rose ('97)	5.25	5.00
		Never hinged	10.50	
		On cover		110.00
80	A39	1c yel grn ('98)	5.25	.35
		Never hinged	10.50	
		On cover		8.00
a.		1c deep green	6.50	.35
		Never hinged	13.00	
		On cover		6.00
b.		Vert. pair, imperf. horiz.	450.00	
		Never hinged	925.00	
81	A40	2c orange ('97)	6.50	4.25
		Never hinged	13.00	
		On cover		100.00
82	A40	2c ver ('98)	11.50	.75
		Never hinged	23.00	
		On cover		12.00
b.		Pair, imperf. between	575.00	
		Never hinged	1,150.	
83	A41	3c orange ('98)	30.00	.75
		Never hinged	60.00	
		On cover		12.00
a.		Vert. pair, imperf. horiz.	500.00	
		Never hinged	1,000.	
c.		3c red orange, *thin bluish* ('98)	50.00	2.25
		Never hinged	100.00	
84	A42	4c violet ('01)	40.00	4.50
		Never hinged	80.00	
		On cover		5.00
		On cover, single franking		200.00
85	A43	5c blue ('99)	45.00	3.00
		Never hinged	90.00	
		On cover		40.00
		Nos. 78-85 (8)	147.75	21.35
		Set, never hinged	295.50	

No. 80b is valued in the grade of fine.

Values on cover for Nos. 79 and 81 are for proper usage from Dec. 4, 1897, to June 18, 1898.

Imperf., Pairs

78a A38 ½c 600.00 *800.00*
Never hinged 1,000.
81a A40 2c *425.00*
On cover *625.00*
82a A40 2c 375.00
Never hinged 800.00
On cover *950.00*
83b A41 3c 425.00
Never hinged 725.00
84a A42 4c 700.00
Never hinged 1,250.

No. 82a used is known only on cover. Three such covers are recorded.

Imperf., Pairs

Newfoundland imperforates virtually always are proofs on stamp paper or "postmaster's perquisites." Most part-perforate varieties also are "postmaster's perquisites." These items were not regularly issued, but rather were sold or given to favored persons.

Map of Newfoundland — A44

1908, Sept.

86 A44 2c rose carmine 50.00 3.50
Never hinged 100.00
On cover 65.00
On postcard 22.50

Guy Issue

James I — A45

Arms of the London and Bristol Co. — A46

John Guy A47

Guy's Ship, the "Endeavour" A48

View of Cupids — A49

Lord Bacon — A50

View of Mosquito — A51

Logging Camp — A52

Paper Mills — A53

Edward VII — A54

George V — A55

Type I

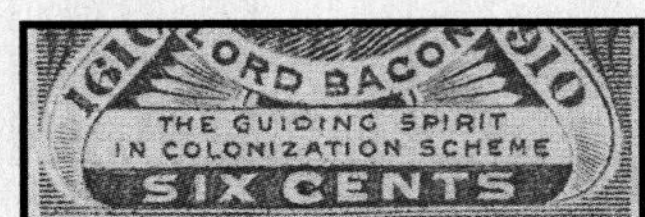

Type II

SIX CENT TYPES
I — "Z" of "COLONIZATION" reversed.
II — "Z" of normal.

1910, Aug. 15 Litho. *Perf. 12*

87 A45 1c deep green, perf. 12x11 2.00 1.10
Never hinged 4.25
On cover 4.75
"NFW" for "NEW" 65.00 60.00
Never hinged 140.00
a. Perf. 12 4.25 1.90
Never hinged 8.50
On cover 7.00
"NFW" for "NEW" 60.00 60.00
Never hinged 120.00
b. Perf. 12x14 7.50 2.25
Never hinged 15.00
On cover 7.00
"NFW" for "NEW" 60.00 60.00
Never hinged 120.00
c. Horiz. pair, imperf. btwn., perf 12x11 400.00 —
Never hinged 800.00
"NFW" for "NEW" 600.00
Never hinged 1,100.
d. Vert. pair, imperf. btwn., perf 12x11 450.00
Never hinged 900.00
e. Horiz. pair, imperf. btwn., perf 12 450.00
Never hinged 900.00
"NFW" for "NEW" 700.00
Never hinged 1,400.
f. Vert. pair, imperf. btwn., perf 12 500.00
Never hinged 1,000.
g. Horiz. pair, imperf. btwn., perf 12x14 750.00 —
Never hinged 1,500.
"NFW" for "NEW" 500.00
Never hinged 1,000.
h. Perf. 12x12x12x11 —
88 A46 2c carmine 11.00 1.15
Never hinged 22.00
On cover 8.00
a. Perf. 12x14 8.50 .85
Never hinged 17.00
On cover 8.00
b. As "a," horiz. pair, imperf. between 900.00
Never hinged 1,750.
c. Perf. 12x11½ 725.00 350.00
Never hinged 1,450.
On cover —
89 A47 3c brown olive 25.00 14.00
Never hinged 50.00
On cover 60.00
90 A48 4c dull violet 25.00 14.00
Never hinged 50.00
On cover 40.00
91 A49 5c ultramarine, perf. 14x12 27.50 4.50
Never hinged 55.00
On cover 24.00
a. Perf. 12 32.50 7.50
Never hinged 65.00
On cover 24.00
92 A50 6c claret, type I 90.00 70.00
Never hinged 180.00
On cover 240.00
92A A50 6c claret, type II 50.00 37.50
Never hinged 100.00
On cover 80.00
b. Imperf., pair 425.00
Never hinged 850.00
93 A51 8c pale brown 75.00 55.00
Never hinged 150.00
On cover 200.00
94 A52 9c olive green 75.00 55.00
Never hinged 150.00
On cover 200.00
95 A53 10c vio black 75.00 55.00
Never hinged 150.00
On cover 200.00
96 A54 12c lilac brown 75.00 55.00
Never hinged 150.00
On cover 240.00
a. Imperf., pair 375.00
Never hinged 750.00
97 A55 15c gray black 80.00 65.00
Never hinged 160.00
On cover 400.00
Nos. 87-97 (12) 610.50 427.25
Set, never hinged 1,211.

Tercentenary of the Colonization of Newfoundland.

On No. 87 printing flaws such as "NFW" and "JANES" exist.

1911 Engr. *Perf. 14*

98 A50 6c brown vio 32.50 22.50
Never hinged 65.00
On cover 80.00
b. Horiz. pair, imperf. btwn. *1,100.*
99 A51 8c bister brn 70.00 67.50
Never hinged 130.00
On cover 200.00
b. Horiz. pair, imperf. btwn. *1,200.*
100 A52 9c olive grn 70.00 60.00
Never hinged 130.00
On cover 200.00
b. Horiz. pair, imperf. btwn. *1,200.*
101 A53 10c violet blk 95.00 95.00
Never hinged 190.00
On cover 250.00
b. Horiz. pair, imperf. btwn. *1,200.*
102 A54 12c red brown 70.00 75.00
Never hinged 140.00
On cover 240.00
b. Horiz. pair, imperf. btwn. —
103 A55 15c slate grn 70.00 75.00
Never hinged 140.00
On cover 575.00
b. Horiz. pair, imperf. btwn. *1,200.*
Nos. 98-103 (6) 407.50 *395.00*
Set, never hinged 795.00

Nos. 100 and 103 are known with papermaker's watermark "E. TOWGOOD FINE." Values, unused or used: No. 100, $800; No. 103, $1,000.

Imperf., Pairs

98a A50 6c 325.00
Never hinged 450.00
99a A51 8c 325.00
Never hinged 450.00
100a A52 9c 325.00
Never hinged 450.00
101a A53 10c 325.00
Never hinged 450.00
102a A54 12c 325.00
Never hinged 450.00
103a A55 15c 325.00
Never hinged 450.00

Nos. 98a-103a were made with and without gum. Values the same.

Royal Family Issue

Queen Mary — A56

George V — A57

Prince of Wales (Edward VIII) — A58

Prince Albert (George VI) — A59

Princess Mary — A60

Prince Henry — A61

Prince George A62

Prince John A63

Queen Alexandra A64

Duke of Connaught A65

Seal of Colony — A66

1911, June 19 *Perf. 13½x14, 14*

104 A56 1c yellow grn 3.00 .25
Never hinged 4.50
On cover 1.60
b. 1c blue green 4.00 .25
Never hinged 7.50
On cover 1.60
105 A57 2c carmine 2.75 1.00
Never hinged 4.50
On cover 1.25
b. 2c rose red (blurred impression) 7.50 .80
Never hinged 15.00
On cover 1.60
106 A58 3c red brown 35.00 19.00
Never hinged 70.00
On cover 24.00
107 A59 4c violet 35.00 13.50
Never hinged 70.00
On cover 20.00
108 A60 5c ultra 22.50 1.90
Never hinged 45.00
On cover 5.00
109 A61 6c black 32.50 22.50
Never hinged 65.00
On cover 25.00
110 A62 8c blue (paper colored through) 80.00 65.00
Never hinged 160.00
On cover 175.00
a. 8c peacock blue 90.00 70.00
Never hinged 180.00
On cover 175.00
111 A63 9c bl violet 35.00 20.00
Never hinged 70.00
On cover 60.00
112 A64 10c dark green 50.00 37.50
Never hinged 100.00
On cover 40.00
113 A65 12c plum 40.00 37.50
Never hinged 80.00
On cover 40.00
114 A66 15c magenta 32.50 *37.50*
Never hinged 65.00
On cover 80.00
Nos. 104-114 (11) 368.25 255.65
Set, never hinged 744.00

Coronation of King George V.

Imperf., Pairs
Without Gum

104a A56 1c 325.00
105a A57 2c 325.00
108a A60 5c 325.00
113a A65 12c 425.00
114a A66 15c 140.00

Trail of the Caribou Issue

Caribou

A67 A68

1919, Jan. 2 *Perf. 14*

115 A67 1c green 2.75 .35
Never hinged 5.50
On cover .75
116 A68 2c scarlet 3.00 .50
Never hinged 6.00
On cover .75
b. 2c carmine red 4.50 .75
Never hinged 9.00
On cover 1.20
117 A67 3c red brown 3.50 .30
Never hinged 7.00
On cover .75
b. 3c brown 3.50 .30
Never hinged 7.00
On cover .75
118 A67 4c violet 5.00 1.40
Never hinged 10.00
On cover 3.25
b. 4c mauve 6.00 1.40
Never hinged 12.00
On cover 3.25
119 A68 5c ultramarine 9.00 1.40
Never hinged 18.00
On cover 2.40
120 A67 6c gray 22.50 22.50
Never hinged 45.00
On cover 24.00
121 A68 8c magenta 25.00 19.00
Never hinged 50.00
On cover 21.00

122 A67 10c dark green 22.50 5.50
Never hinged 45.00
On cover 6.50
123 A68 12c orange 75.00 45.00
Never hinged 150.00
On cover 50.00
124 A67 15c dark blue 42.50 42.50
Never hinged 85.00
On cover 47.50
b. 15c Prussian blue 300.00 150.00
Never hinged 600.00
On cover 200.00
125 A67 24c bister 45.00 42.50
Never hinged 90.00
On cover 42.50
126 A67 36c olive green 37.50 35.00
Never hinged 75.00
On cover 42.50
Nos. 115-126 (12) 293.25 215.95
Set, never hinged 616.50

Services of the Newfoundland contingent in WWI.

Each denomination of type A67 is inscribed with the name of a different action in which Newfoundland troops took part.

For overprint and surcharge see Nos. C1, C5.

A shipment delay of the Trail of the Caribou issue led to trial surcharges of No. 74 reading "TWO / 2 / CENTS" in red. Fifty stamps were so surcharged, including examples with double surcharge. Value, $1,500.

Imperf., Pairs
Without Gum

115a	A67	1c	275.00
116a	A68	2c	275.00
117a	A67	3c red brown	275.00
c.		3c brown	275.00
118a	A67	4c	275.00
119a	A68	5c	275.00
120a	A67	6c	275.00
121a	A68	8c	275.00
122a	A67	10c	275.00
123a	A68	12c	275.00
124a	A67	15c	275.00
125a	A67	24c	275.00
126a	A67	36c	275.00

No. 72 Surcharged in Black

Available Sept. 24 through Sept. 27, 1920

127 A35 2c on 30c slate 5.25 5.50
Never hinged 8.00
On cover 120.00
a. Inverted surcharge 1,100.
Never hinged 2,000.

No. 127 with red surcharge is an unissued color trial. 25 examples are known. Value, $1,250.

Nos. 70 and 73 Surcharged in Black

THREE CENTS
Type I — Bars 10½mm apart.
Type II — Bars 13½mm apart.

Available Sept. 13 through Oct. 3, 1920

128 A33 3c on 15c scar (I) 220.00 240.00
Never hinged 350.00
On cover 350.00
a. Inverted surcharge *2,750.*
Never hinged *5,000.*
129 A33 3c on 15c scar (II) 17.50 11.00
Never hinged 35.00
On cover 40.00
130 A36 3c on 35c red 11.00 9.50
Never hinged 20.00
On cover 40.00
a. Lower bar omitted 140.00 140.00
Never hinged 275.00

Trial surcharges of "THREE CENTS" between bars on No. 66 in red or brown are known. Twenty-five of each were produced, Value, $1,000.

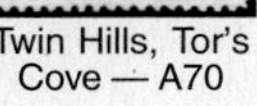

Twin Hills, Tor's Cove — A70

South West Arm, Trinity — A71

War Memorial, St. John's A72

Humber River A73

Coast of Trinity — A74

Upper Steadies, Humber River — A75

Quidi Vidi, near St. John's — A76

Caribou Crossing Lake — A77

Humber River Canyon A78

Shell Bird Island A79

Mt. Moriah, Bay of Islands A80

Humber River near Little Rapids A81

Placentia, from Mt. Pleasant A82

Topsail Falls near St. John's A83

1923-24 Engr. *Perf. 14, 13½x14*

131 A70 1c gray green 1.75 .30
Never hinged 2.75
On cover 10.00
a. Booklet pane of 8 500.00
Never hinged 700.00
132 A71 2c carmine 1.75 .30
Never hinged 2.75
On cover 1.00
a. Booklet pane of 8 300.00
Never hinged 425.00
133 A72 3c brown 2.25 .30
Never hinged 4.25
On cover 1.50
134 A73 4c brn violet 2.60 1.80
Never hinged 4.50
On cover 3.25
135 A74 5c ultramarine 6.50 2.25
Never hinged 11.50
On cover 4.50
136 A75 6c gray black 6.50 6.00
Never hinged 11.50
On cover 12.00
137 A76 8c dull violet 4.75 4.50
Never hinged 8.50
On cover 12.00
138 A77 9c slate green 42.50 27.50
Never hinged 75.00
On cover 55.00
139 A78 10c dark violet 4.25 2.50
Never hinged 7.75
On cover 8.00
b. 10c purple 5.25 2.50
Never hinged 9.50
On cover 8.00
140 A79 11c olive green 7.00 7.00
Never hinged 12.50
On cover 20.00
141 A80 12c lake 7.00 7.50
Never hinged 12.50
On cover 16.00
142 A81 15c deep blue 8.50 8.00
Never hinged 15.00
On cover 20.00
143 A82 20c red brn ('24) 12.00 7.50
Never hinged 22.00
On cover 27.50
144 A83 24c blk brn ('24) 80.00 50.00
Never hinged 130.00
On cover 120.00
Nos. 131-144 (14) 187.35 125.45
Set, never hinged 315.50

For surcharge see No. 160.

Imperf., Pairs

131b	A70	1c	200.00
		Never hinged	300.00
132b	A71	2c	200.00
		Never hinged	300.00
133a	A72	3c	300.00
134a	A73	4c	250.00
135a	A74	5c	250.00
136a	A75	6c	250.00
137a	A76	8c	250.00
138a	A77	9c	250.00
139a	A78	10c	250.00
140a	A79	11c	250.00
		Never hinged	350.00
141a	A80	12c	250.00
142a	A81	15c	160.00

Nos. 133a-139a, 141a-142a are without gum. Others are either with or without gum; values about the same.

Map of Newfoundland A84

Steamship "Caribou" A85

Queen Mary, George V — A86

Prince of Wales — A87

Express Train — A88

Newfoundland Hotel, St. John's — A89

Heart's Content — A90

Cabot Tower, St. John's — A91

War Memorial, St. John's — A92

GPO, St. John's — A93

First Nonstop Transatlantic Flight, 1919 — A94

Colonial Building, St. John's — A95

Grand Falls, Labrador — A96

Perf. 14, 13½x13, 13x13½

1928, Jan. 3

145 A84 1c deep green 1.85 .75
Never hinged 3.75
On cover .80
146 A85 2c deep carmine 2.50 .70
Never hinged 5.00
On cover .80
a. Imperf., pair 300.00
Never hinged *450.00*
147 A86 3c brown 2.75 .50
Never hinged 5.50
On cover .80
148 A87 4c lilac rose 3.50 1.80
Never hinged 7.00
On cover 8.00
a. 4c rose purple ('29) 5.25 2.50
Never hinged 10.50
On cover 8.00
149 A88 5c slate green 10.00 4.25
Never hinged 20.00
On cover 8.00
150 A89 6c ultramarine 5.75 5.00
Never hinged 11.50
On cover 8.00
151 A90 8c lt red brown 7.25 4.50
Never hinged 14.50
On cover 12.00
152 A91 9c myrtle green 7.00 7.00
Never hinged 14.50
On cover 12.00
153 A92 10c dark violet 9.00 4.25
Never hinged 18.00
On cover 12.00
154 A93 12c brn carmine 5.50 5.00
Never hinged 11.00
On cover 16.00
155 A91 14c red brown 10.50 7.00
Never hinged 21.00
On cover 20.00
156 A94 15c dark blue 9.25 7.00
Never hinged 18.50
On cover 16.00
157 A95 20c gray black 12.50 6.50
Never hinged 25.00
On cover 16.00
158 A93 28c gray green 35.00 27.50
Never hinged 700.00
On cover 55.00
159 A96 30c olive brown 17.50 7.50
Never hinged 35.00
On cover 16.00
Nos. 145-159 (15) 139.85 89.25
Set, never hinged 280.25

See Nos. 163-182.

No. 136 Surcharged in Red or Black

Type I — 5mm between "CENTS" and bar.
Type II — 3mm between "CENTS" and bar.

Available Aug. 23-Aug. 30, 1929

160 A75 3c on 6c gray black (II) (R) 4.25 4.25
Never hinged 6.75
On cover 75.00
a. Inverted surcharge (II) 1,000.
Never hinged *1,800.*

Seventy percent of the issue of 100,000 were sold on the first day. Many were used at an incorrect rate as drop covers, for which the proper rate was 2¢. The inland rate was 3¢, and this usage, and other proper rates, warrant the value shown, within the provisional period.

The stamps with black surcharge, type I and II, were trial surcharges, and were not issued. There were 50 examples of each. Value, each $1,750.

Types of 1928 Issue Re-engraved

1c — On No. 145 the lines of the engraving are thinner and the impression is clearer than on No. 163. On the former "C. BAULD" is above "C. NORMAN." On the latter these words are transposed.

2c — On the 1928 stamp the "D" of "NEWFOUNDLAND" is 1mm from the scroll at the right; the flag at the stern is lower than the top of the boat davit. On the 1929 stamp the "D" is ½mm from the scroll and the flag rises above the davits.

3c — On the 1928 stamp the pearls at the top of the crown, the jewels of the tiara and the pillars flanking the portraits are all unshaded. On the reengraved stamp there are small curved lines inside the pearls, the jewels of the tiara are in solid color, and the pillars have vertical shading lines. On the 1928 stamps the tablets with "THREE" and "CENTS" have a background of crossed lines (vertical and horizontal). On the 1929 stamp the background is of horizontal lines only.

4c — On the 1928 stamp the figures "4" have shading of horizontal and diagonal crossed lines. There are six circles at each side of the portrait.

On the 1929 stamp the "4s" have shading of horizontal lines only. There are five roses at each side of the portrait.

5c — The crossbars of the telegraph pole touch the frame at the left on the 1929 stamp but just clear it on the 1928 stamp. In the 1928 issue the foliate ornaments beside and below the figures "5" end in small scrolls and a small spur. These spurs are omitted on the 1929 stamp.

6c — On the re-engraved stamp the columns at right and left of the picture have heavy wavy outlines on the inner sides. There is no period after "JOHNS." The numerals in the lower corners are 1½mm wide instead of 1¼mm.

8c — The impression of the 1928 stamp is clear, that of 1931 is slightly blurred. The 1928 stamp has three horizontal lines above "EIGHT CENTS" and four berries on the laurel branch at the right side. On the 1931 stamp there are two horizontal lines and three berries.

10c — On the re-engraved stamp there is no period after "ST. JOHN'S." The letters of "TEN CENTS" are slightly larger and the numerals "10" slightly smaller than in 1928. Inside the "0" of "10" at the right there are two vertical lines instead of three. The clouds are fainter in 1929 and the cross upheld by the figure on the monument is more distinct. On the 1928 stamp the torch at the left side terminates in a single tongue of flame. On the 1929-30 stamp it terminates in two tongues.

15c — On the 1928 stamp the "N" of "NEWFOUNDLAND" is 1½mm from the left frame, the "L" of "LEAVING" is under the first "A" of "AIRPLANE" and the apostrophe in "JOHN'S" breaks the first line above it.

On the 1929 stamp the "N" of "NEWFOUNDLAND" is 1mm from the left frame, the "L" of "LEAVING" is below the "T" of "FIRST" and the apostrophe in "JOHN'S" does not touch the line above it.

20c — On the 1928 stamp the points of the "W" of "NEWFOUNDLAND" are truncated. The "O" is wide and nearly round. The columns that form the sides of the frame have a shading of evenly spaced horizontal lines at their inner sides.

On the 1929-31 stamp the points of the "W" form sharp angles. The "O" is narrow and has a small opening. Many lines have been added to the shading on the inner sides of the columns, making it almost solid.

30c — 1928 stamp. Size: 19¼x24½mm. At the outer side of the right column there are three strong and two faint vertical lines. Faint period after "FALLS."

1931 stamp. Size: 19x25mm. At the outer side of the right column there are two strong vertical lines and a fragment of the lower end of a faint one. Clear period after "FALLS." A great many of the small lines of the design have been deepened making the whole stamp appear darker.

1929-31 Unwmk. *Perf. 13½ to 14*

163 A84 1c green 2.00 .65
Never hinged 4.00
On cover 1.25
a. Double impression *425.00*
Never hinged *850.00*
b. Vert. pair, imperf. btwn. 210.00
Never hinged *350.00*
164 A85 2c deep carmine 2.00 .70
Never hinged 4.00
On cover 1.25
165 A86 3c dp red brown 2.00 .70
Never hinged 4.00
On cover 1.25
166 A87 4c magenta 3.50 1.25
Never hinged 7.00
On cover 4.00
167 A88 5c slate green 7.00 2.50
Never hinged 14.00
On cover 8.00
168 A89 6c ultramarine 9.00 9.00
Never hinged 18.00
On cover 12.00
169 A92 10c dark violet 8.00 2.25
Never hinged 16.00
On cover 8.00
170 A94 15c deep blue ('30) 45.00 37.50
Never hinged 90.00
On cover 40.00
171 A95 20c gray blk ('31) 70.00 27.50
Never hinged 140.00
On cover 32.50
Nos. 163-171 (9) 148.50 82.05
Set, never hinged 297.00

Imperf., Pairs

163c A84 1c 120.00
Never hinged 200.00
164a A85 2c pale carmine, *cream* 145.00
Never hinged 250.00
b. 2c dark carmine 145.00
165a A86 3c 145.00
Never hinged 250.00
166a A87 4c 145.00
Never hinged 250.00

No. 164b is without gum, others with gum.

Types of 1928 Issue Re-engraved

1931 Wmk. 224 *Perf. 13½x14*

172 A84 1c green, perf. 13½ 2.25 1.30
Never hinged 4.50
On cover 2.00
a. Horiz. pair, imperf. btwn. 450.00
Never hinged *900.00*
173 A85 2c red 7.00 1.30
Never hinged 14.00
On cover 1.60
174 A86 3c red brown 3.50 1.30
Never hinged 7.00
On cover 2.40
175 A87 4c rose 4.25 2.75
Never hinged 8.50
On cover 8.00
176 A88 5c grnsh gray 12.50 7.00
Never hinged 25.00
On cover 12.00
177 A89 6c ultramarine 17.50 17.50
Never hinged 35.00
On cover 24.00
178 A90 8c lt red brn 22.50 17.50
Never hinged 45.00
On cover 20.00
179 A92 10c dk violet 15.00 9.00
Never hinged 30.00
On cover 12.00
180 A94 15c deep blue 45.00 27.50
Never hinged 90.00
On cover 30.00
181 A95 20c gray black 55.00 17.50
Never hinged 110.00
On cover 20.00
182 A96 30c olive brown 45.00 25.00
Never hinged 90.00
On cover 25.00
Nos. 172-182 (11) 229.50 127.65
Set, never hinged 459.00

Codfish — A97

George V — A98

Queen Mary — A99

Prince of Wales — A100

Caribou A101

Princess Elizabeth A102

Salmon Leaping Falls — A103

Newfoundland Dog — A104

Harp Seal Pup — A105

Cape Race — A106

Sealing Fleet — A107

Fishing Fleet Leaving for "The Banks" — A108

Type I

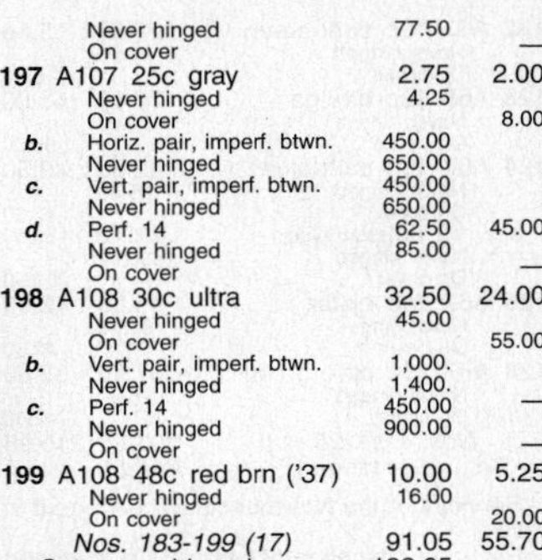

Type II

FIVE CENT
Die I — Antlers even, or equal in height.
Die II — Antler under "T" higher.

1932-37 Engr. *Perf. 13½, 14*

183 A97 1c green 2.75 .50
Never hinged 4.00
On cover 1.20
a. Booklet pane of 4, perf. 13 75.00
Never hinged 110.00
c. Vert. pair, imperf. btwn. 200.00
Never hinged 250.00
184 A97 1c gray black .60 .25
Never hinged .95
On cover .60
a. Bklt. pane of 4, perf. 13½ 57.50
Never hinged 80.00
b. Booklet pane of 4, perf. 14 72.50
Never hinged 90.00
185 A98 2c rose 2.25 .35
Never hinged 3.25
On cover 1.20
a. Booklet pane of 4, perf. 13½ 35.00
Never hinged 50.00
b. Booklet pane of 4, perf. 13 47.50
Never hinged 60.00
186 A98 2c green 1.10 .25
Never hinged 1.75
On cover .60
a. Bklt. pane of 4, perf. 13½ 25.00
Never hinged 32.50
b. Booklet pane of 4, perf. 14 35.00
Never hinged 50.00
d. Horiz. pair, imperf. btwn. 160.00
Never hinged 225.00
187 A99 3c orange brn 1.10 .35
Never hinged 1.75
On cover .60
a. Bklt. pane of 4, perf. 13½ 55.00
Never hinged 75.00
b. Booklet pane of 4, perf. 14 67.50
Never hinged 92.50
c. Booklet pane of 4, perf. 13 75.00
Never hinged 100.00
e. Vert. pair, imperf. btwn. 300.00
Never hinged *450.00*
188 A100 4c deep violet 7.00 2.00
Never hinged 10.50
On cover 2.25
189 A100 4c rose lake .75 .50
Never hinged 1.10
On cover 1.60
b. Vert. pair, imperf. btwn. 120.00
Never hinged 165.00
c. Horiz. pair, imperf. btwn. 120.00
Never hinged 165.00
d. Perf. 14 5.75 4.50
Never hinged 8.50
On cover 6.50
190 A101 5c vio brn, perf. 13½ (Die I) 9.50 2.00
Never hinged 13.00
On cover 3.25
191 A101 5c dp vio, perf. 13½ (Die II) 1.10 .40
Never hinged 1.75
On cover .50
a. 5c dp vio, perf. 13½ (Die I) 14.00 1.25
Never hinged 19.00
On cover 2.00
c. Horiz. pair, imperf. btwn. (I) 240.00
Never hinged 325.00
e. Perf. 14 (Die I) 42.50 20.00
Never hinged 65.00
On cover 65.00
f. Perf. 14 (Die II) 40.00 16.00
Never hinged 57.50
On cover 65.00
g. Horiz. pair, imperf. btwn. (II) 240.00
192 A102 6c dull blue 10.00 11.00
Never hinged 16.00
On cover 24.00
193 A103 10c olive black 1.40 .85
Never hinged 2.25
On cover 1.60
194 A104 14c int black 3.25 2.75
Never hinged 4.50
On cover 8.00
195 A105 15c magenta 2.50 2.25
Never hinged 3.50
On cover 8.00
b. Perf. 14 14.00 7.00
Never hinged 18.00
On cover 12.50
196 A106 20c gray green 2.50 1.00
Never hinged 3.50
On cover 8.00
b. Perf. 14 55.00 37.50
Never hinged 77.50
On cover —
197 A107 25c gray 2.75 2.00
Never hinged 4.25
On cover 8.00
b. Horiz. pair, imperf. btwn. 450.00
Never hinged 650.00
c. Vert. pair, imperf. btwn. 450.00
Never hinged 650.00
d. Perf. 14 62.50 45.00
Never hinged 85.00
On cover —
198 A108 30c ultra 32.50 24.00
Never hinged 45.00
On cover 55.00
b. Vert. pair, imperf. btwn. 1,000.
Never hinged 1,400.
c. Perf. 14 450.00 —
Never hinged 900.00
On cover —
199 A108 48c red brn ('37) 10.00 5.25
Never hinged 16.00
On cover 20.00
Nos. 183-199 (17) 91.05 55.70
Set, never hinged 133.05

Two dies were used for 2c green, one for 2c rose.

See Nos. 253-266.

Imperf., Pairs

183b A97 1c 240.00
Never hinged 350.00
184c A97 1c 47.50
Never hinged 60.00
185c A98 2c 250.00
Never hinged 350.00
186c A98 2c 47.50
Never hinged 60.00
187d A99 3c 95.00
Never hinged 130.00
189a A100 4c 60.00
Never hinged 75.00
190a A101 5c 200.00
Never hinged 300.00
191b A101 5c (II) 75.00
Never hinged 100.00
191d A101 5c (I) 100.00
192a A102 6c 175.00
Never hinged 250.00
193a A103 10c 110.00
Never hinged 160.00
194a A103 14c 130.00
Never hinged 175.00
195a A103 15c 130.00
Never hinged 175.00
196a A106 20c 225.00
Never hinged 300.00
197a A107 25c 225.00
Never hinged 300.00
198a A108 30c 750.00
Never hinged 1,100.
199a A108 48c 120.00
Never hinged 180.00

All with gum. Nos. 186c, 187d, 192a, 193a and 196a also made without gum; values about 10% less.

Queen Elizabeth when Duchess of York — A109

Corner Brook Paper Mills — A110

Loading Iron Ore at Bell Island — A111

1932

208 A109 7c red brown 1.40 1.25
Never hinged 1.75
On cover 8.00
a. Imperf., pair 160.00
Never hinged 225.00
b. Horiz. pair, imperf. between 600.00
Never hinged 850.00
209 A110 8c orange red 1.40 1.10
Never hinged 2.00
On cover 8.00
a. Imperf., pair 140.00
Never hinged 200.00
210 A111 24c light blue 2.75 2.75
Never hinged 4.00
On cover 12.00
a. Imperf., pair 200.00
Never hinged 275.00
b. Double impression 1,750.
Never hinged 2,500.
Nos. 208-210 (3) 5.55 5.10
Set, never hinged 7.75

No. 208a was made both with and without gum. Values about the same.

See Nos. 259, 264.

No. C9 Overprinted Bars and

1933, Feb. 9 **Wmk. 224** ***Perf. 14***

211 AP6 15c brown 11.00 9.50
Never hinged 17.00
On cover 20.00
a. Vert. pair, one without overprint 7,500.
Never hinged *11,500.*
b. Overprint reading up 4,750.
Never hinged *7,500.*

The end of the period of use and availability of No. 211 is unknown.
"L. & S." stands for "Land and Sea."

Sir Humphrey Gilbert Issue

Sir Humphrey Gilbert — A112

Compton Castle, Home of the Gilbert Family — A113

Gilbert Coat of Arms — A114

Eton College — A115

Token from Queen Elizabeth I — A116

Sir Humphrey Receiving Royal Patents for Colonization A117

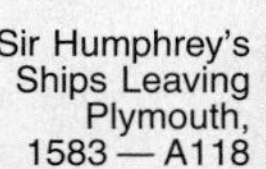

Sir Humphrey's Ships Leaving Plymouth, 1583 — A118

The Ships Arriving at St. John's — A119

Annexation of Newfoundland, Aug. 5, 1583 — A120

Coat of Arms of England A121

Sir Humphrey on the Deck of the "Squirrel" A122

Capt. John Mason's Map of Newfoundland, 1626 — A123

Queen Elizabeth I A124

Gilbert Statue at Truro A125

Wmk. 224

1933, Aug. 3 **Engr.** ***Perf. 13½***

212 A112 1c gray black 1.30 .75
Never hinged 1.70
On cover 1.00
213 A113 2c green 1.30 .75
Never hinged 1.70
On cover 1.00
b. Double impression *600.00*
Never hinged *1,000.*
214 A114 3c yellow brn 2.75 .75
Never hinged 4.00
On cover 3.25
215 A115 4c carmine 2.00 .75
Never hinged 3.00
On cover 3.25
216 A116 5c dull violet 3.25 1.10
Never hinged 4.50
On cover 2.40
217 A117 7c blue 17.50 12.50
Never hinged 32.50
On cover 24.00
b. Perf. 14 14.00 16.00
Never hinged 25.00
On cover 24.00
218 A118 8c orange red 8.50 7.00
Never hinged 11.50
On cover 24.00
a. 8c brownish red (error), never hinged 525.00
219 A119 9c ultramarine 10.00 7.50
Never hinged 14.00
On cover 24.00
b. Perf. 14 80.00 75.00
Never hinged 120.00
On cover 120.00
220 A120 10c red brown 8.50 6.25
Never hinged 11.50
On cover 16.00
b. Perf. 14 110.00 100.00
Never hinged 155.00
On cover 120.00
221 A121 14c black 17.50 15.00
Never hinged 22.00
On cover 26.00
b. Perf. 14 20.00 18.00
Never hinged 30.00
On cover 30.00
222 A122 15c claret 17.50 15.00
Never hinged 22.00
On cover 27.50
223 A123 20c deep green 15.00 10.00
Never hinged 21.50
On cover 20.00
b. Perf. 14 16.50 12.50
Never hinged 25.00
On cover 24.00
224 A124 24c vio brown 27.50 22.50
Never hinged 40.00
On cover 40.00
b. Perf. 14 24.00 24.00
Never hinged 35.00
On cover 40.00
225 A125 32c gray 27.50 22.50
Never hinged 40.00
On cover 40.00
a. Perf. 14 24.00 24.00
Never hinged 35.00
On cover 40.00
Nos. 212-225 (14) 160.10 122.35
Set, never hinged 229.90

350th anniv. of annexation of Newfoundland to England, Aug. 5, 1583, by authority of Letters Patent issued by Queen Elizabeth I to Sir Humphrey Gilbert.

Imperf., Pairs

212a A112 1c 45.00
213a A113 2c 45.00
214a A114 3c 375.00
215a A115 4c 50.00
216a A116 5c 375.00
219a A119 9c 500.00
220a A120 10c 500.00
221a A120 14c 400.00
222a A120 15c 240.00
224a A124 24c 225.00

No. 212a was made both with and without gum. Value of pair without gum about 10% less.

Common Design Types pictured following the introduction.

Silver Jubilee Issue
Common Design Type

1935, May 6 **Wmk. 4** ***Perf. 11x12***

226 CD301 4c bright rose 2.25 .70
Never hinged 2.80
On cover 1.60
227 CD301 5c violet 2.25 .85
Never hinged 2.80
On cover 1.60
228 CD301 7c dark blue 4.00 3.50
Never hinged 5.75
On cover 8.00
229 CD301 24c olive green 9.00 7.00
Never hinged 14.00
On cover 10.00
a. 24c dark olive 16.00 12.00
Never hinged 22.50
On cover 14.00
Nos. 226-229 (4) 17.50 12.05
Set, never hinged 25.35

Coronation Issue
Common Design Type

1937, May 12 ***Perf. 11x11½***

230 CD302 2c deep green 1.75 .70
Never hinged 2.40
On cover 1.60
231 CD302 4c carmine rose 1.75 .70
Never hinged 2.40
On cover 1.60
232 CD302 5c dark violet 3.50 1.40
Never hinged 5.00
On cover 3.25
Nos. 230-232 (3) 7.00 2.80
Set, never hinged 9.80

Codfish A126

Map of Newfoundland — A127

Caribou A128

Corner Brook Paper Mills A129

Salmon A130

Newfoundland Dog — A131

Harp Seal Pup A132

Cape Race A133

Loading Iron Ore at Bell Island A134

Sealing Fleet A135

Fishing Fleet Leaving for "The Banks" A136

Type I

Type II

Two types of the 3c
Type I — Fine impression; no lines on bridge of nose.
Type II — Coarse impression; lines on bridge of nose.

Perf. 13½, 14 (#234-235)

1937, May 12 **Wmk. 224**

233 A126 1c gray black .65 .30
Never hinged 1.00
On cover 1.00
"Fish hook" plate flaw (pos. 23) 15.00 12.00
Never hinged 27.00
On cover 16.00
234 A127 3c org brn, die I 2.75 1.10
Never hinged 4.00
On cover 1.60
a. Die II 2.25 1.10
Never hinged 3.00
On cover 1.60
b. Vert. pair, imperf. btwn. (I) 850.00
Never hinged 1,350.
c. Vert. pair, imperf. btwn. (II) 850.00
Never hinged 1,350.
d. Horiz. pair, imperf. btwn. (I) 575.00
Never hinged 850.00
e. Horiz. pair, imperf. btwn. (II) 575.00
Never hinged 850.00
f. Imperf., pair 240.00
Never hinged 360.00
i. Horiz. pair, imperf. vert., never hinged *1,600.*
235 A128 7c blue 3.00 2.50
Never hinged 4.75
On cover 8.00
236 A129 8c orange red 3.00 2.50
Never hinged 4.75
On cover 8.00
a. Imperf., pair 350.00
Never hinged 600.00
b. Vert. pair, imperf. between 1,400.
Never hinged 1,850.
c. Horiz. pair, imperf. vert. *2,000.*
Never hinged *3,000.*
237 A130 10c olive gray 4.25 4.25
Never hinged 6.50
On cover 8.00
a. Double impression 280.00
Never hinged 560.00
238 A131 14c black 4.25 3.50
Never hinged 7.00
On cover 8.00
a. Imperf., pair 400.00
Never hinged 600.00
239 A132 15c rose lake 4.25 3.50
Never hinged 6.50
On cover 8.00
a. Vert. pair, imperf. between 1,400.
Never hinged *1,850.*
240 A133 20c green 4.25 2.25
Never hinged 6.50
On cover 8.00
a. Vert. pair, imperf. between 1,500.
Never hinged 2,150.
241 A134 24c turq blue 4.25 3.25
Never hinged 6.50
On cover 8.00
a. Vert. pair, imperf. between 2,500.
Never hinged 3,500.
242 A135 25c gray 4.25 3.25
Never hinged 6.50
On cover 8.00
a. Imperf., pair 275.00
Never hinged 300.00

243 A136 48c dark violet 7.00 4.00
Never hinged 11.00
On cover 12.00
a. Vert. pair, imperf. between 2,500.
Never hinged 3,500.
b. Imperf., pair 275.00
Never hinged 360.00
Nos. 233-243 (11) 41.90 30.40
Set, never hinged 64.50

Imperfs are with gum. No. 243b also made without gum; value the same.

Two line-perforating machines were used to produce this set, with exact measurements of 13.7 and 14.1 respectively.

Perf. 13¼

233a A126 1c gray black 16.00 22.00
Never hinged 24.00
On cover 40.00
"Fish hook" plate flaw (pos. 23) *175.00* —
Never hinged *225.00*
On cover —
234g A127 3c org brn, die I 1.60 1.00
Never hinged 2.40
On cover 1.50
h. Die II 2.00 1.25
Never hinged 3.00
On cover 1.60
235a A128 7c blue 400.00 *275.00*
Never hinged 700.00
On cover *800.00*
236d A129 8c orange red 3.75 3.25
Never hinged 5.50
On cover 10.00
237b A130 10c olive gray 5.00 *6.00*
Never hinged 7.50
On cover 10.00
238b A131 14c black *20,000.* —
239b A132 15c rose lake 11.00 11.00
Never hinged 16.00
On cover 20.00
240b A133 20c green 3.25 3.25
Never hinged 5.00
On cover 8.00
241b A134 24c turq blue 11.00 11.00
Never hinged 16.50
On cover 16.00
242b A135 25c gray 11.00 *11.00*
Never hinged 16.50
On cover 16.00
243c A136 48c dark violet 20.00 18.00
Never hinged 27.50
On cover 24.00

This set was produced with a comb perforator with an exact perforation of 13.3x13.2.

Princess Elizabeth — A139

Designs: 2c, King George VI. 3c, Queen Elizabeth. 7c, Queen Mother Mary.

1938, May 12 ***Perf. 13½***
245 A139 2c green 1.75 .25
Never hinged 2.10
On cover 1.60
246 A139 3c dark carmine 1.75 .25
Never hinged 2.10
On cover 1.60
b. Perf. 14 750.00 500.00
Never hinged 1,100.
On cover 750.00
247 A139 4c light blue 2.30 .25
Never hinged 2.80
On cover 1.60
248 A139 7c dark ultra 1.60 1.10
Never hinged 2.40
On cover 4.00
Nos. 245-248 (4) 7.40 1.85
Set, never hinged 9.40

See Nos. 254-256, 258, 269.

Imperf., Pairs

245a A139 2c 120.00
Never hinged 175.00
246a A139 3c 120.00
Never hinged 175.00
247a A139 4c 120.00
Never hinged 175.00
248a A139 7c 120.00
Never hinged 175.00
Set, never hinged 700.00

George VI and Queen Elizabeth A141

1939, June 17 **Unwmk.**
249 A141 5c violet blue 1.25 1.10
Never hinged 1.75
On cover 1.60

Visit of King George and Queen Elizabeth.

No. 249 Surcharged in Brown or Red

Available Nov. 21 and exhausted by Dec. 16, 1939

250 A141 2c on 5c vio blue (Br) 1.40 1.00
Never hinged 1.80
On cover 4.00
251 A141 4c on 5c vio blue (R) 1.00 1.00
Never hinged 1.40
On cover 4.00
Set, never hinged 3.20

There are many varieties of broken letters and figures in the settings of the surcharges.

Sir Wilfred Grenfell and "Strathcona II" — A142

1941, Dec. 1 ***Perf. 12***
252 A142 5c dull blue .40 .30
Never hinged .50
On cover 1.20

Grenfell Mission, 50th anniv.

Types of 1931-38

1941-44 **Wmk. 224** ***Perf. 12½***
253 A97 1c dark gray .35 .25
Never hinged .45
On cover .25
a. Imperf., pair 150.00
Never hinged 275.00
254 A139 2c deep green .35 .25
Never hinged .45
On cover .25
255 A139 3c rose carmine .50 .25
Never hinged .65
On cover .25
a. Imperf., pair 275.00
Never hinged 425.00
256 A139 4c blue .70 .30
Never hinged .90
On cover .40
257 A101 5c violet (Die I) 1.00 .25
Never hinged 1.40
On cover .25
a. Imperf., pair 200.00
Never hinged 260.00
b. Horiz. pair, imperf. vert. 650.00
Never hinged 900.00
c. Double impression 650.00
Never hinged 900.00
258 A139 7c vio blue ('42) 1.20 1.00
Never hinged 1.50
On cover 1.80
259 A110 8c red 1.40 .65
Never hinged 1.75
On cover 1.20
260 A103 10c brownish blk 1.40 .60
Never hinged 1.75
On cover 1.25
261 A104 14c black 2.00 1.75
Never hinged 2.75
On cover 2.40
a. Imperf., pair 240.00
Never hinged 325.00
c. Vert. pair, imperf. horiz. 500.00
Never hinged 750.00
262 A105 15c pale rose vio 2.00 1.40
Never hinged 2.50
On cover 2.25
263 A106 20c green 2.00 1.10
Never hinged 2.50
On cover 1.90
264 A111 24c deep blue 2.25 2.00
Never hinged 2.75
On cover 3.00
265 A107 25c slate 2.25 2.00
Never hinged 2.75
On cover 3.00
266 A108 48c red brown ('44) 3.25 1.75
Never hinged 4.25
On cover 3.50
Nos. 253-266 (14) 20.65 13.55
Set, never hinged 26.35

Nos. 254 and 255 are re-engraved.

Memorial University College A143

1943, Jan. 2 **Unwmk.** ***Perf. 12***
267 A143 30c carmine 1.40 1.00
Never hinged 1.85
On cover 8.00

No. 267 Surcharged in Black

Available Mar. 21 through April 1, 1946

268 A143 2c on 30c carmine .30 .30
Never hinged .40
On cover 25.00

Most of the issue of No. 268 was sold March 21. After that date the stamps were available only for letters handed to postal clerks through April 1. Most examples of No. 268 on cover underpay the drop rate of 3¢ (but not penalized), but a few are known doubled for the inland rate, or with other values for air mail.

Princess Elizabeth — A144

Wmk. 224

1947, Apr. 21 **Engr.** ***Perf. 12½***
269 A144 4c light blue .30 .25
Never hinged .40
On cover .80
a. Imperf., pair 240.00
Never hinged 325.00
b. Horiz. pair, imperf. vert. 400.00
Never hinged 600.00

Princess Elizabeth's 21st birthday.

Deck of the Matthew A145

1947, June 24
270 A145 5c rose violet .30 .25
Never hinged .40
On cover 1.20
a. Horiz. pair, imperf. between 1,350.
Never hinged 2,000.
b. Imperf., pair 240.00
Never hinged 350.00

Cabot's arrival off Cape Bonavista, 450th anniv.

AIR POST STAMPS

No. 117 Overprinted in Black

Manuscript "Aerial Atlantic Mail JAR"

1919, Apr. 12 **Unwmk.** ***Perf. 14***
C1 A67 3c red brown *25,000. 15,000.*
Never hinged *35,000.*
On cover *25,000.*
a. Manuscript "Aerial Atlantic Mail JAR" *75,000. 25,000.*
On cover *35,000.*

No. C1 was issued for the first attempt to cross the Atlantic by air from Newfoundland, by Harry G. Hawker (pilot) and Cdr. K. Mackenzie-Grieve (navigator). The plane took off May 18, but the flight ended by a controlled splash down in the ocean after about 10 hours of flying, the crew being rescued. The plane and mail bag were salvaged five days later by an east-bound U.S. ship. And the envelopes were delivered to England by sea. All stamps are signed "J.A.R." (P.M.G. Robinson initials) on reverse.

Also in April 1919, J.A. Robinson prepared stamps for use on the mail of the "Raymor," Major F.P. Raynham (pilot) and Major C.W.F. Morgan (navigator). Stamps bear at the top a manuscript "Aerial Atlantic Mail," believed to have been written by W. Campbell, the secretary to P.M.G. Robinson, the latter applying his intials "J.A.R" at the bottom. This flight, which took off after the Hawker flight, lasted only a few hundred yards, as did a second attempt in July. Mail from the latter attempt was then taken by sea to London, receiving the Foreign Section F.S. 66 circular date stamp canceled Jan. 7, 1920, on reverse. These stamps are No. C1a.

The unused No. C1a is unique and is from a cover not returned to the Post Office by Major Raynham. No other unused examples can exist. The same manuscript overprint has been noted on Nos. 116 and 119, each unique.

No. 70 Surcharged in Black on Block of 25 with Selvage Removed

1919, June 9 ***Perf. 12***
C2 A33 $1 on 15c scarlet 210.00 210.00
Never hinged 350.00
On cover 1,500.
a. Without comma after "Post" 230.00 *275.00*
Never hinged 350.00
On cover 1,500.
b. As "a," without period after "1919" 450.00 450.00
Never hinged 675.00
On cover 1,700.
c. As "a," "A" of "AIR" under "a" of "Trans" 450.00 450.00
Never hinged 675.00
On cover 1,700.

No. C2 was issued for 1919 attempts to cross the Atlantic, and it was used on three flights: Handley-Page from Harbour Grace (canceled June 9 and 14); Vickers Vimy from St. John's, the successful flight of Capt. J. Alcock and Lt. A.W. Brown (June 10-13); and the second attempt of the "Raymor," (July 12) from St. John's. On-cover values shown are for the Vickers-Vimy and Handley-Page flights, with one exception. Handley-Page covers with an "Atlantic Aerial Mail" handstamps are valued with a 20% premium. Additionally, covers from the "Raymor" are valued at three times the values shown.

No. 73 Overprinted in Black on Block of 25 with Selvage Removed

1921, Nov. 7
C3 A36 35c red, 2½mm between "AIR" and "MAIL" 140.00 *190.00*
Never hinged 240.00
On cover 225.00
a. Inverted overprint *6,000.*
Never hinged *9,000.*
b. With period after "1921" 150.00 *200.00*
Never hinged 250.00
On cover 225.00
c. As "b," inverted overprint *6,500.*
Never hinged *9,500.*
d. "1" of "1921" below "f" of "Halifax" 500.00 500.00
Never hinged 700.00
On cover 750.00
e. As "d," inverted overprint *25,000.* —
Never hinged
f. 35c red, 1½mm between "AIR" and "MAIL" 350.00 350.00
Never hinged 500.00
On cover 400.00
g. As "f," inverted overprint *12,500.*
Never hinged *17,500.*
h. As "f," with period after "1921" 300.00 300.00
Never hinged 400.00
On cover 260.00
i. As "h," inverted overprint *10,000.*
Never hinged *15,000.*
j. As "f," "1" of "1921" below "f" of "Halifax" 500.00 500.00
Never hinged 700.00
On cover 550.00
k. As "j," inverted overprint *22,500.* —
Never hinged

No. C3 was printed in sheets of twenty-five, containing varieties of wide and narrow space between "AIR" and "MAIL," date shifted to right, and with and without period after date.

The "Halifax"-overprinted stamp was issued in connection with an intended flight from Botwood to Halifax by Sydney Cotton. 10,000 stamps were overprinted. The mail was closed on Nov. 26, 1921, in St. John's and sent by rail to Botwood. Values are for covers canceled at St. John's from Nov. 17 to Nov. 26.

No. 74 Overprinted in Red on Block of 50 with Selvage

1927, May 21

C4 A37 60c black 45,000. 20,000.
Never hinged 60,000.
On cover 25,000.
a. Short "7" in "1927" 47,500. 20,000.
Never hinged 67,500.
On cover 25,000.

Francesco de Pinedo, returning from a long voyage through the Americas, landed in Trepassey Bay and accepted four pounds of mail to carry to Italy. 300 stamps were overprinted. Approximately 225 covers should have existed, but only about 85 are recorded.

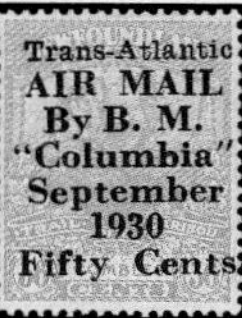

No. 126 Surcharged in Black on Block of 4

1930, Sept. 25 ***Perf. 14***

C5 A67 50c on 36c ol grn 9,500. 9,500.
Never hinged 14,000.
On cover, St. John's Sept. 25, 1930 cancel 14,000.
On cover, Harbour Grace Oct. 9, 1930 cancel 18,000.

Capt. J. Erroll Boyd and Lt. Harry Connor crossed the Atlantic to Croydon Airport (London), arriving Oct. 11, having been delayed in the Scilly Islands due to a shortage of fuel.

300 stamps were surcharged.

Dog Sled and Airplane — AP6

First Transatlantic Mail Airplane and Packet Ship — AP7

Routes of Historic Transatlantic Flights — AP8

1931, Jan. 2 **Engr.** **Unwmk.**

C6 AP6 15c brown 10.00 7.00
Never hinged 15.00
On cover 16.00
a. Horiz. pair, imperf. between 950.00
Never hinged 1,400.
b. Vert. pair, imperf. between 950.00
Never hinged 1,400.
c. Imperf., pair 625.00
Never hinged 1,500.

C7 AP7 50c green 32.50 25.00
Never hinged 55.00
On cover 40.00
a. Horiz. pair, imperf. between 1,350. 825.00
Never hinged 2,000.
b. Vert. pair, imperf. between 1,350.
Never hinged 2,000.
c. Imperf., pair 725.00
Never hinged 1,100.

C8 AP8 $1 blue 70.00 55.00
Never hinged 120.00
On cover 100.00
a. Horiz. pair, imperf. between 1,000.
Never hinged 1,500.
b. Vert. pair, imperf. between 1,000.
Never hinged 1,500.
c. Imperf., pair 725.00
Never hinged 1,100.
Nos. C6-C8 (3) 112.50 87.00
Set, never hinged 190.00

1931 **Wmk. 224 Sideways**

C9 AP6 15c brown 10.00 7.00
Never hinged 15.00
On cover 16.00
a. Horiz. pair, imperf. between 950.00
Never hinged 1,400.
b. Vert. pair, imperf. between 1,100.
Never hinged 1,650.
c. Imperf., pair 600.00
Never hinged 900.00

C10 AP7 50c green 35.00 35.00
Never hinged 65.00
On cover 47.50
a. Horiz. pair, imperf. between 950.00
Never hinged 1,400.
b. Vert. pair, imperf. between 950.00
Never hinged 1,400.
c. Horiz. pair, Imperf. vert. 950.00
Never hinged —

C11 AP8 $1 blue 95.00 90.00
Never hinged 160.00
On cover 120.00
a. Vert. pair, imperf. between 1,000.
Never hinged 1,500.
c. Horiz. pair, imperf. between 1,000.
Never hinged 1,500.
d. Vert. pair, imperf. horiz. 1,000.
Never hinged —
e. Imperf., pair 600.00
Never hinged 900.00
Nos. C9-C11 (3) 140.00 132.00
Set, never hinged 240.00

As the watermark 224 does not show on every stamp in the sheet, pairs are found one with and one without watermark.

For overprint and surcharge see Nos. 211, C12.

No. C11 Surcharged in Red on Block of 4

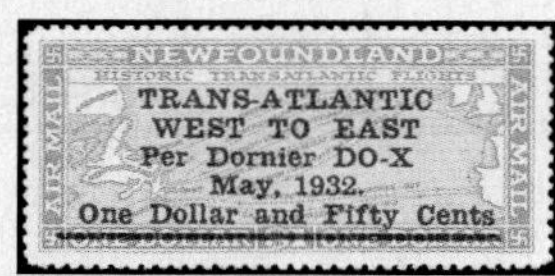

1932, May 19

C12 AP8 $1.50 on $1 blue 275.00 275.00
Never hinged 425.00
On cover (St. John's May 19-20 cancel), to England 400.00
On cover, to other destinations 800.00
a. Inverted surcharge 20,000.
Never hinged 25,000.

The German Dornier DO-X alighted in Trinity Bay waters, not far from St. John's, on May 19, 1932, after a long stay in New York. It took off on May 21 to the Azores Islands, Portugal, England and Germany.

A stamp of this design was produced in the US in 1932 by a private company under contract with Newfoundland authorities. The government canceled the contract and the stamp was not valid for prepayment of postage. Value, $35.

"Put to Flight" — AP9

"Land of Heart's Delight" AP10

"Spotting the Herd" AP11

"News from Home" AP12

"Labrador, The Land of Gold" AP13

Perf. 11½ (10, 60c), 14 (5, 30, 75c)

1933, June 9 **Engr.**

C13 AP9 5c lt brown 10.00 11.00
Never hinged 14.00
On cover 27.50
b. Horiz. pair, imperf. between 1,150.
Never hinged 1,800.
c. Vert. pair, imperf. between 1,150.
Never hinged 1,800.

C14 AP10 10c yellow 17.50 17.50
Never hinged 26.00
On cover 40.00

C15 AP11 30c blue 30.00 30.00
Never hinged 37.50
On cover 47.50

C16 AP12 60c green 65.00 57.50
Never hinged 100.00
On cover 80.00

C17 AP13 75c bister, perf. 14.3 60.00 57.50
Never hinged 92.50
On cover 80.00
b. Horiz. pair, imperf. between 2,500.
Never hinged 3,500.
c. Vert. pair, imperf. between 2,500.
Never hinged 3,500.
d. Perf. 13.8 75.00 75.00
On cover 120.00
Nos. C13-C17 (5) 182.50 173.50
Set, never hinged 270.00

Beware of clever forgeries of Nos. C13b, C13c, C17b and C17c. Certificates of authenticity are highly recommended.

Imperf., Pairs

C13a AP9 5c 275.00
Never hinged 375.00
C14a AP10 10c 200.00
Never hinged 300.00
C15a AP11 30c 725.00
Never hinged 1,000.
C16a AP12 60c 725.00
Never hinged 1,000.
C17a AP13 75c 725.00
Never hinged 1,000.
Set, never hinged 3,150.

No. C17 Surcharged in Black

1933, July 24 ***Perf. 14.3***

C18 AP13 $4.50 on 75c bister 325.00 350.00
Never hinged 500.00
On Balbo flown cover canceled St. John's July 26, 1933 800.00
On Balbo flown cover canceled Shoal Harbour July 27, 1933 1,000.
a. Inverted surcharge 120,000.
Never hinged 150,000.
b. Perf. 13.8 360.00 400.00
On cover 950.00

On return from the Chicago World Fair "Century of Progress" with his "armada" of 24 seaplanes, Gen. Italo Balbo made a stopover in Shoal Harbour and accepted mail to Italy of about 1,150 covers.

No. C18a was not regularly issued.

The $4.50 on No. C14, 10c yellow, is a proof. Value, $62,500.

View of St. John's AP14

1943, June 1 **Unwmk.** ***Perf. 12***

C19 AP14 7c bright ultra .35 .30
Never hinged .45
First day cover 2.75

POSTAGE DUE STAMPS

D1

Perf. 10-10½, Compound

1939-49 **Litho.** **Unwmk.**

J1 D1 1c yellow green, perf. 11 ('49) 4.25 *5.50*
Never hinged 8.25
On cover 400.00
a. Perf. 10-10½ 7.00 5.50
Never hinged 11.00
On cover 350.00

J2 D1 2c vermilion 7.00 5.50
Never hinged 10.50
On cover 350.00
a. Perf. 11x9 ('46) 7.00 5.50
Never hinged 10.50
On cover 550.00

J3 D1 3c ultramarine 7.00 5.50
Never hinged 10.50
On cover 450.00
a. Perf. 11x9 ('49) 7.50 7.50
Never hinged 10.00
On cover 750.00
b. Perf. 9 3,750.
Never hinged 5,000.

J4 D1 4c yel org, perf. 11x9 ('49) 9.50 9.50
Never hinged 16.00
On cover 750.00
a. Perf 10-10½ 15.00 15.00
Never hinged 22.50
On cover 450.00

J5 D1 5c pale brown 15.00 4.25
Never hinged 22.50
On cover 600.00

J6 D1 10c dark violet 7.00 6.50
Never hinged 11.00
On cover 550.00
Nos. J1-J6 (6) 49.75 36.75
Set, never hinged 78.75

1949 **Wmk. 224** ***Perf. 11***

J7 D1 10c dark violet 10.00 *15.00*
Never hinged 17.50
On cover 750.00
"LUE" instead of "DUE" plate flaw 50.00 50.00
Never hinged 75.00
a. Vert. pair, imperf. between 850.00
Never hinged 1,500.

For used examples of Nos. J1-J7 with dated cancels from 1939-49, triple the values shown.

Covers: Cover values are for proper postage due usages on commercial covers prior to April 1, 1949. Note that multiples and combinations are not additive; therefore, for example, a pair of No. J2 on cover is valued at approximately $355 (cover value plus single used value). Values for philatelic covers range from approximately $55 to $100.

POST OFFICE SEAL

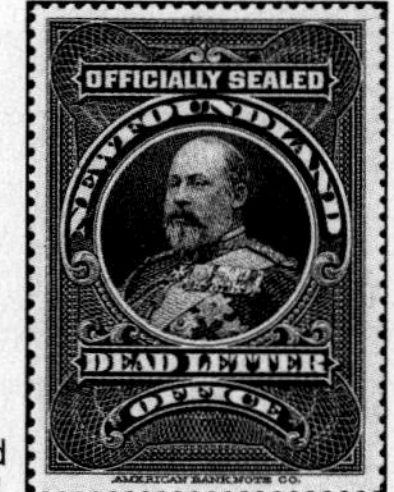
King Edward VII — POS1

1905 **Unwmk.** ***Perf. 12***

OX1 POS1 black, *blue* 750. 500.
Never hinged 1,500.
On cover *2,750.*

No. OX1 used or on cover is valued creased but not torn. Cover value is for presentable cover, with damage to the cover consistent with the application of the seal.

Some examples of No. OX1 show a portion of the papermaker's watermark. Values, unused $1,000, mint never hinged $2,000, used $600.

NOVA SCOTIA

ˌnō-və-ˈskō-shə

LOCATION — Eastern coast of Canada between the Gulf of St. Lawrence and the Atlantic Ocean
GOVT. — British Crown Colony
AREA — 21,428 sq. mi.
POP. — 386,500 (1871)
CAPITAL — Halifax

Nova Scotia joined the Canadian Confederation in 1867 and is now a province of the Dominion. Postage stamps of Canada are used.

12 Pence = 1 Shilling
100 Cents = 1 Dollar (1860)

PRE-STAMP POSTAL MARKINGS

Crowned Circle handstamp type I is pictured in the Crowned Circle Handstamps and Great Britain Used Abroad section.

1845-51
A1 I "Amherst" crowned circle handstamp in red, on cover 1,150.
A2 I "St. Margarets Bay" crowned circle handstamp in red, on cover 11,000.

Values for unused stamps are for examples with original gum as defined in the catalogue introduction except for Nos. 4-7, which are rarely found with any remaining original gum.

Queen Victoria — A1

Crown of Great Britain and Heraldic Flowers of the Empire — A2

Blue Paper

1851-57 Unwmk. Engr. *Imperf.*
1 A1 1p red brown ('53) 2,500. 525.
On cover 2,000.
a. Half used as ½p on cover —
2 A2 3p bright blue 1,750. 250.
On cover 325.
a. Half used as 1½p on cover *3,750.*
b. 3p pale blue ('57) 1,750. 275.
On cover 325.
c. As "b," half used as 1½p on cover *3,750.*
3 A2 3p dark blue 2,250. 300.
On cover 400.
a. Half used as 1½p on cover *4,500.*
4 A2 6p yellow green 5,500. 850.
On cover 1,600.
a. Half used as 3p on cover *4,500.*
5 A2 6p dark green ('57) 11,000. 2,250.
On cover 2,400.
a. Half used as 3p on cover *5,000.*
b. Quarter used as 1½p on cover *47,500.*
6 A2 1sh reddish pur ('57) 25,000. 5,250.
On cover *16,000.*
a. Half used as 6p on cover *30,000.*
b. 1sh deep purple *27,500.* 6,000.
On cover *16,000.*
7 A2 1sh dull violet 25,000. 6,000.
On cover 16,000.
a. Half used as 6p on cover *47,500.*
b. Quarter used as 3p on cover *55,000.*

The 1sh is known with a papermaker's watermark, "T. H. Saunders." Value, $22,500 unused, $7,500 used.

Nos. 2a, 2c, 3a are normally found with a 6p stamp to make up the 7½p rate for a half ounce letter to the United Kingdom.

Reprints are on thin hard white paper. 1p in brown, 3p in blue, 6p dark green, 1sh violet black. Value about $300 per set.

No. 6 was reproduced by the collotype process in a souvenir sheet distributed at the London International Stamp Exhibition 1950.

Queen Victoria — A3

A5

A6

White or Yellowish Paper

1860-63 *Perf. 12*
8 A3 1c black 15.00 7.50
Never hinged 20.00
On cover 200.00
a. White paper 15.00 7.50
Never hinged 20.00
On cover 200.00
b. Half used as ½c on cover *5,750.*
c. Horiz. pair, imperf. vert. 325.00
9 A3 2c lilac 15.00 12.50
Never hinged 20.00
On cover 40.00
a. Yellowish paper 15.00 12.50
Never hinged 20.00
On cover 40.00
b. Half used as 1c on cover *3,250.*
c. 2c grayish purple 17.50 15.00
Never hinged 24.00
10 A3 5c blue 425.00 12.00
Never hinged *1,300.*
On cover 37.50
a. Yellowish paper 425.00 12.00
Never hinged *1,300.*
On cover 37.50
b. Half used as 2½c on cover *5,000.*
c. 5c dark blue 425.00 12.00
Never hinged *1,300.*
11 A5 8½c green 15.00 *22.00*
Never hinged 20.00
On cover *900.00*
a. White paper 15.00 *22.00*
Never hinged 20.00
On cover *900.00*
12 A5 10c vermilion 15.00 12.00
Never hinged 20.00
On cover 80.00
a. Yellowish paper 15.00 12.00
Never hinged 20.00
On cover 80.00
b. Half used as 5c on cover *1,200.*
13 A6 12½c black 42.50 37.50
Never hinged 80.00
On cover 325.00
a. White paper 42.50 37.50
Never hinged 80.00
On cover 325.00
Nos. 8-13 (6) 527.50 103.50
Set, never hinged 1,460.

The stamps of Nova Scotia were replaced by those of Canada.

PRINCE EDWARD ISLAND

ˈprinˌtˌs ˈed-wərd ˈī-lənd

LOCATION — In the Gulf of St. Lawrence, opposite the provinces of New Brunswick and Nova Scotia
GOVT. — British Crown Colony
AREA — 2,184 sq. mi.
POP. — 92,000 (estimated)
CAPITAL — Charlottetown

Originally annexed to Nova Scotia, Prince Edward Island was a separate colony from 1769 to 1873, when it became a part of the Canadian Confederation. Postage stamps of Canada are now used.

12 Pence = 1 Shilling
100 Cents = 1 Dollar (1872)

Values for covers are for examples in fine condition. Very fine covers are extremely scarce and command substantial premiums.

A1

A2

Queen Victoria — A3

1861, Jan. 1 Unwmk. Typo. *Perf. 9*
1 A1 2p dull rose 1,100. 325.
Never hinged *2,500.*
On cover 400.
a. 2p deep rose 1,350. 350.
Never hinged *3,000.*
On cover 400.
b. Rouletted *22,500.*
c. Horiz. pair, imperf. between *6,500.*
d. Diagonal half used as 1p on cover *1,900.*
2 A2 3p blue 2,250. 750.
Never hinged *5,250.*
On cover 1,100.
a. Diagonal half used as 1½p on cover *2,250.*
b. Double impression 4,750.

No. 2b is valued with very small faults.

3 A3 6p yellow green 2,750. 1,200.
Never hinged *6,000.*
On cover 2,800.

A4

A5

White or Yellowish Paper

1862-65 *Perf. 11½-12*
4 A4 1p yellow orange 42.50 35.00
Never hinged 67.50
On cover 350.00
a. 1p brown orange. perf. 11 50.00 35.00
Never hinged 80.00
On cover 375.00
b. Imperf., pair 200.00
Never hinged 300.00
c. Half used as ½p on cover *2,000.*
d. Perf. 11x11½-12 75.00 35.00
Never hinged 150.00
On cover —
5 A1 2p rose 8.50 7.50
Never hinged 12.50
On cover 100.00
a. Yellowish paper 15.00 7.50
Never hinged 21.50
On cover 100.00
b. Imperf., pair 100.00
Never hinged 150.00
c. Horiz. pair, imperf. vert. 275.00
Never hinged 410.00
d. Vert. pair, imperf. horiz. 375.00
Never hinged 560.00
e. Diagonal half used as 1p on cover *1,900.*
f. "TWC" for "TWO" 75.00 60.00
Never hinged 115.00
On cover 175.00
g. Perf. 11x11½-12 8.00 8.00
Never hinged 12.50
On cover 225.00
6 A2 3p blue 16.00 15.00
Never hinged 25.00
On cover 45.00
a. Yellowish paper 32.50 15.00
Never hinged 50.00
On cover 45.00
b. Imperf., pair 150.00
Never hinged 225.00
c. Vert. pair, imperf. horiz. 400.00
Never hinged 650.00
d. Horiz. pair, imperf. vert. 400.00
Never hinged 650.00
e. Diagonal half used as 1½p on cover 250.00
f. Perf. 11x11½-12 45.00 45.00
Never hinged 67.50
On cover 120.00
g. Imperf. pair with gutter btwn. 950.00
h. Imperf. tete-beche pair with gutter btwn. *2,250.*
7 A3 6p yellow green 125.00 95.00
Never hinged 220.00
On cover 475.00
a. 6p blue green 125.00 95.00
Never hinged 220.00
On cover 475.00
c. Diagonal half used as 3p on cover *3,000.*
d. Perf. 11x11½-12 115.00 100.00
Never hinged 225.00
On cover —
8 A5 9p violet 95.00 80.00
Never hinged 140.00
On cover 600.00
a. Imperf., pair 375.00
Never hinged 625.00
b. Horiz. pair, imperf. vert. 450.00
Never hinged 700.00
c. Diagonal half used as 4½p on cover *2,250.*
d. Perf. 11 95.00 80.00

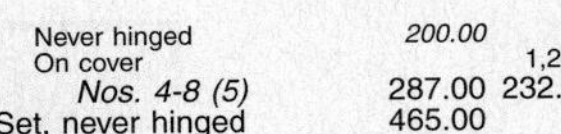
Never hinged *200.00*
On cover 1,200.
Nos. 4-8 (5) 287.00 232.50
Set, never hinged 465.00

Queen Victoria — A6

1868
9 A6 4p black 9.00 19.00
Never hinged 11.00
On cover 200.00
a. Yellowish paper 15.00 20.00
Never hinged 21.00
On cover 200.00
b. Horiz. pair, imperf. vert. 190.00
Never hinged 290.00
c. Diagonal half used as 2p on cover *2,250.*
d. Imperf., pair 140.00
Never hinged 210.00
e. Horiz. pair, imperf. between 160.00
Never hinged 240.00
f. Perf. 11x11½-12 45.00 45.00
Never hinged 75.00
On cover 325.00
g. Horiz. strip of 3, imperf. btwn. *1,100.*

Queen Victoria — A7

1870, June 1 Engr. *Perf. 12*
10 A7 4½p brown 90.00 75.00
Never hinged 200.00
On cover *2,400.*
Without gum 55.00
Block of 4 with horiz. gutter btwn. 550.00
Never hinged *1,100.*
Without gum 360.00

A8

A9

A10

A11

A12

A13

1872, Jan. 1 Typo. *Perf. 12, 12½*
11 A8 1c brown orange 7.00 *7.50*
Never hinged 10.50
On cover 160.00
a. Imperf., pair 240.00
Never hinged 450.00
b. Perf. 12½ 9.00 *9.00*
Never hinged 16.00
On cover 160.00
c. 1c orange, perf. 12x12½ 65.00 *15.00*
Never hinged 110.00
On cover 160.00
12 A9 2c ultra 35.00 *42.50*
Never hinged 47.50
On cover 800.00
a. Imperf., pair 450.00
Never hinged 1,050.
b. Diagonal half used as 1c on cover —
13 A10 3c rose 30.00 22.50
Never hinged 40.00
On cover 60.00
a. Imperf., pair 400.00
Never hinged 725.00
b. Diagonal half used as 1½c on cover —
c. Horiz. or vert. pair, imperf. between 275.00
Never hinged 475.00
d. Perf. 12½ 27.50 22.50
Never hinged 47.50
On cover 120.00
e. Perf. 12x12½ 75.00 24.00
Never hinged 125.00
On cover 50.00

14	A11 4c green	11.50	*16.00*
	Never hinged	16.50	
	On cover		225.00
a.	Imperf., pair	400.00	
	Never hinged	650.00	
b.	Diagonal half used as 2c on cover		2,000.
15	A12 6c black	7.50	*13.00*
	Never hinged	12.00	
	On cover		200.00
a.	Horiz. pair, imperf. btwn.	250.00	
	Never hinged	475.00	
b.	Half used as 3c on cover		*900.00*
c.	Perf. 12½	80.00	*175.00*
	Never hinged	160.00	
	On cover		*375.00*
16	A13 12c violet	7.50	*30.00*
	Never hinged	12.00	
	On cover		*2,000.*
a.	Imperf., pair	425.00	
	Never hinged	650.00	
b.	Half used as 6c on cover		—
	Nos. 11-16 (6)	98.50	*131.50*
	Set, never hinged	138.50	

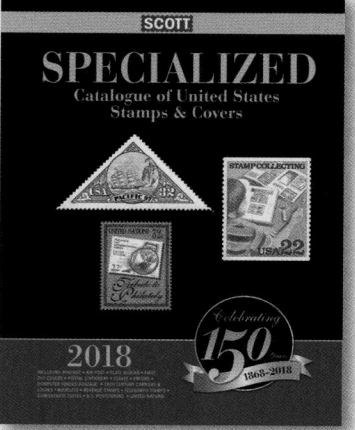

CANADA

'ka-nə-də

LOCATION — Northern part of North American continent, except for Alaska
GOVT. — Self-governing dominion in the British Commonwealth of Nations
AREA — 3,851,809 sq. mi.
POP. — 24,907,100 (est. 1983)
CAPITAL — Ottawa

Included in the dominion are British Columbia, Vancouver Island, Prince Edward Island, Nova Scotia, New Brunswick and Newfoundland, all of which formerly issued stamps.

12 Pence = 1 Shilling
100 Cents = 1 Dollar (1859)

Catalogue values for unused stamps in this country are for Never Hinged items, beginning with Scott 268 in the regular postage section, Scott C9 in the air post section, Scott CE3 in the air post special delivery section, Scott CO1 in the air post official section, Scott E11 in the special delivery section, Scott EO1 in the special delivery official section, Scott J15 in the postage due section, and Scott O1 in the official section.

Values for unused stamps of Nos. 1-33 are for examples with partial original gum. Stamps without gum often trade at prices very close to those of stamps with partial gum. Examples with full original gum and lightly hinged are extremely scarce and generally sell for substantially more than the values listed.

Very fine examples of the perforated issues between Nos. 11-20 will have perforations touching the design or frameline on at least one side due to the narrow spacing of the stamps on the plates. Stamps with perfs clear of the designs on all four sides are extremely scarce and will command much higher prices.

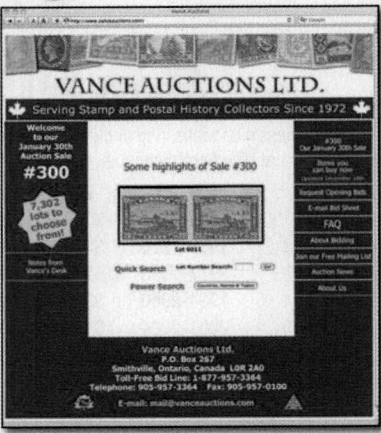

PRE-STAMP POSTAL MARKINGS

Crown Circle Handstamp

Crowned Circle handstamp type II is pictured in the Crowned Circle Handstamps and Great Britain Used Abroad section.

1842-51

A1 II "Quebec" crowned circle handstamp in red, on cover 200.

Crown Circle handstamps exist also from Amherst, Nova Scotia, and St. Margaret's Bay, Nova Scotia, and St. John's, Newfoundland. These are listed under Nova Scotia and Newfoundland respectively.

POSTMASTER PROVISIONAL
New Carlisle, Gaspé

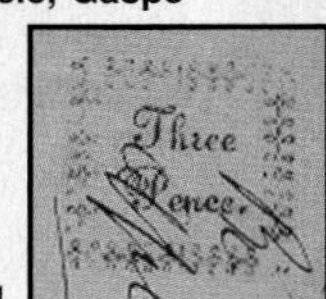

E1

ENVELOPE

1851, Apr. **Typeset**

1X1 E1 3p black, entire —

Only one example of No. 1X1 is recorded, an entire postmarked April 7, 1851, to Toronto.

Province of Canada

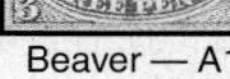

Beaver — A1

Prince Albert — A2

Queen Victoria — A3

1851 Unwmk. Engr. *Imperf.*
Laid Paper

1 A1 3p red *40,000.* 1,000.
No gum *30,000.*
On cover *1,900.*
Double transfer (pos. 47, pane A) 2,400.
On cover *3,250.*
a. 3p orange vermilion 40,000. 1,000.
No gum *30,000.*
On cover *1,900.*
2 A2 6p slate violet *40,000.* 1,650.
No gum *30,000.*
On cover *3,100.*
a. Diagonal half used as 3p on cover *32,500.*
b. 6p grayish purple *40,000.* 1,750.
No gum *30,000.*
On cover *3,100.*
3 A3 12p black *175,000.* *135,000.*
No gum *87,500.*
On cover *300,000.*

On some stamps the laid lines of Nos. 1-3 are practically invisible.

No. 1 double transfer position 47 shows extensive doubling of "EE PEN," above and below "POS," in and below "ANADA THR" and in all four numerals. Pane A is the upper pane.

1852-57 **Wove Paper**

4 A1 3p red 1,500. 225.
No gum 1,250.
On cover 460.
Double transfer (pos. 47, pane A) *4,250.* 850.
No gum *2,750.*
On cover *1,500.*
a. 3p brown red ('53) 1,700. 250.
No gum 1,550.
On cover 500.
b. Diagonal half used as 1½p on cover *32,500.*
c. Ribbed paper 4,500. 575.
No gum 4,000.
On cover 750.00
d. Thin paper 1,600. 225.
No gum 1,450.
On cover 460.

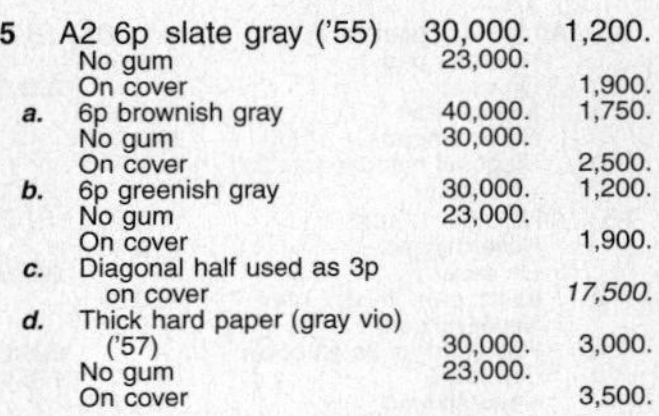

5 A2 6p slate gray ('55) 30,000. 1,200.
No gum 23,000.
On cover 1,900.
a. 6p brownish gray 40,000. 1,750.
No gum 30,000.
On cover 2,500.
b. 6p greenish gray 30,000. 1,200.
No gum 23,000.
On cover 1,900.
c. Diagonal half used as 3p on cover *17,500.*
d. Thick hard paper (gray vio) ('57) 30,000. 3,000.
No gum 23,000.
On cover 3,500.

See note after No. 3 for characteristics of double transfer pos. 47 on No. 4. Pos. 47 is considered the most prominent double transfer, but many others exist. The double transfers exist on all shades and papers; values are for the most common shade and paper.

Most authorities believe the 12p black does not exist on wove paper.

Jacques Cartier — A4

1855

7 A4 10p blue 12,000. 1,650.
No gum 9,250.
On cover 3,250.
a. Thick paper 13,000. 2,250.
No gum 10,000.
On cover 3,500.

Queen Victoria
A5 A6

1857

8 A5 ½p rose 1,100. 700.
No gum 875.
On cover 950.00
On cover, single franking 1,250.
On newspaper or circular 1,000.
a. Horizontally ribbed paper 10,000. 2,500.
No gum 8,500.
On cover 2,750.
b. Vertically ribbed paper 10,000. 3,750.
No gum 8,600.
On cover 4,000.
9 A6 7½p green 10,000. 3,500.
No gum 7,000.
On cover 6,000.
a. 7½p deep green 14,000. 5,000.
No gum 9,000.
On cover 6,250.

Very Thick Soft Wove Paper

10 A2 6p reddish pur 32,500. 7,500.
No gum 20,000.
On cover 9,000.
a. Half used as 3p on cover *25,000.*

1858-59 Wove Paper *Perf. 12*

11 A5 ½p rose 4,250. 1,900.
No gum 3,000.
On cover 2,300.
On cover, single franking 2,500.
On circular, single franking 2,100.
On newspaper, single franking 2,500.
12 A1 3p red 17,500. 1,350.
No gum 12,500.
On cover 1,500.
Double transfer (pos. 47, pane A) *1,250.*
On cover *2,250.*
13 A2 6p brown vio ('59) 22,500. 7,500.
No gum 19,000.
On cover 8,750.
a. 6p gray violet 22,500. 7,500.
No gum 19,000.
On cover 8,750.
b. Diagonal half used as 3p on cover *17,500.*

Nos. 11-13 values are for examples with perfs touching the design.

A7

A8

A9

A10

A11

1859

No.	Type	Description	Unused	Used
14	A7	1c rose	425.00	90.00
		No gum	325.00	
		On cover		180.00
		On cover, single franking		190.00
		On circular		140.00
		On newspaper		240.00
a.		Imperf., pair	5,500.	
b.		1c deep rose	575.00	150.00
		No gum	350.00	
		On cover		350.00
		On cover, single franking		390.00
		On circular		225.00
		On newspaper		475.00
15	A8	5c ver	575.00	37.50
		No gum	425.00	
		On cover		47.50
		Major re-entry (pos. 28)	*2,100.*	*800.00*
		No gum	*1,750.*	
		On cover		*1,200.*
a.		Imperf., pair	15,000.	—
b.		Diagonal half used as 2½c on cover		*6,000.*
c.		5c brick red	625.00	42.50
		No gum	410.00	
		On cover		60.00
16	A9	10c black brn, perf. 11¾	25,000.	6,500.
		No gum	20,000.	
		On cover		*7,000.*
a.		Half used as 5c on cover		*9,000.*
17	A9	10c red lilac	1,400.	175.00
		No gum	1,100.	
		On cover		240.00
a.		10c violet	2,000.	160.00
		No gum	1,600.	
		On cover		225.00
b.		10c brown	1,400.	140.00
		No gum	1,100.	
		On cover		225.00
c.		Imperf., pair	11,000.	
d.		Diagonal half used as 5c on cover		*5,500.*
e.		10c deep red purple	3,250.	1,100.
		No gum	2,100.	
		On cover		1,250.
18	A10	12½c yel green	900.00	130.00
		No gum	750.00	
		On cover		300.00
a.		12½c blue green	1,100.	125.00
		No gum	900.00	
		On cover		375.00
b.		Imperf., pair	5,750.	
19	A11	17c blue	1,250.	200.00
		No gum	950.00	
		On cover		475.00
a.		17c slate blue	1,300.	225.00
		No gum	1,000.	
		On cover		475.00
b.		Imperf., pair	5,250.	

Values for Nos. 14-19 are for examples with perfs touching the design. Imperfs. are without gum.

Re-entries of the 5c are numerous. Many of them are slight and have only small premium value. The major re-entry has many lines of the design double, especially the outlines of the ovals and frame at left.

Nos. 14b, 15c, 16, 17b, 18a and 19 represent the 1st printings of the stamps. No. 17e is from a 2nd printing. All of these gauge closer to perf. 11¾, and this will aid in their proper identification.

No. 15b was used with a 10c for a 12½c rate.

No. 16 should be accompanied by a certificate of authenticity issued by a recognized expertizing authority. Less expensive dark brown shades of the 10c often are offered as the rare black brown.

A12

1864

No.	Type	Description	Unused	Used
20	A12	2c rose	650.00	300.00
		No gum	375.00	
		On cover, single franking		1,600.
		On circular, single franking		1,450.
		On wrapper, single franking		2,700.
a.		2c deep claret rose	750.00	350.00
		No gum	500.00	
		On cover, single franking		1,750.
		On circular, single franking		1,600.
		On wrapper, single franking		2,750.
b.		Imperf., pair	3,500.	

Imperfs. are without gum.

Values are for examples with perfs touching the design.

On cover value is for a single franking on cover, circular or newspaper.

Dominion of Canada

Queen Victoria
A13 A14

A15

A16

A17

A18

A19

A20

1868-76 ***Perf. 12, 11½x12 (5c)***

No.	Type	Description	Unused	Used
21	A13	½c black	110.00	80.00
		No gum	80.00	
		On cover		1,100.
		On cover, single franking		2,250.
a.		Perf. 11½x12 ('73)	150.00	90.00
		No gum	92.50	
		On cover		1,250.
		On cover, single franking		2,500.
b.		Watermarked	*22,500.*	*11,000.*
		No gum	*20,000.*	
c.		Thin paper	150.00	80.00
		No gum	100.00	
		On cover		1,250.
		On cover, single franking		2,500.
22	A14	1c brn red	800.00	160.00
		No gum	550.00	
		On cover		200.00
a.		Watermarked	*3,250.*	500.00
		No gum	*2,150.*	
		On cover		—
b.		Thin paper	950.00	140.00
		No gum	625.00	
		On cover		210.00
23	A14	1c yell org	1,750.	225.00
		No gum	1,400.	
		On cover		240.00
a.		1c deep orange	2,500.	260.00
		No gum	1,900.	
		On cover		275.00
b.		1c yellow	2,000.	260.00
		No gum	1,500.	
		On cover		325.00
24	A15	2c green	1,000.	100.00
		No gum	800.00	
		On cover		275.00
a.		Watermarked	3,250.	425.00
		No gum	2,500.	
		On cover		—
b.		Thin paper	950.00	110.00
		No gum	800.00	
		On cover		320.00
c.		Diagonal half used as 1c on cover		*4,000.*
25	A16	3c red	2,250.	40.00
		No gum	1,900.	
		On cover		50.00
a.		Watermarked	5,250.	475.00
		No gum	4,250.	
		On cover		—
b.		Thin paper	2,500.	55.00
		No gum	2,100.	
		On cover		60.00
26	A17	5c ol grn ('75)	2,000.	225.00
		No gum	1,600.	
		On cover		400.00
a.		Perf. 12	*8,000.*	1,000.
		No gum	*7,250.*	
		On cover		1,300.
b.		Imperf., pair	*32,500.*	

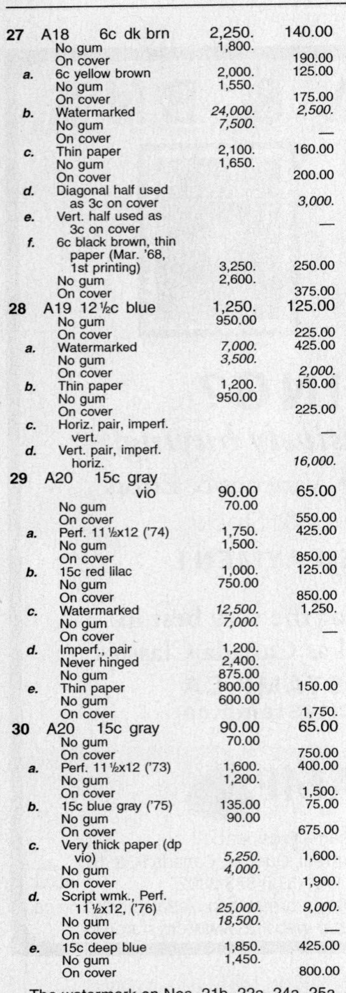

27 A18 6c dk brn 2,250. 140.00
No gum 1,800.
On cover 190.00
a. 6c yellow brown 2,000. 125.00
No gum 1,550.
On cover 175.00
b. Watermarked *24,000.* *2,500.*
No gum *7,500.*
On cover —
c. Thin paper 2,100. 160.00
No gum 1,650.
On cover 200.00
d. Diagonal half used as 3c on cover *3,000.*
e. Vert. half used as 3c on cover —
f. 6c black brown, thin paper (Mar. '68, 1st printing) 3,250. 250.00
No gum 2,600.
On cover 375.00

28 A19 12½c blue 1,250. 125.00
No gum 950.00
On cover 225.00
a. Watermarked *7,000.* 425.00
No gum *3,500.*
On cover *2,000.*
b. Thin paper 1,200. 150.00
No gum 950.00
On cover 225.00
c. Horiz. pair, imperf. vert. —
d. Vert. pair, imperf. horiz. *16,000.*

29 A20 15c gray vio 90.00 65.00
No gum 70.00
On cover 550.00
a. Perf. 11½x12 ('74) 1,750. 425.00
No gum 1,500.
On cover 850.00
b. 15c red lilac 1,000. 125.00
No gum 750.00
On cover 850.00
c. Watermarked *12,500.* 1,250.
No gum *7,000.*
On cover —
d. Imperf., pair 1,200.
Never hinged 2,400.
No gum 875.00
e. Thin paper 800.00 150.00
No gum 600.00
On cover 1,750.

30 A20 15c gray 90.00 65.00
No gum 70.00
On cover 750.00
a. Perf. 11½x12 ('73) 1,600. 400.00
No gum 1,200.
On cover 1,500.
b. 15c blue gray ('75) 135.00 75.00
No gum 90.00
On cover 675.00
c. Very thick paper (dp vio) *5,250.* 1,600.
No gum *4,000.*
On cover 1,900.
d. Script wmk., Perf. 11½x12, ('76) *25,000.* *9,000.*
No gum *18,500.*
On cover —
e. 15c deep blue 1,850. 425.00
No gum 1,450.
On cover 800.00

The watermark on Nos. 21b, 22a, 24a, 25a, 27b, 28a and 29c consists of double-lined letters reading: "E. & G. BOTHWELL CLUTHA MILLS." The script watermark on No. 30d reads in full: "Alexr. Pirie & Sons." Values for all these watermarked stamps are for fine examples. Very fine examples are rare, seldom traded, and generally command premiums of about 100% over the values listed.

No. 21b unused and used, and Nos. 26a and 26b unused are valued in the grade of fine. No. 26b is a unique pair.

The existence of No. 28c has been questioned.

Nos. 21-21c on cover values are for single frankings on cover or circular.

1868 Laid Paper

31 A14 1c brown red *40,000.* *9,000.*
No gum *20,000.*
On cover *11,000.*
32 A15 2c green *250,000.*
33 A16 3c bright red *25,000.* 2,250.
No gum *17,500.*
On cover 3,000.

Only three examples of No. 32 are recorded, none being very fine.

Montreal and Ottawa Printings

A21

A22

A23

A24

A25

A26

A27

1870-89 Wove Paper *Perf. 12*

34 A21 ½c black ('82) 22.50 10.00
Never hinged 45.00
On cover 250.00
On newspaper 275.00
On unaddressed circular 325.00
Pair with vertical gutter between 300.00 —
Never hinged 550.00
On cover *1,500.*
a. Imperf., pair 650.00
Never hinged *1,100.*
b. Horiz. pair, imperf. between 1,000.
Never hinged *1,750.*

35 A22 1c yellow 50.00 1.25
Never hinged 100.00
On cover 8.00
a. 1c orange ('70) 300.00 11.00
Never hinged 600.00
On cover 12.00
b. Imperf., pair 475.00
Never hinged 750.00
c. Diagonal half used as ½c on circular 4,500.

36 A23 2c green ('72) 85.00 2.50
Never hinged 170.00
On cover 12.00
a. Imperf., pair 725.00
Never hinged *1,250.*
b. Diagonal half used as 1c on cover 2,100.
c. Vertical half used as 1c on cover 2,100.
d. 2c blue green ('89) 110.00 5.00
Never hinged 220.00
On cover 12.00
f. Double impression *6,000.* —

37 A24 3c org red ('73) 175.00 1.50
Never hinged 350.00
On cover 8.00
a. 3c rose ('71) 625.00 17.50
Never hinged *1,300.*
On cover 19.00
b. 3c copper red ('70) 1,750. 65.00
Never hinged *3,750.*
On cover 70.00
c. 3c dull red ('72) 175.00 3.25
Never hinged 350.00
On cover 10.00

38 A25 5c sl green ('76) 800.00 27.50
Never hinged *1,600.*
On cover 62.50

39 A26 6c yel brn ('72) 600.00 27.50
Never hinged *1,200.*
On cover 40.00
a. Diagonal half used as 3c on cover 4,500.
c. Imperf., pair 3,500.
d. 6c brown ('75) 725.00 22.50
Never hinged *1,450.*
On cover 40.00

40 A27 10c dull rose lil ('77) 1,600. 90.00
Never hinged *3,000.*
On cover 450.00
a. 10c magenta ('80) 1,600. 90.00
Never hinged *3,000.*
On cover 450.00
b. 10c deep lilac rose 1,600. 90.00
Never hinged *3,000.*
On cover 450.00

No. 34 on cover value is for single franking paying the circular rate.

No. 34a was made with and without gum; values the same.

Examples of Nos. 36b and 36c postmarked "Halifax" are a private speculation.

No. 39c is unique and in the form of a strip of three.

1870 *Perf. 12½*

37d A24 3c copper red (Ottawa) 11,000. 1,500.
Never hinged *22,500.*
On cover 1,700.

1873-79 *Perf. 11½x12*

35d A22 1c orange 500.00 20.00
Never hinged 1,000.
On cover 60.00
36e A23 2c green 750.00 25.00
Never hinged 1,500.
On cover 27.50
37e A24 3c red 450.00 12.50
Never hinged 900.00
On cover 13.00
38a A25 5c slate green 1,250. 52.50
Never hinged *2,500.*
On cover 60.00
39b A26 6c yellow brown 1,000. 65.00
Never hinged *2,000.*
On cover 60.00
40c A27 10c dull rose lilac 1,700. 260.00
Never hinged *3,000.*
On cover 500.00
40d A27 10c magenta 1,700. 240.00
Never hinged *3,000.*
On cover 500.00
40e A27 10c pale milky rose lilac ('74) 3,000. 700.00
Never hinged *5,500.*
On cover 850.00

The gum on Nos. 35d-40c is always dull and usually blotchy or streaky. It is distinct from the earlier clear, smooth gum and from the bright shiny gums of the later periods.

Nos. 38 and 40 were printed at Montreal. Printings of Nos. 34 to 37, and 39 were made at Ottawa or Montreal and can be separated only by differences in paper and gum.

Ottawa Printing

A28

A29

1888-97 *Perf. 12*

41 A24 3c brt vermilion 65.00 .80
Never hinged 135.00
On cover 8.00
a. 3c rose carmine 525.00 15.00
Never hinged *1,150.*
On cover 20.00

42 A25 5c gray 230.00 5.00
Never hinged 500.00
On cover 35.00

43 A26 6c red brown 240.00 12.50
Never hinged 525.00
On cover 40.00
a. 6c chocolate ('90) 400.00 32.50
Never hinged 850.00
On cover 65.00
c. 5c on 6c re-entry *4,000.* *3,750.*

44 A28 8c viol blk ('93) 260.00 7.00
Never hinged 550.00
On cover 25.00
a. 8c blue gray 425.00 8.50
Never hinged 900.00
On cover 27.50
b. 8c slate 300.00 7.00
Never hinged 650.00
On cover 25.00
c. 8c gray 300.00 7.00
Never hinged 650.00
On cover 25.00

45 A27 10c brn red ('97) 725.00 65.00
Never hinged 1,400.
On cover 225.00
a. 10c dull rose 625.00 55.00
Never hinged 1,200.
On cover 225.00
b. 10c pink 725.00 65.00
Never hinged 1,400.
On cover 240.00

46 A29 20c ver ('93) 425.00 125.00
Never hinged 1,000.
On cover 1,000.

47 A29 50c dp blue ('93) 425.00 85.00
Never hinged 1,000.
On cover 1,000.

Stamps of the 1870-93 issues are found on paper varying from very thin to thick, also occasionally on paper showing a distinctly ribbed surface.

The gum on Nos. 41-47 appears bright and shiny, often with a yellowish tint.

Values for Nos. 46-47 on cover are for single frankings paying the correct rate.

No. 43c unused is valued in the grade of fine.

Imperf., Pairs

41b A24 3c 500.
Never hinged 850.
42a A25 5c 750.
Never hinged 1,300.
43b A26 6c 625.
Never hinged 1,050.
44d A28 8c 850.
Never hinged 1,500.
45c A27 10c 625.
Never hinged 1,050.
46a A29 20c 1,500.
Never hinged *2,750.*
47a A29 50c 1,500.
Never hinged *2,750.*

Nos. 41b-45c made with and without gum. Without gum sell for the same as the unused hinged price.

The value for No. 44d is for the pair in the blue gray shade. The imperf. pair also is known in the violet black shade without gum. Value thus, $1,000.

Imperforates and Part-Perforates

From 1859 through 1943 (Nos. 14a/262a), imperforate stamps were printed. The earliest imperforates through perhaps 1917 most likely were from imprimatur sheets (i.e. the first sheets from the approved plates, normally kept in government files) or proof sheets on stamp paper that once were in the post office archives. The imperforates from approximately 1927 to 1943 (often made both with and without gum) were specially created and traded for classic stamps needed for the post office museum, given as gifts to governmental or other dignitaries, or sold or given to favored persons.

The only imperforates from this entire period that were issued to the public were Nos. 90A and 136-138.

Similarly, almost all stamps that are known part-perforate (i.e., horizontal pairs imperforate vertically and vertical pairs imperforate horizontally) were specially made for trading purposes or as presentation items to be given to favored persons. Part-perforate error stamps that are believed to have been actually issued to the public are listed in this catalogue.

See the similar imperforates in the air post, Nos. CE1a and CE2a, special delivery, No. F2c (but not No. F1c which was an issued error), postage dues, and Nos. MR4b and MR4c.

Jubilee Issue

Queen Victoria, "1837" and "1897" — A30

1897, June 19 Unwmk. *Perf. 12*

50 A30 ½c black 110.00 110.00
Never hinged 275.00
On cover 500.00
51 A30 1c orange 30.00 8.00
Never hinged 75.00
On cover 18.00
52 A30 2c green 37.50 15.00
Never hinged 92.50
On cover 25.00
53 A30 3c bright rose 30.00 2.50
Never hinged 75.00
On cover 7.50
54 A30 5c deep blue 70.00 45.00
Never hinged 180.00
On cover 100.00
55 A30 6c yell brn 230.00 175.00
Never hinged 575.00
On cover 325.00
56 A30 8c dark violet 130.00 70.00
Never hinged 325.00
On cover 200.00
57 A30 10c brown violet 175.00 120.00
Never hinged 425.00
On cover 300.00
58 A30 15c steel blue 275.00 190.00
Never hinged 675.00
On cover 350.00
59 A30 20c vermilion 275.00 190.00
Never hinged 650.00
On cover 450.00
60 A30 50c ultra 375.00 190.00
Never hinged 775.00
On cover 450.00
61 A30 $1 lake 1,000. 700.00
Never hinged 2,900.
On cover 1,750.
62 A30 $2 dk purple 1,400. 600.00
Never hinged 4,000.
On cover 1,200.
63 A30 $3 yel bister 1,400. 1,100.
Never hinged 4,000.
On cover 2,200.
64 A30 $4 purple 1,400. 1,100.
Never hinged 4,000.
On cover 2,200.
65 A30 $5 olive green 1,400. 1,100.
Never hinged 4,000.
On cover 2,000.
Nos. 50-60 (11) 1,738. 1,116.
Set, never hinged 4,097.

60th year of Queen Victoria's reign.

Roller and smudged cancels on Nos. 61-65 sell for less.

Covers: Value for No. 50 is for a single franking paying the correct rate. In combination with other postage it is worth much less. Values for Nos. 61-65 are for overfranked items, usually philatelic.

A31

1897-98

66 A31 ½c black 15.00 8.50
Never hinged 37.50
On cover 240.00
67 A31 1c blue green 45.00 2.00
Never hinged 115.00
On cover 3.50
68 A31 2c purple 50.00 2.25
Never hinged 125.00
On cover 6.50
69 A31 3c car ('98) 80.00 2.00
Never hinged 200.00
On cover 4.00
70 A31 5c dk bl, *bluish* 150.00 10.00
Never hinged 375.00
On cover 47.50
71 A31 6c brown 140.00 45.00
Never hinged 350.00
On cover 550.00
72 A31 8c orange 325.00 21.00
Never hinged 800.00
On cover 55.00
73 A31 10c brn vio ('98) 600.00 100.00
Never hinged 1,500.
On cover 800.00
Nos. 66-73 (8) 1,405. 190.75
Set, never hinged 3,503.

Values for Nos. 66, 71 and 73 on cover are for single frankings paying correct rates.
For surcharge see No. 87.

Imperf., Pairs

66a A31 ½c 500.
Never hinged 950.
67a A31 1c 400.
Never hinged 750.
68a A31 2c 500.
Never hinged 950.
69a A31 3c 800.
Never hinged 1,450.
70a A31 5c 500.
Never hinged 800.
71a A31 6c 800.
Never hinged 1,450.
72a A31 8c 700.
Never hinged 1,300.
73a A31 10c 700.
Never hinged 1,300.

Nos. 66a, 67a, 68a and 70a made with and without gum. Specialists can distinguish printings made with and without gum by shade and paper quality. Without gum sell for about 80% of the unused hinged price.

A32

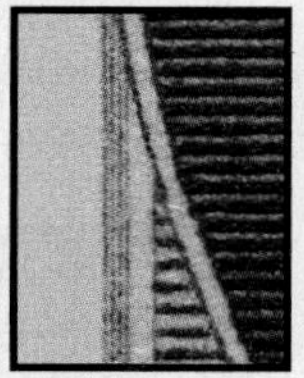
Type I Type II

TWO CENTS:
Type I — Frame of four very thin lines.
Type II — Frame of a thick line between two thin ones.

1898-1902

74 A32 ½c black 12.50 2.75
Never hinged 25.00
On cover *250.00*
75 A32 1c gray green 50.00 .75
Never hinged 100.00
On cover 2.00
76 A32 2c purple (I) 40.00 .75
Never hinged 80.00
On cover 2.00
a. Thick paper ('99) 175.00 12.00
Never hinged 350.00
On cover 24.00
77 A32 2c car (I) ('99) 55.00 .75
Never hinged 110.00
On cover 2.00
a. 2c carmine (II) ('99) 70.00 .60
Never hinged 140.00
On cover 2.50
b. Booklet pane of 6 (II) ('00) 1,600. —
Never hinged 3,000.
Complete booklet, 2 #77b *3,250.*
78 A32 3c carmine 90.00 1.10
Never hinged 180.00
On cover 1.75
79 A32 5c blue, *bluish* ('99) 220.00 3.00
Never hinged 440.00
On cover 47.50
b. Whiter paper ('99) 260.00 3.25
Never hinged 625.00
On cover 47.50
80 A32 6c brown 200.00 57.50
Never hinged 400.00
On cover 550.00
81 A32 7c ol yel ('02) 150.00 22.50
Never hinged 300.00
On cover 67.50
82 A32 8c orange 375.00 27.50
Never hinged 750.00
On cover 80.00
83 A32 10c brown vio 425.00 30.00
Never hinged 850.00
On cover 550.00
84 A32 20c ol grn ('00) 650.00 110.00
Never hinged 1,300.
On cover 1,100.
Nos. 74-84 (11) 2,268. 256.60
Set, never hinged 4,515.

Values for Nos. 74, 80, 83-84 on cover are for single frankings paying correct rates.
For surcharges see Nos. 88-88C.

Imperf., Pairs

74a A32 ½c 500.
Never hinged 800.
75a A32 1c 1,250.
Never hinged 2,250.
77c A32 2c (I) 475.
Never hinged 775.
77d A32 2c (II) *1,250.*
e. As No. 77b, imperf., 2 panes tete beche ('00) *15,000.*
79a A32 5c 1,200.
Never hinged 1,900.
80a A32 6c 1,200.
Never hinged 1,900.
81a A32 7c 600.
82a A32 8c 1,200.
Never hinged 2,000.
83a A32 10c 1,200.
Never hinged 2,000.
84a A32 20c 5,500.

Nos. 77d, 77e, 81a and 84a were made only without gum. No. 80a was made only with gum. Others either with or without gum and of these those without gum sell for about ⅔ of the values shown for unused hinged. Specialists can distinguish printings made with and without gum by shade and paper quality.

Values for complete booklets from No. 77b to No. 219a are for booklets with uncreases and very fine covers containing never-hinged panes with normal centering, which is fine. Booklets with very fine panes will sell for more. Values are for the most common booklet covers; other cover types exist for some booklets from No. 104a to 167a, and these may sell for more.

Imperial Penny Postage Issue

Map of British Empire on Mercator Projection
A33

No. 86

1898, Dec. 7 **Engr. & Typo.**

85 A33 2c black, lav & car 45.00 9.00
Never hinged 100.00
On cover 25.00
a. Imperf., pair 550.00
86 A33 2c black, bl & car 45.00 9.00
Never hinged 100.00
On cover 25.00
a. Imperf., pair 550.00
b. 2c black, deep bl & car 50.00 11.50
Never hinged 100.00
On cover 27.50

Imperfs. are without gum, and known in both the blue and deep blue shades of No. 86 and 86b; values the same.

Nos. 69 and 78 Surcharged in Black

1899, July

87 A31 2c on 3c carmine 17.50 7.50
Never hinged 45.00
On cover 11.00
88 A32 2c on 3c carmine 32.50 6.00
Never hinged 82.50
On cover 10.50

No. 78 Surcharged in Blue or Violet

A32a A32b

1899, Jan. 5

No.	Design	Description	Unused	Used
88B	A32a	1(c) on ⅓ of 3c, on cover (Bl)		7,500.
88C	A32b	2(c) on ⅔ of 3c, on cover (V)		7,000.

Nos. 88B-88C were prepared and used on Jan. 5 only at Port Hood, Nova Scotia, without official authorization.

Nos. 88B-88C must be accompanied by certificates from recognized expertizing organizations. Covers reported to date were backdated and never saw postal use.

King Edward VII — A34

Type I

Type II

Two types of 2c carmine.

Type I — Has breaks in the upper left shading lines above "DA" in Canada.

Type II — Has solid lines, no breaks.

Engr.

1903-08

No.	Design	Description	Unused	Used
89	A34	1c green	45.00	.40
		Never hinged	115.00	
		On cover		1.75
b.		1c deep green	50.00	.40
		Never hinged	125.00	
		On cover		1.75
c.		1c gray green	50.00	.75
		Never hinged	125.00	
		On cover		1.75
d.		1c blue green	50.00	.75
		Never hinged	125.00	
		On cover		1.75
e.		1c yellow green	90.00	.50
		Never hinged	225.00	
		On cover		1.75
90	A34	2c carmine, type II	55.00	.40
		Never hinged	135.00	
		On cover		1.75
		"Hairlines" plate cracks	100.00	7.50
		Never hinged	200.00	
		On cover		10.00
b.		Booklet pane of 6	1,600.	*1,250.*
		Never hinged	*2,750.*	
		Complete booklet, 2 #90b	*3,500.*	
e.		2c carmine, type I	160.00	2.00
		Never hinged	400.00	
f.		Vert. pair, imperf. btwn and at either top or bottom	*5,000.*	
91	A34	5c blue, *blue*	250.00	5.75
		Never hinged	625.00	
		On cover		30.00
b.		Whiter paper	220.00	7.50
		Never hinged	440.00	
		On cover		42.50
92	A34	7c olive bister	275.00	6.25
		Never hinged	675.00	
		On cover		20.00
b.		7c greenish bister	325.00	6.25
		Never hinged	775.00	
		On cover		20.00
c.		7c yellow olive	275.00	6.25
		Never hinged	675.00	
		On cover		20.00
d.		7c straw	250.00	35.00
		Never hinged	625.00	
		On cover		20.00
93	A34	10c brown lilac	450.00	15.00
		Never hinged	1,125.	
		On cover		350.00
b.		10c dull lilac	450.00	15.00
		Never hinged	1,125.	
		On cover		350.00
94	A34	20c ol grn ('04)	800.00	50.00
		Never hinged	2,000.	
		On cover		450.00
a.		20c deep olive green	875.00	57.50
		Never hinged	2,150.	
		On cover		450.00
95	A34	50c purple ('08)	950.00	175.00
		Never hinged	2,350.	
		On cover		1,500.
a.		50c deep purple	950.00	225.00
		Never hinged	2,350.	
		On cover		1,500.
		Nos. 89-95 (7)	2,825.	252.80
		Set, never hinged	7,025.	

Values for Nos. 94 and 95 used are for examples with contemporaneous circular datestamps. Stamps with heavy cancellations or parcel cancellations sell for much less.

Hairlines: a pattern of fine lines across the face of the stamp caused by plate cracks. The values are for stamps with prominent and extensive lines. Values will be less for stamps with less prominent and less extensive cracks. See similar listings for Nos. 104, 104a, 106a, 106c.

Covers: values for Nos. 93-95 are for single frankings paying the correct rate.

Issued: 1c-10c, 7/1/03; 20c, 9/27/04; 50c, 11/19/08.

Imperf., Type II

No.	Design	Description	Unused	Used
90A	A34	2c carmine	40.00	40.00
		Never hinged	80.00	
		On cover		65.00

No. 90A is the only imperforate Canada stamp besides Nos. 136-138 regularly issued to the public. 100,000 were issued.

Imperf., Pairs, Without Gum

No.	Design	Description	Value
89a	A34	1c	725.00
90c	A34	2c Type I	850.00
d.		As No. 90c, imperf, 2 panes tete beche	*20,000.*
91a	A34	5c	1,200.
92a	A34	7c	800.
93a	A34	10c	1,200.

Quebec Tercentenary Issue

Prince and Princess of Wales, 1908 — A35

Jacques Cartier and Samuel de Champlain A36

Queen Alexandra and King Edward A37

Champlain's Home in Quebec A38

Generals Montcalm and Wolfe — A39

View of Quebec in 1700 — A40

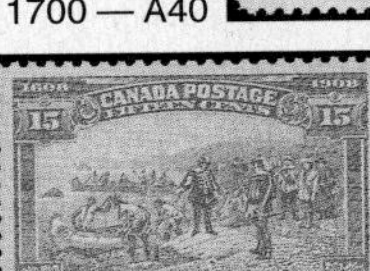

Champlain's Departure for the West — A41

Arrival of Cartier at Quebec A42

1908, July 16 ***Perf. 12***

No.	Design	Description	Unused	Used
96	A35	½c black brown	8.00	5.00
		Never hinged	19.00	
		On cover		275.00
		Re-entry (line through "CANADA" - pos. 44)	50.00	55.00
		Never hinged	120.00	
		On cover		350.00
97	A36	1c blue green	30.00	6.00
		Never hinged	75.00	
		On cover		8.00
98	A37	2c carmine	40.00	3.00
		Never hinged	100.00	
		On cover		8.00
99	A38	5c dark blue	85.00	70.00
		Never hinged	210.00	
		On cover		190.00
100	A39	7c olive green	160.00	100.00
		Never hinged	400.00	
		On cover		120.00
101	A40	10c dark violet	200.00	125.00
		Never hinged	500.00	
		On cover		325.00
102	A41	15c red orange	225.00	160.00
		Never hinged	550.00	
		On cover		400.00
103	A42	20c yellow brown	250.00	225.00
		Never hinged	625.00	
		On cover		500.00
		Nos. 96-103 (8)	998.00	694.00
		Set, never hinged	2,479.	

Covers: values for Nos. 96-103 are for properly franked items in the correct period of use.

Imperf., Pairs

No.	Design	Description	Value
96a	A35	½c	750.
		Never hinged	1,400.
97a	A36	1c	750.
		Never hinged	1,400.
98a	A37	2c	750.
		Never hinged	1,400.
99a	A38	5c	750.
		Never hinged	1,400.
100a	A39	7c	750.
		Never hinged	1,400.
101a	A40	10c	750.
		Never hinged	1,400.
102a	A41	15c	750.
		Never hinged	1,400.
103a	A42	20c	750.
		Never hinged	1,400.

100 pairs of imperfs made, 50 with gum and 50 without. Due to demand, pairs without gum generally sell for 90-95% of the unused hinged price.

WET and DRY PRINTINGS

Before 1922, stamps were printed using dampened paper (wet printing). As the paper dried, it shrank slightly across the grain. In 1922, a new process was introduced that used much drier paper (dry printing) with little or no shrinkage. Additionally, on wet printings the gum does not extend to the edges of the pane and the design is more flat from the gummed side; on dry printings the gum extends to the edges of the pane and the designs shows some embossing effect when viewed from the gummed side.

The King George V Admiral issue, design A43, was printed from 1911 to 1925, and the earlier wet printings generally show a narrower design due to paper shrinkage

King George V — A43

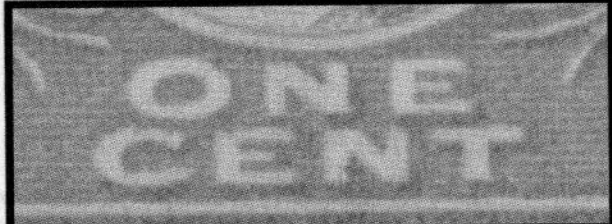

Type I

Type II

Two types of 1c.

Type I — The "N" of "ONE" is separated from the oval above it.

Type II — The "N" of "ONE" almost touches the oval above it.

Type I

Type II

Two types of 3c carmine.

Type I — The "R" of "THREE" is separated from the oval above it. The bottom line of the vignette does not touch the heavy diagonal stroke at right.

Type II — The "R" of "THREE" almost touches the oval above it. The bottom horizontal line of the vignette touches the heavy diagonal stroke at right.

Note that the values for Nos. 104-122 are for sheet stamps with perforations on four sides. Single stamps from booklet panes Nos. 104a, 105a, 105b, 106a, 106d, 107b, 107c, 108a and 109a all have natural straight edges on one or two sides, and (except for No. 107d singles) they are worth much less than the listed sheet stamps.

See note on booklet panes and complete booklets after Nos. 74-84. Values for listed booklet panes throughout this catalog are for very fine panes.

1911-25

No.	Design	Description	Unused	Used
104	A43	1c dark green	25.00	.25
		Never hinged	60.00	
		On cover		1.60
		"Hairlines" plate cracks (horiz.)	37.50	25.00
		Never hinged	92.50	
a.		As "b," booklet pane of 6	150.00	150.00
		Never hinged	300.00	
		Complete booklet, 4 #104a	*750.00*	
b.		1c blue green	30.00	.25
		Never hinged	72.50	
		On cover		1.60
		Major double transfer at lower right (35 LR 12)	*5,000.*	*1,500.*
		On cover		*2,500.*
c.		1c deep blue green	55.00	.25
		Never hinged	110.00	
		On cover		1.60

	Unused	Used
As "c," "hairlines" plate cracks	65.00	7.50
Never hinged	130.00	
On cover		8.00
d. As "c," booklet pane of 6	180.00	180.00
Never hinged	325.00	
Complete booklet, 4 #104d	*875.00*	
e. 1c yellow green	25.00	.25
Never hinged	60.00	
f. As "e," booklet pane of 6	35.00	35.00
Never hinged	70.00	
Complete booklet, 4 #104f	180.00	
105 A43 1c yell, wet printing (I) ('22)	25.00	.25
Never hinged	60.00	
On cover		1.75
a. Booklet pane of 4 + 2 labels	55.00	55.00
Never hinged	110.00	
b. Booklet pane of 6	62.50	62.50
Never hinged	125.00	
Complete booklet, 4 #105b	*375.00*	
d. 1c orange yellow, dry printing (II)	20.00	.25
Never hinged	50.00	
On cover		1.75
e. 1c lemon yellow, wet printing (I)	37.50	6.50
Never hinged	105.00	
On cover		13.00
f. 1c yellow, dry printing (I)	30.00	.50
Never hinged	82.50	
On cover		—
106 A43 2c carmine	25.00	.25
Never hinged	60.00	
On cover		1.75
a. Booklet pane of 6	40.00	40.00
Never hinged	80.00	
Complete booklet, 2 #106a	140.00	
As "a," "hairlines" plate cracks	52.50	52.50
Never hinged	90.00	
b. 2c pink	150.00	18.00
Never hinged	350.00	
On cover		25.00
c. 2c rose carmine	25.00	.25
Never hinged	60.00	
On cover		1.75
As "c," "hairlines" plate cracks	55.00	4.50
Never hinged	110.00	
On cover		8.00
d. As "c," booklet pane of 6	160.00	160.00
Never hinged	320.00	
107 A43 2c yel grn, wet printing ('22)	27.50	.25
Never hinged	65.00	
On cover		2.50
a. Thin paper, wet printing ('24)	20.00	2.50
Never hinged	50.00	
On cover		5.00
b. Booklet pane of 4 + 2 labels ('22)	70.00	*80.00*
Never hinged	140.00	
c. Booklet pane of 6, wet printing ('22)	325.00	*325.00*
Never hinged	575.00	
Complete booklet, 2 #107c	800.00	
e. 2c green, dry printing ('23)	22.50	.25
Never hinged	55.00	
On cover		2.50
f. As "c," dry printing	300.00	300.00
Never hinged	550.00	
108 A43 3c brown, wet printing ('18)	25.00	.40
Never hinged	60.00	
On cover		2.50
a. Booklet pane of 4 + 2 labels	90.00	*95.00*
Never hinged	180.00	
Complete booklet, 2 #108a	550.00	
Complete booklet, #105a, 107b, 108a	*475.00*	
b. 3c yellow brown, wet printing	35.00	.25
Never hinged	82.50	
On cover		2.50
c. 3c brown, dry printing ('23)	25.00	.25
Never hinged	60.00	
On cover		2.50
109 A43 3c car (I) ('23)	17.50	.25
Never hinged	42.50	
On cover		2.50
a. Booklet pane of 4 + 2 labels	70.00	*75.00*
Never hinged	140.00	
Complete booklet, 2 #109a	325.00	
Complete booklet, #105a, 107b, 109a	*350.00*	
c. Die II ('24)	50.00	.25
Never hinged	125.00	
On cover		4.00
d. 3c rose carmine (I) ('23)	30.00	3.50
Never hinged	75.00	
On cover		12.00
110 A43 4c ol bis, wet printing ('22)	47.50	4.50
Never hinged	120.00	
On cover, single franking		27.50
b. 4c olive yellow, wet printing	50.00	4.50
Never hinged	125.00	
On cover, single franking		20.00
c. 4c golden yellow, wet printing	140.00	10.00
Never hinged	350.00	
On cover, single franking		27.50
d. 4c yellow ocher, dry printing ('25)	47.50	4.75
Never hinged	120.00	
On cover, single franking		20.00
111 A43 5c dark blue ('12)	175.00	1.75
Never hinged	450.00	
On cover		40.00
a. 5c indigo	375.00	2.10
Never hinged	825.00	
On cover		40.00
b. 5c gray blue	190.00	1.40
Never hinged	450.00	
On cover		40.00
112 A43 5c violet, wet printing ('22)	40.00	1.00
Never hinged	100.00	
On cover		32.50
a. Thin paper ('24)	35.00	7.50
Never hinged	87.50	
On cover		40.00
c. Dry printing ('25)	52.50	1.60
Never hinged	115.00	
On cover		40.00
113 A43 7c yel ocher ('12)	55.00	3.50
Never hinged	130.00	
On cover		16.00
a. 7c olive bister ('15)	85.00	3.25
Never hinged	220.00	
On cover		16.00
b. 7c straw	200.00	14.00
Never hinged	475.00	
On cover		47.50
c. 7c sage green ('14)	550.00	27.50
Never hinged	1,350.	
On cover		60.00
114 A43 7c red brn, dry printing ('24)	22.50	10.00
Never hinged	55.00	
On cover		20.00
On cover, single franking		40.00
b. 7c red brown, wet printing	30.00	14.50
Never hinged	80.00	
On cover		20.00
On cover, single franking		40.00
115 A43 8c blue ('25)	37.50	10.00
Never hinged	92.50	
On cover		22.50
On cover, single franking		52.50
116 A43 10c plum ('12)	275.00	4.00
Never hinged	675.00	
On cover		27.50
On cover, single franking		55.00
a. 10c reddish purple	310.00	4.00
Never hinged	850.00	
On cover		27.50
On cover, single franking		55.00
117 A43 10c blue, wet printing ('22)	47.50	2.00
Never hinged	115.00	
On cover, single franking		32.50
a. Dry printing	42.50	2.25
Never hinged	110.00	
On cover, single franking		32.50
118 A43 10c bis brn ('25)	40.00	2.00
Never hinged	95.00	
On cover, single franking		32.50
b. 10c yellow brown	60.00	2.25
Never hinged	150.00	
On cover, single franking		32.50
119 A43 20c ol grn, dry printing ('25)	110.00	1.75
Never hinged	275.00	
On cover, single franking		200.00
b. 20c sage green, wet printing	225.00	6.00
Never hinged	550.00	
On cover, single franking		200.00
c. 20c dk olive green, wet printing ('12)	140.00	2.50
Never hinged	300.00	
On cover, single franking		200.00
d. 20c gray green, wet printing	175.00	5.50
Never hinged	425.00	
On cover, single franking		200.00
120 A43 50c blk brn, dry printing ('25)	90.00	3.75
Never hinged	225.00	
On cover, single franking		325.00
a. 50c black, wet printing ('12)	275.00	12.00
Never hinged	650.00	
On cover, single franking		325.00
122 A43 $1 orange, dry printing ('23)	95.00	10.00
Never hinged	240.00	
On cover, single franking		450.00
b. $1 deep orange, wet printing	200.00	14.00
Never hinged	450.00	
On cover, single franking		450.00
Nos. 104-122 (18)	1,180.	55.90
Set, never hinged	2,870.	

For type A43 perforated 12x8 see No. 184.
For surcharges see Nos. 139-140.

Issued: Nos. 104, 106, 12/22/11; No. 105, 6/7/22; No. 108, 8/6/18; No. 109, 12/18/23; 4c, 7/7/22; No. 111, 1/17/12; No. 112, 2/2/22; Nos. 113, 116, 1/12/12; No. 114, 12/12/24; 8c, 9/1/25; No. 117, 2/20/22; No. 118, 8/1/25; 20c, 1/23/12; 50c, 1/26/12; $1, 7/22/23.

Imperf., Panes

105c	As No. 105b, imperf, 2 panes tete beche	*15,000.*
107d	As No. 107c, imperf, 2 panes tete beche	*15,000.*
109b	As No. 109a, imperf, 2 panes tete beche	*15,000.*

Imperf., Pairs

110a	A43	4c	2,250.
		Never hinged	4,250.
112b	A43	5c	2,250.
		Never hinged	4,250.
114a	A43	7c	2,250.
		Never hinged	4,250.
115a	A43	8c	2,250.
		Never hinged	4,250.
118a	A43	10c	2,250.
		Never hinged	4,250.
119a	A43	20c	2,250.
		Never hinged	4,250.
120b	A43	50c	3,000.
		Never hinged	6,000.
122a	A43	$1	2,250.
		Never hinged	4,250.

Nos. 105c and 109b made without gum, others with gum. About half of the No. 120b pairs have creases; value thus $500.

Two pairs of tete beche singles are known from No. 107d; value, unused, $1,750.

Coil Stamps

1913 ***Perf. 8 Horizontally***

	Unused	Used
123 A43 1c dark green	110.00	65.00
Never hinged	275.00	
On cover		75.00
Pair	230.00	140.00
Never hinged	475.00	
On cover		150.00
Paste-up pair	300.00	160.00
Never hinged	600.00	
On cover		175.00
124 A43 2c carmine	110.00	65.00
Never hinged	275.00	
On cover		75.00
Pair	230.00	210.00
Never hinged	475.00	
On cover		225.00
Paste-up pair	300.00	225.00
Never hinged	600.00	
On cover		250.00

1912-24 ***Perf. 8 Vertically***

	Unused	Used
125 A43 1c green	25.00	2.00
Never hinged	50.00	
On cover		4.00
Pair	50.00	4.50
Never hinged	100.00	
On cover		11.00
Paste-up pair	60.00	30.00
Never hinged	120.00	
On cover		40.00
Major double transfer at lower right (35 LR 12)		*4,000.*
126 A43 1c org yell, dry printing (II) ('23)	11.00	7.50
Never hinged	22.00	
On cover		8.50
Pair	22.00	19.00
Never hinged	44.00	
On cover		22.50
Paste-up pair	35.00	31.00
Never hinged	57.50	
On cover		32.50
a. As #126, block of 4 (II)	65.00	50.00
Never hinged	100.00	
On cover, block of 4		62.50
On cover, vert. pair, commercial		27.50
On cover, vert. pair, 1st flight		16.00
b. 1c orange yellow, wet printing (I)	30.00	11.00
Never hinged	60.00	
On cover		16.00
Pair	65.00	25.00
Never hinged	120.00	
On cover		27.50
Paste-up pair	70.00	30.00
Never hinged	130.00	
On cover		40.00
c. As "b," block of 4 (I)	700.00	
Never hinged	1,200.	
d. 1c yellow, dry printing (I)	25.00	10.00
Never hinged	42.50	
On cover		15.00
Pair	52.50	22.50
Never hinged	90.00	
On cover		25.00
Paste-up pair	100.00	50.00
Never hinged	160.00	
On cover		40.00
127 A43 2c carmine	40.00	2.00
Never hinged	80.00	
On cover		4.00
Pair	80.00	7.00
Never hinged	160.00	
On cover		24.00
Paste-up pair	100.00	40.00
Never hinged	185.00	
On cover		42.50
128 A43 2c green ('22)	25.00	1.10
Never hinged	50.00	
On cover		3.75
Pair	50.00	3.25
Never hinged	95.00	
On cover		24.00
Paste-up pair	65.00	16.00
Never hinged	110.00	
On cover		27.50
a. Block of 4	65.00	60.00
Never hinged	100.00	
On cover, block of 4		65.00
On cover, vert. pair, commercial		22.50
On cover, vert. pair, 1st flight		15.00
129 A43 3c brown ('18)	30.00	1.30
Never hinged	60.00	
On cover		4.00
Pair	55.00	4.50
Never hinged	110.00	
On cover		32.50
Paste-up pair	67.50	22.50
Never hinged	140.00	
On cover		25.00

130 A43 3c carmine, wet printing (I) ('24) 70.00 9.00
Never hinged 140.00
On cover 16.00
Pair 140.00 40.00
Never hinged 280.00
On cover, pair alone 65.00
Paste-up pair 175.00 80.00
Never hinged 275.00
On cover 95.00
a. Block of 4 (I) 1,050. 750.00
Never hinged 1,650.
On cover, block of 4 —
On cover, vert. pair, commercial 325.00
On cover, vert. pair, 1st flight 250.00
b. Dry printing, die II 100.00 10.00
Never hinged 200.00
On cover 16.00
Pair 160.00 50.00
Never hinged 325.00
On cover, pair alone 60.00
Paste-up pair 190.00 90.00
Never hinged 375.00
On cover 110.00
Nos. 125-130 (6) 201.00 22.90
Set, never hinged 374.50

Nos. 126a and 128a were issued to the public. Nos. 126c and 130a were issued "by favor" as were the various other imperf and part-perfs of this era.

The used example of No. 125 with major double transfer is unique; it is defective.

Beware of fakes of No. 130a made from No. 138.

1915-24 ***Perf. 12 Horizontally***

131 A43 1c dark green 7.00 6.50
Never hinged 14.00
On cover 9.00
Pair 14.00 15.00
Never hinged 28.00
On cover, pair alone 24.00
Paste-up pair 17.50 19.00
Never hinged 35.00
On cover 27.50
132 A43 2c carmine 40.00 10.00
Never hinged 80.00
On cover 15.00
Pair 80.00 27.50
Never hinged 160.00
On cover, pair alone 50.00
Paste-up pair 100.00 40.00
Never hinged 200.00
On cover 55.00
133 A43 2c yell grn ('24) 85.00 75.00
Never hinged 170.00
On cover 80.00
Pair 170.00 125.00
Never hinged 340.00
On cover, pair alone 160.00
Paste-up pair 210.00 175.00
Never hinged 420.00
On cover 210.00
134 A43 3c brown ('21) 12.50 6.50
Never hinged 25.00
On cover 12.00
Pair 25.00 15.00
Never hinged 50.00
On cover, pair alone 27.50
Paste-up pair 32.50 19.00
Never hinged 65.00
On cover 35.00
Nos. 131-134 (4) 144.50 98.00
Set, never hinged 289.00

"The Fathers of Confederation" — A44

1917, Sept. 15 ***Perf. 12***

135 A44 3c brown 45.00 2.25
Never hinged 115.00
On commercial cover 8.00
1st day cover 325.00
a. Imperf., pair 550.00

50th anniv. of the Canadian Confederation.

Imperfs. are without gum.

Value for No. 135 on commercial cover is for an example with stamp in grade of very fine. Value for grades below very fine are much less than the value shown.

1924 ***Imperf.***

136 A43 1c orange yellow (I) 35.00 35.00
Never hinged 65.00
On cover, single franking 40.00
Pair 87.50 87.50
Never hinged 160.00
On cover 80.00
137 A43 2c green 35.00 35.00
Never hinged 65.00
On cover, single franking 40.00
Pair 87.50 87.50
Never hinged 160.00
On cover 80.00
138 A43 3c carmine (I) 17.50 17.50
Never hinged 32.50
On cover, single franking 20.00
Pair 42.50 42.50
Never hinged 77.50
On cover 45.00
Nos. 136-138 (3) 87.50 87.50
Set, never hinged 162.50

Plate Number Blocks

Before 1958, plate blocks consist of the printer's name and a plate number. As with single stamps, all plate blocks are valued in the grade of very fine, with listings for both hinged and never hinged through Nos. 262, C8, CE2, E10, and J14, and never hinged only from Nos. 268, B1, C9, CE3, C01, E11, EO1, J15, and O1. Some plate numbers and/or positions are worth more than others; only the most common are valued here.

No. 109 Surcharged

a

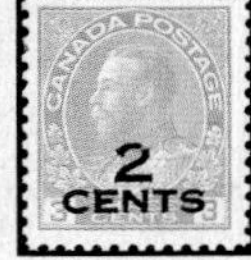

b

1926 ***Perf. 12***

139 A43(a) 2c on 3c carmine (I) 55.00 55.00
Never hinged 90.00
On commercial cover 90.00
On 1st flight cover 62.50
Plate block of 8 600.00
Never hinged 950.00
a. Pair, one without surcharge 725.00
Never hinged 1,150.
b. Double surcharge 275.00
Never hinged 425.00
c. Die II 1,100.
Never hinged 2,250.
140 A43(b) 2c on 3c carmine 27.50 30.00
Never hinged 47.50
On commercial cover 55.00
On 1st flight cover 37.50
Plate block of 8 350.00
Never hinged 550.00
a. Double surcharge 250.00 *250.00*
Never hinged 390.00
b. Triple surcharge 250.00 *275.00*
Never hinged 390.00
c. Double surch., one invtd. 400.00
Never hinged 600.00

First Day Covers

Values for first day covers are for addressed non-cacheted covers through No. 190, addressed cacheted covers from No. 191 to No. 277, and unaddressed covers with the most common cachets from No. 282 and later.

Sir John A. Macdonald A45

Sir Wilfrid Laurier A48

"The Fathers of Confederation" — A46

Parliament Building at Ottawa A47

Map of Canada A49

1927, June 29

141 A45 1c orange 2.75 1.30
Never hinged 5.00
1st day cover 120.00
Plate block of 8 42.50
Never hinged 65.00
142 A46 2c green 2.00 .25
Never hinged 3.75
1st day cover 120.00
Plate block of 4 45.00
Never hinged 67.50
Plate block of 6 25.00
Never hinged 35.00
143 A47 3c brown carmine 8.50 6.50
Never hinged 15.00
1st day cover 120.00
Plate block of 4 65.00
Never hinged 100.00
Plate block of 6 85.00
Never hinged 125.00
144 A48 5c violet 4.25 3.50
Never hinged 8.00
1st day cover 120.00
Plate block of 8 60.00
Never hinged 95.00
145 A49 12c dark blue 22.50 6.50
Never hinged 40.00
1st day cover 160.00
Plate block of 6 200.00
Never hinged 300.00
Nos. 141-145 (5) 40.00 18.05
Set, never hinged 71.75
Set of 5 stamps on one 1st day cover 375.00

60th year of the Canadian Confederation.

Imperf., Pairs

141a A45 1c 125.00
Never hinged 180.00
142a A46 2c 125.00
Never hinged 180.00
143a A47 3c 125.00
Never hinged 180.00
144a A48 5c 125.00
Never hinged 180.00
145a A49 12c 125.00
Never hinged 180.00

Horizontal Pairs, Imperf. Vertically

141b A45 1c 125.00
Never hinged 180.00
142b A46 2c 125.00
Never hinged 180.00
143b A47 3c 125.00
Never hinged 180.00
144b A48 5c 125.00
Never hinged 180.00
145b A49 12c 125.00
Never hinged 180.00

Vertical Pair, Imperf. Horizontally

141c A45 1c 125.00
Never hinged 180.00
142c A46 2c 125.00
Never hinged 180.00
143c A47 3c 125.00
Never hinged 180.00
144c A48 5c 125.00
Never hinged 180.00
145c A49 12c 125.00
Never hinged 180.00

Thomas d'Arcy McGee — A50

Laurier and Macdonald A51

Robert Baldwin and Sir Louis Hypolyte Lafontaine A52

1927, June 29

146 A50 5c violet 4.00 3.00
Never hinged 7.25
1st day cover 120.00
Plate block of 8 (UR) 60.00
Never hinged 90.00
Plate block of 10 (UL) 72.50
Never hinged 110.00
147 A51 12c green 10.00 5.50
Never hinged 18.00
1st day cover 140.00
Plate block of 6 100.00
Never hinged 150.00
148 A52 20c brown carmine 27.50 6.50
Never hinged 50.00
1st day cover 140.00
Plate block of 4 135.00
Never hinged 225.00
Plate block of 6 200.00
Never hinged 325.00
Nos. 146-148 (3) 41.50 15.00
Set, never hinged 75.25

Nos. 146-148 were to have been issued in July, 1926, as a commemorative series, but were withheld and issued June 29, 1927.

Imperf., Pairs

146a A50 5c 125.00
Never hinged 180.00
147a A51 12c 125.00
Never hinged 180.00
148a A52 20c 125.00
Never hinged 180.00

Horizontal Pairs, Imperf. Vertically

146b A50 5c 125.00
Never hinged 180.00
147b A51 12c 125.00
Never hinged 180.00
148b A52 20c 125.00
Never hinged 180.00

Vertical Pairs, Imperf. Horizontally

146c A50 5c 125.00
Never hinged 180.00
147c A51 12c 125.00
Never hinged 180.00
148c A52 20c 125.00
Never hinged 180.00

King George V — A53

Mt. Hurd from Bell-Smith's Painting "The Ice-crowned Monarch of the Rockies" A54

Quebec Bridge A55

Harvesting Wheat A56

Schooner "Bluenose" A57

Parliament Building A58

1928-29

149 A53 1c orange 3.25 .40
Never hinged 6.00
1st day cover (10/29/28) 275.00
Plate block of 8 35.00
Never hinged 60.00
a. Booklet pane of 6 27.50 25.00
Never hinged 40.00
Complete booklet, 4 #149a 150.00
150 A53 2c green 1.90 .25
Never hinged 3.50
1st day cover (10/17/28) 275.00
Plate block of 8 22.50
Never hinged 37.50
a. Booklet pane of 6 27.50 25.00
Never hinged 40.00
Complete booklet, 2 #150a 95.00
151 A53 3c dk carmine 27.50 12.50
Never hinged 50.00
1st day cover (12/12/28) 350.00
Plate block of 8 240.00
Never hinged 450.00
152 A53 4c bister ('29) 22.50 6.00
Never hinged 40.00
1st day cover (8/16/29) 425.00
Plate block of 8 225.00
Never hinged 400.00
153 A53 5c dp violet 16.00 3.00
Never hinged 30.00
1st day cover (12/12/28) 350.00
Plate block of 8 125.00
Never hinged 220.00
a. Booklet pane of 6 200.00 140.00
Never hinged 280.00

Complete booklet, 3 #149a, 2 #150a, 1 #153a 600.00

154 A53 8c blue 18.00 9.00
Never hinged 32.50
1st day cover (12/21/28) 425.00
Plate block of 8 180.00
Never hinged 300.00

155 A54 10c green 20.00 2.50
Never hinged 37.50
1st day cover (12/5/28) 500.00
Plate block of 6 160.00
Never hinged 280.00

156 A55 12c gray ('29) 45.00 9.00
Never hinged 85.00
1st day cover (1/8/29) 500.00
Plate block of 6 225.00
Never hinged 450.00

157 A56 20c dk car ('29) 65.00 12.00
Never hinged 120.00
1st day cover (1/8/29) 550.00
Plate block of 6 500.00
Never hinged 875.00

158 A57 50c dk blue ('29) 225.00 65.00
Never hinged 425.00
1st day cover (1/8/29) 5,000.
Plate block of 4 1,900. —
Never hinged 2,850.
Plate block of 6 2,500.
Never hinged 4,250.
"Man on the Mast" plate flaw 2,000. 1,300.

159 A58 $1 ol grn ('29) 300.00 80.00
Never hinged 575.00
1st day cover (1/8/29) 3,500.
Plate block of 6 2,800.
Never hinged 4,500.

Nos. 149-159 (11) 744.15 199.65
Set, never hinged 1,405.

Imperf., Panes

149c	As No. 149a, imperf, 2 panes tete beche	1,000.
	Never hinged	1,450.
150c	As No. 150a, imperf, 2 panes tete beche	1,000.
	Never hinged	1,450.
153c	As No. 153a, imperf, 2 panes tete beche	1,000.
	Never hinged	1,450.

Imperf., Pairs

149b	A53	1c	100.00
		Never hinged	140.00
150b	A53	2c	100.00
		Never hinged	140.00
151a	A53	3c	120.00
		Never hinged	170.00
152a	A53	4c	120.00
		Never hinged	170.00
153b	A53	5c	100.00
		Never hinged	140.00
154a	A53	8c	120.00
		Never hinged	170.00
155a	A54	10c	200.00
		Never hinged	280.00
156a	A55	12c	200.00
		Never hinged	280.00
157a	A56	20c	200.00
		Never hinged	280.00
158a	A57	50c	800.00
		Never hinged	1,150.
159a	A58	$1	725.00
		Never hinged	1,050.

Horizontal Pairs, Imperf. Vertically

149d	A53	1c	100.00
		Never hinged	140.00
150d	A53	2c	100.00
		Never hinged	140.00
151b	A53	3c	120.00
		Never hinged	170.00
152b	A53	4c	120.00
		Never hinged	170.00
153d	A53	5c	120.00
		Never hinged	170.00
154b	A53	8c	120.00
		Never hinged	170.00
155b	A54	10c	200.00
		Never hinged	280.00
156b	A55	12c	200.00
		Never hinged	280.00
157b	A56	20c	200.00
		Never hinged	280.00
158b	A57	50c	800.00
		Never hinged	1,150.
159b	A58	$1	725.00
		Never hinged	1,050.

Vertical Pairs, Imperf. Horizontally

149e	A53	1c	100.00
		Never hinged	140.00
150e	A53	2c	100.00
		Never hinged	140.00
151c	A53	3c	120.00
		Never hinged	170.00
152c	A53	4c	120.00
		Never hinged	170.00
153e	A53	5c	120.00
		Never hinged	170.00
154c	A53	8c	100.00
		Never hinged	140.00
155c	A54	10c	200.00
		Never hinged	280.00
156c	A55	12c	200.00
		Never hinged	280.00
157c	A56	20c	200.00
		Never hinged	280.00
158c	A57	50c	800.00
		Never hinged	1,150.
159c	A58	$1	725.00
		Never hinged	1,050.

Coil Stamps

1929 *Perf. 8 Vertically*

160 A53 1c orange 40.00 22.50
Never hinged 75.00
On commercial cover 22.50
Pair 80.00 55.00
Never hinged 160.00
On commercial cover 55.00
Paste-up pair 100.00 67.50
Never hinged 200.00
On commercial cover 67.50
Precanceled 22.50

161 A53 2c green 40.00 3.50
Never hinged 75.00
On commercial cover 8.00
Pair 80.00 10.00
Never hinged 160.00
On commercial cover 22.50
Paste-up pair 100.00 35.00
Never hinged 200.00
On commercial cover 37.50

King George V
A59

Library of Parliament
A60

The Citadel at Quebec
A61

Harvesting Wheat
A62

Museum at Grand Pré and Monument to Evangeline
A63

Mt. Edith Cavell
A64

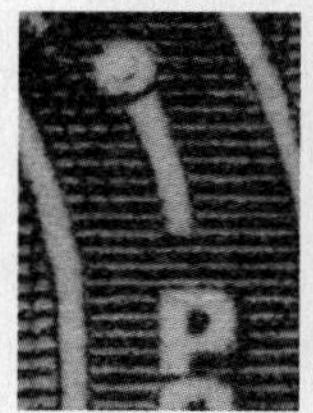
Type I

Type II

Two types of 1c.
Type I — Three thick and one thin colored lines between "P" at right and ornament above it.
Type II — Four thick colored lines. Curved line in ball of ornament at right is longer than in die I.

Type I

Type II

Two types of 2c.
Type I — The top of the letter "P" encloses a tiny dot of color.
Type II — The top of the "P" encloses a larger spot of color than in die I. The "P" appears almost like a "D."

1930-31 *Perf. 11*

162 A59 1c orange 1.25 .70
Never hinged 2.50
1st day cover (7/17/30) 150.00
Plate block of 4 9.00
Never hinged 18.00

163 A59 1c dp grn (II) 2.00 .25
Never hinged 4.00
On commercial cover 1.75
Plate block of 4 12.00
Never hinged 18.00
a. Booklet pane of 4 + 2 labels (II) 120.00 100.00
Never hinged 180.00
b. Die I (12/6/30) 2.00 .25
Never hinged 4.00
1st day cover (12/6/30) 140.00
c. Booklet pane of 6 (I) 22.50 20.00
Never hinged 35.00
Complete booklet, 4 #163c 180.00

164 A59 2c dull green (I) 1.75 .25
Never hinged 3.50
1st day cover (6/6/30) 140.00
Plate block of 4 10.00
Never hinged 20.00
a. Booklet pane of 6 32.50 32.50
Never hinged 47.50
Complete booklet, 2 #164a 180.00

165 A59 2c deep red (I) 1.75 .30
Never hinged 3.50
On commercial cover 2.50
Plate block of 4 10.00
Never hinged 20.00
a. Die II 1.90 .25
Never hinged 3.75
1st day cover (11/17/30) —
Plate block of 4 12.00
Never hinged 24.00
"Extended mustache" variety (65LR8) 100.00 55.00
Never hinged 200.00
On commercial cover 90.00
b. Booklet pane of 6 (I) 25.00 22.50
Never hinged 37.50
Complete booklet, 2 #165b 90.00

166 A59 2c dk brn (II) ('31) 1.75 .25
Never hinged 3.50
On commercial cover 1.60
Plate block of 4 9.50
Never hinged 19.00
"Extended mustache" variety (65LR8) 100.00 55.00
Never hinged 200.00
On commercial cover 90.00
a. Booklet pane of 4 + 2 labels (II) 130.00 130.00
Never hinged 200.00
b. Die I 5.00 4.00
Never hinged 10.00
1st day cover (7/4/31) —
Plate block of 4 30.00
Never hinged 60.00
c. Booklet pane of 6 (I) 57.50 57.50
Never hinged 87.50
Complete booklet, 2 #166c 225.00

167 A59 3c deep red ('31) 2.75 .25
Never hinged 5.50
1st day cover (7/13/31) 210.00
Plate block of 4 20.00
Never hinged 35.00
a. Booklet pane of 4 + 2 labels 40.00 40.00
Never hinged 60.00
Complete booklet, 2 #167a 110.00
Complete booklet, #163a, 166a, 167a 450.00

168 A59 4c yel bister 15.00 7.50
Never hinged 30.00
1st day cover (11/5/30) 210.00
Plate block of 4 75.00
Never hinged 150.00

169 A59 5c dl vio, rotary press, perf. 11¼ x 11 7.00 5.00
Never hinged 14.00
On commercial cover 16.00
Plate block of 4 35.00
Never hinged 70.00
a. Flat plate printing, perf. 11 10.00
Never hinged 20.00
Plate block of 4 40.00
Never hinged 70.00
1st day cover (6/18/30) 210.00

170 A59 5c dull blue 8.50 1.25
Never hinged 17.00
1st day cover (11/13/30) 150.00
On commercial cover 12.00
Plate block of 4 40.00
Never hinged 75.00

171 A59 8c dark blue 27.50 13.50
Never hinged 55.00
1st day cover (8/13/30) 250.00
Plate block of 4 135.00
Never hinged 275.00
172 A59 8c red orange 8.50 5.50
Never hinged 17.00
1st day cover (11/5/30) 110.00
Plate block of 4 52.50
Never hinged 105.00
173 A60 10c olive green 10.00 1.30
Never hinged 20.00
1st day cover (9/15/30) 250.00
Plate block of 4 70.00
Never hinged 140.00
174 A61 12c gray black 30.00 6.50
Never hinged 60.00
1st day cover (12/4/30) 400.00
On commercial cover 12.50
1st flight cover 7.50
Plate block of 4 200.00
Never hinged 375.00
175 A62 20c brown red 47.50 1.40
Never hinged 95.00
1st day cover (12/4/30) 400.00
Plate block of 4 240.00
Never hinged 450.00
176 A63 50c dull blue 175.00 14.00
Never hinged 350.00
1st day cover (12/4/30) 1,000.
Plate block of 4 1,500.
Never hinged 3,000.
177 A64 $1 dk ol green 175.00 27.50
Never hinged 350.00
1st day cover (12/4/30) 1,000.
Plate block of 4 1,500.
Never hinged 3,000.
Nos. 162-177 (16) 515.25 85.45
Set, never hinged 1,029.

No. 169 rotary printing is distinguished unused from No. 169a flat plate printing by the former having gum ridges about 5mm apart.

See No. 201. For surcharge see No. 191. For overprint see No. 203.

Imperf., Pairs

163d A59 1c (II) 1,600.
Never hinged 2,750.
173a A60 10c 1,600.
Never hinged 2,750.
174a A61 12c 900.
Never hinged 1,500.
175a A62 20c 900.
Never hinged 1,500.
176a A63 50c 1,000.
Never hinged 1,600.
177a A64 $1 1,000.
Never hinged 1,600.

Coil Stamps

1930-31 ***Perf. 8½ Vertically***

178 A59 1c orange 12.50 8.00
Never hinged 20.00
On commercial cover 12.00
Pair 25.00 21.00
Never hinged 45.00
On cover 24.00
Joint line pair 37.50 26.00
Never hinged 70.00
On cover 32.50
179 A59 1c deep green 9.00 5.25
Never hinged 17.00
On commercial cover 7.00
Pair 18.00 16.00
Never hinged 32.50
On cover 17.00
Joint line pair 27.50 22.50
Never hinged 50.00
On cover 25.00
180 A59 2c dull green 5.00 2.50
Never hinged 9.00
On commercial cover 3.75
"Cockeyed King" variety 50.00
Never hinged 95.00
On cover 50.00
Pair 10.00 7.50
Never hinged 18.00
On cover 8.00
Joint line pair 17.50 14.00
Never hinged 32.50
On cover 17.50
"Cockeyed King" variety, left stamp in line pair 75.00 67.50
Never hinged 140.00
On cover 80.00
181 A59 2c deep red 20.00 2.00
Never hinged 37.50
On commercial cover 4.00
"Cockeyed King" variety 55.00 52.50
Never hinged 100.00
On cover 55.00
Pair 40.00 6.00
Never hinged 75.00
On cover 12.50
Joint line pair 55.00 15.00
Never hinged 100.00
On cover 17.50
"Cockeyed King" variety, left stamp in line pair 80.00 75.00
Never hinged 150.00
On cover 85.00
182 A59 2c dark brown ('31) 12.50 .65
Never hinged 22.50
On commercial cover 5.50
"Cockeyed King" variety 55.00 45.00
Never hinged 100.00
On cover 47.50
Pair 25.00 2.10
Never hinged 47.50
On cover 12.50
Joint line pair 35.00 6.00
Never hinged 67.50
On cover 14.00
"Cockeyed King" variety, left stamp in line pair 80.00 67.50
Never hinged 150.00
On cover 75.00
183 A59 3c deep red ('31) 18.00 .65
Never hinged 35.00
On commercial cover 2.00
Pair 36.00 1.75
Never hinged 67.50
On cover 20.00
Joint line pair 55.00 7.50
Never hinged 100.00
On cover 25.00
Nos. 178-183 (6) 77.00 19.05
Set, never hinged 141.00

A vertical "jump" in spacing invariably occurs at the line in line pairs of Nos. 178-183. Therefore, a very fine line pair will not contain perfectly centered stamps, but it should show attractive balanced centering. This also applies to the "cockeyed king" variety in a line pair, as this variety occurs on the stamp to the left of the joint line.

George V Type of 1912-25

1931, June 24 ***Perf. 12x8***

184 A43 3c carmine 8.00 4.50
Never hinged 20.00
1st day cover 650.00
Plate block of 8 90.00
Never hinged 180.00

Sir Georges Etienne Cartier — A65

1931, Sept. 30 ***Perf. 11***

190 A65 10c dark green 12.50 .25
Never hinged 27.50
1st day cover 650.00
Plate block of 4 70.00
Never hinged 140.00
a. Imperf., pair 475.00
Never hinged 900.00

First Day Covers

Values for first day covers are for addressed non-cacheted covers through No. 190, addressed cacheted covers from No. 191 to No. 277, and unaddressed covers with the most common cachets from No. 282 and later.

Nos. 165, 165a Surcharged

1932, June 21

191 A59 3c on 2c dp red (II) 1.25 .25
Never hinged 2.00
1st day cover 17.50
Plate block of 4 7.00
Never hinged 12.50
"Extended mustache" variety (65LR8) 100.00 60.00
Never hinged 180.00
On commercial cover 90.00
a. Die I 3.00 1.90
Never hinged 5.00
1st day cover 190.00
Plate block of 4 15.00
Never hinged 27.50

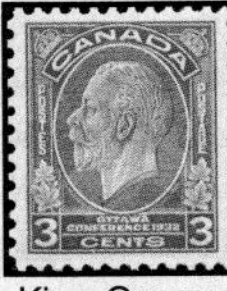

King George V — A66

Edward, Prince of Wales — A67

Allegory of British Empire A68

1932, July 12

192 A66 3c deep red 1.25 .25
Never hinged 2.30
1st day cover 9.00
Plate block of 4 6.00
Never hinged 11.00
193 A67 5c dull blue 7.00 2.50
Never hinged 13.00
1st day cover 12.00
Plate block of 4 50.00
Never hinged 90.00
194 A68 13c deep green 9.00 6.00
Never hinged 17.00
1st day cover 24.00
Plate block of 4 80.00
Never hinged 150.00
Nos. 192-194 (3) 17.25 8.75
Set, never hinged 32.30

Imperial Economic Conference, Ottawa.

Type of 1930 and

King George V — A69

Type I

Type II

Two types of 3c.

Type I — Upper left tip of "3" level with horizontal line to its left.

Type II — Raised "3"; upper left tip of "3" is above horizontal line.

1932, Dec. 1

195 A69 1c dk grn, rotary press, wet printing, perf. 11¼ x 11 1.25 .25
Never hinged 2.25
1st day cover 16.00
Plate block of 4 6.75
Never hinged 13.50
a. Booklet pane of 4 + 2 labels ('33) 90.00 85.00
Never hinged 135.00
b. Booklet pane of 6 ('33) 47.50 47.50
Never hinged 72.50
Complete booklet, 4 #195b 250.00
d. Rotary press dry printing, perf. 11¼ x 11 4.25
Never hinged 6.00
Plate block of 4 19.00
Never hinged 37.50
196 A69 2c black brown 1.30 .25
Never hinged 2.50
1st day cover 16.00
Plate block of 4 7.50
Never hinged 15.00
a. Booklet pane of 4 + 2 labels ('33) 120.00 110.00
Never hinged 180.00
b. Booklet pane of 6 ('33) 90.00 70.00
Never hinged 135.00
Complete booklet, 2 #196b *375.00*
197 A69 3c deep red (I) 1.40 .25
Never hinged 2.70
1st day cover 15.00
Plate block of 4 16.00
Never hinged 32.50
c. Die II 1.50 .25
Never hinged 3.00
On commercial cover 2.40
Plate block of 4 10.50
Never hinged 15.00
d. Booklet pane of 4 + 2 labels, die II ('33) 42.50 37.50
Never hinged 85.00
Complete booklet, 2 #197d 125.00
Complete booklet, #195a, 196a, 197d 250.00
198 A69 4c ocher 50.00 7.00
Never hinged 95.00
1st day cover 24.00
Plate block of 4 300.00
Never hinged 575.00
199 A69 5c dark blue 11.50 .50
Never hinged 20.00
1st day cover 24.00
Plate block of 4 75.00
Never hinged 150.00
a. Horiz. pair, imperf. vert. 1,600.
Never hinged 2,250.
200 A69 8c red orange 40.00 3.50
Never hinged 75.00
1st day cover 27.50
On commercial cover, single franking 55.00
Plate block of 4 250.00
Never hinged 475.00
201 A61 13c dull violet 42.50 3.50
Never hinged 80.00
1st day cover 35.00
Plate block of 4 225.00
Never hinged 425.00
Nos. 195-201 (7) 147.95 15.25
Set, never hinged 277.45
Set of 7, #195-201 on one 1st day cover 35.00

Type A66 has at the foot of the stamp "OTTAWA-CONFERENCE 1932". This inscription does not appear on the stamps of type A69.

Unused examples of No. 195 will show gum ridges about 5mm apart. The gum on No. 195d is flat.

Imperf., Pairs

195c A69 1c 240.00
Never hinged 400.00
196c A69 2c 240.00
Never hinged 400.00
197b A69 3c (I) 240.00
Never hinged 400.00
197e A69 3c (II) *2,250.*
198a A69 4c 240.00
Never hinged 400.00
199b A69 5c 240.00
Never hinged 400.00
200a A69 8c 240.00
Never hinged 400.00
201a A69 13c 800.00
Never hinged 1,300.

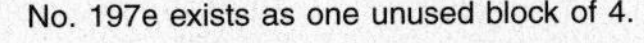

No. 197e exists as one unused block of 4.

Government Buildings, Ottawa — A70

1933, May 18 ***Perf. 11***

202 A70 5c dark blue 10.00 3.75
Never hinged 18.50
1st day cover 27.50
Plate block of 4 65.00
Never hinged 125.00
a. Imperf., pair 625.00
Never hinged 1,050.

Meeting of the Executive Committee of the UPU at Ottawa, May and June, 1933.

No. 175 Overprinted in Blue

1933, July 24

203 A62 20c brown red 45.00 14.00
Never hinged 80.00
1st day cover 55.00
Plate block of 4 240.00
Never hinged 450.00
Broken "X" in "Exhibition" variety (pos. 19) 110.00 60.00
Never hinged 225.00
1st day cover 80.00
a. Imperf., pair 625.00
Never hinged 1,050.
Imperf., pair with one broken "X" *8,500.*
Never hinged *12,000.*

World's Grain Exhibition and Conference at Regina.

Three examples are known of No. 203a with one stamp having the broken "X" variety. Two of these pairs are never hinged.

Steamship Royal William — A71

1933, Aug. 17

204 A71 5c dark blue 11.00 3.75
Never hinged 20.00
1st day cover 26.00
Plate block of 4 55.00
Never hinged 110.00
a. Imperf., pair 700.00
Never hinged 1,150.

Centenary of the linking by steam of the Dominion, then a colony, with Great Britain, the mother country. The Royal William's 1833 voyage was the first Trans-Atlantic passage under steam all the way.

George V Type of 1932 Coil Stamps

1933 ***Perf. 8½ Vertically***

205 A69 1c dark green 12.50 3.00
Never hinged 22.50
On commercial cover 7.25
Pair 25.00 6.00
Never hinged 45.00
On cover 8.00
Joint line pair 35.00 7.50
Never hinged 65.00
On cover 19.00
206 A69 2c black brown 17.50 1.10
Never hinged 32.50
On commercial cover 6.50
Pair 35.00 2.25
Never hinged 65.00
On cover 10.00
Joint line pair 42.50 7.00
Never hinged 80.00
On cover 24.00
207 A69 3c deep red 17.50 .40
Never hinged 32.50
On commercial cover 6.50
Pair 35.00 1.20
Never hinged 65.00
On cover 10.00
Joint line pair 42.50 3.00
Never hinged 80.00
On cover 24.00
Nos. 205-207 (3) 47.50 4.50
Set, never hinged 87.50

Cartier's Arrival at Quebec — A72

1934, July 1 ***Perf. 11***

208	A72 3c blue	4.00	1.40
	Never hinged	7.50	
	1st day cover		20.00
	Plate block of 4	25.00	
	Never hinged	45.00	
	Horiz. strip of 4 with wide vert. gutter btwn. center stamps	275.00	
	Never hinged	550.00	
a.	Imperf., pair	525.00	
	Never hinged	1,050.	

Landing of Jacques Cartier, 400th anniv.

Group from Loyalists Monument, Hamilton, Ontario A73

1934, July 1

209	A73 10c olive green	28.00	7.50
	Never hinged	52.50	
	1st day cover		20.00
	Plate block of 4	175.00	
	Never hinged	325.00	
a.	Imperf., pair	1,400.	
	Never hinged	2,250.	

Emigration of the United Empire Loyalists from the US to Canada, 150th anniv.

Seal of New Brunswick — A74

1934, Aug. 16

210	A74 2c red brown	2.50	2.00
	Never hinged	4.75	
	1st day cover		12.00
	Plate block of 4	17.50	
	Never hinged	32.50	
a.	Imperf., pair	650.00	
	Never hinged	1,150.	

150th anniv. of the founding of the Province of New Brunswick.

Princess Elizabeth A75

Duke of York A76

King George V and Queen Mary — A77

Prince of Wales — A78

Windsor Castle A79

Royal Yacht Britannia A80

1935, May 4 ***Perf. 12***

211	A75 1c green	.65	.35
	Never hinged	1.00	
	1st day cover		6.50
	Plate block of 6	9.00	
	Never hinged	16.00	
	"Weeping Princess" plate flaw (21UR1)	125.00	85.00
	Never hinged	190.00	
	On cover		225.00
212	A76 2c brown	.70	.25
	Never hinged	1.10	
	1st day cover		6.50
	Plate block of 6	10.00	
	Never hinged	15.00	
213	A77 3c carmine	2.00	.25
	Never hinged	3.00	
	1st day cover		6.50
	Plate block of 6	20.00	
	Never hinged	30.00	
214	A78 5c blue	4.00	3.00
	Never hinged	6.00	
	1st day cover		16.00
	Plate block of 6	60.00	
	Never hinged	85.00	
215	A79 10c green	8.50	3.00
	Never hinged	13.50	
	1st day cover		20.00
	Plate block of 6	72.50	
	Never hinged	105.00	
216	A80 13c dark blue	9.00	6.50
	Never hinged	14.00	
	1st day cover		27.50
	Plate block of 6	85.00	
	Never hinged	125.00	
	Plate block of 10 (LL position)	140.00	
	Never hinged	200.00	
	"Shilling mark" plate flaw between "1" and "3" of left "13" (78UR1)	450.00	375.00
	Never hinged	600.00	
	On cover		350.00
	Nos. 211-216 (6)	24.85	13.35
	Set, never hinged	38.60	
	Set of 6, Nos. 211-216 on one 1st day cover		47.50

25th anniv. of the accession to the throne of George V.

Imperf., Pairs

211a	A75 1c	275.00	
	Never hinged	425.00	
212a	A76 2c	275.00	
	Never hinged	425.00	
213a	A77 3c	275.00	
	Never hinged	425.00	
214a	A78 5c	275.00	
	Never hinged	425.00	
215a	A79 10c	275.00	
	Never hinged	425.00	
216b	A80 13c	275.00	
	Never hinged	425.00	

King George V — A81

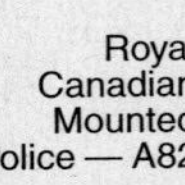

Royal Canadian Mounted Police — A82

Confederation Conference at Charlottetown, 1864 — A83

Niagara Falls — A84

Parliament Buildings, Victoria, B.C. — A85

Champlain Monument, Quebec A86

1935, June 1 ***Perf. 12***

217 A81 1c green .35 .25
Never hinged .50
1st day cover 5.50
Plate block of 6 6.00
Never hinged 9.00
Plate block of 8 (pl. 3) 7.50
Never hinged 11.00
a. Bklt. pane of 4 + 2 labels 70.00 70.00
Never hinged 105.00
b. Booklet pane of 6 50.00 50.00
Never hinged 80.00
Complete booklet, 4 #217b 200.00

218 A81 2c brown .35 .25
Never hinged .50
1st day cover 5.50
Plate block of 6 6.00
Never hinged 9.00
Plate block of 8 7.50
Never hinged 11.00
a. Bklt. pane of 4 + 2 labels 70.00 70.00
Never hinged 105.00
b. Booklet pane of 6 55.00 55.00
Never hinged 82.50
Complete booklet, 2 #218b 130.00

219 A81 3c dk carmine .70 .25
Never hinged 1.00
1st day cover 5.50
Plate block of 6 12.00
Never hinged 17.50
Plate block of 8 14.00
Never hinged 21.00
a. Bklt. pane of 4 + 2 labels 40.00 40.00
Never hinged 60.00
Complete booklet, 2 #219a 100.00
Complete booklet, #217a, 218a, 219a 225.00
c. Printed on gummed side 600.00

220 A81 4c yellowish org 2.50 .55
Never hinged 3.75
1st day cover 8.00
Plate block of 6 52.50
Never hinged 80.00

221 A81 5c blue 3.25 .35
Never hinged 5.00
1st day cover 8.00
Plate block of 6 52.50
Never hinged 80.00
a. Horiz. pair, imperf. vert. 225.00
Never hinged 340.00

222 A81 8c dp orange 2.50 2.25
Never hinged 3.75
1st day cover 12.00
On commercial cover 27.50
On commercial cover, single franking 65.00
Plate block of 6 47.50
Never hinged 72.50

223 A82 10c car rose 8.00 .25
Never hinged 12.50
1st day cover 12.00
Plate block of 6 70.00
Never hinged 100.00
"Broken leg" on mountie variety 1,650. 1,350.
Never hinged *3,000.*

224 A83 13c violet 8.00 .75
Never hinged 12.50
1st day cover 24.00
Plate block of 6 62.50
Never hinged 90.00

225 A84 20c olive green 16.00 .75
Never hinged 24.00
1st day cover 27.50
On commercial cover 16.00
Plate block of 6 175.00
Never hinged 260.00

226 A85 50c dull violet 27.50 6.00
Never hinged 40.00
1st day cover 60.00
Plate block of 6 240.00
Never hinged 350.00

227 A86 $1 deep blue 60.00 11.00
Never hinged 90.00
1st day cover 160.00
Plate block of 6 450.00
Never hinged 600.00
Nos. 217-227 (11) 129.15 22.65
Set, never hinged 193.50
Set of 11, Nos. 217-227 on one 1st day cover 160.00

No. 219c is valued in the grade of fine. Very fine examples are rare and sell for much more.

Imperf., Pairs

217c A81 1c 200.00
Never hinged 290.00
218c A81 2c 200.00
Never hinged 290.00
219b A81 3c 200.00
Never hinged 290.00
220a A81 4c 200.00
Never hinged 290.00
221b A81 5c 200.00
Never hinged 290.00
222a A81 8c 200.00
Never hinged 290.00
223a A82 10c 300.00
Never hinged 450.00
224a A83 13c 300.00
Never hinged 450.00
225a A84 20c 300.00
Never hinged 450.00
226a A85 50c 300.00
Never hinged 450.00
227a A86 $1 350.00
Never hinged 525.00

Coil Stamps

1935 ***Perf. 8 Vertically***

228 A81 1c green 12.50 3.25
Never hinged 19.00
On commercial cover 6.50
Pair 25.00 6.50
Never hinged 37.50
On cover 9.50

229 A81 2c brown 17.00 1.00
Never hinged 26.00
On commercial cover 6.50
Pair 34.00 2.25
Never hinged 50.00
On cover 16.00

230 A81 3c dark carmine 12.50 .60
Never hinged 19.00
On commercial cover 6.50
Pair 25.00 2.50
Never hinged 37.50
On cover 16.00
Nos. 228-230 (3) 42.00 4.85
Set, never hinged 64.00

George VI — A87

1937 ***Perf. 12***

231 A87 1c green .30 .25
Never hinged .45
1st day cover (4/1/37) 4.75
Plate block of 4 2.75
Never hinged 4.10
a. Booklet pane of 4 + 2 labels 20.00 *22.50*
Never hinged 30.00
b. Booklet pane of 6 7.50 *20.00*
Never hinged 11.50

232 A87 2c brown .65 .25
Never hinged 1.00
1st day cover (4/1/37) 4.75
Plate block of 4 3.50
Never hinged 5.25
a. Booklet pane of 4 + 2 labels 20.00 *20.00*
Never hinged 30.00
b. Booklet pane of 6 12.00 *14.00*
Never hinged 18.00

233 A87 3c carmine .65 .25
Never hinged 1.00
1st day cover (4/1/37) 4.75
Plate block of 4 4.00
Never hinged 6.00
a. Booklet pane of 4 + 2 labels 7.00 *14.00*
Never hinged 10.50

234 A87 4c yellow 2.75 .25
Never hinged 4.00
1st day cover (5/10/37) 7.25
Plate block of 4 25.00
Never hinged 37.50

235 A87 5c blue 3.50 .25
Never hinged 5.00
1st day cover (5/10/37) 7.25
Plate block of 4 25.00
Never hinged 37.50

236 A87 8c orange 2.75 .45
Never hinged 4.00
1st day cover (5/10/37) 7.25
On commercial cover 8.50
On commercial cover, single franking 60.00
Plate block of 4 25.00
Never hinged 37.50
Nos. 231-236 (6) 10.60 1.70
Set, never hinged 15.45

Imperf., Pairs

231c A87 1c 300.00
Never hinged 450.00
232c A87 2c 300.00
Never hinged 450.00
233b A87 3c 300.00
Never hinged 450.00
234a A87 4c 300.00
Never hinged 450.00
235a A87 5c 300.00
Never hinged 450.00
236a A87 8c 300.00
Never hinged 450.00

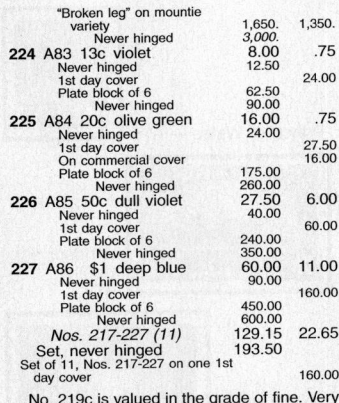

George VI and Queen Elizabeth A88

1937, May 10

237 A88 3c carmine .35 .25
Never hinged .40
1st day cover 3.25
Plate block of 4 3.00
Never hinged 4.50
a. Imperf., pair 625.00
Never hinged 950.00

Coronation of King George VI and Queen Elizabeth.

George VI Types of 1937
Coil Stamps

1937 ***Perf. 8 Vertically***

238 A87 1c green 2.75 1.00
Never hinged 4.00
On commercial cover 6.50
Pair 5.50 2.25
Never hinged 8.25
On cover 8.00

239 A87 2c brown 5.00 .35
Never hinged 7.50
On commercial cover 7.25
Pair 10.00 1.60
Never hinged 15.00
On cover 12.50

240 A87 3c carmine 8.00 .25
Never hinged 12.00
On commercial cover 4.50
Pair 16.00 .80
Never hinged 24.00
On cover 13.50
Nos. 238-240 (3) 15.75 1.60
Set, never hinged 23.50

Memorial Chamber, Parliament Building, Ottawa — A89

Entrance to Halifax Harbor A90

Fort Garry Gate, Winnipeg A91

Vancouver Harbor A92

Chateau de Ramezay, Montreal A93

1938 ***Perf. 12***

241 A89 10c dk carmine 8.50 .25
Never hinged 13.00
1st day cover (7/28/38) 80.00
Plate block of 4 55.00
Never hinged 82.50
a. 10c carmine rose 8.00 .25
Never hinged 12.00
1st day cover (6/15/38) 24.00
Plate block of 4 40.00
Never hinged 60.00

242 A90 13c deep blue 12.00 .60
Never hinged 18.00
1st day cover (11/15/38) 24.00
Plate block of 4 75.00
Never hinged 110.00

243 A91 20c red brown 16.00 .45
Never hinged 24.00
1st day cover (6/15/38) 27.50
Plate block of 4 110.00
Never hinged 165.00

244 A92 50c green 37.50 6.00
Never hinged 55.00
1st day cover (6/15/38) 55.00
Plate block of 4 195.00
Never hinged 290.00

245 A93 $1 dull violet 75.00 7.75
Never hinged 115.00
1st day cover (6/15/38) 100.00
Plate block of 4 450.00
Never hinged 675.00
a. Vert. pair, imperf., horiz. *4,750.*
Never hinged *6,750.*
Nos. 241-245 (5) 149.00 15.05
Set, never hinged 225.00

Imperf., Pairs

241b A89 10c dark carmine 500.00
Never hinged 750.00
241c A89 10c carmine rose 500.00
Never hinged 750.00
242a A90 13c 500.00
Never hinged 750.00
243a A91 20c 500.00
Never hinged 750.00
244a A92 50c 500.00
Never hinged 750.00
245b A93 $1 700.00
Never hinged 1,050.

Princess Elizabeth and Princess Margaret Rose — A94

War Memorial, Ottawa — A95

King George VI and Queen Elizabeth A96

Unwmk.

1939, May 15 **Engr.** ***Perf. 12***

246 A94 1c green & black .35 .25
Never hinged .40
1st day cover 2.40
Plate block of 4 2.25
Never hinged 3.25

247 A95 2c brown & black .35 .25
Never hinged .40
1st day cover 2.40
Plate block of 4 2.25
Never hinged 3.25

248 A96 3c dk car & black .35 .25
Never hinged .40
1st day cover 2.40
Plate block of 4 2.25
Never hinged 3.25
Nos. 246-248 (3) 1.05 .75
Set, never hinged 1.20
Set of 3, #246-248 on 1 1st day cover 3.75

Visit of George VI and Queen Elizabeth to Canada and the US.

This is the first issue of Canada that required the use of two separate plates, and each plate block shows two plate numbers (one for the frame and one for the vignette). 165 different plate number combinations are known, with a few being extremely scarce to rare. The scarcer plate combinations are worth large premiums.

Imperf., Pairs

246a A94 1c 550.00
Never hinged 800.00
247a A95 2c 550.00
Never hinged 800.00
248a A96 3c 550.00
Never hinged 800.00

A97

A98

King George VI — A99

Grain Elevators A100

Farm Scene A101

Parliament Buildings — A102

"Ram" Tank — A103

Corvette A104

Munitions Factory A105

Destroyer A106

1942-43 Engr. *Perf. 12*

No.			Unused	Used
249	A97	1c green	.35	.25
		Never hinged	.45	
		1st day cover (7/1/42)		3.25
		Plate block of 4	2.75	
		Never hinged	4.10	
		Vert. pair with full horiz. gutter betwn. (unique)	*6,000.*	
a.		Booklet pane of 4 + 2 labels	3.50	*3.75*
		Never hinged	5.25	
b.		Booklet pane of 6	5.00	*5.50*
		Never hinged	7.50	
c.		Booklet pane of 3 ('43)	2.50	*5.00*
		Never hinged	3.75	
250	A98	2c brown	.40	.25
		Never hinged	.60	
		1st day cover (7/1/42)		3.50
		Plate block of 4	3.50	
		Never hinged	5.25	
a.		Booklet pane of 4 + 2 labels ('43)	7.00	*8.00*
		Never hinged	10.50	
b.		Booklet pane of 6	10.50	*11.50*
		Never hinged	16.00	
d.		Vert. strip of 3, imperf. horiz.	*5,500.*	
251	A99	3c dk carmine	.60	.25
		Never hinged	.90	
		1st day cover (7/1/42)		3.50
		Plate block of 4	4.00	
		Never hinged	6.00	
a.		Booklet pane of 4 + 2 labels	4.25	*5.25*
		Never hinged	6.50	
252	A99	3c rose violet ('43)	.50	.25
		Never hinged	.70	
		1st day cover (6/30/43)		16.00
		Plate block of 4	4.00	
		Never hinged	6.00	
		Horiz. pair with full vert. gutter btwn.	*2,350.*	
a.		Booklet pane of 4 + 2 labels	3.25	4.50
		Never hinged	5.00	
b.		Booklet pane of 3	3.25	*4.50*
		Never hinged	4.75	
c.		Booklet pane of 6 ('47)	3.75	*4.00*
		Never hinged	5.50	
253	A100	4c greenish black	1.25	.60
		Never hinged	1.90	
		1st day cover (7/1/42)		7.50
		Plate block of 4	13.50	
		Never hinged	20.00	
254	A98	4c dk car ('43)	.70	.25
		Never hinged	1.00	
		1st day cover (4/10/43)		17.50
		Plate block of 4	3.50	
		Never hinged	5.25	
a.		Booklet pane of 6	5.25	*10.00*
		Never hinged	8.00	
b.		Booklet pane of 3	3.25	*4.50*
		Never hinged	4.75	
255	A97	5c deep blue	1.20	.25
		Never hinged	1.80	
		1st day cover (7/1/42)		8.75
		Plate block of 4	10.00	
		Never hinged	15.00	
256	A101	8c red brown	1.60	.50
		Never hinged	2.40	
		1st day cover (7/1/42)		12.00
		Plate block of 4	15.00	
		Never hinged	22.50	
257	A102	10c brown	4.75	.25
		Never hinged	7.00	
		1st day cover (7/1/42)		12.00
		Plate block of 4	40.00	
		Never hinged	60.00	
258	A103	13c dull green	5.00	3.60
		Never hinged	7.50	
		1st day cover (7/1/42)		12.00
		Plate block of 4	45.00	
		Never hinged	67.50	
259	A103	14c dull grn ('43)	7.50	.35
		Never hinged	11.25	
		1st day cover (4/17/43)		24.00
		Plate block of 4	50.00	
		Never hinged	75.00	
260	A104	20c chocolate	9.00	.25
		Never hinged	13.50	
		1st day cover (7/1/42)		16.00
		Plate block of 4	57.50	
		Never hinged	85.00	
261	A105	50c violet	30.00	1.75
		Never hinged	45.00	
		1st day cover (7/1/42)		26.00
		Plate block of 4	180.00	
		Never hinged	275.00	
262	A106	$1 deep blue	65.00	7.50
		Never hinged	100.00	
		1st day cover (7/1/42)		80.00
		Plate block of 4	450.00	
		Never hinged	675.00	
		Nos. 249-262 (14)	127.85	16.30
		Set, never hinged	194.00	

Canada's contribution to the war effort of the Allied Nations.

No. 250d totally imperf horiz. is unique and is valued in the grade of fine. Beware of strips with blind perfs; these sell for much less.

For overprints see Nos. O1-O4.

Imperf., Pairs

249d	A97	1c	300.00
		Never hinged	450.00
250c	A98	2c	300.00
		Never hinged	450.00
251b	A99	3c	300.00
		Never hinged	450.00
252d	A99	3c	300.00
		Never hinged	450.00
253a	A100	4c	300.00
		Never hinged	450.00
254c	A98	4c	300.00
		Never hinged	450.00
255a	A97	5c	300.00
		Never hinged	450.00
256a	A100	8c	300.00
		Never hinged	450.00
257a	A102	10c	450.00
		Never hinged	675.00
258a	A103	13c	450.00
		Never hinged	675.00
259a	A103	14c	450.00
		Never hinged	675.00
260a	A104	20c	450.00
		Never hinged	675.00
261a	A105	50c	450.00
		Never hinged	675.00
262a	A106	$1	600.00
		Never hinged	900.00

Types of 1942
Coil Stamps

1942-43 *Perf. 8 Vertically*

263 A97 1c green ('43)	1.25	.55
Never hinged	1.90	
On commercial cover		5.00
Pair	2.50	1.60
Never hinged	3.80	
On cover		7.00
264 A98 2c brown	2.00	1.10
Never hinged	3.00	
On commercial cover		5.50
Pair	4.00	2.50
Never hinged	6.00	
On cover		10.00
265 A99 3c dark carmine	2.00	1.10
Never hinged	3.00	
On commercial cover		5.00
Pair	4.00	2.50
Never hinged	6.00	
On cover		14.50
266 A99 3c rose violet ('43)	4.00	.40
Never hinged	6.00	
On commercial cover		5.00
Pair	8.00	1.75
Never hinged	12.00	
On cover		14.50
267 A98 4c dk carmine ('43)	5.75	.30
Never hinged	8.75	
On commercial cover		5.00
Pair	11.50	3.50
Never hinged	17.50	
On cover		24.00
Nos. 263-267 (5)	15.00	3.45
Set, never hinged	22.65	

See Nos. 278-281.

Catalogue values for unused stamps in this section, from this point to the end of the section, are for Never Hinged items.

Farm Scene, Ontario
A107

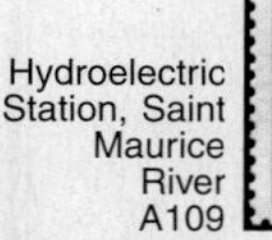
Great Bear Lake, Mackenzie
A108

Hydroelectric Station, Saint Maurice River
A109

Combine
A110

Logging, British Columbia
A111

Train Ferry, Prince Edward Island
A112

1946, Sept. 16 **Engr.** *Perf. 12*

268 A107 8c red brown	2.00	.70
1st day cover		5.50
Plate block of 4	8.00	
269 A108 10c olive	2.75	.25
1st day cover		5.50
Plate block of 4	11.00	
270 A109 14c black brown	4.25	.25
1st day cover		12.00
Plate block of 4	19.00	
271 A110 20c slate black	5.00	.25
1st day cover		16.00
Plate block of 4	22.50	
272 A111 50c dk blue green	20.00	1.75
1st day cover		27.50
Plate block of 4	110.00	
273 A112 $1 red violet	45.00	3.00
1st day cover		55.00
Plate block of 4	210.00	
Nos. 268-273 (6)	79.00	6.20
Set of 6, #268-273 on one 1st day cover		55.00

For overprints see Nos. O6-O10, O21-O23, O25.

Alexander Graham Bell — A113

1947, Mar. 3

274 A113 4c deep blue	.25	.25
1st day cover		2.40
Plate block of 4	1.25	

Birth centenary of Alexander Graham Bell.

Citizen of Canada — A114

1947, July 1

275 A114 4c deep blue	.25	.25
1st day cover		2.40
Plate block of 4	1.25	

Issued on the 80th anniv. of the Canadian Confederation, to mark the advent of Canadian Citizenship.

Princess Elizabeth — A115

1948, Feb. 16

276 A115 4c deep blue	.25	.25
1st day cover		2.40
Plate block of 4	1.25	

Marriage of Princess Elizabeth to Lieut. Philip Mountbatten, R. N., on Nov. 20, 1947.

Parliament Buildings Ottawa
A116

1948, Oct. 1

277 A116 4c gray	.25	.25
1st day cover		2.40
Plate block of 4	1.10	

Centenary of Responsible Government.

George VI Types of 1942
Coil Stamps

1948 *Perf. 9½ Vertically*

278 A97 1c green	7.00	2.00
On commercial cover		5.00
Pair	14.00	6.00
On cover		12.50
279 A98 2c brown	20.00	8.50
On commercial cover		7.00
Pair	40.00	19.00
On cover		20.00
280 A99 3c rose violet	15.00	2.00
On commercial cover		7.00
Pair	30.00	7.75
On cover		19.00
281 A98 4c dark carmine	20.00	2.25
On commercial cover		7.00
Pair	40.00	6.25
On cover		19.00
Nos. 278-281 (4)	62.00	14.75

First Day Covers

Values for first day covers are for addressed non-cacheted covers through No. 190, addressed cacheted covers from No. 191 to No. 277, and unaddressed covers with the most common cachets from No. 282 and later.

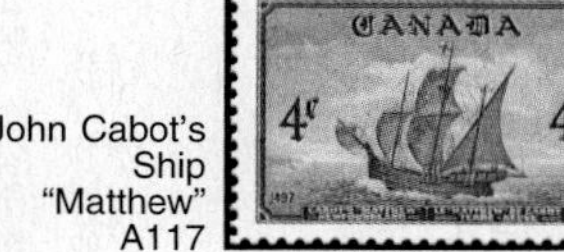
John Cabot's Ship "Matthew"
A117

1949, Apr. 1 **Engr.** *Perf. 12*

282 A117 4c deep green	.25	.25
1st day cover		2.40
Plate block of 4	1.00	

Entry of Newfoundland into confederation with Canada.

"Founding of Halifax, 1749"
A118

1949, June 21 **Unwmk.**

283 A118 4c purple	.25	.25
1st day cover		2.40
Plate block of 4	1.00	

200th anniv. of the founding of Halifax, Nova Scotia.

A119

A120

A121

A122

A123

1949, Nov. 15

284 A119 1c green	.25	.25
1st day cover		6.50
Plate block of 4	1.00	
a. Booklet pane of 3 ('50)	.75	*2.00*
285 A120 2c sepia	.25	.25
1st day cover		6.50
Plate block of 4	1.25	
286 A121 3c rose violet	.35	.25
1st day cover		6.50
Plate block of 4	1.40	
a. Booklet pane of 3 ('50)	2.50	*6.50*
b. Booklet pane of 4 + 2 labels ('50)	3.25	*3.75*
287 A122 4c dk carmine	.55	.25
1st day cover		6.50
Plate block of 4	2.25	
a. Booklet pane of 3 ('50)	12.50	12.50
b. Booklet pane of 6 ('50)	18.00	18.00
288 A123 5c deep blue	1.25	.65
1st day cover		6.50
Plate block of 4	6.25	
Nos. 284-288 (5)	2.65	1.65
Set of 5, #284-288 on one 1st day cover		12.00

Stamps from booklet panes of 3 are imperf. on 2 or 3 sides.

"POSTES POSTAGE" Omitted

1950, Jan. 19

289 A119 1c green	.25	.25
1st day cover		27.50
Plate block of 4	1.10	
290 A120 2c sepia	.35	.25
1st day cover	.35	27.50
Plate block of 4	2.75	
291 A121 3c rose violet	.35	.25
1st day cover		27.50
Plate block of 4	1.90	
292 A122 4c dark carmine	.35	.25
1st day cover		27.50
Plate block of 4	1.90	
293 A123 5c deep blue	1.25	1.00
1st day cover		27.50
Plate block of 4	6.50	
Nos. 289-293 (5)	2.55	2.00
Set of 5, #289-293 on one 1st day cover		45.00

See Nos. 295-300, 305-306, 309-310. For overprints see Nos. O12-O20.

Oil Wells, Alberta
A124

1950, Mar. 1 **Engr.** *Perf. 12*

294 A124 50c dull green	8.50	1.30
1st day cover		32.50
Plate block of 4	42.50	

Development of oil wells in Canada.
For overprints see Nos. O11, O24.

Types of 1949
"POSTES POSTAGE" Omitted
Coil Stamps

1950 *Perf. 9½ Vertically*

295 A119 1c green	.70	.30
On commercial cover		4.50
Pair	1.40	.60
On cover		7.50
296 A121 3c rose violet	1.00	.55
On commercial cover		5.25
Pair	2.00	1.20
On cover		8.50

With "POSTES POSTAGE"
Perf. 9½ Vertically

297 A119 1c green	.40	.25
On commercial cover		4.50
Pair	.80	.50
On cover		8.00
298 A120 2c sepia	3.25	1.30
On commercial cover		6.00
Pair	6.50	2.75
On cover		12.50
299 A121 3c rose violet	2.10	.25
On commercial cover		4.50
Pair	4.20	.50
On cover		11.00
300 A122 4c dark carmine	18.00	.75
On commercial cover		12.50
Pair	36.00	2.25
On cover		32.50
Nos. 297-300 (4)	23.75	2.55

Indians Drying Skins on Stretchers
A125

1950, Oct. 2 *Perf. 12*

301 A125 10c black brown	.90	.25
1st day cover		5.50
Plate block of 4	5.50	

Canada's fur resources. For overprint see No. O26.

Fishing
A126

1951, Feb. 1 **Unwmk.**

302 A126 $1 bright ultra	40.00	10.00
1st day cover		72.50
Plate block of 4	210.00	

Canada's fish resources. For overprint see No. O27.

Sir Robert Laird Borden A127

William L. Mackenzie King A128

1951, June 25 ***Perf. 12***

303 A127 3c turquoise green .25 .25
1st day cover 2.40
Plate block of 4 1.60
304 A128 4c rose pink .25 .25
1st day cover 2.40
Plate block of 4 1.60

George VI Types of 1949

1951 ***Perf. 12***

305 A120 2c olive green .25 .25
On commercial cover .75
Plate block of 4 1.20
306 A122 4c orange vermilion .30 .25
On commercial cover .75
Plate block of 4 1.60
a. Booklet pane of 3 5.25 2.75
b. Booklet pane of 6 5.00 5.00

For overprints see Nos. O28-O29.

Coil Stamps
Perf. 9½ Vertically

309 A120 2c olive green 1.40 .60
On commercial cover 5.50
Pair 2.80 1.50
On cover 9.50
310 A122 4c orange vermilion 2.75 .70
On commercial cover 6.50
Pair 5.50 1.75
On cover 20.00

Trains of 1851 and 1951 — A129

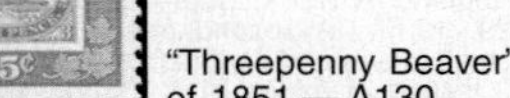

"Threepenny Beaver" of 1851 — A130

Designs: 5c, Steamships City of Toronto and Prince George. 7c, Stagecoach and Plane.

1951, Sept. 24 **Unwmk.** ***Perf. 12***

311 A129 4c dark gray .60 .25
1st day cover 3.50
Plate block of 4 2.75
312 A129 5c purple 1.80 1.25
1st day cover 3.50
Plate block of 4 9.50
313 A129 7c deep blue 1.10 .30
1st day cover 3.50
Plate block of 4 5.50
314 A130 15c bright red 1.20 .30
1st day cover 3.50
Plate block of 4 6.50
Nos. 311-314 (4) 4.70 2.10
Set of 4, #311-314 on one 1st day cover 7.00

Centenary of British North American postal administration.

Princess Elizabeth and Duke of Edinburgh A131

1951, Oct. 26 **Engr.**

315 A131 4c violet .25 .25
1st day cover 2.00
Plate block of 4 1.00

Visit of Princess Elizabeth, Duchess of Edinburgh and the Duke of Edinburgh to Canada and the US.

Symbols of Newsprint Paper Production A132

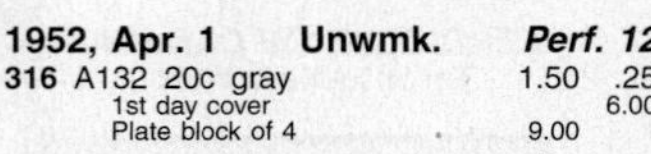

1952, Apr. 1 **Unwmk.** ***Perf. 12***

316 A132 20c gray 1.50 .25
1st day cover 6.00
Plate block of 4 9.00

Canada's paper production. For overprint see No. O30.

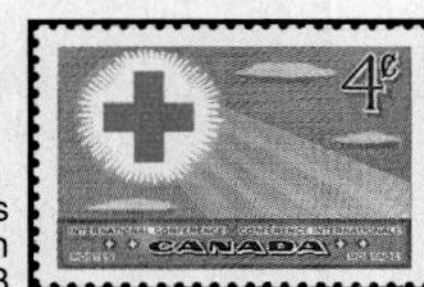
Red Cross on Sun — A133

1952, July 26 **Engr. and Litho.**

317 A133 4c blue & red .25 .25
1st day cover 2.00
Plate block of 4 1.20

18th Intl. Red Cross Conf., Toronto, July 1952.

Sir John J. C. Abbott A134

Alexander Mackenzie A135

1952, Nov. 3 **Engr.**

318 A134 3c rose lilac .25 .25
1st day cover 2.40
Plate block of 4 1.10
319 A135 4c orange vermilion .25 .25
1st day cover 2.40
Plate block of 4 1.10

Canada Goose A136

1952, Nov. 3

320 A136 7c blue .35 .25
1st day cover 6.75
Plate block of 4 1.80

For overprint see No. O31.

AIR POST STAMPS

Allegory of Flight — AP1

Unwmk.

1928, Sept. 21 **Engr.** ***Perf. 12***

C1 AP1 5c brown olive 14.00 5.50
Never hinged 25.00
1st day cover 100.00
Plate block of 6 120.00
Never hinged 225.00
"Swollen breast" variety (4UR2) 85.00 60.00
Never hinged 160.00
On commercial cover 80.00
Plate block of 6 (UR2) 175.00
Never hinged 375.00
a. Imperf., pair 350.00
Never hinged 375.00
b. Horiz. pair, imperf. vert. 225.00
Never hinged 340.00
c. Vert. pair, imperf. horiz. 225.00
Never hinged 340.00

For surcharge see No. C3.

For information on imperforate and part-perforate varieties, see note following No. 47a.

Allegory-Air Mail Circles Globe AP2

1930, Dec. 4 ***Perf. 11***

C2 AP2 5c olive brown 65.00 24.00
Never hinged 110.00
1st day cover 175.00
Plate block of 6 500.00
Never hinged 900.00

For surcharge see No. C4.

No. C1 Surcharged

1932, Feb. 22 ***Perf. 12***

C3 AP1 6c on 5c brown olive 11.00 4.00
Never hinged 20.00
1st day cover 14.50
Plate block of 6 110.00
Never hinged 165.00
"Swollen breast" variety (4UR2) 85.00 60.00
Never hinged 170.00
On commercial cover 80.00
Plate block of 6 (UR2) 175.00
Never hinged 375.00 —
a. Inverted surcharge 225.00
Never hinged 325.00
b. Double surcharge 650.00
Never hinged 925.00
c. Triple surcharge 400.00
Never hinged 550.00
d. Pair, one without surcharge 950.00
Never hinged 1,350.

Counterfeit surcharges exist.
No. C3b is valued in the grade of fine.

No. C2 Surcharged in Dark Blue

1932, July 12 ***Perf. 11***

C4 AP2 6c on 5c olive brown 40.00 14.00
Never hinged 70.00
1st day cover 17.50
Plate block of 4 225.00
Never hinged 450.00

Daedalus AP3

1935, June 1 ***Perf. 12***

C5 AP3 6c red brown 4.25 1.25
Never hinged 6.00
1st day cover 17.50
Plate block of 6 32.50
Never hinged 50.00
a. Horiz. pair, imperf. vert. *7,500.*
b. Imperf., pair 600.00
Never hinged 900.00

No. C5a is unique and is the result of a pre-perforating paper foldover.

Mackenzie River Steamer and Seaplane AP4

1938, June 15

C6 AP4 6c blue 3.75 .40
Never hinged 5.25
1st day cover 16.00
Plate block of 4 22.50
Never hinged 32.50
a. Imperf., pair 650.00
Never hinged 1,000.

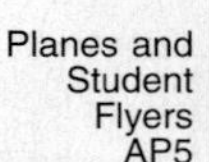

Planes and Student Flyers AP5

1942-43

C7 AP5 6c deep blue 6.00 1.30
Never hinged 7.50
1st day cover (7/1/42) 12.00
Plate block of 4 22.50
Never hinged 32.50
a. Imperf., pair 650.00
Never hinged 1,000.
C8 AP5 7c deep blue ('43) 1.10 .25
Never hinged 1.60
1st day cover (4/16/43) 8.00
Plate block of 4 5.75
Never hinged 8.50
a. Imperf., pair 650.00
Never hinged 1,000.

Canada's contribution to the war effort of the Allied Nations.

Catalogue values for unused stamps in this section, from this point to the end of the section, are for Never Hinged items.

Canada Geese in Flight — AP6

1946, Sept. 16

C9 AP6 7c deep blue 1.10 .25
1st day cover 6.00
Plate block of 4 6.00
a. Booklet pane of 4 4.00 3.50
1st day cover 50.00

For overprints see Nos. CO1, CO2.

AIR POST SPECIAL DELIVERY STAMPS

Trans-Canada Airplane and Aerial View of a City — APSD1

1942-43 **Unwmk.** **Engr.** ***Perf. 12***

CE1 APSD1 16c bright ultra 2.50 2.00
Never hinged 3.50
1st day cover (7/1/42) 14.50
Plate block of 4 13.50
Never hinged 20.00
a. Imperf., pair 650.00
Never hinged 1,025.
CE2 APSD1 17c brt ultra ('43) 3.25 3.00
Never hinged 4.75
1st day cover (4/17/43) 35.00
Plate block of 4 18.00
Never hinged 27.50
a. Imperf., pair 650.00
Never hinged 1,025.

Canada's contribution to the war effort of the Allied Nations.

Catalogue values for unused stamps in this section, from this point to the end of the section, are for Never Hinged items.

DC-4 Transatlantic Mail Plane Over Quebec — APSD2

1946, Sept. 16

CE3 APSD2 17c bright ultra 7.50 4.75
1st day cover 14.50
Plate block of 4 32.50

Circumflex accent on second "E" of "EXPRES."

1946, Dec. 3 **Corrected Die**

CE4 APSD2 17c bright ultra 7.50 6.00
1st day cover 140.00
Plate block of 4 32.50

Grave accent on the 2nd "E" of "EXPRES."

AIR POST OFFICIAL STAMPS

Catalogue values for unused stamps in this section are for Never Hinged items.

All cover values in this section are for uses on commercial covers.

No. C9 Overprinted in Black

1949 **Unwmk.** ***Perf. 12***

CO1 AP6 7c deep blue 12.00 4.75
On cover 24.00
Plate block of 4 50.00
a. No period after "S" 110.00 60.00
On cover 90.00
Plate block of 4 (LL1, LL2) 150.00

Same Overprinted

1950

CO2 AP6 7c deep blue 17.50 13.50
On cover 32.50
Plate block of 4 100.00

AIR POST SEMI-OFFICIAL STAMPS

Mail was first carried by airplane in Canada in 1912, and air clubs and air transport companies pioneered the delivery of mail by air to remote areas of the country, the latter operating under contract with the Canadian Post Office. During 1918-33, labels were issued by both Aero clubs and private companies to frank mail carried on these private flights. Postal regulations required that such labels be affixed to the back of envelopes, and that regular Canadian postage be paid. Generally, hand-stamped cachets bearing the dates or points of the flight were applied to covers flown.

Approximate quantities printed, where known, are noted in parentheses.

AIR CLUBS & SPECIAL FLIGHTS

AERO CLUB OF CANADA
Toronto-Ottawa

Zeppelin on Fire — APL1

1918, Aug. 24 **Litho.** ***Perf. 12***

CLP1 APL1 (25c) black & red *(194)* 1,750. 1,000.
Never hinged 3,500.
Cover, *Aug. 26*, Toronto to Ottawa, green route cancel *(100)* 3,000.
Registered cover, *Aug. 26*, Toronto to Ottawa, green route cancel *(26)* 4,000.
Cover, *Aug. 27*, Ottawa to Toronto, green route cancel *(approx. 35)* 3,800.
Cover, *Aug. 27*, Ottawa to Toronto, black route cancel *(2)* 4,000.
Cover, *Sept. 4*, Toronto to Ottawa, green route cancel 3,400.
Cover, *Sept. 4*, Ottawa to Toronto, green route cancel 3,400.
a. Tête-bêche pair 3,500.
b. Red flame omitted (6) 3,750.

Nos. CLP1 and CLP2 were issued in panes of 2, with the stamps printed tête-bêche. No. CLP1 and a portion of the print run of No. CLP2 were printed on a rough off-white paper. The majority of No. CLP2 was printed on smooth white paper.

A black essay of CLP1 exists on perforated pelure paper, with no gum as issued and no red flame. One recorded. Value, $6,500.

As No. CLP1, Numerals of Value Added — APL2

1918, Aug. 28

CLP2 APL2 25c black & red *(2,800)* 500.00
Never hinged 900.00
Cover, *Sept. 4*, Toronto to Ottawa, green route cancel 4,250.
Cover, *Sept. 4*, Ottawa to Toronto, green route cancel 4,250.
a. Tête-bêche pair 1,200.
Never hinged 2,000.
b. Red flame omitted 1,800.
c. Red flame double (on one stamp in tête-bêche pair) 1,800.
d. On rough off-white paper 750.00
Never hinged 1,000.
e. As "d," tête-bêche 1,600.

Sept. 4 flight covers in both directions bore either CLP1 or CLP2, but no record was kept of which variety was affixed. Total covers flown: Toronto to Ottawa, 44; Ottawa to Toronto, 136.

AERO CLUB OF CANADA
Toronto-New York

APL3

1919

CLP3 APL3 ($1) red & blue *(3,000)* 350.00 125.00
Never hinged 550.00
No gum 125.00
Cover, *Aug. 25*, Toronto to New York *(approx. 300)* 850.00
Return flight, New York to Toronto, without #CLP3 250.00
Commercial cover 1,000.
a. On thin paper, design showing through 350.00

First international air mail service, from the Leaside Aerodrome, Toronto, to Roosevelt Field, Mineola, Long Island, New York.

Printed in panes of 10 (5x2).

Color shift varieties exist.

GRAND ARMY OF CANADA
Toronto-Hamilton and Return

Denomination blocked out — APL4

1920, May 28

CLP4 APL4 ($1) black *14,000.* —
Never hinged —
Pane of 10, without gum —
Flown cover, *May 28*, Toronto to Hamilton *16,000.*
Flown cover, *May 28*, Hamilton to Toronto *16,000.*

Issued in panes of 5, with five stamps in a horizontal strip, surrounded by blank marginal selvage.

Forgeries exist.

ESTEVAN - WINNIPEG PROMOTIONAL ISSUE

APL5

Two types: I, normal spacing between "e" and "w" in "Saskatchewan"; II, wide spacing between "e" and "w" in "Saskatchewan."

1924, Oct. 1 ***Imperf.***

CLP5 APL5 ($1) black *red*, type I *(514)* 350.00 150.00
Never hinged 650.00
On cover, *Oct. 1*, Estevan to Winnipeg *(200-250)* 300.00
a. Inscription inverted *(12)* 2,000. *1,750.*
On flown cover *2,250.*
b. Type II 350.00 150.00
Never hinged 550.00
On cover, *Oct. 1*, Estevan to Winnipeg *(200-250)* 250.00
c. As "b," inscription inverted *(12)* 2,000. *1,750.*
On flown cover *2,250.*
d. Inscription omitted *(4)* 5,000. *1,750.*
On flown cover *5,000.*
e. As #CLP5d, pane of 2 10,000.
f. Pane of 2, #CLP5 + CLP5b 1,500.
Never hinged 2,250.
g. Pane of 2, #CLP5a + CLP5c 4,500.
h. "Aerial" misspelled "Airial" *(2)* 6,500.
First flight cover without #CLP5 (approx. 1,400) 75.00

Issued for first Saskatchewan flight and to publicize the coal-rich area of Estevan.

Issued in vertical panes of 2.

LONDON (Ontario) to LONDON (UK) FLIGHT

Capt. Terrence B. Tully & Lt. James Medcalf — APL6

1927, Aug. ***Perf. 12***

CLP6 APL6 25c green & yellow *(100)* 37,500.
On cover *(1)* *100,000.*

Issued as a result of a Carling Breweries prize offer for the first Canadian or British pilot to fly from London, Ontario, to London, England. A first attempt was aborted on Aug. 29, 1927. A second attempt ended in the crash at sea and death of the pilots on Sept. 6.

Issued in panes of 4. Of the 100 stamps printed, 13 unused single stamps and one example on cover are known.

MOOSE JAW FLYING CLUB
Moose Jaw - Winnipeg

APL7

1928 ***Perf. 11***

CLP7 APL7 ($1) red *(approx. 200)* 3,750.
Never hinged 4,250.
Flight cover, *Aug. 17* *(161)* 3,250.
Pane of 5 20,000.

Issued in vertical panes of 5 stamps (1x5).

PRIVATE COMMERCIAL AIRLINES

LAURENTIDE AIR SERVICE LTD.
Haileybury, Ont. - Rouyn/Angliers, Que.

APL8

1924, Aug. 30 *Rouletted at Left*

CL1 APL8 (25c) green *(200)* 2,000. 1,500.

Never hinged 3,000.

First flight cover, *Sept. 21*, Haileybury to Rouyn or return, *each* 3,000.

Commercial cover 3,500.

a. Booklet pane of 2, with tab at left 4,000.

Never hinged 6,000.

Complete Booklet, 4 #CL1a, stapled at left *(2 known)* *20,000.*

The cover of the No. CL1 booklet is plain, with no printing on front or back.

1924, Sept. 5 *Rouletted at Top*

CL2 APL8 (25c) green *(1,220)* 150.00 100.00

Never hinged 250.00

Sheet of 25 3,750.

First flight cover, *Sept. 21*, Haileybury to Rouyn or return, *each* 2,500.

Flight cover, *Oct. 1*, Angliers to Rouyn 500.00

Flight cover, *Oct. 17*, Haileybury to Rouyn 450.00

Cover, *Jan. 22, 1925*, Three Rivers to Rouyn 250.00

Commercial cover 600.00

a. Booklet pane of 2, tab at top 400.00

Never hinged 650.00

Complete Booklet, 4 #CL2a, stapled at top, printing on front cover 1,800.

Complete Booklet, 4 #CL2a, stapled at top, printing on front and back covers 1,800.

b. (25c) dk blue green (2,400) 200.00

Never hinged 400.00

Flight cover, *Jan. 22, 1925*, Larder Lake to Rouyn 375.00

Commercial cover 600.00

c. As "b," booklet pane of 2, tab at top 425.00

Never hinged 600.00

Complete Booklet, 4 #CL2b, stapled at top, printing on front and back covers *3,000.*

"Canada 1924" Added — APL9

1924, Oct. 1 *Perf. 11½*

CL3 APL9 (25c) red *(3,000)* 140.00

Never hinged 210.00

Pane of 20 2,800.

Flight cover, *Oct. 3*, Haileybury to Rouyn or return, *each* 275.00

Flight cover, *Oct. 24*, Haileybury to Rouyn or return, *each* 375.00

Cover, *Jan. 22, 1925*, Three Rivers to Rouyn Lake 275.00

Commercial cover 500.00

No. CL3 was issued in panes of 20 (4x5).

1924, Oct. 2 *Rouletted at Top*

CL4 APL9 (25c) red *(2,160)* 175.00

Never hinged 260.00

Flight cover, *Oct. 3*, Haileybury to Rouyn or return, *each* 275.00

Flight cover, *Oct. 24*, Haileybury to Rouyn or return, *each* 375.00

Flight cover, *Jan. 22, 1925*, Three Rivers to Rouyn Lake 275.00

Commercial cover 525.00

a. Booklet pane of 2, tab at top 350.00

Never hinged 525.00

Complete booklet, 4 #CL4a 3,000.

b. As "a," top stamp dark red, bottom stamp light red 500.00

Complete booklet, 4 #CL4b 3,000.

Nos. CL4a and CL4b are stapled at top, with printing on both front and back covers.

NORTHERN AIR SERVICE
Haileybury, Ont. - Rouyn, Que.

APL10

1925, June 27 *Perf. 12*

CL5 APL10 (25c) blue *(4,000)* 175.00

Never hinged 260.00

Pane of 20 *3,750.*

Flight cover, *June 27*, Haileybury to Rouyn or return, *each* 175.00

Commercial cover 500.00

a. Tête-bêche pair 700.00

b. Blue dot left of monogram 200.00

Commercial cover 575.00

c. Tête-bêche pair, #CL5 + CL5b 900.00

d. Booklet pane of 4 with tab, top 2 stamps #CL5b 1,500.

Complete booklet, 2 #CL5d 3,000.

No. CL5 was issued both in panes of 20 and in booklet panes of 4.

An experimental flight without No. CL5, but with a special cachet, was made on May 18, 1925, from Haileybury to Rouyn and return. 8 pieces were carried each way. Value, $2,500.

JACK V. ELLIOT AIR SERVICE
Red Lake-Rolling Portage (Hudson) - Sioux Lookout, Ont.

APL11

Yellow background of zig-zag lines

1926, Mar. 6 *Perf. 11½*

CL6 APL11 (25c) red & yellow *(2,500)* 55.00

Never hinged 82.50

Pane of 8 550.00

Flight cover, *Mar. 26*, Rolling Portage to Red Lake or return, *each* 85.00

Commercial cover 225.00

a. Imperf, pair 400.00

b. Tête-bêche gutter pair from sheet of 16 350.00

c. As "b," imperf 700.00

d. Double impression, imperf pair *(2 known)* *1,750.*

e. White spot (position 8, LR) 150.00

On cover 175.00

f. As "e," in pane of 8 650.00

Yellow background of swastikas

1926, Mar. 25

CL7 APL11 (25c) red & yellow *(2,000)* 90.00

Never hinged 135.00

Pane of 8 800.00

Sheet of 16 2,250.

Flight cover, *Mar. 25*, Rolling Portage to Red Lake or return, *each* 85.00

Commercial cover 225.00

a. Imperf, pair 400.00

b. As "a," one stamp with "AIR SERVICE" inverted 550.00

c. Tête-bêche gutter pair from sheet of 16 450.00

d. As "c," imperf 600.00

Nos. CL6 and CL7 were printed in sheets of 16, most of which were cut into two panes of 8, each containing two horizontal rows of 4.

One proof of CL6 exists in black. Value, $50,000.

ELLIOT-FAIRCHILD AIR SERVICE
Service to Red Lake and Rouyn Goldfields

APL12

Yellow background of swastikas

1926, Mar. 21

CL8 APL12 (25c) red & yellow *(2,504)* 40.00

Never hinged 60.00

Pane of 8 350.00

Sheet of 16 2,000.

Flight cover, *Mar. 30*, Rolling Portage to Red Lake or return, *each* 275.00

Flight cover, *April 15*, Rolling Portage to Red Lake or return, *each* 500.00

Flight cover, *May 27*, Rouyn to Haileybury or return, *each* 600.00

Commercial cover 400.00

a. Imperf, pair 225.00

b. Tête-bêche gutter pair from sheet of 16 300.00

c. Tall "r" in "Fairchild," positions 2 and 4 95.00

No. CL8 was printed in sheets of 16 (4x4), with gutter between rows 2 and 3, and cut into panes of 8 (4x2).

ELLIOT-FAIRCHILD AIR SERVICE

APL13

Yellow background of swastikas

1926, Apr. 7

CL9 APL13 (25c) blue & yellow *(5,600)* 30.00

Never hinged 45.00

Pane of 8 275.00

Flight cover, *April 15*, Rolling Portage to Red Lake or return, *each* 250.00

Flight cover, *May 27*, Rouyn to Haileybury or return, *each* 350.00

Commercial cover 500.00

a. Imperf, pair 1,600.

b. Horiz. tete-bêche pair 150.00

c. Vert. tête-bêche pair 150.00

d. Filled-in wing on Pos. 1 100.00

On cover 300.00

No. CL9 was printed in sheets of 16 (4x4) and cut into panes of 8 (4x2).

Panes of 8 with upper-right corner stamp inverted (tete-beche pair at right) sell for a premium.

ELLIOT-FAIRCHILD AIR TRANSPORT LTD.
Rouyn - Haileybury

APL14

1926, Aug. 12

CL10 APL14 (25c) dark red large perfs *(3,000)* 80.00

Never hinged 120.00

Flight cover, *Aug. 12*, Haileybury to Rouyn or return, *each* 225.00

Commercial cover 450.00

a. White dot over "o" of "Elliot," 4th stamp in vert. strip of 5 95.00

First Flight Cover 275.00

Commercial cover 475.00

b. (25c) light red with fine perfs *(2,000)* 80.00

c. As "b," white dot over "o" of "Elliot," 4th stamp in vert. strip of 5 95.00

First Flight Cover 275.00

Commercial cover 475.00

No. CL10 was printed in sheets of 10 (2x5) and cut into panes of 5 (1x5).

FAIRCHILD AIR TRANSPORT LTD.
Northern Ontario to Rouyn Goldfields

APL15

1926, Oct. 19 *Perf. 12*

CL11 APL15 (25c) deep blue *(5,000)* 40.00

Never hinged 60.00

Pane of 10 450.00

Flight cover, *Oct. 20*, Haileybury to Rouyn or return, *each* 90.00

Commercial cover 250.00

a. Vertical tête-bêche pair 85.00

No. CL11 was printed in sheets of 10 (2x5). The pairs of stamps in rows 1, 3 and 5 were normally printed upright, while those in rows 2 and 4 were printed inverted.

CL12 APL15 (25c) ultra *(5,000)* 45.00

Never hinged 67.50

Pane of 10 500.00

a. Horiz. tête-bêche pair, inverted on right 95.00

b. Horiz. tête-bêche pair, one stamp darker shade 150.00

Pane of 10, one column darker shade 1,250.

c. Pane with all stamps tete-beche 2,250.

d. Horiz. tête-bêche pair, inverted on left (from #C12c) 500.00

e. Vert. tête-bêche pair (from #C12c) 350.00

No. CL12 was normally printed in sheets of 10 (2x5), with one column of 5 inverted (No. CL12a). It was also issued with one column in a darker shade (No. CL12b). Within No. CL12c, stamps in positions 1, 4, 5, 8 and 9 are inverted, so that all stamps form tête-bêche pairs with the stamps with which they are contiguous.

No. CL12 was prepared but not issued.

PATRICIA AIRWAYS AND EXPLORATION CO., LTD.
Operated between Sioux Lookout and the Northern Ontario Goldfields, Woman Lake, Pine Ridge, Red Lake, Birch Lake, Ont., and Rouyn, Que.

APL16

Inscribed "Sioux Lookout to Pine Ridge and Red Lake"

1926, July 1

CL13 APL16 (25c) green & red, *yellow* *(12,800)* 65.00

Never hinged 100.00

Sheet of 8 700.00

First flight cover, *July 7*, Sioux Lookout to Red Lake 125.00

Commercial cover 250.00

a. Imperf, pair 375.00

b. Horiz. pair, imperf between, on cover *(4 known)* *900.00*

c. Small "t" in "TO" (pos. 8) 325.00

On cover 575.00

d. No. CL13c in sheet of 8 with 7 #CL13 1,000.

e. Route inscription in black *(488)* 400.00

On cover 500.00

f. As "e," small "t" in "TO" 500.00
On cover 650.00

g. No. CL13f in sheet of 8 with 7 #CL13e 1,200.

h. Handstamped "FED" in red (only known on cover) 1,500.

i. (25c) green & red, *pale yellow* 100.00
Sheet of 8 800.00
On cover 150.00

j. As "i," small "t" in "TO" 750.00
On cover 750.00

k. Route inscription inverted 4,000.
On cover 2,500.

Printed in sheets of 8 (2x4).
Proofs exist in various formats and papers.

No. CL13 Surcharged in Red

1927, Apr. 1

CL14 APL16 10c on (25c) green & red, *yellow, (1,800)* 135.00
Never hinged 200.00
Sheet of 8 1,200.
Cover, *April 9*, Rouyn to Haileybury 350.00

a. On #CL13e 600.00
On flown cover 800.00

b. On #CL13c 1,500.
On flown cover 1,500.

c. Surcharge inverted 550.00

d. Double surcharge, one inverted 850.00

e. 10c on (25c), *buff* 175.00
Sheet of 8 1,500.
On flown cover 350.00

f. Broken "N" in "ROUYN" 175.00
Sheet of 8 1,500.
On flown cover 350.00

g. Surcharge in light red 135.00
Sheet of 8 1,200.
On flown cover 350.00

No. CL13 Surcharged in Black

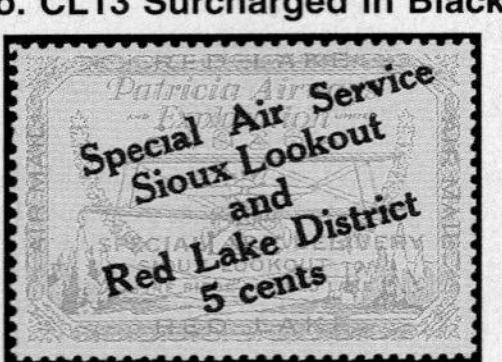

1927, Sept. (?)

CL15 APL16 5c on (25c) green & red, *yellow*, overprint ascending *(200)* 275.00
Never hinged 400.00
Sheet of 8 3,250.
On flown cover 375.00

a. Overprint descending *(8)* 1,750.
On flown cover 2,000.

b. Overprint in red, descending *(200)* 650.00
Sheet of 8 5,200.

c. As "b," malformed "O" in "LOOKOUT" (Plate 1, Pos. 7) 800.00
Sheet of 8, with 7 #CL15 2,800.

No. CL13 Surcharged in Black

1927, Sept. (?)

CL16 APL16 10c on (25c) green & red, *yellow*, overprint ascending 800.00
Never hinged 1,200.
Sheet of 8 5,400.
On flown cover 1,600.

a. Overprint descending 1,000.
Never hinged 1,350.
On flown cover 1,600.

b. Double overprint, descending 1,250.
Never hinged 1,600.

c. Inverted overprint 1,250.

200 stamps were overprinted, which included varieties.

No. CL14 Surcharged in Black

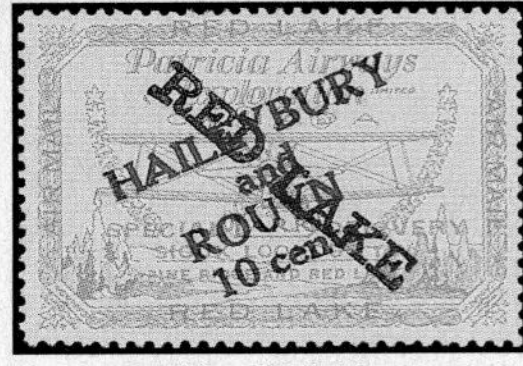

(No. CL17a)

1927, Aug.

CL17 APL16 10c on (25c) green & red, *yellow*, black overprint ascending *(200)* 750.00
Never hinged 1,050.
Sheet of 8 5,500.
On flown cover 850.00

a. Black overprint descending 900.00
Never hinged 1,250.
On flown cover 1,600.

b. As "a," inverted overprint 1,500.

c. Inverted red overprint, descending 1,600.
Never hinged 2,400.

APL17

Inscribed "Woman L Birch L via Sioux Lookout"

1926, July 7

CL18 APL17 (50c) black & red, *blue (1,800)* 200.00
Never hinged 300.
Sheet of 8 1,600.
Flight cover, *Aug. 2*, Sioux Lookout to Woman Lake or return, *each* 250.

a. Imperf, pair 325.

b. Variety "OTT" in "LOOKOUT" 350.
On flown cover 450.

c. Horiz. pair, imperf between 325.

d. As "c," "OTT" variety 450.

e. Additional "FED" in green ink 2,000.
On flown cover 1,400.

f. As "e," "OTT" variety 2,500.
On flown cover 1,750.

g. Missing route inscription 1,500.
Sheet of 8 *12,000.*

No. CL18 on deep blue paper is a trial color proof. Value $500.

No. CL18 Surcharged in Red

1926, July 7

CL19 APL17 10c on (50c) black & red, *blue (770)* 325.00
Never hinged 500.00
Sheet of 8 2,600.
On flown cover 550.00

a. Black overprint 1,200.

b. Dark red overprint 325.00
Sheet of 8 2,600.
On flown cover 550.00

c. Missing red overprint ("Woman Lake" and "Air Mail" on all sides) 5,500.

No. CL18 Surcharged in Black

1926, July 7

CL20 APL17 5c on (50c) black & red, *blue*, ovpt. ascending *(200)* 1,000.
Never hinged 1,500.
Sheet of 8 8,000.
On flown cover 1,000.

a. Overprint descending *(24)* 1,000.
Sheet of 8 8,000.
On flown cover 1,100.

b. Ovpt. in red, ascending *(200)* 750.00
Sheet of 8 6,000.
On flown cover 1,000.

c. Ovpt. in red, descending *(24)* 1,000.
Sheet of 8 8,000.
On flown cover 1,100.

d. As "c," malformed "O" in "LOOKOUT" (Plate 1, Position 7) 1,100.
On flown cover 1,200.
Sheet of 8, 1 #CL20d with 7 #CL20c *7,500.*

No. CL18 Overprinted in Black

1926, July 7

CL21 APL17 (50c) black & red, *blue*, ovpt. descending *(24)* 1,500.
Never hinged 2,300.
On flown cover 1,750.

a. Overprint in violet, ascending *(16)* 2,500.
Never hinged 3,750.
On flown cover 3,000.

b. Overprint in violet, descending *(16)* 2,500.
Never hinged 3,750.
On flown cover 3,000.

c. Double overprint in violet (ascending) 2,500.
Never hinged 3,750.
On flown cover *3,000.*

d. Overprinted in violet, horizontal 2,750.
Never hinged 4,000.
On flown cover 3,500.

No. CL18 Surcharged in Red and Overprinted in Black

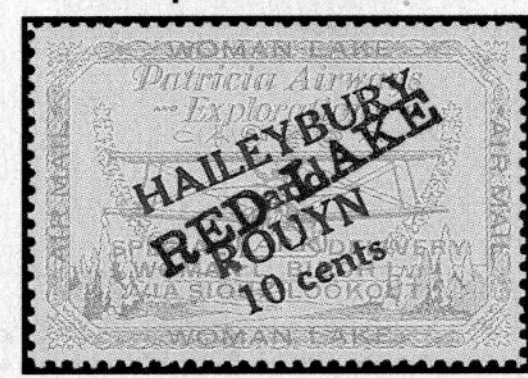

1926, July 7

CL22 APL17 10c on (50c) black & red, *blue*, ovpt. ascending *(24)* 1,750.
Never hinged 2,500.
On flown cover 1,500.

a. Overprint descending (24) 2,250.
Never hinged 3,250.
Sheet of 8 18,000.
On flown cover 1,600.

b. Overprint inverted, ascending (16) 1,750.
Never hinged 2,500.
On flown cover 1,750.

c. Overprint inverted, descending (16) 1,750.
Never hinged 2,500.
On flown cover 1,750.

d. As "a," broken "N" in "ROUYN" 1,750.
Never hinged 2,500.
On flown cover 1,750.

e. As "a," surcharge in light red 1,750.
On flown cover 1,750.

f. As "b," broken "N" in "ROUYN" 1,750.
On flown cover 1,750.

Nos. CL18-CL22 on commercially flown covers are very elusive and command premium prices.

APL18

CL23 APL18 (50c) green & red, *yellow* 700.00
Never hinged 1,000.
Sheet of 8 5,600.

a. Imperf, pair 1,400.
Never hinged 2,000.

CL23 exists with rouletting doubled.

No. CL23 Surcharged in Red

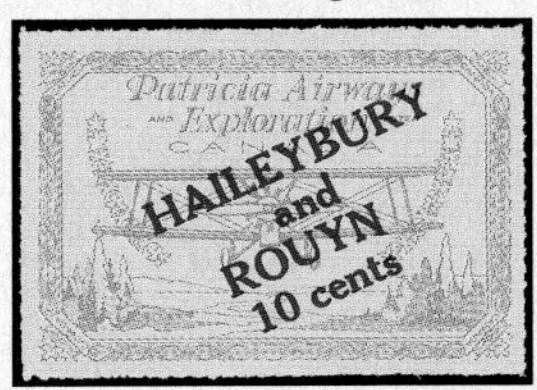

CL24 APL18 10c on (50c) green & red, *yellow (800)* 135.00
Never hinged 200.00
Sheet of 8 1,100.
On flown cover 250.00

No. CL23 Surcharged in Black

CL25 APL18 5c on (50c) green & red, *yellow*, descending *(800)* 65.00
Never hinged 95.00
Sheet of 8 575.00
On flown cover 185.00

a. Overprint in red, descending *(1368)* 45.00
Never hinged 65.00
Sheet of 8 475.00
On flown cover 185.00

b. Overprint in green, descending 45.00
Never hinged 65.00
Sheet of 8 475.00
On flown cover 185.00

c. Overprint in green, ascending *(4448)* 45.00
Never hinged 65.00
Sheet of 8 475.00
On flown cover 185.00

d. As "a," *pale yellow* 175.00

e. As "c," *pale yellow* 175.00

The overprint on Nos. CL25a-CL25c exists with the third "o" in "Lookout" malformed (plate 1, position 7). Values, each: unused $450; on flown cover $500.

No. CL23 Surcharged in Black

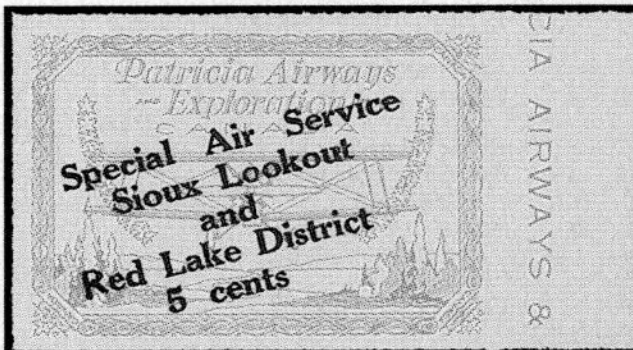

CL26 APL18 5c on (50c) green & red, *yellow*, ascending *(800)* 550.00
Never hinged 175.00
Sheet of 8 1,100.
On flown cover 215.00

a. Inverted overprint 500.00

b. Horiz. pair, left stamp overprinted "RED LAKE" in red, descending 800.00
c. Overprint in red, ascending *(800)* 125.00
Sheet of 8 1,150.
On flown cover 300.00
d. As "c," overprint inverted 500.00
e. Overprint in green *(800)* 135.00
Sheet of 8 1,200.
On flown cover 250.00
f. As "e," overprint inverted 500.00

No. CL24 Surcharged in Black

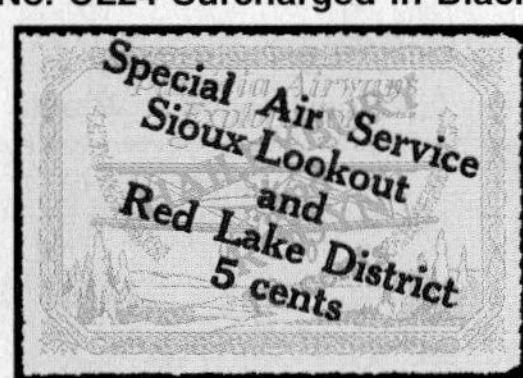

CL27 APL18 5c on 10c on (50c) green & red, *yellow (400)* 400.00
Never hinged 600.00
Sheet of 8 2,800.
On flown cover 550.00
a. Pair, one stamp missing 5c surcharge 1,000.

No. CL24 Surcharged in Black

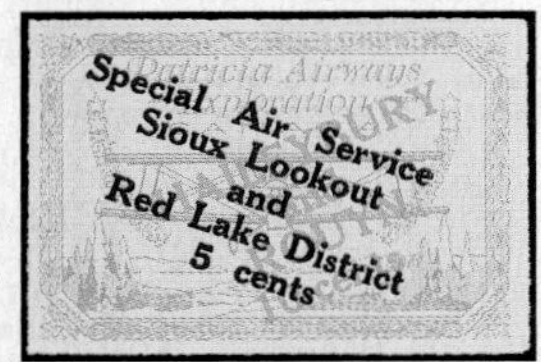

CL28 APL18 5c on 10c on (50c) green & red, *yellow (400-600)* 175.00
Never hinged 250.00
Sheet of 8 1,400.
On flown cover 350.00
a. Black overprint surcharge 450.00
b. On *pale yellow* 375.00
Never hinged 525.00

No. CL24 Ovptd. in Black, Purple or Green

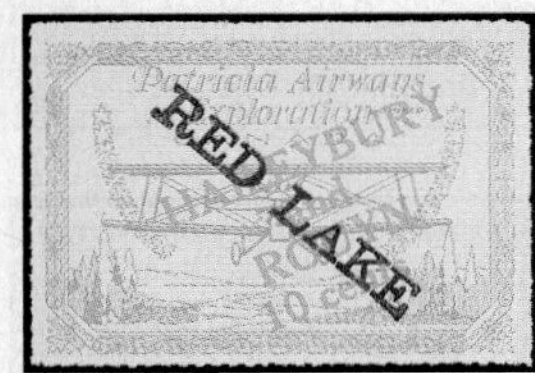

CL29 APL18 10c on (50c) green & red, *yellow,* Black ovpt., descending 200.00
Never hinged 300.00
Sheet of 8 1,600.
On flown cover 350.00
a. Overprint ascending 200.00
Never hinged 300.00
Sheet of 8 1,600.
On flown cover 350.00
b. As #CL29, overprint inverted 250.00
Never hinged 375.00
Sheet of 8 2,000.
On flown cover 375.00
c. As #CL29a, overprint inverted 250.00
Never hinged 375.00
Sheet of 8 2,000.
On flown cover 375.00
d. Overprint in purple, descending 200.00
Never hinged 300.00
Sheet of 8 1,600.
On flown cover 350.00
e. Overprint in purple, ascending 200.00
Never hinged 300.00
Sheet of 8 1,600.
On flown cover 350.00
f. As #CL29d, overprint inverted 250.00
Never hinged 375.00
Sheet of 8 2,000.
On flown cover 375.00
g. As #CL29e, overprint inverted 250.00
Never hinged 375.00
Sheet of 8 2,000.
On flown cover 375.00
h. Overprint in green, descending 200.00
Never hinged 300.00
Sheet of 8 1,600.
On flown cover 350.00
i. Overprint in green, ascending 200.00
Never hinged 300.00
Sheet of 8 1,600.
On flown cover 350.00
j. As #CL29h, overprint inverted 250.00
Never hinged 375.00
Sheet of 8 2,000.
On flown cover 375.00
k. As #CL29i, overprint inverted 250.00
Never hinged 375.00
Sheet of 8 2,000.
On flown cover 375.00

No. CL23 Overprinted in Black, Red, Green or Purple

CL30 APL18 50c green & red, *yellow,* Black ovpt., descending 95.00
Never hinged 150.00
Sheet of 8 800.00
On flown cover 135.00
a. Overprint ascending 95.00
Never hinged 150.00
Sheet of 8 800.00
On flown cover 135.00
b. As #CL30, overprint inverted 175.00
Never hinged 225.00
c. As #CL30a, overprint inverted 175.00
Never hinged 225.00
d. Imperf, pair 400.00
e. Overprint in red, descending 95.00
Sheet of 8 800.00
On flown cover 135.00
f. Overprint in red, ascending 95.00
Sheet of 8 800.00
On flown cover 135.00
g. As #CL30e, overprint inverted 175.00
Never hinged 225.00
h. As #CL30f, overprint inverted 175.00
Never hinged 225.00
i. Imperf, pair 400.00
j. Overprint in green, descending 95.00
Never hinged 150.00
Sheet of 8 800.00
On flown cover 135.00
k. As "j," imperf pair 550.00
l. Overprint in green, ascending 95.00
Never hinged 150.00
Sheet of 8 800.00
On flown cover 135.00
m. As #CL30j, overprint inverted 175.00
Never hinged 225.00
n. As #CL30k, overprint inverted 550.00
Never hinged 675.00
o. Double overprint, one red, one green 450.00
p. Plane inverted, ovpt. in red, descending 2,250.
q. Plane inverted, ovpt. in red, ascending 2,250.
r. As "q," overprint inverted 2,250.
s. As "q," ovpt. in black 3,000.
t. As "q," ovpt. in green 2,250.
u. Overprint in purple 65.00
v. As "u," overprint inverted —
w. As "u," imperf. pair —
x. Overprint in purple, ascending —
y. As "x," ovpt. inverted —
z. As "x," plane inverted —

Nos. CL23-CL30 on commercially flown covers are very elusive and command premium prices.

WESTERN CANADA AIRWAYS SERVICE

APL19

1927, May 1 ***Perf. 12***
CL40 APL19 (10c) black & pink *(36,600)* 7.00
Never hinged 10.00
Pane of 50 400.00
First flight cover, *June 1, 1927,* Lac du Bonnet to Long Lake 250.00
Flight cover, later flight 50.00
Commercial cover 150.00
a. (10c) black & pale rose *(10,000)* 8.50
Never hinged 12.50
Pane of 50 450.00
b. As "a," black double 300.00
c. (10c) black & dark red *(10,000)* 9.00
d. Vertical pair, imperf between 500.00
e. Horizontal pair, imperf between 500.00

Issued in sheets of 200, cut into panes of 50.

The Western Canada Airways Service had bases in northern Ontario, Manitoba, Saskatchewan, Alberta and Northwest Territories. No. CL40 was sold at the Winnipeg post offices and at other Canadian offices, as well as being available from the air service itself.

Jubilee Issue

APL20

1927, July 1 **Thick Paper**
CL41 APL20 (10c) black & orange *(10,000)* 15.00
Never hinged 22.50
Pane of 50 750.00
Jubilee flight cover, *July 1,* Rolling Portage to Red Lake 425.00
Same, printed map on reverse of cover 750.00
Other flight covers, *July 1* 425.00
Commercial cover 600.00
d. Vertical pair, imperf between 550.00

Issued to commemorate the 60th anniversary of Canadian Confederation.

Issued in sheets of 200, cut into panes of 50.

Valid for one day only. Many cachets exist.

YUKON AIRWAYS & EXPLORATION CO., LTD.

APL21

1927, Nov. 11 ***Perf. 12***
CL42 APL21 25c dark blue *(10,000)* 45.00
Never hinged 65.00
Flight cover, *April 2, 1928,* Mayo Landing to White Horse 175.00
Flight cover, *April 13, 1928* 50.00
Commercial cover 450.00
a. Booklet pane of 10, with tab 500.00
Complete booklet of 10 #CL42a *(2 known)* 5,000.
b. Imperf, pair 5,000.
c. "ArRWAYS" variety 275.00
On cover 500.00
d. 25c light blue *(1,200)* 150.00
Never hinged 225.00
On cover 50.00
e. Double print 350.00
f. As "e," "ArRWAYS" variety 550.00
g. As "e," strip of 10 with "ArRWAYS" variety, never hinged 4,500.
h. Horiz. pair, imperf vertically 2,000.
Never hinged 2,500.
Horiz. strip of 16 (8x2) with selvage on both sides *19,000.*

No. CL42 was printed in sheets of 80 and cut into vertical strips of 10 for sale in booklets containing 10 strips with a plain brown cover. The No. CL42h strip of 16 proves the sheet size was 80 stamps (8x10) before cutting into panes for booklet sales.

No. CL42g is unique.

PATRICIA AIRWAYS LTD.

APL22

1928, Mar. 5 ***Rouletted***
CL43 APL22 (10c) green & red, *yellow (3,200)* 50.00
Never hinged 75.00
Sheet of 8 400.00
Flight cover, *Mar. 9, 1928,* Sioux Lookout to Gold Pines 225.00
Flight cover, other flights 225.00
Commercial cover 350.00
a. Plane inverted 1,500.
Never hinged 2,250.
b. Imperf, pair 700.00

Printed in sheets of 8 (2x4)

BRITISH COLUMBIA AIRWAYS LTD. Operated between Vancouver and Victoria, B.C.

APL23

1928, Aug. 3
CL44 APL23 5c ultra *(110,000)* 15.00
Never hinged 17.50
First flight cover, *Aug. 3, 1928,,* Victoria to Vancouver 150.00
Covers flown Aug. 4-25 275.00

Issued in sheets of 220, cut into panes of 55.

KLONDIKE AIRWAYS LTD. Operated between bases in the Yukon

APL24

1928, Oct. 4
CL45 APL24 25c blue (shades) *(110,000)* 65.00
Never hinged 95.00
Pane of 4 with tab 300.00
On cover 400.00

Issued in panes of four (1x4), rouletted between the stamps.

Most covers are addressed to East Orange, New Jersey. These are considered unlikely to have been flown within the Yukon and are worth less than the value shown.

CHERRY RED AIRLINE LTD. Northern Saskatchewan

APL25

1929, July 3 ***Perf. 12***
CL46 APL25 10c black & red *(24,000)* 12.00
Never hinged 15.00
First flight cover, *Dec. 25, 1929,* Prince Albert to Ile a la Crosse 45.00
Other flight covers 40.00

Issued in sheets of 200, cut into panes of 50.

COMMERCIAL AIRWAYS LTD. Northern Alberta and Northwest Territories

APL26

1929, May 18
CL47 APL26 10c black *(3,000)* 125.00
Never hinged 175.00
Pane of 10 1,200.
First flight cover, *May 21, 1929*, Edmonton to Grande Prairie 100.00

APL27

1930, June 2
CL48 APL27 10c black *(2,000)* 15.00
Never hinged 18.50
Pane of 10 150.00
First flight cover, *Dec. 12, 1930*, Edmonton to Peace River or return 50.00
a. 10c deep black on thin paper 15.00
Pane of 10 150.00
b. Imperf, pair 300.00

1930, July 21
CL49 APL26 10c purple *(2,000)* 200.00
Never hinged 275.00
Pane of 10 2,000.
Flight cover, *July 23, 1930*, Edmonton to Ft. McMurray or return 250.00
a. Imperf, pair 450.00
Imperf single on cover 450.00
b. Vertical pair, imperf between 1,400.
c. Broken "C" in "CIAL" 250.00 —
Never hinged 310.00
d. Imperf pair, one stamp the broken "C" variety 500.00 —

Of the 2,000 stamps printed, approximately 700 were destroyed.

1930, Dec. 6
CL50 APL27 10c orange thick paper *(5,000)* 17.50
Never hinged 21.00
Pane of 10 175.00
Flight cover, *Feb. 24, 1931*, Ft. McMurray to Athabaska or return 70.00
a. On thin paper 17.50
Pane of 10 175.00
b. Imperf, pair 300.00

Nos. CL47-CL50 were printed in panes of 10 (2x5).

CANADIAN AIRWAYS LTD. Northern Alberta and Northwest Territories, Manitoba Mining Areas

APL28

1932
CL51 APL28 (10c) blue & orange *(2,000)* 30.00
Never hinged 45.00
Flight cover, *Dec. 30, 1932*, Edmonton to Ft. McMurray or return 70.00
a. Horizontal pair, imperf between *(20 pairs)* 700.00
b. Vertical pair, imperf between *(10 pairs)* 700.00

Printed in sheets of 200, cut into panes of 50.

No. CL51 Surcharged in Black

1934
CL52 APL28 10c on (10c) blue & orange 25.00
Never hinged 32.50
Flight cover, *July 19, 1934*, Edmonton to Ft. McMurray or return 75.00
a. Inverted surcharge *(100)* 1,000.
Never hinged *1,250.*
b. Double surcharge *(10)* 1,500.
c. Pair, one with inverted surcharge 2,000.

Issued in panes of 50.

SCADTA — CONSULAR OVERPRINTS

For Canada (CA) overprints on Colombian stamps for expedited airmail service within Colombia for mail sent from Canada, see the Colombia SCADTA listings in this volume.

SPECIAL DELIVERY STAMPS

All cover values in this section are for uses on commercial covers.

SD1

Unwmk.

1898, June 28 Engr. *Perf. 12*
E1 SD1 10c blue green 125.00 11.00
Never hinged 350.00
On cover 140.00
Plate block of 4 (pl. 2) 650.00
Never hinged 1,500.
Plate block of 6 (pl. 1) 850.00
Never hinged *2,250.*
a. 10c green 110.00 11.00
Never hinged 300.00
On cover 200.00
Plate block of 4 (pl. 2) 550.00
Never hinged 1,400.
Plate block of 6 (pl. 1) 850.00
Never hinged *2,000.*
b. 10c yellow green 150.00 18.50
Never hinged 450.00
On cover 240.00
Plate block of 4 (pl. 2) 750.00
Never hinged 1,500.
Plate block of 6 (pl. 1) 1,100.
Never hinged *2,800.*

Due to plate wear, the last examples of No. E1 printed show no shading in the value tablet areas. Such examples sell for only slightly more than normal stamps, either unused, used or on cover.

SD2

1922, Aug. 21
E2 SD2 20c carmine, dry printing (42½ wide) 100.00 9.00
Never hinged 220.00
On cover 32.50
Plate block of 4 1,100.
Never hinged 1,900.
a. 20c scarlet, wet printing (41mm wide) 180.00 18.00
Never hinged 300.00
On cover 35.00
Plate block of 4 1,150.
Never hinged 2,000.

Five Stages of Mail Transportation SD3

1927, June 29
E3 SD3 20c orange 35.00 22.50
Never hinged 70.00
On cover 55.00
Plate block of 6 250.00
Never hinged 550.00
a. Imperf., pair 225.00
Never hinged 400.00
b. Horiz. pair, imperf. vert. 190.00
Never hinged 275.00
c. Vert. pair, imperf. horiz. 190.00
Never hinged 275.00

No. E3 forms part of the Confederation Commemorative issue.

SD4

1930, Sept. 2 *Perf. 11*
E4 SD4 20c henna brown 65.00 17.50
Never hinged 125.00
On cover 67.50
Plate block of 4 300.00
Never hinged 550.00

SD5

1932, Dec. 24
E5 SD5 20c henna brown 60.00 17.50
Never hinged 115.00
On cover 60.00
Plate block of 4 300.00
Never hinged 550.00
a. Imperf., pair 650.00
Never hinged 950.00

Allegory of Progress — SD6

1935, June 1 *Perf. 12*
E6 SD6 20c dark carmine 12.00 7.50
Never hinged 20.00
On cover 32.50
Plate block of 4 (LL 1) 87.50
Never hinged 130.00
Plate block of 6 120.00
Never hinged 180.00
a. Imperf., pair 650.00
Never hinged 950.00

Arms of Canada — SD7

1938-39
E7 SD7 10c dk green (4/1/39) 9.00 3.50
Never hinged 15.00
On cover 24.00
Plate block of 4 42.50
Never hinged 60.00
a. Imperf., pair 600.00
Never hinged 1,000.
E8 SD7 20c dark carmine (6/15/38) 30.00 25.00
Never hinged 50.00
On cover 50.00
Plate block of 4 (LL 1) 210.00
Never hinged 275.00
Plate block of 6 250.00
Never hinged *350.00*
a. Imperf., pair 600.00
Never hinged 1,000.

No. E8 Surcharged in Black

1939, Mar. 1
E9 SD7 10c on 20c dk car 8.00 6.50
Never hinged 12.00
On cover 27.50
Plate block of 4 (LL 1) 42.50
Never hinged 57.50
Plate block of 6 60.00
Never hinged 85.00

Coat of Arms and Flags SD8

1942, July 1
E10 SD8 10c green 3.50 2.00
Never hinged 5.00
On cover 9.50
Plate block of 4 22.50
Never hinged 30.00
a. Imperf., pair 600.00
Never hinged 950.00

Canada's contribution to the war effort of the Allied Nations.

Catalogue values for unused stamps in this section, from this point to the end of the section, are for Never Hinged items.

Arms of Canada — SD9

1946, Sept. 16
E11 SD9 10c green 4.50 1.25
On cover 8.00
Plate block of 4 19.00

The laurel and olive branches symbolize Victory and Peace.
For overprints see Nos. EO1, EO2.

SPECIAL DELIVERY OFFICIAL STAMPS

Catalogue values for unused stamps in this section are for Never Hinged items.

All cover values in this section are for uses on commercial covers.

No. E11 Overprinted in Black

1950 Unwmk. *Perf. 12*

EO1 SD9 10c green 17.50 12.50
On cover 67.50
Plate block of 4 70.00

Same Overprinted

EO2 SD9 10c green 25.00 17.50
On cover 80.00
Plate block of 4 110.00

REGISTRATION STAMPS

All cover values in this section are for uses on commercial covers.

R1

1875-88 Unwmk. Engr. *Perf. 12*

F1 R1 2c orange 110.00 6.00
Never hinged 240.00
On cover 40.00
a. 2c vermilion 160.00 15.00
Never hinged 350.00
On cover 40.00
b. 2c rose carmine 325.00 110.00
Never hinged 700.00
On cover 85.00
c. As "a," imperf., pair *3,000.*
d. Perf. 12x11½ 550.00 110.00
Never hinged 1,150.
On cover 160.00
F2 R1 5c dark green 140.00 5.50
Never hinged 290.00
On cover 40.00
a. 5c blue green ('88) 160.00 5.50
Never hinged 325.00
On cover 40.00
b. 5c yellow green 225.00 7.00
Never hinged 450.00
On cover 40.00
c. Imperf., pair 1,200.
Never hinged *2,250.*
d. Perf. 12x11½ 2,250. 275.00
Never hinged *4,500.*
On cover 325.00
F3 R1 8c dull blue ('76) 600.00 350.00
Never hinged 1,500.
On cover *12,000.*
a. 8c bright blue 450.00 350.00
Never hinged 1,050.
On cover *12,000.*
Nos. F1-F3 (3) 850.00 361.50

Value for No. F3 on cover is for a correct usage in 1876-1877.

The used No. F1c is unique (fine centering).

POSTAGE DUE STAMPS

All cover values in this section are for uses on commercial covers.

On cover values are for stamps tied by postal cancellations such as datestamps or rollers. Covers with stamps uncanceled or tied by crayon marks sell for much less.

D1

1906-28 Unwmk. Engr. *Perf. 12*

J1 D1 1c violet 25.00 4.75
Never hinged 40.00
On cover 20.00
a. Thin paper ('24) 45.00 7.50
Never hinged 80.00
b. Imperf., pair 400.00
c. 1c reddish violet ('28) 25.00 4.75
Never hinged 40.00
J2 D1 2c violet 25.00 1.00
Never hinged 40.00
On cover 12.00
a. Thin paper ('24) 45.00 11.00
Never hinged 80.00
b. Imperf., pair 400.00
c. 2c reddish violet ('28) 25.00 1.00
Never hinged 40.00
J3 D1 4c violet ('28) 65.00 22.50
Never hinged 110.00
On cover 40.00
J4 D1 5c violet 25.00 2.00
Never hinged 40.00
On cover 40.00
a. As "c," thin paper 35.00 7.50
Never hinged 60.00
b. Imperf., pair 400.00
c. 5c reddish violet ('28) 25.00 2.00
Never hinged 40.00
J5 D1 10c violet ('28) 100.00 14.00
Never hinged 190.00
On cover *80.00*
Nos. J1-J5 (5) 240.00 44.25
Set, never hinged 390.00

In 1924 there was a printing of Nos. J1, J2 and J4 on thin semi-transparent paper. Imperf pairs are without gum.

D2

1930-32 *Perf. 11*

J6 D2 1c dark violet 12.50 4.25
Never hinged 22.50
On cover, single franking 20.00
Plate block of 4 200.00
Never hinged 300.00
J7 D2 2c dark violet 7.00 1.10
Never hinged 12.50
On cover, single franking 16.00
Plate block of 4 150.00
Never hinged 210.00
J8 D2 4c dark violet 15.00 5.50
Never hinged 25.00
On cover, single franking 20.00
Plate block of 4 250.00
Never hinged 325.00
J9 D2 5c dark violet 25.00 6.50
Never hinged 42.50
On cover *40.00*
Plate block of 4 250.00
Never hinged 325.00
J10 D2 10c dark violet ('32) 110.00 10.00
Never hinged 200.00
On cover *50.00*
Plate block of 4 600.00
Never hinged 875.00
a. Vert. pair, imperf. horiz. 1,750. —
Never hinged 2,750.
Nos. J6-J10 (5) 169.50 27.35
Set, never hinged 312.50

No. J10a is valued in the grade of fine.

D3

1933-34

J11 D3 1c dark violet ('34) 15.00 6.50
Never hinged 27.50
On cover, single franking 20.00
Plate block of 4 75.00
Never hinged 115.00
a. Imperf., pair 400.00
Never hinged 575.00
J12 D3 2c dark violet 9.00 1.25
Never hinged 16.50
On cover, single franking 16.00
Plate block of 4 60.00
Never hinged 90.00
J13 D3 4c dark violet 15.00 8.00
Never hinged 27.50
On cover, single franking 20.00
Plate block of 4 70.00
Never hinged 100.00
J14 D3 10c dark violet 35.00 7.25
Never hinged 57.50
On cover *47.50*
Plate block of 4 160.00
Never hinged 230.00
Nos. J11-J14 (4) 74.00 23.00
Set, never hinged 115.50

Catalogue values for unused stamps in this section, from this point to the end of the section, are for Never Hinged items.

D4

1935-65 *Perf. 12*

J15 D4 1c dark violet .30 .25
On cover, single franking 12.00
Plate block of 4 (LL 1) 1.75
Plate block of 6 3.00
Plate block of 10 3.75
a. Imperf., pair 260.00
b. 1c red violet ('40) 2.25 .55
Plate block of 4 (LL 1) 9.00
Plate block of 6 15.00
Plate block of 10 20.00
J16 D4 2c dark violet .30 .25
On cover, single franking 8.00
Plate block of 4 (LL 1) 1.90
Plate block of 6 3.00
Plate block of 10 3.75
a. Imperf., pair 260.00
c. 2c red violet 1.90 .55
Plate block of 4 (LL 1, LL 2) 8.00
Plate block of 6 15.00
Plate block of 10 20.00
J16B D4 3c dark vio ('65) 2.00 1.50
On cover, single franking 40.00
Plate block of 4 (LL 1) 12.50
Plate block of 6 22.50
Plate block of 10 30.00
J17 D4 4c dark violet .35 .25
On cover, single franking 12.00
Plate block of 4 (LL 1) 2.00
Plate block of 6 3.75
Plate block of 10 4.50
a. Imperf., pair 260.00
b. 4c red violet 1.60 .55
Plate block of 4 (LL 1) 9.50
Plate block of 6 16.00
Plate block of 10 22.00
J18 D4 5c dark vio ('48) .40 .35
On cover, single franking 20.00
Plate block of 4 (LL 1) 2.75
Plate block of 6 4.90
Plate block of 10 6.00
a. 5c red violet 3.00 1.10
Plate block of 4 (LL 1) 12.50
Plate block of 6 22.50
Plate block of 10 30.00
J19 D4 6c dark vio ('57) 2.25 1.75
On cover, single franking 16.00
Plate block of 4 (LL 1) 10.00
Plate block of 6 19.00
Plate block of 10 22.50
J20 D4 10c dark violet .40 .25
On cover, single franking 12.00
Plate block of 4 (LL 1) 2.40
Plate block of 6 4.00
Plate block of 10 5.25
a. Imperf., pair 200.00
b. 10c red violet 1.60 .55
Plate block of 4 (LL 1) 12.50
Plate block of 6 19.00
Plate block of 10 26.00
Nos. J15-J20 (7) 6.00 4.60

WAR TAX STAMPS

All cover values in this section are for uses on commercial covers.

WT1

Unwmk.

1915, Mar. 25 Engr. *Perf. 12*

MR1 WT1 1c green 25.00 .40
Never hinged 60.00
On cover 1.60
MR2 WT1 2c carmine 25.00 .40
Never hinged 60.00
On cover 4.00
a. 2c rose carmine 30.00 .60
Never hinged 70.00
On cover 4.00

In 1915 postage stamps of 5, 20 and 50 cents were overprinted "WAR TAX" in two lines. These stamps were intended for fiscal use, the war tax on postal matter being 1 cent. A few of these stamps were used to pay postage.

WT2

Type I

Type II

TWO TYPES:

Type I — There is a colored line between two white lines below the large letter "T."

Type II — The right half of the colored line is replaced by two short diagonal lines and five small dots.

1916

MR3 WT2 2c + 1c car (I) 40.00 .25
Never hinged 100.00
On cover 1.60
a. 2c + 1c carmine (II) 275.00 4.50
Never hinged 625.00
On cover 8.00
b. 2c + 1c rose red (I) 50.00 .40
Never hinged 120.00
On cover 1.60
MR4 WT2 2c + 1c brn (II) 25.00 .25
Never hinged 62.50
On cover 1.20
a. 2c + 1c brown (I) 800.00 10.00
Never hinged 1,500.
On cover 16.00
b. Imperf., pair (I) 175.00
c. Imperf., pair (II) 2,250.

Nos. MR4b and MR4c were made without gum.

Perf. 12x8

MR5 WT2 2c + 1c car (I) 60.00 30.00
Never hinged 130.00
On cover 32.50

Coil Stamps

Perf. 8 Vertically

MR6 WT2 2c + 1c car (I) 140.00 10.00
Never hinged 330.00
On cover 10.00
Pair 280.00 110.00
Never hinged 660.00
On cover *150.00*
Paste-up pair 340.00 —
Never hinged 725.00
MR7 WT2 2c + 1c brn (II) 50.00 2.25
Never hinged 110.00
On cover 8.00
Pair 90.00 15.00
Never hinged 200.00
On cover 15.00
Paste-up pair 250.00 —
Never hinged 450.00
a. 2c + 1c brown (I) 200.00 7.50
Never hinged 500.00
On cover 10.00
Pair 375.00 75.00
Never hinged 750.00
On cover —
Paste-up pair 400.00 —
Never hinged 800.00

OFFICIAL STAMPS

PERFORATED OFFICIAL STAMPS

Stamps perforated "O.H.M.S." (On His Majesty's Service) were introduced in May 1923 for use in the Receiver General's office of the Finance Department and by the Assistant Receiver Generals' offices in provincial cities. In 1935, the Post Office Department became responsible for perforating these stamps, and on March 28, 1939, the Treasury Board ruled that on and after June 30, 1939, all postage stamps used by government offices had to be perforated "O.H.M.S." These stamps continued to be produced until they were replaced by the overprinted "O.H.M.S." stamps in 1949.

The perforated initials can appear either upright, inverted, or sideways reading up or down on any given stamp, and further can be right-reading either from the front of the stamp or from the reverse. Thus, eight varieties are possible for each stamp, though not all stamps are known with all possible varieties. This catalogue values only the most common orientation.

The perfins come in two styles, as shown below. Stamps perforated with five holes in the vertical bars of the "H" are valued only used, because unused examples are rarely seen.

Values are for very fine examples with the stamp itself well centered and the perforations undamaged by encroaching perfin holes. Stamps in a grade below very fine and/or with damaged perforations will sell for less.

Beware of forgeries. On used stamps, be aware that ink from cancellations will tend to "bleed" into the perfin holes of genuine examples, whereas it will not on most forgeries, which almost always were made using already canceled stamps. As with all scarce issues that may be forged, dealing with reputable and knowledgable sources and using recognized expertizing authorities is recommended.

Stamps overprinted "O.H.M.S." or "G" follow No. OE11.

5-HOLE PERFINS

Large "O.H.M.S" 5 Holes in Vertical Bars of "H"

(OA plus Scott No.)

For die types of the 1c and 3c see postage.

1912-25 *Perf. 12*
OA104 A43 1c green 70.00
OA105 A43 1c yellow (I) ('22) 60.00
d. 1c yellow (II) 60.00
OA106 A43 2c carmine 55.00
OA107 A43 2c yel green ('22) 45.00
a. Thin paper ('24) 65.00
OA108 A43 3c brown ('18) 60.00
OA109 A43 3c car (I) ('23) 50.00
c. Die II ('24) 60.00
OA110 A43 4c olive bister ('22) 125.00
OA111 A43 5c dark blue 90.00
OA112 A43 5c violet ('22) 75.00
a. Thin paper ('24) 90.00
OA113 A43 7c yellow ocher 110.00
OA114 A43 7c red brn ('24) 85.00
OA115 A43 8c blue ('25) 140.00
OA116 A43 10c plum 90.00
OA117 A43 10c blue ('22) 85.00
OA118 A43 10c bis brn ('25) 55.00
OA119 A43 20c olive grn ('25) 85.00
OA120 A43 50c blk brn, dry printing ('25) 110.00
a. 50c black, wet printing 150.00
OA122 A43 $1 orange ('23) 125.00

Coil Stamp

1918 *Perf. 8 Vertically*
OA129 A43 3c brown 450.00

50th Anniv. of the Canadian Confederation

1917 *Perf. 12*
OA135 A44 3c brown 475.00

60th Year of the Canadian Confederation

1927
OA141 A45 1c orange 110.00
OA142 A46 2c green 140.00
OA143 A47 3c brown car 140.00
OA144 A48 5c violet 110.00
OA145 A49 12c dark blue 360.00

1927, June 29
OA146 A50 5c violet 110.00
OA147 A51 12c green 360.00
OA148 A52 20c brown car 300.00

Definitives

1928-29
OA149 A53 1c orange 60.00
OA150 A53 2c green 45.00
OA151 A53 3c dk car 125.00
OA152 A53 4c bister ('29) 150.00
OA153 A53 5c dp violet 55.00
OA154 A53 8c blue 150.00
OA155 A54 10c green 45.00
OA156 A55 12c gray ('29) 400.00
OA157 A56 20c dk car ('29) 110.00
OA158 A57 50c dk blue ('29) 650.00
OA159 A58 $1 olive grn ('29) 475.00

1930-31 *Perf. 11*

For die types of the 1c and 2c see postage.

OA162 A59 1c orange 50.00
OA163 A59 1c deep green (II) 35.00
b. Die I (12/6/30) 40.00
OA164 A59 2c dull green (I) 140.00
OA165 A59 2c deep red (I) 45.00
a. Die II 40.00
OA166 A59 2c dk brn (II) ('31) 45.00
b. Die I 50.00
OA167 A59 3c deep red ('31) 40.00
OA168 A59 4c yel bister 125.00
OA169 A59 5c dull violet 67.50
OA170 A59 5c dull blue 55.00
OA171 A59 8c dark blue 110.00
OA172 A59 8c red orange 100.00
OA173 A60 10c olive green 45.00
OA174 A61 12c gray black 300.00
OA175 A62 20c brown red 100.00
OA176 A63 50c dull blue 270.00
OA177 A64 $1 dk ol green 375.00

George V Type of 1912-25

1931 *Perf. 12x8*
OA184 A43 3c carmine 140.00

Sir Georges Etienne Cartier

1931 *Perf. 11*
OA190 A65 10c dark green 65.00

Nos. 165, 165a Surcharged

1932
OA191 A59 3c on 2c dp red (II) 55.00
a. Die I 65.00

Imperial Economic Conference, Ottawa

1932
OA192 A66 3c deep red 55.00
OA193 A67 5c dull blue 110.00
OA194 A68 13c deep green 375.00

Type of 1930 and King George V

For die types of the 3c see postage.

1932
OA195 A69 1c dark green 35.00
OA196 A69 2c black brown 35.00
OA197 A69 3c deep red (I) 35.00
OA198 A69 4c ocher 135.00
OA199 A69 5c dark blue 55.00
OA200 A69 8c red orange 140.00
OA201 A61 13c dull violet 135.00

UPU Executive Meeting, Ottawa

1933
OA202 A70 5c dark blue 135.00

World's Grain Exhibition and Conference at Regina

1933
OA203 A62 20c brown red 200.00

Steamship Royal William

1933
OA204 A71 5c dark blue 135.00

Landing of Jacques Cartier, 400th Anniv.

1934
OA208 A72 3c blue 175.00

Emigration of the United Empire Loyalists from the US to Canada, 150th anniv.

1934
OA209 A73 10c olive green 240.00

150th anniv. of the Founding of the Province of New Brunswick

1934
OA210 A74 2c red brown 210.00

25th anniv. of the accession to the throne of George V

1935 *Perf. 12*
OA211 A75 1c green 100.00
OA212 A76 2c brown 110.00
OA213 A77 3c carmine 135.00
OA214 A78 5c blue 150.00
OA215 A79 10c green 350.00
OA216 A80 13c dark blue 425.00

Definitives

1935
OA217 A81 1c green 40.00
OA218 A81 2c brown 75.00
OA219 A81 3c dk carmine 62.50
OA220 A81 4c yellow 120.00
OA221 A81 5c blue 70.00
OA222 A81 8c dp orange 120.00
OA223 A82 10c car rose 110.00
OA224 A83 13c violet 120.00
OA225 A84 20c olive green 125.00
OA226 A85 50c dull violet 77.50
OA227 A86 $1 deep blue 260.00

King George VI

1937
OA231 A87 1c green 5.50
OA232 A87 2c brown 7.00
OA233 A87 3c carmine 5.50
OA234 A87 4c yellow 22.50
OA235 A87 5c blue 17.50
OA236 A87 8c orange 35.00

Coronation of King George VI and Queen Elizabeth

1937
OA237 A88 3c carmine 110.00

George VI Types of 1937
Coil Stamp

1937 *Perf. 8 Vertically*
OA240 A87 3c carmine 170.00

Pictorials

1938 *Perf. 12*
OA241 A89 10c dk carmine 55.00
a. 10c carmine rose 45.00
OA242 A90 13c deep blue 55.00
OA243 A91 20c red brown 75.00
OA244 A92 50c green 150.00
OA245 A93 $1 dull violet 275.00

Visit of George VI and Queen Elizabeth to Canada and the U.S.

1939
OA246 A94 1c green & black 125.00
OA247 A95 2c brown & black 125.00
OA248 A96 3c dk car & black 125.00

Air Post Issues

1928
OAC1 AP1 5c brown olive 275.00

1930 *Perf. 11*
OAC2 AP2 5c olive brown 425.00

No. C1 Surcharged

1932 *Perf. 12*
OAC3 AP1 6c on 5c brn olive 350.00

No. C2 Surcharged in Dark Blue

1932 *Perf. 11*
OAC4 AP2 6c on 5c olive brn 400.00

Daedalus

1935 *Perf. 12*
OAC5 AP3 6c red brown 400.00

Mackenzie River Steamer and Seaplane

1938
OAC6 AP4 6c blue 55.00

Special Delivery Stamps

OAE1 SD1 10c blue green 525.00

1922
OAE2 SD2 20c carmine 475.00

1927
OAE3 SD3 20c orange 500.00

1930 *Perf. 11*
OAE4 SD4 20c henna brown 350.00

1933
OAE5 SD5 20c henna brown 325.00

1935 *Perf. 12*
OAE6 SD6 20c dark carmine 325.00

Arms of Canada

1938-39
OAE7 SD7 10c dk green ('39) 85.00
OAE8 SD7 20c dark carmine 275.00

No. E8 Surcharged in Black

1939
OAE9 SD7 10c on 20c dk car 240.00

4-HOLE PERFINS

Small "O.H.M.S" 4 Holes in Vertical Bars of "H"

(O plus Scott No.)

Definitives

1935 *Perf. 12*
O223 A82 10c car rose 170.00 100.00
Never hinged 250.00
O224 A83 13c violet 170.00 85.00
Never hinged 250.00
O225 A84 20c olive green 170.00 100.00
Never hinged 250.00
O226 A85 50c dull violet 170.00 100.00
Never hinged 250.00
Nos. O223-O226 (4) 680.00 385.00

George VI and Queen Elizabeth

1937
O231 A87 1c green 2.25 .25
Never hinged 3.40
O232 A87 2c brown 2.50 .25
Never hinged 3.75
O233 A87 3c carmine 2.50 .25
Never hinged 3.75
O234 A87 4c yellow 8.00 4.00
Never hinged 12.00
O235 A87 5c blue 4.50 .25
Never hinged 6.75
O236 A87 8c orange 17.50 9.00
Never hinged 25.00
Nos. O231-O236 (6) 37.25 14.00

Coronation of King George VI and Queen Elizabeth

1937
O237 A88 3c carmine 80.00 75.00
Never hinged 120.00

George VI Types of 1937
Coil Stamps

1937 *Perf. 8 Vertically*
O239 A87 2c brown 130.00 85.00
Never hinged 190.00
O240 A87 3c carmine 130.00 85.00
Never hinged 190.00

Pictorials

1938 *Perf. 12*
O241 A89 10c dk carmine 8.00 .45
Never hinged 12.00
a. 10c carmine rose 60.00 5.00
Never hinged 90.00
O242 A90 13c deep blue 12.50 2.00
Never hinged 18.00
O243 A91 20c red brown 50.00 4.50
Never hinged 75.00
O244 A92 50c green 70.00 12.50
Never hinged 105.00
O245 A93 $1 dull violet 150.00 50.00
Never hinged 225.00
Nos. O241-O245 (5) 290.50 69.45

Visit of George VI and Queen Elizabeth to Canada and the US.

1939
O246 A94 1c grn & blk 120.00 70.00
Never hinged 180.00
O247 A95 2c brn & blk 120.00 70.00
Never hinged 180.00
O248 A96 3c dk car & blk 120.00 70.00
Never hinged 180.00
Nos. O246-O248 (3) 360.00 210.00

Canada's Contribution to the War Effort of the Allied Nations

1942-43
O249 A97 1c green .55 .25
Never hinged .80
O250 A98 2c brown .80 .25
Never hinged 1.20
O251 A99 3c dk carmine 1.60 .50
Never hinged 2.40
O252 A99 3c rose violet ('43) .80 .25
Never hinged 1.20
O253 A100 4c greenish black 3.00 1.00
Never hinged 4.50
O254 A98 4c dk car ('43) .90 .25
Never hinged 1.40
O255 A97 5c deep blue 1.20 .25
Never hinged 1.80
O256 A101 8c red brown 8.00 3.00
Never hinged 12.00
O257 A102 10c brown 5.00 .25
Never hinged 7.50
O258 A103 13c dull green 6.00 5.00
Never hinged 9.00
O259 A103 14c dull grn ('43) 8.00 1.40
Never hinged 12.00
O260 A104 20c chocolate 10.00 1.10
Never hinged 15.00

O261 A105 50c violet 40.00 7.00
Never hinged 60.00
O262 A106 $1 deep blue 130.00 45.00
Never hinged 190.00
Nos. O249-O262 (14) 215.85 65.50

Peace Issue

1946
O268 A107 8c red brown 27.50 8.00
Never hinged 40.00
O269 A108 10c olive 3.25 .45
Never hinged 4.75
O270 A109 14c blk brn 4.25 .80
Never hinged 6.25
O271 A110 20c slate black 5.00 .80
Never hinged 7.50
O272 A111 50c dk bl grn 35.00 7.00
Never hinged 52.50
O273 A112 $1 red violet 75.00 25.00
Never hinged 110.00
Nos. O268-O273 (6) 150.00 42.05

"POSTES POSTAGE"

1949
O285 A120 2c sepia .70 .70
Never hinged 1.00
O286 A121 3c rose violet .70 .70
Never hinged 1.00

Air Post Issues

1928
OC1 AP1 5c brown olive 25.00 12.50
Never hinged 37.50

Daedalus

1935
OC5 AP3 6c red brown 160.00 60.00
Never hinged 240.00

Mackenzie River Steamer and Seaplane

1938
OC6 AP4 6c blue 3.50 1.25
Never hinged 5.25

Canada's Contribution to the War Effort of the Allied Nations

1942-43
OC7 AP5 6c deep blue 3.50 1.50
Never hinged 5.25
OC8 AP5 7c dp bl ('43) 3.50 .40
Never hinged 5.75

Canada Geese in Flight

1946
OC9 AP6 7c deep blue 2.80 .65
Never hinged 4.25

Air Post Special Delivery Canada's Contribution to the War Effort of the Allied Nations

1942-43
OCE1 APSD1 16c brt ultra 25.00 20.00
Never hinged 37.50
OCE2 APSD1 17c brt ultra ('43) 17.50 17.50
Never hinged 26.00

DC-4 Transatlantic Mail Plane

1946-47
OCE3 APSD2 17c bright ultra 40.00 35.00
Never hinged 60.00

Circumflex accent on second "E" of "EXPRES."

Corrected Die

OCE4 APSD2 17c bright ultra ('47) 80.00 80.00
Never hinged 120.00

Grave accent on the 2nd "E" of "EXPRES."

Special Delivery Stamps

1933 *Perf. 11*
OE5 SD5 20c henna brown 425.00 325.00
Never hinged 650.00

1935 *Perf. 12*
OE6 SD6 20c dark carmine 225.00 110.00
Never hinged 340.00

Arms of Canada

1939
OE7 SD7 10c dk green ('39) 17.50 8.00
Never hinged 26.00

No. E8 Surcharged in Black

1939
OE9 SD7 10c on 20c dk car 260.00 140.00
Never hinged 380.00

Canada's Contribution to the War Effort of the Allied Nations

1942
OE10 SD8 10c green 17.50 10.00
Never hinged 26.00

Arms of Canada

1946
OE11 SD9 10c green 11.00 7.00
Never hinged 16.00

OVERPRINTED OFFICIAL STAMPS

Catalogue values for unused stamps in this section are for Never Hinged items.

All cover values in this section are for uses on commercial covers.

Nos. 249, 250, 252 and 254 Overprinted in Black

1949-50 Unwmk. *Perf. 12*
O1 A97 1c green 2.25 1.75
On cover 8.00
Plate block of 4 13.00
a. No period after "S" 150.00 75.00
On cover 120.00
O2 A98 2c brown 10.00 7.50
On cover 24.00
Plate block of 4 160.00
a. No period after "S" 150.00 75.00
On cover 120.00
O3 A99 3c rose violet 2.25 1.25
On cover 8.00
Plate block of 4 13.00
O4 A98 4c dark carmine 3.00 .75
On cover 8.00
Plate block of 4 20.00

Nos. 269 to 273 Overprinted in Black

O6 A108 10c olive 3.50 .60
On cover 15.00
Plate block of 4 27.50
a. No period after "S" 85.00 60.00
Plate block of 4 (LL 1, LL 2) 200.00
O7 A109 14c black brown 6.50 2.25
On cover 15.00
Plate block of 4 42.50
a. No period after "S" 125.00 80.00
Plate block of 4 (LL 1) 170.00
O8 A110 20c slate black 17.50 3.25
On cover 15.00
Plate block of 4 100.00
a. No period after "S" 150.00 80.00
Plate block of 4 (LL 1, LL 2) 180.00
O9 A111 50c dk blue grn 200.00 110.00
On cover 200.00
Plate block of 4 1,400.
a. No period after "S" 1,000. 600.00
Plate block of 4 (LL 1) 1,800. —
O10 A112 $1 red violet 70.00 35.00
On cover 120.00
Plate block of 4 550.00
a. No period after "S" *6,000.* *3,000.*
Plate block of 4 (LL 1) *10,000.*
Nos. O1-O4,O6-O10 (9) 315.00 162.35

The "no period" varieties occur at 47LL1 & 47LL2 on some panes of Nos. O6, O7, O8; on all panes of No. O9; and on just a few panes of No. O10.

It is recommended that a certificate of authenticity be acquired for No. O10a.

Same Overprint on No. 294

1950
O11 A124 50c dull green 40.00 15.00
On cover 95.00
Plate block of 4 225.00

Nos. 284 to 288 Overprinted in Black

1950
O12 A119 1c green .40 .35
On cover 6.50
Plate block of 4 4.50
O13 A120 2c sepia 1.10 .80
On cover 6.50
Plate block of 4 5.50
O14 A121 3c rose violet 1.10 .50
On cover 6.50
Plate block of 4 7.25
O15 A122 4c dk carmine 1.10 .25
On cover 6.50
Plate block of 4 7.25
b. No period after "S" 400.00 275.00
O15A A123 5c deep blue 2.25 1.50
On cover 6.50
Plate block of 4 13.50
c. No period after "S" 80.00 60.00
On cover *95.00*
Nos. O12-O15A (5) 5.95 3.40

The "no period" varieties occur at 52LL1 on #O15 and at 52LL1, 78UL1 & 78UL2 on #O15A.

It is recommended that a certificate of authenticity be acquired for No. O15b.

Stamps of 1946-50 Overprinted in Black

a

b

1950
O16 A119(a) 1c grn (#284) .50 .25
On cover 5.50
Plate block of 4 4.50
O17 A120(a) 2c sep (#285) 1.30 .90
On cover 5.50
Plate block of 4 9.00
O18 A121(a) 3c rose vio (#286) 1.30 .25
On cover 5.50
Plate block of 4 9.00
O19 A122(a) 4c dk car (#287) 1.30 .25
On cover 5.50
Plate block of 4 9.00
O20 A123(a) 5c dp bl (#288) 1.60 .90
On cover 5.50
Plate block of 4 17.00
O21 A108(b) 10c olive 4.25 .50
On cover 11.00
Plate block of 4 18.00
O22 A109(b) 14c black brn 8.50 2.00
On cover 12.00
Plate block of 4 42.50
O23 A110(b) 20c slate blk 14.00 1.00
On cover 12.00
Plate block of 4 110.00
O24 A124(b) 50c dull green 9.00 5.00
On cover 100.00
Plate block of 4 72.50
O25 A112(b) $1 red violet 90.00 85.00
On cover 120.00
Plate block of 4 560.00
Nos. O16-O25 (10) 131.75 96.05

Nos. 301-302 Overprinted Type "b"

1950-51
O26 A125 10c black brown 1.30 .25
On cover 9.00
Plate block of 4 10.00
a. Pair, one without "G" 850.00 600.00
Plate block of 14 (2x7) with one #O26a *1,500.*
O27 A126 $1 brt ultra ('51) 90.00 60.00
On cover 140.00
Plate block of 4 550.00

It is recommended that a certificate of authenticity be acquired for No. O26a.

Nos. 305-306 Overprinted Type "a"

1951-52 Unwmk. *Perf. 12*
O28 A120 2c olive green .60 .25
On cover 4.75
Plate block of 4 3.25
O29 A122 4c orange ver ('52) .95 .25
On cover 4.75
Plate block of 4 5.50

No. 316 Overprinted Type "b"

1952
O30 A132 20c gray 2.25 .25
On cover 9.00
Plate block of 4 18.00

Nos. 320-321 Overprinted Type "b"

1952-53
O31 A136 7c blue 4.00 1.25
On cover 16.00
Plate block of 4 20.00
O32 A137 $1 gray ('53) 11.00 7.50
On cover 45.00
Plate block of 4 80.00

POST OFFICE SEALS

Values for Nos. OX1-OX4 used are for examples that are creased but not torn. Covers: All cover values in this section are for presentable covers with damage to the covers consistent with the application of the seal, which will be creasd but not torn.

POS1

1879 Unwmk. Engr. *Perf. 12*
OX1 POS1 brown 500.00 150.00
Never hinged 1,350.
On cover 2,000.

No. OX1 unused is very scarce with very fine centering, and rare very fine and never hinged; in fine condition values are 25-30% of those given for very fine.

POS2

1902-07
OX2 POS2 black, *bluish* 700.00 275.00
Never hinged 2,250.
On cover 2,400.
a. Imperf., pair 5,000.
OX3 POS2 black ('07) 125.00 55.00
Never hinged 280.00
On cover 2,400.

No. OX2a is without gum.

POS3

1913
OX4 POS3 dark brown 125.00 37.50
Never hinged 280.00
On cover 2,400.

CAPE JUBY

'kāp 'jü-bē

LOCATION — Northwest coast of Africa in Spanish Sahara
GOVT. — Spanish administration
AREA — 12,700 sq. mi.
POP. — 9,836
CAPITAL — Villa Bens (Cape Juby)

By agreement with France, Spain's Sahara possessions were extended to include Cape Juby and in 1916 Spanish troops occupied the territory. It is attached for administrative purposes to Spanish Sahara.

100 Centimos = 1 Peseta

STAMPS OF SPANISH MOROCCO USED IN CAPE JUBY

1915
Cancellations from "CABO JUBI" or "VILLA BENS"

A1 ¼c blue green (#39) 55.00
On cover 160.00
A2 2c dark brown (#40) 55.00
On cover 160.00
A3 5c green (#41) 55.00
On cover 160.00
A4 10c carmine (#42) 55.00
On cover 160.00
A5 15c violet (#43) 55.00
On cover 160.00
A6 20c olive green (#44) 55.00
On cover 160.00
A7 25c deep blue (#45) 55.00
On cover 160.00
A8 30c blue green (#46) 55.00
On cover 160.00
A9 40c rose (#47) 55.00
On cover 160.00
A10 50c slate blue (#48) 55.00
On cover 160.00
A11 1p lake (#49) 160.00
On cover 525.00
A12 4p deep violet (#50) 440.00
On cover 1,350.
A13 10p orange (#51) 440.00
On cover 1,350.
A14 20c red (#E2) 110.00
On cover 275.00

Values for stamps on cover are for philatelic covers, usually overfranked.

1917-19

A15 ¼c blue green (#52) 55.00
On cover 160.00
A16 2c dark brown (#53) 55.00
On cover 160.00
A17 5c green (#54) 55.00
On cover 160.00
A18 10c carmine (#55) 65.00
On cover 190.00
A19 25c deep blue (#58) 65.00
On cover 190.00
A20 30c blue green (#59) 65.00
On cover 225.00

Values for stamps on covers are for philatelic covers, usually overfranked.

Stamps of Rio de Oro, 1914 Surcharged in Violet, Red, Green or Blue

Two Types of Surcharge:
I: "CABO JUBI" in letters without serifs.
II: "CABO JUBI" in thin letters with serifs.

1916 Unwmk. *Perf. 13*
Type I

1 A6 5c on 4p rose (V) 240.00 19.00
Never hinged 315.00
On cover 85.00
On registered cover 125.00
a. Inverted surcharge 250.00 30.00
d. Double surcharge 325.00 50.00
e. As "d," inverted 350.00
2 A6 10c on 10p dl vio (R) 50.00 19.00
Never hinged 62.50
On cover 85.00
On registered cover 125.00
a. Inverted surcharge 55.00 30.00
d. Double surcharge 75.00 50.00
2E A6 10c on 10p dl vio (V) 125.00 72.50
Never hinged 200.00
f. Double surcharge (R, V) 150.00 90.00
2G A6 10c on 10p dl vio (B) 125.00 72.50
Never hinged 200.00
3 A6 15c on 50c dk brn (G) 52.50 30.00
Never hinged 95.00
a. Inverted surcharge 57.50 30.00
4 A6 15c on 50c dk brn (R) 50.00 19.00
Never hinged 62.50
On cover 85.00
On registered cover 140.00
a. Inverted surcharge 55.00 30.00
5 A6 40c on 1p red vio (G) 87.50 35.00
Never hinged 145.00
a. Inverted surcharge 75.00 37.50
6 A6 40c on 1p red vio (R) 85.00 26.00
Never hinged 115.00
On cover 110.00
On registered cover 190.00
a. Inverted surcharge 75.00 42.50
Nos. 1-6 (8) 815.00 293.00
Set, never hinged 1,300.

Type II

1b A6 5c on 4p rose (V) 190.00 100.00
c. Inverted surcharge 425.00 200.00
2b A6 10c on 10p dl vio (R) 190.00 100.00
c. Inverted surcharge 425.00 190.00
3b A6 15c on 50c dk brn (G) 325.00 225.00
c. Inverted surcharge 425.00 200.00
4b A6 15c on 50c dk brn (R) 190.00 100.00
c. Inverted surcharge 425.00 200.00
5b A6 40c on 1p red vio (G) 425.00 —
c. Inverted surcharge 425.00 200.00
6b A6 40c on 1p red vio (R) 190.00 100.00
c. Inverted surcharge 425.00 200.00

Values for stamps in blocks of 4
Type I

1 A6 5c on 4p rose (V) 1,150. 140.00
2 A6 10c on 10p dl vio (R) 260.00 140.00
4 A6 15c on 50c dk brn (R) 260.00 140.00
6 A6 40c on 1p red viol (R) 425.00 200.00

Very fine examples of Nos. 1-6 will be somewhat off center. Well centered examples are uncommon and will sell for more.
Fakes of Nos. 1-6 are plentiful.

Stamps of Spain, 1876-1917, Overprinted in Red or Black

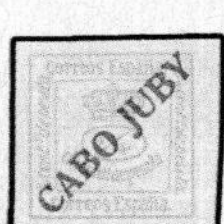

1919 *Imperf.*

7 A21 ¼c bl grn (R) .30 .30
Never hinged .50
On cover 10.00

Perf. 13x12½, 14

8 A46 2c dk brn (Bk) .30 .30
Never hinged .50
On cover 10.00
a. Double overprint 50.00 *60.00*
b. Double overprint (Bk + R) 110.00 110.00
c. Imperf 50.00 50.00
9 A46 5c grn (R) .85 .75
Never hinged 1.50
On cover 12.50
a. Double overprint 50.00 *50.00*
b. Inverted overprint 47.50 *60.00*
c. Imperf (R) 50.00 50.00
d. Imperf (Bk) 100.00 100.00
10 A46 10c car (Bk) 1.00 .70
Never hinged 1.75
On cover 15.00
a. Double overprint (Bk + R) 110.00 80.00
b. Double overprint (Bk) 40.00 *50.00*
c. Imperf 50.00 50.00
11 A46 15c ocher (Bk) 4.00 3.50
Never hinged 8.00
On cover 25.00
b. Double overprint 50.00 *50.00*
c. Red control # 6.50 3.75
As "c," never hinged 13.00
d. As "c," inverted overprint 45.00 45.00
e. Imperf (Bk) 50.00 50.00
f. Imperf (R) 50.00 50.00
12 A46 20c ol grn (R) 27.50 16.00
Never hinged 55.00
On cover 130.00
a. Imperf 160.00 160.00
b. Imperf, control number omitted 225.00 225.00
13 A46 25c dp bl (R) 3.75 3.00
Never hinged 7.50
On cover 40.00
a. Double overprint 50.00 *52.50*
b. Imperf 50.00 50.00
14 A46 30c bl grn (R) 3.75 3.75
Never hinged 7.50
On cover 40.00
15 A46 40c rose (Bk) 4.00 3.75
Never hinged 8.00
On cover 40.00
a. Imperf 50.00 50.00
16 A46 50c sl bl (R) 4.50 4.50
Never hinged 9.00
On cover 55.00
17 A46 1p lake (Bk) 13.00 11.00
Never hinged 25.00
On cover 125.00
a. Imperf 60.00 60.00
18 A46 4p dp vio (R) 57.50 55.00
Never hinged 115.00
On cover 350.00
a. Imperf 70.00 70.00
19 A46 10p org (Bk) 80.00 75.00
Never hinged 155.00
On cover 725.00
a. Imperf 150.00 150.00
Nos. 7-19 (13) 200.45 177.55
Set, never hinged 400.00

Nos. 8-19 have blue control number on back.

Values for stamps in blocks of 4

7 A21 ¼c bl grn(R) 2.00 *2.00*
8 A46 2c dk brn (Bk) 2.00 *2.00*
9 A46 5c grn (R) 3.50 *5.50*
10 A46 10c car (Bk) 4.00 *6.00*
11 A46 15c ocher (Bk) 17.50 *25.00*
12 A46 20c ol grn (R) 110.00 *140.00*
13 A46 25c dp bl (R) 16.00 *22.50*
14 A46 30c bl grn (R) 16.00 *22.50*
15 A46 40c rose (Bk) 16.00 *24.00*
16 A46 50c sl bl (R) 20.00 *28.00*
17 A46 1p lake (Bk) 55.00 *70.00*
18 A46 4p dp vio (R) 230.00 *300.00*
19 A46 10p org (Bk) 320.00 *375.00*

Same on Stamps of Spain, 1920-21

1922 *Imperf.*

20 A47 1c blue green (R) 25.00 14.00
Never hinged 45.00

Engr. *Perf. 13x12½*
Blue Control Number on Back

23 A46 20c violet 145.00 42.50
Never hinged 215.00
On cover 230.00

A 2c and a 15c exist, values $400 and $10, respectively, for unused, hinged examples, $600 and $15 for never hinged. Overprint on 2c privately applied.

Same on Stamps of Spain, 1922-23

1925 *Perf. 13½x13*

25 A49 5c red vio 5.25 3.50
Never hinged 7.00
On cover 30.00
26 A49 10c bl grn 13.00 3.50
Never hinged 22.50
On cover 50.00
28 A49 20c violet 27.50 10.00
Never hinged 42.50
On cover 110.00
Nos. 25-28 (3) 45.75 17.00
Set, never hinged 72.50

Exists on Spain No. 331, 2c olive green. Value $425 unused hinged and $650 never hinged. Overprint was privately applied.

Seville-Barcelona Exposition Issue

Stamps of Spain, 1929, Overprinted in Red or Blue

1929 *Perf. 11*

29 A52 5c rose lake (Bl) .40 .40
Never hinged .80
On cover 22.50
30 A53 10c green (R) .40 .40
Never hinged .80
On cover 22.50
31 A50 15c Prus bl (R) .40 .40
Never hinged .80
On cover 22.50
32 A51 20c pur (R) .40 .40
Never hinged .80
On cover 22.50
33 A50 25c brt rose (Bl) .40 .40
Never hinged .80
On cover 22.50
34 A52 30c blk brn (Bl) .40 .40
Never hinged .80
On cover 22.50
35 A53 40c dk bl (R) .40 .40
Never hinged .80
On cover 22.50
36 A51 50c dp org (Bl) .55 .55
Never hinged 2.00
On cover 32.50
37 A52 1p bl blk (R) 15.00 15.00
Never hinged 32.50
On cover —
38 A53 4p dp rose (Bl) 18.50 19.50
Never hinged 40.00
On cover —
39 A53 10p brn (Bl) 18.50 19.50
Never hinged 40.00
On cover —
Nos. 29-39 (11) 55.35 57.35
Set, never hinged 120.00

Stamps of Spanish Morocco, 1928-33, Overprinted in Black or Red

1934 *Perf. 14*

40 A7 1c brt rose (Bk) .55 .55
Never hinged .75
On cover 18.00
41 A2 2c dk vio (R) 5.00 5.00
Never hinged 9.00
On cover 27.50
42 A2 5c dp bl (R) 5.75 5.75
Never hinged 9.00
On cover 27.50
43 A2 10c dk grn (Bk) 14.00 11.50
Never hinged 22.50
On cover 57.50
43A A10 10c dk grn (R) 3.50 3.50
Never hinged 5.50
On cover 27.50
44 A2 15c org brn (Bk) 32.50 29.00
Never hinged 57.50
On cover 150.00
45 A7 20c sl grn (R) 13.00 10.00
Never hinged 17.00
On cover 55.00
46 A3 25c cop red (Bk) 6.00 5.50
Never hinged 8.50
On cover 27.50
47 A10 30c red brn (Bk) 11.00 10.00
Never hinged 18.00
On cover 62.50
48 A13 40c dp bl (R) 40.00 37.50
Never hinged 65.00
On cover 175.00
49 A13 50c red org (Bk) 80.00 70.00
Never hinged 120.00
On cover 375.00
50 A4 1p yel grn (Bk) 57.50 57.50
Never hinged 97.50
On cover 250.00
51 A5 2.50p red vio (Bk) 120.00 115.00
Never hinged 180.00
On cover 600.00
52 A6 4p ultra (R) 160.00 145.00
Never hinged 290.00
On cover 725.00

No. 43A and 1c, 20c, 30c, 40c, 50c, with control numbers.

Same Overprint in Black on Stamp of Spanish Morocco, 1932

53 A2 1c car rose ("Ct") 2.40 2.40
Never hinged 4.00
On cover 27.50
Nos. 40-53 (15) 551.20 508.20
Set, never hinged 900.00

Stamps of Spanish Morocco, 1933-35, Overprinted in Black, Blue or Red

1935-36

54 A8 2c grn (R) 1.25 1.00
55 A9 5c mag (Bk) 3.50 3.50
55A A10 10c dk grn (R) ('36) 21.00 21.00
56 A11 15c yel (Bl) 8.00 8.00
57 A12 25c crim (Bk) 100.00 85.00
58 A8 1p sl blk (R) 13.50 12.50
59 A9 2.50p brn (Bl) 60.00 47.50
60 A11 4p yel grn (R) 100.00 85.00
61 A12 5p blk (R) 85.00 65.00
Nos. 54-61 (9) 392.25 328.50
Set, never hinged 750.00

Same Overprint in Black or Red on Stamps of Spanish Morocco, 1935

1935 *Perf. 13½*

62 A14 25c vio (R) 4.00 4.00
63 A15 30c crim (Bk) 4.00 4.00
64 A14 40c org (Bk) 5.75 5.25
65 A15 50c brt bl (R) 15.00 11.00
66 A14 60c dk bl grn (R) 17.50 14.00
67 A15 2p brn lake (Bk) 95.00 75.00

Same Overprint on Stamps of Spanish Morocco, 1933

Perf. 13½, 14

68 A7 1c brt rose (Bk) .30 .30

Perf. 14

69 A7 20c slate grn (R) 6.75 6.75
Nos. 62-69 (8) 148.30 120.30
Set, never hinged 200.00

Same Overprint on Stamps of Spanish Morocco, 1937

1937 *Perf. 13½*

70 A21 1c dk bl (Bk) .50 .50
71 A21 2c org brn (Bk) .50 .50
72 A21 5c cer (Bk) .50 .50
73 A21 10c emer (Bk) .50 .50
74 A21 15c brt bl (Bk) .50 .50
75 A21 20c red brn (Bk) .50 .50
76 A21 25c mag (Bk) .50 .50
77 A21 30c red org (Bk) .50 .50
78 A21 40c org (Bk) 1.60 1.60
79 A21 50c ultra (R) 1.60 1.60
80 A21 60c yel grn (Bk) 1.60 1.60
81 A21 1p bl vio (Bk) 1.60 1.60
82 A21 2p Prus bl (Bk) 87.50 87.50
83 A21 2.50p gray blk (R) 87.50 87.50
84 A21 4p dk brn (Bk) 87.50 87.50
85 A22 10p vio blk (R) 87.50 87.50
Nos. 70-85 (16) 360.40 360.40
Set, never hinged 600.00

1st Year of the Revolution.

Same Overprint in Black on Types of Spanish Morocco, 1939

Designs: 5c, Spanish quarter. 10c, Moroccan quarter. 15c, Street scene, Larache. 20c, Tetuan.

1939 Photo. *Perf. 13½*

No.	Type	Description	Unused	Used
86	A25	5c vermilion	.50	.50
87	A25	10c deep green	.50	.50
88	A25	15c brown lake	.50	.50
89	A25	20c bright blue	.50	.50
		Nos. 86-89 (4)	2.00	2.00
		Set, never hinged	4.00	

Same Overprint in Black or Red on Stamps of Spanish Morocco, 1940

1940 *Perf. 11½x11*

No.	Type	Description	Unused	Used
90	A26	1c dk brn (Bk)	.25	.25
91	A27	2c ol grn (R)	.25	.25
92	A28	5c dk bl (R)	.25	.25
93	A29	10c dk red lil (Bk)	.25	.25
94	A30	15c dk grn (R)	.25	.25
95	A31	20c pur (R)	.30	.30
96	A32	25c blk brn (R)	.30	.30
97	A33	30c brt grn (Bk)	.35	.35
98	A34	40c slate grn (R)	.85	.75
99	A35	45c org ver (Bk)	.85	.75
100	A36	50c brn org (Bk)	.90	.90
101	A37	70c saph (R)	2.40	2.25
102	A38	1p ind & brn (Bk)	5.00	5.00
103	A39	2.50p choc & dk grn (Bk)	14.00	12.50
104	A40	5p dk cer & sep (Bk)	14.00	13.00
105	A41	10p dk ol grn & brn org (Bk)	40.00	35.00
		Nos. 90-105 (16)	80.20	72.35
		Set, never hinged	150.00	

Imperfs exist. Value, set $300.

SEMI-POSTAL STAMPS

Types of Semi-Postal Stamps of Spain, 1926, Overprinted

1926 Unwmk. *Perf. 12½, 13*

No.	Type	Description	Unused	Used
B1	SP1	1c orange	11.50	11.50
		Never hinged	22.50	
B2	SP2	2c rose	11.50	11.50
		Never hinged	22.50	
B3	SP3	5c blk brn	3.00	3.00
		Never hinged	4.50	
B4	SP4	10c dk grn	1.60	1.60
		Never hinged	2.25	
B5	SP1	15c dk vio	1.10	1.10
		Never hinged	1.40	
B6	SP4	20c vio brn	1.10	1.10
		Never hinged	1.40	
B7	SP5	25c dp car	1.10	1.10
		Never hinged	1.40	
B8	SP1	30c ol grn	1.10	1.10
		Never hinged	1.40	
B9	SP3	40c ultra	.45	.45
		Never hinged	1.40	
B10	SP2	50c red brn	.45	.45
		Never hinged	1.40	
B11	SP4	1p vermilion	.45	.45
		Never hinged	1.40	
B12	SP3	4p bister	2.00	2.00
		Never hinged	4.25	
B13	SP5	10p lt vio	3.00	3.00
		Never hinged	8.50	
		Nos. B1-B13 (13)	38.35	38.35
		Set, never hinged	65.00	

Nos. B12-B13 surcharged "Alfonso XIII" and new value are listed as Spain Nos. B68-B69. See Spain No. B6a.

AIR POST STAMPS

Spanish Morocco, Nos. C1 to C10 Overprinted "CABO JUBY" as on #54-61

1938, June 1 Unwmk. *Perf. 13½*

No.	Type	Description	Unused	Used
C1	AP1	5c brown	.25	.25
C2	AP1	10c brt grn	.25	.25
C3	AP1	25c crimson	.25	.25
C4	AP1	40c light blue	2.10	2.10
C5	AP2	50c brt mag	.25	.25
C6	AP2	75c dk bl	.25	.25
C7	AP1	1p sepia	.25	.25
C8	AP1	1.50p dp vio	1.90	1.90
C9	AP1	2p dp red brn	2.75	2.75
C10	AP1	3p brn blk	7.25	7.25
		Nos. C1-C10 (10)	15.50	15.50
		Set, never hinged	45.00	

SPECIAL DELIVERY STAMPS

Special Delivery Stamp of Spain Ovptd. "CABO JUBY" as on #7-28

1919 Unwmk. *Perf. 14*

No.	Type	Description	Unused	Used
E1	SD1	20c red (Bk)	3.25	3.25
b.		Double overprint	27.50	13.00

Spanish Morocco #E4 Overprinted "CABO JUBY" as on #40-52 in Red

1934

No.	Type	Description	Unused	Used
E2	SD2	20c black	10.00	10.00

Spanish Morocco No. E5 Overprinted "CABO JUBY" as on Nos. 54-61

1935

No.	Type	Description	Unused	Used
E3	SD3	20c vermilion	3.50	3.50

Same Ovpt. on Spanish Morocco #E6

1937 *Perf. 13½*

No.	Type	Description	Unused	Used
E4	SD4	20c bright carmine	1.10	1.10

1st Year of the Revolution.

Same Ovpt. on Spanish Morocco #E8

1940 *Perf. 11½x11*

No.	Type	Description	Unused	Used
E5	SD5	25c scarlet	.65	.65

SEMI-POSTAL SPECIAL DELIVERY STAMP

Type of Semi-Postal Special Delivery Stamp of Spain, 1926, Overprinted "CABO-JUBY" as on Nos. B1-B13

1926 Unwmk. *Perf. 12½, 13*

No.	Type	Description	Unused	Used
EB1	SPSD1	20c ultra & black	3.50	3.50

CAPE OF GOOD HOPE

'kāp əv 'gud 'hōp

LOCATION — In the extreme southern part of South Africa
GOVT. — British Colony
AREA — 276,995 sq mi. (1911)
POP. — 2,564,965 (1911)
CAPITAL — Cape Town

Cape of Good Hope joined with Natal, the Transvaal and the Orange River Colony in 1910, forming the Union of South Africa.

12 Pence = 1 Shilling

Watermarks

Wmk. 15 — Anchor

Wmk. 16 — Anchor

"Hope" Seated A1

Printed by Perkins, Bacon & Co. Wmk. 15

1853, Sept. 1 Engr. *Imperf.*

No.	Type	Description	Unused	Used
1	A1	1p brick red, bluish paper	3,500.	400.00
a.		1p pale brick red, deeply blued paper	*4,500.*	450.00
b.		1p deep brick red, deeply blued paper	*10,500.*	475.00
f.		1p deep brick red, bluish paper	4,000.	400.00
2	A1	4p deep blue, lightly blued paper	1,750.	170.00
a.		4p deep blue, deeply blued paper	3,500.	375.00
b.		4p blue, bluish paper	3,250.	200.00

Watermark Sideways

No.	Type	Description	Unused	Used
1c	A1	1p As #1	—	450.00
1d	A1	1p As #1a	—	550.00
1e	A1	1p As #1b	—	550.00
1g	A1	1p As #1f	—	450.00
2c	A1	4p As #2	—	400.00
2d	A1	4p As #2a	*5,000.*	400.00
2e	A1	4p As #2b	—	400.00

Values for pairs

No.	Type	Description	Unused	Used
1	A1	1p	—	650.00
1a	A1	1p	—	975.00
1b	A1	1p	—	1,050.
1f	A1	1p	—	900.00
2	A1	4p	*4,750.*	360.00
2a	A1	4p	*9,550.*	825.00
2b	A1	4p	*8,750.*	490.00

Values for Blocks of 4

No.	Type	Description	Unused	Used
1	A1	1p	—	1,400.
1a	A1	1p	—	2,200.
1b	A1	1p	—	2,300.
1f	A1	1p	—	2,000.
2	A1	4p	*10,500.*	800.00
2a	A1	4p	*21,000.*	1,100.
2b	A1	4p	*19,000.*	1,150.

Counterfeits exist.

1855-58 White Paper

No.	Type	Description	Unused	Used
3	A1	1p rose ('57)	850.00	325.00
a.		1p dull red	1,100.	425.00
b.		1p brick red	6,000.	1,050.
		As "b," Rouletted, unofficial		*3,600.*
4	A1	4p blue	700.00	85.00
		Rouletted, unofficial		*2,750.*
a.		Half used as 2p on cover		*42,000.*
b.		4p deep blue	900.00	90.00
e.		4p bright blue	900.00	90.00
5	A1	6p pale lilac ('58)	1,200.	300.00
a.		6p rose lilac	2,500.	400.00
		As "a," Rouletted, unofficial		*1,750.*
b.		6p grayish lilac on bluish paper	5,000.	540.00
c.		6p slate purple on bluish paper	4,150.	1,200.
d.		Half used as 3p on cover		—
6	A1	1sh yellow grn ('58)	*4,000.*	300.00
		Rouletted, unofficial		*3,850.*
a.		1sh dark green	450.00	*600.00*
		As "a," Rouletted, unofficial		*4,150.*
b.		Half used as 6p on cover		—

Unofficially rouletted copies of 3b, 4, 5a, 6 and 6a require certificates of authenticity.

Watermark Sideways

No.	Type	Description	Unused	Used
3c	A1	1p As #3	—	700.00
3d	A1	1p As #3a	—	700.00
4c	A1	4p As#4	2,750.	350.00
4d	A1	4p As #4b	2,750.	350.00
5e	A1	6p As #5	—	1,600.
6c	A1	1sh As #6	—	3,000.

Values for Pairs

No.	Type	Description	Unused	Used
3	A1	1p	2,000.	650.00
3a	A1	1p	2,900.	825.00
3b	A1	1p	*16,250.*	2,900.
4	A1	4p	1,500.	190.00
4b	A1	4p	2,100.	210.00
4e	A1	4p	2,100.	210.00
5	A1	6p	3,150.	1,200.
5a	A1	6p	*6,900.*	1,600.
5b	A1	6p	*14,000.*	2,150.
5c	A1	6p	*11,500.*	4,750.
6	A1	1sh	*10,750.*	*1,100.*
6a	A1	1sh	1,000.	*2,400.*

Values for Blocks of 4

No.	Type	Description	Unused	Used
3	A1	1p	4,400.	1,900.
3a	A1	1p	6,100.	2,400.
3b	A1	1p		—
4	A1	4p	3,300.	540.00
4b	A1	4p	4,700.	575.00
4e	A1	4p	4,500.	575.00
5	A1	6p	6,750.	*2,400.*
5a	A1	6p	*15,000.*	*3,250.*
5b	A1	6p		*4,250.*
5c	A1	6p		*9,500.*
6	A1	1sh	*22,000.*	*2,100.*
6a	A1	1sh	2,100.	*4,750.*

Nos. 3-6 are known rouletted unofficially.
Counterfeits exist.

No. 4 was reproduced by the collotype process in an unwatermarked souvenir sheet distributed at the London Intl. Stamp Exhib. 1950.

A2

Printed by Saul Solomon & Co.

1861 Laid Paper Unwmk. Typo.

No.	Type	Description	Unused	Used
7	A2	1p vermilion	*17,000.*	2,750.
a.		1p carmine	*42,500.*	4,000.
b.		1p red	*50,000.*	5,000.
c.		1p milky blue (error)	*200,000.*	*32,500.*
d.		1p pale blue (error)		*36,000.*
9	A2	4p milky blue	*40,000.*	2,500.
a.		4p pale blue	*42,000.*	3,250.
b.		4p blue	*45,000.*	3,500.
c.		4p dark blue	*120,000.*	5,750.
d.		As #9, right corner retouched		7,750.
e.		As #9a, right corner retouched		7,750.
f.		4p vermilion (error)	*200,000.*	*65,000.*
g.		4p carmine (error)		*112,500.*
h.		Tête bêche pair, cliche error		*225,000.*

Values for Pairs

No.	Type	Description	Unused	Used
7	A2	1p	*50,000.*	*8,300.*
7a	A2	1p	*115,000.*	*12,000.*
7b	A2	1p	*130,000.*	*15,000.*
9	A2	4p	*110,000.*	*15,000.*
9a	A2	4p	*118,000.*	*15,000.*
9b	A2	4p	*140,000.*	*17,500.*
9c	A2	4p	*610,000.*	*30,000.*

Value for Used Blocks of 4

No.	Type	Description	Used
7	A2	1p	*27,000.*
7a	A2	1p	*40,000.*
7b	A2	1p	*50,000.*
9	A2	4p	*29,000.*
9a	A2	4p	*30,000.*
9b	A2	4p	*36,000.*
9c	A2	4p	*59,000.*

Nos. 7 and 9 are usually called Wood Blocks. The plates were made locally and composed of clichés mounted on wood. The errors were caused by a cliché of each value being mounted in the plate of the other value.

No. 9h is the unique pair with the two stamps positioned so that the inscription "POSTAGE" on one stamp is aligned next to the inscription "FOUR PENCE" on the adjoining stamp.

In 1883 plate proofs of both values on white paper, usually called "reprints," were made. The 1p is in dull orange red; the 4p in dark blue. These are known canceled, as a few were misused as stamps. The proofs do not include the errors.

Counterfeits exist.

Printed by De La Rue & Co.

1863-64 Wmk. 15 Engr.

12 A1 1p dark carmine 325.00 *325.00*
 a. 1p reddish brown 650.00 350.00
 b. 1p brownish red 650.00 350.00
13 A1 4p dark blue 325.00 135.00
 a. 4p slate blue 2,500. 600.00
 b. 4p steel blue 2,500. 325.00
 c. 4p pale grayish blue 215.00 75.00
14 A1 6p purple 450.00 *500.00*
15 A1 1sh emerald 675.00 *725.00*
 a. 1sh pale emerald 1,400. —

Watermark Sideways

12c A1 1p As #12 700.00 600.00
12d A1 1p As #12a 800.00 450.00
12e A1 1p As #12b 800.00 400.00
13d A1 4p As #13 1,100. 400.00
14a A1 6p As #14 2,750.

Values for Pairs

12 A1 1p 650.00 *1,050.*
12a A1 1p 1,550. 1,150.
12b A1 1p 1,550. 1,150.
13 A1 4p 650.00 275.00
13a A1 4p *6,000.* 1,900.
13b A1 4p *6,250.* 975.00
13c A1 4p 500.00 250.00
14 A1 6p 850.00 *1,900.*
15 A1 1sh 1,500. *2,500.*
15a A1 1sh *3,500.*

Values for Blocks of 4

12 A1 1p 1,300. *3,250.*
12a A1 1p 3,900. *3,500.*
12b A1 1p 3,500. *3,500.*
13 A1 4p 1,600. *850.00*
13a A1 4p — *6,000.*
13b A1 4p *3,000.*
13c A1 4p 1,200. *775.00*
14 A1 6p 1,450. *5,400.*
15 A1 1sh 3,000. *5,400.*
15a A1 1sh *7,250.*

Nos. 12-15 can be distinguished from Nos. 3-6 not only by colors but because Nos. 12-15 often appear in a granular ink or with the background lightly printed in whole or part.

No. 12a, Wmk. 1, is believed to be a proof. Value, $29,000.

Counterfeits exist.

"Hope" and Symbols of Colony — A3

Frame Line Around Stamp

1864-77 Typo. Wmk. 1 *Perf. 14*

16 A3 1p rose ('65) 130.00 42.50
 a. 1p car red 130.00 35.00
17 A3 4p blue ('65) 210.00 4.50
 a. 4p pale blue 210.00 4.50
 b. 4p dull ultramarine 350.00 65.00
 c. 4p deep blue ('72) 275.00 4.50
18 A3 6p bright vio ('77) 235.00 1.75
 a. 6p dull violet 375.00 8.25
 b. 6p pale lilac 225.00 28.00
19 A3 1sh yellow green 225.00 4.75
 a. 1sh blue green 250.00 6.00
 b. 1sh deep green 650.00 21.50
 Nos. 16-19 (4) 800.00 53.50

Watermark Inverted

16b A3 1p rose 500.00 250.00
17d A3 4p blue 700.00 275.00
18c A3 6p bright violet — 500.00
19d A3 1sh blue green 800.00 175.00

Watermark Reversed

18d A3 6p bright violet black 650.00
19e A3 1sh yellow green —

Imperf. stamps are believed to be proofs.

For surcharges see Nos. 20-21, N3.

For types A3 and A6 with manuscript surcharge of 1d or overprints "G. W." or "G," see Griqualand West listings.

Stamps of 1864 Surcharged in Red or Black

a

b

1868-74 Red Surcharge

20 A3(a) 4p on 6p 625.00 19.00
 a. "Peuce" for "Pence" 2,500. 900.00
 b. "Fonr" for "Four" 850.00
 c. Wmk inverted *550.00*
21 A3(b) 1p on 6p ('74) 800.00 140.00
 a. "E" of "PENNY" omitted 1,800.

Space between words and bars varies from 12½-16mm on No. 20, and 16½-18mm on No. 21.

1876 Black Surcharge

22 A3 (b) 1p on 1sh green 160.00 80.00

"Hope" and Symbols of Colony — A6

Without Frame Line Around Stamp

1871-81 *Perf. 14*

23 A6 ½p gray black ('75) 37.50 17.50
24 A6 1p rose ('72) 55.00 1.25
25 A6 3p lilac rose ('80) 375.00 42.50
26 A6 3p claret ('81) 190.00 4.50
 a. 3p pale claret 275.00 5.50
27 A6 4p blue ('76) 190.00 .90
 a. 4p ultramarine 350.00 60.00
28 A6 5sh orange 650.00 25.00
 Nos. 23-28 (6) 1,498. 91.65

Watermark Inverted

23a A6 ½p gray black 500.00 *200.00*
24a A6 1p rose *500.00 225.00*
25a A6 3p lilac rose — *500.00*
26b A6 3p claret — —
27b A6 4p blue *600.00 175.00*

For surcharges see Nos. 29-32, 39, 55.

No. 27 Surcharged in Red

1879

29 A6 3p on 4p blue 200.00 3.00
 a. "THE.EE" 3,500. 350.00
 b. "PENCB" 4,000. 275.00
 c. Double surcharge *13,000. 4,500.*
 d. As "a," double surcharge — —

Type of 1871 Surcharged in Black

1880

30 A6 3p on 4p lilac rose 145.00 3.25
 a. Wmk. inverted 300.00

No. 25 Surcharged in Black

e f

31 A6(e) 3p on 3p lilac rose 400.00 12.00
 a. Inverted surcharge 13,000. 1,600.
 b. Wmk inverted — *750.00*
32 A6(f) 3p on 3p lilac rose 130.00 2.25
 a. Inverted surcharge 1,600. 47.50
 b. Vert. pair, #31-32 *2,000. 700.00*
 c. Wmk inverted — *300.00*

1882-83 Wmk. 2

33 A6 ½p gray black 47.50 3.25
 a. ½p black 45.00 3.25
 b. Wmk. inverted — *275.00*
34 A6 1p rose 90.00 2.50
 a. 1p dp rose red 90.00 2.50
 b. Wmk inverted — *300.00*
35 A6 2p bister 150.00 1.75
 a. 2p dp bister 160.00 1.75
 b. Wmk inverted — *325.00*
36 A6 3p claret 13.00 1.75
 a. 3p dp claret 20.00 1.00
 b. Wmk. inverted — *200.00*
37 A3 6p bright violet 160.00 1.00
38 A6 5sh orange ('83) 950.00 300.00

For overprint see Rhodesia No. 49.

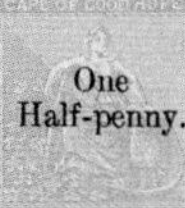

Nos. 26 and 36 Surcharged in Black

1882 Wmk. 1

39 A6 ½p on 3p claret 7,000. 180.00
 a. Hyphen omitted *4,000.*

Wmk. 2

40 A6 ½p on 3p claret 60.00 8.00
 a. "ENNY" 2,500. 825.00
 b. "PENN" 2,000. *800.00*
 c. Hyphen omitted 900.00 425.00
 d. Wmk. inverted 550.00

1884-98 Wmk. 16

41 A6 ½p gray black ('86) 12.00 .25
 a. Wmk. inverted — 650.00
42 A6 ½p yel green ('96) 1.80 .60
 a. ½p green 3.25 .60
43 A6 1p rose ('85) 15.00 .25
 a. Wmk inverted — *325.00*
44 A6 2p bister 15.00 .25
 a. 2p pale bister ('84) 40.00 2.00
 b. As "a," wmk inverted — *275.00*
45 A6 2p choc brown ('97) 4.00 3.50
46 A6 3p red violet ('98) 25.00 1.20
47 A6 4p blue ('90) 26.00 1.50
48 A6 4p pale ol grn ('97) 12.00 4.25
49 A3 6p violet 16.00 .50
 a. 6p reddish purple 72.50 2.00
 b. 6p bright mauve 16.00 .60
 c. As "a," wmk inverted — *550.00*
50 A3 1sh dull bluish grn ('89) 180.00 1.25
 a. 1sh green ('85) 250.00 9.00
 b. Wmk. inverted — *650.00*
51 A6 1sh blue grn ('94) 110.00 8.50
52 A6 1sh yel buff ('96) 19.00 3.25
53 A6 5sh orange ('87) 190.00 9.50
54 A6 5sh brown org ('96) 140.00 5.00
 Nos. 41-54 (14) 765.80 39.80

For surcharges see Nos. 58, 162, 165-166. For overprints see Rhodesia Nos. 43, 45-48.

Type of 1871 Surcharged in Black

1891, Mar.

55 A6 2½p on 3p deep magenta 8.00 .25
 a. "1" of "½" has straight serif 95.00 37.50
 b. 2½p on 3p vio rose 17.50 2.50
 c. As "a," vio rose 90.00 60.00

Hope Seated — A13

1892-96

56 A13 2½p sage green 26.00 .25
 a. 2½p olive green 25.00 .65
57 A13 2½p ultra ('96) 13.00 .25

For surcharge see No. N4. For overprint see Orange River Colony No. 55.

No. 44 Surcharged in Black

1893, Mar.

58 A6 1p on 2p bister 6.00 .60
 a. Double surcharge 600.00
 b. No period after "PENNY" 100.00 25.00
 c. 1p on 2p pale bister (#44a) 17.50 3.25

Hope Standing — A15

1893-1902

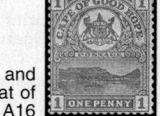

59 A15 ½p green ('98) 11.00 .25
60 A15 1p carmine 4.00 .25
 a. 1p rose red 14.00 3.25
 b. Wmk. inverted — *250.00*
61 A15 3p red violet ('02) 8.00 3.50
 Nos. 59-61 (3) 23.00 4.00

For surcharges see Nos. 163-164, N2. For overprints see Orange River Colony Nos. 54, 56, Rhodesia No. 44, Transvaal Nos. 236-236A.

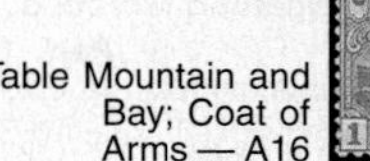

Table Mountain and Bay; Coat of Arms — A16

1900, Jan.

62 A16 1p carmine rose 8.50 .25
 a. Wmk. inverted — 250.00

King Edward VII — A17

Various frames.

1902-04 Wmk. 16

63 A17 ½p emerald 4.00 .25
64 A17 1p car rose 3.50 .25
 a. Wmk. inverted — —
 b. Wmk. inverted and reversed — —
65 A17 2p brown ('04) 24.00 .95
 a. Wmk. inverted — —
66 A17 2½p ultra ('04) 5.75 *13.00*
67 A17 3p red violet ('03) 18.50 1.40
68 A17 4p ol green ('03) 20.00 .80
69 A17 6p violet ('03) 30.00 .60
70 A17 1sh bister 20.00 1.25
71 A17 5sh brown org ('03) 175.00 27.50
 Nos. 63-71 (9) 300.75 46.00

Imperf. stamps are proofs.

Cape of Good Hope stamps were replaced by those of Union of South Africa.

OFFICIAL STAMPS

PERFORATED OFFICIAL STAMPS

Stamps of Cape of Good Hope punched with an 11-hole double triangle device were used by the Stationery and Printed Forms Branch of the Cape of Good Hope Colonial Secretary's Department between 1904 and 1906. They are only known used.

1904-06

On Seated Hope Stamps of 1884/1897

OA1 A6 2p pale bister (#44a) 35.00
OA2 A6 2p choc brown (#45) 35.00
OA3 A6 3p red violet (#46) 45.00
OA4 A6 4p pale bister (#48) 45.00
OA5 A3 6p violet (#49) 45.00

On Standing Hope Stamps of 1898/1902

OA6 A15 ½p green (#59) 45.00
OA7 A15 3p red violet (#61) 37.50

On Table Mountain Stamp of 1900

OA8 A16 1p carmine rose (#62) 32.50

On King Edward VII issue of 1902-04

OA9 A17 ½p emerald (#63) 45.00
OA10 A17 1p car rose (#64) 25.00
OA11 A17 2p brown (#65) 45.00
OA12 A17 3p red violet (#67) 35.00
OA13 A17 4p ol green (#68) 37.50

OA14 A17 6p violet (#69) 40.00
OA15 A17 1sh bister (#70) 55.00
OA16 A17 5sh brown org (#71) 120.00

ISSUED IN MAFEKING

Excellent forgeries of Nos. 162-179 are known.

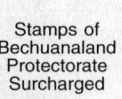

Stamps of Cape of Good Hope Surcharged

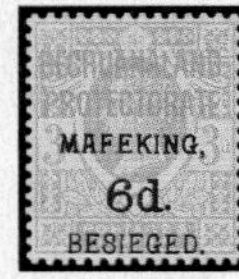

1900, Mar. 24

162 A6 1p on ½p grn 325.00 85.00
163 A15 1p on ½p grn 375.00 125.00
164 A15 3p on 1p rose 325.00 65.00
165 A6 6p on 3p red vio 45,000. 350.00
166 A6 1sh on 4p pale ol grn 8,000. 425.00

Stamps of Bechuanaland Protectorate Surcharged

1900 **Wmk. 30**

167 A54 1p on ½p ver 325.00 85.00
a. Inverted surcharge — 8,000.
b. Vert. pair, surcharge tête bêche 40,000.
168 A40 3p on 1p lilac 1,000. 155.00
a. Double surcharge 37,500.
169 A56 6p on 2p grn & car 3,000. 125.00
170 A58 6p on 3p vio, *yel* 7,500. 425.00
a. Inverted surcharge 42,500.
b. Double surcharge —

The lettering of "Mafeking Besieged" shows varying breaks in various letters, and may have either a period or no punctuation after "Mafeking."

On Stamps of Bechuanaland

Wmk. 29

171 A1 6p on 3p vio & blk 550.00 95.00

Wmk. 30

172 A59 1sh on 4p brn & grn 1,650. 110.00
a. Double surch., one inverted — 30,000.
b. Triple surcharge — 30,000.
c. Inverted surcharge — —
d. Double surcharge — 30,000.

Stamps of Bechuanaland Protectorate Surcharged

173 A40 3p on 1p lil 1,100. 100.00
a. Double surcharge 11,000.
174 A56 6p on 2p grn & car 1,600. 100.00
175 A62 1sh on 6p vio, *rose* 7,500. 130.00

On Stamps of Bechuanaland

176 A62 1sh on 6p vio, *rose* 45,000. 900.00
177 A65 2sh on 1sh green 15,000. 650.00

Sgt. Major Goodyear M1

Gen. Robert S. S. Baden-Powell M2

Wmk. OCEANA FINE
Photographic Print

1900, Apr. ***Perf. 12***

Laid Paper

178 M1 1p blue, *blue* 1,300. 475.00
On cover 12,000.
a. Imperf, pair 27,000.
179 M2 3p blue, *blue*, 18½mm wide 1,900. 525.00
On cover 9,000.
a. Horiz. pair, imperf. between — 120,000.
b. Double impression — 30,000.
c. Reversed design 120,000. 80,000.
180 M2 3p blue, *blue*, 21mm wide 13,000. 1,650.
On cover 16,500.
a. 3p deep blue 15,000. 1,500.
On cover 18,000.

The color of the paper varies from pale to deep blue.

OCEANA FINE is a sheet watermark and does not appear on every stamp.

Imperfs of No. 178 are proofs.

There is one used pair of No. 179a privately owned. A single used, partially imperf. example of No. 179 exists. Value, *$45,000.* There are four used examples of No. 179b reported. There are 2 unused and 6 used examples of No. 179c privately owned.

Issued: No. 179, Apr. 6; Nos. 178 and 180, Apr. 10.

ISSUED IN VRYBURG

Under Boer Occupation

Cape of Good Hope Stamps of 1884-96 Surcharged

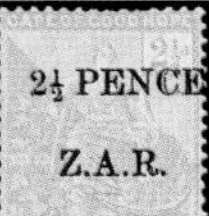

Two Types of Surcharge:

Type I — Surcharge 10mm high. Space between lines 5½mm.

Type II — Surcharge 12mm high. Space between lines 7½mm.

1899, Nov. **Wmk. 16** ***Perf. 14***

N1 A6 ½p on ½p emer (I) 240. 95.00
a. Type II 2,250. 825.
N2 A15 1p on 1p rose (I) 275. 120.
a. Double surcharge — —
b. Type II 2,500. 950.
N3 A3 2p on 6p vio (II) 2,500. 600.
N4 A13 2½p on 2½p ultra (I) 2,000. 500.
a. Type II 15,000. 5,000.

Italic Z in "Z.A.R."

N1b A6 ½p on ½p 2,500. 850.00
N2c A15 1p on 1p 2,750. 950.00
N3a A3 2p on 6p 16,000. 5,000.
N4b A13 2½p on 2½p 16,000. 5,000.

"Z.A.R." stands for Zuid Afrikaansche Republiek (South African Republic).

Under British Occupation

Transvaal Stamps of 1895-96 Handstamped

1900 **Unwmk.** ***Perf. 12½***

N5 A13 ½p green — 3,500.
N6 A13 1p rose & grn 14,000. 6,000.
N7 A13 2p brown & grn — 47,500.
N8 A13 2½p ultra & grn — 47,500.

CAPE VERDE

ˈkāp ˈvərd

LOCATION — A group of 10 islands and five islets in the Atlantic Ocean, about 500 miles due west of Senegal.
GOVT. — Portuguese Territory
AREA — 1,557 sq. mi.
POP. — 296,093 (1980)
CAPITAL — Praia

1000 Reis = 1 Milreis
100 Centavos = 1 Escudo (1913)

BR. POSTAL AGENCY IN CAPE VERDE

FORERUNNERS — British Postal Agency

Crowned Circle handstamp type VII is pictured in the Crowned Circle Handstamps and Great Britain Used Abroad section.

St. Vincent (San Vicente)

1851

A1 VII Crowned circle handstamp on cover, Type VII, inscribed "PAID AT ST. VICENT C. DE V." 6,000.

Crown of Portugal — A1

1877 **Unwmk.** **Typo.** ***Perf. 12½***

1 A1 5r black 6.00 2.00
2 A1 10r yellow 70.00 11.00
b. 10r orange yellow 50.00 11.00
3 A1 20r bister 3.00 1.40
b. 20r pale bister 2.40 1.25
4 A1 25r rose 2.50 1.40
5 A1 40r blue 85.00 50.00
b. Cliche of Mozambique in Cape Verde plate, in pair with #5 2,200. 1,400.
d. 40r pale blue 90.00 50.00
6 A1 50r green 165.00 72.50
b. 50r yellow green 90.00 50.00
7 A1 100r lilac 8.25 3.50
b. 100r pale lilac 9.00 2.25
8 A1 200r orange 6.00 3.75
9 A1 300r brown 7.00 5.25
Nos. 1-9 (9) 352.75 150.80

Perf. 13½

1a A1 5r black 3.50 1.25
2a A1 10r yellow 55.00 13.00
3a A1 20r bister 2.40 1.25
4a A1 25r rose 9.00 4.75
5a A1 40r blue 75.00 40.00
c. Cliche of Mozambique in Cape Verde plate, in pair with #5a 1,500. 1,500.
6a A1 50r green 90.00 50.00
7a A1 100r lilac 7.25 1.75
8a A1 200r orange 9.00 5.75
Nos. 1a-8a (8) 251.15 117.75

1881-85 ***Perf. 12½***

10 A1 10r green 2.75 2.10
11 A1 20r carmine ('85) 5.50 3.75
12 A1 25r violet ('85) 4.00 3.00
13 A1 40r yellow buff 2.40 1.75
a. Imperf. 40.00
b. Cliche of Mozambique in Cape Verde plate, in pair with #13 110.00 110.00
c. As "b," imperf. —
14 A1 50r blue 7.00 4.25
Nos. 10-14 (5) 21.65 14.85

Reprints of the 1877-85 issues are on smooth white chalky paper, ungummed, and on thin white paper with shiny white gum. They are perf 13½.

Perf. 13½

10a A1 10r green 2.40 1.10
11a A1 20r carmine ('85) 45.00 30.00
13d A1 40r yellow buff 4.25 3.00
e. Cliche of Mozambique in Cape Verde plate, in pair with #13d 100.00 75.00
14a A1 50r blue 6.50 3.50

King Luiz — A2

1886 **Embossed** ***Perf. 13½***

Chalk-Surfaced Paper

15 A2 5r black 4.50 3.00
a. Perf 12½ 4.25 2.00
16 A2 10r green 6.75 3.00
a. Perf 12½ 4.75 2.10

Perf. 12½

17 A2 20r carmine 9.00 5.25
a. Perf. 13½ 6.50 4.00
18 A2 25r violet 10.00 5.50
19 A2 40r chocolate 10.00 3.50
a. Perf. 13½ 8.75 4.50
20 A2 50r blue 10.00 3.50
21 A2 100r yel brown 10.00 4.50
22 A2 200r gray lilac 20.00 10.50
23 A2 300r orange 24.00 4.25
Nos. 15-23 (9) 104.25 43.00

The 25r, 50r and 100r have been reprinted in aniline colors with clean-cut Perf. 13½.

For surcharges see Nos. 59-67, 184-187.

King Carlos — A3

1894-95 **Typo.** ***Perf. 11½***

24 A3 5r orange 3.00 1.25
25 A3 10r redsh violet 3.00 1.25
26 A3 15r chocolate 5.00 2.60
27 A3 20r lavender 4.00 2.60
28 A3 25r dp green 4.00 2.25
29 A3 50r lt blue 4.00 2.25
31 A3 80r yel grn ('95) 12.00 6.50
32 A3 100r brn, *buff* ('95) 12.00 5.25
33b A3 150r car, *rose* 70.00 45.00
35 A3 300r dk blue, *sal* ('95) 60.00 17.00

Perf. 12½

26a A3 15r 150.00 120.00
28a A3 25r 4.00 3.25
30 A3 75r carmine ('95) 11.50 5.75
32a A3 100r 100.00 55.00
33a A3 150r 400.00 300.00
34a A3 200r 150.00 120.00

Perf. 13½

29a A3 50r 14.00 4.50
30a A3 75r 55.00 42.00
31a A3 80r 45.00 35.00
33 A3 150r car, *rose* ('95) 50.00 27.00
34 A3 200r dk blue, *lt blue* ('95) 50.00 27.00

For surcharges see Nos. 68-78, 137, 189-193, 201-205.

King Carlos — A4

1898-1903 ***Perf. 11½***

Name and Value in Black except 500r

36 A4 2½r gray .40 .30
37 A4 5r orange .50 .30
38 A4 10r lt green .55 .30
39 A4 15r brown 5.50 2.00
40 A4 15r gray grn ('03) 1.90 1.25
41 A4 20r gray violet 1.60 1.00
42 A4 25r sea green 3.50 1.25
a. Perf 12½ 300.00 180.00
43 A4 25r carmine ('03) 1.00 .40
44 A4 50r dark blue 3.50 1.50
45 A4 50r brown ('03) 3.75 2.40
46 A4 65r slate blue ('03) 60.00 *30.00*
47 A4 75r rose 10.00 3.50
48 A4 75r lilac ('03) 3.50 2.25
49 A4 80r violet 8.50 3.50
50 A4 100r dk blue, *blue* 3.50 2.00
51 A4 115r org brn, *pink* ('03) 15.00 *13.50*
52 A4 130r brown, *straw* ('03) 15.00 *13.50*
53 A4 150r brown, *straw* 10.00 6.75
54 A4 200r red vio, *pnksh* 4.00 3.00
55 A4 300r dk blue, *rose* 10.00 5.00
56 A4 400r dull blue, *straw* ('03) 16.00 10.50
57 A4 500r blk & red, *blue* ('01) 15.00 5.00
58 A4 700r violet, *yelsh* ('01) 30.00 17.50
Nos. 36-58 (23) 222.70 126.70

For overprints and suecharges see Nos. 80-99, 139, 200.

Regular Issues Surcharged in Red or Black

Two spacing types of surcharge. See note above Angola No. 61.

On Issue of 1886

1902, Dec. 1 *Perf. 12½, 13½*

59 A2 65r on 5r black (R) 7.00 3.75
60 A2 65r on 200r gray lil 7.00 3.75
61 A2 65r on 300r orange 7.00 3.75
62 A2 115r on 10r green 7.00 3.75
63 A2 115r on 20r rose 7.00 3.75
a. Perf 13½ 60.00 35.00
64 A2 130r on 50r blue 7.00 3.75
65 A2 130r on 100r brown 7.00 3.75
66 A2 400r on 25r violet 6.00 2.60
67 A2 400r on 40r choc 12.00 3.75
a. Perf 13½ 50.00 35.00

On Issue of 1894

Perf. 11½, 12½, 13½

68 A3 65r on 10r red vio 7.00 3.75
69 A3 65r on 20r lavender 7.00 3.75
70 A3 65r on 100r brn, *buff* 8.50 5.25
a. Perf 12½ 26.00 24.00
71 A3 115r on 5r orange 5.00 3.00
a. Inverted surcharge 60.00 60.00
72 A3 115r on 25r blue grn 4.00 2.10
a. Perf 11½ 55.00 55.00
73 A3 115r on 150r car, *rose* 9.00 6.50
a. Perf 13½ 55.00 25.00
74 A3 130r on 75r car 5.00 3.00
a. Perf 13½ *250.00 200.00*
75 A3 130r on 80r yel grn 4.00 2.00
a. Perf 11½ 2.25 1.90
76 A3 130r on 200r dk blue, *blue* 4.00 2.60
77 A3 400r on 50r lt blue 9.00 3.00
a. Inverted surcharge 65.00 55.00
b. Perf 13½ *300.00 300.00*
78 A3 400r on 300r dk blue, *sal* 4.00 1.75

On Newspaper Stamp of 1893

79 N1 400r on 2½r brown 1.60 1.50
a. Inverted surcharge 30.00
b. Perf 12½ *225.00 200.00*
c. Perf 11½ 1.25 1.00
Nos. 59-79 (21) 135.10 70.80

Reprints of Nos. 59, 66, 67, and 77 have shiny white gum and clean-cut perforation 13½.

For overprint and surcharge see Nos. 137, 205-206.

Overprinted in Black On Nos. 39, 42, 44, 47

1902-03 *Perf. 11½*

80 A4 15r brown 2.00 1.25
81 A4 25r sea green 2.00 1.25
82 A4 50r blue ('03) 2.00 1.25
83 A4 75r rose ('03) 3.75 2.75
a. Inverted overprint 42.50 42.50
Nos. 80-83 (4) 9.75 6.50

For overprint see No. 139.

No. 46 Surcharged in Black

1905, July 1

84 A4 50r on 65r slate blue 6.00 3.00

Stamps of 1898-1903 Overprinted in Carmine or Green

1911, Aug. 20

85 A4 2½r gray .25 .25
86 A4 5r orange .25 .25
87 A4 10r lt green 1.00 .80
88 A4 15r gray green .90 .45
89 A4 20r gray violet 1.50 .80
90 A4 25r carmine (G) .90 .45
91 A4 50r brown 8.50 6.00
92 A4 75r red lilac 1.40 .80
93 A4 100r dk blue, *blue* 1.40 .80
94 A4 115r org brn, *pink* 1.40 .80
95 A4 130r brown, *straw* 1.40 .80
96 A4 200r red vio, *pnksh* 6.50 4.00
97 A4 400r dull bl, *straw* 3.50 1.25
98 A4 500r blk & red, *bl* 3.50 1.25
99 A4 700r violet, *straw* 3.50 1.40
Nos. 85-99 (15) 35.90 20.10

King Manuel II — A5

Overprinted in Carmine or Green

1912 *Perf. 11½x12*

100 A5 2½r violet .25 .25
101 A5 5r black .25 .25
102 A5 10r gray grn .45 .40
103 A5 20r carmine (G) 2.40 1.40
104 A5 25r vio brown .45 .25
105 A5 50r dk blue 5.00 3.50
106 A5 75r bister brn 1.10 1.00
107 A5 100r brown, *lt grn* 1.10 1.00
108 A5 200r dk green, *sal* 1.75 1.10
109 A5 300r black, *azure* 1.75 1.10

Perf. 14½x15

110 A5 400r black & blue 3.75 3.00
111 A5 500r ol grn & vio brn 3.75 3.00
Nos. 100-111 (12) 22.00 16.25

Common Design Types pictured following the introduction.

Vasco da Gama Issue of Various Portuguese Colonies

Common Design Types CD20-CD27 Surcharged

On Stamps of Macao

1913, Feb. 13 *Perf. 12½ to 16*

112 ¼c on ½a blue grn 3.00 .85
113 ½c on 1a red 3.00 .85
114 1c on 2a red violet 3.00 .85
115 2½c on 4a yel grn 3.00 .85
116 5c on 8a dk blue 7.00 6.00
117 7½c on 12a vio brn 5.75 2.40
118 10c on 16a bister brn 2.25 1.60
119 15c on 24a bister 5.75 3.50
Nos. 112-119 (8) 32.75 16.90

On Stamps of Portuguese Africa

Perf. 14 to 15

120 ¼c on 2½r bl grn 2.00 .60
121 ½c on 5r red 2.00 .60
122 1c on 10r red vio 2.00 .60
123 2½c on 25r yel grn 2.00 .60
124 5c on 50r dk blue 2.00 1.50
125 7½c on 75r vio brn 3.75 3.00
126 10c on 100r bis brn 2.00 1.90
127 15c on 150r bister 2.50 2.50
Nos. 120-127 (8) 18.25 11.30

On Stamps of Timor

128 ¼c on ½a bl grn 2.00 .85
129 ½c on 1a red 2.00 .85
130 1c on 2a red vio 2.00 .85
131 2½c on 4a yel grn 2.00 .85
132 5c on 8a dk blue 7.00 5.50
133 7½c On 12a vio brn 5.50 3.00
134 10c on 16a bis brn 2.25 1.90
135 15c on 24a bister 4.50 2.40
Nos. 128-135 (8) 27.25 16.20
Nos. 112-135 (24) 78.25 44.40

For surcharges see Nos. 197-198.

No. 75 Overprinted in Red

1913 *Perf. 11½, 12½, 13½*

137 A3 130r on 80r yel grn 6.00 3.75

Nos. 73 and 76 overprinted but not issued. Values, $20, $25.

Same Overprint on No. 83 in Green

1914 *Perf. 12*

139 A4 75r rose 6.00 3.75
a. "PROVISORIO" double (G and R) 80.00 57.50

Ceres — A6

1914 **Typo.** *Perf. 15x14*

Name and Value in Black

Chalky Paper

144 A6 ¼c olive brn .75 .55
Never hinged 1.20
145 A6 ½c black .45 .30
Never hinged .70
146 A6 1c blue grn 5.25 4.75
Never hinged 8.50
147 A6 1½c lilac brown .75 .55
Never hinged 1.20
148 A6 2c carmine 1.25 .70
Never hinged 2.00
149 A6 2½c lt violet .60 .50
Never hinged .95
150 A6 5c deep blue 1.00 .80
Never hinged 1.60
151 A6 7½c yel brn 1.25 .70
Never hinged 2.00
152 A6 8c slate 1.25 .75
Never hinged 2.00
153 A6 10c orange brn 2.00 .90
Never hinged 3.25
154 A6 15c brn rose ('22) 8.50 5.00
Never hinged 13.50
155 A6 20c yel grn 2.00 .90
Never hinged 3.25
156 A6 30c brown, *grn* 5.00 3.00
Never hinged 6.00
157 A6 40c brown, *pink* 5.00 3.00
Never hinged 6.00
158 A6 50c orange, *sal* 5.00 3.00
Never hinged 6.00
159 A6 1e green, *blue* 3.00 3.00
Never hinged 4.75
Nos. 144-159 (16) 43.05 28.40

1916

Enamel-Surfaced Paper

160 A6 ¼c olive brn .45 .30
Never hinged .70
161 A6 5c deep blue .75 .45
Never hinged 1.20

Ordinary Paper

162 A6 ¼c olive brn .25 .25
Never hinged .40
163 A6 ½c black .25 .25
Never hinged .40
164 A6 1c blue grn .85 .75
Never hinged 1.35
165 A6 1c yel grn ('22) .25 .25
Never hinged .40
166 A6 1½c lilac brown .25 .25
Never hinged .40
167 A6 2c carmine .25 .25
Never hinged .40
168 A6 2½c lt violet .25 .25
Never hinged .40
169 A6 3c org ('22) .30 .25
Never hinged .50
170 A6 4c rose ('22) .25 *.25*
Never hinged .40
171 A6 12c blue grn ('22) .35 .25
Never hinged .55
172 A6 15c plum .90 .75
Never hinged 1.45
Nos. 162-172 (11) 4.15 3.75

1920-26 *Perf. 12x11½*

173 A6 ¼c olive brn .25 .25
Never hinged .40
174 A6 ½c black .25 .25
Never hinged .40
175 A6 1c yel grn ('22) .25 .25
Never hinged .40
176 A6 1½c lilac brown .25 .25
Never hinged .40
177 A6 2c carmine .25 .25
Never hinged .40
178 A6 2c gray ('26) .25 .25
Never hinged .40
179 A6 2½c lt violet .25 .25
Never hinged .40
180 A6 3c org ('22) 2.40 2.25
Never hinged 3.75
181 A6 4c rose ('22) .35 *.50*
Never hinged .55
182 A6 4½c gray ('22) .25 *.50*
Never hinged .40
183 A6 5c brt blue ('22) .25 .25
Never hinged .40
183A A6 6c lilac ('22) .25 .50
Never hinged .40
183B A6 7c ultra ('22) .25 *.50*
Never hinged .40
183C A6 7½c yel brn .25 *.50*
Never hinged .40
183D A6 8c slate .40 .30
Never hinged .65
183E A6 10c orange brn .25 .25
Never hinged .40
183F A6 12c blue grn ('22) .35 .25
Never hinged .55
183G A6 15c plum .30 .30
Never hinged .50
183H A6 20c yel grn .25 .25
Never hinged .40
183I A6 24c ultra ('26) 1.50 1.40
Never hinged 2.40
183J A6 25c choc ('26) 1.50 1.40
Never hinged 2.40
183K A6 30c gray grn ('22) .75 .25
Never hinged 1.20
183L A6 40c turq blue ('22) 2.00 .25
Never hinged 3.00
183M A6 50c violet ('26) 2.00 .30
Never hinged 3.00
183N A6 60c dk blue ('22) 2.00 .45
Never hinged 3.00
183O A6 60c rose ('26) 2.00 .45
Never hinged 3.00
183P A6 80c brt rose ('22) 2.00 1.10
Never hinged 3.25
Nos. 173-183P (27) 21.05 13.70

For surcharge see No. 214.

Glazed Paper

183Q A6 1e rose ('22) 7.00 2.25
Never hinged 11.00
183R A6 1e dp blue ('26) 9.00 1.50
Never hinged 14.50
183S A6 2e dk violet ('22) 10.00 4.00
Never hinged 16.00
183T A6 5e buff ('26) 45.00 12.00
Never hinged 40.00
183U A6 10e pink ('26) 150.00 60.00
Never hinged 160.00
183V A6 20e pale turq ('26) 200.00 80.00
Never hinged 240.00
Nos. 183Q-183V (6) 421.00 159.75

Provisional Issue of 1902 Overprinted in Carmine

1915 *Perf. 11½, 12½, 13½*

184 A2 115r on 10r green (11½) 2.50 2.00
a. Perf. 13½ *100.00 100.00*
185 A2 115r on 20r rose (12½) 2.75 1.75
a. Perf. 13½ 30.00 30.00
186 A2 130r on 50r blue (12½) 2.50 1.25
187 A2 130r on 100r brown (12½) 1.60 1.00
188 A3 115r on 5r org (11½) 1.40 .75
a. Inverted overprint 45.00
189 A3 115r on 25r blue grn (12½) 2.50 1.75
a. Perf. 11½ *70.00 70.00*
190 A3 115r on 150r car, *rose* (11½) 1.00 .75
191 A3 130r on 75r car (12½) 2.50 1.00
192 A3 130r on 80r yel grn (11½) 2.50 1.00
a. Inverted overprint 50.00
193 A3 130r on 200r bl, *bl* (13½) 2.00 1.00
a. Perf. 12½ *90.00 80.00*
Nos. 184-193 (10) 21.25 12.25

War Tax Stamps of Portuguese Africa Srchd.

1921, Feb. 3 *Perf. 15x14*

194 WT1 ¼c on 1c green .60 .40
195 WT1 ½c on 1c green .70 .50
a. "1/2" instead of "½" as shown 17.50 15.00
196 WT1 1c green .65 .50

Perf. 12x11½

194B WT1 ¼c on 1c green 1.20 1.00
195B WT1 ½c on 1c green 1.20 1.00
a. "1/2" instead of "½" as shown 25.00 19.00
196B WT1 1c green 1.10 .95

Nos. 194B-196B also exist on enameled paper. The values are the same.

Nos. 127 and 126 Surcharged

Perf. 14 to 15

No.	Type	Description	Unused	Used
197	CD27	2c on 15c on 150r	2.25	1.50
198	CD26	4c on 10c on 100r	2.75	2.60
a.		On No. 118 (error)	300.00	175.00

The 4c surcharge also exists on No. 134. Value, $500.

No. 50 Surcharged

Perf. 12

No.	Type	Description	Unused	Used
200	A4	6c on 100r dk bl, *bl*	2.75	2.10
a.		No accent on "U" of surcharge	17.50	15.00
		Nos. 194-200 (6)	9.70	7.60

No. 200 has an accent on the "U" of the surcharge.

Stamps of 1913-15 Surcharged

1922, Apr. ***Perf. 11½, 12½, 13½***

On No. 137

No.	Type	Description	Unused	Used
201	A3	4c on 130r on 80r	1.25	1.25

On Nos. 191-193

No.	Type	Description	Unused	Used
202	A3	4c on 130r on 75r	1.60	1.60
203	A3	4c on 130r on 80r	1.25	1.25
204	A3	4c on 130r on 200r	1.00	.80
a.		Perf. 12½	15.00	15.00
		Nos. 201-204 (4)	5.10	4.90

Surcharge of Nos. 201-204 with smaller $ occurs once in sheet of 28. Value eight times normal.

Nos. 78-79 Surcharged

1925 ***Perf. 13½, 11½***

No.	Type	Description	Unused	Used
205	A3	40c on 400r on 300r	1.50	.80
206	N1	40c on 400r on 2½r	1.50	.75

No. 176 Surcharged

1931, Nov. ***Perf. 12x11½***

No.	Type	Description	Unused	Used
214	A6	70c on 80c brt rose	3.75	2.50

Ceres — A7

1934, May 1 **Wmk. 232**

No.	Type	Description	Unused	Used
215	A7	1c bister	.25	*.25*
		Never hinged	.40	
216	A7	5c olive brown	.25	.25
		Never hinged	.40	
217	A7	10c violet	.25	.25
		Never hinged	.40	
218	A7	15c black	.25	.25
		Never hinged	.40	
219	A7	20c gray	.25	.25
		Never hinged	.40	
220	A7	30c dk green	.25	.25
		Never hinged	.40	
221	A7	40c red org	.25	.25
		Never hinged	.40	
222	A7	45c brt blue	2.00	.85
		Never hinged	3.25	
223	A7	50c brown	.90	.55
		Never hinged	1.45	
224	A7	60c olive grn	.90	.55
		Never hinged	1.45	
225	A7	70c brown org	.90	.55
		Never hinged	1.45	
226	A7	80c emerald	.90	.55
		Never hinged	1.45	
227	A7	85c deep rose	4.00	2.60
		Never hinged	6.50	
228	A7	1e maroon	2.75	.50
		Never hinged	4.50	
229	A7	1.40e dk blue	3.75	3.00
		Never hinged	6.00	
230	A7	2e dk violet	4.50	2.60
		Never hinged	7.25	
231	A7	5e apple green	21.00	5.00
		Never hinged	32.50	
232	A7	10e olive bister	32.50	18.00
		Never hinged	52.50	
233	A7	20e orange	60.00	24.00
		Never hinged	95.00	
		Nos. 215-233 (19)	135.85	60.50

For surcharge see No. 256 in *Scott Standard Postage Stamp Catalogue*, Vol. 2.

Vasco da Gama Issue

Common Design Types

1938 **Unwmk.** ***Perf. 13½x13***

Name and Value in Black

No.	Type	Description	Unused	Used
234	CD34	1c gray green	.25	.25
235	CD34	5c orange brn	.25	.25
236	CD34	10c dk carmine	.25	.25
237	CD34	15c dk vio brn	1.00	.85
238	CD34	20c slate	.50	.25
239	CD35	30c rose vio	.50	.25
240	CD35	35c brt green	.50	.25
241	CD35	40c brown	.50	.25
242	CD35	50c brt red vio	.50	.25
243	CD36	60c gray blk	.50	.25
244	CD36	70c brown vio	.50	.25
245	CD36	80c orange	.45	.25
246	CD36	1e red	.60	.25
247	CD37	1.75e blue	1.90	.70
248	CD37	2e dk blue grn	3.50	2.00
249	CD37	5e ol grn	8.00	2.00
250	CD38	10e blue vio	13.00	2.60
251	CD38	20e red brown	37.50	5.00
		Nos. 234-251 (18)	70.20	16.15

For surcharges see Nos. 255, 271-276, 288-292 in *Scott Standard Postage Stamp Catalogue*, Vol. 2.

Outline Map of Africa — A8

1939, June 23 **Litho.** ***Perf. 11½x12***

No.	Type	Description	Unused	Used
252	A8	80c vio, *pale rose*	5.00	3.50
253	A8	1.75e blue, *pale bl*	40.00	30.00
254	A8	20e brown, *buff*	85.00	26.00
		Nos. 252-254 (3)	130.00	59.50

Visit of the President of Portugal in 1939.

AIR POST STAMPS

Common Design Type

Name and Value in Black

Perf. 13½x13

1938, July 26 **Unwmk.**

No.	Type	Description	Unused	Used
C1	CD39	10c red orange	.60	.50
C2	CD39	20c purple	.60	.50
C3	CD39	50c orange	.60	.50
C4	CD39	1e ultra	.60	.50
C5	CD39	2e lilac brown	1.40	.80
C6	CD39	3e dk green	1.75	1.40
C7	CD39	5e red brown	5.50	2.10
C8	CD39	9e rose carmine	9.00	3.75
C9	CD39	10e magenta	9.75	5.00
		Nos. C1-C9 (9)	29.80	15.05
		Set, never hinged	50.00	

No. C7 exists with overprint "Exposicao Internacional de Nova York, 1939-1940" and Trylon and Perisphere.

POSTAGE DUE STAMPS

D1

1904 **Unwmk.** **Typo.** ***Perf. 12***

No.	Type	Description	Unused	Used
J1	D1	5r yellow grn	.40	*.25*
J2	D1	10r slate	.40	*.25*
J3	D1	20r yellow brn	.50	*.40*
J4	D1	30r red orange	1.25	*.40*
J5	D1	50r gray brown	.50	*.35*
J6	D1	60r red brown	9.25	4.25
J7	D1	100r lilac	1.75	1.25
J8	D1	130r dull blue	1.90	1.25
J9	D1	200r carmine	1.60	1.60
J10	D1	500r dull violet	5.00	*3.00*
		Nos. J1-J10 (10)	22.55	*13.00*

Overprinted in Carmine or Green

1911

No.	Type	Description	Unused	Used
J11	D1	5r yellow grn	.30	.25
J12	D1	10r slate	.30	.25
J13	D1	20r yellow brn	.35	.25
J14	D1	30r orange	.35	.25
J15	D1	50r gray brown	.65	.40
J16	D1	60r red brown	.65	.40
J17	D1	100r lilac	.65	.40
J18	D1	130r dull blue	.75	.65
J19	D1	200r carmine (G)	2.00	1.50
J20	D1	500r dull violet	2.50	1.75
		Nos. J11-J20 (10)	8.50	6.10

D2

1921 ***Perf. 11½***

No.	Type	Description	Unused	Used
J21	D2	½c yellow grn	.30	.25
J22	D2	1c slate	.30	.25
J23	D2	2c red brown	.30	.25
J24	D2	3c orange	.30	.25
J25	D2	5c gray brown	.30	.25
J26	D2	6c lt brown	.30	.25
J27	D2	10c red violet	.30	.25
J28	D2	13c dull blue	.55	*.40*
J29	D2	20c carmine	.60	*.50*
J30	D2	50c gray	1.75	*1.10*
		Nos. J21-J30 (10)	5.00	*3.75*

NEWSPAPER STAMP

N1

1893 **Typo.** **Unwmk.** ***Perf. 11½***

No.	Type	Description	Unused	Used
P1	N1	2½r brown	1.50	.60
a.		Perf. 12½	3.00	1.50
b.		Perf. 13½	6.50	3.00

For surcharges see Nos. 79, 206.

POSTAL TAX STAMPS

Pombal Issue

Common Design Types

1925 **Unwmk.** **Engr.** ***Perf. 12½***

No.	Type	Description	Unused	Used
RA1	CD28	15c dull vio & blk	1.25	1.10
RA2	CD29	15c dull vio & blk	1.25	1.10
RA3	CD30	15c dull vio & blk	1.25	1.10
		Nos. RA1-RA3 (3)	3.75	3.30

POSTAL TAX DUE STAMPS

Pombal Issue

Common Design Types

1925 **Unwmk.** ***Perf. 12½***

No.	Type	Description	Unused	Used
RAJ1	CD28	30c dull vio & blk	.75	.70
RAJ2	CD29	30c dull vio & blk	.75	.70
RAJ3	CD30	30c dull vio & blk	.75	.70
		Nos. RAJ1-RAJ3 (3)	2.25	2.10

CAROLINE ISLANDS

ˈkar-ə-ˌlīn ˈī-ləndz

LOCATION — A group of about 549 small islands in the West Pacific Ocean, north of the Equator.
GOVT. — German colony
AREA — 550 sq. mi.
POP. — 40,000 (approx. 1915)

100 Pfennig = 1 Mark

Watermark

Wmk. 125 — Lozenges

Stamps of Germany 1889-90 Overprinted in Black

Overprinted at 56 degree Angle

1900 **Unwmk.** ***Perf. 13½x14½***

No.	Type	Description	Unused	Used
1	A9	3pf dk brown	13.00	*14.00*
		Never hinged	30.00	
		On cover		110.00
		On cover, single franking		125.00
2	A9	5pf green	18.00	*18.00*
		Never hinged	37.50	
		On cover		70.00
		On cover, single franking		85.00
3	A10	10pf carmine	19.00	*19.00*
		Never hinged	50.00	
		On cover		70.00
		On cover, single franking		85.00
4	A10	20pf ultra	24.00	*30.00*
		Never hinged	55.00	
		On cover		150.00
		On cover, single franking		175.00
5	A10	25pf orange	55.00	*65.00*
		Never hinged	145.00	
		On cover		160.00
		On cover, single franking		375.00
6	A10	50pf red brown	55.00	*65.00*
		Never hinged	135.00	
		On cover		125.00
		On cover, single franking		160.00
		Nos. 1-6 (6)	184.00	*211.00*

Overprinted at 48 degree Angle

1899

No.	Type	Description	Unused	Used
1a	A9	3pf light brown	625.00	*750.00*
		Never hinged	1,600.	
		On cover		1,750.
		On cover, single franking		2,100.
2a	A9	5pf green	650.00	650.00
		Never hinged	1,700.	
		On cover		1,400.
		On cover, single franking		1,750.
3a	A10	10pf carmine	65.00	*150.00*
		Never hinged	175.00	
		On cover		300.00
		On cover, single franking		325.00
4a	A10	20pf ultra	65.00	*150.00*
		Never hinged	175.00	
		On cover		300.00
		On cover, single franking		375.00
5a	A10	25pf orange	1,650.	*3,100.*
		Never hinged	3,400.	
		On cover		4,750.
		On cover, single franking		6,750.
6a	A10	50pf red brown	900.00	*1,600.*
		Never hinged	1,500.	
		On cover		2,750.
		On cover, single franking		3,500.

Covers: Values for Nos. 1-5, 1a-5a are for covers paying the correct rates. Nos. 6, 6a are for overfranked complete covers, usually philatelic.

A3

Kaiser's Yacht "Hohenzollern" — A4

1901, Jan. Typo. *Perf. 14*

7 A3 3pf brown 1.10 *1.75*
Never hinged 2.10
On cover 13.00
On cover, single franking 50.00
8 A3 5pf green 1.10 *2.10*
Never hinged 2.10
On cover 17.00
On cover, single franking 21.00
9 A3 10pf carmine 1.10 *5.00*
Never hinged 2.50
On cover 17.50
On cover, single franking 25.00
a. Half used as 5pf on cover, back-stamped in Jaluit ('05) *120.00*
10 A3 20pf ultra 1.25 *9.00*
Never hinged 3.75
On cover 40.00
On cover, single franking 50.00
a. Half used as 10pf on cover ('10) *8,500.*
11 A3 25pf org & blk, *yel* 1.60 *14.50*
Never hinged 4.25
On cover 75.00
On cover, single franking 100.00
12 A3 30pf org & blk, *sal* 1.60 *14.50*
Never hinged 4.25
On cover 75.00
On cover, single franking 100.00
13 A3 40pf lake & blk 1.60 *16.50*
Never hinged 4.25
On cover 75.00
On cover, single franking 100.00
14 A3 50pf pur & blk, *sal* 2.00 *22.50*
Never hinged 5.00
On cover 52.50
On cover, single franking 60.00
15 A3 80pf lake & blk, *rose* 3.00 *25.00*
Never hinged 6.25
On cover 55.00
On cover, single franking 65.00

Engr. *Perf. 14½x14*

16 A4 1m carmine 4.50 *62.50*
Never hinged 11.00
On cover 110.00
On cover, single franking 120.00
17 A4 2m blue 7.25 *87.50*
Never hinged 18.50
On cover 120.00
On cover, single franking 140.00
18 A4 3m black violet 10.00 *150.00*
Never hinged 30.00
On cover 275.00
On cover, single franking 300.00
19 A4 5m slate & car 160.00 550.00
Never hinged 500.00
On cover 875.00
On cover, single franking 1,100.
Nos. 7-19 (13) 196.10 960.85

No. 9a is known as the "typhoon provisional" the stock of 5pf stamps having been destroyed during a typhoon. Covers (cards) without backstamp, value about $72.50.

Forged cancellations are found on #7-19.

Covers: Values for Nos. 14-19 are for over-franked complete envelopes, usually philatelic.

No. 7 Handstamp Surcharged

1910, July 12

20 A3 5pf on 3pf brown *5,500.*
a. Inverted surcharge *7,750.*
b. Double surcharge *11,000.*

Values are for stamps tied to cover. Stamps on piece sell for about 40% less.

1915-19 Wmk. 125 Typo.

21 A3 3pf brown ('19) .90
Never hinged 2.10
22 A3 5pf green 12.50
Never hinged 32.50

Engr.

23 A4 5m slate & carmine (25x17 holes) 35.00
Never hinged 120.00
a. 26x17 holes 42.50
Never hinged 190.00
Nos. 21-23 (3) 48.40

Nos. 21-23 were not placed in use.

CASTELLORIZO

ˌkas-tə-ˈlor-ə-ˌzō

(Castelrosso)

LOCATION — A Mediterranean island in the Dodecanese group lying close to the coast of Asia Minor and about 60 miles east of Rhodes.
GOVT. — Italian Colony
AREA — 4 sq. mi.
POP. — 2,238 (1936)

Formerly a Turkish possession, Castellorizo was occupied by the French in 1915 & ceded to Italy after World War I.

25 Centimes = 1 Piaster
100 Centimes = 1 Franc

Issued under French Occupation

Stamps of French Offices in Turkey Overprinted

1920 Unwmk. *Perf. 14x13½*

1 A2 1c gray 45.00 *65.00*
Never hinged 100.00
On cover *1,000.*
a. Inverted overprint 175.00 *250.00*
b. Double overprint 175.00 *350.00*
f. "Castellorizo" inverted 185.00
g. "Castelloriso" 135.00
2 A2 2c vio brn 50.00 *70.00*
Never hinged 105.00
On cover *1,000.*
a. Double overprint 225.00 *300.00*
f. "Castellorizo" inverted 200.00
g. "Castelloriso" 175.00
3 A2 3c red org 45.00 *65.00*
Never hinged 100.00
On cover *1,000.*
a. Inverted overprint 175.00 *250.00*
f. "Castellorizo" inverted 185.00
g. "Castelloriso" 135.00
4 A2 5c green 75.00 *90.00*
Never hinged 160.00
On cover *1,100.*
a. Inverted overprint 225.00 *300.00*
f. "Castellorizo" inverted 225.00
g. "Castelloriso" 200.00
5 A3 10c rose 90.00 *125.00*
Never hinged 190.00
On cover *1,350.*
f. "Castellorizo" inverted 250.00
g. "Castelloriso" 200.00
6 A3 15c pale red 115.00 *150.00*
On cover *2,000.*
a. Inverted overprint 450.00 *625.00*
f. "Castellorizo" inverted 350.00
g. "Castelloriso" 300.00
7 A3 20c brn vio 125.00 *150.00*
On cover *2,000.*
f. "Castellorizo" inverted 400.00
g. "Castelloriso" 350.00
8 A5 1pi on 25c blue 115.00 125.00
On cover *2,000.*
a. Pair, one without overprint 750.00 800.00
f. "Castellorizo" inverted 375.00
g. "Castelloriso" 300.00
h. Vert. pair, top stamp as "g", bottom stamp ovpt. omitted 2,000.
9 A3 30c lilac 125.00 *150.00*
On cover *2,500.*
f. "Castellorizo" inverted 450.00
g. "Castelloriso" 450.00

Overprint Reading Down

10 A4 40c red & pale bl (down) 200.00 *250.00*
On cover *3,400.*
a. Inverted ovpt (reading up) 850.00 900.00
f. "Castellorizo" inverted 900.00
g. "Castelloriso" 2,000.
11 A6 2pi on 50c bis brn & lav (down) 225.00 *275.00*
On cover *3,400.*
a. Inverted ovpt (reading up) 900.00 1,000.
b. Double overprint 1,250. 1,300.
f. "Castellorizo" inverted 1,000.
g. "Castelloriso" 1,000.
12 A6 4pi on 1fr cl & ol grn (down) 275.00 *350.00*
On cover —
a. Double overprint 1,300. 1,350.
b. Inverted ovpt (reading up) 1,050. 1,100.
f. "Castellorizo" inverted 1,200.
g. "Castelloriso" 1,200.
13 A6 20pi on 5fr dk bl & buff 625.00 *800.00*
On cover —
a. Double overprint 1,850. *2,000.*
f. "Castellorizo" inverted 2,500.
g. "Castelloriso" 2,500.
Nos. 1-13 (13) 2,110. 2,665.
Set, never hinged 4,500.

"S" instead of "Z" in "CASTELLORIZO"

1c A2 1c gray 185.00 185.00
2c A2 2c vio brn 175.00 175.00
3c A2 3c red org 140.00 140.00
4c A2 5c green 200.00 200.00
5c A3 10c rose 200.00 200.00
6c A3 15c pale red 800.00 800.00
7c A3 20c brn vio 800.00 800.00
8c A5 1pi on 25c blue 750.00 750.00
9c A3 30c lilac 800.00 800.00
10c A4 40c red & pale bl (down) 725.00 725.00
11c A6 2pi on 50c bis brn & lav (down) 800.00 800.00
12c A6 4pi on 1fr cl & ol grn (down) 800.00 800.00
13c A6 20pi on 5fr dk bl & buff 1,800. *2,000.*

"CASTELLORIZO" Inverted

1d A2 1c gray 140.00 *140.00*
2d A2 2c vio brn 200.00 *200.00*
3d A2 3c red org 190.00 *190.00*
4d A2 5c green 250.00 250.00
5d A3 10c rose 250.00 250.00
6d A3 15c pale red 1,000. 1,000.
7d A3 20c brn vio 1,000. 1,000.
8d A5 1pi on 25c blue 925.00 925.00
9d A3 30c lilac 1,000. 1,000.

No Dot after "N"

10e A4 40c red & pale bl (down) 640.00 640.00
11e A6 2pi on 50c bis brn & lav (down) 675.00 *675.00*
12e A6 4pi on 1fr cl & ol grn (down) 675.00 *675.00*
13e A6 20pi on 5fr dk bl & buff 1,600. *1,800.*

No. 1-9 were overprinted in blocks of 25. Position 4 had "CASTELLORIZO" inverted and Positions 8 and 18 had "CASTELLORISO." The later variety also occurred in the setting of the form for Nos. 10-13.

"B. N. F." are the initials of "Base Navale Francaise".

Covers: Values for covers are for commercial items. Philatelic covers sell for less.

Overprinted in Black or Red

1920

On Stamps of French Offices in Turkey

14 A2 1c gray 34.00 *40.00*
Never hinged 70.00
On cover 750.00
15 A2 2c vio brn 37.50 *50.00*
Never hinged 80.00
On cover 875.00
16 A2 3c red org 67.50 *80.00*
Never hinged 140.00
On cover 1,100.
17 A2 5c green (R) 32.50 *37.50*
Never hinged 70.00
On cover 750.00
19 A3 10c rose 40.00 *47.50*
Never hinged 90.00
On cover 925.00
20 A3 15c pale red 70.00 *80.00*
Never hinged 150.00
On cover 1,100.
21 A3 20c brn vio 105.00 *110.00*
Never hinged 220.00
On cover 1,750.
22 A5 1pi on 25c bl (R) 67.50 *70.00*
Never hinged 140.00
On cover 925.00
23 A3 30c lilac (R) 77.50 *85.00*
Never hinged 170.00
On cover 1,250.
24 A4 40c red & pale bl 72.50 *75.00*
Never hinged 150.00
On cover 1,100.
25 A6 2pi on 50c bis brn & lav 72.50 *80.00*
Never hinged 150.00
On cover 1,050.
26 A6 4pi on 1fr claret & ol grn 115.00 *140.00*
Never hinged 250.00
On cover 2,000.
28 A6 20pi on 5fr dk bl & buff 400.00 450.00
Never hinged 800.00
On cover 2,500.
Nos. 14-28 (13) 1,192. 1,345.

On Nos. 25, 26 and 28 the two lines of the overprint are set wider apart than on the lower values.

"O.N.F." are the initials of "Occupation Navale Francaise."

Overprint on 5c in black and on 8pi on 2fr (#37) were prepared but not issued. Values: 5c, $1,300; 8pi on 2fr, $1,450.

Covers: Values for covers are for commercial items. Philatelic covers sell for less.

On Stamps of France

30 A22 10c red 50.00 *60.00*
Never hinged 95.00
On cover 1,000.
a. Inverted overprint 200.00 *250.00*
31 A22 25c blue (R) 50.00 *60.00*
Never hinged 90.00
On cover 1,000.
a. Inverted overprint 200.00 *250.00*

"Casetllorizo" instead of "Castellorizo"

14b A2 1c gray 175.00 *175.00*
15b A2 2c vio brn 195.00 *195.00*
16b A2 3c red org 240.00 *240.00*
17b A2 5c green (R) 190.00 190.00
19b A3 10c rose 210.00 210.00
20b A3 15c pale red 300.00 300.00
21b A3 20c brn vio 325.00 325.00
22b A5 1pi on 25c bl (R) 195.00 195.00
23b A3 30c lilac (R) 280.00 280.00

"asetllorizo" instead of "Castellorizo"

14c A2 1c gray 160.00 *160.00*
15c A2 2c vio brn *195.00*
16c A2 3c red org *240.00*
17c A2 5c green (R) 175.00 175.00
19c A3 10c rose 200.00
20c A3 15c pale red 260.00
21c A3 20c brn vio 300.00
22c A5 1pi on 25c bl (R) 200.00 200.00
23c A3 30c lilac (R) 260.00 260.00

No dot over "i" of "Castellorizo"

14d A2 1c gray 175.00 *175.00*
15d A2 2c vio brn 195.00 *195.00*
16d A2 3c red org 240.00 *240.00*
17d A2 5c green (R) 175.00 175.00
19d A3 10c rose 200.00 200.00
20d A3 15c pale red 260.00 260.00
21d A3 20c brn vio 300.00 300.00
22d A5 1pi on 25c bl (R) 225.00 225.00
23d A3 30c lilac (R) 275.00 275.00

This overprint exists on 8 other 1900-1907 denominations of France (5c, 15c, 20c, 30c, 40c, 50c, 1fr, 5fr). These are believed not to have been issued or postally used. Values: 5c, $750; 15c, $750; 20c, $800; 30c, $1,300; 40c, $1,300; 50c, $1,300; 1fr, $1,400; 5fr, $12,500. Varieties exist: 5c, "Casetllorizo" for "Castelorizo," $1,000; 5c, "astellorizo" for "Castellorizo," $1,000; 20c, No dot over "i" of "Castellorizo," $1,200.

Stamps of France, 1900-1907, Handstamped in Black or Violet

1920

33 A22 5c green 175.00 *200.00*
Never hinged 350.00
On cover *1,400.*
a. Overprint inverted (reading up) 1,300.
b. Double overprint *1,000.*
34 A22 10c red 175.00 *200.00*
Never hinged 350.00
On cover *1,400.*
35 A22 20c vio brn 175.00 *200.00*
Never hinged 350.00
On cover *1,000.*
a. Overprint inverted (reading up) *1,500.*
b. Double overprint *1,000.*
36 A22 25c blue 175.00 *200.00*
Never hinged 350.00
On cover *1,400.*
37 A18 50c bis brn & lav 1,000. *1,200.*
Never hinged 2,000.
On cover *2,600.*
a. Double overprint *1,700.*
38 A18 1fr cl & ol grn (V) 1,000. 1,200.
Never hinged 2,000.
On cover *2,600.*
Nos. 33-38 (6) 2,700. 3,200.
Set, never hinged 5,400.

French Offices in Turkey Nos. 25//38 were handstamped as Nos. 33-38 locally by the officers in charge of the French Navy postal facilities but were not issued. Values: 5c, 10c, 15c, 20c, 1pi on 25c, each $1,000; 40c, 2pi on 50c, each $2,000; 4pi on 1fr, $2,350; 20pi on 5fr, $10,000.

Covers: Values for covers are for commercial items. Philatelic covers sell for less.

Forgeries of overprints on Nos. 1-38 exist. They abound of Nos. 33-38.

Issued under Italian Dominion

100 Centesimi = 1 Lira

Italian Stamps of 1906-20 Overprinted

1922, July 22 Wmk. 140 *Perf. 14*

51 A48 5c green 5.00 *30.00*
Never hinged 11.00
On cover 175.00
52 A48 10c claret 3.50 *30.00*
Never hinged 6.50
On cover 160.00
53 A48 15c slate 3.50 *30.00*
Never hinged 12.00
On cover 225.00
54 A50 20c brn org 3.50 *30.00*
Never hinged 9.50
On cover 160.00
a. Double overprint 500.00
b. Vertical pair, one without overprint 2,250.
Never hinged 2,600.
55 A49 25c blue 3.50 *30.00*
Never hinged 9.50
On cover 175.00
56 A49 40c brown 48.00 35.00
Never hinged 130.00
On cover 240.00
57 A49 50c violet 50.00 37.50
Never hinged 130.00
On cover 325.00

58 A49 60c carmine 50.00 *57.50*
Never hinged 130.00
On cover *600.00*
a. Diagonal overprint 800.00
59 A49 85c chocolate 5.50 *65.00*
Never hinged 13.00
On cover *750.00*
Nos. 51-59 (9) 172.50 *345.00*
Set, never hinged 450.00
Complete set, on over-franked cover 525.00

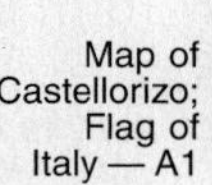

Map of Castellorizo; Flag of Italy — A1

1923, Jan.

60 A1 5c gray green 6.00 *40.00*
Never hinged 15.00
On cover *450.00*
61 A1 10c dull rose 6.00 *40.00*
Never hinged 15.00
On cover *425.00*
62 A1 25c dull blue 6.00 *40.00*
Never hinged 15.00
On cover *375.00*
63 A1 50c gray lilac 6.00 *40.00*
Never hinged 15.00
On cover *375.00*
64 A1 1 l brown 6.00 *40.00*
Never hinged 15.00
On cover *550.00*
Nos. 60-64 (5) 30.00 *200.00*
Set, never hinged 65.00
Complete set, on over-franked cover 525.00

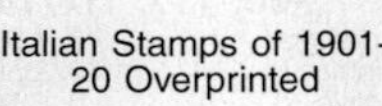

Italian Stamps of 1901-20 Overprinted

1924, March

65 A48 5c green 2.50 *30.00*
Never hinged 6.50
On cover *275.00*
66 A48 10c claret 2.50 *30.00*
Never hinged 6.50
On cover *150.00*
a. Vertical pair, one stamp with albino overprint 1,250.
Never hinged 1,800.
67 A48 15c slate 2.50 *40.00*
Never hinged 6.50
On cover *225.00*
68 A50 20c brn orange 2.50 *40.00*
Never hinged 6.50
On cover *225.00*
a. Double overprint 145.00
69 A49 25c blue 2.50 *30.00*
Never hinged 6.50
On cover *210.00*
70 A49 40c brown 2.50 *30.00*
Never hinged 6.50
On cover *225.00*
71 A49 50c violet 2.50 *40.00*
Never hinged 6.50
On cover *210.00*
72 A49 60c carmine 2.50 *50.00*
Never hinged 6.50
On cover *320.00*
a. Double overprint 450.00
73 A49 85c red brown 2.50 *60.00*
Never hinged 6.50
On cover *550.00*
74 A46 1 l brn & green 2.50 *60.00*
Never hinged 6.50
On cover *675.00*
Nos. 65-74 (10) 25.00 *410.00*
Set, never hinged 55.00
Complete set, on over-franked cover 750.00

Ferrucci Issue

Italian Stamps of 1930, Ovptd. in Red or Blue

1930, Oct. 20 Wmk. Crowns (140)

75 A102 20c violet 10.00 6.00
Never hinged 26.00
On cover *180.00*
76 A103 25c dark green 10.00 *25.00*
Never hinged 26.00
On cover *225.00*
77 A103 50c black 10.00 6.00
Never hinged 26.00
On cover *165.00*
78 A103 1.25 l deep blue 10.00 *25.00*
Never hinged 26.00
On cover *340.00*
79 A104 5 l + 2 l dp car (Bl) 10.00 *77.50*
Never hinged 85.00
On cover —
Nos. 75-79 (5) 50.00 *139.50*
Set, never hinged 150.00
Complete set, on over-franked cover 260.00

Garibaldi Issue

Types of Italian Stamps of 1932, Overprinted like Nos. 75-79 in Red or Blue

1932, Aug. 28

80 A138 10c brown 20.00 *25.00*
Never hinged 62.50
On cover *240.00*
81 A138 20c red brn (Bl) 20.00 *25.00*
Never hinged 62.50
On cover *180.00*
82 A138 25c dp grn 20.00 *25.00*
Never hinged 62.50
On cover *225.00*
83 A138 30c bluish slate 20.00 *25.00*
Never hinged 62.50
On cover *240.00*
84 A138 50c red vio (Bl) 20.00 *25.00*
Never hinged 62.50
On cover *180.00*
85 A141 75c cop red (Bl) 20.00 *25.00*
Never hinged 62.50
On cover *340.00*
86 A141 1.25 l dull blue 20.00 *25.00*
Never hinged 62.50
On cover *490.00*
87 A141 1.75 l + 25c brn 20.00 *25.00*
Never hinged 62.50
On cover —
88 A144 2.55 l + 50c org (Bl) 20.00 *25.00*
Never hinged 62.50
On cover —
89 A145 5 l + 1 l dl vio 20.00 *25.00*
Never hinged 62.50
On cover —
Nos. 80-89 (10) 200.00 *250.00*
Set, never hinged 400.00
Complete set, on over-franked cover 675.00

CAYMAN ISLANDS

ˌkā-ˈman ˈī-ləndz

LOCATION — Three islands in the Caribbean Sea, about 200 miles northwest of Jamaica
GOVT. — Dependency of Jamaica
AREA — 100 sq. mi.
POP. — 18,285 (1982)
CAPITAL — George Town, located on Grand Cayman

12 Pence = 1 Shilling
20 Shilling = 1 Pound

STAMPS OF JAMAICA USED IN CAYMAN ISLANDS

Georgetown, Grand Cayman

Stamps of Jamaica canceled in purple with large double oval "GRAND CAYMAN * POST OFFICE" with date in center.

1889-94

A1 ½p gray green (#16a) 625.
A2 1p lilac & red vio (#24) 625.
A3 2p slate (#20) 8,000.
A4 2p green (#25) 1,100.
A5 2½p lilac & ultra (#26) 1,350.
A6 4p orange brown (#22a) 4,500.

Official Stamps

A7 ½p green, type II, OFFICIAL 17 to 17½mm (#O1) 1,500.
a. 1/2p green, type I, OFFICIAL 16mm (#O1a) 4,000.
A8 1p carmine rose (#O3) 1,600.
A9 2p slate (#O4) 7,000.

Stamps of Jamaica Canceled in purple or black with Single Circle Datestamp "GRAND CAYMAN/P.O." with date in center on two lines

1895-98

A10 ½p gray green (#16a) 750.
A11 1p lilac & red vio (#24) 625.
A12 2½p lilac & ultra (#26) 1,100.
A13 3p olive green (#21) 7,000.

Official Stamps

A14 ½p green, type I (#O1a) 4,500.
A15 1p carmine rose (#O3) 7,000.
A16 2p slate (#O4) 8,000.

Stamps of Jamaica Canceled with Double Circle Datestamp "GRAND CAYMAN * CAYMAN ISLANDS" with date in center on two lines

1898-1901

A17 ½p blue green (#16) 625.
a. 1/2p gray green (#16a) 625.
A18 1p lilac & red violet (#24) 625.
A19 1p red (#31) 700.
A20 2½p lilac & ultra (#26) 900.

Stake Bay, Cayman Brac

Stamps of Jamaica Canceled with Rectangular Postmark: "CAYMAN BRAC/CAYMAN ISLANDS"

1898-1900

A21 ½p gray green (#16a) 5,000.
A22 1p lilac & red vio (#24) 4,500.
A23 2p green (#25) 8,000.
A24 2½p lilac & ultra (#26) 4,500.

Stamps of Jamaica Canceled with Double Circle Datestamp "CAYMAN BRAC * CAYMAN ISLANDS" with date in center in two lines

1900-01

A25 ½p gray green (#16a) 6,000.
A26 1p lilac & red violet (#24) 6,000.
A27 1p red (#31) 6,500.
A28 2½p lilac & ultra (#26) 6,000.

Catalogue values for unused stamps in this country are for Never Hinged items, beginning with Scott 112.

Victoria — A1

1900 Typo. Wmk. 2 *Perf. 14*

1 A1 ½p pale green 15.00 *22.50*
a. ½p green to deep green 22.00 *30.00*
2 A1 1p carmine rose 16.00 4.25
a. 1p carmine 22.00 17.50
Set, Ovptd. "SPECIMEN" 190.00

Edward VII — A2

1901-03

3 A2 ½p green ('02) 5.50 *30.00*
a. Dented frame under "A" of "CAYMAN" (R1/P6) ('02) 325.00
4 A2 1p car rose ('03) 12.00 *12.00*
a. Dented frame under "A" of "CAYMAN" (R1/P6) ('03) 400.00 *400.00*
5 A2 2½p ultramarine 12.00 *21.00*
a. Dented frame under "A" of "CAYMAN" (R1/P6) 450.00
6 A2 6p chocolate 35.00 *70.00*
a. Dented frame under "A" of "CAYMAN" (R1/P6) 800.00 *1,200.*
7 A2 1sh brown orange 72.50 *125.00*
a. Dented frame under "A" of "CAYMAN" (R1/P6) 1,000. *1,500.*
Nos. 3-7 (5) 137.00 *258.00*
Set, Ovptd. "SPECIMEN" 275.00

1905 Wmk. 3

8 A2 ½p green 12.00 *17.50*
a. Dented frame under "A" of "CAYMAN" (R1/P6) 400.00 *450.00*
9 A2 1p carmine rose 24.00 *20.00*
a. Dented frame under "A" of "CAYMAN" (R1/P6) 600.00 *550.00*
10 A2 2½p ultramarine 12.00 5.50
a. Dented frame under "A" of "CAYMAN" (R1/P6) 400.00 *375.00*
11 A2 6p chocolate 19.00 *45.00*
a. Dented frame under "A" of "CAYMAN" (R1/P6) 475.00 *625.00*
12 A2 1sh brown orange 37.50 *55.00*
a. Dented frame under "A" of "CAYMAN" (R1/P6) 700.00
Nos. 8-12 (5) 104.50 *143.00*

For surcharge see No. 17.

1907, Mar. 13

13 A2 4p brown & blue 40.00 *67.50*
a. Dented frame under "A" of "CAYMAN" (R1/P6) 850.00 *1,100.*
14 A2 6p ol green & rose 45.00 *80.00*
a. Dented frame under "A" of "CAYMAN" (R1/P6) 850.00 *1,100.*
15 A2 1sh violet & green 65.00 *95.00*
a. Dented frame under "A" of "CAYMAN" (R1/P6) 1,000.
16 A2 5sh ver & green 225.00 *350.00*
a. Dented frame under "A" of "CAYMAN" (R1/P6) *5,500.* *6,500.*
Nos. 13-16 (4) 375.00 *592.50*
Set, Ovptd. "SPECIMEN" 240.00

Numerals of 4p, 1sh and 5sh of type A2 are in color on colorless tablet.

For surcharges see Nos. 18-20.

Nos. 9, 16, 13 Handstamped

No. 17

No. 18

No. 19

No. 20

1907-08

17 A2 ½p on 1p 60.00 *92.50*
a. Dented frame under "A" of "CAYMAN" (R1/P6) 1,100. *1,500.*
18 A2 ½p on 5sh 325.00 *525.00*
a. Inverted surcharge *100,000.*
b. Double surcharge *12,750.* *12,750.*
c. Double surcharge, one inverted
d. Pair, one without surcharge *100,000.*
e. Dented frame under "A" of "CAYMAN" (R1/P6) 5,500.
19 A2 1p on 5sh 350.00 *525.00*
a. Double surcharge *22,500.* *20,000.*
b. Inverted surcharge *150,000.*
c. Dented frame under "A" of "CAYMAN" (R1/P6) 5,000. 6,000.
20 A2 2½p on 4p ('08) 2,000. *3,750.*
a. Double surcharge *60,000.* *30,000.*
b. Dented frame under "A" of "CAYMAN" (R1/P6) *25,000.*

No. 19b is unique. It exists on the upper left stamp in an upper left corner margin plate no. 1 block of four that is lightly hinged in the top margin only.

The 1p on 4p is a revenue stamp not authorized for postal use, although postally used examples exist. Value for unused is about $300. Varieties exist: surcharge inverted $2,200; surcharge double $3,000; surcharge double, both inverted $3,250.

A3

1907-09 *Perf. 14*

21 A3 ½p green 5.25 *5.50*
22 A3 1p carmine rose 2.10 1.10
23 A3 2½p ultramarine 7.50 3.00

Chalky Paper

24 A3 3p violet, *yellow* 4.50 *3.75*
25 A3 4p blk & red, *yel* 67.50 *100.00*
26 A3 6p purple & br pur 27.50 *52.50*
a. 6p purple & violet purple 37.50 *65.00*
27 A3 1sh black, *grn* 11.00 *32.50*
28 A3 5sh grn & red, *yel* 60.00 *90.00*
Nos. 21-28 (8) 185.35 *288.35*

Issued: ½p, 1p, 12/27/07; 2½p, 3p, 4p, 5sh, 3/30/08; 6d, 10/2/08; 1sh, 4/5/09.

Forged cancellations are found on No. 28.

1908, Mar. 30 Wmk. 2

29 A3 1sh black, *green* 85.00 *125.00*
30 A3 10sh grn & red, *grn* 225.00 *400.00*
Set of 9, #21-26, 28-30, Ovptd. "SPECIMEN" 375.00

Numerals of 3p, 4p, 1sh and 5sh of type A3 are in color on plain tablet.

Forged cancellations are found on No. 30.

A4

1908 Wmk. 3 Ordinary Paper

31 A4 ¼p brown 6.00 1.00
 a. ¼p gray brown ('09) 8.00 1.10
 Ovpted "SPECIMEN" 100.00

King George V — A5

1912-20

32 A5 ¼p brown ('13) 1.25 .50
33 A5 ½p green 3.25 *6.00*
34 A5 1p carmine ('13) 4.00 3.00
35 A5 2p gray 1.25 *12.50*
36 A5 2½p ultra ('14) 8.50 *13.50*
 a. 2½p deep bright blue ('17) 21.00 *29.00*

Chalky Paper

37 A5 3p vio, *yel* ('13) 3.00 *22.50*
 Ovpted "SPECIMEN" 75.00
 a. 3p purple, *yellow* ('14) 17.50 *45.00*
 b. 3p purple, *pale yellow* ('20) 5.00 *35.00*
 c. 3p purple, *orange buff* ('20) 11.50 *35.00*
 d. 3p purple, *buff* ('14) — —
38 A5 4p blk & red, *yel* ('13) 1.25 *12.50*
39 A5 6p vio & red vio ('13) 4.50 *9.00*
40 A5 1sh blk, *grn* ('13) 4.25 *32.50*
 Ovpted "SPECIMEN" 75.00
41 A5 2sh vio & ultra, *bl* 14.50 *65.00*
42 A5 3sh green & vio 22.50 *77.50*
43 A5 5sh grn & red, *yel* ('14) 90.00 *190.00*
44 A5 10sh grn & red, *bl grn, olive back* ('18) 125.00 *250.00*
 a. 10sh green & red, *grn* ('14) 150.00 *250.00*
 Ovpted "SPECIMEN" 120.00
 Nos. 32-44 (13) 283.25 *694.50*

The first printings of the 3p, 1sh and 10sh have a white back.

For surcharges, see Nos. MR1-MR7.

1913, Nov. 19

Surface-colored Paper

45 A5 3p violet, *yel* 4.25 *9.50*
46 A5 1sh black, *green* 4.25 *4.25*
47 A5 10sh grn & red, *grn* 130.00 *190.00*
 Nos. 45-47 (3) 138.50 *203.75*
 Set, ovptd. "SPECIMEN" 100.00

Numeral of ¼p, 2p, 3p, 4p, 1sh, 2sh, 3sh and 5sh of type A5 are in color on plain tablet.

King George V — A6

1921-26 Wmk. 4 *Perf. 14*

50 A6 ¼p yel brown ('22) .60 *1.75*
51 A6 ½p gray green ('22) .60 .35
52 A6 1p rose red ('22) 1.75 *1.00*
53 A6 1½p orange brn 2.10 .35
54 A6 2p gray ('22) 2.10 *4.75*
55 A6 2½p ultramarine ('22) .60 *.60*
56 A6 3p violet, *yel* ('23) 3.25 *5.25*
57 A6 4½p olive grn ('23) 4.00 *3.75*
58 A6 6p claret ('22) 6.50 *37.50*
 a. 6p deep claret 21.00 *45.00*
59 A6 1sh black, *grn* ('25) 11.50 *37.50*
60 A6 2sh violet, *blue* ('22) 17.00 *30.00*
61 A6 3sh violet ('22) 27.50 19.00
62 A6 5sh green, *yel* ('25) 30.00 *55.00*
63 A6 10sh car, *green* ('26) 72.50 *100.00*
 Nos. 50-63 (14) 180.00 *296.80*
 Set, ovptd. "SPECIMEN" 500.00

Issued: 1½p, 4/4/21; ¼p, ½p, 1p, 2p, 2½p, 6p, 2sh, 3sh, 4/1/22; 3p, 4½p, 6/29/23; 5sh, 2/15/25; 1sh, 5/15/25; 10sh, 9/5/26.

1921-22 Wmk. 3

64 A6 3p violet, *org* 1.75 *9.50*
 a. 3p purple, *pale yellow* 50.00 65.00
65 A6 4p red, *yel* 1.25 *6.50*
66 A6 1sh black, *green* 2.25 *11.50*
67 A6 5sh green, *yel* 19.00 *85.00*
 a. 5sh deep green, *pale yellow* 110.00 *170.00*
 a. 5sh deep green, *orange buff* 170.00 *235.00*
68 A6 10sh car, *green* 75.00 *125.00*
 Nos. 64-68 (5) 99.25 *237.50*
 Set, ovptd. "SPECIMEN" 225.00

Issued: 4p, 4/1/22; others, 4/4/21.

King William IV, King George V
A7

Perf. 12½

1932, Dec. 5 Wmk. 4 Engr.

69 A7 ¼p brown 1.90 1.40
70 A7 ½p green 3.25 *11.00*
71 A7 1p carmine 3.25 *15.00*
72 A7 1½p orange 3.25 3.75
73 A7 2p gray 3.25 *4.75*
74 A7 2½p ultramarine 3.25 2.00
75 A7 3p olive green 8.00 *6.75*
76 A7 6p red violet 13.00 *30.00*
77 A7 1sh brn & black 20.00 *42.50*
78 A7 2sh ultra & blk 55.00 *100.00*
79 A7 5sh green & blk 100.00 *160.00*
80 A7 10sh car & black 350.00 *475.00*
 Nos. 69-80 (12) 564.15 *852.15*

Nos. 69 and 72 exist with "A" of "CA" in wmk. omitted. No. 76 exists with watermark reversed.

 Set, never hinged 1,250.
 Set, Perf "SPECIMEN" 650.00

Centenary of the formation of the Cayman Islands Assembly.

Common Design Types pictured following the introduction.

Silver Jubilee Issue

Common Design Type

1935, May 6 *Perf. 13½x14*

81 CD301 ½p green & black .35 *1.50*
82 CD301 2½p blue & brown 5.50 *1.75*
83 CD301 6p ol grn & lt bl 1.60 *4.75*
84 CD301 1sh brt vio & ind 12.50 11.50
 Nos. 81-84 (4) 19.95 19.50
 Set, never hinged 24.00
 Set, Perf "SPECIMEN" 175.00

King George V
A8

Catboat
A9

Red-footed Boobies
A10

Conches and Coconut Palms — A11

Hawksbill Turtles
A12

1935-36 *Perf. 12½*

85 A8 ¼p brown & blk .60 *1.25*
86 A9 ½p yel grn & ultra 1.25 *1.25*
87 A10 1p car & ultra 5.00 3.00
88 A11 1½p org & black 1.75 *2.40*
89 A9 2p brown vio & ultra 4.50 1.50
90 A12 2½p dp blue & blk 4.00 1.60
91 A8 3p ol grn & blk 3.00 *3.75*
92 A12 6p red vio & blk 8.00 6.00
93 A9 1sh org & ultra 7.00 *8.50*
94 A10 2sh black & ultra 55.00 50.00
95 A12 5sh green & blk 60.00 65.00
96 A11 10sh car & black 100.00 *110.00*
 Nos. 85-96 (12) 250.10 254.25
 Set, never hinged 500.00
 Set, perf "SPECIMEN" 375.00

Issued: No. 86, 2½p, 6p, 1sh, 1/1/36; others, 5/1/35.

Coronation Issue

Common Design Type

1937, May 13 *Perf. 11x11½*

97 CD302 ½p deep green .25 *1.50*
98 CD302 1p dark carmine .30 .25
99 CD302 2½p deep ultra .55 .55
 Nos. 97-99 (3) 1.10 2.30
 Set, never hinged 2.25
 Set, Perf "SPECIMEN" 110.00
 Set, Perf "SPECIMEN," never hinged 160.00

Beach View, Grand Cayman
A13

Dolphin — A14

Map of the Islands
A15

Hawksbill Turtles — A16

Cayman Schooner
A17

Perf. 12½; 11½x13 or 13x11½ (A14, #111); 14 (#104, 107)

1938-43 Engr.

100 A13 ¼p red orange .55 *.75*
 a. Perf. 13½x12½ ('43) .25 *.85*
101 A14 ½p yel green .85 *.75*
 a. Perf. 14 ('43) 1.50 *1.75*
102 A15 1p carmine .25 *1.00*
103 A13 1½p black .25 .25
104 A16 2p dp violet ('43) .50 .35
 a. Perf. 11½x13 3.00 .40
105 A17 2½p ultra .40 .25
106 A15 3p orange .40 .25
107 A16 6p dk ol grn ('43) 2.50 2.50
 a. Perf. 11½x13 7.25 5.25
108 A14 1sh reddish brown 5.00 2.00
 a. Perf. 14 ('43) 4.00 2.50
109 A13 2sh green 22.50 18.00
110 A17 5sh deep rose 24.50 19.00
111 A16 10sh dark brown 22.50 12.00
 a. Perf. 14 ('43) 20.00 12.00
 Nos. 100-111 (12) 80.20 57.10
 Set, never hinged 125.00
 Set of 14, #100-111, 114-115, Perf "SPECIMEN" 350.00
 Set, Perf "SPECIMEN," never hinged 500.00

See Nos. 114-115.

Catalogue values for unused stamps in this section, from this point to the end of the section, are for Never Hinged items.

Peace Issue

Common Design Type

1946, Aug. 26 Wmk. 4 *Perf. 13½*

112 CD303 1½p black .30 .40
113 CD303 3p orange .30 .40
 Set, ovptd. "SPECIMEN" 140.00

Types of 1938

1947, Aug. 25 *Perf. 12½*

114 A17 2½p orange 3.50 .65
115 A15 3p ultramarine 3.50 .45

Silver Wedding Issue

Common Design Types

1948, Nov. 29 Photo. *Perf. 14x14½*

116 CD304 ½p dark green .25 1.00

Perf. 11½x11

Engr.; Name Typo.

117 CD305 10sh blue violet 22.50 27.50

UPU Issue

Common Design Types

Engr.; Name Typo. on #119, 120

1949, Oct. 10 *Perf. 13½, 11x11½*

118 CD306 2½p orange .40 *1.00*
119 CD307 3p indigo 1.90 *2.50*
120 CD308 6p olive .85 *2.50*
121 CD309 1sh red brown .85 .40
 Nos. 118-121 (4) 4.00 6.40

Catboat
A18

Designs: ½p, Coconut grove. 1p, Green turtle. 1½p, Thatch rope industry. 2p, Caymanian seamen. 2½p, Map. 3p, Parrot fish. 6p, Bluff, Cayman Brac. 9p, George Town harbor. 1sh, Turtle "crawl". 2sh, Cayman schooner. 5sh, Boat-building. 10sh, Government offices.

Perf. 11½x11

1950, Oct. 2 Wmk. 4 Engr.

122 A18 ¼p rose red & blue .25 *.80*
123 A18 ½p bl grn & red vio .25 *1.75*
124 A18 1p dp blue & olive .75 *1.00*
125 A18 1½p choc & bl grn .45 *1.00*
126 A18 2p rose car & vio 1.75 *2.00*
127 A18 2½p sepia & aqua 1.75 .85
128 A18 3p bl & blue grn 2.10 2.00
129 A18 6p dp bl & org brn 2.50 1.75
130 A18 9p dk grn & rose red 12.00 2.50
131 A18 1sh red org & brn 4.50 3.75
132 A18 2sh red vio & vio 13.00 *14.50*
133 A18 5sh vio & olive 22.50 9.50
134 A18 10sh rose red & blk 27.50 20.00
 Nos. 122-134 (13) 89.30 61.40

WAR TAX STAMPS

No. 36 Surcharged

a

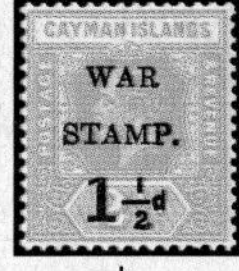

b

1917, Feb. 26 Wmk. 3 *Perf. 14*

MR1 A5(a) 1½p on 2½p 20.00 *25.00*
 a. Fraction bar omitted 275.00 *300.00*
 b. Period missing after "STAMP" 900.00
MR2 A5(b) 1½p on 2½p 2.10 *7.25*
 a. Fraction bar omitted 85.00 *150.00*

On No. 1 the distance between "WAR STAMP" and "1½" varies.

Surcharged

1917, Sept. 4

MR3 A5 1½p on 2½p ultra 850.00 *2,500.*

Surcharged

1917, Sept. 4

MR4 A5 1½p on 2½p ultra .30 *.65*
  a. Ovpted "SPECIMEN" 125.00

No. 33 Overprinted

1919, Feb. 4

MR5 A5 ½p green .70 *3.00*

The "brownish paper" variety comes from the interleaving used for shipment from England.

Type of 1912-16 Surcharged

1919, Feb. 4

MR6 A5 1½p on 2½p orange 1.25 *2.50*
  a. Ovpted "SPECIMEN" 125.00

No. 35 Surcharged

1920, Mar. 10

MR7 A5 1½p on 2p gray 5.50 *9.50*

The "rose-tinted paper" variety comes from the interleaving used for shipment from England.

A surcharge in red was not issued.

CENTRAL LITHUANIA

ˈsen-trəl ˌli-thə-ˈwā-nē-ə

LOCATION — North of Poland and east of Lithuania
CAPITAL — Vilnius

At one time Central Lithuania was a grand duchy of Lithuania but at the end of the 18th Century it fell under Russian rule. After World War I, Lithuania regained her sovereignty but certain areas were occupied by Poland. During the Russo-Polish war this territory was seized by Lithuania whose claim was promptly recognized by the Soviet Government. Under the leadership of the Polish General Zeligowski the territory was recaptured and it was during this occupation the stamps of Central Lithuania came into being. Subsequently the territory became a part of Poland.

100 Fennigi = 1 Markka

Coat of Arms — A1

Perf. 11½, Imperf.

1920-21 Typo. Unwmk.

1 A1 25f red .40 *.55*
2 A1 25f dark grn ('21) .40 *.55*
3 A1 1m blue .40 *.55*
  a. Tête-bêche pair 4.75 4.75
4 A1 1m dark brn ('21) .40 *.55*
  a. Tête-bêche pair 4.75 4.75
5 A1 2m violet .40 *.55*
  a. Tête-bêche pair 4.75 4.75
6 A1 2m orange ('21) .40 *.55*
  Nos. 1-6 (6) 2.40 *3.30*

For surcharges see Nos. B1-B5.

Lithuanian Stamps of 1919 Surcharged in Blue or Black

Perf. 11½x12, 12½x11½, 14

1920, Nov. 23 Wmk. 145

13 A5 2m on 15sk lil 47.50 *55.00*
  a. Inverted surcharge *200.00* *900.00*
14 A5 4m on 10sk red 47.50 *52.50*
  a. Inverted surcharge *150.00*
15 A5 4m on 20sk dl bl (Bk) 47.50 *52.50*
  a. Inverted surcharge *150.00*
16 A5 4m on 30sk buff 47.50 *52.50*
  a. Inverted surcharge *150.00*
17 A6 6m on 50sk lt grn 47.50 *52.50*
  a. 4m on 50sk (error) *200.00*
  b. 10m on 50sk (error) *200.00*
  c. Surcharge inverted —
18 A6 6m on 60sk vio & red 47.50 *52.50*
  a. 4m on 60sk (error) *200.00*
  b. 10m on 60sk (error) *200.00*
19 A6 6m on 75sk bis & red 47.50 *52.50*
  a. 4m on 75sk (error) *200.00*
  b. 10m on 75sk (error) *200.00*
20 A8 10m on 1auk gray & red 95.00 110.00
  a. Inverted surcharge *210.00*
21 A8 10m on 3auk lt brn & red *1,400.* *1,800.*
22 A8 10m on 5auk bl grn & red *1,400.* *1,800.*
  Nos. 13-20 (8) 427.50 *480.00*
  Nos. 13-22 (10) *3,228.* *4,080.*

The overprint on Nos. 17-19 is down-reading, i.e., the top of the overprint is at the right of the original design, the bottom at the left. The inverted overprint on No. 17c is up-reading.

Reprints of Nos. 17a, 17b, 18a, 18b, 19a, 19b. Value, each $45.

Counterfeits of Nos. 21-22 exist.

Lithuanian Girl — A2

Warrior — A3

Holy Gate of Vilnius — A4

Tower and Cathedral, Vilnius — A5

Rector's Insignia — A6

Gen. Lucien Zeligowski — A7

Perf. 11½, Imperf.

1920 Litho. Unwmk.

23 A2 25f gray .25 *.75*
24 A3 1m orange .25 *.75*
25 A4 2m claret .45 *1.00*
26 A5 4m gray grn & buff .60 *1.25*
  a. Tête-bêche pair 24.00 32.50
27 A6 6m rose & gray 2.00 *2.75*
28 A7 10m brown & yellow 3.00 *4.00*
  Nos. 23-28 (6) 6.55 *10.50*

For surcharges see Nos. B13-B14, B17-B19.

St. Anne's Church, Vilnius — A8

St. Stanislas Cathedral, Vilnius — A9

White Eagle, White Knight Vytis — A10

Queen Hedwig and King Ladislas II Jagello — A11

Coat of Arms of Vilnius — A12

Poczobut Astronomical Observatory A13

Union of Lithuania and Poland — A14

Tadeusz Kosciuszko and Adam Mickiewicz A15

1921 ***Perf. 14, Imperf.***

35 A8 1m dk gray & yel .65 *1.10*
36 A9 2m rose & green .65 *1.10*
37 A10 3m dark green .65 *1.10*
38 A11 4m brown & buff .65 *1.10*
39 A12 5m red brown .65 *1.10*
40 A13 6m slate & buff .65 *1.40*
41 A14 10m red vio & buff .90 *2.25*
42 A15 20m blk brn & buff .90 *2.25*
  Nos. 35-42 (8) 5.70 *11.40*

Set, perf. 13½, $150.

Peasant Girl Sowing — A16

White Eagle and Vytis — A17

Great Theater at Vilnius — A18

Allegory: Peace and Industry — A19

Gen. Zeligowski Entering Vilnius — A20

Gen. Zeligowski — A21

1921-22 ***Perf. 11½, Imperf.***

53 A16 10m brown ('22) 3.25 *6.25*
54 A17 25m red & yel ('22) 3.50 *8.00*
55 A18 50m dk blue ('22) 5.00 *12.00*
56 A19 75m violet ('22) 6.00 *22.50*
57 A20 100m bl & bister 2.50 *5.25*
58 A21 150m ol grn & brn 3.50 *6.75*
  Nos. 53-58 (6) 23.75 *60.75*

Opening of the Natl. Parliament, Nos. 53-56; anniv. of the entry of General Zeligowski into Vilnius, Nos. 57-58.

SEMI-POSTAL STAMPS

Nos. 1-6 Surcharged in Black or Red

1921 Unwmk. ***Perf. 11½, Imperf.***

B1 A1 25f + 2m red (Bk) 1.00 *1.75*
B2 A1 25f + 2m dk green 1.00 *1.75*
B3 A1 1m + 2m blue 1.10 *1.75*
B4 A1 1m + 2m dk brown 1.10 *1.75*
B5 A1 2m + 2m violet 1.10 *1.75*
B6 A1 2m + 2m orange 1.10 *1.75*
  Nos. B1-B6 (6) 6.40 *10.50*

The surcharge means "For Silesia 2 marks." The stamps were intended to provide a fund to assist the plebiscite in Upper Silesia.

Nos. 25, 26 Surcharged

a

b

Perf. 11½, Imperf.

B13 A4 (a) 2m + 1(m) claret 1.00 *2.00*
B14 A5 (b) 4m + 1m gray green & buff 1.00 *2.00*

Nos. 25-26, 28 with inset

Perf. 11½, Imperf.

B17 A4 2m + 1m claret .65 *1.25*
B18 A5 4m + 1m gray green & buff .65 *1.25*
B19 A7 10m + 2m brn & yel .90 *1.25*
Nos. B13-B19 (5) 4.20 *7.75*

POSTAGE DUE STAMPS

University, Vilnius — D1

Castle Hill, Vilnius — D2

Castle Ruins, Troki D3

Holy Gate, Vilnius D4

St. Stanislas Cathedral D5

St. Anne's Church, Vilnius D6

1920-21 Unwmk. ***Perf. 11½, Imperf.***

J1 D1 50f red violet .40 *1.25*
J2 D2 1m green .40 *1.25*
J3 D3 2m red violet .50 *1.25*
J4 D4 3m red violet .85 *1.60*
J5 D5 5m red violet 1.00 *2.50*
J6 D6 20m scarlet 2.00 *3.25*
Nos. J1-J6 (6) 5.15 *11.10*

CEYLON

si-'län

LOCATION — An island in the Indian Ocean separated from India by the Gulf of Manaar
GOVT. — British Colony
AREA — 25,332 sq. mi.
POP. — 12,670,000 (est. 1971)
CAPITAL — Colombo

12 Pence = 1 Shilling
100 Cents = 1 Rupee (1872)

Values for unused stamps are for examples with original gum as defined in the catalogue introduction except for Nos. 2, 5, 8-9 which seldom have any remaining trace of their original gum. Many unused stamps of Ceylon, especially between Nos. 59 and 274, have toned gum or tropical stains. Values quoted are for stamps with fresh gum. Toned stamps have lower values, and common stamps with toned gum are worth very little.

Very fine examples of Nos. 1-15 will be cut square, will have small margins, but will show an intact design. Inferior examples with the design partly cut away will sell for much less, and examples with large margins will command higher prices. Very fine examples of Nos. 17-58b will have perforations just cutting into the design on one or more sides due to the narrow spacing of the stamps on the plates and to imperfect perforating methods. Stamps with perfs clear on all four sides are extremely scarce and will command substantially higher prices.

Catalogue values for unused stamps in this country are for Never Hinged items, beginning with Scott 290 in the regular postage section.

Watermarks

Wmk. 1a — 22½mm high, Oval Letters

Wmk. 1b — 21mm high, Round Letters

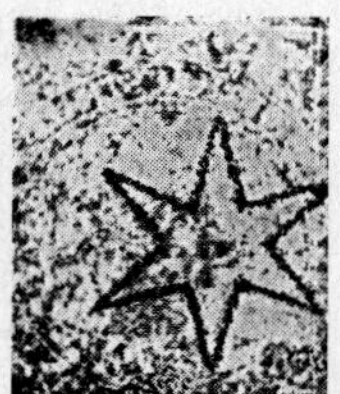

Wmk. 6 — Large Star

Wmk. 290 — Lotus and "Sri" Multiple

Queen Victoria
A1 A2

1857 Engr. Wmk. 6 ***Imperf.***
Blued Paper

1 A1 1p blue — 240.
On cover 1,750.
On cover, single franking 2,100.

2 A1 6p plum *12,500.* 525.
On cover 4,700.
On cover, single franking 5,800.

1857-59 White Paper

3 A1 1p dp turq 1,150. 47.50
a. 1p blue 1,250. 82.50
On cover 325.00
On cover, single franking 575.00
Rouletted, unofficial *10,000.*
4 A1 2p deep grn 210.00 75.00
On cover 525.00
On cover, single franking 4,750.
Rouletted, unofficial *5,250.* *2,650.*
a. 2p yellow green 575.00 105.00
On cover 850.00
On cover, single franking —
5 A2 4p dl rose ('59) *75,000.* 5,250.
On cover *26,500.*
On cover, single franking —
6 A1 5p org brown 1,750. 175.00
On cover with other values 1,150.
On cover, single franking 850.00
6A A1 6p plum *2,850.* 170.00
On cover with other values 725.00
On cover, single franking 575.00
7 A1 6p brown *10,500.* 575.00
On cover 3,750.
On cover, single franking —
a. 6p deep brown 12,500. 1,150.
On cover 7,250.
On cover, single franking —
b. 6p pale brown — 2,150.
On cover —
8 A2 8p brown ('59) *30,000.* 1,750.
On cover *10,500.*
On cover, single franking —
9 A2 9p lil brn ('59) *62,500.* 1,050.
On cover *8,750.*
On cover, single franking *11,500.*
10 A1 10p vermilion 950.00 350.00
On cover with other values 7,500.
On cover, single franking 3,750.
11 A1 1sh violet 5,750. 225.00
On cover with other values 1,425.
On cover, single franking 1,150.
12 A2 1sh9p green ('59) 950.00 925.00
On cover, single franking *21,500.*
Rouletted, unofficial *16,500.*
a. 1sh9p yellow green 5,500. 3,500.
On cover —
13 A2 2sh blue ('59) 6,750. 1,400.
On cover —

Stamps of type A2 frequently have repaired corners.

Beware of Nos. 17-57 trimmed to resemble Nos. 3-13. Values are for stamps with clear margins on all sides.

No. 5 was reproduced by the collotype process in a souvenir sheet distributed at the London International Stamp Exhibition 1950. The paper is unwatermarked.

A3

1857-58 Typo. Unwmk.

14 A3 ½p lilac ('58) 200. *250.*
On cover 2,550.
Rouletted, unofficial *9,000.*
15 A3 ½p lilac, *bluish* 4,250. 650.
On cover 7,500.
On cover, single franking *11,500.*

Values are for stamps without cracking of the surface, and examples showing cracking should be discounted.

Clean-Cut Perf. 14 to 15½

1861 Wmk. 6 Engr.

17 A1 1p blue 210.00 18.00
On cover 425.00
On cover, single franking 425.00
a. 1p pale blue 2,600. 310.00
On cover —
18 A1 2p yel grn 275.00 27.50
On cover —
a. 2p green 290.00 32.50
On cover with other stamps 750.00
b. As "b," vert. pair, imperf between —
19 A2 4p dull rose 2,300. 350.00
On cover with other stamps *8,000.*
20 A1 5p org brown 125.00 10.00
On cover 215.00
On cover, single franking 215.00
20A A1 6p brown 3,200. 190.00
On cover, single franking 1,275.
b. 6p bister brown 2,250. 290.00
On cover, single franking 2,750.
21 A2 8p brown 2,600. 575.00
On cover —
22 A2 9p lilac brown 16,000. 275.00
On cover with other stamps *6,500.*
23 A1 1sh violet 145.00 17.50
On cover 650.00
On cover, single franking 1,000.
24 A2 2sh blue 4,750. 875.00
On cover with other stamps *25,000.*

Rough Perf. 14 to 15½

25 A1 1p blue 170.00 12.50
On cover 215.00
On cover, single franking 215.00
b. Blued paper 850.00 27.50
On cover —
26 A1 2p yel green 475.00 92.50
On cover 900.00
On cover, single franking —
27 A2 4p rose red 600.00 130.00
On cover with other stamps *6,600.*
a. 4p dp rose red 700.00 160.00
28 A1 6p olive brown 1,250. 120.00
On cover, single franking 875.00
On cover with other stamps —
a. 6p deep brown 1,350. 130.00
On cover, single franking 1,100.
On cover with other stamps *1,550.*
b. 6p bister brown 2,300. 200.00
On cover, single franking 1,400.
On cover with other stamps *2,000.*
29 A2 8p brown 1,775. 675.00
On cover —
30 A2 8p yel brown 1,800. 425.00
On cover —
31 A2 9p olive brown 875.00 85.00
On cover 1,100.
On cover, single franking 1,550.
32 A2 9p deep brown 160.00 120.00
On cover, single franking 1,450.
a. 9p light brown 1,350. 130.00
On cover, single franking —
33 A1 10p vermilion 325.00 30.00
On cover, single franking 1,000.
On cover with other stamps —
a. Imperf. vert., pair —
34 A1 1sh violet 300.00 17.50
On cover 425.00
35 A2 1sh9p green 825.00
36 A2 2sh blue 800.00 160.00
On cover —
a. 2sh deep blue 1,100. 200.00
On cover —

The 1sh9p green was never placed in use.

1863 ***Perf. 12½***

37 A1 10p vermilion 340.00 22.50
On cover 425.00
On cover, single franking 650.00

1864 Typo. Unwmk.

38 A3 ½p lilac 260.00 210.00
On cover, single franking *4,250.*

See note following No. 15.

1862 Engr. ***Perf. 13***

39 A1 1p blue 180.00 7.00
On cover 225.00
On cover, single franking 350.00
40 A1 5p car brown 1,850. 175.00
On cover —
41 A1 6p deep brown 210.00 30.00
On cover with other stamps 725.00
On cover, single franking 650.00
a. 6p brown 210.00 30.00
On cover with other stamps 725.00
On cover, single franking 675.00
42 A2 9p brown 1,400. 120.00
On cover, single franking *5,000.*
43 A1 1sh grayish violet 2,100. 95.00
On cover —

Parts of the papermaker's sheet watermark, "T. H. SAUNDERS 1862," may be found on some examples of Nos. 39-43.

Perf. 12

44 A1 1p blue 1,900. 150.00
On cover with other stamps 1,450.

On cover, single franking —
a. Horiz. pair, imperf. btwn. *18,000.*

Two Types of Watermark Crown and CC (1)

1863-67 Typo. Wmk. 1a *Perf. 12½*

45 A3 ½p lilac 80.00 50.00
On cover with other stamps 1,200.
On cover, single franking —
a. ½p reddish lilac 90.00 65.00
On cover with other stamps 1,750.
On cover, single franking 3,600.
b. ½p mauve 55.00 55.00
On cover —

Engr.

46 A1 1p blue 180.00 9.00
On cover 110.00
On cover, single franking 120.00
a. 1p dark blue 180.00 9.00
On cover 110.00
On cover, single franking 125.00
c. Perf. 11½ 3,650. 350.00
On cover 1,500.
On cover, single franking 1,800.
47 A1 2p gray green 100.00 15.00
On cover 200.00
On cover, single franking —
48 A1 2p emerald 190.00 120.00
On cover —
48A A1 2p yel green *10,000.* 475.00
On cover —
48B A1 2p bottle green *4,250.*
49 A1 2p olive 325.00 275.00
On cover —
50 A2 4p rose 550.00 130.00
On cover —
a. 4p carmine rose 900.00 275.00
On cover with other stamps *6,750.*
51 A1 5p car brown 325.00 110.00
On cover 1,200.
On cover, single franking 1,800.
52 A1 5p olive green 1,700. 350.00
On cover *5,000.*
e. 5p deep sage green 2,100. 425.00
On cover *7,500.*
53 A1 6p choc brown 250.00 7.50
On cover 200.00
On cover, single franking 275.00
a. Perf. 13 2,850. 260.00
On cover, single franking —
b. 6p black brown 300.00 11.50
On cover 250.00
On cover, single franking 375.00
c. As "b," double impression *4,500.*
d. 6p reddish brown 350.00 14.00
54 A2 8p red brown 150.00 80.00
On cover 4,000.
On cover, single franking 8,000.
55 A2 9p brown 360.00 52.50
On cover 3,750.
On cover, single franking —
c. Perf. 13 6,750. 1,100.
On cover —
56 A1 10p vermilion 5,000. 70.00
On cover with other stamps 900.00
On cover, single franking 700.00
a. 10p orange 7,500. 500.00
On cover —
58 A2 2sh blue 375.00 45.00
On cover with other stamps *14,500.*

The ½p, 1p blue, 2p olive, 4p and 5p green exist imperf.

Wmk. 1b

46d A1 1p blue 325.00 17.50
On cover 160.00
On cover, single franking 175.00
e. 1p dark blue 275.00 16.00
On cover 160.00
On cover, single franking 175.00
49d A1 2p orange yellow 135.00 8.00
On cover 725.00
On cover, single franking —
e. 2p olive yellow 175.00 14.00
On cover 850.00
On cover, single franking —
f. 2p olive green 175.00 30.00
On cover 2,750.
On cover, single franking —
50b A2 4p rose 325.00 65.00
On cover 1,750.
On cover, single franking *8,500.*
c. 4p carmine rose 125.00 40.00
On cover 1,750.
On cover, single franking —
52b A1 5p myrtle green 160.00 25.00
On cover 1,100.
On cover, single franking 1,100.
c. 5p olive green 150.00 27.50
On cover 2,300.
On cover, single franking 2,300.
d. 5p bronze green 60.00 *60.00*
On cover 2,150.
On cover, single franking 2,150.
53e A1 6p chocolate brown 140.00 11.00
On cover 575.00
On cover, single franking 575.00
f. 6p brown 190.00 9.00
On cover 250.00
On cover, single franking 900.00
54a A2 8p red brown 140.00 80.00
On cover 4,600.
On cover, single franking —
b. 8p chocolate 115.00 72.50
55a A2 9p dark brown 70.00 7.00
On cover 350.00
On cover, single franking 600.00
b. 9p bister brown 975.00 40.00
On cover 725.00
On cover, single franking 1,000.
56b A1 10p orange 150.00 17.00
On cover 675.00
On cover, single franking 625.00
c. 10p orange red 90.00 18.00
On cover 650.00
On cover, single franking 340.00
d. 10p vermilion *5,500.* 170.00
On cover —
On cover, single franking 2,000.
57 A1 1sh purple 150.00 12.00
On cover 440.00
On cover, single franking 450.00
a. 1sh reddish lilac 325.00 32.50
On cover 1,900.
On cover, single franking 1,900.
58a A2 2sh deep blue 160.00 17.50
On cover *13,500.*
On cover, single franking *17,250.*
b. 2sh indigo 300.00 22.50
On cover —

The 1p blue and 6p brown exist imperf.
For overprints see Nos. O2, O4-O7.

A4 A5

1866 Typo. Wmk. 1 *Perf. 12½*

59 A5 3p rose 300.00 105.00
a. Imperf., pair *1,000.*

For overprint see No. O3.

1868 *Perf. 14*

61 A4 1p blue 30.00 12.00
62 A5 3p rose 95.00 52.50
a. 3p bright rose 100.00 57.50

No. 61 exists imperf.
For overprint see No. O1.

A6 A7

A8 A9

A10 A11

A12 A13

A14

A15

1872-80 *Perf. 14*

63 A6 2c brown 32.50 4.50
64 A7 4c gray 50.00 1.75
65 A7 4c lil rose ('80) 75.00 1.60
66 A8 8c orange 55.00 7.25
a. 8c orange yellow 45.00 8.00
67 A9 16c violet 150.00 3.00
68 A10 24c green 90.00 2.25
69 A11 32c slate bl ('77) 190.00 16.00
70 A12 36c blue 210.00 30.00
71 A13 48c rose 110.00 9.50
72 A14 64c red brn ('77) 325.00 77.50
73 A15 96c olive gray 300.00 30.00
Nos. 63-73 (11) 1,588. 183.35

For surcharges see Nos. 83-84, 94A-110, 112-114. For types surcharged see Nos. 124-129.

1872 *Perf. 12½*

74 A6 2c brown *4,750.* 275.00
75 A7 4c gray *3,250.* 350.00

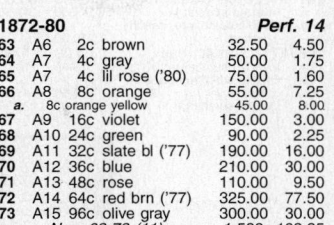

A16

1879 *Perf. 14x12½*

77 A6 2c brown 450.00 75.00
78 A7 4c gray 2,600. 40.00
79 A8 8c orange 500.00 57.50

Perf. 12½x14

82 A16 2r50c claret 825.00 440.00

The 32c and 64c are known perf. 14x12½, but were not regularly issued.
No. 82, perf. 12½, was not regularly issued.
See Nos. 142, 158. For surcharges see Nos. 111, 115, 130. For types surcharged see Nos. 160-161.

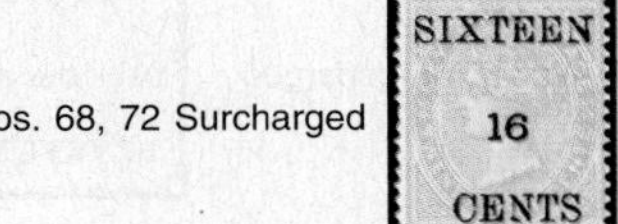

Nos. 68, 72 Surcharged

1882 *Perf. 14*

83 A10 16c on 24c green 42.50 10.00
a. Inverted surcharge —
84 A14 20c on 64c red brn 14.50 10.00
a. Double surcharge 1,850.

1883-99 Wmk. 2

85 A6 2c pale brown 75.00 3.50
86 A6 2c green ('84) 3.25 .25
Ovptd. "SPECIMEN" 500.00
a. Perf. 12 7,000.
87 A6 2c org brn ('99) 5.00 .40
88 A7 4c lilac rose 6.50 .50
89 A7 4c rose ('84) 7.75 *13.50*
Overprinted "SPECIMEN" 475.00
a. Perf. 12 7,250.
90 A7 4c brt rose ('98) 13.00 *15.00*
91 A7 4c yellow ('99) 4.25 4.00
92 A8 8c orange 8.00 *14.00*
a. 8c yellow 5.75 12.50
93 A9 16c violet 2,100. 180.00
94 A10 24c purple brown 1,750.
Overprinted "SPECIMEN" 825.00
b. Perf. 12 *7,750.*

Nos. 86a, 89a, 94 and 94b were never placed in use. A 48c brown, perf. 12, was prepared but not issued.
For surcharges and overprints see Nos.116-123, 143-151D, 155-156. O8-O9.

Issues of 1872-82 Surcharged

a

b

c

d

1885 Wmk. 1 *Perf. 14*

94A A9 (a) 5c on 16c *3,250.*
95 A10 (a) 5c on 24c *6,750.* 115.00
96 A11 (a) 5c on 32c 72.50 20.00
a. Inverted surcharge 3,000.
97 A12 (a) 5c on 36c 325.00 13.50
a. Inverted surcharge *2,850.*
98 A13 (a) 5c on 48c 2,550. 75.00
99 A14 (a) 5c on 64c 145.00 14.00
a. Double surcharge 3,750.
100 A15 (a) 5c on 96c 575.00 75.00
101 A9 (b) 10c on 16c *12,500.* 3,250.
102 A10 (b) 10c on 24c 525.00 145.00
103 A12 (b) 10c on 36c 500.00 290.00
104 A14 (b) 10c on 64c 475.00 275.00
105 A10 (b) 20c on 24c 80.00 30.00
106 A11 (c) 20c on 32c 95.00 80.00
a. 20c on 32c dark gray 115.00 65.00
107 A11 (c) 25c on 32c 27.50 8.25
108 A13 (c) 28c on 48c 45.00 11.50
a. Double surcharge 3,250.
109 A12 (b) 30c on 36c 16.00 12.50
a. Inverted surcharge 350.00 160.00
110 A15 (b) 56c on 96c 37.50 27.50

Perf. 12½

111 A16 (d) 1r12c on 2r50c 750.00 115.00

Perf. 14x12½

112 A11 (a) 5c on 32c 900.00 57.50
113 A14 (a) 5c on 64c 975.00 57.50
114 A14 (b) 10c on 64c 100.00 *175.00*
a. Vert. pair, imperf. btwn. 6,750.

Perf. 12½x14

115 A16 (d) 1r12c on 2r50c 115.00 55.00

Perf. 14
Wmk. 2

117 A7 (a) 5c on 4c rose 27.50 6.00
a. Inverted surcharge *350.00*
118 A8 (a) 5c on 8c org 100.00 12.00
a. Inverted surcharge *4,400.*
b. Double surcharge *4,000.*
119 A9 (a) 5c on 16c vio 190.00 18.00
a. Inverted surcharge *260.00*
120 A10 (a) 5c on 24c pur brn — 600.00
121 A9 (b) 10c on 16c vio 13,500. 1,800.
122 A10 (b) 10c on 24c pur brn 18.50 11.50
123 A9 (b) 15c on 16c vio 15.50 11.50

A 5c on 4c lilac rose and a 5c on 24c green are known to exist and are considered to be a forgeries.

Types of 1872-80 Surcharged

e

f

g

1885-87

124 A 8 (e) 5c on 8c lilac 27.50 1.60
125 A10 (f) 10c on 24c pur brn 14.50 9.00
126 A 9 (f) 15c on 16c org 62.50 15.50
127 A11 (f) 28c on 32c sl bl 30.00 2.75
128 A12 (f) 30c on 36c ol grn 30.00 16.00
129 A15 (f) 56c on 96c ol gray 55.00 18.00

Wmk. 1 Sideways

130 A16 (g) 1r12c on 2r50c cl 62.50 *145.00*
Nos. 124-130 (7) 282.00 207.85

A23

Type I Type II

FIVE CENTS
Type I — Thin lines in background. Hair and curl clear.
Type II — Thicker lines in background. Heavier shading under chin.

1886 **Wmk. 2**
131 A23 5c lilac, type I 4.00 .25
a. Type II 4.00 .25

For overprint see No. O12.

A24

1886-1900
132 A24 3c org brn & green ('93) 7.00 .50
133 A24 3c green ('00) 5.00 .60
134 A24 6c rose & blk ('99) 3.25 .50
135 A24 12c ol grn & car ('00) 5.50 *9.00*
136 A24 15c olive green 9.00 2.40
137 A24 15c ultra ('00) 8.00 1.50
138 A24 25c yel brn 5.75 2.00
a. 25c yel brn, value in ol yel 155.00 90.00
139 A24 28c slate 25.00 1.50
140 A24 30c vio & org brown ('93) 4.75 3.50
141 A24 75c blk & org brown ('00) 9.50 9.50
Nos. 132-141 (10) 82.75 *31.00*

Numeral tablet of 3c, 12c and 75c has lined background with colorless value and "c."
For surcharges & overprints see Nos. 152-154, 157, 159, O10-O11, O13-O17.

1887 **Wmk. 1**
142 A16 1r12c claret 32.50 30.00
Overprinted "SPECIMEN" 165.00

For overprint see No. O18.

Issue of 1883-84 Surcharged

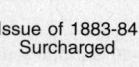

1888-90 **Wmk. 2**
143 A7 2c on 4c lilac rose 1.60 .95
a. Inverted surcharge 25.00 24.00
b. Double surcharge, one invtd. 400.00
144 A7 2c on 4c rose 2.75 .35
a. Inverted surcharge 20.00 *21.00*
b. Double surcharge 400.00

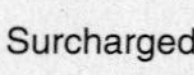

Surcharged

145 A7 2c on 4c lilac rose 1.10 .30
a. Inverted surcharge 42.50 *42.50*
b. Double surcharge 100.00 110.00
c. Double surcharge, one invtd. 85.00 85.00
146 A7 2c on 4c rose 8.00 .25
a. Double surcharge, one invtd. 105.00 *125.00*
b. Double surcharge 110.00 *125.00*
c. Inverted surcharge 425.00

Surcharged

147 A7 2c on 4c lilac rose 82.50 35.00
a. Inverted surcharge 175.00 47.50
b. Double surcharge, one inverted 210.00
148 A7 2c on 4c rose 4.00 1.00
a. Inverted surcharge 19.00 10.00
b. Double surcharge, one inverted 9.50 *15.00*
c. Double surcharge 210.00 175.00

Surcharged

149 A7 2c on 4c lilac rose 67.50 30.00
a. Inverted surcharge 200.00 32.50
150 A7 2c on 4c rose 3.00 1.25
a. Inverted surcharge 19.00 8.50
b. Double surcharge 160.00 150.00
c. Double surcharge, one inverted 19.00 11.00

Surcharged

151 A7 2c on 4c rose 13.50 1.20
a. Inverted surcharge 24.00 7.50
b. Double surcharge 135.00 135.00
c. Double surch., one invtd. 27.50 13.50
i. "S" of "Cents" inverted 525.00 350.00
151D A7 2c on 4c lilac rose 67.50 37.50
e. Inverted surcharge 95.00 42.50
f. Double surcharge 450.00
g. Double surch., one invtd. 150.00 150.00
h. "S" of "Cents" inverted 750.00
i. "POSTAGE" spaced between "T" and "A" 85.00 90.00
j. As "i," inverted surcharge *1,500.*

Counterfeit errors of surcharges of Nos. 143 to 151D are prevalent.

No. 136 Surcharged

1890
152 A24 5c on 15c ol green 4.00 2.75
a. "Five" instead of "Five" 140.00 100.00
b. "REVENUE" omitted 225.00 200.00
c. Inverted surcharge 65.00 *75.00*
d. Double surcharge 125.00 *145.00*
e. As "a," inverted surcharge — 1,800.
f. Inverted "s" in "Cents" 130.00 *120.00*
g. As "f," inverted surcharge 2,200.
h. As "b," invtd. "s" in "Cents" 1,800.

Nos. 138-139 Surcharged

1891
153 A24 15c on 25c brown 20.00 20.00
154 A24 15c on 28c slate 21.00 10.00

Nos. 88, 89 and 139 Surcharged

1892
155 A7 3c on 4c lilac rose 1.10 *3.50*
156 A7 3c on 4c rose 7.25 *11.00*
a. Double surcharge, one invtd.
157 A24 3c on 28c slate 6.25 5.75
a. Double surcharge 180.00
Nos. 155-157 (3) 14.60 *20.25*

Type of 1879

1898
158 A16 2r50c violet, *red* 42.50 *65.00*

No. 136 Surcharged in Black

1899
159 A24 6c on 15c olive green 1.35 *.85*

Surcharged Type "g" in Black

1899 **Wmk. 1**
160 A16 1r50c on 2r50c gray 24.00 *55.00*
161 A16 2r25c on 2r50c yel 50.00 *95.00*

A35

1900 **Wmk. 1**
162 A35 1r50c car rose 35.00 *55.00*
163 A35 2r25c dull blue 37.50 *55.00*

Nos. 166-292 exist in many different shades, representing different printings for each stamp.

King Edward VII
A36 A37

A38

A39

A40

1903-05 **Wmk. 2**
166 A36 2c org brown 2.40 .25
167 A37 3c green 2.40 1.20
168 A37 4c yel & blue 2.40 *6.00*
169 A38 5c dull lilac 2.75 .70
170 A39 6c car rose 11.00 1.75
171 A37 12c ol grn & car 5.50 *11.50*
172 A40 15c ultra 6.75 3.50
173 A40 25c bister 5.00 *12.00*
174 A40 30c vio & green 3.50 *4.25*
175 A37 75c bl & org ('05) 3.50 *24.00*
176 A40 1r50c gray ('04) 67.50 67.50
177 A40 2r25c brn & grn ('04) 95.00 60.00
Nos. 166-177 (12) 207.70 192.65
Set, never hinged 400.00

For overprints see Nos. O19-O24.

1904-10 **Wmk. 3**
178 A36 2c orange brown 2.75 .25
a. 2c orange 1.60 .60
179 A37 3c green 1.75 .25
180 A37 4c yel & blue 3.00 1.75
181 A38 5c dull lilac 3.50 1.50
a. Booklet pane of 12
b. 5c dull lilac, "chalky paper" 7.50 .75
182 A39 6c car rose 5.25 .25
183 A40 10c ol grn & vio ('10) 2.50 3.50
184 A37 12c ol grn & car 1.75 *2.00*
185 A40 15c ultra 3.75 .70
186 A40 25c bister ('05) 6.25 4.00
187 A40 25c slate ('10) 2.75 3.00
188 A40 30c vio & grn ('05) 2.75 *3.25*
189 A40 50c brown ('10) 4.25 *7.75*
190 A37 75c bl & org ('05) 5.50 *8.25*
191 A40 1r vio, *yel* ('10) 8.50 *13.00*
192 A40 1r50c gray ('05) 32.50 14.00
193 A40 2r scar, *yel* ('10) 16.00 *30.00*
194 A40 2r25c brn & grn 26.00 *32.50*
195 A40 5r blk, *grn* ('10) 50.00 *125.00*
196 A40 10r blk, *red* ('10) 150.00 *325.00*
Nos. 178-196 (19) 328.75 *575.95*
Set, never hinged 600.00

A41

A42

1908
197 A41 5c deep red violet 7.75 .25
a. Booklet pane of 12
198 A42 6c carmine rose 3.50 .25

1911, July 5
199 A40 3c green 1.10 .85

A44

King George V — A45

Type I Type II

3 AND 6 CENTS
Type I — Small "c" after value, 2¼mm wide and 2mm high.
Type II — Large "c" after value, 2½mm wide and 2¼mm high.
1, 5 AND 9 CENTS are Type II, other denominations Type I.

For description of dies I and II see "Dies of British Colonial Stamps" in the Table of Contents.

1912-25 **Die I** **Wmk. 3**
200 A44 1c dp brn (Die Ib) ('20) 1.20 .25
201 A44 2c brown org .45 .25
202 A44 3c dp grn (Die Ia, type II) 5.75 .50
a. 3c deep green, die I, type I 6.75 2.40
203 A44 5c red violet 1.20 .70
a. 5c purple 12.00 3.00
204 A44 6c car (Die Ib, type II) 1.75 1.60
a. 6c carmine, die I, type I 20.00 1.25
b. As "a," bklt. pane of 6
205 A44 10c olive green 3.50 2.00
206 A44 15c ultra 3.75 1.50

Chalky Paper

207 A44 25c yel & ultra 2.10 2.10
208 A44 30c green & vio 4.75 3.75
209 A44 50c black & scar 1.75 *2.10*
210 A44 1r violet, *yel* 5.25 4.25
a. Double impression 'Ceylon,' and 'R1' —
211 A44 2r blk & red, *yel* 3.75 *15.00*
212 A44 5r blk, *green* 20.00 *42.50*
a. 5r black, *bl grn*, olive back 25.00 *45.00*
b. 5r blk, *emer* (Die II) ('20) 52.50 *120.00*
213 A44 10r vio & blk, *red* 85.00 *105.00*
a. Die II ('20) 95.00 *165.00*
214 A44 20r blk & red, *bl* 165.00 *175.00*
215 A45 50r dull violet 675.00 *1,300.*
216 A45 100r gray black 3,000.
217 A45 500r gray green *8,000.*
218 A45 1000r vio, *red* ('25) *35,000.*
Nos. 200-214 (15) 305.20 *356.50*
Set, never hinged 600.00

Although Nos. 217 and 218 were theoretically available for postage it is not probable that they were ever used for other than fiscal purposes.
The 1r through 100r with revenue cancellations sell for minimal prices.
For surcharge & overprints see Nos. 223, MR1-MR3.

Die I

1913-14 Surface-colored Paper

220 A44 1r violet, *yellow* 5.00 *5.75*
221 A44 2r black & red, *yel* 3.25 *15.00*
222 A44 5r black, *green* 26.00 *42.50*
Nos. 220-222 (3) 34.25 *63.25*

No. 203 Surcharged

1918

223 A44 1c on 5c red violet 3.50 *3.50*
a. 1c on 5c purple .25 .30

For overprint see No. MR4.

Die I

1921-33 Wmk. 4 Ordinary Paper

225 A44 1c dp brn (Die Ib) ('27) 1.20 .40
226 A44 2c brn org (Die II) .85 .30
227 A44 3c green (Die Ia, type II) 5.75 .90
228 A44 3c slate (Die Ia, type II) ('22) .90 .25
229 A44 5c red vio (Die I) .70 .25
230 A44 6c carmine (Die Ib, type II) 3.50 .90
231 A44 6c vio (Die Ib, type II) ('22) 3.00 .25
232 A44 9c red, *yel* (Die II) ('26) 3.25 .45
233 A44 10c olive green 1.60 .45
a. Die II 2.10 .70
234 A44 12c scarlet, Die II 1.20 *6.00*
a. Die I ('25) 10.00 *12.50*
235 A44 15c ultramarine 4.00 *22.50*
236 A44 15c green, *yel*, Die II 5.00 1.20
a. Die I ('22) 5.75 *6.00*
237 A44 20c ultra, Die II ('24) 4.25 .50
a. Die I ('22) 6.00 *7.25*
238 A44 25c yel & blue 3.25 2.25
a. Die II 5.75 1.50

For surcharges see Nos. 248-249.

Chalky Paper

239 A44 30c green & violet 1.90 *6.75*
a. Die II 6.25 1.50
240 A44 50c blk & scar (Die II) 2.25 .95
a. Die I 65.00 *100.00*
241 A44 1r vio, *yel*, Die II 26.00 *42.50*
a. Die I 16.00 *52.50*
242 A44 2r blk & red, *yel* (Die II) 8.50 *15.00*
243 A44 5r blk, *emer*, (Die II) 52.50 *97.50*
244 A44 20r blk & red, *bl*, (Die II) 260.00 *425.00*
245 A45 50r dull vio 825.00 *1,500.*
246 A45 100r gray black 3,250.
247 A45 100r ultra & dl vio ('27) 2,500.
Nos. 225-244 (20) 389.60 624.30
Set, never hinged 675.00

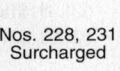

Nos. 228, 231 Surcharged

1926

248 A44 2c on 3c slate 3.50 1.20
a. Double surcharge 85.00
b. Bar omitted 90.00 *100.00*
249 A44 5c on 6c violet 1.25 .45
a. Double surcharge

A46

1927-29 Chalky Paper Wmk. 4

254 A46 1r red vio & dl vio ('28) 3.00 1.50
255 A46 2r car & green ('29) 4.50 3.25
256 A46 5r brn vio & grn ('28) 17.50 *24.00*
257 A46 10r org & green 52.50 *115.00*
258 A46 20r ultra & dl vio 190.00 *340.00*
Nos. 254-258 (5) 267.50 *483.75*
Set, never hinged 450.00

Common Design Types pictured following the introduction.

Silver Jubilee Issue
Common Design Type

1935, May 6 Engr. *Perf. 13½x14*

260 CD301 6c gray blk & ultra .70 .35
261 CD301 9c indigo & green .70 2.50
262 CD301 20c blue & brown 4.00 2.75
263 CD301 50c brt vio & ind 4.75 13.50
Nos. 260-263 (4) 10.15 19.10
Set, never hinged 20.00

Tapping Rubber Tree — A47

Colombo Harbor — A49

Adam's Peak — A48

Picking Tea — A50

Coconut Palms — A53

Rice Terraces A51

River Scene A52

Temple of the Tooth, Kandy A54

Ancient Reservoir A55

Wild Elephants A56

View of Trincomalee A57

Perf. 11x11½ (266, 267), 11½x11 (269, 269, 271, 272, 274), 11½x13 (264, 270), 13x11½ (265), 14 (273)

1935-36 Wmk. 4

264 A47 2c car rose & blk .45 *.55*
a. Perf. 14 12.00 .55
265 A48 3c olive & black .50 *.55*
a. Perf. 14 35.00 *.40*
266 A49 6c blue & black .45 .40
267 A50 9c org red & ol grn 1.50 .90
268 A51 10c dk vio & blk 1.75 *3.25*
269 A52 15c grn & org brn 1.50 .70
270 A53 20c ultra & black 2.50 *3.50*
271 A54 25c choc & dk ultra 2.00 1.75
272 A55 30c green & lake 3.00 *3.75*
273 A56 50c dk vio & blk 15.00 2.50
274 A57 1r brown & vio 35.00 24.00
Nos. 264-274 (11) 63.65 41.85
Set, never hinged 200.00

Issued: 2c, 15c, 25c, 5/1/35; 10c, 6/1/35; 1r, 7/1/35; 30c, 8/1/35; 3c, 10/1/35; 6c, 9c, 20c, 50c, 1/1/36.

Coronation Issue
Common Design Type

1937, May 12 *Perf. 11x11½*

275 CD302 6c dark carmine .75 1.10
a. Booklet pane of 10 20.00
276 CD302 9c deep green 3.00 *4.75*
a. Booklet pane of 10 300.00
277 CD302 20c deep ultra 4.50 *4.50*
Nos. 275-277 (3) 8.25 10.35
Set, never hinged 16.00

Types of 1935 with "Postage & Revenue Removed" and Picturing George VI and

Sigiriya (Lion Rock) — A61

Ancient Guard Stone — A68

George VI — A69

Perf. 11x11½, 11½x11; 12 (#286)

1938-52 Engr. Wmk. 4

278 A47 2c car rose & blk ('44) .45 *1.25*
a. Perf. 13½x13 ('38) 100.00 2.00
b. Perf. 13½ ('38) 2.00 .25
c. Perf. 12 ('49) 1.25 *4.50*
d. Perf. 11½x13 ('38) 10.00 2.75
279 A48 3c dk grn & blk ('42) .50 .25
a. Perf. 13x13½ ('38) 225.00 12.50
b. Perf. 14 ('41) 100.00 1.10
c. Perf. 13½ ('38) 3.50 .25
d. Perf. 12 ('46) .70 *.95*
e. Perf. 13x11½ 8.00 2.50
280 A49 6c blue & black .25 .25
281 A61 10c blue & black 1.75 .25
282 A52 15c red brn & grn 1.25 .25
283 A50 20c dull bl & blk 2.25 .25
284 A54 25c choc & dk ultra 3.25 .30
285 A55 30c dk grn & rose car 8.00 3.75
286 A56 50c dk vio & blk ('46) 2.75 .25
a. Perf. 14 ('42) 90.00 29.00
b. Perf. 13x11½ ('38) 140.00 52.50
c. Perf. 13x13½ ('38) 300.00 3.00
d. Perf. 13½ ('38) 15.00 .55
e. Perf. 11½x11 ('42) 4.00 4.25
287 A57 1r dk brn & bl vio 10.50 1.60
288 A68 2r dark car & blk 9.25 4.00

Perf. 14

Typo.

289 A69 5r brn vio & grn 27.50 13.50
289A A69 10r yel org & dl grn ('52) 50.00 50.00
Nos. 278-289A (13) 117.70 75.90
Set, never hinged 360.00

No. 289A differs from type A69 in having "REVENUE" inscribed vertically at either side of the frame. This revenue 10r was valid for postage Dec. 1, 1952-Mar. 14, 1954.

See Nos. 292, 295. For surcharges see Nos. 290-291.

Catalogue values for unused stamps in this section, from this point to the end of the section, are for Never Hinged items.

No. 283 Surcharged in Black

1940, Nov. 5 *Perf. 11x11½*

290 A50 3c on 20c dull bl & blk *4.50* *4.50*

No. 280 Surcharged

1941, May 10

291 A49 3c on 6c blue & black .65 *1.00*

Coconut Palms — A70

1943-47 Wmk. 4 Engr. *Perf. 12*

292 A70 5c red org & ol grn ('47) 1.75 .35
a. Perf. 13½ ('43) .35 .25

Peace Issue
Common Design Type

1946, Dec. 10 *Perf. 13½x14*

293 CD303 6c deep blue .30 *.35*
294 CD303 15c brown .30 *1.75*

Guard Stone Type of 1938

1947, Mar. 15 *Perf. 11x11½*

295 A68 2r violet & black 2.40 *2.75*

Parliament Building, Colombo — A71

Adam's Peak A72

Dagoba at Anuradhapura A74

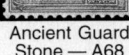

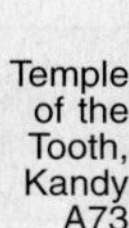

Temple of the Tooth, Kandy
A73

1947, Nov. 25 *Perf. 11x12, 12x11*

296	A71	6c deep ultra & black	.25	.25
297	A72	10c car, orange & black	.25	*.40*
298	A73	15c red vio & grnsh blk	.25	*.80*
299	A74	25c brt green & bister	.25	*1.75*
		Nos. 296-299 (4)	1.00	3.20

New constitution of 1947.

National Flag
A75

D. S. Senanayake
A76

Engr., Flag Typo. (A75); Engr. (A76)
Perf. 12½x12, 12x12½, 13x12½

1949 **Wmk. 4**

300	A75	4c org brn, car & yel	.25	.25
301	A76	5c dark green & brn	.25	.25

Wmk. 290

302	A75	15c red org, car & yel	1.00	.40
303	A76	25c dp blue & brown	.25	1.00
		Nos. 300-303 (4)	1.75	1.90

Size of No. 302: 28x22¼mm.
1st anniv. of Ceylon's independence.
Issued: Nos. 300-301, Feb. 4; Nos. 302-303, Apr. 5.

A77

A78

Design: 15c, Lion Rock and UPU symbols.

Wmk. 290

1949, Oct. 10 **Engr.** *Perf. 12*

304	A77	5c dk green & brown	.85	.25
305	A77	15c dark car & black	1.25	*2.75*
306	A78	25c ultra & black	1.25	1.25
		Nos. 304-306 (3)	3.35	4.25

75th anniv. of the UPU.

Kandyan Dancer
A79

Kiri Vehera, Polonnaruwa
A80

Vesak Orchid — A81

Sigiriya — A82

Ratmalana, Plane — A83

Vatadage Ruins at Madirigiriya
A84

1950, Feb. 4 *Perf. 12x12½*

307	A79	4c bright red & choc	.25	.25
308	A80	5c green	.25	.25
309	A81	15c pur & blue green	2.75	.50
310	A82	30c carmine & yel	.40	*.70*

Perf. 11x11½, 11½x11

311	A83	75c red org & blue	8.50	.25
312	A84	1r red brn & dp blue	2.50	.45
		Nos. 307-312 (6)	14.65	2.40

See Nos. 340-345 in *Scott Standard Postage Stamp Catalogue*, Vol. 2.

Coconut Palms — A85

Star Orchid — A86

1951-52 Unwmk. Photo. *Perf. 11½*

313	A85	10c gray & dark green	1.25	.75
314	A86	35c dk grn & rose brn ('52)	1.50	1.50
a.		Corrected inscription ('54)	6.00	.70

On No. 314a a dot has been added above the third character in the second line of the Tamil inscription.
Issue dates: 10c, Aug. 1; 35c, Feb. 1.
See No. 351 in *Scott Standard Postage Stamp Catalogue*, Vol. 2.

Mace and Symbols of Industry
A87

Perf. 12½x14

1952, Feb. 23 **Wmk. 290**

315	A87	5c green	.25	.30
316	A87	15c brt ultramarine	.40	.60

Colombo Plan Exhibition, February 1952.

WAR TAX STAMPS

Nos. 201, 202, 202a and 203 Overprinted

Die I

1918 **Wmk. 3** *Perf. 14*

MR1	A44	2c brown orange	.25	*.45*
a.		Double overprint	35.00	47.50
b.		Inverted overprint	75.00	*85.00*
MR2	A44	3c dp grn (Die Ia, type II)	4.00	.45
a.		3c dp green (Die I, type I)	.25	*.60*
b.		Double overprint (Die I)	110.00	*130.00*
c.		5c Double overprint (Die Ia, type II)	150.00	
MR3	A44	5c red violet	4.75	3.50
a.		Double overprint	75.00	*85.00*
b.		Inverted overprint	120.00	
c.		5c purple	.60	.35

No. 223 Overprinted in Black

MR4	A44	1c on 5c red violet	3.50	*4.50*
a.		Double overprint	210.00	
b.		1c on No. 223a	.60	.45
		Nos. MR1-MR4 (4)	12.50	8.90

OFFICIAL STAMPS

Regular Issues Overprinted

Black Overprint

1869 **Wmk. 1** *Perf. 12½, 14*

O1	A4	1p blue	77.50
O2	A1	2p yellow	77.50
O3	A5	3p rose	155.00
O4	A2	8p red brown	77.50
O5	A1	1sh gray lilac	175.00

Red Overprint

O6	A1	6p brown	77.50
O7	A2	2sh blue	125.00
a.		Imperf.	*1,150.*
		Nos. O1-O7 (7)	765.00

Nos. O1-O7 were never placed in use.
The overprint measures 15mm on Nos. O1, O3.

Regular Issues Overprinted in Black or Red

1895-1900 **Wmk. 2** *Perf. 14*

O8	A6	2c green	21.00	.75
O9	A6	2c org brn ('00)	13.00	.65
O10	A24	3c org brn & grn	13.00	3.00
O11	A24	3c green ('00)	14.00	5.00
O12	A23	5c lilac	5.75	.35
O13	A24	15c olive green	25.00	.75
O14	A24	15c ultra ('00)	28.00	.75
O15	A24	25c brown	13.50	3.50
O16	A24	30c vio & org brn	13.50	.65
O17	A24	75c blk & org brn (R) ('99)	11.00	*11.00*

Wmk. 1

O18	A16	1r12c claret	100.00	67.50
a.		Double ovpt., one albino	325.00	
		Nos. O8-O18 (11)	257.75	93.90

1903-04 **Wmk. 2**

O19	A36	2c orange brown	24.00	1.75
O20	A37	3c green	17.50	2.40
O21	A38	5c dull lilac	34.00	1.60
O22	A40	15c ultramarine	45.00	3.25
O23	A40	25c bister	40.00	22.50
O24	A40	30c violet & green	22.50	2.25
		Nos. O19-O24 (6)	183.00	33.75

CHAD

'chad

(Tchad)

LOCATION — Central Africa, south of Libya
GOVT. — French Colony
AREA — 495,572 sq. mi.
POP. — 5,122,000 (est. 1984)
CAPITAL — N'djamena

A former dependency of Ubangi-Shari, Chad became a separate French colony in 1920. In 1934, the colonies of Chad, Gabon, Middle Congo and Ubangi-Shari were grouped in a single administrative unit known as French Equatorial Africa, with the capital at Brazzaville.

100 Centimes = 1 Franc

Types of Middle Congo, 1907-17, Overprinted

Perf. 14x13½, 13½x14

1922 Unwmk.

1 A1 1c red & violet .40 .55
Never hinged .80
On cover 75.00
a. Overprint omitted 225.00
Never hinged 340.00
2 A1 2c ol brn & salmon .40 .80
Never hinged .80
On cover 75.00
a. Overprint omitted 260.00
Never hinged 400.00
3 A1 4c ind & vio 1.20 1.60
Never hinged 2.40
On cover 75.00
4 A1 5c choc & grn 1.25 1.60
Never hinged 2.40
On cover 20.00
5 A1 10c dp grn & gray grn 2.40 2.75
Never hinged 4.00
On cover 50.00
6 A1 15c vio & red 2.50 2.75
Never hinged 4.00
On cover 27.50
7 A1 20c grn & vio 4.00 4.75
Never hinged 8.00
On cover 27.50
8 A2 25c ol brn & brn 12.00 12.00
Never hinged 16.00
On cover 30.00
9 A2 30c rose & pale rose 2.40 2.00
Never hinged 4.00
On cover 40.00
On cover, single franking 75.00
10 A2 35c dl bl & dl rose 3.25 3.25
Never hinged 4.00
On cover 32.50
On cover, single franking 50.00
11 A2 40c choc & grn 4.00 4.00
Never hinged 6.50
On cover 32.50
On cover, single franking 50.00
12 A2 45c vio & grn 3.25 3.25
Never hinged 4.00
On cover 62.50
On cover, single franking 110.00
13 A2 50c dk bl & pale bl 3.25 4.00
Never hinged 5.50
On cover 32.50
On cover, single franking 75.00
14 A2 60c on 75c vio, *pnksh* 4.00 4.75
Never hinged 8.00
On cover 40.00
On cover, single franking 62.50
a. "TCHAD" omitted 300.00
Never hinged 450.00
b. "60" omitted 300.00
Never hinged 410.00
15 A1 75c red & violet 4.00 4.00
Never hinged 5.50
On cover 67.50
On cover, single franking 105.00
16 A3 1fr indigo & salmon 12.00 16.00
Never hinged 20.00
On cover 87.50
On cover, single franking 125.00
17 A3 2fr indigo & violet 24.00 24.00
Never hinged 35.00
On cover 105.00
On cover, single franking 190.00
18 A3 5fr ind & olive brn 24.00 24.00
Never hinged 35.00
On cover 140.00
On cover, single franking 225.00
Nos. 1-18 (18) 108.30 116.05

See Nos. 26a, 32a, 38a, 55a.

Stamps of 1922 Overprinted in Various Colors

Nos. 19-28

Nos. 29-50

1924-33

19 A1 1c red & vio .40 .80
Never hinged .80
On cover 55.00
a. "TCHAD" omitted 225.00 *250.00*
Never hinged 340.00
b. Double overprint 300.00
Never hinged 475.00
c. Violet omitted 300.00
Never hinged 450.00
20 A1 2c ol brn & sal .40 *.50*
Never hinged .80
On cover 55.00
a. "TCHAD" omitted 225.00
Never hinged 340.00
b. Double overprint 240.00
Never hinged 350.00
21 A1 4c ind & vio .40 *.50*
Never hinged .80
On cover 55.00
a. "TCHAD" omitted 950.00
22 A1 5c choc & grn (Bl) 1.60 *2.00*
Never hinged 3.25
On cover 27.50
a. "TCHAD" omitted 200.00 225.00
Never hinged 325.00
23 A1 5c choc & grn .80 *.70*
Never hinged 1.20
On cover 27.50
a. "TCHAD" omitted 225.00
Never hinged 340.00
24 A1 10c dp grn & gray grn (Bl) 1.60 1.40
Never hinged 2.00
On cover 21.00
25 A1 10c dp grn & gray grn 1.60 1.40
Never hinged 2.00
On cover 21.00
26 A1 10c red org & blk ('25) .60 .80
Never hinged .80
On cover 30.00
a. "Afrique Equatoriale Française" omitted 225.00 250.00
Never hinged 340.00
b. "TCHAD" omitted 240.00 260.00
Never hinged 375.00
27 A1 15c vio & red .80 .85
Never hinged 1.20
On cover 17.50
28 A1 20c grn & vio .80 .80
Never hinged 1.20
On cover 27.50
a. "TCHAD" omitted 225.00
Never hinged 340.00
b. "Afrique Equatoriale Française" doubled 340.00
Never hinged 450.00
29 A2 25c ol brn & brn .80 .85
Never hinged 1.20
On cover 13.50
a. "Afrique Equatoriale Française" doubled 160.00
Never hinged 240.00
30 A2 30c rose & pale rose .80 1.10
Never hinged 1.20
On cover 32.50
On cover, single franking 75.00
31 A2 30c gray & bl (R) ('25) .40 .80
Never hinged .80
On cover 13.50
32 A2 30c dk grn & grn ('27) 1.20 1.60
Never hinged 2.00
On cover 42.50
a. "Afrique Equatoriale Française" omitted 340.00
Never hinged 450.00
33 A2 35c indigo & dl rose .80 .85
Never hinged 1.20
On cover 40.00
On cover, single franking 67.50
34 A2 40c choc & grn 1.25 1.60
Never hinged 2.00
On cover 45.00
On cover, single franking 75.00
a. Double overprint (R + Bk) 275.00
Never hinged 425.00
35 A2 45c vio & grn 1.20 1.40
Never hinged 1.60
On cover 16.00
On cover, single franking 27.50
a. Double overprint (R + Bk) 275.00
Never hinged 425.00
36 A2 50c dk bl & pale bl (R) 2.40 1.90
Never hinged 4.00
On cover 16.00
On cover, single franking 22.50
a. Inverted overprint 160.00
Never hinged 240.00
37 A2 50c grn & vio ('25) 2.40 2.00
Never hinged 3.50
On cover 13.50
38 A2 65c org brn & bl ('28) 2.40 2.40
Never hinged 4.00
On cover 37.50
On cover, single franking 75.00
a. "Afrique Equatoriale Française" omitted 260.00
Never hinged 400.00
39 A2 75c red & vio (Bl) 2.00 1.90
Never hinged 3.25
On cover 32.50
On cover, single franking 75.00
40 A2 75c dp bl & lt bl (R) ('25) .80 1.20
Never hinged 1.60
On cover 21.00
On cover, single franking 32.50
a. "TCHAD" omitted 260.00
Never hinged 375.00
41 A2 75c rose & dk brn ('28) 3.25 3.25
Never hinged 6.50
On cover 25.00
On cover, single franking 34.00
42 A2 90c brn red & pink ('30) 8.00 12.00
Never hinged 12.00
On cover 67.50
On cover, single franking 160.00
43 A3 1fr ind & salmon 2.40 2.50
Never hinged 4.00
On cover 32.50
On cover, single franking 75.00
44 A3 1.10fr dl grn & bl ('28) 4.00 4.00
Never hinged 6.50
On cover 160.00
On cover, single franking 375.00
45 A3 1.25fr org brn & lt bl ('33) 8.00 9.50
Never hinged 12.00
On cover 50.00
On cover, single franking 125.00
46 A3 1.50fr ultra & bl ('30) 8.00 12.00
Never hinged 12.00
On cover 62.50
On cover, single franking 150.00
47 A3 1.75fr ol brn & vio ('33) 40.00 45.00
Never hinged 65.00
On cover 190.00
On cover, single franking 250.00
48 A3 2fr ind & vio 3.25 3.50
Never hinged 6.50
On cover 62.50
On cover, single franking 110.00
a. Double impression of frame 550.00
Never hinged 875.00
49 A3 3fr red vio ('30) 12.00 16.00
Never hinged 16.00
On cover 100.00
On cover, single franking 190.00
50 A3 5fr ind & ol brn 4.00 4.75
Never hinged 8.00
On cover 67.50
On cover, single franking 125.00
Nos. 19-50 (32) 118.35 139.85

See No. 58a.

Types of 1922 Overprinted like Nos. 29-50 and Surcharged with New Values

1924-27

51 A2 60c on 75c dk vio, *pnksh* .80 1.20
Never hinged 2.40
On cover 20.00
On cover, single franking 32.50
a. "60" omitted 200.00
Never hinged 290.00
52 A3 65c on 1fr brn & ol grn ('25) 2.50 2.00
Never hinged 4.75
On cover 80.00
On cover, single franking 175.00
53 A3 85c on 1fr brn & ol grn ('25) 2.50 2.00
Never hinged 4.75
On cover 67.50
On cover, single franking 140.00
54 A2 90c on 75c brn red & rose red ('27) 2.50 2.00
Never hinged 4.75
On cover 67.50
On cover, single franking 125.00
55 A3 1.25fr on 1fr dk bl & ultra (R) ('26) 1.25 .80
Never hinged 1.90
On cover 75.00
On cover, single franking 150.00
a. "Afrique Equatoriale Francaise" omitted 175.00
Never hinged 260.00
56 A3 1.50fr on 1fr ultra & bl ('27) 2.50 2.00
Never hinged 4.75
On cover 62.50
On cover, single franking 105.00
57 A3 3fr on 5fr org brn & dl red ('27) 6.50 6.00
Never hinged 11.50
On cover 110.00
On cover, single franking 225.00
58 A3 10fr on 5fr ol grn & cer ('27) 16.00 14.50
Never hinged 20.00
On cover 150.00
On cover, single franking 310.00
a. "10fr" omitted 400.00 400.00
Never hinged 575.00
59 A3 20fr on 5fr vio & ver ('27) 20.00 21.00
Never hinged 32.50
On cover 190.00
On cover, single franking 340.00
Nos. 51-59 (9) 54.55 51.50

Common Design Types pictured following the introduction.

Colonial Exposition Issue

Common Design Types

1931 Engr. *Perf. 12½*
Name of Country in Black

60 CD70 40c deep green 5.50 5.50
Never hinged 8.75
On cover 110.00
61 CD71 50c violet 5.50 5.50
Never hinged 8.75
On cover 92.50
62 CD72 90c red orange 5.50 5.50
Never hinged 8.75
On cover 160.00
On cover, single franking 225.00
63 CD73 1.50fr dull blue 5.50 5.50
Never hinged 8.75
On cover 150.00
On cover, single franking 200.00
Nos. 60-63 (4) 22.00 22.00

POSTAGE DUE STAMPS

Postage Due Stamps of France Overprinted

1928 Unwmk. *Perf. 14x13½*

J1 D2 5c light blue .80 1.20
Never hinged 1.20
On cover 100.00
J2 D2 10c gray brown .80 1.20
Never hinged 1.20
On cover 100.00
J3 D2 20c olive green .80 1.20
Never hinged 1.20
On cover 100.00
J4 D2 25c bright rose 1.20 1.60
Never hinged 2.00
On cover 110.00
J5 D2 30c light red 1.20 1.60
Never hinged 2.00
On cover 110.00
J6 D2 45c blue green 1.60 2.00
Never hinged 2.75
On cover 120.00
J7 D2 50c brown violet 2.40 2.40
Never hinged 3.25
On cover 125.00
J8 D2 60c yellow brown 2.40 2.40
Never hinged 3.25
On cover 140.00
J9 D2 1fr red brown 2.40 2.75
Never hinged 4.00
On cover 150.00
J10 D2 2fr orange red 5.50 6.00
Never hinged 8.75
On cover 160.00
J11 D2 3fr bright violet 4.75 5.50
Never hinged 6.50
On cover 180.00
Nos. J1-J11 (11) 23.85 27.85

Huts — D3

Canoe — D4

1930 Typo. *Perf. 14x13½, 13½x14*

J12 D3 5c dp bl & olive .40 .80
Never hinged .80
On cover 50.00
J13 D3 10c dk red & brn .40 .80
Never hinged .80
On cover 50.00
J14 D3 20c grn & brn 1.20 1.60
Never hinged 1.60
On cover 50.00
J15 D3 25c lt bl & brn 1.20 2.40
Never hinged 1.60
On cover 55.00

J16 D3 30c bis brn & Prus bl 1.60 2.00
Never hinged 2.40
On cover 62.50
J17 D3 45c Prus bl & olive 2.40 2.75
Never hinged 3.25
On cover 62.50
J18 D3 50c red vio & brn 2.40 4.00
Never hinged 4.00
On cover 67.50
J19 D3 60c gray lil & bl blk 3.25 4.75
Never hinged 6.50
On cover 75.00
J20 D4 1fr bis brn & bl blk 3.25 4.75
Never hinged 6.50
On cover 87.50
J21 D4 2fr vio & brn 8.00 8.00
Never hinged 12.00
On cover 100.00
J22 D4 3fr dp red & brn 35.00 40.00
Never hinged 55.00
On cover 250.00
Nos. J12-J22 (11) 59.10 71.85

In 1934 stamps of Chad were superseded by those of French Equatorial Africa.

CHILE

ˈchi-lē

LOCATION — Southwest corner of South America
GOVT. — Republic
AREA — 292,135 sq. mi.
POP. — 11,682,260 (est. 1982)
CAPITAL — Santiago

100 Centavos = 1 Peso

STAMPS OF GREAT BRITAIN USED IN CHILE

Values are for clear cancellations on sound, fault-free stamps, with average to fine centering. In many cases, very fine copies are rare or non-existent.

Type A

Numeral Cancellation Type A, C37 (Caldera)

1865-81

A1 1p rose red, plates 71, 72, 88, 90, 95, 195 (#33), *value from* 62.50
A2 1½p lake red, plate 3 (#32a) —
A3 2p blue, plate 9 (#29) 67.50
A4 3p rose (#44) 100.00
A5 3p rose, plates 5, 7 (#49), *value from* *75.00*
A6 3p rose, plates 11, 12, 16-19 (#61), *value from* 62.50
A7 4p vermilion (#34a) —
A8 4p vermilion, plates 8, 11-14 (#43), *value from* 62.50
A9 4p pale olive green, plate 16 (#70) —
A10 6p lilac, plate 4 (#39b) 110.00
A11 6p lilac, plate 5 (#45) 150.00
Plate 6 150.00
A12 6p dull lilac, plate 6 (#50) 100.00
A13 6p violet, plates 8, 9 (#51), *value from* 100.00
A14 6p brown, plate 11 (#59) —
a. 6p pale buff, plate 11 (#59b) —
A15 6p gray, plate 12 (#60) —
A16 6p gray, plates 13-17 (#62), *value from* 62.50
A17 8p orange (#73) 400.00
A18 9p bister (#52) 275.00
A19 10p red brown (#53) 300.00
A20 1sh green, plate 4 (#48) —
A21 1sh green, plates 4-6 (#54), *value from* 62.50
A22 1sh green, plates 8, 10, 11 (#64), *value from* 95.00
Plates 12, 13, *value from, value from* 95.00
A23 2sh blue (#55) 250.00
a. 2sh cobalt blue (#55c) —
A24 2sh brown (#56) *2,250.*
A25 5sh rose, plate 2 (#57) 550.00

Numeral Cancellation Type A, C40 (Coquimbo)

No. A53

1865-81

A26 ½p rose red, plate 14 (#58) —
A27 1p rose red (#20) —
A28 1p rose red, plates 85, 204 (#33) —
A29 2p blue, plate 9 (#29) —
A30 2p blue, plate 14 (#30) —
A31 3p rose (#44) —
A32 3p rose, plate 8 (#49) —
A33 3p rose, plate 9 (#61), *value from* 62.50
A34 4p vermilion, plate 4 (#34a) —
A35 4p vermilion, plates 12, 14, *value from* (#43) 70.00
A36 4p pale olive green, plates 15, 16 (#70), *value from* 225.00
A37 6p lilac, plate 3 (#39) 95.00
a. Hair lines, plate 4 (#39b) —
A38 6p lilac, plate 5 (#45) —
A39 6p dull lilac, plate 6 (#50) 85.00
A40 6p violet, plates 6, 8, 9 (#51), *value from* 80.00
A41 6p brown, plate 11 (#59) —
a. 6p pale buff, plate 11 (#59b) 85.00
Plate 12 *240.00*
A42 6p gray, plate 12 (#60) 240.00
A43 6p gray, plates 13-16 (#62), *value from* 62.50
A44 8p orange (#73) —
A45 9p straw (#40) 350.00
A46 9p bister (#52) 250.00
A47 10p red brown (#53) 375.00
A48 1sh green, plate 4 (#48) 190.00
A49 1sh green, plates 4-6 (#54), *value from* 62.50
A50 1sh green, plates 8-13 (#64), *value from* 90.00
A51 2sh blue (#55) 210.00
a. 2sh cobalt blue (#55c) —
A52 2sh brown (#56) *2,250.*
A53 5sh rose, plate 1 (#57) 550.00
Plate 2 700.00

VALPARAISO
Crowned Circle Handstamps

Crowned Circle handstamp types I and III are pictured in the Crowned Circle Handstamps and Great Britain Used Abroad section.

1846

A54 Crowned circle handstamp on cover, Type III, inscribed "PAID AT VALPARAISO" 450.00
A55 Crowned circle handstamp on cover, Type I, inscribed "PAID AT VALPARAISO" 525.00

Earliest known uses: A54, Oct. 31, 1846; A55, July 16, 1846.

Numeral Cancellation Type B, C30 (Type A)

No. A93

1865-81

A56 ½p rose red, plates 6, 11-14 (#58), *value from* 75.00
A57 1p rose red, plates 80, 84, 85, 89, 91, 101, 106, 113, 122, 123, 138, 140, 141, 148, 149, 152, 157, 158, 162, 167, 175, 178, 181, 185-187, 189, 190, 195, 197-201, 207, 209-215, 217 (#33), *value from* 35.00
A58 1p red brown (#79) —
A59 1½p lake red, plate 1 (#32) *90.00*
Plate 3 60.00
A60 1½p red brown (#80) —
A61 2p blue, plate 9 (#29) 50.00
A62 2p blue, plates 13-15 (#30), *value from* 50.00
A63 2½p claret, plate 2 (#66) 225.00
A64 2½p claret, plates 4, 8 (#67), *value from* 190.00
A65 3p rose (#37) —
A66 3p rose (#44) —
A67 3p rose, plates 5-10 (#49), *value from* 57.50
A68 3p rose, plates 11, 12, 14, 16-19 (#61), *value from* 42.50
A69 4p vermilion, plate 4 (#34a) —
a. Hair lines (#34c) —
A70 4p vermilion, plates 9-14 (#43), *value from* 57.50
A71 4p vermilion, plate 15 (#69) 350.00
A72 4p pale olive green, plate 15 (#70), *value from* *225.00*
Plate 16 225.00
A73 4p gray brown, plate 17 (#71) —
A74 6p lilac, plate 3 (#39) 125.00
a. Hair lines, Plate 4 (#39b) *125.00*
A75 6p lilac, plate 5 (#45) —
Plate 6 —
A76 6p dull violet, plate 6 (#50) —
A77 6p violet, plates 6, 8, 9 (#51), *value from* 80.00
A78 6p brown, plates 11, 12 (#59), *value from* 50.00
a. 6p pale buff, plate 11 (#59b) 85.00
Plate 12 *240.00*
A79 6p gray, plate 12 (#60) 240.00
A80 6p gray, plates 13-17 (#62), *value from* 50.00
A81 6p gray, plate 17 (#86) —
A82 8p orange (#73) 350.00
A83 9p straw (#40) —
a. 9p bister (#40a) —
A84 9p straw (#46) —
A85 9p bister (#52) *225.00*
A86 10p red brown (#53) 300.00
A87 1sh green, plate 4 (#48) —
A88 1sh green, plates 4-6 (#54), *value from* 42.50
Plate 7 60.00
A89 1sh green, plates 8-11 (#64), *value from* 75.00
Plates 12, 13, *value from* 75.00
A90 1sh salmon, plate 13 (#87) 425.00
A91 2sh blue (#55) 150.00
a. 2sh cobalt blue (#55c) *1,700.*
A92 2sh brown (#56) *2,250.*
A93 5sh rose, plate 1 (#57) 550.00
Plate 2 700.00
A94 10sh gray green (#74) *3,100.*
A95 £1 brown lilac (#75) *4,250.*

Issues of the Republic

Values for Nos. 1-14 are for examples with four margins clear of the design. Because these stamps are printed closely together, large margins are not possible, without including portions of adjacent stamps or sheet margin. Values for stamps described as having three margins are for examples with margin touching the design on one side or one corner. Stamps with margins cutting into the design sell for much less than the values shown.

Unused values for Nos. 1-14 are for stamps without gum. Examples with original gum are very scarce and are worth considerably more.

Pen cancellations are common on the 1862-67 issues. Such stamps sell for much less than the quoted values which are for those with handstamped postal cancellations.

Watermarks

1 5 5 5
a b c d

10 10 20
e f g

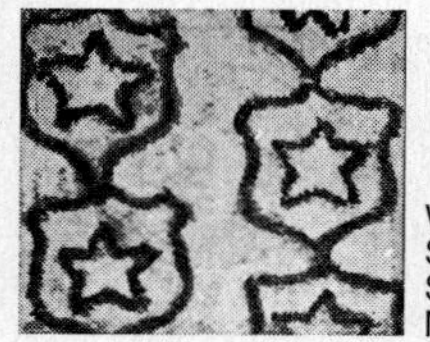

Wmk. 215 — Small Star in Shield, Multiple

Christopher Columbus — A1

London Prints

1853 Wmk. b Engr. *Imperf.*

Blued Paper

1 A1 5c brown red 650.00 150.00
On cover, stamp with three margins 400.00
a. White paper 250.00

Wmk. e

White Paper

2 A1 10c dp brt bl 1,000. 175.00
On cover, stamp with three margins 700.00
a. Blued paper 225.00
b. Diag. half used as 5c on cover 800.00
c. Horiz. half used as 5c on cover 800.00
d. Vert. half used as 5c on cover 800.00

Used examples of Nos. 1-2 with three margins sell for 10-20 percent of the values shown.

Santiago Prints

Impressions Fine and Clear

1854 Wmk. b and e

White Paper

3 A1 5c pale red brn 600.00 67.50
On cover, stamp with three margins 300.00
a. 5c deep red brown 650.00 67.50
b. 5c chestnut 1,000. 200.00
c. 5c chocolate *275.00*
d. Ribbed paper 110.00
e. Double impression 275.00
4 A1 5c burnt sienna 1,800. 300.00
On cover, stamp with three margins 900.00
a. 5c dull chocolate 3,500. 2,000.

On cover, stamp with three margins 900.00
5 A1 10c deep blue 1,200. 275.00
On cover, stamp with three margins 500.00
a. 10c slate blue 275.00
b. 10c greenish blue *475.00*
c. 10c sky blue 190.00
d. Diag. half used as 5c on cover 450.00
e. Horiz. half used as 5c on cover 450.00
f. Vert. half used as 5c on cover 450.00
6 A1 10c lt dl bl 800.00 150.00
On cover, stamp with three margins 325.00
a. 10c pale blue 190.00
b. Diag. half used as 5c on cover 425.00
c. Horiz. half used as 5c on cover 425.00
d. Vert. half used as 5c on cover 425.00

Litho.

7 A1 5c pale brown *1,200.* 300.00
On cover, stamp with three margins 900.00
a. 5c red brown 1,500. 300.00
On cover, stamp with three margins *900.00*
b. 5c deep brown *1,000.* 325.00
On cover, stamp with three margins *900.00*
c. 5c orange brown *1,450.* 325.00
On cover, stamp with three margins *900.00*
d. 5c chocolate brown *1,000.* 325.00
On cover, stamp with three margins *900.00*
e. 5c deep chocolate brown *1,000.* 325.00
On cover, stamp with three margins *900.00*
f. 5c deep red *1,400.* 325.00
On cover, stamp with three margins *900.00*

No. 5b is normally found on ribbed paper.

Used examples of Nos. 3, 5-7 with three margins sell for 15 percent of the values shown. Three-margin examples of No. 4 sell for about 20 percent.

London Print

1855 Blued Paper Wmk. c Engr.

8 A1 5c brown red 220.00 16.00
Fiscal cancellation 2.75
On cover, stamp with three margins 100.00
a. Thin paper 27.50
b. Ivory head 40.00
c. Cream paper without bluing 67.50

Santiago Prints

Impressions Worn and Blurred

1856-62 Wmk. b and e

White Paper

9 A1 5c rose red ('58) 60.00 8.00
Fiscal cancellation 1.40
On cover, stamp with three margins 40.00
On cover, stamp with four margins 55.00
a. 5c carmine red ('62) 90.00 20.00
b. 5c orange red ('61) *225.00* 100.00
c. 5c dull redsh brn ('57) *250.00* 27.50
d. 5c vermilion *125.00* 67.50
e. 5c salmon *125.00* 67.50
f. Printed on both sides *450.00* *250.00*
g. Double impression *450.00* 140.00
h. Very worn plate 20.00
i. Ribbed paper 60.00
10 A1 10c sky blue ('57) 160.00 40.00
Fiscal cancellation 1.40
On cover, stamp with three margins 55.00
On cover, stamp with four margins 140.00
a. 10c deep blue *160.00* 40.00
On cover, stamp with three margins 85.00
On cover, stamp with four margins 150.00
b. 10c light blue ('59) *160.00* 40.00
c. 10c indigo blue ('60) *175.00* 50.00
e. 10c deep slate blue ('57) 27.50
f. 10c greenish blue ('58) 27.50
g. 10c deep gray blue ('58) 27.50
h. 10c slate blue ('59) 27.50
i. 10c blue, *bluish* ('59) 40.00
j. 10c dark blue ('60) 40.00
k. Printed on both sides *350.00*
l. Very worn plate 55.00
m. 10c greenish blue, poor impression 40.00
n. As "j," half used as 5c on cover 165.00
o. Any shade, horiz. half used as 5c on cover 200.00
p. Any shade, vert. half used as 5c on cover 200.00

London Prints

1862 Wmk. a, f and g

11 A1 1c lemon yellow 67.50 40.00
Fiscal cancellation 1.50
On cover, stamp with three margins 550.00
On cover, stamp with four margins 750.00
a. Double impression, one inverted *200.00*
b. 1c greenish yellow 27.50
Fiscally used 5.00
12 A1 10c bright blue 40.00 15.00
Fiscally used 1.50
On cover, stamp with three margins 55.00
On cover, stamp with four margins 90.00
a. 10c deep blue 32.50 21.00
b. Blued paper — 17.50
c. Wmkd. "20" (error) *5,000.* *5,200.*
d. Diag. half used as 5c on cover 110.00
e. Horiz. half used as 5c on cover 125.00
f. Vert. half used as 5c on cover 125.00
13 A1 20c green 160.00 67.50
Fiscally used 6.75
On cover, stamp with three margins 400.00
On cover, stamp with four margins —
a. 20c yellow green 165.00 67.50
On cover, stamp with four margins 400.00
b. 20c intense green — —
Nos. 11-13 (3) 267.50 122.50

No. 11a is only known fiscally used.

Santiago Print

1865 Wmk. d

14 A1 5c rose red 80.00 20.00
Fiscally used 1.50
On cover, stamp with three margins 50.00
On cover, stamp with four margins 90.00
a. 5c carmine red 80.00 20.00
On cover, stamp with four margins 67.50
b. Printed on both sides *375.00* *200.00*
c. Laid paper — *90.00*
d. Double impression, entire stamp *825.00* *160.00*
e. 5c pale red 55.00 13.50
On cover, stamp with four margins 35.00
f. 5c vermilion 37.50 9.25
On cover, stamp with four margins 35.00
g. Vertically laid paper *100.00*
h. Very thin, silky paper 32.50
i. Thick paper (cardboard) 67.50
j. Partial double impression 140.00
k. Very worn plate 21.50

The 5c rose red (shades) on unwatermaked paper, either wove or ribbed, and on paper watermarked Chilean arms in the sheet are reprints made about 1870.

No. 13 has been reprinted in the color of issue and in fancy colors, both from the original engraved plate and from lithographic transfers. The reprints are on paper without watermark or with watermark CHILE and Star.

A2

1867 Unwmk. *Perf. 12*

15 A2 1c orange 70.00 15.00
Never hinged 72.50
On cover, with other stamps 200.00
Pen cancellation 1.25
16 A2 2c black 80.00 30.00
Never hinged 95.00
On cover, with other stamps 200.00
Pen cancellation 2.00
17 A2 5c red 60.00 2.00
Never hinged 70.00
On cover 30.00
Pen cancellation .40
18 A2 10c blue 80.00 6.00
Never hinged 95.00
On cover 50.00
Pen cancellation 1.25
19 A2 20c green 80.00 8.00
Never hinged 95.00
On cover 100.00
Pen cancellation 1.60
Nos. 15-19 (5) 370.00 61.00

Unused values for Nos. 15-19 are for stamps with original gum.

Nos. 15-17 were used during stamp shortages between July 3 and August 28, 1881. So used, they are scarce.

A3

1877 *Rouletted*

20 A3 1c gray 10.00 3.00
Never hinged 15.00
On cover 100.00
Pen cancellation .60
21 A3 2c orange 30.00 3.00
Never hinged 45.00
On cover 100.00
Pen cancellation .60
22 A3 5c dull lake 24.00 2.00
Never hinged 37.50
On cover 20.00
Pen cancellation .40
23 A3 10c blue 18.00 2.75
Never hinged 27.50
On cover 14.00
a. Diagonal half used as 5c on cover —
24 A3 20c green 20.00 4.50
Never hinged 65.00
On cover 37.50
Nos. 20-24 (5) 102.00 15.25

The panel inscribed "CENTAVO" is straight on No. 22.

A4

A5

Columbus — A6

1878-99 *Rouletted*

25 A4 1c green ('81) 1.00 .25
Never hinged 2.50
On cover 3.75
26 A4 2c rose ('81) 1.00 .25
Never hinged 2.50
On cover 3.75
27 A5 5c dull lake ('78) 7.25 .90
Never hinged 18.00
On cover 9.00
28 A5 5c ultra ('83) 1.90 .50
Never hinged 5.50
On cover 3.75
29 A5 10c orange ('85) 2.75 .35
Never hinged 9.25
On cover 12.75
a. 10c yellow 9.00 1.90
Never hinged 27.50
On cover 18.50
30 A5 15c dk grn ('92) 3.00 .55
Never hinged 10.00
On cover 9.00
31 A5 20c gray ('86) 3.00 .55
Never hinged 10.00
On cover 14.00
32 A5 25c org brn ('92) 3.00 .55
Never hinged 10.00
On cover 9.00
33 A5 30c rose car ('99) 7.25 3.75
Never hinged 22.50
On cover 27.50

34 A5 50c lilac ('78) 45.00 27.50
Never hinged 100.00
On cover 135.00
35 A5 50c violet ('85) 3.00 2.00
Never hinged 10.00
On cover 14.50
36 A6 1p dk brn & blk ('92) 19.00 2.75
Never hinged 55.00
On cover 225.00
a. Imperf. horiz. or vert., pair 75.00
Never hinged 150.00
Nos. 25-36 (12) 97.15 39.90

On Nos. 25-26 there is a small colorless ornament at each side of the base of the numeral, above the "E" and "V" of "CENTAVO."

For surcharge and overprint see Nos. 50, O16.

Columbus — A7

No. 25

No. 37

No. 26

No. 38

1894 **Re-engraved**

No.	Type	Description	Unused	Used
37	A7	1c blue green	.90	.25
		Never hinged	2.25	
		On cover		3.75
38	A7	2c carmine lake	.90	.25
		Never hinged	2.25	
		On cover		3.75

On Nos. 37-38 the ornaments on Nos. 25-26 are missing. No. 37 the figure "1" is broader than on No. 25. On No. 38 the head of the figure "2" is formed by a curved line instead of a ball like on No. 26 .

Columbus — A8

Type I

Type II

Type I — There is a heavy shading of short horizontal lines below "Chile" and the adjacent ornaments.

Type II — There is practically no shading below "Chile" and the ornaments.

Type I

1900-01

No.	Type	Description	Unused	Used
39	A8	1c yel grn	.80	.25
		Never hinged	2.10	
		On cover		4.50
40	A8	2c brn rose	1.25	.25
		Never hinged	2.50	
		On cover		4.50
41	A8	5c dp bl	6.50	.35
		Never hinged	27.50	
		On cover		7.50
42	A8	10c violet	6.50	.70
		Never hinged	18.50	
		On cover		9.25
43	A8	20c gray	6.50	2.50
		Never hinged	16.50	
		On cover		12.75
44	A8	30c dp org ('01)	6.50	2.50
		Never hinged	20.00	
		On cover		18.50
45	A8	50c red brn	7.50	2.50
		Never hinged	24.00	
		On cover		27.50
		Nos. 39-45 (7)	35.55	9.05

Type II

No.	Type	Description	Unused	Used
46	A8	1c yel grn ('01)	.85	.25
		Never hinged	2.25	
		On cover		4.50
47	A8	2c rose ('01)	.85	.30
		Never hinged	2.25	
		On cover		4.50
48	A8	5c dull blue ('01)	5.00	.25
		Never hinged	19.00	
		On cover		6.50
a.		Printed on both sides		—
49	A8	10c vio ('01)	6.00	.85
		Never hinged	20.00	
		On cover		13.00
		Nos. 46-49 (4)	12.70	1.65

Nos. 40, 45 and 47 exist in vertical pairs, imperf horizontally, and horizontal pairs, imperf vertically. Nos. 42 and 48 exist in horizontal pairs, imperf between. No.43 exist in vertical pairs, imperf between. Value: unused $22.50, never hinged $45.

For surcharge see No. 57.

No. 33 Surcharged in Black

1900

No.	Type	Description	Unused	Used
50	A5	5c on 30c rose car	1.25	.35
		Never hinged	2.50	
		On cover		6.50
a.		Inverted surcharge	32.50	24.00
		Never hinged	95.00	
b.		Double surcharge	90.00	60.00
		Never hinged	95.00	
c.		Double surcharge, both invtd.	90.00	60.00
		Never hinged	95.00	
d.		Double surcharge, one invtd.	90.00	60.00
		Never hinged	95.00	

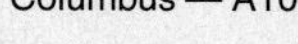
Columbus — A10

1901-02 ***Perf. 12***

No.	Type	Description	Unused	Used
51	A10	1c green	.50	.30
52	A10	2c carmine	.65	.25
53	A10	5c ultra	1.50	.25
54	A10	10c red & blk	2.25	.35
55	A10	30c vio & blk	6.75	.85
56	A10	50c red org & blk	7.25	2.25
		Nos. 51-56 (6)	18.90	4.25

No. 44 Surcharged in Dark Blue

1903 ***Rouletted***

No.	Type	Description	Unused	Used
57	A8	10c on 30c orange	1.90	.75
a.		Inverted surcharge	18.00	12.00
b.		Double surcharge	25.00	15.00
c.		Double surch., one inverted	25.00	15.00
d.		Double surch., both invtd.	25.00	15.00
e.		Stamp design printed on both sides		

Telegraph Stamps Surcharged or Overprinted in Black

Pedro de Valdivia — A11

Coat of Arms — A12

A13

Type I

Type II

Type I — Animal at left has neither mane nor tail.

Type II — Animal at left has mane and tail.

1904 ***Perf. 12***

No.	Type	Description	Unused	Used
58	A11	1c on 20c ultra	.40	.30
a.		Imperf. horiz., pair	40.00	40.00
b.		Inverted surcharge	50.00	50.00
59	A13	2c yel brn, I	.35	.25
a.		Inverted overprint	20.00	20.00
b.		Pair, one without overprint	50.00	50.00
60	A13	5c red, I	.55	.25
a.		Inverted overprint	20.00	20.00
c.		Pair, one without overprint	50.00	50.00
61	A13	10c ol grn, I	1.50	.50
a.		Inverted overprint	50.00	50.00
		Nos. 58-61 (4)	2.80	1.30

Perf. 12½ to 16

No.	Type	Description	Unused	Used
62	A13	2c yel, brn, II	5.25	4.50
63	A11	3c on 5c brn red	37.50	32.50
a.		Inverted surcharge		
64	A12	3c on 1p brn, II	.45	.30
a.		Double surcharge	50.00	50.00
65	A13	5c red, II	6.25	5.50
a.		Inverted overprint		
66	A13	10c ol grn, II	14.50	10.00
67	A11	12c on 5c brn red	1.00	.45
a.		No star at left of "Centavos"	3.00	2.50
b.		Inverted surcharge	40.00	40.00
c.		Double surcharge	50.00	50.00
		Nos. 62-67 (6)	64.95	53.25

Counterfeits exist of the overprint and surcharge varieties of Nos. 57-67.

For overprint see No. O12.

A14

A15

Columbus — A16

1905-09 ***Perf. 12***

No.	Type	Description	Unused	Used
68	A14	1c green	.25	.25
69	A14	2c carmine	.30	.25
70	A14	3c yel brn	.65	.30
71	A14	5c ultra	.70	.25
72	A15	10c gray & blk	1.10	.25
73	A15	12c lake & blk	5.50	2.25
74	A15	15c vio & blk	1.25	.25
75	A15	20c org brn & blk	2.25	.25
76	A15	30c bl grn & blk	3.50	.35
77	A15	50c ultra & blk	3.50	.40
78	A16	1p gold, grn & gray	16.00	11.00
		Nos. 68-78 (11)	35.00	15.80

A 20c dull red and black, type A15, was prepared but not issued. Value $125. "Specimen" examples of Nos. 74, 76-78 exist, punched to prevent postal use.

For surcharges and overprints see Nos. 79-82, O9, O11-O15.

Nos. 73, 78 Surcharged in Blue or Red

a

b

1910

No.	Type	Description	Unused	Used
79	A15 (a)	5c on 12c (Bl)	.50	.25
80	A16 (b)	10c on 1p (R)	1.10	.30
81	A16 (b)	20c on 1p (R)	1.60	.60
82	A16 (b)	1p (R)	3.00	1.10
		Nos. 79-82 (4)	6.20	2.25

The 1p is overprinted "ISLAS DE JUAN FERNANDEZ" only. The use of these stamps throughout Chile was authorized.

Independence Centenary Issue

Oath of Independence — A17

Monument to O'Higgins — A26

Adm. Lord Thomas Cochrane — A29

Designs: 2c, Battle of Chacabuco. 3c, Battle of Roble. 5c, Battle of Maipu. 10c, Naval Engagement of "Lautaro" and "Esmeralda." 12c, Capturing the "Maria Isabel." 15c, First Sortie of Liberating Forces. 20c, Abdication of O'Higgins. 25c, Chile's First Congress. 50c, Monument to José M. Carrera. 1p, Monument to San Martin. 2p, Gen. Manuel Blanco Encalada. 5p, Gen. José Ignacio Zenteno.

1910 **Center in Black**

No.	Type	Description	Unused	Used
83	A17	1c dk green	.25	.25
a.		Center inverted	7,000.	
84	A17	2c lake	1.10	.75
85	A17	3c red brown	.80	.45
86	A17	5c dp blue	.45	.25
87	A17	10c gray brn	1.20	.30
88	A17	12c vermilion	2.50	1.00
89	A17	15c slate	1.90	.55
90	A17	20c red orange	2.50	.85
91	A17	25c ultra	3.25	2.00
92	A26	30c violet	3.25	1.40
93	A26	50c olive grn	6.75	2.25
94	A26	1p yel org	14.00	5.25
95	A29	2p red	14.00	5.25
96	A29	5p yel grn	37.50	17.50
97	A29	10p dk violet	35.00	16.00
		Nos. 83-97 (15)	124.45	54.05

Columbus A32

De Valdivia A33

Mateo de Toro Zambrano A34

Bernardo O'Higgins A35

Ramón Freire — A36

F. A. Pinto — A37

Joaquín Prieto — A38

Manuel Bulnes — A39

Manuel Montt — A40

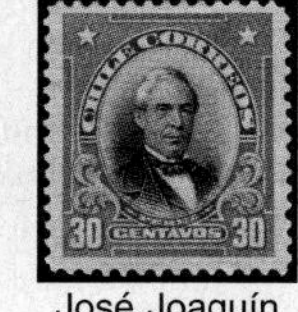
José Joaquín Pérez — A41

Federico Errázuriz Zanartu — A42

José de Balmaceda — A43

Designs: 1p, Anibal Pinto, 2p, Domingo Santa María. 10p, Federico Errázuriz Echaurren.

Outer backgrounds consist of horizontal and diagonal lines

1911 **Engr.** ***Perf. 12***

No.	Type	Description	Unused	Used
98	A32	1c dp green	.25	.25
99	A33	2c scarlet	.25	.25
100	A34	3c sepia	.75	.25
101	A35	5c dk blue	.25	.25
102	A36	10c gray & blk	.75	.25
a.		Center inverted	800.00	600.00
103	A37	12c carmine & blk	1.00	.25
104	A38	15c violet & blk	.90	.25
a.		Center inverted	1,000.	
105	A39	20c org red & blk	1.75	.25
a.		Center inverted	50.00	50.00
106	A40	25c lt blue & blk	2.75	.60
107	A41	30c bis brn & blk	4.00	.30
108	A42	50c myr grn & blk	5.00	.30
109	A43	1p green & blk	9.00	.40
110	A43	2p ver & blk	17.50	1.75
111	A43	5p ol grn & blk	50.00	9.50
112	A43	10p org yel & blk	45.00	8.50
		Nos. 98-112 (15)	139.15	23.35

See Nos. 117, 121, 123, 127-128, 133-141, 143, 155A, 157-161, 165-169,171-172 and designs A47-A55, A57. For overprints see Nos. C6, C6B-C6D, C7-C8, C10-C11, C13-C21, O19-O22, O24-O27, O30-O34, O40.

Columbus
A47

Toro Zambrano
A48

Freire
A49

O'Higgins
A50

1912-13 Engr. *Perf. 12*
113 A47 2c scarlet .25 .25
114 A48 4c black brn .30 .25
115 A49 8c gray 1.00 .25
116 A50 10c blue & blk 1.00 .25
a. Center inverted 500.00 400.00
b. Imperf. horiz. or vert., pair 50.00
117 A37 14c car & blk 1.50 .25
121 A38 40c violet & blk 5.75 .60
123 A40 60c lt blue & blk 14.00 1.75
Nos. 113-123 (7) 23.80 3.60

See Nos. 125-126, 131, 164, 170, 173. For overprints see Nos. C6E, O18, O23, O28, O29.

Cochrane — A52

1915 Engr. *Perf. 13½x14*
124 A52 5c slate blue .60 .35
a. Imperf., pair 11.50

See Nos. 155, 162-163. For overprints see Nos. O17, O37.

1918
125 A49 8c slate 17.50 .80

No. 125 is from a plate made in Chile to resemble No. 115. The top of the head is further from the oval, the spots of color enclosed in the figures "8" are oval instead of round, and there are many small differences in the design.

1921 Worn Plate
126 A49 8c gray 20.00 5.00

No. 126 differs from No. 125 in not having diagonal lines in the frame and only a few diagonal lines above the shoulders (due to wear), while No. 125 has diagonal lines in the oval up to the level of the forehead.

Columbus — A53

1915-25 Typo. *Perf. 13½ to 14½*
127 A32 1c gray green .25 .25
128 A33 2c red .25 .25
129 A53 4c brown ('18) .25 .25

Frame Litho.; Head Engr.
131 A50 10c bl & blk 1.25 .25
a. 10c dark blue & black 1.25 .25
b. Imperf., pair 110.00
c. Center inverted 325.00
133 A38 15c vio & blk .90 .25
134 A39 20c org red & blk 1.40 .25
a. 20c brown orange & blk 1.75 .25
135 A40 25c dl bl & blk .55 .25
136 A41 30c bis brn & blk 1.75 .25
137 A42 50c dp grn & blk 1.75 .25

Perf. 14
138 A43 1p grn & blk 8.00 .25
139 A43 2p red & blk 9.75 .25
a. 2p vermilion & black 32.50 .60
140 A43 5p ol grn & blk ('20) 24.00 .60
141 A43 10p org & blk ('25) 25.00 1.75
Nos. 127-141 (13) 75.10 5.10

The frames have crosshatching on the 15c, 20c, 30c, 2p, 5p and 10p. They have no crosshatching on the 10c, 25c, 50c and 1p.

Nos. 131a and 134a are printed from new head plates which give blacker and heavier impressions. No. 131a exists with; (a) frame litho., head engr.; (b) frame typo., head engr.; (c) frame typo., head litho. No. 134a is with frame typo., head engr.

A 4c stamp with portrait of Balmaceda and a 14c with portrait of Manuel de Salas were prepared but not placed in use. Both stamps were sent to the paper mill at Puente Alto for destruction. They were not all destroyed as some were privately preserved and sold.

Columbus — A54

Types of 1915-20 Redrawn

1918-20 *Perf. 13½x14½*
143 A32 1c gray grn ('20) .30 .25
144 A54 4c brown .50 .25

No. 143 has all the lines much finer and clearer than No. 127. The white shirt front is also much less shaded.

Manuel
Rengifo — A55

1921
145 A55 40c dk vio & blk 2.00 .40

For overprints see Nos. C6A, C9.

Pan-American
Congress
Building — A56

1923, Apr. 25 Typo. *Perf. 14½x14*
146 A56 2c red .25 .25
147 A56 4c brown .25 .25

Typo.; Center Engr.
148 A56 10c blue & blk .25 .25
149 A56 20c orange & blk .75 .25
150 A56 40c dl vio & blk 1.00 .30
151 A56 1p green & blk 1.25 .50
152 A56 2p red & blk 5.00 .60
153 A56 5p dk grn & blk 17.00 4.50
Nos. 146-153 (8) 25.75 6.90

Fifth Pan-American Congress.

Adm. Juan José
Latorre — A57

Typographed; Head Engraved

1927 *Perf. 13½x14½*
154 A57 80c dk brn & blk 2.00 .60

Types of 1915-25 Issues Inscribed: "Chile Correos"

Perf. 13½x14½

1928-31 Engr. Wmk. 215
155 A52 5c slate blue 1.40 .25

Frame Typo.; Center Engr.
155A A38 15c violet & blk 2,200.
156 A55 40c dk vio & blk .60 .25
157 A42 50c dp grn & blk 2.50 .25

Perf. 14
158 A43 1p green & blk 1.00 .25
159 A43 2p red & blk 5.00 .25
160 A43 5p ol grn & blk 9.75 .45
161 A43 10p orange & blk 9.75 1.90
Nos. 155,156-161 (7) 30.00 3.60

Paper of Nos. 155-161 varies from thin to thick.

Types of 1915-25 Issues Inscribed: "Correos de Chile"

1928 Engr. *Perf. 13½x14½*
162 A52 5c deep blue .35 .25

1929 Litho.
163 A52 5c light green .50 .25

Frame Litho.; Center Engr.
164 A50 10c blue & blk 2.00 .25
165 A38 15c violet & blk 2.40 .25
166 A39 20c org red & blk 5.75 .25
167 A40 25c blue & blk .95 .25
168 A41 30c brown & blk .75 .25
169 A42 50c dp grn & blk .65 .25
Nos. 163-169 (7) 13.00 1.75

Redrawn

1929 Frame Typo.; Center Litho.
170 A50 10c blue & blk 3.00 .25
171 A38 15c violet & blk 2.75 .25
172 A39 20c org red & blk 4.25 .25
Nos. 170-172 (3) 10.00 .75

1931 Unwmk.
173 A50 10c blue & blk .70 .25

In the redrawn stamps the lines behind the portraits are heavier and completely fill the ovals. There are strong diagonal lines above the shoulders. On No. 170 the head is larger than on Nos. 164, 173.

A58

Prosperity of Saltpeter Trade
A59 A60

Perf. 13½x14

1930, July 21 Litho. Wmk. 215

Size: 20x25mm
175 A58 5c yellow grn .60 .40
176 A58 10c red brown .60 .30
177 A58 15c violet .60 .30
178 A59 25c deep gray 1.90 .60
179 A60 70c dark blue 4.50 1.50

Perf. 14

Size: 24½x30mm
180 A60 1p dk gray grn 3.75 .75
Nos. 175-180 (6) 11.95 3.85

Cent. of the 1st shipment of saltpeter from Chile, July 21, 1830.

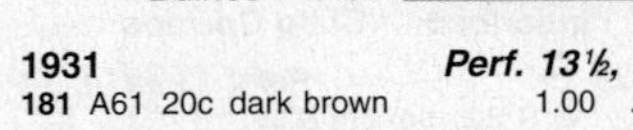
Manuel
Bulnes — A61

1931 *Perf. 13½, 14*
181 A61 20c dark brown 1.00 .30

For overprints see Nos. O35, O39.

Bernardo
O'Higgins — A62

1932
182 A62 10c deep blue 1.50 .45

For overprints see Nos. O36, O38.

Mariano
Egana — A63

Joaquin
Tocornal — A64

1934 *Perf. 13½x14*
183 A63 30c magenta .60 .25

Perf. 14
184 A64 1.20p bright blue 1.00 .25

Centenary of the constitution.

José Joaquín
Pérez — A65

1934 *Perf. 13½x14*
185 A65 30c bright pink 1.60 .35

Atacama
Desert — A66

Designs: 10c, Fishing boats. 20c, Coquito palms. 25c, Sheep. 30c, Mining. 40c, Lonquimay forest. 50c, Colliery at Port Lota. 1p, Shipping at Valparaiso. 1.20p, Puntiagudo volcano. 2p, Diego de Almagro. 5p, Cattle. 10p, Mining saltpeter.

Wmk. 215

1936, Mar. 1 Litho. *Perf. 14*
186 A66 5c vermilion .60 .30
187 A66 10c violet .30 .25
188 A66 20c magenta .40 .25
189 A66 25c grnsh blue 3.00 .80
190 A66 30c lt green .40 .25
191 A66 40c blk, *cream* 3.25 .85
192 A66 50c bl, *bluish* 1.75 .30

Engr.
193 A66 1p dk green 1.75 .50
194 A66 1.20p dp blue 2.00 .70
195 A66 2p dk brown 2.50 .80
196 A66 5p copper red 5.75 2.25
197 A66 10p dk violet 14.00 8.00
Nos. 186-197 (12) 35.70 15.25

400th anniv. of the discovery of Chile by Diego de Almagro.

Laja
Waterfall — A78

Fishing in
Chiloé — A84

Designs: 10c, Agriculture. 15c, Boldo tree. 20c, Nitrate Industry. 30c, Mineral spas. 40c, Copper mine. 50c, Mining. 1.80p, Osorno Volcano. 2p, Mercantile marine. 5p, Lake Villarica. 10p, State railways.

Perf. 13½x14

1938-40 Litho. Wmk. 215
198 A78 5c brn car ('39) .25 .25
199 A78 10c sal pink ('39) .25 .25
200 A78 15c brn org ('40) .25 .25
201 A78 20c light blue .25 .25
202 A78 30c brt pink .25 .25
203 A78 40c lt grn ('39) .25 .25
204 A78 50c violet .25 .25

Engr. *Perf. 14*
205 A84 1p orange brn .25 .25
206 A84 1.80p deep blue .45 .40
207 A84 2p car lake .25 .25
208 A84 5p dk slate grn .35 .25
209 A84 10p rose vio ('40) .90 .25
Nos. 198-209 (12) 3.95 3.15

See Nos. 217-227 in *Scott Standard Postage Stamp Catalogue*, Vol. 2. For surcharge and overprints see Nos. 253, O41-O66, O70-O71 in this catalogue or Scott Standard catalogue, Vol. 2.

Map of the Americas — A89

Unwmk.

1940, Sept. 11 Litho. ***Perf. 14***
210 A89 40c dl grn & yel grn .35 .25

Pan American Union, 50th anniversary.

POSTAL FISCAL STAMPS

Revenue stamps and telegraph stamp authorized for postal use until the end of 1914.

Arms — PF1

1880-91 Engr. Unwmk. ***Perf. 12***
AR1 PF1 1c red 1.75 1.50
Revenue cancel .25
AR2 PF1 2c brown 3.50 2.75
Revenue cancel .25
AR3 PF1 5c blue 3.50 1.50
Revenue cancel .25
AR4 PF1 10c green ('91) 5.25 3.50
Revenue cancel .25
AR5 PF1 20c orange ('91) 7.50 6.25
Revenue cancel .25

Printed by the American Banknote Co. Issued: 1c, 2c, 11/27/80; 5c, 7/3/80; 10c, 20c, 4/1/91.

Arms — PF2

1891, Apr. 21
AR6 PF2 2c yellow brown 3.25 2.00
Telegraph cancel .35
AR7 PF2 10c olive green 1.00 2.50
Telegraph cancel .35
AR8 PF2 20c blue 8.50 3.25
Telegraph cancel .35
AR9 PF2 1p brown 1.50 —
Revenue cancel 1.00

Printed by Bradbury, Wilkinson & Co. Nos. AR6-AR9 are telegraph stamps, authorized for postal use.

PF3

1900-13 ***Perf. 14***
AR10 PF3 1c vermilion 1.00 .25
Revenue cancel .25
AR11 PF3 2c brown ('13) 1.00 .35
Revenue cancel .25
AR12 PF3 5c blue 2.00 .35
Revenue cancel .25

Printed by Waterlow & Sons, London. Issued: 1c, 10/25/00; 2c, 1/21/13; 5c, 12/6/00.

SEMI-POSTAL STAMPS

S. S. Abtao and Captain Policarpo Toro SP1

S. S. Abtao and Brother Eugenio Eyraud SP2

Perf. 14½x15
1940, Mar. 1 Engr. Unwmk.
B1 SP1 80c + 2.20p dk grn & lake 2.50 2.00
B2 SP2 3.60p + 6.40p lake & dk grn 2.50 2.00
a. Pair, #B1-B2 10.00 8.00
Set, never hinged 8.00

50th anniv. of Chilean ownership of Easter Is. Surtax used for charitable institutions.
Sheets containing 15 of each value, with 9 se-tenant pairs.

AIR POST STAMPS

Surcharged in Black

Lithographed; Center Engraved
1927 Unwmk. ***Perf. 13½x14***
Black Brown & Blue
C1 40c on 10c 400.00 50.00
C2 80c on 10c 400.00 65.00
C3 1.20p on 10c 400.00 75.00
C4 1.60p on 10c 400.00 75.00
C5 2p on 10c 400.00 75.00
Nos. C1-C5 (5) 2,000. 340.00

Issued for air post service between Santiago and Valparaiso. The stamps picture Bernardo O'Higgins and are not known without surcharge.

Regular Issues of 1915-28 Overprinted or Surcharged in Black, Red or Blue

Inscribed: "Chile Correos"
1928-29 ***Perf. 13½x14, 14***
C6 A39 20c brn org & blk (Bk) .50 .30
C6A A55 40c dk vio & blk (R) .50 .30
C6B A43 1p grn & blk (Bl) 1.60 .70
C6C A43 2p red & blk (Bl) 2.60 .40
f. 2p ver & blk (Bl) 120.00 30.00
C6D A43 5p ol grn & blk (Bl) 4.00 1.10
C6E A50 6p on 10c dp bl & blk (R) 65.00 22.50
C7 A43 10p org & blk (Bk) ('29) 16.00 4.50
C8 A43 10p org & blk (Bl) 60.00 35.00
Nos. C6-C8 (8) 150.20 64.80

On Nos. C6B to C6D, C7 and C8 the overprint is larger than on the other stamps of the issue.

Same Overprint or Surcharge on Nos. 155, 156, 158-161
Inscribed: "Chile Correos"
1928-32 Wmk. 215
C9 A55 40c vio & blk (R) .70 .40
C10 A43 1p grn & blk (Bl) 1.90 .60
C11 A43 2p red & blk (Bl) 11.00 2.25
C12 A52 3p on 5c sl bl (R) 65.00 40.00
C13 A43 5p ol grn & blk (Bl) 8.50 2.25
C14 A43 10p org & blk (Bk) 45.00 11.00
Nos. C9-C14 (6) 132.10 56.50

Same Overprint on Nos. 166-169, 172 and 158 in Black or Red
Inscribed: "Correos de Chile"
1928-30
C15 A39 20c (#166) ('29) 1.20 .70
C16 A39 20c (#172) ('30) .50 .25
C17 A40 25c bl & blk (R) .60 .25
C18 A41 30c brn & blk .40 .25
a. Double ovpt., one inverted 250.00 250.00
C19 A42 50c dp grn & blk (R) .50 .25
Nos. C15-C19 (5) 3.20 1.70

Inscribed: "Chile Correos"
1932 ***Perf. 13½x14, 14***
C21 A43 1p yel grn & blk (Bk) 2.75 1.50

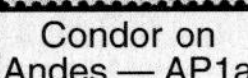

Condor on Andes — AP1a

Airplane Crossing Andes — AP3

Los Cerrillos Airport — AP2

1931 Litho. ***Perf. 13½x14, 14½x14***
C22 AP1a 5c yellow grn .25 .25
C23 AP1a 10c yellow brn .25 .25
C24 AP1a 20c rose .25 .25
C25 AP2 50c dark blue 1.50 .50
C26 AP3 50c black brn .75 .25
C27 AP3 1p purple .60 .25
C28 AP3 2p blue blk .90 .30
a. 2p bluish slate 1.00 .45
C29 AP2 5p lt red 3.00 .30
Nos. C22-C29 (8) 7.50 2.35

For surcharges see Nos. C51-C53.

Airplane over City — AP4

Two Airplanes over Globe — AP9

Designs: 30c, 40c, 50c, Wings over Chile. 60c, Condor. 70c, Airplane and Star of Chile. 80c, Condor and Statue of Canpolican. 3p, 4p, 5p, Seaplane. 6p, 8p, 10p, Airplane. 20p, 30p, Airplane and Southern Cross. 40p, 50p, Airplane and symbols of space.

Perf. 13½x14
1934-39 Engr. Wmk. 215
C30 AP4 10c yel grn ('35) .30 .25
C31 AP4 15c dk grn ('35) .45 .25
C32 AP4 20c dp bl ('36) .25 .25
C33 AP4 30c blk brn ('35) .25 .25
C34 AP4 40c indigo ('38) .25 .25
C35 AP4 50c dk brn ('36) .25 .25
C36 AP4 60c vio blk ('35) .25 .25
C37 AP4 70c blue ('35) .45 .25
C38 AP4 80c ol blk ('35) .25 .25

Perf. 14
C39 AP9 1p slate blk .25 .25
C40 AP9 2p grnsh bl .25 .25
C41 AP9 3p org brn ('35) .30 .25
C42 AP9 4p brn ('35) .30 .25
C43 AP9 5p org red .30 .25
C44 AP9 6p yel brn ('35) .45 .25
a. 6p brown ('39) 2.75 1.90
C45 AP9 8p grn ('35) .40 .25
C46 AP9 10p brn lake .45 .25
C47 AP9 20p olive .45 .25
C48 AP9 30p gray blk .50 .25
C49 AP9 40p gray vio 1.40 .70
C50 AP9 50p brn vio 1.60 .70
Nos. C30-C50 (21) 9.35 6.15

Nos. C30-C50 have been re-issued in slightly different colors, with white gum. The first printings are considerably scarcer.
See Nos. C90-C107B, C148-C154 in *Scott Standard Postage Stamp Catalogue*, Vol. 2.

Types of 1931 Surcharged in Black or Red

Perf. 13½x14, 14½x14
1940 Wmk. 215
C51 AP1a 80c on 20c lt rose .70 .25
C52 AP2 1.60p on 5p lt red 4.25 1.50
C53 AP3 5.10p on 2p sl bl (R) 3.50 1.75
Nos. C51-C53 (3) 8.45 3.50

The surcharge on No. C52 measures 21½mm.

ACKNOWLEDGMENT OF RECEIPT STAMPS

AR1

1894 Unwmk. ***Perf. 11½***
H1 AR1 5c brown .75 .50
a. Imperf., pair 3.00

The black stamp of design similar to AR1 inscribed "Avis de Paiement" was prepared for use on notices of payment of funds but was not regularly issued.

POSTAGE DUE STAMPS

D1

D2

Handstamped
1894 Unwmk. ***Perf. 13***
J1 D1 2c black, *straw* 15.00 8.00
J2 D1 4c black, *straw* 15.00 8.00
J3 D1 6c black, *straw* 15.00 8.00
J4 D1 8c black, *straw* 14.00 8.00
J5 D2 10c black, *straw* 15.00 8.00
J6 D1 16c black, *straw* 15.00 8.00
J7 D1 20c black, *straw* 15.00 8.00
J8 D1 30c black, *straw* 15.00 8.00
J9 D1 40c black, *straw* 15.00 8.00
Nos. J1-J9 (9) 134.00 72.00

J1a D1 2c black, *yellow* 85.00 80.00
J2a D1 4c black, *yellow* 55.00 40.00
J3a D1 6c black, *yellow* 80.00 35.00
J4a D1 8c black, *yellow* 16.00 16.00
J5a D2 10c black, *yellow* 16.00 16.00
J6a D1 16c black, *yellow* 16.00 16.00
J7a D1 20c black, *yellow* 16.00 16.00
J8a D1 30c black, *yellow* 16.00 16.00
J9a D1 40c black, *yellow* 16.00 16.00
Nos. J1a-J9a (9) 316.00 251.00

Counterfeits exist.

D3

1895 Litho. *Perf. 11*

J19	D3	1c red, *yellow*	7.50	3.00
J20	D3	2c red, *yellow*	7.50	3.00
J21	D3	4c red, *yellow*	6.00	3.00
J22	D3	6c red, *yellow*	7.50	3.00
J23	D3	8c red, *yellow*	4.50	3.00
J24	D3	10c red, *yellow*	4.50	4.50
J25	D3	20c red, *yellow*	4.50	2.25
J26	D3	40c red, *yellow*	4.50	3.00
J27	D3	50c red, *yellow*	4.50	3.00
J28	D3	60c red, *yellow*	9.00	4.50
J29	D3	80c red, *yellow*	9.00	6.00
J30	D3	1p red, *yellow*	9.50	6.50
		Nos. J19-J30 (12)	78.50	44.75

Nos. J19-J30 were printed in sheets of 100 (10x10) containing all 12 denominations.

Counterfeits of Nos. J19-J42 exist.

1896 *Perf. 13½*

J31	D3	1c red, *straw*	.90	.50
J32	D3	2c red, *straw*	.90	.50
J33	D3	4c red, *straw*	1.10	.50
J34	D3	6c red, *straw*	2.50	1.00
J35	D3	8c red, *straw*	1.10	.60
J36	D3	10c red, *straw*	.90	.60
J37	D3	20c red, *straw*	.90	.60
J38	D3	40c red, *straw*	18.00	15.00
J39	D3	50c red, *straw*	18.00	15.00
J40	D3	60c red, *straw*	18.00	15.00
J41	D3	80c red, *straw*	25.00	17.50
J42	D3	100c red, *straw*	36.00	30.00
		Nos. J31-J42 (12)	123.30	96.80

D4

1898 *Perf. 13*

J43	D4	1c scarlet	.50	.30
J44	D4	2c scarlet	1.25	.60
J45	D4	4c scarlet	.50	.30
J46	D4	10c scarlet	.50	.30
J47	D4	20c scarlet	.50	.30
		Nos. J43-J47 (5)	3.25	1.80

D5

1924 *Perf. 11½, 12½*

J48	D5	2c blue & red	1.10	.90
J49	D5	4c blue & red	1.10	.90
J50	D5	8c blue & red	1.10	.90
J51	D5	10c blue & red	1.10	.90
J52	D5	20c blue & red	1.10	.60
J53	D5	40c blue & red	1.10	.90
J54	D5	60c blue & red	1.10	.90
J55	D5	80c blue & red	1.10	.90
J56	D5	1p blue & red	1.50	1.10
J57	D5	2p blue & red	2.60	1.90
J58	D5	5p blue & red	2.60	1.90
		Nos. J48-J58 (11)	15.50	11.80

Nos. J48-J58 were printed in sheets of 150 containing all 11 denominations, and a second printing was printed in sheets of 50 containing the five lower denominations, providing various se-tenants. Stamps from the second printing are of a slightly different shade of red.

All values of this issue exist imperforate, also with center inverted, but are not believed to have been regularly issued. Those with inverted centers sell for about 10 times normal stamps.

OFFICIAL STAMPS

For Domestic Postage

O1

Single-lined frame
Control number in violet

1907 Unwmk. *Imperf.*

O1	O1	dl bl, "CARTA" org	125.00	80.00
O2	O1	red, "OFICIO" bl	125.00	80.00
O3	O1	vio, "PAQUETE" red	125.00	80.00
O4	O1	org, *bl*, "EP" vio	125.00	80.00
		Nos. O1-O4 (4)	500.00	320.00

The diagonal inscription in differing color indicates type of usage: CARTA for letters of ordinary weight; OFICIO, heavy letters to 100 grams; PAQUETE, parcels to 100 grams; E P (Encomienda Postal), heavier parcels; C (Certificado), as on No. O8, registration including postage.

Varieties include CARTA, PAQUETE and E P inverted, OFICIO omitted, etc.

Double-lined frame
Large control number in black
Perf. 11

O5	O1	bl, "CARTA" yel	32.50	25.00
O6	O1	red, "OFICIO" bl	50.00	40.00
O7	O1	brn, "PAQUETE" grn	50.00	40.00
O8	O1	grn, "C" red	600.00	600.00
		Nos. O5-O8 (4)	732.50	705.00

Nos. O5-O8 exist in tête bêche pairs; with CARTA, OFICIO or PAQUETE double or inverted, and other varieties.

Counterfeits of Nos. O1-O8 exist.

For Foreign Postage

Regular Issues of 1892-1909 Overprinted in Red — a

On Stamps of 1904-09

1907 *Perf. 12*

O9	A14	1c green	25.00	*40.00*
a.		Inverted overprint	*75.00*	
O10	A12	3c on lp brn	50.00	*60.00*
a.		Inverted overprint	*150.00*	
O11	A14	5c ultra	40.00	*50.00*
a.		Inverted overprint	*120.00*	
O12	A15	10c gray & blk	40.00	*65.00*
O13	A15	15c vio & blk	40.00	*65.00*
O14	A15	20c org brn & blk	40.00	*65.00*
O15	A15	50c ultra & blk	75.00	*100.00*

On Stamp of 1892
Rouletted

O16	A6	1p dk brn & blk	350.00	*500.00*
		Nos. O9-O16 (8)	660.00	*945.00*

Counterfeits of Nos. O9-O16 exist.

Regular Issues of 1915-25 Overprinted in Red or Blue — b

1926 *Perf. 13½x14, 14*

O17	A52	5c slate bl (R)	2.50	.50
O18	A50	10c bl & blk (R)	4.00	.75
O19	A39	20c org red & blk (Bl)	2.00	.40
O20	A42	50c dp grn & blk (Bl)	2.00	.40
O21	A43	1p grn & blk (R)	2.75	.70
O22	A43	2p ver & blk (Bl)	4.00	1.00
		Nos. O17-O22 (6)	17.25	3.75

Nos. O21 and O22 are overprinted vertically at each side.

Nos. O17 to O22 were for the use of the Biblioteca Nacional.

Regular Issue of 1915-25 Overprinted in Red — c

1928 *Perf. 13½x14, 14*

O23	A50	10c bl & blk	6.50	2.00
O24	A39	20c brn org & blk	3.00	1.00
O25	A40	25c dl bl & blk	7.50	1.00
O26	A42	50c dp grn & blk	4.00	1.00
O27	A43	1p grn & blk	5.00	1.50
		Nos. O23-O27 (5)	26.00	6.50

The overprint on Nos. O23 to O26 is 16½mm high; on No. O27 it is 20mm.

Regular Issues of 1928-30 Overprinted in Red — d

On Stamp Inscribed: "Correos de Chile"

1930-31

O28	A50	10c bl & blk	3.00	1.50

Wmk. 215
On Stamps Inscribed: "Correos de Chile"

O29	A50	10c bl & blk	6.00	3.00
O30	A39	20c org red & blk	.75	.50
O31	A40	25c bl & blk	.75	.50
O32	A42	50c dp grn & blk	1.50	.75

On Stamps Inscribed: "Chile Correos"

O33	A42	50c dp grn & blk	1.50	.75
O34	A43	1p grn & blk	1.50	.75
		Nos. O28-O34 (7)	15.00	7.75

Same Overprint on No. 181

1933 *Perf. 13½x14*

O35	A61	20c dk brn	.75	.25

Same Overprint in Red on No. 182

1935 Wmk. 215

O36	A62	10c deep blue	.75	.50

No. 163 Ovptd. Type "b" in Red Inscribed: "Correos de Chile"

1934

O37	A52	5c lt grn	.60	.50

Overprint "b" on No. 182

1935

O38	A62	10c dp bl	.50	.50

Same Overprint in Black on No. 181

1936 Wmk. 215 *Perf. 13½x14*

O39	A61	20c dk brn	10.00	.50

Overprint "b" in Red on No. 158

1938 *Perf. 14*

O40	A43	1p grn & blk	2.50	1.00

Nos. 204 and 205 Overprinted Type "d" in Black

1939 *Perf. 13½x14, 14*

O41	A78	50c violet	4.00	2.50
O42	A84	1p org brn	5.00	4.00

Stamps of 1938-40 Overprinted Type "b" in Black, Red or Blue

1940-46 *Perf. 13½x14, 14*

O43	A78	10c sal pink ('45)	2.00	1.75
O44	A78	15c brn org	1.00	.40
O45	A78	20c lt bl (R) ('42)	1.50	.60
O46	A78	30c brn pink (Bl)	.75	.40
O47	A78	40c lt grn	.75	.40
O48	A78	50c vio ('45)	4.00	.75
O49	A84	1p org brn ('42)	2.50	.75
O50	A84	1.80p dp bl (R) ('45)	10.00	6.00
O51	A84	2p car lake ('42)	2.00	1.25
		Nos. O43-O51 (9)	24.50	12.30

Overprint "b" in Black on Nos. 223, 225

Unwmk.

O58	A84	1p brn org	2.50	1.50
O59	A84	2p car lake ('46)	5.00	2.00

CHINA

'chī-nə

LOCATION — Eastern Asia
GOVT. — Republic
AREA — 2,903,475 sq. mi.
POP. — 462,798,093 (1948)

10 Candareen = 1 Mace
10 Mace = 1 Tael
100 Cents = 1 Dollar (Yuan) (1897)

Watermarks

Wmk. 103 — Yin-Yang Symbol

Wmk. 261 — Character Yu (Post) Multiple

Issues of the Imperial Maritime Customs Post

Imperial Dragon — A1

1878 Unwmk. Typo. *Perf. 12½*
Thin Paper
Stamps printed 2½-3¼mm apart

1	A1	1c green	650.00	550.00
a.		1c dark green	775.00	600.00
2	A1	3c brown red	750.00	450.00
a.		3c vermilion	925.00	500.00
3	A1	5c orange	875.00	400.00
a.		5c bister orange	1,200.	500.00

Imperforate essays of Nos. 1-3 have an extra circle near the dragon's lower left foot. Examples with the circle completely or mostly removed are proofs or unfinished stamps.

1882
Thin or Pelure Paper
Stamps printed 4½mm apart

4	A1	1c green	700.00	400.00
a.		1c dark green	800.00	425.00
5	A1	3c brown red	1,350.	375.00
6	A1	5c orange yellow	25,000.	1,500.

1883 *Rough to smooth Perf. 12½*
Medium to Thick Opaque Paper
Stamps printed 2½ to 3¼mm apart

7	A1	1c green	775.00	475.00
a.		1c dark green	875.00	525.00
b.		1c light green	925.00	575.00
c.		Vert. pair, imperf. between	*160,000.*	
8	A1	3c brown red	1,350.	500.00
a.		3c vermilion	1,600.	400.00
b.		Vert. pair, imperf. between		*230,000.*
9	A1	5c yellow	2,350.	650.00
a.		5c chrome yellow	2,650.	875.00
b.		Horiz. pair, imperf. btwn.		*60,000.*

Nos. 1-9 were printed from plates of 25, 20 or 15 individual copper dies, but only No. 5 exists in the 15-die setting. Many different printings and plate settings exist. All values occur in a wide variety of shades and papers. The effect of climate on certain papers has produced the varieties on so-called toned papers in Nos. 1-15.

Value for No. 8b is for a damaged example.

Counterfeits, frequently with forged cancellations, occur in all early Chinese issues.

Imperial Dragon — A2

1885 Wmk. 103 *Perf. 12½*

10	A2	1c green	190.00	100.00
a.		Vert. pair, imperf. btwn.	*20,000.*	*17,500.*
b.		Horiz. pair, imperf. btwn.		—
11	A2	3c lilac	450.00	130.00
a.		Horiz. pair, imperf. btwn.	*22,000.*	*17,500.*
b.		Vert. pair, imperf. btwn.		*24,000.*
12	A2	5c grnsh yellow	400.00	130.00
a.		5c bister brown	700.00	160.00
b.		Vert. pair, imperf. btwn.	*24,000.*	*24,000.*
c.		Horiz. pair, imperf. btwn.		*52,500.*
		Nos. 10-12 (3)	1,040.	360.00

1888 ***Perf. 11½-12***

13 A2 1c green 100.00 60.00
14 A2 3c lilac 275.00 100.00
b. Double impression *1,100.*
15 A2 5c grnsh yellow 500.00 150.00
b. Horiz. pair, imperf. vert. *50,000.*
c. Double impression 1,100. 1,100.
Nos. 13-15 (3) 875.00 310.00

Nos. 10-15 were printed from plates made of 40 individual copper dies, arranged in two panes of 20 each. Several different settings exist of all values.

Imperforates of Nos. 13-15 are considered proofs by most authorities.

Stamps overprinted "Formosa" in English or Chinese are proofs.

For surcharges see Nos. 25-27, 75-77.

"Shou" and "Wu Fu" — A3

Dragon and Hydrangea Leaves — A4

"Pa Kua" Signs in Corners — A5

Dragon and Peony — A6

Carp, the Messenger Fish — A7

Dragon, "Pa Kua" and Immortelle A8

Dragons and "Shou" A9

Dragons and Giant Peony — A10

Junk on the Yangtse A11

1894 **Lithographed in Shanghai**

16 A3 1c orange red 60.00 *50.00*
a. Vert. pair, imperf. btwn. *2,250.* *2,100.*
b. Horiz. pair, imperf. btwn. *17,500.* *12,000.*
c. Vert. pair, imperf. horiz. *3,250.* *3,250.*
17 A4 2c green 65.00 55.00
a. Horiz. pair, imperf. btwn. *3,750.* *3,500.*
18 A5 3c orange 57.50 30.00
a. Vert. pair, imperf. btwn. *3,350.* *3,500.*
b. Horiz. pair, imperf. btwn. *5,000.* *3,800.*
19 A6 4c rose pink 200.00 *250.00*
a. Horiz. pair, imperf. btwn. *14,000.*
20 A7 5c dull orange 350.00 *400.00*
a. Horiz. pair, imperf. btwn. *18,000.* *18,000.*
21 A8 6c dark brown 150.00 60.00
a. Vert. pair, imperf. btwn. *24,000.*
b. Horiz. pair, imperf. btwn. *12,500.*
22 A9 9c dark green 175.00 120.00
a. Imperf., pair *2,250.*
b. Horiz. pair, imperf. vert. *4,250.* *3,750.*
c. Vert. pair, imperf. horiz. *4,250.*
d. Vert. pair, imperf. btwn. *4,750.* *4,250.*
e. Tete beche pair, vert. *2,000.* *1,800.*
f. Tete beche pair, imperf. horiz. *5,500.*
g. Tete beche pair, imperf. vert. *5,500.* *4,750.*
h. Vert. strip of 3, imperf. btwn. *5,500.*
i. Tete beche pair, horiz. *1,500.* *1,300.*
23 A10 12c orange 650.00 250.00
24 A11 24c carmine 800.00 300.00
a. Vert. pair, imperf. btwn. *30,000.*
Nos. 16-24 (9) 2,508. 1,515.

60th birthday of Tsz'e Hsi, the Empress Dowager. All values exist in several distinct shades.

On Mar. 20, 1896, the Customs Post was changed, by Imperial Edict, effective Jan. 1, 1897, to a National Post and the dollar was adopted as the unit of currency.

Time was required to work out details of the Imperial Post and design new stamps. As a provisional measure, stocks of Nos. 16-24 were ordered surcharged with new values in dollars and cents. It is believed that only the Shanghai office stock of Nos. 16-24 (plus any reserve stock at the printers) was surcharged with small figures of value. Other post offices throughout China were instructed to return all unoverprinted stocks on receipt of the new surcharges.

Early in the year it was apparent that all stamps would be exhausted before the new issues were ready (Nos. 86-97), and since the stones from which Nos. 16-24 had been printed no longer existed, new stones were made from the original transfers. A printing from the new stones was made early in 1897 and surcharged with large figures of value spaced 2½mm below the Chinese characters. During the surcharging, sheets from the 1894 (original) printing were received from outlying post offices and surcharged as they arrived. A small quantity of the 1897 printing reached the public without surcharge (Nos. 16n-24n).

Additional stamps were still required and another printing was made from the new stones and surcharged with large figures, but in a new setting with 1½mm between the Chinese characters and the value. Additional sheets of the 1894 printing were received from the most distant post offices and were also surcharged with the 1½mm setting. Thus there are four different sets of the large-figure surcharges. All these stamps were regularly issued but no attempt was made by the post office to separate printings. Some values are difficult to distinguish as to printing, particularly in used condition.

See No. 73. For surcharges see Nos. 28-72, 74.

1897 **Lithographed in Shanghai**

16n A3 1c pink *1,300.*
17n A4 2c olive green *1,300.*
18n A5 3c chrome yellow *850.00*
p. 3c yellow buff *1,100.*
19n A6 4c pale rose *925.00*
20n A7 5c yellow *1,000.*
21n A8 6c red brown *1,100.*
22n A9 9c yellowish green *3,900.*
p. 9c emerald green —
23n A10 12c yellowish orange *6,000.*
24n A11 24c purplish red *3,900.*

The colors of the 1897 printings are pale or dull; the gum is thin and white. The 1894 printing has a thicker, yellowish gum.

The set of 9 values on thick unwatermarked paper is a special printing of 5,000 sets ordered by P. G. von Mollendorf, a Customs official, for presentation purposes. Value, set $2,400.

For surcharges see Nos. 47-55, 65-72.

Issues of the Chinese Government Post

Preceding Issues Surcharged in Black

Small Numerals 2½mm Below Chinese Characters

Surcharged on Nos. 13-15

1897, Jan. 2 ***Perf. 11½-12***

25 A2 1c on 1c 72.50 *85.00*
26 A2 2c on 3c 300.00 120.00
a. Double surcharge —
27 A2 5c on 5c 100.00 57.50
Nos. 25-27 (3) 472.50 262.50

Surcharged on Nos. 16-24

On No. 28 the ½ is 3mm high.

28 A5 ½c on 3c 45.00 35.00
a. "1" instead of "½" 450.00 450.00
b. Horiz. pair, imperf. btwn. *9,750.*
c. Vert. pair, imperf. horiz. *9,000.* *3,000.*
d. Double surcharge *12,000.* *11,000.*
e. Vert. pair, imperf. btwn. *9,000.*
29 A3 1c on 1c 45.00 30.00
a. Inverted surcharge *50,000.* *10,000.*
30 A4 2c on 2c 40.00 22.50
a. Horiz. pair, imperf. vert. *6,000.*
b. Vert. pair, imperf. btwn. *6,000.*
c. Double surcharge *14,000.*
d. Inverted surcharge — *15,000.*
e. Horiz. pair, imperf. btwn. *2,000.*
31 A6 4c on 4c 45.00 27.50
a. Double surcharge *30,000.* *20,000.*
b. Vert. pair, imperf. btwn. *10,000.* *10,000.*
c. Horiz. pair, imperf. btwn. *10,000.* *10,000.*
32 A7 5c on 5c 50.00 22.50
a. Vert. pair, imperf. btwn. *15,000.* *10,000.*
33 A8 8c on 6c 60.00 35.00
a. Vert. pair, imperf. btwn. *2,750.* *2,250.*
b. Vert. strip of 3, imperf. btwn. *4,200.* *2,100.*
c. Horiz. pair, imperf. btwn. *2,500.* *2,500.*
34 A8 10c on 6c 140.00 90.00
b. Vert. pair, imperf. btwn. *7,500.* *2,500.*
c. Horiz. pair, imperf. vert. *2,400.* *2,400.*
35 A9 10c on 9c 475.00 200.00
a. Double surcharge *40,000.* *40,000.*
b. Inverted surcharge *450,000.* —
36 A10 10c on 12c 500.00 225.00
a. Vert. pair, imperf. horiz. *4,000.*
b. Vert. pair, imperf. btwn. *4,500.* *4,500.*
37 A11 30c on 24c 600.00 240.00
a. Vert. pair, imperf. btwn. *20,000.*
Nos. 28-37 (10) 2,000. 927.50

Small Numerals 4mm Below Chinese Characters

25a A2 1c on 1c green 75.00 *85.00*
28f A4 ½c on 3c orange 60.00 60.00
29b A3 1c on 1c vermilion 75.00 75.00
30f A4 2c on 2c dark green 55.00 55.00
31d A6 4c on 4c dark pink 70.00 55.00
32b A7 5c on 5c dull orange 70.00 55.00
33d A8 8c on 6c brown 100.00 100.00
35c A9 10c on 9c dark green 450.00 375.00
37b A11 30c on 24c dark red 500.00 500.00

Preceding Issues Surcharged in Black

No. 38 the ½ is 4mm high.

Large Numerals Numerals 2½mm below Chinese characters

Surcharged on Nos. 16-24

1897, Mar.

38 A5 ½c on 3c 2,500. 875.00
b. Inverted surcharge *10,000.*
39 A3 1c on 1c 700.00 200.00
40 A4 2c on 2c 375.00 350.00
41 A6 4c on 4c 475.00 375.00
b. Horiz. pair, imperf. btwn. *11,000.*
42 A7 5c on 5c 225.00 200.00
43 A8 8c on 6c 2,250. 1,750.
44 A9 10c on 9c 800.00 375.00
45 A10 10c on 12c *50,000.* 2,850.
46 A11 30c on 24c 1,200. *1,300.*
b. 2mm spacing between "30" and "cents." *15,000.*

Same Surcharge on Nos. 16n-24n

47 A5 ½c on 3c 37.50 *40.00*
a. "cen" for "cent" 850.00 850.00
b. Vert. pair, imperf. btwn. *3,000.* *3,000.*
c. Vert. pair, imperf. horiz. 2,700. 2,700.
d. As "a" and "c" *9,500.* *9,500.*
e. As "a" and "b" *7,500.* *7,500.*
f. Horiz. pair, imperf. btwn. *3,000.* *3,000.*
48 A3 1c on 1c 40.00 25.00
a. Horiz. pair, imperf. btwn. *4,000.*
49 A4 2c on 2c 32.50 19.00
50 A6 4c on 4c 40.00 19.00
a. Horiz. pair, imperf. btwn. *6,000.* *6,000.*
b. Vert. pair, imperf. btwn. *5,000.*
51 A7 5c on 5c 50.00 30.00
52 A8 8c on 6c 600.00 300.00
53 A9 10c on 9c 300.00 125.00
a. 10c on 9c emerald 400.00 150.00
b. Pair, one without surcharge *3,000.* *2,500.*
54 A10 10c on 12c 375.00 90.00
55 A11 30c on 24c 1,200. 400.00
a. 2mm spacing btwn "30" and "cents" *1,500.* 750.00
b. Vert. pair, imperf. btwn. *15,000.*

All recorded unused examples of No. 45 are flawed.

Numerals 1½mm below Chinese characters

1897, May

Surcharged on Nos. 16-24

56 A5 ½c on 3c org yel 550.00 375.00
57 A3 1c on 1c 375.00 300.00
58 A4 2c on 2c 175,000. *5,000.*
59 A6 4c on 4c 300.00 250.00
60 A7 5c on 5c 400.00 300.00
61 A8 8c on 6c 1,600. 1,350.
62 A9 10c on 9c 375.00 250.00
63 A10 10c on 12c 1,750. 1,100.
64 A11 30c on 24c *75,000.* —

Same Surcharge on Nos. 16n-24n

65 A5 ½c on 3c 25.00 *30.00*
a. Inverted surcharge *4,500.* *4,500.*
b. ½mm spacing *3,500.* *3,500.*
66 A3 1c on 1c 40.00 25.00
67 A4 2c on 2c 35.00 17.50
a. Inverted surcharge *25,500.* *8,750.*
b. Vert. pair, imperf. btwn. *20,000.*
68 A6 4c on 4c 300.00 200.00
a. Inverted surcharge 3,500. 3,500.
69 A7 5c on 5c 300.00 225.00
70 A9 10c on 9c 225.00 110.00
a. Inverted surcharge 4,000. 3,000.
71 A10 10c on 12c 400.00 190.00
72 A11 30c on 24c *13,000.* 2,600.

Same Surcharge (1½mm Spacing) on Type A12, and

A12

A12a

Redrawn Designs Printed from New Stones

1897

73 A12 ½c on 3c yel 275.00 200.00
a. ½mm spacing *7,000.* *5,000.*
74 A12a 2c on 2c yel grn 75.00 35.00
a. Horiz. pair, imperf. btwn. *10,000.* *5,000.*

Nos. 73 and 74 were surcharged on stamps printed from new stones, which differ slightly from the originals. On No. 73 the numeral "3" and symbols in the four corner panels have been enlarged and strengthened. On No. 74, the numeral "2" has a thick, flat base.

Surcharged on Nos. 13-15

75 A2 1c on 1c green 500.00 *625.00*
76 A2 2c on 3c lilac 1,000. *1,000.*
77 A2 5c on 5c grnsh yel 350.00 *500.00*

Revenue Stamps Surcharged in Black

A13

a

b

c

d

e

f

g

1 dollar.

1897 **Unwmk.** ***Perf. 12 to 15***

78 A13 (a) 1c on 3c red 525.00 350.00
a. No period after "cent" 600.00 400.00
b. Central character with large "box" 625.00 550.00
79 A13 (b) 2c on 3c red 850.00 450.00
a. Inverted surcharge *40,000.* *30,000.*
b. Inverted "S" in "CENTS" 1,000. 600.00
c. No period after "CENTS" 1,000. 600.00
d. Comma after "CENTS" 950.00 550.00
e. Double surcharge *80,000.* *40,000.*
f. Dbl. surch., both inverted *100,000.*
g. Double surch. (blk & grn) *220,000.*

80 A13 (c) 2c on 3c red 600.00 400.00
81 A13 (d) 4c on 3c red *100,000.* *75,000.*
a. Double surcharge (blk & vio) *250,000.* *250,000.*
82 A13 (e) 4c on 3c red 1,650. 600.00
83 A13 (f) $1 on 3c red *900,000.* —
a. No period after "1" —
84 A13 (g) $1 on 3c red 9,000. 3,500.
85 A13 (g) $5 on 3c red 90,000. 60,000.
a. Inverted surcharge *140,000.* *100,000.*

A few examples of the 3c red exist without surcharge; one canceled. Value, unused $60,000. No. 79 with green surcharge is a trial printing. Value for faulty upper left corner block, $190,000.

No. 79g is unique. The only canceled example of No. 83 is in a museum.

Dragon — A14

Carp — A15

Wild Goose — A16

"Imperial Chinese Post"
Lithographed in Japan
Perf. 11, 11½, 12

1897, Aug. 16 **Wmk. 103**
86 A14 ½c purple brn 5.50 4.50
a. Horiz. pair, imperf. btwn. 800.00
87 A14 1c yellow 7.00 4.00
88 A14 2c orange 6.50 3.75
a. Vert. pair, imperf. horiz. 2,000.
89 A14 4c brown 11.00 3.75
a. Horiz. pair, imperf. btwn. 2,000.
90 A14 5c rose red 14.00 5.00
91 A14 10c dk green 40.00 3.75
92 A15 20c maroon 85.00 19.00
93 A15 30c red 140.00 32.50
94 A15 50c yellow grn 100.00 45.00
a. 50c black green 1,750.
b. 50c blue green 3,600.
95 A16 $1 car & rose 325.00 200.00
a. Horiz. pair, imperf. vert. *4,000.*
96 A16 $2 orange & yel 3,000. 1,400.
a. Horiz. pair, imperf. vert. *15,000.*
97 A16 $5 yel grn & pink 1,800. 1,000.

The inner circular frames and outer frames of Nos. 86-91 differ for each denomination.

No. 97 imperforate was not regularly issued. **Examples have been privately perforated and offered as No. 97.** Shades occur in most values of this issue.

A17

A18

A19

"Chinese Imperial Post"
Engraved in London

1898 **Wmk. 103** ***Perf. 12 to 16***
98 A17 ½c chocolate 6.00 2.75
a. Vert. pair, imperf. btwn. 850.00 475.00
b. Vert. pair, imperf. horiz. 850.00 475.00
99 A17 1c ocher 6.50 2.75
a. Vert. pair, imperf. btwn. 300.00 250.00
b. Horiz. pair, imperf. btwn. 400.00 350.00
100 A17 2c scarlet 8.00 2.75
a. Vert. pair, imperf. btwn. 400.00 200.00
b. Horiz. pair, imperf. vert. 400.00 200.00
101 A17 4c orange brn 7.50 2.75
a. Vert. pair, imperf. btwn. 575.00
b. Horiz. pair, imperf. vert. 500.00 300.00
c. Horiz. pair, imperf. btwn. 700.00 600.00
d. Horiz. strip of 3, imperf. btwn. 2,250. 1,500.
102 A17 5c salmon 11.00 5.00
a. Vert. pair, imperf. btwn. 400.00 300.00
b. Horiz. pair, imperf. btwn. 775.00 500.00
c. Vert. pair, imperf. horiz. 600.00 500.00
d. 5c pale reddish orange 16.00 5.50
e. As "d," vert pair, imperf. btwn. 600.00 500.00
103 A17 10c dk blue grn 17.50 3.00
a. Vert. or horiz, pair, imperf. btwn — —
104 A18 20c claret 70.00 9.00
a. Horiz. pair, imperf. btwn. 850.00 750.00
b. Vert. pair, imperf. horiz. 850.00 750.00
c. Vert. pair, imperf. btwn. 900.00 800.00
105 A18 30c dull rose 60.00 15.00
a. Horiz. pair, imperf. btwn. *2,000.*
b. Vert. pair, imperf. horiz. *1,750.*
c. Vert. pair, imperf. btwn. *1,750.*
106 A18 50c lt green 85.00 20.00
a. Vert. pair, imperf. btwn. *2,250.*
107 A19 $1 red & pale rose 375.00 50.00
108 A19 $2 brn, red & yel 625.00 100.00
109 A19 $5 dp grn & sal 950.00 350.00
a. Horiz. pair, imperf. btwn. *77,500.*
b. Vert. pair, imperf. btwn. *20,000.*
Nos. 98-109 (12) 2,222. 563.00

No. 98 surcharged "B. R. A.-5-Five Cents" in three lines in black or green, was surcharged by British military authorities shortly after the Boxer riots for use from military posts in an occupied area along the Peking-Mukden railway. Usually canceled in violet.

See note following No. 122.

1900(?)-06 **Unwmk.** ***Perf. 12 to 16***
110 A17 ½c brown 4.00 2.75
a. Horiz. pair, imperf. btwn. 400.00 400.00
b. Vert. pair, imperf. btwn. 400.00 400.00
111 A17 1c ocher 4.25 2.75
a. Horiz. pair, imperf. btwn. 350.00 350.00
b. Vert. pair, imperf. btwn. 350.00 350.00
c. Vert. pair, imperf. horiz. 350.00 350.00
112 A17 2c scarlet 6.25 2.75
a. Horiz. pair, imperf. btwn. 300.00 325.00
b. Vert. pair, imperf. btwn. 300.00 300.00
c. Vert. pair, imperf. horiz. 300.00 300.00
d. Horiz. pair, imperf. vert. 300.00 300.00
e. Vert. strip of 3, imperf. btwn. 1,250. 750.00
113 A17 4c orange brn 6.00 3.25
a. Horiz. pair, imperf. btwn. 300.00 300.00
b. Vert. pair, imperf. btwn. 300.00 300.00
114 A17 5c rose red 30.00 5.00
a. Vert. pair, imperf. btwn. 300.00 300.00
b. Vert. pair, imperf. horiz. 275.00 275.00
115 A17 5c orange 35.00 6.00
a. 5c yellow 200.00 27.50
b. Vert. pair, imperf. btwn. 475.00 475.00
c. Horiz. pair, imperf. btwn. 475.00 475.00
116 A17 10c green 20.00 2.75
a. Vert. pair, imperf. btwn. 425.00
b. Horiz. pair, imperf. btwn. 725.00
c. Vert. pair, imperf. horiz. 425.00
d. Vert. strip of 3, imperf. btwn. 700.00
117 A18 20c red brown 30.00 2.75
a. Horiz. pair, imperf. btwn. 600.00
b. Vert. pair, imperf. btwn. 500.00
c. Vert. pair, imperf. horiz. 500.00
118 A18 30c dull red 30.00 2.75
a. Vert. pair, imperf. btwn. 850.00
119 A18 50c yellow grn 55.00 2.75
a. Horiz. pair, imperf. btwn. 1,000.
120 A19 $1 red & pale rose ('06) 175.00 27.50
121 A19 $2 brn red & yel ('06) 375.00 60.00
122 A19 $5 dp grn & sal 600.00 240.00
Nos. 110-122 (13) 1,371. 361.00

See No. 124-130. For surcharges and overprints see Nos. 123, 134-177, J1-J6, Offices in Tibet 1-11.

Diagonal Half of No. 112 Surcharged on Stamp and Envelope

1903
123 A17 1c on half of 2c scarlet, on cover *1,600.*

Used Oct. 22 to Oct. 24. Value is for cover mailed to post office other than sending office (Foochow) and bearing backstamp showing arrival date. Locally addressed or unaddressed covers without backstamps properly used are worth approximately $1,000. Others are worth less.

Forgeries are plentiful, particularly on pieces of cover. Certificates of authenticity are mandatory.

1905-10
124 A17 2c green ('08) 3.25 3.25
a. Horiz. pair, imperf. btwn. 325.00 325.00
b. Vert. pair, imperf. btwn. 325.00 325.00
c. Horiz. pair, imperf. vert. 325.00 325.00
d. Horiz. strip of 4, imperf. btwn. 800.00 *800.00*
125 A17 3c slate grn ('10) 5.00 2.50
a. Horiz. pair, imperf. btwn. 250.00
b. Vert. pair, imperf. btwn. 250.00
126 A17 4c vermilion ('09) 6.75 2.75
127 A17 5c violet 8.50 2.50
a. 5c lilac 10.00 2.75
b. Horiz. pair, imperf. btwn. .55000
c. Vert. pair, imperf. btwn. 1,000.
d. Vert. pair, imperf. horiz. 600.00
128 A17 7c maroon ('10) 20.00 10.00
129 A17 10c ultra ('08) 25.00 2.75
a. Horiz. pair, imperf. btwn. 400.00
b. Vert. pair, imperf. btwn. 400.00
c. Vert. pair, imperf. horiz. 400.00 400.00
130 A18 16c olive grn ('07) 60.00 17.50
Nos. 124-130 (7) 128.50 41.25

Temple of Heaven, Peking — A20

1909 ***Perf. 14***
131 A20 2c orange & green 8.50 *9.00*
132 A20 3c orange & blue 10.00 *17.50*
133 A20 7c orange & brn vio 11.00 12.00
Nos. 131-133 (3) 29.50 *38.50*

1st year of the reign of Hsuan T'ung, who later became Henry Pu-yi and then Emperor Kang Teh of Manchukuo.

Stamps of 1902-10 Overprinted with Chinese Characters
Foochow Issue

Overprinted in Red or Black

1912 ***Perf. 12 to 16***
134 A17 3c slate grn (R) 300. 160.
135 A19 $1 red & pale rose 3,000. 2,500.
136 A19 $2 brn red & yel 5,000. 3,500.
137 A19 $5 dp grn & sal 6,000. 4,000.

The overprint "Ling Shih Chung Li" or "Provisional Neutrality," signified that the P.O. was conducted neutrally by agreement between the Manchu and opposing forces.

Nanking Issue

Overprinted in Red or Black

138 A17 1c ocher (R) 275. 175.
139 A17 3c slate grn (R) 300. 175.
140 A17 7c maroon 550. 375.
141 A18 16c olive grn (R) 2,750. 2,500.
142 A18 50c yellow grn (R) 3,500. 2,250.
143 A19 $1 red & pale rose 3,750. 1,800.
144 A19 $2 brn red & yel 6,000. 4,400.
145 A19 $5 dp green & sal 12,750. 10,000.

Vertical overprint reads: "Chung Hwa Min Kuo" (Republic of China).

Stamps of this issue were also used in Shanghai and Hankow.

Additional values were overprinted but not issued. Excellent forgeries of the overprints of Nos. 134-145 exist.

Issues of the Republic

Overprinted in Black or Red

Overprinted by the Maritime Customs Statistical Department, Shanghai

146 A17 ½c brown 1.50 1.25
a. Inverted overprint 50.00 50.00
b. Double overprint 100.00
147 A17 1c ocher (R) 2.25 1.25
a. Vert. pair, imperf. horiz. 200.00 200.00
b. Inverted overprint 175.00 125.00
c. Double overprint 200.00 175.00
d. Horiz. pair, imperf. btwn. 300.00 250.00
e. Horiz. pair, imperf. vert. 175.00
f. Pair, one without overprint 175.00
148 A17 2c green (R) 2.50 1.75
a. Vert. pair, imperf. btwn. 350.00 300.00
149 A17 3c slate grn (R) 3.00 1.50
a. Inverted overprint 125.00 75.00
b. Horiz.. pair, imperf. btwn. 300.00 300.00
c. Vert. pair, imperf btwn. 300.00 300.00
d. Horiz. pair, imperf. vert. 125.00
e. Horiz. strip of 3, imperf btwn. 450.00
f. Horiz. strip of 5, imperf btwn. 975.00
150 A17 4c vermilion 4.75 1.75
a. Vert. pair, imperf. btwn. 800.00
151 A17 5c violet (R) 6.25 1.75
a. Horiz. pair, imperf. btwn.
152 A17 7c maroon 8.25 3.50
153 A17 10c ultra (R) 8.50 1.75
a. Double overprint 250.00
b. Pair, one without overprint 900.00
c. Brownish red overprint 22.50 9.00
d. Inverted overprint 275.00 275.00
154 A18 16c olive grn (R) 22.50 8.50
155 A18 20c red brown 19.00 5.00
156 A18 30c rose red 24.00 6.00
157 A18 50c yel grn (R) 40.00 6.00
158 A19 $1 red & pale rose 400.00 35.00
a. Inverted overprint *27,500.*
159 A19 $2 brn red & yel 350.00 75.00
a. Inverted overprint 600.00 600.00
160 A19 $5 dp grn & sal 750.00 500.00
Nos. 146-160 (15) 1,643. 650.00

Stamps with blue overprint similar to the preceding were not an official issue but were privately made by a printer in Tientsin.

Overprinted in Red

Overprinted by the Commercial Press, Shanghai.

This type differs in that the top character is shifted slightly to right and the bottom character is larger and has small "legs".

161 A17 1c ocher 7.00 2.00
- *a.* Inverted overprint 375.00 375.00
- *b.* Vert. pair, imperf. btwn. 450.00
- *c.* Double overprint 450.00

162 A17 2c green 37.50 3.50
- *a.* Inverted overprint 1,100. 900.00
- *b.* Vert. pair, imperf. btwn. 800.00
- *c.* Horiz. pair, imperf. btwn. 700.00
- *d.* Horiz. strip of 3, imperf. btwn. 850.00

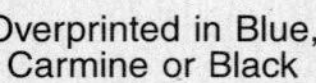

Overprinted in Blue, Carmine or Black

Overprinted by Waterlow & Sons, London

163 A17 ½c brown (Bl) 2.50 2.00
- *a.* Vert. pair, imperf. btwn. 1,400. 1,275.

164 A17 1c ocher (C) 2.50 2.00
- *a.* Horiz. pair, imperf. btwn. 825.00

165 A17 2c green (C) 3.25 2.00
166 A17 3c slate grn (C) 4.00 1.75
- *a.* Inverted overprint 1,750.

167 A17 4c vermilion (Bk) 5.00 2.25
168 A17 5c violet (C) 11.00 2.25
169 A17 7c maroon (Bk) 35.00 *37.50*
170 A17 10c ultra (C) 17.50 2.75
- *a.* Vert. pair, imperf. btwn. 1,500. *2,600.*

171 A18 16c olive grn (R) 50.00 19.00
172 A18 20c red brn (Bk) 32.50 3.50
173 A18 30c dull red (Bk) 100.00 6.75
174 A18 50c yellow grn (R) 150.00 17.50
175 A19 $1 red & pale rose (Bk) 225.00 27.50
176 A19 $2 brn red & yel (Bk) 475.00 225.00
177 A19 $5 dp grn & sal (C) 750.00 525.00
Nos. 163-177 (15) 1,863. 876.75

Due to instructions issued to postmasters throughout China at the time of the Revolution, a number of them prepared unauthorized overprints using the same characters as the overprints prepared by the government. While many were made in good faith, some, like the blue overprints from Tientsin, were bogus, and the status of certain others is extremely dubious.

Dr. Sun Yat-sen — A21

1912, Dec. 14 *Perf. 14½*

178 A21 1c orange 4.75 *3.25*
179 A21 2c yellow grn 4.75 *3.25*
180 A21 3c slate grn 4.75 *3.25*
181 A21 5c rose lilac 9.50 3.25
182 A21 8c dp brown 9.50 5.00
183 A21 10c dull blue 9.50 5.00
184 A21 16c olive grn 27.50 17.50
185 A21 20c maroon 37.50 10.00
186 A21 50c dk green 100.00 40.00
187 A21 $1 brown red 260.00 60.00
188 A21 $2 yellow brn 750.00 300.00
189 A21 $5 gray 275.00 *225.00*
Nos. 178-189 (12) 1,493. 675.50

Honoring the leader of the Revolution.

President Yuan Shih-kai — A22

1912, Dec. 14

190 A22 1c orange 3.00 1.75
191 A22 2c yellow green 3.00 1.75
192 A22 3c slate green 3.00 1.75
193 A22 5c rose lilac 3.75 2.00
194 A22 8c deep brown 11.50 4.00
195 A22 10c dull blue 9.50 2.50
196 A22 16c olive green 10.00 *12.00*
197 A22 20c maroon 9.00 *10.00*
198 A22 50c dark green 55.00 *35.00*
199 A22 $1 brown red 175.00 60.00
200 A22 $2 yellow brown 225.00 75.00
201 A22 $5 gray 675.00 325.00
Nos. 190-201 (12) 1,183. 530.75

Honoring the 1st pres. of the Republic.

Junk — A24

Reaping Rice — A25

Gateway, Hall of Classics, Peking — A26

DESIGN A24

London Printing: Vertical shading lines under top panel fine, junk with clear diagonal shading lines on sails, right pennant of junk usually long, lines in water weak except directly under junk.

Peking Printing: Vertical shading lines under top panel and inner vertical frame line much heavier, water and sails of junk more evenly and strongly colored, white wave over "H" of "CHINA" pointed upward, touching the junk.

DESIGN A25

London: Front hat brim thick and nearly straight, left foot touches shadow.

Peking: Front hat brim thin and strongly upturned, left foot and sickle clearly outlined in white, shadow of middle tree lighter than those of the right and left trees.

DESIGN A26

London: Light colored walk clearly defined almost to the doorway, figure in right doorway "T" shaped with strong horizontal cross-bar, white panel in base of central tower rectangular, vertical stroke in top left character uniformly thick at its base, tree to right of doorway ends in minute dots.

Peking: Walk more heavily shaded near doorway, especially at right; figure in right doorway more like a "Y", white panel at base of central tower is a long oval, right vertical stroke in top left character incurved near its base, tree at right has five prominent dots at top.

London Printing: By Waterlow & Sons, London, perf. 14 to 15.

Peking Printing: By the Chinese Bureau of Engraving and Printing, Peking, perf. 14.

London Printing

1913, May 5 *Perf. 14-15*

202 A24 ½c black brn .75 .40
- *a.* Horiz. or vert. pair, imperf. btwn. 200.00

203 A24 1c orange .75 .40
- *a.* Horiz. pair, imperf. btwn. 250.00
- *b.* Vert. pair, imperf. btwn. 175.00
- *c.* Horiz. strip of 5, imperf. btwn 650.00

204 A24 2c yellow grn 2.75 .40
- *a.* Horiz. pair, imperf. btwn. 400.00

205 A24 3c blue grn 6.75 .45
- *a.* Horiz. pair, imperf. btwn. 200.00
- *b.* Vert. pair, imperf. btwn. 400.00

206 A24 4c scarlet 9.50 .70
207 A24 5c rose lilac 30.00 .60
208 A24 6c gray 5.00 .90
209 A24 7c violet 22.50 8.75
210 A24 8c brown org 42.50 2.50
211 A24 10c dk blue 37.50 1.10
- *a.* Horiz. pair, imperf. btwn. 375.00 375.00
- *b.* Vert. pair, imperf. btwn. 400.00 300.00

212 A25 15c brown 32.50 5.75
213 A25 16c olive grn 17.50 2.25
214 A25 20c brown red 30.00 2.75
215 A25 30c brown vio 32.50 2.00
- *a.* Horiz. pair, imperf. btwn. 400.00 400.00

216 A25 50c green 60.00 3.50
217 A26 $1 ocher & blk 175.00 3.00
218 A26 $2 blue & blk 275.00 19.00
219 A26 $5 scarlet & blk 550.00 125.00
220 A26 $10 yel grn & blk 1,500. 950.00
Nos. 202-220 (19) 2,831. 1,129.

First Peking Printing

1915 *Perf. 14*

221 A24 ½c black brn .80 .35
222 A24 1c orange .80 .35
223 A24 2c yellow grn 1.60 .35
224 A24 3c blue grn 1.75 .35
225 A24 4c scarlet 20.00 .35
226 A24 5c rose lilac 8.50 .35
- *a.* Booklet pane of 4 140.00

227 A24 6c gray 16.00 .35
228 A24 7c violet 25.00 4.50
229 A24 8c brown org 14.00 .40
230 A24 10c dk blue 15.00 .70
- *a.* Booklet pane of 4 140.00

231 A25 15c brown 42.50 4.50
232 A25 16c olive grn 17.50 .70
233 A25 20c brown red 18.50 .70
234 A25 30c brown vio 17.50 .70
235 A25 50c green 42.50 .80
236 A26 $1 ocher & blk 140.00 .85
237 A26 $2 blue & blk 350.00 5.00
- *a.* Center inverted *200,000.* —

238 A26 $5 scarlet & blk 800.00 40.00
239 A26 $10 yel grn & blk 1,100. 275.00
Nos. 221-239 (19) 2,632. 336.30

1919

240 A24 1½c violet 3.75 .60
241 A25 13c brown 9.50 .70
242 A26 $20 yellow & blk 4,900. 3,250.

Nos. 226 and 230 overprinted in red with five characters in vertical column were for postal savings use.

The higher values of the 1913-19 issues are often overprinted with Chinese characters, which are the names of various postal districts. Stamps were frequently stolen while in transit to post offices. The overprints served to protect them, since the stamps could only be used in the districts for which they were overprinted.

Compare designs A24-A26 with designs A29-A31. For surcharges and overprints see Nos. 247, 288, B1-B3, Sinkiang 1-38.

Yeh Kung-cho, Hsu Shi-chang and Chin Yun-peng A27

1921, Oct. 10

243 A27 1c orange 6.00 1.75
244 A27 3c blue green 6.50 1.50
245 A27 6c gray 7.50 5.00
246 A27 10c blue 8.50 4.00
Nos. 243-246 (4) 28.50 12.25

National Post Office, 25th anniversary.
For overprints see Sinkiang Nos. 39-42.

No. 224 Surcharged in Red

1922

247 A24 2c on 3c blue green 3.50 .70
- *a.* Inverted surcharge *175,000.* —

Second Peking Printing

A29

A30

A31

Types of 1913-19 Issues Re-engraved

Type A29: Most of the whitecaps in front of the junk have been removed and the water made darker. The shading lines have been removed from the arabesques and pearls above the top inscription. The inner shadings at the top and sides of the picture have been cut away.

Type A30: The heads of rice in the side panels have a background of crossed lines instead of horizontal lines. The Temple of Heaven is strongly shaded and has a door. There are rows of pearls below the Chinese characters in the upper corners. The arabesques above the top inscription have been altered and are without shading lines.

Type A31: The curved line under the inscription at top is single instead of double. There are four vertical lines, instead of eight, at each side of the picture. The trees at the sides of the temple had foliage in the 1913-19 issues, but now the branches are bare. There are numerous other alterations in the design.

1923 *Perf. 14*

248 A29 ½c black brown 1.75 .30
- *a.* Horiz. pair, imperf. btwn. 175.00 175.00
- *b.* Horiz. pair, imperf. vert. 150.00 150.00

249 A29 1c orange 1.00 .30
- *a.* Imperf., pair 125.00
- *b.* Horiz. pair, imperf. vert. 125.00
- *c.* Booklet pane of 6 90.00
- *d.* Booklet pane of 4 45.00

250 A29 1½c violet 3.50 .90
251 A29 2c yellow grn 2.00 .30
252 A29 3c blue green 6.00 .30
- *a.* Booklet pane of 6 80.00

253 A29 4c gray 27.50 .80
254 A29 5c claret 4.00 .50
- *a.* Booklet pane of 4 100.00

255 A29 6c scarlet 8.50 .50
256 A29 7c violet 8.50 .50
257 A29 8c orange 17.50 .50
258 A29 10c blue 14.50 .30
- *a.* Booklet pane of 6 120.00
- *b.* Booklet pane of 2 150.00

259 A30 13c brown 32.50 .60
260 A30 15c dp blue 10.00 .60
261 A30 16c olive grn 11.00 .60
262 A30 20c brown red 8.50 .40
263 A30 30c purple 32.50 .40
264 A30 50c dp green 60.00 .55
265 A31 $1 org brn & sep 65.00 .65
266 A31 $2 blue & red brn 85.00 1.00
267 A31 $5 red & slate 140.00 4.25
268 A31 $10 green & claret 700.00 70.00
269 A31 $20 plum & blue 1,450. 200.00
Nos. 248-269 (22) 2,689. 284.25

Nos. 249 and 275 exist with webbing watermark from experimental printing.

To prevent speculation and theft, the dollar denominations were overprinted with single characters in red for use in Kwangsi ($1-$20) and Kweichow ($1-$5).

See Nos. 275, 324. For surcharges and overprints see Nos. 274, 289, 311, 325, 330, 339-340, Szechwan 1-3, Yunnan 1-20, Manchuria 1-20, Sinkiang 47-69, 114, C1-C4.

Temple of Heaven, Peking — A32

1923, Oct. 17 *Perf. 14*

270 A32 1c orange 5.00 1.00
271 A32 3c blue green 5.50 2.25
272 A32 4c red 10.50 2.50
273 A32 10c blue 16.50 3.50
Nos. 270-273 (4) 37.50 9.25

Adoption of Constitution, October, 1923.
For overprints see Sinkiang Nos. 43-46.

No. 253 Surcharged in Red

1925

274 A29 3c on 4c gray 3.50 .35
- *a.* Inverted surcharge *300,000.* *275,000.*
- *b.* Vert. pair, imperf. btwn.

Junk Type of 1923

1926

275 A29 4c olive green 1.60 .25
- *a.* Horiz. pair, imperf. vert. 200.00
- *b.* Horiz. pair, imperf. btwn. 200.00
- *c.* Horiz. strip of 3, imperf. btwn. 250.00

Marshal Chang Tso-lin — A34

1928, Mar. 1 *Perf. 14*

276 A34 1c brown orange 1.50 1.50
277 A34 4c olive green 3.00 3.00
278 A34 10c dull blue 7.50 5.50
279 A34 $1 red 60.00 *65.00*
Nos. 276-279 (4) 72.00 75.00

Assumption of office by Marshal Chang Tso-lin. The stamps of this issue were only available for postage in the Provinces of Chihli and

Shantung and at the Offices in Manchuria and Sinkiang.

For overprints see Manchuria Nos. 21-24, Sinkiang 70-73.

President Chiang Kai-shek — A35

1929, May

280 A35 1c brown orange 1.00 .40
281 A35 4c olive green 1.50 .75
282 A35 10c dark blue 12.50 1.50
283 A35 $1 dark red 75.00 55.00
Nos. 280-283 (4) 90.00 57.65

Unification of China.

For overprints see Yunnan Nos. 21-24, Manchuria 25-28, Sinkiang 74-77.

Sun Yat-sen Mausoleum, Nanking — A36

1929, May 30 ***Perf. 14***

284 A36 1c brown orange 1.25 .75
285 A36 4c olive green 1.00 1.25
286 A36 10c dark blue 9.00 2.50
287 A36 $1 dark red 75.00 35.00
Nos. 284-287 (4) 86.25 39.50

The transfer of Dr. Sun Yat-sen's remains from Peiping to the mausoleum at Nanking.

For overprints see Yunnan Nos. 25-28, Manchuria 29-32, Sinkiang 78-81.

Nos. 224 and 252 Surcharged in Red

1930

288 A24 1c on 3c blue green 1.25 *2.25*
289 A29 1c on 3c blue green 1.25 .40
a. No period after "Ct" 18.00 18.00

See Nos. 311, 325, 330.

Dr. Sun Yat-sen — A37

Type I Type II

Type I — Double-lined circle in the sun.

Type II — Heavy, single-lined circle in the sun.

Printed by De la Rue & Co., Ltd., London

Perf. 11½x12½, 12½x13, 12½, 13½

1931, Nov. 12 **Type I** **Engr.**

290 A37 1c orange .55 .30
291 A37 2c olive green .65 .40
292 A37 4c green 1.10 .30
293 A37 20c ultra 1.40 .30
294 A37 $1 org brn & dk brn 12.00 .50
295 A37 $2 blue & org brn 35.00 3.00
296 A37 $5 dull red & blk 50.00 5.00
Nos. 290-296 (7) 100.70 9.80

Stamps issued prior to 1933 were printed by a wet-paper process, and owing to shrinkage such stamps are 1-1½mm narrower than the later dry-printed stamps.

Early printings are perf. 12½x13. Nos. 304, 305 and 306 were later perf. 11½x12½.

1931-37 **Type II**

297 A37 2c olive grn .45 .25
298 A37 4c green .65 .25
299 A37 5c green ('33) .40 .25
300 A37 15c dk green 4.25 1.25
301 A37 15c scarlet ('34) .45 .25
302 A37 20c ultra ('37) .85 .25
303 A37 25c ultra .45 .65
304 A37 $1 org brn & dk brn 14.00 .50
305 A37 $2 blue & org brn 25.00 1.25
306 A37 $5 dull red & blk 47.50 5.00
Nos. 297-306 (10) 94.00 9.90

See Nos. 631-635 in *Scott Standard Postage Stamp Catalogue*, Vol. 2. For surcharges and overprints see Nos. 341, 343, 678, 682, 684-685, 689-691, 768, 843, 1N1, 2N1-2N5, 2N57-2N59, 2N83-2N84, 2N101-2N106, 2N116, 2N124-2N126, 3N1-3N5, 4N1-4N5, 5N1-5N4, 6N1-6N5, 7N1-7N4, 7N54, 8N2-8N3, 8N43-8N44, 8N54, 8N57, 8N69-8N71, 8N85, 9N1-9N5, Taiwan 19, 21-22, Northeastern Provinces 44, Szechwan 4-11, Yunnan 29-44, Sinkiang 82-97 in this catalogue or Scott Standard catalogue, Vol. 2.

"Nomads in the Desert" — A38

1932 **Unwmk.** ***Perf. 14***

307 A38 1c deep orange 29.00 29.00
308 A38 4c olive green 29.00 29.00
309 A38 5c claret 29.00 29.00
310 A38 10c deep blue 29.00 29.00
Nos. 307-310 (4) 116.00 116.00

Northwest Scientific Expedition of Sven Hedin. A small quantity of this issue was sold at face at Peking and several other cities. The bulk of the issue was furnished to Hedin and sold at $5 (Chinese) a set for funds to finance the expedition.

No. 252 Surcharged in Black Like 288

1932

311 A29 1c on 3c blue green 2.50 1.10

Martyrs Issue

Teng Keng A39

Ch'en Ying-shih A40

Chu Chih-hsin A45

Sung Chiao-jen A46

Huang Hsing A47

Liao Chung-kai A48

1932-34 ***Perf. 14***

312 A39 ½c black brown .25 .25
313 A40 1c orange ('34) .25 .25
314 A39 2½c rose lilac ('33) .25 .25
315 A48 3c dp brown ('33) .25 .25
316 A45 8c brown orange .50 .30
317 A46 10c dull violet .60 .30
318 A45 13c blue green .65 .30
319 A46 17c brown olive .55 .30
320 A47 20c brown red 1.10 .30
321 A48 30c brown violet 1.50 .30
322 A47 40c orange 1.40 .35
323 A40 50c green ('34) 5.00 .50
Nos. 312-323 (12) 12.30 3.65

Perfs. 12 to 13 and compound and with secret marks are listed as Nos. 402-439. No. 316 re-drawn is No. 485.

For overprints and surcharge see Nos. 342, 472, 474, 478-479, 486-487, 490, 531-536, 539-541, 544-549, 616, 619, 622-624, 647-659, 662-663, 665, 669, 672, 698, 704, 711, 713-715, 720-721, 831, 846-847, 867, 870, 872, 881-882, J120-J121, 1N14-1N15, 1N59, 2N6-2N9, 2N32-2N56, 2N60, 2N76-2N82, 2N85, 2N87-2N90, 2N107-2N115, 2N118, 2N121-2N123, 3N6-3N10, 3N34-3N55, 3N59, 4N6-4N9, 4N39-4N64, 4N69, 5N5-5N8, 5N34-5N60, 5N65, 6N6-6N8, 6N35-6N61, 6N66, 7N5-7N7, 7N30-7N53, 7N55, 7N59, 8N1, 8N4, 8N28-8N42, 8N45, 8N47-8N50, 8N60-8N61, 8N68, 8N73, 8N76-8N79, 8N89, 8N97, 8N99-8N100, 8N103-8N104, 9N72-9N77, Taiwan 14-17, 20, 28A, 74, Northeastern Provinces 6-8, 11, Szechwan 12-23, Yunnan 49-60, Sinkiang 102-113, 140-161, 197 in this catalogue or *Scott Standard Postage Stamp Catalogue*, Vol. 2.

Junk Type of 1923

1933 ***Perf. 14***

324 A29 6c brown 20.00 1.25

No. 275 Surcharged in Red Like 288

1933

325 A29 1c on 4c olive green 1.75 .35
a. No period after "Ct" 21.00 21.00

Tan Yuan-chang — A49

1933, Jan. 9

326 A49 2c olive green 2.50 1.25
327 A49 5c green 4.00 .40
328 A49 25c ultra 10.00 1.75
329 A49 $1 red 72.50 35.00
Nos. 326-329 (4) 89.00 38.40

Tan Yuan-chang, more commonly known as Tan Yen-kai, a prominent statesman in China since the revolution of 1912 and Pres. of the Executive Dept. of the Natl. Government. Placed on sale Jan. 9, 1933, the date of the ceremony in celebration of the completion of the Tan Yuan-chang Memorial Hall and Tomb at Mukden.

For overprints see Yunnan Nos. 45-48, Sinkiang 98-101.

No. 251 Surcharged in Red Like 288

1935 ***Perf. 14***

330 A29 1c on 2c yellow grn 2.50 .25

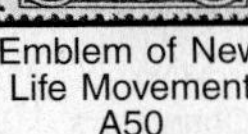

Emblem of New Life Movement A50

Four Virtues of New Life A51

Lighthouse — A52

1936, Jan. 1

331 A50 2c olive green 1.75 .75
332 A50 5c green 2.00 .25
333 A51 20c dark blue 6.00 .70
334 A52 $1 rose red 40.00 11.00
Nos. 331-334 (4) 49.75 12.70

"New Life" movement.

Methods of Mail Transportation A53

Maritime Scene — A54

Shanghai General Post Office — A55

Ministry of Communications, Nanking — A56

1936, Oct. 10

335 A53 2c orange 3.00 .70
336 A54 5c green 1.50 .25
337 A55 25c blue 5.00 .50
338 A56 $1 dk carmine 30.00 9.00
Nos. 335-338 (4) 39.50 10.45

Founding of the Chinese PO, 40th anniv.

Nos. 260 and 261 Surcharged in Red

1936, Oct. 11

339 A30 5c on 15c dp blue 1.75 .50
340 A30 5c on 16c olive grn 3.00 1.00

No. 298 Surcharged in Red

1937

341 A37 1c on 4c green, type II 1.25 .50
a. Upper left character missing

Nos. 322 and 303 Surcharged in Black or Red

1938 ***Perf. 12½, 14***

342 A47 8c on 40c orange (Bk) 2.00 .75
343 A37 10c on 25c ultra (R) 1.75 .30

Dr. Sun Yat-sen — A57

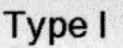

Type I Type II Type III

Type I — Coat button half circle. Six lines of shading above head. Top frame partially shaded with vertical lines.

Type II — Coat button complete circle. Nine lines of shading above head. Top frame partially shaded with vertical lines.

Type III — Coat button complete circle. Nine lines of shading above head. Top frame line fully shaded with vertical lines.

Printed by the Chung Hwa Book Co.
Type I

1938 Unwmk. Engr. ***Perf. 12½***

344	A57	$1	henna & dk brn	85.00	12.00
345	A57	$2	dp blue & org brn	17.50	4.25
346	A57	$5	red & grnsh blk	150.00	19.00
			Nos. 344-346 (3)	252.50	35.25

1939 **Type II**

347	A57	$1	henna & dk brn	16.00	1.00
348	A57	$2	dp blue & org brn	18.00	4.00

1939-43 **Type III**

349	A57	2c	olive green	.25	.25
350	A57	3c	dull claret	.25	.25
351	A57	5c	green	.25	.25
352	A57	5c	olive green	.25	.25
353	A57	8c	olive green	.25	.25
354	A57	10c	green	.25	.25
355	A57	15c	scarlet	1.25	*2.25*
356	A57	15c	dk vio brn ('43)	17.50	*32.50*
357	A57	16c	olive gray	1.75	.45
358	A57	25c	dk blue	.35	*.75*
359	A57	$1	henna & dk brn	2.00	.75
360	A57	$2	dp blue & org brn	4.50	.55
a.			Imperf., pair	300.00	
361	A57	$5	red & grnsh blk	2.75	.50
362	A57	$10	dk green & dull pur	17.50	2.25
363	A57	$20	rose lake & dk blue	60.00	50.00
			Nos. 349-363 (15)	109.10	*91.50*

Several values exist imperforate, but these were not regularly issued. No. 361 imperforate is printer's waste.

See Nos. 368-401, 506-524; for surcharges and overprints see Nos. 440-448, 473, 475-477, 480-481, 482-484, 489, 537-538, 615, 618, 620, 660-661, 664, 666-668, 673-676, 680-681, 686, 688, 699-703, 707-709, 717, 719, 830, J67-J68, M2, M11-M12, 1N2-1N13, 1N23-1N42, 1N57-1N58, 2N10-2N31, 2N61-2N75, 2N86, 2N91-2N93, 2N117, 2N119-2N120, 3N11-3N33, 3N56-3N58, 3N60-3N61, 4N10-4N38, 4N65-4N68, 4N70-4N71, 5N9-5N33, 5N61-5N64, 5N66-5N68, 6N9-6N34, 6N62-6N65, 6N67-6N69, 7N8-7N29, 7N56-7N58, 7N60-7N61, 8N5-8N27, 8N46, 8N51-8N53, 8N55-8N56, 8N58-8N59, 8N62-8N67, 8N72, 8N74-8N75, 8N80-8N84, 8N86-8N88, 8N90, 8N95-8N96, 8N98, 8N101-8N102, 8N105-8N106, 9N6-9N71, 9N97, 9N99, Taiwan 78, 84, Northeastern Provinces 9-10, Sinkiang 115-139, 174-188, 196, 198 in this catalogue or *Scott Standard Postage Stamp Catalogue*, Vol. 2.

Chinese and American Flags and Map of China — A58

Printed by American Bank Note Co.

Frame Engr., Center Litho.
1939, July 4 Unwmk. ***Perf. 12***
Flag in Deep Rose and Ultramarine

364	A58	5c	dark green	1.75	.50
365	A58	25c	deep blue	1.75	.90
366	A58	50c	brown	4.00	1.10
367	A58	$1	rose carmine	6.50	2.25
			Nos. 364-367 (4)	14.00	4.75

150th anniv. of the US Constitution.

Type of 1939-41 Re-engraved

2c, 1939-41 Re-engraved

8c, 1939-41 Re-engraved

1940 ***Perf. 12½***

368	A57	2c	olive green	.25	.25
369	A57	8c	olive green	.25	.25

Type of 1938-41
Type III

1940 Unwmk. ***Perf. 14***

370	A57	2c	olive green	2.50	1.00
371	A57	5c	green	5.00	2.10
372	A57	$1	henna & dk brn	110.00	22.50
373	A57	$2	dp blue & org brn	21.00	5.00
374	A57	$5	red & grnsh blk	26.00	16.50
375	A57	$10	dk grn & dull pur	72.50	12.50
			Nos. 370-375 (6)	237.00	59.60

See surcharge note following No. 363.

Type of 1939-41
1940 Wmk. 261 ***Perf. 12½***
Type III

376	A57	$1	henna & dk brn	7.00	*9.00*
377	A57	$2	dp blue & org brn	9.00	*9.00*
378	A57	$5	red & grnsh blk	10.00	*18.00*
379	A57	$10	dk green & dull pur	15.00	*30.00*
380	A57	$20	rose lake & dp blue	19.00	*30.00*
			Nos. 376-380 (5)	60.00	*96.00*

See surcharge note following No. 363.

Printed by the Dah Tung Book Co.

Five Cent

Type III - Characters joined

Secret Mark - Characters not joined

Eight Cent

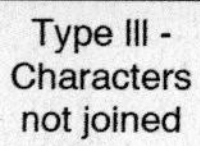

Type III - Characters not joined

Secret Mark - Characters joined

Ten Cent

Type III - Characters sharp and well shaped

Secret Mark - Characters coarse and varying in thickness

Dollar Values

Type III

Secret Mark

1940 Unwmk. ***Perf. 14***
Type III with Secret Marks

381	A57	5c	green	.25	.25
382	A57	5c	olive green	.25	.25
383	A57	8c	olive green	.40	.25
a.			Without "star" in uniform button	1.50	*2.50*
384	A57	10c	green	.25	.25
385	A57	30c	scarlet	.35	.25
386	A57	50c	dk blue	.45	.25
387	A57	$1	org brn & sepia	2.50	.25
388	A57	$2	dp blue & yel brn	1.00	.35
389	A57	$5	red & slate grn	1.00	.45
390	A57	$10	dk grn & dull pur	4.00	2.25
391	A57	$20	rose lake & dk blue	12.00	3.50
			Nos. 381-391 (11)	22.45	8.30

Type III with Secret Marks
1940 Wmk. 261 ***Perf. 14***

392	A57	5c	green	.25	.25
393	A57	5c	olive green	.25	.25
394	A57	10c	green	.35	.25
395	A57	30c	scarlet	.25	.25
396	A57	50c	dk blue	.55	.25
397	A57	$1	org brn & sepia	4.50	2.75
398	A57	$2	dp blue & yel brn	12.50	13.00
399	A57	$5	red & slate grn	11.50	*12.00*
400	A57	$10	dk grn & dull pur	16.00	*17.00*
401	A57	$20	rose lake & dk blue	25.00	20.00
			Nos. 392-401 (10)	71.15	66.00

Nos. 383, 384, 385, 397, 400 and 401 exist perf. 12½, but were not issued with this perforation.

See surcharge note following No. 363.

Types of 1932-34 Martyrs Issue with Secret Mark

1932-34 Issue. In the left Chinese character in bottom row, the two parts are not joined.

Secret Mark, 1940-41 Issue. The two parts are joined

Perf. 12½, 13 and Compound
1940-41 Wmk. 261

402	A39	½c	olive blk	.25	.25
403	A40	1c	orange	.25	.25
404	A46	2c	dp blue ('41)	.25	.25
405	A39	2½c	rose lilac	.25	.25
406	A48	3c	dp yellow brn	.30	.25
407	A39	4c	pale vio ('41)	.30	.25
408	A48	5c	dull red org ('41)	.30	.25
409	A45	8c	dp orange	.25	.25
410	A46	10c	dull violet	.25	.25
411	A45	13c	dp yellow grn	.35	.25
412	A48	15c	brown car	.25	.25
413	A46	17c	brown olive	.25	.25
414	A47	20c	lt blue	.25	.25
415	A45	21c	olive brn ('41)	1.10	*1.25*
416	A40	25c	red vio ('41)	.25	.25
417	A46	28c	olive ('41)	.30	.25
418	A48	30c	brown car	.45	.25
a.			Vert. pair, imperf. btwn.	140.00	
419	A47	40c	orange	.30	.25
420	A40	50c	green	.30	.25

Unwmk.

421	A39	½c	olive black	.25	.25
422	A40	1c	orange	.25	.25
a.			Without secret mark	2.75	2.75
b.			Horiz. pair, imperf. vert.	110.00	
423	A46	2c	dp blue	.25	.25
a.			Vert. pair, imperf. horiz.	100.00	
b.			Horiz. pair, imperf. between	160.00	
424	A39	2½c	rose lilac	.25	.25
425	A48	3c	dp yellow brn	.25	.25
426	A39	4c	pale violet	.25	.25
427	A48	5c	dull red org	.25	.25
428	A45	8c	dp orange	.25	.25
429	A46	10c	dull violet	3.25	.40
430	A45	13c	dp yel grn	.25	.65
431	A48	15c	brown car	.35	.60
432	A46	17c	brn olive	.40	.25
433	A47	20c	lt blue	.30	.25
a.			Vert. pair, imperf. horiz.	125.00	
b.			Horiz. pair, imperf. vert.	125.00	
434	A45	21c	olive brn	.50	.35
435	A40	25c	rose vio	.35	*.50*
436	A46	28c	olive	.70	.50
437	A48	30c	brown car	2.50	2.50
438	A47	40c	orange	.35	.35
439	A40	50c	green	3.50	.40
			Nos. 402-439 (38)	20.65	14.50

Several values exist imperforate, but they were not regularly issued.

Used values are for favor cancels. Postally used examples sell for more.

See surcharge note following No. 323.

Regional Surcharges.

The regional surcharges, Nos. 440-448, 482-484, 486-491, 525-549, have been listed according to the basic stamps, with black or red surcharges. The surcharges of the individual provinces, plus Hong Kong and Shanghai, are noted in small type. The numeral following each letter is the surcharge denomination. These surcharges are identified by the following letters:

a — Hong Kong	i — Kwangsi
b — Shanghai	j — Kwangtung
bx — Anhwei	k — Western Szechwan
c — Hunan	l — Yunnan
d — Kansu	m — Honan
e — Kiangsi	n — Shensi
f — Eastern Szechwan	o — Kweichow
g — Chekiang	p — Hupeh
h — Fukien	

Regional Surcharges on Stamps of 1939-40

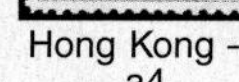

Hong Kong — a4

Shanghai — b3

Hunan — c3

Kansu — d3

Kiangsi — e3

Eastern Szechwan — f3

Chekiang — g3

1940-41 Unwmk. *Perf. 12½, 14*

Carmine Surcharge

440 A57 4c on 5c ol grn (#382) .60 .60
r. Lower right character duplicated at left 30.00 32.50

Black Surcharge

441 A57 3c on 5c grn (#351) (b3) 1.25 *1.40*
442 A57 3c on 5c ol grn (#352) (c3, d3) .65 *2.00*
443 A57 3c on 5c grn (#381) (b3) .60 *1.25*
444 A57 3c on 5c ol grn (#382) (e3) .70 *1.00*
r. Lower left character duplicated at right (Kiangsi) 42.50 42.50
(b3) Shanghai .65 *1.40*
(f3) Eastern Szechwan .65 *1.60*

The Kansu surcharges of No. 442 are of 6 types. Differences include formation of top part of fen character (at left of "3"), fen with low right hook, height of "3" (5-4mm), space between upper and lower characters (6-9mm), etc.

1940-41 Wmk. 261 *Perf. 14*

445 A57 3c on 5c grn (#392) (e3) .60 *1.40*
r. Lower left character duplicated at right (Kiangsi) 35.00 35.00
(b3, c3) Shanghai, Hunan .60 *1.60*
446 A57 3c on 5c ol grn (#393) (f3) .70 *1.75*
(b3) Shanghai .95 *1.75*
r. Lower left character duplicated at right (f3) 60.00 65.00

Red Surcharge

447 A57 3c on 5c grn (#392) (g3) 1.25 3.25
448 A57 3c on 5c ol grn (#393) (g3) 6.00 6.00

SEMI-POSTAL STAMPS

SP1

Red or Blue Surcharge

1920, Dec. 1 Unwmk. *Perf. 14, 15*

B1 SP1 1c on 2c green 5.00 2.00
B2 SP1 3c on 4c scar (B) 8.00 3.00
B3 SP1 5c on 6c gray 12.00 5.00
Nos. B1-B3 (3) 25.00 10.00

The surcharge represents the actual franking value. The extra cent helped victims of the 1919 Yellow River flood.

AIR POST STAMPS

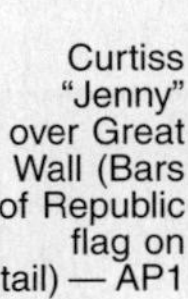

Curtiss "Jenny" over Great Wall (Bars of Republic flag on tail) — AP1

Unwmk.

1921, July 1 Engr. *Perf. 14*

C1 AP1 15c bl grn & blk 50.00 50.00
C2 AP1 30c scar & blk 50.00 50.00
C3 AP1 45c dull vio & blk 50.00 50.00
C4 AP1 60c dk blue & blk 65.00 65.00
C5 AP1 90c ol grn & blk 72.50 72.50
Nos. C1-C5 (5) 287.50 287.50

(Nationalist sun emblem on tail) — AP2

1929, July 5

C6 AP2 15c blue grn & blk 10.00 3.00
C7 AP2 30c dk red & blk 15.00 5.00
C8 AP2 45c dk vio & blk 24.00 10.00
C9 AP2 60c dk blue & blk 27.50 12.00
C10 AP2 90c ol grn & blk 27.50 18.00
Nos. C6-C10 (5) 104.00 48.00

Junkers F-13 over Great Wall AP3

1932-37

C11 AP3 15c gray grn .70 .45
C12 AP3 25c orange ('33) 5.00 3.00
C13 AP3 30c red 10.00 2.50
C14 AP3 45c brown vio 1.00 .45
C15 AP3 50c dk brown ('33) 1.00 .45
C16 AP3 60c dk blue 1.00 .45
C17 AP3 90c olive grn 1.00 .60
C18 AP3 $1 yellow grn ('33) 1.50 .45
C19 AP3 $2 brown ('37) 1.50 .80
C20 AP3 $5 brown car ('37) 4.00 3.00
Nos. C11-C20 (10) 26.70 12.15

See #C21-C40. For surcharges and overprints see #C41-C52, C54-C60, 9N111-9N114, 9NC1-9NC7, Szechwan C1, C3-C6, Sinkiang C5-C19.

Type of 1932-37, with secret mark

1932-37 Issue, Lower part of left character joined

Secret Mark, 1940-41 Issue, Separated

Perf. 12, 12½, 12½x13, 13

1940-41 Wmk. 261

C21 AP3 15c gray green 1.00 .60
C22 AP3 25c yellow org 1.25 .80
C23 AP3 30c red 1.00 .60
a. Vert. pair, imperf. between 500.00
C24 AP3 45c dull rose vio ('41) 1.00 .60
C25 AP3 50c brown 1.00 .60
C26 AP3 60c dp blue ('41) 1.00 .60
C27 AP3 90c olive ('41) 1.00 .70
C28 AP3 $1 apple grn ('41) 1.00 .70
C29 AP3 $2 lt brown ('41) 1.00 .70
C30 AP3 $5 lake 2.50 1.20
Nos. C21-C30 (10) 11.75 7.10

Unwmk.

Perf. 12½, 13, 13½

C31 AP3 15c gray green ('41) .70 .30
C32 AP3 25c lt orange ('41) .70 .30
C33 AP3 30c lt red ('41) .70 .30
C34 AP3 45c dl rose vio ('41) .70 .45
C35 AP3 50c brown .70 .60
C36 AP3 60c blue ('41) .70 .60
C37 AP3 90c lt olive ('41) .70 .60
C38 AP3 $1 apple grn ('41) .70 .70
C39 AP3 $2 lt brown ('41) 3.00 1.50
C40 AP3 $5 lake ('41) 2.00 1.25
Nos. C31-C40 (10) 10.60 6.60

For surcharges see note following No. C20.

SPECIAL DELIVERY STAMPS

Used values of Nos. E1-E8 are for mailer's receipts. Complete unused strips of four are exceptionally scarce because the first section (#1) was to remain in the P.O. booklet.

The mailer received the righthand section (#4), usually canceled, as a receipt. The middle two sections were canceled and attached to the letter. Upon arrival at the destination P.O. they were canceled again, usually on the back, with the righthand copy (#3) retained by that P.O. The lefthand copy (#2) was signed by the recipient and returned to the original P.O. as evidence of delivery. Sections 2 and 3 usually are thin or badly damaged.

Unused strips of three (#2-4) can be found of Nos. E3-E8.

Design: Dragon in irregular oval. Stamp 8x2½ inches, divided into four parts by perforation or serrate rouletting.

"Chinese Imperial Post Office" in lines, repeated to form the background which is usually lighter in color than the rest of the design.

Dragon's head facing downward

Background with period after "POSTOFFICE."

No Date

1905 Unwmk. *Perf. 11*

E1 10c grass green *12,000.* 500.00

Serrate Roulette in Black

E2 10c deep green *15,000.* 500.00

Type, E3-E8

Dragon's head facing forward

Background with no period after "POSTOFFICE"

1907-10 No Date

E3 10c light bluish green *2,000.* 250.00

Background with date at bottom

1909-11

E4 10c grn (Feb. 1909) *1,750.* 200.00
E5 10c bl grn (Jan. 1911) 1,600. 150.00

"IMPERIAL POST OFFICE" in serifed letters repeated to form the background.

No Date, No Border

Background of 30 or 28 lines

1912

E6 10c green (30 lines) 1,400. 130.00
a. 28 lines 1,600. 800.00

Background of 35 lines of sans-serif letters

Colored Border

E8 10c green 1,600. 190.00

On No. E8 the medallion in the third section has Chinese characters in the background instead of the usual English inscriptions. E6 and E8 occur with many types of four-character overprints reading "Republic of China," applied locally but unofficially at various post offices.

Type, E9, E10

Design: Wild Goose. Stamp 7½x2¾ inches, divided into five parts.

"CHINESE POST OFFICE" in sans-serif letters, repeated to form the background of 28 lines. With border.

Serrate Roulette in Black

1913

E9 10c green 900.00 110.00

Unused values for Nos. E9-E10 are for complete strips of five parts. Used values are for single parts.

"CHINESE POST OFFICE" in antique letters, forming a background of 29 or 30 lines. No border.

1914 Serrate Roulette in Green

E10 10c green 325.00 50.00

On No. E9 the background is in sans-serif capitals, the Chinese and English inscriptions are on white tablets and the serial numbers are in black.

On No. E10 the background is in antique capitals and extends under the inscriptions. The serial numbers are in green.

NOTE:

In February, 1916, the Special Delivery Stamps were demonetized and became merely receipts without franking value. To mark this, four of the five sections of the stamp had the letters A, B, C, D either handstamped or printed on them.

POSTAGE DUE STAMPS

Regular Issue of 1902-03 Overprinted in Black

1904 Unwmk. *Perf. 14 to 15*

J1	A17	½c chocolate	14.00	6.00
J2	A17	1c ocher	14.00	5.00
J3	A17	2c scarlet	17.00	6.00
J4	A17	4c red brn	18.00	7.00
J5	A17	5c salmon	20.00	12.00
J6	A17	10c dk blue grn	33.00	20.00
a.		Vert. pair, imperf. btwn.	*2,000.*	*2,000.*
		Nos. J1-J6 (6)	116.00	56.00

D1

1904 Engr.

J7	D1	½c blue	7.00	4.00
a.		Horiz. pair, imperf. btwn.	3,000.	2,000.
J8	D1	1c blue	12.00	4.00
J9	D1	2c blue	12.00	4.00
a.		Horiz. pair, imperf. btwn.	2,000.	1,800.
J10	D1	4c blue	15.00	6.00
J11	D1	5c blue	18.00	7.00
J12	D1	10c blue	20.00	9.00
J13	D1	20c blue	50.00	12.00
J14	D1	30c blue	70.00	40.00
		Nos. J7-J14 (8)	204.00	86.00

Arabic numeral of value at left on Nos. J12-J14.

1911

J15	D1	1c brown	25.00	*18.00*
J16	D1	2c brown	40.00	32.50

The ½c, 4c, 5c and 20c in brown exist but were not issued as they arrived in China after the downfall of the Ching dynasty.

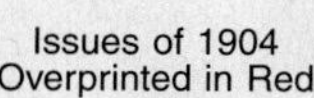

Issues of 1904 Overprinted in Red

1912

J19	D1	½c blue	700.	*1,000.*
J20	D1	4c blue	900.	*1,100.*
J21	D1	5c blue	1,000.	*1,100.*
J22	D1	10c blue	1,500.	1,100.
J23	D1	20c blue	3,000.	*3,200.*
J24	D1	30c blue	3,000.	*3,200.*

Nos. J15-J16 exist with this overprint, but were not regularly issued.

Nos. J1-J14 Overprinted in Red

1912

J25	D1	½c blue	5.00	3.00
J26	D1	1c brown	6.00	3.00
a.		Horiz. pair, imperf. btwn.	3,000.	3,000.
b.		Inverted overprint	550.00	550.00
J27	D1	2c brown	8.00	4.00
J28	D1	4c blue	15.00	6.00
J29	D1	5c blue	275.00	*300.00*
J30	D1	5c brown	20.00	*10.00*
a.		Inverted overprint	320.00	*340.00*
J31	D1	10c blue	25.00	*13.00*
J32	D1	20c blue	27.00	17.00
J33	D1	30c blue	35.00	30.00
		Nos. J25-J33 (9)	416.00	386.00

Issues of 1904 Overprinted in Black

1912

J34	D1	½c blue	15.00	10.00
J35	D1	½c brown	8.00	3.00
J36	D1	1c brown	8.00	3.00
a.		Inverted overprint	350.00	350.00
J37	D1	2c brown	10.00	*5.00*
J38	D1	4c blue	20.00	*9.50*
J39	D1	5c brown	27.50	*14.00*
a.		Horiz. pair, imperf. btwn.	*3,800.*	*3,800.*
J40	D1	10c blue	45.00	*27.50*
J41	D1	20c brown	65.00	*100.00*
J42	D1	30c blue	75.00	65.00
		Nos. J34-J42 (9)	273.50	237.00

D4

Printed by Waterlow & Sons

1913, May *Perf. 14, 15*

J43	D4	½c blue	3.00	1.50
a.		Horiz. pair, imperf. btwn.	*4,000.*	*3,000.*
J44	D4	1c blue	3.50	1.50
J45	D4	2c blue	5.00	3.00
J46	D4	4c blue	8.00	3.00
J47	D4	5c blue	12.00	6.00
J48	D4	10c blue	17.50	8.00
J49	D4	20c blue	27.50	13.00
J50	D4	30c blue	35.00	15.00
		Nos. J43-J50 (8)	111.50	51.00

Printed by the Chinese Bureau of Engraving & Printing

1915 Re-engraved *Perf. 14*

J51	D4	½c blue	3.00	*1.00*
J52	D4	1c blue	3.75	.65
J53	D4	2c blue	4.00	.65
J54	D4	4c blue	5.00	.75
J55	D4	5c blue	7.00	1.50
J56	D4	10c blue	11.00	2.50
J57	D4	20c blue	17.50	8.00
J58	D4	30c blue	50.00	20.00
		Nos. J51-J58 (8)	101.25	35.05

In the upper part of the stamps of type D4 there is an ornament of five marks like the letter "V". Below this is a curved label with an inscription in Chinese characters. On the 1913 stamps there are two complete background lines between the ornament and the label. The 1915 stamps show only one unbroken line at this place. There are other minute differences in the engraving of the stamps of the two issues.

D5

1932 *Perf. 14*

J59	D5	½c orange	.60	*.30*
J60	D5	1c orange	.60	*.30*
J61	D5	2c orange	.60	*.30*
J62	D5	4c orange	.60	*.30*
J63	D5	5c orange	1.50	*1.50*
J64	D5	10c orange	2.00	2.00
J65	D5	20c orange	2.75	3.00
J66	D5	30c orange	4.00	*4.00*
		Nos. J59-J66 (8)	12.65	11.70

See Nos. J69-J79. For surcharges see Nos. 1NJ1, 9NJ1-9NJ4.

Regular Stamps of 1939 Overprinted in Black or Red

1940

J67	A57	$1 henna & dk brn (Bk)	8.00	*25.00*
J68	A57	$2 dl bl & org brn (R)	12.00	*25.00*

Type of 1932
Printed by The Commercial Press, Ltd.

Perf. 12½, 12½x13, 13

1940-41 Engr.

J69	D5	½c yellow orange	.80	*1.00*
J70	D5	1c yellow orange	.80	*1.00*
J71	D5	2c yel org ('41)	.80	*1.00*
J72	D5	4c yellow orange	.80	*1.00*
J73	D5	5c yel org ('41)	1.20	*1.00*
J74	D5	10c yel org ('41)	.80	*1.00*
J75	D5	20c yel org ('41)	.80	*1.00*
J76	D5	30c yellow orange	.80	*1.00*
J77	D5	50c yellow orange	1.00	*1.00*
J78	D5	$1 yellow orange	1.20	*1.00*
J79	D5	$2 yellow orange	1.50	*2.00*
		Nos. J69-J79 (11)	10.50	*12.00*

For surcharge see No. 1NJ1.

SZECHWAN PROVINCE

Re-engraved Issue of China, 1923, Overprinted

1933 Unwmk. *Perf. 14*

1	A29	1c orange	11.00	1.00
2	A29	5c claret	11.00	1.40
3	A30	50c deep green	32.50	6.75
		Nos. 1-3 (3)	54.50	9.15

The overprint reads "For use in Szechwan Province exclusively."

Same on Sun Yat-sen Issue of 1931-37
Type II

1933-34 *Perf. 12½*

4	A37	2c olive grn	2.00	1.00
5	A37	5c green	22.50	2.40
6	A37	15c dk green	7.75	3.50
7	A37	15c scar ('34)	9.00	12.00
8	A37	25c ultra	7.50	1.75
9	A37	$1 org brn & dk brn	22.50	4.00
10	A37	$2 bl & org brn	55.00	6.75
11	A37	$5 dl red & blk	125.00	37.50
		Nos. 4-11 (8)	251.25	68.90

Same on Martyrs Issue of 1932-34

1933 *Perf. 14*

12	A39	½c black brn	.80	.80
13	A40	1c orange	1.25	.55
14	A39	2½c rose lilac	3.50	3.75
15	A48	3c deep brown	3.00	3.00
16	A45	8c brown org	1.75	1.50
17	A46	10c dull violet	4.50	.55
18	A45	13c blue green	5.00	1.00
19	A46	17c brown olive	5.50	1.40
20	A47	20c brown red	8.50	1.00
21	A48	30c brown violet	6.75	1.00
22	A47	40c orange	18.00	1.40
23	A40	50c green	37.50	2.10
		Nos. 12-23 (12)	96.05	18.05

YUNNAN PROVINCE

Stamps of China, 1923-26, Overprinted

The overprint reads "For exclusive use in the Province of Yunnan." It was applied to prevent stamps being purchased in the depreciated currency of Yunnan and used elsewhere.

1926 Unwmk. *Perf. 14*

1	A29	½c blk brn	1.10	.35
2	A29	1c orange	1.75	.35
3	A29	1½c violet	3.75	4.25
4	A29	2c yellow grn	2.75	.50
5	A29	3c blue green	2.75	.35
6	A29	4c olive grn	3.50	.50
7	A29	5c claret	3.50	.50
8	A29	6c red	5.25	1.25
9	A29	7c violet	5.50	1.90
10	A29	8c brown org	4.75	1.40
11	A29	10c dark blue	3.00	.30
12	A30	13c brown	1.75	1.90
13	A30	15c dark blue	1.75	1.90
14	A30	16c olive grn	3.50	1.90
15	A30	20c brown red	8.50	3.25
16	A30	30c brown vio	5.25	5.75
17	A30	50c deep green	5.50	5.75
18	A31	$1 org brn & sep	20.50	14.00
19	A31	$2 blue & red brn	35.00	14.00
20	A31	$5 red & slate	240.00	260.00
		Nos. 1-20 (20)	359.35	320.10

Unification Issue of China, 1929, Overprinted in Red

1929 *Perf. 14*

21	A35	1c brown org	2.25	2.25
22	A35	4c olive grn	3.75	*5.75*
23	A35	10c dark blue	12.00	9.00
24	A35	$1 dark red	120.00	90.00
		Nos. 21-24 (4)	138.00	107.00

Similar Overprint in Black on Sun Yat-sen Mausoleum Issue
Characters 15½-16mm apart

25	A36	1c brown orange	2.25	2.00
26	A36	4c olive green	2.25	*3.75*
27	A36	10c dark blue	9.00	8.50
28	A36	$1 dark red	77.50	*67.50*
		Nos. 25-28 (4)	91.00	*81.75*

London Print Issue of China, 1931-37, Overprinted

1932-34 Unwmk. *Perf. 12½*

Type I (double circle)

29	A37	1c orange	4.00	2.75
30	A37	2c olive grn	5.00	*5.50*
31	A37	4c green	3.25	*5.50*
32	A37	20c ultra	3.25	*3.00*
33	A37	$1 org brn & dk brn	50.00	*55.00*
34	A37	$2 bl & org brn	82.50	*85.00*
35	A37	$5 dl red & blk	250.00	*295.00*
		Nos. 29-35 (7)	398.00	*451.75*

Type II (single circle)

36	A37	2c olive grn	26.00	26.00
37	A37	4c green	17.00	10.75
38	A37	5c green	15.00	10.00
39	A37	15c dk green	8.00	*8.75*
40	A37	15c scar ('34)	8.00	*10.00*
41	A37	25c ultra	11.00	*11.50*
42	A37	$1 org brn & dk brn	67.50	67.50
43	A37	$2 bl & org brn	125.00	125.00
44	A37	$5 dl red & blk	260.00	260.00
		Nos. 36-44 (9)	537.50	529.50

Nos. 36-39, 41-44 were overprinted in London as well as in Peking. The London overprints are 11mm in length; the Peking overprints are 12mm in length. There are other minor differences. Value of London overprints is significantly more than the Peking overprints, which are valued above.

Tan Yuan-chang Issue of China, 1933, Overprinted

1933 *Perf. 14*

45	A49	2c olive green	1.75	1.75
46	A49	5c green	3.00	2.40
47	A49	25c ultra	5.25	*5.50*
48	A49	$1 red	80.00	65.00
		Nos. 45-48 (4)	90.00	74.65

Martyrs Issue of China, 1932-34, Overprinted

1933

No.	Type	Denomination / Color	Unused	Used
49	A39	½c blk brown	1.75	1.60
50	A40	1c orange	3.50	2.75
51	A39	2½c rose lilac	4.00	4.50
52	A48	3c deep brown	6.25	2.25
53	A45	8c brown org	2.75	2.75
54	A46	10c dull vio	4.00	4.50
55	A45	13c blue grn	2.50	1.10
56	A46	17c brn olive	12.50	12.50
57	A47	20c brown red	3.25	3.25
58	A48	30c brown vio	10.00	10.00
59	A47	40c orange	47.50	47.50
60	A40	50c green	47.50	47.50
		Nos. 49-60 (12)	145.50	140.20

China No. 324 was overprinted with characters arranged vertically, like Sinkiang No. 114, but was not issued.

MANCHURIA

Kirin and Heilungkiang Issue

Stamps of China, 1923-26, Overprinted

The overprint reads: "For use in Ki-Hei District" the two names being abbreviated.

The intention of the overprint was to prevent the purchase of stamps in Manchuria, where the currency was depreciated, and their resale elsewhere.

1927 Unwmk. *Perf. 14*

No.	Type	Denomination / Color	Unused	Used
1	A29	½c black brn	1.90	.35
2	A29	1c orange	1.90	.35
3	A29	1½c violet	2.50	1.90
4	A29	2c yellow grn	2.50	1.90
5	A29	3c blue grn	1.75	.75
6	A29	4c olive grn	.85	.35
7	A29	5c claret	1.75	.35
8	A29	6c red	2.50	1.90
9	A29	7c violet	5.25	1.90
10	A29	8c brown org	3.50	1.90
11	A29	10c dk blue	1.90	.50
12	A30	13c brown	4.00	3.00
13	A30	15c dk blue	4.00	3.00
14	A30	16c olive grn	4.00	2.75
15	A30	20c brown red	6.00	3.50
16	A30	30c brown vio	8.75	3.50
17	A30	50c dp green	12.00	4.25
18	A31	$1 org brn & sep	26.00	8.75
19	A31	$2 bl & red brn	70.00	19.00
20	A31	$5 red & slate	325.00	325.00
		Nos. 1-20 (20)	486.05	384.90

Several values of this issue exist with inverted overprint, double overprint and in pairs with one overprint omitted. These "errors" were not regularly issued. Forgeries also exist.

Chang Tso-lin Stamps of 1928 Overprinted in Red or Blue

1928 *Perf. 14*

No.	Type	Denomination / Color	Unused	Used
21	A34	1c brown org (R)	2.75	1.75
22	A34	4c olive grn (R)	1.75	1.75
23	A34	10c dull blue (R)	5.00	3.75
24	A34	$1 red (Bl)	50.00	45.00
		Nos. 21-24 (4)	59.50	52.25

Unification Issue of China, 1929, Overprinted in Red as in 1928

1929

No.	Type	Denomination / Color	Unused	Used
25	A35	1c brown orange	2.00	2.00
26	A35	4c olive green	3.75	3.25
27	A35	10c dark blue	13.00	12.50
28	A35	$1 dark red	110.00	*100.00*
		Nos. 25-28 (4)	128.75	*117.75*

Similar Overprint in Black on Sun Yat-sen Mausoleum Issue of China Characters 15-16mm apart

1929 *Perf. 14*

No.	Type	Denomination / Color	Unused	Used
29	A36	1c brown orange	2.25	*2.50*
30	A36	4c olive green	2.75	*3.00*
31	A36	10c dark blue	8.50	5.25
32	A36	$1 dark red	85.00	65.00
		Nos. 29-32 (4)	98.50	75.75

SINKIANG

Stamps of China, 1913-19, Overprinted in Black or Red

The first character of overprint is ½mm out of alignment, to the left, and the overprint measures 16mm.

1915 Unwmk. *Perf. 14*

No.	Type	Denomination / Color	Unused	Used
1	A24	½c black brn	1.75	.95
2	A24	1c orange	1.75	.70
3	A24	2c yellow grn	2.40	1.25
4	A24	3c slate grn	2.40	.65
5	A24	4c scarlet	4.75	1.10
6	A24	5c rose lilac	3.50	.95
7	A24	6c gray	6.50	2.75
8	A24	7c violet	6.50	*8.50*
9	A24	8c brown orange	5.50	5.50
10	A24	10c dark blue	5.50	2.75
11	A25	15c brown	6.50	3.50
12	A25	16c olive grn	13.00	9.25
13	A25	20c brown red	13.00	7.25
14	A25	30c brown violet	14.50	11.00
15	A25	50c deep green	40.00	18.50
16	A26	$1 ocher & blk (R)	145.00	62.50
a.		Second & third characters of overprint transposed	*70,000.*	
		Nos. 1-16 (16)	272.55	137.10

Stamps of China, 1913-19, Overprinted in Black or Red

The five characters of overprint are correctly aligned and measure 15½mm.

1916-19

No.	Type	Denomination / Color	Unused	Used
17	A24	½c black brn	2.00	2.40
18	A24	1c orange	3.25	1.75
19	A24	1½c violet	4.50	4.00
20	A24	2c yellow grn	3.25	1.75
21	A24	3c slate grn	5.50	.70
22	A24	4c scarlet	5.50	1.25
23	A24	5c rose lilac	5.50	.90
24	A24	6c gray	8.00	1.25
25	A24	7c violet	8.00	*11.00*
26	A24	8c brown org	8.75	8.50
27	A24	10c dark blue	8.75	1.25
28	A25	13c brown	4.75	*8.00*
29	A25	15c brown	6.00	*8.50*
30	A25	16c olive grn	5.50	4.00
31	A25	20c brown red	4.50	3.00
32	A25	30c brown vio	6.75	6.00
33	A25	50c deep green	9.25	5.50
34	A26	$1 ocher & blk (R)	29.00	11.00
35	A26	$2 dk bl & blk (R)	27.50	12.00
36	A26	$5 scar & blk (R)	110.00	37.50
37	A26	$10 yel grn & blk (R)	275.00	175.00
38	A26	$20 yel & blk (R)	1,435.	875.00
		Nos. 17-38 (22)	1,976.	1,180.

For overprint see No. C4.

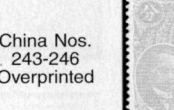

China Nos. 243-246 Overprinted

1921 *Perf. 14*

No.	Type	Denomination / Color	Unused	Used
39	A27	1c orange	1.75	1.75
40	A27	3c blue green	3.50	3.50
41	A27	6c gray	13.50	13.50
42	A27	10c blue	80.00	80.00
		Nos. 39-42 (4)	98.75	98.75

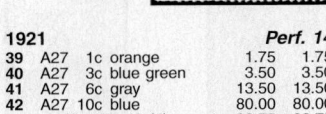

Constitution Issue of China, 1923, Overprinted

1923

No.	Type	Denomination / Color	Unused	Used
43	A32	1c orange	1.55	1.55
44	A32	3c blue green	6.50	6.50
45	A32	4c red	9.75	9.75
46	A32	10c blue	27.50	27.50
		Nos. 43-46 (4)	45.30	45.30

Stamps of China, 1923-26, Overprinted as in 1916-19, in Black or Red

1924

Re-engraved

No.	Type	Denomination / Color	Unused	Used
47	A29	½c black brn	1.50	*3.00*
48	A29	1c orange	1.50	1.25
49	A29	1½c violet	2.75	*5.00*
50	A29	2c yellow grn	4.25	1.40
51	A29	3c blue grn	4.25	1.25
52	A29	4c gray	4.25	*6.75*
53	A29	5c claret	1.40	1.00
54	A29	6c red	7.50	2.75
55	A29	7c violet	8.50	7.50
56	A29	8c org brn	17.00	*15.00*
57	A29	10c dark blue	6.75	1.90
58	A30	13c red brown	6.00	*8.50*
59	A30	15c deep blue	8.75	6.75
60	A30	16c olive grn	10.00	9.75
61	A30	20c brown red	8.50	6.25
62	A30	30c brown vio	9.75	6.75
63	A30	50c deep green	10.00	6.75
64	A31	$1 org brn & sep (R)	18.00	8.50
65	A31	$2 bl & red brn (R)	40.00	12.00
66	A31	$5 red & slate (R)	95.00	19.00
67	A31	$10 grn & claret (R)	300.00	170.00
68	A31	$20 plum & bl (R)	425.00	325.00
		Nos. 47-68 (22)	990.65	626.05

See #69, 114. For overprints see #C1-C3.

Same Overprint on China No. 275

1926

No.	Type	Denomination / Color	Unused	Used
69	A29	4c olive green	5.50	5.50

Chang Tso-lin Stamps of China, 1928, Overprinted in Red or Blue

1928 *Perf. 14*

No.	Type	Denomination / Color	Unused	Used
70	A34	1c brn org (R)	1.75	1.75
71	A34	4c ol grn (R)	2.75	2.75
72	A34	10c dull bl (R)	6.50	6.50
73	A34	$1 red (Bl)	55.00	55.00
		Nos. 70-73 (4)	66.00	66.00

Unification Issue of China, 1929, Overprinted in Red as in 1928

1929

No.	Type	Denomination / Color	Unused	Used
74	A35	1c brown org	2.75	2.75
75	A35	4c olive grn	4.75	4.75
76	A35	10c dk blue	11.50	11.50
77	A35	$1 dk red	90.00	90.00
		Nos. 74-77 (4)	109.00	109.00

Similar Overprint in Black on Sun Yat-sen Mausoleum Issue of China Characters 15mm apart

1929 *Perf. 14*

No.	Type	Denomination / Color	Unused	Used
78	A36	1c brown org	2.25	2.25
79	A36	4c olive grn	3.50	*3.50*
80	A36	10c dark blue	8.00	*8.00*
81	A36	$1 dark red	95.00	95.00
		Nos. 78-81 (4)	108.75	108.75

Stamps of Sun Yat-sen Issue of 1931-37 Overprinted

1932 Type I *Perf. 12½*

No.	Type	Denomination / Color	Unused	Used
82	A37	1c orange	1.75	*4.00*
83	A37	2c olive grn	4.25	*5.75*
84	A37	4c green	2.50	*6.50*
85	A37	20c ultra	4.00	*8.25*
86	A37	$1 org brn & dk brn	12.00	*20.00*
87	A37	$2 bl & org brn	35.00	*42.50*
88	A37	$5 dl red & blk	40.00	*60.00*
		Nos. 82-88 (7)	99.50	*147.00*

No. 83 was overprinted in Shanghai in 1938. The overprint differs in minor details.

1932-38 Type II

No.	Type	Denomination / Color	Unused	Used
89	A37	2c olive grn	.45	*2.00*
90	A37	4c green	1.25	*4.00*
91	A37	5c green	.80	*4.00*
92	A37	15c dk green	1.10	*4.00*
93	A37	15c scar ('34)	1.10	*4.00*
93A	A37	20c ultra ('38)	.80	*2.75*
94	A37	25c ultra	1.25	*4.00*
95	A37	$1 org brn & dk brn	9.50	*11.00*
96	A37	$2 bl & org brn	20.00	*32.50*
97	A37	$5 dl red & blk	40.00	*65.00*
		Nos. 89-97 (10)	76.25	*133.25*

Nos. 89, 90 and 94 were overprinted in London, Peking and Shanghai. Nos. 92, 95-97 exist with London and Peking overprints. Nos. 91 and 93 exist with Peking and Shanghai overprints. No. 93A is a Shanghai overprint. The overprints differ in minor details.

Tan Yuan-chang Issue of China, 1933, Overprinted as in 1928

1933 *Perf. 14*

No.	Type	Denomination / Color	Unused	Used
98	A49	2c olive grn	3.75	3.75
99	A49	5c green	4.75	4.75
100	A49	25c ultra	15.00	15.00
101	A49	$1 red	75.00	65.00
		Nos. 98-101 (4)	98.50	88.50

Stamps of China Martyrs Issue of 1932-34 Overprinted

1933-34

No.	Type	Denomination / Color	Unused	Used
102	A39	½c black brown	.25	*3.50*
103	A40	1c orange	1.10	*4.25*
104	A39	2½c rose lilac	.25	*3.25*
105	A48	3c deep brown	.25	*3.25*
106	A45	8c brown orange	.75	*3.50*
107	A46	10c dull violet	.25	*3.25*
108	A45	13c blue green	.25	*4.50*
109	A46	17c brown olive	.25	*2.50*
110	A47	20c brown red	1.10	*6.50*
111	A48	30c brown violet	.40	*4.50*
112	A47	40c orange	.60	*3.25*
113	A40	50c green	.70	*2.50*
		Nos. 102-113 (12)	6.15	*44.75*

Nos. 102-113 were originally overprinted in Peking. In 1938, Nos. 103-105, 108-112 were overprinted in Shanghai. The two overprints differ in minor details. No. 105, Shanghai overprint, is scarce. Value $35.

China No. 324 Overprinted as in 1916-19

1936 *Perf. 14*

No.	Type	Denomination / Color	Unused	Used
114	A29	6c brown	20.00	*20.00*

Stamps of China, 1939-40 Overprinted in Black Type III

1940-45 Unwmk. *Perf. 12½*

No.	Type	Denomination / Color	Unused	Used
115	A57	2c olive green	.85	*1.00*
116	A57	3c dull claret ('41)	.25	*1.50*
117	A57	5c green	.25	*1.50*
118	A57	5c olive green	.25	*1.50*
119	A57	8c olive green ('41)	.25	*.75*
120	A57	10c green ('41)	.25	*1.10*
121	A57	15c scarlet	.55	*2.50*
122	A57	16c olive gray ('41)	.40	*1.00*
123	A57	25c dark blue	.55	*2.75*
124	A57	$1 hn & dk brn (type II)	6.25	*11.00*
125	A57	$2 dp bl & org brn (type I)	4.50	*11.00*
126	A57	$5 red & grnsh blk	26.00	*32.50*
		Nos. 115-126 (12)	40.35	*68.10*

Perf. 14

With Secret Marks

No.	Type	Denomination / Color	Unused	Used
127	A57	8c ol grn (#383a)	1.10	*1.65*
a.		On #383	19.00	*22.50*
128	A57	10c green ('41)	10.00	*13.00*
129	A57	30c scarlet ('45)	.30	*1.10*
130	A57	50c dk blue ('45)	.55	*1.75*
131	A57	$1 org brn & sep	.55	*2.25*
132	A57	$2 dp bl & org brn	.55	*2.25*
133	A57	$5 red & sl grn	.65	*3.75*
134	A57	$10 dk grn & dl pur	1.90	*2.75*
135	A57	$20 rose lake & dk bl	3.50	*5.50*
		Nos. 127-135 (9)	19.10	*34.00*

Wmk. Character Yu (Post) (261)

Perf. 14

No.	Type	Denomination / Color	Unused	Used
136	A57	5c olive green	.30	*2.50*
137	A57	10c green	.35	*3.75*
138	A57	30c scarlet	.35	*5.00*
139	A57	50c dark blue	.45	*2.50*
		Nos. 136-139 (4)	1.45	*13.75*

AIR POST STAMPS

Sinkiang Nos. 53, 57, 59, 32 Overprinted in Red

1932-33 Unwmk. *Perf. 14*

C1	A29	5c claret ('33)	400.00	290.00
C2	A29	10c dark blue ('33)	400.00	225.00
C3	A30	15c deep blue	2,700.	775.00
C4	A25	30c brown violet	1,170.	990.00

Counterfeits exist of Nos. C1-C4.

OFFICES IN TIBET

12 Pies = 1 Anna
16 Annas = 1 Rupee

Stamps of China, Issues of 1902-10, Surcharged

1911 Unwmk. *Perf. 12 to 16*

1	A17	3p on 1c ocher	27.50	*45.00*
a.		Inverted surcharge	*3,500.*	
2	A17	½a on 2c grn	27.50	*45.00*
3	A17	1a on 4c ver	27.50	*45.00*
4	A17	2a on 7c mar	27.50	*45.00*
5	A17	2½a on 10c ultra	35.00	*55.00*
6	A18	3a on 16c ol grn	70.00	*80.00*
a.		Large "S" in "Annas"	*1,250.*	
7	A18	4a on 20c red brn	70.00	*80.00*
8	A18	6a on 30c rose red	125.00	*140.00*
9	A18	12a on 50c yel grn	325.00	*400.00*
10	A19	1r on $1 red & pale rose	900.00	*900.00*
11	A19	2r on $2 red & yel	1,620.	*1,800.*
		Nos. 1-11 (11)	3,255.	3,635.

Beware of fake overprints.

SHANGHAI

shaŋ'hī

LOCATION — A city on the Whangpoo River, Kiangsu Province, China
POP. — 3,489,998

During 1842-1860, the Chinese government opened a number of ports for foreign trade, and European mercantile colonies were quickly established in these cities. The most active settlement was at Shanghai, where a British settlement was established in 1843, with French and American settlements soon following. The Shanghai Municipal Council was formed in 1854 to administer the foreign settlement. Virtually independent of Chinese control, the Council performed most government functions in Shanghai. Similar autonomous Western commercial settlements were later established in most of the treaty ports. Lack of confidence in existing Chinese postal services and dissatisfaction with the limited service provided by the British Hong Kong Postal Agency prompted the Shanghai Municipal Council to form the Shanghai Local Post in 1863. The first distinctive stamps for this service appeared in 1865, and Shanghai issues continued until 1897. Many of the other Chinese Treaty Ports joined the Shanghai Postal System, and the System handled more mail during its existence than the Imperial Customs Post, the Hong Kong Agencies, and all of the other foreign post offices. Ten of the ports within the system issued stamps during 1893-1897. On Nov. 1, 1897, the Shanghai Local Post was absorbed into the Imperial Chinese Post Office.

Cash Coin System

800-1600 Cash = 1 Tael

Dollar System

10 Cash = 1 Cent
10 Cents = 1 Chiao (Hao)
100 Cents = 1 Dollar (Yuan)
1 Dollar = .72 Tael

Tael System

10 Li = 1 Fen (Candereen)
10 Fen (Candereen) = 1 Ch'ien (Mace)
10 Ch'ien (Mace) = 1 Liang (Tael)

Covers: Although authentic used examples exist of many of Nos. 1-41a, covers are not known.

Margins: While unused stamps normally have wide margins and are valued in that condition, almost all known used examples have very narrow margins or are cut into the design, and are valued in that condition.

Watermark

Wmk. 175 — Kung Pu (Municipal Council)

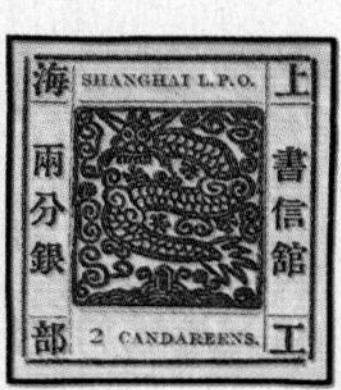

Dragon — A1

Antique Numerals Roman "I" in "I6" "Candareens" Plural

1865-66 Unwmk. Typo. *Imperf.*

Wove Paper

1	A1	2ca black	775.00	*7,500.*
a.		Pelure paper	900.00	
2	A1	4ca yellow	1,000.	*5,250.*
a.		Pelure paper	1,000.	—
b.		Double impression	—	
3	A1	8ca green	700.00	*6,000.*
a.		8ca yellow green	825.00	—
4	A1	16ca scarlet	2,250.	*6,000.*
a.		16ca vermilion	2,250.	
b.		Pelure paper	2,250.	
		Nos. 1-4 (4)	4,725.	24,750.

No. 1: top character of three in left panel as illustrated. No. 5: top character is two horiz. lines.

Nos. 2, 3: center character of three in left panel as illustrated. Nos. 6, 7: center character much more complex.

Antique Numerals "Candareens" Plural

Pelure Paper

5	A1	2ca black	650.00	
a.		Wove paper	650.00	6,250.
6	A1	4ca yellow	825.00	3,750.
7	A1	8ca dp grn	875.00	—
		Nos. 5-7 (3)	2,350.	

Antique Numerals "Candareen" Singular

Laid Paper

8	A1	1ca blue	800.00	*6,000.*
a.		1ca deep blue	375.00	
9	A1	2ca black	11,000.	
10	A1	4ca yellow	3,000.	
		Nos. 8-10 (3)	14,800.	

Wove Paper

11	A1	1ca blue	500.00	*7,750.*
12	A1	2ca black	650.00	*7,750.*
13	A1	4ca yellow	775.00	8,000.
14	A1	8ca ol grn	700.00	—
15	A1	16ca vermilion	700.00	—
a.		"1" of "16" omitted	26,000.	
		Nos. 11-15 (5)	3,325.	

Roman "I," Antique "2" "Candareens" Plural Except on 1ca

Wove Paper

16	A1	1ca blue	1,100.	*3,800.*
17	A1	12ca fawn	375.00	
18	A1	12ca choc	600.00	
		Nos. 16-18 (3)	2,075.	

Antique Numerals "Candareens" Plural Except on 1ca

Wove Paper

19	A1	1ca indigo, pelure paper	450.00	*5,500.*
a.		1ca blue, wove paper	425.00	*5,750.*
b.		1ca indigo, wove paper	175.00	
20	A1	3ca org brn	500.00	*4,250.*
a.		Pelure paper	525.00	*3,750.*
21	A1	6ca red brn	350.00	
22	A1	6ca fawn	875.00	—
23	A1	6ca vermilion	500.00	
24	A1	12ca org brn	325.00	
25	A1	16ca vermilion	325.00	*1,500.*
a.		"1" of "16" omitted	*500.00*	
		Nos. 19-25 (7)	3,325.	

Examples of No. 22 usually have the straight lines cutting through the paper.

Antique Numerals Roman "I" "Candareens" Plural Except on 1ca

Laid Paper

26	A1	1ca blue	*35,000.*	
27	A1	2ca black	*10,000.*	
28	A1	3ca red brn	*30,000.*	—

Examples of No. 28 usually have the straight lines cutting through the paper.

Modern Numerals "Candareen" Singular

29	A1	1ca sl bl	250.00	*4,500.*
a.		1ca dark blue	250.00	*4,250.*
30	A1	3ca red brn	250.00	*5,000.*

"Candareens" Plural Except the 1c

31	A1	2ca gray	225.00	
a.		2ca black	125.00	
32	A1	3ca red brn	225.00	*3,400.*

Coarse Porous Wove Paper

33a	A1	1ca blue	160.00	
34a	A1	2ca black	210.00	
b.		Grayish paper	275.00	
35a	A1	3ca red brown	150.00	
36a	A1	4ca yellow	350.00	
b.		4ca orange yellow	80.00	
37a	A1	6ca olive green	190.00	
b.		6ca bronze green	95.00	
38a	A1	8ca emerald	225.00	
b.		8ca green	95.00	
39a	A1	12ca org ver	160.00	
b.		12ca reddish orange	80.00	
40a	A1	16ca red	250.00	*875.00*
41a	A1	16ca red brown	225.00	*875.00*
		Nos. 33a-41a (9)	1,920.	

Chinese characters change on same denomination stamps.

Nos. 1, 2, 11 and 32 exist on thicker paper, usually toned. Most authorities consider these four stamps and Nos. 33a-41a to be official reprints made to present sample sets to other post offices. The tone in this paper is an acquired characteristic, due to various causes. Many shades and minor varieties exist of Nos. 1-41a.

A2

A3

A4

A5

1866 Litho. *Perf. 12*

42	A2	2c rose	27.50	*35.00*
43	A3	4c lilac	47.50	*60.00*
44	A4	8c gray blue	52.50	*55.00*
45	A5	16c green	82.50	*110.00*
		Nos. 42-45 (4)	210.00	260.00

Nos. 42-45 imperf. are proofs. See No. 50. For surcharges see Nos. 51-61, 67.

A6

A7

A8

A9

1866 *Perf. 15*

46	A6	1ca brown	11.00	17.50
a.		"CANDS"	200.00	200.00
47	A7	3ca orange	45.00	*60.00*
48	A8	6ca slate	47.50	*55.00*
49	A9	12ca olive gray	72.50	*110.00*
		Nos. 46-49 (4)	176.00	242.50

See Nos. 69-77. For surcharges see Nos. 62-66, 68, 78-83.

1872

50	A2	2c rose	170.00	*200.00*

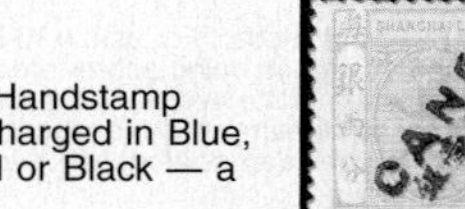

Handstamp Surcharged in Blue, Red or Black — a

1873 *Perf. 12*

51	A2	1ca on 2c rose	60.00	*65.00*
52	A3	1ca on 4c lilac	25.00	*37.50*
a.		Inverted surcharge	625.00	
b.		Double surcharge	725.00	
53	A3	1ca on 4c lilac (R)	*9,000.*	*3,750.*
a.		Double surch., 1 blue	*15,000.*	
54	A3	1ca on 4c lil (Bk)	25.00	*37.50*
a.		Inverted surcharge	300.00	
55	A4	1ca on 8c gray bl	52.50	*55.00*
a.		Double surcharge	625.00	
56	A4	1ca on 8c gray bl (R)	*22,000.*	*16,000.*
57	A5	1ca on 16c green	*4,250.*	*3,250.*
a.		Double surcharge	*15,000.*	
58	A5	1ca on 16c green (R)	*35,000.*	*13,500.*

Perf. 15

59	A2	1ca on 2c rose	72.50	*75.00*

1875 *Perf. 12*

60	A2	3ca on 2c rose	300.00	250.00
61	A5	3ca on 16c green	*4,250.*	*3,250.*

Perf. 15

62	A7	1ca on 3ca org	*38,000.*	*18,000.*
63	A8	1ca on 6ca slate	875.00	650.00
64	A8	1ca on 6ca slate (R)	*12,000.*	*4,500.*
65	A9	1ca on 12ca ol gray	1,100.	900.00
66	A9	1ca on 12ca ol gray (R)	*8,000.*	*4,000.*
67	A2	3ca on 2c rose	875.00	750.00
68	A9	3ca on 12ca olive gray	*6,000.*	*6,000.*

Counterfeits exist of Nos. 51-68.

Types of 1866

1875 *Perf. 15*

69	A6	1ca yel, *yel*	45.00	37.50
70	A7	3ca rose, *rose*	45.00	37.50

Perf. 11½

71	A6	1ca yel, *yel*	900.00	650.00

1876 *Perf. 15*

72	A6	1ca yellow	25.00	*30.00*
73	A7	3ca rose	95.00	*95.00*
74	A8	6ca green	140.00	*160.00*
75	A9	9ca blue	250.00	300.00
76	A9	12ca light brown	275.00	325.00
		Nos. 72-76 (5)	785.00	910.00

1877 Engr. *Perf. 12½*

77	A6	1ca rose	2,250.	*3,000.*

Stamps of 1875-76 Surcharged type "a" in Blue or Red

1877 Litho. *Perf. 15*

78	A7	1ca on 3ca rose, *rose*	550.00	475.00
79	A7	1ca on 3ca rose	170.00	150.00
a.		Double surcharge	2,250.	

80 A8 1ca on 6ca green 300.00 250.00
81 A9 1ca on 9ca blue 550.00 550.00
82 A9 1ca on 12ca lt brn 3,250. 2,000.
83 A9 1ca on 12ca lt brn (R) *8,500. 5,500.*

Counterfeits exist of Nos. 78-83.

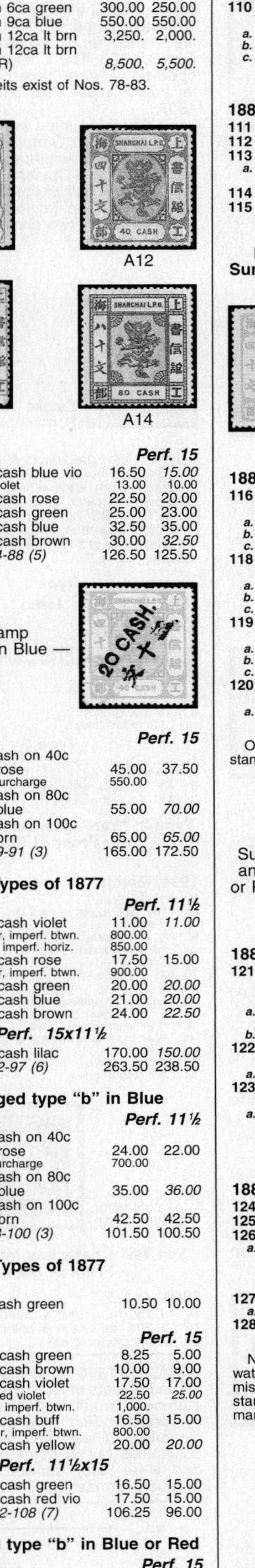

A11 A12

A13 A14

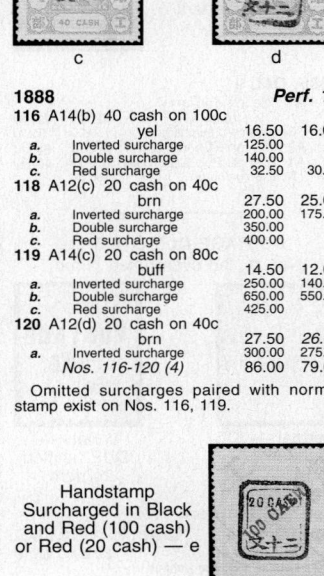

1877 ***Perf. 15***
84 A11 20 cash blue vio 16.50 *15.00*
a. 20 cash violet 13.00 10.00
85 A12 40 cash rose 22.50 20.00
86 A13 60 cash green 25.00 23.00
87 A14 80 cash blue 32.50 35.00
88 A14 100 cash brown 30.00 *32.50*
Nos. 84-88 (5) 126.50 125.50

Handstamp Surcharged in Blue — b

1879 ***Perf. 15***
89 A12 20 cash on 40c rose 45.00 37.50
a. Inverted surcharge 550.00
90 A14 60 cash on 80c blue 55.00 *70.00*
91 A14 60 cash on 100c brn 65.00 *65.00*
Nos. 89-91 (3) 165.00 172.50

Types of 1877

1880 ***Perf. 11½***
92 A11 20 cash violet 11.00 *11.00*
a. Horiz. pair, imperf. btwn. 800.00
b. Vert. pair, imperf. horiz. 850.00
93 A12 40 cash rose 17.50 15.00
a. Horiz. pair, imperf. btwn. 900.00
94 A13 60 cash green 20.00 *20.00*
95 A14 80 cash blue 21.00 *20.00*
96 A14 100 cash brown 24.00 *22.50*

Perf. 15x11½
97 A11 20 cash lilac 170.00 *150.00*
Nos. 92-97 (6) 263.50 238.50

Surcharged type "b" in Blue

1884 ***Perf. 11½***
98 A12 20 cash on 40c rose 24.00 22.00
a. Double surcharge 700.00
99 A14 60 cash on 80c blue 35.00 *36.00*
100 A14 60 cash on 100c brn 42.50 42.50
Nos. 98-100 (3) 101.50 100.50

Types of 1877

1884
101 A11 20 cash green 10.50 10.00

1885 ***Perf. 15***
102 A11 20 cash green 8.25 5.00
103 A12 40 cash brown 10.00 9.00
104 A13 60 cash violet 17.50 17.00
a. 60 cash red violet 22.50 *25.00*
b. Vert. pair, imperf. btwn. 1,000.
105 A14 80 cash buff 16.50 15.00
a. Horiz. pair, imperf. btwn. 800.00
106 A14 100 cash yellow 20.00 *20.00*

Perf. 11½x15
107 A11 20 cash green 16.50 15.00
108 A13 60 cash red vio 17.50 15.00
Nos. 102-108 (7) 106.25 96.00

Surcharged type "b" in Blue or Red

1886 ***Perf. 15***
109 A14 40 cash on 80c buff 13.50 12.00
a. Inverted surcharge 20.00 18.00
b. Red surcharge 550.00

110 A14 60 cash on 100c yellow 20.00 18.00
a. Inverted surcharge 100.00 100.00
b. Double surcharge 225.00
c. Red surcharge 600.00

Types of 1877

1888 ***Perf. 15***
111 A11 20 cash gray 9.50 5.50
112 A12 40 cash black 13.00 *9.50*
113 A13 60 cash rose 20.00 12.00
a. Third character at left lacks dot at top 27.50 *20.00*
114 A14 80 cash green 14.00 10.00
115 A14 100 cash lt blue 20.00 *17.50*
Nos. 111-115 (5) 76.50 54.50

Nos. 106, 103, 105 Handstamp Surcharged in Blue or Red Type "b" or

c d

1888 ***Perf. 15***
116 A14(b) 40 cash on 100c yel 16.50 16.00
a. Inverted surcharge 125.00
b. Double surcharge 140.00
c. Red surcharge 32.50 30.00
118 A12(c) 20 cash on 40c brn 27.50 25.00
a. Inverted surcharge 200.00 175.00
b. Double surcharge 350.00
c. Red surcharge 400.00
119 A14(c) 20 cash on 80c buff 14.50 12.00
a. Inverted surcharge 250.00 140.00
b. Double surcharge 650.00 550.00
c. Red surcharge 425.00
120 A12(d) 20 cash on 40c brn 27.50 *26.00*
a. Inverted surcharge 300.00 275.00
Nos. 116-120 (4) 86.00 79.00

Omitted surcharges paired with normal stamp exist on Nos. 116, 119.

Handstamp Surcharged in Black and Red (100 cash) or Red (20 cash) — e

1889 **Unwmk.**
121 A14(e) 100 cash on 20c on 100c yel 200.00 *225.00*
a. Without the surcharge "100 cash" 500.00
b. Blue & red surcharge 1,800. —
122 A14(c) 20 cash on 80c grn 16.50 15.00
a. Inverted surcharge 140.00
123 A14(c) 20 cash on 100c bl 16.50 15.00
a. Double surcharge 350.00
Nos. 121-123 (3) 233.00 255.00

Counterfeits exist of Nos. 116-123.

1889 **Wmk. 175** ***Perf. 15***
124 A11 20 cash gray 5.75 4.25
125 A12 40 cash black 8.50 7.00
126 A13 60 cash rose 27.50 *27.50*
a. Third character at left lacks dot at top 30.00 *30.00*

Perf. 12
127 A14 80 cash green 11.00 *22.00*
a. Horiz. pair, imperf. btwn. 2,000.
128 A14 100 cash dk bl 17.50 22.00
Nos. 124-128 (5) 70.25 82.75

Nos. 124-126 are sometimes found without watermark. This is caused by the sheet being misplaced in the printing press, so that the stamps are printed on the unwatermarked margin of the sheet.

Shield with Dragon Supporters — A20

1890 **Unwmk.** **Litho.** ***Perf. 15***
129 A20 2c brown 4.25 *4.75*
130 A20 5c rose 12.00 8.00
131 A20 15c blue 27.50 15.00

Nos. 129-131 imperforate are proofs.

Wmk. 175
132 A20 10c black 17.50 12.00
a. Perf. 12 1,000. 550.00
133 A20 15c blue 25.00 18.00
134 A20 20c violet 17.50 14.00
Nos. 129-134 (6) 103.75 71.75

See Nos. 135-141. For surcharges and overprints see Nos. 142-152, J1-J13.

1891 ***Perf. 12***
135 A20 2c brown 3.00 2.00
136 A20 5c rose 13.00 7.00

1892
137 A20 2c green 3.50 2.50
a. Bisect used as 1c on cover —
138 A20 5c red 8.25 7.25
139 A20 10c orange 22.00 *22.00*
140 A20 15c violet 13.50 10.00
141 A20 20c brown 14.50 13.00
Nos. 137-141 (5) 61.75 54.75

No. 130 Handstamp Surcharged in Blue — f

1892 **Unwmk.** ***Perf. 15***
142 A20 2c on 5c rose 175.00 80.00
a. Inverted surcharge 1,000. 850.00

Counterfeits exist of Nos. 142-152.

Stamps of 1892 Handstamp Surcharged in Blue

g h

1893 **Wmk. 175** ***Perf. 12***
143 A20 ½c on 15c violet 20.00 13.00
a. Double surcharge 375.00
b. Vert. pair, imperf. btwn. 350.00 325.00
144 A20 1c on 20c brown 20.00 13.00
a. ½c on 20c brown (error) *26,000.*

Nos. 144 and 144a exist in se-tenant pairs. Example pairs with black surcharge come from a trial printing.

Surcharged in Blue or Red (#152) on Halves of #136 (#145-147), #138 (#148-150), #135 (#151), #137 (#152)

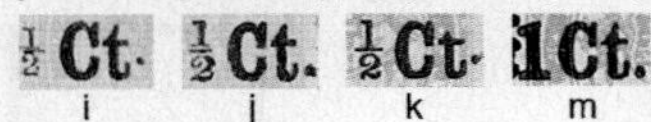

i j k m

145 A20(i) ½c on half of 5c 13.50 10.00
146 A20(j) ½c on half of 5c 13.50 10.00
147 A20(k) ½c on half of 5c 275.00 200.00
148 A20(i) ½c on half of 5c 13.50 10.00
149 A20(j) ½c on half of 5c 13.50 10.00
150 A20(k) ½c on half of 5c 225.00 160.00
151 A20(m) 1c on half of 2c 3.50 3.00
c. Dbl. surch., one in green 1,600. *350.00*
d. Dbl. surch., one in black 1,700. *350.00*
152 A20(m) 1c on half of 2c 16.50 12.00
Nos. 145-152 (8) 574.00 415.00

The ½c surcharge setting of 20 (2x10) covers a vertical strip of 10 unsevered stamps, with horizontal gutter midway. This setting has 11 of type "i," 8 of type "j" and 1 of type "k." Nos. 145-152 are perforated vertically down the middle.

Inverted surcharges exist on Nos. 145-151. Double surcharges, one inverted, are also found in this issue.

Handstamped provisionals somewhat similar to Nos. 145-152 were issued in Foochow by the Shanghai Agency.

Coat of Arms — A24

Typo. (Dot)

Litho. (No Dot)

Frame Inscriptions in Black

1893 **Litho.** ***Perf. 13½x14***
153 A24 ½c orange 7.25 3.00
b. Horiz. pair, imperf vert. 225.00
154 A24 1c brown 7.25 1.75
155 A24 2c vermilion 8.00 2.50
a. Imperf, pair 225.00
156 A24 5c blue 1.10 .65
a. Black inscriptions inverted 1,800.
b. Black inscriptions double 900.00
157 A24 10c green 10.00 *11.00*
158 A24 15c yellow 1.10 .90
159 A24 20c lilac 11.00 9.00
Nos. 153-159 (7) 45.70 28.80

Typographed

153a A24 ½c orange .55 .50
154a A24 1c brown .55 .50

Typo & Litho

157a A24 10c green 2.75 *3.00*
159a A24 20c lilac 3.00 *5.00*

On Nos. 157 and 159, frame inscriptions are lithographed, rest of design typographed.

See Nos. 170-172. For overprints and surcharges see Nos. 160-166, 168-169.

Stamps of 1893 Overprinted in Black

1893, Dec. 14
160 A24 ½c (On #153a) .50 .50
a. Inverted overprint 165.00 150.00
161 A24 1c (On #154a) .65 .65
a. Double overprint 67.50 50.00
162 A24 2c (On #155) .90 .90
a. Inverted overprint 165.00 120.00
163 A24 5c (On #156) 3.50 *5.00*
a. Inverted overprint 325.00
164 A24 10c (On #157a) 11.00 *12.00*
165 A24 15c (On #158) 7.25 6.50
166 A24 20c (On #159) 9.50 *10.00*
Nos. 160-166 (7) 33.30 35.55

50th anniv. of the first foreign settlement in Shanghai.

Mercury — A26

1893, Nov. 11 **Litho.** ***Perf. 13½***
167 A26 2c vermilion & black 1.10 1.00

Nos. 158 and 159 Handstamp Surcharged in Black

1896 *Perf. 13½x14*

168 A24 4c on 15c yel & blk 11.00 8.00
169 A24 6c on 20c lil & blk (#159) 11.00 8.00
a. On #159a 55.00 25.00

Surcharge occurs inverted or double on Nos. 168-169.

Arms Type of 1893

1896

170 A24 2c scarlet & blk .30 *1.60*
a. Black inscriptions inverted 2,000. 1,800.
b. Black inscriptions double 1,400. 1,200.
171 A24 4c org & blk, *yel* 7.25 *5.50*
172 A24 6c car & blk, *rose* 8.25 *8.50*
Nos. 170-172 (3) 15.80 *15.60*

POSTAGE DUE STAMPS

Postage Stamps of 1890-92 Handstamped in Black, Red or Blue

1892 **Unwmk.** ***Perf. 15***

J1 A20 2c brown (Bk) 900.00 *900.00*
a. Inverted overprint 2,500.
J2 A20 5c rose (Bk) 25.00 *14.00*
a. Inverted overprint 425.00
J3 A20 15c blue (Bk) 52.50 47.50
a. Inverted overprint 400.00
b. Blue overprint 425.00

Wmk. 175

J4 A20 10c black (R) 35.00 32.50
J5 A20 15c blue (Bk) 30.00 27.50
a. Inverted overprint 600.00
b. Double overprint 300.00
c. Pair, one without ovpt. 1,300.
J6 A20 20c violet (Bk) 22.50 20.00
Nos. J1-J6 (6) 1,065. 1,042.

1892-93 ***Perf. 12***

J7 A20 2c brown (Bk) 3.75 3.75
a. Inverted overprint 175.00 160.00
b. Double overprint 400.00
c. Pair, one without ovpt. 1,000.
J8 A20 2c brown (Bl) 3.50 *3.00*
J9 A20 5c rose (Bl) 15.50 9.00
a. Inverted overprint 225.00
J10 A20 10c orange (Bk) 250.00 225.00
J11 A20 10c orange (Bl) 20.00 15.00
a. Inverted overprint 325.00
J12 A20 15c violet (R) 32.50 30.00
J13 A20 20c brown (R) 32.50 30.00
Nos. J7-J13 (7) 357.75 *315.75*

D2

1893 **Litho.** ***Perf. 13½***

J14 D2 ½c orange & blk .55 .55

Perf. 14x13½

J15 D2 1c brown & black .65 .55
a. Horiz. pair, imperf. vert. 350.00
J16 D2 2c ver & blk .65 .55
a. Horiz. pair, imperf. vert. 350.00
J17 D2 5c blue & black 1.00 .90
J18 D2 10c green & black 6.00 2.00
J19 D2 15c yellow & black 4.75 4.00
J20 D2 20c violet & black 1.75 1.50
Nos. J14-J20 (7) 15.35 10.05

Stamps of Shanghai were discontinued in 1898.

CHINA TREATY PORTS

Wmk. 402 — Chinese Characters

AMOY

A seaport on an island located off the coast of Fukien Province, in south China. The Shanghai Local Post was handling mail from Amoy as early as 1863, but a formal branch office was not established until 1890. Shanghai stamps were used from 1890 until Mar. 31, 1895, when the post office was taken over by the Amoy Local Council. Amoy stamps were used from June 8, 1895, until Feb. 2, 1897, when mail services came under control of the Imperial Chinese Post Office.

All Amoy issues were printed by Schleicher and Schull, Duren, Germany.

Egrets — A1

Type 1

Type 2

Perf. 11½

1895, June 8-1896 **Unwmk.** **Litho.**

1 A1 ½c green 6.00 *7.00*
2 A1 1c rose red 5.00 3.50
a. 1c aniline rose red 6.00 4.00
3 A1 2c blue, Type 1 80.00 *85.00*
4 A1 2c blue, Type 2 16.00 16.00
5 A1 4c brown 15.00 *16.00*
6 A1 5c orange 16.00 16.00

Two lithographic stones were made for the ½ cent value, with the first used for the June 8, 1895, printing and the second used for a second printing on May 11, 1896, when Nos. 11-13 were printed. Plating details are needed to differentiate the two printings.

No. 1 also exists with papermaker's watermark "C S & S" in script letters.

Nos. 5 and 6 surcharged in two lines, wide "f"

1896, May 8

7 A1 Half Cent on 4c brown 35.00 *45.00*
8 A1 Half Cent on 5c orange 35.00 *45.00*

Nos. 5 and 6 surcharged "1/2"c, "2" with curved foot

1896, May 9

9 A1 ½c on 4c brown 50.00 52.50
a. "2" with straight foot 115.00 *95.00*
10 A1 ½c on 5c orange 45.00 52.50
a. "2" with straight foot 110.00 *85.00*
b. Double surcharge 1,750.
c. Double surcharge, one red 1,600.
d. As "a," double surcharge 1,750.

1896, May 11 **Wmk. 402**

11 A1 15c gray black 40.00 *25.00*
12 A1 20c violet 40.00 *25.00*
13 A1 25c lilac rose 45.00 *35.00*

Nos. 5 and 6 surcharged in two lines, narrow "f"

Surcharged in Blue

1896, May 20 **Unwmk.**

14 A1 ½c on 4c brown 65.00 *100.00*
a. "G" instead of "C" in cent 950.00 *850.00*
15 A1 ½c on 5c orange 65.00 *100.00*
a. "G" instead of "C" in cent 950.00 *850.00*

Surcharged in Black

16 A1 ½c on 4c brown 21.00 *23.00*
17 A1 ½c on 5c orange 21.00 *23.00*

Nos. 11-13 surcharged, dropped "C"

1896, Oct. 1 **Wmk. 402**

18 A1 3c on 15c gray black 22.50 *35.00*
19 A1 6c on 20c violet 22.50 *35.00*
20 A1 10c on 25c lilac rose 22.50 *40.00*
a. Blue surcharge with bar in black *750.00*
b. Blue surcharge —
c. Double surcharge, one blue, one black —

Nos. 11-13 surcharged in red (R) or black, "C" in line with other letters

1896, Oct. 9

21 A1 3c on 15c gray black (R) 40.00 *42.50*
a. Brownish red surcharge 50.00 *55.00*
22 A1 6c on 20c violet (R) 40.00 *45.00*
23 A1 10c on 25c lilac rose 40.00 *45.00*
a. Double surcharge *600.00*

POSTAGE DUE STAMPS

Nos. 1, 3-6 overprinted in red

Normal — "D" under "S"

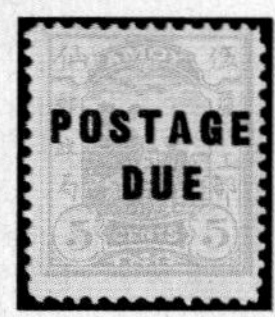

Variety — "DUE" shifted to right

Perf. 11½

1895, Oct. 14 **Unwmk.** **Litho.**

J1 A1 ½c green 30.00 *32.50*
a. Vertical pair, one without ovpt. 575.00
b. Vertical pair, one with red ovpt., one with black —
c. "DUE" shifted to right — —
J2 A1 2c blue, type 1 *525.00 525.00*
a. "DUE" shifted to right —
J3 A1 2c blue, type 2 30.00 *30.00*
a. "DUE" shifted to right 550.00 *550.00*
J4 A1 4c brown 30.00 *30.00*
a. "DUE" shifted to right 550.00 *550.00*
J5 A1 5c orange 30.00 *30.00*
a. "DUE" shifted to right 550.00 *550.00*

Overprinted in Black

J6 A1 ½c green 13.00 *12.00*
a. Double overprint *800.00 600.00*
b. Inverted overprint —
c. "DUE" shifted to right 400.00 *300.00*
J7 A1 1c rose red *9.00 10.00*
a. Double overprint *1,200.*
b. Inverted overprint 600.00 *1,000.*
c. "DUE" shifted to right 550.00 *600.00*
J8 A1 2c blue, type 1 *650.00* —
J9 A1 2c blue, type 2 100.00 *75.00*
a. "DUE" shifted to right 550.00 —
J10 A1 4c brown 52.50 *42.50*
a. "DUE" shifted to right *400.00 400.00*
J11 A1 5c orange 52.50 *42.50*
a. "DUE" shifted to right *400.00 400.00*

No. 2 overprinted in Roman (serifed) Type

1896, June 1

J12 A1 1c rose red *700.00 700.00*

CHEFOO

A seaport in Shantung Province, on the Straits of Pechile. It was opened to foreign trade by the Treaty of Peking in 1860 and by the 1890's had become a bustling city. Because of its pleasant climate, Chefoo became a favorite summer vacation area for foreigners in China. The Chefoo Local Post Committee was formed in mid-1893, and the first stamps for Chefoo were issued on Oct. 6, 1893. The Chefoo Local Post's operations were taken over by the Imperial Chinese Post Office on Feb. 2, 1897.

All Chefoo issues were printed by Schleicher and Schull, Duren, Germany. All were impressed with a faux watermark, the Chinese character for Yan, the first half of the Chinese name for Chefoo, Yan-Tai. Nos. 14-16 are impressed with two characters, for the full city name.

Smoke Tower and Semaphore — A1

Type 1: the right bottom of the "H" and the left bottom of the "E" of "CHEFOO" are clearly separated from each other; the ball of the semaphore is clear. Type 2: the "H" and the "E" of "CHEFOO" are nearly touching; the ball of the semaphore is not clear, and the rim is irregular; there is a hairline in the lower right of the outer frame.

Type 1

1893, Oct. 6 **Litho.** ***Perf. 11½***

1 A1 ½c green 27.50 22.50
2 A1 1c red 9.00 7.00
3 A1 2c ultramarine 27.50 *24.00*
a. Vertical pair, imperf between 950.00
b. 2c pale blue 30.00 *23.00*
4 A1 5c orange 30.00 *30.00*
a. Pair, imperf. 700.00
5 A1 10c brown 30.00 *23.00*
a. 10c reddish brown 32.50 *25.00*

Type 2

1894, Jan.

6 A1 ½c dark gray green 5.00 3.00
7 A1 5c red orange 9.00 8.00

Type 2; "Yan" Character Impressed on Front of Stamp

1894, March

8 A1 ½c green 5.00 2.75
a. "Yan" impression on back of stamp 12.00 12.00
9 A1 1c scarlet 2.75 2.00
a. "Yan" impressed on back of stamp 12.00 12.00
10 A1 1c rose red 4.00 *7.00*
11 A1 2c blue 6.00 *6.00*
a. Pair, imperf between —
12 A1 5c brown orange 9.00 8.00
a. "Yan" impression inverted 30.00
b. "Yan" impression on back of stamp 13.50 12.50
13 A1 10c brown 9.00 9.00
a. 10c reddish brown 12.50 12.50

Harbor Scene — A2

"Yan Tai" Characters Impressed on Front of Stamp

1896, Jan.

14 A2 15c red brown & green 18.00 *22.00*
15 A2 20c red brown & violet 27.50 *24.00*
16 A2 25c violet & red 18.00 *22.00*

In Jan. 1896 a postal clerk overprinted 56 sets of Nos. 1-5 with a handstamped two-line "POSTAGE DUE" overprint, applied either horizontally or diagonally. These were sold from the post office but were never authorized and were later condemned by the Chefoo postmaster.

CHINKIANG

An ancient strategic city on the Yangtze River, 112 miles inland from Shanghai. Chinkiang became a Treaty Port in 1860, and in 1864 a British trading settlement was established in the city. By 1866, Chinkiang was a part of the Shanghai Postal System. On Aug. 6, 1894, postal operations were taken over by the Chinkiang Local Post Office. On Feb. 2, 1897, the Chinkiang mail service was absorbed into the Imperial Chinese Post.

All Chinkiang Local Post stamps were printed by Tokyo Tsukiji Foundry Co., Japan.

Golden Mountain — A1

Perf. 11½

1894, Aug. 6 Unwmk. Litho.

No.	Type	Description	Unused	Used
1	A1	½c rose	5.00	5.50
a.		Horiz. pair, imperf between	175.00	
b.		Vert. pair, imperf between	150.00	
c.		½c aniline rose	7.00	7.00
2	A1	1c blue	2.50	2.50
a.		Horiz. strip of 3, imperf vert.	300.00	300.00
b.		Perf 11½x11	11.00	11.00
3	A1	2c brown	7.50	8.00
a.		Perf 11½x11	10.00	10.00
4	A1	4c yellow	10.00	10.00
a.		Perf 11	11.00	11.00
5	A1	5c green	10.00	11.00
a.		Perf 11½x11	10.00	10.00
b.		Horiz. pair, imperf between	275.00	
c.		Vert. pair, imperf between	300.00	
6	A1	6c mauve	15.00	13.00
a.		Perf 11	13.00	13.50
b.		Perf 11½x11	16.00	16.00
c.		Perf 11x11½	10.00	10.00
d.		Horiz. pair, imperf between	250.00	
7	A1	10c orange	20.00	15.00
a.		Perf 11½x11	22.00	22.00
b.		Perf 11	14.00	14.00
c.		Perf 11x11½	14.00	14.00

Golden Mountain — A2

Type A2 is similar to A1, but clouds have been added to the sky, and shading added to the river.

1895, Apr. 9

No.	Type	Description	Unused	Used
8	A2	½c rose red	13.00	12.00
9	A2	1c blue	11.00	10.00
10	A2	2c brown	35.00	32.50
11	A2	4c yellow	20.00	20.00
12	A2	5c emerald green	20.00	20.00
13	A2	6c mauve	24.00	26.00
a.		Horiz. pair, imperf vert.	300.00	200.00
b.		Horiz. pair, imperf between	325.00	250.00
c.		Imperf, pair	—	
14	A2	10c orange	20.00	20.00
15	A2	15c carmine red	26.00	27.50

POSTAGE DUE STAMPS

Nos. 1-7 overprinted, narrow (1.5mm) spacing between "DUE" and Chinese characters

Perf. 11½

1894, Dec. 21 Unwmk. Litho.

No.	Type	Description	Unused	Used
J1	A1	½c rose	13.00	12.00
a.		Inverted overprint	82.50	72.50
b.		Double overprint	150.00	95.00
J2	A1	1c blue	12.00	9.00
a.		Inverted overprint	87.50	80.00
b.		Double overprint, one inverted	250.00	
J3	A1	2c brown	12.00	11.00
a.		Inverted overprint	85.00	80.00
b.		Double overprint	225.00	225.00
J4	A1	4c yellow	13.00	15.00
a.		Inverted overprint	120.00	95.00
b.		Vert. pair, imperf between	200.00	
c.		Perf 11	14.00	14.00
J5	A1	5c green	13.00	13.00
a.		Inverted overprint	110.00	95.00
J6	A1	6c mauve	16.00	15.00
a.		Inverted overprint	120.00	110.00
b.		Perf 11	14.00	14.00
c.		As "b," inverted overprint	115.00	100.00
d.		Perf 11x11½	20.00	20.00
J7	A1	10c orange	11.00	11.00
a.		Inverted overprint	115.00	100.00
b.		Perf 11x11½	13.00	13.00
c.		Perf 11½x11	13.00	13.00
d.		Vert. pair, imperf between	130.00	

Nos. 1-7, 15 Ovptd., Wide (2.5mm) Spacing Between "DUE" & Chinese Characters

POSTAGE DUE 銀 欠

Split "P" Variety

POSTAGE DUE 銀 欠

1895, Apr. 9 Red Overprint

No.	Type	Description	Unused	Used
J8	A1	½c rose	190.00	160.00
a.		Inverted overprint	250.00	250.00
b.		Pair, one with inverted overprint	450.00	450.00
c.		Split "P"	250.00	250.00
d.		Inverted overprint, Split "P"	325.00	325.00

Overprinted in Black over Red

No.	Type	Description	Unused	Used
J9	A1	½c rose	275.00	310.00
a.		Both overprints inverted	350.00	350.00
b.		Pair, one with inverted overprint	550.00	550.00
J10	A1	1c blue	275.00	310.00
a.		Both overprints inverted	550.00	550.00
b.		Pair, one with inverted overprint	500.00	500.00
J11	A1	2c brown	275.00	310.00
a.		Both overprints inverted	350.00	350.00
J12	A1	4c yellow	275.00	310.00
a.		"DUE" omitted in red ovpt.	350.00	
b.		Both overprints inverted	550.00	550.00
J13	A1	5c green	275.00	310.00
a.		Both overprints inverted	350.00	350.00
J14	A1	6c mauve	275.00	310.00
a.		Both overprints inverted	550.00	550.00
J15	A1	10c orange	275.00	310.00
a.		Both overprints inverted	650.00	650.00
b.		Perf 11½x11	325.00	325.00
c.		Perf 11x11½	375.00	375.00
J16	A1	15c carmine	275.00	310.00
a.		Both overprints inverted	350.00	350.00
b.		Red overprint double	—	

Overprinted in Black over Red, Split "P" Variety

No.	Type	Description	Unused	Used
J9c	A1	½c rose	350.00	350.00
d.		Both overprints inverted	650.00	650.00
J10c	A1	1c blue	350.00	350.00
d.		Both overprints inverted	650.00	650.00
J11b	A1	2c brown	350.00	350.00
c.		Both overprints inverted	650.00	650.00
J12c	A1	4c yellow	350.00	350.00
d.		Both overprints inverted	650.00	650.00
J13b	A1	5c green	350.00	350.00
c.		Both overprints inverted	650.00	650.00
J14b	A1	6c mauve	350.00	350.00
c.		Both overprints inverted	650.00	650.00
J15d	A1	10c orange	350.00	350.00
e.		Both overprints inverted	650.00	650.00
f.		Perf 11x11½	350.00	350.00
J16c	A1	15c carmine	350.00	350.00
d.		Both overprints inverted	650.00	650.00

Black Overprint

No.	Type	Description	Unused	Used
J17	A1	½c rose	9.00	7.00
a.		Inverted overprint	275.00	77.50
b.		Pair, one with inverted overprint	325.00	
c.		"U" of "DUE" omitted	300.00	300.00
d.		"U" of "DUE" handstamped	350.00	
e.		"DU" of "DUE" omitted	350.00	
f.		"DU" handstamped	350.00	
J18	A1	1c blue	9.00	8.00
a.		Inverted overprint	275.00	
b.		Double overprint, one inverted	—	
c.		Pair, one with inverted overprint	300.00	
J19	A1	2c brown	20.00	20.00
a.		Inverted overprint	275.00	
b.		Double overprint	—	
c.		Horiz. pair, imperf between	200.00	200.00
d.		Perf 11½x11	22.50	25.00
J20	A1	4c yellow	15.00	16.00
a.		Inverted overprint	275.00	
J21	A1	5c green	77.50	82.50
a.		Inverted overprint	190.00	
J22	A1	6c mauve	19.00	16.50
a.		Inverted overprint	425.00	
b.		Double overprint, one inverted	—	
J23	A1	10c orange	15.00	42.50
a.		Inverted overprint	275.00	
b.		Perf 11½x11	40.00	40.00
c.		As "b," inverted overprint	275.00	
d.		Perf 11x11½	32.50	32.50
J24	A1	15c carmine	20.00	22.50
a.		Inverted overprint	275.00	
b.		Double overprint, one inverted	350.00	

Overprinted in Black, Split "P" Variety

No.	Type	Description	Unused	Used
J17g	A1	½c rose	65.00	—
h.		Inverted overprint	350.00	
J18d	A1	1c blue	65.00	—
e.		Inverted overprint	350.00	
J19e	A1	2c brown	65.00	—
J20b	A1	4c yellow	77.50	—
J21b	A1	5c green	65.00	—
a.		Inverted overprint	190.00	
J22c	A1	6c mauve	65.00	—
d.		Inverted overprint	500.00	
J23e	A1	10c orange	65.00	—
f.		Inverted overprint	500.00	500.00
g.		Perf 11½x11	65.00	—
h.		Perf 11x11½	65.00	—
i.		As "h," inverted overprint	350.00	
J24c	A1	15c carmine	65.00	—
d.		Inverted overprint	350.00	

Nos. 8-15 overprinted

1895

No.	Type	Description	Unused	Used
J25	A2	½c rose	9.00	9.00
a.		Inverted overprint	60.00	50.00
b.		Double overprint	—	
J26	A2	1c blue	10.00	10.00
a.		Inverted overprint	60.00	50.00
J27	A2	2c brown	35.00	30.00
a.		Inverted overprint	90.00	90.00
b.		Double overprint	—	
J28	A2	4c yellow	27.50	27.50
a.		Inverted overprint	90.00	90.00
J29	A2	5c green	32.50	30.00
a.		Inverted overprint	90.00	90.00
J30	A2	6c mauve	32.50	35.00
a.		Inverted overprint	90.00	90.00
J31	A2	10c orange	30.00	30.00
a.		Inverted overprint	100.00	100.00
J32	A2	15c carmine	45.00	35.00
a.		Inverted overprint	110.00	110.00

Split "P" Variety

No.	Type	Description	Unused	Used
J25c	A2	½c rose	50.00	50.00
J26b	A2	1c blue	50.00	50.00
J27c	A2	2c brown	50.00	50.00
J28b	A2	4c yellow	60.00	60.00
J29b	A2	5c green	60.00	60.00
J30b	A2	6c mauve	60.00	60.00
J31b	A2	10c orange	60.00	60.00
J32b	A2	15c carmine	75.00	75.00

D1

Perf. 11, 11½ (#J33, J36, J39)

1895, Apr. 9

No.	Type	Description	Unused	Used
J33	D1	½c rose	8.00	8.00
a.		Pair, imperf.	200.00	
J34	D1	1c blue	9.00	9.00
a.		Pair, imperf.	200.00	
b.		Vert. pair, imperf between	250.00	250.00
c.		Perf 11½x11	9.00	9.00
J35	D1	2c brown	20.00	20.00
J36	D1	4c yellow	15.00	15.00
J37	D1	5c green	22.50	22.50
a.		Perf 11½	24.00	24.00
J38	D1	6c mauve	20.00	18.00
a.		Pair, imperf.	175.00	
b.		Vert. pair, imperf between	225.00	200.00
J39	D1	10c orange	16.00	17.50
J40	D1	15c carmine	22.50	24.00
a.		Perf 11½	24.00	25.00

Nos. J37, J37a surcharged in red

1895, Sept. 11

No.	Type	Description	Unused	Used
J41	D1	FIVE CENTS on 5c green (#J37a)	40.00	40.00
a.		Inverted surcharge	250.00	190.00
b.		On #J37	45.00	45.00
c.		Inverted surcharge	275.00	275.00

OFFICIAL STAMPS

Nos. 8-15 overprinted

1896

No.	Type	Description	Unused	Used
O1	A2	½c rose	10.00	16.00
a.		Inverted overprint	60.00	
O2	A2	1c blue	16.00	20.00
a.		Inverted overprint	60.00	
O3	A2	2c brown	26.00	16.50
a.		Inverted overprint	60.00	
O4	A2	4c yellow	35.00	26.00
a.		Inverted overprint	100.00	
O5	A2	5c green	35.00	32.50
a.		Inverted overprint	100.00	
O6	A2	6c mauve	27.50	26.00
a.		Inverted overprint	100.00	
O7	A2	10c orange	35.00	32.50
a.		Inverted overprint	100.00	
O8	A2	15c carmine	200.00	190.00
a.		Inverted overprint	200.00	

Inverted overprint with period is probably from a trial printing.

CHUNGKING

An ancient port city on the Yangtze River, some 1,500 miles above Shanghai, which served as a main hub for trade between the interior provinces and the coast. Chungking was opened to foreign trade in 1890. Mail service to the outside world was slow and expensive, and on Nov. 1, 1893, the Chunking Local Post was established to provide improved services at lower rates. It opened offices in Ichang and Shanghai and issued its first stamps in Dec. 1893. It was replaced by the Imperial Chinese Post Office on Feb. 2, 1897, but, because of the lack of government service, the local post continued operations for a few months.

Nos. 1 and 2 were lithographed by Kelly and Walsh, Shanghai. Nos. 3-7 were lithographed by Tokyo Tsukiji Type Foundry Co., Tokyo, Japan, in sheets of 50 (10x5).

Forgeries exist of the rarer Chungking stamps and covers. These should be purchased with certificates of authenticity from knowledgeable authorities.

Pagoda and Junk — A1

Perf. 12½

1893, Dec. Unwmk. Litho.

No.	Type	Description	Unused	Used
1	A1	2c vermilion	95.00	85.00

1894, Mar. ***Imperfx12½***

No.	Type	Description	Unused	Used
2	A1	2c vermilion	30.00	75.00
a.		Horiz. pair, imperf between	—	—

No. 1 was printed in sheets of 40, with stamps perforated on all sides. No. 2 was printed in sheets of 10 stamps, arranged horizontally and perforated vertically only.

Pagoda and Junk, finer design — A2

Perf. 11½

1894, Dec. Unwmk. Litho.

3 A2 2c rose 5.00 *6.50*
 a. Horiz. pair, imperf between 400.00
4 A2 4c blue 9.00 *9.00*
5 A2 8c orange 10.00 *14.00*
 a. Pair, imperf between 500.00
6 A2 16c mauve 11.00 *14.00*
 a. Pair, imperf between —
 b. Vert. strip of 3, imperf between 600.00
7 A2 24c green 12.00 *17.00*

POSTAGE DUE STAMPS

No. 2 handstamped "POSTAGE DUE" in English and Chinese

1895 Unwmk. Litho. *Perf. 11½*

J1 A1 2c vermilion *500.00 500.00*

Nos. 3-7 with this handstamp were made after Feb. 2, 1897, and do not appear to have been used. 2c-24c with black overprint, value $175 each. 2c, 16c and 24c, value $325 each.

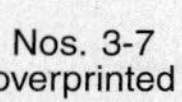

Nos. 3-7 overprinted

Normal spacing between "POSTAGE" and "DUE" is 17.5mm. Narrow spacing is 16.5mm.

1895

J2 A2 2c rose 32.50 *25.00*
 a. Narrow spacing 125.00
 b. Double overprint —
 c. Inverted overprint 175.00
J3 A2 4c blue 32.50 *27.50*
 a. Narrow spacing 125.00
 b. Inverted overprint —
J4 A2 8c orange 32.50 *27.50*
 a. Narrow spacing 125.00
 b. Inverted overprint —
J5 A2 16c mauve 35.00 *27.50*
 a. Narrow spacing 125.00
 b. Inverted overprint —
J6 A2 24c green 40.00 *37.50*
 a. Narrow spacing 125.00
 b. Inverted overprint —

FOOCHOW

A river port on the Min River, Foochow is the capital of Fukien province. It was one of the five original Treaty Ports, opened to foreign trade by the Treaty of Nanking in 1842. Foochow was soon the home of a large foreign community, with a considerable volume of commercial correspondence. By 1863, Shanghai was despatching mail to Foochow and at least as early of 1882 a Shanghai branch agency was operating in the port, using Shanghai stamps.

On Jan. 1, 1895, the Foochow Local Post Office was established, and Shanghai stamps were replaced with a "PAID" handstamp. Distinctive Foochow Local Post stamps were issued on Aug. 1. On Feb. 2, 1897, the Foochow Local Post was merged with the Imperial Chinese Postal Service.

All Foochow issues were lithographed by Waterlow and Sons, London, England, in sheets of 50 (5x10).

Cancellations

The more common cancellation is a circular date stamp inscribed "POSTAL SERVICE FOOCHOW CHINA." Used values are for stamps bearing this cancel. Covers are scarce. Value, $1,000.

Stamps cancelled with "POSTAL SERVICE PAGODA ANCHORAGE" command a $40 premium. Value on cover, $2,500.

Regatta Dragon Boat — A1

Perf. 13½-15

1895, Aug. 1 Unwmk. Litho.

1 A1 ½c blue 4.00 *5.00*
2 A1 1c green 4.00 *5.00*
 a. 1c aniline green 25.00 *26.00*
3 A1 2c orange 15.00 *17.50*
 a. Pair, imperf. 300.00
4 A1 5c ultramarine 20.00 *24.00*
 a. Pair, imperf. 300.00
5 A1 6c carmine 20.00 *24.00*
 a. Pair, imperf. 300.00
6 A1 10c yellow green 24.00 *26.00*
 a. Pair, imperf. 350.00
7 A1 15c yellow brown 32.50 *37.50*
8 A1 20c violet 35.00 *37.50*
9 A1 40c red brown 37.50 *47.50*

New Colors

1896, July

10 A1 ½c yellow 4.00 *3.50*
11 A1 1c brown 4.00 *3.50*

Nos. 1-11 exist with a wide variety of perforations. The following perforations are known:

½c blue: 13½; 13½x14; 14; 14x13½; 14½; 14x14½; 14½x14; 13½x15; 13½x14x14x14.

1c green: 13½; 13½x14; 14; 14x13½; 14½; 14x14½; 15; 14x14½x15; 15x14½; 13½x14x14½14½.

2c orange: 14x14½; 15; 14x15; 15x14½.

5c ultramarine: 14; 14½; 14x14½; 14½; x14; 15; 14x14x14x14½.

6c carmine: 13½; 14; 14x13½; 14x14½.

10c yellow green: 14; 14½; 14½x14; 15; 14½x15; 15x14½; 15x14.

15c yellow brown: 14½; 15.

20c violet: 13½x14; 14; 14x13½; 14½; 14x14½.

40c red brown: 14½; 15.

½c yellow: 13½; 13½x14; 14; 14x13½; 14½; 14x14½; 14½x14; 15; 14½x13½; 14x14.

1c brown: 14; 14½; 15; 14½x15; 15x14½; 13½x14x14½14½.

HANKOW

A river port in Hupeh Province, situated at the junction of the Han and Yangtze Rivers, about 600 miles upriver from Shanghai. An important trading center for tea and other exports, Hankow was served by the Shanghai Local Post as early as 1863, and a Shanghai Agency post office was established in 1878.

The Hankow Municipal Council took over postal operations on Jan. 1, 1893, and the first stamps of the Hankow Local Post were released on May 20. This was the first of the Treaty Port issues. The postal service was absorbed by the Chinese Post Office on Feb. 2, 1897.

Worker Carrying Chests of Tea — A1

Rouletted Horiz. in Color

1893, May 20 Unwmk. Typo.

1 A1 2c violet, *lilac, surfaced paper* 175.00 120.00
2 A1 5c green, *salmon, surfaced paper* 450.00 250.00
 a. Printed on both sides *1,000.*
3 A1 10c claret, *dull rose, unsurfaced paper* 550.00 200.00

Printed in vertical strips of 10 stamps, rouletted horizontally. Ten strips were sold in booklets of 100.

On the 2c and 5c values, the upper left Chinese character ("Hank'ow") is composed of two elements, the first being a four-sided box followed by an apostrophe. Only the second element ("Han") appears on the 10c value.

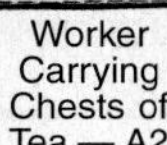

Worker Carrying Chests of Tea — A2

Yellow Stork Tower — A3

Municipal Building — A4

Rouletted Horiz. or Vert. (5c) in Color

1893, May 25-June

4 A2 2c violet, *lilac* 17.50 14.00
 a. Surface colored paper *22.50* 22.50
5 A2 5c green, *salmon* 17.50 14.00
 a. 5c green, *flesh* *27.50* 27.50
 b. Printed on both sides *35.00* —
6 A2 10c carmine rose, *rose, surfaced paper* 27.50 *27.50*
 a. Vertically bisected to pay 5c registration —
7 A3 20c blue, *buff* 35.00 *37.50*
8 A4 30c red, *yellow* 35.00 *35.00*

Nos. 4 and 6-8 were printed in vertical strips of 10, rouletted horizontally. No. 5 was printed in horizontal strips of 10, rouletted vertically.

Issue dates: 20c, 5/25; 30c, 5/26; 5c, 10c, early June; 2c, mid-June.

Faded copies of No. 6 are sometimes mistaken for No. 3. The unsurfaced paper of No. 3 is very rough and porous, while the surfaced paper of No. 6 is smoother and more uniform. Under shortwave ultraviolet light, No. 3 is a dark blue violet, No. 6 a bright red.

Rouletted Horiz. (2c) or Vert. (5c) in Color

1894, June

9 A2 2c violet, *buff* 22.50 17.50
 a. 2c blue violet, *buff* 22.50 17.50
10 A2 5c green, *pale greenish buff* 27.50 17.50

Worker Carrying Chests of Tea — A5

City Gate & Pagoda — A6

Municipal Building — A7

Watermarked Chinese Characters

1894, Sept. *Perf. 15*

11 A5 2c green 14.00 *20.00*
12 A5 5c red brown 20.00 *20.00*
13 A5 10c blue 24.00 22.00
14 A6 20c orange red 32.50 27.50
15 A7 30c violet 35.00 *40.00*

Printed by Waterlow and Sons, London, in sheets of 100 (10x10).

Nos. 13-15 Surcharged

1896, March-May

16 A5 ONE CENT on 10c blue 60.00 *60.00*
 a. Double surcharge, one inverted *1,500.*
17 A6 TWO CENTS on 20c orange red 60.00 *60.00*
 a. Double surcharge *1,200.* *1,200.*
 b. "2" with curved foot *150.00* *150.00*
18 A7 FIVE CENTS on 30c violet 60.00 *60.00*
 a. Double surcharge *1,000.* *1,000.*

Worker Carrying Chests of Tea — A8

City Gate & Pagoda — A9

Municipal Building — A10

Perf. 11½-12

1894, Sept. Unwmk. Litho.

19 A8 2c green 9.00 *10.00*
20 A8 5c red brown 14.00 10.00
 a. Horizontal pair, imperf vertically 600.00
21 A8 10c blue 27.50 *35.00*
 a. 10c dark blue 30.00 *40.00*
 b. Vertical pair, imperf horizontally 425.00
22 A9 20c orange brown 42.50 *35.00*
 a. 20c yellow orange 45.00 35.00
 b. Aniline ink *50.00* *50.00*
23 A10 30c violet 22.50 *30.00*
 a. 30c slate violet 22.50 *30.00*
 b. Short 2nd "L" in "LOCAL" 35.00 35.00
 c. Extra cross bar on "T" of "CENTS" 25.00 25.00
 d. Broken "S" in "CENTS" 27.50 27.50
 e. Horiz. pair, imperf between *600.00* *600.00*

Nos. 21 and 21a printed on both sides, No. 22 in black, No. 23 in black and No. 23 printed on both sides are proofs.

No. 23 Surcharged

1896, August

24 A10 ONE CENT on 30c violet, surcharged vertically 225.00 200.00
 a. Pair, one without surcharge *2,000.*
 b. On #23b 275.00
 c. Vertical pair, imperf horizontally —
 d. Inverted surcharge (reading down) *725.00*
 e. As "a," horiz. pair, imperf between —
25 A10 ONE CENT on 30c violet, surcharged horizontally 24.00 24.00
 a. On 30c slate violent (#23a) 24.00 24.00
 b. On #23b *240.00* 240.00
 c. On #23c 245.00
 d. Broken "O" in "ONE" 30.00 30.00
 e. Inverted surcharge *190.00*
 f. Horiz. pair, imperf between *275.00*
 g. Vertical pair, imperf horizontally *325.00*
 h. Double surcharge *245.00*

Nos. 19-23 Overprinted "P.P.C."

1897, January

26 A8 2c green *200.00* —
27 A8 5c red brown *200.00* —
28 A8 10c blue *200.00* —
29 A9 20c orange brown *200.00* —
30 A10 30c violet *200.00* —

In January, 1897, after being ordered to close its offices on Feb. 2, 1897, the Hankow Local Post Office overprinted the stamps it had on hand with the letters "P.P.C." ("Pour Prendre Congee," French for "to take leave"). These stamps were used during the last few days that the post office was in operation. Covers exist and are very rare.

Dangerous forgeries of this overprint exist.

POSTAGE DUE STAMPS

Nos. 6-10 overprinted, Chinese in "Sung" type characters

1894

J1	A2	2c violet, *buff*	180.00	*250.00*
J2	A2	5c green, *pale green*	180.00	*225.00*
J3	A2	10c carmine, *rose*	180.00	*240.00*
J4	A3	20c blue, *buff*	180.00	*240.00*
J5	A4	30c red, *yellow*	180.00	*275.00*

Nos. 6-10 Overprinted, Chinese in ordinary characters, 2mm space between "POSTAGE" and "DUE"

Type 1 — small top character

Type 2 — large top character

Two types of overprint: Type 1, first vertical radical longer, top of left character 2½mm wide; Type 2, first vertical radical shorter, top of left character 3mm wide.

1894-96

J6	A2	2c violet, *buff*, type 1 ovpt.	22.50	*22.50*
a.		Inverted overprint	350.00	
b.		Double overprint	325.00	
c.		"E" of "POSTAGE" omitted	225.00	
d.		Type 2 ovpt.	240.00	*350.00*
J7	A2	5c green, *pale green*, type 1 ovpt.	30.00	30.00
a.		Inverted overprint	325.00	
b.		Double overprint	325.00	
c.		Double overprint, both inverted	450.00	
d.		Type 2 ovpt.	240.00	*350.00*
J8	A2	10c carmine, *rose* type 1 ovpt.	32.50	30.00
a.		Inverted overprint	400.00	
b.		Double overprint	400.00	
c.		Double overprint, both inverted	725.00	
d.		Type 2 ovpt.	175.00	*200.00*
J9	A3	20c blue, *buff*, type 1 ovpt.	200.00	200.00
a.		Inverted overprint	525.00	
b.		Double overprint	525.00	
c.		"E" of "POSTAGE" omitted	350.00	
d.		Type 2 ovpt.	150.00	—
J10	A4	30c red, *yellow*, type 1 ovpt.	70.00	57.50
a.		Inverted overprint	450.00	
b.		Double overprint	450.00	
c.		Triple overprint	—	
d.		"E" of "POSTAGE" omitted	290.00	*275.00*
e.		Wide space (4¼mm) between Chinese characters	—	
f.		Type 2 ovpt.	125.00	*135.00*

Nos. 6, 7, 9 Overprinted, 3mm Space Between "POSTAGE" and "DUE"

1895

J11	A2	2c violet, *buff*, type 1 ovpt.	*575.00*	575.00
a.		Type 2 ovpt.	625.00	*625.00*
J12	A2	10c carmine, *rose* type 1 ovpt.	525.00	*525.00*
a.		Type 2 ovpt.	625.00	—
J13	A3	20c blue, *buff*, type 1 ovpt.	575.00	575.00
a.		Type 2 ovpt.	625.00	625.00

ICHANG

A river port on the north side of the Yangtze River, about 1,100 miles from Shanghai and 400 miles below Hankow. Ichang was the head of steam navigation on the Yangtze and so was the junction point of trade — most importantly, opium, tung oil and silk — between Szechuan and the rest of China.

Ichang was opened as a Treaty Port in 1876, and the first settlement of foreign traders soon followed, in 1878. The Ichang Local Post Office was estabished in Nov., 1894. Along with the other Treaty Port local posts, it was absorbed into the Chinese Post Office on Feb. 2, 1897.

All Ichang basic issues were lithographed by Tokyo Tsukiji Type Foundry Co., Tokyo, Japan.

Coin-like Design — A1

Brass Cash — A2

Ancient "Ichang" Character — A3

Stylized Pa Kua, "1894" — A4

Modern "Ichang" Character — A5

Pheasant — A6

Otter — A7

Map of the Foreign Settlement in Ichang — A8

Narrow Setting
Stamps Printed 3.5-4mm Apart

Perf. 10¾-11½

1894, Dec. 1 Unwmk. Litho.

1	A1	½ ca. brown	14.00	*18.00*
a.		Horiz. pair, imperf with between	400.00	
2	A2	1 ca. olive brown	14.00	*22.50*
a.		Vert. pair, imperf between	575.00	350.00
3	A3	2 ca. red violet	24.00	*22.50*
4	A4	3 ca. gray	40.00	*29.00*
5	A5	5 ca. brown rose	20.00	*29.00*
a.		Horiz. pair, imperf between	790.00	
6	A6	1 m green	72.50	*115.00*
7	A7	15 ca. blue	70.00	*130.00*
8	A8	3 m carmine	62.50	*85.00*
a.		Vert. pair, imperf between	790.00	

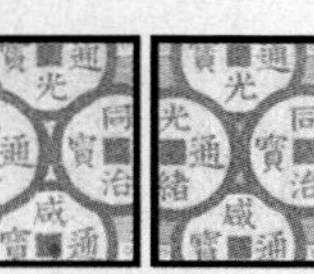

Type A Type B

Two types of 1 ca. value: Type A, 2 small triangles blank, open; Type B, 2 small triangles shaded closed.

Wide Setting
Stamps Printed 5mm Apart

1895

9	A1	½ ca. red brown	17.50	9.00
10	A2	1 ca. bister brown (Type A)	42.50	35.00
11	A2	1 ca. bister brown (Type B)	22.50	*17.50*
12	A4	3 ca. gray lilac	35.00	*22.50*
a.		Horiz. pair, imperf vert.	—	
13	A3	2 ca. red violet	30.00	27.50
14	A8	3 m carmine	57.50	*50.00*

Handstamped in Black

1896 Surcharged in Violet

15	A8	2 ca. on 3m carmine (#8)	*800.00*	*800.00*
16	A8	2 ca. on 3m carmine (#14)	*225.00*	*145.00*

Surcharged in Black

17	A8	2 ca. on 3m carmine (#8)	125.00	*100.00*
18	A8	2 ca. on 3m carmine (#14)	225.00	*145.00*
a.		Pair, one without surcharge	1,450.	
19	A8	2 ca. on 1 ca. bister brown (#10)	35.00	32.50
20	A8	2 ca. on 1 ca. bister brown (#11)	30.00	*22.50*
a.		Inverted surcharge	—	—
b.		Double surcharge	—	—

KEWKIANG

A river port in Kiangsi Province, on the Yangtze River, 458 miles upriver from Shanghai. Kewkiang was opened to foreign trade in 1858 and it appears that at least as early as 1865 an agent of the Shanghai Local Post was receiving and despatching mails. Shanghai Local Post stamps were used from Jan. 1, 1893, to June 1, 1894, when the Kewkiang Local Post took over postal operations. On Feb. 2, 1897, the Chinese Post Office took over postal services between cities, though the Kewkiang Local Post continued limited local delivery until late August.

All basic Kewkiang stamps were typographed by Central China Press, Kewkiang.

Pagoda — A1

Center Stroke Omitted

"Kiang" in Ancient Characters A2

"Kiang" in Modern Characters A3

"Kiang" in Modified Characters — A4

Unwmk.

1894, June 1 Typo. *Perf. 12*

On Native Paper

1	A1	½c black, *rose*	4.00	4.00
a.		Stroke missing in "Kiang"	100.00	85.00
b.		As "a," corrected by hand	110.00	110.00
c.		Double impression	145.00	
2	A1	½c red, *yellow*	4.00	4.00
a.		Stroke missing in "Kiang"	97.50	85.00
b.		As "a," corrected by hand	110.00	110.00
c.		Horiz. pair, imperf vert.	—	—
3	A2	1c gray black	4.00	4.00
4	A3	2c vermilion	8.00	9.00
a.		2c red, on European paper	12.00	11.00
5	A4	5c slate blue, *yellow*	10.00	*9.00*
6	A3	6c yellow	12.00	*12.00*
a.		6c ocher, on European paper	52.50	42.50
7	A2	10c black, *yellow buff*	17.00	17.00
a.		10c black, *yellow*	17.00	17.00
8	A4	15c red, *yellow*	17.00	*20.00*
a.		"1" of "15" omitted	225.00	*175.00*
9	A4	20c blue, *rose*	22.50	*22.50*
10	A3	40c black, *red*	24.00	*27.50*

Lu Shan Hills and Bridge Over Lung K'ai Ho Creek — A5

1894, June 23 On Native Paper

11	A5	½c black, *rose*	4.00	*9.00*
a.		Horiz. pair, imperf between	250.00	
12	A5	½c red, *yellow*	4.00	*9.00*

"Little Orphan Rock" — A6

1894, August On European Paper

13	A6	1c black	5.00	*9.00*
a.		Horiz. pair, imperf between	325.00	
b.		Double impression	350.00	

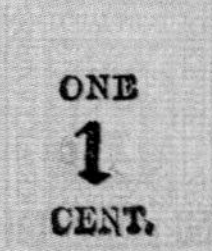

Nos. 6, 8, 9 surcharged in black or blue (#16)

1896, August

14	A4	HALF CENT on 20c	22.50	22.50
a.		Double surcharge	290.00	
b.		"1" of "½" inverted	32.50	32.50
c.		Inverted surcharge	275.00	
d.		Surcharge on reverse	400.00	
15	A4	ONE CENT on 15c	22.50	*22.50*
a.		Blue surcharge	290.00	110.00
b.		Surcharged on both sides	290.00	
c.		Pair, one without surcharge	750.00	
d.		On #8a	325.00	
e.		Wider space (3mm) between "1" and "CENT"	55.00	
16	A3	TWO CENTS on 6c (Bl)	25.00	25.00
a.		Black surcharge	300.00	250.00

POSTAGE DUE STAMPS

Nos. 4a//13 overprinted

Four types of overprint: type A, narrow setting, overprint slope 20 degrees, "D" larger (2½mm) and under "os" of "Postage;" type B, wide setting, overprint slope 20 degrees, "D" larger (2½mm) and under "st" of "Postage;" type C, wide setting, overprint slope 30-35 degrees, "D" smaller (2mm) and under "st" of "Postage;" type D, wide setting, overprint slope 40-45 degrees, "D" smaller (2mm) and under "ta" of "Postage."

1895, Sept. — Overprinted Type A

J1	½c black, *rose*	57.50	*70.00*
a.	"Postag"	325.00	*325.00*
J2	½c red, *yellow*	57.50	*70.00*
a.	"Postag"	325.00	*325.00*
b.	Inverted overprint	—	—
J3	1c black	52.50	*70.00*
a.	"Postag"	325.00	*325.00*
J4	2c red	125.00	*225.00*
a.	"Postag"	650.00	*650.00*
b.	Inverted overprint	—	—

1896 — Overprinted Type B

J5	½c black, *rose*	30.00	17.00
a.	Inverted overprint	325.00	290.00
J6	½c red, *yellow*	22.50	17.00
a.	Inverted overprint	325.00	290.00
J7	1c black	20.00	*16.00*
J8	2c red	22.50	*22.00*
a.	Inverted overprint	325.00	290.00
J9	5c slate blue, *yellow*	30.00	*20.00*
a.	Inverted overprint	325.00	350.00
J10	6c yellow	32.50	*22.00*
J11	10c black, *yellow buff*	35.00	*28.00*
J12	15c red, *yellow*	40.00	*40.00*
a.	On #8a	*350.00*	350.00
J13	20c blue *rose*	57.50	57.50
J14	40c black, *red*	57.50	*57.50*

Overprinted in Red

J15	1c black	175.00	175.00
J16	10c black, *yellow buff*	850.00	*850.00*

Dangerous forgeries of Nos. J15-J16 exist.

Overprinted Type C

J17	½c black, *rose*	30.00	*30.00*
J18	½c red, *yellow*	22.50	*17.00*
J19	1c black	20.00	*16.00*
J20	2c red	22.50	22.00
J21	5c slate blue, *yellow*	30.00	20.00
J22	6c yellow	32.50	*22.50*
J23	10c black, *yellow buff*	35.00	27.50
J24	15c red, *yellow*	40.00	*40.00*
J25	20c blue *rose*	57.50	57.50
J26	40c black, *red*	57.50	*57.50*

Overprinted Type D

J27	½c black, *rose*	*30.00*	27.50
J28	½c red, *yellow*	*32.50*	27.50
J29	1c black	*35.00*	22.50
J30	2c red	*27.50*	27.50
J31	5c slate blue, *yellow*	*30.00*	27.50
J32	6c yellow	*30.00*	27.50
J33	10c black, *yellow buff*	*30.00*	30.00
J34	15c red, *yellow*	*32.50*	32.50
J35	20c blue *rose*	*42.50*	52.50
J36	40c black, *red*	*52.50*	*62.50*

NANKING

A river port on the Yangtze, about 200 miles upriver from Shanghai. An ancient and historical city, Nanking was opened to foreign settlement and trade by the Treaty of Peking in 1860. British and French settlement began in 1865, and a European community gradually developed. Nanking became a center of European missionary and educational work, and in 1885 an office of the Shanghai Agency was established. By 1896 the Nanking Local Post was operating in the city and on Sept. 20, 1896, the first Nanking local stamps were issued. Postal operations were taken over by the Chinese Post Office on Feb. 2, 1897.

All Nanking stamps were lithographed by Tokyo Tsukiji Type Foundry Co., Tokyo, Japan.

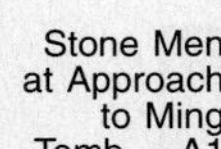
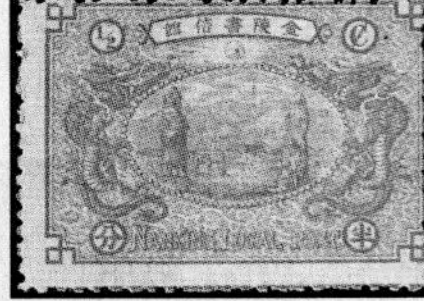

Stone Men at Approach to Ming Tomb — A1

The Drum Tower — A2

Stone Elephants at Approach to Ming Tomb — A3

Lotus Lake Scene — A4

Central Hall of the Confucian Temple — A5

The Great Bell — A6

"NANKING LOCAL POST" in Double-lined Letters

Perf. 11½

1896, Sept. 20 — Unwmk. — Litho.

1	A1 ½c gray	14.00	*16.00*
a.	Horiz. pair, imperf between	650.00	
b.	Vert. pair, imperf between	650.00	
2	A2 1c rose	14.00	*16.00*
a.	Horiz. pair, imperf between	875.00	
3	A3 2c gray green	30.00	*27.50*
a.	Horiz. pair, imperf between	875.00	
4	A4 3c orange yellow	26.00	*20.00*
a.	3c yellow	26.00	*20.00*
5	A5 4c claret	30.00	*30.00*
6	A6 5c violet	32.50	27.50
7	A2 10c yellow green	37.50	27.50
a.	10c deep green	37.50	32.50
8	A2 20c brown	32.50	27.50

Nos. 1-8 were printed in sheets of 25 (5x5)

"NANKING LOCAL POST" in Single-lined Letters

1896

9	A1 ½c salmon rose	13.00	*14.00*

No. 9 was printed in sheets of 25 (5x5).

"NANKING LOCAL POST" in Single-lined Letters

1896 — *Perf. 12½*

10	A1 ½c lilac brown	16.00	*18.00*
11	A2 1c rose	27.50	*22.50*
12	A3 2c green	32.50	27.50
13	A4 3c yellow	35.00	32.50
a.	3c orange yellow	—	
14	A5 4c brown	37.50	35.00
15	A6 5c blue	37.50	*35.00*

1897 — *Imperf*

16	A2 1c rose	12.50	*15.00*

Nos. 10-16 were printed in sheets of 100 (10x10).

WEI HAI WEI

A port in Shantung province which, with adjoining territory, was leased to Great Britain in 1899. The Cornabe Co. operated a private courier post to Chefoo from Dec. 1898 until Mar. 1899, when a Chinese Imperial Post Office was opened. This was replaced by a British Post Office in Sept., 1899, which provided postal service, using Hong Kong stamps, until the territory was returned to China on Oct. 1, 1930.

Although not one of the Treaty Ports, Wei Hai Wei is generally collected with those issues.

A1

A2

Before regular printed stamps were available, provisional stamps were made by impressing a Cornabe & Co. double circle chop on red native paper in black. The 2c stamp was handstamped once and "2c" was handwritten in the top right and left corners; the letters "C," standing for "Courier," and "P," standing for "Post," were written in the left and right lower corners respectively. The 5c stamps were produced by making two impressions of the Cornabe & Co. double circle chop on red native paper, one of which was inverted. "5c" was handwritten in each of the upper corners, and the words "Courier Post" were written below the stamped impressions. These stamps were signed in continuous horizontal rows on the back of the sheet by G.K. Fergusson, the Honorary Postmaster. 8 sheets of 98 stamps (14x7) or 784 stamps of the 2c denomination and 4 sheets of 98 stamps (14x7) or 392 stamps of the 5c denomination were produced.

1898, Dec. 8 — Unwmk. — *Imperf*

1	A1 2c black, *red*	*600.*	*700.*
a.	Vertical signature of G.K. Fergusson	*1,200.*	*1,200.*
b.	"P.C." for "C.P."	*1,500.*	*1,500.*
c.	Chop inverted	—	
d.	Chop double	*1,500.*	
2	A2 5c black, *red*	*2,500.*	*1,700.*
a.	Vertical signature of G.K. Fergusson	*2,100.*	*2,100.*

A3

1899, Jan. 9 — Litho. — *Perf. 11*

3	A3 2c red	175.00	*225.00*
4	A3 5c olive green	275.00	*325.00*
a.	Tete-beche pair	—	
b.	Horiz. pair, imperf between	*3,000.*	3,000.
c.	5c emerald green	350.00	*375.00*
d.	5c green	350.00	*350.00*

Nos. 3-4 were lithographed by Kelly & Walsh, Shanghai, in sheets of 64 (8x8) stamps.

Reprints exist on thin paper.

WUHU

A port city on the Yangtze River, 282 miles from the sea. Wuhu was opened up as a Treaty Port in 1876, and a customs house was established in 1877. The Shanghai Local Post was operating in Wuhu by 1888. In June, 1894, the foreign community, composed mostly of Christian missionaries, established a local post, and stamps were issued in Nov. 1894. The Wuhu Local Post was replaced by the Chinese Post Office on Feb. 2, 1897, although it continued to provide service within the city for a short time after.

All basic Wuhu stamps were printed by the Lithographic Society of Shanghai.

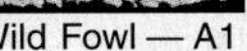

Wild Fowl — A1

Rice Field — A2

Pheasants A3

Wuhu Pagoda A4

"Abundance" ("Fu") — A5

First Printing

11¾, 12¼ and compound

1894, Nov. 26 — Unwmk. — Litho.

1	A1 ½c black	20.00	14.00
a.	Imperf	30.00	20.00
b.	Perf 12	20.00	20.00
2	A2 ½c green	14.00	11.00
a.	Perf 11x11¾	50.00	40.00
3	A3 1c brown	19.00	13.00
a.	Perf 12	24.00	*24.00*
4	A2 2c yellow	16.00	*14.00*
a.	Perf 12	24.00	24.00
5	A4 5c carmine	16.00	*19.00*
a.	Imperf	24.00	*24.00*
6	A5 6c blue	22.50	22.50
7	A3 10c brown red	30.00	*30.00*
8	A4 15c olive green	30.00	*30.00*
9	A5 20c red	30.00	*29.00*
10	A1 40c brown	37.50	37.50

1894 — Second Printing — *Perf. 11*

11	A1 ½c grayish black	12.00	7.00
a.	Imperf	18.00	*12.00*
12	A2 ½c yellow green	10.00	6.00
a.	½c deep green	10.00	6.00
b.	Imperf	20.00	20.00
13	A3 1c grayish brown	16.00	9.00
a.	Imperf	*35.00*	
14	A2 2c orange yellow	14.00	13.00
a.	Imperf	*35.00*	
15	A4 5c red orange	18.00	*20.00*
a.	Imperf	30.00	20.00
16	A5 6c gray blue	18.00	*19.00*
a.	Imperf	30.00	20.00
17	A3 10c brown red	32.50	*26.00*
a.	Imperf	50.00	42.50
18	A4 15c olive green	30.00	*26.00*
a.	Imperf	*40.00*	
19	A5 20c orange red	27.50	24.00
a.	Imperf	*40.00*	
20	A1 40c yellow brown	32.50	32.50
a.	Imperf	*50.00*	

Nos. 1-10 surcharged with denomination in Chinese in black or red (R)

1895 — *11¾, 12¼ and compound*

21	A1 ½c black (R)	22.50	19.00
a.	Perf 12¼	30.00	—
22	A2 ½c green	18.00	16.00
23	A3 1c brown	14.00	11.00
a.	Perf 12	20.00	*16.00*
24	A2 2c yellow	16.00	*14.00*
25	A4 5c carmine	22.00	*22.00*
a.	Inverted surcharge	*240.00*	
26	A5 6c blue	32.50	*32.50*
27	A3 10c brown red	35.00	*32.50*
28	A4 15c olive green	37.50	32.50
29	A5 20c red	47.50	*50.00*
30	A1 40c brown	70.00	70.00

Nos. 11-20 surcharged with denomination in Chinese

31	A1 ½c grayish black (R)	22.00	19.00
a.	Inverted surcharge	240.00	
32	A1 ½c grayish black (Black)	160.00	
a.	Inverted surcharge	*475.00*	
33	A2 ½c green	18.00	16.00
a.	Inverted surcharge	240.00	
34	A3 1c brown	14.00	11.00
a.	Inverted surcharge	240.00	
b.	Horiz. pair, imperf between	450.00	
35	A2 2c orange yellow	16.00	14.00
a.	Inverted surcharge	240.00	
36	A4 5c red orange	22.00	*22.00*
a.	Inverted surcharge	240.00	

37 A5 6c gray blue 32.50 32.50
a. Inverted surcharge 240.00
38 A3 10c brown red 35.00 32.50
a. Inverted surcharge —
39 A4 15c olive green 37.50 32.50
40 A5 20c red 47.50
a. Inverted surcharge 240.00
41 A1 40c yellow brown 70.00 70.00
a. Inverted surcharge 240.00

Nos. 3//14 surcharged in black or red (R)

1895, Nov.

42 A3 ½c on 1c brn, perf 11¾ (R) 26.00 20.00
a. "2" with straight foot 95.00 65.00
b. Perf 11 30.00 27.50
c. As "b," "2" with straight foot 145.00 110.00
d. Perf 12¼ 26.00 20.00
e. As "d," "2" with straight foot 200.00
f. 1c yellow brown, perf 11 275.00 275.00
43 A3 ½c on 1c brn, perf 12¼ (Blk) 375.00
a. On 1c yellow brown, perf 11 375.00
b. Vert. pair, red and black surcharges setenant, perf 11 500.00
c. Vert. pair, red and black surcharges setenant, perf 12¼ 500.00
44 A2 5c on 2c yel, perf 11 30.00 32.50
a. Perf 12 30.00 32.50
b. Double surcharge 725.00

Other stamps with "5 Cent" surcharges, with and without a bar through the original value, exist but are of speculative nature and had no postal validity.

Cranes A6

Chinese Character ("Fortunate") A7

Chinese Characters ("Wuhu") — A8

Designs: 2c, 10c, owl; 6c, 40c stag.

1896, Feb. *Perf. 10-10½*

45 A6 ½c lilac 26.00 19.00
46 A7 ½c yellow 19.00 16.00
47 A8 1c blue 16.00 15.00
48 A6 2c green 37.50 32.50
49 A7 5c yellow green 27.50 25.00
50 A6 6c yellow brown 35.00 32.50
51 A6 10c rose 47.50 45.00
52 A6 15c carmine 50.00 42.50
53 A8 20c rose 32.50 35.00
54 A6 40c carmine 45.00 45.00

Surcharged with values in Chinese characters

55 A6 ½c lilac 32.50 26.00
56 A7 ½c yellow 19.00 19.00
a. Inverted surcharge 190.00 125.00
57 A8 1c blue 16.00 14.00
a. Inverted surcharge 160.00
b. Vert. pair, one stamp with surcharge omitted 325.00
58 A6 2c green 47.50 57.50
a. Inverted surcharge 325.00 225.00
59 A7 5c yellow green 32.50 26.00
a. Inverted surcharge 325.00 325.00
60 A6 6c yellow brown 32.50 35.00
a. Inverted surcharge 190.00 130.00
61 A6 10c rose 77.50 65.00
a. Inverted surcharge 325.00 225.00
62 A6 15c carmine 90.00 65.00
a. Inverted surcharge 300.00 190.00
63 A8 20c rose 50.00 40.00
a. Inverted surcharge 190.00 130.00
64 A6 40c carmine 57.50 37.50
a. Inverted surcharge 190.00 130.00

In Jan. 1897, after being ordered to close its offices on Feb. 2, 1897, the Wuhu Local Post Office overprinted the stamps it had on hand with the letters "P.P.C." ("Pour Prendre Congee," French for "to take leave"). These stamps were used during the last few days that the post office was in operation. Covers exist and are very rare.

Nos. 45-54 overprinted

Nos. 45-54 Overprinted in Black

1897, Jan.

65 A6 ½c lilac 32.50 37.50
66 A7 ½c yellow 32.50 37.50
a. Double overprint — —
67 A8 1c blue 32.50 37.50
68 A6 2c green 45.00 77.50
69 A7 5c yellow green 32.50 37.50
70 A6 6c yellow brown 35.00 47.50
71 A6 10c rose 65.00 77.50
72 A6 15c carmine 45.00 77.50
73 A8 20c rose 30.00 50.00
74 A6 40c carmine 37.50 77.50

Nos. 45-54 Overprinted in Red

75 A6 ½c lilac 37.50 37.50
76 A7 ½c yellow 35.00 45.00
77 A8 1c blue 32.50 65.00
78 A6 2c green 45.00 77.50
79 A7 5c yellow green 32.50 37.50
80 A6 6c yellow brown 37.50 47.50
81 A6 10c rose 77.50 77.50
82 A6 15c carmine 50.00 77.50
83 A8 20c rose 30.00 50.00
84 A6 40c carmine 77.50 77.50

Nos. 55-64 Overprinted in Black Above Chinese Characters

85 A6 ½c lilac 20.00 17.50
86 A7 ½c yellow 14.00 20.00
87 A8 1c blue 20.00 19.00
88 A6 2c green 37.50 45.00
89 A7 5c yellow green 19.00 20.00
90 A6 6c yellow brown 26.00 30.00
91 A6 10c rose 65.00 50.00
92 A6 15c carmine 57.50 50.00
93 A8 20c rose 50.00 57.50
94 A6 40c carmine 50.00 57.50

Nos. 55//62 Overprinted in Red Above Chinese Characters

95 A6 ½c lilac 30.00 25.00
96 A7 ½c yellow 19.00 19.00
97 A8 1c blue 19.00 19.00
98 A6 2c green 57.50 57.50
99 A7 5c yellow green 22.00 24.00
100 A6 6c yellow brown 30.00 32.50
101 A6 15c carmine 70.00 57.50

Nos. 55-64 Overprinted in Black Below Chinese Characters

102 A6 ½c lilac 20.00 18.00
103 A7 ½c yellow 17.00 22.00
104 A8 1c blue 16.00 26.00
105 A6 2c green 35.00 45.00
106 A7 5c yellow green 19.00 20.00
107 A6 6c yellow brown 24.00 30.00
108 A6 10c rose 65.00 50.00
109 A6 15c carmine 57.50 50.00
110 A8 20c rose 45.00 57.50
111 A6 40c carmine 50.00 57.50

Nos. 55//62 Overprinted in Red Below Chinese Characters

112 A6 ½c lilac 30.00 30.00
113 A7 ½c yellow 20.00 24.00
114 A8 1c blue 20.00 24.00
115 A6 2c green 57.50 55.00
116 A7 5c yellow green 24.00 24.00
117 A6 6c yellow brown 27.50 32.50
118 A6 15c carmine 70.00 57.50

POSTAGE DUE STAMPS

Regular postage stamps overprinted in black or red (R)

There are three types of overprint: type 1, "P" longer upright, extending to bottom; type 2, "P" short upright, "P" with loops at left; type 3, "P" short upright, "P" without loops at left. All three types exist on Nos. J1-J20, and types 1 and 2 exist on Nos. J28-J37.

Nos. 1-10 Overprinted

J1 A1 ½c black (R) 12.00 12.00
a. Inverted overprint 175.00
J2 A1 ½c black 190.00
J3 A2 ½c green 13.00 12.00
a. Inverted overprint 175.00
b. Perf 11x11¾ 60.00 60.00
J4 A3 1c brown 27.50 27.50
a. Inverted overprint 175.00
b. Perf 12¼ 27.50 27.50
J5 A2 2c yellow 22.00 16.00
a. Inverted overprint 175.00 175.00
J6 A4 5c carmine 22.00 20.00
J7 A5 6c blue 27.50 26.00
a. Inverted overprint 175.00 175.00
J8 A3 10c brown red 37.50 35.00
a. Inverted overprint 175.00 175.00
J9 A4 15c olive green 37.50 35.00
a. Inverted overprint 175.00 175.00
J10 A5 20c red 52.50 52.50
a. Inverted overprint 175.00 175.00
J11 A1 40c brown 65.00 55.00
a. Inverted overprint 175.00 175.00

Nos. 11-20 Overprinted

J12 A1 ½c black (R) 12.00 12.00
a. Inverted overprint 175.00
J13 A1 ½c black 190.00
J14 A2 ½c green 12.00 12.00
a. Inverted overprint 175.00
b. Perf 11x11¾ 60.00 60.00
J15 A3 1c brown 14.00 12.00
a. Inverted overprint 175.00
J16 A2 2c orange yellow 22.00 16.00
a. Inverted overprint 175.00
J17 A4 5c carmine 19.00 18.00
J18 A5 6c gray blue 27.50 26.00
a. Inverted overprint 175.00 175.00
J19 A3 10c brown red 37.50 35.00
a. Inverted overprint 175.00 175.00
J20 A4 15c olive green 37.50 35.00
a. Inverted overprint 175.00 175.00
b. "a" of "Postage" omitted 275.00
J21 A5 20c red 50.00 50.00
a. Inverted overprint 175.00 175.00
b. Vert. overprint, reading down 500.00 500.00
J22 A1 40c brown 65.00 55.00
a. Inverted overprint 175.00 175.00

Nos. 3//8 Overprinted Type 3

J23 A3 1c brn, perf 11¾ — —
a. Perf 12¼ — —
b. Imperf, "t" of "Postage" omitted — —
J24 A2 2c org yel, imperf, "t" of "Postage" omitted — —
J25 A4 5c car, "t" of "Postage" omitted — —
J26 A3 10c brown red — —
J27 A4 15c ol grn, imperf, overprint inverted — —

Nos. 45-54 Overprinted

J28 A6 ½c lilac 30.00 26.00
a. Inverted overprint 190.00 130.00
J29 A7 ½c yellow 16.00 16.00
a. Inverted overprint 130.00 90.00
J30 A8 1c blue 19.00 22.00
J31 A6 2c green 50.00 45.00
a. Inverted overprint 325.00 240.00
J32 A7 5c yellow green 30.00 26.00
J33 A6 6c yellow brown 37.50 35.00
J34 A6 10c rose 65.00 57.50
a. Inverted overprint 325.00 240.00
J35 A6 15c carmine 110.00 77.50
a. "a" of "Postage" omitted 350.00 87.50
J36 A8 20c rose 65.00 60.00
J37 A6 40c carmine 90.00 77.50

Nos. J28-J37 Overprinted

J38 A6 ½c lilac 30.00 25.00
a. Red overprint 60.00 60.00
b. Overprint reading down —
J39 A7 ½c yellow 25.00 20.00
a. Overprint reading down 175.00 150.00
J40 A8 1c blue 25.00 20.00
a. Red overprint, reading down 175.00 150.00
J41 A6 2c green 45.00 40.00
J42 A7 5c yellow green 30.00 25.00
J43 A6 6c yellow brown 40.00 35.00
J44 A6 10c rose 60.00 50.00
J45 A6 15c carmine 60.00 50.00
J46 A8 20c rose 60.00 50.00
J47 A6 40c carmine 60.00 50.00

CILICIA

sə-ˈli-sh,ē-,ə

LOCATION — A territory of Turkey, in Southeastern Asia Minor
AREA — 6,238 sq. mi.
POP. — 383,645
CAPITAL — Adana

British and French forces occupied Cilicia in 1918 and in 1919 its control was transferred to the French. Eventually part of Cilicia was assigned to the French Mandated Territory of Syria but by the Lausanne Treaty of 1923 which fixed the boundary between Syria and Turkey, Cilicia reverted to Turkey.

40 Paras = 1 Piaster

Issued under French Occupation

Numbers in parentheses are those of basic Turkish or French stamps.

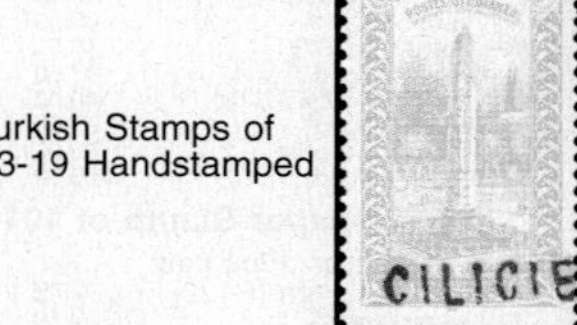

Turkish Stamps of 1913-19 Handstamped

Perf. 11½, 12, 12½, 13½

1919 **Unwmk.**

On Pictorial Issue of 1913

2 A24 2pa red lilac (254) 9.00 9.00
Never hinged 16.00
a. Inverted overprint 20.00 20.00
Never hinged 35.00
b. Double overprint 30.00 30.00
Never hinged 45.00
3 A25 4pa dk brn (255) 7.25 7.25
Never hinged 14.50
a. Inverted overprint 20.00 20.00
Never hinged 35.00
b. Double overprint 22.50 22.50
Never hinged 37.50
4 A27 6pa dk blue (257) 27.50 20.00
Never hinged 52.50
a. Inverted overprint 32.50 32.50
Never hinged 65.00
b. Double overprint 50.00 50.00
Never hinged 100.00
5 A32 1¾pi slate & red brn (262) 8.75 8.75
Never hinged 17.50
a. Inverted overprint 20.00 20.00
Never hinged 35.00
b. Double overprint 22.50 22.50
Never hinged 37.50

On Issue of 1915

6 A17 1pi blue (300) 3.75 3.75
Never hinged 6.25
a. Inverted overprint 10.00 10.00
Never hinged 20.00
b. Double overprint 10.00 10.00
Never hinged 21.00
c. In pair with unovptd. stamp 20.00 20.00
Never hinged 40.00
7 A21 20pa car rose (318) 13.50 12.00
Never hinged 27.50
a. Inverted overprint 20.00 20.00
Never hinged 40.00
b. Double overprint 35.00 35.00
Never hinged 65.00
9 A22 20pa car rose (330) 35.00 32.50
Never hinged 80.00
a. Inverted overprint 45.00 45.00
Never hinged 90.00
b. Double overprint 45.00 45.00
Never hinged 90.00

On Commemorative Issue of 1916

9A A41 5pa grn (345) 130.00 92.50
Never hinged 260.00
10 A41 20pa ultra (347) 7.25 7.25
Never hinged 12.50
a. Double overprint 15.00 15.00
Never hinged 30.00
11 A41 1pi vio & blk (348) 9.50 9.50
Never hinged 12.00
a. Double overprint 27.50 27.50
Never hinged 27.50
b. Perf 12½ 9.50 9.50
Never hinged 17.50
c. In pair with unovptd. stamp 19.00 19.00
Never hinged 37.50
12 A41 5pi yel brn & blk (349) 4.00 4.00
Never hinged 6.25
a. Double overprint 7.50 7.50
Never hinged 15.00

On Issue of 1916-18

13 A44 10pa grn (424) 8.75 8.75
Never hinged 17.50
a. Perf 11½ (424a) 8.75 8.75
Never hinged 17.50
b. Double overprint 24.00 24.00
Never hinged 50.00
14 A47 50pa ultra (428) 45.00 35.00
Never hinged 100.00
a. Perf 11½ (428a) 45.00 35.00
Never hinged 100.00
b. Double overprint 90.00 90.00
Never hinged 210.00
15 A51 25pi car, *straw* (434) 8.75 8.75
Never hinged 17.50
16 A52 50pi car (437) 8.75 8.75
Never hinged 17.50

17 A52 50pi ind (438) 32.50 32.50
Never hinged 67.50

On Issue of 1917

18 A53 5pi on 2pa Prus blue (547) 15.00 15.00
Never hinged 32.50
a. Perf 11½ (547c) 15.00 15.00
Never hinged 32.50

On Issue of 1919

19 A47 50pa ultra (555) 40.00 32.50
Never hinged 87.50
a. Perf 11½ (555a) 40.00 32.50
Never hinged 87.50
b. Double overprint 80.00 80.00
Never hinged 165.00
20 A48 2pi org brn & indigo (556) 40.00 32.50
Never hinged 87.50
21 A49 5pi pale bl & blk (557a) 40.00 32.50
Never hinged 87.50
a. Perf 11½ (557) 40.00 32.50
Never hinged 87.50
b. Perf 11½x12½ (557b) 40.00 32.50
Never hinged 87.50
c. Double overprint 95.00 95.00
Never hinged 200.00

On Newspaper Stamp of 1916

22 A10 5pa on 10pa gray grn (P137) 4.75 4.75
Never hinged 9.50
d. Inverted overprint 11.00 11.00
Never hinged 24.00
e. Double overprint 14.00 14.00
Never hinged 28.00

On Semi-Postal Stamps of 1915

22A A21 20pa car rose (B8) 92.50 80.00
Never hinged 190.00
22B A21 1pi ultra (B9) 2,250. 1,700.
Never hinged —
22C A21 1pi ultra (B13) 1,900. 1,200.

On Semi-Postal Stamps of 1916

23 A17 1pi bl (B19) 10.50 10.50
Never hinged 21.00
a. Inverted overprint 16.00 16.00
Never hinged 32.50
b. Double overprint 16.00 16.00
Never hinged 32.50
c. Perf 13¼ 25.00 25.00
Never hinged 50.00
24 A21 20pa car rose (B28) 3.75 3.75
Never hinged 6.50
a. Inverted overprint 7.50 7.50
Never hinged 15.50
b. Double overprint 10.00 10.00
Never hinged 20.00
25 A21 1pi ultra (B29) 8.75 8.75
Never hinged 17.50
a. Inverted overprint 15.00 15.00
Never hinged 30.00
b. Double overprint 25.00 25.00
Never hinged 50.00

Turkish Stamps of 1913-18 Handstamped

1919 On Pictorial Issue of 1913

31 A24 2pa red lil (254) 4.00 4.00
Never hinged 6.75
a. Inverted overprint 8.00 8.00
Never hinged 16.50
b. Double overprint 12.00 12.00
Never hinged 22.50
c. In pair with unovptd. stamp 16.00 16.00
Never hinged 32.50
32 A25 4pa dk brn (255) 15.00 15.00
Never hinged 32.50
a. Inverted overprint 22.00 22.00
Never hinged 45.00
b. Double overprint 40.00 40.00
Never hinged 80.00

On Issue of 1915

33 A17 1pi blue (300) 13.50 13.50
Never hinged 27.50
a. Inverted overprint 20.00 20.00
Never hinged 40.00
b. Double overprint 35.00 35.00
Never hinged 70.00
34 A22 20pa car rose (330) 5.00 5.00
Never hinged 9.50
a. Inverted overprint 9.50 9.50
Never hinged 20.00
b. Double overprint 15.00 15.00
Never hinged 30.00
c. In pair with unovptd. stamp 20.00 20.00
Never hinged 40.00

On Commemorative Issue of 1916

35 A41 20pa ultra (347) 15.00 15.00
Never hinged 32.50
a. Inverted overprint 30.00 30.00
Never hinged 60.00
b. Perf 12½ (347a) 15.00 15.00
Never hinged 32.50
36 A41 1pi vio & blk (348) 3.25 3.25
Never hinged 5.50
a. Inverted overprint 6.50 6.50
Never hinged 13.50
b. Perf 12½ (348a) 3.25 3.25
Never hinged 5.50

On Issue of 1917

40 A53 5pi on 2pa Prus bl (547) 13.50 13.50
Never hinged 27.50
a. Perf 11½ (547c) 13.50 13.50
Never hinged 27.50

On Newspaper Stamp of 1916

41 A10 5pa on 10pa gray grn (P137) 27.50 27.50
Never hinged 55.00
a. Inverted overprint 50.00 50.00
Never hinged 100.00
b. In pair with unovptd. stamp 60.00 60.00
Never hinged 125.00

On Semi-Postal Stamp of 1915

41A A21 20pa car rose (B8) 210.00 150.00
Never hinged —

On Semi-Postal Stamps of 1916

42 A17 1pi blue (B19) 6.50 6.50
Never hinged 13.50
a. Inverted overprint 12.00 12.00
Never hinged 24.00
b. Double overprint 13.00 13.00
Never hinged 26.00
c. Perf 12 (B19a) 8.00 8.00
Never hinged 16.00
d. Perf 12x13¼ (B19b) 8.00 8.00
Never hinged 16.00
43 A21 20pa car rose (B28) 3.25 3.25
Never hinged 13.50
a. Inverted overprint 8.00 *8.00*
Never hinged 16.00
b. Double overprint 9.00 *9.00*
Never hinged 18.00
Nos. 31-43 (11) 316.50 256.50

Turkish Stamps of 1913-19 Handstamped

1919 On Pictorial Issue of 1913

51 A24 2pa red lil (254) 11.00 11.00
Never hinged 22.50
a. Inverted overprint 16.00 16.00
Never hinged 32.50
b. Double overprint 25.00 25.00
Never hinged 50.00
c. In pair with unovptd. stamp 40.00 40.00
Never hinged 80.00
52 A25 4pa dk brn (255) 3.75 3.75
Never hinged 6.50
a. Inverted overprint 7.50 7.50
Never hinged 17.00
b. Double overprint 10.00 10.00
Never hinged 22.50

On Issue of 1915

53 A17 1pi blue (300) 5.50 5.50
Never hinged 11.00
a. Inverted overprint 11.00 11.00
Never hinged 23.00
b. Double overprint 15.00 15.00
Never hinged 32.50
55 A22 5pa ocher (328) 40.00 35.00
Never hinged 87.50
a. Double overprint 80.00 80.00
Never hinged 165.00
56 A22 20pa car rose (330) 4.00 4.00
Never hinged 7.25
a. Inverted overprint 8.00 8.00
Never hinged 16.00
b. Double overprint 12.00 12.00
Never hinged 26.00
c. In pair with unovptd. stamp 17.50 17.50
Never hinged 35.00

On Commemorative Issue of 1916

57 A41 20pa ultra (347) 4.00 4.00
Never hinged 7.25
a. Inverted overprint 8.00 8.00
Never hinged 16.00
b. Double overprint 12.00 12.00
Never hinged 24.00
c. Double overprint, one inverted 9.50 9.50
Never hinged 20.00
d. In pair with unovptd. stamp 17.50 17.50
Never hinged 35.00
58 A41 1pi vio & blk (348) 3.75 3.75
Never hinged 6.50
a. Inverted overprint 7.50 7.50
Never hinged 16.00
b. Double overprint 10.00 10.00
Never hinged 20.00
59 A41 5pi yel brn & blk (349) 12.00 12.00
Never hinged 24.00
a. Inverted overprint 18.00 18.00
Never hinged 37.50
b. Double overprint 24.00 24.00
Never hinged 47.50

On Issue of 1916

59A A17 1pi blue (372) — —

On Issue of 1916-18

60 A43 5pa org (421) 45.00 40.00
Never hinged 87.50
a. Inverted overprint 70.00 70.00
Never hinged 140.00
b. Perf 11½ (421a) 45.00 40.00
Never hinged 87.50
61 A46 1pi dl vio (426) 13.50 13.50
Never hinged 27.50
a. Inverted overprint 21.00 21.00
Never hinged 45.00
b. Double overprint 35.00 35.00
Never hinged 75.00
63 A52 50pi green, *straw* (439) 35.00 27.50
Never hinged 72.50

On Issue of 1917

64 A53 5pi on 2pa Prus bl (547) 32.50 27.50
Never hinged 67.50
a. Double overprint 75.00 75.00
Never hinged 150.00
b. Perf 11½ (421a) 32.50 27.50
Never hinged 67.50

On Newspaper Stamp of 1916

65 A10 5pa on 10pa gray grn (P137) 8.75 8.75
Never hinged 17.50
a. Inverted overprint 13.50 13.50
Never hinged 27.50
b. Double overprint 24.00 24.00
Never hinged 27.50

On Semi-Postal Stamp of 1915

65A A21 20pa car rose (B8) 1,200. 850.00

On Semi-Postal Stamps of 1916

66 A17 1pi blue (B19) 30.00 30.00
Never hinged 67.50
a. Inverted overprint 55.00 55.00
Never hinged 120.00
67 A19 20pa car (B26) 13.50 13.50
Never hinged 27.50
a. Inverted overprint 17.50 17.50
Never hinged 35.00
b. Double overprint 17.50 17.50
Never hinged 35.00
68 A21 20pa car rose (B28) 180.00 92.50
Never hinged 350.00
69 A21 20pa car rose (B31) 8.00 8.00
Never hinged 16.00
a. Inverted overprint 15.00 15.00
Never hinged 30.00
b. Double overprint 22.50 22.50
Never hinged 45.00
69C A21 1pi ultra (401) 110.00 80.00
Never hinged 225.00
Nos. 51-69C (20) 1,760. 1,270.

Turkey No. 424 Handstamped

1919

71 A44 10pa green (420) 9.50 9.50
Never hinged 20.00
a. Inverted overprint 17.50 17.50
Never hinged 35.00
b. Double overprint 25.00 25.00
Never hinged 50.00
c. Perf 11½ (420a) 11.00 11.00
Never hinged 23.00

"T.E.O." stands for "Territoires Ennemis Occupés."

Turkish Stamps of 1913-19 Overprinted in Black, Red or Blue

In this setting there are various broken and wrong font letters and the letter "i" is sometimes replaced by a "t."

1919 On Pictorial Issue of 1913

75 A30 1pi blue (R) (260) 4.75 4.75
Never hinged 9.50
a. Inverted overprint 11.00 11.00
Never hinged 23.00
b. Double overprint 11.00 11.00
Never hinged 23.00
c. Double overprint, one inverted 20.00 20.00
Never hinged 40.00

On Issue of 1915

76 A21 20pa car rose (318) 8.75 8.75
Never hinged 17.50

On Commemorative Issue of 1916

76A A41 5pa grn (345) 200.00 110.00
77 A41 20pa ultra (347) 13.50 13.50
Never hinged 27.50
a. Inverted overprint 20.00 20.00
Never hinged 40.00
b. Double overprint 30.00 30.00
Never hinged 60.00
c. Perf 12½ (347a) 13.50 13.50
Never hinged 27.50
78 A41 1pi vio & blk (348) 24.00 24.00
Never hinged 47.50
a. Inverted overprint 35.00 35.00
Never hinged 70.00
b. Double overprint 60.00 60.00
Never hinged 120.00
c. Double overprint, one inverted 65.00 65.00
Never hinged 130.00

On Issue of 1916-18

79 A43 5pa org (Bl) (421) 4.75 4.75
Never hinged 9.50
a. Inverted overprint 9.50 9.50
Never hinged 20.00
b. Double overprint 13.00 13.00
Never hinged 27.50
c. Double overprint, one inverted 11.00 11.00
Never hinged 24.00
d. Perf 11½ (421a) 4.75 4.75
Never hinged 9.50
80 A44 10pa grn (424) 8.75 8.75
Never hinged 17.50
a. Inverted overprint 16.00 16.00
Never hinged 32.50
b. Double overprint 22.50 22.50
Never hinged 45.00
c. Double overprint, one inverted 20.00 20.00
Never hinged 40.00
d. Perf 11½ (424a) 8.75 8.75
Never hinged 17.50
81 A45 20pa dp rose (Bk) (425) 27.50 27.50
Never hinged 65.00
a. Double overprint 60.00 60.00
Never hinged 120.00
82 A45 20pa dp rose (Bl) (425) 1.00 1.00
Never hinged 2.00
a. Inverted overprint 5.50 5.50
Never hinged 12.00
b. Double overprint 8.00 8.00
Never hinged 17.50
c. Double overprint, one inverted 10.00 10.00
Never hinged 22.50
83 A48 2pi org brn & indigo (429) 1.60 1.60
Never hinged 2.40
a. Double overprint 5.50 5.50
Never hinged 12.00
b. Perf 11½ (429a) 1.60 1.60
Never hinged 2.50
83C A49 5pi pale blue & black (R) (430) 1.60 1.60
Never hinged 3.25
a. Inverted overprint 9.50 9.50
Never hinged 20.00
b. Double overprint 9.50 9.50
Never hinged 20.00
c. Double overprint, one inverted 12.00 12.00
Never hinged 24.00
d. Perf 11½ (430a) 1.60 1.60
Never hinged 3.25
84 A51 25pi car, *straw* (434) 5.50 5.50
Never hinged 12.00
a. Inverted overprint 15.00 15.00
Never hinged 30.00
b. Double overprint 20.00 20.00
Never hinged 40.00
c. Double overprint, one inverted 13.50 13.50
Never hinged 27.50
85 A52 50pi grn, *straw* (439) 92.50 87.50
Never hinged 190.00
a. Inverted overprint 150.00 150.00
b. Double overprint 150.00 150.00
c. Double overprint, one inverted 160.00 160.00

On Issue of 1917

85A A53 5pi on 2pa Prus bl (547) —
86 A53 5pi on 2pa Prus bl (548) 13.50 13.50
Never hinged 27.50
a. Perf 11½ (548c) 13.50 13.50
Never hinged 27.50

On Newspaper Stamps of 1916-19

87 A10 5pa on 10p gray grn (P137) 2.25 2.25
Never hinged 2.60
a. Inverted overprint 5.50 5.50
Never hinged 12.00
b. Double overprint 7.00 7.00
Never hinged 15.00
c. Double overprint, one inverted 13.50 13.50
Never hinged 27.50
88 A21 5pa on 2pa ol grn (P173) 1.00 1.00
Never hinged 2.00
a. Inverted overprint 5.50 5.50
Never hinged 12.00
b. Double overprint 7.00 7.00
Never hinged 15.00
c. Double overprint, one inverted 6.50 6.50
Never hinged 13.50

On Semi-Postal Stamps of 1915-17

90 A21 20pa car rose (B28) 8.75 8.75
Never hinged 17.50
a. Double overprint 16.00 16.00
Never hinged 32.50
91 A41 10pa car (B42) 3.25 3.25
Never hinged 4.75
a. Inverted overprint 7.25 7.25
Never hinged 14.50
b. Double overprint 9.00 9.00
Never hinged 18.00
c. Double overprint, one inverted 12.00 12.00

Never hinged 24.00
d. Perf 12½ (B42b) 3.25 3.25
Never hinged 4.75
92 A11 10pa on 20pa vio brn (B38) 3.25 3.25
Never hinged 4.75
a. Inverted overprint 9.50 9.50
Never hinged 20.00
b. Double overprint 12.00 12.00
Never hinged 25.00
c. Double overprint, one inverted 14.00 14.00
Never hinged 28.50
93 SP1 10pa red vio (B46) 2.50 2.50
Never hinged 4.00
a. Overprint sideways 8.00 8.00
Never hinged 16.00

It is understood that the newspaper and semi-postal stamps overprinted "Cilicie" were used as ordinary postage stamps.

A1

1920 Blue Surcharge ***Perf. 11½***
98 A1 70pa on 5pa red 2.40 2.40
Never hinged 4.00
a. Double surcharge 40.00 40.00
Never hinged 80.00
b. Triple surcharge 240.00
c. Inverted surcharge 35.00 35.00
Never hinged 72.50
d. Double overprint, one inverted 45.00 45.00
Never hinged 87.50
e. In pair with unovptd. stamp 110.00
Never hinged 190.00
f. "OCCCPATION" for "OCCUPATION" 17.50 17.50
Never hinged 35.00
g. "OCCUPTTION" for "OCCUPATION" 17.50 17.50
Never hinged 35.00
99 A1 3½pi on 5pa red 3.00 2.75
Never hinged 4.00
a. Se-tenant with No. 98, horiz. pair 120.00 120.00
Never hinged 225.00
b. As "a," inverted surcharge 240.00 240.00
c. Double surcharge 40.00 40.00
Never hinged 80.00
d. Inverted surcharge 35.00 35.00
Never hinged 72.50
e. Double surcharge, one inverted 45.00 45.00
Never hinged 87.50
f. "OCCCPATION" for "OCCUPATION" 17.50 17.50
Never hinged 35.00
g. "OCCUPTTION" for "OCCUPATION" 17.50 17.50
Never hinged 35.00
h. "P" of "OCCUPATION" inverted 45.00 45.00
Never hinged 87.50
i. "PIATSRES" for "PIASTERS" 45.00 45.00
Never hinged 87.50

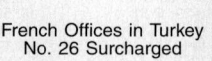

French Offices in Turkey No. 26 Surcharged

1920 ***Perf. 14x13½***
100 A3 20pa on 10c rose red (I) 2.00 2.00
Never hinged 2.00
On cover 24.00
a. "PARAS" omitted 72.50 72.50
Never hinged 130.00
b. Second "A" of "PARAS" omitted 72.50 72.50
Never hinged 130.00
c. "S" of "PARAS" inverted 65.00 65.00
Never hinged 110.00
d. Overprint type II 35.00 35.00
Never hinged 65.00
On cover 120.00
e. Overprint type III 35.00 35.00
Never hinged 65.00
On cover 120.00
f. Pair, #100 + #100c 45.00 45.00
Never hinged 80.00
g. Pair, #100 + #100d 45.00 45.00
Never hinged 80.00
h. Strip, #100 + #100c + #100e 110.00 110.00
Never hinged 180.00

Three types of "20" exist on No. 100: I, "2" bold; II "2" faint; III, "0" distinctly taller than "2."

Stamps of France, 1900-17, Surcharged

1920
101 A16 5pa on 2c vio brn 1.60 1.60
Never hinged 2.75
On cover 47.50
102 A22 10pa on 5c green 2.00 2.00
Never hinged 3.25
On cover 47.50
103 A22 20pa on 10c red 4.00 4.00
Never hinged 6.75
On cover 47.50
On cover, single franking 67.50
104 A22 1pi on 25c blue 2.75 2.25
Never hinged 4.00
On cover 32.50
On cover, single franking 52.50
105 A20 2pi on 15c gray green 12.00 12.00
Never hinged 22.50
On cover 120.00
On cover, single franking 200.00
106 A18 5pi on 40c red & gray bl 26.00 26.00
Never hinged 47.50
On cover 200.00
On cover, single franking 325.00
107 A18 10pi on 50c bis brn & lav 32.50 32.50
Never hinged 52.50
On cover 240.00
On cover, single franking 400.00
108 A18 50pi on 1fr claret & ol grn 180.00 180.00
Never hinged 300.00
On cover 675.00
109 A18 100pi on 5fr dk bl & buff 900.00 900.00
On cover *2,200.*
Nos. 101-109 (9) 1,161. 1,160.

Nos. 106 to 109 surcharged in four lines.
"O.M.F." stands for "Occupation Militaire Francaise."

1917 Stamps of France Surcharged

No. 110

No. 115

1920
110 A16 5pa on 2c vio brn (109b) 13.00
Never hinged 23.00
a. "S" of "EST" inverted 160.00
111 A22 10pa on 5c grn (110b) 13.00
Never hinged 23.00
a. "S" of "EST" inverted 180.00
b. Double surcharge 75.00
Never hinged 125.00
c. On ordinary paper (110) 19.00
Never hinged 35.00
112 A22 20pa on 10c red (162) 9.75
Never hinged 16.00
a. Inverted surcharge 75.00
Never hinged 125.00
b. Double surcharge 67.50
Never hinged 115.00
c. "S" of "EST" inverted 130.00
113 A22 1pi on 25c bl (168d) 6.00
Never hinged 9.50
a. "S" of "EST" inverted 65.00
Never hinged 115.00
b. On ordinary paper (168) 9.50
Never hinged 16.00
114 A20 2pi on 15c gray grn (139c) 27.00
Never hinged 47.50
a. "S" of "EST" inverted 240.00
115 A18 5pi on 40c red & gray bl (121) 50.00
Never hinged 85.00
a. "N" of "SAND." inverted 260.00
116 A18 20pi on 1fr claret & ol grn (125) 190.00
Never hinged 315.00
a. "O.M.F. Cilicie" omitted 625.00
b. Double surcharge 625.00
c. "N" of "SAND." inverted 525.00
Nos. 110-116 (7) 308.75

On Nos. 115 and 116 "SAND. EST" is placed vertically. "Sand. Est" is an abbreviation of Sandjak de l'Est (Eastern County).

Nos. 110-116 were prepared for use, but never issued.

Stamps of France, 1900-17, Surcharged

First Setting: 1.75-2mm spacing between "Cilicie" and figures of value

1920
117 A16 5pa on 2c vio brn, *grayish (GC)* 1.25 1.25
Never hinged 1.60
On cover 32.50
a. Inverted surcharge 32.50 27.50
Never hinged 47.50
b. "Cililie" 35.00 35.00
Never hinged 67.50
c. Surcharge 5pi (error) 60.00 60.00
Never hinged 110.00
d. "5" omitted from surcharge 35.00 35.00
Never hinged 67.50
e. As "c," "e" inverted 27.50 27.50
Never hinged 47.50
f. "S" of "PARAS" inverted 35.00 35.00
Never hinged 67.50
119 A22 10pa on 5c grn, *grayish (GC)* 1.50 1.50
Never hinged 1.50
On cover 22.50
a. Inverted surcharge 30.00 26.00
Never hinged 50.00
b. Surch. 5pa (error), upright 55.00 55.00
Never hinged 100.00
c. Surch. 5pa (error), invtd. 75.00 67.50
Never hinged 140.00
d. "e" in "Cilicie" inverted 32.50 32.50
Never hinged 52.50
e. "S" in "PARAS" inverted 35.00 35.00
Never hinged 67.50
121 A22 20pa on 10c red 1.75 1.75
Never hinged 1.60
On cover 24.00
On cover, single franking 32.50
a. Inverted surcharge 32.50 27.50
Never hinged 52.50
b. Surch. 10pa (error), upright 60.00 60.00
Never hinged 100.00
c. Surch. 10pa (error), invtd. 80.00 72.50
Never hinged 150.00
d. "S" in "PARAS" inverted 35.00 35.00
Never hinged 67.50
122 A22 1pi on 25c bl, *grayish (GC)* 2.00 2.00
Never hinged 2.40
On cover 20.00
On cover, single franking 27.50
a. Double surcharge 72.50 72.50
Never hinged 120.00
b. Inverted surcharge 55.00 52.50
Never hinged 92.50
c. First "S" in "PIASTRE" inverted 45.00 45.00
Never hinged 80.00
123 A20 2pi on 15c gray grn, *grayish (GC)* 2.25 2.25
Never hinged 4.00
On cover 40.00
On cover, single franking 67.50
a. Double surcharge 45.00 45.00
Never hinged 80.00
b. Inverted surcharge 35.00 32.50
Never hinged 67.50
c. Double surcharge, one inverted 55.00 55.00
Never hinged 92.50
d. First "S" in "PIASTRES" inverted 72.50 72.50
Never hinged 120.00
124 A18 5pi on 40c red & gray bl, *grayish (GC)* 4.00 4.00
Never hinged 7.50
On cover 52.50
On cover, single franking 87.50
a. Double surcharge 65.00 65.00
Never hinged 110.00
b. Inverted surcharge 40.00 40.00
Never hinged 72.50
c. First "S" in "PIASTRES" inverted 72.50 72.50
Never hinged 120.00
125 A18 10pi on 50c bis brn & lav, *grayish (GC)* 12.50 12.50
Never hinged 24.00
On cover 100.00
On cover, single franking 175.00
a. Double surcharge 60.00 60.00
Never hinged 110.00
b. Inverted surcharge 55.00 47.50
Never hinged 62.50
c. First "S" in "PIASTRES" inverted 110.00 110.00
Never hinged 180.00
126 A18 50pi on 1fr clar & ol grn, *grayish (GC)* 17.50 17.50
Never hinged 35.00
On cover 140.00
On cover, single franking 240.00
a. Inverted surcharge 130.00
b. Double surcharge 180.00
c. First "S" in "PIASTRES" inverted 180.00
127 A18 100pi on 5fr dk bl & buff 45.00 45.00
Never hinged 80.00
On cover 350.00
On cover, single franking 800.00

a. Inverted surcharge 180.00
b. First "S" in "PIASTRES" inverted 240.00
Nos. 117-127 (9) 87.75 87.75

Second Setting: 1-1.5mm spacing between "Cilicie" and figures of value

117g A16 5pa on 2c vio brn, *grayish (GC)* .65 .65
Never hinged 1.20
On cover 24.00
h. Double surcharge 35.00 35.00
Never hinged 67.50
i. "Cilicie" omitted 32.50 32.50
Never hinged 52.50
j. Surch. "O.M.F. / PARAS / 5 / PARAS" 55.00 55.00
Never hinged 100.00
119f A22 10pa on 5c green, *grayish (GC)* .65 .65
Never hinged 1.20
On cover 20.00
g. On ordinary paper 1.60 1.60
Never hinged 2.40
On cover 24.00
h. Surch. "O.M.F. / PARAS / 10 / PARAS" 55.00 55.00
Never hinged 100.00
121e A22 20pa on 10c red .70 .70
Never hinged 1.20
On cover 20.00
On cover, single franking 27.50
f. Double surcharge 35.00 35.00
Never hinged 65.00
g. Double surcharge, one inverted 47.50 47.50
Never hinged 80.00
122d A22 1pi on 25c blue, *grayish (GC)* .95 .95
Never hinged 1.60
On cover 16.00
On cover, single franking 24.00
e. Inverted surcharge 35.00 32.50
Never hinged 67.50
f. On ordinary paper 2.40 2.40
Never hinged 4.00
On cover 20.00
On cover, single franking 27.50
123e A20 2pi on 15c gray grn, *grayish (GC)* 1.00 1.00
Never hinged 1.60
On cover 27.50
On cover, single franking 40.00
f. Second "S" in "PIASTRES" omitted 21.00 21.00
Never hinged 35.00
124d A18 5pi on 40c red & gray bl, *grayish (GC)* 3.25 3.25
Never hinged 5.50
On cover 47.50
On cover, single franking 80.00
e. "PIASRTES" 72.50 72.50
Never hinged 120.00
125d A18 10pi on 50c bis brn & lavender, *grayish (GC)* 3.25 3.25
Never hinged 5.50
On cover 60.00
On cover, single franking 100.00
e. "PIASRTES" 72.50 72.50
Never hinged 120.00
f. On ordinary paper 8.00 8.00
Never hinged 13.50
On cover 80.00
On cover, single franking 130.00
126d A18 50pi on 1fr claret & ol grn, *grayish (GC)* 13.50 13.50
Never hinged 25.00
On cover 120.00
On cover, single franking 225.00
e. "PIASRTES" 87.50
Never hinged 150.00
f. "50" omitted 87.50
Never hinged 150.00
127c A18 100pi on 5fr dk bl & buff 300.00 300.00
On cover *1,200.*
On cover, single franking —
d. "PIASRTES" *925.00*
Nos. 117g-127c (9) 323.95 323.95

This surcharge has "O.M.F." in thicker letters than the preceding issues.

Most of the French stamps overprinted for this issue were from the wartime printings, on poor quality grayish paper (GC, or *Grande Consommation* paper).

For overprints see Nos. C1-C2.

AIR POST STAMPS

Nos. 123 and 124 Handstamped

Perf. 14x13½
1920, July 15 **Unwmk.**
C1 A20 2pi on 15c gray grn *9,250.* 9,250.
On cover 35,000.
C2 A18 5pi on 40c red & gray blue 9,500. 9,500.
On cover 35,000.
a. "PIASRTES"

A very limited number of Nos. C1 and C2 were used on two air mail flights between

Adana and Aleppo. At a later date impressions from a new handstamp were struck "to oblige" on stamps of the regular issue of 1920 (Nos. 123, 124, 125 and 126) that were in stock at the Adana Post Office.

Counterfeits exist.

POSTAGE DUE STAMPS

Turkish Postage Due Stamps of 1914 Handstamped

Handstamped

1919	**Unwmk.**	***Perf. 12***	
J1	D1 5pa claret	22.00	22.00
	Never hinged	45.00	
a.	Inverted overprint	35.00	35.00
	Never hinged	70.00	
b.	Double overprint	50.00	50.00
	Never hinged	100.00	
J2	D2 20pa red	22.50	22.50
	Never hinged	45.00	
a.	Inverted overprint	35.00	35.00
	Never hinged	70.00	
b.	Double overprint	50.00	50.00
	Never hinged	100.00	
J3	D3 1pi dark blue	35.00	35.00
	Never hinged	72.50	
a.	Inverted overprint	50.00	50.00
	Never hinged	100.00	
J4	D4 2pi slate	45.00	45.00
	Never hinged	90.00	
a.	Inverted overprint	65.00	65.00
	Never hinged	130.00	
	Nos. J1-J4 (4)	124.50	124.50

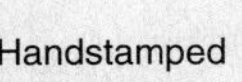

Handstamped

J5	D1 5pa claret	26.00	26.00
	Never hinged	52.50	
a.	Inverted overprint	40.00	40.00
	Never hinged	80.00	
b.	Double overprint	55.00	55.00
	Never hinged	110.00	
J6	D2 20pa red	30.00	30.00
	Never hinged	60.00	
a.	Inverted overprint	45.00	45.00
	Never hinged	87.50	
b.	Double overprint	60.00	60.00
	Never hinged	120.00	
J7	D3 1pi dark blue	35.00	35.00
	Never hinged	72.50	
a.	Inverted overprint	47.50	47.50
	Never hinged	95.00	
J8	D4 2pi slate	35.00	35.00
	Never hinged	72.50	
a.	Inverted overprint	47.50	47.50
	Never hinged	95.00	
	Nos. J5-J8 (4)	126.00	126.00

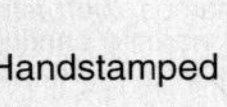

Handstamped

J9	D1 5pa claret	22.00	22.00
	Never hinged	45.00	
a.	Inverted overprint	32.50	32.50
	Never hinged	65.00	
b.	Double overprint	32.50	32.50
	Never hinged	65.00	
J10	D2 20pa red	22.50	22.50
	Never hinged	45.00	
a.	Inverted overprint	32.50	32.50
	Never hinged	65.00	
b.	Double overprint	35.00	35.00
	Never hinged	65.00	
J11	D3 1pi dark blue	35.00	35.00
	Never hinged	67.50	
a.	Inverted overprint	47.50	47.50
	Never hinged	95.00	
J12	D4 2pi slate	22.00	22.00
	Never hinged	45.00	
a.	Inverted overprint	32.50	32.50
	Never hinged	65.00	
	Nos. J9-J12 (4)	101.50	101.50

Postage Due Stamps of France Surcharged

1921			
J13	D2 1pi on 10c choc	11.00	11.00
	Never hinged	18.00	
a.	Inverted overprint	130.00	
	Never hinged	225.00	
b.	Period after "O" omitted	35.00	
	Never hinged	65.00	
c.	Period after "M" omitted	35.00	
	Never hinged	65.00	
J14	D2 2pi on 20c olive grn	11.00	11.00
	Never hinged	18.00	
a.	Inverted overprint	130.00	
	Never hinged	225.00	
b.	Period after "M" omitted	35.00	
	Never hinged	65.00	
c.	First "S" in "PIASTRES" inverted	32.50	
	Never hinged	60.00	
J15	D2 3pi on 30c red	11.00	11.00
	Never hinged	17.50	
a.	Inverted overprint	92.50	
	Never hinged	150.00	
b.	Period after "O" omitted	35.00	
	Never hinged	65.00	
c.	Period after "M" omitted	35.00	
	Never hinged	65.00	
J16	D2 4pi on 50c vio brn	10.50	10.50
	Never hinged	17.50	
a.	Inverted overprint	92.50	
	Never hinged	150.00	
	Nos. J13-J16 (4)	43.50	43.50

COCHIN CHINA

'kō-chən 'chī-nə

LOCATION — The southernmost state of French Indo-China in the Cambodian Peninsula.
GOVT. — French Colony
AREA — 26,476 sq. mi.
POP. — 4,615,968
CAPITAL — Saigon

100 Centimes = 1 Franc

Surcharged in Black on Stamps of French Colonies

a

b

c

1886-87	**Unwmk.**	***Perf. 14x13½***	
1	A9(a) 5c on 25c yel, *straw*	225.00	120.00
	No gum	160.00	
	On cover		*2,000.*
2	A9(b) 5c on 2c brn, *buff*	40.00	*32.50*
	No gum	30.00	
	On cover		*1,500.*
a.	9¼mm between "5" and "C. CH."	*90.00*	*60.00*
3	A9(b) 5c on 25c yel, *straw*	32.50	27.50
	No gum	26.00	
	On cover		*1,200.*
a.	Inverted surcharge	*275.00*	*275.00*
b.	9¼mm between "5" and "C. CH."	*90.00*	*60.00*
4	A9(c) 5c on 25c blk, *rose* ('87)	60.00	47.50
	No gum	45.00	
	On cover		*1,500.*
a.	Double surch., one of type b	*3,750.*	*2,750.*
b.	Triple surch., two of type b	—	—
c.	Inverted surcharge	375.00	375.00
d.	Double surch., both type "a"	*2,750.*	*3,250.*
e.	Triple surch., types "a," "b" and "c"		*8,750.*
	Nos. 1-4 (4)	357.50	227.50

The space between "5" and "C. CH." on Nos. 2 and 3 is normally 8½mm. The wider spacing occurs in six positions on each pane.

Covers: Values for covers are for commercial items with proper rates.

1888			
5	A9 15c on half of 30c brn, *bis*	125.00	
	No gum	90.00	

No. 5 was prepared but not issued.

The so-called Postage Due stamps were never issued.

Stamps of Cochin China were superseded by those of Indo-China in 1892.

COLOMBIA

kə-'ləm-bē-ə

LOCATION — On the northwest coast of South America, bordering on the Caribbean Sea and the Pacific Ocean
GOVT. — Republic
AREA — 456,535 sq. mi.
POP. — 28,240,000 (est. 1984)
CAPITAL — Bogota

In 1810 the Spanish Viceroyalty of New Granada gained its independence and with Venezuela and Ecuador formed the State of Greater Colombia. In 1832 this state split into three independent units as Venezuela, Ecuador and the Republic of New Granada. The name of the country has been, successively, Granadine Confederation (1858-61), United States of New Granada (1861), United States of Colombia (1861-65), and the Republic of Colombia (1885 to date).

100 Centavos = 1 Peso

In the earlier days many towns did not have handstamps for canceling and stamps were canceled with pen and ink. Pen cancellations, therefore, do not indicate fiscal use. (Postage stamps were not used for revenue purposes.) Used values for Nos. 1-128 are for stamps with illegible manuscript cancels or handstamp cancels of Bogota or Medellin. Stamps with legible manuscript or other handstamped town-name cancels sell for more.

Fractions of many Colombian stamps of both early and late issues are found canceled, their use to pay postage having been tolerated even though forbidden by the postal laws and regulations. Many are known to have been made for philatelic purposes.

Watermarks

Wmk. 116 — Crosses and Circles

Wmk. 127 — Quatrefoils

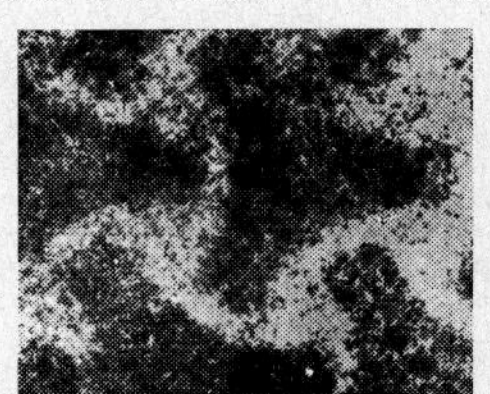

Wmk. 194 — Multiple Curvilinear Triangles

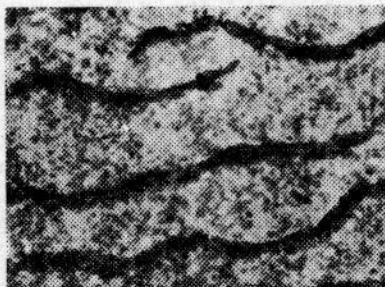

Wmk. 229 — Wavy Lines

Wmk. 255 — Wavy Lines and C Multiple

STAMPS OF GREAT BRITAIN USED IN COLOMBIA

Crowned Circle handstamp types and numeral cancellation types A and B are pictured in the Crowned Circle Handstamps and Great Britain Used Abroad section.

Values are for clear cancellations on sound, fault-free stamps, with average to fine centering. In many cases, very fine examples are rare or non-existent.

CARTAGENA

Pre-Stamp Postal Markings

1841		
A1	Crowned Circle handstamp Type II, on cover, inscribed "PAID AT CARTHAGENA" in red	*1,500.*
A2	Crowned Circle handstamp Type I, on cover, inscribed "PAID AT CARTHAGENA" in black	1,100.

Earliest known uses: A1, 1/15/41; A2, 7/1/46.

Stamps of Great Britain, Canceled C56, Type A

1865-84		
A3	½p rose red (#58 P 10)	—
A4	1p rose red (#33, P 78, 87, 100, 111, 113, 117, 119, 125, 172, 189, 217) *value from*	62.50
A5	2p blue (#29, P 9)	62.50
A6	2p blue (#30, P 14)	82.50
A7	3p rose (#44)	—
A8	3p rose (#49, P 4, 5)	—
A9	3p rose (#61, P 12, 17, 18) *value from*	62.50
A10	4p vermilion (#43, P 7-14) *value from*	62.50
A11	4p vermilion (#69, P 15)	350.00
A12	4p pale olive green (#70, P 15, 16)	225.00
A13	6p lilac (#45, P 5, 6)	—
A14	6p dull violet (#50, P 6)	85.00
A15	6p violet (#51, P 8)	87.50
A16	6p gray (#60, P 12)	240.00
A17	6p gray (#62, P 13-16) *value from*	62.50
A18	8p orange (#73)	375.00
A19	9p straw (#46)	—
A20	1sh green (#48, P 4)	—
A21	1sh green (#54, P 4, 5, 7) *value from*	70.00
A22	1sh green (#64, P 12, 13) *value from*	80.00
	Plates 8-11 *value from*	80.00
A23	1sh salmon (#87)	—
A24	2sh blue (#55)	325.00
A25	5sh rose (#57, P 1)	650.00

Stamps of Great Britain, Canceled C65, Type B

A26	½p rose red (#58, P 10)	—
A27	1p rose red (#33, P 100, 106, 111, 123) *value from*	85.00
A28	1½p dull rose (#32)	—
A29	2p blue (#29, P 9)	85.00
A30	2p lilac rose (#81)	—

A31 2½p blue (#68) —
A32 3p rose (#49, P 9) —
A33 3p rose (#61, P 14, 17, 19, 20) —
A34 4p vermilion (#43, P 7-9, 11-14) *value from* 70.00
A35 4p vermilion (#69, P 15) 350.00
A36 4p pale olive green (#70, P 15, 16) 225.00
A37 6p dull violet (#50, P 6) 105.00
A38 6p violet (#51, P 8) 105.00
A39 6p pale buff (#51, P 8) —
A40 6p gray (#60, P 12) 240.00
A41 6p gray (#60, P 13, 15-17) *value from* 70.00
A42 8p orange (#73) 450.00
A43 9p straw (#46) 510.00
A44 1sh green (#48, P 4) 150.00
A45 1sh green (#54, P 4-7) *value from* 75.00
A46 1sh green (#64, P 12, 13) *value from* 85.00
Plates 8, 11 *value from* 85.00
A47 1sh salmon (#87) —
A48 2sh blue (#55) 750.00
A49 2sh brown (#56) *2,750.*
A50 5sh pale rose (#57a, P 1) 575.00
Plate 2 725.00
A51 5sh rose (#57, P 1) 600.00
Plate 2 725.00

The C65 canceler was supplied to the British post office in Cartagena in error. C56 was the obliterator assigned to Cartagena.

CHAGRES

Pre-Stamp Postal Markings

A52 Crowned Circle handstamp Type I, on cover, inscribed "PAID AT CHAGRES" in black —

Chagres is located in what is now the Republic of Panama. It was the chief Atlantic port of the isthmus from the 18th century and activity reached a zenith during the 1840s-1850s, when it was the Atlantic terminus for the trans-Isthmian route for miners en route to California.

Earliest known use: 9/16/46.

COLON

Pre-Stamp Postal Marking

A53 Crowned Circle handstamp Type VI, on cover, inscribed "PAID AT COLON" in red *5,500.*

Colon is located in what is now the Republic of Panama.

Earliest known use: 6/21/54.

Stamps of Great Britain, Canceled E88, Type B

1865-81

A54 1p rose red (#33, see footnote) *value from* 57.50

#A54 plate numbers 107, 121-123, 125, 127, 130, 131, 133, 136, 142, 150-153, 155-158, 160, 169-171, 174, 176, 178, 179, 184, 187, 188, 194, 195, 201, 209, 213, 214, 217.

A55 1p red brown (#79) 125.00
A56 1½p dull rose (#32, P 3) *125.00*
A57 2p blue (#30, P 14, 15) *value from* 57.50
A58 2p lilac rose (#81) —
A59 3p rose (#49, P 6, 9) —
A60 3p rose (#61, P 11, 12, 16, 18-20) *value from* 65.00
A61 4p vermilion (#43, P 10-14) *value from* 65.00
A62 4p vermilion (#69, P 15) —
A63 4p pale olive green (#70, P 15, 16) *value from* 225.00
A64 4p gray brown (#71, P 17) *375.00*
A65 4p gray brown (#84, P 17) *85.00*
A66 6p violet (#51, P 6, 8, 9) —
A67 6p pale buff (#59b, P 11) —
A68 6p brown (#59, P 11) 75.00
A69 6p gray (#60, P 12) —
A70 6p gray (#62, P 13-17) *value from* 62.50
A71 8p orange (#73) —
A72 9p bister (#52) 260.00
A73 10p red brown (#53) —
A74 1sh green (#54, P 4-7) *value from* 57.50
A75 1sh green (#64, P 8-13) *value from* 75.00
A76 1sh salmon (#65) *425.00*
A77 1sh salmon (#87, P 13) *175.00*
A78 2sh blue (#55) 175.00
A79 2sh brown (#56) *2,500.*
A80 5sh pale rose (#57a, P 1) 575.00
Plate 2 700.00
A81 5sh rose (#57, P 1) 575.00
Plate 2 700.00

PANAMA

Pre-Stamp Postal Marking

1846

A82 Crowned Circle handstamp Type I, on cover, inscribed "PAID AT PANAMA" in red *2,200.*

Panama is located in what is now the Republic of Panama.

Earliest known use: 8/24/46.

Stamps of Great Britain, Canceled C35, Type A or B

No. A128

1865-81

A83 ½p rose red (#58 P 10-15, 19) *value from* 57.50
A84 1p rose red (#33, see footnote) *value from* 37.50

#A84 plate numbers 71, 72, 76, 81, 85, 87-89, 93, 95, 96, 101, 104, 114, 122, 124, 130, 138, 139, 142, 159, 168, 171, 172, 174, 179, 180, 184, 185, 187, 189, 191-193, 196, 197, 200, 203-205, 207-211, 213-215, 218, 224.

A85 1p red brown (#79) 65.00
A86 1½p lake red (#32a, P 3) 75.00
A87 1½p red brown (#80) —
A88 2p blue (#29, P 9) 42.50
Plate 12 80.00
A89 2p blue (#30, P 13-15) *value from* 42.50
A90 2p blue (#81) 110.00
A91 2½p claret (#66, P 1) 225.00
A92 2½p claret (#67, P 4, 12, 16) 200.00
A93 2½p blue (#68, P 19) —
A94 2½p blue (#82, P 22, 23) —
A95 3p rose (#37) 290.00
A96 3p rose (#44) —
A97 3p rose (#49, P 4-9) *value from* 57.50
A98 3p rose (#61, P 12, 14-20) *value from* 42.50
A99 3p rose (#83, P 20, 21) —
A100 4p vermilion (#34a, P4) 125.00
A101 4p vermilion, "hair-lines" (#34c, P 4) —
A102 4p vermilion (#43, P 7-14) *value from* 57.50
A103 4p vermilion (#69, P 15) 350.00
A104 4p pale olive green (#70, P 16) 225.00
Plate 15 *275.00*
A105 4p gray brown (#84, P 17, 18) *value from* 57.50
A106 5p deep indigo (#85) *220.00*
A107 6p lilac (#39, P 3) 110.00
A108 6p lilac (#39b, P 4) *150.00*
A109 6p lilac (#45, P 5) 85.00
Plate 6 *150.00*
A110 6p dull violet (#50, P 6) —
A111 6p violet (#51, P 6, 8, 9) *value from* 80.00
A112 6p pale buff (#59b, P 11) 85.00
Plate 12 *250.00*
A113 6p brown (#59, P 11) 57.50
A114 6p gray (#60, P 12) 240.00
A115 6p gray (#62, P 13-17) *value from* 57.50
A116 6p gray (#86, P 17) 80.00
A117 8p orange (#73) 350.00
A118 9p straw (#40) 400.00
A119 9p bister (#52) 290.00
A120 10p red brown (#53) 310.00
A121 1sh green (#48, P 4) 160.00
A122 1sh green (#54, P 4-6) *value from* 52.50
Plate 7 65.00
A123 1sh green (#64, P 12, 13) *value from* 70.00
Plates 8-11 *value from* 75.00
A124 1sh salmon (#65, P 13) 450.00
A125 1sh salmon (#87, P 13) *125.00*
A126 2sh blue (#55) 150.00
A127 2sh brown (#56) *2,500.*
A128 5sh pale rose (#57a, P 1) 550.00
Plate 2 700.00
A129 5sh rose (#57, P 1) 575.00
Plate 2 700.00

Later stamps of Great Britain are also known canceled "C35." These originate on mail posted aboard British civilian ships, and on other forms of ship mail which transited through Panama.

SANTA MARTHA

Pre-Stamp Postal Marking

1841

A130 Crowned Circle handstamp Type V, on cover, inscribed "PAID AT SANTA MARTHA" in red *2,200.*

Earliest known use: 12/15/41.

Stamps of Great Britain, Canceled C62, Type A

1865-81

A131 ½p rose red (#58 P 8) *110.00*
A132 1p rose red (#33, P 33) 75.00
A133 2p blue (#29, P 9) 110.00
A134 2p blue (#30, P 14) 110.00
A135 4p vermilion (#43, P 7-9, 11-14) *value from* 70.00
A136 4p pale olive green (#70, P 15) 225.00
A137 4p gray brown (#71, P 17) *375.00*
A138 4p gray brown (#84, P 17) 85.00
A139 6p lilac (#45, P 5) 115.00
A140 6p gray (#60, P 12) —
A141 6p gray (#62, P 14) —
A142 8p orange (#73) 400.00
A143 9p straw (#40) —
A144 1sh green (#48, P 4) 180.00
A145 1sh green (#54, P 5, 7) *value from* 85.00
A146 1sh green (#64, P 8) —
A147 2sh blue (#55) 350.00
A148 5sh rose (#57, P 2) 725.00

SAVANILLA (BARRANQUILLA)

Stamps of Great Britain, Canceled F69, Type B

1872-81

A149 ½p rose red (#58 P 6) 105.00
A150 1p rose red (#33, P 122, 171) *value from* 75.00
A151 1½p lake red (#32a, P 3) 125.00
A152 3p rose (#49, P 7) —
A153 3p rose (#61, P 20) 115.00
A154 3p rose (#83, P 20) 115.00
A155 4p ver (#43, P 12-14) *value from* 70.00
A156 4p ver (#69, P 15) 350.00
A157 4p pale ol grn (#70, P 16) 260.00
Plate 15 *290.00*
A158 4p gray brn (#71, P 17) *425.00*
A159 4p gray brn (#84, P 17) 85.00
A160 6p pale buff (#59b, P 11) —
A161 6p gray (#86, P 16, 17) *value from* 90.00
A162 8p org (#73) 450.00
A163 1sh grn (#54, P 5, 7) *value from* 85.00
A164 1sh grn (#64, P 8, 11-13) *value from* 90.00
A165 1sh salmon (#65, P 13) 450.00
A166 2sh blue (#55) 260.00
A167 5sh rose (#57, P 2) 725.00

ISSUES OF COLOMBIA

Granadine Confederation

Coat of Arms — A1

Type A1 — Asterisks in frame. Wavy lines in background.

Type A2 — Diamond-shaped ornaments in frame. Straight lines in background. Numerals larger.

1859 Unwmk. Litho. *Imperf.*

Wove Paper

1	A1 2½c green	120.00	120.00
a.	2½c yellow green	120.00	120.00
b.	2½c olive green	90.00	90.00
c.	2½c deep green	90.00	90.00
d.	2½c ochre	*125.00*	*125.00*
2	A1 5c blue	140.00	87.50
a.	Tête bêche pair	*4,500.*	*7,250.*
b.	"50" instead of "5"		*7,500.*
3	A1 5c violet	375.00	120.00
a.	Tête bêche pair	*6,000.*	*6,000.*
b.	"50" instead of "5"		*15,000.*
c.	50c blue violet	225.00	90.00
d.	50c lilac	225.00	90.00
e.	50c slate	250.00	100.00
4	A1 10c red brown	140.00	80.00
a.	10c buff	140.00	80.00
b.	10c bister brown	100.00	62.50
c.	10c yellow	100.00	62.50
d.	10c orange chestnut	100.00	62.50
e.	10c red orange	*125.00*	*125.00*
6	A1 20c blue	120.00	67.50
a.	20c gray blue	120.00	67.50
b.	Se-tenant with 5c	—	—
c.	Tête bêche pair	*40,000.*	*32,500.*
d.	20c pale ultramarine	*100.00*	*70.00*
7	A1 1p carmine	72.50	*120.00*
a.	1p rose	110.00	150.00
8	A1 1p rose, *bluish*	350.00	

The 2½c brown and 10c green are essays.

Reprints of No. 7 are in brown rose or brown red. Wavy lines of background are much broken; no dividing lines between stamps.

Coat of Arms — A2

1860 Laid Paper

9 A2 5c lilac 325.00 210.00

Wove Paper

10 A2 5c gray lilac 85.00 65.00
a. 5c lilac 85.00 65.00
11 A2 10c yellow buff 85.00 55.00
a. Tête bêche pair *7,000.* *7,000.*
12 A2 20c blue 210.00 140.00

United States of New Granada

Arms of New Granada — A3

1861

13 A3 2½c black 1,450. 400.00
14 A3 5c yellow 400.00 175.00
a. 5c buff 400.00 175.00
16 A3 10c blue 1,250. 175.00
17 A3 20c red 500.00 475.00
18 A3 1p pink 1,250. 375.00

There are 54 varieties of the 5c, 20c, and 1 peso.

Forgeries exist of Nos. 13-18.

United States of Colombia

Coat of Arms — A4

1862

19 A4 10c blue 250.00 125.00
20 A4 20c red *4,500.* 725.00
21 A4 50c green 250.00 175.00
22 A4 1p red lilac 600.00 175.00
23 A4 1p red lil, *bluish* *5,500.* *1,750.*

No. 23 is on a thinner, coarser wove paper than Nos. 19-22.

Coat of Arms — A5

1863

24 A5 5c orange 100.00 65.00
a. Star after "Cent" 110.00 72.50
25 A5 10c blue 175.00 24.00
a. Period after "10" 200.00 30.00
26 A5 20c red 225.00 75.00
a. Star after "Cent" 250.00 82.50
b. Transfer of 50c in stone of 20c *18,500* *5,500.*

Bluish Paper

28 A5 10c blue 175.00 32.50
a. Period after "10" 190.00 35.00
29 A5 50c green 210.00 75.00
a. Star after "Cent" 210.00 77.50

Ten varieties of each.

Coat of Arms — A6

1864 Wove Paper

30 A6 5c orange 60.00 37.50
a. Tête bêche pair 475.00 400.00
31 A6 10c blue 55.00 15.00
a. Period after 10 55.00 15.00
32 A6 20c scarlet 100.00 55.00
33 A6 50c green 85.00 55.00
34 A6 1p red violet 350.00 175.00

Two varieties of each.

Arms of Colombia
A7 A9

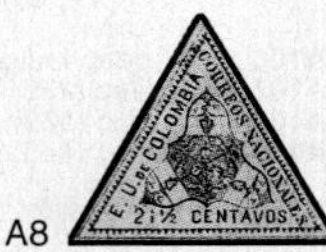

A8

1865

35 A7 1c rose 10.00 10.00
a. bluish pelure paper 30.00 21.00
36 A8 2½c black, *lilac* 21.00 14.00
37 A9 5c yellow 47.50 20.00
a. 5c orange 47.50 20.00
38 A9 10c violet 67.50 4.50
39 A9 20c blue 67.50 20.00
40 A9 50c green 120.00 52.50
41 A9 50c grn (small figures) 120.00 52.50
42 A9 1p vermilion 125.00 18.00
a. 1p rose red 125.00 18.00
b. Period after "PESO" 150.00 20.00

Ten varieties of each of the 5c, 10c, 20c, and 50c, and six varieties of the 1 peso. No. 36 was used as a carrier stamp.

A10 A11 A12

A13 A14

A15 A16

1866 White Wove Paper

45 A10 5c orange 72.50 27.50
46 A11 10c lilac 17.00 5.25
a. Pelure paper 21.00 11.50
47 A12 20c light blue 42.50 21.00
a. Pelure paper 67.50 52.50
48 A13 50c green 17.00 13.00
49 A14 1p rose red, *bluish* 92.50 32.50
a. 1p vermilion 92.50 32.50
51 A15 5p blk, *green* 500.00 210.00
52 A16 10p blk, *vermilion* 350.00 200.00

There are several varieties of the 1 peso having the letters "U," "N," "S" and "O" smaller.

A17 A18

A19 A20

A21

TEN CENTAVOS:

Type I — "B" of "COLOMBIA" over "V" of "CENTAVOS".

Type II — "B" of "COLOMBIA" over "VO" of "CENTAVOS."

ONE PESO:

Type I — Long thin spear heads. Diagonal lines in lower part of shield.

Type II — Short thick spear heads. Horizontal and a few diagonal lines in lower part of shield.

Type III — Short thick spear heads. Crossed lines in lower part of shield. Ornaments at each side of circle are broken. (See No. 97.)

1868

53 A17 5c orange 67.50 52.50
54 A18 10c lilac (I) 4.25 1.10
a. 10c red violet (I) 4.25 1.10
b. 10c lilac (II) 4.25 1.10
c. 10c red violet (II) 4.25 1.10
d. Printed on both sides 7.50 2.50
55 A19 20c blue 3.00 1.25
56 A20 50c yellow green 3.50 2.40
57 A21 1p ver (II) 4.25 2.10
a. Tête bêche pair 140.00 100.00
b. 1p rose red (I) 60.00 27.50
c. 1p rose red (II) 4.00 2.10
Nos. 53-57 (5) 82.50 59.35

See Nos. 83-84, 96-97.

Counterfeits or reprints.

10c — There is a large white dot at the upper left between the circle enclosing the "X" and the ornament below.

50c — There is a shading of dots instead of dashes below the ribbon with motto. There are crossed lines in the lowest section of the shield instead of diagonal or horizontal ones.

1p — The ornaments in the lettered circle are broken. There are crossed lines in the lowest section of the shield. These counterfeits, or reprints, are on white paper, wove and laid, on colored wove paper and in fancy colors.

A22

Two varieties

1869-70 Wove Paper

59 A22 2½c black, *violet* 4.75 2.50
a. Laid paper ('70) 325.00 250.00
b. Laid batonné paper ('70) 30.00 24.00

Nos. 59, 59a, 59b were used as carrier stamps.

Counterfeits, or reprints, are on magenta paper wove or ribbed.

A23 A24

1870 Wove Paper

62 A23 5c orange 2.00 1.25
a. 5c yellow 2.00 1.25
63 A24 25c black, *blue* 16.00 13.00

See No. 89.

In the counterfeits, or reprints, of No. 63, the top of the "2" of "25" does not touch the down stroke. The counterfeits are on paper of various colors.

A25 A26

5 pesos — The ornament at the left of the "C" of "Cinco" cuts into the "C," and the shading of the flag is formed of diagonal lines.

10 pesos — The stars have extra rays between the points, and the central part of the shield has some horizontal lines of shading at each end.

Surface Colored, Chalky Paper

1870

64 A25 5p blk, *green* 100.00 67.50
65 A26 10p blk, *vermilion* 120.00 67.50

See Nos. 77-79, 125-126.

A27 A28

A29

TEN CENTAVOS:

Type I — "S" of "CORREOS" 2½mm high. First "N" of "NACIONALES" small.

Type II — "S" of "CORREOS" 2mm high. First "N" of "NACIONALES" wide.

1871-74 Thin Porous Paper

66 A27 1c green ('72) 3.50 3.50
67 A27 1c rose ('73) 3.50 3.50
a. 1c carmine ('73) 3.50 3.50
68 A28 2c brown 1.60 1.60
a. 2c red brown 1.60 1.60
69 A29 10c vio (I) ('74) 2.50 2.50
a. 10c lilac (I) ('74) 2.50 2.50
b. 10c violet (II) ('74) 2.50 2.50
c. 10c lilac (II) ('74) 2.50 2.50
d. As #69, laid paper ('72) 140.00 140.00
e. As "b," laid paper ('72) 140.00 140.00
Nos. 66-69 (4) 11.10 11.10

Counterfeits or reprints.

1c — The outer frame of the shield is broken near the upper left corner and the "A" of "Colombia" has no cross-bar.

2c — There are scratches across "DOS" and many white marks around the letters on the large "2." The counterfeits, or reprints, are on white wove and bluish white laid paper.

Condor — A30

Liberty Head
A31 A32

5 pesos, redrawn — The ornament at the left of the "C" only touches the "C," and the shading of the flag is formed of vertical and diagonal lines.

10 pesos, redrawn — The stars are distinctly five pointed, and there is no shading in the central part of the shield.

1877 Wove Paper

73 A30 5c purple 7.25 2.10
a. 5c lilac 7.25 2.10
74 A31 10c bister brown 3.50 .90
a. 10c red brown 3.50 .90
b. 10c violet brown 3.50 .90
75 A32 20c blue 4.25 1.40
a. 20c violet blue 25.00 3.50
77 A26 10p blk, *rose* 120.00 67.50
78 A25 5p blk, *lt grn*, redrawn 42.50 32.50
79 A26 10p blk, *rose*, redrawn 17.00 2.75
a. 10p blk, *dark rose*, redrawn 17.00 2.75
Nos. 73-79 (6) 194.50 107.15

Stamps of the issues of 1871-77 are known with private perforations of various gauges, also with sewing machine perforation.

In the counterfeits, or reprints, of the 5 pesos the ornament at the left of the "C" of "Cinco" is separated from the "C" by a black line.

In the counterfeits, or reprints, of the 10 pesos the outer line of the double circle containing "10" is broken at the top, below "OS" of "Unidos," and the vertical lines of shading contained in the double circle are very indistinct. There is a colorless dash below the loop of the "P" of "Pesos."

1876-79 Laid Paper

80 A30 5c lilac 85.00 65.00
81 A31 10c brown 47.50 2.75
82 A32 20c blue 100.00 67.50
83 A20 50c green ('79) 97.50 65.00

84 A21 1p pale red (II) ('79) 62.50 15.00
Nos. 80-84 (5) 392.50 215.25

1879 **Wove Paper**
89 A24 25c green 32.50 32.50

1881 **Blue Wove Paper**
93 A30 5c violet 20.00 13.00
a. 5c lilac 20.00 13.00
94 A31 10c brown 12.00 2.50
95 A32 20c blue 12.00 3.75
96 A20 50c yellow green 12.50 7.50
97 A21 1p ver (III) 17.00 7.50
Nos. 93-97 (5) 73.50 34.25

For types of 1p, see note over No. 53.

Reprints of the 10c and 20c are much worn. On the 10c the letters "TAVOS" of "CENTAVOS" often touch. On the 20c the letters "NT" of "VEINTE" touch and the left arm of the "T" is too long. Reprints of the 25c, 50c and 1p have the characteristics previously described. The reprints are on white wove or laid paper, on colored papers, and in fancy colors. Stamps on green paper exist only as reprints.

A34

A35

A36

1 centavo — The period before "UNION" is round and there are rays between the stars and the condors.

2 centavos — The "2's" and "C's" in the corners are placed upright.

5 centavos — The last star at the right almost touches the frame.

10 centavos — The letters of the inscription are thin; there are rays between the stars and the condor.

1881 **White Wove Paper** ***Imperf.***
103 A34 1c green 5.00 4.00
104 A35 2c vermilion 2.10 1.60
a. 2c rose 2.50 1.60
106 A34 5c blue 5.00 1.60
a. Printed on both sides
107 A36 10c violet 4.25 1.25
108 A34 20c black 4.75 2.00
Nos. 103-108 (5) 21.10 10.45

The stamps of this issue are found with perforations of various gauges, also sewing machine perforation, all of which are unofficial.

See Nos. 112, 114-115.

Liberty Head — A37

1881 ***Imperf.***
109 A37 1c blk, *green* 3.50 *5.00*
110 A37 2c blk, *lilac rose* 3.50 *5.00*
111 A37 5c blk, *lilac* 8.50 1.75
Nos. 109-111 (3) 15.50 *11.75*

Nos. 109 to 111 are found with regular or sewing machine perforation, unofficial.

Reprints:

1c — The top line of the stamp and the top frame extend to the left. 2c — There is a curved line over the scroll below the "AV" of "CENTAVOS."

5c — There are scratches across the "5" in the upper left corner. All three values were reprinted on the three colors of paper of the originals.

A37a

Redrawn

1 centavo — The period before "UNION" is square and the rays between the stars and the condor have been wholly or partly erased.

2 centavos — The "2's" and "C's" in the corners are placed diagonally.

5 centavos — The last star at the right touches the wing of the condor.

10 centavos — The letters of the inscription are thick; there are no rays under the stars; the last star at the right touches the wing of the condor and this wing touches the frame.

1883 ***Imperf.***
112 A34 1c green 4.75 4.25
113 A37a 2c rose 2.10 1.75
114 A34 5c blue 4.00 1.00
a. 5c ultramarine 4.00 1.00
b. Printed on both sides, reverse ultra 25.00 20.00
115 A36 10c violet 5.00 1.40
Nos. 112-115 (4) 15.85 8.40

The stamps of this issue are found with regular or sewing machine perforation, privately applied.

A38

A39

1883 ***Perf. 10½, 12, 13½***
116 A38 1c gray grn, *grn* 1.00 1.00
a. Imperf., pair 5.00 5.00
117 A39 2c red, *rose* 1.00 *1.25*
a. 2c org red, *rose* 1.00 *1.25*
b. 2c red, *buff* 12.00 12.00
c. Imperf., pair (#117 or 117a) 7.75 7.75
d. "DE LOS" in very small caps 15.00 15.00
118 A38 5c blue, *bluish* 2.50 1.50
a. 5c dk bl, *bluish* 2.50 1.00
b. 5c blue 3.25 2.50
c. Imperf., pair (#118 or 118a) 7.75 7.75
d. As "b," imperf., pair 12.00 12.00
119 A39 10c org, *yel* 1.25 *1.40*
a. "DE LOS" in large caps 60.00 26.00
b. Imperf., pair 16.00 16.00
120 A39 20c vio, *lilac* 1.40 1.40
a. Imperf., pair 16.00 16.00
122 A38 50c brn, *buff* 3.00 3.25
a. Perf. 12 3.00 3.25
123 A38 1p claret, *bluish* 5.50 1.90
a. Imperf., pair 16.00 16.00
Nos. 116-123 (7) 15.65 11.70

Redrawn Types of 1877

1883 (?) ***Perf. 10½, 12***
125 A25 5p orange brown 10.00 6.00
126 A26 10p black, *gray* 10.00 7.25

1886 ***Perf. 10½, 11½, 12***
127 A38 5p brown, *straw* 10.00 5.50
a. Imperf., pair 32.50 32.50
128 A38 10p black, *rose* 10.00 5.50
a. Imperf., pair 32.50 32.50

Republic of Colombia

A40

Simón Bolívár — A41

Pres. Rafael Núñez — A42

1886 ***Perf. 10½ and 13½***
129 A40 1c grn, *grn* 1.75 .70
a. Imperf., pair 6.75 6.75
130 A41 5c blue, *bl* 1.75 .40
a. 5c ultra, *blue* 1.75 .40
b. Imperf., pair (#130) 6.75 6.75
131 A42 10c orange 3.50 .70
a. Imperf., pair 9.25 9.25
b. Pelure paper 4.50 1.00
Nos. 129-131 (3) 7.00 1.80

Gen. Antonio Jose de Sucre y Alcala — A43

Gen. Antonio Nariño — A44

1887
133 A43 2c org red, *rose* 2.25 1.00
a. 2c orange red, *yellowish* 6.00 6.00
b. 2c orange red 7.25 7.25
c. Imperf., pair (#133) 10.00 10.00
134 A44 20c pur, *grysh* 3.00 1.10
a. Imperf., pair 8.50 8.50
b. Pelure paper 3.50 2.25

Impressions of No. 134 on white, blue or greenish blue paper were not regularly issued.

Arms — A45

1888
135 A45 50c brn, *buff* 1.75 *1.90*
a. Imperf., pair 6.00 6.00
136 A45 1p claret, *bluish* 8.00 2.10
137 A45 1p claret 3.50 1.60
138 A45 5p org brn 8.50 6.50
139 A45 5p black 14.50 9.50
140 A45 10p black, *rose* 21.00 6.75
Nos. 135-140 (6) 57.25 28.35

See Nos. 155, 158-159.

Nariño — A46

1889
141 A46 20c pur, *grayish* 1.90 1.25
a. Imperf., pair 9.25 9.25

Impressions on white, blue or greenish blue paper were not regularly issued.

A47

A48

A49

A50

A51

1890-91 ***Perf. 10½, 13½, 11***
142 A47 1c grn, *grn* 1.90 1.60
143 A48 2c org red, *rose* .95 .95
144 A49 5c bl, *grnsh bl* 1.40 .40
a. 5c deep blue, *blue* 1.40 .40
b. Imperf., pair 5.50 5.50
146 A50 10c brn, *yel* 1.00 .40
a. 10c brown, *buff* 1.00 .40
147 A51 20c vio, pelure paper 3.50 *3.50*
Nos. 142-147 (5) 8.75 *6.85*

A52

A52a

A53

A53a

A54

Perf. 10½, 12, 13½, 14 to 15½

1892-99 **Ordinary Paper**
148 A47 1c red, *yel* .85 .40
149 A52 2c red, *rose* 42.50 42.50
150 A52 2c green .50 .30
a. 2c yellow green .50 .30
151 A49 5c blk, *buff* 13.00 .35
152 A52a 5c org brn, *pale buff* 1.00 .30
a. 5c red brown, *salmon* ('97) 1.00 .30
153 A50 10c bis brn, *rose* .75 .40
a. 10c brown, *brownish* 2.00 1.60
154 A53 20c brn, *bl* .75 .40
a. 20c red brown, *blue* .75 .40
b. 20c yel brn, *grnsh bl* ('97) 5.50 *13.00*
c. 20c brown, *buff* ('97) 19.00 13.00
155 A45 50c vio, *vio* 1.25 .75
156 A53a 50c red vio, *vio* ('99) 1.75
157 A54 1p bl, *grnsh* 2.10 .90
a. 1p blue, *buff* 2.10 .90
158 A45 5p red, *pale rose* 8.50 3.25
159 A45 10p blue 16.00 3.25
a. Thin, pale rose paper 27.50 7.25
Nos. 148-159 (12) 88.95
Nos. 148-155,157-159 (11) 52.80

Type A53a is a redrawing of type A45. The letters of the inscriptions are slightly larger and the numerals "50" slightly smaller than in type A45.

The 20c brown on white paper is believed to be a chemical changeling.

Nos. 148, 150-152a, 153-155, 157, 159 exist imperf. Value per pair, $6-9.

A56

1899
162 A56 1c red, *yellow* .70 .35
163 A56 5c red brn, *sal* .70 .35
164 A56 10c brn, *lil rose* 2.00 .95
165 A56 50c blue, *lilac* 1.40 1.25
Nos. 162-165 (4) 4.80 2.90

Cartagena Issues

A57

1899 **Blue Overprint** ***Imperf.***
167 A57 5c red, *buff* 30.00 30.00
a. Sewing machine perf. 30.00 30.00
168 A57 10c ultra, *buff* 30.00 30.00
a. Sewing machine perf. 30.00 30.00

Nos. 167 and 167a differ slightly from the illustration.

Bolivar No. 55 Overprinted with 7 Parallel Wavy Lines and

A58

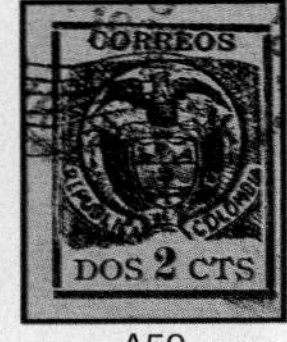
A59

A60

A61

Perf. 14 (#169), Sewing Machine Perf.

1899		**Purple Overprint**		
169	A18	1c black	60.00	60.00
170	A58	1c brn, *buff*	20.00	20.00
a.		Altered from 10c	30.00	30.00
171	A59	2c blk, *buff*	20.00	20.00
a.		Altered from 10c	30.00	30.00
172	A60	5c mar, *grnsh bl*	18.00	18.00
a.		Perf. 12	18.00	18.00
b.		Without overprint	10.50	10.50
173	A61	10c red, *sal*	18.00	18.00
a.		Perf. 12	18.00	18.00
		Nos. 169-173 (5)	136.00	136.00

Types A58 and A59 illustrate Nos. 170a and 171a, which were made from altered plates of the 10c (No. 168). Nos. 170 and 171 were made from altered plate of the 5c denomination (No. 167), show part of the top flag of the "5" and differ slightly from the illustrations.

Nos. 170-173 exist imperf. Values about same as perf.

A62

1900		**Purple Overprint** *Imperf.*		
174	A62	5c red	25.00	25.00
a.		Perf. 12	35.00	35.00

A63

A64

"Gobierno Provisorio" at Top

1900		**Litho.** *Perf. 12 Vertically*		
175	A63	1c (ctvo) blk, *bl grn*	47.50	8.00
a.		"cvo."	120.00	14.50
b.		"cvos."	47.50	8.00
c.		"centavo"	55.00	47.50
176	A63	2c black	26.00	6.00
177	A63	5c blk, *pink*	26.00	6.00
a.		Name at side (V)	62.50	9.00
178	A63	10c blk, *pink*	26.00	6.00
a.		Name at side (V)	62.50	9.00
179	A63	20c blk, *yellow*	47.50	8.00
a.		Name at side (G)	92.50	12.00
		Nos. 175-179 (5)	173.00	34.00

"Gobierno Provisional" at Top Name at Side in Black or Green

No.	Type	Description	Unused	Used
180	A64	1c (ctvo.) blk, *bl grn*	47.50	8.00
a.		"centavo"	125.00	47.50
181	A64	2c blk, *bl grn*	30.00	5.00
182	A64	5c blk (G)	30.00	5.00
a.		"ctvos." smaller	47.50	9.00
183	A64	10c blk, *pink*	30.00	5.00
184	A64	20c blk, *yel* (G)	47.50	8.00
		Nos. 180-184 (5)	185.00	31.00

Issues of the rebel provisional government in Cucuta.

A65

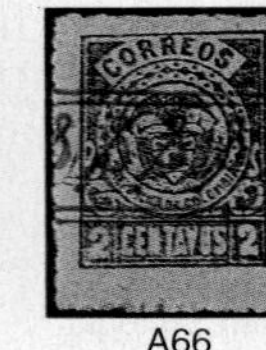
A66

Purple Overprint

1901		*Sewing Machine Perf.*		
185	A65	1c black	1.00	1.00
a.		Without overprint	2.25	2.25
b.		Double overprint	2.50	2.50
c.		Imperf., pair	2.50	2.50
d.		Inverted overprint	1.25	1.25
186	A66	2c blk, *rose*	1.00	1.00
a.		Imperf., pair	2.50	2.50
b.		Without overprint	2.25	2.25
c.		Double overprint	2.50	2.50

A67

A68

1901		**Rose Overprint**		
187	A67	1c blue	1.00	1.00
a.		Imperf., pair	4.00	4.00
188	A68	2c brown	1.00	1.00
a.		Imperf., pair	4.00	4.00
b.		Without overprint	1.00	1.00

A69

A70

Sewing Machine or Regular Perf. 12, 12½

1902		**Magenta Overprint**		
189	A69	5c violet	2.25	2.25
a.		Without overprint	2.25	2.25
b.		Double overprint	2.25	2.25
c.		Imperf., pair	4.75	4.75
190	A70	10c yel brn	2.25	2.25
a.		Double overprint	2.25	2.25
b.		Imperf., pair	4.75	4.75
c.		Without overprint	2.25	2.25
d.		Printed on both sides	3.25	3.25

A71

A72

1902		**Magenta Overprint**		
191	A71	5c yel brn	2.25	2.25
a.		Without overprint	2.10	2.10
b.		Imperf., pair	6.00	6.00
192	A71	10c black	1.75	1.75
a.		Without overprint	1.50	1.50
b.		Imperf., pair	9.00	9.00
193	A72	20c maroon	5.50	4.50
b.		Imperf., pair	15.00	15.00
		Nos. 191-193 (3)	9.50	8.50

Nos. 191-193 exist tête bêche. Value of 10c and 20c, each $15.

Washed examples of Nos. 167-174, 185-193 are offered as "without overprint."

Barranquilla Issues

Magdalena River — A75

Iron Quay at Sabanilla — A76

La Popa Hill — A77

1902-03		*Imperf.*		
194	A75	2c green	1.60	1.60
195	A75	2c dk bl	1.60	1.60
196	A75	2c rose	22.50	22.50
197	A76	10c scarlet	1.10	1.10
198	A76	10c orange	13.00	13.00
199	A76	10c rose	1.75	1.75
200	A76	10c maroon	1.90	1.90
201	A76	10c claret	1.90	1.90
202	A77	20c violet	3.50	3.50
a.		Laid paper		9.50
203	A77	20c dl bl	9.50	9.50
204	A77	20c dl bl, *pink*	*125.00*	*125.00*
205	A77	20c car rose	20.00	20.00
		Nos. 194-205 (12)	*203.35*	*203.35*

Sewing Machine Perf. and Perf. 12

No.	Type	Description	Unused	Used
194a	A75	2c green	9.50	9.50
195a	A75	2c dark blue	9.50	9.50
196a	A75	2c carmine	*47.50*	*47.50*
197a	A76	10c scarlet	4.75	4.75
198a	A76	10c orange	*35.00*	*35.00*
199a	A76	10c rose	6.50	6.50
200a	A76	10c maroon	6.50	6.50
201a	A76	10c claret	6.00	6.00
202b	A77	20c purple	.70	.70
c.		20c lilac	.70	.70
203a	A77	20c dull blue	9.50	9.50
204a	A77	20c dull blue, *rose*	*150.00*	*150.00*
205b	A77	20c carmine rose	*72.50*	*72.50*
		Nos. 194a-205b (12)	*357.95*	*357.95*

See Nos. 240-245.

Cruiser "Cartagena" — A78

Bolívar — A79

General Próspero Pinzón — A80

A81

A82

1903-04		*Imperf.*		
209	A78	5c blue	2.75	2.75
210	A78	5c bister	4.50	4.50
211	A79	50c yellow	3.75	3.75
212	A79	50c green	4.50	4.50
213	A79	50c scarlet	4.50	4.50
214	A79	50c carmine	4.50	4.50
a.		50c rose	4.50	4.50
215	A79	50c pale brown	4.50	4.50
216	A80	1p yellow brn	1.60	1.60
217	A80	1p rose	2.50	2.50
218	A80	1p blue	2.50	2.50
219	A80	1p violet	25.00	25.00
220	A81	5p claret	5.50	5.50
221	A81	5p pale brown	8.00	8.00
222	A81	5p blue green	7.50	7.50
223	A82	10p pale green	7.75	7.75
224	A82	10p claret	25.00	25.00
		Nos. 209-224 (16)	114.35	114.35

Nos. 216 and 217 measure 20½x26½mm and No. 218, 18x24mm. Stamps of this issue exist with forged perforations.

Perf. 12

No.	Type	Description	Unused	Used
209a	A78	5c blue	9.50	9.50
210a	A78	5c bister	9.50	9.50
211a	A79	50c yellow	9.50	9.50
b.		50c orange	25.00	25.00
212a	A79	50c green	25.00	25.00
213a	A79	50c scarlet	11.50	11.50
214b	A79	50c rose	11.50	11.50
215a	A79	50c pale brown	11.50	11.50
216a	A80	1p yellow brown	5.25	5.25
217a	A80	1p rose	7.50	7.50
218a	A80	1p blue	9.50	7.50
219a	A80	1p violet	62.50	62.50
220a	A81	5p claret	20.00	20.00
221a	A81	5p pale brown	22.50	22.50
222a	A81	5p blue green	22.50	22.50
223a	A82	10p pale green	30.00	30.00
224a	A82	10p claret	77.50	77.50
		Nos. 209a-224a (16)	345.25	343.25

		Laid Paper *Imperf.*		
240	A76	10c dk bl, *lil*	6.25	6.25
241	A76	10c dk bl, *bluish*	3.75	3.75
242	A76	10c dk bl, *brn*	3.75	3.75
243	A76	10c dk bl, *sal*	9.25	9.25
244	A76	10c dk bl, *grnsh bl*	5.00	5.00
245	A76	10c dk bl, *dp rose*	3.75	3.75
		Nos. 240-245 (6)	31.75	31.75

Perf. 12

No.	Type	Description	Unused	Used
240a	A76	10c dk bl, *lilac*	13.50	13.50
241a	A76	10c dk bl, *bluish*	9.25	9.25
242a	A76	10c dk bl, *brn*	9.25	9.25
243a	A76	10c dk bl, *salmon*	72.50	72.50
244a	A76	10c dk bl, *grnsh bl*	20.00	20.00
245a	A76	10c dk bl, *deep rose*	9.25	9.25
		Nos. 240a-245a (6)	133.75	133.75

A82a

Imperf., Sewing Machine Perf.

1902		**Typeset**		
255	A82a	10c black, *rose*	3.50	3.50
256	A82a	20c blk, *orange*	2.50	2.50

This issue was printed in either Cali or Popayan.

Medellin Issue

A83

1902				
257	A83	1c grn, *straw*	.35	*.50*
258	A83	2c salmon, *rose*	.35	*.50*
259	A83	5c dp bl, *grnsh*	.35	*.50*
260	A83	10c pale brn, *straw*	.35	*.50*
261	A83	20c pur, *rose*	.45	*.50*
262	A83	50c dl rose, *grnsh*	2.25	*3.00*
263	A83	1p blk, *yellow*	4.50	*6.75*
264	A83	5p slate, *blue*	35.00	35.00
265	A83	10p dk brn, *rose*	22.50	22.50
		Nos. 257-265 (9)	66.10	69.75

For overprint see No. L8.

Imperf., Pairs

No.	Type	Denomination	Unused	Used
257a	A83	1c	11.00	11.00
258a	A83	2c	11.00	11.00
259a	A83	5c	11.00	11.00
260a	A83	10c	11.00	11.00
261a	A83	20c	11.00	11.00
262a	A83	50c	11.00	11.00
263a	A83	1p	27.50	27.50
264a	A83	5p	80.00	80.00
265a	A83	10p	50.00	50.00

Regular Issue

A84

A85

A86

A87

A88

A89

A90

A91

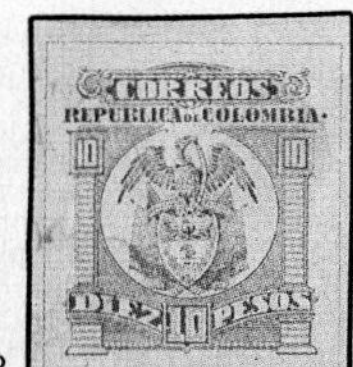
A92

1902				*Imperf.*
266	A84	2c blk, *rose*	.25	.25
267	A85	4c red, *grn*	.25	.25
268	A86	5c grn, *grn*	.25	.25
269	A87	10c blk, *pink*	.25	.25
c.		10c blk, *rose*	1.10	1.10
270	A88	20c brn, *buff*	.25	.25
271	A89	50c dk grn, *rose*	1.40	1.40
272	A90	1p pur, *buff*	.60	.60
273	A91	5p grn, *bl*	4.25	4.25
274	A92	10p grn, *pale grn*	13.00	6.50
		Nos. 266-274 (9)	20.50	14.00

For overprint see No. H4.

Sewing Machine Perf.

266a	A84	2c blk, *rose*	1.90	1.90
267a	A85	4c red, *grn*	1.60	1.60
268a	A86	5c grn, *blue*	1.90	1.90
269a	A87	10c blk, *pink*	1.90	1.90
270a	A88	20c brn, *buff*	3.25	2.50
271a	A89	50c dk grn, *rose*	6.50	5.25
272a	A90	1p pur, *buff*	7.75	6.50
273a	A91	5p grn, *blue*	35.00	35.00
274a	A92	10p grn, *pale grn*	65.00	65.00
		Nos. 266a-274a (9)	124.80	121.55

1903				*Perf. 12*
266b	A84	2c blk, *rose*	1.40	1.40
269b	A87	10c blk, *pink*	1.60	1.60
270b	A88	20c brn, *buff*	1.60	1.60
272b	A90	1p pur, *buff*	3.25	3.25
273b	A91	5p grn, *blue*	27.50	27.50
274b	A92	10p grn, *pale grn*	52.50	45.00
		Nos. 266b-274b (6)	87.85	80.35

1903				*Imperf.*
284	A85	4c blue, *grn*	.35	.35
285	A86	5c blue, *blue*	.35	.35
286	A88	20c blue,*buff*	.35	.35
288	A89	50c blue, *rose*	1.75	1.75
		Nos. 284-288 (4)	2.80	2.80

Sewing Machine Perf.

284a	A85	4c blue, *grn*	2.25	1.75
285a	A86	5c blue, *blue*	2.25	1.75
286a	A88	20c blue, *buff*	3.25	2.50
288a	A89	50c blue, *rose*	6.50	5.75
		Nos. 284a-288a (4)	14.25	11.75

Perf. 12

284b	A85	4c blue, *grn*	2.50	2.50
285b	A86	5c blue, *blue*	2.50	2.50
286b	A88	20c blue, *buff*	3.50	3.50
288b	A89	50c blue, *rose*	9.75	9.75
		Nos. 284b-288b (4)	18.25	18.25

A93

1904		Pelure Paper		*Imperf.*
303	A93	½c yellow brn	1.10	1.10
304	A90	1c blue green	1.10	1.10
a.		1c yellow green	1.10	1.10
306	A84	2c blue	.90	.65
307	A86	5c carmine	1.00	1.00
308	A87	10c violet	1.10	.90
		Nos. 303-308 (5)	5.20	4.75

For overprint see No. H13.

1904				*Perf. 13*
303a	A93	½c yellow brown	4.25	4.25
304b	A90	1c blue green	5.50	5.00
c.		1c yellow green	7.50	7.00
306a	A84	2c blue	2.50	2.50

Perf. 12

307a	A86	5c carmine	2.25	2.25
308a	A87	10c violet	2.25	2.25
		Nos. 303a-308a (5)	16.75	16.25

A94

A95

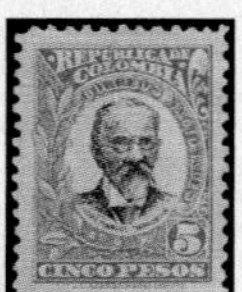
Pres. José Manuel Marroquín — A96

Imprint: "Lit. J.L.Arango Medellin. Col."

1904		Wove Paper		*Perf. 12*
314	A94	½c yellow	.85	.25
315	A94	1c green	.85	.25
316	A94	2c rose	.85	.25
317	A94	5c blue	1.40	.25
318	A94	10c violet	1.75	.25
319	A94	20c black	1.75	.25
320	A95	1p brown	19.00	3.00
321	A96	5p red & blk, *yel*	60.00	60.00
322	A96	10p bl & blk, *grnsh*	60.00	60.00
		Nos. 314-322 (9)	146.45	124.50

Redrawn

314a	A94	½c	.85	.25
315a	A94	1c	.85	.25
316a	A94	2c	.85	.25
317a	A94	5c	1.40	.25
319a	A94	20c	1.75	.25
		Nos. 314a-319a (5)	5.70	1.25

Imperf., Pairs

314b	A94	½c	3.25	3.25
315b	A94	1c	2.50	2.50
316b	A94	2c	3.25	3.25
317b	A94	5c	3.25	3.25
318a	A94	10c	4.25	4.25
319b	A94	20c	7.75	7.75
320a	A95	1p	65.00	65.00
		Nos. 314b-320a (7)	89.25	89.25

On the redrawn types, the imprint is close to the base of the design instead of being spaced from it. On the redrawn 2c and 5c, the lower end of the vertical white line below "OR" of "CORREOS" forms a hook which turns to the right instead of to the left as in the originals.

See Nos. 325-330. For surcharges see Nos. 351-354, L1-L7, L9-L13, L15-L25.

A97

100p has different frame.

1903				*Imperf.*
323	A97	50p org yel, *pale pink*	92.50	92.50
324	A97	100p dk bl, *dk rose*	77.50	77.50

Imprint: "Lit. Nacional"
Perf. 10, 13, 13½ and Compound

1908				
325	A94	½c orange	.85	.25
a.		½c yellow	.85	.25
b.		Imperf., pair	2.50	1.90
c.		Without imprint	5.25	5.25
326	A94	1c yel grn	.75	.25
a.		Without imprint	.75	.25
d.		Imperf., pair	4.00	3.25
327	A94	2c red	.75	.25
a.		2c carmine	.75	.25
b.		Imperf., pair	4.00	3.25
328	A94	5c blue	.60	.25
a.		Imperf., pair	4.25	5.25
329	A94	10c violet	*50.00*	1.00
330	A94	20c gray blk	*50.00*	1.00
		Nos. 325-330 (6)	102.95	3.00

The above stamps may be easily distinguished from those of 1904 by the perforation, by the height of the design, 24mm instead of 23mm, and by the "Lit. Nacional" imprint.

Camilo Torres
A99

Policarpa Salavarrieta
A100

Bolívar Demanding Liberation of Slaves — A105

Designs: 2c, Nariño. 5c, Bolívar. 10c, Francisco José de Caldas. 20c, Francisco de Paula Santander. 10p, Bolívar Resigning.

1910, Aug.		Engr.		*Perf. 12*
331	A99	½c violet & blk	.50	.30
a.		Center inverted	425.00	425.00
332	A100	1c deep green	.40	.25
333	A100	2c scarlet	.40	.25
334	A100	5c deep blue	1.25	.45
335	A100	10c plum	10.00	5.00
336	A100	20c black brn	15.00	5.50
337	A105	1p dk violet	85.00	25.00
338	A105	10p claret	325.00	250.00
		Nos. 331-338 (8)	437.55	286.75

Colombian independence centenary.

Caldas
A107

Monument to Battle of Boyacá
A113

View of Cartagena
A114

Coat of Arms
A118

Designs: 1c, Torres. 2c, Narino. 4c, Santander. 5c, Bolivar. 10c, Jose Maria Cordoba. 1p, Sucre. 2p, Rufino Cuervo. 5p, Antonio Ricaurte y Lozano.

1917		Engr.		*Perf. 14*
339	A107	½c bister	.35	.25
340	A107	1c green	.30	.25
341	A107	2c car rose	.30	.25
342	A107	4c violet	.90	.30
343	A107	5c dull blue	3.00	.25
344	A107	10c gray	3.00	.25
345	A113	20c red	1.50	.25
346	A114	50c carmine	1.75	.25
347	A107	1p brt blue	12.00	.40
348	A107	2p orange	13.50	.45
349	A107	5p gray	40.00	11.00
350	A118	10p dk brown	47.50	11.50
		Nos. 339-350 (12)	124.10	25.40

The 1c, 5c, 10c, 50c, 2p, 5p and 10p also exist perf. 11½ and 11½ compounded with 14.

Litho. varieties of Nos. 343, 345 and 346 are counterfeits made to defraud the government.

Imperforate examples of Nos. 339-350 are not known to have been regularly issued.

See Nos. 373-374, 400-405. For overprints and surcharges see Nos. 369-370, 377, 409-410, 440, C1, O3, O5-O9.

Nos. 318-319, 329-330 Surcharged in Red

1918				On Issue of 1904
351	A94	½c on 20c black	1.25	.35
352	A94	3c on 10c violet	3.00	.60
		On Issue of 1908		
353	A94	½c on 20c gray blk	10.00	6.25
354	A94	3c on 10c violet	15.00	5.00
		Nos. 351-354 (4)	29.25	12.20

Nos. 351-354 inclusive exist with surcharge reading up or down. On one stamp in each sheet the letter "S" in "Especie" is omitted. All denominations exist with a small zero before the decimal in the surcharge.

A119

1918		Litho.		*Perf. 13½*
358	A119	3c red	.95	.25
a.		Imperf., pair	5.00	5.00

A120

1920		Engr.		*Perf. 14*
359	A120	3c red, *org*	.40	.25
a.		Imperf., pair	3.75	3.75

See No. 371-372. For surcharge see No. 453.

A121

A122

A123

Perf. 10, 13½ and Compound

1920-21				Litho.
360	A121	½c yellow	1.40	.50
361	A121	1c green	.85	.25
362	A121	2c red	.65	.25
363	A122	3c green	.65	.25
a.		3c yellow green	.65	.25
364	A121	5c blue	1.25	.25
365	A121	10c violet	6.00	1.50
366	A121	20c deep green	6.75	4.00
367	A123	50c dark red	8.50	4.00
		Nos. 360-367 (8)	26.05	11.00

The tablet with "PROVISIONAL" was added separately to each design on the various lithographic stones and its position varies slightly on different stamps in the sheet. For some values there were two or more stones, on which the tablet was placed at various angles.

Nos. 360-366 exist imperf.

See No. 375.

No. 342 Surcharged in Red

a

(15mm wide) — b

1921

No.	Type	Description	Unused	Used
369	A107 (a)	3c on 4c violet	.95	.25
a.		Double surcharge	15.00	
370	A107 (b)	3c on 4c violet	3.75	2.00

See No. 377.

Types of 1917-21

1923-24 Engr. *Perf. 13½*

No.	Type	Description	Unused	Used
371	A120	1½c chocolate	1.25	.60
372	A120	3c blue	.50	.25
373	A107	5c claret ('24)	3.00	.25
374	A107	10c blue	9.25	.50

Litho.

No.	Type	Description	Unused	Used
375	A121	10c dark blue	12.50	7.25
		Nos. 371-375 (5)	26.50	8.85

No. 342 Surcharged in Red

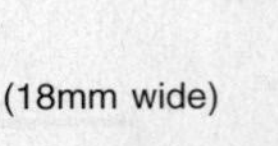

(18mm wide)

1924

No.	Type	Description	Unused	Used
377	A107	3c on 4c vio	3.75	1.50
a.		Double surcharge	15.00	
b.		Double surch., one invtd.	15.00	
c.		With added surch. "3cs." in red		

A124

1924-25 Litho. *Perf. 10, 10x13½*

No.	Type	Description	Unused	Used
379	A124	1c red	.85	.25
380	A124	3c dp blue ('25)	.85	.25

Exist imperf. Value, each pair $6.25.

A125

A126

Black, Red or Green Srch. & Ovpt.

Imprint of Waterlow & Sons

1925 *Perf. 14, 14½*

No.	Type	Description	Unused	Used
382	A125	1c on 3c bis brn	.70	.25
383	A126	4c violet (R)	.50	.25
a.		Inverted surcharge	8.75	8.75

Imprint of American Bank Note Co.

Perf. 12

No.	Type	Description	Unused	Used
384	A125	1c on 3c bis brn	7.50	6.25
a.		Inverted surcharge	19.00	19.00
385	A126	4c violet (G)	.50	.30
a.		Inverted overprint	9.50	9.50
		Nos. 382-385 (4)	9.20	7.05

Correos

Provisional

Revenue stamps of basic types A125 and A126 were handstamped as above in violet or blue by the Cali post office in 1925, but were not authorized by the government. Denominations so overprinted are 1c, 2c, 3c, 4c and 5c.

A127

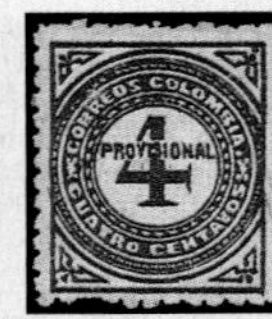

A128

Perf. 10, 13½x10

1926 Litho. Wmk. 194

No.	Type	Description	Unused	Used
395	A127	1c gray green	.50	.25
396	A128	4c deep blue	.55	.25

Exist imperf. Value, each pair $5.

Types of 1917 and

Sabana Station — A129

1926-29 Unwmk. Engr. *Perf. 14*

No.	Type	Description	Unused	Used
400	A107	4c deep blue	.50	.25
401	A118	8c dark blue	.60	.25
402	A107	30c olive bister	6.00	.70
403	A129	40c brn & yel brn	9.25	1.25
404	A107	5p violet	9.25	.90
a.		Perf. 11 ('29)	12.00	1.00
405	A118	10p green	15.00	2.50
a.		Perf. 11 ('29)	30.00	4.75
		Nos. 400-405 (6)	40.60	5.85

For surcharges & overprint see Nos. 409-410, 453, O4.

Death of Bolívar A130

1930, Dec. 17 *Perf. 12½*

No.	Type	Description	Unused	Used
408	A130	4c dk blue & blk	.60	.35

Cent. of the death of Simón Bolívar. See Nos. C80-C82.

Nos. 400 and 402 Surcharged in Red or Dark Blue

1932, Jan. 20 *Perf. 14*

No.	Type	Description	Unused	Used
409	A107	1c on 4c dp bl (R)	.30	.25
a.		Inverted surcharge	5.25	5.25
410	A107	20c on 30c ol bis	10.00	.70
a.		Inverted surcharge	21.00	
b.		Double surcharge	21.00	

Emerald Mine — A131

Oil Wells — A132

Coffee Cultivation A133

Platinum Mine — A134

Gold Mining — A135

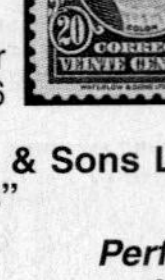

Christopher Columbus — A136

Imprint: "Waterlow & Sons Ltd. Londres"

1932 Wmk. 229 *Perf. 12½*

No.	Type	Description	Unused	Used
411	A131	1c green	.60	.25
412	A132	2c red	.60	.25
413	A133	5c brown	.70	.25
414	A134	8c blue blk	4.75	.60
415	A135	10c yellow	3.50	.25
416	A136	20c dk blue	10.00	.40
		Nos. 411-416 (6)	20.15	2.00

See Nos. 441-442, 464-466a, 517. For surcharges see Nos. 455, 527, O10-O11, O13, RA30. Post 1940 issues in *Scott Standard Postage Stamp Catalogue*, Vol. 2.

Pedro de Heredia — A137

Perf. 11½

1934, Jan. 10 Unwmk. Litho.

No.	Type	Description	Unused	Used
417	A137	1c dark green	3.00	.80
418	A137	5c chocolate	3.75	.65
419	A137	8c dark blue	3.00	.80
		Nos. 417-419 (3)	9.75	2.25

Cartagena, 400th anniv. See Nos. C111-C114.

Coffee Picking — A138

1934, Dec. Engr. *Perf. 12*

No.	Type	Description	Unused	Used
420	A138	5c brown	3.00	.25

Soccer — A139

Condor — A145

Allegory of Olympic Games at Barranquilla — A140

Foot Race A141

Tennis A142

Pier at Puerto Colombia A143

View of the Bay A144

Designs: 4c, Discus Thrower. 10c, Hurdling. 15c, Athlete in stadium. 18c, Baseball. 24c, Swimming. 50c, View of Barranquilla. 1p, Post and Telegraph Building. 2p, Monument to Flag. 5p, Coat of Arms.

1935, Jan. 26 Litho. *Perf. 11½*

No.	Type	Description	Unused	Used
421	A139	2c bluish grn & buff	1.60	.50
422	A139	4c deep green	1.60	.50
423	A140	5c dk brn & yel	1.60	.50
a.		Horiz. pair, imperf. btwn.	240.00	
424	A141	7c dk carmine	3.00	1.75
425	A142	8c blk & pink	2.50	2.50
426	A141	10c brown & bl	3.50	1.75
427	A143	12c indigo	4.25	3.00
428	A141	15c bl & red brn	7.25	5.50
429	A141	18c dk vio & buff	10.00	8.25
430	A144	20c purple & grn	8.50	7.00
431	A144	24c bluish grn & ultra	8.50	6.75
432	A144	50c ultra & buff	13.00	10.00
433	A145	1p drab & blue	120.00	62.50
434	A145	2p dull grn & gray	140.00	110.00
435	A145	5p pur blk & bl	475.00	500.00
436	A145	10p black & gray	550.00	575.00
		Nos. 421-436 (16)	1,350.	1,296.

3rd Natl. Olympic Games, Barranquilla. Counterfeits of 10p exist.

Oil Wells — A155

Gold Mining — A157

Imprint: "American Bank Note Co."

1935, Mar. Unwmk. Engr. *Perf. 12*

No.	Type	Description	Unused	Used
437	A155	2c carmine rose	.45	.25
439	A157	10c deep orange	25.00	.25

See Nos. 468, 470, 498, 516. For surcharge and overprints see Nos. 496, 596, O2. Post 1940 issues in *Scott Standard Postage Stamp Catalogue*, Vol. 2.

No. 347 Surcharged in Black

1935, Aug. *Perf. 14*

No.	Type	Description	Unused	Used
440	A107	12c on 1p brt bl	4.75	1.50

Types of 1932

Imprint: "Lit. Nacional Bogotá"

1935-36 Litho. *Perf. 11, 11½, 12½*

No.	Type	Description	Unused	Used
441	A131	1c lt green	.25	.25
a.		Imperf., pair	4.25	
442	A133	5c brown ('36)	.70	.25
a.		Imperf., pair	4.75	4.00

For overprint, see No. O1. For surcharge see No. 527 in *Scott Standard Postage Stamp Catalogue*, Vol. 2.

Bolívar A159

Tequendama Falls A160

Wmk. Wavy Lines. (229)

1937 **Engr.** ***Perf. 12½***

443	A159	1c deep green	.25	.25
a.		Perf. 14	.25	.25
444	A160	12c deep blue	3.25	1.10

See No. 570. For surcharges and overprints see Nos. 454, 456, C231, C326, O12. Post 1940 issues in *Scott Standard Postage Stamp Catalogue*, Vol. 2.

Soccer Player A161

Discus Thrower A162

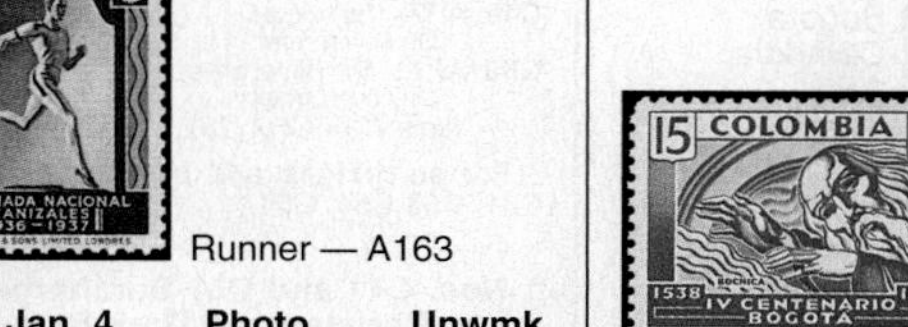
Runner — A163

1937, Jan. 4 **Photo.** **Unwmk.**

445	A161	3c lt green	1.40	.85
446	A162	10c carmine rose	3.75	1.75
447	A163	1p black	35.00	26.00
		Nos. 445-447 (3)	40.15	28.60

National Olympic Games, Manizales. For surcharge see No. 452.

Exposition Palace — A164

Stadium at Barranquilla A165

Monument to the Colors A166

1937, Jan. 4

448	A164	5c violet brown	2.75	.40
449	A165	15c blue	6.75	4.50
450	A166	50c orange brn	19.00	9.75
		Nos. 448-450 (3)	28.50	14.65

Barranquilla National Exposition.

Stamps of 1926-37 Surcharged in Black

Perf. 12½, 14 (#453)

1937-38 **Unwmk.**

452	A161	1c on 3c lt grn	1.00	1.00
a.		Inverted surcharge	2.25	2.25
453	A118	5c on 8c dk bl	.50	.45
a.		Inverted surcharge	2.25	2.25

Wmk. 229

454	A160	2c on 12c dp bl	.50	.40
455	A134	5c on 8c bl blk	.60	*.65*
a.		Invtd. surcharge	2.00	2.00
456	A160	10c on 12c dp bl ('38)	5.50	1.00
a.		Dbl. surcharge	11.00	11.00
		Nos. 452-456 (5)	8.10	3.50

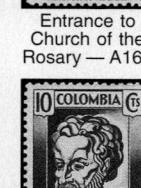

Calle del Arco — A168

Entrance to Church of the Rosary — A169

Arms of Bogotá A170

Gonzálo Jiménez de Quesada A171

Bochica A172

Santo Domingo Convent A173

Mass of the Conquistadors — A174

1938, July 27 **Unwmk.** ***Perf. 12½***

457	A168	1c yellow green	.25	.25
458	A169	2c scarlet	.25	.25
459	A170	5c brown blk	.35	.25
460	A171	10c brown	.75	.40
461	A172	15c brt blue	3.75	1.60
462	A173	20c brt red vio	3.75	1.60
463	A174	1p red brown	50.00	29.00
		Nos. 457-463 (7)	59.10	33.35

Bogotá, 400th anniversary.

Types of 1932
Imprint: "Litografia Nacional Bogotá"

1938, Dec. 5 **Litho.** ***Perf. 10½, 11***

464	A132	2c rose	1.00	.35
465	A135	10c yellow	2.50	.35
466	A136	20c dull blue	10.00	1.25
a.		20c dark blue, perf. 12½ ('44)	62.50	6.25
		Nos. 464-466 (3)	13.50	1.95

Types of 1935 and

Bolívar A175

Coffee Picking A176

Arms of Colombia A177

Christopher Columbus A178

Caldas A179

Sabana Station A180

Imprint: "American Bank Note Co."

Wmk. 255

1939, Mar. 3 **Engr.** ***Perf. 12***

467	A175	1c green	.25	.25
468	A155	2c car rose	.25	.25
469	A176	5c dull brown	.25	.25
470	A157	10c deep orange	.50	.25
471	A177	15c dull blue	1.75	.25
472	A178	20c violet blk	19.00	.25
473	A179	30c olive bister	5.50	.35
474	A180	40c bister brn	17.00	3.75
		Nos. 467-474 (8)	44.50	5.60

See Nos. 497-499, 515, 518, 574. For surcharges and overprints see Nos. 506-507, 520-522, 596, RA26, RA47. Post 1940 listings are in Scott Standard catalogue, Vol. 2.

Gen. Santander A181

Allegory A182

Gen. Santander A183

Statue at Cúcuta A184

Birthplace of Santander A185

Church at Rosario A186

Paya — A187

Bridge at Boyacá — A188

Death of General Santander A189

Invasion of the Liberators A190

Perf. 13x13½, 13½x13

1940, May 6 **Engr.** **Wmk. 229**

475	A181	1c olive green	.25	.25
476	A182	2c dk carmine	.50	.35
477	A183	5c sepia	.25	.25
478	A184	8c carmine	1.75	1.75
479	A185	10c orange yel	.80	.60
480	A186	15c dark blue	2.10	1.40
481	A187	20c green	2.75	2.10
482	A188	50c violet	6.50	6.00
483	A189	1p deep rose	20.00	20.00
484	A190	2p orange	65.00	65.00
		Nos. 475-484 (10)	99.90	97.70

Death of General Francisco Santander, cent.

Tobacco Plant A194

Gen. Santander A195

Garcia Rovira — A196

R. Galan — A197

Antonio Sucre — A198

1940-43 **Engr.** **Wmk. 255** ***Perf. 12***

488	A194	8c rose car & grn	1.25	.65
489	A195	15c dp blue ('43)	1.25	.25
490	A196	20c slate ('41)	4.75	.50
491	A197	40c brown bis ('41)	2.75	.50
492	A198	1p black	5.00	1.25
		Nos. 488-492 (5)	15.00	3.15

See Nos. 500, 554, RA28 (overprint) in Scott Standard catalogue, Vol. 2.

AIR POST STAMPS

No. 341 Overprinted

1919 **Unwmk.** ***Perf. 14***

C1	A107	2c car rose	3,500.	1,700.
a.		Numerals "1" with serifs	*7,250.*	*4,250.*

Used for the first experimental flight from Barranquilla to Puerto Colombia, 6/18/19. Values are for faulty stamps.

Issued by Compania Colombiana de Navegacion Aerea

From 1920 to 1932 the internal airmail service of Colombia was handled by the Compania Colombiana de Navegacion Aerea (1920) and the Sociedad Colombo-Alemana de Transportes Aéreos, known familiarly as "SCADTA" (1920-1932).

These organizations, under government contracts, operated and maintained their own post offices and issued stamps which were the only legal franking for airmail service during this period, both in the internal and international mails. All letters had to bear government stamps as well.

Woman and Boy Watching Plane — AP1

Designs: No. C3, Clouds and small biplane at top. No. C4, Tilted plane viewed close-up from above. No. C5, Flier in plane watching biplane. No. C6, Lighthouse. No. C7, Fuselage and tail of biplane. No. C8, Condor on cliff. No. C9, Plane at rest; pilot foreground. No. C10, Ocean liner.

1920, Feb. Unwmk. Litho. *Imperf.*
Without Gum

C2	AP1	10c multi	3,000.	1,875.
C3	AP1	10c multi	3,800.	1,875.
C4	AP1	10c multi	4,600.	1,875.
C5	AP1	10c multi	3,500.	1,875.
C6	AP1	10c multi	3,000.	1,875.
C7	AP1	10c multi	11,000.	3,800.
C8	AP1	10c multi	6,000.	3,000.
C9	AP1	10c multi	3,500.	1,875.
C10	AP1	10c multi	4,600.	2,750.

Nos. C2-C10 were overprinted on the nine lighter-colored varieties of a set of 18 publicity labels produced by the Curtiss Co. for inclusion with packs of cigarettes. These labels were printed setenant, in panes of 18 (3x6). Value for the set of 18 values without overprint: $4,000.

Flier in Plane Watching Biplane — AP2

1920, Mar.

C11	AP2	10c green	60.00	*92.50*

Four other 10c stamps, similar to No. C11, have two designs showing plane, mountains and water. They are printed in deep green or light brown red. Some authorities state that these four were not used regularly.

Issued by Sociedad Colombo-Alemana de Transportes Aereos (SCADTA)

Seaplane over Magdalena River — AP3

1920-21 Litho. *Perf. 12*

C12	AP3	10c yellow ('21)	60.00	47.50
C13	AP3	15c blue ('21)	65.00	52.50
C14	AP3	30c blk, *rose*	30.00	16.00
C15	AP3	30c rose ('21)	60.00	45.00
C16	AP3	50c pale green	60.00	47.50
		Nos. C12-C16 (5)	275.00	208.50

For surcharges see Nos. C17-C24, C36-C37.

No. C16 Handstamp Surcharged in Violet or Black

a

b

c

d

e

f

g

1921

C17	AP3 (a)	10c on 50c	1,250.	1,200.
C18	AP3 (b)	10c on 50c	1,250.	1,200.
C19	AP3 (c)	10c on 50c	1,250.	1,200.
C20	AP3 (b)	30c on 50c	925.	625.
C21	AP3 (d)	30c on 50c	925.	625.
C22	AP3 (e)	30c on 50c	1,850.	1,450.
C23	AP3 (f)	30c on 50c	1,850.	1,450.
C24	AP3 (g)	30c on 50c	1,850.	1,450.

No. C16 with Typwritten Surcharge in Red

1921

C24A	AP3	10c on 50c	—	*1,500.*
		On cover		*2,000.*
C24B	AP3	30c on 50c		—
		On cover		—

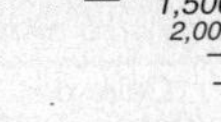

Plane over Magdalena River — AP4

Plane over Bogota Cathedral AP5

1921 *Perf. 11½*

C25	AP4	5c orange yellow	4.50	4.00
		On cover, *from*		27.50
C26	AP4	10c slate green	2.10	1.50
		On cover, *from*		27.50
C27	AP4	15c orange brown	2.10	1.60
		On cover, *from*		27.50
C28	AP4	20c red brown	4.50	2.10
		On cover, *from*		27.50
a.		Horiz. pair, imperf. vert.	*210.00*	
C29	AP4	30c green	2.10	1.10
		On cover, *from*		25.00
C30	AP4	50c blue	3.25	1.25
		On cover, *from*		30.00
C31	AP4	60c vermilion	85.00	32.50
		On cover, *from*		*100.00*
C32	AP5	1p gray black	22.50	5.00
		On cover, *from*		80.00
C33	AP5	2p rose	42.50	20.00
		On cover, *from*		100.00
C34	AP5	3p violet	125.00	72.50
		On cover, *from*		200.00
C35	AP5	5p olive green	325.00	300.00
		On cover, *from*		*500.00*
		Nos. C25-C35 (11)	618.55	441.55

Exist imperf.

For surcharge see No. C52.

Nos. C16 and C12 Handstamp Surcharged

h

i

1921-22 *Perf. 12*

C36	AP3 (h)	20c on 50c	3,750.	2,500.
C37	AP3 (i)	30c on 10c	850.	575.

Seaplane over Magdalena River — AP6

Plane over Bogota Cathedral AP7

1923-28 Wmk. 116 *Perf. 14x14½*

C38	AP6	5c orange yellow	1.75	.25
		On cover, *from*		20.00
C39	AP6	10c green	1.75	.25
		On cover, *from*		20.00
C40	AP6	15c carmine	1.75	.25
		On cover, *from*		20.00
C41	AP6	20c gray	1.75	.25
		On cover, *from*		17.50
C42	AP6	30c blue	1.75	.25
		On cover, *from*		17.50
C43	AP6	40c purple ('28)	12.50	8.00
		On cover, *from*		25.00
C44	AP6	50c green	2.10	.25
		On cover, *from*		20.00
C45	AP6	60c brown	3.25	.25
		On cover, *from*		22.50
C46	AP6	80c olive grn ('28)	32.50	30.00
		On cover, *from*		40.00
C47	AP7	1p black	14.50	3.25
		On cover, *from*		40.00
C48	AP7	2p red orange	21.00	6.00
		On cover, *from*		80.00
C49	AP7	3p violet	37.50	25.00
		On cover, *from*		175.00
C50	AP7	5p olive green	67.50	32.50
		On cover, *from*		250.00
		Nos. C38-C50 (13)	199.60	106.50

For surcharges and overprints see Nos. C51, C53-C54, CF1.

Nos. C41 and C31 Surcharged in Carmine and Dark Blue

No. C51

No. C52

1923

C51	AP6	30c on 20c gray (C)	92.50	57.50
C52	AP4	30c on 60c ver	85.00	37.50
		On cover, *from*		125.00

Nos. C41-C42 Overprinted in Black

1928 Wmk. 116 *Perf. 14x14½*

C53	AP6	20c gray	80.00	62.50
C54	AP6	30c blue	80.00	62.50

Goodwill flight of Lt. Benjamin Mendez from New York to Bogota.

Magdalena River and Tolíma Volcano AP8

Columbus' Ship and Plane AP9

1929, June 1 Wmk. 127 *Perf. 14*

C55	AP8	5c yellow org	1.25	.25
		On cover, *from*		20.00
C56	AP8	10c red brown	1.25	.25
		On cover, *from*		20.00
C57	AP8	15c deep green	1.25	.25
		On cover, *from*		20.00

C58 AP8 20c carmine 1.25 .25
On cover, *from* 15.00
C59 AP8 30c gray blue 1.25 .25
On cover, *from* 15.00
C60 AP8 40c dull violet 1.25 .25
On cover, *from* 30.00
C61 AP8 50c dk olive grn 2.50 .25
On cover, *from* 25.00
C62 AP8 60c orange brown 3.75 .25
On cover, *from* 25.00
C63 AP8 80c green 11.00 3.25
On cover, *from* 40.00
C64 AP9 1p blue 12.00 2.50
On cover, *from* 50.00
C65 AP9 2p brown orange 18.00 5.75
On cover, *from* 80.00
C66 AP9 3p pale rose vio 42.50 18.00
On cover, *from* 175.00
C67 AP9 5p olive green 100.00 37.50
On cover, *from* 250.00
Nos. C55-C67 (13) 197.25 69.00

For surcharges and overprints see Nos. C80-C95, CF2, CF4.

For International Airmail

AP10 AP11

1929, June 1 Wmk. 127 *Perf. 14*
C68 AP10 5c yellow org 6.25 *7.25*
Never hinged 9.50
C69 AP10 10c red brown 1.25 *3.00*
Never hinged 1.80
C70 AP10 15c deep green 1.25 *3.00*
Never hinged 1.80
C71 AP10 20c carmine 1.25 *3.75*
Never hinged 1.80
C72 AP10 25c violet blue 1.25 .85
Never hinged 1.80
C73 AP10 30c gray blue 1.25 .95
Never hinged 1.80
C74 AP10 50c dk olive grn 1.25 *1.90*
Never hinged 1.80
C75 AP10 60c brown 2.50 *3.00*
Never hinged 3.60
C76 AP11 1p blue 5.50 *7.25*
Never hinged 7.50
C77 AP11 2p red orange 8.50 *10.00*
Never hinged 12.50
C78 AP11 3p violet 100.00 100.00
Never hinged 135.00
C79 AP11 5p olive green 125.00 *140.00*
Never hinged 165.00
Nos. C68-C79 (12) 255.25 *280.95*

This issue was sold abroad for use on correspondence to be flown from coastal to interior points of Colombia. Cancellations are those of the country of origin rather than Colombia.

For overprint see No. CF3.

Nos. C63, C66 and C64 Surcharged in Black

m

n

1930, Dec. 15
C80 AP8(m) 10c on 80c 7.25 7.25
C81 AP9(n) 20c on 3p 13.50 13.50
C82 AP9(n) 30c on 1p 17.00 13.50
Nos. C80-C82 (3) 37.75 *34.25*

Simon Bolivar (1783-1830).

Colombian Government Issues

Nos. C55-C67 Overprinted in Black

o

p

Wmk. 127

1932, Jan. 1 Typo. *Perf. 14*
C83 AP8(o) 5c yellow org 10.00 10.00
On cover, *from* 25.00
C84 AP8(o) 10c red brown 2.25 .60
On cover, *from* 25.00
C85 AP8(o) 15c deep green 3.75 3.75
On cover, *from* 25.00
C86 AP8(o) 20c carmine 1.90 .35
On cover, *from* 17.50
C87 AP8(o) 30c gray blue 1.90 .60
On cover, *from* 17.50
C88 AP8(o) 40c dull violet 2.50 1.25
On cover, *from* 35.00
C89 AP8(o) 50c dk ol grn 5.00 3.75
On cover, *from* 30.00
C90 AP8(o) 60c orange brn 4.25 3.75
On cover, *from* 30.00
C91 AP8(o) 80c green 17.00 17.00
On cover, *from* 50.00
C92 AP9(p) 1p blue 14.50 12.00
On cover, *from* 60.00
C93 AP9(p) 2p brown org 37.50 35.00
On cover, *from* *100.00*
C94 AP9(p) 3p pale rose vio 77.50 65.00
On cover, *from* *200.00*
C95 AP9(p) 5p olive green 125.00 *140.00*
On cover, *from* 400.00
Nos. C83-C95 (13) 303.05 293.05

Coffee AP12 Gold AP16

Designs: 10c, 50c, Cattle. 15c, 60c, Petroleum. 20c, 40c, Bananas. 3p, 5p, Emerald.

1932-39 Wmk. 127 Photo. *Perf. 14*
C96 AP12 5c org & blk brn .90 .25
C97 AP12 10c lake & blk 1.00 .25
C98 AP12 15c bl grn & vio blk .50 .25
C99 AP12 15c ver & vio blk ('39) 4.00 .25
C100 AP12 20c car & ol blk .85 .25
C101 AP12 20c turq grn & ol blk ('39) 4.25 .35
C102 AP12 30c dk bl & blk brn 2.40 .25
C103 AP12 40c dk vio & ol bis 1.10 .25
C104 AP12 50c dk grn & brnsh blk 6.75 1.50
C105 AP12 60c dk brn & blk vio 1.40 .25
C106 AP12 80c grn & blk brn 9.50 2.00
C107 AP16 1p dk bl & ol bis 10.00 1.25
C108 AP16 2p org brn & ol bis 16.00 2.75
C109 AP16 3p dk vio & emer 26.00 7.25
C110 AP16 5p gray blk & emer 57.50 21.00
Nos. C96-C110 (15) 142.15 38.10

For overprint see No. CF5.

Nos. C104, C106-C108 Surcharged

a

b

1934, Jan. 5
C111 AP12(a) 10c on 50c 4.50 4.50
C112 AP12(a) 15c on 80c 6.25 6.25
C113 AP16(b) 20c on 1p 6.50 6.50
C114 AP16(b) 30c on 2p 7.25 7.25
Nos. C111-C114 (4) 24.50 24.50

400th anniversary of Cartagena.

Nos. C100 and C103 Surcharged in Black or Carmine

1939, Jan. 15
C115 AP12 5c on 20c (Bk) .35 .35
C116 AP12 5c on 40c (C) .35 .25
C117 AP12 15c on 20c (Bk) 1.50 .50
a. Double surcharge 12.00
b. Pair, one with dbl. surch. 14.00
c. Inverted surcharge 12.00 12.00

No. CF5 Surcharged in Black

C118 AP12 5c on 20c .70 .70
Nos. C115-C118 (4) 2.90 1.80

Nos. C102-C103 Surcharged in Black or Red

1940, Oct. 20
C119 AP12 15c on 30c 1.25 .50
a. Inverted surcharge 12.00
C120 AP12 15c on 40c (R) 2.00 .75
a. Double surcharge 12.00

AIR POST REGISTRATION STAMPS

Issued by Sociedad Colombo-Alemana de Transportes Aereos (SCADTA)

No. C41 Overprinted in Red

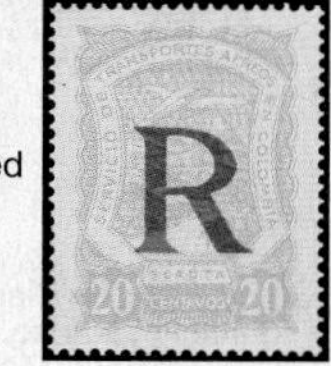

1923 Wmk. 116 *Perf. 14x14½*
CF1 AP6 20c gray 4.75 1.10

No. C58 Overprinted in Black

1929 Wmk. 127 *Perf. 14*
CF2 AP8 20c carmine 8.00 7.00
Never hinged 12.00

Same Overprint on No. C71

CF3 AP10 20c carmine 6.50 6.00

Colombian Government Issues

No. C86 Overprinted in Black

1932
CF4 AP8 20c carmine 6.50 6.00

No. C100 Overprinted

CF5 AP12 20c car & ol blk 6.00 1.25

For surcharge see No. C118.

UNITED STATES DISPATCH FOR EXPEDITED AIRMAIL SERVICE WITHIN COLOMBIA

Colombia (SCADTA) Consular Overprints Sociedad Colombo-Alemana de Transportes Aereos (S.C.A.D.T.A.)

Establishing an office in New York, the SCADTA Company sold the following two issues, each bearing the agent's signature, "G Mejia" (Gonzalo Mejia), in red ink, to designate use from the United States.

SCADTA — CONSULAR OVERPRINTS

The Sociedad Colombo-Alemana de Transportes Aéreos (SCADTA) was established in Colombia in December 1919 by a group of Colombian and German businessmen, with the aim of organizing efficient and reliable airline service within Colombia. In 1920 the Colombian government granted SCADTA the monopoly for carrying mail within the country and authorized it to establish and maintain its own post offices and to print its own stamps. These stamps represented the company's fees for air service, and all proceeds from their sale were retained by SCADTA. Airmail articles also required regular postage stamps, those of Colombia for domestic mail and, initially, for mail from abroad, or, later, stamps of the country of origin.

In order to encourage foreign airmail to Colombia, SCADTA made its stamps available at Colombian consular offices and trade missions, and through its own agents. For accounting purposes and to prevent speculation due to the frequent currency fluctuations of the period, one or two-letter control overprints were applied denoting the country of origin.

These stamps were superseded by Colombia Nos. C68-C79, which were sold abroad in the equivalent of U.S. gold dollars, thus eliminating the need to identify the various sales offices because of changes in rates of exchange.

NOTE: In order to maintain integrity of presentation, and for the convenience of the collector, the Scott editors have included SCADTA consular overprinted air post registration stamps within the air post sets with which they were issued.

UNITED STATES Nos. C14, C16 with ms "G Mejia" in red

Quantity printed of each value in parentheses.

1920, November
CLEU1 AP3 30c blk, *rose* (5,000) 100.00 350.00
Never hinged 150.00
On cover 2,000.

CLEU2 AP3 50c green (1,000) 100.00 500.00
Never hinged 150.00
On cover — 5,000.
a. Black signature —

Two examples of No. CLEU2 on cover are known. Nos. CLEU1 and CLEU2 exist together on a unique cover.

E.U. or EU - STAMPS FOR USE IN THE UNITED STATES

Colombia Nos. C25-C35 Hstmp. Ovptd. in Black

Letters 6½mm high

1921-23

CLEU3 AP4 5c org yel 15.00 15.00
Never hinged 20.00
On cover 75.00
CLEU4 AP4 10c sl grn 15.00 15.00
Never hinged 20.00
On cover 75.00
CLEU5 AP4 15c org brn 15.00 15.00
Never hinged 20.00
On cover 110.00
CLEU6 AP4 20c red brown 15.00 15.00
Never hinged 20.00
On cover 75.00
CLEU7 AP4 30c green 10.00 10.00
Never hinged 15.00
On cover 150.00
CLEU8 AP4 50c blue 15.00 15.00
Never hinged 20.00
On cover 125.00
CLEU9 AP4 60c vermilion 22.50 25.00
Never hinged 30.00
On cover 225.00
CLEU10 AP5 1p gray black 30.00 30.00
Never hinged 40.00
On cover 175.00
CLEU11 AP5 2p rose 62.50 70.00
Never hinged 100.00
On cover 225.00
CLEU12 AP5 3p violet 87.50 100.00
Never hinged 125.00
On cover 260.00
CLEU13 AP5 5p ol grn 375.00 400.00
Never hinged 500.00
On cover 600.00
Nos. CLEU3-CLEU13 (11) 662.50 710.00
Nos. CLEU3-CLEU13, never hinged 910.00

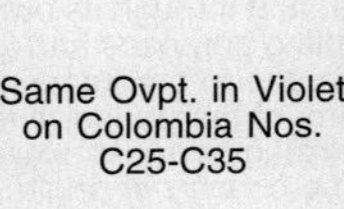
Same Ovpt. in Violet on Colombia Nos. C25-C35

1921-23

CLEU14 AP4 5c org yel 15.00 17.50
Never hinged 20.00
On cover 80.00
CLEU15 AP4 10c sl grn 12.50 17.50
Never hinged 17.50
On cover 80.00
CLEU16 AP4 15c org brn 12.50 17.50
Never hinged 17.50
On cover 150.00
CLEU17 AP4 20c red brown 12.50 17.50
Never hinged 17.50
On cover 80.00
CLEU18 AP4 30c green 9.00 12.00
Never hinged 12.50
On cover 125.00
a. Double overprint 750.00
b. Double overprint, vert. —
CLEU19 AP4 50c blue 12.50 17.50
Never hinged 17.50
On cover 90.00
CLEU20 AP4 60c vermilion 30.00 25.00
Never hinged 40.00
On cover 125.00
CLEU21 AP5 1p gray black 27.50 37.50
Never hinged 40.00
On cover 150.00
CLEU22 AP5 2p rose 62.50 72.50
Never hinged 90.00
On cover 200.00
CLEU23 AP5 3p violet 112.50 125.00
Never hinged 165.00
On cover 300.00
CLEU24 AP5 5p ol grn 375.00 400.00
Never hinged 500.00
On cover 600.00
Nos. CLEU14-CLEU24 (11) 681.50 759.50
Nos. CLEU14-CLEU24, never hinged 937.50

Same overprint in black on Colombia Nos. C38//51, CF1

No. CLEU29

No. CLEU32

1923

CLEU25 AP6 5c org yel 12.50 12.50
Never hinged 17.50
On cover 75.00
CLEU26 AP6 10c green 12.50 12.50
Never hinged 17.50
On cover 75.00
CLEU27 AP6 15c carmine 15.00 15.00
Never hinged 20.00
On cover 75.00
CLEU28 AP6 20c gray 15.00 15.00
Never hinged 22.50
On cover 75.00
CLEU29 AP6 30c blue 5.00 5.00
Never hinged 7.50
On cover 75.00
CLEU30 AP6 50c green 10.00 10.00
Never hinged 15.00
On cover 175.00
CLEU31 AP6 60c brown 10.00 10.00
Never hinged 15.00
On cover 200.00
CLEU32 AP7 1p black 20.00 20.00
Never hinged 30.00
On cover 200.00
CLEU33 AP7 2p red org 27.50 27.50
Never hinged 37.50
On cover 250.00
CLEU34 AP7 3p violet 50.00 50.00
Never hinged 75.00
On cover 275.00
CLEU35 AP7 5p ol grn 87.50 87.50
Never hinged 125.00
On cover 400.00
CFLEU1 AP6 20c gray 37.50 37.50
Never hinged 125.00
On cover 300.00
Nos. CLEU25-CLEU35, CFLEU1 (12) 302.50 302.50
Nos. CLEU25-CLEU35, CFLEU1, never hinged 432.50

Same Ovpt. in Black on Colombia No. C51

1923

CLEU36 AP6 30c on 20c gray (C) *1,250.* 450.00
On cover *600.00*
a. "60" instead of "30" at left, on cover —

No. CLEU36a is unique.

Same Overprint in Violet on Colombia Nos. C38//C50, CF1

1923

CLEU37 AP6 5c org yel 12.50 12.50
Never hinged 17.50
On cover 75.00
CLEU38 AP6 10c green 12.50 12.50
Never hinged 17.50
On cover 75.00
CLEU39 AP6 15c carmine 12.50 12.50
Never hinged 17.50
On cover 75.00
CLEU40 AP6 20c gray 12.50 12.50
Never hinged 17.50
On cover 75.00
CLEU41 AP6 30c blue 5.00 5.00
Never hinged 7.50
On cover 75.00
CLEU42 AP6 50c green 10.00 10.00
Never hinged 15.00
On cover 150.00
CLEU43 AP6 60c brown 10.00 10.00
Never hinged 15.00
On cover 175.00
CLEU44 AP7 1p black 20.00 20.00
Never hinged 30.00
On cover 175.00
CLEU45 AP7 2p red org 25.00 25.00
Never hinged 35.00
On cover 200.00
CLEU46 AP7 3p violet 50.00 50.00
Never hinged 75.00
On cover 225.00
CLEU47 AP7 5p ol grn 125.00 87.50
Never hinged 175.00
On cover 350.00
CFLEU2 AP6 20c gray 50.00 50.00
Never hinged 75.00
On cover 200.00
Nos. CLEU37-CLEU47, CFLEU2 (12) 345.00 307.50
Nos. CLEU37-CLEU47, CFLEU2, never hinged 500.00

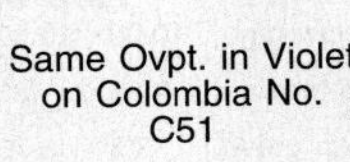
Same Ovpt. in Violet on Colombia No. C51

1923

CLEU48 AP6 30c on 20c gray (C) 45.00 22.50
Never hinged 65.00
On cover 100.00

Same Overprint in Red on Colombia No. C41

1923

CLEU49 AP6 20c gray 60.00 *60.00*
Never hinged 90.00
On cover 200.00

Colombia Nos. C38//C50, CF1 Lithograph Overprinted in Black, by the Reichsdruckerei, Berlin, Germany

No. CLEU50

No. CLEU60

Quantity printed of each value in parentheses.

Letters 10mm high

1923, June 4

CLEU50 AP6 5c org yel (7500) 4.50 4.50
Never hinged 7.50
On cover 75.00
CLEU51 AP6 10c green (15,000) 2.00 2.00
Never hinged 3.00
On cover 75.00
CLEU52 AP6 15c carmine (11,600) 3.00 3.00
Never hinged 4.00
On cover 75.00
CLEU53 AP6 20c gray (45,000) 6.00 6.00
Never hinged 9.00
On cover 75.00
CLEU54 AP6 30c blue (170,000) 2.00 2.00
Never hinged 3.00
On cover 50.00
CLEU55 AP6 50c green (5,000) 5.00 5.00
Never hinged 7.50
On cover 75.00
CLEU56 AP6 60c brown (55,000) 2.75 2.75
Never hinged 4.00
On cover 125.00
CLEU57 AP7 1p black (8,400) 6.75 6.00
Never hinged 8.00
On cover 150.00
a. Double impression of basic stamp *1,250.*
CLEU58 AP7 2p red org (3,800) 17.50 17.50
Never hinged 25.00
On cover 175.00
CLEU59 AP7 3p violet (3,200) 37.50 40.00
Never hinged 50.00
On cover 175.00
CLEU60 AP7 5p ol grn (3,400) 55.00 55.00
Never hinged 75.00
On cover 250.00

CFLEU3 AP6 20c gray (2,000) 25.00 12.50
Never hinged 50.00
On cover 180.00
Nos. CLEU50-CLEU60, CFLEU3 (12) 167.00 156.25
Nos. CLEU50-CLEU60, CFLEU3, never hinged 221.00

Colombia Nos. C40, C42 Litho. Ovptd. in Black

Letters 10mm high

1928, Sept. 25

CLEU61 AP6 15c carmine (1,500) 15.00 15.00
Never hinged 22.50
On cover 75.00
a. Inverted overprint *300.00 200.00*
CLEU62 AP6 30c blue (49,000) 5.00 5.00
Never hinged 7.50
On cover 35.00
a. Inverted overprint *450.00 450.00*
b. Double overprint *500.00 500.00*

Nos. CLEU61 and CLEU62 were lithograph overprinted in New York in a slightly different font by Fleming & Benedict for the New York agency. There were two printings of the 30c value, the first generally centered toward the top of the stamp, the second toward the bottom.

ARGENTINA & URUGUAY

Nos. C38//C50, CF1 Handstamped in Black

A-U.

Letters 5mm high

1923

CLAU1 AP6 5c org yel 90.00 *90.00*
CLAU2 AP6 10c green 90.00 *90.00*
CLAU3 AP6 15c carmine 90.00 *90.00*
CLAU4 AP6 20c gray 90.00 *90.00*
CLAU5 AP6 30c blue 75.00 *75.00*
CLAU6 AP6 50c green 90.00 *90.00*
CLAU7 AP6 60c brown 90.00 *90.00*
CLAU8 AP7 1p black 125.00 *150.00*
CLAU9 AP7 2p red org 175.00 *200.00*
CLAU10 AP7 3p violet 400.00 *450.00*
CLAU11 AP7 5p ol grn 450.00 *500.00*
CFLAU1 AP6 20c gray 175.00 *200.00*

Nos. C38//C50, CF1 Hstmpd. in Black

Letters 7½mm high

CLAU12 AP6 5c org yel 90.00 *90.00*
CLAU13 AP6 10c green 90.00 *90.00*
CLAU14 AP6 15c carmine 90.00 *90.00*
CLAU15 AP6 20c gray 90.00 *90.00*
CLAU16 AP6 30c blue 75.00 *75.00*
On cover, *from* 800.00
CLAU17 AP6 50c green 90.00 *90.00*
CLAU18 AP6 60c brown 90.00 *90.00*
CLAU19 AP7 1p black 125.00 *150.00*
CLAU20 AP7 2p red org 175.00 *200.00*
CLAU21 AP7 3p violet 400.00 *450.00*
CLAU22 AP7 5p ol grn 450.00 *500.00*
CFLAU2 AP6 20c gray 175.00 *200.00*

BARBADOS

No. C15 with Manuscript Overprint "G.M. Allayn" in Black

1921, November

No.	Type	Description	Unused	Used
CLBA1	AP3	30c rose		
		On cover		—

BELGIUM

Nos. C38//50, CF1 Ovptd. in Black

Letters 10mm high

1923, Aug. 1

No.	Type	Description	Unused	Used
CLB1	AP6	5c org yel	6.00	6.00
CLB2	AP6	10c green	4.00	4.00
CLB3	AP6	15c carmine	6.00	6.00
CLB4	AP6	20c gray	3.50	3.50
CLB5	AP6	30c blue	3.50	3.50
		On cover, *from*		250.00
CLB6	AP6	50c green	6.00	6.00
CLB7	AP6	60c brown	6.00	6.00
CLB8	AP7	1p black	15.00	16.00
CLB9	AP7	2p red org	20.00	22.50
CLB10	AP7	3p violet	75.00	80.00
CLB11	AP7	5p ol grn	87.50	90.00

"R" 12mm high

No.	Type	Description	Unused	Used
CFLB1	AP6	20c gray	100.00	100.00
a.		Overprint "R" 10mm high	37.50	37.50

Nos. CLB1-CFLB1 were lithograph overprinted by the Reichsdruckerei Berlin.

BOLIVIA

Nos. C38//50, CF1 Hstmpd. in Black

Letters 6½mm high

1923

No.	Type	Description	Unused	Used
CLBO1	AP6	5c org yel	15.00	—
CLBO2	AP6	10c green	15.00	—
CLBO3	AP6	15c carmine	15.00	—
CLBO4	AP6	20c gray	15.00	—
CLBO5	AP6	30c blue	10.00	—
CLBO6	AP6	50c green	20.00	—
CLBO7	AP6	60c brown	30.00	—
CLBO8	AP7	1p black	37.50	—
CLBO9	AP7	2p red org	67.50	—
CLBO10	AP7	3p violet	87.50	—
CLBO11	AP7	5p ol grn	140.00	—
CFLBO1	AP6	20c gray	40.00	—

Nos. CLBO1-CFLBO1 were prepared but not issued. All used examples are either canceled by favor or are forgeries.

BRAZIL

Nos. C38//50, CF1 Handstamped in Black

Br.

Letters 9½mm high

1923

No.	Type	Description	Unused	Used
CLBR1	AP6	5c org yel	20.00	20.00
CLBR2	AP6	10c green	20.00	20.00
CLBR3	AP6	15c carmine	20.00	20.00
CLBR4	AP6	20c gray	30.00	30.00
CLBR5	AP6	30c blue	20.00	20.00
CLBR6	AP6	50c green	40.00	40.00
CLBR7	AP6	60c brown	50.00	50.00
CLBR8	AP7	1p black	67.50	67.50
CLBR9	AP7	2p red org	100.00	*110.00*
CLBR10	AP7	3p violet	175.00	*190.00*
CLBR11	AP7	5p ol grn	375.00	*400.00*
CFLBR2	AP6	20c gray	67.50	*67.50*

Nos. C38//50, CF1 Hstmpd. in Black

Letters 7mm high

1923

No.	Type	Description	Unused	Used
CLBR12	AP6	5c org yel	27.50	27.50
CLBR13	AP6	10c green	27.50	27.50
CLBR14	AP6	15c carmine	27.50	27.50
CLBR15	AP6	20c gray	37.50	37.50
CLBR16	AP6	30c blue	22.50	22.50
		On cover, *from*		800.00
CLBR17	AP6	50c green	40.00	40.00
CLBR18	AP6	60c brown	40.00	40.00
CLBR19	AP7	1p black	50.00	55.00
CLBR20	AP7	2p red org	140.00	*150.00*
CLBR21	AP7	3p violet	225.00	*250.00*
CLBR22	AP7	5p ol grn	500.00	*550.00*
CFLBR3	AP6	20c gray	40.00	*45.00*

CANADA

Nos. C38//50, CF1 Hstmpd. in Black

Letters 7mm high

1923

No.	Type	Description	Unused	Used
CLCA1	AP6	5c org yel	275.00	*175.00*
		Never hinged	*380.00*	
		On cover		*2,500.*
CLCA2	AP6	10c green	275.00	*175.00*
		Never hinged	*380.00*	
		On cover		*2,500.*
a.		Double overprint		*750.00*
CLCA3	AP6	15c carmine	275.00	*150.00*
		Never hinged	*380.00*	
		On cover, *from*		*7,500.*
CLCA4	AP6	20c gray	180.00	*110.00*
		Never hinged	*245.00*	
		On cover		—
CLCA5	AP6	30c blue	115.00	*75.00*
		Never hinged	*160.00*	
		On cover		*2,000.*
a.		Double overprint		—
CLCA6	AP6	50c green	275.00	*210.00*
		Never hinged	*380.00*	
		On cover		—
a.		Inverted overprint		—
CLCA7	AP6	60c brown	275.00	*175.00*
		Never hinged	*380.00*	
		On cover		*3,500.*
CLCA8	AP7	1p black	275.00	*175.00*
		Never hinged	*380.00*	
		On cover		—
CLCA9	AP7	2p red org	275.00	*175.00*
		Never hinged	*380.00*	
		On cover		—
CLCA10	AP7	3p violet	1,000.	*350.00*
		Never hinged	*1,250.*	
		On cover		—
CLCA11	AP7	5p ol grn	1,000.	*450.00*
		Never hinged	*1,250.*	
		On cover		—
CFLCA1	AP6	20c gray	900.00	*550.00*
		Never hinged	*1,225.*	
		On cover, *from*		*7,000.*
a.		With manuscript red "R" overprint		—

On No. CFLCA1, the "R" is machine overprinted, while on No. CFLCA1a it is hand-written. The unique example of No. CFLCA1a is on cover.

CANAL ZONE

No. C42 Overprinted "P", 10mm (#CLP60), and Handstamped "C.Z." in Violet

1923 **Letters 6mm High**

No.	Type	Description	Unused	Used
CLCZ1	AP6	30c blue	*5,000.*	*5,000.*
		On cover		—

Five examples of No. CLCZ1 are known, three of them on cover. Forgeries exist.

CHILE

Nos. C38//50, CF1 Hstmpd. in Black

Letters 7mm high

1923

No.	Type	Description	Unused	Used
CLCH1	AP6	5c org yel	20.00	20.00
CLCH2	AP6	10c green	20.00	20.00
CLCH3	AP6	15c carmine	20.00	17.50
CLCH4	AP6	20c gray	20.00	20.00
CLCH5	AP6	30c blue	15.00	12.50
		On cover, *from*		*800.00*
CLCH6	AP6	50c green	20.00	20.00
CLCH7	AP6	60c brown	20.00	20.00
CLCH8	AP7	1p black	37.50	37.50
CLCH9	AP7	2p red org	45.00	45.00
CLCH10	AP7	3p violet	87.50	87.50
CLCH11	AP7	5p ol grn	175.00	175.00
CFLCH1	AP6	20c gray	50.00	50.00

COSTA RICA

Nos. C38//50, CF1 Hstmpd. in Black

Letters 7½mm high

1923

No.	Type	Description	Unused	Used
CLCR1	AP6	5c org yel	15.00	15.00
CLCR2	AP6	10c green	15.00	15.00
CLCR3	AP6	15c carmine	20.00	20.00
CLCR4	AP6	20c gray	20.00	20.00
CLCR5	AP6	30c blue	10.00	5.00
		On cover, *from*		*650.00*
CLCR6	AP6	50c green	40.00	40.00
CLCR7	AP6	60c brown	50.00	50.00
CLCR8	AP7	1p black	50.00	50.00
CLCR9	AP7	2p red org	75.00	75.00
CLCR10	AP7	3p violet	100.00	100.00
CLCR11	AP7	5p ol grn	175.00	175.00
CFLCR1	AP6	20c gray	50.00	50.00
		On cover, *from*		*1,000.*

CUBA

Nos. C38//50, CF1 Hstmpd. in Black

Letters 7mm High Without Period, or 8mm High With Period

1923

No.	Type	Description	Unused	Used
CLC1	AP6	5c org yel	20.00	20.00
CLC2	AP6	10c green	20.00	20.00
a.		Inverted overprint	—	—
CLC3	AP6	15c carmine	20.00	20.00
CLC4	AP6	20c gray	20.00	20.00
CLC5	AP6	30c blue	10.00	10.00
		On cover, *from*		*600.00*
CLC6	AP6	50c green	30.00	30.00
CLC7	AP6	60c brown	30.00	30.00
CLC8	AP7	1p black	35.00	35.00
CLC9	AP7	2p red org	45.00	50.00
CLC10	AP7	3p violet	90.00	100.00
CLC11	AP7	5p ol grn	175.00	200.00
CFLC1	AP6	20c gray	40.00	45.00

No. C42 Handstamped in Violet, 8mm High

No.	Type	Description	Unused	Used
CLC12	AP6	30c blue	*75.00*	*75.00*

DENMARK, NORWAY & SWEDEN

Nos. C38//50, CF1 Handstamped in Violet

D

Letters 10½mm high

1923

No.	Type	Description	Unused	Used
CLD1	AP6	5c org yel	62.50	*62.50*
CLD2	AP6	10c green	62.50	*62.50*
CLD3	AP6	15c carmine	100.00	*100.00*
CLD4	AP6	20c gray	62.50	*62.50*
CLD5	AP6	30c blue	30.00	*30.00*
CLD6	AP6	50c green	50.00	*50.00*
CLD7	AP6	60c brown	60.00	*60.00*
CLD8	AP7	1p black	100.00	*100.00*
CLD9	AP7	2p red org	120.00	*120.00*
CLD10	AP7	3p violet	275.00	*275.00*
CLD11	AP7	5p ol grn	375.00	*375.00*
CFLD1	AP6	20c gray	75.00	*75.00*

No. C42 Handstamped in Black, 10½mm High

No.	Type	Description	Unused	Used
CLD12	AP6	30c blue	*125.00*	*125.00*

Nos. CLD1-CLD12 were overprinted in Copenhagen.

Nos. C38//50, CF1 Handstamped in Violet

D

Letters 7 or 8mm high

1923

No.	Type	Description	Unused	Used
CLD13	AP6	5c org yel	—	—
CLD14	AP6	10c green	—	—
CLD15	AP6	15c carmine	30.00	30.00
CLD16	AP6	20c gray	30.00	30.00
CLD17	AP6	30c blue	32.50	32.50
CLD18	AP6	50c green	62.50	62.50
CLD19	AP6	60c brown	75.00	75.00
CLD20	AP7	1p black	100.00	100.00
CLD21	AP7	2p red org	125.00	140.00
CLD22	AP7	3p violet	210.00	240.00
CLD23	AP7	5p ol grn	250.00	275.00
CFLD2	AP6	20c gray	—	—

Handstamped in Red

No.	Type	Description	Unused	Used
CLD24	AP6	5c org yel	30.00	30.00
CLD25	AP6	10c green	40.00	40.00
CLD26	AP6	15c carmine	30.00	30.00
CLD27	AP6	20c gray	40.00	40.00
CLD28	AP6	30c blue	32.50	32.50
CLD29	AP6	50c green	—	—
CLD30	AP6	60c brown	—	—
CLD31	AP7	1p black	—	—
CLD32	AP7	2p red org	—	—
CLD33	AP7	3p violet	—	—
CLD34	AP7	5p ol grn	—	—
CFLD3	AP6	20c gray	82.50	90.00

Nos. CLD13-CFLD3 were overprinted in Barranquilla.

Nos. C38//50, CF1 Ovptd. in Black

Letters 10mm high

1927, June 1

No.	Type	Description	Unused	Used
CLD35	AP6	5c org yel	6.00	6.00
CLD36	AP6	10c green	6.00	6.00
CLD37	AP6	15c carmine	10.00	10.00
CLD38	AP6	20c gray	10.00	10.00
CLD39	AP6	30c blue	6.00	6.00
		On cover, *from*		*400.00*
CLD40	AP6	50c green	6.00	6.00
CLD41	AP6	60c brown	10.00	10.00
CLD42	AP7	1p black	10.00	10.00
CLD43	AP7	2p red org	40.00	40.00
CLD44	AP7	3p violet	50.00	50.00
CLD45	AP7	5p ol grn	87.50	100.00
CFLD4	AP6	20c gray	17.50	17.50

Nos. CLD35-CFLD4 were lithograph overprinted by the Reichsdruckerei Berlin.

FRANCE

Nos. C25-C35 Hstmpd. in Black

Letters 8mm high

1921-23

No.	Type	Description	Unused	Used
CLF1	AP4	5c org yel	20.00	25.00
CLF2	AP4	10c sl grn	20.00	25.00
CLF3	AP4	15c org brn	20.00	25.00
CLF4	AP4	20c red brown	—	—
CLF5	AP4	30c green	17.50	22.50
CLF6	AP4	50c blue	12.50	17.50

CLF7 AP4 60c vermilion 22.50 25.00
CLF8 AP5 1p gray black 75.00 35.00
CLF9 AP5 2p rose 67.50 75.00
CLF10 AP5 3p violet 75.00 85.00
CLF11 AP5 5p ol grn *1,000.*

Nos. C25-C35 Handstamped in Red, Letters 8mm High With or Without Period

1923

CLF12 AP4 5c org yel 25.00 25.00
CLF13 AP4 10c sl grn 15.00 15.00
CLF14 AP4 15c org brn 12.50 12.50
CLF15 AP4 20c red brown 25.00 25.00
CLF16 AP4 30c green 30.00 30.00
CLF17 AP4 50c blue 25.00 25.00
CLF18 AP4 60c vermilion 40.00 40.00
CLF19 AP5 1p gray black 20.00 20.00
CLF20 AP5 2p rose 45.00 50.00
CLF21 AP5 3p violet 80.00 90.00
CLF22 AP5 5p ol grn 275.00 300.00

Nos. C25-C35 Handstamped in Violet, Letters 8mm High With or Without Period

CLF23 AP4 5c org yel 300.00 300.00
CLF24 AP4 10c sl grn 12.50 12.50
CLF25 AP4 15c org brn 20.00 20.00
CLF26 AP4 20c red brown 150.00 150.00
CLF27 AP4 30c green 15.00 15.00
CLF28 AP4 50c blue 12.50 12.50
CLF29 AP4 60c vermilion 20.00 20.00
CLF30 AP5 1p gray black 30.00 30.00
CLF31 AP5 2p rose 67.50 75.00
CLF32 AP5 3p violet 87.50 100.00
CLF33 AP5 5p ol grn 800.00 *1,000.*

No. C29 Handstamped in Blue, Letters 8mm High With Period

CLF34 AP4 30c green *100.00*

Nos. C38//C50, CF1 Handstamped in Black, Letters 6½ or 8mm High Without Period

CLF35 AP6 5c org yel 15.00 15.00
CLF36 AP6 10c green 12.50 12.50
CLF37 AP6 15c carmine 30.00 30.00
CLF38 AP6 20c gray 12.50 12.50
CLF39 AP6 30c blue 10.00 10.00
CLF40 AP6 50c green 12.50 12.50
CLF41 AP6 60c brown 12.50 12.50
CLF42 AP7 1p black 20.00 20.00
CLF43 AP7 2p red org 20.00 25.00
CLF44 AP7 3p violet 50.00 55.00
CLF45 AP7 5p ol grn 75.00 85.00
CFLF1 AP6 20c gray 25.00 27.50

Nos. C38//C50, CF1 Handstamped in Black

F.

Letters 6½ or 8mm High, With Period

1923

CLF46 AP6 5c org yel — —
CLF47 AP6 10c green *12.50 12.50*
CLF48 AP6 15c carmine *30.00 30.00*
CLF49 AP6 20c gray *12.50 12.50*
CLF50 AP6 30c blue *10.00 10.00*
CLF51 AP6 50c green *12.50 12.50*
CLF52 AP6 60c brown *15.00 15.00*
CLF53 AP7 1p black — —
CLF54 AP7 2p red org *30.00 35.00*
CLF55 AP7 3p violet *50.00 60.00*
CLF56 AP7 5p ol grn *90.00 100.00*
CFLF2 AP6 20c gray *25.00 27.50*

Nos. C38//C50, CF1 Handstamped in Violet, Letters 6½ or 8mm High, Without Period

CLF57 AP6 5c org yel 12.00 12.00
CLF58 AP6 10c green 9.00 9.00
CLF59 AP6 15c carmine 12.00 12.00
CLF60 AP6 20c gray 9.00 9.00
CLF61 AP6 30c blue 10.00 10.00
CLF62 AP6 50c green 20.00 20.00
CLF63 AP6 60c brown 20.00 20.00
CLF64 AP7 1p black 20.00 20.00
CLF65 AP7 2p red org 12.00 14.00
CLF66 AP7 3p violet 100.00 *110.00*
CLF67 AP7 5p ol grn 110.00 *120.00*
CFLF3 AP6 20c gray 25.00 27.50

Nos. C38//C50, CF1 Handstamped in Violet, Letters 6½ or 8mm High, With Period

CLF68 AP6 5c org yel — —
CLF69 AP6 10c green 12.00 12.00
CLF70 AP6 15c carmine 12.00 12.00
CLF71 AP6 20c gray 12.00 12.00
CLF72 AP6 30c blue 10.00 10.00
CLF73 AP6 50c green 20.00 20.00
CLF74 AP6 60c brown 20.00 20.00
CLF75 AP7 1p black — —
CLF76 AP7 2p red org 27.50 27.50
CLF77 AP7 3p violet 100.00 *110.00*
CLF78 AP7 5p ol grn 110.00 *120.00*
CFLF4 AP6 20c gray 25.00 5.00

Nos. C42-C43 Handstamped in Red, Letters 6½ or 8mm High

CLF79 AP6 30c blue 30.00 30.00
CLF80 AP6 50c green 37.50 37.50

Nos. C38//50, CF1 Ovptd. in Black

Letters 10mm high

1923, June 4

CLF81 AP6 5c org yel 15.00 17.50
CLF82 AP6 10c green 10.00 10.00
CLF83 AP6 15c carmine 7.50 7.50
CLF84 AP6 20c gray 10.00 10.00
On cover, *from* *275.00*
a. On 20c black 190.00
CLF85 AP6 30c blue 6.50 6.50
CLF86 AP6 50c green 10.00 10.00
CLF87 AP6 60c brown 10.00 10.00
CLF88 AP7 1p black 15.00 15.00
CLF89 AP7 2p red org 30.00 32.50
CLF90 AP7 3p violet 67.50 75.00
CLF91 AP7 5p ol grn 87.50 90.00
CFLF5 AP6 20c gray 30.00 30.00

Nos. CLF81-CFLF5 were lithograph overprinted by the Reichsdruckerei Berlin.

GERMANY, AUSTRIA, CZECHOSLOVAKIA AND, LATER, HUNGARY & YUGOSLAVIA

Nos. C25-C35 Hstmpd. in Black or Blue-black

Letters 20mm high

1921-23

CLA1 AP4 5c org yel 17.00 20.00
CLA2 AP4 10c sl grn 10.00 17.50
a. Overprint inverted —
CLA3 AP4 15c org brn 17.00 15.00
CLA4 AP4 20c red brown 12.50 17.50
a. Horizontal pair, imperf vertically *1,000.*
b. Vertical pair, imperf horizontally —
CLA5 AP4 30c green 12.50 11.00
On cover, *from* *350.00*
CLA6 AP4 50c blue 15.00 22.50
CLA7 AP4 60c vermilion 45.00 50.00
CLA8 AP5 1p gray black 50.00 55.00
CLA9 AP5 2p rose 55.00 65.00
CLA10 AP5 3p violet 100.00 110.00
CLA11 AP5 5p ol grn 500.00 *600.00*

No. CLA4 Overprinted "R" in Red

CFLA1 AP4 20c red brown *1,250.*
On cover, *from* *2,500.*

Nos. CLA1-CFLA1 were overprinted in Berlin prior to receipt of overprinted stamps from Barranquilla (Nos. CLA12-CLA22).

Three examples of No. CFLA1 are known. All are used.

Nos. C25-C35 Handstamped in Violet

Letters 6½mm high

1921-23

CLA12 AP4 5c org yel 12.50 —
CLA13 AP4 10c sl grn 9.00 —
CLA14 AP4 15c org brn 20.00 —
CLA15 AP4 20c red brown 12.50 —
CLA16 AP4 30c green 10.00 12.50
CLA17 AP4 50c blue 12.50 17.50
CLA18 AP4 60c vermilion — —
CLA19 AP5 1p gray black — —
CLA20 AP5 2p rose 70.00 75.00
CLA21 AP5 3p violet 110.00 —
CLA22 AP5 5p ol grn 500.00 —

Nos. C38//50, CF1 Ovptd. in Black

Letters 12mm high

1923, June 4

CLA23 AP6 5c org yel 5.00 5.50
CLA24 AP6 10c green 5.00 5.50
a. Overprint inverted 300.00
CLA25 AP6 15c carmine 4.00 4.00
CLA26 AP6 20c gray 4.00 4.00
CLA27 AP6 30c blue 1.50 1.50
On cover, *from* *50.00*
CLA28 AP6 50c green 5.00 5.00
CLA29 AP6 60c brown 5.00 5.00
CLA30 AP7 1p black 6.00 6.00
CLA31 AP7 2p red org 17.50 18.00
CLA32 AP7 3p violet 37.50 37.50
CLA33 AP7 5p ol grn 67.50 70.00
CFLA2 AP6 20c gray 5.00 5.50
On cover, *from* *125.00*

Nos. CLA23-CFLA2 were lithograph overprinted by the Reichsdruckerei Berlin.

Nos. C38 Overprinted in Black

Letters 10mm high

1923 (?)

CLA34 AP6 5c org yel — —

No. CLA34 was a proof, printed by the Reichsdruckerei Berlin, that was later put into service when supplies of No. CLA23 were depleted.

GREAT BRITAIN

Nos. C25-C35 Handstamped in Violet

Letters 6½mm high

1921-23

CLGB1 AP4 5c org yel 12.50 16.00
CLGB2 AP4 10c sl grn 10.00 12.50
a. Pair, one stamp without ovpt. —
CLGB3 AP4 15c org brn 10.00 12.50
a. Double overprint —
CLGB4 AP4 20c red brown 12.50 16.00
CLGB5 AP4 30c green 10.00 12.50
On cover, *from* *300.00*
a. Imperf *200.00*
CLGB6 AP4 50c blue 25.00 30.00
CLGB7 AP4 60c vermilion —
CLGB8 AP5 1p gray black 50.00 55.00
CLGB9 AP5 2p rose 110.00 125.00
CLGB10 AP5 3p violet 150.00 175.00
a. Double overprint —
CLGB11 AP5 5p ol grn 400.00 *450.00*

Handstamped in Black

CLGB12 AP4 10c sl grn 20.00 *20.00*
CLGB13 AP4 60c vermilion 37.50 *37.50*
CLGB14 AP5 1p gray black 30.00 *55.00*
CLGB15 AP5 2p rose 175.00 *175.00*
CLGB16 AP5 3p violet 175.00 *175.00*

Handstamped in Red

CLGB17 AP4 50c blue *45.00 50.00*

Nos. C38//50, CF1 Handstamped in Black, Letters 6mm High

1923

CLGB18 AP6 5c org yel 15.00 15.00
CLGB19 AP6 10c green 10.00 10.00
CLGB20 AP6 15c carmine 10.00 10.00
CLGB21 AP6 20c gray 10.00 10.00
CLGB22 AP6 30c blue 5.00 5.00
CLGB23 AP6 50c green 15.00 15.00
CLGB24 AP6 60c brown 15.00 15.00
CLGB25 AP7 1p black 20.00 20.00
CLGB26 AP7 2p red org 50.00 50.00
CLGB27 AP7 3p violet 75.00 75.00
CLGB28 AP7 5p ol grn 125.00 125.00
CFLGB1 AP6 20c gray 25.00 25.00

Handstamped in Violet

CLGB29 AP6 5c org yel 15.00 15.00
CLGB30 AP6 10c green 10.00 10.00
CLGB31 AP6 15c carmine 10.00 10.00
CLGB32 AP6 20c gray 10.00 10.00
CLGB33 AP6 30c blue 5.00 5.00
CLGB34 AP6 50c green 15.00 15.00
CLGB35 AP6 60c brown 15.00 15.00
CLGB36 AP7 1p black 17.50 17.50
CLGB37 AP7 2p red org 50.00 50.00
CLGB38 AP7 3p violet 75.00 75.00
CLGB39 AP7 5p ol grn 125.00 140.00
CFLGB2 AP6 20c gray 17.50 20.00

Handstamped in Red

CLGB40 AP6 5c org yel 15.00 15.00
CLGB41 AP6 10c green 10.00 10.00
CLGB42 AP6 15c carmine 15.00 10.00
CLGB43 AP6 20c gray 15.00 15.00
CLGB44 AP6 30c blue 10.00 10.00
CLGB45 AP6 50c green 15.00 11.50
CLGB46 AP6 60c brown 20.00 20.00
CLGB47 AP7 1p black 20.00 20.00
CLGB48 AP7 2p red org 50.00 55.00
CLGB49 AP7 3p violet *175.00 190.00*
CLGB50 AP7 5p ol grn *250.00 275.00*
CFLGB3 AP6 20c gray 25.00 25.00

Nos. C38//50, CF1 Ovptd. in Black

Letters 10mm high

1923, June 4

CLGB51 AP6 5c org yel 20.00 22.50
CLGB52 AP6 10c green 15.00 18.00
CLGB53 AP6 15c carmine 15.00 18.00
CLGB54 AP6 20c gray 15.00 18.00
CLGB55 AP6 30c blue 8.00 8.00
On cover, *from* *175.00*
CLGB56 AP6 50c green 8.00 8.00
CLGB57 AP6 60c brown 8.00 8.00
CLGB58 AP7 1p black 20.00 22.50
a. Double impression of basic stamp *1,250.*
CLGB59 AP7 2p red org 50.00 60.00
CLGB60 AP7 3p violet 100.00 110.00
CLGB61 AP7 5p ol grn 150.00 160.00
CFLGB4 AP6 20c gray 60.00 60.00

Nos. CLGB51-CFLGB4 were lithograph overprinted by the Reichsdruckerei Berlin.

ITALY

Nos. C25-C35 Handstamped in Red

Letter 7½mm high

1921-23

CLIT1 AP4 5c org yel 20.00 20.00
CLIT2 AP4 10c sl grn 15.00 15.00
CLIT3 AP4 15c org brn 15.00 15.00
CLIT4 AP4 20c red brown 20.00 20.00
CLIT5 AP4 30c green 10.00 10.00
CLIT6 AP4 50c blue 40.00 40.00
CLIT7 AP4 60c vermilion 62.50 62.50
CLIT8 AP5 1p gray black *75.00 75.00*
CLIT9 AP5 2p rose *110.00 125.00*
CLIT10 AP5 3p violet *160.00 175.00*
CLIT11 AP5 5p ol grn *750.00 900.00*

Handstamped in Violet

CLIT12 AP4 5c org yel 17.50 17.50
CLIT13 AP4 10c sl grn 15.00 15.00
CLIT14 AP4 15c org brn 15.00 15.00
CLIT15 AP4 20c red brown 25.00 25.00
CLIT16 AP4 30c green 10.00 10.00
CLIT17 AP4 50c blue 50.00 50.00
CLIT18 AP4 60c vermilion 50.00 50.00
CLIT19 AP5 1p gray black *100.00 100.00*
CLIT20 AP5 2p rose *150.00 175.00*
CLIT21 AP5 3p violet *300.00 350.00*
CLIT22 AP5 5p ol grn *750.00 900.00*

Nos. C38//50, CF1 Ovptd. in Black

Letter 12mm high

1923, Dec. 11

CLIT23 AP6 5c org yel 11.00 12.50
CLIT24 AP6 10c green 5.00 5.50
CLIT25 AP6 15c carmine 5.00 5.50
CLIT26 AP6 20c gray 5.00 5.50
CLIT27 AP6 30c blue 4.00 5.00
On cover, *from* *400.00*
a. Double ovpt., 10mm, 8mm —
CLIT28 AP6 50c green 7.50 7.50
CLIT29 AP6 60c brown 7.50 7.50
CLIT30 AP7 1p black 15.00 16.00
CLIT31 AP7 2p red org 20.00 20.00
CLIT32 AP7 3p violet 50.00 50.00
CLIT33 AP7 5p ol grn 67.50 75.00

"R" 12mm high

CFLIT1 AP6 20c gray 17.50 19.00

"R" 10mm high

CFLIT2 AP6 20c gray 30.00 30.00

Nos. C47-C50 Overprinted in Black, Letter 8mm High

CLIT34 AP7 1p black 25.00 30.00
CLIT35 AP7 2p red org 35.00 37.50
CLIT36 AP7 3p violet 75.00 85.00
CLIT37 AP7 5p ol grn 100.00 110.00

Nos. CLIT23-CFLIT37 were lithograph overprinted by the Reichsdruckerei Berlin.

MEXICO

The typewritten overprint "De Mexico" is known on postal stationery and reported on stamps of the 1923 issue.

NETHERLANDS & NETHERLANDS ANTILLES

Nos. C25-C35 Handstamped in Violet

H.

Letters 6mm High With or Without Period

1921-23

CLH1 AP4 5c org yel 15.00 16.00
CLH2 AP4 10c sl grn 15.00 16.00
CLH3 AP4 15c org brn 15.00 16.00
CLH4 AP4 20c red brown 20.00 22.50
CLH5 AP4 30c green 10.00 11.00
CLH6 AP4 50c blue 30.00 32.50
CLH7 AP4 60c vermilion, ovpt. with period 37.50 40.00
a. Overprint without period —
CLH8 AP5 1p gray black 110.00 125.00
CLH9 AP5 2p rose 150.00 175.00
CLH10 AP5 3p violet 210.00 240.00
CLH11 AP5 5p ol grn *900.00*

Nos. C38//50, CF1 Handstamped in Black, Letter 6mm High

1923

CLH12 AP6 5c org yel 30.00 30.00
CLH13 AP6 10c green 20.00 20.00
CLH14 AP6 15c carmine 20.00 20.00
CLH15 AP6 20c gray 32.50 32.50
CLH16 AP6 30c blue 25.00 25.00
CLH17 AP6 50c green 25.00 25.00
CLH18 AP6 60c brown 40.00 40.00
CLH19 AP7 1p black 50.00 50.00
CLH20 AP7 2p red org 250.00 *275.00*
CLH21 AP7 3p violet 150.00 *175.00*
CLH22 AP7 5p ol grn 300.00 *325.00*
CFLH1 AP6 20c gray 50.00 50.00

Nos. C38//50, CF1 Handstamped in Violet, Letter 7mm High Without Period

1923

CLH23 AP6 5c org yel 25.00 25.00
CLH24 AP6 10c green 20.00 20.00
CLH25 AP6 15c carmine 20.00 20.00
CLH26 AP6 20c gray 17.50 17.50
CLH27 AP6 30c blue 12.50 12.50
CLH28 AP6 50c green 12.50 12.50
CLH29 AP6 60c brown 20.00 20.00
CLH30 AP7 1p black 30.00 30.00
CLH31 AP7 2p red org 30.00 35.00
CLH32 AP7 3p violet 50.00 55.00
CLH33 AP7 5p ol grn 100.00 *125.00*
CFLH1A AP6 20c gray 30.00 32.50

Nos. C42, C47 Handstamped in Red

CLH34 AP6 30c blue 25.00 25.00
CLH35 AP7 3p violet 100.00 *125.00*

Nos. C38//50, CF1 Handstamped in Black, Letter 8mm High

1923

CLH36 AP6 5c org yel *25.00 25.00*
CLH37 AP6 10c green *20.00 22.50*
CLH38 AP6 15c carmine *20.00 22.50*
CLH39 AP6 20c gray *20.00 22.00*
CLH40 AP6 30c blue *15.00 17.50*
CLH41 AP6 50c green *25.00 27.50*
CLH42 AP6 60c brown *25.00 27.50*
CLH43 AP7 1p black *40.00 45.00*
CLH44 AP7 2p red org *60.00 65.00*
CLH45 AP7 3p violet *90.00 100.00*
CLH46 AP7 5p ol grn *160.00 175.00*
CFLH2 AP6 20c gray *40.00 45.00*

Nos. C38//50, CF1 Ovptd. in Black

Letter 10mm high

1923

CLH47 AP6 5c org yel 15.00 17.50
CLH48 AP6 10c green 6.00 7.00
CLH49 AP6 15c carmine 6.00 7.00
CLH50 AP6 20c gray 6.00 7.00
CLH51 AP6 30c blue 5.00 6.00
On cover, *from* 400.00
CLH52 AP6 50c green 6.00 7.00
CLH53 AP6 60c brown 6.00 7.00
CLH54 AP7 1p black 10.00 12.50
CLH55 AP7 2p red org 20.00 22.50
CLH56 AP7 3p violet 45.00 50.00
CLH57 AP7 5p ol grn 75.00 85.00

"R" 12mm high

CFLH3 AP6 20c gray 17.50 20.00
a. "R" 10mm high 37.50 40.00

Nos. CLH47-CFLH3 were lithograph overprinted by the Reichsdruckerei Berlin.

PANAMA & CANAL ZONE

Nos. C25-C35 Handstamped in Violet

P.

Letters 7½mm high

1921-23

CLP1 AP4 5c org yel 15.00 17.50
CLP2 AP4 10c sl grn 12.50 15.00
CLP3 AP4 15c org brn 12.50 15.00
CLP4 AP4 20c red brown 10.00 12.50
CLP5 AP4 30c green 10.00 12.50
CLP6 AP4 50c blue 17.50 20.00
CLP7 AP4 60c vermilion 20.00 22.50
CLP8 AP5 1p gray black 50.00 55.00
CLP9 AP5 2p rose 110.00 *125.00*
CLP10 AP5 3p violet 190.00 *225.00*
CLP11 AP5 5p ol grn 375.00 *400.00*

Handstamped in Black

CLP12 AP4 5c org yel 25.00 27.50
CLP13 AP4 10c sl grn 20.00 22.50
CLP14 AP4 15c org brn 20.00 22.50
CLP15 AP4 20c red brown 35.00 40.00
CLP16 AP4 30c green 30.00 32.50
CLP17 AP4 50c blue 40.00 45.00
CLP18 AP4 60c vermilion 25.00 27.50
CLP19 AP5 1p gray black 80.00 90.00
CLP20 AP5 2p rose 225.00 *250.00*
CLP21 AP5 3p violet 275.00 *300.00*
CLP22 AP5 5p ol grn 350.00 *400.00*

Handstamped in Red

CLP23 AP4 5c org yel 15.00 17.50
CLP24 AP4 10c sl grn 20.00 22.50
CLP25 AP4 15c org brn 20.00 22.50
CLP26 AP4 20c red brown 20.00 22.50
CLP27 AP4 30c green 10.00 12.50
CLP28 AP4 50c blue 15.00 17.50
CLP29 AP4 60c vermilion 25.00 27.50
CLP30 AP5 1p gray black 40.00 45.00
CLP31 AP5 2p rose 175.00 *190.00*
CLP32 AP5 3p violet 275.00 *300.00*
CLP33 AP5 5p ol grn 575.00 *650.00*

Nos. C38//50, CF1 Handstamped in Violet, Letter 6½mm High

1923

CLP34 AP6 5c org yel 15.00 17.50
CLP35 AP6 10c green 15.00 17.50
CLP36 AP6 15c carmine 10.00 12.50
CLP37 AP6 20c gray 20.00 20.00
CLP38 AP6 30c blue 15.00 15.00
CLP39 AP6 50c green 15.00 17.50
CLP40 AP6 60c brown 20.00 22.50
CLP41 AP7 1p black 20.00 22.50
CLP42 AP7 2p red org 20.00 22.50
CLP43 AP7 3p violet 50.00 55.00
CLP44 AP7 5p ol grn 100.00 110.00
CFLP1 AP6 20c gray 32.50 35.00

Handstamped in Red

CLP45 AP6 5c org yel 25.00 27.50
CLP46 AP6 10c green 20.00 22.50
CLP47 AP6 15c carmine 20.00 22.50
CLP48 AP6 20c gray 20.00 22.50
CLP49 AP6 30c blue 15.00 17.50
CLP50 AP6 50c green 50.00 55.00
CLP51 AP6 60c brown 50.00 55.00
CLP52 AP7 1p black 70.00 *80.00*
CLP53 AP7 2p red org 100.00 *120.00*
CLP54 AP7 3p violet 150.00 *175.00*
CLP55 AP7 5p ol grn 300.00 *375.00*
CFLP2 AP6 20c gray 110.00 *125.00*

Nos. C38//50, CF1 Ovptd. in Black

Letter 10mm high

1923, June 4

CLP56 AP6 5c org yel 7.50 7.50
CLP57 AP6 10c green 7.50 7.50
CLP58 AP6 15c carmine 7.50 7.50
CLP59 AP6 20c gray 7.50 7.50
CLP60 AP6 30c blue 2.50 2.50
On cover, *from* 150.00
On cover, used in Canal Zone, *from* 500.00
CLP61 AP6 50c green 12.50 12.50
CLP62 AP6 60c brown 7.50 7.50
CLP63 AP7 1p black 12.50 12.50
CLP64 AP7 2p red org 17.50 19.00
CLP65 AP7 3p violet 30.00 35.00
CLP66 AP7 5p ol grn 55.00 65.00
CFLP3 AP6 20c gray 10.00 12.50

Nos. CLP56-CFLP3 were lithograph overprinted by the Reichsdruckerei Berlin.

PERU

Nos. C38//50, CF1 Handstamped in Black

Letter 7mm high

1923

CLPE1 AP6 5c org yel 15.00 15.00
CLPE2 AP6 10c green 15.00 15.00
CLPE3 AP6 15c carmine 12.00 12.00
CLPE4 AP6 20c gray 12.00 12.00
CLPE5 AP6 30c blue 12.00 12.00
On philatelic flight cover, *from* 150.00
CLPE6 AP6 50c green 20.00 20.00
CLPE7 AP6 60c brown 20.00 20.00
CLPE8 AP7 1p black 30.00 *32.50*
CLPE9 AP7 2p red org 90.00 *100.00*
CLPE10 AP7 3p violet 90.00 *100.00*
CLPE11 AP7 5p ol grn 100.00 *125.00*
CFLPE1 AP6 20c gray 22.50 *25.00*

Nos. C38//47 Handstamped in Red, Letter 6½mm High

1923

CLPE12 AP6 5c org yel 50.00 55.00
CLPE13 AP6 15c carmine *40.00 45.00*
CLPE14 AP6 20c gray *45.00 50.00*
CLPE15 AP6 50c green *40.00 45.00*
CLPE16 AP6 60c brown *60.00 65.00*
CLPE17 AP7 1p black *87.50 95.00*

SPAIN

Nos. C25-C35 Handstamped in Violet

E

Letters 6½mm High Without Period, Except for 30c

1921-23

CLE1 AP4 5c org yel 14.00 17.50
a. Pair, one with period, one without —
CLE2 AP4 10c sl grn 10.00 12.50
CLE3 AP4 15c org brn 20.00 22.00
CLE4 AP4 20c red brown 12.00 12.00
CLE5 AP4 30c green 12.50 16.00
CLE6 AP4 50c blue 18.00 22.00
CLE7 AP4 60c vermilion 37.50 40.00
CLE8 AP5 1p gray black 50.00 55.00
CLE9 AP5 2p rose 62.50 *70.00*
CLE10 AP5 3p violet 125.00 *150.00*
CLE11 AP5 5p ol grn 500.00 *600.00*

No. CLE1a is unique.

Handstamped in Red

CLE12 AP4 5c org yel 25.00 *30.00*
CLE13 AP4 10c sl grn 25.00 *30.00*
CLE14 AP4 15c org brn 25.00 *30.00*
CLE15 AP4 20c red brown 25.00 *30.00*
CLE16 AP4 30c green 25.00 *30.00*
CLE17 AP4 50c blue 37.50 *45.00*
CLE18 AP4 60c vermilion 40.00 *50.00*
CLE19 AP5 1p gray black 62.50 *75.00*
CLE20 AP5 2p rose 75.00 *85.00*
CLE21 AP5 3p violet 125.00 *140.00*
CLE22 AP5 5p ol grn 625.00 *750.00*

Handstamped in Black

CLE23 AP4 5c org yel 22.50 *25.00*

Nos. C38//50, CF1 Ovptd. in Black

Letter 10mm high

1923, June 4

CLE24 AP6 5c org yel 15.00 17.50
CLE25 AP6 10c green 10.00 12.50
CLE26 AP6 15c carmine 15.00 17.50
a. Double overprint —
CLE27 AP6 20c gray 15.00 17.50
CLE28 AP6 30c blue 10.00 10.00
On cover, *from* 375.00
CLE29 AP6 50c green 12.50 14.00
CLE30 AP6 60c brown 15.00 17.50
CLE31 AP7 1p black 20.00 22.50
CLE32 AP7 2p red org 45.00 55.00
CLE33 AP7 3p violet 62.50 75.00
CLE34 AP7 5p ol grn 80.00 85.00

"R" 12mm high

CFLE1 AP6 20c gray 62.50 75.00
a. "R" 10mm high 75.00 90.00

Nos. CLE24-CFLE1 were lithograph overprinted by the Reichsdruckerei Berlin.

SWEDEN & NORWAY

Nos. C38//50, CF1 Ovptd. in Black

Letter 10mm high

1927, March 10

CLSU1 AP6 5c org yel 10.00 12.00
CLSU2 AP6 10c green 7.50 7.50
CLSU3 AP6 15c carmine 7.50 7.50
CLSU4 AP6 20c gray 10.00 12.00
CLSU5 AP6 30c blue 6.00 6.00
On cover, *from* 600.00
CLSU6 AP6 50c green 7.50 7.50
CLSU7 AP6 60c brown 7.50 7.50
CLSU8 AP7 1p black 10.00 12.00
CLSU9 AP7 2p red org 27.50 30.00
CLSU10 AP7 3p violet 50.00 55.00
CLSU11 AP7 5p ol grn 65.00 70.00
CFLSU1 AP6 20c gray 17.50 17.50

Nos. CLSU1-CFLSU1 were lithograph overprinted by the Reichsdruckerei Berlin.

SWITZERLAND & LIECHTENSTEIN

Nos. C25-C35 Handstamped in Violet

S

Letters 8mm High Without Period, Except for 30c

1921-23

CLS1 AP4 5c org yel 15.00 17.50
CLS2 AP4 10c sl grn 15.00 17.50
CLS3 AP4 15c org brn 15.00 17.50
CLS4 AP4 20c red brown — —
CLS5 AP4 30c green, ovpt. with period 10.00 12.50
CLS6 AP4 50c blue 22.50 22.50
CLS7 AP4 60c vermilion 37.50 42.50
CLS8 AP5 1p gray black 62.50 70.00
CLS9 AP5 2p rose 62.50 70.00
CLS10 AP5 3p violet 325.00 *375.00*
CLS11 AP5 5p ol grn 450.00 *525.00*

Handstamped in Black

CLS12 AP4 60c vermilion — —
CLS13 AP5 2p rose 325.00 *375.00*
CLS14 AP5 3p violet 650.00 *750.00*
CLS15 AP5 5p ol grn — —

Nos. C38//50, CF1 Ovptd. in Black

Letter 10mm high

1924, Jan. 1

No.	Type	Description	Unused	Used
CLS16	AP6	5c org yel	10.00	12.00
CLS17	AP6	10c green	6.00	7.50
CLS18	AP6	15c carmine	6.00	7.50
CLS19	AP6	20c gray	6.00	7.50
CLS20	AP6	30c blue	3.00	3.75
		On cover, *from*		*400.00*
CLS21	AP6	50c green	7.50	9.00
CLS22	AP6	60c brown	6.00	7.50
CLS23	AP7	1p black	10.00	12.00
CLS24	AP7	2p red org	30.00	32.50
CLS25	AP7	3p violet	40.00	45.00
CLS26	AP7	5p ol grn	55.00	60.00

"R" 12mm high

No.	Type	Description	Unused	Used
CFLS1	AP6	20c gray	10.00	12.50
		On cover, *from*		*1,500.*
a.		"R" 10mm high	27.50	30.00

Nos. CLS16-CFLS1 were lithograph overprinted by the Reichsdruckerei Berlin.

VENEZUELA

Nos. C25-C35 Handstamped in Black

Letters 8mm high

1921-23

No.	Type	Description	Unused	Used
CLV1	AP4	5c org yel	25.00	30.00
CLV2	AP4	10c sl grn	*20.00*	*25.00*
CLV3	AP4	15c org brn	20.00	25.00
CLV4	AP4	20c red brown	20.00	25.00
CLV5	AP4	30c green, ovpt. with period	17.50	20.00
CLV6	AP4	50c blue	*25.00*	*30.00*
CLV7	AP4	60c vermilion	25.00	30.00
CLV8	AP5	1p gray black	*90.00*	*100.00*
CLV9	AP5	2p rose	300.00	*350.00*
CLV10	AP5	3p violet	450.00	*500.00*
CLV11	AP5	5p ol grn	*1,250.*	*1,500.*

Handstamped in Violet

No.	Type	Description	Unused	Used
CLV12	AP4	5c org yel	20.00	25.00
CLV13	AP4	10c sl grn	20.00	22.50
CLV14	AP4	15c org brn	20.00	22.50
CLV15	AP4	20c red brown	20.00	22.50
CLV16	AP4	30c green, ovpt. with period	22.50	25.00
CLV17	AP4	50c blue	*35.00*	*35.00*
CLV18	AP4	60c vermilion	50.00	50.00
CLV19	AP5	1p gray black	90.00	100.00
CLV20	AP5	2p rose	350.00	*400.00*
CLV21	AP5	3p violet	450.00	*500.00*
CLV22	AP5	5p ol grn	*800.00*	*1,000.*

Handstamped in Red

No.	Type	Description	Unused	Used
CLV23	AP4	5c org yel	*17.50*	*25.00*
CLV24	AP4	10c sl grn	25.00	27.50
CLV25	AP4	15c org brn	*30.00*	*32.50*
CLV26	AP4	20c red brown	*30.00*	*32.50*
CLV27	AP4	30c green, ovpt. with period	*32.50*	*35.00*
CLV28	AP4	50c blue	35.00	40.00
CLV29	AP4	60c vermilion	*60.00*	*70.00*
CLV30	AP5	1p gray black	140.00	150.00
CLV31	AP5	2p rose	*400.00*	*450.00*
CLV32	AP5	3p violet	*650.00*	*750.00*
CLV33	AP5	5p ol grn	*1,000.*	*1,200.*

Nos. C38//50, CF1 Handstamped in Black

Letter 8mm high

1923

No.	Type	Description	Unused	Used
CLV34	AP6	5c org yel	22.50	22.50
CLV35	AP6	10c green	17.50	17.50
CLV36	AP6	15c carmine	17.50	17.50
CLV37	AP6	20c gray	17.50	17.50
CLV38	AP6	30c blue	17.50	17.50
CLV39	AP6	50c green	40.00	40.00
CLV40	AP6	60c brown	40.00	40.00
CLV41	AP7	1p black	70.00	70.00
CLV42	AP7	2p red org	150.00	*175.00*
CLV43	AP7	3p violet	300.00	*350.00*
CLV44	AP7	5p ol grn	300.00	*350.00*

No.	Type	Description	Unused	Used
CFLV1	AP6	20c gray	30.00	35.00

Nos. C42//C50 Hstmpd. in Violet

No.	Type	Description	Unused	Used
CLV45	AP6	30c blue	*45.00*	*45.00*
CLV46	AP6	50c green	40.00	40.00
CLV47	AP7	1p black	50.00	50.00
CLV48	AP7	2p red org	90.00	*100.00*
CLV49	AP7	3p violet	100.00	*125.00*
CLV50	AP7	5p ol grn	125.00	*150.00*

Nos. C44//C48 Handstamped in Red

No.	Type	Description	Unused	Used
CLV51	AP6	50c green	40.00	45.00
CLV52	AP7	1p black	50.00	55.00
CLV53	AP7	2p red org	90.00	*100.00*

No. C42 With Blue-black Locally Handstamp Overprint, 12mm High

No.	Type	Description	Unused	Used
CLV54	AP6	30c blue		*200.00*

No. CLV54 was used mostly at Puerto Cabello.

Nos. C38//50, CF1 Ovptd. in Black

Letter 10mm high

1923, June 4

No.	Type	Description	Unused	Used
CLV55	AP6	5c org yel	22.50	22.50
CLV56	AP6	10c green	22.50	22.50
CLV57	AP6	15c carmine	15.00	15.00
CLV58	AP6	20c gray	15.00	15.00
CLV59	AP6	30c blue	15.00	15.00
		On cover, *from*		*500.00*
CLV60	AP6	50c green	15.00	15.00
CLV61	AP6	60c brown	15.00	15.00
CLV62	AP7	1p black	22.50	22.50
CLV63	AP7	2p red org	45.00	52.50
CLV64	AP7	3p violet	85.00	*100.00*
CLV65	AP7	5p ol grn	180.00	*225.00*
CFLV2	AP6	20c gray	26.00	*30.00*

Nos. CLV55-CFLV2 were lithograph overprinted by the Reichsdruckerei Berlin.

SPECIAL DELIVERY STAMPS

Special Delivery Messenger — SD1

1917 Unwmk. Engr. *Perf. 14*

No.	Type	Description	Unused	Used
E1	SD1	5c dark green	*60.00*	*150.00*

REGISTRATION STAMPS

R1

R2

1865 Unwmk. Litho. *Imperf.*

No.	Type	Description	Unused	Used
F1	R1	5c black	87.50	47.50
F2	R2	5c black	110.00	50.00

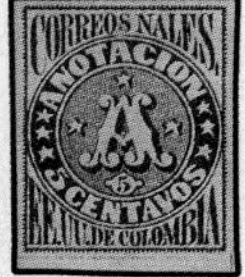

R3

R4

Vertical Lines in Background

1870 White Paper

No.	Type	Description	Unused	Used
F3	R3	5c black	3.00	2.50
F4	R4	5c black	3.00	2.50

Horizontal Lines in Background

No.	Type	Description	Unused	Used
F5	R3	5c black	10.00	8.50
F6	R4	5c black	3.00	2.50
		Nos. F3-F6 (4)	19.00	16.00

Reprints of Nos. F3 to F6 show either crossed lines or traces of lines in background.

R5

1881 *Imperf.*

No.	Type	Description	Unused	Used
F7	R5	10c violet	60.00	52.50
a.		Sewing machine perf.	67.50	60.00
b.		Perf. 11	75.00	62.50

R6

1883 *Perf. 12, 13½*

No.	Type	Description	Unused	Used
F8	R6	10c red, *orange*	2.00	*2.50*

R7

1889-95 *Perf. 12, 13½*

No.	Type	Description	Unused	Used
F9	R7	10c red, *grysh*	9.50	4.50
F10	R7	10c red, *yelsh*	9.50	4.50
F11	R7	10c dp brn, *rose buff* ('95)	2.00	1.60
F12	R7	10c yel brn, *lt buff* ('92)	2.00	1.60
		Nos. F9-F12 (4)	23.00	12.20

Nos. F9-F12 exist imperf.

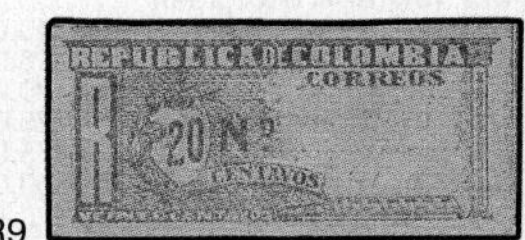

R9

1902 *Imperf.*

No.	Type	Description	Unused	Used
F13	R9	20c red brown, *blue*	1.60	1.60
a.		Sewing machine perf.	4.75	4.75
b.		Perf. 12	4.75	4.75

Medellin Issue

R10

1902 Laid Paper *Perf. 12*

No.	Type	Description	Unused	Used
F16	R10	10c blk vio	15.00	15.00
a.		Wove paper	21.00	21.00

Regular Issue
Imperf

1903

No.	Type	Description	Unused	Used
F17	R9	20c blue, *blue*	1.60	1.60
a.		Sewing machine perf.	4.75	4.75
b.		Perf. 12	4.75	4.75

R11

1904 Pelure Paper *Imperf.*

No.	Type	Description	Unused	Used
F19	R11	10c purple	3.75	3.75
a.		Sewing machine perf.	5.00	3.75
b.		Perf. 12	6.25	5.00

R12

Imprint: "J. L. Arango"

1904 Wove Paper *Perf. 12*

No.	Type	Description	Unused	Used
F20	R12	10c purple	2.50	.60
a.		Imperf., pair	7.75	7.75

Imprint: "Lit. Nacional"

1909 *Perf. 10, 14, 10x14, 14x10*

No.	Type	Description	Unused	Used
F21	R12	10c purple	2.75	.85
a.		Imperf., pair	6.25	6.25

For overprints see Nos. LF1-LF4.

Execution at Cartagena in 1816 — R13

1910, July 20 Engr. *Perf. 12*

No.	Type	Description	Unused	Used
F22	R13	10c red & black	21.00	*90.00*

Centenary of National Independence.

Pier at Puerto Colombia — R14

Tequendama Falls — R15

Perf. 11, 11½, 14, 11½x14

1917, Aug. 25

No.	Type	Description	Unused	Used
F23	R14	4c green & ultra	.55	*3.50*
a.		Center inverted	575.00	575.00
F24	R15	10c deep blue	8.00	.60

R16

1925 Litho. *Perf. 10x13½*

No.	Type	Description	Unused	Used
F25	R16	(10c) blue	4.25	1.90
a.		Imperf., pair	15.00	12.50
b.		Perf. 13½x10	7.50	5.00

INSURED LETTER STAMPS ("CUBIERTAS")

The following stamps were affixed to the back of letters which contained valuables (normally, money) and were therefore insured through the post office. The origin and date of dispatch were written in the appropriate lines, and a description of the values enclosed and destination were penned in the appropriate cartouche below. The denomination indicated the payment of insurance and functioned as a receipt. Often, the recipient signed the stamp and handed it back to the postman, indicating completed delivery. Scott G1 is an exception in that it represented only the payment for registration exclusive of insurance.

Beware of deceiving forgeries which exist for most of the Cubiertas.

ESTADOS UNIDOS DE COLOMBIA

IL1

Unwmk.

1865, July 1 Litho. *Imperf.*

Flag colors handpainted with watercolors

G1 IL1 25c brn, bister, yel, bl & red 25.00 25.00
G2 IL1 50c brn, bister, yel, bl & red 62.50 80.00

IL2

1867 Litho. Unwmk. *Imperf.*

Flag colors handpainted with watercolors

G3 IL2 50c blk, yel, bl & red 25.00 25.00

IL3

"COLOMBIA" AND "CINCUENTA" in White. "CENTAVOS" with White Shading (No. G4)

1870 Litho. *Imperf.*

G4 IL3 50c blk, yel, bl & red 30.00 25.00
G5 IL3 50c As G4, white shading of "CENTAVOS" removed 35.00 30.00

IL4

White Words and Shading Removed. "50" Without Horizontal Shading

1873-77 Litho. *Imperf.*

G6 IL4 50c blk, yel, bl & red 80.00 75.00
a. blk, yel, pale bl & red 80.00 75.00
b. blk, yel, very dp bl & red — 125.00

IL5

"50" With Horizontal Shading. Dateline Ends in "de18".

1880 Litho. Unwmk. *Imperf.*

G7 IL5 50c blk, golden yel, bl & red 100.00 80.00
a. Wmk. "ESTADO SOBERANO" — 125.00
b. Wmk. "ARMS OF CUNDINAMARCA" — 125.00

IL6

Inscribed "ESTADOS UNIDOS DE COLOMBIA".

1883-86 Litho. *Imperf.*

G8 IL6 50c rose, on white wove paper 20.00 12.50
a. Deep carmine, white wove paper 20.00 12.50
b. Red, bluish wove paper 27.50 20.00

REPUBLICA DE COLOMBIA

IL7

Inscribed "REPUBLICA DE COLOMBIA".

1887-88 Litho. *Imperf.*

G9 IL7 50c rose, on white wove paper 17.50 12.50
a. Violet red (shades), bluish wove paper 20.00 20.00

IL8

Dateline ends in "de18".

1890 Litho. *Imperf.*

G10 IL8 10c blue 11.00 16.50
G11 IL8 20c blue 11.00 16.50
G12 IL8 30c blue 11.00 16.50
G13 IL8 40c blue 16.50 22.50
G14 IL8 50c blue 19.00 25.00
G15 IL8 60c blue 19.00 25.00
G16 IL8 70c blue 32.50 35.00
G17 IL8 80c blue 32.50 32.50
G18 IL8 90c blue 37.50 45.00
G19 IL8 1p blue 45.00 *55.00*

Denominations represent payment of 1% of the declared value of the letter.

IL9

Dateline ends in "de189".

1890 Litho. *Imperf.*

Dateline ends in "de189"

G20 IL9 10c black, *rose* 8.00 12.00
G21 IL9 20c black, *yellow* 8.00 12.00
G22 IL9 30c black, *fawn* 8.00 12.00
G23 IL9 40c black, *blue green* 12.00 16.00
G24 IL9 50c black, *green* 14.00 18.00
G25 IL9 60c orange 14.00 18.00
a. 60c Yellow 35.00
b. 60c Orange red 15.00
c. 60c Orange brown 30.00
G26 IL9 70c blue 16.00 37.50
a. 70c Deep blue 27.50
G27 IL9 80c dp bluish green 20.00 40.00
a. 80c Deep green 20.00 40.00
b. 80c Yellow green 20.00 40.00
G28 IL9 90c brown 28.00 32.50
G29 IL9 1p bright scarlet vermilion 32.50 *55.00*
a. 1p Pale red 32.50 50.00
b. "PESOS" instead of "PESO" in left inscription 32.50

No. G29b is found in Position 5 in the plate of 10 subjects, and is constant throughout the printing.

IL10

1892-93 Litho. *Imperf.*

G30 IL10 10c black, *rose* 10.00 10.00
a. 10c Black, *pale rose* 10.00 10.00
G31 IL10 20c black, *buff* 10.00 *12.50*
a. 20c Black, *yellow* 20.00 *12.50*
b. 20c Black, *very pale buff (almost white)* 25.00 *12.50*
G32 IL10 30c black, *buff* 10.00 *12.50*
a. 30c Black, *pale salmon* 10.00 *15.00*
G33 IL10 40c blk, *pale gray bl* 12.50 *15.00*
G34 IL10 50c blk, *gray grn* 17.50 *15.00*
a. 1p Black, *br green* 20.00 *20.00*
b. 1p Black, *bluish green* 20.00 *20.00*
c. 1p Black, *buff* (error) — —

IL11

Two types of condor:
Type I: With wings 38mm long.
Type II: With wings 28mm long.

1905 Litho. *Perf. 13½*

G35 IL11 5c blk, *yel* (II) 8.00 12.00
a. Type I *16.00 24.00*
G36 IL11 10c blk, *bl grn* (II) 12.00 14.00
G37 IL11 15c black, *buff* (II) 14.00 16.00
G38 IL11 20c blk, *bluish gray* (II) 20.00 24.00
G39 IL11 25c blk, *dp dull rose* (II) 28.00 40.00

New Design

Arms at left; large "50" in scrollin center, small "50" in scroll at right. Dateline ends in "DE190".
Two types of "50c":
Type I: "50" at right in circular scroll.
Type II: "50" at right in oblong scroll.

1905 Litho. *Perf. 13½*

G40 50c red (I) *50.00 50.00*
a. Type II *50.00 50.00*
G41 1p pale yellow brown *50.00 75.00*
a. 1p Deep yellow brown *50.00 75.00*

The editors would like to examine and photograph an example of Nos. G40-G41.

OFFICIAL INSURED LETTER STAMPS

Official Insured Letter Stamps carry no denomination. Used examples often have a manuscript specification of the amount of insurance required.

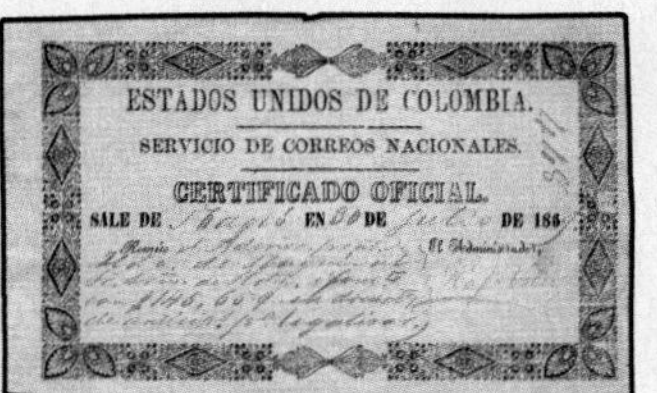

ILO1

Inscribed "ESTADOS UNIDOS DE COLOMBIA."

1867 *Imperf.*

Size: About 136x85mm

GO1 ILO1 black, *blue batonne paper* 120.00 60.00
a. Black, *blue* wove ruled paper *120.00 60.00*
GO2 ILO1 black 120.00 60.00
a. Black wove ruled paper *120.00 60.00*

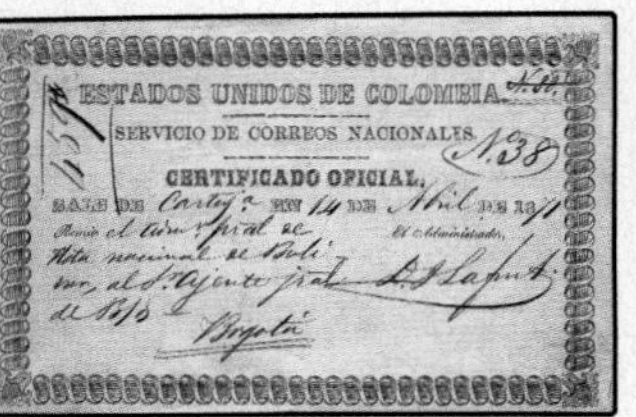

ILO2

1870 *Imperf.*

Size: About 142x92mm

GO3 ILO2 black *120.00* 65.00
a. Black, ruled paper *140.00 90.00*

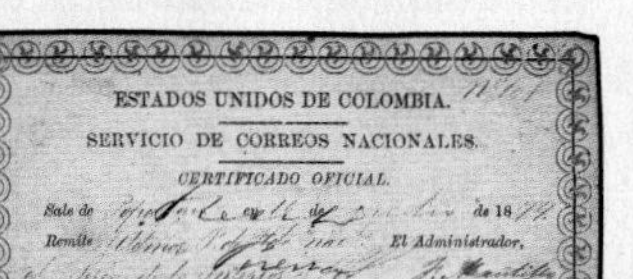

ILO3

1874 *Imperf.*

Size: About 141x84mm

GO4 ILO3 black *75.00* 50.00
a. Black, ruled paper 75.00
b. As "a," vertical ruled lines — —

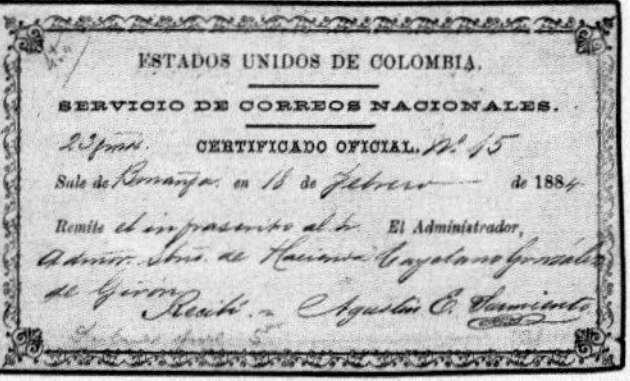

ILO4

1881 *Imperf.*

Size: About 143x96mm

GO5 ILO4 black *60.00* 40.00
a. Black, ruled paper *60.00* 40.00
b. As "a," vertical ruled lines *60.00* 40.00
c. Black, batonne paper *150.00* 100.00

ILO5

Special Issue for Cartago

1882 *Imperf.*

GO6 ILO5 black, *yellow* — 175.00

New Design

Double-lined letters with floral decorations

1884 *Imperf.*

Size: About 140x80mm

GO7 black — —
a. Black, ruled paper — —

The editors would like to examine and photograph an example of either Nos. GO7 or GO7a.

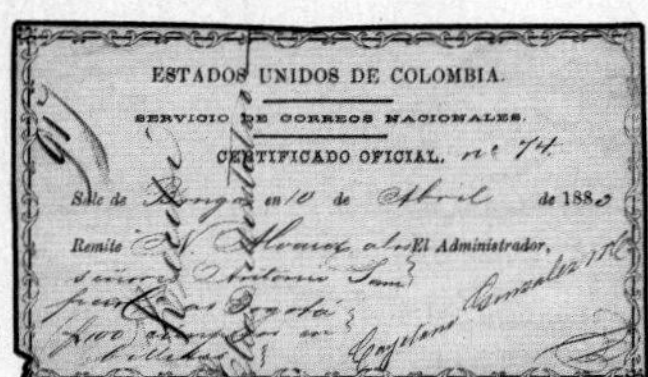

ILO7

Dateline ends in "de188".
Two types of inscriptions:

Type I: "SERVICIO DE CORREOS NACIONALES" 83mm long.
Type II: "SERVICIO DE CORREOS NACIONALES" 109mm long.

1884 ***Imperf.***

GO8	ILO7	black (I)	*75.00*	50.00
a.		Black, ruled paper (I)	*75.00*	50.00
b.		Type II	*75.00*	50.00
c.		Type II, ruled paper	*75.00*	50.00
d.		Type II, laid paper	*125.00*	*100.00*

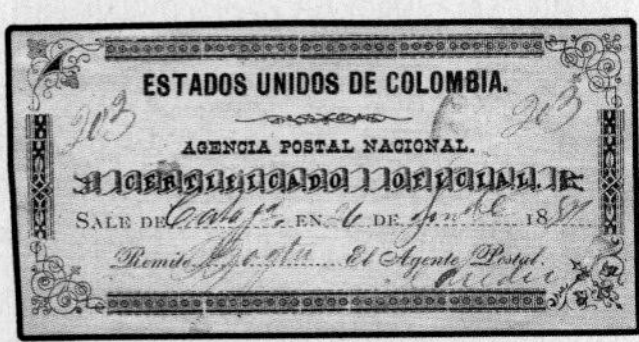

ILO8

1884 ***Imperf.***

Size: About 105x52mm

GO9	ILO8	black	*200.00*	150.00
GO10	ILO8	Blk, *lemon yel*		250.00

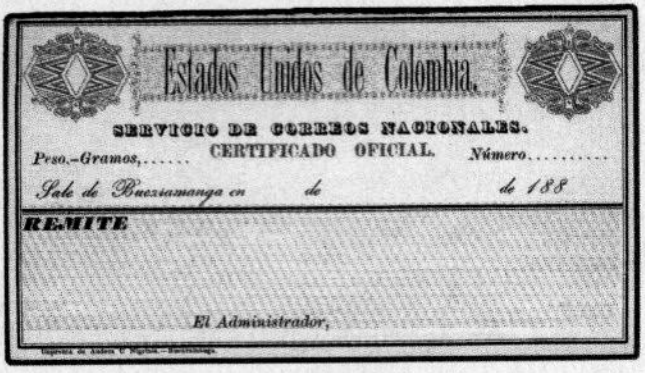

ILO9

Dateline reads: "Sale de Bucaramanga en.. de..de 188..".

Special Issue for Bucaramanga

1886 **Unwmk.** ***Imperf.***

Ribbed Paper

GO11	ILO9	blk, red vio & bister	50.00	—
a.		Watermarked	75.00	—

Wove Paper

GO12	ILO9	blk, red vio & bister	—	—
GO13	ILO9	As #GO12, "BUCARAMANGA" omitted from dateline	—	—

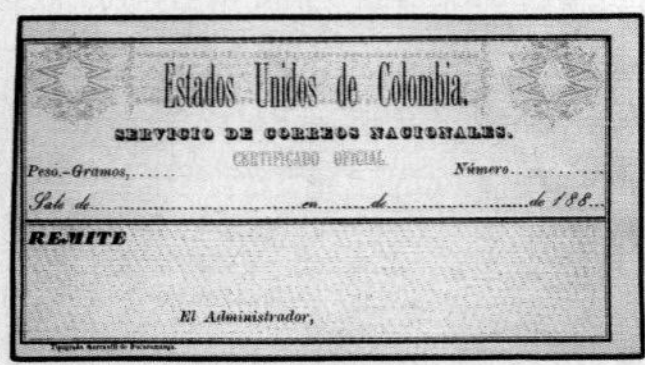

ILO10

Dateline reads: "Sale de... en.. de..de 188..". "CERTIFICADO OFICIAL" is narrower than on No. GO13, and is made up of tall, thin letters.

Special Issue for Bucaramanga

1886 **Unwmk.** ***Imperf.***

Ribbed Paper

GO14	ILO10	blk, pink & bister	50.00	—
a.		Watermarked	60.00	—

ILO11

Inscribed "REPúBLICA DE COLOMBIA."
Dateline reads "Sale de.. en.. de.. de 188..."

1886 ***Imperf.***

Size: About 130x84mm

GO15	ILO11	black	—	100.00
a.		Black, ruled paper	—	100.00

ILO12

Dateline reads "Sale de Mompos en.. de.. de 188..."

Special Issue for Mompos

1886 ***Imperf.***

GO16	ILO12	black	—	200.00

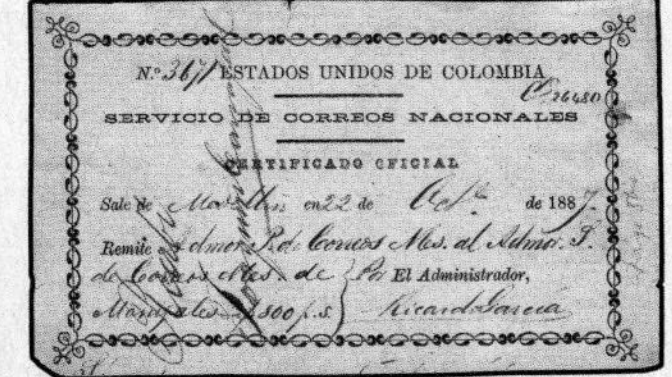

ILO13

Inscribed "No....ESTADOS UNIDOS DE COLOMBIA"

1887 ***Imperf.***

Size: About 135x85mm

GO17	ILO13	black	—	150.00

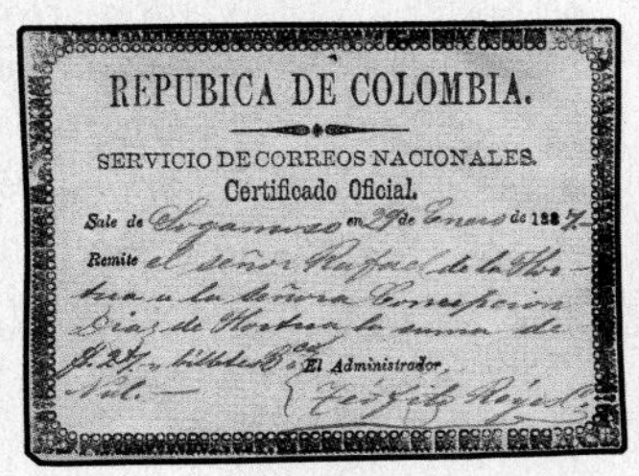

ILO14

Inscribed "REPUBLICA DE COLOMBIA."

Special Issue for Sagamoso

1887 ***Imperf.***

Size: About 108x80mm

GO18	ILO14	black	—	175.00

New Design

As. No. GO14, inscribed "REPUBLICA DE COLOMBIA". Dateline reads: "Sale de... en.. de..de 188..".

Special Issue for Bucaramanga

1886 **Unwmk.** ***Imperf.***

Ribbed Paper

GO19		blk, pink & bister	—	—
a.		Black, pink & bister, on wove paper	—	—

The editors would like to examine and photograph and example of either No. GO19 or GO19a.

ILO16

Inscribed "No. ..." at right. Dateline reads: "Sale de Bucaramanga en.. de..de 188..".

Special Issue for Bucaramanga

1888 **Unwmk.** ***Imperf.***

GO20	ILO16	violet, *buff*	40.00	150.00
a.		"BACARAMANGA" in dateline	—	—
b.		"BUCARAMANGA" removed from dateline	—	—

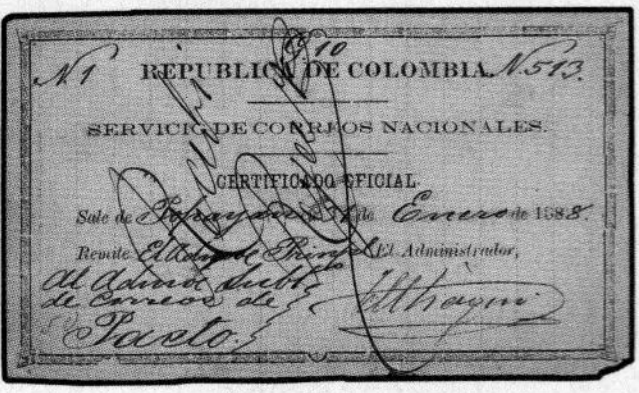

ILO17

Inscribed "CERTIFICADO OFICIAL"
Dateline reads: "Sale de... en... de... de 1888"

Special Issue for Popayan

1888 ***Imperf.***

GO21	ILO17	black, with vertical ruling	—	—
a.		Partial year date "188"	—	—
b.		Plain paper	—	—

ILO18

Inscribed "CERTIFICACIÓN OFICIAL."
Dateline reads: "Salió de Popayán, en...de....de 18..."

Special Issue for Popayan

1888 ***Imperf.***

GO22	ILO18	black	*200.00*	*175.00*
a.		Black, laid batonne paper	*200.00*	*175.00*

ILO19

Frame with Simple Arabesque
Inscribed "CERTIFICADO OFFICIAL"
Dateline reads: "Sale de Popayán...de 1888"

Special Issue for Popayan

1888 ***Imperf.***

Size: About 132x78mm

GO23	ILO19	black, *gray*	—	—
a.		Black, creme horiz. laid paper	—	—

ILO21

Thick-thin double line border.
Inscribed "CERTIFICADO OFICIAL."
Dateline reads: "Sale de... en..de.. de 18.."

Special Issue for Bogota

1889 ***Imperf.***

Size: About 132x85mm

GO25	ILO21	black		125.00

ILO22

As No. GO25, dateline reads: "Sale de Bogotá... en.. de.. de 18.."

Special Issue for Bogota

1889 ***Imperf.***

Size: About 132x85mm

GO26	ILO22	black		150.00

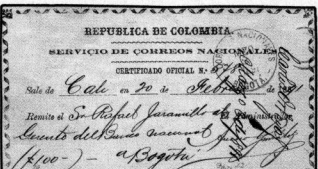

ILO23

Dateline reads: "Sale de ... en.. de.. de 188.."

Special Issue for Cali

1889 ***Imperf.***

Thin, Vertically Ribbed Paper

GO27	ILO23	black	—	100.00

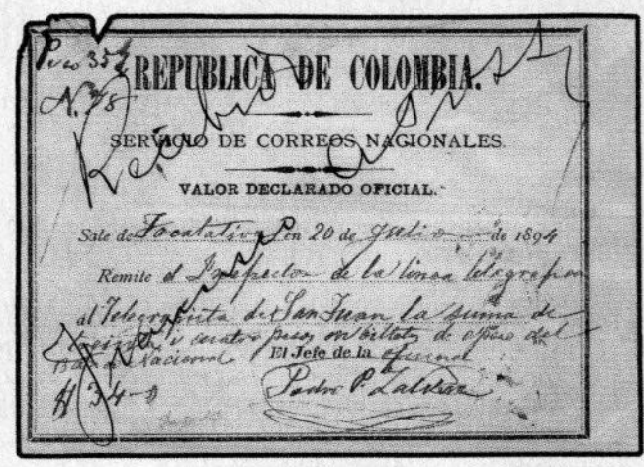

ILO24

Thick-thin double-line border.
Elaborate ornaments separate lines of text.
Inscribed "VALOR DECLARADO OFICIAL."
Dateline reads: "Sale de... en.. de.. de 189..."

Special Issue for Bogota

1890 ***Imperf.***

GO28	ILO24	black		200.00

ILO25

Thick-thin double-line border.
Bold, heavy ornaments separate lines of text.
Inscribed "REPUBLICA DE COLOMBIA." in bold, tall letters.

Special Issue for Bogota

1890 ***Imperf.***

GO29	ILO25	black		200.00

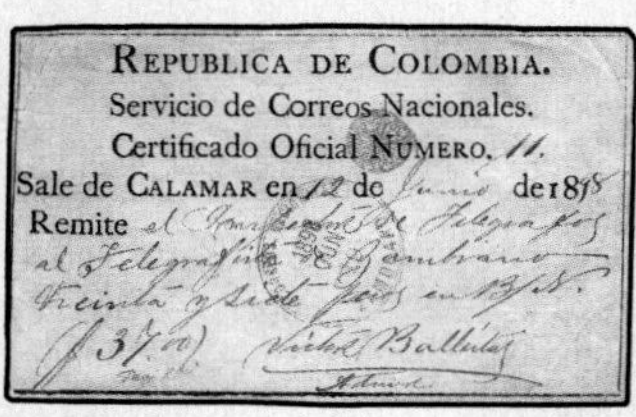

ILO26

Single-line border. Simple typographed text.

Special Issue for Calamar.

1890 ***Imperf.***

Vertically Laid Paper

GO30 ILO26 black — 250.00

New Design

Heavy border, coiling around bars, with double rectangular frame inside. Eagle and arms at center.

Inscribed at UR: "Servicio Postal Interior", and below: "Certificacion Oficial".

1890 ***Imperf.***

Size: About 143x97mm

GO31 black — —

The editors would like to examine and photograph an example of No. GO31.

New Designs

Double-line rectangular frame.

Inscribed "REPUBLICA DE COLOMBIA" in small letters.

Third line of text reads: "SERVICIO DE CORREOS NACIONALES"

1890 ***Imperf.***

Size: About 132x85mm

GO32 black *75.00 75.00*
a. Black, ruled laid paper *75.00 75.00*

Letters & Ornaments Frame Small Ornaments Separate Lines of Text

GO33 black, ruled paper *75.00 75.00*
a. Black, *bluish* ruled paper *72.50 75.00*

As No. GO22, Ornaments bolder

GO34 black *75.00 75.00*
a. Black, *bluish* ribbed paper *75.00 75.00*

The editors would like to examine and photograph examples of Nos. GO32-GO34.

Type ILO16 Redrawn

"Numero" at UR.

Special Issue for Bucamaranga

1891 ***Imperf.***

GO35 ILO16 black — —

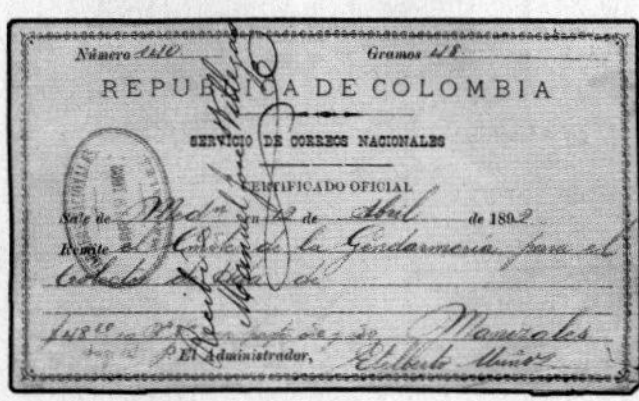

ILO31

Thin, scalloped frame. "GRAMOS..." added at UR.

1892 ***Imperf.***

Size: About 155x94mm

GO36 ILO31 black *75.00 75.00*

New Design

Rope-like frame. Inscriptions same as No. GO36, but "C" of "COLOMBIA" is from a fancy font.

1894 ***Imperf.***

Size: About 152x93mm

GO37 ILO32 black

The editors would like to examine and photograph an example of No. GO37.

ACKNOWLEDGMENT OF RECEIPT STAMPS

AR1

1893 Unwmk. Litho. ***Perf. 13½***

H1 AR1 5c ver, *blue* 4.75 4.75

1894 ***Perf. 12***

H2 AR1 5c vermilion 4.50 *5.00*

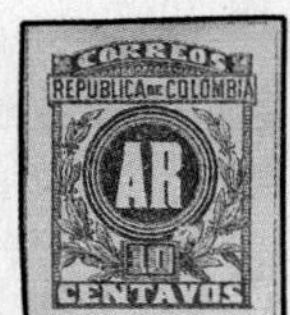

AR2

1902-03 ***Imperf.***

H3 AR2 10c blue, *blue* 3.50 5.00
a. 10c, blue, *greenish blue* 3.50 5.00
b. Sewing machine perf. 3.50 5.00
c. Perf. 12 3.50 5.00

The handstamp "AR" in circle is believed to be a postmark.

AR2a

Purple Handstamp

1903 ***Imperf.***

H4 AR2a 10c black, *pink* 25.00 25.00

AR3

1904 Pelure Paper ***Imperf.***

H12 AR3 5c pale blue 10.50 10.50
a. Perf. 12 10.50 10.50

No. 307 Overprinted in Black, Green or Violet

H13 A86 5c carmine 17.50 17.50

AR4

1904 ***Perf. 12***

H16 AR4 5c blue 3.25 2.75
a. Imperf., pair 8.75 8.75

For overprints see Nos. LH1-LH2.

General José Acevedo y Gómez — AR5

1910, July 20 **Engr.**

H17 AR5 5c orange & green 7.00 *17.50*

Centenary of National Independence.

Sabana Station AR6

Map of Colombia AR7

1917 ***Perf. 14***

H18 AR6 4c bister brown 5.50 *6.00*
H19 AR7 5c orange brown 5.50 *4.50*
a. Imperf., pair 14.00

LATE FEE STAMPS

LF1

1886 Unwmk. Litho. ***Perf. 10½***

I1 LF1 2½c blk, *lilac* 4.00 3.25
a. Imperf., pair 15.00 15.00

LF2

1892 ***Perf. 12, 13½***

I2 LF2 2½c dk bl, *rose* 3.50 2.50
a. Imperf., pair 15.00
I3 LF2 2½c ultra, *pink* 3.50 2.50

LF3

1902 ***Imperf.***

I4 LF3 5c purple, *rose* 1.00 1.00
a. Perf. 12 2.10 2.10

LF4

1914 ***Perf. 10, 13½***

I6 LF4 2c vio brown 5.00 5.00
I7 LF4 5c blue green 5.00 4.25

Overprints illustrated above are unauthorized and of private origin.

POSTAGE DUE STAMPS

These are not, strictly speaking, postage due stamps but were issued to cover an additional fee, "Sobreporte," charged on mail to foreign countries with which Colombia had no postal conventions.

D1

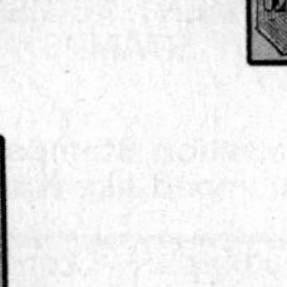

D2

D3

1866 Unwmk. Litho. ***Imperf.***

J1 D1 25c black, *blue* 80.00 55.00
J2 D2 50c black, *yellow* 55.00 *80.00*
J3 D3 1p black, *rose* 160.00 *125.00*
Nos. J1-J3 (3) 295.00 260.00

DEPARTMENT STAMPS

These stamps are said to be for interior postage, to supersede the separate issues for the various departments.

Regular Issues Handstamped in Black, Violet, Blue or Green — a

On Stamps of 1904

1909 Unwmk. ***Perf. 12***

L1 A94 ½c yellow 2.50 2.50
a. Imperf., pair 7.50 7.50
L2 A94 1c yel grn 3.75 2.50
L3 A94 2c red 5.50 3.75
a. Imperf., pair 15.00 15.00
L4 A94 5c blue 6.25 4.00
L5 A94 10c violet 8.75 8.75
L6 A94 20c black 14.00 14.00
L7 A95 1p brown 22.50 21.00

On Stamp of 1902

L8 A83 10p dk brn, *rose* 25.00 25.00
Nos. L1-L8 (8) 88.25 81.50

On Stamps of 1908

Perf. 10, 13, 13½ and Compound

L9 A94 ½c orange 2.90 2.90
a. Imperf., pair 7.50 7.50
L10 A94 1c green 5.00 5.00
a. Without imprint 6.25 6.25
L11 A94 2c red 5.50 5.50
a. Imperf., pair
L12 A94 5c blue 5.50 5.50
a. Imperf., pair 15.00 15.00
L13 A94 10c violet 8.75 8.75

On Tolima Stamp of 1888

Perf. 10½

L14 A23 1p red brn 27.50 27.50
Nos. L9-L14 (6) 55.15 55.15

Regular Issues Handstamped — b

On Stamps of 1904

Perf. 12

L15	A94	½c yellow	2.50	2.50
L16	A94	1c yellow grn	4.25	4.25
L17	A94	2c red	7.50	7.50
L18	A94	5c blue	7.50	7.50
L19	A94	10c violet	10.00	10.00
L20	A94	20c black	14.00	14.00
L21	A94	1p brown	25.00	25.00
		Nos. L15-L21 (7)	70.75	70.75

On Stamps of 1908

Perf. 10, 13, 13½

L22	A94	½c orange	2.75	2.75
L23	A94	1c yellow grn	7.75	7.75
L24	A94	2c red	6.25	6.25
a.		Imperf., pair	15.00	15.00
L25	A94	5c light blue	7.50	7.50
		Nos. L22-L25 (4)	24.25	24.25

The handstamps on Nos. L1-L25 are, as usual, found inverted and double.

DEPARTMENT REGISTRATION STAMPS

Registration Stamps of 1904 Handstamped like Nos. L1-L25

1909 Unwmk. *Perf. 12*

LF1	R12 (a)	10c purple	30.00	30.00
LF2	R12 (b)	10c purple	30.00	30.00

On Registration Stamp of 1909

Perf. 10, 13

LF3	R12 (a)	10c purple	30.00	30.00
LF4	R12 (b)	10c purple	30.00	30.00
		Nos. LF1-LF4 (4)	120.00	120.00

Nos. LF1-LF4 exist imperf. Value per pair, $125.

DEPARTMENT ACKNOWLEDGMENT OF RECEIPT STAMPS

Acknowledgment of Receipt Stamp of 1904 Hstmpd.

1909 Unwmk. *Perf. 12*

LH1	AR4 (a)	5c blue	30.00	30.00
a.		Imperf., pair	125.00	
LH2	AR4 (b)	5c blue	30.00	30.00
a.		Imperf., pair	125.00	

LOCAL STAMPS FOR THE CITY OF BOGOTA

A1

Pelure Paper

1889 Unwmk. Litho. *Perf. 12*

LX1	A1	½c black	1.10	1.10
a.		Imperf., pair	7.25	7.25

Impressions on bright blue and blue-gray paper were not regularly issued.

A2

White Wove Paper

1896 ***Perf. 12, 13½***

LX2	A2	½c black	1.10	1.10

A3

1903 ***Imperf.***

LX3	A3	10c black, *pink*	7.25	1.40
a.		Perf. 12	7.25	1.40

OFFICIAL STAMPS

Stamps of 1917-1937 Overprinted in Black or Red

a

b

1937 Unwmk. *Perf. 11, 12, 13½*

O1	A131 (a)	1c green	.25	.25
O2	A157 (a)	10c dp org	.25	.25
O3	A107 (b)	30c olive bis	2.10	1.00
O4	A129 (b)	40c brn & yel brn	1.60	.80
O5	A114 (b)	50c car	1.60	.80
O6	A107 (b)	1p lt bl	13.00	5.50
O7	A107 (b)	2p org	15.00	6.50
O8	A107 (b)	5p gray	47.50	*52.50*
O9	A118 (b)	10p dk brn	110.00	*125.00*

Wmk. 229

Perf. 12½

O10	A132 (a)	2c red	.25	.25
O11	A133 (a)	5c brn	.25	.25
O12	A160 (a)	12c dp bl (R)	1.00	.50
O13	A136 (b)	20c dk bl (R)	1.60	.80
		Nos. O1-O13 (13)	194.40	194.40

Tall, wrong font "I's" in OFICIAL exist on all stamps with "a" overprint.

REGISTERED PARCEL STAMPS

PP1

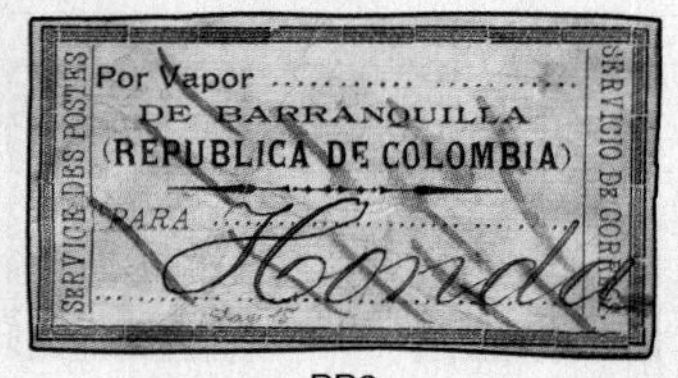

PP2

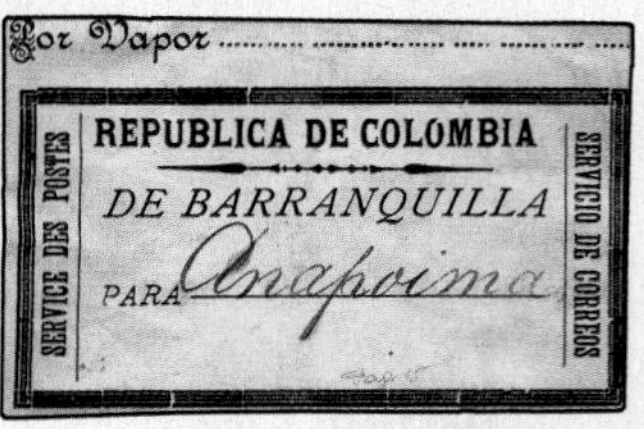

PP3

PP4

Inscribed "Por Vapor" and "de BARRANQUILLA."

QF1	PP1	black	—	75.00
QF2	PP2	black	—	75.00
QF3	PP3	black	—	75.00

Inscribed "De CALI para", "Por Vapor" removed.

QF4	PP4	black	—	200.00

POSTAL TAX STAMPS

"Greatest Mother" PT1

Perf. 11½

1935, May 27 Unwmk. Litho.

RA1	PT1	5c olive blk & scar	4.00	1.25

Required on all mail during Red Cross Week in 1935 (May 27-June 3) and in 1936.

Mother and Child — PT2

Perf. 10½, 10½x11

1937, May 24 Unwmk.

RA2	PT2	5c red	2.75	.90

Required on all mail during Red Cross Week. The tax was for the Red Cross.

Ministry of Posts and Telegraphs Building — PT3

1939-45 Litho. *Perf. 10½, 12½*

RA3	PT3	¼c dp bl	.25	.25
RA3A	PT3	¼c dk vio brn ('45)	.25	.25
RA4	PT3	½c pink	.25	.25
RA5	PT3	1c violet	.30	.25
RA5A	PT3	1c yel org ('45)	1.75	.70
RA6	PT3	2c pck grn	.55	.25
RA7	PT3	20c lt brn	4.50	1.50
		Nos. RA3-RA7 (7)	7.85	3.45

Obligatory on all mail. The tax was for the construction of the new Communications Building.

The 25c of type PT3 and PT4 were not usable on postal matter.

For overprint see No. 561 in Scott Standard catalogue, Vol. 2.

Ministry of Posts and Telegraphs Building — PT4

Perf. 12½x13

1940, Jan. 20 Engr. Wmk. 229

RA8	PT4	¼c ultra	.25	.25
RA9	PT4	½c carmine	.25	.25
RA10	PT4	1c violet	.25	.25
RA11	PT4	2c bl grn	.30	.25
RA12	PT4	20c brown	1.25	.25
		Nos. RA8-RA12 (5)	2.30	1.25

See note after No. RA7. See No. RA18 in Scott Standard catalogue, Vol. 2.

"Protection" — PT5

1940, Apr. 25 Wmk. 255 *Perf. 12*

RA13	PT5	5c rose carmine	.30	.25

See No. RA17.

ANTIOQUIA

ant-ē-'ō-kē-ə

Originally a State, now a Department of the Republic of Colombia. Until the revolution of 1885, the separate states making up the United States of Colombia were sovereign governments in their own right. On August 4, 1886, the National Council of Bogotá, composed of two delegates from each state, adopted a new constitution which abolished the sovereign rights of states, which then became departments with governors appointed by the President of the Republic. The nine original states represented at the Bogotá Convention retained some of their previous rights, as management of their own finances, and all issued postage stamps until as late as 1904. For Panama's issues, see Panama Nos. 1-30.

Coat of Arms

A1 A2

A3

A4

Wove Paper

1868 Unwmk. Litho. *Imperf.*

1	A1	2½c blue	*1,000.*	*750.*
2	A2	5c green	*750.*	*575.*
3	A3	10c lilac	*3,000.*	*1,000.*
4	A4	1p red	*675.*	*750.*

Reprints of Nos. 1, 3 and 4 are on a bluish white paper and all but No. 3 have scratches across the design.

A5

A6

A7

A8

A9

A10

1869

5 A5 2½c blue 3.75 3.25
6 A6 5c green 5.50 5.00
7 A7 5c green 5.50 5.00
8 A8 10c lilac 7.25 3.50
9 A9 20c brown 7.25 3.50
10 A10 1p rose red 14.50 13.00
a. 1p vermilion 27.50 25.00
Nos. 5-10 (6) 43.75 33.25

Reprints of Nos. 7, 8 and 10 are on a bluish white paper; reprints of Nos. 5 and 10a on white paper. The 10c blue is believed to be a reprint.

A11

A12

A13

A14

A15

A16

A17 A18

1873

12 A11 1c yellow grn 5.25 4.00
a. 1c green 5.25 4.00
13 A12 5c green 8.75 6.50
14 A13 10c lilac 25.00 21.00
15 A14 20c yellow brn 8.75 7.50
a. 20c dark brown 8.75 7.50
16 A15 50c blue 2.00 1.75
17 A16 1p vermilion 3.75 3.00
18 A17 2p black, *yellow* 8.75 8.00
19 A18 5p black, *rose* 65.00 55.00

A19

A20

Liberty Head
A21 A22

Pedro Justo Berrio — A23

1875-85

20 A19 1c blk, *grn*, unglazed ('76) 1.60 2.40
a. Glazed paper 2.60 3.25
b. 1c blk, *lt grn*, laid paper ('85) 3.75 3.50
21 A19 1c black ('76) 1.10 1.00
a. Laid paper 160.00 110.00
22 A19 1c bl grn ('85) 2.50 4.00
23 A19 1c red lil, laid paper ('85) 2.50 4.00
24 A20 2½c blue 2.50 1.90
a. Pelure paper ('78) *1,500.* *1,100.*
25 A21 5c green 16.00 14.50
a. Laid paper 160.00 87.50
26 A22 5c green 16.00 14.50
a. Laid paper 160.00 87.50
27 A23 10c lilac 25.00 21.00
a. Laid paper 160.00 125.00
28 A20 10c vio, pelure paper ('78) *900.00* 675.00

Arms — A24

Liberty — A25

A26

A27

1878-85

29 A24 2½c blue, pelure paper 2.75 2.50
30 A24 2½c green ('83) 2.50 2.10
a. Laid paper ('83) 80.00 55.00
31 A24 2½c blk, *buff* ('85) 7.25 6.50
32 A25 5c green ('83) 4.50 4.00
a. Pelure paper 32.50 27.50
b. Laid paper ('82) 40.00 13.00
33 A25 5c violet ('83) 9.50 7.50
a. 5c blue violet ('83) 9.50 7.50
34 A26 10c vio, laid paper ('82) 190.00 65.00
35 A26 10c scar ('83) 2.50 2.10
a. Tete beche pair 110.00 110.00
36 A27 20c brown ('83) 4.50 4.00
a. Laid paper ('82) 6.00 5.50

A28

A29

Liberty — A30

1883-85

37 A28 5c brown 5.25 3.50
a. Laid paper 225.00 87.50
38 A28 5c green ('85) 140.00 45.00
a. Laid paper ('85) 160.00 75.00
39 A28 5c yel, laid paper ('85) 5.50 4.50
40 A29 10c bl grn, laid paper 5.50 4.75
41 A29 10c bl, *bl* ('85) 5.50 4.50

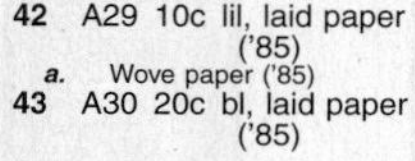
42 A29 10c lil, laid paper ('85) 12.00 7.50
a. Wove paper ('85) 125.00 80.00
43 A30 20c bl, laid paper ('85) 4.50 4.00

Coat of Arms — A31

1886 **Wove Paper**

55 A31 1c grn, *pink* .65 .55
56 A31 2½c blk, *orange* .65 .55
57 A31 5c ultra, *buff* 2.00 1.75
a. 5c blue, *buff* 3.75 3.25
58 A31 10c rose, *buff* 1.75 1.60
a. Transfer of 50c in stone of 10c 140.00 140.00
59 A31 20c dk vio, *buff* 1.75 1.60
61 A31 50c yel brn, *buff* 3.25 2.75
62 A31 1p yel, *grn* 5.25 4.50
63 A31 2p green, *vio* 5.25 4.50
Nos. 55-63 (8) 20.55 17.80

1887-88

64 A31 1c red, *vio* .50 .45
65 A31 2½c lil, *pale lil* .50 *.60*
66 A31 5c car, *buff* .65 .65
67 A31 5c red, *grn* 3.75 1.75
68 A31 10c brn, *grn* .65 *.80*
Nos. 64-68 (5) 6.05 4.25

Medellin Issue

A32

A33

A34

1888 **Typeset**

69 A32 2½c blk, *yellow* 16.00 14.50
70 A33 5c blk, *yellow* 8.75 7.50
71 A34 5c red, *yellow* 5.25 4.50
Nos. 69-71 (3) 30.00 26.50

Two varieties of No. 69, six of No. 70 and ten of No. 71.

A35

1889

72 A35 2½c red 8.00 6.75

Ten varieties including "eentavos."

Regular Issue

Coat of Arms — A36

1889 **Litho.** ***Perf. 13½***

73 A36 1c blk, *rose* .25 .25
74 A36 2½c blk, *blue* .25 .25
75 A36 5c blk, *yellow* .30 .30
76 A36 10c blk, *green* .30 .30
Nos. 73-76 (4) 1.10 1.10

A37

A38

A39

A40

Coat of Arms — A41

1890

78 A37 20c blue 1.40 1.40
79 A38 50c vio brn 2.50 2.50
a. Transfer of 20c in stone of 50c 95.00 95.00
80 A38 50c green 2.25 2.25
81 A39 1p red 2.00 2.00
82 A40 2p blk, *mag* 14.50 14.50
83 A41 5p blk, *org red* 22.50 22.50
Nos. 78-83 (6) 45.15 45.15

Nos. 73-76, 82-83 exist imperf.

The so-called "errors" of Nos. 73 to 76, printed on paper of wrong colors, are essays or, possibly, reprints. They exist perforated and imperforate.

See No. 96.

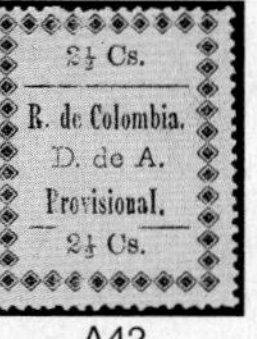
A42

A43

A44 A45

1890 **Typeset** ***Perf. 14***

84 A42 2½c blk, *buff* 2.25 2.25
85 A43 5c blk, *orange* 2.25 2.25
86 A44 10c blk, *buff* 7.00 7.00
87 A44 10c blk, *rose* 9.00 9.00
88 A45 20c blk, *orange* 9.00 9.00
Nos. 84-88 (5) 29.50 29.50

20 varieties of the 5c, 10 each of the other values.

A46

1892 **Litho.** ***Perf. 13½***

89 A46 1c brn, *brnsh* .40 .40
90 A46 2½c pur, *lil* .40 .40
92 A46 5c blk, *gray* 1.10 .55
a. Transfer of 2½c in stone of 5c 200.00
Nos. 89-92 (3) 1.90 1.35

1893

93 A46 1c blue .25 .25
94 A46 2½c green .40 .40
95 A46 5c vermilion .25 .25
96 A36 10c pale brown .25 .25
Nos. 93-96 (4) 1.15 1.15

A47

1896 *Perf. 14*

No.	Type	Denomination	Color	Unused	Used
97	A47	2c	gray	.25	.25
98	A47	2c	lilac rose	.25	.25
99	A47	2½c	brown	.25	.25
100	A47	2½c	steel blue	.25	.25
101	A47	3c	orange	.25	.25
102	A47	3c	olive grn	.25	.25
103	A47	5c	green	.25	.25
104	A47	5c	yellow buff	.30	.30
105	A47	10c	brown vio	.55	.55
106	A47	10c	violet	.55	.55
107	A47	20c	brown org	1.40	1.40
108	A47	20c	blue	1.40	1.40
109	A47	50c	gray brn	1.40	1.40
110	A47	50c	rose	1.40	1.40
111	A47	1p	blue & blk	17.50	17.50
112	A47	1p	rose red & blk	17.50	17.50
113	A47	2p	orange & blk	55.00	55.00
114	A47	2p	dk grn & blk	55.00	55.00
115	A47	5p	red vio & blk	95.00	95.00
116	A47	5p	purple & blk	95.00	95.00
			Nos. 97-116 (20)	343.75	343.75

#115-116 with centers omitted are proofs.

General José María Córdoba — A48

1899 *Perf. 11*

No.	Type	Denomination	Color	Unused	Used
117	A48	½c	grnsh bl	.25	.25
118	A48	1c	slate blue	.25	.25
119	A48	2c	slate brown	.25	.25
120	A48	3c	red	.25	.25
121	A48	4c	bister brown	.25	.25
122	A48	5c	green	.25	.25
123	A48	10c	scarlet	.25	.25
124	A48	20c	gray violet	.25	.25
125	A48	50c	olive bister	.25	.25
126	A48	1p	greenish blk	.25	.25
127	A48	2p	olive gray	.25	.25
			Nos. 117-127 (11)	2.75	2.75

Numerous part-perf. and imperf. varieties of Nos. 117-127 exist.

Used values for Nos. 117-127 are for favor-canceled stamps with oval cancels in violet. Postally used examples are valued at $1.75 each.

A49

A50

A50a

1901 **Typeset** *Perf. 12*

No.	Type	Denomination	Color	Unused	Used
128	A49	1c	red	.25	.25
129	A50	1c	ultra	.65	.65
130	A50	1c	bister	.65	.65
130A	A50a	1c	dull red	.65	.65
130B	A50a	1c	ultra	4.50	4.50
			Nos. 128-130B (5)	6.70	6.70

Eight varieties of No. 128, four varieties of Nos. 129-130B.

A51

A52

Atanasio Girardot A53

Dr. José Félix Restrepo A54

1902 **Litho.** **Wove Paper**

No.	Type	Denomination	Color	Unused	Used
131	A51	1c	brt rose	.25	.25
a.			Laid paper	.65	.65
b.			Imperf., pair	2.75	
132	A51	2c	blue	.25	.25
a.			Transfer of 3c in stone of 2c	6.00	6.00
133	A51	3c	green	.25	.25
a.			Imperf., pair	5.00	
134	A51	4c	dull violet	.25	.25
135	A52	5c	rose red	.25	.25
136	A53	10c	rose lilac	.25	.25
a.			Small head	5.75	5.75
b.			10c rose	.25	.25
137	A53	20c	gray green	.25	.25
138	A53	30c	brt rose	.25	.25
139	A53	40c	blue	.25	.25
140	A53	50c	brn, *yel*	.25	.25

Laid Paper

No.	Type	Denomination	Color	Unused	Used
141	A54	1p	purple & blk	.80	.80
142	A54	2p	rose & blk	.80	.80
143	A54	5p	sl bl & blk	1.50	1.50
			Nos. 131-143 (13)	5.60	5.60

1903 **Wove Paper**

No.	Type	Denomination	Color	Unused	Used
143A	A51	1c	blue	.25	.25
144	A51	2c	violet	.25	.25
a.			Imperf.	3.00	

A55

A56

A57

Designs: 1p, Francisco Antonio Zea. 2p, Custodio Garcia Rovira. 3p, La Pola (Policarpa Salavarrieta). 4p, J. M. Restrepo. 5p, José Fernández Madrid. 10p, Juan del Corral.

1903-04

No.	Type	Denomination	Color	Unused	Used
145	A55	4c	yellow brn	.35	.30
146	A55	5c	blue	.35	.30
147	A56	10c	yellow	.35	.30
148	A56	20c	purple	.35	.30
149	A56	30c	brown	.90	.85
150	A56	40c	green	.90	.85
151	A56	50c	rose	.35	.30
152	A57	1p	olive gray	.90	.85
153	A57	2p	purple	.90	.85
154	A57	3p	dark blue	.90	.85
155	A57	4p	dull red	1.50	1.50
156	A57	5p	red brown	4.50	2.10
157	A57	10p	scarlet	9.25	5.25
			Nos. 145-157 (13)	21.50	14.60

Nos. 145-146, 151, 153-157 exist imperf. Value of pairs, $4 to $5.

Manizales Issue

Stamps of these designs are local private post issues.

OFFICIAL STAMPS Stamps of 1903-04 with overprint "OFICIAL" were never issued.

REGISTRATION STAMPS

R1

1896 **Unwmk.** **Litho.** *Perf. 14*

No.	Type	Denomination	Color	Unused	Used
F1	R1	2½c	rose	1.25	1.25
F2	R1	2½c	dull blue	1.25	1.25

Córdoba R2

R3

1899 *Perf. 11*

No.	Type	Denomination	Color	Unused	Used
F3	R2	2½c	dull blue	.25	.25
F4	R3	10c	red lilac	.25	.25

R4

1902 *Perf. 12*

No.	Type	Denomination	Color	Unused	Used
F5	R4	10c	purple, *blue*	.30	.30
a.			Imperf.	—	

ACKNOWLEDGMENT OF RECEIPT STAMPS

AR1

1902-03 **Unwmk.** **Litho.** *Perf. 12*

No.	Type	Denomination	Color	Unused	Used
H1	AR1	5c	black, *rose*	1.10	1.10
H2	AR1	5c	slate ('03)	.35	.35

LATE FEE STAMPS

Córdoba — LF1

1899 **Unwmk.** **Litho.** *Perf. 11*

No.	Type	Denomination	Color	Unused	Used
I1	LF1	2½c	dark green	.30	.30
a.			Imperf., pair	3.00	

LF2

1901 **Typeset** *Perf. 12*

No.	Type	Denomination	Color	Unused	Used
I2	LF2	2½c	red violet	.80	.80
a.			2½c purple	.80	.80

LF3

1902 **Litho.**

No.	Type	Denomination	Color	Unused	Used
I3	LF3	2½c	violet	.25	.25

City of Medellin

Stamps of the designs shown were not issued by any governmental agency but by the Sociedad de Mejoras Publicas.

BOLIVAR

bə-ˈlē-ˌvär

Originally a State, now a Department of the Republic of Colombia. (See Antioquia.)

A1

1863-66 **Unwmk.** **Litho.** *Imperf.*

No.	Type	Denomination	Color	Unused	Used
1	A1	10c	green	*1,200.*	*600.00*
a.			Five stars below shield	*2,500.*	*2,400.*
2	A1	10c	red ('66)	27.50	*30.00*
a.			Diagonal half used as 5c on cover		120.00
b.			Five stars below shield	80.00	72.50
3	A1	1p	red	6.75	*7.75*

Fourteen varieties of each. Counterfeits of Nos. 1 and 1a exist.

Coat of Arms
A2 A3

A4

A5

1873

No.	Type	Denomination	Color	Unused	Used
4	A2	5c	blue	7.25	7.25
5	A3	10c	violet	7.25	7.25
6	A4	20c	yellow green	32.50	32.50
7	A5	80c	vermilion	65.00	65.00
			Nos. 4-7 (4)	112.00	112.00

A6

A7

A8

1874-78

No.	Type	Description	Unused	Used
8	A6	5c blue	27.50	14.00
9	A7	5c blue ('78)	8.00	7.25
10	A8	10c violet ('77)	4.00	3.75
		Nos. 8-10 (3)	39.50	25.00

Bolívar — A9

Dated "1879"

1879 White Wove Paper *Perf. 12½*

No.	Type	Description	Unused	Used
11	A9	5c blue	.30	.30
a.		Imperf., pair	.90	
12	A9	10c violet	.25	.25
13	A9	20c red	.30	.30
a.		20c green (error)	11.00	11.00

Bluish Laid Paper

No.	Type	Description	Unused	Used
15	A9	5c blue	.30	.30
a.		Imperf., pair	2.25	
16	A9	10c violet	1.60	1.60
a.		Imperf., pair	4.50	
17	A9	20c red	.40	.40
a.		Imperf., pair	2.00	
		Nos. 11-17 (6)	3.15	3.15

Stamps of 80c and 1p on white wove paper and 1p on bluish laid paper were prepared but not placed in use.

Dated "1880"

1880 White Wove Paper *Perf. 12½*

No.	Type	Description	Unused	Used
19	A9	5c blue	.30	.30
a.		Imperf., pair	1.60	
20	A9	10c violet	.40	.40
a.		Imperf., pair	1.60	
21	A9	20c red	.40	.40
a.		20c green (error)	14.00	14.00
23	A9	80c green	2.50	2.50
24	A9	1p orange	2.75	2.75
a.		Imperf., pair	5.50	
		Nos. 19-24 (5)	6.35	6.35

Bluish Laid Paper

No.	Type	Description	Unused	Used
25	A9	5c blue	.30	.30
a.		Imperf., pair	1.40	
26	A9	10c violet	2.50	2.50
27	A9	20c red	.40	.40
a.		Imperf., pair	3.00	
28	A9	1p orange	450.00	
a.		Imperf.	*475.00*	

A11

A12

A13 A15

A16

Dated "1882"

White Wove Paper

1882 *Perf. 12, 16x12*

No.	Type	Description	Unused	Used
29	A11	5c blue	.35	.35
30	A12	10c lilac	.25	.25
31	A13	20c red	.35	.35
33	A15	80c green	.65	.65
34	A16	1p orange	.65	.65
		Nos. 29-34 (5)	2.25	2.25

Nos. 29, 30 and 34 are known imperforate. They are printer's waste and were not issued through post offices.

A17

1882 Engr. *Perf. 12*

No.	Type	Description	Unused	Used
35	A17	5p blue & rose red	.65	.65
a.		Imperf., pair	5.25	
b.		Perf. 16	8.00	6.75
c.		Perf. 14	6.75	6.75
36	A17	10p brown & blue	1.75	1.75
a.		Imperf., pair	8.75	
b.		Perf. 16	7.25	6.00
c.		Rouletted	8.75	8.75

Dated "1883"

1883 Litho. *Perf. 12, 16x12*

No.	Type	Description	Unused	Used
37	A11	5c blue	.25	.25
a.		Imperf., pair	1.00	
b.		Perf. 12	12.00	2.40
38	A12	10c lilac	.30	.30
39	A13	20c red	.30	.30
41	A15	80c green	.30	.30
42	A16	1p orange	1.60	1.60
a.		Perf. 16x12	2.25	2.25
		Nos. 37-42 (5)	2.75	2.75

1884 Dated "1884"

No.	Type	Description	Unused	Used
43	A11	5c blue	.30	.30
a.		Perf. 12	16.00	16.00
44	A12	10c lilac	.25	.25
45	A13	20c red	.25	.25
a.		Perf. 12	8.00	8.00
47	A15	80c green	.30	.35
a.		Perf. 12	4.00	4.00
48	A16	1p orange	.30	.30
		Nos. 43-48 (5)	1.40	1.45

1885 Dated "1885"

No.	Type	Description	Unused	Used
49	A11	5c blue	.25	.25
50	A12	10c lilac	.25	.25
51	A13	20c red	.25	.25
53	A15	80c green	.25	.25
54	A16	1p orange	.30	.30
		Nos. 49-54 (5)	1.30	1.30

The note after No. 34 will also apply to imperforate stamps of the 1884-85 issues.

A18

1891 *Perf. 14*

No.	Type	Description	Unused	Used
55	A18	1c black	.30	.30
56	A18	5c orange	.30	.30
a.		Imperf., pair	.90	
57	A18	10c carmine	.30	.30
58	A18	20c blue	.65	.65
59	A18	50c green	.95	.95
60	A18	1p purple	.95	.95
		Nos. 55-60 (6)	3.45	3.45

For overprint see Colombia No. 169.

Bolívar A19

José Fernández Madrid A20

Manuel Rodriguez Torices A21

José María García de Toledo A22

1903 Laid Paper *Imperf.*

No.	Type	Description	Unused	Used
62	A19	50c dk bl, *pink*	.65	.65
a.		Bluish paper	.65	.65
63	A19	50c sl grn, *pink*	.65	.65
a.		Rose paper	2.25	2.25
b.		Greenish blue paper	3.25	3.25
c.		Yellow paper	4.50	4.50
d.		Brown paper	4.50	4.50
e.		Salmon paper	8.00	8.00
64	A19	50c pur, *pink*	2.25	2.25
a.		White paper	4.50	4.50
b.		Brown paper	4.50	4.50
c.		Greenish blue paper	4.50	4.50
d.		Lilac paper	4.50	4.50
e.		Rose paper	4.00	4.00
f.		Yellow paper	4.50	4.50
g.		Salmon paper	6.50	6.50
h.		As "a," wove paper	9.75	9.75
65	A20	1p org, *sal*	.65	.65
a.		Yellow paper	5.00	5.00
b.		Greenish blue paper	16.00	16.00
66	A20	1p gray grn, *lil*	1.60	1.60
a.		Yellow paper	7.00	7.00
b.		Salmon paper	8.00	8.00
c.		Green paper	8.00	8.00
d.		White wove paper	12.00	
67	A21	5p car rose, *lil*	.65	.65
a.		Brown paper	1.25	1.25
b.		Yellow paper	1.25	1.25
c.		Greenish blue paper	5.00	5.00
d.		Bluish paper	6.50	6.50
e.		Salmon paper	8.00	8.00
f.		Rose paper	9.75	9.75
68	A22	10p dk bl, *bluish*	1.40	1.40
a.		Greenish blue paper	1.40	1.40
b.		Rose paper	8.00	8.00
c.		Salmon paper	8.00	8.00
d.		Yellow paper	8.00	8.00
e.		Brown paper	9.00	9.00
f.		Lilac paper	12.00	12.00
g.		White paper	9.75	9.75
69	A22	10p pur, *grnsh bl*	3.75	3.75
a.		Bluish paper	8.00	8.00
b.		Rose paper	7.25	7.25
c.		Yellow paper	8.00	8.00
d.		Brown paper	8.00	8.00
		Nos. 62-69 (8)	11.60	11.60

Sewing Machine Perf.

Laid Paper

No.	Type	Description	Unused	Used
70	A19	50c dk bl, *pink*	1.10	1.10
a.		Bluish paper	1.10	1.10
71	A19	50c sl grn, *pink*	2.25	2.25
72	A19	50c pur, *grnsh bl*	4.50	4.50
a.		White paper	4.50	4.50
b.		White wove paper	8.00	
73	A20	1p org, *sal*	2.25	2.25
74	A20	1p gray grn, *lil*	9.75	9.75
a.		Yellow paper	9.75	9.75
75	A21	5p car rose, *yel*	1.75	1.75
a.		Lilac paper	4.50	4.50
b.		Brown paper	4.50	4.50
c.		Bluish paper	6.00	6.00
d.		White wove paper	9.75	
76	A22	10p dk bl, *grnsh bl*	5.00	5.00
a.		Bluish paper	7.50	7.50
b.		Yellow paper	9.75	9.75
c.		As "b," wove paper	12.00	
77	A22	10p pur, *grnsh bl*	7.50	7.50
a.		Bluish paper	13.00	13.00
b.		Rose paper	8.50	8.50
c.		Yellow paper	13.00	13.00
		Nos. 70-77 (8)	34.10	34.10

José María del Castillo y Rada — A23

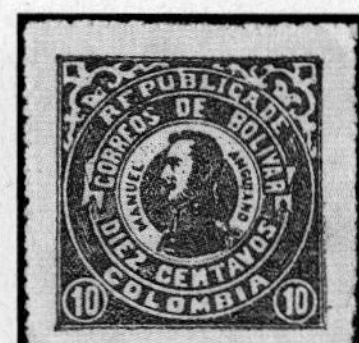
Manuel Anguiano — A24

Pantaleón C. Ribón — A25

1904 *Sewing Machine Perf.*

No.	Type	Description	Unused	Used
89	A23	5c black	.25	.25
90	A24	10c brown	.25	.25
91	A25	20c red	.30	.30
92	A25	20c red brown	.65	.65
		Nos. 89-92 (4)	1.45	1.45

Imperf., pairs

No.	Type	Description	Unused	Used
89a	A23	5c black	4.00	4.00
90a	A24	10c brown	3.00	3.00
91a	A25	20c red	7.25	7.25
92a	A25	20c red brown	7.25	7.25

A26

A27

A28

1904 *Imperf.*

No.	Type	Description	Unused	Used
93	A26	½c black	.65	.65
a.		Tête bêche pair	3.75	3.75
94	A27	1c blue	1.25	1.25
95	A28	2c purple	1.40	1.40
		Nos. 93-95 (3)	3.30	3.30

REGISTRATION STAMPS

Simón Bolívar — R1

White Wove Paper

Perf. 12½, 16x12

1879 Unwmk. Litho.

No.	Type	Description	Unused	Used
F1	R1	40c brown	.75	.75

Bluish Laid Paper

No.	Type	Description	Unused	Used
F2	R1	40c brown	.75	.75
a.		Imperf., pair	3.50	

Dated "1880"

1880 White Wove Paper

No.	Type	Description	Unused	Used
F3	R1	40c brown	.35	.35

Bluish Laid Paper

No.	Type	Description	Unused	Used
F4	R1	40c brown	.75	.75
a.		Imperf., pair	3.50	

Simón Bolívar — R2

Dated "1882" to "1885"

White Wove Paper

1882-85 *Perf. 16x12*

No.	Type	Description	Unused	Used
F5	R2	40c brown (1882)	.35	.35
F6	R2	40c brown (1883)	.30	.30
F7	R2	40c brown (1884)	.30	.30
F8	R2	40c brown (1885)	.30	.30
		Nos. F5-F8 (4)	1.25	1.25

Perf. 12

No.	Type	Description	Unused	Used
F5a	R2	40c	19.00	
F6a	R2	40c	16.00	
F7a	R2	40c	16.00	
F8a	R2	40c	16.00	
		Nos. F5a-F8a (4)	67.00	

R3

1903 Laid Paper *Imperf.*

F9 R3 20c orange, *rose*	.65	.65
a. Salmon paper	1.25	1.25
b. Greenish blue paper	6.50	6.50

Sewing Machine Perf.

F10 R3 20c orange, *rose*	2.75	2.75
a. Salmon paper	2.75	2.75
b. Greenish blue paper	6.50	6.50

R4

1904

Wove Paper

F11 R4 5c black	3.25	3.25

ACKNOWLEDGMENT OF RECEIPT STAMPS

AR1

1903 Unwmk. Litho. *Imperf.*

Laid Paper

H1 AR1 20c org, *rose*	2.75	2.75
a. Yellow paper	1.40	1.40
b. Greenish blue paper	5.50	5.50
H2 AR1 20c dk bl, *yel*	2.25	2.25
a. Brown paper	3.75	3.75
b. Rose paper	2.75	2.75
c. Salmon paper	7.50	7.50
d. Greenish blue paper	7.50	7.50

Sewing Machine Perf.

H3 AR1 20c org, *grnsh bl*	6.75	6.75
a. Yellow paper	7.75	7.75
H4 AR1 20c dk bl, *yel*	7.75	7.75
a. Lilac paper	7.75	7.75
Nos. H1-H4 (4)	19.50	19.50

AR2

1904 Wove Paper

H5 AR2 2c red	1.25	1.25

LATE FEE STAMPS

LF1

1903 Unwmk. Litho. *Imperf.*

Laid Paper

I1 LF1 20c car rose, *bluish*	.65	.65
I2 LF1 20c pur, *bluish*	.65	.65
a. Rose paper	2.25	2.25
b. Brown paper	2.25	2.25
c. Lilac paper	2.25	2.25
d. Yellow paper	7.00	7.00

Sewing Machine Perf.

I3 LF1 20c car rose, *bluish*	3.75	3.75
I4 LF1 20c pur, *bluish*	3.75	3.75
a. Rose paper	6.50	6.50
b. Lilac paper	6.50	6.50
c. Yellow paper	12.00	12.00
Nos. I1-I4 (4)	8.80	8.80

BOYACA

bō-yä-cä

Originally a State, now a Department of the Republic of Colombia. (See Antioquia.)

Diego Mendoza Pérez — A1

1902 Unwmk. Litho. *Perf. 13½*

Wove Paper

1 A1 5c blue green	.80	.80
a. Bluish paper	95.00	95.00
b. Imperf., pair	16.00	16.00

Laid Paper

Perf. 12

2 A1 5c green	110.00	110.00

Coat of Arms
A2 A3

Gen. Próspero Pinzón — A4

A5

Monument of Battle of Boyacá — A6

President José Manuel Marroquin — A7

1903 Litho. *Imperf.*

4 A2 10c dark gray	.30	.30
5 A3 20c red brown	.35	.35
6 A5 1p red	3.25	3.25
a. 1p claret	3.75	3.75
8 A6 5p black, *rose*	1.25	1.25
a. 5p black, *buff*	12.00	12.00
9 A7 10p black, *buff*	1.25	1.25
a. 10p black, *rose*	12.00	12.00
b. As "a," tête bêche pair	24.00	
Nos. 4-9 (5)	6.40	6.40

Perf. 12

10 A2 10c dark gray	.35	.35
11 A3 20c red brown	.40	.40
12 A4 50c green	.35	.35
13 A4 50c dull blue	2.50	2.50
14 A5 1p red	.35	.35
a. 1p claret	3.00	3.00
16 A6 5p black, *rose*	11.00	11.00
a. 5p black, *buff*	9.50	9.50
17 A7 10p black, *buff*	1.10	1.10
a. 10p black, *rose*	11.00	11.00
b. Tête bêche pair	12.00	12.00
Nos. 10-17 (7)	16.05	16.05

Statue of Bolívar — A8

1904

18 A8 10c orange	.25	.25
a. Imperf., pair	3.75	3.75

CAUCA

Stamps of these designs were issued by a provincial post between 1879(?) and 1890.

Stamps of this design are believed to be of private origin and without official sanction.

Items inscribed "No hay estampillas" (No stamps available) and others inscribed "Manuel E. Jiménez" are considered by specialists to be receipt labels, not postage stamps.

CUNDINAMARCA

kün-di-nə-'mär-kə

Originally a State, now a Department of the Republic of Colombia. (See Antioquia.)

Coat of Arms
A1 A2

1870 Unwmk. Litho. *Imperf.*

1 A1 5c blue	5.25	5.25
2 A2 10c red	16.00	16.00

The counterfeits, or reprints, show traces of the cuts made to deface the dies.

A3

A4

A5

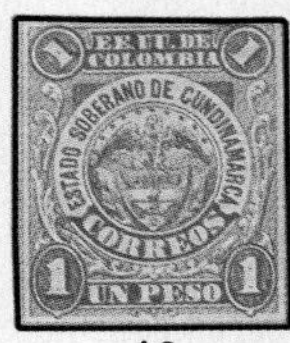
A6

1877-82

3 A3 10c red ('82)	3.50	3.50
a. Laid paper ('77)	4.50	4.50
4 A4 20c green ('82)	7.50	7.50
a. Laid paper ('77)	12.00	12.00
7 A5 50c purple ('82)	8.25	8.25
8 A6 1p brown ('82)	12.00	12.00
Nos. 3-8 (4)	31.25	31.25

A7

Redrawn

1884

10 A7 5c blue	.80	.80
11 A7 5c blue (redrawn)	.80	.80
a. Tête bêche pair	80.00	80.00

The redrawn stamp has no period after "COLOMBIA."

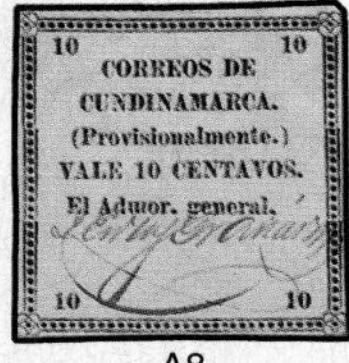

A8

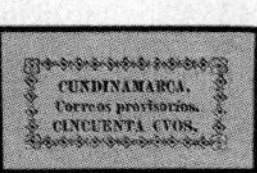

A9

A10

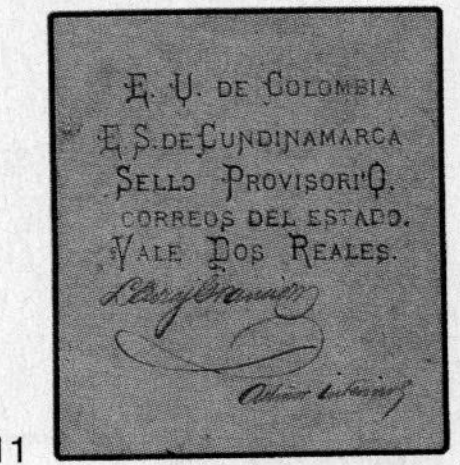

A11

1883 Typeset

13 A8 10c black, *yellow*	14.00	14.00
14 A9 50c black, *rose*	14.00	14.00
15 A10 1p black, *brown*	37.50	37.50
16 A11 2r black, *green*	*2,200.*	

Typeset varieties exist: 4 of the 10c, 2 each of 50c and 1p.

Some experts doubt that No. 16 was issued. The variety without signature and watermarked "flowers" is believed to be a proof. Forgeries exist.

A12

1886 Litho.

17 A12 5c blue	.80	.80
18 A12 10c red	5.00	5.00
19 A12 10c red, *lilac*	2.75	2.75
20 A12 20c green	4.25	4.25
a. 20c yellow green	5.00	5.00

21	A12	50c purple	5.50	5.50
22	A12	1p orange brown	5.75	5.75
		Nos. 17-22 (6)	24.05	24.05

Nos. 17 to 22 have been reprinted. The colors are aniline and differ from those of the original stamps. The impression is coarse and blurred.

A13

A14

A15

A16

A17 A18

A19 A20

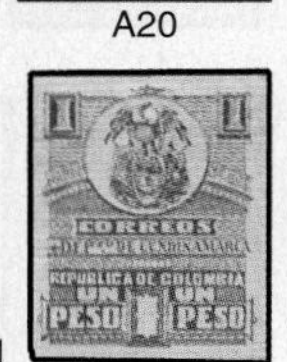
A21

1904 ***Perf. 10½, 12***

23	A13	1c orange	.25	.25
24	A14	2c gray blue	.25	.25
25	A15	3c rose	.35	.35
26	A15	5c olive grn	.35	.35
27	A16	10c pale brn	.35	.35
28	A17	15c pink	.35	.35
29	A18	20c blue, *grn*	.35	.35
30	A18	20c blue	.60	.60
31	A19	40c blue	.60	.60
32	A19	40c blue, *buff*	21.00	21.00
33	A20	50c red vio	.60	.60
34	A21	1p gray grn	.60	.60
		Nos. 23-34 (12)	25.65	25.65

Imperf

23a	A13	1c orange	.75	.75
24a	A14	2c blue	.75	.75
b.		2c slate	6.50	6.50
25a	A15	3c rose	.90	.90
26a	A15	5c olive green	1.60	1.60
27a	A16	10c pale brown	2.00	2.00
28a	A17	15c pink	.50	.50
29a	A18	20c blue, *green*	2.00	2.00
30a	A18	20c blue	2.00	2.00
31a	A19	40c blue	.70	.70
32a	A19	40c blue, *buff*	21.00	21.00
33a	A20	50c red violet	.70	.70
34a	A21	1p gray green	.70	.70
		Nos. 23a-34a (12)	33.60	33.60

REGISTRATION STAMPS

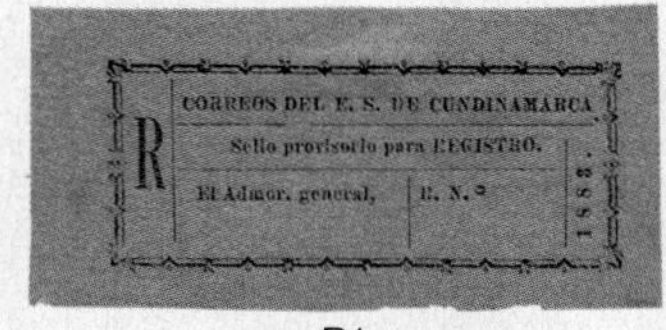
R1

1883 **Unwmk.** ***Imperf.***

F1	R1	black, *orange*	17.00	17.00

R2

1904 ***Perf. 12***

F2	R2	10c bister	.85	.85
a.		Imperf.	3.75	3.75

INSURED LETTER STAMP

IL1

1883 ***Imperf.***

Thin Paper with Vertical Mesh

G1	IL1	20c blk, *emerald grn*	80.00	120.00

Magdalena

Items inscribed "No hay estampillas" (No stamps available) are considered by specialists to be not postage stamps but receipt labels.

Panama

Issues of Panama as a state and later Department of Colombia are listed with the Republic of Panama issues (Nos. 1-30).

SANTANDER

săn-ˌtän-ˈdeˌəˌr

Originally a State, now a Department of the Republic of Colombia. (See Antioquia.)

Coat of Arms
A1 A2

1884 **Unwmk.** **Litho.** ***Imperf.***

1	A1	1c blue	.30	.30
a.		1c gray blue	.50	.50
2	A2	5c red	.50	.50
3	A2	10c bluish purple	1.90	1.90
a.		Tête bêche pair	—	
		Nos. 1-3 (3)	2.70	2.70

No. 2 exists unofficially perforated 14.

A3

1886 ***Imperf.***

4	A3	1c blue	.90	.90
5	A3	5c red	.30	.30
6	A3	10c red violet	.50	.50
a.		10c deep violet	.50	.50
b.		Inscribed "CINCO CENTAVOS"	26.00	26.00
		Nos. 4-6 (3)	1.70	1.70

The numerals in the upper corners are omitted on No. 5, while on No. 6 there are no numerals in the side panels. No. 6 exists unofficially perforated 12.

A4

1887

7	A4	1c blue	.25	.25
a.		1c ultramarine	1.75	1.75
8	A4	5c red	1.75	1.75
9	A4	10c violet	5.50	5.50
		Nos. 7-9 (3)	7.50	7.50

A5

A6

A7

1889 ***Perf. 11½ and 13½***

10	A5	1c blue	.35	.35
11	A6	5c red	1.25	1.25
12	A7	10c purple	.45	.45
a.		Imperf., pair	16.00	*20.00*
		Nos. 10-12 (3)	2.05	2.05

A8

1892 ***Perf. 13½***

13	A8	5c red, *rose buff*	1.00	1.00

A9

1895-96

14	A9	5c brown	.70	.70
15	A9	5c yel grn ('96)	.70	.70

A10

A11

A12

1899 ***Perf. 10***

16	A10	1c black, *green*	.35	.35
17	A11	5c black, *pink*	.35	.35

Perf. 13½

18	A12	10c blue	.70	.70
a.		Perf. 12	1.00	1.00
		Nos. 16-18 (3)	1.40	1.40

A13

1903 ***Imperf.***

19	A13	50c red	.60	.60
a.		50c rose	.60	.60
b.		"SANTENDER"	2.50	2.50
c.		"Corrcos"	2.50	2.50
d.		"Corceos"	2.50	2.50
e.		Tête bêche pair	4.75	4.75
f.		Pair, one without overprint	2.75	2.75

The overprint "Correos de Departmento Bucaramanga" on the 50c red revenue stamp has been proved to be a cancellation.

A14

A15

Arms
A16

Locomotive
A17

A18

A19

A20

1904 ***Imperf.***

22	A14	5c dark green	.25	.25
a.		5c yellow green	.40	.40
24	A15	10c rose	.25	.25
25	A16	20c brown violet	.25	.25
26	A17	50c yellow	.25	.25
27	A18	1p black	.25	.25
28	A19	5p dark blue	.35	.35
29	A20	10p carmine	.40	.40
		Nos. 22-29 (7)	2.00	2.00

1905

30	A14	5c pale blue	.45	.45
31	A15	10c red brown	.45	.45
32	A16	20c yellow green	.45	.45
33	A17	50c red violet	.60	.60
34	A18	1p dark blue	.60	.60
35	A19	5p pink	.60	.60
36	A20	10p red	1.60	1.60
		Nos. 30-36 (7)	4.75	4.75

A21

1907 ***Imperf.***

37	A21	½c on 50c rose	.80	*1.60*

City of Cucuta

Stamps of these and similar designs on white and yellow paper, with and without surcharges of ½c, 1c or 2c, are believed to have been produced without government authorization.

TOLIMA

tə-lē-mə

Originally a State, now a Department of the Republic of Colombia.
(See Antioquia.)

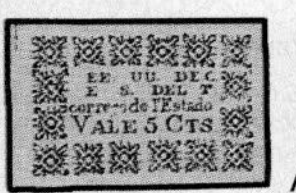
A1

1870 Unwmk. Typeset *Imperf.*

White Wove Paper

1	A1	5c black	62.50	62.50
2	A1	10c black	75.00	75.00
a.		Vert. se-tenant pair	1,500.	1,500.

Printed from two settings. Setting I, ten types of 5c. Setting II, six types of 5c and four types of 10c.

Blue Laid Batonné Paper

3	A1	5c black	*950.00*	

Buff Laid Batonné Paper

4	A1	5c black	150.00	100.00

Blue Wove Paper

5	A1	5c black	70.00	45.00

Blue Vertically Laid Paper

6	A1	5c black	110.00	70.00
a.		Paper with ruled blue vertical lines		

Blue Horizontally Laid Paper

7	A1	5c black	100.00	75.00

Blue Quadrille Paper

8	A1	5c black	150.00	80.00

Ten varieties each of Nos. 3-5 and 7; 20 varieties each of Nos. 6 and 8.

Official imitations were made in 1886 from new settings of the type. There are only 2 varieties of each value. They are printed on blue and white paper, wove, batonné, laid, etc.

A2

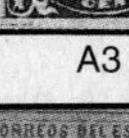
A3

A4

A5

Yellowish White Wove Paper

1871 Litho. *Imperf.*

9	A2	5c deep brown	2.25	2.25
a.		5c red brown	2.25	2.25
b.		Value reads "CINGO"	40.00	40.00
10	A3	10c blue	6.25	6.25
11	A4	50c green	8.00	8.00
12	A5	1p carmine	13.00	13.00
		Nos. 9-12 (4)	29.50	29.50

The 5p stamps, type A2, are bogus varieties made from an altered die of the 5c.

The 10c, 50c and 1 peso stamps have been reprinted on bluish white wove paper. They are from new plates and most copies show traces of fine lines with which the dies had been defaced. Reprints of the 5c have a large cross at the top. The 10c on laid batonné paper is known only as a reprint.

A6

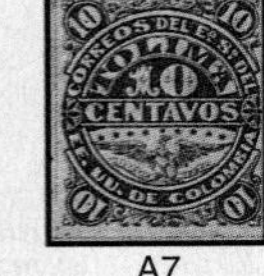
A7

A8

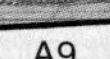
A9

1879

Grayish or White Wove Paper

14	A6	5c yellow brown	.45	.45
a.		5c purple brown	.45	.45
15	A7	10c blue	.50	.50
16	A8	50c green, *bluish*	.50	.50
a.		White paper	1.60	1.60
17	A9	1p vermilion	2.25	2.25
a.		1p carmine rose	9.00	9.00
		Nos. 14-17 (4)	3.70	3.70

A10

1883 *Imperf.*

18	A6	5c orange	.45	.45
19	A7	10c vermilion	.95	.95
20	A10	20c violet	1.50	1.50
		Nos. 18-20 (3)	2.90	2.90

Coat of Arms — A12

1884 *Imperf.*

23	A12	1c gray	.25	.25
24	A12	2c rose lilac	.25	.25
a.		2c slate	.25	.25
25	A12	2½c dull orange	.25	.25
26	A12	5c brown	.25	.25
27	A12	10c blue	.35	.35
a.		10c slate	.25	.25
28	A12	20c lemon	.35	.35
a.		Laid paper	5.00	5.00
29	A12	25c black	.30	.30
30	A12	50c green	.30	.30
31	A12	1p vermilion	.40	.40
32	A12	2p violet	.60	.60
a.		Value omitted	30.00	30.00
33	A12	5p yellow	.40	.40
34	A12	10p lilac rose	1.10	1.10
a.		Laid paper	30.00	30.00
b.		10p gray	*175.00*	
		Nos. 23-34 (12)	4.80	4.80

A13

A14

Condor with Long Wings Touching Flagstaffs
A15 A16

1886 Litho. *Perf. 10½, 11*

White Paper

36	A13	5c brown	1.40	1.40
a.		5c yellow brown	1.40	1.40
b.		Imperf., pair	17.50	
37	A14	10c blue	3.75	3.75
a.		Imperf., pair	17.50	
38	A15	50c green	3.25	3.25
a.		Imperf., pair	17.50	
39	A16	1p vermilion	2.75	2.75
a.		Imperf., pair	26.00	
		Nos. 36-39 (4)	11.15	11.15

No. 38 has been reprinted in pale gray green, perforated 10½, and No. 39 in bright vermilion, perforated 11½. The impressions show many signs of wear.

Lilac Tinted Paper

36c	A13	5c orange brown	12.50	12.50
37b	A14	10c blue	12.50	12.50
38b	A15	50c green	9.25	9.25
39b	A16	1p vermilion	8.25	8.25
		Nos. 36c-39b (4)	42.50	42.50

Items similar to A15 and A16 but with condor with long wings and upper flagstaffs omitted are forgeries.

A17

A18

Condor with Short Wings
A19 A20

1886 White Paper *Perf. 12*

44	A19	1c gray	6.25	6.25
45	A17	2c rose lilac	6.50	6.50
46	A18	2½c dull org	19.00	19.00
47	A19	5c brown	8.50	8.00
48	A20	10c blue	8.00	8.00
49	A20	20c lemon	6.50	6.50
a.		Tête bêche pair	275.00	275.00
50	A20	25c black	6.25	6.25
51	A20	50c green	3.75	3.75
52	A20	1p vermilion	5.00	4.25
53	A20	2p violet	7.25	7.25
b.		Tête bêche pair	190.00	190.00
54	A20	5p orange	13.00	13.00
55	A20	10p lilac rose	7.50	7.50
		Nos. 44-55 (12)	97.50	96.25

Imperf., Pairs

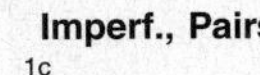

44a	A19	1c	17.00
47a	A19	5c	29.00
48a	A20	10c	29.00
52a	A20	1p	21.00
53a	A20	2p	26.00
54a	A20	5p	40.00
55a	A20	10p	17.00

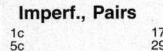

A23

1888 *Perf. 10½*

62	A23	5c red	.25	.25
63	A23	10c green	.30	.30
64	A23	50c blue	.75	.75
65	A23	1p red brown	1.90	1.90
		Nos. 62-65 (4)	3.20	3.20

For overprint see Colombia No. L14.

1895 *Perf. 12, 13½*

66	A23	1c blue, *rose*	.25	.25
67	A23	2c grn, *lt grn*	.25	.25
68	A23	5c red	.25	.25
69	A23	10c green	.50	.50
70	A23	20c blue, *yellow*	.30	.30
71	A23	1p brown	2.10	2.10
		Nos. 66-71 (6)	3.65	3.65

Imperf., Pairs

62a	A23	5c	8.75	
63a	A23	10c	12.00	
64a	A23	50c	14.50	14.50
65a	A23	1p	21.00	
66a	A23	1c	21.00	
67a	A23	2c	21.00	
70a	A23	20c	24.00	

"No Hay Estampillas"

Items inscribed "No hay estampillas" (No stamps available) are considered by specialists to be not postage stamps but receipt labels.

"Honda Issue"

This item seems to be of private origin.

A24

A25

A26

A27

A28

A29

A30

A31

Sewing Machine or Regular Perf. 12

1903-04 Litho.

79	A24	4c black, *green*	.25	.25
80	A25	10c dull blue	.25	.25
81	A26	20c orange	.50	.50
82	A27	50c black, *rose*	.25	.25
a.		50c black, *buff*	.25	.25
84	A28	1p brown	.25	.25
85	A29	2p gray	.25	.25
86	A30	5p red	.25	.25
a.		Tête bêche pair	8.00	*12.00*
87	A31	10p black, *blue*	.25	.25
a.		10p black, *light green*	.25	.25
b.		10p black, *grn*, glazed	3.75	3.75
		Nos. 79-87 (8)	2.25	2.25

Imperf

79a	A24	4c black, *green*	.25	.25
80a	A25	10c dull blue	.25	.25
81a	A26	20c orange	1.25	1.25
82b	A27	50c black, *rose*	1.75	1.75
c.		50c black, *buff*	1.75	1.75
84a	A28	1p brown	.25	.25
85a	A29	2p gray	.25	.25
86b	A30	5p red	.25	.25
c.		Tête bêche pair	12.00	*16.00*
87c	A31	10p black, *blue*	2.50	2.50
d.		Tête bêche pair		
e.		10p black, *light green*	3.75	3.75
f.		10p black, *green*, glazed	19.00	19.00
		Nos. 79a-87c (8)	6.75	6.75

INSURED LETTER STAMPS

IL1

IL2

Dateline ends with "de...187...".

1879			*Imperf.*	
G1	IL1	5c yellow ochre	40.00	40.00
G2	IL2	10c blk, *yel, bl & red*	75.00	75.00
G3	IL2	50c blk, *yel, bl & red*	75.00	*100.00*

Types of 1879 Redrawn

Dateline ends with "de...18...".

1879, Dec.			*Imperf.*	
G4	IL1	5c red brown	40.00	40.00
G5	IL2	10c blk, *yel, bl & red*	60.00	60.00
G6	IL2	50c blk, *yel, bl & red*	60.00	*90.00*

IL3

Dateline ends with "de...188...".

Wmk. With or Without Sheet Watermark "188"

1886			*Imperf.*	
G7	IL3	5c blk, *yel, bl & red*	75.00	80.00
G8	IL3	10c blk, *yel, bl & red*	75.00	80.00
G9	IL3	50c blk, *yel, bl & red*	150.00	120.00

1886

White Wove Paper

G10	IL3	5c yellow	20.00	*40.00*
a.		5c Orange	12.00	*25.00*
b.		5c Light brown	12.00	*25.00*
G11	IL3	10c light blue	12.00	*25.00*
a.		10c Blue	12.00	*25.00*
b.		10c Ultramarine	12.00	*25.00*
G12	IL3	50c red	20.00	*40.00*
a.		50c Brick red	25.00	*55.00*

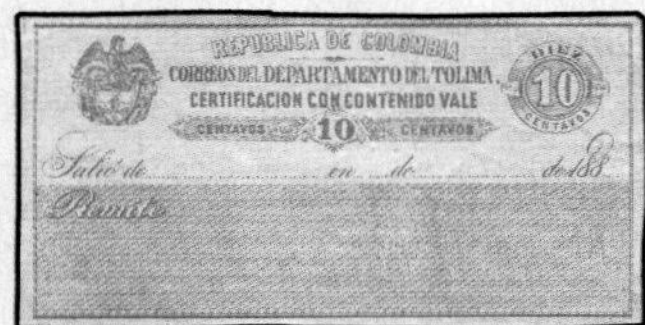

IL4

Dateline ends with "de...188...".

1888			*Imperf.*	
G13	IL4	5c brown	25.00	*40.00*
G14	IL4	10c red	25.00	*40.00*
G15	IL4	50c blue	37.50	*60.00*

Type of 1888 Redrawn

Dateline ends with "de...18...".

1890			*Imperf.*	
G16	IL4	5c brown	35.00	*52.50*
G17	IL4	10c red	40.00	*200.00*
G18	IL4	50c blue	100.00	*250.00*

IL5

Dateline ends with "de...189...".

1896			*Imperf.*	
G19	IL5	20c brown	25.00	*50.00*
G20	IL5	30c blue green	25.00	*50.00*
a.		30c Olive green	25.00	*50.00*
G21	IL5	40c brown orange	25.00	*50.00*
G22	IL5	50c blue	25.00	*50.00*
G23	IL5	60c black, *yellow*	25.00	*50.00*
G24	IL5	70c blk, *pale brn*	25.00	*55.00*
G25	IL5	80c black, *green*	25.00	*55.00*
G26	IL5	90c black, *pale blue*	25.00	*55.00*
G27	IL5	1p black, *rose pink*	35.00	*55.00*

COOK ISLANDS

'kuk 'ī-ləndz

(Rarotonga)

LOCATION — South Pacific Ocean, northeast of New Zealand
GOVT. — Dependency of New Zealand
AREA — 117 sq. mi.
POP. — 17,754 (1981)
CAPITAL — Rarotonga

Fifteen islands in Northern and Southern groups extend over 850,000 square miles of ocean.

Separate stamp issues used by Aitutaki (1903-32) and Penrhyn Islands (1902-32). Niue is included geographically, but administered separately. It issues separate stamps.

12 Pence = 1 Shilling
20 Shillings = 1 Pound

Catalogue values for unused stamps in this country are for Never Hinged items, beginning with Scott 127 in the regular postage section.

Watermarks

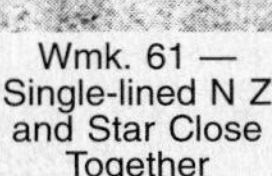

Wmk. 61 — Single-lined N Z and Star Close Together

Wmk. 62 — Single-lined N Z and Star Wide Apart

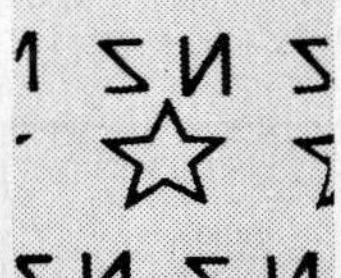

Wmk. 253 — Multiple N Z and Star

A1

1892	Unwmk.	Typo.	*Perf. 12½*	
		Toned Paper		
1	A1	1p black	35.00	30.00
2	A1	1½p violet	50.00	45.00
a.		Imperf, pair	*19,000.*	
3	A1	2½p blue	47.50	45.00
4	A1	10p carmine	160.00	150.00
		Nos. 1-4 (4)	292.50	270.00
		White Paper		
5	A1	1p black	35.00	30.00
a.		Vert. pair, imperf. between	*11,000.*	
6	A1	1½p violet	50.00	45.00
7	A1	2½p blue	47.50	45.00
8	A1	10p carmine	160.00	150.00
		Nos. 5-8 (4)	292.50	270.00

Nos. 1-8 were printed in sheets of 60 (6x10), from a setting of six slightly different cliches.

Queen Makea Takau — A2

1893-94	Wmk. 62		*Perf. 12x11½*	
9	A2	1p brown	50.00	*55.00*
10	A2	1p blue ('94)	13.00	2.50
a.		Perf. 12½ with 12x11½	—	1,900.
11	A2	1½p brt violet	19.00	8.50
12	A2	2½p rose	55.00	27.50
a.		Perf. 12½ with 12x11½	2,750.	—
b.		2½p rose carmine	70.00	55.00
13	A2	5p olive gray	24.00	16.00
14	A2	10p green	85.00	57.50
		Nos. 9-14 (6)	246.00	*167.00*

Perf. 12½ examples of Nos. 10, 12 are from a part of the normal perf. 12x11½ sheets. They were caused by a partial deviation of the original perforating.

Wrybill (Torea) — A3

1898-1900			*Perf. 11*	
15	A3	½p blue ('00)	6.50	*15.00*
a.		"d" omitted at upper right	*1,750.*	
b.		½p steel blue (1st setting)	37.50	*52.50*
c.		½p steel blue (2nd setting)	23.00	*25.00*
16	A2	1p brown	32.50	21.00
a.		1p bistre brown ('00)	25.00	25.00
17	A2	1p blue	6.00	5.50
18	A2	1½p violet	19.00	7.50
a.		1½p deep mauve ('00)	11.00	7.50
19	A3	2p chocolate ('00)	15.00	8.50
a.		2p brown, thin toned paper ('00)	14.00	7.50
20	A2	2½p car rose ('00)	25.00	13.00
a.		2½p pale rose	55.00	45.00
21	A2	5p olive gray	30.00	21.00
22	A3	6p red violet ('00)	24.00	*29.00*
a.		6p purple, thin toned paper	29.00	*32.50*
23	A2	10p green	26.00	*57.50*
24	A3	1sh car rose ('00)	57.50	57.50
a.		1sh red, thin toned paper	70.00	*80.00*
		Nos. 15-24 (10)	241.50	*235.50*

The first setting of No. 15 is distinguished by the misplacement of the "½d" in each corner. In the second setting, these values are correctly positioned.

No. 17 Surcharged in Black

1899				
25	A2	½p on 1p blue	40.00	*50.00*
a.		Double surcharge	1,000.	*1,200.*
b.		Inverted surcharge	1,200.	1,100.

No. 16 Overprinted in Black

1901				
26	A2	1p brown	210.00	160.00
a.		Inverted overprint	2,400.	1,900.
c.		Double overprint	1,900.	1,900.

Some single stamps were overprinted by favor. Other varieties could exist.

Forgeries exist.

Types of 1893-98

1902			**Unwmk.**	
27	A3	½p green	10.00	10.00
a.		Vert. pair, imperf. horiz.	*1,400.*	
b.		½p blue green	7.50	*8.25*
28	A2	1p rose	16.00	*21.00*
a.		1p rose lake	12.50	7.50
29	A2	2½p dull blue	15.00	*25.00*
		Nos. 27-29 (3)	41.00	*56.00*

1902	Wmk. 61		*Perf. 11*	
30	A3	½p green	4.25	*3.75*
a.		½p gray green	25.00	*55.00*
31	A2	1p rose	4.75	*3.50*
32	A2	1½p brt violet	4.75	*10.00*
33	A3	2p chocolate	11.00	*12.00*
a.		Figures of value omitted	*2,750.*	*3,600.*
b.		Perf. 11x14	*2,600.*	
34	A2	2½p dull blue	4.50	*8.25*
35	A2	5p olive gray	42.50	*57.50*
36	A3	6p purple	37.50	*32.50*
37	A2	10p blue green	55.00	*120.00*
38	A3	1sh car rose	55.00	*82.50*
a.		Perf. 11x14	*3,000.*	
		Nos. 30-38 (9)	219.25	*330.00*

1909-19		*Perf. 14, 14x14½, 14½x14*		
39	A3	½p green, perf 14½x14 ('11)	13.00	*9.50*
a.		½p dp grn, perf 14 ('15)	42.50	*17.50*
b.		As "a," wmk upright	14.00	*22.50*
40	A2	1p red, wmk. sideways ('09)	15.00	5.00
a.		1p red, wmk. upright, perf 14	40.00	35.00
b.		1p red, chalky paper, perf 14	7.50	4.25
c.		1p red, chalky paper, perf 14x14½	6.50	*7.00*
41	A2	1½p purple, perf 14x15 ('16)	21.00	4.75
a.		1½p purple, perf 14 ('15)	87.50	47.50
42	A3	2p dp brown ('19)	6.00	*57.50*
43	A2	10p dp green ('18)	40.00	*110.00*
44	A3	1sh car rose ('19)	32.50	*110.00*
		Nos. 39-44 (6)	127.50	*296.75*

Nos. 39-40 are on both ordinary and chalky paper; Nos. 41-44 on chalky paper.

New Zealand Stamps of 1909-19 Surcharged in Dark Blue or Red

1919		Typo.	*Perf. 14x15*	
48	A43	½p yel green (R)	.45	*1.25*
a.		Pair, one without surcharge		
49	A42	1p carmine	1.25	*5.00*
50	A47	1½p brown org (R)	.60	*.90*
51	A43	2p yellow (R)	1.75	*2.00*
52	A43	3p chocolate	3.25	*15.00*
		Engr.	*Perf. 14x14½*	
53	A44	2½p dull blue (R)	2.75	2.50
a.		Perf 14x13½	2.75	*7.50*
54	A45	3p violet brown	3.00	2.00
a.		Perf 14x13½	2.25	*9.50*
55	A45	4p purple	2.25	*4.25*
a.		Perf 14x13½	2.25	*6.50*
56	A44	4½p dark green	2.25	*9.50*
a.		Perf 14x13½	2.25	*8.00*
57	A45	6p car rose	2.00	*5.50*
a.		Perf 14x13½	3.50	*10.00*
58	A44	7½p red brown, perf 14x13½	2.10	*6.50*
59	A45	9p ol green (R)	3.75	*17.50*
a.		Perf 14x13½	3.75	*17.50*
60	A45	1sh vermilion	3.25	*30.00*
a.		Perf 14x13½	13.00	*35.00*
		Nos. 48-60 (13)	28.65	*101.90*

The Polynesian surcharge restates the denomination of the basic stamp.

Vertical Pairs, Perf 14x14½ and 14x13½

53b	#53 + #53a	23.00	*52.50*
	Block of four, never hinged	65.00	
54b	#54 + #54a	25.00	*57.50*
	Block of four, never hinged	77.50	
55b	#55 + #55a	23.00	*65.00*
	Block of four, never hinged	67.50	
56b	#56 + #56a	23.00	*75.00*
	Block of four, never hinged	67.50	
57b	#57 + #57a	45.00	*100.00*
	Block of four, never hinged	140.00	
59b	#59 + #59a	45.00	*125.00*
	Block of four, never hinged	140.00	
60b	#60 + #60a	55.00	*140.00*
	Block of four, never hinged	175.00	

The Polynesian surcharge restates the denomination of the basic stamp.

Landing of Capt. Cook A4

Avarua Waterfront A5

Capt. James Cook — A6

Palm — A7

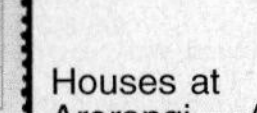
Houses at Arorangi — A8

Avarua Harbor — A9

1920 Unwmk. Engr. *Perf. 14*

61 A4 ½p green & black 4.75 *30.00*
62 A5 1p car & black 5.50 *30.00*
  a. Center inverted *875.00*
63 A6 1½p blue & black 10.00 10.00
64 A7 3p red brn & blk 2.50 *6.50*
65 A8 6p org & red brn 4.25 *10.00*
66 A9 1sh vio & black 8.00 *20.00*
  a. Center inverted *875.00*
  Nos. 61-66 (6) 35.00 *106.50*

The stamps overprinted or inscribed "Rarotonga" were used throughout the Cook Islands.

For surcharges see Nos. 78, 79.

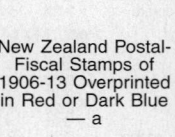

New Zealand Postal-Fiscal Stamps of 1906-13 Overprinted in Red or Dark Blue — a

Perf. 14, 14½, 14x14½

1921 Typo. Wmk. 61

67 PF1 2sh blue (R) 32.50 *65.00*
68 PF1 2sh6p brown 22.50 *60.00*
69 PF1 5sh green (R) 32.50 *77.50*
70 PF1 10sh claret 90.00 *140.00*
71 PF2 £1 rose 150.00 *260.00*
  Nos. 67-71 (5) 327.50 *602.50*

Types of 1920 Issue

1924-26 Engr. *Perf. 14*

72 A4 ½p yel grn & black 5.25 10.00
73 A5 1p carmine & black 7.00 2.50

Issued: ½p, May 13, 1926; 1p, Nov. 10, 1924.

New Zealand Stamps of 1926 Overprinted in Red

1926-28 Typo. *Perf. 14, 14½x14*

74 A56 2sh blue ('27) 19.00 *47.50*
  a. 2sh dark blue 12.00 *47.50*
75 A56 3sh violet ('28) 19.00 *50.00*

Rarotongan Chief (Te Po) — A10

Avarua Harbor — A11

1927, Oct. 15 Engr. *Perf. 14*

76 A10 2½p dk bl & red brn 8.00 *29.00*
77 A11 4p dull vio & bl grn 13.00 *20.00*

No. 63 Surcharged in Red

1931 Unwmk.

78 A6 2p on 1½p blue & blk 11.00 4.75

Same Surcharge on Type of 1920

Wmk. 61

79 A6 2p on 1½p blue & blk 5.50 *13.00*

No. 79 was not issued without surcharge.

New Zealand Postal-Fiscal Stamps of 1931-32 Overprinted Type "a" in Blue or Red

1931, Nov. 12 Typo.

80 PF5 2sh6p dp brown (Bl) 16.00 *26.00*
81 PF5 5sh green (R) 27.50 *65.00*
82 PF5 10sh dk car (Bl) 45.00 *110.00*
83 PF5 £1 pink (Bl) ('32) 125.00 *200.00*
  Nos. 80-83 (4) 213.50 *401.00*

See Nos. 103-108, 124A-126C.

Landing of Capt. Cook — A12

Capt. James Cook — A13

Double Canoe — A14

Islanders Unloading Ship — A15

View of Avarua Harbor — A16

R.M.S. Monowai — A17

King George V — A18

Unwmk.

1932, Mar. 16 Engr. *Perf. 13*

Center in Black

84 A12 ½p deep green 4.00 *19.00*
  a. Perf. 14 32.50 *105.00*
85 A13 1p brown lake 7.75 5.25
  a. Center inverted *9,500.* *9,500.*
  b. Perf. 14 17.50 *32.50*
86 A14 2p brown 3.50 *8.75*
  b. Perf. 14 10.00 *24.00*
87 A15 2½p dark ultra 27.50 *70.00*
  b. Perf. 14 20.00 *65.00*

Perf. 14

88 A16 4p ultra 12.00 *65.00*
  a. Perf. 13 32.50 *75.00*
  b. Perf. 14x13 35.00 *130.00*
89 A17 6p orange 5.00 *17.50*
  a. Perf. 13 30.00 *57.50*
90 A18 1sh deep violet 24.00 *26.00*
  Nos. 84-90 (7) 83.75 *211.50*

Nos. 84 to 90 were available for postage in Aitutaki, Penrhyn and Rarotonga and replaced the special issues for those islands.

Inverted centers of the ½p (value $1,000), 1p (value $550), and 2p (value $3,500) are from printers waste.

1933-36 Wmk. 61 *Perf. 14*

91 A12 ½p dp grn & blk 1.20 *5.25*
92 A13 1p dk car & black ('35) 1.50 *2.40*
93 A14 2p brn & blk ('36) 1.75 .60
94 A15 2½p dk ultra & blk 1.75 *2.50*
95 A16 4p blue & black 1.75 .60
96 A17 6p org & blk ('36) 2.00 *2.50*
97 A18 1sh dp vio & black ('36) 27.50 *42.50*
  Nos. 91-97 (7) 37.45 *56.35*

See Nos. 116-121.

Silver Jubilee Issue

Types of 1932 Overprinted in Black or Red

1935, May 7

98 A13 1p dk car & brn red .65 *1.50*
99 A15 2½p dk ultra & bl (R) 2.00 *3.50*
100 A17 6p dull org & green 7.00 *7.00*
  Nos. 98-100 (3) 9.65 *12.00*
  Set, never hinged 16.00

The vertical spacing of the overprint is wider on No. 100.

New Zealand Stamps of 1926 Overprinted in Black — b

1936, July 15 Typo. *Perf. 14*

101 A56 2sh blue 15.00 *50.00*
102 A56 3sh violet 16.00 *80.00*

1931-35 New Zealand Postal-Fiscal Stamps Ovptd. Type "b" in Black or Red

1932-36

103 PF5 2sh6p brown ('36) 47.50 *110.00*
104 PF5 5sh grn (R) ('36) 52.50 *130.00*
105 PF5 10sh dk car ('36) 92.50 *250.00*
106 PF5 £1 pink ('36) 125.00 *275.00*
107 PF5 £3 lt grn (R) 500.00 *900.00*
108 PF5 £5 dk blue (R) 250.00 *400.00*
  Nos. 103-108 (6) 1,068. *2,065.*

Issue dates: Mar. 1932, July 15, 1936.

New Zealand Stamps of 1937 Overprinted in Black

Perf. 14x13½

1937, June 1 Engr. Wmk. 253

109 A78 1p rose carmine .25 .25
110 A78 2½p dark blue .25 .25
111 A78 6p vermilion .35 .30
  Nos. 109-111 (3) .85 .80
  Set, never hinged 2.25

King George VI A19

Village and Palms A20

Coastal Scene with Canoe — A21

1938, May 2 Wmk. 61 *Perf. 14*

112 A19 1sh dp violet & blk 6.00 *13.00*
113 A20 2sh dk red brn & blk 12.00 16.00
114 A21 3sh yel green & blue 32.50 *40.00*
  Nos. 112-114 (3) 50.50 69.00
  Set, never hinged 90.00

See Nos. 122-124.

Mt. Ikurangi behind Avarua — A22

Perf. 13½x14

1940, Sept. 2 Engr. Wmk. 253

115 A22 3p on 1½p violet & blk .80 .70

Issued only with surcharge. Stamps without surcharge are from the printer's archives. Value $275.

Types of 1932-38

1944-46 Engr. *Perf. 14*

116 A12 ½p dk ol grn & blk ('45) 1.00 *4.50*
117 A13 1p dk car & blk ('45) 1.50 1.25
118 A14 2p brn & blk ('46) .90 *7.00*
119 A15 2½p dk bl & blk ('45) .60 *2.00*
120 A16 4p blue & black 2.50 *15.00*
121 A17 6p org & black 1.00 *2.50*
122 A19 1sh dp vio & blk 1.00 *3.50*
123 A20 2sh dk red brn & blk 27.50 *50.00*
124 A21 3sh yel green & blue ('45) 25.00 *40.00*
  Nos. 116-124 (9) 61.00 125.75
  Set, never hinged 100.00

New Zealand Nos. AR76, AR78, AR86 and Type of 1931 Postal-Fiscal Stamps Overprinted Type "b" in Black or Red

1943-50 Wmk. 253 Typo. *Perf. 14*

124A PF5 2sh6p brn ('51) 37.50 *37.50*
125 PF5 5sh green (R) 8.25 *37.50*
126 PF5 10sh dp pink ('51) 42.50 *100.00*
126A PF5 £1 pink ('54) 42.50 *110.00*
126B PF5 £3 lt grn (R) ('53) 40.00 *175.00*
126C PF5 £5 dk bl (R) ('54) 200.00 *400.00*
  Nos. 124A-126C (6) 370.75 *860.00*

Values for Nos. 124A-126C are for the second printing with watermarks inverted.

Set, never hinged 550.00

For surcharges see Nos. 192-194 in Scott Standard catalogue, Vol. 2.

Catalogue values for unused stamps in this section, from this point to the end of the section, are for Never Hinged items.

Peace Issue

New Zealand Nos. 248, 250, 254 and 255 Overprinted in Black or Blue

c

d

Perf. 13x13½, 13½x13

1946, June 1 **Engr.**

No.	Type	Denom.	Description	Unused	Used
127	A94 (c)	1p	emerald	.30	.25
128	A96 (d)	2p	rose vio (Bl)	.35	.35
129	A100(c)	6p	org red & red brn	.80	.70
130	A101(c)	8p	brn lake & blk (Bl)	.55	.55
			Nos. 127-130 (4)	2.00	1.85

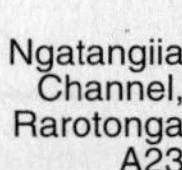

Ngatangiia Channel, Rarotonga A23

Capt. James Cook Statue and Map of Cook Islands — A24

Designs: 1p, Cook and map of Hervey Isls. 2p, Rev. John Williams, his ship Messenger of Peace, and map of Rarotonga. 3p, Aitutaki map and palms. 5p, Mail plane landing at Rarotonga airport. 6p, Tongareva (Penrhyn) scene. 8p, Islander's house, Rarotonga. 2sh, Thatched house, mat weaver. 3sh, Steamer Matua offshore.

Perf. 13½x13, 13x13½

1949, Aug.1 **Engr.** **Wmk. 253**

No.	Type	Denom.	Description	Unused	Used
131	A23	½p	brown & violet	.25	*1.25*
132	A23	1p	green & orange	3.00	3.00
133	A23	2p	carmine & brn	1.75	3.00
134	A23	3p	ultra & green	4.50	*1.75*
135	A23	5p	purple & grn	5.00	1.25
136	A23	6p	car rose & blk	5.25	2.25
137	A23	8p	orange & olive	.65	*2.25*
138	A24	1sh	chocolate & bl	3.50	3.00
139	A24	2sh	rose car & brn	5.00	*11.00*
140	A24	3sh	bl grn & lt ultra	17.50	*27.50*
			Nos. 131-140 (10)	46.40	*56.25*

For surcharge see No. 147 in Scott Standard catalogue, Vol 2.

CORFU

kor-'fü

LOCATION — An island in the Ionian Sea opposite the Greek-Albanian border
GOVT. — A department of Greece
AREA — 245 sq. mi.
POP. — 114,620 (1938)
CAPITAL — Corfu

In 1923 Italy occupied Corfu (Kerkyra) during a controversy with Greece over the assassination of an Italian official in Epirus.

100 Centesimi = 1 Lira
100 Lepta = 1 Drachma

Watermark

Wmk. 140 — Crown

ISSUED UNDER ITALIAN OCCUPATION

Italian Stamps of 1901-23 Overprinted

1923, Sept. 20 **Wmk. 140** ***Perf. 14***

No.	Type	Denom.	Description	Unused	Used
N1	A48	5c	green	6.00	*11.00*
			Never hinged	14.00	
			On cover		80.00
N2	A48	10c	claret	6.00	*11.00*
			Never hinged	14.00	
			On cover		80.00
N3	A48	15c	slate	6.00	*11.00*
			Never hinged	14.50	
			On cover		90.00
N4	A50	20c	brown orange	6.00	*11.00*
			Never hinged	14.50	
			On cover		90.00
N5	A49	30c	orange brown	6.00	*11.00*
			Never hinged	14.50	
			On cover		125.00
N6	A49	50c	violet	6.00	*11.00*
			Never hinged	14.50	
			On cover		80.00
N7	A49	60c	blue	6.00	*11.00*
			Never hinged	14.50	
			On cover		100.00
a.			Vert. pair, one without overprint	*1,500.*	
N8	A46	1 l	brown & green	6.00	*11.00*
			Never hinged	14.50	
			On cover		175.00
			Nos. N1-N8 (8)	48.00	*88.00*
			Set, never hinged	115.00	

Italian Stamps of 1901-23 Surcharged

1923, Sept. 24

No.	Type	Surcharge	Description	Unused	Used
N9	A48	25 l	on 10c claret	60.00	45.00
			Never hinged	110.00	
			On cover		140.00
N10	A49	60 l	on 25c blue	10.00	
			Never hinged	16.00	
N11	A49	70 l	on 30c org brn	10.00	
			Never hinged	16.00	
N12	A49	1.20d	on 50c violet	25.00	*45.00*
			Never hinged	50.00	
			On cover		140.00
N13	A46	2.40d	on 1 l brn & grn	25.00	*45.00*
			Never hinged	50.00	
			On cover		175.00
N14	A46	4.75d	on 2 l grn & org	15.00	
			Never hinged	25.00	
			Nos. N9-N14 (6)	145.00	
			Set, never hinged	267.00	
			#N9, N12-N13 on overfranked philatelic cover		600.00

Nos. N10, N11, N14 were not placed in use.

COSTA RICA

ˌkōs-tə-'rē-kə

LOCATION — Central America between Nicaragua and Panama
GOVT. — Republic
AREA — 19,344 sq. mi.
POP. — 2,450,226 (1984)
CAPITAL — San Jose

8 Reales = 100 Centavos = 1 Peso
100 Centimos = 1 Colon (1900)

Watermarks

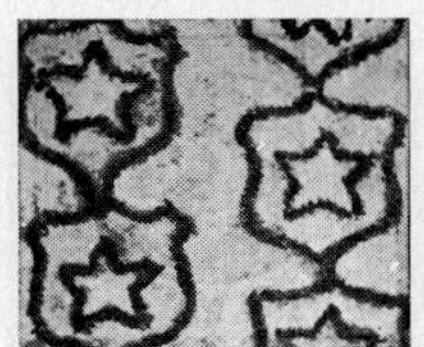

Wmk. 215 — Small Star in Shield, Multiple

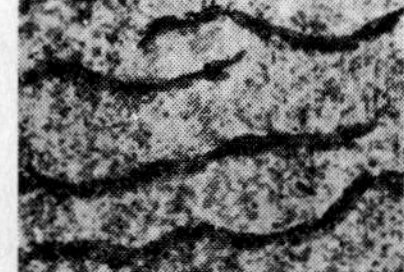
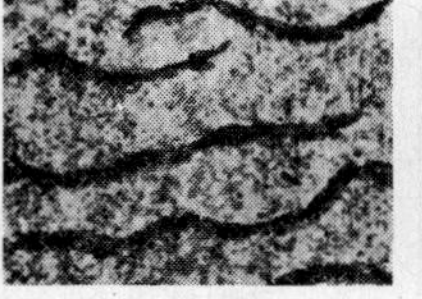

Wmk. 229 — Wavy Lines

Values for unused stamps are for examples with original gum as defined in the catalogue introduction. Very fine examples of Nos. 1-22 will have perforations just clear of the design on one or more sides due to the placement of the stamps on the plates and to imperfect perforating methods.

Coat of Arms — A1

1863 **Unwmk.** **Engr.** ***Perf. 12***

No.	Type	Denom.	Description	Unused	Used
1	A1	½r	blue	.40	*1.10*
a.			½r light blue	.40	*1.10*
b.			Pair, imperf. horiz.	*6,000.*	
2	A1	2r	scarlet	1.75	*2.25*
3	A1	4r	green	16.00	*16.00*
4	A1	1p	orange	42.50	*42.50*
			Nos. 1-4 (4)	60.65	61.85

The ½r was printed from two plates. The second is in light blue with little or no sky over the mountains.

Imperforate stamps of Nos. 1-2 are corner stamps from poorly perforated sheets.

Nos. 1-3 Surcharged in Red or Black

a

b

c

d

e

1881-82 **Red or Black Surcharge**

No.	Type	Description	Unused	Used
7	A1(a)	1c on ½r ('82)	3.00	*6.00*
a.		On No. 1a	15.00	—
8	A1(b)	1c on ½r ('82)	18.00	*30.00*
9	A1(c)	2c on ½r, #1a	3.00	2.75
a.		On No. 1	8.00	—
12	A1(c)	5c on ½r	15.00	
13	A1(d)	5c on ½r ('82)	65.00	
14	A1(d)	10c on 2r (Bk) ('82)	72.50	—
15	A1(e)	20c on 4r ('82)	300.00	—

Overprints with different fonts and "OFICIAL" were never placed in use, and are said to have been surcharged to a dealer's order. The ½r surcharged "DOS CTS" is not a postage stamp. It probably is an essay.

Postally used examples of Nos. 7-15 are rare. Nos. 13-15 exist with a favor cancel having a hyphen between "San" and "Jose." Values same as unused. Fake cancellations exist.

Counterfeits exist of surcharges on Nos. 7-15.

Gen. Prospero Fernández — A6

1883, Jan. 1

No.	Type	Denom.	Description	Unused	Used
16	A6	1c	green	3.00	1.50
17	A6	2c	carmine	3.25	1.50
18	A6	5c	blue violet	32.50	2.00
19	A6	10c	orange	150.00	12.00
20	A6	40c	blue	3.00	*3.00*
			Nos. 16-20 (5)	191.75	20.00

Unused examples of 40c usually lack gum.

For overprints see Nos. O1-O20, O24, Guanacaste 1-38, 44.

President Bernardo Soto Alfaro — A7

1887

No.	Type	Denom.	Description	Unused	Used
21	A7	5c	blue violet	7.00	.50
22	A7	10c	orange	4.00	3.00

Unused examples of 5c usually lack gum.

For overprints see Nos. O22-O23, Guanacaste 42-43, 45.

A8

A9

1889 **Black Overprint**

No.	Type	Denom.	Description	Unused	Used
23	A8	1c	rose	5.00	3.00
24	A9	5c	brown	7.00	3.00

Vertical and inverted overprints are fakes.

For overprints see Guanacaste Nos. 47-54.

President Soto Alfaro

A10 A11

A12

A13

A14

A15

A16

A17

A18

A19

1889 ***Perf. 14-16 & Compound***

25	A10	1c brown	.35	*.45*
a.		Horiz. pair, imperf. vert	*150.00*	
b.		Imperf. pair	*150.00*	
c.		Horiz. or vert. pair, imperf. btwn.	*150.00*	
26	A11	2c dark green	.35	*.45*
a.		Imperf., pair	50.00	
b.		Vert. pair, imperf. horiz.	125.00	
c.		Horiz. pair, imperf. btwn.	125.00	
27	A12	5c orange	.45	.35
a.		Imperf., pair		*750.00*
b.		Horiz. pair, imperf. btwn.	*350.00*	
28	A13	10c red brown	.40	.35
a.		Vert. or horiz. pair, imperf. btwn.	*150.00*	*500.00*
29	A14	20c yellow green	.30	*.35*
a.		Vert. pair, imperf. horiz.	200.00	
b.		Horizontal pair, imperf. btwn.	*150.00*	
30	A15	50c rose red	1.00	
		Telegram cancel		.75
31	A16	1p blue	1.25	
		Telegram cancel		.75
32	A17	2p dull violet	6.00	
a.		2p slate	6.00	
		Telegram cancel		4.00
33	A18	5p olive green	25.00	
		Telegram cancel		10.00
34	A19	10p black	100.00	
		Telegram cancel		45.00
		Nos. 25-34 (10)	135.10	1.95

Nos. 30-34 normally were used on telegrams and most examples were removed from the forms and sold by the government.

Most unused examples of No. 34 have no gum or only part gum. These sell for somewhat less.

For overprints see Nos. O25-O30, Guanacaste 55-67.

Arms of Costa Rica
A20 A21

A22

A23

A24 A25

A26 A27

A28 A29

1892 ***Perf. 12-15 & Compound***

35	A20	1c grnsh blue	.30	*.40*
36	A21	2c yellow	.30	*.40*
37	A22	5c red lilac	.30	.25
a.		5c violet	60.00	.30
38	A23	10c lt green	.80	.35
a.		Horiz. pair, imperf. btwn.	—	*100.00*
39	A24	20c scarlet	12.00	.25
a.		Horiz. pair, imperf. btwn.	—	*100.00*
40	A25	50c gray blue	4.00	*4.25*
41	A26	1p green, *yel*	1.25	1.00
42	A27	2p brown red, *lilac*	3.00	1.00
a.		2p rose red, *pale lil*	12.00	1.00
43	A28	5p dk blue, *blue*	2.00	1.00
44	A29	10p brown, *pale buff*	35.00	5.00
a.		10p brown, *yellow*	8.00	
		Nos. 35-44 (10)	58.95	13.90

Imperfs. of Nos. 35-44 are proofs.
For overprints see Nos. O31-O36.

Statue of Juan Santamaría
A30

Juan Mora Fernández
A31

View of Port Limón — A32

Braulio Carrillo ("Branlio" on stamp) — A33

National Theater — A34

José M. Castro — A35

Birris Bridge — A36

Juan Rafael Mora — A37

Jesús Jiménez — A38

Coat of Arms — A39

1901, Jan. ***Perf. 12-15½***

45	A30	1c green & blk	3.25	.30
a.		Horiz. pair, imperf. btwn.	*150.00*	
46	A31	2c ver & blk	1.25	.30
47	A32	5c gray blue & blk	3.25	.30
a.		Vert. pair, imperf. btwn.	—	*300.00*
48	A33	10c ocher & blk	3.25	.35
49	A34	20c lake & blk	22.50	.25
a.		Vert. pair, imperf. btwn.	*1,000.*	
50	A35	50c dull lil & dk bl	5.50	1.00
51	A36	1col ol bis & blk	110.00	3.50
52	A37	2col car rose & dk grn	16.00	3.00
53	A38	5col brown & blk	75.00	3.50
54	A39	10col yel grn & brn red	29.00	3.00
		Nos. 45-54 (10)	269.00	15.50

The 2c exists with center inverted. Value $77,500.

Nos. 45-57 in other colors are private reprints made in 1948. They have little value.

For surcharge and overprints see Nos. 58, 78, O37-O44.

Remainders

In 1914 the government sold a large quantity of stamps at very much less than face value. The lot included most regular issues from 1901 to 1911 inclusive, postage due stamps of 1903 and Official stamps of 1901-03. These stamps were canceled with groups of thin parallel bars. The higher valued used stamps, such as Nos. 64, 65-68a, sell for much less than the values quoted, which are for stamps with regular postal cancellations. A few sell for much higher prices.

José M. Cañas — A40

Julián Volio — A41

Eusebio Figueroa Oreamuno — A42

1903 ***Perf. 13½, 14, 15***

55	A40	4c red vio & blk	2.00	.70
56	A41	6c olive grn & blk	7.25	4.00
57	A42	25c gray lil & brn	16.00	.30
		Nos. 55-57 (3)	25.25	5.00

See note on private reprints following No. 54.
For overprints see Nos. 81, O45-O47.

No. 49 Surcharged in Black:

1905

58	A34	1c on 20c lake & blk	.60	.60
a.		Inverted surcharge	10.00	10.00
b.		Diagonal surcharge	.60	.60

Examples surcharged in other colors are proofs.

Statue of Juan Santamaría
A43

Juan Mora Fernández
A44

José M. Cañas
A45

Mauro Fernández
A46

Braulio Carrillo — A47

Julián Volio — A48

Eusebio Figueroa Oreamuno
A49

José M. Castro
A50

Jesús Jiménez — A51

Juan Rafael Mora — A52

Perf. 11x14, 14 (1c, 5c, 10c, 25c)

1907 **Unwmk.**

59	A43	1c red brn & ind	8.00	.40
a.		Perf. 11x14	60.00	3.00
b.		Imperf pair	15.00	—
60	A44	2c yel grn & blk	3.00	.30
a.		Perf. 14	3.00	.30
b.		Imperf pair	15.00	—
61	A45	4c car & indigo	12.00	2.50
a.		Perf. 14	500.00	45.00
b.		Imperf pair	15.00	—
62	A46	5c yel & dull bl	3.00	.30
a.		Perf. 11x14	60.00	1.00
b.		Imperf pair	15.00	—
63	A47	10c blue & blk	10.00	.50
a.		Perf. 11x14	20.00	1.00
b.		Imperf pair	30.00	—
64	A48	20c olive grn & blk	25.00	6.00
a.		Perf. 14	25.00	6.00
		Remainder cancel		2.00
b.		Imperf pair	—	
65	A49	25c gray lil & blk	3.00	3.00
		Remainder cancel		1.00
a.		Perf. 11x14	150.00	50.00
b.		Imperf pair	—	
66	A50	50c red lil & blue	75.00	25.00
		Remainder cancel		2.00
a.		Perf. 14	175.00	50.00
b.		Imperf pair	100.00	
67	A51	1col brown & blk	25.00	20.00
a.		Perf. 14	25.00	20.00
		Remainder cancel		2.00
b.		Imperf pair	—	
68	A52	2col claret & grn	160.00	100.00
		Remainder cancel		3.00
a.		Perf. 14	300.00	150.00
b.		Imperf pair	200.00	
		Nos. 59-68 (10)	324.00	158.00

The remainder cancel value applies to both perforations.

The imperforate varieties of the above set are valued without gum. Ungummed stamps were probably placed on the market in London, while gummed stamps appear to have been sent to Costa Rica and accepted for postal use. There is a small premium for gummed stamps.

The 1c, 2c, 5c, 20c, 50c, 1 col and 2 col exist with center inverted. Value, set $62,500.

Nos. 59-68 exist with papermaker's watermark.

No. 65b with brown vignette is a proof. Value, pair $40. The actual No. 65b (black vignette) is worth much more.

For overprints see Nos. 77, 79-80, 82-84, O48-O55, O60-O64.

Statue of Juan Santamaria
A53

Juan Mora Fernández
A54

José M. Cañas
A55

Mauro Fernández
A56

Braulio Carrillo — A57

Julián Volio — A58

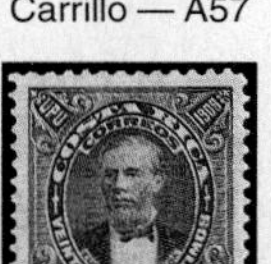
Eusebio Figueroa Oreamuno A59

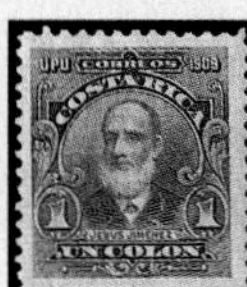
Jesús Jiménez A60

1910 *Perf. 12*

69 A53 1c brown .25 .25
70 A54 2c dp green .30 .25
71 A55 4c scarlet .35 .35
72 A56 5c orange 1.00 .25
73 A57 10c deep blue .40 .25
74 A58 20c olive grn .50 .35
75 A59 25c dp violet 17.00 1.50
76 A60 1col dk brown .50 .50
Nos. 69-76 (8) 20.30 3.70

For overprints and surcharge see Nos. 111C-111J, B1, C2, O56-O59.

No. 60a Overprinted in Red

1911 *Perf. 14*

77 A44 2c yel grn & blk 3.00 1.10
a. Inverted overprint 6.00 5.00
b. Double overprint, both inverted 45.00

Stamps of 1901-07 Overprinted in Red or Black

78 A30 1c grn & blk (R) 3.00 1.00
a. Black overprint 32.50 18.00
b. Inverted overprint
79 A43 1c red brn & ind (Bk) 1.25 .40
a. Inverted overprint 4.50 3.50
b. Double overprint 5.50 5.00
80 A44 2c yel grn & blk (Bk) 1.00 .40
a. Inverted overprint 3.75 3.50
b. Dbl. ovpt., one as on No. 77 40.00 27.50
c. Double overprint, one inverted 15.00 15.00
d. Pair, one stamp No. 77 25.00 18.00
e. Perf. 11x14 30.00 *1.00*

No. 55 Overprinted in Black

81 A40 4c red vio & blk 1.50 .65

Stamps of 1907 Overprinted in Blue, Black or Rose

Perf. 14, 11x14 (#83, 84)

82 A46 5c yel & bl (Bl) 2.00 .25
a. "Habilitada" 3.25 2.50
b. "2911" 5.50 3.25
c. Roman "I" in "1911" 4.00 2.50
d. Double overprint 5.50 5.00
e. Inverted overprint 6.00 3.75
f. Black overprint *250.00* 2.00
g. Triple overprint 6.00
h. Vert. pair, imperf. horiz. *100.00*
83 A47 10c blue & blk (Bk) 5.00 1.40
a. As #83, Roman "I" in "1911" 7.00 5.00
c. As #83, double overprint 20.00 11.50
d. Perf. 14 45.00 5.25
84 A47 10c blue & blk (R) 15.00 13.50
a. Roman "I" in "1911" *100.00 100.00*
c. Perf. 14 *100.00 100.00*
Nos. 77-84 (8) 31.75 18.70

Many counterfeits of overprint exist.

Telegraph Stamps Surcharged in Rose, Blue or Black

A61

A62

A63

1911 *Perf. 12*

86 A61 1c on 10c bl (R) .50 .25
a. "Coereos" 7.75 6.00
b. Inverted surcharge
87 A61 1c on 10c bl (Bk) *210.00 87.50*
88 A61 1c on 25c vio (Bk) .50 .25
a. "Coereos" 8.75 6.00
b. Pair, one without surcharge 20.00
c. Double surcharge 9.00
e. Double surch., one inverted 12.50
89 A61 1c on 50c red brn (Bl) .55 .40
a. Inverted surcharge 5.50 5.00
b. Double surcharge 4.50
90 A61 1c on 1col brn (R) .55 .40
91 A61 1c on 5col red (Bl) 1.00 .55
92 A61 1c on 10col dk brn (R) 1.50 .70

Perf. 14

93 A62 2c on 5c brn org (Bk) 3.50 1.90
a. Inverted surcharge *9.00 3.75*
b. "Correos" inverted *17.50*
c. Double surcharge 9.00

Perf. 14x11

94 A62 2c on 10c bl (R) 100.00 100.00
a. Perf. 14 *350.00 350.00*
b. "Correos" inverted 2,000.
c. As "b," perf. 14 —
95 A62 2c on 50c cl (Bk) 1.00 .55
a. Inverted surcharge 4.50 3.25
b. Double surcharge 12.50
c. Perf. 14 45.00 20.00
96 A62 2c on 1col brn (Bk) 1.25 .70
a. Inverted surcharge 12.50
b. Double surcharge 16.00
c. Perf. 14 2.00 .80
97 A62 2c on 2col car (Bk) 1.25 .60
a. Inverted surcharge 8.00 5.00
b. "Correos" inverted 10.00 5.50
c. Double surcharge
d. Perf. 14 27.50 16.00
98 A62 2c on 5col grn (Bk) 1.00 .70
a. Inverted surcharge 10.00 7.00
b. "Correos" inverted *16.00 4.25*
c. Perf. 14 6.00 3.00
99 A62 2c on 10col mar (Bk) 1.50 .70
a. "Correos" inverted *400.00*
b. Perf. 14 6.00 3.00

Perf. 12

100 A63 5c on 5c org (Bl) .40 .25
a. Double surcharge 27.50 16.00
b. Inverted surcharge 27.50 9.50
c. Pair, one without surcharge 16.00

Counterfeits exist of Nos. 87, 94 and all minor varieties. Genuine used examples of No. 94 are rare and have a cancel only used on registered mail. Genuine "Coereos" errors do not exist on No. 87. Used examples of No. 94 with target cancels are counterfeits. No. 94c is unique. All examples of Nos. 94b and 94c have stains and are valued thus.

Nos. 93-99 exist with papermaker's watermark.

Coffee Plantation — A64

1921, June 17 **Litho.** *Perf. 11½*

103 A64 5c bl & blk 3.00 3.00
a. Tête bêche pair 15.00 6.50
b. Imperf., pair *40.00*
c. As "a," imperf. *150.00*

Centenary of coffee raising in Costa Rica.

Liberty with Torch of Freedom — A65

1921 **Typo.** *Perf. 11*

104 A65 5c violet 1.00 .40
a. Imperf, pair *100.00*

Cent. of Central American independence.

Beware of trimmed singles that look like No. 104a.

For overprint see No. 111.

Juan Mora and Julio Acosta — A66

1921, Sept. 15 *Perf. 11½*

105 A66 2c orange & blk 2.00 2.00
106 A66 3c green & blk 2.00 2.00
107 A66 6c scarlet & blk 3.75 3.75
108 A66 15c dk blue & blk 8.00 8.00
109 A66 30c orange brn & blk 10.00 10.00
Nos. 105-109 (5) 25.75 25.75

Centenary of Central American independence. Issue requested by Costa Rican Philatelic Society. Authorized by decree calling for 2,000 of 30c and 5,000 each of other values. Nos. 105-109 imperf were not regularly issued. Inverted centers exist of both perf and imperf. They are rare. Used values are for Independence commemorative cancel.

Each sheet of 20 (4x5) contains 5 tête-bêche pairs. Value, set of 5 pairs $40.

Simón Bolívar — A67

1921 **Engr.** *Perf. 12*

110 A67 15c deep violet .75 .25

For overprint see No. 111H. For surcharge see No. 148.

No. 104 Overprinted

1922 *Perf. 11*

111 A65 5c violet .75 .40
a. Inverted overprint 10.00
b. Double overprint 15.00

Stamps of 1910-1921 Overprinted in Blue, Red, Black or Gold

1922 *Perf. 12*

111C A53 1c brown (Bl) .30 .25
111D A54 2c deep green (R) .40 .25
111E A55 4c scarlet .30 .25
111F A56 5c orange 3.00 .40
111G A57 10c deep blue (R) .75 .40
111H A67 15c deep violet (G) 5.50 2.00
Nos. 111C-111H (6) 10.25 3.55

Inverted overprints occur on all values. Value, set $20. Counterfeits predominate.

No. 72 Overprinted

1923

111J A56 5c orange 3.00 .75
k. "VD." for "UD." *75.00 75.00*

Jesús Jiménez — A68

1923, June 18 **Litho.** *Perf. 11½*

112 A68 2c brown .40 .40
113 A68 4c green .40 .40
114 A68 5c blue .60 .40
115 A68 20c carmine .85 .50
116 A68 1col violet 1.10 1.25
Nos. 112-116 (5) 3.35 2.95

Pres. Jesús Jiménez (1823-98).

Nos. 112-116, imperf, were not regularly issued. Value, set $5.

For overprints see Nos. O65-O69.

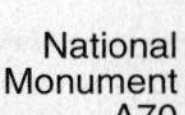
National Monument A70

Harvesting Coffee — A71

Banana Growing — A73

General Post Office A74

Columbus Soliciting Aid of Isabella A75

Christopher Columbus A76

Columbus at Cariari A77

Map of Costa Rica — A78

Manuel M. Gutiérrez — A79

1923-26 **Engr.** ***Perf. 12***

117	A70	1c violet	.25	.25
118	A71	2c yellow	.50	.25
119	A73	4c deep green	.75	.30
120	A74	5c light blue	1.50	.25
121	A74	5c yellow grn ('26)	.50	.25
122	A75	10c red brown	3.00	.25
123	A75	10c car rose ('26)	.50	.25
124	A76	12c carmine rose	10.00	3.00
125	A77	20c deep blue	10.00	.65
126	A78	40c orange	11.00	3.00
127	A79	1col olive green	2.40	.80
		Nos. 117-127 (11)	40.40	9.25

See Nos. 151-156. For surcharges & overprints see Nos. 136-140, 147, 189, 218 (in Scott Standard catalogue, Vol. 2), C2.

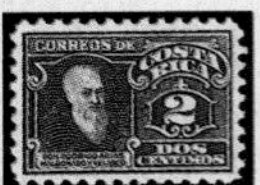
Rodrigo Arias Maldonado — A80

1924 ***Perf. 12½***

128	A80	2c dark green	.25	.25
a.		Perf. 14	.50	.25

See No. 162.

Map of Guanacaste A81

Mission at Nicoya A82

1924 **Litho.** ***Perf. 12***

129	A81	1c carmine rose	.30	.25
130	A81	2c violet	.40	.25
131	A81	5c green	.40	.25
132	A81	10c orange	2.25	.50
133	A82	15c light blue	1.00	.50
134	A82	20c gray black	2.00	1.00
135	A82	25c light brown	3.00	1.50
		Nos. 129-135 (7)	9.35	4.25

Centenary of annexation of Province of Guanacaste to Costa Rica.
Exist imperf. Value, set, $50.

Stamps of 1923 Surcharged

a

b

1925

136	A74(a)	3c on 5c lt blue	.30	.25
137	A75(a)	6c on 10c red brn	.40	.25
138	A78(a)	30c on 40c orange	1.50	.40
139	A79(b)	45c on 1col ol grn	1.75	.50
a.		Double surcharge	*250.00*	
		Nos. 136-139 (4)	3.95	1.40

No. 124 Surcharged

1926

140	A76	10c on 12c car rose	1.50	.30

College of San Luis, Cartago A83

Chapui Asylum, San José — A84

Normal School, Heredia A85

Ruins of Ujarrás A86

1926 **Unwmk.** **Engr.** ***Perf. 12½***

143	A83	3c ultra	.55	.25
144	A84	6c dark brown	.55	.25
145	A85	30c deep orange	3.00	.40
146	A86	45c black violet	5.00	1.60
		Nos. 143-146 (4)	9.10	2.50

For surcharges see Nos. 190-190D, 217 (in Scott Standard catalogue, Vol. 2).

No. 124 Surcharged in Black

1928, Jan. 7 ***Perf. 12***

147	A76	10c on 12c car rose	4.75	4.75

Issued in honor of Col. Charles A. Lindbergh during his Good Will Tour of Central America.
The surcharge was privately reprinted using an original die. Reprints can be distinguished by distinct dots under the "10s." All errors and inverted surcharges are reprints.

No. 110 Surcharged

1928

148	A67	5(c) on 15c dp violet	.25	.25
a.		Inverted surcharge	35.00	

Type I — A88

Type II

Type III

Type IV

Type V

Surcharge Typo. (I-V) & Litho. (V)

1929 ***Perf. 12½***

149	A88	5c on 2col car (I)	.50	.25
a.-d.		Types II-V	.60	.25
e.		Type V (litho.)	3.00	3.00

Telegraph Stamp Surcharged for Postage as in 1929, Surcharge Lithographed

1929

150	A88	13c on 40c deep grn	.35	.25
a.		Inverted surcharge	1.00	1.00

Excellent counterfeits exist of No. 150a.

Types of 1923-26 Issues Dated "1929" Imprint of Waterlow & Sons

1930 **Size: 26x21½mm** ***Perf. 12½***

151	A70	1c dark violet	.70	.25
155	A74	5c green	.70	.25
156	A75	10c carmine rose	.70	.25
		Nos. 151-156 (3)	2.10	.75

Juan Rafael Mora — A89

1931, Jan. 29

157	A89	13c carmine rose	.60	.25

For surcharge see No. 209 in Scott Standard catalogue, Vol. 2.

Seal of Costa Rica Philatelic Society ("Octubre 12 de 1932") — A90

1932, Oct. 12 ***Perf. 12***

158	A90	3c orange	.25	.25
159	A90	5c dark green	.40	.25
160	A90	10c carmine rose	.50	.25
161	A90	20c dark blue	.85	.40
		Nos. 158-161 (4)	2.00	1.15

Phil. Exhib., Oct. 12, 1932. See Nos. 179-183.

Maldonado Type of 1924

1934, Aug. 11 ***Perf. 12½***

162	A80	3c dark green	.25	.25

Red Cross Nurse — A91

1935, May 31 ***Perf. 12***

163	A91	10c rose carmine	7.50	.25

50th anniv. of the founding of the Costa Rican Red Cross Society.

Air View of Cartago A92

Miraculous Statuette and View of Cathedral A93

Vision of 1635 — A94

1935, Aug. 1 ***Perf. 12½***

164	A92	5c green	.25	.25
165	A93	10c carmine	.25	.25
166	A92	30c orange	.25	.25
167	A94	45c dark violet	1.00	.55
168	A93	50c blue black	1.00	1.00
		Nos. 164-168 (5)	2.75	2.30

Tercentenary of the Patron Saint, Our Lady of the Angels, of Costa Rica.

Map of Cocos Island A95

1936, Jan. 29 ***Perf. 14, 11½ (25c)***

169	A95	4c ocher	.50	.25
170	A95	8c dark violet	.65	.25
171	A95	25c orange	.80	.25
172	A95	35c brown vio	.95	.25
173	A95	40c brown	1.25	.40
174	A95	50c yellow	1.50	.60
175	A95	2col yellow grn	11.00	10.00
176	A95	5col green	30.00	25.00
		Nos. 169-176 (8)	46.65	37.00

Exist imperf. Value, set, $50.
For surcharges see Nos. 196-200 (in Scott Standard catalogue, Vol. 2), C55-C56.

Map of Cocos Island and Ships of Columbus A96

1936, Dec. 5 ***Perf. 12***

177	A96	5c green	.40	.25
178	A96	10c carmine rose	.55	.25

For overprints see Nos. 247 (in Scott Standard catalogue, Vol. 2), O80-O81.

Seal of Costa Rica Philatelic Society ("Diciembre 1937") — A97

1937, Dec. 15

179 A97 2c dark brown .45 .25
180 A97 3c black .45 .25
181 A97 5c green .45 .25
182 A97 10c orange red .45 .25
Nos. 179-182 (4) 1.80 1.00

Souvenir Sheet

Imperf

183 Sheet of 4 6.50 4.00
a. A97 2c dark brown .25 .25
b. A97 3c black .25 .25
c. A97 5c green .25 .25
d. A97 10c orange red .25 .25

Phil. Exhib., Dec. 1937.

Purple Guaria Orchid, National Flower — A98

Tuna — A99

Native with Donkey Carrying Bananas A101

3c, Cacao pod. 10c, Coffee harvesting.

1937-38 Wmk. 229 *Perf. 12½*

184 A98 1c green & vio ('38) .55 .25
185 A98 3c chocolate ('38) .55 .25

Unwmk. *Perf. 12*

186 A99 2c olive gray .40 .25
187 A101 5c dark green .55 .25
188 A101 10c carmine rose .90 .25
Nos. 184-188 (5) 2.95 1.25

National Exposition.

No. 125 Overprinted in Black

1938, Sept. 23 Unwmk. *Perf. 12*

189 A77 20c deep blue 1.50 .30

No. 146 Surcharged in Red

a

b

c

d

e

1940 *Perf. 12½*

190 A86(a) 15c on 45c blk vio .60 .30
190A A86(b) 15c on 45c blk vio .60 .30
190B A86(c) 15c on 45c blk vio .60 .30
190C A86(d) 15c on 45c blk vio .60 .30
190D A86(e) 15c on 45c blk vio .60 .30
Nos. 190-190D (5) 3.00 1.50

No. 190D exists with inverted surcharge. Value, $5.

Allegory A103

Black Overprint

1940, Dec. 2 Engr. *Perf. 12*

191 A103 5c green .35 .25
192 A103 10c rose carmine .75 .25
193 A103 20c deep blue 2.00 1.00
194 A103 40c brown 6.00 2.75
195 A103 55c orange yellow 15.00 10.00
Nos. 191-195 (5) 24.10 14.25

Pan-American Health Day. See Nos. C46-C54.
Exist without overprint.

POSTAL-FISCAL STAMPS

From April 1884 through September 1889 revenue stamps were permitted for postal use, when post offices exhausted supplies of regular postage stamps.

Used values are for stamps with postal cancels.

PF1

1884 Engr. *Perf. 12*

AR1 PF1 1c rose .50 *5.00*
AR2 PF1 2c light blue *20.00* 5.00

PF2

1888

AR3 PF2 5c brown .50 *3.00*
AR4 PF2 10c blue *.25* 3.00

Nos. AR2-AR4 are normally found without gum.

SEMI-POSTAL STAMPS

No. 72 Surcharged in Red

1922 Unwmk. *Perf. 12*

B1 A56 5c + 5c orange 1.00 .40

Issued for the benefit of the Costa Rican Red Cross Society. In 1928, owing to a temporary shortage of the ordinary 5c stamp, No. B1 was placed on sale as a regular 5c stamp, the surtax being disregarded.

Discus Thrower SP1

Trophy SP2

Parthenon SP3

1924 Litho. *Imperf.*

B2 SP1 5c dark green 1.60 *2.00*
B3 SP2 10c carmine 1.60 *2.00*
B4 SP3 20c dark blue 20.00 *20.00*
a. Tête bêche pair 60.00 *60.00*

Perf. 12

B5 SP1 5c dark green 1.60 *2.25*
B6 SP2 10c carmine 1.60 *2.25*
B7 SP3 20c dark blue 3.50 *4.00*
a. Tête bêche pair 16.00 *20.00*
Nos. B2-B7 (6) 29.90 *32.50*

These stamps were sold at a premium of 10c each, to help defray the expenses of athletic games held at San José in Dec. 1924.

AIR POST STAMPS

Airplane AP1

Perf. 12½

1926, June 4 Unwmk. Engr.

C1 AP1 20c ultramarine 3.00 .65

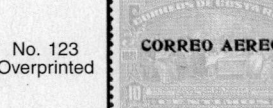

No. 123 Overprinted

1930, Mar. 14 *Perf. 12*

C2 A75 10c carmine rose 2.00 .25

Inverted or double overprints are fakes.

AP3

1930-32 *Perf. 12½*

C3 AP3 5c on 10c dk brn ('32) .40 .25
C4 AP3 20c on 50c ultra .50 .25
C5 AP3 40c on 50c ultra .60 .25
Nos. C3-C5 (3) 1.50 .75

The existence of genuine inverted or double surcharges of Nos. C3-C5 is in doubt.

Telegraph Stamp Overprinted

1930, Mar. 19

C6 AP3 1col orange 2.00 .50

No. O79 Surcharged in Red

1930, Mar. 11

C7 O7 8c on 1col lilac & blk .80 .65
C8 O7 20c on 1col lilac & blk 1.25 .70
C9 O7 40c on 1col lilac & blk 2.40 1.50
C10 O7 1col on 1col lilac & blk 3.50 2.00
Nos. C7-C10 (4) 7.95 4.85

AP6

Red Surcharge on Revenue Stamps

1931-32 *Perf. 12*

C11 AP6 2col on 2col gray grn 35.00 35.00
C12 AP6 3col on 5col lil brn 35.00 35.00
C13 AP6 5col on 10col gray blk 35.00 35.00
Nos. C11-C13 (3) 105.00 105.00

There were two printings of this issue which were practically identical in the colors of the stamps and the surcharges.

Nos. C11 and C13 have the date "1929" on the stamp, No. C12 has "1930."

AP7

Black Overprint on Telegraph Stamp

1932, Mar. 8 *Perf. 12½*

C14 AP7 40c green 3.00 .30
a. Inverted overprint 32.50 27.50

Unofficial "proofs," inverts and double overprints were made from a defaced plate.

Mail Plane about to Land AP8

Allegory of Flight
AP9

1934, Mar. 14 *Perf. 12*

C15 AP8 5c green .25 .25
C16 AP8 10c carmine rose .25 .25
C17 AP8 15c chocolate .40 .25
C18 AP8 20c deep blue .40 .25
C19 AP8 25c deep orange .55 .25
C20 AP8 40c olive blk 1.75 .25
C21 AP8 50c gray blk .85 .25
C22 AP8 60c orange yel 1.50 .25
C23 AP8 75c dull violet 2.75 .50
C24 AP9 1col deep rose 1.50 .25
C25 AP9 2col lt blue 7.50 .95
C26 AP9 5col black 7.50 4.75
C27 AP9 10col red brown 10.00 8.00
Nos. C15-C27 (13) 35.20 16.45

Nos. C15-C27 with holes punched through were for use of government officials.

See Nos. C216-C219. For overprints see Nos. C67-C73, C92-C93, C103-C116, CO1-CO13. Post 1940 issues in Scott Standard catalogue, Vol. 2.

Airplane over Poás Volcano — AP10

1937, Feb. 10

C28 AP10 1c black .45 .35
C29 AP10 2c brown .45 .35
C30 AP10 3c dk violet .45 .35
Nos. C28-C30 (3) 1.35 1.05

First Fair of Costa Rica.

Puntarenas — AP11

Perf. 12, 12½

1937, Dec. 15 **Unwmk.**

C31 AP11 2c black gray .25 .25
C32 AP11 5c green .30 .25
C33 AP11 20c deep blue .30 .25
C34 AP11 1.40col olive brn 2.50 2.50
Nos. C31-C34 (4) 3.35 3.25

National Bank
AP12

1938, Jan. 11 **Wmk. 229** *Perf. 12½*

C35 AP12 1c purple .25 .25
C36 AP12 3c red orange .25 .25
C37 AP12 10c carmine rose .30 .25
C38 AP12 75c brown 2.50 2.00
Nos. C35-C38 (4) 3.30 2.75

Nos. C31-C38 for the Natl. Products Exposition held at San José, Dec. 1937.

Airport Administration Building, La Sabana — AP13

1940, May 2 **Engr.** **Unwmk.**

C39 AP13 5c green .30 .25
C40 AP13 10c rose pink .30 .25
C41 AP13 25c lt blue .40 .25
C42 AP13 35c red brown .40 .25
C43 AP13 60c red org .55 .40
C44 AP13 85c violet 1.40 1.00
C45 AP13 2.35col turq grn 6.50 5.50
Nos. C39-C45 (7) 9.85 7.90

Opening of the Intl. Airport at La Sabana.

Duran Sanatorium
AP14

Overprinted in Black

1940, Dec. 2 *Perf. 12*

C46 AP14 10c scarlet .25 .25
C47 AP14 15c purple .25 .25
C48 AP14 25c lt blue .50 .40
C49 AP14 35c bister brn .70 .65
C50 AP14 60c pck green 1.00 .95
C51 AP14 75c olive 2.75 2.50
C52 AP14 1.35col red org 8.75 8.00
C53 AP14 5col sepia 45.00 40.00
C54 AP14 10col red lilac 140.00 100.00
Nos. C46-C54 (9) 199.20 153.00

Pan-American Health Day. Nos. C46-C54 exist without overprint. Value, set $5,000.

No. 174 Surcharged in Black or Blue

1940, Dec. 17 *Perf. 14*

C55 A95 15c on 50c yel (Bk) 1.00 1.00
C56 A95 30c on 50c yel (Bl) 1.00 1.00

Pan-American Aviation Day, proclaimed by President F. D. Roosevelt.

The 15c surcharge exists normal and inverted on No. 171, Value, normal $30. Inverted surcharge is worth more.

AIR POST OFFICIAL STAMPS

Air Post Stamps of 1934 Ovptd. in Red

1934 **Unwmk.** *Perf. 12*

CO1 AP8 5c green .25 .25
CO2 AP8 10c car rose .25 .25
CO3 AP8 15c chocolate .50 .50
CO4 AP8 20c deep blue .80 .80
CO5 AP8 25c deep org .80 .80
CO6 AP8 40c olive blk .80 .80
CO7 AP8 50c gray blk .80 .80
CO8 AP8 60c org yel .95 .95
CO9 AP8 75c dull vio .95 .95
CO10 AP9 1col deep rose 1.60 1.60
CO11 AP9 2col light blue 4.75 4.75
CO12 AP9 5col black 8.00 8.00
CO13 AP9 10col red brown 12.00 12.00
Nos. CO1-CO13 (13) 32.45 32.45

For overprints see Nos. C103-C116 in Scott Standard catalogue, Vol 2.

POSTAGE DUE STAMPS

D1

1903 **Unwmk.** **Engr.** *Perf. 14*

Numerals in Black

J1 D1 5c slate blue 6.75 1.25
J2 D1 10c brown orange 6.75 1.25
J3 D1 15c yellow green 3.50 1.75
J4 D1 20c carmine 4.75 1.75
J5 D1 25c slate gray 4.75 2.40
J6 D1 30c brown 6.00 2.50
J7 D1 40c olive bister 6.75 2.50
J8 D1 50c red violet 6.75 2.50
Nos. J1-J8 (8) 46.00 15.90

D2

1915 **Litho.** *Perf. 12*

J9 D2 2c orange 1.25 .55
J10 D2 4c dark blue 1.25 .55
J11 D2 8c gray green 1.25 .55
J12 D2 10c violet 1.25 .55
J13 D2 20c brown 1.25 .55
Nos. J9-J13 (5) 6.25 2.75

OFFICIAL STAMPS

Values for unused stamps are for examples with original gum as defined in the catalogue introduction. Examples without gum have probably been used and are so regarded.

Very fine examples of Nos. O1-O24 will have perforations just clear of the design on one or more sides.

Nos. O1-O55, to about 1915, normally were not canceled when affixed to official mail. Occasionally they were canceled in a foreign country of destination. Used values are for favor-canceled stamps or for stamps without gum.

Regular Issues Overprinted

Overprinted in Red, Black, Blue or Green

1883-85 **Unwmk.** *Perf. 12*

O1 A6 1c green (R) 2.00 1.10
O2 A6 1c green (Bk) 4.00 1.10
O3 A6 2c carmine (Bk) 4.00 1.40
O4 A6 2c carmine (Bl) 2.40 1.60
O5 A6 5c blue vio (R) 7.00 3.00
O6 A6 10c orange (G) 10.00 4.00
O7 A6 40c blue (R) 10.00 4.00
Nos. O1-O7 (7) 39.40 16.20

Overprinted

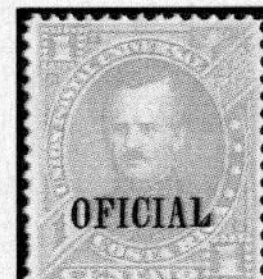

1886

O8 A6 1c green (Bk) 3.50 1.10
O9 A6 2c carmine (Bk) 3.50 1.60
O10 A6 5c blue vio (R) 24.00 11.00
O11 A6 10c orange (Bk) 24.00 11.00
Nos. O8-O11 (4) 55.00 24.70

Overprinted

O12 A6 1c green (Bk) 3.50 1.00
O13 A6 2c carmine (Bk) 3.50 1.40
O14 A6 5c blue vio (R) 24.00 11.00
O15 A6 10c orange (Bk) 24.00 11.00
Nos. O12-O15 (4) 55.00 24.40

Nos. O8-O11 and O12-O15 exist se-tenant in vertical pairs.

Overprinted in Black

O16 A6 5c blue vio 60.00 35.00
O17 A6 10c orange — 275.00

Overprinted

1887

O18 A6 1c green 1.25 .55
O19 A6 2c carmine 1.25 .50
O21 A6 10c orange 37.50 24.00
c. Double overprint 42.50
O22 A7 5c blue vio 12.00 3.50
O23 A7 10c orange .90 .50
c. Double overprint 27.50
O24 A6 40c olive blue 1.25 .50
Nos. O18-O24 (6) 54.15 29.55

Overprinted "OFICAL"

O18a A6 1c green
O19a A6 2c carmine *14.50 14.50*
O22a A7 5c blue violet *14.50*
O23a A7 10c orange *14.50 3.50*
O24a A6 40c blue *17.00 17.00*
Nos. O18a-O24a (5) *60.50*

Dangerous counterfeits exist of Nos. O18a-O24a.

Without Period

O18b A6 1c green 14.50 10.00
O19b A6 2c carmine 14.50 10.00
O22b A7 5c blue violet 14.50 10.00
O23b A7 10c orange 14.50 10.00
Nos. O18b-O23b (4) 58.00 40.00

Nos. O18b-O23b are from a separate plate without periods. No. O23 exists without period (position 32). These must be collected in pairs.

Issues of 1889-1901 Overprinted

1889 *Perf. 14, 15*

O25 A10 1c brown .25 .25
O26 A11 2c dk green .25 .25
O27 A12 5c orange .25 .25
O28 A13 10c red brown .25 .25
O29 A14 20c yellow grn .40 .25
O30 A15 50c rose red 1.40 1.40
Nos. O25-O30 (6) 2.80 2.65

1892

O31 A20 1c grnsh blue .25 .25
O32 A21 2c yellow .25 .25
O33 A22 5c violet .25 .25
O34 A23 10c lt green 3.50 1.60
O35 A24 20c scarlet .25 .25
O36 A25 50c gray blue .65 .55
Nos. O31-O36 (6) 5.15 3.15

1901-02

O37 A30 1c green & blk .40 .40
O38 A31 2c ver & blk .40 .40
O39 A32 5c gray bl & blk .40 .40
O40 A33 10c ocher & blk .80 .80
O41 A34 20c lake & blk 1.25 1.25
O42 A35 50c lilac & dk bl 10.00 4.00
O43 A36 1col ol bis & blk 17.50 10.00
Nos. O37-O43 (7) 30.75 17.25

No. 46 Overprinted in Green

1903

O44 A31 2c ver & blk 3.00 3.00
b. "PROVISIORO" 10.00 10.00
d. Inverted overprint 10.00 10.00
f. As "b," inverted 13.00 10.00

Counterfeit overprints exist.

Regular Issue of 1903 Overprinted Like Nos. O25-O43

1903 ***Perf. 14, 12½x14***

O45	A40	4c red vio & blk	1.40	1.40
O46	A41	6c ol grn & blk	1.75	1.75
O47	A42	25c gray lil & brn	9.50	6.00
		Nos. O45-O47 (3)	12.65	9.15

Counterfeit overprints exist.

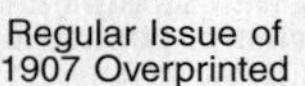

Regular Issue of 1907 Overprinted

1908 ***Perf. 14***

O48	A43	1c red brn & ind	.25	.25
O49	A44	2c yel grn & blk	.25	.25
O50	A45	4c car & ind	.25	.25
O51	A46	5c yel & dull bl	.25	.25
O52	A47	10c blue & blk	.80	.80
O53	A49	25c gray lil & blk	.30	.25
O54	A50	50c red lil & bl	.55	.55
O55	A51	1col brown & blk	1.25	1.25
		Nos. O48-O55 (8)	3.90	3.85

Various varieties of the overprint and basic stamps exist.

Imperf examples of Nos. O48, O49, O53 were found in 1970.

Regular Issue of 1910 Overprinted in Black

1917

O56	A56	5c orange	.40	.40
a.		Inverted overprint	6.00	3.50
O57	A57	10c deep blue	.25	.25
a.		Inverted overprint	3.50	3.50

No. 74 Surcharged

1920 **Red Surcharge** ***Perf. 12***

O58	A58	15c on 20c olive grn	.55	.55

Nos. 72, 61, 59, 65-67 Surcharged or Overprinted

1921 **Black Surcharge** ***Perf. 12***

O59	A56	10c on 5c orange	.50	.50
a.		"10 CTS." inverted	17.50	

Perf. 14

O60	A45	4c car & indigo	.40	.40
a.		"1291" for "1921"	12.00	
O61	A43	6c on 1c red brn & ind	.55	.55
O62	A49	20c on 25c gray lil & blk	.55	.55

Overprinted like No. O60

O63	A50	50c red lil & bl	2.50	1.75
O64	A51	1col brown & blk	5.00	3.00
		Nos. O59-O64 (6)	9.50	6.75

Nos. O60 to O64 exist with date and new values inverted. These may be printer's waste but probably were deliberately made.

Regular Issue of 1923 Overprinted

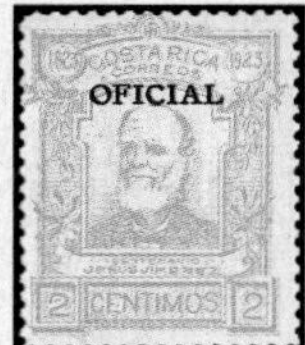

1923 ***Perf. 11½***

O65	A68	2c brown	.25	.25
O66	A68	4c green	.25	.25
O67	A68	5c blue	.40	.40
O68	A68	20c carmine	.25	.25
O69	A68	1col violet	.50	.50
		Nos. O65-O69 (5)	1.65	1.65

Nos. O65 to O69 exist imperforate but were not regularly issued in that condition.

O7

1926 **Unwmk.** **Engr.** ***Perf. 12½***

O70	O7	2c ultra & blk	.25	.25
O71	O7	3c mag & blk	.25	.25
O72	O7	4c lt bl & blk	.25	.25
O73	O7	5c grn & blk	.25	.25
O74	O7	6c ocher & blk	.25	.25
O75	O7	10c rose red & blk	.25	.25
O76	O7	20c ol grn & blk	.25	.25
O77	O7	30c red org & blk	.25	.25
O78	O7	45c brown & blk	.25	.25
O79	O7	1col lilac & blk	.50	.50
		Nos. O70-O79 (10)	2.75	2.75

See Nos. O82-O94. For surcharges see Nos. C7-C10.

Regular Issue of 1936 Overprinted in Black

1936 **Unwmk.** ***Perf. 12***

O80	A96	5c green	.25	.25
O81	A96	10c carmine rose	.25	.25

Type of 1926

1937 ***Perf. 12½***

O82	O7	2c vio & blk	.25	.25
O83	O7	3c bis brn & blk	.25	.25
O84	O7	4c rose car & blk	.25	.25
O85	O7	5c ol grn & blk	.25	
O86	O7	8c blk brn & blk	.25	
O87	O7	10c rose lake & blk	.25	
O88	O7	20c ind & blk	.25	.25
O89	O7	40c red org & blk	.25	.25
O90	O7	55c dk vio & blk	.25	
O91	O7	1col brn vio & blk	.30	.30
O92	O7	2col gray bl & blk	.70	.70
O93	O7	5col dl yel & blk	3.00	3.00
O94	O7	10col blue & blk	45.00	20.00
		Nos. O82-O94 (13)	51.25	

Nine stamps of this series exist with perforated star (2c, 3c, 4c, 20c, 40c, 1col, 2col, 5col, 10col). These were issued to officials for postal purposes. Unpunched stamps were sold to collectors but had no franking power. Values for unused are for unpunched.

POSTAL TAX STAMPS

The 1927 postal tax stamps covered the 10c per book charge for books sent by mail. The stamps were sold at the post office and applied to any package containing books.

Regular Stamps and Revenue Stamps Overprinted in Black

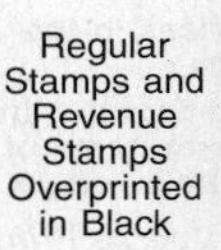

Nos. RA1B-RA1D Overprinted

1927, Mar. 17

RA1A	A75	10c red brown	25.00	5.00
RA1B		50c brown (overprinted on revenue stamp)	35.00	10.00
RA1C	A79	1col olive green	35.00	10.00
RA1D		2col blue green (overprinted on revenue stamp)	*750.00*	*400.00*
		Nos. RA1A-RA1D (4)	845.00	425.00

No. 124 Surcharged in Black

1927, Dec. 23

RA1E	A76	10c on 12c carmine rose	25.00	5.00

GUANACASTE

ˌgwä-nə-ˈkäs-tā

(A province of Costa Rica)

LOCATION — Northwestern coast of Central America
AREA — 4,000 sq. mi. (approx.)
POP. — 69,531 (estimated)
CAPITAL — Liberia

Residents of Guanacaste were allowed to buy Costa Rican stamps, overprinted "Guanacaste," at a discount from face value because of the province's isolation and climate, which make it difficult to keep mint stamps. Use was restricted to the province.

Counterfeits of most Guanacaste overprints are plentiful.

For 1c and 2c stamps between Nos. 1-20, unused values are for examples with or without gum. For 5c stamps between Nos. 5-21, unused examples without gum sell for slightly more than the used value.

Very fine examples of Nos. 1-54 will have perforations just clear of the design on one or more sides.

Dangerous counterfeits exist of Nos. 1-54.

On Issue of 1883

16mm

1885 **Unwmk.** ***Perf. 12***

Overprinted Horizontally in Black

1	A6	1c green	4.00	3.25
2	A6	2c carmine	4.00	3.25
a.		"Gnanacaste"	*250.00*	
3	A6	10c orange	35.00	21.00
a.		"Gnanacaste"	*500.00*	

Same Overprint in Red

4	A6	1c green	4.00	3.25
a.		"Gnanacaste"	*200.00*	
b.		Overprinted in black & red	*300.00*	
5	A6	5c blue violet	30.00	4.00
a.		"Gnanacaste"	*350.00*	
6	A6	40c blue	25.00	21.00

17½mm

Overprinted Horizontally in Black

7	A6	1c green	10.00	7.00
8	A6	2c carmine	10.00	7.00
9	A6	5c blue violet	60.00	15.00
10	A6	10c orange	75.00	35.00
11	A6	40c blue	75.00	60.00

Same Overprint in Red

12	A6	5c blue violet	*2,000.*	250.00
13	A6	40c blue	*2,000.*	

18½mm — c

Overprinted Horizontally in Black

14	A6	2c carmine	10.00	7.00
15	A6	10c orange	100.00	75.00

Same Overprint in Red

16	A6	1c green	7.00	7.00
a.		Double ovpt., one in blk	250.00	
17	A6	5c blue violet	45.00	15.00
18	A6	40c blue	75.00	75.00

Same Overprint, Vertically in Black

19	A6	1c green	*5,000.*	
20	A6	2c carmine	*4,250.*	
21	A6	5c blue violet	800.00	200.00
22	A6	10c orange	200.00	200.00

e

f

g

h

i

Overprinted Type e, Vertically

23	A6	1c green	3,000.	2,000.
24	A6	2c carmine	1,500.	300.00
25	A6	5c blue violet	400.00	75.00
26	A6	10c orange	75.00	75.00

Overprinted Type f, Vertically

27	A6	1c green	2,000.	2,000.
28	A6	2c carmine	1,000.	400.00
29	A6	5c blue violet	400.00	125.00
30	A6	10c orange	100.00	100.00

Overprinted Type g, Vertically

31	A6	1c green	3,000.	2,500.
32	A6	2c carmine	1,500.	1,000.
33	A6	5c blue violet	800.00	250.00
34	A6	10c orange	200.00	150.00

Overprinted Type h, Vertically

35	A6	1c green	3,000.	1,500.
36	A6	2c carmine	1,000.	300.00
37	A6	5c blue violet	600.00	75.00
38	A6	10c orange	100.00	60.00

Overprinted Type i, Vertically

39	A6	1c green		*500.00*
39A	A6	2c carmine		*300.00*
40	A6	5c blue violet		20.00
41	A6	10c orange		*250.00*

On Issues of 1883-87

Overprinted Horizontally in Black

1888-89

42	A7	5c blue violet	15.00	3.00

Overprinted Horizontally in Black

43	A7	5c blue violet	15.00	3.00

Overprinted Horizontally in Black

44	A6	2c carmine	4.00	
45	A7	10c orange	4.00	

Inverted overprints are fakes.

On Issue of 1889

Overprinted Like Nos. 7-13

1889 **Horizontally**

47	A8	2c blue	25.00

Vertically

48	A8	2c blue (c)	250.00
49	A8	2c blue (e)	100.00
51	A8	2c blue (f)	100.00
52	A8	2c blue (g)	350.00
54	A8	2c blue (h)	100.00

Nos. 47-54 are overprinted "Correos." Stamps without "Correos" are known postally used. Unused examples are valued the same as Nos. 47-54, unused. The 1c without "Correos" is known postally used. The 1c with "Correos" is counterfeit.

On Nos. 25-33 Overprinted Horizontally in Black

1889 ***Perf. 14 and 15***

55	A10	1c brown	10.00	3.50
56	A11	2c dark green	4.50	1.50
57	A12	5c orange	6.75	2.10
58	A13	10c red brown	6.75	2.10
59	A14	20c yellow green	1.00	.70
60	A15	50c rose red	1.75	1.50
61	A16	1p blue	4.50	4.50
62	A17	2p violet	13.00	6.75
63	A18	5p olive green	60.00	37.50
		Nos. 55-63 (9)	108.25	60.15

Overprinted "GUAGACASTE"

60a	A15	50c rose red	*325.00*	*325.00*
61a	A16	1p blue	*325.00*	*325.00*
62a	A17	2p violet	*400.00*	*400.00*
63a	A18	5p olive green	*600.00*	*600.00*

Values for Nos. 60a-63a used are for examples with remainder cancels.

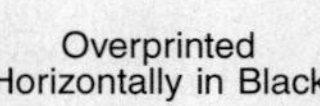

Overprinted Horizontally in Black

64	A10	1c brown	2.25	1.50
a.		Vert. pair, imperf. between		
65	A11	2c dark green	2.25	1.50
66	A12	5c orange	2.25	1.50
67	A13	10c red brown	2.25	1.50
		Nos. 64-67 (4)	9.00	6.00

CRETE

'krēt

LOCATION — An island in the Mediterranean Sea south of Greece
GOVT. — A department of Greece
AREA — 3,235 sq. mi.
POP. — 336,150 (1913)
CAPITAL — Canea

Formerly Crete was a province of Turkey. After an extended period of civil wars, France, Great Britain, Italy and Russia intervened and declaring Crete an autonomy, placed it under the administration of Prince George of Greece as High Commissioner. In October, 1908, the Cretan Assembly voted for union with Greece and in 1913 the union was formally effected.

40 Paras = 1 Piaster
4 Metallik = 1 Grosion (1899)
100 Lepta = 1 Drachma (1900)

AUSTRIAN POST IN CRETE

The Austrian Empire maintained post offices in three cities in Crete.

Post Office	Open	Close
Candia	1858	1914
Canea	1845	1914
Rettimo	1858	1914

Values in the first column for Nos. 2A1-2A185 are for stamps without defects tied to piece with legible partial strikes of town cancellations; values in the second column are for stamps without defects tied to cover by complete strikes of town cancellations. Stamps with legible town cancellations off cover sell for 25-50% of the on-piece value.

Issue dates refer to dates of stamps' issue, not necessarily to their usage with specific Albanian postal markings.

CANDIA

Stamps of Lombardy-Venetia

Canceled in black or red brown with single circle date stamp with post office name, month and date, without year

1863 ***Perf. 14***

2A1	2s yellow (#15)	450.00	1,500.
2A2	3s green (#16)	400.00	1,650.
2A3	5s rose (#17)	400.00	1,450.
2A4	10s blue (#18)	350.00	1,200.
2A5	15s yel brn (#19)	425.00	1,300.

1864-65 ***Perf. 9½***

2A6	2s yellow (#20)	450.00	1,500.
2A7	3s green (#21)	200.00	850.00
2A8	5s rose (#22)	150.00	700.00
2A9	10s blue (#23)	125.00	500.00
2A10	15s yel brn (#24)	160.00	600.00

Stamps of Austrian Offices in the Turkish Empire

Canceled in black or red brown with single circle date stamp with post office name, month and date, without year

1867-83 ***Coarse Print***

2A11	2s yellow (#1)	37.50	450.00
2A12	3s green (#2)	57.50	400.00
2A13	5s red (#3)	27.50	140.00
2A14	10s blue (#4)	20.00	92.50
2A15	15s brown (#5)	24.00	100.00
2A16	25s gray lilac (#6)	50.00	700.00
2A17	50s brown (#7)	57.50	*3,750.*

Fine Print

2A18	2s yellow (#7C)	1,150.	—
2A19	3s green (#7D)	35.00	275.00
2A20	5s red (#7E)	32.50	150.00
2A21	10s blue (#7F)	20.00	87.50
2A22	15s org brown (#7I)	135.00	775.00
2A23	25s gray lilac (#7J)	250.00	*5,000.*

Stamps of Austrian Offices in the Turkish Empire

Canceled in blue with single circle date stamp with post office name, month and date, without year

1867-83 ***Coarse Print***

2A24	2s yellow (#1)	125.00	825.00
2A25	3s green (#2)	150.00	750.00
2A26	5s red (#3)	120.00	500.00
2A27	10s blue (#4)	115.00	450.00
2A28	15s brown (#5)	120.00	475.00
2A29	25s gray lilac (#6)	145.00	1,100.
2A30	50s brown (#7)	150.00	*4,250.*

Fine Print

2A31	2s yellow (#7C)	1,250.	—
2A32	3s green (#7D)	125.00	625.00
2A33	5s red (#7E)	125.00	525.00
2A34	10s blue (#7F)	115.00	450.00
2A35	15s org brown (#7I)	225.00	1,125.
2A36	25s gray lilac (#7J)	350.00	*5,500.*

Stamps of Austrian Offices in the Turkish Empire

Canceled in black with circular date stamp with post office name, month and date, with year date

1867-83 ***Coarse Print***

2A37	2s yellow (#1)	37.50	450.00
2A38	3s green (#2)	57.50	400.00
2A39	5s red (#3)	27.50	140.00
2A40	10s blue (#4)	20.00	92.50
2A41	15s brown (#5)	24.00	100.00
2A42	25s gray lilac (#6)	50.00	700.00
2A43	50s brown (#7)	57.50	*3,750.*

Fine Print

2A44	2s yellow (#7C)	1,150.	—
2A45	3s green (#7D)	35.00	275.00
2A46	5s red (#7E)	32.50	150.00
2A47	10s blue (#7F)	20.00	87.50
2A48	15s org brown (#7I)	135.00	775.00
2A49	25s gray lilac (#7J)	250.00	*5,000.*

Stamps of Austrian Offices in the Turkish Empire

Canceled in blue with circular date stamp with post office name, month and date, with year date

1867-83 ***Coarse Print***

2A50	2s yellow (#1)	300.00	1,325.
2A51	3s green (#2)	325.00	1,250.
2A52	5s red (#3)	285.00	1,000.
2A53	10s blue (#4)	275.00	950.00
2A54	15s brown (#5)	280.00	975.00
2A55	25s gray lilac (#6)	300.00	1,575.
2A56	50s brown (#7)	325.00	*4,750.*

Fine Print

2A57	2s yellow (#7C)	1,400.	—
2A58	3s green (#7D)	300.00	1,125.
2A59	5s red (#7E)	285.00	1,000.
2A60	10s blue (#7F)	275.00	950.00
2A61	15s org brown (#7I)	385.00	1,625.
2A62	25s gray lilac (#7J)	500.00	*6,000.*

Candia Agencia del Lloyd Austriaco

Stamps of Lombardy-Venetia

Canceled with with oval postmark with ornaments in blue

1863 ***Perf. 14***

2A63	2s yellow (#15)	—	—
2A64	3s green (#16)	—	—
2A65	5s rose (#17)	3,150.	12,000.
2A66	10s blue (#18)	3,100.	11,050.
2A67	15s yel brn (#19)	3,250.	12,000.

CANEA

Stamps of Lombardy-Venetia

Canceled in black or red brown with straight-line postmark with name of post office and date in italic letters

1863 ***Perf. 14***

2A68	2s yellow (#15)	350.00	1,250.
2A69	3s green (#16)	300.00	1,350.
2A70	5s rose (#17)	300.00	1,100.
2A71	10s blue (#18)	250.00	850.00
2A72	15s yel brn (#19)	325.00	1,000.

1864-65 ***Perf. 9½***

2A73	2s yellow (#20)	375.00	1,100.
2A74	3s green (#21)	110.00	475.00
2A75	5s rose (#22)	60.00	325.00
2A76	10s blue (#23)	32.50	120.00
2A77	15s yel brn (#24)	65.00	240.00

Stamps of Austrian Offices in the Turkish Empire

Canceled in black or red brown with straight-line postmark with name of post office and date in italic letters

1867-83 ***Coarse Print***

2A78	2s yellow (#1)	30.00	425.00
2A79	3s green (#2)	47.50	350.00
2A80	5s red (#3)	18.75	100.00
2A81	10s blue (#4)	11.50	55.00
2A82	15s brown (#5)	15.00	62.50
2A83	25s gray lilac (#6)	40.00	675.00
2A84	50s brown (#7)	47.50	*3,800.*

Fine Print

2A85	2s yellow (#7C)	1,150.	—
2A86	3s green (#7D)	27.50	225.00
2A87	5s red (#7E)	22.50	115.00
2A88	10s blue (#7F)	11.00	50.00
2A89	15s org brown (#7I)	125.00	725.00
2A90	25s gray lilac (#7J)	235.00	*5,000.*

Stamps of Lombardy-Venetia

Canceled in blue with straight-line postmark with name of post office and date in italic letters

1863 ***Perf. 14***

2A91	2s yellow (#15)	450.00	1,500.
2A92	3s green (#16)	400.00	1,650.
2A93	5s rose (#17)	400.00	1,450.
2A94	10s blue (#18)	350.00	1,200.
2A95	15s yel brn (#19)	425.00	1,300.

1864-65 ***Perf. 9½***

2A96	2s yellow (#20)	625.00	1,950.
2A97	3s green (#21)	375.00	1,350.
2A98	5s rose (#22)	325.00	1,200.
2A99	10s blue (#23)	300.00	1,000.
2A100	15s yel brn (#24)	325.00	1,100.

Stamps of Austrian Offices in the Turkish Empire

Canceled in blue with straight-line postmark with name of post office and date in italic letters

1867-83 ***Coarse Print***

2A101	2s yellow (#1)	130.00	825.00
2A102	3s green (#2)	150.00	750.00
2A103	5s red (#3)	120.00	500.00
2A104	10s blue (#4)	115.00	450.00
2A105	15s brown (#5)	120.00	475.00
2A106	25s gray lilac (#6)	145.00	1,100.
2A107	50s brown (#7)	150.00	*4,250.*

Fine Print

2A108	2s yellow (#7C)	1,250.	—
2A109	3s green (#7D)	130.00	625.00
2A110	5s red (#7E)	125.00	525.00
2A111	10s blue (#7F)	115.00	450.00
2A112	15s org brown (#7I)	225.00	1,125.
2A113	25s gray lilac (#7J)	340.00	*5,500.*

Stamps of Austrian Offices in the Turkish Empire

Canceled in black with circular date stamp with post office name, month and date, with year date

1867-83 ***Coarse Print***

2A114	2s yellow (#1)	30.00	425.00
2A115	3s green (#2)	47.50	350.00
2A116	5s red (#3)	18.75	100.00
2A117	10s blue (#4)	1.50	55.000
2A118	15s brown (#5)	15.00	62.50
2A119	25s gray lilac (#6)	40.00	675.00
2A120	50s brown (#7)	47.50	*3,800.*

Fine Print

2A121	2s yellow (#7C)	1,150.	—
2A122	3s green (#7D)	27.50	225.00
2A123	5s red (#7E)	22.50	115.00
2A124	10s blue (#7F)	11.00	55.00
2A125	15s org brown (#7I)	125.00	725.00
2A126	25s gray lilac (#7J)	235.00	*5,000.*

RETTIMO

Stamps of Lombardy-Venetia

Canceled in black with single circle date stamp with post office name, month and date, without year

1863 ***Perf. 14***

2A127	2s yellow (#15)	450.00	1,500.
2A128	3s green (#16)	400.00	1,650.
2A129	5s rose (#17)	400.00	1,450.
2A130	10s blue (#18)	350.00	1,200.
2A131	15s yel brn (#19)	425.00	1,300.

1864-65 ***Perf. 9½***

2A132	2s yellow (#20)	425.00	1,275.
2A133	3s green (#21)	160.00	675.00
2A134	5s rose (#22)	110.00	525.00
2A135	10s blue (#23)	85.00	325.00
2A136	15s yel brn (#24)	115.00	450.00

Stamps of Austrian Offices in the Turkish Empire

Canceled in black or red brown with single circle date stamp with post office name, month and date, without year

1867-83 ***Coarse Print***

2A137	2s yellow (#1)	37.50	450.00
2A138	3s green (#2)	57.50	400.00
2A139	5s red (#3)	27.50	140.00

2A140 10s blue (#4) 20.00 92.50
2A141 15s brown (#5) 24.00 100.00
2A142 25s gray lilac (#6) 50.00 700.00
2A143 50s brown (#7) 57.50 *3,850.*

Fine Print

2A144 2s yellow (#7C) 1,150. —
2A145 3s green (#7D) 35.00 275.00
2A146 5s red (#7E) 32.50 150.00
2A147 10s blue (#7F) 20.00 87.50
2A148 15s org brown (#7I) 135.00 775.00
2A149 25s gray lilac (#7J) 250.00 *5,000.*

Stamps of Lombardy-Venetia

Canceled in blue with single circle date stamp with post office name, month and date, without year

1863 ***Perf. 14***

2A150 2s yellow (#15) 575.00 2,000.
2A151 3s green (#16) 525.00 2,200.
2A152 5s rose (#17) 525.00 2,000.
2A153 10s blue (#18) 500.00 1,750.
2A154 15s yel brn (#19) 575.00 1,850.

1864-65 ***Perf. 9½***

2A155 2s yellow (#20) 625.00 1,950.
2A156 3s green (#21) 375.00 1,350.
2A157 5s rose (#22) 325.00 1,200.
2A158 10s blue (#23) 300.00 1,000.
2A159 15s yel brn (#24) 325.00 1,100.

Stamps of Austrian Offices in the Turkish Empire

Canceled in blue with single circle date stamp with post office name, month and date, without year

1867-83 ***Coarse Print***

2A160 2s yellow (#1) 87.50 650.00
2A161 3s green (#2) 110.00 600.00
2A162 5s red (#3) 77.50 340.00
2A163 10s blue (#4) 70.00 300.00
2A164 15s brown (#5) 75.00 300.00
2A165 25s gray lilac (#6) 100.00 900.00
2A166 50s brown (#7) 110.00 *4,000.*

Fine Print

2A167 2s yellow (#7C) 1,200. —
2A168 3s green (#7D) 85.00 475.00
2A169 5s red (#7E) 82.50 350.00
2A170 10s blue (#7F) 70.00 290.00
2A171 15s org brown (#7I) 180.00 975.00
2A172 25s gray lilac (#7J) 300.00 *5,250.*

Stamps of Austrian Offices in the Turkish Empire

Canceled in black with single circle date stamp with post office name, month and date, with year

1867-83 ***Coarse Print***

2A173 2s yellow (#1) 30.00 425.00
2A174 3s green (#2) 47.50 350.00
2A175 5s red (#3) 18.75 100.00
2A176 10s blue (#4) 11.50 55.00
2A177 15s brown (#5) 15.00 62.50
2A178 25s gray lilac (#6) 40.00 675.00
2A179 50s brown (#7) 45.00 *3,800.*

Fine Print

2A180 2s yellow (#7C) 1,150. —
2A181 3s green (#7D) 27.50 225.00
2A182 5s red (#7E) 22.50 115.00
2A183 10s blue (#7F) 11.00 50.00
2A184 15s org brown (#7I) 125.00 725.00
2A185 25s gray lilac (#7J) 235.00 *5,000.*

Issued Under Joint Administration of France, Great Britain, Italy and Russia

British Sphere of Administration District of Heraklion (Candia)

A1

Handstamped

1898 **Unwmk.** ***Imperf.***

1 A1 20pa violet 400.00 225.00
Never hinged 1,250.

A2

1898 **Litho.** ***Perf. 11½***

2 A2 10pa blue 6.50 2.00
Never hinged 17.50
a. Horiz. pair, imperf. btwn. *200.00*
b. Imperf., pair *225.00*
c. Horiz. pair, imperf. vert. —
3 A2 20pa green 6.50 2.00
Never hinged 24.00
a. Imperf., pair 225.00

1899

4 A2 10pa brown 6.50 2.00
Never hinged 18.00
a. Horiz. pair, imperf. btwn. *200.00*
b. Imperf., pair *225.00*
5 A2 20pa rose 8.00 2.00
Never hinged 31.00
a. Imperf., pair 225.00

Used values for Nos. 2-5 are for stamps canceled by the straight-line "Heraklion" town postmark. Stamps canceled with any other postmark used for postal duty are scarce and worth much more. Other cancellations, values from: Ag. Thomas, $65; Ag. Myron, $70; Arkanais, $90; Episkopi, $170; Kastelli, $175; Moirais, $175; Xarakas, $190; Chersonissos, $235; and Moxos.

Counterfeits exist of Nos. 1-5.

Russian Sphere of Administration District of Rethymnon

Coat of Arms
A3 A4

1899 **Handstamped** ***Imperf.***

Laid paper

No Gum

10 A3 1m green 13.50 5.50
m. 2m blue — —
11 A3 2m black 11.00 4.00
a. Double impression — —
12 A3 2m rose 325.00 225.00
a. 2m carmine 340.00 190.00
b. 2m vermilion — —
c. 2m pale grayish rose — 525.00
d. 2m violet — 600.00
f. 2m red 340.00 300.00
13 A4 1m blue 100.00 75.00

Wove paper

10E A3 1m green 13.00 5.00
f. 1m blue — 400.00
g. 1m violet — —
h. As No. 10Ef, printed on both sides 600.00 —
11E A3 2m black 13.00 5.00
a. 2m pale gray rose 120.00 60.00
b. 2m blue 750.00 550.00
f. 2m Double impression 350.00 350.00
12E A3 2m rose 225.00 165.00
f. 2m Very thin paper *600.00* *450.00*
g. 2m blue *750.00* *550.00*
h. 2m lilac — —
i. 2m violet — —
13E A4 1m blue 100.00 60.00
f. 1m violet — —
g. 1m Double impression — —

Quadrille paper

10J A3 1m green 350.00 —
k. 1m violet — *650.00*
l. 1m blue — *650.00*
11J A3 2m black 350.00 80.00
k. 2m blue — *800.00*
l. 2m brown — *1,300.*
m. 2m violet *800.00* *600.00*
n. 2m pale gray rose *500.00*
12J A3 2m rose 500.00
13J A4 1m violet 650.00

Nos. 10-13 normally have a circular control mark applied in violet or blue on blocks of four stamps. They also are known without this control mark (errors) and occasionally with the small round control marks of the next issue, in blue or violet (probably proofs). They are sometimes found with pin-perforations. Other varieties exist.

Counterfeits exist.

Poseidon's Trident — A5a
A5

1899 **Litho.** ***Perf. 11½***

With Control Mark Overprinted in Violet

Without Stars at Sides

14 A5 1m orange 175.00 115.00
Never hinged 300.00
15 A5 2m orange 175.00 115.00
Never hinged 300.00
16 A5 1gr orange 175.00 115.00
Never hinged 300.00
17 A5 1m green 175.00 115.00
Never hinged 300.00
18 A5 2m green 175.00 115.00
Never hinged 300.00
19 A5 1gr green 175.00 115.00
Never hinged 300.00
20 A5 1m yellow 175.00 115.00
Never hinged 300.00
21 A5 2m yellow 175.00 115.00
Never hinged 300.00
22 A5 1gr yellow 175.00 115.00
Never hinged 300.00
23 A5 1m rose 175.00 115.00
Never hinged 300.00
24 A5 2m rose 175.00 115.00
Never hinged 300.00
25 A5 1gr rose 175.00 115.00
Never hinged 300.00
26 A5 1m violet 175.00 115.00
Never hinged 300.00
27 A5 2m violet 175.00 115.00
Never hinged 300.00
28 A5 1gr violet 175.00 115.00
Never hinged 300.00
29 A5 1m blue 175.00 115.00
Never hinged 300.00
30 A5 2m blue 175.00 115.00
Never hinged 300.00
31 A5 1gr blue 175.00 115.00
Never hinged 300.00
32 A5 1m black 1,250. 1,150.
Never hinged 2,000.
33 A5 2m black 1,250. 1,150.
Never hinged 2,000.
34 A5 1gr black 1,250. 1,150.
Never hinged 2,000.

With Stars at Sides

35 A5a 1m blue 37.50 30.00
Never hinged 75.00
a. Imperf., pair 325.00
36 A5a 2m blue 15.00 12.50
Never hinged 30.00
37 A5a 1gr blue 13.00 8.50
Never hinged 26.00
38 A5a 1m rose 160.00 70.00
Never hinged 320.00
39 A5a 2m rose 15.00 12.00
Never hinged 25.00
40 A5a 1gr rose 12.50 8.50
Never hinged 27.00
a. Imperf., pair 325.00
41 A5a 1m green 37.50 30.00
Never hinged 75.00
a. Imperf., pair 325.00
42 A5a 2m green 15.00 12.00
Never hinged 30.00
43 A5a 1gr green 12.50 8.50
Never hinged 25.00
44 A5a 1m violet 37.50 30.00
Never hinged 75.00
45 A5a 2m violet 15.00 12.00
Never hinged 30.00
46 A5a 1gr violet 12.50 8.50
Never hinged 25.00
a. Horiz. pair, imperf. btwn. 250.00
b. Vert. pair, imperf. horiz. 190.00
Nos. 35-46 (12) 383.00 242.50

Almost all of Nos. 14 to 46 may be found without control mark, with double control marks and in various colors.

Used values for Nos. 10-46 are for stamps with postmarks of Rethymnon. Thirteen other post offices existed, and stamps with postmarks other than Rethymnon are scarce and command significant premiums: Ag. Galini, $125; Amari, $90; Anogeia, $525; Garazo, $160; Damasta, $550; Kastelli, $125; Margaritais, $550; Melampes, $375; Pigi, $125; Roystika, $70; Xenia, $105; Spili, $105; Fodede, $550.

Counterfeits exist of Nos. 14-46.

Imperf., Pairs

14a A5 1m orange 1,150.
15a A5 2m orange 1,150.
16a A5 1gr orange 1,150.
17a A5 1m green 1,150.
18a A5 2m green 1,150.
19a A5 1gr green 1,150.
20a A5 1m yellow 1,150.
21a A5 2m yellow 1,150.
22a A5 1gr yellow 1,150.
23a A5 1m rose 1,150.
24a A5 2m rose 1,150.
25a A5 1gr rose 1,150.
26a A5 1m violet 1,150.
27a A5 2m violet 1,150.
28a A5 1gr violet 1,150.
29a A5 1m blue 1,150.
30a A5 2m blue 1,150.
31a A5 1gr blue 1,150.

Issued by the Cretan Government

Hermes — A6

Hera — A7

Prince George of Greece — A8

1900, Mar. 1 **Engr.** ***Perf. 14***

50 A6 1 l violet brown .40 .45
Never hinged 1.35
51 A7 5 l green 1.80 .45
Never hinged 5.75
52 A8 10 l red 1.35 .45
Never hinged 4.75
53 A7 20 l carmine rose 5.00 2.00
Never hinged 17.00
Nos. 50-53 (4) 8.55 3.35

See #64-71. For overprints and surcharges see #54-63, 72-73, 85, 88, 93, 97-99, 108, 111.

Overprinted

Red Overprint

54 A8 25 l blue .80 1.00
Never hinged 1.60
55 A6 50 l lilac 2.00 1.35
Never hinged 4.00
56 A9 1d gray violet 11.00 13.50
Never hinged 22.50
57 A10 2d brown 35.00 32.50
Never hinged 70.00
58 A11 5d green & blk 185.00 200.00
Never hinged 325.00
Nos. 54-58 (5) 233.80 248.35

Black Overprint

59 A8 25 l blue 1.60 .75
Never hinged 3.25
60 A6 50 l lilac 1.60 1.50
Never hinged 3.25
61 A9 1d gray violet 8.75 5.75
Never hinged 17.50
a. Inverted overprint *350.00* *350.00*
62 A10 2d brown 23.00 17.00
Never hinged 47.50
63 A11 5d green & blk 100.00 110.00
Never hinged 210.00
Nos. 59-63 (5) 134.95 135.00

Talos — A9

Minos — A10

St. George and the Dragon — A11

1901 **Without Overprint**

64 A6 1 l bister 1.00 1.15
Never hinged 2.25
65 A7 20 l orange 3.00 1.15
Never hinged 6.25
66 A8 25 l blue 8.75 .85
Never hinged 19.00
67 A6 50 l lilac 37.50 27.50
Never hinged 80.00
68 A6 50 l ultra 13.00 13.00
Never hinged 27.50
69 A9 1d gray violet 40.00 27.50
Never hinged 85.00
70 A10 2d brown 13.00 11.50
Never hinged 27.50
71 A11 5d green & blk 16.50 13.00
Never hinged 35.00
Nos. 64-71 (8) 132.75 95.65

No. 64 is a revenue stamp that was used for postage for short periods in 1901 and 1904.

Types A6 to A8 in olive yellow, and types A9 to A11 in olive yellow and black are revenue stamps.

See note following No. 53.

Surcharges with the year "1922" on designs A6, A8, A9, A11, A13, A15-A23 and D1 are listed under Greece.

No. 66 Overprinted in Black

1901

72 A8 25 l blue 22.50 .75
Never hinged 60.00
a. First letter of ovpt. invtd. 475.00 300.00
Never hinged 725.00
b. Inverted overprint 700.00 350.00
Never hinged 1,100.
c. "S" of "PROSORINON" omitted 200.00 80.00
Never hinged 350.00

No. 65 Surcharged in Black

1904, Dec.

73 A7 5 l on 20 l orange 2.25 .75
Never hinged 4.75
a. Without "5" at right *150.00* *150.00*

Mycenaean Seal — A12

Britomartis (Cortyna Coin) — A13

Prince George — A14

Kydon and Dog (Cydonia Coin) — A15

Triton (Itanos Coin) — A16

Ariadne (Knossos Coin) — A17

Zeus as Bull Abducting Europa (Cortyna Coin) A18

Palace of Minos Ruins, Knossos A19

Arkadi Monastery and Mt. Ida — A20

1905, Feb. 15

74 A12 2 l dull violet 1.25 .35
Never hinged 3.00
75 A13 5 l yellow grn 1.50 .35
Never hinged 4.00
76 A14 10 l red 1.50 .75
Never hinged 4.00
77 A15 20 l blue grn 5.50 1.00
Never hinged 15.00
78 A16 25 l ultra 7.00 1.00
Never hinged 17.50
79 A17 50 l yellow brn 7.50 3.25
Never hinged 20.00
80 A18 1d rose car & dp brn 72.50 62.50
Never hinged 175.00
81 A19 3d orange & blk 50.00 40.00
Never hinged 110.00
82 A20 5d ol grn & blk 25.00 25.00
Never hinged 57.50
Nos. 74-82 (9) 171.75 134.20

For overprints see Nos. 86-87, 89, 91-92, 94-95, 104, 106, 109-110, 112-113, 115-120.

The so-called revolutionary stamps of 1905 were issued for sale to collectors and, so far as can be ascertained, were of no postal value.

A. T. A. Zaimis A21

Prince George Landing at Suda A22

1907, Aug. 28

83 A21 25 l blue & blk 36.00 .85
Never hinged 90.00
84 A22 1d green & blk 9.00 7.00
Never hinged 20.00

Administration under a High Commissioner.
For overprints see Nos. 90, 105, 107.

Stamps of 1900-1907 Overprinted in Black

1908, Sept. 21

85 A6 1 l violet brn .55 .40
Never hinged 1.90
a. Inverted overprint —
86 A12 2 l dull violet .55 .40
Never hinged 1.90
a. Pair, one without ovpt. —
87 A13 5 l yellow grn .55 .40
Never hinged 1.90
88 A8 10 l red 1.15 .80
Never hinged 3.75
a. Pair, one without ovpt. —
89 A15 20 l blue grn 3.00 1.00
Never hinged 9.50
90 A21 25 l blue & blk 8.50 2.50
Never hinged 25.00
91 A17 50 l yellow brn 11.50 4.25
Never hinged 35.00
a. Inverted overprint —
92 A18 1d rose car & dp brn 95.00 67.50
Never hinged 290.00
93 A10 2d brown 10.00 8.00
Never hinged 32.50
94 A19 3d orange & blk 45.00 37.50
Never hinged 125.00
95 A20 5d ol grn & blk 35.00 30.00
Never hinged 110.00
Nos. 85-95 (11) 210.80 152.75

This overprint exists inverted and double, as well as with incorrect, reversed, misplaced and omitted letters. Similar errors are found on the Postage Due and Official stamps with this overprint.

Hermes by Praxiteles — A23

1908

96 A23 10 l brown red 2.75 .80
a. Pair, one without overprint 150.00 150.00
b. Inverted overprint —
c. Double overprint —

Nos. 96 and 114 were not regularly issued without overprint.
For overprints see Nos. 103, 114.

No. 53 Surcharged

1909

97 A7 5 l on 20 l car rose 220.00 *245.00*

Forgeries exist of No. 97.

On No. 65

98 A7 5 l on 20 l orange 1.25 1.10
a. Inverted surcharge 150.00 150.00
b. Double surcharge 120.00 120.00

Overprinted on Nos. 64, J1

99 A6 1 l bister 3.50 3.50
100 D1 1 l red 1.25 1.25

No. J4 Surcharged

101 D1 2 l on 20 l red 1.25 1.25
b. Inverted surcharge 75.00
c. Second letter of surcharge "Δ" instead of "P" 50.00 50.00

No. J4 Surcharged

102 D1 2 l on 20 l red 1.25 1.25
a. Double overprint *125.00* *125.00*
b. Half used as 1 l, on piece 17.50

No. 102b was valid for use Feb. 15-28, 1909.

Overprinted in Black

a

b

c

103 A23(a) 10 l brown red 3.00 1.00
Never hinged 6.50
a. Inverted overprint 110.00
Never hinged 270.00
104 A15(a) 20 l blue grn 4.00 1.00
Never hinged 9.00
105 A21(c) 25 l blue & blk 5.00 2.00
Never hinged 11.50
106 A17(a) 50 l yellow brn 7.00 4.00
Never hinged 16.00
107 A22(b) 1d green & blk 12.50 7.00
Never hinged 27.50
108 A10(a) 2d brown 12.50 10.00
Never hinged 27.50
109 A19(b) 3d org & blk 125.00 115.00
Never hinged 260.00
110 A20(b) 5d ol grn & blk 52.50 52.50
Never hinged 110.00
Nos. 103-110 (8) 221.50 192.50

Stamps of 1900-08 Overprinted in Red or Black

1909-10

111 A6 1 l violet brown .35 .25
Never hinged 1.00
112 A12 2 l dull violet .35 .25
Never hinged 1.00
113 A13 5 l yellow green .35 .25
Never hinged 1.00
114 A23 10 l brown red (Bk) .60 .60
Never hinged 1.50
115 A15 20 l blue green 2.00 .70
Never hinged 4.75
116 A16 25 l ultra 2.50 .75
Never hinged 6.50
117 A17 50 l yellow brn 7.00 2.00
Never hinged 17.50
118 A18 1d rose car & dp brn (Bk) 100.00 100.00
Never hinged 225.00
119 A19 3d orange & blk 85.00 85.00
Never hinged 185.00
120 A20 5d ol grn & blk 55.00 55.00
Never hinged 125.00
Nos. 111-120 (10) 253.15 244.80

POSTAGE DUE STAMPS

D1

1901 Unwmk. Litho. *Perf. 14*

J1 D1 1 l red .30 .30
Never hinged .75
J2 D1 5 l red .50 .30
Never hinged 1.25
J3 D1 10 l red .75 .40
Never hinged 1.75
J4 D1 20 l red 1.00 *.50*
Never hinged 2.50
J5 D1 40 l red 11.50 11.50
Never hinged 25.00
J6 D1 50 l red 11.50 11.50
Never hinged 25.00
J7 D1 1d red 22.50 22.50
Never hinged 50.00
J8 D1 2d red 14.00 12.50
Never hinged 30.00
Nos. J1-J8 (8) 62.05 59.50

For overprints and surcharges see Nos. 100-102, J9-J26.

Surcharged in Black

1901

J9 D1 1d on 1d red 11.00 10.00
Never hinged 22.50

Overprinted in Black

1908

No.	Type	Description	Unused	Used
J10	D1	1 l red	.35	.35
		Never hinged	.80	
J11	D1	5 l red	.60	.60
		Never hinged	1.50	
J12	D1	10 l red	.60	.60
		Never hinged	1.50	
J13	D1	20 l red	2.00	2.00
		Never hinged	4.75	
J14	D1	40 l red	8.25	7.50
		Never hinged	19.00	
J15	D1	50 l red	10.50	9.00
		Never hinged	24.00	
J16	D1	1d red	475.00	475.00
		Never hinged	1,100.	
a.		Pair, one without ovpt.		—
J17	D1	1d on 1d red	11.50	10.00
		Never hinged	25.00	
J18	D1	2d red	19.00	10.00
		Never hinged	45.00	
		Nos. J10-J18 (9)	527.80	515.05

Nos. J10-J18 exist with inverted overprint. See note after No. 95.

Counterfeits of No. J16 exist.

Overprinted in Black

1910

No.	Type	Description	Unused	Used
J19	D1	1 l red	.45	.30
		Never hinged	1.00	
J20	D1	5 l red	1.00	.35
		Never hinged	2.25	
J21	D1	10 l red	1.00	.35
		Never hinged	2.25	
J22	D1	20 l red	3.25	1.75
		Never hinged	7.00	
J23	D1	40 l red	11.00	6.00
		Never hinged	24.00	
J24	D1	50 l red	16.50	12.00
		Never hinged	35.00	
J25	D1	1d red	27.50	27.50
		Never hinged	57.50	
J26	D1	2d red	27.50	27.50
		Never hinged	57.50	
		Nos. J19-J26 (8)	88.20	75.75

OFFICIAL STAMPS

O1

O2

Unwmk.

1908, Jan. 14 Litho. ***Perf. 14***

No.	Type	Description	Unused	Used
O1	O1	10 l dull claret	18.00	1.50
		Never hinged	40.00	
O2	O2	30 l blue	37.50	1.50
		Never hinged	70.00	

Nos. O1-O2 exist imperf.

Nos. O1-O2 Overprinted

No.	Type	Description	Unused	Used
O3	O1	10 l dull claret	13.00	1.20
		Never hinged	27.50	
a.		Inverted overprint	100.00	100.00
O4	O2	30 l blue	27.50	1.20
		Never hinged	57.50	
a.		Inverted overprint	200.00	200.00

See note after No. 95.

Nos. O1-O2 Overprinted

1910

No.	Type	Description	Unused	Used
O5	O1	10 l dull claret	2.25	1.10
		Never hinged	4.25	
O6	O2	30 l blue	2.25	1.10
		Never hinged	4.25	

Nos. O5-O6 remained in use until 1922, nine years after union with Greece.

CUBA

'kyü-bə

LOCATION — The largest island of the West Indies; south of Florida
GOVT. — Republic
AREA — 44,206 sq. mi.
POP. — 6,743,000 (est. 1960)
CAPITAL — Havana

Formerly a Spanish possession, Cuba made several unsuccessful attempts to gain her freedom, which finally led to the intervention of the US in 1898. In that year under the Treaty of Paris, Spain relinquished the island to the US in trust for its inhabitants. In 1902 a republic was established and the Cuban Congress took over the government from the military authorities.

8 Reales Plata = 1 Peso
100 Centesimos = 1 Escudo or Peseta (1867)
1000 Milesimas = 100 Centavos = 1 Peso

Catalogue values for unused stamps in this country are for Never Hinged items, beginning with Scott RA1 in the postal tax section.

Pen cancellations are common on the earlier stamps of Cuba. Stamps so canceled sell for very much less than those with postmark cancellations.

Watermarks

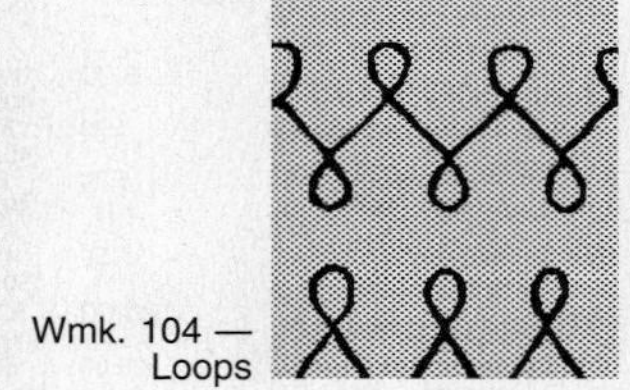
Wmk. 104 — Loops

Loops from different rows may or may not be directly opposite each other.

Wmk. 105 — Crossed Lines

Wmk. 106 — Star

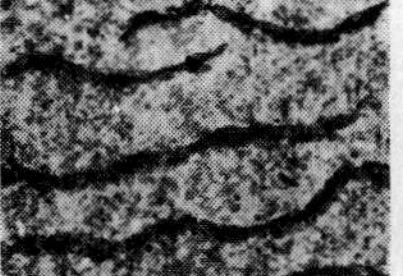
Wmk. 229 — Wavy Lines

FORERUNNERS

Crowned Circle handstamp types are pictured in the Crowned Circle Handstamps and Great Britain Used Abroad section.

BRITISH POST OFFICES IN CUBA

Havana

British P.O. opened 1762; stamps supplied 1865; closed May 30, 1877

Pre-Stamp Postal Markings

1841

No.	Description	Value
A1	Crowned Circle handstamp Type II, on cover, inscribed "PAID AT HAVANA"	1,150.
A2	Crowned Circle handstamp Type IV, on cover, inscribed "PAID AT HAVANA" in black	1,150.
A3	Crowned Circle handstamp Type V, on cover, inscribed "PAID AT HAVANA"	950.00

Earliest known uses: A1, 11/13/41; A2, 1848; A3, 7/14/48

Stamps of Great Britain, Canceled C58, or with Circular Date Stamp

1865-77

No.	Description	Value
A4	½p rose red (#58 P 6, 12), *value from*	85.00
A5	1p rose red (#33, P 86, 90, 93, 115, 120, 123, 144, 146, 171, 174, 208), *value from*	70.00
A6	2p blue (#29, P 9)	85.00
A7	2p blue (#30, P 14, 15), *value from*	90.00
A8	3p rose (#49, P 4)	160.00
A9	3p rose (#61, P 18, 19)	—
A10	4p vermilion (#43, P 7, 8, 10-14), *value from*	75.00
A11	4p vermilion (#69, P 15)	350.00
A12	6p lilac (#45, P 5)	—
A13	6p gray (#62, P 15)	—
A14	8p orange (#73)	—
A15	9p bister (#52)	310.00
A16	10p red brown (#53)	350.00
A17	1sh green (#48, P 4)	185.00
A18	1sh green (#54, P 4, 5), *value from*	75.00
	Plate 7	*125.00*
A19	1sh green (#64, P 10, 12, 13), *value from*	105.00
A20	2sh blue (#55)	275.00
A21	5sh rose (#57, P 1)	600.00
	Plate 2	750.00
a.	5sh pale rose (#57a, P 1)	600.00
	Plate 2	750.00

St. Jago de Cuba

British P.O. opened 1841; stamps supplied 1866; closed May 30, 1877

Pre-Stamp Postal Markings

1841

No.	Description	Value
A22	Crowned Circle handstamp Type III, on cover, inscribed "PAID AT ST JAGO-DE-CUBA" in red	*7,000.*

Earliest known use: 12/15/41.

Stamps of Great Britain, Canceled C88

1866-77

No.	Description	Value
A23	½p rose red (#58 P 4, 6, 14)	—
A24	1p rose red (#33, P 100, 105, 106, 109, 111, 120, 123, 138, 144, 146-148, 171, 208) *value from*	175.00
A25	1 ½p lake red (#32 P 3)	—

A26 2p blue (#29, P 13, 14) —
A27 2p blue (#30, P 13, 14) 175.00
A28 3p rose (#49, P 5) 175.00
A29 4p vermilion (#43, P 9-14) *value from* 185.00
A30 4p vermilion (#69, P 15) 625.00
A31 6p violet (#51, P 6, 8, 9) *value from* 425.00
A32 6p pale buff (#59b, P 11) —
A33 9p straw (#46) —
A34 9p bister (#52) —
A35 10p red brown (#53) 575.00
A36 1sh green (#54, P 4-6) *value from* 375.00
A37 1sh green (#64, P 9-13) —
A38 2sh blue (#55) 425.00
A39 5sh rose (#57) —

Issued under Spanish Dominion

Used also in Puerto Rico: Nos. 1-3, 9-14, 17-21, 32-34, 35A-37, 39-41, 43-45, 47-49, 51-53, 55-57.
Used also in the Philippines: Nos. 2-3.
Identifiable cancellations of those countries will increase the value of the stamps.

Queen Isabella II — A1

Blue Paper

1855 Typo. Wmk. 104 *Imperf.*
1 A1 ½r p blue green 100.00 7.50
On cover 40.00
a. ½r p blackish green 250.00 30.00
On cover 150.00
2 A1 1r p gray green 100.00 6.50
On cover 40.00
3 A1 2r p carmine 1,000. 15.00
On cover 500.00
4 A1 2r p orange red 1,500. 20.00
On cover —
a. 2r p vermilion 1,600. 22.00
On cover —
Nos. 1-4 (4) 2,700. 49.00

See Nos. 9-14. For surcharges see Nos. 5-8, 15.

Counterfeit surcharges are plentiful.

Nos. 3-4 Surcharged
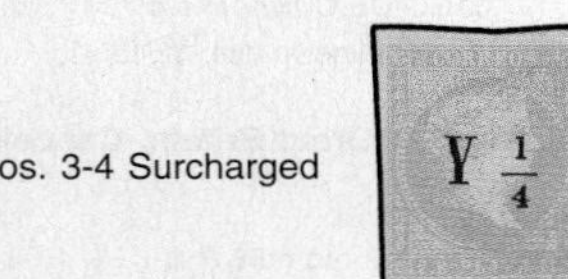

1855-56
5 A1 ¼r p on 2r p car 1,500. 400.00
On cover 1,750.
a. Without fraction bar *3,000.* 2,000.
6 A1 ¼r p on 2r p org red *4,000.* 800.00
On cover 2,250.
a. Without fraction bar — *3,000.*

Surcharged
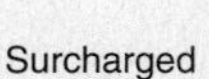

7 A1 ¼r p on 2r p car 1,250. 300.00
On cover *1,250.*
a. Without fraction bar *2,500.* 1,500
8 A1 ¼r p on 2r p org red 1,800. 600.00
On cover *1,500.*
a. Without fraction bar — —

The "Y ¼" surcharge met the "Ynterior" rate for delivery within the city of Havana.

Rough Yellowish Paper

1856 Wmk. 105
9 A1 ½r p yellow grn 10.00 2.00
On cover 75.00
a. ½r p greenish blue 10.00 2.00
On cover 75.00
b. ½r p olive green 10.00 2.00
On cover 75.00
c. "CORRFOS" instead of "CORREOS" — —
On cover —
10 A1 1r p green 1,250. 30.00
On cover 600.00
a. 1r p emerald *1,750.* 100.00
On cover 900.00
b. 1r p olive green *1,250.* 90.00
On cover 750.00
11 A1 2r p orange red 700.00 40.00
On cover 800.00

White Smooth Paper

1857 Unwmk.
12 A1 ½r p blue 5.00 1.00
On cover 30.00
a. ½r p ultramarine 8.00 1.25
On cover 30.00
b. ½r p dark blue 5.00 1.00
On cover 30.00
c. ½r p milky blue (cleaned plate) 5.75 1.00
On cover 30.00
d. "CORRFOS" instead of "CORREOS" — —
On cover —
e. As "c," "CORRFOS" instead of "CORREOS" — —
On cover —
13 A1 1r p gray green 5.00 1.00
On cover 40.00
a. 1r p pale yellow green 5.00 3.25
On cover 40.00
b. 1r p dark green 5.00 .70
On cover 40.00
c. 1r p pale green (cleaned plate) 6.50 1.25
On cover 50.00
14 A1 2r p dull rose 25.00 5.00
On cover 600.00
a. 2r p carmine 25.00 5.00
On cover 600.00
b. 2r p orange red 25.00 5.00
On cover 600.00
Nos. 12-14 (3) 35.00 7.00

Surcharged

1860
15 A1 ¼r p on 2r p dl rose 300.00 100.00
On cover 750.00
a. 1 of ¼ inverted 500.00 200.00
On cover 1,500.
b. "Y ⅛" instead of "1 ¼" —

Queen Isabella II
A2 A3

1862-64 *Imperf.*
16 A2 ¼r p black 30.00 *60.00*
On cover 800.00
17 A3 ¼r p blk, *buff* ('64) 30.00 *60.00*
On cover 800.00
18 A3 ½r p green ('64) 5.00 1.00
On cover 30.00
19 A3 ½r p grn, *pale rose* ('64) 15.00 3.00
On cover 75.00
a. ½r p grn, *rose lilac* 15.00 2.00
On cover 15.00
20 A3 1r p bl, *sal* ('64) 6.00 2.00
On cover 40.00
a. Diagonal half used as ½r p on cover 300.00
21 A3 2r p ver, *buff* ('64) 30.00 8.00
On cover 800.00
a. 2r p red, *buff* 35.00 15.00
On cover 900.00
Nos. 16-21 (6) 116.00 134.00

No. 17 Overprinted in Black

1866
22 A3 ¼r p black, *buff* 85.00 *120.00*
On cover *600.00*

Exists with handstamped "1866."

A5

1866
23 A5 5c dull violet 50.00 60.00
On cover 400.00
24 A5 10c blue 6.00 1.10
On cover 300.00
25 A5 20c green 4.00 1.10
On cover 30.00
a. Diag. half used as 10c on cover —
26 A5 40c rose 50.00 60.00
On cover 900.00
a. 40c deep rose 50.00 55.00
On cover 900.00
Nos. 23-26 (4) 110.00 122.20

For the Type A5 20c in dull lilac, see Spain No. 87.

Stamps Dated "1867"

1867 *Perf. 14*
27 A5 5c dull violet 40.00 35.00
On cover 400.00
28 A5 10c blue 35.00 4.00
On cover 30.00
a. Imperf., pair 110.00 *6.50*
b. Diagonal half used as 5c on cover 300.00
29 A5 20c green 30.00 5.00
On cover 40.00
a. Imperf., pair 110.00 75.00
b. Diag. half used as 10c on cover 325.00
30 A5 40c rose 20.00 30.00
On cover 1,000.
a. Without dot after "1867" 25.00 35.00
Nos. 27-30 (4) 125.00 74.00

A6

1868 Stamps Dated "1868"
31 A6 5c dull violet 30.00 20.00
On cover 200.00
32 A6 10c blue 5.00 2.00
On cover 30.00
a. Diagonal half used as 5c on cover 250.00
33 A6 20c green 10.00 4.00
On cover 40.00
a. Diag. half used as 10c on cover 275.00
b. 20c yellow green 10.50 4.50
On cover 18.50
c. As "b," diag. half used as 10c on cover 300.00
34 A6 40c rose 25.00 15.00
On cover 250.00
a. Diag. half used as 20c on cover 175.00
b. 40c carmine rose 27.50 16.50
On cover 250.00
c. As "b," diag. half used as 10c on cover 175.00
Nos. 31-34 (4) 70.00 41.00

Nos. 31-34 Overprinted in Black

1868
35 A6 5c dull violet 75.00 32.50
On cover —
35A A6 10c blue 75.00 32.50
On cover —
36 A6 20c green 75.00 32.50
On cover —
37 A6 40c rose 75.00 32.50
On cover —
Nos. 35-37 (4) 300.00 130.00

1869 Stamps Dated "1869"
38 A6 5c rose 50.00 40.00
On cover 300.00
39 A6 10c red brown 5.00 2.00
On cover 30.00
a. Diagonal half used as 5c on cover 140.00
40 A6 20c orange 10.00 3.00
On cover 50.00
41 A6 40c dull violet 40.00 30.00
On cover —
Nos. 38-41 (4) 105.00 75.00

Nos. 38-41 Ovptd. Like Nos. 35-37

42 A6 5c rose 100.00 40.00
On cover —
43 A6 10c red brown 100.00 40.00
On cover 2,500.
44 A6 20c orange 100.00 40.00
On cover —
45 A6 40c dull violet 100.00 40.00
On cover —
Nos. 42-45 (4) 400.00 160.00

"Espana" — A8

1870 *Perf. 14*
46 A8 5c blue 250.00 125.00
On cover 750.00
47 A8 10c green 5.00 2.00
On cover 30.00
a. Diagonal half used as 5c on cover 250.00
48 A8 20c red brown 4.00 3.00
On cover 40.00
a. Diag. half used as 10c on cover 300.00
49 A8 40c rose 300.00 100.00
On cover 750.00

Forgeries of No. 46 exist.

"Espana" — A9

1871
50 A9 12c red lilac 25.00 12.00
On cover 200.00
a. Imperf., pair 100.00 —
b. 12c gray lilac 27.50 12.50
51 A9 25c ultra 3.00 1.00
On cover 25.00
a. Imperf., pair 50.00 —
b. Diagonal half used as 12c on cover 125.00
52 A9 50c gray green 4.00 2.00
On cover 30.00
a. Imperf., pair 75.00 —
b. Diagonal half used as 25c on cover 250.00
c. 50c pale green, carton paper 5.00 3.50
53 A9 1p yel brown 40.00 15.00
On cover 600.00
a. Imperf., pair 125.00 —
b. 1p pale brown 42.50 16.50
Nos. 50-53 (4) 72.00 30.00

King Amadeo — A10

1873 *Perf. 14*
54 A10 12½c dark green 40.00 30.00
On cover 200.00
55 A10 25c gray 3.00 1.00
On cover 30.00
a. Diagonal half used as 12½c on cover 120.00
b. 25c lilac 10.00 4.00
On cover 40.00
c. As "b," half used as 12½c on cover 150.00
d. As "b," imperf., pair 50.00 —
56 A10 50c brown 3.00 1.00
On cover 30.00
a. Imperf., pair 75.00 —
b. Half used as 25c on cover 200.00
c. 50c dark brown 1.50 .50
On cover 15.00
d. As "c," half used as 25c on cover 75.00
57 A10 1p red brown 450.00 75.00
On cover 1,500.
a. Diagonal half used as 50c on cover 750.00

"España" — A11

1874
58 A11 12½c brown 30.00 25.00
On cover 300.00
a. Half used as 5c on cover 500.00
59 A11 25c ultra 1.00 .60
On cover 30.00
a. Diagonal half used as 12½c on cover 100.00
b. 25c blue 1.20 .75
On cover 32.50
c. As "b," diagonal half used as 12½c on cover 110.00
d. 25c blue lilac 1.25 .75
On cover 32.50
e. As "d," diagonal half used as 12½c on cover 110.00
60 A11 50c dp violet 2.00 5.00
On cover 60.00
a. Diagonal half used as 25c on cover 200.00
b. "1374" instead of "1874" — —
61 A11 50c gray 5.00 2.00
On cover 60.00
a. Diagonal half used as 25c on cover 175.00
62 A11 1p carmine 350.00 400.00
On cover —
a. Imperf., pair 700.00 *250.00*
Nos. 58-62 (5) 388.00 432.60

Examples of Nos. 61, 63-65, 67-87 with fine impressions in slightly different colors are proofs.

Coat of Arms — A12

1875
63 A12 12½c lt violet 1.50 2.00
On cover 100.00
a. Imperf., pair 100.00
64 A12 25c ultra 1.25 1.60
On cover 30.00
a. Imperf., pair 100.00 —
b. Diagonal half used as 12½c on cover 100.00
65 A12 50c blue green 1.00 2.00
On cover 30.00
a. Imperf., pair 100.00
b. Diag. half used as 25c on cover 80.00
66 A12 1p brown 15.00 10.00
On cover 400.00
b. Diag. half used as 50c on cover 135.00
Nos. 63-66 (4) 18.75 15.60

King Alfonso XII — A13

1876
67 A13 12½c green 3.00 6.00
On cover 75.00
a. 12½c emerald green 3.75 6.00
On cover 75.00
b. 12½c yellow green 1.50 6.00
On cover 75.00
c. 12½c bright green, fine impression 75.00 —
68 A13 25c gray 4.00 3.00
On cover 30.00
a. Diagonal half used as 12½c on cover 100.00
b. 25c pale violet 4.50 3.25
On cover 32.50
c. As "b," half used as 12½c on cover 100.00
d. 25c bluish gray 4.50 3.25
On cover 32.50
e. As "d" half used as 12½c on cover 100.00
f. 25c bright violet, fine impression 10.00 —
69 A13 50c ultra 3.00 6.00
On cover 30.00
a. Imperf., pair 75.00 16.00
b. Diag. half used as 25c on cover 100.00
c. 50c pale blue, fine impression 10.00 —
d. "1870" instead of "1876" 15.00 10.00
On cover 90.00
70 A13 1p black 15.00 25.00
a. Imperf., pair 40.00 40.00
b. Diag. half used as 50c on cover 125.00
c. 1p jet black 17.50 —
Nos. 67-70 (4) 25.00 40.00

King Alfonso XII — A14

1877
71 A14 10c lt green 40.00 —
72 A14 12½c gray 6.00 12.50
On cover 200.00
a. Imperf., pair 100.00 —
b. Diagonal half used on cover 300.00
73 A14 25c dk green 1.00 .50
On cover 30.00
a. Imperf., pair 100.00 —
b. Diagonal half used as 12½c on cover 75.00
74 A14 50c black 1.00 1.50
On cover 30.00
a. Imperf., pair 100.00 —
b. Half used as 25c on cover 100.00
75 A14 1p brown 30.00 25.00
On cover —
Nos. 71-75 (5) 78.00

Fine Impressions
71e A14 10c bright green 32.50
72e A14 12½c gray violet 12.50
73e A14 25c bright green 6.25
74e A14 50c jet black 6.50
75e A14 1p jet black 20.00

No. 71 was not placed in use.

1878 Stamps Dated "1878"
76 A14 5c blue 1.00 2.00
On cover 100.00
b. 5c dark blue 1.00 2.00
On cover 100.00
77 A14 10c black 100.00
78 A14 12½c brown bis 6.00 10.00
On cover 100.00
a. 12½c olive brown 6.00 10.00
On cover 100.00
c. Diagonal half used on cover 200.00
d. As "a," diagonal half used on cover 200.00
79 A14 25c yel green 1.00 2.00
On cover 30.00
b. No. 79, diagonal half used as 12½c on cover 100.00
c. 25c deep green 1.00 2.00
On cover 30.00
d. As "c," diagonal half used on cover 200.00
e. No dot between "CUBA" and "1878" *2.00* *3.00*
On cover 45.00
80 A14 50c dk blue grn 1.00 2.00
On cover 40.00
b. Diagonal half used as 25c on cover 100.00
81 A14 1p carmine 25.00 15.00
b. 1p rose 16.00 *500.00*
c. Diagonal half used as 50c on cover *900.00*
Nos. 76-81 (6) 134.00 31.00

No. 77 was not placed in use.

Imperf., Pairs
76a A14 5c blue 100.00
77a A14 10c black 400.00
78b A14 12½c brown bister 100.00
79a A14 25c deep green 100.00
80a A14 50c dk blue green 200.00
81a A14 1p carmine 150.00

1879 Stamps Dated "1879"
82 A14 5c slate black 1.00 3.00
On cover 150.00
83 A14 10c orange 200.00 *75.00*
84 A14 12½c rose 1.00 3.00
On cover 75.00
85 A14 25c ultra 1.00 2.00
On cover 30.00
a. Diagonal half used as 12½c on cover 100.00
b. Imperf., pair 75.00
86 A14 50c gray 1.00 1.00
On cover 30.00
a. Diag. half used as 25c on cover 100.00
87 A14 1p olive bister 25.00 30.00
On cover *600.00*
Nos. 82-87 (6) 229.00 114.00

Forgeries exist of No. 83.

A15

1880
88 A15 5c green 1.00 2.00
On cover, single franking 100.00
a. 5c dark green 1.25 2.50
On cover, single franking *125.00*
89 A15 10c lake 125.00 —
a. Double impression of frame and lettering 200.00
90 A15 12½c gray 1.00 .50
On cover 75.00
91 A15 25c gray blue 1.00 .50
On cover 30.00
a. Diagonal half used as 12½c on cover 100.00
b. Deformed "5" 7.75 7.50
c. "CU" of "CUBA" missing — —
92 A15 50c brown 1.00 .50
On cover 30.00
a. Diagonal half used as 25c on cover 100.00
93 A15 1p yellow brn 8.00 5.00
a. Diagonal half used as 50c on cover 400.00
Nos. 88-93 (6) 137.00 8.50

No. 89 was not placed in use.

A16

1881
94 A16 1c green 1.00 .50
On cover 100.00
95 A16 2c lake 50.00
96 A16 2½c olive bister 1.00 .50
On cover 50.00
97 A16 5c gray blue .50 .25
On cover 25.00
a. Diag. half used as 2½c on cover 100.00
b. 5c bluish gray .75 .30
On cover 27.50
98 A16 10c yellow brown .50 .25
On cover 30.00
a. Diagonal half used as 5c on cover 100.00
b. 10c pale brown .50 .25
On cover 30.00
c. As "b," diagonal half used as 5c on cover 100.00
99 A16 20c dark brown 6.00 10.00
On cover 200.00
Nos. 94-99 (6) 59.00 11.50

No. 95 was not placed in use.

A17

1882
100 A17 1c green .75 .50
On cover 30.00
a. Diag. half used as ½c on cover 150.00
101 A17 2c lake 5.00 3.00
On cover 50.00
a. Diag. half used as 1c on cover 100.00
b. 2c rose 7.50 3.75
On cover 60.00
c. As "b," diag. half used as 1c on cover 110.00
102 A17 2½c dk brown 10.00 5.00
On cover 75.00
a. Diag. half used as 1c on cover *50.00*
b. 2½c dk olive brown 9.00 5.00
On cover 75.00
103 A17 5c gray blue 8.00 .50
On cover 25.00
a. Diag. half used as 2½c on cover 100.00
b. 5c dark gray blue 9.00 .65
On cover 27.50
c. As "b," diag. half used as 2½c on cover 110.00
104 A17 10c olive bister .75 .50
On cover 25.00
a. Diag. half used as 5c on cover 100.00
105 A17 20c red brown 130.00 50.00
On cover 1,000.
a. Diag. half used as 10c on cover 500.00
Nos. 100-105 (6) 154.50 59.50

See Nos. 121-131. For surcharges see Nos. 106-120.

Issue of 1882 Surcharged or Overprinted in Black, Blue or Red

a

b

c

d

e

1883 Type "a"
106 A17 5 on 5c (R) 3.00 2.00
On cover 150.00
a. Triple surcharge
b. Double surcharge 25.00 25.00
c. Inverted surcharge 30.00 30.00
d. Without "5" in surcharge 20.00 20.00
e. Dbl. surch., types "a" & "d" 75.00 —
107 A17 10 on 10c (Bl) 3.50 2.50
On cover 150.00
a. Inverted surcharge 75.00
b. Double surcharge 30.00 30.00
108 A17 20 on 20c 45.00 75.00
On cover 1,000.
a. "10" instead of "20" 75.00 *75.00*
b. Double surcharge 75.00
c. As "a," inverted surcharge *90.00* *90.00*

Type "b"
109 A17 5 on 5c (R) 3.00 2.00
On cover 150.00
a. Inverted surcharge 30.00 30.00
b. Double surcharge 25.00 25.00
110 A17 10 on 10c (Bl) 10.00 12.00
On cover 250.00
a. Inverted surcharge 35.00 35.00
b. Double surcharge 35.00 35.00
111 A17 20 on 20c 120.00 150.00
On cover —
a. Double surcharge
b. Dbl. surch., types "b" & "c"

Type "c"
112 A17 5 on 5c (R) 2.50 2.00
On cover 175.00
a. Inverted surcharge 35.00 35.00
b. Dbl. surch., types "c" & "d" —
c. Dbl. surch., types "c" & "a"
113 A17 10 on 10c (Bl) 10.00 12.00
On cover 250.00
a. Inverted surcharge 40.00 40.00
b. Double surcharge 40.00 40.00
114 A17 20 on 20c 60.00 100.00
On cover 1,000.
a. "10" instead of "20" 100.00 120.00
b. Double surcharge 100.00 120.00
c. Dbl. surch., types "a" & "c" 100.00 120.00

Type "d"
115 A17 5 on 5c (R) 3.00 2.00
On cover 150.00
a. Inverted surcharge 35.00 35.00
b. Double surcharge 30.00 30.00
116 A17 10 on 10c (Bl) 4.00 3.00
On cover 300.00
a. Inverted surcharge 40.00 40.00
b. Double surcharge 40.00 40.00
c. Dbl. surch., types "d" & "c" — —
117 A17 20 on 20c 85.00 100.00
On cover 1,000.
a. Dbl. surch., types "a" & "d" — —

Type "e"
118 A17 5c gray blue (R) 4.00 3.00
On cover 200.00
a. Double overprint 40.00 40.00
119 A17 10c olive bis (Bl) 12.00 15.00
On cover 300.00
a. Double overprint 40.00 40.00
120 A17 20c red brown 250.00 300.00
On cover —
a. Double overprint 300.00 300.00
Nos. 106-120 (15) 615.00 780.50

Handstamped overprints and surcharges are counterfeits.

Numerous other varieties exist.

Type of 1882

Original

1st retouch

2nd retouch

The differences between the stamps of 1882 and the various retouches are as follows:

Original state: The medallion is surrounded by a heavy line of color of nearly even thickness, touching the horizontal line below the word "Cuba" (or "Filipinas," "Puerto Rico," as the case may be); the opening in the hair above the temple is narrow and pointed.

1st retouch: The line around the medallion is thin, except at the upper right, and does not touch the horizontal line above it; the opening in the hair is slightly wider and a trifle rounded; the lock of hair above the forehead is shaped like a broad "V" and ends in a point; there is a faint white line below it, which is not found on the stamps in the original state. Owing to wear of the plate the shape of the lock of hair and the width of the white line below it vary.

2nd retouch: The opening in the hair forms a semi-circle; the lock above the forehead is nearly straight, having only a slight wave, and the white line is much broader than before.

1883-86
121 A17 1c grn, 2nd retouch 150.00 40.00
On cover 300.00
122 A17 2½c olive bister .50 .30
On cover 60.00
124 A17 2½c violet 1.00 .40
On cover 75.00
a. 2½c red lilac ('85) 1.00 .40
On cover 75.00
b. 2½c ultramarine 125.00 150.00
125 A17 5c gray bl, 1st retouch 100.00 .50
On cover 25.00
a. Diag. half used as 2½c on cover 75.00
126 A17 5c gray bl, 2nd retouch 120.00 2.00
On cover 50.00
a. Diag. half used as 2½c on cover 125.00
127 A17 10c brn, 1st retouch 3.00 1.00
On cover 40.00
a. Diagonal half used as 5c on cover 75.00
b. 10c reddish brn, ist retouch 3.00 1.25
On cover 42.50
c. Imperf, pair 300.00 —
128 A17 20c olive bister 15.00 10.00
On cover 100.00
Nos. 121-128 (7) 389.50 54.20

1888
129 A17 2½c red brown 1.75 .85
On cover 10.00
a. 2½c pale brn, 1st retouch 2.00 1.00
On cover 10.00

130 A17 10c blue 1.50 1.00
On cover 25.00
a. Diagonal half used as 5c on cover 175.00
131 A17 20c brnsh gray 15.00 10.00
On cover 125.00
Nos. 129-131 (3) 18.25 11.85

King Alfonso XIII — A18

1890-97

132 A18 1c gray brown 20.00 6.50
On cover 50.00
133 A18 1c ol gray ('91) 10.00 4.00
On cover 50.00
134 A18 1c ultra ('94) 5.00 .50
On cover 40.00
135 A18 1c dk vio ('96) 1.50 .50
On cover 40.00
136 A18 2c slate blue 10.00 3.00
On cover 75.00
137 A18 2c lilac brn ('91) 2.00 .75
On cover 75.00
138 A18 2c rose ('94) 35.00 5.00
On cover 125.00
139 A18 2c claret ('96) 9.00 5.00
On cover 150.00
140 A18 2½c emerald 12.50 5.00
On cover 75.00
141 A18 2½c salmon ('91) 60.00 5.00
On cover 200.00
142 A18 2½c lilac ('94) 4.00 3.00
On cover 75.00
143 A18 2½c rose ('96) 4.00 6.00
On cover 175.00
144 A18 5c olive gray 1.00 .75
On cover 30.00
b. Diagonal half used as 2½c on cover 500.00
145 A18 5c emerald ('91) 1.00 .50
On cover 30.00
b. Diagonal half used as 2½c on cover 500.00
146 A18 5c sl blue ('96) .75 1.00
On cover 30.00
b. Diagonal half used as 2½c on cover 600.00
147 A18 10c brown violet 6.00 1.00
On cover 30.00
b. Diagonal half used as 5c on cover 500.00
148 A18 10c claret ('91) 2.50 .50
On cover 30.00
b. Diagonal half used as 5c on cover 400.00
149 A18 10c emerald ('96) 1.00 1.50
On cover 30.00
150 A18 20c dk violet 2.00 1.00
On cover 75.00
151 A18 20c ultra ('91) 25.00 8.00
On cover 400.00
152 A18 20c red brn ('94) 20.00 30.00
On cover 300.00
153 A18 20c violet ('96) 15.00 10.00
On cover 200.00
b. Diagonal half used as 10c on cover 600.00
154 A18 40c orange brn ('97) 40.00 35.00
On cover 2,500.
155 A18 80c lilac brn ('97) 80.00 70.00
On cover 2,500.
Nos. 132-155 (24) 367.25 203.50

Imperf., Pairs

134a A18 1c ultramarine 100.00
135a A18 1c dark violet 100.00
138a A18 2c rose 100.00
139a A18 2c claret 100.00
142a A18 2½c lilac 100.00
143a A18 2½c rose 100.00
145a A18 5c emerald 100.00
146a A18 5c slate blue 100.00
148a A18 10c claret 100.00
149a A18 10c emerald 100.00
152a A18 20c red brown 135.00
153a A18 20c violet 125.00
154a A18 40c orange brown 115.00
155a A18 80c red brown 175.00

King Alfonso XIII — A19

1898

156 A19 1m orange brn .75 1.00
On cover 150.00
157 A19 2m orange brn .30 1.00
On cover 150.00
158 A19 3m orange brn .30 1.00
On cover 150.00
159 A19 4m orange brn 6.00 12.00
On cover 500.00
160 A19 5m orange brn .30 1.00
On cover 150.00
161 A19 1c black vio .30 1.00
On cover 75.00
162 A19 2c dk blue grn .30 1.00
On cover 50.00
163 A19 3c dk brown .30 1.00
On cover 50.00
164 A19 4c orange 16.00 12.00
On cover 1,000.
165 A19 5c car rose 1.25 .50
On cover 40.00
166 A19 6c dk blue .50 1.50
On cover 75.00
167 A19 8c gray brown 2.00 4.00
On cover 300.00
168 A19 10c vermilion 1.30 .75
On cover 1,000.
169 A19 15c slate green 6.00 10.00
On cover 400.00
170 A19 20c maroon 4.00 1.00
On cover 200.00
171 A19 40c dark lilac 5.00 8.00
On cover 600.00
172 A19 60c black 10.00 20.00
On cover 800.00
173 A19 80c red brown 20.00 25.00
174 A19 1p yel green 20.00 25.00
175 A19 2p slate blue 35.00 40.00
Nos. 156-175 (20) 129.60 166.75

Nos. 156-160 were issued for use on newspapers.

Nos. 156-175 exist imperf. Value, unused pairs, $7,500. Only one set of pairs is currently known.

For surcharges see Nos. 176-189C, 196-200.

Issued under Administration of the United States
Puerto Principe Issue

Issues of Cuba of 1898 and 1896 Surcharged

a

b

1898-99

176 (a) 1c on 1m org brn 100.00 60.00
On cover —
177 (b) 1c on 1m org brn 600.00 115.00
On cover *7,000.*
a. Broken figure "1" *3,000.* 275.00
b. Inverted surcharge *500.00*
d. As "a," inverted *1,500.*

c

d

178 (c) 2c on 2m org brn 65.00 62.50
On cover *5,000.*
a. Inverted surcharge 500.00 100.00
179 (d) 2c on 2m org brn 82.50 77.50
On cover *5,500.*
a. Inverted surcharge 350.00 *500.00*

k

l

179B (k) 3c on 1m org brn 300. 175.
On cover *4,000.*
c. Double surcharge 1,500. *3,000.*

An unused example is known with "cents" omitted.

179D (l) 3c on 1m org brn *1,350. 675.00*

e

f

179F (e) 3c on 2m org brn *1,500.*

Value is for example with minor faults.

179G (f) 3c on 2m org brn — *2,000.*

Value is for example with minor faults.

180 (e) 3c on 3m org brn 150. *100.*
On cover *5,000.*
a. Inverted surcharge 375.
181 (f) 3c on 3m org brn 600. 400.
a. Inverted surcharge *750.*

g

h

i

j

182 (g) 5c on 1m org brn 1,000. 170.
On cover *5,750.*
a. Inverted surcharge — *1,000.*
183 (h) 5c on 1m org brn *1,500. 1,000.*
a. Inverted surcharge — *1,500.*
184 (g) 5c on 2m org brn 1,000. 275.
185 (h) 5c on 2m org brn 1,500. 600.
186 (g) 5c on 3m org brn 1,500. 350.
a. Inverted surcharge 1,200. 700.
187 (h) 5c on 3m org brn — 500.
a. Inverted surcharge — 1,000.
188 (g) 5c on 5m org brn 145. 230.
a. Inverted surcharge 400. 200.
On cover *6,000.*
b. Double surcharge — —
189 (h) 5c on 5m org brn 3,000. 425.
a. Inverted surcharge *3,000. 900.*
b. Double surcharge — —

The 2nd printing of Nos. 188-189 has shiny ink. Values are for the 1st printing.

189C (i) 5c on 5m org brn *7,500.*

No. 191

Black Surcharge on No. P25

190 (g) 5c on ½m bl grn 375. 115.
a. Inverted surcharge 1,000. 210.
b. Pair, one without surcharge 500.

Value for 190b is for pair with unsurcharged stamp at right. Also exists with unsurcharged stamp at left.

191 (h) 5c on ½m bl grn 1,000. 275.
a. Inverted surcharge *1,000.*
192 (i) 5c on ½m bl grn 3,000. 100.
a. Dbl. surch., one diagonal *3,500. 11,500.*
193 (j) 5c on ½m bl grn 900. 500.

Red Surcharge on No. 161

196 (k) 3c on 1c blk vio 150. 125.
On cover *3,000.*
a. Inverted surcharge 500.
197 (l) 3c on 1c blk vio 250. 200.
On cover *3,000.*
a. Inverted surcharge *1,500.*
198 (i) 5c on 1c blk vio 92.50 72.50
On cover *6,000.*
a. Inverted surcharge 500.
b. Surcharge vert. reading up *3,500.*
c. Double surcharge *600.* 500.
d. Double invtd. surch. — 2,750.

Value for No. 198b is for surcharge reading up. One example is known with surcharge reading down.

199 (j) 5c on 1c blk vio 150. 115.
a. Inverted surcharge *3,000.*
b. Vertical surcharge — *2,000.*
c. Double surcharge *3,000. 3,000.*

m

200 (m) 10c on 1c blk vio 62.50 *92.50*
a. Broken figure "1" 160.00 *225.00*

Black Surcharge on Nos. P26-P30

201 (k) 3c on 1m bl grn 350. 350.
On cover *5,800.*
a. Inverted surcharge 450.
b. "EENTS" 600. 450.
c. As "b", inverted 850.
202 (l) 3c on 1m bl grn 1,000. 400.
a. Inverted surcharge 850.
203 (k) 3c on 2m bl grn 1,650. 400.
a. "EENTS" 1,650. 500.
b. Inverted surcharge 1,500.
c. As "a," inverted *2,750.*
204 (l) 3c on 2m bl grn 2,750. 600.
a. Inverted surcharge *1,500.*
205 (k) 3c on 3m bl grn 900. 400.
a. Inverted surcharge 750.
b. "EENTS" 1,250. 450.
c. As "b," inverted *2,750.*
206 (l) 3c on 3m bl grn 1,500. 550.
a. Inverted surcharge *1,000.*
211 (i) 5c on 1m bl grn 1,800.
a. "EENTS" — 3,000.
212 (j) 5c on 1m bl grn 3,000. 2,250.
213 (i) 5c on 2m bl grn 1,800.
a. "EENTS" 3,000. 3,000.
214 (j) 5c on 2m bl grn 3,000. 1,750.
215 (i) 5c on 3m bl grn 550.
a. "EENTS" 1,000.
216 (j) 5c on 3m bl grn 3,000. 1,000.
217 (i) 5c on 4m bl grn *3,000.* 900.
a. "EENTS" *3,000.* 1,500.
b. Inverted surcharge *2,000.*
c. As "a," inverted 3,000.
218 (j) 5c on 4m bl grn 3,000. *1,500.*
a. Inverted surcharge *2,000.*
219 (i) 5c on 8m bl grn *2,500.* 1,250.
a. Inverted surcharge 1,500.
b. "EENTS" 3,000. 2,750.
c. As "b," inverted 2,500.
220 (j) 5c on 8m bl grn 2,000.
a. Inverted surcharge 2,500.

Beware of forgeries of the Puerto Principe issue. Obtaining expert opinions is recommended.

United States Stamps Nos. 279, 267, 267b, 279Bf, 279Bh, 268, 281, 282C and 283 Surcharged in Black

1899 **Wmk. 191** ***Perf. 12***

221 A87 1c on 1c yel grn 4.50 .40
Never hinged 11.50
On cover 15.00
222 A88 2c on 2c reddish car, type III 10.00 .75
Never hinged 25.00
On cover 22.50
b. 2c on 2c vermilion, type III 10.00 .75
222A A88 2c on 2c reddish car, type IV 6.00 .40
Never hinged 15.00
On cover 12.50
c. 2c on 2c vermilion, type IV 6.00 .40
d. As No. 222A, inverted surcharge *5,500. 4,000.*
223 A88 2½c on 2c reddish car, type III 6.00 .80
Never hinged 15.00
On cover 20.00
b. 2½c on 2c vermilion, type III 6.00 .80
223A A88 2½c on 2c reddish car, type IV 3.50 .50
Never hinged 8.75
On cover 12.50
c. 2½c on 2c vermilion 3.50 .50

224 A89 3c on 3c pur 12.00 1.75
Never hinged 30.00
On cover 25.00
a. Period between "B" and "A" 40.00 35.00
225 A91 5c on 5c bl 12.50 2.00
Never hinged 30.00
On cover 30.00
226 A94 10c on 10c brn, type I 25.00 6.00
On cover - 110.00
b. "CUBA" omitted *7,000. 4,000.*
226A A94 10c on 10c brn, type II *6,000.*
Nos. 221-226 (8) 79.50 12.60

The 2½c was sold and used as a 2c stamp. Excellent counterfeits of this and the preceding issue exist, especially inverted and double surcharges.

Issues of the Republic under US Military Rule

Statue of Columbus A20

Royal Palms A21

"Cuba" A22

Ocean Liner A23

Cane Field — A24

1899 Wmk. US-C (191C) *Perf. 12*

227 A20 1c yel grn 3.50 .25
Never hinged 8.75
On cover 2.00
228 A21 2c carmine 3.50 .25
Never hinged 8.75
On cover 2.00
a. scarlet 3.50 .25
b. Booklet pane of 6 *5,500.*
229 A22 3c purple 3.50 .30
Never hinged 8.75
On cover 4.00
230 A23 5c blue 4.50 .30
Never hinged 11.00
On cover 4.00
231 A24 10c brown 11.00 .80
Never hinged 27.50
On cover 6.50
Nos. 227-231 (5) 26.00 1.90

No. 228b was issued by the Republic.
See Nos. 233-237. For surcharge see No. 232.

Issues of the Republic

No. 229 Surcharged in Carmine

1902, Sept. 30

232 A22 1c on 3c purple 2.75 .50
a. Inverted surcharge 150.00 150.00
b. Surcharge sideways (numeral horizontal) 200.00 200.00
c. Double surcharge 200.00 200.00

Counterfeits of the errors are plentiful.

Re-engraved

The re-engraved stamps of 1905-07 may be distinguished from the issue of 1899 as follows:

ORIGINAL RE-ENGRAVED

1c — The ends of the label inscribed "Centavo" are rounded instead of square.
2c — The foliate ornaments, inside the oval disks bearing the numerals of value, have been removed.
5c — Two lines forming a right angle have been added in the upper corners of the label bearing the word "Cuba."
10c — A small ball has been added to each of the square ends of the label bearing the word "Cuba."

1905 Unwmk. *Perf. 12*

233 A20 1c green 1.75 .25
234 A21 2c rose 1.20 .25
a. Booklet pane of 6 150.00
236 A23 5c blue 42.50 1.00
237 A24 10c brown 3.50 .50
Nos. 233-237 (4) 48.95 2.00

Maj. Gen. Antonio Maceo — A26

1907

238 A26 50c gray bl & blk 1.75 .80

Bartolomé Masó A27

Máximo Gómez A28

Julio Sanguily A29

Ignacio Agramonte A30

Calixto García A31

José M. Rodriquez y Rodriquez (Mayia) A32

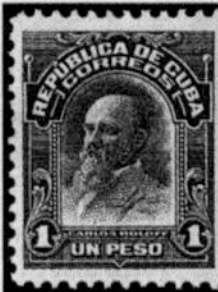

Carlos Roloff — A33

1910, Feb. 1

239 A27 1c grn & vio 1.00 .30
a. Center inverted 260.00 260.00
240 A28 2c car & grn 1.90 .30
a. Center inverted 575.00 575.00
241 A29 3c vio & bl 1.35 .30
242 A30 5c bl & grn 20.00 .80
243 A31 8c ol & vio 1.35 .30
244 A32 10c brn & bl 8.00 .65
a. Center inverted 850.00
245 A26 50c vio & blk 1.90 .50
246 A33 1p slate & blk 9.25 4.00
Nos. 239-246 (8) 44.75 7.15
Set, never hinged 72.50

1911-13

247 A27 1c green 1.00 .25
248 A28 2c car rose 1.35 .25
a. Booklet pane of 6 ('13) 82.50
250 A30 5c ultra 3.75 .25
251 A31 8c ol grn & blk 2.00 .60
252 A33 1p black 9.50 2.00
Nos. 247-252 (5) 17.60 3.35
Set, never hinged 25.00

Map of Cuba — A34

1914-15

253 A34 1c green .80 .25
a. Booklet pane of 6 100.00
254 A34 2c car rose .95 .25
a. Booklet pane of 6 100.00
255 A34 2c red ('15) 1.50 .25
a. Booklet pane of 6 100.00
256 A34 3c violet 4.75 .35
257 A34 5c blue 6.50 .25
258 A34 8c ol grn 5.25 .70
259 A34 10c brown 9.50 .35
260 A34 10c ol grn ('15) 11.50 .55
261 A34 50c orange 75.00 10.00
262 A34 1p gray 110.00 24.00
Nos. 253-262 (10) 225.75 36.95
Set, never hinged 400.00

Complete set of eight 1914 stamps, imperf. pairs, value $1,500.
Nos. 253, 254, 256 and E5 exist with "1917 GOB./CONSTITUCIONAL/CAMAGUEY" overprint. These were not authorized.

Gertrudis Gómez de Avellaneda, Cuban Poetess (1814-73) A34a

1914

263 A34a 5c blue 18.00 5.00
Never hinged 30.00

José Martí A35

Máximo Gómez A36

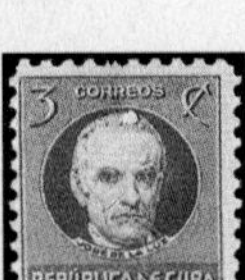

José de la Luz Caballero A37

Calixto García A38

Ignacio Agramonte A39

Tomás Estrada Palma A40

José A. Saco — A41

Antonio Maceo — A42

Carlos Manuel de Céspedes — A43

1917-18 Unwmk. *Perf. 12*

264 A35 1c bl grn 1.00 .25
a. Booklet pane of 6 40.00
b. Booklet pane of 30 250.00
265 A36 2c rose 1.05 .25
a. Booklet pane of 6 50.00
b. Booklet pane of 30 210.00
266 A36 2c lt red ('18) .85 .25
a. Booklet pane of 6 50.00
267 A37 3c violet 1.10 .25
a. Imperf. pair 275.00
b. Booklet pane of 6 50.00
268 A38 5c dp bl 1.05 .25
269 A39 8c red brn 5.50 .25
270 A40 10c yel brn 3.25 .25
271 A41 20c gray grn 18.50 1.60
272 A42 50c dl rose 18.50 .70
273 A43 1p black 19.00 .70
Nos. 264-273 (10) 69.80 4.75
Set, never hinged 110.00

1925-28 Wmk. 106 *Perf. 12*

274 A35 1c bl grn 1.10 .25
a. Booklet pane of 6 350.00
275 A36 2c brt rose 1.20 .25
a. Booklet pane of 6 75.00
b. Booklet pane of 30 350.00
276 A38 5c dp bl 2.50 .25
277 A39 8c red brn ('28) 5.75 .65
278 A40 10c yel brn ('27) 7.00 .70
279 A41 20c olive grn 11.00 1.10
Nos. 274-279 (6) 28.55 3.20
Set, never hinged 50.00

1926 *Imperf.*

280 A35 1c blue green 2.75 2.00
281 A36 2c brt rose 2.75 2.00
282 A38 5c deep blue 3.50 2.75
Nos. 280-282 (3) 9.00 6.75
Set, never hinged 10.00

See Nos. 304-310. For overprint and surcharge see Nos. 317-318, 644 (in Scott Standard catalogue, Vol. 2).

Arms of Republic A44

1927, May 20 Unwmk. *Perf. 12*

283 A44 25c violet 18.00 3.50
Never hinged 27.50

25th anniversary of the Republic.
For surcharges see Nos. 355, C3.

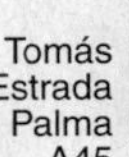

Tomás Estrada Palma A45

Designs: 2c, Gen. Gerardo Machado. 5c, Morro Castle. 8c, Havana Railway Station. 10c, Presidential Palace. 13c, Tobacco Plantation. 20c, Treasury Building. 30c, Sugar Mill. 50c, Havana Cathedral. 1p, Galician Clubhouse, Havana.

1928, Jan. 2 **Wmk. 106**

No.	Type	Description	Unused	Used
284	A45	1c deep green	.60	.30
285	A45	2c brt rose	.60	.30
286	A45	5c deep blue	1.75	.50
287	A45	8c lt red brn	3.75	1.10
288	A45	10c bister brn	1.50	.80
289	A45	13c orange	2.10	.80
290	A45	20c olive grn	2.50	.95
291	A45	30c dk violet	5.25	.75
292	A45	50c carmine rose	8.00	2.75
293	A45	1p gray black	16.00	6.25
		Nos. 284-293 (10)	42.05	14.50
		Set, never hinged	67.50	

Sixth Pan-American Conference.

Capitol, Havana
A55

1929, May 18

No.	Type	Description	Unused	Used
294	A55	1c green	.50	.35
295	A55	2c carmine rose	.50	.30
296	A55	5c blue	.65	.40
297	A55	10c bister brn	1.35	.50
298	A55	20c violet	4.50	2.75
		Nos. 294-298 (5)	7.50	4.30
		Set, never hinged	12.00	

Opening of the Capitol, Havana.

Hurdler — A56

1930, Mar. 15 **Engr.**

No.	Type	Description	Unused	Used
299	A56	1c green	.95	.45
300	A56	2c carmine	.95	.50
301	A56	5c deep blue	1.25	.50
302	A56	10c bister brn	2.50	.95
303	A56	20c violet	15.00	3.25
		Nos. 299-303 (5)	20.65	5.65
		Set, never hinged	32.50	

2nd Central American Athletic Games.

Types of 1917 Portrait Issue
Flat Plate Printing

1930-45 Wmk. 106 Engr. *Perf. 10*

No.	Type	Description	Unused	Used
304	A35	1c blue green	.80	.25
a.		Booklet pane of 6	50.00	
b.		Booklet pane of 30	—	
305	A36	2c brt rose	75.00	—
a.		Booklet pane of 6	1,200.	
305B	A37	3c dk rose vio ('42)	4.00	.75
c.		Booklet pane of 6	42.50	
306	A38	5c dk blue	2.75	.25
306A	A39	8c red brn ('45)	2.75	.25
307	A40	10c brown	2.75	.25
a.		10c yellow brown ('35)	3.50	.75
307B	A41	20c olive grn ('41)	4.75	.75
		Nos. 304-307B (7)	92.80	2.50

Nos. 305 and 305B were printed for booklet panes and all examples have straight edges.

For surcharge see No. 644.

Rotary Press Printing

No.	Type	Description	Unused	Used
308	A35	1c blue grn	1.10	.25
309	A36	2c brt rose	1.10	.25
a.		Booklet pane of 50		
310	A37	3c violet	1.50	.25
a.		3c dull violet ('38)	1.10	.25
b.		3c rose violet ('41)	1.10	.25
c.		Booklet pane of 50		
		Nos. 308-310 (3)	3.70	.75

Flat plate stamps measure 18½x21½mm; rotary press, 19x22mm.

The Mangos of Baragua — A57

War Memorial — A61

Battle of Mal Tiempo
A58

Battle of Coliseo
A59

Maceo, Gómez and Zayas
A60

Wmk. 229

1933, Apr. 23 **Photo.** ***Perf. 12½***

No.	Type	Description	Unused	Used
312	A57	3c dk brown	2.00	.30
313	A58	5c dk blue	1.75	.40
314	A59	10c emerald	3.50	.40
315	A60	13c red	4.00	1.10
316	A61	20c black	7.75	3.00
		Nos. 312-316 (5)	19.00	5.20
		Set, never hinged	29.00	

War of Independence and dedication of the "Soldado Invasor" (the American Army that came to the aid of the revolution against Spain) monument.

Types of 1917 Issues with Carmine or Black Overprint Reading Up or Down

Rotary Press Printing

Wmk. 106

1933, Dec. 23 **Engr.** ***Perf. 10***

No.	Type	Description	Unused	Used
317	A35	1c blue green (C)	1.50	.25

With Additional Surcharge of New Value and Bars

No.	Type	Description	Unused	Used
318	A37	2c on 3c vio (Bk)	1.50	.25

Establishment of a revolutionary junta.

Catalogue values for Nos. 317-318 unused are for examples with overprint reading up. Values for overprint reading down, $4.

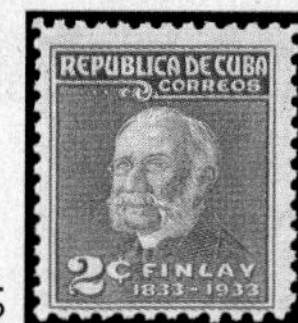

Dr. Carlos J. Finlay — A62

1934, Dec. 3 **Engr.** ***Perf. 10***

No.	Type	Description	Unused	Used
319	A62	2c dark carmine	1.35	.50
320	A62	5c dark blue	3.75	1.50
		Set, never hinged	8.00	

Cent. of the birth of Dr. Carlos J. Finlay (1833-1915), physician-biologist who found that a mosquito transmitted yellow fever.

Pres. José Miguel Gómez — A63

Gómez Monument
A64

1936, May ***Perf. 10***

No.	Type	Description	Unused	Used
322	A63	1c green	2.25	.40
323	A64	2c carmine	3.25	.50
		Set, never hinged	8.00	

Unveiling of a monument to Gen. José Miguel Gómez, ex-president.

Matanzas Issue

Map of Cuba
A65

2c, Map of Free Zone. 4c, S. S. "Rex" in Matanzas Bay. 5c, Ships in Matanzas Bay. 8c, Caves of Bellamar. 10c, Valley of Yumuri. 20c, Yumuri River. 50c, Ships Leaving Port.

Wmk. 229

1936, May 5 **Photo.** ***Perf. 12½***

No.	Type	Description	Unused	Used
324	A65	1c blue green	.45	.25
325	A65	2c red	.70	.25
326	A65	4c claret	1.20	.25
327	A65	5c ultra	1.75	.25
328	A65	8c orange brn	3.00	.70
329	A65	10c emerald	3.25	.70
330	A65	20c brown	6.25	2.50
331	A65	50c slate	11.50	3.50
		Nos. 324-331,C18-C21,CE1,E8 (14)	55.70	21.85
		Set, never hinged	92.50	

Exist imperf. Value 20% more.

"Peace and Work"
A73

Máximo Gómez Monument — A74

Torch — A75

"Independence" — A76

"Messenger of Peace" — A77

1936, Nov. 18 ***Perf. 12½***

No.	Type	Description	Unused	Used
332	A73	1c emerald	.75	.25
333	A74	2c crimson	.90	.30
334	A75	4c maroon	1.05	.30
335	A76	5c ultra	4.00	.55
336	A77	8c dk green	6.00	1.20
		Nos. 332-336,C22-C23,E9 (8)	26.55	7.20
		Set, never hinged	48.00	

Maj. Gen. Máximo Gómez, birth centenary.

Issued both perf and imperf. Values for imperfs are approx. 400% higher.

Sugar Cane — A78

Primitive Sugar Mill — A79

Modern Sugar Mill — A80

Wmk. 106

1937, Oct. 2 **Engr.** ***Perf. 10***

No.	Type	Description	Unused	Used
337	A78	1c yellow green	1.75	.40
338	A79	2c red	1.00	.25
339	A80	5c bright blue	2.25	.40
		Nos. 337-339 (3)	5.00	1.05
		Set, never hinged	8.50	

Cuban sugar cane industry, 400th anniv.

Argentine Emblem — A81

Mountain Scene (Bolivia) — A82

Arms of Brazil — A83

Canadian Scene — A84

Camilo Henriquez (Chile)
A85

Gen, Francisco de Paula Santander (Colombia)
A86

Natl. Monument (Costa Rica) — A87

Autograph of José Marti (Cuba) — A88

Columbus Lighthouse (Dominican Rep.) — A89

Juan Montalvo (Ecuador) — A90

Abraham Lincoln (US) A91

Quetzal and Scroll (Guatemala) A92

Arms of Haiti A93

Francisco Morazán (Honduras) A94

Fleet of Columbus — A95

Wmk. 106

1937, Oct. 13 Engr. *Perf. 10*

340 A81 1c deep green .75 .75
341 A82 1c green .75 .75
342 A83 2c carmine .75 .75
343 A84 2c carmine .75 .75
344 A85 3c violet 1.75 1.75
345 A86 3c violet 1.75 1.75
346 A87 4c bister brown 2.10 2.10
347 A88 4c bister brown 3.75 3.75
348 A89 5c blue 1.90 1.90
349 A90 5c blue 1.90 1.90
350 A91 8c citron 7.00 7.00
351 A92 8c citron 3.25 3.25
352 A93 10c maroon 3.25 3.25
353 A94 10c maroon 3.25 3.25
354 A95 25c rose lilac 35.00 35.00
Nos. 340-354,C24-C29,E10-E11 (23) 132.90 132.90
Set, never hinged 170.00

Nos. 340-354 were sold by the Cuban PO for 3 days, Oct. 13-15, during which no other stamps were sold. They were postally valid for the full face value. Proceeds from their three-day sale above 30,000 pesos were paid by the Cuban POD to the Assoc. of American Writers and Artists. Remainders were overprinted "SVP" (Without Postal Value).

No. 283 Surcharged in Green

1937, Nov. 19 Unwmk. *Perf. 12*

355 A44 10c on 25c violet 16.00 4.00
Never hinged 22.50

Centenary of Cuban railroads.

Ciboney Indian and Cigar — A96

Cigar and Globe — A97

Tobacco Plant and Cigars — A98

1939, Aug. 28 Wmk. 106 *Perf. 10*

356 A96 1c yellow green .75 .25
357 A97 2c red 1.00 .25
358 A98 5c brt ultra 1.75 .30
Nos. 356-358 (3) 3.50 .80
Set, never hinged 5.25

General Calixto García
A99 A100

1939, Nov. 6 *Perf. 10, Imperf.*

359 A99 2c dark red .95 .25
360 A100 5c deep blue 1.25 .40
Set, never hinged 3.50

Birth centenary of General Garcia.

Values are for perf examples. Value of imperfs approx. 20% higher.

Gonzalo de Quesada — A101

1940, Apr. 30 Engr. *Perf. 10*

361 A101 2c rose red 1.75 .50
Never hinged 2.75

Pan American Union, 50th anniversary.

Rotary Club Emblem, Cuban Flag and Tobacco Plant — A102

1940, May 18 Wmk. 106 *Perf. 10*

362 A102 2c rose red 2.75 .75
Never hinged 4.00

Rotary Intl. Convention held at Havana.

Lions Emblem, Cuban Flag and Royal Palms — A103

1940, July 23

363 A103 2c orange vermilion 2.75 .75
Never hinged 4.00

Lions International Convention, Havana.

Dr. Nicolás J. Gutiérrez A104

1940, Oct. 28

364 A104 2c orange ver 1.90 .30
365 A104 5c blue 2.50 .30
a. Sheet of four, imperf., unwmkd. 8.50 3.00
Never hinged 12.00
b. As "a," black overprint ('51) 11.00 4.75
Never hinged 17.00
Set, never hinged 5.50

100th anniv. of the publication of the 1st Cuban Medical Review, "El Repertorio Medico Habanero."

No. 365a contains 2 each of Nos. 364-365 imperf. and sold for 25c.

For overprint see No. C43A.

In 1951 No. 365a was overprinted in black: "50 Aniversario Descubrimiento Agente Transmisor de la Flebre Amarilla por el Dr. Carlos J. Finlay Honor a los Martires de la Ciencia 1901 1951." The overprint is illustrated over No. C43A, but does not include the plane and "Correo Aereo."

SEMI-POSTAL STAMPS

Common Design Types pictured following the introduction.

Curie Issue

Common Design Type

Wmk. 106

1938, Nov. 23 Engr. *Perf. 10*

B1 CD80 2c + 1c salmon 4.25 1.00
B2 CD80 5c + 1c deep ultra 4.25 1.40
Set, never hinged 12.00

40th anniv. of the discovery of radium by Pierre and Marie Curie. Surtax for the benefit of the Intl. Union for the Control of Cancer.

AIR POST STAMPS

Seaplane over Havana Harbor AP1

Wmk. 106

1927, Nov. 1 Engr. *Perf. 12*

C1 AP1 5c dark blue 8.00 1.00
Never hinged 13.50

For overprint see No. C30.

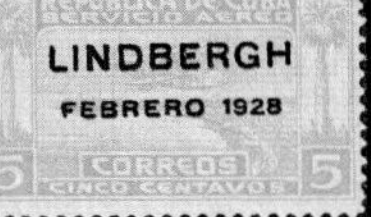

Type of 1927 Issue Overprinted

1928, Feb. 8

C2 AP1 5c carmine rose 6.25 1.60
Never hinged 10.00

No. 283 Surcharged in Red

1930, Oct. 27 Unwmk.

C3 A44 10c on 25c violet 5.75 1.60
Never hinged 8.50

Airplane and Coast of Cuba — AP3

For Foreign Postage

1931, Feb. 26 Wmk. 106 *Perf. 10*

C4 AP3 5c green .45 .25
C5 AP3 10c dk blue .45 .25
C6 AP3 15c rose .90 .30
C7 AP3 20c brown .90 .25
C8 AP3 30c dk violet 1.25 .25
C9 AP3 40c dp orange 4.00 .35
C10 AP3 50c olive grn 6.75 .35
C11 AP3 1p black 10.00 .90
Nos. C4-C11 (8) 24.70 2.90
Set, never hinged 37.50

See No. C40. For surcharges see Nos. C16-C17, C203, C225. Post 1940 issues in Scott Standard catalogue, Vol. 2.

Airplane AP4

For Domestic Postage

1931-46

C12 AP4 5c rose vio ('32) .40 .25
a. 5c brown violet ('36) .40 .25
C13 AP4 10c gray blk .40 .25
C14 AP4 20c car rose 3.25 .90
C14A AP4 20c rose pink ('46) 1.40 .25
C15 AP4 50c dark blue 5.25 .90
Nos. C12-C15 (5) 10.70 2.55
Set, never hinged 17.00

See No. C130. For overprints see Nos. C31, E29-E30. Post 1940 issues in Scott Standard catalogue, Vol. 2.

Type of 1931 Surcharged in Black

1935, Apr. 24 *Perf. 10*

C16 AP3 10c + 10c red 15.00 9.50
Never hinged 20.00
a. Double surcharge 110.00

Imperf

C17 AP3 10c + 10c red 40.00 40.00
Never hinged 55.00 55.00

Matanzas Issue

Air View of Matanzas AP5

10c, Airship "Macon." 20c, Airplane "The Four Winds." 50c, Air View of Fort San Severino.

Wmk. 229

1936, May 5 Photo. *Perf. 12½*

C18 AP5 5c violet .85 .30
C19 AP5 10c yellow orange 1.00 .50
C20 AP5 20c green 3.75 1.90
C21 AP5 50c greenish slate 9.00 3.75
Nos. C18-C21 (4) 14.60 6.45
Set, never hinged 22.50

Exist imperf. Value 20% more.

"Lightning" AP9

Allegory of Flight AP10

1936, Nov. 18

C22 AP9	5c violet	2.10	1.10
C23 AP10	10c orange brown	2.75	1.50
	Set, never hinged	6.00	

Major Gen. Maximo Gomez, birth cent.

Flat Arch (Panama) — AP11

Carlos Antonio López (Paraguay) — AP12

Inca Gate, Cuzco (Peru) — AP13

Atlacatl (Salvador) AP14

José Enrique Rodó (Uruguay) AP15

Simón Bolívar (Venezuela) AP16

Wmk. 106

1937, Oct. 13 Engr. *Perf. 10*

C24 AP11	5c red	7.75	7.75
C25 AP12	5c red	7.75	7.75
C26 AP13	10c blue	7.75	7.75
C27 AP14	10c blue	7.75	7.75
C28 AP15	20c green	10.00	10.00
C29 AP16	20c green	10.00	10.00
	Nos. C24-C29 (6)	51.00	51.00
	Set, never hinged	67.50	

See note after No. 354.

Type of 1927 Ovptd. in Black

1938, May Wmk. 106

C30 AP1	5c dark orange	7.25	1.60
	Never hinged	10.00	

1st airplane flight from Key West to Havana, made by Domingo Rosillo, 1913.

Type of 1931-32 Overprinted

1939, Oct. 15

C31 AP4	10c emerald	32.50	6.50
	Never hinged	55.00	

Issued in connection with an experimental postal rocket flight held at Havana.

Sir Rowland Hill, Map of Cuba and First Stamps of Britain, Spanish Cuba and Republic of Cuba — AP17

1940, Nov. 28 Engr. Wmk. 106

C32 AP17	10c brown	6.75	2.00
	Never hinged	11.00	

Souvenir Sheet

Unwmk. *Imperf.*

C33	Sheet of 4	22.50	22.50
	Never hinged	35.00	
a.	AP17 10c light brown	5.50	3.50
	Never hinged	8.00	

Cent. of the 1st postage stamp.

Sheet sold for 60c.

No. C33 exists with each of the four stamps overprinted in black: "Exposicion de la ACNU/24 de Octubre de 1951/Dia de las Naciones" and "Historia de la Aviacion" in lower margin. Value, $80.

For overprints see Nos. C39, C211 in Scott Standard catalogue, Vol. 2.

Poet José Heredia and Palms AP18

Heredia and Niagara Falls — AP19

1940, Dec. 30 Wmk. 106

C34 AP18	5c emerald	3.25	1.00
C35 AP19	10c greenish slate	4.00	1.60
	Set, never hinged	11.00	

Death cent. of José Maria Heredia y Campuzano (1803-39), poet and patriot.

AIR POST SPECIAL DELIVERY STAMPS

Matanzas Issue

Matanzas Harbor APSD1

Wmk. 229

1936, May 5 Photo. *Perf. 12½*

CE1 ASPD1	15c light blue	5.00	3.50
	Never hinged	8.00	

Exists imperf. Value $6.50 unused, $4.50 used.

SPECIAL DELIVERY STAMPS

Issued under Administration of the United States

US No. E5 Surcharged in Red

1899 Wmk. 191 *Perf. 12*

E1 SD3	10c blue	130.	100.
	Never hinged	300.	
a.	No period after "CUBA"	575.	400.
b.	Five dots in curved frame above messenger's head (Pl. 882)	*2,500.*	

Issue of the Republic under US Military Rule

Special Delivery Messenger SD2

Printed by the US Bureau of Engraving and Printing

1899 Wmk. US-C (191C)

Inscribed: "Immediata"

E2 SD2	10c orange	52.50	15.00
	Never hinged	120.00	

Issues of the Republic Inscribed: "Inmediata"

1902 *Perf. 12*

E3 SD2	10c orange	3.00	1.00

J. B. Zayas SD3

1910 Unwmk.

E4 SD3	10c orange & blue	20.00	3.25
	Never hinged	30.00	
a.	Center inverted	1,250.	

Airplane and Morro Castle SD4

1914, Feb. 24 *Perf. 12*

E5 SD4	10c dark blue	15.00	1.25

Exists imperf. Value, pair $500.

1927 Wmk. Star (106)

E6 SD4	10c deep blue	12.00	.50
	Never hinged	18.00	

1935 *Perf. 10*

E7 SD4	10c blue	12.00	.40
	Never hinged	15.00	

Matanzas Issue

Mercury SD5

Wmk. Wavy Lines (229)

1936, May 5 Photo. *Perf. 12½*

E8 SD5	10c deep claret	8.00	3.50
	Never hinged	9.50	

Exists imperf. Value $7.50 unused, $5 used.

"Triumph of the Revolution" — SD6

1936, Nov. 18

E9 SD6	10c red orange	9.00	2.00
	Never hinged	11.00	

Maj. Gen. Máximo Gómez (1836-1905).

Temple of Quetzalcoatl (Mexico) SD7

Ruben Dario (Nicaragua) SD8

Wmk. 106

1937, Oct. 13 Engr. *Perf. 10*

E10 SD7	10c deep orange	7.00	7.00
E11 SD8	10c deep orange	7.00	7.00
	Set, never hinged	18.00	

Issued for the benefit of the Association of American Writers and Artists. See note after No. 354.

POSTAGE DUE STAMPS

Issued under Administration of the United States

Postage Due Stamps of the United States Nos. J38, J39, J41 and J42 Srchd. in Black Like Nos. 221-226A

1899 Wmk. 191 *Perf. 12*

J1 D2	1c dp claret	45.00	5.25
	Never hinged	110.00	
J2 D2	2c dp claret	45.00	5.25
	Never hinged	110.00	
a.	Inverted surcharge		*3,500.*
J3 D2	5c dp claret	42.50	5.25
	Never hinged	105.00	
J4 D2	10c dp claret	25.00	2.50
	Never hinged	60.00	
	Nos. J1-J4 (4)	157.50	18.25

Issues of the Republic

D1

1914 Unwmk. Engr. *Perf. 12*

J5 D1	1c carmine rose	8.00	1.25
J6 D1	2c carmine rose	10.00	1.25
J7 D1	5c carmine rose	15.00	2.50
	Nos. J5-J7 (3)	33.00	5.00

1927-28

J8 D1	1c rose red	5.50	.90
J9 D1	2c rose red	8.50	.90
J10 D1	5c rose red	10.00	1.25
	Nos. J8-J10 (3)	24.00	3.05

NEWSPAPER STAMPS

Issued under Spanish Dominion

N1

1888 Unwmk. Typo. *Perf. 14*

P1	N1	½m black	.25	*.25*
P2	N1	1m black	.25	*.30*
P3	N1	2m black	.25	*.30*
P4	N1	3m black	1.60	1.00
P5	N1	4m black	2.10	*2.00*
P6	N1	8m black	8.00	*8.50*
		Nos. P1-P6 (6)	12.45	12.35

N2

1890

P7	N2	½m red brown	.55	*.65*
P8	N2	1m red brown	.55	*.65*
P9	N2	2m red brown	.90	*.95*
P10	N2	3m red brown	1.10	*1.10*
P11	N2	4m red brown	8.25	5.50
P12	N2	8m red brown	8.25	5.50
		Nos. P7-P12 (6)	19.60	14.35

1892

P13	N2	½m violet	.25	*.30*
P14	N2	1m violet	.25	*.30*
P15	N2	2m violet	.25	*.30*
P16	N2	3m violet	1.10	.35
P17	N2	4m violet	4.25	1.90
P18	N2	8m violet	8.75	3.00
		Nos. P13-P18 (6)	14.85	6.15

1894

P19	N2	½m rose	.25	*.30*
a.		Imperf. pair	40.00	40.00
P20	N2	1m rose	.50	.35
P21	N2	2m rose	.55	.35
P22	N2	3m rose	2.10	1.40
P23	N2	4m rose	3.50	1.60
P24	N2	8m rose	6.00	4.00
		Nos. P19-P24 (6)	12.90	8.00

1896

P25	N2	½m blue green	.25	*.30*
P26	N2	1m blue green	.25	*.30*
P27	N2	2m blue green	.25	*.30*
P28	N2	3m blue green	2.75	1.50
P29	N2	4m blue green	5.75	*7.00*
P30	N2	8m blue green	10.50	*10.00*
		Nos. P25-P30 (6)	19.75	19.40

For surcharges see Nos. 190-193, 201-220.

POSTAL TAX STAMPS

Catalogue values for unused stamps in this section are for Never Hinged items.

Mother and Child — PT1

Wmk. Star. (106)

1938, Dec. 1 Engr. *Perf. 10*

RA1	PT1	1c bright green	.90	.25

The tax benefited the National Council of Tuberculosis fund for children's hospitals. Obligatory on all mail during December and January. This note applies also to Nos. RA2-RA4, RA7-RA10, RA12-RA15, RA17-RA21. Post 1940 issues in Scott Standard catalogue, Vol. 2.

Nurse with Child — PT2

1939, Dec. 1

RA2	PT2	1c orange vermilion	.90	.25

"Health" Protecting Children — PT3

1940, Dec. 1

RA3	PT3	1c deep blue	.90	.25

CYPRUS

ˈsī-prəs

LOCATION — An island in the Mediterranean Sea off the coast of Turkey
GOVT. — British Colony
AREA — 3,572 sq. mi.
POP. — 645,500 (1982)
CAPITAL — Nicosia

12 Pence = 1 Shilling
40 Paras = 1 Piaster
9 Piasters = 1 Shilling
20 Shillings = 1 Pound

Catalogue values for unused stamps in this country are for Never Hinged items, beginning with Scott 156 in the regular postage section.

STAMPS OF GREAT BRITAIN USED IN CYPRUS

Numeral cancellations on stamps of Great Britain.

When more than one plate number is shown, value is for the least expensive.

1878-81

982 (Famagusta)

A1	½p rose (#58, P11, 13), *value from*	800.
A2	1p rose red (#33, P145, 174, 181, 193, 202, 206, 215), *value from*	550.
A3	2p blue (#30, P13-15), *value from*	1,100.
A4	2½p claret (#67, P13, 16), *value from*	1,275.
A5	6p gray (#62, P15)	
A6	1sh green (#64, P12)	3,000.
A7	1sh salmon (#87, P14)	—

974 (Kyrenia)

A8	½p rose (#58, P13)	1,050.
A9	1p rose red (#33, P168, 171, 193, 196, 206, 207, 209, 220), *value from*	675.
A10	2p blue (#30, P13, 15), *value from*	1,150.
A11	2½p claret (#67, P12-15), *value from*	1,150.
A12	4p pale ol grn (#64, P16)	
A13	6p gray (#62, P16)	

942 (Larnaca)

A14	½p rose (#58, P11-15, 19-20), *value from*	300.
A15	1p rose red (#33), *value from*	195.

#A15 plate numbers: 129, 131, 146, 154, 170, 171, 174-179, 181-184, 187, 188, 190-210, 212-218, 220-222, 225.

A16	1½p lake red (#32, P3)	2,150.
A17	2p blue (#29, P9)	325.
A18	2p blue (#30, P13-15), *value from*	260.
A19	2½p claret (#67, P4-6, 8, 10, 12-17), *value from*	80.
A20	2½p ultra (#68, P17-20), *value from*	575.
A21	2½p ultra (#82, P21)	—
A22	4p pale ol grn (#64, P15-16), *value from*	640.
A23	6p gray (#62, P15-17), *value from*	575.
A24	6p pale buff (#59b, P11)	2,900.
A25	8p orange (#73)	*6,500.*
A26	1sh green (#64, P12-13), *value from*	1,100.
A27	1sh salmon (#87, P14)	—
A28	5sh rose (#90, P4)	*6,500.*

975 (Limassol)

A29	½p rose (#58, P11, 13, 15, 19), *value from*	525.
A30	1p rose red (#33), *value from*	325.

#A30 plate numbers: 160, 171, 173-175, 177, 179, 184, 187, 190, 191, 193, 195-198, 200, 202, 206-210, 213, 215, 216, 218, 220-222, 225.

A31	1½p lake red (#32, P3)	2,750.
A32	2p blue (#30, P14, 15), *value from*	575.
A33	2½p claret (#67, P11-16), *value from*	275.
A34	2½p ultra (#68, P17, 19, 20), *value from*	1,400.
A35	4p pale ol grn (#64, P16)	950.

969 (Nicosia)

A36	½p rose (#58, P12-15, 20), *value from*	525.
A37	1p rose red (#33), *value from*	325.
A37A	1½p lake red (#32, P3)	3,500.

#A37 plate numbers: 170, 171, 174, 189, 190, 192, 193, 195, 196, 198, 200, 202, 203, 205-207, 210, 212, 214, 215, 218, 221, 222, 225.

A38	2p blue (#30, P14, 15), *value from*	525.
A39	2½p claret (#67, P10-16), *value from*	225.
A40	2½p ultra (#68, P20)	850.
A41	4p pale ol grn (#70, P16)	950.
A42	6p gray (#62, P16)	1,100.

981 (Paphos)

A43	½p rose (#58, P13, 15)	
A44	1p rose red (#33, P196, 201, 202, 204, 206, 213, 217), *value from*	675.
A45	2p blue (#30, P15), *value from*	1,150.
A46	2½p claret (#67, P13-16), *value from*	625.

AUSTRIAN OFFICES IN CYPRUS

Values in the first column for Nos. 2A1-2A78 are for stamps without defects tied to piece with legible partial strikes of town cancellations; values in the second column are for stamps without defects tied to cover by complete strikes of town cancellations. Stamps with legible town cancellations off cover sell for 25-50% of the on-piece value.

Issue dates refer to dates of stamps' issue, not necessarily to their usage with specific Cyprian postal markings.

Larnaca

Stamps of Lombardy-Venetia canceled in black with straight-line postmark with name of post office and date, italic lettering

1863 *Perf. 14*

2A1	2s yellow (#15)	*2,100.*	*7,000.*
2A2	3s green (#16)	*1,950.*	*7,200.*
2A3	5s rose (#17)	*1,950.*	*7,000.*
2A4	10s blue (#18)	*1,900.*	*6,600.*
2A5	15s yel brn (#19)	*2,000.*	*6,750.*

1864-65 *Perf. 9½*

2A6	2s yellow (#20)	1,175.	*3,650.*
2A7	3s green (#21)	775.00	*2,850.*
2A8	5s rose (#22)	725.00	2,625.
2A9	10s blue (#23)	675.00	2,400.
2A10	15s yel brn (#24)	725.00	2,300.

Stamps of Lombardy-Venetia canceled in blue with straight-line postmark with name of post office and date, italic lettering

1863 *Perf. 14*

2A11	5s rose (#17)	*2,950.*	*11,500.*
2A12	10s blue (#18)	*2,900.*	*11,000.*
2A13	15s yel brn (#19)	*3,000.*	*11,500.*

1864-65 *Perf. 9½*

2A14	2s yellow (#20)	1,600.	*5,000.*
2A15	3s green (#21)	1,200.	*4,250.*
2A16	5s rose (#22)	1,150.	4,000.
2A17	10s blue (#23)	1,100.	3,800.
2A18	15s yel brn (#24)	1,150.	3,900.

Larnacca di Cipro

Stamps of Lombardy-Venetia canceled in black with single circle date stamp with post office name, month and date, without year

1863 *Perf. 14*

2A19	2s yellow (#15)	950.00	3,150.
2A20	3s green (#16)	800.00	3,250.
2A21	5s rose (#17)	800.00	3,000.
2A22	10s blue (#18)	750.00	1,600.
2A23	15s yel brn (#19)	850.00	2,800.

1864-65 *Perf. 9½*

2A24	2s yellow (#20)	900.00	2,800.
2A25	3s green (#21)	525.00	2,000.
2A26	5s rose (#22)	450.00	1,850.
2A27	10s blue (#23)	425.00	1,550.
2A28	15s yel brn (#24)	450.00	1,700.

Stamps of Austrian Offices In the Turkish Empire

Canceled in black or red brown with single circle date stamp with post office name, month and date, without year

1867-83

Coarse Print

2A29	2s yellow (#1)	300.00	1,325.
2A30	3s green (#2)	325.00	1,250.
2A31	5s red (#3)	285.00	1,000.
2A32	10s blue (#4)	275.00	950.
2A33	15s brown (#5)	280.00	975.
2A34	25s gray lilac (#6)	300.00	1,575.
2A35	50s brown (#7)	325.00	*4,750.*

Fine Print

2A36	2s yellow (#7C)	1,400.	—
2A37	3s green (#7D)	300.00	1,125.
2A38	5s red (#7E)	285.00	1,000.
2A39	10s blue (#7F)	275.00	950.
2A40	15s org brown (#7I)	385.00	1,625.
2A41	25s gray lilac (#7J)	500.00	*6,000.*

Stamps of Austria

Canceled in black or red brown with single circle date stamp with post office name, month and date, without year

1867-83

Coarse Print

2A42	2kr yellow (#27)	625.00	—
2A43	3kr green (#28)	625.00	—
2A44	5kr red (#29)	625.00	—
2A45	10kr blue (#30)	625.00	*2,250.*
2A46	15kr brown (#31)	625.00	*2,250.*
2A47	25kr gray lilac (#32)	625.00	—
2A48	50kr brown (#33)	700.00	—

Fine Print

2A49	2kr yellow (#34)	625.00	—
2A50	3kr green (#35)	625.00	—
2A51	5kr red (#36)	625.00	—
2A52	10kr blue (#37)	625.00	*2,250.*
2A53	15kr org brown (#38)	625.00	*2,250.*
2A54	25kr gray (#39)	725.00	
2A55	50kr brown (#40)	750.00	—

Stamps of Austrian Offices In the Turkish Empire

Canceled in blue with single circle date stamp with post office name, month and date, without year

1867-83

Coarse Print

2A56	2s yellow (#1)	300.00	1,325.
2A57	3s green (#2)	325.00	1,250.
2A58	5s red (#3)	285.00	1,000.
2A59	10s blue (#4)	275.00	950.
2A60	15s brown (#5)	280.00	975.
2A61	25s gray lilac (#6)	300.00	1,575.
2A62	50s brown (#7)	325.00	*4,750.*

Fine Print

2A63	2s yellow (#7C)	1,400.	—
2A64	3s green (#7D)	300.00	1,125.
2A65	5s red (#7E)	285.00	1,000.
2A66	10s blue (#7F)	275.00	950.
2A67	15s org brown (#7I)	385.00	1,625.
2A68	25s gray lilac (#7J)	500.00	*6,000.*

1863 *Perf. 14*

2A69	2s yellow (#15)	—	—
2A70	3s green (#16)	3,000.	—
2A71	5s rose (#17)	*2,950.*	*11,500.*
2A72	10s blue (#18)	*2,900.*	*11,000.*
2A73	15s yel brn (#19)	*3,000.*	*11,500.*

1864-65 *Perf. 9½*

2A74	2s yellow (#20)	2,350.	7,500.
2A75	3s green (#21)	1,950.	6,750.
2A76	5s rose (#22)	1,900.	6,750.
2A77	10s blue (#23)	1,850.	6,350.
2A78	15s yel brn (#24)	1,900.	6,500.

BRITISH ADMINISTRATION

Values for unused stamps are for examples with original gum as defined in the catalogue introduction. Very fine examples of Nos. 1, 2 and 7-10 will have perforations touching the design on at least one or more sides due to the narrow spacing of the stamps on the plates and to imperfect perforation methods. Stamps with perfs clear on all four sides are scarce and will command higher prices.

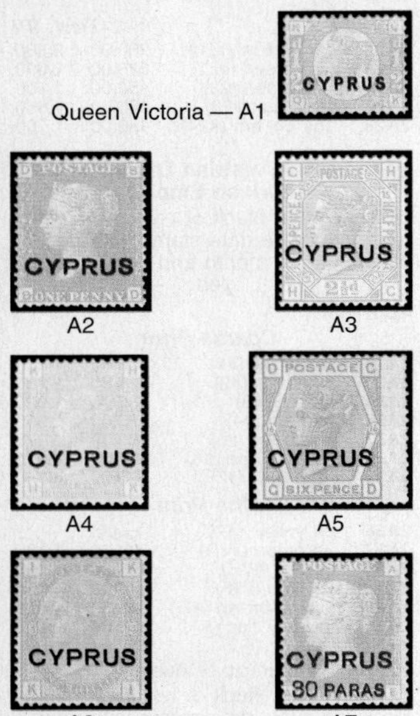
Queen Victoria — A1
A2
A3
A4
A5
A6
A7

Various Watermarks as in Great Britain (#20, 23, 25, 27 & 29)

1880 Typo. *Perf. 14*

1 A1 ½p rose (P 15) 125.00 115.00
Plate 12 240.00 300.00
Plate 19 5,750. 950.00
b. Double overprint (P 15) 45,000.
2 A2 1p red (P 216) 22.50 55.00
Plate 217 22.50 60.00
Plate 174 1,500. 1,500.
Plate 181 525.00 210.00
Plate 184 22,000. 3,500.
Plate 193 840.00
Plate 196 725.00
Plate 201 27.50 57.50
Plate 205 90.00 57.50
Plate 208 135.00 65.00
Plate 215 22.50 57.50
Plate 218 32.50 65.00
Plate 220 550.00 475.00
b. Double overprint (P 218) 5,400.
Double overprint (P 208) 27,500.
c. Pair, one without ovpt. (P 208) 27,500.
3 A3 2½p claret (P 14) 4.50 19.00
Plate 15 8.00 50.00
4 A4 4p lt ol grn (P 16) 150.00 240.00
5 A5 6p ol gray (P 16) 575.00 750.00
6 A6 1sh green (P 13) 900.00 525.00

Black Surcharge

7 A7 30 paras on 1p red (P 216) 150.00 95.00
Plate 201 180.00 110.00
Plate 217 210.00 210.00
Plate 220 175.00 190.00
b. Dbl. surch., one invtd. (P 220) 2,000. 1,500.
Dbl. surch., one invtd. (P 216) 7,750.

No. 2 Surcharged

18mm Long

1881

8 A2 ½p on 1p (205, 216) 82.50 100.00
Plate 174 225.00 400.00
Plate 181 210.00 260.00
Plate 201 115.00 140.00
Plate 205 85.00 100.00
Plate 208 225.00 375.00
Plate 215 840.00 1,000.
Plate 217 1,000. 900.00
Plate 218 550.00 675.00
Plate 220 325.00 450.00
a. "HALFPENN" (P216) 3,250. 3,000.

16mm Long

9 A2 ½p on 1p (P 201) 140.00 190.00
Plate 216 400.00 460.00
Plate 218 17,500.
a. Double surcharge (P 201, 216) 3,750. 3,000.

13mm Long

10 A2 ½p on 1p red (P 215) 52.50 75.00
Plate 205 425.00
Plate 217 175.00 105.00
Plate 218 90.00 125.00
c. Double surcharge (P 215) 550.00 700.00
Double surcharge (P 205) 875.00
e. Triple surcharge (P 215) 875.00
Triple surcharge (P 205) 4,750.
Triple surcharge (P 217) —
Triple surcharge (P 218) 4,750.
h. Quadruple surch. (P 205, 215) 7,500.
j. "CYPRUS" double (P 218) 6,000.

A8

1881, July Typo. Wmk. 1

11 A8 ½pi emerald green 210.00 52.50
12 A8 1pi rose 425.00 37.50
13 A8 2pi ultramarine 525.00 37.50
14 A8 4pi olive green 1,050. 325.00
15 A8 6pi olive gray 1,900. 500.00

Postage and revenue stamps of Cyprus with "J.A.B." (the initials of Postmaster J.A. Bulmer) in manuscript, or with "POSTAL SURCHARGE" (with or without "J. A. B."), were not Postage Due stamps but were employed for accounting purposes between the chief PO at Larnaca and the sub-offices.

See Nos. 19-25, 28-37. For surcharges see Nos. 16-18, 26-27.

Stamps of 1881-1894 Surcharged in Black

1882 Wmk. 1

16 A8 ½pi on ½pi grn 750.00 92.50
17 A8 30pa on 1pi rose 1,750. 140.00
a. Double surcharge, one inverted 1,400. 850.00

1884 Wmk. 2

18 A8 ½pi on ½pi green 190.00 10.00
a. Double surcharge 3,200.

See Nos. 26, 27.

1882-94 Die B

For description of Dies A and B see "Dies of British Colonial Stamps" in Table of Contents.

19 A8 ½pi green 16.00 2.50
20 A8 30pa violet 11.00 14.00
21 A8 1pi rose 15.50 8.50
22 A8 2pi blue 17.50 2.10
23 A8 4pi pale ol grn 20.00 40.00
b. 4pi olive green 57.50 42.50
24a A8 6pi 275.00 800.00
25a A8 12pi 190.00 450.00
Nos. 19-25a (7) 545.00 1,317.

Die A

19a A8 ½pi 22.50 3.25
b. ½pi emerald 6,000. 525.00
20a A8 30pa lilac 85.00 27.50
21a A8 1pi 110.00 4.00
22a A8 2pi 170.00 4.00
23a A8 4pi 375.00 35.00
c. 4pi deep olive green ('83) 575.00 47.50
24 A8 6pi olive gray 75.00 21.00
25 A8 12pi brown org 225.00 45.00
Overprinted "SPECIMEN" 1,200.
Nos. 19a-25 (7) 1,063. 139.75

A11

Type I — Figures "½" 8mm apart.
Type II — Figures "½" 6mm apart.
The space between the fraction bars varies from 5½ to 8½mm but is usually 6 or 8mm.

Black Surcharge Type I

1886 Wmk. 2

26 A11 ½pi on ½pi grn 525.00 16.00
a. Type II 325.00 100.00
b. Double surcharge, type II

Wmk. 1

27 A11 ½pi on ½pi grn 8,750. 500.00
a. Type II 24,000.

No. 27a probably is a proof.

1894-96 Wmk. 2

28 A8 ½pi grn & car rose 5.25 1.75
29 A8 30pa violet & green 4.75 5.00
30 A8 1pi rose & ultra 8.50 1.75
31 A8 2pi ultra & mar 17.50 1.75
32 A8 4pi ol green & vio 21.00 17.50
33 A8 6pi ol gray & grn 22.50 40.00
34 A8 9pi brown & rose 29.00 35.00
35 A8 12pi brn org & blk 25.00 67.50
36 A8 18pi slate & brown 60.00 62.50
37 A8 45pi dk vio & ultra 125.00 165.00
Nos. 28-37 (10) 318.50 397.75
Set, optd. "SPECIMEN" 375.00

King Edward VII — A12

1903 Typo.

38 A12 ½pi grn & car rose 13.00 1.40
39 A12 30pa violet & green 26.00 5.50
a. 30pa mauve & green 25.00 9.50
40 A12 1pi car rose & ultra 40.00 7.50
41 A12 2pi ultra & mar 90.00 18.00
42 A12 4pi ol grn & vio 57.50 27.50
43 A12 6pi ol brn & grn 52.50 145.00
44 A12 9pi brn & car rose 125.00 275.00
45 A12 12pi org brn & blk 37.50 87.50
46 A12 18pi blk & brn 100.00 175.00
47 A12 45pi dk vio & ultra 250.00 600.00
Nos. 38-47 (10) 791.50 1,342.
Set, optd. "SPECIMEN" 500.00

1904-07 Wmk. 3

48 A12 5pa bis & blk ('07) 1.25 2.00
49 A12 10pa org & grn ('07) 6.00 1.90
a. 10pa yellow & green 47.50 6.25
50 A12 ½pi grn & car rose 12.00 1.60
51 A12 30pa redsh vio & grn 20.00 2.75
a. 30pa violet & green ('10) 22.50 2.90
52 A12 1pi car rose & ultra 16.00 1.10
53 A12 2pi ultra & mar 20.00 2.00
54 A12 4pi ol grn & red vio 30.00 20.00
55 A12 6pi ol brn & grn 30.00 17.00
56 A12 9pi brn & car rose 52.50 9.75
a. 9pi yel brn & car rose 57.50 27.50
57 A12 12pi org brn & blk 40.00 67.50
58 A12 18pi blk & brn 55.00 15.00
59 A12 45pi dk vio & ultra 120.00 175.00
Nos. 48-59 (12) 402.75 315.60

King George V — A13

1912

61 A13 10pa org & grn 5.25 2.90
a. 10pa org yel & br green ('15) 2.75 1.60
62 A13 ½pi grn & car rose 2.90 .35
a. ½pi yel green & carmine 8.50 2.25
63 A13 30pa vio & grn 3.25 2.40
64 A13 1pi car & ultra 5.75 1.90
a. 1pi carmine & blue ('15) 15.00 4.50
65 A13 2pi ultra & mar 8.50 2.25
66 A13 4pi ol grn & red vio 5.50 5.25
67 A13 6pi ol brn & grn 6.00 11.50
68 A13 9pi brn & car rose 42.50 28.00
a. 9pi yellow brown & carmine 24.00 32.50
69 A13 12pi org brn & blk 25.00 57.50
70 A13 18pi blk & brn 50.00 50.00
71 A13 45pi dl vio & ultra 130.00 170.00
Nos. 61-71 (12) 287.40 333.65
Set, optd. "SPECIMEN" 550.00

1921-23 Wmk. 4

72 A13 10pa org & grn 16.00 13.50
73 A13 10pa gray & yel 16.00 9.50
74 A13 30pa violet & grn 3.75 2.00
75 A13 30pa green 9.00 1.75
76 A13 1pi rose & ultra 26.00 45.00
77 A13 1pi violet & car 4.00 5.00
78 A13 1½pi org & blk 12.50 7.25
79 A13 2pi ultra & red vio 35.00 25.00
80 A13 2pi rose & ultra 16.00 27.50
81 A13 2¾pi ultra & red vio 11.00 12.00
82 A13 4pi ol grn & red vio 19.00 26.00
83 A13 6pi ol brn & grn 37.50 80.00
84 A13 9pi brn & car 47.50 95.00
a. 9pi yel brn & car 125.00 165.00
85 A13 18pi black & brn 90.00 175.00
86 A13 45pi dl vio & ultra 275.00 325.00
Nos. 72-86 (15) 618.25 849.50
Set, optd. "SPECIMEN" 700.00

Wmk. 3

87 A13 10sh grn & red, *yel* 425.00 900.00
88 A13 £1 vio & blk, *red* 1,400. 3,250.
Nos. 87-88, optd. "SPECIMEN" 625.00

Years of issue: Nos. 73, 75, 77-78, 80-81, 87-88, 1923; others, 1921.

Forged cancellations exist on Nos. 83-88, including a dangerous "LIMASSOL 14 MR 25" fake postmark.

A14

1924-28 Chalky Paper Wmk. 4

89 A14 ¼pi gray & brn org 2.10 .55
90 A14 ½pi gray blk & blk 6.25 14.50
91 A14 ½pi grn & dp grn ('25) 2.50 1.10
92 A14 ¾pi grn & dp grn 4.25 1.10
93 A14 ¾pi gray blk & blk ('25) 4.50 1.10
94 A14 1pi brn vio & org brn 2.40 2.10
95 A14 1½pi org & blk 3.50 14.50
96 A14 1½pi car ('25) 5.25 1.60
97 A14 2pi car & grn 4.25 21.00
98 A14 2pi org & blk ('25) 15.00 4.25
99 A14 2½pi ultra ('25) 9.00 1.90
100 A14 2¾pi ultra & dl vio 3.75 5.00
101 A14 4pi ap grn & vio 5.25 5.25
102 A14 4½pi blk & yel, *emer* 4.00 5.25
103 A14 6pi grn ol & grn 5.25 9.00
104 A14 9pi brn & dk vio 9.00 5.75
105 A14 12pi org brn & blk 14.50 65.00
106 A14 18pi blk & org 29.00 5.75
Revenue cancel 1.00
107 A14 45pi gray vio & ultra 65.00 45.00
Revenue cancel 1.50
108 A14 90pi grn & red, *yel* 125.00 270.00
Revenue cancel 3.75
109 A14 £5 blk, *yel* ('28) 3,750. 8,000.
On cover (overfranked) 275.00
Overprinted "SPECIMEN" 1,100.
Revenue cancel 275.00

Wmk. 3

110 A14 £1 vio & blk, *red* 350.00 900.00
Revenue cancel 12.50
Nos. 89-108 (20) 319.75 479.70

Nos. 96 and 99 are on ordinary paper.

Silver Coin of Amathus — A15

Philosopher Zeno — A16

Map of Cyprus — A17

Discovery of Body of St. Barnabas — A18

Cloisters of Bella Paise Monastery — A19

Badge of the Colony — A20

Hospice of Umm Haram at Larnaca — A21

Statue of Richard Coeur de Lion, London — A22

St. Nicholas Cathedral, Famagusta — A23

King George V — A24

Perf. 12

1928, Feb. 1 Engr. Wmk. 4

114 A15	¾pi	dark violet	3.75	1.60
115 A16	1pi	Prus bl & blk	4.00	2.00
116 A17	1½pi	red	7.50	2.25
117 A18	2½pi	ultramarine	4.75	2.75
118 A19	4pi	dp red brown	9.50	9.50
119 A20	6pi	dark blue	14.00	*32.50*
120 A21	9pi	violet brown	11.00	*17.50*
121 A22	18pi	dk brn & blk	30.00	*35.00*
122 A23	45pi	dp blue & vio	52.50	*62.50*
123 A24	£1	ol brn & dp blue	275.00	*400.00*
		Nos. 114-123 (10)	412.00	*565.60*
		Set, optd. "SPECIMEN"	750.00	

50th year of Cyprus as a British colony.

Ruins of Vouni Palace — A25

Columns at Salamis — A26

Peristerona Church — A27

Soli Theater — A28

Kyrenia Castle and Harbor — A29

Kolossi Castle — A30

St. Sophia Cathedral — A31

Bairakdar Mosque — A32

Queen's Window, St. Hilarion Castle — A33

Buyuk Khan, Nicosia — A34

Forest Scene — A35

1934, Dec. 1 Engr. *Perf. 12½*

125 A25	¼pi	yel brn & ultra	1.40	1.10
		Never hinged	2.10	
a.		Vert. pair, imperf. between	*52,500.*	*35,000.*
126 A26	½pi	green	1.90	1.25
		Never hinged	2.10	
a.		Vert. pair, imperf. between	*18,000.*	*20,000.*
127 A27	¾pi	vio & blk	3.50	.45
		Never hinged	4.50	
a.		Vert. pair, imperf. between	*52,500.*	
128 A28	1pi	brn & blk	3.00	2.50
		Never hinged	4.50	
a.		Vert. pair, imperf. between	*26,000.*	*26,000.*
b.		Horiz. pair, imperf. btwn.	*19,000.*	
129 A29	1½pi	rose red	4.00	2.10
		Never hinged	6.00	
130 A30	2½pi	dk ultra	5.25	2.40
		Never hinged	7.75	
131 A31	4½pi	dk car & blk	5.25	5.00
		Never hinged	14.00	
132 A32	6pi	blue & blk	12.50	*20.00*
		Never hinged	26.00	
133 A33	9pi	dl vio & blk brn	20.00	8.50
		Never hinged	32.50	
134 A34	18pi	ol grn & blk	55.00	50.00
		Never hinged	120.00	
135 A35	45pi	blk & emer	120.00	85.00
		Never hinged	225.00	
		Nos. 125-135 (11)	231.80	*178.30*
		Set, never hinged	405.00	
		Set, perf "SPECIMEN"	575.00	

Common Design Types pictured following the introduction.

Silver Jubilee Issue
Common Design Type

1935, May 6 *Perf. 11x12*

136 CD301	¾pi	gray blk & ultra	4.25	1.50
		Never hinged	6.25	
137 CD301	1½pi	car & dk bl	6.25	3.00
		Never hinged	9.00	
138 CD301	2½pi	ultra & brn	5.25	1.90
		Never hinged	10.00	
139 CD301	9pi	brn vio & ind	24.00	*28.00*
		Never hinged	35.00	
		Nos. 136-139 (4)	39.75	*34.40*
		Set, never hinged	60.00	
		Set, perf "SPECIMEN"	210.00	

Coronation Issue
Common Design Type

1937, May 12 *Perf. 11x11½*

140 CD302	¾pi	dark gray	1.00	1.00
		Never hinged	2.00	
141 CD302	1½pi	dark car	1.25	*2.50*
		Never hinged	2.00	
142 CD302	2½pi	deep ultra	1.50	*3.00*
		Never hinged	3.25	
		Nos. 140-142 (3)	3.75	6.50
		Set, never hinged	7.75	
		Set, perf "SPECIMEN"	140.00	
		Same, never hinged	200.00	

Ruins of Vouni Palace — A36

Columns at Salamis — A37

Peristerona Church — A38

Soli Theater — A39

Kyrenia Castle and Harbor — A40

Kolossi Castle — A41

Map of Cyprus — A42

Bairakdar Mosque — A43

Citadel, Famagusta — A44

Buyuk Khan — A45

Forest Scene A46

King George VI A47

1938-44 Wmk. 4 *Perf. 12½*

143 A36	¼pi	yel brn & ultra	.60	.60
		Never hinged	1.75	
144 A37	½pi	green	.80	.50
		Never hinged	2.40	
145 A38	¾pi	violet & blk	7.25	1.75
		Never hinged	22.00	
146 A39	1pi	orange	.90	.40
		Never hinged	2.50	
a.		Perf. 13½x12½ ('44)	375.00	30.00
		Never hinged	575.00	
147 A40	1½pi	rose car	3.25	2.00
		Never hinged	6.25	
147A A40	1½pi	lt vio ('43)	.90	.75
		Never hinged	2.50	
147B A38	2pi	car & blk ('42)	.90	.45
		Never hinged	2.90	
c.		Perf. 12½x13½ ('44)	2.00	*12.50*
		Never hinged	3.25	
148 A41	2½pi	ultramarine	15.00	4.50
		Never hinged	45.00	
148A A41	3pi	dp ultra ('42)	1.25	.60
		Never hinged	3.50	

149 A42 4½pi gray .90 .40
Never hinged 2.50
150 A43 6pi blue & blk 1.25 *1.10*
Never hinged 3.75
151 A44 9pi dk vio & blk 1.00 .80
Never hinged 2.90
152 A45 18pi ol grn & blk 5.00 1.75
Never hinged 14.50
153 A46 45pi blk & emer 16.00 5.00
Never hinged 47.50
154 A47 90pi blk & brt vio 21.00 8.00
Never hinged 37.50
155 A47 £1 ind & dl red 45.00 32.50
Never hinged 67.50
Nos. 143-155 (16) 121.00 61.10
Set, never hinged 275.00
Set, perf "SPECIMEN" 450.00
Same, never hinged 725.00

See Nos. 164-166.

Catalogue values for unused stamps in this section, from this point to the end of the section, are for Never Hinged items.

Peace Issue
Common Design Type

1946, Oct. 21 Engr. *Perf. 13½x14*
156 CD303 1½pi purple .50 .25
157 CD303 3pi deep blue .50 .45

Silver Wedding Issue
Common Design Types

1948, Dec. 20 Photo. *Perf. 14x14½*
158 CD304 1½pi purple 1.00 .55

Engr.; Name Typo.
Perf. 11½x11
159 CD305 £1 dark blue 57.50 *77.50*

UPU Issue
Common Design Types
Perf. 13½, 11x11½

1949, Oct. 10 Engr. Wmk. 4
160 CD306 1½pi violet .65 *1.60*
161 CD307 2pi deep carmine 1.75 1.60
162 CD308 3pi indigo 1.10 1.10
163 CD309 9pi rose violet 1.10 4.00
Nos. 160-163 (4) 4.60 8.30

Types of 1938-43

1951, July 2 Engr. *Perf. 12½*
164 A37 ½pi purple 3.25 .75
165 A40 1½pi deep green 6.25 1.25
166 A41 4pi deep ultra 4.75 1.40
Nos. 164-166 (3) 14.25 3.40

CYRENAICA

ˌsir-ə-ˈnā-ə-kə

LOCATION — In northern Africa bordering on the Mediterranean Sea
GOVT. — Italian colony
AREA — 75,340 sq. mi.
POP. — 225,000 (approx. 1934)
CAPITAL — Bengasi (Benghazi)

100 Centesimi = 1 Lira

Used values in italics are for postally used stamps. CTO's sell for about the same as unused, hinged stamps.

Watermark

Wmk. 140 — Crown

Propaganda of the Faith Issue
Italy Nos. 143-146 Overprinted

1923, Oct. 24 Wmk. 140 *Perf. 14*
1 A68 20c ol grn & brn org 9.50 *42.50*
Never hinged 22.50
On overfranked cover —
2 A68 30c claret & brn org 9.50 *42.50*
Never hinged 22.50
On overfranked cover —
a. Vert. pair, imperf between and at bottom *1,050.*
b. Vert. strip of 3, imperf between and at bottom *1,200.*
3 A68 50c violet & brn org 6.00 *47.50*
Never hinged 15.00
On overfranked cover —
4 A68 1 l blue & brn org 6.00 *75.00*
Never hinged 15.00
On overfranked cover —
a. Vert. pair, imperf between *1,050.*
b. Vert. strip of 3, imperf between and at bottom *1,200.*
Nos. 1-4 (4) 31.00 *207.50*
Set, never hinged 75.00
Set on overfranked cover —

Fascisti Issue

Italy Nos. 159-164 Overprinted in Red or Black

1923, Oct. 29 Unwmk. *Perf. 14*
5 A69 10c dk grn (R) 8.50 *15.00*
Never hinged 20.00
On commercial cover *300.00*
6 A69 30c dk vio (R) 8.50 *15.00*
Never hinged 20.00
On commercial cover *300.00*
7 A69 50c brn car 8.50 *21.00*
Never hinged 20.00
On commercial cover *300.00*

Wmk. 140
8 A70 1 l blue 8.50 *40.00*
Never hinged 20.00
On commercial cover *560.00*
9 A70 2 l brown 8.50 *47.50*
Never hinged 20.00
On commercial cover *825.00*
10 A71 5 l blk & bl (R) 8.50 *72.50*
Never hinged 20.00
On commercial cover —
Nos. 5-10 (6) 51.00 *211.00*
Set, never hinged 120.00
Set on overfranked cover *650.00*

Manzoni Issue

Italy Nos. 165-170 Ovptd. in Red

1924, Apr. 1 *Perf. 14*
11 A72 10c brn red & blk 9.00 *60.00*
Never hinged 27.50
12 A72 15c bl grn & blk 9.00 *60.00*
Never hinged 27.50
13 A72 30c blk & slate 9.00 *60.00*
Never hinged 27.50
14 A72 50c org brn & blk 9.00 *60.00*
Never hinged 27.50
15 A72 1 l bl & blk 55.00 *350.00*
Never hinged 140.00
a. Double overprint *1,200.*
Never hinged *1,800.*
16 A72 5 l vio & blk 350.00 *2,700.*
Never hinged 875.00
Nos. 11-16 (6) 441.00 *3,290.*
Set, never hinged 1,125.
Set on overfranked cover —

Vertical overprints on Nos. 11-14 are essays. On Nos. 15-16 the overprint is vertical at the left.

All examples of No. 15a are poorly centered.

Commercial covers of this issue are very rare.

Victor Emmanuel Issue

Italy Nos. 175-177 Overprinted

1925-26 Unwmk. *Perf. 11*
17 A78 60c brn car 1.60 *11.00*
Never hinged 3.00
On commercial cover *200.00*
18 A78 1 l dark blue 1.60 *11.00*
Never hinged 3.00
On commercial cover *325.00*
19 A78 1.25 l dk bl ('26) 4.75 *24.00*
Never hinged 14.00
On commercial cover *475.00*
a. Perf. 13½ 350.00 *1,000.*
Never hinged 900.00
Nos. 17-19 (3) 7.95 *46.00*
Set, never hinged 20.00

Issue dates: Nov. 1925, July 1926.

Saint Francis of Assisi Issue

Italian Stamps of 1926 Ovptd.

1926, Apr. 12 Wmk. 140 *Perf. 14*
20 A79 20c gray green 1.80 *11.00*
Never hinged 4.50
On commercial cover 125.00
21 A80 40c dark violet 1.80 *11.00*
Never hinged 4.50
On commercial cover 160.00
22 A81 60c red brown 1.80 *19.00*
Never hinged 4.50
On commercial cover *160.00*

Ovptd. in Red

Unwmk.
23 A82 1.25 l dk bl, perf. 11 1.80 *20.00*
Never hinged 4.50
On commercial cover *275.00*
a. Pair, one with albino surcharge *1,900.*
Never hinged *3,500.*
24 A83 5 l + 2.50 l ol grn 6.00 *55.00*
Never hinged 12.00
On commercial cover —
a. Double surcharge, one black, one red *2,400.*
Never hinged *4,500.*
Nos. 20-24 (5) 13.20 *116.00*
Set, never hinged 30.00
Set on overfranked cover 475.00

Volta Issue

Type of Italy 1927, Overprinted

1927, Oct. 10 Wmk. 140 *Perf. 14*
25 A84 20c purple 4.75 *30.00*
Never hinged 12.00
On commercial cover 275.00
a. Overprint omitted *4,250.*
Never hinged *6,500.*
26 A84 50c dp org 7.25 *40.00*
Never hinged 18.00
On commercial cover 275.00
a. Dot omitted after figures of value 55.00 *95.00*
b. Double overprint *200.00*
c. Overprinted "Cirenaica" and "Eritrea" (inverted) *550.00*
27 A84 1.25 l brt bl 11.00 *47.50*
Never hinged 25.00
On commercial cover 520.00
Nos. 25-27 (3) 23.00 *117.50*
Set, never hinged 55.00
Set on overfranked cover 380.00

Monte Cassino Issue

Types of 1929 Issue of Italy, Ovptd. in Red or Blue

1929, Oct. 14
28 A96 20c dk grn (R) 4.75 *17.00*
Never hinged 12.00
On commercial cover 275.00
29 A96 25c red org (Bl) 4.75 *17.00*
Never hinged 12.00
On commercial cover 200.00
30 A98 50c + 10c crim (Bl) 4.75 *18.00*
Never hinged 12.00
On commercial cover 160.00
31 A98 75c + 15c ol brn (R) 4.75 *18.00*
Never hinged 12.00
On commercial cover 275.00
32 A96 1.25 l + 25c dk vio (R) 11.00 *32.50*
Never hinged 25.00
On commercial cover 340.00
33 A98 5 l + 1 l saph (R) 11.00 *28.50*
Never hinged 25.00

Overprinted in Red

Unwmk.
34 A100 10 l + 2 l gray brn 11.00 *45.00*
Never hinged 25.00
Nos. 28-34 (7) 52.00 *176.00*
Set, never hinged 123.00
Set on overfranked cover 475.00

Royal Wedding Issue

Type of Italian Stamps of 1930 Overprinted

1930, Mar. 17 Wmk. 140
35 A101 20c yel grn 2.40 *8.50*
Never hinged 6.50
On commercial cover 140.00
a. Without overprint *42,500.*
Never hinged *65,000.*
36 A101 50c + 10c dp org 1.80 *8.50*
Never hinged 4.75
On commercial cover 190.00
37 A101 1.25 l + 25c rose red 1.80 *14.50*
Never hinged 4.75
On commercial cover 300.00
Nos. 35-37 (3) 6.00 *31.50*
Set, never hinged 16.00
Set on overfranked cover 180.00

Ferrucci Issue

Types of Italian Stamps of 1930, Ovptd. in Red or Blue

1930, July 26
38 A102 20c violet (R) 6.50 *6.50*
Never hinged 16.00
On commercial cover 160.00
39 A103 25c dk grn (R) 6.50 *6.50*
Never hinged 16.00
On commercial cover 190.00
40 A103 50c black (R) 6.50 *12.00*
Never hinged 16.00
On commercial cover 160.00
41 A103 1.25 l dp bl (R) 6.50 *22.50*
Never hinged 16.00
On commercial cover 350.00
42 A104 5 l + 2 l dp car 14.50 *47.50*
Never hinged 30.00
Nos. 38-42 (5) 40.50 *95.00*
Set, never hinged 94.00
Set on overfranked cover 350.00

Virgil Issue

Italian Stamps of 1930 Ovptd. in Red or Blue

1930, Dec. 4

43 A106 15c vio blk .90 *9.00*
Never hinged 2.25
On commercial cover 175.00
44 A106 20c org brn (Bl) .90 *3.50*
Never hinged 2.25
On commercial cover 100.00
45 A106 25c dk grn .90 *3.50*
Never hinged 2.25
On commercial cover 95.00
46 A106 30c lt brn (Bl) .90 *3.50*
Never hinged 2.25
On commercial cover 100.00
47 A106 50c dl vio .90 *3.50*
Never hinged 2.25
On commercial cover 87.50
48 A106 75c rose red (Bl) .90 *8.50*
Never hinged 2.25
On commercial cover 210.00
49 A106 1.25 l gray bl .90 *9.00*
Never hinged 2.25
On commercial cover 300.00

Unwmk.

50 A106 5 l + 1.50 l dk vio 3.50 *35.00*
Never hinged 7.00
On commercial cover —
51 A106 10 l + 2.50 l ol brn (Bl) 3.50 *55.00*
Never hinged 7.00
Nos. 43-51 (9) 13.30 *130.50*
Set, never hinged 30.00
Set on overfranked cover 475.00

Saint Anthony of Padua Issue

Italian Stamps of 1931 Ovptd. in Blue or Red

1931, May 7 **Wmk. 140**

52 A116 20c brown (Bl) 1.25 *22.50*
Never hinged 2.75
On commercial cover 120.00
53 A116 25c green (R) 1.25 *8.00*
Never hinged 2.75
On commercial cover 120.00
54 A118 30c gray brn (Bl) 1.25 *8.00*
Never hinged 2.75
On commercial cover 180.00
55 A118 50c dl vio (Bl) 1.25 *8.00*
Never hinged 2.75
On commercial cover 120.00
56 A120 1.25 l slate bl (R) 1.25 *22.50*
Never hinged 2.75
On commercial cover 400.00

Overprinted like Nos. 23-24 in Red or Black

Unwmk.

57 A121 75c blk, Ovpt. Type 1 (R) 1.25 *22.50*
Never hinged 2.75
On commercial cover 325.00
a. Overprint Type 2 *65.00* *100.00*
58 A122 5 l + 2.50 l dk brn, Ovpt. Type 1 11.00 *80.00*
Never hinged 19.50
a. Overprint Type 2 *120.00* *260.00*
Nos. 52-58 (7) 18.50 *171.50*
Set, never hinged 36.00
Set on overfranked cover 540.00

Overprint on Nos. 57-58: Type 1, 14½mm wide; Type 2, 13mm wide.

Carabineer A1

1934, Oct. 16 **Photo.** **Wmk. 140**

59 A1 5c dk ol grn & brn 4.25 *17.00*
Never hinged 10.00
On commercial cover 350.00
60 A1 10c brn & blk 4.25 *17.00*
Never hinged 10.00
On commercial cover 300.00
61 A1 20c scar & indigo 4.25 *15.00*
Never hinged 10.00
On commercial cover 300.00
62 A1 50c pur & brn 4.25 *15.00*
Never hinged 10.00
On commercial cover 275.00
63 A1 60c org brn & ind 4.25 *21.00*
Never hinged 10.00
On commercial cover 350.00
64 A1 1.25 l dk bl & grn 4.25 *35.00*
Never hinged 10.00
On commercial cover 450.00
Nos. 59-64 (6) 25.50 *120.00*
Set, never hinged 60.00
Set on overfranked cover 350.00

2nd Colonial Art Exhibition held at Naples. See Nos. C24-C29.

SEMI-POSTAL STAMPS

Many issues of Italy and Italian Colonies include one or more semipostal denominations. To avoid splitting sets, these issues are generally listed as regular postage unless all values carry a surtax.

Holy Year Issue

Italian Semi-Postal Stamps of 1924 Overprinted in Black or Red

1925, June 1 **Wmk. 140** ***Perf. 12***

B1 SP4 20c + 10c dk grn & brn 3.00 *18.00*
Never hinged 6.75
On commercial cover 225.00
B2 SP4 30c + 15c dk brn & brn 3.00 *19.00*
Never hinged 6.75
On commercial cover 225.00
B3 SP4 50c + 25c vio & brn 3.00 *18.00*
Never hinged 6.75
On commercial cover 225.00
B4 SP4 60c + 30c dp rose & brn 3.00 *24.00*
Never hinged 6.75
On commercial cover 300.00
B5 SP8 1 l + 50c dp bl & vio (R) 3.00 *30.00*
Never hinged 6.75
B6 SP8 5 l + 2.50 l org brn & vio (R) 3.00 *45.00*
Never hinged 6.75
Nos. B1-B6 (6) 18.00 *154.00*
Set, never hinged 40.50
Set on overfranked cover 500.00

Colonial Institute Issue

"Peace" Substituting Spade for Sword — SP1

1926, June 1 **Typo.** ***Perf. 14***

B7 SP1 5c + 5c brown .90 *7.25*
Never hinged 2.50
On commercial cover 180.00
B8 SP1 10c + 5c olive grn .90 *7.25*
Never hinged 2.50
On commercial cover 140.00
B9 SP1 20c + 5c blue grn .90 *7.25*
Never hinged 2.50
On commercial cover 110.00
B10 SP1 40c + 5c brown red .90 *7.25*
Never hinged 2.50
On commercial cover 110.00
B11 SP1 60c + 5c orange .90 *7.25*
Never hinged 3.00
On commercial cover 180.00
B12 SP1 1 l + 5c blue .90 *15.00*
Never hinged 3.00
On commercial cover 300.00
Nos. B7-B12 (6) 5.40 *51.25*
Set, never hinged 16.00
Set on overfranked cover 260.00

Surtax for Italian Colonial Institute.

Types of Italian Semi-Postal Stamps of 1926 Overprinted like Nos. 17-19

1927, Apr. 21 **Unwmk.** ***Perf. 11***

B13 SP10 40c + 20c dk brn & blk 4.00 *45.00*
Never hinged 10.00
On commercial cover 190.00
B14 SP10 60c + 30c brn red & ol brn 4.00 *45.00*
Never hinged 10.00
On commercial cover 225.00
B15 SP10 1.25 l + 60c dp bl & blk 4.00 *65.00*
Never hinged 10.00
On commercial cover 400.00
a. Double overprint *1,750.*
Never hinged *2,600.*
B16 SP10 5 l + 2.50 l dk grn & blk 6.50 *100.00*
Never hinged 13.00
Nos. B13-B16 (4) 18.50 *255.00*
Set, never hinged 43.00
Set on overfranked cover 600.00

The surtax on these stamps was for the charitable work of the Voluntary Militia for Italian National Defense.

Allegory of Fascism and Victory — SP2

1928, Oct. 15 **Wmk. 140** ***Perf. 14***

B17 SP2 20c + 5c bl grn 3.25 *14.50*
Never hinged 8.00
On commercial cover 190.00
B18 SP2 30c + 5c red 3.25 *14.50*
Never hinged 8.00
On commercial cover 190.00
B19 SP2 50c + 10c purple 3.25 *24.00*
Never hinged 8.00
On commercial cover 190.00
B20 SP2 1.25 l + 20c dk bl 4.00 *32.50*
Never hinged 10.00
On commercial cover 525.00
Nos. B17-B20 (4) 13.75 *85.50*
Set, never hinged 34.00
Set on overfranked cover 325.00

46th anniv. of the Societa Africana d'Italia. The surtax aided that society.

Types of Italian Semi-Postal Stamps of 1926 Overprinted in Red or Black like Nos. 52-56

1929, Mar. 4 **Unwmk.** ***Perf. 11***

B21 SP10 30c + 10c red & blk 4.75 *27.50*
Never hinged 12.00
On commercial cover 225.00
B22 SP10 50c + 20c vio & blk 4.75 *30.00*
Never hinged 12.00
On commercial cover 225.00
B23 SP10 1.25 l + 50c brn & bl 7.25 *52.50*
Never hinged 18.00
On commercial cover 475.00
B24 SP10 5 l + 2 l ol grn & blk (Bk) 7.25 *100.00*
Never hinged 18.00
Nos. B21-B24 (4) 24.00 *210.00*
Set, never hinged 60.00
Set on overfranked cover 600.00

Surtax for the charitable work of the Voluntary Militia for Italian Natl. Defense.

Types of Italian Semi-Postal Stamps of 1926 Overprinted in Black or Red like Nos. 52-56

1930, Oct. 20 ***Perf. 14***

B25 SP10 30c + 10c dk grn & bl grn (Bk) 35.00 *65.00*
Never hinged 87.50
On commercial cover 325.00
B26 SP10 50c + 10c dk grn & vio 35.00 *100.00*
Never hinged 87.50
On commercial cover 350.00
B27 SP10 1.25 l + 30c ol brn & red brn 35.00 *100.00*
Never hinged 87.50
On commercial cover 550.00
B28 SP10 5 l + 1.50 l ind & grn 120.00 *275.00*
Never hinged 300.00
On commercial cover —
Nos. B25-B28 (4) 225.00 *540.00*
Set, never hinged 562.50
Set on overfranked cover 1,000.

Surtax for the charitable work of the Voluntary Militia for Italian Natl. Defense.

Sower — SP3

1930, Nov. 27 **Photo.** **Wmk. 140**

B29 SP3 50c + 20c ol brn 3.00 *21.00*
Never hinged 7.00
On commercial cover 210.00
B30 SP3 1.25 l + 20c dp bl 3.00 *21.00*
Never hinged 7.00
On commercial cover 300.00
B31 SP3 1.75 l + 20c green 3.00 *24.00*
Never hinged 7.00
On commercial cover 375.00
B32 SP3 2.55 l + 50c purple 11.00 *35.00*
Never hinged 16.00
On commercial cover 600.00
B33 SP3 5 l + 1 l dp car 11.00 *55.00*
Never hinged 16.00
Nos. B29-B33 (5) 31.00 *156.00*
Set, never hinged 53.00
Set on overfranked cover *350.00*

25th anniv. of the Italian Colonial Agricultural Institute. The surtax was for the aid of that institution.

AIR POST STAMPS

Air Post Stamps of Tripolitania, 1931, Overprinted in Blue like Nos. 38-42

1932, Jan. 7 **Wmk. 140** ***Perf. 14***

C1 AP1 50c rose car 1.25 .30
Never hinged 3.00
On commercial cover 20.00
C2 AP1 60c dp org 4.75 *7.25*
Never hinged 10.50
On commercial cover 250.00
C3 AP1 80c dl vio 4.75 *17.00*
Never hinged 10.50
On commercial cover 375.00
Nos. C1-C3 (3) 10.75 *24.55*
Set, never hinged 24.00
Set on overfranked cover 225.00

Air Post Stamps of Tripolitania, 1931, Overprinted in Blue

1932, May 12

C4 AP1 50c rose car 1.60 2.00
Never hinged 4.00
On commercial cover 18.00
C5 AP1 80c dull violet 6.50 *27.50*
Never hinged 12.50
On commercial cover 350.00
Set, never hinged 16.50
Set on flight cover 200.00

This overprint was also applied to the 60c, Tripolitania No. C9. The overprinted stamp was never used in Cyrenaica, but was sold at Rome in 1943 by the Postmaster General for the Italian Colonies. Value $10.

Arab on Camel — AP2

Airplane in Flight AP3

1932, Aug. 8 **Photo.**

C6 AP2 50c purple 12.00 .25
Never hinged 35.00
On commercial cover 4.00
C7 AP2 75c brn rose 12.00 *12.00*
Never hinged 35.00
On commercial cover *175.00*
C8 AP2 80c deep blue 12.00 *23.00*
Never hinged 35.00
On commercial cover *250.00*
C9 AP3 1 l black 4.25 .25
Never hinged 14.00
On commercial cover 6.50
C10 AP3 2 l green 4.25 *12.00*
Never hinged 14.00
On commercial cover *475.00*
C11 AP3 5 l deep car 8.50 *24.00*
Never hinged 27.00
On commercial cover *800.00*
Nos. C6-C11 (6) 53.00 *71.50*
Set, never hinged 160.00
Set on flight cover *325.00*

For surcharges and overprint see Nos. C20-C23.

Graf Zeppelin Issue

Zeppelin and Clouds forming Pegasus AP4

Zeppelin and Ancient Galley AP5

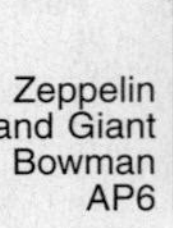

Zeppelin and Giant Bowman AP6

1933, Apr. 15

C12 AP4 3 l dk brn 10.00 *100.00*
Never hinged 22.50
On commercial cover *450.00*
C13 AP5 5 l purple 10.00 *100.00*
Never hinged 22.50
On commercial cover *600.00*
C14 AP6 10 l dp grn 10.00 *180.00*
Never hinged 22.50
On commercial cover *875.00*
C15 AP5 12 l deep blue 10.00 *200.00*
Never hinged 22.50
On commercial cover *1,100.*
C16 AP4 15 l carmine 10.00 *200.00*
Never hinged 22.50
On commercial cover *1,100.*
C17 AP6 20 l black 10.00 *275.00*
Never hinged 22.50
On commercial cover *1,100.*
Nos. C12-C17 (6) 60.00 *1,055.*
Set, never hinged 135.00
Set on flight cover *4,600.*
Set on 6 flight covers *5,250.*

North Atlantic Crossing Issue

Airplane Squadron and Constellations — AP7

1933, June 1

C18 AP7 19.75 l grn & dp bl 16.00 *500.00*
Never hinged 52.50
On commercial cover *2,750.*
C19 AP7 44.75 l red & indigo 16.00 *500.00*
Never hinged 52.50
On commercial cover *2,750.*
Set, never hinged 105.00
Set on flight cover *5,400.*

Type of 1932 Ovptd. and Srchd.

1934, Jan. 20

C20 AP3 2 l on 5 l org brn 4.75 *95.00*
Never hinged 12.00
On commercial cover 350.00
C21 AP3 3 l on 5 l yel grn 4.75 *95.00*
Never hinged 12.00
On commercial cover 350.00
C22 AP3 5 l ocher 4.75 *110.00*
Never hinged 12.00
On commercial cover 450.00
C23 AP3 10 l on 5 l rose 6.50 *110.00*
Never hinged 16.00
On commercial cover 600.00
Nos. C20-C23 (4) 20.75 *410.00*
Set, never hinged 52.00
Set on flight cover *1,800.*

For use on mail to be carried on a special flight from Rome to Buenos Aires.

Transport Plane AP8

Venus of Cyrene AP9

1934, Oct. 9

C24 AP8 25c sl bl & org red 4.25 *17.00*
Never hinged 10.00
On commercial cover 350.00
C25 AP8 50c dk grn & ind 4.25 *15.00*
Never hinged 10.00
On commercial cover 225.00
C26 AP8 75c dk brn & org red 4.25 *15.00*
Never hinged 10.00
On commercial cover 300.00
a. Imperf. 3,250.
Never hinged 4,850.
C27 AP9 80c org brn & ol grn 4.25 *17.00*
Never hinged 10.00
On commercial cover 350.00
C28 AP9 1 l scar & ol grn 4.25 *21.00*
Never hinged 10.00
On commercial cover 400.00
C29 AP9 2 l dk bl & brn 4.25 *35.00*
Never hinged 10.00
On commercial cover 550.00
Nos. C24-C29 (6) 25.50 *120.00*
Set, never hinged 60.00
Set on flight cover 450.00

2nd Colonial Arts Exhib. held at Naples.

AIR POST SEMI-POSTAL STAMPS

King Victor Emmanuel III SPAP1

Wmk. 104

1934, Nov. 5 **Photo.** ***Perf. 14***

CB1 SPAP1 25c + 10c gray grn 9.50 *27.50*
Never hinged 24.00
On cover 325.00
CB2 SPAP1 50c + 10c brn 9.50 *27.50*
Never hinged 24.00
On cover 325.00
CB3 SPAP1 75c + 15c rose red 9.50 *27.50*
Never hinged 24.00
On cover 350.00
CB4 SPAP1 80c + 15c brn blk 9.50 *27.50*
Never hinged 24.00
On cover 450.00
CB5 SPAP1 1 l + 20c red brn 9.50 *27.50*
Never hinged 24.00
On cover 475.00
CB6 SPAP1 2 l + 20c brt bl 9.50 *27.50*
Never hinged 24.00
CB7 SPAP1 3 l + 25c pur 27.50 *130.00*
Never hinged 67.50
CB8 SPAP1 5 l + 25c org 27.50 *130.00*
Never hinged 67.50
CB9 SPAP1 10 l + 30c dp vio 27.50 *130.00*
Never hinged 67.50
CB10 SPAP1 25 l + 2 l dp grn 27.50 *130.00*
Never hinged 67.50
Nos. CB1-CB10 (10) 167.00 *685.00*
Set, never hinged 415.00
Set on flown cover 1,900.

65th birthday of King Victor Emmanuel III and the non-stop flight, Rome-Mogadiscio.

AIR POST SEMI-POSTAL OFFICIAL STAMP

Type of Air Post Semi-Postal Stamps, 1934, Overprinted Crown and "SERVIZIO DI STATO" in Black

1934, Nov. 5 **Wmk. 140** ***Perf. 14***

CBO1 SPAP1 25 l + 2 l cop red *1,900.*
Never hinged *4,000.*
On flight cover *3,250.*

CZECHOSLOVAKIA

ˌche-kə-slō-ˈvä-kē-ə

LOCATION — Central Europe
GOVT. — Republic
AREA — 49,355 sq. mi.
POP. — 15,395,970 (1983)
CAPITAL — Prague

The Czechoslovakian Republic consists of Bohemia, Moravia and Silesia, Slovakia and Ruthenia (Carpatho-Ukraine). In March 1939, a German protectorate was established over Bohemia and Moravia, as well as over Slovakia which had meanwhile declared its independence. Ruthenia was incorporated in the territory of Hungary. These territories were returned to the Czechoslovak Republic in 1945, except for Ruthenia, which was ceded to Russia.

100 Haleru = 1 Koruna

Catalogue values for unused stamps in this country are for Never Hinged items, beginning with Scott 142 in the regular postage section, Scott B144 in the semi-postal section, Scott EX1 in the personal delivery section, and Scott P14 in the newspaper section.

Watermarks

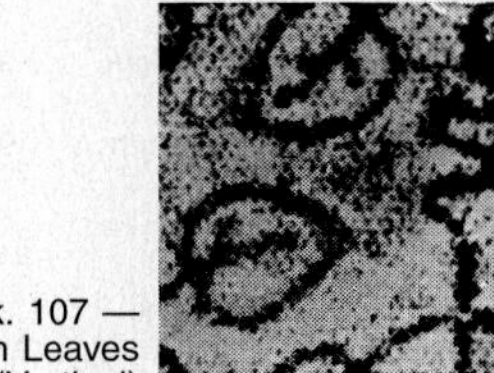
Wmk. 107 — Linden Leaves (Vertical)

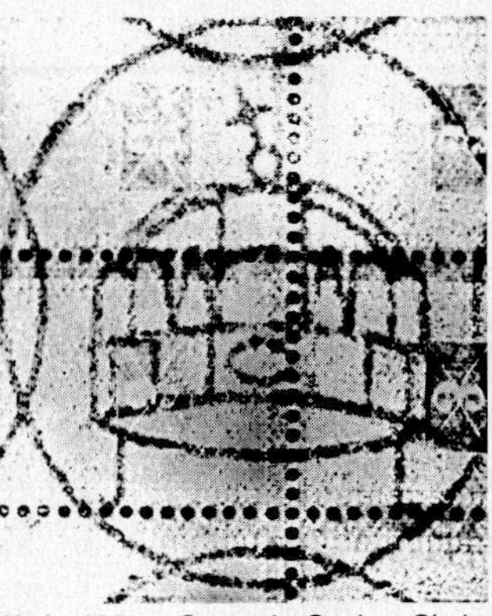
Wmk. 135 — Crown in Oval or Circle, Sideways

Wmk. 136

Wmk. 136a

Stamps of Austria overprinted "Ceskoslovenska Republika," lion and "Cesko Slovensky Stat," "Provisorni Ceskoslovenska Vlada" and Arms, and "Ceskoslovenska Statni Posta" and Arms were made privately. A few of them were passed through the post but all have been pronounced unofficial and unauthorized by the Postmaster General.

During the occupation of part of Northern Hungary by the Czechoslovak forces, stamps of Hungary were overprinted "Cesko Slovenska Posta," "Ceskoslovenska Statni Posta" and Arms, and "Slovenska Posta" and Arms. These stamps were never officially issued though examples have passed the post.

Hradcany at Prague — A1

1918-19 **Unwmk.** **Typo.** ***Imperf.***

1 A1 3h red violet .25 .25
2 A1 5h yellow green .25 .25
a. 5h green .95 .60
3 A1 10h rose .25 .25
a. 10h dark red .95 .30
4 A1 20h bluish green .25 .25
5 A1 25h deep blue .25 .25
a. 25h light blue 1.15 .25
b. 25h dark blue .75 .25
c. 25h ultramarine 19.00 12.50
6 A1 30h bister .45 .25
7 A1 40h red orange .45 .25
8 A1 100h brown 1.25 .25
9 A1 200h ultra 2.25 .25
a. 200h violet blue 19.00 25.00
b. 200h blue 11.00 .25
10 A1 400h purple 3.50 .25

On the 3h-40h "Posta Ceskoslovenska" is in white on a colored background; on the higher values the words are in color on a white background.

No. 5c was not valid for postage.

Nos. 1-6 exist as tete-beche gutter pairs.

See Nos. 368, 1554, 1600 in Scott Standard catalogue, Vol. 2. For surcharges see Nos. B130, C1, C4, J15, J19-J20, J22-J23, J30.

Perf. 11½, 13½

13 A1 5h yellow green .80 .25
a. Perf. 11½x10¾ 2.50 .55
14 A1 10h rose .40 .25
15 A1 20h bluish green .40 .25
a. Perf. 11½ .40 .25

16 A1 25h deep blue .60 .25
a. Perf. 11½ 1.50 .65
20 A1 200h ultra 4.25 .25
Nos. 1-10,13-16,20 (15) 15.60 3.75

All values of this issue exist with various private perforations and examples have been used on letters.

The 3h, 30h, 40h, 100h and 400h formerly listed are now known to have been privately perforated.

For overprints see Eastern Silesia Nos. 2, 5, 7-8, 14, 16, 18, 30.

A2

Type II

Type III

Type IV

Type II — Sun behind cathedral. Colorless foliage in foreground.

Type III — Without sun. Shaded foliage in foreground.

Type IV — No foliage in foreground. Positions of buildings changed. Letters redrawn.

1919 ***Imperf.***

23 A2 1h dark brown (II) .25 .25
25 A2 5h blue green (IV) .40 .25
a. 5h dark blue green 7.50 —
b. 5h dark green 57.50 —
27 A2 15h red (IV) .85 .25
29 A2 25h dull violet (IV) .65 .25
a. 25h red violet 90.00 5.00
30 A2 50h dull violet (II) .40 .25
31 A2 50h dark blue (IV) .40 .25
32 A2 60h orange (III) 1.60 .25
33 A2 75h slate (IV) 1.20 .25
34 A2 80h olive grn (III) .95 .25
36 A2 120h gray black (IV) 2.50 .35
a. 120h light gray 19.00 .25
b. 120h silver gray 350.00 —
38 A2 300h dark green (III) 8.00 .65
39 A2 500h red brown (IV) 8.50 .50
40 A2 1000h violet (III) 19.00 1.20
a. 1000h bluish violet 42.50 2.40
Nos. 23-40 (13) 44.70 4.95

For overprints see Eastern Silesia Nos. 1, 3-4, 6, 9-13, 15, 17, 20-21.

1919-20 ***Perf. 11½, 13¾, 13¾x11½***

41 A2 1h dk brown (II) .25 .25
42 A2 5h blue grn (IV), perf. 13½ .75 .25
a. Perf. 11½ 25.00 4.00
43 A2 10h yellow grn (IV) .40 .25
a. Imperf. 25.00 19.00
b. Perf. 11¾ 13.00 1.25
44 A2 15h brick red (IV) .40 .25
a. Perf. 11½x10¾ 30.00 4.50
b. Perf. 11½x13¾ 85.00 22.50
c. Perf. 13¾x10¾ 125.00 26.00
d. 15h brown red 9.00 *10.00*
e. 15h red 55.00 52.50
f. 15h carmine — 750.00
g. 15h vermilion red 37.50 —
45 A2 20h rose (IV) .40 .25
a. Imperf. 100.00 95.00
46 A2 25h dull vio (IV), perf. 11½ .65 .25
a. Perf. 11½x10¾ 5.00 1.10
b. Perf. 13¾x10¾ 175.00 40.00
47 A2 30h red violet (IV) .35 .25
a. Imperf. 190.00 190.00
b. Perf. 13¾x13½ 550.00 175.00
c. 30h deep violet .70 .25
d. As "c," perf. 13¾x13½ 625.00 190.00
e. As "c," imperf. 190.00 140.00
50 A2 60h orange (III) .30 .25
a. Perf. 13¾x13½ 25.00 6.25
53 A2 120h gray black (IV) 3.75 .95
Nos. 41-53 (9) 7.25 2.95

Nos. 43a, 45a, 47a and 47e were imperforate by accident and not issued in quantities as were Nos. 23 to 40.

Rouletted stamps of the preceding issues are said to have been made by a postmaster in a branch post office at Prague, or by private firms, but without authority from the Post Office Department.

The 50, 75, 80, 300, 500 and 1000h have been privately perforated.

Unlisted color varieties of types A1 and A2 were not officially released, and some are printer's waste.

For surcharges and overprints see Nos. B131, C2-C3, C5-C6, J16-J18, J21, J24-J29, J31, J42-J43, Eastern Silesia 22-29.

Pres. Thomas Garrigue Masaryk — A4

1920 ***Perf. 13½***

61 A4 125h gray blue 2.00 .25
a. 125h ultramarine 40.00 19.00
62 A4 500h slate, *grysh* 5.00 2.50
a. Imperf. 20.00 7.00
63 A4 1000h blk brn, *brnsh* 10.00 5.00
Nos. 61-63 (3) 17.00 7.75

Nos. 61, 61a, 63 imperf. were not regularly issued. Values: unused singles, No. 61 $30; No. 61a $150; No. 63 $40.

For surcharge and overprints, see Nos. B131, Eastern Silesia 31-32.

Carrier Pigeon with Letter — A5

Czechoslovakia Breaking Chains to Freedom — A6

Hussite Priest — A7

Agriculture and Science — A8

Type I

Type II

Two types of 40h:
Type I: 9 leaves by woman's hip.
Type II: 10 leaves by woman's hip.

1920 ***Perf. 14***

65 A5 5h dark blue .25 .25
a. Perf. 13¾ *325.00* *150.00*
66 A5 10h blue green .25 .25
a. Perf. 13¾ *225.00* 110.00
67 A5 15h red brown .25 .25
68 A6 20h rose .25 .25
69 A6 25h lilac brown .25 .25
70 A6 30h red violet .25 .25
71 A6 40h red brown (I) .60 .25
a. As "b," tête bêche pair 6.75 2.00
b. Perf. 13½ 1.50 .25
c. Type II .25 .25
72 A6 50h carmine .50 .25
73 A6 60h dark blue .50 .25
a. As "b," tête bêche pair 6.00 4.00
b. Perf. 13½ 2.00 .25

Photo.

74 A7 80h purple .25 .25
75 A7 90h black brown .30 .25

Typo.

Perf. 13¾

76 A8 100h dark green 1.00 .25
77 A8 200h violet 1.50 .25
78 A8 300h vermilion 3.50 .25
a. Perf. 13¾x13½ 7.00 .35
79 A8 400h brown 6.00 .45
80 A8 500h deep green 7.00 .45
a. Perf. 13¾x13½ 100.00 5.50
81 A8 600h deep violet 9.00 .45
a. Perf. 13¾x13½ 275.00 7.00
Nos. 65-81 (17) 31.65 4.85

No. 69 has background of horizontal lines.

Imperfs. were not regularly issued.

Nos. 71 and 73 exist as tete-beche gutter pairs.

For surcharges and overprint see Nos. C7-C9, J44-J56.

Type I

Type II

Two types of 20h:
Type I: Base of 2 is long, interior of 0 is angular.
Type II: Base of 2 is short, interior of 0 is an oval.

Type I

Type II

Two types of 25h:
Type I: Top of 2 curves up.
Type II: Top of 2 curves down.

1920-25 ***Perf. 14***

82 A5 5h violet .25 .25
a. As "b," tête bêche pair 2.00 1.00
b. Perf. 13½ 1.00 .35
83 A5 10h olive bister .25 .25
a. As "b," tête bêche pair 2.25 1.50
b. Perf. 13½ .80 .25
84 A5 20h deep orange (II) .25 .25
a. As "b," tête bêche pair 30.00 14.00
b. Perf. 13½ 6.00 .60
c. Type I — —
85 A5 25h blue green (I) .25 .25
a. Type II .25 .25
86 A5 30h deep violet ('25) 3.00 .25
87 A6 50h yellow green 1.00 .25
a. As "b," tête bêche pair 60.00 27.50
b. Perf. 13½ 12.00 2.00
88 A6 100h dark brown 1.00 .25
a. Perf. 13½ 15.00 .25
89 A6 150h rose 4.50 .50
a. Perf. 13½ 80.00 1.10
90 A6 185h orange 3.00 .25
91 A6 250h dark green 5.00 .25
Nos. 82-91 (10) 18.50 2.75

Imperfs. were not regularly issued.

Nos. 82-84, 87 exist as tete-beche gutter pairs.

Type of 1920 Issue Redrawn

Type I

Type II

Type III

Type I — Rib of leaf below "O" of POSTA is straight and extends to tip. White triangle above book is entirely at left of twig. "P" has a stubby, abnormal appendage.

Type II — Rib is extremely bent; does not reach tip. Triangle extends at right of twig. "P" like Type I.

Type III — Rib of top left leaf is broken in two. Triangle like Type II. "P" has no appendage.

1923 ***Perf. 13¾, 13¾x13½***

92 A8 100h red, *yellow*, III, perf. 14x13½ 1.00 .25
a. Type I, perf. 13¾ 1.25 .25
b. Type I, perf. 13¾x13½ 1.25 .25
c. Type II, perf. 13¾ 1.50 .25
d. Type II, perf. 13¾x13½ 1.50 .25
e. Type III, perf. 13¾ 7.00 .25
93 A8 200h blue, *yellow*, II, perf. 14 5.00 .25
a. Type II, perf. 13¾x13½ 8.50 .25
b. Type III, perf. 13¾ 8.50 .25
c. Type III, perf. 13¾x13½ 52.50 .50
94 A8 300h violet, *yellow*, I, perf. 13¾ 3.75 .25
a. Type II, perf. 13¾ 35.00 .25
b. Type II, perf. 13¾x13½ 50.00 .50
c. Type III, perf. 13¾x13½ 7.00 .25
d. Type III, perf. 13¾ 24.00 .35
Nos. 92-94 (3) 9.75 .75

President Masaryk
A9 A10

Perf. 13¾x13½, 13¾

1925 **Photo.** **Wmk. 107**

Size: 19½x23mm

95 A9 40h brown orange .75 .25
96 A9 50h olive green 1.50 .25
97 A9 60h red violet 1.75 .25
Nos. 95-97 (3) 4.00 .75

Distinctive Marks of the Engravings.

I, II, III — Background of horizontal lines in top and bottom tablets. Inscriptions in Roman letters with serifs.

IV — Crossed horizontal and vertical lines in the tablets. Inscriptions in Antique letters without serifs.

I, II, IV — Shading of crossed diagonal lines on the shoulder at the right.

III — Shading of single lines only.

I — "T" of "Posta" over middle of "V" of "Ceskoslovenska." Three short horizontal lines in lower part of "A" of "Ceskoslovenska."

II — "T" over right arm of "V." One short line in "A."

III — "T" as in II. Blank space in lower part of "A."

IV — "T" over left arm of "V."

Wmk. Horizontally (107)

Engr.

I. First Engraving

Size: 19¾x22½mm

98 A10 1k carmine .85 .25
99 A10 2k deep blue 2.00 .25
100 A10 3k brown 4.00 .65
101 A10 5k blue green 1.40 .45
Nos. 98-101 (4) 8.25 1.60

Wmk. Vertically (107)

Size: 19¼x23mm

101A A10 1k carmine 100.00 4.00
101B A10 2k deep blue 100.00 12.50
101C A10 3k brown 250.00 12.50
101D A10 5k blue green 5.00 2.00
Nos. 101A-101D (4) 455.00 31.00

II. Second Engraving

Wmk. Horizontally (107)

Size: 19x21½mm

102 A10 1k carmine 50.00 .50
103 A10 2k deep blue 3.50 .25
104 A10 3k brown 3.50 .50
Nos. 102-104 (3) 57.00 1.25

III. Third Engraving

Size: 19-19½x21½-22mm

Perf. 10

105 A10 1k carmine rose 1.00 .25
a. Perf. 14 15.00 .25

IV. Fourth Engraving

Size: 19x22mm

1926 ***Perf. 10***

106 A10 1k carmine rose 1.00 .25

Perf. 14

108 A10 3k brown 4.50 .25

There is a 2nd type of No. 106: with long mustache. Same values. See No. 130, design SP3.

Karlstein Castle — A11

1926, June 1 **Engr.** ***Perf. 10***

109 A11 1.20k red violet .50 .30
110 A11 1.50k car rose .30 .25
111 A11 2.50k dark blue 3.00 .30
Nos. 109-111 (3) 3.80 .85

See Nos. 133, 135.

Karlstein Castle — A12

Pernstein Castle — A13

Orava Castle A14

Masaryk A15

Strahov Monastery — A16

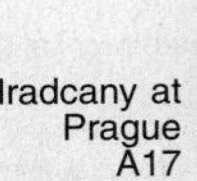

Hradcany at Prague A17

Great Tatra — A18

Short Mustache

Long, Wavy Mustache

1926-27 Engr. Wmk. 107

No.	Type	Description	Unused	Used
114	A13	30h gray green	1.25	.25
115	A14	40h red brown	.50	.25
116	A15	50h deep green	.50	.25
117	A15	60h red vio, *lil*	.85	.25
118	A16	1.20k red violet	4.00	1.50

Perf. 13½

No.	Type	Description	Unused	Used
119	A17	2k blue	.75	.25
a.		2k ultramarine	6.00	.75
120	A17	3k deep red	1.50	.25
121	A18	4k brn vio ('27)	4.75	.40
122	A18	5k dk grn ('27)	14.00	2.25
		Nos. 114-122 (9)	28.10	5.65

No. 116 exists in two types. The one with short, straight mustache at left sells for several times as much as that with longer wavy mustache.

See Nos. 137-140.

Coil Stamps

Perf. 10 Vertically

No.	Type	Description	Unused	Used
123	A12	20h brick red	.50	.40
a.		Vert. pair, imperf. horiz.	100.00	
124	A13	30h gray green	.35	.25
a.		Vert. pair, imperf. horiz.	100.00	
125	A15	50h deep green	.25	.25
		Nos. 123-125 (3)	1.10	.90

See No. 141.

Short Mustache

Long, Wavy Mustache

1927-31 Unwmk. *Perf. 10*

No.	Type	Description	Unused	Used
126	A13	30h gray green	.25	.25
127	A14	40h deep brown	.70	.25
128	A15	50h deep green	.25	.25
129	A15	60h red violet	.70	.25
130	A10	1k carmine rose	1.10	.25
131	A15	1k deep red	.75	.25
132	A16	1.20k red violet	.40	.25

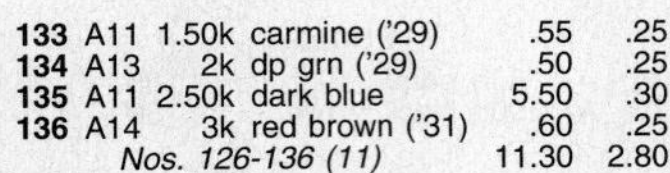

No.	Type	Description	Unused	Used
133	A11	1.50k carmine ('29)	.55	.25
134	A13	2k dp grn ('29)	.50	.25
135	A11	2.50k dark blue	5.50	.30
136	A14	3k red brown ('31)	.60	.25
		Nos. 126-136 (11)	11.30	2.80

No. 130 exists in two types. The one with longer mustache at right sells for several times as much as that with the short mustache.

1927-28 *Perf. 13½*

No.	Type	Description	Unused	Used
137	A17	2k ultra	.85	.25
138	A17	3k deep red ('28)	1.90	.65
139	A18	4k brown violet ('28)	6.00	1.00
140	A18	5k dark green ('28)	6.25	.50
		Nos. 137-140 (4)	15.00	2.40

Coil Stamp

1927 *Perf. 10 Vertically*

No.	Type	Description	Unused	Used
141	A12	20h brick red	.50	.25

Catalogue values for unused stamps in this section, from this point to the end of the section, are for Never Hinged items.

Hradec Castle A19

Brno Cathedral A25

Masaryk — A27

10th anniv. of Czech. independence: 40h, Town Hall, Levoca. 50h, Telephone exchange, Prague. 60h, Town of Jasina. 1k, Hluboka Castle. 1.20k, Pilgrims' House, Velehrad. 2.50k, Great Tatra. 5k, Old City Square, Prague.

1928, Oct. 22 *Perf. 13½*

No.	Type	Description	Unused	Used
142	A19	30h black	.25	.25
143	A19	40h red brown	.30	.25
144	A19	50h dark green	.35	.35
145	A19	60h orange red	.40	.40
146	A19	1k carmine	.55	.55
147	A19	1.20k brown vio	1.25	1.25
148	A25	2k ultra	1.30	1.30
149	A19	2.50k dk blue	4.00	3.25
150	A27	3k dark brown	2.25	2.25
151	A25	5k deep violet	4.25	4.25
		Nos. 142-151 (10)	14.90	14.10

From one to three sheets each of Nos. 142-148, perf 12½, appeared on the market in the early 1950's.

Coat of Arms — A29

1929-37 *Perf. 10*

No.	Type	Description	Unused	Used
152	A29	5h dark ultra ('31)	.25	.25
153	A29	10h bister brn ('31)	.25	.25
154	A29	20h red	.25	.25
155	A29	25h green	.25	.25
156	A29	30h red violet	.25	.25
157	A29	40h dk brown ('37)	1.50	.25
a.		40h red brown ('29)	4.00	.25
		Nos. 152-157 (6)	2.75	1.50

Coil Stamp

Perf. 10 Vertically

No.	Type	Description	Unused	Used
158	A29	20h red	.25	.25

For overprints, see Bohemia and Moravia Nos. 1-5, Slovakia Nos. 2-6.

St. Wenceslas A30

Founding St. Vitus' Cathedral A31

Design: 3k, 5k, St. Wenceslas martyred.

1929, May 14 *Perf. 13½*

No.	Type	Description	Unused	Used
159	A30	50h gray green	.50	.25
160	A30	60h slate violet	.80	.25
161	A31	2k dull blue	1.50	.50
162	A30	3k brown	2.00	.50
163	A30	5k brown violet	7.50	4.00
		Nos. 159-163 (5)	12.30	5.50

Millenary of the death of St. Wenceslas.

Statue of St. Wenceslas and National Museum, Prague — A33

1929 *Perf. 10*

No.	Type	Description	Unused	Used
164	A33	2.50k deep blue	1.00	.25

Brno Cathedral A34

Tatra Mountain Scene A35

Design: 5k, Old City Square, Prague.

1929, Oct. 15 *Perf. 13½*

No.	Type	Description	Unused	Used
165	A34	3k red brown	3.00	.25
166	A35	4k indigo	9.50	.55
167	A35	5k gray green	11.00	.50
		Nos. 165-167 (3)	23.50	1.30

See No. 183.

A37

Type I

Type II

Two types of 50h:

I — A white space exists across the bottom of the vignette between the coat, shirt and tie and the "HALERU" frame panel.

II — An extra frame line has been added just above the "HALERU" panel which finishes off the coat and tie shading evenly.

1930, Jan. 2 *Perf. 10*

No.	Type	Description	Unused	Used
168	A37	50h myrtle green (II)	.25	.25
a.		Type I	1.25	.25
169	A37	60h brown violet	1.00	.25
170	A37	1k brown red	.40	.25
		Nos. 168-170 (3)	1.65	.75

See No. 234.

Coil Stamp

1931 *Perf. 10 Vertically*

No.	Type	Description	Unused	Used
171	A37	1k brown red	1.25	.65

President Masaryk — A38

1930, Mar. 1 *Perf. 13½*

No.	Type	Description	Unused	Used
175	A38	2k gray green	2.00	.50
176	A38	3k red brown	3.25	.50
177	A38	5k slate blue	8.00	2.00
178	A38	10k gray black	22.50	5.00
		Nos. 175-178 (4)	35.75	8.00

Eightieth birthday of President Masaryk.

Nos. 175-178 were each issued in sheets with ornamental tabs at the bottom. Value, set with tabs $65.50.

St. Nicholas' Church, Prague — A39

1931, May 15

No.	Type	Description	Unused	Used
183	A39	10k black violet	18.00	3.25

Krivoklat Castle — A40

Krumlov Castle — A42

Design: 4k, Orlik Castle.

1932, Jan. 2 *Perf. 10*

No.	Type	Description	Unused	Used
184	A40	3.50k violet	4.50	1.50
185	A40	4k deep blue	4.50	.75
186	A42	5k gray green	5.50	.75
		Nos. 184-186 (3)	14.50	3.00

A43

A44

1932, Mar. 16

No.	Type	Description	Unused	Used
187	A43	50h yellow green	.75	.25
188	A43	1k brown carmine	2.00	.25
189	A44	2k dark blue	12.00	.60
190	A44	3k red brown	17.50	.60
		Nos. 187-190 (4)	32.25	1.70

Miroslav Tyrs — A45

1933, Feb. 1

No.	Type	Description	Unused	Used
191	A45	60h dull violet	.30	.25

Miroslav Tyrs (1832-84), founder of the Sokol movement; and the 9th Sokol Congress (Nos. 187-190).

First Christian Church at Nitra
A46 A47

1933, June 20

192	A46	50h yellow green	.60	.30
193	A47	1k carmine rose	9.00	.60

Prince Pribina who introduced Christianity into Slovakia and founded there the 1st Christian church in A.D. 833.

All gutter pairs are vertical. Values unused: No. 192 $350; No. 193 $10,000.

Bedrich Smetana, Czech Composer and Pianist, 50th Death Anniv. — A48

1934, Mar. 26 **Engr.** ***Perf. 10***

194	A48	50h yellow green	.40	.25

Consecration of Legion Colors at Kiev, Sept. 21, 1914 — A49

Ensign Heyduk with Colors A51

Legionnaires A52

1k, Legion receiving battle flag at Bayonne.

1934, Aug. 15 ***Perf. 10***

195	A49	50h green	.75	.25
196	A49	1k rose lake	.90	.25
197	A51	2k deep blue	4.00	.60
198	A52	3k red brown	6.75	.75
		Nos. 195-198 (4)	12.40	1.85

20th anniv. of the Czechoslovakian Legion which fought in WWI.

Antonin Dvorák, (1841-1904), Composer — A53

1934, Nov. 22

199	A53	50h green	.40	.25

Pastoral Scene — A54

1934, Dec. 17 ***Perf. 10***

200	A54	1k claret	.80	.25
a.		Souv. sheet of 15, perf. 13½	200.00	*300.00*
b.		As "a," single stamp	10.00	*12.50*
201	A54	2k blue	2.25	.80
a.		Souv. sheet of 15, perf. 13½	1,000.	*1,000.*
b.		As "a," single stamp	42.50	29.00

Centenary of the National Anthem.

Nos. 200-201 were each issued in sheets of 100 stamps and 12 blank labels. Value, set with attached labels: mint $24; used $8.

Nos. 200a & 201a have thick paper, darker shades, no gum. Forgeries exist.

President Masaryk
A55 A56

1935, Mar. 1

202	A55	50h green, *buff*	.35	.25
203	A55	1k claret, *buff*	.40	.25
204	A56	2k gray blue, *buff*	2.00	.60
205	A56	3k brown, *buff*	3.25	.60
		Nos. 202-205 (4)	6.00	1.70

85th birthday of President Masaryk.

Nos. 204-205 were each issued in sheets of 100 stamps and 12 blank labels. Value with attached labels: mint $30; used $10.

See No. 235.

Monument to Czech Heroes at Arras, France — A57

1935, May 4

206	A57	1k rose	.85	.25
207	A57	2k dull blue	3.00	.75

20th anniversary of the Battle of Arras.

Nos. 206-207 were each issued in sheets of 100 stamps and 12 blank labels. Value, set with attached labels: mint $22.50; used $22.50.

Gen. Milan Stefánik — A58

1935, May 18

208	A58	50h green	.25	.25

Sts. Cyril and Methodius — A59

1935, June 22

209	A59	50h green	.40	.25
210	A59	1k claret	.55	.25
211	A59	2k deep blue	2.00	.50
		Nos. 209-211 (3)	2.95	1.00

Millenary of the arrival in Moravia of the Apostles Cyril and Methodius.

Masaryk — A60

1935, Oct. 20 ***Perf. 12½***

212	A60	1k rose lake	.25	.25

No. 212 exists imperforate. See Bohemia and Moravia No. 1A. For overprints see Bohemia and Moravia Nos. 9-10, Slovakia 12.

Statue of Macha, Prague — A61

1936, Apr. 30

213	A61	50h deep green	.25	.25
214	A61	1k rose lake	.50	.25

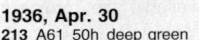

Karel Hynek Macha (1810-1836), Bohemian poet.

Nos. 213-214 were each issued in sheets of 100 stamps and 12 blank labels. Value, set with attached labels: mint $2; used 80c.

Jan Amos Komensky (Comenius) — A61a

Pres. Eduard Benes A62

Gen. Milan Stefánik A63

1936

215	A61a	40h dark blue	.25	.25
216	A62	50h dull green	.25	.25
217	A63	60h dull violet	.25	.25
		Nos. 215-217 (3)	.75	.75

See no. 252, Slovakia 23A. For overprints see Bohemia and Moravia Nos. 6, 8, Slovakia 7, 9-11.

Castle Palanok near Mukacevo A64

Town of Banska Bystrica A65

Castle at Zvikov — A66

Ruins of Castle at Strecno — A67

Castle at Cesky Raj A68

Palace at Slavkov (Austerlitz) A69

Statue of King George of Podebrad A70

Town Square at Olomouc — A71

Castle Ruins at Bratislava A72

1936, Aug. 1

218	A64	1.20k rose lilac	.25	.25
219	A65	1.50k carmine	.25	.25
220	A66	2k dark blue green	.25	.25
221	A67	2.50k dark blue	.40	.25
222	A68	3k brown	.40	.25
223	A69	3.50k dark violet	1.60	.55
224	A70	4k dark violet	.65	.25
225	A71	5k green	.65	.25
226	A72	10k blue	1.10	.55
		Nos. 218-226 (9)	5.55	2.85

Nos. 224-226 were each issued in sheets of 100 stamps and 12 blank labels. Value, with attached labels: mint $7; used $2.75.

For overprints and surcharge see Nos. 237-238, 254A, Bohemia and Moravia 11-12, 14-19, Slovakia 13-14, 16-23.

President Benes — A73

1937, Apr. 26 **Unwmk.** ***Perf. 12½***

227	A73	50h deep green	.25	.25

For overprints see Nos. 236, Slovakia 8.

Soldiers of the Czech Legion — A74

1937, June 15

228	A74	50h deep green	.25	.25
229	A74	1k rose lake	.40	.25

20th anniv. of the Battle of Zborov.

Nos. 228-229 were each issued in sheets of 100 stamps and 12 blank labels. Value, set with attached labels: mint $4; used $2.

Cathedral at Prague — A75

1937, July 1

230	A75	2k green	1.00	.25
231	A75	2.50k blue	1.50	.80

Founding of the "Little Entente," 16th anniv.

Nos. 230-231 were each issued in sheets with blank labels. Value, set with attached labels: mint $22.50; used $11.

Jan Evangelista Purkyne — A76

1937, Sept. 2

232	A76	50h slate green	.25	.25
233	A76	1k dull rose	.30	.25

150th anniv. of the birth of Purkyne, Czech physiologist.

Nos. 232-233 were printed in sheets of 100 with 12 decorated labels. Value, set with labels, $2.50.

Masaryk Types of 1930-35

1937, Sept. ***Perf. 12½***

234	A37	50h black	.25	.25

With date "14.IX. 1937" in design

235	A56	2k black	.30	.25

Death of former President Thomas G. Masaryk on Sept. 14, 1937.

No. 235 was issued in sheets of 100 stamps and 12 inscribed labels. Value, with attached label: mint $3.50; used $3.50.

International Labor Bureau Issue

Stamps of 1936-37 Overprinted in Violet or Black

1937, Oct. 6		*Perf. 12½*	
236 A73	50h dp green (Bk)	.55	.50
237 A65	1.50k carmine (V)	.55	.50
238 A66	2k dp green (V)	.95	.60
	Nos. 236-238 (3)	2.05	1.60

Bratislava Philatelic Exhibition Issue
Souvenir Sheet

A77

1937, Oct. 24		*Perf. 12½*	
239 A77	Sheet of 2	2.50	*3.25*
a.	50h dark blue	.80	1.20
b.	1k brown carmine	.80	1.20

The stamps show a view of Poprad Lake (50h) and the tomb of General Milan Stefanik (1k).

No. 239 overprinted with the Czechoslovak arms and "Czecho-Slovak Participation New York World's Fair 1939, Czecho-Slovak Pavilion" were privately produced to finance Czechoslovak participation in the exhibition. The overprint exists in black, green, red, blue, gold and silver.

No. 239 overprinted "Liberation de la Tchechoslovaquie, 28-X-1945" etc., was sold at a philatelic exhibition in Brussels, Belgium.

St. Barbara's Church, Kutna Hora — A79

1937, Dec. 4			
240 A79	1.60k olive green	.25	.25

For overprints see Bohemia and Moravia Nos. 13, Slovakia 15.

Peregrine Falcon, Sokol Emblem — A80

1938, Jan. 21			
241 A80	50h deep green	.25	.25
242 A80	1k rose lake	.25	.25

10th Intl. Sokol Games.

Nos. 241-242 were each issued in sheets of 100 stamps and 12 inscribed labels. Value, set with attached labels: mint $1.50; used $2.50.

Imperf. examples of No. 242 are essays.

Legionnaires

A81 A82

Legionnaire — A83

1938			
243 A81	50h deep green	.25	.25
244 A82	50h deep green	.25	.25
245 A83	50h deep green	.25	.25
	Nos. 243-245 (3)	.75	.75

20th anniv. of the Battle of Bachmac, Vouziers and Doss Alto.

Nos. 243-245 were each issued in sheets of 100 stamps and 12 inscribed labels. Value, set with attached labels $2, mint or used.

Jindrich Fügner, Co-Founder of Sokol Movement — A84

1938, June 18		*Perf. 12½*	
246 A84	50h deep green	.25	.25
247 A84	1k rose lake	.25	.25
248 A84	2k slate blue	.40	.25
	Nos. 246-248 (3)	.90	.75

10th Sokol Summer Games.

Nos. 246-248 were each issued in sheets of 100 stamps and 12 inscribed labels. Value, set with attached labels: mint $2.50; used $2.

View of Pilsen — A85

1938, June 24			
249 A85	50h deep green	.25	.25

Provincial Economic Council meeting, Pilsen.

No. 249 was issued in sheets of 150 stamps and 10 labels depicting a flower within a cogwheel. Value, with attached label $1, mint or used.

For overprint see Bohemia & Moravia No. 7.

Cathedral of Kosice — A86

1938, July 15		*Perf. 12½*	
250 A86	50h deep green	.25	.25

Kosice Cultural Exhibition.

No. 250 was issued in sheets of 150 stamps and 10 labels depicting grapes. Value, with attached label $1, $7.50 mint, $4.50 used.

Prague Philatelic Exhibition Issue
Souvenir Sheet

Vysehrad Castle — Hradcany — A87

1938, June 26		*Perf. 12½*	
251 A87	Sheet of 2	5.00	5.00
a.	50h dark blue	1.50	1.50
b.	1k deep carmine	1.50	1.50

See No. 3036 in Scott Standard catalogue, Vol. 2.

Stefánik Type of 1936

1938, Nov. 21			
252 A63	50h deep green	.25	.25

Allegory of the Republic — A89

1938, Dec. 19		**Unwmk.**	
253 A89	2k lt ultra	.30	.25
254 A89	3k pale brown	.50	.40

20th anniv. of Independence.

Nos. 253-254 were each issued in sheets of 100 stamps and 12 blank labels. Value, set with attached labels $2.50, mint or used.

See No. B153.

"Wir sind frei!"

Stamps of Czechoslovakia, 1918-37, overprinted with a swastika in black or red and "Wir sind frei!" were issued locally and unofficially in 1938 as Czech authorities were evacuating and German authorities arriving. They appeared in the towns of Asch, Karlsbad, Reichenberg-Maffersdorf, Rumburg, etc.

The overprint, sometimes including a surcharge or the town name (as in Karlsbad), exists on many values of postage, air post, semi-postal, postage due and newspaper stamps.

No. 226 Surcharged in Orange Red

1939, Jan. 18	**Unwmk.**	*Perf. 12½*	
254A A72	300h on 10k blue	1.60	*2.25*

Opening of the Slovakian Parliament.

No. 254A was issued in sheets of 100 stamps with 12 blank labels. Value with attached labels, mint $4.

View of Jasina — A89a

Perf. 12½

1939, Mar. 15	**Engr.**	**Unwmk.**	
254B A89a	3k ultra	*8.00*	*40.00*

Inauguration of the Carpatho-Ukraine Diet, Mar. 2, 1939.

Printed for use in the province of Carpatho-Ukraine but issued in Prague at the same time.

No. 254B was issued in sheets of 100 stamps with 12 blank labels. Values with attached labels: mint $12, used $80. Used value is for red commemorative cancel.

The stamps formerly listed as Czechoslovakia Nos. 255, 256 and C18 are now listed with Bohemia and Moravia and Slovakia. No. 255 is now Slovakia 23A. No. 256 and C18 are now listed as Bohemia and Moravia 1A and C1, respectively.

SEMI-POSTAL STAMPS

Nos. B1-B123 were sold at 1½ times face value at the Philatelists' Window of the Prague P.O. for charity benefit. They were available for ordinary postage.

Almost all stamps between Nos. B1-B123 are known with misplaced or inverted overprints and/or in pairs with one stamp missing the overprint.

The overprints of Nos. B1-B123 have been well forged.

Austrian Stamps of 1916-18 Overprinted in Black or Blue — a

Two sizes of type A40:
Type I: 25x30mm.
Type II: 26x29mm.

1919			*Perf. 12½*	
B1	A37	3h brt violet	.25	*.25*
B2	A37	5h lt green	.25	*.25*
B3	A37	6h dp orange (Bl)	.60	*.80*
B4	A37	6h dp orange (Bk)	*2,000.*	*2,000.*
B5	A37	10h magenta	.80	*1.00*
B6	A37	12h lt blue	.80	.80
B7	A42	15h dull red	.25	*.25*
B8	A42	20h dark green	.25	*.25*
a.		20h green	55.00	40.00
B9	A42	25h blue	.35	.25
B10	A42	30h dull violet	.35	.25
B11	A39	40h olive grn	.40	.40
B12	A39	50h dk green	.40	.40
B13	A39	60h dp blue	.40	.40
B14	A39	80h orange brn	.40	.40
B15	A39	90h red violet	.80	.80
B16	A39	1k car, *yel* (Bl)	.60	.60
B17	A39	1k car, *yel* (Bk)	62.50	62.50
B18	A40	2k light blue (I)	3.25	3.25
a.		2k dark blue (II)	3,000.	2,000.
b.		2k light blue (II)	1.90	1.90
c.		2k dark blue (I)	8,500.	4,000.
B19	A40	3k car rose (I)	37.50	32.50
a.		3k claret (I)	2,500.	900.00
b.		3k carmine rose (II)	2,000.	1,000.
c.		3k claret (II)	5,500.	4,000.
B20	A40	4k yellow grn (I)	20.00	15.00
a.		4k deep green (I)	55.00	45.00
b.		4k yellow grn (II)	45.00	40.00
B21	A40	10k violet	300.00	160.00
a.		10k deep violet	375.00	275.00
b.		10k black violet	450.00	300.00

The used value of No. B18a is for a stamp that has only a Czechoslovakian cancellation. Some examples of Austria No. 160, which were officially overprinted with type "a" and sold by the post office, had previously been used and lightly canceled with Austrian cancellations. These canceled-before-overprinting stamps, which were postally valid, sell for about one-fourth as much.

Granite Paper

B22 A40	2k light blue	4.00	2.90
B23 A40	3k carmine rose	10.00	8.25

The 4k and 10k on granite paper with this overprint were not regularly issued.

Excellent counterfeits of Nos. B1-B23 exist.

Austrian Newspaper Stamps Overprinted — b

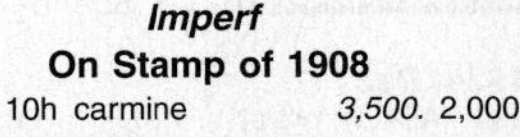

Imperf

On Stamp of 1908

B26 N8	10h carmine	*3,500.*	2,000.

On Stamps of 1916

B27 N9	2h brown	.25	.25
B28 N9	4h green	.40	.40
B29 N9	6h deep blue	.40	.40
B30 N9	10h orange	5.00	5.00
B31 N9	30h claret	1.60	1.60
	Nos. B27-B31 (5)	7.65	7.65

Austrian Special Handling Stamps Overprinted in Blue or Black — c

Perf. 12½

Stamps of 1916 Overprinted

B32 SH1 2h claret, *yel* (Bl) 25.00 25.00
B33 SH1 5h dp grn, *yel* (Bk) *1,900.* *825.00*

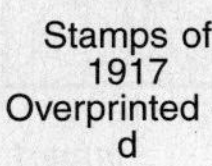

Stamps of 1917 Overprinted — d

B34 SH2 2h cl, *yel* (Bl) .25 *.35*
a. Vert. pair, imperf. btwn. *250.00*
B35 SH2 2h cl, *yel* (Bk) 60.00 35.00
B36 SH2 5h grn, *yel* (Bk) .25 .25

Austrian Air Post Stamps, #C1-C3, Overprinted Type "c" Diagonally

B37 A40 1.50k on 2k lil 175.00 175.00
B38 A40 2.50k on 3k ocher 175.00 175.00
B39 A40 4k gray 1,500. 800.00

1919

Austrian Postage Due Stamps of 1908-13 Overprinted Type "b"

B40 D3 2h carmine *6,500.* *2,750.*
B41 D3 4h carmine 25.00 15.00
B42 D3 6h carmine 12.50 8.00
B43 D3 14h carmine 90.00 35.00
B44 D3 25h carmine 45.00 20.00
B45 D3 30h carmine 600.00 300.00
B46 D3 50h carmine 1,200. 825.00

Austria Nos. J49-J56 Overprinted Type "b"

B47 D4 5h rose red .25 *.30*
B48 D4 10h rose red .25 *.30*
B49 D4 15h rose red .25 *.30*
B50 D4 20h rose red 2.00 2.00
B51 D4 25h rose red 2.00 2.00
B52 D4 30h rose red .65 .65
B53 D4 40h rose red 2.00 2.00
B54 D4 50h rose red 600.00 250.00

Austria Nos. J57-J59 Overprinted Type "a"

B55 D5 1k ultra 12.50 10.00
B56 D5 5k ultra 55.00 35.00
B57 D5 10k ultra 475.00 200.00

Austria Nos. J47-J48, J60-J63 Overprinted Type "c" Diagonally

B58 A22 1h gray 32.50 30.00
B59 A23 15h on 2h vio 150.00 110.00
B60 A38 10h on 24h blue 120.00 85.00
B61 A38 15h on 36h vio 1.00 1.00
B62 A38 20h on 54h org 90.00 85.00
B63 A38 50h on 42h choc 1.00 1.00

Hungarian Stamps Ovptd. Type "b"

1919 **Wmk. 137** ***Perf. 15***

On Stamps of 1913-16

B64 A4 1f slate 4,000. 1,600.
B65 A4 2f yellow 3.50 2.50
B66 A4 3f orange 45.00 25.00
B67 A4 6f olive green 4.50 4.50
B68 A4 50f lake, *bl* 1.25 1.00
B69 A4 60f grn, *sal* 50.00 20.00
B70 A4 70f red brn, *grn* 4,000. 1,600.

On Stamps of 1916

B71 A8 10f rose 475.00 175.00
B72 A8 15f violet 250.00 100.00

On Stamps of 1916-18

B73 A9 2f brown orange .25 .25
B74 A9 3f red lilac .25 .25
B75 A9 5f green .25 .25
B76 A9 6f grnsh blue .60 .60
B77 A9 10f rose red 1.40 *2.25*
B78 A9 15f violet .25 .25
B79 A9 20f gray brown 14.00 14.00
B80 A9 25f dull blue 1.00 .80
B81 A9 35f brown 10.00 10.00
B82 A9 40f olive green 3.25 2.50

Overprinted Type "d"

B83 A10 50f red vio & lil 1.25 *1.60*
B84 A10 75f brt bl & pale bl 1.25 *1.60*
B85 A10 80f yel grn & pale grn 1.25 *1.60*
B86 A10 1k red brn & cl 2.50 2.00
B87 A10 2k ol brn & bis 10.00 10.00
B88 A10 3k dk vio & ind 37.50 37.50
B89 A10 5k dk brn & lt brn 140.00 90.00
B90 A10 10k vio brn & vio 1,800. 800.00

Overprinted Type "b"

On Stamps of 1918

B91 A11 10f scarlet .25 .25
B92 A11 20f dark brown .30 .30
B93 A11 25f deep blue 1.40 1.25
B94 A12 40f olive grn 4.00 3.25
B95 A12 50f lilac 67.50 25.00

On Stamps of 1919

B96 A13 10f red 10.00 8.00
B97 A13 20f dk brn *10,000.* —

Same Overprint On Hungarian Newspaper Stamp of 1914

Imperf

B98 N5 (2f) orange .25 *.30*

Same Overprint On Hungarian Special Delivery Stamp

Perf. 15

B99 SD1 2f gray grn & red .25 *.35*

Same Ovpt. On Hungarian Semi-Postal Stamps

B100 SP3 10f + 2f rose red .80 .80
B101 SP4 15f + 2f violet 1.25 1.25
B102 SP5 40f + 2f brn car 7.00 3.50
Nos. B98-B102 (5) 9.55 6.20

Hungarian Postage Due Stamps of 1903-18 Overprinted Type "b"

1919 **Wmk. 135** ***Perf. 11½, 12***

B103 D1 50f green & black *525.00* *525.00*

Wmk. Crown (136, 136a)

Perf. 11½x12, 15

B104 D1 1f green & black *1,200.* *1,000.*
B105 D1 2f green & black *1,000.* *750.*
B106 D1 12f green & black *4,250.* *3,000.*
B107 D1 50f green & black *275.* 150.

Wmk. Double Cross (137)

Perf. 15

On Stamps of 1914

B110 D1 1f green & black 1,250. 600.
B111 D1 2f green & black 700. 550.
B112 D1 5f green & black 1,325. 900.
B113 D1 12f green & black *5,250.* *4,000.*
B114 D1 50f green & black 275. 150.

On Stamps of 1915-18

B115 D1 1f green & red 175.00 140.00
B116 D1 2f green & red 1.00 .80
B117 D1 5f green & red 12.50 10.00
B118 D1 6f green & red 1.50 1.50
B119 D1 10f green & red .60 .60
a. Pair, one without overprint
B120 D1 12f green & red 2.00 2.00
B121 D1 15f green & red 7.50 5.00
B122 D1 20f green & red 1.00 1.00
B123 D1 30f green & red 80.00 70.00
Nos. B115-B123 (9) 281.10 230.90

Excellent counterfeits of Nos. B1-B123 exist.

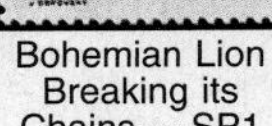
Bohemian Lion Breaking its Chains — SP1

Mother and Child — SP2

Perf. 11½, 13¾ and Compound

1919 **Typo.** **Unwmk.**

Pinkish Paper

B124 SP1 15h gray green .25 .25
a. 15h light green 32.50 25.00
B125 SP1 25h dark brown .25 .25
a. 25h light brown *5.00* 4.00
B126 SP1 50h dark blue .25 .25

Photo.

Yellowish Paper

B127 SP2 75h slate .25 .25
B128 SP2 100h brn vio .25 .25
B129 SP2 120h vio, *yel* .25 .25
Nos. B124-B129 (6) 1.50 1.50

Values are for perf 13¾. Other perfs are valued higher.

Nos. B124-B126 commemorate the 1st anniv. of Czechoslovak independence. Nos. B127-B129 were sold for the benefit of Legionnaires' orphans. Imperforates exist.

See No. 1581 in Scott Standard catalogue, Vol. 2.

Regular Issues of Czechoslovakia Surcharged in Red

a

b

1920 ***Perf. 13¾***

B130 A1(a) 40h + 20h bister 1.25 *.90*
B131 A2(a) 60h + 20h green 1.25 *.90*
B132 A4(b) 125h + 25h gray bl 5.75 *2.75*
Nos. B130-B132 (3) 8.25 *4.55*

President Masaryk — SP3

Wmk. Linden Leaves (107)

1923 **Engr.** ***Perf. 13¾x14¾***

B133 SP3 50h gray green .90 .55
B134 SP3 100h carmine 1.10 .90
B135 SP3 200h blue 3.50 3.00
B136 SP3 300h dark brown 3.50 4.25
Nos. B133-B136 (4) 9.00 8.70

5th anniv. of the Republic.

The gum was applied through a screen and shows the monogram "CSP" (Ceskoslovenska Posta). These stamps were sold at double their face values, the excess being given to the Red Cross and other charitable organizations.

International Olympic Congress Issue

Semi-Postal Stamps of 1923 Overprinted in Blue or Red

1925

B137 SP3 50h gray green 10.00 8.50
B138 SP3 100h carmine 14.50 12.00
B139 SP3 200h blue (R) 72.50 55.00
Nos. B137-B139 (3) 97.00 75.50
Set, never hinged 175.00

These stamps were sold at double their face values, the excess being divided between a fund for post office clerks and the Olympic Games Committee.

Sokol Issue

Semi-Postal Stamps of 1923 Overprinted in Blue or Red

1926

B140 SP3 50h gray green 1.60 *4.00*
B141 SP3 100h carmine 3.25 *4.00*
B142 SP3 200h blue (R) 15.00 12.50
a. Double overprint
B143 SP3 300h dk brn (R) 20.00 20.00
Nos. B140-B143 (4) 39.85 40.50
Set, never hinged 140.00

These stamps were sold at double their face values, the excess being given to the Congress of Sokols, June, 1926.

Catalogue values for unused stamps in this section, from this point to the end of the section, are for Never Hinged items.

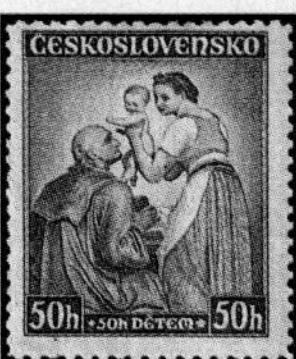

Midwife Presenting Newborn Child to its Father; after a Painting by Josef Manes

SP4 SP5

1936 **Unwmk.** **Engr.** ***Perf. 12½***

B144 SP4 50h + 50h green .75 .75
B145 SP5 1k + 50h claret 1.25 1.25
B146 SP4 2k + 50h blue 2.75 2.75
Nos. B144-B146 (3) 4.75 4.75

Nos. B144-B146 were each issued in sheets of 100 with 12 labels. Value, set $40.

SP6

"Lullaby" by Stanislav Suchարda SP7

1937 ***Perf. 12½***

B147 SP6 50h + 50h dull green .60 .35
B148 SP6 1k + 50h rose lake 1.10 1.10
B149 SP7 2k + 1k dull blue 2.60 1.75
Nos. B147-B149 (3) 4.30 3.20

Nos. B147-B149 were each issued in sheets of 100 with 12 labels. Value, set of singles with attached labels hinged mint $5; used $5.

President Masaryk and Little Girl in Native Costume — SP8

1938 ***Perf. 12½***

B150 SP8 50h + 50h deep green .95 .95
B151 SP8 1k + 50h rose lake 1.25 1.25

Souvenir Sheet

Imperf

B152 SP8 2k + 3k black 6.25 6.25

88th anniv. of the birth of Masaryk (1850-1937).

Nos. B150-B151 were each issued in sheets of 100 stamps and 12 blank labels. Value, set of singles with attached labels: mint $6; used $4.

Allegory of the Republic Type

Souvenir Sheet

1938 ***Perf. 12½***

B153 A89 2k (+ 8k) dark blue 4.00 4.00

The surtax was devoted to national relief for refugees.

AIR POST STAMPS

Nos. 9, 39-40, 20, and Types of 1919 Srchd. in Red, Blue or Green

1920 **Unwmk.** ***Imperf.***

C1 A1 14k on 200h (R) 21.00 18.00
a. Inverted surcharge 125.00

C2 A2 24k on 500h (Bl) 50.00 30.00
a. Inverted surcharge 225.00
C3 A2 28k on 1000h (G) 32.50 30.00
a. Inverted surcharge 150.00
b. Double surcharge 200.00
Nos. C1-C3 (3) 103.50 78.00

Perf. 13¾

C4 A1 14k on 200h (R) 22.50 *30.00*
a. Perf. 13¾x13½ 95.00 95.00
C5 A2 24k on 500h (Bl) 45.00 *70.00*
a. Perf. 13¾x13½ 100.00 100.00

Perf. 13¾x13½

C6 A2 28k on 1000h (G) 20.00 27.50
a. Inverted surcharge 400.00 —
b. Perf. 13¾ 475.00 700.00
c. As "b," invtd. surcharge 350.00 —
Nos. C4-C6 (3) 87.50 127.50
Nos. C1-C6 (6) 191.00 205.50

Excellent counterfeits of the overprint are known.

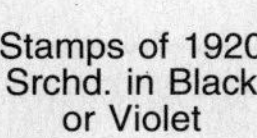
Stamps of 1920 Srchd. in Black or Violet

1922, June 15 ***Perf. 13¾***

C7 A8 50h on 100h dl grn 1.50 1.50
a. Inverted surcharge 150.00
b. Double surcharge 160.00
C8 A8 100h on 200h vio 4.00 3.25
a. Inverted surcharge 150.00
C9 A8 250h on 400h brn (V) 6.00 7.50
a. Inverted surcharge 275.00
Nos. C7-C9 (3) 11.50 12.25
Set, never hinged 20.00

Fokker Monoplane AP3

Smolik S 19 AP4

Smolik S 19 — AP5

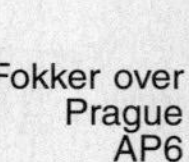
Fokker over Prague AP6

1930, Dec. 16 **Engr.** ***Perf. 13½***

C10 AP3 50h deep green .25 .25
C11 AP3 1k deep red .30 *.45*
C12 AP4 2k dark green .70 *1.10*
C13 AP4 3k red violet 1.50 1.30
C14 AP5 4k indigo 1.40 1.30
C15 AP5 5k red brown 2.75 *4.25*
C16 AP6 10k vio blue 5.00 4.25
a. 10k ultra 13.50 12.00
C17 AP6 20k gray violet 5.25 5.25
Nos. C10-C17 (8) 17.15 18.15

Two types exist of the 50h, 1k and 2k, and three types of the 3k, differing chiefly in the size of the printed area. A "no hill at left" variety of the 3k exists.

Imperf. examples of Nos. C10-C17 are proofs.

See Bohemia and Moravia No. C1.

Perf. 12

C10a AP3 50h deep green 3.25 *5.00*
C11a AP3 1k deep red 18.00 *22.50*
C12a AP4 2k dark green 18.00 *22.50*
C14a AP5 4k indigo 2.75 *3.75*
C17a AP6 20k gray violet 3.50 *7.50*

Perf. 12x13½, 13½x12

C11b AP3 1k deep red 4.00 *7.50*
C12b AP4 2k dark green 12.00 *20.00*

Perf. 13¾x12¼

C17b AP6 20k gray violet *1,750.*

Perf. 12½

C15a AP5 5k red brown *2,000.*

SPECIAL DELIVERY STAMPS

Doves — SD1

1919-20 **Unwmk.** **Typo.** ***Imperf.***

E1 SD1 2h red vio, *yel* .25 .25
E2 SD1 5h yel grn, *yel* .25 .25
E3 SD1 10h red brn, *yel* ('20) .80 .80
Nos. E1-E3 (3) 1.30 1.30

For overprints and surcharge see Nos. P11-P13, Eastern Silesia E1-E2.

1921 **White Paper**

E1a SD1 2h red violet 9.50
E2a SD1 5h yellow green 6.50
E3a SD1 10h red brown 140.00
Nos. E1a-E3a (3) 156.00

It is doubted that Nos. E1a-E3a were regularly issued.

PERSONAL DELIVERY STAMPS

Catalogue values for unused stamps in this section are for Never Hinged items.

PD1

Design: No. EX2, "D" in each corner.

1937 **Unwmk.** **Photo.** ***Perf. 13½***

EX1 PD1 50h blue .25 *.25*
EX2 PD1 50h carmine .25 *.25*

POSTAGE DUE STAMPS

D1

1918-20 **Unwmk.** **Typo.** ***Imperf.***

J1 D1 5h deep bister .25 .25
J2 D1 10h deep bister .25 .25
J3 D1 15h deep bister .25 .25
J4 D1 20h deep bister .30 .25
J5 D1 25h deep bister .45 .25
J6 D1 30h deep bister .45 .25
J7 D1 40h deep bister .60 .25
J8 D1 50h deep bister .75 .25
J9 D1 100h blk brn 1.50 .25
J10 D1 250h orange 11.00 1.40
J11 D1 400h scarlet 15.00 1.40
J12 D1 500h gray grn 7.50 .25
J13 D1 1000h purple 7.50 .25
J14 D1 2000h dark blue 22.50 .60
Nos. J1-J14 (14) 68.30 6.15

For surcharges and overprints see Nos. J32-J41, J57, Eastern Silesia J1-J11.

Nos. 1, 33-34, 10 Surcharged in Blue

1922

J15 A1 20h on 3h red vio .30 .25
J16 A2 50h on 75h slate 1.50 .25
J17 A2 60h on 80h olive grn .80 .25
J18 A2 100h on 80h olive grn 3.00 .25
J19 A1 200h on 400h purple 4.00 .25
Nos. J15-J19 (5) 9.60 1.25

Same Surcharge on Nos. 1, 10, 30-31, 33-34, 36, 40 in Violet

1923-26

J20 A1 10h on 3h red vio .25 .25
J21 A1 20h on 3h red vio .30 .25
J22 A1 30h on 3h red vio .25 .25
J23 A1 40h on 3h red vio .25 .25
J24 A2 50h on 75h slate 1.25 .25
J25 A2 60h on 50h dk vio ('26) 4.00 1.25
J26 A2 60h on 50h dk bl ('26) 4.00 1.50
J27 A2 60h on 75h slate .50 .25
J28 A2 100h on 80h ol grn 27.50 .25
J29 A2 100h on 120h gray blk 1.00 .25
J30 A1 100h on 400h pur ('26) 1.00 .25
J31 A2 100h on 1000h dp vio ('26) 1.60 .25
Nos. J20-J31 (12) 41.90 5.25

Postage Due Stamp of 1918-20 Surcharged in Violet

1924

J32 D1 50h on 400h scar .90 .25
J33 D1 60h on 400h scar 3.25 .60
J34 D1 100h on 400h scar 2.00 .25
Nos. J32-J34 (3) 6.15 1.10

Postage Due Stamps of 1918-20 Surcharged with New Values in Violet as in 1924

1925

J35 D1 10h on 5h bister .25 .25
J36 D1 20h on 5h bister .25 .25
J37 D1 30h on 15h bister .25 .25
J38 D1 40h on 15h bister .25 .25
J39 D1 50h on 250h org 1.10 .25
J40 D1 60h on 250h org 1.50 .60
J41 D1 100h on 250h org 2.25 .25
Nos. J35-J41 (7) 5.85 2.10

Stamps of 1918-19 Surcharged with New Values in Violet as in 1922

1926 ***Perf. 14, 11½***

J42 A2 30h on 15h red .50 .30
J43 A2 40h on 15h red .50 .30

Surcharged in Violet

1926 ***Perf. 14***

J44 A8 30h on 100h dk grn .25 .25
J45 A8 40h on 200h violet .25 .25
J46 A8 40h on 300h ver .95 .25
a. Perf. 14x13½ 60.00
J47 A8 50h on 500h dp grn .50 .25
a. Perf. 14x13½ 2.75
J48 A8 60h on 400h brown 1.00 .25
J49 A8 100h on 600h dp vio 2.50 .35
a. Perf. 14x13½ 30.00 1.25
Nos. J44-J49 (6) 5.45 1.60

Surcharged in Violet

1927

J50 A6 100h dark brown .55 .25
a. Perf. 13½ *200.00* 10.00

Surcharged in Violet

J51 A6 40h on 185h org .25 .25
J52 A6 50h on 20h car .25 .25
a. 50h on 50h carmine (error) *55,000.*
J53 A6 50h on 150h rose .25 .25
a. Perf. 13½ 12.50 2.00
J54 A6 60h on 25h brown .25 .25
J55 A6 60h on 185h orange .55 .25
J56 A6 100h on 25h brown .55 .25
Nos. J50-J56 (7) 2.65 1.75

No. J52a is known only used.

No. J12 Surcharged in Deep Violet

1927 ***Imperf.***

J57 D1 200h on 500h gray grn 8.00 2.50

Catalogue values for unused stamps in this section, from this point to the end of the section, are for Never Hinged items.

D5

1928 ***Perf. 14x13½***

J58 D5 5h dark red .25 .25
J59 D5 10h dark red .25 .25
J60 D5 20h dark red .25 .25
J61 D5 30h dark red .25 .25
J62 D5 40h dark red .25 .25
J63 D5 50h dark red .25 .25
J64 D5 60h dark red .25 .25
J65 D5 1k ultra .25 .25
J66 D5 2k ultra .50 .25
J67 D5 5k ultra .75 .25
J68 D5 10k ultra 1.90 .25
J69 D5 20k ultra 3.75 .30
Nos. J58-J69 (12) 8.90 3.05

LOCAL OFFICIAL STAMPS

Coat of Arms — L1

Typo. & Embossed

1918, Nov. 7 ***Die Cut Perf 12***

OL1 L1 10h blue 19.50 *11.50*
Never hinged 27.50
On cover 135.00
a. 10h pale blue 32.50 57.50
Never hinged 50.00
On cover 250.00
OL2 L1 20h bright carmine 19.50 11.00
Never hinged 27.50
On cover 135.00

In the first weeks of independence, the Czechoslovak National Council employed the Czech Scouts to maintain a local post in Prague, and Nos. OL1-OL2 were issued for this service. These stamps were in use Nov. 7-25, after which regular postal operations were resumed.

Nos. OL1 and OL2 were printed on grayish paper with yellow gum. A later printing on white paper with white gum was made for sale to collectors. These reprints sell for substantially less than the values above.

The scout delivery service was revived for one day, December 21, 1918, as part of the celebration of Thomas G. Masaryk's arrival in Czechoslovakia. 600 copies of No. OL1 and 1,000 examples of OL2 were overprinted "Prijezd presidenta Masaryka." ("Arrival of President Masaryk") in three lines. Values: overprint on No. OL1, unused $2,450, used $1,200, on cover $4,400; on OL1a, unused $8,250, used $3,850, on cover $11,000; on OL2, unused $2,450, used $1,000, on cover $3,300.

NEWSPAPER STAMPS

Windhover — N1

1918-20 Unwmk. Typo. ***Imperf.***

P1 N1 2h gray green .25 .25
P2 N1 5h green ('20) .25 .25
a. 5h dark green .40 .25
P3 N1 6h red .30 .25
P4 N1 10h dull violet .25 .25
P5 N1 20h blue .25 .25
P6 N1 30h gray brown .25 .25
P7 N1 50h orange ('20) .30 .25
P8 N1 100h red brown ('20) .40 .25
Nos. P1-P8 (8) 2.25 2.00

Nos. P1-P8 exist privately perforated.
For surcharges and overprints see Nos. P9-P10, P14-P16, Eastern Silesia P1-P5.

Stamps of 1918-20 Surcharged in Violet

1925-26

P9 N1 5h on 2h gray green .50 .40
P10 N1 5h on 6h red ('26) .25 *.40*

Special Delivery Stamps of 1918-20 Overprinted in Violet

1926

P11 SD1 5h apple grn, *yel* .25 .25
a. 5h dull green, *yellow* .50 .40
P12 SD1 10h red brn, *yel* .25 .25

With Additional Surcharge of New Value

P13 SD1 5h on 2h red vio, *yel* .35 .35
Nos. P11-P13 (3) .85 .85

Catalogue values for unused stamps in this section, from this point to the end of the section, are for Never Hinged items.

Newspaper Stamps of 1918-20 Overprinted in Violet

1934

P14 N1 10h dull violet .25 .25
P15 N1 20h blue .25 .25
P16 N1 30h gray brown .25 .25
Nos. P14-P16 (3) .75 .75

Overprinted for use by commercial firms only.

Carrier Pigeon — N2

1937 ***Imperf.***

P17 N2 2h bister brown .25 .25
P18 N2 5h dull blue .25 .25
P19 N2 7h red orange .25 .25
P20 N2 9h emerald .25 .25
P21 N2 10h henna brown .25 .25
P22 N2 12h ultra .25 .25
P23 N2 20h dark green .25 .25
P24 N2 50h dark brown .25 .25
P25 N2 1k olive gray .25 .25
Nos. P17-P25 (9) 2.25 2.25

For overprint see Slovakia Nos. P1-P9.

Bratislava Philatelic Exhibition Issue
Souvenir Sheet

1937 ***Imperf.***

P26 N2 10h henna brn, sheet of 25 4.00 4.00

CZECHOSLOVAK LEGION POST

The Czechoslovak Legion in Siberia issued these stamps for use on its mail and that of local residents. Forgeries exist.

Russia No. 79 Overprinted

1918 Typo. ***Perf. 14x14½***

A1 A15 10k dark blue 2,500. —

No. A1 was sold for a few days in Chelyabinsk. It was withdrawn because of a spelling error ("CZESZKJA," instead of "CZESZKAJA").

This overprint was also applied to Russia Nos. 73-78, 80-81, 83-85, 119-121, 123 and 130-131. These were trial printings, never sold to the public, although favor-cancelled covers exist.

Urn and Cathedral at Irkutsk — A1

Armored Railroad Car — A2

Sentinel — A3

1919-20 Litho. ***Imperf.***

1 A1 25k carmine 10.50 —
Never hinged 21.00
a. Perf 11½ ('20) 15.00 —
Never hinged 30.00
2 A2 50k yellow green 10.50 —
Never hinged 21.00
a. Perf 11½ ('20) 15.00 —
Never hinged 30.00
3 A3 1r red brown 19.00 —
Never hinged 37.50
a. Perf 11½ ('20) 22.50 —
Never hinged 52.50

Nos. 1-3 were printed by Makusin & Posochin in Irkutsk and were delivered to the Czech Field Post, imperforate and ungummed, in Dec. 1919. A crackled yellow gum was applied to stamps sold at Field Post offices. In Jan. 1920 a quantity of sheets was perforated 11½.

Nos. 1 and 2 exist in wide horizontal gutter pairs, containing one of each denomination. Value, $700 unused, $1,000 never hinged. No. 3 exists in wide vertical gutter pairs. Value, $1,700 unused, $3,000 never hinged.

Later, ungummed imperforate remainders were sent to Prague, where a smooth white gum was applied. Some of these remainder sheets were perforated 11½ and a large proportion were perforated 13¼. Value, set: $3 unused; $6 never hinged.

Nos. 1-3 and 1a-3a exist overprinted "Balicky do vlasti 50R" ("Packages to the homeland, 50 Rubles") and "Prvi Jugoslavenski puk u Sibiriji" ("First Jugoslav Regiment in Siberia"). Nos. 1-3 also exist overprinted "Vlak cs cerv.krize" ("Train of the Czechoslovak Red Cross"). All are rare.

Lion of Bohemia — A4

Type 1

Type 2

Two types: 1 — 6 points on star-like mace head at right of goblet; large saber handle; measures 20x25¼mm. 2 — 5 points on mace head; small saber handle; measures 19½x25mm.

Perce en Arc in Blue

1920 Embossed

4 A4 (25k) blue & rose, ty 1 3.00 —
Never hinged 4.00
a. Type 2 3.00 —
Never hinged 4.00

1st, 2nd

3rd

No. 4 was printed in Prague in 1919 and received in Siberia in 1920. It was overprinted "1920" (No. 5), which was in turn surcharged in various denominations (Nos. 6-14).

There were three printings of No. 4, all of which received the subsequent overprintings. The first printing has a steel blue frame and carmine center. The second printing has a gray-blue frame and red center. The first and second printings were sent to Siberia, apparently in similar quantities, and values for Nos. 4-14 are for examples from these printings.

A third printing was made in Prague in the 1920s to create stamps for sale to collectors. Stamps of the third printing have a deep blue frame and carmine center, with heavy carmine inking at the top of the oval. Values for examples of Nos. 4-14 from this philatelic printing are much lower.

No. 4 Overprinted

1920

5 A4 (25k) bl & rose, type 1 10.00 —
Never hinged 15.00
a. Type 2 10.00 —
Never hinged 15.00

Both types of No. 4 received overprint.

No. 5 (type 1) Surcharged with New Values in Green

6 A4 2k bl & rose 35.00
Never hinged 52.50
7 A4 3k bl & rose 35.00
Never hinged 52.50
8 A4 5k bl & rose 35.00
Never hinged 52.50
9 A4 10k bl & rose 35.00
Never hinged 52.50
10 A4 15k bl & rose 35.00
Never hinged 52.50
11 A4 25k bl & rose 35.00
Never hinged 52.50
12 A4 35k bl & rose 35.00
Never hinged 52.50
13 A4 50k bl & rose 35.00
Never hinged 52.50
14 A4 1r bl & rose 35.00
Never hinged 52.50
Nos. 6-14 (9) 315.00
Set, never hinged 475.00

Surcharged on No. 5a (type 2)

6a A4 2k bl & rose 35.00
Never hinged 52.50
7a A4 3k bl & rose 35.00
Never hinged 52.50
8a A4 5k bl & rose 35.00
Never hinged 52.50
9a A4 10k bl & rose 35.00
Never hinged 52.50
10a A4 15k bl & rose 35.00
Never hinged 52.50
11a A4 25k bl & rose 35.00
Never hinged 52.50
12a A4 35k bl & rose 35.00
Never hinged 52.50
13a A4 50k bl & rose 35.00
Never hinged 52.50
14a A4 1r bl & rose 35.00
Never hinged 52.50
Nos. 6a-14a (9) 315.00
Set, never hinged 475.00

BOHEMIA AND MORAVIA

Catalogue values for unused stamps in this country are for never hinged items, beginning with Scott 20 in the regular postage section, Scott B1 in the semi-postal section, Scott J1 in the postage due section, and Scott P1 in the newspaper section.

Masaryk Type of Czechoslovakia with hyphen in "Cesko-Slovensko" A60

1939, Apr. 23

1A A60 1k rose lake .25 .25

Prepared by Czechoslovakia prior to the German occupation March 15, 1939. Subsequently issued for use in Bohemia and Moravia.

See No. C1.

German Protectorate

Stamps of Czechoslovakia, 1928-39, Overprinted in Black

Perf. 10, 12½, 12x12½

1939, July 15 Unwmk.

1 A29 5h dk ultra .25 *1.25*
2 A29 10h brown .25 *1.25*
3 A29 20h red .25 *1.25*
4 A29 25h green .25 *1.25*
5 A29 30h red vio .25 *1.25*
6 A61a 40h dk bl 2.50 *5.00*
7 A85 50h dp grn .25 *1.25*
8 A63 60h dl vio 2.50 *5.00*
9 A60 1k rose lake (#212) .75 *1.75*
10 A60 1k rose lake .30 *1.25*
11 A64 1.20k rose lilac 3.00 *5.00*
12 A65 1.50k carmine 2.50 *5.75*
13 A79 1.60k olive grn 5.00 *5.75*
a. "Mähnen" 32.50 *75.00*
14 A66 2k dk bl grn 1.10 *4.00*
15 A67 2.50k dk bl 3.00 *5.00*
16 A68 3k brown 3.00 *5.75*
17 A70 4k dk vio 9.50 *6.50*
18 A71 5k green 3.50 *10.00*
19 A72 10k blue 4.75 *15.00*
Nos. 1-19 (19) 42.90 *83.25*
Set, never hinged 60.00

The size of the overprint varies, Nos. 1-10 measure 17½x15½mm, Nos. 11-16 19x18mm, Nos. 17 and 19 28x17½mm and No. 18 23½x23mm.

Catalogue values for unused stamps in this section, from this point to the end of the section, are for never hinged items.

Linden Leaves and Closed Buds — A1

1939-41 Photo. ***Perf. 14***

20 A1 5h dark blue .25 *.30*
21 A1 10h blk brn .25 *.40*
22 A1 20h crimson .25 *.30*
23 A1 25h dk bl grn .25 *.30*
24 A1 30h dp plum .25 *.30*

No.	Type	Description	Unused	Used
24A	A1	30h golden brn ('41)	.25	*.30*
25	A1	40h orange ('40)	.25	.25
26	A1	50h slate grn ('40)	.25	.25
		Nos. 20-26 (8)	2.00	2.40

See Nos. 49-51.

Castle at Zvikov — A2

Karlstein Castle — A3

St. Barbara's Church, Kutna Hora — A4

Cathedral at Prague — A5

Brno Cathedral — A6

Town Square, Olomouc — A7

1939 **Engr.** ***Perf. 12½***

No.	Type	Description	Unused	Used
27	A2	40h dark blue	.25	*.30*
28	A3	50h dk bl grn	.25	*.30*
29	A4	60h dl vio	.25	*.30*
30	A5	1k dp rose	.25	*.30*
31	A6	1.20k rose lilac	.40	*.60*
32	A6	1.50k rose car	.25	*.30*
33	A7	2k dk bl grn	.25	*.50*
34	A7	2.50k dark blue	.25	*.30*
		Nos. 27-34 (8)	2.15	*2.90*

No. 31 measures 23½x29½mm, No. 42 measures 18½x23mm.

See nos. 52-53, 53B, 60-61 (overprints) in Scott Standard catalog, Vol. 2.

Zlin — A8

Iron Works at Moravská Ostrava — A9

Prague — A10

1939-40

No.	Type	Description	Unused	Used
35	A8	3k dl rose vio	.25	*.30*
36	A9	4k slate ('40)	.25	*.40*
37	A10	5k green	.50	*.80*
38	A10	10k lt ultra	.40	*1.00*
39	A10	20k yel brn	1.25	*2.00*
		Nos. 35-39 (5)	2.65	*4.50*

Types of 1939 and

Neuhaus A11

Pernstein Castle A12

Pardubice Castle — A13

Lainsitz Bridge near Bechyne A14

Samson Fountain, Budweis — A15

Kromeriz A16

Wallenstein Palace, Prague — A17

1940 **Engr.** ***Perf. 12½***

No.	Type	Description	Unused	Used
40	A11	50h dk bl grn	.25	.25
41	A12	80h dp bl	.25	*.40*
42	A6	1.20k vio brn	.40	.25
43	A13	2k gray grn	.25	.25
44	A14	5k dk bl grn	.25	.25
45	A15	6k brn vio	.25	*.50*
46	A16	8k slate grn	.25	*.30*
47	A17	10k blue	.45	.30
48	A10	20k sepia	1.10	*1.60*
		Nos. 40-48 (9)	3.45	*4.10*

No. 42 measures 18½x23mm; No. 31, 23½x29½mm.

SEMI-POSTAL STAMPS

Catalogue values for unused stamps in this section are for never hinged items.

Nurse and Wounded Soldier — SP1

Perf. 13½

1940, June 29 **Photo.** **Unwmk.**

No.	Type	Description	Unused	Used
B1	SP1	60h + 40h indigo	.90	*1.10*
B2	SP1	1.20k + 80h deep plum	.90	*1.25*

Surtax for German Red Cross.

Labels alternate with stamps in sheets of Nos. B1-B2.

AIR POST STAMP

Catalogue values for unused stamps in this section are for never hinged items.

Type of Czechoslovakia 1930 with hyphen in "Cesko-Slovensko"

Fokker Monoplane — AP3

1939, Apr. 22 ***Perf. 13½***

No.	Type	Description	Unused	Used
C1	AP3	30h rose lilac	.25	.25

Prepared by Czechoslovakia prior to the German occupation March 15, 1939. Subsequently issued for use in Bohemia and Moravia. See No. 1A.

PERSONAL DELIVERY STAMPS

PD1

1939-40 **Unwmk.** **Photo.** ***Perf. 13½***

No.	Type	Description	Unused	Used
EX1	PD1	50h indigo & blue ('40)	1.25	*2.00*
EX2	PD1	50h carmine & rose	1.60	*2.50*

POSTAGE DUE STAMPS

Catalogue values for unused stamps in this section are for never hinged items.

D1

1939-40 **Unwmk.** **Typo.** ***Perf. 14***

No.	Type	Description	Unused	Used
J1	D1	5h dark carmine	.25	*.30*
J2	D1	10h dark carmine	.25	*.30*
J3	D1	20h dark carmine	.25	*.30*
J4	D1	30h dark carmine	.25	*.30*
J5	D1	40h dark carmine	.25	*.30*
J6	D1	50h dark carmine	.25	*.30*
J7	D1	60h dark carmine	.25	*.30*
J8	D1	80h dark carmine	.25	*.30*
J9	D1	1k bright ultra	.25	*.40*
J10	D1	1.20k brt ultra ('40)	.30	*.40*
J11	D1	2k bright ultra	1.00	*1.25*
J12	D1	5k bright ultra	1.10	*1.60*
J13	D1	10k bright ultra	1.60	*2.00*
J14	D1	20k bright ultra	3.25	*3.25*
		Nos. J1-J14 (14)	9.50	*11.30*

NEWSPAPER STAMPS

Catalogue values for unused stamps in this section are for never hinged items.

Carrier Pigeon — N1

1939 **Unwmk.** **Typo.** ***Imperf.***

No.	Type	Description	Unused	Used
P1	N1	2h ocher	.25	*.30*
P2	N1	5h ultra	.25	*.30*
P3	N1	7h red orange	.25	*.30*
P4	N1	9h emerald	.25	*.30*
P5	N1	10h henna brown	.25	*.30*
P6	N1	12h dark ultra	.25	*.30*
P7	N1	20h dark green	.25	*.30*
P8	N1	50h red brown	.25	*.40*
P9	N1	1k greenish gray	.25	*.80*
		Nos. P1-P9 (9)	2.25	3.30

No. P5 Overprinted in Black

1940

No.	Type	Description	Unused	Used
P10	N1	10h henna brown	.40	*.65*

Overprinted for use by commercial firms.

DAHOMEY

də-ˈhō-mē

LOCATION — West coast of Africa
AREA — 43,483 sq. mi.
POP. — 3,030,000 (est. 1974)
CAPITAL — Porto-Novo

Formerly a native kingdom including Benin, Dahomey was annexed by France in 1894. It became part of the colonial administrative unit of French West Africa in 1895.

100 Centimes = 1 Franc

See French West Africa No. 71 for stamp inscribed "Dahomey" and "Afrique Occidentale Francaise."

Navigation and Commerce — A1

Perf. 14x13½

1899-1905 **Typo.** **Unwmk.**

Name of Colony in Blue or Carmine

No.	Type	Description	Unused	Used
1	A1	1c black, *lil bl* ('01)	1.60	.80
		Never hinged	4.00	
		On cover		125.00
2	A1	2c brown, *buff* ('04)	1.60	.80
		Never hinged	4.00	
		On cover		150.00
3	A1	4c claret, *lav* ('04)	2.40	2.40
		Never hinged	4.00	
		On cover		150.00
4	A1	5c yellow grn ('04)	6.50	4.00
		Never hinged	12.00	
		On cover		87.50
5	A1	10c red ('01)	8.00	4.00
		Never hinged	12.00	
		On cover		80.00
6	A1	15c gray ('01)	4.00	4.00
		Never hinged	8.00	
		On cover		50.00
7	A1	20c red, *grn* ('04)	20.00	16.00
		Never hinged	40.00	
		On cover		140.00
		On cover, single franking		250.00
8	A1	25c black, *rose* ('99)	24.00	24.00
		Never hinged	55.00	
		On cover		500.00
9	A1	25c blue ('01)	20.00	16.00
		Never hinged	40.00	
		On cover		105.00
10	A1	30c brown, *bis* ('04)	24.00	12.00
		Never hinged	40.00	
		On cover		140.00
		On cover, single franking		200.00
11	A1	40c red, *straw* ('04)	24.00	16.00
		Never hinged	47.50	
		On cover		140.00
		On cover, single franking		200.00
12	A1	50c brn, *az* (name in red) ('01)	40.00	24.00
		Never hinged	55.00	
		On cover		200.00
		On cover, single franking		250.00
12A	A1	50c brn, *az* (name in bl) ('05)	32.50	24.00
		Never hinged	60.00	
		On cover		210.00
		On cover, single franking		275.00
13	A1	75c dp vio, *org* ('04)	85.00	55.00
		Never hinged	170.00	
		On cover		475.00
		On cover, single franking		725.00
14	A1	1fr brnz grn, *straw* ('04)	40.00	32.50
		Never hinged	80.00	
		On cover		525.00
		On cover, single franking		775.00
15	A1	2fr violet, *rose* ('04)	110.00	72.50
		Never hinged	225.00	
		On cover		725.00
		On cover, single franking		925.00

16 A1 5fr red lilac, *lav* ('04) 135.00 105.00
Never hinged 280.00
On cover 840.00
On cover, single franking 1,100.
Nos. 1-16 (17) 578.60 413.00

Perf. 13½x14 stamps are counterfeits.
For surcharges see Nos. 32-41.

Gen. Louis Faidherbe A2

Oil Palm — A3

Dr. Noel Eugène Ballay A4

1906-07 ***Perf. 13½x14***

Name of Colony in Red or Blue

17 A2 1c slate 1.60 .80
Never hinged 4.00
On cover 100.00
18 A2 2c chocolate 2.40 .80
Never hinged 4.00
On cover 100.00
19 A2 4c choc, *gray bl* 4.00 3.25
Never hinged 8.00
On cover 100.00
20 A2 5c green 8.00 3.25
Never hinged 20.00
On cover 50.00
21 A2 10c carmine (B) 24.00 4.00
Never hinged 50.00
On cover 32.50
22 A3 20c black & red, *azure* 16.00 12.00
Never hinged 30.00
On cover 42.50
23 A3 25c blue, *pnksh* 16.00 12.00
Never hinged 35.00
On cover 55.00
On cover, single franking 150.00
24 A3 30c choc, *pnksh* 16.00 16.00
Never hinged 35.00
On cover 62.50
On cover, single franking 110.00
25 A3 35c black, *yellow* 87.50 12.00
Never hinged 190.00
On cover 67.50
On cover, single franking 105.00
26 A3 45c choc, *grnsh* ('07) 24.00 16.00
Never hinged 45.00
On cover 87.50
On cover, single franking 140.00
27 A3 50c deep violet 20.00 20.00
Never hinged 45.00
On cover 87.50
On cover, single franking 190.00
28 A3 75c blue, *orange* 24.00 24.00
Never hinged 55.00
On cover 125.00
On cover, single franking 260.00
29 A4 1fr black, *azure* 32.00 24.00
Never hinged 65.00
On cover 140.00
On cover, single franking 275.00
30 A4 2fr blue, *pink* 110.00 110.00
Never hinged 225.00
On cover 340.00
On cover, single franking 400.00
31 A4 5fr car, *straw* (B) 95.00 110.00
Never hinged 210.00
On cover 340.00
On cover, single franking 460.00
Nos. 17-31 (15) 480.50 368.10

Nos. 2-3, 6-7, 9-13 Surcharged in Black or Carmine

Spacing between figures of surcharge 1.5mm (5c), 2mm (10c)

1912 ***Perf. 14x13½***

32 5c on 2c brn, *buff* 2.00 *2.40*
Never hinged 3.75
On cover 87.50
33 5c on 4c claret, *lav* (C) 1.60 *2.00*
Never hinged 3.25
On cover 67.50
a. Double surcharge 275.00
34 5c on 15c gray (C) 2.00 *2.40*
Never hinged 4.00
On cover 87.50
35 5c on 20c red, *grn* 2.00 *2.40*
Never hinged 4.00
On cover 87.50
36 5c on 25c blue (C) 2.00 *2.40*
Never hinged 4.00
On cover 87.50
a. Inverted surcharge 240.00
b. Pair, one without surcharge 1,200.
37 5c on 30c brown, *bis* (C) 2.00 *2.40*
Never hinged 4.00
On cover 92.50
38 10c on 40c red, *straw* 2.00 *2.40*
Never hinged 4.00
On cover 92.50
a. Inverted surcharge 325.00
39 10c on 50c brn, *az*, name in bl (C) 2.40 2.75
Never hinged 4.75
On cover 140.00
40 10c on 50c brn, *az*, name in red (C) 1,125. 1,300.
41 10c on 75c violet, *org* 8.00 8.00
Never hinged 16.00
On cover 150.00
a. Double surcharge *5,500.*
Nos. 32-39,41 (9) 24.00 27.15

Spacing between figures of surcharge 2.25mm (5c), 2.75mm (10c)

32a 5c on 2c brn, *buff* 12.00 12.00
Never hinged 20.00
33b 5c on 4c claret, *lav* (C) 9.50 9.50
Never hinged 16.00
c. Double surcharge, both wider spacing 2,000.
d. Double surcharge, one narrow and one wide spacing 5,000.
34a 5c on 15c gray (C) 12.00 12.00
Never hinged 20.00
35a 5c on 20c red, *grn* 12.00 12.00
Never hinged 20.00
36c 5c on 25c blue (C) 12.00 12.00
Never hinged 20.00
d. Inverted surcharge 2,200.
37a 5c on 30c brown, *bis* (C) 12.00 12.00
Never hinged 20.00
38b 10c on 40c red, *straw* 80.00 80.00
Never hinged 145.00
c. Inverted surcharge 2,800.
39a 10c on 50c brn, *az*, name in bl (C) 150.00 150.00
40a 10c on 50c brn, *az*, name in red (C) 11,000.
41b 10c on 75c violet, *org* 230.00 230.00
Nos. 32a-39a,41b (9) 529.50 529.50

Man Climbing Oil Palm — A5

1913-39 ***Perf. 13½x14***

42 A5 1c violet & blk .40 .30
Never hinged .80
On cover 80.00
a. Chalky paper .80 .80
Never hinged 1.20
On cover 80.00
43 A5 2c choc & rose .40 .40
Never hinged .80
On cover 80.00
44 A5 4c black & brn .40 .40
Never hinged .80
On cover 80.00
a. Chalky paper 1.20 1.20
Never hinged 1.60
On cover 80.00
45 A5 5c yel grn & bl grn 1.20 .55
Never hinged 2.40
On cover 37.50
a. Chalky paper 2.75 1.60
Never hinged 4.75
On cover 32.50
46 A5 5c vio brn & vio ('22) .40 .80
Never hinged .80
On cover 30.00
47 A5 10c org red & rose 1.60 .80
Never hinged 3.25
On cover 21.00
a. Half used as 5c on wrapper or printed matter —
b. Chalky paper 2.40 1.25
Never hinged 4.00
On cover 25.00
48 A5 10c yel grn & bl grn ('22) .80 .80
Never hinged 1.25
On cover 55.00
49 A5 10c red & ol ('25) .40 .40
Never hinged .80
On cover 21.00
50 A5 15c brn org & dk vio ('17) .80 .80
Never hinged 1.25
On cover 20.00
a. Chalky paper .95 .95
Never hinged 1.60
On cover 20.00
51 A5 20c gray & red brown .80 .75
Never hinged 1.60
On cover 32.50
a. Chalky paper 2.00 1.20
Never hinged 3.25
On cover 40.00
b. 20c gray & sepia 1.20 .80
Never hinged 2.00
On cover 32.50
c. As "b," chalky paper 3.25 1.75
Never hinged 5.25
On cover 40.00
52 A5 20c bluish grn & grn ('26) .40 .40
Never hinged .80
On cover 15.00
53 A5 20c mag & blk ('27) .40 .40
Never hinged .80
On cover 37.50
54 A5 25c ultra & dp blue 2.00 1.60
Never hinged 4.00
On cover 42.50
On cover, single franking 100.00
a. Chalky paper 3.25 2.40
Never hinged 5.50
On cover 50.00
55 A5 25c vio brn & org ('22) 1.20 .80
Never hinged 1.60
On cover 13.50
56 A5 30c choc & vio 2.75 2.40
Never hinged 5.50
On cover 45.00
On cover, single franking 125.00
a. Chalky paper 4.00 3.25
Never hinged 7.25
On cover 50.00
57 A5 30c red org & rose ('22) 3.25 3.25
Never hinged 5.50
On cover 42.50
On cover, single franking 75.00
58 A5 30c yellow & vio ('25) .40 .40
Never hinged .80
On cover 12.50
59 A5 30c dl grn & grn ('27) .40 .40
Never hinged .80
On cover 37.50
60 A5 35c brown & blk .80 .80
Never hinged 1.60
On cover 45.00
On cover, single franking 105.00
a. Chalky paper 1.60 1.20
Never hinged 2.40
On cover 50.00
61 A5 35c bl grn & grn ('38) .40 .30
Never hinged .55
On cover 37.50
62 A5 40c black & red org .80 .80
Never hinged 1.60
On cover 55.00
On cover, single franking 125.00
a. Chalky paper 1.60 1.25
Never hinged 2.40
On cover 62.50
63 A5 45c gray & ultra .80 .80
Never hinged 1.60
On cover 67.50
On cover, single franking 140.00
a. Chalky paper 1.60 1.25
Never hinged 2.40
On cover 62.50
64 A5 50c chocolate & brn 6.50 6.00
Never hinged 12.00
On cover 67.50
On cover, single franking 150.00
a. Half used as 25c on cover *500.00*
b. Chalky paper 6.50 6.00
Never hinged 12.00
On cover 67.50
c. 50c dk brown & brn, chalky paper 12.00 9.50
Never hinged 20.00
On cover 80.00
65 A5 50c ultra & bl ('22) 1.60 1.60
Never hinged 2.75
On cover 37.50
On cover, single franking 67.50
66 A5 50c brn red & bl ('26) 1.20 1.20
Never hinged 2.00
On cover 12.50
67 A5 55c gray grn & choc ('38) .80 .55
Never hinged 1.20
On cover 12.50
68 A5 60c vio, *pnksh* ('25) .40 .40
Never hinged .80
On cover 30.00
On cover, single franking 75.00
69 A5 65c yel brn & ol grn ('26) 1.20 1.20
Never hinged 2.00
On cover 19.00
On cover, single franking 30.00
70 A5 75c blue & violet 1.20 1.20
Never hinged 2.40
On cover 55.00
On cover, single franking 140.00
a. Chalky paper 2.40 1.60
Never hinged 3.25
On cover 55.00
71 A5 80c henna brn & ultra ('38) .40 .40
Never hinged .75
On cover 62.50
On cover, single franking 105.00
72 A5 85c dk bl & ver ('26) 1.60 1.60
Never hinged 3.25
On cover 37.50
On cover, single franking 62.50
73 A5 90c rose & brn red ('30) .80 .80
Never hinged 1.60
On cover 50.00
On cover, single franking 92.50
74 A5 90c yel bis & red org ('39) 1.20 .80
Never hinged 1.60
On cover 42.50
On cover, single franking 92.50
75 A5 1fr blue grn & blk 1.20 1.20
Never hinged 2.40
On cover 75.00
On cover, single franking 175.00
a. Chalky paper 2.75 2.00
Never hinged 4.75
On cover 87.50
76 A5 1fr dk bl & ultra ('26) 1.60 1.60
Never hinged 3.25
On cover 25.00
On cover, single franking 50.00
77 A5 1fr yel brn & lt red ('28) 1.60 1.20
Never hinged 3.25
On cover 27.50
On cover, single franking 42.50
78 A5 1fr dk red & red org ('38) 1.05 .95
Never hinged 1.60
On cover 37.50
On cover, single franking 67.50
79 A5 1.10fr vio & bis ('28) 5.50 *6.00*
Never hinged 9.50
On cover 150.00
On cover, single franking 340.00
80 A5 1.25fr dp bl & dk brn ('33) 17.50 7.25
Never hinged 27.50
On cover 40.00
On cover, single franking 105.00
81 A5 1.50fr dk bl & lt bl ('30) 1.60 .80
Never hinged 2.40
On cover 42.50
On cover, single franking 80.00
82 A5 1.75fr dk brn & dp buff ('33) 4.00 2.00
Never hinged 6.50
On cover 27.50
On cover, single franking 42.50
83 A5 1.75fr ind & ultra ('38) 1.60 .95
Never hinged 2.00
On cover 37.50
On cover, single franking 62.50
84 A5 2fr yel org & choc 1.20 *1.60*
Never hinged 2.40
On cover 92.50
On cover, single franking 200.00
a. Chalky paper 2.40 2.00
Never hinged .3025
On cover 92.50
85 A5 3fr red violet ('30) 2.40 1.75
Never hinged 5.50
On cover 87.50
On cover, single franking 190.00
86 A5 5fr violet & dp bl 2.40 2.75
Never hinged 4.75
On cover 110.00
On cover, single franking 210.00
a. Chalky paper 3.25 3.50
Never hinged 5.50
On cover 110.00
Nos. 42-86 (45) 79.35 62.15

The 1c gray and yellow green and 5c dull red and black are Togo Nos. 193a, 196a.

Nos. 47a and 64a were authorized for use in Paouignan during the last part of November 1921. Other values exist as bisects but were not authorized.

For surcharges see Nos. 87-96, B1, B8-B11. Post 1940 issues in Scott Standard catalogue, Vol. 2.

Type of 1913 Surcharged

1922-25

87 A5 60c on 75c vio, *pnksh* 1.20 1.20
Never hinged 2.40
On cover 27.50
On cover, single franking 42.50
a. Double surcharge 200.00
Never hinged 320.00
88 A5 65c on 15c brn org & dk vio ('25) 2.00 2.00
Never hinged 3.25
On cover 75.00
On cover, single franking 160.00
a. On #50a 5.25 5.25
Never hinged 8.75
On cover 80.00
89 A5 85c on 15c brn org & dk vio ('25) 2.00 2.00
Never hinged 3.25
On cover 55.00
On cover, single franking 105.00
Nos. 87-89 (3) 5.20 5.20

Stamps and Type of 1913-39 Surcharged with New Value and Bars

1924-27

90 A5 25c on 2fr org & choc 1.20 1.20
Never hinged 2.40
On cover 13.50
a. On #84a 2.40 2.40
Never hinged 4.00
On cover 21.00
91 A5 90c on 75c cer & brn red ('27) 2.00 2.00
Never hinged 3.25
On cover 62.50
On cover, single franking 100.00
92 A5 1.25fr on 1fr dk bl & ultra (R) ('26) 1.60 1.60
Never hinged 2.40
On cover 62.50
On cover, single franking 110.00
93 A5 1.50fr on 1fr dk bl & grnsh bl ('27) 2.75 2.75
Never hinged 4.75
On cover 50.00
On cover, single franking 80.00
94 A5 3fr on 5fr olvn & dp org ('27) 10.50 10.50
Never hinged 16.00
On cover 105.00
On cover, single franking 210.00
95 A5 10fr on 5fr bl vio & red brn ('27) 8.00 8.00
Never hinged 16.00
On cover 110.00
On cover, single franking 225.00
96 A5 20fr on 5fr ver & dl grn ('27) 8.75 8.75
Never hinged 16.00
On cover 125.00
On cover, single franking 250.00
Nos. 90-96 (7) 34.80 34.80

Common Design Types pictured following the introduction.

Colonial Exposition Issue
Common Design Types

1931 **Engr.** ***Perf. 12½***

Name of Country in Black

97 CD70 40c deep green 6.50 6.50
Never hinged 12.00
On cover 110.00
98 CD71 50c violet 6.50 6.50
Never hinged 12.00
On cover 100.00
99 CD72 90c red orange 6.50 6.50
Never hinged 12.00
On cover 165.00
On cover, single franking 240.00
100 CD73 1.50fr dull blue 6.50 6.50
Never hinged 12.00
On cover 150.00
On cover, single franking 210.00
Nos. 97-100 (4) 26.00 26.00

Paris International Exposition Issue
Common Design Types

1937 **Engr.** ***Perf. 13***

101 CD74 20c deep violet 2.00 2.00
Never hinged 3.25
On cover 110.00
102 CD75 30c dark green 2.00 2.00
Never hinged 3.25
On cover 80.00
103 CD76 40c car rose 2.00 2.00
Never hinged 3.25
On cover 87.50
104 CD77 50c dark brown 1.60 1.60
Never hinged 2.75
On cover 80.00
105 CD78 90c red 1.60 1.60
Never hinged 2.75
On cover 120.00
On cover, single franking 200.00
106 CD79 1.50fr ultra 2.40 2.40
Never hinged 4.00
On cover 105.00
On cover, single franking 190.00
Nos. 101-106 (6) 11.60 11.60

Souvenir Sheet

Imperf

107 CD77 3fr dp blue & blk 12.00 *16.00*
Never hinged 16.00
On cover 140.00
On cover, single franking 200.00
a. Inscription inverted 1,600. 1,600.
Never hinged 2,100.

Caillié Issue
Common Design Type

1939, Apr. 5 **Engr.** ***Perf. 12½x12***

108 CD81 90c org brn & org .40 1.20
Never hinged .80
On cover 13.50
109 CD81 2fr brt violet .40 1.20
Never hinged .80
On cover 32.50
On cover, single franking 55.00
110 CD81 2.25fr ultra & dk blue .40 1.20
Never hinged .80
On cover 42.50
On cover, single franking 67.50
Nos. 108-110 (3) 1.20 3.60

New York World's Fair Issue
Common Design Type

1939 **Engr.**

111 CD82 1.25fr car lake .80 1.60
Never hinged 1.20
On cover 87.50
On cover, single franking 175.00
112 CD82 2.25fr ultra .80 1.60
Never hinged 1.20
On cover 87.50
On cover, single franking 150.00

SEMI-POSTAL STAMPS

Regular Issue of 1913 Surcharged in Red

1915 **Unwmk.** ***Perf. 14x13½***

B1 A5 10c + 5c orange red & rose 1.60 1.60
Never hinged 2.40
On cover 60.00

Curie Issue
Common Design Type

1938 ***Perf. 13***

B2 CD80 1.75fr + 50c brt ultra 9.50 9.50
Never hinged 16.00
On cover 110.00
On cover, single franking 190.00

French Revolution Issue
Common Design Type

1939 **Photo.**

Name and Value Typo. in Black

B3 CD83 45c + 25c green 9.50 9.50
Never hinged 16.00
On cover 150.00
B4 CD83 70c + 30c brown 9.50 9.50
Never hinged 16.00
On cover 110.00
B5 CD83 90c + 35c red org 9.50 9.50
Never hinged 16.00
On cover 100.00
B6 CD83 1.25fr + 1fr rose pink 9.50 9.50
Never hinged 16.00
On cover 165.00
On cover, single franking 250.00
B7 CD83 2.25fr + 2fr blue 9.50 9.50
Never hinged 16.00
On cover 160.00
On cover, single franking 225.00
Nos. B3-B7 (5) 47.50 47.50

AIR POST STAMPS

Common Design Type

1940 **Unwmk.** **Engr.** ***Perf. 12½***

C1 CD85 1.90fr ultra .40 .40
Never hinged .80
On cover 50.00
C2 CD85 2.90fr dk red .40 .40
Never hinged .80
On cover 50.00
C3 CD85 4.50fr dk gray grn .80 .80
Never hinged 1.00
On cover 55.00
C4 CD85 4.90fr yel bister .80 .80
Never hinged 1.25
On cover 67.50
C5 CD85 6.90fr deep org 1.60 1.60
Never hinged 2.00
On cover 87.50
Nos. C1-C5 (5) 4.00 4.00

POSTAGE DUE STAMPS

Dahomey Natives — D1

1906 **Unwmk.** **Typo.** ***Perf. 14x13½***

J1 D1 5c grn, *grnsh* 4.00 4.00
Never hinged 8.00
On cover 105.00
J2 D1 10c red brn 4.00 4.00
Never hinged 8.00
On cover 105.00
J3 D1 15c dark blue 8.00 8.00
Never hinged 16.00
On cover 110.00
J4 D1 20c blk, *yellow* 8.00 8.00
Never hinged 16.00
On cover 105.00
J5 D1 30c red, *straw* 12.00 12.00
Never hinged 20.00
On cover 110.00
J6 D1 50c violet 24.00 24.00
Never hinged 55.00
On cover 150.00
J7 D1 60c blk, *buff* 16.00 16.00
Never hinged 27.50
On cover 140.00
J8 D1 1fr blk, *pinkish* 52.50 40.00
Never hinged 100.00
On cover 275.00
Nos. J1-J8 (8) 128.50 116.00

D2

1914

J9 D2 5c green .25 .25
Never hinged .40
On cover 55.00
J10 D2 10c rose .55 .55
Never hinged .80
On cover 55.00
J11 D2 15c gray .55 .55
Never hinged .80
On cover 55.00
J12 D2 20c brown 1.10 1.10
Never hinged 1.60
On cover 62.50
J13 D2 30c blue 1.40 1.40
Never hinged 2.00
On cover 62.50
J14 D2 50c black 1.60 1.60
Never hinged 2.00
On cover 67.50
J15 D2 60c orange 2.00 2.00
Never hinged 2.75
On cover 80.00
J16 D2 1fr violet 2.10 2.10
Never hinged 3.25
On cover 105.00
Nos. J9-J16 (8) 9.55 9.55

Type of 1914 Issue Surcharged

1927

J17 D2 2fr on 1fr lilac rose 5.50 5.50
Never hinged 8.75
On cover 140.00
a. Period after "F" omitted 27.50 24.00
Never hinged 40.00
J18 D2 3fr on 1fr org brn 5.50 5.50
Never hinged 8.75
On cover 150.00

DALMATIA

dal-'mā-shē-ə

LOCATION — A promontory in the northwestern part of the Balkan Peninsula, together with several small islands in the Adriatic Sea.
GOVT. — Part of the former Austro-Hungarian crownland of the same name.
AREA — 113 sq. mi.
POP. — 18,719 (1921)
CAPITAL — Zara.

Stamps were issued during Italian occupation. This territory was subsequently annexed by Italy.

100 Centesimi = 1 Corona = 1 Lira

Used values are for postally used stamps.

Issued under Italian Occupation

Italy No. 87 Surcharged

1919, May 1 **Wmk. 140** ***Perf. 14***

1 A46 1cor on 1 l brn & grn 3.50 *15.00*
Never hinged 8.75
On cover 200.00
a. Pair, one without surcharge *1,050.* *1,050.*

Italian Stamps of 1906-08 Surcharged — a

Italian Stamps of 1901-10 Surcharged — b

1921-22

2 A48 5c on 5c green 3.50 *4.75*
Never hinged 8.75
On cover 140.00
3 A48 10c on 10c claret 3.50 *4.75*
Never hinged 8.75
On cover 95.00
a. Pair, one without surcharge 875.00
4 A49 25c on 25c blue ('22) 6.00 *7.25*
Never hinged 15.00
On cover 80.00
5 A49 50c on 50c vio ('22) 6.00 *7.25*
Never hinged 15.00
On cover 160.00
a. Double surcharge *250.00*
b. Pair, one without surcharge *1,050.*
6 A46 1cor on 1 l brn & grn ('22) 8.00 *24.00*
Never hinged 20.00
On cover 360.00
7 A46 5cor on 5 l bl & rose ('22) 45.00 *120.00*
Never hinged 110.00
On cover 800.00
8 A51 10cor on 10 l gray grn & red ('22) 45.00 *120.00*
Never hinged 110.00
On cover 140.00
Nos. 2-8 (7) 117.00 *288.00*

Surcharges similar to these but differing in style or arrangement of type were used in Austria under Italian occupation.

SPECIAL DELIVERY STAMPS

Italian Special Delivery No. E1 Srchd. Type "a"

1921 **Wmk. 140** ***Perf. 14***

E1 SD1 25c on 25c rose red 3.50 *15.00*
Never hinged 8.75
a. Double surcharge 400.00 *650.00*

Italian Special Delivery Stamp Surcharged

1922

E2 SD2 1.20 l on 1.20 l 240.00
Never hinged 600.00

No. E2 was not placed in use.

POSTAGE DUE STAMPS

Italian Postage Due Stamps and Type Surcharged types "a" or "b"

1922 Wmk. 140 ***Perf. 14***

J1	D3 (a) 50c on 50c buff & mag	4.00	*9.00*
	Never hinged	10.00	
	On cover		95.00
J2	D3 (b) 1cor on 1 l bl & red	9.00	*32.50*
	Never hinged	22.50	
	On cover		125.00
J3	D3 (b) 2cor on 2 l bl & red	55.00	*135.00*
	Never hinged	135.00	
	On cover		450.00
J4	D3 (b) 5cor on 5 l bl & red	55.00	*135.00*
	Never hinged	135.00	
	Nos. J1-J4 (4)	123.00	*311.50*

DANISH WEST INDIES

ˈdā-nish ˈwest ˈin-dēs

LOCATION — A group of islands in the West Indies, lying east of Puerto Rico
GOVT. — Danish Colony
AREA — 132 sq. mi.
POP. — 27,086 (1911)
CAPITAL — Charlotte Amalie

The U.S. bought these islands in 1917 and they became the US Virgin Islands, using U.S. stamps and currency. However, for the first six months of U.S. ownership, until September 30, 1917, a postal transition period existed. During this period, either U.S., D.W.I. or mixed frankings could be used. The domestic printed matter or postcard rate was 5 bits or 1 cent, and the foreign printed matter or postcard rate was 10 bits, 2 cents, or 5 bits + 1 cent. The domestic minimum-weight letter rate was 10 bits, 2 cents, or 5 bits + 1 cent, while the foreign minimum letter rate was 25 bits, 5 cents, or any combination of U.S. and D.W.I. stamps that together totaled 25 bits or 5 cents.

Letters posted to foreign destinations during the transition period are rare because of World War I. Values for covers listed here are for the period before the transition. Transition-period covers, including those with mixed franking, sell for much more.

100 Cents = 1 Dollar
100 Bit = 1 Franc (1905)

FORERUNNERS

Crowned Circle handstamp types are pictured in the Crowned Circle Handstamps and Great Britain Used Abroad section.

BRITISH POST OFFICES IN DANISH WEST INDIES

St. Thomas

British P.O. opened Jan., 1809; stamps supplied July 3, 1865; closed to the public Sept. 1, 1877; closed for receiving mail in transit 1879

Pre-Stamp Postal Markings

1849-55

A1	Crowned Circle handstamp Type I, on cover, inscribed "PAID AT ST. THOMAS"	575.
A2	Crowned Circle handstamp Type IX, on cover, inscribed "PAID AT ST. THOMAS" in black	1,900.

Earliest known uses: A1, 2/20/49; A2, 5/1/55.

Stamps of Great Britain, Canceled C51, or with Circular Date Stamp (Several Types Exist)

No. A32

1865-79

A3	½p rose red (#58 P 5, 6, 8, 10-12), *value from*	42.50
A4	1p rose red (#20)	—
A5	1p rose red (#33, P 71, 72, 79, 81, 84-90, 93-102, 105-114, 116-125, 127, 129-131, 133, 134, 136-142, 144-152, 154-167, 169-182, 184-187, 189, 190, 197) *value from*	30.00
A6	1 ½p lake red (#32, P1, 3), *value from*	75.00
A7	2p blue (#29, P 9)	35.00
	Plate 12	*350.00*
A8	2p blue (#30, P 13-15), *value from*	35.00
A9	3p rose (#44, P 4)	100.00
A10	3p rose (#49, P 4-10)	50.00
A11	3p rose (#61, P 11-12, 14-19), *value from*	35.00
A12	4p vermilion (#34)	85.00
	a. Hair-lines (#34c)	100.00
A13	4p vermilion (#43, P 7-14), *value from*	57.50
A14	4p vermilion (#69, P 15)	350.00
A15	4p pale olive green (#70, P 15, 16)	225.00
A16	6p lilac (#39c, P 4)	175.00
A17	6p lilac (#45, P 5)	85.00
	Plate 6	160.00
A18	6p dull violet (#50, P 6)	85.00
A19	6p violet (#51, P 6, 8, 9), *value from*	80.00
A20	6p brown (#59, P 11)	50.00
	a. 6p pale buff (#59b, P 11)	100.00
	Plate 12	250.00
A21	6p gray (#60, P 12)	240.00
A22	6p gray (#62, P 13-16), *value from*	50.00
A23	8p orange (#73)	310.00
A24	9p straw (#40)	325.00
	a. 9p bister (#40a)	350.00
A25	9p straw (#46)	425.00
A26	9p bister (#52)	325.00
A27	10p red brown (#53)	310.00
A28	1sh green (#48, P 4)	160.00
A29	1sh green (#54, P 4-7) *value from*	35.00
A30	1sh green (#64, P 8-13) *value from*	70.00
A31	2sh blue (#55)	150.00
A32	5sh rose (#57, P 1)	550.00
	Plate 2	700.00

Issued under Danish Dominion Watermarks

Wmk. 111 — Small Crown

Wmk. 112 — Crown

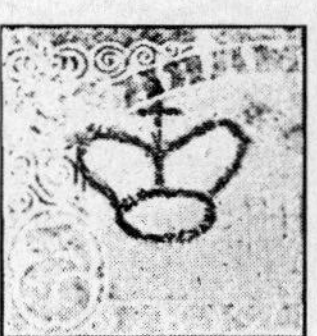

Wmk. 113 — Crown

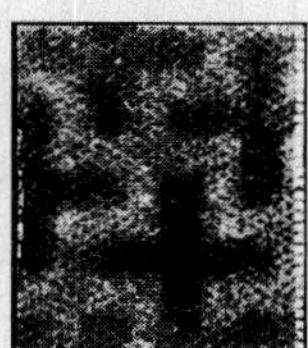

Wmk. 114 — Multiple Crosses

Coat of Arms — A1

Yellowish Paper
Yellow Wavy-line Burelage, UL to LR

1856 Typo. Wmk. 111 ***Imperf.***

1	A1 3c dark carmine, brown gum	200.	*275.*
	On cover		3,000.
a.	3c dark carmine, yellow gum	225.	*275.*
	On cover		3,000.
b.	3c carmine, white gum	*4,250.*	—

The brown and yellow gums were applied locally.

Reprint: 1981, carmine, back-printed across two stamps ("Reprint by Dansk Post og Telegrafmuseum 1978"), value, pair, $10.

White Paper

1866

Yellow Wavy-line Burelage UR to LL

2	A1 3c rose	40.	*65.*
	On cover		3,000.

No. 2 reprints, unwatermarked: 1930, carmine, value $100. 1942, rose carmine, back-printed across each row ("Nytryk 1942 G. A. Hagemann Danmark og Dansk Vestindiens Frimaerker Bind 2"), value $50.

1872 ***Perf. 12½***

3	A1 3c rose	100.	*275.*
	On cover		*7,500.*

1873 Without Burelage

4	A1 4c dull blue	250.	*475.*
	On cover		—
a.	Imperf., pair	775.	
b.	Horiz. pair, imperf. vert.	575.	

The 1930 reprint of No. 4 is ultramarine, unwatermarked and imperf., value $100.

The 1942 4c reprint is blue, unwatermarked, imperf. and has printing on back (see note below No. 2), value $60.

A2

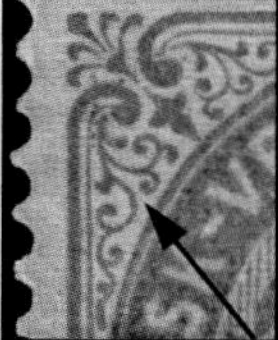

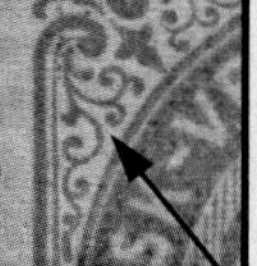

Normal Frame

Inverted Frame

The arabesques in the corners have a main stem and a branch. When the frame is in normal position, in the upper left corner the branch leaves the main stem half way between two little leaflets. In the lower right corner the branch starts at the foot of the second leaflet. When the frame is inverted the corner designs are, of course, transposed.

White Wove Paper
Varying from Thin to Thick

1874-79 Wmk. 112 ***Perf. 14x13½***

Values for inverted frames, covers and blocks are for the cheapest variety.

5	A2 1c green & brown red	22.50	*30.00*
	On cover		250.00
a.	1c green & rose lilac, thin paper	80.00	*125.00*
b.	1c green & red violet, medium paper	45.00	*65.00*
c.	1c green & claret, thick paper	20.00	*30.00*
e.	As "c," inverted frame	25.00	*32.50*
f.	As "a," inverted frame	*475.00*	

No. 5 exists with a surcharge similar to the surcharge on No. 15, with 10 CENTS value and 1895 date. This stamp is an essay.

6	A2 3c blue & carmine	27.50	20.00
	On cover		225.00
a.	3c light blue & rose carmine, thin paper	65.00	50.00
b.	3c deep blue & dark carmine, medium paper	40.00	17.00
c.	3c greenish blue & lake, thick paper	32.50	17.00
d.	Imperf., pair	375.00	—
e.	Inverted frame, thick paper	30.00	20.00
f.	As "a," inverted frame	*350.00*	
7	A2 4c brown & dull blue	16.00	*19.00*
	On cover		225.00
b.	4c brown & ultramarine, thin paper	225.00	*225.00*
c.	Diagonal half used as 2c on cover		140.00
d.	As "b," inverted frame	*900.00*	*1,400.*
8	A2 5c grn & gray ('76)	30.00	20.00
	On cover		250.00
a.	5c yellow green & dark gray, thin paper	55.00	32.50
b.	Inverted frame, thick paper	30.00	20.00
9	A2 7c lilac & orange	35.00	*95.00*
	On cover		1,100.
a.	7c lilac & yellow	90.00	*100.00*
b.	Inverted frame	65.00	*150.00*
10	A2 10c blue & brn ('76)	30.00	25.00
	On cover		300.00
a.	10c dark blue & black brown, thin paper	70.00	40.00
b.	Period between "t" & "s" of "cents"	35.00	25.00
c.	Inverted frame	27.50	*32.50*
11	A2 12c red lil & yel grn ('77)	42.50	*175.00*
	On cover		1,750.
a.	12c lilac & deep green	160.00	*200.00*
12	A2 14c lilac & green	650.00	*1,250.*
	On cover		
13	A2 50c vio, thin paper ('79)	190.00	*300.00*
	On cover		2,500.
a.	50c gray violet, thick paper	250.00	*375.00*
	Nos. 5-13 (9)	1,044.	1,934.

The central element in the fan-shaped scrollwork at the outside of the lower left corner of Nos. 5a and 7b looks like an elongated diamond.

See Nos. 16-20. For surcharges see Nos. 14-15, 23-28, 40.

No. 9 Surcharged in Black

a

1887

14	A2 (a) 1c on 7c lilac & orange	100.00	*200.00*
	On cover		3,000.
a.	1c on 7c lilac & yellow	120.00	*225.00*
b.	Double surcharge	250.00	*500.00*
c.	Inverted frame	110.00	*350.00*

No. 13 Surcharged in Black

b

1895

15	A2 (b) 10c on 50c violet, thin paper	42.50	*67.50*
	On cover		275.00

The "b" surcharge also exists on No. 5, with "10" found in two sizes. These are essays.

Type of 1873

1896-1901 ***Perf. 13***

16	A2 1c grn & red vio, inverted frame ('98)	15.00	*22.50*
	On cover		150.00
a.	Normal frame	300.00	*450.00*
17	A2 3c blue & lake, inverted frame ('98)	12.00	*17.50*
	On cover		150.00
a.	Normal frame	250.00	*425.00*
18	A2 4c bister & dull blue ('01)	17.50	11.00
	On cover		150.00
a.	Diagonal half used as 2c on cover		100.00
b.	Inverted frame	60.00	*80.00*
	On cover		250.00
c.	As "b," diagonal half used as 2c on cover		350.00
19	A2 5c green & gray, inverted frame	35.00	35.00
	On cover		325.00
a.	Normal frame	800.00	*1,200.*
20	A2 10c blue & brn ('01)	80.00	*150.00*
	On cover		1,150.
a.	Inverted frame	1,000.	*2,000.*
b.	Period between "t" and "s" of "cents"	170.00	160.00
	Nos. 16-20 (5)	159.50	*236.00*

Arms — A5

1900
21 A5 1c light green 3.00 3.00
On cover 80.00
On cover, single franking 300.00
22 A5 5c light blue 17.50 25.00
On cover 300.00

See Nos. 29-30. For surcharges see Nos. 41-42.

Nos. 6, 17, 20 Surcharged

c

Surcharge "c" in Black

1902 *Perf. 14x13½*
23 A2 2c on 3c blue & carmine, inverted frame 700.00 *900.00*
On cover *4,000.*
a. "2" in date with straight tail 750.00 *950.00*
b. Normal frame —
24 A2 2c on 3c blue & lake, inverted frame 10.00 *27.50*
On cover 160.00
a. "2" in date with straight tail 12.00 *32.50*
b. Dated "1901" 750.00 750.00
c. Normal frame 175.00 *300.00*
d. Dark green surcharge 2,750.
e. As "d" & "a" — —
f. As "d" & "c" —

The overprint on No. 24b exists in two types: with "1901" measuring 2.5 mm or 2.2 mm high.
Only one example of No. 24f can exist.

25 A2 8c on 10c blue & brown 25.00 *42.50*
On cover 225.00
a. "2" with straight tail 30.00 *45.00*
b. On No. 20b 32.50 *45.00*
c. Inverted frame 250.00 *425.00*

d

Surcharge "d" in Black

1902 *Perf. 13*
27 A2 2c on 3c blue & lake, inverted frame 12.00 *32.50*
On cover 500.00
a. Normal frame 240.00 *425.00*
28 A2 8c on 10c blue & brown 12.00 12.00
On cover 175.00
a. On No. 20b 18.50 *25.00*
b. Inverted frame 225.00 *400.00*
Nos. 23-28 (5) 759.00 1,015.

1903 **Wmk. 113**
29 A5 2c carmine 8.00 *22.50*
On cover 125.00
30 A5 8c brown 27.50 *35.00*
On cover 250.00

King Christian IX — A8

St. Thomas Harbor — A9

1905 **Typo.**
31 A8 5b green 3.75 3.25
On cover 35.00
32 A8 10b red 3.75 3.25
On cover 35.00
33 A8 20b green & blue 8.75 8.75
On cover 150.00
34 A8 25b ultramarine 8.75 *10.50*
On cover 85.00
35 A8 40b red & gray 8.25 *9.50*
On cover 225.00
36 A8 50b yellow & gray 10.00 10.00
On cover 250.00

Perf. 12
Wmk. Two Crowns (113)
Frame Typographed, Center Engraved
37 A9 1fr green & blue 17.50 *40.00*
On cover 625.00
38 A9 2fr orange red & brown 30.00 *55.00*
On cover 1,100.
39 A9 5fr yellow & brown 77.50 *275.00*
On cover 1,750.
Nos. 31-39 (9) 168.25 *415.25*

On cover values are for commercial usages, usually parcel address cards. Philatelic covers are valued at approximately 25% of these values.

Nos. 18, 22 and 30 Surcharged in Black

1905 **Wmk. 112**
40 A2 5b on 4c bister & dull blue 16.00 *50.00*
On cover 250.00
a. Inverted frame 45.00 *90.00*
41 A5 5b on 5c light blue 10.00 *47.50*
On cover 250.00

Wmk. 113
42 A5 5b on 8c brown 12.50 *50.00*
On cover 250.00
Nos. 40-42 (3) 38.50 147.50

Favor cancels exist on Nos. 40-42. Value 25% less.

Frederik VIII — A10

Frame Typographed, Center Engraved

1908 **Wmk. 113** ***Perf. 13***
43 A10 5b green 1.90 1.90
On cover 22.50
44 A10 10b red 1.90 1.90
On cover 22.50
45 A10 15b violet & brown 3.75 *4.50*
On cover 125.00
46 A10 20b green & blue 30.00 27.50
On cover 110.00
47 A10 25b blue & dark blue 1.90 *2.50*
On cover 35.00
48 A10 30b claret & slate 50.00 *52.50*
On cover 350.00
49 A10 40b vermilion & gray 5.75 *9.50*
On cover 210.00
50 A10 50b yellow & brown 5.75 *14.00*
On cover 210.00
Nos. 43-50 (8) 100.95 114.30

Christian X — A11

1915 **Wmk. 114** ***Perf. 14x14½***
51 A11 5b yellow green 4.00 *5.50*
On cover 45.00
52 A11 10b red 4.00 *55.00*
On cover 110.00
53 A11 15b lilac & red brown 4.00 *55.00*
On cover 300.00
54 A11 20b green & blue 4.00 *55.00*
On cover 350.00
55 A11 25b blue & dark blue 4.00 *17.50*
On cover 110.00
56 A11 30b claret & black 4.00 *100.00*
On cover 900.00
57 A11 40b orange & black 4.00 *100.00*
On cover 550.00
58 A11 50b yellow & brown 3.75 *100.00*
On cover 650.00
Nos. 51-58 (8) 31.75 *488.00*

Forged and favor cancellations exist.

POSTAGE DUE STAMPS

Royal Cipher, "Christian 9 Rex" D1

1902 **Litho.** **Unwmk.** ***Perf. 11½***
J1 D1 1c dark blue 5.00 *17.50*
On cover 400.00
J2 D1 4c dark blue 12.50 *22.50*
On cover 350.00
J3 D1 6c dark blue 22.50 *60.00*
On cover 450.00
J4 D1 10c dark blue 20.00 *65.00*
On cover 400.00
Nos. J1-J4 (4) 60.00 *165.00*

There are five types of each value. On the 4c they may be distinguished by differences in the figure "4"; on the other values differences are minute.
Used values of Nos. J1-J8 are for canceled stamps. Uncanceled stamps without gum have probably been used. Value 60% of unused. On cover values are for stamps tied by cancellation.
Excellent counterfeits of Nos. J1-J4 exist.

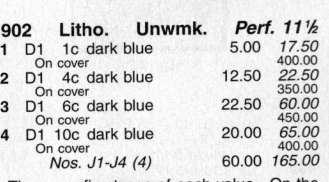

Numeral of value — D2

1905-13 ***Perf. 13***
J5 D2 5b red & gray 4.50 *6.75*
On cover *450.00*
J6 D2 20b red & gray 7.50 *14.00*
On cover *450.00*
J7 D2 30b red & gray 6.75 *14.00*
On cover *450.00*
J8 D2 50b red & gray 6.00 *30.00*
On cover *900.00*
a. Perf. 14x14½ ('13) 37.50 *140.00*
b. Perf. 11½ 325.00

All values of this issue are known imperforate, but were not regularly issued.
Used values of Nos. J5-J8 are for canceled stamps. Uncanceled examples without gum have probably been used. Value 60% of unused.
On cover values are for stamps tied by cancellation.
Counterfeits of Nos. J5-J8 exist.
Danish West Indies stamps were replaced by those of the U.S. in 1917, after the U.S. bought the islands.

DANZIG

'dan,t,-sig

LOCATION — In northern Europe bordering on the Baltic Sea
AREA — 754 sq. mi.
POP. — 407,000 (approx. 1939)
CAPITAL — Danzig

Established as a "Free City and State" under the protection of the League of Nations in 1920, Danzig was seized by Germany in 1939.

100 Pfennig = 1 Gulden (1923)
100 Pfennig = 1 Mark

Watermarks

Wmk. 108 — Honeycomb

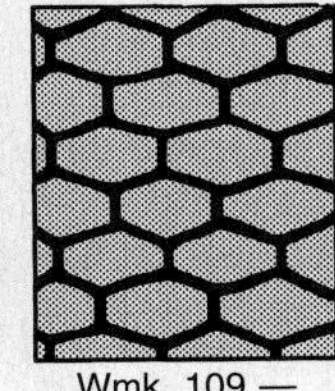
Wmk. 109 — Webbing

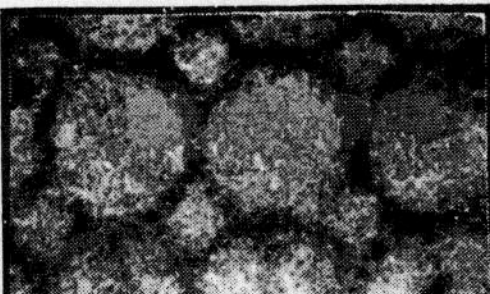
Wmk. 110 — Octagons

Wmk. 125 — Lozenges

Wmk. 237 — Swastikas

Used Values of 1920-23 are for favor-canceled stamps unless otherwise noted. Postally used examples bring much higher prices.

German Stamps of 1906-20 Overprinted in Black

Perf. 14, 14½, 15x14½

1920 **Wmk. 125**
1 A16 5pf green .30 *.50*
Never hinged 1.75
Postally used *2.00*
On cover 5.00
a. Pair, one without overprint 100.00
Never hinged 240.00
b. Double overprint —
2 A16 10pf car rose .30 .30
Never hinged 1.25
Postally used *2.00*
On cover 5.00
a. 10pf deep carmine 34.00 *30.00*
Never hinged 120.00
Postally used *150.00*
On cover 200.00
3 A22 15pf violet brown .30 .30
Never hinged 1.75
Postally used *3.75*
On cover 6.25
4 A16 20pf blue violet .30 *1.10*
Never hinged 1.25
Postally used *3.75*
On cover 8.50
5 A16 30pf org & blk, *buff* .30 .30
Never hinged 1.25
Postally used *2.50*
On cover 8.50
a. Pair, one without overprint — —
6 A16 40pf car rose .30 .30
Never hinged 1.25
Postally used *1.75*
On cover 8.50
7 A16 50pf pur & blk, *buff* .50 .30
Never hinged 1.40
Postally used *3.90*
On cover 8.50
a. Pair, one without overprint 175.00
Never hinged 425.00
8 A17 1m red .50 .60
Never hinged 2.50
Postally used *4.50*
On cover 10.00
a. Pair, one without overprint 100.00
Never hinged 250.00
9 A17 1.25m green .50 .60
Never hinged 2.50
Postally used *4.50*
On cover 10.00
a. 1.25m deep bluish green 60.00 34.00
Never hinged 210.00
Postally used *190.00*
On cover 225.00
10 A17 1.50m yellow brn .90 *1.60*
Never hinged 4.25
Postally used *6.00*
On cover 14.50
11 A21 2m blue 3.25 *7.25*
Never hinged 14.50
Postally used *26.00*
On cover 50.00
a. Double overprint *375.00*
Never hinged 825.00
b. 2m blue black 125.00 125.00
Never hinged 375.00
Postally used *1,250.*
On cover *1,600.*

12 A21 2.50m lilac rose 3.00 *4.50*
Never hinged 11.25
Postally used *12.50*
On cover 25.00
a. 2.50m deep lilac rose 3.00 *6.00*
Never hinged 17.00
Postally used *17.00*
On cover 37.50
b. 2.50m lake rose 100.00 *110.00*
Never hinged 300.00
Postally used *850.00*
On cover 1,100.
c. Double overprint 1,000.
13 A19 3m black violet 7.50 *10.50*
Never hinged 40.00
Postally used *110.00*
On cover 375.00
a. 3m blackish slate-violet 67.50 *135.00*
Never hinged 220.00
Postally used *1,000.*
On cover *1,250.*
b. Double overprint
14 A16 4m black & rose 4.75 *6.00*
Never hinged 27.50
Postally used *37.50*
On cover 92.50
15 A20 5m slate & car (25x17 holes) 2.50 *3.75*
Never hinged 10.00
Postally used *37.50*
On cover 85.00
a. Center & "Danzig" invtd. *15,000.*
Never hinged —
b. Inverted overprint *20,000.*
c. 5m slate & car (26x17 holes) *2,500.*
Never hinged *7,250.*
Nos. 1-15 (15) 25.20 37.90
Set, never hinged 122.50

The 5pf brown, 10pf orange and 40pf lake and black with this overprint were not regularly issued. Value for trio, $450.

For surcharges see Nos. 19-23, C1-C3.

Issued: 40pf, 9/13; 1.50m, 3m 7/20; 4m, 12/21; others 6/14.

Nos. 5, 4 Surcharged in Various Sizes

1920

19 A16 5pf on 30pf (V) .25 .25
Never hinged 1.00
Postally used *2.10*
On cover 4.25
20 A16 10pf on 20pf (R) .25 .25
Never hinged 1.40
Postally used *2.00*
On cover 4.25
a. Double surcharge 110.00 —
Never hinged 250.00
21 A16 25pf on 30pf (G) .25 .25
Never hinged 1.40
Postally used *2.00*
On cover 6.25
a. Inverted surcharge 85.00 *275.00*
Never hinged 250.00
22 A16 60pf on 30pf (Br) .70 *1.00*
Never hinged 4.00
Postally used *5.00*
On cover 10.00
a. Double surcharge 85.00 *290.00*
Never hinged 250.00
b. Pair, one without surcharge *75.00* —
23 A16 80pf on 30pf (V) .70 *1.00*
Never hinged 4.00
Postally used *5.00*
On cover 10.00

Issued: No. 21, 8/10. No. 20, 8/17. Nos. 19, 22-23, 11/1.

German Stamps Surcharged in Various Styles

No. 25

No. 27

No. 30

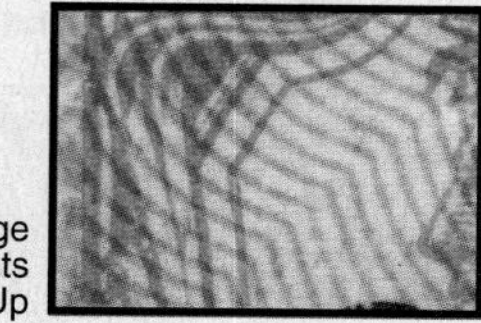

Burelage With Points Up

Gray Burelage with Points Up

25 A16 1m on 30pf org & blk, *buff* (Bk) .85 *1.50*
Never hinged 4.25
Postally used *4.25*
On cover 17.00
a. Pair, one without surcharge
e. Double burlage, both pointing up 75.00 *150.00*
Never hinged 250.00
Postally used *850.00*
26 A16 1¼m on 3pf brn (R) 1.00 *1.50*
Never hinged 4.50
Postally used *5.00*
On cover 18.00
e. Double burelage, both pointing up 75.00 *150.00*
Never hinged 250.00
Postally used *500.00*
27 A22 2m on 35pf red brn (Bl) 1.50 1.50
Never hinged 6.75
Postally used *5.00*
On cover 17.00
d. Surcharge omitted 70.00 —
Never hinged 260.00
e. Double burelage, both pointing up 110.00 *170.00*
Never hinged 340.00
Postally used *675.00*
28 A22 3m on 7½pf org (G) 1.00 *1.50*
Never hinged 4.50
Postally used *8.50*
On cover 21.00
d. Double surcharge 170.00
Never hinged 425.00
e. Double burelage, both pointing up 67.50 *125.00*
Never hinged 200.00
Postally used *500.00*
29 A22 5m on 2pf gray (R) 1.00 *2.00*
Never hinged 4.50
Postally used *10.00*
On cover 25.00
30 A22 10m on 7½pf org (Bk) 3.00 *7.00*
Never hinged 27.50
Postally used *22.00*
On cover 135.00
d. Double surcharge 42.50
Never hinged 250.00
e. Double burelage, both pointing up 75.00 *125.00*
Never hinged 210.00
Postally used *600.00*
Nos. 19-30 (11) 10.50 *17.75*
Set, never hinged 64.00

Gray Burelage with Points Down

26a A16 1¼m on 3pf brown 36.00 *42.50*
Never hinged 115.00
Postally used *100.00*
On cover 150.00
f. Double burelage, both pointing down 42.50 *160.00*
Never hinged 300.00
Postally used *675.00*
27a A22 2m on 35pf red brn 400.00 325.00
Never hinged *1,650.*
Postally used *750.00*
On cover *1,000.*
28a A22 3m on 7½pf orange 25.00 17.00
Never hinged 140.00
Postally used *50.00*
On cover 85.00
29a A22 5m on 2pf gray 25.00 *30.00*
Never hinged 140.00
Postally used *140.00*
On cover 210.00
30a A22 10m on 7½pf orange 5.75 *11.00*
Never hinged 32.50
Postally used *45.00*
On cover 150.00
Nos. 26a-30a (5) 491.75 *425.50*
Set, never hinged 2,100.

Violet Burelage with Points Up

25b A16 1m on 30pf org & blk, *buff* 85.00 30.00
Never hinged 350.00
Postally used *75.00*
On cover 170.00
26b A16 1¼m on 3pf brown 4.50 *6.50*
Never hinged 17.50
Postally used *21.00*
On cover 50.00
g. Double burelage, both pointing up 210.00 *250.00*
Never hinged 850.00
27b A22 2m on 35pf red brn 11.50 *37.50*
Never hinged 45.00
Postally used *140.00*
On cover 210.00
f. Double burelage, both pointing up 210.00 *250.00*
Never hinged 850.00
28b A22 3m on 7½pf orange 2.50 *2.50*
Never hinged 11.50
Postally used *10.00*
On cover 42.50
f. Double burelage, both pointing up 210.00 *250.00*
Never hinged 850.00
29b A22 5m on 2pf gray 1.25 *2.50*
Never hinged 4.25
Postally used *12.50*
On cover *42.50*

30b A22 10m on 7½pf orange 1.25 *2.50*
Never hinged 4.25
Postally used *13.50*
On cover 42.50
g. Double burelage, both pointing up 210.00 *250.00*
Never hinged 850.00
h. Double overprint 70.00
Nos. 25b-30b (6) 106.00 *81.50*
Set, never hinged 430.00

Burelage with Points Down

Violet Burelage with Points Down

25c A16 1m on 30pf org & blk, *buff* 1.25 2.50
Never hinged 4.25
Postally used *15.50*
On cover 24.00
d. Double burelage, both pointing down 210.00 *250.00*
Never hinged 850.00
26c A16 1¼m on 3pf brown 6.50 *11.00*
Never hinged 30.00
Postally used *45.00*
On cover 82.50
d. Double burelage, both pointing down 210.00 *250.00*
Never hinged 850.00
e. Double overprint 450.00
27c A22 2m on 35pf red brn 30.00 *50.00*
Never hinged 95.00
Postally used *275.00*
On cover 340.00
g. Double burelage, both pointing down 210.00 *250.00*
Never hinged 850.00
28c A22 3m on 7½pf orange 40.00 *85.00*
Never hinged 175.00
Postally used *340.00*
On cover 425.00
g. Double burelage, both pointing down 210.00 *250.00*
Never hinged 850.00
29c A22 5m on 2pf gray 6.50 *8.50*
Never hinged 22.50
Postally used *37.50*
On cover 500.00
e. Double burelage, both pointing down 210.00 *250.00*
Never hinged 850.00
30c A22 10m on 7½pf orange 13.50 *29.00*
Never hinged 55.00
Postally used *110.00*
On cover 150.00
h. Double burelage, both pointing down 210.00 *250.00*
Never hinged 850.00
i. Double burelage, one pointing up, one down 210.00 *250.00*
Never hinged 850.00
Nos. 25c-30c (6) 97.75 *186.00*
Set, never hinged 380.00

Burelage Omitted

25f A16 1m on 30pf org & blk, *buff* 3.25 *6.00*
Never hinged 12.50
Postally used *21.00*
On cover 50.00
26h A16 1¼m on 3pf brown 110.00 *175.00*
Never hinged 340.00
Postally used *750.00*
On cover 1,000.
27h A22 2m on 35pf red brn 135.00 *175.00*
Never hinged 425.00
Postally used *925.00*
On cover 1,500.
28h A22 3m on 7½pf orange 240.00 *375.00*
Never hinged 850.00
Postally used *850.00*
On cover 1,350.
29f A22 5m on 2pf gray 240.00 *375.00*
Never hinged 850.00
Postally used *850.00*
On cover 1,350.
30j A22 10m on 7½pf orange 9.25 *21.00*
Never hinged 21.00
Postally used *100.00*
On cover 135.00

Excellent counterfeits of the surcharges are known.

German Stamps of 1906-20 Overprinted in Blue

1920

31 A22 2pf gray 110.00 *200.00*
Never hinged 375.00
Postally used *450.00*
On cover *2,100.*
32 A22 2½pf gray 150.00 *300.00*
Never hinged 550.00
Postally used *600.00*
On cover *3,400.*
33 A16 3pf brown 11.00 *17.00*
Never hinged 37.50
Postally used *50.00*
On cover 125.00
a. Double overprint 75.00 —
Never hinged 180.00

34 A16 5pf green .60 *.70*
Never hinged 2.25
Postally used *2.50*
On cover 7.50
a. Double overprint 85.00
Never hinged 200.00
35 A22 7½pf orange 40.00 *57.50*
Never hinged 150.00
Postally used *150.00*
On cover 300.00
36 A16 10pf carmine 3.75 *7.00*
Never hinged 15.00
Postally used *30.00*
On cover 67.50
a. 10pf dark rose red 22.50 37.50
Never hinged 85.00
Postally used *175.00*
On cover 250.00
b. Double overprint 75.00
37 A22 15pf dk violet .60 *.70*
Never hinged 2.90
Postally used *5.25*
On cover 9.00
a. 15pf deep brownish violet 55.00 *67.50*
Never hinged 225.00
Postally used *225.00*
On cover 260.00
b. Double overprint 85.00
Never hinged 200.00
38 A16 20pf blue violet .60 *.70*
Never hinged 2.90
Postally used *2.90*
On cover 8.50

Overprinted in Carmine or Blue

39 A16 25pf org & blk, *yel* .60 *.70*
Never hinged 2.90
Postally used *2.60*
On cover 8.50
40 A16 30pf org & blk, *buff* 50.00 *92.50*
Never hinged 160.00
Postally used *200.00*
On cover 425.00
42 A16 40pf lake & blk 2.25 *2.50*
Never hinged 7.50
Postally used *18.50*
On cover 67.50
a. Inverted overprint 210.00
b. Double overprint 425.00
c. 40pf red & black 19.00 *30.00*
Never hinged 100.00
Postally used *110.00*
On cover 150.00
43 A16 50pf pur & blk, *buff* 175.00 *300.00*
Never hinged 550.00
Postally used *850.00*
On cover *3,000.*
44 A16 60pf mag (Bl) 1,250. *2,100.*
Never hinged 2,500.
Postally used *3,400.*
On cover —
45 A16 75pf green & blk .60 *.70*
Never hinged 2.75
Postally used *5.00*
On cover 11.00
a. Double overprint *450.00*
46 A16 80pf lake & blk, *rose* 2.40 *4.25*
Never hinged 8.50
Postally used *37.50*
On cover 125.00
47 A17 1m carmine 1,200. *2,100.*
Never hinged 2,500.
Postally used *3,400.*
On cover —
a. Double overprint *4,250.*

Overprinted in Carmine

48 A21 2m gray blue 1,200. *2,100.*
Never hinged 2,500.
Postally used *3,400.*
On cover —

Counterfeit overprints of Nos. 31-48 exist.

Nos. 44, 47 and 48 were issued in small quantities and usually affixed directly to the mail by the postal clerk.

For surcharge see No. 62.

Issued: 5pf, 15pf, 20pf, 25pf, 75pf, 8/20. Others, 8/30.

A8

Hanseatic Trading Ship — A9

Serrate Roulette 13½

1921, Jan. 31 Typo. Wmk. 108

49 A8 5pf brown & violet .25 .25
Never hinged 1.50
Postally used *1.90*
On cover 3.40

50 A8 10pf orange & dk vio .25 .25
Never hinged 1.50
Postally used 1.90
On cover 4.25
51 A8 25pf green & car rose .50 .65
Never hinged 2.25
Postally used 1.90
On cover 4.25
52 A8 40pf carmine rose 3.75 3.25
Never hinged 15.00
Postally used 6.00
On cover 12.50
53 A8 80pf ultra .50 .50
Never hinged 2.25
Postally used 7.00
On cover 12.50
54 A9 1m car rose & blk 1.60 *2.00*
Never hinged 7.50
Postally used 6.75
On cover 17.00
55 A9 2m dk blue & dk grn 5.00 5.00
Never hinged 21.00
Postally used 21.00
On cover 37.50
56 A9 3m blk & grnsh bl 2.00 *2.00*
Never hinged 8.25
Postally used 9.75
On cover 17.00
57 A9 5m indigo & rose red 2.00 *2.00*
Never hinged 8.25
Postally used 9.25
On cover 21.00
58 A9 10m dk grn & brn org 2.50 *4.50*
Never hinged 15.00
Postally used 34.00
On cover 50.00
Nos. 49-58 (10) 18.35 *20.40*
Set, never hinged 82.50

Issued in honor of the Constitution.

Nos. 49 and 50 with center in red instead of violet and Nos. 49-51, 54-58 with center inverted are probably proofs. All values of this issue exist imperforate but are not known to have been regularly issued in that condition.

1921, Mar. 11 ***Perf. 14***

59 A8 25pf green & car rose .50 *.85*
Never hinged 4.00
Postally used 1.75
On cover 9.25
60 A8 40pf carmine rose .50 .85
Never hinged 4.00
Postally used 2.60
On cover 9.25
61 A8 80pf ultra 5.50 *10.00*
Never hinged 26.00
Postally used 23.00
On cover 37.50
Nos. 59-61 (3) 6.50 *11.70*
Set, never hinged 34.00

No. 45 Surcharged in Black

1921, May 6 **Wmk. 125**

62 A16 60pf on 75pf .95 .90
Never hinged 5.50
Postally used 4.25
On cover 9.50
a. Double surcharge 100.00 *110.00*
Never hinged 250.00
Postally used 600.00
b. Pair, one stamp without "Danzig" overprint 42.50 *175.00*
Never hinged 125.00
Postally used —
c. Double surcharge, one inverted 85.00 75.00
Never hinged 210.00
Postally used 300.00
d. Surcharge "60" in center of design 17.00 *42.50*
Never hinged 60.00
Postally used 85.00
On cover 175.00

Surcharge on No. 62 normally appears at top of design.

Arms — A11

Coat of Arms — A12

Wmk. 108 (Upright or Sideways)

1921-22 ***Perf. 14***

63 A11 5(pf) orange .25 .25
Never hinged .90
Postally used 3.50
On cover 5.00
64 A11 10(pf) dark brown .25 .25
Never hinged .70
Postally used 2.00
On cover 5.00
65 A11 15(pf) green .25 .25
Never hinged .70
Postally used 1.60
On cover 4.25
66 A11 20(pf) slate .25 .25
Never hinged .70
Postally used 1.60
On cover 4.25
67 A11 25(pf) dark green .25 .25
Never hinged .70
Postally used 1.60
On cover 4.25
68 A11 30(pf) blue & car .25 .25
Never hinged .85
Postally used 1.60
On cover 4.25
a. Center inverted 75.00 *150.00*
Never hinged 225.00
69 A11 40pf green & car .25 .25
Never hinged .85
Postally used 1.60
On cover 3.40
a. Center inverted 75.00 *150.00*
Never hinged 225.00
70 A11 50pf dk grn & car .25 .25
Never hinged .85
Postally used 1.60
On cover 3.50
71 A11 60pf carmine .45 .45
Never hinged 1.50
Postally used 3.00
On cover 6.25
72 A11 80pf black & car .35 *.45*
Never hinged .85
Postally used 3.40
On cover 7.50

Paper With Faint Gray Network

73 A11 1m org & car .50 .40
Never hinged 1.40
Postally used 2.10
On cover 4.25
a. Center inverted 75.00 150.00
Never hinged 225.00
b. Background omitted 5.75 *30.00*
Never hinged 15.00
On cover 75.00
74 A11 1.20m blue violet 1.25 1.25
Never hinged 6.75
Postally used 3.75
On cover 12.50
a. Background omitted 7.50 *30.00*
Never hinged 24.00
On cover 110.00
75 A11 2m gray & car 3.25 *4.25*
Never hinged 11.00
Postally used 7.50
On cover 15.00
a. Background omitted 15.00 *45.00*
Never hinged 45.00
On cover 125.00
76 A11 3m violet & car 9.00 10.00
Never hinged 32.50
Postally used 29.00
On cover 50.00

Serrate Roulette 13½

Wmk. 108 Upright

77 A12 5m grn, red & blk 1.25 *3.00*
Never hinged 6.00
Postally used 17.00
On cover 34.00
78 A12 9m rose, red & org ('22) 3.00 *8.50*
Never hinged 14.50
Postally used 150.00
On cover 210.00
a. Background omitted 42.50
Never hinged 125.00
79 A12 10m ultra, red & blk 1.25 *3.00*
Never hinged 6.00
Postally used 25.00
On cover 42.50
a. Background omitted 67.50
Never hinged 200.00 3.00
80 A12 20m red & black 1.25 *3.00*
Never hinged 6.00
Postally used 50.00
On cover 85.00
a. Background omitted 67.50
Never hinged 200.00
Nos. 63-80 (18) 23.55 *36.30*
Set, never hinged 85.00

Wmk. 108 Sideways

77a A12 5m grn, red & blk 1.25 *2.75*
Never hinged 6.00
Postally used 67.50
On cover 80.00
78b A12 9m rose, red & org 2.75 *8.00*
Never hinged 14.50
Postally used 175.00
On cover 240.00
79b A12 10m ultra, red & blk 1.25 *2.75*
Never hinged 5.50
Postally used 72.50
On cover 105.00
80b A12 20m red & blk 1.25 *2.75*
Never hinged 6.00
Postally used 140.00
On cover 190.00

In this and succeeding issues the mark values usually have the face of the paper covered with a gray network. This network is often very faint and occasionally is omitted.

Nos. 64-76 exist imperf. Value, each $16-$50 unused, $50-$150 never hinged.

See Nos. 81-93, 99-105. For surcharges and overprints see Nos. 96-98, O1-O33.

Issued: Nos. 63-76, 6/3/21. Nos. 77, 79-80, 8/1/21. No. 78, 2/1/22. Nos. 77a-80a, 3/1922.

Type of 1921 and

A13

Coat of Arms — A13a

1922 **Wmk. 108 Upright** ***Perf. 14***

81 A11 75(pf) deep vio .25 *.25*
Never hinged .75
Postally used 1.60
On cover 4.00
82 A11 80(pf) green .25 *.25*
Never hinged .75
Postally used 32.50
On cover 60.00
83 A11 1.25m vio & car .25 *.25*
Never hinged .75
Postally used 2.00
On cover 4.00
84 A11 1.50m slate gray .25 *.40*
Never hinged .75
Postally used 2.00
On cover 4.00
On cover 4.00
85 A11 2m car rose .25 *.25*
Never hinged .75
Postally used 1.60
a. Gray network double 70.00
Never hinged 150.00
86 A11 2.40m dk brn & car 1.15 *2.00*
Never hinged 5.25
Postally used 32.50
On cover 65.00
87 A11 3m car lake .25 *.40*
Never hinged .75
Postally used 2.00
On cover 4.00
a. dark carmine red 64.00 *67.50*
Never hinged 240.00
Postally used 525.00
On cover 600.00
88 A11 4m dark blue 1.15 *2.00*
Never hinged 5.50
Postally used 9.00
On cover 13.50
89 A11 5m deep grn .25 *.35*
Never hinged .75
Postally used 1.60
On cover 4.00
a. Wmk. sideways 16.00 *55.00*
Never hinged 65.00
Postally used 275.00
On cover 475.00
90 A11 6m car lake .25 *.35*
Never hinged .75
Postally used 1.60
On cover 4.00
a. 6m car rose, wmk. 109 sideways *1,800.*
Never hinged *3,900.*
91 A11 8m light blue .45 *1.60*
Never hinged 2.25
Postally used 20.00
On cover 27.50
92 A11 10m orange .25 *.35*
Never hinged .75
Postally used 1.60
On cover 4.00
93 A11 20m org brn .25 *.35*
Never hinged .75
Postally used 1.60
On cover 4.00
94 A13 50m gold & car 2.00 *6.50*
Never hinged 9.00
Postally used 175.00
On cover 210.00
a. 50m gold & red 57.50 *120.00*
Never hinged 220.00
Postally used 525.00
On cover 725.00
95 A13a 100m metallic grn & red 3.25 *6.00*
Never hinged 14.00
Postally used *2,400.*
On cover *3,500.*
Nos. 81-95 (15) 10.50 *21.30*
Set, never hinged 42.50

Wmk. 108 Sideways

94b A13 50m gold & car 2.00 *12.00*
Never hinged 9.00
Postally used 175.00
On cover 240.00
c. As "a" 7.25 *12.50*
Never hinged 26.00
Postally used 175.00
On cover 210.00
95b A13a 100m metallic grn & red 3.00 *5.00*
Never hinged 10.50
Postally used 210.00
On cover 350.00

No. 95 has buff instead of gray network.

Nos. 81-83, 85-86, 88 exist imperf. Value, each $12.50.

Nos. 94-95 exist imperf. Value, each $60

Issued: 75pf, 80pf, 1.25m, 2m, 2.40m, 4m, 2/1. 50m, 100m, 3/10. 1.50m, 3m, 8m, 7/29. 6m, 20m, 10/30. 5m, 10m, 11/9.

Nos. 87, 88 and 91 Surcharged in Black or Carmine

1922

96 A11 6m on 3m car lake .35 *.60*
Never hinged 1.40
Postally used 2.50
On cover 4.00
a. Double surcharge
97 A11 8m on 4m dk blue .35 *.85*
Never hinged 1.20
Postally used 16.00
On cover 24.00
a. Double surcharge 70.00 *145.00*
Never hinged 140.00
b. Pair, one without surcharge 150.00
Never hinged 325.00
98 A11 20m on 8m lt bl (C) .35 *.60*
Never hinged 1.75
Postally used 15.00
On cover 24.00
Nos. 96-98 (3) 1.05 *2.05*
Set, never hinged 4.00

Issued: No. 97, 5/15. Nos. 96, 98, 10/2.

Wmk. 109 Sideways

1922-23 ***Perf. 14***

99 A11 4m dark blue .25 *.40*
Never hinged .90
Postally used 2.40
On cover 8.00
100 A11 5m dark green .25 *.40*
Never hinged .90
Postally used 1.90
On cover 4.00
a. Wmk. 110 *2,750.*
Never hinged *4,000.*
b. Wmk. 109 upright .45 *.80*
Never hinged 2.10
Postally used 4.75
On cover 8.00
102 A11 10m orange .25 *.40*
Never hinged .90
Postally used 1.60
On cover 4.00
b. Wmk. 109 upright .45 *.80*
Never hinged 1.90
Postally used 4.00
On cover 8.00
103 A11 20m orange brn .25 *.40*
Never hinged .90
Postally used 2.00
On cover 4.00
b. Wmk. 109 upright .45 *.80*
Never hinged 1.90
Postally used 3.50
On cover 8.50

Paper Without Network

Wmk. 109 Upright

104 A11 40m pale blue .25 *.60*
Never hinged .90
Postally used 10.00
On cover 20.00
105 A11 80m red .25 *.60*
Never hinged .90
Postally used 52.50
On cover 80.00
Nos. 99-105 (6) 1.50 *2.80*
Set, never hinged 5.40

Nos. 100, 102 and 103 also exist with watermark vertical. Values slightly higher.

Nos. 104-105 exist imperf. Value, each $12.50 unused, $32.50 never hinged.

Issued: No. 99, 12/16/22. Nos. 104-105, 5/15/1923. Others, 1/1923.

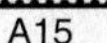
A15

A15a

Coat of Arms
A16

1922-23 Wmk. 109 Upright *Perf. 14*

Paper With Gray Network

106 A15 50m pale bl & red .25 *.40*
Never hinged .90
Postally used *1.75*
On cover 4.00
a. Wmk. sideways .45 *.80*
Never hinged 1.75
Postally used *4.00*
On cover 8.00
107 A15a 100m dk grn & red .25 *.40*
Never hinged .90
Postally used *1.75*
On cover 4.00
a. Wmk. sideways .75 *.80*
Never hinged 3.75
Postally used *4.75*
On cover 10.00
108 A15a 150m violet & red .25 *.40*
Never hinged .90
Postally used *3.25*
On cover 8.00
109 A16 250m violet & red .40 *.40*
Never hinged 2.25
Postally used *80.00*
On cover *105.00*
110 A16 500m gray blk & red .40 *.40*
Never hinged 2.25
Postally used *32.50*
On cover 65.00
111 A16 1000m brn & red .40 *.40*
Never hinged 2.25
Postally used *21.00*
On cover 40.00
112 A16 5000m silver & red 1.50 *6.00*
Never hinged 7.50
Postally used *65.00*
On cover 105.00

Paper Without Network

113 A15 50m pale blue .40 *.60*
Never hinged .90
Postally used *140.00*
On cover 190.00
114 A15a 100m deep green .40 *.60*
Never hinged .90
Postally used *4.75*
On cover 9.50
115 A15 200m orange .40 *.60*
Never hinged .90
Postally used *2.25*
On cover 6.00
Nos. 106-115 (10) 4.65 *10.20*
Set, never hinged 19.00

Nos. 108-112 exist imperf. Value, each $50 unused, $125 never hinged.

Nos. 113-115 exist imperf. Value, each $35 unused, $92.50 never hinged.

See Nos. 123-125. For surcharges and overprints see Nos. 126, 137-140, 143, 156-167, O35-O38.

Issued: No. 106, 11/21/22. No. 107, 12/14/22. 150m, 250m, 500m, 1000m, 1/24/23. 5000m, 2/27/23. No. 113, 200m, 7/20/23. No. 114, 4/27/23.

A17

1923 *Perf. 14*

Paper With Gray Network

117 A17 250m violet & red .25 *.55*
Never hinged .75
Postally used *12.00*
On cover 24.00
118 A17 300m bl grn & red .25 *.55*
Never hinged .65
Postally used *2.75*
On cover 6.00
119 A17 500m gray & red .25 *.55*
Never hinged .75
Postally used *2.50*
On cover 6.00
120 A17 1000m brown & red .25 *.55*
Never hinged .75
Postally used *2.50*
On cover 6.00
121 A17 3000m violet & red .25 *.55*
Never hinged .75
Postally used *14.00*
On cover 24.00
123 A16 10,000m orange & red .60 .60
Never hinged 3.00
Postally used *14.50*
On cover 20.00
124 A16 20,000m pale bl & red .60 *1.00*
Never hinged 3.00
Postally used *25.00*
On cover 32.50
125 A16 50,000m green & red .60 *1.00*
Never hinged 3.00
Postally used *21.00*
On cover 27.50
Nos. 117-125 (8) 3.05 *5.35*
Set, never hinged 12.50

Nos. 117, 119-121 exist imperf. Value, each $19 unused, $45 never hinged; Nos. 123-125 also exist imperf. Values each, $25 unused, $85 never hinged.

See Nos. 127-135. For surcharges & overprints see Nos. 141-142, 144-155, O39-O41.

Issued: 300m, 3/22. 250m, 5/15. 500m, 6/29. 1000m, 7/29. 3000m, 8/3. 10,000m, 8/8. 20,000m, 8/13. 50,000m, 8/20.

Network Omitted

117a A17 250m 19.00 16.50
Never hinged 45.00
Postally used *90.00*
118a A17 300m 19.00 *16.50*
Never hinged 45.00
Postally used *90.00*
119a A17 500m 19.00 16.50
Never hinged 45.00
Postally used *90.00*
120a A17 1000m 19.00 *16.50*
Never hinged 45.00
Postally used *90.00*
121a A17 3000m 19.00 *16.50*
Never hinged 45.00
Postally used *90.00*
123a A16 10,000m 22.50 *22.50*
Never hinged 75.00
Postally used *150.00*
124a A16 20,000m 22.50 *27.50*
Never hinged 75.00
Postally used *240.00*
125a A16 50,000m 22.50 *27.50*
Never hinged 75.00
Postally used *240.00*

Nos. 117a, 119a-121a exist imperf. Value each, $19 unused, $45 never hinged.

No. 124 Surcharged in Red

1923, Aug. 14

126 A16 100,000m on #124 1.00 *6.00*
Never hinged 4.50
Postally used *110.00*
On cover 140.00
a. On #124a 6.00 16.00
Never hinged 16.00
Postally used *325.00*
On cover —

No. 126 exists imperf. Value $50 unused, $125 never hinged.

1923 *Perf. 14*

Paper Without Network

127 A17 1000m brown .25 *.40*
Never hinged .70
Postally used *4.00*
On cover 9.50
129 A17 5000m rose .25 *.40*
Never hinged .70
Postally used *1.75*
On cover 6.00
131 A17 20,000m pale blue .25 *.40*
Never hinged .70
Postally used *1.75*
On cover 6.00
132 A17 50,000m green .25 *.40*
Never hinged .70
Postally used *1.75*
On cover 6.00
a. Wmk. 110 —
b. Wmk. two vert. interlaced ribbons *4,000.*
Never hinged *7,500.*

Paper With Gray Network

133 A17 100,000m deep blue .25 *.40*
Never hinged .70
Postally used *2.10*
On cover 8.00
a. Network omitted 8.00 *16.00*
Never hinged 24.00
Postally used *55.00*
b. Double impression 80.00
134 A17 250,000m violet .25 *.40*
Never hinged .70
Postally used *2.10*
On cover 10.00
a. Network omitted 8.00 *16.00*
Never hinged 24.00
Postally used *55.00*
135 A17 500,000m slate .25 *.40*
Never hinged .70
Postally used *2.10*
On cover 6.00
a. Network omitted 8.00 *16.00*
Never hinged 24.00
Postally used *55.00*
Nos. 127-135 (7) 1.75 2.80
Set, never hinged 5.00

Nos. 127, 129, 131-135 exist imperf. Value each, $40 unused, $100 never hinged. Nos. 133a-135a also exist imperf, Value each, $50 unused, $135.00 never hinged.

Issued: No. 127, 7/24. Nos. 129, 131, 8/25. No. 132, 9/1. No. 133, 9/11. No. 135, 9/16.

Abbreviations:
th=(tausend) thousand
mil=million

Nos. 115, 114, 132, and Type of 1923 Surcharged

1923 *Perf. 14*

Paper Without Network

137 A15 40th m on 200m .85 *2.00*
Never hinged 5.25
Postally used *190.00*
On cover 240.00
a. Double surcharge 85.00
Never hinged 160.00
b. Pair, one without surch. —
138 A15 100th m on 200m .85 *2.00*
Never hinged 4.75
Postally used *26.00*
On cover 47.50
139 A15 250th m on 200m 6.25 *13.00*
Never hinged 30.00
Postally used *250.00*
On cover 350.00
140 A15a 400th m on 100m .60 .60
Never hinged 3.00
Postally used *12.00*
On cover 16.00
a. Pair, one without surch. —
141 A17 500th m on #132 .40 *.60*
Never hinged 2.10
Postally used *5.25*
On cover 8.00

On 10,000m

142 A17 1mil m org 3.75 *6.25*
Never hinged 15.00
Postally used *440.00*
On cover 550.00

The surcharges on Nos. 140-142 differ in details from those on Nos. 137-139.

Type of 1923 Surcharged

Paper With Gray Network

On 1,000,000m

143 A16 10mil m org .40 *1.25*
Never hinged 3.00
Postally used *95.00*
On cover 125.00
a. Network omitted 24.00 20.00
Never hinged *65.00*
Postally used *475.00*
Nos. 137-143 (7) 13.10 *25.70*
Set, never hinged 60.00

Nos. 142-143 exist imperf. Values: No. 142 unused $50, never hinged $125; No. 143 unused $25, never hinged $85.

Issued: Nos. 137-139, 9/1. No. 141, 9/8. No. 142, 9/13. No. 143, 10/1.

Type of 1923 Surcharged

Wmk. 109 Upright

Perf. 14

10,000m rose on paper without Network

144 A17 1mil m on 10,000m .25 *.60*
Never hinged 1.00
Postally used *1.90*
On cover 6.00
145 A17 2mil m on 10,000m .25 *.60*
Never hinged 1.00
Postally used *2.25*
On cover 6.00
146 A17 3mil m on 10,000m .25 *.60*
Never hinged 1.00
Postally used *2.25*
On cover 6.00
147 A17 5mil m on 10,000m .35 *.60*
Never hinged 1.50
Postally used *1.90*
On cover 6.00
b. Double surcharge 85.00
Never hinged 160.00

10,000m gray lilac on paper without Network

148 A17 10mil m on 10,000m .40 *.75*
Never hinged 1.60
Postally used *7.25*
On cover 16.00
149 A17 20mil m on 10,000m .40 *.75*
Never hinged 1.60
Postally used *8.75*
On cover 20.00
150 A17 25mil m on 10,000m .25 *.75*
Never hinged 1.40
Postally used *32.50*
On cover 47.50
151 A17 40mil m on 10,000m .25 *.75*
Never hinged 1.40
Postally used *32.50*
On cover 47.50
a. Double surcharge 52.50
Never hinged 160.00
152 A17 50mil m on 10,000m .25 *.75*
Never hinged 1.40
Postally used *11.00*
On cover 20.00

Type of 1923 Surcharged in Red

10,000m gray lilac on paper without Network

153 A17 100mil m on 10,000m .25 *.75*
Never hinged 1.40
Postally used *4.00*
On cover 8.00
154 A17 300mil m on 10,000m .25 *.75*
Never hinged 1.40
Postally used *12.00*
On cover 20.00
155 A17 500mil m on 10,000m .25 *.75*
Never hinged 1.40
Postally used *2.75*
On cover 8.00
Nos. 144-155 (12) 3.40 *8.40*
Set, never hinged 15.00

Nos. 144-147 exist imperf. Value, each $25 unused, $85 never hinged. Nos. 148-155 exist imperf. Value, each $32.50 unused, $85 never hinged.

Issued: Nos. 148-150, 152, 10/15. No. 153, 10/22. Nos. 151, 154-155, 10/23.

Types of 1923 Surcharged

1923, Oct. 31 Wmk. 110 *Perf. 14*

156 A15 5pf on 50m .45 .40
Never hinged 2.25
Postally used *2.00*
On cover 4.00
157 A15 10pf on 50m .45 .40
Never hinged 2.25
Postally used *2.00*
On cover 4.00
158 A15a 20pf on 100m .45 .40
Never hinged 2.25
Postally used *2.00*
On cover 4.00
159 A15 25pf on 50m 3.50 *9.00*
Never hinged 16.00
Postally used *32.50*
On cover 52.50
160 A15 30pf on 50m 3.50 2.00
Never hinged 16.00
Postally used *5.25*
On cover 12.00
161 A15a 40pf on 100m 2.25 2.00
Never hinged 11.00
Postally used *8.75*
On cover 16.00
162 A15a 50pf on 100m 2.25 *3.00*
Never hinged 13.50
Postally used *12.00*
On cover 20.00
163 A15a 75pf on 100m 8.00 *16.00*
Never hinged 30.00
Postally used *55.00*
On cover 80.00

Type of 1923 Surcharged

1923, Nov. 5

164 A16 1g on 1mil m rose 4.50 *6.25*
Never hinged 24.00
Postally used *14.50*
On cover 47.50
165 A16 2g on 1mil m rose 12.00 *17.50*
Never hinged 35.00
Postally used *60.00*
On cover 160.00
166 A16 3g on 1mil m rose 22.00 *62.50*
Never hinged 110.00
Postally used *160.00*
On cover 350.00
167 A16 5g on 1mil m rose 25.00 *67.50*
Never hinged 125.00
Postally used *550.00*
On cover *800.00*
Nos. 156-167 (12) 84.35 *186.95*
Set, never hinged 400.00

Issued: Nos. 156-163, 10/31. Nos. 164-167, 11/5.

Coat of Arms — A19

1924-37 Wmk. 109 Perf. 14

168 A19 3pf brn, *yelsh* ('35) 1.25 *1.50*
Never hinged 4.75
On cover 6.00
a. 3pf dp brn, *white* ('27) 2.10 1.90
Never hinged 9.50
On cover 6.00
b. As #168, imperf. 27.50
Never hinged 80.00
c. As "a," imperf. 27.50
Never hinged 80.00
170 A19 5pf org, *yelsh* 3.25 .55
Never hinged 6.50
On cover 4.00
a. White paper 8.50 2.00
Never hinged 45.00
On cover 4.00
c. Tête bêche pair 375.00
Never hinged 725.00
d. Syncopated perf., #170 10.50 9.25
Never hinged 30.00
On cover 27.50
e. Syncopated perf., #170a 25.00 22.50
Never hinged 120.00
On cover 27.50
171 A19 7pf yel grn ('33) 1.60 *3.00*
Never hinged 4.25
On cover 10.50
172 A19 8pf yel grn ('37) 1.60 *6.00*
Never hinged 6.50
On cover 17.50
173 A19 10pf grn, *yelsh* 5.50 .50
Never hinged 15.50
On cover 4.00
a. White paper 11.50 2.50
Never hinged 47.50
On cover 4.00
c. 10pf blue grn, *yellowish* 7.75 1.10
Never hinged 27.50
On cover 4.00
d. Tête bêche pair 325.00
Never hinged 750.00
e. Syncopated perf., #173 18.00 11.00
Never hinged 55.00
On cover 40.00
f. Syncopated perf., #173a 27.50 13.00
Never hinged 110.00
On cover 40.00
g. Syncopated perf., #173c 11.00 *14.50*
Never hinged 37.50
On cover —
175 A19 15pf gray 3.75 .65
Never hinged 21.00
On cover 4.00
a. 15pf dark greenish gray 12.00 4.50
Never hinged 52.50
On cover 8.00
176 A19 15pf red, *yelsh* ('35) 2.10 1.10
Never hinged 9.50
On cover 4.00
a. White paper ('25) 4.50 1.10
Never hinged 25.00
On cover 4.00
177 A19 20pf carmine & red 15.00 .65
Never hinged 34.50
On cover 4.00
a. 20pf dp lilac red & rose red 32.50 12.00
Never hinged 130.00
On cover 27.50
178 A19 20pf gray ('35) 2.25 *2.50*
Never hinged 5.50
On cover 9.50
179 A19 25pf slate & red 27.00 3.75
Never hinged 100.00
On cover 12.00
180 A19 25pf carmine ('35) 16.00 1.60
Never hinged 52.50
On cover 6.00
181 A19 30pf green & red 14.00 .85
Never hinged 47.50
On cover 7.00
a. 30pf dk grn & dk rose red 32.50 12.50
Never hinged 160.00
On cover 55.00
182 A19 30pf dk violet ('35) 2.25 *4.25*
Never hinged 5.25
On cover 12.00
183 A19 35pf ultra 4.50 1.50
Never hinged 11.00
On cover 10.00
a. 35pf grayish ultra 14.50 5.50
Never hinged 40.00
On cover 12.00
184 A19 40pf dk blue & blue 12.00 1.00
Never hinged 27.50
On cover 12.00
185 A19 40pf yel brn & red 6.50 *12.50*
Never hinged 30.00
On cover 40.00
186 A19 40pf dk blue ('35) 2.25 *3.75*
Never hinged 5.50
On cover 18.00
a. Imperf. 60.00
Never hinged 170.00
187 A19 50pf blue & red 16.00 7.50
Never hinged 67.50
On cover 24.00
a. Yellowish paper 17.50 *32.50*
Never hinged 57.50
On cover 80.00
b. 50pf dk ultra & dk rose red 24.00 11.00
Never hinged 110.00
On cover 40.00
188 A19 55pf plum & scar 5.00 *14.50*
Never hinged 17.50
On cover 67.50
189 A19 60pf dk grn & red 6.25 *17.50*
Never hinged 30.00
On cover 47.50
190 A19 70pf yel grn & red ('35) 2.25 *7.50*
Never hinged 10.50
On cover 47.50
191 A19 75pf violet & red, *yellowish* 7.50 *29.00*
Never hinged 17.50
On cover 120.00
a. White paper 10.00 8.50
Never hinged 47.50
On cover 40.00
b. 75pf dk pur & dk rose red 16.00 16.00
Never hinged 55.00
On cover 40.00
192 A19 80pf dk org brn & red ('35) 2.25 *7.50*
Never hinged 10.50
On cover 47.50
Nos. 168-192 (23) 160.05 *129.15*
Set, never hinged 675.00

The 5pf and 10pf with syncopated perforations (Netherlands type C) are coils.

See Nos. 225-232. For overprints and surcharges see Nos. 200-209, 211-215, 241-252, B9-B11, O42-O52.

Issued: No. 168, 10/1935. No. 168a, 2/19/27. No. 170, 2/1935. Nos. 170a, 173a, 175a, 1/19/24. Nos. 170d, 173e, 173g, 1937. Nos. 170e, 173f, 1932. No. 171, 4/27/33. No. 172, 8/14/37. No. 173, 3/1935. No. 173c, 6/24/37. No. 175, 3/1924. No. 176, 1936. No. 176a, 8/20/25. No. 177, 1/26/24. No. 178, 186, 6/20/35. Nos. 179, 181, 187, 191a, 3/12/24. No. 180, 6/5/25. No. 181a, 9/1930. No. 182, 8/21/35. No. 183, 1925. No. 183a, 1930. No. 184, 2/14/24. Nos. 185, 189, 4/15/35. No. 187a, 3/1938. No. 187b, 2/1930. No. 188, 4/17/37. Nos. 190, 192, 9/5/35. No. 191, 2/1937. No. 191b, 4/1932.

Oliva Castle and Cathedral A20

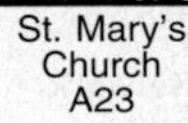

St. Mary's Church A23

Council Chamber on the Langenmarkt A24

2g, Mottlau River & Krantor. 3g, View of Zoppot.

1924-32 Engr. Wmk. 125

193 A20 1g yel grn & blk 21.00 *45.00*
Never hinged 105.00
On cover 120.00
Parcel post cancel 20.00
194 A20 1g org & gray blk ('32) 17.00 3.75
Never hinged 67.50
On cover 12.00
Parcel post cancel 1.00
a. 1g red orange & blk 17.00 11.00
Never hinged 67.50
On cover 60.00
Parcel post cancel 1.00
195 A20 2g red vio & blk 45.00 *110.00*
Never hinged 205.00
On cover 240.00
Parcel post cancel 40.00
196 A20 2g rose & blk 3.75 *8.00*
Never hinged 14.50
On cover 21.00
Parcel post cancel 1.75
197 A20 3g dk blue & blk 4.75 *5.00*
Never hinged 24.00
On cover 40.00
Parcel post cancel 2.25
198 A23 5g brn red & blk 4.75 *8.50*
Never hinged 24.00
On cover 72.50
Parcel post cancel 1.90
199 A24 10g dk brn & blk 21.00 *110.00*
Never hinged 110.00
On cover 600.00
Parcel post cancel 18.00
Nos. 193-199 (7) 117.25 *290.25*
Set, never hinged 600.00

See No. 233. For overprints and surcharges see Nos. 210, 253-254, C31-C35.

Issued: Nos. 193, 195, 9/22/24. Nos. 194, 196, 11/28/24. No. 194a, 5/1932.

Stamps of 1924-25 Overprinted in Black, Violet or Red

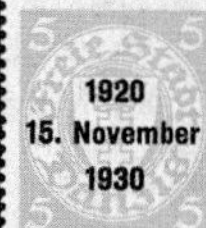

1930, Nov. 15 Typo. Wmk. 109

200 A19 5pf orange 2.50 *3.50*
Never hinged 9.50
On cover 10.00
201 A19 10pf yellow grn (V) 3.50 4.25
Never hinged 14.00
On cover 10.00
202 A19 15pf red 6.00 *10.00*
Never hinged 19.00
On cover 24.00
203 A19 20pf carmine & red 3.00 *5.50*
Never hinged 9.50
On cover 10.00
204 A19 25pf slate & red 4.25 *10.00*
Never hinged 24.00
On cover 24.00
205 A19 30pf green & red 8.50 *22.50*
Never hinged 34.00
On cover 47.50
206 A19 35pf ultra (R) 32.50 *90.00*
Never hinged 145.00
On cover 225.00
207 A19 40pf dk bl & bl (R) 11.50 *35.00*
Never hinged 42.50
On cover 60.00
208 A19 50pf dp blue & red 32.50 *75.00*
Never hinged 125.00
On cover 160.00
209 A19 75pf violet & red 32.50 *82.50*
Never hinged 130.00
On cover 160.00

Engr. Wmk. (125)

210 A20 1g orange & blk (R) 32.50 *75.00*
Never hinged 125.00
On cover 160.00
Nos. 200-210 (11) 169.25 *413.25*
Set, never hinged 675.00

10th anniv. of the Free State. Counterfeits exist.

Nos. 171 and 183 Surcharged in Red, Blue or Green

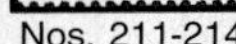

Nos. 211-214 No. 215

1934-36

211 A19 6pf on 7pf (R) 1.00 *1.50*
Never hinged 3.75
On cover 6.00
212 A19 8pf on 7pf (Bl) 2.00 *2.25*
Never hinged 7.75
On cover 9.50
213 A19 8pf on 7pf (R) 1.15 *2.40*
Never hinged 5.75
On cover 9.50
214 A19 8pf on 7pf (G) .75 *2.40*
Never hinged 4.50
On cover 9.50
215 A19 30pf on 35pf (Bl) 11.00 *24.50*
Never hinged 40.00
On cover 40.00
a. on #183a 24.00 *72.50*
Never hinged 90.00
On cover 100.00
Nos. 211-215 (5) 15.90 *33.05*
Set, never hinged 60.00

Issued: Nos. 211, 215-216, 215a, 12/28/34. No. 212, 6/5/35. No. 213, 7/13/36. No. 214, 12/23/36.

Bathing Beach, Brösen A25

View of Brösen Beach A26

War Memorial at Brösen — A27

1936, June 23 Typo. Wmk. 109

216 A25 10pf deep green .70 *.70*
Never hinged 3.00
On commercial cover 12.00
a. 10pf dark opal green 12.00 *32.50*
Never hinged 60.00
On commercial cover 65.00
On first day cover 80.00
217 A26 25pf rose red 1.25 *2.40*
Never hinged 3.00
On commercial cover 12.00
On first day cover 40.00
218 A27 40pf bright blue 2.25 *4.50*
Never hinged 7.50
On commercial cover 20.00
On first day cover 40.00
Nos. 216-218 (3) 4.20 *7.60*
Set, never hinged 15.00

Village of Brösen, 125th anniversary.

Exist imperf. Value each, $40 unused, $110 never hinged.

Skyline of Danzig — A28

1937, Mar. 27

219 A28 10pf dark blue .50 *1.40*
Never hinged 2.25
On cover 4.75
220 A28 15pf violet brown 1.60 *2.00*
Never hinged 6.00
On cover 8.00
Set, never hinged 11.25
Set of 2, #219-220 on one 1st day cover 20.00

Air Defense League.

Danzig Philatelic Exhibition Issue

Souvenir Sheet

St. Mary's Church — A29

1937, June 6 Wmk. 109 Perf. 14

221 A29 50pf dark opal green 4.00 *20.00*
Never hinged 11.00
On commercial cover 80.00
With Exhibition cancel 20.00
a. 10pf blackish green 16.00 *42.50*
Never hinged 40.00
On commercial cover 160.00
With Exhibition cancel 47.50
On first day cover 120.00

Danzig Philatelic Exhib., June 6-8, 1937.

No. 221a is the first printing (June 6); No. 221 is the second printing (October).

Arthur Schopenhauer
A30 A31

Design: 40pf, Full-face portrait, white hair.

Unwmk.

1938, Feb. 22 Photo. Perf. 14

222 A30 15pf dull blue 1.35 *2.40*
Never hinged 4.00
On commercial cover 8.00
223 A31 25pf sepia 3.25 *8.00*
Never hinged 12.00
On commercial cover 16.00
224 A31 40pf orange ver 1.35 *3.25*
Never hinged 4.00
On commercial cover 12.00
Nos. 222-224 (3) 5.95 *13.65*
Set, never hinged 20.00
Set of 3, #222-224 on one 1st day cover 37.50

150th anniv. of the birth of Schopenhauer.

Type of 1924-35

1938-39 Typo. Wmk. 237 Perf. 14

225 A19 3pf brown .90 *7.25*
Never hinged 2.75
On cover 16.00
226 A19 5pf orange .90 *2.00*
Never hinged 2.75
On cover 16.00
b. Syncopated perf. 1.40 *7.50*

Never hinged 5.50
On cover 13.00
227 A19 8pf yellow grn 4.00 *32.50*
Never hinged 16.50
On cover 47.50
228 A19 10pf blue green .90 *2.00*
Never hinged 2.75
On cover 4.00
b. Syncopated perf. 3.00 *10.00*
Never hinged 14.00
On cover 20.00
229 A19 15pf scarlet 1.60 *10.00*
Never hinged 5.50
On cover 20.00
230 A19 25pf carmine 2.10 *7.50*
Never hinged 10.00
On cover 24.00
231 A19 40pf dark blue 2.10 *27.50*
Never hinged 10.00
On cover 55.00
232 A19 50pf brt bl & red 2.10 *130.00*
Never hinged 10.00
On cover 200.00

Engr.

233 A20 1g red org & blk 6.75 *110.00*
Never hinged 25.00
On cover 200.00
Nos. 225-233 (9) 21.35 *328.75*
Set, never hinged 90.00

Sizes: No. 233, 32½x21¼mm; No. 194, 31x21mm.

Nos. 226b and 228b are coils with Netherlands type C perforation.

Issued: 3pf, 7/1938. 5pf, 25pf, 7/23/38. 8pf, 9/1938. 10pf, 15pf, 1g, 10/1938. 40pf, 7/19/38. 50pf, 6/1939. No. 226b, 8/24/38. No. 228b, 7/18/38.

Knights in Tournament, 1500 — A33

French Leaving Danzig, 1814 — A35

Stamp Day: 10pf, Signing of Danzig-Sweden neutrality treaty, 1630. 25pf, Battle of Weichselmünde, 1577.

Unwmk.

1939, Jan. 7 Photo. *Perf. 14*

234 A33 5pf dark green .40 *2.00*
Never hinged 2.00
On commercial cover 8.00
235 A33 10pf copper brown .85 *2.25*
Never hinged 2.90
On commercial cover 8.00
236 A35 15pf slate black 1.25 *2.75*
Never hinged 3.75
On commercial cover 9.50
237 A35 25pf brown violet 1.60 *3.75*
Never hinged 4.50
On commercial cover 17.50
Nos. 234-237 (4) 4.10 *10.75*
Set, never hinged 14.00
Set of 4, #234-237 on one 1st day cover 30.00

Gregor Mendel — A37

15pf, Dr. Robert Koch. 25pf, Wilhelm Roentgen.

1939, Apr. 29 Photo. *Perf. 13x14*

238 A37 10pf copper brown .65 *.85*
Never hinged 1.60
On commercial cover 6.00
239 A37 15pf indigo .65 *2.00*
Never hinged 2.75
On commercial cover 6.00
240 A37 25pf dark olive green 1.25 *2.75*
Never hinged 2.75
On commercial cover 9.50
Nos. 238-240 (3) 2.55 *5.60*
Set, never hinged 7.25
Set of 3, #238-240 on one 1st day cover 20.00

Issued in honor of the achievements of Mendel, Koch and Roentgen.

Issued under German Administration

Stamps of Danzig, 1925-39, Surcharged in Black

a

b

c

1939 Wmk. 109 *Perf. 14*

241 A19(b) 4rpf on 35pf ultra .75 *2.25*
Never hinged 2.00
On cover 4.75
242 A19(b) 12rpf on 7pf yel grn 1.50 *2.25*
Never hinged 4.50
On cover 4.75
243 A19(a) 20rpf gray 3.00 *8.50*
Never hinged 9.00
On cover 12.00

Wmk. 237

244 A19(a) 3rpf brown .75 *2.40*
Never hinged 2.25
On cover 4.75
245 A19(a) 5rpf orange .65 *3.00*
Never hinged 2.00
On cover 4.75
246 A19(a) 8rpf yellow grn 1.10 *4.25*
Never hinged 3.50
On cover 8.00
247 A19(a) 10rpf blue grn 2.25 *4.25*
Never hinged 7.00
On cover 8.00
248 A19(a) 15rpf scarlet 6.00 *11.00*
Never hinged 19.00
On cover 17.50
249 A19(a) 25rpf carmine 4.50 *10.00*
Never hinged 14.50
On cover 16.00
250 A19(a) 30rpf dk violet 2.00 *4.50*
Never hinged 6.00
On cover 8.75
251 A19(a) 40rpf dk blue 2.75 *6.00*
Never hinged 7.50
On cover 12.00
252 A19(a) 50rpf brt bl & red 4.00 *7.00*
Never hinged 12.00
On cover 13.50

Thick Paper

253 A20(c) 1rm on 1g red org & blk 14.00 *57.50*
Never hinged 45.00
On cover 80.00
a. Thin white paper 42.50 *160.00*
Never hinged 160.00
On cover 225.00

Wmk. 125

Thin White Paper

254 A20(c) 2rm on 2g rose & blk 20.00 *62.50*
Never hinged 55.00
On cover 95.00
a. Thick paper 18.00 *67.50*
Never hinged 60.00
On cover 95.00
b. As "a," "Deutsches Reich" omitted from surcharge *1,000.* —
Never hinged *1,750.*
c. As "a," "2 Reichmark" omitted from surcharge *1,000.* *1,750.*
Never hinged *1,750.*
Nos. 241-254 (14) 63.25 *185.40*
Set, never hinged 190.00

Nos. 241-254 were valid throughout Germany.

SEMI-POSTAL STAMPS

St. George and Dragon — SP1

Wmk. 108

1921, Oct. 16 Typo. *Perf. 14*

Size: 19x22mm

B1 SP1 30pf + 30pf grn & org .45 .95
Never hinged 1.50
Postally used *110.00*
On cover 160.00
B2 SP1 60pf + 60pf rose & org 1.25 *1.60*
Never hinged 5.25
Postally used *110.00*
On cover 160.00

Size: 25x30mm

Serrate Roulette 13½

B3 SP1 1.20m + 1.20m dk bl & org 2.00 *2.25*
Never hinged 8.25
Postally used *110.00*
On cover 160.00
Nos. B1-B3 (3) 3.70 4.80
Set, never hinged 16.00

Nos. B1-B3 exist imperf. Value each, $45 unused, $125 never hinged.

Aged Pensioner SP2

1923, Mar. Wmk. 109 *Perf. 14*

Paper With Gray Network

B4 SP2 50m + 20m lake .25 *.60*
Never hinged 1.10
Postally used *42.50*
On cover 100.00
B5 SP2 100m + 30m red vio .25 *.60*
Never hinged 1.10
Postally used *42.50*
On cover 100.00
Set, never hinged 2.50

Nos. B4-B5 exist imperf. Value each, $50 unused, $30 used, $210 never hinged.

Philatelic Exhibition Issue

Neptune Fountain — SP3

Various Frames.

1929, July 7 Engr. Unwmk.

B6 SP3 10pf yel grn & gray 2.40 1.60
Never hinged 8.25
Exhibition cancellation 6.00
On cover 24.00
B7 SP3 15pf car & gray 2.40 1.60
Never hinged 8.25
Exhibition cancellation 6.00
On cover 35.00
B8 SP3 25pf ultra & gray 8.50 *13.00*
Never hinged 27.50
Exhibition cancellation 47.50
On cover 65.00
a. 25pf violet blue & black 25.00 *80.00*
Never hinged 92.50
On cover 110.00
b. 25pf deep gray bl & blk 47.50 *225.00*
Never hinged 175.00
On cover 275.00
Nos. B6-B8 (3) 13.30 16.20
Set, never hinged 45.00
Set of 3, #B6-B8 on one 1st day cover 200.00

These stamps were sold exclusively at the Danzig Philatelic Exhibition, June 7-14, 1929, at double their face values, the excess being for the aid of the exhibition.

Regular Issue of 1924-25 Surcharged in Black

1934, Jan. 15 Wmk. 109

B9 A19 5pf + 5pf orange 9.50 *19.00*
Never hinged 42.50
On cover 60.00
B10 A19 10pf + 5pf yel grn 22.50 *45.00*
Never hinged 100.00
On cover 110.00
B11 A19 15pf + 5pf carmine 13.50 *35.00*
Never hinged 77.50
On cover 80.00
Nos. B9-B11 (3) 45.50 *99.00*
Set, never hinged 220.00

Surtax for winter welfare. Counterfeits exist.

Stock Tower — SP4

George Hall — SP6

City Gate, 16th Century SP5

1935, Dec. 16 Typo. *Perf. 14*

B12 SP4 5pf + 5pf orange .65 *1.50*
Never hinged 2.10
On cover 5.50
B13 SP5 10pf + 5pf green 1.10 *2.25*
Never hinged 3.25
On cover 9.50
B14 SP6 15pf + 10pf scarlet 2.75 *3.50*
Never hinged 9.00
On cover 16.00
Nos. B12-B14 (3) 4.50 *7.25*
Set, never hinged 16.00
Set of 3, #B12-B14 on one 1st day cover 40.00

Surtax for winter welfare.

Milk Can Tower SP7

Frauentor SP8

Krantor — SP9

Langgarter Gate — SP10

High Gate SP11

1936, Nov. 25

B15 SP7 10pf + 5pf dk bl 1.60 *4.50*
Never hinged 11.00
On cover 16.00
a. Imperf. 75.00
Never hinged 180.00
B16 SP8 15pf + 5pf dull grn 1.60 *5.75*
Never hinged 11.00
On cover 16.00

B17 SP9 25pf + 10pf red brn 2.25 *9.00*
Never hinged 14.50
On cover 24.00
B18 SP10 40pf + 20pf brn & red brn 3.00 *10.00*
Never hinged 17.50
On cover 27.50
B19 SP11 50pf + 20pf bl & dk bl 5.25 *15.00*
Never hinged 21.00
On cover 40.00
Nos. B15-B19 (5) 13.70 *44.25*
Set, never hinged 80.00

Surtax for winter welfare.

SP12

SP13

1937, Oct. 30 Wmk. 109 Sideways
B20 SP12 25pf + 25pf dk car 2.75 *5.25*
Never hinged 14.00
On cover 47.50
a. Wmk. upright 10.50 *40.00*
Never hinged 35.00
On cover 95.00

Wmk. 109 Upright
B21 SP13 40pf + 40pf blue & red 2.75 *5.25*
Never hinged 13.00
On cover 45.00
a. Souvenir sheet of 2, #B20a-B21 60.00 *110.00*
Never hinged 110.00
Exposition cancellation 90.00
On cover 275.00
Set, never hinged 27.50

Founding of Danzig community at Magdeburg. No. B21a exists imperf. Value, $1,600 unused, $3,250 never hinged.

Madonna SP14

Mercury SP15

Weather Vane, Town Hall SP16

Neptune Fountain SP17

St. George and Dragon — SP18

1937, Dec. 13
B23 SP14 5pf + 5pf brt violet 2.50 *7.50*
Never hinged 7.50
On cover 15.00
B24 SP15 10pf + 10pf dk brn 2.50 *5.75*
Never hinged 7.50
On cover 12.00
B25 SP16 15pf + 5pf bl & yel brn 2.50 *8.25*
Never hinged 7.50
On cover 15.00
B26 SP17 25pf + 10pf bl grn & grn 3.25 *11.00*
Never hinged 11.00
On cover 20.00
B27 SP18 40pf + 25pf brt car & bl 5.75 *15.00*
Never hinged 21.00
On cover 40.00
Nos. B23-B27 (5) 16.50 *47.50*
Set, never hinged 65.00
Set of 5, #B23-B27 on one 1st day cover 100.00

Surtax for winter welfare. Designs are from frieze of the Artushof.

"Peter von Danzig" Yacht Race — SP19

Ships: 10pf+5pf, Dredger Fu Shing. 15pf+10pf, S. S. Columbus. 25pf+10pf, S. S. City of Danzig. 40pf+15pf, Peter von Danzig, 1472.

1938, Nov. 28 Photo. Unwmk.
B28 SP19 5pf + 5pf dk bl grn 1.40 *1.50*
Never hinged 6.00
On cover 16.00
B29 SP19 10pf + 5pf gldn brn 1.40 *3.00*
Never hinged 6.00
On cover 20.00
B30 SP19 15pf + 10pf ol grn 1.60 *3.00*
Never hinged 7.50
On cover 12.00
B31 SP19 25pf + 10pf indigo 2.50 *4.00*
Never hinged 9.00
On cover 13.50
B32 SP19 40pf + 15pf vio brn 3.00 *6.75*
Never hinged 12.50
On cover 20.00
Nos. B28-B32 (5) 9.90 *18.25*
Set, never hinged 50.00
Set of 5, #B28-B32 on one 1st day cover 60.00

Surtax for winter welfare.

AIR POST STAMPS

No. 6 Surcharged in Blue or Carmine

1920, Sept. 29 Wmk. 125 *Perf. 14*
C1 A16 40pf on 40pf 1.25 *2.60*
Never hinged 4.50
Postally used *10.50*
On flight cover 24.00
On commercial flown cover 45.00
a. Double surcharge 160.00 *250.00*
Never hinged 450.00
C2 A16 60pf on 40pf (C) 1.25 *2.60*
Never hinged 4.50
Postally used *11.00*
On flight cover 120.00
On commercial flown cover 225.00
a. Double surcharge 125.00 *250.00*
Never hinged 350.00
C3 A16 1m on 40pf 1.25 *2.60*
Never hinged 4.50
Postally used *14.50*
On flight cover 27.50
On commercial flown cover 55.00
a. Double surcharge 125.00 250.00
Never hinged 350.00
Nos. C1-C3 (3) 3.75 *7.80*
Set, never hinged 13.50

Plane faces left on No. C2.

AP3

Plane over Danzig AP4

Wmk. (108) Upright
1921-22 Typo. *Perf. 14*
C4 AP3 40(pf) blue green .25 *.45*
Never hinged 1.20
Postally used *5.50*
On commercial flown cover 27.50
C5 AP3 60(pf) dk violet .25 *.45*
Never hinged 1.20
Postally used *4.75*
On commercial flown cover 9.50
C6 AP3 1m carmine .25 *.45*
Never hinged 1.20
Postally used *4.75*
On commercial flown cover 12.00
C7 AP3 2m org brn .25 *.45*
Never hinged 1.20
Postally used *4.75*
On commercial flown cover 12.00

Serrate Roulette 13½
Size: 34½x23mm
C8 AP4 5m violet blue 1.25 *2.25*
Never hinged 4.75
Postally used *9.50*
On commercial flown cover 20.00
C9 AP4 10m dp grn 2.00 *4.25*
Never hinged 8.00
Postally used *40.00*
On commercial flown cover 65.00
Nos. C4-C9 (6) 4.25 *8.30*
Set, never hinged 18.00

Nos. C4-C9 exist imperf. Value, each $32.50 unused, $125 never hinged.

Issued: Nos. C4-C5, C7-C8, 5/3/21. No. C6, 4/3/21. No. C9, 5/15/22.

Wmk. 108 Sideways
C4a AP3 40(pf) 25.00 *8.00*
Never hinged 55.00
C5a AP3 60(pf) 65.00 *80.00*
Never hinged 190.00
C6a AP3 1m —
C7a AP3 2m 80.00 *175.00*
Never hinged 200.00
C8a AP4 5m 1,400. *2,400.*
Never hinged *2,800.*
b. imperf *2,000.* *3,250.*
Never hinged 4,000.
Postally used —
C9a AP4 10m 24.00 *80.00*
Never hinged 60.00

Issued: Nos. C4a-C5a, C7a-C8a, 5/3/21. No. C6a, 4/3/21. No. C9a, 5/15/22.

1923 Wmk. (109) Upright *Perf. 14*
C10 AP3 40(pf) blue green .55 *1.90*
Never hinged 2.60
Postally used *240.00*
On commercial flown cover 350.00
C11 AP3 60(pf) dk violet .55 *1.90*
Never hinged 2.60
Postally used *250.00*
On commercial flown cover 350.00
a. Double impression —
C12 AP3 1m carmine .55 *1.90*
Never hinged 2.60
Postally used *140.00*
On commercial flown cover 240.00
C13 AP3 2m org brown .55 *1.90*
Never hinged 2.60
Postally used *120.00*
On commercial flown cover 160.00
C14 AP3 25m pale blue .40 *.70*
Never hinged 2.25
Postally used *4.25*
On commercial flown cover 10.00

Serrate Roulette 13½
Size: 34½x23mm
C15 AP4 5m violet blue .55 *1.00*
Never hinged 2.75
Postally used *120.00*
On commercial flown cover 200.00
C16 AP4 10m deep green .55 *1.00*
Never hinged 2.75
Postally used *120.00*
On commercial flown cover 160.00

Paper With Gray Network
C17 AP4 20m org brn .55 *1.00*
Never hinged 2.75
Postally used *27.50*
On commercial flown cover 60.00

Size: 40x23mm
C18 AP4 50m orange .40 *.70*
Never hinged 2.25
Postally used *24.00*
On commercial flown cover 40.00
C19 AP4 100m red .40 *.70*
Never hinged 2.25
Postally used *3.25*
On commercial flown cover 8.00
C20 AP4 250m dark brown .60 *.70*
Never hinged 2.25
Postally used *32.50*
On commercial flown cover 60.00
C21 AP4 500m car rose .60 *.70*
Never hinged 2.25
Postally used *24.00*
On commercial flown cover 40.00
Nos. C10-C21 (12) 6.25 *14.10*
Set, never hinged 30.00

Nos. C11, C12, C14-C21 exist imperf. Value, Nos. C11, C12, C15-C17, each $8.50 unused, $32.50 never hinged. Value, Nos. C14, C18-C21, each $40 unused, $125 never hinged.

Issued: Nos. C10, C13, C15-C16, 1/3/23. Nos. C14, C18, C20-C21, 4/27/23. Nos. C17, 1/10/23. No. C19, 2/5/23.

Nos. C18, C19 and C21 exist with wmk. sideways, both perf and imperf. Value each, $60 unused, $160 never hinged.

Network Omitted
C18a AP4 50m 20.00 *16.00*
Never hinged 55.00
Postally used *120.00*
C19a AP4 100m 8.75 *24.00*
Never hinged 24.00
Postally used *120.00*
C20a AP4 250m 8.75 *24.00*
Never hinged 24.00
Postally used *200.00*
C21a AP4 500m 14.00 16.00
Never hinged 40.00
Postally used *160.00*

Issued: Nos. C18a, C20a-C21a, 4/27/23. No. C19a, 2/5/23.

Post Horn and Airplanes — AP5

1923, Oct. 18 *Perf. 14*
Paper Without Network
C22 AP5 250,000m scarlet .35 *1.25*
Never hinged 1.10
Postally used *350.00*
On commercial flown cover 400.00
C23 AP5 500,000m scarlet .35 *1.25*
Never hinged 1.10
Postally used *350.00*
On commercial flown cover 400.00

Exist imperf. Value, each: $50 unused; $125 never hinged.

Surcharged

On 100,000m
C24 AP5 2mil m scarlet .35 *1.25*
Never hinged 1.10
Postally used *350.00*
On commercial flown cover 400.00

On 50,000m
C25 AP5 5mil m scarlet .35 *1.25*
Never hinged 1.10
Postally used *350.00*
On commercial flown cover 400.00
b. Cliché of 10,000m in sheet of 50,000m 32.50 *160.00*
Never hinged 130.00
Postally used *4,000.*
c. As "b," surcharge omitted *6,250.*
Never hinged *10,500.*

Exist imperf. Value, each $125 unused, $290 never hinged.

Nos. C24 and C25 were not regularly issued without surcharge, although examples have been passed through the post. Values: C24 unused $8.50, never hinged $32.50; C25 unused $12, never hinged $21.

Plane over Danzig
AP6 AP7

1924
C26 AP6 10(pf) vermilion 21.00 3.50
Never hinged 85.00
On commercial flown cover 13.50
C27 AP6 20(pf) carmine rose 2.10 1.50
Never hinged 6.50
On commercial flown cover 9.50
C28 AP6 40(pf) olive brown 3.00 1.75
Never hinged 9.25
On commercial flown cover 11.50
C29 AP6 1g deep green 3.00 3.00
Never hinged 9.25
On commercial flown cover 16.00

C30 AP7 2½g violet brown 17.50 *32.50*
Never hinged 65.00
On commercial flown cover 95.00
Nos. C26-C30 (5) 46.60 *42.25*
Set, never hinged 175.00

Exist imperf. Value Nos. C26, C30, $85 unused, $200 never hinged; others, each $40 unused, $110 never hinged.

Issued: Nos. C26-C27, C29, 6/6. No. C28, 6/4. No. C30, 6/7.

Nos. 193, 195, 197-199 Srchd. in Various Colors

1932 **Wmk. 125**

C31 A20 10pf on 1g (G) 9.00 *21.00*
Never hinged 40.00
On commercial flown cover 60.00
C32 A20 15pf on 2g (V) 9.00 *21.00*
Never hinged 40.00
On commercial flown cover 60.00
C33 A20 20pf on 3g (Bl) 9.00 *21.00*
Never hinged 40.00
On commercial flown cover 60.00
C34 A23 25pf on 5g (R) 9.00 *21.00*
Never hinged 40.00
On commercial flown cover 60.00
C35 A24 30pf on 10g (Br) 9.00 *21.00*
Never hinged 40.00
On commercial flown cover 60.00
Nos. C31-C35 (5) 45.00 *105.00*
Set, never hinged 200.00

Intl. Air Post Exhib. of 1932. The surcharges were variously arranged to suit the shapes and designs of the stamps. The stamps were sold at double their surcharged values, the excess being donated to the exhibition funds.

No. C31 exists with inverted surcharge and with double surcharge. Value each, $85 unused, $210 never hinged.

Airplane
AP8 AP9

1935, Oct. 24 **Wmk. 109**

C36 AP8 10pf scarlet 1.75 .85
Never hinged 7.50
On commercial flown cover 2.90
C37 AP8 15pf yellow 1.75 1.25
Never hinged 7.50
On commercial flown cover 6.00
C38 AP8 25pf dark green 1.75 1.50
Never hinged 7.50
On commercial flown cover 9.50
C39 AP8 50pf gray blue 9.00 *9.25*
Never hinged 22.50
On commercial flown cover 32.50
C40 AP9 1g magenta 3.50 *13.00*
Never hinged 16.00
On commercial flown cover 32.50
Nos. C36-C40 (5) 17.75 *25.85*
Set, never hinged 65.00
Set of 5, #C36-C40 on one 1st day cover 60.00

Nos. C36 and C40 exist imperf. Values: C36 unused $20, never hinged $62.50; C40 unused $29, never hinged $85.

See Nos. C42-C45.

Souvenir Sheet

St. Mary's Church — AP10

1937, June 6 ***Perf. 14***

C41 AP10 50pf dark grayish blue 3.75 *16.00*
Never hinged 10.50
On commerical cover 80.00
Exhibition cancellation 26.00
a. 50pf dark ultramarine 16.00 *140.00*
Never hinged 40.00
On commerical cover 150.00
Exhibition cancellation 57.50
On first day cover 115.00

C41a is the first printing (June 6); C41 is the second printing (October).

Danzig Phil. Exhib., June 6-8, 1937.

Type of 1935

1938-39 **Wmk. 237**

C42 AP8 10pf scarlet 1.25 *3.75*
Never hinged 5.25
On commercial flown cover 12.00
C43 AP8 15pf yellow ('39) 2.00 *12.00*
Never hinged 13.00
On commercial flown cover 40.00
C44 AP8 25pf dark green 1.60 *6.50*
Never hinged 7.75
On commercial flown cover 32.50
C45 AP8 50pf gray blue ('39) 4.00 *57.50*
Never hinged 19.00
On commercial flown cover 95.00
Nos. C42-C45 (4) 8.85 *79.75*
Set, never hinged 42.50

Issued: Nos. C42, C44, 7/1938. No. C43, 7/8/38. No. C44, 2/13/39.

POSTAGE DUE STAMPS

Danzig Coat of Arms — D1

1921-22 **Typo.** **Wmk. (108)** ***Perf. 14***

Paper Without Network

J1 D1 10(pf) deep violet .35 *.45*
Never hinged .90
Postally used *9.50*
On cover 47.50
J2 D1 20(pf) deep violet .35 *.45*
Never hinged .90
Postally used *9.50*
On cover 47.50
J3 D1 40(pf) deep violet .35 *.45*
Never hinged .90
Postally used *12.50*
On cover 47.50
J4 D1 60(pf) deep violet .35 *.45*
Never hinged .90
Postally used *12.50*
On cover 47.50
J5 D1 75(pf) dp violet ('22) .35 *.45*
Never hinged .90
Postally used *24.00*
On cover 95.00
J6 D1 80(pf) deep violet .35 *.45*
Never hinged .90
Postally used *12.00*
On cover 47.50
J7 D1 120(pf) deep violet .35 *.45*
Never hinged .90
Postally used *16.00*
On cover 47.50
J8 D1 200(pf) dp violet ('22) .95 *1.00*
Never hinged 3.25
Postally used *32.50*
On cover 80.00
J9 D1 240(pf) deep violet .35 *1.00*
Never hinged 1.50
Postally used *24.00*
On cover 60.00
J10 D1 300(pf) dp violet ('22) .95 *1.00*
Never hinged 3.25
Postally used *21.00*
On cover 80.00
J11 D1 400(pf) deep violet .95 *1.00*
Never hinged 3.25
Postally used *21.00*
On cover 95.00
J12 D1 500(pf) deep violet .95 *1.00*
Never hinged 3.25
Postally used *21.00*
On cover 40.00
J13 D1 800(pf) deep violet ('22) .95 *1.00*
Never hinged 3.25
Postally used *55.00*
On cover 105.00
J14 D1 20m dp violet ('22) .95 *1.00*
Never hinged 3.25
Postally used *45.00*
On cover 95.00
Nos. J1-J14 (14) 8.50 *10.15*
Set, never hinged 27.50

Nos. J1-J14 exist imperf. Value, each $30 unused, $75 never hinged.

1923 **Wmk. 109 Sideways**

J15 D1 100(pf) deep violet .60 *.75*
Never hinged 2.25
Postally used *725.00*
On cover *800.00*
J16 D1 200(pf) deep violet 2.50 *3.75*
Never hinged 7.50
Postally used *1,050.*
On cover *1,200.*
J17 D1 300(pf) deep violet .60 *.75*
Never hinged 2.25
Postally used *1,050.*
On cover *1,200.*
J18 D1 400(pf) deep violet .60 *.75*
Never hinged 2.25
Postally used *1,050.*
On cover *1,200.*
J19 D1 500(pf) deep violet .60 *.75*
Never hinged 2.00
Postally used *240.00*
On cover *350.00*
a. Wmk. Upright .65 1.10
Never hinged 2.25
Postally used *175.00*
On cover *250.00*
J20 D1 800(pf) deep violet 1.25 *3.75*
Never hinged 7.50
Postally used *1,750.*
On cover *2,000.*
J21 D1 10m deep violet .60 *1.00*
Never hinged 2.25
Postally used *24.00*
On cover 60.00
a. Wmk. Upright .60 1.00
Never hinged 2.25
Postally used *160.00*
On cover 200.00
J22 D1 20m deep violet .60 *.75*
Never hinged 2.25
Postally used *65.00*
On cover *110.00*
J23 D1 50m deep violet .60 *.75*
Never hinged 2.25
Postally used *16.00*
On cover *80.00*

Paper With Gray Network

J24 D1 100m deep violet .60 *1.00*
Never hinged 2.25
Postally used *24.00*
On cover 80.00
J25 D1 500m deep violet .60 *1.00*
Never hinged 2.25
Postally used *16.00*
On cover 80.00
Nos. J15-J25 (11) 9.15 15.00
Set, never hinged 25.00

Nos. J15, J17, J22-J25 exist imperf. Value each, $12.50 unused, $40 never hinged.

Issued: Nos. J15, J21, J23, 1/10. Nos. J16-J20, J22, 1/1923. Nos. J19a, J21a, J24-J25, 4/3.

Nos. J22-J23 and Type of 1923 Surcharged

1923, Oct. 1

Paper without Network

J26 D1 5000m on 50m .40 *.75*
Never hinged 2.00
Postally used *1,250.*
On cover —
J27 D1 10,000m on 20m .40 *.75*
Never hinged 2.00
Postally used *1,250.*
On cover —
J28 D1 50,000m on 500m .40 *.75*
Never hinged 2.00
Postally used *1,250.*
On cover —
J29 D1 100,000m on 20m .85 *1.25*
Never hinged 2.00
Postally used *1,300.*
On cover —
Nos. J26-J29 (4) 2.05 *3.50*
Set, never hinged 8.00

On No. J26 the numerals of the surcharge are all of the larger size.

A 1000(m) on 100m deep violet was prepared but not issued. Value, $145, never hinged $350.

Nos. J26-J28 exist imperf. Value each, $18 unused, $45 never hinged.

Danzig Coat of Arms — D2

1923-28 **Wmk. 110**

J30 D2 5(pf) blue & blk .85 .75
Never hinged 2.50
On cover 35.00
J31 D2 10(pf) blue & blk .40 *.75*
Never hinged 2.50
On cover 24.00
J32 D2 15(pf) blue & blk 1.25 1.10
Never hinged 5.25
On cover 60.00
J33 D2 20(pf) blue & blk 1.25 *2.00*
Never hinged 4.00
On cover 72.50
J34 D2 30(pf) blue & blk 9.00 2.00
Never hinged 21.00
On cover 72.50
J35 D2 40(pf) blue & blk 2.10 *3.00*
Never hinged 6.00
On cover 120.00
J36 D2 50(pf) blue & blk 2.10 *2.25*
Never hinged 6.00
On cover 65.00
J37 D2 60(pf) blue & blk 13.00 *18.00*
Never hinged 37.50
On cover 240.00
J38 D2 100(pf) blue & blk 17.50 9.75
Never hinged 55.00
On cover 140.00
J39 D2 3g blue & car 10.00 *40.00*
Never hinged 40.00
On cover 350.00
a. "Guldeu" instead of "Gulden" 325.00 *1,050.*
Never hinged 1,050.
Nos. J30-J39 (10) 57.45 *79.60*
Set, never hinged 225.00

Used values of Nos. J30-J39 are for postally used stamps.

See Nos. J43-J47.

Postage Due Stamps of 1923 Issue Surcharged in Red

1932, Dec. 20

J40 D2 5pf on 40(pf) 4.25 *7.50*
Never hinged 11.00
On cover 175.00
J41 D2 10pf on 60(pf) 32.50 9.00
Never hinged 110.00
On cover 160.00
J42 D2 20pf on 100(pf) 2.75 *7.50*
Never hinged 11.00
On cover 175.00
Nos. J40-J42 (3) 39.50 *24.00*
Set, never hinged 160.00

Type of 1923

1938-39 **Wmk. 237** ***Perf. 14***

J43 D2 10(pf) bl & blk ('39) 1.25 *62.50*
Never hinged 5.50
On cover *325.00*
J44 D2 30(pf) bl & blk 2.25 *50.00*
Never hinged 8.00
On cover *325.00*
J45 D2 40(pf) bl & blk ('39) 6.75 *100.00*
Never hinged 27.50
On cover *600.00*
J46 D2 60(pf) bl & blk ('39) 6.75 *100.00*
Never hinged 40.00
On cover *600.00*
J47 D2 100(pf) bl & blk 11.00 *72.50*
Never hinged 40.00
On cover *725.00*
Nos. J43-J47 (5) 28.00 *385.00*
Set, never hinged 125.00

OFFICIAL STAMPS

Regular Issues of 1921-22 Overprinted — a

1921-22 **Wmk. 108** ***Perf. 14x14½***

O1 A11 5(pf) orange .25 .25
Never hinged .60
Postally used *27.50*
On cover 110.00
O2 A11 10(pf) dark brown .25 .25
Never hinged .60
Postally used *6.50*
On cover 72.50
a. Inverted overprint 60.00
Never hinged 170.00
O3 A11 15(pf) green .25 .25
Never hinged .60
Postally used *6.50*
On cover 72.50
O4 A11 20(pf) slate .25 .25
Never hinged .60
Postally used *6.50*
On cover 80.00
O5 A11 25(pf) dark green .25 .25
Never hinged .60
Postally used *6.00*
On cover 72.50
a. Pair, one without oveprint 170.00
Never hinged 425.00
O6 A11 30(pf) blue & car .60 .60
Never hinged 1.35
Postally used *6.00*
On cover 72.50
O7 A11 40(pf) grn & car .25 .25
Never hinged .60
Postally used *12.00*
On cover 72.50
O8 A11 50(pf) dk grn & car .25 .25
Never hinged .60
Postally used *5.25*
On cover 55.00

O9 A11 60(pf) carmine .25 .25
Never hinged .60
Postally used *4.75*
On cover 52.50
O10 A11 75(pf) dp vio .25 *.40*
Never hinged .75
Postally used *2.75*
On cover 40.00
O11 A11 80(pf) black & car .85 .85
Never hinged 2.90
Postally used *16.00*
On cover 72.50
O12 A11 80(pf) green .25 *2.40*
Never hinged .75
Postally used *210.00*
On cover *325.00*

Paper With Faint Gray Network

O14 A11 1m org & car .25 .25
Never hinged .75
Postally used *3.25*
On cover 40.00
O15 A11 1.20m blue violet 1.25 1.25
Never hinged 4.00
Postally used *24.00*
On cover 95.00
O16 A11 1.25m vio & car .25 *.40*
Never hinged .75
Postally used *80.00*
On cover —
O17 A11 1.50m slate gray .25 *.40*
Never hinged .90
Postally used *7.25*
On cover 40.00
O18 A11 2m gray & car 16.00 12.00
Never hinged 62.50
Postally used *60.00*
On cover 120.00
a. Inverted overprint 110.00
Never hinged 250.00
O19 A11 2m car rose .25 *.40*
Never hinged .75
Postally used *3.25*
On cover 47.50
O20 A11 2.40m dk brn & car 1.25 *2.40*
Never hinged 9.00
Postally used *65.00*
On cover 120.00
O21 A11 3m violet & car 8.50 *10.00*
Never hinged 37.50
Postally used *55.00*
On cover 110.00
O22 A11 3m car lake .25 *.40*
Never hinged .90
Postally used *12.00*
On cover 47.50
O23 A11 4m dk blue 1.25 .85
Never hinged 9.00
Postally used *75.00*
On cover 120.00
O24 A11 5m dp grn .25 *.40*
Never hinged .90
Postally used *32.50*
On cover 80.00
O25 A11 6m car lake .25 *.40*
Never hinged .90
Postally used *14.50*
On cover 72.50
O26 A11 10m orange .25 *.40*
Never hinged .90
Postally used *10.50*
On cover 60.00
O27 A11 20m org brn .25 *.40*
Never hinged .90
Postally used *20.00*
On cover 80.00
Nos. O1-O27 (26) 34.45 *36.20*
Set, never hinged 175.00

Double overprints exist on Nos. O1-O2, O5-O7, O10 and O12.

Issued: Nos. O10, O12, O16-O17, O19-O20, O22-O27, 1922. Values start at $30 each. Nos. O1-O4, O8, O10-O14 exist imperf. Values start at $40 each.

Same Overprint on No. 96

O28 A11 6m on 3m .35 *.75*
Never hinged 1.00
Postally used *14.50*
On cover 72.50
a. Inverted overprint 30.00
Never hinged 85.00

No. 77 Overprinted

Serrate Roulette 13½

1922 Wmk. 108 Sideways

O29 A12 5m grn, red & blk 3.75 *6.00*
Never hinged 18.00
Postally used *105.00*
On cover *160.00*
a. Wmk. upright 4.25 *10.50*
Never hinged 20.00
Postally used *95.00*
On cover *140.00*

Nos. 99-103, 106-107 Overprinted Type "a"

1922-23 Wmk. 109 *Perf. 14*

O30 A11 4m dark blue .25 *.60*
Never hinged 1.40
Postally used *35.00*
On cover 120.00
O31 A11 5m dark green .25 *.60*
Never hinged 1.40
Postally used *42.50*
On cover 100.00
O32 A11 10m orange .25 *.60*
Never hinged 1.40
Postally used *8.00*
On cover 60.00
O33 A11 20m orange brn .25 *.60*
Never hinged 1.40
Postally used *8.00*
On cover 87.50
O34 A15 50m pale blue & red .25 *.60*
Never hinged 1.40
Postally used *7.25*
On cover 32.50
O35 A15a 100m dk grn & red .25 *.60*
Never hinged 1.40
Postally used *12.50*
On cover 60.00

Nos. 113-115, 118-120 Overprinted Type "a"

O36 A15 50m pale blue .25 *.75*
Never hinged 1.40
Postally used *1,350.*
On cover *1,600.*
a. Inverted overprint 25.00
Never hinged 62.50
O37 A15a 100m dark green .25 *.75*
Never hinged 1.40
Postally used *350.00*
On cover 525.00
O38 A15 200m orange .25 *.75*
Never hinged 1.40
Postally used *32.50*
On cover 200.00
a. Inverted overprint 25.00
Never hinged 62.50

Paper With Gray Network

O39 A17 300m bl grn & red .25 *.60*
Never hinged 1.40
Postally used *325.00*
On cover 475.00
O40 A17 500m gray & red .25 *.75*
Never hinged 1.40
Postally used *450.00*
On cover *800.00*
a. Network omitted 14.00 *5.75*
Never hinged 37.50
O41 A17 1000m brn & red .25 *.75*
Never hinged 1.40
Postally used *95.00*
On cover 240.00
a. Network omitted 14.50 *8.00*
Never hinged 40.00
Nos. O30-O41 (12) 3.00 *7.95*
Set, never hinged 16.80

Issued: No. O30, 12/16/22. Nos. O31-O34, 1/10/23. Nos. O36-O40, 7/20/23. No. O41, 7/29/23.

Regular Issue of 1924-25 Overprinted

1924-25 *Perf. 14x14½*

O42 A19 5pf red orange 2.10 *3.25*
Never hinged 6.75
On cover 24.00
a. 5pf orange 15.00 *9.50*
Never hinged 52.50
On cover 40.00
O43 A19 10pf green 2.10 *9.00*
Never hinged 22.50
On cover 22.50
a. 10pf dark green 2.00 *3.00*
Never hinged 6.25
On cover 13.50
O44 A19 15pf gray 2.10 3.25
Never hinged 7.00
On cover 16.00
a. 15pf dk greenish gray 5.25 4.25
Never hinged 17.50
On cover 27.50
O45 A19 15pf red 19.00 10.00
Never hinged 60.00
On cover 20.00
O46 A19 20pf car & red 2.10 2.10
Never hinged 7.00
On cover 20.00
O47 A19 25pf slate & red 19.00 27.50
Never hinged 55.00
On cover 120.00
O48 A19 30pf green & red 3.00 *3.75*
Never hinged 8.50
On cover 24.00
a. 30pf dk grn & rose red 27.50 11.00
Never hinged 110.00
On cover 60.00
O49 A19 35pf ultra 60.00 50.00
Never hinged 175.00
On cover 105.00
O50 A19 40pf dk bl & dull bl 7.00 *8.50*
Never hinged 19.00
On cover 72.50
O51 A19 50pf dp blue & red 21.00 *42.50*
Never hinged 65.00
On cover 275.00
O52 A19 75pf violet & red 42.50 *120.00*
Never hinged 150.00
On cover 325.00
Nos. O42-O52 (11) 179.90 *279.85*
Set, never hinged 640.00

Double overprints exist on Nos. O42-O44, O47, O50-O52.

Issued: Nos. O42-O43, O44a, O46, O50, 3/1/24. Nos. O42a, O45, O49, 1925. Nos. O48, O51-O52, 3/12/24.

DENMARK

'den-,märk

LOCATION — Northern part of a peninsula which separates the North and Baltic Seas, and includes the surrounding islands
GOVT. — Kingdom
AREA — 16,631 sq. mi.
POP. — 5,112,130 (1984)
CAPITAL — Copenhagen

96 Skilling = 1 Rigsbank Daler
100 Ore = 1 Krone (1875)

Values for unused stamps are for examples with original gum as defined in the catalogue introduction. Very fine examples of Nos. 9-37 and O1-O9 will have perforations clear of the framelines but with the design noticeably off center. Well centered stamps are quite scarce and will command substantial premiums.

Watermarks

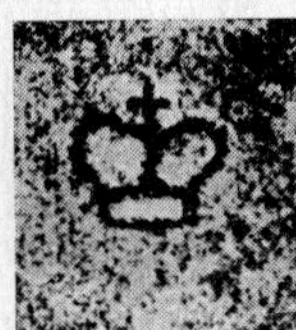
Wmk. 111 — Small Crown

Wmk. 112 — Crown

Wmk. 113 — Crown

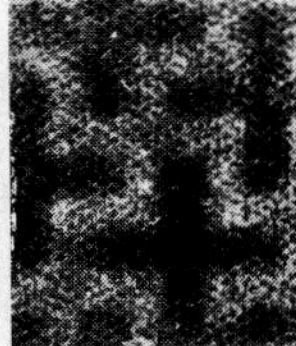
Wmk. 114 — Multiple Crosses

A1

Royal Emblems — A2

1851 Typo. Wmk. 111 *Imperf.*
With Yellow Brown Burelage

1 A1 2rs blue *3,500.* 1,000.
On cover 2,200.
a. First printing *8,250.* *2,400.*
On cover 7,250.
2 A2 4rs brown 600.00 40.00
On cover 120.00
a. First printing 600.00 40.00
On cover 160.00
b. 4rs yellow brown 875.00 55.00
On cover 125.00
c. 4rs chestnut (4th printing) 2,400. 250.00
On cover 500.00

Full margins = 1mm.

The first printing of Nos. 1 and 2 had the burelage printed from a copper plate, giving a clear impression with the lines in slight relief. The subsequent impressions had the burelage typographed, with the lines fainter and not rising above the surface of the paper.

Nos. 1-2 were reprinted in 1885 and 1901 on heavy yellowish paper, unwatermarked and imperforate, with a brown burelage. No. 1 was also reprinted without burelage, on both yellowish and white paper. Value for least costly reprint of No. 1, $50.

No. 2 was reprinted in 1951 in 10 shades with "Colour Specimen 1951" printed on the back. It was also reprinted in 1961 in 2 shades without burelage and with "Farve Nytryk 1961" printed on the back. Value for least costly reprint of No. 2, $8.50.

Numeral Postmarks on No. 2

Values in the left column are for very fine used stamps with clear, legible numeral cancels. Values in the right column are for very fine stamps with clear, legible numeral cancels on complete covers.

1 Kjobenhavn	40.00	120.00
2 Hamburg	350.00	—
3 Lübeck	500.00	—
4 Aalborg	40.00	145.00
5 Aarhus	40.00	120.00
6 Aabenraa	52.50	150.00
7 Assens	52.50	150.00
8 Bogense	52.50	145.00
9 Bredstedt	95.00	375.00
10 Burg	62.50	200.00
11 Cappeln	62.50	200.00
12 Christiansfeld	62.50	200.00
13 Ebeltoft	52.50	135.00
14 Eckernförde	52.50	150.00
15 Faaborg	52.50	150.00
16 Flensburg	52.50	135.00
17 Fredericia	52.50	135.00
18 Frederiksborg	52.50	150.00
19 Frederikshavn	52.50	135.00
20 Frederikssund	52.50	135.00
21 Friedrichstad	62.50	135.00
22 Grenaae	50.00	135.00
23 Haderslev	50.00	135.00
24 Helsingor	40.00	145.00
25 Horsholm	52.50	135.00
26 Hjoring	52.50	135.00
27 Hobroe	52.50	135.00
28 Holbek	52.50	135.00
29 Holstebro	52.50	135.00
30 Horsens	52.50	135.00
31 Husum	62.50	225.00
32 Kallundborg	52.50	150.00
33 Kjerteminde	52.50	150.00
34 Kbhvns. jernb. postkontor	40.00	150.00
35 Kjoge	52.50	145.00
36 Kolding	52.50	145.00
37 Korsoer	52.50	145.00
38 Lemvig	52.50	150.00
39 Lyngbye	100.00	160.00
40 Logstoer	52.50	140.00
41 Mariboe	52.50	140.00
42 Middelfart	52.50	140.00
43 Nakskov	52.50	140.00
44 Nestved	52.50	150.00
45 Nibe	52.50	140.00
46 Nyborg	52.50	140.00
47 Nykjobing, Falster	52.50	140.00
48 Nykjobing, Jylland	62.50	200.00
49 Nykjobing, Sjaelland	52.50	150.00
50 Nysted	52.50	125.00
51 Odense	40.00	125.00
52 Praestöe	52.50	190.00
53 Randers	40.00	140.00
54 Rendsburg	52.50	190.00
55 Ribe	52.50	175.00
56 Ringkjobing	52.50	140.00
57 Ringsted	52.50	140.00
58 Roeskilde	40.00	135.00
59 Rudkjobing	52.50	140.00
60 Rodby	52.50	160.00
61 Ronne	52.50	210.00
62 Saxkjobing	52.50	160.00
63 Skanderborg	52.50	140.00
64 Skive	52.50	140.00
65 Slagelse	52.50	140.00
66 Schleswig	52.50	150.00
67 Soro	52.50	140.00
68 Stege	52.50	140.00
69 Stubbekjobing	52.50	130.00
70 Svendborg	52.50	150.00
71 Sonderborg	62.50	150.00
72 Thisted	52.50	140.00
73 Tonder	52.50	260.00
74 Tonning	62.50	260.00
75 Varde	52.50	175.00
76 Vejle	52.50	130.00
77 Viborg	52.50	125.00
78 Vordingborg	52.50	125.00
79 Wyck	95.00	300.00
80 Aeroeskjobing	95.00	750.00
81 Aarosund	750.00	—
82 Frederiksvaerk	62.50	130.00
83 Garding	72.50	275.00
84 Herning	52.50	130.00
85 Hojer	150.00	550.00
86 Leck	100.00	375.00
87 Logumkloster	62.50	260.00
88 Mariager	52.50	150.00
89 Marstal	125.00	475.00
90 Ronnede	52.50	150.00
91 Silkeborg	52.50	140.00
92 Skjelskjor	52.50	125.00
93 Storehedinge	52.50	150.00
94 Taastrup	92.50	450.00
95 Aakirkeby	190.00	1,500.
96 Allinge	190.00	1,000.
97 Augustenborg	140.00	1,200.
98 Fjerritslev	52.50	125.00
99 Fredensborg	52.50	150.00
100 Gaabense	95.00	125.00
101 Graasten	75.00	225.00
102 Gudhjem	*2,000.*	—
103 Hasle	260.00	—
104 Nexo	160.00	450.00
105 Nordborg	250.00	550.00
106 Skagen	52.50	150.00
107 Skjernbro	52.50	160.00
108 Skodborghuus	—	—
109 Snoghoi	—	—
110 Stokkemarke	100.00	825.00
111 Svaneke	125.00	1,000.
112 Saeby	52.50	175.00
113 Altona	52.50	130.00
114 Elmshorn	625.00	—
115 Eutin	100.00	375.00
116 Glückstadt	52.50	260.00
117 Heide	62.50	325.00
118 Heiligenhafen	52.50	375.00
119 Itzehoe	52.50	160.00
120 Kellinghusen	95.00	475.00
121 Kiel	52.50	130.00
122 Lütjenburg	95.00	525.00
123 Meldorf	95.00	425.00
124 Neumünster	62.50	160.00
125 Neustadt	150.00	425.00
126 Nortoft	160.00	—
127 Oldenburg	62.50	275.00
128 Oldesloe	75.00	375.00
129 Pinneberg	75.00	275.00
130 Plön	75.00	275.00
131 Preetz	62.50	225.00
132 Remmels	250.00	550.00
133 Segeberg	62.50	175.00
134 Uetersen	75.00	175.00

135 Ahrensbock 160.00 350.00
136 Ahrensburg 325.00 1,100.
137 Barmstedt 125.00 875.00
138 Bornhöved 72.50 450.00
139 Bramstedt 100.00 300.00
140 Brunsbüttel 100.00 300.00
141 Crempe 425.00 —
142 Horst 750.00
143 Lunden 175.00 325.00
144 Reinbeck 225.00 325.00
145 Schwartau 175.00 300.00
146 Wandsbeck 125.00 275.00
147 Wilster 75.00 175.00
148 Lauenburg 75.00 375.00
149 Mölln 175.00 400.00
150 Ratzeburg 190.00 275.00
151 Büchen 525.00 1,300.
152 Schwarzenbeck 425.00 900.00
153 Friedrichsruhe 950.00 1,275.
154 L.P. No. 5 Blankenese (Blankenese-Altona) 325.00 1,275.
155 Bordesholm 190.00 1,275.
156 L.P. No. 2 (Hanerau-Itzenhoe) 325.00 1,100.
157 L.P. No. 4 (Kaltenkirchen-Bramstedt) 525.00 1,100.
158 Lensahn 525.00 1,100.
159 L.P. No. 3 (Schonfeld-Itzenhoe) — 1,150.
160 L.P. Schönwalde 950.00 1,275.
161 Bahnhof Rendsburg 95.00 350.00
162 Altona Bahnhof 95.00 200.00
163 Bandholm 95.00 175.00
164 Vedbaeck
165 Slangerup — —
166 Humlebaek 275.00 750.00
167 Rungsted — —
168 Holstenske Jb. postkontor — —
169 Holstenske Jb. postkontor — —
170 Holstenske Jb. postkontor 275.00 925.00
171 Gettorf 525.00 1,550.
172 Marne 325.00 650.00
173 Trittau 325.00 1,750.

The initials "L.P." are short for "Land Postrute," which means a rural post route.

Dotting in Spandrels — A3

1854-57

3 A3 2s blue ('55) 75.00 60.00
Never hinged 150.00
On cover 210.00
4 A3 4s brown 325.00 15.00
Never hinged 650.00
On cover 30.00
a. 4s yellow brown 350.00 15.00
Never hinged 700.00
On cover 30.00
5 A3 8s green ('57) 300.00 67.50
Never hinged 600.00
On cover 300.00
On cover, single franking 350.00
a. 8s yellow green 300.00 80.00
Never hinged 600.00
On cover 300.00
On cover, single franking 350.00
6 A3 16s gray lilac ('57) 525.00 190.00
Never hinged 1,100.
On cover 900.00
On cover, single franking 1,000.
Nos. 3-6 (4) 1,225. 332.50

Full margins = 1mm.

See No. 10. For denominations in cents see Danish West Indies Nos. 1-4.

Wavy Lines in Spandrels — A4

1858-62

7 A4 4s yellow brown 65.00 8.50
Never hinged 140.00
On cover 24.00
a. 4s brown 67.50 8.00
Never hinged 150.00
On cover 24.00
b. Wmk. 112 ('62) 62.50 9.00
Never hinged 140.00
On cover 27.50
8 A4 8s green 800.00 82.50
Never hinged 2,000.
On cover 475.00
On cover, single franking 540.00

Full margins = 1mm.

Nos. 2 to 8 inclusive are known with unofficial perforation 12 or 13, and Nos. 4, 5, 7 and 8 with unofficial roulette 9½.

Nos. 3, 6-8 were reprinted in 1885 on heavy yellowish paper, unwatermarked, imperforate and without burelage. Nos. 4-5 were reprinted in 1924 on white paper, unwatermarked, imperforate, gummed and without burelage. Value for No. 3, $15; Nos. 4-5, each $110; No. 6, $20; Nos. 7-8, each $15.

1863 Wmk. 112 *Rouletted 11*

9 A4 4s brown 100.00 15.00
Never hinged 175.00
On cover 35.00
a. 4s deep brown 100.00 15.00
Never hinged 175.00
On cover 35.00
b. 4s red brown 100.00 15.00
Never hinged 175.00
On cover 35.00

10 A3 16s violet 1,400. 650.00
On cover 4,750.
On cover, single franking 5,400.

Royal Emblems — A5

1864-68 *Perf. 13*

11 A5 2s blue ('65) 65.00 35.00
Never hinged 210.00
On cover 72.50
12 A5 3s red vio ('65) 80.00 75.00
Never hinged 260.00
On cover 350.00
On cover, single franking 725.00
13 A5 4s red 40.00 8.00
Never hinged 85.00
On cover 18.00
14 A5 8s bister ('68) 275.00 95.00
Never hinged 725.00
On cover 350.00
15 A5 16s olive green 475.00 175.00
Never hinged 1,200.
On cover 350.00
On cover, single franking 540.00
Nos. 11-15 (5) 935.00 388.00

Nos. 11-15 were reprinted in 1886 on heavy yellowish paper, unwatermarked, imperforate and without gum. The reprints of all values except the 4s were printed in two vertical rows of six, inverted with respect to each other, so that horizontal pairs are always tête bêche. Value $12 each.

Nos. 13 and 15 were reprinted in 1942 with printing on the back across each horizontal row: "Nytryk 1942. G. A. Hagemann: Danmarks og Vestindiens Frimaerker, Bind 2." Value, $70 each.

Imperf, single

11a A5 2s blue 95.00 95.00
As "a," pair 240.00 240.00
12a A5 3s red violet 140.00
As "a," pair 475.00
13a A5 4s red 77.50 90.00
On cover *2,000.*
As "a," pair 240.00 —
14a A5 8s bister 375.00
As "a," pair 900.00
15a A5 16s olive green 450.00
As "a," pair 975.00

1870 *Perf. 12½*

11b A5 2s blue 275.00 350.00
Never hinged 600.00
On cover 500.00
12b A5 3s red violet 475.00 650.00
Never hinged 950.00
On cover 1,200.
14b A5 8s bister 475.00 475.00
Never hinged 1,300.
On cover 1,100.
15b A5 16s olive green 725.00 *1,450.*
Never hinged 1,450.
On cover 3,600.
Nos. 11b-15b (4) 1,950. 2,925.

A6

Normal Frame Inverted Frame

The arabesques in the corners have a main stem and a branch. When the frame is in normal position, in the upper left corner the branch leaves the main stem half way between two little leaflets. In the lower right corner the branch starts at the foot of the second leaflet. When the frame is inverted the corner designs are, of course, transposed.

1870-71 Wmk. 112 *Perf. 14x13½*

Paper Varying from Thin to Thick

16 A6 2s gray & ultra ('71) 70.00 27.50
Never hinged 180.00
On cover 72.50
a. 2s gray & blue 70.00 27.50
Never hinged 180.00
On cover 72.50
17 A6 3s gray & brt lil ('71) 100.00 110.00
Never hinged 240.00
On cover 200.00
18 A6 4s gray & car 40.00 10.00
Never hinged 180.00
On cover 21.00
19 A6 8s gray & brn ('71) 200.00 75.00
Never hinged 725.00
On cover 240.00
20 A6 16s gray & grn ('71) 275.00 175.00
Never hinged 850.00
On cover 725.00
On cover, single franking 900.00

Perf. 12½

21 A6 2s gray & bl ('71) 2,000. *3,250.*
Never hinged 6,000.
On cover 6,500.
On cover, single franking 7,000.
22 A6 4s gray & car 150.00 125.00
Never hinged 450.00
On cover 150.00
24 A6 48s brn & lilac 450.00 275.00
Never hinged 1,300.
On cover *2,400.*
On cover, single franking *2,600.*

Nos. 16-20, 24 were reprinted in 1886 on thin white paper, unwatermarked, imperforate and without gum. These were printed in sheets of 10 in which 1 stamp has the normal frame (value $32.50 each) and 9 the inverted (value $11 each).

Imperf, single

16b A6 2s *250.*
17a A6 3s *240.*
18a A6 4s *200.*
19a A6 8s *250.*
20a A6 16s *400.*
24a A6 48s *425.* —

Inverted Frame

16c A6 2s 1,000. 775.
17b A6 3s 2,500. 2,000.
18b A6 4s 775. 87.50
On cover *250.*
19b A6 8s 1,750. 900.
20b A6 16s 2,000. 1,750.
24b A6 48s 2,750. 1,900.

1875-79 *Perf. 14x13½*

25 A6 3o gray blue & gray 18.00 15.00
Never hinged 36.00
On cover 37.50
On cover, single franking 75.00
a. 1st "A" of "DANMARK" missing 60.00 150.00
Never hinged 190.00
b. Imperf *750.00*
c. Inverted frame 18.00 16.00
Never hinged 36.00
On cover 50.00
26 A6 4o slate & blue 25.00 .50
Never hinged 85.00
On cover 3.75
a. 4o gray & blue 25.00 1.10
Never hinged 95.00
On cover 3.75
b. 4o slate & ultra 90.00 17.00
Never hinged 425.00
On cover 40.00
c. 4o gray & ultra 75.00 16.00
Never hinged 425.00
On cover 40.00
d. Imperf 75.00 —
On cover —
Pair —
e. As #26, inverted frame 25.00 .50
Never hinged 85.00
On cover 3.50
f. As "b," inverted frame 400.00 240.00
On cover —
27 A6 5o rose & blue ('79) 30.00 72.50
Never hinged 60.00
On cover 725.00
On cover, single franking 900.00
a. Ball of lower curve of large "5" missing 125.00 300.00
Never hinged 300.00
b. Inverted frame 1,000. *2,250.*
Never hinged 2,100.
28 A6 8o slate & car 22.50 .50
Never hinged 105.00
On cover 2.75
a. 8o gray & carmine 75.00 5.00
Never hinged 260.00
On cover 16.00
b. Imperf 150.00 —
On cover —
Pair —
c. Inverted frame 22.50 .50
Never hinged 95.00
On cover 2.75
d. 8o gray & aniline red ('86) 72.50 9.50
Never hinged 260.00
On cover 25.00
e. As "d," imperf 150.00 —
On cover —
f. As "d," inverted frame (pos. 69) 750.00 190.00
29 A6 12o sl & dull lake 10.00 4.00
Never hinged 20.00
On cover 55.00
On cover, single franking 72.50
a. 12o gray & bright lilac 65.00 8.00
Never hinged 180.00
On cover 72.50
b. 12o gray & dull magenta 72.50 10.00
Never hinged 180.00
On cover 95.00
c. Inverted frame 14.00 4.00
Never hinged 35.00
On cover 42.50
30 A6 16o slate & brn 77.50 6.50
Never hinged 220.00
On cover 47.50
On cover, single franking 77.50
a. 16o light gray & brown 77.50 17.00
Never hinged 220.00
On cover 52.50
On cover, single franking 85.00
b. Inverted frame 52.50 4.50
Never hinged 145.00
On cover 52.50
c. As "a," inverted frame 120.00 45.00
Never hinged 250.00
On cover 120.00

31 A6 20o rose & gray 90.00 32.50
Never hinged 425.00
On cover 175.00
a. 20o carmine & gray 90.00 32.50
Never hinged 350.00
On cover 130.00
b. Inverted frame 90.00 32.50
Never hinged 350.00
On cover 130.00
32 A6 25o gray & green 65.00 40.00
Never hinged 140.00
On cover 260.00
On parcel post receipt card 240.00
a. Inverted frame 77.50 62.50
Never hinged 325.00
On cover 450.00
33 A6 50o brown & vio 70.00 37.50
Never hinged 225.00
On cover 240.00
On parcel post receipt card 190.00
a. 50o brown & blue violet 400.00 175.00
Never hinged 1,000.
On cover 1,200.
b. Inverted frame 70.00 32.50
Never hinged 240.00
On cover 225.00
34 A6 100o gray & org ('77) 110.00 60.00
Never hinged 350.00
On cover 300.00
On parcel post receipt card 300.00
a. Imperf, single 375.00
b. Inverted frame 150.00 60.00
Never hinged 425.00
On cover 275.00
c. 100o greenish gray & orange yellow ('87) 130.00 60.00
Never hinged 350.00
On cover 290.00
d. 100o bluish gray & orange yellow ('91) 130.00 60.00
Never hinged 350.00
On cover 350.00
Nos. 25-34 (10) 518.00 269.00
Set, never hinged 1,625.

The stamps of this issue on thin semi-transparent paper are far scarcer than those on thicker paper.

See Nos. 41-42, 44, 46-47, 50-52. For surcharges see Nos. 55, 79-80, 136.

Arms — A7

Two types of numerals in corners

Small Numerals

Large Numerals

1882

Small Corner Numerals

35 A7 5o green 240.00 100.00
Never hinged 725.00
On cover 950.00
On cover, single franking 1,100.
37 A7 20o blue 190.00 70.00
Never hinged 650.00
On cover 160.00

1884-88

Larger Corner Numerals

38 A7 5o green 15.00 3.50
Never hinged 75.00
On cover 18.00
a. Imperf —
39 A7 10o carmine ('85) 16.00 2.50
Never hinged 95.00
On cover 18.00
a. Small numerals in corners ('88) 550.00 *725.00*
Never hinged 1,200.
On cover *3,000.*
b. Imperf, single 175.00
c. Pair, Nos. 39, 39a 600.00 *875.00*
Never hinged 1,200.
40 A7 20o blue 30.00 5.00
Never hinged 110.00
On cover 24.00
a. Pair, Nos. 37, 40 400.00 *875.00*
Never hinged 825.00
On cover 2,750.
b. Imperf —
Nos. 38-40 (3) 61.00 11.00
Set, never hinged 285.00

Stamps with large corner numerals have white line around crown and lower oval touches frame.

The plate for No. 39, was damaged and 3 clichés in the bottom row were replaced by clichés for post cards, which had small numerals in the corners.

Two clichés with small numerals were inserted in the plate of No. 40.

See Nos. 43, 45, 48-49, 53-54. For surcharge see No. 56.

1895-1901 Wmk. 112 *Perf. 13*

41 A6 3o blue & gray 10.00 7.25
Never hinged 21.00
On cover 24.00

42 A6 4o slate & bl ('96) 4.50 .40
Never hinged 10.50
On cover 2.40
43 A7 5o green 12.00 .75
Never hinged 35.00
On cover 3.00
44 A6 8o slate & car 4.50 .45
Never hinged 12.00
On cover 2.40
45 A7 10o rose car 24.00 .65
Never hinged 60.00
On cover 4.00
46 A6 12o sl & dull lake 7.00 4.00
Never hinged 15.00
On cover 47.50
47 A6 16o slate & brown 19.00 4.50
Never hinged 35.00
On cover 47.50
48 A7 20o blue 30.00 2.40
Never hinged 85.00
On cover 12.00
49 A7 24o brown ('01) 7.00 6.00
Never hinged 18.00
On cover 120.00
On cover, single franking 240.00
50 A6 25o gray & grn ('98) 110.00 19.50
Never hinged 240.00
On cover 150.00
51 A6 50o brown & vio ('97) 60.00 24.00
Never hinged 150.00
On cover 140.00
On cover, single franking 300.00
52 A6 100o slate & org 90.00 35.00
Never hinged 200.00
On cover 140.00
On cover, single franking 300.00
Nos. 41-52 (12) 378.00 104.90
Set, never hinged 875.00

Inverted Frame

41b A6 3o 12.00 7.00
Never hinged 24.00
On cover 19.00
42a A6 4o 4.50 .45
Never hinged 10.50
On cover 2.40
44a A6 8o 4.50 .50
Never hinged 12.00
On cover 2.40
46a A6 12o 14.00 4.50
Never hinged 24.00
On cover 47.50
47a A6 16o 30.00 5.00
Never hinged 47.50
On cover 65.00
50a A6 25o 60.00 27.50
Never hinged 120.00
On cover 160.00
51a A6 50o 95.00 32.50
Never hinged 200.00
On cover 160.00
52a A6 100o 90.00 57.50
Never hinged 200.00
On cover 160.00
Nos. 41b-52a (8) 310.00 134.95
Set, never hinged 635.00

1902-04 **Wmk. 113**

41c A6 3o blue & gray 2.75 3.00
Never hinged 6.00
On cover 18.00
42b A6 4o slate & blue 17.00 20.00
Never hinged 35.00
On cover 42.50
43a A7 5o green 2.00 .25
Never hinged 6.00
On cover 2.75
44d A6 8o slate & carmine 525.00 425.00
Never hinged 1,050.
On cover —
45a A7 10o rose carmine 3.00 .25
Never hinged 9.00
On cover 3.00
48a A7 20o blue 20.00 4.75
Never hinged 47.50
On cover 18.00
50b A6 25o gray & green 10.50 4.50
Never hinged 26.00
On cover 105.00
51b A6 50o brown & violet 27.50 20.00
Never hinged 72.50
On cover 130.00
On cover, single franking 260.00
52b A6 100o slate & orange 30.00 15.00
Never hinged 72.50
On cover 130.00
On cover, single franking 300.00
Nos. 41c-52b (9) 637.75 492.75
Set, never hinged 1,325.

Inverted Frame

41d A6 3o 75.00 130.00
Never hinged 240.00
On cover 180.00
42c A6 4o 140.00 130.00
Never hinged 425.00
On cover 180.00
50c A6 25o 210.00 60.00
Never hinged 540.00
On cover 140.00
51c A6 50o 260.00 240.00
Never hinged 650.00
On cover 175.00
52c A6 100o 225.00 240.00
Never hinged 650.00
On cover 300.00
Nos. 41d-52c (5) 910.00 800.00
Set, never hinged 2,500.

1902 **Wmk. 113**

53 A7 1o orange .75 .65
Never hinged 1.50
On cover 3.50
a. Imperf — —
54 A7 15o lilac 11.00 .75
Never hinged 30.00
On cover 21.00
a. Imperf, single *4,250.*

Nos. 44d, 44, 49 Surcharged

a

b

1904-12 **Wmk. 113**

55 A6(a) 4o on 8o sl & car 3.50 4.00
Never hinged 6.00
On cover 24.00
a. Wmk. 112 ('12) 21.00 *60.00*
Never hinged 42.50
On cover 140.00
b. As "a," inverted frame — *6,000.*
Never hinged —

Wmk. 112

56 A7(b) 15o on 24o brown 5.75 17.50
Never hinged 6.00
On cover 42.50
a. Short "15" at right 27.50 *105.00*
Never hinged 60.00
Set, never hinged 16.00

A10

1905-17 **Wmk. 113** ***Perf. 13***

57 A10 1o orange ('06) 2.25 .75
Never hinged 7.50
On cover 3.00
58 A10 2o carmine 4.75 .40
Never hinged 17.50
On cover 6.00
a. Perf. 14x14½ ('17) 3.75 *19.00*
Never hinged 7.50
On cover 45.00
59 A10 3o gray 9.75 .65
Never hinged 30.00
On cover 2.25
60 A10 4o dull blue 7.00 .60
Never hinged 21.00
On cover 5.25
a. Perf. 14x14½ ('17) 11.00 *37.50*
Never hinged 22.50
On cover 75.00
61 A10 5o dp green ('12) 5.25 .35
Never hinged 13.00
On cover 1.50
62 A10 10o dp rose ('12) 6.75 .35
Never hinged 21.00
On cover 2.25
63 A10 15o lilac 25.00 2.25
Never hinged 65.00
On cover 15.00
64 A10 20o dk blue ('12) 35.00 .90
Never hinged 105.00
On cover 15.00
Nos. 57-64 (8) 95.75 6.25
Set, never hinged 310.00

The three wavy lines in design A10 are symbolical of the three waters which separate the principal Danish islands.

See Nos. 85-96, 1338-1342A, 1468-1473. For surcharges and overprints see Nos. 163, 181, J1, J38, Q1-Q2.

King Christian IX — A11

1904-05 **Engr.**

65 A11 10o scarlet 4.00 .65
Never hinged 11.00
On cover 2.25
66 A11 20o blue 22.50 3.00
Never hinged 52.50
On cover 9.00
67 A11 25o brown ('05) 27.50 8.00
Never hinged 110.00
On cover 67.50
On cover, single franking 75.00
68 A11 50o dull vio ('05) 110.00 *120.00*
Never hinged 350.00
On cover 375.00
On cover, single franking 425.00
69 A11 100o ocher ('05) 13.00 *60.00*
Never hinged 42.50
On cover 375.00
On cover, single franking 500.00
Nos. 65-69 (5) 177.00 *191.65*
Set, never hinged 565.00

1905-06 **Re-engraved**

70 A11 5o green 4.50 .35
Never hinged 8.50
71 A11 10o scarlet ('06) 21.00 .60
Never hinged 47.50
Set, never hinged 56.00

The re-engraved stamps are much clearer than the originals, and the decoration on the king's left breast has been removed.

King Frederik VIII — A12

1907-12

72 A12 5o green 1.75 .40
Never hinged 3.50
a. Imperf. —
73 A12 10o red 4.25 .40
Never hinged 6.75
a. Imperf. —
74 A12 20o indigo 19.00 .65
Never hinged 42.50
a. 20o bright blue ('11) 40.00 2.75
Never hinged 80.00
75 A12 25o olive brn 35.00 1.25
Never hinged 87.50
76 A12 35o dp org ('12) 6.00 *10.00*
Never hinged 12.50
77 A12 50o claret 35.00 7.00
Never hinged 85.00
78 A12 100o bister brn 100.00 5.00
Never hinged 300.00
Nos. 72-78 (7) 201.00 24.70
Set, never hinged 525.00

Nos. 47, 31 and O9 Surcharged

c

d

Dark Blue Surcharge

1912 **Wmk. 112** ***Perf. 13***

79 A6(c) 35o on 16o 17.00 *50.00*
Never hinged 35.00
a. Inverted frame 325.00 *625.00*
Never hinged 725.00

Perf. 14x13½

80 A6(c) 35o on 20o 30.00 *85.00*
Never hinged 60.00
a. Inverted frame 130.00 *325.00*
Never hinged 300.00

Black Surcharge

81 O1(d) 35o on 32o 42.50 *120.00*
Never hinged 90.00
Nos. 79-81 (3) 89.50 *255.00*
Set, never hinged 185.00

General Post Office, Copenhagen — A15

1912 **Engr.** **Wmk. 113** ***Perf. 13***

82 A15 5k dark red 500.00 200.00
Never hinged 1,500.

See Nos. 135, 843 (in Scott Standard Catalogue Vol. 2).

Perf. 14x14½

1913-30 **Typo.** **Wmk. 114**

85 A10 1o dp orange ('14) .40 .45
Never hinged 1.00
a. Bklt. pane, 2 ea #85, 91 + 2 labels 20.00
86 A10 2o car ('13) 3.75 .35
Never hinged 11.00
a. Imperf 150.00 *300.00*
b. Booklet pane, 4 + 2 labels 27.50
87 A10 3o gray ('13) 6.75 .40
Never hinged 16.00
88 A10 4o blue ('13) 8.00 .45
Never hinged 18.00
a. Half used as 2o on cover 1,250.
89 A10 5o dk brown ('21) .75 .35
Never hinged 2.25
a. Imperf 190.00
b. Booklet pane, 4 + 2 labels 14.00
90 A10 5o lt green ('30) 1.50 .40
Never hinged 6.00
a. Booklet pane, 4 + 2 labels 16.00
b. Booklet pane of 50
91 A10 7o apple grn ('26) 5.75 *7.25*
Never hinged 13.50
a. Booklet pane, 4 + 2 labels 20.00
92 A10 7o dk violet ('30) 16.00 6.50
Never hinged 42.50
93 A10 8o gray ('21) 7.00 3.25
Never hinged 14.00
94 A10 10o green ('21) .85 .35
Never hinged 2.75
a. Imperf 225.00
b. Booklet pane, 4 + 2 labels 37.50
95 A10 10o bister brn ('30) 2.25 .35
Never hinged 9.00
a. Booklet pane, 4 + 2 labels 16.00
b. Booklet pane of 50

96 A10 12o violet ('26) 25.00 9.75
Never hinged 65.00
Nos. 85-96 (12) 78.00 29.85
Set, never hinged 200.00

No. 88a was used with No. 97 in Faroe Islands, Jan. 3-23, 1919.

See surcharge and overprint note following No. 64.

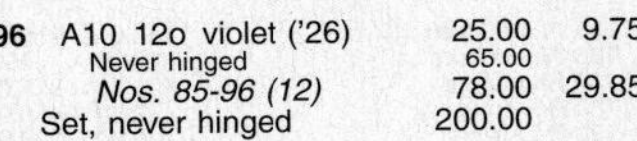
King Christian X — A16

1913-28 **Typo.** ***Perf. 14x14½***

97 A16 5o green 1.40 .35
Never hinged 5.25
a. Bklt. pane of 4, with P# *400.00*
98 A16 7o orange ('18) 2.25 *2.75*
Never hinged 9.75
99 A16 8o dk gray ('20) 14.00 6.50
Never hinged 37.50
100 A16 10o red 2.40 .40
Never hinged 7.50
a. Imperf 300.00
b. Bklt. pane of 4, with P# *500.00*
101 A16 12o gray grn ('18) 7.50 *10.00*
Never hinged 13.00
102 A16 15o violet 3.25 .40
Never hinged 8.50
103 A16 20o dp blue 13.00 .35
Never hinged 47.50
104 A16 20o brown ('21) 1.25 .40
Never hinged 3.00
105 A16 20o red ('26) 1.50 .40
Never hinged 3.75
106 A16 25o dk brown 13.50 .50
Never hinged 67.50
107 A16 25o brn & blk ('20) 85.00 8.75
Never hinged 210.00
108 A16 25o red ('22) 4.25 .95
Never hinged 7.50
109 A16 25o yel grn ('25) 3.00 .50
Never hinged 7.50
110 A16 27o ver & blk ('18) 30.00 *50.00*
Never hinged 75.00
111 A16 30o green & blk ('18) 35.00 3.25
Never hinged 105.00
112 A16 30o orange ('21) 3.00 2.00
Never hinged 7.50
113 A16 30o dk blue ('25) 1.75 1.00
Never hinged 4.25
114 A16 35o orange 29.00 7.50
Never hinged 95.00
115 A16 35o yel & blk ('19) 9.00 6.50
Never hinged 18.00
116 A16 40o vio & blk ('18) 18.00 4.00
Never hinged 75.00
117 A16 40o gray bl & blk ('20) 37.50 7.50
Never hinged 120.00
118 A16 40o dk blue ('22) 6.00 1.60
Never hinged 12.00
119 A16 40o orange ('25) 1.50 *1.50*
Never hinged 4.50
120 A16 50o claret 37.50 5.75
Never hinged 110.00
121 A16 50o claret & blk ('19) 75.00 2.50
Never hinged 225.00
122 A16 50o lt gray ('22) 9.25 .40
Never hinged 37.50
a. 50o olive gray ('21) 75.00 8.00
Never hinged 210.00
123 A16 60o brn & bl ('19) 60.00 3.75
Never hinged 225.00
a. 60o brown & ultra ('19) 225.00 12.50
Never hinged 750.00
124 A16 60o grn bl ('21) 9.00 .75
Never hinged 37.50
125 A16 70o brn & grn ('20) 26.00 2.25
Never hinged 90.00
126 A16 80o bl grn ('15) 50.00 22.50
Never hinged 120.00
127 A16 90o brn & red ('20) 18.00 3.25
Never hinged 50.00
128 A16 1k brn & bl ('22) 75.00 3.00
Never hinged 120.00
129 A16 2k gray & cl ('25) 67.50 15.00
Never hinged 140.00
130 A16 5k vio & brn ('27) 7.00 *5.75*
Never hinged 10.00
131 A16 10k ver & yel grn ('28) 325.00 65.00
Never hinged 975.00
Nos. 97-131 (35) 1,082. 247.00
Set, never hinged 3,085.

No. 97 surcharged "2 ORE" is Faroe Islands No. 1. Two of the 14 printings of No. 97a have no P# in the selvage. These sell for more.

Nos. 87 and 98, 89 and 94, 89 and 104, 90 and 95, 97 and 103, 100 and 102 exist se-tenant in coils for use in vending machines.

For surcharges and overprints see Nos. 161-162, 176-177, 182-184, J2-J8, M1-M2, Q3-Q10.

King Christian X — A17

1913-20 **Engr.**

132 A17 1k yellow brown 95.00 1.25
  Never hinged 375.00
133 A17 2k gray 150.00 7.00
  Never hinged 525.00
134 A17 5k purple ('20) 15.00 10.00
  Never hinged 37.50
  Nos. 132-134 (3) 260.00 18.25
  Set, never hinged 940.00

For overprint see No. Q11.

G.P.O. Type of 1912
Perf. 14x14½

1915 **Wmk. 114** **Engr.**

135 A15 5k dark red ('15) 500.00 175.00
  Never hinged 1,500.

Nos. 46 and O10 Surcharged in Black type "c" and

e

1915 **Wmk. 112** **Typo.** ***Perf. 13***

136 A6 (c) 80o on 12o 40.00 *100.00*
  Never hinged 65.00
  a. Inverted frame 600.00 *1,100.*
  Never hinged 825.00
137 O1 (e) 80o on 8o 47.50 *140.00*
  Never hinged 90.00
  a. "POSTERIM" 95.00 *325.00*
  Never hinged 140.00
  Set, never hinged 155.00

Newspaper Stamps Surcharged

On Issue of 1907

1918 **Wmk. 113** ***Perf. 13***

138 N1 27o on 1o olive 105.00 *325.00*
  Never hinged 225.00
139 N1 27o on 5o blue 105.00 *325.00*
  Never hinged 225.00
140 N1 27o on 7o car 105.00 *325.00*
  Never hinged 225.00
141 N1 27o on 10o dp lil 105.00 *325.00*
  Never hinged 225.00
142 N1 27o on 68o yel brn 7.50 *37.50*
  Never hinged 13.00
143 N1 27o on 5k rose & yel grn 6.75 *26.00*
  Never hinged 13.00
144 N1 27o on 10k bis & bl 7.50 *35.00*
  Never hinged 17.00
  Nos. 138-144 (7) 441.75 *1,399.*
  Set, never hinged 940.00

On Issue of 1914-15
Wmk. Multiple Crosses (114)
Perf. 14x14½

145 N1 27o on 1o ol gray 5.00 *15.50*
  Never hinged 7.50
146 N1 27o on 5o blue 7.50 *30.00*
  Never hinged 15.00
147 N1 27o on 7o rose 5.00 *12.50*
  Never hinged 7.50
148 N1 27o on 8o green 7.50 *16.00*
  Never hinged 10.50
149 N1 27o on 10o dp lil 3.25 *17.00*
  Never hinged 7.50
150 N1 27o on 20o green 8.00 *16.50*
  Never hinged 10.50
151 N1 27o on 29o org yel 3.25 *14.50*
  Never hinged 7.50
152 N1 27o on 38o orange 32.50 *110.00*
  Never hinged 55.00
153 N1 27o on 41o yel brn 7.50 *45.00*
  Never hinged 18.00
154 N1 27o on 1k bl grn & mar 5.00 *14.50*
  Never hinged 10.00
  Nos. 145-154 (10) 84.50 *291.50*
  Set, never hinged 150.00

Kronborg Castle — A20

Sonderborg Castle — A21

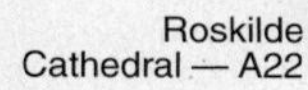

Roskilde Cathedral — A22

Perf. 14½x14, 14x14½

1920, Oct. 5 **Typo.**

156 A20 10o red 7.00 .50
  Never hinged 12.00
157 A21 20o slate 5.00 .50
  Never hinged 7.50
158 A22 40o dark brown 17.00 4.50
  Never hinged 32.50
  Nos. 156-158 (3) 29.00 5.50
  Set, never hinged 52.00

Reunion of Northern Schleswig with Denmark.

See Nos. 159-160. For surcharges see Nos. B1-B2.

1921

159 A20 10o green 9.00 .55
  Never hinged 24.00
160 A22 40o dark blue 67.50 11.50
  Never hinged 150.00
  Set, never hinged 174.00

Stamps of 1918 Surcharged in Blue

1921-22

161 A16 8o on 7o org ('22) 2.25 *5.00*
  Never hinged 7.50
162 A16 8o on 12o gray grn 2.25 *15.00*
  Never hinged 8.25
  Set, never hinged 15.75

No. 87 Surcharged

1921

163 A10 8o on 3o gray 3.75 *5.25*
  Never hinged 8.25

Christian X A23

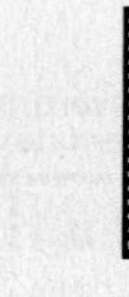

Christian IV A24

A25

A26

1924, Dec. 1 ***Perf. 14x14½***

164 A23 10o green 7.50 *7.00*
  Never hinged 15.00
165 A24 10o green 7.50 *7.00*
  Never hinged 15.00
166 A25 10o green 7.50 *7.00*
  Never hinged 15.00
167 A26 10o green 7.50 *7.00*
  Never hinged 15.00
  a. Block of 4, #164-167 37.50 *50.00*
  Never hinged 75.00
168 A23 15o violet 7.50 *7.00*
  Never hinged 15.00
169 A24 15o violet 7.50 *7.00*
  Never hinged 15.00
170 A25 15o violet 7.50 *7.00*
  Never hinged 15.00
171 A26 15o violet 7.50 *7.00*
  Never hinged 15.00
  a. Block of 4, #168-171 37.50 *50.00*
  Never hinged 75.00
172 A23 20o dark brown 7.50 *7.00*
  Never hinged 15.00
173 A24 20o dark brown 7.50 *7.00*
  Never hinged 15.00
174 A25 20o dark brown 7.50 *7.00*
  Never hinged 15.00
175 A26 20o dark brown 7.50 *7.00*
  Never hinged 15.00
  a. Block of 4, #172-175 37.50 *50.00*
  Never hinged 75.00
  Nos. 164-175 (12) 90.00 84.00
  Set, never hinged 180.00
  #167a, 171a, 175a, never hinged 225.00

300th anniv. of the Danish postal service.

Stamps of 1921-22 Surcharged

k

l

1926

176 A16 (k) 20o on 30o org 6.75 *15.00*
  Never hinged 16.00
177 A16 (l) 20o on 40o dk bl 9.00 *18.00*
  Never hinged 15.00
  Set, never hinged 31.00

A27

A28

1926, Mar. 11 ***Perf. 14x14½***

178 A27 10o dull green 1.50 .45
  Never hinged 3.00
179 A28 20o dark red 2.00 .45
  Never hinged 4.50
180 A28 30o dark blue 8.50 1.50
  Never hinged 17.00
  Nos. 178-180 (3) 12.00 2.40
  Set, never hinged 24.50

75th anniv. of the introduction of postage stamps in Denmark.

Stamps of 1913-26 Surcharged in Blue or Black

No. 181

Nos. 182-184

1926-27 ***Perf. 14x14½***

181 A10 7o on 8o gray (Bl) 1.50 *4.75*
  Never hinged 4.25
182 A16 7o on 27o ver & blk 4.50 *17.00*
  Never hinged 10.50
183 A16 7o on 20o red ('27) .75 *2.50*
  Never hinged 1.50
184 A16 12o on 15o violet 2.25 *6.00*
  Never hinged 5.50

Surcharged on Official Stamps of 1914-23

185 O1 (e) 7o on 1o org 4.00 *16.00*
  Never hinged 8.00
186 O1 (e) 7o on 3o gray 7.50 *32.50*
  Never hinged 15.00
187 O1 (e) 7o on 4o blue 3.75 *7.75*
  Never hinged 7.50
188 O1 (e) 7o on 5o grn 52.50 *150.00*
  Never hinged 100.00
189 O1 (e) 7o on 10o grn 4.50 *15.50*
  Never hinged 9.00
190 O1 (e) 7o on 15o vio 4.50 *15.50*
  Never hinged 7.00
191 O1 (e) 7o on 20o ind 19.00 *77.50*
  Never hinged 30.00
  a. Double surcharge 750.00 *975.00*
  Never hinged 1,000.
  Nos. 181-191 (11) 104.75 *345.00*
  Set, never hinged 155.00

Caravel — A30

1927 **Typo.** ***Perf. 14x14½***

192 A30 15o red 6.00 .40
  Never hinged 15.00
193 A30 20o gray 11.00 2.40
  Never hinged 35.00
194 A30 25o light blue 1.25 .40
  Never hinged 4.00
195 A30 30o ocher 1.25 .40
  Never hinged 4.75
196 A30 35o red brown 25.00 1.50
  Never hinged 75.00
197 A30 40o yel green 25.00 .40
  Never hinged 70.00
  Nos. 192-197 (6) 69.50 5.50
  Set, never hinged 200.00

See Nos. 232-238J. For surcharges & overprints see Nos. 244-245, 269-272, Q12-Q14, Q19-Q25.

Christian X — A31

1930, Sept. 26

210 A31 5o apple grn 2.50 .35
  Never hinged 4.50
  a. Booklet pane, 4 + 2 labels 18.00
211 A31 7o violet 6.75 3.00
  Never hinged 17.00
212 A31 8o dk gray 22.50 32.50
  Never hinged 67.50
213 A31 10o yel brn 5.00 .35
  Never hinged 8.25
  a. Booklet pane, 4 + 2 labels 29.00
214 A31 15o red 10.00 .35
  Never hinged 40.00
215 A31 20o lt gray 25.00 9.75
  Never hinged 57.50
216 A31 25o lt blue 8.50 1.25
  Never hinged 21.00
217 A31 30o yel buff 9.00 1.75
  Never hinged 21.00
218 A31 35o red brown 12.00 4.50
  Never hinged 27.50
219 A31 40o dp green 10.00 1.25
  Never hinged 30.00
  Nos. 210-219 (10) 111.25 55.05
  Set, never hinged 295.00

60th birthday of King Christian X.

Wavy Lines and Numeral of Value — A32

Type A10 Redrawn

1933-40 **Unwmk.** **Engr.** ***Perf. 13***

220 A32 1o gray blk .45 .30
  Never hinged .75
221 A32 2o scarlet .35 .30
  Never hinged .60
222 A32 4o blue .40 .35
  Never hinged 1.20
223 A32 5o yel grn 1.00 .35
  Never hinged 2.25
  a. 5o gray green 37.50 *60.00*
  Never hinged 50.00
  b. Tête bêche gutter pair 8.00 *15.50*
  Never hinged 24.00
  c. Booklet pane of 4 11.00
  d. Bklt. pane, 1 #223a, 3 #B6 37.50 70.00
  Never hinged 60.00
  e. As "b," without gutter 17.50 *27.50*
  Never hinged 35.00
224 A32 5o rose lake ('38) .30 .30
  Never hinged .40
  a. Booklet pane of 4 1.20
  b. Booklet pane of 10 12.00
224C A32 6o orange ('40) .30 .30
  Never hinged .55
225 A32 7o violet 2.00 .35
  Never hinged 5.00
226 A32 7o yel grn ('38) 1.10 .45
  Never hinged 2.25
226A A32 7o lt brown ('40) .35 .35
  Never hinged .75
227 A32 8o gray .45 .50
  Never hinged .90
227A A32 8o yellow grn ('40) .30 .35
  Never hinged .85
228 A32 10o yellow org 12.50 .35
  Never hinged 25.00
  a. Tête bêche gutter pair 50.00 55.00
  Never hinged 80.00
  b. Booklet pane of 4 110.00
  c. As "a," without gutter 60.00 *70.00*
  Never hinged 100.00
229 A32 10o lt brown ('37) 9.50 .35
  Never hinged 35.00
  a. Booklet pane of 4 100.00
  b. Booklet pane of 4, 1 #229, 3 #B7 32.50 45.00
230 A32 10o violet ('38) .75 .35
  Never hinged 1.50
  a. Booklet pane of 4 2.75
  b. Bklt. pane, 2 #230, 2 #B10 2.50 7.00
  Never hinged 6.00
  Nos. 220-230 (14) 29.75 4.95
  Set, never hinged 75.00

Design A10 was typographed. They had a solid background with groups of small hearts below the heraldic lions in the upper corners and below "DA" and "RK" of "DANMARK." The numerals of value were enclosed in single-lined ovals.

Design A32 is line-engraved and has a background of crossed lines. The hearts have been removed and the numerals of value are now in double-lined ovals. Two types exist of some values.

The 1ö, No. 220, was issued on fluorescent paper in 1969.

No. 230 with wide margins is from booklet pane No. 230b.

Surcharges of 20, 50 & 60öre on #220, 224 and 224C are listed as Faroe Islands #2-3, 5-6.

See Nos. 318, 333, 382, 416, 437-437A, 493-498, 629, 631, 688-695, 793-795, 883-

886, 1111-1113, 1116, 1295B. For overprints and surcharges see Nos. 257, 263, 267-268, 355-356, Q15-Q17, Q31, Q43. Post 1940 issues in Scott Standard catalogue, Vol. 2.

Certain tête-bêche pairs of 1938-55 issues which reached the market in 1971, and were not regularly issued, are not listed. This group comprises 24 different major-number vertical pairs of types A32, A47, A61 and SP3 (13 with gutters, 11 without), and pairs of some minor numbers and shades. They were removed from booklet pane sheets.

Type of 1927 Issue
Type I

Type I — Two columns of squares between sail and left frame line.

1933-34 Engr. *Perf. 13*

232	A30 20o gray		15.00	.35
	Never hinged		30.00	
233	A30 25o blue		85.00	30.00
	Never hinged		210.00	
234	A30 25o brown ('34)		30.00	.35
	Never hinged		60.00	
235	A30 30o orange yel		1.50	1.40
	Never hinged		3.00	
236	A30 30o blue ('34)		1.50	.40
	Never hinged		3.00	
237	A30 35o violet		.60	.35
	Never hinged		1.50	
238	A30 40o yellow grn		6.25	.35
	Never hinged		19.00	
	Nos. 232-238 (7)		139.85	33.20
	Set, never hinged		325.00	

Type II

Type II — One column of squares between sail and left frame line.

1933-40

238A	A30 15o deep red		3.00	.35
	Never hinged		6.00	
k.	Booklet pane of 4		26.00	
l.	Bklt. pane, 1 #238A, 3 #B8		45.00	
	Never hinged		115.00	
238B	A30 15o yel grn ('40)		9.00	.40
	Never hinged		22.50	
238C	A30 20o gray blk ('39)		4.50	.70
	Never hinged		11.00	
238D	A30 20o red ('40)		.90	.35
	Never hinged		1.50	
238E	A30 25o dp brown ('39)		.90	.35
	Never hinged		1.75	
238F	A30 30o blue ('39)		2.25	.70
	Never hinged		6.00	
238G	A30 30o orange ('40)		.75	.35
	Never hinged		2.00	
238H	A30 35o violet ('40)		1.00	.35
	Never hinged		2.75	
238I	A30 40o yel grn ('39)		15.00	.35
	Never hinged		37.50	
238J	A30 40o blue ('40)		1.40	.35
	Never hinged		3.00	
	Nos. 238A-238J (10)		38.70	4.25
	Set, never hinged		95.00	

Nos. 232-238J, engraved, have crosshatched background. Nos. 192-197, typographed, have solid background.

For No. 238A surcharged 20 ore see Denmark No. 271, Faroe Islands No. 4.

See note on surcharges and overprints following No. 197.

King Christian X — A33

1934-41 *Perf. 13*

239	A33 50o gray		1.20	.30
	Never hinged		3.00	
240	A33 60o blue grn		2.40	.35
	Never hinged		8.00	
240A	A33 75o dk blue ('41)		.45	.35
	Never hinged		.75	
241	A33 1k lt brown		3.75	.35
	Never hinged		18.00	
242	A33 2k dull red		6.00	1.00
	Never hinged		15.00	
243	A33 5k violet		9.00	3.50
	Never hinged		30.00	
	Nos. 239-243 (6)		22.80	5.85
	Set, never hinged		75.00	

For overprints see Nos. Q26-Q27.

Nos. 233, 235 Surcharged in Black

1934, June 9

244	A30 4o on 25o blue		.50	.50
	Never hinged		1.50	
245	A30 10o on 30o org yel		2.40	*3.25*
	Never hinged		6.00	
	Set, never hinged		7.50	

"The Ugly Duckling" A34

Andersen A35

"The Little Mermaid" — A36

1935, Oct. 1 *Perf. 13*

246	A34 5o lt green		3.00	.30
	Never hinged		6.25	
a.	Tête bêche gutter pair		15.00	*22.50*
	Never hinged		30.00	
b.	Booklet pane of 4		40.00	
c.	As "a," without gutter		17.00	*21.00*
	Never hinged		45.00	
247	A35 7o dull vio		2.50	*2.50*
	Never hinged		5.00	
248	A36 10o orange		4.50	.30
	Never hinged		12.00	
a.	Tête bêche gutter pair		18.00	*32.50*
	Never hinged		48.00	
b.	Booklet pane of 4		65.00	
c.	As "a," without gutter		20.00	*40.00*
	Never hinged		65.00	
249	A35 15o red		11.00	.30
	Never hinged		30.00	
a.	Tête bêche gutter pair		45.00	*52.50*
	Never hinged		100.00	
b.	Booklet pane of 4		160.00	
c.	As "a," without gutter		42.50	*75.00*
	Never hinged		110.00	
250	A35 20o gray		9.50	1.25
	Never hinged		27.50	
251	A35 30o dl bl		3.00	.35
	Never hinged		5.50	
	Nos. 246-251 (6)		33.50	*5.00*
	Set, never hinged		87.50	

Centenary of the publication of the earliest installment of Hans Christian Andersen's "Fairy Tales."

Nikolai Church A37

Hans Tausen A38

Ribe Cathedral — A39

1936 *Perf. 13*

252	A37 5o green		1.40	.40
	Never hinged		3.50	
a.	Booklet pane of 4		21.00	
253	A37 7o violet		2.00	*4.50*
	Never hinged		4.00	
254	A38 10o lt brown		2.00	.40
	Never hinged		5.00	
a.	Booklet pane of 4		25.00	
255	A38 15o dull rose		3.00	.30
	Never hinged		7.50	
256	A39 30o blue		16.00	1.40
	Never hinged		42.50	
	Nos. 252-256 (5)		24.40	7.00
	Set, never hinged		62.50	

Church Reformation in Denmark, 400th anniv.

No. 229 Overprinted in Blue

1937, Sept. 17

257	A32 10o lt brown		1.50	*1.60*
	Never hinged		2.00	

Jubilee Exhib. held by the Copenhagen Phil. Club on their 50th anniv. The stamps were on sale at the Exhib. only, each holder of a ticket of admission (1k) being entitled to purchase 20 stamps at face value; of a season ticket (5k), 100 stamps.

Yacht and Summer Palace, Marselisborg A40

Christian X in Streets of Copenhagen A41

Equestrian Statue of Frederik V and Amalienborg Palace — A42

1937, May 15 *Perf. 13*

258	A40 5o green		1.40	.30
	Never hinged		4.50	
a.	Booklet pane of 4		15.00	
259	A41 10o brown		1.40	.30
	Never hinged		2.60	
a.	Booklet pane of 4		15.00	
260	A42 15o scarlet		1.40	.30
	Never hinged		2.60	
a.	Booklet pane of 4		17.00	
261	A41 30o blue		15.00	2.40
	Never hinged		32.50	
	Nos. 258-261 (4)		19.20	3.30
	Set, never hinged		42.50	

25th anniv. of the accession to the throne of King Christian X.

Emancipation Column, Copenhagen — A43

1938, June 20 *Perf. 13*

262	A43 15o scarlet		.60	.30
	Never hinged		1.40	

Abolition of serfdom in Denmark, 150th anniv.

No. 223 Overprinted in Red on Alternate Stamps

1938, Sept. 2

263	A32 5o yellow grn, pair		3.25	*7.00*
	Never hinged		4.50	

10th Danish Philatelic Exhibition.

Bertel Thorvaldsen A44

Statue of Jason A45

1938, Nov. 17 Engr. *Perf. 13*

264	A44 5o rose lake		.45	.30
	Never hinged		.65	
265	A45 10o purple		.45	.30
	Never hinged		.65	
266	A44 30o dark blue		1.50	.60
	Never hinged		3.50	
	Nos. 264-266 (3)		2.40	1.20
	Set, never hinged		5.25	

The return to Denmark in 1838 of Bertel Thorvaldsen, Danish sculptor.

Stamps of 1933-39 Surcharged with New Values in Black

a

b

c

1940

267	A32 (a) 6o on 7o yel grn		.30	*.35*
	Never hinged		.40	
268	A32 (a) 6o on 8o gray		.45	*.35*
	Never hinged		.85	
269	A30 (b) 15o on 40o #238		.90	*6.00*
	Never hinged		2.25	
270	A30 (b) 15o on 40o #238I		.75	*.95*
	Never hinged		1.75	
271	A30 (c) 20o on 15o dp red		1.10	.30
	Never hinged		2.00	
272	A30 (b) 40o on 30o #238F		1.00	.35
	Never hinged		2.00	
	Nos. 267-272 (6)		4.50	*8.30*

Stamps previously listed as Denmark No. 273-276 are listed as Faroe Islands Nos. 2-6 .

Set, never hinged 9.25

SEMI-POSTAL STAMPS

Nos. 159, 157 Surcharged in Red

Wmk. Multiple Crosses (114)

1921, June 17 *Perf. 14½x14*

B1	A20 10o + 5o green		27.50	*60.00*
	Never hinged		67.50	
	On cover			160.00
B2	A21 20o + 10o slate		30.00	*77.50*
	Never hinged		100.00	
	On cover			85.00
	Set, never hinged		167.50	

Crown and Staff of Aesculapius — SP1

1929, Aug. 1 Engr.

B3	SP1 10o yellow green		4.50	*7.00*
	Never hinged		8.50	
	On cover			15.00
a.	Booklet pane of 2		27.50	
B4	SP1 15o brick red		9.00	*12.00*
	Never hinged		18.00	
	On cover			19.00
a.	Booklet pane of 2		32.50	
B5	SP1 25o deep blue		25.00	*40.00*
	Never hinged		50.00	
	On cover			75.00
a.	Booklet pane of 2		135.00	
	Nos. B3-B5 (3)		38.50	*59.00*
	Set, never hinged		100.00	

These stamps were sold at a premium of 5 øre each for benefit of the Danish Cancer Committee.

Dybbol Mill — SP2

1937, Jan. 20 Unwmk. *Perf. 13*

B6	SP2 5o + 5o green		.60	*1.40*
	Never hinged		1.00	
B7	SP2 10o + 5o lt brown		2.25	*9.00*
	Never hinged		6.00	

B8 SP2 15o + 5o carmine 3.25 *9.00*
Never hinged 6.00
Nos. B6-B8 (3) 6.10 *19.40*
Set, never hinged 13.00

The surtax was for a fund in memory of H. P. Hanssen, statesman.

Nos. 223a and B6, Nos. 229 and B7, Nos. 238A and B8 are found se-tenant in booklets. For booklet panes, see Nos. 223d, 229b and 238Al.

Queen Alexandrine — SP3

1939-40 ***Perf. 13***
B9 SP3 5o + 3o rose lake & red ('40) .25 .35
Never hinged .35
a. Booklet pane of 4 2.00 2.00
B10 SP3 10o + 5o dk violet & red .35 .25
Never hinged .50
B11 SP3 15o + 5o scarlet & red .30 *.50*
Never hinged .50
Nos. B9-B11 (3) .90 1.10
Set, never hinged 1.35

The surtax was for the Danish Red Cross.

Nos. 230 and B10 have been issued se-tenant in booklets. See No. 230b. In this pane No. 230 measures 23½x31mm from perf. to perf.

AIR POST STAMPS

Airplane and Plowman — AP1

Wmk. Multiple Crosses (114)
1925-29 **Typo.** ***Perf. 12x12½***
C1 AP1 10o yellow green 27.50 *50.00*
Never hinged 67.50
C2 AP1 15o violet ('26) 70.00 *110.00*
Never hinged 175.00
C3 AP1 25o scarlet 45.00 *72.50*
Never hinged 110.00
C4 AP1 50o lt gray ('29) 130.00 *315.00*
Never hinged 350.00
C5 AP1 1k choc ('29) 105.00 *300.00*
Never hinged 275.00
Nos. C1-C5 (5) 377.50 *847.50*
Set, never hinged 975.00

Towers of Copenhagen — AP2

Unwmk.
1934, June 9 **Engr.** ***Perf. 13***
C6 AP2 10o orange .75 *1.10*
Never hinged 1.50
C7 AP2 15o red 2.60 *5.50*
Never hinged 6.00
C8 AP2 20o Prus blue 2.60 *5.50*
Never hinged 6.00
C9 AP2 50o olive black 2.60 *5.50*
Never hinged 6.00
C10 AP2 1k brown 10.50 *19.00*
Never hinged 20.00
Nos. C6-C10 (5) 19.05 *36.60*
Set, never hinged 40.00

LATE FEE STAMPS

LF1

Perf. 14x14½
1923 **Typo.** **Wmk. 114**
I1 LF1 10o green 17.00 5.25
Never hinged 50.00
a. Double overprint *3,000.*

No. I1 was, at first, not a postage stamp but represented a tax for the services of the post office clerks in filling out postal forms and writing addresses. In 1923 it was put into use as a Late Fee stamp.

Coat of Arms — LF2

1926-31
I2 LF2 10o green 13.50 1.00
Never hinged 37.50
I3 LF2 10o brown ('31) 9.00 .70
Never hinged 22.50
Set, never hinged 60.00

1934 **Unwmk.** **Engr.** ***Perf. 13***
I4 LF2 5o green .35 .30
Never hinged .65
I5 LF2 10o orange .35 .30
Never hinged .65
Set, never hinged 1.30

POSTAGE DUE STAMPS

Regular Issues of 1913-20 Overprinted

Perf. 14x14½
1921, May 1 **Wmk. 114**
J1 A10 1o deep orange 2.50 7.00
Never hinged 6.75
J2 A16 5o green 7.00 7.00
Never hinged 18.00
J3 A16 7o orange 4.50 8.50
Never hinged 10.50
J4 A16 10o red 30.00 17.00
Never hinged 75.00
J5 A16 20o deep blue 22.50 14.00
Never hinged 60.00
J6 A16 25o brown & blk 30.00 10.00
Never hinged 100.00
J7 A16 50o claret & blk 13.50 8.50
Never hinged 30.00
Nos. J1-J7 (7) 110.00 72.00
Set, never hinged 300.00

Same Overprint in Dark Blue On Military Stamp of 1917
1921, Nov. 23
J8 A16 10o red 15.00 20.00
Never hinged 37.50
a. "S" inverted 175.00 240.00
Never hinged 350.00

Numeral of Value — D1

Typographed (Solid Panel)
1921-30 ***Perf. 14x14½***
J9 D1 1o orange ('22) 2.00 2.50
Never hinged 5.50
J10 D1 4o blue ('25) 3.75 3.25
Never hinged 8.25
J11 D1 5o brown ('22) 3.25 2.50
Never hinged 9.00
J12 D1 5o lt green ('30) 3.75 2.50
Never hinged 7.50
J13 D1 7o apple grn ('27) 18.00 24.00
Never hinged 52.50
J14 D1 7o dk violet ('30) 50.00 40.00
Never hinged 110.00
J15 D1 10o yellow grn ('22) 4.50 2.25
Never hinged 12.50
J16 D1 10o lt brown ('30) 4.50 2.25
Never hinged 6.75
J17 D1 20o grnsh blue ('21) 3.50 3.25
Never hinged 6.00
a. Double impression 2,700.
J18 D1 20o gray ('30) 4.75 5.00
Never hinged 9.75
J19 D1 25o scarlet ('23) 4.50 6.00
Never hinged 21.00
J20 D1 25o violet ('26) 3.75 7.75
Never hinged 10.00
J21 D1 25o lt blue ('30) 7.25 10.75
Never hinged 16.50
J22 D1 1k dk blue ('21) 90.00 20.00
Never hinged 250.00
J23 D1 1k brn & dk bl ('25) 10.00 18.00
Never hinged 30.00
J24 D1 5k purple ('25) 22.50 18.00
Never hinged 60.00
Nos. J9-J24 (16) 236.00 168.00
Set, never hinged 615.00

Engraved (Lined Panel)
1934-55 **Unwmk.** ***Perf. 13***
J25 D1 1o slate .30 .30
Never hinged .40
J26 D1 2o carmine .35 .30
Never hinged .75
J27 D1 5o yellow green .45 .30
Never hinged .80
J28 D1 6o dk olive ('41) .45 .30
Never hinged 1.00
J29 D1 8o magenta ('50) 2.00 *4.00*
Never hinged 4.00
J30 D1 10o orange .35 .30
Never hinged .60
J31 D1 12o dp ultra ('55) .55 1.50
Never hinged .75
J32 D1 15o lt violet ('54) .85 .30
Never hinged 1.00
J33 D1 20o gray .65 .30
Never hinged .85
J34 D1 25o blue .75 .30
Never hinged 1.00
J35 D1 30o green ('53) .50 .30
Never hinged .75
J36 D1 40o claret ('49) .60 .25
Never hinged 1.20
J37 D1 1k brown .80 .30
Never hinged 1.60
Nos. J25-J37 (13) 8.60 *8.75*
Set, never hinged 14.50

No. 96 Surcharged in Black

1934 **Wmk. 114** ***Perf. 14x14½***
J38 A10 15o on 12o violet 6.00 4.50
Never hinged 18.00

MILITARY STAMPS

Nos. 97 and 100 Overprinted in Blue

1917 **Wmk. 114** ***Perf. 14x14½***
M1 A16 5o green 19.00 *40.00*
Never hinged 37.50
a. "S" inverted 300.00 *375.00*
Never hinged 525.00
M2 A16 10o red 16.00 *27.00*
Never hinged 32.50
a. "S" inverted 225.00 *375.00*
Never hinged 450.00
Set, never hinged 70.00
#M1a, M2a, never hinged 975.00

The letters "S F" are the initials of "Soldater Frimaerke" (Soldier's Stamp).

For overprint see No. J8.

OFFICIAL STAMPS

Small State Seal — O1

Wmk. Crown (112)
1871 **Typo.** ***Perf. 14x13½***
O1 O1 2s blue 275.00 200.00
Never hinged 750.00
On cover 225.00
a. 2s ultra 275.00 200.00
Never hinged 750.00
On cover 225.00
b. Imperf *450.00*
As "b," pair *1,200.*
O2 O1 4s carmine 77.50 40.00
Never hinged 275.00
On cover 37.50
a. Imperf *450.00*
As "a," pair *1,250.*
O3 O1 16s green 450.00 350.00
Never hinged 1,300.
On cover 2,100.
a. Imperf *450.00*
As "a," pair *1,250.*

Perf. 12½
O4 O1 4s carmine 6,500. 650.00
On cover 750.00
O5 O1 16s green 450.00 600.00
Never hinged 1,250.
On cover 2,400.
#O1-O3, O5, never hinged 3,575.

Nos. O4-O5 values are for stamps with defective perfs.

Nos. O1-O3 were reprinted in 1886 upon white wove paper, unwatermarked and imperforate. Value $10 each.

1875 ***Perf. 14x13½***
O6 O1 3o violet 15.00 *55.00*
Never hinged 60.00
On cover 150.00
O7 O1 4o grnsh blue 18.00 6.25
Never hinged 52.50
On cover 22.50
O8 O1 8o carmine 15.00 2.00
Never hinged 52.50
On cover 11.00
a. Imperf —
O9 O1 32o green 32.50 *30.00*
Never hinged 80.00
On cover 225.00
Nos. O6-O9 (4) 80.50 *93.25*
Set, never hinged 245.00

For surcharge see No. 81.

1899-02 ***Perf. 13***
O9A O1 3o red lilac ('02) 4.50 *15.00*
Never hinged 10.00
On cover 37.50
c. Imperf *400.00*
As "c," pair *1,100.*
O9B O1 4o blue 3.75 *4.50*
Never hinged 10.00
On cover 35.00
O10 O1 8o carmine 20.00 *26.00*
Never hinged 65.00
On cover 72.50
Nos. O9A-O10 (3) 28.25 45.50
Set, never hinged 85.00

For surcharge see No. 137.

1902-06 **Wmk. 113**
O11 O1 1o orange 2.25 *3.25*
Never hinged 6.75
On cover 18.00
O12 O1 3o red lilac ('06) 1.50 *1.90*
Never hinged 4.50
On cover 18.00
O13 O1 4o blue ('03) 3.00 *4.50*
Never hinged 7.50
On cover 19.00
O14 O1 5o green 3.00 .85
Never hinged 7.50
On cover 10.00
O15 O1 10o carmine 4.50 3.50
Never hinged 10.00
On cover 18.00
Nos. O11-O15 (5) 14.25 14.00
Set, never hinged 36.00

1914-23 **Wmk. 114** ***Perf. 14x14½***
O16 O1 1o orange 1.25 *2.75*
Never hinged 2.75
On cover 22.50
O17 O1 3o gray ('18) 4.50 *17.00*
Never hinged 12.00
On cover 75.00
O18 O1 4o blue ('16) 30.00 *60.00*
Never hinged 65.00
On cover 150.00
O19 O1 5o green ('15) 3.00 2.25
Never hinged 7.50
On cover 11.00
O20 O1 5o choc ('23) 7.50 *30.00*
Never hinged 18.00
Postally used 17.00
On cover —
O21 O1 10o red ('17) 15.00 8.00
Never hinged 35.00
On cover 30.00
O22 O1 10o green ('21) 5.25 *6.00*
Never hinged 15.00
On cover 30.00
O23 O1 15o violet ('19) 20.00 *37.50*
Never hinged 37.50
On cover 120.00
O24 O1 20o indigo ('20) 22.50 20.00
Never hinged 60.00
On cover 67.50
Nos. O16-O24 (9) 109.00 *183.50*
Set, never hinged 250.00

For surcharges see Nos. 185-191.

No. O20 is valued CTO.

Official stamps were discontinued Apr. 1, 1924.

NEWSPAPER STAMPS

Postal documents as listed below were official Post Office forms supplied to publishers. Newspaper stamps were affixed to the forms to pay postage for the delivery of bundles of papers.

Numeral of Value — N1

1907 Typo. Wmk. 113 *Perf. 13*

P1 N1 1o olive 20.00 3.00
Never hinged 60.00
On postal document 375.00
P2 N1 5o blue 30.00 15.00
Never hinged 100.00
On postal document 375.00
P3 N1 7o carmine 18.00 1.25
Never hinged 60.00
On postal document 300.00
P4 N1 10o deep lilac 57.50 5.00
Never hinged 160.00
On postal document 375.00
P5 N1 20o green 45.00 1.50
Never hinged 175.00
On postal document 375.00
P6 N1 38o orange 62.50 2.50
Never hinged 175.00
On postal document 450.00
P7 N1 68o yellow brown 150.00 27.50
Never hinged 450.00
On postal document 550.00
P8 N1 1k bl grn & claret 37.50 6.00
Never hinged 150.00
On postal document 375.00
P9 N1 5k rose & yel grn 225.00 45.00
Never hinged 825.00
On postal document 600.00
P10 N1 10k bister & blue 225.00 45.00
Never hinged 900.00
On postal document 600.00
Nos. P1-P10 (10) 870.50 151.75
Set, never hinged 3,050.

For surcharges see Nos. 138-144.

1914-15 Wmk. 114 *Perf. 14x14½*

P11 N1 1o olive gray 18.00 2.00
Never hinged 75.00
On postal document 375.00
P12 N1 5o blue 45.00 12.50
Never hinged 160.00
On postal document 375.00
P13 N1 7o rose 45.00 3.00
Never hinged 160.00
On postal document 300.00
P14 N1 8o green ('15) 45.00 7.00
Never hinged 160.00
On postal document 375.00
P15 N1 10o deep lilac 75.00 3.00
Never hinged 300.00
On postal document 375.00
P16 N1 20o green 300.00 3.25
Never hinged 900.00
On postal document 375.00
a. Imperf., pair *1,200.*
P17 N1 29o orange yel ('15) 75.00 8.00
Never hinged 350.00
On postal document 375.00
P18 N1 38o orange 2,000. 190.00
Never hinged 3,500.
On postal document —
P19 N1 41o yellow brn ('15) 95.00 5.75
Never hinged 450.00
On postal document 375.00
P20 N1 1k blue grn & mar 125.00 3.25
Never hinged 650.00
On postal document 300.00
Nos. P11-P17,P19-P20 (9) 823.00 47.75
Set, never hinged 3,200.

For surcharges see Nos. 145-154.

PARCEL POST STAMPS

These stamps were for use on postal packets sent by the Esbjerg-Fano Ferry Service.

Regular Issues of 1913-30 Overprinted

1919-41 Wmk. 114 *Perf. 14x14½*

Q1 A10 10o green ('22) 20.00 20.00
Never hinged 75.00
Q2 A10 10o bister brn ('30) 15.00 8.50
Never hinged 50.00
Q3 A16 10o red 45.00 *90.00*
Never hinged 120.00
a. "POSFFAERGE" 200.00 *500.00*
Never hinged 450.00
Q4 A16 15o violet 20.00 *35.00*
Never hinged 60.00
a. "POSFFAERGE" 250.00 *525.00*
Never hinged 450.00
Q5 A16 30o orange ('22) 22.50 *47.50*
Never hinged 60.00
Q6 A16 30o dk blue ('26) 4.50 8.00
Never hinged 9.50
Q7 A16 50o cl & blk ('20) 300.00 *350.00*
Never hinged 600.00
Q8 A16 50o lt gray ('22) 30.00 30.00
Never hinged 90.00
a. 50o olive gray ('22) 225.00 *450.00*
Never hinged 600.00
Q9 A16 1k brn & bl ('24) 60.00 30.00
Never hinged 225.00
Q9A A16 5k vio & brn ('41) 3.75 *3.25*
Never hinged 5.00
Q10 A16 10k ver & grn ('30) 80.00 *150.00*
Never hinged 150.00

Engr.

Q11 A17 1k yellow brn 120.00 *225.00*
Never hinged 300.00
a. "POSFFAERGE" 1,500. *2,600.*
Never hinged 2,250.
Nos. Q1-Q11 (12) 720.75 *997.25*
Set, never hinged 1,750.

1927-30

Q12 A30 15o red ('27) 27.00 15.00
Never hinged 45.00
Q13 A30 30o ocher ('27) 18.00 *20.00*
Never hinged 45.00
Q14 A30 40o yel grn ('30) 27.00 17.00
Never hinged 90.00
Nos. Q12-Q14 (3) 72.00 52.00
Set, never hinged 180.00

Overprinted on Regular Issues of 1933-40

1936-42 Unwmk. *Perf. 13*

Q15 A32 5o rose lake ('42) .35 .35
Never hinged .40
Q16 A32 10o yellow org 35.00 *35.00*
Never hinged 65.00
Q17 A32 10o lt brown ('38) 1.50 *2.75*
Never hinged 3.00
Q18 A32 10o purple ('39) .35 .35
Never hinged .50
Q19 A30 15o deep red 1.50 *2.00*
Never hinged 2.25
Q20 A30 30o blue, I 4.50 *7.50*
Never hinged 9.50
Q21 A30 30o blue, II ('40) 15.00 *32.50*
Never hinged 30.00
Q22 A30 30o org, II ('42) .60 *1.25*
Never hinged 1.00
Q23 A30 40o yel grn, I 4.50 *7.00*
Never hinged 12.00
Q24 A30 40o yel grn, II ('40) 15.00 *32.50*
Never hinged 30.00
Q25 A30 40o blue, II ('42) .60 *1.10*
Never hinged 1.20
Q26 A33 50o gray 1.20 *2.40*
Never hinged 2.25
Q27 A33 1k lt brown 1.40 *1.40*
Never hinged 2.25
Nos. Q15-Q27 (13) 81.50 *126.10*
Set, never hinged 160.00

DIEGO-SUAREZ

dē-ˌā-gō ˈswär-əs

LOCATION — A town at the northern end of Madagascar
GOVT. — French Colony
POP. — 12,237

From 1885 to 1896 Diego-Suarez, (Antsirane), a French naval base, was a separate colony and issued its own stamps. These were succeeded by stamps of Madagascar.

100 Centimes = 1 Franc

Values for unused stamps are for examples with original gum as defined in the catalogue introduction except for Nos. 6-10 and J1-J2 which are valued without gum.

Stamps of French Colonies Handstamp Surcharged in Violet

1890 Unwmk. *Perf. 14x13½*

1 A9 15c on 1c blk, *bl* 300.00 100.00
On cover 625.00
2 A9 15c on 5c grn, *grnsh* 650.00 100.00
On cover 650.00
3 A9 15c on 10c blk, *lav* 300.00 92.50
On cover 625.00
4 A9 15c on 20c red, *grn* 650.00 80.00
On cover 550.00
5 A9 15c on 25c blk, *rose* 130.00 52.50
On cover 250.00

Inverted Surcharge

1a A9 15c on 1c blk, *bl* 475.00 225.00
2a A9 15c on 5c grn, *grnsh* 1,200. 325.00
3a A9 15c on 10c blk, *lav* 1,200. 450.00
4a A9 15c on 20c red, *grn* 1,200. 325.00
5a A9 15c on 25c blk, *rose* 550.00 250.00

Double Surcharge

1b A9 15c on 1c blk, *bl* 750.00 375.00
2b A9 15c on 5c grn, *grnsh* 3,000. 3,000.
3b A9 15c on 10c blk, *lav* 1,400. 475.00
4b A9 15c on 20c red, *grn* 1,400. 475.00
c. Dble. surch., both inverted 950.00
5b A9 15c on 25c blk, *rose* 550.00 250.00

Counterfeits exist.

Ship Flying French Flag — A2

France — A5

Symbolical of Union of France and Madagascar
A3 A4

1890 Litho. *Imperf.*

6 A2 1c black 1,150. 240.00
On cover 1,050.
7 A3 5c black 1,100. 200.00
On cover 875.00
8 A4 15c black 210.00 95.00
On cover 300.00
9 A5 25c black 225.00 110.00
On cover 375.00

Counterfeits exist of Nos. 6-9.

A6

1891

10 A6 5c black 350.00 100.00
On cover 1,050.

Excellent counterfeits exist of No. 10.

Stamps of French Colonies Surcharged in Red or Black

No. 11

No. 12

1892 *Perf. 14x13½*

11 A9 5c on 10c blk, *lav* (R) 210.00 105.00
On cover 1,100.
a. Inverted surcharge 475.00 400.00
12 A9 5c on 20c red, *grn* 190.00 72.50
On cover 1,000.
a. Inverted surcharge 450.00 400.00

Stamps of French Colonies Overprinted in Black or Red

1892

13 A9 1c blk, *lilac blue* (R) 32.50 20.00
Never hinged 55.00
On cover 190.00
14 A9 2c brown, *buff* 32.50 20.00
Never hinged 55.00
On cover 190.00
15 A9 4c claret, *lav* 55.00 45.00
Never hinged 105.00
On cover 225.00
16 A9 5c green, *grnsh* 120.00 80.00
Never hinged 225.00
On cover 275.00
17 A9 10c black, *lavender* 40.00 32.50
Never hinged 80.00
On cover 100.00
b. Double overprint 240.00 180.00
18 A9 15c blue, *pale blue* 32.50 20.00
Never hinged 55.00
On cover 80.00
19 A9 20c red, *grn* 40.00 32.50
Never hinged 80.00
On cover 150.00
20 A9 25c black, *rose* 36.00 20.00
Never hinged 65.00
On cover 75.00
21 A9 30c brown, *bis* (R) 1,300. 925.00
22 A9 35c black, *yellow* 1,300. 925.00
23 A9 75c carmine, *rose* 72.50 52.50
Never hinged 145.00
On cover 425.00
a. Double overprint 400.00
24 A9 1fr brnz grn, *straw* (R) 80.00 52.50
Never hinged 175.00
On cover 550.00
a. Double overprint 240.00 210.00

Inverted Overprint

13a A9 1c 225.00 190.00
14a A9 2c 225.00 190.00
15a A9 4c 325.00
16a A9 5c 240.00 200.00
17a A9 10c 240.00 200.00
20a A9 25c 240.00 200.00
21a A9 30c 1,700.
22a A9 35c 1,700.

Navigation and Commerce
A10 A11

1892 Typo. *Perf. 14x13½*

Name of Colony in Blue or Carmine

25 A10 1c black, *blue* 2.00 2.00
Never hinged 3.25
On cover 150.00
26 A10 2c brown, *buff* 2.75 2.75
Never hinged 5.00
On cover 150.00
27 A10 4c claret, *lav* 3.25 3.25
Never hinged 5.75
On cover 125.00
28 A10 5c green, *grnsh* 6.50 6.50
Never hinged 12.00
On cover 67.50
29 A10 10c black, *lavender* 8.75 7.25
Never hinged 16.00
On cover 62.50
30 A10 15c bl, quadrille paper 16.50 11.00
Never hinged 30.00
On cover 62.50
31 A10 20c red, *green* 22.50 16.00
Never hinged 45.00
On cover 110.00
On cover, single franking 200.00
32 A10 25c black, *rose* 17.50 14.50
Never hinged 32.50
On cover 62.50
33 A10 30c brown, *bister* 22.50 16.00
Never hinged 45.00
On cover 100.00
On cover, single franking 150.00
34 A10 40c red, *straw* 27.50 21.00
Never hinged 55.00
On cover 105.00
On cover, single franking 150.00
35 A10 50c carmine, *rose* 45.00 35.00
Never hinged 92.50
On cover 150.00
On cover, single franking 210.00
36 A10 75c violet, *org* 52.50 45.00
Never hinged 110.00
On cover 250.00
On cover, single franking 425.00
37 A10 1fr brnz grn, *straw* 75.00 60.00
Never hinged 150.00
On cover 375.00
On cover, single franking 625.00
Nos. 25-37 (13) 302.25 240.25

Perf. 13½x14 stamps are counterfeits.

1894 *Perf. 14x13½*

38 A11 1c black, *blue* 2.00 2.00
Never hinged 3.25
On cover 105.00
39 A11 2c brown, *buff* 2.75 2.40
Never hinged 4.75
On cover 105.00
40 A11 4c claret, *lav* 3.25 2.75
Never hinged 5.50
On cover 100.00
41 A11 5c green, *grnsh* 5.50 4.75
Never hinged 10.00
On cover 50.00
42 A11 10c black, *lavender* 7.25 7.25
Never hinged 12.50
On cover 37.50

43 A11 15c blue, quadrille paper 12.00 6.50
Never hinged 24.00
On cover 37.50
44 A11 20c red, *grn* 20.00 13.50
Never hinged 40.00
On cover 105.00
On cover, single franking 160.00
45 A11 25c black, *rose* 12.00 9.50
Never hinged 24.00
On cover 50.00
46 A11 30c brown, *bister* 13.50 6.50
Never hinged 27.50
On cover 92.50
On cover, single franking 120.00
47 A11 40c red, *straw* 13.50 6.50
Never hinged 27.50
On cover 92.50
On cover, single franking 120.00
48 A11 50c carmine, *rose* 20.00 13.50
Never hinged 40.00
On cover 110.00
On cover, single franking 150.00
49 A11 75c violet, *org* 12.00 8.75
Never hinged 24.00
On cover 150.00
On cover, single franking 250.00
50 A11 1fr brnz grn, *straw* 27.50 24.00
Never hinged 55.00
On cover 275.00
On cover, single franking 400.00
Nos. 38-50 (13) 151.25 107.90

Bisected stamps of type A11 are mentioned in note after Madagascar No. 62.

For surcharges see Madagascar Nos. 56-57, 61-62.

Perf. 13½x14 stamps are counterfeits.

POSTAGE DUE STAMPS

D1

D2

1891 Unwmk. Litho. *Imperf.*
J1 D1 5c violet 240.00 120.00
On cover 800.00
J2 D2 50c black 260.00 140.00
On cover 825.00

Excellent counterfeits exist of Nos. J1-J2.

Postage Due Stamps of French Colonies Ovptd. Like Nos. 13-24

1892
J3 D1 1c black 130.00 72.50
On cover 525.00
J4 D1 2c black 130.00 65.00
On cover 475.00
a. Inverted overprint 450.00 300.00
J5 D1 3c black 130.00 65.00
On cover 475.00
J6 D1 4c black 130.00 60.00
On cover 475.00
J7 D1 5c black 130.00 72.50
On cover 525.00
J8 D1 10c black 40.00 32.50
On cover 190.00
a. Inverted overprint 460.00 450.00
J9 D1 15c black 36.00 32.50
On cover 190.00
a. Double overprint 575.00 500.00
J10 D1 20c black 200.00 135.00
On cover 725.00
a. Double overprint 600.00 500.00
J11 D1 30c black 120.00 60.00
On cover 475.00
a. Inverted overprint 450.00 300.00
J12 D1 60c black 1,200. 775.00
J13 D1 1fr brown 2,800. 1,500.

DOMINICA

ˌdä-mə-ˈnē-kə

LOCATION — The largest island of the Windward group in the West Indies. Southeast of Puerto Rico.
AREA — 290 sq. mi.
POP. — 74,859 (1981)
CAPITAL — Roseau

Formerly a Presidency of the Leeward Islands, Dominica became a separate colony under the governor of the Windward Islands on January 1, 1940.

12 Pence = 1 Shilling
20 Shillings = 1 Pound
100 Cents = 1 Dollar (1949)

Catalogue values for unused stamps in this country are for Never Hinged items, beginning with Scott 112.

PRE-STAMP POSTAL MARKINGS

Crowned Circle handstamp type I is pictured in the Crowned Circle Handstamps and Great Britain Used Abroad section.

1845
A1 I "Dominica" crowned circle handstamp in red, on cover 625.00

This marking was used in black as a cancel from 1874 to 1883.

STAMPS OF GREAT BRITAIN USED IN DOMINICA

Numeral cancellation type A is pictured in the Crowned Circle Handstamps and Great Britain Used Abroad section.

1858-60

A07 (Roseau)
A2 A 1p rose red (#20) 320.00
A3 A 2p blue (#29, P7) 1,000.
A4 A 4p rose (#26) 375.00
A5 A 6p lilac (#27) 350.00
A6 A 1sh green (#28) 1,900.

Queen Victoria — A1

Perf. 12½
1874, May 4 Typo. Wmk. 1
1 A1 1p violet 170.00 55.00
a. Vertical half used as ½p on cover 9,000.
2 A1 6p green 625.00 115.00
3 A1 1sh deep lilac rose 375.00 80.00
Nos. 1-3 (3) 1,170. 250.00

During 1875-87 some issues were manuscript dated with village names. These are considered postally used. Stamps with entire village names sell for much more, starting at $100.

1877-79 *Perf. 14*
4 A1 ½p bister ('79) 19.00 62.50
5 A1 1p violet 20.00 3.75
a. Diagonal or vertical half used as ½p on cover 2,600.
6 A1 2½p red brown ('79) 275.00 45.00
7 A1 4p blue ('79) 130.00 4.00
8 A1 6p green 170.00 22.50
9 A1 1sh dp lilac rose 140.00 57.50
Nos. 4-9 (6) 754.00 195.25

For surcharges see Nos. 10-15.

No. 5 Bisected and Surcharged in Black or Red

a b c

1882
10 A1(a) ½p on half of 1p 240.00 57.50
a. Inverted surcharge 1,150. 900.00
b. Surcharge tete beche pair 2,600. 2,000.
11 A1(b) ½p on half of 1p 72.50 42.50
a. Surch. reading downward 72.50 42.50
b. Double surcharge 900.00
12 A1(c) ½p on half of 1p (R) 35.00 20.00
a. Inverted surcharge 1,150. 550.00
b. Double surcharge 1,850. 750.00
Nos. 10-12 (3) 347.50 120.00

The existence of genuine examples of No. 10b has been questioned.

Nos. 8 and 9 Surcharged in Black

1886
13 A1 ½p on 6p green 12.00 13.00
14 A1 1p on 6p green *45,000.* *12,500.*
15 A1 1p on 1sh 22.00 *22.00*
a. Double surcharge 11,500. 4,250.

All examples of No. 14 may have small pin marks which may have been part of the surcharging process.

1883-89 Wmk. 2
16 A1 ½p bister ('83) 7.00 *11.50*
17 A1 ½p green ('86) 5.75 *6.25*
18 A1 1p violet ('86) 60.00 16.00
a. Half used as ½p on cover 2,350.
19 A1 1p dp carmine ('89) 4.25 *14.00*
a. 1p rose ('87) 19.00 *26.00*
b. Vert. half used as ½p on cover 2,100.
20 A1 2½p red brn ('84) 160.00 4.00
21 A1 2½p ultra ('88) 4.25 *8.50*
22 A1 4p gray ('86) 7.75 *7.75*
23 A1 6p orange ('88) 21.00 *92.50*
24 A1 1sh dp lil rose ('88) 200.00 *500.00*
Nos. 16-24 (9) 470.00 *660.50*

Roseau, Capital of Dominica — A6

King Edward VII — A7

1903 Wmk. 1 *Perf. 14*
Ordinary Paper
25 A6 ½p gray green 5.25 4.75
26 A6 1p car & black 17.50 .80
27 A6 2p brn & gray grn 6.00 *8.00*
28 A6 2½p ultra & blk 11.50 5.25
29 A6 3p black & vio 10.50 4.50
30 A6 6p org brn & blk 15.00 *22.50*
31 A6 1sh gray grn & red vio 42.50 *52.50*
32 A6 2sh red vio & blk 40.00 *35.00*
33 A6 2sh6p ocher & gray grn 23.00 *92.50*
34 A7 5sh brown & blk 125.00 *175.00*
Nos. 25-34 (10) 296.25 *400.80*
Set, ovptd "SPECIMEN" 190.00

1906-07 Chalky Paper
25a ½p gray green 24.00 *24.00*
26a 1p car & black 50.00 8.50
27a 2p brn & gray grn 45.00 *55.00*
28a 2½p ultra & blk ('07) 32.50 *65.00*
29a 3p black & vio 55.00 *37.50*
31a 1sh gray grn & red vio 85.00 *175.00*

1907-20 Chalky Paper Wmk. 3
35 A6 ½p gray green 15.00 11.00
36 A6 1p car & black 2.50 .55
37 A6 2p brn & gray grn 16.00 *24.00*
38 A6 2½p ultra & black 5.50 27.50
39 A6 3p black & vio 5.00 *20.00*
40 A6 3p vio, *yel,* chalky paper ('09) 3.75 *5.25*
a. 3p vio, *yel,* ordinary paper ('12) 3.50 5.00
b. 3p vio, *pale yel,* ordinary paper ('20) 9.75 20.00
41 A6 6p org brn & blk ('08) 65.00 *100.00*
42 A6 6p vio & dl vio, chalky paper ('09) 12.50 *19.00*
a. 6p vio & dl vio, ordinary paper ('15) 4.00 *20.00*
43 A6 1sh gray grn & red vio 4.75 *67.50*
44 A6 1sh blk, *green,* chalky paper ('10) 3.75 5.00
a. 1sh blk, *green,* ordinary paper ('15) 4.25 *4.50*
45 A6 2sh red vio & blk ('08) 30.00 *40.00*
46 A6 2sh ultra & vio, *bl* ('19) 32.50 *110.00*
47 A6 2sh6p ocher & gray grn ('08) 27.50 *75.00*
48 A6 2sh6p red & blk, *bl* ('20) 32.50 *125.00*
49 A7 5sh brn & blk ('08) 75.00 75.00
Nos. 35-49 (15) 331.25 *704.80*

For type surcharged see No. 55.

1908-09 Ordinary Paper
50 A6 ½p green 9.50 6.25
a. ½p deep green 3.75 2.50
51 A6 1p scarlet 2.00 .75
a. 1p carmine 4.50 .45
52 A6 2p gray ('09) 4.50 *17.50*
53 A6 2½p ultramarine 9.50 *9.75*
a. 2½p bright blue ('18) 5.75 *10.50*
Nos. 50-53 (4) 25.50 *34.25*

King George V — A8

1914 Chalky Paper *Perf. 14*
54 A8 5sh grn & scar, *yel* 70.00 *100.00*

Type of 1903 Surcharged

1920
55 A6 1½p on 2½p orange 7.50 4.75

1921 Ordinary Paper Wmk. 4
56 A6 ½p green 3.50 *25.00*
57 A6 1p rose red 3.00 *4.00*
58 A6 1½p orange 4.75 *18.00*
59 A6 2p gray 4.25 *4.00*
60 A6 2½p ultra 3.25 *17.50*
61 A6 6p vio & dl vio 5.00 *50.00*
62 A6 2sh ultra & vio, *bl* 50.00 *145.00*
63 A6 2sh6p red & blk, *bl* 45.00 *165.00*
Nos. 56-63 (8) 118.75 *428.50*
Set, ovptd. "SPECIMEN" 175.00

No. 61 is on chalky paper.

Seal of Colony and George V — A9

1923-33 Chalky Paper Wmk. 4
65 A9 ½p green & blk 2.50 .85
66 A9 1p violet & blk 7.50 2.25
67 A9 1p scar & black 18.00 1.40
68 A9 1½p car & black 6.75 .90
69 A9 1½p dp brn & blk 15.50 .95
70 A9 2p gray & black 4.50 .65
71 A9 2½p org & black 4.50 *10.00*
72 A9 2½p ultra & black 7.75 2.25
73 A9 3p ultra & black 4.50 *19.00*
74 A9 3p red & blk, *yel* 4.50 1.40
75 A9 4p brown & blk 5.25 *7.25*
76 A9 6p red vio & blk 5.50 *9.00*
77 A9 1sh blk, *emerald* 3.50 *3.75*
78 A9 2sh ultra & blk, *bl* 26.00 *40.00*
79 A9 2sh6p red & blk, *bl* 27.50 *40.00*
80 A9 3sh vio & blk, *yel* 4.50 *15.00*
81 A9 4sh red & blk, *emer* 22.00 *40.00*
82 A9 5sh grn & blk, *yel* 40.00 *62.50*
Nos. 65-82 (18) 210.25 *257.15*

Issue years: Nos. 80, 82, 1927; Nos. 72, 74, 1928; Nos. 67, 69, 1933; others, 1923.

Many values of this set are known with a forged G.P.O. cancellation dated "MY 19 27".

1923 **Wmk. 3**

83 A9 3sh vio & blk, *yel* 5.75 *72.50*
84 A9 5sh grn & blk, *yel* 10.00 *65.00*
85 A9 £1 vio & blk, *red* 260.00 *375.00*
Nos. 83-85 (3) 275.75 *512.50*

Common Design Types pictured following the introduction.

Silver Jubilee Issue
Common Design Type
Perf. 13½x14

1935, May 6 **Wmk. 4** **Engr.**

90 CD301 1p car & blue 1.60 .35
91 CD301 1½p gray blk & ultra 5.75 3.25
92 CD301 2½p blue & brn 5.75 *4.75*
93 CD301 1sh brt vio & ind 5.75 *11.50*
Nos. 90-93 (4) 18.85 19.85
Set, never hinged 27.50
Set, perf. "SPECIMEN" 120.00

Coronation Issue
Common Design Type

1937, May 12 ***Perf. 11x11½***

94 CD302 1p dark carmine .25 .25
95 CD302 1½p brown .25 .25
96 CD302 2½p deep ultra .35 *1.90*
Nos. 94-96 (3) .85 2.40
Set, never hinged 1.50
Set, perf. "SPECIMEN" 120.00

Fresh-Water Lake — A10

Layou River — A11

Picking Limes — A12

Boiling Lake — A13

1938-47 **Wmk. 4** ***Perf. 12½***

97 A10 ½p grn & red brn .25 .25
98 A11 1p car & gray .25 .25
99 A12 1½p rose vio & grn .25 *.75*
100 A13 2p brn blk & dp rose .35 *2.25*
101 A12 2½p ultra & rose vio .25 *2.25*
a. 2½p bl & rose vio 2.75 1.90
102 A11 3p red brn & ol .25 *.60*
103 A12 3½p red vio & brt ultra 1.00 *2.10*
104 A10 6p vio & yel grn .50 *1.60*
105 A10 7p org brn & grn 1.00 *1.60*
106 A13 1sh olive & vio 2.50 1.60
107 A11 2sh red vio & blk 4.50 *12.50*
108 A10 2sh6p scar ver & blk 10.00 5.75
109 A11 5sh dk brn & bl 8.00 *12.00*
110 A13 10sh dl org & blk 10.00 *22.50*
Nos. 97-110 (14) 39.10 *66.00*
Set, never hinged 80.00

Issued: No. 101, 8/42; 3½p, 7p, 2sh, 10sh, 10/15/47; others, 8/15/38.

King George VI — A14

1940, Apr. 15 **Photo.** ***Perf. 14½x14***

111 A14 ¼p brown violet 1.00 *.25*
a. Ordinary paper ('42) .25 *1.50*

No. 111 is on chalky paper.

Catalogue values for unused stamps in this section, from this point to the end of the section, are for Never Hinged items.

Peace Issue
Common Design Type

1946, Oct. 14 **Engr.** ***Perf. 13½x14***

112 CD303 1p carmine .25 .25
113 CD303 3½p deep blue .25 .25

Silver Wedding Issue
Common Design Types

1948, Dec. 1 **Photo.** ***Perf. 14x14½***

114 CD304 1p scarlet .25 .25

Engraved; Name Typographed
Perf. 11½x11

115 CD305 10sh orange brn 25.00 *32.50*

UPU Issue
Common Design Types
Engr.: Name Typo. on 6c and 12c

1949, Oct. 10 ***Perf. 13½, 11x11½***

116 CD306 5c blue .25 .25
117 CD307 6c chocolate 1.25 *3.00*
118 CD308 12c rose violet .50 *2.10*
119 CD309 24c olive .30 .30
Nos. 116-119 (4) 2.30 5.65

University Issue
Common Design Types

1951, Feb. 16 **Engr.** ***Perf. 14x14½***

120 CD310 3c purple & green .60 *1.25*
121 CD311 12c dp car & dk bl grn .80 .50

George VI A15

Drying Cocoa A16

Picking Oranges — A17

Designs: 2c and 60c, Carib Baskets. 3c and 48c, Lime Plantation. 4c, Picking Oranges. 5c, Bananas. 6c, Botanical Gardens. 8c, Drying Vanilla Beans. 12c and $1.20, Fresh Water Lake. 14c, Layou River. 24c, Boiling Lake.

Perf. 14½x14

1951, July 1 **Photo.** **Wmk. 4**

122 A15 ½c brown .25 .25

Perf. 13x13½
Engr.

123 A16 1c red org & blk .25 .30
124 A16 2c dp grn & red brn .25 .25
125 A16 3c red vio & bl grn .25 *3.50*
126 A16 4c dk brn & brn org .75 *3.75*
127 A16 5c rose red & blk .85 .30
128 A16 6c org brn & ol grn 1.00 .30
129 A16 8c dp bl & dp grn 3.00 1.75
130 A16 12c emer & gray .75 *1.25*
131 A16 14c pur & blue 1.25 *3.50*
132 A16 24c rose car & red vio 1.00 .40
133 A16 48c red org & bl grn 5.00 *13.50*
134 A16 60c gray & car 4.00 *9.25*
135 A16 $1.20 gray & emer 8.25 *7.25*

Perf. 13½x13

136 A17 $2.40 gray & org 30.00 *52.50*
Nos. 122-136 (15) 56.85 *98.05*

Nos. 125, 127, 129 and 131 Overprinted in Black or Carmine

1951, Oct. 15 ***Perf. 13x13½***

137 A16 3c red vio & bl green .25 *.60*
138 A16 5c rose red & black .25 *1.75*
139 A16 8c dp blue & dp grn (C) .30 .25
140 A16 14c purple & blue (C) 1.75 .30
Nos. 137-140 (4) 2.55 2.90

Adoption of a new constitution for the Windward Islands, 1951.

WAR TAX STAMPS

No. 50 Surcharged in Red

1916 **Wmk. 3** ***Perf. 14***

MR1 A6 ½p on ½p green 3.50 .85

No. 50 Overprinted in Black

1918

MR2 A6 ½p green 7.50 *6.25*

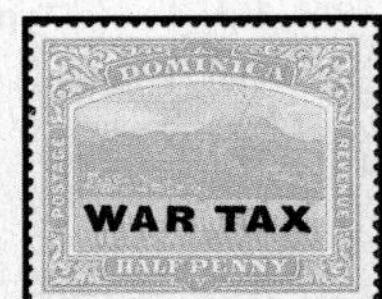

Nos. 50, 40 in Black or Red

1918

MR3 A6 ½p green .25 *.30*
MR4 A6 3p violet, *yel* (R) 5.50 *4.50*

Type of 1908-09 Surcharged in Red

1919

MR5 A6 1½p on 2½p orange .25 *.60*

DOMINICAN REPUBLIC

də-'mi-ni-kən ri-'pə-blik

LOCATION — Comprises about two-thirds of the island of Hispaniola in the West Indies.
GOVT. — Republic
AREA — 18,700 sq. mi.
POP. — 5,982,000 (est. 1983)
CAPITAL — Santo Domingo

8 Reales = 1 Peso
100 Centavos = 1 Peso (1880)
100 Centimos = 1 Franco (1883)
100 Centavos = 1 Peso (1885)

Watermarks

Wmk. 115 — Diamonds

Wmk. 116 — Crosses and Circles

FORERUNNERS

BRITISH POST OFFICES IN DOMINICAN REPUBLIC

Puerto Plata

British P.O. opened by 1867; closed 1871; reopened 1876; closed 1881

Stamps of Great Britain, Canceled C86, or with Circular Date Stamp

1876-81

A1 ½p rose red (#58, P 10, 12, 14), *value from* 85.00
A2 1p rose red (#33, P 123, 130, 136, 146, 151, 178, 199, 200, 205, 217) *value from* 70.00
A3 1½p lake red (#32, P 3) 125.00
A4 2p blue (#30, P 13, 14), *value from* 85.00
A5 2½p claret (#67, P 13, 14), *value from* 250.00
A6 3p rose (#61, P 18) 110.00
A7 4p vermilion (#43, P 14) 110.00
A8 4p vermilion (#69, P 15) 375.00
A9 4p pale olive green (#70, P 15) 290.00
A10 6p violet (#51, P 8) —
A11 6p gray (#62, P 15) 95.00
A12 8p orange (#73) 450.00
A13 1sh green (#54, P 4, 7) *value from* 85.00
A14 1sh green (#64, P 11-13) *value from* 90.00
A15 2sh blue (#55) 310.00
A16 5sh rose (#57, P 2) —

Santo Domingo

British P.O. opened by 1867; closed 1871; reopened 1876; closed 1881

Stamps of Great Britain, Canceled C87, or with Circular Date Stamp

1876-81

A17 ½p rose red (#58, P 5, 6, 8, 10, 11, 13), *value from* 105.00
A18 1p rose red (#33, P 146, 154, 171, 173, 174, 176, 178, 186, 190, 197, 220) *value from* 80.00
A19 1½p lake red (#32, P 3) 125.00
A20 2p blue (#30, P 13, 14), *value from* 125.00
A21 3p rose (#61, P 18) —
A22 4p vermilion (#43, P 11, 12, 14) 125.00
A23 4p vermilion (#69, P 15) 510.00
A24 4p pale olive green (#70, P 15) 325.00
A25 6p gray (#62, P 15) —
A26 8p orange (#73) —
A27 9p bister (#52) —
A28 1sh green (#54, P 4) —
A29 1sh green (#64, P 10-13) *value from* 130.00
A30 2sh blue (#55) —

Dominican Republic

Coat of Arms
A1 A2

1865 Unwmk. Typo. *Imperf.*

Wove Paper

1 A1 ½r black, *rose* 700. 650.
2 A1 1r black, *dp green* 1,100. 1,000.

Twelve varieties of each.

Laid Paper

3 A2 ½r black, *pale green* 550. 475.
4 A2 1r black, *straw* 1,800. 1,200.

Twelve varieties of the ½r, ten of the 1r.

A3

A4

1866 Laid Paper Unwmk.

5 A3 ½r black, *straw* 200.00 160.00
6 A3 1r black, *pale green* 2,500. 2,000.
7 A4 1r black, *pale green* 175.00 125.00

Nos. 5-8 have 21 varieties (sheets of 21).

Wmk. 115

8 A3 1r black, *pale green* 13,000. 13,000.
a. "CORREOS" and "Un Real" doubled 21,000.

The unique example of No. 8a is centered in the grade of fine, has a shallow thin spot and pinhole.

1866-67 Wove Paper Unwmk.

9 A3 ½r black, *rose* ('67) 60.00 60.00
10 A3 1r blk, *pale green* 85.00 75.00
a. Inscription dbl., top & bottom *400.00* *400.00*
11 A3 1r black, *blue* ('67) 60.00 37.50
a. 1r black, *light blue* ('67) 50.00 30.00
b. No space btwn. "Un" and "real" *600.00* 500.00
c. Without inscription at top & bottom *1,500.* 1,000.
d. Inscription invtd., top & bottom —
Nos. 9-11 (3) 205.00 172.50

1867-71 Pelure Paper

13 A3 ½r black, *rose* 150.00 75.00
15 A3 ½r black, *lav* ('68) 250.00 210.00
a. Without inscription at top and bottom 525.00
b. Dbl. inscriptions, one invtd. *425.00*
16 A3 ½r black, *grnsh gray* ('68) 260.00 225.00
17 A3 ½r black, *yellow* ('68) 12,000.
18 A3 ½r black, *ol* ('69) 3,000. 5,500.
22 A3 1r black, *blue* 4,000.
23 A3 1r black, *lavender* 225.00 200.00
24 A4 1r black, *rose* ('68) 225.00 225.00
25 A4 1r black, *mag* ('69) 2,250. 1,300.
26 A4 1r black, *sal* ('71) 300.00 225.00

Value for No. 17 is for an example with very fine centering and small faults. Value for No. 22 is for a faulty example with very fine centering and appearance.

1870-73 Ordinary Paper

27 A3 ½r black, *magenta* 2,500. 4,750.
28 A3 ½r blue, *rose* (blk inscription) ('71) 50.00 42.50
a. Blue inscription 500.00 500.00
b. Without inscription at top and bottom
29 A3 ½r black, *yel* ('73) 30.00 21.00
a. Without inscription at top and bottom 700.00 700.00
30 A4 1r black, *vio* ('73) 30.00 21.00
a. Without inscription at top and bottom 700.00 700.00
31 A4 1r black, *dk grn* 60.00 50.00

Nos. 9-31 have 21 varieties (sheets of 21). Nos. 29 and 30 are known pin-perforated, unofficially.

Bisects are known of several of the early 1r stamps.

A5

1879 *Perf. 12½x13*

32 A5 ½r violet 3.00 2.10
a. Imperf., pair 9.00 9.00
b. Horiz. pair, imperf. vert. 17.00
33 A5 ½r violet, *bluish* 2.50 1.80
a. Imperf., pair 9.00 7.50
34 A5 1r carmine 4.50 2.10
a. Imperf., pair 11.50 9.00
b. Perf. 13 11.50 7.50
c. Perf. 13x12½ 11.50 7.50
35 A5 1r carmine, *sal* 2.50 1.50
a. Imperf., pair 8.25 8.25
Nos. 32-35 (4) 12.50 7.50

In 1891 15 stamps of 1879-83 were surcharged "U P U," new values and crossed diagonal lines.

A6

1880 Typo. *Rouletted in Color*

36 A6 1c green 1.40 .90
b. Laid paper 50.00 50.00
37 A6 2c red 1.00 .75
a. Pelure paper 40.00 40.00
b. Laid paper 40.00 40.00
38 A6 5c blue 1.50 .70
39 A6 10c rose 3.25 .90
40 A6 20c brown 2.00 .85
41 A6 25c violet 2.25 1.25
42 A6 50c orange 3.00 1.75
43 A6 75c ultra 5.75 3.00
a. Laid paper 40.00 40.00
44 A6 1p gold 7.50 4.50
a. Laid paper 50.00 50.00
b. Double impression 42.50 42.50
Nos. 36-44 (9) 27.65 14.60

1881 Network Covering Stamp

45 A6 1c green .90 .50
46 A6 2c red .90 .50
47 A6 5c blue 1.25 .50
48 A6 10c rose 1.50 .65
49 A6 20c brown 1.50 .90
50 A6 25c violet 1.75 1.00
51 A6 50c orange 2.00 1.40
52 A6 75c ultra 6.00 4.50
53 A6 1p gold 8.00 7.00
Nos. 45-53 (9) 23.80 16.95

Preceding Issues (Type A6) Srch. with Value in New Currency

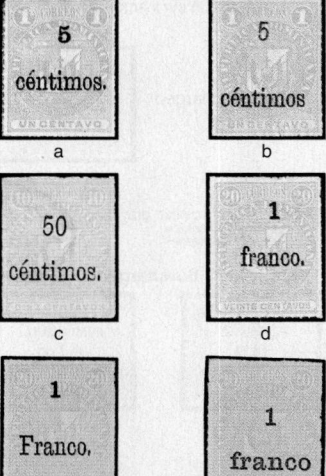

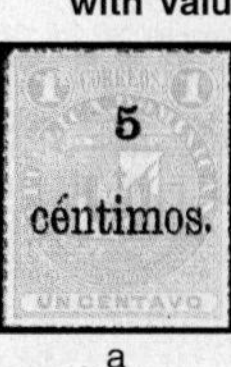
a

b

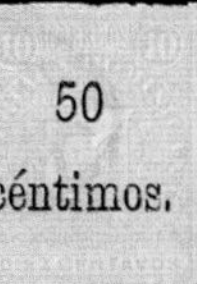
c

d

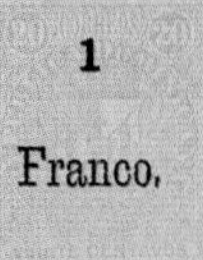
e

f

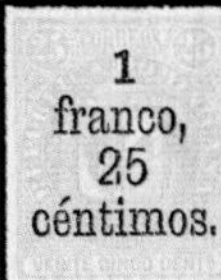
g

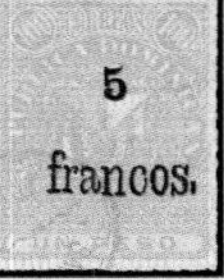
h

i

1883 Without Network

54 (a) 5c on 1c green 1.50 1.60
b. Inverted surcharge 21.00 21.00
c. Surcharged "25 céntimos" 50.00 50.00
d. Surcharged "10 céntimos" 27.50 27.50
55 (b) 5c on 1c green 25.00 9.00
b. Double surcharge 100.00
c. Inverted surcharge 65.00 65.00
56 (c) 5c on 1c green 17.00 9.50
b. Surcharged "10 céntimos" 35.00 35.00
c. Surcharged "25 céntimos" 37.50 37.50
57 (a) 10c on 2c red 5.00 3.00
a. Inverted surcharge 27.50 27.50
d. Surcharged "5 céntimos" 52.50 52.50
e. Surcharged "25 céntimos" 75.00 75.00
58 (c) 10c on 2c red 4.50 3.50
a. "Céntimso"
b. Inverted surcharge 37.50 37.50
c. Surcharged "25 céntimos" 60.00 60.00
d. "10" omitted 60.00
59 (a) 25c on 5c blue 7.00 4.50
a. Surcharged "5 céntimos" 52.50
b. Surcharged "10 céntimos" 52.50 52.50
c. Surcharged "50 céntimos" 75.00 75.00
d. Inverted surcharge 50.00 50.00
60 (c) 25c on 5c blue 7.50 3.50
a. Inverted surcharge 45.00 37.50
b. Surcharged "10 céntimos" 45.00 37.50
e. "25" omitted 75.00
f. Surcharged on back 75.00
61 (a) 50c on 10c rose 27.50 12.50
a. Inverted surcharge 50.00 45.00
62 (c) 50c on 10c rose 35.00 17.50
a. Inverted surcharge 52.50 52.50
63 (d) 1fr on 20c brown 15.00 9.75
64 (e) 1fr on 20c brown 17.50 9.75
a. Comma after "Franco," 27.50 27.50
65 (f) 1fr on 20c brown 25.00 17.50
a. Inverted surcharge 75.00
66 (g) 1fr25c on 25c violet 21.00 15.00
a. Inverted surcharge 65.00 65.00
67 (g) 2fr50c on 50c orange 16.00 12.00
a. Inverted surcharge 35.00 27.50
68 (g) 3fr75c on 75c ultra 27.50 25.00
b. Inverted surcharge 60.00 60.00
c. Laid paper 75.00 75.00
70 (i) 5fr on 1p gold 550.00 500.00
a. "s" of "francos" inverted 700.00 700.00

With Network

71 (a) 5c on 1c green 3.00 2.50
b. Inverted surcharge 22.50 22.50
c. Double surcharge 22.50 22.50
d. Surcharged "25 céntimos" 42.50 42.50
e. "5" omitted 75.00 75.00
72 (b) 5c on 1c green 21.00 9.00
b. Inverted surcharge 60.00 60.00
73 (c) 5c on 1c green 27.50 11.50
b. Surcharged "10 céntimos" 50.00 42.50
c. Surcharged "25 céntimos" 60.00
74 (a) 10c on 2c red 3.75 2.25
a. Surcharged "5 céntimos" 52.50 45.00
b. Surcharged "25 céntimos" 67.50 67.50
c. "10" omitted 57.50
75 (c) 10c on 2c red 3.00 2.00
a. Inverted surcharge 30.00 17.00
76 (a) 25c on 5c blue 7.50 3.50
a. Surcharged "10 céntimos" 75.00
b. Surcharged "5 céntimos" 60.00
c. Surcharged "50 céntimos" 67.50
77 (c) 25c on 5c blue 60.00 30.00
a. Inverted surcharge
b. Surcharged on back
78 (a) 50c on 10c rose 25.00 7.50
a. Inverted surcharge 50.00 30.00
b. Surcharged "25 céntimos" 60.00
79 (c) 50c on 10c rose 30.00 9.50
a. Inverted surcharge 60.00
80 (d) 1fr on 20c brown 12.00 9.75
81 (e) 1fr on 20c brown 14.50 12.50
a. Comma after "Franco" 35.00 35.00
b. Inverted surcharge 75.00
82 (f) 1fr on 20c brown 25.00 20.00
83 (g) 1fr25c on 25c violet 45.00 30.00
a. Inverted surcharge 75.00
84 (g) 2fr50c on 50c orange 19.00 12.50
a. Inverted surcharge 35.00 27.50
85 (g) 3fr75c on 75c ultra 45.00 42.50
86 (h) 5fr on 1p gold 140.00 140.00
a. Inverted surcharge
87 (i) 5fr on 1p gold 190.00 190.00

Many minor varieties exist in Nos. 54-87: accent on "i" of "centimos"; "5" with straight top; "1" with straight serif.

A7

A7a

1885-91 Engr. *Perf. 12*

88 A7 1c green 1.00 .50
89 A7 2c vermilion 1.00 .50
90 A7 5c blue 1.40 .50
91 A7a 10c orange 2.25 .65
92 A7a 20c dark brown 2.25 .80
93 A7a 50c violet ('91) 7.50 6.50
94 A7 1p carmine ('91) 20.00 13.50
95 A7 2p red brown ('91) 25.00 16.00
Nos. 88-95 (8) 60.40 38.95

Nos. 93, 94, 95 were issued without gum.
Imperf. varieties are proofs.
For surcharges see Nos. 166-168.

Coat of Arms — A8

1895 *Perf. 12½x14*

96 A8 1c green 1.25 .50
97 A8 2c orange red 1.25 .50
98 A8 5c blue 1.40 .50
99 A8 10c orange 3.25 1.60
Nos. 96-99 (4) 7.15 3.10

Exist imperforate but were not issued.

1897 *Perf. 14*

96a A8 1c green 1.40 .50
97a A8 2c orange red 8.00 .75
98a A8 5c blue 1.40 .75
99a A8 10c orange 2.75 1.50
Nos. 96a-99a (4) 13.55 3.50

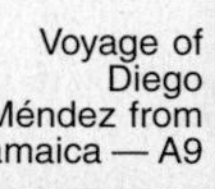
Voyage of Diego Méndez from Jamaica — A9

Enriquillo's Revolt — A10

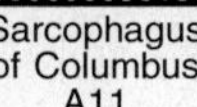
Sarcophagus of Columbus A11

"Española" Guarding Remains of Columbus A12

Toscanelli Replying to Columbus A13

Bartolomé de las Casas Defending Indians — A14

Columbus at Salamanca A15

Columbus' Mausoleum A16

1899, Feb. 27 Litho. *Perf. 11½*

100 A9 1c brown violet 7.25 5.25
102 A10 2c rose red 1.75 .70
103 A11 5c blue 2.00 .70
104 A12 10c orange 5.00 1.60
a. Tête bêche pair 42.50 42.50
105 A13 20c brown 10.00 8.25
106 A14 50c yellow green 11.50 9.75
a. Tête bêche pair 60.00 60.00
107 A15 1p black, *gray bl* 27.00 22.00
108 A16 2p bister brown 45.00 47.50

1900, Jan.

109 A11 ¼c black .75 *1.60*
110 A15 ½c black .75 *1.60*
110A A9 1c gray green .75 .65
Nos. 100-110A (11) 111.75 99.60

Nos. 100-110A were issued to raise funds for a Columbus mausoleum.

Imperf., Pairs

100a A9 1c brown violet 16.50 16.50
102a A10 2c rose red 5.00
103a A11 5c blue 5.75
104b A12 10c orange 8.75
105a A13 20c brown 15.00
106b A14 50c yellow green 17.50
c. As "b," tête bêche pair 125.00
107a A15 1p black, *gray blue* 42.50
108a A16 2p bister brown 70.00
109a A11 ¼c black 3.75 *4.25*
110b A15 ½c black 3.75 *4.25*
110c A9 1c gray green 3.50

Map of Hispaniola A17

1900, Oct. 21 Unwmk. *Perf. 14*

111 A17 ¼c dark blue .75 .40
112 A17 ½c rose .75 .40
113 A17 1c olive green .75 .40
114 A17 2c deep green .75 .40
115 A17 5c red brown .75 .40
a. Vertical pair, imperf. between 17.50

Perf. 12

116 A17 10c orange .75 .40
117 A17 20c lilac 3.00 2.50
a. 20c rose (error) 6.00 6.00
118 A17 50c black 2.75 2.50
119 A17 1p brown 3.00 2.50
Nos. 111-119 (9) 13.25 9.90

Several varieties in design are known in this issue. They were deliberately made. Counterfeits of Nos. 111-119 abound.

A18

1901-06 Typo. *Perf. 14*

120 A18 ½c carmine & vio .70 .40
121 A18 ½c blk & org ('05) 1.80 .95
122 A18 ½c grn & blk ('06) .85 .30
123 A18 1c ol grn & vio .70 .25
124 A18 1c blk & ultra ('05) 1.80 .85
125 A18 1c car & blk ('06) 1.00 .45
126 A18 2c dp grn & vio .80 .25
127 A18 2c blk & vio ('05) 2.25 .70
128 A18 2c org brn & blk ('06) 1.40 .25
129 A18 5c org brn & vio .80 .25
130 A18 5c black & cl ('05) 2.50 1.25
131 A18 5c blue & blk ('06) 1.25 .30
132 A18 10c orange & vio 1.40 .45
133 A18 10c blk & grn ('05) 4.25 2.25
134 A18 10c red vio & blk ('06) 1.40 .40
135 A18 20c brn vio & vio 2.50 .95
136 A18 20c blk & ol ('05) 13.50 8.75
137 A18 20c ol grn & blk ('06) 7.25 3.25
138 A18 50c gray blk & vio 8.00 5.50
139 A18 50c blk & red brn ('05) 47.50 34.00
140 A18 50c brn & blk ('06) 8.75 7.75
141 A18 1p brn & vio 18.00 10.00
142 A18 1p blk & gray ('05) 200.00 *225.00*
143 A18 1p violet & blk ('06) 21.00 13.50
Nos. 120-143 (24) 349.40 318.00

Issued: 11/15/01; 5/11/05; 8/17/06.

See Nos. 172-176. For surcharges see Nos.151-156.

Francisco Sánchez — A19

Juan Pablo Duarte — A20

Ramón Mella — A21

Ft. Santo Domingo — A22

1902, Feb. 25 Engr. *Perf. 12*

144 A19 1c dk green & blk .35 .35
145 A20 2c scarlet & blk .35 .35
146 A20 5c blue & blk .35 .35
147 A19 10c orange & blk .35 .35
148 A21 12c purple & blk .35 .35
149 A21 20c rose & blk .60 .60
150 A22 50c brown & blk .90 .90
Nos. 144-150 (7) 3.25 3.25

Center Inverted

144a A19 1c 17.50 *17.50*
145a A20 2c 17.50 *17.50*
146a A20 5c 17.50 *17.50*
148a A21 12c 17.50 *17.50*
149a A21 20c 17.50 *17.50*
150a A22 50c 17.50 *17.50*
Nos. 144a-150a (6) 105.00 *105.00*

400th anniversary of Santo Domingo.

Imperforate varieties of Nos. 144 to 150 were never sold to the public.

Nos. 138, 141 Surcharged in Black

1904, Aug.

151 A18 2c on 50c 9.25 7.25
152 A18 2c on 1p 13.50 9.25
b. "2" omitted 50.00 50.00
153 A18 5c on 50c 4.25 2.25
154 A18 5c on 1p 5.25 4.00
155 A18 10c on 50c 8.25 6.75
156 A18 10c on 1p 8.75 6.75
Nos. 151-156 (6) 49.25 36.25

Inverted Surcharge

151a A18 2c on 50c 15.00 15.00
152a A18 2c on 1p 15.00 15.00
c. As "a," "2" omitted 85.00 85.00
153a A18 5c on 50c 5.50 5.50
154a A18 5c on 1p 7.00 6.50
155a A18 10c on 50c 14.00 14.00
156a A18 10c on 1p 10.00 10.00
Nos. 151a-156a (6) 66.50 66.00

Official Stamps of 1902 Overprinted

1904, Aug. 16 Red Overprint

157 O1 5c dk blue & blk 5.75 3.00
a. Inverted overprint 7.25 5.75

Black Overprint

158 O1 2c scarlet & blk 17.00 5.25
a. Inverted overprint 20.00 6.50
159 O1 5c dk blue & blk 3,500. 3,500.
160 O1 10c yellow grn & blk 10.50 10.50
a. Inverted overprint 14.00 14.00

Official Stamps of 1902 Surcharged

161 O1 1c on 20c yellow & blk 4.75 3.00
a. Inverted surcharge 7.25 5.50

Nos. J1-J2 Surcharged or Overprinted in Black

1904-05 Surcharged "CENTAVOS"

162 D1 1c on 2c olive gray 250.00 200.00
a. "entavos" —
b. "Dominican" 350.00 300.00
c. "Centavo" 350.00 300.00

Carmine Surcharge or Overprint

163 D1 1c on 2c olive gray 3.50 1.10
a. Inverted surcharge 4.75 2.50
b. "Domihicana" 15.00 15.00
c. As "b," inverted 40.00 40.00
d. "Dominican" 10.50 10.50
e. "Centavos" omitted 30.00 30.00
g. "entavos" 30.00
163F D1 1c on 4c olive gray 35.00 7.00
164 D1 2c olive gray .95 .60
a. "Domihicana" 11.00 11.00
b. Inverted overprint 1.90 1.90
c. As "a," inverted 25.00 25.00
d. "Dominican" 5.75 5.75
e. "Centavo" omitted 12.50 10.00
f. "entavos" 12.50 12.50
g. As "f," inverted 40.00 40.00
h. As "d," inverted 40.00 40.00

Surcharged "CENTAVO"

165 D1 1c on 4c olive gray .95 .70
a. "Domihicana" 10.00 10.00
c. Inverted surcharge 1.75 1.75
d. "1" omitted 3.50 3.50
e. As "a," inverted 32.50 32.50
f. As "d," inverted 40.00 40.00
g. Double surcharge 30.00 30.00

No. 92 Surcharged in Red

1905, Apr. 4

166 A7a 2c on 20c dk brown 8.75 7.25
a. Inverted surcharge 15.00 15.00
167 A7a 5c on 20c dk brown 4.75 2.50
a. Inverted surcharge 16.00 16.00
b. Double surcharge 25.00 25.00
168 A7a 10c on 20c dk brown 8.75 7.25
Nos. 166-168 (3) 22.25 17.00

Nos. 166-168 exist with inverted "A" for "V" in "CENTAVOS" in surcharge.

No. J2 Surcharged in Red

1906, Jan. 16 *Perf. 14*

169 D1 1c on 4c olive gray .95 .50
a. Inverted surcharge 10.50 10.50
b. Double surcharge 25.00

Nos. J4, J3 Surcharged in Black

1906, May 1

170 D1 1c on 10c olive gray 1.10 .40
a. Inverted surcharge 10.50 10.50
b. Double surcharge 14.00 14.00
c. "OMINICANA" 20.00 20.00
d. As "c," inverted 150.00
171 D1 2c on 5c olive gray 1.10 .40
a. Inverted surcharge 10.50 10.50
b. Double surcharge 35.00

The varieties small "C" or small "A" in "REPUBLICA" are found on Nos.169, 170, 171.

Arms Type of 1901-06

1907-10 Wmk. 116

172 A18 ½c grn & blk ('08) .85 .25
173 A18 1c carmine & blk .85 .25
174 A18 2c orange brn & blk .85 .25
175 A18 5c blue & blk .85 .25
176 A18 10c red vio & blk ('10) 8.00 1.00
Nos. 172-176 (5) 11.40 2.00

No. O6 Overprinted in Red

1911, July 11 *Perf. 13½x14, 13½x13*

177 O2 2c scarlet & black 1.60 .60
a. "HABILITAOO" 8.75 6.00
b. Inverted overprint 21.00
c. Double overprint 21.00

A23

1911-13 Center in Black *Perf. 14*

178 A23 ½c orange ('13) .25 .25
179 A23 1c green .25 .25
180 A23 2c carmine .25 .25
181 A23 5c gray blue ('13) .80 .25
182 A23 10c red violet 1.60 .45
183 A23 20c olive green 11.50 11.50
184 A23 50c yellow brn ('12) 3.75 3.75
185 A23 1p violet ('12) 5.75 4.25
Nos. 178-185 (8) 24.15 20.95

See Nos. 230-232.

Juan Pablo Duarte — A24

1914, Apr. 13 *Perf. 13x14*

Background Red, White and Blue

186 A24 ½c orange & blk .60 .30
187 A24 1c green & blk .60 .30
188 A24 2c rose & blk .60 .30
189 A24 5c slate & blk .60 .40
190 A24 10c magenta & blk 1.40 .70
191 A24 20c olive grn & blk 2.50 1.90
192 A24 50c brown & blk 3.50 2.75
193 A24 1p dull lilac & blk 5.50 4.00
Nos. 186-193 (8) 15.30 10.65

Cent. of the birth of Juan Pablo Duarte (1813-1876), patriot and revolutionary.

Official Stamps of 1909-12 Surcharged in Violet or Overprinted in Red

a

b

1915, Feb. *Perf. 13½x13, 13½x14*

194 O2 (a) ½c on 20c orange & blk .50 .35
a. Inverted surcharge 6.00 6.00
b. Double surcharge 8.75 8.75
c. "Habilitado" omitted 5.25 5.25
195 O2 (b) 1c blue grn & blk .80 .25
a. Inverted overprint 6.00 6.00
b. Double overprint 7.00
c. Overprinted "1915" only 12.50
196 O2 (b) 2c scarlet & blk 1.25 .25
a. Inverted overprint 5.25 5.25
b. Double overprint 7.75 7.75
c. Overprinted "1915" only 8.75
d. "1915" double
197 O2 (b) 5c dk blue & blk 1.00 .25
a. Inverted overprint 7.00 7.00
b. Double overprint 8.75 8.75

c. Double ovpt., one invtd. 27.50
d. Overprinted "1915" only 8.50
198 O2 (b) 10c yel grn & blk 2.75 2.50
a. Inverted overprint 15.00
199 O2 (b) 20c orange & blk 9.25 7.25
a. "Habilitado" omitted
Nos. 194-199 (6) 15.55 10.85

Nos. 194, 196-198 are known with both perforations. Nos. 195, 199 are only perf. 13½x13.

The variety capital "I" for "1" in "Habilitado" occurs once in each sheet in all denominations.

Type of 1911-13 Redrawn

A25

SMALL LETTERS

LARGE LETTERS

TWO CENTAVOS:
Type I — "DOS" in small letters.
Type II — "DOS" in larger letters with white dot at each end of the word.

Overprinted "1915" in Red

1915 Unwmk. Litho. *Perf. 11½*
200 A25 ½c violet & blk .85 .25
a. Imperf., pair 5.75
201 A25 1c yel brn & blk .85 .25
a. Imperf., pair 6.50
b. Vert. pair, imperf. horiz. 10.50
c. Horiz. pair, imperf. vert. 10.50
202 A25 2c ol grn & blk (I) 3.75 .25
a. Imperf., pair 10.00
203 A25 2c ol grn & blk (II) 6.00 .25
a. Center omitted 87.50
b. Frame omitted 87.50
c. Imperf., pair 15.00
d. Horiz. pair, imperf. vert. 15.00
204 A25 5c magenta & blk 3.75 .25
a. Pair, one without overprint 65.00
b. Imperf., pair 6.50
205 A25 10c gray blue & blk 3.75 .50
a. Imperf., pair 7.75
b. Horiz. pair, imperf. vert. 35.00
206 A25 20c rose red & blk 8.25 1.40
a. Imperf., pair 12.50
207 A25 50c green & blk 10.50 4.00
a. Imperf., pair 25.00
208 A25 1p orange & blk 21.00 7.00
a. Imperf., pair 52.50
Nos. 200-208 (9) 58.70 14.15

Type of 1915 Overprinted "1916" in Red

1916
209 A25 ½c violet & blk 2.25 .25
a. Imperf., pair 21.00
210 A25 1c green & blk 3.25 .25
a. Imperf., pair 21.00

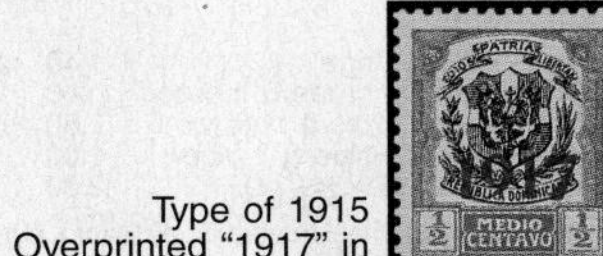

Type of 1915 Overprinted "1917" in Red

1917-19
213 A25 ½c red lilac & blk 3.50 .30
a. Horiz. pair, imperf. btwn. 47.50 47.50
214 A25 1c yellow grn & blk 1.60 .25
a. Vert. pair, imperf. btwn. 50.00
215 A25 2c olive grn & blk 2.25 .25
a. Imperf., pair 35.00
216 A25 5c magenta & blk 23.00 .85
Nos. 213-216 (4) 30.35 1.65

Type of 1915 Overprinted "1919" in Red

1919
219 A25 2c olive grn & blk 17.00 .25

Type of 1915 Overprinted "1920" in Red

1920-27
220 A25 ½c lilac rose & blk .60 .25
a. Horiz. pair, imperf. btwn. 25.00 25.00
b. Inverted overprint
c. Double overprint
d. Double overprint, one invtd.
221 A25 1c yellow grn & blk .75 .25
a. Overprint omitted 70.00
b. Horiz. pair, imperf. btwn. 40.00
222 A25 2c olive grn & blk .75 .25
a. Vertical pair, imperf. between 27.50
223 A25 5c dp rose & blk 9.00 .50
224 A25 10c blue & black 5.75 .25
225 A25 20c rose red & blk ('27) 7.75 .50
226 A25 50c green & blk ('27) 65.00 21.00
Nos. 220-226 (7) 89.60 23.00

Type of 1915 Overprinted "1921" in Red

1921
227 A25 1c yellow grn & blk 5.25 .30
a. Horiz. pair, imperf. btwn. 45.00 45.00
b. Imperf., pair 45.00 45.00
228 A25 2c olive grn & blk 5.75 .40
a. Vert. pair, imperf. btwn. 45.00

Redrawn Design of 1915 without Overprint

1922
230 A25 1c green 3.75 .25
231 A25 2c carmine (II) 3.75 .25
232 A25 5c blue 5.75 .25
Nos. 230-232 (3) 13.25 .75

Nos. 230-232 exist imperf.

A26

Type I

Type II

TEN CENTAVOS:
Type I — Numerals 2mm high. "DIEZ" in thick letters with large white dot at each end.
Type II — Numerals 3mm high. "DIEZ" in thin letters with white dot with colored center at each end.

1924-27 Second Redrawing
233 A26 1c green 1.60 .25
a. Vert. pair, imperf. btwn. 35.00 35.00
234 A26 2c red .85 .25
235 A26 5c blue 2.25 .25
236 A26 10c pale bl & blk (I) ('26) 12.00 3.00
236A A26 10c pale bl & blk (II) 22.50 1.10
236B A26 50c gray grn & blk ('26) 60.00 33.00
237 A26 1p orange & blk ('27) 19.00 12.50
Nos. 233-237 (7) 118.20 50.35

In the second redrawing the shield has a flat top and the design differs in many details from the stamps of 1911-13 and 1915-22.

A27

1927
238 A27 ½c lilac rose & blk .30 .25

Exhibition Pavilion — A28

1927 Unwmk. *Perf. 12*
239 A28 2c carmine 1.10 .50
240 A28 5c ultra 2.10 .50

Natl. and West Indian Exhib. at Santiago de los Caballeros.

Ruins of Columbus' Fortress A29

1928
241 A29 ½c lilac rose .95 .35
242 A29 1c deep green .70 .25
a. Horiz. pair, imperf. btwn. 25.00
243 A29 2c red .95 .25
244 A29 5c dark blue 2.75 .35
245 A29 10c light blue 2.75 .30
246 A29 20c rose 4.75 .40
247 A29 50c yellow green 13.50 8.25
248 A29 1p orange yellow 35.00 27.00
Nos. 241-248 (8) 61.35 37.15

Reprints exist of 1c, 2c and 10c.
Issued: 1c, 2c, 10c, Oct. 1; others, Dec.

Horacio Vasquez — A30

1929, May-June
249 A30 ½c dull rose .60 .30
250 A30 1c gray green .60 .25
251 A30 2c red .70 .25
252 A30 5c dark ultra 1.40 .35
253 A30 10c pale blue 2.10 .50
Nos. 249-253 (5) 5.40 1.65

Signing of the "Frontier" treaty with Haiti. Issue dates: 2c, May; others, June.

Imperf., Pairs

249a A30 ½c 12.50
250a A30 1c 12.50
251a A30 2c 12.50
252a A30 5c 14.00

Convent of San Ignacio de Loyola — A31

1930, May 1 *Perf. 11½*
254 A31 ½c red brown .70 .45
a. Imperf., pair 55.00 55.00
255 A31 1c deep green .65 .25
256 A31 2c vermilion .65 .25
a. Imperf., pair 60.00
257 A31 5c deep blue 2.10 .35
258 A31 10c light blue 4.25 1.25
Nos. 254-258 (5) 8.35 2.55

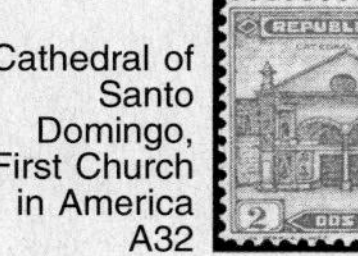

Cathedral of Santo Domingo, First Church in America A32

1931 *Perf. 12*
260 A32 1c deep green .85 .25
a. Imperf., pair 50.00
261 A32 2c scarlet .60 .25
a. Imperf., pair 50.00
262 A32 3c violet .85 .25
263 A32 7c dark blue 2.50 .25
264 A32 8c bister 3.00 .85
265 A32 10c light blue 5.75 1.25
a. Imperf., pair 35.00
Nos. 260-265 (6) 13.55 3.10

Issued: 3c-7c, Aug. 1; others, July 11.
For overprint see No. RAC8.

A33

Overprinted or Surcharged in Black

1932, Dec. 20 *Perf. 12*
Cross in Red
265B A33 1c yellow green .55 .50
265C A33 3c on 2c violet .80 .60
265D A33 5c blue 4.50 4.75
265E A33 7c on 10c turq bl 6.00 6.25
Nos. 265B-265E (4) 11.85 12.10

Proceeds of sale given to Red Cross. Valid Dec. 20 to Jan. 5, 1933.

Inverted and pairs, one without surcharge or overprint, exist on Nos. 265B-265D, as well as missing letters.

Fernando Arturo de Merino (1833-1906) as President — A35

Cathedral of Santo Domingo A36

Designs: ½c, 5c, 8c, Tomb of Merino. 1c, 3c, 10c, as Archbishop.

1933, Feb. 27 Engr. *Perf. 14*
266 A35 ½c lt violet .45 .35
267 A35 1c yellow green .60 .25
268 A35 2c lt red 1.00 .75
269 A35 3c deep violet .70 .30
270 A35 5c dark blue .80 .35
271 A35 7c ultra 1.40 .50
272 A35 8c dark green 1.75 1.00
273 A35 10c orange yel 1.50 .60
274 A35 20c carmine rose 3.00 1.75
275 A36 50c lemon 11.25 7.75
276 A36 1p dark brown 26.00 19.00
Nos. 266-276 (11) 48.45 32.60

For surcharges see Nos. G1-G7.

Tower of Homage, Ozama Fortress — A37

1932 Litho. *Perf. 12*

278 A37 1c green 1.75 .25
279 A37 3c violet 1.10 .25

Issue dates: 1c, July 2; 3c, June 22.

"CORREOS" added at left

1933, May 28

283 A37 1c dark green .50 .25

President Rafael L. Trujillo
A38 A39

1933, Aug. 16 Engr. *Perf. 14*

286 A38 1c yellow grn & blk .75 .35
287 A39 3c dp violet & blk .90 .35
288 A38 7c ultra & blk 2.00 .75
Nos. 286-288 (3) 3.65 1.45

42nd birthday of President Rafael Leonidas Trujillo Molina.

San Rafael Bridge — A40

1934 Litho. *Perf. 12*

289 A40 ½c dull violet .70 .40
290 A40 1c dark green 1.00 .25
291 A40 3c violet 1.75 .25
Nos. 289-291 (3) 3.45 .90

Opening of San Rafael Bridge.
Issue dates: ½c, 3c, Mar. 3; 1c, Feb. 17.

Trujillo Bridge A41

1934

292 A41 ½c red brown .70 .25
293 A41 1c green 1.00 .25
294 A41 3c purple 1.40 .25
Nos. 292-294 (3) 3.10 .75

Opening of the General Trujillo Bridge near Ciudad Trujillo.
Issue dates: 1c, Aug. 24. Others, Sept. 7.

Ramfis Bridge A42

1935, Apr. 6

295 A42 1c green .70 .25
296 A42 3c yellow brown .70 .25
297 A42 5c brown violet 2.10 1.00
298 A42 10c rose 4.25 1.40
Nos. 295-298 (4) 7.75 2.90

Opening of the Ramfis Bridge over the Higuamo River.

President Trujillo — A43

A44

A45

1935 *Perf. 11*

299 A43 3c yellow & brown .30 .25
300 A44 5c org red, bl, red & bis .40 .25
301 A45 7c ultra, bl, red & brn .60 .25
302 A44 10c red vio, bl, red & bis 1.00 .25
Nos. 299-302 (4) 2.30 1.00

Ratification of a treaty setting the frontier between Dominican Republic and Haiti.
Issued: 3c, 10/29; 5c, 10c, 11/25; 7c, 11/8.

National Palace A46

1935, Apr. 1 *Perf. 11½*

303 A46 25c yellow orange 3.75 .30

Obligatory for all mail addressed to the president and cabinet ministers.

Post Office, Santiago A47

1936

304 A47 ½c bright violet .30 .35
305 A47 1c green .30 .25

Issue dates: ½c, Jan. 14; 1c, Jan. 4.

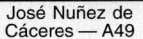

George Washington Ave., Ciudad Trujillo — A48

1936, Feb. 22

306 A48 ½c brn & vio brn .40 .45
a. Imperf., pair 52.50
307 A48 2c carmine & brn .40 .30
308 A48 3c yellow org & red brn .70 .25
309 A48 7c ultra, blue & brn 1.60 1.25
a. Imperf., pair 52.50
Nos. 306-309 (4) 3.10 2.25

Dedication of George Washington Avenue, Ciudad Trujillo.

José Nuñez de Cáceres — A49

Felix M. del Monte — A55

Proposed National Library — A56

1c, Gen. Gregorio Luperon. 2c, Emiliano Tejera. 3c, Pres. Trujillo. 5c, Jose Reyes. 7c, Gen. Antonio Duverge. 25c, Francisco J. Peynado. 30c, Salome Urena. 50c, Gen. Jose M. Cabral. 1p, Manuel de Jesus Galvan. 2p, Gaston F. Deligne.

1936 Unwmk. Engr. *Perf. 13½, 14*

310 A49 ½c dull violet .40 .25
311 A49 1c dark green .30 .25
312 A49 2c carmine .30 .25
313 A49 3c violet .40 .25
314 A49 5c deep ultra .70 .30
315 A49 7c slate blue 1.25 .60
316 A55 10c orange 1.25 .30
317 A56 20c olive green 5.75 3.00
318 A55 25c gray violet 6.75 8.75
319 A55 30c scarlet 8.25 11.50
320 A55 50c black brown 9.75 6.25
321 A55 1p black 27.50 35.00
322 A55 2p yellow brown 80.00 90.00
Nos. 310-322 (13) 142.60 156.70

The funds derived from the sale of these stamps were returned to the National Treasury Fund for the erection of a building for the National Library and Archives.
Issued: 3c, 7c, Mar. 18; others, May 22.

President Trujillo and Obelisk — A62

1937, Jan. 11 Litho. *Perf. 11½*

323 A62 1c green .30 .25
324 A62 3c violet .40 .25
325 A62 7c blue & turq blue 1.10 1.10
Nos. 323-325 (3) 1.80 1.60

1st anniv. of naming Ciudad Trujillo.

Discus Thrower and Flag — A63

Flag in Red and Blue

1937, Aug. 14

326 A63 1c dark green 11.50 1.00
327 A63 3c violet 14.50 1.00
328 A63 7c dark blue 26.00 5.25
Nos. 326-328 (3) 52.00 7.25

1st Natl. Olympic Games, Aug. 16, 1937.

Symbolical of Peace, Labor and Progress — A64

1937, Sept. 18 *Perf. 12*

329 A64 3c purple .50 .25

"8th Year of the Benefactor."

Monument to Father Francisco Xavier Billini (1837-90) — A65

1937, Dec. 29

330 A65 ½c deep orange .25 .25
331 A65 5c purple .60 .25

Globe and Torch of Liberty — A66

1938, Feb. 22 *Perf. 11½*

332 A66 1c green .50 .25
333 A66 3c purple .70 .25
334 A66 10c orange 1.40 .25
Nos. 332-334 (3) 2.60 .75

150th anniv. of the Constitution of the US.

Pledge of Trinitarians, City Gate and National Flag — A67

1938, July 16 *Perf. 12*

335 A67 1c green, red & dk bl .50 .25
336 A67 3c purple, red & bl .60 .25
337 A67 10c orange, red & bl 1.25 .40
Nos. 335-337 (3) 2.35 .90

Trinitarians and patriots, Francisco Del Rosario Sanchez, Matías Ramón Mella and Juan Pablo Duarte, who helped free their country from foreign domination.

Seal of the University of Santo Domingo — A68

1938, Oct. 28

338 A68 ½c orange .40 .25
339 A68 1c dp green & lt green .40 .25
340 A68 3c purple & pale vio .50 .25
341 A68 7c dp blue & lt blue 1.00 .50
Nos. 338-341 (4) 2.30 1.25

Founding of the University of Santo Domingo, on Oct. 28, 1538.

Trylon and Perisphere, Flag and Proposed Columbus Lighthouse — A69

Flag in Blue and Red

1939, Apr. 30	**Litho.**	***Perf. 12***	
342 A69	½c red org & org	.35	.25
343 A69	1c green & lt green	.40	.25
344 A69	3c purple & pale vio	.40	.25
345 A69	10c orange & yellow	1.40	.65
	Nos. 342-345,C33 (5)	4.55	2.25

New York World's Fair.

A70

1939, Sept.		**Typo.**	
346 A70	½c black & pale gray	.40	.25
347 A70	1c black & yel grn	.50	.25
348 A70	3c black & yel brn	.50	.25
349 A70	7c black & dp ultra	1.10	.90
350 A70	10c black & brt red vio	2.10	.40
	Nos. 346-350 (5)	4.60	2.05

José Trujillo Valdez (1863-1935), father of President Trujillo Molina.

A71

Map of the Americas and flags of 21 American republics.

Flags in National Colors

1940, Apr. 14	**Litho.**	***Perf. 11½***	
351 A71	1c deep green	.35	.25
352 A71	2c carmine	.45	.25
353 A71	3c red violet	.60	.25
354 A71	10c orange	1.25	.25
355 A71	1p chestnut	18.00	13.50
	Nos. 351-355 (5)	20.65	14.50

Pan American Union, 50th anniv.

Sir Rowland Hill — A72

1940, May 6		***Perf. 12***	
356 A72	3c brt red vio & rose lil	3.25	.40
357 A72	7c dk blue & lt blue	6.75	1.75

Centenary of first postage stamp.

Julia Molina Trujillo A73

1940, May 26			
358 A73	1c grn, lt grn & dk grn	.40	.25
359 A73	2c brt red, buff & dp rose	.40	.25
360 A73	3c org, dl org & brn org	.55	.25
361 A73	7c bl, pale bl & dk bl	1.10	.35
	Nos. 358-361 (4)	2.45	1.10

Issued in commemoration of Mother's Day.

Map of Caribbean A74

1940, June 6		***Perf. 11½***	
362 A74	3c brt car & pale rose	.50	.25
363 A74	7c dk blue & lt blue	1.00	.25
364 A74	1p yel grn & pale grn	10.00	9.00
	Nos. 362-364 (3)	11.50	9.50

2nd Inter-American Caribbean Conf. held at Ciudad Trujillo, May 31 to June 6.

Marion Military Hospital — A75

1940, Dec. 24			
365 A75	½c chestnut & fawn	.25	.25

AIR POST STAMPS

Map of Hispaniola — AP1

Perf. 11½

1928, May 31	**Litho.**	**Unwmk.**	
C1 AP1	10c deep ultra	5.25	2.50

1930			
C2 AP1	10c ocher	3.50	3.00
a.	Vert. pair, imperf. btwn.	*600.00*	
C3 AP1	15c scarlet	6.75	4.00
C4 AP1	20c dull green	3.25	.85
C5 AP1	30c violet	6.75	4.50
	Nos. C2-C5 (4)	20.25	12.35

Nos. C2-C5 have only "CENTAVOS" in lower panel. Issued: 10c, 20c, 1/24; 15c, 30c, 2/14.

1930			
C6 AP1	10c light blue	1.75	.60
C7 AP1	15c blue green	3.25	1.00
C8 AP1	20c yellow brown	3.50	.85
a.	Horiz. pair, imperf. vert.	450.00	450.00
C9 AP1	30c chocolate	6.25	1.75
	Nos. C6-C9 (4)	14.75	4.20

Issue dates: 10c, 15c, 20c, Sept.; 30c, Oct.

Batwing Sundial Erected in 1753 — AP2

1931-33		***Perf. 12***	
C10 AP2	10c carmine	3.50	.50
C11 AP2	10c light blue	1.75	.50
C12 AP2	10c dark green	6.25	2.75
C13 AP2	15c rose lilac	2.75	.50
C14 AP2	20c dark blue	6.25	2.25
a.	Numerals reading up at left and down at right	5.75	2.75
b.	Imperf., pair	250.00	
C15 AP2	30c green	2.50	.25
C16 AP2	50c red brown	6.25	.50
C17 AP2	1p deep orange	10.00	2.75
	Nos. C10-C17 (8)	39.25	10.00

Issued: No. C11, 7/2/32; No. C12, 5/28/33; others 8/16.

Airplane and Ozama Fortress AP3

1933, Nov. 20			
C18 AP3	10c dark blue	3.50	.60

Airplane and Trujillo Bridge AP4

1934, Sept. 20			
C19 AP4	10c dark blue	3.00	.50

Symbolic of Flight AP5

1935, Apr. 29			
C20 AP5	10c lt blue & dk blue	1.60	.50

AP6

1936, Feb. 11		***Perf. 11½***	
C21 AP6	10c dk bl & turq bl	2.50	.50

Allegory of Flight AP7

1936, Oct. 17			
C22 AP7	10c dk bl, bl & turq bl	2.25	.40

Macoris Airport AP8

1937, Oct. 22			
C23 AP8	10c green	1.00	.25

Fleet of Columbus AP9

Air Fleet AP10

Proposed Columbus Lighthouse — AP11

1937, Nov. 9		***Perf. 12***	
C24 AP9	10c rose red	1.75	1.40
C25 AP10	15c purple	1.40	.95
C26 AP11	20c dk bl & lt bl	1.40	1.25
C27 AP10	25c red violet	2.00	1.25
C28 AP11	30c yellow green	1.75	1.25
C29 AP10	50c brown	3.50	1.75
C30 AP11	75c dk olive grn	10.50	10.50
C31 AP9	1p orange	6.25	2.50
	Nos. C24-C31 (8)	28.55	20.85

Goodwill flight to all American countries by the planes "Colon," "Pinta," "Nina" and "Santa Maria."

No. C30 was reproduced imperf. on No. 1019.

Pan American Clipper AP12

1938, July 30			
C32 AP12	10c green	1.25	.25

Trylon and Perisphere, Plane and Proposed Columbus Lighthouse — AP13

1939, Apr. 30			
C33 AP13	10c green & lt green	2.00	.85

New York World's Fair.

Airplane AP14

1939, Oct. 18			
C34 AP14	10c green & dp green	1.60	.25
a.	Pair, imperf. btwn.	*450.00*	

Proposed Columbus Lighthouse, Plane and Caravels — AP15

Christopher Columbus and Proposed Lighthouse — AP16

Proposed Lighthouse — AP17

Christopher Columbus — AP18

Caravel — AP19

1940, Oct. 12

C35 AP15 10c sapphire & lt bl 1.10 .60
C36 AP16 15c org brn & brn 1.60 1.00
C37 AP17 20c rose red & red 1.60 1.00
C38 AP18 25c brt red lil & red vio 1.60 .50
C39 AP19 50c green & lt green 3.00 1.75
Nos. C35-C39 (5) 8.90 4.85

Discovery of America by Columbus and proposed Columbus memorial lighthouse in Dominican Republic.

AIR POST OFFICIAL STAMPS

Nos. O13-O14 Overprinted in Blue

Unwmk.

1930, Dec. 3 Typo. *Perf. 12*

CO1 O3 10c light blue 25.00 *27.50*
a. Pair, one without ovpt. *1,100.*
CO2 O3 20c orange 25.00 *27.50*

SPECIAL DELIVERY STAMPS

Biplane SD1

Perf. 11½

1920, Apr. Unwmk. Litho.

E1 SD1 10c deep ultra 6.75 1.40
a. Imperf., pair

Special Delivery Messenger — SD2

1925

E2 SD2 10c dark blue 21.00 5.75

SD3

1927

E3 SD3 10c red brown 6.75 1.40
a. "E EXPRESO" at top 55.00 55.00

INSURED LETTER STAMPS

Merino Issue of 1933 Surcharged in Red or Black

1935, Feb. 1 Unwmk. *Perf. 14*

G1 A35 8c on 7c ultra .60 .25
a. Inverted surcharge 18.00
G2 A35 15c on 10c org yel .65 .25
a. Inverted surcharge 18.00
G3 A35 30c on 8c dk green 2.25 .90
G4 A35 45c on 20c car rose (Bk) 3.25 1.10
G5 A36 70c on 50c lemon 7.75 1.75
Nos. G1-G5 (5) 14.50 4.25

Merino Issue of 1933 Surcharged in Red

1940

G6 A35 8c on ½c lt vio 2.75 2.75
G7 A35 8c on 7c ultra 3.25 3.25

Coat of Arms — IL1

1940-45 Litho. *Perf. 11½*

Arms in Black

G8 IL1 8c brown red .85 .25
a. 8c dk red, no shading on inner frame 1.10 .25
G9 IL1 15c dp orange ('45) 1.75 .25
G10 IL1 30c dk green ('41) 2.00 .25
a. 30c yellow green 2.00 .25
G11 IL1 45c ultra ('44) 2.25 .30
G12 IL1 70c olive brn ('44) 2.10 .30
Nos. G8-G12 (5) 8.95 1.35

See Nos. G13-G16, G24-G27 in Scott Standard catalogue, Vol. 2.

POSTAGE DUE STAMPS

D1

1901 Unwmk. Typo. *Perf. 14*

J1 D1 2c olive gray .90 .25
J2 D1 4c olive gray 1.10 .25
J3 D1 5c olive gray 1.90 .30
J4 D1 10c olive gray 3.25 .95
Nos. J1-J4 (4) 7.15 1.75

For surcharges and overprint see Nos. 162-165, 169-171.

1909 Wmk. 116

J5 D1 2c olive gray 1.50 .50
J6 D1 4c olive gray 1.50 .50
J7 D1 6c olive gray 2.00 .75
J8 D1 10c olive gray 4.00 2.50
Nos. J5-J8 (4) 9.00 4.25

1913

J9 D1 2c olive green .60 .30
J10 D1 4c olive green .70 .40
J11 D1 6c olive green 1.10 .50
J12 D1 10c olive green 1.25 .60
Nos. J9-J12 (4) 3.65 1.80

1922 Unwmk. Litho. *Perf. 11½*

J13 D1 1c olive green .70 .70

OFFICIAL STAMPS

Bastion of February 27 O1

Unwmk.

1902, Feb. 25 Litho. *Perf. 12*

O1 O1 2c scarlet & blk .65 .30
O2 O1 5c dk blue & blk .85 .25
O3 O1 10c yel grn & blk 1.00 .55
O4 O1 20c yellow & blk 1.25 .55
a. Imperf., pair 11.00
Nos. O1-O4 (4) 3.75 1.65

For overprints and surcharge see Nos. 157-161.

Bastion of Feb. 27 — O2

Perf. 13½x13, 13½x14

1909-12 Wmk. 116 Typo.

O5 O2 1c blue grn & blk .40 .25
O6 O2 2c scarlet & blk .50 .30
O7 O2 5c dk blue & blk 1.00 .40
O8 O2 10c yel grn & blk ('12) 1.60 .95
O9 O2 20c orange & blk ('12) 2.75 2.25
Nos. O5-O9 (5) 6.25 4.15

The 2c, 5c are found in both perforations; 1c, 20c perf. 13½x13; 10c perf. 13½x14.

For overprints and surcharge see Nos. 177, 194-199.

Columbus Lighthouse — O3

1928 Unwmk. *Perf. 12*

O10 O3 1c green .40 .40
O11 O3 2c red .40 .40
O12 O3 5c ultramarine .50 .50
O13 O3 10c light blue .60 .60
O14 O3 20c orange .90 .90
Nos. O10-O14 (5) 2.80 2.80

For overprints see Nos. CO1-CO2.

Proposed Columbus Lighthouse O4

1937 Litho. *Perf. 11½*

O15 O4 3c dark purple 1.50 .50
O16 O4 7c indigo & blue 1.75 .60
O17 O4 10c orange yellow 2.00 .85
Nos. O15-O17 (3) 5.25 1.95

Proposed Columbus Lighthouse O5

1939-41

O18 O5 1c dp grn & lt grn .75 .40
O19 O5 2c crim & pale pink .75 .40
O20 O5 3c purple & lt vio .75 .40
O21 O5 5c dk bl & lt bl ('40) 1.00 .60
O21A O5 5c lt blue ('41) 2.00 1.25
O22 O5 7c brt bl & lt bl ('41) 1.75 .40
O23 O5 10c yel org & pale org ('41) 1.75 .60
O24 O5 20c brn org & buff ('41) 5.75 1.00
O25 O5 50c brt red lil & pale lil ('41) 7.00 3.00
Nos. O18-O25 (9) 21.50 8.05

POSTAL TAX STAMPS

Santo Domingo after Hurricane PT1

Hurricane's Effect on Capital PT2

1930, Dec. Unwmk. Litho. *Perf. 12*

RA1 PT1 1c green & rose .25 .25
RA2 PT1 2c red rose .25 .25
RA3 PT2 5c ultra & rose .30 .25
RA4 PT2 10c yellow & rose .40 .30

Imperf

RA5 PT1 1c green & rose .40 .30
RA6 PT1 2c red & rose .50 .30
RA7 PT2 5c ultra & rose .60 .50
RA8 PT2 10c yellow & rose .90 .75
Nos. RA1-RA8 (8) 3.60 2.90

For surcharges see Nos. RAC1-RAC7.

Tête bêche Pairs

RA1a PT1 1c green & rose 1.75 1.75
RA2a PT1 2c red rose 1.75 1.50
RA3a PT1 5c ultra & rose 1.75 2.10
RA4a PT1 10c yellow & rose 2.10 2.10
RA5a PT1 1c green & rose 1.75 1.75
RA6a PT1 2c red & rose 1.75 1.75
RA7a PT1 5c ultra & rose 2.10 2.10
RA8a PT1 10c yellow & rose 2.10 2.10
Nos. RA1a-RA8a (8) 15.05 15.15

POSTAL TAX AIR POST STAMPS

Postal Tax Stamps Surcharged in Red or Gold

1930, Dec. 3 Unwmk. *Perf. 12*

RAC1 PT2 5c + 5c blk & rose (R) 27.00 31.00
a. Tête bêche pair 125.00
b. "Habilitado Para" missing 52.50
RAC2 PT2 10c + 10c blk & rose (R) 27.00 31.00
a. Tête bêche pair 125.00
b. "Habilitado Para" missing 52.50
c. Gold surcharge 95.00 95.00
d. As "c," tête bêche pair 450.00
e. As "c" and "b" 250.00

Nos. RAC1-RAC2 were on sale one day.

RAC4 PT2 5c + 5c ultra & rose (R) 6.75 6.75
a. Tête bêche pair 45.00
b. Inverted surcharge 42.50
c. Tête bêche pair, inverted surcharge 600.00

d. Pair, one without surcharge 190.00
e. "Habilitado Para" missing 15.00
RAC5 PT2 10c + 10c yel & rose (G) 5.25 5.25
a. Tête bêche pair 42.50
b. "Habilitado Para" missing 18.00

Imperf

RAC6 PT2 5c + 5c ultra & rose (R) 6.75 6.75
a. Tête bêche pair 52.50
b. "Habilitado Para" missing 18.00
RAC7 PT2 10c + 10c yel & rose (G) 6.75 6.75
a. Tête bêche pair 52.50
b. "Habilitado Para" missing 18.00
Nos. RAC1-RAC7 (6) 79.50 87.50

It was obligatory to use Nos. RA1-RA8 and RAC1-RAC7 on all postal matter, in amounts equal to the ordinary postage.

This surtax was for the aid of sufferers from the hurricane of Sept. 3, 1930.

No. 261 Overprinted in Green

1933, Oct. 11

RAC8 A32 2c scarlet .50 .40
a. Double overprint 9.00
b. Pair, one without overprint 375.00

By official decree this stamp, in addition to the regular postage, had to be used on every letter, etc., sent by the internal air post service.

EAST AFRICA & UGANDA PROTECTORATES

ˈest ˈa-fri-kə and ü-ˈgan-də prə-ˈtek-t̹ə-ˌrəts

LOCATION — Central East Africa, bordering on the Indian Ocean
GOVT. — Former British Protectorate
AREA — 350,000 sq. mi. (approx.)
POP. — 6,503,507 (approx.)
CAPITAL — Mombasa

This territory, formerly administered by the British East Africa Colony, was divided between Kenya Colony and the Uganda Protectorate. See Kenya, Uganda and Tanzania.

16 Annas = 1 Rupee
100 Cents = 1 Rupee (1907)

A1

A2

King Edward VII

1903 Typo. Wmk. 2 *Perf. 14*

1 A1 ½a gray green 6.50 *22.50*
2 A1 1a car & black 2.25 1.50
3 A1 2a vio & dull vio 10.50 3.00
4 A1 2½a ultramarine 14.50 *60.00*
5 A1 3a gray grn & brn 30.00 *70.00*
6 A1 4a blk & gray grn 13.50 *27.50*
7 A1 5a org brn & blk 22.50 *60.00*
8 A1 8a pale blue & blk 26.00 *50.00*

Wmk. 1

9 A2 1r gray green 25.00 *65.00*
a. On chalky paper 87.50 *135.00*
10 A2 2r vio & dull vio 92.50 *100.00*
11 A2 3r blk & gray grn 175.00 *325.00*
12 A2 4r lt green & blk 175.00 *350.00*
13 A2 5r car & black 175.00 *350.00*
14 A2 10r ultra & black 475.00 *675.00*
a. On chalky paper 575.00 *650.00*
15 A2 20r ol gray & blk 825.00 *1,950.*
Overprinted "SPECIMEN" 150.00
16 A2 50r org brn & blk 2,600. *4,750.*
Overprinted "SPECIMEN" 350.00
Nos. 1-14 (14) 1,243. *2,160.*
Set, ovptd "SPECIMEN" 500.00

1904-07 Wmk. 3 Chalky Paper

17 A1 ½a gray green 16.00 3.75
18 A1 1a car & black 16.00 2.00
19 A1 2a vio & dull vio 3.50 3.25
21 A1 3a gray grn & brn 4.75 *45.00*
22 A1 4a blk & gray grn 9.25 *22.50*
23 A1 5a org brn & blk 8.00 *32.50*
24 A1 8a pale blue & blk 8.75 *22.50*
25 A2 1r gray green 35.00 *75.00*
26 A2 2r vio & dl vio 50.00 *77.50*
27 A2 3r blk & gray grn 100.00 *160.00*
28 A2 4r lt green & blk 140.00 *200.00*
29 A2 5r car & black 175.00 *700.00*
29A A2 10r ultra & black 400.00 *450.00*
30 A2 20r ol gray & blk 875.00 *1,600.*
30A A2 50r org brn & blk 2,750. *4,500.*
Nos. 17-29 (12) 566.25 *1,344.*

Ordinary Paper

17a ½a gray green 9.00 3.50
18a A1 1a car & black 11.00 1.00
19a 2a vio & dull vio 3.25 3.00
20 A1 2½a blue 10.00 37.50
a. 2½a blue & ultramarine 9.50 *35.00*
21a 3a gray grn & brn 5.00 *47.50*
22a 4a blk & gray grn 8.50 *20.00*
23a 5a org brn & blk 9.25 *17.50*
24a A1 8a pale blue & blk 8.75 *10.50*

1907-08

31 A1 1c brown ('08) 3.00 .25
32 A1 3c gray green 22.50 .80
a. 3c blue green 25.00 4.25
33 A1 6c carmine 3.25 .25
a. 6c carmine, single plate ('10) 25.00 .35
34 A1 10c citron & violet 11.00 10.00
35 A1 12c red vio & dl vio 12.00 3.50
36 A1 15c ultramarine 34.00 11.00
37 A1 25c blk & blue green 22.50 *8.50*
38 A1 50c org brn & green 17.50 16.00
39 A1 75c pale bl & gray blk ('08) 5.50 *40.00*
Nos. 31-39 (9) 131.25 *90.30*
Set, ovptd "SPECIMEN" 210.00

Nos. 31-33, 36 are on ordinary paper.

On No. 33a, there is a distinct white line separating the lower tablets from the rest of the design. This is not present on No. 33. The word "PROTECTORATE" is in taller letters on No. 33a.

King George V
A3 A4

1912-18 Ordinary Paper Wmk. 3

40 A3 1c black .40 *2.10*
41 A3 3c green 2.50 .75
a. Booklet pane of 6
b. 3c deep blue green ('17) 5.00 1.75
42 A3 6c carmine 1.50 .70
a. Booklet pane of 6
b. 6c scarlet ('17) 25.00 3.25
43 A3 10c yel orange 2.50 .65
a. 10c orange ('21) 14.00 6.50
44 A3 12c gray 3.25 .65
45 A3 15c ultramarine 3.25 1.00

Chalky Paper

46 A3 25c scar & blk, *yel* .65 *1.60*
a. 25c scar & blk, *lemon* ('16) 12.50 12.50
Overprinted "SPECIMEN" 40.00
b. 25c scar & blk, *org buff* ('21) 50.00 19.00
c. 25c scar & blk, *pale yel* ('21) 15.00 7.00
47 A3 50c violet & black 1.90 1.60
48 A3 75c black, *green* 1.90 *21.00*
a. 75c black, *emerald* 13.50 *65.00*
b. 75c blk, *bl grn, olive back* 9.25 9.25
c. 75c blk, *emer, olive back* 50.00 *175.00*
49 A4 1r black, *green* 2.25 *5.25*
a. 1r black, *emerald* 6.00 *60.00*
50 A4 2r blk & red, *bl* 24.50 *45.00*
51 A4 3r gray grn & vio 27.50 *130.00*
52 A4 4r grn & red, *yel* 65.00 *130.00*
a. 4r grn & red, *pale yellow* 150.00 *200.00*
53 A4 5r dl vio & ultra 65.00 *160.00*
54 A4 10r grn & red, *grn* 180.00 *275.00*
55 A4 20r vio & blk, *red* 425.00 425.00
56 A4 20r bl & violet, *blue* ('18) 500.00 *550.00*
57 A4 50r gray grn & rose red 900.00 *975.00*
Overprinted "SPECIMEN" 275.00
a. 50r dull green & dull rose, ordinary paper 1,400. *1,400.*
58 A4 100r blk & vio, *red* *9,750.* *4,000.*
Overprinted "SPECIMEN" 600.00
59 A4 500r red & grn, *grn* *40,000.*
Overprinted "SPECIMEN" 1,400.
Nos. 40-54 (15) 382.10 *775.30*
Nos. 40-54 (15), ovptd "SPECIMEN" 1,000.

1914 Surface-colored Paper

60 A3 25c scarlet & blk, *yel* .65 *5.50*
61 A3 75c black, *green* 1.25 *19.50*
Nos. 60-61, ovptd "SPECIMEN" 75.00

Stamps of types A3 and A4 with watermark 4 are listed under Kenya, Uganda and Tanzania.

The 1r through 50r with revenue cancellations sell for minimal prices. The 100r and 500r were available for postage but were nearly always used fiscally.

For surcharge see No. 62.

No. 42 Surcharged

1919

62 A3 4c on 6c carmine 1.50 .25
Handstamped "SPECIMEN" 70.00
a. Double surcharge 150.00 *240.00*
b. Without squares over old value 50.00 *85.00*
c. Pair, one without surcharge 2,000. *2,250.*
d. Inverted surcharge 350.00 *475.00*
e. Surcharged on back 500.00

For later issues see Kenya, Uganda and Tanzania.

For stamps of East Africa and Uganda overprinted "G. E. A." see German East Africa.

EASTERN RUMELIA

ˈē-stərn rü-ˈmēl-yə

(South Bulgaria)

LOCATION — In southern Bulgaria
GOVT. — An autonomous unit of the Turkish Empire.
CAPITAL — Philippopolis (Plovdiv)

In 1885 the province of Eastern Rumelia revolted against Turkish rule and united with Bulgaria, adopting the new name of South Bulgaria. This union was assured by the Treaty of Bucharest in 1886, following the war between Serbia and Bulgaria.

40 Paras = 1 Piaster

Counterfeits of all overprints are plentiful.

Stamps of Turkey, 1876-84, Overprinted in Blue

No. 1

A2

A3

1880 Unwmk. *Perf. 13½*

1 A5 ½pi on 20pa yel grn 67.50 57.50
a. Horiz. pair, one without overprint *400.00*
3 A2 10pa blk & rose *55.00*
4 A2 20pa vio & grn 87.50 67.50
6 A2 2pi blk & buff 115.00 100.00
7 A2 5pi red & bl 450.00 *500.00*
8 A3 10pa blk & red lil 57.50

Nos. 3 & 8 were not placed in use.

Inverted and double overprints of all values exist.

Same, with Extra Overprint "R. O."

9 A3 10pa blk & red lil 97.50 95.00

Crescent and Turkish Inscriptions of Value — A4

1881 Typo. *Perf. 13½*

10 A4 5pa blk & olive 17.00 1.35
11 A4 10pa blk & green 65.00 1.35
12 A4 20pa blk & rose 1.75 1.25
b. Cliché of 10pa in plate of 20pa *625.00*
In pair with No. 12 *1,000.*
13 A4 1pi blk & blue 5.75 4.50
14 A4 5pi rose & blue 57.50 *82.50*

Tête bêche pairs and imperforates were not placed in use, and were found only in the remainder stock. This is true also of No. 12b, and of a cliché of Turkey No. 63 in the 1pi plate.

Perf. 11½

10a A4 5pa blk & olive 30.00
11a A4 10pa blk & green 30.00
12a A4 20pa blk & rose 30.00
13a A4 1pi blk & blue 30.00
14a A4 5pi rose & blue 45.00

Nos. 10a-14a were not placed in use, and were found only in the remainder stock.

1884 *Perf. 11½*

15 A4 5pa lil & pale lil .75 .45
16 A4 10pa grn & pale grn .25 .45
17 A4 20pa car & pale rose .55
18 A4 1pi bl & pale bl 1.15
19 A4 5pi brn & pale brn *400.00*

Nos. 17-19 were not placed in use, and were found only in the remainder stock.

Nos. 15-19 imperf. are from remainders.

For overprints see Turkey Nos. 542-545.

Perf. 13½

15a A4 5pa lil & pale lil 1.15 *3.50*
16a A4 10pa grn & pale grn 17.50 17.00
17a A4 20pa car & pale rose 20.00
18a A4 1pi bl & pale bl 20.00
19a A4 5pi brn & pale brn *475.00*

Nos. 17a-19a were not placed in use, and were found only in the remainder stock.

South Bulgaria

Counterfeits of all overprints are plentiful.

Nos. 10-14 Overprinted in Two Types

a

b

Type a — Four toes on each foot.
Type b — Three toes on each foot.

Blue Overprint

1885 Unwmk. *Perf. 13½*

20 A4 (a) 5pa blk & olive *325.00* *375.00*
21 A4 (a) 10pa blk & grn *875.00* *825.00*
22 A4 (a) 20pa blk & rose 325.00 —
a. Type "b" 325.00 —
b. Type "a," perf. 11½ 325.00 *375.00*
c. Type "b," perf. 11½ 225.00 —
23 A4 (a) 1pi blk & blue 37.50 *72.50*
a. Type "b" 82.50 *97.50*

No.	Type	Description	Unused	Used
24	A4 (b)	5pi rose & blue	1,100.	—
a.		Type "a"	725.00	—

Black Overprint

No.	Type	Description	Unused	Used
24B	A4 (a)	20pa blk & rose	275.00	—
25	A4 (a)	1pi blk & bl	55.00	115.00
a.		Type "b"	65.00	82.50
26	A4 (b)	5pi rose & bl	675.00	—

Same Overprint on Nos. 15-17

Blue Overprint

Perf. 11½

No.	Type	Description	Unused	Used
27	A4 (b)	5pa lil & pale lil, type "b"	22.50	57.50
a.		Type "a"	35.00	82.50
b.		Perf. 13½, type "b"	87.50	97.50
c.		Perf. 13½, type "a"	225.00	250.00
28	A4 (b)	10pa grn & pale grn	40.00	75.00
a.		Type "a"	57.50	115.00
29	A4 (b)	20pa car & pale rose	275.00	375.00
a.		Type "a"	325.00	375.00

Black Overprint

Perf. 13½

No.	Type	Description	Unused	Used
30	A4 (b)	5pa lil & pale lil	40.00	67.50
a.		Type "a"	40.00	67.50
b.		Type "b," perf. 11½	55.00	65.00

Perf. 11½

No.	Type	Description	Unused	Used
31	A4 (a)	10pa grn & pale grn	42.50	85.00
a.		Type "b"	65.00	—
b.		Type "a," perf. 13½	60.00	115.00
32	A4 (b)	20pa car & pale rose	55.00	65.00
a.		Type "a"	55.00	82.50

Nos. 10-17 Handstamped in Black in Two Types

a

b

Type a — First letter at top circular.
Type b — First letter at top oval.

1885 ***Perf. 13½***

No.	Type	Description	Unused	Used
33	A4 (b)	5pa blk & olive	300.00	250.00
a.		Type "a"	250.00	
34	A4 (b)	10pa blk & grn	225.00	250.00
a.		Type "a"	300.00	
35	A4 (b)	20pa blk & rose	72.50	85.00
a.		Type "a"	135.00	170.00
36	A4 (a)	1pi blk & bl	87.50	115.00
a.		Type "b"	90.00	125.00
37	A4 (a)	5pi rose & blue, type "a"	2,500.	—
a.		Type "b"	—	—

Perf. 13½

No.	Type	Description	Unused	Used
38	A4 (a)	5pa lil & pale lil	26.00	44.00
a.		Type "b"	32.50	44.00
b.		Perf. 11½, type "a"	225.00	275.00
c.		Perf. 11½, type "b"	225.00	275.00

Perf. 11½

No.	Type	Description	Unused	Used
39	A4 (a)	10pa grn & pale grn	29.00	35.00
a.		Type "b"	57.50	57.50
40	A4 (a)	20pa car & pale rose	29.00	50.00
a.		Type "b"	29.00	28.00

Nos. 20-40 exist with inverted and double handstamps. Overprints in unlisted colors are proofs.

The stamps of South Bulgaria were superseded in 1886 by those of Bulgaria.

EASTERN SILESIA

'ē-stərn sī-'lē-zh,ē-,ə

LOCATION — In central Europe
GOVT. — Former Austrian crownland
AREA — 1,987 sq. mi.
POP. — 680,422 (estimated 1920)
CAPITAL — Troppau

After World War I, this territory was occupied by Czechoslovakia and eventually was divided between Poland and Czechoslovakia, the dividing line running through Teschen.

100 Heller = 1 Krone
100 Fennigi = 1 Marka

Plebiscite Issues

Stamps of Czechoslovakia 1918-20, Overprinted in Black, Blue, Violet or Red

1920 **Unwmk.** ***Imperf.***

No.	Type	Description	Unused	Used
1	A2	1h dark brown	.25	.30
2	A1	3h red violet	.25	.25
3	A2	5h blue green	23.50	22.50
4	A2	15h red	11.50	11.00
5	A1	20h blue green	.25	.25
6	A2	25h dull violet	.75	.75
7	A1	30h bister (R)	.25	.25
8	A1	40h red orange	.30	.30
9	A2	50h dull violet	.60	.45
10	A2	50h dark blue	2.60	1.50
11	A2	60h orange (Bl)	.75	.75
12	A2	75h slate (R)	.50	.75
13	A2	80h olive grn (R)	.50	.75
14	A1	100h brown	1.10	1.10
15	A2	120h gray blk (R)	1.60	2.25
16	A1	200h ultra (R)	1.60	2.00
17	A2	300h green (R)	6.25	7.50
18	A1	400h purple (R)	2.60	3.00
20	A2	500h red brn (Bl)	5.25	6.00
a.		Black overprint	6.25	9.00
21	A2	1000h violet (Bl)	13.00	13.50
a.		Black overprint	62.50	75.00
		Nos. 1-21 (20)	73.40	75.15

Perf. 11½, 13¾

No.	Type	Description	Unused	Used
22	A2	1h dark brown	.25	.25
23	A2	5h blue green	.30	.25
24	A2	10h yellow green	.30	.25
a.		Imperf.	260.00	210.00
25	A2	15h red	.50	.25
26	A2	20h rose	.50	.35
a.		Imperf.	300.00	250.00
27	A2	25h dull violet	.50	.35
28	A2	30h red violet (Bl)	.35	.35
29	A2	60h orange (Bl)	.50	.50
30	A1	200h ultra (R)	3.00	3.00
		Nos. 22-30 (9)	6.20	5.55

The letters "S. O." are the initials of "Silésie Orientale."

Forged cancellations are found on Nos. 1-30.

Overprinted in Carmine or Violet

No.	Type	Description	Unused	Used
31	A4	500h sl, *grysh* (C)	40.00	
32	A4	1000h blk brn, *brnsh*	40.00	

Excellent counterfeits of this overprint exist.

Stamps of Poland, 1919, Overprinted

1920 ***Perf. 11½***

No.	Type	Description	Unused	Used
41	A10	5f green	.25	.25
42	A10	10f red brown	.25	.25
43	A10	15f light red	.25	.25
44	A11	25f olive green	.25	.25
45	A11	50f blue green	.25	.25

Overprinted

No.	Type	Description	Unused	Used
46	A12	1k deep green	.25	.25
47	A12	1.50k brown	.25	.25
48	A12	2k dark blue	.25	.25
49	A13	2.50k dull violet	.30	.25
50	A14	5k slate blue	.50	.25
		Nos. 41-50 (10)	2.80	2.50

SPECIAL DELIVERY STAMPS

Czechoslovakia Special Delivery Stamps Ovptd. in Blue

1920 **Unwmk.** ***Imperf.***

No.	Type	Description	Unused	Used
E1	SD1	2h red violet, *yel*	.25	.25
a.		Black overprint	4.75	.80
E2	SD1	5h yellow green, *yel*	.25	.25
a.		Black overprint	8.00	5.00

Nos. E1-E2a exist on white paper.

POSTAGE DUE STAMPS

Czechoslovakia Postage Due Stamps Overprinted In Blue or Red

1920 **Unwmk.** ***Imperf.***

No.	Type	Description	Unused	Used
J1	D1	5h deep bis (Bl)	.25	.25
a.		Black overprint	72.50	62.50
J2	D1	10h deep bister	.25	.25
J3	D1	15h deep bister	.25	.25
J4	D1	20h deep bister	.25	.25
J5	D1	25h deep bister	.25	.25
J6	D1	30h deep bister	.25	.25
J7	D1	40h deep bister	.50	.25
J8	D1	50h deep bister	2.60	3.00
J9	D1	100h blk brn (R)	2.60	3.00
J10	D1	500h gray grn (R)	5.75	4.50
J11	D1	1000h purple (R)	8.50	11.50
		Nos. J1-J11 (11)	21.45	23.75

Forged cancellations exist.

NEWSPAPER STAMPS

Czechoslovakia Newspaper Stamps Overprinted in Black like Nos. 1-30

1920 **Unwmk.** ***Imperf.***

No.	Type	Description	Unused	Used
P1	N1	2h gray green	.30	.30
P2	N1	6h red	.25	.25
P3	N1	10h dull violet	.40	.25
P4	N1	20h blue	.65	.25
P5	N1	30h gray brown	.65	.25
		Nos. P1-P5 (5)	2.25	1.30

ECUADOR

'e-kwə-,dor

LOCATION — Northwest coast of South America, bordering on the Pacific Ocean
GOVT. — Republic
AREA — 116,270 sq. mi.
POP. — 8,420,000 (est. 1984)
CAPITAL — Quito

The Republic of Ecuador was so constituted on May 11, 1830, after the Civil War that separated the original members of the Republic of Colombia, founded by Simon Bolivar by uniting the Presidency of Quito with the Viceroyalty of New Grenada and the Captaincy of Venezuela. The Presidency of Quito became the Republic of Ecuador.

8 Reales = 1 Peso
100 Centavos = 1 Sucre (1881)

Watermarks

Wmk. 117 — Liberty Cap

Wmk. 127 — Quatrefoils

Wmk. 233 — "Harrison & Sons, London" in Script Letters

STAMPS OF GREAT BRITAIN USED IN ECUADOR

Guayaquil

Stamps of Great Britain cancelled Type A "C41"

1865-80

No.	Description	Value
A1	½p rose red, plates 5, 6 (#58), *value from*	70.00
A2	1p rose red ('57) (#20)	—
A3	1p rose red, plates 74, 78, 85, 92, 94, 105, 110, 115, 133, 140, 145, 166, 174, 180, 216 (#33), *value from*	50.00
A4	1½p lake red, plate 3 (#32)	100.00
A5	2p blue, plate 9 (#29)	55.00
A6	2p blue, plates 13, 14 (#30), *value from*	50.00
A7	3p rose ('62) (#37)	290.00
A8	3p rose ('65) (#44)	140.00
A9	3p rose ('67-'73), plates 6, 7, 9, 10 (#49), *value from*	57.50
A10	3p rose ('73-'80), plates 11, 12, 15-20 (#61), *value from*	57.50
A11	4p vermilion ('62), plate 4 (#34a)	140.00
A12	4p vermilion ('62), "hair lines" (#34c)	140.00
A13	4p vermilion ('65-'73), plates 7-14 (#43), *value from*	57.50
A14	4p vermilion ('76), plate 15 (#69)	350.00
A15	4p pale olive green, plate 15 (#70)	225.00
A16	4p pale olive green, plate 16 (#70)	225.00
A17	6p lilac, plate 4 (#39b)	175.00
A18	6p lilac ('65-'67), plate 5 (#45)	85.00
A19	6p lilac ('65-'67), plate 6 (#45)	85.00
A20	6p dull violet ('67), plate 6 (#50)	—
A21	6p violet ('67-'70), plates 6, 8, 9 (#51), *value from*	80.00
A22	6p pale buff ('72-'73), plate 11 (#59b)	92.50
A23	6p pale buff ('72-'73), plate 12 (#59b)	225.00
A24	6p brown ('72), plates 11, 12 (#59)	—
A25	6p gray ('73), plate 12 (#60)	—
A26	6p gray ('73), plates 13-16 (#60), *value from*	57.50
A27	8p orange ('76) (373)	375.00
A28	9p straw ('62) (#40)	310.00
A29	9p bister ('67) (#52)	225.00
A30	10p red brown ('67) (#53)	350.00
A31	1sh green ('65) (#48)	185.00
A32	1sh green ('67-'73), plates 4-6 (#54), *value from*	50.00
A33	1sh green ('67-'73), plate 7 (#54)	85.00
A34	1sh green ('73-'77), plates 8-11 (#64), *value from*	90.00
A35	1sh green ('73-'77), plates 12, 13 (#64), *value from*	85.00
A36	2sh blue ('67) (#55)	175.00
A37	2sh brown ('80) (#56)	*2,600.*
A38	5sh rose ('67-'74), plate 1 (#57)	550.00
A39	5sh rose ('67-'74), plate 2 (#57)	700.00

Issues of the Republic

Coat of Arms
A1 A2

1865-72 Unwmk. Typo. *Imperf.*

Quadrille Paper

1 A1 1r yellow ('72) 60.00 55.00
On wrapper 150.00
On cover 300.00

Wove Paper

2 A1 ½r ultra 40.00 20.00
On wrapper 125.00
On cover 250.00
a. ½r gray blue ('67) 40.00 15.00
On wrapper 100.00
On cover 125.00
b. Batonne paper ('70) 50.00 25.00
c. Blue paper ('72) 250.00 100.00
d. Embossed arms — 400.00
e. Watermarked — 1,000.
3 A1 1r buff 25.00 18.00
On wrapper 150.00
On cover 300.00
a. 1r orange buff 30.00 20.00
On wrapper 175.00
On cover 325.00
4 A1 1r yellow 25.00 15.00
On wrapper 125.00
On cover 250.00
a. 1r olive yellow ('66) 32.50 22.50
On wrapper 175.00
On cover 400.00
b. Laid paper 175.00 110.00
c. Half used as ½r on cover 900.00
d. Batonne paper 40.00 30.00
e. Embossed arms — 500.00
f. Watermarked — 1,000.
5 A1 1r green 300.00 55.00
On wrapper 150.00
On cover 300.00
a. Half used as ½r on cover *900.00*
b. Embossed arms — *700.00*
c. Watermarked — *1,000.*
6 A2 4r red ('66) 500.00 200.00
On wrapper *700.00*
On cover *1,000.*
a. 4r red brown ('66) 700.00 200.00
On wrapper *700.00*
On cover *1,100.*
b. Arms in circle 500.00 250.00
c. Printed on both sides 550.00 —
d. Half used as 2r on cover 1,600.
e. Embossed arms — *900.00*
f. Watermarked — *2,000.*
Nos. 1-6 (6) 950.00 363.00

Letter paper embossed with arms of Ecuador was used in printing a number of sheets of Nos. 2, 4-6.

Papermakers' watermarks on No. 2e, 4f, 5c and 6f reads "Rolland Freres".

On the 4r the oval holding the coat of arms is usually 13½-14mm wide, but on about one-fifth of the stamps in the sheet it is 15-15½mm wide, almost a circle.

The 2r, 8r and 12r, type A1, are bogus.

Proofs of the ½r, type A1, are known in black and green.

An essay of type A2 shows the condor's head facing right.

1871-72 Blue-surface Paper

7 A1 ½r ultra 50.00 25.00
On wrapper 175.00
On cover 350.00
8 A1 1r yellow 300.00 100.00
On wrapper *750.00*
On cover

Unofficial reprints of types A1-A2 differ in color, have a different sheet makeup and lack gum. Type A1 reprints usually have a double frameline at left. All stamps on blue paper with horiz. blue lines are reprints.

A3 A4

1872 White Paper Litho. *Perf. 11*

9 A3 ½r blue 30.00 5.00
10 A4 1r orange 40.00 7.00
11 A3 1p rose 5.00 *25.00*
Nos. 9-11 (3) 75.00 *37.00*

The 1r surcharged 4c is fraudulent.

 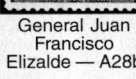

A5 A6

A7 A8

A9 A10

1881, Nov. 1 Engr. *Perf. 12*

12 A5 1c yellow brn .40 .25
13 A6 2c lake .40 .25
14 A7 5c blue 10.00 .50
15 A8 10c orange .40 .25
16 A9 20c gray violet .40 .25
17 A10 50c blue green 2.00 *3.00*
Nos. 12-17 (6) 13.60 *4.50*

The 1c surcharged 3c, and 20c surcharged 5c are fraudulent.

For overprints see Nos. O1-O6.

No. 17 Surcharged in Black

1883, Apr.

18 A10 10c on 50c blue grn 50.00 30.00
a. Double surcharge

Dangerous forgeries exist.

A12 A13

A14 A15

1887

19 A12 1c blue green .50 .40
20 A13 2c vermilion 1.00 .40
21 A14 5c blue 3.00 .50
22 A15 80c olive green 6.00 *15.00*
Nos. 19-22 (4) 10.50 *16.30*

For overprints see Nos. O7-O10.

President Juan Flores — A16

1892

23 A16 1c orange .30 1.00
24 A16 2c dk brown .30 1.00
25 A16 5c vermilion .30 1.00
26 A16 10c green .30 1.00
27 A16 20c red brown .30 1.00
28 A16 50c maroon .30 *2.00*
29 A16 1s blue .30 *4.00*
30 A16 5s purple 1.00 *8.00*
Nos. 23-30 (8) 3.10 *19.00*

The issues of 1892, 1894, 1895 and 1896 were printed by the Hamilton Bank Note Co., New York, to the order of N. F. Seebeck, who held a contract for stamps with the government of Ecuador.

No. 30 in green is said to be an essay or color trial.

For surcharges and overprints see Nos. 31-37, O11-O17.

Nos. 29 and 30 Surcharged in Black

1893

Surcharge Measures 25½x2½mm

31 A16 5c on 1s blue 6.00 6.00
32 A16 5c on 5s purple 10.00 9.00
a. Double surcharge

Surcharge Measures 24x2¼mm

33 A16 5c on 1s blue 3.00 3.00
a. Double surcharge, one inverted
34 A16 5c on 5s purple 12.00 10.00
a. Double surcharge, one invtd.

Nos. 28-30 Surcharged in Black

35 A16 5c on 50c maroon 2.00 2.00
a. Inverted surcharge 5.00
36 A16 5c on 1s blue 2.50 2.00
37 A16 5c on 5s purple 10.00 10.00
Nos. 31-37 (7) 45.50 42.00

Pres. Juan Flores — A19

38 A19 5c on 5s lake 4.00 4.00

It is stated that No. 38 was used exclusively as a postage stamp and not for telegrams.

Pres. Vicente Rocafuerte — A20

Dated "1894"

1894 Various Frames *Perf. 12*

39 A20 1c blue .40 .40
40 A20 2c yellow brn .40 .40
41 A20 5c green .40 .40
b. Perf. 14 6.00 2.00
42 A20 10c vermilion .70 .60
43 A20 20c black 1.10 .70
44 A20 50c orange 6.00 2.00
45 A20 1s carmine 9.50 4.00
46 A20 5s dark blue 12.00 6.00
Nos. 39-46 (8) 30.50 14.50

1895 Same, Dated "1895"

47 A20 1c blue .90 .70
48 A20 2c yellow brn .90 .70
49 A20 5c green .70 .50
50 A20 10c vermilion .70 .40
51 A20 20c black 1.00 1.00
52 A20 50c orange 3.50 2.25
53 A20 1s carmine 21.00 8.00
54 A20 5s dark blue 8.50 4.00
Nos. 47-54 (8) 37.20 17.55

Reprints of the 2c, 10c, 50c, 1s and 5s of the 1894-95 issues are generally on thick paper. Original issues are on thin to medium thick paper. To distinguish reprints from originals, a comparison of paper thickness, paper color, gum, printing clarity and direction of paper weave is necessary. Value 20 cents each.

For overprints see Nos. 77-112, O20-O33, O50-O91.

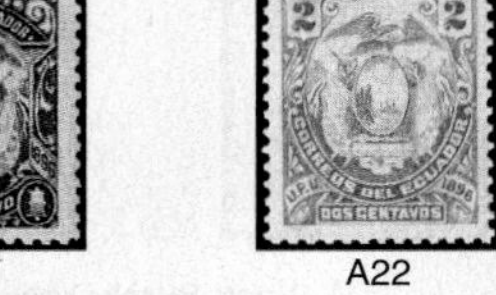

A21 A22

A23 A24

A25 A26

A27 A28

1896 Wmk. 117

55 A21 1c dk green .70 .60
56 A22 2c red .70 .40
57 A23 5c blue .70 .40
58 A24 10c bister brn .60 *.90*
59 A25 20c orange 1.40 *2.00*
60 A26 50c dark blue 5.00 3.00
61 A27 1s yellow brn 4.00 *4.00*
62 A28 5s violet 14.00 5.50
Nos. 55-62 (8) 27.10 *16.80*

Unwmk.

62A A21 1c dk green 1.00 .40
62B A22 2c red 1.10 .40
62C A23 5c blue 1.10 .70
62D A24 10c bister brn .70 *1.40*
62E A25 20c orange 6.00 5.50
62F A26 50c dark blue 2.00 *2.75*
62G A27 1s yellow brn 6.00 *8.00*
62H A28 5s violet 15.00 6.00
Nos. 62A-62H (8) *32.90* *25.15*

Reprints of Nos. 55-62H are on very thick paper, with paper weave direction vertical. Value 20 cents each.

For surcharges and overprints see Nos. 74, 76, 113-114, O34-O49.

Vicente Roca, Diego Noboa and José Olmedo — A28a

General Juan Francisco Elizalde — A28b

Perf. 11½

1896, Oct. 9 Unwmk. Litho.

63 A28a 1c rose .55 .55
64 A28b 2c blue .55 .55
65 A28a 5c green .75 .75
66 A28b 10c ocher .75 .75
67 A28a 20c red 1.10 *3.25*
68 A28b 50c violet 1.75 *4.75*
69 A28a 1s orange 3.25 *8.00*
Nos. 63-69 (7) 8.70 *18.60*

Success of the Liberal Party in 1845 & 1895.

For overprints see Nos. 115-125.

A29

Black Surcharge

1896, Nov. *Perf. 12*

No.	Type	Description	Unused	Used
70	A29	1c on 1c ver, "1893-1894"	1.00	.60
a.		Inverted surcharge	2.50	2.00
b.		Double surcharge	8.00	7.00
71	A29	2c on 2c bl, "1893-1894"	2.00	1.75
a.		Inverted surcharge	4.00	3.50
72	A29	5c on 10c org, "1887-1888"	2.00	.60
a.		Inverted surcharge	4.00	1.75
b.		Double surcharge	7.00	4.00
c.		Surcharged "2cts"	1.00	.80
d.		"1893-1894"	6.00	5.00
73	A29	10c on 4c brn, "1887-1888"	2.00	1.10
a.		Inverted surcharge	4.00	1.75
b.		Double surcharge	6.00	3.50
c.		Double surcharge, one inverted		
d.		Surcharged "1 cto"	2.00	*2.75*
e.		"1891-1892"	17.00	13.50
		Nos. 70-73 (4)	7.00	4.05

Similar surcharges of type A29 include: Dated "1887-1888" — 1c on 1c blue green, 1c on 2c red, 1c on 4c brown, 1c on 10c yellow; 2c on 2c red, 2c on 10c yellow; 10c on 1c green.

Dated "1891-1892" — 1c on 1c blue green, 1c on 4c brown.

Dated "1893-1894" — 2c on 10c yellow; 10c on 1c vermilion, 10c on 10s black.

For overprints see Nos. O18-O19.

Nos. 59-60 Surcharged in Black or Red

1896, Oct. **Wmk. 117**

No.	Type	Description	Unused	Used
74	A25	5c on 20c orange	40.00	40.00
76	A26	10c on 50c dk bl (R)	50.00	50.00
a.		Double surcharge		

The surcharge is diag., horiz. or vert.

Nos. 39-54 Overprinted

On Issue of 1894

1897 **Unwmk.**

No.	Type	Description	Unused	Used
77	A20	1c blue	2.25	2.25
78	A20	2c yellow brn	1.90	1.30
79	A20	5c green	.90	.90
80	A20	10c vermilion	2.75	2.25
81	A20	20c black	3.00	2.75
82	A20	50c orange	6.50	3.25
83	A20	1s carmine	19.00	6.50
84	A20	5s dark blue	110.00	90.00
		Nos. 77-84 (8)	146.30	109.20

On Issue of 1895

No.	Type	Description	Unused	Used
85	A20	1c blue	6.00	5.50
86	A20	2c yellow brn	2.25	2.25
87	A20	5c green	1.90	1.60
88	A20	10c vermilion	7.00	6.00
89	A20	20c black	1.90	1.75
90	A20	50c orange	32.50	13.00
91	A20	1s carmine	14.50	7.50
92	A20	5s dark blue	14.50	14.50
		Nos. 85-92 (8)	80.55	52.10

Nos. 39-54 Overprinted

On Issue of 1894

No.	Type	Description	Unused	Used
93	A20	1c blue	1.40	.90
94	A20	2c yellow brn	1.20	.75
95	A20	5c green	.60	.50
96	A20	10c vermilion	3.50	1.75
97	A20	20c black	3.75	2.50
98	A20	50c orange	7.00	2.75
99	A20	1s carmine	13.00	8.50
100	A20	5s dark blue	115.00	85.00
		Nos. 93-100 (8)	145.45	102.65

On Issue of 1895

No.	Type	Description	Unused	Used
101	A20	1c blue	3.25	1.60
102	A20	2c yellow brn	1.60	1.60
103	A20	5c green	1.75	1.00
104	A20	10c vermilion	5.50	4.50
105	A20	20c black	5.00	1.20
106	A20	50c orange	1.75	1.75
107	A20	1s carmine	8.00	7.00
108	A20	5s dark blue	9.50	9.50
		Nos. 101-108 (8)	36.35	28.15

Overprints on Nos. 77-108 are to be found reading upward from left to right and downward from left to right, as well as inverted.

Overprinted

1897 **On Issue of 1894**

No.	Type	Description	Unused	Used
109	A20	10c vermilion	—	—

On Issue of 1895

No.	Type	Description	Unused	Used
110	A20	2c yellow brn	—	—
111	A20	1s carmine	—	—
112	A20	5s dark blue	—	—

Nos. 56, 59 Overprinted like Nos. 93-108

1897, June **Wmk. 117**

No.	Type	Description	Unused	Used
113	A22	2c red	—	—
114	A25	20c orange	—	—

Many forged overprints on Nos. 77-114 exist, made on original stamps and reprints.

Stamps or Types of 1896 Overprinted in Black

1897 **Unwmk.** *Perf. 11½*

No.	Type	Description	Unused	Used
115	A28a	1c rose	3.75	3.75
116	A28b	2c blue	3.00	3.00
117	A28b	10c ocher	3.00	3.00
118	A28a	1s yellow	15.00	15.00
		Nos. 115-118 (4)	24.75	24.75

No. 63 Overprinted in Black

1897

No.	Type	Description	Unused	Used
119	A28a	1c rose	.60	.50

Nos. 63-66 Overprinted in Black

1897

No.	Type	Description	Unused	Used
122	A28a	1c rose	4.50	4.00
123	A28b	2c blue	4.50	4.00
124	A28a	5c green	4.50	4.00
125	A28b	10c ocher	4.50	4.00
a.		Double overprint	10.50	9.50
		Nos. 122-125 (4)	18.00	16.00

The 20c, 50c and 1s with this overprint in black and all values of the issue overprinted in blue are reprints.

Overprint Inverted

No.	Type	Description	Unused	Used
122a	A28a	1c	6.00	5.50
123a	A28b	2c	6.00	5.50
124a	A28a	5c	6.00	5.50
125b	A28b	10c	6.00	5.50

Coat of Arms — A33

1897, June 23 **Engr.** *Perf. 14-16*

No.	Type	Description	Unused	Used
127	A33	1c dk yellow grn	.35	.25
128	A33	2c orange red	.35	.25
129	A33	5c lake	.35	.25
130	A33	10c dk brown	.35	.25
131	A33	20c yellow	.45	.40
132	A33	50c dull blue	.45	*.65*
133	A33	1s gray	.90	*1.25*
134	A33	5s dark lilac	4.00	*5.00*
		Nos. 127-134 (8)	7.20	*8.30*

No. 135

No. 136

1899, May

No.	Type	Description	Unused	Used
135	A33	1c on 2c orange red	3.00	1.50
136	A33	5c on 10c brown	2.50	1.00
a.		Double surcharge		

Luis Vargas Torres A36

Abdón Calderón A37

Juan Montalvo A38

José Mejia A39

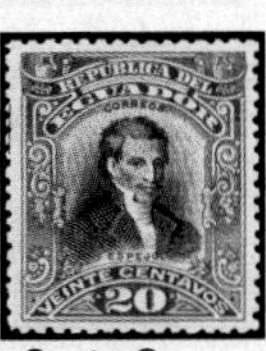
Santa Cruz y Espejo — A40

Pedro Carbo — A41

José Joaquin Olmedo A42

Pedro Moncayo A43

1899 *Perf. 12½-16*

No.	Type	Description	Unused	Used
137	A36	1c gray blue & blk	.40	.25
a.		Horiz. pair, imperf. vert.		
138	A37	2c brown lil & blk	.40	.25
139	A38	5c lake & blk	.70	.25
140	A39	10c violet & blk	.70	.25
141	A40	20c green & blk	.70	.25
142	A41	50c lil rose & blk	1.75	.55
143	A42	1s ocher & blk	8.00	2.75
144	A43	5s lilac & blk	14.50	7.50
		Nos. 137-144 (8)	27.15	12.05

1901

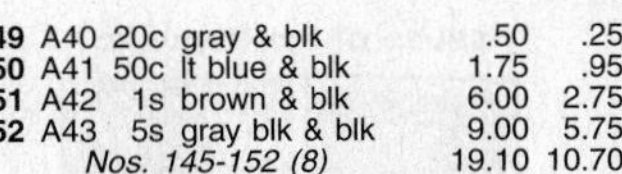

No.	Type	Description	Unused	Used
145	A36	1c scarlet & blk	.45	.25
146	A37	2c green & blk	.45	.25
147	A38	5c gray lil & blk	.45	.25
148	A39	10c dp blue & blk	.50	.25
149	A40	20c gray & blk	.50	.25
150	A41	50c lt blue & blk	1.75	.95
151	A42	1s brown & blk	6.00	2.75
152	A43	5s gray blk & blk	9.00	5.75
		Nos. 145-152 (8)	19.10	10.70

In July, 1902, following the theft of a quantity of stamps during a fire at Guayaquil, the Government authorized the governors of the provinces to handstamp their stocks. Many varieties of these handstamps exist.

Other control marks were used in 1907.

For overprints see Nos. O103-O106, O167.

A44

Surcharged on Revenue Stamp Dated 1901-1902

1903-06 *Perf. 14, 15*

No.	Type	Description	Unused	Used
153	A44	1c on 5c gray lil ('06)	.75	.40
154	A44	1c on 20c gray ('06)	10.00	4.50
155	A44	1c on 25c yellow	1.50	.40
a.		Double surcharge		
156	A44	1c on 1s bl ('06)	77.50	50.00
157	A44	3c on 5c gray lil ('06)	10.00	4.00
158	A44	3c on 20c gray ('06)	25.00	15.00
159	A44	3c on 25c yel ('06)	24.00	15.00
159A	A44	3c on 1s blue ('06)	3.75	2.25
		Nos. 153-159A (8)	152.50	91.55

Counterfeits are plentiful.

See Nos. 191-197.

Capt. Abdón Calderón
A45 A46

1904, July 31 *Perf. 12*

No.	Type	Description	Unused	Used
160	A45	1c red & blk	.45	.30
161	A45	2c blue & blk	.50	.35
162	A46	5c yellow & blk	1.90	1.00
163	A45	10c red & blk	6.00	2.00
164	A45	20c blue & blk	10.00	8.00
165	A46	50c yellow & blk	85.00	*120.00*
		Nos. 160-165 (6)	103.85	131.65

Centenary of the birth of Calderón.

Presidents

Vicente Roca — A47

Diego Noboa — A48

Francisco Robles — A49

José M. Urvina — A50

García Moreno — A51

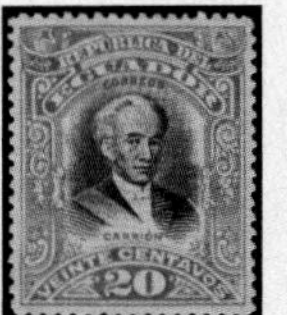
Jerónimo Carrión — A52

Javier Espinoza A53

Antonio Borrero A54

1907, July ***Perf. 14, 15***

No.	Type	Description	Unused	Used
166	A47	1c red & blk	1.00	.25
167	A48	2c pale blue & blk	2.00	.25
168	A49	3c orange & blk	3.00	.25
169	A50	5c lilac rose & blk	3.75	.25
170	A51	10c dp blue & blk	7.50	.25
171	A52	20c yellow grn & blk	10.00	.35
172	A53	50c violet & blk	22.50	.70
173	A54	1s green & blk	30.00	2.00
		Nos. 166-173 (8)	79.75	4.30

The stamps of the 1907 issue frequently have control marks similar to those found on the 1899 and 1901 issues. These marks were applied to distinguish the stamps issued in the various provinces and to serve as a check on local officials.

Locomotive — A55

García Moreno — A56

Gen. Eloy Alfaro — A57

Abelardo Moncayo — A58

Archer Harman — A59

James Sivewright — A60

Mt. Chimborazo A61

1908, June 25

No.	Type	Description	Unused	Used
174	A55	1c red brown	1.10	*2.10*
175	A56	2c blue & blk	1.30	*2.25*
176	A57	5c claret & blk	2.75	*5.25*
177	A58	10c ocher & blk	1.75	*2.75*
178	A59	20c green & blk	1.75	*3.75*
179	A60	50c gray & blk	1.75	*3.75*
180	A61	1s black	3.50	*8.00*
		Nos. 174-180 (7)	13.90	*27.85*

Opening of the Guayaquil-Quito Railway.

José Mejía Vallejo — A62

Principal Exposition Building — A70

Designs: 2c, Francisco J. E. Santa Cruz y Espejo. 3c, Francisco Ascásubi. 5c, Juan Salinas. 10c, Juan Pio de Montúfar, el Marques de Selva Alegre. 20c, Carlos de Montúfar. 50c, Juan de Dios Morales. 1s, Manuel R. de Quiroga.

1909, Aug. 10 ***Perf. 12***

No.	Type	Description	Unused	Used
181	A62	1c green	.35	*.65*
182	A62	2c blue	.35	*.65*
183	A62	3c orange	.35	*.75*
184	A62	5c claret	.35	*.75*
185	A62	10c yellow brn	.45	*.75*
186	A62	20c gray	.45	*1.10*
187	A62	50c vermilion	.45	*1.10*
188	A62	1s olive grn	.45	*1.40*
189	A70	5s violet	1.25	*2.75*
		Nos. 181-189 (9)	4.45	*9.90*

National Exposition of 1909.

No. 187 Surcharged

1909

No.	Type	Description	Unused	Used
190	A62	5c on 50c vermilion	.90	.75

Revenue Stamps Surcharged as in 1903

1910 ***Perf. 14, 15***

No.	Type	Description	Unused	Used
		Stamps Dated 1905-1906		
191	A44	1c on 5c green	2.25	1.75
192	A44	5c on 20c blue	9.50	2.00
193	A44	5c on 25c violet	18.00	3.50
		Stamps Dated 1907-1908		
194	A44	1c on 5c green	.40	.40
195	A44	5c on 20c blue	14.00	9.50
196	A44	5c on 25c violet	1.20	.40
		Stamp Dated 1909-1910		
197	A44	5c on 20c blue	*80.00*	*60.00*
		Nos. 191-197 (7)	*125.35*	*77.55*

Presidents

Roca — A71

Noboa — A72

Robles — A73

Urvina — A74

Moreno — A75

Borrero — A76

1911-28 ***Perf. 12***

No.	Type	Description	Unused	Used
198	A71	1c scarlet & blk	.80	.25
199	A71	1c orange ('16)	.80	.25
200	A71	1c lt blue ('25)	.40	.25
201	A72	2c blue & blk	1.10	.25
202	A72	2c green ('16)	1.10	.25
203	A72	2c dk violet ('25)	1.10	.25
204	A73	3c orange & blk ('13)	2.25	.30
205	A73	3c black ('15)	1.50	.25
206	A74	5c scarlet & blk	1.90	.25
207	A74	5c violet ('15)	1.90	.25
208	A74	5c rose ('25)	.70	.25
209	A74	5c dk brown ('28)	.70	.25
210	A75	10c dp blue & blk	2.25	.25
211	A75	10c dp blue ('15)	2.25	.25
212	A75	10c yellow grn ('25)	.70	.25
213	A75	10c black ('28)	1.60	.25
214	A76	1s green & blk	12.00	1.50
215	A76	1s orange & blk ('27)	8.00	.25
		Nos. 198-215 (18)	41.05	5.80

For overprints see Nos. 260-262, 264-265, O107-O122, O124-O134, O156-O157, O160-O162, O164-O166, O168-O173, O175-O178, O183-O184, O189, RA1.

A77

1912 ***Perf. 14, 15***

No.	Type	Description	Unused	Used
216	A77	1c on 1s green	1.00	1.00
217	A77	2c on 2s carmine	2.50	1.50
218	A77	2c on 5s dull blue	1.50	1.50
219	A77	2c on 10s yellow	5.00	5.00
a.		Inverted surcharge	16.00	12.00
		Nos. 216-219 (4)	10.00	9.00

No. 216 exists with narrow "V" and small "U" in "UN" and Nos. 217, 218 and 219 with "D" with serifs or small "O" in "DOS."

Enrique Váldez — A78

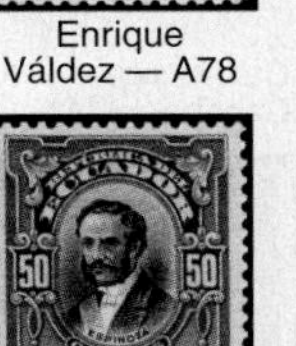

Jerónimo Carrión — A79

Javier Espinoza — A80

1915-17 ***Perf. 12***

No.	Type	Description	Unused	Used
220	A78	4c red & blk	.40	.25
221	A79	20c green & blk ('17)	3.50	.25
222	A80	50c dp violet & blk	6.00	.45
		Nos. 220-222 (3)	9.90	.95

For overprints see Nos. O123, O135, O163, O174.

Olmedo — A86

Monument to "Fathers of the Country" — A95

Laurel Wreath and Star — A104

Designs: 2c, Rafael Ximena. 3c, Roca. 4c, Luis F. Vivero. 5c, Luis Febres Cordero. 6c, Francisco Lavayen. 7c, Jorge Antonio de Elizalde. 8c, Baltazar Garcia. 9c, Jose de Antepara. 15c, Luis Urdaneta. 20c, Jose M. Villamil. 30c, Miguel Letamendi. 40c, Gregorio Escobedo. 50c, Gen. Antonio Jose de Sucre. 60c, Juan Illingworth. 70c, Roca. 80c, Rocafuerte. 1s, Simon Bolivar.

1920

No.	Type	Description	Unused	Used
223	A86	1c yellow grn	.35	.25
224	A86	2c carmine	.35	.25
225	A86	3c yellow brn	.35	.25
226	A86	4c myrtle green	.55	.25
227	A86	5c pale blue	.55	.25
228	A86	6c red orange	.90	.30
229	A86	7c brown	2.25	.75
230	A86	8c apple green	1.25	.35
231	A86	9c lake	4.25	1.50
232	A95	10c lt blue	1.50	.25
233	A86	15c dk gray	2.25	.35
234	A86	20c dk violet	2.25	.25
235	A86	30c brt violet	4.25	1.40
236	A86	40c dk brown	7.50	2.10
237	A86	50c dk green	5.25	.55
238	A86	60c dk blue	9.50	2.10
239	A86	70c gray	16.00	4.75
240	A86	80c orange yel	16.50	4.75
241	A104	90c green	17.00	4.75
242	A86	1s pale blue	24.00	8.50
		Nos. 223-242 (20)	116.80	33.90

Cent. of the independence of Guayaquil.

For overprints and surcharges see Nos. 263, 274-292, O136-O155, O179-O182, O185-O188.

Postal Tax Stamp of 1924 Overprinted

1925

No.	Type	Description	Unused	Used
259	PT6	20c bister brown	4.00	1.50

Stamps of 1915-25 Overprinted in Black or Red Upright (1c, 3c, 5c) or Inverted (2c, 4c, 10c)

1926

No.	Type	Description	Unused	Used
260	A71	1c lt blue	12.50	10.50
261	A72	2c dk violet	12.50	10.50
262	A73	3c black (R)	12.50	10.50
263	A86	4c myrtle green	12.50	10.50
264	A74	5c rose	17.50	10.50
265	A75	10c yellow grn	17.50	10.50
		Nos. 260-265 (6)	85.00	63.00

Quito-Esmeraldas railway opening.

Upright overprints on 2c, 4c, 10c and inverted overprints on 1c, 3c, 5c sell for more.

Postal Tax Stamps of 1920-24 Overprinted

1927

No.	Type	Description	Unused	Used
266	PT6	1c olive green	.50	.25
a.		"POSTAI"	1.40	.85
b.		Double overprint	2.00	.85
c.		Inverted overprint	2.00	.85
267	PT6	2c deep green	.50	.25
a.		"POSTAI"	1.40	.85
b.		Double overprint	2.00	.85
268	PT6	20c bister brown	1.00	.25
a.		"POSTAI"	8.50	5.00
		Nos. 266-268 (3)	2.00	.75

Quito Post Office — A109

1927, June

No.	Type	Description	Unused	Used
269	A109	5c orange	.50	.25
270	A109	10c dark green	.70	.25
271	A109	20c violet	.80	.25
		Nos. 269-271 (3)	2.00	.75

Opening of new Quito P.O.

For overprint see No. O190.

Postal Tax Stamp of 1924 Overprinted in Dark Blue

1928

273 PT6 20c bister brown .50 .25
a. Double overprint, one inverted 2.00 .70

See No. 339 for 10c with same overprint.

Nos. 235, 239-240 Ovptd. in Red Brown and Srchd. in Dark Blue

1928, July 8

274 A86 10c on 30c violet 16.00 16.00
275 A86 50c on 70c gray 20.00 20.00
276 A86 1s on 80c org yel 22.50 22.50
Nos. 274-276 (3) 58.50 58.50

Quito-Cayambe railway opening.

Stamps of 1920 Surcharged

1928, Oct. 9

277 A86 1c on 1c yel grn 15.00 15.00
278 A86 1c on 2c car .30 .30
279 A86 2c on 3c yel brn 2.25 2.25
a. Dbl. surch., one reading up 30.00 30.00
280 A86 2c on 4c myr grn 1.50 1.50
281 A86 2c on 5c lt blue .60 .45
a. Dbl. surch., one reading up 30.00 30.00
282 A86 2c on 7c brown 75.00 75.00
283 A86 5c on 6c red org .40 .30
a. "5 ctvos." omitted 37.50 37.50
284 A86 10c on 7c brown 1.25 1.25
285 A86 20c on 8c apple grn .35 .30
a. Double surcharge
286 A95 40c on 10c blue 4.25 4.25
287 A86 40c on 15c dk gray 1.25 1.25
288 A86 50c on 20c dk vio 13.25 13.25
289 A86 1s on 40c dk brown 4.50 4.50
290 A86 5s on 50c dk green 5.25 5.25
291 A86 10s on 60c dk blue 19.50 19.50

With Additional Surcharge in Red

292 A86 10c on 2c on 7c brn .55 .55
a. Red surcharge double 30.00 30.00
Nos. 277-292 (16) 145.20 144.90

National Assembly of 1928.
Counterfeit overprints exist of Nos. 277-291.

A111

Surcharged in Various Colors

1928, Oct. 31 ***Perf. 14***

293 A111 5c on 20c gray lil (Bk) 3.00 1.75
294 A111 10c on 20c gray lil (R) 3.00 1.75
295 A111 20c on 1s grn (O) 3.00 1.75
296 A111 50c on 1s grn (Bl) 3.75 1.40
297 A111 1s on 1s grn (V) 4.75 1.75
298 A111 5s on 2s red (G) 15.00 9.00
299 A111 10s on 2s red (Br) 18.00 12.00
a. Black surcharge 15.00 10.00
Nos. 293-299 (7) 50.50 29.40

Quito-Otavalo railway opening.
See Nos. 586-587 in Scott Standard catalogue, Vol. 2.

Postal Tax Stamp of 1924 Overprinted in Red

1929 ***Perf. 12***

302 PT6 2c deep green .50 .25

There are two types of overprint on No. 302 differing slightly.

A112

1929 **Red Overprint**

303 A112 1c dark blue .50 .25
a. Overprint reading down .75 .50

See Nos. 586-587 in Scott Standard catalogue, Vol. 2.

Plowing — A113

Cultivating Cacao — A114

Cacao Pod — A115

Growing Tobacco — A116

Exportation of Fruits — A117

Landscape — A118

Loading Sugar Cane — A119

Scene in Quito A120

Scene in Quito A121

Olmedo — A122

Monument to Simón Bolívar — A125

Designs: 2s, Sucre. 5s, Bolivar.

1930, Aug. 1 ***Perf. 12½***

304 A113 1c yellow & car .30 .25
305 A114 2c yellow & grn .30 .25
306 A115 5c dp grn & vio brn .35 .25
307 A116 6c yellow & red .45 .25
308 A117 10c orange & ol grn .45 .25
309 A118 16c red & yel grn .55 .25
310 A119 20c ultra & yel .90 .25
311 A120 40c orange & sepia 1.10 .35
312 A121 50c orange & sepia 1.10 .40
313 A122 1s dp green & blk 4.25 .45
314 A122 2s dk blue & blk 6.50 2.00
315 A122 5s dk violet & blk 11.50 3.00
316 A125 10s car rose & blk 40.00 6.50
Nos. 304-316 (13) 67.75 14.45

Centenary of founding of republic.
For surcharges and overprints see Nos. 319-320, 331-338, RA25, RA33, RA43.

A126 A127

1933 **Red Overprint** ***Perf. 15***

317 A126 10c olive brown 1.15 .25

Blue Overprint

318 A127 10c olive brown .70 .25
a. Inverted overprint 5.00 5.00

For overprint see No. 339.

Nos. 307, 309 Surcharged in Black

1933 ***Perf. 12½***

319 A116 5c on 6c yellow & red 1.00 .25
320 A118 10c on 16c red & yel grn 2.00 .25
a. Inverted overprint 4.00 4.00

Landscape A128

Mt. Chimborazo A129

1934-45 ***Perf. 12***

321 A128 5c violet 1.40 .55
322 A128 5c blue 1.40 .55
323 A128 5c dark brown 1.40 .55
323A A128 5c slate blk ('45) 1.40 .55
324 A128 10c rose 1.40 .55
325 A128 10c dark green 1.40 .55
326 A128 10c brown 1.40 .55
327 A128 10c orange 1.40 .55
328 A128 10c olive green 1.40 .55
329 A128 10c gray blk ('35) 1.40 .55
329A A128 10c red lilac ('44) 1.40 .55

Perf. 14

330 A129 1s carmine rose 1.60 .55
Nos. 321-330 (12) 17.00 6.60

Stamps of 1930 Srchd. or Ovptd. in various colors

1935 ***Perf. 12½***

331 A116 5c on 6c (Bl) .90 .35
332 A116 10c on 6c (G) 1.25 .35
333 A119 20c (R) 1.75 .35
334 A120 40c (G) 2.50 .35
335 A121 50c (G) 3.00 .45
336 A122 1s on 5s (Gold) 7.00 1.25
337 A122 2s on 5s (Gold) 9.50 1.75
338 A125 5s on 10s (Bl) 12.00 5.00
Nos. 331-338,C35-C38 (12) 87.90 29.85

Unveiling of a monument to Bolivar at Quito, July 24, 1935.

A129a

1935, Oct. 13 **Photo.** ***Perf. 11½x11***

338A A129a 5c ultra & black .25 .25
338B A129a 10c orange & blue .25 .25
338C A129a 40c dk carmine & red .25 *.30*

338D	A129a	1S blue green & red	.30	*.70*
338E	A129a	2S violet & red	.55	*1.20*
		Nos. 338A-338E,C38A-C38E (10)	4.35	*7.60*

Columbus Day. Nos. 338A-338E and C38A-C38E were prepared by the Sociedad Colombista Panamericana and were sold by the Ecuadorian post office through Oct. 30.

Telegraph Stamp Overprinted Diagonally in Red like No. 273

1935 ***Perf. 14½***

339	A126	10c olive brown	.75	.25

Map of Galápagos Islands A130

Galapagos Land Iguana A131

Galápagos Tortoise — A132

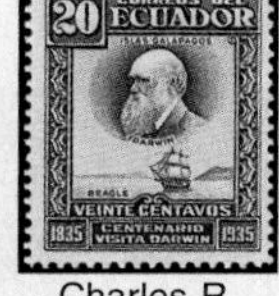

Charles R. Darwin — A133

Columbus A134

Island Scene A135

1936 ***Perf. 14***

340	A130	2c black	1.00	.25
341	A131	5c olive grn	1.25	.25
342	A132	10c brown	2.40	.30
343	A133	20c dk violet	2.75	.45
344	A134	1s dk carmine	5.00	.85
345	A135	2s dark blue	7.75	1.40
		Nos. 340-345 (6)	20.15	3.50

Cent. of the visit of Charles Darwin to the Galápagos Islands, Sept. 17, 1835.

For overprints see Nos. O191-O195.

Tobacco Stamp Overprinted in Black

1936 ***Rouletted 7***

346	PT7	1c rose red	.50	.25
a.		Horiz. pair, imperf. vert.		
b.		Double surcharge		

No. 346 is similar to type PT7 but does not include "CASA CORREOS."

Louis Godin, Charles M. de la Condamine and Pierre Bouguer A136

Portraits: 5c, 20c, Antonio Ulloa, La Condamine and Jorge Juan.

1936 **Engr.** ***Perf. 12½***

347	A136	2c deep blue	.50	.30
348	A136	5c dark green	.50	.30
349	A136	10c deep orange	.50	.30
350	A136	20c violet	.80	.30
351	A136	50c dark red	1.25	.30
		Nos. 347-351,C39-C42 (9)	6.60	2.60

Bicentenary of Geodesical Mission to Quito.

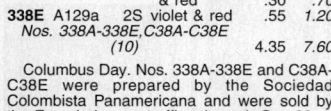

Independence Monument — A137

1936 ***Perf. 13½x14***

352	A137	2c green	2.25	1.25
353	A137	5c dark violet	2.25	1.25
354	A137	10c carmine rose	2.25	1.25
355	A137	20c black	2.25	1.25
356	A137	50c blue	3.25	2.10
357	A137	1s dark red	3.75	3.25
		Nos. 352-357,C43-C50 (14)	50.50	41.35

1st Intl. Philatelic Exhibition at Quito.

Coat of Arms — A138

Overprint in Black or Red

1937 ***Perf. 12½***

359	A138	5c olive green	2.00	.30
360	A138	10c dark blue (R)	2.00	.25

For overprint see No. 562.

Andean Landscape A139

Atahualpa, the Last Inca A140

Hat Weavers — A141

Coast Landscape A142

Gold Washing A143

1937, Aug. 19 ***Perf. 11½***

361	A139	2c green	.50	.25
362	A140	5c deep rose	.50	.25
363	A141	10c blue	.50	.25
364	A142	20c deep rose	1.50	.30
365	A143	1s olive green	2.00	.35
		Nos. 361-365 (5)	5.00	1.40

For overprints see Nos. O196-O200.

"Liberty" Carrying Flag of Ecuador — A144

Engraved and Lithographed

1938, Feb. 22 ***Perf. 12***

Center Multicolored

366	A144	2c blue	.25	.25
367	A144	5c violet	.35	.25
368	A144	10c black	.55	.25
369	A144	20c brown	.65	.25
370	A144	50c black	1.10	.25
371	A144	1s olive blk	1.75	.30
372	A144	2s dk brn	3.25	.55
		Nos. 366-372,C57-C63 (14)	22.40	4.50

US Constitution, 150th anniversary.

For overprints and surcharges see Nos. 413-415, 444-446, RA46, RA52. Post 1940 issues in Scott Standard catalogue, Vol. 2.

A145

A146

A147

A148

Designs: 10c, Winged figure holding globe. 50c, Cactus, winged wheel. 1s, "Communications." 2s, "Construction."

Perf. 13, 13x13½

1938, Oct. 30 **Engr.**

373	A145	10c bright ultra	.40	.25
374	A146	50c deep red violet	.40	.25
375	A147	1s copper red	.70	.25
376	A148	2s dark green	1.10	.25
		Nos. 373-376 (4)	2.60	1.00

Progress of Ecuador Exhibition.

For overprints see Nos. C105-C113 in Scott Standard catalogue, Vol. 2.

Parade of Athletes — A149

Runner — A150

Basketball — A151

Wrestlers A152

Diver A153

1939, Mar. ***Perf. 12***

377	A149	5c carmine rose	3.00	.55
378	A150	10c deep blue	3.50	.65
379	A151	50c gray olive	5.75	.85
380	A152	1s dull violet	7.75	.85
381	A153	2s dull olive green	12.50	.95
		Nos. 377-381,C65-C69 (10)	78.35	6.15

First Bolivarian Games (1938), Bogota.

Dolores Mission — A154

1939, June 16 ***Perf. 12½x13***

382	A154	2c blue green	.50	.25
383	A154	5c rose red	.50	.25
384	A154	10c ultra	.50	.25
385	A154	50c yellow brown	1.20	.25
386	A154	1s black	1.90	.25
387	A154	2s purple	1.25	.40
		Nos. 382-387,C73-C79 (13)	11.25	3.40

Golden Gate International Exposition.

For surcharges see Nos. 429, 436 in Scott Standard catalogue, Vol. 2.

Trylon and Perisphere — A155

1939, June 30

388	A155	2c lt olive green	.80	.35
389	A155	5c red orange	.80	.35
390	A155	10c ultra	.80	.35
391	A155	50c slate gray	1.10	.35
392	A155	1s rose carmine	1.90	.35
393	A155	2s black brown	2.25	.40
		Nos. 388-393,C80-C86 (13)	16.55	4.20

New York World's Fair.

For surcharge see No. 437.

Flags of the 21 American Republics — A156

1940 ***Perf. 12***

394	A156	5c dp rose & blk	1.00	.25
395	A156	10c dk blue & blk	.40	.25
396	A156	50c Prus green & blk	.60	.25
397	A156	1s dp violet & blk	1.00	.30
		Nos. 394-397,C87-C90 (8)	8.30	2.75

Pan American Union, 50th anniversary.

AIR POST STAMPS

In 1928-30, the internal airmail service of Ecuador was handled by the Sociedad Colombo-Alemana de Transportes Aereos ("SCADTA") under government sanction. During this period SCADTA issued stamps which were the only legal franking for airmail service except that handled under contract with Pan American-Grace Airways. SCADTA issues are Nos. C1-C6, C16-C25, CF1-CF2.

Colombia Air Post Stamps of 1923 Surcharged in Carmine

"Provisional" at 45 degree Angle

Perf. 14x14½

1928, Aug. 28 **Wmk. 116**

C1	AP6	50c on 10c green	110.00	70.00
C2	AP6	75c on 15c car	210.00	160.00
C3	AP6	1s on 20c gray	70.00	42.50
C4	AP6	1½s on 30c blue	45.00	35.00
C5	AP6	3s on 60c brown	85.00	52.50
		Nos. C1-C5 (5)	520.00	360.00

"Provisional" at 41 degree Angle

1929, Mar. 20

C1a	*AP6*	*50c on 10c green*	*125.00*	*110.00*
C2a	*AP6*	*75c on 15c carmine*	*225.00*	*175.00*
C3a	*AP6*	*1s on 20c gray*	*225.00*	*175.00*
		Nos. C1a-C3a (3)	*575.00*	*460.00*

C6	AP6	50c on 10c green	*700.00*	*1,700.*

A 75c on 15c carmine with "Cts." between the surcharged numerals exists. There is no evidence that it was regularly issued or used.

For overprints see Nos. CF1-CF1a.

Plane over River Guayas — AP1

Unwmk.

1929, May 5 Engr. *Perf. 12*

C8	AP1	2c black	.40	.25
C9	AP1	5c carmine rose	.40	.25
C10	AP1	10c deep brown	.40	.25
C11	AP1	20c dark violet	.90	.25
C12	AP1	50c deep green	1.60	.45
C13	AP1	1s dark blue	6.00	2.75
C14	AP1	5s orange yellow	25.00	11.00
C15	AP1	10s orange red	135.00	57.50
		Nos. C8-C15 (8)	169.70	72.70

Establishment of commercial air service in Ecuador. The stamps were available for all forms of postal service and were largely used for franking ordinary letters.

Nos. C13-C15 show numerals in color on white background. Counterfeits of No. C15 exist.

See Nos. C26-C31. For overprints and surcharge see Nos. C32-C38, C287 (in Scott Standard catalogue, Vol. 2), CO1-CO12.

Jesuit Church La Compania AP2

Mount Chimborazo AP3

Wmk. 127

1929, Apr. 1 Litho. *Perf. 14*

C16	AP2	50c red brown	4.50	2.25
C17	AP2	75c green	4.50	2.25
C18	AP2	1s rose	7.00	2.25
C19	AP2	1⅛s gray blue	7.00	2.25
C20	AP2	2s violet	11.50	4.50
C21	AP2	3s brown	11.50	4.50
C22	AP3	5s lt blue	50.00	15.00
C23	AP3	10s lt red	100.00	32.50
C24	AP3	15s violet	160.00	65.00
C25	AP3	25s olive green	225.00	75.00
		Nos. C16-C25 (10)	581.00	205.50

For overprint see No. CF2.

Plane Type of 1929

1930-44 Unwmk. Engr. *Perf. 12*

C26	AP1	1s carmine lake	6.50	.55
C27	AP1	1s green ('44)	1.00	.25
C28	AP1	5s olive green	10.00	3.75
C29	AP1	5s purple ('44)	2.00	.25
C30	AP1	10s black	30.00	5.50
C31	AP1	10s brt ultra ('44)	4.50	.30
		Nos. C26-C31 (6)	54.00	10.60

Nos. C26-C31 show numerals in color on white background.

For surcharge see No. C287 in Scott Standard catalogue, Vol. 2.

Type of 1929 Overprinted in Various Colors

AP4

1930, June 4

C32	AP4	1s car lake (Bk)	22.50	22.50
a.		Double ovpt. (R Br + Bk)	75.00	
C33	AP4	5s olive grn (Bl)	22.50	22.50
C34	AP4	10s black (R Br)	22.50	22.50
		Nos. C32-C34 (3)	67.50	67.50

Flight of Capt. Benjamin Mendez from Bogota to Quito, bearing a crown of flowers for the tomb of Grand Marshal Sucre.

Air Post Official Stamps of 1929-30 Ovptd. in Various Colors or Srchd. Similarly in Upper & Lower Case

1935, July 24

C35	AP1	50c deep green (Bl)	12.50	5.00
C36	AP1	50c olive brn (R)	12.50	5.00
C37	AP1	1s on 5s ol grn (Bk)	12.50	5.00
a.		Double surcharge	95.00	
C38	AP1	2s on 10s black (R)	12.50	5.00
		Nos. C35-C38 (4)	50.00	20.00

Unveiling of a monument to Bolívar at Quito, July 24th, 1935.

AP5

1935, Oct. 13 Photo. *Perf. 11½x11*

C38A	AP5	5c ultra & red	.25	*.30*
C38B	AP5	10c brown & black	.25	*.50*
C38C	AP5	50c green & red	.25	*.50*
C38D	AP5	1S carmine & blue	.80	*1.20*
C38E	AP5	5S gray grn & red	1.20	*2.40*
		Nos. C38A-C38E (5)	2.75	*4.90*

Columbus Day. Nos. 338A-338E and C38A-C38E were prepared by the Sociedad Colombista Panamericana and were sold by the Ecuadorian post office through Oct. 30. Nos. C38B-C38E exist imperf.

Geodesical Mission Issue

Nos. 349-351 Overprinted in Blue or Black and Type of Regular issue

1936, July 3 *Perf. 12½*

C39	A136	10c deep orange (Bl)	.60	.25
C40	A136	20c violet (Bk)	.60	.25
C41	A136	50c dark red (Bl)	.60	.25
C42	A136	70c black	1.25	.35
		Nos. C39-C42 (4)	3.05	1.10

For surcharge see No. RA42.

Philatelic Exhibition Issue

Type of Regular Issue Overprinted "AEREA"

1936, Oct. 20 *Perf. 13½x14*

C43	A137	2c rose	5.00	5.00
C44	A137	5c brown orange	5.00	5.00
C45	A137	10c brown	5.00	5.00
C46	A137	20c ultra	5.00	5.00
C47	A137	50c red violet	5.00	5.00
C48	A137	1s green	5.00	5.00
		Nos. C43-C48 (6)	30.00	30.00

Condor and Plane — AP6

Perf. 13½

C49	AP6	70c orange brown	2.25	.50
C50	AP6	1s dull violet	2.25	.50

Nos. C43-C50 were issued for the 1st Intl. Phil. Exhib. at Quito.

Condor over "El Altar" — AP7

1937-46 *Perf. 11½, 12*

C51	AP7	10c chestnut	5.00	.25
C52	AP7	20c olive black	6.50	.25
C53	AP7	40c rose car ('46)	6.50	.25
C54	AP7	70c black brown	9.00	.25
C55	AP7	1s gray black	14.00	.25
C56	AP7	2s dark violet	24.00	.65
		Nos. C51-C56 (6)	65.00	1.90

Issue dates: 40c, Oct. 7; others, Aug. 19.

For overprints see Nos. 463-464 (in Scott Standard catalogue, Vol. 2), CO13-CO17.

Portrait of Washington, American Eagle and Flags — AP8

Engraved and Lithographed

1938, Feb. 9 *Perf. 12*

Center Multicolored

C57	AP8	2c brown	.40	.25
C58	AP8	5c black	.40	.25
C59	AP8	10c brown	.40	.25
C60	AP8	20c dark blue	.80	.25
C61	AP8	50c violet	1.75	.25
C62	AP8	1s black	3.25	.25
C63	AP8	2s violet	7.50	.90
		Nos. C57-C63 (7)	14.50	2.40

150th anniv. of the US Constitution.

In 1947, Nos. C61-C63 were overprinted in dark blue: "Primero la Patria!" and plane. These revolutionary propaganda stamps were later renounced by decree. Value $20.

For overprints see Nos. C102-C104, C139-C141 in Scott Standard catalogue, Vol. 2.

No. RA35 Surcharged in Red

1938, Nov. 16 *Perf. 13½*

C64	PT12	65c on 3c ultra	.40	.25

A national airmail concession was given to the Sociedad Ecuatoriano de Transportes Aereos (SEDTA) in July, 1938. No. RA35 was surcharged for SEDTA postal requirements. SEDTA operated through 1940.

Army Horseman — AP9

Woman Runner — AP10

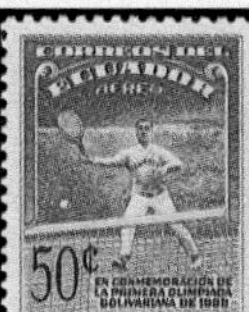

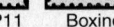

Tennis — AP11

Boxing — AP12

Olympic Fire — AP13

1939, Mar. Engr. *Perf. 12*

C65	AP9	5c lt green	1.60	.25
C66	AP10	10c salmon	2.25	.25
C67	AP11	50c redsh brown	11.50	.25
C68	AP12	1s black brown	13.50	.45
C69	AP13	2s rose carmine	17.00	1.10
		Nos. C65-C69 (5)	45.85	2.30

First Bolivarian Games (1938).

Plane over Chimborazo AP14

1939, May 1 *Perf. 13x12½*

C70	AP14	1s yellow brown	.40	.25
C71	AP14	2s rose violet	.70	.25
C72	AP14	5s black	1.90	.25
		Nos. C70-C72 (3)	3.00	.75

Golden Gate Bridge and Mountain Peak — AP15

1939 *Perf. 12½x13*

C73	AP15	2c black	.40	.25
C74	AP15	5c rose red	.40	.25
C75	AP15	10c indigo	.40	.25
C76	AP15	50c rose violet	.40	.25
C77	AP15	1s chocolate	.80	.25
C78	AP15	2s yellow brown	1.00	.25
C79	AP15	5s emerald	2.00	.25
		Nos. C73-C79 (7)	5.40	1.75

Golden Gate International Exposition.

For surcharge & overprint see Nos. 434 (in Scott Standard catalogue, Vol. 2), CO18.

Empire State Building and Mountain Peak — AP16

1939

C80	AP16	2c brown orange	.65	.30
C81	AP16	5c dark carmine	.65	.25
C82	AP16	10c indigo	.65	.30
C83	AP16	50c slate green	.65	.30
C84	AP16	1s deep orange	1.30	.30
C85	AP16	2s dk red violet	1.50	.30
C86	AP16	5s dark gray	3.50	.30
		Nos. C80-C86 (7)	8.90	2.05

New York World's Fair.

For surcharge see No. 435 in Scott Standard catalogue, Vol. 2.

Map of the Americas and Airplane — AP17

1940, July 9
C87 AP17 10c red org & blue .45 .25
C88 AP17 70c sepia & blue .45 .25
C89 AP17 1s copper brn & blue .90 .25
C90 AP17 10s black & blue 3.50 .95
Nos. C87-C90 (4) 5.30 1.70

Pan American Union, 50th anniversary.

AIR POST REGISTRATION STAMPS

Issued by Sociedad Colombo-Alemana de Transportes Aereos (SCADTA)

Nos. C3 and C3a Overprinted in Carmine

1928-29 Wmk. 116 *Perf. 14x14½*
CF1 AP6 1s on 20c (#C3) 110.00 100.00
a. 1s on 20c (#C3a) ('29) 140.00 110.00

No. C18 Overprinted in Black

1929, Apr. 1 Wmk. 127 *Perf. 14*
CF2 AP2 1s rose 85.00 55.00

AIR POST OFFICIAL STAMPS

Nos. C8-C15 Overprinted in Red or Black

1929, May Unwmk. *Perf. 12*
CO1 AP1 2c black (R) 1.00 .50
CO2 AP1 5c carmine rose 1.00 .50
CO3 AP1 10c deep brown 1.00 .50
CO4 AP1 20c dark violet 1.00 .50
CO5 AP1 50c deep green 4.00 2.00
CO6 AP1 1s dark blue 4.00 2.00
a. Inverted overprint 240.00
CO7 AP1 5s orange yellow 18.00 7.75
CO8 AP1 10s orange red 210.00 75.00
Nos. CO1-CO8 (8) 240.00 88.75

Establishment of commercial air service in Ecuador.
Counterfeits of No. CO8 exist.
See Nos. CO9-CO12. For overprints and surcharges see Nos. C35-C38.

1930, Jan. 9
CO9 AP1 50c olive brown 3.50 1.75
CO10 AP1 1s carmine lake 4.50 2.25
CO11 AP1 5s olive green 11.00 5.50
CO12 AP1 10s black 21.00 10.50
Nos. CO9-CO12 (4) 40.00 20.00

For surcharges and overprint see Nos. C36-C38.

Air Post Stamps of 1937 Overprinted in Black

1937, Aug. 19
CO13 AP7 10c chestnut .50 .25
CO14 AP7 20c olive black .50 .25
CO15 AP7 70c black brown .60 .25
CO16 AP7 1s gray black .70 .25
CO17 AP7 2s dark violet .70 .30
Nos. CO13-CO17 (5) 3.00 1.30

For overprints see Nos. 463-464 in Scott Standard catalogue, Vol. 2.

No. C79 Overprinted in Black

1940, Aug. 1 *Perf. 12½x13*
CO18 AP15 5s emerald 2.00 .60

SPECIAL DELIVERY STAMPS

SD1

1928 Unwmk. *Perf. 12*
E1 SD1 2c on 2c blue 8.00 *9.00*
E2 SD1 5c on 2c blue 7.00 *9.00*
E3 SD1 10c on 2c blue 7.00 6.00
a. "10 CTVOS" inverted 21.00 *25.00*
E4 SD1 20c on 2c blue 10.00 9.00
E5 SD1 50c on 2c blue 12.00 9.00
Nos. E1-E5 (5) 44.00 *42.00*

POSTAGE DUE STAMPS

Numeral — D1

1896 Engr. Wmk. 117 *Perf. 12*
J1 D1 1c blue green 6.00 *6.50*
J2 D1 2c blue green 6.00 *6.50*
J3 D1 5c blue green 6.00 *6.50*
J4 D1 10c blue green 6.00 *6.50*
J5 D1 20c blue green 6.00 *8.50*
J6 D1 50c blue green 6.00 *13.00*
J7 D1 100c blue green 6.00 *17.00*
Nos. J1-J7 (7) 42.00 *64.50*

Reprints are on very thick paper with distinct watermark and vertical paper-weave direction. Value 15c each.

Unwmk.
J8 D1 1c blue green *5.00 6.00*
J9 D1 2c blue green *5.00 6.00*
J10 D1 5c blue green *5.00 6.00*
J11 D1 10c blue green *5.00 6.00*
J12 D1 20c blue green *5.00 7.50*
J13 D1 50c blue green *5.00 10.50*
J14 D1 100c blue green *5.00 15.00*
Nos. J8-J14 (7) 35.00 *57.00*

Coat of Arms — D2

1929
J15 D2 5c deep blue .40 .40
J16 D2 10c orange yellow .40 .40
J17 D2 20c red .60 .60
Nos. J15-J17 (3) 1.40 1.40

OFFICIAL STAMPS

Regular Issues of 1881 and 1887 Handstamped in Black

1886 Unwmk. *Perf. 12*
O1 A5 1c yellow brown 2.50 2.50
O2 A6 2c lake 3.00 3.00
O3 A7 5c blue 6.75 *8.75*
O4 A8 10c orange 5.25 3.25
O5 A9 20c gray violet 5.25 5.25
O6 A10 50c blue green 15.00 11.50
Nos. O1-O6 (6) 37.75 34.25

1887
O7 A12 1c green 3.25 2.50
O8 A13 2c vermilion 3.25 3.25
O9 A14 5c blue 5.25 2.50
O10 A15 80c olive green 17.50 10.00
Nos. O7-O10 (4) 29.25 18.25

Nos. O1-O10 are known with red handstamp but these are believed to be speculative.
The overprint on the 1886-87 issues is handstamped and is found in various positions.

Flores — O1

1892 Carmine Overprint
O11 O1 1c ultramarine .25 *.40*
O12 O1 2c ultramarine .25 *.40*
O13 O1 5c ultramarine .25 *.40*
O14 O1 10c ultramarine .25 *.60*
O15 O1 20c ultramarine .25 *.90*
O16 O1 50c ultramarine .25 *.90*
O17 O1 1s ultramarine .35 *1.00*
Nos. O11-O17 (7) 1.85 4.60

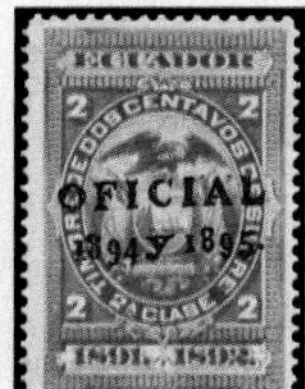
Arms — O1a

1894
O18 O1a 1c slate green (R) 15.00
O19 O1a 2c lake (Bk) 20.00

Nos. O18 and O19 were not placed in use.

Rocafuerte — O2

Dated "1894"

1894 Carmine Overprint
O20 O2 1c gray black .60 *1.00*
O21 O2 2c gray black .60 .60
O22 O2 5c gray black .60 .60
O23 O2 10c gray black .75 *1.00*
O24 O2 20c gray black 1.00 1.00
O25 O2 50c gray black 3.75 3.75
O26 O2 1s gray black 6.00 6.00
Nos. O20-O26 (7) 13.30 13.95

Dated "1895"

1895 Carmine Overprint
O27 O2 1c gray black 5.25 5.25
O28 O2 2c gray black 7.50 7.50
O29 O2 5c gray black 1.50 1.50
O30 O2 10c gray black 7.50 7.50
O31 O2 20c gray black 11.00 10.50
O32 O2 50c gray black *75.00 75.00*
O33 O2 1s gray black 3.75 3.75
Nos. O27-O33 (7) *111.50 111.00*

Reprints of 1894-95 issues are on very thick paper with paper weave found both horizontal and vertical for all denominations. Generally they are blacker than originals.
For overprints see Nos. O50-O91.

Types of 1896 Overprinted in Carmine

1896 Wmk. 117
O34 A21 1c olive bister 1.00 1.00
O35 A22 2c olive bister 1.00 1.00
O36 A23 5c olive bister 1.00 1.00
O37 A24 10c olive bister 1.00 1.00
O38 A25 20c olive bister 1.00 1.00
O39 A26 50c olive bister 1.00 1.00
O40 A27 1s olive bister 3.00 3.00
O41 A28 5s olive bister 6.00 6.00
Nos. O34-O41 (8) 15.00 15.00

Reprints of Nos. O34-O41 are on thick paper with vertical paper weave direction.

Unwmk.
O42 A21 1c olive bister 3.00 3.00
O43 A22 2c olive bister 3.00 3.00
O44 A23 5c olive bister 3.00 3.00
O45 A24 10c olive bister 3.00 3.00
O46 A25 20c olive bister 3.00 3.00
O47 A26 50c olive bister 3.00 *3.00*
O48 A27 1s olive bister 7.50 7.50
O49 A28 5s olive bister 10.50 10.50
Nos. O42-O49 (8) 36.00 36.00

Reprints of Nos. O42-O49 all have overprint in black. Value 20 cents each.

Nos. O20-O26 Overprinted

1897-98
O50 O2 1c gray black *20.00 20.00*
O51 O2 2c gray black *35.00 35.00*
O52 O2 5c gray black *200.00 200.00*
O53 O2 10c gray black *30.00 30.00*
O54 O2 20c gray black *20.00 20.00*
O55 O2 50c gray black *35.00 35.00*
O56 O2 1s gray black *55.00 55.00*
Nos. O50-O56 (7) *395.00 395.00*

Nos. O20-O26 Overprinted

O57 O2 1c gray black *4.00 4.00*
O58 O2 2c gray black *9.00 9.00*
O59 O2 5c gray black *90.00 90.00*
O60 O2 10c gray black *100.00 100.00*
O61 O2 20c gray black *25.00 25.00*
O62 O2 50c gray black *15.00 15.00*
O63 O2 1s gray black *165.00 165.00*
Nos. O57-O63 (7) *408.00 408.00*

Nos. O20-O26 Overprinted

O64 O2 1c gray black *40.00 40.00*
O65 O2 2c gray black *40.00 40.00*
O66 O2 5c gray black *40.00 40.00*
O67 O2 10c gray black *40.00 40.00*
O68 O2 20c gray black *40.00 40.00*
O69 O2 50c gray black *40.00 40.00*
O70 O2 1s gray black *40.00 40.00*
Nos. O64-O70 (7) *280.00 280.00*

Nos. O27-O33 Overprinted in Black like Nos. O50-O56

O71 O2 1c gray black *20.00 20.00*
O72 O2 2c gray black *20.00 20.00*
O73 O2 5c gray black *20.00 20.00*
O74 O2 10c gray black *20.00 20.00*
O75 O2 20c gray black *30.00 30.00*
O76 O2 50c gray black *275.00 275.00*
O77 O2 1s gray black *100.00 100.00*
Nos. O71-O77 (7) 485.00 485.00

Nos. O27-O33 Overprinted

O78 O2 1c gray black *35.00 35.00*
O79 O2 2c gray black *30.00 30.00*
O80 O2 5c gray black *30.00 30.00*
O81 O2 10c gray black *32.50 32.50*
O82 O2 20c gray black *42.50 42.50*
O83 O2 50c gray black *30.00 30.00*
O84 O2 1s gray black *30.00 30.00*
Nos. O78-O84 (7) *230.00 230.00*

Nos. O27-O33 Overprinted like #O64-O70

O85 O2 1c gray black *90.00 90.00*
O86 O2 2c gray black *20.00 20.00*
O87 O2 5c gray black *80.00 80.00*
O88 O2 10c gray black *80.00 80.00*
O89 O2 20c gray black *140.00 140.00*
O90 O2 50c gray black *85.00 85.00*
O91 O2 1s gray black *165.00 165.00*
Nos. O85-O91 (7) *660.00 660.00*

Many forged overprints of Nos. O50-O91 exist, made on the original stamps and reprints.

O3

1898-99 ***Perf. 15, 16***

Black Surcharge

O92 O3 5c on 50c lilac 10.00 10.00
a. Inverted surcharge 25.00 25.00
O93 O3 10c on 20s org 15.00 15.00
a. Double surcharge 40.00 30.00
O94 O3 10c on 50c lilac *140.00 140.00*
O95 O3 20c on 50c lilac 30.00 30.00
O96 O3 20c on 50s green 30.00 30.00
Nos. O92-O96 (5) *225.00 225.00*

Green Surcharge

O97 O3 5c on 50c lilac 10.00 10.00
a. Double surcharge 5.00
b. Double surcharge, blk and grn 12.00
c. Same as "b," blk surch. invtd. 5.00

1899 **Red Surcharge**

O98 O3 5c on 50c lilac 10.00 10.00
a. Double surcharge 20.00
b. Dbl. surch., blk and red 25.00
O99 O3 20c on 50s green 15.00 15.00
a. Inverted surcharge 40.00
b. Dbl. surch., red and blk 60.00

Similar Surcharge in Black Value in Words in Two Lines

O100 O3 1c on 5c blue *650.00*

Red Surcharge

O101 O3 2c on 5c blue *1,150.*
O102 O3 4c on 20c blue *800.00*

Types of Regular Issue of 1899 Ovptd. in Black

1899 ***Perf. 14, 15***

O103 A37 2c orange & blk .70 *1.60*
O104 A39 10c orange & blk .70 *1.60*
O105 A40 20c orange & blk .50 *2.50*
O106 A41 50c orange & blk .50 *3.25*
Nos. O103-O106 (4) 2.40 *8.95*

For overprint see No. O167.

The above overprint was applied to remainders of the postage stamps of 1904 with the idea of increasing their salability. They were never regularly in use as official stamps.

Regular Issue of 1911-13 Overprinted in Black

1913 ***Perf. 12***

O107 A71 1c scarlet & blk 3.50 3.50
O108 A72 2c blue & blk 3.50 3.50
O109 A73 3c orange & blk 2.25 2.25
O110 A74 5c scarlet & blk 4.50 4.50
O111 A75 10c blue & blk 4.50 4.50
Nos. O107-O111 (5) 18.25 18.25

Regular Issue of 1911-13 Overprinted

1916-17 **Overprint 22x3½mm**

O112 A72 2c blue & blk 25.00 18.00
O113 A74 5c scarlet & blk 25.00 18.00
O114 A75 10c blue & blk 15.00 12.00
Nos. O112-O114 (3) 65.00 48.00

Overprint 25x4mm

O115 A71 1c scarlet & blk 1.10 1.10
O116 A72 2c blue & blk 1.60 1.60
a. Inverted overprint 5.00 5.00
O117 A73 3c orange & blk 1.00 1.00
O118 A74 5c scarlet & blk 1.60 1.60
O119 A75 10c blue & blk 1.60 1.60
Nos. O115-O119 (5) 6.90 6.90

Same Overprint On Regular Issue of 1915-17

O120 A71 1c orange 1.40 1.40
O121 A72 2c green 1.40 1.40
O122 A73 3c black 2.25 2.25
O123 A78 4c red & blk 2.25 2.25
a. Inverted overprint 15.00
O124 A74 5c violet 1.40 1.40
O125 A75 10c blue 2.75 2.75
O126 A79 20c green & blk 15.00 15.00
Nos. O120-O126 (7) 26.45 26.45

Regular Issues of 1911-17 Overprinted in Black or Red

O127 A71 1c orange .90 .90
O128 A72 2c green .70 .70
O129 A73 3c black (Bk) .90 .90
O130 A73 3c black (R) .90 .70
a. Inverted overprint
O131 A78 4c red & blk .90 .90
O132 A74 5c violet 1.75 .90
O133 A75 10c blue & blk 4.50 1.75
O134 A75 10c blue .90 .90
O135 A79 20c green & blk 4.50 1.75
Nos. O127-O135 (9) 15.95 9.40

Regular Issue of 1920 Overprinted

1920

O136 A86 1c green 1.25 1.25
a. Inverted overprint 17.00 —
O137 A86 2c carmine 1.00 1.00
O138 A86 3c yellow brn 1.25 1.25
O139 A86 4c dark green 2.00 2.00
a. Inverted overprint 17.00 —
O140 A86 5c blue 2.00 2.00
O141 A86 6c orange 1.25 1.25
O142 A86 7c brown 2.00 2.00
O143 A86 8c yellow green 2.50 2.50
O144 A86 9c red 3.25 3.25
O145 A95 10c blue 2.00 2.00
O146 A86 15c gray 11.00 11.00
O147 A86 20c deep violet 14.50 14.50
O148 A86 30c violet 17.00 17.00
O149 A86 40c dark brown 21.00 21.00
O150 A86 50c dark green 14.50 14.50
O151 A86 60c dark blue 17.00 17.00
O152 A86 70c gray 17.00 17.00
O153 A86 80c yellow 21.00 21.00
O154 A104 90c green 21.00 21.00
O155 A86 1s blue 45.00 45.00
Nos. O136-O155 (20) 217.50 217.50

Cent. of the independence of Guayaquil.

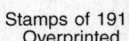

Stamps of 1911 Overprinted

1922

O156 A71 1c scarlet & blk 9.00 9.00
O157 A72 2c blue & blk 4.50 4.50

Revenue Stamps of 1919-1920 Overprinted like Nos. O156 and O157

1924

O158 PT3 1c dark blue 2.00 2.00
O159 PT3 2c green 12.50 12.50

Regular Issues of 1911-17 Overprinted

1924

O160 A71 1c orange 7.00 7.00
a. Inverted overprint 15.00

Overprinted in Black or Red

O161 A72 2c green .60 .60
O162 A73 3c black (R) .80 .80
O163 A78 4c red & blk 1.25 1.25
O164 A74 5c violet 1.25 1.25
O165 A75 10c deep blue 1.25 1.25
O166 A76 1s green & blk 7.00 7.00
Nos. O160-O166 (7) 19.15 19.15

No. O106 with Additional Overprint

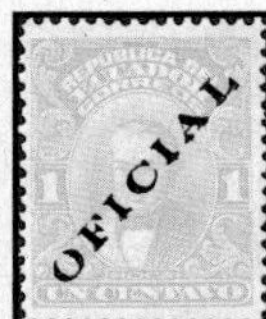

1924 ***Perf. 14, 15***

O167 A41 50c orange & blk 2.25 2.25

Nos. O160-O167 exist with inverted overprint.

No. 199 Overprinted

1924 ***Perf. 12***

O168 A71 1c orange 5.50 5.50

Regular Issues of 1911-25 Overprinted

1925

O169 A71 1c scarlet & blk 10.00 4.25
a. Inverted overprint 15.00
O170 A71 1c orange .60 .60
a. Inverted overprint 4.00
O171 A72 2c green .60 .60
a. Inverted overprint 4.00
O172 A73 3c black (Bk) .60 .60
O173 A73 3c black (R) 1.10 1.10
O174 A78 4c red & blk .60 .60
O175 A74 5c violet .80 .80
O176 A74 5c rose .80 .80
O177 A75 10c deep blue .60 .60
Nos. O169-O177 (9) 15.70 9.95

Regular Issues of 1916-25 Ovptd. Vertically Up or Down

1927, Oct.

O178 A71 1c orange 2.00 2.00
O179 A86 2c carmine 2.00 2.00
O180 A86 3c yellow brown 2.00 2.00
O181 A86 4c myrtle green 2.00 2.00
O182 A86 5c pale blue 2.00 2.00
O183 A75 10c yellow green 2.00 2.00
Nos. O178-O183 (6) 12.00 12.00

Regular Issues of 1920-27 Overprinted

1928

O184 A71 1c lt blue 1.25 1.25
O185 A86 2c carmine 1.25 1.25
O186 A86 3c yellow brown 1.25 1.25
a. Inverted overprint 5.00
O187 A86 4c myrtle green 1.25 1.25
O188 A86 5c lt blue 1.25 1.25
O189 A75 10c yellow green 1.25 1.25
O190 A109 20c violet 11.00 2.50
a. Overprint reading up 3.50 2.25
Nos. O184-O190 (7) 18.50 10.00

The overprint is placed vertically reading down on No. O190.

Regular Issue of 1936 Overprinted in Black

1936 ***Perf. 14***

O191 A131 5c olive green 1.50 1.50
O192 A132 10c brown 1.50 1.50
O193 A133 20c dark violet 1.90 .70
O194 A134 1s dark carmine 2.25 1.10
O195 A135 2s dark blue 2.50 1.75
Nos. O191-O195 (5) 9.65 6.55

Regular Postage Stamps of 1937 Overprinted in Black

OFICIAL

1937 ***Perf. 11½***

O196 A139 2c green .40 .40
O197 A140 5c deep rose .40 .40
O198 A141 10c blue .40 .40
O199 A142 20c deep rose .40 .40
O200 A143 1s olive green .40 .40
Nos. O196-O200 (5) 2.00 2.00

POSTAL TAX STAMPS

CASA de CORREOS

Roca — PT1

1920 **Unwmk.** ***Perf. 12***

RA1 PT1 1c orange .75 .30

PT2

PT3

RA2 PT2 1c red & blue 1.10 .25
a. "de" inverted 10.50 5.25
b. Double overprint 10.00 .60
c. Inverted overprint 10.00 .60
RA3 PT3 1c deep blue 1.25 .25
a. Inverted overprint 6.00 1.00
b. Double overprint 6.00 1.00

For overprints see Nos. O158-O159.

PT4

PT5

Red or Black Surcharge or Overprint

Stamp Dated 1911-1912

RA4 PT4 20c deep blue — 30.00

Stamp Dated 1913-1914

RA5 PT4 20c deep blue (R) 2.25 .35

Stamp Dated 1917-1918

RA6 PT4 20c olive green (R) 6.50 .55
a. Dated 1919-20 *25.00*
RA7 PT5 1c on 2c green .90 .25

Stamp Dated 1911-1912

RA8 PT5 1c on 5c green .90 .25
a. Double surcharge

Stamp Dated 1913-1914

RA9 PT5 1c on 5c green 8.00 .55
a. Double surcharge 12.00 4.00

On Nos. RA7, RA8 and RA9 the surcharge is found reading upward or downward.
For surcharges see Nos. RA15-RA16.

Post Office — PT6

1920-24 **Engr.**

RA10 PT6 1c olive green .40 .25
RA11 PT6 2c deep green .40 .25
RA12 PT6 20c bister brn ('24) 1.75 .25
RA13 PT6 2s violet 11.50 3.25
RA14 PT6 5s blue 20.00 5.75
Nos. RA10-RA14 (5) 34.05 9.75

For overprints and surcharge see Nos. 259, 266-268, 273, 302, RA17, RA28.

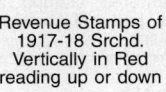

Revenue Stamps of 1917-18 Srchd. Vertically in Red reading up or down

1921-22

RA15 PT5 20c on 1c dk blue 55.00 6.50
RA16 PT5 20c on 2c green 55.00 6.50

No. RA12 Surcharged in Green

1924

RA17 PT6 2c on 20c bis brn .60 .25
a. Inverted surcharge 14.00 5.00
b. Double surcharge 4.00 2.00

PT7

1924 ***Rouletted 7***

RA18 PT7 1c rose red .90 .25
a. Inverted overprint 3.50

Similar Design, Eagle at left

Perf. 12

RA19 PT7 2c blue .90 .25
a. Inverted overprint 3.50 1.75

For overprints and surcharges see Nos. 346, O201, RA32, RA34, RA37, RA44-RA45, RA47.

PT8

Inscribed "Timbre Fiscal"

1924

RA20 PT8 1c yellow 4.50 .85
RA21 PT8 2c dark blue 1.40 .35

Inscribed "Region Oriental"

RA22 PT8 1c yellow .70 .30
RA23 PT8 2c dark blue 1.40 .35
Nos. RA20-RA23 (4) 8.00 1.85

Overprint on No. RA22 reads down or up.

Revenue Stamp Overprinted in Blue

1934

RA24 2c green .50 .25
a. Blue overprint inverted 3.50 1.75
b. Blue ovpt. dbl., one invtd. 4.00 1.25

Postage Stamp of 1930 Overprinted in Red

Perf. 12½

RA25 A119 20c ultra & yel .50 .25

Telegraph Stamp Overprinted in Red, like No. RA24, and Surcharged diagonally in Black

1934 ***Perf. 14***

RA26 2c on 10c olive brn .70 .25
a. Double surcharge 5.50

Overprint Blue, Surcharge Red

RA27 2c on 10c olive brn .70 .25

PT9

1934-36 ***Perf. 12***

RA28 PT9 2c green .60 .25
a. Both overprints in red ('36) .60 .25

Postal Tax stamp of 1920-24, overprinted in red "POSTAL" has been again overprinted "CASA de Correos y Teleg. de Guayaquil" in black.

PT10

Perf. 14½x14

1934 **Photo.** **Wmk. 233**

RA29 PT10 2c yellow green .50 .25

For the rebuilding of the GPO at Guayaquil.
For surcharge see No. RA31.

Symbols of Post and Telegraph Service PT11

1935

RA30 PT11 20c claret .50 .25

For the rebuilding of the GPO at Guayaquil.

No. RA29 Surcharged in Red and Overprinted in Black

1935

RA31 PT10 3c on 2c yel grn .40 .25
a. Double surcharge

Social and Rural Workers' Insurance Fund.

Tobacco Stamp Surcharged in Black

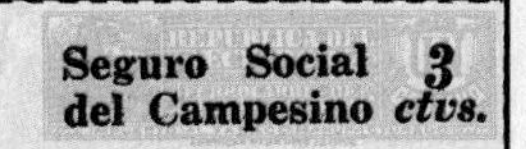

1936 **Unwmk.** ***Rouletted 7***

RA32 PT7 3c on 1c rose red .60 .25
a. Lines of words reversed 2.00 .25
b. Horiz. pair, imperf. vert.

Issued for the Social and Rural Workers' Insurance Fund.

No. 310 Overprinted in Black

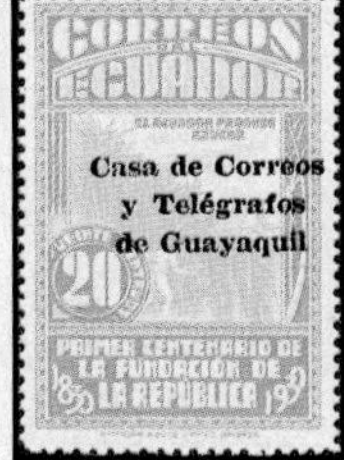

1936 ***Perf. 12½***

RA33 A119 20c ultra & yel .60 .25
a. Double overprint

Tobacco Stamp Surcharged in Black

SEGURO SOCIAL DEL CAMPESINO 3 ctvs.

1936 ***Rouletted 7***

RA34 PT7 3c on 1c rose red .60 .25

Social and Rural Workers' Insurance Fund.

Worker — PT12

1936 **Engr.** ***Perf. 13½***

RA35 PT12 3c ultra .40 .25

Social and Rural Workers' Insurance Fund.
For surcharges see Nos. C64, RA36, RA53-RA54 (in Scott Standard catalogue, Vol. 2).

Surcharged in Black

1936

RA36 PT13 5c on 3c ultra .60 .25

This combines the 2c for the rebuilding of the post office with the 3c for the Social and Rural Workers' Insurance Fund.

National Defense Issue

Tobacco Stamp Surcharged in Black

1936 ***Rouletted 7***

RA37 PT7 10c on 1c rose .90 .25
a. Double surcharge

Symbolical of Defense — PT14

1937-42 ***Perf. 12½***

RA38 PT14 10c deep blue .90 .25

A 1s violet and 2s green exist in type PT14.
For surcharge see No. RA40.

Overprinted or Surcharged in Black

PT15

1937 **Engr. & Typo.** ***Perf. 13½***

RA39 PT15 5c lt brn & red 2.00 .25
d. Inverted overprint 20.00

No. RA38 Surcharged in Red

1937 **Engr.** ***Perf. 12½***

RA40 PT14 5c on 10c dp blue 1.10 .25

Map of Ecuador — PT16

1938 ***Perf. 14x13½***

RA41 PT16 5c carmine rose .70 .25

Social and Rural Workers' Insurance Fund.

No. C42 Surcharged in Red

1938 *Perf. 12½*

RA42 A136 20c on 70c black 1.10 .25

No. 307 Surcharged in Red

1938

RA43 A116 5c on 6c yel & red .40 .25

This stamp was obligatory on all mail from Nov. 23rd to 30th, 1938. The tax was for the Intl. Union for the Control of Cancer.

Tobacco Stamp Surcharged in Black

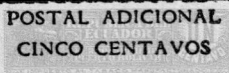

POSTAL ADICIONAL
CINCO CENTAVOS

1939 *Rouletted*

RA44 PT7 5c on 1c rose .70 .25
- *a.* Double surcharge
- *b.* Triple surcharge

Tobacco Stamp Surcharged in Blue

CASAS DE CORREOS
Y TELEGRAFOS
CINCO CENTAVOS

1940

RA45 PT7 5c on 1c rose red 1.00 .25
- *a.* Double surcharge 3.50 3.50

No. 370 Surcharged in Carmine

1940 *Perf. 11½*

RA46 A144 20c on 50c blk & multi .50 .25
- *a.* Double surcharge, one inverted

Tobacco Stamp Surcharged in Black

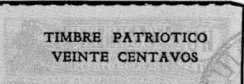

TIMBRE PATRIOTICO
VEINTE CENTAVOS

1940 *Rouletted*

RA47 PT7 20c on 1c rose red 6.00 .50

Farmer Plowing — PT17

1940 *Perf. 13x13½*

RA48 PT17 5c carmine rose .70 .25

Communication Symbols — PT18

1940-43 *Perf. 12*

RA49 PT18 5c copper brown .70 .25
RA49A PT18 5c green ('43) .70 .25

For overprint and surcharges see #534, E6, I1 in Scott Standard catalogue, Vol. 2.

EGYPT

'ē-jəpt

LOCATION — Northern Africa, bordering on the Mediterranean and the Red Sea
GOVT. — Monarchy
AREA — 386,900 sq. mi.
POP. — 46,000,000 (est. 1984)
CAPITAL — Cairo

Modern Egypt was a part of Turkey until 1914 when a British protectorate was declared over the country and the Khedive was deposed in favor of Hussein Kamil under the title of sultan. In 1922 the protectorate ended and the reigning sultan was declared king of the new monarchy.

40 Paras = 1 Piaster
1000 Milliemes = 100 Piasters = 1 Pound (1888)

Catalogue values for unused stamps in this country are for Never Hinged items, beginning with Scott B1 in the semi-postal section.

Watermarks

Wmk. 118 — Pyramid and Star

Wmk. 119 — Crescent and Star

Wmk. 120 — Triple Crescent and Star

Wmk. 195 — Multiple Crown and Arabic F

"F" in watermark stands for Fuad.

GREAT BRITAIN POST OFFICES IN EGYPT

PRE-STAMP POSTAL MARKINGS

Crowned Circle handstamps types I, II and VII are pictured in the Crowned Circle Handstamps and Great Britain Used Abroad section.

Alexandria

1843, May 13

A1 II "Alexandria" crowned circle handstamp in red, on cover *3,500.*

Cairo

1859, Mar. 23

A2 VII "Cairo" crowned circle handstamp in red, on cover *5,000.*
A3 VII "Cairo" crowned circle handstamp in black, on cover *5,000.*

Suez

1847, July 16

A4 I "Suez" crowned circle handstamp in red, on cover *6,000.*
A5 I "Suez" crowned circle handstamp in black, on cover *6,000.*

STAMPS OF GREAT BRITAIN USED IN EGYPT ALEXANDRIA / CAIRO

Stamps of Great Britain Cancelled with barred oval "BO1" obliterator

1859-78

A6 ½p rose (#58, P5, 6, 8, 10, 13-15, 19-20), *from* 23.00
A7 1p rose red (#20) *8.00*
- *a.* 1p red brown (#20b) —

A8 1p rose red (#33, see footnote), *from* 11.50
A9 2p blue (#29, P7-9), *from* 12.50
A10 2p blue (#30, P13-15), *from* 12.50
A11 2½p claret (#66, P1-3) 40.00
- *a.* Bluish paper (#66a, P1) 70.00
- As "a," P2 *1,500.*
- *b.* Lettered "LH-FL" (#66b) *1,800.*

A12 2½p claret (#67, P3-9), *from* 29.00
A13 3p rose (#37) 140.00
A14 3p rose (#44) 70.00
A15 3p rose (#49, P4-9), *from* 30.00
A16 3p rose (#61, P11-12, 14-16, 18, 19), *from* 30.00
A17 4p rose (#26) 47.50
A18 4p vermilion (#34) 47.50
- *a.* Hairlines (#34b) 47.50

A19 4p vermilion (#43, P7-14), *from* 32.50
A20 4p vermilion (#69, P15) 225.00
A21 4p pale ol grn (#70, P15) 150.00
A22 6p lilac (#27) 55.00
A23 6p lilac (#39, P3) 47.50
- *a.* Hairlines (#39b) 90.00

A24 6p lilac (#45, P5) 37.50
- Plate 6 90.00

A25 6p dull violet (#50, P6) 47.50
A26 6p violet (#51, P8-9) 45.00
- *a.* Imperf. (#51b, P8) *5,000.*

A27 6p brown (#59, P11) 32.00
- *a.* 6p pale buff (#59b, P11) 80.00
- As "a," plate 12 225.00

A28 6p gray (#60) 100.00
A29 6p gray (#62, P13-15), *from* 27.50
A30 9p straw (#40) 175.00
- *a.* 9p bister (#40a) —

A31 9p straw (#46) —
A32 9p bister (#52) —
A33 10p red brown (#53) 160.00
A34 1sh green (#28) 140.00
A35 1sh green (#42) 85.00
A36 1sh green (#48) 40.00
A37 1sh green (#54, P4-6) 17.50
- Plate 7 50.00

A38 1sh green (#64, P12-13) 32.00
- Plates 8-11 45.00

A39 2sh blue (#55) 150.00
- *a.* 2sh pale blue (#55a) 200.00

A40 5sh rose (#57, P1) 550.00
- Plate 2 700.00

When more than one plate number is shown, value is for the least expensive.

A8 plate numbers: 71-74, 76, 78-99, 101-104, 106-115, 117-125, 127, 129-131, 133, 134, 136-140, 142-150, 152, 154, 156, 157, 159, 160, 162, 163, 165, 168-172, 174, 175, 177, 179-183, 185, 188, 190, 198, 200, 203, 206, 210, 220.

SUEZ

Stamps of Great Britain Cancelled with "BO2" Type A or B obliterator or with circular date stamp

1859-78

A41 ½p rose (#58, P6, 10-14), *from* 40.00
A42 1p rose red (#20) 13.00
A43 1p rose red (#33, see footnote) 16.00
A44 2p blue (#29, P9) 20.00
- Plate 8 27.50

A45 2p blue (#30, P13) 20.00
- Plates 14-15 27.50

A46 2½p claret (#66, P1-2) 45.00
- Plate 3 55.00
- *a.* Bluish paper (#66a, P1) 80.00
- Plates 2-3 —
- *b.* Lettered "LH-FL" (#66b) *2,500.*

A47 2½p claret (#67, P3-9), *from* 32.50
- Plate 10 37.50

A48 3p rose (#37) 160.00
A49 3p rose (#44) 85.00
A50 3p rose (#49, P5-8, 10), *from* 35.00
A51 3p rose (#61, P12, 16) 35.00
A52 4p rose (#26) 70.00
A53 4p vermilion (#34) 60.00
- *a.* Hairlines (#34b) 65.00

A54 4p vermilion (#43, P7-14), *from* 35.00
A55 4p vermilion (#69, P15) —
A56 4p pale ol grn (#70, P15) 225.00
A57 6p lilac (#27) 70.00
A58 6p lilac (#39, P3) 55.00
- *a.* Hairlines (#39b) 95.00

A59 6p lilac (#45, P5) 45.00
- Plate 6 100.00

A60 6p dull violet (#50, P6) 55.00
A61 6p violet (#51, P8-9) 45.00
A62 6p brown (#59, P11) 40.00
- *a.* 6p pale buff (#59b, P11) 85.00
- As "a," plate 12 3,250.

A63 6p gray (#60) 110.00
A64 6p gray (#62, P15-16) 35.00
- Plates 13-14 35.00

A65 8p orange (#73) —
A66 9p straw (#40) 300.00
- *a.* 9p bister (#40a) —

A67 9p bister (#52) —
A68 10p red brown (#53) 275.00
A69 1sh green (#28) 175.00
A70 1sh green (#42) 97.50
A71 1sh green (#48) 60.00
A72 1sh green (#54, P4-6) 27.50
- Plate 7 45.00

A73 1sh green (#64, P12) 40.00
- Plates 8-11 42.50

A74 2sh blue (#55) 200.00
- *a.* 2sh pale blue (#55a) 225.00

A75 5sh rose (#57, P1) 550.00
- Plate 2 700.00

When more than one plate number is shown, value is for the least expensive.

A8 plate numbers: 73-74, 78-81, 83-84, 86-87, 90-91, 93-94, 96-97, 100-101, 106-108, 110, 113, 118-125, 129-131, 134, 136-138, 140, 142-145, 147-154, 156, 158-168, 170, 174, 176-182, 184-187, 189-190, 198, 205.

Values for unused stamps are for examples with original gum as defined in the catalogue introduction. Very fine examples of Nos. 1-15 will have perforations that are clear of the framelines but with the design noticeably off center. Well centered stamps are extremely scarce and will command substantial premiums.

Turkish Numerals

Turkish Suzerainty

A1

A2

A3

A4

A5

A6

A7

Surcharged in Black

Wmk. 118

1866, Jan. 1 Litho. *Perf. 12½*

No.	Type	Description	Unused	Used
1	A1	5pa greenish gray	62.50	37.50
		Never hinged	125.00	
a.		Imperf., pair	250.00	
b.		Pair, imperf. between	400.00	
c.		Perf. 12½x13	82.50	62.50
d.		Perf. 13	325.00	365.00
e.		5pa gray	57.50	37.50
2	A2	10pa brown	75.00	37.50
		Never hinged	150.00	
a.		Imperf., pair	210.00	
b.		Pair, imperf. between	525.00	
c.		Perf. 13	290.00	325.00
d.		Perf. 12½x15	325.00	350.00
e.		Perf. 12½x13	100.00	62.50
3	A3	20pa blue	105.00	40.00
		Never hinged	210.00	
a.		Imperf., pair	300.00	
b.		Pair, imperf. between	500.00	
c.		Perf. 12½x13	140.00	95.00
d.		Perf. 13	575.00	375.00
e.		20pa greenish blue	105.00	40.00
4	A4	2pi yellow	125.00	52.50
		Never hinged	250.00	
a.		Imperf.	150.00	125.00
b.		Imperf. vert. or horiz., pair	500.00	425.00
c.		Perf. 12½x15	210.00	
d.		Diagonal half used as 1pi on cover		3,000.
e.		Perf. 12½x13, 13x12½	200.00	75.00
f.		Pair, imperf. between	625.00	525.00
5	A5	5pi rose	325.00	250.00
		Never hinged	650.00	
a.		Imperf.	425.00	375.00
b.		Imperf. vert. or horiz., pair	1,250.	
d.		Inscription of 10pi, imperf.	1,100.	950.00
e.		Perf. 12½x13, 13x12½	350.00	275.00
f.		As "d," perf. 12½x15	1,050.	1,000.
g.		Perf. 13	825.00	
6	A6	10pi slate bl	375.00	325.00
		Never hinged	750.00	
a.		Imperf.	550.00	450.00
b.		Pair, imperf. between	2,500.	
c.		Perf. 12½x13, 13x12½	550.00	550.00
d.		Perf. 13	2,000.	

Unwmk.

Typo.

No.	Type	Description	Unused	Used
7	A7	1pi rose lilac	80.00	5.50
		Never hinged	160.00	
a.		Imperf.	125.00	
b.		Horiz. pair, imperf. vert.	500.00	
c.		Perf. 12½x13, 13x12½	110.00	25.00
d.		Perf. 13	450.00	300.00
e.		Perf. 12½x15	350.00	
		Nos. 1-7 (7)	1,148.	748.00

Single imperforates of types A1-A10 are sometimes simulated by trimming wide-margined examples of perforated stamps.

No. 4d must be dated between July 16 and July 31, 1867.

Proofs of Nos. 1-7 are on smooth white paper, unwatermarked and imperforate. Proofs of No. 7 are on thinner paper than No. 7a.

Sphinx and Pyramid — A8

Perf. 15x12½

1867 Litho. Wmk. 119

No.	Type	Description	Unused	Used
8	A8	5pa orange	42.50	11.00
		Never hinged	65.00	
a.		Imperf.	250.00	—
b.		Horiz. pair, imperf between	190.00	
c.		Vert. pair, imperf between	—	
9	A8	10pa lilac ('69)	70.00	11.00
		Never hinged	100.00	
a.		10pa violet	95.00	14.00
b.		Half used as 5pa on newspaper piece		850.00
11	A8	20pa yellow green ('69)	135.00	14.00
		Never hinged	210.00	
a.		20pa blue green	135.00	17.00
13	A8	1pi rose red	27.50	1.10
		Never hinged	42.50	
a.		Imperf, pair	150.00	
b.		Pair, imperf. between	300.00	
d.		Rouletted	70.00	
e.		1pi lake red	175.00	32.50
14	A8	2pi blue	150.00	18.00
		Never hinged	225.00	
a.		Imperf.	325.00	
b.		Horiz. pair, imperf. vert.	500.00	
d.		Perf. 12½	275.00	
15	A8	5pi brown	375.00	200.00
		Never hinged	575.00	
		Nos. 8-15 (6)	800.00	255.10

There are 4 types of each value, so placed that any block of 4 contains all types.

A9

Clear Impressions
Thick Opaque Paper
Typographed by the Government at Boulac

Perf. 12½x13½ Clean-cut

1872 Wmk. 119

No.	Type	Description	Unused	Used
19	A9	5pa brown	10.00	5.50
		Never hinged	15.00	
20	A9	10pa lilac	9.00	3.75
		Never hinged	13.50	
21	A9	20pa blue	67.50	4.75
		Never hinged	105.00	
22	A9	1pi rose red	72.50	2.25
		Never hinged	110.00	
h.		Half used as 20pa on cover		750.00
23	A9	2pi dull yellow	100.00	15.00
		Never hinged	150.00	
j.		Half used as 1p on cover		1,200.
24	A9	2½pi dull violet	95.00	25.00
		Never hinged	145.00	
25	A9	5pi green	325.00	42.50
		Never hinged	500.00	
i.		Tête bêche pair	8,000.	
		Nos. 19-25 (7)	679.00	98.75

Perf. 13½ Clean-cut

No.	Type	Description	Unused	Used
19a	A9	5pa brown	27.50	10.00
20a	A9	10pa dull lilac	7.00	3.50
21a	A9	20pa blue	95.00	22.00
22a	A9	1pi rose red	95.00	4.00
23a	A9	2pi dull yellow	20.00	4.50
24a	A9	2½pi dull violet	800.00	225.00
25a	A9	5pi green	325.00	62.50

Litho.

No.	Type	Description	Unused	Used
21m	A9	20pa blue, perf. 12½x13½	160.00	80.00
21n	A9	20pa blue, perf. 13½	250.00	65.00
21p	A9	20pa blue, imperf.	—	
21q	A9	20pa blue, pair, imperf. between	—	2,000.
22m	A9	1pi rose red, perf. 12½x13½	550.00	20.00
22n	A9	1pi rose red, perf. 13½	875.00	50.00

A10

Blurred Impressions
Thinner Paper

Perf. 12½ Rough

1874-75 Typo. Wmk. 119

No.	Type	Description	Unused	Used
26	A10	5pa brown ('75)	22.50	3.75
		Never hinged	35.00	
e.		Imperf.	200.00	200.00
f.		Vert. pair, imperf. horiz.	1,000.	—
g.		Tête bêche pair	45.00	45.00
20b	A9	10pa gray lilac	16.00	3.75
g.		Tête bêche pair	225.00	225.00
21b	A9	20pa gray blue	105.00	4.00
k.		Half used as 10pa on cover		—
22b	A9	1pi vermilion	12.00	1.75
f.		Imperf.	—	150.00
g.		Tête bêche pair	150.00	125.00
23b	A9	2pi yellow	90.00	5.75
i.		Tête bêche pair	600.00	600.00
24b	A9	2½pi deep violet	9.25	6.25
e.		Imperf.	—	
f.		Tête bêche pair	600.00	600.00
25b	A9	5pi yellow green	65.00	22.50
e.		Imperf.	400.00	—

No. 26f normally occurs tête-bêche.

Perf. 13½x12½ Rough

No.	Type	Description	Unused	Used
26c	A10	5pa brown	24.00	4.50
i.		Tête bêche pair	62.50	62.50
20c	A9	10pa gray lilac	37.50	3.50
i.		Tête bêche pair	225.00	225.00
21c	A9	20pa gray blue	11.00	3.75
h.		Pair, imperf. between	350.00	
22c	A9	1pi vermilion	90.00	3.25
i.		Tête bêche pair	500.00	500.00
23c	A9	2pi yellow	10.00	6.25
g.		Tête bêche pair	500.00	500.00
k.		Half used as 1pi on cover		4,000.

Perf. 12½x13½ Rough

No.	Type	Description	Unused	Used
23d	A9	2pi yellow ('75)	80.00	17.00
h.		Tête bêche pair	1,250.	
24d	A9	2½pi dp violet ('75)	80.00	20.00
i.		Tête bêche pair	1,150.	800.00
25d	A9	5pi yel green ('75)	375.00	300.00

Nos. 24b, 24d Surcharged in Black

1879, Jan. 1 *Perf. 12½ Rough*

No.	Type	Description	Unused	Used
27	A9	5pa on 2½pi dull vio	10.00	12.00
		Never hinged	15.00	
a.		Imperf.	450.00	450.00
b.		Tête bêche pair	7,500.	
c.		Inverted surcharge	125.00	75.00
d.		Perf. 12½x13½ rough	12.00	12.00
e.		As "d," tête bêche pair	7,500.	
f.		As "d," inverted surcharge	150.00	150.00
28	A9	10pa on 2½pi dull vio	12.50	12.50
		Never hinged	20.00	
a.		Imperf.	400.00	400.00
b.		Tête bêche pair	2,500.	
c.		Inverted surcharge	125.00	82.50
d.		Perf. 12½x13½ rough	17.00	17.00
e.		As "d," tête bêche pair	3,000.	
f.		As "d," inverted surcharge	150.00	125.00

A11

A12

A13

A14

A15

A16

1879-1902 Typo. *Perf. 14x13½*

Ordinary Paper

No.	Type	Description	Unused	Used
29	A11	5pa brown	4.25	1.25
30	A12	10pa violet	57.50	5.00
31	A12	10pa lilac rose ('81)	70.00	10.00
32	A12	10pa gray ('82)	8.00	1.75
33	A12	10pa green ('84)	2.50	2.00
34	A13	20pa ultra	67.50	2.25
35	A13	20pa rose ('84)	22.00	1.25
36	A14	1pi rose	42.50	.30
37	A14	1pi ultra ('84)	5.75	.30
38	A15	2pi orange yel	42.50	1.50
39	A15	2pi orange brn	27.50	.50
40	A16	5pi green	77.50	11.50
41	A16	5pi gray ('84)	25.00	.50
		Nos. 29-41 (13)	452.50	38.10

Chalky Paper

No.	Type	Description	Unused	Used
37a	A14	1pi ultra ('02)	3.50	.25
39a	A15	2pi orange brn ('02)	13.50	.25
41a	A16	5pi gray ('02)	18.00	.25

Nos. 29-31, 35-41 imperf are proofs.

For overprints see Nos. 42, O6-O7.

A17

1884, Feb. 1

No.	Type	Description	Unused	Used
42	A17	20pa on 5pi green	14.00	2.25
a.		Inverted surcharge	70.00	62.50
b.		Double surcharge		—

A18

A19

A20

A21

A22

A23

1888-1906 Ordinary Paper

No.	Type	Description	Unused	Used
43	A18	1m brown	3.50	.25
44	A19	2m green	3.00	.25
45	A20	3m maroon ('92)	8.00	2.25
46	A20	3m orange ('93)	5.75	.25
48	A22	5m carmine rose	6.50	.25
a.		5m rose, aniline ink	6.00	.25
49	A23	10p purple ('89)	35.00	1.00
a.		10m purple, aniline ink	20.00	1.00
		Nos. 43-49 (6)	61.75	4.25

Chalky Paper

No.	Type	Description	Unused	Used
43a	A18	1m pale brown ('02)	4.00	.25
44a	A19	2m green ('02)	1.25	.25
46a	A20	3m yel org ('02)	3.00	.25
47	A21	4m brown red ('06)	4.75	.25
a.		Half used as 2m on cover		—
48b	A22	5m rose ('02)	3.00	.25
49b	A23	10p mauve ('02)	22.50	.55

Nos. 43-44, 47-48 imperf are proofs.

For overprints see Nos. O2-O5, O8-O10, O14-O15.

Boats on Nile A24

Cleopatra A25

Ras-el-Tin Palace A26

Giza Pyramids A27

Sphinx A28

Colossi of Thebes A29

Pylon of Karnak and Temple of Khonsu — A30

Citadel at Cairo — A31

Rock Temple of Abu Simbel — A32

Aswan Dam — A33

Perf. 13½x14

1914, Jan. 8 Wmk. 119

Chalk-surfaced Paper

50 A24 1m olive brown 1.25 *.80*
51 A25 2m dp green 3.75 .25
52 A26 3m orange 3.50 .50
53 A27 4m red 4.50 .75
54 A28 5m lake 4.25 .25
a. Booklet pane of 6 250.00
55 A29 10m dk blue 7.50 .40

Perf. 14

56 A30 20m olive grn 8.00 .70
57 A31 50m red violet 24.00 1.10
58 A32 100m black 25.00 1.40
59 A33 200m plum 42.50 4.00
Nos. 50-59 (10) 124.25 10.15

All values of this issue exist imperforate on both watermarked and unwatermarked paper but are not known to have been issued in that condition.

See Nos. 61-69, 72-74. For overprints and surcharge see Nos. 60, 78-91, O11-O13, O16-O27, O30.

British Protectorate

No. 52 Surcharged

1915, Oct. 15

60 A26 2m on 3m orange 1.25 2.25
a. Inverted surcharge 250.00 250.00

Scenic Types of 1914 and

Statue of Ramses II
A34 A35

1921-22 Wmk. 120 *Perf. 13½x14*

Chalk-surfaced Paper

61 A24 1m olive brown 1.50 *3.00*
62 A25 2m dp green 9.00 4.75
63 A25 2m red ('22) 6.00 2.50
64 A26 3m orange 9.00 6.00
65 A27 4m green ('22) 8.00 *6.50*
66 A28 5m lake 7.00 1.75
67 A28 5m pink 14.00 .25
68 A29 10m dp blue 12.00 .70
69 A29 10m lake ('22) 3.50 .70
70 A34 15m indigo ('22) 10.00 .30
71 A35 15m indigo ('22) 40.00 5.00

Perf. 14

72 A30 20m olive green 12.50 .40
73 A31 50m maroon 10.00 1.25
74 A32 100m black 95.00 7.50
Nos. 61-74 (14) 237.50 40.60

For overprints see Nos. O28-O29.

Independent Kingdom

Stamps of 1921-22 Overprinted

1922, Oct. 10

78 A24 1m olive brown 1.50 1.10
a. Inverted overprint 475.00 450.00
b. Double overprint 225.00 —
79 A25 2m red 1.10 .65
a. Double overprint 225.00 —
80 A26 3m orange 2.25 1.10
81 A27 4m green 1.50 1.00
b. Inverted overprint 225.00 —
82 A28 5m pink 2.75 .25
83 A29 10m lake 2.75 .25
84 A34 15m indigo 5.75 1.10
85 A35 15m indigo 4.50 1.10

Perf. 14

86 A30 20m olive green 6.00 1.10
a. Inverted overprint 200.00 —
b. Double overprint 300.00 —
87 A31 50m maroon 9.00 1.10
a. Inverted overprint 400.00 500.00
88 A32 100m black 22.50 1.25
a. Inverted overprint 500.00 160.00
b. Double overprint 400.00 150.00
Nos. 78-88 (11) 59.60 10.00

Same Overprint on Nos. 58-59

Wmk. Crescent and Star (119)

90 A32 100m black 90.00 50.00
91 A33 200m plum 30.00 1.60

Proclamation of the Egyptian monarchy.

The overprint signifies "The Egyptian Kingdom, March 15, 1922." It exists in four types, one lithographed and three typographed on Nos. 78-87, but lithographed only on Nos. 88-91.

A36

King Fuad — A37

Wmk. 120

1923-24 Photo. *Perf. 13½*

Size 18x22½mm

92 A36 1m orange .35 .25
93 A36 2m black 1.10 .25
94 A36 3m brown 1.00 .65
a. Imperf., pair 225.00
95 A36 4m yellow grn .90 .50
96 A36 5m orange brn .45 .25
a. Imperf., pair 50.00
97 A36 10m rose 2.00 .25
98 A36 15m ultra 3.25 .25

Perf. 14

Size: 22x28mm

99 A36 20m dk green 6.25 .25
100 A36 50m myrtle grn 10.00 .25
101 A36 100m red violet 25.00 .55
102 A36 200m violet ('24) 45.00 2.00
a. Imperf., pair 325.00
103 A37 £1 ultra & dk vio ('24) 175.00 27.50
a. Imperf., pair 1,750.
Nos. 92-103 (12) 270.30 32.95

For overprints & surcharge see Nos. 167, O31-O38.

Thoth Carving Name of King Fuad — A38

1925, Apr. Litho. *Perf. 11*

105 A38 5m brown 11.00 6.00
Never hinged 13.50
106 A38 10m rose 22.50 12.50
Never hinged 27.00
107 A38 15m ultra 22.50 14.00
Never hinged 30.00
Nos. 105-107 (3) 56.00 32.50

International Geographical Congress, Cairo.

Nos. 106-107 exist with both white and yellowish gum.

Oxen Plowing A39

1926 Wmk. 195 *Perf. 13x13½*

108 A39 5m lt brown 3.00 2.00
Never hinged 4.50
109 A39 10m brt rose 2.75 2.00
Never hinged 4.00
110 A39 15m dp blue 3.00 2.00
Never hinged 4.50
111 A39 50m Prus green 14.00 5.00
Never hinged 20.00
112 A39 100m brown vio 22.50 8.00
Never hinged 30.00
113 A39 200m brt violet 32.50 17.50
Never hinged 45.00
Nos. 108-113 (6) 77.75 36.50

12th Agricultural and Industrial Exhibition at Gezira.

For surcharges see Nos. 115-117.

King Fuad — A40

Perf. 14x14½

1926, Apr. 2 Photo. Wmk. 120

114 A40 50p brn vio & red vio 140.00 22.50
Never hinged 210.00

58th birthday of King Fuad.

For overprint and surcharge see Nos. 124, 166.

Nos. 111-113 Surcharged

Perf. 13x13½

1926, Aug. 24 Wmk. 195

115 A39 5m on 50m Prus green 2.50 2.50
Never hinged 3.50
116 A39 10m on 100m brown vio 2.50 2.50
Never hinged 3.50
117 A39 15m on 200m brt violet 2.50 2.50
Never hinged 8.50
a. Double surcharge 300.00
Nos. 115-117 (3) 7.50 7.50

Ship of Hatshepsut — A41

1926, Dec. 9 Litho. *Perf. 13x13½*

118 A41 5m brown & blk 3.00 1.40
Never hinged 3.25
119 A41 10m dp red & blk 3.50 1.50
Never hinged 4.50
120 A41 15m dp blue & blk 4.00 1.50
Never hinged 4.75
Nos. 118-120 (3) 10.50 4.40

International Navigation Congress, Cairo.

For overprints see Nos. 121-123.

Nos. 118-120, 114 Overprinted — a

No. 114 Overprinted — b

1926, Dec. 21

121 A41 (a) 5m 300.00 250.00
122 A41 (a) 10m 300.00 250.00
123 A41 (a) 15m 300.00 250.00

Perf. 14x14½

Wmk. 120

124 A40 (b) 50p 1,600. *875.00*

Inauguration of Port Fuad opposite Port Said.

Nos. 121-123 have a block over "Le Caire" at lower left.

Forgeries of Nos. 121-124 exist.

Branch of Cotton A42

Perf. 13x13½

1927, Jan. 25 Wmk. 195

125 A42 5m dk brown & sl grn 1.75 .80
Never hinged 2.75
126 A42 10m dp red & slate grn 2.75 1.50
Never hinged 3.50
127 A42 15m dp blue & slate grn 3.50 1.50
Never hinged 5.25
Nos. 125-127 (3) 8.00 3.80

International Cotton Congress, Cairo.

King Fuad
A43 A44

A45

A46

Type I Type II

Early printings of the seven values indicated were printed from plates with screens of vertical dots in the vignettes (type I). All values were printed later from plates with screens of diagonal dots (type II).

Perf. 13x13½
1927-37 Wmk. 195 Photo.
Type II

128 A43 1m orange .35 .25
a. Type I 3.25 .60
129 A43 2m black .35 .25
a. Type I 11.00 6.00
130 A43 3m olive brn .35 .55
a. Type I 2.50 1.00
131 A43 3m dp green ('30) .65 .25
132 A43 4m yellow grn 1.25 1.10
a. Type I 65.00 12.50
133 A43 4m brown ('30) 1.10 .55
134 A43 4m dp green ('34) .85 .40
135 A43 5m dk red brn ('29) .95 .40
a. Type I 3.50 1.00
136 A43 10m dk red ('29) 1.40 .25
a. 10m orange red, type I 2.50 .45
137 A43 10m purple ('34) 3.75 .25
138 A43 13m car rose ('32) 1.50 .40
139 A43 15m ultra 2.50 .25
a. Type I 12.00 .65
140 A43 15m dk violet ('34) 5.25 .25
141 A43 20m ultra ('34) 9.25 .30

Perf. 13½x14

142 A44 20m olive grn 3.25 .40
143 A44 20m ultra ('32) 7.50 .25
144 A44 40m olive brn ('32) 4.25 .25
145 A44 50m Prus green 3.50 .25
a. 50m greenish blue 6.00 .35
146 A44 100m brown vio 10.00 .35
a. 100m claret 14.00 .50
147 A44 200m deep violet 9.00 1.25

Printings of Nos. 142, 145 and 146, made in 1929 and later, were from new plates with stronger impressions and darker colors.

Lithographed; Center Photogravure
Perf. 13x13½

148 A45 500m choc & Prus bl, entirely photo ('32) 100.00 25.00
a. Frame litho, vignette photo 125.00 11.50
149 A46 £1 dk grn & org brn, entirely photo ('37) 125.00 8.25
a. Frame litho, vignette photo 140.00 7.00
Nos. 128-149 (22) 292.00 41.45

Statue of Amenhotep, Son of Hapu — A47

1927, Dec. 29 Photo. Perf. 13½x13

150 A47 5m orange brown 1.50 1.00
151 A47 10m copper red 2.00 1.00
152 A47 15m deep blue 3.25 1.00
Nos. 150-152 (3) 6.75 3.00

Statistical Congress, Cairo.

Imhotep — A48

Mohammed Ali Pasha — A49

1928, Dec. 15

153 A48 5m orange brown 1.10 .65
154 A49 10m copper red 1.25 .65

Intl. Congress of Medicine at Cairo and the cent. of the Faculty of Medicine at Cairo.

Prince Farouk — A50

1929, Feb. 11 Litho.

155 A50 5m choc & gray 2.00 1.40
156 A50 10m dull red & gray 3.00 1.50
157 A50 15m ultra & gray 3.00 1.50
158 A50 20m Prus blue & gray 3.50 1.50
Nos. 155-158 (4) 11.50 5.90

Ninth birthday of Prince Farouk.

Nos. 155-158 with black or brown centers are trial color proofs. They were sent to the UPU, but were never placed on sale to the public, although some are known used.

Tomb Fresco at El-Bersheh — A51

1931, Feb. 15 Perf. 13x13½

163 A51 5m brown 1.50 1.00
164 A51 10m copper red 2.50 1.75
165 A51 15m dark blue 3.50 2.00
Nos. 163-165 (3) 7.50 4.75

14th Agricultural & Industrial Exhib., Cairo.

Nos. 114 and 103 Surcharged in Black

1932 Wmk. 120 Perf. 14x14½

166 A40 50m on 50p 20.00 3.00

Perf. 14

167 A37 100m on £1 250.00 190.00

Locomotive of 1852 — A52

Perf. 13x13½
1933, Jan. 19 Litho. Wmk. 195

168 A52 5m shown 14.00 8.00
169 A52 13m 1859 21.00 12.00
170 A52 15m 1862 21.00 12.00
171 A52 20m 1932 21.00 12.00
Nos. 168-171 (4) 77.00 44.00

International Railroad Congress, Heliopolis.

Commercial Passenger Airplane — A56

Dornier Do-X A57

Graf Zeppelin A58

1933, Dec. 20 Photo.

172 A56 5m brown 6.50 4.00
173 A56 10m brt violet 15.00 12.00
174 A57 13m brown car 18.00 15.00
175 A57 15m violet 18.00 13.00
176 A58 20m blue 24.00 20.00
Nos. 172-176 (5) 81.50 64.00

International Aviation Congress, Cairo.

A59

Khedive Ismail Pasha — A60

1934, Feb. 1 Perf. 13½

177 A59 1m dp orange .60 *1.10*
178 A59 2m black .60 *1.10*
179 A59 3m brown .75 *1.25*
180 A59 4m blue green 1.25 .40
181 A59 5m red brown 1.40 .25
182 A59 10m violet 2.50 .35
183 A59 13m copper red 4.00 2.25
184 A59 15m dull violet 4.50 1.75
185 A59 20m ultra 3.00 .40
186 A59 50m Prus blue 9.50 .65
187 A59 100m olive grn 9.50 1.25
188 A59 200m dp violet 75.00 7.25

Perf. 13½x13

189 A60 50p brown 225.00 95.00
190 A60 £1 Prus blue 400.00 150.00
Nos. 177-190 (14) 737.60 263.00

10th Congress of UPU, Cairo.

King Fuad — A61

1936-37 Perf. 13½

191 A61 1m dull orange .55 *.90*
Never hinged .85
192 A61 2m black 1.75 .25
Never hinged 2.60
193 A61 4m dk green 2.00 .25
Never hinged 3.00
194 A61 5m chestnut 1.40 .55
Never hinged 2.10
195 A61 10m purple ('37) 2.50 .35
Never hinged 3.75
196 A61 15m brown violet 2.75 .50
Never hinged 4.00
197 A61 20m sapphire 3.25 .35
Never hinged 5.00
Nos. 191-197 (7) 14.20 3.15

Entrance to Agricultural Building — A62

Agricultural Building — A63

Design: 15m, 20m, Industrial Building.

1936, Feb. 15 Perf. 13½x13

198 A62 5m brown 1.75 1.25
Never hinged 2.75

Perf. 13x13½

199 A63 10m violet 2.00 1.50
Never hinged 3.00
200 A63 13m copper red 3.25 2.50
Never hinged 5.00
201 A63 15m dark violet 1.75 1.25
Never hinged 2.75
202 A63 20m blue 3.75 2.25
Never hinged 5.50
Nos. 198-202 (5) 12.50 8.75

15th Agricultural & Industrial Exhib., Cairo.

Signing of Treaty — A65

1936, Dec. 22 Perf. 11

203 A65 5m brown .80 .80
Never hinged 1.45
204 A65 15m dk violet 1.00 1.00
Never hinged 1.50
205 A65 20m sapphire 1.75 1.75
Never hinged 2.75
Nos. 203-205 (3) 3.55 3.55

Signing of Anglo-Egyptian Treaty, Aug. 26, 1936.

King Farouk — A66

1937-44 Wmk. 195 Perf. 13x13½

206 A66 1m brown org .30 .25
Never hinged .40
207 A66 2m vermilion .30 .25
Never hinged .40
208 A66 3m brown .30 .25
Never hinged .40
209 A66 4m green .30 .25
Never hinged .40
210 A66 5m red brown .50 .25
Never hinged .65
211 A66 6m lt yel grn ('40) .60 .25
Never hinged .75
212 A66 10m purple .30 .25
Never hinged .40
213 A66 13m rose car .60 .35
Never hinged .75
214 A66 15m dk vio brn .50 .25
Never hinged .65
215 A66 20m blue .75 .35
Never hinged .95
216 A66 20m lil gray ('44) .75 .25
Never hinged .95
Nos. 206-216 (11) 5.20 2.95

For overprints see Nos. 301, 303, 345, 348, 360E, N3, N6, N8, N22, N25, N27 in Scott Standard catalogue, Vol. 2.

Medal for Montreux Conf. — A67

1937, Oct. 15 Perf. 13½x13

217 A67 5m red brown .75 .55
Never hinged 1.50
218 A67 15m dk violet 1.25 1.10
Never hinged 2.25
219 A67 20m sapphire 1.50 1.25
Never hinged 2.25
Nos. 217-219 (3) 3.50 2.90

Intl. Treaty signed at Montreux, Switzerland, under which foreign privileges in Egypt were to end in 1949.

Eye of Ré — A68

1937, Dec. 8 Perf. 13x13½

220 A68 5m brown 1.25 .80
Never hinged 1.60
221 A68 15m dk violet 1.50 .90
Never hinged 1.90
222 A68 20m sapphire 1.75 1.00
Never hinged 1.90
Nos. 220-222 (3) 4.50 2.70

15th Ophthalmological Congress, Cairo, December, 1937.

King Farouk, Queen Farida — A69

1938, Jan. 20 *Perf. 11*

223	A69 5m red brown	6.50	5.00
	Never hinged	10.00	

Royal wedding of King Farouk and Farida Zulficar.

Inscribed: "11 Fevrier 1938"

1938, Feb. 11

224	A69 £1 green & sepia	200.00	*150.00*

King Farouk's 18th birthday.

Cotton Picker — A70

1938, Jan. 26 *Perf. 13½x13*

225	A70 5m red brown	.75	.75
226	A70 15m dk violet	2.25	1.50
227	A70 20m sapphire	2.00	1.75
	Nos. 225-227 (3)	5.00	4.00

18th International Cotton Congress at Cairo.

Pyramids of Giza and Colossus of Thebes A71

1938, Feb. 1 *Perf. 13x13½*

228	A71 5m red brown	1.40	1.00
229	A71 15m dk violet	2.00	1.25
230	A71 20m sapphire	2.25	1.25
	Nos. 228-230 (3)	5.65	3.50

Intl. Telecommunication Conf., Cairo.

Branch of Hydnocarpus — A72

1938, Mar. 21 *Perf. 13x13½*

231	A72 5m red brown	1.50	1.25
232	A72 15m dk violet	2.25	1.25
233	A72 20m sapphire	2.50	1.25
	Nos. 231-233 (3)	6.25	3.75

International Leprosy Congress, Cairo.

King Farouk and Pyramids — A73

King Farouk
A74 A75

Backgrounds: 40m, Hussan Mosque. 50m, Cairo Citadel. 100m, Aswan Dam. 200m, Cairo University.

1939-46 Photo. *Perf. 14x13½*

234	A73	30m gray	.75	.25
a.		30m slate gray	.75	.25
234B	A73	30m ol grn ('46)	.80	.25
235	A73	40m dk brown	.85	.25
236	A73	50m Prus green	1.00	.25
237	A73	100m brown vio	1.40	.50
238	A73	200m dk violet	5.00	.50

Perf. 13½x13

239	A74	50p green & sep	11.00	4.00
240	A75	£1 dp bl & dk brn	26.00	7.00
		Nos. 234-240 (8)	46.80	13.00

For £1 with A77 portrait, see No. 269D. See Nos. 267-269D.

For overprints see Nos. 310-314, 316, 355-358, 360, 363-364, N13-N19, N32-N38. These issues in Scott Standard catalogue, Vol. 2.

SEMI-POSTAL STAMPS

Catalogue values for unused stamps in this section are for Never Hinged items.

Princess Ferial — SP1

Perf. 13½x14

1940, May 17 Photo. Wmk. 195

B1	SP1 5m + 5m copper brown	4.50	1.25

AIR POST STAMPS

Mail Plane in Flight AP1

Perf. 13x13½

1926, Mar. 10 Wmk. 195 Photo.

C1	AP1 27m deep violet	30.00	30.00

1929, July 17

C2	AP1 27m orange brown	9.00	2.25

Zeppelin Issue

No. C2 Surcharged in Blue or Violet

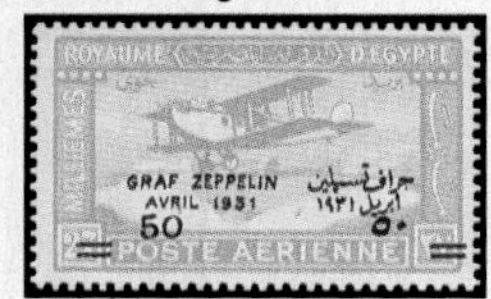

1931, Apr. 6

C3	AP1	50m on 27m (Bl)	85.00	75.00
a.		"1951" instead of "1931"	110.00	100.00
C4	AP1	100m on 27m (V)	85.00	*80.00*

Airplane over Giza Pyramids AP2

1933-38 Litho. *Perf. 13x13½*

C5	AP2	1m orange & blk	.30	.50
C6	AP2	2m gray & blk	.80	1.50
C7	AP2	2m org red & blk ('38)	2.75	2.00
C8	AP2	3m ol brn & blk	.60	.35
C9	AP2	4m green & blk	.90	.90
C10	AP2	5m dp brown & blk	.75	.25
C11	AP2	6m dk green & blk	1.50	1.25
C12	AP2	7m dk blue & blk	1.25	1.00
C13	AP2	8m violet & blk	.80	.25
C14	AP2	9m dp red & blk	2.00	1.50
C15	AP2	10m violet & brn	.75	.70
C16	AP2	20m dk green & brn	.60	.25
C17	AP2	30m dull blue & brn	.75	.25
C18	AP2	40m dp red & brn	15.00	.60
C19	AP2	50m orange & brn	13.00	.25
C20	AP2	60m gray & brn	6.00	1.10
C21	AP2	70m dk blue & bl grn	3.50	1.00
C22	AP2	80m ol brn & bl grn	3.50	1.00
C23	AP2	90m org & bl grn	4.00	1.00
C24	AP2	100m vio & bl grn	9.00	.80
C25	AP2	200m dp red & bl grn	12.00	1.75
		Nos. C5-C25 (21)	79.75	18.20

See Nos. C34-C37. For overprint see No. C38. These issues in Scott Standard catalogue, Vol. 2.

AIR POST STAMPSSPECIAL DELIVERY STAMPS

Motorcycle Postman — SD1

Perf. 13x13½

1926, Nov. 28 Photo. Wmk. 195

E1	SD1 20m dark green	35.00	9.50

1929, Sept.

E2	SD1 20m brown red & black	6.75	1.75

POSTAGE DUE STAMPS

D1

Wmk. Crescent and Star (119)

1884, Jan. 1 Litho. *Perf. 10½*

J1	D1	10pa red	57.50	9.50
a.		Horiz. pair, imperf. vert.	150.00	
J2	D1	20pa red	175.00	50.00
J3	D1	1pi red	145.00	52.50
J4	D1	2pi red	240.00	12.50
J5	D1	5pi red	20.00	*60.00*
		Nos. J1-J5 (5)	637.50	184.50

1886, Aug. 1 Unwmk.

J6	D1	10pa red	75.00	17.50
a.		Horiz. pair, imperf. vert.	135.00	
J7	D1	20pa red	260.00	50.00
J8	D1	1pi red	37.50	10.00
a.		Pair, imperf. between	200.00	135.00
J9	D1	2pi red	37.50	5.00
a.		Pair, imperf. between	175.00	
		Nos. J6-J9 (4)	410.00	82.50

D2

1888, Jan. 1 *Perf. 11½*

J10	D2	2m green	22.50	*27.50*
a.		Horiz. pair, imperf. between	225.00	200.00
J11	D2	5m rose red	45.00	27.50
J12	D2	1pi blue	145.00	40.00
a.		Pair, imperf. between	300.00	
J13	D2	2pi yellow	155.00	20.00
J14	D2	5pi gray	240.00	210.00
a.		Period after "PIASTRES"	325.00	250.00
		Nos. J10-J14 (5)	607.50	325.00

Excellent counterfeits of #J1-J14 are plentiful.

There are 4 types of each of Nos. J1-J14, so placed that any block of 4 contains all types.

D3

Perf. 14x13½

1889 Wmk. 119 Typo.

J15	D3	2m green	10.00	.70
a.		Half used as 1m on cover		350.00
J16	D3	4m maroon	3.75	.70
J17	D3	1pi ultra	7.75	.70
J18	D3	2pi orange	7.50	1.00
a.		Half used as 1p on cover		—
		Nos. J15-J18 (4)	29.00	3.10

Nos. J15-J18 exist on both ordinary and chalky paper. Imperf. examples of Nos. J15-J17 are proofs.

Black Surcharge

Type I — D4

Type II

Type I: the spacing between the last two Arabic characters at the right is 2mm. Type II: spacing is 3mm, and there is an added sign on top of the second character from the right.

1898

J19	D4	3m on 2pi orange (I)	2.10	*6.25*
a.		Inverted surcharge	65.00	*82.50*
b.		Pair, one without surcharge		—
c.		Arabic "3" over "2"	125.00	
d.		3m on 2pi orange (II)	5.50	18.00
e.		As "d," inverted surcharge	57.50	*70.00*
f.		As "d," double surcharge	225.00	—

D5

D6

1921 Wmk. 120 *Perf. 14x13½*

J20	D5	2m green	3.75	*6.75*
J21	D5	4m vermilion	7.50	*19.00*
J22	D6	10m deep blue	12.50	*25.00*
		Nos. J20-J22 (3)	23.75	50.75

1921-22

J23	D5	2m vermilion	1.00	*2.25*
J24	D5	4m green	6.00	2.00
J25	D6	10m lake ('22)	6.50	1.50
		Nos. J23-J25 (3)	13.50	5.75

Nos. J18, J23-J25 Overprinted

1922, Oct. 10 Wmk. 119

J26	D3	2pi orange	7.50	*10.50*
a.		Overprint right side up	30.00	*30.00*

Wmk. 120

J27	D5	2m vermilion	1.00	*3.00*
J28	D5	4m green	1.60	*3.00*
J29	D6	10m lake	2.50	1.90
		Nos. J26-J29 (4)	12.60	18.40

Overprint on Nos. J26-J29 is inverted.

Arabic Numeral — D7

Perf. 13x13½

1927-56 Litho. Wmk. 195

Size: 18x22½mm

J30	D7	2m slate	.85	.50
J31	D7	2m orange ('38)	1.00	1.10
J32	D7	4m green	.85	.55
J33	D7	4m ol brn ('32)	8.00	5.25
J34	D7	5m brown	4.25	1.10
J35	D7	6m gray grn ('41)	2.75	2.10
J36	D7	8m brn vio	1.60	.65
J37	D7	10m brick red ('29)	1.25	.35
a.		10m deep red	1.90	1.00
J38	D7	12m rose lake ('41)	1.90	*3.75*
J38A	D7	20m dk red ('56)	2.50	2.50

Perf. 13½x14

Size: 22x28mm

J39	D7	30m purple	5.25	3.75
		Nos. J30-J39 (11)	30.20	21.60

See Nos. J47-J59, Nos. J40-J46 and NJ1-NJ7 (overprints) in Scott Standard catalogue, Vol. 2.

LOCAL STAMPS

SUEZ CANAL COMPANY

Steamship — L1

1868, July 8 **Litho.** ***Imperf.***

L1 L1 1c black 275.00 *1,150.*
On cover *22,500.*
L2 L1 5c green 100.00 *575.00*
On cover *11,500.*
L3 L1 20c blue 90.00 *575.00*
On cover *11,500.*
L4 L1 40c pink 150.00 *850.00*
On cover *17,000.*

Nos. L1-L4 were issued by the Suez Canal Co. for use on letters and printed matter carried between canal ports. Items addressed to further destinations required additional French or Egyptian postage.

These issues were recognized officially by the French Consulate Offices at Port Said and Suez but not by the Egyptian Post Office, which suppressed their use at the end of August 1868.

Nos. L1-L4 exist with portions of the papermaker's watermark, "LA + F" (La Croix Freres).

Many forgeries exist of the stamps of the Suez Canal Co., including excellent counterfeits created from the genuine plate of the 40c value, stolen from the company's archives.

MILITARY STAMPS

The "British Forces" and "Army post" stamps were special issues provided at a reduced rate for the purchase and use by the British military forces in Egypt and their families for ordinary letters sent to Great Britain and Ireland by a concessionary arrangement made with the Egyptian government. From Nov. 1, 1932 to Feb. 29, 1936, in order to take advantage of the concessionary rate, it was mandatory to use #M1-M11 by affixing them to the backs of envelopes. An "Egypt Postage Prepaid" handstamp was applied to the face of the envelopes. Envelopes bearing these stamps were to be posted only at British military post boxes. Envelopes bearing the 1936-39 "Army Post" stamps (#M12-M15, issued by the Egyptian Postal Administration) also were sold at the concessionary rate and also were to be posted only at British military post boxes. The "Army Post" stamps were withdrawn in 1941, but the concession continued without the use of special stamps. The concession was finally canceled in 1951.

Imperf examples of Nos. M1-M4, M6, M9 (without overprint) and M10 are proofs.

M1

Unwmk.

1932, Nov. 1 **Typo.** ***Perf. 11***

M1 M1 1pi red & blue 70.00 4.50

For similar design see No. M3.

M2

1932, Nov. 26 **Typo.** ***Perf. 11½***

M2 M2 3m blk, *sage grn* 57.50 *80.00*

See Nos. M4, M6, M10.

M3

1933, Aug. **Typo.** ***Perf. 11***

M3 M3 1pi red & blue 47.50 1.10

Camel Type of 1932

1933, Nov. 13 **Typo.** ***Perf. 11½***

M4 M2 3m brown lake 40.00 *57.50*

M4

1934, June 1 **Photo.** ***Perf. 14½x14***

M5 M4 1pi bright carmine 40.00 1.25

See Nos. M7-M8. For overprint and surcharge see Nos. M9, M11.

Camel Type of 1932

1934, Nov. 17 **Typo.** ***Perf. 11½***

M6 M2 3m deep blue 8.25 *30.00*

Type of 1934

1934, Dec. 5 **Photo.** ***Perf. 14½x14***

M7 M4 1pi green 6.00 6.00

Type of 1934

1935, Apr. 24 ***Perf. 13½x14***

M8 M4 1pi bright carmine 2.90 *3.75*

Type of 1934 Overprinted in Red

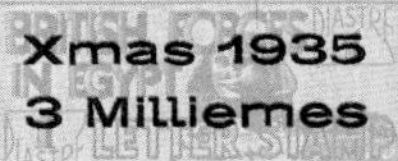

1935, May 6 ***Perf. 14***

M9 M4 1pi ultramarine 350.00 275.00

Camel Type of 1932

1935, Nov. 23 **Typo.** ***Perf. 11½***

M10 M2 3m vermilion 30.00 *45.00*

No. M8 Surcharged

Xmas 1935
3 Milliemes

1935, Dec. 16 **Photo.** ***Perf. 13½x14***

M11 M4 3m on 1pi brt car 25.00 *100.00*

Fuad Type of 1927

Inscribed "Army Post" — M5

1936, Mar. 1 **Wmk. 195**

M12 M5 3m green 2.50 2.50
M13 M5 10m carmine 7.00 .25

King Farouk — M6

1939, Dec. 16 ***Perf. 13x13½***

M14 M6 3m green 6.00 *12.00*
M15 M6 10m carmine rose 8.00 .25

OFFICIAL STAMPS

O1

Wmk. Crescent and Star (119)

1893, Jan. 1 **Typo.** ***Perf. 14x13½***

O1 O1 orange brown 3.75 .25
Never hinged 6.50

No. O1 exists on ordinary and chalky paper. Imperf. examples of No. O1 are proofs.

Regular Issues of 1884-93 Overprinted

1907

O2 A18 1m brown 2.40 .35
Never hinged 4.20
O3 A19 2m green 4.25 .25
Never hinged 7.50
O4 A20 3m orange 4.75 1.25
Never hinged 8.00
O5 A22 5m car rose 7.75 .25
Never hinged 13.50
O6 A14 1pi ultra 4.75 .25
Never hinged 8.00
O7 A16 5pi gray 17.00 6.00
Never hinged 30.00
Nos. O2-O7 (6) 40.90 8.35

Nos. O2-O3, O5-O7 imperf. are proofs.

No. 48 Overprinted

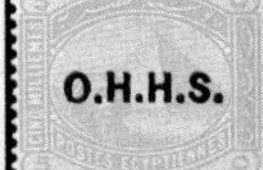

1913

O8 A22 5m carmine rose 9.50 .70
Never hinged 16.50
a. Inverted overprint 90.00
b. No period after "S" 65.00 19.00

Regular Issues Overprinted

1914-15 **On Issues of 1888-1906**

O9 A19 2m green 5.00 *10.00*
Never hinged 7.50
a. Inverted overprint 42.50 42.50
b. Double overprint 450.00
c. No period after "S" 16.00 16.00
O10 A21 4m brown red 7.50 5.50
Never hinged 11.25
a. Inverted overprint 225.00 160.00

On Issue of 1914

O11 A24 1m olive brown 2.50 *5.00*
Never hinged 3.75
a. No period after "S" 14.00 *30.00*
O12 A26 3m orange 3.75 *6.00*
Never hinged 5.50
a. No period after "S" 16.00 *30.00*
O13 A28 5m lake 4.75 2.75
Never hinged 7.15
a. No period after "S" 17.50 *26.00*
b. Two periods after "S" 17.50 *26.00*
Nos. O9-O13 (5) 23.50 29.25

Regular Issues Overprinted

1915, Oct. **On Issues of 1888-1906**

O14 A19 2m green 5.50 *5.00*
Never hinged 8.25
a. Inverted overprint 24.00 24.00
b. Double overprint 30.00
O15 A21 4m brown red 11.00 *11.00*
Never hinged 16.50

On Issue of 1914

O16 A28 5m lake 15.00 1.75
Never hinged 22.50
a. Pair, one without overprint 325.00
Nos. O14-O16 (3) 31.50 17.75

Nos. 50, 63, 52, 67 Overprinted

1922 **Wmk. 120**

O17 A24 1m olive brown 4.25 *16.00*
Never hinged 6.50
O18 A25 2m red 10.00 *24.00*
Never hinged 15.00
O19 A26 3m orange 77.50 *150.00*
Never hinged 115.00
O20 A28 5m pink 21.00 6.00
Never hinged 31.50
Nos. O17-O20 (4) 112.75 196.00

Regular Issues of 1921-22 Overprinted

1922

O21 A24 1m olive brn 1.50 *3.25*
Never hinged 2.25
O22 A25 2m red 2.00 *4.50*
Never hinged 3.00
O23 A26 3m orange 3.25 *5.00*
Never hinged 5.00
O24 A27 4m green 7.00 *9.00*
Never hinged 10.50
a. Two periods after "H" none after "S" 175.00 175.00
O25 A28 5m pink 4.00 1.00
Never hinged 6.00
a. Two periods after "H" none after "S" 75.00 75.00
O26 A29 10m deep blue 7.00 *8.00*
Never hinged 10.50
O27 A29 10m lake ('23) 10.00 4.00
Never hinged 15.00
a. Two periods after "H" none after "S" 100.00 100.00
O28 A34 15m indigo 8.00 7.00
Never hinged 12.00
O29 A35 15m indigo 160.00 160.00
Never hinged 240.00
a. Two periods after "H" none after "S" 250.00 250.00
O30 A31 50m maroon 20.00 18.00
Never hinged 30.00

Regular Issue of 1923 Overprinted in Black or Red

1924 ***Perf. 13½x14***

O31 A36 1m orange 2.10 *2.25*
Never hinged 3.15
O32 A36 2m gray (R) 2.75 *3.50*
Never hinged 4.15
O33 A36 3m brown 6.75 *6.75*
Never hinged 10.25
O34 A36 4m yellow green 8.50 8.50
Never hinged 12.75
O35 A36 5m orange brown 2.00 1.05
Never hinged 3.00
O36 A36 10m rose 5.50 4.00
Never hinged 8.25
O37 A36 15m ultra 9.25 6.75
Never hinged 14.00

Perf. 14

O38 A36 50m myrtle green 25.00 13.50
Never hinged 37.50
Nos. O31-O38 (8) 61.85 46.30

O2

Perf. 13x13½

1926-35 **Litho.** **Wmk. 195**

Size: 18½x22mm

O39 O2 1m lt orange 1.05 .55
Never hinged 1.55
O40 O2 2m black .70 .40
Never hinged 1.00
O41 O2 3m olive brn 2.00 1.35
Never hinged 3.00
O42 O2 4m lt green 1.75 1.60
Never hinged 2.65
O43 O2 5m brown 2.10 .55
Never hinged 3.15
O44 O2 10m dull red 5.25 .55
Never hinged 8.00
O45 O2 10m brt vio ('34) 3.00 .60
Never hinged 4.50
O46 O2 15m dp blue 5.25 1.25
Never hinged 8.00

O47	O2 15m brown vio ('34)	5.25	1.10
	Never hinged	8.00	
O48	O2 20m dp blue ('35)	5.50	1.60
	Never hinged	8.25	

Perf. 13½

Size: 22½x27½mm

O49	O2 20m olive green	7.50	2.75
	Never hinged	11.25	
O50	O2 50m myrtle green	10.00	2.00
	Never hinged	15.00	
	Nos. O39-O50 (12)	49.35	14.30

O3

1938, Dec. **Size: 22½x19mm**

O51	O3 1m orange	.35	.35
	Never hinged	.50	
O52	O3 2m red	.35	.35
	Never hinged	.50	
O53	O3 3m olive brown	1.60	1.60
	Never hinged	2.40	
O54	O3 4m yel green	1.00	1.00
	Never hinged	1.50	
O55	O3 5m brown	.50	.50
	Never hinged	.75	
O56	O3 10m brt violet	.60	.60
	Never hinged	.90	
O57	O3 15m rose violet	1.60	1.60
	Never hinged	2.40	
O58	O3 20m blue	1.60	1.60
	Never hinged	2.40	

Perf. 14x13½

Size: 26½x22mm

O59	O3 50m myrtle green	3.75	3.00
	Never hinged	5.25	
	Nos. O51-O59 (9)	11.35	10.60

ELOBEY, ANNOBON & CORISCO

ˌel-ə-ˈbā, ˌan-ə-ˈbän and kə-ˈris-ˌkō

LOCATION — A group of islands near the Guinea Coast of western Africa.
GOVT. — Spanish colonial possessions administered as part of the Continental Guinea District. A second district under the same governor-general included Fernando Po.
AREA — 13¾ sq. mi.
POP. — 2,950 (estimated 1910)
CAPITAL — Santa Isabel

100 Centimos = 1 Peseta

King Alfonso XIII — A1

1903 Unwmk. Typo. *Perf. 14*
Control Numbers on Back

1 A1 ¼c carmine .75 .55
2 A1 ½c dk violet .75 .55
3 A1 1c black .75 .55
4 A1 2c red .75 .55
5 A1 3c dk green .75 .55
6 A1 4c dk blue grn .75 .55
7 A1 5c violet .75 .55
8 A1 10c rose lake 1.50 1.60
9 A1 15c orange buff 4.50 1.75
10 A1 25c dark blue 7.75 6.00
11 A1 50c red brown 9.00 10.50
12 A1 75c black brn 9.00 *14.50*
13 A1 1p orange red 15.00 *20.00*
14 A1 2p chocolate 40.00 *60.00*
15 A1 3p olive grn 60.00 *75.00*
16 A1 4p claret 140.00 100.00
17 A1 5p blue green 165.00 110.00
18 A1 10p dull blue 300.00 165.00
Nos. 1-18 (18) 757.00 568.20
Set, never hinged 1,500.

Dated "1905"

1905 Control Numbers on Back

19 A1 1c carmine 1.25 .70
20 A1 2c dp violet 5.00 .70
21 A1 3c black 1.25 .70
22 A1 4c dull red 1.25 .70
23 A1 5c dp green 1.25 .70
24 A1 10c blue grn 4.50 .90
25 A1 15c violet 5.00 4.75
26 A1 25c rose lake 5.00 4.75
27 A1 50c orange buff 9.00 7.25
28 A1 75c dark blue 9.00 7.25
29 A1 1p red brown 18.50 16.00
30 A1 2p black brn 20.00 22.50
31 A1 3p orange red 20.00 23.00
32 A1 4p dk brown 150.00 72.50
33 A1 5p bronze grn 160.00 80.00
34 A1 10p claret 350.00 225.00
Nos. 19-34 (16) 761.00 467.40
Set, never hinged 1,500.

Nos. 19-22 Surcharged in Black or Red

1906

35 A1 10c on 1c rose (Bk) 11.50 6.50
a. Inverted surcharge 11.50 6.50
b. Value omitted 30.00 16.00
c. Frame omitted 16.00 7.50
d. Double surcharge 11.50 6.50
e. Surcharged "15 cents" 30.00 16.00
f. Surcharged "25 cents" 52.50 22.50
g. Surcharged "50 cents" 37.50 22.50
h. "1906" omitted 17.50 7.50
36 A1 15c on 2c dp vio (R) 11.50 6.50
a. Frame omitted 12.50 6.50
b. Surcharged "25 cents" 16.00 9.00
c. Inverted surcharge 11.50 6.50
d. Double surcharge 11.50 6.50
37 A1 25c on 3c blk (R) 11.50 6.50
a. Inverted surcharge 11.50 6.50
b. Double surcharge 11.50 6.50
c. Surcharged "15 cents" 16.00 6.50
d. Surcharged "50 cents" 25.00 11.00
38 A1 50c on 4c red (Bk) 11.50 6.50
a. Inverted surcharge 11.50 6.50
b. Value omitted 35.00 17.50
c. Frame omitted 17.50 8.00
e. Double surcharge 11.50 6.50
f. "1906" omitted 17.50 8.00
g. Surcharged "10 cents" 32.50 16.00
h. Surcharged "25 cents" 32.50 16.00
Nos. 35-38 (4) 46.00 26.00

Eight other surcharges were prepared but not issued: 10c on 50c, 75c, 1p, 2p and 3p; 15c on 50c and 5p; 50c on 5c.

Exist with surcharges in different colors; #35 in blue, red or violet, #36 in black or violet, #37 in black or violet, #38 in blue, violet or red. Value, set of 10, $135.

King Alfonso XIII — A2

1907 Control Numbers on Back

39 A2 1c dk violet .55 .45
40 A2 2c black .55 .45
41 A2 3c red orange .55 .45
42 A2 4c dk green .55 .45
43 A2 5c blue green .55 .45
44 A2 10c violet 6.00 5.50
45 A2 15c carmine 1.75 1.75
46 A2 25c orange 1.75 1.75
47 A2 50c blue 1.75 1.75
48 A2 75c brown 6.50 2.75
49 A2 1p black brn 10.00 4.75
50 A2 2p orange red 13.50 8.00
51 A2 3p dk brown 13.00 9.00
52 A2 4p bronze grn 20.00 8.50
53 A2 5p claret 25.00 10.00
54 A2 10p rose 50.00 27.50
Nos. 39-54 (16) 152.00 83.50
Set, never hinged 350.00

Stamps of 1907 Surcharged

1908-09 Black Surcharge

55 A2 5c on 3c red org ('09) 2.25 1.25
56 A2 5c on 4c dk grn ('09) 2.25 1.25
57 A2 5c on 10c violet 4.50 5.00
58 A2 25c on 10c violet 30.00 15.00
Nos. 55-58 (4) 39.00 22.50

1910 Red Surcharge

59 A2 5c on 1c dark violet 1.75 .90
60 A2 5c on 2c black 1.75 .90

Nos. 55-60 exist with surcharge inverted (value set, $125 unused or used); with double surcharge, one black, one red (value set, $300 unused or used); with "PARA" omitted (value set, $150.00 unused or used)

The same 5c surcharge was also applied to Nos. 45-54, but these were not issued (value set, $250).

In 1909, stamps of Spanish Guinea replaced those of Elobey, Annobon and Corisco.

Revenue stamps surcharged as above were unauthorized although some were postally used.

For postally valid examples similar to the item shown above see Rio de Oro Nos. 44-45 and Spanish Guinea Nos. 98-101C.

For revenue stamps with the arms at the left surcharged for postal use see Spanish Guinea Nos. 8A-8J.

EPIRUS

i-ˈpī-rəs

LOCATION — A region of southeastern Europe, now divided between Greece and Albania.

During the First Balkan War (1912-13), this territory was occupied by the Greek army, and the local Greek majority wished to be united with Greece. Italy and Austria-Hungary favored its inclusion in the newly created Albania, however, which both powers expected to dominate. Greek forces were withdrawn subsequently in early 1914. The local population resisted inclusion in Albania and established the Autonomous Republic of Northern Epirus on Feb. 28, 1914. Resistance to Albanian control continued until October, when Greece reoccupied the country. Northern Epirus was administered as an integral part of Greece, and it was expected that Greece's annexation of the territory would become official following World War I. Instead, in 1916, Italian pressure and its own military reverses in Anatolia caused Greece to withdraw from Epirus and to formally cede the territory to Albania.

100 Lepta = 1 Drachma

Chimarra Issue

Double-headed Eagle, Skull and Crossbones — A1

Handstamped
1914, Feb. 10 Unwmk. *Imperf.*
Control Mark in Blue
Without Gum

1 A1 1 l black & blue *475.00* 250.00
a. Tête-bêche pair 3,000.
2 A1 5 l blue & red *475.00* 250.00
3 A1 10 l red & blk *475.00* 250.00
4 A1 25 l blue & red *475.00* 250.00
Nos. 1-4 (4) *1,900.* 1,000.
Set, on over-franked cover or postcard *1,750.*

All values exist without control mark. This mark is a solid blue oval, about 12x8mm, containing the colorless Greek letters "SP," the first two letters of Spiromilios, the Chimarra commander.

All four exist with denomination inverted and the 1 l, 5 l and 10 l with denomination double.

The values above are for the first printing on somewhat transparent shiny, white, thin, wove paper, which is sometimes known as "rice paper."

A second printing was made from original handstamps, on similar thin wove paper, but not transluscent, known as "Spetsiotis Reprints." Value, unused or canceled to order, each $55. Later printings were made from original handstamps on other papers, generally thicker and whiter, sometimes surfaced. Value, unused or canceled to order, each $45.

Values above are for genuine stamps expertized by knowledgeable authorities. Most of the stamps offered as Nos. 1-4 in the marketplace are forgeries. Most resemble the stamps from the second reprinting, but the designs differ in details of the lettering, monogram and skull. Such forgeries have only nominal commercial value.

Some experts question the official character of this issue.

Argyrokastro Issues

Stamps of Turkey surcharged "AUTONOMOUS EPIRUS" and new denominations in several formats in Greek currency.

On Turkish stamps of 1908

No. 4A

No. 4B

1914, Mar. 2

4A A19 1d on 2½pi (#137) 10.00 11.00
Never hinged 20.00
4B A19 2d on 2½pi (#137) 10.00 11.00
Never hinged 20.00
a. Horiz. pair, #4A, 4B 35.00

No. 4C
No. 4D

4C A19 5d on 25pi (#140) 77.50 90.00
Never hinged 155.00
4D A19 5d on 50pi (#141) 125.00 135.00
Never hinged 250.00

On Turkish stamps of 1909-10

4E A21 5 l on 5pa (#151) 77.50 —
Never hinged 150.00

No. 4F

No. 4G

4F A21 5 l on 10pa (#152) 3.25 *3.75*
Never hinged 6.50
4G A21 10 l (oval "O") on 20pa (#153) 2.25 *2.50*
Never hinged 4.50
a. Double surcharge 77.50

No. 4H

No. 4I

4H A21 10 l (round "O") on 20pa (#153) 2.25 *2.50*
Never hinged 4.50
a. Double surcharge 77.50
b. Horiz. pair (#4G, 4H) 14.50
c. Horiz. pair (#4Ga, 4Ha) 375.00
4I A21 20 l on 1pi (#154) 2.25 *2.50*
Never hinged 4.50
a. Double surcharge 77.50

No. 4J

No. 4K

4J A21 25 l on 1pi (#154) 2.25 *2.50*
Never hinged 4.50
a. Double surcharge 77.50
b. Horiz. pair (#4I, 4J) 14.50
c. Horiz. pair (#4Ia, 4Ja) 375.00
4K A21 40 l on 2pi (#155) 3.25 *3.75*
Never hinged 6.50

No. 4L
No. 4M

4L A21 80 l on 2pi (#155) 3.25 *3.75*
Never hinged 6.50
a. Horiz. pair (#4K, 4L) 18.50
b. Double surcharge *80.00*
4M A21 1d on 5pi (#157) 12.50 *13.50*
Never hinged 25.00

No. 4N

No. 4O

4N A21 2d on 5pi (#157) 12.50 13.50
Never hinged 25.00
a. Horiz. pair (#4M, 4N) 37.50
4O A21 5d on 10pi (#158) 77.50 *90.00*
Never hinged 155.00
a. Double surcharge
4P A21 5d on 10pa (#152) 135.00 *165.00*
Never hinged 270.00

4Q A21 5d on 20pa (#153) 135.00 *165.00*
Never hinged 270.00
4R A21 5d on 1pi (#154) 135.00 *165.00*
Never hinged 270.00
4RR A21 5d on 2½pi (#156) 135.00 *165.00*
Never hinged 270.00
4S A21 5d on 50pi (#160) 135.00 *165.00*
Never hinged 250.00

On Turkish stamps of 1909-11 (with "Béhié")

4T A21 5 l on 10pa (#161) 77.50
Never hinged 155.00
4U A21 10 l (oval "O") on 20pa (#162) 77.50
Never hinged 155.00
4V A21 10 l (round "O") on 20pa (#162) 77.50
Never hinged 155.00
a. Horiz. pair (#4U, 4V) 400.00
4W A21 20 l on 1pi (#163) 77.50
Never hinged 155.00
4X A21 25 l on 1pi (#163) 77.50
Never hinged 155.00
a. Horiz. pair (#4W, 4X) 400.00
4Y A21 40 l on 2pi (#164) 77.50
Never hinged 155.00
4Z A21 80 l on 2pi (#164) 77.50
Never hinged 155.00
a. Horiz. pair (#4Y, 4Z) 400.00
4AA A21 5d on 10pa (#161) 135.00
Never hinged 270.00
4BB A21 5d on 20pa (#162) 135.00
Never hinged 270.00
4CC A21 5d on 1pi (#163) 135.00
Never hinged 270.00
4CA A21 5d on 2pi (#164) 135.00
Never hinged 250.00

On Turkish Newspaper Stamps of 1910-11

No. 4DD

No. 4EE

4DD A21 30 l on 2pa on 5pa (#P67) 85.00
Never hinged 170.00
4EE A21 50 l on 2pa on 5pa (#P67) 85.00
Never hinged 170.00
a. Horiz. pair (#4DD, 4EE) 150.00

No. 4FF

4FF A21 30 l on 2pa (#P68) 2.25 *2.50*
Never hinged 4.50
4GG A21 50 l on 2pa (#P68) 2.25 *2.50*
Never hinged 4.50
a. Horiz. pair (#4FF, 4GG) 15.00

Covers exist, starting at $50 for the most common (Nos. 4G, 4H, 4I, 4J).

Tête-bêche pairs exist for Nos. 4A-4GG. Value, double the value of the individual stamps combined.

Provisional Government Issues

Infantryman with Rifle
A2 A3

Serrate Roulette 13½

1914, Mar. **Litho.**

5 A2 1 l orange .45 *.90*
Never hinged .90
a. Imperf., pair 60.00
6 A2 5 l green .45 1.00
Never hinged .90
a. Imperf., pair 60.00
7 A3 10 l carmine .45 1.00
Never hinged .90
8 A3 25 l deep blue .45 1.00
Never hinged .90
on registered cover *175.00*
9 A2 50 l brown 1.35 1.45
Never hinged 2.75
On overfranked cover *50.00*
10 A2 1d violet 2.00 2.25
Never hinged 4.00
On overfranked cover *50.00*
11 A2 2d blue 13.50 13.50
Never hinged 27.00
on overfranked cover *100.00*
12 A2 5d gray green 17.50 18.50
Never hinged 35.00
On overfranked cover *100.00*
Nos. 5-12 (8) 36.15 39.60
Set on philatelic cover 200.00

Issue dates: 10 l, 25 l, Mar. 5; balance of set, Mar. 26.

Flag of Epirus — A5

1914, Aug. 28

15 A5 1 l brown & blue .35 *.40*
Never hinged .70
16 A5 5 l green & blue .35 *.40*
Never hinged .70
17 A5 10 l rose red & blue .40 *.65*
Never hinged 1.00
18 A5 25 l dk blue & blue 1.00 1.10
Never hinged 2.25
19 A5 50 l violet & blue 1.00 1.10
Never hinged 2.25
20 A5 1d carmine & blue 5.75 *6.50*
Never hinged 12.00
21 A5 2d orange & blue 1.50 *2.25*
Never hinged 3.25
a. Double impression, one inverted *1,000.*
22 A5 5d dk green & blue 9.50 11.00
Never hinged 20.00
a. Double impression 1,000.
Nos. 15-22 (8) 19.85 *23.40*

Nos. 16 and 21 exist with the blue color inverted.

Koritsa Issue

A7

1914, Sept. 25

26 A7 25 l dk blue & blue 6.00 5.25
Never hinged 12.00
27 A7 50 l violet & blue 12.00 *13.50*
Never hinged 24.00

Nos. 26 and 27 were issued at Koritsa (Korce) to commemorate that city's occupation by Epirot forces.

Chimarra Issues

King Constantine I — A8

1914, Oct.

28 A8 1 l yellow green 135.00 77.50
Never hinged 300.00
29 A8 2 l red 115.00 42.50
Never hinged 275.00
30 A8 5 l dark blue 115.00 77.50
Never hinged 275.00
31 A8 10 l orange brown 80.00 30.00
Never hinged 175.00
a. 10 l red brown (Nov.) 140.00 110.00
Never hinged 350.00
32 A8 20 l carmine 87.50 62.50
Never hinged 200.00
a. 20 l rose carmine 140.00
Never hinged 350.00
33 A8 25 l gray blue 115.00 77.50
Never hinged 275.00
33A A8 50 l yellow green 170.00 90.00
Never hinged 400.00
33B A8 1d carmine 170.00 90.00
Never hinged 400.00
a. 1d rose carmine 225.00
Never hinged 500.00
33C A8 2d pale yellow green 255.00 125.00
Never hinged 550.00
33D A8 5d orange brown 425.00 290.00
Never hinged 1,000.
Nos. 28-33D (10) 1,668. 962.50

Nos. 28-33D were printed by Papachrysanthou, Athens. The papermaker's watermark "PARCHIMINE JOHANNOT" appears on some stamps in the set.

1911-23 Issues of Greece Overprinted

1914, Aug. 24 ***Perf. 11 ½***

34 A24 1 l green 55.00 62.50
Never hinged 130.00
35 A25 2 l carmine 45.00 52.50
Never hinged 110.00
36 A24 3 l vermilion 45.00 52.50
Never hinged 110.00
37 A26 5 l green 45.00 52.50
Never hinged 110.00
38 A24 10 l carmine 60.00 65.00
Never hinged 135.00
39 A25 20 l slate 80.00 87.50
Never hinged 190.00
40 A25 25 l blue 175.00 185.00
Never hinged 400.00
41 A26 50 l violet brn 220.00 225.00
Never hinged 500.00
Nos. 34-41 (8) 725.00 782.50

The 2 l and 3 l are engraved stamps of the 1911-21 issue; the others are lithographed stamps of the 1912-23 issue.

Overprint reads: "Greek Chimarra 1914."

Stamps of this issue are with or without a black monogram (S.S., for S. Spiromilios) in manuscript. Counterfeits are plentiful.

Moschopolis Issue

Arms A9

Ancient Epirot Coins/Medals A10

1914, Sept. **Engr.** ***Perf. 14 ½***

42 A9 1 l yellow brown .75 *3.25*
Never hinged 1.75
a. Imperf., pair 40.00
Never hinged 60.00
b. 1 l yellow 25.00 20.00
Never hinged 40.00
43 A9 2 l black .75 *3.25*
Never hinged 1.75
a. Imperf., pair 40.00
Never hinged 60.00
b. 2 l blue black 25.00 20.00
Never hinged 40.00
44 A9 3 l yellow .75 *3.25*
Never hinged 1.75
a. Imperf., pair 40.00
Never hinged 60.00
b. 3 l yellow brown 25.00 20.00
Never hinged 40.00
c. 3 l brown 25.00 20.00
Never hinged 40.00
45 A9 5 l green .75 *3.25*
Never hinged 1.75
a. Imperf., pair 40.00
46 A9 10 l red .75 *3.25*
Never hinged 1.75
a. Imperf., pair 40.00
Never hinged 60.00
47 A9 25 l deep blue .75 *3.25*
Never hinged 1.75
a. Imperf., pair 40.00
Never hinged 60.00
b. 25 l blue green 25.00 20.00
Never hinged 40.00
48 A9 30 l violet .75 *3.25*
Never hinged 1.75
a. Imperf., pair 40.00
Never hinged 60.00
b. 30 l deep violet 25.00 20.00
Never hinged 40.00
c. 30 l green 35.00
Never hinged 50.00
49 A9 40 l olive gray .75 *3.25*
Never hinged 1.75
a. Imperf., pair 40.00
Never hinged 60.00
b. 40 l gray brown 25.00 20.00
Never hinged 40.00
c. 40 l blue green 35.00
Never hinged 50.00
d. 40 l deep brown 35.00
Never hinged 50.00
50 A9 50 l violet black .75 *3.25*
Never hinged 1.75
a. Imperf., pair 40.00
Never hinged 60.00
b. 50 l brown black 25.00 20.00
Never hinged 40.00
51 A10 1d yellow brown & olive 5.00 *10.00*
Never hinged 10.00
a. Imperf., pair 80.00
Never hinged 120.00
b. 1d olive green & rose 25.00
Never hinged 37.50
52 A10 2d carmine & gray 5.00 *10.50*
Never hinged 10.00
a. Imperf., pair 80.00
Never hinged 120.00
b. 2d orange & blue 25.00
53 A10 3d gray green & red brown 5.00 *10.50*
Never hinged 10.00
a. Imperf., pair 80.00
Never hinged 120.00
b. 3d blue gray & brownish red 25.00
54 A10 5d olive & yellow brown 5.00 *10.50*
Never hinged 10.00
a. Imperf., pair 80.00
Never hinged 120.00
b. 5d blue gray & yellow brown 25.00
55 A10 10d orange & blue 5.00 *14.00*
Never hinged 10.00
a. Imperf., pair 80.00
Never hinged 120.00
b. 10d red & blue 25.00
Never hinged 37.50
56 A10 25d violet & black 5.00 *19.00*
Never hinged 10.00
a. Imperf., pair 80.00
Never hinged 120.00
b. 25d brown violet & black 25.00 25.00
Never hinged 45.00
c. 25d green & red brown 25.00
Never hinged 45.00
Nos. 42-56 (15) 36.75 *103.75*

Nos. 42-56 were privately printed in early 1914. In June 1914, the Epirots occupied Moschopolis (Voskopoje), and these stamps were authorized for use by the local military commander in Sept. After the occupation of Moschopolis by Greek forces in Nov., remaining stocks of this issue were sent to Athens, where they were destroyed in 1931.

The 1d exists with center omitted. Value $100. The 1d, 2d, 10d and 25d exist with center inverted. Values, each $65.

Stamps of the following designs were locals, privately produced. Issued primarily for propaganda and for philatelic purposes, their postal use is in dispute. The 1917 and 1920 designs are fantasy items, created long after Epirus was annexed by Albania.

From 1914: 1st design, 3 varieties. 2nd design, 6 varieties. 3rd design, 7 varieties.

From 1917: 4th design, 8 varieties, + 1 surcharged; perforated and imperforate.

From 1920: 5th design, 4 varieties.

OCCUPATION STAMPS

Issued under Greek Occupation

Greek Occupation Stamps of 1913 Overprinted Horizontally

Serrate Roulette 13½

1914-15 Black Overprint Unwmk.

N1 O1 1 l brown .80 .80
Never hinged 2.75
b. Inverted overprint 25.00 25.00
Never hinged 35.00
c. Double overprint 25.00 25.00
Never hinged 35.00
d. Double overprint, one inverted 25.00 25.00
Never hinged 37.50
N2 O2 2 l red .80 .80
Never hinged 2.75
b. 2 l rose 1.25 1.25
Never hinged 4.00
c. As #N2, inverted overprint 25.00 25.00
Never hinged 35.00
d. As "b", inverted overprint 30.00 30.00
Never hinged 42.50
e. As #N2, double overprint 25.00 *30.00*
Never hinged 35.00
f. As "b", double overprint 30.00 30.00
Never hinged 42.50
g. As #N2, double overprint, one inverted 25.00 25.00
Never hinged 37.50
N4 O2 3 l orange .80 .80
Never hinged 2.75
b. Inverted overprint 19.00 16.50
Never hinged 29.00
c. Double overprint 19.00 16.50
Never hinged 29.00
d. Double overprint, one inverted 25.00 25.00
Never hinged 37.50
N5 O1 5 l green 2.00 2.00
Never hinged 4.50
b. Inverted overprint 35.00 35.00
Never hinged 50.00
N6 O1 10 l rose red 2.75 2.75
Never hinged 10.00
a. Inverted overprint 50.00 50.00
Never hinged 70.00
b. Double overprint 50.00 50.00
Never hinged 70.00
N7 O1 20 l violet 6.50 6.50
Never hinged 16.50
a. Inverted overprint 50.00 50.00
Never hinged 72.50
b. Double overprint 85.00 65.00
Never hinged 120.00
N8 O2 25 l pale blue 2.75 3.00
Never hinged 10.00
N9 O1 30 l gray green 14.00 14.50
Never hinged 50.00
N10 O2 40 l indigo 19.00 20.00
Never hinged 65.00
N11 O1 50 l dark blue 21.00 23.00
Never hinged 72.50
N12 O2 1d violet brown 135.00 145.00
Never hinged 465.00
a. Inverted overprint 300.00 *225.00*
Never hinged 450.00
b. Double overprint 375.00 *300.00*
Never hinged 550.00
Nos. N1-N12 (11) 205.40 219.15

Red Overprint

N1a O1 1 l brown 5.75
Never hinged 11.50
N2a O2 2 l red 5.75
Never hinged 11.50
N4a O2 3 l orange 5.75
Never hinged 11.50
N5a O1 5 l green 5.75
Never hinged 11.50

Nos. N1a-N5a were not issued. Exist canceled.

Regular Issues of Greece, 1911-23, Ovptd. Reading Up

On Issue of 1911-21

1916 Engr.

N17 A24 3 l vermilion 11.50 11.50
Never hinged 22.50
a. Overprint reading down 14.50
Never hinged 29.00
N18 A26 30 l carmine rose 40.00 40.00
Never hinged 55.00
a. Overprint reading down 225.00
Never hinged 450.00
N19 A27 1d ultra 85.00 85.00
Never hinged 170.00
N20 A27 2d vermilion 95.00 95.00
Never hinged 190.00
N21 A27 3d carmine rose 130.00 130.00
Never hinged 250.00
N22 A27 5d ultra — —
Never hinged —
a. Double overprint 1,950. 1,950.
Never hinged 1,900.
b. Overprint reading down 725.00
Never hinged 1,375.
Nos. N17-N22 (6) 361.50 361.50

On Issue of 1912-23

1916 Litho.

N23 A24 1 l green 2.75 2.75
Never hinged 5.50
a. Overprint reading down 9.50
Never hinged 19.00
b. As #N23, "I" omitted 20.00
Never hinged 30.00
c. As #N23, inverted "L" in place of "E" in "Epirus" 20.00
Never hinged 30.00
N24 A25 2 l carmine 2.75 2.75
Never hinged 5.50
a. Overprint reading down 9.50
Never hinged 19.00
b. As #N24, "I" omitted 20.00
Never hinged 30.00
c. As #N24, inverted "L" in place of "E" in "Epirus" 20.00
Never hinged 30.00
N25 A24 3 l vermilion 2.75 2.75
Never hinged 5.50
a. Overprint reading down 14.00
Never hinged 28.00
b. As #N25, 'I' omitted 20.00
Never hinged 30.00
c. As #N25, inverted "L" in place of "E" in "Epirus" 20.00
Never hinged 30.00
N26 A26 5 l green 2.75 2.75
Never hinged 5.50
a. Overprint reading down 14.00
Never hinged 28.00
b. As #N26, 'I' omitted 24.00
Never hinged 35.00
c. As #N27, inverted "L" in place of "E" in "Epirus" 24.00
Never hinged 35.00
N27 A24 10 l carmine 2.75 2.75
Never hinged 5.50
a. Overprint reading down 27.50
Never hinged 55.00
b. As #N27, "I" omitted 27.50
Never hinged 42.50
c. As #N27, inverted "L" in place of "E" in "Epirus" 27.50
Never hinged 42.50
N28 A25 20 l slate 2.75 2.75
Never hinged 5.50
a. As #N28, "I" omitted 35.00
Never hinged 50.00
b. As #N28, inverted "L" in place of "E" in "Epirus" 35.00
Never hinged 50.00
N29 A25 25 l blue 3.75 3.75
Never hinged 7.50
a. As #N29, "I" omitted 35.00
Never hinged 50.00
b. As #N29, inverted "L" in place of "E" in "Epirus" 35.00
Never hinged 50.00
N30 A26 30 l rose 21.00 21.00
Never hinged 42.00
a. Overprint reading down 250.00
Never hinged 450.00
b. As #N30, "I" omitted 95.00
Never hinged 145.00
c. As #N30, inverted "L" in place of "E" in "Epirus" 95.00
Never hinged 145.00
N31 A25 40 l indigo 16.00 16.00
Never hinged 28.00
a. Overprint reading down 475.00
Never hinged 450.00
b. As #N31, "I" omitted 95.00
Never hinged 145.00
c. As #N31, inverted "L" in place of "E" in "Epirus" 95.00
Never hinged 145.00
N32 A26 50 l violet brown 25.00 25.00
Never hinged 50.00
a. As #N32, "I" omitted 110.00
Never hinged 160.00
b. As #N32, inverted "L" in place of "E" in "Epirus" 110.00
Never hinged 160.00
Nos. N23-N32 (10) 82.25 82.25

In each sheet, there are two varieties in the overprint: the "I" in "Epirus" omitted and an inverted "L" in place of the first letter of the word.

Counterfeits exist of Nos. N1-N32.

Postage stamps issued in 1940-41, during Greek occupation, are listed under Greece.

ERITREA

ˌer-ə-ˈtrē-ə

LOCATION — In northeast Africa, bordering on the Red Sea
GOVT. — Italian Colony
AREA — 15,754 sq. mi. (1936)
POP. — 600,573 (1931)
CAPITAL — Asmara

Eritrea was incorporated as a State of Italian East Africa in 1936.

100 Centesimi = 1 Lira

All used values to about 1916 are for postally used stamps. From 1916, used values in italics are for postally used stamps. CTO's, for stamps valued postally used, sell for about the same as unused, hinged stamps.

Watermark

Wmk. 140 — Crown

Stamps of Italy Overprinted

a

b

1892 Wmk. 140 *Perf. 14*

Overprinted Type "a" in Black

1 A6 1c bronze grn 10.00 10.00
Never hinged 24.00
No gum 2.50
On cover 120.00
a. Inverted overprint 675.00 675.00
Never hinged —
b. Double overprint 1,900.
Never hinged 2,400.
c. Vert. pair, one without overprint 4,500.
Never hinged 5,750.
2 A7 2c org brn 5.00 5.00
Never hinged 12.00
No gum 1.40
On cover 95.00
a. Inverted overprint 600.00 600.00
Never hinged —
b. Double overprint 1,900.
Never hinged 2,400.
3 A33 5c green 160.00 17.50
Never hinged 400.00
No gum 40.00
On cover 87.50
a. Inverted overprint 8,000. 4,500.
Never hinged 10,000.

Overprinted Type "b" in Black

4 A17 10c claret 210.00 17.50
Never hinged 525.00
No gum 40.00
On cover 87.50
5 A17 20c orange 375.00 12.00
Never hinged 950.00
No gum 75.00
On cover 60.00
6 A17 25c blue 1,450. 55.00
Never hinged 3,500.
No gum 325.00
On cover 400.00
7 A25 40c brown 13.50 *32.50*
Never hinged 32.50
No gum 3.25
On cover 325.00
8 A26 45c slate grn 13.50 *32.50*
Never hinged 32.50
No gum 3.25
On cover 350.00
9 A27 60c violet 13.50 72.50
Never hinged 40.00
No gum 3.25
On cover 725.00
10 A28 1 l brn & yel 65.00 *80.00*
Never hinged 160.00
No gum 9.00
On cover 950.00
11 A38 5 l bl & rose 650.00 550.00
Never hinged 1,625.
No gum 140.00
On cover *8,400.*
Nos. 1-11 (11) 2,966. *884.50*
Set, never hinged *7,300.*

1895-99

Overprinted type "a" in Black

12 A39 1c brown ('99) 22.50 12.00
Never hinged 55.00
No gum 3.25
On cover 120.00
13 A40 2c org brn ('99) 4.75 2.40
Never hinged 12.00
No gum .60
On cover 95.00
14 A41 5c green 4.75 2.40
Never hinged 12.00
No gum .60
On cover 47.50
a. Inverted overprint 525.00 *4,250.*
Never hinged —

Overprinted type "b" in Black

15 A34 10c claret ('98) 4.75 2.40
Never hinged 12.00
No gum .60
On cover 72.50
16 A35 20c orange 4.75 3.25
Never hinged 12.00
No gum .80
On cover 55.00
17 A36 25c blue 4.75 4.75
Never hinged 12.00
No gum .80
On cover 240.00
18 A37 45c olive grn 37.50 *27.50*
Never hinged 100.00
No gum 6.50
On cover 550.00
Nos. 12-18 (7) 83.75 *54.70*
Set, never hinged 215.00

1903-28

Overprinted type "a" in Black

19 A42 1c brown 1.60 *1.25*
Never hinged 4.00
On cover 16.00
a. Inverted overprint 125.00 125.00
20 A43 2c orange brn 1.60 .60
Never hinged 4.00
On cover 16.00
21 A44 5c blue green 120.00 .60
Never hinged 300.00
On cover 9.50
22 A45 10c claret 140.00 .60
Never hinged 350.00
On cover 9.50
23 A45 20c orange 6.50 1.25
Never hinged 16.00
On cover 14.50
24 A45 25c blue 1,200. 18.00
Never hinged 3,000.
On cover 140.00
a. Double overprint 1,100. —
Never hinged —
25 A45 40c brown 1,300. 30.00
Never hinged 3,300.
On cover 325.00
26 A45 45c olive grn 8.00 *10.00*
Never hinged 20.00
On cover 200.00
27 A45 50c violet 475.00 32.50
Never hinged 1,200.
On cover 475.00
28 A46 75c dk red & rose ('28) 80.00 20.00
Never hinged 200.00
On cover 120.00
29 A46 1 l brown & grn 8.00 .85
Never hinged 20.00
On cover 110.00
30 A46 1.25 l bl & ultra ('28) 40.00 20.00
Never hinged 100.00
On cover 275.00
31 A46 2 l dk grn & org ('25) 87.50 *100.00*
Never hinged 210.00
On cover 475.00
32 A46 2.50 l dk grn & org ('28) 175.00 72.50
Never hinged 425.00
On cover 725.00
33 A46 5 l blue & rose 55.00 *45.00*
Never hinged 140.00
On cover *4,000.*
Nos. 19-33 (15) 3,698. 353.15
Set, never hinged 9,250.

Surcharged in Black

1905

34 A45 15c on 20c orange 80.00 20.00
Never hinged 200.00
On cover 100.00

1908-28

Overprinted type "a" in Black

35 A48 5c green 1.20 1.00
Never hinged 3.50
On cover 8.00
36 A48 10c claret ('09) 1.20 1.00
Never hinged 3.50
On cover 14.50
37 A48 15c slate ('20) 22.50 14.50
Never hinged 55.00
On cover 80.00
38 A49 20c green ('25) 16.00 11.00
Never hinged 40.00
On cover 65.00
39 A49 20c lilac brn ('28) 8.00 3.25
Never hinged 20.00
On cover 87.50
40 A49 25c blue ('09) 6.50 2.25
Never hinged 15.00
On cover 35.00
41 A49 30c gray ('25) 16.00 14.50
Never hinged 40.00
On cover 120.00

42 A49 40c brown ('16) 55.00 40.00
Never hinged 140.00
On cover 125.00
43 A49 50c violet ('16) 16.00 2.10
Never hinged 40.00
On cover 160.00
44 A49 60c brown car ('18) 27.50 *28.00*
Never hinged 70.00
On cover 120.00
a. Printed on both sides *1,750.*
45 A49 60c brown org ('28) 110.00 *225.00*
Never hinged 275.00
On cover 600.00
46 A51 10 l gray grn & red ('16) 425.00 *775.00*
Never hinged 1,050.
Nos. 35-46 (12) 704.90 *1,118.*
Set, never hinged 1,750.

See No. 53.

A1

Government Building at Massaua — A2

1910-29 Unwmk. Engr. *Perf. 13½*

47 A1 15c slate 390.00 30.00
Never hinged 975.00
On cover 175.00
a. Perf. 11 ('29) 40.00 *55.00*
Never hinged 100.00
On cover 600.00
48 A2 25c dark blue 7.25 *17.50*
Never hinged 18.00
On cover 250.00
a. Perf. 12 875.00 875.00

For surcharges see Nos. 51-52.

A3

Farmer Plowing — A4

1914-28

49 A3 5c green 1.20 *2.50*
Never hinged 2.00
On cover 65.00
a. Perf. 11 ('28) 210.00 75.00
Never hinged 525.00
On cover 525.00
50 A4 10c carmine 4.75 *4.25*
Never hinged 12.00
On cover 80.00
a. Perf. 11 ('28) 12.00 *47.50*
Never hinged 30.00
On cover 450.00
b. Perf. 13½x14 62.50 62.50
Never hinged 140.00
On cover *450.00*

No. 47 Surcharged in Red or Black

1916

51 A1 5c on 15c slate (R) 8.75 *15.00*
Never hinged 22.00
On cover 240.00
52 A1 20c on 15c slate 4.00 4.25
Never hinged 10.00
On cover 120.00
a. "CEN" for "CENT" 47.50 47.50
Never hinged 120.00
b. "CENT" omitted 190.00 190.00
Never hinged 450.00
c. "ENT" 47.50 *47.50*
Never hinged 120.00
Set, never hinged 32.00

Italy No. 113 Overprinted in Black — f

1921 Wmk. 140 *Perf. 14*

53 A50 20c brown orange 4.75 *15.00*
Never hinged 12.00
On cover 52.50

Victory Issue

Italian Victory Stamps of 1921 Overprinted type "f" 13mm long

1922

54 A64 5c olive green 2.00 *7.25*
Never hinged 5.00
On cover 125.00
55 A64 10c red 2.00 *7.25*
Never hinged 5.00
On cover 240.00
56 A64 15c slate green 2.00 *11.00*
Never hinged 5.00
On cover 250.00
57 A64 25c ultra 2.00 *11.00*
Never hinged 5.00
On cover 300.00
Nos. 54-57 (4) 8.00 *36.50*
Set, never hinged 20.00
Set on overfranked, philatelic cover 180.00

Somalia Nos. 10-16 Overprinted In Black g

1922 Wmk. 140

58 A1 2c on 1b brn 4.75 *17.50*
Never hinged 12.00
On cover 120.00
a. Pair, one missing "ERITREA" 2,250.
Never hinged 3,000.
59 A1 5c on 2b bl grn 4.75 *13.00*
Never hinged 12.00
On cover 80.00
60 A2 10c on 1a claret 4.75 2.40
Never hinged 12.00
On cover 80.00
61 A2 15c on 2a brn org 4.75 2.40
Never hinged 12.00
On cover 80.00
62 A2 25c on 2½a blue 4.75 2.40
Never hinged 12.00
On cover 120.00
63 A2 50c on 5a yellow 22.50 13.50
Never hinged 55.00
On cover 250.00
a. "ERITREA" double *1,600.*
64 A2 1 l on 10a lilac 22.50 22.50
Never hinged 55.00
On cover 450.00
a. "ERITREA" double 1,600. 1,600.
Never hinged 2,000.
b. Pair, one missing "ERITREA" *3,000.*
Never hinged *4,000.*
Nos. 58-64 (7) 68.75 *73.70*
Set, never hinged 170.00

See Nos. 81-87.

Propagation of the Faith Issue

Italy Nos. 143-146 Overprinted

1923

65 A68 20c ol grn & brn org 12.00 *52.50*
Never hinged 30.00
66 A68 30c claret & brn org 12.00 *52.50*
Never hinged 30.00
67 A68 50c vio & brn org 8.00 *60.00*
Never hinged 20.00
68 A68 1 l bl & brn org 8.00 *92.50*
Never hinged 20.00
Nos. 65-68 (4) 40.00 *257.50*
Set, never hinged 100.00

Fascisti Issue

Italy Nos. 159-164 Overprinted in Red or Black — j

1923 Unwmk. *Perf. 14*

69 A69 10c dk green (R) 11.00 *20.00*
Never hinged 27.50
On cover 325.00
70 A69 30c dk violet (R) 11.00 *20.00*
Never hinged 27.50
On cover 325.00
71 A69 50c brown carmine 11.00 *27.50*
Never hinged 27.50
On cover 325.00

Wmk. 140

72 A70 1 l blue 11.00 *52.50*
Never hinged 27.50
On cover 600.00
73 A70 2 l brown 11.00 *65.00*
Never hinged 27.50
On cover 875.00
74 A71 5 l black & blue (R) 11.00 *95.00*
Never hinged 27.50
Nos. 69-74 (6) 66.00 *280.00*
Set, never hinged 165.00
Set on overfranked, philatelic cover 775.00

Manzoni Issue

Italy Nos. 165-170 Overprinted in Red

1924 *Perf. 14*

75 A72 10c brown red & blk 12.00 *80.00*
Never hinged 30.00
76 A72 15c blue grn & blk 12.00 *80.00*
Never hinged 30.00
77 A72 30c black & slate 12.00 *80.00*
Never hinged 30.00
78 A72 50c org brn & blk 12.00 *80.00*
Never hinged 30.00
79 A72 1 l blue & blk 72.50 *475.00*
Never hinged 180.00
80 A72 5 l violet & blk 475.00 *3,250.*
Never hinged 1,200.
Nos. 75-80 (6) 595.50 *4,045.*
Set, never hinged 1,500.

On Nos. 79 and 80 the overprint is placed vertically at the left side.

Somalia Nos. 10-16 Overprinted type "g" in Blue or Red

1924

Bars over Original Values

81 A1 2c on 1b brn 17.50 *27.50*
Never hinged 45.00
On cover 175.00
a. Pair, one without "ERITREA" 2,400.
Never hinged 2,750.
82 A1 5c on 2b bl grn (R) 17.50 *17.50*
Never hinged 45.00
On cover 110.00
83 A2 10c on 1a rose red 9.50 *16.00*
Never hinged 24.00
On cover 87.50
84 A2 15c on 2a brn org 9.50 *16.00*
Never hinged 24.00
On cover 110.00
a. Pair, one without "ERITREA" 2,400.
Never hinged 3,000.
b. "ERITREA" inverted 1,750. 1,750.
Never hinged 2,250.
85 A2 25c on 2½a bl (R) 9.50 *11.00*
Never hinged 24.00
On cover 140.00
a. Double surcharge 1,200.
Never hinged 1,500.
86 A2 50c on 5a yellow 9.50 *20.00*
Never hinged 24.00
On cover 240.00
87 A2 1 l on 10a lil (R) 9.50 *27.50*
Never hinged 24.00
On cover 475.00
Nos. 81-87 (7) 82.50 *135.50*
Set, never hinged 200.00

Stamps of Italy, 1901-08 Overprinted type "j" in Black

1924

88 A42 1c brown 9.50 *9.50*
Never hinged 23.00
On cover 72.50
a. Inverted overprint 325.00
b. Vertical pair, one without ovpt. 1,750.
Never hinged 2,400.
89 A43 2c orange brown 6.50 *8.00*
Never hinged 14.00
On cover 72.50
b. Vertical pair, one without ovpt. 1,750.
Never hinged 2,400.
90 A48 5c green 9.50 *8.75*
Never hinged 23.00
On cover 47.50
Nos. 88-90 (3) 25.50 *26.25*
Set, never hinged 60.00

Victor Emmanuel Issue

Italy Nos. 175-177 Overprinted — k

1925-26 Unwmk. *Perf. 11*

91 A78 60c brown car 2.40 *9.50*
Never hinged 6.00
On cover 140.00
a. Perf. 13½ 13.00 40.00
Never hinged 32.50
On cover 450.00
92 A78 1 l dark blue 2.40 *14.50*
Never hinged 6.00
On cover 260.00
a. Perf. 13½ *24,000. 9,500.*
Never hinged *36,000.*

Perf. 13½

93 A78 1.25 l dk blue ('26) 4.00 *32.50*
Never hinged 10.00
On cover 600.00
a. Perf. 11 8.00 *40.00*
Never hinged 20.00
On cover 525.00
Nos. 91-93 (3) 8.80 *56.50*
Set, never hinged 22.00

Saint Francis of Assisi Issue

Italian Stamps of 1926 Overprinted

1926 Wmk. 140 *Perf. 14*

94 A79 20c gray green 2.40 *14.00*
Never hinged 6.00
On cover 125.00
95 A80 40c dark violet 2.40 *14.00*
Never hinged 6.00
On cover 160.00
96 A81 60c red violet 2.40 *26.00*
Never hinged 6.00
On cover 160.00

Overprinted in Red

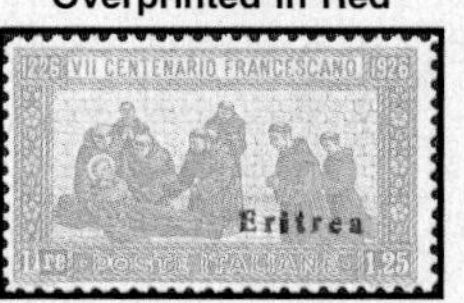

Unwmk. *Perf. 11*

97 A82 1.25 l dark blue 2.40 *36.00*
Never hinged 6.00
On cover 275.00

Perf. 14

98 A83 5 l + 2.50 l ol grn 8.00 *72.50*
Never hinged 20.00
Nos. 94-98 (5) 17.60 *162.50*
Set, never hinged 44.00
Set on overfranked philatelic cover 475.00

Italian Stamps of 1926 Overprinted type "f" in Black

1926 Wmk. 140 *Perf. 14*

99 A46 75c dk red & rose 80.00 20.00
Never hinged 200.00
On cover 120.00
a. Double overprint 450.00

100 A46 1.25 l blue & ultra 40.00 20.00
Never hinged 100.00
On cover 275.00
101 A46 2.50 l dk green & org 175.00 72.50
Never hinged 425.00
On cover 725.00
Nos. 99-101 (3) 295.00 112.50
Set, never hinged 725.00

Volta Issue

Type of Italy, 1927, Overprinted — o

1927
102 A84 20c purple 6.50 *40.00*
Never hinged 16.00
On cover 275.00
103 A84 50c deep orange 9.50 *27.50*
Never hinged 24.00
On cover 275.00
a. Double overprint 200.00
Never hinged 320.00
104 A84 1.25 l brt blue 14.00 *65.00*
Never hinged 35.00
On cover 525.00
Nos. 102-104 (3) 30.00 *132.50*
Set, never hinged 75.00

Italian Stamps of 1925-28 Overprinted type "a" in Black

1928-29
105 A86 7½c lt brown ('29) 24.00 *72.50*
Never hinged 60.00
On cover 325.00
106 A86 50c brt violet 87.50 65.00
Never hinged 210.00
On cover 160.00
Set, never hinged 270.00

Italian Stamps of 1927-28 Overprinted type "f"

1928-29
107 A86 50c brt violet 72.50 *60.00*
Never hinged 175.00
On cover 140.00

Unwmk. ***Perf. 11***
107A A85 1.75 l deep brown 95.00 52.50
Never hinged 240.00
On cover 190.00

Italy No. 192 Overprinted type "o"

1928 **Wmk. 140** ***Perf. 14***
108 A85 50c brown & slate 24.00 12.00
Never hinged 60.00
On cover 65.00

Monte Cassino Issue

Types of 1929 Issue of Italy Overprinted in Red or Blue

1929 ***Perf. 14***
109 A96 20c dk green (R) 6.50 *22.50*
Never hinged 16.00
On cover 275.00
110 A96 25c red orange (Bl) 6.50 *22.50*
Never hinged 16.00
On cover 200.00
111 A98 50c + 10c crim (Bl) 6.50 *24.00*
Never hinged 16.00
On cover 160.00
112 A98 75c + 15c ol brn (R) 6.50 *24.00*
Never hinged 16.00
On cover 275.00
113 A96 1.25 l + 25c dl vio (R) 14.50 *45.00*
Never hinged 35.00
On cover 340.00
114 A98 5 l + 1 l saph (R) 14.50 *47.50*
Never hinged 35.00

Overprinted in Red

Unwmk.
115 A100 10 l + 2 l gray brn 14.50 *72.50*
Never hinged 35.00
Nos. 109-115 (7) 69.50 *258.00*
Set, never hinged 170.00
Set on overfranked philatelic cover 475.00

Royal Wedding Issue

Type of Italian Stamps of 1930 Overprinted

1930 **Wmk. 140**
116 A101 20c yellow green 3.25 *9.50*
Never hinged 8.00
On cover 140.00
117 A101 50c + 10c dp orange 2.40 *9.50*
Never hinged 6.00
On cover 190.00
118 A101 1.25 l + 25c rose red 2.40 *19.00*
Never hinged 6.00
On cover 300.00
Nos. 116-118 (3) 8.05 *38.00*
Set, never hinged 20.00
Set on overfranked, philatelic cover 175.00

Lancer — A5

Scene in Massaua A6

2c, 35c, Lancer. 5c, 10c, Postman. 15c, Lineman. 25c, Askari (infantryman). 2 l, Railroad viaduct. 5 l, Asmara Deghe Selam. 10 l, Camels.

1930 **Wmk. 140** **Litho.** ***Perf. 14***
119 A5 2c brt bl & blk 4.75 *20.00*
Never hinged 11.00
On cover 160.00
120 A5 5c dk vio & blk 8.00 2.40
Never hinged 20.00
On cover 87.50
121 A5 10c yel brn & blk 8.00 1.25
Never hinged 20.00
On cover 47.50
122 A5 15c dk grn & blk 8.00 1.60
Never hinged 20.00
On cover 87.50
123 A5 25c gray grn & blk 8.00 1.25
Never hinged 20.00
On cover 55.00
124 A5 35c red brn & blk 12.50 *35.00*
Never hinged 30.00
On cover 200.00
125 A6 1 l dk bl & blk 8.00 1.25
Never hinged 20.00
On cover 55.00
126 A6 2 l choc & blk 12.50 *40.00*
Never hinged 30.00
On cover 375.00
127 A6 5 l ol grn & blk 24.00 *52.50*
Never hinged 60.00
On cover 1,100.
128 A6 10 l dl bl & blk 32.50 *100.00*
Never hinged 80.00
Nos. 119-128 (10) 126.25 *255.25*
Set, never hinged 310.00
Set on overfranked philatelic cover 475.00

Ferrucci Issue
Types of Italian Stamps of 1930 Overprinted type "f" in Red or Blue

1930
129 A102 20c violet (R) 6.50 *6.50*
Never hinged 16.00
On cover 160.00
130 A103 25c dk green (R) 6.50 *6.50*
Never hinged 16.00
On cover 190.00
131 A103 50c black (R) 6.50 *12.00*
Never hinged 16.00
On cover 160.00
132 A103 1.25 l dp blue (R) 6.50 *22.50*
Never hinged 16.00
On cover 350.00
133 A104 5 l + 2 l dp car (Bl) 14.50 *47.50*
Never hinged 30.00
Nos. 129-133 (5) 40.50 *95.00*
Set, never hinged 99.00
Set on overfranked philatelic cover 350.00

Virgil Issue
Types of Italian Stamps of 1930 Overprinted in Red or Blue

1930 **Photo.**
134 A106 15c violet black 1.25 *12.00*
Never hinged 3.25
On cover 175.00
135 A106 20c orange brown 1.25 *4.75*
Never hinged 3.25
On cover 100.00
136 A106 25c dark green 1.25 *4.75*
Never hinged 3.25
On cover 95.00
137 A106 30c lt brown 1.25 *4.75*
Never hinged 3.25
On cover 100.00
138 A106 50c dull violet 1.25 *4.75*
Never hinged 3.25
On cover 87.50
139 A106 75c rose red 1.25 *9.50*
Never hinged 3.25
On cover 210.00
140 A106 1.25 l gray blue 1.25 *12.00*
Never hinged 3.25
On cover 300.00

Unwmk. **Engr.**
141 A106 5 l + 1.50 l dk vio 4.75 *47.50*
Never hinged 11.00
142 A106 10 l + 2.50 l ol brn 4.75 *72.50*
Never hinged 11.00
Nos. 134-142 (9) 18.25 *172.50*
Set, never hinged 44.00
Set on overfranked philatelic cover 475.00

Saint Anthony of Padua Issue
Types of Italian Stamps of 1931 Overprinted type "f" in Blue, Red or Black

1931 **Photo.** **Wmk. 140**
143 A116 20c brown (Bl) 1.60 *22.50*
Never hinged 4.50
On cover 120.00
144 A116 25c green (R) 1.60 *8.00*
Never hinged 4.50
On cover 120.00
145 A118 30c gray brn (Bl) 1.60 *8.00*
Never hinged 4.50
On cover 180.00
146 A118 50c dl violet (Bl) 1.60 *8.00*
Never hinged 4.50
On cover 120.00
147 A120 1.25 l slate bl (R) 1.60 *40.00*
Never hinged 5.00
On cover 400.00

Unwmk. **Engr.**
148 A121 75c black (R) 1.60 *22.50*
Never hinged 5.00
On cover 325.00
149 A122 5 l + 2.50 l dk brn (Bk) 11.00 *80.00*
Never hinged 27.50
Nos. 143-149 (7) 20.60 *189.00*
Set, never hinged 55.00
Set on overfranked philatelic cover 540.00

Victor Emmanuel III — A13

1931 **Photo.** **Wmk. 140**
150 A13 7½c olive brown 1.60 *6.50*
Never hinged 4.00
On cover 80.00
151 A13 20c slate bl & car 1.60 .25
Never hinged 4.00
On cover 2.50
152 A13 30c ol grn & brn vio 1.60 .25
Never hinged 4.00
On cover 2.50
153 A13 40c bl & yel grn 2.40 .25
Never hinged 6.00
On cover 14.50
154 A13 50c bis brn & ol 1.60 .25
Never hinged 4.00
On cover 2.50
155 A13 75c carmine rose 4.75 .25
Never hinged 12.00
On cover 14.50
156 A13 1.25 l violet & indigo 6.50 6.50
Never hinged 16.00
On cover 14.50
157 A13 2.50 l dull green 6.50 14.50
Never hinged 16.00
On cover 225.00
Nos. 150-157 (8) 26.55 28.75
Set, never hinged 65.00
Set on overfranked philatelic cover 140.00

Camel A14

Temple Ruins — A18

Designs: 2c, 10c, Camel. 5c, 15c, Shark fishery. 25c, Baobab tree. 35c, Pastoral scene. 2 l, African elephant. 5 l, Eritrean man. 10 l, Eritrean woman.

1934 **Photo.** **Wmk. 140**
158 A14 2c deep blue 2.40 *4.75*
Never hinged 6.00
On cover 35.00
159 A14 5c black 4.00 .40
Never hinged 10.00
On cover 3.25
160 A14 10c brown 4.00 .35
Never hinged 10.00
On cover 3.25
161 A14 15c orange brn 4.75 *1.60*
Never hinged 12.00
On cover 32.50
162 A14 25c gray green 4.00 .35
Never hinged 10.00
On cover 3.25
163 A14 35c purple 12.50 *9.50*
Never hinged 30.00
On cover 52.50
164 A18 1 l dk blue gray .80 .35
Never hinged 2.00
On cover 3.25
165 A14 2 l olive black 35.00 3.25
Never hinged 87.50
On cover 20.00
166 A18 5 l carmine rose 19.00 6.50
Never hinged 47.50
On cover 260.00
167 A18 10 l red orange 27.50 *22.50*
Never hinged 67.50
On cover 525.00
Nos. 158-167 (10) 113.95 *49.55*
Set, never hinged 275.00
Set on overfranked philatelic cover 275.00

Abruzzi Issue

Types of 1934 Issue Overprinted in Black or Red

1934
168 A14 10c dull blue (R) 22.50 *32.50*
Never hinged 55.00
On cover *400.00*
169 A14 15c blue 16.00 *32.50*
Never hinged 40.00
On cover *400.00*
170 A14 35c green (R) 9.50 *32.50*
Never hinged 24.00
On cover *450.00*
171 A18 1 l copper red 9.50 *32.50*
Never hinged 24.00
On cover *450.00*
172 A14 2 l rose red 27.50 *32.50*
Never hinged 67.50
173 A18 5 l purple (R) 19.00 *55.00*
Never hinged 47.50
174 A18 10 l olive grn (R) 19.00 *72.50*
Never hinged 47.50
Nos. 168-174 (7) 123.00 *290.00*
Set, never hinged 300.00
Set on overfranked philatelic cover 550.00

Grant's Gazelle A22

1934 **Photo.**

175 A22 5c ol grn & brn 5.50 *22.50*
Never hinged 13.50
On cover *350.00*
176 A22 10c yel brn & blk 5.50 *22.50*
Never hinged 13.50
On cover *300.00*
177 A22 20c scar & indigo 5.50 *20.00*
Never hinged 13.50
On cover *300.00*
178 A22 50c dk vio & brn 5.50 *20.00*
Never hinged 13.50
On cover *275.00*
179 A22 60c org brn & ind 5.50 *27.50*
Never hinged 13.50
On cover *350.00*
180 A22 1.25 l dk bl & grn 5.50 *47.50*
Never hinged 13.50
On cover *450.00*
Nos. 175-180 (6) 33.00 *160.00*
Set, never hinged 80.00
Set on overfranked philatelic cover 350.00

Second Colonial Arts Exhibition, Naples. See Nos. C1-C6.

SEMI-POSTAL STAMPS

Many issues of Italy and Italian Colonies include one or more semipostal denominations. To avoid splitting sets, these issues are generally listed as regular postage, airmail, etc., unless all values carry a surtax.

Italy Nos. B1-B3 Overprinted type "f"

1915-16 **Wmk. 140** ***Perf. 14***

B1 SP1 10c + 5c rose 4.00 *16.00*
Never hinged 10.00
On cover 120.00
a. "EPITREA" 32.50 *45.00*
b. Inverted overprint 800.00 800.00
B2 SP2 15c + 5c slate 32.50 *27.50*
Never hinged 80.00
On cover 225.00
B3 SP2 20c + 5c orange 4.75 *35.00*
Never hinged 12.00
On cover 325.00
a. "EPITREA" 80.00 *110.00*
b. Inverted overprint 800.00 800.00
c. Pair, one without ovpt. — *4,500.*
Nos. B1-B3 (3) 41.25 *78.50*
Set, never hinged 102.00

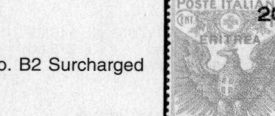

No. B2 Surcharged

1916

B4 SP2 20c on 15c+5c slate 32.50 *35.00*
Never hinged 80.00
On cover 325.00
a. "EPITREA" 80.00 *110.00*
b. Pair, one without overprint 2,000.
Never hinged 2,500.
Nos. B1-B4 on overfranked philatelic cover *275.00*

Counterfeits exist of the minor varieties of Nos. B1, B3-B4.

Holy Year Issue
Italy Nos. B20-B25 Overprinted in Black or Red

1925 ***Perf. 12***

B5 SP4 20c + 10c dk grn & brn 4.00 *24.00*
Never hinged 10.00
On cover 225.00
B6 SP4 30c + 15c dk brn & brn 4.00 *27.50*
Never hinged 10.00
On cover 225.00
a. Double overprint
B7 SP4 50c + 25c vio & brn 4.00 *24.00*
Never hinged 10.00
On cover 225.00
B8 SP4 60c + 30c dp rose & brn 4.00 *32.50*
Never hinged 10.00
On cover 300.00
a. Inverted overprint
B9 SP8 1 l + 50c dp bl & vio (R) 4.00 *40.00*
Never hinged 10.00
B10 SP8 5 l + 2.50 l org brn & vio (R) 4.00 *60.00*
Never hinged 10.00
Nos. B5-B10 (6) 24.00 *208.00*
Set, never hinged 60.00
Set on overfranked philatelic cover 500.00

Colonial Institute Issue

"Peace" Substituting Spade for Sword — SP1

1926 **Typo.** ***Perf. 14***

B11 SP1 5c + 5c brown 1.20 *9.50*
Never hinged 3.00
On cover 180.00
B12 SP1 10c + 5c olive grn 1.20 *9.50*
Never hinged 3.00
On cover 140.00
B13 SP1 20c + 5c blue grn 1.20 *9.50*
Never hinged 3.00
On cover 110.00
B14 SP1 40c + 5c brown red 1.20 *9.50*
Never hinged 3.00
On cover 110.00
B15 SP1 60c + 5c orange 1.20 *9.50*
Never hinged 3.00
On cover 180.00
B16 SP1 1 l + 5c blue 1.20 *20.00*
Never hinged 3.00
On cover 300.00
Nos. B11-B16 (6) 7.20 *67.50*
Set, never hinged 18.00
Set on overfranked philatelic cover 260.00

The surtax of 5c on each stamp was for the Italian Colonial Institute.

Italian Semi-Postal Stamps of 1926 Overprinted

1927 **Unwmk.** ***Perf. 11½***

B17 SP10 40c + 20c dk brn & blk 4.00 *45.00*
Never hinged 10.00
On cover 190.00
B18 SP10 60c + 30c brn red & ol brn 4.00 *45.00*
Never hinged 10.00
On cover 225.00
B19 SP10 1.25 l + 60c dp bl & blk 4.00 *65.00*
Never hinged 10.00
On cover 400.00
B20 SP10 5 l + 2.50 l dk grn & blk 6.50 *100.00*
Never hinged 16.00
Nos. B17-B20 (4) 18.50 *255.00*
Set, never hinged 46.00
Set on overfranked philatelic cover 600.00

The surtax on these stamps was for the charitable work of the Voluntary Militia for Italian National Defense.

Fascism and Victory — SP2

1928 **Wmk. 140** **Typo.** ***Perf. 14***

B21 SP2 20c + 5c blue grn 3.25 *14.00*
Never hinged 8.00
On cover 190.00
B22 SP2 30c + 5c red 3.25 *14.00*
Never hinged 8.00
On cover 190.00
B23 SP2 50c + 10c purple 3.25 *24.00*
Never hinged 8.00
On cover 190.00
B24 SP2 1.25 l + 20c dk blue 4.00 *32.50*
Never hinged 10.00
On cover 525.00
Nos. B21-B24 (4) 13.75 *84.50*
Set, never hinged 34.00
Set on overfranked philatelic cover 325.00

The surtax was for the Society Africana d'Italia, whose 46th anniv. was commemorated by the issue.

Types of Italian Semi-Postal Stamps of 1928 Overprinted type "f"

1929 **Unwmk.** ***Perf. 11***

B25 SP10 30c + 10c red & blk 4.75 *27.50*
Never hinged 12.00
On cover 225.00
B26 SP10 50c + 20c vio & blk 4.75 *30.00*
Never hinged 12.00
On cover 225.00
B27 SP10 1.25 l + 50c brn & bl 7.25 *52.50*
Never hinged 18.00
On cover 475.00
B28 SP10 5 l + 2 l olive grn & blk 7.25 *100.00*
Never hinged 18.00
Nos. B25-B28 (4) 24.00 *210.00*
Set, never hinged 60.00
Set on overfranked philatelic cover 600.00

Surtax for the charitable work of the Voluntary Militia for Italian Natl. Defense.

Types of Italian Semi-Postal Stamps of 1930 Overprinted type "f" in Black or Red

1930 ***Perf. 14***

B29 SP10 30c + 10c dk grn & bl grn (Bk) 35.00 *65.00*
Never hinged 87.50
On cover 325.00
B30 SP10 50c + 10c dk grn & vio 35.00 *100.00*
Never hinged 87.50
On cover 360.00
B31 SP10 1.25 l + 30c ol brn & red brn 35.00 *100.00*
Never hinged 87.50
On cover 550.00
B32 SP10 5 l + 1.50 l ind & grn 120.00 *275.00*
Never hinged 300.00
Nos. B29-B32 (4) 225.00 *540.00*
Set, never hinged 560.00
Set on overfranked philatelic cover 1,050.

Surtax for the charitable work of the Voluntary Militia for Italian Natl. Defense.

Agriculture — SP3

1930 **Photo.** **Wmk. 140**

B33 SP3 50c + 20c ol brn 4.00 *25.00*
Never hinged 10.00
On cover 210.00
B34 SP3 1.25 l + 20c dp bl 4.00 *25.00*
Never hinged 10.00
On cover 300.00
B35 SP3 1.75 l + 20c green 4.00 *27.50*
Never hinged 10.00
On cover 375.00
B36 SP3 2.55 l + 50c purple 9.50 *45.00*
Never hinged 23.00
On cover 600.00
B37 SP3 5 l + 1 l dp car 9.50 *67.50*
Never hinged 23.00
Nos. B33-B37 (5) 31.00 *190.00*
Set, never hinged 76.00
Set on overfranked philatelic cover 350.00

Italian Colonial Agricultural Institute, 25th anniv. The surtax aided that institution.

AIR POST STAMPS

Desert Scene AP1

Design: 80c, 1 l, 2 l, Plane and globe.

Wmk. Crowns (140)

1934, Oct. 17 **Photo.** ***Perf. 14***

C1 AP1 25c sl bl & org red 5.50 *22.50*
Never hinged 13.50
On cover 350.00
C2 AP1 50c grn & indigo 5.50 *20.00*
Never hinged 13.50
On cover 225.00
C3 AP1 75c brn & org red 5.50 *20.00*
Never hinged 13.50
On cover 300.00
C4 AP1 80c org brn & ol grn 5.50 *22.50*
Never hinged 13.50
On cover 350.00
C5 AP1 1 l scar & ol grn 5.50 *27.50*
Never hinged 13.50
On cover 400.00
C6 AP1 2 l dk bl & brn 5.50 *47.50*
Never hinged 13.50
On cover 550.00
Nos. C1-C6 (6) 33.00 *160.00*
Set, never hinged 81.00
Set on overfranked philatelic cover 450.00

Second Colonial Arts Exhibition, Naples.

Plowing AP3

Plane and Cacti AP6

Designs: 25c, 1.50 l, Plowing. 50c, 2 l, Plane over mountain pass. 60c, 5 l, Plane and trees. 75c, 10 l, Plane and cacti. 1 l, 3 l, Bridge.

1936 **Photo.**

C7 AP3 25c deep green 4.75 *4.75*
Never hinged 12.00
On cover 72.50
C8 AP3 50c dark brown 3.25 .35
Never hinged 8.00
On cover 2.50
C9 AP3 60c brown orange 6.50 *16.00*
Never hinged 16.00
On cover 240.00
C10 AP6 75c orange brown 4.75 1.60
Never hinged 12.00
On cover 20.00
C11 AP3 1 l deep blue 1.60 .35
Never hinged 4.00
On cover 2.50
C12 AP3 1.50 l purple 6.50 .85
Never hinged 16.00
On cover 40.00
C13 AP3 2 l gray blue 6.50 *3.25*
Never hinged 16.00
On cover 120.00
C14 AP3 3 l copper red 25.00 27.50
Never hinged 62.50
On cover 250.00
C15 AP3 5 l green 19.00 8.00
Never hinged 47.50
On cover 550.00
C16 AP6 10 l rose red 45.00 27.50
Never hinged 110.00
On cover *1,050.*
Nos. C7-C16 (10) 122.85 90.15
Set, never hinged 300.00
Set on overfranked philatelic cover 450.00

AIR POST SEMI-POSTAL STAMPS

King Victor Emmanuel III — SPAP1

1934 Wmk. 140 Photo. *Perf. 14*

CB1 SPAP1 25c + 10c 9.50 *27.50*
Never hinged 24.00
On cover *325.00*
CB2 SPAP1 50c + 10c 9.50 *27.50*
Never hinged 24.00
On cover *325.00*
CB3 SPAP1 75c + 15c 9.50 *27.50*
Never hinged 24.00
On cover *350.00*
CB4 SPAP1 80c + 15c 9.50 *27.50*
Never hinged 24.00
On cover *450.00*
CB5 SPAP1 1 l + 20c 9.50 *27.50*
Never hinged 24.00
On cover *475.00*
CB6 SPAP1 2 l + 20c 9.50 *27.50*
Never hinged 24.00
CB7 SPAP1 3 l + 25c 27.50 *125.00*
Never hinged 67.50
CB8 SPAP1 5 l + 25c 27.50 *125.00*
Never hinged 67.50
CB9 SPAP1 10 l + 30c 27.50 *125.00*
Never hinged 67.50
CB10 SPAP1 25 l + 2 l 27.50 *125.00*
Never hinged 67.50
Nos. CB1-CB10 (10) 167.00 *665.00*
Set, never hinged 410.00
Set on overfranked philatelic flown cover 1,900.

65th birthday of King Victor Emmanuel III and the nonstop flight from Rome to Mogadiscio. Used values are for stamps canceled to order.

AIR POST SEMI-POSTAL OFFICIAL STAMP

Type of Air Post Semi-Postal Stamps, 1934, Overprinted in Black

1934 Wmk. 140 *Perf. 14*

CBO1 SPAP1 25 l + 2 l cop red *2,800.*
Never hinged *5,500.*
On flight cover 3,250.

SPECIAL DELIVERY STAMPS

Special Delivery Stamps of Italy, Overprinted type "a"

1907 Wmk. 140 *Perf. 14*

E1 SD1 25c rose red 24.00 20.00
Never hinged 60.00
On cover *180.00*
a. Double overprint — —

1909

E2 SD2 30c blue & rose 145.00 *240.00*
Never hinged 375.00
On cover *675.00*

1920

E3 SD1 50c dull red 4.00 *24.00*
Never hinged 10.00
On cover *275.00*

"Italia" SD1

1924 Engr. Unwmk.

E4 SD1 60c dk red & brn 6.50 *24.00*
Never hinged 16.00
On cover *180.00*
a. Perf. 13½ 14.00 *40.00*
Never hinged 35.00
On cover —

E5 SD1 2 l dk blue & red 17.50 *27.50*
Never hinged 42.50
On cover *525.00*
Set, never hinged 59.00

For surcharges see Nos. E6-E8.

Nos. E4 and E5 Surcharged in Dark Blue or Red

v

w

1926

E6 SD1 70c on 60c (Bl) 6.50 *16.00*
Never hinged 17.50
On cover *180.00*
E7 SD1 2.50 l on 2 l (R) 17.50 *27.50*
Never hinged 42.50
On cover *600.00*
Set, never hinged 60.00

Type of 1924 Surcharged in Blue or Black

1927-35 *Perf. 11*

E8 SD1 1.25 l on 60c dk red & brn (Bl) 16.00 4.00
Never hinged 40.00
On cover *12.00*
a. Perf. 14 (Bl) ('35) 110.00 24.00
Never hinged 275.00
On cover *200.00*
b. Perf. 11 (Bk) ('35) *9,500.* 1,250.
Never hinged *14,500.*
On cover *4,750.*
c. Perf. 14 (Bk) ('35) 400.00 65.00
Never hinged 1,000.
On cover *450.00*

AUTHORIZED DELIVERY STAMP

Authorized Delivery Stamp of Italy, No. EY2, Overprinted Type "f" in Black

1939-41 Wmk. 140 *Perf. 14*

EY1 AD2 10c dk brown ('41) .80
Never hinged 2.00
a. 10c reddish brown 27.50 *47.50*
Never hinged 72.50
On cover *475.00*

On No. EY1a, which was used in Italian East Africa, the overprint hits the figures "10." On No. EY1, which was sold in Rome, the overprint falls above the 10's.

POSTAGE DUE STAMPS

Postage Due Stamps of Italy Overprinted type "a" at Top

1903 Wmk. 140 *Perf. 14*

J1 D3 5c buff & mag 24.00 *47.50*
Never hinged 47.50
On cover *550.00*
a. Double overprint 550.00
J2 D3 10c buff & mag 16.00 *47.50*
Never hinged 32.50
On cover *325.00*
J3 D3 20c buff & mag 16.00 *32.50*
Never hinged 32.50
On cover *325.00*
J4 D3 30c buff & mag 24.00 *35.00*
Never hinged 47.50
On cover *475.00*
J5 D3 40c buff & mag 80.00 *72.50*
Never hinged 160.00
On cover *475.00*
J6 D3 50c buff & mag 87.50 72.50
Never hinged 175.00
On cover *325.00*
J7 D3 60c buff & mag 24.00 *72.50*
Never hinged 47.50
On cover *725.00*
J8 D3 1 l blue & mag 16.00 *40.00*
Never hinged 32.50
On cover *550.00*
J9 D3 2 l blue & mag 200.00 *180.00*
Never hinged 400.00
On cover *1,250.*
J10 D3 5 l blue & mag 325.00 340.00
Never hinged 650.00
J11 D3 10 l blue & mag 3,600. 875.00
Never hinged 7,200.
Set, #J1-J10, never hinged 1,600.

Same with Overprint at Bottom

1920-22

J1b D3 5c buff & magenta 4.75 *16.00*
Never hinged 9.50
On cover *540.00*
c. Numeral and ovpt. inverted 550.00 550.00
Never hinged —
J2a D3 10c buff & magenta 8.00 *16.00*
Never hinged 16.00
On cover *260.00*
J3a D3 20c buff & magenta 950.00 475.00
Never hinged 1,900.
On cover *3,000.*
J4a D3 30c buff & magenta 65.00 65.00
Never hinged 130.00
On cover *460.00*
J5a D3 40c buff & magenta 47.50 52.50
Never hinged 95.00
On cover *525.00*
J6a D3 50c buff & magenta 24.00 *47.50*
Never hinged 47.50
On cover *260.00*
J7a D3 60c buff & magenta 24.00 *47.50*
Never hinged 47.50
On cover *650.00*
J8a D3 1 l blue & magenta 40.00 47.50
Never hinged 80.00
On cover *525.00*
J9a D3 2 l blue & magenta 1,900. 1,450.
Never hinged 3,750.
On cover *11,000.*
J10a D3 5 l blue & magenta 475.00 350.00
Never hinged 950.00
J11a D3 10 l blue & magenta 47.50 *100.00*
Never hinged 95.00
Set, never hinged 7,125.

1903 Wmk. 140

J12 D4 50 l yellow 875.00 300.00
Never hinged 1,750.
J13 D4 100 l blue 475.00 180.00
Never hinged 950.00
Set, never hinged 2,700.

1927

J14 D3 60c buff & brown 160.00 *240.00*
Never hinged 325.00
On cover *725.00*

Postage Due Stamps of Italy, 1934, Overprinted type "j" in Black

1934

J15 D6 5c brown .80 *16.00*
Never hinged 2.00
On cover *550.00*
J16 D6 10c blue .80 *3.25*
Never hinged 2.00
On cover *275.00*
J17 D6 20c rose red 4.00 *4.75*
Never hinged 10.00
On cover *260.00*
a. Inverted overprint — —
J18 D6 25c green 4.00 *6.50*
Never hinged 10.00
On cover *260.00*
J19 D6 30c red orange 4.00 *16.00*
Never hinged 10.00
On cover *400.00*
J20 D6 40c black brown 4.00 *16.00*
Never hinged 10.00
On cover *475.00*
J21 D6 50c violet 4.00 2.40
Never hinged 10.00
On cover *200.00*
J22 D6 60c black 8.00 *24.00*
Never hinged 20.00
On cover *550.00*
J23 D7 1 l red orange 4.00 3.25
Never hinged 10.00
On cover *400.00*
a. Inverted overprint 550.00 —
Never hinged 800.00
J24 D7 2 l green 16.00 *47.50*
Never hinged 40.00
On cover *550.00*
J25 D7 5 l violet 28.00 *55.00*
Never hinged 70.00
J26 D7 10 l blue 32.50 *65.00*
Never hinged 82.50
J27 D7 20 l carmine rose 40.00 *72.50*
Never hinged 100.00
a. Inverted overprint 550.00 —
Never hinged 800.00
Nos. J15-J27 (13) 150.10 *332.15*
Set, never hinged 375.00

PARCEL POST STAMPS

These stamps were used by affixing them to the way bill so that one half remained on it following the parcel, the other half staying on the receipt given the sender. Most used halves are right halves. Complete stamps were obtainable canceled, probably to order. Both unused and used values are for complete stamps.

Parcel Post Stamps of Italy, 1914-17, Overprinted type "j" in Black on Each Half

1916 Wmk. 140 *Perf. 13½*

Q1 PP2 5c brown 145.00 *225.00*
Never hinged 290.00
Q2 PP2 10c deep blue *2,600.* *4,250.*
Never hinged 5,250.
Q3 PP2 25c red 290.00 *350.00*
Never hinged 575.00
Q4 PP2 50c orange 72.50 *225.00*
Never hinged 145.00
Q5 PP2 1 l violet 145.00 *225.00*
Never hinged 290.00
Q6 PP2 2 l green 110.00 *225.00*
Never hinged 225.00
Q7 PP2 3 l bister 875.00 *625.00*
Never hinged 1,750.
Q8 PP2 4 l slate 875.00 *625.00*
Never hinged 1,750.
Set #Q1, Q3-Q8, never hinged 5,200.

Halves Used, Each

Q1	4.25
Q2	85.00
Q3	5.50
Q4	3.00
Q5	3.00
Q6	8.50
Q7	19.00
Q8	19.00

Overprinted type "f" on Each Half

1917-24

Q9 PP2 5c brown 3.25 *8.00*
Never hinged 6.50
On parcel post receipt card *250.00*
Q10 PP2 10c deep blue 3.25 *8.00*
Never hinged 6.50
Q11 PP2 20c black 3.25 *8.00*
Never hinged 6.50
Q12 PP2 25c red 3.25 *8.00*
Never hinged 6.50
On parcel post receipt card *120.00*
Q13 PP2 50c orange 6.50 *12.00*
Never hinged 13.00
On parcel post receipt card *120.00*
Q14 PP2 1 l violet 6.50 *12.00*
Never hinged 13.00
On parcel post receipt card *160.00*
Q15 PP2 2 l green 6.50 *12.00*
Never hinged 13.00
Q16 PP2 3 l bister 6.50 *12.00*
Never hinged 13.00
Q17 PP2 4 l slate 6.50 *20.00*
Never hinged 13.00
Q18 PP2 10 l rose lil ('24) 87.50 *190.00*
Never hinged 175.00
Q19 PP2 12 l red brn ('24) 240.00 *375.00*
Never hinged 475.00
Q20 PP2 15 l olive grn ('24) 240.00 *375.00*
Never hinged 475.00
Q21 PP2 20 l brn vio ('24) 325.00 *525.00*
Never hinged 650.00
Nos. Q9-Q21 (13) 938.00 *1,565.*
Set, never hinged 1,860.

Halves Used, Each

Q9	1.20
Q10	1.20
Q11	1.20
Q12	1.20
Q13	1.20
Q14	1.20
Q15	1.60
Q16	4.25
Q17	4.25
Q18	8.50
Q19	12.50
Q20	12.50
Q21	17.00

Parcel Post Stamps of Italy, 1927-39, Overprinted type "f" on Each Half

1927-37

Q21A PP3 10c dp blue ('37) *8,750.* 1,250.
Never hinged *13,500.*
Q22 PP3 25c red ('37) 550.00 72.50
Never hinged 1,100.
Q23 PP3 30c ultra ('29) 4.00 *24.00*
Never hinged 8.00
On parcel post receipt card *200.00*
Q24 PP3 50c orange ('36) 725.00 47.50
Never hinged 1,450.
Q25 PP3 60c red ('29) 4.00 *24.00*
Never hinged 8.00
On parcel post receipt card *200.00*
Q26 PP3 1 l brown vio ('36) 325.00 47.50
Never hinged 650.00
a. 1 l lilac 400.00 47.50
Never hinged 800.00
On parcel post receipt card *125.00*

Q27 PP3 2 l green ('36) 325.00 47.50
Never hinged 650.00
On parcel post receipt card *150.00*
Q28 PP3 3 l bister 9.50 *40.00*
Never hinged 19.00
Q29 PP3 4 l gray 9.50 *40.00*
Never hinged 19.00
Q30 PP3 10 l rose lilac ('36) 525.00 800.00
Never hinged 1,050.
Q31 PP3 20 l lilac brn ('36) 525.00 800.00
Never hinged 1,050.
Nos. Q22-Q31 (10) 3,002.
Set, never hinged 6,000.
Nos. Q21A-Q31 (11) 3,193.

Halves Used, Each

Q21A	27.50
Q22	1.20
Q23	.65
Q24	1.70
Q25	.85
Q26	1.25
Q26a	1.25
Q27	1.25
Q28	1.25
Q29	1.25
Q30	37.50
Q31	37.50

ESTONIA

e-ˈstō-nē-ə

LOCATION — Northern Europe, bordering on the Baltic Sea and the Gulf of Finland
GOVT. — Republic
AREA — 18,353 sq. mi.
POP. — 1,542,000 (1986)
CAPITAL — Tallinn

Formerly a part of Russia, Estonia declared its independence in 1918. In 1940 it was incorporated in the Union of Soviet Socialist Republics.

100 Kopecks = 1 Ruble (1918)
100 Penni = 1 Mark (1919)
100 Sents = 1 Kroon (1928)

Watermark

Wmk. 207 — Arms of Finland in the Sheet

Watermark covers a large part of sheet.

A1

A2

1918-19 Unwmk. Litho. *Imperf.*
1 A1 5k pale red 1.00 .85
2 A1 15k bright blue 1.00 .85
3 A2 35p brown ('19) 1.00 .90
a. Printed on both sides 200.00
b. 35p olive 80.00 80.00
4 A2 70p olive grn ('19) 1.60 *2.10*
Nos. 1-4 (4) 4.60 4.70

Nos. 1-4 exist privately perforated.

Russian Stamps of 1909-17 Handstamped in Violet or Black

1919, May 7 *Perf. 14, 14½x15, 13½*
8 A14 1k orange *5,500.* *5,500.*
9 A14 2k green 45.00 *45.00*
10 A14 3k red 52.50 *52.50*
11 A14 5k claret 45.00 *45.00*
12 A15 10k dk bl (Bk) 85.00 *85.00*
13 A15 10k dk bl 500.00 *500.00*
14 A14 10k on 7k lt bl *1,500.* *1,500.*
15 A11 15k red brn & bl 67.50 *67.50*
16 A11 25k grn & vio 77.50 *77.50*
17 A11 35k red brn & grn 5,500. *5,500.*
18 A8 50k vio & grn 190.00 190.00
19 A9 1r pale brn, brn & org 325.00 325.00
20 A13 10r scar, yel & gray *9,500.* *9,500.*

Imperf
21 A14 1k orange 62.50 *62.50*
22 A14 2k green *950.00* *950.00*
23 A14 3k red 85.00 85.00
24 A9 1r pale brn, brn & red org *425.00* *425.00*
25 A12 3½r maroon & grn *1,200.* *1,200.*
26 A13 5r dk bl, grn & pale bl *1,500.* *1,500.*

Provisionally issued at Tallinn. This overprint has been extensively counterfeited. Values are for genuine examples competently expertized.
No. 20 is always creased.

Gulls — A3

1919, May 13 *Imperf.*
27 A3 5p yellow 2.50 *5.50*

A4 A5 A6

A7

Viking Ship — A8

1919-20 *Perf. 11½*
28 A4 10p green .45 .80

Imperf
29 A4 5p orange .25 .25
30 A4 10p green .25 .25
31 A5 15p rose .25 .30
32 A6 35p blue .25 .30
33 A7 70p dl vio ('20) .25 .30
34 A8 1m bl & blk brn 4.25 1.60
a. Gray granite paper ('20) 1.60 .80
35 A8 5m yel & blk 6.25 4.75
a. Gray granite paper ('20) 3.25 1.25
36 A8 15m yel grn & vio ('20) 3.50 2.40
37 A8 25m ultra & blk brn ('20) 6.50 5.50
Nos. 28-37 (10) 22.20 16.45
Set, never hinged 32.50

The 5m exists with inverted center. Not a postal item.
See Nos. 76-77. For surcharges see Nos. 55, 57.

Skyline of Tallinn — A9

1920-24 Pelure Paper *Imperf.*
39 A9 25p green .35 .40
40 A9 25p yellow ('24) .35 .30
41 A9 35p rose .40 .40
42 A9 50p green ('21) .40 .25
43 A9 1m vermilion 1.25 .80
44 A9 2m blue .80 .40
45 A9 2m ultramarine 1.00 1.25
46 A9 2.50m blue 1.25 .80
Nos. 39-46 (8) 5.80 4.60
Set, never hinged 16.50

Nos. 39-46 with sewing machine perforation are unofficial.
For surcharge see No. 56.

Stamps of 1919-20 Surcharged

1920 *Imperf.*
55 A5 1m on 15p rose .50 .50
56 A9 1m on 35p rose .70 .50
57 A7 2m on 70p dl vio .85 .60
Nos. 55-57 (3) 2.05 1.60
Set, never hinged 4.25

Weaver A10

Blacksmith A11

1922-23 Typo. *Imperf.*
58 A10 ½m orange ('23) 2.75 *8.00*
59 A10 1m brown ('23) 4.75 *11.00*
60 A10 2m yellow green 4.75 *8.00*
61 A10 2½m claret 5.50 *8.00*
62 A11 5m rose 8.00 8.00
63 A11 9m red ('23) 12.00 *24.00*
64 A11 10m deep blue 6.00 *16.00*
Nos. 58-64 (7) 43.75 83.00
Set, never hinged 105.00

1922-25 *Perf. 14*
65 A10 ½m orange ('23) 1.25 .80
66 A10 1m brown ('23) 2.40 .80
67 A10 2m yellow green 2.40 .40
68 A10 2½m claret 4.75 .80
69 A10 3m blue green ('24) 2.00 .40
70 A11 5m rose 2.75 .40
71 A11 9m red ('23) 4.75 1.60
72 A11 10m deep blue 6.00 .40
73 A11 12m red ('25) 6.00 1.75
74 A11 15m plum ('25) 8.00 1.40
75 A11 20m ultra ('25) 20.00 .80
Nos. 65-75 (11) 60.30 9.55
Set, never hinged 130.00

See No. 89. For surcharges see Nos. 84-88.

Viking Ship Type of 1920

1922, June 8 *Perf. 14x13½*
76 A8 15m yel grn & vio 8.00 .80
77 A8 25m ultra & blk brn 10.00 3.25
Set, never hinged 35.00

Map of Estonia — A13

1923-24 Paper with Lilac Network
78 A13 100m ol grn & bl 20.00 3.50

Paper with Buff Network
79 A13 300m brn & bl ('24) 72.50 17.50
Set, never hinged 210.00

For surcharges see Nos. 106-107.

National Theater, Tallinn — A14

Paper with Blue Network

1924, Dec. 9 *Perf. 14x13½*
81 A14 30m violet & blk 10.00 4.00

Paper with Rose Network
82 A14 70m car rose & blk 15.00 8.00
Set, never hinged 50.00

For surcharge see No. 105.

Vanemuine Theater, Tartu — A15

Paper with Lilac Network

1927, Oct. 25
83 A15 40m dp bl & ol brn 10.00 3.50
Never hinged 20.00

Stamps of 1922-25 Surcharged in New Currency in Red or Black

1928 *Perf. 14*
84 A10 2s yellow green 1.50 1.25
85 A11 5s rose red (B) 1.50 1.25
86 A11 10s deep blue 2.40 1.25
a. Imperf., pair *1,300.* —
87 A11 15s plum (B) 6.50 1.25
88 A11 20s ultra 4.50 1.25
Nos. 84-88 (5) 16.40 6.25
Set, never hinged 35.00

10th anniversary of independence.

3rd Philatelic Exhibition Issue
Blacksmith Type of 1922-23

1928, July 6
89 A11 10m gray 4.50 *7.50*
Never hinged 9.00

Sold only at Tallinn Philatelic Exhibition. Exists imperf. Value $1,000.

Arms — A16

Paper with Network in Parenthesis

1928-40 *Perf. 14, 14½x14*
90 A16 1s dk gray (bl) .50 .25
a. Thick gray-toned laid paper ('40) 10.00 *27.50*
91 A16 2s yel grn (org) .60 .25
92 A16 4s grn (brn) ('29) 1.25 .25
93 A16 5s red (grn) .35 .25
a. 5 feet on lowest lion 45.00 32.50
94 A16 8s vio (buff) ('29) 3.00 .25
95 A16 10s lt bl (lilac) 3.00 .25
96 A16 12s crimson (grn) 2.25 .25
97 A16 15s yel (blue) 3.00 .25
98 A16 15s car (gray) ('35) 14.50 1.75
99 A16 20s slate bl (red) 4.25 .25
100 A16 25s red vio (grn) ('29) 10.50 .25
101 A16 25s bl (brn) ('35) 12.00 1.75
102 A16 40s red org (bl) ('29) 11.00 .60
103 A16 60s gray (brn) ('29) 15.00 .60
104 A16 80s brn (bl) ('29) 15.00 .60
Nos. 90-104 (15) 96.20 7.80
Set, never hinged 175.00

Types of 1924 Issues Surcharged

1930, Sept. 1 *Perf. 14x13½*

Paper with Green Network

105 A14 1k on 70m car & blk 12.00 5.50

Paper with Rose Network

106 A13 2k on 300m brn & bl 30.00 16.00

Paper with Blue Network

107 A13 3k on 300m brn & bl 60.00 27.50
Nos. 105-107 (3) 102.00 49.00
Set, never hinged 210.00

University Observatory A17

University of Tartu A18

Paper with Network as in Parenthesis

1932, June 1 *Perf. 14*

108 A17 5s red (yellow) 5.25 .80
109 A18 10s light bl (lilac) 2.40 .80
110 A17 12s car (blue) 8.25 4.00
111 A18 20s dk bl (green) 6.00 1.60
Nos. 108-111 (4) 21.90 7.20
Set, never hinged 55.00

University of Tartu tercentenary.

Narva Falls — A19

1933, Apr. 1 **Photo.** *Perf. 14x13½*

112 A19 1k gray black 7.00 3.00
Never hinged 15.00

See No. 149.

Ancient Bard Playing Harp — A20

Paper with Network as in Parenthesis

1933, May 29 **Typo.** *Perf. 14*

113 A20 2s green (orange) 1.60 .30
114 A20 5s red (green) 2.75 .30
115 A20 10s blue (lilac) 3.50 .30
Nos. 113-115 (3) 7.85 .90
Set, never hinged 17.00

Tenth National Song Festival.
Nos. 113-115 exist imperf. Value $125.

Woman Harvester — A21

1935, Mar. 1 **Engr.** *Perf. 13½*

116 A21 3k black brown .80 6.50
Never hinged 1.60

Pres. Konstantin Päts — A22

1936-40 **Typo.** *Perf. 14*

117 A22 1s chocolate .80 .25
118 A22 2s yellow green .80 .25
119 A22 3s dp org ('40) 8.00 6.00
120 A22 4s rose vio 1.25 .80
121 A22 5s lt blue grn 1.50 .30
122 A22 6s rose lake 1.25 .25
123 A22 6s dp green ('40) 27.50 42.00
124 A22 10s greenish blue 1.50 .25
125 A22 15s crim rose ('37) 1.90 .40
126 A22 15s dp bl ('40) 3.25 2.50
127 A22 18s dp car ('39) 20.00 7.00
128 A22 20s brt vio 3.00 .35
129 A22 25s dk bl ('38) 8.00 1.25
130 A22 30s bister ('38) 14.00 1.25
131 A22 30s ultra ('39) 16.00 5.00
132 A22 50s org brn 7.00 1.00
133 A22 60s brt pink 16.00 4.50
Nos. 117-133 (17) 131.75 73.35
Set, never hinged 255.00

St. Brigitta Convent Entrance A23

Ruins of Convent, Pirita River A24

Front View of Convent — A25

Seal of Convent — A26

Paper with Network as in Parenthesis

1936, June 10 *Perf. 13½*

134 A23 5s green (buff) .40 .40
135 A24 10s blue (lil) .40 .40
136 A25 15s red (org) 1.25 *4.00*
137 A26 25s ultra (brn) 1.60 *5.50*
Nos. 134-137 (4) 3.65 *10.30*
Set, never hinged 8.00

St. Brigitta Convent, 500th anniversary.

Harbor at Tallinn — A27

1938, Apr. 11 **Engr.** *Perf. 14*

138 A27 2k blue 1.00 *8.00*
Never hinged 1.75

Friedrich R. Faehlmann A28

Friedrich R. Kreutzwald A29

1938, June 15 **Typo.** *Perf. 13½*

139 A28 5s dark green .70 .50
140 A29 10s deep brown .70 .50
141 A29 15s dark carmine 1.00 .90
142 A28 25s ultra 1.60 1.40
a. Sheet of 4, #139-142 10.00 *80.00*
Nos. 139-142 (4) 4.00 3.30
Set, never hinged 10.00

Society of Estonian Scholars centenary.

Hospital at Pärnu — A30

Beach Hotel — A31

1939, June 20 **Typo.** *Perf. 14x13½*

144 A30 5s dark green 1.60 1.60
145 A31 10s deep red violet .80 1.60
146 A30 18s dark carmine 1.50 *5.50*
147 A31 30s deep blue 1.75 *7.25*
a. Sheet of 4, #144-147 15.00 *87.50*
Nos. 144-147 (4) 5.65 15.95
Set, never hinged 11.00

Cent. of health resort and baths at Pärnu.

Narva Falls Type of 1933

1940, Apr. 15 **Engr.**

149 A19 1k slate green 1.40 *12.00*
Never hinged 2.50

The sky consists of heavy horizontal lines and the background consists of horizontal and vertical lines.

Carrier Pigeon and Plane — A32

1940, July 30 **Typo.**

150 A32 3s red orange .25 .25
151 A32 10s purple .25 .25
152 A32 15s rose brown .25 .25
153 A32 30s dark blue 1.60 1.25
Nos. 150-153 (4) 2.35 2.00
Set, never hinged 5.00

SEMI-POSTAL STAMPS

Assisting Wounded Soldier — SP1

Offering Aid to Wounded Hero — SP2

1920, June **Unwmk.** **Litho.** ***Imperf.***

B1 SP1 35p + 10p red & ol grn .75 *2.00*
B2 SP2 70p + 15p dp bl & brn .75 *2.00*

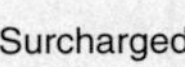

Surcharged

1920

B3 SP1 1m on No. B1 .50 .30
B4 SP2 2m on No. B2 .50 .30

Nurse and Wounded Soldier — SP3

1921, Aug. 1 ***Imperf.***

B5 SP3 2½ (3½)m org, brn & car 2.00 *7.25*
B6 SP3 5 (7)m ultra, brn & car 2.00 *7.25*

1922, Apr. 26 *Perf. 13½x14*

B7 SP3 2½ (3½)m org, brn & car 2.00 *7.25*
a. Vert. pair, imperf. horiz. 30.00 *80.00*
B8 SP3 5 (7)m ultra, brn & car 2.00 *7.25*
a. Vert. pair, imperf. horiz. 30.00 *80.00*

Nos. B5-B8 Overprinted

1923, Oct. 8 ***Imperf.***

B9 SP3 2½ (3½)m 60.00 *160.00*
B10 SP3 5 (7)m 60.00 *160.00*

Perf. 13½x14

B11 SP3 2½ (3½)m 60.00 *160.00*
a. Vert. pair, imperf. horiz. 200.00 *800.00*
B12 SP3 5 (7)m 60.00 *160.00*
a. Vert. pair, imperf. horiz. 200.00 *800.00*
Nos. B9-B12 (4) 240.00 640.00

Excellent forgeries are plentiful.

Nos. B7 and B8 Surcharged

1926, June 15

B13 SP3 5 (6)m on #B7 3.75 *8.00*
a. Vert. pair, imperf. horiz. 24.00 *120.00*
B14 SP3 10 (12)m on #B8 4.50 *8.00*
a. Vert. pair, imperf. horiz. 24.00 *120.00*

Nos. B5-B14 had the franking value of the lower figure. They were sold for the higher figure, the excess going to the Red Cross Society.

Kuressaare Castle SP4

Tartu Cathedral SP5

Tallinn Castle SP6

Narva Fortress SP7

View of Tallinn — SP8

Laid Paper

Perf. 14½x14

1927, Nov. 19 **Typo.** **Wmk. 207**

B15 SP4 5m + 5m bl grn & ol, *grysh* .90 *8.00*
B16 SP5 10m + 10m dp bl & brn, *cream* .90 *8.00*
B17 SP6 12m + 12m rose red & ol grn, *bluish* .90 *8.00*

Perf. 14x13½

B18 SP7 20m + 20m bl & choc, *gray* 1.75 *8.00*
B19 SP8 40m + 40m org brn & slate, *buff* 1.75 *8.00*
Nos. B15-B19 (5) 6.20 *40.00*

The money derived from the surtax was donated to the Committee for the commemoration of War for Liberation.

Red Cross Issue

Symbolical of Succor to Injured — SP9

Symbolical of "Light of Hope" — SP10

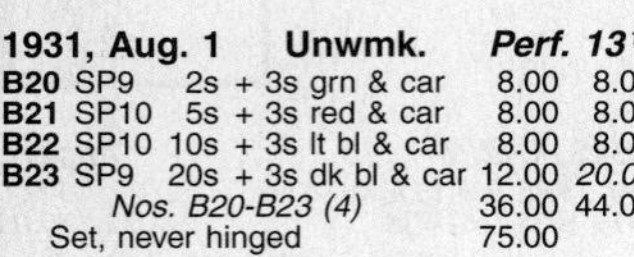

1931, Aug. 1 **Unwmk.** ***Perf. 13½***

B20 SP9	2s + 3s grn & car	8.00	8.00
B21 SP10	5s + 3s red & car	8.00	8.00
B22 SP10	10s + 3s lt bl & car	8.00	8.00
B23 SP9	20s + 3s dk bl & car	12.00	*20.00*
	Nos. B20-B23 (4)	36.00	44.00
	Set, never hinged	75.00	

Nurse and Child SP11

Taagepera Sanatorium SP12

Lorraine Cross and Flower — SP13

Paper with Network as in Parenthesis

1933, Oct. 1 ***Perf. 14, 14½***

B24 SP11	5s + 3s ver (grn)	*6.00*	*8.00*
B25 SP12	10s + 3s lt bl & red (vio)	6.00	*8.00*
B26 SP13	12s + 3s rose & red (grn)	8.00	*12.00*
B27 SP12	20s + 3s dk bl & red (org)	10.00	*16.00*
	Nos. B24-B27 (4)	30.00	44.00
	Set, never hinged	72.50	

The surtax was for a fund to combat tuberculosis.

Coats of Arms

Narva — SP14

Pärnu — SP15

Tartu — SP16

Tallinn — SP17

Paper with Network as in Parenthesis

1936, Feb. 1 ***Perf. 13½***

B28 SP14	10s + 10s grn & ultra (gray)	3.50	*8.00*
B29 SP15	15s + 15s car & bl (gray)	3.50	*12.00*
B30 SP16	25s + 25s gray bl & red (brn)	4.50	*16.00*
B31 SP17	50s + 50s blk & dl org (ol)	17.00	*52.50*
	Nos. B28-B31 (4)	28.50	*88.50*
	Set, never hinged	52.50	

Paide SP18

Rakvere SP19

Valga SP20

Viljandi SP21

Paper with Network as in Parenthesis

1937, Jan. 2 ***Perf. 13½x14***

B32 SP18	10s + 10s grn (gray)	3.00	*6.50*
B33 SP19	15s + 15s red brn (gray)	3.00	*6.50*
B34 SP20	25s + 25s dk bl (lil)	5.00	*9.50*
B35 SP21	50s + 50s dk vio (gray)	9.00	*24.00*
	Nos. B32-B35 (4)	20.00	*46.50*
	Set, never hinged	40.00	

Baltiski — SP22

Võru — SP23

Haapsalu SP24

Kuressaare SP25

Designs are the armorial bearings of various cities

1938, Jan. 21

Paper with Gray Network

B36 SP22	10s + 10s dk brn	3.00	*8.00*
B37 SP23	15s + 15s car & grn	3.50	12.00
B38 SP24	25s + 25s dk bl & car	5.00	20.00
B39 SP25	50s + 50s blk & org yel	8.00	*40.00*
a.	Sheet of 4, #B36-B39	35.00	*80.00*
	Nos. B36-B39 (4)	19.50	*80.00*
	Set, never hinged	40.00	

Annual charity ball, Tallinn, Jan. 2, 1938.

Viljandimaa SP27

Pärnumaa SP28

Tartumaa SP29

Harjumaa SP30

Designs are the armorial bearings of various cities

1939, Jan. 10 ***Perf. 13½***

Paper with Gray Network

B41 SP27	10s + 10s dk bl grn	3.50	*8.00*
B42 SP28	15s + 15s carmine	4.00	*8.00*
B43 SP29	25s + 25s dk blue	5.50	*20.00*
B44 SP30	50s + 50s brn lake	14.00	*47.50*
a.	Sheet of 4, #B41-B44	45.00	*175.00*
	Nos. B41-B44 (4)	27.00	*83.50*
	Set, never hinged	47.50	

Võrumaa SP32

Järvamaa SP33

Läänemaa SP34

Saaremaa SP35

Designs are the armorial bearings of various cities

1940, Jan. 2 **Typo.** ***Perf. 13½***

Paper with Gray Network

B46 SP32	10s + 10s dp grn & ultra	2.50	*12.00*
B47 SP33	15s + 15s dk car & ultra	2.50	*16.00*
B48 SP34	25s + 25s dk bl & scar	3.00	*24.00*
B49 SP35	50s + 50s ocher & ultra	8.00	*32.50*
	Nos. B46-B49 (4)	16.00	*84.50*
	Set, never hinged	30.00	

AIR POST STAMPS

Airplane AP1

Unwmk.

1920, Mar. 13 **Typo.** ***Imperf.***

C1 AP1	5m yel, blk & lt grn	3.00	*5.50*
	Never hinged	7.00	

No. C1 Overprinted "1923" in Red

1923, Oct. 1

C2 AP1	5m multicolored	8.00	*32.50*
	Never hinged	15.00	

No. C1 Surcharged in Red

1923, Oct. 1

C3 AP1	15m on 5m multi	16.00	*47.50*
	Never hinged	30.00	

Pairs of No. C1 Surcharged in Black or Red

1923, Oct.

C4 AP1	10m on 5m+5m (B)	10.00	*35.00*
C5 AP1	20m on 5m+5m	20.00	*55.00*
C6 AP1	45m on 5m+5m	80.00	*200.00*

Rough Perf. 11½

C7 AP1	10m on 5m+5m (B)	*550.00*	*1,200.*
C8 AP1	20m on 5m+5m	*200.00*	*525.00*
	Nos. C4-C8 (5)	*860.00*	*2,015.*
	Set, never hinged	*1,700.*	

The pairs comprising Nos. C7 and C8 are imperforate between. Forged surcharges and perforations abound. Authentication is required.

Monoplane in Flight — AP2

Designs: Various views of planes in flight.

1924, Feb. 12 ***Imperf.***

C9 AP2	5m yellow & blk	2.00	*8.00*
C10 AP2	10m blue & blk	2.00	*8.00*
C11 AP2	15m red & blk	2.00	*8.00*
C12 AP2	20m green & blk	2.00	*8.00*
C13 AP2	45m violet & blk	2.00	*16.00*
	Nos. C9-C13 (5)	10.00	*48.00*
	Set, never hinged	15.00	

The paper is covered with a faint network in pale shades of the frame colors. There are four varieties of the frames and five of the pictures.

1925, July 15 ***Perf. 13½***

C14 AP2	5m yellow & blk	1.50	*8.00*
C15 AP2	10m blue & blk	1.50	*8.00*
C16 AP2	15m red & blk	1.50	*8.00*
C17 AP2	20m green & blk	1.50	*8.00*
C18 AP2	45m violet & blk	1.50	*16.00*
	Nos. C14-C18 (5)	7.50	*48.00*
	Set, never hinged	11.00	

Counterfeits of Nos. C1-C18 are plentiful.

OCCUPATION STAMPS

Issued under German Occupation

For Use in Tartu (Dorpat)

Russian Stamps of 1909-12 Surcharged

1918 **Unwmk.** ***Perf. 14x14½***

N1 A15	20pf on 10k dk bl	35.00	*80.00*
a.	20pf on 10k light blue	225.00	
N2 A8	40pf on 20k bl & car	35.00	*80.00*
	Set, Never Hinged	130.00	

Forged overprints exist.

ETHIOPIA

ˌē-thē-ˈō-pē-ə

(Abyssinia)

LOCATION — Northeastern Africa
GOVT. — Monarchy
AREA — 471,800 sq. mi.
POP. — 40,000,000 (est. 1984)
CAPITAL — Addis Ababa

During the Italian occupation (1936-1941) Nos. N1-N7 were used, also stamps of Italian East Africa, Eritrea and Somalia.

16 Guerche = 1 Menelik Dollar or 1 Maria Theresa Dollar
100 Centimes = 1 Franc (1905)
40 Paras = 1 Piaster (1908)
16 Mehalek = 1 Thaler or Talari (1928)
100 Centimes = 1 Thaler (1936)

Watermarks

Wmk. 140 — Crown

Wmk. 282 — Ethiopian Star and Amharic Characters, Multiple

Excellent forgeries of Nos. 1-86 exist.

Very Fine examples of Nos. 1-86 and J1-J42 will have perforations touching the design on one or more sides due to the narrow spacing of the stamps on the plates and imperfect perforating methods. Stamps with margins clear on all sides are scarce and command high premiums.

On March 9, 1894 Menelik II awarded Alfred Ilg a concession to develop a railway, including postal service. Ilg's stamps, Nos. 1-79, were valid locally and to Djibouti. Mail to other countries had to bear stamps of Obock, Somali Coast, etc.

Ethiopia joined the UPU Nov. 1, 1908.

Menelik II
A1

Lion of Judah
A2

Amharic numeral "8"

Perf. 14x13½

1895, Jan. Unwmk. Typo.

1	A1	¼g green	4.00	2.00
2	A1	½g red	4.00	2.00
3	A1	1g blue	4.00	2.00
4	A1	2g dark brown	4.00	2.00
5	A2	4g lilac brown	4.00	2.00
6	A2	8g violet	4.00	2.00
7	A2	16g black	4.00	2.00
		Nos. 1-7 (7)	28.00	14.00

For 4g, 8g and 16g stamps of type A1, see Nos. J3a, J4a and J7a.

Earliest reported use is Jan. 29, 1895.

Forged cancellations are plentiful.

For overprints see Nos. 8-86, J8-J28, J36-J42. For surcharges see Nos. 94-100, J29-J35.

Nos. 1-7 Handstamped in Violet or Blue

Overprint 9¼x2½mm, Serifs on "E"

1901, July 18

8	A1	¼g green	27.50	27.50
9	A1	½g red	27.50	27.50
10	A1	1g blue	27.50	27.50
11	A1	2g dark brown	27.50	27.50
12	A2	4g lilac brown	32.50	32.50
13	A2	8g violet	47.50	47.50
14	A2	16g black	60.00	60.00
		Nos. 8-14 (7)	250.00	250.00

Violet overprints were issued July 18, 1901, for postal use, while the blue overprints were issued in Jan. 5 1902 for philatelic purposes. The blue overprints were not used in the mails. Values for unused stamps are for examples with blue overprints. The blue overprints became valid for postage in 1908 only. Unused stamps with violet overprints are worth much more.

Overprints 8¼mm wide are unofficial reproductions.

Nos. 1-7 Handstamped in Violet, Blue or Black

Overprint 11x3mm, Low Colons

1902, Apr. 1

15	A1	¼g green	6.00	6.00
16	A1	½g red	9.00	7.00
17	A1	1g blue	10.00	10.00
18	A1	2g dark brown	14.00	14.00
19	A2	4g lilac brown	24.00	24.00
20	A2	8g violet	30.00	30.00
21	A2	16g black	55.00	55.00
		Nos. 15-21 (7)	148.00	146.00

The handstamp reads "Bosta" (Post).

Overprints 10¾mm and 11mm wide with raised colons are unofficial reproductions.

Nos. 1-7 Handstamped in Black

1903, Jan. 9 Overprint 16x3¾mm

22	A1	¼g green	7.50	7.50
23	A1	½g red	12.00	12.00
24	A1	1g blue	15.00	15.00
25	A1	2g dark brown	19.00	19.00
26	A2	4g lilac brown	27.50	27.50
27	A2	8g violet	37.50	37.50
28	A2	16g black	57.50	57.50
		Nos. 22-28 (7)	176.00	176.00

The handstamp reads "Malekt." (Also "Melekt," message).

Original stamps have blurred colons. Unofficial reproductions have clean colons.

Nos. 22-28 have black overprints only. All other colors are fakes.

Nos. 1-7 Handstamped in Violet or Blue

Overprint 18¼mm Wide

1904, Dec.

36	A1	¼g green	15.00	15.00
37	A1	½g red	20.00	
38	A1	1g blue	25.00	
39	A1	2g dark brown	27.50	
40	A2	4g lilac brown	35.00	
41	A2	8g violet	57.50	
42	A2	16g black	75.00	
		Nos. 36-42 (7)	255.00	

The handstamp reads "Malekathe" (message). This set was never issued.

Preceding Issues Surcharged with New Values in French Currency in Blue, Violet, Rose or Black

a

b

On Nos. 1-7

1905, Jan. 1 Overprint 3mm High

43	A1 (a)	5c on ¼g	10.00	10.00
44	A1 (a)	10c on ½g	10.00	10.00
45	A1 (a)	20c on 1g	10.00	10.00
46	A1 (a)	40c on 2g	11.00	11.00
47	A2 (a)	80c on 4g	21.00	21.00
48	A2 (b)	1.60fr on 8g	22.50	22.50
49	A2 (b)	3.20fr on 16g	40.00	40.00
		Nos. 43-49 (7)	124.50	124.50

Nos. 48-49 exist with period or comma.

1905, Feb.

On No. 8, "Ethiopie" in Blue

50	A1 (a)	5c on ¼g	120.00	100.00

On No. 15, "Bosta" in Black

51	A1 (a)	5c on ¼g	40.00	40.00

On No. 22, "Malekt" in Black

52	A1 (a)	5c on ¼g	140.00	75.00

Unofficial reproductions exist of Nos. 50, 51, 52. The 5c on No. 36, 10c, 20c, 40c, 80c, and 1.60fr surcharges exist as unofficial reproductions only.

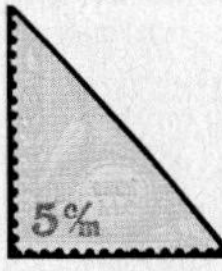

c

d

1905 On No. 2

54	A1 (c)	5c on half of ½g	10.00	10.00

On No. 21, "Bosta" in Black

55	A2 (d)	5c on 16g blk	200.00	100.00

On No. 55, "Bosta" is in black.

On No. 28, "Malekt" in Black

56	A2 (d)	5c on 16g blk	250.00	250.00
		Nos. 54-56 (3)	460.00	360.00

No. 54 issued in March. Nos. 55-56 issued Mar. 30.

The overprints and surcharges on Nos. 8 to 56 inclusive were handstamped, the work being very roughly done.

As is usual with handstamped overprints and surcharges there are many inverted and double, but most of them are fakes or unofficial reproductions.

Surcharged with New Values in Various Colors and in Violet

Overprint 14¾x3½mm

1906, Jan. 1

57	A1	5c on ¼g green	10.00	10.00
58	A1	10c on ½g red	12.00	12.00
59	A1	20c on 1g blue	12.00	12.00
60	A1	40c on 2g dk brn	12.00	12.00
61	A2	80c on 4g lilac brn	18.00	18.00
62	A2	1.60fr on 8g violet	27.50	27.50
63	A2	3.20fr on 16g black	45.00	45.00
		Nos. 57-63 (7)	136.50	136.50

Two types of the 4-character overprint ("Menelik"): 14x¾x3½mm and 16x4mm.

Surcharged in Violet Brown

1906, July 1 Overprint 16x4¼mm

64	A1	5c on ¼g grn	9.25	9.25
a.		Surcharged "20"	75.00	75.00
65	A1	10c on ½g red	11.00	11.00
66	A1	20c on 1g blue	17.50	17.50
67	A1	40c on 2g dk brn	17.50	17.50
68	A2	80c on 4g lil brn	25.00	25.00
69	A2	1.60fr on 8g vio	25.00	25.00
70	A2	3.20fr on 16g blk	60.00	60.00
		Nos. 64-70 (7)	165.25	165.25

The control overprint reads "Menelik."

Surcharged in Violet

e

f

1907, June 21

71	A1 (e)	¼ on ¼g grn	8.75	8.75
72	A1 (e)	½ on ½g red	8.75	8.75
73	A1 (f)	1 on 1g blue	11.00	11.00
74	A1 (f)	2 on 2g dk brn	12.00	12.00
a.		Surcharged "40"	65.00	
75	A2 (f)	4 on 4g lil brn	13.00	13.00
a.		Surcharged "80"	57.50	
76	A2 (f)	8 on 8g vio	30.00	30.00
77	A2 (f)	16 on 16g blk	37.50	37.50
		Nos. 71-77 (7)	121.00	121.00

Nos. 71-72 are also found with stars farther away from figures.

The control overprint reads "Dagmawi" ("Second"), meaning Emperor Menelik II.

On stamps with "1" in surcharge, genuine examples have straight serifs, forgeries have curved serifs.

Nos. 2, 23 Surcharged in Bluish Green

1908, Aug. 14

78	A1	1pi on ½g red (#2)	15.00	15.00
79	A1	1pi on ½g red (#23)	*850.00*	—

Official reproductions exist. Value, set $25.

Forgeries exist.

The surcharges on Nos. 57-78 are handstamped and are found double, inverted, etc.

Surcharged in Black

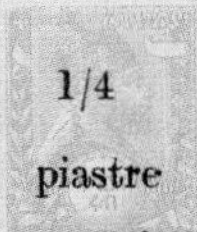

1908, Nov. 1

80	A1	¼p on ¼g grn	1.50	1.50
81	A1	½p on ½g red	1.50	1.50
82	A1	1p on 1g blue	2.25	2.25
83	A1	2p on 2g dk brn	3.75	3.75
84	A2	4p on 4g lil brn	5.25	5.25
85	A2	8p on 8g vio	12.50	12.50
86	A2	16p on 16g blk	18.00	18.00
		Nos. 80-86 (7)	44.75	44.75

Surcharges on Nos. 80-85 are found double, inverted, etc. Forgeries exist.

These are the 1st stamps valid for international mail.

King Solomon's Throne — A3

Menelik in Native Costume — A4

Menelik in Royal Dress — A5

1909, Jan. 29 *Perf. 11½*

87 A3 ¼g blue green 1.10 .85
88 A3 ½g rose 1.25 .85
89 A3 1g green & org 6.25 2.50
90 A4 2g blue 4.75 3.00
91 A4 4g green & car 7.00 5.50
92 A5 8g ver & dp grn 15.00 10.00
93 A5 16g ver & car 22.50 16.50
Nos. 87-93 (7) 57.85 39.20

For overprints see Nos. 101-115, J43-J49, J55-J56. For surcharges see Nos. 116-119.

Nos. 1-7 Handstamped and Surcharged in ms.

1911, Oct. 1 *Perf. 14x13½*

94 A1 ¼g on ¼g grn 50.00
95 A1 ½g on ½g red 50.00
96 A1 1g on 1g blue 50.00
97 A1 2g on 2g dk brn 50.00
98 A2 4g on 4g lil brn 50.00
99 A2 8g on 8g violet 50.00
100 A2 16g on 16g black 50.00
Nos. 94-100 (7) 350.00

Nos. 94-100 were produced as a philatelic speculation by the postmaster at Dire-Dawa. The overprint is abbreviated from "Affranchissement Exceptionnel Faute Timbres" (Special Franking Lacking Stamps). The overprints and surcharges were applied to stamps on cover and then canceled. These covers were then sold to dealers in Europe. No. 98 is known postally used on a small number of commercial covers.

Nos. 94-100 without surcharge are forgeries.

Stamps of 1909 Handstamped in Violet or Black

Nos. 101-102

Nos. 104-107

1917, Mar. 30 *Perf. 11½*

101 A3 ¼g blue grn (V) 7.50 6.75
102 A3 ½g rose (V) 7.50 6.75
104 A4 2g blue (Bk) 10.00 8.25
105 A4 4g grn & car (Bk) 15.00 17.00
106 A5 8g ver & dp grn (Bk) 25.00 22.50
107 A5 16g ver & car (Bk) 40.00 35.00
Nos. 101-107 (6) 105.00 96.25

Coronation of Empress Zauditu and appointment of Prince Tafari as Regent and Heir to the throne.

Exist with overprint inverted and double.

Stamps of 1909 Overprinted in Blue, Black or Red

Nos. 108-111

Nos. 112-115

1917, Apr. 5-Oct. 1

108 A3 ¼g blue grn (Bl) 1.25 1.25
109 A3 ½g rose (Bl) 1.25 1.25
110 A3 1g grn & org (Bl) 2.25 2.25
111 A4 2g blue (R) 82.50 87.25
112 A4 2g blue (Bk) 1.25 1.25
113 A4 4g grn & car (Bl) 1.25 1.25
a. Black overprint 11.00 11.00
114 A5 8g ver & dp grn (Bl) 1.25 1.25
115 A5 16g ver & car (Bl) 2.25 2.25
Nos. 108-115 (8) 93.25 98.00

Coronation of Empress Zauditu.

Nos. 108-115 all exist with double overprint, inverted overprint, double overprint, one inverted, and various combinations.

Nos. 114-115 with Additional Surcharge

k

l

m

n

1917, May 28

116 A5 (k) ¼g on 8g 5.00 4.00
117 A5 (l) ½g on 8g 5.00 4.00
118 A5 (m) 1g on 16g 11.00 8.00
119 A5 (n) 2g on 16g 12.00 9.00
Nos. 116-119 (4) 33.00 25.00

Nos. 116-119 all exist with the numerals double and inverted and No. 116 with the Amharic surcharge missing.

Sommering's Gazelle — A6

Prince Tafari — A9

Cathedral of St. George A12

Empress Waizeri Zauditu — A18

⅛g, Giraffes. ½g, Leopard. 2g, Prince Tafari, diff. 4g, Prince Tafari, diff. 8g, White rhinoceros. 12g, Somali ostriches. 1t, African elephant. 2t, Water buffalo. 3t, Lions. 5t, 10t, Empress Zauditu.

1919, June 16 **Typo.** *Perf. 11½*

120 A6 ⅛g violet & brn .25 .25
121 A6 ¼g bl grn & drab .25 .25
122 A6 ½g scar & ol grn .25 .25
123 A9 1g rose lil & gray grn .25 .25
124 A9 2g dp ultra & fawn .25 .25
125 A9 4g turq bl & org .25 *2.50*
126 A12 6g lt blue & org .25 .25
127 A12 8g ol grn & blk brn .35 .25
128 A12 12g red vio & gray .50 .30
129 A12 1t rose & gray blk .90 .40
130 A12 2t black & brown 2.50
131 A12 3t grn & dp org 2.50 1.90
132 A18 4t brn & lil rose 3.00 2.50
133 A18 5t carmine & gray 4.00 4.00
134 A18 10t gray grn & bis 8.00 5.25
Nos. 120-134 (15) 23.50
Nos. 120-129,131-134 (14) 18.25

No. 130 was not issued.

For overprints see Nos. J50-J54. For surcharges see Nos. 135-154.

Reprints have brownish gum that is cracked diagonally. Originals have smooth, white gum. Reprints exist imperf. and some values with inverted centers. Value for set, unused or canceled, $5.

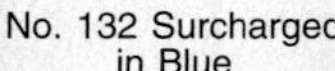

No. 132 Surcharged in Blue

1919, July

135 A18 4g on 4t brn & lil rose 3.50 3.50

Nos. 135-154

The Amharic surcharge indicates the new value and, therefore, varies on Nos. 135-154. There are numerous defective letters and figures, several types of the "2" of "½," the errors "guerhce," "gnerche," etc.

Many varieties of surcharge, such as double, inverted, lines transposed or omitted, and inverted "2" in "½," exist.

There are many irregularly produced settings in imitation of Nos. 136-154 which differ slightly from the originals. These may be essays or proofs.

Stamps of 1919 Surcharged

1921

136 A6 ½g on ⅛g vio & brn 1.00 1.00
137 A6 1g on ¼g grn & db 2.50 1.00
138 A9 2g on 1g lil brn & gray grn 1.00 1.50
139 A18 2g on 4t brn & lil rose 35.00 15.00
140 A6 2½g on ½g scar & ol grn 1.00 *1.50*
141 A9 4g on 2g ultra & fawn 1.00 *1.25*
Nos. 136-141 (6) 41.50 21.25

Forgeries of No. 139 exist.

Stamps and Type of 1919 Surcharged

1925-26

142 A12 ½g on 1t rose & gray blk ('26) 1.00 1.00
a. Without colon ('26) 12.50 12.50
143 A18 ½g on 5t car & gray ('26) 2.00 1.00
144 A12 1g on 6g bl & org 1.00 1.00
145 A12 1g on 12g lil & gray 400.00 400.00
146 A12 1g on 3t grn & org ('26) 22.50 16.00
147 A18 1g on 10t gray grn & bis ('26) 1.00 *1.00*
Nos. 142-147 (6) 427.50 420.00

On No. 142 the surcharge is at the left side of the stamp, reading upward. On No. 142a it is at the right, reading downward. The two surcharges are from different, though similar, settings. On No. 146 the surcharge is at the right, reading upward. See note following No. 154.

Type of 1919 Srchd.

1925, Oct.

147A A12 1g on 12g lil & gray 400.00

Forgeries exist.

Nos. 126-128 Srchd.

1926

148 A12 ½g on 8g 3.00 1.25
149 A12 1g on 6g 80.00 50.00
150 A12 1g on 12g 350.00
Nos. 148-150 (3) 433.00 51.25

The Amharic line has 7 (½g) or 6 characters (1g).

Nos. 126-128, 131 Srchd.

1925-27

151 A12 ½g on 8g ('27) 1.50 1.50
152 A12 1g on 6g ('27) 60.00 40.00
153 A12 1g on 12g ('27) 5.00 1.50
154 A12 1g on 3t 400.00
Nos. 151-154 (4) 466.50 43.00

The Amharic line has 7 (½g) or 4 characters (1g). No. 152 has the lines closer together than do the others.

Forgeries of No. 154 exist.

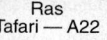

Ras Tafari — A22

Empress Zauditu — A23

1928, Sept. 5 **Typo.** *Perf. 13½x14*

155 A22 ⅛m org & lt bl 1.50 1.40
156 A23 ¼m ind & red org .90 *1.40*
157 A22 ½m gray grn & blk 1.50 1.40
158 A23 1m dk car & blk .90 *1.40*
159 A22 2m dk bl & blk .90 *1.40*
160 A23 4m yel & olive .90 *1.40*
161 A22 8m vio & olive 2.40 1.40
162 A23 1t org brn & vio 2.75 1.40
163 A22 2t grn & bister 4.25 3.25
164 A23 3t choc & grn 6.75 3.75
Nos. 155-164 (10) 22.75 18.20

For overprints and surcharges see Nos. 165-209, 217-230, C1-C10.

Preceding Issue Overprinted in Black, Violet or Red

1928, Sept. 1

165	A22	⅛m (Bk)	3.25	3.25
166	A23	¼m (V)	3.25	3.25
167	A22	½m (V)	3.25	3.25
168	A23	1m (V)	3.25	3.25
169	A22	2m (R)	3.25	3.25
170	A23	4m (Bk)	3.25	3.25
171	A22	8m (R)	3.25	3.25
172	A23	1t (Bk)	4.50	4.50
173	A22	2t (R)	6.00	6.00
174	A23	3t (R)	6.00	6.00
		Nos. 165-174 (10)	39.25	39.25

Opening of General Post Office, Addis Ababa.

Exist with overprint inverted, double, double, one inverted, etc.

Nos. 155, 157, 159, 161, 163 Handstamped in Violet, Red or Black

1928, Oct. 7

175	A22	⅛m (V)	4.25	4.25
176	A22	½m (R)	4.25	4.25
177	A22	2m (R)	4.25	4.25
178	A22	8m (Bk)	4.25	4.25
179	A22	2t (V)	4.25	4.25
		Nos. 175-179 (5)	21.25	21.25

Crowning of Prince Tafari as king (Negus) on Oct. 7, 1928.

Nos. 175-177 exist with overprint vertical, inverted, double, etc.

Forgeries exist.

Nos. 155-164 Overprinted in Red or Green

1930, Apr. 3

180	A22	⅛m org & lt bl (R)	1.40	1.40
181	A23	¼m ind & red org (G)	1.40	1.40
182	A22	½m gray grn & blk (R)	1.40	1.40
183	A23	1m dk car & blk (G)	1.40	1.40
184	A22	2m dk bl & blk (R)	1.40	1.40
185	A23	4m yel & ol (R)	2.10	2.10
186	A22	8m vio & ol (R)	3.00	3.00
187	A23	1t org brn & vio (R)	5.00	5.00
188	A22	2t grn & bis (R)	6.00	6.00
189	A23	3t choc & grn (R)	8.00	8.00
		Nos. 180-189 (10)	31.10	31.10

Proclamation of King Tafari as King of Kings of Abyssinia under the name "Haile Selassie."

A similar overprint, set in four vertical lines, was printed on all denominations of the 1928 issue. It was not considered satisfactory and was rejected. The trial impressions were not placed on sale to the public, but some stamps reached private hands and have been passed through the post.

Nos. 155-164 Overprinted in Red or Olive Brown

1930, Apr. 3

190	A22	⅛m orange & lt bl	1.40	1.40
191	A23	¼m ind & red org (OB)	1.40	1.40
192	A22	½m gray grn & blk	1.40	1.40
193	A23	1m dk car & blk (OB)	1.40	1.40
194	A22	2m dk blue & blk	1.40	1.40
195	A23	4m yellow & ol	2.10	2.10
196	A22	8m violet & ol	3.00	3.00
197	A23	1t org brn & vio	5.00	5.00
198	A22	2t green & bister	6.00	6.00
199	A23	3t chocolate & grn	8.00	8.00
		Nos. 190-199 (10)	31.10	31.10

Proclamation of King Tafari as Emperor Haile Selassie.

All stamps of this series exist with "H" of "HAILE" omitted and with many other varieties.

Nos. 155-164 Handstamped in Violet or Red

1930, Nov. 2

200	A22	⅛m (V)	1.10	1.10
201	A23	¼m (V)	1.10	1.10
202	A22	½m (R)	1.10	1.10
203	A23	1m (V)	1.10	1.10
204	A22	2m (R)	1.10	1.10
205	A23	4m (V)	1.10	1.10
206	A22	8m (V or R)	1.90	1.90
207	A23	1t (V)	3.00	3.00
208	A22	2t (V or R)	4.50	4.50
209	A23	3t (V or R)	6.50	6.50
		Nos. 200-209 (10)	22.50	22.50

Coronation of Emperor Haile Selassie, Nov. 2, 1930.

Haile Selassie Coronation Monument, Symbols of Empire — A24

1930, Nov. Engr. *Perf. 12½*

210	A24	1g orange	1.00	1.00
211	A24	2g ultra	1.00	1.00
212	A24	4g violet	1.00	1.00
213	A24	8g dull green	1.00	1.00
214	A24	1t brown	1.25	1.25
215	A24	3t green	2.00	2.00
216	A24	5t red brown	2.00	2.00
		Nos. 210-216 (7)	9.25	9.25

Coronation of Emperor Haile Selassie.

Issued: 4g, 11/2; others, 11/23.

Reprints of Nos. 210 to 216 exist. Colors are more yellow and the ink is thicker and slightly glossy. Ink on the originals is dull and granular. Value 35c each.

Nos. 158-160, 164 Surcharged in Green, Red or Blue

Type I

Type II

1931 ***Perf. 13½x14***

217	A23	⅛m on 1m	.80	.80
218	A22	⅛m on 2m (R)	.80	.80
219	A23	⅛m on 4m	.80	.80
220	A23	¼m on 1m (Bl)	.80	.80
221	A22	¼m on 2m (R)	1.50	1.50
222	A23	¼m on 4m	1.50	1.50
225	A23	½m on 1m (Bl)	1.50	1.50
226	A22	½m on 2m (R)	1.50	1.50
227	A23	½m on 4m, type II	1.50	1.50
a.		½m on 4m, type I	10.00	10.00
228	A23	½m on 3t (R)	12.00	12.00
230	A22	1m on 2m (R)	3.00	3.00
		Nos. 217-230 (11)	25.70	25.70

The ½m on ⅛m orange & light blue and ½m on ¼m indigo & red orange were clandestinely printed and never sold at the post office.

No. 230 with double surcharge in red and blue is a color trial.

Many varieties exist.

Issued: 1m, Apr.; others, 3/20.

Ras Makonnen A25

Empress Menen A27

View of Hawash River and Railroad Bridge A26

Designs: 2g, 8g, Haile Selassie (profile). 4g, 1t, Statue of Menelik II. 3t, Empress Menen (full face). 5t, Haile Selassie (full face).

Perf. 12½, 12x12½, 12½x12

1931, June 27 Engr.

232	A25	⅛g red	.40	.40
233	A26	¼g olive green	1.10	1.10
234	A25	½g dark violet	1.10	1.10
235	A27	1g red orange	1.10	1.10
236	A27	2g ultra	1.10	1.10
237	A25	4g violet	1.25	1.25
238	A27	8g blue green	2.00	2.00
239	A25	1t chocolate	24.00	10.00
240	A27	3t yellow green	7.00	3.00
241	A27	5t red brown	12.00	5.50
		Nos. 232-241 (10)	51.05	26.55

For overprints see Nos. B1-B5. For surcharges see Nos. 242-246.

Reprints of Nos. 232-236, 238-240 are on thinner and whiter paper than the originals. On originals the ink is dull and granular. On reprints, heavy, caked and shiny. Value 20c each.

Nos. 232-236 Surcharged in Blue or Carmine

1936, Jan. 29 ***Perf. 12x12½, 12½x12***

242	A25	1c on ⅛g red	2.00	1.00
243	A26	2c on ¼g ol grn (C)	2.00	1.00
244	A25	3c on ½g dk vio	2.00	1.10
245	A27	5c on 1g red org	2.50	1.50
246	A27	10c on 2g ultra (C)	3.25	1.90
		Nos. 242-246 (5)	11.75	6.50

SEMI-POSTAL STAMPS

Types of 1931, Overprinted in Red at Upper Left

Perf. 12x12½, 12½x12

1936, Feb. 24 Unwmk.

B1	A27	1g light green	.60	.60
B2	A27	2g rose	.60	.60
B3	A25	4g blue	.60	.60
B4	A27	8g brown	.85	.85
B5	A25	1t purple	.85	.85
		Nos. B1-B5 (5)	3.50	3.50

Nos. B1-B5 were sold at twice face value, the surtax going to the Red Cross.

AIR POST STAMPS

Regular Issue of 1928 Handstamped in Violet, Red, Black or Green

Perf. 13½x14

1929, Aug. 17 Unwmk.

C1	A22	⅛m orange & lt bl	.90	*1.00*
C2	A23	¼m ind & red org	.90	*1.00*
C3	A22	½m gray grn & blk	.90	*1.00*
C4	A23	1m dk car & blk	.90	*1.00*
C5	A22	2m dk blue & blk	1.00	*1.25*
C6	A23	4m yellow & olive	1.00	*1.25*
C7	A22	8m violet & olive	1.00	*1.25*
C8	A23	1t org brn & vio	1.25	*1.25*
C9	A22	2t green & bister	1.60	*2.00*
C10	A23	3t choc & grn	1.75	*2.00*
		Nos. C1-C10 (10)	11.20	*13.00*

The overprint signifies "17 August 1929-Airplane of the Ethiopian Government." The stamps commemorate the arrival at Addis Ababa of the 1st airplane of the Ethiopian Government.

There are 3 types of the overprint: (I) 19½mm high; "colon" at right of bottom word. (II) 20mm high; same "colon." (III) 19½mm high; no "colon." Many errors exist.

Symbols of Empire, Airplane and Map — AP1

1931, June 17 Engr. *Perf. 12½*

C11	AP1	1g orange red	.25	*.25*
C12	AP1	2g ultra	.25	*.30*
C13	AP1	4g violet	.25	*.40*
C14	AP1	8g blue green	.50	*.80*
C15	AP1	1t olive brown	1.25	*1.00*
C16	AP1	2t carmine	2.25	*3.75*
C17	AP1	3t yellow green	3.25	*5.00*
		Nos. C11-C17 (7)	8.00	*11.50*

Nos. C11 to C17 exist imperforate.

Reprints of C11 to C17 exist. Paper is thinner and gum whiter than the originals and the ink is heavy and shiny. Originals have ink that is dull and granular. Reprints usually sell at about one-tenth of above values.

POSTAGE DUE STAMPS

Very Fine examples of Nos. J1-J42 will have perforations touching the design on one or more sides.

Nos. 1-4 and unissued values Overprinted

Perf. 14x13½

1896, June 10 Unwmk.

Black Overprint

J1 A1 ¼g green 1.45
J2 A1 ½g red 1.45
J3 A1 4g lilac brown 1.00
a. Without overprint 1.00
J4 A1 8g violet 1.00
a. Without overprint 1.00

Red Overprint

J5 A1 1g blue 1.45
J6 A1 2g dark brown 1.45
J7 A1 16g black 1.00
a. Without overprint 1.00
Nos. J1-J7 (7) 8.80

Nos. J1-J7 were not issued. Forgeries exist.

Nos. 1-7 Handstamped in Various Colors

a

1905, Apr.

J8 A1 (a) ¼g green 55.00 55.00
J9 A1 (a) ½g red 55.00 55.00
J10 A1 (a) 1g blue 55.00 55.00
J11 A1 (a) 2g dk brown 55.00 55.00
J12 A2 (a) 4g lilac brown 55.00 55.00
J13 A2 (a) 8g violet 55.00 55.00
J14 A2 (a) 16g black 55.00 55.00
Nos. J8-J14 (7) 385.00 385.00

b

1905, Aug.

J15 A1 (b) ¼g green 55.00 55.00
J16 A1 (b) ½g red 55.00 55.00
J17 A1 (b) 1g blue 55.00 55.00
J18 A1 (b) 2g dark brown 55.00 55.00
J19 A2 (b) 4g lilac brown 55.00 55.00
J20 A2 (b) 8g violet 55.00 55.00
J21 A2 (b) 16g black 55.00 55.00
Nos. J15-J21 (7) 385.00 385.00

Excellent forgeries of Nos. J8-J42 exist.

Nos. 1-7 Handstamped in Blue or Violet

1905, Sept.

J22 A1 ¼g green 14.50 14.50
J23 A1 ½g red 14.50 14.50
J24 A1 1g blue 14.50 14.50
J25 A1 2g dark brown 14.50 14.50
J26 A2 4g lilac brown 14.50 14.50
J27 A2 8g violet 21.00 21.00
J28 A2 16g black 25.00 25.00
Nos. J22-J28 (7) 118.50 118.50

Nos. J22-J27 exist with inverted overprint, also No. J22 with double overprint.
Forgeries exist.

With Additional Surcharge of Value Handstamped as on Nos. 71-77

1907, July 1

J29 A1 (e) ¼ on ¼g grn 14.00 14.00
J30 A1 (e) ½ on ½g red 14.00 14.00
J31 A1 (f) 1 on 1g blue 14.00 14.00
J32 A1 (f) 2 on 2g dk brown 14.00 14.00
J33 A2 (f) 4 on 4g lilac brn 14.00 14.00
J34 A2 (f) 8 on 8g violet 14.00 14.00
J35 A2 (f) 16 on 16g blk 22.50 22.50
Nos. J29-J35 (7) 106.50 106.50

Nos. J30-J35 exist with inverted surcharge. Nos. J30, J33-J35 exist with double surcharge.

Nos. 1-7 Handstamped in Black

1908, Dec. 1

J36 A1 ¼g green 1.40 1.25
J37 A1 ½g red 1.40 1.25
J38 A1 1g blue 1.40 1.25
J39 A1 2g dark brown 1.75 1.50
J40 A2 4g lilac brown 2.50 2.50
J41 A2 8g violet 5.50 6.25
J42 A2 16g black 17.50 20.00
Nos. J36-J42 (7) 31.45 34.00

Nos. J36 to J42 exist with inverted overprint and Nos. J36, J37, J38 and J40 with double overprint.
Forgeries of Nos. J36-J56 exist.

Same Handstamp on Nos. 87-93

1912, Dec. 1 *Perf. 11½*

J43 A3 ¼g blue green 1.75 1.25
J44 A3 ½g rose 1.75 1.50

1913, July 1

J45 A3 1g green & org 6.00 4.25
J46 A4 2g blue 7.00 6.00
J47 A4 4g green & car 11.00 7.00
J48 A5 8g ver & dp grn 14.00 11.00
J49 A5 16g ver & car 35.00 27.50
Nos. J43-J49 (7) 76.50 58.50

Nos. J43-J49, all exist with inverted, double and double, one inverted overprint.

Same Handstamp on Nos. 120-124 in Blue Black

1925-27 *Perf. 11½*

J50 A6 ⅛g violet & brn *18.00 18.00*
J51 A6 ¼g bl grn & db *18.00 18.00*
J52 A6 ½g scar & ol grn *20.00 20.00*
J53 A9 1g rose lil & gray grn *20.00 20.00*
J54 A9 2g dp ultra & fawn *20.00 20.00*
Nos. J50-J54 (5) *96.00 96.00*

Same Handstamp on Nos. 110, 112

1917 (?)

J55 A3 (i) 1g green & org *30.00 30.00*
J56 A4 (j) 2g blue *30.00 30.00*

The status of Nos. J55-J56 is questioned.

OCCUPATION STAMPS

Issued under Italian Occupation

100 Centesimi = 1 Lira

OS1

Emperor Victor Emmanuel III — OS2

1936 Wmk. 140 *Perf. 14*

N1 OS1 10c org brn 16.00 9.50
Never hinged 35.00
On cover 140.00
N2 OS1 20c purple 14.50 4.00
Never hinged 30.00
On cover 125.00
N3 OS2 25c dark green 9.50 .80
Never hinged 20.00
On cover 40.00
N4 OS2 30c dark brown 9.50 1.60
Never hinged 20.00
On cover 40.00
N5 OS2 50c rose car 4.00 .40
Never hinged 8.00
On cover 32.50
N6 OS1 75c deep orange 36.00 8.00
Never hinged 67.50
On cover 225.00
N7 OS1 1.25 l deep blue 36.00 12.00
Never hinged 67.50
On cover 300.00
Nos. N1-N7 (7) 125.50 36.30
Set, never hinged 300.00

Issued: Nos. N3-N5, May 22; others Dec. 5.
For later issues see Italian East Africa.

FALKLAND ISLANDS

ˈfol-klənd ˈī-ləndz

LOCATION — A group of islands about 300 miles east of the Straits of Magellan at the southern limit of South America
GOVT. — British Crown Colony
AREA — 4,700 sq. mi.
POP. — 1,813 (1980)
CAPITAL — Stanley

12 Pence = 1 Shilling
20 Shillings = 1 Pound

Catalogue values for unused stamps in this country are for Never Hinged items, beginning with Scott 97 in the regular postage section, Scott 1L1 in Falkland Island Dependencies regular issues, and Scott 2L1, 3L1, 4L1, 5L1 in the Issues for Separate Islands.

Values for unused stamps are for examples with original gum as defined in the catalogue introduction.

Nos. 1-4, 7-8, and some printings of Nos. 5-6, exist with straight edges on one or two sides, being the imperforate margins of the sheets. This occurs in 24 out of 60 stamps. Catalogue values are for stamps with perforations on all sides.

Queen Victoria — A1

1878-79 Unwmk. Engr. *Perf. 14*

1 A1 1p claret 850.00 500.00
2 A1 4p dark gray ('79) 1,400. 200.00
3 A1 6p green 125.00 85.00
4 A1 1sh bister brown 85.00 80.00

No. 2 is known with paper maker's watermark "TURNER, CHAFFORD MILLS," in double-lined capital letters. Values, unused $2,500, used $475.

1883-95 Wmk. 2

5 A1 1p brt claret ('94) 130.00 95.00
a. 1p claret 425.00 190.00
b. Horiz. pair, imperf. vert. *90,000.*
c. 1p red brown ('91) 300.00 95.00
d. Diag. half of #5c used as ½p on cover *4,250.*
6 A1 4p ol gray ('95) 14.00 27.50
a. 4p gray black 750.00 100.00
b. 4p olive gray black ('89) 200.00 65.00
c. 4p brownish black ('94) 1,300. 400.00

No. 6c has watermark reversed.
For surcharge see No. 19E.

1886 Wmk. 2 Sideways

7 A1 1p claret 95.00 65.00
a. 1p brownish claret 125.00 80.00
b. Diagonal half of #7a used as ½p on cover *4,250.*
8 A1 4p olive gray 525.00 60.00
a. 4p pale gray black 840.00 90.00

For surcharge see No. 19.

1891-1902 Wmk. 2

9 A1 ½p green ('92) 19.00 18.00
a. ½p blue green 27.50 *32.50*
10 A1 ½p yel green ('99) 2.25 *3.50*
11 A1 1p orange brown 130.00 85.00
a. Diagonal half used as ½p on cover *4,250.*
11B A1 1p pale red ('99) 9.00 3.50
12 A1 1p org red ('02) 17.50 4.75
a. 1p Venetian red ('95) 32.50 20.00
13 A1 2p magenta ('96) 7.00 14.00
14 A1 2½p deep blue ('94) 275.00 160.00
15 A1 2½p ultra ('94) 50.00 14.00
a. 2½p pale ultra ('98) 50.00 20.00
b. 2½p dull blue 350.00 35.00
c. 2½p deep ultra ('01) 50.00 42.50
d. 2½p pale chalky ultra 240.00 60.00
16 A1 6p yellow ('96) 52.50 55.00
a. 6p orange ('92) 325.00 225.00
17 A1 9p ver ('95) 55.00 *65.00*
a. 9p salmon ('96) 60.00 *70.00*
18 A1 1sh gray brn ('95) 80.00 65.00
a. 1sh bis brn ('96) 75.00 55.00
Nos. 9-18 (11) 697.25 487.75

Nos. 7 and 5a Surcharged in Black

1891 Wmk. 2 Sideways

19 A1 ½p on half of 1p, #7 725.00 360.00
d. Unsevered pair 3,750. 1,600.

Wmk. 2

19E A1 ½p on half of 1p, #5a 825.00 325.00
f. Unsevered pair 4,750. 1,800.

Genuine used bisects should be canceled with a segmented circular cork cancel. Any other cancel must be linked by date to known mail ship departures. This surcharge exists on "souvenir" bisects, including examples of No. 11, and can be found inverted, double and sideways.

A3

A4

1898 Wmk. 1

20 A3 2sh6p dark blue 290.00 290.00
21 A4 5sh brown red 260.00 260.00
Set of two, ovptd. "SPECIMEN" 575.00

A5

A6

King Edward VII

1904-07 Wmk. 3 *Perf. 14*

22 A5 ½p yellow green 9.00 1.75
23 A5 1p red, wmk. sideways ('07) 1.50 *4.25*
a. Wmk. upright ('04) 17.00 *1.75*
b. Thick paper ('08) 22.50 2.00
24 A5 2p dull vio ('04) 25.00 *32.50*
a. 2p reddish pur ('12) 260.00 310.00
25 A5 2½p ultramarine 35.00 10.00
a. 2½p deep blue 300.00 200.00
26 A5 6p orange ('05) 50.00 *57.50*
27 A5 1sh bis brn ('05) 50.00 40.00
28 A6 3sh gray green 180.00 160.00
a. 3sh green 160.00 140.00
29 A6 5sh dull red ('05) 240.00 160.00
Nos. 22-29 (8) 590.50 466.00
Nos. 22-29 (8), ovptd. "SPECIMEN" 700.00

A7

A8

King George V

1912-14 *Perf. 13¾x14, 14 (#36-40)*

30 A7 ½p yel grn 3.00 3.75
a. ½p dp yel grn, perf. 14 ('14) 20.00 40.00
b. ½p dp ol, perf. 14 ('18) 25.00 160.00

No.	Type	Description	Unused	Used
c.		½p As "b" printed on both sides		7,500.
d.		½p dl yel grn, thick grayish paper ('20)	5.00	40.00
31	A7	1p red	5.50	2.75
a.		1p org ver, perf. 14 ('14)	50.00	2.75
b.		1p vermilion ('18)		950.00
c.		1p org ver ('19)	7.50	3.25
d.		1p org ver, thick grayish paper ('20)	7.50	2.25
32	A7	2p brn vio	27.50	*24.00*
a.		2p dp redsh pur, perf. 14 ('14)	350.00	160.00
b.		2p brn vio, perf. 14 ('18)	375.00	175.00
c.		2p dp redsh pur ('19)	9.00	17.00
33	A7	2½p deep ultra	27.50	*25.00*
a.		2½p dp ultra, perf. 14 ('14)	45.00	52.50
b.		2½p dp blue, perf. 14 ('16)	550.00	65.00
c.		2½p deep blue	7.50	17.50
34	A7	6p orange	17.50	*22.50*
a.		6p brn org ('19)	16.00	45.00
35	A7	1sh bis brn	40.00	*37.50*
a.		1sh pale bister brn ('19)	100.00	140.00
b.		1sh brn, thick grayish paper ('20)	40.00	160.00
36	A8	3sh dark green	100.00	*95.00*
37	A8	5sh brown red	120.00	*120.00*
38	A8	5sh plum ('14)	300.00	*300.00*
a.		5sh maroon	140.00	150.00
39	A8	10sh red, *green*	200.00	*275.00*
40	A8	£1 black, *red*	550.00	*600.00*
		Nos. 30-40 (11)	1,391.	*1,506.*

For overprints see Nos. MR1-MR3.

1921-29 Wmk. 4 *Perf. 14*

No.	Type	Description	Unused	Used
41	A7	½p yellow green	3.50	*4.50*
a.		½p green	3.50	4.50
42	A7	1p red ('24)	6.00	2.10
a.		1p org ver ('25)	6.00	1.40
43	A7	2p brown vio ('23)	26.00	8.50
a.		2p brn vio ('27)	55.00	30.00
b.		2p reddish mar ('28)	11.00	25.00
44	A7	2½p dark blue	22.00	*20.00*
a.		2½p Prussian blue ('29)	*375.00*	*550.00*
45	A7	2½p vio, *yel* ('23)	6.00	*42.50*
a.		2½p pale vio, pale yel ('25)	6.00	42.50
46	A7	6p orange ('25)	11.00	*45.00*
47	A7	1sh bister brown	24.00	*57.50*
48	A8	3sh dk green ('23)	100.00	*190.00*
		Nos. 41-48 (8)	198.50	*370.10*

Some specialists call into question No. 44a. The editors would like to see authenticated evidence of its existence.

No. 43 Surcharged

1928

No.	Type	Description	Unused	Used
52	A7	2½p on 2p brn vio	*1,300.*	*1,400.*
a.		Double surcharge	*60,000.*	

Beware of forged surcharges.

King George V — A9

1929-31 *Perf. 14*

No.	Type	Description	Unused	Used
54	A9	½p green	1.40	*4.25*
55	A9	1p scarlet	4.25	.90
56	A9	2p gray	6.00	3.75
57	A9	2½p blue	6.00	2.50
58	A9	4p deep orange	23.00	15.00
59	A9	6p brown violet	24.00	19.00
60	A9	1sh black, *green*	27.50	*37.50*
a.		1sh black, *emerald*	*25.00*	*37.50*
61	A9	2sh6p red, *blue*	70.00	70.00
62	A9	5sh green, *yel*	105.00	*120.00*
63	A9	10sh red, *green*	225.00	*275.00*

Wmk. 3

No.	Type	Description	Unused	Used
64	A9	£1 black, *red*	350.00	425.00
		Nos. 54-64 (11)	842.15	972.90
		Nos. 54-64 (11), Ovptd. "SPECIMEN"	*1,100.*	

Issue dates: 4p, 1931, others, Sept. 2.

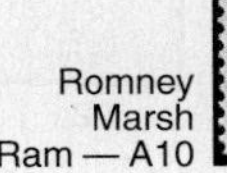

Romney Marsh Ram — A10

Iceberg A11

Whaling Ship — A12

Port Louis A13

Map of the Islands A14

South Georgia A15

Blue Whale A16

Government House A17

Battle Memorial — A18

King Penguin — A19

Coat of Arms — A20

King George V — A21

1933, Jan. 2 Wmk. 4 *Perf. 12*

No.	Type	Description	Unused	Used
65	A10	½p grn & blk	4.00	*12.00*
66	A11	1p dl red & blk	3.75	2.50
67	A12	1½p lt bl & blk	21.00	*27.50*
68	A13	2p ol brn & blk	17.50	*32.50*
69	A14	3p dl vio & blk	27.00	*35.00*
70	A15	4p org & blk	26.00	*27.50*
71	A16	6p gray & blk	70.00	*90.00*
72	A17	1sh ol grn & blk	75.00	*100.00*
73	A18	2sh6p dp vio & blk	250.00	*400.00*
74	A19	5sh yel & blk	950.00	*1,500.*
a.		5sh yellow orange & black	3,000.	*3,500.*
75	A20	10sh lt brn & blk	850.00	*1,500.*
76	A21	£1 rose & blk	2,500.	*3,500.*
		Nos. 65-76 (12)	4,794.	*7,227.*
		Set (12), Ovptd. "SPECIMEN"	*4,500.*	

Cent. of the permanent occupation of the islands as a British colony.

Common Design Types pictured following the introduction.

Silver Jubilee Issue

Common Design Type

1935, May 7 *Perf. 11x12*

No.	Type	Description	Unused	Used
77	CD301	1p car & blue	3.50	.50
78	CD301	2½p ultra & brn	12.50	2.25
79	CD301	4p indigo & grn	20.00	7.00
80	CD301	1sh brn vio & ind	15.00	4.00
		Nos. 77-80 (4)	51.00	13.75
		Set, never hinged	75.00	
		Set (4), Ovptd. "SPECIMEN"	*475.00*	

Coronation Issue

Common Design Type

1937, May 12 *Perf. 11x11½*

No.	Type	Description	Unused	Used
81	CD302	½p deep green	.25	.25
82	CD302	1p dark carmine	.75	*.55*
83	CD302	2½p deep ultra	1.90	*1.50*
		Nos. 81-83 (3)	2.90	*2.30*
		Set, never hinged	4.00	
		Set (3), Ovptd. "SPECIMEN"	*450.00*	

Whale Jawbones (Centennial Monument) — A22

Nos. 85, 86A, Black-necked swan. Nos. 85B, 86, Battle memorial. 2½p, 3p, Flock of sheep. 4p, Upland goose. 6p, R.R.S. "Discovery II." 9p, R.R.S. "William Scoresby." 1sh, Mt. Sugar Top. 1sh3p, Turkey vultures. 2sh6p, Gentoo penguins. 5sh, Sea lions. 10sh, Deception Island. £1, Arms of Colony.

1938-46 *Perf. 12*

No.	Type	Description	Unused	Used
84	A22	½p green & blk	.25	.75
85	A22	1p red & black	2.50	1.00
a.		1p rose carmine & black	22.50	1.00
85B	A22	1p dk vio & blk ('41)	2.00	2.00
a.		1p red vio & blk	8.00	3.50
86	A22	2p dk vio & blk	1.30	1.00
86A	A22	2p rose car & black ('41)	1.40	4.00
b.		2p red & black	3.00	3.00
87	A22	2½p ultra & blk	1.00	.50
b.		2½p blue & blk	5.00	8.00
87A	A22	3p blue & blk ('41)	5.50	6.50
c.		3p dp blue & blk	12.50	4.50
88	A22	4p rose vio & black	2.75	1.75
89	A22	6p sepia & blk	7.50	4.25
a.		6p dp brn & blk	19.50	2.50
90	A22	9p sl bl & blk	17.50	5.00
91	A22	1sh lt dl blue	25.00	5.50
a.		1sh dl grnsh blue	40.00	5.00
b.		1sh dl blue, grayish paper	30.00	150.00
c.		1sh dp dl blue, grayish paper ('48)	50.00	140.00
92	A22	1sh3p car & blk	2.00	*1.50*
93	A22	2sh6p gray black	40.00	22.50
94	A22	5sh org brn & ultra	100.00	90.00
a.		5sh yel brown & indigo	650.00	150.00
b.		5sh yel brn & dl bl, grayish paper ('49)	850.00	500.00
c.		5sh duff & steel bl, thin paper ('50)	250.00	65.00
95	A22	10sh org & blk	100.00	62.50
a.		10sh org brn & blk	150.00	65.00
b.		10sh red org & blk, grayish paper ('49)	90.00	450.00
c.		10sh dp red org & blk, thin paper ('50)	450.00	475.00
96	A22	£1 dk vio & blk	120.00	75.00
		Nos. 84-96 (16)	428.70	283.75
		Set, never hinged	600.00	
		Set (16), perf. "SPECIMEN"	*2,500.*	

Issued: Nos. 85B, 86A, 3p, 7/14/41; 1sh3p, 12/10/46; No. 94a, 1942; others, 1/3/38.

See Nos. 101-102. For overprints see Nos. 2L1-2L8, 3L1-3L8, 4L1-4L8.

Catalogue values for unused stamps in this section, from this point to the end of the section, are for Never Hinged items.

Peace Issue

Common Design Type

Perf. 13½x14

1946, Oct. 7 Engr. Wmk. 4

No.	Type	Description	Unused	Used
97	CD303	1p purple	.35	*.80*
98	CD303	3p deep blue	.55	.55
		Set (2), perf. "SPECIMEN"	*425.00*	

Silver Wedding Issue

Common Design Types

1948, Nov. 1 Photo. *Perf. 14x14½*

No.	Type	Description	Unused	Used
99	CD304	2½p bright ultra	2.10	1.10

Engr.; Name Typo.

Perf. 11½x11

No.	Type	Description	Unused	Used
100	CD305	£1 purple	110.00	82.50

Types of 1938-46

2½p, Upland goose. 6p, R.R.S. "Discovery II."

Perf. 12

1949, June 15 Engr. Wmk. 4

No.	Type	Description	Unused	Used
101	A22	2½p dp blue & black	7.50	*8.50*
102	A22	6p gray black	6.75	4.75

UPU Issue

Common Design Types

Engr.; Name Typo. on 3p, 1sh3p

1949, Oct. 10 *Perf. 13½, 11x11½*

No.	Type	Description	Unused	Used
103	CD306	1p violet	1.90	1.10
104	CD307	3p indigo	5.25	4.25
105	CD308	1sh3p green	3.75	3.00
106	CD309	2sh blue	4.00	8.75
		Nos. 103-106 (4)	14.90	17.10

Sheep
A35

Arms of the Colony — A36

Designs: 1p, R.M.S. Fitzroy. 2p Upland goose. 2½p, Map. 4p, Auster plane. 6p, M.S.S. John Biscoe. 9p, "Two Sisters" peaks. 1sh, Gentoo penguins. 1sh 3p, Kelp goose and gander. 2sh 6p, Sheep shearing. 5sh, Battle memorial. 10sh, Sea lion and clapmatch. £1, Hulk of "Great Britain."

Perf. 13½x13, 13x13½

1952, Jan. 2 Engr. Wmk. 4

107 A35 ½p green 1.30 *1.00*
108 A35 1p red 2.60 .55
109 A35 2p violet 4.75 *3.00*
110 A35 2½p ultra & blk 2.10 .70
111 A36 3p deep ultra 2.40 *1.10*
112 A35 4p claret 12.50 1.75
113 A35 6p yellow brn 14.00 1.10
114 A35 9p orange yel 12.50 2.25
115 A36 1sh black 26.00 1.10
116 A35 1sh3p red orange 19.00 *7.00*
117 A36 2sh6p olive 22.50 *12.50*
118 A36 5sh red violet 20.00 *11.00*
119 A35 10sh gray 30.00 *19.00*
120 A35 £1 black 40.00 *25.00*
Nos. 107-120 (14) 209.65 *87.05*

WAR TAX STAMPS

Regular Issue of 1912-14 Overprinted

1918-20 Wmk. 3 *Perf. 14*

MR1 A7 ½p dp ol grn .55 *7.25*
a. ½p yel grn ('19) 30.00 750.00
b. As "a," albino ovpt. 2,500.
c. ½p dl yel grn, thick grayish paper ('20) 8.00 55.00
MR2 A7 1p org ver ('19) .55 *4.00*
a. Double overprint *3,750.*
b. 1p vermilion 2.00 18.00
c. As "b," double ovpt, one albino 400.00
d. 1p org ver, thick grayish paper ('20) 125.00 200.00
MR3 A7 1sh bis brn 6.50 *52.50*
a. Pair, one without overprint 16,500.
b. Double ovpt., one albino 2,000.
c. 1sh brn, thick grayish paper ('20) 6.00 50.00
d. As "c," double ovpt., one albino 2,000.
Nos. MR1-MR3 (3) 7.60 *63.75*

No. MR3a probably is caused by a foldover and is not constant.

FALKLAND ISLANDS DEPENDENCIES

Catalogue values for unused stamps in this section are for Never Hinged items.

Map of Falkland Islands — A1

Engr., Center Litho. in Black

1946, Feb. 1 Wmk. 4 *Perf. 12*

1L1 A1 ½p yellow green 1.10 *3.50*
1L2 A1 1p blue violet 1.30 *1.90*
1L3 A1 2p deep carmine 1.30 *2.60*
1L4 A1 3p ultramarine 1.90 *5.25*
1L5 A1 4p deep plum 2.40 *5.00*
1L6 A1 6p orange yellow 3.75 *5.25*
1L7 A1 9p brown 2.25 *4.00*
1L8 A1 1sh rose violet 3.00 *5.00*
Nos. 1L1-1L8 (8) 17.00 *32.50*

Nos. 1L1-1L8 were reissued in 1948, printed on more opaque paper with the lines of the map finer and clearer. Value for set, unused or used $120.

See No. 1L13.

Common Design Types pictured following the introduction.

Peace Issue
Common Design Type

1946, Oct. 4 *Perf. 13½x14*

1L9 CD303 1p purple .50 .50
1L10 CD303 3p deep blue .90 .50

Silver Wedding Issue
Common Design Types

1948, Dec. 6 Photo. *Perf. 14x14½*

1L11 CD304 2½p brt ultra 1.75 3.25

Perf. 11½x11
Engr.

1L12 CD305 1sh blue violet 2.50 2.75

Type of 1946

1949, Mar. 6 *Perf. 12*
Center Litho. in Black

1L13 A1 2½p deep blue 8.00 4.25

UPU Issue
Common Design Types
Engr.; Name Typo. on 2p, 3p

1949, Oct. 10 *Perf. 13½, 11x11½*

1L14 CD306 1p violet 1.25 3.50
1L15 CD307 2p deep carmine 5.25 4.00
1L16 CD308 3p indigo 4.00 2.25
1L17 CD309 6p red orange 5.00 4.25
Nos. 1L14-1L17 (4) 15.50 14.00

ISSUES FOR THE SEPARATE ISLANDS

Graham Land

Nos. 84, 85B, 86A, 87A, 88-91 Overprinted in Red

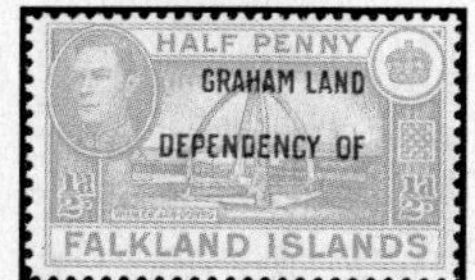

1944, Feb. 12 Wmk. 4 *Perf. 12*

2L1 A22 ½p green & black .50 2.10
a. ½p grn & blue blk 1,500. 900.00
2L2 A22 1p dk vio & black .50 1.10
2L3 A22 2p rose car & blk .60 1.10
2L4 A22 3p deep bl & blk .60 1.10
2L5 A22 4p rose vio & blk 2.00 1.90
2L6 A22 6p brown & black 21.00 2.75
a. 6p brn & blue blk ('45) 21.00
2L7 A22 9p slate bl & blk 1.50 1.50
2L8 A22 1sh dull blue 1.50 1.50
Nos. 2L1-2L8 (8) 28.20 13.05

South Georgia

1944, Apr. 3 Wmk. 4 *Perf. 12*

3L1 A22 ½p green & black .40 2.25
3L2 A22 1p dark vio & blk .40 1.10
3L3 A22 2p rose car & blk .60 1.10
3L4 A22 3p deep bl & blk .60 1.10
3L5 A22 4p rose vio & blk 2.00 2.00
3L6 A22 6p brown & black 21.00 2.50
a. 6p brn & blue blk ('45) 21.00
3L7 A22 9p slate bl & blk 1.50 1.50
3L8 A22 1sh dull blue 1.50 1.50
Nos. 3L1-3L8 (8) 28.00 13.05

South Orkneys

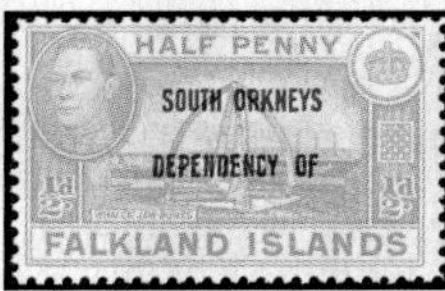

1944, Feb. 21 Wmk. 4 *Perf. 12*

4L1 A22 ½p green & black .50 2.10
4L2 A22 1p dark vio & blk .50 1.10
4L3 A22 2p rose car & blk .80 1.10
4L4 A22 3p deep bl & blk .80 1.10
4L5 A22 4p rose vio & blk 2.00 2.00
4L6 A22 6p brown & black 21.00 2.50
a. 6p brn & blue blk ('45) 21.00
4L7 A22 9p slate bl & blk 1.50 1.50
4L8 A22 1sh dull blue 1.50 1.50
Nos. 4L1-4L8 (8) 28.60 12.90

South Shetlands

1944 Wmk. 4 *Perf. 12*

5L1 A22 ½p green & black .50 2.10
5L2 A22 1p dark vio & blk .50 1.10
5L3 A22 2p rose car & blk .60 1.10
5L4 A22 3p deep bl & blk .60 1.10
5L5 A22 4p rose vio & blk 2.00 2.00
5L6 A22 6p brown & black 21.00 2.50
a. 6p brn & blue blk ('45) 21.00
5L7 A22 9p slate bl & blk 1.50 1.50
5L8 A22 1sh dull blue 1.50 1.50
Nos. 5L1-5L8 (8) 28.20 12.90

FAR EASTERN REPUBLIC

ˈfär ˈē-stərn ri-ˈpə-blik

LOCATION — In Siberia east of Lake Baikal
GOVT. — Republic
AREA — 900,745 sq. mi.
POP. — 1,560,000 (approx. 1920)
CAPITAL — Chita

A short-lived independent government was established here in 1920.

100 Kopecks = 1 Ruble

Watermark

Wmk. 171 — Diamonds

Vladivostok Issue
Russian Stamps Surcharged or Overprinted

a

b

c

On Stamps of 1909-17

Perf. 14, 14½x15, 13½

1920 Unwmk.

2 A14(a) 2k green 10.00 *15.00*
3 A14(a) 3k red 10.00 *10.00*
4 A11(b) 3k on 35k red brn & grn 40.00 50.00
5 A15(a) 4k carmine 10.00 *12.00*
6 A11(b) 4k on 70k brn & org 10.00 *15.00*
8 A11(b) 7k on 15k red brn & bl 2.00 2.00
a. Inverted surcharge 100.00
b. Pair, one ovptd. "DBP" only *100.00*
9 A15(a) 10k dark blue 75.00 *55.00*
a. Overprint on back 90.00
10 A12(c) 10k on 3½r mar & lt grn 25.00 *25.00*
11 A11(a) 14k blue & rose 50.00 35.00
12 A11(a) 15k red brn & bl 30.00 25.00
13 A8(a) 20k blue & car 150.00 *100.00*
14 A11(b) 20k on 14k bl & rose 10.00 *8.00*
a. Surcharge on back 30.00
15 A11(a) 25k green & vio 25.00 15.00
16 A11(a) 35k red brn & grn 50.00 35.00
17 A8(a) 50k brn vio & grn 10.00 *12.00*
18 A9(a) 1r pale brn, dk brn & org *750.00 750.00*

On Stamps of 1917
Imperf

21 A14(a) 1k orange 25.00 *10.00*
22 A14(a) 2k gray grn 20.00 10.00
23 A14(a) 3k red 20.00 *10.00*
25 A11(b) 7k on 15k red brn & dp bl 2.00 *5.00*
a. Pair, one without surcharge *100.00*
b. Pair, one ovptd. "DBP" only *100.00*
26 A12(c) 10k on 3½r mar & lt grn 27.50 *15.00*
27 A9(a) 1r pale brn, brn & red org 40.00 *20.00*

On Stamps of Siberia 1919
Perf. 14, 14½x15

30 A14(a) 35k on 2k green 5.00 *8.00*
a. "DBP" on back 25.00 *50.00*

Imperf

31 A14(a) 35k on 2k green 35.00 25.00
32 A14(a) 70k on 1k orange 7.50 *10.00*

Counterfeit surcharges and overprints abound, including digital forgeries.

On Russia Nos. AR2, AR3

A1

Perf. 14½x15
Wmk. 171

35 A1(b) 1k on 5k green, *buff* 30.00 20.00
36 A1(b) 2k on 10k brown, *buff* 40.00 30.00

The letters on these stamps resembling "DBP," are the Russian initials of "Dalne Vostochnaya Respublika" (Far Eastern Republic).

Chita Issue

A2

A2a

1921 Unwmk. Typo. *Imperf.*

38 A2 2k gray green 1.50 1.50
39 A2a 4k rose 3.00 3.00
40 A2 5k claret 3.00 3.00
41 A2a 10k blue 2.50 2.50
Nos. 38-41 (4) 10.00 10.00

For overprints see Nos. 62-65.

Blagoveshchensk Issue

A3

1921 Litho. *Imperf.*
42 A3 2r red 2.75 2.00
43 A3 3r dark green 2.75 2.00
44 A3 5r dark blue 2.75 2.00
a. Tête bêche pair 45.00 *50.00*
45 A3 15r dark brown 2.75 2.00
46 A3 30r dark violet 2.75 2.00
a. Tête bêche pair 35.00 *15.00*
Nos. 42-46 (5) 13.75 10.00

Remainders of Nos. 42-46 were canceled in colored crayon or by typographed bars. These sell for half of foregoing values.

Chita Issue

A4

A5

1922 Litho. *Imperf.*
49 A4 1k orange 1.00 *.85*
50 A4 3k dull red .40 *.45*
51 A5 4k dp rose & buff .40 *.45*
52 A4 5k orange brown .80 .45
53 A4 7k light blue 1.50 *1.50*
a. Perf. 11½ 2.00 2.50
b. Rouletted 9 3.00 3.00
c. Perf. 11½x rouletted 6.50 6.50
54 A5 10k dk blue & red .60 *.65*
55 A4 15k dull rose .80 *1.10*
56 A5 20k blue & red .80 *1.10*
57 A5 30k green & red org 1.25 *1.10*
58 A5 50k black & red org 3.00 *2.25*
Nos. 49-58 (10) 10.55 *9.90*

The 4k exists with "4" omitted. Value $100.

Vladivostok Issue

Stamps of 1921 Overprinted in Red

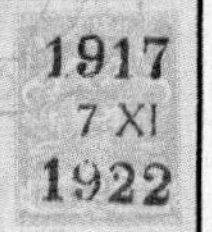

1922 *Imperf.*
62 A2 2k gray green 35.00 25.00
a. Inverted overprint 250.00
63 A2a 4k rose 35.00 25.00
a. Inverted overprint 250.00
b. Double overprint 250.00
64 A2 5k claret 35.00 35.00
a. Inverted overprint 100.00
b. Double overprint 350.00
65 A2a 10k blue 35.00 35.00
a. Inverted overprint 250.00
Nos. 62-65 (4) 140.00 120.00

Russian revolution of Nov. 1917, 5th anniv.
Once in the setting the figures "22" of 1922 have the bottom stroke curved instead of straight. Value, each $75.

Vladivostok Issue

Russian Stamps of 1922-23 Surcharged in Black or Red

1923 *Imperf.*
66 A50 1k on 100r red .40 *1.00*
a. Inverted surcharge 60.00
67 A50 2k on 70r violet .40 *.75*
68 A49 5k on 10r blue (R) .40 *.75*
69 A50 10k on 50r brown .90 *1.25*
a. Inverted surcharge 250.00

Perf. 14½x15
70 A50 1k on 100r red .90 *1.25*
Nos. 66-70 (5) 3.00 *5.00*

OCCUPATION STAMPS

Issued under Occupation of General Semenov
Chita Issue
Russian Stamps of 1909-12 Surcharged

a

b

c

1920 Unwmk. *Perf. 14, 14x15½*
N1 A15 (a) 1r on 4k car 150.00 *100.00*
N2 A8 (b) 2r50k on 20k bl & car 40.00 30.00
N3 A14 (c) 5r on 5k claret 25.00 *50.00*
a. Double surcharge 200.00
N4 A11 (a) 10r on 70k brn & org 20.00 *25.00*
Nos. N1-N4 (4) 235.00 *205.00*

FAROE ISLANDS

'far-ˌō 'ī-lənds

(The Faroes)

LOCATION — North Atlantic Ocean
GOVT. — Part of the Kingdom of Denmark
AREA — 540 sq. mi.
POP. — 52,347 (1984)
CAPITAL — Thorshavn

100 Ore = 1 Krone

Denmark No. 97 Handstamp Surcharged

1919, Jan. Typo. *Perf. 14x14½*
1 A16 2o on 5o green 1,400. 475.00
Never hinged 3,900.

Counterfeits of surcharge exist.
Denmark No. 88a, the bisect, was used with Denmark No. 97 in Faroe Islands Jan. 3-23, 1919.

Denmark Nos. 220, 224, 238A, 224C Surcharged in Blue or Black

Nos. 2, 5-6

No. 3

No. 4

1940-41 Engr. *Perf. 13*
2 A32 20o on 1o ('41) 40.00 110.00
3 A32 20o on 5o ('41) 40.00 35.00
4 A30 20o on 15o (Bk) 60.00 22.50
5 A32 50o on 5o (Bk) 275.00 90.00
6 A32 60o on 6o (Bk) 125.00 *250.00*
Nos. 2-6 (5) 540.00 507.50
Set, never hinged 1,150.

Issued during British administration.

FERNANDO PO

fər-'nan-ˌdō 'pō

LOCATION — An island in the Gulf of Guinea off west Africa.
GOVT. — Spanish Colony
AREA — 800 sq. mi.
POP. — 62,612 (1960)
CAPITAL — Santa Isabel

Together with the islands of Elobey, Annobon and Corisco, Fernando Po came under the administration of Spanish Guinea. Postage stamps of Spanish Guinea were used until 1960.

100 Centimos = 1 Escudo = 2.50 Pesetas
100 Centimos = 1 Peseta
1000 Milesimas = 100 Centavos = 1 Peso (1882)

FORERUNNERS

Crowned Circle handstamp type VII and Numeral Cancellation type B are pictured in the Crowned Circle Handstamps and Great Britain Used Abroad section.

P.O. at St. Thomas opened Apr. 1, 1858; canceler supplied 1874; closed in 1877

1859
A1 I Crowned circle handstamp Type VII inscribed "FERNANDO-P" in red, on cover 6,250.
Earliest known use: 2/19/59.

STAMPS OF GREAT BRITAIN USED IN FERNANDO PO
Canceled "247"

1874-77
A2 4p vermilion (#43, P 13, 14) —
A3 4p vermilion (#69, P 15) —
A4 6p gray (#62, P 13-16) —

Issued under Spanish Dominion

Isabella II — A1

1868 Unwmk. Typo. *Perf. 14*
1 A1 20c brown 400.00 140.00
a. 20c red brown 525.00 140.00

No. 1 is valued in the grade of fine, as illustrated. Examples with very fine centering are uncommon and sell for more.
Forgeries exist.

Alfonso XII — A2

1879 Centimos de Peseta
2 A2 5c green 57.50 15.00
3 A2 10c rose 42.50 15.00
4 A2 50c blue 100.00 15.00
Nos. 2-4 (3) 200.00 45.00

1882-89 Centavos de Peso
5 A2 1c green 9.50 5.50
6 A2 2c rose 18.00 8.75
7 A2 5c gray blue 60.00 12.00
8 A2 10c dk brown ('89) 82.50 6.75
Nos. 5-8 (4) 170.00 33.00

Nos. 5-7 Handstamp Surcharged in Blue, Black or Violet — a

1884-95
9 A2 50c on 1c green ('95) 120.00 19.00
11 A2 50c on 2c rose 32.00 6.00
12 A2 50c on 5c blue ('87) 150.00 25.00
Nos. 9-12 (3) 302.00 50.00

Values above are for examples surcharged in black. Stamps surcharged in violet or blue are worth about 25% more.
Inverted and double surcharges exist. No. 12 exists overprinted in carmine. Value $100.

King Alfonso XIII — A4

1894-97 *Perf. 14*
13 A4 ⅛c slate ('96) 22.00 3.00
14 A4 2c rose ('96) 15.50 2.50
15 A4 5c blue grn ('97) 16.00 2.50
16 A4 6c dk violet ('96) 13.00 3.00
17 A4 10c blk vio ('94) 450.00 115.00
17A A4 10c dark brown ('94) 30.00 5.00
18 A4 10c lake ('95) 50.00 8.75
19 A4 10c org brn ('96) 10.50 2.50
20 A4 12½c dk brown ('96) 11.50 3.00
21 A4 20c slate bl ('96) 11.50 3.00
22 A4 25c claret ('96) 23.00 3.00
Nos. 13-22 (10) 623.00 146.25

Most exist imperf. Value, set, pairs Nos. 13-16 and Nos. 18-22, $2,500.

Stamps of 1894-97 Handstamped in Blue, Black or Red

b

c

Type "b" Surcharge

1896-98
22A A4 5c on ⅛c slate (Bl) 100.00 27.50
23 A4 5c on 2c rose (Bl) 50.00 16.50
23A A4 5c on 6c dk vio (Bl) 180.00 45.00
24 A4 5c on 10c brn vio (Bl) 180.00 45.00
24A A4 5c on 10c org brn (Bl) 180.00 45.00
24B A4 5c on 10c dk brn (Bk) 67.50 27.50
25 A4 5c on 12½c brn (Bl) 37.50 13.00
a. Black surcharge 37.50 13.00
25B A4 5c on 20c sl bl (R) 180.00 45.00
25C A4 5c on 25c claret (Bk) 180.00 35.00
Nos. 22A-25C (9) 1,155. 299.50

Type "c" Surcharge
26 A4 5c on ⅛c slate (Bk) 32.50 6.75
27 A4 5c on 2c rose (Bl) 32.50 6.75
a. Black surcharge 32.50 6.75
28 A4 5c on 5c green (R) 160.00 22.00
29 A4 5c on 6c dk vio (R) 23.00 14.00
a. Violet surcharge 24.00 15.50
30 A4 5c on 10c org brn (Bk) 210.00 27.50
30A A4 5c on 10c dk brn (Bk) 160.00 26.00
30B A4 5c on 10c lake (Bl) 400.00 110.00
31 A4 5c on 12½c brn (R) 70.00 11.00
32 A4 5c on 20c sl bl (R) 40.00 10.50
33 A4 5c on 25c claret (Bk) 37.50 11.00
a. Blue surcharge 37.50 13.50
Nos. 26-33 (10) 1,166. 245.50

Exist surcharged in other colors.

Type "a" Srch. in Blue or Black

1898-99
34 A4 50c on 2c rose 92.50 11.50
35 A4 50c on 10c brn vio 220.00 33.00
36 A4 50c on 10c lake 230.00 33.00
37 A4 50c on 10c org brn 220.00 33.00
38 A4 50c on 12½c brn (Bk) 190.00 22.00

The "a" surch. also exists on ⅛c, 5c & 25c. Values, $325, $225 and $210, respectively.

Revenue Stamps Privately Handstamped in Blue

Arms

A5 A6

1897-98			*Imperf.*	
39	A5	5c on 10c rose	28.00	12.50
40	A6	10c rose	24.00	11.00

Revenue Stamps Handstamped in Black or Red

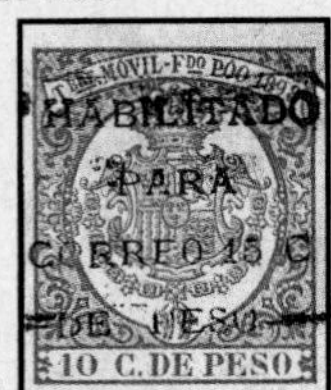

A7

A8

A9

Arms — A9a

1899			*Imperf.*	
41	A7	15c on 10c green	45.00	23.00
a.		Blue surcharge, vertical	39.00	21.00
42	A8	10c on 25c green	120.00	65.00
43	A9	15c on 25c green	190.00	120.00
43A	A9a	15c on 25c green (R)	*1,800.*	*1,100.*
b.		Black surcharge	*1,800.*	*1,100.*

Surcharge on No. 41 is either horizontal, inverted or vertical.

On No. 42 "CORREOS" is ovptd. in red.

On Nos. 43A and 43Ab, the signature is always in black.

King Alfonso XIII — A10

Double-lined shaded letters at sides.

1899			*Perf. 14*	
44	A10	1m orange brn	2.40	.45
45	A10	2m orange brn	2.40	.45
46	A10	3m orange brn	2.40	.45
47	A10	4m orange brn	2.40	.45
48	A10	5m orange brn	2.40	.45
49	A10	1c black vio	2.40	.45
50	A10	2c dk blue grn	2.40	.45
51	A10	3c dk brown	2.40	.45
52	A10	4c orange	13.00	1.10
53	A10	5c carmine rose	2.50	.45
54	A10	6c dark blue	2.50	.45
55	A10	8c gray brn	8.00	.45
56	A10	10c vermilion	5.25	.45
57	A10	15c slate grn	5.25	.45
58	A10	20c maroon	14.50	1.10
59	A10	40c violet	100.00	19.00
60	A10	60c black	100.00	19.00
61	A10	80c red brown	100.00	19.00
62	A10	1p yellow grn	325.00	92.50
63	A10	2p slate blue	325.00	95.00
		Nos. 44-63 (20)	1,020.	252.55

Nos. 44-63 exist imperf. Value for set, $3,500.

See Nos. 66-85. For surcharges see Nos. 64-65, 88-88B.

1900			Surcharged type "a"	
64	A10	50c on 20c maroon	16.00	2.50
a.		Blue surcharge	32.00	4.75

Surcharged type "b"

64B	A10	5c on 20c maroon	300.00	40.00

Surcharged type "c"

65	A10	5c on 20c maroon	9.50	2.40
		Nos. 64-65 (3)	325.50	44.90

1900 Dated "1900"

Solid letters at sides.

66	A10	1m black	3.00	.50
67	A10	2m black	3.00	.50
68	A10	3m black	3.00	.50
69	A10	4m black	3.00	.50
70	A10	5m black	3.00	.50
71	A10	1c green	3.00	.50
72	A10	2c violet	3.00	.50
73	A10	3c rose	3.00	.50
74	A10	4c black brn	3.00	.50
75	A10	5c blue	3.00	.50
76	A10	6c orange	3.00	.50
77	A10	8c bronze grn	3.00	.50
78	A10	10c claret	3.00	.50
79	A10	15c dk violet	3.00	.50
80	A10	20c olive brn	3.00	.50
81	A10	40c brown	7.75	2.25
82	A10	60c green	16.50	2.50
83	A10	80c dark blue	17.50	3.75
84	A10	1p red brown	110.00	30.00
85	A10	2p orange	190.00	62.50
		Nos. 66-85 (20)	386.75	108.50
		Set, never hinged	750.00	

Nos. 66-85 exist imperf. Value, set *$3,500.*

Revenue Stamps Overprinted or Surcharged with Handstamp in Red or Black

A11

A12

1900			*Imperf.*	
86	A11	10c blue (R)	37.50	17.50
87	A12	5c on 10c blue	100.00	40.00
		Set, never hinged	175.00	

Nos. 52 and 80 Surcharged type "a" in Violet or Black

1900				
88	A10	50c on 4c orange (V)	14.00	4.00
a.		Green surcharge	22.50	12.00
88B	A10	50c on 20c ol brn	14.00	3.50
		Set, never hinged	37.50	

A13

1901			*Perf. 14*	
89	A13	1c black	3.00	.90
90	A13	2c orange brn	3.00	.90
91	A13	3c dk violet	3.00	.90
92	A13	4c lt violet	3.00	.90
93	A13	5c orange red	1.75	.90
94	A13	10c violet brn	1.75	.90
95	A13	25c dp blue	1.75	.90
96	A13	50c claret	3.00	.90
97	A13	75c dk brown	2.25	.90
98	A13	1p blue grn	67.50	7.50
99	A13	2p red brown	42.50	10.00
100	A13	3p olive grn	42.50	14.00
101	A13	4p dull red	42.50	14.00
102	A13	5p dk green	52.50	14.00
103	A13	10p buff	125.00	40.00
		Nos. 89-103 (15)	395.00	107.60
		Set, never hinged	850.00	

Dated "1902"

1902 Control Numbers on Back

104	A13	5c dk green	2.60	.45
105	A13	10c slate	2.90	.50
106	A13	25c claret	6.25	1.00
107	A13	50c violet brn	15.00	3.25
108	A13	75c lt violet	15.00	3.25
109	A13	1p car rose	18.50	4.00
110	A13	2p olive grn	40.00	9.50
111	A13	5p orange red	57.50	20.00
		Nos. 104-111 (8)	157.75	41.95
		Set, never hinged	250.00	

Exist imperf. Value for set, *$1,500.*

A14

Dated "1903"

1903 *Perf. 14*

Control Numbers on Back

112	A14	¼c dk violet	.45	.25
113	A14	½c black	.45	.25
114	A14	1c scarlet	.45	.25
115	A14	2c dk green	.45	.30
116	A14	3c blue grn	.45	.30
117	A14	4c violet	.45	.30
118	A14	5c rose lake	.50	.30
119	A14	10c orange buff	.60	.45
120	A14	15c blue green	2.50	1.00
121	A14	25c red brown	2.75	1.25
122	A14	50c black brn	4.50	2.00
123	A14	75c carmine	16.50	3.50
124	A14	1p dk brown	25.00	6.00
125	A14	2p dk olive grn	32.50	7.50
126	A14	3p claret	32.50	7.50
127	A14	4p dark blue	40.00	12.50
128	A14	5p dp dull blue	60.00	16.00
129	A14	10p dull red	130.00	27.50
		Nos. 112-129 (18)	350.05	87.15
		Set, never hinged	600.00	

Dated "1905"

1905 Control Numbers on Back

136	A14	1c dp violet	.40	.30
137	A14	2c black	.40	.30
138	A14	3c vermilion	.40	.30
139	A14	4c dp green	.40	.30
140	A14	5c blue grn	.45	.35
141	A14	10c violet	1.60	.75
142	A14	15c car lake	1.60	.75
143	A14	25c orange buff	12.50	2.25
144	A14	50c green	8.00	2.75
145	A14	75c red brown	11.00	7.50
146	A14	1p dp gray brn	12.50	7.50
147	A14	2p carmine	20.00	12.50
148	A14	3p deep brown	32.50	14.00
149	A14	4p bronze grn	40.00	18.00
150	A14	5p claret	62.50	25.00
151	A14	10p deep blue	90.00	35.00
		Nos. 136-151 (16)	294.25	127.55
		Set, never hinged	600.00	

King Alfonso XIII — A15

1907 Control Numbers on Back

152	A15	1c blue black	.30	.25
153	A15	2c car rose	.30	.25
154	A15	3c dp violet	.40	.25
155	A15	4c black	.40	.25
156	A15	5c orange buff	.40	.25
157	A15	10c maroon	2.00	.80
158	A15	15c bronze grn	.55	.35
159	A15	25c dk brown	65.00	15.00
160	A15	50c blue green	.45	.30
161	A15	75c vermilion	.45	.30
162	A15	1p dull blue	3.00	.60
163	A15	2p brown	11.00	4.00
164	A15	3p lake	11.00	4.00
165	A15	4p violet	11.00	4.00
166	A15	5p black brn	11.00	4.00
167	A15	10p orange brn	11.00	4.00
		Nos. 152-167 (16)	128.25	38.60
		Set, never hinged	350.00	

No. 157 Handstamp Surcharged in Black, Blue or Red

1908				
168	A15	5c on 10c mar (Bk)	2.75	2.00
a.		Blue surcharge	10.00	5.50
b.		Red surcharge	30.00	10.00
169	A15	25c on 10c mar (Bk)	60.00	20.00
		Set, never hinged	77.50	

The surcharge on Nos. 168-169 exist inverted, double, etc. The surcharge also exists on other stamps.

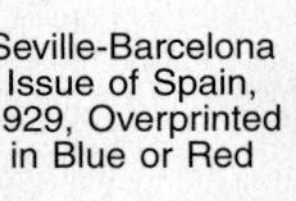

Seville-Barcelona Issue of Spain, 1929, Overprinted in Blue or Red

1929			*Perf. 11*	
170	A52	5c rose lake	.25	.25
171	A53	10c green (R)	.25	.25
a.		Perf. 14	.65	.65
172	A50	15c Prus bl (R)	.25	.25
173	A51	20c purple (R)	.25	.25
174	A50	25c brt rose	.25	.25
175	A52	30c black brn	.25	.25
176	A53	40c dk blue (R)	.50	.50
177	A51	50c dp orange	1.10	1.10
178	A52	1p blue blk (R)	4.25	4.25
179	A53	4p deep rose	22.50	22.50
180	A53	10p brown	27.50	27.50
		Nos. 170-180 (11)	57.35	57.35
		Set, never hinged	100.00	

FIJI

ˈfē-ˌjē

LOCATION — Group of 332 islands (106 inhabited) in the South Pacific Ocean east of New Hebrides
GOVT. — British Colony
AREA — 7,078 sq. mi.
POP. — 646,561 (1981)
CAPITAL — Suva

12 Pence = 1 Shilling
20 Shillings = 1 Pound
100 Cents = 1 Dollar (1872-74)

Catalogue values for unused stamps in this country are for Never Hinged items, beginning with Scott 137 in the regular postage section and Scott B1 in the semi-postal section.

Values for unused stamps are for examples with original gum as defined in the catalogue introduction except for Nos. 1-10 which are valued without gum. Additionally, Nos. 1-10 are valued with roulettes showing on two or more sides, but expect small faults that do not detract from the appearance of the stamps. Very few examples of Nos. 1-10 will be found free of faults, and these will command substantial premiums.

Watermark

Wmk. 17 — FIJI POSTAGE Across Center Row of Sheet

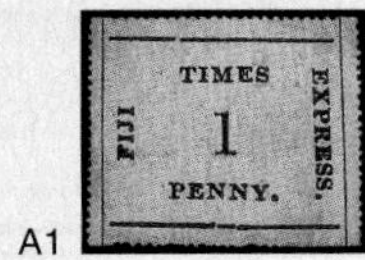

A1

1870 Unwmk. Typeset *Rouletted*
Thin Quadrille Paper

1 A1 1p black, *pink* 4,500. 4,750.
2 A1 3p black, *pink* 5,500. 5,000.
 a. Comma after "EXPRESS" *8,000. 8,000.*
3 A1 6p black, *pink* 2,750. 2,750.
5 A1 1sh black, *pink* 2,250. 2,500.

1871 Thin Vertically Laid Paper

6 A1 1p black, *pink* 1,150. 2,100.
7 A1 3p black, *pink* 1,900. 3,400.
8 A1 6p black, *pink* 1,600. 2,100.
9 A1 9p black, *pink* 3,400. 4,000.
 a. Comma after "EXPRESS" *4,250.*
10 A1 1sh black, *pink* 1,900. 1,900.

This service was established by the *Fiji Times*, a weekly newspaper, for the delivery of the newspaper. Since there was no postal service to the other islands, delivery of letters to agents of the newspaper on the islands was offered to the public.

Nos. 1-5 were printed in the same sheet, one horizontal row of 6 of each (6p, 1sh, 1p, 3p). Nos. 6-10 were printed from the same plate with three 9p replacing three 3p.

The rose tint of the paper is somewhat fugitive and is partially or totally lost on most surviving examples.

A vertical se-tenant strip of four of No. 5 on yellow paper is in the Royal Collection and is considered to be a proof or specimen, ex-Ferrari, and is unique.

A vertical se-tenant strip of four of Nos. 6, 8, 9, 10 exists. Value about $45,000.

A single 1p stamp of the 1871 setting on white wove ordinary paper is in the Royal Collection.

Most used examples have pen cancels.

Covers: Covers bearing Nos. 1-5 are very rare, values starting at about $30,000. Covers bearing Nos 6-10 are very rare, values starting at about $27,500.

As with most 19th-century laid papers, there are perpendicular lines widely spaced apart, which represent the supports in the paper-making grid. These lines are clearly visible and only occasionally are entirely missing on one stamp.

Up to three sets of imitations exist. One on pink laid paper, pin-perforated, measuring 22½x16mm. Originals measure 22½x18½mm. A later printing was made on pink wove paper.
Forgeries also exist plus fake cancellations.

Crown and "CR" (Cakobau Rex)
A2 A3

A4

1871 Typo. Wmk. 17 *Perf. 12½*
Wove Paper

15 A2 1p blue 62.50 140.00
16 A3 3p green 125.00 400.00
17 A4 6p rose 170.00 325.00
 Nos. 15-17 (3) 357.50 865.00

Sheets of 50 (10x5).

For overprints and surcharges see Nos. 18-39.

Forgeries exist.

Stamps of 1871 Surcharged in Black

1872, Jan. 13

18 A2 2c on 1p blue 60.00 *65.00*
 a. 2c on 1p pale blue 62.50 *75.00*
19 A3 6c on 3p green 90.00 90.00
20 A4 12c on 6p rose 125.00 90.00
 Nos. 18-20 (3) 275.00 245.00

Nos. 18-20 with Additional Overprint in Black

b

c

1874, Oct. 10

21 A2(b) 2c on 1p blue 1,250. 340.00
 a. No period after "R" 3,250. 1,150.
22 A2(c) 2c on 1p blue 1,150. 300.00
 a. Invtd. "A" instead of "V" 3,250. 1,500.
 b. Period after "R" is a Maltese Cross 3,250. 1,500.
 c. No period after "R" 3,250. 1,500.
 d. Round raised period after "V" 3,250. 1,500.
 e. Round raised period after "V" and "R" 3,250. 1,500.
23 A3(b) 6c on 3p green 3,250. 1,000.
 a. No period after "R" 5,500. 2,000.
24 A3(c) 6c on 3p green 2,750. 750.00
 a. Inverted "A" 2,100. 1,900.
 b. Period after "R" is a Maltese Cross 5,250. 2,000.
 c. No period after "R" 5,500. 2,000.
 d. Round raised period after "V" 5,500. 2,000.
 e. Round raised period after "V" and "R" 5,500. 2,000.
 f. Vert. pair, one type b and one type c 14,000.
25 A4(b) 12c on 6p rose 1,050. 260.00
 a. "V.R." inverted 7,500.
 b. No period after "R" 3,000. 1,150.
26 A4(c) 12c on 6p rose 1,000. 250.00
 a. Inverted "A" 2,900. 1,350.
 b. Period after "R" is a Maltese Cross 3,000. 1,350.
 c. "V.R." inverted — 7,000.
 d. No period after "R" 3,000. 1,350.
 e. Round raised period after "V" 3,000. 1,350.
 f. Round raised period after "V" and "R" 3,000. 1,350.
 g. Vert. pair, one type b and one type c 7,500.

Forged overprints exist on both forged stamps and on genuine stamps.

Types "b" and "c" were in the same sheet.

Nos. 23-26 with Additional Surcharge in Black or Red

1875

27 A3(b) 2p on 6c on 3p 2,750. 800.00
 a. Period btwn. "2" and "d" 4,500. 1,600.
 b. "V.R." double 5,000. 4,500.
 c. No period after "R" 4,500. 1,600.
28 A3(b) 2p on 6c on 3p (R) 900.00 325.00
 a. Period btwn. "2" and "d" 2,250. 850.00
 b. No period after "R" 2,250. 900.00
29 A3(c) 2p on 6c on 3p 1,900. 600.00
 a. Inverted "A" 4,750. 1,600.
 b. Period after "R" is a Maltese Cross 4,750. 1,600.
 c. No period after "2d" 4,750. 1,600.
 d. No period after "R" 2,250. 900.00
 e. Round raised period after "V" 4,750. 1,600.
 f. Round raised period after "V" and "R" 4,750. 1,600.
30 A3(c) 2p on 6c on 3p (R) 750.00 250.00
 a. Inverted "A" 2,100. 850.00
 b. Period after "R" is a Maltese Cross 2,250. 875.00
 c. No period after "2d" 2,250. 875.00
 d. No period after "R" 2,250. 875.00
 e. Round raised period after "V" 2,250. 875.00
 f. Round raised period after "V" and "R" 2,250. 875.00
31 A4(b) 2p on 12c on 6p 3,250. 1,000.
 a. Period btwn. "2" and "d"
 b. No period after "2d"
 c. "2d, VR" double 5,500.
32 A4(c) 2p on 12c on 6p 3,000. 900.00
 a. Inverted "A" 4,500. 1,400.
 b. No period after "2d"
 c. "2d, VR" double 5,500.
 d. Round raised period after "R" — 1,200.
 e. Round raised period after "R" — 1,200.
 f. As "a," with raised period after "V" 3,000. 1,000.
 g. As "a," with raised period after "V" and "R" 4,500. 1,500.

Forged overprints exist on both forged stamps and on genuine stamps.

Types of 1871 Overprinted or Surcharged in Black

e

f

1876, Jan. 31 Unwmk.
Wove Paper

33 A2(e) 1p ultramarine 60.00 60.00
 a. Inverted surcharge
 b. Dbl. impression of stamp 1,000.
 c. Horiz. pair, imperf vert. 1,000.
34 A3(e+f) 2p on 3p dk grn 60.00 *65.00*
 a. Dbl. surch. "Two Pence"
 b. 2p on 3p pale green 70.00 *65.00*
35 A4(e) 6p rose 70.00 65.00
 a. 6p carmine rose 70.00 65.00
 b. Surcharge inverted
 c. Dbl. impression of stamp 2,850.
 Nos. 33-35 (3) 190.00 190.00

1877 Laid Paper

36 A2(e) 1p ultramarine 32.50 *50.00*
 a. Horiz. pair, imperf. vert. 1,100.
 b. 1p deep blue 30.00 *50.00*
37 A3(e+f) 2p on 3p dk grn 80.00 *85.00*
 a. 2p on 3p yellow green 80.00 *80.00*
 b. Perf 10 400.00
 c. Perf 11 375.00
 d. Horiz. pair, imperf. vert. 1,100.
 e. Horiz. pair, imperf. between 1,000.
38 A3(e+f) 4p on 3p lilac 110.00 27.50
 a. Horiz. pair, imperf. vert. 1,000.
39 A4(e) 6p rose 60.00 37.50
 a. Horiz. pair, imperf. vert. 800.00
 b. 6p carmine rose 60.00 45.00
 Nos. 36-39 (4) 282.50 200.00

Many of the preceding stamps are known imperforate. They are printer's waste and were never issued.

A12

A13

Queen Victoria
A14 A15

Perf. 10-13½ & Compound

1878-90 Wove Paper Typo.

40 A12 1p ultra ('79) 20.00 20.00
 a. 1p blue 65.00 6.50
41 A12 2p green 40.00 1.75
 b. 2p ultramarine (error) *40,000.*
42 A12 4p brt vio ('90) 16.00 9.00
 a. 4p mauve 27.50 12.00
43 A13 6p brt rose ('80) 16.00 4.75
 a. Printed on both sides 2,500. 2,000.
44 A14 1sh yel brn ('81) 60.00 12.50
 a. 1sh deep brown 100.00 32.50

Litho. & Typo.

45 A15 5sh blk & red brn ('82) 75.00 50.00
 Nos. 40-45 (6) 227.00 98.00

No. 41b was not put on sale. All examples were supposed to be destroyed.

A quantity of No. 45 was sold as remainders, canceled-to-order with the following Suva dates: 15.DEC.00; 22.DE.1900; 28.DEC.1900; 12.DEC.01; 15.DEC.01; 16.DE.1901; 21.JUN.02; 15.DEC.02; 15. DE. 1902; and 21.DE.1902. Examples so canceled are worth less than postally used examples.

No. 45 imperf was sold only as a remainder, canceled "Suva, 15.DEC.00."

A late printing of the 5sh, made from an electrotyped plate, exists in gray black and red orange, perf 10, differing from No. 45 in many details. It was also sold only as a remainder, canceled "Suva, 15.DEC.00." It is scarce.

For surcharges see Nos. 46-52.

Nos. 40-45 exist with sheetmaker's watermark. Watermarked stamps are scarcer than unwatermarked.

1881-90 *Perf. 10*

40d A12 1p ultramarine 30.00 3.50

Surcharged type "f" in Black

1878-90 Typo.

46 A12 2p on 3p green 12.00 *42.50*
47 A12 4p on 1p vio ('90) 75.00 60.00
48 A12 4p on 2p lilac ('83) 100.00 16.00
 Nos. 46-48 (3) 187.00 118.50

Nos. 40-43 Surcharged in Black

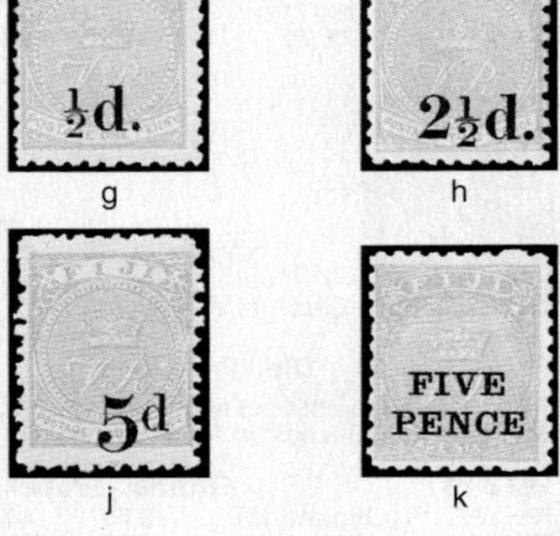

g h j k

1891-92 *Perf. 10*

49 A12(g) ½p on 1p ('92) 62.50 *80.00*
50 A12(h) 2½p on 2p 52.50 *55.00*
 a. Wider space (2mm) between "2" and "½" 150.00 *150.00*
51 A12(j) 5p on 4p ('92) 62.50 *80.00*
52 A13(k) 5p on 6p ('92) 67.50 *75.00*
 a. "FIVE" and "PENCE" 3mm apart 75.00 *85.00*
 Nos. 49-52 (4) 245.00 *290.00*

A18

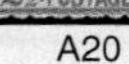

A20

Fijian Canoe — A19

1891-96 ***Perf. 10-12 & Compound***

No.	Type	Description	Unused	Used
53	A18	½p grnsh blk ('92)	2.75	7.00
a.		½p gray	3.75	7.00
54	A19	1p black ('93)	18.00	8.50
55	A19	1p lilac rose ('96)	5.00	1.10
56	A19	2p green ('93)	9.00	.85
a.		Perf. 10x12 ('94)	800.00	425.00
57	A20	2½ red brown	6.50	5.50
58	A19	5p ultra ('93)	25.00	8.00
		Nos. 53-58 (6)	66.25	30.95

Edward VII — A22

1903, Feb. 1 **Wmk. 2** ***Perf. 14***

No.	Type	Description	Unused	Used
59	A22	½p gray grn & pale grn	3.25	2.25
60	A22	1p vio & blk, *red*	20.00	.65
61	A22	2p vio & orange	4.50	1.40
62	A22	2½p vio & ultra, *bl*	15.00	3.50
63	A22	3p vio & red vio	1.60	*4.00*
64	A22	4p violet & blk	1.60	*2.75*
65	A22	5p vio & green	1.60	*2.75*
66	A22	6p vio & car rose	1.60	*2.00*
67	A22	1sh grn & car rose	17.50	*80.00*
68	A22	5sh green & blk	85.00	*170.00*
69	A22	£1 gray & ultra	400.00	*475.00*
		Revenue cancel		75.00
		Nos. 59-68 (10)	151.65	*269.30*

Numerals of 2p, 4p, 6p and 5sh of type A22 are in color on plain tablet.

1904-12 **Ordinary Paper** **Wmk. 3**

No.	Type	Description	Unused	Used
70	A22	½p grn & pale grn ('04)	16.50	3.25
70A	A22	½p green ('08)	15.00	3.50
71	A22	1p vio & black, *red* ('04)	32.50	.25
72	A22	1p carmine ('06)	16.50	.25
73	A22	2½p ultra ('10)	6.75	*7.75*

Chalky Paper

No.	Type	Description	Unused	Used
74	A22	6p violet ('10)	30.00	*50.00*
75	A22	1sh grn & car rose ('09)	32.50	*42.50*
76	A22	1sh black, *green* ('11)	11.00	*16.00*
77	A22	5sh grn & scarlet, *yel* ('11)	72.50	*105.00*
78	A22	£1 vio & black, *red* ('12)	360.00	300.00
		Nos. 70-77 (9)	233.25	*228.50*

George V — A23

Die I

For description of Dies I and II see "Dies of British Colonial Stamps" in Table of Contents.

1912-23 **Ordinary Paper**

No.	Type	Description	Unused	Used
79	A23	¼p brown ('16)	2.75	.40
80	A23	½p green	2.75	1.10
81	A23	1p scarlet	2.75	.50
a.		1p carmine ('16)	2.25	.25
82	A23	2p gray ('14)	2.00	.25
83	A23	2½p ultra ('14)	3.50	3.75
84	A23	3p violet, *yel*	4.50	*9.00*
a.		Die II ('21)	3.25	*32.00*
85	A23	4p black & red, *yel* ('14)	24.00	*22.50*
a.		Die II ('23)	3.25	*35.00*

Chalky Paper

No.	Type	Description	Unused	Used
86	A23	5p dl vio & ol grn ('14)	5.50	*12.50*
87	A23	6p dl vio & red vio ('14)	2.40	*6.00*
88	A23	1sh black, *green*	1.30	*14.50*
a.		1sh black, *blue green, ol back*	3.25	*11.00*
b.		1sh black, *emerald* ('21)	5.50	*67.50*
c.		Die II ('22)	3.25	*37.50*

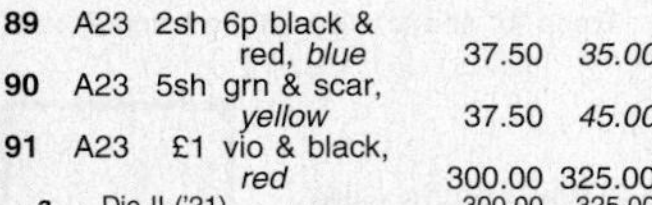

No.	Type	Description	Unused	Used
89	A23	2sh 6p black & red, *blue*	37.50	*35.00*
90	A23	5sh grn & scar, *yellow*	37.50	*45.00*
91	A23	£1 vio & black, *red*	300.00	325.00
a.		Die II ('21)	300.00	325.00
		Revenue cancel		52.50

Surface-colored Paper

No.	Type	Description	Unused	Used
92	A23	1sh black, *green*	1.25	*14.50*
		Nos. 79-90,92 (13)	127.70	*165.00*

Numerals of ¼p, 1½p, 2p, 4p, 6p, 2sh, 2sh6p and 5sh of type A23 are in color on plain tablet.

For overprints see Nos. MR1-MR2.

Die II

1922-27 **Wmk. 4** **Ordinary Paper**

No.	Type	Description	Unused	Used
93	A23	¼p dark brown	3.75	*27.50*
94	A23	½p green	1.10	*1.50*
95	A23	1p rose red	5.75	1.00
96	A23	1p violet ('27)	1.40	.25
97	A23	1½p rose red ('27)	4.50	1.50
98	A23	2p gray	1.40	.25
a.		"2d" and value tablet omitted	28,000.	
99	A23	3p ultra ('23)	3.00	1.20
100	A23	4p blk & red, *yel*	16.00	7.00
101	A23	5p dl vio & ol green	1.75	*2.25*
102	A23	6p dl vio & red violet	2.40	1.50

Chalky Paper

No.	Type	Description	Unused	Used
103	A23	1sh blk, *emerald*	11.00	4.00
104	A23	2sh vio & ultra, *bl* ('27)	30.00	*72.50*
105	A23	2sh6p blk & red, *bl*	12.50	*35.00*
106	A23	5sh grn & scar, *yellow*	55.00	*90.00*
		Nos. 93-106 (14)	149.55	*245.45*

The only known example of No. 98a is the center stamp of an unused block of nine.

Common Design Types pictured following the introduction.

Silver Jubilee Issue

Common Design Type

1935, May 6 ***Perf. 13½x14***

No.	Type	Description	Unused	Used
110	CD301	1½p carmine & blue	1.00	*9.00*
111	CD301	2p gray blk & ultra	1.50	.50
112	CD301	3p blue & brown	2.75	*4.50*
113	CD301	1sh brt vio & indigo	10.00	*15.00*
		Nos. 110-113 (4)	15.25	29.00
		Set, never hinged	24.00	

Coronation Issue

Common Design Type

1937, May 12 ***Perf. 11x11½***

No.	Type	Description	Unused	Used
114	CD302	1p dark violet	.45	1.25
115	CD302	2p gray black	.45	*2.25*
116	CD302	3p indigo	.45	*2.25*
		Nos. 114-116 (3)	1.35	5.75
		Set, never hinged	2.00	

Outrigger Canoe — A24

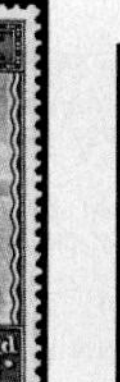

Fijian Village — A25

Outrigger Canoe A26

Map of Fiji Islands A27

Government Buildings — A27a

Canoe and Arms of Fiji — A28

Sugar Cane — A29

Spear Fishing at Night — A30

Arms of Fiji — A31

Suva Harbor — A32

River Scene — A33

Fijian House — A34

Papaya Tree — A35

Bugler — A36

8p, 1sh5p, 1sh6p, Arms of Fiji.

Perf. 13½, 12½ (1p)

1938-55 **Engr.** **Wmk. 4**

No.	Type	Description	Unused	Used
117	A24	½p green	.25	1.00
		Never hinged	.25	
c.		Perf. 14 ('41)	16.00	4.75
		Never hinged	21.00	
d.		Perf. 12 ('48)	.80	*4.00*
		Never hinged	1.30	
118	A25	1p blue & brn	.40	.25
		Never hinged	.55	
119	A26	1½p rose car (empty canoe)	12.00	.50
		Never hinged	16.00	
120	A27	2p grn & org brn (no "180 degree")	30.00	.50
		Never hinged	42.50	
121	A27a	2p mag & grn	.45	.80
		Never hinged	.55	
a.		Perf. 12 ('46)	1.25	.90
		Never hinged	2.10	

Perf. 12½, 13x12 (6p), 14 (8p)

No.	Type	Description	Unused	Used
122	A28	3p dp ultra	.80	.40
		Never hinged	1.60	
123	A29	5p rose red & blue	32.50	13.00
		Never hinged	45.00	
124	A29	5p rose red & yel grn	.25	.40
		Never hinged	.25	
125	A27	6p blk (no "180 degree")	45.00	16.00
		Never hinged	62.50	
126	A31	8p rose car	1.40	3.00
		Never hinged	2.75	
a.		Perf. 13 ('50)	.55	*3.50*
		Never hinged	.75	
127	A30	1sh black & yel	.75	.90
		Never hinged	1.90	

Perf. 14

No.	Type	Description	Unused	Used
128	A31	1sh5p car & black	.25	.25
		Never hinged	.30	
128A	A31	1sh6p ultra	2.75	3.50
		Never hinged	3.75	
b.		Perf. 13 ('55)	1.10	*20.00*
		Never hinged	1.30	

Perf. 12½

No.	Type	Description	Unused	Used
129	A32	2sh vio & org	2.00	.55
		Never hinged	2.75	
130	A33	2sh6p brn & grn	2.75	2.00
		Never hinged	5.25	
131	A34	5sh dk vio & grn	2.75	2.25
		Never hinged	5.25	
131A	A35	10sh emer & brn org	27.50	*52.50*
		Never hinged	45.00	
131B	A36	£1 car & ultra	37.50	*65.00*
		Never hinged	52.50	
		Nos. 117-131B (18)	199.30	*162.80*

Issued: 1sh5p, 6/13/40; 5p, 10/1/40; No. 121, 5/19/42; 8p, 11/15/48; 10sh, £1, 3/13/50; 1sh6p, 8/1/50; others, 4/5/38.

Types of 1938-40 Redrawn

Man in Canoe — A36a

180 Degree Added to the Lower Right Hand Corner of the Design — A36b

Perf. 13½ (1½p, 2p, 6p), 14 (2½p)

1940-49 **Wmk. 4**

No.	Type	Description	Unused	Used
132	A36a	1½p rose carmine	1.00	*3.00*
a.		Perf. 12 ('49)	.80	*1.60*
b.		Perf. 14 ('42)	14.50	*22.50*
133	A36b	2p grn & org brn ("180 degree")	12.50	*17.50*
134	A36b	2½p grn & org brn	.50	1.25
a.		Perf. 12 ('48)	.80	.60
b.		Perf. 13½ ('42)	.55	1.00
135	A36b	6p blk ("180 degree")	2.50	2.40
a.		Perf. 12 ('47)	1.40	1.75
		Nos. 132-135 (4)	16.50	24.15

Issued: 2½p, Jan. 6, 1942; others Oct. 1, 1940.

No. 133 Surcharged in Black

1941, Feb. 10 ***Perf. 13½***

No.	Type	Description	Unused	Used
136	A27	2½p on 2p grn & org brn	1.50	1.00
		Never hinged	2.50	

Catalogue values for unused stamps in this section, from this point to the end of the section, are for Never Hinged items.

Peace Issue

Common Design Type

1946, Aug. 17 ***Perf. 13½***

No.	Type	Description	Unused	Used
137	CD303	2½p bright green	.25	*1.50*
138	CD303	3p deep blue	.25	.25

Silver Wedding Issue
Common Design Types

1948, Dec. 17 Photo. *Perf. 14x14½*
139 CD304 2½p dark green .70 1.75

Engr.; Name Typo.
Perf. 11½x11
140 CD305 5sh blue violet 17.50 9.00

UPU Issue
Common Design Types
Engr.; Name Typo. on 3p, 8p
Perf. 13½, 11x11½

1949, Oct. 10 Wmk. 4
141 CD306 2p red violet .35 .75
142 CD307 3p indigo 2.25 5.75
143 CD308 8p dp carmine .35 *4.50*
144 CD309 1sh6p blue .40 *3.00*
Nos. 141-144 (4) 3.35 14.00

SEMI-POSTAL STAMPS

Catalogue values for unused stamps in this section are for Never Hinged items.

Children at Play — SP1

Rugby Player — SP2

Perf. 13x13½
1951, Sept. 17 Engr. Wmk. 4
B1 SP1 1p + 1p brown .30 *1.60*
B2 SP2 2p + 1p deep green .45 *1.10*

POSTAGE DUE STAMPS

D1

D2

D3

1917 Unwmk. Typeset *Perf. 11*
Laid Papers; Without Gum
J1 D1 ½p black 1,300. 500.00
J2 D2 ½p black 550.00 300.00
J3 D3 1p black 500.00 140.00
a. Narrow setting 375.00
J4 D3 2p black 350.00 80.00
a. Narrow setting 1,250.
J5 D3 3p black 525.00 120.00
J6 D3 4p black 1,250. 550.00
a. Strip of 8, 3 #J3, 1 ea. #J1 and #J6, and 3 #J5 *19,000.*
Nos. J1-J6 (6) 4,475. 1,690.

There were two printings of this issue. In the first printing, the 2d was printed in sheets of 84 (7x12), and the other four values were printed together in sheets of 96 (8x12), with each row consisting of three 1p, one ½p, one 4p and three 3p values. Setenant multiples exist. Sheets were not perforated on the margins, so that marginal stamps were not perforated on the outer edge. Examples from the first printing are 25mm wide (including margins).

In the second printing, the ½p, 1p and 2p were printed in separate sheets of 84 (7x12). The clichés were set a little closer, so that examples of this printing are 23mm wide.

D4

Perf. 14
1918, June 1 Typo. Wmk. 3
J7 D4 ½p black 3.25 *30.00*
On cover *500.00*
J8 D4 1p black 3.75 *5.50*
On cover *150.00*
J9 D4 2p black 3.50 *8.00*
On cover *150.00*
J10 D4 3p black 3.50 *52.50*
On cover *2,000.*
J11 D4 4p black 6.50 *30.00*
On cover *750.00*
Nos. J7-J11 (5) 20.50 *126.00*

Cover values for Nos. J7-J11 are for properly franked commercial items. Philatelic usages also exist and sell for less.

D5

1940 Wmk. 4 *Perf. 12½*
J12 D5 1p bright green 5.00 *72.50*
On cover *600.00*
J13 D5 2p bright green 10.00 *72.50*
On cover *600.00*
J14 D5 3p bright green 11.00 *80.00*
On cover *600.00*
J15 D5 4p bright green 12.00 *85.00*
On cover *650.00*
J16 D5 5p bright green 14.00 *90.00*
On cover *850.00*
J17 D5 6p bright green 15.00 *90.00*
On cover *750.00*
J18 D5 1sh dk carmine 15.00 *115.00*
On cover *750.00*
J19 D5 1sh6p dk carmine 15.00 *175.00*
On cover *750.00*
Nos. J12-J19 (8) 97.00 *780.00*
Set, never hinged 140.00

Virtually all covers with Nos. J12-J19 are overfranked and of philatelic origin. The values above are for such covers.

WAR TAX STAMPS

Regular Issue of 1912-16 Overprinted

Die I
1916 Wmk. 3 *Perf. 14*
MR1 A23 ½p green 1.90 *9.00*
a. Inverted overprint 700.00
b. Double overprint
MR2 A23 1p scarlet 3.50 .80
a. 1p carmine 37.50 26.00
b. Pair, one without ovpt. *8,000.*
c. Inverted overprint 800.00

Most examples of #MR2b are within horiz. strips of 12.

FINLAND

'fin-lənd

(Suomi)

LOCATION — Northern Europe bordering on the Gulfs of Bothnia and Finland
GOVT. — Republic
AREA — 130,119 sq. mi.
POP. — 4,869,858 (1984)
CAPITAL — Helsinki

Finland was a Grand Duchy of the Russian Empire from 1809 until December 1917, when it declared its independence.

100 Kopecks = 1 Ruble
100 Pennia = 1 Markka (1866)

Catalogue values for unused stamps in this country are for Never Hinged items, beginning with Scott B39 in the semi-postal section.

Unused stamps are valued with original gum as defined in the catalogue introduction except for Nos. 1-3B which are valued without gum. Used values for Nos. 1-3B are for pen-canceled examples.

Very fine examples of the serpentine rouletted issues, Nos. 4-13c, will have roulettes cutting the design slightly on one or more sides and will have all "teeth" complete and intact. Stamps with roulettes clear of the design on all four sides are extremely scarce and sell for substantial premiums.

Watermarks

Wmk. 121 — Multiple Swastika

Wmk. 208 — Post Horn

Wmk. 168 — Wavy Lines and Letters

Issues under Russian Empire

Coat of Arms — A1

1856-58 Unwmk. Typo. *Imperf.*
Small Pearls in Post Horns
Wove Paper
1 A1 5k blue *6,750.* 1,600.
On cover, pen cancellation 5,750.
Pen and town cancellation 1,900.
On cover 8,000.
Town cancellation 3,250.
On cover 10,000.
a. Tête bêche pair *80,000.* *80,000.*
Pen and town cancellation *75,000.*
Town cancellation 120,000.
2 A1 10k rose 8,750. 400.
On cover, pen cancellation 975.
Pen and town cancellation 575.
On cover 1,850.
Town cancellation 925.
On cover 2,850.
a. Tête bêche pair *80,000.* *65,000.*
Pen and town cancellation *75,000.*
Town cancellation *120,000.*
e. 10k carmine 8,750. 450.
Pen and town cancellation 650.
Town cancellation 900.
f. 10k dark carmine 9,250. 500.
Pen and town cancellation 725.
Town cancellation 950.
g. 10k lilac red — 725.
Pen and town cancellation 1,200.
Town cancellation 1,800.

Cut to shape
1 A1 5k blue 150.
On cover, pen cancellation 1,000.
Pen and town cancellation 200.
On cover 1,200.
Town cancellation 250.
On cover 1,750.
2 A1 10k rose 65.
On cover, pen cancellation 550.
Pen and town cancellation 90.
On cover 600.
Town cancellation 100.
On cover 700.

Wide Vertically Laid Paper
2C A1 10k rose ('58) — 1,400.
Pen and town cancellation 1,800.
Town cancellation 2,500.
d. Tête bêche pair —

Cut to shape
2C A1 10k rose 200.
Pen and town cancellation 250.
Town cancellation 300.

Narrow Vertically Laid Paper
2C A1 10k carmine 625.
Pen and town cancellation 800.
Town cancellation 1,100.

Full margins = 1½mm.

The wide vertically laid paper has 13-14 distinct lines per 2 centimeters. The narrow laid paper has lines that sometimes are indistinct.

A 5k blue with small pearls exists on narrow vertically laid paper. It is rare.

Stamps on diagonally laid paper are envelope cut squares. Envelope cut squares also exist on unwatermarked wove paper.

Large Pearls in Post Horns
1858 Wove Paper
3 A1 5k blue *11,000.* 1,800.
On cover, pen cancellation 4,000.
Pen and town cancellation 1,550.
On cover 7,250.
Town cancellation 2,500.
On cover 8,500.
a. Tête bêche pair *60,000.*
Pen and town cancellation *65,000.*

Cut to shape
3 A1 5k blue 125.00
On cover, pen cancellation 750.00
Pen and town cancellation 150.00
On cover 1,250.
Town cancellation 200.00
On cover 1,750.

Full margins = 1½mm.

1859 Wide Vertically Laid Paper
3B A1 5k blue — *18,000.*
Pen and town cancellation *25,000.*

Cut to shape
3B A1 5k blue 2,000.
Pen and town cancellation *2,500.*

Reprints of Nos. 2 and 3, made in 1862, are on brownish paper, on vertically laid paper, and in tête bêche pairs on normal and vertically laid paper. Reprints of 1871, 1881 and 1893 are on yellowish or white paper. Value for least costly of each, $85.

In 1956, Nos. 2 and 3 were reprinted for the Centenary with post horn watermark and gum. Value, $85 each.

Coat of Arms — A2

I — Depth 1-1¼mm

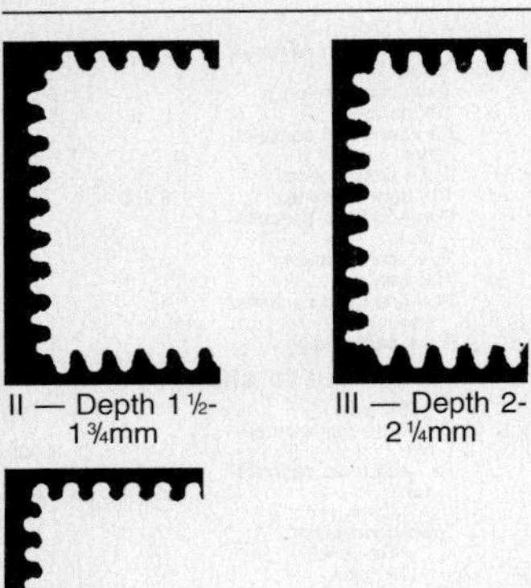

II — Depth 1½-1¾mm

III — Depth 2-2¼mm

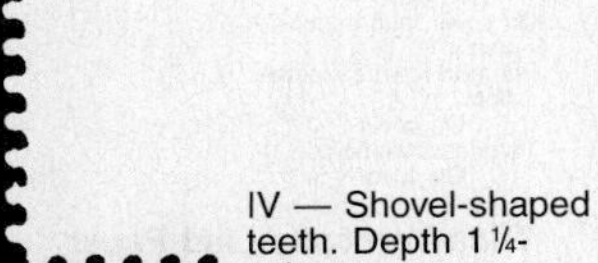

IV — Shovel-shaped teeth. Depth 1¼-1½mm

Wove Paper

1860 *Serpentine Roulette 7½, 8*

4 A2 5k blue, *bluish*, I 850.00 200.00
On cover 1,200.
a. Roulette II 800.00 225.00
On cover 1,600.
b. Perf. vert.
5 A2 10k rose, *pale rose*, I 575.00 57.50
On cover 260.00
a. Roulette II 1,150. 160.00
On cover 850.00

Four types of indentation are noted:

A3

A4

1866-74 *Serpentine Roulette*

6 A3 5p pur brn, *lil*, I ('73) 375.00 170.00
On cover 1,250.
a. Roulette II 4,000.
On cover —
b. 5p red brn, *lil*, III ('71) 350.00 180.00
On cover 1,300.
7 A3 8p blk, *grn*, III ('67) 275.00 170.00
On cover 2,850.
a. Ribbed paper, III ('72) 1,150. 925.00
On cover —
b. Roulette II ('74) 340.00 275.00
On cover 2,850.
c. As "b," ribbed paper ('74) 340.00 225.00
On cover 2,300.
d. Roulette I ('73) 525.00 325.00
On cover 2,850.
e. As "d," ribbed paper 1,050. 400.00
On cover —
f. Serpentine roulette 10½ ('67) 13,500.
On cover —
8 A3 10p blk, *yel*, III ('70) 675.00 350.00
On cover 2,000.
a. 10p blk, *buff*, II 800.00 450.00
On cover 2,000.
b. 10p blk, *buff*, I ('73) 750.00 375.00
On cover 2,300.
9 A3 20p bl, *bl*, III 575.00 57.50
On cover 190.00
a. Roulette II 575.00 90.00
On cover 290.00
b. Roulette I ('73) 675.00 115.00
On cover 225.00
c. Roulette IV ('74) — 1,150.
On cover —
d. Perf. horiz. —
e. Printed on both sides (40p blue on back) 10,500.
10 A3 40p rose, *lil rose*, III 525.00 67.50
On cover 260.00
a. Ribbed paper, III ('73) 675.00 200.00
On cover 525.00
b. Roulette II 525.00 85.00
On cover 260.00
c. As "b," ribbed paper ('73) 675.00 170.00
On cover 450.00
d. Roulette I 750.00 170.00
On cover 525.00
e. As "d," ribbed paper 675.00 115.00
On cover 400.00
f. Roulette IV — 2,275.
g. As "f," ribbed paper — —
h. Serpentine roulette 10½ —

11 A4 1m yel brn, III ('67) 2,250. 850.00
On cover 15,000.
a. Roulette II 2,850. 1,700.
On cover —

Nos. 7f and 10h are private roulettes and are also known in compound serpentine roulette 10½ and 7½.

Nos. 4-11 were reprinted in 1893 on thick wove paper. Colors differ from originals. Roulette type IV. Value for Nos. 4-5, each $40, Nos. 6-10, each $50. Value for No. 11, $55.

Thin or Thick Laid Paper

12 A3 5p red brn, *lil*, III 290.00 160.00
On cover 900.00
a. Roulette II 300.00 300.00
On cover 1,750.
b. Roulette I 290.00 300.00
On cover 1,750.
d. 5p blk, *buff*, roul. III (error) 20,000.
e. Tête bêche pair —
On cover 300,000.
13 A3 10p black, *buff*, III 675.00 290.00
On cover 1,900.
a. 10p black, *yel*, II 850.00 290.00
On cover 1,900.
b. 10p black, *yel*, I 1,150. 750.00
On cover 2,850.
c. 10p red brown, *lil*, III (error) 8,000. 7,000.
On cover —

Forgeries of Nos. 11 and 13c exist.

Cover values for Nos. 6-13 are for covers bearing stamps with full teeth.

Nos. 6-13 with Short Teeth

Values below are for used stamps with one or two short roulettes. Stamps with teeth entirely missing or with several short roulettes are worth much less.

6 62.50
6a 2,100.
6b 50.00
7 50.00
7a 300.00
7b 80.00
7c 45.00
7d 90.00
7e 180.00
7f 14,000.
8 80.00
8a 115.00
8b 125.00
9 19.00
9a 32.50
9b 40.00
9c 525.00
10 21.00
10a 110.00
10b 21.00
10c 85.00
10d 45.00
10e 45.00
10f 1,000.
10g 1,400.
11 225.00
11a 600.00
12 45.00
12a 70.00
12b 70.00
12d 15,000.
13 80.00
13a 85.00
13b 160.00
13c 3,500.

A5

1875 *Perf. 14x13½*

16 A5 32p lake 2,400. 425.00
On cover 15,500.

Forgeries exist of No. 16 that have been created by perforating cut squares.

1875-82 *Perf. 11*

17 A5 2p gray 62.50 70.00
Never hinged 120.00
On cover 800.00
On cover, single franking 575.00
On postal stationery 625.00
18 A5 5p orange 140.00 15.00
Never hinged 300.00
On cover 170.00
On cover, single franking 200.00
a. 5p yellow org 160.00 18.00
Never hinged 300.00
On cover 170.00
On cover, single franking 200.00
19 A5 8p blue green 300.00 90.00
Never hinged 450.00
On cover 4,000.
On newsprint, single franking 7,000.
a. 8p yellow green 275.00 70.00
Never hinged 450.00
On cover 4,000.
On newsprint, single franking 7,000.
20 A5 10p brown ('81) 700.00 70.00
On cover 2,100.
On cover, single franking 3,750.
21 A5 20p ultra 175.00 3.50
Never hinged 300.00
On cover 42.50
a. 20p blue 175.00 5.00
Never hinged 300.00
On cover 45.00
b. 20p Prussian blue 400.00 45.00
On cover 350.00
c. Tête bêche pair 3,500.
22 A5 25p carmine ('79) 350.00 17.00
Never hinged 600.00
On cover 300.00
a. 25p rose ('82) 475.00 75.00
On cover 600.00
23 A5 32p carmine 400.00 60.00
On cover 600.00
a. 32p rose 450.00 62.50
Never hinged 775.00
On cover 575.00
24 A5 1m violet ('77) 1,000. 160.00
On cover 13,000.
Nos. 17-24 (8) 3,128. 485.50

A souvenir card issued in 1974 for NORDIA 1975 reproduced a block of four of the unissued "1 MARKKAA" design.

Nos. 19, 23 were reprinted in 1892-93, perf. 12½. Value $25.00 each. They exist imperf.

1881-83 *Perf. 12½*

25 A5 2p gray 20.00 20.00
Never hinged 35.00
On cover 425.00
a. Imperf., pair 600.00 600.00
26 A5 5p orange 62.50 6.25
Never hinged 92.50
On cover 145.00
a. Tête bêche pair 8,250. 4,750.
b. Imperf. vert., pair —
c. Imperf. horiz., pair —
27 A5 10p brown 100.00 27.00
Never hinged 180.00
On cover 1,450.
On cover, single franking 2,850.
28 A5 20p ultra 65.00 2.00
Never hinged 95.00
On cover 29.00
a. 20p blue 65.00 2.00
Never hinged 95.00
On cover 30.00
b. Tête bêche pair — 2,500.
c. Imperf., pair —
29 A5 25p rose ('82) 55.00 12.00
Never hinged 90.00
On cover 300.00
a. 25p carmine 55.00 21.00
Never hinged 100.00
On cover 300.00
b. Tête bêche pair 15,000. —
30 A5 1m violet ('82) 450.00 55.00
Never hinged 600.00
On cover 11,000.
Nos. 25-30 (6) 752.50 122.25

Nos. 27-29 were reprinted in 1893 in deeper shades, perf. 12½. Value $40 each.

Most examples of No. 28c are from printer's waste.

1881 *Perf. 11x12½*

26d A5 5p orange 450.00 90.00
On cover 1,700.
27a A5 10p brown 925.00 225.00
On cover 5,750.
28d A5 20p ultra 575.00 42.50
On cover 1,900.
28e A5 20p blue 575.00 42.50
On cover 1,700.
29c A5 25p rose 675.00 190.00
On cover —
29d A5 25p carmine 650.00 125.00
On cover —
30a A5 1m violet 1,450.
On cover —

1881 *Perf. 12½x11*

26e A5 5p orange 450.00 90.00
On cover 1,800.
27b A5 10p brown — 325.00
On cover —
28f A5 20p ultra 575.00 45.00
On cover 1,800.
28g A5 20p blue 575.00 45.00
On cover 1,800.
29e A5 25p rose — 290.00
On cover —
29f A5 25p carmine 575.00 115.00
On cover —

1885 *Perf. 12½*

31 A5 5p emerald 20.00 8.00
Never hinged 35.00
On cover 24.00
a. 5p yellow green 24.00 1.10
Never hinged 42.50
On cover 30.00
b. Tête bêche pair 14,000. 11,000.
32 A5 10p carmine 30.00 3.50
Never hinged 45.00
On cover 75.00
a. 10p rose 50.00 3.50
Never hinged 45.00
On cover 75.00
33 A5 20p orange 35.00 .65
Never hinged 57.50
On cover 15.00
a. 20p yellow 47.50 2.50
Never hinged 60.00
On cover 17.50
b. Tête bêche pair — 3,500.
34 A5 25p ultra 70.00 4.25
Never hinged 90.00
On cover 100.00
a. 25p blue 70.00 3.00
Never hinged 90.00
On cover 100.00
35 A5 1m gray & rose 37.50 25.00
Never hinged 55.00
On cover 3,750.
36 A5 5m green & rose 500.00 500.00
Never hinged 1,100.
On cover —
37 A5 10m brown & rose 625.00 750.00
Never hinged 1,200.
On cover —

Denomination on No. 35 is spelled "MARKKA". Denomination on Nos. 36-37 is spelled "MARKKAA".

A6

1889-92 *Perf. 12½*

38 A6 2p slate ('90) .75 1.25
Never hinged 1.40
On cover 60.00
39 A6 5p green ('90) 40.00 .50
Never hinged 65.00
On cover 8.50
40 A6 10p carmine ('90) 70.00 .50
Never hinged 120.00
On cover 10.00
a. 10p rose ('90) 90.00 .75
Never hinged 130.00
On cover 18.00
b. Imperf. 110.00
Never hinged 145.00
41 A6 20p orange ('92) 95.00 .50
Never hinged 120.00
On cover 6.00
a. 20p yellow ('89) 95.00 1.25
Never hinged 140.00
On cover 30.00
42 A6 25p ultra ('91) 80.00 .85
Never hinged 130.00
On cover 27.50
a. 25p blue 80.00 1.15
Never hinged 140.00
On cover 27.50
43 A6 1m slate & rose ('92) 6.00 3.25
Never hinged 9.50
On cover 120.00
a. 1m brnsh gray & rose ('90) 35.00 4.00
Never hinged 40.00
On cover 120.00
44 A6 5m green & rose ('90) 32.50 *77.50*
Never hinged 47.50
On cover *11,000.*
45 A6 10m brown & rose ('90) 40.00 *90.00*
Never hinged 65.00
On cover *6,000.*
Nos. 38-45 (8) 364.25 *174.35*

The 2p slate, perf. 14x13, is believed to be an essay.

See Nos. 60-63.

See Russia for types similar to A7-A18.

Finnish stamps have "dot in circle" devices or are inscribed "Markka," "Markkaa," "Pen." or "Pennia."

Imperial Arms of Russia

A7 A8 A9

A10

A11

Laid Paper

1891-92 **Wmk. 168** *Perf. 14½x15*

46 A7 1k orange yel 6.50 *11.00*
Never hinged 9.50
On cover 150.00
47 A7 2k green 6.50 *11.00*
Never hinged 11.00
On cover 85.00
48 A7 3k carmine 12.00 *18.00*
Never hinged 18.00
On cover 75.00

49 A8 4k rose 14.00 18.00
Never hinged 20.00
On cover 55.00
50 A7 7k dark blue 8.00 2.25
Never hinged 14.50
On cover 30.00
51 A8 10k dark blue 17.50 *18.00*
Never hinged 32.50
On cover 150.00
52 A9 14k blue & rose 20.00 *30.00*
Never hinged 35.00
On cover 650.00
53 A8 20k blue & car 20.00 24.00
Never hinged 27.50
On cover 425.00
54 A9 35k violet & grn 30.00 *60.00*
Never hinged 40.00
On cover 2,100.
55 A8 50k violet & grn 35.00 42.50
Never hinged 62.50
On cover 1,500.

Perf. 13½

56 A10 1r brown & org 90.00 67.50
Never hinged 140.00
On cover 2,400.
57 A11 3½r black & gray 325.00 *550.00*
Never hinged 475.00
On cover 9,000.
a. 3½r black & yellow (error) *15,000.* *18,000.*
58 A11 7r black & yellow 250.00 *350.00*
Never hinged 375.00
On cover 15,000.
Nos. 46-58 (13) 834.50 *1,202.*

Forgeries of Nos. 57, 57a, 58 exist.

Type of 1889-90
Wove Paper

1895-96 Unwmk. *Perf. 14x13*

60 A6 5p green .80 .50
Never hinged 2.25
On cover 4.25
61 A6 10p carmine .80 .50
Never hinged 2.25
On cover 9.00
a. 10p rose 60.00 5.00
Never hinged 140.00
On cover 22.00
62 A6 20p orange .80 .50
Never hinged 2.25
On cover 6.00
a. 20p yellow .70 .45
Never hinged 2.75
On cover 5.00
b. Imperf. 160.00 —
Never hinged 190.00
63 A6 25p ultra 1.25 .70
Never hinged 2.25
On cover 12.00
a. 25p blue 1.25 .70
Never hinged 3.50
On cover 7.50
b. Imperf. 125.00 —
Never hinged 140.00
Nos. 60-63 (4) 3.65 2.20

A12 A13

A14 A15

1901 Litho. *Perf. 14½x15*
Chalky Paper

64 A12 2p yellow 6.00 8.00
Never hinged 13.00
On cover 15.00
65 A12 5p green 12.50 2.00
Never hinged 26.00
On cover 4.25
66 A13 10p carmine 27.50 3.25
Never hinged 47.50
On cover 4.00
67 A12 20p dark blue 70.00 1.50
Never hinged 100.00
On cover 3.00
68 A14 1m violet & grn 350.00 10.00
Never hinged 575.00
On cover 60.00

Perf. 13½

69 A15 10m black & gray 325.00 350.00
Never hinged 625.00
On cover 1,700.
Nos. 64-69 (6) 791.00 374.75

Imperf sheets of 10p and 20p, stolen during production, were privately perforated 11½ to defraud the P.O. Uncanceled imperfs. of Nos. 65-68 are believed to be proofs.

See Nos. 70-75, 82.

Types of 1901 Redrawn

No. 64

No. 70

2p. On No. 64, the "2" below "II" is shifted slightly leftward. On No. 70, the "2" is centered below "II."

No. 65

No. 71

5p. On No. 65, the frame lines are very close. On No. 71, a clear white space separates them.

Nos. 66, 67 Nos. 72, 73

10p, 20p. On Nos. 66-67, the horizontal central background lines are faint and broken. On Nos. 72-73, they are clear and solid, though still thin.

20p. On No. 67, "H" close to "2" with period midway. On No. 73 they are slightly separated with period close to "H."

No. 68

Nos. 74, 74a

1m. On No. 68, the "1" following "MARKKA" lacks serif at base. On Nos. 74-74a, this "1" has serif.

No. 69

No. 75

10m. On No. 69, the serifs of "M" and "A" in top and bottom panels do not touch. On No. 75, the serifs join.

Perf. 14¼x14¾, 14¼x14

1901-14 Typo. Ordinary Paper

70 A12 2p orange 1.00 1.50
Never hinged 1.40
On cover 7.00
71 A12 5p green 2.00 .60
Never hinged 4.00
On cover 2.00
a. Perf 14¼x14 ('06) 3.50 .75
Never hinged 4.00
On cover 3.00
72 A13 10p carmine 14.00 .60
Never hinged 21.00
On cover 2.00
a. Perf 14¼x14 ('07) 90.00 .95
Never hinged 92.50
On cover 2.00
b. Background inverted, perf 14¼x14¾ 17.50 5.00
Never hinged 35.00
c. Background inverted, perf 14¼x14 95.00 2.75
Never hinged 140.00
73 A12 20p dark blue 10.00 .60
Never hinged 15.00
On cover 2.00
a. Perf 14¼x14 ('06) 82.50 1.25
Never hinged 115.00
On cover 4.25
74 A14 1m lil & grn, perf. 14¼x14 ('14) 1.10 .60
Never hinged 3.50
On cover 12.00
a. 1m violet & blue green, perf. 14¼x14¾ ('02) 10.00 .90
Never hinged 22.50
On cover 12.00
Nos. 70-74 (5) 28.10 3.90
Set, never hinged 45.00

Perf. 13½

75 A15 10m blk & drab ('03) 160.00 60.00
Never hinged 275.00
On cover 725.00

Imperf Pairs

70a A12 2p 375.00 *525.00*
Never hinged 400.00
71b A12 5p 100.00 *200.00*
Never hinged 100.00
72d A13 10p 110.00 *225.00*
Never hinged 120.00
73b A12 20p 200.00 *225.00*
Never hinged 210.00
74b A14 1m 190.00 *210.00*
Never hinged 190.00
Nos. 70a-74b (5) 975.00 1,385.

A16 A17 A18

1911-16 *Perf. 14, 14¼x14¾*

77 A16 2p orange .30 *.90*
Never hinged .70
On cover 4.00
78 A16 5p green .35 .40
Never hinged .70
On cover 1.75
a. Imperf. —
Never hinged —
b. Perf. 14¼x14¾ 1,400. 140.00
Never hinged 675.00
On cover *1,750.*
79 A17 10p rose ('15) .30 .75
Never hinged .60
On cover 1.75
a. Imperf. 110.00 225.00
Never hinged 110.00
On cover *475.00*
b. Perf. 14¼x14¾ ('16) 3.50 *5.50*
Never hinged 9.50
On cover 8.50
80 A16 20p deep blue .40 *.60*
Never hinged .50
On cover 2.00
a. Imperf. 180.00 140.00
Never hinged —
On cover 200.00
b. Perf. 14¼x14¾ 27.50 3.50
Never hinged 21.00
On cover 4.00
81 A18 40p violet & blue .40 .40
Never hinged .50
On cover 4.50
a. Perf. 14¼x14¾ 6,000. 4,000.
Nos. 77-81 (5) 1.75 3.05
Set, never hinged 3.00

There are three minor types of No. 79. Values are for the least expensive type.

Perf. 14½

82 A15 10m blk & grnsh gray ('16) 160.00 210.00
Never hinged 275.00
On cover 1,100.
a. Horiz. pair, imperf. vert. 3,900.

Republic
Helsinki Issue

Arms of the Republic — A19

Type I

Type II

Two types of the 40p.
Type I — Thin figures of value.
Type II — Thick figures of value.

Perf. 14, 14¼x14¾

1917-30 Unwmk.

83 A19 5p green .35 .35
Never hinged .30
On cover 1.60
84 A19 5p gray ('19) .35 .35
Never hinged .30
On cover 1.60
85 A19 10p rose .35 *.45*
Never hinged .50
On cover 1.60
a. Imperf., pair 250.00 *400.00*
Never hinged 290.00
86 A19 10p green ('19) 1.50 .55
Never hinged 2.75
On cover 2.50
a. Perf. 14¼x14¾ *3,000.*
87 A19 10p brt blue ('21) .40 *.45*
Never hinged .50
On cover 2.50
a. 10p grysh ultra .40 .50
Never hinged .50
On cover 2.50
88 A19 20p buff .40 *.50*
Never hinged .50
On cover 2.50
89 A19 20p rose ('20) .40 *.45*
Never hinged 1.00
On cover 2.50
90 A19 20p brown ('24) 1.00 *.90*
Never hinged 2.10
On cover 5.25
a. Perf. 14¼x14¾ .65 *25.00*
Never hinged 1.50
On cover 700.00
91 A19 25p blue .40 *.45*
Never hinged .50
On cover 5.25
92 A19 25p lt brown ('19) .40 .40
Never hinged .30
On cover 2.50
93 A19 30p green ('23) .40 *.55*
Never hinged .80
On cover 2.50
94 A19 40p violet (I) .40 .35
Never hinged .50
a. Perf. 14¼x14¾ 400.00 27.50
Never hinged 850.00
On cover 52.50
95 A19 40p bl grn (II) ('29) .50 *3.00*
Never hinged .70
On cover 4.00
a. Type I ('24) 14.00 6.00
Never hinged 24.00
On cover 13.00
b. Perf. 14¼x14¾ 1.25 *21.00*
Never hinged 2.50
On cover 35.00
96 A19 50p orange brn .45 *.45*
Never hinged .80
On cover 5.25
97 A19 50p dp blue ('19) 4.00 .45
Never hinged 7.00
On cover 4.50
a. Perf. 14¼x14¾ 2,200.
98 A19 50p green ('21) 4.50 .40
Never hinged 16.00
On cover 2.50
a. Perf. 14¼x14¾ .40 *1.50*
Never hinged .50
On cover 4.00
99 A19 60p red vio ('21) .60 .40
Never hinged 2.25
On cover 1.60
a. Imperf., pair — —
100 A19 75p yellow ('21) .40 *.75*
Never hinged .30
On cover 9.75
101 A19 1m dull rose & blk 16.00 .30
Never hinged 26.00
On cover 1.50
102 A19 1m red org ('25) 9.00 *30.00*
Never hinged 21.00
On cover 45.00
a. Perf. 14 ('30) .25 *550.00*
Never hinged .65
On cover *1,500.*
103 A19 1½m bl grn & red vio ('29) .25 *2.50*
Never hinged .65
a. Perf. 14¼x14¾ .40 *1.25*
Never hinged .65
On cover 4.00
104 A19 2m green & blk ('21) 3.50 .70
Never hinged 6.00
On cover 7.00
105 A19 2m dk blue & ind ('22) 2.50 .45
Never hinged 6.00
On cover 7.25
a. Perf. 14¼x14¾ .65 *4.00*
Never hinged 1.50
On cover 47.50
106 A19 3m blue & blk ('21) 25.00 .50
Never hinged 105.00
On cover 7.00
107 A19 5m red vio & blk 17.50 .45
Never hinged 32.50
On cover 7.50
108 A19 10m brn & gray blk, perf. 14 1.00 *1.25*
Never hinged 2.10
On cover 775.00
a. 10m light brown & black, perf. 14¼x14¾ ('29) 3.50 *400.00*
Never hinged 7.00
On cover *1,750.*
110 A19 25m dull red & yel ('21) .90 *26.00*
Never hinged 1.25
On cover 325.00
Nos. 83-108,110 (27) 92.45 *73.35*
Set, never hinged 260.00

Examples of a 2½p gray of this type exist. They are proofs from the original die which were distributed through the UPU. No plate was made for this denomination.

See Nos. 127-140, 143-152. For surcharge and overprints see Nos. 119-126, 153-154.

Vasa Issue

Arms of the Republic — A20

1918 Litho. *Perf. 11½*

111 A20 5p green .75 *1.25*
Never hinged .90
On cover 8.50
112 A20 10p red .75 *1.25*
Never hinged .90
On cover 8.50

113 A20 30p slate 1.25 *4.50*
Never hinged 1.40
On cover 57.50
114 A20 40p brown vio .70 *1.75*
Never hinged .65
On cover 13.00
115 A20 50p orange brn .75 *5.00*
Never hinged .90
On cover 80.00
116 A20 70p gray brown 2.25 *32.50*
Never hinged 3.50
On cover 115.00
117 A20 1m red & gray .75 *2.50*
Never hinged .90
On cover 35.00
118 A20 5m red violet & gray 45.00 *125.00*
Never hinged 85.00
On cover 1,450.
Nos. 111-118 (8) 52.20 *173.75*
Set, never hinged 92.50

Nos. 111-118 exist imperforate but were not regularly issued in that condition.

Sheet margin examples, perf. on 3 sides, imperf. on margin side, were sold by post office.

Stamps and Type of 1917-29 Surcharged

1919 ***Perf. 14***
119 A19 10p on 5p green .50 .55
Never hinged 1.00
On cover 3.50
120 A19 20p on 10p rose .50 .55
Never hinged 1.00
On cover 3.50
121 A19 50p on 25p blue 1.00 .55
Never hinged 2.50
On cover 8.00
122 A19 75p on 20p orange .50 *.85*
Never hinged 1.00
On cover 9.00
Nos. 119-122 (4) 2.50 2.50
Set, never hinged 5.75

Stamps and Type of 1917-29 Surcharged

Nos. 123-125

No. 126

1921
123 A19 30p on 10p green .65 .65
Never hinged 1.40
On cover 3.50
124 A19 60p on 40p red violet 3.75 1.25
Never hinged 7.00
On cover 4.50
125 A19 90p on 20p rose .40 .50
Never hinged .45
On cover 10.50
126 A19 1½m on 50p blue 1.40 .50
Never hinged 4.00
On cover 9.50
a. Thin "2" in "½" 12.50 11.00
Never hinged 24.00
b. Imperf., pair 300.00 *500.00*
Never hinged 350.00
Nos. 123-126 (4) 6.20 2.90
Set, never hinged 13.00

Arms Type of 1917-29
Perf. 14, 14¼x14¾

1925-29 **Wmk. 121**
127 A19 10p ultra ('27) .50 *2.75*
Never hinged .70
On cover 7.00
128 A19 20p brown .50 *2.00*
Never hinged .70
On cover 5.25
129 A19 25p brn org ('29) 1.00 *90.00*
Never hinged 1.75
On cover 350.00
130 A19 30p yel green .40 *.95*
Never hinged .25
On cover 4.00
a. Perf. 14¼x14¾ 7.00 1.50
Never hinged 7.50
131 A19 40p blue grn (I) ('26) 9.50 1.40
Never hinged 8.00
On cover 1.75
a. Perf. 14¼x14¾ ('26) 9.50 1.40
Never hinged 15.00
On cover 2.25
b. Type II ('28) *140.00* *82.50*
Never hinged 290.00
On cover 85.00
c. As "b," perf. 14¼x14¾ ('28) 9.50 1.40
Never hinged 13.50
On cover 2.25
132 A19 50p gray grn ('26) 1.25 .80
Never hinged 2.25
On cover 2.25
a. Perf. 14¼x14¾ ('26) .55 *.55*
Never hinged 2.00
On cover 2.25
133 A19 60p red violet .40 *.95*
Never hinged .25
On cover 2.25
134 A19 1m dp orange 7.00 .40
Never hinged 10.50
On cover 2.25
a. Perf. 14¼x14¾ 100.00 1.25
Never hinged 250.00
On cover 3.50

Perf. 14¼x14¾
135 A19 1½m blue green & red violet ('26) 6.25 .60
Never hinged 14.00
On cover 2.00
a. Perf. 14 ('26) 60.00 .50
Never hinged 80.00
On cover 1.50
136 A19 2m dk blue & indigo ('27) 1.00 *.50*
Never hinged 1.35
On cover 3.50
a. Perf. 14 1.00 .50
Never hinged 2.25
On cover 3.00
137 A19 3m chlky blue & blk ('26) 1.00 .50
Never hinged 2.00
On cover 4.00
138 A19 5m red violet & blk ('27) .50 .50
Never hinged 1.15
On cover 6.25
a. Perf. 14 1.25 .50
Never hinged 2.75
On cover 4.00
139 A19 10m lt brn & blk ('27) 4.00 *32.50*
Never hinged 5.75
On cover 200.00
140 A19 25m dp org & yel ('27) 20.00 *400.00*
Never hinged 35.00
On cover
Nos. 127-140 (14) 53.30 *533.85*
Set, never hinged 100.00

No. 130a is not known cancelled during the period in which it was valid for postal use.

A21

Wmk. 208
1927, Dec. 6 **Typo.** ***Perf. 14***
141 A21 1½m deep violet .30 *.60*
Never hinged .25
On cover 7.50
142 A21 2m deep blue .30 *2.00*
Never hinged .25
On cover 16.00

10th anniv. of Finnish independence.

Arms Type of 1917-29
Perf. 14, 14¼x14¾

1927-29 **Wmk. 208**
143 A19 20p lt brown ('29) 2.00 *40.00*
Never hinged 2.50
On cover 32.50
144 A19 40p bl grn (II) ('28) .40 *.65*
Never hinged .25
On cover 1.25
145 A19 50p gray grn ('28) .40 *.75*
Never hinged .55
On cover 3.00
146 A19 1m dp orange .40 *1.00*
Never hinged .45
On cover 1.75
a. Imperf., pair 115.00 *200.00*
Never hinged 175.00
On cover 675.00
b. Perf. 14 1.25 1.25
Never hinged 2.00
On cover 2.25
147 A19 1½m bl grn & red vio ('28) 3.00 .70
Never hinged 2.25
On cover 5.25
a. Perf. 14 1,000. 26.00
Never hinged 1,750.
On cover 32.50
148 A19 2m dk bl & ind ('28) .45 *.65*
Never hinged .55
On cover 3.50
149 A19 3m chlky bl & blk .50 *.65*
Never hinged .65
On cover 3.25
a. Perf. 14 1.60 *5.00*
Never hinged 2.75
On cover 11.50
150 A19 5m red vio & blk ('28) .50 .60
Never hinged .65
On cover 4.00
151 A19 10m lt brown & blk 2.00 *35.00*
Never hinged 2.50
On cover 350.00
152 A19 25m brown org & yel 2.25 *400.00*
Never hinged 2.50
On cover 1,150.
Nos. 143-152 (10) 11.90 *480.00*

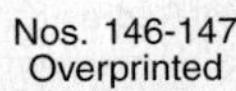
Nos. 146-147 Overprinted

1928, Nov. 10 **Litho.** **Wmk. 208**
153 A19 1m deep orange 10.00 *19.00*
Never hinged 14.00
On cover 40.00
154 A19 1½m bl grn & red vio 10.00 *19.00*
Never hinged 14.00
On cover 40.00
Set, never hinged 35.00

Nos. 153 and 154 were sold exclusively at the Helsinki Philatelic Exhibition, Nov. 10-18, 1928, and were valid only during that period.

S. S. "Bore" Leaving Turku — A23

Turku Cathedral — A24

Turku Castle — A25

Wmk. 208
1929, May 22 **Typo.** ***Perf. 14***
155 A23 1m olive green 1.50 *5.00*
Never hinged 4.00
On cover 11.50
156 A24 1½m chocolate 2.25 *4.00*
Never hinged 7.25
On cover 10.50
157 A25 2m dark gray .45 *4.50*
Never hinged 1.25
On cover 16.00
Nos. 155-157 (3) 4.20 *13.50*
Set, never hinged 12.50

Founding of the city of Turku (Abo), 700th anniv.

A26

1930-46 **Unwmk.** ***Perf. 14***
158 A26 5p chocolate .50 *.50*
Never hinged .25
On cover 3.50
159 A26 10p dull violet .50 .50
Never hinged .25
On cover 3.50
160 A26 20p yel grn .50 *.50*
Never hinged .65
On cover 8.50
161 A26 25p yel brn .50 .50
Never hinged .25
On cover 1.75
162 A26 40p blue grn 2.00 .25
Never hinged 5.25
On cover 3.50
163 A26 50p yellow .50 .50
Never hinged 1.35
On cover 3.50
164 A26 50p blue grn ('32) .45 .45
Never hinged .25
On cover 1.00
b. Imperf., pair 150.00 *200.00*
Never hinged 175.00
165 A26 60p dark gray .50 *.65*
Never hinged .80
On cover 8.50
165A A26 75p dp org ('42) .55 *.75*
Never hinged .90
On cover 1.35
166 A26 1m red org .50 .50
Never hinged .90
On cover 1.35
166B A26 1m yel grn ('42) .50 .50
Never hinged .35
On cover 1.00
167 A26 1.20m crimson .55 *1.75*
Never hinged .65
On cover 11.50
168 A26 1.25m yel ('32) .50 .50
Never hinged .55
On cover 1.50
169 A26 1½m red vio 2.00 .50
Never hinged 5.75
On cover 1.35
170 A26 1½m car ('32) .50 .50
Never hinged .55
On cover 2.25
170A A26 1½m sl ('40) .50 .50
Never hinged .55
On cover 2.25
170B A26 1.75m org yel ('40) .90 .70
Never hinged 1.35
On cover 2.25
171 A26 2m indigo .50 .50
Never hinged .55
On cover 4.00
172 A26 2m dp vio ('32) 6.00 .50
Never hinged 12.50
On cover .80
173 A26 2m car ('36) .50 .50
Never hinged .55
On cover 1.35
Complete booklet, panes of 4 #161, 164, 166, 168, 173 5.75
173B A26 2m yel org ('42) .50 .50
Never hinged .25
On cover .80
173C A26 2m blue grn ('45) .50 .50
Never hinged .45
On cover 4.50
174 A26 2½m brt blue ('32) 4.75 .55
Never hinged 7.00
On cover 5.75
174A A26 2½m car ('42) .50 .50
Never hinged .45
On cover 2.75
174B A26 2.75m rose vio ('40) .50 .50
Never hinged .25
On cover .80
175 A26 3m olive blk 35.00 .65
Never hinged 57.50
On cover 4.00
175B A26 3m car ('45) 1.00 .50
Never hinged .55
On cover 2.25
175C A26 3m yel ('45) .50 *.80*
Never hinged .65
On cover 17.50
176 A26 3½m brt bl ('36) 9.00 .50
Never hinged 21.00
On cover 4.50
176A A26 3½m olive ('42) .50 .50
Never hinged .25
On cover .80
176B A26 4m olive ('45) 1.10 .50
Never hinged 1.00
On cover 2.25
176C A26 4½m saph ('42) .50 .50
Never hinged .25
On cover 7.00
176D A26 5m saph ('45) .50 .50
Never hinged 1.35
On cover 2.25
176E A26 5m pur ('45) 1.50 .50
Never hinged 1.35
On cover 4.50
j. Imperf., pair 150.00 *200.00*
Never hinged 185.00
176F A26 5m yel ('46) 1.25 .55
Never hinged 1.75
On cover .80
k. Imperf., pair 150.00 *200.00*
Never hinged 185.00
176G A26 6m car ('45) 1.20 .50
Never hinged 1.15
On cover 1.75
m. Imperf., pair 200.00 *275.00*
Never hinged 225.00
176H A26 8m pur ('46) .50 .50
Never hinged .45
On cover .90
176I A26 10m saph ('45) 1.75 .50
Never hinged 2.50
On cover 3.50
Nos. 158-176I (38) 80.00 21.10

See Nos. 257-262, 270-274, 291-296, 302-304. For surcharges and overprints see Nos. 195-196, 212, 221-222, 243, 250, 275, M2-M3. Post 1940 issues in Scott Standard catalogue, Vol. 2.

Stamps of types A26-A29 overprinted "ITA KARJALA" are listed under Karelia, Nos. N1-N15 in Scott Standard catalogue, Vol. 2.

Castle in Savonlinna A27

Lake Saima — A28

Woodchopper A29

1930 Engr.

177 A27 5m blue 1.50 *.65*
Never hinged .45
On cover 3.50
178 A28 10m gray lilac 55.00 4.75
Never hinged 125.00
On cover 135.00
179 A29 25m black brown 1.00 .50
Never hinged 2.25
On cover 3.50
Nos. 177-179 (3) 57.50 5.90
Set, never hinged 150.00

See Nos. 205, 305 (in Scott Standard catalogue, Vol. 2). For overprint see No. C1.

Elias Lönnrot — A30

Seal of Finnish Literary Society — A31

1931, Jan. 1 Typo.

180 A30 1m olive brown 2.50 *5.75*
Never hinged 5.25
On cover 8.00
181 A31 1½m dull blue 12.50 6.25
Never hinged 45.00
On cover 11.50

Centenary of Finnish Literary Society.

A32

1931, Feb. 28

182 A32 1½m red 2.75 *9.50*
Never hinged 6.00
On cover 12.50
183 A32 2m blue 2.75 *11.50*
Never hinged 6.00
On cover 20.00

1st use of postage stamps in Finland, 75th anniv.

Nos. 162-163 Surcharged

1931, Dec.

195 A26 50p on 40p blue grn 2.75 1.20
Never hinged 8.50
On cover 3.50
196 A26 1.25m on 50p yellow 4.00 3.50
Never hinged 13.00
On cover 5.75

Svinhufvud — A33

1931, Dec. 15

197 A33 2m gray blue & blk 1.50 *3.25*
Never hinged 5.25
On cover 8.00

Pres. Pehr Eyvind Svinhufvud, 70th birthday.

Lake Saima Type of 1930

1932-43 Re-engraved

205 A28 10m red violet ('43) .70 .50
Never hinged 1.60
On cover 5.00
a. 10m dark violet 20.00 .70
Never hinged 40.00
On cover 25.00

On Nos. 205 and 205a the lines of the islands, the clouds and the foliage are much deeper and stronger than on No. 178.

Alexis Kivi — A34

1934, Oct. 10 Typo.

206 A34 2m red violet 2.25 *4.50*
Never hinged 5.50
On cover 7.50

Alexis Kivi, Finnish poet (1834-1872).

Bards Reciting the "Kalevala" A35

Goddess Louhi, As Eagle Seizing Magic Mill — A36

Kullervo — A37

1935, Feb. 28 Engr.

207 A35 1¼m brown lake 2.00 *2.50*
Never hinged 4.00
On cover 6.00
208 A36 2m black 4.50 2.00
Never hinged 12.50
On cover 5.00
209 A37 2½m blue 3.00 3.00
Never hinged 10.00
On cover 11.50
Nos. 207-209 (3) 9.50 7.50
Set, never hinged 26.50

Cent. of the publication of the "Kalevala" (Finnish National Epic).

No. 170 Surcharged in Black

1937, Feb.

212 A26 2m on 1½m car 8.00 1.40
Never hinged 14.00
On cover 5.00

Gustaf Mannerheim — A38

1937, June 4 Photo. *Perf. 14*

213 A38 2m ultra 1.00 *1.45*
Never hinged 2.50
On cover 3.50

70th birthday of Field Marshal Baron Carl Gustaf Mannerheim, June 4th, 1937.

Swede-Finn Co-operation in Colonization A39

1938, June 1

214 A39 3½m dark brown .90 *2.75*
Never hinged 3.00
On cover 7.50

Tercentenary of the colonization of Delaware by Swedes and Finns.

Early Post Office — A40

Designs: 1¼m, Mail delivery in 1700. 2m, Modern mail plane. 3½m, Helsinki post office.

1938, Sept. 6 Photo. *Perf. 14*

215 A40 50p green .35 .55
Never hinged .65
On cover 3.00
216 A40 1¼m dk blue 1.15 *3.25*
Never hinged 3.25
On cover 5.75
217 A40 2m scarlet 1.15 1.25
Never hinged 6.25
On cover 3.50
218 A40 3½m slate black 3.25 *8.00*
Never hinged 8.75
On cover 12.50
Nos. 215-218 (4) 5.90 13.05
Set, never hinged 19.00

300th anniv. of the Finnish Postal System.

Margin strips of each denomination (3 of No. 215, 2 each of Nos. 216, 217, 218) were pasted on to advertising sheets and stapled into a booklet. Value, $120.

Post Office, Helsinki — A44

1939-42 Photo.

219 A44 4m brown black .40 *.45*
Never hinged 1.10
On cover 3.50

Engr.

219A A44 7m black brn ('42) .50 *.45*
Never hinged 1.90
On cover 7.50
219B A44 9m rose lake ('42) .60 .50
Never hinged 1.60
On cover 7.50
Nos. 219-219B (3) 1.50 1.40
Set, never hinged 3.50

See No. 248 in Scott Standard catalogue, Vol. 2.

Catalogue values for unused stamps in this section, from this point to the end of the section, are for Never Hinged items.

University of Helsinki — A45

1940, May 1 Photo.

220 A45 2m dp blue & blue .75 *.90*
On cover 5.00

300th anniv. of the founding of the University of Helsinki.

Nos. 168 and 173 Surcharged in Black

1940, June 16 Typo.

221 A26 1.75m on 1.25m yel 4.00 *3.25*
On cover 7.50
222 A26 2.75m on 2m carmine 10.00 .90
On cover 6.00

SEMI-POSTAL STAMPS

Arms — SP1

Unwmk.

1922, May 15 Typo. *Perf. 14*

B1 SP1 1m + 50p gray & red .90 *10.00*
Never hinged 2.00
a. Perf. 13x13½ *11.00*
Never hinged *22.50*

Red Cross Standard SP2

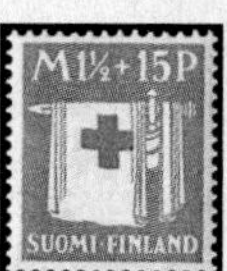

Symbolic SP3

Ship of Mercy — SP4

1930, Feb. 6

B2 SP2 1m + 10p red org & red 1.75 *11.50*
Never hinged 4.50
On cover 24.00
B3 SP3 1½m + 15p grysh grn & red 1.10 *11.50*
Never hinged 3.25
On cover 24.00
B4 SP4 2m + 20p dk bl & red 3.00 *50.00*
Never hinged 6.25
On cover 80.00
Nos. B2-B4 (3) 5.85 *73.00*
Set, never hinged 14.00

The surtax on this and subsequent similar issues was for the benefit of the Red Cross Society of Finland.

Church in Hattula — SP5

Designs: 1½m+15p, Castle of Hameenlinna. 2m+20p, Fortress of Viipuri.

1931, Jan. 1 Cross in Red Engr.

B5 SP5 1m + 10p gray grn 1.90 *14.00*
Never hinged 4.25
On cover 20.00
B6 SP5 1½m + 15p lil brn 11.50 *16.50*
Never hinged 35.00
On cover 20.00
B7 SP5 2m + 20p dull bl 1.90 *35.00*
Never hinged 3.50
On cover 75.00
Nos. B5-B7 (3) 15.30 *65.50*
Set, never hinged 42.50

SP8

1931, Oct. 15 Typo. ***Rouletted 4, 5***

B8 SP8 1m + 4m black 12.50 *45.00*
Never hinged 20.00
On cover 85.00

The surtax was to assist the Postal Museum of Finland in purchasing the Richard Granberg collection of entire envelopes.

Helsinki University Library SP9

Nikolai Church at Helsinki SP10

2½m+25p, Parliament Building, Helsinki.

1932, Jan. 1 ***Perf. 14***

B9 SP9 1¼m + 10p ol bis & red 1.50 *12.50*
Never hinged 4.75
On cover 18.00
B10 SP10 2m + 20p dp vio & red .40 *6.50*
Never hinged 1.00
On cover 12.50
B11 SP9 2½m + 25p lt blue & red 1.00 *25.00*
Never hinged 2.50
On cover 57.50
Nos. B9-B11 (3) 2.90 *44.00*
Set, never hinged 8.25

Bishop Magnus Tawast SP12

Michael Agricola SP13

Design: 2½m+25p, Isacus Rothovius.

1933, Jan. 20 **Engr.**

B12 SP12 1¼m + 10p blk brn & red 3.25 *16.00*
Never hinged 11.00
On cover 24.00
B13 SP13 2m + 20p brn vio & red 1.25 *4.50*
Never hinged 2.75
On cover 5.75
B14 SP13 2½m + 25p indigo & red 1.25 *8.75*
Never hinged 2.75
On cover 17.50
Nos. B12-B14 (3) 5.75 *29.25*
Set, never hinged 16.50

Evert Horn — SP15

Designs: 2m+20p, Torsten Stalhandske. 2½m+25p, Jakob (Lazy Jake) de la Gardie.

1934, Jan. **Cross in Red**

B15 SP15 1¼m + 10p brown 1.10 *4.50*
Never hinged 2.75
On cover 12.00
B16 SP15 2m + 20p gray lil 2.10 *8.00*
Never hinged 11.00
On cover 11.00
B17 SP15 2½m + 25p gray 1.10 *4.50*
Never hinged 2.75
On cover 16.00
Nos. B15-B17 (3) 4.30 *17.00*
Set, never hinged 16.50

Mathias Calonius — SP18

Designs: 2m+20p, Henrik C. Porthan. 2½m+25p, Anders Chydenius.

1935, Jan. 1 **Cross in Red**

B18 SP18 1¼m + 15p brown .90 *3.25*
Never hinged 2.10
On cover 12.00
B19 SP18 2m + 20p gray lil 2.00 *5.75*
Never hinged 5.75
On cover 12.00
B20 SP18 2½m + 25p gray bl .75 *3.25*
Never hinged 1.75
On cover 20.00
Nos. B18-B20 (3) 3.65 *12.25*
Set, never hinged 9.60

Robert Henrik Rehbinder — SP21

2m+20p, Count Gustaf Mauritz Armfelt. 2½m+25p, Count Arvid Bernard Horn.

1936, Jan. 1 **Cross in Red**

B21 SP21 1¼m + 15p dk brn .75 *2.40*
Never hinged 1.35
On cover 12.00
B22 SP21 2m + 20p vio brn 3.00 *7.25*
Never hinged 9.00
On cover 12.00
B23 SP21 2½m + 25p blue .75 *3.50*
Never hinged 1.60
On cover 20.00
Nos. B21-B23 (3) 4.50 *13.15*
Set, never hinged 12.00

Type "Uusimaa" SP24

Type "Turunmaa" SP25

Design: 3½m+35p, Type "Hameenmaa."

1937, Jan. 1 **Cross in Red**

B24 SP24 1¼m + 15p brown .70 *3.00*
Never hinged 2.00
On cover 12.00
B25 SP25 2m + 20p brn lake 13.00 9.00
Never hinged 50.00
On cover 12.00
B26 SP24 3½m + 35p indigo 1.00 *3.50*
Never hinged 2.75
On cover 24.00
Nos. B24-B26 (3) 14.70 15.50
Set, never hinged 54.00

Aukuste Makipeska — SP27

Designs: 1¼m+15p, Robert Isidor Orn. 2m+20p, Edward Bergenheim. 3½m+35p, Johan Mauritz Nordenstam.

1938, Jan. 5 **Cross in Red** **Engr.**

B27 SP27 50p + 5p dk grn .50 *1.35*
Never hinged .95
On cover 6.00
B28 SP27 1¼m + 15p dk brn .80 *2.25*
Never hinged 2.00
On cover 12.00
B29 SP27 2m + 20p rose lake 7.00 *7.50*
Never hinged 15.00
On cover 10.00
B30 SP27 3½m + 35p dk blue .55 *3.50*
Never hinged 1.25
On cover 15.00
Nos. B27-B30 (4) 8.85 *14.60*
Set, never hinged 19.00

Skiing — SP31

Designs: 2m+1m, Ski jumper. 3.50m+1.50m, Skier.

1938, Jan. 18

B31 SP31 1.25m + 75p sl grn 3.00 *13.00*
Never hinged 7.50
On cover 20.00
B32 SP31 2m + 1m dk car 3.00 *13.00*
Never hinged 7.50
On cover 20.00
B33 SP31 3.50m + 1.50m dk blue 3.00 *13.00*
Never hinged 7.50
On cover 20.00
Nos. B31-B33 (3) 9.00 *39.00*
Set, never hinged 22.50

Ski championships held at Lahti.

Soldier — SP34

1938, May 16

B34 SP34 2m + ½m blue 1.40 *5.00*
Never hinged 4.00
On cover 8.00

Victory of the White Army over the Red Guards. The surtax was for the benefit of the members of the Union of the Finnish Front.

Battlefield at Solferino SP35

1939, Jan. 2 **Cross in Scarlet**

B35 SP35 50p + 5p dk grn .85 *2.10*
Never hinged 1.75
On cover 8.50
B36 SP35 1¼m + 15p dk brn 1.00 *2.75*
Never hinged 1.50
On cover 8.50
B37 SP35 2m + 20p lake 14.00 *17.50*
Never hinged 32.50
On cover 17.50
B38 SP35 3½m + 35p dk bl .85 *3.50*
Never hinged 1.75
On cover 17.50
Nos. B35-B38 (4) 16.70 25.85
Set, never hinged 37.50

Intl. Red Cross Soc., 75th anniv.

Catalogue values for unused stamps in this section, from this point to the end of the section, are for Never Hinged items.

Soldiers with Crossbows — SP36

1¼m+15p, Cavalryman. 2m+20p, Soldier of Charles XII of Sweden. 3½m+35p, Officer and soldier of War with Russia, 1808-1809.

1940, Jan. 3 **Cross in Red**

B39 SP36 50p + 5p dk grn 1.40 *1.75*
On cover 6.00
B40 SP36 1¼m + 15p dk brn 3.50 3.00
On cover 7.00
B41 SP36 2m + 20p lake 5.50 3.50
On cover 8.00
B42 SP36 3½m + 35p dp ultra 3.50 *4.25*
On cover 12.00
Nos. B39-B42 (4) 13.90 12.50

The surtax aided the Finnish Red Cross.

Arms of Finland — SP40

1940, Feb. 15 **Litho.**

B43 SP40 2m +2m indigo .50 *1.75*
On cover 6.00

The surtax was given to a fund for the preservation of neutrality.

AIR POST STAMPS

No. 178 Overprinted in Red

1930, Sept. 24 **Unwmk.** ***Perf. 14***

C1 A28 10m gray lilac 140.00 *290.00*
Never hinged 225.00
On cover 300.00
a. 1830 for 1930 2,500. *12,000.*
Never hinged 3,250.
On cover *16,500.*

Overprinted expressly for use on mail carried in "Graf Zeppelin" on return flight from Finland to Germany on Sept. 24, 1930, after which trip the stamps ceased to be valid for postage. Forgeries are almost always on No. 205, rather than No. 178.

FIUME

'fyü-ˌmā

LOCATION — A city and surrounding territory on the Adriatic Sea
AREA — 8 sq. mi.
POP. — 44,956 (estimated 1924)

Fiume was under Hapsburg rule after 1466 and was transferred to Hungarian control after 1870. Of mixed Italian and Croatian population and strategically important, it was Hungary's only international seaport. Following World War I, Fiume was disputed between Italy and the newly created Kingdom of the Serbs, Croats and Slovenes (later Yugoslavia). A force of Allied troops occupied the city in Nov. 1918, while its future status was negotiated at the Paris Peace Conference.

In Sept. 1919, the Italian nationalist poet Gabriele d'Annunzio organized his legionnaires and seized Fiume, together with the islands of Arbe, Carnaro and Veglia, in the name of Italy. D'Annunzio established an autonomous administration, which soon came into conflict with the Italian government. There followed several years of instability, with three Italian interventions after 1920. In Jan. 1924, the Treaty of Rome between Italy and Yugoslavia established formal Italian sovereignty over Fiume, and Fiume stamps were replaced by those of Italy after March 31, 1924.

100 Filler = 1 Korona
100 Centesimi = 1 Corona (1919)
100 Centesimi = 1 Lira

The overprints on Nos. 1-23a have been extensively forged. Even the inexpensive values are difficult to find with genuine overprints. Forgeries of many later issues also exist, most created for the packet trade in the 1920s. Values are for genuine stamps. Collectors should be aware that stamps sold "as is" are likely to be forgeries, and unexpertized collections should be assumed to consist of mostly forged stamps. Education plus working with knowledgeable dealers is mandatory in this collecting area. More valuable stamps should be expertized.

Hungarian Stamps of 1916-18 Typograph Overprinted, Bold Sans Serif Letters

1918, Dec. 2 Wmk. 137 *Perf. 15*

On Stamps of 1916

Colored Numerals

1A A9 20f gray brown 4,000. 2,500.
Never hinged 8,000.
On cover 4,000.

Hungarian Stamps of 1916-18 Typograph Overprinted

On Stamps of 1916

White Numerals

1 A8 10f rose — —
b. Handstamped overprint 100.00 47.50
Never hinged 200.00
2 A8 15f violet 47.50 40.00
Never hinged 120.00
On cover 100.00

No. 1 with typographed overprint is unique.

Typographed Overprint On Stamps of 1916-18

Colored Numerals

3 A9 2f brown orange 4.75 2.40
Never hinged 8.75
On cover 45.00
4 A9 3f red violet 4.75 2.40
Never hinged 8.75
On cover 45.00
5 A9 5f green 4.75 2.40
Never hinged 8.75
On cover 45.00
6 A9 6f grnsh blue 4.75 2.40
Never hinged 8.75
On cover 45.00
7 A9 10f rose red, inverted ovpt. *24,000.* *11,000.*
Never hinged *36,000.*
On cover —
8 A9 15f violet 4.75 2.40
Never hinged 8.75
On cover 45.00
9 A9 20f gray brown 4.75 2.40
Never hinged 8.75
On cover 45.00
10 A9 25f deep blue 16.00 3.25
Never hinged 32.50
On cover 75.00
11 A9 35f brown 9.50 4.75
Never hinged 16.00
On cover 100.00
12 A9 40f olive green 95.00 40.00
Never hinged 225.00
On cover 200.00

White Numerals

13 A10 50f red vio & lil 6.50 4.00
Never hinged 10.50
On cover 50.00
14 A10 75f brt bl & pale bl 13.00 4.75
Never hinged 25.00
On cover 50.00
15 A10 80f grn & pale grn 13.00 4.00
Never hinged 25.00
On cover 50.00
16 A10 1k red brn & claret 40.00 9.50
Never hinged 85.00
On cover 120.00
17 A10 2k ol brn & bis 6.50 4.50
Never hinged 10.50
On cover 200.00
18 A10 3k dk vio & ind 55.00 27.50
Never hinged 110.00
On cover *350.00*
19 A10 5k dk brn & lt brn 145.00 27.50
Never hinged 275.00
On cover *500.00*
20 A10 10k vio brn & vio 8,750. 3,250.
Never hinged *12,500.*
On cover —

Handstamped Overprint

3a A9 2f brown orange 24.00 24.00
Never hinged 47.50
4a A9 3f red violet 24.00 24.00
Never hinged 47.50
5a A9 5f green 24.00 24.00
Never hinged 47.50
6a A9 6f grnsh blue 35.00 24.00
Never hinged 70.00
7a A9 10f rose red *72.50* *27.50*
Never hinged *100.00*
8a A9 15f violet 45.00 27.50
Never hinged 90.00
9a A9 20f gray brown 300.00 120.00
Never hinged 600.00
10a A9 25f deep blue 72.50 24.00
Never hinged 160.00
11a A9 35f brown 72.50 24.00
Never hinged 150.00
12a A9 40f olive green 45.00 24.00
Never hinged 85.00

White Numerals

13a A10 50f red vio & lil 24.00 24.00
Never hinged 50.00
14a A10 75f brt bl & pale bl 105.00 24.00
Never hinged 210.00
15a A10 80f grn & pale grn 105.00 24.00
Never hinged 210.00
16a A10 1k red brn & claret 47.50 24.00
Never hinged 85.00
17a A10 2k ol brn & bis 80.00 32.50
Never hinged 160.00
18a A10 3k dk vio & ind 1,050. 95.00
Never hinged 2,000.
19a A10 5k dk brn & lt brn 950.00 95.00
Never hinged 1,800.
20a A10 10k vio brn & vio 475.00 240.00
Never hinged *900.00*

Inverted or double overprints exist on most of Nos. 4-15. No. 7 only exists with inverted overprint.

Typographed Overprint On Stamps of 1918

21 A11 10f scarlet 4.00 4.00
Never hinged 8.25
On cover 30.00
22 A11 20f dark brown 3.25 2.40
Never hinged 6.25
On cover 35.00
23 A12 40f olive green 27.50 11.00
Never hinged 67.50
On cover 50.00

Handstamped Overprint On Stamps of 1918

21a A11 10f scarlet 24.00 24.00
Never hinged 47.50
22a A11 20f dark brown 27.50 24.00
Never hinged 55.00
23a A12 40f olive green 37.50 20.00
Never hinged 75.00

The overprint on Nos. 3-23a was applied by 2 printing plates and 6 handstamps. Values are for the less costly. All genuine printed overprints on No. 7 are inverted and are extremely scarce.

Postage Due Stamps of Hungary, 1915-20 Ovptd. & Surcharged in Black

1919, Jan.

24 D1 45f on 6f green & red 20.00 16.00
Never hinged 60.00
On cover 75.00
a. Pair, one with inverted surcharge *1,450.*
25 D1 45f on 20f green & red 60.00 16.00
Never hinged 140.00
On cover 87.50
Set, never hinged 200.00

Hungarian Savings Bank Stamp Surcharged in Black

A2

1919, Jan. 29

26 A2 15f on 10f dk violet 24.00 20.00
Never hinged 60.00
On cover 60.00

Overprints on Nos. 24-26 are typographed.

"Italy" — A3

Italian Flag on Clock-Tower in Fiume — A4

"Revolution" A5

Sailor Raising Italian Flag at Fiume (1918) A6

Nos. 30-43 exist on three types of paper: (A) grayish, porous paper, printed in sheets of 70 stamps (Jan, Feb. printings); (B) translucent or semi-translucent good quality white paper, printed in sheets of 70 stamps (March printing); and (C) good quality medium white paper, plain and opaque, sometimes grayish or yellowish, printed in sheets of 100 (April printing).

Perf. 11½

1919, April Unwmk. Litho.

Good Quality Medium White Paper (C)

27 A3 2c dull blue 2.40 2.40
Never hinged 5.00
On cover 35.00
28 A3 3c gray brown 2.40 2.40
Never hinged 5.00
On cover 40.00
a. Perf 10½ *1,000.*
Never hinged *2,000.*
29 A3 5c yellow green 2.40 2.40
Never hinged 5.00
On cover 35.00
30 A4 10c rose 40.00 27.50
Never hinged 100.00
On cover 42.50
31 A4 15c violet 2.40 2.40
Never hinged 4.25
On cover 35.00
32 A4 20c green 95.00 *140.00*
Never hinged 240.00
On cover *600.00*
33 A5 25c dark blue 3.25 2.40
Never hinged 6.25
On cover 35.00
34 A6 30c deep violet 3.25 2.40
Never hinged 6.25
On cover 35.00
a. Perf 10½ *1,000.*
Never hinged *2,000.*
35 A5 40c brown 3.25 2.40
Never hinged 6.25
On cover 35.00
36 A5 45c orange 3.25 2.40
Never hinged 6.25
On cover 35.00
37 A6 50c yellow green 3.25 2.40
Never hinged 6.25
On cover 35.00
a. Perf 10½ —
38 A6 60c claret 3.25 2.40
Never hinged 6.25
On cover 35.00
39 A6 1cor brown orange 4.75 2.40
Never hinged 10.50
On cover 35.00
40 A6 2cor brt blue 4.75 2.40
Never hinged 10.50
On cover 45.00
a. Perf 10½ *1,000.*
Never hinged *2,000.*
41 A6 3cor orange red 6.50 2.40
Never hinged 12.50
On cover 60.00
a. Perf 10½ *2,400.*
Never hinged *4,800.*
42 A6 5cor deep brown 40.00 40.00
Never hinged 85.00
On cover 90.00
a. Perf 10½ —
Never hinged 4,800.
43 A6 10cor olive green 135.00 90.00
Never hinged 340.00
On cover *600.00*
Nos. 27-43 (17) 355.10 328.70

1919, Jan.-Feb.

Poor Quality Grayish Paper (A)

30a A4 10c rose 25.00 16.00
Never hinged 62.50
On cover 45.00
31a A4 15c violet 32.50 *40.00*
Never hinged 80.00
On cover 50.00
32a A4 20c emerald green 4.00 *4.00*
Never hinged 10.00
On cover *45.00*
33a A5 25c light blue 16.00 2.40
Never hinged 40.00
On cover 45.00
36a A5 45c bister orange 4.00 4.00
Never hinged 10.00
On cover 45.00
b. Perf 10½ — *1,600.*
38a A6 60c claret 32.50 20.00
Never hinged 80.00
On cover 45.00
39a A6 1cor brown orange 8.00 4.00
Never hinged 20.00
On cover —
b. Perf 10½ — —
40b A6 2cor cobalt blue — —
Never hinged —
42b A6 5cor deep brown — —
Never hinged —
43a A6 10cor olive green 47.50 *80.00*
Never hinged 120.00
On cover *175.00*

1919, Mar.

Good Quality Translucent White Paper (B)

27a A3 2c dull blue 2.40 *4.00*
Never hinged 6.00
On cover 25.00
28b A3 3c gray brown 2.40 *4.00*
Never hinged 6.00
On cover 25.00
29a A3 5c yellow green 2.40 *4.00*
Never hinged 6.00
On cover 25.00
30b A4 10c car rose — —
31b A4 15c violet 3.25 *16.00*
Never hinged 8.00
On cover 35.00
33b A5 25c blue 3.25 *6.50*
Never hinged 8.00
On cover 35.00
35a A5 40c brown 3.25 *4.00*
Never hinged 8.00
On cover 30.00
36c A5 45c orange 200.00 *240.00*
Never hinged 500.00
On cover *500.00*
40c A6 2cor cobalt blue 12.00 *16.00*
Never hinged 30.00
On cover *550.00*
d. Perf 10½ *1,200.*
Never hinged *1,800.*
41b A6 3cor org vermilion 12.00 *16.00*
Never hinged 30.00
On cover *550.00*
c. Perf 10½ —
42c A6 5cor choc brown 100.00 100.00
Never hinged 250.00
On cover
43b A6 10cor olive green 110.00 *80.00*
Never hinged 275.00
On cover *550.00*

Part-perf. examples of most of this series are known.

For surcharges see Nos. 58, 60, 64, 66-69.

A7

A8

A9

A10

1919, July 28 *Perf. 11½*

46 A7 5c yellow green 2.40 1.60
Never hinged 4.50
On cover 45.00
47 A8 10c rose 2.40 1.60
Never hinged 4.50
On cover 35.00
48 A9 30c violet 11.00 4.00
Never hinged 26.00
On cover 45.00
49 A10 40c yellow brown 2.40 *2.40*
Never hinged 26.00
On cover 40.00
50 A10 45c orange 11.00 8.00
Never hinged 26.00
On cover 40.00
51 A9 50c yellow green 11.00 8.00
Never hinged 26.00
On cover 40.00
52 A9 60c claret 11.00 8.00
Never hinged 27.00
On cover 90.00
a. Perf. 13x12½ 190.00
Never hinged 475.00
b. Perf. 10½ 350.00
Never hinged 875.00
53 A9 10cor olive green 11.00 *22.50*
Never hinged 27.00
On cover 450.00
a. Perf. 13x12½ 65.00 *105.00*
Never hinged 160.00
On cover 600.00
b. Perf. 10½ 350.00 *375.00*
Never hinged 875.00
On cover 750.00
Nos. 46-53 (8) 62.20 56.10
Set, never hinged 145.00

Five other denominations (25c, 1cor, 2cor, 3cor and 5cor) were not officially issued. Some examples of the 25c are known canceled, a few examples having been sold at post offices along with full sets of Nos. 46-53. Values: 25c blue, $1,050 unused, $1,875 never hinged, $3,000 used; 1cor brown orange, perf 11½, $160 unused, $400 never hinged; 1cor brown orange, perf 12½-13, unused $30, never hinged $75; 2cor blue, perf 11½, unused $72.50, never hinged $180; 2cor blue, perf 12½-13, unused $30, never hinged $75; 3cor vermilion, perf 11½, unused $55, never hinged, $140; 3cor vermilion, perf 12½-13, unused $105, never hinged $260; 5cor brown, perf 11½, unused $160, never hinged $400; 5cor brown, perf 12½-13, unused $190, never hinged $460.

For surcharges see Nos. 59, 61-63, 65, 70.

Stamps and Types of 1919 Handstamp Surcharged

1919-20

58 A4 5c on 20c grn ('20) 2.40 2.40
Never hinged 4.50
59 A9 5c on 25c blue 2.40 2.40
Never hinged 4.50
60 A5 10c on 45c orange 2.40 2.40
Never hinged 4.50
61 A9 15c on 30c vio ('20) 2.40 2.40
Never hinged 4.50
62 A10 15c on 45c orange 2.40 2.40
Never hinged 4.50
63 A9 15c on 60c cl ('20) 2.40 2.40
Never hinged 4.50
64 A6 25c on 50c yel grn ('20) 20.00 *35.00*
Never hinged 47.50
65 A9 25c on 50c yel grn ('20) 2.40 2.40
Never hinged 4.50
66 A6 55c on 1cor brn org 40.00 40.00
Never hinged 100.00
67 A6 55c on 2cor brt bl 6.50 *9.50*
Never hinged 12.50
68 A6 55c on 3cor org red 6.50 8.00
Never hinged 12.50
69 A6 55c on 5cor dp brn 6.50 8.00
Never hinged 12.50
70 A9 55c on 10cor ol grn 32.50 35.00
Never hinged 82.50
Nos. 58-70 (13) 128.80 *152.30*
Set, never hinged 300.00

Semi-Postal Stamps of 1919 Surcharged

a

b

1919-20

73 SP6(a) 5c on 5c green 2.40 2.40
Never hinged 5.00
74 SP6(a) 10c on 10c rose 2.40 2.40
Never hinged 5.00
75 SP6(a) 15c on 15c gray 2.40 2.40
Never hinged 5.00
76 SP6(a) 20c on 20c org 2.40 2.40
Never hinged 5.00
77 SP9(a) 25c on 25c bl ('20) 2.40 2.40
Never hinged 5.00
78 SP7(b) 45c on 45c ol grn 4.00 4.00
Never hinged 7.50
79 SP7(b) 60c on 60c rose 4.00 4.00
Never hinged 7.50
80 SP7(b) 80c on 80c violet 2.40 2.40
Never hinged 5.00
81 SP7(b) 1cor on 1cor sl 4.00 4.00
Never hinged 7.50
82 SP8(a) 2cor on 2cor red brn 6.50 6.50
Never hinged 13.00
83 SP8(a) 3cor on 3cor blk brn 8.00 8.00
Never hinged 22.00
84 SP8(a) 5cor on 5cor yel brn 9.50 9.50
Never hinged 25.00
85 SP8(a) 10cor on 10cor dk vio ('20) 4.00 4.00
Never hinged 7.50
Nos. 73-85 (13) 54.40 54.40
Set, never hinged 120.00

Double or inverted surcharges, or imperf. varieties, exist on most of Nos. 73-85.

There were three settings of the surcharges on Nos. 73-85 except No. 77 which is known only with one setting.

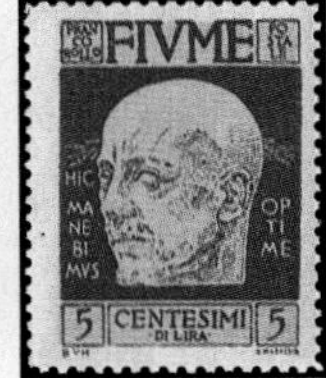

Gabriele d'Annunzio — A11

1920, Sept. 12 **Typo.** *Perf. 11½*

Pale Buff Background

86 A11 5c green 2.40 2.40
Never hinged 5.00
On commercial cover, from *50.00*
a. Imperf. 65.00 65.00
Never hinged 100.00
b. Pair, imperf. vert. 35.00 35.00
Never hinged 55.00
c. Horiz. pair, imperf. btwn. 240.00 —
Never hinged 360.00
87 A11 10c carmine 2.40 2.40
Never hinged 5.00
On commercial cover, from *50.00*
a. Imperf. 22.50 22.50
Never hinged 32.50
b. Double impression, one inverted 75.00 —
Never hinged 115.00
88 A11 15c dark gray 2.40 2.40
Never hinged 5.00
On commercial cover, from *50.00*
a. Imperf. 55.00 55.00
Never hinged 82.50
b. Pair, imperf. vert. 35.00 —
Never hinged 55.00
c. Vert. pair, imperf. btwn. 300.00 300.00
Never hinged 450.00
d. Double impression 25.00 25.00
Never hinged 37.50
89 A11 20c orange 2.40 2.40
Never hinged 5.00
On commercial cover, from *50.00*
a. Imperf. 22.50 22.50
Never hinged 32.50
b. Pair, imperf. vert. 65.00 65.00
Never hinged 100.00
90 A11 25c dark blue 3.25 3.25
Never hinged 7.00
On commercial cover, from *50.00*
a. Imperf. 22.50 22.50
Never hinged 32.50
b. Pair, imperf. horiz. 55.00 *65.00*
Never hinged 82.50
c. Horiz. pair, imperf. btwn. 210.00 210.00
Never hinged 315.00
d. Vert. pair, imperf. btwn. 300.00 —
Never hinged 450.00
e. 25c carmine, imperf. 425.00
Never hinged 1,050.
91 A11 30c red brown 3.25 3.25
Never hinged 7.00
On commercial cover, from *75.00*
a. Imperf. 22.50 22.50
Never hinged 32.50
92 A11 45c olive gray 4.75 4.75
Never hinged 10.00
On commercial cover, from *90.00*
a. Imperf. 22.50 22.50
Never hinged 32.50
b. Pair, imperf. horiz. 55.00 *65.00*
Never hinged 82.50
c. Pair, imperf. vert. 35.00 35.00
Never hinged 55.00
d. Vert. pair, imperf. btwn. 175.00 175.00
Never hinged 275.00
e. Double impression 150.00 —
Never hinged 225.00
f. Double impression, one inverted 65.00 65.00
Never hinged 100.00
93 A11 50c lilac 4.75 4.75
Never hinged 10.00
On commercial cover, from *75.00*
a. Imperf. 55.00 55.00
Never hinged 82.50
b. Double impression 150.00 —
Never hinged 225.00
c. Double impression, one inverted 15.00 15.00
Never hinged 22.50
94 A11 55c bister 4.75 4.75
Never hinged 10.00
On commercial cover, from *175.00*
a. Imperf. 27.50 27.50
Never hinged 40.00
95 A11 1 l black 20.00 *27.50*
Never hinged 47.50
On commercial cover, from 325.00
a. Imperf. 95.00 95.00
Never hinged 150.00
b. Horiz. pair, imperf. btwn. 360.00 —
Never hinged 725.00
c. Double impression 240.00 —
Never hinged 360.00
96 A11 2 l red violet 20.00 *27.50*
Never hinged 47.50
On commercial cover, from *325.00*
a. Double impression — —
Never hinged —
97 A11 3 l dark green 20.00 *27.50*
Never hinged 47.50
On commercial cover, from *400.00*
98 A11 5 l brown 80.00 55.00
Never hinged 200.00
On commercial cover, from *750.00*
a. Double impression 175.00 175.00
Never hinged 275.00
99 A11 10 l gray violet 20.00 *27.50*
Never hinged 47.50
On commercial cover, from *900.00*
Nos. 86-99 (14) 190.35 *195.35*
Set, never hinged 450.00

The background print, pale buff, also exists doubly printed or shifted on several denominations.

Counterfeits of Nos. 86 to 99 are plentiful.

For overprints see Nos. 134-148.

Severing the Gordian Knot — A12

Designs: 10c, Ancient emblem of Fiume. 20c, Head of "Fiume." 25c, Hands holding daggers.

1920, Sept. 12

100 A12 5c green 42.50 27.50
Never hinged 135.00
a. Imperf. 145.00
Never hinged 285.00
b. Horiz. pair, imperf. between 375.00
Never hinged 725.00
101 A12 10c deep rose 27.50 22.50
Never hinged 85.00
a. Imperf. 95.00
Never hinged 190.00
102 A12 20c brown orange 42.50 22.50
Never hinged 135.00
103 A12 25c indigo 27.50 *47.50*
Never hinged 85.00
a. Imperf. 180.00
Never hinged 360.00
b. Double impression, imperf. 1,075.
Never hinged 2,150.
c. Horiz. pair, imperf. between 550.00
Never hinged 1,075.
d. 25c blue 95.00 *100.00*
Never hinged 325.00
e. As "d," imperf. 400.00
Never hinged 800.00
f. As "d," horiz. pair, imperf. between 1,075.
Never hinged 2,150.
Nos. 100-103 (4) 140.00 120.00
Set, never hinged 440.00

Anniv. of the occupation of Fiume by d'Annunzio. They were available for franking the correspondence of the legionnaires on the day of issue only, Sept. 12, 1920.

Counterfeits of Nos. 100-103 are plentiful.

For overprints and surcharges see Nos. 104-133, E4-E9.

Nos. 100-103 Overprinted or Surcharged in Black or Red

1920, Nov. 20

104 A12 1c on 5c green 2.40 2.40
Never hinged 5.00
a. Inverted overprint 55.00 55.00
b. Double overprint 200.00
105 A12 2c on 25c indigo (R) 2.40 2.40
Never hinged 5.00
a. Inverted overprint 55.00 55.00
b. Double overprint 72.50 72.50
c. 2c on 25c blue (R) 80.00 80.00
Never hinged 200.00
106 A12 5c green 20.00 2.40
Never hinged 57.50
a. Inverted overprint 47.50 47.50
b. Double overprint 72.50 72.50
107 A12 10c rose 20.00 2.40
Never hinged 57.50
a. Inverted overprint 55.00 55.00
b. Double overprint 72.50 72.50
108 A12 15c on 10c rose 2.40 2.40
Never hinged 5.00
a. Inverted overprint 65.00 65.00
b. Double overprint 72.50 72.50
109 A12 15c on 20c brn org 2.40 *2.40*
Never hinged 5.00
a. Inverted overprint 65.00 65.00
b. Double overprint 72.50 72.50
110 A12 15c on 25c indigo (R) 2.40 *2.40*
Never hinged 5.00
a. Inverted overprint 65.00 65.00
b. Double overprint 72.50 72.50
c. 15c on 25c blue (R) 225.00 225.00
Never hinged 550.00
d. As "c," inverted overprint 475.00 475.00
e. As "c," double overprint 475.00
111 A12 20c brown orange 2.40 2.40
Never hinged 5.00
a. Inverted overprint 27.50 27.50
b. Double overprint 125.00 125.00
112 A12 25c indigo (R) 2.40 2.40
Never hinged 5.00
a. Inverted overprint 24.00 24.00
b. 25c blue (R) 8.00 8.00
Never hinged 19.00
113 A12 25c indigo (Bk) 175.00 175.00
Never hinged 500.00
a. Inverted overprint 450.00 350.00
b. 25c blue (Bk) 240.00 240.00
Never hinged 560.00
c. As "b," inverted overprint 725.00
114 A12 25c on 10c rose 2.40 4.75
Never hinged 5.00
a. Double overprint 72.50 72.50
115 A12 50c on 20c brn org 5.00 2.40
Never hinged 14.00
a. Double overprint 72.50 72.50
116 A12 55c on 5c green 21.00 4.75
Never hinged 57.50
a. Inverted overprint 95.00 95.00
b. Double overprint 72.50 72.50
117 A12 1 l on 10c rose 47.50 40.00
Never hinged 120.00
a. Inverted overprint 275.00 275.00
b. Double overprint 275.00
118 A12 1 l on 25c indigo (R) 100.00 100.00
Never hinged 290.00
a. 1 l on 25c blue (R) 600.00 600.00
Never hinged 1,500.
b. As "a," inverted overprint 875.00 725.00
119 A12 2 l on 5c green 47.50 40.00
Never hinged 120.00
a. Inverted overprint 325.00
b. Double overprint 200.00
120 A12 5 l on 10c rose 225.00 *240.00*
Never hinged 600.00
a. Inverted overprint 725.00 725.00
b. Double overprint 725.00
121 A12 10 l on 20c brn org 700.00 550.00
Never hinged 2,000.
a. Inverted overprint 1,600. 800.00
b. Double overprint 1,600. 800.00
Nos. 104-121 (18) 1,380. 1,179.
Set, never hinged 3,850.

The Fiume Legionnaires of d'Annunzio occupied the islands of Arbe and Veglia in the Gulf of Carnaro Nov. 13, 1920-Jan. 5, 1921.

Varieties of overprint or surcharge exist for most of Nos. 104-121.

Nos. 113, 117-121, 125, 131 have a backprint.

Nos. 106-107, 111, 113, 115-116 Overprinted or Surcharged at top

1920, Nov. 28

"ARBE" 11mm wide

122 A12 5c green 35.00 24.00
Never hinged 82.50
123 A12 10c rose 45.00 *52.50*
Never hinged 105.00
124 A12 20c brown org 87.50 52.50
Never hinged 215.00
125 A12 25c deep blue 52.50 *52.50*
Never hinged 115.00
126 A12 50c on 20c brn org 95.00 52.50
Never hinged 240.00
127 A12 55c on 5c green 95.00 52.50
Never hinged 240.00
Nos. 122-127 (6) 410.00 286.50
Set, never hinged 1,000.

The overprint on Nos. 122-125 comes in two widths: 11mm and 14mm. Values are for the 11mm width.

"ARBE" 14mm wide

122a A12 5c green 400.00 225.00
Never hinged 900.00
123a A12 10c rose 400.00 225.00
Never hinged 925.00
124a A12 20c brown org 400.00 225.00
Never hinged 925.00
125a A12 25c deep blue 900.00 445.00
Never hinged 2,050.
Nos. 122a-125a (4) 2,100. 1,120.
Set, never hinged 4,800.

Nos. 122a-125a issued Nov. 13.

Nos. 106-107, 111, 113, 115-116 Overprinted or Surcharged at top

1920, Nov. 28

"VEGLIA" 17mm wide

128 A12 5c green 35.00 24.00
Never hinged 85.00
129 A12 10c rose 45.00 *52.50*
Never hinged 105.00
130 A12 20c brown orange 87.50 52.50
Never hinged 210.00
131 A12 25c deep blue 52.50 *52.50*
Never hinged 120.00
132 A12 50c on 20c brn org 95.00 52.50
Never hinged 240.00
133 A12 55c on 5c green 95.00 52.50
Never hinged 240.00
Nos. 128-133 (6) 410.00 286.50
Set, never hinged 1,000.

"VEGLIA" 19mm wide

128a A12 5c green 400.00 225.00
Never hinged 900.00
129a A12 10c rose 400.00 225.00
Never hinged 900.00
130a A12 20c brown org 400.00 225.00
Never hinged 900.00
131a A12 25c deep blue 875.00 450.00
Never hinged 2,100.
Nos. 128a-131a (4) 2,075. 1,125.
Set, never hinged 4,800.

Nos. 122a-125a issued Nov. 13.

Nos. 122-133 exist with double and inverted overprints.
Counterfeits of these overprints exist.

Nos. 86-99 Overprinted

1921, Feb. 2

"Provvisorio" 20mm wide

Space between lines 3mm

Pale Buff Background

134 A11 5c green 2.40 2.40
Never hinged 5.50
On cover 32.50
a. Inverted overprint 27.50 27.50
Never hinged 40.00
b. Double overprint 52.50 52.50
135 A11 10c carmine 2.40 2.40
Never hinged 5.50
On cover 32.50
a. Inverted overprint 27.50 27.50
Never hinged 40.00
b. Double overprint 52.50 52.50
136 A11 15c dark gray 2.40 *2.40*
Never hinged 5.50
On cover 37.50
a. Inverted overprint 27.50 27.50
Never hinged 40.00
b. Double overprint 52.50 52.50
137 A11 20c orange 4.00 4.00
Never hinged 9.00
On cover 37.50
a. Inverted overprint 27.50 27.50
Never hinged 40.00
b. Double overprint 27.50 27.50
138 A11 25c dark blue 4.00 4.00
Never hinged 9.00
On cover 40.00
a. Inverted overprint 27.50 27.50
Never hinged 40.00
b. Double overprint 52.50 52.50
139 A11 30c red brown 4.00 4.00
Never hinged 9.00
On cover 35.00
a. Inverted overprint 27.50 27.50
Never hinged 40.00
b. Double overprint 27.50 27.50
140 A11 45c olive gray 2.40 2.40
Never hinged 5.50
On cover 37.50
a. Inverted overprint 55.00 55.00
Never hinged 82.50
b. Double overprint 40.00 40.00
141 A11 50c lilac 4.00 4.00
Never hinged 9.00
On cover 37.50
a. Inverted overprint 27.50 27.50
Never hinged 40.00
142 A11 55c bister 4.00 4.00
Never hinged 9.00
On cover 55.00
a. Inverted overprint 16.00 16.00
Never hinged 24.00
143 A11 1 l black 145.00 *180.00*
Never hinged 325.00
On cover 850.00
a. Inverted overprint 350.00 350.00
Never hinged 500.00
144 A11 2 l red violet 95.00 95.00
Never hinged 215.00
On cover 225.00
145 A11 3 l dark green 95.00 95.00
Never hinged 225.00
On cover 375.00
146 A11 5 l brown 95.00 95.00
Never hinged 215.00
On cover 600.00
147 A11 10 l gray violet 95.00 95.00
Never hinged 240.00
On cover 675.00

With Additional Surcharge

148 A11 1 l on 30c red brown 2.50 2.50
Never hinged 4.50
a. Inverted overprint 27.50 27.50
Never hinged 42.50
b. Double overprint 55.00 55.00
Nos. 134-148 (15) 557.10 592.10
Set, never hinged 1,400.

See Nos. E10-E11.

Second Printing, Milan

"Provvisorio" 21mm wide

Space between overprint lines 4mm

1921, Dec. 18

148A A11 5c yellow green 50.00 *57.50*
Never hinged 125.00
On cover 300.00
148B A11 10c carmine 135.00 40.00
Never hinged 340.00
On cover 300.00
c. Vert. pair, imperf. between *650.00*

First Constituent Assembly

Nos. B4-B15 Overprinted

1921, Apr. 24

149 SP6 5c blue green 6.50 4.75
Never hinged 12.50
150 SP6 10c rose 6.50 4.75
Never hinged 12.50
a. Inverted overprint 65.00 65.00
151 SP6 15c gray 6.50 4.75
Never hinged 12.50
152 SP6 20c orange 6.50 4.75
Never hinged 12.50
153 SP7 45c olive green 17.50 12.00
Never hinged 37.50
154 SP7 60c car rose 17.50 12.00
Never hinged 37.50
a. Inverted overprint 47.50 47.50
155 SP7 80c brt violet 27.50 24.00
Never hinged 62.50

With Additional Overprint "L"

156 SP7 1 l on 1cor dk slate 32.50 *35.00*
Never hinged 85.00
a. Inverted overprint 80.00 80.00
157 SP8 2 l on 2cor red brn 120.00 4.25
Never hinged 300.00
a. Inverted overprint 325.00 160.00
158 SP8 3 l on 3cor black brn 120.00 *130.00*
Never hinged 300.00
159 SP8 5 l on 5cor yel brn 120.00 4.25
Never hinged 300.00
160 SP8 10 l on 10cor dk vio 175.00 175.00
Never hinged 450.00
a. Inverted overprint 475.00 400.00
Nos. 149-160 (12) 656.00 415.50
Set, never hinged 1,625.

The overprint exists inverted on several denominations.

Second Constituent Assembly

"Constitution" Issue of 1921 With Additional Overprint "1922"

1922

161 SP6 5c blue green 4.75 3.25
Never hinged 11.00
a. Inverted overprint 24.00 24.00
162 SP6 10c rose 2.40 *2.40*
Never hinged 4.25
a. Inverted overprint 24.00 24.00
b. Double overprint, one inverted 40.00 40.00
163 SP6 15c gray 20.00 12.00
Never hinged 50.00
164 SP6 20c orange 2.40 2.40
Never hinged 4.50
a. Inverted overprint 32.50 32.50
b. Double overprint 40.00 40.00
c. Double overprint, one inverted — —
165 SP7 45c olive grn 13.00 12.00
Never hinged 30.00
a. Double overprint 40.00 40.00
166 SP7 60c car rose 2.40 *3.25*
Never hinged 4.50
167 SP7 80c brt violet 2.40 *3.25*
Never hinged 4.50
168 SP7 1 l on 1cor dk slate 2.40 *2.40*
Never hinged 4.50
a. Inverted overprint 55.00 55.00
b. Double overprint 40.00 40.00
169 SP8 2 l on 2cor red brn 20.00 16.00
Never hinged 47.50
170 SP8 3 l on 3cor blk brn 2.50 *3.25*
Never hinged 4.50
171 SP8 5 l on 5cor yel brn 2.50 *3.25*
Never hinged 4.50
Nos. 161-171 (11) 74.75 63.45
Set, never hinged 170.00

Nos. 161-171 have the overprint in heavier type than Nos. 149-160 and "IV" in Roman instead of sans-serif numerals.

Venetian Ship — A16

Roman Arch — A17

St. Vitus — A18

Rostral Column — A19

1923, Mar. 23 ***Perf. 11½***

Pale Buff Background

172 A16 5c blue green 2.40 2.40
Never hinged 4.25
173 A16 10c violet 2.40 2.40
Never hinged 4.25
174 A16 15c brown 2.40 2.40
Never hinged 4.25
175 A17 20c orange red 2.40 2.40
Never hinged 4.25
176 A17 25c dark gray 2.40 2.40
Never hinged 4.25
177 A17 30c dark green 2.40 2.40
Never hinged 4.25
178 A18 50c dull blue 2.40 2.40
Never hinged 4.25
179 A18 60c rose 4.00 *4.00*
Never hinged 6.25
180 A18 1 l dark blue 4.00 *4.00*
Never hinged 6.25
181 A19 2 l violet brown 65.00 20.00
Never hinged 175.00
182 A19 3 l olive bister 55.00 45.00
Never hinged 125.00
183 A19 5 l yellow brown 55.00 52.50
Never hinged 125.00
Nos. 172-183 (12) 199.80 142.30
Set, never hinged 465.00

Nos. 172-183 Overprinted

1924, Feb. 22

Pale Buff Background

184 A16 5c blue green 2.40 *12.00*
Never hinged 4.25
a. Inverted overprint 20.00 *40.00*
b. Double overprint 130.00
185 A16 10c violet 2.40 *12.00*
Never hinged 4.25
a. Inverted overprint 16.00 *40.00*
186 A16 15c brown 2.40 *12.00*
Never hinged 4.25
a. Inverted overprint 17.00 *40.00*
187 A17 20c orange red 2.40 *12.00*
Never hinged 4.25
a. Inverted overprint 21.00 *40.00*
b. Double overprint 260.00
188 A17 25c dk gray 2.40 *12.00*
Never hinged 4.25
189 A17 30c dk green 2.40 *12.00*
Never hinged 4.25
a. Inverted overprint 42.50
190 A18 50c dull blue 2.40 *12.00*
Never hinged 4.25
a. Inverted overprint 42.50 42.50
191 A18 60c red 2.40 *12.00*
Never hinged 4.25
a. Inverted overprint 87.50
192 A18 1 l dark blue 2.40 *12.00*
Never hinged 4.25
a. Inverted overprint 21.00 *40.00*
193 A19 2 l violet brown 4.00 *32.50*
Never hinged 8.75
a. Inverted overprint 130.00 *160.00*
194 A19 3 l olive 6.00 *40.00*
Never hinged 17.00
195 A19 5 l yellow brown 6.00 *40.00*
Never hinged 17.00
Nos. 184-195 (12) 37.60 *220.50*
Set, never hinged 80.00

The overprint exists inverted on almost all values.

Nos. 172-183 Overprinted

1924, Mar. 1

Pale Buff Background

196 A16 5c blue green 2.40 *20.00*
Never hinged 4.25
197 A16 10c violet 2.40 *20.00*
Never hinged 4.25
198 A16 15c brown 2.40 *20.00*
Never hinged 4.25
199 A17 20c orange red 2.40 *20.00*
Never hinged 4.25
200 A17 25c dark gray 2.40 *20.00*
Never hinged 4.25
201 A17 30c dark green 2.40 *20.00*
Never hinged 4.25
202 A18 50c dull blue 2.40 *20.00*
Never hinged 4.25
203 A18 60c red 2.40 *20.00*
Never hinged 4.50
204 A18 1 l dark blue 2.40 *20.00*
Never hinged 4.50
205 A19 2 l violet brown 4.00 *27.50*
Never hinged 7.25
206 A19 3 l olive 4.00 *27.50*
Never hinged 8.00

207 A19 5 l yellow brown 4.00 *27.50*
Never hinged 8.00
Nos. 196-207 (12) 33.60 *262.50*
Set, never hinged 62.50

Postage stamps of Fiume were superseded by stamps of Italy.

SEMI-POSTAL STAMPS

Semi-Postal Stamps of Hungary, 1916-17 Overprinted

1918, Dec. 2 Wmk. 137 *Perf. 15*

Typographed Overprint

B1 SP3 10f + 2f rose 8.00 8.00
Never hinged 17.50
a. Inverted overprint 72.50 40.00
b. Double overprint 240.00 120.00
B2 SP4 15f + 2f dl vio 8.00 8.00
Never hinged 17.50
a. Inverted overprint 145.00 40.00
b. Double overprint 145.00 47.50
B3 SP5 40f + 2f brn car 14.50 8.00
Never hinged 37.50
a. Inverted overprint 87.50 37.50
Nos. B1-B3 (3) 30.50 24.00
Set, never hinged 72.50

Handstamped Overprint

B1c SP3 10f + 2f rose 125.00 80.00
Never hinged 250.00
B2c SP4 15f + 2f dl vio 90.00 60.00
Never hinged 180.00
B3c SP5 40f + 2f brn car 27.50 27.50
Never hinged 45.00
Nos. B1c-B3c (3) 242.50 167.50
Set, never hinged 525.00

Statue of Romulus and Remus Being Suckled by Wolf — SP6

Venetian Galley — SP7

Church of St. Mark's, Venice — SP8

Perf. 11½

1919, May 18 Unwmk. Typo.

B4 SP6 5c +5 l bl grn 47.50 32.50
Never hinged 120.00
B5 SP6 10c +5 l rose 47.50 32.50
Never hinged 120.00
B6 SP6 15c +5 l dk gray 47.50 32.50
Never hinged 120.00
B7 SP6 20c +5 l orange 47.50 32.50
Never hinged 120.00
B8 SP7 45c +5 l ol grn 47.50 32.50
Never hinged 120.00
B9 SP7 60c +5 l car rose 47.50 32.50
Never hinged 120.00
B10 SP7 80c +5 l lilac 47.50 32.50
Never hinged 120.00
B11 SP7 1cor +5 l dk slate 47.50 32.50
Never hinged 120.00
B12 SP8 2cor +5 l red brn 47.50 32.50
Never hinged 120.00
B13 SP8 3cor +5 l blk brn 47.50 32.50
Never hinged 120.00
B14 SP8 5cor +5 l yel brn 47.50 32.50
Never hinged 120.00
B15 SP8 10cor +5 l dk vio 47.50 32.50
Never hinged 120.00
Nos. B4-B15 (12) 570.00 390.00
Set, never hinged 1,450.

200th day of peace. The surtax aided Fiume students in Italy. "Posta di Fiume" is printed on the back of Nos. B4-B16.

The surtax is shown on the stamps as "LIRE 5" but actually was 5cor.

For surcharges and overprints see Nos. 73-76, 78-85, 149-171, J15-J26.

Dr. Antonio Grossich — SP9

1919, Sept. 20

B16 SP9 25c + 2 l blue 3.25 3.25
Never hinged 8.00

Surtax for the Dr. Grossich Foundation.
For overprint and surcharge, see No. 77.

SPECIAL DELIVERY STAMPS

1916 Special Delivery Stamp of Hungary Overprinted

1918, Dec. 2 Wmk. 137 *Perf. 15*

Typographed Overprint

E1 SD1 2f gray green & red 4.75 4.75
Never hinged 12.00
a. Double overprint 190.00 175.00

Handstamped overprints sell for more.

Handstamped Overprint

E1c SD1 2f gray green & red 85.00 27.50
Never hinged 170.00

SD3

Perf. 11½

1920, Sept. 12 Unwmk. Typo.

E2 SD3 30c slate blue 25.00 25.00
Never hinged 62.50
E3 SD3 50c rose 25.00 25.00
Never hinged 62.50
Set, never hinged 125.00

For overprints see Nos. E10-E11.

Nos. 102 and 100 Surcharged

1920, Nov.

E4 A12 30c on 20c brn org 190.00 175.00
Never hinged 500.00
a. Inverted overprint 625.00
b. Double overprint 625.00
E5 A12 50c on 5c green 290.00 125.00
Never hinged 700.00
a. Inverted overprint 1,000.
b. Double overprint 1,000.
c. Double overprint, one inverted 1,100.

Nos. E4-E5 have a backprint.

Same Surcharge as on Nos. 124, 122

E6 A12 30c on 20c brn org 275.00 180.00
Never hinged 560.00
E7 A12 50c on 5c green 210.00 180.00
Never hinged 425.00
a. Double overprint 950.00

Overprint on Nos. E6-E7 is 11mm wide.

Same Surcharge as on Nos. 130, 128

E8 A12 30c on 20c brn org 275.00 180.00
Never hinged 560.00
E9 A12 50c on 5c green 210.00 180.00
Never hinged 425.00
a. Double overprint 950.00 950.00
Nos. E4-E9 (6) 1,450. 1,020.
Set, never hinged 2,900.

Overprint on Nos. E8-E9 is 17mm wide.

Nos. E2 and E3 Overprinted

1921, Feb. 2

E10 SD3 30c slate blue 11.00 12.00
Never hinged 25.00
a. Inverted overprint 120.00 120.00
b. Double overprint 40.00 40.00
E11 SD3 50c rose 15.00 12.00
Never hinged 37.50
a. Inverted overprint 27.50 27.50
b. Double overprint 105.00 105.00
Set, never hinged 62.50

Fiume in 16th Century SD4

1923, Mar. 23 *Perf. 11, 11½*

E12 SD4 60c rose & buff 24.00 24.00
Never hinged 60.00
E13 SD4 2 l dk bl & buff 24.00 24.00
Never hinged 60.00
Set, never hinged 120.00

Nos. E12-E13 Overprinted

1924, Feb. 22

E14 SD4 60c car & buff 3.25 *20.00*
Never hinged 8.00
E15 SD4 2 l dk bl & buff 3.25 *20.00*
Never hinged 8.00
a. Inverted overprint 130.00 *160.00*
Set, never hinged 16.00

Nos. E12-E13 Overprinted

1924, Mar. 1

E16 SD4 60c car & buff 4.00 *80.00*
Never hinged 10.00
E17 SD4 2 l dk bl & buff 4.00 *80.00*
Never hinged 10.00
Set, never hinged 20.00

POSTAGE DUE STAMPS

Postage Due Stamps of Hungary, 1915-1916, Overprinted

1918, Dec. Wmk. 137 *Perf. 15*

Typographed Overprint

J1 D1 6f green & black 525.00 175.00
Never hinged 1,100.
a. Inverted overprint 1,050.
J2 D1 12f green & black 800.00 400.00
Never hinged 1,600.
a. Double overprint 950.00
J3 D1 50f green & black 225.00 125.00
Never hinged 450.00
a. Double overprint 950.00
Set, never hinged 3,150.

Handstamped Overprint

J1c D1 6f green & black 190.00 105.00
Never hinged 380.00
d. Double overprint — 1,450.
J2c D1 12f green & black 180.00 72.50
Never hinged 360.00
d. Double overprint 1,450.
J3c D1 50c green & black 65.00 35.00
Never hinged 130.00
d. Double overprint 1,450.
Set, never hinged 870.00

Typographed Overprint

J4 D1 1f green & red 175.00 240.00
Never hinged 350.00
J5 D1 2f green & red 6.50 6.50
Never hinged 13.00
a. Inverted overprint 52.50 45.00
b. Double overprint 175.00
J6 D1 5f green & red 72.50 72.50
Never hinged 145.00
a. Inverted overprint 175.00 130.00
J7 D1 6f green & red 6.50 6.50
Never hinged 13.00
a. Inverted overprint 25.00 25.00
b. Double overprint 27.50
J8 D1 10f green & red 90.00 27.50
Never hinged 180.00
a. Inverted overprint 440.00
J9 D1 12f green & red 6.50 6.50
Never hinged 13.00
J10 D1 15f green & red 650.00 550.00
Never hinged 1,300.
J11 D1 20f green & red 6.50 6.50
Never hinged 13.00
a. Double overprint 45.00 32.50
J12 D1 30f green & red 1,600. 1,300.
Never hinged 3,200.
Nos. J4-J12 (9) 2,614. 2,216.
Set, never hinged 5,225.

Handstamped Overprint

J4c D1 1f green & red 40.00 24.00
Never hinged 77.50
d. Inverted overprint 425.00
e. Double overprint 525.00 190.00
J5c D1 2f green & red 120.00 72.50
Never hinged 300.00
d. Inverted overprint 440.00
e. Double overprint —
J6c D1 5f green & red 40.00 *47.50*
Never hinged 80.00
d. Inverted overprint 320.00 440.00
e. Double overprint *525.00* 525.00
J7c D1 6f green & red 77.50 72.50
Never hinged 155.00
d. Inverted overprint 440.00
e. Double overprint — 950.00
J8c D1 10f green & red 32.50 32.50
Never hinged 65.00
d. Inverted overprint 475.00 475.00
J9c D1 12f green & red 77.50 72.50
Never hinged 160.00
d. Inverted overprint 800.00
J10c D1 15f green & red 32.50 32.50
Never hinged 65.00
d. Inverted overprint 800.00
e. Double overprint 440.00 440.00
J11c D1 20f green & red 725.00 145.00
Never hinged 1,450.
d. Inverted overprint 1,275. 550.00
J12c D1 30f green & red 32.50 32.50
Never hinged 65.00
d. Inverted overprint 900.00
e. Double overprint 950.00 950.00
Nos. j4c-j12c (9) 1,178. 531.50
Set, never hinged 2,350.

Six minor varieties of the handstamp exist. Some are sought by specialists at much higher values. Excellent forgeries exist.

Eagle — D2

Perf. 11½

1919, July 28 Unwmk. Typo.

J13 D2 2c brown 2.40 2.40
Never hinged 6.00
J14 D2 5c brown 2.40 2.40
Never hinged 6.00
Set, never hinged 12.00

Semi-Postal Stamps of 1919 Overprinted and Surcharged

1921, Mar. 21

No.	Description	Unused	Used
J15	SP6 2c on 15c gray	6.50	6.50
	Never hinged	14.50	
J16	SP6 4c on 10c rose	4.75	4.75
	Never hinged	12.00	
J17	SP9 5c on 25c blue	4.75	4.75
	Never hinged	12.00	
J18	SP6 6c on 20c orange	4.75	4.75
	Never hinged	12.00	
J19	SP6 10c on 20c orange	6.50	6.50
	Never hinged	14.50	

Nos. B8-B11 Surcharged

No.	Description	Unused	Used
J20	SP7 20c on 45c olive grn	2.40	*4.75*
	Never hinged	5.75	
J21	SP7 30c on 1cor dk slate	12.00	*12.00*
	Never hinged	24.00	
J22	SP7 40c on 80c violet	4.75	*6.50*
	Never hinged	12.00	
J23	SP7 50c on 60c carmine	4.75	*6.50*
	Never hinged	12.00	
J24	SP7 60c on 45c olive grn	2.40	*4.75*
	Never hinged	5.75	
J25	SP7 80c on 45c olive grn	2.40	*4.75*
	Never hinged	5.75	

Surcharged like Nos. J15-J19

No.	Description	Unused	Used
J26	SP8 1 l on 2cor red brown	24.00	*24.00*
	Never hinged	60.00	
	Nos. J15-J26 (12)	79.95	*90.50*
	Set, never hinged	190.00	

See note below No. 85 regarding settings of "Valore Globale" overprint.

NEWSPAPER STAMPS

Newspaper Stamp of Hungary, 1914, Overprinted like Nos. 1-23

1918, Dec. 2 Wmk. 137 *Imperf.*

Typographed Overprint

No.	Description	Unused	Used
P1	N5 (2f) orange	4.75	3.25
	Never hinged	15.00	
a.	Inverted overprint	55.00	52.50
b.	Double overprint	210.00	190.00

Handstamped Overprint

No.	Description	Unused	Used
P1c	N5 (2f) orange	72.50	27.50
	Never hinged	145.00	
d.	Double overprint	875.00	875.00

Handstamped overprints sell for more.

Eagle N1

1919 Unwmk. *Perf. 11½*

No.	Description	Unused	Used
P2	N1 2c deep buff	9.50	*14.50*
	Never hinged	24.00	

Re-engraved

No.	Description	Unused	Used
P3	N1 2c deep buff	9.50	*14.50*
	Never hinged	24.00	
	Set, never hinged	48.00	

In the re-engraved stamp the top of the "2" is rounder and broader, the feet of the eagle show clearly and the diamond at bottom has six lines instead of five.

Steamer — N2

1920, Sept. 12

No.	Description	Unused	Used
P4	N2 1c gray green	4.00	3.25
	Never hinged	10.00	
a.	Imperf	24.00	24.00

FRANCE

'fran‿t‿s

LOCATION — Western Europe
GOVT. — Republic
AREA — 210,033 sq. mi.
POP. — 54,539,000 (est. 1984)
CAPITAL — Paris

100 Centimes = 1 Franc

Catalogue values for unused stamps in this country are for Never Hinged items, beginning with Scott 299 in the regular postage section, Scott B42 in the semi-postal section, Scott S1 for franchise stamps, and Scott N27 for occupation stamps.

Ceres — A1

FORTY CENTIMES

40 Type I   40 Type II

1849-50 Typo. Unwmk. *Imperf.*

No.	Description	Unused	Used
1	A1 10c bis, *yelsh* ('50)	*1,500.*	210.00
	No gum	800.00	
	On cover, single franking		500.00
a.	10c dark bister, *yelsh*	1,825.	240.00
	No gum	900.00	
	On cover, single franking		575.00
b.	10c greenish bister	2,350.	600.00
	No gum	1,200.	
	On cover, single franking		*975.00*
c.	10c deep greenish bister	3,950.	675.00
	No gum	1,700.	
	On cover, single franking		1,300.
d.	As #1, tête beche pair	*85,000.*	*18,000.*
	No gum	45,000.	
	On cover		*34,000.*
e.	As #1a, tête beche pair	*100,000.*	*19,000.*
	On cover		*34,000.*
f.	As #1b, tête beche pair	*100,000.*	*18,500.*
	On cover		*33,500.*
2	A1 15c green, *grnsh*	*21,500.*	800.00
	No gum	10,500.	
	On cover, single franking		1,325.
a.	15c yellow green, *grnsh* ('50)	*20,000.*	700.00
	No gum	11,000.	
	On cover, single franking		1,350.
b.	15c dark green	*22,500.*	950.00
	No gum	11,000.	
	On cover, single franking		1,550.
c.	Tête bêche pair	—	
	On cover front		*260,000.*
3	A1 20c blk, *yelsh*	340.00	34.00
	No gum	170.00	
	On cover, single franking		72.50
a.	20c black	375.00	50.00
	No gum	185.00	
	On cover, single franking		105.00
b.	20c black, *buff*	1,100.	135.00
	No gum	450.00	
	On cover, single franking		240.00
c.	Tête bêche pair	*9,250.*	*6,500.*
	On cover		*12,000.*
4	A1 20c dark blue	*2,400.*	
a.	20c blue, *bluish*	*2,050.*	
b.	20c blue, *yelsh*	*2,750.*	
	No gum	2,500.	
c.	Tête bêche pair	*60,000.*	
e.	As "a," tête bêche pair	*55,000.*	
f.	As "b", tête bêche pair	*85,000.*	
6	A1 25c lt bl, *bluish*	*5,400.*	30.00
	No gum	2,750.	
	On cover, single franking		54.00
a.	25c blue, *bluish* ('50)	*5,400.*	30.00
	No gum	2,750.	
	On cover, single franking		54.00
b.	25c blue, *yelsh*	*6,250.*	40.00
	No gum	3,100.	
	On cover, single franking		65.00
c.	Tête bêche pair	*155,000.*	*12,500.*
	No gum	75,000.	
	On cover		*27,500.*
7	A1 40c org, *yelsh* (I) ('50)	*2,950.*	360.00
	No gum	1,500.	
	With dark brownish gum	2,150.	
	On cover, single franking		575.00
a.	40c org ver, *yelsh* (I)	*3,500.*	475.00
	No gum	1,850.	
	On cover, single franking		750.00
b.	40c orange, *yelsh* (II)	*20,750.*	*5,250.*
	No gum	10,500.	
	On cover, single franking		*10,000.*
c.	Pair, types I and II	*31,000.*	*12,500.*
	No gum	15,500.	
	On cover		*17,750.*
f.	Pair, type II	*87,500.*	*42,000.*
	No gum	43,500.	
	On cover		*70,000.*
g.	Vertical half used as 20c on cover		*260,000.*
h.	40c deep orange	*3,750.*	*625.00*
	No gum	1,850.	
	On cover		*1,100.*
i.	40c dp red org	*3,750.*	*625.00*
	No gum	1,850.	
	On cover		*1,000.*
8	A1 1fr vermilion, *yelsh*	*92,500.*	*13,750.*
	No gum	45,000.	
	On cover, single franking		*21,000.*
a.	1fr dull orange red	*95,000.*	*17,000.*
	No gum	46,000.	
	On cover, single franking		*28,000.*
b.	Tête bêche pair, no gum	*750,000.*	*210,000.*
	On cover		*215,000.*
c.	1fr pale ver ("Vervelle")	*20,000.*	
d.	As "c," tête bêche pair	*450,000.*	
9	A1 1fr light carmine	*8,750.*	650.00
	No gum	4,250.	
	On cover, single franking		1,350.
a.	Tête bêche pair	*200,000.*	*23,250.*
	On cover		*63,250.*
b.	1fr brown carmine	*10,000.*	800.00
	No gum	5,000.	
	On cover, single franking		1,150.
c.	1fr dark carmine, *yelsh*	*12,250.*	1,075.
	No gum	6,000.	
	On cover, single franking		1,550.
e.	1fr red brown	*11,500.*	900.00
	No gum	5,250.	
	On cover, single franking, *from*		1,250.

Full margins = ¾mm.

No. 4 was printed but not yet gummed when the rate change to 25c made them unnecessary. An essay with a red "25" surcharge on No. 4 was rejected. No. 7 exists in blue (unissued) from Jan. 1, 1849. Value, $28,000.

An ungummed sheet of No. 8c was found in 1895 among the effects of Anatole A. Hulot, the printer. It was sold to Ernest Vervelle, a Parisian dealer, by whose name the stamps are known.

No. 9e exists used from the beginning of 1849. On-cover values: January to March dates, $6,000; April and May dates, $3,300; June and later dates, $2,500.

See Nos. 329-329e, 612-613, 624. Compare with Type A2412. Post 1940 issues in Scott Standard catalogue, Vol. 2.

Values for blocks of 4

No.	Description	Unused	Used
1	A1 10c bis, *yelsh*	*7,250.*	*9,000.*
	On cover		*13,750.*
b.	10c greenish bister	*11,750.*	*10,500.*
	On cover		*18,000.*
2	A1 15c green, *grnsh*	*105,000.*	*60,000.*
	On cover		*105,000.*
b.	15c dark green	*112,500.*	*68,000.*
	On cover		*115,000.*
3	A1 20c blk, *yelsh*	*1,600.*	*4,000.*
	On cover		*9,000.*
a.	20c black	*2,000.*	*4,750.*
	On cover		*10,250.*
4	A1 20c dark blue	*11,000.*	
a.	20c blue, *bluish*	*12,000.*	
b.	20c blue, *yelsh*	*13,500.*	
6	A1 25c lt bl, *bluish*	*27,500.*	*4,250.*
	On cover		*7,500.*
a.	25c blue, *bluish* ('50)	*27,500.*	*4,250.*
	On cover		*7,500.*
7	A1 40c org, *yelsh* (I)	*19,000.*	*15,000.*
	On cover		*23,000.*
a.	40c org ver, *yelsh* (I)	*23,000.*	19,500.
	On cover		*27,500.*
b.	40c org, *yelsh* (I)	*23,000.*	*19,500.*
	On cover		*27,500.*
8	A1 1fr vermilion, *yelsh*	—	—
a.	1fr dull orange red	—	—
c.	1fr pale ver ("Vervelle")	*135,000.*	
9b	A1 1fr brown carmine	*52,500.*	*12,000.*
	On cover		*21,500.*
c.	1fr dark carmine, *yelsh*	*60,000.*	*14,500.*
	On cover		*23,500.*
e.	1fr red brown	*47,500.*	*11,000.*
	On cover		*21,500.*

Values for used pairs

No.	Description	Used
1	A1 10c bis, *yelsh*	600.
a.	10c dark bister, *yelsh*	650.
b.	10c greenish bister	900.
c.	10c deep greenish bister	1,900.
2	A1 15c green, *grnsh*	1,825.
a.	15c yellow green, *grnsh*	1,825.
b.	15c dark green	2,200.
3	A1 20c blk, *yelsh*	92.50
a.	20c black	110.
b.	20c black, *buff*	350.
6	A1 25c lt bl, *bluish*	80.
a.	25c blue, *bluish* ('50)	82.50
b.	25c blue, *yelsh*	120.
7	A1 40c org, *yelsh* (I)	900.
a.	40c org ver, *yelsh* (I)	950.
c.	Pair, types I and II	*11,000.*
f.	Pair, type II	*43,500.*
8	A1 1fr vermilion, *yelsh*	*47,500.*
a.	1fr dull orange red	*48,000.*
9	A1 1fr light carmine	1,525.
b.	1fr brown carmine	1,950.
c.	1fr dark carmine, *yelsh*	2,400.
e.	1fr red brown	*2,250.*

Values for pairs on cover

1	A1	10c bis, *yelsh*	1,150.
a.		10c dark bister, *yelsh*	1,200.
b.		10c greenish bister	1,500.
c.		10c deep greenish bister	2,600.
2	A1	15c green, *grnsh*	4,000.
		Pair on cover, alone	36,000.
a.		15c yellow green, *grnsh*	4,000.
		Pair on cover, alone	36,000.
b.		15c dark green	4,600.
		Pair on cover, alone	45,000.
3	A1	20c blk, *yelsh*	200.
a.		20c black	250.
b.		20c black, *buff*	625.
6	A1	25c lt bl, *bluish*	200.
a.		25c blue, *bluish* ('50)	190.
b.		25c blue, *yelsh*	210.
7	A1	40c org, *yelsh* (I)	1,150.
a.		40c org ver, *yelsh* (I)	1,400.
c.		Pair, types I and II	18,000.
f.		Pair, type II	72,500.
8	A1	1fr vermilion, *yelsh*	80,000.
a.		1fr dull orange red	80,000.
9	A1	1fr light carmine	2,700.
b.		1fr brown carmine	3,200.
c.		1fr dark carmine, *yelsh*	4,400.
e.		1fr red brown ('49)	—

Nos. 1, 4a, 6a, 7 and 13 are of similar designs and colors to French Colonies Nos. 9, 11, 12, 14, and 8. There are numerous shades of each. Identification by those who are not experts can be difficult, though cancellations can be used as a guide for used stamps.

Because of the date of issue the Colonies stamps are similar in shades and papers to the perforated French stamps, Nos. 23a, 54, 57-59, and are not as clearly printed. Except for No. 13, unused, the French Colonies stamps sell for much less than the values shown here for properly identified French versions.

Expertization of these stamps is recommended.

1862 **Re-issue**

1g	A1	10c bister	435.
		No gum	250.
2d	A1	15c yellow green	560.
		No gum	290.
3d	A1	20c black, *yellowish*	375.
		No gum	160.
4d	A1	20c blue	340.
		No gum	155.
6d	A1	25c blue	400.
		No gum	200.
7d	A1	40c orange (I)	575.
		No gum	270.
7e	A1	40c orange (II)	11,000.
		No gum	3,800.
h.		Pair, types I and II	15,000.
		No gum	5,000.
i.		Pair, type II	32,000.
		No gum	11,000.
9d	A1	1fr pale lake	600.
		No gum	285.

The re-issues are fine impressions in lighter colors and on whiter paper than the originals. An official imitation of the essay, 25c on 20c blue, also in a lighter shade and on whiter paper, was made at the same time as the re-issues.

Values for blocks of 4

1d	A1	10c bister	2,200.
2d	A1	15c yellow green	3,000.
3d	A1	20c black, *yellowish*	1,900.
4d	A1	20c blue	1,900.
6d	A1	25c blue	2,000.
7d	A1	40c orange (I)	2,700.
9d	A1	1fr pale lake	2,800.

President Louis Napoleon — A2

1852

10	A2	10c pale bister, *yelsh*	30,000.	450.00
		No gum	9,000.	
		On cover, single franking		750.00
a.		10c dark bister, *yelsh*	30,000.	525.00
		No gum	9,500.	
		On cover, single franking		850.00
c.		10c dark brownish bister	37,500.	800.00
		No gum	11,000.	
		On cover, single franking		1,350.
11	A2	25c blue, *bluish*	2,450.	32.50
		No gum	1,000.	
		On cover, single franking		50.00
b.		25c dark blue, *bluish*	2,900.	50.00
		No gum	1,100.	
		On cover, single franking		90.00
c.		25c greenish blue	3,000.	80.00
		No gum	1,200.	
		On cover, single franking		155.00

Full margins = ¾mm.

Values for used pairs

10	A2	10c pale bister, *yelsh*	1,150.
11	A2	25c blue, *bluish*	95.00

A sheet margin pair of 10 centimes, No. 10, realized the equivalent of U.S. $20,000 at a Geneva auction in 2004.

Values for pairs on cover

10	A2	10c pale bister, *yelsh*	2,075.
a.		10c dark bister, *yelsh*	2,400.
c.		10c dark brownish bister	3,100.
11	A2	25c blue, *bluish*	275.
b.		25c dark blue, *bluish*	325.
c.		25c greenish blue	450.

Values for used strips of 3

10	A2	10c pale bister, *yelsh*	2,750.
11	A2	25c blue, *bluish*	250.

Values for used strips of 4

10	A2	10c pale bister, *yelsh*	4,250.
11	A2	25c blue, *bluish*	550.

Values for used strips of 5

10	A2	10c pale bister, *yelsh*	8,000.
11	A2	25c blue, *bluish*	1,250.

Values for blocks of 4

10	A2	10c pale bister, *yelsh*	180,000.	47,500.
		On cover		72,500.
11	A2	25c blue, *bluish*	13,500.	2,150.
		On cover		3,600.

1862 **Re-issue**

10b	A2	10c bister	525.00
		No gum	250.00
11a	A2	25c blue	350.00
		No gum	160.00

The re-issues are in lighter colors and on whiter paper than the originals.

Values for blocks of 4

10b	A2	10c bister	2,500.
11a	A2	25c blue	2,000.

Emperor Napoleon III — A3

Die I. The curl above the forehead directly below "R" of "EMPIRE" is made up of two lines very close together, often appearing to form a single thick line. There is no shading across the neck.

Die II. The curl is made of two distinct, more widely separated lines. There are lines of shading across the upper neck.

1853-60 ***Imperf.***

12	A3	1c ol grn, *pale bl* ('60)	165.00	62.50
		No gum	77.50	
		On cover		175.00
		On cover, single franking		320.00
a.		1c bronze grn, *pale bluish*	155.00	67.50
		No gum	77.50	
		On cover		190.00
		On cover, single franking		340.00
b.		1c dp ol grn, *pale blue* ('60)	220.00	65.00
		No gum	110.00	
		On cover		175.00
		On cover, single franking		310.00
13	A3	5c grn, *grnsh* (I) ('54)	630.00	62.50
		No gum	315.00	
		On cover		125.00
		On cover, single franking		200.00
a.		5c dark green	1,500.	175.00
		No gum	750.00	
		On cover		185.00
		On cover, single franking		290.00
b.		5c pale green, *grnsh*	1,025.	115.00
		No gum	515.00	
		On cover		140.00
		On cover, single franking		185.00
14	A3	10c bis, *yelsh* (I)	360.00	6.50
		No gum	175.00	
		On cover, single franking		11.50
a.		10c yellow, *yelsh* (I)	1,200.	27.50
		No gum	525.00	
		On cover, single franking		45.00
b.		10c bister brn, *yelsh* (I)	450.00	18.50
		No gum	225.00	
		On cover, single franking		31.00
c.		10c bister, *yelsh* (II) ('60)	450.00	19.00
		No gum	225.00	
		On cover, single franking		32.50
d.		10c dark brn (III) ('62)	675.00	45.00
		No gum	340.00	
		On cover, single franking		75.00
e.		Half used as 5c on cover		130,000.
15	A3	20c bl, *bluish* (I) ('54)	150.00	1.35
		No gum	75.00	
		On cover, single franking		2.50
a.		20c dark bl, *bluish* (I)	220.00	1.35
		No gum	110.00	
		On cover, single franking		2.50
b.		20c milky blue (I)	225.00	10.00
		No gum	110.00	
		On cover, single franking		15.00
c.		20c blue, *lilac* (I)	4,250.	62.50
		No gum	2,150.	
		On cover		100.00
d.		20c blue, *bluish* (II) ('60)	285.00	4.00
		No gum	140.00	
		On cover		6.00
e.		Half used as 10c on cover		16,000.
f.		Tête bêche pair	155,000.	—
		No gum		
16	A3	20c bl, *grnsh* (II)	5,250.	150.00
		No gum	2,650.	
		On cover, single franking		225.00
a.		20c blue, *greenish* (I)	4,250.	100.00
		No gum	2,000.	
		On cover		175.00
17	A3	25c bl, *bluish* (I)	2,050.	165.00
		No gum	1,000.	
		On cover, single franking		325.00
a.		25c milky blue (I)	2,000.	185.00
		No gum	1,000.	
		On cover, single franking		325.00
b.		25c deep blue (I)	2,100.	195.00
		No gum	1,050.	
		On cover, single franking		340.00
18	A3	40c org, *yelsh* (I)	2,000.	10.00
		No gum	1,000.	
		On cover, single franking		17.00
a.		40c org ver, *yellowish*	2,850.	16.00
		No gum	1,375.	
		On cover, single franking		27.50
b.		Half used as 20c on cover		110,000.
d.		40c dp orange	2,850.	18.50
		No gum	1,375.	
		On cover, single franking		28.00
19	A3	80c lake, *yelsh* (I) ('54)	2,800.	40.00
		No gum	1,400.	
		On cover, single franking		170.00
a.		Tête bêche pair	340,000.	22,000.
		On cover		35,000.
b.		Half used as 40c on cover		50,000.
c.		80c dp car lake ('55)	4,100.	62.50
		No gum	2,000.	
		On cover, single franking		90.00
d.		80c pale car lake ('57)	2,800.	40.00
		No gum	1,400.	
		On cover, single franking		62.50
20	A3	80c rose, *pnksh* (I) ('60)	1,875.	42.50
		No gum	950.00	
		On cover, single franking		75.00
a.		Tête-bêche pair	49,500.	10,000.
		On cover, single franking		18,000.
b.		80c bright rose	2,175.	52.50
		No gum	1,100.	
		On cover, single franking		95.00
d.		80c pale rose	1,875.	37.50
		No gum	925.00	
		On cover, single franking		70.00
e.		80c bright gooseberry red ("groseille")	4,100.	185.00
		No gum	2,000.	
		On cover, single franking		275.00
21	A3	1fr lake, *yelsh* (I)	7,450.	2,475.
		No gum	3,100.	
		On cover		7,500.
		On cover, single franking		7,500.
a.		Tête bêche pair	300,000.	135,000.
		On cover		195,000.
b.		1fr pale lake	7,450.	2,175.
		No gum	2,800.	
		On cover		6,800.
		On cover, single franking		7,000.
c.		1fr deep lake	8,750.	3,400.
		No gum	4,000.	
		On cover		8,000.
		On cover, single franking		8,000.

Full margins = ¾mm.

Most values of the 1853-60 issue are known privately rouletted, pin-perf., perf. 7 and percé en scie.

Values for bisected stamps on cover

14d	A3	10c	Nangis, *5/7/55*	130,000.
15e	A3	20c	Bordeaux, *Feb. '56*	15,500.
15e	A3	20c	Marines, *Sep. '56*	20,000.
15e	A3	20c	Meru, *Sep. '56*	20,000.
15e	A3	20c	Sainte-Sigolene, *Feb. '56*	21,000.
15e	A3	20c	Vebron, *June '61-Jan '62*	22,000.
15e	A3	20c	Villars-de-Lans, *Jan '58*	21,000.
18b	A3	40c	Mostaganem, *May '60*	115,000.
19b	A3	80c	Givors	50,000.

Nos. 14d and 18b are unique.

Values for pairs

12	A3	1c ol grn, *pale bl,*	400.00	175.00
a.		1c bronze grn, *pale bluish,*	400.00	180.00
13	A3	5c grn, *grnsh* (I)	1,450.	160.00
a.		5c dark green	3,400.	400.00
14	A3	10c bis, *yelsh* (I)	810.00	18.00
a.		10c yellow, *yelsh* (I)	3,250.	105.00
b.		10c bister brn, *yelsh* (I)	1,625.	72.50
c.		10c bister, *yelsh* (II)	1,000.	50.00
15	A3	20c bl, *bluish* (I)	360.00	4.25
a.		20c dark bl, *bluish* (I)	600.00	14.00
b.		20c milky blue (I)	575.00	27.00
c.		20c blue, *lilac* (I)	10,000.	180.00
d.		20c blue, *bluish* (II)	800.00	12.00
16	A3	20c bl, *grnsh* (II)	11,250.	400.00
a.		20c blue, *greenish* (I)	9,000.	250.00
17	A3	25c bl, *bluish* (I)	4,500.	475.00
a.		25c milky blue (I)	4,500.	500.00
18	A3	40c org, *yelsh* (I)	4,500.	29.00
a.		40c org ver, *yellowish*	6,750.	40.00
19	A3	80c lake, *yelsh* (I)	8,000.	105.00
20	A3	80c rose, *pnksh* (I)	4,500.	105.00
21	A3	1fr lake, *yelsh* (I)	18,000.	6,250.

Values for pairs on cover

12	A3	1c ol grn, *pale bl,* on cover, paying 2c rate	425.00
a.		1c bronze grn, *pale bluish,* on cover, paying 2c rate	450.00
13	A3	5c grn, *grnsh* (I) on cover, paying 10c rate	225.00
a.		5c dark green, on cover, paying 10c rate	500.00
14	A3	10c bis, *yelsh* (I)	20.00
a.		10c yellow, *yelsh* (I)	100.00
b.		10c bister brn, *yelsh* (I)	80.00
c.		10c bister, *yelsh* (II)	72.50
15	A3	20c bl, *bluish* (I)	5.50
a.		20c dark bl, *bluish* (I)	5.50
b.		20c milky blue (I)	54.00
c.		20c blue, *lilac* (I)	250.00
d.		20c blue, *bluish* (II)	12.50
16	A3	20c bl, *grnsh* (II)	575.00
a.		20c blue, *greenish* (I)	450.00
17	A3	25c bl, *bluish* (I)	900.00
a.		25c milky blue (I)	1,000.
18	A3	40c org, *yelsh* (I)	45.00
a.		40c org ver, *yellowish*	70.00
19	A3	80c lake, *yelsh* (I)	225.00
20	A3	80c rose, *pnksh* (I)	200.00
		Strip of 3 on cover	325.00
		Strip of 4 on cover	400.00
		Strip of 5 on cover	675.00
21	A3	1fr lake, *yelsh* (I)	18,500.

Blocks of 4

12	A3	1c ol grn, *pale bl,*	775.00	950.00
		On cover		2,100.
13	A3	5c grn, *grnsh* (I)	3,200.	1,000.
		On cover		2,000.
a.		5c dark green	5,750.	1,450.
		On cover		2,250.
14	A3	10c bister, *yellowish* (I)	1,725.	250.00
		On cover		450.00
c.		10c bister, *yellowish* (II)	2,400.	400.00
		On cover		675.00
15	A3	20c blue, *bluish* (I)	725.00	80.00
		On cover		150.00
a.		20c dark blue, *bluish* (I)	1,175.	105.00
		On cover		190.00
d.		20c blue, *bluish* (II)	1,500.	400.00
		On cover		575.00
16	A3	20c blue, *greenish* (II)		2,600.
		On cover		4,100.
a.		20c blue, *greenish* (I)		1,475.
		On cover		2,400.
17	A3	25c bl, *bluish* (I)	10,000.	2,150.
		On cover		3,250.
18	A3	40c orange, *yellowish* (I)	10,000.	650.00
		On cover		1,100.
19	A3	80c lake, *yellowish* (I)	15,000.	500.00
		On cover		900.00
20	A3	80c rose, *pinkish* (I)	10,000.	500.00
		On cover		900.00

21 A3 1fr lake, *yellowish* (I) 50,000. 28,000.
On cover 45,000.

1862 **Re-issue**

17c A3 25c blue (I) 450.
No gum 170.00
19c A3 80c lake (I) 1,800.
No gum 800.00
21c A3 1fr lake (I) 1,500.
No gum 750.00
d. Tête bêche pair 27,500.

Blocks of 4

17c A3 25c blue (I) 2,200.
19c A3 80c lake (I) 9,500.
21c A3 1fr lake (I) 8,500.
d. Tête bêche pair in block 36,000.

The re-issues are in lighter colors and on whiter paper than the originals.

1862-71 ***Perf. 14x13½***

22 A3 1c ol grn, *pale bl* (II) 140.00 30.00
No gum 50.00
On cover 65.00
On cover, single franking 135.00
a. 1c bronze grn, *pale bl* (II) 140.00 35.00
No gum 50.00
On cover 75.00
On cover, single franking 150.00
b. 1c bronze gold ("mordore") 300.00
No gum 85.00
On cover 175.00
On cover, single franking 325.00
23 A3 5c yel grn, *grnsh* (I) 190.00 10.00
No gum 75.00
On cover 20.00
On cover, single franking 100.00
a. 5c deep green, *grnsh* (I) 225.00 12.50
No gum 82.50
On cover 27.50
On cover, single franking 90.00
24 A3 5c grn, *pale bl* ('71) (I) 1,800. 110.00
No gum 500.00
On cover 165.00
On cover, single franking 315.00
25 A3 10c bis, *yelsh* (II) 1,350. 3.75
No gum 325.00
On cover, single franking 5.00
a. 10c yel brn, *yelsh* (II) 1,750. 8.50
No gum 475.00
On cover, single franking 12.50
26 A3 20c bl, *bluish* (II) 200.00 1.25
No gum 65.00
On cover, single franking 2.25
a. Tête bêche pair (II) 4,000. 1,000.
On cover 2,250.
b. 20c dark blue 250.00 1.75
No gum 95.00
On cover, single franking 2.25
c. 20c pale blue 225.00 2.25
No gum 85.00
On cover, single franking 4.00
d. 20c blue, *azure* 325.00 2.00
No gum 115.00
On cover, single franking 3.25
27 A3 40c org, *yelsh* (I) 1,200. 6.50
No gum 375.00
On cover, single franking 10.00
a. 40c pale orange 1,200. 6.75
No gum 375.00
On cover, single franking 10.00
b. 40c yellow orange 1,200. 7.50
No gum 400.00
On cover, single franking 10.00
c. 40c bright orange 1,650. 9.00
No gum 525.00
On cover, single franking 12.50
28 A3 80c rose, *pnksh* (I) 1,100. 30.00
No gum 375.00
On cover 52.50
On cover, single franking 70.00
a. 80c bright rose, *pinkish* (I) 1,300. 35.00
No gum 425.00
On cover 65.00
On cover, single franking 95.00
b. 80c carmine rose (I) 1,650. 65.00
No gum 550.00
On cover 100.00
On cover, single franking 135.00
c. Tête bêche pair (I) 17,500. 7,750.
On cover 19,500.

No. 26a imperf is from a trial printing.

Values for used pairs

22 A3 1c ol grn, *pale bl* (II) 70.00
a. 1c bronze grn, *pale bl* (II) 70.00
23 A3 5c yel grn, *grnsh* (I) 27.50
a. 5c deep green, *grnsh* (I) 25.00
24 A3 5c green, *pale bl* (I) 225.00
a. 5c dp grn, *brt bluish* (I) 500.00
25 A3 10c bis, *yelsh* (II) 8.00
a. 10c yel brn, *yelsh* (II) 16.50
b. 10c bis brn ('66-'67) 35.00
26 A3 20c bl, *bluish* (II) 3.00
b. 20c dark blue 3.50
c. 20c pale blue 4.00
d. 20c blue, *azure* 4.00
27 A3 40c org, *yelsh* (I) 18.00
a. 40c pale orange 18.00
b. 40c yellow orange 19.00
c. 40c bright orange 21.00
28 A3 80c rose, *pnksh* (I) 80.00
a. 80c bright rose, *pinkish* (I) 90.00
b. 80c carmine rose (I) 140.00

Values for pairs on cover

22 A3 1c ol grn, *pale bl* (II) 450.00
a. 1c bronze grn, *pale bl* (II) 450.00
23 A3 5c yel grn, *grnsh* (I) 50.00
a. 5c deep green, *grnsh* (I) 42.50
24 A3 5c green, *pale bl* (I) 375.00
a. 5c dp grn, *brt bluish* (I) 625.00
25 A3 10c bis, *yelsh* (II) 11.50
a. 10c yel brn, *yelsh* (II) 27.50
b. 10c bis brn ('66-'67) 55.00
26 A3 20c bl, *bluish* (II) 4.00
b. 20c dark blue 4.00
c. 20c pale blue 7.00
d. 20c blue, *azure* 6.50
27 A3 40c org, *yelsh* (I) 25.00
a. 40c pale orange 25.00
b. 40c yellow orange 27.50
c. 40c bright orange 32.50
28 A3 80c rose, *pnksh* (I) 115.00
a. 80c bright rose, *pinkish* (I) 140.00
b. 80c carmine rose (I) 250.00

Values for strips of 3

22 A3 1c ol grn, *pale bl* (II) 110.00
On cover 450.00
23 A3 5c yel grn, *grnsh* (I) 37.50
On cover 55.00
24 A3 5c green, *pale bl* (I) 325.00
On cover 425.00
a. 5c dp grn, *brt bluish* (I) 725.00
On cover 1,000.
25 A3 10c bis, *yelsh* (II) 20.00
On cover 27.50
26 A3 20c bl, *bluish* (II) 5.50
On cover 12.50
27 A3 40c org, *yelsh* (I) 32.50
On cover 75.00
28 A3 80c rose, *pnksh* (I) 150.00
On cover 200.00
Strip of 4 300.00
On cover 425.00
Strip of 5 450.00
On cover 750.00

Values for blocks of 4

22 A3 1c ol grn, *pale bl* (II) 675.00 325.00
On cover 575.00
b. 1c bronze-gold ("mordore") ('65) 1,400.
23 A3 5c yel grn, *grnsh* (I) 750.00 200.00
On cover 350.00
24 A3 5c green, *pale bl* (I) 10,500. 900.00
On cover 1,450.
25 A3 10c bis, *yelsh* (II) 5,750. 125.00
On cover 275.00
a. 10c yel brn, *yelsh* (II) 8,000. 250.00
On cover 500.00
b. 10c bis brn ('66-'67) 8,500. 325.00
On cover 750.00
26 A3 20c bl, *bluish* (II) 850.00 80.00
On cover 135.00
27 A3 40c org, *yelsh* (I) 5,250. 240.00
On cover 500.00
28 A3 80c rose, *pnksh* (I) 5,000. 400.00
On cover 750.00

A4 A5

Napoleon III — A6

1863-70 ***Perf. 14x13½***

29 A4 1c brnz grn, *pale bl* ('70) 37.50 16.00
No gum 16.00
On cover 25.00
On cover, single franking 70.00
a. 1c olive green, *pale blue* 37.50 16.00
No gum 16.00
On cover 25.00
On cover, single franking 70.00
b. 1c olive grn, *grnsh* ('71) 37.50 16.00
No gum 16.00
On cover 25.00
On cover, single franking 70.00
30 A4 2c red brn, *yelsh* 105.00 25.00
No gum 47.50
On cover 50.00
On cover, single franking 70.00
a. 2c chocolate ('62) 135.00 32.50
No gum 52.50
On cover 35.00
On cover, single franking 65.00
b. Half used as 1c on cover 36,000.
31 A4 4c gray 165.00 37.50
No gum 52.50
On cover 75.00
On cover, single franking 275.00
a. Tete beche pair 17,500. 11,000.
On cover 30,000.
b. 4c lilac gray 47.50 3.25
No gum 37.50
On cover 75.00
On cover, single franking 300.00
d. Half used as 2c on cover 50,000.
32 A5 10c bis, *yelsh* ('67) 215.00 5.00
No gum 62.50
On cover, single franking 7.25
a. 10c dk bister 275.00 6.00
No gum 95.00
On cover, single franking 8.00
c. Half used as 5c on cover with other stamps 3,750.
d. Half used as 5c on cover, single franking 22,500.
33 A5 20c bl, *bluish* ('67) 175.00 1.55
No gum 60.00
On cover, single franking 4.00
c. Half used as 10c on cover 62,500.
d. 20c pale blue ('68) 210.00 2.40
No gum 70.00
On cover, single franking 4.00
e. 20c dark blue ('67) 275.00 3.25
No gum 140.00
On cover, single franking 4.00
34 A5 30c brn, *yelsh* ('67) 625.00 12.50
No gum 185.00
On cover 20.00
On cover, single franking 25.00
a. 30c dk brn, *yellowish* 1,000. 30.00
No gum 375.00
On cover 45.00
On cover, single franking 52.50
b. 30c pale brn 650.00 12.50
No gum 185.00
On cover 20.00
On cover, single franking 25.00
35 A5 40c pale org, *yelsh* 700.00 8.00
No gum 185.00
On cover, single franking 10.00
a. 40c org, *yelsh* ('68) 700.00 8.00
No gum 185.00
On cover, single franking 10.00
b. 40c brt orange 1,050. 4.50
No gum 250.00
On cover, single franking 20.00
c. Half used as 20c on cover 35,000.
36 A5 80c rose, *pnksh* ('68) 800.00 20.00
No gum 225.00
On cover 25.00
On cover, single franking 30.00
a. 80c carmine, *yellowish* 950.00 24.00
No gum 325.00
On cover 27.50
On cover, single franking 40.00
b. 80c pale rose 825.00 20.00
No gum 225.00
On cover 25.00
On cover, single franking 30.00
c. 80c brt rose 925.00 22.50
No gum 315.00
On cover 27.50
On cover, single franking 32.50
d. Half used as 40c on cover 42,500.
e. Quarter used as 20c on cover 50,000.
37 A6 5fr gray lil, *lav* ('69) 6,000. 750.00
No gum 1,750.
On cover 1,450.
On cover, single franking 18,000.
a. "5" and "F" omitted 90,000.
c. 5fr bluish gray, *lavender* 6,000. 875.00
No gum 1,750.
On cover 1,525.
On cover, single franking 18,000.
d. As #37, "5" and "F" in light blue 6,800. 900.00
No gum 2,000.
On cover 19,000.
e. As #37, "5" and "F" in black 3,250.
f. Larger figure "5" 1,475.
No gum 2,500.
g. Background double 9,000. 1,250.
No gum 2,000.
h. Imperf, optd. "SPECIMEN" 2,250.

No. 33 exists in two types, differing in the size of the dots at either side of POSTES.

On No. 37, the "5" and "F" vary in height from 3¾mm to 4½mm. These figures normally appear in gray but exist in blue or black.

All known examples of No. 37a are more or less damaged.

No. 29 was reprinted in 1887 by authority of Granet, Minister of Posts. The reprints show a yellowish shade under the ultraviolet lamp. Value $850.

For surcharge see No. 49.

Values for blocks of 4

29 A4 1c brnz green, *pale blue* ('70) 165.00 130.00
On cover 200.00
a. 1c olive green, *pale blue* 185.00 150.00
On cover 235.00
30 A4 2c red brn, *yelsh* 420.00 280.00
On cover 400.00
31 A4 4c gray 725.00 500.00
On cover 800.00
32 A5 10c bis, *yelsh* ('67) 925.00 65.00
On cover, single franking 115.00
33 A5 20c bl, *bluish* ('67) 775.00 47.50
On cover, single franking 82.50
34 A5 30c brn, *yelsh* ('67) 2,850. 275.00
On cover 480.00
a. 30c dk brn, *yellowish* 5,750. 510.00
On cover 975.00
b. 30c pale brn 2,850. 275.00
On cover 480.00
35 A5 40c pale org, *yelsh* 3,000. 315.00
On cover, single franking 550.00
a. 40c org, *yelsh* ('68) 3,000. 325.00
On cover, single franking 550.00
36 A5 80c rose, *pnksh* ('68) 3,600. 215.00
On cover 450.00
a. 80c carmine, *yellowish* 5,000. 425.00
On cover 750.00
37 A6 5fr gray lil, *lav* ('69) 22,500. 6,900.
On cover 11,000.
c. 5fr bluish gray, *lavender* 25,000. 6,900.
On cover 11,000.

Values for blocks of 4 Original Issue Imperfs

31c A4 4c gray 270.00 —
No gum 115.00
32b A5 10c bis, *yelsh* 360.00 —
No gum 155.00
33b A5 20c bl, *bluish* 270.00 —
No gum 75.00
On cover 13,250.
36c A5 80c rose, *pnksh* — —
On cover —
37b A6 5fr gray lil, *lav* 7,800.
No gum 2,400.
Block of 4 40,000.

Imperfs, "Rothschild" Re-issue Paper Colors are the Same

29b A4 1c olive green 1,050.
No gum 450.00
30a A4 2c pale red brown 200.00
No gum 80.00
31b A4 4c pale gray 185.00
No gum 62.50
32a A5 10c pale bister 160.00
No gum 62.50
33a A5 20c pale blue 250.00
No gum 110.00
34c A5 30c pale brown 190.00
No gum 62.50
35b A5 40c pale orange 225.00
No gum 80.00
36b A5 80c rose 400.00
No gum 155.00

The re-issues constitute the "Rothschild Issue." These stamps were authorized exclusively for the banker to use on his correspondence. Used examples exist.

The listings for Ballons Montes covers that appeared following Scott 41 have been moved. They now appear after the Semi-Postal stamp listings.

Ceres

A7 A8

A9 A10

A11

Bordeaux Issue

On the lithographed stamps, except for type I of the 20c, the shading on the cheek and neck is in lines or dashes, not in dots. On the typographed stamps the shading is in dots. The 2c, 5c, 10c and 20c (types II and III) occur in two or more types. The most easily distinguishable are:

2c — Type A. To the left of and within the top of the left "2" are lines of shading composed of dots.

2c — Type B. These lines of dots are replaced by solid lines.

5c — Type A. The head and hairline merge with the background of the medallion, without a distinct separation.

5c — Type B. A white line separates the contour of the head and hairline from the background of the medallion.

10c — Type A. The inner frame lines are of the same thickness as all other frame lines.

10c — Type B. The inner frame lines are much thicker than the others.

Three Types of the 20c.

A9 — The inscriptions in the upper and lower labels are small and there is quite a space between the upper label and the circle containing the head. There is also very little shading under the eye and in the neck.

A10 — The inscriptions in the labels are similar to those of the first type, the shading under the eye and in the neck is heavier and the upper label and circle almost touch.

A11 — The inscriptions in the labels are much larger than those of the two preceding types, and are similar to those of the other values of the same type in the set.

1870-71 Litho. *Imperf.*

38 A7 1c ol grn, *pale bl*	125.00	1.00
No gum	60.00	
On cover		150.00
On cover, single franking		900.00
a. 1c bronze green, *pale blue*	160.00	155.00
No gum	75.00	
On cover		225.00
On cover, single franking		1,150.
39 A7 2c red brn, *yelsh* (B)	225.00	225.00
No gum	110.00	
On cover		350.00
On cover, single franking		1,900.
a. 2c brick red, *yelsh* (B)	800.00	700.00
No gum	300.00	
On cover		900.00
On cover, single franking		2,500.
b. 2c chestnut, *yelsh* (B)	1,350.	700.00
No gum	500.00	
On cover		900.00
On cover, single franking		2,000.
c. 2c chocolate, *yelsh* (A)	750.00	700.00
No gum	275.00	
On cover		1,000.
On cover, single franking		2,500.
40 A7 4c gray	250.00	200.00
No gum	125.00	
On cover		550.00
On cover, single franking		*12,500.*
41 A8 5c yel green, *greenish* (B)	250.00	160.00
No gum	125.00	
On cover		375.00
On cover, single franking		3,000.
a. 5c grn, *grnsh* (B)	325.00	175.00
No gum	125.00	
On cover		375.00
On cover, single franking		3,000.
b. 5c emerald, *greenish* (B)	3,500.	1,250.
No gum	175.00	
On cover		2,200.
On cover, single franking		6,000.

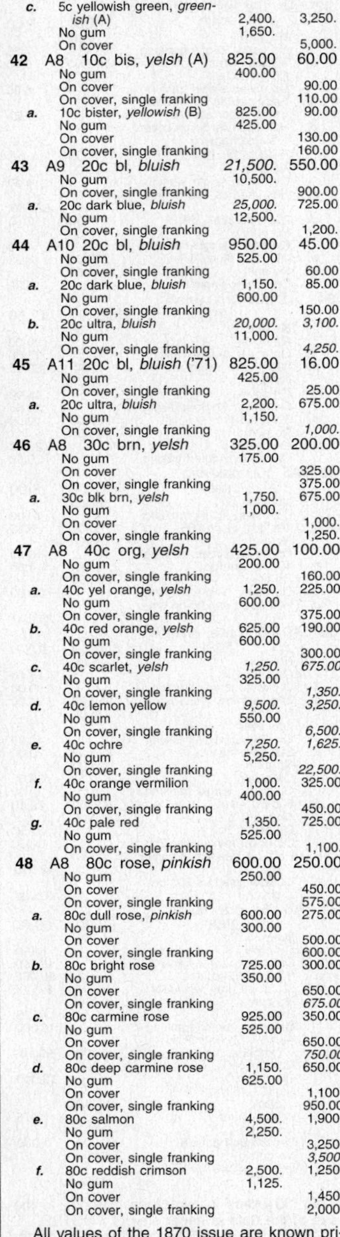

c. 5c yellowish green, *greenish* (A)	2,400.	3,250.
No gum	1,650.	
On cover		5,000.
42 A8 10c bis, *yelsh* (A)	825.00	60.00
No gum	400.00	
On cover		90.00
On cover, single franking		110.00
a. 10c bister, *yellowish* (B)	825.00	90.00
No gum	425.00	
On cover		130.00
On cover, single franking		160.00
43 A9 20c bl, *bluish*	*21,500.*	550.00
No gum	10,500.	
On cover, single franking		900.00
a. 20c dark blue, *bluish*	*25,000.*	725.00
No gum	12,500.	
On cover, single franking		1,200.
44 A10 20c bl, *bluish*	950.00	45.00
No gum	525.00	
On cover, single franking		60.00
a. 20c dark blue, *bluish*	1,150.	85.00
No gum	600.00	
On cover, single franking		150.00
b. 20c ultra, *bluish*	*20,000.*	*3,100.*
No gum	11,000.	
On cover, single franking		*4,250.*
45 A11 20c bl, *bluish* ('71)	825.00	16.00
No gum	425.00	
On cover, single franking		25.00
a. 20c ultra, *bluish*	2,200.	675.00
No gum	1,150.	
On cover, single franking		*1,000.*
46 A8 30c brn, *yelsh*	325.00	200.00
No gum	175.00	
On cover		325.00
On cover, single franking		375.00
a. 30c blk brn, *yelsh*	1,750.	675.00
No gum	1,000.	
On cover		1,000.
On cover, single franking		1,250.
47 A8 40c org, *yelsh*	425.00	100.00
No gum	200.00	
On cover, single franking		160.00
a. 40c yel orange, *yelsh*	1,250.	225.00
No gum	600.00	
On cover, single franking		375.00
b. 40c red orange, *yelsh*	625.00	190.00
No gum	600.00	
On cover, single franking		300.00
c. 40c scarlet, *yelsh*	*1,250.*	*675.00*
No gum	325.00	
On cover, single franking		*1,350.*
d. 40c lemon yellow	*9,500.*	*3,250.*
No gum	550.00	
On cover, single franking		*6,500.*
e. 40c ochre	*7,250.*	*1,625.*
No gum	5,250.	
On cover, single franking		*22,500.*
f. 40c orange vermilion	1,000.	325.00
No gum	400.00	
On cover, single franking		450.00
g. 40c pale red	1,350.	725.00
No gum	525.00	
On cover, single franking		1,100.
48 A8 80c rose, *pinkish*	600.00	250.00
No gum	250.00	
On cover		450.00
On cover, single franking		575.00
a. 80c dull rose, *pinkish*	600.00	275.00
No gum	300.00	
On cover		500.00
On cover, single franking		600.00
b. 80c bright rose	725.00	300.00
No gum	350.00	
On cover		650.00
On cover, single franking		*675.00*
c. 80c carmine rose	925.00	350.00
No gum	525.00	
On cover		650.00
On cover, single franking		*750.00*
d. 80c deep carmine rose	1,150.	650.00
No gum	625.00	
On cover		1,100.
On cover, single franking		950.00
e. 80c salmon	4,500.	1,900.
No gum	2,250.	
On cover		3,250.
On cover, single franking		*3,500.*
f. 80c reddish crimson	2,500.	1,250.
No gum	1,125.	
On cover		1,450.
On cover, single franking		2,000.

All values of the 1870 issue are known privately rouletted, pin-perf and perf. 14.

See Nos. 50-53.

A12

Dark Blue Surcharge

1871 Typo. *Perf. 14x13½*

49 A12 10c on 10c bister	1,400.	
No gum	700.00	
Block of 4, with gum	*6,750.*	
a. Pale blue surcharge	1,900.	
No gum	1,050.	
Block of 4, with gum	*10,500.*	

No. 49 was never placed in use. Counterfeits exist.

A13

Two types of the 40c as in the 1849-50 issue.

1870-73 Typo. *Perf. 14x13½*

50 A7 1c ol grn, *pale bl*	40.00	11.50
No gum	13.50	
On cover		35.00
On cover, single franking		80.00
a. 1c bronze grn, *pale bl* ('72)	47.50	14.00
No gum	16.00	
On cover		45.00
On cover, single franking		110.00
51 A7 2c red brn, *yelsh* ('70)	80.00	13.50
No gum	27.50	
On cover		40.00
On cover, single franking		80.00
52 A7 4c gray ('70)	250.00	40.00
No gum	85.00	
On cover		135.00
On cover, single franking		170.00
53 A7 5c yel grn, *pale bl* ('72)	150.00	7.50
No gum	45.00	
On cover		18.00
On cover, single franking		25.00
a. 5c green	150.00	7.50
No gum	45.00	
On cover		18.00
On cover, single franking		25.00
54 A13 10c bis, *yelsh*	540.00	55.00
No gum	170.00	
On cover		125.00
On cover, single franking		180.00
a. Tête beche pair	*5,500.*	*2,250.*
On cover		*5,000.*
b. Half used as 5c on cover		*4,500.*
55 A13 10c bis, *rose* ('73)	265.00	9.50
No gum	110.00	
On cover		15.00
On cover, single franking		18.00
a. Tête bêche pair	3,750.	1,750.
No gum	1,450.	
On cover		*3,000.*
56 A13 15c bis, *yelsh* ('71)	300.00	4.50
No gum	90.00	
On cover		7.25
a. Tête bêche pair	*37,500.*	*12,000.*
No gum	*11,000.*	
On cover		*26,500.*
57 A13 20c dl bl, *bluish*	225.00	6.75
No gum	72.50	
On cover		9.00
a. 20c bright blue, *bluish*	350.00	8.00
No gum	100.00	
On cover		12.50
b. Tête bêche pair	3,750.	1,450.
No gum	2,400.	
On cover		3,500.
c. Half used as 10c on cover		*55,000.*
d. Quarter used as 5c on cover		*52,500.*
58 A13 25c bl, *bluish* ('71)	110.00	1.10
No gum	32.50	
On cover		1.50
a. 25c dk bl, *bluish*	135.00	1.10
No gum	40.00	
On cover		1.50
b. Tête bêche pair	*6,750.*	*3,000.*
On cover		*9,000.*
59 A13 40c org, *yelsh* (I)	475.00	6.00
No gum	160.00	
On cover		10.00
a. 40c orange yel, *yelsh* (I)	575.00	9.00
No gum	175.00	
On cover		12.50
b. 40c orange, *yelsh* (II)	3,150.	130.00
No gum	1,000.	
On cover		150.00
c. 40c orange yel, *yelsh* (II)	3,150.	130.00
No gum	1,000.	
On cover		250.00
d. Pair, types I and II	*6,500.*	525.00
No gum	1,800.	
On cover		1,000.
e. Pair, both type II	*19,000.*	2,250.
No gum	5,500.	
On cover		3,500.
f. Half used as 20c on circular		*20,000.*
g. Half used as 20c on cover		*40,000.*

No. 58 exists in three main plate varieties, differing in one or another of the flower-like corner ornaments.

Margins on this issue are extremely small.

Nos. 54, 57 and 58 were reprinted imperf. in 1887. See note after No. 37.

Imperf.

50b A7 1c	270.00
No gum	100.00
51a A7 2c	350.00
No gum	120.00
52a A7 4c	450.00
No gum	125.00
53b A7 5c yel grn, *pale bl*	260.00
No gum	110.00
55b A13 10c	350.00
No gum	145.00
56b A13 15c	375.00
No gum	145.00

A14

1872-75 *Perf. 14x13½*

Larger Numerals

60 A14 10c bis, *rose* ('75)	325.00	11.00
No gum	100.00	
On cover		12.50
On cover, single franking		15.00
a. Cliché of 15c in plate of 10c	*3,750.*	*4,250.*
No gum	1,800.	
On cover		*20,000.*
b. Pair, #60, 60a	*6,750.*	*8,500.*
On cover		*52,000.*
61 A14 15c bister ('73)	320.00	3.25
No gum	100.00	
On cover		5.50
62 A14 30c brn, *yelsh*	550.00	5.25
No gum	140.00	
On cover		7.25
On cover, single franking		8.00
63 A14 80c rose, *pnksh*	640.00	11.50
No gum	200.00	
On cover		25.00
On cover, single franking		32.50
b. 80c carmine rose	675.00	15.00
No gum	210.00	
On cover		25.00
On cover, single franking		35.00
c. 80c bright carmine	925.00	22.50
No gum	250.00	
On cover		35.00
On cover, single franking		50.00

Imperf.

62a A14 30c	475.00
No gum	125.00
63a A14 80c	650.00
No gum	225.00

Values for Nos. 64-240 are for stamps with all perforations clear of the framelines. Stamps with perforations touching the framelines on one or two sides are worth about 35% less than the values quoted. Values for stamps on cover are for average stamps on very fine, clean, complete covers.

Peace and Commerce ("Type Sage") — A15

Type I. The "N" of "INV" is under the "B" of "REPUBLIQUE."

Type II. The "N" of "INV" is under the "U" of "REPUBLIQUE."

Type I

1876-78 *Perf. 14x13½*

64 A15 1c grn, *grnsh*	125.00	70.00
Never hinged	210.00	
No gum	50.00	
On cover		240.00
On cover, single franking		700.00
65 A15 2c grn, *grnsh*	1,425.	240.00
Never hinged	2,200.	
No gum	375.00	
On cover		375.00
On cover, single franking		625.00
66 A15 4c grn, *grnsh*	145.00	55.00
Never hinged	225.00	
No gum	50.00	
On cover		230.00
On cover, single franking		680.00
67 A15 5c grn, *grnsh*	650.00	45.00
Never hinged	1,100.	
No gum	235.00	
On cover		62.50
On cover, single franking		90.00
68 A15 10c grn, *grnsh*	800.00	21.00
Never hinged	1,325.	
No gum	260.00	
On cover		32.50
On cover, single franking		45.00
69 A15 15c gray lil, *grysh*	800.00	17.50
Never hinged	1,325.	
No gum	260.00	
On cover		25.00
On cover, single franking		45.00
70 A15 20c red brn, *straw*	575.00	17.50
Never hinged	875.00	
No gum	175.00	
On cover		32.50
On cover, single franking		82.50
71 A15 20c bl, *bluish*	*27,500.*	
No gum	17,500.	
Ovptd. "SPECIMEN," no gum	*12,500.*	
72 A15 25c ultra, *bluish*	*7,750.*	55.00
Never hinged	*12,000.*	
No gum	1,900.	
On cover		75.00
On cover, single franking		82.50
73 A15 30c brn, *yelsh*	425.00	8.25
Never hinged	650.00	
No gum	165.00	
On cover		10.00
On cover, single franking		11.50
74 A15 40c red, *straw* ('78)	600.00	35.00
Never hinged	950.00	
No gum	260.00	
On cover		50.00
On cover, single franking		55.00
75 A15 75c car, *rose*	950.00	12.50
Never hinged	1,500.	
No gum	255.00	
On cover		20.00
On cover, single franking		37.50
76 A15 1fr brnz grn, *straw*	925.00	10.00
Never hinged	1,450.	
On cover		37.50
On cover, single franking		100.00

No. 71 was never put into use.

The reprints of No. 71 are type II. They are imperforate or with forged perforation.

For overprints and surcharges see Offices in China Nos. 1-17, J7-J10, J20-J22, Offices in Egypt, Alexandria 1-15, Port Said 1-17, Offices in Turkish Empire 1-7, Cavalle 1-8, Dedeagh 1-8, Port Lagos 1-5, Vathy 1-9,

Offices in Zanzibar 1-33, 50-54, French Morocco 1-8, and Madagascar 14-27.

Values for blocks of 4

No.	Description	Unused	Used
64	A15 1c grn, *grnsh*	725.00	375.00
	Never hinged	1,000.	
	On cover		950.00
65	A15 2c grn, *grnsh*	6,750.	2,350.
	Never hinged	10,500.	
	On cover		3,500.
66	A15 4c grn, *grnsh*	725.00	450.00
	Never hinged	1,100.	
	On cover		1,650.
67	A15 5c grn, *grnsh*	3,200.	375.00
	Never hinged	5,000.	
	On cover		625.00
68	A15 10c grn, *grnsh*	4,000.	375.00
	Never hinged	6,250.	
	On cover		575.00
69	A15 15c gray lil, *grnsh*	4,000.	350.00
	Never hinged	6,250.	
	On cover		575.00
70	A15 20c red brn, *straw*	2,600.	360.00
	Never hinged	4,400.	
	On cover		700.00
72	A15 25c ultra, *bluish*	*37,500.*	2,200.
	Never hinged	*50,000.*	
	On cover		3,250.
73	A15 30c brn, *yelsh*	1,800.	145.00
	Never hinged	2,900.	
	On cover		150.00
74	A15 40c red, *straw* ('78)	2,750.	275.00
	Never hinged	4,500.	
	On cover		440.00
75	A15 75c car, *rose*	4,250.	175.00
	Never hinged	7,250.	
	On cover		300.00
76	A15 1fr brnz grn, *straw*	4,250.	165.00
	Never hinged	7,250.	
	On cover		400.00

Imperf.

No.	Description	Unused	Used
64a	A15 1c	150.00	
	Never hinged	250.00	
65a	A15 2c	1,000.	
	Never hinged	1,500.	
66a	A15 4c	160.00	
	Never hinged	250.00	
67a	A15 5c	525.00	
	Never hinged	900.00	
68a	A15 10c	575.00	
	Never hinged	900.00	
69a	A15 15c	575.00	
	Never hinged	900.00	
70a	A15 20c	375.00	
	Never hinged	600.00	
73a	A15 30c	275.00	
	Never hinged	450.00	
74a	A15 40c	250.00	
	Never hinged	400.00	
75a	A15 75c	550.00	
	Never hinged	900.00	
76a	A15 1fr	400.00	
	Never hinged	625.00	

Beware of French Colonies Nos. 24-29.

Type II

1876-77 ***Perf. 14x13½***

No.	Description	Unused	Used
77	A15 2c grn, *grnsh*	115.00	19.00
	Never hinged	175.00	
	On cover		42.50
	On cover, single franking		90.00
78	A15 5c grn, *grnsh*	25.00	.60
	Never hinged	37.50	
	On cover		1.00
a.	Imperf.	175.00	
	Never hinged	275.00	
79	A15 10c grn, *grnsh*	1,100.	240.00
	Never hinged	1,600.	
	On cover		290.00
	On cover, single franking		390.00
80	A15 15c gray lil, *grysh*	675.00	1.90
	Never hinged	1,050.	
	On cover		2.50
	On cover, single franking		2.75
81	A15 25c ultra, *bluish*	425.00	1.00
	Never hinged	750.00	
	On cover		1.35
	On cover, single franking		1.65
a.	25c blue, *bluish*	475.00	1.50
	Never hinged	725.00	
	On cover		2.00
	On cover, single franking		2.50
b.	Pair, types I & II	*60,000.*	*17,500.*
	No gum	*20,000.*	
	On cover		*52,500.*
c.	Imperf.	325.00	
	Never hinged	525.00	
d.	25c ultramarine, *pale greenish*		*675.00*
	On cover		*1,100.*
	On cover, single franking		*1,350.*
82	A15 30c yel brn, *yelsh*	82.50	1.40
	Never hinged	135.00	
	On cover		2.25
	On cover, single franking		5.00
a.	30c brown, *yellowish*	90.00	1.40
	Never hinged	140.00	
	On cover		2.25
	On cover, single franking		5.00
b.	Imperf.	525.00	
	Never hinged	800.00	
83	A15 75c car, *rose* ('77)	1,775.	110.00
	Never hinged	2,700.	
	On cover		225.00
	On cover, single franking		500.00
84	A15 1fr brnz grn, *straw* ('77)	145.00	7.50
	Never hinged	220.00	
	On cover		32.50
	On cover, single franking		105.00
a.	Imperf.	1,100.	
	Never hinged	1,650.	
b.	1fr deep olive green, *straw*	155.00	10.00
	Never hinged	250.00	
	On cover		45.00
	On cover, single franking		115.00

Beware of French Colonies Nos. 31, 35.

1877-80

No.	Description	Unused	Used
86	A15 1c blk, *lil bl*	3.75	1.65
	Never hinged	5.75	
	On cover		2.90
	On cover, single franking		4.25
a.	1c black, *gray blue*	3.75	1.65
	Never hinged	5.75	
	On cover, single franking		2.90
	On cover		4.25
b.	Imperf.	75.00	
	Never hinged	115.00	
87	A15 1c blk, *Prus bl* ('80)	*11,000.*	*4,350.*
	Never hinged	*16,000.*	
	No gum	4,250.	
	On cover		*20,000.*
	On cover, single franking		*18,750.*

Values for No. 87 are for examples with the perfs touching the design on at least one side.

No.	Description	Unused	Used
88	A15 2c brn, *straw*	4.50	1.90
	Never hinged	7.50	
	On cover		3.00
	On cover, single franking		7.00
a.	2c brown, *yellow*	4.50	1.90
	Never hinged	7.50	
	On cover		3.00
	On cover, single franking		7.00
b.	Imperf.	210.00	
	Never hinged	290.00	
89	A15 3c yel, *straw* ('78)	200.00	42.50
	Never hinged	310.00	
	On cover		425.00
	On cover, single franking		900.00
a.	Imperf.	150.00	
	Never hinged	225.00	
90	A15 4c claret, *lav*	5.00	1.90
	Never hinged	7.50	
	On cover		11.50
	On cover, single franking		110.00
a.	4c vio brown, *lavender*	8.25	4.50
	Never hinged	12.50	
	On cover		15.00
	On cover, single franking		145.00
b.	Imperf.	60.00	
	Never hinged	95.00	
91	A15 10c blk, *lavender*	35.00	1.00
	Never hinged	52.50	
	On cover		1.65
	On cover, single franking		2.10
a.	10c black, *rose lilac*	37.50	1.00
	Never hinged	57.50	
	On cover		2.10
	On cover, single franking		2.10
b.	10c black, *lilac*	37.50	1.00
	Never hinged	57.50	
	On cover		2.10
	On cover, single franking		2.10
c.	Imperf.	70.00	
	Never hinged	115.00	
92	A15 15c blue ('78)	22.50	.60
	Never hinged	32.50	
	On cover		.85
	On cover, single franking		1.00
a.	Imperf.	95.00	
	Never hinged	150.00	
b.	15c blue, *bluish*	435.00	15.00
	Never hinged	660.00	
	On cover		16.50
	On cover, single franking		25.00
93	A15 25c blk, *red* ('78)	1,075.	25.00
	Never hinged	1,675.	
	No gum	310.00	
	On cover		40.00
	On cover, single franking		45.00
a.	Imperf.	675.00	
	Never hinged	1,075.	
94	A15 35c blk, *yel* ('78)	525.00	35.00
	Never hinged	825.00	
	On cover		75.00
	On cover, single franking		135.00
a.	35c blk, *yel org*	525.00	35.00
	Never hinged	825.00	
	On cover		77.50
	On cover, single franking		135.00
b.	Imperf.	250.00	
	Never hinged	400.00	
95	A15 40c red, *straw* ('80)	90.00	2.10
	Never hinged	145.00	
	On cover		7.00
	On cover, single franking		7.50
a.	As #95, imperf.	240.00	
	Never hinged	360.00	
b.	40c pale orange red, *straw*	90.00	2.10
	Never hinged	145.00	
	On cover		7.00
	On cover, single franking		7.50
96	A15 5fr vio, *lav*	440.00	70.00
	Never hinged	725.00	
	On cover		400.00
	On cover, single franking		*3,500.*
a.	As #96, imperf.	750.00	
	Never hinged	1,250.	
b.	5fr red lilac, *lavender*	650.00	100.00
	Never hinged	975.00	
	On cover		500.00
	On cover, single franking		*4,000.*
c.	5fr bright violet, *lavender*	650.00	90.00
	Never hinged	975.00	
	On cover		475.00
	On cover, single franking		4,000.

Beware of French Colonies Nos. 38-40, 42, 44.

1879-90

No.	Description	Unused	Used
97	A15 3c gray, *grysh* ('80)	3.00	1.65
	Never hinged	4.25	
	On cover		11.00
	On cover, single franking		82.50
a.	Imperf.	67.50	
	Never hinged	100.00	
98	A15 20c red, *yel grn*	37.50	4.25
	Never hinged	57.50	
	On cover		27.50
	On cover, single franking		140.00
a.	20c red, *deep green* ('84)	72.50	6.00
	Never hinged	110.00	
	On cover		32.50
	On cover, single franking		145.00
b.	Imperf.	100.00	
	Never hinged	155.00	
99	A15 25c yel, *straw*	340.00	5.00
	Never hinged	525.00	
	On cover		11.50
	On cover, single franking		12.50
a.	Imperf.	250.00	
	Never hinged	400.00	
100	A15 25c blk, *pale rose* ('86)	72.50	1.00
	Never hinged	115.00	
	On cover		2.65
	On cover, single franking		3.60
a.	Imperf.	155.00	
	Never hinged	240.00	
101	A15 50c rose, *rose* ('90)	210.00	2.65
	Never hinged	325.00	
	On cover		11.50
	On cover, single franking		29.00
a.	50c carmine, *rose*	225.00	3.50
	Never hinged	350.00	
	On cover		12.50
	On cover, single franking		30.00
102	A15 75c dp vio, *org* ('90)	215.00	35.00
	Never hinged	350.00	
	On cover		110.00
	On cover, single franking		250.00
a.	75c deep violet, *yellow*	265.00	45.00
	Never hinged	400.00	
	On cover		115.00
	On cover, single franking		300.00
	Nos. 97-102 (6)	878.00	49.55

Beware of French Colonies No. 43.

1892 **Quadrille Paper**

No.	Description	Unused	Used
103	A15 15c blue	12.50	.35
	Never hinged	18.00	
	On cover		1.35
	On cover, single franking		4.50
a.	Imperf.	175.00	
	Never hinged	275.00	

1898-1900 **Ordinary Paper**

No.	Description	Unused	Used
104	A15 5c yel grn	16.00	1.30
	Never hinged	25.00	
	On cover		2.00
	On cover, single franking		4.75
a.	Imperf.	82.50	
	Never hinged	135.00	

Type I

No.	Description	Unused	Used
105	A15 5c yel grn	14.00	1.30
	Never hinged	21.00	
	On cover		2.00
	On cover, single franking		2.25
a.	Imperf.	575.00	
	Never hinged	925.00	
	No gum	190.00	
106	A15 10c blk, *lavender*	21.00	2.50
	Never hinged	35.00	
	On cover		3.75
	On cover, single franking		4.25
a.	Imperf.	275.00	
	Never hinged	400.00	
	No gum	82.50	
107	A15 50c car, *rose*	200.00	30.00
	Never hinged	315.00	
	On cover		65.00
	On cover, single franking		110.00
108	A15 2fr brn, *azure* ('00)	110.00	40.00
	Never hinged	165.00	
	On cover		440.00
	On cover, single franking		4,500.
b.	Imperf.	2,250.	
	Never hinged	3,350.	
	No gum	850.00	
	Nos. 104-108 (5)	361.00	75.10

See No. 226.

Reprints of A15, type II, were made in 1887 and left imperf. See note after No. 37. Value for set of 27, $4,000.

Liberty, Equality, Fraternity A16

"The Rights of Man" A17

Liberty and Peace A18

1900-29 ***Perf. 14x13½***

No.	Description	Unused	Used
109	A16 1c gray	.55	.40
	Never hinged	.90	
	On cover		.85
	On cover, single franking		2.10
b.	Grayish paper (GC) ('16)	.65	.55
	Never hinged	1.10	
	On cover		1.20
110	A16 2c violet brn	.70	.25
	Never hinged	1.35	
	On cover		1.00
	On cover, single franking		4.25
b.	Grayish (GC) paper ('17)	1.60	.25
	Never hinged	3.00	
	On cover		1.00
111	A16 3c orange	.45	.45
	Never hinged	.90	
	On cover		2.50
	On cover, single franking		8.25
a.	3c red	19.00	7.50
	Never hinged	32.50	
	On cover		22.50
c.	Grayish (GC) paper ('17)	.55	.55
	Never hinged	1.00	
	On cover		2.75
112	A16 4c yellow brn	3.00	1.60
	Never hinged	4.00	
	On cover		3.50
	On cover, single franking		55.00
113	A16 5c green	2.00	.35
	Never hinged	4.25	
	On cover		.70
	On cover, single franking		1.65
b.	Booklet pane of 10	330.00	
114	A16 7½c lilac ('26)	.60	.45
	Never hinged	1.25	
115	A16 10c lilac ('29)	4.00	.60
	Never hinged	6.50	
	On cover		7.00
	On cover, single franking		60.00
116	A17 10c carmine	25.00	1.50
	Never hinged	75.00	
	On cover		10.00
	On cover, single franking		15.00
a.	Numerals printed separately	24.00	10.00
	Never hinged	67.50	
	On cover		15.00
	On cover, single franking		18.00

117 A17 15c orange 8.00 .60
Never hinged 20.00
On cover .70
On cover, single franking .85
118 A17 20c brown vio 55.00 9.25
Never hinged 150.00
On cover 17.50
On cover, single franking 42.50
119 A17 25c blue 125.00 1.65
Never hinged 340.00
On cover 4.50
On cover, single franking 9.50
a. Numerals printed separately 115.00 9.25
Never hinged 340.00
On cover 12.50
On cover, single franking 20.00
120 A17 30c violet 70.00 6.00
Never hinged 210.00
On cover 17.50
On cover, single franking 42.50
121 A18 40c red & pale bl 15.00 .85
Never hinged 52.50
On cover 1.65
On cover, single franking 2.10
b. Grayish (GC) paper ('16) 25.00 1.20
Never hinged 67.50
On cover 2.75
122 A18 45c green & bl ('06) 29.00 2.10
Never hinged 105.00
On cover 7.25
On cover, single franking 9.25
b. Grayish (GC) paper ('16) 45.00 4.00
Never hinged 110.00
On cover 8.75
123 A18 50c bis brn & gray 100.00 1.65
Never hinged 325.00
On cover 3.50
On cover, single franking 3.75
b. Grayish paper (GC) ('16) 200.00 2.00
Never hinged 375.00
On cover 4.50
124 A18 60c vio & ultra ('20) 1.00 1.15
Never hinged 1.85
On cover 5.00
125 A18 1fr claret & ol grn 26.50 .85
Never hinged 95.00
On cover 3.00
On cover, single franking 5.00
b. Grayish paper (GC) ('16) 52.50 .95
Never hinged 130.00
On cover 4.50
126 A18 2fr gray vio & yel 625.00 75.00
Never hinged 2,150.
On cover 275.00
On cover, single franking 1,675.
127 A18 2fr org & pale bl ('20) 42.50 .60
Never hinged 140.00
On cover 9.25
On cover, single franking 30.00
128 A18 3fr vio & bl ('25) 27.50 7.50
Never hinged 52.50
On cover 20.00
On cover, single franking 60.00
129 A18 3fr brt vio & rose ('27) 55.00 2.80
Never hinged 130.00
On cover 26.00
On cover, single franking 50.00
130 A18 5fr dk bl & buff 85.00 5.00
Never hinged 300.00
On cover 35.00
On cover, single franking 145.00
131 A18 10fr grn & red ('26) 125.00 17.00
Never hinged 325.00
On cover 37.50
On cover, single franking 100.00
132 A18 20fr mag & grn ('26) 200.00 37.50
Never hinged 500.00
On cover 135.00
On cover, single franking 400.00
Nos. 109-132 (24) 1,626. 175.10

In the 10c and 25c values, the first printings show the numerals to have been impressed by a second operation, whereas, in later printings, the numerals were inserted in the plates. Two operations were used for all 20c and 30c, and one operation for the 15c.

No. 114 was issued precanceled only. Values for precanceled stamps in first column are for those which have not been through the post and have original gum. Values in the second column are for postally used, gumless stamps.

See Offices in China Nos. 34, 40-44, Offices in Crete 1-5, 10-15, Offices in Egypt, Alexandria 16-20, 26-30, 77, 84-86, Port Said 18-22, 28-32, 83, 90-92, Offices in Turkish Empire 21-26, 31-33, Cavalle 9, Dedeagh 9.

For overprints and surcharge see Nos. 197, 246, C1-C2, M1, P7. Offices in China 57, 62-65, 71, 73, 75, 83-85, J14, J27, Offices in Crete 17-20, Offices in Egypt, Alexandria 31-32, 34-35, 40-48, 57-64, 66, 71-73, Port Said 33, 35-40, 43, 46-57, 59, 65-71, 73, 78-80, Offices in Turkish Empire 35-38, 47-49, Cavalle 13-15, Dedeagh 16-18, Offices in Zanzibar 39, 45-49, 55, Offices in Morocco 11-15, 20-22, 26-29, 35-41, 49-54, 72-76, 84-85, 87-89, B6.

Imperf.

109a A16 1c 55.00
Never hinged 90.00
110a A16 2c 67.50 60.00
Never hinged 105.00
No gum 50.00
111b A16 3c 55.00
Never hinged 90.00
112a A16 4c 150.00
Never hinged 220.00
No gum 125.00
113a A16 5c 75.00
Never hinged 120.00
No gum 60.00
116b A17 10c #116 or 116a 235.00 *135.00*
Never hinged 375.00
No gum 140.00
117a A17 15c 190.00 *165.00*
Never hinged 300.00
No gum 125.00
119b A17 25c #119 or 119a 500.00
Never hinged 775.00
No gum 290.00
121a A18 40c 190.00 *155.00*
Never hinged 325.00
No gum 120.00
122a A18 45c 260.00
Never hinged 400.00
No gum 170.00
123a A18 50c 375.00 *375.00*
Never hinged 650.00
No gum 275.00
124a A18 60c 525.00
Never hinged 950.00
No gum 390.00
125a A18 1fr 250.00 *225.00*
Never hinged 360.00
No gum 180.00
126a A18 2fr No gum *1,300.*
127a A18 2fr 475.00
Never hinged 875.00
No gum 400.00
128a A18 3fr *725.00* 500.00
Never hinged *1,175.*
129a A18 3fr 425.00
Never hinged 675.00
130a A18 5fr 950.00
Never hinged 1,450.
No gum 425.00

Flat Plate & Rotary Press

The following stamps were printed by both flat plate and rotary press: Nos. 109-113, 144-146, 163, 166, 168, 170, 175, 177-178, 185, 192 and P7.

"Rights of Man" — A19

1902

133 A19 10c rose red 32.50 .90
Never hinged 150.00
On cover 1.40
On cover, single franking 3.00
134 A19 15c pale red 11.00 .60
Never hinged 37.50
On cover .65
On cover, single franking .85
135 A19 20c brown violet 82.50 14.00
Never hinged 225.00
On cover 22.50
On cover, single franking 62.50
136 A19 25c blue 100.00 2.25
Never hinged 390.00
On cover 5.50
On cover, single franking 10.00
137 A19 30c lilac 250.00 14.50
Never hinged 575.00
On cover 22.50
On cover, single franking 50.00
Nos. 133-137 (5) 476.00 32.25

Imperf.

133a A19 10c rose red 450.00 *275.00*
Never hinged 650.00
No gum 200.00
134a A19 15c pale red 450.00 *325.00*
Never hinged 650.00
No gum 250.00
135a A19 20c brown violet 800.00 *475.00*
Never hinged 1,250.
No gum 350.00
136a A19 25c blue 950.00 *625.00*
Never hinged 1,450.
137a A19 30c lilac *1,100.* 675.00
Never hinged 1,475.

See Offices in China Nos. 35-39, Offices in Crete 6-10, Offices in Egypt, Alexandria 21-25, 81-82, Port Said 23-27, 87-88, Offices in Turkish Empire 26-30, Cavalle 10-11, Dedeagh 10-11.

For overprints and surcharges see Nos. M2, Offices in China 45, 58-61, 66-70, 76-82, J15-J16, J28-J30, Offices in Crete 16, Offices in Egypt, Alexandria 33, 36-39, 49-50, 52-56, 65, 67-70, B1-B4, Port Said 34, 41-42, 44-45, 57, 60-64, 77, 74-77, B1-B4, Offices in Turkish Empire 34, 39, Cavalle 12, Dedeagh 15, Offices in Zanzibar 40-44, 56-59, Offices in Morocco 16-19, 30-34, 42-48, 77-83, 86, B1-B5, B7, B9.

Sower — A20

1903-38

138 A20 10c rose 8.00 .40
Never hinged 18.00
On cover .85
139 A20 15c slate grn 4.00 .25
Never hinged 9.00
On cover .75
b. Booklet pane of 10 450.00
c. Grayish (GC) paper ('16) 4.50 .25
Never hinged 9.50
On cover .75
140 A20 20c violet brn 67.50 1.90
Never hinged 150.00
On cover 9.00
On cover, single franking 40.00
141 A20 25c dull blue 75.00 1.40
Never hinged 160.00
On cover 4.25
On cover, single franking 6.50
142 A20 30c violet 175.00 5.25
Never hinged 375.00
On cover 13.00
On cover, single franking 30.00
143 A20 45c lt violet ('26) 6.00 1.90
Never hinged 11.50
On cover 7.00
On cover, single franking 45.00
144 A20 50c dull blue ('21) 27.50 1.40
Never hinged 62.50
On cover 7.00
On cover, single franking 10.00
145 A20 50c gray grn ('26) 6.25 1.25
Never hinged 11.50
On cover 3.00
On cover, single franking 22.50
146 A20 50c vermilion ('26) 1.25 .25
Never hinged 2.25
On cover .50
On cover, single franking .50
a. Booklet pane of 10 40.00
147 A20 50c grnsh bl ('38) 1.00 .35
Never hinged 1.90
On cover 2.10
On cover, single franking 5.75
148 A20 60c lt vio ('24) 6.25 2.10
Never hinged 13.00
On cover 7.50
On cover, single franking 16.50
149 A20 65c rose ('24) 3.00 1.75
Never hinged 5.25
On cover 5.75
On cover, single franking 42.50
150 A20 65c gray grn ('27) 6.50 2.10
Never hinged 14.00
On cover 10.00
On cover, single franking 55.00
151 A20 75c rose lil ('26) 5.25 .60
Never hinged 10.00
On cover 2.50
On cover, single franking 4.50
152 A20 80c ver ('25) 26.50 9.50
Never hinged 52.50
On cover 14.00
On cover, single franking 50.00
153 A20 85c ver ('24) 13.50 3.25
Never hinged 27.00
On cover 5.75
On cover, single franking 10.00
154 A20 1fr dull blue ('26) 6.00 .75
Never hinged 13.00
On cover 4.25
On cover, single franking 18.00
Nos. 138-154 (17) 438.50 34.40
Set, never hinged 940.00

See Nos. 941, 942A. For surcharges and overprints see Nos. 229-230, 232-233, 236, 256, B25, B29, B32, B36, B40, M3-M4, M6, Offices in Turkish Empire 46, 54.

Imperf.

138a A20 10c 175.00
Never hinged 275.00
No gum 105.00
139a A20 15c 140.00 55.00
Never hinged 200.00
No gum 62.50
140a A20 20c 300.00 160.00
Never hinged 460.00
No gum 115.00
141a A20 25c 350.00
Never hinged 525.00
No gum 110.00
142a A20 30c 625.00
Never hinged 925.00
No gum 225.00
144a A20 50c 140.00
Never hinged 200.00
145a A20 50c 125.00
Never hinged 190.00
146b A20 50c No gum 70.00
147a A20 50c 67.50
Never hinged 110.00
149a A20 65c 300.00
Never hinged 500.00
151a A20 75c 450.00
Never hinged 650.00
154a A20 1fr *1,000.*
Never hinged 1,400.

Ground — A21

1906, Apr. 13
With Ground Under Feet of Figure

155 A21 10c red 2.50 1.75
Never hinged 4.25
On cover 5.00
On cover, single franking 5.50
a. Imperf. pair, no gum 275.00 225.00
As "a," with gum 450.00
Never hinged 775.00

No Ground — A22

TEN AND THIRTY-FIVE CENTIMES

Type I — Numerals and letters of the inscriptions thin.
Type II — Numerals and letters thicker.

No Ground Under the Feet

1906-37

156 A22 1c olive bis ('33) .25 .30
Never hinged .40
On cover 3.25
On cover, single franking 50.00
a. 1c bistre brown ('36) .25 .25
Never hinged .40
On cover 3.25
On cover, single franking 40.00
157 A22 2c dk green ('33) .25 .30
Never hinged .40
On cover 2.50
On cover, single franking 45.00
158 A22 3c ver ('33) .25 .30
Never hinged .40
On cover 18.00
On cover, single franking 82.50
159 A22 5c green ('07) 1.50 .25
Never hinged 2.75
On cover .55
On cover, single franking .65
a. Imperf., pair 40.00 30.00
Never hinged 60.00
No gum 18.00
b. Booklet pane of 10 100.00
c. Grayish (GC) paper ('16) 2.75 .35
Never hinged 30.00
On cover .80
160 A22 5c orange ('21) 1.25 .30
Never hinged 2.50
On cover 1.00
On cover, single franking 3.00
a. Booklet pane of 10 72.50
161 A22 5c cerise ('34) .25 .25
Never hinged .40
On cover 4.00
On cover, single franking 120.00
162 A22 10c red (II) ('07) 1.50 .25
Never hinged 2.75
On cover .60
On cover, single franking .65
a. Imperf., pair 37.50 115.00
Never hinged 65.00
No gum 13.50
b. 10c red (I) ('06) 8.25 1.00
Never hinged 29.00
On cover 2.75
On cover, single franking 3.00
c. As #162b, imperf., pair 37.50 115.00
Never hinged 40.00
d. Booklet pane of 10 (I) 125.00
e. Booklet pane of 10 (II) 75.00
f. Booklet pane of 6 (II) 240.00
g. Grayish (GC) paper ('16) 12.00 2.10
Never hinged 19.00
On cover 3.50
163 A22 10c grn (II) ('21) 1.00 .55
Never hinged 1.60
On cover .60
On cover, single franking 1.00
a. 10c green (I) ('27) 32.50 37.50
Never hinged 45.00
On cover 75.00
On cover, single franking 175.00
b. Booklet pane of 10 (II, "Phena") 350.00
c. Booklet pane of 10 (I, "Mineraline") 3,200.
164 A22 10c ultra ('32) 1.40 .25
Never hinged 2.40
On cover 1.60
On cover, single franking 20.00
165 A22 15c red brn ('26) .25 .25
Never hinged .50
On cover .40
On cover, single franking .40
a. Booklet pane of 10 27.50
166 A22 20c brown 3.00 .65
Never hinged 7.00
On cover 2.00
On cover, single franking 2.50
a. Imperf., pair 82.50 100.00
Never hinged 105.00
No gum 27.50
b. 20c black brown 6.00 2.00
Never hinged 13.00
On cover 3.75
On cover, single franking 4.00
c. Grayish (GC) paper ('17) 6.50 .80
Never hinged 12.00
On cover 3.25
167 A22 20c red vio ('26) .25 .25
Never hinged .50
On cover .50
On cover, single franking .65
a. Booklet pane of 10 7.50
168 A22 25c blue 2.40 .25
Never hinged 4.50
On cover .50
On cover, single franking .65
a. Booklet pane of 10 37.50
b. Imperf, pair (dark blue) 45.00 60.00
Never hinged 75.00
c. Imperf, pair (pale blue) 180.00 120.00
Never hinged 290.00
d. Grayish (GC) paper ('17) 4.00 1.20
Never hinged 6.75
On cover 2.40
169 A22 25c yel brown ('27) .25 .25
Never hinged .40
On cover .65
On cover, single franking 1.00
a. 25c red brown .30 .25
Never hinged .65
On cover .80
170 A22 30c orange 13.50 1.40
Never hinged 30.00
On cover 2.50
On cover, single franking 6.25
a. Imperf, pair 200.00 175.00
Never hinged 300.00
No gum 80.00
b. Grayish (GC) paper ('16) 15.00 1.75
Never hinged 32.50
On cover 2.75
171 A22 30c red ('21) 6.50 2.25
Never hinged 15.00
On cover 7.00
On cover, single franking 10.00

172 A22 30c cerise ('25) 1.25 .80
Never hinged 2.10
On cover 3.50
On cover, single franking 9.00
a. Booklet pane of 10 13.50
b. Imperf, pair 575.00
Never hinged 900.00
173 A22 30c lt blue ('25) 3.75 .60
Never hinged 5.75
On cover 2.50
On cover, single franking 9.00
a. Booklet pane of 10 35.00
b. Imperf, pair 2,200.
174 A22 30c cop red ('37) .25 .30
Never hinged .65
On cover 1.00
On cover, single franking 2.00
a. Booklet pane of 10 9.00
175 A22 35c vio (II) ('07) 8.25 .90
Never hinged 15.00
On cover 2.00
On cover, single franking 2.50
a. Imperf, pair 150.00 120.00
Never hinged 225.00
No gum 72.50
b. 35c violet (I) ('06) 150.00 7.50
Never hinged 310.00
On cover 22.00
On cover, single franking 26.00
c. As "b," Imperf, pair, no gum *575.00*
176 A22 35c grn ('37) .50 .55
Never hinged 1.00
On cover 3.00
On cover, single franking 6.00
a. Imperf, pair 750.00
Never hinged 1,050.
177 A22 40c olive ('25) 1.40 .55
Never hinged 3.25
On cover 2.50
On cover, single franking 5.00
b. Booklet pane of 10 30.00
178 A22 40c ver ('26) 2.50 .80
Never hinged 4.50
On cover 2.50
On cover, single franking 3.50
a. Booklet pane of 10 25.00
179 A22 40c violet ('27) 2.00 .90
Never hinged 3.50
On cover 1.60
On cover, single franking 2.00
180 A22 40c lt ultra ('28) 1.25 .50
Never hinged 2.25
On cover 1.50
On cover, single franking 1.60
a. 40c gray blue 1.60 .85
Never hinged 2.90
On cover 2.00
181 A22 1.05fr ver ('25) 9.50 5.25
Never hinged 18.50
On cover 13.00
On cover, single franking 50.00
182 A22 1.10fr cerise ('27) 11.50 2.50
Never hinged 22.00
On cover 9.00
On cover, single franking 32.50
a. 1.10fr bright rose 16.50 4.00
Never hinged 29.00
On cover 11.50
183 A22 1.40fr cerise ('26) 20.00 22.50
Never hinged 37.50
On cover 120.00
On cover, single franking 750.00
a. 1.40fr bright rose 25.00 25.00
Never hinged 45.00
184 A22 2fr Prus grn ('31) 14.00 1.75
Never hinged 24.00
On cover 16.50
On cover, single franking 62.50
a. 2fr blackish green 18.00 3.00
Never hinged 31.00
On cover 20.00
Nos. 156-184 (29) 109.95 45.95
Set, never hinged 225.00

The 10c and 35c, type I, were slightly retouched by adding thin white outlines to the sack of grain, the underside of the right arm and the back of the skirt. It is difficult to distinguish the retouches except on clearly-printed stamps. The white outlines were made stronger on the stamps of type II.

Stamps of types A16, A18, A20 and A22 were printed in 1916-20 on paper of poor quality, usually grayish and containing bits of fiber. This is called G. C. (Grande Consommation) paper. These wartime printings are noted (GC) in the descriptions above.

Nos. 160, 162b, 163, 175b and 176 also exist imperf.

See Nos. 241-241b. For surcharges and overprint see Nos. 227-228, 234, 238, 240, 400, B1, B24, B28, B31, B35, B37, B39, B41, M5, P8, Offices in Turkish Empire 40-45, 52, 55.

Louis Pasteur — A23

1923-26

185 A23 10c green .55 .30
Never hinged 1.25
On cover 1.00
On cover, single franking 1.60
a. Booklet pane of 10 15.00
186 A23 15c green ('24) 1.40 .30
Never hinged 3.00
On cover 1.00
On cover, single franking 3.75
187 A23 20c green ('26) 2.75 .90
Never hinged 4.50
On cover 4.25
On cover, single franking 5.75
188 A23 30c red .90 *1.50*
Never hinged 1.50
On cover 3.75
On cover, single franking 6.50
189 A23 30c green ('26) .55 .50
Never hinged 1.25
On cover 3.25
On cover, single franking 6.50
190 A23 45c red ('24) 1.90 2.10
Never hinged 3.50
On cover 4.50
On cover, single franking 9.00
191 A23 50c blue 4.50 .50
Never hinged 7.75
On cover 4.50
On cover, single franking 14.00
192 A23 75c blue ('24) 3.75 1.00
Never hinged 6.00
On cover 3.25
On cover, single franking 6.50
a. Imperf., pair 250.00
Never hinged 410.00
No gum 250.00
193 A23 90c red ('26) 11.00 3.50
Never hinged 20.00
On cover 5.25
On cover, single franking 9.00
194 A23 1fr blue ('25) 21.00 .50
Never hinged 40.00
On cover 4.50
On cover, single franking 29.00
195 A23 1.25fr blue ('26) 25.00 8.00
Never hinged 41.00
On cover 22.00
On cover, single franking 52.50
196 A23 1.50fr blue ('26) 5.25 .50
Never hinged 15.00
On cover 2.00
On cover, single franking 4.00
Nos. 185-196 (12) 78.55 19.60
Set, never hinged 150.00

Nos. 185, 188 and 191 were issued to commemorate the cent. of the birth of Pasteur.

For surcharges and overprint see Nos. 231, 235, 257, B26, B30, B33, C4.

No. 125 Overprinted in Blue

1923, June 15

197 A18 1fr claret & ol grn 440.00 500.00
Never hinged 825.00
On cover 650.00
On cover, single franking 650.00

Allegory of Olympic Games at Paris
A24

The Trophy
A25

Milo of Crotona — A26

Victorious Athlete — A27

1924, Apr. 1 ***Perf. 14x13½, 13½x14***

198 A24 10c gray grn & yel grn 2.25 1.25
Never hinged 6.25
On cover 2.90
On cover, single franking 5.75
199 A25 25c rose & dk rose 3.00 .80
Never hinged 7.50
On cover 2.90
On cover, single franking 5.75
200 A26 30c brn red & blk 9.50 11.00
Never hinged 21.00
On cover 29.00
On cover, single franking 60.00
201 A27 50c ultra & dk bl 26.00 5.75
Never hinged 90.00
On cover 37.50
On cover, single franking 100.00
Nos. 198-201 (4) 40.75 18.80
Set, never hinged 125.00

Imperf Singles

198a A24 10c 1,000.
Never hinged 1,500.
199a A25 25c 1,000. *725.*
Never hinged 1,500.
200a A26 30c 1,000.
Never hinged 1,500.
201a A27 50c 1,000. 1,000.
Never hinged 1,500.
On cover *6,500.*

8th Olympic Games, Paris.

Pierre de Ronsard (1524-85), Poet — A28

1924, Oct. 6 ***Perf. 14x13½***

219 A28 75c blue, *bluish* 1.90 1.40
Never hinged 2.75
On cover 10.50
On cover, single franking 20.00

"Light and Liberty" Allegory
A29

Majolica Vase — A30

Potter Decorating Vase — A31

Terrace of Château
A32

1924-25 ***Perf. 14x13½, 13½x14***

220 A29 10c dk grn & yel ('25) .55 .75
Never hinged 1.25
On cover 2.00
On cover, single franking 5.00
221 A30 15c ind & grn ('25) .55 .85
Never hinged 1.25
On cover 2.00
On cover, single franking *5.00*
a. Imperf. *400.00*
Never hinged *640.00*
b. As "a," setenant with normal *500.00*
Never hinged *775.00*
222 A31 25c vio brn & garnet .80 .50
Never hinged 1.80
On cover 2.50
On cover, single franking 6.25
a. Imperf, se-tenant with normal *2,050.*
Never hinged *2,750.*
223 A32 25c gray bl & vio ('25) 1.60 .65
Never hinged 2.25
On cover 2.50
On cover, single franking 6.25
a. Imperf. *450.00* 150.00
Never hinged *700.00*
b. As "a," setenant with normal *575.00*
Never hinged *900.00*
224 A31 75c indigo & ultra 3.50 2.25
Never hinged 6.50
On cover 6.50
On cover, single franking 16.50
a. Imperf, no gum 150.00
225 A29 75c dk bl & lt bl ('25) 18.00 6.50
Never hinged 37.50
On cover 19.00
On cover, single franking 32.50
a. Imperf. *375.00*
Never hinged *650.00*
b. As "a," setenant with normal *550.00*
Never hinged *1,000.*
Nos. 220-225 (6) 25.00 11.50
Set, never hinged 52.50

Intl. Exhibition of Decorative Modern Arts at Paris, 1925.

Philatelic Exhibition Issue
Souvenir Sheet

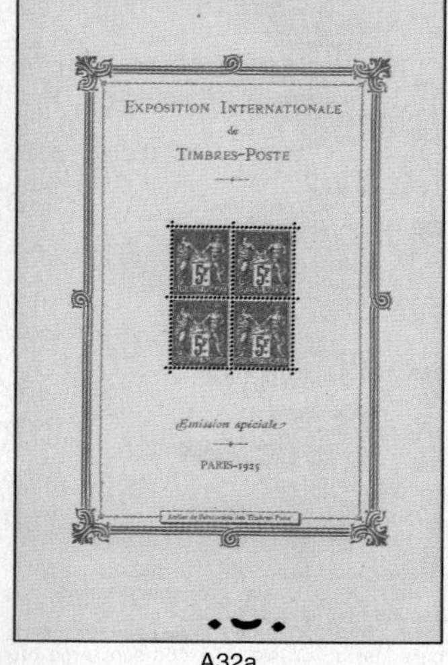

A32a

1925, May 2 ***Perf. 14x13½***

226 A32a Sheet of 4, A15 II 1,100. 1,100.
Never hinged 3,750.
On cover *2,000.*
a. Imperf. sheet 5,000. 1,750.
Never hinged 7,750.
b. 5fr carmine, perf. 125.00 140.00
Never hinged 225.00
On cover 250.00
On cover, single franking 250.00
c. 5fr carmine, imperf. 900.00
Never hinged 1,325.

These were on sale only at the Intl. Phil. Exhib., Paris, May, 1925. Size: 140x220mm.

Nos. 148-149, 152-153, 173, 175, 181, 183, 192, 195 Surcharged

1926-27

227 A22 25c on 30c lt bl .25 .50
Never hinged .50
On cover 3.25
On cover, single franking 5.75
a. Pair, one without surcharge 1,050. 925.00
Never hinged 1,500.
228 A22 25c on 35c violet .25 .50
Never hinged .50
On cover 3.75
On cover, single franking 6.50
a. Double surcharge 525.00 350.00
Never hinged 750.00
b. Pair, one without surcharge 550.00 *925.00*
Never hinged 825.00
229 A20 50c on 60c lt vio ('27) 1.40 1.10
Never hinged 2.50
On cover 4.25
On cover, single franking 6.00
a. Pair, one without surcharge 525.00 *925.00*
Never hinged 750.00
230 A20 50c on 65c rose ('27) .75 .55
Never hinged 1.50
On cover 3.75
On cover, single franking 8.25
a. Inverted surcharge *1,225.* *1,400.*
Never hinged *1,850.*
b. Pair, one without surcharge 675.00 *925.00*
Never hinged 1,100.
231 A23 50c on 75c blue 3.25 1.50
Never hinged 5.25
On cover 4.00
On cover, single franking 8.25
232 A20 50c on 80c ver ('27) 1.25 1.10
Never hinged 2.25
On cover 5.25
On cover, single franking 27.50
a. Pair, one without surcharge 475.00 *925.00*
Never hinged 675.00
233 A20 50c on 85c ver ('27) 2.25 1.00
Never hinged 5.00
On cover 4.25
On cover, single franking 10.00
234 A22 50c on 1.05fr ver 1.25 .75
Never hinged 2.25
On cover 4.25
On cover, single franking 8.25

a. Pair, one without surcharge 475.00 *925.00*
Never hinged 700.00

235 A23 50c on 1.25fr blue 2.75 2.25
Never hinged 5.25
On cover 5.00
On cover, single franking 12.50
a. Pair, one without surcharge 525.00 *925.00*
Never hinged 750.00

236 A20 55c on 60c lt vio 125.00 52.50
Never hinged 240.00
On cover 160.00
On cover, single franking 160.00

238 A22 90c on 1.05fr ver ('27) 2.25 2.75
Never hinged 3.75
On cover 5.00
On cover, single franking 11.00
a. Pair, one without surcharge *1,000.* 925.00
Never hinged *1,500.*

240 A22 1.10fr on 1.40fr cer 1.00 1.10
Never hinged 1.90
On cover 7.50
On cover, single franking 45.00
a. Pair, one without surcharge 575.00 *925.00*
Never hinged 825.00
Nos. 227-240 (12) 141.65 65.60
Set, never hinged 275.00

Issue dates: Nos. 229-230, 232-234, 1927.

No. 236 is known only precanceled. See second note after No. 132.

Nos. 229, 230, 234, 238 and 240 have three bars instead of two. The 55c surcharge has thinner, larger numerals and a rounded "c." Width, including bars, is 17mm, instead of 13mm.

The 55c was used only precanceled at the Magasins du Louvre department store in Paris, August 1926.

Strasbourg Exhibition Issue

Souvenir Sheet

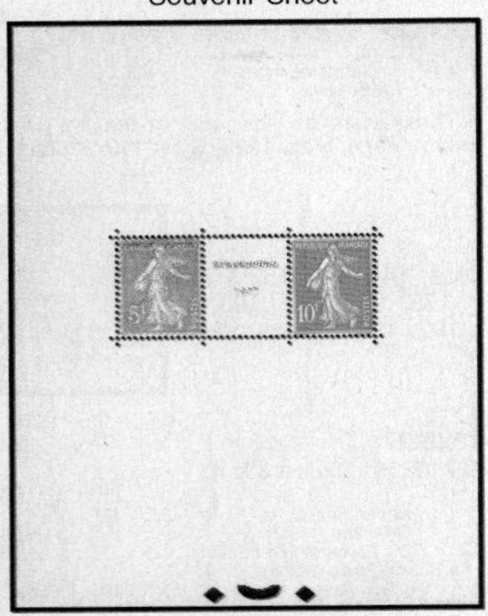

A32b

1927, June 4

241 A32b Sheet of 2 1,000. 1,000.
Never hinged 2,300.
On cover *1,400.*
a. 5fr light ultra (A22) 250.00 250.00
Never hinged 400.00
On cover *300.00*
b. 10fr carmine rose (A22) 250.00 250.00
Never hinged 400.00
On cover *300.00*
In pair with #241a and label 500.00 540.00
Never hinged 800.00

Sold at the Strasbourg Philatelic Exhibition as souvenirs. Size: 111x140mm.

Marcelin Berthelot (1827-1907), Chemist and Statesman — A33

1927, Sept. 7

242 A33 90c dull rose 1.90 .60
Never hinged 3.00
On cover 3.00
On cover, single franking 4.25

For surcharge see No. C3.

Lafayette, Washington, S. S. Paris and Airplane "Spirit of St. Louis" — A34

1927, Sept. 15

243 A34 90c dull red 1.25 1.75
Never hinged 2.50
On cover 5.75
On cover, single franking 9.00
a. Value omitted 2,000. 1,725.
Never hinged *2,600.*
On cover 2,200.

244 A34 1.50fr deep blue 4.00 2.50
Never hinged 7.50
On cover 5.75
On cover, single franking 9.00
a. Value omitted 1,450.
Never hinged *1,850.*
Set, never hinged 10.00

Visit of American Legionnaires to France, September, 1927. Exist imperf.

Joan of Arc — A35

1929, Mar.

245 A35 50c dull blue 1.90 .25
Never hinged 2.75
On cover .85
On cover, single franking 2.00
a. Booklet pane of 10 50.00
Never hinged 160.00
b. Imperf. 140.00
Never hinged 210.00

500th anniv. of the relief of Orleans by the French forces led by Joan of Arc.

No. 127 Overprinted in Blue

1929, May 18

246 A18 2fr org & pale bl 600.00 600.00
Never hinged 1,325.
On cover 750.00
On cover, single franking 750.00

Sold exclusively at the Intl. Phil. Exhib., Le Havre, May, 1929, for 7fr, which included a 5fr admission ticket.

Excellent counterfeits of No. 246 exist.

Reims Cathedral — A37

Die I, II, III

Die IV

Die I Die II Die III

Die I — The window of the 1st turret on the left is made of 2 lines. The horizontal line of the frame surrounding 3F is not continuous.

Die II — Same as Die I but the line under 3F is continuous.

Die III — Same as Die II but there is a deeply cut line separating 3 and F.

Die IV — Same as Die III but the window of the first turret on the left is made of three lines.

Mont-Saint-Michel — A38

Die I

Die II

Die I — The line at the top of the spire is broken.

Die II — The line is unbroken.

Port of La Rochelle A39

Dies I & II

Die III

Die I — The top of the "E" of "POSTES" has a serif. The oval of shading inside the "0" of "10 fr" and the outer oval are broken at their bases.

Die II — The same top has no serif. Interior and exterior of "0" broken as in Die I.

Die III — Top of "E" has no serif. Interior and exterior of "0" complete.

Pont du Gard, Nimes A40

Dies I & II

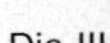

Die III

Die I — Shading of the first complete arch in the left middle tier is made of horizontal lines. Size 36x20¾mm. Perf. 13½.

Die II — Same, size 35½x21mm. Perf. 11.

Die III — Shading of same arch is made of three diagonal lines. Thin paper. Perf. 13.

1929-33 Engr. ***Perf. 11, 13, 13½***

247 A37 3fr dk gray ('30) (I) 62.50 2.40
Never hinged 115.00
On cover 6.25
On cover, single franking 25.00

247A A37 3fr dk gray ('30) (II) 125.00 3.50
Never hinged 200.00
On cover 10.00
On cover, single franking 37.50

247B A37 3fr dk gray ('30) (III) 375.00 24.00
Never hinged 600.00
On cover *45.00*
On cover, single franking *70.00*

248 A37 3fr bluish sl ('31) (IV) 60.00 2.40
Never hinged 115.00
On cover 6.25
On cover, single franking 25.00

249 A38 5fr brn ('30) (I) 24.00 4.25
Never hinged 40.00
On cover 6.50
On cover, single franking 22.00

250 A38 5fr brn ('31) (II) 21.00 .75
Never hinged 32.50
On cover 5.75
On cover, single franking 19.00

251 A39 10fr lt ultra (I) 95.00 15.00
Never hinged 160.00
On cover 25.00
On cover, single franking 45.00

251A A39 10fr ultra (II) 140.00 26.00
Never hinged 225.00
On cover 40.00
On cover, single franking 60.00

252 A39 10fr dk ultra ('31) (III) 70.00 6.50
Never hinged 140.00
On cover 19.00
On cover, single franking 40.00

253 A40 20fr red brown (I) 275.00 40.00
Never hinged 500.00
On cover 100.00
On cover, single franking 300.00
a. 20fr pale red brown (I) 1,250. 350.00
Never hinged 2,000.

254 A40 20fr brt red brn ('30) (II) 1,000. 350.00
Never hinged 1,650.
On cover 750.00
On cover, single franking 1,350.

254A A40 20fr org brn ('31) (III) 250.00 35.00
Never hinged 450.00
On cover 82.50
On cover, single franking 275.00
b. 20fr pale orange brown (III) 240.00 30.00
Never hinged 475.00
Nos. 247-254A (12) 2,498. 509.80

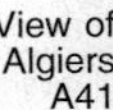

View of Algiers A41

1929, Jan. 1 **Typo.**

255 A41 50c blue & rose red 2.40 .50
Never hinged 5.50
On cover 1.40
On cover, single franking 4.50
a. Imperf 210.00 130.00
Never hinged 310.00

Cent. of the 1st French settlement in Algeria.

Nos. 146 and 196 Overprinted

1930, Apr. 23 ***Perf. 14x13½***

256 A20 50c vermilion 3.00 3.25
Never hinged 6.50
On cover 8.25
On cover, single franking 18.00

257 A23 1.50fr blue 20.00 14.50
Never hinged 40.00
On cover 29.00
On cover, single franking 37.50
Set, never hinged 47.50

Intl. Labor Bureau, 48th Congress, Paris.

Colonial Exposition Issue

Fachi Woman — A42

French Colonials A43

1930-31 Typo. ***Perf. 14x13½***

258 A42 15c gray black 1.10 .30
Never hinged 2.25
On cover 1.00
On cover, single franking 3.25

259 A42 40c dark brown 2.40 .30
Never hinged 4.75
On cover 1.00
On cover, single franking 2.00

260 A42 50c dark red .65 .25
Never hinged 1.10
On cover 1.00
On cover, single franking 1.00
a. Booklet pane of 10 12.50

261 A42 1.50fr deep blue 9.00 .65
Never hinged 21.00
On cover 2.75
On cover, single franking 4.50

Perf. 13½
Photo.

262 A43 1.50fr dp blue ('31) 45.00 2.75
Never hinged 95.00
On cover 4.00
On cover, single franking 6.50
Nos. 258-262 (5) 58.15 4.25
Set, never hinged 125.00

No. 260 has two types: type 1 shows four short downward hairlines near top of head, type 2 has no lines. Booklet stamps are type 2.

Arc de Triomphe A44

1931 **Engr.** ***Perf. 13***

263 A44 2fr red brown 40.00 1.25
Never hinged 80.00
On cover 5.00
On cover, single franking 11.00

Peace with Olive Branch — A45

1932-39 **Typo.** ***Perf. 14x13½***

264 A45 30c dp green 1.00 .55
Never hinged 2.00
On cover 2.00
On cover, single franking 5.75
265 A45 40c brt violet .30 .30
Never hinged .55
On cover 1.40
On cover, single franking 2.50
266 A45 45c yellow brown 1.75 1.00
Never hinged 3.75
On cover 10.00
On cover, single franking 40.00
267 A45 50c rose red .25 .25
Never hinged .30
On cover .40
On cover, single franking .40
a. Imperf., pair 140.00
Never hinged 210.00
b. Booklet pane of 10 5.50
Never hinged 10.00
268 A45 55c dull vio ('37) .60 .25
Never hinged 1.25
On cover 1.00
On cover, single franking 2.75
269 A45 60c ocher ('37) .30 .25
Never hinged .50
On cover 4.50
On cover, single franking 26.00
270 A45 65c violet brown .50 .50
Never hinged 1.00
On cover .80
On cover, single franking 4.50
271 A45 65c brt ultra ('37) .25 .25
Never hinged .50
On cover .80
On cover, single franking .90
a. Booklet pane of 10 7.00
Never hinged 10.00
272 A45 75c olive green .25 .30
Never hinged .30
On cover .85
On cover, single franking 3.75
273 A45 80c orange ('38) .25 .25
Never hinged .30
On cover 1.00
On cover, single franking 4.50
274 A45 90c dk red 32.50 2.00
Never hinged 62.50
On cover 5.25
On cover, single franking 10.00
275 A45 90c brt green ('38) .25 .25
Never hinged .30
On cover 1.25
On cover, single franking 5.25
276 A45 90c ultra ('38) .90 .25
Never hinged 1.50
On cover .50
On cover, single franking 1.00
a. Booklet pane of 10 8.50
Never hinged 12.00
b. Imperf 260.00
Never hinged 450.00
277 A45 1fr orange 3.25 .25
Never hinged 6.25
On cover 2.00
On cover, single franking 6.50
278 A45 1fr rose pink ('38) 3.25 .50
Never hinged 5.75
On cover 1.40
On cover, single franking 4.50
279 A45 1.25fr brown ol 75.00 4.75
Never hinged 160.00
On cover 6.25
On cover, single franking 32.50
280 A45 1.25fr rose car ('39) 1.90 2.25
Never hinged 3.50
On cover 3.75
On cover, single franking 10.00
281 A45 1.40fr brt red vio ('39) 5.75 5.25
Never hinged 11.00
On cover 13.00
On cover, single franking 60.00
282 A45 1.50fr deep blue .30 .30
Never hinged .55
On cover 1.00
On cover, single franking 4.00
283 A45 1.75fr magenta 4.00 .50
Never hinged 9.50
On cover 1.00
On cover, single franking 4.00
Nos. 264-283 (20) 132.55 20.20
Set, never hinged 275.00

The 50c is found in 4 types, differing in the lines below belt and size of "c."

For surcharges and overprints see Nos. 298, 333, 401-403, 405-409, M7-M9, S1.

Le Puy-en-Velay — A46

1933 **Engr.** ***Perf. 13***

290 A46 90c rose 3.00 1.10
Never hinged 5.75
On cover 2.00
On cover, single franking 4.00

Aristide Briand A47

Paul Doumer A48

Victor Hugo — A49

1933, Dec. 11 **Typo.** ***Perf. 14x13½***

291 A47 30c blue green 17.00 8.00
Never hinged 32.50
On cover 11.00
On cover, single franking 16.50
292 A48 75c red violet 27.50 1.90
Never hinged 62.50
On cover 2.75
On cover, single franking 8.25
a. Imperf 825.00
293 A49 1.25fr claret 6.00 2.25
Never hinged 11.00
On cover 5.75
On cover, single franking 27.50
Nos. 291-293 (3) 50.50 12.15
Set, never hinged 110.00

Dove and Olive Branch — A50

1934, Feb. 20

294 A50 1.50fr ultra 50.00 15.00
Never hinged 95.00
On cover 29.00
On cover, single franking 50.00

Joseph Marie Jacquard — A51

1934, Mar. 14 **Engr.** ***Perf. 14x13***

295 A51 40c blue 3.00 1.10
Never hinged 4.50
On cover 1.60
On cover, single franking 3.25

Jacquard (1752-1834), inventor of an improved loom for figured weaving.

Jacques Cartier A52

1934, July 18 ***Perf. 13***

296 A52 75c rose lilac 30.00 2.25
Never hinged 87.50
On cover 5.00
On cover, single franking 16.50
297 A52 1.50fr blue 50.00 4.25
Never hinged 130.00
On cover 5.25
On cover, single franking 13.00
Set, never hinged 210.00

Cartier's discovery of Canada, 400th anniv.

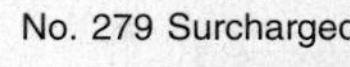

No. 279 Surcharged

1934, Nov. ***Perf. 14x13½***

298 A45 50c on 1.25fr brn ol 3.75 .65
Never hinged 7.00
On cover 2.75
On cover, single franking 13.00

Catalogue values for unused stamps in this section, from this point to the end of the section, are for Never Hinged items.

Breton River Scene A53

1935, Feb. **Engr.** ***Perf. 13***

299 A53 2fr blue green 70.00 1.00
Hinged 32.50
On cover 4.50
On cover, single franking 16.50

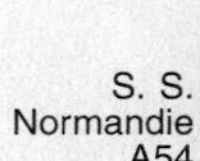

S. S. Normandie A54

1935, Apr.

300 A54 1.50fr dark blue 29.00 2.00
Hinged 14.00
On cover 5.00
On cover, single franking 8.25
a. 1.50fr pale blue ('36) 145.00 19.00
Hinged 55.00
On cover 40.00
On cover, single franking 65.00
b. 1.50fr blue green ('36) *30,000.* *12,500.*
Hinged *19,000.*
c. 1.50fr turquoise ('36) 400.00 40.00
Hinged 275.00
On cover 90.00
On cover, single franking 140.00
d. As #300, imperf 300.00
Hinged 200.00

Maiden voyage of the transatlantic steamship, the "Normandie."

Benjamin Delessert A55

1935, May 20

301 A55 75c blue green 47.50 1.75
Hinged 17.50
On cover 4.00
On cover, single franking 12.50

Opening of the International Savings Bank Congress, May 20, 1935.

View of St. Trophime at Arles — A56

1935, May 3

302 A56 3.50fr dark brown 70.00 4.25
Hinged 27.50
On cover 9.00
On cover, single franking 25.00

Victor Hugo (1802-85) — A57

1935, May 30 ***Perf. 14x13***

303 A57 1.25fr magenta 8.25 2.00
Hinged 4.00
On cover 5.75
On cover, single franking 29.00

Cardinal Richelieu — A58

1935, June 12 ***Perf. 13***

304 A58 1.50fr deep rose 70.00 1.75
Hinged 20.00
On cover 3.25
On cover, single franking 6.50

Tercentenary of the founding of the French Academy by Cardinal Richelieu.

Jacques Callot — A59

1935, Nov. ***Perf. 14x13***

305 A59 75c red 19.00 .75
Hinged 10.00
On cover 2.50
On cover, single franking 6.50

300th anniv. of the death of Jacques Callot, engraver.

André Marie Ampère (1775-1836), Scientist, by Louis Boilly — A60

1936, Feb. 27 ***Perf. 13***

306 A60 75c brown 37.50 2.00
Hinged 17.50
On cover 3.25
On cover, single franking 8.25

Windmill at Fontvielle, Immortalized by Daudet — A61

1936, Apr. 27

307 A61 2fr ultra 5.75 .40
Hinged 3.00
On cover 3.25
On cover, single franking 9.00

Publication, in 1866, of Alphonse Daudet's "Lettres de mon Moulin," 75th anniv.

Pilâtre de Rozier and his Balloon A62

1936, June 4

308 A62 75c Prus blue 37.50 2.75
Hinged 19.00
On cover 5.75
On cover, single franking 14.00

150th anniversary of the death of Jean Francois Pilâtre de Rozier, balloonist.

Rouget de Lisle — A63

"La Marseillaise" — A64

1936, June 27

309 A63 20c Prus green 5.75 2.00
Hinged 3.25
On cover 3.25
On cover, single franking 5.00

310 A64 40c dark brown 11.50 3.25
Hinged 5.50
On cover 5.00
On cover, single franking 5.75

Cent. of the death of Claude Joseph Rouget de Lisle, composer of "La Marseillaise."

Canadian War Memorial at Vimy Ridge A65

1936, July 26

311 A65 75c henna brown 25.00 2.00
Hinged 9.50
On cover 5.75
On cover, single franking 32.50

312 A65 1.50fr dull blue 32.50 9.50
Hinged 16.00
On cover 16.50
On cover, single franking 29.00

Unveiling of the Canadian War Memorial at Vimy Ridge, July 26, 1936.

A66

Jean Léon Jaurès A67

1936, July 30

313 A66 40c red brown 5.75 1.40
Hinged 4.00
On cover 2.00
On cover, single franking 5.00

314 A67 1.50fr ultra 32.50 3.75
Hinged 13.00
On cover 5.00
On cover, single franking 10.00

Assassination of Jean Léon Jaurès (1859-1914), socialist and politician.

Herald — A68

Allegory of Exposition A69

1936, Sept. 15 Typo. *Perf. 14x13½*

315 A68 20c brt violet 1.00 .50
Hinged .30
On cover 2.00
On cover, single franking 7.75

316 A68 30c Prus green 4.00 1.75
Hinged 2.40
On cover 2.75
On cover, single franking 28.00

317 A68 40c ultra 2.50 .50
Hinged 1.00
On cover 1.60
On cover, single franking 5.00

318 A68 50c red orange 2.25 .25
Hinged 1.00
On cover .85
On cover, single franking 1.00

319 A69 90c carmine 25.00 7.50
Hinged 11.00
On cover 15.00
On cover, single franking 29.00

320 A69 1.50fr ultra 67.50 4.00
Hinged 30.00
On cover 7.50
On cover, single franking 25.00

Nos. 315-320 (6) 102.25 14.50

Publicity for the 1937 Paris Exposition.

"Peace" A70

1936, Oct. 1 Engr. *Perf. 13*

321 A70 1.50fr blue 27.50 4.00
Hinged 12.50
On cover 7.50
On cover, single franking 18.00

Skiing A71

1937, Jan. 18

322 A71 1.50fr dark blue 14.00 1.75
Hinged 7.00
On cover 4.00
On cover, single franking 8.25

Intl. Ski Meet at Chamonix-Mont Blanc.

Pierre Corneille, Portrait by Charles Le Brun — A72

1937, Feb. 15

323 A72 75c brown carmine 3.75 1.40
Hinged 1.90
On cover 2.75
On cover, single franking 6.50

300th anniv. of the publication of "Le Cid."

Paris Exposition Issue

Exposition Allegory A73

1937, Mar. 15

324 A73 1.50fr turq blue 4.00 1.25
Hinged 2.25
On cover 2.75
On cover, single franking 6.50

Jean Mermoz (1901-36), Aviator A74

Memorial to Mermoz — A75

1937, Apr. 22

325 A74 30c dk slate green 1.00 .55
Hinged .50
On cover 2.75
On cover, single franking 8.25

326 A75 3fr dark violet 13.50 3.75
Hinged 6.25
On cover 12.50
On cover, single franking 32.50

a. 3fr violet 15.00 4.50
Hinged 6.75
On cover 13.00

b. 3fr gray violet (non-Fluorescent) 325.00 100.00
Hinged 200.00

Electric Train A76

Streamlined Locomotive A77

1937, May 31

327 A76 30c dk green 1.40 1.75
Hinged 1.00
On cover 3.25
On cover, single franking 5.75

328 A77 1.50fr dk ultra 15.00 8.25
Hinged 7.25
On cover 14.00
On cover, single franking 37.50

13th International Railroad Congress.

Intl. Philatelic Exhibition Issue

Souvenir Sheet

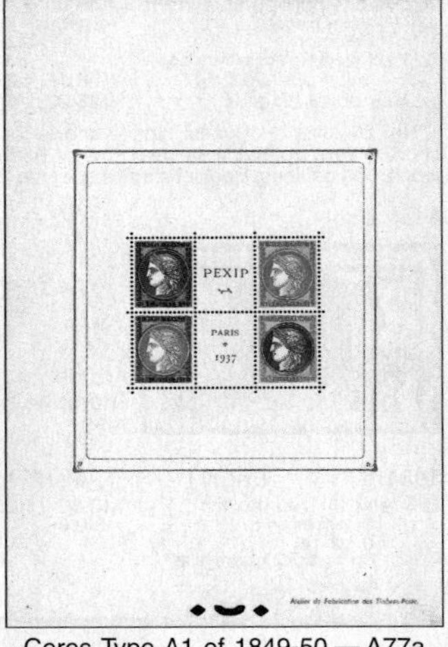

Ceres Type A1 of 1849-50 — A77a

1937, June 18 Typo. *Perf. 14x13½*

329 A77a Sheet of 4 700.00 300.00
Lightly hinged in margins 360.00
On cover *475.00*

a. 5c ultra & dark brown 90.00 47.50
Lightly hinged 40.00
On cover *160.00*

b. 15c red & rose red 90.00 47.50
Lightly hinged 40.00
On cover *160.00*

c. 30c ultra & rose red 90.00 47.50
Lightly hinged 40.00
On cover *160.00*

d. 50c red & dark brown 90.00 47.50
Lightly hinged 40.00
On cover *160.00*

e. Sheet of 4, imperf 3,000.
Lightly hinged in margins 2,350.

Issued in sheets measuring 150x220mm.

The sheets were sold only at the exhibition in Paris, a ticket of admission being required for each sheet purchased.

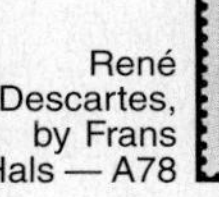

René Descartes, by Frans Hals — A78

1937, June Engr. *Perf. 13*

Inscribed "Discours sur la Méthode"

330 A78 90c copper red 3.25 1.40
Hinged 1.90
On cover 3.25
On cover, single franking 10.00

Inscribed "Discours de la Méthode"

331 A78 90c copper red 11.00 1.75
Hinged 5.50
On cover 3.25
On cover, single franking 12.50

3rd centenary of the publication of "Discours de la Méthode" by René Descartes.

France Congratulating USA — A79

1937, Sept. 17

332 A79 1.75fr ultra 4.50 2.00
Hinged 2.50
On cover 3.25
On cover, single franking 5.00

150th anniv. of the US Constitution.

No. 277 Surcharged in Red

1937, Oct. ***Perf. 14x13½***
333 A45 80c on 1fr orange 1.90 .85
Hinged .80
On cover 13.00
On cover, single franking 65.00
a. Inverted surcharge *1,225.*
Hinged *825.00*

Mountain Road at Iseran A80

1937, Oct. 4 Engr. ***Perf. 13***
334 A80 90c dark green 3.75 .30
Hinged 1.90
On cover 1.25
On cover, single franking 4.50

Issued in commemoration of the opening of the mountain road at Iseran, Savoy.

Ceres — A81

1938-40 Typo. ***Perf. 14x13½***
335 A81 1.75fr dk ultra 1.40 .55
Hinged .55
On cover 1.00
On cover, single franking 5.25
336 A81 2fr car rose ('39) .30 .30
Hinged .25
On cover 1.10
On cover, single franking 13.00
337 A81 2.25fr ultra ('39) 15.00 1.10
Hinged 8.00
On cover 1.25
On cover, single franking 5.25
338 A81 2.50fr green ('39) 3.00 .50
Hinged 1.25
On cover 1.25
On cover, single franking 5.25
339 A81 2.50fr vio blue ('40) 1.25 .75
Hinged .65
On cover 1.25
On cover, single franking 6.25
340 A81 3fr rose lilac ('39) 1.25 .50
Hinged .55
On cover 1.25
On cover, single franking 4.50
Nos. 335-340 (6) 22.20 3.70

For surcharges see Nos. 397-399.

Léon Gambetta (1838-82), Lawyer and Statesman — A82

1938, Apr. 2 Engr. ***Perf. 13***
341 A82 55c dark violet .55 .40
Hinged .35
On cover 1.40
On cover, single franking 4.50

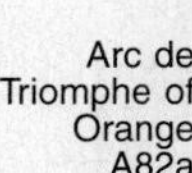

Arc de Triomphe of Orange A82a

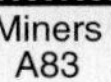

Miners A83

Keep and Gate of Vincennes A86

Palace of the Popes, Avignon A84

Medieval Walls of Carcassonne — A85

Port of St. Malo — A87

1938
342 A82a 2fr brown black 1.75 1.25
Hinged .55
On cover 3.75
On cover, single franking 16.50
343 A83 2.15fr violet brn 9.50 1.00
Hinged 4.75
On cover 1.60
On cover, single franking 5.00
344 A84 3fr car brown 26.50 5.00
Hinged 12.50
On cover 11.00
On cover, single franking 40.00
345 A85 5fr deep ultra 1.50 .40
Hinged .75
On cover 2.90
On cover, single franking 18.00
346 A86 10fr brown, *blue* 3.25 1.90
Hinged 1.50
On cover 4.00
On cover, single franking 45.00
347 A87 20fr dk blue green 80.00 19.00
Hinged 37.50
On cover 30.00
On cover, single franking 57.50
Nos. 342-347 (6) 122.50 28.55

For surcharges see Nos. 410-413.

Clément Ader, Air Pioneer A88

1938, June 16
348 A88 50fr ultra (thin paper) 150.00 65.00
Hinged 95.00
On cover 200.00
On cover, single franking 450.00
a. 50fr dark ultra (thick paper) 175.00 77.50
Hinged 100.00
On cover 200.00
On cover, single franking 450.00

For surcharge, see No. 414.

Soccer Players A89

1938, June 1
349 A89 1.75fr dark ultra 29.00 13.50
Hinged 13.50
On cover 26.00
On cover, single franking 60.00

World Cup Soccer Championship.

Costume of Champagne Region — A90

1938, June 13
350 A90 1.75fr dark ultra 7.50 4.50
Hinged 3.75
On cover 6.50
On cover, single franking 12.50

Tercentenary of the birth of Dom Pierre Pérignon, discoverer of the champagne process.

Jean de La Fontaine — A91

1938, July 8
351 A91 55c dk blue green 1.00 .80
Hinged .65
On cover 1.40
On cover, single franking 2.75

Jean de La Fontaine (1621-1695) the fabulist.

Seal of Friendship and Peace, Victoria Tower and Arc de Triomphe A92

1938, July 19
352 A92 1.75fr ultra 1.25 .80
Hinged .65
On cover 2.90
On cover, single franking 5.25

Visit of King George VI and Queen Elizabeth of Great Britain to France.

Mercury — A93

1938-42 Typo. ***Perf. 14x13½***
353 A93 1c dark brown ('39) .25 .25
Hinged .25
On cover 11.00
On cover, single franking 90.00
354 A93 2c slate grn ('39) .25 .25
Hinged .25
On cover 26.00
On cover, single franking 130.00
355 A93 5c rose .25 .25
Hinged .25
On cover 11.00
On cover, single franking 60.00
356 A93 10c ultra .25 .25
Hinged .25
On cover 2.75
On cover, single franking 30.00
357 A93 15c red orange .25 .25
Hinged .25
On cover 2.75
On cover, single franking 57.50
358 A93 15c orange brn ('39) 1.00 .50
Hinged .55
On cover 3.75
On cover, single franking 57.50
359 A93 20c red violet .25 .25
Hinged .25
On cover 3.75
On cover, single franking 26.00
360 A93 25c blue green .25 .25
Hinged .25
On cover 7.00
On cover, single franking 30.00
361 A93 30c rose red ('39) .25 .25
Hinged .25
On cover 1.10
On cover, single franking 3.75
362 A93 40c dk violet ('39) .25 .25
Hinged .25
On cover 1.00
On cover, single franking 2.75
363 A93 45c lt green ('39) .80 .50
Hinged .50
On cover 7.75
On cover, single franking 13.00
364 A93 50c deep blue ('39) 4.00 .40
Hinged 2.25
On cover 3.75
On cover, single franking 20.00
365 A93 50c dk green ('41) .55 .35
Hinged .30
On cover 3.75
On cover, single franking 25.00
366 A93 50c grnsh blue ('42) .25 .25
Hinged .25
On cover 1.00
On cover, single franking 4.50
367 A93 60c red orange ('39) .25 .25
Hinged .25
On cover 3.25
On cover, single franking 15.00
368 A93 70c magenta ('39) .25 .25
Hinged .25
On cover 1.00
On cover, single franking 2.75
369 A93 75c dk org brn ('39) 7.50 2.50
Hinged 3.75
On cover 32.50
On cover, single franking 130.00
Nos. 353-369 (17) 16.85 7.25

No. 366 exists imperforate. See Nos. 455-458. For overprints and surcharge see Nos. 404, 499-502. Post 1940 issues in Scott Standard catalogue, Vol. 2.

Self-portrait — A95

1939, Mar. 15 Engr. ***Perf. 13***
370 A95 2.25fr Prussian blue 8.25 3.50
Hinged 3.50
On cover 5.00
On cover, single franking 9.00

Paul Cézanne (1839-1906), painter.

Georges Clemenceau and Battleship Clemenceau — A96

1939, Apr. 18
371 A96 90c ultra 1.00 .75
Hinged .50
On cover 2.00
On cover, single franking 4.50

Laying of the keel of the warship "Clemenceau," Jan. 17, 1939.

Statue of Liberty, French Pavilion, Trylon and Perisphere A97

1939-40
372 A97 2.25fr ultra 17.00 6.50
Hinged 8.00
On cover 10.00
On cover, single franking 16.50
373 A97 2.50fr ultra ('40) 22.50 9.50
Hinged 8.50
On cover 14.50
On cover, single franking 20.00

New York World's Fair.

Joseph Nicéphore Niepce and Louis Jacques Mandé Daguerre A98

1939, Apr. 24
374 A98 2.25fr dark blue 16.00 7.00
Hinged 7.00
On cover 10.00
On cover, single franking 16.50

Centenary of photography.

Iris — A99

1939-44 Typo. *Perf. 14x13½*

375 A99 80c red brown ('40) .25 .25
Hinged .25
On cover .65
On cover, single franking 8.25
376 A99 80c yellow grn ('44) .25 .25
Hinged .25
On cover 3.00
On cover, single franking 12.00
377 A99 1fr green 1.00 .25
Hinged .55
On cover .65
On cover, single franking 1.25
378 A99 1fr crimson ('40) .40 .35
Hinged .25
On cover .65
On cover, single franking 1.25
a. Booklet pane of 10 7.50
379 A99 1fr grnsh blue ('44) .25 .25
Hinged .25
On cover 2.00
On cover, single franking 7.50
380 A99 1.20fr violet ('44) .25 .25
Hinged .25
On cover 1.25
On cover, single franking 2.50
381 A99 1.30fr ultra ('40) .25 .25
Hinged .25
On cover 3.75
On cover, single franking 16.50
382 A99 1.50fr red org ('41) .25 .25
Hinged .25
On cover 1.25
On cover, single franking 12.50
383 A99 1.50fr henna brn ('44) .25 .25
Hinged .25
On cover 1.25
On cover, single franking 5.75
384 A99 2fr violet brn ('44) .25 .25
Hinged .25
On cover 1.25
On cover, single franking 5.25
385 A99 2.40fr car rose ('44) .25 .25
Hinged .25
On cover 3.00
On cover, single franking 140.00
386 A99 3fr orange ('44) .25 .25
Hinged .25
On cover 2.00
On cover, single franking 10.00
387 A99 4fr ultra ('44) .25 .25
Hinged .25
On cover 3.00
On cover, single franking 15.00
Nos. 375-387 (13) 4.15 3.35

Pumping Station at Marly A100

1939 Engr. *Perf. 13*

388 A100 2.25fr brt ultra 25.00 5.00
Hinged 11.00
On cover 7.50
On cover, single franking 16.50

France's participation in the International Water Exposition at Liège.

St. Gregory of Tours — A101

1939, June 10

389 A101 90c red .90 .55
Hinged .50
On cover 1.60
On cover, single franking 3.75

14th centenary of the birth of St. Gregory of Tours, historian and bishop.

"The Oath of the Tennis Court" by Jacques David A102

1939, June 20

390 A102 90c deep slate green 3.50 1.90
Hinged 1.90
On cover 2.50
On cover, single franking 4.00

150th anniversary of French Revolution.

Cathedral of Strasbourg — A103

1939, June 23

391 A103 70c brown carmine 1.50 1.00
Hinged .75
On cover 1.60
On cover, single franking 4.00

500th anniv. of the completion of Strasbourg Cathedral.

Porte Chaussée, Verdun A104

1939, June 23

392 A104 90c black brown 1.00 .80
Hinged .80
On cover 1.60
On cover, single franking 3.75

23rd anniv. of the Battle of Verdun.

View of Pau A105

1939, Aug. 25

393 A105 90c brt rose, *gray bl* 1.25 1.25
Hinged .80
On cover 3.75
On cover, single franking 10.00

Maid of Languedoc A106

Bridge at Lyons A107

1939

394 A106 70c black, *blue* .50 .40
Hinged .40
On cover 3.75
On cover, single franking 25.00
395 A107 90c dull brown vio 1.00 *1.25*
Hinged .90
On cover 4.50
On cover, single franking 25.00

Imperforates

Nearly all French stamps issued from 1940 onward exist imperforate. Officially 20 sheets, ranging from 25 to 100 subjects, were left imperforate.

Georges Guynemer (1894-1917), World War I Ace — A108

1940, Nov. 7

396 A108 50fr ultra 16.00 9.00
Hinged 8.00
On cover 77.50
On cover, single franking 240.00

Stamps of 1938-39 Surcharged in Carmine

1940-41 *Perf. 14x13½*

397 A81 1fr on 1.75fr dk ultra .30 .30
Hinged .25
On cover 1.25
On cover, single franking 4.00
398 A81 1fr on 2.25fr ultra ('41) .30 .30
Hinged .25
On cover 1.25
On cover, single franking 4.50
399 A81 1fr on 2.50fr grn ('41) 1.40 1.40
Hinged .65
On cover 1.60
On cover, single franking 4.50
Nos. 397-399 (3) 2.00 2.00

Stamps of 1932-39 Surcharged in Carmine, Red (#408) or Black (#407)

1940-41 *Perf. 13, 14x13½*

400 A22 30c on 35c grn ('41) .30 .30
Hinged .25
On cover 2.00
On cover, single franking 12.50
401 A45 50c on 55c dl vio ('41) .30 .30
Hinged .25
On cover 1.25
On cover, single franking 18.00
a. Inverted surcharge *1,000.*
Lightly hinged *575.00*
402 A45 50c on 65c brt ultra ('41) .30 .30
Hinged .25
On cover 1.25
On cover, single franking 18.00
403 A45 50c on 75c ol grn ('41) .30 .30
Hinged .25
On cover 1.25
On cover, single franking 18.00
404 A93 50c on 75c dk org brn ('41) .30 .30
Hinged .25
On cover 1.25
On cover, single franking 37.50
405 A45 50c on 80c org ('41) .30 .30
Hinged .25
On cover 1.25
On cover, single franking 20.00
406 A45 50c on 90c ultra ('41) .30 .30
Hinged .25
On cover 1.25
On cover, single franking 18.00
a. Inverted surcharge *550.00*
Lightly hinged *375.00*
b. "05" instead of "50" *9,000.* 6,400.
Lightly hinged *6,400.*
407 A45 1fr on 1.25fr rose car (Bk) ('41) .30 .30
Hinged .25
On cover 1.25
On cover, single franking 4.00
408 A45 1fr on 1.40fr brt red vio (R) ('41) .40 .40
Hinged .25
On cover 1.25
On cover, single franking 5.00
a. Double surcharge *1,600.*
Lightly hinged *1,150.*
409 A45 1fr on 1.50fr dk bl ('41) 1.40 1.40
Hinged .25
On cover 1.25
On cover, single franking 4.00
410 A83 1fr on 2.15fr vio brn .40 .40
Hinged .25
On cover 1.25
On cover, single franking 3.75
a. Inverted surcharge *12,000.* *5,250.*
On cover *10,000.*
411 A85 2.50fr on 5fr dp ultra ('41) .40 .40
Hinged .25
On cover 5.25
On cover, single franking 25.00
a. Double surcharge *350.00* 190.00
Lightly hinged *240.00*
412 A86 5fr on 10fr brn, *bl* ('41) 1.90 1.90
Hinged 1.00
On cover 6.00
On cover, single franking 52.50
413 A87 10fr on 20fr dk bl grn ('41) 1.60 1.60
Hinged 1.00
On cover 77.50
On cover, single franking 210.00
414 A88 20fr on 50fr dk ultra (#348a) ('41) 70.00 37.50
Hinged 29.00
On cover 110.00
On cover, single franking 325.00
a. 20fr on 50fr ultra, thin paper (#348) 75.00 50.00
On cover 125.00
On cover, single franking 325.00
Nos. 400-414 (15) 78.50 46.00

Issued: No. 410, 1940; others, 1941

SEMI-POSTAL STAMPS

No. 162 Surcharged in Red

and

SP2

1914 Unwmk. Typo. *Perf. 14x13½*

B1 A22 10c + 5c red 5.00 4.25
Never hinged 7.00
On cover 9.50
On cover, single franking 17.50
B2 SP2 10c + 5c red 32.50 3.25
Never hinged 90.00
On cover 10.50
On cover, single franking 17.00
a. Booklet pane of 10 600.00
Never hinged 800.00

Issue dates: No. B1, Aug. 11; No. B2, Sept. 10.

See Nos. B746a, B746b.

For overprint see Offices in Morocco No. B8.

Widow at Grave SP3

War Orphans SP4

Woman Plowing — SP5

"Trench of Bayonets" SP6

Lion of Belfort SP7

"La Marseillaise" — SP8

1917-19

B3 SP3 2c + 3c vio brn 4.50 5.00
Never hinged 10.00
On cover 7.50
B4 SP4 5c + 5c grn ('19) 21.00 9.50
Never hinged 60.00
On cover 13.50
B5 SP5 15c + 10c gray green 30.00 27.50
Never hinged 85.00
On cover 35.00
B6 SP5 25c + 15c dp bl 80.00 57.50
Never hinged 175.00
On cover 87.50
B7 SP6 35c + 25c slate & vio 135.00 125.00
Never hinged 350.00
On cover 200.00

B8 SP7 50c + 50c pale brn & dk brn 225.00 180.00
Never hinged 650.00
On cover 300.00
B9 SP8 1fr + 1fr cl & mar 425.00 400.00
Never hinged 1,100.
On cover 550.00
B10 SP8 5fr + 5fr dp bl & blk 1,600. 1,550.
Never hinged 4,000.
On cover 2,000.
Nos. B3-B10 (8) 2,521. 2,355.

See No. B20-B23. For surcharges see No. B12-B19.

Hospital Ship and Field Hospital SP9

1918, Aug.
B11 SP9 15c + 5c sl & red 125.00 60.00
Never hinged 250.00
On cover 95.00

See No. B746d.

Semi-Postal Stamps of 1917-19 Surcharged

1922, Sept. 1
B12 SP3 2c + 1c violet brn .50 .80
Never hinged 1.00
On cover 2.75
B13 SP4 5c + 2½c green .80 1.25
Never hinged 1.50
On cover 2.75
B14 SP5 15c + 5c gray grn 1.25 1.60
Never hinged 2.60
On cover 4.00
B15 SP5 25c + 5c deep bl 2.30 2.50
Never hinged 4.75
On cover 5.50
B16 SP6 35c + 5c slate & vio 13.00 15.00
Never hinged 30.00
On cover 27.50
B17 SP7 50c + 10c pale brn & dk brn 19.00 24.00
Never hinged 39.00
On cover 40.00
a. Pair, one without surcharge
B18 SP8 1fr + 25c cl & mar 32.50 37.50
Never hinged 60.00
On cover 110.00
B19 SP8 5fr + 1fr bl & blk 150.00 155.00
Never hinged 275.00
On cover 300.00
Nos. B12-B19 (8) 219.35 237.65
Set, never hinged 415.00

Style and arrangement of surcharge differs for each denomination.

Types of 1917-19

1926-27
B20 SP3 2c + 1c violet brn 1.50 1.40
Never hinged 4.00
On cover 4.50
B21 SP7 50c + 10c ol brn & dk brn 20.00 12.50
Never hinged 72.50
On cover 27.50
B22 SP8 1fr + 25c dp rose & red brn 55.00 42.50
Never hinged 150.00
On cover 100.00
B23 SP8 5fr + 1fr sl bl & blk 105.00 100.00
Never hinged 240.00
On cover 300.00
Nos. B20-B23 (4) 181.50 156.40

Sinking Fund Issues

Types of Regular Issues of 1903-07 Surcharged in Red or Blue

1927, Sept. 26
B24 A22 40c + 10c lt blue (R) 5.75 5.75
Never hinged 10.50
On cover 20.00
a. Missing first "e" in "Amortissement" 150.00 160.00
Never hinged 240.00
B25 A20 50c + 25c green (Bl) 8.25 9.00
Never hinged 14.00
On cover 27.50
a. Missing dot on "i" of "Caisse" 85.00 92.50
Never hinged 125.00

Surcharge on No. B25 differs from illustration.

Type of Regular Issue of 1923 Surcharged in Black

B26 A23 1.50fr + 50c orange 14.50 14.00
Never hinged 37.50
On cover 40.00
a. Pair, one without surcharge 2,000.
Never hinged 2,700.
Nos. B24-B26 (3) 28.50 28.75

See Nos. B28-B33, B35-B37, B39-B41.

Industry and Agriculture SP10

1928, May Engr. *Perf. 13½*
B27 SP10 1.50fr + 8.50fr dull blue 140.00 150.00
Never hinged 225.00
On cover 225.00
On cover, single franking 300.00
a. Blue green 500.00 550.00
Never hinged 725.00

Types of 1903-23 Issues Surcharged like Nos. B24-B26

1928, Oct. 1 *Perf. 14x13½*
B28 A22 40c + 10c gray lilac (R) 13.00 14.00
Never hinged 32.50
On cover 25.00
a. Missing first "e" in "Amortissement" 160.00 180.00
Never hinged 275.00
B29 A20 50c + 25c orange brn (Bl) 32.50 29.00
Never hinged 60.00
On cover 55.00
a. Missing dot on "i" of "Caisse" 110.00 120.00
Never hinged 175.00
B30 A23 1.50fr + 50c rose lilac (Bk) 52.50 42.50
Never hinged 100.00
On cover 72.50
Nos. B28-B30 (3) 98.00 85.50

Types of 1903-23 Issues Surcharged like Nos. B24-B26

1929, Oct. 1
B31 A22 40c + 10c green 18.00 19.00
Never hinged 37.50
On cover 30.00
a. Missing first "e" in "Amortissement" 175.00 200.00
Never hinged 300.00
b. Missing dot on "i" of "Caisse" 72.50 80.00
Never hinged 120.00
B32 A20 50c + 25c lilac rose 30.00 30.00
Never hinged 60.00
On cover 52.50
a. Missing dot on "i" of "Caisse" 130.00 140.00
Never hinged 180.00
B33 A23 1.50fr + 50c chestnut 60.00 65.00
Never hinged 130.00
On cover 110.00
Nos. B31-B33 (3) 108.00 114.00

"The Smile of Reims" SP11

1930, Mar. 15 Engr. *Perf. 13*
B34 SP11 1.50fr + 3.50fr red vio 80.00 82.50
Never hinged 130.00
On cover 125.00
On cover, single franking 225.00
a. Booklet pane of 4 300.00
Never hinged 525.00
b. Booklet pane of 8 600.00
Never hinged 1,050.
Complete booklet, #B34b 1,100.

Booklets containing No. B34 have two panes of 4 (No. B34a) connected by a gutter, the complete piece constituting #B34b, which is stapled into the booklet through the gutter. See footnote after No. 4642.

Types of 1903-07 Issues Surcharged like Nos. B24-B25

1930 Oct. 1 *Perf. 14x13½*
B35 A22 40c + 10c cerise 20.00 21.00
Never hinged 70.00
On cover 32.50
a. Missing dot on "i" of "Caisse" 72.50 75.00
Never hinged 110.00
B36 A20 50c + 25c gray brown 37.50 42.50
Never hinged 120.00
On cover 67.50
a. Missing dot on "i" of "Caisse" 120.00 120.00
Never hinged 175.00
b. Missing dot on "i" of "Amortissement" 120.00 120.00
Never hinged 175.00
B37 A22 1.50fr + 50c violet 65.00 70.00
Never hinged 190.00
On cover 100.00
a. "C" below "t" of "Amortissement" 200.00 200.00
Never hinged 260.00
Nos. B35-B37 (3) 122.50 133.50

Allegory, French Provinces SP12

1931, Mar. 1 *Perf. 13*
B38 SP12 1.50fr + 3.50fr green 125.00 140.00
Never hinged 300.00
On cover 240.00
On cover, single franking 325.00

Types of 1903-07 Issues Surcharged like Nos. B24-B25

1931, Oct. 1 *Perf. 14x13½*
B39 A22 40c + 10c ol grn 40.00 45.00
Never hinged 100.00
On cover 75.00
a. Missing dot on "i" of "Caisse" 110.00 92.50
Never hinged 160.00
B40 A20 50c + 25c gray vio 100.00 110.00
Never hinged 235.00
On cover 175.00
a. Missing first "e" in "Amortissement" 190.00 210.00
Never hinged 300.00
B41 A22 1.50fr + 50c deep red 100.00 110.00
Never hinged 200.00
On cover 160.00
a. "C" below "t" of "Amortissement" 230.00 230.00
Never hinged 310.00
Nos. B39-B41 (3) 240.00 265.00

Catalogue values for unused stamps in this section, from this point to the end of the section, are for Never Hinged items.

"France" Giving Aid to an Intellectual SP13

Symbolic of Music SP14

1935, Dec. 9 Engr. *Perf. 13*
B42 SP13 50c + 10c ultra 4.00 2.50
Hinged 2.50
On cover 4.75
On cover, single franking 8.75
B43 SP14 50c + 2fr dull red 125.00 45.00
Hinged 55.00
On cover 65.00
On cover, single franking 110.00

The surtax was for the aid of distressed and exiled intellectuals.
For surcharge see No. B47.

Statue of Liberty — SP15

1936-37
B44 SP15 50c + 25c dk blue ('37) 7.50 5.00
Hinged 4.00
On cover 8.75
On cover, single franking 17.50
B45 SP15 75c + 50c violet 20.00 10.00
Hinged 9.50
On cover 16.00
On cover, single franking 27.50

Surtax for the aid of political refugees.
For surcharge see No. B47.

Children of the Unemployed SP16

1936, May
B46 SP16 50c + 10c copper red 7.50 5.00
Hinged 4.50
On cover 8.75
On cover, single franking 13.50

The surtax was for the aid of children of the unemployed.

No. B43 Surcharged in Black

1936, Nov.
B47 SP14 20c on 50c + 2fr dull red 4.75 3.50
Hinged 3.25
On cover 5.50
On cover, single franking 9.50

Jacques Callot SP17

Anatole France (Jacques Anatole Thibault) — SP18

Hector Berlioz SP19

Victor Hugo SP20

Auguste Rodin SP21

Louis Pasteur SP22

1936-37 **Engr.**

B48 SP17 20c + 10c brown car 4.50 2.50
Hinged 2.25
On cover 6.50
On cover, single franking 14.50

B49 SP18 30c + 10c emer ('37) 5.00 2.75
Hinged 2.25
On cover 5.50
On cover, single franking 9.50

B50 SP19 40c + 10c emer 4.50 2.75
Hinged 2.25
On cover 6.75
On cover, single franking 11.00

B51 SP20 50c + 10c copper red 8.75 3.75
Hinged 3.75
On cover 6.75
On cover, single franking 8.75

B52 SP21 90c + 10c rose red ('37) 13.00 6.50
Hinged 6.00
On cover 10.50
On cover, single franking 16.00

B53 SP22 1.50fr + 50c deep ultra 40.00 20.00
Hinged 20.00
On cover 30.00
On cover, single franking 52.50
Nos. B48-B53 (6) 75.75 38.25

The surtax was used for relief of unemployed intellectuals.

1938

B54 SP18 30c + 10c brown car 3.00 1.75
Hinged 1.75
On cover 5.25
On cover, single franking 11.00

B55 SP17 35c + 10c dull green 3.50 2.40
Hinged 2.40
On cover 5.25
On cover, single franking 10.50

B56 SP19 55c + 10c dull vio 10.00 4.00
Hinged 6.00
On cover 6.50
On cover, single franking 10.50

B57 SP20 65c + 10c ultra 11.50 4.00
Hinged 6.00
On cover 6.50
On cover, single franking 10.50

B58 SP21 1fr + 10c car lake 8.50 4.50
Hinged 4.75
On cover 6.75
On cover, single franking 14.50

B59 SP22 1.75fr + 25c dp blue 35.00 17.00
Hinged 17.00
On cover 25.00
On cover, single franking 40.00
Nos. B54-B59 (6) 71.50 33.65

Tug of War SP23

Foot Race SP24

Hiking — SP25

1937, June 16

B60 SP23 20c + 10c brown 3.00 2.25
Hinged 1.60
On cover 4.50
On cover, single franking 11.00

B61 SP24 40c + 10c red brown 3.00 2.25
Hinged 1.60
On cover 4.50
On cover, single franking 10.50

B62 SP25 50c + 10c black brn 3.00 2.25
Hinged 1.60
On cover 4.50
On cover, single franking 10.50
Nos. B60-B62 (3) 9.00 6.75

The surtax was for the Recreation Fund of the employees of the Post, Telephone and Telegraph.

Pierre Loti (Louis Marie Julien Viaud) SP26

1937, Aug.

B63 SP26 50c + 20c rose car 7.50 5.00
Hinged 3.75
On cover 10.50
On cover, single franking 27.50

The surtax was for the Pierre Loti Monument Fund.

"France" and Infant SP27

1937-39

B64 SP27 65c + 25c brown vio 5.25 2.75
Hinged 3.25
On cover 5.25
On cover, single franking 7.50

B65 SP27 90c + 30c pck bl ('39) 3.50 2.75
Hinged 2.10
On cover 6.50
On cover, single franking 16.00

The surtax was used for public health work.

Winged Victory of Samothrace — SP28

1937, Aug.

B66 SP28 30c blue green 175.00 40.00
Hinged 65.00
On cover 67.50
On cover, single franking 110.00

B67 SP28 55c red 175.00 40.00
Hinged 65.00
On cover 67.50
On cover, single franking 110.00

On sale at the Louvre for 2.50fr. The surtax of 1.65fr was for the benefit of the Louvre Museum.

Jean Baptiste Charcot — SP29

1938-39

B68 SP29 65c + 35c dk bl grn 3.00 3.00
Hinged 1.60
On cover 5.25
On cover, single franking 8.75

B69 SP29 90c + 35c brt red vio ('39) 30.00 13.50
Hinged 11.00
On cover 17.50
On cover, single franking 40.00

Surtax for the benefit of French seamen.

Palace of Versailles SP30

1938, May 9

B70 SP30 1.75fr + 75c dp bl 37.50 19.00
Hinged 19.00
On cover 30.00
On cover, single franking 47.50

Natl. Exposition of Painting and Sculpture at Versailles.

The surtax was for the benefit of the Versailles Concert Society.

French Soldier — SP31

1938, May 16

B71 SP31 55c + 70c brown vio 8.50 5.25
Hinged 4.75
On cover 9.50
On cover, single franking 27.50

B72 SP31 65c + 1.10fr pck bl 8.50 5.25
Hinged 4.75
On cover 9.50
On cover, single franking 27.50

The surtax was for a fund to erect a monument to the glory of the French Infantrymen.

Monument — SP32

1938, May 25

B73 SP32 55c + 45c vermilion 22.50 12.50
Hinged 10.00
On cover 25.00
On cover, single franking 52.50

The surtax was for a fund to erect a monument in honor of the Army Medical Corps.

Reims Cathedral — SP33

1938, July 10

B74 SP33 65c + 35c ultra 17.50 10.50
Hinged 8.50
On cover 19.00
On cover, single franking 29.00

Completion of the reconstruction of Reims Cathedral, July 10, 1938.

"France" Welcoming Her Sons — SP34

1938, Aug. 8

B75 SP34 65c + 60c rose car 8.50 5.75
Hinged 4.00
On cover 10.50
On cover, single franking 24.00

The surtax was for the benefit of French volunteers repatriated from Spain.

Curie Issue
Common Design Type

1938, Sept. 1

B76 CD80 1.75fr + 50c dp ultra 21.00 12.50
Hinged 8.75
On cover 21.00
On cover, single franking 32.50

Victory Parade Passing Arc de Triomphe SP36

1938, Oct. 8

B77 SP36 65c + 35c brown car 5.75 4.50
Hinged 3.25
On cover 8.75
On cover, single franking 20.00

20th anniversary of the Armistice.

Student and Nurse — SP37

1938, Dec. 1

B78 SP37 65c + 60c pck blue 15.00 8.25
Hinged 8.00
On cover 14.50
On cover, single franking 27.50

The surtax was for Student Relief.

Blind Man and Radio SP38

1938, Dec.

B79 SP38 90c + 25c brown vio 15.00 9.00
Hinged 8.00
On cover 14.50
On cover, single franking 20.00

The surtax was used to help provide radios for the blind.

Civilian Facing Firing Squad — SP39

1939, Feb. 1

B80 SP39 90c + 35c black brn 17.00 10.50
Hinged 8.75
On cover 17.00
On cover, single franking 22.50

The surtax was used to erect a monument to civilian victims of World War I.

Red Cross Nurse — SP40

1939, Mar. 24

B81 SP40 90c + 35c dk sl grn, turq bl & red 13.00 8.25
Hinged 6.75
On cover 12.50
On cover, single franking 17.50

75th anniv. of the Intl. Red Cross Society. See No. B746c.

Army Engineer SP41

1939, Apr. 3

B82 SP41 70c + 50c vermilion 12.50 8.25
Hinged 6.00
On cover 12.50
On cover, single franking 52.50

Army Engineering Corps. The surtax was used to erect a monument to those members who died in World War I.

Ministry of Post, Telegraph and Telephone SP42

1939, Apr. 8

B83 SP42 90c + 35c turq blue 37.50 20.00
Hinged 19.00
On cover 30.00
On cover, single franking 47.50

The surtax was used to aid orphans of employees of the postal system. Opening of the new building for the Ministry of Post, Telegraph and Telephones.

Mother and Child — SP43

1939, Apr. 24

B84 SP43 90c + 35c red 3.75 2.50
Hinged 2.40
On cover 5.25
On cover, single franking 8.75

The surtax was used to aid children of the unemployed.

50th Anniv. of the Eiffel Tower — SP44

1939, May 5

B85 SP44 90c + 50c red violet 15.00 9.00
Hinged 8.75
On cover 12.50
On cover, single franking 20.00

The surtax was used for celebration festivities.

Puvis de Chavannes — SP45

Claude Debussy SP46

Honoré de Balzac SP47

Claude Bernard SP48

1939-40

B86 SP45 40c + 10c ver 1.75 1.00
Hinged .80
On cover 4.00
On cover, single franking 9.50

B87 SP46 70c + 10c brn vio 8.25 2.50
Hinged 3.50
On cover 5.25
On cover, single franking 11.00

B87A SP46 80c + 10c brn vio ('40) 9.00 7.50
Hinged 4.25
On cover 12.00
On cover, single franking 16.00

B88 SP47 90c + 10c brt red vio 7.25 2.50
Hinged 3.25
On cover 5.25
On cover, single franking 10.50

B88A SP47 1fr + 10c brt red vio ('40) 9.00 7.50
Hinged 4.25
On cover 12.00
On cover, single franking 16.00

B89 SP48 2.25fr + 25c brt ultra 28.00 11.50
Hinged 14.50
On cover 19.00
On cover, single franking 27.50

B89A SP48 2.50fr + 25c brt ultra ('40) 9.00 7.50
Hinged 4.25
On cover 13.50
On cover, single franking 21.00

Nos. B86-B89A (7) 72.25 40.00

The surtax was used to aid unemployed intellectuals.

Mothers and Children
SP49 SP50

1939, June 15

B90 SP49 70c + 80c bl, grn & vio 5.25 4.50
Hinged 3.25
On cover 8.75
On cover, single franking 16.00

B91 SP50 90c + 60c dk brn, dl vio & brn 8.50 5.25
Hinged 4.75
On cover 8.75
On cover, single franking 16.00

The surtax was used to aid France's repopulation campaign.

"The Letter" by Jean Honoré Fragonard — SP51

1939, July 6

B92 SP51 40c + 60c multi 4.25 2.75
Hinged 2.40
On cover 5.25
On cover, single franking 8.00

The surtax was used for the Postal Museum. See footnote after No. 4642.

Statue of Widow and Children — SP52

1939, July 20

B93 SP52 70c + 30c brown vio 25.00 12.00
Hinged 12.00
On cover 18.00
On cover, single franking 32.50

Surtax for the benefit of French seamen.

French Soldier SP53

Colonial Trooper SP54

1940, Feb. 15

B94 SP53 40c + 60c sepia 3.25 2.75
Hinged 1.50
On cover 7.25
On cover, single franking 14.50

B95 SP54 1fr + 50c turq blue 3.25 2.75
Hinged 1.50
On cover 7.25
On cover, single franking 14.50

The surtax was used to assist the families of mobilized men.

World Map Showing French Possessions — SP55

1940, Apr. 15

B96 SP55 1fr + 25c scarlet 2.50 1.50
Hinged 1.50
On cover 5.25
On cover, single franking 8.00

Marshal Joseph J. C. Joffre SP56

Marshal Ferdinand Foch — SP57

Gen. Joseph S. Gallieni SP58

Woman Plowing SP59

1940, May 1

B97 SP56 80c + 45c choc 6.00 3.75
Hinged 3.00
On cover 10.50
On cover, single franking 20.00

B98 SP57 1fr + 50c dk vio 4.50 3.00
Hinged 2.50
On cover 10.50
On cover, single franking 20.00

B99 SP58 1.50fr + 50c brown red 4.50 3.00
Hinged 2.50
On cover 10.50
On cover, single franking 17.50

B100 SP59 2.50fr + 50c indigo & dl bl 12.00 7.50
Hinged 6.00
On cover 18.00
On cover, single franking 47.50

Nos. B97-B100 (4) 27.00 17.25

The surtax was used for war charities. See footnote after No. 4642.

Doctor, Nurse, Soldier and Family SP60

Nurse and Wounded Soldier SP61

1940, May 12

B101 SP60 80c + 1fr dk grn & red 7.25 3.50
Hinged 3.50
On cover 12.50
On cover, single franking 72.50

B102 SP61 1fr + 2fr sep & red 9.00 3.50
Hinged 3.50
On cover 11.00
On cover, single franking 21.00

The surtax was used for the Red Cross. See Nos. B747a, B747e.

Nurse with Injured Children — SP62

1940, Nov. 12

B103 SP62 1fr + 2fr sepia 1.25 .80
Hinged .80
On cover 3.25
On cover, single franking 8.75

The surtax was used for victims of the war.

Wheat Harvest SP63

Sowing SP64

Picking Grapes SP65

Grazing Cattle SP66

1940, Dec. 2

B104	SP63	80c + 2fr brn blk	3.00	1.50
		Hinged	1.40	
		On cover		6.50
		On cover, single franking		67.50
B105	SP64	1fr + 2fr chestnut	3.00	1.50
		Hinged	1.40	
		On cover		6.50
		On cover, single franking		21.00
B106	SP65	1.50fr + 2fr brt vio	3.00	1.50
		Hinged	1.40	
		On cover		6.50
		On cover, single franking		52.50
B107	SP66	2.50fr + 2fr dp grn	3.25	1.75
		Hinged	1.75	
		On cover		6.50
		On cover, single franking		52.50
		Nos. B104-B107 (4)	12.25	6.25

The surtax was for national relief.

BALLONS MONTES

"Ballons Montes" are letters which left Paris between Sept. 23, 1870, and Jan. 28, 1871, toward the end of the Franco-Prussian War. Placed under siege by the German army, the French capital was isolated from the rest of the world. With all other means of communication severed, Parisians took to the air, inaugurating what many consider to be the world's first air mail. Of the 67 balloons that were launched from Paris, 56 carried mail that passed through the Paris Post Office, including private letters, newspapers and official documents. While some balloons were unmanned, most carried at least a single person in addition to the 225-275 pounds of mail.

Ballons Montes can usually be identified by examination of the dates of posting, transit and arrival postmarks. Carried by capricious winds, each balloon landed in a different and unexpected location. Some crashed, some fell into the English Channel and many came down in German-controlled territory. When balloons landed in French territory or countries friendly to France, postal authorities enthusiastically aided the Parisians by sending the recovered mail by the most direct and efficient route to its destination. This use of a bewildering variety of postal routes is reflected in the unusual postal markings found on most Ballon Montes. While mail that fell into German hands was usually confiscated, on some occasions, German authorities actually helped deliver the mail to its intended destination. Mail confiscated by the Germans was posted following the conclusion of hostilities.

Ballon Montes are valued according to five criteria, three of which are reflected in the listings that follow. The base value is determined by the balloon that carried the cover. Values for the destination and the franking used to pay the postage are then added to the base value as premiums. Not reflected in the listings are premiums for the nature and contents of the cover and any postmarks applied to the cover prior to its departure on the balloon. **Covers are valued in Very Fine condition.**

Balloon Name & Base Value

Sept. 23 Departure 08:00 a.m.
BM1 *Neptune* 10,500.

Sept. 25 Departure 11:00 a.m.
BM2 *Ville de Florence* 700.

Sept. 29 Departure 10:30 a.m.
BM3 *Etats-Unis* 550.
a. With transit pmk: *Gare de Mantes Sept. 29* 3,250.

Sept. 30 Departure 09:30 a.m.
BM4 *Celeste* 425.

Sept. 30 Departure noon
BM5 Unnamed #1 325.

Oct. 7 Departure 11:10 a.m.
BM6 *Armand-Barbes* 275.

Oct. 7 Departure 11:10 a.m.
BM7 *George-Sand* 4,000.

Oct. 7 Departure 02:15 p.m.
BM8 Unnamed #2 350.

Shortly after take-off, No. BM8 crashed inside the French defensive lines and within sight of the encircling German forces. The mail carried by No. BM8 was salvaged and returned to Paris where it was re-posted on subsequent balloons.

Oct. 12 Departure 08:00 a.m.
BM9 *Washington* 275.
a. With transit pmk: *Douai Oct. 13* 2,750.

Oct. 12 Departure 09:00 a.m.
BM10 *Louis-Blanc* 275.
a. With Traveling Post Office pmk: *Lille a Paris Oct. 12* 1,850.

Oct. 14 Departure 10:00 a.m.
BM11 *Godefroy-Caraignac* 325.
a. With transit pmk: *Chaumont Oct. 16* 2,500.

Oct. 14 Departure 01:15 p.m.
BM12 *Jean-Bart #1* 440.

Oct. 16 Departure 07:30 a.m.
BM13 *Jules-Favre #1* 250.

Oct. 16 Departure 09:50 a.m.
BM14 *Jean-Bart #2* 250.

Oct. 18 Departure 11:45 a.m.
BM15 *Victor Hugo* 325.

Oct. 19 Departure 09:15 a.m.
BM16 *Republique Universelle* 350.
a. With transit pmk: *Renwez* 3,200.
b. With transit pmk: *Rocroi Oct. 16* 3,200.

No. BM16 was also named *La Lafayette.*

Oct. 22 Departure 11:30 a.m.
BM17 *Garibaldi* 325.

Oct. 25 Departure 08:30 a.m.
BM18 *Montgolfier* 2,400.

Oct. 27 Departure 09:00 a.m.
BM19 *Vauban* 325.
a. With transit pmk: *Bar-le-Duc* 2,750.

Oct. 27 Departure 02:10 p.m.
BM20 *Bretagne* 16,000.

No. BM20 was also named *le Normandie (A).*

Oct. 29 Departure noon
BM21 *Colonel Charras* 300.

Nov. 2 Departure 08:45 a.m.
BM22 *Fulton* 325.

Nov. 4 Departure 09:30 a.m.
BM23 *Ferdinand Flocon* 275.
a. With transit pmk: *Nantes* 675.

Nov. 4 Departure 02:00 p.m.
BM24 *Galilee* 425.

Nov. 6 Departure 09:45 a.m.
BM25 *Ville de Chateaudun* 275.

Nov. 7 Departure 10:00 a.m.
BM26 Unnamed #3 10,500.

Nov. 8 Departure 08:20 a.m.
BM27 *Gironde* 350.

Nov. 12 Departure 09:00 a.m.
BM28 *Daguerre* 325.

Nov. 12 Departure 09:15 a.m.
BM29 *Niepce* 6,250.

Nov. 18 Departure 11:15 p.m.
BM30 *General Ulrich* 275.
a. With transit pmk: *Luzarches* 1,500.

Nov. 21 Departure 00:45 a.m.
BM31 *Archimede* 325.

Nov. 24 Departure 11:30 a.m.
BM32 *Egalite* 7,750.

Nov. 24 Departure 11:30 p.m.
BM33 *Ville d'Orleans* 500.
a. Re-posted from Norway 1,000.
b. With transit pmk: *London Dec. 2/Dec. 4* 1,350.

Nov. 28 Departure 11:00 p.m.
BM34 *Jacquard* 2,250.
a. With transit pmk: *Falmouth* 7,000.
b. Re-posted from La Rochelle Dec. 21 6,000.

Nov. 30 Departure 11:30 p.m.
BM35 *Jules-Favre #2* 300.

Dec. 1 Departure 05:15 a.m.
BM36 *Bataille de Paris* 5,500.

Dec. 2 Departure 08:00 a.m.
BM37 *Volta* 55,000.

No mail is known from No. BM37.

Dec. 5 Departure 01:00 p.m.

BM38 *Franklin* 350.
a. With transit pmk: *Nantes* 1,800.

Dec. 5 Departure 06:00 a.m.

BM39 *Armee de Bretagne* *4,500.*

Dec. 7 Departure 01:00 a.m.

BM40 *Denis-Papin* 400.

Dec. 11 Departure 02:15 a.m.

BM41 *General Renault* 350.
a. With transit pmk: *Foucarmont* 3,250.

Dec. 15 Departure 04:45 a.m.

BM42 *Ville de Paris* 450.
a. Re-posted at Paris, July 1871 1,100.

Dec. 17 Departure 01:15 a.m.

BM43 *Parmentier* 325.

Dec. 17 Departure 01:25 a.m.

BM44 *Gutenberg* *4,000.*

Dec. 18 Departure 05:00 a.m.

BM45 *Davy* 500.
a. With transit pmk: *Beaune* 2,750.

Dec. 20 Departure 02:00 a.m.

BM46 *General Chanzy* *975.*

Dec. 22 Departure 02:30 a.m.

BM47 *Lavoisier* 325.

Dec. 23 Departure 04:30 a.m.

BM48 *Delivrance* 350.
a. With transit pmk: *Roche-sur-Yon* 475.

Dec. 24

BM49 *Rouget-de-L'isle* *5,500.*

Dec. 27 Departure 04:00 a.m.

BM50 *Tourville* 325.

Dec. 27 Departure 04:00 a.m.

BM51 *Merlin de Douai* *40,000.*

Dec. 29 Departure 04:00 a.m.

BM52 *Bayard* 350.

Dec. 31 Departure 05:00 a.m.

BM53 *Armee de la Loire* 350.

Jan. 4 Departure 01:00 a.m.

BM54 *Newton* 325.

Jan. 9 Departure 03:00 a.m.

BM55 *Duquesne* 285.

Jan. 10 Departure 04:15 a.m.

BM56 *Gambetta* 350.

Jan. 11 Departure 03:00 a.m.

BM57 *Kepler* 350.
a. With transit pmk: *Paris a Brest* 475.

Jan. 13 Departure 00:30 a.m.

BM58 *Monge* *27,500.*

Jan. 13 Departure 03:30 a.m.

BM59 *General Faidherbe* 350.
a. With transit pmk: *Ste Foy* 925.

Jan. 15 Departure 03:00 a.m.

BM60 *Vaucanson* 350.

Jan. 16 Departure 07:00 a.m.

BM61 *Steenackers* *42,500.*

Nos. BM20, BM26, BM29, BM32, BM36, BM44, BM46, BM49, BM58 and BM61 only carried "Plis Conflies," which did not pass through the Paris Post Office, but were delivered to either the balloon, the balloon company or the balloon's pilot directly. These covers normally carry postage and were canceled on transit or arrival.

Jan. 18 Departure 03:00 a.m.

BM62 *Poste de Paris* 375.

Jan. 20 Departure 05:15 a.m.

BM63 *General Bourbaki* 350.

Jan. 22 Departure 04:00 a.m.

BM64 *General Daumesnil* 325.

Jan. 24 Departure 03:00 a.m.

BM65 *Torricelli* 425.

Jan. 27 Departure 03:30 a.m.

BM66 *Richard Wallace* *2,600.*

Jan. 28 Departure 05:45 a.m.

BM667 *General Cambronne* 1,100.

Destinations of Mail Carried by Ballons Montes

The Premium Value listed by destination is combined with the premium for the stamp used (shown in the following listings) and added to the base value for each Ballon Montes listed above.

French Area

Rate, Destination & Premium

D1 20c French Occupied Territory (without arrival pmk.) +225.
a. With French arrival pmk. +1,150.
b. With German arrival pmk. +3,250.
D2 20c Island of Corsica +1,750.
D3 20c Algeria +1,250.
D4 70c West Indies +9,000.
D5 80c Gabon *+35,000.*
D6 50c Guadeloupe +16,000.
D7 50c Martinique *+14,000.*
D8 20c Monaco +8,500.
D9 70c New Caledonia *+17,000.*
D10 50c Reunion +25,000.
D11 50c Senegal *+25,000.*
D12 40c Tunisia *+22,500.*

Europe

D13 60c Austria *+2,500.*
D14 30c Baden *+3,250.*
D15 40c Bavaria *+2,400.*
D16 30c Belgium +200.
D17 50c Bremen *+3,500.*
D18 50c Brunswick *+3,500.*
D19 50c Bulgaria *+18,500.*
D20 40c Canary Islands *+14,000.*
a. 80c Via England *+10,500.*
D21 40c Cyprus *+15,500.*
D22 50c Denmark *+8,250.*
a. 70c Via Thurn & Taxis *+10,500.*
D23 40c, 50c Germany 3,250.
a. With arrival pmk *+3,500.*
D24 40c Gibraltar *+17,500.*
D25 30c Great Britain +200.
D26 60c Greece (Sea post) *+27,500.*
D27 30c Isle of Wight +1,750.
D28 30c Ireland *+2,400.*
D29 40c Italy *+1,250.*
D30 30c Jersey +875.
D31 60c Liechtenstein *+21,000.*
D32 25c Luxembourg *+8,250.*
D33 80c Madeira *+12,000.*
D34 40c Malta *+15,500.*
D35 60c Montenegro *+16,500.*
D36 40c Netherlands +750.
D37 70c Norway *+13,750.*
a. 1fr Via Denmark *+17,500.*
D38 80c Poland *+17,500.*
D39 40c Portugal *+3,500.*
D40 40c Prussia *+2,750.*
D41 40c Rhodes *+17,500.*
D42 50c Roman States *+2,750.*
D43 40c Romania *+19,000.*
a. 80c By land post *+24,000.*
D44 80c Russia (without arrival pmk.) *+2,250.*
a. With arrival pmk. *+13,750.*
D45 1fr South Russia (without arrival pmk.) *+2,750.*
a. With arrival pmk. *+21,000.*
D46 50c Saxony *+2,750.*
D47 30c Scotland *+2,500.*
D48 40c Spain *+3,500.*
D49 60c Sweden (via Denmark) *+10,500.*
a. 70 Via Thurn & Taxis *+12,000.*
D50 30c Switzerland +150.
D51 40c Turkey (sea post) *+4,250.*
a. 80 Land post *+5,500.*
D52 50c Walachia *+18,500.*

Other Areas

D53 80c Argentina *+13,750.*
D54 80c Australia *+45,000.*
D55 1fr Bolivia *+25,000.*
D56 80c Brazil *+17,500.*
D57 80c Canada (via England) *+14,000.*
a. Canada *+45,000.*
D58 80c Cape of Good Hope *+35,000.*
D59 80c Ceylon *+21,000.*
D60 80c Chile *+16,500.*
D61 80c China *+55,000.*
D62 80c Cuba *+17,500.*
D63 40c Egypt *+5,000.*
D64 80c Haiti *+22,500.*
D65 80c Hong Kong *+55,000.*
D66 80c India *+14,500.*
D67 80c Jamaica *+21,000.*
D68 80c Japan *+45,000.*
D69 80c Malaysia *+22,500.*
D70 80c Mauritius *+25,000.*
D71 80c Mexico *+16,000.*
a. 1fr Via Panama *+17,500.*
D72 80c Newfoundland *+22,500.*
D73 80c Panama *+17,500.*
D74 80c Paraguay *+17,500.*
D75 1fr Peru *+25,000.*
D76 80c Philippines *+20,000.*
D77 80c Puerto Rico *+22,500.*
D78 40c Tangier *+12,500.*
D79 70c, 80c United States *+5,250.*
a. 1fr Interior *+9,500.*
D80 80c Uruguay *+17,500.*
D81 80c Venezuela *+21,500.*
D82 70c West Indies *+17,500.*

Franking used on Mail Carried by Ballons Montes

The Premium Value shown for the stamp used is combined with the premium value of the destination and then added to the base value for each of the Ballon Montes listed above. Stamps shown without a value attach no premium to the base value of the cover.

1853-1860

France Scott Number & Premium

15 20c blue, *bluish* *+6,000.*
18 40c org, *yelsh* *+7,000.*

1862-71

22 1c ol grn, *pale bl* *+3,250.*
23 5c yel grn, *grnish* +975.
25 10c bis, *yelsh* +700.
26 20c bl, *bluish* +350.
27 40c org, *yelsh* +1,250.
28 80c rose, *pinkish* *+2,800.*

1863-70

29 1c bronze grn, *pale bl* *+2,600.*
30 2c red brn, *yelsh* *+3,000.*
31 4c grey *+3,000.*
32 10c bis, *yelsh* +75.
33 20c bl, *bluish* no premium
34 30c brn, *yelsh* no premium
35 40c org, *yelsh* +150.
36 80c rose, *pinkish* +475.

1870

54 10c bis, *yelsh* +200
a. tete beche pair *+11,000.*
57 20c bl, *bluish* no premium
b. tete beche pair *+11,000.*

AIR POST STAMPS

Nos. 127, 130 Overprinted in Dark Blue or Black

Perf. 14x13½

1927, June 25 **Unwmk.**

C1 A18 2fr org & bl (DB) 200.00 225.00
Never hinged 400.00
On cover, stamp very fine 525.00
C2 A18 5fr dk bl & buff 200.00 225.00
Never hinged 400.00
On cover, stamp very fine 525.00

On sale only at the Intl. Aviation Exhib. at Marseilles, June, 1927. One set could be purchased by each holder of an admission ticket. Excellent counterfeits exist.

Stamps centered in the grade of fine sell for about 30 percent less.

Nos. 242, 196 Surcharged

1928, Aug. 23

C3 A33 10fr on 90c 2,400. 1,800.
Never hinged 3,500.
On cover 2,200.
a. Inverted surcharge 16,500. 16,500.
Never hinged 25,000.
On cover 19,000.
b. Space between "10" and bars 6½mm 3,100. 3,100.
Never hinged 5,100.
On cover 3,900.
C4 A23 10fr on 1.50fr 10,000. 8,250.
Never hinged 14,000.
On cover 10,500.
a. Space between "10" and bars 6½mm 13,000. 13,000.
Never hinged 20,000.
On cover 12,500.
b. Vert. pair, Nos. C4, C4a 23,000.

Nos. C3-C4 received their surcharge in New York by order of the French consul general. They were for use in paying the 10fr fee for letters leaving the liner Ile de France on a catapulted hydroplane when the ship was one day off the coast of France on its eastward voyage.

The normal space between "10" and bars is 4½mm, but on 10 stamps in each pane of 50 the space is 6½mm. Counterfeits exist.

View of Marseille, Church of Notre Dame at Left — AP1

1930-31 **Engr.** ***Perf. 13***

C5 AP1 1.50fr dp carmine 21.00 4.00
Never hinged 40.00
On cover 5.50
On cover, single franking 16.00
a. With perf. initials "E.I.P.A.30" 2,750. 3,750.
Never hinged 3,600.
b. Pair, C5, C5a 3,400.
Never hinged 5,500.
C6 AP1 1.50fr dk bl ('31) 19.00 2.25
Never hinged 35.00
On cover 4.75
On cover, single franking 6.50
a. 1.50fr ultramarine 50.00 21.00
Never hinged 90.00
On cover 32.50
On cover, single franking 47.50
b. As "a," with perf. initials "E.I.P.A.30" 450.00 350.00
Never hinged 700.00
On cover 450.00
c. Pair, C6a, C6b 600.00
Never hinged 1,100.
d. 1.50fr bright ultra 290.00 175.00
Never hinged 450.00

Nos. C5a, C6a were sold at the Intl. Air Post Exhib., Paris, Nov. 6-20, 1930, at face value plus 5fr, the price of admission.

Forgeries abound of Nos. C5a and C6b. Certificates from recognized authorities are recommended.

Blériot's Monoplane AP2

1934, Sept. 1 ***Perf. 13***

C7 AP2 2.25fr violet 24.00 6.00
Never hinged 32.50
On cover 12.00
On cover, single franking 24.00

1st flight across the English Channel, by Louis Blériot.

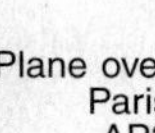

Plane over Paris AP3

1936

C8 AP3 85c deep green 2.25 2.25
Never hinged 6.50
On cover 5.50
On cover, single franking 16.00
a. 85c green 14.00 4.00
Never hinged 20.00
C9 AP3 1.50fr blue 10.50 5.50
Never hinged 18.00
On cover 8.75
On cover, single franking 14.50
C10 AP3 2.25fr violet 18.00 7.00
Never hinged 35.00
On cover 10.00
On cover, single franking 17.50
C11 AP3 2.50fr rose 32.50 8.25
Never hinged 45.00
On cover 12.00
On cover, single franking 21.00
C12 AP3 3fr ultra 26.00 2.50
Never hinged 37.50
On cover 5.50
On cover, single franking 20.00
C13 AP3 3.50fr orange brn 62.50 24.00
Never hinged 105.00
On cover 32.50
On cover, single franking 60.00

C14 AP3 50fr emerald 825.00 325.00
Never hinged 1,450.
On cover 525.00
On cover, single franking 1,200.
a. 50fr deep green 1,000. 525.00
Never hinged 1,650.
b. 50fr green 850.00 350.00
Never hinged 1,500.
Nos. C8-C14 (7) 976.75 374.50

Monoplane over Paris — AP4

Paper with Red Network Overprint

1936, July 10 ***Perf. 12½***
C15 AP4 50fr ultra 625.00 310.00
Never hinged 1,700.
On cover 525.00
On cover, single franking 1,200.
a. Red network inverted 800.00 375.00
Never hinged 1,300.

Airplane and Galleon — AP5

Airplane and Globe AP6

1936, Aug. 17 ***Perf. 13***
C16 AP5 1.50fr dk ultra 17.50 5.25
Never hinged 35.00
On cover 7.50
On cover, single franking 21.00
C17 AP6 10fr Prus green 290.00 130.00
Never hinged 700.00
On cover 175.00
On cover, single franking 240.00

100th air mail flight across the South Atlantic.

POSTAGE DUE STAMPS

D1

1859-70 Unwmk. Litho. *Imperf.*
J1 D1 10c black 30,500. 240.00
No gum 7,250.
On cover 625.00
J2 D1 15c black ('70) 140.00 *250.00*
No gum 40.00
On cover 1,300.

Full margins = 1mm.

In the lithographed stamps the central bar of the "E" of "CENTIMES" is very short, and the accent on "a" slants at an angle of 30 degree, for the 10c and 17 degree for the 15c, while on the typographed the central bar of the "E" is almost as wide as the top and bottom bars and the accent on the "a" slants at an angle of 47 degree.

No. J2 is known rouletted unofficially.

1859-78 **Typo.**
J3 D1 10c black 30.00 17.50
No gum 8.75
On cover 32.50
J4 D1 15c black ('63) 35.00 15.00
No gum 9.50
On cover 32.50
J5 D1 20c black ('77) 4,100.
No gum 3,250.
J6 D1 25c black ('71) 150.00 50.00
No gum 47.50
On cover 110.00
a. Double impression 6,000.
J7 D1 30c black ('78) 225.00 125.00
No gum 72.50
On cover 250.00
J8 D1 40c blue ('71) 325.00 *425.00*
No gum 105.00
On cover 2,350.
a. 40c ultramarine 6,500. 5,700.
No gum 3,250.
On cover *24,000.*
b. 40c Prussian blue 2,600.
No gum 1,300.
J9 D1 60c bister ('71) 475.00 *1,050.*
No gum 225.00
On cover *9,500.*
J10 D1 60c blue ('78) 60.00 *110.00*
No gum 20.00
On cover 1,350.
a. 60c dark blue 600.00 *725.00*
No gum 225.00
On cover *2,250.*
J10B D1 60c black 2,700.
No gum 1,600.

Full margins = 1¼mm.

The 20c & 60c black were not put into use.

Nos. J3, J4, J6, J8 and J9 are known rouletted unofficially and Nos. J4, J6, J7 and J10 pin-perf. unofficially.

D2

1882-92 ***Perf. 14x13½***
J11 D2 1c black 2.50 2.50
On cover 20.00
J12 D2 2c black 30.00 26.00
On cover 450.00
J13 D2 3c black 30.00 25.00
On cover 550.00
J14 D2 4c black 60.00 40.00
On cover 525.00
J15 D2 5c black 130.00 32.50
On cover 60.00
J16 D2 10c black 110.00 2.50
On cover 25.00
J17 D2 15c black 77.50 10.50
On cover 35.00
J18 D2 20c black 350.00 140.00
On cover 400.00
J19 D2 30c black 210.00 2.50
On cover 30.00
J20 D2 40c black 140.00 60.00
On cover 160.00
J21 D2 50c blk ('92) 600.00 175.00
On cover 425.00
J22 D2 60c blk ('84) 600.00 57.50
On cover 290.00
J23 D2 1fr black 750.00 350.00
On cover *3,400.*
J24 D2 2fr blk ('84) 1,400. 825.00
On cover *8,000.*
J25 D2 5fr blk ('84) 3,000. 1,600.
On cover —

Excellent counterfeits exist of Nos. J23-J25.

See Nos. J26-J45A. For overprints and surcharges see Offices in China Nos. J1-J6, J33-J40, Offices in Egypt, Alexandria J1-J5, Port Said J1-J8, Offices in Zanzibar 60-62, J1-J5, Offices in Morocco 9-10, 24-25, J1-J5, J10-J12, J17-J22, J35-J41.

1884
J26 D2 1fr brown 400.00 90.00
On cover 1,700.
J27 D2 2fr brown 190.00 130.00
On cover *7,000.*
J28 D2 5fr brown 450.00 325.00
On cover —

1893-1941
J29 D2 5c blue ('94) .25 .30
Never hinged .55
On cover .80
J30 D2 10c brown .25 .30
Never hinged .55
On cover .80
J31 D2 15c lt grn ('94) 28.00 1.40
Never hinged 50.00
On cover 3.50
J32 D2 20c ol grn ('06) 6.50 .65
Never hinged 11.00
On cover 2.00
J33 D2 25c rose ('23) 6.50 3.75
Never hinged 11.00
On cover 6.75
J34 D2 30c red ('94) .25 .25
Never hinged .55
On cover .80
J35 D2 30c org red ('94) 475.00 85.00
Never hinged 875.00
J36 D2 40c rose ('25) 11.50 4.50
Never hinged 21.00
On cover 7.25
J37 D2 45c grn ('24) 9.00 5.25
Never hinged 19.00
On cover 8.75
J38 D2 50c brn vio ('95) .50 .30
Never hinged .85
On cover 1.20
a. 50c lilac .50 .30
Never hinged .85
On cover 1.20
J39 D2 60c bl grn ('25) 1.00 .55
Never hinged 1.60
On cover 1.20
J40 D2 1fr rose, *straw* ('96) 475.00 375.00
Never hinged 875.00
On cover 550.00
J41 D2 1fr red brn, *straw* ('20) 9.50 .30
Never hinged 19.00
On cover 1.20
J42 D2 1fr red brn ('35) 1.25 .40
Never hinged 2.25
On cover 1.20
J43 D2 2fr red org ('10) 225.00 65.00
Never hinged 425.00
On cover 150.00
J44 D2 2fr brt vio ('26) .65 *.75*
Never hinged 1.20
On cover 4.00
J45 D2 3fr magenta ('26) .65 *.75*
Never hinged 1.20
On cover 4.75
J45A D2 5fr red org ('41) 1.40 *2.25*
Never hinged 2.50
On cover 9.50

D3

1908-25
J46 D3 1c olive grn 1.00 *1.25*
Never hinged 2.10
On cover 9.50
J47 D3 10c violet 1.10 .30
Never hinged 2.60
On cover 5.50
a. Imperf., pair 175.00
Never hinged 275.00
J48 D3 20c bister ('19) 40.00 1.25
Never hinged 75.00
On cover 8.75
J49 D3 30c bister ('09) 14.00 .40
Never hinged 27.50
On cover 4.75
J50 D3 50c red ('09) 275.00 60.00
Never hinged 550.00
On cover 200.00
J51 D3 60c red ('25) 2.75 *3.75*
Never hinged 5.50
On cover 16.00
Nos. J46-J51 (6) 333.85 66.95

"Recouvrements" stamps were used to recover charges due on undelivered or refused mail which was returned to the sender.

For surcharges see Offices in Morocco Nos. J6-J9, J13-J16, J23-J26, J42-J45.

Nos. J49-J50 Surcharged

1917
J52 D3 20c on 30c bister 20.00 4.00
Never hinged 40.00
On cover 12.50
J53 D3 40c on 50c red 10.50 4.00
Never hinged 22.50
On cover 12.50
a. Double surcharge 475.00
Never hinged 600.00

In Jan. 1917 several values of the current issue of postage stamps were handstamped "T" in a triangle and used as postage due stamps.

Recouvrements Stamps of 1908-25 Surcharged

1926
J54 D3 50c on 10c lilac 3.50 3.25
Never hinged 6.75
On cover 12.50
J55 D3 60c on 1c ol grn 7.00 5.00
Never hinged 12.50
On cover 16.00
J56 D3 1fr on 60c red 18.00 10.00
Never hinged 35.00
On cover 32.50
J57 D3 2fr on 60c red 18.00 10.50
Never hinged 35.00
On cover 32.50
Nos. J54-J57 (4) 46.50 28.75

D4

1927-31
J58 D4 1c olive grn ('28) 1.00 1.00
Never hinged 1.90
On cover 8.00
J59 D4 10c rose ('31) 1.90 1.40
Never hinged 3.75
On cover 9.50
J60 D4 30c bister 4.50 .50
Never hinged 10.50
On cover 5.50
J61 D4 60c red 4.50 .50
Never hinged 10.50
On cover 4.75
J62 D4 1fr violet 14.00 3.25
Never hinged 27.50
On cover 16.00
J63 D4 1fr Prus grn ('31) 17.00 .55
Never hinged 35.00
On cover 7.25
J64 D4 2fr blue 80.00 42.50
Never hinged 175.00
On cover 110.00
J65 D4 2fr olive brn ('31) 150.00 26.00
Never hinged 275.00
On cover 92.50
Nos. J58-J65 (8) 272.90 75.70

Nos. J62 to J65 have the numerals of value double-lined.

Nos. J64, J62 Surcharged in Red or Black

1929
J66 D4 1.20fr on 2fr blue 42.50 11.00
Never hinged 105.00
On cover 40.00
J67 D4 5fr on 1fr vio (Bk) 65.00 15.00
Never hinged 140.00
On cover 47.50

No. J61 Surcharged

1931
J68 D4 1fr on 60c red 30.00 2.75
Never hinged 60.00
On cover 12.50

MILITARY STAMPS

Regular Issue Overprinted in Black or Red

1901-39 Unwmk. *Perf. 14x13½*
M1 A17 15c orange ('01) 65.00 6.00
Never hinged 160.00
On cover 20.00
a. Inverted overprint 300.00 150.00
b. Imperf., pair 425.00
M2 A19 15c pale red ('03) 65.00 6.00
Never hinged 200.00
On cover 16.00
M3 A20 15c slate grn ('04) 52.50 6.00
Never hinged 130.00
On cover 16.00
a. No period after "M" 110.00 57.50
Never hinged 190.00
b. Imperf., pair 290.00
Never hinged 400.00
M4 A20 10c rose ('06) 30.00 8.25
Never hinged 80.00
On cover 17.50
a. No period after "M" 82.50 45.00
Never hinged 150.00
b. Imperf., pair 350.00
Never hinged 475.00
M5 A22 10c red ('07) 1.75 1.00
Never hinged 2.75
On cover 4.75
a. Inverted overprint 105.00 65.00
Never hinged 140.00
b. Imperf., pair 190.00
Never hinged 275.00
M6 A20 50c vermilion ('29) 4.75 1.00
Never hinged 9.25
On cover 4.75
a. No period after "M" 32.50 18.00
Never hinged 55.00
b. Period in front of F 32.50 18.00
Never hinged 55.00
M7 A45 50c rose red ('34) 2.75 .55
Never hinged 7.25
On cover 4.00
a. No period after "M" 29.00 16.00
b. Inverted overprint 150.00 110.00
Never hinged 210.00
M8 A45 65c brt ultra (R) ('38) .30 .30
Never hinged .70
On cover 3.25
a. No period after "M" 29.00 16.00
Never hinged 45.00

M9 A45 90c ultra (R) ('39) .40 .35
Never hinged .70
On cover 12.00
Nos. M1-M9 (9) 222.45 29.45

"F. M." are initials of Franchise Militaire (Military Frank). See No. S1.

NEWSPAPER STAMPS

Coat of Arms — N1

1868 Unwmk. Typo. *Imperf.*
P1 N1 2c lilac 300.00 65.00
No gum 150.00
On newspaper 240.00
P2 N1 2c (+ 2c) blue 600.00 275.00
No gum 275.00
On newspaper *1,050.*

Perf. 12½
P3 N1 2c lilac 52.50 25.00
No gum 20.00
On newspaper 72.50
P4 N1 2c (+ 4c) rose 250.00 100.00
No gum 72.50
On newspaper 425.00
P5 N1 2c (+ 2c) blue 75.00 35.00
No gum 27.50
On newspaper 110.00
P6 N1 5c lilac 1,250. 550.00
No gum 400.00
On newspaper *3,500.*

Nos. P2, P4, and P5 were sold for face plus an added fiscal charge indicated in parenthesis. Nos. P1, P3 and P6 were used simply as fiscals.

The 2c rose and 5c lilac imperforate and the 5c rose and 5c blue, both imperforate and perforated, were never put into use.

Nos. P1-P6 were reprinted for the 1913 Ghent Exhibition and the 1937 Paris Exhibition (PEXIP).

No. 109 Surcharged in Red

1919 *Perf. 14x13½*
P7 A16 ½c on 1c gray .30 .30
Never hinged .65
On cover 35.00
On printed matter, single franking 600.00
a. Inverted surcharge 1,200. 1,150.
Never hinged 1,900.
b. Double surcharge *7,500.*

No. 156 Surcharged

1933
P8 A22 ½c on 1c olive bister .30 .30
Never hinged .65
a. ½c on 1c brown bister .55 *.80*
Never hinged 1.00

PARCEL POST STAMPS

Inscribed "I APPORT A LA GARE" — PP1

Perfs As Noted
1892 Unwmk. Typo.
Q1 PP1 25c brown, *yel*, perf 13½ 825.00 290.00
Never hinged 1,500.
Q2 PP1 25c brown, *yel*, perf 11 30.00 24.00
Never hinged 45.00
On postal document —
a. Printed on both sides 400.00
Never hinged 650.00

Inscribed "II VALEUR DECLAREE" — PP2

Q3 PP2 10c red, perf 13½ 1,000. 275.00
Never hinged 1,750.
On postal document 1,000.
Q4 PP2 10c red, perf 10x13½ 875.00 325.00
Never hinged 1,600.
Q5 PP2 10c org red, perf 11 30.00 14.00
Never hinged 42.50
On postal document 115.00
Q6 PP2 10c red, imperf 22.50 16.50
Never hinged 32.50
On postal document 140.00

Inscribed "III LIVRAISON PAR EXPRESS" — PP3

Q7 PP3 25c green, perf 13½ 57.50 32.50
Never hinged 115.00
On postal document 180.00
Q8 PP3 25c green, perf 11 45.00 24.00
Never hinged 70.00
On postal document 140.00

See Nos. Q22-Q26.

Locomotive — PP4

A set of six stamps, in the design above, was prepared in 1901 as postal tax stamps for expedited parcels but were not issued. All are perf 14x13½. Values: 5c gray, $3, never hinged $4; 10c yellow green, $3, never hinged $5; 20c rose, $20, never hinged $29; 50c blue, $7, never hinged $11.50; 1fr brown, $8, never hinged $12; 2fr brown red, $37.50, never hinged $57.50.

PP5

1918 *Perf. 11*
Type I: Large Trefoil Under "N" of "MAJORATION"
Q9 PP5 5c black 1.25 .85
Never hinged 2.00
On postal document 42.50
Q10 PP5 15c brn lilac 1.25 .85
Never hinged 2.00
On postal document 42.50

Imperforate
Q11 PP5 5c black 3.25 2.50
Never hinged 6.25
On postal document 42.50
Q12 PP5 15c brn lilac 9.00 4.25
Never hinged 14.00
On postal document 45.00
Nos. Q9-Q12 (4) 14.75 8.45

40c values, perforated 11 and imperf, in orange, were prepared but not issued. Value, perf or imperf, $375.

Type II: Small Trefoil Under "O" of "MAJORATION"
Perf. 11
Q13 PP5 5c black 140.00 45.00
Never hinged 275.00
On postal document 325.00
Q14 PP5 35c red 3.75 2.50
Never hinged 5.00
On postal document 37.50
Q15 PP5 50c vio blue 4.50 1.60
Never hinged 7.00
On postal document 45.00
Q16 PP5 1fr yellow 4.25 1.60
Never hinged 7.00
On postal document 50.00

Imperforate
Q17 PP5 5c black 130.00 45.00
Never hinged 260.00
On postal document 350.00
Q18 PP5 15c brn lilac 30.00 16.50
Never hinged 50.00
On postal document 90.00
Q19 PP5 35c red 3.25 2.50
Never hinged 6.75
On postal document 42.50
Q20 PP5 50c vio blue 24.00 14.00
Never hinged 40.00
On postal document 75.00
Q21 PP5 1fr yellow 18.50 12.50
Never hinged 30.00
On postal document 75.00
Nos. Q13-Q21 (9) 358.25 141.20

See Nos. Q41-Q44, Q143-Q145.
For surcharges, see Nos. Q28-Q40.

Type of 1892
1918-23 *Perf. 10½x11*
Q22 PP1 30c brn, *yel* 37.50 16.50
Never hinged 55.00
On postal document 140.00
a. Imperf 200.00
Never hinged 290.00
Q23 PP1 60c brn, *straw* ('23) 47.50 30.00
Never hinged 70.00
On postal document 180.00
a. Imperf 190.00
Never hinged 275.00
Q24 PP2 15c vermilion ('22) 16.00 11.00
Never hinged 23.00
On postal document 65.00
Q25 PP3 30c green 40.00 21.00
Never hinged 57.50
On postal document 140.00
a. Imperf 240.00
Never hinged 325.00
Q26 PP3 60c green ('23) 75.00 50.00
Never hinged 110.00
On postal document 325.00
Nos. Q22-Q26 (5) 216.00 128.50

PP6

1924, Oct. *Perf. 14*
Q27 PP6 15c rose & blue 4.00 3.75
Never hinged 5.00
a. Imperf 550.00
Never hinged 750.00

No. Q27 is a postal tax stamp, issued to show the collection of a new 15c excise fee on rail parcels. On July 3, 1925, its use was extended to all fiscal categories.

Surcharged in Black or Red (R) on Nos. Q9//Q16 and Types of 1918

1926 *Perf. 13*
Q28 PP5 20c on 2fr rose 1.90 1.10
Never hinged 2.75
On postal document 42.50
Q29 PP5 30c on 2fr yellow 1.90 1.10
Never hinged 2.75
On postal document 42.50
a. "0f30" omitted 190.00
Never hinged 250.00
Q30 PP5 40c on 3fr gray 1.90 1.40
Never hinged 2.75
On postal document 42.50
Q31 PP5 45c on 3fr orange 1.90 1.40
Never hinged 2.75
On postal document 42.50
a. Period after "f" omitted 19.00 19.00
Never hinged 30.00
Q32 PP5 95c on 1fr yel 8.00 2.75
Never hinged 12.50
On postal document 70.00
a. Imperf 90.00
Never hinged 150.00
Q33 PP5 1.35fr on 3fr vio 10.50 4.50
Never hinged 14.00
On postal document 70.00
a. Imperf 150.00
Never hinged 225.00
Q34 PP5 1.45fr on 5fr black (R) 1.90 1.00
Never hinged 2.75
On postal document 45.00
Q35 PP5 1.75fr on 2fr blue 10.50 4.50
Never hinged 14.00
On postal document 75.00
Q36 PP5 1.85fr on 10c orange 1.90 1.20
Never hinged 2.75
On postal document 50.00
Q37 PP5 1.95fr on 15c lilac ben 2.50 1.75
Never hinged 3.50
On postal document 50.00
a. Imperf 110.00
Never hinged 175.00
Q38 PP5 2.35fr on 25c green 1.90 1.00
Never hinged 2.75
On postal document 50.00
a. Imperf 110.00
Never hinged 175.00
Q39 PP5 2.90fr on 35c red 2.50 1.00
Never hinged 3.50
On postal document 50.00
a. Dots before and after "f" 140.00
Never hinged 200.00
b. Imperf 125.00
Never hinged 190.00
Q40 PP5 3.30fr on 50c blue violet (R) 2.50 1.25
Never hinged 3.50
On postal document 50.00
a. Double surcharge 250.00
Never hinged 375.00
b. Imperf 90.00
Never hinged 140.00
Nos. Q28-Q40 (13) 49.80 23.95

Type of 1918
1926 *Perf. 11*
Q41 PP5 10c orange 2.00 1.25
Never hinged 3.75
On postal document 42.50
a. Imperf 4.00
Never hinged 6.50
Q42 PP5 25c pale green 2.00 1.25
Never hinged 3.75
On postal document 42.50
a. Imperf 4.00
Never hinged 6.50
Q43 PP5 2fr pale blue 25.00 14.50
Never hinged 42.50
On postal document 130.00
a. Imperf 50.00
Never hinged 80.00
Q44 PP5 3fr violet 110.00 67.50
Never hinged 190.00
On postal document 325.00
a. Imperf 225.00
Never hinged 360.00
Nos. Q41-Q44 (4) 139.00 84.50

Inscribed "APPORT A LA GARE" — PP7

1926
Q45 PP7 1fr on 60c brn, *yel* 13.50 10.50
Never hinged 24.00
On postal document 75.00
a. Imperf 190.00
Never hinged 300.00
Q46 PP7 1fr brn, *yel* 17.50 13.00
Never hinged 30.00
On postal document 75.00
Q47 PP7 1.30fr on 1fr brn, *yel* 17.50 12.50
Never hinged 30.00
On postal document 80.00
Q48 PP7 1.50fr brn, *yel* 20.00 11.50
Never hinged 32.50
On postal document 75.00
Q49 PP7 1.65fr brn, *yel* 15.00 12.50
Never hinged 24.00
On postal document 75.00
Q50 PP7 1.90fr on 1fr brn, *yel* 17.50 12.50
Never hinged 30.00
On postal document 80.00
Q51 PP7 2.10fr on 1.65fr brn, *yel* 17.50 12.50
Never hinged 30.00
On postal document 80.00
Nos. Q45-Q51 (7) 118.50 85.00

See Nos. Q91-Q95, footnote following No. Q102, Q143-Q145.

For overprints and surcharges, see Nos. Q76-Q78, Q83-Q86, Q91-Q92, boxed note following Q95, Q96-Q99, Q107-QQ109, boxed note following Q159.

PP8

Type I Type II Type III

1926-38

Q52 PP8 15c brown, *yel*, type I 7.50 3.00
Never hinged 11.00
On postal document 55.00
a. Imperf 180.00
Never hinged 275.00
Q53 PP8 15c brown, *yel*, type II ('32) 8.00 4.25
Never hinged 11.50
On postal document 70.00
a. Type III ('38) 210.00
Never hinged 275.00
b. As "a," imperf 240.00
Never hinged 300.00

Nos. Q52-Q53a were issued for use in Paris only. No. Q53a was prepared but not issued.

Inscribed "VALEUR DECLAREE" — PP9

The additional numerals overprinted on Nos. Q56-Q63 and on Nos. Q72-Q75 indicate the weight category of the parcels being sent.

1926

Q54 PP9 50c on 15c red 3.00 1.60
Never hinged 5.00
On postal document 45.00
a. Imperf 180.00
Never hinged 275.00
Q55 PP9 50c red 750.00 750.00
Never hinged 1,200.
a. Imperf 1,200.
Never hinged 1,650.
Q56 PP9 50c red, ovptd. "1" 4.50 2.00
Never hinged 7.00
On postal document 45.00
a. Imperf 200.00
Never hinged 300.00
b. Double overprint "1" 300.00
Never hinged 400.00
Q57 PP9 55c on 15c red, ovptd. "1" 6.75 5.00
Never hinged 11.50
On postal document 50.00
a. Imperf 190.00 —
Never hinged
Q58 PP9 55c on 50c red, ovptd. "1" 6.75 5.00
Never hinged 11.50
On postal document 50.00
Q59 PP9 65c on 50c red 2.50 2.50
Never hinged 4.25
On postal document 40.00
Q60 PP9 65c on 50c red, ovptd. "1" 15.00 8.25
Never hinged 27.50
On postal document 45.00
Q61 PP9 1.50fr on 50c red, ovptd. "3" 7.00 5.00
Never hinged 12.00
On postal document 50.00
a. Imperf 275.00
Never hinged 375.00
Q62 PP9 2.00fr on 50c red, ovptd. "4" 8.25 3.75
Never hinged 14.00
On postal document 55.00
Q63 PP9 2.50fr on 50c red, ovptd. "5" 15.00 8.25
Never hinged 26.50
On postal document 75.00
Nos. Q54-Q63 (10) 818.75 791.35

See Nos. Q79, Q93, Q150-Q152.

For overprints and surcharges, see No. Q87, boxed note following No. Q95, Q100, Q110, Q123-Q124, Q138.

Inscribed "LIVRAISON PAR EXPRESS" — PP10

Q64 PP10 1.00fr on 60c grn 13.50 10.50
Never hinged 24.00
On postal document 75.00
a. Imperf 225.00
Never hinged 325.00
Q65 PP10 1.00fr green 125.00 75.00
Never hinged 250.00
On postal document —
Q66 PP10 1.30fr on 1fr grn 16.50 12.50
Never hinged 29.00
On postal document 85.00
Q67 PP10 1.50fr green 16.50 15.00
Never hinged 32.50
On postal document 70.00
Q68 PP10 1.65fr green 16.50 15.00
Never hinged 32.50
On postal document 70.00
Q69 PP10 1.90fr on 1.50fr grn 16.50 12.50
Never hinged 30.00
On postal document 85.00
Q70 PP10 2.10fr on 1.65fr grn 30.00 14.00
Never hinged 50.00
On postal document 85.00
Nos. Q64-Q70 (7) 234.50 154.50

For overprints and surcharges, see Nos. Q80-Q82, Q88-Q90, Q94, boxed note following Q95, Q101-Q105, Q111-Q113, Q125-Q132, Q139-Q141, Q146-Q149.

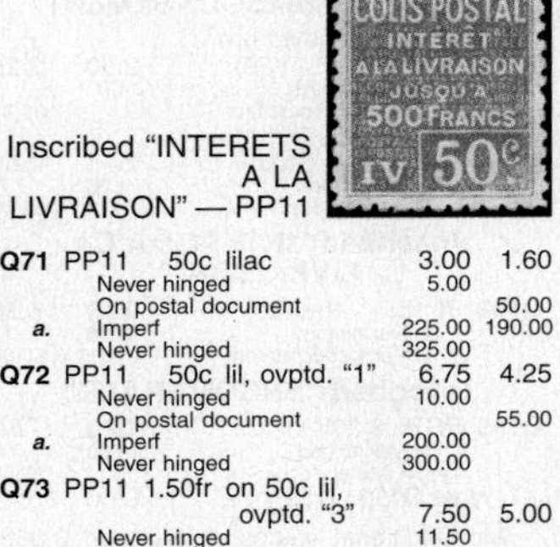

Inscribed "INTERETS A LA LIVRAISON" — PP11

Q71 PP11 50c lilac 3.00 1.60
Never hinged 5.00
On postal document 50.00
a. Imperf 225.00 190.00
Never hinged 325.00
Q72 PP11 50c lil, ovptd. "1" 6.75 4.25
Never hinged 10.00
On postal document 55.00
a. Imperf 200.00
Never hinged 300.00
Q73 PP11 1.50fr on 50c lil, ovptd. "3" 7.50 5.00
Never hinged 11.50
On postal document 55.00
a. Imperf 200.00
Never hinged 300.00
Q74 PP11 2.00fr on 50c lil ovptd. "4" 10.00 7.00
Never hinged 16.00
On postal document 75.00
Q75 PP11 2.50fr on 50c lil ovptd. "5" 10.00 7.00
Never hinged 16.50
On postal document 80.00
a. Imperf 210.00
Never hinged 310.00
Nos. Q71-Q75 (5) 37.25 24.85

1926 Issues Overprinted

1928

Inscribed "APPORT A LA GARE"

Q76 PP7 1.00fr brn, *yel* 16.50 14.00
Never hinged 25.00
On postal document 80.00
a. Imperf 190.00 190.00
Never hinged 300.00
Q77 PP7 1.50fr brn, *yel* 16.50 13.00
Never hinged 25.00
On postal document 80.00
Q78 PP7 1.65fr brn, *yel* 16.50 13.00
Never hinged 25.00
On postal document 80.00

Inscribed "VALEUR DECLAREE"

Q79 PP9 50c red 5.75 4.25
Never hinged 8.25
On postal document 45.00
a. Imperf 190.00 190.00
Never hinged 300.00
b. Inverted overprint 210.00
Never hinged 310.00

Inscribed "LIVRAISON PAR EXPRESS"

Q80 PP10 1.00fr green 17.00 13.50
Never hinged 26.00
On postal document 80.00
Q81 PP10 1.50fr green 17.00 13.50
Never hinged 26.00
On postal document 80.00
Q82 PP10 1.65fr green 17.00 13.50
Never hinged 27.50
On postal document 80.00
Nos. Q76-Q82 (7) 106.25 84.75

1926 Issues Surcharged

1928

Inscribed "APPORT A LA GARE"

Q83 PP7 1.45fr on 60c brn, *yel* 7.00 6.75
Never hinged 10.00
On postal document 55.00
Q84 PP7 1.45fr on 1fr brn, *yel* 40.00 32.50
Never hinged 70.00
On postal document 125.00
Q85 PP7 2.15fr on 1.50fr brn, *yel* 62.50 42.50
Never hinged 105.00
On postal document 200.00
Q86 PP7 2.35fr on 1.65fr brn, *yel* 62.50 42.50
Never hinged 105.00
On postal document 180.00

Inscribed "VALEUR DECLAREE"

Q87 PP9 75c on 50c red 2.10 1.60
Never hinged 3.25
On postal document 40.00
a. Imperf 210.00
Never hinged 400.00

Inscribed "LIVRAISON PAR EXPRESS"

Q88 PP10 1.45fr on 1fr green 62.50 42.50
Never hinged 105.00
On postal document 200.00
Q89 PP10 2.15fr on 1.50fr green 62.50 42.50
Never hinged 105.00
On postal document 200.00
Q90 PP10 2.35fr on 1.65fr green 62.50 42.50
Never hinged 105.00
On postal document 200.00
Nos. Q83-Q90 (8) 361.60 253.35

Types of 1926 and

PP12

1933-34

Inscribed "APPORT A LA GARE"

Q91 PP7 1.45fr brn, *yel* 55.00 25.00
Never hinged 82.50
On postal document 100.00
Q92 PP7 2.35fr brn, *yel* 1,400.
Never hinged 1,900.

A 2.15fr value, brown on yellow paper, was prepared but not issued without overprint or surcharge.

For overprints and surcharges, see Nos. Q96, Q98, Q99, Q107-Q109, Q115, Q116, Q118, Q120-Q122, Q135-Q137.

Inscribed "VALEUR DECLAREE"

Q93 PP9 75c red 18.00 3.25
Never hinged 22.50
On postal document 15.00
a. Imperf 180.00

For overprints and surcharges on No. Q93, see Nos. Q110, Q123, Q124, Q138.

A 1.15fr black in this design, imperf, was prepared but not issued. Value, $400.

Inscribed "LIVRAISON PAR EXPRESS"

Q94 PP10 1.45fr yel grn 450.00 300.00
Never hinged 675.00

Two other values, 2.15fr and 2.35fr were prepared but not issued without overprint or surcharge.

For overprints and surcharges, see Nos. Q101, Q103, Q105, Q111-Q113, Q125, Q126, Q128, Q130-Q132, Q139-Q141.

Inscribed "COLIS ENCOMBRANT"

Q95 PP12 2fr blue ('34) 45.00 21.00
Never hinged 70.00
On postal document 115.00

For overprints and surcharges, see Nos. Q106, Q114, Q133, Q134, Q142.

Nos. Q46, Q48, Q49, Q55, Q65, Q67 and Q68 overprinted "B" were not issued. Values: 1fr (No. Q46), $95; never hinged $130; 1.50fr (No. Q48), $95, never hinged $130; 1.65fr (No. Q49), $95, never hinged $130; 50c (No. Q55), $95, never hinged $130; 1fr (No. Q65), $92.50, never hinged $140; 1.50fr (No. Q67), $92.50, never hinged $140; 1.65fr (No. Q68), $92.50, never hinged $140.

Stamps and Types of 1926-34 Overprinted

1937

Inscribed "APPORT A LA GARE"

Q96 PP7 1.45fr brn, *yel* 6.75 6.75
Never hinged 10.00
On postal document 65.00
Q97 PP7 2.15fr on 1.50fr brn, *yel* 37.50 31.00
Never hinged 57.50
On postal document 150.00
Q98 PP7 2.15fr brn, *yel* 25.00 19.00
Never hinged 37.50
On postal document 125.00
Q99 PP7 2.35fr brn, *yel* 25.00 19.00
Never hinged 37.50
On postal document 125.00

Inscribed "VALEUR DECLAREE"

Q100 PP9 75c red 17.50 16.50
Never hinged 25.00
On postal document 95.00
a. Imperf 225.00
Never hinged 325.00

Inscribed "LIVRAISON PAR EXPRESS"

Q101 PP10 1.45fr green 17.50 16.50
Never hinged 25.00
On postal document 100.00
Q102 PP10 2.15fr on 1.50fr grn 17.50 16.50
Never hinged 25.00
On postal document 100.00
Q103 PP10 2.15fr green 42.50 30.00
Never hinged 67.50
On postal document 150.00
a. Imperf 210.00
Never hinged 315.00
Q104 PP10 2.35fr on 1.65fr grn 250.00 110.00
Never hinged 350.00
On postal document —
Q105 PP10 2.35fr green 17.50 12.50
Never hinged 26.00
On postal document 100.00

Inscribed "COLIS ENCOMBRANT"

Q106 PP12 2fr blue 37.50 35.00
Never hinged 57.50
On postal document 180.00
Nos. Q96-Q106 (11) 494.25 312.75

For overprints and surcharges, see Nos. Q146-Q149.

Types of 1933-34 Surcharged

1937

Inscribed "APPORT A LA GARE"

Q107 PP7 1.85fr on 1.45fr brn, *yel* 15.00 12.50
Never hinged 26.00
On postal document 57.50
Q108 PP7 2.75fr on 2.15fr brn, *yel* 26.00 17.50
Never hinged 45.00
On postal document 125.00
Q109 PP7 3.05fr on 2.55fr brn, *yel* 50.00 26.00
Never hinged 90.00
On postal document 140.00

Inscribed "VALEUR DECLAREE"

Q110 PP9 .95fr on 75c red 42.50 25.00
Never hinged 67.50
On postal document 125.00

Inscribed "LIVRAISON PAR EXPRESS"

Q111 PP10 1.85fr on 1.45fr grn 70.00 45.00
Never hinged 120.00
On postal document 210.00
Q112 PP10 2.75fr on 2.15fr grn 70.00 45.00
Never hinged 120.00
On postal document 210.00
Q113 PP10 3.05fr on 2.35fr grn 70.00 45.00
Never hinged 120.00
On postal document 210.00

Inscribed "COLIS ENCOMBRANT"

Q114 PP12 2.60fr on 2fr bl 17.50 17.50
Never hinged 26.00
On postal document 85.00
Nos. Q107-Q114 (8) 361.00 233.50

Stamps and Types of 1926-34 Overprinted

1937

Inscribed "APPORT A LA GARE"

Q115 PP7 1.45fr brn, *yel* 3.00 2.50
Never hinged 4.50
On postal document 45.00
Q116 PP7 1.85fr on 1.45fr brn, *yel* 3.00 2.50
Never hinged 4.50
On postal document 45.00
Q117 PP7 2.15fr on 1.50fr brn, *yel* 2.50 2.50
Never hinged 4.25
On postal document 45.00
Q118 PP7 2.15fr brn, *yel* 42.50 35.00
Never hinged 62.50
On postal document 140.00
Q119 PP7 2.35fr on 1.65fr brn, *yel* 575.00 475.00
Never hinged 800.00
On postal document —
Q120 PP7 2.35fr brn, *yel* 3.00 2.50
Never hinged 4.50
On postal document 45.00
Q121 PP7 2.75fr on 2.15fr brn, *yel* 3.25 2.50
Never hinged 5.75
On postal document 45.00
Q122 PP7 3.05fr on 2.35fr brn, *yel* 6.50 6.25
Never hinged 10.00
On postal document 50.00

Inscribed "VALEUR DECLAREE"

Q123 PP9 75c red 3.75 3.50
Never hinged 5.50
On postal document 45.00
a. Pair, one without overprint 225.00
Never hinged 350.00
Q124 PP9 95c on 75c red 3.00 3.00
Never hinged 3.75
On postal document 45.00

Inscribed "LIVRAISON PAR EXPRESS"

Q125 PP10 1.45fr green 4.25 3.25
Never hinged 6.25
On postal document 42.50
Q126 PP10 1.85fr on 1.45fr brn, *yel* 5.75 4.25
Never hinged 8.25
On postal document 50.00
Q127 PP10 2.15fr on 1.50fr grn 375.00 325.00
Never hinged 500.00
On postal document —
Q128 PP10 2.15fr green 18.50 16.50
Never hinged 27.50
On postal document 95.00
Q129 PP10 2.35fr on 1.65fr grn 675.00 725.00
Never hinged 775.00
On postal document —
Q130 PP10 2.35fr green 11.00 10.50
Never hinged 15.00
On postal document 62.50
Q131 PP10 2.75fr on 2.15fr grn 35.00 45.00
Never hinged 55.00
On postal document 115.00
Q132 PP10 3.05fr on 2.35fr grn 35.00 45.00
Never hinged 55.00
On postal document 115.00

Inscribed "COLIS ENCOMBRANT"

Q133 PP12 2fr blue 3.00 2.10
Never hinged 4.50
On postal document 50.00
a. Pair, imperf between 130.00
Never hinged 210.00
Q134 PP12 2.60fr on 2fr bl 3.25 2.50
Never hinged 5.50
On postal document 50.00
Nos. Q115-Q134 (20) 1,811. 1,714.

For additional surcharges, see Nos. Q146-Q149.

Stamps and Types of 1933-34 Surcharged

1938

Inscribed "APPORT A LA GARE"

Q135 PP7 2.30fr on 1.45fr brn, *yel* 3.75 3.00
Never hinged 5.50
On postal document 42.50
Q136 PP7 3.45fr on 2.15fr brn, *yel* 3.75 3.00
Never hinged 5.50
On postal document 42.50
Q137 PP7 3.85fr on 1.45fr brn, *yel* 3.75 3.00
Never hinged 5.50
On postal document 42.50

Inscribed "VALEUR DECLAREE"

Q138 PP9 1.15fr on 75c red 1.60 1.60
Never hinged 2.50
On postal document 42.50

Inscribed "LIVRAISON PAR EXPRESS"

Q139 PP10 2.30fr on 1.45fr grn 3.75 3.00
Never hinged 5.50
On postal document 45.00
Q140 PP10 3.45fr on 2.15fr grn 3.75 3.00
Never hinged 5.50
On postal document 45.00
Q141 PP10 3.85fr on 2.35fr grn 3.75 3.00
Never hinged 5.50
On postal document 45.00

Inscribed "COLIS ENCOMBRANT"

Q142 PP12 3.25fr on 2fr bl 1.60 1.60
Never hinged 2.50
On postal document 50.00
Nos. Q135-Q142 (8) 25.70 21.20

For Nos. Q135-Q138, Q140-Q142 overprinted "E," see editor's note following No. Q159.

Type of 1918

1938 ***11, Imperf (#Q161)***

Q143 PP5 10c gray black 17.50 16.00
Never hinged 26.00
On postal document 350.00
a. Imperf 26.00
Never hinged 42.50
Q144 PP5 20c brown lilac 17.50 16.00
Never hinged 26.00
On postal document 400.00
a. Imperf 42.50
Never hinged 62.50
Q145 PP5 25c green, imperf *50.00* *20.00*
Never hinged *80.00*
Nos. Q143-Q145 (3) 85.00 52.00

Two additional values, a 10c rose lilac and a 15c ultramarine, were prepared with this set but not issued. Values, each stamp: $90, never hinged $150. Both stamps also exist imperf. Values, each: $82.50; never hinged $150.

Nos. Q103, Q105, Q112, Q113 Overprinted

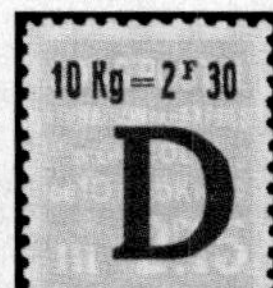

1938 ***Perf. 11***

Q146 PP10 2.30fr on 2.15fr green 62.50 62.50
Never hinged 80.00
On postal document 250.00
Q147 PP10 2.30fr on 2.35fr green 62.50 62.50
Never hinged 80.00
On postal document 250.00
Q148 PP10 2.30fr on 2.75fr on 2.15fr green 125.00 100.00
Never hinged 175.00
On postal document 350.00
Q149 PP10 2.30fr on 3.05fr on 2.35fr green 125.00 100.00
Never hinged 175.00
On postal document 350.00
Nos. Q146-Q149 (4) 375.00 325.00

Types of 1926 and

PP13

PP14

PP15

PP16

1938-39

Inscribed "VALEUR DECLAREE"

Q150 PP9 1fr red ('39) 2.50 2.50
Never hinged 4.00
On postal document 35.00
Q151 PP9 1.15fr red 1.25 1.25
Never hinged 2.10
On postal document 40.00
Imperf 140.00
Never hinged 225.00
Q152 PP9 5fr red ('39) 2.50 *2.75*
Never hinged 4.00
On postal document 40.00

Inscribed "AU DESSUS DE 10"

Q153 PP13 2.40fr brown, *yel* 2.50 *2.75*
Never hinged 4.00
On postal document 37.50
Q154 PP13 3.50fr brown, *yel* 2.50 *2.75*
Never hinged 4.00
On postal document 37.50
Q155 PP13 3.80fr brown, *yel* 2.50 *2.75*
Never hinged 4.00
On postal document 37.50
Imperf 125.00
Never hinged 190.00

Inscribed "REMBOURSEMENT"

Q156 PP14 2.50fr yel grn ('39) 2.50 2.25
Never hinged 4.00
On postal document 35.00
Q157 PP14 7.50fr yel grn ('39) 2.75 2.50
Never hinged 4.25
On postal document 35.00

Inscribed "INTERET A LA LIVRAISON"

Q158 PP15 1fr lilac ('39) 9.50 6.75
Never hinged 14.00
On postal document 50.00

Inscribed "ENCOMBRANT"

Q159 PP16 3.20fr blue 11.00 7.50
Never hinged 16.00
On postal document 55.00
Nos. Q150-Q159 (10) 39.50 33.75

Two additional values, 3.45fr and 3.85fr, type PP7, brown on yellow paper, imperforate, were prepared but not issued. Values, each: $140; never hinged, $225.

Nos. Nos. Q135-Q138, Q140-Q142 were overprinted "E" in 1939, in anticipation of new rates to take effect April 1, but were not issued. Values: 2.30fr on 1.45fr, $675, never hinged $1,000; 3.45fr on 2.15fr, $875, never hinged $1,300; 3.85fr on 2.35fr, $875, never hinged $1,300; 1.15fr on 75c, $300, never hinged $450; 3.45fr on 2.15fr, $2,800, never hinged $4,000; 3.85fr on 2.35fr, $2,800, never hinged $4,000; 3.25fr on 2fr, $675, never hinged $1,000.

FRANCHISE STAMPS

No. 276 Overprinted "F"

1939 **Unwmk.** ***Perf. 14x13½***

S1 A45 90c ultramarine 1.90 *2.50*
Never hinged 2.75
On cover 16.00
a. Period following "F" 30.00 30.00
Never hinged 50.00

No. S1 was for the use of Spanish refugees in France. "F" stands for "Franchise."

OCCUPATION STAMPS

FRANCO-PRUSSIAN WAR
Issued under German Occupation (Alsace and Lorraine)

OS1

1870 **Typo.** **Unwmk.** ***Perf. 13½x14***

Network with Points Up

N1 OS1 1c bronze green 75.00 *100.00*
Never hinged 110.00
On cover 215.00
On cover, single franking —
a. 1c olive grn 75.00 *100.00*
Never hinged 110.00
On cover 215.00
On cover, single franking —
N2 OS1 2c dark brown 125.00 *175.00*
Never hinged 180.00
On cover 315.00
On cover, single franking 950.00
a. 2c red brown 115.00 *175.00*
Never hinged 170.00
On cover 315.00
On cover, single franking 950.00
N3 OS1 4c gray 135.00 100.00
Never hinged 190.00
On cover 215.00
On cover, single franking 650.00
N4 OS1 5c yel grn 125.00 14.00
Never hinged 180.00
On cover 82.50
On cover, single franking 150.00
a. 5c deep green 130.00 15.00
Never hinged 190.00
On cover 87.50
On cover, single franking 160.00
N5 OS1 10c bistre brn 110.00 5.75
Never hinged 160.00
On cover 40.00
On cover, single franking 45.00
a. 10c yellow brown 110.00 6.50
Never hinged 160.00
On cover 45.00
On cover, single franking 50.00
b. Network lemon yellow 135.00 10.00
Never hinged 200.00
On cover 90.00
On cover, single franking 100.00
N6 OS1 20c ultra 115.00 16.50
Never hinged 170.00
On cover 65.00
On cover, single franking 77.50
a. 20c milky blue 115.00 15.00
Never hinged 170.00
On cover 70.00
On cover, single franking 82.50
N7 OS1 25c brown 150.00 100.00
Never hinged 215.00
On cover 275.00
On cover, single franking 325.00
a. 25c black brown 145.00 100.00
Never hinged 210.00
On cover 275.00
On cover, single franking 325.00

There are three varieties of the 4c and two of the 10c, differing in the position of the figures of value, and several other setting varieties.

Network with Points Down

N8 OS1 1c olive grn 350.00 *625.00*
Never hinged 550.00
On cover 1,600.
N9 OS1 2c red brn 150.00 *550.00*
Never hinged 250.00
On cover 1,100.
On cover, single franking 2,000.
N10 OS1 4c gray 150.00 200.00
Never hinged 250.00
On cover 350.00
On cover, single franking 825.00
N11 OS1 5c yel grn 6,500. 650.00
Never hinged —
On cover 1,750.
On cover, single franking 2,600.
N12 OS1 10c bister 150.00 21.50
Never hinged 250.00
On cover 100.00
On cover, single franking 115.00
a. Network lemon yellow 225.00 50.00
Never hinged 300.00
On cover 200.00
On cover, single franking 250.00
N13 OS1 20c ultra 225.00 90.00
Never hinged 300.00
On cover 250.00
On cover, single franking 275.00
N14 OS1 25c brown 450.00 300.00
Never hinged 650.00
On cover 650.00
On cover, single franking 825.00

Official imitations have the network with points downward. The "P" of "Postes" is 2½mm from the border in the imitations and 3mm in the originals.

The word "Postes" measures 12¾ to 13mm on the imitations, and from 11 to 12½mm on the originals.

The imitations are perf. 13½x14½; originals, perf. 13½x14¼.

The stamps for Alsace and Lorraine were replaced by stamps of the German Empire on Jan. 1, 1872.

WORLD WAR I
German Stamps of 1905-16 Surcharged

1916 **Wmk. 125** ***Perf. 14, 14½***

N15 A16 3c on 3pf brown 1.25 1.25
Never hinged 2.90
On cover 100.00
N16 A16 5c on 5pf green 1.25 1.25
Never hinged 2.90
On cover 100.00
N17 A22 8c on 7½pf org 2.00 2.00
Never hinged 3.75
On cover 105.00
N18 A16 10c on 10pf car 2.00 2.00
Never hinged 3.75
On cover 100.00
N19 A22 15c on 15pf yel brn 1.25 1.25
Never hinged 2.90
On cover 100.00

N20 A16 25c on 20pf blue 1.25 1.25
Never hinged 2.90
On cover 100.00
a. 25c on 20pf ultramarine 2.00 2.00
Never hinged 5.25
On cover 160.00
N21 A16 40c on 30pf org & blk, *buff* 2.90 2.75
Never hinged 6.00
On cover 180.00
N22 A16 50c on 40pf lake & blk 2.90 2.75
Never hinged 7.00
On cover 250.00
N23 A16 75c on 60pf mag 12.50 12.50
Never hinged 35.00
On cover 600.00
N24 A16 1fr on 80pf lake & blk, *rose* 12.50 12.50
Never hinged 35.00
On cover 600.00

N25 A17 1fr25c on 1m car 47.50 47.50
Never hinged 150.00
a. Double surcharge —
N26 A21 2fr50c on 2m gray bl 47.50 47.50
Never hinged 150.00
a. Double surcharge —
Nos. N15-N26 (12) 134.80 134.50

These stamps were also used in parts of Belgium occupied by the German forces.

Catalogue values for unused stamps in this section, from this point to the end of the section, are for Never Hinged items.

WORLD WAR II
Alsace
Issued under German Occupation

Values for unused copies of N27-N58 are for never hinged stamps.

Stamps of Germany 1933-36 Overprinted in Black

1940 Wmk. 237 *Perf. 14*

N27 A64 3pf olive bister .80 *.55*
On cover 4.00
On cover, single franking 12.50
N28 A64 4pf dull blue .80 *.55*
On cover 4.00
On cover, single franking 20.00
N29 A64 5pf brt green .80 *.55*
On cover 3.25
On cover, single franking 20.00
N30 A64 6pf dark green .80 *.55*
On cover 2.75
On cover, single franking —
a. Inverted overprint 1,500.
N31 A64 8pf vermilion .80 *.55*
On cover .40
On cover, single franking 12.50
a. Inverted overprint 4,000.
N32 A64 10pf chocolate .80 *.55*
On cover 5.00
On cover, single franking 82.50
N33 A64 12pf dp carmine 1.00 *.55*
On cover 3.75
On cover, single franking —
N34 A64 15pf maroon 1.00 *.55*
On cover 8.25
On cover, single franking 77.50
N35 A64 20pf brt blue 1.65 *.75*
On cover 11.50
On cover, single franking 50.00
N36 A64 25pf ultra 1.65 *.75*
On cover 11.50
On cover, single franking 40.00
N37 A64 30pf olive grn 1.65 *.75*
On cover 12.50
On cover, single franking 82.50
N38 A64 40pf red violet 2.90 *1.00*
On cover 16.50
On cover, single franking 40.00
N39 A64 50pf dk grn & blk 7.00 *3.25*
On cover 29.00
On cover, single franking 50.00
N40 A64 60pf claret & blk 7.00 *3.25*
On cover 29.00
On cover, single franking 50.00
N41 A64 80pf dk blue & blk 17.50 *7.00*
On cover 52.50
On cover, single franking 65.00
N42 A64 100pf orange & blk 17.50 7.00
On cover 62.50
On cover, single franking 125.00
Nos. N27-N42 (16) 63.65 28.15

Lorraine
Issued under German Occupation

Stamps of Germany 1933-36 Overprinted in Black

1940 Wmk. 237 *Perf. 14*

N43 A64 3pf olive bister 1.00 .75
On cover 5.00
On cover, single franking 14.00
N44 A64 4pf dull blue 1.00 .75
On cover 5.00
On cover, single franking 22.00
N45 A64 5pf brt green 1.00 *4.00*
On cover 22.50
On cover, single franking —
N46 A64 6pf dark green 1.00 .75
On cover 3.75
On cover, single franking —
N47 A64 8pf vermilion 1.00 .75
On cover 5.00
On cover, single franking 14.00
N48 A64 10pf chocolate 1.50 .85
On cover 6.00
On cover, single franking 90.00
N49 A64 12pf deep carmine 1.50 .85
On cover 3.75
On cover, single franking —
N50 A64 15pf maroon 1.50 .75
On cover 10.00
On cover, single franking 90.00
a. Inverted surcharge —
N51 A64 20pf brt blue 1.65 1.00
On cover 12.50
On cover, single franking 52.50
N52 A64 25pf ultra 1.40 1.00
On cover 12.50
On cover, single franking 45.00
N53 A64 30pf olive grn 2.10 1.00
On cover 14.00
On cover, single franking 90.00
N54 A64 40pf red violet 2.50 1.25
On cover 18.00
On cover, single franking 45.00
N55 A64 50pf dk grn & blk 6.00 3.00
On cover 27.50
On cover, single franking 52.50
N56 A64 60pf claret & blk 6.00 3.00
On cover 27.50
On cover, single franking 52.50
N57 A64 80pf dk blue & blk 18.00 7.50
On cover 60.00
On cover, single franking 75.00
N58 A64 100pf orange & blk 18.00 7.50
On cover 65.00
On cover, single franking 125.00
Nos. N43-N58 (16) 65.15 *34.70*

Besetztes Gebiet Nordfrankreich
These three words, in a rectangular frame covering two stamps, were handstamped in black on Nos. 267, 367 and 369 and used in the Dunkerque region in July-August, 1940. The German political officer of Dunkerque authorized the overprint. The prevalence of forgeries and later favor overprints make expertization mandatory.

FRANCE OFFICES ABROAD

OFFICES IN CHINA

Prior to 1923 several of the world powers maintained their own post offices in China for the purpose of sending and receiving overseas mail. French offices were maintained in Canton, Hoi Hao (Hoihow), Kwangchowan (Kouangtchéou-wan), Mongtseu (Mong-tseu), Packhoi (Paknoi), Tong King (Tchongking), Yunnan Fou (Yunnanfu).

100 Centimes = 1 Franc
100 Cents = 1 Piaster
100 Cents = 1 Dollar

Peace and Commerce Stamps of France Ovptd. in Red, Carmine or Black

1894-1900 Unwmk. *Perf. 14x13½*

1 A15 5c green, *greenish* (R) 3.25 3.00
Never hinged 7.25
On cover 50.00
a. 5c green, *greenish* (C) 1.25 1.10
Never hinged 5.75
On cover 50.00
2 A15 5c yel grn, I (R) ('00) 4.25 3.00
Never hinged 7.50
On cover 50.00
a. Type II 47.50 32.50
Never hinged 105.00
On cover 350.00
3 A15 10c blk, *lav*, I (R) 9.25 3.00
Never hinged 17.00
On cover 32.50
a. Type II 27.50 *17.50*
On cover 190.00
b. Type II (C) 17.50 11.00
On cover 140.00
4 A15 15c bl (R) 12.50 4.25
Never hinged 26.00
On cover 32.50
a. Black overprint —
b. Carmine overprint 12.50 4.00
Never hinged 26.00
On cover 32.50
5 A15 20c red, *grn* 7.50 5.00
Never hinged 15.00
On cover 60.00
On cover, single franking 160.00
6 A15 25c blk, *rose* (C) 9.25 2.50
Never hinged 17.50
On cover 52.50
On cover, single franking 70.00
a. Double overprint 225.00
b. Pair, one without overprint 550.00
c. Red overprint 17.50 3.25
Never hinged 40.00
d. Imperf 120.00 45.00
Never hinged 260.00
7 A15 30c brn, *bis* 9.25 6.25
Never hinged 18.00
On cover 72.50
On cover, single franking 90.00
8 A15 40c red, *straw* 9.25 7.50
Never hinged 18.00
On cover 85.00
On cover, single franking 175.00
9 A15 50c car, *rose*, I 26.00 17.50
Never hinged 52.50
On cover 150.00
On cover, single franking 200.00
a. Carmine overprint 62.50
Never hinged 115.00
b. Type II (Bk) 25.00 16.00
Never hinged 60.00
On cover 200.00
On cover, single franking 325.00
10 A15 75c dp vio, *org* (R) 80.00 60.00
Never hinged 160.00
On cover 525.00
On cover, single franking 900.00
a. Carmine overprint 80.00 60.00
Never hinged 160.00
On cover 525.00
On cover, single franking 900.00
11 A15 1fr brnz grn, *straw* 17.00 8.50
Never hinged 37.50
On cover 200.00
On cover, single franking 275.00
a. Double overprint 425.00 *450.00*
12 A15 2fr brn, *az* ('00) 30.00 29.00
Never hinged 65.00
On cover 400.00
On cover, single franking 650.00
12A A15 5fr red lil, *lav* 75.00 60.00
Never hinged 160.00
On cover 650.00
On cover, single franking 1,050.
b. Red overprint 525.00
Never hinged —
Nos. 1-12A (13) 292.50 209.50

For surcharges and overprints see Nos. 13-17, J7-J10, J20-J23.

Stamps of Indo-China Surcharged in Black

Two types of Nos. 18-33: type I, 13mmx3mm, "C" and "H" wide, "E" with fine serifs; type II, 12½mmx2¾mm, "C" and "H" narrower, "E" with heavy serifs.

1902-04

Type I ('02)

18 A3 1c blk, *lil bl* 4.00 4.00
Never hinged 8.00
On cover 110.00
19 A3 2c brn, *buff* 4.25 4.25
Never hinged 8.00
On cover 110.00
20 A3 4c claret, *lav* 5.50 5.50
Never hinged 12.00
On cover 110.00
21 A3 5c yellow grn 6.50 5.50
Never hinged 14.00
On cover 85.00
22 A3 10c red 6.75 6.00
Never hinged 14.00
On cover 75.00
23 A3 15c gray 7.50 6.75
Never hinged 16.00
On cover 70.00
24 A3 20c red, *grn* 18.00 16.00
Never hinged 42.50
On cover 210.00
On cover, single franking 375.00
25 A3 25c blk, *rose* 16.00 12.50
Never hinged 37.50
On cover 160.00
On cover, single franking 225.00
27 A3 30c brn, *bis* 27.50 27.50
Never hinged 70.00
On cover 325.00
On cover, single franking 450.00
28 A3 40c red, *straw* 60.00 50.00
Never hinged 150.00
On cover 700.00
On cover, single franking 1,000.
29 A3 50c car, *rose* 67.50 67.50
Never hinged 160.00
On cover 1,000.
On cover, single franking 1,250.
31 A3 75c vio, *org* 60.00 60.00
Never hinged 150.00
On cover 1,100.
On cover, single franking 1,600.
32 A3 1fr brnz grn, *straw* 87.50 87.50
Never hinged 210.00
On cover 1,200.
On cover, single franking 2,000.
33 A3 5fr red lil, *lavender* 110.00 110.00
Never hinged 260.00
On cover 1,300.
On cover, single franking 2,400.
Nos. 18-33 (14) 481.00 463.00

Type II ('04)

18a A3 1c blk, *lil bl* 2.50 2.50
Never hinged 4.75
On cover 62.50
19a A3 2c brn, *buff* 8.25 7.25
Never hinged 17.50
On cover 100.00
20a A3 4c claret, *lav* 4.25 3.40
Never hinged 8.00
On cover 65.00
21a A3 5c yellow grn 5.00 3.40
Never hinged 8.50
On cover 50.00
22a A3 10c red 8.50 8.00
Never hinged 17.50
On cover 65.00
24a A3 20c red, *grn* 9.25 8.50
Never hinged 17.50
On cover 65.00
25a A3 25c blk, *rose* 12.50 12.50
Never hinged 22.50
On cover 100.00
On cover, single franking 150.00
26 A3 25c blue 10.00 8.50
Never hinged 20.00
On cover 75.00
On cover, single franking 110.00
27a A3 30c brn, *bis* 9.25 8.50
Never hinged 17.50
On cover 75.00
On cover, single franking 100.00
28a A3 40c red, *straw* 25.00 21.00
Never hinged 47.50
On cover 110.00
On cover, single franking 160.00
30 A3 50c brn, *azure* 10.00 9.25
Never hinged 20.00
On cover 125.00
On cover, single franking 210.00
31a A3 75c vio, *org* 40.00 37.50
Never hinged 75.00
On cover 325.00
On cover, single franking 525.00
32a A3 1fr brnz grn, *straw* 45.00 42.50
Never hinged 85.00
On cover 475.00
On cover, single franking 625.00
33a A3 5fr red lil, *lavender* 97.50 90.00
Never hinged 180.00
On cover 625.00
On cover, single franking 1,200.
Nos. 18a-33a (14) 287.00 262.80

The Chinese characters surcharged on Nos. 18-33 are the Chinese equivalents of the French values and therefore differ on each denomination. Many varieties of surcharge exist.

No. 11 Surcharged in Black

13 A15 25c on 1fr brnz grn, *straw* 125.00 75.00
On cover 625.00
On cover, single franking 1,050.

No. 6 Surcharged in Red

1901

14 A15 2c on 25c blk, *rose* 1,100. 340.00
On cover *1,900.*
15 A15 4c on 25c blk, *rose* 1,350. 450.00
On cover *2,250.*
16 A15 6c on 25c blk, *rose* 1,100. 375.00
On cover *1,900.*
17 A15 16c on 25c blk, *rose* 325.00 200.00
On cover *1,250.*
a. Black surcharge *7,250.*
Nos. 14-17 (4) 3,875. 1,365.

Liberty, Equality and Fraternity
A3

"Rights of Man"
A4

A5

1902-03 **Typo.**

34 A3 5c green 6.00 3.75
Never hinged 9.50
On cover 65.00
35 A4 10c rose red ('03) 3.00 2.10
Never hinged 5.50
On cover 40.00
36 A4 15c pale red 3.00 2.10
Never hinged 5.50
On cover 32.50
37 A4 20c brn vio ('03) 8.50 7.25
Never hinged 16.00
On cover 100.00
On cover, single franking 150.00
38 A4 25c blue ('03) 6.75 3.40
Never hinged 13.50
On cover 50.00
On cover, single franking 70.00
39 A4 30c lilac ('03) 9.25 7.50
Never hinged 16.00
On cover 50.00
On cover, single franking 80.00
40 A5 40c red & pale bl 19.00 16.00
Never hinged 35.00
On cover 110.00
On cover, single franking 150.00
41 A5 50c bis brn & lav 23.00 19.00
Never hinged 47.50
On cover 125.00
On cover, single franking 200.00
42 A5 1fr claret & ol grn 30.00 19.00
Never hinged 60.00
On cover 150.00
On cover, single franking 250.00
43 A5 2fr gray vio & yel 62.50 45.00
Never hinged 125.00
On cover 325.00
On cover, single franking 475.00
44 A5 5fr dk bl & buff 92.50 72.50
Never hinged 175.00
On cover 400.00
On cover, single franking 625.00
Nos. 34-44 (11) 263.50 197.60

For surcharges and overprints see Nos. 45, 57-85, J14-J16, J27-J30.

Surcharged in Black

1903

45 A4 5c on 15c pale red 17.50 12.00
Never hinged 32.50
On cover 90.00
a. Inverted surcharge 135.00 75.00
Never hinged 250.00

Stamps of Indo-China, 1904-06, Surcharged as Nos. 18-33 in Black

Two types of overprint on 15c: type I, "China" above Chinese characters (2nd printing); type II, "China" below Chinese characters (1st printing).

1904-05

46 A4 1c olive grn 2.10 2.10
Never hinged 3.25
On cover 70.00
47 A4 2c vio brn, *buff* 2.10 2.10
Never hinged 3.25
On cover 70.00
47A A4 4c cl, *bluish* 975.00 800.00
On cover *2,250.*
48 A4 5c deep grn 2.10 2.10
Never hinged 3.25
On cover 30.00
49 A4 10c carmine 3.00 3.00
Never hinged 4.75
On cover 40.00
50 A4 15c org brn, *bl* (I) 3.00 3.00
Never hinged 4.50
On cover 50.00
a. Type II 4.00 2.90
Never hinged 7.25
On cover 55.00
51 A4 20c red, *grn* 11.50 11.00
Never hinged 19.00
On cover 80.00
On cover, single franking 125.00
52 A4 25c deep blue 10.00 6.00
Never hinged 17.50
On cover 50.00
On cover, single franking 80.00
53 A4 40c blk, *bluish* 8.50 6.00
Never hinged 15.00
On cover 50.00
On cover, single franking 80.00
54 A4 1fr pale grn 360.00 300.00
On cover 1,100.
On cover, single franking 1,750.
55 A4 2fr brn, *org* 42.50 37.50
Never hinged 75.00
On cover 325.00
On cover, single franking 750.00
56 A4 10fr org brn, *grn* 165.00 155.00
Never hinged 300.00
On cover 900.00
On cover, single franking 1,750.
Nos. 46-56 (12) 1,585. 1,328.

Many varieties of the surcharge exist.

Stamps of 1902-03 Surcharged in Black

1907

57 A3 2c on 5c green 2.50 1.60
Never hinged 4.00
On cover 30.00
a. Perf 11 160.00
Never hinged 260.00
58 A4 4c on 10c rose red 2.50 1.75
Never hinged 4.00
On cover 30.00
a. Pair, one without surcharge —
b. Perf 11 160.00
Never hinged 260.00
59 A4 6c on 15c pale red 3.40 2.50
Never hinged 5.25
On cover 40.00
60 A4 8c on 20c brn vio 6.00 6.00
Never hinged 11.00
On cover 80.00
a. "8" inverted 75.00 75.00
Never hinged 150.00
61 A4 10c on 25c blue 2.10 1.25
Never hinged 3.50
On cover 30.00
62 A5 20c on 50c bis brn & lav 6.25 3.75
Never hinged 12.00
On cover 50.00
a. Double surcharge
b. Triple surcharge 440.00 440.00
63 A5 40c on 1fr claret & ol grn 22.00 13.50
Never hinged 40.00
On cover 100.00
64 A5 2pi on 5fr dk bl & buff 23.00 13.50
Never hinged 40.00
On cover 125.00
a. Double surcharge *2,300.* *1,900.*
Nos. 57-64 (8) 67.75 43.85

Stamps of 1902-03 Surcharged in Black

1911-22

65 A3 2c on 5c green 2.10 1.50
Never hinged 3.50
On cover 30.00
66 A4 4c on 10c rose red 2.50 1.75
Never hinged 4.75
On cover 30.00
67 A4 6c on 15c org 5.00 2.10
Never hinged 8.50
On cover 40.00
68 A4 8c on 20c brn vio 2.10 1.80
Never hinged 3.50
On cover 70.00
69 A4 10c on 25c bl ('21) 4.25 2.10
Never hinged 8.50
On cover 30.00
70 A4 20c on 50c bl ('22) 55.00 55.00
Never hinged 100.00
On cover 500.00
71 A5 40c on 1fr cl & ol grn 7.50 6.00
Never hinged 13.50
On cover 80.00

No. 44 Surcharged

73 A5 $2 on 5fr bl & buff ('22) 175.00 *200.00*
Never hinged 300.00
On cover 850.00
Nos. 65-73 (8) 253.45 270.25

Types of 1902-03 Surcharged like Nos. 65-71

1922

75 A3 1c on 5c org 6.00 *6.75*
Never hinged 10.50
On cover 100.00
On cover, single franking *225.00*
76 A4 2c on 10c grn 6.75 *7.50*
Never hinged 12.00
On cover 110.00
On cover, single franking *225.00*
77 A4 3c on 15c org 9.25 *11.00*
Never hinged 16.00
On cover 125.00
On cover, single franking *225.00*
78 A4 4c on 20c red brn 11.00 *13.50*
Never hinged 20.00
On cover 200.00
79 A4 5c on 25c dk vio 6.00 6.00
Never hinged 10.50
On cover 62.50
On cover, single franking *225.00*
80 A4 6c on 30c red 12.00 11.00
Never hinged 23.00
On cover 100.00
On cover, single franking *225.00*
82 A4 10c on 50c blue 14.50 12.00
Never hinged 26.00
On cover 125.00
On cover, single franking *225.00*
83 A5 20c on 1fr claret & ol grn 35.00 *40.00*
Never hinged 700.00
On cover 400.00
On cover, single franking *500.00*
84 A5 40c on 2fr org & pale bl 45.00 *55.00*
Never hinged 80.00
On cover 700.00
On cover, single franking *800.00*
85 A5 $1 on 5fr dk bl & buff 150.00 *160.00*
Never hinged 250.00
On cover 850.00
On cover, single franking —
Nos. 75-85 (10) 295.50 322.75

POSTAGE DUE STAMPS

Postage Due Stamps of France Handstamped in Red or Black

1901-07 **Unwmk.** ***Perf. 14x13½***

J1 D2 5c lt bl (R) 7.50 4.25
Never hinged 16.00
On cover 100.00
a. Double overprint 160.00
Never hinged 300.00
J2 D2 10c choc (R) 11.00 6.00
Never hinged 21.00
On cover *650.00*
a. Double overprint 160.00
Never hinged 300.00
J3 D2 15c lt grn (R) 11.00 7.50
Never hinged 21.00
On cover *250.00*
a. Pair, one stamp without ovpt. 275.00
b. Imperf, single 160.00
J4 D2 20c ol grn (R) ('07) 12.50 11.00
Never hinged 22.50
On cover 650.00
J5 D2 30c carmine 17.00 12.00
Never hinged 35.00
On cover 650.00
a. Double overprint 160.00
J6 D2 50c lilac 17.00 12.50
Never hinged 35.00
On cover 650.00
a. Triple overprint 160.00
b. Pair, one stamp without overprint 275.00
Nos. J1-J6 (6) 76.00 53.25

Stamps of 1894-1900 Handstamped in Carmine

1903

J7 A15 5c yel grn — 2,250.
a. Purple handstamp — —
b. 5c green, *greenish* —
J8 A15 10c blk, *lavender* — —
a. Purple handstamp — —
J9 A15 15c blue *2,750.* 1,250.
a. Purple handstamp — —
J10 A15 30c brn, *bister* *1,500.* 350.00
On cover *3,250.*
a. Purple handstamp — —

Same Handstamp on Stamps of 1902-03 in Carmine

1903

J14 A3 5c green — 2,000.
a. Purple handstamp — —
J15 A4 10c rose red 750. 425.00
On cover *3,500.*
a. Purple handstamp — —
J16 A4 15c pale red 750. 325.00
a. Purple handstamp — —

Stamps of 1894-1900 Handstamped in Carmine

1903

J20 A1 5c yellow green — 1,100.
On cover *3,500.*
a. Purple handstamp — —
b. 5c green, *greenish* —
J21 A1 10c blk, *lavender* — —
a. Purple handstamp — —
J22 A1 15c blue 1,250. 350.
a. Purple handstamp — —
J23 A1 30c brn, *bister* 600. 325.
On cover *3,250.*
a. Purple handstamp — —

Same Handstamp on Stamps of 1902-03 in Carmine or Purple

1903

J27 A3 5c green (C) — 1,750.
a. Purple handstamp —
J28 A4 10c rose red (C) 340. 225.
On cover *3,500.*
a. Purple handstamp — —
J29 A4 15c pale red (C) 675. 225.
a. Purple handstamp — —
J30 A4 30c lilac (P) — —

The handstamps on Nos. J7-J30 are found inverted, double, etc.

The cancellations on these stamps should have dates between Sept. 1, and Nov. 30, 1903, to be genuine.

Postage Due Stamps of France, 1893-1910 Surcharged like Nos. 65-71

1911

J33 D2 2c on 5c blue 3.00 2.50
Never hinged 5.25
On cover *625.00*
a. Double surcharge 140.00 —
Never hinged 240.00
J34 D2 4c on 10c choc 3.00 2.50
Never hinged 5.25
On cover *625.00*
a. Double surcharge 140.00 —
Never hinged 240.00
J35 D2 8c on 20c ol grn 3.40 3.00
Never hinged 6.50
On cover *625.00*
a. Double surcharge 140.00 —
Never hinged 240.00
J36 D2 20c on 50c lilac 3.40 3.00
Never hinged 6.50
On cover *625.00*
Nos. J33-J36 (4) 12.80 11.00

1922

J37 D2 1c on 5c blue 82.50 *95.00*
Never hinged 145.00
J38 D2 2c on 10c brn 145.00 *165.00*
Never hinged 250.00
J39 D2 4c on 20c ol grn 145.00 *165.00*
Never hinged 250.00
J40 D2 10c on 50c brn vio 125.00 *185.00*
Never hinged 225.00
Nos. J37-J40 (4) 497.50 610.00

CANTON

Stamps of Indo-China, 1892-1900, Overprinted in Red

1901 **Unwmk.** ***Perf. 14x13½***

1 A3 1c blk, *lil bl* 2.10 2.10
Never hinged 4.50
On cover 100.00
1A A3 2c brn, *buff* 2.50 2.50
Never hinged 5.00
On cover 100.00
2 A3 4c claret, *lav* 4.25 4.25
Never hinged 8.50
On cover 100.00
2A A3 5c grn, *grnsh* 600.00 600.00
Never hinged 1,100.
On cover 2,000.
3 A3 5c yel grn 3.40 3.40
Never hinged 7.25
On cover 65.00
4 A3 10c blk, *lavender* 7.25 7.25
Never hinged 13.50
On cover 85.00
5 A3 15c blue, quadrille paper 6.75 6.75
Never hinged 14.00
On cover 70.00

6 A3 15c gray 7.50 7.50
Never hinged 16.00
On cover 85.00
a. Double overprint 19.00
7 A3 20c red, *grn* 22.50 22.50
Never hinged 45.00
On cover 300.00
On cover, single franking 600.00
8 A3 25c blk, *rose* 13.50 13.50
Never hinged 27.50
On cover 160.00
On cover, single franking 225.00
9 A3 30c brn, *bister* 32.50 32.50
Never hinged 65.00
On cover 325.00
On cover, single franking 450.00
10 A3 40c red, *straw* 32.50 32.50
Never hinged 65.00
On cover 325.00
On cover, single franking 450.00
11 A3 50c car, *rose* 35.00 35.00
Never hinged 75.00
On cover 600.00
On cover, single franking 900.00
12 A3 75c dp vio, *org* 35.00 35.00
Never hinged 75.00
On cover 600.00
On cover, single franking 900.00
13 A3 1fr brnz grn, *straw* 45.00 45.00
Never hinged 95.00
On cover 700.00
On cover, single franking 1,100.
14 A3 5fr red lil, *lav* 250.00 250.00
On cover 1,600.
On cover, single franking 2,600.
Nos. 1-14 (16) 1,100. 1,100.

The Chinese characters in the overprint on Nos. 1-14 read "Canton." On Nos. 15-64, they restate the denomination of the basic stamp.

Surcharged in Black

1903-04

15 A3 1c blk, *lil bl* 4.25 4.25
Never hinged 8.50
On cover 120.00
16 A3 2c brn, *buff* 4.50 4.25
Never hinged 9.50
On cover 120.00
17 A3 4c claret, *lav* 4.50 4.25
Never hinged 9.50
On cover 120.00
18 A3 5c yellow green 4.25 4.25
Never hinged 8.50
On cover 85.00
19 A3 10c rose red 4.50 4.25
Never hinged 9.50
On cover 70.00
20 A3 15c gray 4.50 4.25
Never hinged 9.50
On cover 65.00
21 A3 20c red, *grn* 21.00 17.50
Never hinged 45.00
On cover 225.00
On cover, single franking 475.00
22 A3 25c blue 7.50 7.50
Never hinged 16.00
On cover 85.00
On cover, single franking 110.00
23 A3 25c blk, *rose* ('04) 10.00 8.50
Never hinged 21.00
On cover 85.00
On cover, single franking 110.00
24 A3 30c brn, *bister* 27.50 21.00
Never hinged 57.50
On cover 110.00
On cover, single franking 140.00
25 A3 40c red, *straw* 67.50 55.00
Never hinged 140.00
On cover 400.00
On cover, single franking 525.00
26 A3 50c car, *rose* 340.00 310.00
On cover 975.00
On cover, single franking 1,300.
27 A3 50c brn, *az* ('04) 85.00 72.50
On cover 525.00
On cover, single franking 800.00
28 A3 75c dp vio, *org* 67.50 67.50
On cover 575.00
On cover, single franking 900.00
a. "INDO-CHINE" inverted 55,000.
29 A3 1fr brnz grn, *straw* 67.50 67.50
On cover 625.00
On cover, single franking 1,100.
30 A3 5fr red lil, *lav* 67.50 67.50
On cover 800.00
On cover, single franking 1,300.
Nos. 15-30 (16) 787.50 720.00

Many varieties of the surcharge exist on Nos. 15-30.

Stamps of Indo-China, 1892-1906, Surcharged in Red or Black

A second printing of the 1906 surcharges of Canton, Hoi Hao, Kwangchowan, Mongtseu, Packhoi, Tong King and Yunnan Fou was made in 1908. The inks are grayish instead of full black and vermilion instead of carmine.

Values are for the cheaper variety which usually is the second printing.

The 4c and 50c of the 1892 issue of Indo-China are known with this surcharge and similarly surcharged for other cities in China. The surcharges on these two stamps are always inverted. It is stated that they were irregularly produced and never issued.

1906

31 A4 1c ol grn (R) 2.50 2.50
Never hinged 4.50
On cover 50.00
32 A4 2c vio brn, *buff* 2.50 2.50
Never hinged 4.50
On cover 50.00
33 A4 4c cl, *bluish* (R) 2.50 2.50
Never hinged 4.50
On cover 50.00
34 A4 5c dp grn (R) 2.10 2.10
Never hinged 3.50
On cover 37.50
35 A4 10c carmine 3.00 3.00
Never hinged 5.25
On cover 37.50
36 A4 15c org brn, *bl* 22.50 22.50
Never hinged 50.00
On cover 200.00
37 A4 20c red, *grn* 12.50 12.50
Never hinged 26.00
On cover 210.00
On cover, single franking 260.00
38 A4 25c deep blue 5.00 5.00
Never hinged 8.75
On cover 65.00
On cover, single franking 110.00
39 A4 30c pale brn 17.00 17.00
Never hinged 35.00
On cover 240.00
On cover, single franking 300.00
40 A4 35c blk, *yel* (R) 12.50 12.50
Never hinged 26.00
On cover 100.00
On cover, single franking 130.00
41 A4 40c blk, *bluish* (R) 21.00 21.00
Never hinged 45.00
On cover 325.00
On cover, single franking 450.00
42 A4 50c bister brn 14.50 14.50
Never hinged 32.50
On cover 200.00
On cover, single franking 325.00
43 A3 75c dp vio, *org* (R) 67.50 67.50
On cover 65.00
On cover, single franking 800.00
44 A4 1fr pale grn 30.00 30.00
Never hinged 60.00
On cover 650.00
On cover, single franking 850.00
45 A4 2fr brn, *org* (R) 42.50 42.50
Never hinged 87.50
On cover 725.00
On cover, single franking 900.00
46 A3 5fr red lil, *lav* 92.50 92.50
On cover 850.00
On cover, single franking 1,300.
47 A4 10fr org brn, *grn* 85.00 85.00
On cover 900.00
On cover, single franking 2,000.
Nos. 31-47 (17) 435.10 435.10

Surcharge exists inverted on 1c, 25c & 1fr.

Stamps of Indo-China, 1907, Srchd. in Red or Blue

Chinese Characters

1908

48 A5 1c ol brn & blk 1.25 1.25
Never hinged 2.40
On cover 32.50
49 A5 2c brn & blk 1.25 1.25
Never hinged 2.40
On cover 32.50
50 A5 4c bl & blk 2.50 1.25
Never hinged 4.50
On cover 32.50
51 A5 5c grn & blk 2.50 2.10
Never hinged 4.50
On cover 20.00
52 A5 10c red & blk (Bl) 3.40 2.50
Never hinged 6.50
On cover 20.00
53 A5 15c vio & blk 4.25 3.40
Never hinged 8.00
On cover 20.00
54 A6 20c vio & blk 5.00 5.00
Never hinged 9.50
On cover 22.50
55 A6 25c bl & blk 5.00 4.25
Never hinged 9.50
On cover 32.50
On cover, single franking 52.50
56 A6 30c brn & blk 8.50 8.50
Never hinged 16.00
On cover 60.00
On cover, single franking 100.00
57 A6 35c ol grn & blk 8.50 8.50
Never hinged 16.00
On cover 52.50
On cover, single franking 72.50
58 A6 40c brn & blk 11.00 8.50
Never hinged 22.50
On cover 65.00
On cover, single franking 110.00
59 A6 50c car & blk (Bl) 11.00 8.50
Never hinged 22.50
On cover 72.50
On cover, single franking 120.00
60 A7 75c ver & blk (Bl) 11.00 10.00
Never hinged 22.50
On cover 80.00
On cover, single franking 130.00
61 A8 1fr car & blk (Bl) 18.00 15.00
Never hinged 35.00
On cover 150.00
On cover, single franking 300.00
62 A9 2fr grn & blk 45.00 37.50
Never hinged 87.50
On cover 175.00
On cover, single franking 350.00
63 A10 5fr bl & blk 62.50 55.00
Never hinged 120.00
On cover 260.00
On cover, single franking 525.00
64 A11 10fr pur & blk 92.50 92.50
Never hinged 175.00
On cover 425.00
On cover, single franking 800.00
Nos. 48-64 (17) 293.15 265.00

Nos. 48-64 Surcharged with New Values in Cents or Piasters in Black, Red or Blue

1919

65 A5 ⅖c on 1c 1.25 1.25
Never hinged 2.40
On cover 32.50
66 A5 ⅘c on 2c 1.25 1.25
Never hinged 2.40
On cover 32.50
67 A5 1⅗c on 4c (R) 1.25 1.25
Never hinged 2.40
On cover 32.50
68 A5 2c on 5c 1.60 1.60
Never hinged 3.25
On cover 20.00
69 A5 4c on 10c (Bl) 2.10 1.60
Never hinged 3.50
On cover 20.00
a. Chinese "2" instead of "4" 42.50 42.50
70 A5 6c on 15c 2.50 2.10
Never hinged 4.50
On cover 16.00
71 A6 8c on 20c 4.25 2.10
Never hinged 7.25
On cover 22.50
72 A6 10c on 25c 5.00 1.60
Never hinged 8.75
On cover 27.50
73 A6 12c on 30c 2.10 2.10
Never hinged 3.50
On cover 29.00
a. Double surcharge 140.00 140.00
Never hinged 240.00
74 A6 14c on 35c 2.10 1.60
Never hinged 3.50
On cover 29.00
a. Closed "4" 10.00 10.00
Never hinged 17.50
On cover 65.00
75 A6 16c on 40c 2.50 1.60
Never hinged 4.75
On cover 45.00
76 A6 20c on 50c (Bl) 2.50 2.10
Never hinged 4.75
On cover 45.00
77 A7 30c on 75c (Bl) 2.50 2.10
Never hinged 4.75
On cover 52.50
a. Double surcharge 750.00 750.00
78 A8 40c on 1fr (Bl) 12.50 7.50
Never hinged 22.50
On cover 52.50
79 A9 80c on 2fr (R) 19.00 12.00
Never hinged 32.50
On cover 95.00
80 A10 2pi on 5fr (R) 32.50 32.50
Never hinged 65.00
On cover 525.00
81 A11 4pi on 10fr (R) 32.50 32.50
Never hinged 65.00
On cover 600.00
Nos. 65-81 (17) 127.40 106.75

HOI HAO

Stamps of Indo-China Overprinted in Red

1901 Unwmk. *Perf. 14x13½*

1 A3 1c blk, *lil bl* 3.40 3.40
Never hinged 6.50
On cover 120.00
2 A3 2c brn, *buff* 4.25 4.25
Never hinged 8.00
On cover 120.00
3 A3 4c claret, *lav* 4.25 4.25
Never hinged 8.00
On cover 120.00
4 A3 5c yel grn 5.00 5.00
Never hinged 8.75
On cover 85.00
5 A3 10c blk, *lavender* 13.50 12.00
Never hinged 32.50
On cover 100.00
6 A3 15c blue 1,850. 800.00
On cover 2,000.
7 A3 15c gray 7.50 5.00
Never hinged 15.00
On cover 72.50
8 A3 20c red, *grn* 32.50 25.00
Never hinged 75.00
On cover 300.00
On cover, single franking 600.00
9 A3 25c blk, *rose* 17.00 12.50
Never hinged 35.00
On cover 160.00
On cover, single franking 225.00
10 A3 30c brn, *bister* 67.50 67.50
On cover 650.00
On cover, single franking 900.00
11 A3 40c red, *straw* 67.50 67.50
On cover 650.00
On cover, single franking 900.00
12 A3 50c car, *rose* 67.50 67.50
On cover 800.00
On cover, single franking 1,200.
13 A3 75c dp vio, *org* 250.00 225.00
On cover 1,000.
On cover, single franking 1,500.
14 A3 1fr brnz grn, *straw* 800.00 740.00
On cover 2,750.
On cover, single franking 4,500.
15 A3 5fr red lil, *lav* 800.00 675.00
On cover 2,750.
On cover, single franking 5,250.
Nos. 1-15 (15) 3,990. 2,714.

The Chinese characters in the overprint on Nos. 1-15 read "Hoi Hao." On Nos. 16-66, they restate the denomination of the basic stamp.

Surcharged in Black

1903-04

16 A3 1c blk, *lil bl* 2.50 2.50
Never hinged 4.50
On cover 100.00
17 A3 2c brn, *buff* 2.50 2.50
Never hinged 4.50
On cover 100.00
18 A3 4c claret, *lav* 4.25 4.25
Never hinged 7.25
On cover 100.00
19 A3 5c yel grn 4.25 4.25
Never hinged 7.25
On cover 80.00
20 A3 10c red 4.25 4.25
Never hinged 7.25
On cover 65.00
21 A3 15c gray 5.00 5.00
Never hinged 8.75
On cover 65.00
22 A3 20c red, *grn* 7.50 7.50
Never hinged 15.00
On cover 11.00
On cover, single franking 200.00
23 A3 25c blue 5.00 5.00
Never hinged 8.75
On cover 85.00
On cover, single franking 110.00
24 A3 25c blk, *rose* ('04) 8.50 8.50
Never hinged 16.00
On cover 85.00
On cover, single franking 110.00
25 A3 30c brn, *bister* 6.75 6.75
Never hinged 14.00
On cover 100.00
On cover, single franking 140.00
26 A3 40c red, *straw* 32.50 32.50
Never hinged 72.50
On cover 160.00
On cover, single franking 240.00
27 A3 50c car, *rose* 30.00 30.00
Never hinged 60.00
On cover 175.00
On cover, single franking 275.00
28 A3 50c brn, *az* ('04) 170.00 170.00
On cover 725.00
On cover, single franking 1,050.
29 A3 75c dp vio, *org* 50.00 50.00
Never hinged 105.00
On cover 600.00
On cover, single franking 900.00
a. "INDO-CHINE" inverted 45,000.
30 A3 1fr brnz grn, *straw* 67.50 67.50
Never hinged 130.00
On cover 650.00
On cover, single franking 1,100.
31 A3 5fr red lil, *lav* 225.00 225.00
On cover 1,100.
On cover, single franking 1,600.
Nos. 16-31 (16) 625.50 625.50

Many varieties of the surcharge exist on Nos. 1-31.

Stamps of Indo-China, 1892-1906, Surcharged in Red or Black

1906

32 A4 1c ol grn (R) 8.50 8.50
Never hinged 17.50
On cover 130.00
33 A4 2c vio brn, *buff* 8.50 8.50
Never hinged 17.50
On cover 130.00
34 A4 4c cl, *bluish* (R) 8.50 8.50
Never hinged 17.50
On cover 130.00
35 A4 5c dp grn (R) 8.50 8.50
Never hinged 17.50
On cover 100.00
36 A4 10c carmine 8.50 8.50
Never hinged 17.50
On cover 100.00
37 A4 15c org brn, *bl* 32.50 32.50
Never hinged 75.00
On cover 260.00

86 A15 8c gray grn (R) 1.25 1.25
Never hinged 2.50
On cover 16.00
a. Accent omitted on "TCHÉOU" 1.60 1.60
Never hinged 2.75
87 A15 9c red violet 1.70 1.70
Never hinged 2.75
On cover 16.00
a. Accent omitted on "TCHÉOU" 2.40 2.40
Never hinged 4.00
111 A21 5c dp violet .95 .95
Never hinged 1.40
On cover 8.00
a. Accent omitted on "TCHÉOU" 1.40 1.40
Never hinged 2.40
112 A21 5c dp green ('41) .50 .50
Never hinged .75
On cover 13.00
a. Accent omitted on "TCHÉOU" .75 .75
Never hinged 1.00

Name and Value typo. in Black

B1 CD83 6c + 2c green 9.25 9.25
Never hinged 15.00
On cover 120.00
B2 CD83 7c + 3c brown 9.25 9.25
Never hinged 15.00
On cover 85.00
B3 CD83 9c + 4c red org 9.25 9.25
Never hinged 15.00
On cover 72.50

Never hinged 22.50
On cover 150.00
On cover, single franking 215.00
24 A4 30c pale brn 13.50 13.50
Never hinged 28.00
On cover 240.00
On cover, single franking 300.00
25 A4 35c blk, *yel* (R) 12.50 12.50
Never hinged 28.00
On cover 260.00
On cover, single franking 350.00

38 A4 20c red, *grn* 13.50 13.50
Never hinged 27.50
On cover 200.00
On cover, single franking 260.00
39 A4 25c deep blue 11.00 11.00
Never hinged 24.00

70 A5 2c on 5c 2.50 2.50
Never hinged 4.50
On cover 20.00
71 A5 4c on 10c (Bl) 3.00 3.00
Never hinged 5.25
On cover 16.00

17 A4 10fr org brn, *grn* 275.00 275.00
On cover 1,000.
On cover, single franking 2,000.
Nos. 1-17 (17) 845.00 845.00
Various varieties of the surcharge exist on

44 A6 12c on 30c 3.40 3.40
Never hinged 6.50
On cover 47.50
45 A6 14c on 35c 3.40 3.40
Never hinged 6.50
On cover 60.00

26 A4 40c blk, *bluish* (R) 20.00 20.00
Never hinged 35.00
On cover 325.00
On cover, single franking 475.00
27 A4 50c bister brn 21.00 21.00
Never hinged 45.00
On cover 350.00
On cover, single franking 525.00
28 A3 75c dp vio, *org* (R) 67.50 67.50
Never hinged 65.00
On cover 650.00
On cover, single franking 800.00
a. "INDO-CHINE" inverted *67,500.*
29 A4 1fr pale grn 42.50 42.50
Never hinged 90.00
On cover 625.00
On cover, single franking 900.00
30 A4 2fr brn, *org* (R) 55.00 55.00
Never hinged 125.00
On cover 825.00
On cover, single franking 1,050.
31 A3 5fr red lil, *lav* 140.00 140.00
On cover 850.00
On cover, single franking 1,300.
32 A4 10fr org brn, *grn* 150.00 150.00
On cover 1,000.
On cover, single franking 2,000.
a. Chinese characters inverted 1,750. *2,100.*
Nos. 16-32 (17) 606.50 606.50

Inverted varieties of the surcharge exist on Nos. 19, 22 and 32.

Stamps of Indo-China, 1907, Srchd. in Red or Blue

Value in Chinese

1908

33 A5 1c ol brn & blk 1.25 1.25
Never hinged 2.40
On cover 32.50
34 A5 2c brn & blk 1.25 1.25
Never hinged 2.40
On cover 32.50
35 A5 4c bl & blk 1.25 1.25
Never hinged 2.40
On cover 32.50
36 A5 5c grn & blk 1.25 1.25
Never hinged 2.40
On cover 20.00
37 A5 10c red & blk (Bl) 3.00 3.00
Never hinged 5.25
On cover 20.00
38 A5 15c vio & blk 3.00 3.00
Never hinged 5.25
On cover 26.00
39 A6 20c vio & blk 6.00 6.00
Never hinged 10.50
On cover 32.50
40 A6 25c bl & blk 15.00 15.00
Never hinged 27.50
On cover 100.00
On cover, single franking 160.00
41 A6 30c brn & blk 6.75 6.75
Never hinged 13.50
On cover 65.00
On cover, single franking 110.00
42 A6 35c ol grn & blk 7.50 7.50
Never hinged 16.00
On cover 60.00
On cover, single franking 87.50
43 A6 40c brn & blk 5.00 5.00
Never hinged 9.00
On cover 65.00
On cover, single franking 110.00
45 A6 50c car & blk (Bl) 6.75 6.75
Never hinged 13.50
On cover 80.00
On cover, single franking 130.00
46 A7 75c ver & blk (Bl) 14.50 14.50
Never hinged 27.50
On cover 90.00
On cover, single franking 160.00
47 A8 1fr car & blk (Bl) 13.50 13.50
Never hinged 24.00
On cover 160.00
On cover, single franking 325.00
48 A9 2fr grn & blk 19.00 19.00
Never hinged 32.50
On cover 200.00
On cover, single franking 350.00
49 A10 5fr bl & blk 105.00 105.00
Never hinged 210.00
On cover 350.00
On cover, single franking 600.00
50 A11 10fr pur & blk 125.00 125.00
Never hinged 240.00
On cover 400.00
On cover, single franking 725.00
Nos. 33-50 (17) 335.00 335.00

The Chinese characters overprinted on Nos. 1 to 50 repeat the denomination of the basic stamp.

Nos. 33-50 Srchd. in Cents or Piasters in Black, Red or Blue

1919

51 A5 ⅖c on 1c 1.70 1.70
Never hinged 2.40
On cover 32.50
52 A5 ⅘c on 2c 1.70 1.70
Never hinged 2.40
On cover 32.50
53 A5 1⅗c on 4c 1.70 1.70
Never hinged 2.40
On cover 32.50
54 A5 2c on 5c 1.70 1.70
Never hinged 2.40
On cover 20.00
55 A5 4c on 10c (Bl) 3.00 3.00
Never hinged 5.25
On cover 16.00
56 A5 6c on 15c 3.00 3.00
Never hinged 5.25
On cover 16.00
57 A6 8c on 20c 6.75 6.75
Never hinged 12.00
On cover 26.00
58 A6 10c on 25c 5.00 5.00
Never hinged 9.00
On cover 40.00
59 A6 12c on 30c 5.00 5.00
Never hinged 9.00
On cover 40.00
60 A6 14c on 35c 3.40 3.40
Never hinged 35.00
a. Closed "4" 21.00 21.00
61 A6 16c on 40c 4.25 4.25
Never hinged 8.00
On cover 47.50
63 A6 20c on 50c (Bl) 5.00 5.00
Never hinged 9.00
On cover 60.00
64 A7 30c on 75c (Bl) 9.25 9.25
Never hinged 16.00
On cover 72.50
65 A8 40c on 1fr (Bl) 10.00 10.00
Never hinged 17.50
On cover 90.00
66 A9 80c on 2fr (R) 10.00 10.00
Never hinged 17.50
On cover 105.00
a. Triple surch., one inverted 550.00 550.00
67 A10 2pi on 5fr (R) 200.00 200.00
Never hinged 375.00
On cover 650.00
a. Triple surch., one inverted 625.00 625.00
b. Double surcharge 925.00 925.00
68 A11 4pi on 10fr (R) 30.00 30.00
Never hinged 65.00
On cover 200.00
Nos. 51-68 (17) 301.45 301.45

PAKHOI

Stamps of Indo-China Surcharged in Black

1903-04 Unwmk. *Perf. 14x13½*

1 A3 1c blk, *lil bl* 6.75 6.75
Never hinged 12.00
On cover 120.00
2 A3 2c brn, *buff* 6.75 6.75
Never hinged 12.00
On cover 120.00
3 A3 4c claret, *lav* 6.75 6.75
Never hinged 12.00
On cover 120.00
4 A3 5c yel grn 5.00 5.00
Never hinged 9.50
On cover 85.00
5 A3 10c red 5.00 5.00
Never hinged 9.50
On cover 80.00
6 A3 15c gray 5.00 5.00
Never hinged 9.50
On cover 72.50
7 A3 20c red, *grn* 11.00 11.00
Never hinged 20.00
On cover 110.00
On cover, single franking 175.00
8 A3 25c blue 9.25 9.25
Never hinged 15.00
On cover 100.00
On cover, single franking 120.00
9 A3 25c blk, *rose* ('04) 6.75 6.75
Never hinged 11.00
On cover 100.00
On cover, single franking 120.00
10 A3 30c brn, *bister* 8.50 8.50
Never hinged 15.00
On cover 120.00
On cover, single franking 160.00
11 A3 40c red, *straw* 57.50 57.50
Never hinged 110.00
On cover 200.00
On cover, single franking 260.00
12 A3 50c car, *rose* 340.00 340.00
On cover 1,100.
On cover, single franking 1,300.
13 A3 50c brn, *az* ('04) 47.50 47.50
Never hinged 90.00
On cover 260.00
On cover, single franking 450.00
14 A3 75c dp vio, *org* 67.50 67.50
On cover 600.00
On cover, single franking 850.00
a. "INDO-CHINE" inverted *47,500.*
15 A3 1fr brnz grn, *straw* 67.50 67.50
On cover 650.00
On cover, single franking 1,100.
16 A3 5fr red lil, *lav* 135.00 135.00
On cover 800.00
On cover, single franking 1,300.
Nos. 1-16 (16) 785.75 785.75

Many varieties of the surcharge exist.

Stamps of Indo-China 1892-1906, Surcharged in Red or Black

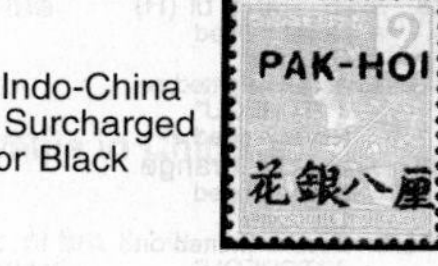

1906

17 A4 1c ol grn (R) 8.50 8.50
Never hinged 17.50
On cover 130.00
18 A4 2c vio brn, *buff* 8.50 8.50
Never hinged 17.50
On cover 130.00
19 A4 4c cl, *bluish* (R) 8.50 8.50
Never hinged 17.50
On cover 130.00
20 A4 5c dp grn (R) 8.50 8.50
Never hinged 17.50
On cover 100.00
21 A4 10c carmine 8.50 8.50
Never hinged 17.50
On cover 100.00
22 A4 15c org brn,*bl* 32.50 32.50
Never hinged 75.00
On cover 260.00
23 A4 20c red, *grn* 13.50 13.50
Never hinged 27.50
On cover 200.00
On cover, single franking 260.00
24 A4 25c deep blue 11.00 11.00
Never hinged 22.50
On cover 150.00
On cover, single franking 260.00
25 A4 30c pale brn 13.50 13.50
Never hinged 27.50
On cover 250.00
On cover, single franking 300.00
26 A4 35c blk, *yel* (R) 21.00 21.00
Never hinged 45.00
On cover 260.00
On cover, single franking 360.00
27 A4 40c blk, *bluish*(R) 21.00 21.00
Never hinged 45.00
On cover 325.00
On cover, single franking 475.00
28 A4 50c bister brn 21.00 21.00
Never hinged 45.00
On cover 360.00
On cover, single franking 525.00
29 A3 75c dp vio, *org* (R) 67.50 67.50
30 A4 1fr pale grn 42.50 42.50
31 A4 2fr brn, *org*(R) 55.00 55.00
32 A3 5fr red lil, *lav* 140.00 140.00
33 A4 10fr org brn, *grn* 150.00 150.00
Nos. 17-33 (17) 631.00 631.00

Various surcharge varieties exist on Nos. 17-24.

Stamps of Indo-China, 1907, Surcharged "PAKHOI" and Value in Chinese in Red or Blue

1908

34 A5 1c ol brn & blk 1.25 1.25
Never hinged 2.40
On cover 32.50
35 A5 2c brn & blk 1.25 1.25
Never hinged 2.40
On cover 32.50
36 A5 4c bl & blk 1.25 1.25
Never hinged 2.40
On cover 32.50
37 A5 5c grn & blk 1.70 1.70
Never hinged 3.25
On cover 20.00
38 A5 10c red & blk (Bl) 1.70 1.70
Never hinged 3.25
On cover 20.00
39 A5 15c vio & blk 2.10 2.10
Never hinged 4.00
On cover 26.00
40 A6 20c vio & blk 2.50 2.50
Never hinged 4.75
On cover 32.50
41 A6 25c bl & blk 3.00 3.00
Never hinged 5.50
On cover 40.00
On cover, single franking 65.00
42 A6 30c brn & blk 3.40 3.40
Never hinged 6.00
On cover 65.00
On cover, single franking 105.00
43 A6 35c ol grn & blk 3.40 3.40
Never hinged 6.00
On cover 60.00
On cover, single franking 87.50
44 A6 40c brn & blk 3.40 3.40
Never hinged 6.00
On cover 65.00
On cover, single franking 110.00
46 A6 50c car & blk (Bl) 3.40 3.40
Never hinged 6.00
On cover 80.00
On cover, single franking 130.00
47 A7 75c ver & blk (Bl) 7.25 7.25
Never hinged 12.00
On cover 95.00
On cover, single franking 150.00
48 A8 1fr car & blk (Bl) 7.50 7.50
Never hinged 15.00
On cover 160.00
On cover, single franking 325.00
49 A9 2fr grn & blk 16.00 16.00
Never hinged 35.00
On cover 200.00
On cover, single franking 360.00
50 A10 5fr bl & blk 85.00 85.00
Never hinged 150.00
On cover 325.00
On cover, single franking 525.00
51 A11 10fr pur & blk 150.00 150.00
Never hinged 275.00
On cover 450.00
On cover, single franking 800.00
Nos. 34-51 (17) 294.10 294.10

The Chinese characters overprinted on Nos. 1 to 51 repeat the denomination of the basic stamps.

Nos. 34-51 Surcharged with New Values in Cents or Piasters in Black, Red or Blue

1919

52 A5 ⅖c on 1c 1.25 1.25
Never hinged 2.40
On cover 32.50
a. "PAK-HOI" and Chinese double 170.00
Never hinged 300.00
53 A5 ⅘c on 2c 1.25 1.25
Never hinged 2.40
On cover 32.50
54 A5 1⅗c on 4c (R) 1.25 1.25
Never hinged 2.40
On cover 32.50
55 A5 2c on 5c 2.50 2.50
Never hinged 4.50
On cover 20.00
a. "S" omitted from "CENTS" 72.50 70.00
Never hinged 140.00
56 A5 4c on 10c (Bl) 3.40 3.40
Never hinged 6.50
On cover 20.00
57 A5 6c on 15c 1.70 1.70
Never hinged 3.25
On cover 27.50
58 A6 8c on 20c 3.40 3.40
Never hinged 6.50
On cover 27.50
59 A6 10c on 25c 5.00 5.00
Never hinged 8.50
On cover 40.00
60 A6 12c on 30c 1.70 1.70
Never hinged 3.25
On cover 40.00
a. "12 CENTS" double 675.00
Never hinged 350.00
61 A6 14c on 35c 1.25 1.25
Never hinged 2.40
On cover 40.00
a. Closed "4" 14.50 14.50
Never hinged 26.00
62 A6 16c on 40c 3.00 3.00
Never hinged 5.25
On cover 47.50
64 A6 20c on 50c (Bl) 2.10 2.10
Never hinged 4.00
On cover 60.00
65 A7 30c on 75c (Bl) 9.25 9.25
Never hinged 17.50
On cover 75.00
66 A8 40c on 1fr (Bl) 12.50 12.50
Never hinged 22.50
On cover 95.00
67 A9 80c on 2fr (R) 10.00 10.00
Never hinged 17.50
On cover 105.00
68 A10 2pi on 5fr (R) 16.00 16.00
Never hinged 32.50
On cover 130.00
69 A11 4pi on 10fr (R) 35.00 35.00
Never hinged 70.00
On cover 200.00
Nos. 52-69 (17) 110.55 110.55

TCHONGKING (CHUNGKING)

Stamps of Indo-China Surcharged in Black

1903-04 Unwmk. *Perf. 14x13½*

1 A3 1c blk, *lil bl* 5.00 5.00
Never hinged 9.50
On cover 120.00
2 A3 2c brn, *buff* 5.00 5.00
Never hinged 9.50
On cover 120.00
3 A3 4c claret, *lav* 6.00 6.00
Never hinged 10.50
On cover 120.00
4 A3 5c yel grn 6.00 6.00
Never hinged 10.50
On cover 87.50
5 A3 10c red 6.00 6.00
Never hinged 10.50
On cover 80.00
6 A3 15c gray 6.00 6.00
Never hinged 10.50
On cover 75.00
7 A3 20c red, *grn* 8.50 8.50
Never hinged 16.00
On cover 120.00
On cover, single franking 180.00
8 A3 25c blue 55.00 55.00
Never hinged 110.00
On cover 300.00
On cover, single franking 400.00
9 A3 25c blk, *rose* ('04) 10.00 10.00
Never hinged 19.00
On cover 100.00
On cover, single franking 120.00
10 A3 30c brn, *bister* 15.00 15.00
Never hinged 32.50
On cover 200.00
On cover, single franking 450.00

11 A3 40c red, *straw* 62.50 62.50
Never hinged 120.00
On cover 400.00
On cover, single franking 525.00
12 A3 50c car, *rose* 225.00 225.00
On cover 800.00
On cover, single franking 1,100.
13 A3 50c brn, *az* ('04) 140.00 140.00
On cover 650.00
On cover, single franking 900.00
14 A3 75c vio, *org* 45.00 45.00
Never hinged 95.00
On cover 525.00
On cover, single franking 850.00
15 A3 1fr brnz grn, *straw* 60.00 60.00
On cover 650.00
On cover, single franking 1,100.
16 A3 5fr red lil, *lav* 105.00 105.00
On cover 800.00
On cover, single franking 1,300.
Nos. 1-16 (16) 760.00 760.00

Many surcharge varieties exist on Nos. 1-14.

Stamps of Indo-China and French China, issued in 1902 with similar overprint, but without Chinese characters, were not officially authorized.

Stamps of Indo-China, 1892-1906, Surcharged in Red or Black

1906

17 A4 1c ol grn (R) 8.50 8.50
Never hinged 12.50
On cover 130.00
a. "T" omitted from "TCH'ONG" 160.00 160.00
18 A4 2c vio brn, *buff* 8.50 8.50
Never hinged 12.50
On cover 130.00
a. "T" omitted from "TCH'ONG" 160.00 160.00
19 A4 4c cl, *bluish* (R) 8.50 8.50
Never hinged 12.50
On cover 130.00
a. "T" omitted from "TCH'ONG" 140.00 140.00
20 A4 5c dp grn (R) 8.50 8.50
Never hinged 12.50
On cover 100.00
a. "T" omitted from "TCH'ONG" 160.00 160.00
21 A4 10c carmine 8.50 8.50
Never hinged 12.50
On cover 100.00
a. "T" omitted from "TCH'ONG" 160.00 160.00
22 A4 15c org brn, *bl* 32.50 32.50
Never hinged 80.00
On cover 260.00
a. "T" omitted from "TCH'ONG" 400.00 400.00
23 A4 20c red, *grn* 13.50 13.50
Never hinged 27.50
On cover 200.00
On cover, single franking 260.00
a. "T" omitted from "TCH'ONG" 240.00 240.00
24 A4 25c deep blue 11.00 11.00
Never hinged 24.00
On cover 150.00
On cover, single franking 225.00
a. "T" omitted from "TCH'ONG" 160.00 160.00
25 A4 30c pale brn 13.50 13.50
Never hinged 27.50
On cover 250.00
On cover, single franking 325.00
a. "T" omitted from "TCH'ONG" 240.00 240.00
26 A4 35c blk, *yellow* (R) 21.00 21.00
Never hinged 45.00
On cover 275.00
On cover, single franking 375.00
a. "T" omitted from "TCH'ONG" 240.00 240.00
27 A4 40c blk, *bluish* (R) 21.00 21.00
Never hinged 45.00
On cover 325.00
On cover, single franking 475.00
a. "T" omitted from "TCH'ONG" 240.00 240.00
28 A4 50c bis brn 25.00 25.00
Never hinged 52.50
On cover 375.00
On cover, single franking 525.00
a. "T" omitted from "TCH'ONG" 275.00 275.00
29 A3 75c dp vio, *org* (R) 67.50 67.50
On cover 650.00
On cover, single franking 800.00
a. "T" omitted from "TCH'ONG" 675.00 675.00
30 A4 1fr pale grn 42.50 42.50
Never hinged 90.00
On cover 650.00
On cover, single franking 900.00
a. "T" omitted from "TCH'ONG" 475.00 475.00
31 A4 2fr brn, *org* (R) 55.00 55.00
Never hinged 120.00
On cover 750.00
On cover, single franking 1,000.
a. "T" omitted from "TCH'ONG" 550.00 550.00
32 A3 5fr red lil, *lav* 140.00 140.00
On cover 850.00
On cover, single franking 1,300.
a. "T" omitted from "TCH'ONG" 1,000. 1,000.
33 A4 10fr org brn, *grn* 150.00 150.00
On cover 1,000.
On cover, single franking 2,000.
a. "T" omitted from "TCH'ONG" 1,200. 1,200.
Nos. 17-33 (17) 635.00 635.00

Other surcharge varieties exist. Inverted surcharge on 1c and 2c are of private origin.

Stamps of Indo-China, 1907, Surcharged "TCHONGKING" and Value in Chinese in Red or Blue

1908

34 A5 1c ol brn & blk .85 .85
Never hinged 1.60
On cover 32.50
35 A5 2c brn & blk .85 .85
Never hinged 1.60
On cover 32.50
36 A5 4c bl & blk 1.25 1.25
Never hinged 2.40
On cover 32.50
37 A5 5c grn & blk 2.10 2.10
Never hinged 3.75
On cover 20.00
38 A5 10c red & blk (Bl) 2.10 2.10
Never hinged 3.75
On cover 20.00
39 A5 15c vio & blk 3.00 3.00
Never hinged 5.25
On cover 27.50
40 A6 20c vio & blk 3.00 3.00
Never hinged 5.25
On cover 32.50
41 A6 25c bl & blk 5.50 5.50
Never hinged 11.00
On cover 47.50
On cover, single franking 65.00
42 A6 30c brn & blk 3.40 3.40
Never hinged 6.50
On cover 65.00
On cover, single franking 110.00
43 A6 35c ol grn & blk 7.50 7.50
Never hinged 14.00
On cover 60.00
On cover, single franking 85.00
44 A6 40c brn & blk 15.00 15.00
Never hinged 27.50
On cover 65.00
On cover, single franking 110.00
45 A6 50c car & blk (Bl) 12.00 12.00
Never hinged 20.00
On cover 80.00
On cover, single franking 130.00
46 A7 75c ver & blk (Bl) 10.00 10.00
Never hinged 17.50
On cover 85.00
On cover, single franking 140.00
47 A8 1fr car & blk (Bl) 13.50 13.50
Never hinged 26.00
On cover 160.00
On cover, single franking 325.00
48 A9 2fr grn & blk 85.00 85.00
Never hinged 160.00
On cover 325.00
On cover, single franking 525.00
49 A10 5fr bl & blk 37.50 37.50
Never hinged 72.50
On cover 240.00
On cover, single franking 475.00
50 A11 10fr pur & blk 225.00 225.00
Never hinged 400.00
On cover 600.00
On cover, single franking 1,000.
Nos. 34-50 (17) 427.55 427.55

The Chinese characters overprinted on Nos. 1 to 50 repeat the denomination of the basic stamp.

Nos. 34-50 Surcharged with New Values in Cents or Piasters in Black, Red or Blue

1919

51 A5 ⅖c on 1c 1.25 1.25
Never hinged 2.40
On cover 32.50
52 A5 ⅘c on 2c 1.25 1.25
Never hinged 2.40
On cover 32.50
53 A5 1⅗c on 4c (R) 1.25 1.25
Never hinged 2.40
On cover 32.50
54 A5 2c on 5c 1.70 1.70
Never hinged 3.25
On cover 20.00
55 A5 4c on 10c (Bl) 1.25 1.25
Never hinged 2.40
On cover 16.00
56 A5 6c on 15c 1.70 1.70
Never hinged 3.25
On cover 16.00
57 A6 8c on 20c 3.00 1.25
Never hinged 5.25
On cover 27.50
58 A6 10c on 25c 8.50 8.50
Never hinged 16.00
On cover 40.00
59 A6 12c on 30c 3.00 1.25
Never hinged 5.25
On cover 40.00
60 A6 14c on 35c 2.10 1.70
Never hinged 3.75
On cover 40.00
a. Closed "4" 35.00 35.00
Never hinged 62.50
61 A6 16c on 40c 2.10 1.70
Never hinged 5.50
On cover 47.50
a. "16 CENTS" double 125.00 125.00
Never hinged 225.00
62 A6 20c on 50c (Bl) 11.00 10.00
Never hinged 19.00
On cover 60.00
63 A7 30c on 75c (Bl) 9.25 6.75
Never hinged 17.50
On cover 75.00
64 A8 40c on 1fr (Bl) 9.25 6.75
Never hinged 17.50
On cover 95.00
65 A9 80c on 2fr (R) 9.25 6.75
Never hinged 17.50
On cover 110.00
66 A10 2pi on 5fr (R) 9.25 9.25
Never hinged 17.50
On cover 120.00
67 A11 4pi on 10fr (R) 17.50 17.50
Never hinged 32.50
On cover 200.00
Nos. 51-67 (17) 92.60 79.80

YUNNAN FOU

(Formerly Yunnan Sen, later known as Kunming)

Stamps of Indo-China Surcharged in Black

1903-04 Unwmk. *Perf. 14x13½*

1 A3 1c blk, *lil bl* 6.75 6.75
Never hinged 12.00
On cover 110.00
2 A3 2c brn, *buff* 6.75 6.75
Never hinged 12.00
On cover 110.00
3 A3 4c claret, *lav* 7.50 7.50
Never hinged 15.00
On cover 110.00
4 A3 5c yel green 6.75 6.75
Never hinged 12.00
On cover 75.00
5 A3 10c red 7.50 7.50
Never hinged 15.00
On cover 65.00
6 A3 15c gray 7.50 7.50
Never hinged 15.00
On cover 65.00
7 A3 20c red, *grn* 12.50 12.50
Never hinged 24.00
On cover 100.00
On cover, single franking 175.00
8 A3 25c blue 7.50 7.50
Never hinged 15.00
On cover 90.00
On cover, single franking 120.00
9 A3 30c brn, *bister* 12.50 12.50
Never hinged 25.00
On cover 110.00
On cover, single franking 160.00
10 A3 40c red, *straw* 75.00 60.00
On cover 160.00
On cover, single franking 240.00
11 A3 50c car, *rose* 350.00 350.00
On cover 900.00
On cover, single franking 1,200.
12 A3 50c brn, *az* ('04) 180.00 180.00
On cover 500.00
On cover, single franking 800.00
13 A3 75c dp vio, *org* 67.50 62.50
On cover 500.00
On cover, single franking 1,000.
a. "INDO-CHINE" inverted 47,500.
14 A3 1fr brnz grn, *straw* 67.50 62.50
On cover 600.00
On cover, single franking 1,000.
15 A3 5fr red lil, *lav* 125.00 125.00
On cover 650.00
On cover, single franking 1,200.
Nos. 1-15 (15) 940.25 915.25

The Chinese characters overprinted on Nos. 1 to 15 repeat the denomination of the basic stamp.

Many varieties of the surcharge exist.

Stamps of Indo-China, 1892-1906, Surcharged in Red or Black

1906 Unwmk. *Perf. 14x13½*

17 A4 1c ol grn (R) 5.00 5.00
Never hinged 9.00
On cover 100.00
18 A4 2c vio brn, *buff* 5.00 5.00
Never hinged 9.00
On cover 100.00
19 A4 4c cl, *bluish* (R) 5.00 5.00
Never hinged 9.00
On cover 100.00
20 A4 5c dp grn (R) 5.00 5.00
Never hinged 9.00
On cover 75.00
21 A4 10c carmine 5.00 5.00
Never hinged 9.00
On cover 75.00
22 A4 15c org brn, *bl* 35.00 35.00
Never hinged 75.00
On cover 240.00
23 A4 20c red, *grn* 13.50 13.50
Never hinged 27.50
On cover 160.00
On cover, single franking 240.00
24 A4 25c deep blue 11.00 11.00
Never hinged 24.00
On cover 130.00
On cover, single franking 200.00
25 A4 30c pale brn 13.50 13.50
Never hinged 27.50
On cover 200.00
On cover, single franking 275.00
26 A4 35c blk, *yel* (R) 17.00 17.00
Never hinged 35.00
On cover 240.00
On cover, single franking 325.00
27 A4 40c blk, *bluish* (R) 17.00 17.00
Never hinged 35.00
On cover 300.00
On cover, single franking 400.00
28 A4 50c bister brn 21.00 21.00
Never hinged 45.00
On cover 325.00
On cover, single franking 475.00
29 A3 75c dp vio, *org* (R) 67.50 67.50
On cover 525.00
On cover, single franking 750.00
30 A4 1fr pale grn 42.50 42.50
On cover 525.00
On cover, single franking 800.00
31 A4 2fr brn, *org* (R) 55.00 55.00
On cover 600.00
On cover, single franking 900.00
32 A3 5fr red lil, *lav* 140.00 140.00
On cover 750.00
On cover, single franking 1,200.
33 A4 10fr org brn, *grn* 150.00 150.00
On cover 875.00
On cover, single franking 1,800.
Nos. 17-33 (17) 608.00 608.00

Various varieties of the surcharge exist on Nos. 18, 20, 21 and 27.

Stamps of Indo-China, 1907, Surcharged "YUNNANFOU," and Value in Chinese in Red or Blue

1908

34 A5 1c ol brn & blk 1.25 1.25
Never hinged 2.40
On cover 32.50
35 A5 2c brn & blk 1.25 1.25
Never hinged 2.40
On cover 32.50
36 A5 4c bl & blk 2.10 2.10
Never hinged 4.00
On cover 32.50
37 A5 5c grn & blk 3.00 3.00
Never hinged 5.25
On cover 20.00
38 A5 10c red & blk (Bl) 3.00 3.00
Never hinged 5.25
On cover 20.00
39 A5 15c vio & blk 6.75 6.75
Never hinged 12.00
On cover 22.50
40 A6 20c vio & blk 6.25 6.25
Never hinged 11.00
On cover 32.50
41 A6 25c bl & blk 9.25 9.25
Never hinged 17.50
On cover 40.00
On cover, single franking 65.00
42 A6 30c brn & blk 7.50 7.50
Never hinged 15.00
On cover 65.00
On cover, single franking 110.00
43 A6 35c ol grn & blk 7.50 7.50
Never hinged 15.00
On cover 55.00
On cover, single franking 80.00
44 A6 40c brn & blk 8.50 8.50
Never hinged 16.00
On cover 60.00
On cover, single franking 110.00
45 A6 50c car & blk (Bl) 9.25 9.25
Never hinged 17.50
On cover 65.00
On cover, single franking 120.00
46 A7 75c ver & blk (Bl) 11.00 11.00
Never hinged 22.50
On cover 80.00
On cover, single franking 130.00
47 A8 1fr car & blk (Bl) 17.00 17.00
Never hinged 32.50
On cover 130.00
On cover, single franking 250.00
48 A9 2fr grn & blk 29.00 29.00
Never hinged 47.50
On cover 160.00
On cover, single franking 325.00
a. "YUNANNFOU" 2,500. 2,500.
b. Pair, #48, #48a 3,000.
49 A10 5fr bl & blk 60.00 60.00
Never hinged 110.00
On cover 250.00
On cover, single franking 400.00
a. "YUNANNFOU" 2,500. 2,500.
b. Pair, #49, #49a 3,000.
50 A11 10fr pur & blk 120.00 120.00
Never hinged 200.00
On cover 400.00
On cover, single franking 650.00
a. "YUNANNFOU" 2,500. 2,500.
b. Pair, #50, #50a 3,000.
Nos. 34-50 (17) 302.60 302.60

The Chinese characters overprinted on Nos. 17-50 repeat the denomination of the basic stamp.

Nos. 34-50 Surcharged with New Values in Cents or Piasters in Black, Red or Blue

1919

51 A5 ⅖c on 1c 1.25 1.25
Never hinged 2.40
On cover 32.50
a. New value double 140.00
Never hinged 350.00
52 A5 ⅘c on 2c 1.25 1.25
Never hinged 2.40
On cover 32.50
53 A5 1⅗c on 4c (R) 1.25 1.25
Never hinged 2.40
On cover 32.50
54 A5 2c on 5c 2.10 2.10
Never hinged 3.50
On cover 20.00
a. Triple surcharge 210.00
55 A5 4c on 10c (Bl) 1.70 1.70
Never hinged 3.25
On cover 20.00
56 A5 6c on 15c 3.00 3.00
Never hinged 5.25
On cover 20.00
57 A6 8c on 20c 2.10 2.10
Never hinged 3.50
On cover 27.50
58 A6 10c on 25c 3.75 3.75
Never hinged 7.25
On cover 40.00
59 A6 12c on 30c 9.25 9.25
Never hinged 27.50
On cover 47.50

60 A6 14c on 35c 14.50 14.50
Never hinged 40.00
On cover 60.00
a. Closed "4" 140.00 140.00
Never hinged 240.00
61 A6 16c on 40c 9.25 9.25
Never hinged 17.50
On cover 65.00
62 A6 20c on 50c (Bl) 3.00 3.00
Never hinged 5.25
On cover 65.00
63 A7 30c on 75c (Bl) 9.25 9.25
Never hinged 17.50
On cover 65.00
64 A8 40c on 1fr (Bl) 35.00 35.00
Never hinged 72.50
On cover 130.00
65 A9 80c on 2fr (R) 14.50 14.50
Never hinged 27.50
On cover 90.00
a. Triple surch., one inverted 250.00
66 A10 2pi on 5fr (R) 67.50 67.50
Never hinged 130.00
On cover 250.00
67 A11 4pi on 10fr (R) 35.00 35.00
Never hinged 72.50
On cover 190.00
Nos. 51-67 (17) 213.65 213.65

OFFICES IN CRETE

Austria, France, Italy and Great Britain maintained their own post offices in Crete during the period when that country was an autonomous state.

100 Centimes = 1 Franc

Liberty, Equality and Fraternity A1

"Rights of Man" A2

Liberty and Peace (Symbolized by Olive Branch) — A3

Perf. 14x13½

1902-03 Unwmk. Typo.

1 A1 1c dark gray 2.50 2.75
Never hinged 5.25
On cover 100.00
a. A1 1c light gray 2.50 2.75
Never hinged 5.25
On cover 100.00
2 A1 2c violet brown 2.50 2.75
Never hinged 5.25
On cover 100.00
3 A1 3c red orange 2.50 2.75
Never hinged 5.25
On cover 100.00
4 A1 4c yellow brown 2.50 2.75
Never hinged 5.25
On cover 100.00
5 A1 5c green 2.50 2.75
Never hinged 5.25
On cover 65.00
6 A2 10c rose red 3.00 2.75
Never hinged 6.25
On cover 65.00
7 A2 15c pale red ('03) 4.25 3.00
Never hinged 8.50
On cover 65.00
8 A2 20c brown vio ('03) 5.25 4.00
Never hinged 9.50
On cover 100.00
On cover, single franking 175.00
9 A2 25c blue ('03) 7.00 4.50
Never hinged 13.00
On cover 80.00
On cover, single franking 110.00
10 A2 30c lilac ('03) 7.00 4.50
Never hinged 12.00
On cover 80.00
On cover, single franking 100.00
11 A3 40c red & pale bl 13.00 13.00
Never hinged 22.50
On cover 90.00
On cover, single franking 110.00
12 A3 50c bis brn & lav 18.00 15.00
Never hinged 32.50
On cover 150.00
On cover, single franking 240.00
13 A3 1fr claret & ol grn 25.00 22.50
Never hinged 40.00
On cover 275.00
On cover, single franking 475.00
14 A3 2fr gray vio & yel 40.00 37.50
Never hinged 77.50
On cover 525.00
On cover, single franking 625.00
a. Imperf, pair 675.00
15 A3 5fr dk blue & buff 65.00 60.00
Never hinged 120.00
On cover 600.00
On cover, single franking 875.00
Nos. 1-15 (15) 200.00 180.50
Set, never hinged 375.00

A4

A5

1903 Black Surcharge

16 A4 1pi on 25c blue 55.00 47.50
Never hinged 92.50
On cover 275.00
On cover, single franking 400.00
a. Ovptd. "PIASRTE" 325.00 225.00
17 A5 2pi on 50c bis brn & lav 75.00 57.50
Never hinged 120.00
On cover 300.00
On cover, single franking 475.00
18 A5 4pi on 1fr claret & ol grn 110.00 100.00
Never hinged 160.00
On cover 475.00
On cover, single franking 725.00
19 A5 8pi on 2fr gray vio & yel 140.00 *145.00*
Never hinged 225.00
On cover 525.00
On cover, single franking 875.00
20 A5 20pi on 5fr dk bl & buff 235.00 220.00
On cover 875.00
On cover, single franking 1,300.
Nos. 16-20 (5) 615.00 570.00

OFFICES IN EGYPT

French post offices formerly maintained in Alexandria and Port Said.

100 Centimes = 1 Franc

ALEXANDRIA

Stamps of France Ovptd. in Red, Blue or Black

1899-1900 Unwmk. *Perf. 14x13½*

1 A15 1c blk, *lil bl* (R) 2.10 2.10
Never hinged 4.00
On cover 65.00
a. Double overprint 150.00
b. Triple overprint 180.00
2 A15 2c brn, *buff* (Bl) 3.25 2.50
Never hinged 6.00
On cover 65.00
3 A15 3c gray, *grysh* (Bl) 3.25 2.50
Never hinged 6.00
On cover 65.00
4 A15 4c cl, *lav* (Bl) 4.25 3.25
Never hinged 7.25
On cover 65.00
5 A15 5c yel grn, (I) (R) 6.00 3.25
Never hinged 11.50
On commercial cover 65.00
a. Type II (R) 160.00 97.50
Never hinged 325.00
On cover 525.00
6 A15 10c blk, *lav,* (I) (R) 9.25 7.50
Never hinged 20.00
On cover 47.50
On commercial cover 75.00
a. Type II (R) 62.50 37.50
Never hinged 140.00
On cover 275.00
7 A15 15c blue (R) 9.25 4.25
Never hinged 17.00
On cover 20.00
On commercial cover 75.00
8 A15 20c red, *grn* 14.50 7.50
Never hinged 27.50
On cover 55.00
On cover, single franking 100.00
9 A15 25c blk, *rose* (R) 7.50 4.25
Never hinged 14.00
On cover 32.50
On cover, single franking 50.00
On commercial cover 75.00
a. Inverted overprint 97.50
b. Double ovpt., one invtd. 160.00
10 A15 30c brn, *bis* 15.00 12.00
Never hinged 29.00
On cover 50.00
On cover, single franking 75.00
11 A15 40c red, *straw* 13.50 13.50
Never hinged 26.00
On cover 55.00
On cover, single franking 75.00
12 A15 50c car, *rose* (II) 35.00 17.50
Never hinged 70.00
On cover 90.00
On cover, single franking 120.00
a. Type I 150.00 27.50
Never hinged 325.00
On cover 110.00
On cover, single franking 150.00
13 A15 1fr brnz grn, *straw* 32.50 22.50
Never hinged 67.50
On cover 110.00
On cover, single franking 220.00
On commercial cover 750.00
14 A15 2fr brn, *az* ('00) 82.50 80.00
Never hinged 175.00
On cover 325.00
On cover, single franking 525.00
15 A15 5fr red lil, *lav* 120.00 110.00
Never hinged 250.00
On cover 400.00
On cover, single franking 650.00
Nos. 1-15 (15) 357.85 292.60

Covers: Values for commercial covers are for covers with correct postage rates. Postcards sell for somewhat less than covers.

A2

A3

A4

1902-13

16 A2 1c pale gray .80 .65
Never hinged 1.40
On cover 45.00
a. 1c gray ('13) .80 .80
Never hinged 1.60
On cover 45.00
b. 1c slate ('20) 1.60 1.20
Never hinged 2.75
On cover 52.50
c. Grayish paper (GC) ('18) 1.20 .80
Never hinged 2.00
On cover 52.50
17 A2 2c violet brn .75 .75
Never hinged 1.40
On cover 50.00
18 A2 3c red orange .75 .75
Never hinged 1.40
On cover 50.00
19 A2 4c yellow brn 1.00 .85
Never hinged 1.75
On cover 52.50
20 A2 5c green 5.00 4.25
Never hinged 8.75
On cover 13.00
On commercial cover 40.00
21 A3 10c rose red 1.50 .75
Never hinged 2.75
On cover 10.00
On commercial cover 40.00
22 A3 15c orange ('13) 1.75 1.25
Never hinged 3.25
On cover 13.00
On commercial cover 35.00
a. 15c pale red ('03) 4.75 1.60
Never hinged 8.00
On cover 16.00
On commercial cover 37.50
23 A3 20c brn vio ('03) 3.00 1.50
Never hinged 5.25
On cover 20.00
On cover, single franking 26.00
On commercial cover 52.50
24 A3 25c blue ('03) 1.75 .75
Never hinged 3.25
On cover 16.00
On cover, single franking 26.00
On commercial cover 35.00
a. 25c dark blue 1.50 .50
On commercial cover 52.50
25 A3 30c violet ('03) 7.50 4.25
Never hinged 15.00
On cover 16.00
On cover, single franking 21.00
a. 30c lilac ('13) 11.00 6.75
Never hinged 19.00
On cover 16.00
On cover, single franking 20.00
b. Grayish paper (GC) ('18) 9.50 5.25
Never hinged 17.00
On cover 20.00
26 A4 40c red & pale bl 5.00 2.50
Never hinged 8.75
On cover 20.00
On cover, single franking 27.50
27 A4 50c bis brn & lav 11.00 3.00
Never hinged 22.50
On cover 27.50
On cover, single franking 50.00
a. Grayish paper (GC) 13.00 4.50
Never hinged 25.00
On cover 27.50
28 A4 1fr cl & ol grn 10.00 4.25
Never hinged 19.00
On cover 40.00
On cover, single franking 100.00
29 A4 2fr gray vio & yel 24.00 12.00
a. 2fr deep violet & yellow — —
30 A4 5fr dk bl & buff 29.00 17.00
Never hinged 62.50
On cover 85.00
On cover, single franking 175.00
Nos. 16-30 (15) 102.80 54.50

The 2c, 5c, 10c, 20c and 25c exist imperf. Value, each: $55 unused, $100 never hinged.

See Nos. 77-86. For surcharges see Nos. 31-73, B1-B4.

Covers: Values for commercial covers are for covers with correct postage rates. Postcards sell for somewhat less than covers.

Stamps of 1902-03 Surcharged Locally in Black

1921

31 A2 2m on 5c green 7.50 5.00
Never hinged 14.00
On cover 65.00
32 A2 3m on 3c red org 14.50 12.00
Never hinged 26.00
On cover 65.00
a. Larger numeral 140.00 125.00
Never hinged 250.00
On cover 525.00
33 A3 4m on 10c rose 6.75 6.00
Never hinged 11.00
On cover 65.00
34 A2 5m on 1c gray 14.50 12.00
Never hinged 26.00
On cover 95.00
a. On #16b (GC) 62.50 130.00
35 A2 5m on 4c yel brn 19.00 13.50
Never hinged 35.00
On cover 110.00
36 A3 6m on 15c orange 6.75 6.00
Never hinged 11.50
On cover 52.50
a. Larger numeral 110.00 110.00
Never hinged 210.00
On cover 475.00
37 A3 8m on 20c brn vio 7.50 6.00
Never hinged 14.00
On cover 65.00
a. Larger numeral 80.00 60.00
Never hinged 140.00
On cover 275.00
38 A3 10m on 25c blue 4.25 4.25
Never hinged 6.25
On cover 27.50
a. Inverted surcharge 45.00 45.00
Never hinged 80.00
b. Double surcharge 45.00 45.00
Never hinged 80.00
39 A3 12m on 30c vio 17.50 17.50
Never hinged 32.50
On cover 120.00
a. Grayish paper (GC) 21.00 22.50
Never hinged 35.00
40 A2 15m on 2c vio brn 14.50 14.50
Never hinged 26.00
On cover 110.00

Nos. 26-30 Surcharged

41 A4 15m on 40c 25.00 19.00
Never hinged 40.00
On cover 130.00
42 A4 15m on 50c (#27a) 12.00 12.00
Never hinged 22.50
On cover 100.00
a. White paper (#29) 37.50 40.00
Never hinged 70.00
43 A4 30m on 1fr 175.00 175.00
Never hinged 290.00
On cover 800.00
44 A4 60m on 2fr 250.00 250.00
On cover 1,200.
a. Larger numeral 1,050. 1,050.
On cover 2,600.
45 A4 150m on 5fr 350.00 350.00
On cover 1,450.

Port Said Nos. 20 and 19 Surcharged like Nos. 32 and 40

45A A2 3m on 3c red org 150.00 150.00
Never hinged 240.00
46 A2 15m on 2c vio brn 150.00 150.00
Never hinged 260.00
Nos. 31-46 (17) 1,225. 1,203.

Alexandria No. 28 Srchd.

1921

46A A4 30m on 15m on 1fr 1,200. *1,350.*

The surcharge "15 Mill." was made in error and is canceled by a bar.

The surcharges were lithographed on Nos. 31, 33, 38, 39 and 42 and typographed on the other stamps of the 1921 issue. Nos. 34, 36 and 37 were surcharged by both methods.

Alexandria Stamps of 1902-03 Surcharged in Paris

1921-23

47	A2 1m on 1c slate	3.25	2.50
	Never hinged	5.25	
	On cover		40.00
48	A2 2m on 5c green	2.25	1.90
	Never hinged	5.50	
	On cover		40.00
49	A3 4m on 10c rose	2.75	2.50
	Never hinged	4.50	
	On cover		32.50
50	A3 4m on 10c green ('23)	2.50	2.50
	Never hinged	4.75	
	On cover		27.50
51	A2 5m on 3c red org ('23)	6.75	5.00
	Never hinged	10.50	
	On cover		52.50
52	A3 6m on 15c orange	2.25	1.90
	Never hinged	3.50	
	On cover		27.50
53	A3 8m on 20c brn vio	2.25	1.25
	Never hinged	3.50	
	On cover		24.00
54	A3 10m on 25c blue	1.40	1.25
	Never hinged	2.40	
	On cover		20.00
55	A3 10m on 30c vio	4.25	3.25
	Never hinged	6.50	
	On cover		32.50
56	A3 15m on 50c bl ('23)	3.25	3.00
	Never hinged	5.25	
	On cover		32.50

Nos. 27-30 and Type of 1902 Surcharged

57	A4 15m on 50c	5.00	3.25
	Never hinged	7.50	
	On cover		32.50
a.	Grayish paper (GC)	6.50	5.50
	Never hinged	11.50	
	On cover		47.50
58	A4 30m on 1fr	4.25	3.00
	Never hinged	6.75	
	On cover		40.00
59	A4 60m on 2fr	2,250.	*2,400.*
60	A4 60m on 2fr org & pale bl ('23)	13.50	13.00
	Never hinged	21.00	
	On cover		52.50
61	A4 150m on 5fr	13.50	8.50
	Never hinged	21.00	
	On cover		62.50
	Nos. 47-58,60-61 (14)	67.15	52.80

Stamps and Types of 1902-03 Surcharged with New Values and Bars in Black

1925

62	A2 1m on 1c slate	1.25	1.25
	Never hinged	2.40	
	On cover		47.50
63	A2 2m on 5c orange	1.25	1.25
	Never hinged	2.40	
	On cover		47.50
64	A2 2m on 5c green	1.75	1.75
	Never hinged	2.00	
	On cover		40.00
65	A3 4m on 10c green	1.10	.85
	Never hinged	2.00	
	On cover		40.00
66	A2 5m on 3c red org	1.50	1.25
	Never hinged	2.75	
	On cover		32.50
67	A3 6m on 15c orange	1.40	1.25
	Never hinged	2.40	
	On cover		32.50
68	A3 8m on 20c brn vio	1.75	1.40
	Never hinged	2.75	
	On cover		32.50
69	A3 10m on 25c blue	1.10	1.00
	Never hinged	2.00	
	On cover		27.50
70	A3 15m on 50c blue	2.40	1.40
	Never hinged	3.50	
	On cover		27.50
71	A4 30m on 1fr cl & ol grn	3.50	2.90
	Never hinged	6.50	
	On cover		32.50
72	A4 60m on 2fr org & pale bl	4.25	3.50
	Never hinged	7.50	
	On cover		47.50
73	A4 150m on 5fr dk bl & buff	6.00	5.00
	Never hinged	9.50	
	On cover		52.50
	Nos. 62-73 (12)	27.25	22.80

Types of 1902-03 Issue

1927-28

77	A2 3m orange ('28)	2.50	2.10
	Never hinged	3.50	
	On cover		47.50
81	A3 15m slate blue	2.50	2.10
	Never hinged	3.50	
	On cover		27.50
82	A3 20m rose lil ('28)	6.75	5.00
	Never hinged	11.50	
	On cover		40.00
84	A4 50m org & blue	11.00	9.35
	Never hinged	19.00	
	On cover		52.50
85	A4 100m sl bl & buff	15.00	12.00
	Never hinged	25.00	
	On cover		65.00
86	A4 250m gray grn & red	25.00	16.00
	Never hinged	45.00	
	On cover		90.00
	Nos. 77-86 (6)	62.75	46.55

SEMI-POSTAL STAMPS

Regular Issue of 1902-03 Surcharged in Carmine

1915 Unwmk. *Perf. 14x13½*

B1	A3 10c + 5c rose	1.25	1.25
	Never hinged	2.25	
	On cover		15.00

Sinking Fund Issue

Type of 1902-03 Issue Surcharged in Blue or Black

1927-30

B2	A3 15m + 5m deep org	6.00	6.00
	Never hinged	10.50	
	On cover		52.50
B3	A3 15m + 5m red vio ('28)	9.25	9.25
	Never hinged	16.00	
	On cover		65.00
a.	15m + 5m violet ('30)	15.00	15.00
	Never hinged	25.00	
	On cover		90.00

Type of 1902-03 Issue Surcharged as in 1927-28

1929

B4	A3 15m + 5m fawn	12.00	12.00
	Never hinged	19.00	
	On cover		75.00

POSTAGE DUE STAMPS

Postage Due Stamps of France, 1893-1920, Surcharged in Paris in Black

1922 Unwmk. *Perf. 14x13½*

J1	D2 2m on 5c blue	2.50	2.50
	Never hinged	4.50	
	On cover		52.50
J2	D2 4m on 10c brown	2.50	2.50
	Never hinged	4.50	
	On cover		52.50
J3	D2 10m on 30c rose red	3.00	3.00
	Never hinged	5.50	
	On cover		52.50
J4	D2 15m on 50c brn vio	3.25	3.25
	Never hinged	6.50	
	On cover		60.00
J5	D2 30m on 1fr red brn, *straw*	4.50	4.50
	Never hinged	8.00	
	On cover		75.00
	Nos. J1-J5 (5)	15.75	15.75

D3

1928 Typo.

J6	D3 1m slate	1.60	1.60
	Never hinged	2.75	
	On cover		47.50
J7	D3 2m light blue	1.25	1.25
	Never hinged	2.40	
	On cover		47.50
J8	D3 4m lilac rose	1.75	1.75
	Never hinged	3.25	
	On cover		32.50
J9	D3 5m gray green	2.00	2.00
	Never hinged	4.00	
	On cover		27.50
J10	D3 10m light red	2.50	2.50
	Never hinged	4.00	
	On cover		27.50
J11	D3 20m violet brn	2.25	2.25
	Never hinged	3.00	
	On cover		27.50
J12	D3 30m green	5.00	5.00
	Never hinged	7.50	
	On cover		47.50
J13	D3 40m lt violet	6.25	6.25
	Never hinged	9.50	
	On cover		65.00
	Nos. J6-J13 (8)	22.60	22.60

Nos. J6-J13 were also available for use in Port Said.

PORT SAID

Stamps of France Overprinted in Red, Blue or Black

1899-1900 Unwmk. *Perf. 14x13½*

1	A15 1c blk, *lil bl* (R)	2.10	1.70
	Never hinged	3.50	
	On cover		62.50
2	A15 2c brn, *buff* (bl)	2.10	1.70
	Never hinged	3.50	
	On cover		62.50
3	A15 3c gray, *grysh* (Bl)	2.10	2.10
	Never hinged	3.50	
	On cover		62.50
4	A15 4c claret, *lav* (Bl)	1.75	*2.10*
	Never hinged	3.50	
	On cover		62.50
5	A15 5c yel grn (I) (R)	11.00	5.00
	Never hinged	17.50	
	On cover		32.50
	On cover, single franking		110.00
a.	Type II (R)	55.00	25.00
	Never hinged	100.00	
	On cover		100.00
6	A15 10c blk, *lav* (I) (R)	14.00	12.50
	Never hinged	25.00	
	On cover		47.50
	On cover, single franking		110.00
a.	Type II (R)	72.50	55.00
	Never hinged	130.00	
	On cover		325.00
7	A15 15c blue (R)	14.00	8.50
	Never hinged	25.00	
	On cover		40.00
	On cover, single franking		110.00
8	A15 20c red, *grn*	17.00	11.00
	Never hinged	30.00	
	On cover		65.00
	On cover, single franking		110.00
9	A15 25c blk, *rose* (R)	14.00	5.00
	Never hinged	26.00	
	On cover		32.50
	On cover, single franking		47.50
	On commercial cover		110.00
a.	Double overprint	300.00	
b.	Inverted overprint	300.00	
10	A15 30c brn, *bister*	17.00	14.00
	Never hinged	32.50	
	On cover		47.50
	On cover, single franking		60.00
a.	Inverted overprint	325.00	
11	A15 40c red, *straw*	14.00	14.00
	Never hinged	26.00	
	On cover		52.50
	On cover, single franking		75.00
12	A15 50c car, *rose* (II)	20.00	14.00
	Never hinged	35.00	
	On cover		75.00
	On cover, single franking		100.00
a.	Type I	300.00	100.00
b.	Double overprint (II)	425.00	
13	A15 1fr brnz grn, *straw*	30.00	17.50
	Never hinged	57.50	
	On cover		100.00
	On cover, single franking		160.00
	On commercial cover		725.00
14	A15 2fr brn, *az* ('00)	75.00	65.00
	Never hinged	140.00	
	On cover		325.00
	On cover, single franking		525.00
15	A15 5fr red lil, *lav*	120.00	92.50
	Never hinged	225.00	
	On cover		400.00
	On cover, single franking		650.00
	Nos. 1-15 (15)	354.05	266.60

Covers: Values for commercial covers are for covers with correct postage rates. Postcards sell for somewhat less than covers.

Regular Issue Surcharged in Red

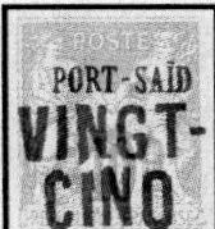

1899

16	A15 25c on 10c blk, *lav*	130.00	32.50
	Never hinged	325.00	
	On cover		260.00
a.	Inverted surcharge		250.00

With Additional Surcharge "25" in Red

17	A15 25c on 10c blk, *lav*	475.00	160.00
	Never hinged	1,000.	
a.	"25" inverted	1,500.	1,400.
b.	"25" in black		2,600.
c.	As "b," "VINGT CINQ" inverted		3,400.
d.	As "b," "25" vertical		3,400.
e.	As "c" and "d"		3,400.

A2 A3 A4

1902-03 Typo.

18	A2 1c pale gray ('16)	.65	.65
	Never hinged	1.60	
	On cover		47.50
a.	1c gray ('02)	.80	.80
	Never hinged	1.60	
	On cover		47.50
b.	1c slate ('20)	.80	.80
	Never hinged	1.60	
	On cover		47.50
19	A2 2c violet brn	.75	.75
	Never hinged	1.60	
	On cover		47.50
a.	Grayish paper (GC) ('18)	1.20	1.20
	Never hinged	2.40	
	On cover		52.50
20	A2 3c red orange	.85	.75
	Never hinged	1.60	
	On cover		47.50
21	A2 4c yellow brown	1.10	.90
	Never hinged	2.00	
	On cover		52.50
22	A2 5c blue green ('04)	1.20	.85
	Never hinged	2.00	
	On cover		13.00
	On commercial cover		50.00
a.	5c yellow green	5.00	3.00
	Never hinged	8.75	
	On cover		13.00
23	A3 10c rose red	1.60	1.10
	Never hinged	3.25	
	On cover		11.00
	On commercial cover		50.00
24	A3 15c pale red ('03)	3.25	2.25
	Never hinged	6.50	
	On cover		11.00
	On commercial cover		40.00
a.	15c orange	5.00	3.00
	Never hinged	8.75	
	On cover		16.00
	On commercial cover		40.00
25	A3 20c brn vio ('03)	3.25	2.25
	Never hinged	6.50	
	On cover		24.00
	On cover, single franking		47.50
	On commercial cover		50.00
26	A3 25c blue ('03)	2.50	1.60
	Never hinged	4.50	
	On cover		16.00
	On cover, single franking		26.00
	On commercial cover		45.00
a.	25c dark blue	4.25	3.50
27	A3 30c gray violet ('03)	6.75	5.00
	Never hinged	11.50	
	On cover		21.00
	On cover, single franking		26.00
a.	30c red violet ('09)	6.75	5.00
	Never hinged	11.50	
	On cover		16.00
	On cover, single franking		21.00
28	A4 40c red & pale bl	6.00	4.25
	Never hinged	11.00	
	On cover		27.50
	On cover, single franking		35.00
29	A4 50c bis brn & lav	9.25	6.75
	Never hinged	17.50	
	On cover		47.50
	On cover, single franking		65.00
30	A4 1fr claret & ol grn	12.00	9.25
	Never hinged	22.50	
	On cover		60.00
	On cover, single franking		95.00
31	A4 2fr gray vio & yel	15.00	15.00
	Never hinged	35.00	
	On cover		75.00
	On cover, single franking		110.00
a.	2fr dark violet & yellow	9.75	
32	A4 5fr dk bl & buff	35.00	32.50
	Never hinged	80.00	
	On cover		120.00
	On cover, single franking		240.00
	Nos. 18-32 (15)	99.15	83.85

See Nos. 83-92. For surcharges see Nos. 33-80, B1-B4.

Stamps of 1902-03 Surcharged Locally

1921

33	A2 2m on 5c green	10.00	10.00
	Never hinged	22.50	
	On cover		100.00
a.	Inverted surcharge	50.00	50.00
	Never hinged	90.00	

34 A3 4m on 10c rose 9.25 9.25
Never hinged 19.00
On cover 85.00
a. Inverted surcharge 50.00 50.00
Never hinged 90.00
35 A2 5m on 1c slate 14.00 14.00
Never hinged 26.00
On cover 100.00
a. Inverted surcharge 92.50 92.50
Never hinged 175.00
b. 5m on 1c light gray 26.00 26.00
Never hinged 45.00
On cover 110.00
c. Surcharged "2 Milliemes" on #35 67.50 67.50
Never hinged 130.00
d. As "c," surcharge inverted 175.00 175.00
Never hinged 300.00
36 A2 5m on 2c 24.00 24.00
Never hinged 40.00
On cover 110.00
a. Surcharged "2 Milliemes" 75.00 75.00
Never hinged 150.00
b. As "a," inverted 160.00 160.00
Never hinged 190.00
37 A2 5m on 3c 15.00 15.00
Never hinged 32.50
On cover 100.00
a. Inverted surcharge 62.50 62.50
b. On Alexandria #18 400.00 400.00
38 A2 5m on 4c 11.00 11.00
Never hinged 25.00
On cover 75.00
a. Inverted surcharge 80.00 80.00
Never hinged 160.00
39 A2 10m on 2c 25.00 25.00
Never hinged 45.00
On cover 110.00
40 A2 10m on 4c 35.00 35.00
Never hinged 75.00
On cover 160.00
a. Inverted surcharge 85.00 85.00
Never hinged 225.00
b. Double surcharge 100.00 105.00
Never hinged 200.00
41 A3 10m on 25c 9.25 9.25
Never hinged 22.50
On cover 60.00
a. Inverted surcharge 85.00 85.00
Never hinged 160.00
42 A3 12m on 30c 42.50 42.50
Never hinged 90.00
On cover 60.00
43 A2 15m on 4c 10.00 10.00
Never hinged 22.50
On cover 75.00
a. Inverted surcharge 85.00 85.00
Never hinged 160.00
b. Double surcharge 92.50 97.50
Never hinged 175.00
44 A3 15m on 15c pale red 67.50 67.50
Never hinged 130.00
On cover 250.00
a. Inverted surcharge 160.00 160.00
Never hinged 310.00
45 A3 15m on 20c 67.50 67.50
Never hinged 130.00
On cover 250.00
a. Inverted surcharge 160.00 160.00
Never hinged 310.00
46 A4 30m on 50c 300.00 300.00
On cover 1,000.
47 A4 60m on 50c 350.00 350.00
On cover 1,100.
48 A4 150m on 50c 400.00 400.00
On cover 1,300.

Nos. 46, 47 and 48 have a bar between the numerals and "Millièmes," which is in capital letters.

Same Surcharge on Stamps of French Offices in Turkey, 1902-03

49 A2 2m on 2c vio brn 160.00 160.00
Never hinged 30.00
50 A2 5m on 1c gray 150.00 150.00
Never hinged 260.00
a. "5" inverted 7,250.
Nos. 33-50 (18) 1,700. 1,700.

Nos. 28-32 Surcharged

51 A4 15m on 40c 60.00 60.00
Never hinged 130.00
On cover 260.00
52 A4 15m on 50c 85.00 85.00
Never hinged 175.00
On cover 360.00
b. Bar below 15 50.00 50.00
Never hinged 105.00
On cover 240.00
53 A4 30m on 1fr 300.00 300.00
On cover 1,000.
54 A4 60m on 2fr 85.00 *92.50*
Never hinged 260.00
On cover 300.00
55 A4 150m on 5fr 250.00 *275.00*
Never hinged 575.00
On cover 1,200.
Nos. 51-55 (5) 780.00 812.50

Overprinted "MILLtEMES"

51a A4 15m on 40c 425.00 425.00
Never hinged 800.00
52a A4 15m on 50c 500.00 500.00
Never hinged 950.00
53a A4 30m on 1fr 1,400. 1,400.
Never hinged 2,600.
54a A4 60m on 2fr 400.00 400.00
Never hinged 750.00
55a A4 150m on 5fr 1,050. 1,050.
Never hinged 2,000.
Nos. 51a-55a (5) 3,775. 3,775.

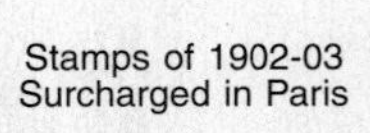

Stamps of 1902-03 Surcharged in Paris

1921-23

56 A2 1m on 1c slate 1.60 1.60
Never hinged 2.50
On cover 27.50
57 A2 2m on 5c green 1.60 1.60
Never hinged 2.75
On cover 27.50
58 A3 4m on 10c rose 2.50 2.50
Never hinged 4.50
On cover 27.50
59 A2 5m on 3c red org 9.25 9.25
Never hinged 16.00
On cover 75.00
60 A3 6m on 15c orange 3.25 3.25
Never hinged 6.50
On cover 40.00
a. 6m on 15c pale red 14.00 14.00
Never hinged 26.00
On cover 80.00
61 A3 8m on 20c brn vio 5.00 5.00
Never hinged 8.75
On cover 40.00
62 A3 10m on 25c blue 2.50 2.50
Never hinged 4.75
On cover 20.00
63 A3 10m on 30c violet 7.50 7.50
Never hinged 14.00
On cover 65.00
64 A3 15m on 50c blue 6.75 6.75
Never hinged 11.00
On cover 47.50

Nos. 29-32 and Type of 1902 Surcharged

65 A4 15m on 50c 6.00 6.00
Never hinged 9.50
On cover 20.00
66 A4 30m on 1fr 9.25 9.25
Never hinged 17.50
On cover 65.00
67 A4 60m on 2fr 130.00 130.00
Never hinged 240.00
On cover 475.00
68 A4 60m on 2fr org & pale blue 12.50 12.50
Never hinged 24.00
On cover 60.00
69 A4 150m on 5fr 20.00 20.00
Never hinged 35.00
On cover 130.00
Nos. 56-69 (14) 217.70 217.70

Stamps and Types of 1902-03 Surcharged

1925

70 A2 1m on 1c light gray .75 .75
Never hinged 1.20
On cover 47.50
a. 1m on 1c slate 2.00 2.00
Never hinged 3.25
71 A2 2m on 5c green 1.10 1.10
Never hinged 2.00
On cover 47.50
72 A3 4m on 10c rose red .90 .90
Never hinged 1.60
On cover 40.00
73 A2 5m on 3c red org 1.10 1.10
Never hinged 2.00
On cover 32.50
74 A3 6m on 15c orange 1.10 1.10
Never hinged 2.00
On cover 32.50
75 A3 8m on 20c brn vio 1.00 1.00
Never hinged 1.60
On cover 30.00
76 A3 10m on 25c blue 1.40 1.40
Never hinged 1.75
On cover 27.50
77 A3 15m on 50c blue 1.60 1.60
Never hinged 2.75
On cover 30.00
78 A4 30m on 1fr cl & ol grn 2.75 2.75
Never hinged 4.50
On cover 32.50
79 A4 60m on 2fr org & pale blue 2.50 2.50
Never hinged 4.50
On cover 32.50
80 A4 150m on 5fr dk bl & buff 4.25 4.25
Never hinged 7.50
On cover 52.50
Nos. 70-80 (11) 18.45 18.45

Type of 1902-03 Issue and

A5

1927-28

83 A5 3m orange ('28) 2.10 2.10
Never hinged 3.25
On cover 47.50
87 A3 15m slate bl 2.50 2.50
Never hinged 3.50
On cover 27.50
88 A3 20m rose lil ('28) 2.50 2.50
Never hinged 3.50
On cover 32.50
90 A4 50m org & blue 4.50 4.50
Never hinged 8.00
On cover 47.50
91 A4 100m slate bl & buff 6.00 6.00
Never hinged 9.50
On cover 52.50
92 A4 250m gray grn & red 9.25 9.25
Never hinged 16.00
On cover 65.00
Nos. 83-92 (6) 26.85 26.85

SEMI-POSTAL STAMPS

Regular Issue of 1902-03 Surcharged in Carmine

1915 Unwmk. *Perf. 14x13½*

B1 A3 10c + 5c rose 1.60 1.60
Never hinged 2.75
On cover 15.00

Sinking Fund Issue

Type of 1902-03 Issue Surcharged like Alexandria Nos. B2-B3 in Blue or Black

1927-30

B2 A3 15m + 5m dp org (Bl) 5.00 5.00
Never hinged 8.75
On cover 52.50
a. Dot omitted from "i" in "Caisse" 95.00 100.00
Never hinged 160.00
B3 A3 15m + 5m red vio ('28) 8.50 8.50
Never hinged 14.50
On cover 65.00
a. Dot omitted from "i" in "Caisse" 105.00 110.00
Never hinged 175.00
b. 15m + 5m violet ('30) 14.00 14.00
Never hinged 26.00
On cover 90.00
c. As "b," dot omitted from "i" in "Caisse" 150.00 160.00
Never hinged 225.00
B4 A3 15m + 5m fawn ('29) 10.00 10.00
Never hinged 17.50
On cover 75.00
a. Dot omitted from "i" in "Caisse" 120.00 125.00
Never hinged 225.00
Nos. B2-B4 (3) 23.50 23.50

POSTAGE DUE STAMPS

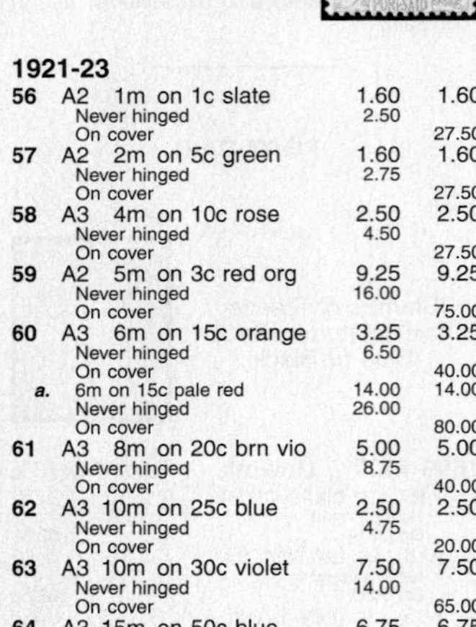

Postage Due Stamps of France, 1893-1906, Srchd. Locally in Black

1921 Unwmk. *Perf. 14x13½*

J1 D2 12m on 10c brown 62.50 *67.50*
Never hinged 150.00
On cover 325.00
J2 D2 15m on 5c blue 92.50 *105.00*
Never hinged 225.00
On cover 600.00
J3 D2 30m on 20c ol grn 92.50 *105.00*
Never hinged 225.00
On cover 600.00
a. Inverted surcharge 1,100. 1,100.
J4 D2 30m on 50c red vio 3,000. 3,400.

Same Surcharged in Red or Blue

1921

J5 D2 2m on 5c bl (R) 55.00 *60.00*
Never hinged 120.00
On cover 300.00
a. Blue surcharge 300.00 300.00
b. Accent omitted from "è" of "Millièmes" 190.00 200.00
c. Second "m" of "Millièmes" inverted 190.00 200.00
d. "S" of "Millièmes" omitted 190.00 225.00
J6 D2 4m on 10c brn (Bl) 55.00 *62.50*
Never hinged 120.00
On cover 300.00
a. Surcharged "15 Millièmes" 725.00 725.00
b. Accent omitted from "è" of "MILLlèMES" 190.00 200.00
c. Second "m" of "Millièmes" inverted 190.00 200.00
d. "S" of "Millièmes" omitted 190.00 225.00
J7 D2 10m on 30c red (Bl) 55.00 *60.00*
Never hinged 120.00
On cover 300.00
a. Inverted surcharge 160.00 160.00
b. Accent omitted from "è" of "Millièmes" 190.00 190.00
c. Second "M" of "Millièmes" inverted 190.00 190.00
d. "S" of "Millièmes" omitted 190.00 225.00
e. "Q" for "0" in surcharge (1Qm) 1,450. 1,500.
J8 D2 15m on 50c brn vio (Bl) 67.50 *72.50*
Never hinged 140.00
On cover 360.00
a. Inverted surcharge 160.00 160.00
b. Accent omitted from "è" of "Millièmes" 190.00 190.00
c. Second "m" of "Millièmes" inverted 190.00 190.00
d. "S" of "Millièmes" omitted 210.00 240.00
e. As "a," accent omitted from è of "Millièmes" 425.00
Never hinged 675.00
Nos. J5-J8 (4) 232.50 255.00

Alexandria Nos. J6-J13 were also available for use in Port Said.

OFFICES IN TURKEY (LEVANT)

Various powers maintained post offices in the Turkish Empire before World War I by authority of treaties which ended with the signing of the Treaty of Lausanne in 1923. The foreign post offices were closed Oct. 27, 1923.

100 Centimes = 1 Franc
25 Centimes = 40 Paras = 1 Piaster

Stamps of France Surcharged in Black or Red

1885-1901 Unwmk. *Perf. 14x13½*

1 A15 1pi on 25c yel, *straw* 550.00 16.00
On cover 75.00
On cover, single franking 110.00
a. Inverted surcharge 2,500. 2,400.
2 A15 1pi on 25c blk, *rose* (R) ('86) 4.25 1.25
Never hinged 8.00
On cover 13.00
On cover, single franking 20.00
a. Inverted surcharge 400.00 325.00
3 A15 2pi on 50c car, *rose* (II) ('90) 18.00 3.00
Never hinged 35.00
On cover 32.50
On cover, single franking 52.50
a. Type I ('01) 375.00 50.00
Never hinged 725.00
On cover 525.00
On cover, single franking 875.00
4 A15 3pi on 75c car, *rose* 30.00 15.00
Never hinged 60.00
On cover 85.00
On cover, single franking 120.00
5 A15 4pi on 1fr brnz grn, *straw* 30.00 15.00
Never hinged 60.00
On cover 100.00
On cover, single franking 160.00
6 A15 8pi on 2fr brn, *az* ('00) 37.50 25.00
Never hinged 67.50
On cover 200.00
On cover, single franking 325.00

7 A15 20pi on 5fr red lil, *lav* ('90) 110.00 60.00
Never hinged 225.00
On cover 650.00
On cover, single franking 1,050.
Nos. 1-7 (7) 779.75 135.25

A2 A3

A4

Nos. 29, 32, 36 and Types of A4 Surcharged

No. 34

No. 35

1902-07 Typo. *Perf. 14x13½*

21 A2 1c gray .65 .65
Never hinged 1.25
On cover 47.50
a. 1c pale gray ('11) .65 .65
Never hinged 1.25
On cover 47.50
b. 1c slate ('20) .80 .80
Never hinged 1.50
On cover 47.50
c. Grayish paper (GC) ('18) 1.25 1.00
Never hinged 2.00
On cover 52.50
22 A2 2c vio brn .65 .65
Never hinged 1.25
On cover 47.50
a. Grayish paper (GC) ('18) 1.25 1.00
Never hinged 2.00
On cover 52.50
23 A2 3c red org .65 .65
Never hinged 1.25
On cover 47.50
a. Grayish paper (GC) ('18) 1.25 1.00
Never hinged 2.00
On cover 52.50
24 A2 4c yel brn 3.00 1.10
Never hinged 4.75
On cover 65.00
a. Imperf., pair 90.00
25 A2 5c grn ('06) 1.00 .65
Never hinged 1.60
On cover 13.00
26 A3 10c rose red 1.00 .65
Never hinged 1.60
On cover 10.00
27 A3 15c pale red ('03) 3.00 1.25
Never hinged 4.75
On cover 11.00
28 A3 20c brn vio ('03) 3.25 2.00
Never hinged 6.00
On cover 27.50
29 A3 25c blue ('07) 45.00 *60.00*
Never hinged 80.00
On cover 37.50
a. Imperf., pair 425.00
30 A3 30c lilac ('03) 6.00 3.00
Never hinged 9.50
On cover 13.00
On cover, single franking 20.00
31 A4 40c red & pale bl 6.00 3.25
Never hinged 9.50
On cover 20.00
On cover, single franking 27.50
32 A4 50c bis brn & lav ('07) 190.00 *225.00*
On cover 5,000.
a. Imperf., pair 925.00
33 A4 1fr claret & ol grn ('07) 425.00 450.00
On cover 6,000.
a. Imperf., pair 1,100.

Black Surcharge

34 A3 1pi on 25c bl ('03) 1.20 .65
Never hinged 2.00
On cover 16.00
On cover, single franking 27.50
a. Second "I" omitted 32.50 25.00
Never hinged 55.00
b. Double surcharge 72.50 60.00
Never hinged 130.00
35 A4 2pi on 50c bis brn & lavender 4.25 1.60
Never hinged 7.25
On cover 27.50
On cover, single franking 47.50
36 A4 4pi on 1fr cl & ol grn 5.00 2.10
Never hinged 9.00
On cover 32.50
On cover, single franking 65.00
a. Imperf., pair 750.00
37 A4 8pi on 2fr gray vio & yel 20.00 15.00
Never hinged 35.00
On cover 65.00
On cover, single franking 110.00
38 A4 20pi on 5fr dk bl & buff 10.00 6.00
Never hinged 16.00
On cover 55.00
On cover, single franking 125.00
Nos. 21-38 (18) 725.65 774.20

Nos. 29, 32-33 were used during the early part of 1907 in the French Offices at Harar and Diredawa, Ethiopia. Djibouti and Port Said stamps were also used.

No. 27 Surcharged in Green

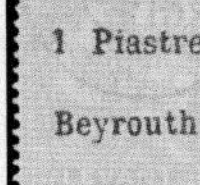

1905

39 A3 1pi on 15c pale red 2,100. 325.
On cover 1,750.
a. "Piastte" 6,500. 1,450.
b. Se-tenant pair, #39, #39a 11,000. 2,600.
Never hinged 16.00
On cover 5,500.

Stamps of France 1900-21 Surcharged

On A22 On A20

On A18

1921-22

40 A22 30pa on 5c grn 1.00 1.00
Never hinged 1.60
On cover 16.00
41 A22 30pa on 5c org 1.00 .85
Never hinged 1.60
On cover 16.00
42 A22 1pi20pa on 10c red 1.10 1.10
Never hinged 1.60
On cover 13.00
43 A22 1pi20pa on 10c grn 1.10 .85
Never hinged 1.60
On cover 16.00
44 A22 3pi30pa on 25c bl 1.60 1.00
Never hinged 2.40
On cover 11.00
45 A22 4pi20pa on 30c org 1.60 1.10
Never hinged 2.40
On cover 16.00
a. "4" omitted 1,050.
46 A20 7pi20pa on 50c bl 1.60 1.25
Never hinged 2.40
On cover 20.00
On cover, single franking 27.50
47 A18 15pi on 1fr car & ol grn 3.00 2.10
Never hinged 4.00
On cover 27.50
On cover, single franking 40.00
48 A18 30pi on 2fr org & pale bl 12.50 10.00
Never hinged 20.00
On cover 47.50
On cover, single franking 75.00
49 A18 75pi on 5fr dk bl & buff 11.00 7.50
Never hinged 17.50
On cover 52.50
On cover, single franking 100.00
Nos. 40-49 (10) 35.50 26.75

Stamps of France, 1903-07, Handstamped

1923

52 A22 1pi20pa on 10c red 62.50 60.00
Never hinged 110.00
On cover 275.00
54 A20 3pi30pa on 15c gray grn (GC) 25.00 25.00
Never hinged 40.00
On cover 120.00
a. On normal paper 52.50 52.50
Never hinged 87.50
55 A22 7pi20pa on 35c vio 30.00 30.00
Never hinged 47.50
On cover 130.00
a. Grayish paper (GC) 47.50 47.50
Never hinged 80.00
b. 1pi20pa on 35c violet 1,400. 1,400.
c. Se-tenant pair, #55, #55b 2,600.
Nos. 52-55 (3) 117.50 115.00

CAVALLE (CAVALLA)

Stamps of France Ovptd. or Srchd. in Carmine, Red, Blue or Black

1893-1900 Unwmk. *Perf. 14x13½*

1 A15 5c grn, *grnsh* (R) 25.00 21.00
Never hinged 47.50
On cover 160.00
a. Type II (C) 25.00 21.00
2 A15 5c yel grn (I) ('00) (R) 21.00 20.00
Never hinged 35.00
On cover 150.00
3 A15 10c blk, *lav* (II) 25.00 25.00
Never hinged 47.50
On cover 165.00
a. 10c black, *lavender* (I) 175.00 145.00
On cover 525.00
4 A15 15c blue (R) 47.50 30.00
Never hinged 75.00
On cover 150.00
a. 15c blue (C) 47.50 30.00
5 A15 1pi on 25c blk, *rose* 27.50 19.00
Never hinged 47.50
On cover 275.00
On cover, single franking 400.00
a. Dot omitted from "i" in "Piastre" 67.50 67.50
6 A15 2pi on 50c car, *rose* 90.00 62.50
Never hinged 175.00
On cover 800.00
On cover, single franking 1,000.
a. Dot omitted from "i" in "Piastres" 245.00 245.00
7 A15 4pi on 1fr brnz grn, *straw* (R) 95.00 85.00
Never hinged 175.00
On cover 1,000.
On cover, single franking 1,200.
a. Dot omitted from "i" in "Piastres" 245.00 245.00
b. 4pi on 1fr brnz grn, *straw* (C) 95.00 85.00
8 A15 8pi on 2fr brn, *az* ('00) (Bk) 115.00 115.00
On cover 1,100.
On cover, single franking 1,600.
a. Dot omitted from "i" in "Piastres" 300.00 300.00
Nos. 1-8 (8) 446.00 377.50
Set, never hinged 1,000.

A3 A4

A5

A6

1902-03

9 A3 5c green 2.25 1.75
Never hinged 3.50
On cover 100.00
a. 5c yel grn 2.50 2.00
10 A4 10c rose red ('03) 2.25 1.75
Never hinged 3.50
On cover 100.00
11 A4 15c orange 2.25 1.75
Never hinged 4.00
On cover 100.00
a. 15c pale red ('03) 12.50 12.50
Never hinged 21.00
On cover 165.00

Surcharged in Black

12 A5 1pi on 25c bl 4.75 3.00
Never hinged 7.25
On cover 130.00
On cover, single franking 180.00
13 A6 2pi on 50c bis brn & lav 13.00 7.00
Never hinged 19.00
On cover 160.00
On cover, single franking 225.00
14 A6 4pi on 1fr cl & ol grn 16.00 13.00
Never hinged 24.00
On cover 200.00
On cover, single franking 300.00
15 A6 8pi on 2fr gray vio & yel 21.00 19.00
Never hinged 32.50
On cover 240.00
On cover, single franking 425.00
Nos. 9-15 (7) 61.50 47.25

DEDEAGH (DEDEAGATCH)

Stamps of France Ovptd. or Srchd. in Carmine, Red, Blue or Black

1893-1900 Unwmk. *Perf. 14x13½*

1 A15 5c grn, *grnsh* (II) (R) 17.50 15.00
Never hinged 40.00
On cover 130.00
a. Type II (C) 17.50 15.00
Never hinged 27.50
On cover 130.00
2 A15 5c yel grn (I) ('00) (R) 14.00 14.00
Never hinged 35.00
On cover 130.00
3 A15 10c blk, *lav* (II) 26.50 20.00
Never hinged 65.00
On cover 130.00
a. Type I 45.00 32.50
Never hinged 75.00
On cover 165.00
b. As "a," double overprint 300.00
4 A15 15c blue (II) (R) 35.00 30.00
Never hinged 87.50
On cover 120.00
a. Type II (C) 35.00 30.00
Never hinged 87.50
On cover 120.00
5 A15 1pi on 25c blk, *rose* 40.00 35.00
Never hinged 97.50
On cover 325.00
On cover, single franking 475.00
a. Dot omitted from "i" in "Piastre" 120.00 120.00
6 A15 2pi on 50c car, *rose* 67.50 47.50
Never hinged 160.00
On cover 525.00
On cover, single franking 875.00
a. Dot omitted from "i" in "Piastres" 200.00 200.00
7 A15 4pi on 1fr brnz grn, *straw* (R) 80.00 70.00
Never hinged 220.00
On cover 875.00
On cover, single franking 1,100.
a. Dot omitted from "i" in "Piastres" 240.00 240.00
8 A15 8pi on 2fr brn, *az* ('00) (Bk) 115.00 95.00
Never hinged 290.00
On cover 1,000.
On cover, single franking 1,500.
a. Dot omitted from "i" in "Piastres" 340.00 340.00
Nos. 1-8 (8) 395.50 326.50
Set, never hinged 1,000.

A3 A4

A5

A6

1902-03

9 A3 5c green ('03) 3.00 2.50
Never hinged 7.50
On cover 100.00
a. 5c yellow green 3.50 3.00
Never hinged 8.00
On cover 110.00
10 A4 10c rose red ('03) 3.50 2.75
Never hinged 7.50
On cover 100.00

11 A4 15c orange 5.00 3.75
Never hinged 17.50
On cover 130.00
a. 15c rose red ('03) 7.00 6.00
Never hinged 24.00
On cover 140.00

Black Surcharge

15 A5 1pi on 25c bl ('03) 3.50 2.75
Never hinged 8.75
On cover 130.00
On cover, single franking 180.00
16 A6 2pi on 50c bis brn & lav 11.50 10.00
Never hinged 30.00
On cover 175.00
On cover, single franking 260.00
a. Double surcharge 300.00
17 A6 4pi on 1fr cl & ol grn 22.50 18.50
Never hinged 52.50
On cover 225.00
On cover, single franking 360.00
18 A6 8pi on 2fr gray vio & yel 32.50 27.50
Never hinged 52.50
On cover 225.00
On cover, single franking 360.00
Never hinged 52.50
On cover 300.00
On cover, single franking 500.00
Nos. 9-18 (7) 81.50 67.75
Set, never hinged 175.00

PORT LAGOS

Stamps of France Ovptd. or Srchd. in Carmine, Red or Blue

1893 Unwmk. *Perf. 14x13½*

1 A15 5c grn, *grnsh* (R) 30.00 30.00
Never hinged 55.00
On cover 325.00
a. 5c grn, *grnsh* (C) 30.00 30.00
Never hinged 55.00
On cover 325.00
2 A15 10c blk, *lav* 62.50 47.50
Never hinged 110.00
On cover 525.00
3 A15 15c blue (R) 90.00 70.00
Never hinged 160.00
On cover 600.00
a. 15c blue (C) 95.00 75.00
Never hinged 160.00
On cover 600.00
4 A15 1pi on 25c blk, *rose* 75.00 60.00
Never hinged 140.00
On cover 85.00
On cover, single franking 1,200.
a. Dot omitted from "i" in "Piastres" 225.00 225.00
5 A15 2pi on 50c car, *rose* 185.00 95.00
On cover 1,100.
On cover, single franking 1,750.
a. Dot omitted from "i" in "Piastres" 550.00 425.00
6 A15 4pi on 1fr brnz grn, *straw* (R) 112.50 95.00
On cover 1,500.
On cover, single franking 2,300.
a. Dot omitted from "i" in "Piastres" 340.00 340.00
Nos. 1-6 (6) 555.00 397.50
Set, never hinged 1,300.

VATHY (SAMOS)

Stamps of France Ovptd. or Srchd. in Carmine, Red, Blue or Black

1894-1900 Unwmk. *Perf. 14x13½*

1 A15 5c grn, *grnsh* (R) 8.50 7.50
Never hinged 15.50
On cover 110.00
a. 5c grn, *grnsh* (II) (C) 10.00 8.00
Never hinged 17.00
On cover 110.00
2 A15 5c yel grn (I) ('00) (R) 8.50 7.50
Never hinged 17.00
On cover 110.00
a. Type II 85.00 85.00
Never hinged 160.00
On cover 675.00
b. Vert. pair, #2, #2a 2,000.
3 A15 10c blk, *lav* (I) 17.50 14.00
Never hinged 35.00
On cover 110.00
a. Type II 50.00 45.00
Never hinged 100.00
On cover 525.00
4 A15 15c blue (R) 17.50 14.00
Never hinged 32.00
On cover 110.00

5 A15 1pi on 25c blk, *rose* 17.50 11.00
Never hinged 24.00
On cover 100.00
On cover, single franking 130.00
a. Dot omitted from "i" in "Piastres" 52.50 52.50
Never hinged 450.00
6 A15 2pi on 50c car, *rose* 30.00 26.00
Never hinged 57.50
On cover 300.00
On cover, single franking 475.00
a. Dot omitted from "i" in "Piastres" 90.00 90.00
Never hinged 290.00
7 A15 4pi on 1fr brnz grn, *straw* (R) 40.00 35.00
Never hinged 72.50
On cover 525.00
On cover, single franking 725.00
a. Dot omitted from "i" in "Piastres" 120.00 120.00
Never hinged 290.00
b. Left "4" omitted 800.00
8 A15 8pi on 2fr brn, *az* ('00) (Bk) 72.50 72.50
Never hinged 150.00
On cover 1,000.
On cover, single franking 1,500.
a. Dot omitted from "i" in "Piastres" 215.00 215.00
Never hinged 290.00
9 A15 20pi on 5fr lil, *lav* ('00) (Bk) 105.00 105.00
Never hinged 200.00
On cover 1,100.
On cover, single franking 1,600.
a. Dot omitted from "i" in "Piastres" 315.00 315.00
Never hinged 575.00
Nos. 1-9 (9) 317.00 292.50
Set, never hinged 600.00

OFFICES IN ZANZIBAR

Until 1906 France maintained post offices in the Sultanate of Zanzibar, but in that year Great Britain assumed direct control over this protectorate and the French withdrew their postal system.

16 Annas = 1 Rupee

Stamps of France Surcharged in Red, Carmine, Blue or Black

1894-96 Unwmk. *Perf. 14x13½*

1 A15 ½a on 5c grn, *grnsh* 10.00 7.50
2 A15 1a on 10c blk, *lav* (Bl) 15.00 12.50
3 A15 1½a on 15c bl ('96) 22.50 21.00
a. "ANNAS" 100.00 92.50
b. Carmine surcharge 19.00 15.00
4 A15 2a on 20c red, *grn* ('96) (Bk) 19.00 15.00
a. "ANNA" 2,300. 2,300.
5 A15 2½a on 25c blk, *rose* (Bl) 12.50 9.25
a. Double surcharge 250.00 250.00
6 A15 3a on 30c brn, *bis* ('96) (Bk) 21.00 18.00
7 A15 4a on 40c red, *straw* ('96) (Bk) 29.00 25.00
8 A15 5a on 50c car, *rose* (Bl) 37.50 32.50
9 A15 7½a on 75c vio, *org* ('96) 500.00 400.00
10 A15 10a on 1fr brnz grn, *straw* 67.50 55.00
a. Carmine surcharge 50.00
11 A15 50a on 5fr red lil, *lav* ('96) (Bk) 325.00 260.00
Nos. 1-11 (11) 1,059. 855.75

1894

12 A15 ½a & 5c on 1c blk, *lil bl* (R) 200.00 *220.00*
13 A15 1a & 10c on 3c gray, *grysh* (R) 180.00 *200.00*
a. "1" before "ANNA" omitted —
14 A15 2½a & 25c on 4c cl, *lav* (Bk) 230.00 *275.00*
15 A15 5a & 50c on 20c red, *grn* (Bk) 250.00 *275.00*

16 A15 10a & 1fr on 40c red, *straw* (Bk) 475.00 *525.00*
Nos. 12-16 (5) 1,335. 1,495.

There are two distinct types of the figures 5c, four of the 25c and three of each of the others of this series.

Stamps of France Srchd. in Red, Carmine, Blue or Black

1896-1900

17 A15 ½a on 5c grn, *grnsh* (R) 11.00 8.50
a. Carmine surcharge 11.00 8.50
18 A15 ½a on 5c yel grn (I) (R) 7.50 6.75
a. Type II 9.25 7.50
19 A15 1a on 10c blk, *lav* (II) (Bl) 9.25 7.50
a. Type I 22.50 19.00
20 A15 1½a on 15c bl (R) 11.00 9.25
21 A15 2a on 20c red, *grn* 9.25 9.25
a. "ZANZIBAR" double 210.00 210.00
b. "ZANZIBAR" triple 210.00 210.00
22 A15 2½a on 25c blk, *rose* (Bl) 11.00 9.25
a. Inverted surcharge 275.00 210.00
23 A15 3a on 30c brn, *bis* 11.00 9.25
24 A15 4a on 40c red, *straw* 13.50 10.00
25 A15 5a on 50c rose, *rose* (II) (Bl) 45.00 32.50
a. Type I 125.00 100.00
26 A15 10a on 1fr brnz grn, *straw* (R) 29.00 25.00
a. Carmine surcharge 12.50 11.50
27 A15 20a on 2fr brn, *az* 35.00 29.00
a. "ZANZIBAS" 675.00 *750.00*
b. "ZANZIBAR" triple 1,600.
28 A15 50a on 5fr lil, *lav* 67.50 62.50
a. "ZANZIBAS" *9,250.*
Nos. 17-28 (12) 260.00 218.75

For surcharges see Nos. 50-54.

A4

A5

1897

29 A4 2½a & 25c on ½a on 5c grn, *grnsh* 1,300. 240.
30 A4 2½a & 25c on 1a on 10c *lav* *4,500.* 1,100.
31 A4 2½a & 25c on 1½a on 15c blue *4,400.* 950.
32 A5 5a & 50c on 3a on 30c brn, *bis* *4,400.* 950.
33 A5 5a & 50c on 4a on 40c red, *straw* *4,500.* 1,300.

Printed on the Margins of Sheets of French Stamps

A6

A7

Perf. 14x13½ on one or more sides
1897

34 A6 2½a & 25c grn, *grnsh* 1,300.
35 A6 2½a & 25c blk, *lav* *4,000.*
36 A6 2½a & 25c blue *3,000.*
37 A7 5a & 50c brn, *bis* *2,900.*
38 A7 5a & 50c red, *straw* *4,000.*

There are 5 varieties of figures in the above surcharges.

Surcharged in Red or Black

A8

A9

A10

1902-03 *Perf. 14x13½*

39 A8 ½a on 5c grn (R) 6.75 6.00
40 A9 1a on 10c rose red ('03) 7.50 7.50
41 A9 1½a on 15c pale red ('03) 15.00 14.00
42 A9 2a on 20c brn vio ('03) 18.00 15.00
43 A9 2½a on 25c bl ('03) 18.00 15.00
44 A9 3a on 30c lil ('03) 13.00 13.00
a. 5a on 30c (error) 325.00 *375.00*
45 A10 4a on 40c red & pale bl 30.00 25.00
46 A10 5a on 50c bis brn & lav 25.00 21.00
47 A10 10a on 1fr cl & ol grn 32.50 29.00
48 A10 20a on 2fr gray vio & yel 85.00 75.00
49 A10 50a on 5fr dk bl & buff 100.00 92.50
Nos. 39-49 (11) 350.75 313.00

For see Reunion Nos. 55-59.

Nos. 23-24 Surcharged in Black

a

b

c

1904

50 A15 (a) 25c & 2½a on 4a on 40c 1,000.
51 A15 (b) 50c & 5a on 3a on 30c 1,200.
52 A15 (b) 50c & 5a on 4a on 40c 6,500. 1,200.
53 A15 (c) 1fr & 10a on 3a on 30c 2,000.
54 A15 (c) 1fr & 10a on 4a on 40c 2,000.

Nos. 39-40, 44 Surcharged in Red or Black

d

e

f

g

55 A8 (d) 25c & 2a on ½a on 5c (R) 3,100. 140.00
56 A9 (e) 25c & 2½a on 1a on 10c 6,500. 150.00
a. Inverted surcharge 1,500.
57 A9 (e) 25c & 2½a on 3a on 30c 2,400.
a. Inverted surcharge 4,100.
b. Double surch., both invtd. 2,600.

58 A9 (f) 50c & 5a on 3a on 30c 1,250.
59 A9 (g) 1fr & 10a on 3a on 30c 2,000.

No. J1-J3 With Various Surcharges Overprinted: "Timbre" in Red

60 D1 ½a on 5c blue 450.00

Overprinted "Affrancht" in Black

61 D1 1a on 10c brown 450.00

With Red Bars Across "CHIFFRE" and "TAXE"

62 D1 1½a on 15c green 1,000.

The illustrations are not exact reproductions of the new surcharges but are merely intended to show their relative positions and general styles.

POSTAGE DUE STAMPS

Postage Due Stamps of France Srchd. in Red, Blue or Black Like Nos. 17-28

1897 Unwmk. *Perf. 14x13½*

J1 D2 ½a on 5c blue (R)	21.00	12.50
J2 D2 1a on 10c brn (Bl)	21.00	12.50
a. Inverted surcharge	160.00	*190.00*
J3 D2 1½a on 15c grn (R)	32.50	12.50
J4 D2 3a on 30c car (Bk)	29.00	21.00
J5 D2 5a on 50c lil (Bl)	32.50	25.00
a. 2½a on 50c lilac (Bl)	1,400.	1,300.
Nos. J1-J5 (5)	136.00	83.50

For overprints see Nos. 60-62.

FRENCH COLONIES

ˈfrench ˈkä-lə-nēz

From 1859 to 1906 and in 1944 and 1945 special stamps were issued for use in all French Colonies which did not have stamps of their own.

100 Centimes = 1 Franc

Perforations: Nos. 1-45 are known variously perforated privately.

Gum: Many of Nos. 1-45 were issued without gum. Some were gummed locally.

Reprints: Nos. 1-7, 9-12, 24, 26-42, 44 and 45 were reprinted officially in 1887. These reprints are ungummed and the colors of both design and paper are deeper or brighter than the originals. Value for Nos. 1-6, $20 each.

Eagle and Crown — A1

1859-65 Unwmk. Typo. *Imperf.*

1 A1 1c ol grn, *pale bl* ('62)	24.00	*27.50*
On cover		275.00
2 A1 5c yel grn, *grnsh* ('62)	24.00	16.00
On cover		110.00
3 A1 10c bister, *yel*	32.50	8.00
On cover		35.00
a. Pair, one sideways	1,000.	525.00
On cover		*1,600.*
4 A1 20c bl, *bluish* ('65)	35.00	13.50
On cover		42.50
5 A1 40c org, *yelsh*	27.50	13.50
On cover		52.50
6 A1 80c car rose, *pnksh* ('65)	110.00	60.00
On cover		250.00
Nos. 1-6 (6)	253.00	138.50

Values for stamps on cover are for covers paying ordinary rates and emanating from the most populated colonies such as Martinique and Guadeloupe. Covers originating from more remote areas command premiums.

Values for blocks of 4

1	A1	1c ol grn, *pale bl*	140.00	*250.00*
2	A1	5c yel grn, *grnsh*	120.00	*200.00*
3	A1	10c bister, *yel*	160.00	60.00
a.		Block, one sideways	—	—
4	A1	20c bl, *bluish*	175.00	175.00
5	A1	40c org, *yelsh*	140.00	130.00
6	A1	80c car rose, *pnksh*	540.00	*600.00*

Napoleon III
A2 A3

Ceres A4 Napoleon III A5

1871-72 *Imperf.*

7 A2 1c ol grn, *pale bl* ('72)	80.00	80.00
On cover		290.00
8 A3 5c yel grn, *grnsh* ('72)	1,000.	400.00
On cover		1,650.
9 A4 10c bis, *yelsh*	375.00	130.00
On cover		350.00
a. Tête bêche pair	*55,000.*	*22,500.*
On cover		*60,000.*
10 A4 15c bis, *yelsh* ('72)	325.00	13.00
On cover		57.50
11 A4 20c blue, *bluish*	525.00	125.00
On cover		450.00
a. Tête bêche pair	—	18,000.
On cover		*40,000.*
12 A4 25c bl, *bluish* ('72)	175.00	13.00
On cover		110.00
13 A5 30c brn, *yelsh*	175.00	60.00
On cover		140.00
14 A4 40c org, *yelsh* (I)	250.00	13.00
On cover		52.50
a. Type II	*3,500.*	*650.00*
On cover		*1,400.*
b. Pair, types I & II	*7,250.*	*1,750.*
On cover		*3,900.*
c. Type II, pair	*22,000.*	*7,250.*
On cover		*27,000.*
15 A5 80c rose, *pnksh*	1,100.	115.00
On cover		450.00
Nos. 7-15 (9)	4,005.	949.00

For 40c types I-II see illustrations over France #1.

See note after France No. 9 for additional information on Nos. 8-9, 11-12, 14.

Values for blocks of 4

7	A2	1c ol grn, *pale bl*	400.00	*650.00*
8	A3	5c yel grn, *grnsh*	7,750.	*8,750.*
9	A4	10c bis, *yelsh*	1,850.	1,700.
a.		Tête bêche pair	—	—
10	A4	15c bis, *yelsh*	1,600.	140.00
11	A4	20c blue, *bluish*	2,600.	1,500.
a.		Tête bêche pair	—	—
12	A4	25c bl, *bluish*	900.00	130.00
13	A5	30c brn, *yelsh*	940.00	400.00
14	A4	40c org, *yelsh* (I)	1,800.	525.00
a.		Type II	—	—
b.		Block, 1 type II	—	—
c.		Block, 2 type II	—	—
15	A5	80c rose, *pnksh*	5,400.	2,900.

Ceres
A6 A7

1872-77 *Imperf.*

16 A6 1c ol grn, *pale bl* ('73)	13.00	*14.50*
Never hinged	25.00	
On cover		260.00
17 A6 2c red brn, *yelsh* ('76)	475.00	750.00
On cover		*10,750.*
18 A6 4c gray ('76)	*11,000.*	475.00
On cover		*16,000.*
19 A6 5c grn, *pale bl*	17.50	9.50
Never hinged	35.00	
On cover		175.00
20 A7 10c bis, *rose* ('76)	240.00	13.00
On cover		35.00
21 A7 15c bister ('77)	525.00	100.00
On cover		600.00
22 A7 30c brn, *yelsh*	130.00	21.00
On cover		57.50
23 A7 80c rose, *pnksh* ('73)	625.00	140.00
On cover		650.00

No. 17 was used only in Cochin China, 1876-77. Excellent forgeries of Nos. 17 and 18 exist.

With reference to the stamps of France and French Colonies in the same designs and colors see the note after France No. 9.

Values for blocks of 4

16	A6	1c ol grn, *pale bl*	65.	100.
		Never hinged	130.	
17	A6	2c red brn, *yelsh*	2,500.	
18	A6	4c gray	—	
19	A6	5c grn, *pale bl*	100.	100.
		Never hinged	200.	
20	A7	10c bis, *rose*	1,250.	225.
21	A7	15c bister	2,500.	1,250.
22	A7	30c brn, *yelsh*	625.	200.
23	A7	80c rose, *pnksh*	3,100.	1,100.

Peace and Commerce — A8

1877-78 Type I *Imperf.*

24 A8 1c grn, *grnsh*	35.00	*45.00*
Never hinged	70.00	
On cover		350.00
25 A8 4c grn, *grnsh*	24.00	14.50
Never hinged	47.50	
On cover		350.00
26 A8 30c brn, *yelsh* ('78)	52.50	52.50
Never hinged	105.00	
On cover		175.00
27 A8 40c ver, *straw*	35.00	21.00
Never hinged	70.00	
On cover		80.00
28 A8 75c rose, *rose* ('78)	75.00	*100.00*
On cover		290.00
a. 75c carmine, *rose*	110.00	95.00
On cover		525.00
29 A8 1fr brnz grn, *straw*	60.00	67.50
Never hinged	120.00	
On cover		100.00
Nos. 24-29 (6)	281.50	300.50

Type II

30 A8 2c grn, *grnsh*	17.50	11.00
Never hinged	35.00	
On cover		250.00
31 A8 5c grn, *grnsh*	24.00	5.50
Never hinged	47.50	
On cover		87.50
32 A8 10c grn, *grnsh*	125.00	24.00
Never hinged	250.00	
On cover		175.00
33 A8 15c gray, *grnsh*	250.00	72.50
On cover		290.00
34 A8 20c red brn, *straw*	52.50	9.50
Never hinged	105.00	
On cover		92.50
35 A8 25c ultra *bluish*	52.50	8.75
Never hinged	105.00	
On cover		87.50
a. 25c blue, *bluish* ('78)	*4,250.*	175.00
On cover		*450.00*
36 A8 35c vio blk, *org* ('78)	67.50	32.50
On cover		175.00
Nos. 30-36 (7)	589.00	163.75
Nos. 24-36 (13)	870.50	464.25

Values for blocks of 4

24	A8	1c grn, *grnsh*	225.00	*260.00*
25	A8	4c grn, *grnsh*	125.00	130.00
26	A8	30c brn, *yelsh*	150.00	210.00
		Never hinged	500.00	
27	A8	40c ver, *straw*	90.00	175.00
28	A8	75c rose, *rose*	290.00	375.00
a.		75c carmine, *rose*	625.00	600.00
29	A8	1fr brnz grn, *straw*	175.00	190.00

Type II

30	A8	2c grn, *grnsh*	87.50	65.00
		Never hinged	180.00	
31	A8	5c grn, *grnsh*	120.00	75.00
		Never hinged	240.00	
32	A8	10c grn, *grnsh*	575.00	160.00
33	A8	15c gray, *grnsh*	1,450.	1,300.
34	A8	20c red brn, *straw*	250.00	240.00
35	A8	25c ultra, *bluish*	250.00	100.00
a.		25c blue, *bluish*	—	3,250.
36	A8	35c vio blk, *org*	340.00	275.00

Type II

1878-80

38 A8 1c blk, *lil bl*	21.00	21.00
Never hinged	42.50	
On cover		175.00
39 A8 2c brn, *buff*	21.00	*24.00*
Never hinged	42.50	
On cover		175.00
40 A8 4c claret, *lav*	32.50	*45.00*
Never hinged	65.00	
On cover		175.00
41 A8 10c blk, *lav* ('79)	120.00	27.50
Never hinged	240.00	
On cover		130.00
42 A8 15c blue ('79)	35.00	17.50
Never hinged	70.00	
On cover		67.50
43 A8 20c red, *grn* ('79)	87.50	17.50
Never hinged	175.00	
On cover		87.50
44 A8 25c blk, *red* ('79)	600.00	275.00
On cover		1,200.
45 A8 25c yel, *straw* ('80)	725.00	32.50
On cover		100.00
Nos. 38-45 (8)	1,642.	460.00

No. 44 was used only in Mayotte, Nossi-Be and New Caledonia. Forgeries exist.

The 3c yellow, 3c gray, 15c yellow, 20c blue, 25c rose and 5fr lilac were printed together with the reprints, and were never issued.

For stamps of type A8 surcharged and with "SPM" see St. Pierre & Miquelon Nos. 1-8.

Values for blocks of 4

38	A8	1c blk, *lil bl*	110.00	*180.00*
39	A8	2c brn, *buff*	87.50	125.00
40	A8	4c claret, *lav*	160.00	*240.00*
		Never hinged	325.00	
41	A8	10c blk, *lav*	600.00	240.00
42	A8	15c blue	190.00	*200.00*
43	A8	20c red, *grn*	450.00	200.00
44	A8	25c blk, *red*	*3,100.*	—
45	A8	25c yel, *straw*	*3,500.*	425.00

Commerce — A9

1881-86 *Perf. 14x13½*

46 A9 1c blk, *lil bl*	5.50	4.75
Never hinged	11.00	
On cover		60.00
47 A9 2c brn, *buff*	5.50	4.75
Never hinged	11.00	
On cover		60.00
48 A9 4c claret, *lav*	5.50	5.50
Never hinged	11.00	
On cover		60.00
49 A9 5c grn, *grnsh*	6.50	3.25
Never hinged	13.00	
On cover		40.00
50 A9 10c blk, *lavender*	11.00	4.75
Never hinged	22.50	
On cover		52.50
51 A9 15c blue	16.00	3.25
Never hinged	32.50	
On cover		32.50
52 A9 20c red, *yel grn*	52.50	18.00
Never hinged	105.00	
On cover		110.00
53 A9 25c yel, *straw*	17.50	5.50
Never hinged	35.00	
On cover		52.50
54 A9 25c blk, *rose* ('86)	24.00	3.25
Never hinged	47.50	
On cover		32.50

55 A9 30c brn, *bis* 45.00 21.00
Never hinged 90.00
On cover 110.00
56 A9 35c vio blk, *yel org* 40.00 30.00
Never hinged 80.00
On cover 160.00
a. 35c violet black, *yellow* 100.00 52.50
Never hinged 200.00
On cover 250.00
57 A9 40c ver, *straw* 45.00 27.50
Never hinged 90.00
On cover 160.00
58 A9 75c car, *rose* 120.00 60.00
Never hinged 240.00
On cover 275.00
59 A9 1fr brnz grn, *straw* 80.00 45.00
Never hinged 160.00
On cover 275.00
Nos. 46-59 (14) 474.00 236.50

Nos. 46-59 exist imperforate. They are proofs and were not used for postage, except the 10c.

For stamps of type A9 surcharged with numerals see: Cochin China, Diego Suarez, Gabon, Malagasy (Madagascar), Nossi-Be, New Caledonia, Reunion, Senegal, Tahiti.

For stamps of type A9 surcharged and with "MQE" see Martinique Nos. 3-4. For stamps of type A9 surcharged and with "SPM" see St. Pierre & Miquelon Nos. 9-11, 15-18.

Values for blocks of 4

46 A9 1c blk, *lil bl* 32.50 87.50
Never hinged 47.50
47 A9 2c brn, *buff* 32.50 87.50
Never hinged 47.50
48 A9 4c claret, *lav* 32.50 87.50
Never hinged 47.50
49 A9 5c grn, *grnsh* 35.00 52.50
Never hinged 72.50
50 A9 10c blk, *lavender* 60.00 87.50
Never hinged 120.00
51 A9 15c blue 87.50 87.50
Never hinged 175.00
52 A9 20c red, *yel grn* 240.00 240.00
Never hinged 475.00
53 A9 25c yel, *straw* 87.50 87.50
Never hinged 175.00
54 A9 25c blk, *rose* 120.00 87.50
Never hinged 240.00
55 A9 30c brn, *bis* 200.00 210.00
56 A9 35c vio blk, *yel org* 200.00 250.00
a. 35c violet black, *yellow* 475.00 475.00
57 A9 40c ver, *straw* 225.00 240.00
58 A9 75c car, *rose* 600.00 925.00
59 A9 1fr brnz grn, *straw* 400.00 400.00

POSTAGE DUE STAMPS

D1

1884-85 Unwmk. Typo. *Imperf.*

J1 D1 1c black 4.00 4.00
Never hinged 8.00
J2 D1 2c black 4.00 4.00
Never hinged 8.00
J3 D1 3c black 4.00 4.00
Never hinged 8.00
J4 D1 4c black 4.75 4.00
Never hinged 9.50
J5 D1 5c black 6.50 3.25
Never hinged 12.50
J6 D1 10c black 8.75 6.50
Never hinged 17.50
J7 D1 15c black 13.00 10.50
Never hinged 25.00
J8 D1 20c black 16.00 10.50
Never hinged 32.50
J9 D1 30c black 17.50 8.75
Never hinged 35.00
J10 D1 40c black 21.00 8.75
Never hinged 42.50
J11 D1 60c black 27.50 16.00
Never hinged 55.00
J12 D1 1fr brown 35.00 27.50
Never hinged 72.50
a. 1fr black 300.00
J13 D1 2fr brown 35.00 27.50
Never hinged 72.50
a. 2fr black 300.00 *325.00*
J14 D1 5fr brown 110.00 67.50
a. 5fr black 425.00 *450.00*

Values for blocks of 4

J1 D1 1c black 24.00 *72.50*
Never hinged 47.50
J2 D1 2c black 24.00 *72.50*
Never hinged 47.50
J3 D1 3c black 24.00 *72.50*
Never hinged 47.50
J4 D1 4c black 25.00 *75.00*
Never hinged 52.50
J5 D1 5c black 35.00 *45.00*
Never hinged 72.50
J6 D1 10c black 47.50 *65.00*
Never hinged 95.00
J7 D1 15c black 65.00 *100.00*
Never hinged 130.00
J8 D1 20c black 80.00 *100.00*
Never hinged 160.00
J9 D1 30c black 87.50 *92.50*
Never hinged 175.00
J10 D1 40c black 100.00 *120.00*
Never hinged 200.00
J11 D1 60c black 130.00 *160.00*
Never hinged 275.00
J12 D1 1fr brown 180.00 *200.00*
Never hinged 360.00
a. 1fr black 300.00
J13 D1 2fr brown 180.00 *200.00*
Never hinged 360.00
a. 2fr black 300.00 *325.00*
J14 D1 5fr brown 540.00 750.00
a. 5fr black 425.00 *450.00*

Nos. J12a, J13a and J14a were not regularly issued.

1894-1906

J15 D1 5c pale blue 1.60 1.60
Never hinged 2.75
J16 D1 10c gray brown 1.60 1.60
Never hinged 2.75
J17 D1 15c pale green 1.60 1.60
Never hinged 2.75
J18 D1 20c olive grn ('06) 1.60 1.60
Never hinged 2.75
J19 D1 30c carmine 2.75 1.60
Never hinged 4.75
J20 D1 50c lilac 2.75 1.60
Never hinged 4.75
J21 D1 60c brown, *buff* 4.50 2.75
Never hinged 8.00
a. 60c dark violet, *buff* 4.75 2.75
Never hinged 9.50
J22 D1 1fr red, *buff* 7.50 4.50
Never hinged 11.00
a. 1fr rose, *buff* 27.50 19.00
Never hinged 47.50
Nos. J15-J22 (8) 23.90 16.85

Values for blocks of 4

J15 D1 5c pale blue 8.00 *22.50*
Never hinged 14.00
J16 D1 10c gray brown 8.00 *22.50*
Never hinged 14.00
J17 D1 15c pale green 8.00 *22.50*
Never hinged 14.00
J18 D1 20c olive grn ('06) 8.00 *22.50*
Never hinged 14.00
J19 D1 30c carmine 12.00 *25.00*
Never hinged 22.50
J20 D1 50c lilac 12.00 *25.00*
Never hinged 22.50
J21 D1 60c brown, *buff* 20.00 *40.00*
Never hinged 40.00
a. 60c dark violet, *buff* 24.00 *40.00*
Never hinged 47.50
J22 D1 1fr red, *buff* 35.00 *65.00*
Never hinged 55.00
a. 1fr rose, *buff* 140.00 *160.00*
Never hinged 240.00

For overprints see New Caledonia Nos. J1-J8.

FRENCH CONGO

ˈfrench ˈkäŋ-ˌgō

LOCATION — Central Africa
GOVT. — French possession

French Congo was originally a separate colony, but was joined in 1888 to Gabon and placed under one commissioner-general with a lieutenant-governor presiding in Gabon and another in French Congo. In 1894 the military holdings in Ubangi were attached to French Congo, and in 1900 the Chad military protectorate was added. Postal service was not established in Ubangi or Chad, however, at that time. In 1906 Gabon and Middle Congo were separated and French Congo ceased to exist as such. Chad and Ubangi remained attached to Middle Congo as the joint dependency of "Ubangi-Chari-Chad," and Middle Congo stamps were used there.

100 Centimes = 1 Franc

Watermarks

Wmk. 122 Thistle Branch

Wmk. 123 — Rose Branch

Wmk. 124 Olive Branch

Stamps of French Colonies Surcharged Horizontally in Red or Black

1891 Unwmk. *Perf. 14x13½*

1 A9 5c on 1c blk, *lil bl* (R) *6,500.* *4,750.*
On cover *12,500.*
a. Double surcharge 20,000.
2 A9 5c on 1c blk, *lil bl* 200.00 110.00
On cover 775.00
a. Double surcharge 650.00 425.00
3 A9 5c on 15c blue 350.00 180.00
On cover 1,000.
a. Double surcharge 725.00 375.00
5 A9 5c on 25c blk, *rose* 130.00 52.50
On cover 460.00
a. Inverted surcharge
b. Surcharge vertical 275.00 115.00
c. Double surcharge 600.00 600.00

The error, No. 3a, occurred when paper meant for printing No. 6 was inadvertently placed in the stack intended for printing No. 3.

First "O" of "Congo" is a Capital, "Francais" with Capital "F"

1891-92

6 A9 5c on 20c red, *grn* 1,300. 425.00
On cover 2,800.
7 A9 5c on 25c blk, *rose* 200.00 100.00
On cover 625.00
a. Surcharge vertical 250.00 110.00
8 A9 10c on 25c blk, *rose* 240.00 67.50
On cover 600.00
a. Inverted surcharge 400.00 160.00
On cover 1,500.
b. Surcharge vertical 300.00 100.00
On cover 625.00
d. Double surcharge 400.00 225.00
On cover 1,100.
9 A9 10c on 40c red, *straw* 2,750. 400.00
On cover 2,600.
10 A9 15c on 25c blk, *rose* 225.00 52.50
On cover 500.00
a. Surcharge vertical 260.00 92.50
On cover 875.00
c. Double surcharge 400.00 200.00

First "O" of Congo small Surcharge Vert., Down or Up No Period

11 A9 5c on 25c blk, *rose* 300.00 135.00
On cover *350.00*
12 A9 10c on 25c blk, *rose* —
13 A9 15c on 25c blk, *rose* 425.00 190.00
On cover *950.00*

The listings Nos. 5a and 12 are being re-evaluated. The Catalogue Editors would appreciate any information on these stamps.

Postage Due Stamps of French Colonies Surcharged in Red or Black Reading Down or Up

1892 *Imperf.*

14 D1 5c on 5c blk (R) 200.00 140.00
On cover 750.00
a. Double surcharge 1,450.
On cover —
15 D1 5c on 20c blk (R) 200.00 140.00
On cover 750.00
16 D1 5c on 30c blk (R) 260.00 180.00
On cover 750.00
17 D1 10c on 1fr brown 200.00 140.00
On cover 625.00
a. Double surcharge 4,100.
b. Surcharge horiz. *2,400.*
c. "Congo" omitted *475.00*
Nos. 14-17 (4) 860.00 600.00

Excellent counterfeits of Nos. 1-17 exist.

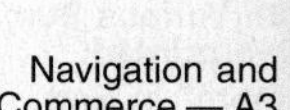
Navigation and Commerce — A3

1892-1900 Typo. *Perf. 14x13½*
Colony Name in Blue or Carmine

18 A3 1c blk, *lil bl* 1.60 1.60
Never hinged 3.25
On cover 150.00
a. Name double 225.00 175.00
19 A3 2c brn, *buff* 4.00 3.25
Never hinged 6.50
On cover 150.00
a. Name double 225.00 175.00
20 A3 4c claret, *lav* 4.00 3.25
Never hinged 6.50
On cover 140.00
a. Name in blk and in blue 225.00 175.00
21 A3 5c grn, *grnsh* 8.00 8.00
Never hinged 12.00
On cover 87.50
22 A3 10c blk, *lavender* 24.00 20.00
Never hinged 40.00
On cover 125.00
a. Name double 850.00 600.00
23 A3 10c red ('00) 4.00 4.00
Never hinged 5.50
On cover 45.00
24 A3 15c blue, quadrille paper 55.00 20.00
Never hinged 120.00
On cover 125.00
25 A3 15c gray ('00) 12.00 8.00
Never hinged 16.00
On cover 67.50
26 A3 20c red, *grn* 24.00 20.00
Never hinged 40.00
On cover 150.00
On cover, single franking 260.00
27 A3 25c blk, *rose* 24.00 16.00
Never hinged 40.00
On cover 92.50
28 A3 25c blue ('00) 12.00 *12.00*
Never hinged 22.50
On cover 100.00
29 A3 30c brn, *bis* 40.00 24.00
Never hinged 55.00
On cover 250.00
On cover, single franking 340.00
30 A3 40c red, *straw* 55.00 32.50
Never hinged 120.00
On cover 260.00
On cover, single franking 375.00
31 A3 50c car, *rose* 55.00 40.00
Never hinged 110.00
On cover 210.00
On cover, single franking 310.00
32 A3 50c brn, *az* ('00) 16.00 16.00
Never hinged 27.50
On cover 150.00
On cover, single franking 200.00
a. Name double 775.00 775.00
33 A3 75c dp vio, *org* 47.50 40.00
Never hinged 95.00
On cover 310.00
On cover, single franking 500.00
34 A3 1fr brnz grn, *straw* 55.00 40.00
Never hinged 120.00
On cover 375.00
On cover, single franking 625.00
Nos. 18-34 (17) 441.10 308.60

Perf. 13½x14 stamps are counterfeits.

For surcharges see Nos. 50-51.

No. 21 exists in yellow green on pale green. The stamp was prepared but not issued. Value, $4,000.

Leopard — A4

Type I

Type II

Bakalois Woman — A5 Coconut Grove — A6

Design A4 exists in two types. Type 1: end of left tusk extends behind and above right tusk. Type 2: end of left tusk does not appear behind right tusk. Type 2 of design A4 appears in position 91 of each pane of 100.

1900-04 Wmk. 122 *Perf. 11*

Thick Paper

35 A4 1c brn vio & gray lilac (1) .80 .80
Never hinged 1.60
On cover 75.00
a. Background inverted 75.00 75.00
Never hinged 140.00
b. Value doubled 47.50 47.50
Never hinged 87.50
c. Type 2 52.50 52.50
Never hinged 80.00
d. Pair, types 1 and 2 55.00 55.00
Never hinged 87.50
e. Thin paper, perf 11½ ('04) 1.60 1.60
Never hinged 2.75

36 A4 2c brn & yel (1) .80 .80
Never hinged 1.60
On cover 75.00
a. Imperf., pair 80.00 *80.00*
Never hinged 125.00
b. Pair, imperf between 100.00 *110.00*
c. Type 2 52.50 52.50
Never hinged 80.00
d. Pair, types 1 and 2 55.00 55.00
Never hinged 87.50
e. Thin paper, perf 11½ ('04) 1.60 1.60
Never hinged 2.75
f. 2c dark red & red (1) (error) 180.00 *260.00*
g. As "f," type 2 800.00
h. As "f," imperf single 1,000.

37 A4 4c scar & gray bl 1.60 1.20
Never hinged 3.25
On cover 75.00
a. Background inverted 95.00 87.50
Never hinged 170.00
b. Type 2 55.00 55.00
Never hinged 87.50
c. Pair, types 1 and 2 65.00 65.00
Never hinged 100.00
d. Thin paper, perf 11½ ('04) 3.25 2.75
Never hinged 5.50
e. 4c dark red & red (1) (error) 725.00
f. As "e," type 2 2,400.

38 A4 5c grn & gray grn (1) 2.75 1.60
Never hinged 4.00
On cover 75.00
a. Imperf., pair 140.00 140.00
Never hinged 250.00
b. Pair, imperf between 87.50
Never hinged 145.00
c. Type 2 55.00 55.00
Never hinged 87.50
d. Pair, types 1 and 2 65.00 65.00
Never hinged 100.00
e. Thin paper, perf 11½ ('04) 6.50 4.00
Never hinged 11.00

39 A4 10c red & rose pink (1) 8.00 3.25
Never hinged 16.00
On cover 105.00
a. Imperf., pair 140.00 140.00
Never hinged 250.00
b. Type 2 125.00 125.00
Never hinged 190.00
c. Pair, types 1 and 2 145.00 145.00
Never hinged 210.00
d. Thin paper, perf 11½ ('04) 8.75 4.00
Never hinged 14.00

40 A4 15c dl vio & ol grn (1) 2.40 1.20
Never hinged 4.00
On cover 95.00
a. Imperf. pair 110.00
Never hinged 190.00
b. Type 2 67.50 67.50
Never hinged 110.00
c. Pair, types 1 and 2 75.00 75.00
Never hinged 110.00
d. Thin paper, perf 11½ ('04) 3.25 1.60
Never hinged 5.50

Wmk. 123

41 A5 20c yel grn & org 2.40 2.00
Never hinged 4.00
On cover 105.00
On cover, single franking 175.00
a. Center double 145.00
Never hinged 240.00
b. Thin paper, perf 11½ ('04) 4.75 4.00
Never hinged 8.00

42 A5 25c bl & pale bl 3.50 2.40
Never hinged 5.50
On cover 80.00
a. Thin paper, perf 11½ ('04) 4.75 4.50
Never hinged 8.00

43 A5 30c car rose & org 5.50 2.40
Never hinged 8.00
On cover 140.00
On cover, single franking 225.00
a. Thin paper, perf 11½ ('04) 8.75 4.75
Never hinged 16.00

44 A5 40c org brn & brt grn 8.00 2.75
Never hinged 12.00
On cover 150.00
On cover, single franking 225.00
a. Imperf., pair 110.00 110.00
Never hinged 190.00
b. Center and value inverted 200.00 170.00
c. Thin paper, perf 11½ ('04) 7.25 4.00
Never hinged 13.00

45 A5 50c gray vio & lil 8.00 6.50
Never hinged 16.00
On cover 110.00
On cover, single franking 150.00
a. Thin paper, perf 11½ ('04) 12.50 11.00
Never hinged 24.00

46 A5 75c red vio & org 20.00 11.00
Never hinged 32.50
On cover 190.00
On cover, single franking 310.00
a. Imperf., pair 110.00 110.00
Never hinged 190.00
b. Pair, imperf between 140.00
Never hinged 240.00
c. Thin paper, perf 11½ ('04) 32.50 20.00
Never hinged 55.00

Wmk. 124

47 A6 1fr gray lil & ol 24.00 20.00
Never hinged 45.00
On cover 250.00
On cover, single franking 440.00
a. Center and value inverted 300.00 300.00
b. Imperf., pair 140.00 140.00
Never hinged 250.00

48 A6 2fr car & brn 47.50 32.50
Never hinged 105.00
On cover 310.00
On cover, single franking 550.00
a. Imperf., pair 300.00 300.00
Never hinged 550.00
b. Frame double 260.00

49 A6 5fr brn org & gray 87.50 72.50
Never hinged 200.00
On cover 375.00
On cover, single franking 625.00
a. 5fr ocher & gray 750.00 *950.00*
b. Center and value inverted 450.00 450.00
c. Wmk. 123 500.00 500.00
d. Imperf., pair 800.00 800.00
e. Center and value double 400.00 400.00
Nos. 35-49 (15) 222.75 160.90

For surcharges see Nos. 52-53.

Nos. 26 and 29 Surcharged in Black

1900 Unwmk. *Perf. 14x13½*

50 A3 5c on 20c red, *grn* 26,000. *6,000.*
a. Double surcharge *18,000.*

51 A3 15c on 30c brn, *bis* 20,000. *2,600.*
On cover *7,500.*
a. Double surcharge *6,000.*

Nos. 43 and 48 Surcharged in Black

a

b

1903 Wmk. 123 *Perf. 11*

52 A5 5c on 30c 325.00 160.00
On cover *550.00*
a. Inverted surcharge *2,750.*
b. Ovptd. "SPECIMEN" in violet 400.00

Wmk. 124

53 A6 10c on 2fr 375.00 160.00
On cover *550.00*
a. Inverted surcharge *2,750.*
b. Double surcharge *3,250.*
c. Ovptd. "SPECIMEN" in violet 550.00

Counterfeits of the preceding surcharges are known.

FRENCH EQUATORIAL AFRICA

'french ,ē-kwə-'tōr-ē-əl 'a-fri-kə

LOCATION — North of Belgian Congo and south of Libya.
GOVT. — French Colony
AREA — 959,256 square miles
POP. — 4,491,785
CAPITAL — Brazzaville

In 1910 Gabon and Middle Congo, with its military dependencies, were politically united as French Equatorial Africa. The component colonies were granted administrative autonomy. In 1915 Ubangi-Chari-Chad was made an autonomous civilian colony and in 1920 Chad was made a civil colony. In 1934 the four colonies were administratively united as one colony, but this federation was not completed until 1936. Each colony had its own postal administration until 1936. The postal issues of the former colonial subdivisions are listed under the names of those colonies.

100 Centimes = 1 Franc

Stamps of Gabon, 1932, Overprinted "Afrique Equatoriale Francaise" and Bars Similar to "a" and "b" in Black

Perf. 13x13½, 13½x13

1936 Unwmk.

1 A16 1c brown violet .40 *.80*
Never hinged .80
On cover 37.50

2 A16 2c black, *rose* .80 *.80*
Never hinged 1.20
On cover 37.50

3 A16 4c green 1.20 1.60
Never hinged 2.40
On cover 37.50

4 A16 5c grnsh blue 1.20 1.60
Never hinged 2.40
On cover 30.00

5 A16 10c red, *yel* 1.20 1.60
Never hinged 2.40
On cover 30.00

6 A17 40c brown violet 4.00 3.25
Never hinged 6.75
On cover 12.50

7 A17 50c red brown 3.25 2.40
Never hinged 4.00
On cover 6.25

8 A17 1fr yel grn, *bl* 32.50 16.00
Never hinged 47.50
On cover 50.00
On cover, single franking 75.00

9 A18 1.50fr dull blue 8.00 4.00
Never hinged 16.00
On cover 25.00
On cover, single franking 55.00

10 A18 2fr brown red 20.00 16.00
Never hinged 50.00
On cover 42.50
On cover, single franking 55.00
Nos. 1-10 (10) 72.55 48.05

Stamps of Middle Congo, 1933 Overprinted in Black

a

b

c

1936

11 A4 (b) 1c lt brown .40 *.50*
Never hinged .80
On cover 37.50

12 A4 (b) 2c dull blue .40 *.50*
Never hinged .80
On cover 37.50

13 A4 (b) 4c olive green 1.60 1.60
Never hinged 2.40
On cover 37.50

14 A4 (b) 5c red violet .80 1.00
Never hinged 1.20
On cover 27.50

15 A4 (b) 10c slate 1.60 1.25
Never hinged 2.40
On cover 27.50

16 A4 (b) 15c dk violet 2.00 1.60
Never hinged 3.25
On cover 25.00

17 A4 (b) 20c red, *pink* 2.00 1.60
Never hinged 3.25
On cover 30.00

18 A4 (b) 25c orange 4.00 2.40
Never hinged 6.00
On cover 12.50

19 A5 (a) 40c orange brn 5.50 2.75
Never hinged 8.00
On cover 12.50

20 A5 (c) 50c black violet 5.50 2.40
Never hinged 8.00
On cover 6.25

21 A5 (c) 75c black, *pink* 5.50 4.75
Never hinged 8.00
On cover 12.50

22 A5 (a) 90c carmine 5.50 4.00
Never hinged 8.00
On cover 30.00
On cover, single franking 75.00

23 A5 (c) 1.50fr dark blue 4.75 2.00
Never hinged 8.00
On cover 19.00
On cover, single franking 50.00

24 A6 (a) 5fr slate blue 55.00 35.00
Never hinged 87.50
On cover 140.00
On cover, single franking 225.00

25 A6 (a) 10fr black 35.00 30.00
Never hinged 55.00
On cover 140.00
On cover, single franking 250.00

26 A6 (a) 20fr dark brown 35.00 32.50
Never hinged 55.00
On cover 165.00
On cover, single franking 310.00
Nos. 11-26 (16) 164.55 123.85

Other overprints inscribed "Afrique Equitoriale Française" in a different type font on earlier Middle Congo stamps are listed under Middle Congo.

Common Design Types pictured following the introduction.

Paris International Exposition Issue

Common Design Types

1937, Apr. 15 Engr. *Perf. 13*

27 CD74 20c dark violet 2.40 2.40
Never hinged 3.25
On cover 92.50

28 CD75 30c dark green 2.40 2.40
Never hinged 3.25
On cover 75.00

29 CD76 40c carmine rose 2.40 2.40
Never hinged 3.25
On cover 67.50

30 CD77 50c dk brn & bl 2.40 2.40
Never hinged 3.25
On cover 62.50
31 CD78 90c red 3.25 3.25
Never hinged 4.00
On cover 92.50
On cover, single franking 150.00
32 CD79 1.50fr ultra 3.25 3.25
Never hinged 4.00
On cover 80.00
On cover, single franking 140.00
Nos. 27-32 (6) 16.10 16.10

Logging on Loéme River — A1

People of Chad — A2

Pierre Savorgnan de Brazza A3

Emile Gentil — A4

Paul Crampel A5

Governor Victor Liotard A6

Two types of 25c:
Type I — Wide numerals (4mm).
Type II — Narrow numerals (3½mm).

1937-40 Photo. *Perf. 13½x13*
33 A1 1c brown & yel .25 .25
Never hinged .40
On cover 27.50
34 A1 2c violet & grn .25 .25
Never hinged .40
On cover 27.50
35 A1 3c blue & yel ('40) .25 .30
Never hinged .40
On cover 27.50
36 A1 4c magenta & bl .25 .30
Never hinged .40
On cover 25.00
37 A1 5c dk & lt green .25 .30
Never hinged .40
On cover 25.00
38 A2 10c magenta & blue .25 .30
Never hinged .40
On cover 25.00
39 A2 15c blue & buff .25 .30
Never hinged .40
On cover 30.00
40 A2 20c brown & yellow .25 *.30*
Never hinged .40
On cover 19.00
41 A2 25c cop red & bl (I) .80 .30
Never hinged 1.20
On cover 12.50
a. Type II 2.75 2.00
Never hinged 4.00
On cover 27.50
42 A3 30c gray grn & grn .80 .55
Never hinged 1.20
On cover 19.00
43 A3 30c chlky bl, ind & buff ('40) .40 .50
Never hinged .80
On cover 12.50
44 A2 35c dp grn & yel ('38) .80 .80
Never hinged 1.20
On cover 30.00
45 A3 40c cop red & bl .40 .30
Never hinged .80
On cover 6.25
46 A3 45c dk bl & lt grn 4.75 3.50
Never hinged 5.50
On cover 42.50
47 A3 45c dp grn & yel grn ('40) .40 .80
Never hinged .80
On cover 25.00
48 A3 50c brown & yellow .50 .25
Never hinged .80
On cover 12.50
49 A3 55c pur & bl ('38) .80 .80
Never hinged 1.20
On cover 7.50
50 A3 60c mar & gray bl ('40) .80 .85
Never hinged 1.20
On cover 21.00
51 A4 65c dk bl & lt grn .80 .40
Never hinged 1.20
On cover 6.25
52 A4 70c dp vio & buff ('40) .80 .95
Never hinged 1.20
On cover 25.00
53 A4 75c ol blk & dl yel 5.50 4.50
Never hinged 9.50
On cover 19.00
54 A4 80c brn & yel ('38) .40 .80
Never hinged .80
On cover 50.00
On cover, single franking 80.00
55 A4 90c copper red & buff .55 .40
Never hinged .80
On cover 12.50
On cover, single franking 19.00
56 A4 1fr dk vio & lt grn 2.40 1.20
Never hinged 4.00
On cover 37.50
On cover, single franking 62.50
57 A3 1fr cer & dl org ('38) 4.00 1.60
Never hinged 4.75
On cover 32.50
On cover, single franking 62.50
58 A4 1fr bl grn & sl grn ('40) .40 .55
Never hinged .80
On cover 6.25
59 A5 1.25fr cop red & buff 2.40 1.20
Never hinged 4.00
On cover 37.50
On cover, single franking 100.00
60 A5 1.40fr dk brn & pale grn ('40) 1.20 1.25
Never hinged 2.00
On cover 37.50
On cover, single franking 80.00
61 A5 1.50fr dk & lt blue 1.60 .80
Never hinged 4.00
On cover 30.00
On cover, single franking 67.50
62 A5 1.60fr dp vio & buff ('40) 1.60 1.25
Never hinged 2.40
On cover 37.50
On cover, single franking 92.50
63 A5 1.75fr brn & yel 2.00 1.20
Never hinged 4.00
On cover 25.00
On cover, single franking 42.50
64 A4 1.75fr bl & lt bl ('38) .80 .80
Never hinged 1.60
On cover 30.00
On cover, single franking 50.00
65 A5 2fr dk & lt green 1.60 .80
Never hinged 3.25
On cover 25.00
On cover, single franking 50.00
66 A6 2.15fr brn, vio & yel ('38) 1.20 .80
Never hinged 2.40
On cover 37.50
On cover, single franking 42.50
67 A6 2.25fr bl & lt bl ('39) 1.60 1.60
Never hinged 2.00
On cover 55.00
On cover, single franking 110.00
68 A6 2.50fr rose lake & buff ('40) 2.00 1.40
Never hinged 2.40
On cover 30.00
On cover, single franking 50.00
69 A6 3fr dk blue & buff .80 .50
Never hinged 1.60
On cover 37.50
On cover, single franking 105.00
70 A6 5fr dk & lt green 1.60 1.20
Never hinged 2.40
On cover 37.50
On cover, single franking 80.00
71 A6 10fr dk violet & bl 3.25 3.25
Never hinged 5.50
On cover 42.50
On cover, single franking 92.50
72 A6 20fr ol blk & dl yel 4.00 3.50
Never hinged 5.50
On cover 50.00
On cover, single franking 110.00
Nos. 33-72 (40) 52.95 40.90

For overprints and surcharges see Nos. 80-127, 129-141, B2-B3, B10-B13, B22-B23. Post 1940 issues in Scott Standard catalogue, Vol. 2.

Colonial Arts Exhibition Issue
Souvenir Sheet
Common Design Type

1937 *Imperf.*
73 CD79 3fr red brown 12.00 *16.00*
Never hinged 16.00
On cover 110.00
On cover, single franking 165.00

Count Louis Edouard Bouet-Willaumez and His Ship "La Malouine" — A7

1938, Dec. 5 *Perf. 13½*
74 A7 65c gray brown 1.25 1.25
Never hinged 1.60
On cover 45.00
75 A7 1fr deep rose 1.25 1.25
Never hinged 1.60
On cover 55.00
On cover, single franking 100.00
76 A7 1.75fr blue 1.60 1.60
Never hinged 2.40
On cover 55.00
On cover, single franking 100.00
77 A7 2fr dull violet 2.40 2.40
Never hinged 3.25
On cover 62.50
On cover, single franking 105.00
Nos. 74-77 (4) 6.50 6.50
Set, never hinged 8.85

Centenary of Gabon.

New York World's Fair Issue
Common Design Type

1939, May 10 Engr. *Perf. 12½x12*
78 CD82 1.25fr carmine lake .80 1.60
Never hinged 1.20
On cover 67.50
On cover, single franking 150.00
79 CD82 2.25fr ultra .80 1.60
Never hinged 1.20
On cover 67.50
On cover, single franking 140.00
Set, never hinged 2.40

Stamps of 1936-40, Overprinted in Carmine or Black

Nos. 80-82, 84-88, 93

Nos. 83, 89-92, 94-125

1940-41 *Perf. 13½x13*
80 A1 1c brn & yel (C) 4.00 4.00
Never hinged 6.50
On cover 125.00
81 A1 2c vio & grn (C) 4.00 4.00
Never hinged 6.50
On cover 125.00
82 A1 3c blue & yel (C) 4.00 4.00
Never hinged 6.50
On cover 125.00
83 A4 4c ol grn (No. 13) 24.00 16.00
Never hinged 32.50
On cover 300.00
b. Inverted overprint 120.00 *150.00*
Never hinged 190.00
84 A1 5c dk grn & lt grn (C) 4.00 4.00
Never hinged 6.50
On cover 125.00
85 A2 10c magenta & bl 4.00 4.00
Never hinged 6.50
On cover 150.00
86 A2 15c blue & buff (C) 4.00 4.00
Never hinged 6.50
On cover 150.00
87 A2 20c brn & yel (C) 4.00 4.00
Never hinged 6.50
On cover 150.00
88 A2 25c cop red & bl 4.00 4.00
Never hinged 6.50
On cover 200.00
89 A3 30c gray grn & grn (C) 16.00 16.00
Never hinged 24.00
On cover 260.00
90 A3 30c gray grn & grn ('41) 16.00 16.00
Never hinged 20.00
On cover 190.00
91 A3 30c chlky bl, ind & buff (C) ('41) 16.00 16.00
Never hinged 20.00
On cover 225.00
92 A3 30c chlky bl, ind & buff ('41) 16.00 16.00
Never hinged 30.00
On cover 225.00
93 A2 35c dp grn & yel (C) 4.00 4.00
Never hinged 6.50
On cover 150.00
94 A3 40c cop red & bl 4.00 4.00
Never hinged 6.50
On cover 125.00
b. Inverted overprint *100.00*
95 A3 45c dp grn & yel grn (C) 4.00 4.00
Never hinged 6.50
On cover 125.00
96 A3 45c dp grn & yel grn ('41) 16.00 16.00
Never hinged 20.00
On cover 175.00
97 A3 50c brn & yel (C) 4.00 4.00
Never hinged 6.50
On cover 175.00
98 A3 50c brn & yel ('41) 8.00 8.00
Never hinged 16.00
On cover 180.00
99 A3 55c pur & bl (C) 4.00 4.00
Never hinged 6.50
On cover 125.00
100 A3 55c pur & bl ('41) 16.00 16.00
Never hinged 20.00
On cover 180.00
101 A3 60c mar & gray bl 4.00 4.00
Never hinged 6.50
On cover 125.00
102 A4 65c dk bl & lt grn 4.00 4.00
Never hinged 6.50
On cover 125.00
103 A4 70c dp vio & buff 4.00 4.00
Never hinged 6.50
On cover 125.00
104 A4 75c ol blk & dl yel 80.00 80.00
Never hinged 160.00
On cover 460.00
105 A4 80c brown & yellow 4.00 4.00
Never hinged 6.50
On cover 125.00
106 A4 90c cop red & buff 4.00 4.00
Never hinged 6.50
On cover 125.00
107 A4 1fr bl grn & sl grn 8.00 8.00
Never hinged 16.00
On cover 200.00
108 A4 1fr bl grn & sl grn (C) ('41) 20.00 20.00
Never hinged 32.50
On cover 300.00
109 A3 1fr cer & dl org 4.00 4.00
Never hinged 6.50
On cover 125.00
110 A5 1.40fr dk brn & pale grn 4.00 4.00
Never hinged 6.50
On cover 125.00
111 A5 1.50fr dk bl & lt bl 4.00 4.00
Never hinged 6.50
On cover 125.00
112 A5 1.60fr dp vio & buff 4.00 4.00
Never hinged 6.50
On cover 125.00
113 A5 1.75fr brown & yel 4.00 4.00
Never hinged 6.50
On cover 150.00
114 A6 2.15fr brn, vio & yel 4.00 4.00
Never hinged 6.50
On cover 150.00
115 A6 2.25fr bl & lt bl (C) 4.00 4.00
Never hinged 6.50
On cover 125.00
116 A6 2.25fr bl & lt bl ('41) 16.00 16.00
Never hinged 20.00
On cover 210.00
117 A6 2.50fr rose lake & buff 4.00 4.00
Never hinged 6.50
On cover 150.00
118 A6 3fr dk bl & buff (C) 4.00 4.00
Never hinged 6.50
On cover 125.00
119 A6 3fr dk bl & buff ('41) 16.00 16.00
Never hinged 20.00
On cover 200.00
120 A6 5fr dk grn & lt grn (C) 4.00 4.00
Never hinged 6.50
On cover 150.00
121 A6 5fr dk grn & lt grn ('41) 140.00 140.00
Never hinged 225.00
On cover 375.00
122 A6 10fr dk vio & bl (C) 3.25 3.25
Never hinged 5.50
On cover 2.50
On cover, single franking 80.00
123 A6 10fr dk vio & bl ('41) 130.00 130.00
Never hinged 200.00
On cover 400.00
124 A6 20fr ol blk & dl yel (C) 4.00 4.00
Never hinged 6.50
On cover 150.00
125 A6 20fr ol blk & dl yel ('41) 16.00 16.00
Never hinged 20.00
On cover 275.00
Nos. 80-125 (46) 673.25 665.25

For overprints and surcharges see Nos. 129-132, B12-B13, B22-B23.

For types of Nos. 38/61 without "RF," see Nos. 155A-155B in the *Scott Standard Postage Stamp Catalogue,* Vol. 2.

Double Overprint

80a	A1	1c	325.00	225.00
		Never hinged	475.00	
81a	A1	2c	32.50	
		Never hinged	55.00	
82a	A1	3c	32.50	
		Never hinged	55.00	
83a	A4	4c	75.00	
		Never hinged	125.00	
84a	A1	5c	32.50	
		Never hinged	55.00	
85a	A2	10c	32.50	40.00
		Never hinged	55.00	
86a	A2	15c	32.50	
		Never hinged	55.00	
87a	A2	20c	32.50	
		Never hinged	55.00	

88a A2 25c 55.00
Never hinged 100.00
89a A3 30c 110.00 120.00
Never hinged 200.00
On cover 425.00
90a A3 30c 47.50 55.00
Never hinged 80.00
91a A3 30c 47.50 47.50
Never hinged 80.00
93a A2 35c 250.00
Never hinged 400.00
94a A3 40c 47.50
Never hinged 72.50
96a A3 45c 75.00
Never hinged 120.00
98a A3 50c 110.00 75.00
Never hinged 200.00
100a A3 55c 75.00
Never hinged 120.00
102a A4 65c 45.00
Never hinged 72.50
103a A4 70c 47.50
Never hinged 80.00
104a A4 75c 175.00
Never hinged 325.00
105a A4 80c 47.50
Never hinged 80.00
106a A4 90c 45.00
Never hinged 72.50
b. one inverted 120.00
Never hinged 190.00
109a A4 1fr One inverted 120.00
Never hinged 190.00
110a A5 1.40fr 47.50
Never hinged 80.00
111a A5 1.50fr 47.50
Never hinged 80.00
114a A6 2.15fr 40.00
Never hinged 67.50
115a A6 2.25fr 60.00
Never hinged 100.00
116a A6 2.25fr 47.50
Never hinged 80.00
117a A6 2.50fr 47.50
Never hinged 80.00
119a A6 3fr 60.00
Never hinged 100.00
123a A6 10fr 60.00 *67.50*
Never hinged 100.00
124a A6 20fr 60.00
Never hinged 100.00
Nos. 96a-124a (17) 1,035.

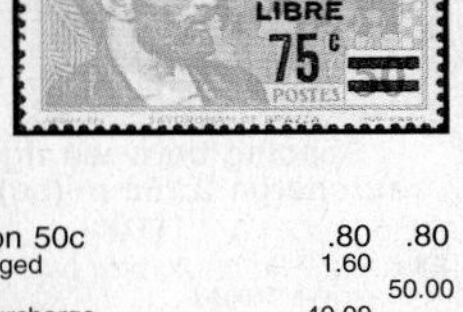

Nos. 48, 51 Surcharged in Black or Carmine

1940
126 A3 75c on 50c .80 .80
Never hinged 1.60
On cover 50.00
a. Double surcharge 40.00
Never hinged 60.00
127 A4 1fr on 65c (C) .80 .80
Never hinged 1.60
On cover 4.00
a. Double surcharge 32.50
Never hinged 47.50
Set, never hinged 3.20

Middle Congo No. 67 Overprinted in Carmine like No. 80
Perf. 13½
128 A4 4c olive green 65.00 65.00
Never hinged 100.00
On cover 200.00

Stamps of 1940 With Additional Overprint in Black

1940 ***Perf. 13½x13***
129 A4 80c brown & yel 24.00 16.00
On card 140.00
a. Overprint without "2" 150.00
130 A4 1fr bl grn & sl grn 24.00 20.00
On card 160.00
131 A3 1fr cer & dull org 24.00 16.00
On card 165.00
132 A5 1.50fr dk bl & lt bl 24.00 16.00
On card 190.00
Nos. 129-132 (4) 96.00 68.00

Arrival of General de Gaulle in Brazzaville, capital of Free France, Oct. 24, 1940.

These stamps were sold affixed to post cards and at a slight increase over face value to cover the cost of the cards. Values for unused stamps are for examples without gum.

For surcharges see Nos. B12-B13, B22-B23 in Scott Standard catalogue, Vol. 2.

SEMI-POSTAL STAMPS

Common Design Type

1938, Oct. 24 **Engr.**
B1 CD80 1.75fr + 50c brt ultra 24.00 24.00
Never hinged 32.50
On cover 105.00
On cover, single franking 190.00

Nos. 51, 64 Surcharged in Black or Red

1938, Nov. 7 ***Perf. 13x13½***
B2 A4 65c + 35c dk bl & lt grn (R) 2.40 2.40
Never hinged 4.00
On cover 55.00
On cover, single franking 125.00
B3 A4 1.75fr + 50c bl & lt bl 4.00 4.00
Never hinged 8.00
On cover 67.50
On cover, single franking 190.00
Set, never hinged 12.00

The surtax was for welfare.

French Revolution Issue
Common Design Type
Name and Value Typo. in Black

1939, July 5 **Photo.**
B4 CD83 45c + 25c green 16.00 16.00
Never hinged 24.00
On cover 120.00
B5 CD83 70c + 30c brown 16.00 16.00
Never hinged 24.00
On cover 87.50
B6 CD83 90c + 35c red org 16.00 16.00
Never hinged 24.00
On cover 75.00
B7 CD83 1.25fr + 1fr rose pink 16.00 16.00
Never hinged 24.00
On cover 140.00
On cover, single franking 225.00
B8 CD83 2.25fr + 2fr blue 16.00 16.00
Never hinged 125.00
On cover 190.00
On cover, single franking 120.00
Nos. B4-B8 (5) 80.00 80.00
Set, never hinged 120.00

Surtax used for the defense of the colonies.

AIR POST STAMPS

Hydroplane over Pointe-Noire — AP1

Trimotor over Stanley Pool — AP2

1937 **Unwmk.** **Photo.** ***Perf. 13½***
C1 AP1 1.50fr ol blk & yel .40 .40
Never hinged 1.60
On cover 32.50
C2 AP1 2fr mag & blue .55 .55
Never hinged 1.60
On cover 27.50
C3 AP1 2.50fr grn & buff .55 .55
Never hinged 1.60
On cover 40.00
C4 AP1 3.75fr brn & lt grn .80 .80
Never hinged 1.60
On cover 45.00
C5 AP2 4.50fr cop red & bl .90 .90
Never hinged 4.00
On cover 50.00
C6 AP2 6.50fr bl & lt grn 1.60 1.60
Never hinged 4.00
On cover 50.00
C7 AP2 8.50fr red brn & yel 1.60 1.60
Never hinged 4.00
On cover 55.00
C8 AP2 10.75fr vio & lt grn 1.60 1.60
Never hinged 4.00
On cover 62.50
Nos. C1-C8 (8) 8.00 8.00

For overprints and surcharges see Nos. C9-C16, CB6 (in Scott Standard catalog, Vol. 2).

Nos. C1, C3-C7 Overprinted in Black like Nos. 133-141

No. C10

1940-41
C9 AP1 1.50fr ('41) 240.00 240.00
Never hinged 450.00
On cover 690.00
C10 AP1 2.50fr 4.00 4.00
Never hinged 8.00
On cover 125.00
a. Double overprint 275.00 275.00
Never hinged 400.00
b. Inverted overprint 275.00 275.00
Never hinged 400.00
C11 AP1 3.75fr ('41) 240.00 240.00
Never hinged 450.00
On cover 690.00
C12 AP2 4.50fr 4.50 4.50
Never hinged 8.00
On cover 150.00
a. Double overprint 275.00 275.00
Never hinged 400.00
C13 AP2 6.50fr 4.00 4.00
Never hinged 8.00
On cover 150.00
a. Double overprint 130.00 130.00
Never hinged 200.00
C14 AP2 8.50fr 4.00 4.00
Never hinged 8.00
On cover 150.00

No. C8 Surcharged in Carmine

C15 AP2 50fr on 10.75fr 12.00 12.00
Never hinged 20.00
On cover 200.00

No. C3 Surcharged in Black

C16 AP1 10fr on 2.50fr ('41) 95.00 95.00
Never hinged 150.00
On cover 340.00
Nos. C9-C16 (8) 603.50 603.50

Counterfeits of Nos. C9 and C11 exist.

See note following No. 141 in Scott Standard catalogue, Vol. 2.

AIR POST SEMI-POSTAL STAMP

French Revolution Issue
Common Design Type

1939 **Unwmk.** **Photo.** ***Perf. 13***
Name and Value Typo. in Orange
CB1 CD83 4.50fr + 4fr brn blk 40.00 40.00
Never hinged 65.00
On cover 140.00
On cover, single franking 250.00

POSTAGE DUE STAMPS

Numeral of Value on Equatorial Butterfly — D1

1937 **Unwmk.** **Photo.** ***Perf. 13***
J1 D1 5c redsh pur & lt bl .25 .40
Never hinged .40
On cover 30.00
J2 D1 10c cop red & buff .25 .40
Never hinged .40
On cover 30.00
J3 D1 20c dk grn & grn .30 .50
Never hinged .50
On cover 30.00
J4 D1 25c red brn & buff .30 .50
Never hinged .50
On cover 30.00
J5 D1 30c cop red & lt bl .50 .55
Never hinged .55
On cover 30.00
J6 D1 45c mag & yel grn .75 .80
Never hinged .95
On cover 37.50
J7 D1 50c dk ol grn & buff .80 .95
Never hinged 1.20
On cover 37.50
J8 D1 60c redsh pur & yel .95 1.10
Never hinged 1.25
On cover 42.50
J9 D1 1fr brown & yel 1.00 1.20
Never hinged 1.40
On cover 42.50
J10 D1 2fr dk bl & buff 1.40 1.50
Never hinged 1.75
On cover 55.00
J11 D1 3fr red brn & lt grn 1.50 1.75
Never hinged 2.10
On cover 67.50
Nos. J1-J11 (11) 8.00 9.65
Set, never hinged 12.00

FRENCH GUIANA

ˈfrench gē-ˈa-nə

LOCATION — On the northeast coast of South America bordering on the Atlantic Ocean.
GOVT. — French colony
AREA — 34,740 sq. mi.
POP. — 28,537 (1946)
CAPITAL — Cayenne

100 Centimes = 1 Franc

Stamps of French Colonies Surcharged in Black

1886, Dec. **Unwmk.** ***Imperf.***
1 A8 5c on 2c grn, *grnsh*, srchg 12mm high 750.00 675.00
a. Double surcharge 1,900. 1,900.
b. Surcharge 10½mm high 900.00 825.00
c. No "f" after "O" 950.00 850.00

Perf. 14x13½
2 A9 5c on 2c brn, *buff*, srchg 12mm high 650.00 600.00
a. No "f" after "O" 525.00 450.00
b. As "a," double surcharge 1,700. 1,700.

Nos. 1-2 unused are valued without gum.

Stamps of French Colonies Overprinted in Black

"Av" of Date Line Inverted-Reversed
1887, Apr. ***Imperf.***
4 A8 20c on 35c blk, *org* 70.00 57.50
On cover 1,500.
a. Double surcharge 225.00 225.00
b. No "f" after "O" 150.00 150.00

Date Line Reads "Avril 1887"
5 A8 5c on 2c grn, *grnsh* 175.00 125.00
a. Double surcharge 900.00 900.00
b. No "f" after "O" 375.00 375.00
c. Pair, one stamp without surcharge 1,500.
6 A8 20c on 35c blk, *org* 375.00 375.00
a. Double surcharge 1,250. 1,250.
b. No "f" after "O" 850.00 850.00
c. Vertical pair, #6 + #4 2,200.
7 A7 25c on 30c brn, *yelsh* 55.00 47.50
On cover *2,500.*
a. Double surcharge 900.00 900.00
b. No "f" after "O" 275.00 275.00

Nos. 4-7 unused are valued without gum.

French Colonies Nos. 22 and 26 Surcharged

8 A7 5c on 30c brn, *yelsh* 155.00 140.00
On cover 3,000.
a. Double surcharge 800.00 800.00
b. Inverted surcharge 1,200. 1,200.
c. Pair, one without surcharge 1,600.
9 A8 5c on 30c brn, *yelsh* 1,500. 1,500.

Nos. 8-9 unused are valued without gum.

French Colonies Nos. 22 and 28 Surcharged

1888

No.	Description	Unused	Used
10	A7 5c on 30c brn, *yelsh*	155.00	140.00
	On cover		*3,750.*
b.	Double surcharge	500.00	500.00
c.	Inverted surcharge	600.00	600.00
11	A8 10c on 75c car, *rose*	400.00	290.00
	No gum	290.00	
a.	Double surcharge	1,100.	1,100.
b.	Pair, one stamp without surcharge	2,500.	

No. 10 unused is valued without gum.

Stamps of French Colonies Overprinted in Black

1892, Feb. 20 ***Imperf.***

No.	Description	Unused	Used
12	A8 2c grn, *grnsh*	850.00	*975.00*
	On cover		2,250.
a.	Inverted overprint	3,500.	
13	A7 30c brn, *yelsh*	155.00	155.00
	On cover	625.00	
a.	Inverted overprint	575.00	575.00
14	A8 35c blk, *orange*	*2,850.*	*3,000.*
15	A8 40c red, *straw*	175.00	140.00
	No gum	130.00	
	On cover		675.00
16	A8 75c car, *rose*	180.00	140.00
	No gum	140.00	
	On cover		1,050.
a.	Inverted overprint	625.00	550.00
	No gum	500.00	
17	A8 1fr brnz grn, *straw*	210.00	160.00
	No gum	180.00	
a.	Inverted overprint	800.00	800.00
b.	Double overprint	800.00	800.00
c.	Triple overprint	1,800.	1,800.

Nos. 12-14 unused are valued without gum.

1892 ***Perf. 14x13½***

No.	Description	Unused	Used
18	A9 1c blk, *lil bl*	47.50	35.00
	Never hinged	100.00	
	On cover		600.00
19	A9 2c brn, *buff*	45.00	37.50
	Never hinged	95.00	
	On cover		600.00
20	A9 4c claret, *lav*	42.50	37.50
	Never hinged	105.00	
	On cover		725.00
21	A9 5c grn, *grnsh*	47.50	35.00
	Never hinged	100.00	
	On cover		375.00
a.	Inverted overprint	150.00	150.00
b.	Double overprint	150.00	150.00
22	A9 10c blk, *lavender*	67.50	40.00
	Never hinged	160.00	
	On cover		350.00
a.	Inverted overprint	200.00	200.00
b.	Double overprint	275.00	275.00
23	A9 15c blue	67.50	45.00
	Never hinged	160.00	
	On cover		350.00
a.	Double overprint	275.00	200.00
24	A9 20c red, *grn*	55.00	42.50
	Never hinged	125.00	
	On cover		375.00
a.	Inverted overprint	225.00	225.00
25	A9 25c blk, *rose*	75.00	35.00
	On cover		475.00
a.	Double overprint	275.00	275.00
b.	Triple overprint	300.00	300.00
26	A9 30c brn, *bis*	47.50	40.00
	Never hinged	100.00	
	On cover		475.00
27	A9 35c blk, *orange*	225.00	225.00
	On cover		1,500.
a.	Inverted overprint	575.00	575.00
28	A9 40c red, *straw*	135.00	135.00
	On cover		675.00
a.	Inverted overprint	300.00	300.00
29	A9 75c car, *rose*	145.00	125.00
	On cover		925.00
30	A9 1fr brnz grn, *straw*	250.00	220.00
	On cover		1,150.
a.	Double overprint	375.00	
	Nos. 18-30 (13)	1,250.	1,053.

French Colonies No. 51 Surcharged

1892, Dec.

No.	Description	Unused	Used
31	A9 5c on 15c blue	70.00	47.50
	On cover		325.00
	On cover, single franking		1,500.
a.	Double surcharge	300.00	275.00
b.	No "f" after "O"	160.00	135.00
c.	Pair, one stamp without surcharge	1,700.	1,700.

Navigation and Commerce — A12

1892-1904 Typo. ***Perf. 14x13½***

Name of Colony in Blue or Carmine

No.	Description	Unused	Used
32	A12 1c blk, *lil bl*	2.00	1.75
	Never hinged	3.00	
	On cover		160.00
33	A12 2c brn, *buff*	1.45	1.45
	Never hinged	1.90	
	On cover		160.00
34	A12 4c claret, *lav*	2.00	1.90
	Never hinged	3.00	
	On cover		125.00
a.	"GUYANE" double	275.00	
35	A12 5c grn, *grnsh*	12.50	11.00
	Never hinged	20.00	
	On cover		62.50
36	A12 5c yel grn ('04)	2.40	1.60
	Never hinged	3.75	
	On cover		40.00
37	A12 10c blk, *lavender*	13.50	8.25
	Never hinged	20.00	
	On cover		50.00
38	A12 10c red ('00)	4.75	1.60
	Never hinged	8.00	
	On cover		45.00
39	A12 15c blue, quadrille paper	42.50	4.00
	Never hinged	77.50	
	On cover		35.00
40	A12 15c gray, *lt gray* ('00)	122.50	110.00
	Never hinged	245.00	
	On cover		625.00
41	A12 20c red, *grn*	25.00	18.00
	Never hinged	47.50	
	On cover		85.00
	On cover, single franking		175.00
42	A12 25c blk, *rose*	20.00	5.50
	Never hinged	40.00	
	On cover		42.50
	On cover, single franking		97.50
43	A12 25c blue ('00)	22.50	*22.50*
	Never hinged	37.50	
	On cover		240.00
	On cover, single franking		325.00
44	A12 30c brn, *bis*	24.00	18.00
	Never hinged	45.00	
	On cover		42.50
	On cover, single franking		72.50
45	A12 40c red, *straw*	24.00	16.00
	Never hinged	45.00	
	On cover		85.00
	On cover, single franking		175.00
46	A12 50c car, *rose*	35.00	18.00
	Never hinged	65.00	
	On cover		175.00
	On cover, single franking		300.00
47	A12 50c brn, *az* ('00)	26.00	26.00
	Never hinged	45.00	
	On cover		275.00
	On cover, single franking		425.00
48	A12 75c dp vio, *org*	37.50	27.50
	Never hinged	75.00	
	On cover		175.00
	On cover, single franking		325.00
49	A12 1fr brn grn, *straw*	18.00	14.00
	Never hinged	37.50	
	On cover		190.00
	On cover, single franking		350.00
50	A12 2fr vio, *rose* ('02)	180.00	16.00
	Never hinged	375.00	
	On cover		400.00
	On cover, single franking		850.00
	Nos. 32-50 (19)	615.60	323.05

Perf. 13½x14 stamps are counterfeits.

For surcharges see Nos. 87-93.

Great Anteater — A13

Washing Gold — A14

Palm Grove at Cayenne A15

1905-28

No.	Description	Unused	Used
51	A13 1c black	.40	.40
	Never hinged	.65	
	On cover		45.00
	On cover, single franking		160.00
52	A13 2c blue	.40	.40
	Never hinged	.65	
	On cover		40.00
	On cover, single franking		140.00
a.	Imperf	57.50	
	Never hinged	105.00	
53	A13 4c red brn	.40	.40
	Never hinged	.65	
	On cover		40.00
	On cover, single franking		120.00
54	A13 5c green	1.25	1.10
	Never hinged	1.75	
	On cover		32.50
55	A13 5c org ('22)	.40	*.45*
	Never hinged	.65	
	On cover		40.00
	On cover, single franking		100.00
56	A13 10c rose	1.50	1.10
	Never hinged	2.10	
	On cover		32.50
57	A13 10c grn ('22)	.65	.40
	Never hinged	1.10	
	On cover		32.50
58	A13 10c red, *bluish* ('25)	.45	.45
	Never hinged	.70	
	On cover		27.50
59	A13 15c violet	1.75	1.25
	Never hinged	2.40	
	On cover		40.00
60	A14 20c red brn	.65	.65
	Never hinged	.95	
	On cover		32.50
61	A14 25c blue	3.00	1.60
	Never hinged	4.75	
	On cover		47.50
	On cover, single franking		120.00
62	A14 25c vio ('22)	.60	.50
	Never hinged	1.10	
	On cover		27.50
63	A14 30c black	2.50	1.00
	Never hinged	4.00	
	On cover		40.00
	On cover, single franking		120.00
64	A14 30c rose ('22)	.50	*.60*
	Never hinged	1.00	
	On cover		40.00
65	A14 30c red org ('25)	.45	.45
	Never hinged	.70	
	On cover		24.00
66	A14 30c dk grn, *grnsh* ('28)	1.35	1.35
	Never hinged	2.00	
	On cover		47.50
67	A14 35c blk, *yel* ('06)	.65	.65
	Never hinged	1.00	
	On cover		40.00
	On cover, single franking		150.00
68	A14 40c rose	1.50	.85
	Never hinged	2.50	
	On cover		40.00
	On cover, single franking		92.50
69	A14 40c black ('22)	.40	*.45*
	Never hinged	.65	
	On cover		32.50
	On cover, single franking		100.00
70	A14 45c olive ('07)	1.00	.95
	Never hinged	1.50	
	On cover		40.00
	On cover, single franking		80.00
71	A14 50c violet	4.25	3.50
	Never hinged	6.50	
	On cover		40.00
	On cover, single franking		120.00
72	A14 50c blue ('22)	.55	*.65*
	Never hinged	1.00	
	On cover		40.00
	On cover, single franking		100.00
73	A14 50c gray ('25)	.80	.80
	Never hinged	1.20	
	On cover		47.50
	On cover, single franking		110.00
74	A14 60c lil, *rose* ('25)	.65	.65
	Never hinged	.95	
	On cover		45.00
	On cover, single franking		100.00
75	A14 65c myr grn ('26)	.85	.80
	Never hinged	1.20	
	On cover		60.00
	On cover, single franking		110.00
76	A14 75c green	1.60	1.40
	Never hinged	2.40	
	On cover		55.00
	On cover, single franking		180.00
77	A14 85c magenta ('26)	.85	.80
	Never hinged	1.30	
	On cover		67.50
	On cover, single franking		120.00
78	A15 1fr rose	.90	.85
	Never hinged	1.50	
	On cover		47.50
	On cover, single franking		100.00
a.	Imperf	82.50	
	Never hinged	135.00	
79	A15 1fr bl, *bluish* ('25)	.85	.80
	Never hinged	1.30	
	On cover		55.00
	On cover, single franking		120.00
80	A15 1fr bl, *yel grn* ('28)	2.75	2.75
	Never hinged	4.00	
	On cover		52.50
	On cover, single franking		80.00
81	A15 1.10fr lt red ('28)	1.50	1.50
	Never hinged	2.25	
	On cover		60.00
	On cover, single franking		110.00
82	A15 2fr blue	1.35	1.35
	Never hinged	2.50	
	On cover		60.00
	On cover, single franking		120.00
83	A15 2fr org red, *yel* ('26)	2.75	2.40
	Never hinged	4.50	
	On cover		67.50
	On cover, single franking		140.00
84	A15 5fr black	8.50	6.50
	Never hinged	15.00	
	On cover		80.00
	On cover, single franking		180.00
a.	Imperf	82.50	
	Never hinged	135.00	
85	A15 10fr grn, *yel* ('24)	14.00	*14.50*
	Never hinged	22.00	
	On cover		80.00
	On cover, single franking		180.00
a.	Printed on both sides	140.00	
	Never hinged	240.00	
b.	Chalky paper	14.50	*16.00*
	Never hinged	24.00	
86	A15 20fr brn lake ('24)	17.50	17.50
	Never hinged	24.00	
	On cover		110.00
	On cover, single franking		225.00
a.	Chalky paper	21.00	*19.00*
	Never hinged	32.50	
	Nos. 51-86 (36)	79.45	71.75

For surcharges see Nos. 94-108, B1-B2.

Issue of 1892 Surcharged in Black or Carmine

1912

Spacing between figures of surcharge 1.5mm (5c), 2mm (10c)

No.	Description	Unused	Used
87	A12 5c on 2c brn, *buff*	1.60	*2.00*
	Never hinged	2.75	
	On cover		90.00
88	A12 5c on 4c cl, *lav* (C)	1.20	*1.60*
b.	Chalky paper	14.50	*16.00*
	Never hinged	2.10	
	On cover		90.00
89	A12 5c on 20c red, *grn*	1.75	*1.90*
	Never hinged	3.00	
	On cover		90.00
90	A12 5c on 25c blk, *rose* (C)	4.00	4.75
	Never hinged	6.50	
	On cover		120.00
91	A12 5c on 30c brn, *bis* (C)	1.75	*1.90*
	Never hinged	3.00	
	On cover		90.00
92	A12 10c on 40c red, *straw*	1.40	*1.90*
	Never hinged	2.40	
	On cover		90.00
a.	Pair, one stamp without surcharge	1,250.	
93	A12 10c on 50c car, *rose*	4.25	*5.25*
	Never hinged	7.00	
	On cover		120.00
a.	Double surcharge	550.00	
	Nos. 87-93 (7)	15.95	*19.30*

Spacing between figures of surcharge 2.25mm (5c), 2.75mm (10c)

No.	Description	Unused	Used
87a	A12 5c on 2c brn, *buff*	21.00	21.00
	Never hinged	45.00	
88a	A12 5c on 4c cl, *lav* (C)	12.50	12.50
	Never hinged	24.00	
89a	A12 5c on 20c red, *grn*	21.00	21.00
	Never hinged	40.00	
90a	A12 5c on 25c blk, *rose* (C)	35.00	35.00
	Never hinged	67.50	
91a	A12 5c on 30c brn, *bis* (C)	21.00	21.00
	Never hinged	40.00	
92b	A12 10c on 40c red, *straw*	140.00	140.00
	Never hinged	275.00	
93b	A12 10c on 50c car, *rose*	300.00	300.00
	Never hinged	550.00	
	Nos. 87a-93b (7)	550.50	550.50

No. 59 Surcharged in Various Colors

1922

No.	Description	Unused	Used
94	A13 1c on 15c vio (Bk)	.65	*.75*
	Never hinged	.95	
	On cover		60.00
	On cover, single franking		160.00
a.	Double surcharge	90.00	
	Never hinged	135.00	
95	A13 2c on 15c vio (Bl)	.65	*.75*
	Never hinged	.95	
	On cover		60.00
	On cover, single franking		150.00
a.	Inverted surcharge	97.50	
	Never hinged	155.00	
b.	In pair with unovptd. stamp	250.00	
	Never hinged	425.00	
c.	No. 95a, in pair with unovptd. stamp	850.00	
	Never hinged	1,275.	
96	A13 4c on 15c vio (G)	.65	*.75*
	Never hinged	.95	
	On cover		52.50
	On cover, single franking		140.00
a.	Double surcharge	90.00	
	Never hinged	135.00	
b.	In pair with unovptd. stamp	275.00	
	Never hinged	475.00	
97	A13 5c on 15c vio (R)	.65	*.75*
	Never hinged	.95	
	On cover		45.00
	On cover, single franking		100.00
a.	In pair with unovptd. stamp	275.00	
	Never hinged	475.00	
	Nos. 94-97 (4)	2.60	3.00

Type of 1905-28 Srchd. in Blue

1923
98 A15 10fr on 1fr grn, *yel* 22.50 *24.00*
Never hinged 32.50
On cover 100.00
On cover, single franking 225.00
99 A15 20fr on 5fr lilac, *rose* 22.50 *24.00*
Never hinged 32.50
On cover 125.00
On cover, single franking 260.00

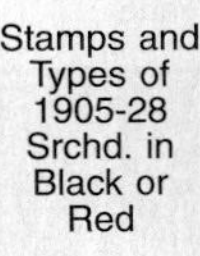
Stamps and Types of 1905-28 Srchd. in Black or Red

1924-27
100 A13 25c on 15c vio ('25) .85 *.85*
Never hinged 1.20
On cover 32.50
a. Triple surcharge 130.00 130.00
Never hinged 205.00
b. In pair with unovptd. stamp 260.00
Never hinged 425.00
101 A15 25c on 2fr bl ('24) .90 *.95*
Never hinged 1.60
On cover 32.50
a. Double surcharge 140.00
Never hinged 225.00
b. Triple surcharge 150.00
Never hinged 240.00
102 A14 65c on 45c ol (R) ('25) 1.75 *1.90*
Never hinged 2.75
On cover 60.00
On cover, single franking 130.00
103 A14 85c on 45c ol (R) ('25) 1.75 *1.90*
Never hinged 2.75
On cover 67.50
On cover, single franking 140.00
104 A14 90c on 75c red ('27) 1.50 1.50
Never hinged 2.50
On cover 65.00
On cover, single franking 140.00
105 A15 1.05fr on 2fr lt yel brn ('27) 1.50 1.50
Never hinged 2.50
On cover 72.50
On cover, single franking 160.00
106 A15 1.25fr on 1fr ultra (R) ('26) 1.60 *1.75*
Never hinged 2.75
On cover 45.00
On cover, single franking 80.00
107 A15 1.50fr on 1fr lt bl ('27) 1.60 *1.75*
Never hinged 2.75
On cover 47.50
On cover, single franking 120.00
108 A15 3fr on 5fr vio ('27) 1.75 *2.00*
Never hinged 3.00
On cover 55.00
On cover, single franking 130.00
a. No period after "F" 12.00 12.00
Never hinged 20.00
Nos. 100-108 (9) 13.20 14.10

Carib Archer — A16

Shooting Rapids, Maroni River A17

Government Building, Cayenne — A18

1929-40 ***Perf. 13½x14***
109 A16 1c gray lil & grnsh bl .25 .25
Never hinged .40
On cover 55.00
a. Imperf 35.00
Never hinged 50.00
110 A16 2c dk red & bl grn .25 .25
Never hinged .40
On cover 52.50
a. Imperf 35.00
Never hinged 50.00
111 A16 3c gray lil & grnsh bl ('40) .30 .30
Never hinged .50
On cover 52.50
112 A16 4c ol brn & red vio .30 .30
Never hinged .55
On cover 52.50
113 A16 5c Prus bl & red org .30 .30
Never hinged .55
On cover 47.50
114 A16 10c mag & brn .30 .30
Never hinged .55
On cover 45.00
115 A16 15c yel brn & red org .30 .30
Never hinged .55
On cover 40.00
a. Imperf 35.00
Never hinged 50.00
116 A16 20c dk bl & ol grn .30 .30
Never hinged .55
On cover 32.50
117 A16 25c dk red & dk brn .50 .50
Never hinged .75
On cover 27.50

Perf. 14x13½
118 A17 30c dl & lt grn .70 .70
Never hinged 1.00
On cover 32.50
119 A17 30c grn & brn ('40) .50 .50
Never hinged .70
On cover 472.50
120 A17 35c Prus grn & ol grn ('38) 1.10 1.10
Never hinged 1.40
On cover 32.50
121 A17 40c org brn & ol gray .30 .30
Never hinged .55
On cover 32.50
122 A17 45c grn & dk brn 1.20 1.20
Never hinged 1.60
On cover 32.50
123 A17 45c ol grn & lt grn ('40) .70 .70
Never hinged 1.00
On cover 45.00
124 A17 50c dk bl & ol gray .40 .40
Never hinged .55
On cover 27.50
a. Imperf 35.00
Never hinged 50.00
125 A17 55c vio bl & car ('38) 1.50 1.50
Never hinged 2.00
On cover 35.00
126 A17 60c sal & grn ('40) .75 .75
Never hinged 1.05
On cover 40.00
a. Imperf 47.50
Never hinged 67.50
127 A17 65c sal & grn 1.10 1.10
Never hinged 1.40
On cover 40.00
128 A17 70c ind & sl bl ('40) 1.30 1.30
Never hinged 1.90
On cover 32.50
129 A17 75c ind & sl bl 1.15 1.15
Never hinged 1.75
On cover 35.00
130 A17 80c blk & vio bl ('38) .80 .80
Never hinged 1.00
On cover 35.00
131 A17 90c dk red & ver 1.10 1.10
Never hinged 1.50
On cover 40.00
On cover, single franking 80.00
132 A17 90c red vio & brn ('39) 1.30 1.30
Never hinged 1.60
On cover 32.50
133 A17 1fr lt vio & brn .70 .70
Never hinged 1.00
On cover 40.00
On cover, single franking 72.50
134 A17 1fr car & lt red ('38) 2.10 2.10
Never hinged 3.00
On cover 47.50
On cover, single franking 80.00
135 A17 1fr blk & vio bl ('40) .80 .80
Never hinged 1.00
On cover 32.50
136 A18 1.05fr ver & olivine 6.25 6.25
Never hinged 9.75
On cover 60.00
On cover, single franking 110.00
137 A18 1.10fr ol brn & red vio 7.25 5.75
Never hinged 11.50
On cover 67.50
On cover, single franking 140.00
138 A18 1.25fr blk brn & bl grn ('33) .80 .80
Never hinged 1.20
On cover 40.00
On cover, single franking 67.50
139 A18 1.25fr rose & lt red ('39) 1.10 1.10
Never hinged 1.40
On cover 72.50
On cover, single franking 110.00
140 A18 1.40fr ol brn & red vio ('40) 1.30 1.30
Never hinged 1.75
On cover 52.50
On cover, single franking 80.00
141 A18 1.50fr dk bl & lt bl .40 .40
Never hinged .65
On cover 47.50
On cover, single franking 100.00
142 A18 1.60fr ol brn & bl grn ('40) 1.30 1.30
Never hinged 1.75
On cover 52.50
On cover, single franking 110.00
143 A18 1.75fr brn red & blk brn ('33) 2.25 2.25
Never hinged 3.00
On cover 55.00
On cover, single franking 110.00
144 A18 1.75fr vio bl ('38) 1.75 1.75
Never hinged 2.40
On cover 47.50
On cover, single franking 80.00
145 A18 2fr dk grn & rose red .65 .65
Never hinged 1.00
On cover 40.00
On cover, single franking 67.50
146 A18 2.25fr vio bl ('39) 1.30 1.30
Never hinged 1.60
On cover 65.00
On cover, single franking 100.00
147 A18 2.50fr cop red & brn ('40) 1.30 1.30
Never hinged 1.75
On cover 65.00
On cover, single franking 100.00
148 A18 3fr brn red & red vio .75 .75
Never hinged 1.20
On cover 55.00
On cover, single franking 110.00
149 A18 5fr dl vio & yel grn 1.25 1.25
Never hinged 2.00
On cover 65.00
On cover, single franking 110.00
150 A18 10fr ol gray & dp ultra 1.50 1.50
Never hinged 2.10
On cover 87.50
On cover, single franking 160.00
151 A18 20fr indigo & ver 2.50 2.50
Never hinged 3.50
On cover 95.00
On cover, single franking 180.00
Nos. 109-151 (43) 51.95 50.45

For types A16-A18 without "RF," see Nos. 170C-170E.

Common Design Types pictured following the introduction.

Colonial Exposition Issue
Common Design Types

1931 **Engr.** ***Perf. 12½***
Name of Country in Black
152 CD70 40c dp green 5.50 5.50
Never hinged 7.50
On cover 65.00
153 CD71 50c violet 5.50 5.50
Never hinged 7.50
On cover 47.50
154 CD72 90c red orange 5.50 5.50
Never hinged 7.50
On cover 80.00
On cover, single franking 120.00
155 CD73 1.50fr dull blue 5.50 5.50
Never hinged 7.50
On cover 72.50
On cover, single franking 110.00
Nos. 152-155 (4) 22.00 22.00

Recapture of Cayenne by d'Estrées, 1676 — A19

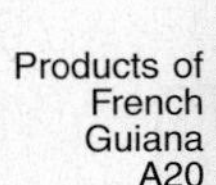
Products of French Guiana A20

1935, Oct. 21 ***Perf. 13***
156 A19 40c gray brn 5.75 5.75
Never hinged 8.00
On cover 65.00
157 A19 50c dull red 10.00 8.00
Never hinged 14.00
On cover 47.50
158 A19 1.50fr ultra 5.75 5.75
Never hinged 8.00
On cover 72.50
On cover, single franking 110.00
159 A20 1.75fr lilac rose 12.50 11.50
Never hinged 19.00
On cover 65.00
On cover, single franking 92.50
160 A20 5fr brown 10.00 9.00
Never hinged 14.00
On cover 65.00
On cover, single franking 92.50
161 A20 10fr blue green 10.50 10.00
Never hinged 16.00
On cover 80.00
On cover, single franking 140.00
Nos. 156-161 (6) 54.50 50.00

Tercentenary of the founding of French possessions in the West Indies.

Paris International Exposition Issue
Common Design Types

1937, Apr. 15
162 CD74 20c deep violet 1.75 1.75
Never hinged 2.50
On cover 60.00
163 CD75 30c dark green 1.75 1.75
Never hinged 2.50
On cover 47.50
164 CD76 40c carmine rose 1.75 1.75
Never hinged 2.50
On cover 45.00
165 CD77 50c dark brown 1.75 1.75
Never hinged 2.50
On cover 40.00
166 CD78 90c red 1.75 1.75
Never hinged 2.75
On cover 80.00
On cover, single franking 140.00
167 CD79 1.50fr ultra 2.25 2.25
Never hinged 3.50
On cover 72.50
On cover, single franking 120.00
Nos. 162-167 (6) 11.00 11.00

Colonial Arts Exhibition Issue
Souvenir Sheet
Common Design Type

1937 ***Imperf.***
168 CD75 3fr violet 11.50 *13.50*
Never hinged 16.00
On cover 100.00
On cover, single franking 150.00
a. Marginal inscription inverted 2,600.
Never hinged 3,400.

New York World's Fair Issue
Common Design Type

1939, May 10 **Engr.** ***Perf. 12½x12***
169 CD82 1.25fr car lake 1.30 1.30
Never hinged 1.75
On cover 80.00
On cover, single franking 130.00
170 CD82 2.25fr ultra 1.30 1.30
Never hinged 1.75
On cover 72.50
On cover, single franking 110.00

SEMI-POSTAL STAMPS

Regular Issue of 1905-28 Surcharged in Red

1915 **Unwmk.** ***Perf. 13½x14***
B1 A13 10c + 5c rose 17.50 *18.00*
Never hinged 29.00
On cover 175.00
a. Inverted surcharge 250.00 250.00
b. Double surcharge 250.00 250.00

Regular Issue of 1905-28 Surcharged in Rose

B2 A13 10c + 5c rose 1.60 1.60
Never hinged 2.40
On cover 25.00

Curie Issue
Common Design Type

1938 ***Perf. 13***
B3 CD80 1.75fr + 50c brt ultra 13.50 13.50
Never hinged 19.50

French Revolution Issue
Common Design Type

1939 **Photo.**
Name and Value in Black
B4 CD83 45c + 25c green 11.50 11.50
Never hinged 17.00
On cover 92.50
B5 CD83 70c + 30c brown 11.50 11.50
Never hinged 17.00
On cover 67.50
B6 CD83 90c + 35c red org 11.50 11.50
Never hinged 17.00
On cover 65.00
B7 CD83 1.25fr + 1fr rose pink 11.50 11.50
Never hinged 17.00
On cover 110.00
On cover, single franking 160.00
B8 CD83 2.25fr + 2fr blue 11.50 11.50
Never hinged 17.00
On cover 100.00
On cover, single franking 140.00
Nos. B4-B8 (5) 57.50 57.50

AIR POST STAMPS

Cayenne AP1

Perf. 13½

1933, Nov. 20 Unwmk. Photo.

C1 AP1 50c orange brn .30 .30
Never hinged .50
On cover 52.50
C2 AP1 1fr yellow grn .50 .50
Never hinged .90
On cover 35.00
C3 AP1 1.50fr dk blue .70 .70
Never hinged 1.05
On cover 55.00
On cover, single franking 110.00
C4 AP1 2fr orange .70 .70
Never hinged 1.05
On cover 55.00
On cover, single franking 110.00
C5 AP1 3fr black .85 .85
Never hinged 1.10
On cover 65.00
On cover, single franking 110.00
C6 AP1 5fr violet .85 .85
Never hinged 1.10
On cover 72.50
On cover, single franking 120.00
C7 AP1 10fr olive grn .85 .85
Never hinged 1.10
On cover 92.50
On cover, single franking 160.00
C8 AP1 20fr scarlet 1.25 1.25
Never hinged 2.00
On cover 100.00
On cover, single franking 160.00
Nos. C1-C8 (8) 6.00 6.00

For No. C1 without "RF," see No. C8A.

A 20fr violet exists, but was not regularly issued. Value, $175.

AIR POST SEMI-POSTAL STAMP

French Revolution Issue
Common Design Type
Unwmk.
1939, July 5 Photo. *Perf. 13*
Name & Value Typo. in Orange

CB1 CD83 5fr + 4fr brn blk 22.00 22.00
Never hinged 35.00
On cover 47.50
On cover, single franking 100.00

SOCIETE DE TRANSPORTS AERIENS GUYANAIS

During 1920-22, a pioneering airline, *La Société des Transports Aériens Guyanais,* maintained service between Cayenne, Saint Laurent du Maroni and Inini, with less regular flights to Paramaribo, Surinam. During July-Oct. 1921, T.A.G. produced stamps to prepay the 75c internal airmail fee, under contract with the postal authorities. After October, these stamps were replaced by regular French Guiana issues.

Nos CL1-CL15 were issued without gum.

APSO1

1921, July 8 *Imperf.*

CL1 APSO1 75c red vio, *bluish* 1,600. 1,750.
On cover *3,750.*
Block of 4 *7,000.* *7,750.*

1921, July 9 *Pin-Perf*

CL2 APSO1 75c red vio, *org brn* 2,600. 2,300.
On cover 5,000.
Block of 4 10,500. 10,500.

Nos CL1-CL2 were for use on the St. Laurent du Maroni-Cayenne Route. Used examples were usually cancelled by a manuscript signature in red ink.

All stamps were overprinted in red violet with a large oval inscribed "Societe Des Transports Aeriens Guyanais" on the front, and by a similar overprint, inscribed "St. Laurent du Maroni" on the reverse. Because the overprint covers four stamps, each individual stamp shows approximately one-fourth of the oval.

APSO2

1921, July 8 *Imperf.*

CL3 APSO2 75c blk, *grayish* 1,200. 750.00
On cover 1,500.
Tête-beche pair *12,000.* *12,000.*
CL4 APSO2 75c blk, *bluish* 1,250. 800.00
On cover 1,550.
Tête-beche pair *12,000.* *12,000.*
CL5 APSO2 75c blk, *sal* 1,350. 850.00
On cover 1,750.

For flights from Cayene, St. Laurent du Maroni and return. Flown letters bearing Nos. CL3-CL15 were cancelled "Avion"

Because the letters "T.A.G." and the denomination "0.75" were printed separately from the rest of the design, their position on the stamp varies.

APSO3

Two Die Types:

Type I, lower part of right frame line straight.

Type II, lower part of right frame line curved outward.

There are many minor differences between the two dies, but the angle of the frame line is sufficient for identification.

1921, Sept.

CL6 APSO3 75c blk, *gray* (I) 1,350. 975.00
On cover 2,100.
Tête-beche pair *12,000.* *12,000.*
CL7 APSO3 75c blk, *bluish* (I) 1,400. 1,050.
On cover 2,100.
Tête-beche pair *12,000.* *12,000.*
CL8 APSO3 75c blk, *sal* (I) *15,000.*
CL9 APSO3 75c blk, *rose* (II) 1,700. 1,250.
On cover 2,400.

For flights from Cayenne to St. Laurent du Maroni and return and from St. Laurent du Maroni to Inini and return.

APSO4

1921, Sept.

CL10 APSO4 75c blk, *gray* 2,900. 2,750.
On cover *5,500.*
CL11 APSO4 75c blk, *bluish* 3,000.
CL12 APSO4 75c blk, *sal* 1,400. 1,200.
On cover *2,400.*
CL13 APSO4 75c blk, *rose* 1,800. 1,500.
On cover *3,000.*
CL14 APSO4 75c blk, *yel* 1,900. 1,800.
On cover *3,600.*
CL15 APSO4 75c blk, *straw* 1,900. 1,800.
On cover *3,600.*

Nos. CL10-CL15 were for use on all T.A.G. flights.

POSTAGE DUE STAMPS

Postage Due Stamps of France, 1893-1926, Overprinted

1925-27 Unwmk. *Perf. 14x13½*

J1 D2 5c light blue .70 *.75*
Never hinged 1.30
On cover. *from* 200.00
a. In pair with unovptd. stamp 375.00
J2 D2 10c brown 1.00 *1.10*
Never hinged 1.75
On cover. *from* 200.00
J3 D2 20c olive green 1.10 *1.25*
Never hinged 2.10
On cover. *from* 200.00
J4 D2 50c violet brown 1.50 *1.60*
Never hinged 2.60
On cover. *from* 200.00
J5 D2 3fr magenta ('27) 11.00 *12.50*
Never hinged 27.00
On cover. *from* 200.00

Surcharged in Black

J6 D2 15c on 20c ol grn 1.00 *1.10*
Never hinged 1.75
On cover. *from* 200.00
a. Blue surcharge 67.50
Never hinged 105.00
J7 D2 25c on 5c lt bl 1.30 *1.40*
Never hinged 2.50
a. In pair with unovptd. stamp 375.00
On cover. *from* 200.00
J8 D2 30c on 20c ol grn 1.50 *1.60*
Never hinged 2.60
On cover. *from* 200.00
J9 D2 45c on 10c brn 1.50 *1.60*
Never hinged 2.60
On cover. *from* 200.00
J10 D2 60c on 5c lt bl 1.50 *1.60*
Never hinged 2.60
On cover. *from* 200.00
J11 D2 1fr on 20c ol grn 2.25 *2.40*
Never hinged 3.75
On cover. *from* 250.00
J12 D2 2fr on 50c vio brn 2.25 *2.40*
Never hinged 3.75
On cover. *from* 250.00
Nos. J1-J12 (12) 26.60 *29.30*

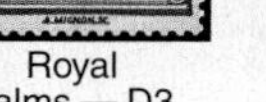

Royal Palms — D3

Guiana Girl — D4

1929, Oct. 14 Typo. *Perf. 13½x14*

J13 D3 5c indigo & Prus bl .45 *.50*
Never hinged .60
On cover. *from* 300.00
J14 D3 10c bis brn & Prus grn .45 *.50*
Never hinged .60
On cover. *from* 300.00
J15 D3 20c grn & rose red .45 *.50*
Never hinged .60
On cover. *from* 300.00
J16 D3 30c ol brn & rose red .45 *.50*
Never hinged .60
On cover. *from* 300.00
J17 D3 50c vio & ol brn .95 *1.00*
Never hinged 1.25
On cover. *from* 300.00
J18 D3 60c brn red & ol brn 1.30 *1.40*
Never hinged 2.00
On cover. *from* 300.00
J19 D4 1fr dp bl & org brn 1.75 *1.90*
Never hinged 2.60
On cover. *from* 300.00
J20 D4 2fr brn red & bluish grn 2.00 *2.10*
Never hinged 3.00
On cover. *from* 300.00
J21 D4 3fr violet & blk 4.25 *4.50*
Never hinged 5.75
On cover. *from* 300.00
Nos. J13-J21 (9) 12.05 *12.90*

FRENCH GUINEA

'french 'gi-nē

LOCATION — On the coast of West Africa, between Portuguese Guinea and Sierra Leone.
GOVT. — Former French colony
AREA — 89,436 sq. mi.
POP. — 2,058,442 (est. 1941)
CAPITAL — Conakry

French Guinea stamps were replaced by those of French West Africa around 1944-45. French Guinea became the Republic of Guinea Oct. 2, 1958.

100 Centimes = 1 Franc

Navigation and Commerce — A1

Perf. 14x13½

1892-1900 Typo. Unwmk.
Name of Colony in Blue or Carmine

1 A1 1c black, *lilac bl* 2.40 1.60
Never hinged 4.00
On cover 150.00
2 A1 2c brown, *buff* 2.40 2.00
Never hinged 4.00
On cover 150.00
3 A1 4c claret, *lav* 3.25 2.00
Never hinged 4.00
On cover 140.00
4 A1 5c green, *grnsh* 8.00 8.00
Never hinged 16.00
On cover 80.00
5 A1 10c blk, *lavender* 8.00 4.75
Never hinged 14.50
On cover 75.00
6 A1 10c red ('00) 45.00 40.00
Never hinged 85.00
On cover 175.00
7 A1 15c blue, quadrille paper 16.00 8.00
Never hinged 27.50
On cover 80.00
8 A1 15c gray, *lt gray* ('00) 100.00 87.50
Never hinged 200.00
On cover 375.00
9 A1 20c red, *grn* 20.00 16.00
Never hinged 40.00
On cover 140.00
On cover, single franking 240.00
10 A1 25c black, *rose* 16.00 8.00
Never hinged 27.50
On cover 67.50
11 A1 25c blue ('00) 24.00 24.00
Never hinged 40.00
On cover 190.00
12 A1 30c brown, *bis* 40.00 32.50
Never hinged 72.50
On cover 140.00
On cover, single franking 210.00
13 A1 40c red, *straw* 40.00 32.50
Never hinged 72.50
On cover 140.00
On cover, single franking 210.00
a. "GUINEE FRANCAISE" double 475.00 475.00
14 A1 50c car, *rose* 47.50 35.00
Never hinged 80.00
On cover 190.00
On cover, single franking 250.00
15 A1 50c brown, *az* ('00) 40.00 40.00
Never hinged 72.50
On cover 300.00
On cover, single franking 400.00
16 A1 75c dp vio, *org* 65.00 47.50
Never hinged 115.00
On cover 340.00
On cover, single franking 525.00
17 A1 1fr brnz grn, *straw* 50.00 40.00
Never hinged 100.00
On cover 375.00
On cover, single franking 625.00
Nos. 1-17 (17) 527.55 429.35

Perf. 13½x14 stamps are counterfeits.

For surcharges see Nos. 48-54.

Fulah Shepherd — A2

1904

18 A2 1c black, *yel grn* 1.20 1.20
Never hinged 1.60
On cover 110.00
19 A2 2c vio brn, *buff* 1.20 1.20
Never hinged 1.60
On cover 110.00
20 A2 4c carmine, *bl* 1.60 1.60
Never hinged 2.40
On cover 105.00
21 A2 5c green, *grnsh* 1.60 1.60
Never hinged 2.40
On cover 62.50
22 A2 10c carmine 4.00 2.40
Never hinged 8.00
On cover 50.00

23 A2 15c violet, *rose* 12.00 5.50
Never hinged 16.00
On cover 55.00
24 A2 20c carmine, *grn* 16.00 16.00
Never hinged 25.00
On cover 105.00
On cover, single franking 200.00
25 A2 25c blue 16.00 10.00
Never hinged 32.50
On cover 50.00
26 A2 30c brown 24.00 24.00
Never hinged 40.00
On cover 100.00
On cover, single franking 135.00
27 A2 40c red, *straw* 35.00 24.00
Never hinged 65.00
On cover 100.00
On cover, single franking 135.00
28 A2 50c brown, *az* 32.50 24.00
Never hinged 72.50
On cover 92.50
On cover, single franking 125.00
29 A2 75c green, *org* 32.50 32.50
Never hinged 72.50
On cover 160.00
On cover, single franking 225.00
30 A2 1fr brnz grn, *straw* 47.50 47.50
Never hinged 100.00
On cover 250.00
On cover, single franking 425.00
31 A2 2fr red, *org* 87.50 87.50
Never hinged 200.00
On cover 375.00
On cover, single franking 625.00
32 A2 5fr green, *yel grn* 120.00 120.00
Never hinged 240.00
On cover 500.00
On cover, single franking 800.00
Nos. 18-32 (15) 432.60 399.00

For surcharges see Nos. 55-62.

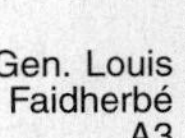

Gen. Louis Faidherbé
A3

Oil Palm — A4

Dr. Noel Eugène Ballay
A5

1906-07

Name of Colony in Red or Blue

33 A3 1c gray .80 .80
Never hinged 1.60
On cover 87.50
34 A3 2c brown 1.20 1.20
Never hinged 2.00
On cover 87.50
35 A3 4c brown, *bl* 1.60 1.60
Never hinged 2.75
On cover 87.50
36 A3 5c green 4.00 2.00
Never hinged 5.50
On cover 40.00
37 A3 10c carmine (B) 24.00 1.60
Never hinged 47.50
On cover 21.00
38 A4 20c black, *blue* 8.00 4.00
Never hinged 16.00
On cover 30.00
39 A4 25c blue, *pnksh* 8.00 6.50
Never hinged 12.00
On cover 50.00
On cover, single franking 135.00
40 A4 30c brown, *pnksh* 8.00 4.00
Never hinged 16.00
On cover 50.00
On cover, single franking 87.50
41 A4 35c black, *yellow* 6.50 2.40
Never hinged 12.00
On cover 50.00
On cover, single franking 67.50
42 A4 45c choc, *grnsh gray* 8.00 4.00
Never hinged 12.00
On cover 55.00
On cover, single franking 100.00
43 A4 50c dp violet 16.00 12.00
Never hinged 27.50
On cover 67.50
On cover, single franking 125.00
44 A4 75c blue, *org* 12.00 4.00
Never hinged 16.00
On cover 100.00
On cover, single franking 200.00
45 A5 1fr black, *az* 20.00 24.00
Never hinged 40.00
On cover 120.00
On cover, single franking 225.00
46 A5 2fr blue, *pink* 40.00 *45.00*
Never hinged 90.00
On cover 190.00
On cover, single franking 350.00
47 A5 5fr car, *straw* (B) 60.00 *65.00*
Never hinged 125.00
On cover 200.00
On cover, single franking 400.00
Nos. 33-47 (15) 218.10 *178.10*

Regular Issues Surcharged in Black or Carmine

1912

Spacing between figures of surcharge 1.5mm (5c), 2mm (10c)

On Issue of 1892-1900

48 A1 5c on 2c brown, *buff* 1.60 *2.00*
Never hinged 2.75
On cover 80.00
49 A1 5c on 4c cl, *lav* (C) 1.25 *1.60*
Never hinged 2.00
On cover 55.00
50 A1 5c on 15c blue (C) 1.25 *1.60*
Never hinged 2.00
On cover 62.50
51 A1 5c on 20c red, *grn* 4.00 *5.25*
Never hinged 6.50
On cover 100.00
52 A1 5c on 30c brn, *bis* (C) 5.50 *6.50*
Never hinged 8.75
On cover 120.00
53 A1 10c on 40c red, *straw* 2.40 *3.25*
Never hinged 4.50
On cover 87.50
54 A1 10c on 75c dp vio, *org* 8.00 *9.50*
Never hinged 14.00
On cover 120.00
a. Double surcharge, inverted 325.00

On Issue of 1904

55 A2 5c on 2c vio brn, *buff* 1.20 *1.20*
Never hinged 1.60
On cover 50.00
a. Pair, one without surcharge 650.00
b. Inverted surcharge 210.00
56 A2 5c on 4c car, *blue* 1.20 *1.20*
Never hinged 2.10
On cover 55.00
57 A2 5c on 15c violet, *rose* 1.20 *1.20*
Never hinged 2.10
On cover 55.00
58 A2 5c on 20c car, *grn* 1.60 1.60
Never hinged 2.40
On cover 67.50
59 A2 5c on 25c blue (C) 1.60 *2.00*
Never hinged 2.40
On cover 75.00
60 A2 5c on 30c brown (C) 2.00 *3.25*
Never hinged 3.25
On cover 80.00
61 A2 10c on 40c red, *straw* 2.00 *3.25*
Never hinged 4.00
On cover 80.00
62 A2 10c on 50c brn, *az* (C) 5.50 *6.50*
Never hinged 10.00
On cover 105.00
Nos. 48-62 (15) 40.30 49.90

Spacing between figures of surcharge 2.25mm (5c), 2.75mm (10c)

48a A1 5c on 2c brown, *buff* 100.00 100.00
Never hinged 175.00
49a A1 5c on 4c cl, *lav* (C) 40.00 40.00
Never hinged 65.00
50a A1 5c on 15c blue (C) 52.50 52.50
Never hinged 87.50
51a A1 5c on 20c red, *grn* 225.00 225.00
52a A1 5c on 30c brn, *bis* (C) 625.00 625.00
53a A1 10c on 40c red, *straw* 52.50 52.50
Never hinged 87.50
54b A1 10c on 75c dp vio, *org* 200.00 200.00
c. Double surcharge, inverted 3,800.

On Issue of 1904

55c A2 5c on 2c vio brn, *buff* 35.00 35.00
Never hinged 55.00
56a A2 5c on 4c car, *blue* 35.00 35.00
Never hinged 55.00
57a A2 5c on 15c violet, *rose* 35.00 35.00
Never hinged 55.00
58a A2 5c on 20c car, *grn* 50.00 50.00
Never hinged 87.50
59a A2 5c on 25c blue (C) 125.00 125.00
Never hinged 200.00
60a A2 5c on 30c brown (C) 160.00 160.00
Never hinged 240.00
61a A2 10c on 40c red, *straw* 50.00 50.00
Never hinged 87.50
62a A2 10c on 50c brn, *az* (C) 67.50 67.50
Never hinged 110.00
Nos. 48a-62a (15) 1,853. 1,853.

Ford at Kitim — A6

1913-33 ***Perf. 13½x14***

63 A6 1c violet & bl .25 .25
Never hinged .40
On cover 67.50
a. Imperf. 72.50
Never hinged 120.00
64 A6 2c brn & vio brn .25 .25
Never hinged .40
On cover 67.50
a. Double impression of vio brn 160.00
Never hinged 260.00
65 A6 4c gray & black .25 .25
Never hinged .40
On cover 67.50
66 A6 5c yel grn & bl grn 1.20 .40
Never hinged 2.00
On cover 27.50
a. Booklet pane of 4 —
Complete booklet, 10 #66a 275.00
b. Chalky paper 1.20 .40
Never hinged 2.00
On cover 27.50
67 A6 5c brn vio & grn ('22) .40 .25
Never hinged .65
On cover 22.50
68 A6 10c red org & rose 1.20 .40
Never hinged 1.60
On cover 16.00
a. Booklet pane of 4 —
Complete booklet, 10 #68a 550.00
b. Chalky paper 1.00 .40
Never hinged 1.60
On cover 16.00
69 A6 10c yel grn & bl grn ('22) .55 .25
Never hinged .85
On cover 40.00
70 A6 10c vio & ver ('25) .80 .40
Never hinged 1.25
On cover 45.00
a. Imperf. 45.00
Never hinged 67.50
71 A6 15c vio brn & rose, chalky paper ('16) .80 .40
Never hinged 1.25
On cover 16.00
a. Booklet pane of 4 —
Complete booklet, 10 #71a 1,200.
72 A6 15c gray grn & yel grn ('25) .40 .40
Never hinged .80
On cover 16.00
73 A6 15c red brn & rose lil ('27) .40 .30
Never hinged .80
On cover 27.50
74 A6 20c brown & violet .40 .40
Never hinged .80
On cover 27.50
75 A6 20c grn & bl grn ('26) .80 .80
Never hinged 1.20
On cover 13.00
76 A6 20c brn red & brn ('27) .80 .50
Never hinged 1.60
On cover 32.50
77 A6 25c ultra & blue 2.75 1.60
Never hinged 4.75
On cover 27.50
On cover, single franking 67.50
a. Chalky paper 4.50 3.25
Never hinged 8.00
On cover 27.50
78 A6 25c black & vio ('22) .80 .80
Never hinged 1.25
On cover 5.50
79 A6 30c vio brn & grn 1.60 1.20
Never hinged 2.75
On cover 32.50
On cover, single franking 87.50
80 A6 30c red org & rose ('22) 1.20 1.10
Never hinged 2.40
On cover 32.50
On cover, single franking 62.50
81 A6 30c rose red & grn ('25) .30 .30
Never hinged .50
On cover 8.75
82 A6 30c dl grn & bl grn ('28) 1.60 1.60
Never hinged 3.25
On cover 40.00
83 A6 35c blue & rose .55 .55
Never hinged 1.20
On cover 40.00
On cover, single franking 87.50
84 A6 40c green & gray 1.20 1.20
Never hinged 1.60
On cover 45.00
On cover, single franking 100.00
85 A6 45c brown & red 1.20 1.20
Never hinged 1.60
On cover 55.00
On cover, single franking 125.00
86 A6 50c ultra & black 6.50 4.75
Never hinged 11.00
On cover 62.50
On cover, single franking 140.00
87 A6 50c ultra & bl ('22) 1.60 .80
Never hinged 2.40
On cover 30.00
On cover, single franking 62.50
88 A6 50c yel brn & ol ('25) .80 .80
Never hinged 1.25
On cover 30.00
89 A6 60c vio, *pnksh* ('25) .80 .80
Never hinged 1.20
On cover 27.50
On cover, single franking 80.00
90 A6 65c yel brn & sl bl ('26) 2.00 1.20
Never hinged 3.25
On cover 16.00
On cover, single franking 27.50
91 A6 75c red & ultra 1.60 1.60
Never hinged 2.00
On cover 45.00
On cover, single franking 120.00
92 A6 75c indigo & dl bl ('25) .80 1.20
Never hinged 2.00
On cover 27.50
On cover, single franking 62.50
93 A6 75c mag & yel grn ('27) 1.60 1.20
Never hinged 3.25
On cover 20.00
94 A6 85c ol grn & red brn ('26) 1.20 1.20
Never hinged 2.00
On cover 32.50
On cover, single franking 125.00
95 A6 90c brn red & rose ('30) 5.50 4.75
Never hinged 9.50
On cover 55.00
On cover, single franking 140.00
96 A6 1fr violet & black 1.60 2.40
Never hinged 2.75
On cover 67.50
On cover, single franking 150.00
97 A6 1.10fr vio & ol brn ('28) 8.00 8.00
Never hinged 14.00
On cover 125.00
On cover, single franking 300.00
98 A6 1.25fr vio & yel brn ('33) 2.40 1.60
Never hinged 4.00
On cover 27.50
On cover, single franking 87.50
99 A6 1.50fr dk bl & lt bl ('30) 6.50 2.40
Never hinged 10.00
On cover 50.00
On cover, single franking 125.00
100 A6 1.75fr ol brn & vio ('33) 1.75 1.60
Never hinged 2.40
On cover 21.00
On cover, single franking 27.50
101 A6 2fr orange & vio brn 4.00 4.00
Never hinged 6.50
On cover 80.00
On cover, single franking 175.00
102 A6 3fr red violet ('30) 8.00 5.50
Never hinged 14.00
On cover 92.50
On cover, single franking 175.00
103 A6 5fr black & vio 16.00 16.00
Never hinged 25.00
On cover 105.00
On cover, single franking 210.00
104 A6 5fr dl bl & blk ('22) 4.00 2.40
Never hinged 4.75
On cover 67.50
On cover, single franking 125.00
Nos. 63-104 (42) 94.35 77.00

For surcharges see Nos. 105-115, B1.

Nos. 66, 68 and 77 pasted on colored cardboard and overprinted "VALEUR D'ECHANGE" were used as emergency currency in 1920.

Type of 1913-33 Surcharged

1922

105 A6 60c on 75c violet, *pnksh* .40 .40
Never hinged .80
On cover 20.00
On cover, single franking 32.50

Stamps and Type of 1913-33 Surcharged

1924-27

106 A6 25c on 2fr org & brn (R) .40 .40
Never hinged .80
On cover 10.00

107 A6 25c on 5fr dull bl & blk .40 .40
Never hinged .80
On cover 10.00

108 A6 65c on 75c rose & ultra ('25) 1.60 1.60
Never hinged 2.00
On cover 62.50
On cover, single franking 140.00

109 A6 85c on 75c rose & ultra ('25) 2.40 2.00
Never hinged 3.25
On cover 45.00
On cover, single franking 87.50

110 A6 90c on 75c brn red & cer ('27) 3.25 3.25
Never hinged 4.75
On cover 50.00
On cover, single franking 87.50

111 A6 1.25fr on 1fr dk bl & ultra ('26) 1.20 1.60
Never hinged 2.00
On cover 55.00
On cover, single franking 105.00

112 A6 1.50fr on 1fr dp bl & lt bl ('27) 2.40 2.40
Never hinged 3.25
On cover 40.00
On cover, single franking 67.50

113 A6 3fr on 5fr mag & sl ('27) 4.00 4.00
Never hinged 6.50
On cover 80.00
On cover, single franking 160.00

114 A6 10fr on 5fr bl & bl grn, *bluish* ('27) 8.00 8.00
Never hinged 16.00
On cover 100.00
On cover, single franking 200.00

115 A6 20fr on 5fr rose lil & brn ol, *pnksh* ('27) 20.00 20.00
Never hinged 32.50
On cover 150.00
On cover, single franking 275.00
Nos. 106-115 (10) 43.65 43.65

Common Design Types pictured following the introduction.

Colonial Exposition Issue
Common Design Types

1931 Engr. *Perf. 12½*
Name of Country in Black

116 CD70 40c deep green 4.75 4.75
Never hinged 8.00
On cover 100.00
a. "GUINÉE FRANCAISE" omitted 55.00 *67.50*
Never hinged 92.50
On cover 160.00

117 CD71 50c violet 4.75 4.75
Never hinged 8.00
On cover 80.00

118 CD72 90c red orange 4.75 4.75
Never hinged 8.00
On cover 125.00
On cover, single franking 200.00
a. "GUINÉE FRANCAISE" omitted 55.00 *70.00*
Never hinged 92.50
On cover 250.00

119 CD73 1.50fr dull blue 5.50 5.50
Never hinged 8.00
On cover 110.00
On cover, single franking 175.00
a. "GUINÉE FRANCAISE" omitted 55.00 *67.50*
Never hinged 92.50
On cover 250.00
Nos. 116-119 (4) 19.75 19.75
Set, never hinged 32.00

Paris International Exposition Issue
Common Design Types

1937 *Perf. 13*

120 CD74 20c deep violet 2.00 2.00
Never hinged 3.25
On cover 100.00

121 CD75 30c dark green 2.00 2.00
Never hinged 3.25
On cover 87.50

122 CD76 40c carmine rose 2.40 2.40
Never hinged 3.25
On cover 75.00

123 CD77 50c dark brown 1.60 1.60
Never hinged 3.25
On cover 67.50

124 CD78 90c red 1.60 1.60
Never hinged 3.25
On cover 100.00
On cover, single franking 160.00

125 CD79 1.50fr ultra 2.40 2.40
Never hinged 4.00
On cover 87.50
On cover, single franking 150.00
Nos. 120-125 (6) 12.00 12.00
Set, never hinged 20.25

Colonial Arts Exhibition Issue
Souvenir Sheet
Common Design Type

1937 *Imperf.*

126 CD76 3fr Prussian green 12.00 *16.00*
Never hinged 16.00
On cover 110.00
On cover, single franking 160.00

Guinea Village A7

Hausa Basket Workers A8

Forest Waterfall A9

Guinea Women — A10

1938-40 *Perf. 13*

128 A7 2c vermilion .25 .25
Never hinged .40
On cover 32.50

129 A7 3c ultra .25 .25
Never hinged .40
On cover 32.50

130 A7 4c green .25 .25
Never hinged .40
On cover 32.50

131 A7 5c rose car .25 .25
Never hinged .40
On cover 27.50

132 A7 10c peacock blue .25 .25
Never hinged .40
On cover 27.50

133 A7 15c violet brown .25 .25
Never hinged .40
On cover 22.50

134 A8 20c dk carmine .30 .25
Never hinged .50
On cover 15.00

135 A8 25c pck blue .40 .25
Never hinged .65
On cover 20.00

136 A8 30c ultra .40 .25
Never hinged .65
On cover 12.50

137 A8 35c green .55 .50
Never hinged .80
On cover 32.50

138 A8 40c blk brn ('40) .40 .40
Never hinged .80
On cover 12.50

139 A8 45c dk green ('40) .40 .40
Never hinged .80
On cover 30.00

140 A8 50c red brown .55 .50
Never hinged .80
On cover 16.00

141 A9 55c dk ultra 1.20 .80
Never hinged 1.60
On cover 8.75

142 A9 60c dk ultra ('40) 1.20 1.20
Never hinged 1.75
On cover 25.00

143 A9 65c green 1.20 .80
Never hinged 1.60
On cover 6.25

144 A9 70c green ('40) 1.20 1.20
Never hinged 1.60
On cover 30.00

145 A9 80c rose violet .80 .55
Never hinged 1.20
On cover 55.00
On cover, single franking 100.00

146 A9 90c rose vio ('39) 1.25 1.25
Never hinged 1.60
On cover 42.50
On cover, single franking 92.50

147 A9 1fr orange red 2.40 2.00
Never hinged 3.50
On cover 42.50
On cover, single franking 80.00

148 A9 1fr brn blk ('40) .40 .40
Never hinged .80
On cover 6.25

149 A9 1.25fr org red ('39) 1.40 1.40
Never hinged 1.90
On cover 62.50
On cover, single franking 125.00

150 A9 1.40fr brown ('40) 1.20 1.20
Never hinged 1.60
On cover 42.50
On cover, single franking 92.50

151 A9 1.50fr violet 2.40 2.00
Never hinged 3.50
On cover 25.00
On cover, single franking 50.00

152 A10 1.60fr org red ('40) 1.60 1.60
Never hinged 2.00
On cover 42.50
On cover, single franking 105.00

153 A10 1.75fr ultra .80 .80
Never hinged 1.25
On cover 32.50
On cover, single franking 67.50

154 A10 2fr magenta 1.20 .80
Never hinged 1.60
On cover 20.00
On cover, single franking 32.50

155 A10 2.25fr brt ultra ('39) 1.75 1.75
Never hinged 2.40
On cover 55.00
On cover, single franking 110.00

156 A10 2.50fr brn blk ('40) 1.60 1.60
Never hinged 2.00
On cover 37.50
On cover, single franking 75.00

157 A10 3fr peacock blue .95 .40
Never hinged 1.20
On cover 50.00
On cover, single franking 87.50

158 A10 5fr rose violet .95 .80
Never hinged 1.20
On cover 50.00
On cover, single franking 87.50

159 A10 10fr slate green 1.60 1.60
Never hinged 2.00
On cover 55.00
On cover, single franking 100.00

160 A10 20fr chocolate 2.40 2.40
Never hinged 3.50
On cover 67.50
On cover, single franking 120.00
Nos. 128-160 (33) 32.00 28.60
Set, never hinged 45.00

For surcharges see Nos. B8-B11 in Scott Standard catalogue, Vol. 2.

Caillié Issue
Common Design Type

1939 Engr. *Perf. 12½x12*

161 CD81 90c org brn & org .40 .80
Never hinged .80
On cover 8.75

162 CD81 2fr brt violet .40 1.20
Never hinged .80
On cover 27.50
On cover, single franking 50.00

163 CD81 2.25fr ultra & dk bl .40 1.20
Never hinged .80
On cover 32.50
On cover, single franking 55.00
Nos. 161-163 (3) 1.20 3.20
Set, never hinged 2.40

René Caillié, French explorer, death cent.

New York World's Fair Issue
Common Design Type

1939

164 CD82 1.25fr carmine lake .80 1.60
Never hinged 1.20
On cover 75.00
On cover, single franking 150.00

165 CD82 2.25fr ultra .80 1.60
Never hinged 1.20
On cover 75.00
On cover, single franking 140.00

SEMI-POSTAL STAMPS

Regular Issue of 1913 Surcharged in Red

1915 Unwmk. *Perf. 13½x14*

B1 A6 10c + 5c org & rose 1.60 1.60
Never hinged 2.40
On cover 55.00
a. Chalky paper 2.00 2.00
Never hinged 3.25
On cover 55.00

Curie Issue
Common Design Type

1938 Engr. *Perf. 13*

B2 CD80 1.75fr + 50c brt ultra 8.75 8.75
Never hinged 14.00
On cover 100.00
On cover, single franking 160.00

French Revolution Issue
Common Design Type

1939 Photo.
Name and Value Typo. in Black

B3 CD83 45c + 25c green 9.50 9.50
Never hinged 16.00
On cover 140.00

B4 CD83 70c + 30c brown 9.50 9.50
Never hinged 16.00
On cover 105.00

B5 CD83 90c + 35c red org 9.50 9.50
Never hinged 16.00
On cover 92.50

B6 CD83 1.25fr + 1fr rose pink 9.50 9.50
Never hinged 16.00
On cover 150.00
On cover, single franking 225.00

B7 CD83 2.25fr + 2fr blue 9.50 9.50
Never hinged 16.00
On cover 140.00
On cover, single franking 210.00
Nos. B3-B7 (5) 47.50 47.50
Set, never hinged 80.00

AIR POST STAMPS

Common Design Type

1940 Unwmk. Engr. *Perf. 12½x12*

C1 CD85 1.90fr ultra .40 .40
Never hinged .80
On cover 40.00

C2 CD85 2.90fr dark red .40 .40
Never hinged .80
On cover 40.00

C3 CD85 4.50fr dk gray grn .80 .80
Never hinged 1.10
On cover 50.00

C4 CD85 4.90fr yellow bis .80 .80
Never hinged 1.20
On cover 55.00

C5 CD85 6.90fr dp orange 1.60 1.60
Never hinged 2.00
On cover 67.50
Nos. C1-C5 (5) 4.00 4.00
Set, never hinged 6.00

POSTAGE DUE STAMPS

Fulah Woman — D1

1905 Unwmk. Typo. *Perf. 14x13½*

J1 D1 5c blue 1.60 *3.25*
Never hinged 4.00
On cover 110.00

J2 D1 10c brown 2.40 *3.25*
Never hinged 4.00
On cover 110.00

J3 D1 15c green 8.00 6.50
Never hinged 12.00
On cover 135.00

J4 D1 30c rose 8.00 6.50
Never hinged 12.00
On cover 135.00

J5 D1 50c black 12.00 *13.00*
Never hinged 16.00
On cover 110.00

J6 D1 60c dull orange 12.00 *16.00*
Never hinged 32.50
On cover 160.00

J7 D1 1fr violet 40.00 *47.50*
Never hinged 80.00
On cover 225.00
Nos. J1-J7 (7) 84.00 96.00

Heads and Coast — D2

1906-08

J8 D2 5c grn, *grnsh* ('08) 20.00 13.00
Never hinged 40.00
On cover 135.00

J9 D2 10c violet brn ('08) 8.00 5.50
Never hinged 12.00
On cover 110.00

J10 D2 15c dk blue ('08) 8.00 5.50
Never hinged 12.00
On cover 110.00

J11 D2 20c blk, *yellow* 8.00 5.50
Never hinged 12.00
On cover 115.00

J12 D2 30c red, *straw* ('08) 27.50 26.00
Never hinged 62.50
On cover 200.00

J13 D2 50c violet ('08) 24.00 *26.00*
Never hinged 55.00
On cover 200.00

J14 D2 60c blk, *buff* ('08) 24.00 21.00
Never hinged 45.00
On cover 160.00

J15 D2 1fr blk, *pnksh* ('08) 16.00 13.50
Never hinged 27.00
On cover 150.00
Nos. J8-J15 (8) 135.50 116.00

D3

1914
J16 D3 5c green .40 *.55*
Never hinged .80
On cover 50.00
J17 D3 10c rose .40 *.65*
Never hinged .80
On cover 50.00
J18 D3 15c gray .40 *.80*
Never hinged .80
On cover 50.00
J19 D3 20c brown .80 .80
Never hinged 1.20
On cover 55.00
J20 D3 30c blue .80 .80
Never hinged 1.20
On cover 55.00
J21 D3 50c black 1.00 *1.25*
Never hinged 1.60
On cover 62.50
J22 D3 60c orange 2.00 *2.40*
Never hinged 2.75
On cover 67.50
J23 D3 1fr violet 2.00 *2.40*
Never hinged 2.75
On cover 55.00
Nos. J16-J23 (8) 7.80 9.65

Type of 1914 Issue Surcharged

1927
J24 D3 2fr on 1fr lil rose 8.00 *8.00*
Never hinged 12.00
On cover 110.00
a. No period after "F" 27.50 *32.50*
Never hinged 45.00
J25 D3 3fr on 1fr org brn 8.00 *8.00*
Never hinged 12.00
On cover 125.00

D4

1938 **Engr.**
J26 D4 5c dk violet .25 .30
Never hinged .40
On cover 42.50
J27 D4 10c carmine .25 .30
Never hinged .40
On cover 42.50
J28 D4 15c green .25 .30
Never hinged .40
On cover 42.50
J29 D4 20c red brown .25 .40
Never hinged .40
On cover 42.50
J30 D4 30c rose violet .25 .40
Never hinged .40
On cover 42.50
J31 D4 50c chocolate .80 .70
Never hinged 1.20
On cover 50.00
J32 D4 60c peacock blue .80 1.10
Never hinged 1.20
On cover 55.00
J33 D4 1fr vermilion .80 1.10
Never hinged 1.20
On cover 55.00
J34 D4 2fr ultra .80 1.10
Never hinged 1.20
On cover 67.50
J35 D4 3fr black 1.60 1.60
Never hinged 2.00
On cover 87.50
Nos. J26-J35 (10) 6.05 7.30

A 10c of type D4 without "RF" was issued in 1944 by the Vichy Government. See Scott No. J36 in Vol. 2 of the *Scott Standard Postage Stamp Catalogue*.

FRENCH INDIA

'french 'in-dē-ə

LOCATION — East coast of India bordering on Bay of Bengal.
GOVT. — French Territory
AREA — 196 sq. mi.
POP. — 323,295 (1941)
CAPITAL — Pondichéry

French India was an administrative unit comprising the five settlements of Chandernagor, Karikal, Mahé, Pondichéry and Yanaon.

100 Centimes = 1 Franc
24 Caches = 1 Fanon (1923)
8 Fanons = 1 Rupie

Navigation and Commerce — A1

Perf. 14x13½
1892-1907 **Typo.** **Unwmk.**
Colony Name in Blue or Carmine

1 A1 1c blk, *lil bl* 1.40 1.00
Never hinged 2.40
On cover 60.00
2 A1 2c brn, *buff* 2.40 1.50
Never hinged 3.75
On cover 60.00
3 A1 4c claret, *lav* 3.00 2.50
Never hinged 5.25
On cover 60.00
4 A1 5c grn, *grnsh* 6.00 3.75
Never hinged 10.00
On cover 32.50
5 A1 10c blk, *lavender* 13.50 2.75
Never hinged 23.00
On cover 20.00
6 A1 10c red ('00) 5.00 2.40
Never hinged 8.75
On cover 14.00
7 A1 15c blue, quadrille paper 16.00 5.50
Never hinged 28.00
On cover 24.00
8 A1 15c gray, *lt gray* ('00) 30.00 30.00
Never hinged 55.00
On cover 80.00
9 A1 20c red, *grn* 8.00 5.50
Never hinged 13.00
On cover 40.00
On cover, single franking 67.50
10 A1 25c blk, *rose* 5.25 2.75
Never hinged 8.75
On cover 35.00
On cover, single franking 60.00
11 A1 25c blue ('00) 19.00 16.00
Never hinged 35.00
On cover 100.00
On cover, single franking 160.00
12 A1 30c brn, *bis* 57.50 50.00
Never hinged 110.00
On cover 180.00
On cover, single franking 240.00
13 A1 35c blk, *yel* ('06) 19.00 9.00
Never hinged 32.50
On cover 40.00
On cover, single franking 52.50
14 A1 40c red, *straw* 7.50 7.25
Never hinged 13.00
On cover 40.00
On cover, single franking 55.00
15 A1 45c blk, *gray grn* ('07) 5.25 *6.00*
Never hinged 8.75
On cover 45.00
On cover, single franking 65.00
16 A1 50c car, *rose* 7.25 7.25
Never hinged 11.00
On cover 52.50
On cover, single franking 80.00
17 A1 50c brn, *az* ('00) 16.00 *17.50*
Never hinged 30.00
On cover 150.00
On cover, single franking 240.00
18 A1 75c dp vio, *org* 9.75 *9.50*
Never hinged 17.50
On cover 92.50
On cover, single franking 160.00
19 A1 1fr brnz grn, *straw* 14.00 *14.50*
Never hinged 23.00
On cover 140.00
On cover, single franking 240.00
Nos. 1-19 (19) 245.80 *194.65*

Perf. 13½x14 stamps are counterfeits.

Nos. 10 and 16 Surcharged in Carmine or Black

1903
20 A1 5c on 25c blk, *rose* 400.00 240.00
On cover 350.00
21 A1 10c on 25c blk, *rose* 375.00 225.00
On cover 340.00
22 A1 15c on 25c blk, *rose* 125.00 115.00
Never hinged 250.00
On cover 160.00
23 A1 40c on 50c car, *rose* (Bk) 525.00 425.00
On cover 550.00
On cover, single franking 675.00
Nos. 20-23 (4) 1,425. 1,005.

Counterfeits of Nos. 20-23 abound.

A2

Revenue Stamp Surcharged in Black

1903
24 A2 5c gray blue 30.00 30.00
Never hinged 52.50
On cover 80.00

The bottom of the revenue stamps were cut off.

Brahma — A5

Kali Temple near Pondichéry A6

1914-22 *Perf. 13½x14, 14x13½*
25 A5 1c gray & blk .30 .30
Never hinged .55
On cover 32.50
a. 1c light gray & black .55 .55
Never hinged .95
On cover 32.50
26 A5 2c brn vio & blk .30 .30
Never hinged .55
On cover 32.50
27 A5 2c grn & brn vio ('22) .45 .45
Never hinged .70
On cover 27.50
28 A5 3c brown & blk .40 .40
Never hinged .65
On cover 32.50
29 A5 4c orange & blk .40 .40
Never hinged .65
On cover 32.50
30 A5 5c bl grn & blk .70 .70
Never hinged 1.20
On cover 14.50
31 A5 5c vio brn & blk ('22) .60 .60
Never hinged .70
On cover 12.00
32 A5 10c dp rose & blk 1.25 1.25
Never hinged 2.10
On cover 8.00
33 A5 10c grn & blk ('22) .90 .90
Never hinged 1.40
On cover 20.00
34 A5 15c vio & blk 1.10 1.10
Never hinged 1.90
On cover 8.00
35 A5 20c org red & blk 2.00 2.00
Never hinged 3.50
On cover 11.00
36 A5 25c blue & blk 2.00 2.00
Never hinged 3.50
On cover 8.00
On cover, single franking 9.50
37 A5 25c ultra & fawn ('22) 1.60 1.60
Never hinged 2.25
On cover 6.50
38 A5 30c ultra & blk 4.00 4.00
Never hinged 6.00
On cover 20.00
On cover, single franking 45.00
39 A5 30c rose & blk ('22) 1.75 1.75
Never hinged 2.90
On cover 16.00
On cover, single franking 27.50
40 A6 35c choc & blk 2.25 2.25
Never hinged 4.00
On cover 9.50
On cover, single franking 16.00
41 A6 40c org red & blk 2.25 2.25
Never hinged 4.00
On cover 12.00
On cover, single franking 20.00
42 A6 45c bl grn & blk 2.25 2.25
Never hinged 4.00
On cover 27.50
On cover, single franking 65.00
43 A6 50c dp rose & blk 2.25 2.25
Never hinged 4.00
On cover 32.50
On cover, single franking 72.50
44 A6 50c ultra & bl ('22) 3.00 3.00
Never hinged 4.75
On cover 14.50
On cover, single franking 27.50
45 A6 75c blue & blk 4.50 4.50
Never hinged 7.75
On cover 24.00
On cover, single franking 45.00
46 A6 1fr yellow & blk 4.50 4.50
Never hinged 7.75
On cover 32.50
On cover, single franking 80.00
47 A6 2fr violet & blk 6.75 6.75
Never hinged 11.00
On cover 45.00
On cover, single franking 87.50
48 A6 5fr ultra & blk 3.50 3.50
Never hinged 5.75
On cover 47.50
On cover, single franking 92.50
49 A6 5fr rose & blk ('22) 5.50 5.50
Never hinged 8.00
On cover 45.00
On cover, single franking 80.00
Nos. 25-49 (25) 54.50 54.50

For surcharges see Nos. 50-79, 113-116, 156A, B1-B5. Post 1940 issues in Scott Standard catalogue, Vol. 2.

No. 34 Surcharged in Various Colors

1922
50 A5 1c on 15c (Bk) .80 .80
Never hinged 1.25
On cover 40.00
51 A5 2c on 15c (Bl) .80 .80
Never hinged 1.40
On cover 40.00
53 A5 5c on 15c (R) .80 .80
Never hinged 1.40
On cover 40.00
Nos. 50-53 (3) 2.40 2.40

Stamps and Types of 1914-22 Surcharged with New Values in Caches, Fanons and Rupies in Black, Red or Blue

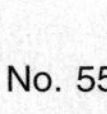
No. 55

No. 69

No. 78

1923-28
54 A5 1ca on 1c gray & blk (R) .30 .30
Never hinged .55
On cover 27.50
a. Imperf. 50.00 50.00
55 A5 2ca on 5c vio brn & blk .50 .50
Never hinged .70
On cover 20.00
a. Horizontal pair, imperf. between —
b. Imperf. 45.00 45.00
56 A5 3ca on 3c brn & blk .55 .55
Never hinged .85
On cover 20.00
57 A5 4ca on 4c org & blk .80 .80
Never hinged 1.40
On cover 16.00
58 A5 6ca on 10c grn & blk .95 .95
Never hinged 1.50
On cover 12.00
a. Double surcharge 175.00
59 A6 6ca on 45c bl grn & blk (R) .95 .95
Never hinged 1.50
On cover 12.00
60 A5 10ca on 20c dp red & bl grn ('28) 2.50 2.50
Never hinged 4.00
On cover 20.00
61 A5 12ca on 15c vio & blk .95 .95
Never hinged 1.50
On cover 12.00

62 A5 15ca on 20c org & blk 1.50 1.50
Never hinged 2.25
On cover 9.50
63 A6 16ca on 35c lt bl & yel brn ('28) 2.60 2.60
Never hinged 4.00
On cover 20.00
64 A5 18ca on 30c rose & blk 2.40 2.40
Never hinged 4.00
On cover 13.50
65 A6 20ca on 45c grn & dl red ('28) 2.00 1.50
Never hinged 3.00
On cover 13.50
66 A5 1fa on 25c dp grn & rose red ('28) 3.50 3.50
Never hinged 6.00
On cover 24.00
67 A6 1fa3ca on 35c choc & blk (Bl) 1.10 1.10
Never hinged 1.75
On cover 9.50
68 A6 1fa6ca on 40c org & blk (R) 1.50 1.25
Never hinged 2.40
On cover 12.00
69 A6 1fa12ca on 50c ultra & bl (Bl) 1.75 1.50
Never hinged 2.90
On cover 14.50
70 A6 1fa12ca on 75c bl & blk (Bl) 1.25 1.25
Never hinged 4.75
On cover 24.00
a. Double surcharge 145.00
Never hinged 250.00
71 A6 1fa16ca on 75c brn red & grn ('28) 3.50 3.00
Never hinged 6.00
On cover 20.00
72 A5 2fa9ca on 25c ultra & fawn (Bl) 1.50 1.20
Never hinged 2.40
On cover 13.50
73 A6 2fa12ca on 1fr vio & dk brn ('28) 3.00 3.00
Never hinged 5.25
On cover 24.00
74 A6 3fa3ca on 1fr yel & blk (R) 1.75 1.45
Never hinged 2.90
On cover 16.00
a. Double surcharge 145.00
Never hinged 250.00
75 A6 6fa6ca on 2fr vio & blk (Bl) 5.25 4.50
Never hinged 8.75
On cover 40.00
76 A6 1r on 1fr grn & dp bl (R) ('26) 9.50 7.75
Never hinged 17.50
On cover 47.50
77 A6 2r on 5fr rose & blk (R) 7.50 7.00
Never hinged 15.00
On cover 24.00
a. Double surcharge 145.00
Never hinged 250.00
78 A6 3r on 2fr gray & bl vio (R) ('26) 21.00 19.00
Never hinged 37.50
On cover 52.50
79 A6 5r on 5fr rose & blk, *grnsh* ('26) 27.50 24.00
Never hinged 45.00
On cover 80.00
Nos. 54-79 (26) 105.60 95.00

Nos. 60, 63, 66 and 73 have the original value obliterated by bars.

A7

A8

1929
80 A7 1ca dk gray & blk .25 .25
Never hinged .40
On cover 20.00
81 A7 2ca vio brn & blk .25 .25
Never hinged .40
On cover 16.00
82 A7 3ca brn & blk .25 .25
Never hinged .40
On cover 16.00
83 A7 4ca org & blk .30 .30
Never hinged .45
On cover 12.00
84 A7 6ca gray grn & grn .30 .30
Never hinged .45
On cover 9.50
85 A7 10ca brn, red & grn .30 .30
Never hinged .45
On cover 8.00
86 A8 12ca grn & lt grn .75 .70
Never hinged 1.20
On cover 8.00
87 A7 16ca brt bl & blk .95 .95
Never hinged 1.35
On cover 7.25
88 A7 18ca brn red & ver .95 .95
Never hinged 1.35
On cover 6.50
89 A7 20ca dk bl & grn, *bluish* .75 .75
Never hinged 1.20
On cover 6.50
90 A8 1fa gray grn & rose red .75 .70
Never hinged 1.20
On cover 8.00
91 A8 1fa6ca red org & blk .75 .70
Never hinged 1.20
On cover 8.00
92 A8 1fa12ca dp bl & ultra .75 .70
Never hinged 1.20
On cover 9.50
93 A8 1fa16ca rose red & grn .95 .95
Never hinged 1.35
On cover 11.00
94 A8 2fa12ca brt vio & brn 1.20 1.00
Never hinged 2.00
On cover 12.00
95 A8 6fa6ca dl vio & blk 1.20 1.00
Never hinged 1.75
On cover 14.50
a. Imperf. 50.00
96 A8 1r gray grn & dp bl 1.10 1.00
Never hinged 1.80
On cover 16.00
a. Imperf. 50.00
97 A8 2r rose & blk 1.60 1.20
Never hinged 2.60
On cover 20.00
a. Imperf. 50.00
98 A8 3r lt gray & gray lil 3.00 2.25
Never hinged 4.75
On cover 27.50
99 A8 5r rose & blk, *grnsh* 3.00 2.40
Never hinged 5.00
On cover 32.50
Nos. 80-99 (20) 19.35 16.90

For overprints and surcharges see Nos. 117-134, 157-176, 184-209G in the *Scott Standard Postage Stamp Catalogue*, Vol. 2.

Common Design Types pictured following the introduction.

Colonial Exposition Issue
Common Design Types

1931 **Engr.** ***Perf. 12½***
100 CD70 10ca deep green 4.50 *4.50*
Never hinged 6.00
On cover 52.50
101 CD71 12ca violet 4.50 *4.50*
Never hinged 6.75
On cover 45.00
102 CD72 18ca red orange 4.50 *4.50*
Never hinged 6.75
On cover 72.50
On cover, single franking 105.00
103 CD73 1fa12ca dull blue 4.50 *4.50*
Never hinged 6.75
On cover 65.00
On cover, single franking 92.50
Nos. 100-103 (4) 18.00 *18.00*

Paris International Exposition Issue
Common Design Types

1937 ***Perf. 13***
104 CD74 8ca dp violet 2.00 *4.00*
Never hinged 3.00
On cover 60.00
105 CD75 12ca dk green 2.25 *4.00*
Never hinged 3.25
On cover 52.50
106 CD76 16ca car rose 2.25 *4.00*
Never hinged 3.25
On cover 45.00
107 CD77 20ca dk brown 1.40 *4.00*
Never hinged 2.25
On cover 40.00
108 CD78 1fa12ca red 1.75 *4.00*
Never hinged 2.60
On cover 65.00
On cover, single franking 100.00
109 CD79 2fa12ca ultra 2.25 *4.00*
Never hinged 3.25
On cover 55.00
On cover, single franking 92.50
Nos. 104-109 (6) 11.90 *24.00*

For overprints see Nos. 135-139, 177-181 in the *Scott Standard Postage Stamp Catalogue*, Vol. 2.

Colonial Arts Exhibition Issue
Souvenir Sheet
Common Design Type

1937 ***Imperf.***
110 CD79 5fa red violet 9.25 *12.50*
Never hinged 14.50
On cover 72.50
On cover, single franking 105.00

For overprint see No. 140 in the *Scott Standard Postage Stamp Catalogue*, Vol. 2.

New York World's Fair Issue
Common Design Type

1939 **Engr.** ***Perf. 12½x12***
111 CD82 1fa12ca car lake 1.25 *4.00*
Never hinged 2.00
On cover 40.00
On cover, single franking 80.00
112 CD82 2fa12ca ultra 1.75 *4.00*
Never hinged 2.40
On cover 40.00
On cover, single franking 72.50

For overprints see Nos. 141-142, 182-183 in the *Scott Standard Postage Stamp Catalogue*, Vol. 2.

SEMI-POSTAL STAMPS

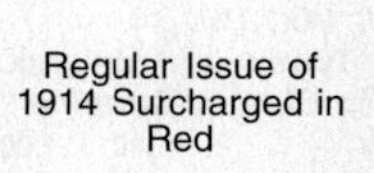
Regular Issue of 1914 Surcharged in Red

Two printings: 1st, surcharge at bottom of stamp; 2nd, surcharge centered toward top.

1915 **Unwmk.** ***Perf. 14x13½***
B1 A5 10c + 5c rose & blk (1st) 2.10 2.10
Never hinged 4.00
On cover 20.00
a. Second printing 2.00 2.00
Never hinged 3.50
On cover 20.00
b. As "a," inverted surcharge 210.00 210.00

Issued: No. B1, 6/15/15; No. B1a, 11/15.

Regular Issue of 1914 Surcharged in Red

1916
B2 A5 10c + 5c rose & blk 21.00 21.00
Never hinged 40.00
On cover 67.50
a. Inverted surcharge 210.00 210.00
b. Double surcharge 210.00 210.00

No. 32 Surcharged

B3 A5 10c + 5c rose & blk 3.50 3.50
Never hinged 6.00
On cover 27.50

No. 32 Surcharged

B4 A5 10c + 5c rose & blk 1.60 1.60
Never hinged 2.75
On cover 16.00

No. 32 Surcharged

B5 A5 10c + 5c rose & blk 2.25 2.25
Never hinged 3.50
On cover 20.00

Curie Issue
Common Design Type

1938 **Engr.** ***Perf. 13***
B6 CD80 2fa12ca + 20ca brt ultra 10.00 10.00
Never hinged 13.50
On cover 47.50
On cover, single franking 80.00

French Revolution Issue
Common Design Type

1939 **Photo.**
Name and Value Typo. in Black
B7 CD83 18ca + 10ca grn 5.75 *6.50*
Never hinged 12.50
On cover 72.50
B8 CD83 1fa6ca + 12ca brn 5.75 *6.50*
Never hinged 12.50
On cover 55.00
B9 CD83 1fa12ca + 16ca red org 5.75 *6.50*
Never hinged 12.50
On cover 47.50
B10 CD83 1fa16ca + 1fa16ca rose pink 5.75 *6.50*
Never hinged 12.50
On cover 80.00
On cover, single franking 125.00
B11 CD83 2fa12ca + 3fa blue 5.75 *6.50*
Never hinged 12.50
On cover 80.00
On cover, single franking 110.00
Nos. B7-B11 (5) 28.75 *32.50*

POSTAGE DUE STAMPS

Postage Due Stamps of France Surcharged like Nos. 54-75 in Black, Blue or Red

1923 **Unwmk.** ***Perf. 14x13½***
J1 D2 6ca on 10c brn 1.25 1.25
Never hinged 2.00
On cover 60.00
J2 D2 12ca on 25c rose (Bk) 1.25 1.25
Never hinged 2.00
On cover 60.00
J3 D2 15ca on 20c ol grn (R) 1.60 1.60
Never hinged 2.75
On cover 60.00
J4 D2 1fa6ca on 30c red 1.60 1.60
Never hinged 2.75
On cover 65.00
J5 D2 1fa12a on 50c brn vio 2.75 2.75
Never hinged 4.75
On cover 67.50
J6 D2 1fa15ca on 5c bl (Bk) 3.00 3.00
Never hinged 4.75
On cover 72.50
J7 D2 3fa3ca on 1fr red brn, *straw* 3.25 3.25
Never hinged 5.50
On cover 80.00
Nos. J1-J7 (7) 14.70 14.70

Types of Postage Due Stamps of French Colonies, 1884-85, Surcharged with New Values as in 1923 in Red or Black Bars over Original Values

1928
J8 D1 4ca on 20c gray lil 1.60 1.60
Never hinged 2.40
On cover 52.50
J9 D1 1fa on 30c orange 3.25 3.25
Never hinged 4.75
On cover 60.00
J10 D1 1fa16ca on 5c bl blk (R) 3.25 3.25
Never hinged 4.75
On cover 65.00
J11 D1 3fa on 1fr lt grn 3.75 3.75
Never hinged 6.50
On cover 72.50
Nos. J8-J11 (4) 11.85 11.85

D3

1929 **Typo.**

J12 D3 4ca deep red .50 .50
Never hinged .80
On cover 20.00
J13 D3 6ca blue .65 .65
Never hinged 1.00
On cover 20.00
J14 D3 12ca green .65 .65
Never hinged 1.00
On cover 20.00
J15 D3 1fa brown 1.25 1.25
Never hinged 1.90
On cover 24.00
J16 D3 1fa12ca lilac gray 1.25 1.25
Never hinged 1.90
On cover 24.00
J17 D3 1fa16ca buff 1.75 1.75
Never hinged 2.75
On cover 27.50
J18 D3 3fa lilac 2.10 2.10
Never hinged 3.25
On cover 32.50
Nos. J12-J18 (7) 8.15 8.15

FRENCH MOROCCO

'french mə-'rä-ˌkō

LOCATION — Northwest coast of Africa
GOVT. — French Protectorate
AREA — 153,870 sq. mi.
POP. — 8,340,000 (estimated 1954)
CAPITAL — Rabat

100 Centimos = 1 Peseta
100 Centimes = 1 franc (1917)

French Offices in Morocco

Stamps of France Surcharged in Red or Black

Type I. The "N" of "INV" is under the "B" of "REPUBLIQUE."
Type II. The "N" of "INV" is under the "U" of "REPUBLIQUE."

1891-1900 **Unwmk.** ***Perf. 14x13½***

1 A15 5c on 5c grn, *grnsh* (R) 16.00 4.00
Never hinged 32.50
On cover 62.50
a. Imperf., pair 175.00
Never hinged 320.00
2 A15 5c on 5c yel grn (II) (R) ('99) 32.50 27.50
Never hinged 65.00
On cover 340.00
a. Type I 32.50 27.50
Never hinged 65.00
On cover 375.00
3 A15 10c on 10c blk, *lav* (II) (R) 32.50 4.00
Never hinged 65.00
On cover 75.00
a. Type I 45.00 20.00
Never hinged 87.50
On cover 275.00
b. 10c on 25c black, *rose* 1,100. 1,200.
4 A15 20c on 20c red, *grn* 40.00 32.50
Never hinged 80.00
On cover 300.00
On cover, single franking 400.00
5 A15 25c on 25c blk, *rose* (R) 32.50 4.00
Never hinged 72.50
On cover 140.00
On cover, single franking 190.00
a. Double surcharge 225.00
b. Imperf., pair 175.00
Never hinged 325.00
6 A15 50c on 50c car, *rose* (II) 105.00 47.50
Never hinged 210.00
On cover 425.00
On cover, single franking 500.00
a. Type I 375.00 260.00
On cover 1,050.
On cover, single franking 1,250.
7 A15 1p on 1fr brnz grn, *straw* 120.00 80.00
Never hinged 240.00
On cover 500.00
On cover, single franking 550.00
8 A15 2p on 2fr brn, *az* (Bk) ('00) 240.00 240.00
Never hinged 475.00
On cover 925.00
On cover, single franking 1,100.
Nos. 1-8 (8) 618.50 439.50

No. 3b was never sent to Morocco.

France Nos. J15-J16 Overprinted in Carmine

1893

9 D2 5c black 3,250. 1,200.
On cover *2,500.*
10 D2 10c black 2,900. 800.
On cover *2,050.*

Counterfeits exist.

Surcharged in Red or Black

A3

A4

A5

1902-10

11 A3 1c on 1c gray (R) ('08) 2.40 1.20
Never hinged 4.00
On cover 37.50
12 A3 2c on 2c vio brn ('08) 2.40 1.20
Never hinged 4.00
On cover 37.50
13 A3 3c on 3c red org ('08) 3.25 1.60
Never hinged 5.50
On cover 37.50
14 A3 4c on 4c yel brn ('08) 13.00 8.00
Never hinged 23.00
On cover 55.00
15 A3 5c on 5c grn (R) 12.00 4.00
Never hinged 16.00
On cover 62.50
a. Double surcharge 340.00
b. Triple surcharge 340.00
16 A4 10c on 10c rose red ('03) 8.00 4.00
Never hinged 16.00
On cover 45.00
a. Surcharge omitted 225.00
Never hinged 390.00
17 A4 20c on 20c brn vio ('03) 40.00 24.00
Never hinged 55.00
On cover 120.00
On cover, single franking 190.00
18 A4 25c on 25c bl ('03) 40.00 4.00
Never hinged 55.00
On cover 67.50
On cover, single franking 92.50
19 A4 35c on 35c vio ('10) 40.00 24.00
Never hinged 67.50
On cover 67.50
20 A5 50c on 50c bis brn & lav ('03) 67.50 16.00
Never hinged 110.00
On cover 92.50
On cover, single franking 125.00
21 A5 1p on 1fr cl & ol grn ('03) 120.00 80.00
Never hinged 200.00
On cover 275.00
On cover, single franking 350.00
22 A5 2p on 2fr gray vio & yel ('03) 160.00 120.00
Never hinged 240.00
On cover 340.00
On cover, single franking 425.00
Nos. 11-22 (12) 508.55 288.00

Nos. 11-14 exist spelled CFNTIMOS or GENTIMOS.
The 25c on 25c with surcharge omitted is listed as No. 81a.
For overprints and surcharges see Nos. 26-37, 72-79, B1, B3.

Postage Due Stamps Nos. J1-J2 Handstamped

1903

24 D2 5c on 5c light blue 1,500. 1,400.
On postcard *4,250.*
25 D2 10c on 10c chocolate 2,800. 2,600.
On postcard *5,900.*

Nos. 24 and 25 were used only on Oct. 10, 1903. Used stamps were not canceled, the overprint serving as a cancellation.
Numerous counterfeits exist.

Types of 1902-10 Issue Surcharged in Red or Blue

1911-17

26 A3 1c on 1c gray (R) 1.20 .90
Never hinged 1.60
On cover 25.00
27 A3 2c on 2c vio brn 1.20 1.20
Never hinged 1.60
On cover 25.00
28 A3 3c on 3c orange 1.20 1.20
Never hinged 1.60
On cover 25.00
29 A3 5c on 5c green (R) 1.20 .80
Never hinged 1.60
On cover 12.50
30 A4 10c on 10c rose 1.20 .80
Never hinged 1.60
On cover 8.75
a. Imperf., pair 275.00
Never hinged 450.00
31 A4 15c on 15c org ('17) 3.50 2.40
Never hinged 6.50
On cover 10.00
32 A4 20c on 20c brn vio 5.50 4.00
Never hinged 8.00
On cover 18.00
33 A4 25c on 25c blue (R) 2.40 1.60
Never hinged 4.00
On cover 25.00
On cover, single franking 37.50
34 A4 35c on 35c violet (R) 12.00 5.50
Never hinged 16.00
On cover 25.00
On cover, single franking 30.00
35 A5 40c on 40c red & pale bl ('17) 8.00 5.50
Never hinged 12.00
On cover 30.00
On cover, single franking 37.50
36 A5 50c on 50c bis brn & lav (R) 27.50 16.00
Never hinged 35.00
On cover 50.00
On cover, single franking 92.50
37 A5 1p on 1fr cl & ol grn 24.00 12.00
Never hinged 35.00
On cover 42.50
On cover, single franking 125.00
Nos. 26-37 (12) 88.90 51.90

For surcharges see Nos. B1, B3.

The Administration Cherifinne des Postes, Telegraphes et Telephones was formed in 1911 under French guidance, and stamps of this design were issued by the Cherifien posts in 1912-13. See listings under "Morocco."

French Protectorate
Issue of 1911-17 Overprinted "Protectorat Francais"

A6

A7

A8

1914-21

38 A6 1c on 1c lt gray .40 .50
Never hinged .80
On cover 12.50
a. 1c dk gray ('22) .55 .80
Never hinged .80
On cover 12.50
39 A6 2c on 2c vio brn .80 .50
Never hinged 1.20
On cover 12.50
40 A6 3c on 3c orange 1.20 .65
Never hinged 1.60
On cover 12.50
41 A6 5c on 5c green 1.20 .50
Never hinged 1.60
On cover 7.50
a. New value omitted 275.00 275.00
Never hinged 410.00
42 A7 10c on 10c rose .80 .30
Never hinged 1.20
On cover 3.25
a. New value omitted 550.00 550.00
43 A7 15c on 15c org ('17) .80 .80
Never hinged 1.60
On cover 5.00
a. New value omitted 120.00 120.00
Never hinged 175.00
44 A7 20c on 20c brn vio 4.75 3.50
Never hinged 8.00
On cover 12.50
a. "Protectorat Francais" double 300.00 300.00
Never hinged 425.00
45 A7 25c on 25c blue 3.25 .80
Never hinged 5.50
On cover 15.00
On cover, single franking 21.00
a. New value omitted 350.00 350.00
Never hinged 525.00
46 A7 25c on 25c violet ('21) 1.25 .40
Never hinged 2.00
On cover 3.75
a. "Protectorat Francais" omitted 80.00 80.00
Never hinged 120.00
b. "Protectorat Francais" double 175.00 175.00
Never hinged 250.00
c. "Protectorat Francais" dbl. (R + Bk) 175.00 175.00
Never hinged 250.00
47 A7 30c on 30c vio ('21) 20.00 9.00
Never hinged 27.50
On cover 37.50
On cover, single franking 62.50
48 A7 35c on 35c violet 4.75 1.60
Never hinged 8.00
On cover 15.00
On cover, single franking 21.00
49 A8 40c on 40c red & pale bl 20.00 8.75
Never hinged 27.50
On cover 42.50
On cover, single franking 55.00
a. New value omitted 375.00 375.00
Never hinged 540.00
50 A8 45c on 45c grn & bl ('21) 55.00 40.00
Never hinged 80.00
On cover 125.00
On cover, single franking 180.00
51 A8 50c on 50c bis brn & lav 2.40 .80
Never hinged 4.00
On cover 19.00
On cover, single franking 30.00
a. "Protectorat Francais" invtd. 200.00 200.00
Never hinged 290.00
b. "Protectorat Francais" double 450.00 450.00
Never hinged 650.00
c. New value omitted 260.00 260.00
Never hinged 350.00
52 A8 1p on 1fr cl & ol grn 5.50 .80
Never hinged 8.00
On cover 15.00
On cover, single franking 42.50
a. "Protectorat Francais" invtd. 350.00 350.00
Never hinged 525.00
b. New value double 200.00 200.00
Never hinged 260.00
c. New value dbl., one invtd. 210.00 210.00
Never hinged 300.00
53 A8 2p on 2fr gray vio & yel 8.00 4.00
Never hinged 12.00
On cover 21.00
On cover, single franking 62.50
a. New value omitted 175.00 175.00
Never hinged 260.00
b. "Protectorat Francais" omitted 110.00 110.00
Never hinged 160.00
c. New value double 225.00
d. New value dbl., one invtd.
54 A8 5p on 5fr dk bl & buff 15.00 8.00
Never hinged 24.00
On cover 25.00
On cover, single franking 80.00
Nos. 38-54 (17) 145.10 80.90

For surcharges see Nos. B2, B4-B5.

Tower of Hassan, Rabat — A9

Mosque of the Andalusians, Fez — A10

City Gate Chella
A11

Koutoubiah, Marrakesh
A12

Bab Mansour, Meknes
A13

Roman Ruins, Volubilis
A14

1917 Engr. *Perf. 13½x14, 14x13½*

55 A9 1c grnsh gray .40 .40
Never hinged .80
On cover 16.00
56 A9 2c brown lilac .40 .40
Never hinged .80
On cover 13.00
57 A9 3c orange brn .40 .80
Never hinged .80
On cover 15.00
a. Imperf., pair 87.50
Never hinged 140.00
58 A10 5c yellow grn .40 .40
Never hinged .80
On cover 10.00
59 A10 10c rose red .80 .40
Never hinged 1.20
On cover 6.25
60 A10 15c dark gray .80 .40
Never hinged 1.20
On cover 3.75
a. Imperf., pair 65.00
Never hinged 95.00
61 A11 20c red brown 4.00 2.40
Never hinged 5.50
On cover 8.75
62 A11 25c dull blue 4.00 1.25
Never hinged 5.50
On cover 7.50
On cover, single franking 25.00
63 A11 30c gray violet 4.75 3.25
Never hinged 6.50
On cover 10.50
On cover, single franking 19.00
64 A12 35c orange 4.75 4.00
Never hinged 6.50
On cover 13.00
On cover, single franking 25.00
65 A12 40c ultra 1.60 1.60
Never hinged 2.40
On cover 10.00
On cover, single franking 17.50
66 A12 45c gray green 32.50 16.00
Never hinged 47.50
On cover 42.50
On cover, single franking 67.50
67 A13 50c dk brown 5.50 4.00
Never hinged 8.00
On cover 12.50
On cover, single franking 19.00
a. Imperf., pair 65.00
Never hinged 95.00
68 A13 1fr slate 16.00 4.00
Never hinged 20.00
On cover 16.00
On cover, single franking 29.00
a. Imperf., pair 65.00
Never hinged 95.00
69 A14 2fr black brown 160.00 95.00
Never hinged 275.00
On cover 340.00
70 A14 5fr dk gray grn 47.50 40.00
Never hinged 67.50
On cover 135.00
On cover, single franking 275.00
71 A14 10fr black 47.50 40.00
Never hinged 72.50
On cover 140.00
On cover, single franking 275.00
Nos. 55-71 (17) 331.30 214.30

See note following No. 115. See Nos. 93-105. For surcharges see Nos. 120-121.

Types of the 1902-10 Issue Overprinted

1918-24 *Perf. 14x13½*

72 A3 1c dk gray .40 .80
Never hinged .80
On cover 13.00
a. 1c light gray .95 .95
Never hinged 1.40
On cover 15.00
b. Grayish paper ('18) 1.40 1.40
Never hinged 2.00
On cover 16.00
73 A3 2c violet brn .40 .80
Never hinged .80
On cover 13.00
74 A3 3c red orange 1.20 1.20
Never hinged 1.60
On cover 15.00
a. Grayish paper ('19) 1.60 1.60
Never hinged 2.40
On cover 15.00
75 A3 5c green 1.20 1.20
Never hinged 1.60
On cover 12.50
76 A3 5c orange ('23) 2.40 2.00
Never hinged 4.00
On cover 12.50
77 A4 10c rose 2.40 1.60
Never hinged 3.25
On cover 7.50
78 A4 10c green ('24) 2.40 1.60
Never hinged 4.00
On cover 7.50
79 A4 15c orange 1.60 1.20
Never hinged 2.40
On cover 6.25
80 A4 20c violet brn 2.40 2.40
Never hinged 4.00
On cover 13.50
81 A4 25c blue 2.40 2.40
Never hinged 4.00
On cover 12.50
a. "TANGER" omitted 450.00 450.00
82 A4 30c red org ('24) 4.00 2.75
Never hinged 8.00
On cover 13.50
On cover, single franking 27.50
83 A4 35c violet 4.00 2.40
Never hinged 7.50
On cover 12.50
On cover, single franking 19.00
84 A5 40c red & pale bl 4.00 2.40
Never hinged 5.00
On cover 12.50
On cover, single franking 15.00
85 A5 50c bis brn & lav 27.50 16.00
Never hinged 45.00
On cover 50.00
On cover, single franking 62.50
86 A4 50c blue ('24) 24.00 13.50
Never hinged 32.50
On cover 27.50
On cover, single franking 42.50
87 A5 1fr claret & ol grn 16.00 8.00
Never hinged 24.00
On cover 30.00
On cover, single franking 87.50
88 A5 2fr org & pale bl ('24) 80.00 72.50
Never hinged 130.00
On cover 200.00
On cover, single franking 275.00
89 A5 5fr dk bl & buff ('24) 67.50 65.00
Never hinged 110.00
On cover 200.00
On cover, single franking 300.00
Nos. 72-89 (18) 243.80 197.75

Types of 1917 and

Tower of Hassan, Rabat — A15

Bab Mansour, Meknes
A16

Roman Ruins, Volubilis
A17

1923-27 Photo. *Perf. 13½*

90 A15 1c olive green .25 .25
Never hinged .40
On cover 13.50
91 A15 2c brown vio .25 .25
Never hinged .40
On cover 13.50
92 A15 3c yellow brn .25 .25
Never hinged .40
On cover 13.50
93 A10 5c orange .25 .25
Never hinged .40
On cover 10.00
94 A10 10c yellow grn .25 .25
Never hinged .40
On cover 11.00
95 A10 15c dk gray .25 .25
Never hinged .40
On cover 6.25
96 A11 20c red brown .25 .25
Never hinged .40
On cover 5.00
97 A11 20c red vio ('27) .40 .40
Never hinged .80
On cover 12.50
98 A11 25c ultra .40 .40
Never hinged .80
On cover 3.75
99 A11 30c deep red .40 .40
Never hinged .80
On cover 3.75
100 A11 30c turq bl ('27) 1.20 .80
Never hinged 1.60
On cover 12.50
101 A12 35c violet 1.20 .80
Never hinged 1.60
On cover 12.50
On cover, single franking 21.00
102 A12 40c orange red .25 .25
Never hinged .40
On cover 8.75
103 A12 45c deep green .40 .40
Never hinged .80
On cover 12.50
On cover, single franking 15.00
104 A16 50c dull turq .40 .40
Never hinged .80
On cover 12.50
On cover, single franking 30.00
105 A12 50c olive grn ('27) .80 .40
Never hinged 1.20
On cover 3.75
106 A16 60c lilac 1.20 .80
Never hinged 1.60
On cover 10.00
On cover, single franking 18.00
107 A16 75c red vio ('27) .80 .40
Never hinged 1.20
On cover 6.25
On cover, single franking 8.75
108 A16 1fr deep brown .80 .80
Never hinged 1.20
On cover 13.50
On cover, single franking 32.50
109 A16 1.05fr red brn ('27) 1.60 .80
Never hinged 2.40
On cover 18.00
On cover, single franking 42.50
110 A16 1.40fr dull rose ('27) .80 .80
Never hinged 1.20
On cover 13.50
On cover, single franking 22.50
111 A16 1.50fr turq bl ('27) 1.20 .40
Never hinged 2.00
On cover 16.00
On cover, single franking 32.50
112 A17 2fr olive brn 1.60 1.20
Never hinged 2.00
On cover 30.00
On cover, single franking 140.00
113 A17 3fr dp red ('27) 1.60 1.20
Never hinged 2.40
On cover 22.50
On cover, single franking 30.00
114 A17 5fr dk gray grn 4.00 2.75
Never hinged 4.75
On cover 50.00
On cover, single franking 200.00
115 A17 10fr black 12.00 4.75
Never hinged 16.00
On cover 67.50
On cover, single franking 250.00
Nos. 90-115 (26) 32.80 19.90

Nos. 90-110, 112-115 exist imperf. The stamps of 1917 were line engraved. Those of 1923-27 were printed by photogravure and have in the margin at lower right the imprint "Helio Vaugirard."

See No. B36 in Scott Standard catalogue, Vol. 2. For surcharges see Nos. 122-123.

No. 102 Surcharged in Black

1930

120 A12 15c on 40c orange red 1.60 1.60
Never hinged 2.40
On cover 5.00
a. Surcharge bars omitted 72.50 72.50
Never hinged 115.00
b. Pair, one with surcharge omitted 350.00
Never hinged 500.00

Nos. 100, 106 and 110 Surcharged in Blue Similarly to No. 176

1931

121 A11 25c on 30c turq blue 2.50 2.10
Never hinged 4.00
On cover 7.50
a. Inverted surcharge 140.00 140.00
Never hinged 200.00
122 A16 50c on 60c lilac 1.20 .40
Never hinged 1.60
On cover 3.75
a. Inverted surcharge 150.00 150.00
Never hinged 210.00
b. Double surcharge 150.00 150.00
Never hinged 210.00
c. Surcharge bars omitted 90.00
Never hinged 140.00
123 A16 1fr on 1.40fr rose 3.25 1.60
Never hinged 4.00
On cover 7.50
On cover, single franking 12.50
a. Inverted surcharge 150.00 150.00
Never hinged 225.00
b. Surcharge bars omitted 90.00
Never hinged 140.00
Nos. 121-123 (3) 6.95 4.10

Old Treasure House and Tribunal, Tangier
A18

Roadstead at Agadir
A19

Post Office at Casablanca
A20

Moulay Idriss of the Zehroun
A21

Kasbah of the Oudayas, Rabat
A22

Court of the Medersa el Attarine at Fez — A23

Kasbah of Si Madani el Glaoui at Ouarzazat
A24

Saadiens' Tombs at Marrakesh — A25

1933-34 Engr. *Perf. 13*

124 A18 1c olive blk .25 .25
Never hinged .40
On cover 8.75
125 A18 2c red violet .25 .25
Never hinged .40
On cover 8.75
126 A19 3c dark brown .25 .25
Never hinged .40
On cover 8.75
127 A19 5c brown red .25 .25
Never hinged .40
On cover 7.50
128 A20 10c blue green .30 .30
Never hinged .50
On cover 6.25
129 A20 15c black .40 .30
Never hinged .80
On cover 6.25
130 A20 20c red brown .40 .30
Never hinged .80
On cover 6.25
131 A21 25c dark blue .40 .30
Never hinged .80
On cover 6.25

132 A21 30c emerald .40 .30
Never hinged .80
On cover 7.50
133 A21 40c black brn .40 .30
Never hinged .80
On cover 3.75
134 A22 45c brown vio .80 .65
Never hinged 1.20
On cover 8.00
135 A22 50c dk blue grn .80 .30
Never hinged 1.20
On cover 2.50
a. Booklet pane of 10 —
b. Booklet pane of 20 —
Complete booklet, #135b 2,000.
136 A22 65c brown red .40 .30
Never hinged .50
On cover 10.00
a. Booklet pane of 10 —
b. Booklet pane of 20 —
Complete booklet, #136b 65.00
137 A23 75c red violet .80 .30
Never hinged 1.20
On cover 3.75
138 A23 90c orange red .40 .30
Never hinged .80
On cover 7.50
On cover, single franking 18.00
139 A23 1fr deep brown 1.20 .50
Never hinged 1.60
On cover 5.00
On cover, single franking 6.25
140 A23 1.25fr black ('34) 1.60 1.50
Never hinged 2.00
On cover 5.00
On cover, single franking 16.00
141 A24 1.50fr ultra .40 .30
Never hinged .80
On cover 7.50
On cover, single franking 15.00
142 A24 1.75fr myr grn ('34) .80 .40
Never hinged 1.20
On cover 5.00
On cover, single franking 11.00
143 A24 2fr yellow brn 4.75 .80
Never hinged 6.50
On cover 5.00
On cover, single franking 10.00
144 A24 3fr car rose 55.00 6.50
Never hinged 80.00
On cover 21.00
On cover, single franking 37.50
145 A25 5fr red brown 12.00 2.50
Never hinged 20.00
On cover 13.50
On cover, single franking 27.50
146 A25 10fr black 10.00 6.50
Never hinged 16.00
On cover 21.00
On cover, single franking 42.50
147 A25 20fr bluish gray 9.50 7.25
Never hinged 14.00
On cover 21.00
On cover, single franking 50.00
Nos. 124-147 (24) 101.75 30.90

Booklets containing Nos. 135 and 136 each have two panes of 10 (Nos. 135a, 136a) connected by a gutter, the complete piece constituting No. 135b or 136b, which is stapled into the booklet through the gutter.

For surcharges see Nos. 148, 176, B13-B20.

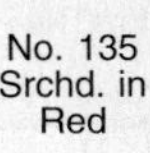

No. 135 Srchd. in Red

1939

148 A22 40c on 50c dk bl grn .95 .50
Never hinged 1.20
On cover 3.75

Mosque of Salé — A26

Sefrou — A27

Cedars — A28

Goatherd A29

Ramparts of Salé — A30

Scimitar-horned Oryxes — A31

Valley of Draa A32

Fez — A33

1939-42

149 A26 1c rose violet .25 .25
Never hinged .30
On cover 7.50
150 A27 2c emerald .25 .25
Never hinged .30
On cover 7.50
151 A27 3c ultra .25 .25
Never hinged .30
On cover 7.50
152 A26 5c dk bl grn .25 .25
Never hinged .30
On cover 6.25
153 A27 10c brt red vio .25 .25
Never hinged .30
On cover 6.25
154 A28 15c dk green .25 .25
Never hinged .30
On cover 6.25
155 A28 20c black grn .25 .25
Never hinged .30
On cover 6.25
156 A29 30c deep blue .25 .25
Never hinged .30
On cover 5.00
157 A29 40c chocolate .25 .25
Never hinged .30
On cover 2.50
158 A29 45c Prus green .50 .50
Never hinged .65
On cover 10.00
159 A30 50c rose red 1.40 .90
Never hinged 1.60
On cover 11.00
159A A30 50c Prus grn ('40) .30 .25
Never hinged .40
On cover 8.75
160 A30 60c turq blue 1.25 .75
Never hinged 1.50
On cover 7.50
160A A30 60c choc ('40) .30 .25
Never hinged .40
On cover 6.25
161 A31 70c dk violet .25 .25
Never hinged .30
On cover 2.50
162 A32 75c grnsh blk .50 .50
Never hinged .65
On cover 6.75
163 A32 80c pck bl ('40) .30 .25
Never hinged .40
On cover 3.75
163A A32 80c dk grn ('42) .40 .25
Never hinged .80
On cover 7.50
164 A30 90c ultra .30 .25
Never hinged .40
On cover 2.50
165 A28 1fr chocolate .30 .25
Never hinged .40
On cover 2.50
165A A32 1.20fr rose vio ('42) .80 .40
Never hinged 1.20
On cover 2.50
166 A32 1.25fr henna brn 1.10 .65
Never hinged 1.40
On cover 7.50
On cover, single franking 21.00
167 A32 1.40fr rose violet .65 .30
Never hinged .80
On cover 9.25
On cover, single franking 21.00
168 A30 1.50fr cop red ('40) .30 .25
Never hinged .40
On cover 7.50
On cover, single franking 21.00
168A A30 1.50fr rose ('42) .25 .25
Never hinged .40
On cover 2.50
169 A33 2fr Prus green .25 .25
Never hinged .30
On cover 6.25
On cover, single franking 13.50
170 A33 2.25fr dark blue .65 .50
Never hinged .80
On cover 7.50
On cover, single franking 15.00
170A A26 2.40fr red ('42) .30 .30
Never hinged .40
On cover 12.50
On cover, single franking 37.50
171 A26 2.50fr scarlet .90 .70
Never hinged 1.10
On cover 5.00
On cover, single franking 8.75
171A A26 2.50fr dp blue ('40) 1.10 .65
Never hinged 1.60
On cover 7.50
On cover, single franking 15.00
172 A33 3fr black brown .50 .30
Never hinged .65
On cover 5.00
On cover, single franking 8.75
172A A26 4fr dp ultra ('42) .40 .40
Never hinged .80
On cover 5.00
On cover, single franking 25.00
172B A32 4.50fr grnsh blk ('42) .80 .80
Never hinged 1.20
On cover 5.00
On cover, single franking 7.50
173 A31 5fr dark blue .65 .50
Never hinged .85
On cover 5.00
On cover, single franking 12.50
174 A31 10fr red 1.25 .90
Never hinged 1.60
On cover 10.00
On cover, single franking 21.00
174A A31 15fr Prus grn ('42) 4.75 4.00
Never hinged 6.50
On cover 12.00
On cover, single franking 30.00
175 A31 20fr dk vio brn 2.00 1.75
Never hinged 2.60
On cover 12.00
On cover, single franking 27.50
Nos. 149-175 (37) 24.70 19.55
Set, never hinged 32.50

See Nos. 197-219 in Scott Standard catalogue, Vol. 2. For surcharges see Nos. 244, 261-262, B21-B24, B26, B28, B32 in Scott Standard catalogue, Vol. 2.

No. 136 Srchd. in Black

1940

176 A22 35c on 65c brown red 1.75 .95
Never hinged 2.40
On cover 6.25
a. Pair, one without surcharge 3.25 2.40
Never hinged 4.50
On cover 6.25

The surcharge was applied on alternate rows in the sheet, making No. 176a. This was done to make a pair equal 1fr, the new rate.

SEMI-POSTAL STAMPS

French Protectorate

No. 30 Surcharged in Red

1914 Unwmk. *Perf. 14x13½*

B1 A4 10c + 5c on 10c *24,000. 28,000.*

Known only with inverted red surcharge.

No. 42 Surcharged in Red

B2 A7 10c + 5c on 10c rose 6.50 6.50
Never hinged 9.50
On cover 21.00
a. Double surcharge 175.00 175.00
Never hinged 275.00
b. Inverted surcharge 225.00 225.00
Never hinged 310.00
c. "c" omitted 110.00 110.00
Never hinged 160.00

On Nos. B1 and B2 the cross is set up from pieces of metal (quads), the horizontal bar being made from two long pieces, the vertical bar from two short pieces. Each cross in the setting of twenty-five differs from the others.

No. 30 Handstamp Surcharged in Red

B3 A4 10c + 5c on 10c rose *1,650. 1,300.*
On cover *4,250.*

No. B3 was issued at Oujda. The surcharge ink is water-soluble.

No. 42 Surcharged in Vermilion or Carmine

B4 A7 10c + 5c on 10c (V) 25.00 25.00
Never hinged 35.00
On cover 55.00
a. Double surcharge 240.00 240.00
Never hinged 350.00
b. Inverted surcharge 240.00 240.00
Never hinged 350.00
c. Double surch., one invtd. 200.00 200.00
Never hinged 300.00
B5 A7 10c +5c on 10c (C) 475.00 525.00
Never hinged 800.00
On cover 1,100.
a. Inverted surcharge 1,600. 1,600.

On Nos. B4-B5 the horizontal bar of the cross is single and not as thick as on Nos. B1-B2.

No. B5 was sold largely at Casablanca.

Carmine Surcharge SP1

Black Overprint SP2

1915

B6 SP1 5c + 5c green 3.25 2.40
Never hinged 4.75
On cover 8.75
a. Inverted surcharge 300.00 300.00
Never hinged 450.00
B7 SP2 10c + 5c rose 4.75 4.75
Never hinged 7.25
On cover 13.50

No. B6 was not issued without the Red Cross surcharge. No. B7 was used in Tangier.

France No. B2 Overprinted in Black

B8 SP2 10c + 5c red 7.50 7.50
Never hinged 10.50
On cover 21.00

No. 30 Surcharged in Carmine — SP4

1917

B9 SP4 10c + 5c on 10c rose 3.25 3.25
Never hinged 4.75
On cover 8.75

On No. B9 the horizontal bar of the cross is made from a single, thick piece of metal.

Marshal Hubert Lyautey — SP5

1935, May 15 Photo. *Perf. 13x13½*

B10 SP5 50c + 50c red 9.50 9.50
Never hinged 13.50
On cover 25.00
B11 SP5 1fr + 1fr dk grn 11.00 11.00
Never hinged 17.00
On cover 30.00
B12 SP5 5fr + 5fr blk brn 45.00 45.00
Never hinged 67.50
On cover 200.00
Nos. B10-B12 (3) 65.50 65.50
Set, never hinged 98.00

Stamps of 1933-34 Surcharged in Blue or Red

1938 *Perf. 13*

B13 A18 2c + 2c red vio 5.50 5.50
Never hinged 8.00
On cover 20.00
B14 A19 3c + 3c dk brn 5.50 5.50
Never hinged 8.00
On cover 20.00
B15 A20 20c + 20c red brn 5.50 5.50
Never hinged 8.00
On cover 16.00
B16 A21 40c + 40c blk brn (R) 5.50 5.50
Never hinged 8.00
On cover 13.50
B17 A22 65c + 65c brn red 5.50 5.50
Never hinged 8.00
On cover 13.50
B18 A23 1.25fr + 1.25fr blk (R) 5.50 5.50
Never hinged 8.00
On cover 30.00
B19 A24 2fr + 2fr yel brn 5.50 5.50
Never hinged 8.00
On cover 25.00
B20 A25 5fr + 5fr red brn 5.50 5.50
Never hinged 8.00
On cover 42.50
Nos. B13-B20 (8) 44.00 44.00
Set, never hinged 64.00

AIR POST STAMPS

French Protectorate

Biplane over Casablanca AP1

1922-27 Photo. Unwmk. *Perf. 13½*

C1 AP1 5c dp orange ('27) .50 .50
Never hinged .80
On cover 8.75
C2 AP1 25c dp ultra 1.20 1.20
Never hinged 2.00
On cover 4.25
C3 AP1 50c grnsh blue .40 .40
Never hinged .80
On cover 12.50
C4 AP1 75c dp blue 80.00 16.00
Never hinged 120.00
On cover 42.50
C5 AP1 75c dp green .80 .40
Never hinged 1.60
On cover 11.00
C6 AP1 80c vio brn ('27) 2.40 .80
Never hinged 3.25
On cover 8.75
C7 AP1 1fr vermilion 1.20 .80
Never hinged 1.60
On cover 12.50
C8 AP1 1.40fr brn lake ('27) 2.40 1.25
Never hinged 4.00
On cover 6.25
C9 AP1 1.90fr dp blue ('27) 2.75 1.60
Never hinged 4.00
On cover 8.75
C10 AP1 2fr black vio 2.40 1.20
Never hinged 4.00
On cover 25.00
a. 2fr deep violet 2.25 1.40
Never hinged 3.40
On cover 27.50
C11 AP1 3fr gray blk 2.75 2.00
Never hinged 4.00
On cover 25.00
Nos. C1-C11 (11) 96.80 26.15

The 25c, 50c, 75c deep green and 1fr each were printed in two of three types, differing in frameline thickness, or hyphen in "Helio-Vaugirard" imprint. Values are for the more common types.

Imperf., Pairs

C1a AP1 5c 65.00 65.00
Never hinged 95.00
C2a AP1 25c 72.50 72.50
Never hinged 105.00
C3a AP1 50c 72.50 72.50
Never hinged 105.00
C4a AP1 75c 550.00 550.00
Never hinged 775.00
C5a AP1 75c 72.50 72.50
Never hinged 105.00
C6a AP1 80c 72.50 72.50
Never hinged 105.00
C7a AP1 1fr 90.00 90.00
Never hinged 125.00
C10b AP1 2fr 225.00 225.00
Never hinged 350.00

Nos. C8-C9 Srchd. in Blue or Black

1931, Apr. 10

C12 AP1 1fr on 1.40fr (B) 2.40 2.40
Never hinged 3.25
On cover 10.00
a. Inverted surcharge 310.00 310.00
Never hinged 425.00
C13 AP1 1.50fr on 1.90fr (Bk) 2.40 2.40
Never hinged 3.25
On cover 12.50

Rabat and Tower of Hassan AP2

Casablanca AP3

1933, Jan. Engr.

C14 AP2 50c dark blue .80 .80
Never hinged 1.20
On cover 3.00
C15 AP2 80c orange brn .80 .65
Never hinged 1.20
On cover 4.25
C16 AP2 1.50fr brown red .80 .80
Never hinged 1.20
On cover 8.75
C17 AP3 2.50fr carmine rose 6.50 1.20
Never hinged 9.50
On cover 7.50
C18 AP3 5fr violet 3.25 1.75
Never hinged 4.00
On cover 7.50
C19 AP3 10fr blue green 1.20 1.20
Never hinged 1.60
On cover 8.75
Nos. C14-C19 (6) 13.35 6.40

For surcharges see Nos. CB22-CB23.

Storks and Minaret, Chella — AP4

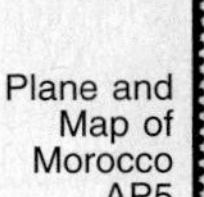

Plane and Map of Morocco AP5

1939-40 *Perf. 13*

C20 AP4 80c Prus green .25 .25
Never hinged .30
On cover 3.75
C21 AP4 1fr dk red .25 .25
Never hinged .30
On cover 3.00
C22 AP5 1.90fr ultra .40 .30
Never hinged .50
On cover 6.25
C23 AP5 2fr red vio ('40) .40 .30
Never hinged .50
On cover 15.00
C24 AP5 3fr chocolate .50 .25
Never hinged .65
On cover 4.25
C25 AP4 5fr violet 1.40 .80
Never hinged 1.75
On cover 11.00
C26 AP5 10fr turq blue 1.25 .55
Never hinged 1.60
On cover 21.00
Nos. C20-C26 (7) 4.45 2.70

AIR POST SEMI-POSTAL STAMPS

French Protectorate

Moorish Tribesmen SPAP1

Designs: 25c, Moor plowing with camel and burro. 50c, Caravan nearing Saffi. 75c, Walls, Marrakesh. 80c, Sheep grazing at Azrou. 1fr, Gate at Fez. 1.50fr, Aerial view of Tangier. 2fr, Aerial view of Casablanca. 3fr, Storks on old wall, Rabat. 5fr, Moorish fete.

Perf. 13½

1928, July 26 Photo. Unwmk.

CB1 SPAP1 5c dp blue 5.25 5.25
Never hinged 8.75
On cover 20.00
CB2 SPAP1 25c brn org 5.25 5.25
Never hinged 8.75
On cover 13.50
CB3 SPAP1 50c red 5.25 5.25
Never hinged 8.75
On cover 12.50
CB4 SPAP1 75c org brn 5.25 5.25
Never hinged 8.75
On cover 15.00
CB5 SPAP1 80c olive grn 5.25 5.25
Never hinged 8.75
On cover 20.00
CB6 SPAP1 1fr orange 5.25 5.25
Never hinged 8.75
On cover 18.00
CB7 SPAP1 1.50fr Prus bl 5.25 5.25
Never hinged 8.75
On cover 29.00
CB8 SPAP1 2fr dp brown 5.25 5.25
Never hinged 8.75
On cover 21.00
CB9 SPAP1 3fr dp violet 5.25 5.25
Never hinged 8.75
On cover 40.00
CB10 SPAP1 5fr brown blk 5.25 5.25
Never hinged 8.75
On cover 55.00
Nos. CB1-CB10 (10) 52.50 52.50

These stamps were sold in sets only and at double their face value. The money received for the surtax was divided among charitable and social organizations. The stamps were not sold at post offices but solely by subscription to the Moroccan Postal Administration.

Overprinted in Red or Blue (25c, 50c, 75c, 1fr)

1929, Feb. 1

CB11 SPAP1 5c dp blue 5.25 5.25
Never hinged 8.75
On cover 20.00
CB12 SPAP1 25c brown org 5.25 5.25
Never hinged 8.75
On cover 13.50
CB13 SPAP1 50c red 5.25 5.25
Never hinged 8.75
On cover 12.50
CB14 SPAP1 75c org brn 5.25 5.25
Never hinged 8.75
On cover 15.00
CB15 SPAP1 80c olive grn 5.25 5.25
Never hinged 8.75
On cover 20.00
CB16 SPAP1 1fr orange 5.25 5.25
Never hinged 8.75
On cover 19.00
CB17 SPAP1 1.50fr Prus bl 5.25 5.25
Never hinged 8.75
On cover 29.00
CB18 SPAP1 2fr dp brown 5.25 5.25
Never hinged 8.75
On cover 21.00
CB19 SPAP1 3fr dp violet 5.25 5.25
Never hinged 8.75
On cover 40.00
CB20 SPAP1 5fr brown blk 5.25 5.25
Never hinged 8.75
On cover 55.00
Nos. CB11-CB20 (10) 52.50 52.50

These stamps were sold at double their face values and only in Tangier. The surtax benefited various charities.

Marshal Hubert Lyautey SPAP10

1935, May 15 *Perf. 13½*

CB21 SPAP10 1.50fr + 1.50fr blue 20.00 20.00
Never hinged 32.50
On cover 80.00

Nos. C14, C19 Surcharged in Red

1938 *Perf. 13*

CB22 AP2 50c + 50c dk bl 8.00 8.00
Never hinged 12.00
On cover 25.00
CB23 AP3 10fr + 10fr bl grn 5.50 5.50
Never hinged 12.00
On cover 30.00

POSTAGE DUE STAMPS

French Offices in Morocco

France Postage Due Stamps and Types Surcharged in Red or Black

1896 Unwmk. *Perf. 14x13½*

On Stamps of 1891-93

J1 D2 5c on 5c lt bl (R) 12.00 5.50
Never hinged 16.00
On cover 105.00
J2 D2 10c on 10c choc (R) 16.00 6.50
Never hinged 27.50
On cover 105.00
J3 D2 30c on 30c car 32.50 24.00
Never hinged 60.00
On cover 340.00
a. Pair, one without surcharge
J4 D2 50c on 50c lilac 32.50 27.50
Never hinged 60.00
On cover 340.00
a. "S" of "CENTIMOS" omitted 340.00 250.00
J5 D2 1p on 1fr lil brn 350.00 325.00
On cover 1,200.

1909-10 On Stamps of 1908-10

J6 D3 1c on 1c ol grn (R) 4.00 4.00
Never hinged 8.00
On cover 50.00
J7 D3 10c on 10c violet 40.00 32.50
Never hinged 72.50
On cover 460.00
J8 D3 30c on 30c bister 55.00 40.00
Never hinged 80.00
On cover 500.00
J9 D3 50c on 50c red 80.00 72.50
Never hinged 125.00
On cover 625.00
Nos. J6-J9 (4) 179.00 149.00

Postage Due Stamps of France Surcharged in Red or Blue

1911 On Stamps of 1893-96
J10 D2 5c on 5c blue (R) 4.75 4.75
Never hinged 8.00
On cover 37.50
J11 D2 10c on 10c choc (R) 16.00 16.00
Never hinged 27.50
On cover 45.00
a. Double surcharge 225.00 *260.00*
Never hinged 325.00
J12 D2 50c on 50c lil (Bl) 20.00 20.00
Never hinged 40.00
On cover 55.00

On Stamps of 1908-10
J13 D3 1c on 1c ol grn (R) 4.00 3.25
Never hinged 4.75
On cover 30.00
J14 D3 10c on 10c vio (R) 8.00 8.00
Never hinged 16.00
On cover 50.00
J15 D3 30c on 30c bis (R) 12.00 12.00
Never hinged 16.00
On cover 55.00
J16 D3 50c on 50c red (Bl) 16.00 16.00
Never hinged 32.50
On cover 75.00
Nos. J10-J16 (7) 80.75 80.00

For surcharges see Nos. J23-J26.

French Protectorate

France Postage Due Stamps of 1911 Issue Overprinted

1915-17
J17 D4 1c on 1c black .80 .80
Never hinged 1.20
On cover 30.00
a. New value double 175.00
Never hinged 260.00
J18 D4 5c on 5c blue 3.25 2.00
Never hinged 4.00
On cover 30.00
a. Grayish paper ('17) 3.25 3.25
Never hinged 4.75
J19 D4 10c on 10c choc 4.00 2.00
Never hinged 5.50
On cover 37.50
J20 D4 20c on 20c ol grn 4.00 2.00
Never hinged 5.50
On cover 37.50
J21 D4 30c on 30c rose red, *grayish* 8.00 5.50
Never hinged 12.00
On cover 50.00
J22 D4 50c on 50c vio brn 12.00 8.00
Never hinged 20.00
On cover 55.00
Nos. J17-J22 (6) 32.05 20.30

Nos. J13 to J16 With Additional Overprint "Protectorat Francais"

1915
J23 D3 1c on 1c ol grn 1.60 1.60
Never hinged 2.50
On cover 30.00
a. "s" in "Francais" inverted 12.00 12.00
Never hinged 20.00
On cover 120.00
J24 D3 10c on 10c violet 4.00 3.25
Never hinged 4.75
On cover 37.50
a. "s" in "Francais" inverted 24.00 24.00
Never hinged 40.00
On cover 120.00
J25 D3 30c on 30c bister 4.00 4.00
Never hinged 4.75
On cover 37.50
a. "s" in "Francais" inverted 32.50 32.50
Never hinged 55.00
On cover 120.00
J26 D3 50c on 50c red 4.00 4.00
Never hinged 4.75
On cover 37.50
a. "s" in "Francais" inverted 40.00 40.00
Never hinged 55.00
On cover 120.00
Nos. J23-J26 (4) 13.60 12.85

D5

1917-26 Typo.
J27 D5 1c black .25 .25
Never hinged .40
On cover 21.00
a. Grayish paper ('17) .50 .50
Never hinged .80
On cover 25.00
J28 D5 5c deep blue .40 .25
Never hinged .80
On cover 21.00
a. Grayish paper ('17) .80 .65
Never hinged 1.20
On cover 25.00
J29 D5 10c brown .40 .40
Never hinged .80
On cover 21.00
J30 D5 20c olive green 2.50 1.60
Never hinged 3.25
On cover 27.50
J31 D5 30c rose .40 .40
Never hinged .80
On cover 21.00
a. Grayish paper ('17) 1.00 1.00
Never hinged 1.60
On cover 27.50
J32 D5 50c lilac brown .80 .40
Never hinged 1.20
On cover 19.00
J33 D5 1fr red brn, *straw* ('26) .85 .80
Never hinged 1.60
On cover 21.00
J34 D5 2fr violet ('26) 2.40 1.60
Never hinged 3.25
On cover 27.50
Nos. J27-J34 (8) 8.00 5.70

See #J49-J56, Morocco #J1-J4 in Scott Standard catalogue, Vol. 2. For surcharges see #J46-J48 in Scott Standard catalogue, Vol. 2.

Postage Due Stamps of France, 1882-1906 Overprinted

1918
J35 D2 1c black 1.20 1.20
Never hinged 1.60
On cover 21.00
J36 D2 5c blue 2.40 2.40
Never hinged 3.25
On cover 27.50
a. Grayish paper ('17) 4.00 4.00
Never hinged 5.25
On cover 42.50
J37 D2 10c chocolate 2.00 2.00
Never hinged 2.75
On cover 27.50
a. Grayish paper ('17) 4.75 4.75
Never hinged 7.25
On cover 42.50
J38 D2 15c green, *grayish* 4.75 4.75
Never hinged 8.00
On cover 42.50
J39 D2 20c olive green 6.50 6.50
Never hinged 9.50
On cover 42.50
J40 D2 30c rose red, *grayish* 16.00 16.00
Never hinged 24.00
On cover 75.00
J41 D2 50c violet brown 24.00 24.00
Never hinged 40.00
On cover 92.50
Nos. J35-J41 (7) 56.85 56.85

Postage Due Stamps of France, 1908-19 Overprinted

1918
J42 D3 1c olive green 1.20 1.20
Never hinged 1.60
On cover 21.00
a. Grayish paper 2.00 2.00
Never hinged 2.75
On cover 27.50
J43 D3 10c violet 2.75 2.75
Never hinged 4.00
On cover 27.50
a. Grayish paper ('17) 2.25 2.25
Never hinged 3.75
On cover 25.00
J44 D3 20c bister, *grayish* 8.00 8.00
Never hinged 14.00
On cover 50.00
J45 D3 40c red 20.00 20.00
Never hinged 32.50
On cover 87.50
Nos. J42-J45 (4) 31.95 31.95

PARCEL POST STAMPS

French Protectorate

PP1

1917 Unwmk. *Perf. 13½x14*
Q1 PP1 5c green 1.20 .80
Never hinged 1.60
Q2 PP1 10c carmine 1.20 .80
Never hinged 1.60
Q3 PP1 20c lilac brown 1.20 1.00
Never hinged 1.60
Q4 PP1 25c blue 1.60 .80
Never hinged 2.75
Q5 PP1 40c dark brown 2.40 1.60
Never hinged 3.50
Q6 PP1 50c red orange 4.00 .80
Never hinged 4.75
Q7 PP1 75c pale slate 4.00 2.40
Never hinged 6.50
Q8 PP1 1fr ultra 5.50 .80
Never hinged 9.50
Q9 PP1 2fr gray 12.00 1.60
Never hinged 16.00
Q10 PP1 5fr violet 12.00 1.60
Never hinged 20.00
Q11 PP1 10fr black 20.00 1.60
Never hinged 27.50
Nos. Q1-Q11 (11) 65.10 13.80

FRENCH OCEANIA

ˈfrench ˌpä-lə-ˈnē-zhə

(French Polynesia)

LOCATION — South Pacific Ocean
GOVT. — French Overseas Territory
AREA — 1,522 sq. mi.
POP. — 172,000 (est. 1984)
CAPITAL — Papeete

In 1903 various French Establishments in the South Pacific were united to form a single colony. Most important of the island groups are the Society Islands, Marquesas Islands, the Tuamotu group and the Gambier, Austral, and Rapa Islands. Tahiti, largest of the Society group, ranks first in importance.

100 Centimes = 1 Franc

Navigation and Commerce — A1

Perf. 14x13½
1892-1907 Typo. Unwmk.
Name of Colony in Blue or Carmine
1 A1 1c black, *lil bl* 1.60 1.60
Never hinged 2.40
On cover or postcard, in combination 115.00
2 A1 2c brown, *buff* 2.75 2.75
Never hinged 4.50
On cover or postcard, in combination 115.00
3 A1 4c claret, *lav* 4.50 4.00
Never hinged 8.25
On cover or postcard, in combination 115.00
4 A1 5c green, *grnsh* 13.50 9.50
Never hinged 20.00
On cover 80.00
On commercial cover 150.00
5 A1 5c yellow grn ('06) 5.00 2.40
Never hinged 9.00
On cover 100.00
On commercial cover 135.00
6 A1 10c blk, *lavender* 30.00 12.50
Never hinged 57.50
On cover 100.00
On commercial cover 200.00
7 A1 10c red ('00) 5.00 2.40
Never hinged 9.00
On cover 60.00
On commercial cover 175.00
8 A1 15c blue, quadrille paper 35.00 12.00
Never hinged 65.00
On cover 80.00
On commercial cover 200.00
9 A1 15c gray, *lt gray* ('00) 10.00 7.25
Never hinged 22.00
On cover 67.50
On commercial cover 300.00
10 A1 20c red, *grn* 17.50 16.00
Never hinged 35.00
On cover 80.00
On cover, single franking 140.00
On commercial cover 400.00
11 A1 25c black, *rose* 60.00 30.00
Never hinged 120.00
On cover 160.00
On cover, single franking 240.00
12 A1 25c blue ('00) 32.50 16.00
Never hinged 65.00
On cover 130.00
On cover, single franking 160.00
On commercial cover 290.00
13 A1 30c brown, *bis* 16.00 14.50
Never hinged 32.50
On cover 92.50
On cover, single franking 120.00
On commercial cover 600.00
14 A1 35c black, *yel* ('06) 11.00 9.50
Never hinged 22.00
On cover 120.00
On cover, single franking 160.00
On commercial cover 600.00
15 A1 40c red, *straw* 132.50 80.00
Never hinged 275.00
On cover 360.00
On cover, single franking 525.00
On commercial cover 800.00
16 A1 45c blk, *gray grn* ('07) 6.75 *6.75*
Never hinged 13.00
On cover 105.00
On cover, single franking 150.00
On commercial cover 900.00
17 A1 50c car, *pale rose* 10.00 10.00
Never hinged 19.50
On cover 240.00
On cover, single franking 350.00
a. 50c rose, *pale rose* 10.00 9.00
Never hinged 19.50
On cover 225.00
On cover, single franking 350.00
18 A1 50c brown, *az* ('00) 275.00 250.00
On cover 600.00
On cover, single franking 725.00
On commercial cover *2,250.*
19 A1 75c dp vio, *org* 12.00 12.00
Never hinged 26.00
On cover 260.00
On cover, single franking 400.00
On commercial cover 625.00
20 A1 1fr brnz grn, *straw* 13.50 13.50
Never hinged 27.50
On cover 260.00
On cover, single franking 400.00
Nos. 1-20 (20) 694.10 512.65

Perf. 13½x14 stamps are counterfeits.
For overprint and surcharge see Nos. 55, B1.

Tahitian Girl — A2

Kanakas — A3

Fautaua Valley — A4

1913-30
21 A2 1c violet & brn .25 .25
Never hinged .40
On cover 60.00
22 A2 2c brown & blk .25 .25
Never hinged .40
On cover 60.00
23 A2 4c orange & bl .35 .35
Never hinged .45
On cover 52.50
24 A2 5c grn & yel grn 1.60 .90
Never hinged 3.00
On cover 30.00
a. Double impression of yel grn 500.00
25 A2 5c bl & blk ('22) .50 .50
Never hinged .65
On cover 45.00
On commercial cover 55.00
26 A2 10c rose & org 2.25 2.25
Never hinged 3.75
On cover 32.50
On commercial cover 55.00
27 A2 10c bl grn & yel grn ('22) 1.25 1.25
Never hinged 1.60
On cover 40.00
On commercial cover 55.00
28 A2 10c org red & brn red, *bluish* ('26) 1.40 1.40
Never hinged 2.10
On cover 47.50
On commercial cover 60.00
29 A2 15c org & blk ('15) .85 .65
Never hinged 1.30
On cover 27.50
On commercial cover 60.00
a. Imperf., pair 175.00
Never hinged, pair 275.00
Single on cover 92.50
30 A2 20c black & vio 1.10 1.00
Never hinged 1.90
On cover 27.50
On commercial cover 60.00
a. Imperf., pair 175.00
Never hinged 350.00
31 A2 20c grn & bl grn ('26) 1.00 1.00
Never hinged 1.60
On cover 40.00
On commercial cover 62.50
32 A2 20c brn red & dk brn ('27) 1.60 1.60
Never hinged 1.80
On cover 40.00
On commercial cover 65.00
33 A3 25c ultra & blue 1.50 1.25
Never hinged 2.50
On cover 40.00
On cover, single franking 60.00
34 A3 25c vio & rose ('22) .75 .75
Never hinged 1.20
On cover 27.50
On commercial cover 55.00
35 A3 30c gray & brown 5.00 4.00
Never hinged 8.00
On cover 55.00
On cover, single franking 80.00

a. Imperf., pair 325.00
Never hinged 525.00

36 A3 30c rose & red org ('22) 3.25 3.25
Never hinged 5.25
On cover 60.00
On cover, single franking 75.00

37 A3 30c blk & red org ('26) .75 .75
Never hinged 1.050
On cover 27.50
On cover, single franking 60.00

38 A3 30c slate bl & bl grn ('27) 1.75 1.75
Never hinged 2.50
On cover 40.00
On cover, single franking 65.00

39 A3 35c green & rose 1.25 1.25
Never hinged 2.10
On cover 40.00
On cover, single franking 75.00

40 A3 40c black & green 1.10 1.10
Never hinged 1.80
On cover 40.00
On cover, single franking 60.00

41 A3 45c orange & red 1.10 1.10
Never hinged 1.90
On cover 47.50
On cover, single franking 67.50

42 A3 50c dk brown & blk 17.50 13.50
Never hinged 29.00
On cover 52.50
On cover, single franking 75.00

43 A3 50c ultra & bl ('22) 1.25 1.25
Never hinged 1.65
On cover 52.50
On cover, single franking 75.00

44 A3 50c gray & bl vio ('26) 1.10 1.10
Never hinged 1.50
On cover 35.00
On cover, single franking 60.00

45 A3 60c green & blk ('25) 1.25 1.25
Never hinged 2.00
On cover 60.00
On cover, single franking 75.00

46 A3 65c ol brn & red vio ('27) 3.25 3.25
Never hinged 5.00
On cover 47.50
On cover, single franking 75.00

47 A3 75c vio brn & vio 2.50 2.50
Never hinged 4.00
On cover 40.00
On cover, single franking 60.00

48 A3 90c brn red & rose ('30) 16.50 16.50
Never hinged 22.50
On cover 67.50
On cover, single franking 100.00
a. Imperf., pair 225.00

49 A4 1fr rose & black 6.25 4.25
Never hinged 10.50
On cover 40.00
On cover, single franking 60.00

50 A4 1.10fr vio & dk brn ('28) 1.60 1.60
Never hinged 2.40
On cover 60.00
On cover, single franking 160.00

51 A4 1.40fr bis brn & vio ('29) 4.00 4.00
Never hinged 6.50
On cover 47.50
On cover, single franking 67.50

52 A4 1.50fr ind & bl ('30) 16.50 16.50
Never hinged 23.00
On cover 47.50
On cover, single franking 60.00

53 A4 2fr dk brown & grn 6.25 4.25
Never hinged 10.50
On cover 60.00
On cover, single franking 80.00

54 A4 5fr violet & bl 11.00 11.00
Never hinged 18.50
On cover 80.00
On cover, single franking 120.00
a. Imperf., pair 500.00
Nos. 21-54 (34) 117.80 107.55

For surcharges see Nos. 56-71, B2-B4.

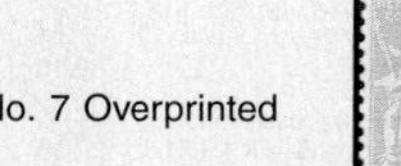

No. 7 Overprinted

1915

55 A1 10c red 6.75 6.75
Never hinged 11.50
On cover 120.00
a. Inverted overprint 225.00 225.00
Never hinged 365.00

For surcharge see No. B1.

No. 29 Surcharged

1916

56 A2 10c on 15c org & blk 3.50 3.50
Never hinged 5.25
On cover 40.00

Nos. 22, 41 and 29 Surcharged

1921

57 A2 5c on 2c brn & blk 36.00 36.00
Never hinged 55.00
On cover 120.00

58 A3 10c on 45c org & red 36.00 36.00
Never hinged 55.00
On cover 120.00

59 A2 25c on 15c org & blk 9.00 9.00
Never hinged 15.00
On cover 52.50
Nos. 57-59 (3) 81.00 81.00

On No. 58 the new value and date are set wide apart and without bar.

Types of 1913-30 Issue Surcharged in Black or Red

1923-27

60 A3 60c on 75c bl & brn .75 .75
Never hinged 1.10
On cover 60.00
On cover, single franking 80.00

61 A4 65c on 1fr dk bl & ol (R) ('25) 2.25 2.25
Never hinged 3.00
On cover 60.00
On cover, single franking 80.00

62 A4 85c on 1fr dk bl & ol (R) ('25) 2.25 2.25
Never hinged 3.00
On cover 60.00
On cover, single franking 80.00

63 A3 90c on 75c brn red & cer ('27) 3.00 3.00
Never hinged 4.50
On cover 67.50
On cover, single franking 92.50
Nos. 60-63 (4) 8.25 8.25

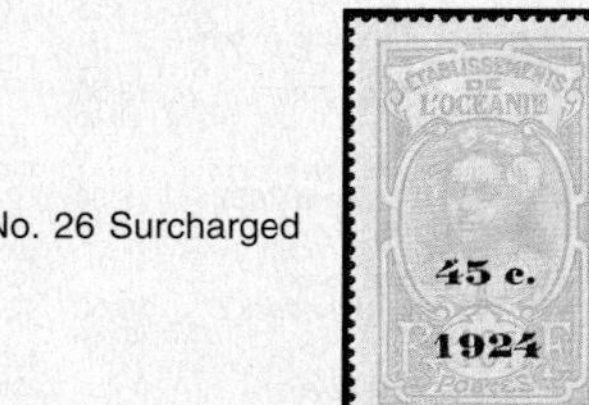

No. 26 Surcharged

1924

64 A2 45c on 10c rose & org 3.00 3.00
Never hinged 5.00
On cover 40.00
a. Inverted surcharge *2,400.* *2,400.*

Stamps and Type of 1913-30 Surcharged with New Value and Bars in Black or Red

1924-27

65 A4 25c on 2fr dk brn & grn 1.10 1.10
Never hinged 1.60
On cover 40.00

66 A4 25c on 5fr vio & bl 1.10 1.10
Never hinged 1.60
On cover 40.00

67 A4 1.25fr on 1fr dk bl & ultra (R) ('26) 1.20 1.20
Never hinged 1.75
On cover 67.50
On cover, single franking 80.00

68 A4 1.50fr on 1fr dk bl & lt bl ('27) 4.00 4.00
Never hinged 6.00
On cover 80.00
On cover, single franking 120.00

69 A4 20fr on 5fr org & brt vio ('27) 32.50 26.00
Never hinged 47.50
On cover 130.00
On cover, single franking 190.00
Nos. 65-69 (5) 39.90 33.40

Surcharged in Black or Red

1926

70 A4 3fr on 5fr gray & blue 3.25 2.50
Never hinged 5.00
On cover 72.50
On cover, single franking 110.00

71 A4 10fr on 5fr grn & blk (R) 7.25 7.25
Never hinged 11.00
On cover 100.00
On cover, single franking 160.00

Papetoai Bay, Moorea
A5

1929, Mar. 25

72 A5 3fr green & dk brn 8.00 8.00
Never hinged 12.00
On cover 40.00
On cover, single franking 52.50

73 A5 5fr lt blue & dk brn 15.00 15.00
Never hinged 22.00
On cover 60.00
On cover, single franking 80.00

74 A5 10fr lt red & dk brn 45.00 45.00
Never hinged 70.00
On cover 100.00
On cover, single franking 160.00

75 A5 20fr lilac & dk brn 57.50 57.50
Never hinged 87.50
On cover 125.00
On cover, single franking 180.00
Nos. 72-75 (4) 125.50 125.50

For overprints see Nos. 128, 130, 132, 134 in Scott Standard catalogue, Vol. 2.

Common Design Types pictured following the introduction.

Colonial Exposition Issue
Common Design Types

1931, Apr. 13 Engr. *Perf. 12½*
Name of Country Printed in Black

76 CD70 40c deep green 7.50 7.50
Never hinged 12.50
On cover 40.00

77 CD71 50c violet 7.50 7.50
Never hinged 12.50
On cover 32.50

78 CD72 90c red orange 7.50 7.50
Never hinged 12.50
On cover 60.00
On cover, single franking 87.50

79 CD73 1.50fr dull blue 7.50 7.50
Never hinged 12.50
On cover 52.50
On cover, single franking 80.00
Nos. 76-79 (4) 30.00 30.00

Spear Fishing
A12

Tahitian Girl — A13

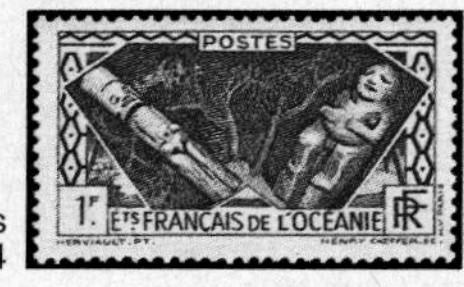

Idols
A14

1934-40 Photo. *Perf. 13½, 13½x13*

80 A12 1c gray black .25 .25
Never hinged .40
On cover 60.00

81 A12 2c claret .35 .35
Never hinged .55
On cover 60.00

82 A12 3c lt blue ('40) .35 .35
Never hinged .55
On cover 52.50

83 A12 4c orange .60 .60
Never hinged .75
On cover 52.50

84 A12 5c violet .90 .90
Never hinged 1.25
On cover 40.00

85 A12 10c dark brown .40 .40
Never hinged .60
On cover 40.00

86 A12 15c green .60 .60
Never hinged .80
On cover 32.50

87 A12 20c red .60 .60
Never hinged .80
On cover 24.00

88 A13 25c gray blue .90 .90
Never hinged 1.25
On cover 35.00

89 A13 30c yellow green 1.20 1.20
Never hinged 1.75
On cover 35.00

90 A13 30c orange brn ('40) .80 .80
Never hinged 1.10
On cover 24.00

91 A14 35c dp green ('38) 4.00 4.00
Never hinged 6.00
On cover 52.50

92 A13 40c red violet .60 .60
Never hinged .80
On cover 20.00

93 A13 45c brown orange 9.00 9.00
Never hinged 13.00
On cover 60.00

94 A13 45c dk green ('39) 1.60 1.60
Never hinged 2.25
On cover 32.50

95 A13 50c violet .60 .60
Never hinged .80
On cover 20.00

96 A13 55c blue ('38) 6.75 6.75
Never hinged 9.00
On cover 47.50

97 A13 60c black ('39) .75 .75
Never hinged 1.05
On cover 32.50

98 A13 65c brown 3.25 3.25
Never hinged 4.25
On cover 52.50

99 A13 70c brt pink ('39) 1.40 1.40
Never hinged 1.80
On cover 20.00

100 A13 75c olive green 9.00 9.00
Never hinged 12.50
On cover 45.00

101 A13 80c violet brn ('38) 2.00 2.00
Never hinged 2.75
On cover 35.00

102 A13 90c rose red .90 .90
Never hinged 1.25
On cover 32.50
On cover, single franking 60.00

103 A14 1fr red brown .90 .90
Never hinged 1.25
On cover 27.50
On cover, single franking 52.50

104 A14 1.25fr brown violet 8.25 8.25
Never hinged 12.00
On cover 52.50
On cover, single franking 67.50

105 A14 1.25fr rose red ('39) 1.25 1.25
Never hinged 1.60
On cover 32.50
On cover, single franking 60.00

106 A14 1.40fr orange yel ('39) 1.25 1.25
Never hinged 1.75
On cover 32.50
On cover, single franking 60.00

107 A14 1.50fr blue .90 .90
Never hinged 1.25
On cover 32.50
On cover, single franking 52.50

108 A14 1.60fr dull vio ('39) 1.40 1.40
Never hinged 2.00
On cover 32.50
On cover, single franking 60.00

109 A14 1.75fr olive 6.75 6.75
Never hinged 9.00
On cover 60.00
On cover, single franking 80.00

110 A14 2fr red 1.10 1.10
Never hinged 1.40
On cover 45.00
On cover, single franking 60.00

111 A14 2.25fr deep blue ('39) 1.25 1.25
Never hinged 1.60
On cover 32.50
On cover, single franking 52.50

112 A14 2.50fr black ('39) 1.25 1.25
Never hinged 1.60
On cover 32.50
On cover, single franking 60.00

113 A14 3fr brown org ('39) 1.50 1.50
Never hinged 2.00
On cover 40.00
On cover, single franking 67.50

114 A14 5fr red violet ('39) 1.00 1.00
Never hinged 1.20
On cover 47.50
On cover, single franking 80.00

115 A14 10fr dark green ('39) 3.00 3.00
Never hinged 4.00
On cover 55.00
On cover, single franking 92.50

116 A14 20fr dark brown ('39) 3.50 3.50
Never hinged 4.75
On cover 65.00
On cover, single franking 120.00
Nos. 80-116 (37) 80.10 80.10

For overprints see Nos. 126-127, 129, 131, 133, 135 in Scott Standard catalogue, Vol. 2.

Paris International Exposition Issue
Common Design Types

1937 Engr. *Perf. 13*

117 CD74 20c deep violet 3.50 3.50
Never hinged 5.00
On cover 52.50
118 CD75 30c dark green 3.50 3.50
Never hinged 5.00
On cover 52.50
119 CD76 40c carmine rose 3.50 3.50
Never hinged 5.00
On cover 52.50
120 CD77 50c dk brown & blue 4.25 4.25
Never hinged 6.50
On cover 60.00
121 CD78 90c red 4.25 4.25
Never hinged 6.50
On cover 60.00
On cover, single franking 80.00
122 CD79 1.50fr ultra 5.00 5.00
Never hinged 7.75
On cover 52.50
On cover, single franking 72.50
Nos. 117-122 (6) 24.00 24.00

Colonial Arts Exhibition Issue
Souvenir Sheet
Common Design Type

1937 *Imperf.*

123 CD78 3fr emerald 36.00 *52.50*
Never hinged 55.00
On cover 120.00
On cover, single franking 160.00

New York World's Fair Issue
Common Design Type

1939, May 10 Engr. *Perf. 12½x12*

124 CD82 1.25fr carmine lake 2.40 2.40
Never hinged 4.00
On cover 52.50
On cover, single franking 72.50
125 CD82 2.25fr ultra 2.40 2.40
Never hinged 4.00
On cover 52.50
On cover, single franking 72.50
Set, never hinged 8.00

SEMI-POSTAL STAMPS

Nos. 55 and 26 Surcharged in Red

1915 Unwmk. *Perf. 14x13½*

B1 A1 10c + 5c red 32.50 32.50
Never hinged 55.00
On cover 80.00
a. "e" instead of "c" 87.50 87.50
Never hinged 140.00
b. Inverted surcharge 225.00 225.00
Never hinged 350.00
c. Double surcharge 525.00 525.00
B2 A2 10c + 5c rose & org 12.50 12.50
Never hinged 21.00
On cover 72.50
a. "e" instead of "c" 65.00 65.00
Never hinged 110.00
b. "c" inverted 65.00 65.00
Never hinged 110.00
c. Inverted surcharge 300.00 300.00
Never hinged 475.00
d. As "a," inverted surcharge 400.00
e. As "b," inverted surcharge 400.00

Surcharged in Carmine

B3 A2 10c + 5c rose & org 5.50 5.50
Never hinged 9.50
On cover 52.50
a. "e" instead of "c" 45.00 45.00
Never hinged 72.50
b. Inverted surcharge 200.00 200.00
Never hinged 340.00
c. Double surcharge 200.00 200.00
Never hinged 340.00
d. As "a," inverted surcharge 325.00

Surcharged in Carmine

1916

B4 A2 10c + 5c rose & org 5.50 5.50

Curie Issue
Common Design Type

1938 Engr. *Perf. 13*

B5 CD80 1.75fr + 50c brt ultra 20.00 20.00
Never hinged 32.50
On cover 60.00
On cover, single franking 92.50

French Revolution Issue
Common Design Type

1939 Photo.
Name and Value Typo. in Black

B6 CD83 45c + 25c grn 17.50 17.50
Never hinged 29.00
On cover 80.00
B7 CD83 70c + 30c brn 17.50 17.50
Never hinged 29.00
On cover 67.50
B8 CD83 90c + 35c red org 17.50 17.50
Never hinged 29.00
On cover 60.00
B9 CD83 1.25fr + 1fr rose pink 17.50 17.50
Never hinged 29.00
On cover 80.00
On cover, single franking 120.00
B10 CD83 2.25fr + 2fr blue 17.50 17.50
Never hinged 29.00
On cover 72.50
On cover, single franking 110.00
Nos. B6-B10 (5) 87.50 87.50
Set, never hinged 145.00

AIR POST STAMP

Seaplane in Flight AP1

Perf. 13½

1934, Nov. 5 Unwmk. Photo.

C1 AP1 5fr green 1.25 1.25
Never hinged 1.60
On cover 47.50

For overprint see No. C2 in Scott Standard catalogue, Vol. 2.

For Type AP1 without "RF," see Nos. C1A-C1D in Scott Standard catalogue, Vol. 2.

AIR POST SEMI-POSTAL STAMP

French Revolution Issue
Common Design Type
Unwmk.

1939, July 5 Photo. *Perf. 13*
Name and Value Typo. in Orange

CB1 CD83 5fr + 4fr brn blk 35.00 35.00
Never hinged 60.00
On cover 87.50
On cover, single franking 125.00

POSTAGE DUE STAMPS

Postage Due Stamps of French Colonies, 1894-1906, Overprinted

1926-27 Unwmk. *Perf. 14x13½*

J1 D1 5c light blue .95 .95
Never hinged 1.60
On cover 60.00
J2 D1 10c brown .95 .95
Never hinged 1.60
On cover 55.00
J3 D1 20c olive green 1.40 1.40
Never hinged 2.40
On cover 55.00
J4 D1 30c dull red 1.60 1.60
Never hinged 2.75
On cover 52.50
J5 D1 40c rose 3.50 3.50
Never hinged 6.50
On cover 60.00
J6 D1 60c blue green 3.50 3.50
Never hinged 6.50
On cover 60.00
J7 D1 1fr red brown, *straw* 3.75 3.75
Never hinged 7.00
On cover 60.00
J8 D1 3fr magenta ('27) 15.00 15.00
Never hinged 29.00
On cover 80.00

With Additional Surcharge of New Value

J9 D1 2fr on 1fr orange red 4.00 4.75
Never hinged 7.25
On cover 65.00
Nos. J1-J9 (9) 34.65 35.40

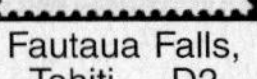

Fautaua Falls, Tahiti — D2

Tahitian Youth — D3

1929 Typo. *Perf. 13½x14*

J10 D2 5c lt blue & dk brn .75 .75
Never hinged 1.20
On cover 60.00
J11 D2 10c vermilion & grn .75 .75
Never hinged 1.20
On cover 60.00
J12 D2 30c dk brn & dk red 1.75 1.75
Never hinged 2.60
On cover 52.50
J13 D2 50c yel grn & dk brn 1.40 1.40
Never hinged 2.00
On cover 52.50
J14 D2 60c dl vio & yel grn 4.00 4.00
Never hinged 6.00
On cover 60.00
J15 D3 1fr Prus bl & red vio 3.50 3.50
Never hinged 5.25
On cover 60.00
J16 D3 2fr brn red & dk brn 2.00 2.10
Never hinged 3.25
On cover 67.50
J17 D3 3fr bl vio & bl grn 2.10 2.40
Never hinged 3.25
On cover 80.00
Nos. J10-J17 (8) 16.25 16.65

FRENCH SUDAN

'french sü-'dan

LOCATION — In northwest Africa, north of French Guinea and Ivory Coast
GOVT. — French Colony
AREA — 590,966 sq. mi.
POP. — 3,794,270 (1941)
CAPITAL — Bamako

In 1899 French Sudan was abolished as a separate colony and was divided among Dahomey, French Guinea, Ivory Coast, Senegal and Senegambia and Niger. Issues for French Sudan were resumed in 1921.

From 1906 to 1921 a part of this territory was known as Upper Senegal and Niger. A part of Upper Volta was added in 1933.

100 Centimes = 1 Franc

French Colonies Nos. 58-59 Srchd. in Black

Perf. 14x13½

1894, Apr. 12 Unwmk.

1 A9 15c on 75c car, *rose* 4,600. 2,300.
On cover 7,200.
2 A9 25c on 1fr brnz grn, *straw* 5,000. 1,700.
On cover 4,750.

The imperforate stamp like No. 1 was made privately in Paris from a fragment of the lithographic stone which had been used in the Colony for surcharging No. 1.

Counterfeit surcharges exist.

Navigation and Commerce — A2

1894-1900 Typo. *Perf. 14x13½*
Name of colony in Blue or Carmine

3 A2 1c blk, *lil bl* 1.60 2.00
Never hinged 4.00
On cover 225.00
4 A2 2c brn, *buff* 2.40 2.75
Never hinged 4.00
On cover 225.00
5 A2 4c claret, *lav* 8.00 6.50
Never hinged 12.00
On cover 220.00
6 A2 5c grn, *grnsh* 12.00 12.00
Never hinged 20.00
On cover 105.00
7 A2 10c blk, *lav* 24.00 24.00
Never hinged 40.00
On cover 92.50
8 A2 10c red ('00) 8.00 8.00
Never hinged 12.00
On cover 80.00
9 A2 15c blue, quadrille paper 8.00 8.00
Never hinged 12.00
On cover 100.00
10 A2 15c gray, *lt gray* ('00) 8.00 8.00
Never hinged 12.00
On cover 80.00
11 A2 20c red, *grn* 40.00 35.00
Never hinged 60.00
On cover 190.00
On cover, single franking 340.00
12 A2 25c blk, *rose* 32.50 27.50
Never hinged 52.50
On cover 110.00
13 A2 25c blue ('00) 8.00 8.75
Never hinged 16.00
On cover 87.50
14 A2 30c brn, *bister* 40.00 40.00
Never hinged 80.00
On cover 140.00
On cover, single franking 200.00
15 A2 40c red, *straw* 40.00 35.00
Never hinged 80.00
On cover 140.00
On cover, single franking 200.00
16 A2 50c car, *rose* 55.00 65.00
Never hinged 120.00
On cover 225.00
On cover, single franking 275.00
17 A2 50c brn, *az* ('00) 16.00 16.00
Never hinged 27.50
On cover 150.00
On cover, single franking 220.00
18 A2 75c dp vio, *org* 55.00 55.00
Never hinged 105.00
On cover 350.00
On cover, single franking 525.00
19 A2 1fr brnz grn, *straw* 12.00 12.00
Never hinged 24.00
On cover 375.00
On cover, single franking 625.00
Nos. 3-19 (17) 370.50 365.50

Perf. 13½x14 stamps are counterfeits.

Nos. 8, 10, 13, 17 were issued in error. They were accepted for use in the other colonies.

Covers: Values are for commercial with correct frankings. Philatelic covers sell for less.

Stamps and Types of Upper Senegal and Niger, 1914-17, Overprinted

1921-30 *Perf. 13½x14*

21 A4 1c brn vio & vio .25 .40
Never hinged .40
On cover 80.00
22 A4 2c dk gray & dl vio .30 .50
Never hinged .40
On cover 80.00
23 A4 4c blk & blue .30 .50
Never hinged .40
On cover 80.00
24 A4 5c ol brn & dk brn .30 .40
Never hinged .40
On cover 42.50
25 A4 10c yel grn & bl grn .90 .55
Never hinged 1.60
On cover 87.50

26 A4 10c red vio & bl ('25) .40 .50
Never hinged .80
On cover 27.50
27 A4 15c red brn & org .50 .55
Never hinged .65
On cover 50.00
28 A4 15c yel grn & dp grn ('25) .40 .40
Never hinged .80
On cover 19.00
29 A4 15c org brn & vio ('27) 1.60 1.60
Never hinged 2.40
On cover 27.50
30 A4 20c brn vio & blk .50 .55
Never hinged .80
On cover 42.50
31 A4 25c blk & bl grn 1.25 .80
Never hinged 2.00
On cover 37.50
a. Booklet pane of 4 —
Complete booklet, 5 #31a 650.00
Complete booklet, overprint omitted on one pane 16,000.
32 A4 30c red org & rose 1.60 1.60
Never hinged 2.75
On cover 62.50
On cover, single franking 125.00
33 A4 30c bl grn & blk ('26) .80 .70
Never hinged 1.60
On cover 15.00
34 A4 30c dl grn & bl grn ('28) 2.00 2.00
Never hinged 2.75
On cover 42.50
35 A4 35c rose & vio .40 .55
Never hinged .55
On cover 55.00
On cover, single franking 75.00
36 A4 40c gray & rose 1.25 1.25
Never hinged 2.00
On cover 42.50
On cover, single franking 62.50
37 A4 45c bl & ol brn 1.25 1.25
Never hinged 2.40
On cover 75.00
On cover, single franking 125.00
38 A4 50c ultra & bl 1.60 1.25
Never hinged 3.25
On cover 50.00
On cover, single franking 135.00
39 A4 50c red org & bl ('26) 1.25 1.25
Never hinged 2.40
On cover 16.00
40 A4 60c vio, *pnksh* ('26) 1.25 1.25
Never hinged 2.40
On cover 42.50
On cover, single franking 110.00
41 A4 65c bis & pale bl ('28) 1.60 1.60
Never hinged 2.40
On cover 50.00
On cover, single franking 87.50
42 A4 75c org & ol brn 1.60 2.00
Never hinged 2.75
On cover 55.00
On cover, single franking 135.00
43 A4 90c brn red & pink ('30) 5.50 5.50
Never hinged 9.50
On cover 55.00
On cover, single franking 110.00
44 A4 1fr dk brn & dl vio 1.60 2.00
Never hinged 3.25
On cover 75.00
On cover, single franking 150.00
45 A4 1.10fr gray lil & red vio ('28) 3.25 4.00
Never hinged 5.50
On cover 200.00
On cover, single franking 400.00
46 A4 1.50fr dp bl & bl ('30) 5.50 5.50
Never hinged 9.50
On cover 50.00
On cover, single franking 100.00
47 A4 2fr grn & bl 2.40 2.75
Never hinged 4.00
On cover 92.50
On cover, single franking 190.00
48 A4 3fr red vio ('30) 12.00 12.00
Never hinged 20.00
On cover 105.00
On cover, single franking 190.00
a. Double overprint 190.00
Never hinged 300.00
49 A4 5fr vio & blk 8.00 7.25
Never hinged 12.00
On cover 110.00
On cover, single franking 210.00
Nos. 21-49 (29) 59.55 60.45

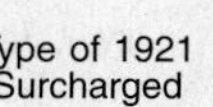
Type of 1921 Surcharged

1922, Sept. 28
50 A4 60c on 75c vio, *pnksh* .80 .80
Never hinged 1.20
On cover 42.50
On cover, single franking 62.50

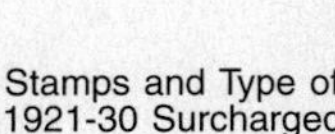
Stamps and Type of 1921-30 Surcharged

1925-27
51 A4 25c on 45c .80 .80
Never hinged 1.20
On cover 20.00
52 A4 65c on 75c 2.00 2.40
Never hinged 3.25
On cover 87.50
On cover, single franking 165.00
53 A4 85c on 2fr 2.00 2.40
Never hinged 3.25
On cover 75.00
On cover, single franking 140.00
54 A4 85c on 5fr 2.00 2.40
Never hinged 3.25
On cover 75.00
On cover, single franking 140.00
55 A4 90c on 75c brn red & sal pink ('27) 2.40 2.75
Never hinged 4.00
On cover 80.00
On cover, single franking 140.00
56 A4 1.25fr on 1fr dp bl & lt bl (R) ('26) 1.25 1.60
Never hinged 2.00
On cover 80.00
On cover, single franking 140.00
57 A4 1.50fr on 1fr dp bl & ultra ('27) 1.60 2.00
Never hinged 2.75
On cover 62.50
On cover, single franking 110.00
58 A4 3fr on 5fr dl red & brn org ('27) 6.50 5.50
Never hinged 11.00
On cover 110.00
On cover, single franking 225.00
59 A4 10fr on 5fr brn red & bl grn ('27) 24.00 21.00
Never hinged 35.00
On cover 125.00
On cover, single franking 250.00
60 A4 20fr on 5fr vio & ver ('27) 29.00 29.00
Never hinged 47.50
On cover 140.00
On cover, single franking 275.00
Nos. 51-60 (10) 71.55 69.85

Sudanese Woman — A4

Entrance to the Residency at Djenné — A5

Sudanese Boatman — A6

1931-40 Typo. *Perf. 13x14*
61 A4 1c dk red & blk .25 .25
Never hinged .40
On cover 67.50
62 A4 2c dp blue & org .25 .25
Never hinged .40
On cover 67.50
63 A4 3c dk red & blk ('40) .25 .25
Never hinged .40
On cover 37.50
64 A4 4c gray lil & rose .25 .25
Never hinged .40
On cover 67.50
65 A4 5c indigo & grn .25 .25
Never hinged .40
On cover 67.50
66 A4 10c ol grn & rose .25 .25
Never hinged .40
On cover 32.50
67 A4 15c blk & brt vio .40 .30
Never hinged .50
On cover 25.00
68 A4 20c hn brn & lt bl .40 .30
Never hinged .50
On cover 27.50
69 A4 25c red vio & lt red .40 .30
Never hinged .50
On cover 27.50
70 A5 30c grn & lt grn .80 .50
Never hinged .95
On cover 37.50
71 A5 30c dk bl & red org ('40) .30 .30
Never hinged .40
On cover 19.00
72 A5 35c ol grn & grn ('38) .40 .40
Never hinged .80
On cover 37.50
73 A5 40c ol grn & pink .40 .30
Never hinged .50
On cover 13.50
74 A5 45c dk bl & red org 1.20 .65
Never hinged 1.40
On cover 32.50
75 A5 45c ol grn & grn ('40) .50 .50
Never hinged .80
On cover 25.00
76 A5 50c red & black .40 .30
Never hinged .50
On cover 13.50
77 A5 55c ultra & car ('38) .40 .40
Never hinged .80
On cover 12.50
78 A5 60c brt bl & brn ('40) 1.20 1.20
Never hinged 1.65
On cover 25.00
79 A5 65c brt vio & blk .80 .55
Never hinged .90
On cover 50.00
80 A5 70c vio bl & car rose ('40) .80 .80
Never hinged 1.60
On cover 30.00
81 A5 75c brt bl & ol brn 2.40 2.00
Never hinged 3.50
On cover 22.50
82 A5 80c car & brn ('38) .80 .80
Never hinged 1.60
On cover 62.50
On cover, single franking 105.00
83 A5 90c dp red & red org 1.60 .80
Never hinged 2.00
On cover 37.50
On cover, single franking 87.50
84 A5 90c brt vio & sl blk ('39) .90 1.00
Never hinged 1.25
On cover 42.50
On cover, single franking 100.00
85 A5 1fr indigo & grn 8.00 2.40
Never hinged 12.00
On cover 27.50
On cover, single franking 40.00
86 A5 1fr rose red ('38) 5.50 1.60
Never hinged 7.25
On cover 37.50
On cover, single franking 67.50
87 A5 1fr car & brn ('40) .80 .80
Never hinged 1.60
On cover 8.75
88 A6 1.25fr vio & dl vio ('33) .80 .80
Never hinged 1.20
On cover 25.00
On cover, single franking 67.50
89 A6 1.25fr red ('39) .90 1.00
Never hinged 1.25
On cover 62.50
On cover, single franking 125.00
90 A6 1.40fr brt vio & blk ('40) .90 .90
Never hinged 1.60
On cover 42.50
On cover, single franking 92.50
91 A6 1.50fr dk bl & ultra .80 .55
Never hinged 1.20
On cover 37.50
On cover, single franking 75.00
92 A6 1.60fr brn & dp bl ('40) .90 .90
Never hinged 1.60
On cover 37.50
On cover, single franking 92.50
93 A6 1.75fr dk brn & dp bl ('33) .80 .80
Never hinged 1.20
On cover 19.00
On cover, single franking 27.50
94 A6 1.75fr vio bl ('38) .80 .80
Never hinged 1.60
On cover 37.50
On cover, single franking 62.50
95 A6 2fr org brn & grn .80 .55
Never hinged 1.60
On cover 32.50
On cover, single franking 62.50
96 A6 2.25fr vio bl & ultra ('39) 1.00 1.10
Never hinged 1.60
On cover 55.00
On cover, single franking 110.00
97 A6 2.50fr lt brown ('40) 1.60 1.60
Never hinged 2.40
On cover 30.00
On cover, single franking 55.00
98 A6 3fr Prus grn & brn .80 .40
Never hinged 1.60
On cover 45.00
On cover, single franking 105.00
99 A6 5fr red & blk 2.00 1.20
Never hinged 3.25
On cover 50.00
On cover, single franking 100.00
100 A6 10fr dull bl & grn 2.40 2.00
Never hinged 3.25
On cover 55.00
On cover, single franking 105.00
101 A6 20fr red vio & brn 3.25 2.40
Never hinged 4.00
On cover 67.50
On cover, single franking 120.00
Nos. 61-101 (41) 47.65 32.70

For surcharges see Nos. B7-B10 in Scott Standard catalogue, Vol. 2.

For 10c and 30c, without "RF," see Nos. 120-121 in Scott Standard catalogue, Vol. 2.

Common Design Types pictured following the introduction.

Colonial Exposition Issue
Common Design Types

1931, Apr. 13 Engr. *Perf. 12½*
Name of Country Printed in Black
102 CD70 40c deep green 4.75 4.75
Never hinged 7.25
On cover 105.00
103 CD71 50c violet 4.75 4.75
Never hinged 7.25
On cover 87.50
104 CD72 90c red orange 4.75 4.75
Never hinged 7.25
On cover 150.00
On cover, single franking 220.00
105 CD73 1.50fr dull blue 4.75 4.75
Never hinged 7.25
On cover 140.00
On cover, single franking 190.00
Nos. 102-105 (4) 19.00 19.00
Set, never hinged 29.00

Paris International Exposition Issue
Common Design Types

1937, Apr. 15 *Perf. 13*
106 CD74 20c deep violet 2.00 2.00
Never hinged 3.25
On cover 120.00
107 CD75 30c dark green 2.00 2.00
Never hinged 3.25
On cover 100.00
108 CD76 40c carmine rose 2.40 2.40
Never hinged 3.25
On cover 87.50
109 CD77 50c dark brown 1.60 1.60
Never hinged 3.25
On cover 80.00
110 CD78 90c red 1.60 1.60
Never hinged 3.25
On cover 120.00
On cover, single franking 220.00
111 CD79 1.50fr ultra 2.40 2.40
Never hinged 4.00
On cover 105.00
On cover, single franking 160.00
Nos. 106-111 (6) 12.00 12.00
Set, never hinged 20.25

Colonial Arts Exhibition Issue
Souvenir Sheet
Common Design Type

1937 Engr. *Imperf.*
112 CD77 3fr magenta & blk 12.00 *16.00*
Never hinged 16.00
On cover 140.00
On cover, single franking 220.00

Caillie Issue
Common Design Type

1939, Apr. 5 *Perf. 12½x12*
113 CD81 90c org brn & org .40 .80
Never hinged .80
On cover 13.50
114 CD81 2fr brt violet .40 1.20
Never hinged .80
On cover 32.50
On cover, single franking 55.00
115 CD81 2.25fr ultra & dk bl .40 1.20
Never hinged .80
On cover 40.00
On cover, single franking 67.50
Nos. 113-115 (3) 1.20 3.20
Set, never hinged 2.40

New York World's Fair Issue
Common Design Type

1939, May 10
116 CD82 1.25fr car lake .80 1.60
Never hinged 1.20
On cover 87.50
On cover, single franking 160.00
117 CD82 2.25fr ultra .80 1.60
Never hinged 1.20
On cover 87.50
On cover, single franking 155.00
Set, never hinged 2.40

SEMI-POSTAL STAMPS

Curie Issue
Common Design Type
Unwmk.

1938, Oct. 24 Engr. *Perf. 13*
B1 CD80 1.75fr + 50c brt ultra 12.50 12.50
Never hinged 21.00
On cover 110.00
On cover, single franking 190.00

French Revolution Issue
Common Design Type

1939, July 5 Photo.
Name and Value Typo. in Black

B2	CD83 45c + 25c green	10.00	10.00
	Never hinged	17.50	
	On cover		150.00
B3	CD83 70c + 30c brown	10.00	10.00
	Never hinged	17.50	
	On cover		120.00
B4	CD83 90c + 35c red org	10.00	10.00
	Never hinged	17.50	
	On cover		105.00
B5	CD83 1.25fr + 1fr rose pink	10.00	10.00
	Never hinged	17.50	
	On cover		160.00
	On cover, single franking		250.00
B6	CD83 2.25fr + 2fr blue	10.00	10.00
	Never hinged	17.50	
	On cover		150.00
	On cover, single franking		225.00
	Nos. B2-B6 (5)	50.00	50.00
	Set, never hinged	87.50	

AIR POST STAMPS

Common Design Type
Perf. 12½x12

1940, Feb. 8 Unwmk. Engr.

C1	CD85 1.90fr ultra	.40	.40
	Never hinged	.80	
	On cover		42.50
C2	CD85 2.90fr dark red	.40	.40
	Never hinged	.80	
	On cover		42.50
C3	CD85 4.50fr dk gray green	.80	.80
	Never hinged	1.20	
	On cover		50.00
C4	CD85 4.90fr yellow bister	.80	.80
	Never hinged	1.20	
	On cover		62.50
C5	CD85 6.90fr deep orange	1.60	1.60
	Never hinged	2.00	
	On cover		75.00
	Nos. C1-C5 (5)	4.00	4.00
	Set, never hinged	5.20	

POSTAGE DUE STAMPS

Postage Due Stamps of Upper Senegal and Niger Overprinted — D1

Perf. 14x13½

1921, Dec. Unwmk. Typo.

J1	D1 5c green	.40	.40
	Never hinged	.80	
	On cover		62.50
J2	D1 10c rose	.40	.40
	Never hinged	.80	
	On cover		62.50
J3	D1 15c gray	.40	.80
	Never hinged	.80	
	On cover		62.50
J4	D1 20c brown	1.20	1.20
	Never hinged	1.60	
	On cover		67.50
J5	D1 30c blue	1.20	1.20
	Never hinged	1.60	
	On cover		67.50
J6	D1 50c black	2.00	2.40
	Never hinged	3.25	
	On cover		75.00
J7	D1 60c orange	2.40	2.40
	Never hinged	3.25	
	On cover		87.50
J8	D1 1fr violet	2.40	3.25
	Never hinged	4.00	
	On cover		105.00
	Nos. J1-J8 (8)	10.40	12.05

Type of 1921 Issue Surcharged

1927, Oct. 10

J9	D1 2fr on 1fr lilac rose	8.00	8.00
	Never hinged	12.00	
J10	D1 3fr on 1fr org brown	8.00	8.00
	Never hinged	12.00	

D2

1931, Mar. 9

J11	D2 5c green	.25	.30
	Never hinged	.40	
	On cover		50.00
J12	D2 10c rose	.25	.30
	Never hinged	.40	
	On cover		50.00
J13	D2 15c gray	.25	.50
	Never hinged	.40	
	On cover		55.00
J14	D2 20c dark brown	.25	.50
	Never hinged	.40	
	On cover		55.00
J15	D2 30c dark blue	.40	.55
	Never hinged	.80	
	On cover		55.00
J16	D2 50c black	.40	.55
	Never hinged	.80	
	On cover		62.50
J17	D2 60c deep orange	.80	.80
	Never hinged	1.20	
	On cover		67.50
J18	D2 1fr violet	1.20	1.20
	Never hinged	1.60	
	On cover		80.00
J19	D2 2fr lilac rose	1.60	1.60
	Never hinged	2.00	
	On cover		100.00
J20	D2 3fr red brown	1.60	1.60
	Never hinged	2.40	
	On cover		110.00
	Nos. J11-J20 (10)	7.00	7.90

FUNCHAL

fün-ˈshäl

LOCATION — A city and administrative district in the Madeira island group in the Atlantic Ocean northwest of Africa

GOVT. — A part of the Republic of Portugal

POP. — 150,574 (1900)

Postage stamps of Funchal were superseded by those of Portugal.

1000 Reis = 1 Milreis

STAMPS OF PORTUGAL USED IN FUNCHAL

Barred Numeral "51"

Queen Maria II

1853

A1	5r orange brown (#1)	1,425.
A2	25r blue (#2)	92.50
A3	50r deep yellow green (#3)	1,400.
a.	50r blue green (#3a)	—
A4	100r lilac (#4)	3,000.

1855 King Pedro V (Straight Hair)

A5	5r red brown (#5)	1,425.
A6	25r blue, type II (#6)	72.50
a.	Type I (#6a)	67.50
A7	50r green (#7)	110.00
A8	100r lilac (#8)	115.00

1856-58
King Pedro V (Curled Hair)

A9	5r brown (#9)	175.00
A10	25r blue, type II (#10)	110.00
a.	Type I (#10a)	110.00
A11	25r rose, type II (#11) ('58)	36.00

1862-64 King Luiz

A12	5r brown (#12)	110.00
A13	10r orange (#13)	115.00
A14	25r rose (#14)	40.00
A15	50r yellow green (#15)	110.00
A16	100r lilac (#16) ('64)	100.00

1866-67 King Luiz
Imperf.

A17	5r black (#17)	115.00
A18	10r yellow (#18)	175.00
A19	20r bister (#19)	175.00
A20	25r rose (#20) ('67)	132.50
A21	50r green (#21)	175.00
A22	80r orange (#22)	175.00
A23	100r dark lilac (#23) ('67)	225.00
A24	120r blue (#24)	115.00

Perf. 12½

A28	25r rose (#28)	95.00

King Carlos — A1

1892-93 Typo. Unwmk.
Enamel Surfaced Paper,
Perf. 12½

1	A1 5r yellow	4.00	2.00
	Never hinged	5.75	
a.	Half used as 2½r on entire newspaper		17.50
2	A1 10r red violet	3.00	2.00
	Never hinged	4.25	
3	A1 15r chocolate	4.00	2.50
	Never hinged	6.00	
4	A1 20r lavender	5.00	2.50
	Never hinged	6.00	
a.	Perf. 13½	10.00	7.50
5	A1 25r dark green	8.00	1.35
	Never hinged	12.00	
6	A1 50r ultramarine	9.00	2.50
	Never hinged	18.50	
7	A1 75r carmine	10.00	6.00
	Never hinged	11.00	
8	A1 80r yellow green	15.00	11.00
	Never hinged	20.00	
9	A1 100r brn, *yel* ('93)	12.00	5.00
	Never hinged	12.50	
a.	Diagonal half used as 50r on cover		70.00
11	A1 200r dk bl, *bl* ('93)	75.00	45.00
	Never hinged	90.00	
12	A1 300r dk bl, *sal* ('93)	80.00	55.00
	Never hinged	120.00	
	Nos. 1-12 (11)	225.00	134.85

Enamel Surfaced Paper,
Perf. 13½

1c	A1 5r yellow	3.00	1.50
	Never hinged	4.00	
2a	A1 10r red violet	3.25	2.10
	Never hinged	4.75	
3a	A1 15r chocolate	4.50	2.10
	Never hinged	6.25	
4b	A1 20r lavendar	8.75	6.25
	Never hinged	12.50	
6a	A1 50r ultramarine	8.75	5.50
	Never hinged	12.50	
7a	A1 75r carmine	8.75	5.50
	Never hinged	12.50	
8a	A1 80r yellow green	17.50	12.00
	Never hinged	20.00	
10	A1 150r car, *rose* ('93)	60.00	30.00
	Never hinged	72.50	

Enamel Surfaced Paper,
Perf. 11½

1b	A1 5r yellow	4.00	2.75
5a	A1 25r dark green	8.00	1.00
6b	A1 50r ultramarine	4.75	2.10

Chalky Paper,
Perf. 12½

3b	A1 15r chocolate	14.00	10.00
	Never hinged	20.00	
8b	A1 80r yellow green	16.00	11.00
	Never hinged	22.50	

Chalky Paper,
Perf. 13½

6c	A1 50r ultramarine	12.50	7.25
	Never hinged	19.00	

Nos. 1-12 were issued on two types of paper: enamel surfaced, which is white, with a uniform low gloss; and chalky, which bears a low-gloss application in a pattern of tiny lozenges, producing a somewhat duller appearance.

The reprints of this issue have shiny white gum and clean-cut perforation 13½. The shades differ from those of the originals and the uncolored paper is thin.

King Carlos — A2

Name and Value in Black except Nos. 25 and 34

1897-1905 ***Perf. 11¾***

13	A2 2½r gray	.50	.35
	Never hinged	.60	
14	A2 5r orange	.50	.35
	Never hinged	.60	
15	A2 10r light green	.50	.35
	Never hinged	.60	
16	A2 15r brown	5.50	5.00
	Never hinged	8.00	
17	A2 15r gray grn ('99)	3.75	2.75
	Never hinged	5.25	
18	A2 20r gray vio	1.40	.75
	Never hinged	1.75	
19	A2 25r sea green	2.75	.75
	Never hinged	3.75	
20	A2 25r car rose ('99)	1.40	.55
	Never hinged	1.75	
a.	Booklet pane of 6	—	
21	A2 50r dark blue	10.00	5.00
	Never hinged	12.00	
a.	Perf. 12½	25.00	9.00
	Never hinged	18.00	
22	A2 50r ultra ('05)	1.50	.90
	Never hinged	1.75	
23	A2 65r slate blue ('98)	1.25	.90
	Never hinged	1.50	
24	A2 75r rose	2.00	.95
	Never hinged	2.75	
25	A2 75r brn & red, *yel* ('05)	8.00	1.40
	Never hinged	9.25	
26	A2 80r violet	1.40	1.10
	Never hinged	2.00	
27	A2 100r dark blue, *blue*	1.40	1.10
	Never hinged	2.00	
a.	Diagonal half used as 50r on cover		*75.00*
28	A2 115r org brn, *pink* ('98)	5.00	1.40
	Never hinged	6.50	
29	A2 130r gray brown, *buff* ('98)	6.00	1.40
	Never hinged	7.75	
30	A2 150r lt brn, *buff*	6.00	1.25
	Never hinged	7.75	
31	A2 180r sl, *pnksh* ('98)	6.00	1.40
	Never hinged	7.75	
32	A2 200r red vio, *pale lil*	6.00	2.10
	Never hinged	7.75	
33	A2 300r blue, *rose*	6.00	2.10
	Never hinged	7.75	
34	A2 500r blk & red, *bl*	10.00	2.40
	Never hinged	12.00	
a.	Perf. 12½	20.00	7.75
	Never hinged	17.50	
	Nos. 13-34 (22)	86.85	34.25

Yellowish Paper

13a	A2 2½r gray	.50	.35
	Never hinged	.60	
14a	A2 5r orange	.50	.35
	Never hinged	.60	
15a	A2 10r lightt green	.50	.35
	Never hinged	.60	
17a	A2 15r gray grn ('99)	3.25	2.25
	Never hinged	4.75	
18a	A2 20r gray vio	1.40	.75
	Never hinged	1.75	
20b	A2 25r car rose ('99)	1.40	.55
	Never hinged	1.75	
23a	A2 65r slate blue ('98)	1.25	.90
	Never hinged	1.50	
24a	A2 75r rose	1.40	.95
	Never hinged	2.00	

GABON

ga-'bōn

LOCATION — West coast of Africa, at the equator
GOVT. — French colony
AREA — 102,089 sq. mi.
POP. — 1,367,000 (est. 1984)
CAPITAL — Libreville

Gabon originally was under the control of French West Africa. In 1886, it was united with French Congo. In 1904, Gabon was granted a certain degree of colonial autonomy which prevailed until 1934, when it merged with French Equatorial Africa.

100 Centimes = 1 Franc

Stamps of French Colonies of 1881-86 Handstamp Surcharged in Black

a

b

1886 Unwmk. *Perf. 14x13½*

1 A9 (a) 5c on 20c red, *grn* 575.00 *625.00*
On cover —
a. "5" double *3,850.*
2 A9 (b) 10c on 20c red, *grn* 550.00 *575.00*
On cover —
a. "0" double *1,400.* *1,250.*
b. "10" double *1,400.* *1,250.*
3 A9 (b) 25c on 20c red, *grn* 100.00 75.00
On cover 260.00
a. "25" double *750.00* *525.00*
b. "25" omitted *1,200.* *1,200.*
c. "GAB" inverted *1,100.* *925.00*
d. "GAB" double *550.00* *450.00*
e. 56-dot diamond grid around "GAB" *6,750.* 2,100.
On cover —
4 A9 (b) 50c on 15c bl 1,500. *2,100.*
On cover —
a. "GAB" omitted *3,200.*
5 A9 (b) 75c on 15c bl 1,900. *2,300.*
On cover —
a. "75" double *5,000.*

On Nos. 3 and 5 the surcharge slants down; on No. 4 it slants up. The number of dots varies.

Counterfeits of Nos. 1-15 exist.

Covers: Values are for commercial covers with correct frankings.

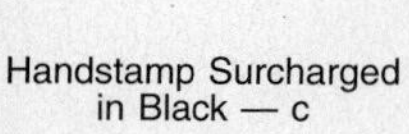
Handstamp Surcharged in Black — c

1888-89

6 A9 15c on 10c blk, *lav* *6,000.* 1,500.
On cover —
7 A9 15c on 1fr brnz grn, *straw* *2,400.* 1,200.
On cover —
8 A9 25c on 5c grn, *grnsh* 1,500. 325.00
On cover 1,800.
a. Double surcharge *4,000.* *4,000.*
9 A9 25c on 10c blk, *lav* *6,000.* 1,900.
On cover —
10 A9 25c on 75c car, *rose* *4,000.* 2,100.
On cover —

Official reprints exist.

Postage Due Stamps of French Colonies Handstamp Surcharged in Black — d

1889 *Imperf.*

11 D1 15c on 5c black 325.00 275.00
On cover 1,400.
a. "TIMBRE" omitted 1,000. 675.00
b. "TIMBRE" double 650.00
c. "15" omitted 1,000. 625.00
d. "15" double 650.00
e. "GABON" double 650.00
12 D1 15c on 30c black *5,000.* *3,800.*
On cover —
a. "GABON" omitted *6,500.*
b. "15" omitted *6,500.*
13 D1 25c on 20c black 150.00 120.00
On cover 475.00
a. "25" double 325.00 325.00
b. "GABON" double 325.00
c. "TIMBRE" double 325.00

A8

1889 Typeset

14 A8 15c blk, *rose* 1,900. 1,200.
On cover *4,750.*
a. "GAB" omitted *8,500.*
a. "GAB" double *3,250.*
15 A8 25c blk, *green* 1,200. 950.
On cover *3,600.*
a. "GAB" omitted *5,750.*
b. "GAB" inverted *2,850.*
c. "GAB" double *2,850.*

Ten varieties of each. Nos. 14-15 exist with small "f" in "Francaise."

Navigation and Commerce — A9

Name of Colony in Blue or Carmine

1904-07 Typo. *Perf. 14x13½*

16 A9 1c blk, *lil bl* 1.40 1.40
Never hinged 2.10
On cover 190.00
a. "GABON" double 360.00 360.00
17 A9 2c brn, *buff* 2.10 1.40
Never hinged 3.00
On cover 190.00
18 A9 4c claret, *lav* 2.75 2.10
Never hinged 5.50
On cover 190.00
19 A9 5c yellow green 3.25 2.40
Never hinged 5.00
On cover 75.00
20 A9 10c rose 10.00 7.50
Never hinged 15.00
On cover 92.50
21 A9 15c gray 11.00 7.50
Never hinged 18.50
On cover 92.50
22 A9 20c red, *grn* 15.00 14.00
Never hinged 25.00
On cover 190.00
On cover, single franking 300.00
23 A9 25c blue 14.00 7.50
Never hinged 27.00
On cover 85.00
24 A9 30c yel brn 16.00 15.00
Never hinged 30.00
On cover 250.00
On cover, single franking 350.00
25 A9 35c blk, *yel* ('06) 24.00 24.00
Never hinged 45.00
On cover 225.00
On cover, single franking 310.00
26 A9 40c red, *straw* 25.00 20.00
Never hinged 40.00
On cover 250.00
On cover, single franking 340.00
27 A9 45c blk, *gray grn* ('07) 37.50 32.50
Never hinged 80.00
On cover 310.00
On cover, single franking 400.00
28 A9 50c brn, *az* 16.00 14.00
Never hinged 30.00
On cover 190.00
On cover, single franking 250.00
29 A9 75c dp vio, *org* 25.00 25.00
Never hinged 42.50
On cover 340.00
On cover, single franking 550.00
30 A9 1fr brnz grn, *straw* 40.00 40.00
Never hinged 80.00
On cover 400.00
On cover, single franking 690.00
31 A9 2fr vio, *rose* 80.00 80.00
Never hinged 140.00
On cover 625.00
On cover, single franking 900.00
32 A9 5fr lil, *lav* 127.50 127.50
Never hinged 225.00
On cover 800.00
On cover, single franking 1,125.
Nos. 16-32 (17) 450.50 421.80

Perf. 13½x14 stamps are counterfeits.
For surcharges see Nos. 72-84.

Covers: Values are for commercial covers with correct frankings. Philatelic covers sell for less.

Fang Warrior — A10

Fang Woman — A12

Libreville A11

Inscribed: "Congo Français"

1910 *Perf. 13½x14*

33 A10 1c choc & org 2.00 2.00
Never hinged 3.75
On cover 110.00
34 A10 2c black & choc 2.75 2.75
Never hinged 3.75
On cover 110.00
35 A10 4c vio & dp bl 2.50 2.50
Never hinged 3.50
On cover 110.00
36 A10 5c ol gray & grn 4.00 4.00
Never hinged 7.00
On cover 50.00
37 A10 10c red & car 5.75 5.75
Never hinged 7.25
On cover 37.50
38 A10 20c choc & dk vio 8.00 8.00
Never hinged 14.00
On cover 80.00
39 A11 25c dp bl & choc 8.00 8.00
Never hinged 14.00
On cover 80.00
On cover, single franking 190.00
40 A11 30c gray blk & red 40.00 40.00
Never hinged 80.00
On cover 175.00
On cover, single franking 250.00
41 A11 35c dk vio & grn 24.00 24.00
Never hinged 45.00
On cover 140.00
On cover, single franking 200.00
42 A11 40c choc & ultra 32.50 32.50
Never hinged 57.50
On cover 190.00
On cover, single franking 275.00
43 A11 45c car & vio 52.50 52.50
Never hinged 90.00
On cover 200.00
On cover, single franking 340.00
44 A11 50c bl grn & gray 75.00 75.00
Never hinged 140.00
On cover 275.00
On cover, single franking 475.00
45 A11 75c org & choc 130.00 130.00
Never hinged 260.00
On cover 400.00
On cover, single franking 600.00
46 A12 1fr dk brn & bis 130.00 130.00
Never hinged 260.00
On cover 400.00
On cover, single franking 625.00
47 A12 2fr car & brn 325.00 325.00
On cover 650.00
On cover, single franking 925.00
48 A12 5fr blue & choc 325.00 325.00
Never hinged 550.00
On cover 690.00
On cover, single franking 950.00
Nos. 33-48 (16) 1,167. 1,167.

Inscribed: "Afrique Equatoriale"

1910-22 Dull Cream Paper

49 A10 1c choc & org .35 *.40*
Never hinged .70
On cover 87.50
a. White paper 1.00 *1.20*
Never hinged 1.75
On cover 87.50
b. Center double 130.00
Never hinged 225.00
c. 1c gray brown & orange .40 .50
Never hinged .70
On cover 87.50
50 A10 2c black & choc .35 *.40*
Never hinged .70
On cover 87.50
a. White paper 1.00 *1.20*
Never hinged 1.75
On cover 87.50
b. 2c gray black & deep olive .65 *.80*
Never hinged 1.00
On cover 87.50
51 A10 4c vio & dp bl .35 *.50*
Never hinged 1.40
On cover 87.50
a. White paper 1.00 *1.20*
Never hinged 1.75
On cover 87.50
b. 4c violet & blue black .90 *1.00*
Never hinged 1.75
On cover 87.50
52 A10 5c ol gray & grn .95 .55
Never hinged 1.60
On cover 32.50
53 A10 5c gray blk & ocher ('22) 1.40 1.40
Never hinged 2.00
On cover 30.00
54 A10 10c red & car 1.40 1.00
Never hinged 2.40
On cover 21.00
a. White paper 3.25 2.75
Never hinged 5.25
On cover 25.00
b. 10c vermilion & carmine 3.50 3.25
Never hinged 6.00
On cover 25.00
55 A10 10c yel grn & bl grn ('22) 1.40 1.40
Never hinged 2.00
On cover 50.00
56 A10 15c brn vio & rose ('18) 1.25 .80
Never hinged 1.90
On cover 19.00
57 A10 20c ol brn & dk vio 6.50 5.50
Never hinged 11.00
On cover 42.50
a. 20c brown & dk vio 17.00 13.50
Never hinged 30.00
On cover 75.00
58 A11 25c dp bl & choc 1.40 1.00
Never hinged 2.50
On cover 40.00
On cover, single franking 105.00
59 A11 25c Prus bl & blk ('22) 1.60 1.60
Never hinged 2.25
On cover 15.00
60 A11 30c gray blk & red 1.60 1.60
Never hinged 2.60
On cover 50.00
On cover, single franking 125.00
61 A11 30c rose & red ('22) 2.00 *2.40*
Never hinged 3.00
On cover 40.00
On cover, single franking 80.00
62 A11 35c dk vio & grn 1.40 1.25
Never hinged 1.75
On cover 45.00
On cover, single franking 67.50
a. White paper 1.40 1.25
Never hinged 2.00
On cover 45.00
63 A11 40c choc & ultra 1.60 1.60
Never hinged 2.60
On cover 55.00
On cover, single franking 80.00
64 A11 45c carmine & vio 1.60 1.60
Never hinged 2.40
On cover 67.50
On cover, single franking 80.00
a. White paper 4.00 3.50
Never hinged 7.50
On cover 80.00
65 A11 45c blk & red ('22) 2.75 *3.25*
Never hinged 4.00
On cover 55.00
On cover, single franking 92.50
66 A11 50c bl grn & gray 2.00 2.00
Never hinged 3.00
On cover 67.50
On cover, single franking 150.00
a. White paper 3.50 3.50
Never hinged 6.00
On cover 80.00
67 A11 50c dk bl & bl ('22) 1.60 1.60
Never hinged 2.75
On cover 32.50
On cover, single franking 62.50
68 A11 75c org & choc 7.00 5.00
Never hinged 11.00
On cover 80.00
On cover, single franking 140.00
69 A12 1fr dk brn & bis 3.50 2.75
Never hinged 5.25
On cover 87.50
On cover, single franking 165.00
70 A12 2fr car & brn 7.00 *6.50*
Never hinged 11.00
On cover 92.50
On cover, single franking 200.00
71 A12 5fr blue & choc 7.00 *8.50*
Never hinged 15.00
On cover 110.00
On cover, single franking 210.00
Nos. 49-71 (23) 56.00 52.60

For overprints & surcharges see Nos. 85-119, B1-B3.

Stamps of 1904-07 Surcharged in Black or Carmine

Spacing between figures of surcharge 1.5mm (5c), 2mm (10c)

1912

72 A9 5c on 2c brn, *buff* 1.60 *2.00*
Never hinged 2.50
On cover 92.50
73 A9 5c on 4c cl, *lav* (C) 1.60 *2.00*
Never hinged 2.50
On cover 92.50
74 A9 5c on 15c gray (C) 1.25 1.25
Never hinged 1.75
On cover 55.00
75 A9 5c on 20c red, *grn* 1.25 *1.60*
Never hinged 2.00
On cover 75.00
76 A9 5c on 25c bl (C) 1.25 *1.60*
Never hinged 2.00
On cover 67.50
77 A9 5c on 30c pale brn (C) 1.60 *2.00*
Never hinged 2.50
On cover 100.00

78 A9 10c on 40c red, *straw* 1.25 *1.60*
Never hinged 1.75
On cover 62.50
a. Double surcharge 2,400.
79 A9 10c on 45c blk, *gray grn* (C) 1.25 *1.60*
Never hinged 1.75
On cover 62.50
80 A9 10c on 50c brn, *az* (C) 1.60 *2.00*
Never hinged 2.50
On cover 92.50
81 A9 10c on 75c dp vio, *org* 1.60 *2.00*
Never hinged 2.50
On cover 100.00
82 A9 10c on 1fr brnz grn, *straw* 1.60 *2.00*
Never hinged 3.50
On cover 92.50
83 A9 10c on 2fr vio, *rose* 1.60 *2.00*
Never hinged 3.50
On cover 92.50
a. Inverted surcharge 340.00 340.00
Never hinged 500.00
84 A9 10c on 5fr lil, *lav* 4.00 *4.25*
Never hinged 7.00
On cover 120.00
Nos. 72-84 (13) 21.45 25.90

Spacing between figures of surcharge 2.25mm (5c), 2.75mm (10c)

72a A9 5c on 2c brn, *buff* 10.50 10.50
Never hinged 14.00
73a A9 5c on 4c cl, *lav* (C) 10.50 10.50
Never hinged 14.00
74a A9 5c on 15c gray (C) 7.00 7.00
Never hinged 14.00
75a A9 5c on 20c red, *grn* 10.50 10.50
Never hinged 14.00
76a A9 5c on 25c bl (C) 10.50 10.50
Never hinged 14.00
77a A9 5c on 30c pale brn (C) 14.00 14.00
Never hinged 21.00
78a A9 10c on 40c red, *straw* 35.00 35.00
Never hinged 52.50
79a A9 10c on 45c blk, *gray grn* (C) 35.00 35.00
Never hinged 52.50
80a A9 10c on 50c brn, *az* (C) 45.00 45.00
Never hinged 70.00
81a A9 10c on 75c dp vio, *org* 70.00 70.00
Never hinged 120.00
82a A9 10c on 1fr brnz grn, *straw* 70.00 70.00
Never hinged 120.00
83b A9 10c on 2fr vio, *rose* 70.00 70.00
Never hinged 120.00
c. Inverted surcharge 4,000. 4,000.
84a A9 10c on 5fr lil, *lav* 160.00 160.00
Nos. 72a-84a (13) 548.00 548.00

Se-tenant pairs
Se-tenant Pairs, Both Ovpt. Settings

72b A9 5c on 2c, #72 + #72a 14.00 14.00
Never hinged 20.00
73b A9 5c on 4c, #73 + #73a 14.00 14.00
Never hinged 20.00
74b A9 5c on 15c, #74 + #74a 10.50 10.50
Never hinged 17.50
75b A9 5c on 20c, #75 + #75a 11.00 11.00
Never hinged 19.00
76b A9 5c on 25c, #76 + #76a 11.00 11.00
Never hinged 19.00
77b A9 5c on 30c, #77 + #77a 16.00 16.00
Never hinged 27.50
78b A9 10c on 40c, #78 + #78a 35.00 35.00
Never hinged 52.50
79b A9 10c on 45c, #79 + #79a 35.00 35.00
Never hinged 60.00
80b A9 10c on 50c, #80 + #80a 50.00 50.00
Never hinged 70.00
81b A9 10c on 75c, #81 + #81a 75.00 75.00
Never hinged 135.00
82b A9 10c on 1fr, #82 + #82a 75.00 75.00
Never hinged 135.00
83d A9 10c on 2fr, #83 + #83b 75.00 75.00
Never hinged 135.00
84b A9 10c on 5fr, #84 + #84a 180.00 180.00
Nos. 72b-84b (13) 601.50 601.50

Stamps of 1910-22 Overprinted in Black, Blue or Carmine

On A10, A12

On A11

1924-31
85 A10 1c brn & org .35 *.35*
Never hinged .70
On cover 67.50
a. White paper (#49a) .80 .80
Never hinged 1.20
On cover 67.50
86 A10 2c blk & choc (Bl) .35 *.70*
Never hinged .70
On cover 67.50
a. White paper (#50a) 1.05 1.05
Never hinged 1.60
On cover 67.50
87 A10 4c violet & ind .25 *.35*
Never hinged .35
On cover 67.50
a. White paper (#51a) .80 .80
Never hinged 1.20
On cover 67.50
88 A10 5c gray blk & ocher .35 *.70*
Never hinged .70
On cover 30.00
89 A10 10c yel grn & bl grn .70 1.10
Never hinged 1.40
On cover 22.50
a. Double overprint (Bk & Bl) 175.00
Never hinged 260.00
90 A10 10c dk bl & brn ('26) (C) .40 .40
Never hinged .70
On cover 30.00
a. Overprint omitted 350.00 350.00
Never hinged 550.00
b. Double overprint 475.00
91 A10 15c brn vio & rose (Bl) 1.00 1.00
Never hinged 1.40
On cover 20.00
92 A10 15c rose & brn vio ('31) (Bl) 1.25 1.25
Never hinged 1.60
On cover 12.50
a. Overprint omitted 250.00
Never hinged 325.00
93 A10 20c ol brn & dk vio (C) .70 1.10
Never hinged 1.40
On cover 30.00
a. Inverted overprint 180.00 180.00
Never hinged 260.00
b. Double overprint 400.00
c. Double overprint, both inverted 525.00
Never hinged 800.00
94 A11 25c Prus bl & blk (C) .70 1.10
Never hinged 1.40
On cover 13.50
95 A11 30c rose & red (Bl) .70 *1.10*
Never hinged 1.40
On cover 40.00
On cover, single franking 92.50
96 A11 30c blk & org ('26) .70 .85
Never hinged 1.40
On cover 16.00
a. Overprint omitted —
97 A11 30c dk grn & bl grn ('28) 1.25 1.25
Never hinged 1.75
On cover 42.50
a. Overprint omitted 1,800.
98 A11 35c dk vio & grn (Bl) .70 *1.10*
Never hinged 1.10
On cover 50.00
On cover, single franking 87.50
a. White paper (#62a) 1.60 1.60
Never hinged 2.75
On cover 50.00
99 A11 40c choc & ultra (C) .75 *.75*
Never hinged 1.05
On cover 55.00
On cover, single franking 92.50
a. In pair with unovptd. stamp (#63) 3,600.
100 A11 45c blk & red (Bl) 1.50 2.10
Never hinged 2.10
On cover 20.00
On cover, single franking 30.00
101 A11 50c dk bl & bl (C) 1.00 1.00
Never hinged 1.40
On cover 16.00
On cover, single franking 30.00
a. White paper (#67a) 2.00 2.00
Never hinged 3.25
On cover 16.00
102 A11 50c car & grn ('26) .70 .90
Never hinged 1.40
On cover 16.00
103 A11 65c dp bl & red org ('27) 3.50 3.50
Never hinged 6.00
On cover 32.50
On cover, single franking 75.00
104 A11 75c org & brn (Bl) 2.25 2.25
Never hinged 3.25
On cover 40.00
On cover, single franking 87.50
105 A11 90c brn red & rose ('30) 2.75 2.75
Never hinged 4.50
On cover 62.50
On cover, single franking 110.00
106 A12 1fr dk brn & bis 1.40 1.75
Never hinged 2.25
On cover 40.00
On cover, single franking 87.50
107 A12 1.10fr dl grn & rose red ('28) 6.00 *7.50*
Never hinged 10.50
On cover 165.00
On cover, single franking 375.00
108 A12 1.50fr pale bl & dk bl ('30) 1.25 1.25
Never hinged 2.00
On cover 55.00
On cover, single franking 100.00
a. Overprint omitted 290.00
Never hinged 475.00
109 A12 2fr rose & brn 2.25 *2.75*
Never hinged 3.50
On cover 67.50
On cover, single franking 140.00
110 A12 3fr red vio ('30) 7.00 7.00
Never hinged 12.00
On cover 92.50
On cover, single franking 190.00
a. Overprint omitted 275.00
Never hinged 450.00
111 A12 5fr dp bl & choc 7.00 5.50
Never hinged 10.50
On cover 75.00
On cover, single franking 150.00
Nos. 85-111 (27) 46.75 51.35

Types of 1924-31 Issues Surcharged with New Values in Black or Carmine

1925-28
112 A12 65c on 1fr ol grn & brn 1.25 1.25
Never hinged 2.00
On cover 80.00
On cover, single franking 190.00
113 A12 85c on 1fr ol grn & brn 1.25 1.25
Never hinged 1.90
On cover 67.50
On cover, single franking 140.00
114 A11 90c on 75c brn red & cer ('27) 1.75 1.75
Never hinged 2.60
On cover 67.50
On cover, single franking 125.00
a. "90" omitted 240.00
Never hinged 375.00
115 A12 1.25fr on 1fr dk bl & ultra (C) 1.25 1.25
Never hinged 1.90
On cover 75.00
On cover, single franking 150.00
116 A12 1.50fr on 1fr lt bl & dk bl ('27) 2.00 2.00
Never hinged 3.25
On cover 62.50
On cover, single franking 110.00
117 A12 3fr on 5fr mag & ol brn 7.00 8.00
Never hinged 12.00
On cover 110.00
On cover, single franking 225.00
a. Period after "F" omitted 32.50 32.50
Never hinged 55.00
118 A12 10fr on 5fr org brn & grn ('27) 12.00 *12.50*
Never hinged 17.50
On cover 140.00
On cover, single franking 275.00
a. Period after "F" omitted 40.00 40.00
Never hinged 67.50
119 A12 20fr on 5fr red vio & org red ('27) 16.00 *17.50*
Never hinged 21.00
On cover 150.00
On cover, single franking 310.00
a. Period after "F" omitted 45.00 45.00
Never hinged 67.50
Nos. 112-119 (8) 42.50 45.50

Bars cover the old denominations on Nos. 114-119.

Common Design Types pictured following the introduction.

Colonial Exposition Issue
Common Design Types

1931 ***Perf. 12½***

Name of Country in Black

120 CD70 40c dp green 4.00 4.00
Never hinged 5.50
On cover 110.00
121 CD71 50c violet 4.00 4.00
Never hinged 5.50
On cover 92.50
122 CD72 90c red orange 4.00 4.00
Never hinged 5.50
On cover 165.00
On cover, single franking 240.00
123 CD73 1.50fr dull blue 5.50 5.50
Never hinged 7.25
On cover 150.00
On cover, single franking 200.00
Nos. 120-123 (4) 17.50 17.50

Timber Raft on Ogowe River
A16

Count Savorgnan de Brazza — A17

Village of Setta Kemma
A18

1932-33 **Photo.** ***Perf. 13x13½***
124 A16 1c brown violet .25 .25
Never hinged .40
On cover 27.50
125 A16 2c blk, *rose* .25 .25
Never hinged .40
On cover 27.50
126 A16 4c green .30 .30
Never hinged .70
On cover 27.50
127 A16 5c grnsh blue .70 .50
Never hinged .80
On cover 20.00
128 A16 10c red, *yel* .55 .55
Never hinged .80
On cover 16.00
129 A16 15c red, *grn* .70 .65
Never hinged 1.00
On cover 20.00
130 A16 20c deep red .70 .65
Never hinged 1.00
On cover 16.00
131 A16 25c brown red .70 .50
Never hinged 1.00
On cover 30.00
132 A17 30c yellow grn 2.00 1.60
Never hinged 3.50
On cover 42.50
133 A17 40c brown vio 2.25 1.10
Never hinged 3.50
On cover 13.50
134 A17 45c blk, *dl grn* 3.50 2.40
Never hinged 4.75
On cover 50.00
135 A17 50c red brown 1.60 1.25
Never hinged 2.10
On cover 9.50
136 A17 65c Prus blue 6.50 6.50
Never hinged 11.00
On cover 80.00
137 A17 75c blk, *red org* 4.00 3.25
Never hinged 5.75
On cover 16.00
138 A17 90c rose red 4.00 3.25
Never hinged 5.75
On cover 42.50
On cover, single franking 100.00
139 A17 1fr yel grn, *bl* 27.50 24.00
Never hinged 50.00
On cover 80.00
On cover, single franking 110.00
140 A18 1.25fr dp vio ('33) 2.25 2.00
Never hinged 3.00
On cover 32.50
On cover, single franking 92.50
141 A18 1.50fr dull blue 11.00 7.25
Never hinged 18.50
On cover 67.50
On cover, single franking 190.00
142 A18 1.75fr dp grn ('33) 2.50 2.00
Never hinged 3.50
On cover 32.50
On cover, single franking 50.00
143 A18 2fr brn red 52.50 45.00
Never hinged 110.00
On cover 200.00
On cover, single franking 275.00
144 A18 3fr yel grn, *bl* 6.00 4.50
Never hinged 10.50
On cover 67.50
On cover, single franking 125.00
145 A18 5fr red brown 15.00 13.50
Never hinged 25.00
On cover 80.00
On cover, single franking 140.00
146 A18 10fr blk, *red org* 32.50 27.50
Never hinged 60.00
On cover 165.00
On cover, single franking 275.00
147 A18 20fr dk violet 47.50 40.00
Never hinged 87.50
On cover 190.00
On cover, single franking 325.00
Nos. 124-147 (24) 224.75 188.75

For overprints see French Equatorial Africa Nos. 1-10.

SEMI-POSTAL STAMPS

No. 37 Surcharged in Red

1916 Unwmk. *Perf. 13½x14*

B1 A10 10c + 5c red & car 30.00 30.00
Never hinged 60.00
On cover 140.00
a. Double surcharge 200.00 225.00
Never hinged 300.00
b. "5" omitted 80.00 80.00
Never hinged 140.00
c. Cross omitted 260.00
d. In pair with unsurcharged stamp 550.00

Same Surcharge on No. 54 in Red

B2 A10 10c + 5c red & car 37.50 37.50
Never hinged 85.00
On cover 165.00
a. Double surcharge 200.00 225.00
Never hinged 340.00
b. Inverted surcharge 175.00
Never hinged 340.00
c. Double surcharge, one inverted 175.00 200.00
Never hinged 340.00
d. In pair with unsurcharged stamp 550.00

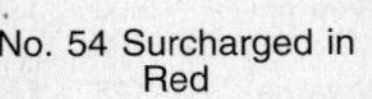

No. 54 Surcharged in Red

1917

B3 A10 10c + 5c red & car 2.40 2.40
Never hinged 3.25
On cover 67.50

POSTAGE DUE STAMPS

Postage Due Stamps of France Overprinted

1928 Unwmk. *Perf. 14x13½*

J1 D2 5c light blue .40 *.55*
Never hinged .70
On cover 92.50
J2 D2 10c gray brown .40 *.65*
Never hinged .70
On cover 92.50
J3 D2 20c olive green 1.05 *1.60*
Never hinged 1.40
On cover 92.50
J4 D2 25c bright rose 1.05 *1.40*
Never hinged 1.40
On cover 100.00
J5 D2 30c light red 1.60 *2.00*
Never hinged 2.50
On cover 100.00
J6 D2 45c blue green 2.00 *2.40*
Never hinged 3.00
On cover 105.00
J7 D2 50c brown violet 3.00 *3.25*
Never hinged 4.25
On cover 110.00
a. Period omitted after "F" 17.50 17.50
Never hinged 32.50
J8 D2 60c yellow brown 3.00 *3.25*
Never hinged 4.25
On cover 120.00
J9 D2 1fr red brown 3.00 *3.25*
Never hinged 4.25
On cover 125.00
J10 D2 2fr orange red 3.50 4.25
Never hinged 6.50
On cover 140.00
J11 D2 3fr bright violet 4.25 5.00
Never hinged 7.50
On cover 150.00
Nos. J1-J11 (11) 23.25 27.60

Chief Makoko, de Brazza's Aide — D3

Count Savorgnan de Brazza — D4

1930 Typo. *Perf. 13½x14*

J12 D3 5c dk bl & olive .70 1.10
Never hinged 1.40
On cover 42.50
J13 D3 10c dk red & brn .70 1.10
Never hinged 1.40
On cover 42.50
J14 D3 20c green & brn 1.40 1.40
Never hinged 2.10
On cover 42.50
J15 D3 25c lt bl & brn 1.40 1.40
Never hinged 2.10
On cover 50.00
J16 D3 30c bis brn & Prus bl 2.25 2.00
Never hinged 3.50
On cover 50.00
J17 D3 45c Prus bl & ol 2.75 3.25
Never hinged 3.50
On cover 55.00
J18 D3 50c red vio & brn 3.50 4.00
Never hinged 7.00
On cover 55.00
J19 D3 60c gray lil & bl blk 7.00 6.50
Never hinged 10.50
On cover 62.50
J20 D4 1fr bis brn & bl blk 7.00 10.00
Never hinged 14.00
On cover 80.00
J21 D4 2fr violet & brn 10.50 14.00
Never hinged 17.50
On cover 92.50
J22 D4 3fr dp red & brn 17.50 15.00
Never hinged 25.00
On cover 105.00
Nos. J12-J22 (11) 54.70 59.75

Fang Woman — D5

1932 Photo. *Perf. 13x13½*

J23 D5 5c dk bl, *bl* 1.10 1.40
Never hinged 1.75
On cover 42.50
J24 D5 10c red brown 1.40 1.75
Never hinged 2.25
On cover 42.50
J25 D5 20c chocolate 1.75 2.00
Never hinged 2.75
On cover 42.50
J26 D5 25c yel grn, *bl* 1.75 2.00
Never hinged 2.75
On cover 42.50
J27 D5 30c car rose 1.75 2.10
Never hinged 2.75
On cover 50.00
J28 D5 45c red org, *yel* 7.00 7.00
Never hinged 10.00
On cover 75.00
J29 D5 50c dk violet 2.75 2.75
Never hinged 4.00
On cover 55.00
J30 D5 60c dull blue 3.75 3.75
Never hinged 5.50
On cover 55.00
J31 D5 1fr blk, *red org* 8.50 9.50
Never hinged 12.00
On cover 92.50
J32 D5 2fr dark green 11.00 12.00
Never hinged 14.00
On cover 92.50
J33 D5 3fr rose lake 9.00 11.50
Never hinged 12.50
On cover 100.00
Nos. J23-J33 (11) 49.75 55.75

GAMBIA

'gam-bē-ə

LOCATION — Extending inland from the mouth of the Gambia River on the west coast of Africa

GOVT. — Republic in British Commonwealth

AREA — 4,068 sq. mi.

POP. — 695,886 (1983)

CAPITAL — Banjul

The British Crown Colony and Protectorate of Gambia became independent in 1965 and a republic in 1970.

12 Pence = 1 Shilling

Catalogue values for unused stamps in this country are for Never Hinged items, beginning with Scott 144.

Queen Victoria — A1

Typographed and Embossed

1869, Jan. Unwmk. *Imperf.*

1 A1 4p pale brown 575.00 240.00
No gum 400.00
a. 4p brown 675.00 240.00
No gum 475.00
2 A1 6p blue 675.00 240.00
No gum 450.00
a. 6p deep blue *650.00* *240.00*
No gum 475.00
b. 6p pale blue *3,400.* *1,250.*
No gum 2,500.

1874, Aug. Wmk. 1

3 A1 4p brown 450.00 240.00
No gum 300.00
a. 4p pale brown 475.00 250.00
No gum 300.00
4 A1 6p blue 425.00 240.00
No gum 290.00
a. 6p deep blue 475.00 250.00
No gum 290.00
b. Panel sloping down from left to right 975.00 525.00
No gum 650.00

Nos. 1-4 are often seen with flat embossing. Unused values for are for fine-very fine examples with sharp, detailed embossing. Values for unused stamps without gum and used stamps are for examples with average embossing.

The name panel sloping down variety, No. 4b, is from a top right corner position. A top left corner position exists with a less noticeable sloping of the panel down from right to left; it is worth less. **Covers:** Nos. 1-4 on cover are rare. Values start at about $7,500.

1880, June *Perf. 14*

5 A1 ½p orange 19.00 *27.50*
6 A1 1p maroon 11.00 *7.00*
7 A1 2p rose 67.50 12.50
8 A1 3p ultra 80.00 37.50
9 A1 4p pale brown 350.00 25.00
a. 4p brown 350.00 26.00
10 A1 6p blue 140.00 52.50
a. Panel sloping down from left to right 375.00 175.00
11 A1 1sh green 300.00 165.00
a. 1sh deep green 400.00 200.00
Nos. 5-11 (7) 967.50 327.00

The watermark on Nos. 5-11 exists both upright and sideways.

See footnote following No. 4.

1886-93 Wmk. 2 Sideways

12 A1 ½p gray grn 6.50 3.50
a. ½p deep green ('87) 6.50 2.50
13 A1 1p rose car ('87) 10.50 *12.50*
b. 1p aniline rose car 8.50 *14.00*
c. 1p pale carmine 8.50 *14.00*
14 2p dp org 4.50 *10.50*
b. 2p orange 15.00 5.75
15 A1 2½p dp brt blue 12.50 1.75
a. 2½ ultramarine ('87) 14.00 2.25
16 A1 3p gray 14.00 *17.00*
a. 3p slate gray ('86) 14.00 *16.00*
17 A1 4p dp brown 13.00 2.50
a. 4p brown ('87) 14.00 2.25
18 A1 6p sl grn ('93) 20.00 *67.50*
a. 6p pale olive green ('86) 110.00 60.00
b. 6p bronze green ('89) 47.50 *72.50*
c. As "a," panel sloping down from left to right 325.00 150.00
d. As "b," panel sloping down from left to right 95.00 *180.00*
e. 6p olive green ('87) 85.00 75.00
f. As "e," panel sloping down from left to right 275.00 190.00
g. 6p dp bronze grn ('89) 50.00 *75.00*
h. As "g," panel sloping down from left to right 100.00 190.00
19 A1 1sh violet 10.00 *24.00*
a. 1sh purple 5.00 *22.50*
b. 1sh aniline violet 1,250.
Nos. 12-19 (8) 91.00 *139.25*

See footnote following No. 4.

Queen Victoria — A2

1898, Jan. Typo. Wmk. 2

20 A2 ½p gray green 3.25 2.00
21 A2 1p carmine rose 3.50 .85
22 A2 2p brn org & pur 7.00 4.00
23 A2 2½p ultramarine 5.25 *2.75*
24 A2 3p red vio & ultra 50.00 14.00
25 A2 4p brown & ultra 20.00 *37.50*
26 A2 6p ol grn & car rose 19.00 *50.00*
27 A2 1sh vio & green 45.00 *85.00*
Nos. 20-27 (8) 153.00 *196.10*
Set, ovptd. "SPECIMEN" 225.00

King Edward VII — A3

1902-05 *Perf. 14*

28 A3 ½p green 6.75 *2.75*
29 A3 1p car rose 15.00 1.10
30 A3 2p org & pur 3.75 2.25
31 A3 2½p ultramarine 52.50 20.00
32 A3 3p red vio & ultra 23.00 4.00
33 A3 4p brn & ultra 10.00 *42.50*
34 A3 6p ol grn & rose 18.50 *14.50*
35 A3 1sh bluish vio & green 50.00 *92.50*
36 A3 1sh6p grn & red, *yel* 13.00 *26.00*
37 A3 2sh black & org 55.00 *75.00*
38 A3 2sh6p pur & brn, *yel* 16.00 *75.00*
39 A3 3sh red & grn, *yel* 22.50 *72.50*
Nos. 28-39 (12) 286.00 *428.10*
Set, ovptd. "SPECIMEN" 275.00

Numerals of 5p, 7½p, 10p, 1sh6p, 2sh, 2sh6p and 3sh of type A3 are in color on plain tablet.

Issue dates: 1p, Mar. 13. ½p, 3p, Apr. 19. 2p, 2½p, 4p, 6p, 1sh, 2sh, June 14. 1sh6p, 2sh6p, 3sh, Apr. 6, 1905.

For surcharges, see Nos. 65-66.

1904-09 Wmk. 3

41 A3 ½p green 5.25 .35
a. ½p blue green ('09) 15.00 7.00
42 A3 1p car rose 5.25 .25
a. 1p carmine ('09) 17.50 .25
43 A3 2p org & pur ('06) 14.00 2.50
44 A3 2p gray ('09) 2.25 12.50
45 A3 2½p brt blue ('05) 17.50 5.50
a. 2½ ultra & brt blue 21.00 *29.00*
46 A3 3p red vio & ultra 20.00 3.00
47 A3 3p vio, *yel* ('09) 7.50 1.10
a. 3p violet, *lemon yellow* 6.25 2.00
48 A3 4p brn & ultra ('06) 25.00 *50.00*
49 A3 4p blk & red, *yel* ('09) 3.75 .75
50 A3 5p gray & black 19.00 *30.00*
51 A3 5p org & vio ('09) 3.75 1.60
52 A3 6p ol grn & rose ('06) 26.00 *75.00*
53 A3 6p dull vio ('09) 2.75 2.50
54 A3 7½p blue grn & red 21.00 *65.00*
55 A3 7½p brn & ultra ('09) 5.00 2.75
56 A3 10p ol bis & red 32.50 *52.50*
57 A3 10p ol grn & car rose ('09) 7.00 *8.00*
58 A3 1sh violet & grn 42.50 *62.50*
59 A3 1sh blk, *grn* ('09) 7.50 *20.00*
60 A3 1sh 6p vio & grn ('09) 32.50 *80.00*
61 A3 2sh black & org 100.00 *125.00*
62 A3 2sh vio & bl, *bl* ('09) 16.00 *22.50*
63 A3 2sh 6p blk & red, *bl* ('09) 25.00 22.50
64 A3 3sh yel & grn ('09) 45.00 *55.00*
Nos. 41-64 (24) 486.00 *700.80*

Nos. 38-39 Surcharged in Black

Type I

Type II

Type I — The word "PENNY" is 5mm from the horizontal bars.

Type II — "PENNY" is 4mm from the bars.

1906, Apr. Wmk. 2

65 A3 ½p on 2sh6p, type I 57.50 *70.00*
a. Type II 62.50 *75.00*
66 A3 1p on 3sh 62.50 35.00
a. Double surcharge *2,150.* *5,750.*

King George V — A4

1912-22 **Wmk. 3**

70 A4 ½p dp green 3.75 *1.75*
a. ½p green 4.00 1.75
b. ½p pale green ('16) 6.50 3.75
71 A4 1p carmine 3.00 1.25
a. 1p scarlet ('16) 11.00 1.00
b. 1p rose red 5.00 .35
72 A4 1½p ol brn & grn .85 .35
73 A4 2p gray .85 *3.25*
74 A4 2½p dp brt blue 5.00 3.50
a. 2½p bright blue 5.00 2.75
75 A4 3p violet, *yel* 1.75 .35
a. 3p violet, *lemon* ('17) 16.00 *20.00*
b. 3p violet, *org buff* ('20) 11.50 *9.50*
c. 3p violet, *pale yellow* 1.60 *13.00*
76 A4 4p blk & red, *yel* 1.10 *11.50*
a. 4p blk & red, *lemon* ('17) 4.00 *8.50*
b. 4p blk & red, *org buff* ('20) 10.00 *13.00*
c. 4p blk & red, *pale yellow* 1.75 *13.00*
77 A4 5p orange & vio 2.00 *2.25*
78 A4 6p dl vio & red violet 3.00 *2.75*
79 A4 7½p brn & ultra 6.00 *16.00*
80 A4 10p ol grn & car rose 6.25 *20.00*
a. 10p dp ol grn & car rose 4.25 *17.50*
81 A4 1sh blk, *green* 4.25 1.10
a. 1sh black, *emerald* 3.75 *28.00*
82 A4 1sh6p vio & green 22.50 11.50
83 A4 2sh vio & bl, *bl* 10.00 *7.00*
84 A4 2sh6p blk & red, *bl* 10.00 *16.00*
85 A4 3sh yel & green 18.00 *50.00*
86 A4 5sh grn & red, *yel* ('22) *130.00 200.00*
Nos. 70-86 (17) *228.30 348.55*
Set, ovptd. "SPECIMEN" 400.00

Numerals of 1½p, 5p, 7½p, 10p, 1sh6p, 2sh, 2sh6p, 3sh, 4sh and 5sh of type A3 are in color on colorless tablet. No. 86 is on chalky paper.

1921-22 **Wmk. 4**

87 A4 ½p green .35 *22.50*
88 A4 1p carmine 2.75 *11.00*
89 A4 1½p ol grn & bl grn 3.00 *24.00*
90 A4 2p gray 1.50 *2.75*
91 A4 2½p ultramarine .75 *13.00*
92 A4 5p org & violet 2.00 *26.00*
93 A4 6p dl vio & red vio 3.50 *22.50*
94 A4 7½p brn & ultra 3.25 *57.50*
95 A4 10p yel grn & car rose 12.00 *27.50*
96 A4 4sh gray & red ('22) *110.00 225.00*
Nos. 87-96 (10) *139.10 431.75*
Set, ovptd. "SPECIMEN" 240.00

No. 96 is on chalky paper.

George V and Elephant — A5

George V — A6

1922-27 **Engr.** **Wmk. 4**
Head and Shield in Black

102 A5 ½p green .65 .65
a. ½p deep green ('25) 8.50 2.25
103 A5 1p brown 1.10 .30
104 A5 1½p carmine 1.10 .30
105 A5 2p gray 1.75 *5.00*
106 A5 2½p orange 3.00 *15.00*
107 A5 3p ultramarine 1.10 .25
108 A5 4p car, *org* ('27) 27.50 *39.00*
109 A5 5p yellow green 4.50 *17.50*
110 A5 6p claret 1.50 1.00
111 A5 7½p vio, *yel* ('27) 24.00 *95.00*
112 A5 10p blue 7.50 *24.00*
113 A6 1sh vio, *org* ('24) 5.25 2.50
a. 1sh dk violet, *yel buff* ('29) 75.00 50.00
114 A6 1sh6p blue 25.00 23.00
115 A6 2sh vio, *blue* 15.00 8.50
116 A6 2sh6p dark green 15.00 *14.00*
117 A6 3sh aniline vio 34.00 *95.00*
a. 3sh black purple 290.00 *475.00*
118 A6 4sh brown 35.00 *24.00*
119 A6 5sh dk grn, *yel* ('26) 52.50 *82.50*
120 A6 10sh yellow green 85.00 *150.00*
Nos. 102-120 (19) 340.45 *597.50*
Set, ovptd. "SPECIMEN" 600.00

1922, Sept. 1 **Wmk. 3**
Head & Shield in Black

121 A5 4p carmine, *yel* 7.25 *7.25*
122 A5 7½p violet, *yel* 9.50 *11.50*
123 A6 1sh violet, *orange* 42.50 *52.50*
124 A6 5sh dk green, *yel* 77.50 *260.00*
Nos. 121-124 (4) 136.75 *331.25*
Set, ovptd. "SPECIMEN" 190.00

The Specimen overprint on No. 124 is handstamped.

Common Design Types pictured following the introduction.

Silver Jubilee Issue
Common Design Type

1935, May 6 **Wmk. 4** ***Perf. 11x12***

125 CD301 1½p carmine & bl .55 *2.75*
Never hinged 1.10
126 CD301 3p ultra & brn 1.00 *2.50*
Never hinged 1.75
127 CD301 6p ol grn & lt bl 1.90 *7.00*
Never hinged 3.75
128 CD301 1sh brn vio & ind 8.75 *13.00*
Never hinged 17.00
Nos. 125-128 (4) 12.20 *25.25*
Set, never hinged 22.50
Set, perf "SPECIMEN" 140.00

Coronation Issue
Common Design Type

1937, May 12 ***Perf. 11x11½***

129 CD302 1p brown .25 *1.10*
Never hinged .35
130 CD302 1½p dark carmine .25 *1.10*
Never hinged .35
131 CD302 3p deep ultra .45 *1.75*
Never hinged .75
Nos. 129-131 (3) .95 3.95
Set, never hinged 1.45
Set, perf "SPECIMEN" 125.00

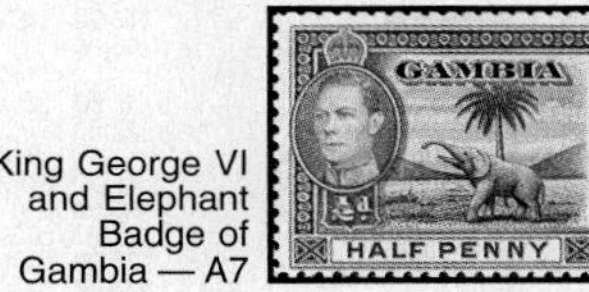

King George VI and Elephant Badge of Gambia — A7

1938-46 ***Perf. 12***

132 A7 ½p bl grn & blk .25 *.70*
Never hinged .25
133 A7 1p brn & red vio .25 *.55*
Never hinged .25
134 A7 1½p rose red & brn lake .25 2.00
Never hinged .25
b. 1½ scarlet & brn lake 4.00 5.75
Never hinged .25
c. 1½ br car & brn lake 175.00 14.00
Never hinged 210.00
134A A7 1½p gray blk & ultra ('44) .25 1.50
Never hinged .30
135 A7 2p gray blk & ultra 8.50 3.50
Never hinged 16.00
135A A7 2p rose red & brn lake ('43) .95 2.25
Never hinged 1.40
136 A7 3p blue & brt bl .25 .25
Never hinged .40
136A A7 5p dk vio brn & olive ('41) .45 .60
Never hinged .60
137 A7 6p plum & ol grn 1.75 .40
Never hinged 3.00
138 A7 1sh vio & sl blk 2.75 .25
Never hinged 5.00
138A A7 1sh3p bl & choc ('46) 2.25 *2.50*
Never hinged 4.25
139 A7 2sh bl & dp rose 7.50 3.25
Never hinged 12.00
140 A7 2sh6p sl grn & sep 9.50 2.50
Never hinged 16.00
141 A7 4sh dk vio & red orange 21.00 2.50
Never hinged 35.00
142 A7 5sh org red & dk blue 21.00 4.00
Never hinged 35.00
143 A7 10sh blk & yel org 22.50 8.50
Never hinged 40.00
Nos. 132-143 (16) 99.40 35.25
Set, never hinged 170.00
Set, perf "SPECIMEN" 575.00

Issued: 5p, 3/13; No. 135A, 10/1; No. 134A, 1/22; 1sh3p, 11/28; others, 4/1.

Catalogue values for unused stamps in this section, from this point to the end of the section, are for Never Hinged items.

Peace Issue
Common Design Type

1946, Aug. 6 **Engr.** ***Perf. 13½***

144 CD303 1½p black .25 .50
145 CD303 3p deep blue .25 .45
Set, perf "SPECIMEN" 110.00

Silver Wedding Issue
Common Design Types

1948, Dec. 24 **Photo.** ***Perf. 14x14½***

146 CD304 1½p black .25 .25

Perf. 11½x11
Engr.; Name Typo.

147 CD305 £1 purple 21.00 *21.00*

UPU Issue
Common Design Types
Engr.; Name Typo. on 3p, 6p
Perf. 13½, 11x11½

1949, Oct. 10 **Wmk. 4**

148 CD306 1½p slate .35 *1.50*
149 CD307 3p indigo 1.50 2.00
150 CD308 6p red lilac .75 3.00
151 CD309 1sh violet .50 .60
Nos. 148-151 (4) 3.10 7.10

GEORGIA

'jor-jə

LOCATION — In the southern part of Russia, bordering on the Black Sea and occupying the entire western part of Trans-Caucasia
GOVT. — A Soviet Socialist Republic
AREA — 25,760 sq. mi. (1920)
POP. — 2,372,403 (1920)
CAPITAL — Tbilisi (Tiflis)

Georgia was formerly a province of the Russian Empire and later a part of the Transcaucasian Federation of Soviet Republics. Stamps of Georgia were replaced in 1923 by those of Transcaucasian Federated Republics.

100 Kopecks = 1 Ruble

Tiflis

A 6k local stamp, imperforate and embossed without color on white paper, was issued in November, 1857, at Tiflis by authority of the viceroy. The square design shows a coat of arms.

National Republic

St. George
A1 A2

1919 **Litho.** **Unwmk.** ***Perf. 11½***

1 A1 10k blue .80 .80
2 A1 40k red orange .80 .80
a. Tête bêche pair 50.00 50.00
3 A1 50k emerald .80 .80
4 A1 60k red .80 .80
5 A1 70k claret .80 *.80*
6 A2 1r orange brown .80 *.80*
Nos. 1-6 (6) 4.80 4.80

Imperf

7 A1 10k blue .80 .80
8 A1 40k red orange .80 .80
a. Tête bêche pair 50.00 50.00
9 A1 50k emerald .80 .80
10 A1 60k red .80 .80
11 A1 70k claret .80 *.80*
12 A2 1r orange brown .80 *.80*
Nos. 7-12 (6) 4.80 4.80

Queen Thamar — A3

1920 ***Perf. 11½***

13 A3 2r red brown .65 1.25
14 A3 3r gray blue .65 1.25
15 A3 5r orange .65 1.25
Nos. 13-15 (3) 1.95 3.75

Imperf

16 A3 2r red brown .65 1.25
17 A3 3r gray blue .65 1.25
18 A3 5r orange .65 1.25
Nos. 16-18 (3) 1.95 3.75

Nos. 1-18 with parts of design inverted, sideways or omitted are fraudulent varieties.

Overprints meaning "Day of the National Guard, 12, 12, 1920" (5 lines) and "Recognition of Independence, 27, 1, 1921" (4 lines) were applied, probably in Italy, to remainders taken by government officials who fled when Russian forces occupied Georgia. Value, set $30.

"Constantinople" and new values were unofficially surcharged on stamps of 1919-20 by a consul in Turkey.

Soviet Socialist Republic

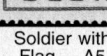

Soldier with Flag — A5

Peasant Sowing Grain — A6

Industry and Agriculture — A7

1922 **Unwmk.** ***Perf. 11½***

26 A5 500r rose 8.00 5.00
27 A6 1000r bister brown 8.00 5.00
28 A7 2000r slate 11.50 8.00
29 A7 3000r brown 11.50 8.00
30 A7 5000r green 11.50 8.00
Nos. 26-30 (5) 50.50 34.00

Forgeries exist of Nos. 26-30.

Nos. 26 to 30 exist imperforate but were not so issued. Value for set, $200.

Nos. 26-30 Handstamped with New Values in Violet

1923

36 A6 10,000r on 1000r 7.50 6.50
a. Black surcharge 25.00 *25.00*
b. 20,000r on 1000r 200.00
37 A7 15,000r on 2000r, blk surch. 7.75 *8.50*
a. Violet surcharge 30.00 30.00
38 A5 20,000r on 500r 7.75 *8.50*
a. Black surcharge 15.00 7.50
39 A7 40,000r on 5000r 7.50 5.50
a. Black surcharge 15.00 *15.00*
40 A7 80,000r on 3000r 7.75 *8.50*
a. Black surcharge 15.00 *17.50*
Nos. 36-40 (5) 38.25 *37.50*

There were two types of the handstamped surcharges, with the numerals 5½mm and 6½mm high. The impressions are often too indistinct to measure or even to distinguish the numerals.

Double and inverted surcharges exist, as is usual with handstamps.

Surcharged in Black

43 A6 10,000r on 1000r 7.00 7.00
44 A7 15,000r on 2000r 4.50 4.50
45 A5 20,000r on 500r 2.25 2.25
46 A7 40,000r on 5000r 4.50 4.50
47 A7 80,000r on 3000r 4.50 4.50
Nos. 43-47 (5) 22.75 *22.75*

Nos. 43, 45, 46 and 47 exist imperforate but were not so issued. Value $25 each.

Russian Stamps of 1909-18 Handstamp Surcharged

Type I — Surcharge 20x5½mm.
Type II — Surcharge 22x7¼mm.

1923 ***Perf. 14½x15***

No.	Type	Description	Unused	Used
48	A14	10,000r on 7k lt bl	150.00	150.00
49	A11	15,000r on 15k red brn & bl (I)	15.00	15.00
a.		Type II	10.00	10.00

Type I Surcharge Handstamped on Armenia No. 141

No.	Type	Description	Unused	Used
50	A11	15,000r on 5r on 15k red brn & bl	500.00	*500.00*
a.		Type II		500.00
		Nos. 48-50 (3)	*665.00*	*665.00*

Russian Stamps and Types of 1909-18 Surcharged in Dark Blue or Black

1923 ***Perf. 11½, 14½x15***

No.	Type	Description	Unused	Used
51	A14	75,000r on 1k org	3.00	*4.25*
a.		Imperf.	150.00	*150.00*
52	A14	200,000r on 5k cl	4.00	*5.00*
53	A8	300,000r on 20k bl & car (Bk)	4.00	*5.00*
a.		Dark blue surcharge	70.00	*100.00*
54	A14	350,000r on 3k red	7.00	*8.00*
a.		Imperf.	7.00	*7.25*

Imperf

No.	Type	Description	Unused	Used
55	A14	700,000r on 2k grn	7.00	*10.00*
a.		Perf. 14½x15	27.50	*32.50*
		Nos. 51-55 (5)	25.00	*32.25*

SEMI-POSTAL STAMPS

Surcharge in Red or Black

SP1

SP2

SP3

SP4

1922 **Unwmk.** ***Perf. 11½***

No.	Type	Description	Unused	Used
B1	SP1	1000r on 50r vio (R)	.75	*3.00*
B2	SP2	3000r on 100r brn red	.75	*3.00*
B3	SP3	5000r on 250r gray grn	.75	*3.00*
B4	SP4	10,000r on 25r blue (R)	.75	*3.00*
		Nos. B1-B4 (4)	3.00	*12.00*

Nos. B1-B4 exist imperf but were not so issued. Value slightly more than perforated examples.

GERMAN EAST AFRICA

'jər-mən 'ēst 'a-fri-kə

LOCATION — In East Africa, bordering on the Indian Ocean
GOVT. — German Colony
AREA — 384,180 sq. mi.
POP. — 7,680,132 (1913)
CAPITAL — Dar-es Salaam

Following World War I, the greater part of this German Colonial possession was mandated to Great Britain. The British ceded to the Belgians the provinces of Ruanda and Urundi. The Kionga triangle was awarded to the Portuguese and became part of the Mozambique Colony. The remaining area became the British Mandated Territory of Tanganyika.

64 Pesa = 1 Rupee
100 Heller = 1 Rupee (1905)
100 Centimes = 1 Franc (1916)

Stamps of Germany Surcharged in Black

1893 **Unwmk.** ***Perf. 13½x14½***

Surcharge 15¼mm long

No.	Type	Description	Unused	Used
1	A9	2pes on 3pf brown	37.50	*47.50*
		Never hinged	170.00	
		On cover		340.00
a.		Surcharge 16¾mm long	—	
		Never hinged	—	
2	A9	3pes on 5pf green	45.00	*47.50*
		Never hinged	225.00	
		On cover		340.00
a.		Surcharge 14¼mm long	*850.00*	
		Never hinged	*2,000.*	
b.		Surcharge 16¼mm long	*1,100.*	
		Never hinged	*2,200.*	
3	A10	5pes on 10pf car	35.00	27.50
		Never hinged	190.00	
		On cover		175.00
a.		Surcharge 14¼mm long	*2,100.*	
		Never hinged	*6,000.*	
b.		Surcharge 16¼mm long	*2,100.*	
		Never hinged	*6,000.*	

Surcharge 16¼mm long

No.	Type	Description	Unused	Used
4	A10	10pes on 20pf ultra	27.50	14.00
		Never hinged	120.00	
		On cover		80.00

Surcharge 16¾mm long

No.	Type	Description	Unused	Used
5	A10	25pes on 50pf red brn	35.00	27.50
		Never hinged	125.00	
		On cover		140.00
a.		Surcharge 17½mm long	*100.00*	*42.50*
		Never hinged	*300.00*	
		On cover		150.00
		Nos. 1-5 (5)	180.00	164.00

Covers: Value for No. 5 is for overfranked complete covers, usually philatelic.

Stamps of Germany Surcharged in Black

1896

No.	Type	Description	Unused	Used
6	A9	2pes on 3pf dk brn	2.10	*37.50*
		Never hinged	6.75	
		On cover		175.00
a.		2pes on 3pf light brown	28.00	*45.00*
		Never hinged	100.00	
		On cover		210.00
b.		2pes on 3pf grayish brown	11.50	11.50
		Never hinged	35.00	
		On cover		67.50
c.		2pes on 3pf reddish brown	110.00	*200.00*
		Never hinged	450.00	
		On cover		750.00
7	A9	3pes on 5pf green	2.50	*4.50*
		Never hinged	6.00	
		On cover		35.00
8	A10	5pes on 10pf car	4.75	4.50
		Never hinged	12.50	
		On cover		35.00
9	A10	10pes on 20pf ultra	5.25	5.25
		Never hinged	15.00	
		On cover		42.50
10	A10	25pes on 50pf red brn	23.00	*28.00*
		Never hinged	92.50	
		On cover		85.00
		Nos. 6-10 (5)	37.60	*79.75*

Covers: Value for No. 10 is for overfranked complete covers, usually philatelic.

A5

Kaiser's Yacht "Hohenzollern" — A6

1900 **Typo.** ***Perf. 14***

No.	Type	Description	Unused	Used
11	A5	2p brown	2.75	1.60
		Never hinged	7.50	
		On cover		67.50
12	A5	3p green	2.75	2.00
		Never hinged	7.50	
		On cover		30.00
13	A5	5p carmine	3.25	2.50
		Never hinged	11.00	
		On cover		35.00
14	A5	10p ultra	5.25	4.75
		Never hinged	17.00	
		On cover		60.00
15	A5	15p org & blk, *sal*	5.25	*6.50*
		Never hinged	19.00	
		On cover		85.00
16	A5	20p lake & blk	7.25	*14.00*
		Never hinged	27.50	
		On cover		85.00
17	A5	25p pur & blk, *sal*	7.25	*14.00*
		Never hinged	24.00	
		On cover		42.50
18	A5	40p lake & blk, *rose*	8.75	*22.50*
		Never hinged	27.50	
		On cover		72.50

Engr.

Perf. 14½x14

No.	Type	Description	Unused	Used
19	A6	1r claret	19.00	*47.50*
		Never hinged	60.00	
		On cover		120.00
20	A6	2r yel green	9.50	*80.00*
		Never hinged	27.50	
		On cover		240.00
21	A6	3r car & slate	200.00	*300.00*
		Never hinged	450.00	
		On cover		500.00
a.		red & slate	120.00	180.00
		Never hinged	300.00	
		On cover		425.00
		Nos. 11-21 (11)	271.00	*495.35*

Covers: Values for Nos. 17-21 are for overfranked complete covers, usually philatelic.

Value in Heller

1905 **Typo.** ***Perf. 14***

No.	Type	Description	Unused	Used
22	A5	2½h brown	4.00	1.75
		Never hinged	13.50	
		On cover		21.00
23	A5	4h dk olive green	14.00	5.50
		Never hinged	45.00	
		On cover		21.00
a.		4h green	14.00	1.60
		Never hinged	35.00	
		On cover		55.00
b.		4h dark yellowish green	27.50	*20.00*
		Never hinged	100.00	
		On cover		45.00
24	A5	7½h carmine	14.00	1.60
		Never hinged	35.00	
		On cover		17.00
25	A5	15h ultra	24.00	6.00
		Never hinged	60.00	
		On cover		25.00
a.		15h violet blue	47.50	16.00
		Never hinged	150.00	
		On cover		45.00
26	A5	20h org & blk, *yel*	14.00	*16.00*
		Never hinged	35.00	
		On cover		45.00
27	A5	30h lake & blk	14.00	6.00
		Never hinged	35.00	
		On cover		19.00
28	A5	45h pur & blk	27.50	*35.00*
		Never hinged	60.00	
		On cover		85.00
29	A5	60h lake & blk, *rose*	35.00	*95.00*
		Never hinged	120.00	
		On cover		275.00
		Nos. 22-29 (8)	146.50	*166.85*

Covers: Values for Nos. 27-29 are for overfranked complete covers, usually philatelic.

1905-16 **Wmk. Lozenges (125)**

No.	Type	Description	Unused	Used
31	A5	2½h brn ('06)	.95	.95
		Never hinged	3.00	
		On cover		25.00
32	A5	4h grn ('06)	.95	.65
		Never hinged	3.25	
		On cover		17.00
b.		Booklet pane of 4 + 2 labels	45.00	
		Never hinged	100.00	
c.		Booklet pane of 5 + label	*400.00*	
		Never hinged	700.00	
33	A5	7½h car ('06)	1.10	*1.60*
		Never hinged	4.75	
		On cover		17.00
b.		Booklet pane of 4 + 2 labels	45.00	
		Never hinged	100.00	
c.		Booklet pane of 5 + label	*400.00*	
		Never hinged	700.00	
34	A5	15h dk blue ('08)	2.25	1.50
		Never hinged	10.00	
		On cover		21.00
a.		15h ultramarine ('06)	10.00	11.00
		Never hinged	25.00	
		On cover		42.50
35	A5	20h org & blk, *yel* ('11)	2.50	*20.00*
		Never hinged	9.25	
		On cover		67.50
36	A5	30h lake & blk ('09)	2.60	*8.00*
		Never hinged	9.25	
		On cover		50.00
37	A5	45h pur & blk ('06)	5.50	*55.00*
		Never hinged	20.00	
		On cover		300.00
38	A5	60h lake & blk, *rose*	30.00	*190.00*
		Never hinged	75.00	
		On cover		425.00

Engr.

Perf. 14½x14

No.	Type	Description	Unused	Used
39	A6	1r red ('16)	12.00	*25,000.*
		Never hinged	85.00	
		On cover		*55,000.*
40	A6	2r yel grn	47.50	
		Never hinged	110.00	
41	A6	3r car & sl ('08)	47.50	*240.00*
		Never hinged	140.00	
		On cover		500.00
a.		3r red & blackish green ('08)	160.00	*400.00*
		Never hinged	475.00	
		On cover		675.00
		Nos. 31-41 (11)	152.85	25,518.

No. 40 was never placed in use.

The frame of No. 41a fluoresces bright orange under ultra-violet light.

Booklet panes of 6 made from sheet stamps exist of the 4h and 7½h.

Forged cancellations are found on Nos. 35-39, 41.

Covers: Values for Nos. 37-38, 41 are for overfranked complete covers, usually philatelic.

In early 1916, German East African authorities ordered supplies of provisional stamps, printed by the press of the Evangelical Mission in Wuga. Three values in denominations most urgently needed were produced in March, but before they could be issued, new stocks of regular stamps were received from Germany. To prevent their capture by the British, the provisionals were buried until 1922, when they were retrieved by the German government and sold at auction. Because of their long storage in the tropical climate, 90-95% of the stamps were destroyed and those surviving are usually brittle and somewhat faded.

Values: 2½h violet brown, $55; 7½h, carmine, $25; 1r pink, $1,400.

OCCUPATION STAMPS

Issued Under Belgian Occupation
Stamps of Belgian Congo, 1915, Handstamped "RUANDA" in Black, Blue or Red Violet

1916 **Unwmk.** ***Perf. 13½ to 15***

No.	Type	Description	Unused
N1	A29	5c green & blk	65.00
N2	A30	10c carmine & blk	65.00
N3	A21	15c blue grn & blk	125.00
N4	A31	25c blue & blk	65.00
N5	A23	40c brown red & blk	65.00
N6	A24	50c brown lake & blk	75.00
N7	A25	1fr olive bis & blk	400.00
N8	A27	5fr ocher & blk	*4,000.*
		Nos. N1-N7 (7)	860.00

Stamps of Belgian Congo, 1915, Handstamped "URUNDI" in Black, Blue or Red Violet

No.	Type	Description	Unused
N9	A29	5c green & blk	65.00
N10	A30	10c carmine & blk	65.00
N11	A21	15c bl grn & blk	125.00
N12	A31	25c blue & blk	65.00
N13	A23	40c brn red & blk	65.00
N14	A24	50c brn lake & blk	75.00
N15	A25	1fr ol bis & blk	400.00
N16	A27	5fr ocher & blk	*4,000.*
		Nos. N9-N15 (7)	860.00

Stamps of Belgian Congo overprinted "Karema," "Kigoma" and "Tabora" were not officially authorized.

Nos. N1-N16 exist with forged overprint.

Stamps of Belgian Congo, 1915, Ovptd. in Dark Blue

1916 *Perf. 12½ to 15*

N17 A29 5c green & blk 1.00 .30
On cover —
b. Inverted overprint 225.00 —
N18 A30 10c carmine & blk 1.25 .50
On cover 32.50
a. Inverted overprint 225.00
N19 A21 15c bl grn & blk 1.00 .30
On cover 27.50
N20 A31 25c blue & blk 7.25 1.75
On cover 37.50
N21 A23 40c brn red & blk 20.00 6.00
On cover 70.00
N22 A24 50c brn lake & blk 27.50 6.00
On cover 45.00
N23 A25 1fr olive bis & blk 3.00 .75
On cover —
a. Double overprint
N24 A27 5fr ocher & blk 3.50 1.75
On cover —
Nos. N17-N24 (8) 64.50 17.35

Nos. N17-N18, N20-N22 Surcharged in Black or Red

1922

N25 A24 5c on 50c brn lake & blk .75 .45
Never hinged 1.50
On cover —
N26 A29 10c on 5c grn & blk (R) .75 .40
Never hinged 1.50
On cover 22.50
N27 A23 25c on 40c brn red & blk (R) 3.75 2.75
Never hinged 16.50
On cover 27.50
N28 A30 30c on 10c car & blk .75 .30
Never hinged 1.50
On cover 27.50
N29 A31 50c on 25c bl & blk (R) .75 .30
Never hinged 1.50
On cover 27.50
Nos. N25-N29 (5) 6.75 4.20

No. N25 has the surcharge at each side.

ISSUED UNDER BRITISH OCCUPATION

Stamps of Nyasaland Protectorate, 1913-15 Overprinted

1916 **Wmk. 3** *Perf. 14*

N101 A3 ½p green 1.75 9.50
a. Double overprint (R & Bk)
N102 A3 1p carmine 1.75 3.75
N103 A3 3p violet, *yel* 27.50 18.00
a. Double overprint 26,000.
N104 A3 4p scar & blk, *yel* 52.50 42.00
N105 A3 1sh black, *green* 72.50 72.50
Nos. N101-N105 (5) 156.00 145.75
Set, ovptd. "SPECIMEN" 190.00

"N.F." stands for "Nyasaland Force."

Stamps of East Africa and Uganda, 1912-14, Overprinted in Black or Red

1917

N106 A3 1c black (R) .25 .95
N107 A3 3c blue green .25 .25
N108 A3 6c carmine .25 .25
N109 A3 10c brown orange .60 .70
N110 A3 12c gray .60 3.00
N111 A3 15c ultramarine 1.90 3.50
N112 A3 25c scar & blk, *yel* .90 4.50
N113 A3 50c violet & blk 2.50 5.00
N114 A3 75c blk, *bl grn, olive back* (R) 1.25 4.50
a. 75c black, *emerald* (R) 3.75 52.50

Overprinted

N115 A4 1r blk, *green* (R) 6.50 8.00
a. 1r black, *emerald* (R) 14.00 65.00
N116 A4 2r blk & red, *bl* 15.00 62.50
N117 A4 3r gray grn & vio 17.50 95.00
N118 A4 4r grn & red, *yel* 27.50 120.00
N119 A4 5r dl vio & ultra 52.50 140.00
N120 A4 10r grn & red, *grn* 160.00 450.00
a. 10r grn & red, *emerald* 210.00 700.00
N121 A3 20r vio & blk, *red* 325.00 700.00
N122 A3 50r gray grn & red 750.00 1,200.
Nos. N106-N120 (15) 287.50 898.15

See Tanganyika for "G.E.A." overprints on stamps inscribed "East Africa and Uganda Protectorates" with watermark 4.

SEMI-POSTAL STAMPS

Issued under Belgian Occupation

Semi-Postal Stamps of Belgian Congo, 1915, Overprinted

1918 **Unwmk.** *Perf. 14, 15*

NB1 A29 5c + 10c grn & bl .50 .50
Never hinged 1.25
NB2 A30 10c + 15c car & bl .80 .50
Never hinged 1.60
NB3 A21 15c + 20c bl grn & bl 1.00 .50
Never hinged 2.00
NB4 A31 25c + 25c dp & pale bl 1.50 .50
Never hinged 3.00
NB5 A23 40c + 40c brn red & bl 1.00 .75
Never hinged 3.75
NB6 A24 50c + 50c brn lake & bl 1.50 1.00
Never hinged 4.50
NB7 A25 1fr + 1fr ol bis & bl 3.00 3.00
Never hinged 4.25
NB8 A27 5fr + 5fr ocher & bl 10.00 10.00
Never hinged 17.00
NB9 A28 10fr + 10fr grn & bl 95.00 95.00
Never hinged 200.00
Nos. NB1-NB9 (9) 114.30 111.75

The letters "A.O." are the initials of "Afrique Orientale" (East Africa).

MAFIA ISLAND

Mafia is a small island on the Indian Ocean coast of German East Africa, near the mouth of the Rufiji River. It was captured by the British in December, 1914, and in January, 1915, the military authorities began to overprint stamps for the use of civilian personnel on the island. Overprinted stamps were used, until the island's transfer to Tanganyikan administration in 1918.

Stamps of German East Africa with Manuscript Overpint "G R Mafia J D M."

1915

NL1 A5 2½h brown 3,750.
NL2 A5 4h green 3,750.
a. Mss. "JDM GR Mafia" 4,250.
NL3 A5 7½h carmine 3,750.
a. Mss. "JDM GR Mafia"
NL4 A5 15h ultra 3,750.
NL5 A5 20h org & blk, *yel* —
NL6 A5 30h lake & blk —
NL7 A5 45h pur & blk —
NL8 A6 2r yel grn —

Initials are those of Lt. Col. J.D. Mackay, Military Governor.

German East Africa #31//41, Zanzibar #141//146 Handstamped

1915, Jan. **Black Overprint**

NL9 A5 2½h brown 1,200.
NL10 A5 4h green 1,050.
a. Double ovpt. —
NL11 A5 7½h carmine 625.00
a. Pair, one without ovpt. 8,250.
NL12 A5 15h ultra 675.00
NL13 A5 20h org & blk, *yel* 975.00
NL14 A5 30h lake & blk 1,100.
a. Pair, one without ovpt. 9,000.
NL15 A5 45h pur & blk 1,100.
a. Pair, one without ovpt. 9,000.
NL16 A6 1r red 16,500.
NL17 A6 2r yel grn 18,000.
NL18 A6 3r car & slate 19,500.

Deep Purple Overprint

NL19 A5 4h green 1,350.
NL20 A5 7½h carmine 825.00
NL21 A5 15h ultra 1,050.
NL22 A5 20h org & blk, *yel* 1,200.
a. Pair, one without ovpt. 7,500.
b. Double ovpt. —
NL23 A5 30h lake & blk 1,650.
a. Double ovpt. —
NL24 A5 45h pur & blk 1,650.

Reddish Violet Overprint

NL25 A5 2½h brown 300.00
a. Pair, one without ovpt. 4,850.
b. Initialled "JDM" 2,250.
NL26 A5 4h green 450.00
a. Pair, one without ovpt. 4,850.
b. Initialled "JDM" 2,250.
NL27 A5 7½h carmine 150.00
a. Pair, one without ovpt. 3,750.
b. Initialled "JDM" 2,250.
NL28 A5 15h ultra 250.00
a. Pair, one without ovpt. 4,250.
b. Initialled "JDM" 2,250.
NL29 A5 20h org & blk, *yel* 500.00
a. Pair, one without ovpt. 5,000.
b. Initialled "JDM" 2,000.
NL30 A5 30h lake & blk 550.00
a. Pair, one without ovpt. 5,000.
b. Initialled "JDM" 2,500.
NL31 A5 45h pur & blk 675.00
a. Pair, one without ovpt. 5,500.
b. Initialled "JDM" 2,500.
NL32 A6 1r red 11,000.
NL33 A6 2r yel grn 12,500.
NL34 A6 3r car & slate 14,500.

The reddish violet overprint is often underinked and may be faint.

On Zanzibar 1915 Issue

Surcharge in Black

NL35 1c gray (#141) —
NL36 3c yel grn (#142) —
NL37 6c carmine (#143) 1,650. 1,500.
NL38 15c ultra (#146) —

German East Africa #13//41, Zanzibar #141, 143 With Handstamped Ovpt. & Srchd.

No. NL44

No. NL49

1915, May

On 1900 Issue

NL39 A5 6c on 5p carmine —
NL40 A5 6c on 20p lake & blk —
NL41 A5 6c on 40p car —

On 1905-16 Issues

Surcharge in Green, Violet or Black

NL42 A5 6c on 2½h brown 2,400. 2,550.
a. Pair, one without surcharge 9,750.
b. Inverted surcharge
c. Double surcharge
NL43 A5 6c on 4h green 2,550. 2,750.
a. Pair, one without surcharge 9,750.
b. Inverted surcharge
c. Double surcharge
NL44 A5 6c on 7½h car 2,450. 2,750.
a. Pair, one without surcharge
b. Inverted surcharge
c. Double surcharge
NL45 A5 6c on 15h ultra 2,250. 2,750.
a. Double surcharge
b. Triple surcharge
c. Inverted surcharge
NL46 A5 6c on 20h org & blk, *yel* 3,350. 3,400.
a. Inverted surcharge
NL47 A5 6c on 30h lake & blk 4,100. 4,500.
a. Inverted surcharge
NL48 A5 6c on 45h pur & blk 4,100. 4,100.
a. Pair, one without surcharge
b. Inverted surcharge
NL49 A6 6c on 1r red 57,500.
a. Double surcharge
NL50 A6 6c on 2r yel grn 62,500.
a. Double surcharge
NL51 A6 6c on 3r car & slate 72,500.

On Zanzibar 1914 Issue

Surcharge in Black

NL52 6c on 1c gray (#141) —
NL53 6c on 6c car (#143) —

German East Africa Fiscal Stamps Handstamped in Bluish Green or Violet

No. NL56

Inscribed "Statistik Des Waaren-Verkehrs"

1915, Sept.

NL54 24p ver, *buff* 1,100. 1,650.
NL55 12½p brown 1,200. 1,800.
a. Pair, one without overprint 15,000.
NL56 25h dull green 1,200. 1,800.
NL57 50h slate 1,200. 1,800.
a. Pair, one without overprint 15,000.
NL58 1r lilac 1,200. 1,800.

No. NL59

Inscribed "Ubersetzungs Gebuhren"

NL59 25h gray 1,200. 1,800.

Handstamped in three lines, serifed type

1915, Sept. **On Nos. NL55-60**

NL60 24p ver, *buff*, (#55) 1,650.
NL61 12½p brn (#56) 1,800.
a. "G.R. POST MAFIA" inverted
NL62 25h dl grn (#57) 1,800.
NL63 50h slate (#58) 1,800.
NL64 1r lilac (#59) 1,800.

NL65 25h gray (#60) 1,800.
a. Pair, one without overprint *11,250.*

No. NL67

On unoverprinted Fiscal Stamps

NL66 24p ver, *buff* —
NL67 12½p brown —
NL68 25h dull grn —
NL69 50h slate —
NL70 1r lilac —
NL71 25h gray —
a. Inverted ovpt.

On German East African Stamps in Green, Violet or Black

NL72 A5 7½h carmine —
NL73 A5 20h org & blk, *yel* —
NL74 A5 30h lake & blk —

On Zanzibar Stamps in Green, Violet or Black

NL75 1c gray (#141) —
NL76 3c yel grn (#142) —
NL77 6c car (#143) —
NL78 15c ultra (#146) —

On Indian Expeditionary Force Stamps (India #M34-M43) in Green, Greenish Black or Blue

NL79 3p gray (#M34) 55.00 *125.00*
a. Pair, one without overprint *2,750.*
NL80 ½a grn (#M35) 82.50 *135.00*
a. Pair, one without overprint 3,500. *2,750.*
NL81 1a car rose (#M36) 90.00 *135.00*
NL82 2a vio (#M37) 125.00 *225.00*
NL83 2½a ultra (#M38) 180.00 *275.00*
NL84 3a org brn (#M39) 195.00 *275.00*
a. Pair, one without overprint 4,500.
NL85 4a ol grn (#M40) 225.00 *375.00*
NL86 8a pur (#M41) 410.00 *600.00*
a. Pair, one without overprint *5,000.*
NL87 12a dl clar (#M42) 475.00 *750.00*
NL88 1r grn & red brn (#M43) 550.00 *825.00*
a. Double overprint, one inverted *2,750.*

Handstamp exists inverted, double and sideways.

Handstamped in three lines, sans-serif italic type, in green, greenish black or blue

On Indian Expeditionary Force Stamps (India #M34-M43)

1916, Oct.

NL89 3p gray (#M34) *250.00* *250.00*
NL90 ½a green (#M35) *275.00* *275.00*
NL91 1a car rose (#M36) *225.00* *250.00*
NL92 2a violet (#M37) *300.00* *300.00*
NL93 2½a ultra (#M38) *300.00* *350.00*
NL94 3a org brn (#M39) *325.00* *500.00*
NL95 4a ol grn (#M40) *500.00* *500.00*
NL96 8a pur (#M41) *600.00* *675.00*
NL97 12a dl clar (#M42) *700.00* *800.00*
NL98 1r grn & red brn (#M43) *1,000.* *1,000.*

Some values exist with handstamp inverted.

GERMAN NEW GUINEA

ˈjər-mən ˈnü ˈgi-nē

LOCATION — A group of islands in the west Pacific Ocean, including a part of New Guinea and adjacent islands of the Bismarck Archipelago.
GOVT. — German Protectorate
AREA — 93,000 sq. mi.
POP. — 601,427 (1913)
CAPITAL — Herbertshohe (later Kokopo)

The islands were occupied by Australian troops during World War I and renamed "New Britain." By covenant of the League of Nations they were made a mandated territory of Australia in 1920. The old name of "New Guinea" has since been restored. Postage stamps were issued under all regimes.

For other listings see New Britain (1914-15), North West Pacific Islands (1915-22) and New Guinea.

100 Pfennig = 1 Mark

Stamps of Germany Overprinted in Black

1897-99 Unwmk. *Perf. 13½x14½*

1 A9 3pf brown 8.00 *8.00*
Never hinged 20.00
On cover 85.00
a. 3pf reddish brown ('99) 135.00 *240.00*
Never hinged 500.00
On cover 600.00
b. 3pf yellow brown ('98) 30.00 *57.50*
Never hinged 92.50
On cover 125.00
2 A9 5pf green 4.00 *5.00*
Never hinged 7.50
On cover 75.00
3 A10 10pf carmine 6.50 *8.00*
Never hinged 13.50
On cover 100.00
4 A10 20pf ultra 9.00 *12.00*
Never hinged 22.00
On cover 175.00
5 A10 25pf orange ('98) 29.00 *52.50*
Never hinged 67.50
On cover 175.00
a. Inverted overprint *2,250.*
Never hinged *4,500.*
6 A10 50pf red brown 32.50 *50.00*
Never hinged 85.00
On cover 100.00
Nos. 1-6 (6) 89.00 *135.50*

Covers: Value for No. 6 is for overfranked complete cover, usually philatelic.

A3

Kaiser's Yacht "Hohenzollern" — A4

1901 Typo. *Perf. 14*

7 A3 3pf brown 1.25 1.25
Never hinged 2.50
On cover 102.00
8 A3 5pf green 6.50 1.25
Never hinged 17.00
On cover 42.50
9 A3 10pf carmine 20.00 3.00
Never hinged 67.50
On cover 50.00
10 A3 20pf ultra 1.50 *3.00*
Never hinged 4.25
On cover 85.00
11 A3 25pf org & blk, *yel* 1.75 *16.00*
Never hinged 4.25
On cover 175.00
12 A3 30pf org & blk, *sal* 1.75 *20.00*
Never hinged 4.25
On cover 175.00
13 A3 40pf lake & blk 1.75 *23.00*
Never hinged 4.25
On cover 175.00
14 A3 50pf pur & blk, *sal* 2.00 *20.00*
Never hinged 4.25
On cover 60.00
15 A3 80pf lake & blk, *rose* 3.75 *27.50*
Never hinged 6.75
On cover 85.00

Engr.
Perf. 14½x14

16 A4 1m carmine 8.00 *52.50*
Never hinged 25.00
On cover 100.00
17 A4 2m blue 8.00 *77.50*
Never hinged 25.00
On cover 140.00
18 A4 3m blk vio 11.00 *150.00*
Never hinged 35.00
On cover 210.00
19 A4 5m slate & car 160.00 *500.00*
Never hinged 425.00
On cover 800.00
Nos. 7-19 (13) 227.25 *895.00*

Fake cancellations exist on Nos. 10-19.
Covers: Values for Nos. 14-19 are for overfranked complete cover, usually philatelic.

A5

A6

Nos. 21-23 have "NEUGUINEA" as one word without a hyphen.

Wmk. Lozenges (125)

1914-19 Typo. *Perf. 14*

20 A3 3pf brown ('19) .80
Never hinged 1.75
21 A5 5pf green 1.75
Never hinged 3.50
22 A5 10pf carmine 1.75
Never hinged 3.50

Engr.
Perf. 14½x14

23 A6 5m slate & carmine 32.50
Never hinged 120.00
Nos. 20-23 (4) 36.80

Nos. 20-23 were never placed in use.

GERMAN SOUTH WEST AFRICA

ˈjər-mən ˈsauth ˈwest ˈa-fri-kə

LOCATION — In southwest Africa, bordering on the South Atlantic.
GOVT. — German Colony
AREA — 322,450 sq. mi. (1913)
POP. — 94,372 (1913)
CAPITAL — Windhoek

The Colony was occupied by South African troops during World War I and in 1920 was mandated to the Union of South Africa by the League of Nations. See South-West Africa.

100 Pfennig = 1 Mark

Stamps of Germany Overprinted

1897 Unwmk. *Perf. 13½x14½*

1 A9 3pf dark brown 8.25 *12.00*
Never hinged 30.00
On cover 75.00
a. 3pf yellow brown 50.00 *2,800.*
Never hinged 160.00
On cover —
b. 3pf olive brown 60.00
Never hinged 190.00
c. 3pf reddish brown — *2,500.*
Never hinged
2 A9 5pf green 4.50 4.75
Never hinged 12.50
On cover 30.00
3 A10 10pf carmine 21.00 15.00
Never hinged 62.50
On cover 85.00
4 A10 20pf ultra 5.75 5.25
Never hinged 25.00
On cover 35.00
5 A10 25pf orange 225.00 *29,000.*
Never hinged 640.00
6 A10 50pf red brown 225.00 *29,000.*
Never hinged 640.00
Nos. 1-4 (4) 39.50 37.00

Nos. 5 and 6 were prepared for issue but were not sent to the Colony.

Overprinted in Black on 2 lines

1898-99

7 A9 3pf dark brown 4.00 *12.00*
Never hinged 17.00
On cover 110.00
a. 3pf reddish brown 52.50 *160.00*
Never hinged 190.00
On cover 640.00
b. 3pf yellow brown 7.00 *12.00*
Never hinged 22.50
On cover 55.00
8 A9 5pf green 3.25 3.25
Never hinged 11.00
On cover 21.00
9 A10 10pf carmine 3.25 4.00
Never hinged 11.00
On cover 21.00
10 A10 20pf ultra 11.50 *15.00*
Never hinged 47.50
On cover 50.00
11 A10 25pf orange 350.00 400.00
Never hinged 1,000.
On cover 850.00
12 A10 50pf red brown 12.00 12.00
Never hinged 50.00
On cover 50.00

Covers: Value for No. 12 is for overfranked complete covers, usually philatelic.

Kaiser's Yacht "Hohenzollern"
A3 A4

1901 Typo. *Perf. 14*

13 A3 3pf brown 4.00 1.60
Never hinged 10.00
On cover 67.50
14 A3 5pf green 20.00 1.60
Never hinged 50.00
On cover 17.00
15 A3 10pf carmine 14.00 .80
Never hinged 50.00
On cover 17.00
16 A3 20pf ultra 30.00 1.50
Never hinged 80.00
On cover 17.00
17 A3 25pf org & blk, *yel* 1.50 *5.50*
Never hinged 6.00
On cover 25.00
18 A3 30pf org & blk, *sal* 72.50 2.75
Never hinged 225.00
On cover 17.00
19 A3 40pf lake & blk 1.75 *3.25*
Never hinged 6.00
On cover 17.00
20 A3 50pf pur & blk, *sal* 2.10 2.10
Never hinged 6.75
On cover 17.00
21 A3 80pf lake & blk, *rose* 2.10 *9.00*
Never hinged 6.75
On cover 37.50

Engr.

Perf. 14½x14

No.	Type	Description	Unused	Used
22	A4	1m carmine	110.00	30.00
		Never hinged	375.00	
		On cover		67.50
23	A4	2m blue	30.00	*37.50*
		Never hinged	100.00	
		On cover		75.00
24	A4	3m blk vio	32.50	*50.00*
		Never hinged	125.00	
		On cover		92.50
25	A4	5m slate & car	200.00	160.00
		Never hinged	400.00	
		On cover		375.00
		Nos. 13-25 (13)	520.45	*305.60*

Covers: Values for Nos. 20-25 are for over-franked complete covers, usually philatelic.

Wmk. Lozenges (125)

1906-19 Typo. *Perf. 14*

No.	Type	Description	Unused	Used
26	A3	3pf dk brn ('07)	.80	*3.75*
		Never hinged	2.10	
		On cover		50.00
a.		3pf yellow brown ('13)	.80	*2.90*
		Never hinged	2.00	
		On cover		32.50
27	A3	5pf green	.80	*1.50*
		Never hinged	2.10	
		On cover		21.00
b.		Bklt. pane of 6 (2 #27, 4 #28)	65.00	
		Never hinged	75.00	
c.		Booklet pane of 5 + label	*600.00*	
		Never hinged	*390.00*	
28	A3	10pf lt rose	1.00	*1.50*
		Never hinged	4.50	
		On cover		17.00
a.		10pf red ('13)	3.50	*17.00*
		Never hinged	12.50	
		On cover		100.00
b.		Booklet pane of 5 + label	*600.00*	
		Never hinged	*800.00*	
29	A3	20pf ultra ('11)	1.00	*3.75*
		Never hinged	4.25	
		On cover		25.00
30	A3	30pf org & blk, *pale yel* ('11)	16.00	*52.50*
		Never hinged	60.00	
		On cover		1,000.
a.		30pf orange & black, *pale orange* ('13)	6.50	—
		Never hinged	17.00	
		On cover		—

Engr.

Perf. 14½x14

No.	Type	Description	Unused	Used
31	A4	1m carmine ('12)	13.00	*80.00*
		Never hinged	55.00	
		On cover		300.00
32	A4	2m blue ('11)	13.00	*80.00*
		Never hinged	55.00	
		On cover		300.00
33	A4	3m blk vio ('19)	15.00	
		Never hinged	50.00	
a.		3m gray violet	40.00	
		Never hinged	150.00	
34	A4	5m slate & car	37.50	*325.00*
		Never hinged	130.00	
		On cover		850.00
a.		5m slate & rose red	65.00	
		Never hinged	225.00	
		Nos. 26-34 (9)	98.10	548.00

Nos. 33, 33a, 34a were never placed in use.

Booklet panes of 6 made from sheet stamps exist of the 5pf and 10pf.

Forged cancellations are found on Nos. 30-32, 34.

Covers: Values for Nos. 31-34 are for over-franked complete covers, usually philatelic.

GERMAN STATES

'jər-mən 'stāts

Watermarks

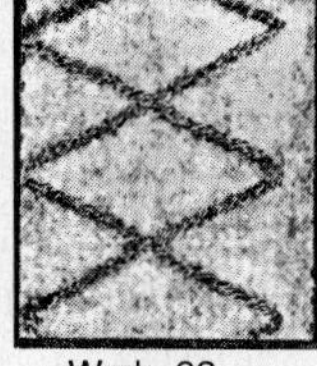

Wmk. 92 — 17mm wide

Wmk. 93 — 14mm wide

Wmk. 94 — Horiz. WavyLines Wide Apart

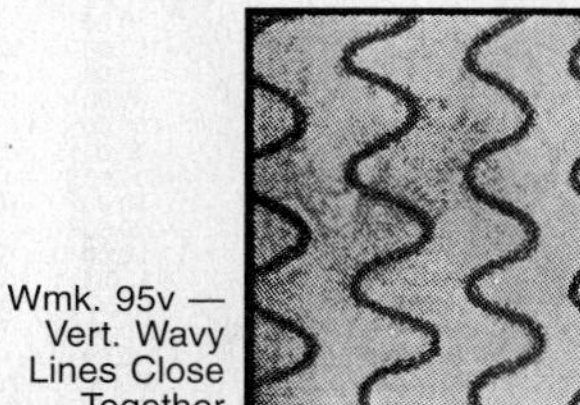

Wmk. 95v — Vert. Wavy Lines Close Together

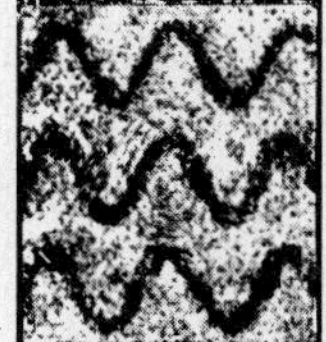

Wmk. 95h — Horiz. Wavy Lines Close Together

Wmk. 102 — Post Horn

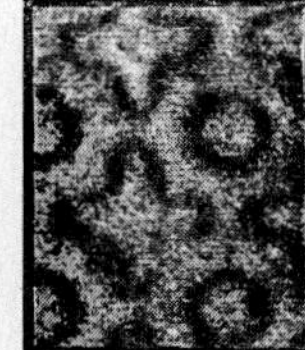

Wmk. 116 — Crosses and Circles

Wmk. 128 — Wavy Lines

Wmk. 130 — Wreath of Oak Leaves

Wmk. 148 — Small Flowers

Wmk. 162 — Laurel Wreath

Wmk. 192 — Circles

BADEN

LOCATION — In southwestern Germany

GOVT. — Former Grand Duchy

AREA — 5,817 sq. mi.

POP. — 1,432,000 (1864)

CAPITAL — Karlsruhe (Principal city)

Baden was a member of the German Confederation. In 1870 it became part of the German Empire.

60 Kreuzer = 1 Gulden

Values for unused stamps are for examples with original gum as defined in the catalogue introduction except for Nos. 1-9 which are valued without gum. Very fine examples of Nos. 1-9 will have one or two margins touching the framelines due to the very narrow spacing of the stamps on the plates. Stamps with margins clear of the framelines on all four sides are scarce and sell for considerably more.

A1

1851-52 Unwmk. Typo. *Imperf.*

No.	Type	Description	Unused	Used
1	A1	1kr blk, *dk buff*	275.00	250.00
		With gum	490.00	
		On cover		600.00
2	A1	3kr blk, *yellow*	140.00	16.00
		With gum	240.00	
		On cover		40.00
3	A1	6kr blk, *yel grn*	440.00	45.00
		With gum	800.00	
		On cover		125.00
4	A1	9kr blk, *lil rose*	90.00	26.00
		With gum	200.00	
		On cover		95.00
		Nos. 1-4 (4)	945.00	337.00

Thin Paper (First Printing, 1851)

No.	Type	Description	Unused	Used
1a	A1	1kr black, *buff*	2,000.	800.00
		With gum	9,000.	
		On cover		1,750.
2a	A1	3kr blk, *org*	675.00	35.00
		With gum	1,600.	
		On cover		95.00
3a	A1	6kr blk, *blue grn*	2,250.	90.00
		With gum	3,600.	
		On cover		250.00
4a	A1	9kr blk, *dp rose*	2,800.	160.00
		With gum	4,500.	
		On cover		475.00

Nos. 1a-4a range in paper thickness between 0.05-0.08mm. Nos. 1-4 range in paper thickness between 0.07-0.09mm. The shades also vary slightly between printings. The crucial difference is the porosity of the printing. The numerals of Nos. 1-4 are porus, filled with tiny white flecks, while Nos. 1a-4a are black with few or no white flecks.

Nos. 1 and 1a are often forged by dipping No. 6 in coffee or other dying fluid. Under UV these forgeries will often appear mottled, and will vary slightly in shade compared to genuine examples.

Official reprints exist on carton paper.

Forgeries exist.

No. 4b

No.	Type	Description	Unused	Used
4b	A1	9kr blk, *bl grn* (error)		1,300,000.
		On cover		*2,000,000.*

Only three examples of No. 4b are known: one on cover, two off. Excellent forgeries exist.

Values for pairs

No.	Type	Description	Unused	Used
1	A1	1kr blk, *dk buff*	1,600.	550.00
		With gum	3,200.	
		On cover		1,500.
2	A1	3kr blk, *yellow*	360.00	52.50
		With gum	875.00	
		On cover		95.00
		Gutter pair (10)		*8,000.*
		On cover		*40,000.*
3	A1	6kr blk, *yel grn*	1,200.	160.00
		With gum	2,750.	
		On cover		275.00
		Gutter pair (2)		*30,000.*
4	A1	9kr blk, *lil rose*	240.00	145.00
		With gum	600.00	
		On cover		650.00

Thin Paper

No.	Type	Description	Unused	Used
1a	A1	1kr black, *buff*	—	2,000.
		On cover		3,000.
		Gutter pair (1)		*115,000.*
2a	A1	3kr blk, *org*	2,200.	160.00
		With gum	*4,800.*	
		On cover		200.00
3a	A1	6kr blk, *blue grn*	3,750.	325.00
		With gum	*9,500.*	
		On cover		800.00
4a	A1	9kr blk, *dp rose*	—	1,600.
		With gum	*10,400.*	

Values for strips of 3

No.	Type	Description	Unused	Used
1	A1	1kr blk, *dk buff*		960.00
		On cover		1,600.
2	A1	3kr blk, *yellow*	960.00	180.00
		With gum	1,750.	
		On cover		*400.00*
3	A1	6kr blk, *yel grn*		600.00
		On cover		*1,300.*
4	A1	9kr blk, *lil rose*	400.00	400.00
		With gum	960.00	
		On cover		800.00

Thin Paper

No.	Type	Description	Unused	Used
1a	A1	1kr black, *buff*		2,900.
		On cover		*4,000.*
2a	A1	3kr blk, *org*	3,200.	550.00
		With gum	*6,800.*	
		On cover		800.00
3a	A1	6kr blk, *blue grn*		1,450.
		On cover		*2,600.*
4a	A1	9kr blk, *dp rose*		4,800.

Values for blocks of 4

No.	Type	Description	Unused	Used
1	A1	1kr blk, *dk buff*	—	*4,000.*
2	A1	3kr blk, *yellow*	—	*1,450.*
		With gum	*5,200.*	
3	A1	6kr blk, *yel grn*	—	*4,000.*
		With gum	*8,000.*	
4	A1	9kr blk, *lil rose*	600.00	*3,000.*
		With gum	*2,000.*	

Thin Paper

No.	Type	Description	Unused	Used
1a	A1	1kr black, *buff*	—	4,000.
2a	A1	3kr blk, *org*	*4,800.*	*2,550.*
		With gum	*9,600.*	
3a	A1	6kr blk, *blue grn*	—	—
		With gum	*24,000.*	
4a	A1	9kr blk, *dp rose*	—	—
		With gum	*24,000.*	

1853-58

No.		Description	Unused	Used
6		A1 1kr black	160.00	27.50
		With gum	440.00	
		On cover		110.00
	a.	Tête bêche gutter pair		*35,000.*
7		A1 3kr black, *green*	160.00	14.00
		With gum	320.00	
		On cover		25.00
8		A1 3kr black, *bl* ('58)	675.00	30.00
		With gum	1,450.	
		On cover		110.00
	a.	Printed on both sides		
9		A1 6kr black, *yellow*	250.00	27.50
		With gum	550.00	
		On cover		67.50
		Nos. 6-9 (4)	1,245.	99.00

The paper of No. 6 is 0.06-0.095mm thick.

Values for pairs

No.		Description	Unused	Used
6	A1	1kr black	575.00	120.00
		With gum	1,650.	
		On cover		225.00
7	A1	3kr blk, *green*		32.50
		With gum	1,900.	
		On cover		47.50
8	A1	3kr blk, *blue*, (58)	1,550.	145.00
		With gum	3,100.	
		On cover		200.00
9	A1	6kr blk, *yellow*		240.00
		With gum	2,000.	
		On cover		1,100.

Values for used strips of 3

No.		Description	Used
6	A1	1kr black	175.00
		On cover	290.00
7	A1	3kr blk, *green*	95.00
		On cover	120.00
8	A1	3kr blk, *blue*, (58)	360.00
		On cover	600.00
9	A1	6kr blk, *yellow*	800.00

Values for blocks of 4

No.		Description	Unused	Used
6	A1	1kr black	—	*1,450.*
		With gum	4,800.	
7	A1	3kr blk, *green*		*2,250.*
		With gum	4,800.	
		On cover		*3,200.*
8	A1	3kr blk, *blue*, (58)		*2,400.*
		With gum	8,000.	
9	A1	6kr blk, *yellow*		*8,900.*
		With gum	7,200.	

Full margins of Nos. 1-4, 6-9 = ½mm.

Reissues (1865) of Nos. 1, 2, 3, 6, 7 and 8 exist on thick paper and No. 9 on thin paper; the color of the last is brighter than that of the original.

Covers: Values for Nos. 1-9 on cover are for covers bearing stamps with one or more margins touching, but not into the design. Covers bearing stamps with full clear margins are rare and command substantial premiums.

5-Ring Numeral Postmarks

Values are for neat and clearly legible numeral cancellations in five concentric circles struck on the imperforate issues of Baden (#1-9).

The left column is for fairly complete strikes on sound single stamps. The right column is for complete covers.

All values are premiums to be added to the value of the stamps or stamps on covers, upon which the cancels are struck.

Postmark	Stamp	Cover
1 Aach	+40.00	+100.00
1 Aach (red)	+1,100.	+4,000.
2 Achern	+5.00	+20.00
3 Adelsheim	+20.00	+50.00
3 Adelsheim (blue)	+220.00	+60.00
4 Aglasterhausen	+25.00	+60.00
4 Aglasterhausen (blue)	+180.00	+500.00
5 Allensbach	+200.00	+500.00
5 Allensbach (red)	+1,100.	+3,750.
6 Altbreisach	+5.00	+10.00
7 Appenweier	+25.00	+80.00
8 Baden	0.00	0.00
8 Baden (red)	+800.00	+800.00
9 Beroldzheim	+300.00	+1,000.
9 Beroldzheim (red)	+1,500.	+4,250.
10 Beuggen (blue)	+400.00	+1,200.
Rheinfelden	+40.00	+80.00
11 Biberach	+50.00	+120.00
11 Biberach (blue)	+300.00	+1,000.
12 Bischofsheim a. Rh.	+10.00	+30.00
12 bischofsheim a. Rh. (blue)	+250.00	+800.00
13 Bischofsheim a. T.	+10.00	+20.00
13 Bischofsheim a. T. (blue)	+180.00	+500.00
14 Blumberg	+80.00	+250.00
14 Blumberg (red)	+900.00	+3,500.
15 Blumenfeld	+50.00	+200.00
15 Blumenfeld (blue)	+200.00	+750.00
16 Bonndorf	+5.00	+15.00
16 Bonndorf (red)	+750.00	+2,500.
16 Bonndorf (blue)	+250.00	+600.00
17 Boxberg	+10.00	+30.00
17 Boxberg (red)	+500.00	+1,500.
17 Boxberg (blue)	+120.00	+350.00
18 Bretten	+5.00	+10.00
19 Bruchsal	0.00	0.00
19 Bruchsal (red)	+400.00	+1,000.
20 Buchen	+5.00	+20.00
20 Buchen (blue)	+150.00	+500.00
21 Buehl	+5.00	+10.00
21 Buehl (blue)	+200.00	+500.00
22 Burg	+200.00	+450.00
22 Burg (blue)	+1,100.	+3,750.
23 Burkheim	+100.00	+250.00
23 Burkheim (red)	+1,000.	+3,500.
24 Carlsruhe	0.00	0.00
24 Carlsruhe (red)	+1,000.	+4,500.
25 Constanz	0.00	0.00
25 Constanz (red)	+400.00	+1,000.
26 Dinglingen	+15.00	+50.00
27 Donaueschingen	0.00	0.00
28 Durlach	0.00	0.00
28 Durlach (red)	+50.00	+150.00
29 Durmersheim	+250.00	+1,350.
29 Durmersheim (red)	+1,100.	+3,750.
30 Dürrheim	+80.00	+250.00
31 Eberbach	+5.00	+10.00
31 Eberbach (red)	+450.00	+1,200.
32 Efringen	+40.00	+100.00
32 Efringen (red)	+400.00	+1,000.
32 Efringen (blue)	+400.00	+1,000.
33 Eichtersheim	+25.00	+80.00
33 Eichtersheim (blue)	+400.00	+1,000.
34 Eigeltingen	+50.00	+120.00
34 Eigeltingen (red)	+300.00	+750.00
35 Elzach	+30.00	+80.00
35 Elzach (blue)	+450.00	+1,200.
36 Emmendingen	0.00	0.00
36 Emmendingen (blue)	+200.00	+500.00
37 Endingen	+10.00	+40.00
37 Endingen (blue)	+250.00	+600.00
38 Engen	+5.00	+20.00
38 Engen (blue)	+200.00	+500.00
39 Eppingen	+10.00	+30.00
39 Eppingen (red)	+1,000.	+3,000.
39 Eppingen (blue)	+80.00	+250.00
40 Ernstthal	+300.00	+750.00
40 Ernstthal (blue)	+1,000.	+2,500.
41 Ettenheim	+5.00	+10.00
41 Ettenheim (blue)	+250.00	+600.00
42 Ettlingen	0.00	0.00
42 Ettlingen (blue)	+400.00	+1,200.
43 Freiburg	0.00	0.00
43 Freiburg (red)	+800.00	+2,500.
44 Freudenberg	+150.00	+400.00
44 Freudenberg (red)	+500.00	+1,800.00
45 Furtwangen	+15.00	+40.00
45 Furtwangen (red)	+600.00	+2,000.
46 Gaggenau	+80.00	+150.00
47 Geisingen	+30.00	+80.00
47 Geisingen (blue)	+1,500.	+3,500.
48 Gengenbach	+25.00	+60.00
48 Gengenbach (red)	+300.00	+1,200.
49 Gerlachsheim	+15.00	+40.00
50 Gernsbach	+10.00	+30.00
51 Graben	+500.00	+1,500.
51 Graben (red)	+1,500.	*+10,000.*
51 Neckaretz	—	—
52 Griesbach	+80.00	+250.00
52 Greisbach (red)	+700.00	+2,500.
53 Haltingen	+30.00	+60.00
53 Haltingen (red)	+700.00	+2,000.
54 Hardheim	+80.00	+250.00
54 Hardheim (red)	+800.00	+2,500.
55 Haslach	+15.00	+40.00
55 Haslach (blue)	+250.00	+600.00
56 Hausach	+15.00	+40.00
57 Heidelberg	0.00	0.00
58 Heiligenberg	+40.00	+80.00
58 Heiligenberg (red)	+350.00	+1,200.
59 Heitersheim	+30.00	+60.00
60 Hilzingen	+40.00	+100.00
60 Hilzingen (blue)	+300.00	+800.00
61 Höllsteig	+60.00	+200.00
61 Höllsteig (red)	+800.00	+3,000.
61 Höllsteig (blue)	+800.00	+2,500.
62 Hornberg	+15.00	+40.00
62 Hornberg (blue)	+150.00	+400.00
63 Hüfingen	+10.00	+30.00
63 Hüfingen (red)	+400.00	+1,200.
63 Hüfingen (blue)	+500.00	+1,200.
64 Hundheim	+700.00	+4,500.
64 Hernsbach		*+4,500.*
65 Ichenheim	+700.00	+3,000.
65 Ichenheim (blue)	+1,500.	+4,500.
66 Jestetten	+30.00	+80.00
66 Jestetten (blue)	+40.00	+100.00
67 Kandern	+30.00	+80.00
68 Kehl	+5.00	+10.00
68 Kehl (red)	+400.00	+1,000.
69 Kenzingen	+5.00	+10.00
69 Kenzingen (red)	+700.00	+2,500.
70 Kippenheim	+10.00	+20.00
71 Kleinlaufenburg	+25.00	+50.00
71 Kleinlaufenburg (blue)	+120.00	+300.00
72 Kork	+20.00	+30.00
72 Kork (blue)	+400.00	+1,000.
73 Krautheim	+25.00	+50.00
73 Krautheim (red)	+600.00	+1,250.
74 Krotzingen	+40.00	+150.00
74 Krotzingen (blue)	+60.00	+150.00
75 Königschaffhausen	+30.00	+80.00
76 Königshofen	+120.00	+400.00
77 Külsheim	+180.00	+500.00
77 Meckesheim	—	—
78 Ladenburg	+20.00	+50.00
78 Ladenburg (red)	+1,000.	+3,000.
79 Lahr	0.00	0.00
80 Langenbrücken	+30.00	+80.00
81 Langendenzlingen	+25.00	+60.00
82 Lenzkirch	+10.00	+30.00
82 Lenzkirch (red)	+600.00	+1,500.
82 Lenzkirch (blue)	+150.00	+400.00
83 Löffingen	+15.00	+40.00
83 Löffingen (blue)	+150.00	+350.00
84 Lörrach	0.00	0.00
84 Lörrach (red)	+120.00	+350.00
85 Ludwigshafen	+25.00	+50.00
85 Ludwigshafen (blue)	+400.00	+1,200.
86 Malsch	+60.00	+250.00
86 Malsch (blue)	+400.00	+1,200.
87 Mannheim	0.00	0.00
88 Markdorf	+25.00	+70.00
88 Markdorf (red)	+700.00	+2,000.
89 Meersburg	+20.00	+50.00
90 Merchingen	+25.00	+60.00
90 Merchingen (blue)	+400.00	+1,000.
91 Moehringen	+30.00	+60.00
91 Moehringen (blue)	+400.00	+1,000.
92 Möskirch	+5.00	+10.00
92 Möskirch (red)	+200.00	+500.00
92 Möskirch (blue)	+60.00	+150.00
92 Möskirch (green)	—	—
93 Mosbach	+5.00	+20.00
93 Mosbach (red)	+200.00	+600.00
93 Mosbach (blue)	+300.00	+700.00
94 Mühlburg	+30.00	+80.00
95 Müllheim	0.00	0.00
95 Müllheim (red)	+700.00	+2,000.
96 Muggensturm	+120.00	+400.00
96 Muggensturm (blue)	*+1,000.*	*+5,000.*
97 Munzingen	+150.00	+400.00
97 Munzingen (red)	+500.00	+1,500.
97 Munzingen (blue)	+200.00	+600.00
98 Neckarbischofsheim	+20.00	+40.00
98 Neckarbischofsheim (blue)	+500.00	+1,500.
99 Neckargemünd	+20.00	+40.00
99 Neckargemünd (red)	+700.00	+2,500.
99 Neckargemünd (blue)	+250.00	+600.00
100 Neustadt	+5.00	+10.00
100 Neustadt (red)	+400.00	+1,200.
100 Neustadt (blue)	+150.00	+350.00
101 Oberkirch	+10.00	+40.00
101 Oberkirch (red)	+300.00	+800.00
102 Oberlauchringen	+40.00	+150.00
103 Oberschefflenz	+40.00	+150.00
103 Oberschefflenz (blue)	+500.00	+1,500.
104 Offenburg	0.00	0.00
104 Offenburg (blue)	+150.00	+350.00
105 Oppenau	+20.00	+40.00
106 Orschweier	+30.00	+100.00
107 Osterburken	+60.00	+150.00
107 Osterburken (red)	+700.00	+2,500.
107 Osterburken (blue)	+500.00	+1,500.
108 Petersthal	+50.00	+150.00
108 Petersthal (blue)	+600.00	+1,500.
109 Pforzheim	0.00	0.00
109 Pforzheim (red)	+1,200.	+3,500.
109 Pforzheim (blue)	+1,500.	+4,500.
110 Pfullendorf	+20.00	+60.00
110 Pfullendorf (red)	+500.00	+1,500.
110 Pfullendorf (blue)	+80.00	+200.00
111 Philippsburg	+30.00	+100.00
111 Philippsburg (blue)	+300.00	+800.00
112 Radolfzell	+5.00	+20.00
112 Radolfzell (red)	*+1,500.*	*+8,000.*
113 Randegg	+50.00	+150.00
113 Randegg (red)	+800.00	+3,000.
113 Randegg (blue)	+160.00	+500.00
113 Gailingen	—	—
114 Rappenau	+40.00	+100.00
114 Rappenau (blue)	+250.00	+800.00
115 Rastatt	0.00	0.00
115 Rastatt (red)	+50.00	+100.00
115 Rastatt (blue)	+300.00	+800.00
116 Renchen	+20.00	+40.00
116 Renchen (blue)	+400.00	+1,000.
117 Riedern	+350.00	+1,200.
117 Riedern (blue)	+200.00	+400.00
117 Gottmadingen	—	—
117 Gottmadingen (blue)	—	—
118 Riegel	+10.00	+30.00
118 Riegel (red)	+400.00	+1,000.
118 Riegel (blue)	+400.00	+1,000.
119 Rippoldsau	+150.00	+300.00
119 Rippoldsau (red)	+400.00	+1,000.
119 Rippoldsau (blue)	+300.00	+600.00
120 Rothenfels	+200.00	+500.00
120 Rothenfels (red)	+500.00	+1,500.
121 Sackingen	0.00	0.00
121 Sackingen (red)	+300.00	+700.00
121 Sackingen (blue)	+400.00	+1,000.
122 Salem	+20.00	+40.00
122 Salem (red)	+500.00	+1,500.
122 Salem (blue)	+350.00	+1,000.
123 St. Blasien	+15.00	+40.00
123 St. Blasien (red)	*+1,000.*	*+6,000.*
123 St. Blasien (blue)	+500.00	+1,200.
124 St. Georgen	+25.00	+60.00
125 Schallstadt	+80.00	+200.00
125 Schallstadt (blue)	+150.00	+300.00
126 Schappach	*+2,000.*	*+7,500.*
126 Schappach (blue)	+400.00	+1,000.
127 Schiltach	+15.00	+40.00
127 Schiltach (red)	+400.00	+1,200.
128 Schleingen	+15.00	+50.00
128 Schleingen (red)	+500.00	+1,500.
128 Schleingen (blue)	+500.00	+1,500.
129 Schönau	+20.00	+50.00
130 Schopfheim	+5.00	+10.00
130 Schopfheim (red)	*+1,000.*	*+7,000.*
130 Schopfheim (blue)	+100.00	+250.00
131 Schwetzingen	+5.00	+10.00
131 Schwetzingen (blue)	+300.00	+700.00
132 Singen	+10.00	+30.00
132 Singen (red)	+700.00	+2,000.
133 Sinsheim	+5.00	+10.00
133 Sinsheim (red)	+600.00	+1,900.
134 Stadel		*+50,000.*
134 Brennet	+40.00	+150.00
135 Staufen	+5.00	+10.00
136 Steinen	+30.00	+60.00
136 Steinen (red)	+1,000.	+3,000.
136 Steinen (blue)	+1,000.	+3,000.
137 Steißlingen	+1,200.	+5,000.
137 Steißlingen (red)	+2,500.	*+10,000.*
138 Stetten A.K.M.	+60.00	+180.00
138 Stetten A.K.M. (blue)	+400.00	+1,200.
139 Stockach	0.00	0.00
139 Stockach (red)	+500.00	+2,000.
140 Stollhofen	+250.00	+1,200.
140 Lichtenau	+50.00	+150.00
141 Stühlingen	+15.00	+80.00
141 Stühlingen (red)	+600.00	+2,000.
141 Stühlingen (blue)	+400.00	+1,000.
142 Sulzburg	+15.00	+50.00
142 Sulzburg (blue)	+400.00	+1,200.
143 Todtnau	+25.00	+100.00
143 Todtnau (red)	+500.00	+2,500.
144 Thiengen	+15.00	+50.00
144 Thiengen (red)	—	—
144 Thiengen (blue)	+150.00	+300.00
145 Triberg	+10.00	+20.00
145 Triberg (red)	+600.00	+2,000.
145 Triberg (blue)	+400.00	+1,200.
146 Überlingen	+5.00	+10.00
146 Überlingen (red)	+500.00	+1,500.
147 Uihlingen	+500.00	+2,500.
147 Uihlingen (red)	+1,500.	*+5,500.*
147 Albbruck	—	—
148 Villingen	0.00	0.00
149 Vöhrenbach	+20.00	+50.00
149 Vöhrenbach (red)	+700.00	+2,500.
150 Waghäusel	+20.00	+50.00
150 Waghäusel (red)	+100.00	+350.00
151 Waibstadt	+25.00	+80.00
151 Waibstadt (blue)	—	—
152 Waldkirch	+10.00	+30.00
153 Waldshut	0.00	0.00
153 Waldshut (red)	+100.00	+300.00
154 Walldürn	+20.00	+50.00
154 Walldürn (red)	+500.00	+2,000.
155 Weingarten	+50.00	+150.00
155 Weingarten (red)	+500.00	+2,000.
156 Weinheim	+5.00	+10.00
157 Wertheim	+5.00	+10.00
157 Wertheim (blue)	+100.00	+300.00
158 Wiesenbach	+500.00	+1,500.
158 Wiesenbach (red)	+1,500.	+5,000.
158 Wiesenbach (blue)	+1,200.	+3,500.
159 Wiesloch	+5.00	+10.00
159 Wiesloch (red)	+500.00	+2,500.
160 Wilferdingen	+100.00	+250.00
161 Wolfach	+10.00	+30.00
161 Wolfach (blue)	+400.00	+1,200.
162 Zell a.H.	+10.00	+40.00
162 Zell a.H. (blue)	+60.00	+150.00
163 Zell i.W.	+10.00	+20.00
163 Zell i.W. (blue)	+300.00	+700.00
164 Bahnpost	+250.00	+3,000.
165 Rittersbach	+1,200.	+5,000.
165 Rittersbach (blue)	+4,000.	*+15,000.*
166 Gondelsheim	+150.00	+400.00
167 Heidelsheim	+80.00	+400.00
167 Heidelsheim (red)	+600.00	+2,500.
168 Dertingen	+8,000.	*+50,000.*
169 Werbach	+600.00	+3,000.
170 Basel, Bad, Bahnhof	+1,200.	*+4,750.*
171 Badenweiler	+80.00	+200.00
171 Badenweiler (blue)	+1,200.	+4,000.
172 Weiterdingen	+2,000.	*+10,000.*
172 Weiterdingen (blue)	+4,000.	*+15,000.*
173 Steinbach	+120.00	+300.00
174 Mannheim Bhf.	+40.00	+150.00
175 Baden Bhf.	+50.00	+100.00
176 Bronnbach	+1,500.	*+10,000.*
177 Karlsruhe Stadtpost	+10.00	+40.00

Coat of Arms — A2

1860-62 *Perf. 13½*

No.		Description	Unused	Used
10		A2 1kr black	87.50	30.00
		No gum	32.50	
		Never hinged	300.00	
		On cover		72.50
		On cover, single franking		110.00
12		A2 3kr ultra ('61)	87.50	22.00
		No gum	37.50	
		Never hinged	250.00	
		On cover		55.00
	a.	3kr Prussian blue	275.00	72.50
		No gum	110.00	
		Never hinged	725.00	
		On cover		180.00
	b.	3kr violet ultramarine	375.00	175.00
		No gum	145.00	
		Never hinged	875.00	
		On cover		440.00
13		A2 6kr red org ('61)	95.00	72.50
		No gum	37.50	
		Never hinged	450.00	
		On cover		180.00
	a.	6kr yellow orange ('62)	180.00	87.50
		No gum	90.00	
		Never hinged	675.00	
		On cover		225.00
14		A2 9kr rose ('61)	250.00	175.00
		No gum	95.00	
		Never hinged	900.00	
		On cover		440.00
		Nos. 10-14 (4)	520.00	299.50

Examples of Nos. 10-14 and 18 with all perforations intact sell for considerably more.

Values for pairs

No.		Description	Unused	Used
10	A2	1kr black	145.00	60.00
		No gum	80.00	
		On cover		110.00
12	A2	3kr ultra	300.00	60.00
		No gum	110.00	
		On cover		130.00
a.		3kr Prussian blue	1,100.	225.00
		No gum	300.00	
		On cover		375.00
b.		3kr violet ultramarine	1,100.	550.00
		No gum	325.00	
		On cover		875.00
13	A2	6kr red org	300.00	175.00
		No gum	110.00	
		On cover		375.00
a.		6kr yellow orange	475.00	225.00
		No gum	180.00	
		On cover		400.00
14	A2	9kr rose	550.00	440.00
		No gum	225.00	
		On cover		800.00

Values for strips of 3

No.		Description	Unused	Used
10	A2	1kr black	290.00	100.00
		No gum	125.00	
		On cover		145.00
12	A2	3kr ultra	440.00	110.00
		No gum	160.00	
		On cover		160.00
a.		3kr Prussian blue	1,825.	600.00
		No gum	725.00	
		On cover		725.00
b.		3kr violet ultramarine		1,100.
		On cover		1,600.
13	A2	6kr red org	525.00	375.00
		No gum	250.00	
		On cover		650.00
a.		6kr yellow orange	650.00	400.00
		No gum	250.00	
		On cover		650.00
14	A2	9kr rose	875.00	*1,000.*
		No gum	375.00	
		On cover		1,450.

Values for blocks of 4

No.		Description	Unused	Used
10	A2	1kr black	400.00	*875.00*
		No gum	180.00	
12	A2	3kr ultra	550.00	*725.00*
		No gum	225.00	
a.		3kr Prussian blue	3,250.	2,200.
		No gum	875.00	
b.		3kr violet ultramarine		—
13	A2	6kr red org	725.00	*1,600.*
		No gum	300.00	
a.		6kr yellow orange	875.00	*2,200.*
		No gum	375.00	
14	A2	9kr rose	1,800.	*2,750.*
		No gum	725.00	

Coat of Arms — A3

1862 *Perf. 10*

No.		Description	Unused	Used
15		A2 1kr black	65.00	87.50
		No gum	22.50	
		Never hinged	180.00	
		On cover		180.00
		On cover, single franking		375.00
	a.	1kr silver gray	6,500.	*6,500.*
		No gum	4,500.	
		On cover		*13,500.*
	b.	1kr gray black	725.00	*800.00*

No gum 300.00
On cover 1,800.
16 A2 6kr Prus bl ('62) 125.00 235.00
Never hinged 450.00
On cover 150.00
a. 6kr blue ('63) 145.00 95.00
No gum 50.00
Never hinged 550.00
On cover 190.00
17 A2 9kr brown 80.00 72.50
No gum 30.00
Never hinged 450.00
On cover 145.00
a. 9kr dark brown 325.00 250.00
No gum 130.00
Never hinged 1,100.
On cover 550.00
b. 9kr bister 110.00 *240.00*
No gum 45.00
Never hinged 650.00
On cover 300.00

Perf. 13½

18 A3 3kr rose 2,250. 290.00
No gum 725.00
On cover 525.00

Values for pairs

15 A2 1kr black 140.00 *190.00*
No gum 45.00
On cover 275.00
a. 1kr silver gray *18,000.*
b. 1kr gray black 1,800.
On cover *2,500.*
16 A2 6kr Prus bl 290.00 240.00
No gum 110.00
On cover 300.00
a. 6kr blue 325.00 275.00
No gum 130.00
On cover 360.00
17 A2 9kr brown 275.00 180.00
No gum 100.00
On cover 290.00
a. 9kr dark brown 900.00 720.00
No gum 360.00
On cover 850.00
b. 9kr bister 340.00 *575.00*
No gum 145.00
On cover 650.00
18 A3 3kr rose *5,400.* 850.00
No gum 1,800.
On cover 1,150.

Values for strips of 3

15 A2 1kr black 200.00 *360.00*
No gum 72.50
On cover 500.00
a. 1kr silver gray
b. 1kr gray black 3,900.
On cover 5,000.
16 A2 6kr Prus bl 400.00 360.00
No gum 145.00
On cover 600.00
a. 6kr blue 475.00 425.00
No gum 180.00
On cover 725.00
17 A2 9kr brown 400.00 400.00
No gum 145.00
On cover 725.00
a. 9kr dark brown 1,350. 1,200.
No gum 500.00
On cover 1,700.
b. 9kr bister 1,100.
No gum 250.00
On cover 1,700.
18 A3 3kr rose 1,350.
On cover 2,500.

Values for blocks of 4

15 A2 1kr black 275.00 *1,300.*
No gum 100.00
a. 1kr silver gray — —
b. 1kr gray black — —
16 A2 6kr Prus bl 1,300. 1,300.
No gum 215.00
a. 6kr blue 1,450. 1,450.
No gum 275.00
17 A2 9kr brown 2,500. *2,900.*
No gum 360.00
a. 9kr dark brown 2,900. *2,900.*
No gum 700.00
b. 9kr bister 2,500. *2,900.*
No gum 250.00
18 A3 3kr rose — 2,150.
strip of 4 — —

1862-65 ***Perf. 10***

19 A3 1kr black ('64) 47.50 15.00
No gum 16.00
Never hinged 120.00
On cover 32.50
On cover, single franking 140.00
a. 1kr silver gray *2,250.*
On cover *4,000.*
b. 1kr gray black 440.00 300.00
On cover 560.00
20 A3 3kr rose 62.50 4.00
No gum 16.00
Never hinged 150.00
On cover 8.00
a. Imperf. *40,000.* *40,000.*
On cover *100,000.*
22 A3 6kr ultra ('65) 11.00 *27.50*
No gum 4.00
Never hinged 30.00
On cover 60.00
a. 6kr Prussian blue ('64) *575.00* 70.00
No gum 175.00
Never hinged 2,000.
On cover 175.00
23 A3 9kr brn ('64) 16.00 30.00
No gum 6.00
Never hinged 35.00
On cover 72.50
a. 9kr bister 375.00 90.00
No gum 110.00
Never hinged 800.00
On cover 175.00
b. Printed on both sides *6,500.*
c. 9kr dark brown 500.00 *440.00*
No gum 175.00
Never hinged 1,500.
On cover *1,400.*
24 A3 18kr green 400.00 575.00
No gum 125.00
Never hinged 1,200.
On cover 2,400.

On cover, single franking 2,900.
a. 18kr dark green 1,400. 1,600.
No gum 360.00
Never hinged 4,000.
On cover *8,800.*
On cover, single franking *8,800.*
25 A3 30kr dp org 32.50 *2,250.*
No gum 12.00
Never hinged 72.50
On cover *7,200.*
On cover, single franking *19,000.*
a. 30kr yellow orange 140.00 *2,400.*
No gum 52.50
Never hinged 600.00
On cover *8,250.*
On cover, single franking *9,000.*

Forged cancellations are known on No. 25.

Values for pairs

19 A3 1kr black 140.00 40.00
On cover 55.00
a. 1kr silver gray *5,200.*
On cover *6,400.*
b. 1kr gray black *800.00*
On cover 1,200.
20 A3 3kr rose 125.00 8.00
On cover 15.00
22 A3 6kr ultra 24.00 *72.50*
On cover 95.00
a. 6kr Prussian blue 1,750. 175.00
On cover 360.00
23 A3 9kr brown 40.00 *80.00*
On cover 160.00
a. 9kr bister 960.00 240.00
On cover 475.00
c. 9kr dark brown 1,400. 1,100.
On cover 2,000.
24 A3 18kr green 1,600. 1,600.
On cover 6,400.
a. 18kr dark green 4,000. 3,600.
On cover *21,000.*
25 A3 30kr deep orange 80.00 *5,200.*
On cover *14,500.*
a. 30kr yellow orange 400.00 *6,000.*
On cover *22,500.*

Values for strips of 3

19 A3 1kr black 200.00 72.50
On cover 90.00
a. 1kr silver gray *8,000.*
On cover *9,500.*
b. 1kr gray black 1,400.
On cover 2,000.
20 A3 3kr rose 175.00 22.50
On cover 40.00
22 A3 6kr ultra 35.00 *240.00*
On cover 360.00
a. 6kr Prussian blue 2,500. *675.00*
On cover 1,200.
23 A3 9kr brown 60.00 *225.00*
On cover 400.00
a. 9kr bister 400.00
On cover 640.00
c. 9kr dark brown 2,200. 1,800.
On cover 3,000.
24 A3 18kr green 4,400. —
a. 18kr dark green —
25 A3 30kr deep orange 125.00 *7,500.*
a. 30kr yellow orange 600.00

Values for blocks of 4

19 A3 1kr black 300.00 *800.00*
Never hinged 640.00
20 A3 3kr rose 260.00 *800.00*
Never hinged 600.00
22 A3 6kr ultra 52.50 *1,600.*
Never hinged 95.00
a. 6kr Prussian blue 3,600. 2,000.
23 A3 9kr brown 80.00 *1,400.*
Never hinged 160.00
c. 9kr dark brown 3,200. —
Never hinged 6,400.
24 A3 18kr green 4,400. —
25 A3 30kr deep orange 160.00 —
Never hinged 325.00
a. 30kr yellow orange 960.00 —
Never hinged 2,800.

A4

1868

26 A4 1kr green 4.00 *9.00*
Never hinged 9.50
On cover 16.00
On wrapper, single franking 70.00
27 A4 3kr rose 2.75 4.50
Never hinged 5.25
On cover 8.00
28 A4 7kr dull blue 20.00 *35.00*
Never hinged 47.50
On cover 100.00
a. 7kr sky blue 42.50 *100.00*
Never hinged 90.00
On cover 300.00
On cover, single franking *700.00*
Nos. 26-28 (3) 26.75 48.50

Forged cancellations are known on No. 28a.

Values for pairs

26 A4 1kr green 9.50 *20.00*
On cover 32.50
27 A4 3kr rose 4.75 *9.50*
On cover 20.00
28 A4 7kr dull blue 45.00 *100.00*
On cover 200.00
a. 7kr sky blue 100.00 400.00
On cover 1,300.

Values for strips of 3

26 A4 1kr green 14.50 *27.50*
On cover 40.00
27 A4 3kr rose 8.00 *40.00*
On cover 60.00
28 A4 7kr dull blue 65.00 *325.00*
On cover 475.00
a. 7kr sky blue 160.00 *1,200.*
On cover 2,200.

Values for blocks of 4

26 A4 1kr green 17.50 *400.00*
Never hinged 45.00
27 A4 3kr rose 9.50 *1,800.*
Never hinged 20.00
28 A4 7kr dull blue 90.00 *3,000.*
Never hinged 200.00
a. 7kr sky blue 225.00 —
Never hinged 400.00

The postage stamps of Baden were superseded by those of the German Empire on Jan. 1, 1872, but Official stamps were used during the year 1905.

RURAL POSTAGE DUE STAMPS

RU1

1862 **Unwmk.** ***Perf. 10***

Thin Paper

LJ1 RU1 1kr blk, *yellow* 5.00 *325.00*
Never hinged 8.00
On cover 575.00
a. Thick paper 140.00 *600.00*
Never hinged 275.00
On cover 1,400.
LJ2 RU1 3kr blk, *yellow* 2.75 *125.00*
Never hinged 5.50
On cover 240.00
a. Thick paper 120.00 *400.00*
Never hinged 225.00
On cover 960.00
LJ3 RU1 12kr blk, *yellow* 35.00 *13,500.*
Never hinged 72.50
On cover *32,500.*
a. Half used as 6kr on cover *25,000.*
b. Quarter used as 3kr on cover —
Nos. LJ1-LJ3 (3) 42.75 13,950.

On No. LJ3, "LAND-POST" is a straight line.
Paper of #LJ1a, LJ2a is darker yellow.
Forged cancellations abound on Nos. LJ1-LJ3.

Values for pairs

LJ1 RU1 1kr blk, *yellow* 11.00 *800.00*
On cover 960.00
a. Thick paper 300.00 *1,400.*
On cover 2,100.
LJ2 RU1 3kr blk, *yellow* 6.00 *275.00*
On cover 440.00
a. Thick paper 240.00 *960.00*
On cover 1,800.
LJ3 RU1 12kr blk, *yellow* 110.00 *32,000.*
On cover *60,000.*

Values for strips of 3

LJ1 RU1 1kr blk, *yellow* 16.00 *1,200.*
On cover 1,600.
a. Thick paper 475.00 *2,200.*
On cover 3,000.
LJ2 RU1 3kr blk, *yellow* 9.50 *475.00*
On cover 525.00
a. Thick paper 400.00 *1,600.*
On cover 2,200.
LJ3 RU1 12kr blk, *yellow* 160.00 —

Values for blocks of 4

LJ1 RU1 1kr blk, *yellow* 24.00 *2,000.*
Never hinged 40.00
a. Thick paper 640.00 *3,200.*
Never hinged 1,300.
LJ2 RU1 3kr blk, *yellow* 12.00 *1,600.*
Never hinged 24.00
a. Thick paper 525.00 *2,800.*
Never hinged 1,100.
LJ3 RU1 12kr blk, *yellow* 210.00 —
Never hinged 400.00

A used single of the 12kr stamp (Scott No. LJ3) tied to a small piece by a neat c.d.s., sold for the equivalent of U.S. $24,400 at a German auction in 2003.

OFFICIAL STAMPS

See Germany Nos. OL16-OL21.

BAVARIA

LOCATION — In southern Germany
GOVT. — Kingdom
AREA — 30,562 sq. mi. (1920)
POP. — 7,150,146 (1919)
CAPITAL — Munich

Bavaria was a member of the German Confederation and became part of the German Empire in 1870. After World War I, it declared itself a republic. It lost its postal autonomy on Mar. 31, 1920.

60 Kreuzer = 1 Gulden
100 Pfennig = 1 Mark (1874)

Values for unused stamps are for examples with original gum as defined in the catalogue introduction. Unused examples of the 1849-78 issues without gum sell for about 50-60% of the figures quoted.

A1

Broken Circle — A1a

Two plates used for No. 1:
Plate I: Rough impression, framelines around figure "1" broken or incomplete.
Plate II: Fine impression, framelines around "1" complete.

1849 **Unwmk.** **Typo.** ***Imperf.***

1 A1 1kr black (I) 1,000. *2,250.*
Pen & postmark cancels 1,400.
Pen cancel 1,400.
On cover, postmark cancel 4,750.
On cover, pen cancel 5,500.
On cover, pen & postmark cancels 4,000.
On printed matter, single franking 7,250.
On printed matter, pair *13,000.*
Pair with gutter between *19,000.* *90,000.*
a. 1kr deep black (I) 2,800. *3,000.*
Pen cancel 1,900.
Pen & postmark cancels 2,000.
On cover, pen & postmark cancels 5,800.
b. Tête bêche pair *125,000.*
c. 1kr black (II) 2,800. 2,600.
Pen cancel 2,000.
Pen & postmark cancels 1,600.
On cover, pen & postmark cancels 4,800.
On cover, pen cancel 6,500.
On cover, postmark cancel 6,600.
On printed matter, single franking *8,000.*
d. 1kr deep black (II) 4,800. 4,000.
On cover, pen & postmark cancels 8,000.

Full margins = 1mm.
There are dividing lines between stamps.

With Silk Thread

2 A1a 3kr blue 60.00 3.50
On cover 12.00
On printed matter, single franking 225.00
Pair with gutter between *2,750.* *12,000.*
On cover *26,000.*
a. 3kr greenish blue 60.00 3.50
On cover 12.00
b. 3kr deep blue 60.00 3.50
On cover 12.00
3 A1a 6kr brown *7,000.* 240.00
Pen cancel 240.00
Pen & postmark cancels 160.00
On cover 500.00
Pair with gutter between — *30,000.*

Full margins = 1mm.
There are dividing lines between stamps.

No. 1 exists with silk thread, from a single proof sheet, value about $4,000.

Values for pairs

1 A1 1kr black (I) 2,200. *5,200.*
Pen & postmark cancels 4,000.
On cover 14,500.
a. 1kr deep black (I) 6,400. *8,000.*
Pen & postmark cancels 6,400.
On cover 16,000.
c. 1kr black (II) 5,600.
d. 1kr deep black (II) 9,600.
2 A1a 3kr blue 140.00 16.00
On cover 40.00
a. 3kr greenish blue 140.00 16.00
On cover 40.00
b. 3kr deep blue 140.00 16.00
On cover 40.00
3 A1a 6kr brown *20,000.* 1,200.
On cover 2,400.

Values for strips of 3

1 A1 1kr black (I) 3,600. *8,800.*
Pen & postmark cancels 7,200.
On cover *20,800.*
a. 1kr deep black (I) 8,800. *13,600.*
Pen & postmark cancels 10,400.
On cover 22,400.
c. 1kr black (II) 10,400.

On cover 20,800.
d. 1kr deep black (II) 14,400.
2 A1a 3kr blue 200.00 72.50
On cover 140.00
a. 3kr greenish blue 200.00 72.50
On cover 140.00
b. 3kr deep blue 225.00 82.50
On cover 160.00
3 A1a 6kr brown —

Values for blocks of 4

1 A1 1kr black (I) 4,800. 58,000.
a. 1kr deep black — —
2 A1a 3kr blue 325.00 1,450.
a. 3kr greenish blue 325.00 1,450.
b. 3kr deep blue 325.00 1,450.
3 A1a 6kr brown — —

Complete circle — A2

1850-58 With Silk Thread

4 A2 1kr pink 95.00 22.50
Never hinged 160.00
On cover 72.50
On wrapper, single franking 160.00
On cover, single franking, local delivery 300.00
Pair with gutter between 2,500. 25,000.
On cover 52,000.
a. 1kr lilac rose 400.00 50.00
Never hinged 640.00
On cover 95.00
5 A2 6kr brown 50.00 6.50
Never hinged 90.00
On cover 27.50
Pair with gutter between 4,000. 16,000.
On cover 36,000.
a. Half used as 3kr on cover 16,000.
6 A2 9kr yellow green 70.00 16.00
Never hinged 130.00
On cover 45.00
Pair with gutter between 2,600. 16,000.
On cover 48,000.
a. 9kr blue green ('53) 11,000. 150.00
On cover 500.00
Pair with gutter between — —
b. 9kr pale blue green 6,500. 45.00
On cover 140.00
Pair with gutter between — 21,750.
On cover 47,500.
7 A2 12kr red ('58) 150.00 140.00
Never hinged 275.00
On cover 600.00
On cover, single franking 700.00
Pair with gutter between 4,000. 26,000.
8 A2 18kr yel ('54) 140.00 190.00
Never hinged 325.00
On cover 960.00
On cover, single franking 1,200.
Pair with gutter between 2,500. 26,000.
Nos. 4-8 (5) 505.00 375.00

Full margins = 1mm.
There are dividing lines between stamps.

Values for pairs

4 A2 1kr pink 240.00 125.00
On cover 325.00
a. 1kr lilac rose — 200.00
On cover 400.00
5 A2 6kr brown 125.00 47.50
On cover 80.00
6 A2 9kr yel grn 160.00 160.00
On cover 300.00
a. 9kr blue green — 800.00
On cover 1,400.
b. 9kr pale blue green — 275.00
On cover 525.00
7 A2 12kr red 360.00 875.00
On cover 1,400.
8 A2 18kr yellow 300.00 960.00
On cover 1,600.

Values for strips of 3

4 A2 1kr pink 350.00 175.00
On cover 425.00
a. 1kr lilac rose — 250.00
On cover 500.00
5 A2 6kr brown 175.00 475.00
On cover 675.00
6 A2 9kr yel grn 300.00 350.00
On cover 625.00
a. 9kr blue green 1,600.
On cover 2,800.
b. 9kr pale blue green 550.00
On cover 950.00
7 A2 12kr red 500.00 2,200.
On cover 3,200.
8 A2 18kr yellow 475.00 2,200.
On cover 2,400.

Values for blocks or strips of 4

4 A2 1kr pink 500.00 2,400.
a. 1kr lilac rose 3,200.
5 A2 6kr brown 275.00 2,800.
6 A2 9kr yel grn 400.00 3,200.
a. 9kr blue green 9,600.
b. 9kr pale blue green 7,200.
7 A2 12kr red 800.00 8,000.
8 A2 18kr yellow 875.00 6,000.

1862

9 A2 1kr yellow 80.00 20.00
Never hinged 110.00
On cover 95.00
On wrapper, single franking 190.00
On cover, single franking, local delivery 410.00
Pair with gutter between 3,000. 25,000.
10 A1a 3kr rose 140.00 4.00
Never hinged 260.00
On cover 12.00
On printed matter, single franking 225.00
On wrapper, single franking 300.00
a. 3kr carmine 52.50 6.00
Never hinged 95.00
On cover 14.50
Pair with gutter between 2,400. 13,000.
On cover 30,000.
11 A2 6kr blue 70.00 12.00
Never hinged 110.00
On cover 35.00
Pair with gutter between 2,400. 16,000.
On cover 48,000.
a. 6kr ultra 2,400. 9,000.
b. Half used as 3kr on cover 10,000.
12 A2 9kr bister 110.00 16.00
Never hinged 200.00
On cover 55.00
Pair with gutter between 3,000. 21,000.
13 A2 12kr yel grn 95.00 70.00
Never hinged 175.00
On cover 260.00
On cover, single franking 400.00
Pair with gutter between 3,000.
a. Half used as 6kr on cover 32,000.
14 A2 18kr ver red 900.00 140.00
Never hinged 1,650.
On cover 1,200.
On cover, single franking 2,400.
a. 18kr pale red 190.00 450.00
Never hinged 260.00
On cover 2,000.
On cover, single franking 4,800.
Pair with gutter between 3,000.
Nos. 9-14 (6) 1,395. 262.00

Full margins = 1mm.
There are dividing lines between stamps.

No. 11a was not put in use.

Values for pairs

9 A2 1kr yellow 200.00 110.00
On cover 325.00
10 A1a 3kr rose 640.00 16.00
On cover 35.00
a. 3kr carmine 125.00 24.00
On cover 40.00
11 A2 6kr blue 160.00 160.00
On cover 360.00
12 A2 9kr bister 260.00 160.00
On cover 360.00
13 A2 12kr yel grn 210.00 400.00
On cover 875.00
14 A2 18kr ver red 2,800. 600.00
On cover 2,000.
a. 18kr pale red 475.00 1,400.
On cover 3,600.

Values for strips of 3

9 A2 1kr yellow 300.00 200.00
On cover 525.00
10 A1a 3kr rose 960.00 47.50
On cover 80.00
a. 3kr carmine 175.00 55.00
On cover 90.00
11 A2 6kr blue 550.00 400.00
On cover 675.00
12 A2 9kr bister 400.00 800.00
On cover 1,400.
13 A2 12kr yel grn 325.00 960.00
On cover 1,750.
14 A2 18kr ver red 2,400.
On cover 4,000.
a. 18kr pale red 725.00 —

Values for blocks or strips of 4

9 A2 1kr yellow 400.00 2,400.
10 A1a 3kr rose 1,200. 960.00
a. 3kr carmine 240.00 1,400.
11 A2 6kr blue 400.00 2,000.
12 A2 9kr bister 525.00 8,000.
13 A2 12kr yel grn 440.00 —
14 A2 18kr ver red — 6,000.
a. 18kr pale red 875.00 —

Coat of Arms — A3

1867-68 Embossed

15 A3 1kr yel grn 65.00 12.00
Never hinged 100.00
On cover 40.00
On wrapper, single franking 125.00
On cover, single franking, local delivery 200.00
Pair with gutter between 2,600. 13,000.
a. 1kr dark blue green 300.00 52.50
Never hinged 525.00
On cover 175.00
Pair with gutter between 14,000.
16 A3 3kr rose 70.00 2.40
Never hinged 110.00
On cover 8.00
Pair with gutter between 3,000. 12,000.
a. Printed on both sides 5,000.
17 A3 6kr ultra 45.00 19.00
Never hinged 72.50
On cover 125.00
Pair with gutter between 1,600.
a. Half used as 3kr on cover 75,000.
18 A3 6kr bis ('68) 80.00 50.00
Never hinged 140.00
On cover 300.00
On cover, single franking 4,000.
Pair with gutter between 3,400.
a. Half used as 3kr on cover 32,000.
19 A3 7kr ultra ('68) 400.00 16.00
Never hinged 800.00
On cover 60.00
Pair with gutter between 8,000.
a. 7kr Prus bl ('69) 3,300. 800.00
On cover 2,400.
b. 7kr royal bl ('69) 2,000. 525.00
Never hinged 2,400.
On cover 1,400.
20 A3 9kr bister 45.00 35.00
Never hinged 72.50
On cover 175.00
Pair with gutter between 1,900.
21 A3 12kr lilac 350.00 95.00
Never hinged 960.00
On cover 450.00
Pair with gutter between 8,000.
22 A3 18kr red 140.00 175.00
Never hinged 240.00
On cover 2,600.
On cover, single franking 3,600.
Pair with gutter between 2,400.
Nos. 15-22 (8) 1,195. 404.40

Full margins = 1¼mm.

The paper of the 1867-68 issues often shows ribbed or laid lines.

Values for pairs

15 A3 1kr yellow green 140.00 32.50
On cover 160.00
a. 1kr dk blue green 640.00 160.00
On cover 340.00
16 A3 3kr rose 140.00 14.50
On cover 47.50
17 A3 6kr ultra 95.00 160.00
On cover 360.00
18 A3 6kr bister 175.00 300.00
On cover 640.00
19 A3 7kr ultra 1,200. 240.00
On cover 360.00
a. 7kr Prussian blue 2,700.
b. 7kr royal blue 1,800.
On cover 2,200.
20 A3 9kr bister 95.00 275.00
On cover 600.00
21 A3 12kr lilac 800.00 525.00
On cover 960.00
22 A3 18kr red 290.00 960.00
On cover 4,000.

Values for strips of 3

15 A3 1kr yellow green 225.00 55.00
On cover 125.00
a. 1kr dk blue green 960.00 250.00
On cover 440.00
16 A3 3kr rose 225.00 80.00
On cover 160.00
17 A3 6kr ultra 175.00 725.00
On cover 1,200.
18 A3 6kr bister 275.00 960.00
On cover 1,600.
19 A3 7kr ultra 2,000. 800.00
On cover 1,450.
20 A3 9kr bister 175.00 1,200.
On cover 2,000.
21 A3 12kr lilac 1,450. 1,750.
On cover 3,200.
22 A3 18kr red 450.00 2,400.
On cover 6,000.

Values for blocks of 4

15 A3 1kr yellow green 400.00 1,600.
16 A3 3kr rose 600.00 800.00
On cover 2,000.
17 A3 6kr ultra 250.00 3,600.
18 A3 6kr bister 400.00 4,500.
19 A3 7kr ultra 3,400. 2,400.
20 A3 9kr bister 250.00
21 A3 12kr lilac 4,800. 5,600.
22 A3 18kr red 640.00

1870-72 Wmk. 92 *Perf. 11½*

Without Silk Thread

23 A3 1kr green 12.00 1.60
Never hinged 22.00
On cover 8.00
Pair with gutter between 325.00
Never hinged 475.00
b. Unwmk. 240.00 95.00
Never hinged 440.00
c. 1kr deep yellow green 32.50 4.75
Never hinged 55.00
On cover 16.00
Pair with gutter between 400.00
Never hinged 640.00
24 A3 3kr rose 24.00 1.60
Never hinged 45.00
On cover 6.40
Pair with gutter between 300.00
Never hinged 440.00
b. Unwmk. 150.00 65.00
Never hinged 200.00
25 A3 6kr bister 30.00 30.00
Never hinged 65.00
On cover 125.00
On cover, single franking 1,350.
Pair with gutter between 600.00
Never hinged 960.00
b. Unwmk. 160.00 125.00
Never hinged 275.00
26 A3 7kr ultra 3.50 4.50
Never hinged 7.25
On cover 24.00
Pair with gutter between 325.00
Never hinged 560.00
a. 7kr Prussian blue 20.00 14.00
Never hinged 34.00
On cover 50.00
c. 7kr dk ultra 640.00 175.00
On cover 725.00
d. 7kr ultra, unwmk. 160.00 125.00
Never hinged 275.00
27 A3 9kr pale brn ('72) 5.50 4.00
Never hinged 11.50
On cover 175.00
On parcel post receipt card, single franking 350.00
Pair with gutter between 525.00
Never hinged 875.00
28 A3 10kr yellow 6.50 15.00
Never hinged 13.00
On cover 150.00
On parcel post receipt card, single franking 325.00
On parcel post receipt card, two singles 325.00
On cover, two singles 440.00
Pair with gutter between 440.00
Never hinged 575.00
b. 10kr yellowish orange 15.00 42.50
Never hinged 30.00
On cover 250.00
On parcel post receipt card, single franking 350.00
On parcel post receipt card, two singles 400.00
On cover, two singles 625.00
Pair with gutter between 525.00
Never hinged 800.00
29 A3 12kr lilac 1,200. 4,800.
Never hinged 2,000.
Pair with gutter between 7,200.
Never hinged 9,000.
30 A3 18kr dull brick red 16.00 16.00
Never hinged 32.00
On cover —
On parcel post receipt card 875.00
Pair with gutter between 560.00
Never hinged 800.00
b. 18kr dark brick red 120.00 70.00
Never hinged 325.00
On cover —
On parcel post receipt card 1,100.

The paper of the 1870-75 issues frequently appears to be laid with the lines either close or wide apart.
See Nos. 33-37.
Reprints exist.

Values for blocks of 4

23 A3 1kr green 65.00 275.00
Never hinged 130.00
b. 1kr deep yellow green 190.00 400.00
Never hinged 360.00
24 A3 3kr rose 140.00 200.00
Never hinged 260.00
25 A3 6kr bister 175.00 875.00
Never hinged 300.00
26 A3 7kr ultra 20.00 640.00
Never hinged 35.00
a. 7kr Prussian blue 125.00 7,000.
Never hinged 240.00
27 A3 9kr pale brown 50.00 600.00
Never hinged 80.00
28 A3 10kr yellow 32.50 800.00
Never hinged 60.00
b. 10kr yellowish orange 110.00
Never hinged 200.00
29 A3 12kr 6,000. 25,000.
Never hinged —
30 A3 18kr dull brick red 65.00 475.00
Never hinged 125.00
b. 18kr dark brick red 675.00

Imperf

23d A3 1kr 1,600.
24c A3 3kr 1,600. 1,600.
25c A3 6kr 2,400.
26e A3 7kr 2,400.
30d A3 18kr 2,400.

Wmk. 93

23a A3 1kr green 100.00 9.50
Never hinged 190.00
On cover 27.50
e. 1kr deep yellow green 160.00 35.00
Never hinged 290.00
On cover 80.00
24a A3 3kr rose 95.00 2.40
Never hinged 160.00
On cover 12.00
25a A3 6kr bister 175.00 70.00
Never hinged 325.00
On cover 260.00
On cover, single franking 1,750.
26b A3 7kr ultra 140.00 35.00
Never hinged 260.00
On cover 125.00
g. 7kr dk ultra 300.00
On cover 1,200.
27a A3 9kr pale brown 290.00 475.00
Never hinged 525.00
On parcel post receipt card 1,100.
On cover, single franking 2,200.
28a A3 10kr yellow 240.00 360.00
Never hinged 440.00
On parcel post receipt card 875.00
On cover, single franking 1,400.
On parcel post receipt card, two singles 1,400.
On cover, two singles 2,000.
c. 10kr yellowish orange 325.00 400.00
Never hinged 600.00
On parcel post receipt card 900.00
On cover, single franking 1,300.
On parcel post receipt card, two singles 1,600.
29a A3 12kr lilac 360.00 1,125.
Never hinged 640.00
On cover 3,600.
On cover, single franking 7,200.
Pair with gutter between
30a A3 18kr dull brick red 300.00 190.00
Never hinged 625.00
On cover —
On parcel post receipt card 1,250.
c. 18kr dark brick red 400.00 225.00
Never hinged 675.00
On cover —
On parcel post receipt card 1,400.

Values for blocks of 4

23a A3 1kr green 640.00 475.00
e. 1kr deep yellow green 1,200.
24a A3 3kr rose 560.00 450.00
25a A3 6kr bister 1,000.
26b A3 7kr ultra 950.00
27a A3 9kr pale brown 2,200.
28a A3 10kr yellow 1,450.
c. 10kr yelsh org 2,800.
29a A3 12kr lilac, wmk. 92 1,750. 26,000.
30c A3 18kr dull brick red 1,900.

Imperf

23f A3 1kr 1,800.
24d A3 3kr 1,800.
26f A3 7kr 2,800.
30e A3 18kr 2,800.

A4

1874-75 Wmk. 92 *Imperf.*

31 A4 1m violet 675.00 85.00
Never hinged 1,000.
On cover, single franking *7,250.*
On parcel post receipt card *1,400.*
a. 1m deep violet 2,000. 200.00
Never hinged 3,200.
On cover *8,750.*
On parcel post receipt card *1,750.*

Perf. 11½

32 A4 1m violet ('75) 200.00 55.00
Never hinged 350.00
On cover, single franking *2,850.*
On parcel post receipt card 950.00
a. 1m deep violet 475.00 125.00
Never hinged 800.00
On cover, single franking *3,200.*
On parcel post receipt card 1,600.

Values for blocks of 4

31 A4 1m violet 8,000. 1,400.
31a A4 1m deep violet 8,750. 1,800.
32 A4 1m violet 1,600. 950.00
32a A4 1m deep violet 2,800.

See Nos. 46-47, 54-57, 73-76.

1875 Wmk. 94

33 A3 1kr green .80 *24.00*
Never hinged 1.60
On cover 125.00
Pair with gutter between 12.00
Never hinged 22.50
34 A3 3kr rose .80 *8.00*
Never hinged 1.50
On cover 40.00
Pair with gutter between 9.50
Never hinged 17.50
35 A3 7kr ultra 5.25 *275.00*
Never hinged 10.00
On cover 1,400.
Pair with gutter between 95.00
Never hinged 175.00
36 A3 10kr yellow 30.00 *250.00*
Never hinged 70.00
On cover *1,600.*
Two singles on cover 3,250.
Pair with gutter between 475.00
Never hinged 800.00
37 A3 18kr red 24.00 *60.00*
Never hinged 47.50
On cover *27,500.*
On parcel post receipt card *22,000.*
Pair with gutter between 325.00
Never hinged 600.00
Nos. 33-37 (5) 60.85 617.00

Values for blocks of 4

33 A3 1kr green 3.50 *1,300.*
Never hinged 7.25
34 A3 3kr rose 4.00 *400.00*
Never hinged 7.25
35 A3 7kr ultra 27.50 *4,800.*
Never hinged 52.50
36 A3 10kr yel 200.00 *4,800.*
Never hinged 400.00
37 A3 18kr red 160.00 *2,600.*
Never hinged 300.00

False cancellations exist on Nos. 29, 29a, 33-37.

A5

1876-78 Embossed *Perf. 11½*

38 A5 3pf lt grn 35.00 1.60
Never hinged 90.00
On cover 16.00
a. 3pf lt yel grn 80.00 24.00
Never hinged 175.00
On cover 60.00
39 A5 5pf dk grn 90.00 16.00
Never hinged 225.00
On cover 40.00
On cover, single franking 100.00
a. 5pf dk bluish grn 325.00 20.00
Never hinged 1,200.
On cover 55.00
40 A5 5pf lilac ('78) 160.00 20.00
Never hinged 375.00
On cover 95.00
a. 5pf lt reddish vio 275.00 52.50
Never hinged 560.00
On cover 140.00
41 A5 10pf rose 190.00 1.25
Never hinged 640.00
On cover 9.50
a. 10pf dk magenta 360.00 160.00
Never hinged 875.00
On cover 325.00
42 A5 20pf ultra 190.00 3.25
Never hinged 600.00
On cover 25.00
On postcard, single franking 160.00
a. 20pf gray blue 450.00 80.00
Never hinged 950.00
On cover 120.00
43 A5 25pf yel brn 175.00 6.50
Never hinged 450.00
On cover 725.00
On postcard, single franking 725.00
On cover, single franking 750.00
44 A5 50pf scarlet 55.00 7.25
Never hinged 125.00
On cover 1,500.
On parcel post receipt card 1,100.
45 A5 50pf brn ('78) 800.00 27.50
Never hinged 2,000.
On cover 1,500.
On parcel post receipt card 700.00
46 A4 1m violet 1,900. 90.00
Never hinged 3,600.
On cover 3,500.
On parcel post receipt card 675.00
47 A4 2m orange 24.00 12.00
Never hinged 52.50
On cover 2,200.
On parcel post receipt card 275.00

The paper of the 1876-78 issue often shows ribbed lines.

See Nos. 48-53, 58-72. For overprints and surcharge see Nos. 237, O1-O5.

Values for blocks of 4

38 A5 3pf green 160.00 125.00
Never hinged 325.00
On cover 325.00
a. 3pf lt yel grn 360.00 —
Never hinged 800.00
39 A5 5pf dk green 360.00 160.00
Never hinged 1,000.
On cover 1,200.
a. 5pf dk bluish green 1,400. 200.00
On cover 1,200.
40 A5 5pf lilac 800.00 600.00
Never hinged 1,900.
On cover 2,000.
a. 5pf lt reddish violet 1,400. 800.00
Never hinged 2,800.
On cover 2,800.
41 A5 10pf rose 800.00 200.00
On cover 1,200.
42 A5 20pf ultramarine 160.00
a. 20pf gray blue 600.00
43 A5 25pf yel brn 325.00
44 A5 50pf scarlet 275.00 *525.00*
Never hinged 550.00
45 A5 50pf brown *6,000.*
46 A4 1m violet 9,600. *6,000.*
47 A4 2m orange 125.00 60.00
Never hinged 275.00

1881-1911 Wmk. 95v *Perf. 11½*

48 A5 3pf green 12.00 .80
Never hinged 28.00
On cover 12.00
49 A5 5pf lilac 17.50 1.25
Never hinged 35.00
On cover 16.00
50 A5 10pf carmine 12.50 .65
Never hinged 27.50
On cover 4.00
b. 10pf magenta 24.00 4.00
Never hinged 60.00
On cover 25.00
51 A5 20pf ultramarine 14.00 .80
Never hinged 30.00
On cover 9.50
52 A5 25pf yellow brown 125.00 3.50
Never hinged 240.00
On cover 400.00
On postal card, single franking 500.00
On cover, single franking, local delivery 740.00
On parcel post receipt card 290.00
53 A5 50pf deep brown 145.00 3.25
Never hinged 275.00
On cover 300.00
Two singles on cover 775.00
On parcel post receipt card 275.00
On cover, single franking 500.00
54 A4 1m rose lil ('00) 4.50 3.50
Never hinged 9.50
On cover 300.00
On parcel post receipt card 45.00
Two singles on parcel post receipt card 475.00
a. 1m brownish lilac, toned paper 52.50 4.00
Never hinged 110.00
On cover 300.00
On cover, single franking 1,100.
On parcel post receipt card 75.00
b. 1m brownish pur, toned paper 1,100. 110.00
Never hinged 2,250
On cover 1,600.
On cover, single franking 2,600.
On parcel post receipt card 900.00
c. 1m brownish lilac, white paper 32.50
Never hinged 65.00
On cover 575.00
On parcel post receipt card 175.00
Two singles on parcel post receipt card 400.00
55 A4 2m orange ('01) 5.50 *8.00*
Never hinged 13.00
On cover 875.00
On cover, single franking 1,400.
Two singles on cover 2,300.
On parcel post receipt card 175.00
a. Toned paper ('90) 90.00 14.00
Never hinged 190.00
On cover 1,300.
On cover, single franking 1,800.
Two singles on cover 2,900.
On parcel post receipt card 325.00
56 A4 3m olive gray ('00) 24.00 *30.00*
Never hinged 47.50
On cover 2,200.
On cover, single franking 2,200.
On parcel post receipt card 600.00
a. White paper ('06) 175.00 *400.00*
Never hinged 300.00
On cover 2,900.
On cover, single franking 3,600.
On parcel post receipt card 1,300.
b. Yellowish translucent paper ('11) 110.00 *550.00*
Never hinged 175.00
On cover 2,200.
On cover, single franking *2,500.*
On parcel post receipt card *875.00*
57 A4 5m yel grn ('00) 24.00 *30.00*
Never hinged 47.50
On cover 2,200.
On cover, single franking 2,200.
On parcel post receipt card 800.00
a. White paper ('06) 150.00 *350.00*
Never hinged 275.00
On cover 2,900.
On cover, single franking 3,600.
On parcel post receipt card 1,400.
b. Yellowish translucent paper ('11) 80.00 *150.00*
Never hinged 125.00
On cover *2,200.*
On cover, single franking 2,500.
On parcel post receipt card 950.00
Nos. 48-57 (10) 384.00 81.75

Nos. 54-55 are on white paper. Nos. 56-57 are on toned paper. A 2m lilac was not regularly issued.

Values for blocks of 4

48 A5 3pf green 72.50 60.00
Never hinged 150.00
On cover 125.00
49 A5 5pf lilac 87.50 40.00
Never hinged 175.00
On cover 125.00
50 A5 10pf carmine 60.00 40.00
Never hinged 140.00
On cover 60.00
b. 10pf magenta 160.00 60.00
Never hinged 400.00
51 A5 20pf ultramarine 70.00 55.00
Never hinged 140.00
52 A5 25pf yellow brown 600.00 95.00
Never hinged 1,200.
53 A5 50pf deep brown 640.00 125.00
Never hinged 1,300.
54 A4 1m rose 22.50 *40.00*
Never hinged 47.50
a. 1m brownish lilac, toned paper 325.00 80.00
Never hinged 800.00
e. 1m brownish lilac, white paper 250.00 —
Never hinged 550.00
55 A4 2m orange 18.00 *37.50*
Never hinged 35.00
a. Toned paper 475.00 80.00
Never hinged 1,000.

Imperf.

48a A5 3pf 400.00 *2,000.*
Never hinged 800.00
49a A5 5pf 2,000.
Never hinged 3,200.
50a A5 10pf 400.00 *2,000.*
Never hinged 800.00
On cover *2,500.*
51a A5 20pf 1,600.
Never hinged 3,600.
52a A5 25pf 1,600.
Never hinged 3,600.
53a A5 50pf 1,600.
Never hinged 3,600.
54d A4 1m rose 140.00
Never hinged 275.00
e. As "a." 4,000.
Never hinged 6,400.
55b A4 2m org 75.00
Never hinged 150.00
56c A4 3m As "a." 300.00
Never hinged 600.00
57c A4 5m As "a." 300.00
Never hinged 600.00

1888-1900 Wmk. 95h *Perf. 14½*

White Paper

58 A5 2pf gray ('00) 2.40 .55
Never hinged 5.50
On cover 7.25
60 A5 3pf brown ('00) .30 *.65*
Never hinged .80
On cover 2.40
b. 3pf black brown 9.75 8.00
Never hinged 25.00
On cover 25.00
62 A5 5pf dk grn ('00) .30 *.65*
Never hinged .80
On cover 2.00
63 A5 10pf carmine .40 *.80*
Never hinged .80
On cover 2.00
64 A5 20pf ultra .40 *.80*
Never hinged .80
On cover 3.25
On postal card, single franking *28.00*
b. 20pf grayish blue .65 *1.60*
Never hinged 1.25
On cover 8.00
66 A5 25pf orange ('00) .60 *1.10*
Never hinged .95
On cover 22.50
On cover, single franking 67.50
67 A5 30pf ol grn ('00) .80 *1.40*
Never hinged 2.00
On cover 24.00
On postal card, single franking 75.00
68 A5 40pf yellow ('00) .80 *1.10*
Never hinged 2.00
On cover 35.00
70 A5 50pf maroon ('00) .50 *1.60*
Never hinged .95
On cover 35.00
On cover, single franking 47.50
On parcel post receipt card 20.00
71 A5 80pf lilac ('00) 3.25 *4.00*
Never hinged 7.25
On cover 175.00
On cover, single franking 275.00
On parcel post receipt card 55.00
Nos. 58-71 (10) 9.75 12.65

Nos. 59, 61, 65, 69 and 70 are on toned paper; Nos. 67-68 on white.

Values for blocks of 4

58 A5 2pf gray 65.00 *80.00*
Never hinged 175.00
On cover *125.00*
63 A5 10pf carmine 2.00 *3.25*
Never hinged 3.50
On cover *9.50*
64 A5 20pf ultra 2.00 *6.50*
Never hinged 3.50
On cover *9.50*
b. 20pf grayish blue 3.50 *16.00*
Never hinged 8.00
On cover 32.50

Imperf

58b A5 2pf 72.50
Never hinged 175.00
60c A5 3pf 72.50
Never hinged 160.00
62b A5 5pf 75.00
Never hinged 160.00
63c A5 10pf 72.50
Never hinged 160.00
64c A5 20pf 75.00
Never hinged 160.00
66b A5 25pf 75.00
Never hinged 200.00
70b A5 50pf 130.00
Never hinged 260.00

1888-99 Toned Paper

58a A5 2pf gray ('99) 12.00 5.25
Never hinged 35.00
On cover 16.00
59 A5 3pf green 9.25 2.10
Never hinged 35.00
On cover 12.00
60a A5 3pf dk ocher brn ('90) 9.25 .40
Never hinged 23.00
On cover 3.25
d. 3pf yel brn 26.00 6.75
Never hinged 65.00
On cover 13.50
61 A5 5pf lilac 24.00 5.50
Never hinged 67.50
On cover 20.00
a. 5pf brownish violet 20.00 7.50
Never hinged 60.00
On cover 30.00
62a A5 5pf dk green ('90) 10.00 .65
Never hinged 25.00
On cover 3.25
d. Imperf 600.00 *1,200.*
On cover *3,200.*
63a A5 10pf car red 6.75 .80
Never hinged 17.50
On cover 3.25
b. Imperf. 72.50 *175.00*
Never hinged 225.00
On cover 525.00
d. 10pf lilac red 20.00 8.00
Never hinged 60.00
On cover 20.00
64a A5 20pf ultra 10.00 1.25
Never hinged 30.00
On cover 5.50
d. 20pf grayish blue 14.00 4.00
Never hinged 40.00
On cover 12.00
65 A5 25pf yel brn 32.50 6.75
Never hinged 90.00
On cover 190.00
On cover, single franking 250.00
On parcel post receipt card 90.00
66a A5 25pf org ('90) 16.50 1.60
Never hinged 55.00
On cover 22.50
69 A5 50pf dp brn 60.00 6.75
Never hinged 160.00
On cover 160.00
On cover, single franking 190.00
On parcel post receipt card 82.50
70a A5 50pf mar ('90) 47.50 2.40
Never hinged 95.00
On cover 65.00
On parcel post receipt card 24.00
71a A5 80pf lilac ('99) 32.50 12.00
Never hinged 95.00
On cover 275.00
On cover, single franking 375.00
On parcel post receipt card 80.00

Values for blocks of 4

58a A5 2pf gray 55.00 *70.00*
On cover 110.00
59 A5 3pf green 50.00 35.00
Never hinged 150.00
60a A5 3pf dk ocher brn ('90) 70.00 7.00
Never hinged 150.00
On cover 21.00
d. 3pf yel brn 160.00 62.50
Never hinged 375.00
61 A5 5pf lilac 125.00 37.50
Never hinged 325.00
On cover 125.00
a. 5pf brownish violet 125.00 95.00
Never hinged 325.00
On cover 190.00
62a A5 5pf dk green 80.00 8.00
Never hinged 175.00
On cover 24.00
63a A5 10pf car red 30.00 8.00
Never hinged 90.00
On cover 16.00
d. 10pf lilac red 125.00 95.00
Never hinged 325.00
On cover 200.00
64a A5 20pf ultra 55.00 20.00
Never hinged 160.00
On cover 60.00
d. 20pf grayish blue 80.00 47.50
Never hinged 240.00
On cover 95.00
65 A5 25pf yel brn 160.00 47.50
Never hinged 440.00
66a A5 25pf org ('90) 95.00 15.00
Never hinged 300.00
On cover 77.50
69 A5 50pf dp brn 275.00 60.00
Never hinged 800.00
70a A5 50pf mar ('90) 275.00 35.00
Never hinged 540.00
On parcel post receipt card 130.00
71a A5 80pf lilac 175.00 125.00
Never hinged 450.00

1911, Jan. 23 Wmk. 95v

72 A5 5pf dark green .65 *13.50*
Never hinged 1.50
On cover *20.00*
On registered cover *60.00*
On first day cover *40.00*

1911, Jan. Wmk. 95h *Perf. 11½*

73 A4 1m rose lilac 4.00 *27.50*
Never hinged 7.00
On cover *350.00*
On parcel post receipt card *425.00*

74 A4 2m orange 17.00 *37.50*
Never hinged 20.00
On cover *1,400.*
On parcel post receipt card *875.00*
75 A4 3m olive gray 17.00 *57.50*
Never hinged 22.00
On cover *2,900.*
On parcel post receipt card *1,300.*
76 A4 5m pale yel grn 17.00 *57.50*
Never hinged 22.00
On cover *2,900.*
On parcel post receipt card *1,300.*
Nos. 73-76 (4) 55.00 180.00

See note after No. 91 concerning used values.

Values for canceled to order and on philatelic covers

73 A4 1m rose lilac 92.50
On overfranked cover 65.00
74 A4 2m orange 14.00
On overfranked cover 82.50
75 A4 3m olive gray 22.00
On overfranked cover 140.00
76 A4 5m pale yellow green 22.00
On overfranked cover 210.00

See note after No. 91 concerning used values.

A6

A7

A8

Prince Regent Luitpold

Perf. 14x14½

1911 Wmk. 95h Litho.

77 A6 3pf brn, *gray brn* .30 .30
Never hinged 1.25
On cover 1.25
a. "911" for "1911" *325.00* *325.00*
Never hinged *525.00*
78 A6 5pf dk grn, *grn* .30 .30
Never hinged 1.25
On cover 1.25
a. Tête bêche pair 4.50 *10.50*
b. Booklet pane of 4 + 2 labels 100.00 *150.00*
c. Bklt. pane of 5 + label 225.00 *375.00*
d. Bklt. pane of 6 35.00
79 A6 10pf scar, *buff* .30 .30
Never hinged .80
On cover 1.25
a. Tête bêche pair 5.75 *62.50*
b. "911" for "1911" 15.00 15.00
Never hinged 25.00
d. Booklet pane of 5 + label 65.00 30.00
80 A6 20pf dp bl, *bl* 2.00 .75
Never hinged 9.00
On cover 3.75
81 A6 25pf vio brn, *buff* 3.25 1.25
Never hinged 12.00
On cover 14.00

Perf. 11½

Wmk. 95v

82 A7 30pf org buff, *buff* 2.25 1.25
Never hinged 7.50
On cover 14.00
83 A7 40pf ol grn, *buff* 4.00 1.25
Never hinged 13.50
On cover 14.00
84 A7 50pf cl, *gray brn* 3.25 *3.25*
Never hinged 11.00
On cover 25.00
84A A7 60pf dk grn, *buff* 3.25 *3.25*
Never hinged 11.00
On cover 27.50
85 A7 80pf vio, *gray brn* 9.00 *11.00*
Never hinged 29.00
On cover 80.00
86 A8 1m brn, *gray brn* 3.25 *4.00*
Never hinged 11.00
On parcel post receipt card 27.50
87 A8 2m dk grn, *grn* 4.75 *12.00*
Never hinged 14.00
On parcel post receipt card *40.00*
88 A8 3m lake, *buff* 13.00 *65.00*
Never hinged 28.00
On parcel post receipt card 160.00
89 A8 5m dk bl, *buff* 13.00 *45.00*
Never hinged 32.50
On parcel post receipt card *300.00*
90 A8 10m org, *yel* 22.50 *65.00*
Never hinged 47.50
On parcel post receipt card *400.00*
91 A8 20m blk brn, *yel* 25.00 *32.50*
Never hinged 50.00
On parcel post receipt card 475.00
Nos. 77-91 (16) 109.40 *246.40*

90th birthday of Prince Regent Luitpold.
All values exist in 2 types except No. 84A.
Used values: Nos. 73-76 and 77-91 often were canceled en masse for accounting purposes. These cancels are perfectly clear, and used values are for stamps canceled thus. Postally used examples are worth about twice as much.

Imperf

77b A6 3pf 32.50
Never hinged 50.00
78e A6 5pf 12.50
Never hinged 24.00
79e A6 10pf 27.50
Never hinged 47.50
80a A6 20pf 27.50
Never hinged 47.50
81a A6 25pf 30.00
Never hinged 50.00
82a A7 30pf 30.00
Never hinged 50.00
83a A7 40pf 50.00
Never hinged 60.00
84b A7 50pf 32.50 *95.00*
Never hinged 47.50
85a A7 80pf 50.00 *120.00*
Never hinged 65.00
86a A8 1m 275.00
Never hinged 450.00
87a A8 2m 960.00
Never hinged 1,400.
88a A8 3m *600.00*
89a A8 5m 400.00
Never hinged 600.00
90a A8 10m 400.00
Never hinged 600.00
91a A8 20m 400.00
Never hinged 600.00

Prince Regent Luitpold — A9

1911, June 10 Unwmk.

92 A9 5pf grn, yel & blk .80 *1.40*
Never hinged 1.40
On cover 4.00
b. Horiz. pair, imperf. btwn. 140.00 *225.00*
93 A9 10pf rose, yel & blk 1.25 *2.40*
Never hinged 2.40
On cover 6.50
b. Pair, imperf. between 140.00 *225.00*

Silver Jubilee of Prince Regent Luitpold.

Used values of Nos. 94-275, B1-B3 are for postally used stamps. Canceled-to-order stamps, which abound, sell for same prices as unused.

A10

A11

King Ludwig III — A12

Perf. 14x14½

1914-20 Wmk. 95h Photo.

Wartime & Later Printings ('16-'20)

Coarse Impressions, Dull Colors

94 A10 2pf gray ('18) .25 2.00
Never hinged .65
On cover 2.40
95 A10 3pf brown .25 *2.00*
Never hinged .65
On cover 2.40
96 A10 5pf yellow grn 1.10 *2.00*
Never hinged 3.25
On cover 2.40
a. 5pf dark green 1.10 *2.00*
Never hinged 3.25
On cover 2.40
b. Tête bêche pair 3.50 *16.50*
c. Booklet pane of 5 + 1 label 16.00 *60.00*
97 A10 7½pf dp grn ('16) .25 *2.00*
On cover 2.40
a. Tête bêche pair 2.40 *11.00*
b. Booklet pane of 6 16.00
98 A10 10pf vermilion 1.40 *2.00*
Never hinged 3.25
On cover 2.40
a. Tête bêche pair 3.50 *16.50*
b. Booklet pane of 5 + 1 label 16.00 *60.00*
99 A10 10pf car rose ('16) .25 *2.00*
Never hinged .65
On cover 2.40
100 A10 15pf ver ('16) .25 *2.00*
Never hinged .65
On cover 2.40
a. Tête bêche pair 2.40 *11.00*
b. Booklet pane of 5 + 1 label 6.75 *24.00*
101 A10 15pf car ('20) 1.50 *27.50*
Never hinged 3.50
On cover 47.50
102 A10 20pf blue .25 *2.00*
Never hinged .65
On cover 2.40
103 A10 25pf gray .25 *2.00*
Never hinged .65
On cover 2.75
104 A10 30pf orange 1.25 *2.00*
Never hinged 2.75
On cover 2.40
105 A10 40pf olive grn .25 *2.00*
Never hinged .65
On cover 2.40
106 A10 50pf red brn .25 *2.00*
Never hinged .65
On cover 2.40
107 A10 60pf blue grn .80 *2.00*
Never hinged 2.75
On cover 3.50
108 A10 80pf violet .25 *2.00*
Never hinged .65
On cover 5.50

Perf. 11½

Wmk. 95v

109 A11 1m brown .25 *2.00*
Never hinged .70
On cover 9.50
110 A11 2m violet .30 *2.75*
Never hinged .80
On cover 14.50
111 A11 3m scarlet .40 *5.50*
Never hinged .95
On cover 27.50

Wmk. 95h

112 A12 5m deep blue .55 *20.00*
Never hinged 1.25
On cover 35.00
113 A12 10m yellow grn 1.75 *55.00*
Never hinged 4.00
On cover 125.00
114 A12 20m brown 3.25 *80.00*
Never hinged 6.50
On cover 190.00
Nos. 94-114 (21) 15.05 *220.75*

Pre-war Printings ('14-'15)

Clear Impressions, Bright Colors

Values for used stamps, covers and parcel post receipt cards with dated cancellations between Mar. 30, 1914, and Dec. 31, 1915.

95c A10 3pf brown 1.40
On cover 2.10
96d A10 5pf yellow grn 1.50
On cover 2.10
96e A10 5pf dark green 1.50
On cover 1.90
98c A10 10pf vermilion 1.50
On cover 2.10
102a A10 20pf blue 2.25
On cover 5.50
103a A10 25pf gray 8.50
On cover 24.00
104a A10 30pf orange 5.00
On cover 20.00
105a A10 40pf olive grn 8.50
On cover 20.00
106a A10 50pf red brn 8.50
On cover 20.00
107a A10 60pf blue grn 11.00
On cover 20.00
108a A10 80pf violet 11.00
On cover 32.50
109a A11 1m brown 7.00
On cover 27.50
110a A11 2m violet 14.00
On parcel post receipt card 65.00
111a A11 3m scarlet 5.50
On parcel post receipt card 27.50
112a A12 5m deep blue 77.50
On parcel post receipt card 275.00
113a A12 10m yellow grn 275.00
On parcel post receipt card 625.00
114a A12 20m brown 250.00
On parcel post receipt card 625.00
Nos. 95c-114a (17) 689.65

See Nos. 117-135. For overprints and surcharges see Nos. 115, 136-175, 193-236, B1-B3.

No. 94 Surcharged

1916 Wmk. 95h *Perf. 14x14½*

115 A10 2½pf on 2pf gray .25 2.00
a. Double surcharge

Ludwig III Types of 1914-20

1916-20 *Imperf.*

117 A10 2pf gray .25 *14.50*
118 A10 3pf brown .25 *14.50*
119 A10 5pf pale yel grn .25 *14.50*
120 A10 7½pf dp green .25 *14.50*
a. Tête bêche pair 3.25 *25.00*
121 A10 10pf car rose .25 *14.50*
122 A10 15pf vermilion .25 *14.50*
a. Tête bêche pair 3.25 *25.00*
123 A10 20pf blue .25 *14.50*
124 A10 25pf gray .25 *14.50*
125 A10 30pf orange .25 *14.50*
126 A10 40pf olive grn .25 *14.50*
127 A10 50pf red brown .25 *14.50*
128 A10 60pf dark green .25 *16.00*
129 A10 80pf violet .25 *16.00*
130 A11 1m brown .35 *16.00*
131 A11 2m violet .35 *20.00*
132 A11 3m scarlet .50 *27.50*
133 A12 5m deep blue .95 *45.00*
134 A12 10m yellow green 1.60 *65.00*
135 A12 20m brown 2.25 *110.00*
Nos. 117-135 (19) 9.25 *475.00*

Stamps and Type of 1914-20 Overprinted

a

b

Wmk. 95h or 95v

1919 *Perf. 14x14½*

Overprint "a"

136 A10 3pf brown .25 *2.00*
137 A10 5pf yellow grn .25 *2.00*
138 A10 7½pf deep green .25 *2.00*
139 A10 10pf car rose .25 *2.00*
140 A10 15pf vermilion .25 *2.00*
141 A10 20pf blue .25 *2.00*
142 A10 25pf gray .25 *2.00*
143 A10 30pf orange .25 *2.00*
144 A10 35pf orange .25 *2.50*
a. Without overprint 100.00
145 A10 40pf olive grn .25 *2.00*
146 A10 50pf red brown .25 *2.00*
147 A10 60pf dark green .25 *2.00*
148 A10 75pf red brown .25 *2.00*
a. Without overprint 22.50 *225.00*
149 A10 80pf violet .25 *2.00*

Perf. 11½

Overprint "a"

150 A11 1m brown .25 *2.00*
151 A11 2m violet .25 *2.00*
152 A11 3m scarlet .45 *4.75*

Overprint "b"

153 A12 5m deep blue .90 *12.00*
154 A12 10m yellow green 1.40 *50.00*
155 A12 20m dk brown 2.50 *50.00*
Nos. 136-155 (20) 9.25 *149.25*

Inverted overprints exist on Nos. 137-143, 145-147, 149. Value, each $15.
Double overprints exist on Nos. 137, 139, 143, 145, 150. Values, $30-$75.

Imperf

Overprint "a"

156 A10 3pf brown .25 *20.00*
157 A10 5pf pale yel grn .25 *20.00*
158 A10 7½pf dp green .25 *20.00*
159 A10 10pf car rose .25 *20.00*
160 A10 15pf vermilion .25 *20.00*
161 A10 20pf blue .25 *20.00*
162 A10 25pf gray .25 *20.00*
163 A10 30pf orange .25 *20.00*
164 A10 35pf orange .25 *20.00*
a. Without overprint 13.00
165 A10 40pf olive grn .25 *20.00*
166 A10 50pf red brown .25 *20.00*
167 A10 60pf dk green .25 *20.00*
168 A10 75pf red brown .25 *20.00*
a. Without overprint 190.00
169 A10 80pf violet .25 *20.00*
170 A11 1m brown .25 *24.00*
171 A11 2m violet .50 *27.50*
172 A11 3m scarlet .70 *45.00*

Overprint "b"

173 A12 5m deep blue .95 *55.00*
174 A12 10m yellow grn 1.40 *80.00*
175 A12 20m brown 2.75 *80.00*
Nos. 156-175 (20) 10.05 591.50

Stamps of Germany 1906-19 Overprinted

1919 Wmk. 125 *Perf. 14, 14½*

176 A22 2½pf gray .25 *2.00*
177 A16 3pf brown .25 *2.00*
178 A16 5pf green .25 *2.00*
179 A22 7½pf orange .25 *2.00*

180 A16 10pf carmine .25 *2.00*
181 A22 15pf dk violet .25 *2.00*
a. Double overprint 375.00 *1,050.*
182 A16 20pf ultra .25 *2.00*
183 A16 25pf org & blk, *yel* .25 *2.00*
184 A22 35pf red brown .25 *2.00*
185 A16 40pf lake & blk .40 *2.00*
186 A16 75pf green & blk .55 *2.40*
187 A16 80pf lake & blk, *rose* .55 *3.25*
188 A17 1m car rose 1.25 *4.75*
189 A21 2m dull blue 1.60 *11.00*
190 A19 3m gray violet 1.60 *13.00*
191 A20 5m slate & car 1.60 *13.00*
a. Inverted overprint *3,575.*
Nos. 176-191 (16) 9.80 *67.40*

Bavarian Stamps of 1914-16 Overprinted

c d

Wmk. 95h or 95v

1919-20 ***Perf. 14x14½***

Overprint "c"

193 A10 3pf brown .25 *2.00*
194 A10 5pf yellow grn .25 *2.00*
195 A10 7½pf dp green .25 *16.00*
196 A10 10pf car rose .25 *2.00*
197 A10 15pf vermilion .25 *2.00*
198 A10 20pf blue .25 *2.00*
199 A10 25pf gray .25 *2.00*
200 A10 30pf orange .25 *2.00*
201 A10 40pf olive grn .25 *14.50*
202 A10 50pf red brown .25 *2.00*
203 A10 60pf dk green .25 *14.50*
204 A10 75pf olive bister .40 *14.50*
205 A10 80pf violet .25 *3.50*

Perf. 11½

Overprint "c"

206 A11 1m brown .25 *3.50*
207 A11 2m violet .25 *4.25*
208 A11 3m scarlet .35 *6.00*

Overprint "d"

209 A12 5m deep blue 1.10 *17.50*
210 A12 10m yellow grn 2.00 *35.00*
211 A12 20m dk brown 2.40 *60.00*
Nos. 193-211 (19) 9.75 205.25

Imperf

Overprint "c"

212 A10 3pf brown .25 *12.00*
213 A10 5pf pale yel grn .25 *12.00*
214 A10 7½pf deep green .25 *22.50*
215 A10 10pf car rose .25 *12.00*
216 A10 15pf vermilion .25 *12.00*
217 A10 20pf blue .25 *12.00*
a. Double overprint 50.00
218 A10 25pf gray .25 *12.00*
219 A10 30pf orange .25 *13.50*
220 A10 40pf olive grn .25 *14.50*
221 A10 50pf red brn .25 *14.50*
222 A10 60pf dk green .25 *14.50*
223 A10 75pf olive bis .25 *35.00*
a. Without overprint 5.00
224 A10 80pf violet .25 *14.50*
225 A11 1m brown .25 *22.50*
226 A11 2m violet .25 *22.50*
227 A11 3m scarlet .65 *27.50*

Overprint "d"

228 A12 5m deep blue 1.10 *40.00*
229 A12 10m yellow grn 2.00 *70.00*
230 A12 20m brown 2.40 *110.00*
Nos. 212-230 (19) 9.90 493.50

Ludwig Type of 1914, Printed in Various Colors and Surcharged

1919 ***Perf. 11½***

231 A11 1.25m on 1m yel grn .25 *2.40*
232 A11 1.50m on 1m orange .25 *3.25*
233 A11 2.50m on 1m gray .45 *6.50*
Nos. 231-233 (3) .95 *12.15*

1920 ***Imperf.***

234 A11 1.25m on 1m yel grn .30 *35.00*
a. Without surcharge 400.00
235 A11 1.50m on 1m org .30 *35.00*
a. Without surcharge 8.00
236 A11 2.50m on 1m gray .65 *35.00*
a. Without surcharge 8.00
Nos. 234-236 (3) 1.25 *105.00*

No. 60 Surcharged in Dark Blue

1920 ***Perf. 14½***

237 A5 20pf on 3pf brown .25 *2.00*
a. Inverted surcharge 9.00 *30.00*
b. Double surcharge 95.00 *225.00*

Plowman A14

"Electricity" Harnessing Light to a Water Wheel A15

Sower — A16

Madonna and Child — A17

von Kaulbach's "Genius" — A18

TWENTY PFENNIG
Type I — Foot of "2" turns downward.
Type II — Foot of "2" turns upward.

Perf. 14x14½

1920 **Wmk. 95h** **Typo.**

238 A14 5pf yellow grn .25 *2.40*
239 A14 10pf orange .25 *2.40*
240 A14 15pf carmine .25 *2.40*
241 A15 20pf violet (I) .25 *2.40*
a. 20pf violet (II) 10.00 *1,400.*
242 A15 30pf dp blue .25 *3.25*
243 A15 40pf brown .25 *2.40*
244 A16 50pf vermilion .25 *2.40*
245 A16 60pf blue green .25 *2.40*
246 A16 75pf lilac rose .25 *2.40*

Perf. 12x11½

Wmk. 95v

247 A17 1m car & gray .35 *2.40*
248 A17 1¼m ultra & ol bis .25 *2.40*
249 A17 1½m dk grn & gray .25 *3.25*
250 A17 2½m blk & gray .25 *32.50*

Perf. 11½x12

Wmk. 95h

251 A18 3m pale blue .55 *14.50*
252 A18 5m orange .55 *14.50*
253 A18 10m deep green .95 *25.00*
254 A18 20m black 1.40 *32.50*
Nos. 238-254 (17) 6.80 149.50

Imperf. Pairs

238a A14 5pf yellow grn 65.00 *450.00*
239a A14 10pf orange 160.00
241b A15 20pf violet (I) 65.00
243a A15 40pf brown 140.00
244a A16 50pf vermilion 80.00
245a A16 60pf blue green 47.50
246a A16 75pf lilac rose 47.50
247a A17 1m car & gray 8.00 *32.50*
248a A17 1¼m ultra & ol bis 8.00 *32.50*
249a A17 1½m dk grn & gray 8.00 *32.50*
250a A17 2½m blk & gray 18.00 *160.00*
251a A18 3m pale blue 14.00 *80.00*
252a A18 5m orange 14.00 *80.00*
253a A18 10m deep green 14.00 *95.00*
254a A18 20m black 14.00 *125.00*

Perf. 12x11½

1920 **Litho.** **Wmk. 95v**

255 A17 2½m black & gray .50 *65.00*

On No. 255 the background dots are small, hazy and irregularly spaced. On No. 250 they are large, clear, round, white and regularly spaced in rows. The backs of the typo. stamps usually show a raised impression of parts of the design.

Stamps and Types of Preceding Issue Overprinted

1920

256 A14 5pf yellow green .25 *1.60*
a. Inverted overprint 30.00
b. Imperf., pair 37.50 *375.00*
257 A14 10pf orange .25 *1.60*
a. Imperf., pair 37.50 *375.00*
b. Inverted overprint 30.00 *600.00*
258 A14 15pf carmine .25 *1.60*
a. Inverted overprint 30.00
259 A15 20pf violet .25 *1.60*
a. Inverted overprint 30.00 *750.00*
b. Double overprint 13.00
c. Imperf., pair 50.00
260 A15 30pf deep blue .25 *1.60*
a. Inverted overprint 30.00
b. Imperf., pair 50.00 *375.00*
261 A15 40pf brown .25 *1.60*
a. Inverted overprint 30.00 *750.00*
b. Imperf., pair 50.00
262 A16 50pf vermilion .25 *2.40*
a. Inverted overprint 30.00 *900.00*
263 A16 60pf blue green .50 *1.40*
264 A16 75pf lilac rose .40 *5.25*
a. Inverted overprint 30.00
265 A16 80pf dark blue .40 *2.75*
a. Without overprint *100.00*
b. Imperf., pair 50.00

Overprinted in Black or Red

266 A17 1m car & gray .50 *2.75*
a. Imperf., pair 50.00 *375.00*
b. Inverted overprint 52.50
267 A17 1¼m ultra & ol bis .50 *2.75*
a. Imperf., pair 47.50
268 A17 1½m dk grn & gray .50 *3.50*
a. Imperf., pair 47.50
269 A17 2m vio & ol bis .80 *4.00*
a. Without overprint 32.50
b. Imperf., pair 50.00
270 A17 2½m (#250) (R) .25 *2.75*
c. Imperf., pair 50.00
270A A17 2½m (#255) (R) .95 *95.00*
b. Imperf., pair 50.00

Nos. 251-254 Overprinted

271 A18 3m pale blue 3.25 *9.50*
272 A18 4m dull red 3.25 *10.00*
a. Without overprint 47.50
273 A18 5m orange 3.25 *9.50*
274 A18 10m dp green 5.25 *16.00*
275 A18 20m black 6.00 *13.00*
Nos. 256-275 (21) 27.55 190.15

Nos. 256-275 were available for postage through all Germany, but were used almost exclusively in Bavaria.

SEMI-POSTAL STAMPS

Regular Issue of 1914-20 Surcharged in Black

1919 **Wmk. 95h** ***Perf. 14x14½***

B1 A10 10pf + 5pf car rose .40 *2.00*
a. Inverted surcharge 26.00 *65.00*
b. Surcharge on back 50.00
c. Imperf., pair 325.00
B2 A10 15pf + 5pf ver .40 *2.00*
a. Inverted surcharge 26.00 *65.00*
b. Imperf., pair *190.00*
B3 A10 20pf + 5pf blue .40 *2.40*
a. Inverted surcharge 26.00 *65.00*
b. Imperf., pair *375.00*
Nos. B1-B3 (3) 1.20 *6.40*

Surtax was for wounded war veterans.

AIR POST SEMI-OFFICIAL STAMPS

Symbol of Bavarian Air Club — CL1

1912, October **Unwmk.** ***Perf. 11½***

CL1 APL1 25pf dp Prus bl 150.00 300.00
Never hinged 300.00
On flight cover, canceled *Munich* 375.00
On flight cover, canceled *Nurnberg* 750.00

No. CL1 was issued under the auspices of the Aero Club of Bavaria for its inaugural flight. The stamp paid the airmail fee, but postal regulations required that Bavarian stamps also be affixed to covers and postcards to pay regular Bavarian postage.

Forgeries exist.

POSTAGE DUE STAMPS

D1

With Silk Thread

1862 **Typeset** **Unwmk.** ***Imperf.***

J1 D1 3kr black 125.00 *325.00*
Never hinged 175.00
No gum 57.50
Pen cancel *87.50*
On cover *875.00*
On cover, pen cancel *275.00*
Pair with gutter between 1,300.
Never hinged 2,000.
No gum 700.00
a. "Empfange" 375.00 *1,000.*
Never hinged 600.00
On cover *2,200.*

Values for Multiples

J1 D1 3kr Pair 275.00 *1,200.*
Never hinged 475.00
On cover *1,600.*
J1 D1 3kr Strip of 3 440.00 *2,400.*
Never hinged 725.00
On cover *3,200.*
J1 D1 3kr Block or strip of 4 725.00 *4,800.*
Never hinged 1,100.

Full margins = 1¼mm at sides, ¾mm at top and bottom. There are vertical dividing lines between stamps.

Without Silk Thread

1870 **Typo.** **Wmk. 93** ***Perf. 11½***

J2 D1 1kr black 12.00 *800.00*
Never hinged 20.00
On cover *1,600.*
Pair with gutter between 95.00
Never hinged 200.00
a. Wmk. 92 55.00 *1,750.*
Never hinged 110.00
On cover *2,800.*
Pair with gutter between 225.00
Never hinged 400.00
J3 D1 3kr black 12.00 *475.00*
Never hinged 20.00
On cover *960.00*
Pair with gutter between 125.00
Never hinged 225.00
a. Wmk. 92 55.00 *960.00*
Never hinged 110.00
On cover *1,900.*
Pair with gutter between 240.00
Never hinged 425.00

Type of 1876 Regular Issue Overprinted in Red "Vom Empfänger zahlbar"

D2

1876 **Wmk. 94**

J4 D2 3pf gray 16.00 40.00
Never hinged 45.00
On cover 95.00
Pair with gutter between 200.00
J5 D2 5pf gray 10.00 17.00
Never hinged 40.00
On cover 72.50
Pair with gutter between 175.00
J6 D2 10pf gray 3.25 1.25
Never hinged 16.00
On cover 16.00
Pair with gutter between 95.00
a. Vert. half used as 5pf on cover 2,800.
Nos. J4-J6 (3) 29.25 58.25

1883 **Wmk. 95v**

J7 D2 3pf gray 90.00 100.00
Never hinged 200.00
On cover 400.00
Pair with gutter between 600.00
J8 D2 5pf gray 55.00 70.00
Never hinged 110.00
On cover 200.00
Pair with gutter between 400.00
J9 D2 10pf gray 2.40 .80
Never hinged 8.00
On cover 8.00
Pair with gutter between 160.00
a. "Empfanper" 140.00 140.00
Never hinged 275.00
On cover 275.00
b. "zahlhar" 80.00 80.00
Never hinged 200.00
On cover 200.00
c. Imperf. 95.00
Never hinged 160.00
Nos. J7-J9 (3) 147.40 170.80

1895-1903 **Wmk. 95h** **Perf. 14½**

J10 D2 2pf gray .80 2.40
Never hinged 1.60
On cover 12.00
Pair with gutter between 8.00 40.00
Never hinged 16.00
J11 D2 3pf gray ('03) .80 2.50
Never hinged 1.60
On cover 16.00
Pair with gutter between 12.00 40.00
Never hinged 20.00
J12 D2 5pf gray ('03) 1.00 1.75
Never hinged 2.10
On cover 13.50
Pair with gutter between 7.00 37.50
Never hinged 14.00
J13 D2 10pf gray ('03) .60 .90
Never hinged 1.25
On cover 10.00
Pair with gutter between 7.00 37.50
Never hinged 10.50
Nos. J10-J13 (4) 3.20 7.55

Imperf

J10b D2 2pf 60.00
Never hinged 95.00
Pair with gutter between 300.00
Never hinged 475.00
J11c D2 3pf 60.00
Never hinged 95.00
Pair with gutter between 300.00
Never hinged 475.00
J12b D2 5pf 60.00
Never hinged 95.00
Pair with gutter between 300.00
Never hinged 475.00
J13c D2 10pf 60.00
Never hinged 95.00
Pair with gutter between 300.00
Never hinged 475.00

1888 **Rose-toned Paper**

J10a D2 2pf gray 2.00 4.75
Never hinged 4.50
On cover 14.00
Pair with gutter between 16.00 47.50
Never hinged 32.50
J11a D2 3pf gray 2.60 2.40
Never hinged 6.50
On cover 13.50
Pair with gutter between 70.00
b. Inverted overprint 2,200.
On cover 3,500.
J12a D2 5pf gray 2.60 2.60
Never hinged 6.50
On cover 13.50
Pair with gutter between 72.50
J13a D2 10pf gray 2.60 1.25
Never hinged 6.50
On cover 9.00
Pair with gutter between 90.00
b. As "a," double overprint 2,200.
On cover 3,500.
Nos. J10a-J13a (4) 9.80 11.00

No. J13b was used at Pirmasens.

Surcharged in Red in Each Corner

1895

J14 D2 2pf on 3pf gray 150,000.

Six used examples of No. J14 exist, all used in Aichach. There are two covers (each bearing two examples) and two loose stamps.

OFFICIAL STAMPS

Nos. 77-81, 84, 95-96, 98-99, 102 perforated with a large E were issued for official use in 1912-16.

Regular Issue of 1888-1900 Overprinted

1908 **Wmk. 95h** **Perf. 14½**

O1 A5 3pf dk brown (R) .75 4.50
O2 A5 5pf dk green (R) .25 .40
O3 A5 10pf carmine (G) .25 .40
O4 A5 20pf ultra (R) .50 .80
O5 A5 50pf maroon 4.50 8.00
Nos. O1-O5 (5) 6.25 14.10

Nos. O1-O5 were issued for the use of railway officials. "E" stands for "Eisenbahn."

Coat of Arms — O1

1916-17 **Typo.** **Perf. 11½**

O6 O1 3pf bister brn .25 .80
O7 O1 5pf yellow grn .25 .80
O8 O1 7½pf grn, *grn* .25 .50
O9 O1 7½pf grn ('17) .25 1.20
O10 O1 10pf deep rose .25 1.20
O11 O1 15pf red, *buff* .30 1.20
O12 O1 15pf red ('17) .25 1.20
O13 O1 20pf dp bl, *bl* 2.00 2.25
O14 O1 20pf dp blue ('17) .25 1.20
O15 O1 25pf gray .25 .65
O16 O1 30pf orange .25 .65
O17 O1 60pf dark green .25 1.25
O18 O1 1m dl vio, *gray* .95 3.25
O19 O1 1m maroon ('17) 2.75 475.00
Nos. O6-O19 (14) 8.50 491.15

Used values of Nos. O6-O69 are for postally used stamps. Canceled-to-order stamps, which abound, sell for same prices as unused.

Official Stamps and Type of 1916-17 Overprinted

1918

O20 O1 3pf bister brn .25 13.50
O21 O1 5pf yellow green .25 2.00
O22 O1 7½pf gray green .25 13.00
O23 O1 10pf deep rose .25 2.25
O24 O1 15pf red .25 2.25
O25 O1 20pf blue .25 2.25
O26 O1 25pf gray .25 2.25
O27 O1 30pf orange .25 2.25
O28 O1 35pf orange .25 2.25
O29 O1 50pf olive gray .25 2.50
O30 O1 60pf dark green .30 13.50
O31 O1 75pf red brown .35 3.50
O32 O1 1m dl vio, *gray* 1.10 14.50
O33 O1 1m maroon 4.00 375.00
Nos. O20-O33 (14) 8.25 451.00

O2

O3

O4

1920 **Typo.** **Perf. 14x14½**

O34 O2 5pf yellow grn .25 6.50
O35 O2 10pf orange .25 6.50
O36 O2 15pf carmine .25 6.50
O37 O2 20pf violet .25 6.50
O38 O2 30pf dark blue .25 7.25
O39 O2 40pf bister .25 7.25

Perf. 14½x14

Wmk. 95v

O40 O3 50pf vermilion .25 22.50
O41 O3 60pf blue green .25 9.50
O42 O3 70pf dk violet .25 27.50
a. Imperf., pair 26.00
O43 O3 75pf deep rose .25 35.00
O44 O3 80pf dull blue .25 35.00
O45 O3 90pf olive green .25 55.00
O46 O4 1m dark brown .25 50.00
a. Imperf., pair 72.50
O47 O4 1¼m green .25 65.00
O48 O4 1½m vermilion .25 65.00
a. Imperf. pair 25.00
O49 O4 2½m deep blue .25 70.00
a. Imperf. pair 72.50
O50 O4 3m dark red .25 100.00
a. Imperf. pair 20.00
O51 O4 5m black 1.50 125.00
a. Imperf., pair 72.50
Nos. O34-O51 (18) 5.75 700.00

Stamps of Preceding Issue Overprinted

1920, Apr. 1

O52 O2 5pf yellow green .25 3.25
a. Imperf., pair 26.00
O53 O2 10pf orange .25 1.90
O54 O2 15pf carmine .25 2.00
O55 O2 20pf violet .25 1.60
O56 O2 30pf dark blue .25 1.60
O57 O2 40pf bister .25 1.60
O58 O3 50pf vermilion .25 2.00
a. Imperf., pair 26.00
O59 O3 60pf blue green .25 1.60
O60 O3 70pf dark violet 2.00 2.75
O61 O3 75pf deep rose .35 1.40
O62 O3 80pf dull blue .25 1.40
O63 O3 90pf olive green 1.60 3.50

Similar Ovpt., Words 8mm apart

O64 O4 1m dark brown .25 2.00
a. Imperf., pair 26.00
O65 O4 1¼m green .25 2.00
O66 O4 1½m vermilion .25 2.00
O67 O4 2½m deep blue .25 2.00
a. Imperf., pair 37.50
O68 O4 3m dark red .25 2.00
O69 O4 5m black 8.75 25.00
Nos. O52-O69 (18) 16.20 59.60

Nos. O52-O69 could be used in all parts of Germany, but were almost exclusively used in Bavaria.

BERGEDORF

LOCATION — A town in northern Germany.
POP. — 2,989 (1861)

Originally Bergedorf belonged jointly to the Free City of Hamburg and the Free City of Lübeck. In 1867 it was purchased by Hamburg.

16 Schillings = 1 Mark

Values for unused stamps are for examples with original gum as defined in the catalogue introduction. Copies without gum sell for about 40% of the figures quoted. Values for used stamps are for examples canceled with parallel bars. Copies bearing dated town postmarks sell for more.

Combined Arms of Lübeck and Hamburg

A1 A2 A3

A4 A5

1861-67 **Unwmk.** **Litho.** **Imperf.**

1 A1 ½s blk, *pale bl* 45.00 725.00
Never hinged 90.00
No gum 16.00
On cover 3,600.
Pair with gutter between 225.00
Never hinged 325.00
No gum 87.50
a. ½s black, *blue* ('67) 125.00 4,750.
Never hinged 240.00
No gum 47.50
On cover 26,000.
Pair with gutter between 500.00
Never hinged 875.00
No gum 225.00
2 A3 1s blk, *white* 45.00 375.00
Never hinged 80.00
No gum 16.00
On cover 2,600.
Pair with gutter between 160.00
Never hinged 300.00
No gum 65.00
a. Tête bêche pair, vert. 225.00
Never hinged 340.00
No gum 87.50
b. Tête bêche pair, horiz. 300.00
Never hinged 550.00
No gum 120.00
3 A4 1½s blk, *yellow* 20.00 1,600.
Never hinged 40.00
No gum 8.00
On cover 5,200.
Pair with gutter between 175.00
Never hinged 300.00
No gum 72.50
a. Tête bêche pair 125.00
Never hinged 225.00
No gum 55.00
Pair with gutter between 300.00
Never hinged 550.00
No gum 125.00
4 A2 3s blue, *pink* 25.00 2,000.
Never hinged 45.00
No gum 8.00
On cover 12,000.
Pair with gutter between 175.00
Never hinged 325.00
No gum 80.00
5 A5 4s blk, *brown* 25.00 2,250.
Never hinged 45.00
No gum 8.00
On cover 23,500.
Pair with gutter between 175.00
Never hinged 325.00
No gum 80.00
Nos. 1-5 (5) 160.00 6,950.

Full margins Nos. 1-3 = 1½mm; No. 4 = ¾mm; No. 5 = 1mm. There are vertical dividing lines between stamps.

Values for pairs

1 A1 ½s blk, *pale bl* 95.00 1,800.
Never hinged 190.00
a. ½s black, *blue* 300.00 14,500.
Never hinged 575.00
2 A3 1s blk, *white* 95.00 1,600.
Never hinged 175.00
3 A4 1½s blk, *yellow* 47.50 3,500.
Never hinged 95.00
4 A2 3s blue, *pink* 52.50 —
Never hinged 95.00
5 A5 4s blk, *brown* 52.50 15,000.
Never hinged 95.00

Values for strips of 3

1 A1 ½s blk, *pale bl* 150.00 10,000.
Never hinged 275.00
a. ½s black, *blue* 500.00 —
Never hinged 875.00
2 A3 1s blk, *white* 150.00 8,000.
Never hinged 275.00
3 A4 1½s blk, *yellow* 72.50 —
Never hinged 140.00
4 A2 3s blue, *pink* 80.00 —
Never hinged 140.00
5 A5 4s blk, *brown* 80.00 —
Never hinged 140.00

Values for blocks or strips of 4

1 A1 ½s blk, *pale bl* 210.00 16,000.
Never hinged 360.00
a. ½s black, *blue* 650.00 —
Never hinged 1,200.
2 A3 1s blk, *white* 200.00 12,000.
Never hinged 360.00
3 A4 1½s blk, *yellow* 95.00 —
Never hinged 190.00
4 A2 3s blue, *pink* 110.00 —
Never hinged 200.00
5 A5 4s blk, *brown* 110.00 —
Never hinged 200.00

Counterfeit cancellations are plentiful.

No. 3 exists in a tête bêche gutter pair. Value, unused $310.

The ½s on violet and 3s on rose, listed previously, as well as a 1s and 1½s on thick paper and 4s on light rose brown, come from proof sheets and were never placed in use. A 1½ "SCHILLINGE" (instead of SCHILLING) also exists only as a proof.

No. 3 exists as a tête bêche pair with 'SCHILLING' and 'SCHILLINGE', this is a forgery, value $250.

All five issues exist in five colors (black, blue, red, green, and brown) on white paper, these are proofs, value $150.

REPRINTS

½ SCHILLING

There is a dot in the upper part of the right branch of "N" of "EIN." The upper part of the shield is blank or almost blank. The horizontal bar of "H" in "HALBER" is generally defective.

1 SCHILLING

The "1" in the corners is generally with foot. The central horizontal bar of the "E" of "EIN" is separated from the vertical branch by a black line. The "A" of "POSTMARKE" has the horizontal bar incomplete or missing. The horizontal bar of the "H" of "SCHILLING" is separated from the vertical branches by a dark line at each side, sometimes the bar is missing.

1½ SCHILLINGE

There is a small triangle under the right side of the tower, exactly over the "R" of "POSTMARKE."

3 SCHILLINGE

The head of the eagle is not shaded. The horizontal bar of the second "E" of "BERGEDORF" is separated from the vertical branch by a thin line. There is generally a colored dot in the lower half of the "S" of "POSTMARKE."

4 SCHILLINGE

The upper part of the shield is blank or has two or three small dashes. In most of the reprints there is a diagonal dash across the wavy lines of the groundwork at the right of "I" and "E" of "VIER."

Reprints, value $1 each.

These stamps were superseded by those of the North German Confederation in 1868.

BREMEN

LOCATION — In northwestern Germany
AREA — 99 sq. mi.
POP. — 122,402 (1871)

Bremen was a Free City and member of the German Confederation. In 1870 it became part of the German Empire.

22 Grote = 10 Silbergroschen.

Values for unused stamps are for examples with original gum as defined in the catalogue introduction.

Coat of Arms — A1

I

II

III

Type I. The central part of the scroll below the word Bremen is crossed by one vertical line.
Type II. The center of the scroll is crossed by two vertical lines.
Type III. The center of the scroll is crossed by three vertical lines.

1855 Unwmk. Litho. *Imperf.*

Horizontally Laid Paper

1 A1 3gr black, *blue* 200.00 *290.00*
Never hinged 400.00
No gum 110.00
On cover 2,000.

Vertically Laid Paper

1A A1 3gr black, *blue* 450.00 *600.00*
Never hinged 950.00
No gum 150.00
On cover 2,500.

Full margins = 1½mm.

No. 1 can be found with parts of a papermaker's watermark, consisting of lilies. Value: unused $700; unused, no gum, $400; used $1,000; on cover $4,000.

See Nos. 9-10.

Values for pairs

1 A1 3gr black, *blue* 500.00 —
Never hinged 875.00
No gum 300.00
1A A1 3gr black, *blue* 1,500. —
Never hinged 2,500.
No gum 1,000.

Values for strips of 3

1 A1 3gr black, *blue* 950.00 —
No gum 500.00
Types I, II and III — —
1A A1 3gr black, *blue* 2,500. —
No gum 1,000.
Types I, II and III — —

Values for blocks of 4

1 A1 3gr black, *blue* *1,450.* —
Never hinged *2,250.*
No gum *800.00*
1A A1 3gr black, *blue* — —

A2

A3

FIVE GROTE

Type I. The shading at the left of the ribbon containing "funf Grote" runs downward from the shield.
Type II. The shading at the left of the ribbon containing "funf Grote" runs upward.

1856-60 Wove Paper

2 A2 5gr blk, *rose* 150.00 *300.00*
Never hinged 325.00
No gum 80.00
On cover 3,200.
a. Printed on both sides 4,000.
b. "Marken" (not issued) 12.00
Never hinged 20.00
No gum 8.00
3 A2 7gr blk, *yel* ('60) 240.00 *725.00*
Never hinged 475.00
No gum 95.00
On cover *4,500.*
a. Thin paper 560.00 900.00
Never hinged —
No gum 240.00
On cover *4,800.*
4 A3 5sgr green ('59) 500.00 *300.00*
Never hinged 500.00
No gum 150.00
On cover 2,500.
a. Chalky paper 60.00 *2,000.*
Never hinged 95.00
No gum 30.00
b. 5sgr yellow green 160.00 *300.00*
Never hinged 225.00
No gum 65.00
On cover 2,600.

Full margins: No. 2 = 1¼mm; No. 3 = 1½mm; No. 5 = 1mm. There are vertical dividing lines between stamps.

See Nos. 6, 8, 12-13, 15.

Values for pairs

2 A2 5gr black, *rose* 400.00 *2,000.*
Never hinged 725.00
No gum 225.00
3 A2 7gr black, *yel* 575.00 —
Never hinged 1,100.
No gum 300.00
4 A3 5sgr green 600.00 —
Never hinged 1,200.
No gum 400.00
a. Chalky paper 130.00 —
Never hinged 225.00
No gum 72.50
b. 5sgr yellow green 325.00 *1,500.*
Never hinged 575.00
No gum 175.00

Values for strips of 3

2 A2 5gr black, *rose* 640.00
Never hinged 1,200.
No gum 325.00
3 A2 7gr black, *yel* 1,100.
Never hinged 1,800.
No gum 500.00
4 A3 5sgr green 1,200.
Never hinged 2,000.
No gum 600.00
a. Chalky paper 225.00
Never hinged 375.00
No gum 110.00
b. 5sgr yellow green 575.00
Never hinged 1,100.
No gum 325.00

Values for blocks of 4

2 A2 5gr blk, *rose* 875.00
Never hinged 1,700.
No gum 575.00
3 A2 7gr blk, *yel* 1,450.
Never hinged 2,600.
No gum 650.00
4 A3 5sgr green 1,750.
Never hinged —
No gum 900.00
a. Chalky paper 300.00
Never hinged 500.00
No gum 175.00
b. 5sgr yellow green 800.00
Never hinged 1,450.
No gum 450.00

A4

A5

1861-63 *Serpentine Roulette*

5 A4 2gr orange ('63) 400.00 *2,000.*
No gum 240.00
On cover 5,750.
a. 2gr red orange 800.00 *3,500.*
No gum 400.00
On cover *8,500.*
b. Chalky paper 350.00 *3,250.*
No gum 210.00
On cover 7,000.
c. as "a," chalky paper 800.00 *3,500.*
No gum 400.00
On cover 12,000.
6 A2 5gr blk, *rose* ('62) 350.00 *225.00*
No gum 110.00
On cover 900.00
Two singles on cover *2,500.*
a. Horiz. pair, imperf between —
b. Double impression —
7 A5 10gr black 700.00 *950.00*
No gum 350.00
On cover 2,800.
Two singles on cover *7,000.*
8 A3 5sgr yellow green ('63) 1,100. 200.00
No gum 625.00
On cover 900.00
a. Chalky paper 600.00 450.00
No gum 325.00
On cover 1,400.
b. 5sgr green 925.00 225.00
No gum 550.00
On cover 1,000.

Full margins of No. 5 = 1mm. There are dividing lines between stamps.

See Nos. 11, 14.

Values for pairs

5 A4 2gr orange 1,000. *5,200.*
No gum 550.00
a. 2gr red orange 2,000. —
No gum 1,000.
b. Chalky paper 2,000. —
No gum 1,000.
c. as "a," chalky paper 1,800. —
No gum 1,100.
6 A2 5gr blk, *rose* 1,000. *1,000.*
No gum 600.00
7 A5 10gr black 2,500. *2,450.*
No gum 1,250.
8 A3 5sgr green —
a. Chalky paper —
b. 5sgr yellow green —

Values for strips of 3

5 A4 2gr orange 1,150.
No gum 900.00
a. 2gr red orange —
No gum —
b. Chalky paper —
No gum —
c. as "a," chalky paper 3,000.
No gum 2,000.
6 A2 5gr blk, *rose* —
7 A5 10gr black *5,000.*
8 A3 5sgr green —
a. Chalky paper —
b. 5sgr yellow green —

Values for blocks of 4

5 A4 2gr orange 2,100.
No gum 1,250.
a. 2gr red orange —
No gum —
b. Chalky paper —
No gum —
c. as "a," chalky paper 4,500.
No gum 3,000.
6 A2 5gr blk, *rose* —
7 A5 10gr black — *11,000.*
8 A3 5sgr green —
a. Chalky paper —
b. 5sgr yellow green —

1863

Horizontally (H) or Vertically (V) Laid Paper

9 A1 3gr blk, *blue* (V) 650.00 725.00
No gum 400.00
On cover 2,400.
a. 3gr black, *blue* (H) 2,250. *4,000.*
No gum 1,250.
On cover *12,500.*

Values for pairs

9 A1 3gr blk, *blue* (V) 1,500. *2,500.*
No gum 850.00
a. 3gr black, *blue* (H) —

1866-67 *Perf. 13*

10 A1 3gr black, *blue* 80.00 *325.00*
Never hinged 125.00
No gum 35.00
On cover *1,400.*

Wove Paper

11 A4 2gr orange 95.00 *325.00*
Never hinged 175.00
No gum 47.50
On cover *1,200.*
Pair with gutter between 3,250.
Never hinged 5,000.
No gum 2,000.
a. 2gr red orange 450.00 *800.00*
Never hinged 650.00
No gum 125.00
On cover *1,900.*
b. Horiz. pair, imperf. btwn. 3,250.
12 A2 5gr blk, *rose* 125.00 *325.00*
Never hinged 225.00
No gum 65.00
On cover *3,250.*
a. Horiz. pair, imperf. btwn. 1,250. —
No gum 700.00
13 A2 7gr blk, *yel* ('67) 150.00 *4,500.*
Never hinged 240.00
No gum 80.00
On cover *16,000.*
14 A5 10gr black ('67) 190.00 *1,125.*
Never hinged 360.00
No gum 110.00
On cover *4,000.*
15 A3 5sgr green 140.00 *3,750.*
Never hinged 360.00
No gum 72.50
On cover 40,000.
a. 5sgr yellow green 450.00 175.00
Never hinged 700.00
No gum 250.00
On cover 1,250.
b. As "a," chalky paper 450.00 275.00
Never hinged 800.00
No gum 250.00
On cover 3,250.

Values for pairs

10 A1 3gr black, *blue* 225.00 —
Never hinged 400.00
No gum 125.00
11 A4 2gr orange 225.00 *1,250.*
Never hinged 400.00
No gum 125.00
a. 2gr red orange — —
12 A2 5gr blk, *rose* 325.00 *1,200.*
Never hinged 560.00
No gum 160.00
13 A2 7gr blk, *yel* ('67) 525.00 —
Never hinged 960.00
No gum 275.00
14 A5 10gr black ('67) 475.00 *3,200.*
Never hinged 800.00
No gum 275.00
15 A3 5sgr green 650.00 —
Never hinged 1,200.
No gum 400.00
a. 5sgr yellow green —
b. As "a," chalky paper —

Values for Blocks of 4

10 A1 3gr black, *blue* 800.00
Never hinged 1,400.
No gum 475.00
11 A4 2gr orange 525.00
Never hinged 960.00
No gum 275.00
12 A2 5gr blk, *rose* 800.00
Never hinged 960.00
No gum 400.00
13 A2 7gr blk, *yel* ('67) 1,100.
Never hinged 2,100.
No gum 725.00
14 A5 10gr black ('67) 1,000.
Never hinged 1,800.
No gum 640.00
15 A3 5sgr green 1,900.
Never hinged 3,000.
No gum 1,100.

The stamps of Bremen were superseded by those of the North German Confederation on Jan. 1, 1868.

BRUNSWICK

LOCATION — In northern Germany
GOVT. — Former duchy
AREA — 1,417 sq. mi.
POP. — 349,367 (1880)
CAPITAL — Brunswick

Brunswick was a member of the German Confederation and, in 1870 became part of the German Empire.

12 Pfennigs = 1 Gutegroschen
30 Silbergroschen (Groschen) = 24 Gutegroschen = 1 Thaler

Values for unused stamps are for examples with original gum as defined in the catalogue introduction except for Nos. 1-3 which are valued without gum. Nos. 1-3 with original gum sell for much higher prices.

The "Leaping Saxon Horse" — A1

The ½gr has white denomination and "Gr" in right oval.

1852 Unwmk. Typo. *Imperf.*

1 A1 1sgr rose 2,200. 300.00
On cover 1,200.
2 A1 2sgr blue 1,450. 250.00
On cover 960.00
a. Half used as 1sgr on cover —
3 A1 3sgr vermilion 1,450. 250.00
On cover 900.00

Full margins = 1¼mm.

Values for used pairs

1 A1 1sgr rose 1,400.
On cover *3,000.*
2 A1 2sgr blue 2,800.
3 A1 3sgr vermilion 2,800.

Values for used strip of 3

1 A1 1sgr *6,000.*
On cover *9,600.*

See Nos. 4-11, 13-22.

1853-63 Wmk. 102

4 A1 ¼ggr blk, *brn* ('56) 800.00 250.00
No gum 400.00
On cover 960.00
On cover, single franking, local post *13,000.*
5 A1 ⅓sgr black ('56) 140.00 325.00
No gum 60.00
On cover 2,600.
On cover, single franking, local post *7,250.*
6 A1 ½gr blk, *grn* ('63) 25.00 *240.00*
Never hinged 50.00
No gum 9.50
On cover *725.00*
On cover, single franking 1,100.
a. Thin paper (.065mm) 40.00 *400.00*
Never hinged 80.00

No gum 20.00
On cover 650.00
7 A1 1sgr blk, *orange* 400.00 55.00
No gum 240.00
On cover 150.00
a. 1sgr black, *orange buff* 400.00 65.00
No gum 260.00
On cover 175.00
8 A1 1sgr blk, *yel* ('61) 400.00 50.00
No gum 240.00
On cover 125.00
a. Diagonal half used as ½sgr on cover 18,000.
9 A1 2sgr blk, *blue* 325.00 65.00
No gum 200.00
On cover 175.00
a. Diagonal half used as 1sgr on cover 9,600.
b. Vertical half used as 1sgr on cover 18,000.
c. 2sgr black, *pale blue* — 160.00
On cover 440.00
d. As "c," half used as 1sgr on cover 14,000.
e. Thick paper (.13mm) — 225.00
On cover 475.00
f. Wmk. inverted 3,600. 1,450.
10 A1 3sgr blk, *rose* 475.00 80.00
No gum 325.00
On cover 240.00
11 A1 3sgr rose ('62) 600.00 200.00
No gum 325.00
On cover 475.00
a. 3sgr carmine — 275.00
On cover 560.00

Full margins = 1mm.

Values for pairs

4 A1 ¼ggr blk, *brn* 2,000. 725.00
On cover 1,400.
5 A1 ⅓sgr black 600.00 1,200.
On cover 8,000.
6 A1 ½gr blk, *grn* 60.00 675.00
No gum 24.00
Never hinged 125.00
On cover 1,000.
7 A1 1sgr blk, *orange* 200.00
On cover 325.00
a. 1sgr black, *orange buff* 1,600. 200.00
On cover 325.00
8 A1 1sgr blk, *yel* 210.00
On cover 360.00
9 A1 2sgr blk, *blue* 800.00 400.00
On cover 800.00
c. 2sgr black, *pale blue* —
e. Thick paper (.13mm) —
10 A1 3sgr blk, *rose* — 360.00
On cover 800.00
11 A1 3sgr rose 1,600. 725.00
No gum 960.00
On cover 1,200.
a. 3sgr carmine 800.00
On cover 1,600.

Values for strips of 3

4 A1 ¼ggr blk, *brn* — 1,200.
On cover 1,800.
5 A1 ⅓sgr black 1,600. 2,200.
On cover 4,000.
6 A1 ½gr blk, *grn* 90.00 1,300.
No gum 40.00
7 A1 1sgr blk, *orange* — 360.00
On cover 960.00
a. 1sgr black, *orange buff* — 360.00
On cover 960.00
8 A1 1sgr blk, *yel* — 1,200.
9 A1 2sgr blk, *blue* — 1,200.
10 A1 3sgr blk, *rose* — 1,200.
11 A1 3sgr rose — 1,200.
a. 3sgr carmine — 1,200.

Values for blocks or strips of 4

4 A1 ¼ggr blk, *brn* — 2,000.
On cover 2,800.
6 A1 ½gr blk, *grn* 125.00 2,400.
Never hinged 240.00
No gum 60.00
7 A1 1sgr blk, *orange* — 3,000.
8 A1 1sgr blk, *yel* 3,600. 3,200.
No gum 2,000.
9 A1 2sgr blk, *blue* 2,000.
On cover 6,000.
10 A1 3sgr blk, *rose* 2,400.
11 A1 3sgr rose 4,000.
a. 3sgr carmine 6,000.

A3

1857
12 A3 Four ¼ggr blk, *brn* ('57) 40.00 95.00
No gum 16.00
Single on cover 150.00
Two ¼ggr on cover 110.00
Three ¼ggr on cover 150.00
Four ¼ggr on cover 240.00
Five ¼ggr on cover 310.00
Ten ¼ggr on cover 1,400.
a. Four ¼ggr blk, *yel brown* — 210.00
On cover 440.00

Full margins = 1mm.

Values for pairs

12 A3 Four ¼ggr blk, *brn* 95.00 325.00
Never hinged 240.00
No gum 40.00
On cover 800.00
a. Four ¼ggr blk, *yel brown* 640.00

Values for strips of 3

12 A3 Four ¼ggr blk, *brn* 160.00
Never hinged 400.00
No gum 125.00

Values for blocks of 4

12 A3 Four ¼ggr blk, *brn* 300.00
No gum 125.00

Covers: Each multiple corresponds to a rate based on distance and destination. Values are for covers correctly franked.

The bister on white paper was not issued. Value $6.

1864 *Serpentine Roulette 16*
13 A1 ⅓sgr black 475.00 2,250.
No gum 275.00
On cover 4,800.
14 A1 ½gr blk, *green* 190.00 3,000.
No gum 110.00
On cover 11,000.
15 A1 1sgr blk, *yellow* 2,850. 1,425.
No gum 1,800.
On cover 7,250.
16 A1 1sgr yellow 400.00 145.00
No gum 240.00
On cover 325.00
17 A1 2sgr blk, *blue* 400.00 340.00
No gum 240.00
On cover 960.00
a. Half used as 1sgr on cover 12,000.
e. Thick paper (.13mm) — 800.00
On cover —
18 A1 3sgr rose 800.00 525.00
No gum 475.00
On cover 1,000.

Rouletted 12
20 A1 1sgr blk, *yellow* 11,000.
21 A1 1sgr yellow 600.00 325.00
On cover 875.00
22 A1 3sgr rose — 2,500.

Nos. 13, 16, 18, 21-22 are on white paper.
Faked roulettes of Nos. 13-22 exist.

Values for pairs

13 A1 ⅓sgr black 5,600.
16 A1 1sgr yellow 475.00
On cover 800.00
17 A1 2sgr blk, *blue* 960.00 1,400.
No gum 560.00
18 A1 3sgr rose 2,400. 1,600.
No gum 1,600.
21 A1 1sgr yellow 700.00
On cover 1,500.

Values for strips of 3

13 A1 ⅓sgr black 8,000.
On cover 14,500.
16 A1 1sgr yellow 800.00
17 A1 2sgr blk, *blue* 1,600.
No gum 960.00
18 A1 3sgr rose 4,000.
21 A1 1sgr yellow 1,100.

Values for blocks or strips of 4

13 A1 ⅓sgr black 3,200.
No gum 2,400.
17 A1 2sgr blk, *blue* 3,200.
18 A1 3sgr rose 4,000.

A4

Serpentine Roulette
1865 **Embossed** **Unwmk.**
23 A4 ⅓gr black 27.50 350.00
Never hinged 55.00
On cover 1,600.
On wrapper or newsprint, single franking 3,200.
24 A4 1gr carmine 3.00 50.00
Never hinged 4.75
On cover 140.00
25 A4 2gr ultra 8.75 125.00
Never hinged 16.00
On cover 360.00
a. 2gr gray blue 8.75 125.00
Never hinged 16.00
On cover 360.00
c. Half used as 1sgr on cover 20,000.
26 A4 3gr brown 8.00 160.00
Never hinged 16.00
On cover 475.00
Nos. 23-26 (4) 47.25 685.00

Faked cancellations of Nos. 5-26 exist.

Values for pairs

23 A4 ⅓gr black 65.00 960.00
Never hinged 140.00
24 A4 1gr carmine 5.50 175.00
Never hinged 9.50
25 A4 2gr ultra 19.00 400.00
Never hinged 35.00
a. 2gr gray blue 19.00 400.00
Never hinged 35.00
26 A4 3gr brown 20.00 475.00
Never hinged 32.50

Values for strips of 3

23 A4 ⅓gr black 95.00 1,600.
Never hinged 200.00
24 A4 1gr carmine 8.75 360.00
Never hinged 16.00
25 A4 2gr ultra 27.50 640.00
Never hinged 52.50
a. 2gr gray blue 27.50 640.00
Never hinged 52.50
26 A4 3gr brown 27.50 875.00
Never hinged 47.50

Values for blocks or strips of 4

23 A4 ⅓gr black 140.00 4,000.
Never hinged 275.00
24 A4 1gr carmine 12.00
Never hinged 22.50
25 A4 2gr ultra 47.50
Never hinged 72.50
a. 2gr gray blue 47.50
Never hinged 72.50
26 A4 3gr brown 40.00
Never hinged 65.00

Imperf., Pairs

23a A4 ⅓gr 110.00
Never hinged 150.00
24a A4 1gr 32.50
Never hinged 47.50
25b A4 2gr 92.50
Never hinged 150.00
26a A4 3gr 110.00
Never hinged 175.00

Stamps of Brunswick were superseded by those of the North German Confederation on Jan. 1, 1868.

Numeral Postmarks

These values are premiums to be added to the used value of the stamp.
The left column has the premium for Nos. 1-22, the right column has the premium to be added for Nos. 23-26.

	Nos. 1-22	Nos. 23-26
1 Badenhausen	+120.00	+225.00
2 Bahrdorf	+700.00	
3 Bevern	+225.00	+310.00
4 Blankenburg	+22.50	+310.00
5 Bodenburg	+120.00	+82.50
6 Boerssum	+92.50	+125.00
7 Braunlage	+67.50	+92.50
7 Braunlage (red)	+5,400.	
8 Braunschweig		+9.25
9 Braunschweig, Small 9 ('52-'63)		—
9 Braunschweig, Large 9 ('63-'67)		+14.00
10 Calvoerde	+92.50	+120.00
11 Delligsen	+140.00	+190.00
12 Eschershausen	+47.50	+70.00
13 Fuerstenberg	+250.00	+375.00
14 Gandersheim	+37.50	+62.50
15 Gittelde	+92.50	+110.00
16 Greene (to 10/10/65)	+225.00	
16 Naensen (after 10/10/65)		+340.00
17 Gross-Winnigstedt	+250.00	+310.00
18 Halle am der Weser	+150.00	+190.00
19 Harzburg	+55.00	+110.00
20 Hasselfelde	+70.00	+100.00
21 Helmstedt	+22.50	+2,000.
22 Hessen	+140.00	+225.00
23 Hohengeiss	+190.00	+225.00
24 Holzminden	+28.00	+82.50
25 Jerxheim	+55.00	+82.50
26 Immendorf (to 12/31/60)	+475.00	
26 Hehlen (from 11/1/62)	+340.00	+460.00
27 Kleine Rheuden (to Oct. '64)	+200.00	
27 Bornum b. Seesen (after Oct. '64)	+225.00	+290.00
28 Koenigslutter	+37.50	+47.50
29 Kreinensen	+55.00	+82.50
30 Langelsheim	+92.50	+125.00
31 Lehre	+190.00	+225.00
32 Lutter a Bge.	+82.50	+110.00
33 Oker	+92.50	+150.00
34 Ottenstein	+225.00	+460.00
35 Ruebeland	+460.00	+625.00
36 Salder, thick lines	+150.00	
36 Salder, thin lines	+92.50	+110.00
37 Schoeningen	+22.50	+55.00
38 Schoeppenstedt	+47.50	+92.50
39 Seesen	+32.50	+47.50
40 Stadtoldendorf	+47.50	+70.00
41 Tanne	+625.00	+825.00
42 Thedinghausen	+140.00	+250.00
43 Vechelde	+70.00	+92.50
44 Velpke	+225.00	+140.00
45 Vorsfelde	+82.50	+110.00
46 Walkenreid	+700.00	
47 Wolfenbuettel		+19.00
48 Zorge	+775.00	+1,100.
49 Mainzholzen (to 10/10/65)	+1,400.	
49 Vorwohle (from 10/10/65)		+1,800.
50 Braunschweig	+8,750.	

Stamps of Brunswick were superseded by those of the North German Confederation on Jan. 1, 1868.

HAMBURG

LOCATION — Northern Germany
GOVT. — A former Free City
AREA — 160 sq. mi.
POP. — 453,869 (1880)
CAPITAL — Hamburg

Hamburg was a member of the German Confederation and became part of the German Empire in 1870.

16 Schillings = 1 Mark

Values for unused stamps are for examples with original gum as defined in the catalogue introduction.

Value Numeral on Arms — A1

1859 **Typo.** **Wmk. 128** ***Imperf.***
1 A1 ½s black 100.00 600.00
No gum 45.00
On cover 6,400.
On cover, single franking 10,300.
2 A1 1s brown 100.00 95.00
No gum 45.00
On cover 900.00
a. Period betweenn "M" and "B" 240.00 475.00
No gum 140.00
3 A1 2s red 100.00 100.00
No gum 45.00
On cover 800.00
4 A1 3s blue 100.00 125.00
No gum 45.00
On cover 1,100.
5 A1 4s yellow green 80.00 1,450.
No gum 47.50
On cover 16,000.
a. 4s green 125.00 1,300.
No gum 80.00
On cover 14,500.
b. Double impression —
6 A1 7s orange 100.00 47.50
No gum 55.00
On cover 325.00
7 A1 9s yellow 200.00 2,000.
No gum 125.00
On cover 14,500.

Full margins = 1¾mm at sides, ¾mm at top and bottom. There are vertical dividing lines between stamps.

See Nos. 13-21.

Values for pairs

1 A1 ½s black 450.00 2,000.
2 A1 1s brown 960.00 325.00
On cover 1,100.
3 A1 2s red 450.00 725.00
On cover 1,600.
4 A1 3s blue 960.00 800.00
On cover 2,400.
5 A1 4s yellow green 200.00 7,200.
a. 4s green 725.00 7,200.
6 A1 7s orange 400.00 200.00
On cover 1,300.
7 A1 9s yellow 725.00 8,000.

Values for strips of 3

1 A1 ½s black 600.00
2 A1 1s brown 1,500. 800.00
3 A1 2s red 600.00 3,200.
4 A1 3s blue 1,500. 4,000.
5 A1 4s yellow green 325.00 —
a. 4s green 1,000.
6 A1 7s orange 960.00 640.00
7 A1 9s yellow 1,100. 11,500.

Values for blocks of 4, Unused without gum and used

1 A1 ½s black 400.00
2 A1 1s brown 900.00
3 A1 2s red 400.00
4 A1 3s blue 900.00
5 A1 4s yellow green 240.00
a. 4s green 640.00
6 A1 7s orange 400.00
7 A1 9s yellow 760.00 18,000.

A2

A3

1864 **Litho.**
9 A2 1¼s gray 90.00 80.00
No gum 52.50
On cover 325.00
a. 1¼s lilac 150.00 85.00
No gum 90.00
On cover 360.00
b. 1¼s red lilac 125.00 72.50
No gum 72.50
On cover 360.00
c. 1¼s blue 425.00 850.00
No gum 310.00
On cover 3,600.
d. 1¼s greenish gray 110.00 200.00
No gum 72.50
On cover 360.00
e. 1¼s mauve(1st printing) 475.00 850.00
No gum 290.00
On cover 2,400.
12 A3 2½s green 140.00 140.00
No gum 82.50
On cover 560.00

Full margins = 1¼mm.

See Nos. 22-23.

The 1¼s and 2½s have been reprinted on watermarked and unwatermarked paper.

Values for pairs

9 A2 1¼s gray 1,350. 250.00
On cover 525.00
a. 1¼s lilac 1,350. 390.00
b. 1¼s red lilac 1,350. 250.00
On cover 475.00
c. 1¼s blue 1,500. —
d. 1¼s greenish gray 475.00 360.00
e. 1¼s mauve(1st printing) 1,500. 2,400.
12 A3 2½s green 560.00 450.00

Values for strips of 3

9 A2 1¼s gray 2,000. 810.00
a. 1¼s lilac 2,000. —
b. 1¼s red lilac 2,000. 775.00
c. 1¼s blue —
d. 1¼s greenish gray 725.00 *1,200.*
e. 1¼s mauve(1st printing) 2,500. *4,750.*
12 A3 2½s green 950.00 *1,100.*

Values for unused blocks of 4

9 A2 1¼s gray 2,600.
No gum 1,250.
a. 1¼s lilac 2,600.
No gum 1,250.
b. 1¼s red lilac 2,600.
No gum 1,250.
c. 1¼s blue —
d. 1¼s greenish gray 1,050.
No gum 475.00
e. 1¼s mauve(1st printing) 4,050.
No gum 2,000.
12 A3 2½s green 1,600.
No gum 725.00

1864-65 Typo. *Perf. 13½*

13 A1 ½s black 8.00 *12.00*
No gum 4.00
On cover 72.50
a. Horiz. pair, imperf between 72.50
No gum 35.00
14 A1 1s brown 13.00 *17.50*
No gum 6.50
On cover 60.00
a. Half used as ½s on cover *16,000.*
b. Horiz. pair, imperf between 450.00 *650.00*
15 A1 2s red 16.00 *20.00*
No gum 8.00
On cover 95.00
17 A1 3s ultra 40.00 40.00
No gum 24.00
On cover 160.00
a. Imperf., pair 140.00
No gum 70.00
b. Horiz. pair, imperf. vert. —
c. 3s blue 42.50 29.00
No gum 22.50
On cover 140.00
d. 3s Prussian blue 140.00 110.00
No gum 55.00
On cover 540.00
18 A1 4s green 12.00 20.00
No gum 7.75
On cover 190.00
a. 4s blue green 210.00 40.00
No gum 110.00
On cover 190.00
19 A1 7s orange 160.00 125.00
No gum 90.00
On cover 560.00
20 A1 7s vio ('65) 11.50 16.00
No gum 5.50
On cover 95.00
a. Imperf, pair 275.00
No gum 140.00
21 A1 9s yellow 25.00 *2,000.*
No gum 13.50
On cover *20,000.*
a. Vert. pair, imperf btwn. 400.00

Litho.

22 A2 1¼s lilac 95.00 12.00
No gum 55.00
On cover 30.00
a. 1¼s red lilac 95.00 12.00
No gum 55.00
On cover 30.00
b. 1¼s violet 95.00 12.00
No gum 55.00
On cover 32.50
c. As "a," imperf, pair 140.00
No gum 110.00
23 A3 2½s yel grn, blurred printing 125.00 35.00
No gum 60.00
On cover 80.00
a. 2½s blue green, blurred printing 125.00 35.00
No gum 60.00
On cover 80.00
b. 2½s green, fine printing 125.00 30.00
No gum 80.00
On cover 100.00

The 1¼s has been reprinted on watermarked and unwatermarked paper; the 2½s on unwatermarked paper.

Values for used pairs

13 A1 ½s black 42.50
14 A1 1s brown 45.00
15 A1 2s red 72.50
17 A1 3s ultra 115.00
c. 3s blue 125.00
d. 3s Prussian blue 510.00
18 A1 4s green 72.50
a. 4s blue green 125.00
19 A1 7s orange 300.00
20 A1 7s violet 60.00
21 A1 9s yellow *7,500.*
22 A2 1¼s lilac 32.50
a. 1¼s red lilac 32.50
b. 1¼s violet 30.00
23 A3 2½s yel grn 100.00
a. 2½s blue green 125.00
b. 2½s green 140.00

Values for used strips of 3

13 A1 ½s black 100.00
14 A1 1s brown 125.00
15 A1 2s red 160.00
17 A1 3s ultra 260.00
d. 3s Prussian blue 990.00
18 A1 4s green 210.00
a. 4s blue green 425.00
19 A1 7s orange
20 A1 7s violet 160.00
21 A1 9s yellow *10,800.*
22 A2 1¼s lilac 160.00
b. 1¼s violet 160.00
23 A3 2½s yel grn 260.00
b. 2½s green 260.00

Values for Blocks of 4, unused without gum

13 A1 ½s black 17.50 *990.00*
14 A1 1s brown 42.50 *1,800.*
15 A1 2s red 27.50 *1,600.*
17 A1 3s ultra 110.00
c. 3s blue 100.00
d. 3s Prussian blue 500.00
18 A1 4s green 22.50
19 A1 7s orange 625.00
20 A1 7s violet 25.00
21 A1 9s yellow 57.50 *20,000.*
22 A2 1¼s lilac 390.00 *1,700.*
b. 1¼s violet 425.00
23 A3 2½s yel grn 325.00
b. 2½s green 350.00 *1,700.*

A4

A5

Rouletted 10

1866 Unwmk. Embossed

24 A4 1¼s violet 40.00 35.00
No gum 21.00
On cover 125.00
a. 1¼s red violet 72.50 72.50
No gum 40.00
On cover 140.00
25 A5 1½s rose 12.50 *125.00*
No gum 6.25
On cover *600.00*

Values for used pairs

24 A4 1¼s violet 100.00
a. 1¼s red violet 175.00
25 A5 1½s rose *340.00*

Values for used strips of 3

24 A4 1¼s violet 325.00
a. 1¼s red violet 475.00
25 A5 1½s rose *725.00*

Values for unused blocks of 4, without gum

24 A4 1¼s violet 110.00
a. 1¼s red violet 225.00
25 A5 1½s rose 22.50

REPRINTS

1¼s: The rosettes between the words of the inscription have a well-defined open circle in the center of the originals, while in the reprints this circle is filled up.

In the upper part of the top of the "g" of "Schilling", there is a thin vertical line which is missing in the reprints.

The two lower lines of the triangle in the upper left corner are of different thicknesses in the originals while in the reprints they are of equal thickness.

The labels at the right and left containing the inscriptions are 2¾mm in width in the originals while they are 2½mm in reprints.

1½s: The originals are printed on thinner paper than the reprints. This is easily seen by turning the stamps over, when on the originals the color and impression will clearly show through, which is not the case in the reprints.

The vertical stroke of the upper part of the "g" in Schilling is very short on the originals, scarcely crossing the top line, while in the reprints it almost touches the center of the "g."

The lower part of the "g" of Schilling in the originals, barely touches the inner line of the frame, in some stamps it does not touch it at all, while in the reprints the whole stroke runs into the inner line of the frame.

A6

1867 Typo. Wmk. 128 *Perf. 13½*

26 A6 2½s dull green 12.50 *80.00*
No gum 6.50
On cover *175.00*
a. 2½s dark green 65.00 *100.00*
No gum 32.50
On cover *250.00*
b. Imperf., pair 225.00
No gum 87.50
c. Horiz. pair, imperf between 92.50
No gum 44.00

Values for used pairs

26 A6 2½s dull green *200.00*
a. 2½s dark green *260.00*

Values for used strips of 3

26 A6 2½s dull green *375.00*
a. 2½s dark green *440.00*

Values for unused blocks of 4, without gum

26 A6 2½s dull green 27.50
a. 2½s dark green 160.00

Forged cancellations exist on almost all stamps of Hamburg, especially on Nos. 4, 7, 21 and 25.

Nos. 1-23 and 26 exist without watermark, but they come from the same sheets as the watermarked stamps.

The stamps of Hamburg were superseded by those of the North German Confederation on Jan. 1, 1868.

HANOVER

LOCATION — Northern Germany
GOVT. — A former Kingdom
AREA — 14,893 sq. mi.
POP. — 3,191,000
CAPITAL — Hanover

Hanover was a member of the German Confederation and became in 1866 a province of Prussia.

10 Pfennigs = 1 Groschen
24 Gute Groschen = 1 Thaler
30 Silbergroschen = 1 Thaler (1858)

Values for unused stamps are for examples with original gum as defined in the catalogue introduction. Examples without gum sell for about 50-60% of the figures quoted.

Coat of Arms — A1

Wmk. Square Frame

1850 Rose Gum Typo. *Imperf.*

1 A1 1gg blk, *gray bl* 3,250. 50.00
On cover, single franking 160.00
On cover, multiple franking 400.00

Full margins = 1mm.

See Nos. 2, 11.

The reprints have white gum and no watermark.

Values for multiples

1 A1 1gg horiz. pair 190.00
1 A1 1gg vert. pair 4,000. 160.00
On cover *475.00*
1 A1 1gg horiz. strip of 3 *800.00*
1 A1 1gg vert. strip of 3 *1,450.* *800.00*
On cover *2,000.*
1 A1 1gg vert. strip of 4 *4,500.*
1 A1 1gg horiz.. strip of 4 —
On cover *10,000.*
1 A1 1gg block of 4 *8,000.*
On cover *32,000.*

Horizontal multiples are particularly scarce as the stamps were dispensed to the public in vertical strips

The off-cover vert. strip of 4 is unique.

Coat of Arms — A2

1851-55 Wmk. 130

2 A1 1gg blk, *gray grn* 80.00 9.00
No gum 40.00
On cover, single franking 20.00
On cover, multiple franking 30.00
On cover with #3 *3,250.*
On cover with #3a *3,300.*
a. 1gg black, *yellow green* 950.00 32.50
No gum 325.00
On cover, single franking 95.00
On cover, multiple franking 125.00
b. Wmk. inverted *500.00* 240.00
On cover 475.00
c. As "a," wmk inverted 600.00
On cover 1,600.
3 A2 1/30th blk, *salmon* 95.00 50.00
No gum 55.00
On cover, single franking 120.00
On cover, multiple franking 240.00
On cover with other stamps 600.00
a. 1/30th black, *crimson* ('55) 95.00 50.00
No gum 55.00
On cover, single franking 95.00
On cover, multiple franking 240.00
On cover with other stamps 600.00
b. Bisect on cover —
c. Wmk. inverted 1,600.
d. As "a," wmk. inverted 460.00 240.00
On cover 600.00
5 A2 1/15th blk, *gray bl* 160.00 80.00
No gum 80.00
On cover, single franking 200.00
On cover, multiple franking 475.00
On cover with other stamps 590.00
a. Bisect on cover —
b. Wmk inverted *1,000.*
On cover *2,800.*
6 A2 1/10th blk, *yellow* 240.00 60.00
No gum 125.00
On cover, single franking 125.00
On cover, multiple franking 610.00
On cover with other stamps 775.00
a. 1/10th black, *orange* 240.00 60.00
No gum 125.00
On cover, single franking 125.00
On cover, multiple franking 610.00
On cover with other stamps 775.00
b. Wmk. inverted 1,600.
c. As "a," wmk. inverted 1,600.
Nos. 2-6 (4) 575.00 199.00

Full margins = 1mm.

Bisects Nos. 3b, 5a, 12a and 13a were used for ½g.

See Nos. 8, 12-13.

The 1/10th has been reprinted on unwatermarked paper, with white gum.

Values for horizontal pairs

2 A1 1gg black, *gray grn* 475.00 27.50
On cover *57.50*
On registered cover *175.00*
a. 1gg black, *yellow green* 150.00
On cover 390.00
On first telegraph form ('52) *20,000.*
On telegraph form ('56) *5,750.*
3 A2 1/30th black, *salmon* 475.00 27.50
No gum 300.00
On cover 775.00
a. 1/30th black, *crimson* 475.00 150.00
No gum 300.00
On cover 325.00
5 A2 1/15th black, *gray bl* 725.00 450.00
No gum 300.00
On cover 1,400.
6 A2 1/10th black, *yellow* 990.00 360.00
No gum 300.00
On cover 1,400.
a. 1/10th black, *orange* 990.00 360.00
No gum 300.00
On cover 1,200.

Values for vertical pairs

2 A1 1gg black, *gray grn* 400.00 24.00
On cover 47.50
a. 1gg black, *yellow green* 125.00
On cover 325.00
3 A2 1/30th black, *salmon* 400.00 200.00
No gum 240.00
On cover 650.00
a. 1/30th black, *crimson* 400.00 125.00
No gum 240.00
On cover 275.00
5 A2 1/15th black, *gray bl* 600.00 375.00
No gum 240.00
On cover 1,200.
6 A2 1/10th black, *yellow* 825.00 300.00
No gum 240.00
On cover 1,000.
a. 1/10th black, *orange* 825.00 300.00
No gum 240.00
On cover 1,000.

Values for horizontal strips of 3

2 A1 1gg black, *gray grn* *760.00* 125.00
On cover 290.00
a. 1gg black, *yellow green* 675.00 675.00
On cover 1,200.
3 A2 1/30th black, *salmon* 900.00 900.00
On cover 2,400.
a. 1/30th black, *crimson* 390.00 875.00
On cover 2,400.
5 A2 1/15th black, *gray bl* 3,000. *2,900.*
On cover 7,200.
6 A2 1/10th black, *yellow* 2,000. 2,000.
On cover 3,900.
a. 1/10th black, *orange* 2,100. 1,950.
On cover 3,900.

Values for vertical strips of 3

2 A1 1gg black, *gray grn* *640.00* 100.00
On cover 240.00
a. 1gg black, *yellow green* 560.00 560.00
On cover 1,000.
3 A2 1/30th black, *salmon* 750.00 725.00
On cover 2,000.
a. 1/30th black, *crimson* 325.00 350.00
On cover 825.00
5 A2 1/15th black, *gray bl* 2,500. 2,450.
On cover 6,000.
6 A2 1/10th black, *yellow* 1,650. 1,650.
On cover 3,250.
a. 1/10th black, *orange* 1,725. 1,625.
On cover 3,250.

Values for vertical strips of 4

2 A1 1gg black, *gray grn* 850.00 *500.00*
On cover *1,300.*
6 A2 1/10th black, *yellow* *4,000.*

Values for vertical strips of 5

2 A1 1gg black, *gray grn* — *1,150.*

Values for blocks of 4

2 A1 1gg black, *gray grn* 1,600. *2,000.*
On cover 8,000.
a. 1gg black, *yellow green* 5,000.
3 A2 1/30th black, *salmon* 2,400.
a. 1/30th black, *crimson* 2,125.
5 A2 1/15th black, *gray bl* 3,200.
6 A2 1/10th black, *yellow* 1,750.
a. 1/10th black, *orange* 1,750.

Crown and Numeral — A3

1853 Wmk. 130

7 A3 3pf rose 400.00 300.00
No gum 250.00
On cover 800.00
a. 3pf dark lilac rose 2,000. 960.00
No gum 875.00
On cover 2,250.

Full margins = 1mm.

See Nos. 9, 16-17, 25.

The reprints of No. 7 have white gum.

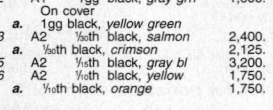

Values for horizontal pairs

7 A3 3pf rose 1,200. 800.00
On cover 1,600.
a. 3pf dark lilac rose — 2,800.
On cover 4,800.

Values for used vertical pairs

7 A3 3pf rose 1,600.
a. 3pf dark lilac rose 3,000.

Values for used horizontal strips of 3

7 A3 3pf rose *1,900.*
a. 3pf dark lilac rose *3,600.*

Values for blocks of 4

7 A3 3pf rose — *4,000.*
a. 3pf dark lilac rose *8,000.*

Fine Network in Second Color

1855 Unwmk.

8 A2 1/10th blk & org 200.00 160.00
No gum 140.00
On cover 400.00
a. 1/10th black & yellow 400.00 275.00
No gum 240.00
On cover 725.00

Full margins = 1mm.

No. 8 with olive yellow network and other values with fine network are essays.

Values for horizontal pairs

8 A2 1/10th blk & org 800.00 600.00
No gum 475.00
On cover 1,600.
a. 1/10th black & yellow 800.00

Values for vertical pairs

8 A2 1/10th blk & org 640.00
a. 1/10th black & yellow —

Values for strips of 3

8 A2 1/10th blk & org 1,300.
a. 1/10th black & yellow 1,625.

Large Network in Second Color

1856-57

9 A3 3pf rose & blk 275.00 275.00
No gum 85.00
On cover 525.00
a. 3pf rose & gray 400.00 350.00
No gum 130.00
On cover 800.00
11 A1 1gg blk & grn 55.00 12.00
No gum 19.00
On cover 32.50
12 A2 1/30th blk & rose 125.00 32.50
No gum 45.00
On cover 80.00
a. Bisect on cover *13,500.*
b. 1/30th black & carmine 950.00 475.00
No gum 350.00
On cover 950.00
13 A2 1/15th blk & bl 95.00 72.50
No gum 30.00
On cover 200.00
a. Bisect on cover *12,000.*
14 A2 1/10th blk & org ('57) 725.00 55.00
No gum 320.00
On cover 160.00

Full margins = 1mm.

The reprints have white gum, and the network does not cover all the outer margin.

Values for pairs

9 A3 3pf rose & blk 950.00 650.00
On cover 1,350.
a. 3pf rose & gray 1,600. 800.00
On cover 1,600.
11 A1 1gg blk & grn 250.00 47.50
On cover 125.00
12 A2 1/30th blk & rose 400.00 100.00
On cover 200.00
b. 1/30th black & carmine 1,400.
On cover
13 A2 1/15th blk & bl 275.00 *325.00*
On cover 1,200.
14 A2 1/10th blk & org 275.00
On cover 1,000.

Values for horizontal strips of 3

9 A3 3pf rose & blk 1,000.
a. 3pf rose & gray 1,400.
11 A1 1gg blk & grn 400.00 250.00
On cover 600.00
12 A2 1/30th blk & rose 950.00 250.00
On cover 600.00
b. 1/30th black & carmine —
13 A2 1/15th blk & bl 475.00 *1,600.*
14 A2 1/10th blk & org 1,600.

Values for blocks of 4

9 A3 3pf rose & blk 1,600. 1,600.
On cover 4,000.
a. 3pf rose & gray 2,000. *2,000.*
On cover *4,800.*
11 A1 1gg blk & grn 950.00 *2,000.*
12 A2 1/30th blk & rose 1,100. *1,500.*
b. 1/30th black & carmine —
13 A2 1/15th blk & bl 1,400. —
14 A2 1/10th blk & org —

1859-63 Without Network

16 A3 3pf pink 140.00 *100.00*
Never hinged 250.00
No gum 65.00
On cover 400.00
a. 3pf carmine rose 80.00 *90.00*
Never hinged 160.00
No gum 32.50
On cover 250.00
17 A3 3pf grn (Drei Zehntel) ('63) 400.00 *950.00*
Never hinged 800.00
On cover 3,200.
On cover, single franking, local delivery *4,000.*

Full margins = 1mm.

Values for pairs

16 A3 3pf pink 325.00 *475.00*
16a A3 3pf carmine rose 175.00 *250.00*
17 A3 3pf green 950.00 *2,400.*

Values for horizontal strips of 3

16 A3 3pf pink 475.00 *800.00*
16a A3 3pf carmine rose 275.00 *475.00*
On cover 1,600.
17 A3 3pf green 1,600. *4,000.*
On cover *8,000.*

Values for blocks of 4

16 A3 3pf pink 650.00 *1,200.*
16a A3 3pf carmine rose 400.00 *950.00*
On cover 6,000.
17 A3 3pf green 3,200. *7,500.*

Examples of No. 25 with rouletting trimmed off are sometimes offered as No. 17. Minimum size of No. 17 acknowledged as genuine: 21 1/2x24 1/2mm.

The reprints of No. 16 have pink gum instead of red; the extremities of the banderol point downward instead of outward.

Crown and Post Horn — A7

King George V — A8

1859-61 *Imperf.*

18 A7 1/2g black ('60) 120.00 200.00
Never hinged 325.00
On cover 600.00
a. Rose gum 400.00 *325.00*
Never hinged 800.00
On cover 900.00
19 A8 1g rose 4.00 4.50
Never hinged 9.50
On cover 8.00
a. 1g vio rose 20.00 20.00
Never hinged 32.50
On cover 47.50
b. 1g carmine 80.00 32.50
Never hinged 140.00
On cover 80.00
c. Half used as 1/3g on cover *12,000.*
20 A8 2g ultra 16.00 40.00
Never hinged 26.00
On cover 95.00
a. Half used as 1g on cover *8,000.*
b. 2g dark blue 16.00 *45.00*
Never hinged 26.00
On cover 125.00
22 A8 3g yellow 260.00 60.00
Never hinged 450.00
On cover 160.00
a. 3g orange yellow 160.00 95.00
Never hinged 275.00
On cover 250.00
23 A8 3g brown ('61) 27.50 50.00
Never hinged 52.50
On cover 125.00
a. One third used as 1g on cover —
b. 3g gray brown ('61) 80.00 *250.00*
Never hinged 140.00
On cover 475.00
c. 3g black brown ('61) 400.00 *400.00*
Never hinged 800.00
On cover 800.00
24 A8 10g green ('61) 275.00 875.00
Never hinged 400.00
On cover 4,800.
On cover, single franking 6,000.

Full margins = 1mm.

Reprints of 1/2g are on thick toned paper with yellowish gum. Originals are on white paper with rose or white gum. Reprints exist tête bêche.

Reprints of 3g yellow and 3g brown have white or pinkish gum. Originals have rose or orange gum.

Values for pairs

18 A7 1/2g black 400.00 *475.00*
On cover 1,300.
a. Rose gum 1,000. 800.00
On cover 2,250.
19 A8 1g rose 9.50 *11.00*
On cover 32.50
a. 1g vio rose 45.00 *47.50*
On cover 125.00
b. 1g carmine 200.00 *80.00*
On cover 250.00
20 A8 2g ultra 45.00 *110.00*
On cover 325.00
b. 2g dark blue 35.00 *140.00*
On cover 400.00
22 A8 3g yellow 550.00 140.00
On cover 480.00
a. 3g orange yellow 400.00 200.00
On cover 600.00
23 A8 3g brown 60.00 *250.00*
On cover 725.00
b. 3g gray brown 200.00 *600.00*
On cover 1,400.
c. 3g black brown 950.00 950.00
24 A8 10g green 525.00 *2,800.*
On cover *12,000.*

Values for horizontal strips of 3

18 A7 1/2g black 1,000. *2,400.*
a. Rose gum 1,600. —
19 A8 1g rose 13.50 *47.50*
On cover 100.00
a. 1g vio rose 72.50 *140.00*
On cover 325.00
b. 1g carmine *140.00*
On cover 400.00
20 A8 2g ultra 72.50 *475.00*
b. 2g dark blue 55.00 *800.00*
22 A8 3g yellow 900.00 250.00
a. 3g orange yellow 725.00 350.00
23 A8 3g brown 95.00 *900.00*
On cover 2,000.
b. 3g gray brown 325.00 *700.00*
c. 3g black brown —
24 A8 10g green 800.00 —

Values for blocks of 4

18 A7 1/2g black 3,200. *6,400.*
a. Rose gum 2,200. *3,500.*
19 A8 1g rose 22.50 *2,000.*
a. 1g vio rose 125.00
b. 1g carmine 110.00 *1,050.*
20 A8 2g ultra 130.00 *2,400.*
b. 2g dark blue 90.00
22 A8 3g yellow 1,600. 400.00
a. 3g orange yellow 1,200. 460.00
23 A8 3g brown 125.00 *3,200.*
b. 3g gray brown 475.00 —
c. 3g black brown — —
24 A8 10g green 1,200. *7,200.*

1864 White Gum *Perce en Arc 16*

25 A3 3pf grn (Drei Zehntel) 30.00 60.00
Never hinged 65.00
On cover 150.00
26 A7 1/2g black 275.00 275.00
Never hinged 475.00
On cover 600.00
27 A8 1g rose 12.00 8.00
Never hinged 25.00
On cover 12.00
28 A8 2g ultra 125.00 60.00
Never hinged 240.00
On cover 160.00
a. Half used as 1g on cover 16,000.
29 A8 3g brown 70.00 70.00
Never hinged 125.00
On cover 175.00
Nos. 25-29 (5) 512.00 473.00

Reprints of 3g are percé en arc 13 1/2.

Rose Gum

25a A3 3pf green 80.00 80.00
Never hinged 140.00
On cover 200.00
26a A7 1/2g black 475.00 450.00
On cover 1,000.
27a A8 1g rose 40.00 25.00
Never hinged 60.00
On cover 47.50
29a A8 3g brown *1,200.* *1,200.*
On cover 2,400.

Used examples of Nos. 25a-29a retain the rose color on the reverse after the gum has been removed.

Values for pairs

25 A3 3pf green 80.00 *200.00*
On cover 400.00
26 A7 1/2g black 725.00 600.00
On cover 1,200.
27 A8 1g rose 25.00 25.00
On cover 47.50
28 A8 2g ultra 325.00 160.00
On cover 400.00
29 A8 3g brown 160.00 *200.00*
On cover 400.00

Rose Gum

25a A3 3pf green 250.00 250.00
On cover 550.00
26a A7 1/2g black 1,200. 1,000.
On cover 2,000.
27a A8 1g rose 95.00 60.00
On cover 125.00
29a A8 3g brown *3,200.* *4,050.*

Values for horizontal strips of 3

25 A3 3pf green 125.00 *325.00*
26 A7 1/2g black 1,000. *1,000.*
27 A8 1g rose 47.50 *80.00*
On cover 200.00
28 A8 2g ultra 600.00 *1,000.*
On cover 1,600.
29 A8 3g brown 250.00 *600.00*

Rose Gum

25a A3 3pf green 350.00 *400.00*
26a A7 1/2g black 1,750. *1,750.*
27a A8 1g rose 200.00 140.00
On cover 325.00
29a A8 3g brown —

Values for blocks of 4

25 A3 3pf green 150.00 *950.00*
On cover 2,000.
26 A7 1/2g black 1,750. *2,700.*
27 A8 1g rose 90.00 *1,200.*
28 A8 2g ultra 800.00 *1,150.*
29 A8 3g brown 340.00 *2,000.*

Rose Gum

25a A3 3pf green 800.00 *950.00*
On cover 2,000.
26a A7 1/2g black 3,200. *3,400.*
27a A8 1g rose 350.00 *1,600.*
29a A8 3g brown *6,000.* —

The stamps of Prussia superseded those of Hanover on Oct. 1, 1866.

LUBECK

LOCATION — Situated on an arm of the Baltic Sea between the former German States of Holstein and Mecklenburg.
GOVT. — Former Free City and State
AREA — 115 sq. mi.
POP. — 136,413
CAPITAL — Lubeck

Lubeck was a member of the German Confederation and became part of the German Empire in 1870.

16 Schillings = 1 Mark

Values for Nos. 1-7 unused are for stamps without gum. Nos. 6 and 7 with gum sell for about twice the figures quoted. Values for Nos. 8-14 unused are for examples with original gum as defined in the catalogue introduction. Nos. 8-14 without gum sell for about 50-60% of the figures quoted.

Coat of Arms — A1

1859 Litho. Wmk. 148 *Imperf.*

1 A1 1/2g gray lilac 475.00 *2,000.*
With original gum 2,200.
On cover 6,400.
On cover, single franking 9,500.
2 A1 1s orange 475.00 *2,000.*
With original gum 2,400.
On cover *4,000.*
3 A1 2s brown 27.50 *240.00*
With original gum 120.00
On cover 800.00
a. Value in words reads "ZWEI EIN HALB" 400.00 *7,200.*
On cover *56,000.*
4 A1 2 1/2s rose 50.00 *800.00*
With original gum 200.00
On cover 2,000.
5 A1 4s green 27.50 *600.00*
With original gum 100.00
On cover 1,400.
a. 4s yellow green 32.50

Full margins = 3/4mm.

The 1872 reprints of the 1859 issue are unwatermarked and printed in bright colors. Values: unused, $240 each; never hinged, $550 each.

Values for pairs

1 A1 1/2g gray lilac 1,600. —
2 A1 1s orange 1,600. 5,600.
On cover 6,500.
3 A1 2s brown 52.50 *1,200.*
On cover *2,800.*
a. Value in words reads "ZWEI EIN HALB" 950.00 —
4 A1 2 1/2s rose 125.00 *4,800.*
On cover 6,900.
5 A1 4s green 52.50 —
On cover 5,000.
a. 4s yellow green 80.00

Values for blocks of 4

1 A1 1/2g gray lilac —
2 A1 1s orange —
3 A1 2s brown 90.00
a. Value in words reads "ZWEI EIN HALB" —
4 A1 2 1/2s rose 325.00
5 A1 4s green 110.00
5a A1 4s yel grn 190.00

1862 Unwmk.

6 A1 1/2s lilac 17.50 *1,600.*
With original gum 40.00
On cover 4,000.
On cover, single franking 7,700.
7 A1 1s yellow orange 30.00 *1,600.*
With original gum 90.00
On cover 4,000.

Full margins = 3/4mm.

Values for pairs

6 A1 1/2s lilac 35.00 *4,800.*
7 A1 1s yellow orange 72.50 *4,800.*

Values for strips of 3

6 A1 1/2s lilac 55.00
7 A1 1s yellow orange 100.00

Values for blocks of 4

6 A1 1/2s lilac 80.00
7 A1 1s yellow orange 140.00

A2

1863 *Rouletted 11½*

Eagle embossed

8 A2 ½s green 50.00 *72.50*
Never hinged *95.00*
No gum 16.00
On cover 400.00
On cover, single franking 400.00
9 A2 1s orange 125.00 *160.00*
Never hinged 275.00
No gum 52.50
On cover 350.00
a. Rouletted 10 200.00 *475.00*
Never hinged 475.00
No gum 80.00
On cover 3,200.
10 A2 2s rose 27.50 *65.00*
Never hinged 65.00
No gum 12.00
On cover 240.00
11 A2 2½s ultra 125.00 *400.00*
Never hinged 240.00
No gum 65.00
On cover 1,200.
12 A2 4s bister 55.00 *100.00*
Never hinged 100.00
No gum 27.50
On cover 325.00
Nos. 8-12 (5) 382.50 *797.50*

The 1872 reprints are imperforate and without embossing. Values: unused, $120 each; never hinged, $225 each.

Values for pairs

8 A2 ½s green 85.00 *200.00*
Never hinged 260.00
On cover 400.00
9 A2 1s orange 260.00 *275.00*
Never hinged 725.00
a. Rouletted 10 650.00 *2,750.*
10 A2 2s rose 55.00 *150.00*
Never hinged 140.00
On cover 275.00
11 A2 2½s ultra 300.00 *1,200.*
Never hinged 650.00
On cover 2,550.
12 A2 4s bister 110.00 *325.00*
Never hinged 250.00
On cover 900.00

Values for strips of 3

8 A2 ½s green 150.00 *250.00*
Never hinged 400.00
On cover 1,200.
9 A2 1s orange 600.00 *450.00*
Never hinged 1,400.
a. Rouletted 10 1,000. *10,000.*
10 A2 2s rose 90.00 *800.00*
Never hinged 200.00
11 A2 2½s ultra 475.00 *1,800.*
Never hinged 1,350.
12 A2 4s bister 240.00 *950.00*
Never hinged 375.00

Values for blocks of 4

8 A2 ½s green 225.00 *800.00*
Never hinged 550.00
On cover 2,400.
9 A2 1s orange 800.00
a. Rouletted 10 1,350.
10 A2 2s rose 125.00
Never hinged 275.00
11 A2 2½s ultra 600.00
12 A2 4s bister 225.00
Never hinged 550.00

A3

1864 **Litho.** *Imperf.*

13 A3 1¼s dark brown 45.00 *55.00*
Never hinged 110.00
No gum 20.00
On cover 200.00
a. 1¼s reddish brown 32.50 *125.00*
Never hinged 55.00
No gum 14.50
On cover 360.00

Values for pairs

13 A3 1¼s dark brown 125.00 *240.00*
Never hinged 250.00
No gum 47.50
a. 1¼s reddish brown 80.00 *400.00*
Never hinged 150.00
No gum 32.50

Values for used strips of 3

13 A3 1¼s dark brown 175.00 *800.00*
Never hinged 375.00
No gum 72.50
a. 1¼s reddish brown 150.00 *1,200.*
Never hinged 325.00
No gum 52.50

Values for blocks of 4

13 A3 1¼s dark brown 250.00
No gum 100.00
a. 1¼s reddish brown 200.00
No gum 72.50

A4

1865 *Rouletted 11½*

Eagle embossed

14 A4 1½s red lilac 30.00 *85.00*
Never hinged 55.00
No gum 14.50
On cover 225.00

Value for pair

14 A4 1½s red lilac 72.50 *290.00*
Never hinged 140.00
No gum 32.50

Value for strip of 3

14 A4 1½s red lilac 100.00 *950.00*
Never hinged 200.00
No gum 47.50

Value for block of 4

14 A4 1½s red lilac 140.00
Never hinged 300.00
No gum 72.50

The 1872 reprints are imperforate and without embossing. Values: unused, $120; never hinged, $225.

Counterfeit cancellations are found on Nos. 1-14.

The stamps of Lübeck were superseded by those of the North German Confederation on Jan. 1, 1868.

MECKLENBURG-SCHWERIN

LOCATION — In northern Germany, bordering on the Baltic Sea.
GOVT. — Grand Duchy
AREA — 5,065 sq. mi. (approx.)
POP. — 674,000 (approx.)
CAPITAL — Schwerin

Mecklenburg-Schwerin was a member of the German Confederation and became part of the German Empire in 1870.

48 Schillings = 1 Thaler

Values for unused stamps are for examples with original gum as defined in the catalogue introduction. Examples without gum sell for about 70% of the figures quoted.

Coat of Arms
A1 A2

A1 has dots in background.

1856 **Unwmk.** **Typo.** *Imperf.*

1 A1 Four ¼s red 150.00 125.00
Never hinged 260.00
No gum 95.00
On cover 250.00
a. ¼s red 14.50 12.00
No gum 8.00
Single on cover 225.00
Two ¼s on cover 160.00
Two ¼s on postal envelope 200.00
Three ¼s on cover 260.00
Five ¼s on cover 390.00
Six ¼s on cover —
Seven ¼s on cover —
2 A2 3s yellow 95.00 55.00
Never hinged 160.00
No gum 55.00
On cover 200.00
a. 3s orange 80.00 55.00
Never hinged 160.00
No gum 65.00
On cover 200.00
3 A2 5s blue 225.00 275.00
Never hinged 400.00
No gum 150.00
On cover 1,000.
Nos. 1-3 (3) 470.00 455.00

Full margins: No. 1 = ¾mm; Nos. 2-3 = 1¼mm.

Covers: Each multiple of No. 1a corresponds to a rate based on distance and destination. Values are for covers correctly franked.

See Nos. 4, 6-8.

Values for pairs

1 A1 Four ¼s red 800.00 400.00
No gum 475.00
On cover 800.00
a. ¼s red 32.50 24.00
No gum 20.00
On cover 160.00
2 A2 3s yellow 325.00 300.00
No gum 190.00
On cover 800.00
a. 3s orange 325.00 300.00
No gum 190.00
On cover 800.00
3 A2 5s blue 1,400. *1,750.*
No gum 900.00
On cover *4,000.*

A3

A3 has no dots in background.

1864-67 *Rouletted 11½*

4 A1 Four ¼s red *2,800.* *1,900.*
No gum 1,900.
Four ¼s on cover 4,800.
a. ¼s red 175.00 240.00
No gum 125.00
Single on cover 1,350.
b. Pair of ¼s red 600.00
On cover 2,000.
On postal stationery 2,400.
5 A3 Four ¼s red 70.00 60.00
Never hinged 120.00
No gum 37.50
Four ¼s on cover 160.00
a. ¼s red 9.50 9.50
Never hinged 16.00
No gum 4.00
¼s on cover or postal stationery 120.00
Two ¼s on cover 125.00
6 A2 2s gray lil ('67) 140.00 *1,600.*
Never hinged 260.00
No gum 67.50
On cover *11,200.*
a. 2s red violet ('66) 240.00 240.00
Never hinged 400.00
No gum 110.00
On cover 1,100.
7 A2 3s org yel, wide margin ('67) 45.00 *300.00*
Never hinged 72.50
No gum 22.50
On cover 950.00
a. Narrow margin ('65) 160.00 125.00
Never hinged 275.00
No gum 80.00
Single on cover 800.00
8 A2 5s bister brn 160.00 *240.00*
Never hinged 225.00
No gum 72.50
On cover 1,200.
a. Thick paper 240.00 *340.00*
Never hinged 400.00
No gum 125.00
On cover 1,450.
b. Ribbed paper 250.00 250.00
Never hinged 475.00
No gum 160.00
On cover 1,350.

The overall size of No. 7, including margin, is 24½x24½mm. That of No. 7a is 23½x23mm.

Covers: Each multiple of Nos. 4-5 corresponds to a rate based on distance and destination. Values are for covers correctly franked.

The bister on white paper was not issued. Value $12.

Values for pairs

4 A1 Four ¼s red *5,500.*
On cover *16,000.*
5 A3 Four ¼s red 140.00 125.00
Never hinged 260.00
On cover 230.00
6 A2 2s gray lil ('67) 350.00 —
No gum 160.00
a. 2s red violet ('66) 650.00 1,450.
No gum 300.00
On cover 4,000.
7 A2 3s org yel, wide margin ('67) 140.00 *1,350.*
No gum 52.50
On cover 3,600.
a. Narrow margin ('65) 725.00 350.00
No gum 340.00
On cover 1,450.
8 A2 5s bister brn 350.00 *1,100.*
No gum 175.00
On cover 1,600.
a. Thick paper 650.00 *1,350.*
No gum 325.00
On cover 1,750.
b. Ribbed paper —

Counterfeit cancellations exist on those stamps valued higher used than unused.

These stamps were superseded by those of the North German Confederation on Jan. 1, 1868.

MECKLENBURG-STRELITZ

LOCATION — In northern Germany, divided by Mecklenburg-Schwerin
GOVT. — Grand Duchy
AREA — 1,131 sq. mi.
POP. — 106,347
CAPITAL — Neustrelitz

Mecklenburg-Strelitz was a member of the German Confederation and became part of the German Empire in 1870.

30 Silbergroschen = 48 Schillings = 1 Thaler

Values for unused stamps are for examples with original gum as defined in the catalogue introduction. Examples without gum sell for about 50% of the figures quoted.

Coat of Arms
A1 A2

Rouletted 11½

1864 **Unwmk.** **Embossed**

1 A1 ¼sg orange 175.00 *2,400.*
Never hinged 275.00
No gum 80.00
On cover *80,000.*
a. ¼sg yellow orange 340.00 *4,000.*
Never hinged 600.00
No gum 190.00
On cover —
2 A1 ⅓sg green 80.00 *1,350.*
Never hinged 140.00
No gum 32.50
On cover *10,500.*
a. ⅓sg dark green 140.00 *2,400.*
Never hinged 300.00
No gum 72.50
On cover *13,500.*
3 A1 1sch violet 290.00 *3,200.*
Never hinged 550.00
No gum 130.00
On cover *9,600.*
4 A2 1sg rose 140.00 190.00
Never hinged 275.00
No gum 65.00
On cover 525.00
5 A2 2sg ultra 40.00 *800.00*
Never hinged 95.00
No gum 13.50
On cover 2,000.
6 A2 3sg bister 40.00 *1,275.*
Never hinged 90.00
No gum 16.50
On cover 4,800.

Counterfeit cancellations abound.

Values for pairs

1 A1 ¼sg orange 375.00 *5,600.*
No gum 175.00
a. ¼sg yellow orange 1,000. —
No gum 475.00
2 A1 ⅓sg green 175.00 *2,800.*
No gum 80.00
On cover *11,000.*
a. ⅓sg dark green 350.00 *5,500.*
No gum 175.00
On cover *14,500.*
3 A1 1sch violet 650.00 —
No gum 325.00
4 A2 1sg rose 325.00 *525.00*
No gum 140.00
On cover *1,000.*
5 A2 2sg ultra 95.00 *2,000.*
Never hinged 200.00
No gum 40.00
6 A2 3sg bister 72.50 *3,600.*
No gum 32.50
On cover *20,000.*

These stamps were superseded by those of the North German Confederation in 1868.

OLDENBURG

LOCATION — In northwestern Germany, bordering on the North Sea.
GOVT. — Grand Duchy
AREA — 2,482 sq. mi.
POP. — 483,042 (1910)
CAPITAL — Oldenburg

Oldenburg was a member of the German Confederation and became part of the German Empire in 1870.

30 Silbergroschen = 1 Thaler
30 Groschen = 1 Thaler

Values for unused stamps are for examples with original gum as defined in the catalogue introduction. Examples without gum sell for about 50% of the figures quoted.

A1 A2

1852-55 **Unwmk.** **Litho.** *Imperf.*

1 A1 1/30th blk, *blue* 350.00 27.50
No gum 190.00
On cover 80.00
2 A1 1/15th blk, *rose* 800.00 80.00
No gum 475.00
On cover 200.00
3 A1 1/10th blk, *yellow* 800.00 95.00
No gum 475.00
On cover 200.00

No.	Type	Description	Unused	Used
4	A2	⅓sgr blk, *grn* ('55)	1,275.	1,100.
		No gum	675.00	
		On newspaper or circular		*2,400.*
		On cover		*5,500.*

Full margins = 1mm.

There are three types of Nos. 1 and 2.

Values for pairs

No.	Type	Description	Unused	Used
1	A1	1/30th black, *blue*	1,200.	400.00
		No gum	650.00	
		On cover		950.00
2	A1	1/15th black, *rose*	8,000.	550.00
		No gum	4,500.	
		On cover		2,200.
3	A1	1/10th black, *yellow*		1,300.
		On cover		2,400.
4	A2	⅓sgr black, *grn*	6,000.	2,800.
		No gum	3,200.	

Values for strips of 3

No.	Type	Description	Unused	Used
1	A1	1/30th black, *blue*	2,400.	640.00
		No gum	1,600.	
		On cover		1,600.
2	A1	1/15th black, *rose*		2,800.
3	A1	1/10th black, *yellow*		2,400.
4	A2	⅓sgr black, *grn*	*12,000.*	*8,000.*
		No gum	7,200.	
		On cover		16,000.

Values for blocks of 4

No.	Type	Description	Unused	Used
1	A1	1/30th blk, *blue*	3,600.	—
		No gum	2,000.	
2	A1	1/15th black, *rose*	—	—
		On cover		*40,000.*
3	A1	1/10th black, *yellow*	—	—
		On cover		*40,000.*
4	A2	⅓sgr black, *grn*	*21,500.*	
		No gum	*12,000.*	

A3

1859

No.	Type	Description	Unused	Used
5	A3	⅓g blk, *green*	2,600.	*2,900.*
		On cover		*31,500.*
		On newspaper or circular		*20,000.*
6	A3	1g blk, *blue*	725.00	45.00
		On cover		95.00
7	A3	2g blk, *rose*	1,050.	600.00
		On cover		*2,500.*
8	A3	3g blk, *yellow*	1,050.	600.00
		On cover		*2,400.*
a.		"OLBENBURG"	1,600.	1,200.
		On cover		*4,000.*

Full margins = 1½mm.

See Nos. 10, 13-15.

Values for pairs

No.	Type	Description	Unused	Used
5	A3	⅓g black, *green*		*12,000.*
6	A3	1g black, *blue*		160.00
7	A3	2g black, *rose*		*2,800.*
8	A3	3g black, *yellow*		*4,000.*

Values for strips of 3

No.	Type	Description	Unused	Used
5	A3	⅓g black, *green*		*26,000.*
6	A3	1g black, *blue*		550.00
7	A3	2g black, *rose*		*16,000.*
8	A3	3g black, *yellow*		*16,500.*

A4

1861

No.	Type	Description	Unused	Used
9	A4	¼g orange	300.00	*4,000.*
		On cover		*28,000.*
10	A3	⅓g green	475.00	*875.00*
		On cover		*8,000.*
		On cover, single franking		*15,000.*
a.		⅓g bluish green	475.00	*875.00*
		On cover		*8,000.*
		On cover, single franking		*15,000.*
b.		⅓g moss green	1,600.	*2,800.*
		On cover		*14,000.*
		On cover, single franking		*20,000.*
c.		"OLDEIBURG"	*875.00*	*1,450.*
d.		"Dritto"	*875.00*	*1,450.*
e.		"Drittd"	*875.00*	*1,450.*
f.		Printed on both sides		*5,000.*
12	A4	½g redsh brn	450.00	525.00
		On cover		*2,400.*
a.		½g dark brown	450.00	525.00
		On cover		*2,400.*
13	A3	1g blue	240.00	160.00
		On cover		350.00
a.		1g gray blue	475.00	250.00
		On cover		600.00
b.		Printed on both sides		*3,750.*
14	A3	2g red	450.00	450.00
		On cover		*1,750.*
15	A3	3g yellow	450.00	450.00
		On cover		*2,200.*
a.		"OLDEIBURG"	*800.00*	*875.00*
b.		Printed on both sides		*5,000.*

Full margins = 1mm.

Forged cancellations are found on Nos. 9, 10, 12 and their minor varieties.

Coat of Arms — A5

1862 Embossed *Rouletted 11½*

No.	Type	Description	Unused	Used
16	A5	⅓g green	200.00	190.00
		On cover		950.00
17	A5	½g orange	200.00	110.00
		On cover		250.00
a.		½g orange red	250.00	160.00
		On cover		400.00
18	A5	1g rose	110.00	16.00
		On cover		40.00
19	A5	2g ultra	200.00	50.00
		On cover		125.00
20	A5	3g bister	210.00	52.50
		On cover		125.00

1867 *Rouletted 10*

No.	Type	Description	Unused	Used
21	A5	⅓g green	32.50	*725.00*
		On cover		*4,800.*
22	A5	½g orange	40.00	*360.00*
		On cover		*1,600.*
23	A5	1g rose	20.00	*55.00*
		On cover		*140.00*
a.		Half used as ½g on cover		—
24	A5	2g ultra	20.00	*475.00*
		On cover		*4,800.*
25	A5	3g bister	45.00	*400.00*
		On cover		*4,400.*
		Nos. 21-25 (5)	157.50	*2,015.*

Forged cancellations are found on Nos. 21-25.

The stamps of Oldenburg were replaced by those of the North German Confederation on Jan. 1, 1868.

PRUSSIA

LOCATION — The greater part of northern Germany.
GOVT. — Independent Kingdom
AREA — 134,650 sq. mi.
POP. — 40,165,219 (1910)
CAPITAL — Berlin

Prussia was a member of the German Confederation and became part of the German Empire in 1870.

12 Pfennigs = 1 Silbergroschen
60 Kreuzer = 1 Gulden (1867)

Values for unused stamps are for examples with original gum as defined in the catalogue introduction. Examples without gum sell for about 50% of the figures quoted.

King Frederick William IV
A1 A2

1850-56 Engr. Wmk. 162 *Imperf.*
Background of Crossed Lines

No.	Type	Description	Unused	Used
1	A1	4pf yel grn ('56)	110.00	72.50
		On cover		225.00
a.		4pf dark green	160.00	125.00
		On cover		300.00
2	A1	6pf (½sg) red org	90.00	52.50
		On cover		200.00
3	A2	1sg black, *rose*	80.00	14.00
		On cover		20.00
a.		1sg black, *bright red*	*20,000.*	450.00
		On cover		*1,400.*
4	A2	2sg black, *blue*	110.00	16.00
		On cover		57.50
a.		Half used as 1sg on cover		—
5	A2	3sg black, *yellow*	110.00	16.00
		On cover		32.50
a.		3sg black, *orange buff*	325.00	37.50
		On cover		95.00
		Nos. 1-5 (5)	500.00	171.00

Full margins = ½mm.

See Nos. 10-13.

Values for pairs

No.	Type	Description	Unused	Used
1	A1	4pf yellow green	240.00	150.00
		On cover		550.00
1a	A1	4pf dark green	475.00	275.00
		On cover		725.00
2	A1	6pf (½ sgr) red orange	240.00	125.00
		On cover		450.00
3	A1	1sg black, *rose*	200.00	25.00
		On cover		47.50
a.		1sg black, *bright red*		1,000.
		On cover		2,500.
4	A2	2sg black, *blue*	250.00	90.00
		On cover		175.00
5	A2	3sg black, *yellow*	250.00	57.50
		On cover		125.00
a.		3sg black, *orange buff*		125.00
		On cover		475.00

Reprints exist on watermarked and unwatermarked paper.

A3

Solid Background

1857 Typo. Unwmk.

No.	Type	Description	Unused	Used
6	A3	1sg rose	325.00	35.00
		On cover		72.50
a.		1sg carmine rose	360.00	50.00
		On cover		110.00
7	A3	2sg blue	1,280.	90.00
		On cover		250.00
a.		2sg dark blue	1,750.	125.00
		On cover		400.00
b.		Half used as 1sg on cover		—
8	A3	3sg orange	160.00	40.00
		On cover		125.00
a.		3sg yellow	1,600.	95.00
		On cover		350.00
b.		3sg deep orange	800.00	120.00
		On cover		400.00
		Nos. 6-8 (3)	1,765.	165.00

Full margins = 1¾mm.

The reprints of Nos. 6-8 have a period instead of a colon after "SILBERGR."

Thin translucent paper

No.	Type	Description	Unused	Used
6b	A3	1sg rose	650.00	110.00
6c	A3	1sg carmine rose	600.00	125.00
7c	A3	2sg blue		110.00
7d	A3	2sg dark blue	2,000.	110.00
8c	A3	3sg orange	325.00	47.50
8d	A3	3sg yellow		250.00
8e	A3	3sg deep orange		600.00

Values for pairs

No.	Type	Description	Unused	Used
6	A3	1sg rose	800.00	80.00
		On cover		200.00
a.		1sg carmine rose	950.00	110.00
		On cover		250.00
7	A3	2sg blue		250.00
		On cover		800.00
a.		2sg dark blue		475.00
8	A3	3sg orange	475.00	125.00
		On cover		350.00
a.		3sg yellow		400.00
		On cover		725.00
b.		3sg deep orange		325.00
		On cover		800.00

A4

Background of Crossed Lines

1858-60 Typo.

No.	Type	Description	Unused	Used
9	A4	4pf green	80.00	32.50
		On cover		140.00

Engr.

No.	Type	Description	Unused	Used
10	A1	6pf (½sg) org ('59)	190.00	160.00
		On cover		550.00
a.		6pf (½sg) brick red	275.00	225.00
		On cover		800.00

Typo.

No.	Type	Description	Unused	Used
11	A2	1sg rose	32.50	4.00
		On cover		11.50
12	A2	2sg blue	110.00	17.50
		On cover		80.00
a.		2sg dark blue	160.00	42.50
		On cover		140.00
b.		Half used as 1sg on cover		—
13	A2	3sg orange	95.00	16.00
		On cover		55.00
a.		3sg yellow	140.00	20.00
		On cover		65.00
		Nos. 9-13 (5)	507.50	230.00

Full margins: Nos. 9, 11-13 = ¾mm; No. 10 = ½mm.

Values for pairs

No.	Type	Description	Unused	Used
9	A4	4pf green	200.00	90.00
		On cover		250.00
10	A1	6pf (½sgr) orange	475.00	350.00
		On cover		800.00
a.		6pf (½sgr) brick red	650.00	475.00
		On cover		1,000.
11	A2	1sg rose	80.00	9.50
		On cover		25.00
12	A2	2sg blue	275.00	60.00
		On cover		140.00
a.		2sg dark blue	400.00	125.00
		On cover		325.00
13	A2	3sg orange	225.00	40.00
		On cover		100.00
a.		3sg yellow	350.00	55.00
		On cover		110.00

Coat of Arms
A6 A7

1861-67 Embossed *Rouletted 11½*

No.	Type	Description	Unused	Used
14	A6	3pf red lilac ('67)	27.50	45.00
		On cover		160.00
a.		3pf red violet ('65)	325.00	275.00
		On cover		725.00
15	A6	4pf yellow green	12.00	12.00
		On cover		52.50
a.		4pf green	42.50	55.00
		On cover		140.00
16	A6	6pf orange	12.00	14.50
		On cover		55.00
a.		6pf vermilion	125.00	65.00
		On cover		150.00
17	A7	1sg rose	3.50	1.60
		On cover		3.50
18	A7	2sg ultra	12.00	1.60
		On cover		8.50
a.		2sg blue	400.00	27.50
		On cover		125.00
20	A7	3sg bister	8.75	2.00
		On cover		8.00
a.		3sg gray brown ('65)	—	29.00
		On cover		125.00
		Nos. 14-20 (6)	75.75	76.70

Values for pairs

No.	Type	Description	Unused	Used
14	A6	3pf red lilac	60.00	*125.00*
		On cover		290.00
a.		3pf red violet	675.00	*800.00*
		On cover		2,100.
15	A6	4pf yellow green	27.50	*27.50*
		On cover		200.00
a.		4pf green	100.00	*140.00*
		On cover		400.00
16	A6	6pf orange	27.50	*35.00*
		On cover		80.00
a.		6pf vermilion	300.00	175.00
		On cover		325.00
17	A7	1sg rose	9.50	4.00
		On cover		9.50
18	A7	2sg ultramarine	25.00	4.75
		On cover		45.00
a.		2sg blue	950.00	125.00
		On cover		450.00
20	A7	3sg bistre	25.00	8.00
		On cover		32.50
a.		3sg gray brown	—	95.00
		On cover		200.00

A8 A9

Typographed in Reverse on Paper Resembling Goldbeater's Skin

1866 *Rouletted 10*

No.	Type	Description	Unused	Used
21	A8	10sg rose	95.00	*105.00*
		Never hinged	250.00	
		On cover		650.00
		On cover, single franking		1,400.
		On parcel post receipt card		650.00
22	A9	30sg blue	110.00	*225.00*
		Never hinged	250.00	
		On cover		1,600.
		On parcel post receipt card		2,500.

Values for pairs

No.	Type	Description	Unused	Used
21	A8	10sg rose	200.00	225.00
		Never hinged	525.00	
		On parcel post receipt card		*4,800.*
22	A9	30sg blue	250.00	475.00
		Never hinged	550.00	
		On parcel post receipt card		*4,600.*

Values for blocks of 4

No.	Type	Description	Unused	Used
21	A8	10sg rose	475.00	*1,300.*
		Never hinged	1,100.	
22	A9	30sg blue	600.00	*1,600.*
		Never hinged	1,200.	

Perfect examples of Nos. 21-22 are extremely rare.

Covers: Values for Nos. 21-22 on covers and parcel post receipt cards are for stamps used in 1866-1867. Later items are worth considerably less. Covers bearing stamps in perfect condition are extremely rare and are worth much more than the value stated.

See Nos. 4, 6-8.

A10

1867 Embossed *Rouletted 16*

No.	Type	Description	Unused	Used
23	A10	1kr green	30.00	*45.00*
		Never hinged	95.00	
		On cover		200.00
24	A10	2kr orange	45.00	*95.00*
		Never hinged	140.00	
		On cover		475.00

25 A10 3kr rose 24.00 *27.50*
Never hinged 65.00
On cover 80.00
26 A10 6kr ultra 24.00 *45.00*
Never hinged 87.50
On cover 160.00
27 A10 9kr bister brown 27.50 *47.50*
Never hinged 72.50
On cover 160.00
Nos. 23-27 (5) 150.50 *260.00*

Values for pairs

23 A10 1kr green 60.00 *95.00*
On cover 325.00
24 A10 2kr orange 95.00 *225.00*
On cover 1,000.
25 A10 3kr rose 55.00 *125.00*
On cover 400.00
26 A10 6kr ultramarine 55.00 *125.00*
On cover 450.00
27 A10 9kr bister brown 80.00 *125.00*
On cover 475.00

Imperforate stamps of the above sets are proofs.

The stamps of Prussia were superseded by those of the North German Confederation on Jan. 1, 1868.

OFFICIAL STAMPS
See Germany Nos. OL1-OL15.

SAXONY

LOCATION — In central Germany
GOVT. — Kingdom
AREA — 5,787 sq. mi.
POP. — 2,500,000 (approx.)
CAPITAL — Dresden

Saxony was a member of the German Confederation and became a part of the German Empire in 1870.

10 Pfennings = 1 Neu-Groschen
30 Neu-Groschen = 1 Thaler

Values for unused stamps are for examples with original gum as defined in the catalogue introduction. Examples without gum sell for about 50-60% of the figures quoted.

A1

1850 Unwmk. Typo. *Imperf.*

1 A1 3pf brick red *8,000.* *6,500.*
No gum 4,000.
On cover or wrapper *20,000.*
a. 3pf cherry red *12,000.* *13,600.*
No gum 6,850.
On cover or wrapper *32,000.*
b. 3pf brown red *12,000.* *10,500.*
No gum 6,850.
On cover or wrapper *28,000.*

Full margins = 1mm.

There are vertical dividing lines between stamps.

Values for pairs

1 A13pf brick red *20,000.* *22,400.*
No gum *11,000.*
On cover or wrapper *36,000.*
1a A13pf cherry red *30,500.* *48,000.*
No gum *21,000.*
On cover or wrapper *80,000.*
1b A13pf brown red *30,500.* *40,000.*
No gum *21,000.*
On cover or wrapper *71,000.*

Values for strips of 3

1 A13pf brick red *48,000.* *52,000.*

Values for strips of 4 or blocks of 4

1 A13pf brick red *145,000.* *200,000.*
1b A13pf brown red *175,000.*

Cancellations and usages

1 A13pf brick red, *pen cancelled* *6,800.*
On cover, wrapper or circular *28,000.*
1 A13pf brick red, *with mute canceller* *7,200.*
On cover, wrapper or circular *28,000.*
1 A13pf brick red, *with numeral cancellation, from* *9,000.*
On cover, wrapper or circular —
1 A13pf brick red, pair or two singles on local delivery cover *40,000.*

Coat of Arms — A2

1851

2 A2 3pf green 125.00 95.00
No gum 65.00
On cover 190.00
On local cover, single franking 600.00
On cover, pen canceled (railway) 240.00
a. 3pf yellow green 1,750. 800.00
No gum 975.00
On cover 1,350.

Nos. 2 and 2a are valued with the margin just touching the design in one or two places. Stamps with margins all around sell for considerably more.

Stamps with very fine impressions, from the first printing, command substantial premiums.

Frederick Augustus II — A3

1851-52 Engr.

3 A3 ½ng black, *gray* 72.50 12.00
No gum 25.00
On cover 35.00
a. ½ng black, *pale blue* (error) *20,000.*
5 A3 1ng black, *rose* 95.00 12.00
No gum 40.00
On cover 27.50
6 A3 2ng black, *pale bl* 250.00 70.00
No gum 100.00
On cover 160.00
7 A3 2ng blk, *dk bl* ('52) 725.00 55.00
No gum 400.00
On cover 125.00
8 A3 3ng black, *yellow* 160.00 25.00
No gum 72.50
On cover 60.00
Nos. 3-8 (5) 1,303. 174.00

Full margins = ¾mm.

The error No. 3a occurred when paper meant for printing No. 6 was inadvertently placed in the stack of paper for printing No. 3.

King John I — A4

1855-60

9 A4 ½ng black, *gray* 16.00 8.00
No gum 6.50
On cover 9.50
a. "1/20" at left or right — —
On cover 1,300.
10 A4 1ng black, *rose* 16.00 8.00
No gum 6.50
On cover 9.50
11 A4 2ng black, *dark blue* 24.00 20.00
No gum 9.50
On cover 40.00
a. 2ng black, *blue* 72.50 47.50
No gum 32.50
On cover 95.00
12 A4 3ng black, *yellow* 24.00 16.00
No gum 7.50
On cover 27.50
13 A4 5ng ver ('56) 90.00 65.00
No gum 32.50
On cover 160.00
a. 5ng orange brown ('60) 325.00 *325.00*
No gum 115.00
On cover 950.00
b. 5ng deep brown ('57) *725.00* 175.00
No gum 260.00
On cover 625.00
14 A4 10ng milky blue ('56) 225.00 225.00
No gum 95.00
On cover 1,100.
On cover, single franking 2,200.
a. 10ng dk blue ('59) 275.00 300.00
No gum 125.00
On cover 1,450.
On cover, single franking 3,200.

Full margins = ¾mm.

The ½ng is found in 3 types, the 1ng in 2.

In 1861 the 5ng and 10ng were printed on hard, brittle, translucent paper.

A5

A6

Typo.; Arms Embossed

1863 *Perf. 13*

15 A5 3pf blue green 4.00 *40.00*
No gum 1.60
On cover 95.00
a. 3pf yellow green 95.00 *125.00*
No gum 22.50
On cover 240.00
16 A5 ½ng orange 4.00 *2.75*
No gum 1.60
On cover 8.00
a. ½ng red orange 24.00 6.00
No gum 9.25
On cover 11.00
17 A6 1ng rose 1.60 2.40
No gum .50
On cover 8.00
a. Vert. pair, imperf. between *225.00*
b. Horiz. pair, imperf. between *375.00*
18 A6 2ng blue 2.75 8.00
No gum .75
On cover 19.00
a. 2ng dark blue 12.00 32.50
No gum 4.75
On cover 80.00
19 A6 3ng red brown 4.50 12.00
No gum 1.75
On cover 25.00
a. 3ng bister brown 24.00 9.50
No gum 9.25
On cover 19.00
20 A6 5ng dull violet 30.00 *47.50*
No gum 12.00
On cover 130.00
a. 5ng gray violet 16.00 *450.00*
No gum 6.00
On cover 875.00
b. 5ng gray blue 30.00 *72.50*
No gum 11.00
On cover 225.00
c. 5ng slate 22.50 *250.00*
No gum 11.00
On cover 550.00

The stamps of Saxony were superseded on Jan. 1, 1868, by those of the North German Confederation.

SCHLESWIG-HOLSTEIN

LOCATION — In northern Germany.
GOVT. — Duchies
AREA — 7,338 sq. mi.
POP. — 1,519,000 (approx.)
CAPITAL — Schleswig

Schleswig-Holstein was an autonomous territory from 1848 to 1851 when it came under Danish rule. In 1864, it was occupied by Prussia and Austria, and in 1866 it became a province of Prussia.

16 Schillings = 1 Mark

Values for unused stamps are for examples with original gum as defined in the catalogue introduction. Stamps without gum sell for about 50% of the figures quoted.

Coat of Arms — A1

Typographed; Arms Embossed

1850 Unwmk. *Imperf.*
With Silk Threads

1 A1 1s dl bl & grnsh bl 325.00 *5,600.*
No gum 175.00
On cover *9,600.*
a. 1s Prussian blue 725.00
No gum 400.00
b. Double silk thread 1,200.
No gum 800.00
2 A1 2s rose & pink 560.00 *7,200.*
No gum 325.00
On cover *20,000.*
On cover, #1 and 2 *55,000.*
a. 2s deep pink & rose 725.00
No gum 350.00
b. Double embossing *3,100.*
No gum 1,600.

Full margins = ½mm.

Values for stamps with legible town postmarks

1 A1 1s dull blue & greenish blue, *from* *14,500.*
On cover *24,000.*
2 A1 2s rose & pink, *from* *16,000.*

Values for stamps with legible town cancellations start at the figure above.

Values for pairs

1 A1 1s dull blue & greenish blue 875.00 *13,500.*
No gum 525.00
1a A1 1s prussian blue 1,750.
No gum 950.00
2 A1 2s rose & pink 1,350. *30,500.*
No gum 800.00
2a A1 2s deep pink & rose 1,900.
No gum 1,100.

Values for strips of 3

1 A1 1s dull blue & greenish blue 1,450.
No gum 800.00
1a A1 1s prussian blue 2,550.
No gum 1,600.
2 A1 2s rose & pink 2,000.
No gum 1,300.
2a A1 2s deep pink & rose 2,800.
No gum 1,750.

Values for blocks or strips of 4

1 A1 1s dull blue & greenish blue 1,750.
No gum 1,100.
1a A1 1s prussian blue 3,350.
No gum 1,750.
2 A1 2s rose & pink 2,800.
No gum 1,750.
2a A1 2s deep pink & rose 4,000.
No gum 2,400.

Forged cancellations are found on Nos. 1-2, 5-7, 9, 16 and 19.

A2

A3

1865 Typo. *Rouletted 11½*

3 A2 ⅛s rose 40.00 *45.00*
On cover 225.00
On cover, single franking 240.00
4 A2 1⅓s green 20.00 *20.00*
On cover 35.00
5 A3 1⅓s red lilac 45.00 *125.00*
On cover 600.00
On cover, single franking *12,000.*
6 A2 2s ultra 50.00 *240.00*
On cover 600.00
7 A3 4s bister 65.00 *1,300.*
On cover *6,000.*
Nos. 3-7 (5) 220.00 1,730.

Schleswig

A4

1864 Typo. *Rouletted 11½*

8 A4 1⅓s green 45.00 20.00
On cover 32.50
9 A4 4s carmine 95.00 *450.00*
On cover 800.00

A5

1865 *Rouletted 10, 11½*

10 A4 ⅛s green 32.50 *55.00*
On cover 225.00
On cover, single franking 240.00
11 A4 1⅓s red lilac 55.00 25.00
On cover 32.50
a. 1⅓s gray lilac ('67) 255.00 47.50
On cover 95.00
b. Half of #11a used as ⅔s on cover *32,000.*
12 A5 1⅓s rose 27.50 *60.00*
On cover 300.00
On cover, single franking 1,900.
13 A4 2s ultra 27.50 *60.00*
On cover 90.00
14 A4 4s bister 32.50 *80.00*
On cover 160.00
Nos. 10-14 (5) 175.00 *280.00*

Holstein

A6

Type I — Small lettering in frame. Wavy lines in spandrels close together.
Type II — Small lettering in frame. Wavy lines wider apart.
Type III — Larger lettering in frame and no periods after "H R Z G." Wavy lines as II.

1864 Litho. *Imperf.*

15 A6 1¼s bl & gray, I 52.50 *55.00*
On cover 160.00
a. Half used as ⅛s on cover *9,500.*
16 A6 1¼s bl & gray, II 800.00 *2,400.*
On cover *32,000.*
a. Half used as ⅛s on cover *24,000.*
17 A6 1¼s bl & gray, III 45.00 *55.00*
On cover 110.00
With town datestamp 200.00
On cover, with town datestamp 400.00
a. Half used as ⅛s on cover *8,000.*

Full margins = ¾mm.

A7

1864 Typo. *Rouletted 8*

18 A7 1¼s blue & rose 45.00 20.00
On cover 40.00
a. Half used as ⅛s on cover *2,000.*

A8

1865 *Rouletted 8*

19 A8 ½s green 65.00 *95.00*
On cover 325.00
On cover, single franking 340.00
20 A8 1¼s red lilac 47.50 25.00
On cover 35.00
21 A8 2s blue 52.50 47.50
On cover 120.00
Nos. 19-21 (3) 165.00 167.50

A9

A10

1865-66 *Rouletted 7 and 8*

22 A9 1¼s red lilac ('66) 72.50 25.00
On cover 35.00
a. Half used as ⅛s on cover *24,000.*
23 A10 1⅓s carmine 60.00 45.00
On cover 300.00
On cover, single franking *2,000.*
24 A9 2s blue ('66) 145.00 *160.00*
On cover 335.00
25 A10 4s bister 65.00 *80.00*
On cover 160.00
Nos. 22-25 (4) 342.50 310.00

These stamps were superseded by those of North German Confederation on Jan. 1, 1868.

THURN AND TAXIS

A princely house which, prior to the formation of the German Empire, enjoyed the privilege of a postal monopoly. These stamps were superseded on July 1, 1867, by those of Prussia, followed by those of the North German Postal District on Jan. 1, 1868, and later by stamps of the German Empire on Jan. 1, 1872.

Values are for stamps with four complete margins just clear of the framelines. Stamps with margins just touching the framelines on one or two sides are worth approximately 60% of the values quoted. Stamps with four large margins are rare and command premiums of up to 500% over the values quoted.

Values for unused stamps are for examples with original gum as defined in the catalogue introduction. Stamps without gum sell for about 50% of the figures quoted.

NORTHERN DISTRICT

30 Silbergroschen or Groschen = 1 Thaler

A1

1852-58 Unwmk. Typo. *Imperf.*

1 A1 ¼sgr blk, *red brn* ('54) 265.00 60.00
No gum 175.00
On cover 160.00
On cover tied by town datestamp 550.00
On cover, single franking 690.00
On news wrapper, single franking 1,000.
2 A1 ⅓sgr blk, *buff* ('58) 125.00 250.00
No gum 80.00
On cover 690.00
On cover tied by town datestamp 1,350.
3 A1 ½sgr blk, *green* 725.00 40.00
No gum 500.00
On cover 160.00
On newspaper wrapper 690.00
a. ½sgr black, *olive green* 650.00 27.50
No gum 575.00
On cover 125.00
On newspaper wrapper 675.00
4 A1 1sgr blk, *dk bl* 1,325. 140.00
No gum 875.00
On cover 325.00
5 A1 1sgr blk, *lt bl* ('53) 800.00 22.50
No gum 525.00
On cover 82.50
6 A1 2sgr blk, *rose* 850.00 32.50
No gum 575.00
On cover 100.00
a. Half used as 1sgr on cover *10,000.*
7 A1 3sgr blk, *brownish yellow* 1,000. 30.00
No gum 675.00
On cover 60.00
a. 3sgr blk, *pale orange yellow* 1,000. 80.00
No gum 675.00
On cover 175.00

Full margins = ¼mm.

Reprints of Nos. 1-12, 15-20, 23-24, were made in 1910. They have "ND" in script on the back. Value, $6.50 each.

A2

1859-60

8 A1 ¼sgr red ('60) 67.50 67.50
Never hinged 140.00
No gum 42.50
On cover 160.00
On cover, single franking 400.00
9 A1 ½gr green 300.00 95.00
Never hinged 525.00
No gum 200.00
On cover 300.00
On cover, four clear margins 550.00
10 A1 1sgr blue 300.00 45.00
Never hinged 525.00
No gum 200.00
On cover 100.00
On cover, four clear margins 160.00
11 A1 2sgr rose ('60) 145.00 80.00
Never hinged 240.00
No gum 95.00
On cover 210.00
On cover, four clear margins 410.00
12 A1 3sgr red brn ('60) 145.00 110.00
Never hinged 240.00
No gum 95.00
On cover 325.00
On cover, four clear margins 625.00
13 A2 5sgr lilac 2.75 *400.00*
Never hinged 4.00
No gum 1.75
On cover *1,000.*
On cover, four clear margins 2,200.
14 A2 10sgr orange 2.75 *875.00*
Never hinged 4.00
No gum 1.75
On cover *4,750.*
On cover, four clear margins 10,250.
On cover, single franking *18,500.*

Full margins = ¼mm.

Excellent forged cancellations exist on Nos. 13 and 14. For reprints, see note after No. 7.

1862-63

15 A1 ¼sgr black ('63) 35.00 *75.00*
Never hinged 57.50
No gum 25.00
On cover 200.00
On cover, four clear margins 300.00
On cover, single franking 600.00
Single franking on newspaper 700.00
16 A1 ⅓sgr green ('63) 50.00 *250.00*
Never hinged 82.50
No gum 30.00
On cover 550.00
On cover, four clear margins 1,100.
On newsprint, single franking 1,100.
17 A1 ½sgr org yel 100.00 47.50
Never hinged 175.00
No gum 65.00
On cover 210.00
On cover, four clear margins 210.00
18 A1 1sgr rose ('63) 67.50 27.50
Never hinged 110.00
No gum 42.50
On cover 160.00
On cover, four clear margins 160.00
19 A1 2sgr blue ('63) 60.00 *100.00*
Never hinged 100.00
No gum 18.00
On cover 250.00
On cover, four clear margins 500.00
20 A1 3sgr bister ('63) 27.50 *55.00*
Never hinged 55.00
No gum 18.00
On cover 190.00
On cover, four clear margins 190.00
Nos. 15-20 (6) 340.00 *555.00*

Full margins = ¼mm.

For reprints, see note after No. 7.

1865 *Rouletted*

21 A1 ¼sgr black 7.50 *400.00*
Never hinged 13.00
On cover *825.00*
On cover, single franking 2,200.
22 A1 ⅓sgr green 11.00 *240.00*
Never hinged 22.50
On cover *875.00*
On cover, single franking 1,350.
23 A1 ½sgr yellow 22.50 *37.50*
Never hinged 40.00
On cover *92.50*
24 A1 1sgr rose 25.00 25.00
Never hinged 40.00
On cover 62.50
25 A1 2sgr blue 1.50 *67.50*
Never hinged 2.75
On cover *140.00*
26 A1 3sgr bister 2.75 *27.50*
Never hinged 4.50
On cover *82.50*
Nos. 21-26 (6) 70.25 *797.50*

For reprints, see note after No. 7.

1866 *Rouletted in Colored Lines*

27 A1 ¼sgr black 2.00 *1,250.*
Never hinged 3.00
On cover *3,250.*
On cover, single franking 7,500.
28 A1 ⅓sgr green 2.00 *600.00*
Never hinged 3.00
On cover *2,250.*
29 A1 ½sgr yellow 2.00 *120.00*
Never hinged 3.00
On cover *275.00*
30 A1 1sgr rose 1.50 *60.00*
Never hinged 2.75
On cover *140.00*
a. Horizontal pair without rouletting between 150.00 1,500.
b. Half used as ½sgr on cover *52,500.*
31 A1 2sgr blue 1.50 *600.00*
Never hinged 2.75
On cover *1,300.*
32 A1 3sgr bister 1.50 *150.00*
Never hinged 2.75
On cover *375.00*
Nos. 27-32 (6) 10.50 *2,780.*

Forged cancellations on Nos. 2, 13-14, 15-16, 21-22, 25-32 are plentiful.

SOUTHERN DISTRICT

60 Kreuzer = 1 Gulden

A1

1852-53 Unwmk. *Imperf.*

42 A1 1kr blk, *lt grn* 240.00 15.00
No gum 160.00
On cover 60.00
On cover, four clear margins 115.00
On cover, single franking 140.00
On newsprint, single franking 175.00
a. 9kr black, *black* 500.00 40.00
No gum 500.00
On cover 300.00
On cover, four clear margins 325.00
On cover, single franking 300.00
43 A1 3kr blk, *dk bl* 925.00 50.00
No gum 575.00
On cover 125.00
On cover, four clear margins 275.00
44 A1 3kr blk, *bl* ('53) 800.00 20.00
No gum 525.00
On cover 75.00
On cover, four clear margins 140.00
45 A1 6kr blk, *rose* 800.00 11.00
No gum 525.00
On cover 60.00
On cover, four clear margins 110.00
46 A1 9kr blk, *brnish yell* 875.00 17.50
No gum 550.00
On cover 60.00
On cover, four clear margins 120.00
a. 9kr blk, *pale orange yellow* 750.00 45.00
No gum 500.00
On cover 90.00
On cover, four clear margins 160.00

Full margins = ¼mm.

Reprints of Nos. 42-50, 53-56 were made in 1910. Each has "ND" in script on the back. Value, each $6.50.

A2

1859

47 A1 1kr green 25.00 10.00
Never hinged 37.50
No gum 16.00
On cover 35.00
On cover, four clear margins 70.00
On cover, single franking 120.00
Single franking, printed matter 135.00
48 A1 3kr blue 560.00 25.00
Never hinged 1,100.
On cover 80.00
On cover, four clear margins 160.00
49 A1 6kr rose 560.00 67.50
Never hinged 1,100.
On cover 185.00
On cover, four clear margins 375.00
50 A1 9kr yellow 560.00 67.50
Never hinged 1,150.
On cover 350.00
On cover, four clear margins 700.00
51 A2 15kr lilac 2.75 *175.00*
Never hinged 4.00
On cover *525.00*
On cover, four clear margins 1,150.
52 A2 30kr orange 2.75 *475.00*
Never hinged 4.00
No gum 1.90
On cover *1,500.*
On cover, four clear margins 3,400.
On cover, single franking *13,500.*

Forged cancellations exist on Nos. 51 and 52. For reprints, see note after No. 46.

1862

53 A1 3kr rose 13.50 30.00
Never hinged 27.50
On cover 75.00
On cover, four clear margins 160.00
54 A1 6kr blue 13.50 30.00
Never hinged 27.50
On cover 80.00
On cover, four clear margins 160.00
55 A1 9kr bister 13.50 35.00
Never hinged 27.50
On cover 115.00
On cover, four clear margins 190.00
Nos. 53-55 (3) 40.50 95.00

For reprints, see note after No. 46.

1865 *Rouletted*

56 A1 1kr green 12.50 13.50
Never hinged 22.50
On cover 35.00
On cover, single franking 140.00
Single franking on printed matter 140.00
57 A1 3kr rose 18.50 7.50
Never hinged 30.00
On cover 27.50
58 A1 6kr blue 1.50 *20.00*
Never hinged 2.50
On cover 50.00

59 A1 9kr bister 2.25 *22.50*
Never hinged 3.75
On cover 60.00
Nos. 56-59 (4) 34.75 *63.50*

For reprint of No. 56, see note after No. 46.

1866 *Rouletted in Colored Lines*

60 A1 1kr green 1.50 *22.50*
Never hinged 2.50
On cover 65.00
On cover, single franking 200.00
61 A1 3kr rose 1.50 *20.00*
Never hinged 2.50
On cover 65.00
62 A1 6kr blue 1.50 *37.50*
Never hinged 2.50
On cover 77.50
63 A1 9kr bister 1.50 *32.50*
Never hinged 2.50
On cover 100.00
Nos. 60-63 (4) 6.00 *112.50*

Forged cancellations exist on Nos. 51-52, 58-63.

The Thurn & Taxis Stamps, Northern and Southern Districts, were replaced on July 1, 1867, by those of Prussia.

WURTTEMBERG

LOCATION — In southern Germany
GOVT. — Kingdom
AREA — 7,530 sq. mi.
POP. — 2,580,000 (approx.)
CAPITAL — Stuttgart

Württemberg was a member of the German Confederation and became a part of the German Empire in 1870. It gave up its postal autonomy on March 31, 1902, but official stamps were issued until 1923.

16 Kreuzer = 1 Gulden
100 Pfennigs = 1 Mark (1875)

Values for unused stamps are for examples with original gum as defined in the catalogue introduction. Unused stamps without gum of Nos. 1-46 sell for about 60-70% of the figures quoted. Unused stamps without gum of Nos. 47-54 sell for about 50% of the figures quoted.

A1

A1a

1851-52 Unwmk. Typo. *Imperf.*

1 A1 1kr blk, *buff* 1,125. 95.00
On cover 375.00
a. 1kr black, *straw* 3,500. 500.00
On cover 950.00
2 A1 3kr blk, *yellow* 275.00 7.25
On cover 19.00
a. 3kr black, *orange* 3,000. 300.00
On cover 750.00
4 A1 6kr blk, *yel grn* 1,450. 32.50
On cover 90.00
a. 6kr black, *blue green* 2,600. 50.00
On cover 130.00
5 A1 9kr blk, *rose* *4,800.* 37.50
On cover 90.00
6 A1a 18kr blk, *dl vio* ('52) 1,750. 725.00
On cover 1,750.
On cover, single franking 3,200.

Values for Pairs

1 A1 1kr blk, *buff* *400.00*
1a A1 1kr blk, *straw* *1,750.*
2 A1 3kr blk, *yellow* 60.00
2a A1 3kr blk, *orange* *2,200.*
4 A1 6kr blk, *yel grn* *475.00*
4a A1 6kr blk, *yel grn* *500.00*
5 A1 9kr blk, *rose* *675.00*
6 A1a 18kr blk, *dl vio* ('52) *2,400.*

Values for Strips of 3

1 A1 1kr blk, *buff* *1,200.*
1a A1 1kr blk, *straw* *3,250.*
2 A1 3kr blk, *yellow* 275.00
2a A1 3kr blk, *orange* —
4 A1 6kr blk, *yel grn* *2,800.*
4a A1 6kr blk, *yel grn* *2,800.*
5 A1 9kr blk, *rose* *3,000.*
6 A1a 18kr blk, *dl vio* ('52) *6,000.*

Full margins = 1mm.

On the "reprints" the letters of "Württemberg" are smaller, especially the first "e"; the right branch of the "r's" of Württemberg runs upward in the reprints and downward in the originals.

Coat of Arms — A2

With Orange Silk Threads

Typographed and Embossed

1857

7 A2 1kr yel brn 800.00 80.00
On cover 250.00
a. 1kr dark brown 1,100. 225.00
On cover 350.00
9 A2 3kr yel org 400.00 14.00
On cover 27.50
10 A2 6kr green 800.00 65.00
On cover 175.00
11 A2 9kr car rose 1,925. 70.00
On cover 175.00
a. 9kr dk lilac red 950.00
On cover 2,400.
12 A2 18kr blue 3,350. 1,350.
On cover 3,200.
On cover, single franking 6,000.

Values for Pairs

7 A2 1kr yellow brown 250.00
On traveled printed matter 800.00
a. 1kr dark brown 500.00
9 A2 3kr yellow orange 45.00
10 A2 6kr green 325.00
11 A2 9kr carmine rose 650.00
a. 9kr dk lilac red 4,500.
12 A2 18kr blue 4,500.

Full margins = ¼mm.

Very fine examples of Nos. 7-12 with have one or two margins touching, but not cutting, the frameline.

See Nos. 13-46, 53.

The reprints have red or yellow silk threads and are printed 2mm apart, while the originals are ¾mm apart.

1859 Without Silk Threads

13 A2 1kr brown 650.00 100.00
On cover 325.00
a. 1kr dark brown 2,000. 725.00
On cover 1,600.
15 A2 3kr yel org 275.00 14.00
On cover 25.00
16 A2 6kr green *9,600.* 125.00
On cover 250.00
17 A2 9kr car rose 1,275. 80.00
On cover 140.00
a. 9kr dk reddish lilac 1,000.
On cover 2,000.
18 A2 18kr dark blue 3,000. 1,450.
On cover 5,000.
On cover, single franking 9,500.

Values for Pairs

13 A2 1kr brown 325.00
On traveled printed matter 900.00
a. 1kr dark brown 1,750.
15 A2 3kr yellow org 55.00
16 A2 6kr green 800.00
17 A2 9kr car rose 600.00
18 A2 18kr dark blue *4,800.*

Full margins = ¾mm.

The colors of the reprints are brighter; they are also printed 2mm apart instead of 1¼mm.

1860 *Perf. 13½*

19 A2 1kr brown 1,125. 125.00
On cover 475.00
20 A2 3kr yel org 325.00 9.50
On cover 25.00
21 A2 6kr green 3,000. 100.00
On cover 250.00
22 A2 9kr carmine 1,200. 120.00
On cover 450.00
a. 9kr dk lake red 2,000.
On cover 4,000.

Values for Pairs

19 A2 1kr brown 450.00
On traveled printed matter 900.00
20 A2 3kr yellow org 72.50
21 A2 6kr green 325.00
22 A2 9kr carmine 600.00
a. 9kr dk lake red *6,000.*

1861 Thin Paper

23 A2 1kr brown 950.00 275.00
On cover 600.00
a. 1kr black brown 1,000. 250.00
On cover 600.00
25 A2 3kr yel org 200.00 65.00
On cover 140.00
26 A2 6kr green 400.00 110.00
On cover 225.00
27 A2 9kr rose 1,275. 275.00
On cover 600.00
a. 9kr claret 1,500. 350.00
On cover 725.00
29 A2 18kr dark blue 3,000. 2,250.
On cover 4,000.
On cover, single franking 6,000.

Values for Pairs

23 A2 1kr brown 600.00
On traveled printed matter 1,000.
a. 1kr black brown 650.00
25 A2 3kr yellow org 160.00
26 A2 6kr green 325.00
27 A2 9kr rose 1,200.
a. 9kr claret 1,750.
29 A2 18kr dark blue 4,600.

Examples of Nos. 23-29 with all perforations intact sell for considerably more.

1862 *Perf. 10*

30 A2 1kr blk brn 650.00 440.00
On cover 1,200.
31 A2 3kr yel org 800.00 47.50
On cover 200.00
32 A2 6kr green 525.00 160.00
On cover 360.00
33 A2 9kr claret 4,000. 800.00
On cover 2,200.

Values for Pairs

30 A2 1kr black brown 1,450.
On traveled printed matter 1,850.
31 A2 3kr yellow orange 200.00
32 A2 6kr green 525.00
33 A2 9kr claret 3,600.

1863

34 A2 1kr yel grn 45.00 13.50
On cover 25.00
a. 1kr green 400.00 95.00
On cover 250.00
36 A2 3kr rose 325.00 5.50
On cover 9.50
a. 3kr dark claret 1,600. 275.00
On cover 600.00
37 A2 6kr blue 160.00 55.00
On cover 145.00
39 A2 9kr yel brn 750.00 175.00
On cover 475.00
a. 9kr red brown 260.00 52.50
On cover 240.00
b. 9kr black brown 1,200. 190.00
On cover 600.00
40 A2 18kr orange 1,200. 400.00
On cover 950.00
On cover, single franking 1,750.

Values for Pairs

34 A2 1kr yellow grn 27.50
On traveled printed matter 125.00
a. 1kr green 275.00
36 A2 3kr rose 9.00
a. 3kr dark claret 950.00
37 A2 6kr blue 175.00
39 A2 9kr yellow brn 600.00
a. 9kr red brown 250.00
b. 9kr black brown 600.00
40 A2 18kr orange 1,200.

1865-68 *Rouletted 10*

41 A2 1kr yel grn 45.00 12.00
On cover 25.00
a. 1kr dark green 575.00 275.00
On cover 800.00
42 A2 3kr rose 45.00 3.25
On cover 7.00
a. 3kr claret 1,900. 2,250.
On cover 4,000.
43 A2 6kr blue 275.00 52.50
On cover 140.00
44 A2 7kr slate bl ('68) 960.00 125.00
On cover 325.00
45 A2 9kr bis brn 1,500. 120.00
On cover 200.00
a. 9kr red brown 1,150. 80.00
On cover 150.00
46 A2 18kr orange ('67) 1,800. 950.00
On cover 2,750.
On cover, single franking 4,000.

Values for Pairs

41 A2 1kr yellow grn 32.50
On traveled printed matter 140.00
a. 1kr dark green 725.00
42 A2 3kr rose 12.00
a. 3kr claret 6,000.
43 A2 6kr blue 175.00
44 A2 7kr slate bl ('68) 400.00
45 A2 9kr bister brn ('66) 360.00
a. 9kr red brown 240.00
46 A2 18kr orange ('67) 2,500.

A3

1869-73 Typo. & Embossed

47 A3 1kr yel grn 32.50 2.40
On cover 8.00
a. 1kr bl grn 225.00 72.50
On cover 200.00
48 A3 2kr orange 175.00 140.00
On cover 400.00
49 A3 3kr rose 16.00 1.60
On cover 4.00
50 A3 7kr blue 67.50 17.50
On cover 40.00
51 A3 9kr lt brn ('73) 80.00 40.00
On cover 240.00
a. 9kr org brn 240.00 225.00
On cover 600.00
52 A3 14kr orange 88.00 45.00
On cover 325.00
On cover, single franking 700.00
a. 14kr lemon yellow 1,500. 1,500.
On cover 4,000.
On cover, single franking 4,800.
b. 14kr dp yel org 240.00 125.00
On cover 675.00
On cover, single franking 1,000.
Nos. 47-52 (6) 459.00 246.50

Values for Pairs

47 A3 1kr yellow grn 8.00
On cover 32.50
On traveled printed matter 80.00
On traveled printed matter abroad, *from,* 90.00
a. 1kr bl grn 240.00
On cover 350.00
48 A3 2kr orange 350.00
On cover 675.00
49 A3 3kr rose 4.00
On cover 20.00
50 A3 7kr blue 60.00
On cover 140.00
51 A3 9kr lt brn ('73) 125.00
On cover 600.00
a. 9kr org brn 140.00
52 A3 14kr orange 140.00
a. 14kr lemon yellow 4,000.
b. 14kr dp yel org 400.00

See No. 54.

1873 *Imperf.*

53 A2 70kr red violet 1,750. 4,000.
On parcel post receipt card *50,000.*
a. 70kr violet 2,900. 5,250.
On parcel post receipt card *52,000.*

Values for Pairs

53 A2 70kr red violet *11,000.*
a. 70kr violet *12,000.*

Nos. 53 and 53a have single or double lines of fine black dots printed in the gutters between the stamps.

1874 *Perf. 11½x11*

54 A3 1kr yellow green 110.00 40.00
On cover 125.00
Pair 125.00

A4

A5

1875-1900 Typo.

55 A4 2pf sl gray ('93) 2.00 .95
Never hinged 4.00
On cover 8.00
56 A4 3pf green 20.00 1.60
Never hinged 47.50
On cover 16.00
57 A4 3pf brn ('90) .80 .55
Never hinged 1.75
On cover 2.00
a. Imperf., pair 160.00
Never hinged 330.00
58 A4 5pf violet 9.50 .80
Never hinged 19.00
On cover 2.40
59 A4 5pf grn ('90) 1.60 .55
Never hinged 3.25
On cover 2.00
a. 5pf blue green 300.00 24.00
Never hinged 600.00
On cover 80.00
b. Imperf., pair 175.00
Never hinged 315.00
60 A4 10pf carmine 1.60 .80
Never hinged 3.00
On cover 2.40
a. 10pf rose 85.00 1.25
Never hinged 185.00
On cover 6.50
b. Imperf., pair 80.00
Never hinged 160.00
61 A4 20pf ultra 1.60 1.60
Never hinged 4.00
On cover 4.00
a. 20pf dull blue 1.60 1.60
Never hinged 4.00
On cover 3.75
b. Imperf., pair 175.00
Never hinged 350.00
62 A4 25pf red brn 125.00 12.00
Never hinged 250.00
On cover 55.00
63 A4 25pf org ('90) 2.75 1.60
Never hinged 5.50
On cover 20.00
a. Imperf., pair 175.00
Never hinged 350.00
64 A5 30pf org & blk ('00) 4.00 5.50
Never hinged 9.00
On cover 40.00
65 A5 40pf dp rose & blk ('00) 4.00 6.50
Never hinged 8.00
On cover 95.00
66 A4 50pf gray 725.00 40.00
Never hinged 1,450.
On cover 725.00
On parcel post receipt card 395.00
67 A4 50pf gray grn 65.00 6.50
Never hinged 135.00
On cover 80.00
On parcel post receipt car 25.00
68 A4 50pf pur brn ('90) 3.25 .95
Never hinged 8.50
On cover 80.00
a. 50pf red brown 640.00 65.00
Never hinged 1,200.
On cover 800.00
On parcel post receipt card 275.00

b. As #68, imperf., pair 175.00
Never hinged *350.00*
69 A4 2m yellow 800.00 260.00
Never hinged 1,400.
On cover 3,250.
On parcel post receipt card 2,000.
70 A4 2m ver, *buff* ('79) 2,800. 125.00
Never hinged —
On cover 3,250.
On parcel post receipt card 2,000.
71 A5 2m org & blk ('86) 8.00 12.00
Never hinged 15.00
Telegraph cancel 4.50
On cover 325.00
On parcel post receipt card 65.00
a. 2m yellow & black 450.00 72.50
Never hinged 800.00
On cover 500.00
On parcel post receipt card 150.00
b. Imperf., pair 125.00
Never hinged 325.00
72 A5 5m bl & blk ('81) 45.00 *160.00*
Never hinged 65.00
Telegraph cancel 72.50
On cover —
On parcel post receipt card 6,000.
a. Double impression of figure of value 200.00
Never hinged 400.00

No. 70 has "Unverkauflich" (not for sale) printed on its back to remind postal clerks that it, like No. 69, was for their use and not to be sold to the public.

The regular postage stamps of Württemberg were superseded by those of the German Empire in 1902. Official stamps were in use until 1923.

WURTTEMBERG OFFICIAL STAMPS

For the Communal Authorities

O1

Perf. 11½x11

1875-1900 Typo. Unwmk.
O1 O1 2pf sl gray ('00) 3.00 2.00
Never hinged 7.50
On cover 3.00
O2 O1 3pf brn ('96) 3.00 2.00
Never hinged 6.75
On cover 4.50
O3 O1 5pf violet 37.50 2.40
Never hinged 80.00
On cover 12.00
a. Imperf., pair *3,000.*
O4 O1 5pf bl grn ('90) 1.60 2.00
Never hinged 4.00
On cover 3.25
a. Imperf., pair 55.00
Never hinged 105.00
O5 O1 10pf rose 7.50 2.25
Never hinged 16.00
On cover 4.75
a. Imperf., pair 90.00
Never hinged 160.00
O6 O1 25pf org ('00) 22.50 8.00
Never hinged 60.00
On cover 12.00
Nos. O1-O6 (6) 75.10 18.65

See Nos. O12-O32. For overprints and surcharges see Nos. O7-O11, O40-O52, O59-O93.

Used Values
When italicized, used values for Nos. O7-O183 are for favor-canceled stamps. Postally used stamps command a premium.

Stamps of Previous Issues Overprinted in Black

1906, Jan. 30
O7 O1 2pf slate gray 45.00
Never hinged 80.00
Postally used 65.00
On cover *95.00*
O8 O1 3pf dk brown 14.00 *9.25*
Never hinged 27.50
Postally used 12.00
On cover 20.00
O9 O1 5pf green 6.50 *4.75*
Never hinged 13.00
Postally used 9.25
On cover 8.00
O10 O1 10pf deep rose 6.50 *4.75*
Never hinged 13.00
Postally used 3.75
On cover 8.00
O11 O1 25pf orange 47.50 *72.50*
Never hinged 87.50
Postally used 72.50
On cover 140.00
Nos. O7-O11 (5) 119.50 *91.25*

Centenary of Kingdom of Württemberg.
Nos. O7-O11 also exist imperf but it is doubtful if they were ever issued in that condition.

1906-21 Wmk. 116
O12 O1 2pf slate gray 4.00 .40
Never hinged 8.00
Postally used 9.25
On cover 16.00
O13 O1 2½pf gray blk ('16) .80 .25
Never hinged 1.60
Postally used 2.00
On cover 3.50
O14 O1 3pf dk brown .95 .40
Never hinged 2.00
Postally used 2.00
On cover 2.75
O15 O1 5pf green .80 .40
Never hinged 1.60
Postally used 2.00
On cover 2.50
O16 O1 7½pf orange ('16) .80 .25
Never hinged 1.60
Postally used 2.00
On cover 3.50
O17 O1 10pf dp rose .80 .40
Never hinged 1.60
Postally used 2.00
On cover 2.50
O18 O1 10pf orange ('21) .30 *.30*
Never hinged .55
Postally used 2.00
On cover 2.50
O19 O1 15pf yellow brn ('16) 2.40 .25
Never hinged 4.75
Postally used 2.00
On cover 4.00
O20 O1 15pf purple ('17) 1.25 .25
Never hinged 2.40
Postally used 2.25
On cover 5.50
a. 15pf blackish violet ('21) .30 *1.40*
Never hinged .55
Postally used 2.00
On cover 2.50
O21 O1 20pf dp ultra ('11) 1.60 .40
Never hinged 3.25
Postally used *2.25*
On cover 4.00
O22 O1 20pf dp green ('21) .30 .30
Never hinged .55
Postally used 2.00
On cover 2.60
O23 O1 25pf orange .95 .40
Never hinged 2.40
Postally used 2.00
On cover 4.00
O24 O1 25pf brn & blk ('17) 1.25 .25
Never hinged 2.40
Postally used 2.25
On cover 8.00
O25 O1 35pf brown ('19) 1.60 .95
Never hinged 3.25
Postally used 37.50
On cover 95.00
O26 O1 40pf rose red ('21) .30 .30
Never hinged .55
Postally used 2.00
On cover 2.50
O27 O1 50pf rose lake ('11) 14.50 .40
Never hinged 25.00
Postally used 12.50
On cover 55.00
O28 O1 50pf vio brn ('21) .30 .30
Never hinged .80
Postally used 2.00
On cover 2.50
O29 O1 60pf olive grn ('21) .50 .30
Never hinged 1.25
Postally used 2.00
On cover 2.50
O30 O1 1.25m emerald ('21) .30 .30
Never hinged .80
Postally used 2.00
On cover 2.60
O31 O1 2m gray ('21) .30 .30
Never hinged .80
Postally used 2.00
On cover 2.60
O32 O1 3m brown ('21) .50 .30
Never hinged .80
Postally used 2.00
On cover 2.60
Nos. O12-O32 (21) 34.50 7.40

No. O24 contains solid black numerals.
Nos. O12-O32 exist imperf. Value, each pair, $6-$16.

O3

Perf. 14½x14

1916, Oct. 6 Typo. Unwmk.
O33 O3 2½pf slate 1.60 1.60
Never hinged 2.50
Postally used 9.25
On cover 18.50
O34 O3 7½pf orange 1.60 1.60
Never hinged 2.50
Postally used 3.00
On cover 4.00
O35 O3 10pf car rose 1.60 1.60
Never hinged 2.50
Postally used 4.75
On cover 16.00
O36 O3 15pf yellow brn 1.60 1.60
Never hinged 2.50
Postally used 2.00
On cover 6.25
O37 O3 20pf blue 1.60 1.60
Never hinged 2.50
Postally used 5.00
On cover 18.50
O38 O3 25pf gray blk 4.00 1.60
Never hinged 3.50
Postally used 15.00
On cover 27.50
O39 O3 50pf red brown 8.00 1.60
Never hinged 2.50
Postally used 62.50
On cover 155.00
Nos. O33-O39 (7) 20.00 11.20

25th year of the reign of King Wilhelm II.

Stamps of 1900-06 Surcharged

Perf. 11½x11

1916, Sept. 10 Wmk. 116
O40 O1 25pf on 25pf orange 4.00 .95
Never hinged 6.25
Postally used 15.50
On cover 37.50

No. O13 Surcharged in Blue

1919 Wmk. 116
O42 O1 2pf on 2½pf gray blk .80 .50
Never hinged 1.25
Postally used 2.75
On cover 7.50

Official Stamps of 1906-19 Overprinted

1919
O43 O1 2½pf gray blk .40 *.60*
Never hinged .65
Postally used 2.00
On cover 4.00
O44 O1 3pf dk brown 12.00 .60
Never hinged 16.00
Postally used 18.50
On cover 32.50
O45 O1 5pf green .30 .60
Never hinged .50
Postally used 2.00
On cover 2.50
O46 O1 7½pf orange 1.00 .60
Never hinged 2.25
Postally used 3.25
On cover 6.25
O47 O1 10pf rose .30 .60
Never hinged .50
Postally used 2.00
On cover 2.50
O48 O1 15pf purple .30 .60
Never hinged .50
Postally used 2.00
On cover 2.50
O49 O1 20pf ultra .40 .60
Never hinged 1.00
Postally used 2.00
On cover 2.50
O50 O1 25pf brown & blk .40 .60
Never hinged .65
Postally used 6.25
On cover 10.00
O51 O1 35pf brown 4.00 .60
Never hinged 6.25
Postally used 10.00
On cover 18.50
O52 O1 50pf red brown 5.50 .60
Never hinged 9.25
Postally used 10.00
On cover 25.00
Nos. O43-O52 (10) 24.60 *6.00*

Stag — O4

Wmk. 192

1920, Mar. 19 Litho. *Perf. 14½*
O53 O4 10pf maroon 1.45 *1.60*
Never hinged 2.00
Postally used 6.50
On cover 35.00
O54 O4 15pf brown 1.45 *1.60*
Never hinged 2.00
Postally used *3.75*
On cover 18.50
O55 O4 20pf indigo 1.45 *1.60*
Never hinged 2.00
Postally used 2.00
On cover 25.00
O56 O4 30pf deep green 1.45 *1.60*
Never hinged 2.00
Postally used 11.00
On cover 75.00
O57 O4 50pf yellow 3.25 *1.60*
Never hinged 4.00
Postally used 25.00
On cover 125.00
O58 O4 75pf bister 3.25 *1.60*
Never hinged 4.00
Postally used 52.00
On cover 300.00
Nos. O53-O58 (6) 12.30 *9.60*

Official Stamps of 1906-19 Overprinted

Perf. 11½x11

1920, Apr. 1 Wmk. 116
O59 O1 5pf green 4.00 10.00
Never hinged 9.50
On cover 12.50
O60 O1 10pf deep rose 2.40 4.75
Never hinged 6.50
On cover 7.50
O61 O1 15pf dp violet 2.40 5.25
Never hinged 6.75
On cover 7.50
O62 O1 20pf ultra 4.00 8.75
Never hinged 10.00
On cover 9.50
a. Wmk. 192 4.75 8.75
Never hinged 12.50
On cover 9.50
O63 O1 50pf red brown 6.50 20.00
Never hinged 18.50
On cover 22.50
Nos. O59-O63 (5) 19.30 48.75

Nos. O59 to O63 were available for official postage throughout all Germany but were used almost exclusively in Württemberg.

Stamps of 1917-21 Surcharged in Black, Red or Blue

1923
O64 O1 5m on 10pf orange .25 *.50*
Never hinged .40
Postally used 2.00
On cover 2.50
O65 O1 10m on 15pf dp violet .25 *.50*
Never hinged .40
Postally used 2.00
On cover 2.50
O66 O1 12m on 40pf rose red .25 *.50*
Never hinged .40
Postally used 2.00
On cover 2.50
O67 O1 20m on 10pf orange .80 *.50*
Never hinged 1.25
Postally used 5.50
On cover 10.00
O68 O1 25m on 20pf green .25 *.50*
Never hinged .40
Postally used 2.00
On cover 2.50
O69 O1 40m on 20pf green .25 *.50*
Never hinged .40
Postally used 4.75
On cover 9.50
O70 O1 50m on 60pf olive grn .25 *.50*
Never hinged .40
Postally used 2.00
On cover 2.50

Surcharged

O71 O1 60m on 1.25m emer .25 *.50*
Never hinged .40
Postally used 2.00
On cover 2.50
O72 O1 100m on 40pf rose red .25 *.50*
Never hinged .40
Postally used 2.00
On cover 2.50
O73 O1 200m on 2m gray (R) .25 *.50*
Never hinged .40
Postally used 2.00
On cover 3.25

O74 O1 300m on 50pf red brn (Bl) .25 *.50*
Never hinged .40
Postally used 2.00
On cover 3.25
O75 O1 400m on 3m brn (Bl) .25 *.50*
Never hinged .40
Postally used *2.00*
On cover 3.25
O76 O1 1000m on 60pf ol grn .25 *.50*
Never hinged .65
Postally used 2.00
On cover 5.00
O77 O1 2000m on 1.25m emer .25 *.50*
Never hinged .50
Postally used 2.00
On cover 4.00
Nos. O64-O77 (14) 4.05 *7.00*

Abbreviations:
Th = (Tausend) Thousand
Mil = (Million) Million
Mlrd = (Milliarde) Billion

Surcharged

1923
O78 O1 5th m on 10pf orange .25 *.50*
Never hinged .50
Postally used 8.00
On cover 16.00
O79 O1 20th m on 40pf rose red .25 *.50*
Never hinged .50
Postally used 4.00
On cover 12.50
O80 O1 50th m on 15pf violet 1.00 .50
Never hinged 2.50
Postally used 13.50
On cover 75.00
O81 O1 75th m on 2m gray 1.60 .50
Never hinged 4.50
Postally used 2.00
On cover 3.50
O82 O1 100th m on 20pf green .25 *.50*
Never hinged .40
Postally used 5.50
On cover 11.00
O83 O1 250th m on 3m brown .25 *.50*
Never hinged .40
Postally used 2.00
On cover 6.25

Surcharged

O84 O1 1mil m on 60pf ol grn 1.25 .50
Never hinged 3.00
Postally used 20.00
On cover 45.00
O85 O1 2mil m on 50pf red brn .25 *.50*
Never hinged .40
Postally used 2.00
On cover 6.25
O86 O1 5mil m on 1.25m emer .35 *.50*
Never hinged .75
Postally used 5.00
On cover 50.00

Surcharged

O87 O1 4 mlrd m on 50pf red brn 4.50 .50
Never hinged 12.50
Postally used 87.50
On cover 375.00
O88 O1 10 mlrd m on 3m brn 3.25 .50
Never hinged 8.00
Postally used 15.00
On cover 225.00
Nos. O78-O88 (11) 13.20 5.50

No. O23 Surcharged in Rentenpfennig as

1923, Dec.
O89 O1 3pf on 25pf orange .50 .40
Never hinged 1.00
Postally used 7.00
On cover 16.00
O90 O1 5pf on 25pf orange .40 .40
Never hinged .75
Postally used 2.00
On cover 2.50
O91 O1 10pf on 25pf orange .40 .40
Never hinged .75
Postally used 2.00
On cover 2.50
O92 O1 20pf on 25pf orange .50 .40
Never hinged 1.00
Postally used 2.50
On cover 5.00
O93 O1 50pf on 25pf orange .40 .40
Never hinged .75
Postally used 625.00
On cover 1,550.
Nos. O89-O93 (5) 2.20 2.00

For the State Authorities

O6

Perf. 11½x11

1881-1902 Typo. Unwmk.
O94 O6 2pf sl gray ('96) 1.60 1.60
Never hinged 2.75
On cover 2.50
O95 O6 3pf green 25.00 4.50
Never hinged 42.50
On cover 12.50
O96 O6 3pf dk brn ('90) 1.60 2.00
Never hinged 2.50
On cover 2.50
O97 O6 5pf violet 8.00 2.00
Never hinged 12.50
On cover 12.50
O98 O6 5pf green ('90) 2.40 2.00
Never hinged 1.85
On cover 2.50
O99 O6 10pf rose 8.00 1.90
Never hinged 5.00
On cover 2.50
O100 O6 20pf ultra 1.00 2.40
Never hinged 1.55
On cover 3.00
O101 O6 25pf brown 35.00 6.50
Never hinged 57.50
On cover 30.00
O102 O6 25pf orange ('90) 5.25 1.40
Never hinged 8.00
On cover 9.25
O103 O6 30pf org & blk ('02) 2.00 3.25
Never hinged 3.75
On cover 9.25
O104 O6 40pf dp rose & blk ('02) 2.25 3.25
Never hinged 3.75
On cover 32.00
O105 O6 50pf gray grn 6.50 8.75
Never hinged 10.50
On cover 62.50
O106 O6 50pf maroon ('91) 1.60 4.00
Never hinged 3.00
On cover 37.50
a. 50pf red brown ('90) 240.00 *1,750.*
Never hinged 300.00
On cover 5,500.
O107 O6 1m yellow 72.50 175.00
Never hinged 145.00
On cover 925.00
O108 O6 1m violet ('90) 5.50 16.00
Never hinged 12.50
On cover 55.00
Nos. O94-O108 (15) 178.20 234.55

See #O119-O135. For overprints & surcharges see #O109-O118, O146-O164, O176-O183.

Overprinted in Black

1906
O109 O6 2pf slate gray 27.00 5.00
Never hinged 40.00
Postally used 40.00
On cover 75.00
O110 O6 3pf dk brown 5.50 *5.00*
Never hinged 10.00
Postally used 3.00
On cover 6.00
O111 O6 5pf green 4.75 *5.00*
Never hinged 8.75
Postally used 2.00
On cover 3.75
O112 O6 10pf dp rose 4.50 *5.00*
Never hinged 8.00
Postally used 2.50
On cover 4.00
O113 O6 20pf ultra 4.75 *5.00*
Never hinged 8.00
Postally used 3.50
On cover 6.00
a. 20pf pale grayish ultra 600.00 185.00
Never hinged 925.00
Postally used 500.00
On cover 1,050.
O114 O6 25pf orange 11.00 6.00
Never hinged 18.50
Postally used 8.50
On cover 25.00
O115 O6 30pf org & blk 9.50 7.50
Never hinged 13.50
Postally used 8.00
On cover 50.00
O116 O6 40pf dp rose & blk 32.50 7.50
Never hinged 50.00
Postally used 40.00
On cover 125.00
O117 O6 50pf red brown 32.50 7.50
Never hinged 45.00
Postally used 40.00
On cover 125.00
O118 O6 1m purple 65.00 7.50
Never hinged 100.00
Postally used 67.50
On cover 275.00
Nos. O109-O118 (10) 197.00 *61.00*

Cent. of the kingdom of Wüttemberg.

Nos. O109 to O118 are also found imperforate, but it is doubtful if they were ever issued in that condition. Value, each: unused $45; never hinged $90.

1906-19 Wmk. 116
O119 O6 2pf slate gray .50 .40
Never hinged 1.00
Postally used 2.00
On cover 3.00
O120 O6 2½pf gray blk ('16) .55 .40
Never hinged .80
Postally used 2.00
On cover 2.50
O121 O6 3pf dk brown .50 .40
Never hinged .90
Postally used 2.00
On cover 2.50
O122 O6 5pf green .50 .40
Never hinged .90
Postally used 2.00
On cover 2.50
O123 O6 7½pf orange ('16) .55 .40
Never hinged .80
Postally used 2.00
On cover 3.00
O124 O6 10pf deep rose .50 .40
Never hinged .75
Postally used 2.00
On cover 2.50
O125 O6 15pf yel brn ('16) .65 .40
Never hinged .50
Postally used 2.00
On cover 3.00
O126 O6 15pf purple ('17) 1.25 .40
Never hinged 1.85
Postally used 2.00
On cover 2.50
O127 O6 20pf ultra .65 .40
Never hinged 1.25
Postally used 2.00
On cover 2.50
a. 20pf pale brt bl (1st ptg.) 185.00 —
Never hinged 500.00
Postally used *550.00*
On cover *1,550.*
O128 O6 25pf orange .60 .40
Never hinged 1.85
Postally used 2.00
On cover 2.50
O129 O6 25pf brn & blk ('17) .50 .40
Never hinged .90
Postally used 2.00
On cover 3.00
O130 O6 30pf org & blk .50 .40
Never hinged .75
Postally used 2.00
On cover 3.00
O131 O6 35pf brown ('19) 1.60 *2.40*
Never hinged 2.50
Postally used 25.00
On cover 50.00
O132 O6 40pf dp rose & blk .50 .40
Never hinged .75
Postally used 2.00
On cover 6.00
O133 O6 50pf red brown .65 .40
Never hinged 1.25
Postally used 2.75
On cover 6.25
O134 O6 1m purple 5.50 .40
Never hinged 12.50
Postally used 18.50
On cover —
O135 O6 1m sl & blk ('17) 11.00 1.55
Never hinged 23.50
Postally used 34.00
On cover —
Nos. O119-O135 (17) 26.50 *9.95*

King Wilhelm II — O8

1916 Unwmk. Typo. *Perf. 14*
O136 O8 2½pf slate .80 .65
Never hinged 1.85
Postally used 5.50
On cover 12.50
O137 O8 7½pf orange .80 .45
Never hinged 1.55
Postally used 2.00
On cover 3.50
O138 O8 10pf carmine .80 .45
Never hinged 1.85
Postally used 2.25
On cover 6.25
O139 O8 15pf yellow brn .80 .45
Never hinged 1.55
Postally used 2.00
On cover 3.00
O140 O8 20pf blue .80 .45
Never hinged 1.85
Postally used 2.50
On cover 12.50
O141 O8 25pf gray blk 1.60 .65
Never hinged 3.00
Postally used 5.50
On cover 15.00
O142 O8 30pf green 1.60 1.25
Never hinged 3.00
Postally used 12.50
On cover 25.00
O143 O8 40pf claret 2.40 1.25
Never hinged 5.00
Postally used 12.50
On cover 50.00
O144 O8 50pf red brn 3.25 1.85
Never hinged 5.50
Postally used 25.00
On cover 60.00
O145 O8 1m violet 3.25 2.50
Never hinged 5.50
Postally used 37.50
On cover 110.00
Nos. O136-O145 (10) 16.10 9.95

25th year of the reign of King Wilhelm II.

Stamps of 1890-1906 Surcharged

1916-19 Wmk. 116 *Perf. 11½x11*
O146 O6 25pf on 25pf org 2.75 .80
Never hinged 5.00
Postally used 6.00
On cover 15.00
a. Without watermark 35.00 13,400.
Never hinged 50.00
O147 O6 50pf on 50pf red brn 1.60 1.10
Never hinged 2.50
Postally used 15.00
On cover 62.50
a. Inverted surcharge 32.50
Never hinged 50.00

Beware of fake cancels on No. O146a.
No. O147a is considered a proof.

No. O120 Surcharged in Blue

1919 Wmk. 116
O149 O6 2pf on 2½pf gray blk 1.60 1.60
Never hinged 2.50
Postally used 5.00
On cover 10.00

Official Stamps of 1890-1919 Overprinted

1919
O150 O6 2½pf gray blk .55 .40
Never hinged .85
Postally used 2.00
On cover 6.50
O151 O6 3pf dk brown 7.25 .80
Never hinged 11.00
Postally used 20.00
On cover 37.50
a. Without watermark 52.50
Never hinged 92.50
O152 O6 5pf green .40 .40
Never hinged .60
Postally used 2.00
On cover 6.00
O153 O6 7½pf orange .40 .40
Never hinged .75
Postally used 2.75
On cover 6.25
O154 O6 10pf rose .40 .40
Never hinged .65
Postally used 2.00
On cover 2.50
O155 O6 15pf purple .40 .40
Never hinged .65
Postally used 2.00
On cover 2.50
O156 O6 20pf ultra .40 .40
Never hinged .75
Postally used 2.00
On cover 2.50
O157 O6 25pf brn & blk .40 .40
Never hinged 1.50
Postally used 2.00
On cover 9.50
a. Inverted overprint 95.00 240.00
Never hinged 185.00
O158 O6 30pf org & blk .80 .40
Never hinged 1.25
Postally used 2.25
On cover 9.25
a. Inverted overprint 475.00 —
Never hinged 625.00
O159 O6 35pf brown .55 .40
Never hinged .85
Postally used 5.50
On cover 10.00
O160 O6 40pf rose & blk .55 .40
Never hinged .85
Postally used 2.75
On cover 15.00

O161 O6 50pf claret .80 .65
Never hinged 1.25
Postally used 5.00
On cover 12.50
O162 O6 1m slate & blk .80 .80
Never hinged 1.35
Postally used 50.00
On cover —
Nos. O150-O162 (13) 13.70 6.25

Nos. O151, O151a Surcharged in Carmine

1920 **Wmk. 116**
O164 O6 75pf on 3pf dk brn 1.25 1.25
Never hinged 6.00
Postally used 30.00
On cover 125.00
a. Without watermark 80.00 *20.00*
Never hinged 125.00

View of Stuttgart
O9

10pf, 50pf, 2.50m, 3m, View of Stuttgart. 15pf, 75pf, View of Ulm. 20pf, 1m, View of Tubingen. 30pf, 1.25m, View of Ellwangen.

Wmk. 192
1920, Mar. 25 Typo. ***Perf. 14½***
O166 O9 10pf maroon .55 *1.20*
Never hinged 1.00
Postally used 7.50
On cover 55.00
O167 O9 15pf brown .55 *1.20*
Never hinged 1.00
Postally used 6.00
On cover 50.00
O168 O9 20pf indigo .55 *1.20*
Never hinged 1.00
Postally used 3.00
On cover 30.00
O169 O9 30pf blue grn .55 *1.20*
Never hinged 1.00
Postally used 15.50
On cover 105.00
O170 O9 50pf yellow .55 *1.20*
Never hinged 1.00
Postally used 25.00
On cover 450.00
O171 O9 75pf bister .55 *1.20*
Never hinged 1.00
Postally used 25.00
On cover 450.00
O172 O9 1m orange red .80 *1.20*
Never hinged 1.25
Postally used 25.00
On cover 850.00
O173 O9 1.25m dp violet .80 *1.20*
Never hinged 1.25
Postally used 32.50
On cover 850.00
O174 O9 2.50m dark ultra 2.00 1.20
Never hinged 3.75
Postally used 32.50
On cover 1,100.
O175 O9 3m yellow grn 2.40 1.20
Never hinged 3.75
Postally used 50.00
On cover 1,250.
Nos. O166-O175 (10) 9.30 *12.00*

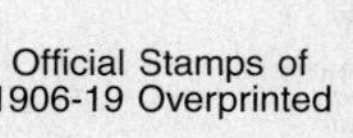

Official Stamps of 1906-19 Overprinted

1920 Wmk. 116 ***Perf. 11½x11***
O176 O6 5pf green 2.40 4.00
Never hinged 6.75
On cover 7.50
O177 O6 10pf deep rose 1.60 3.25
Never hinged 5.00
On cover 5.50
O178 O6 15pf purple 1.60 3.25
Never hinged 5.00
On cover 5.50
O179 O6 20pf ultra 1.60 1.60
Never hinged 5.00
On cover 4.75
a. Wmk. 192 125.00 325.00
Never hinged 275.00
On cover 550.00
O180 O6 30pf orange & blk 1.60 4.00
Never hinged 5.00
On cover 6.25
O181 O6 40pf dp rose & blk 1.60 3.25
Never hinged 5.00
On cover 7.50
O182 O6 50pf red brown 1.60 4.00
Never hinged 5.00
On cover 6.25
O183 O6 1m slate & blk 2.40 8.00
Never hinged 6.75
On cover 12.50
Nos. O176-O183 (8) 14.40 31.35

The note after No. O63 will also apply to Nos. O176-O183.

NORTH GERMAN CONFEDERATION

Northern District
30 Groschen = 1 Thaler
Southern District
60 Kreuzer = 1 Gulden
Hamburg
16 Schillings = 1 Mark

Values for unused stamps are for examples with original gum as defined in the catalogue introduction. Stamps without gum sell for about 50% of the figures quoted.

A1

A2

Rouletted 8½ to 10, 11 to 12½ and Compound

1868 Typo. Unwmk.
1 A1 ¼gr violet 15.00 15.00
Never hinged 50.00
On cover 55.00
On cover, single franking 150.00
b. ¼gr red lilac 35.00 22.00
On cover 57.50
On cover, single franking 150.00
c. ¼gr gray violet 65.00 37.50
On cover 160.00
On cover, single franking 550.00
2 A1 ⅓gr green 30.00 4.00
Never hinged 65.00
On cover 16.00
3 A1 ½gr orange 30.00 2.50
Never hinged 65.00
On cover 8.00
4 A1 1gr rose 20.00 1.60
Never hinged 40.00
On cover 4.25
b. Half used as ½gr on cover —
5 A1 2gr ultra 80.00 3.25
Never hinged 125.00
On cover 8.00
6 A1 5gr bister 80.00 9.50
Never hinged 125.00
On cover 65.00
7 A2 1kr green 35.00 8.00
Never hinged 60.00
On cover 25.00
8 A2 2kr orange 55.00 55.00
Never hinged 90.00
On cover 140.00
9 A2 3kr rose 35.00 3.25
Never hinged 60.00
On cover 8.00
10 A2 7kr ultra 160.00 11.00
Never hinged 260.00
On cover 47.50
11 A2 18kr bister 35.00 65.00
Never hinged 65.00
On cover 200.00
Nos. 1-11 (11) 575.00 178.10

See Nos. 13-23.

Imperf

1a	A1	¼gr red lilac	200.00	—
2a	A1	⅓gr green	95.00	—
3a	A1	½gr orange	140.00	—
4a	A1	1gr rose	80.00	—
5a	A1	2gr ultra	275.00	—
6a	A1	5gr bister	275.00	—
7a	A2	1kr green	72.50	*125.00*
8a	A2	2kr orange	200.00	95.00
9a	A2	3kr rose	80.00	100.00
10a	A2	7kr ultra	350.00	*675.00*
11a	A2	18kr bister	350.00	*675.00*

A3

1868
12 A3 (½s) lilac brown 110.00 55.00
Never hinged 200.00
On cover 125.00
a. ½gr reddish brown 110.00 55.00
Never hinged 200.00
On cover 125.00
b. ½gr dark carmine brown 140.00 140.00
On cover 325.00
c. ½gr violet brown 200.00 *200.00*
On cover 360.00
d. Imperf 200.00
Never hinged 350.00

See No. 24.

1869 ***Perf. 13½x14***
13 A1 ¼gr lilac 14.50 16.00
Never hinged 35.00
On cover 40.00
a. ¼gr red violet 25.00 20.00
Never hinged 40.00
On cover 52.50
14 A1 ⅓gr green 5.25 2.75
Never hinged 10.00
On cover 8.00
15 A1 ½gr orange 5.25 3.50
Never hinged 10.00
On cover 6.50
16 A1 1gr rose 4.00 1.60
Never hinged 7.25
On cover 4.00
17 A1 2gr ultra 7.25 2.00
Never hinged 16.00
On cover 6.50
18 A1 5gr bister 8.75 10.00
Never hinged 19.00
On cover 40.00
19 A2 1kr green 12.75 10.00
Never hinged 25.00
On cover 16.00
20 A2 2kr orange 40.00 *110.00*
Never hinged 95.00
On cover *250.00*
21 A2 3kr rose 7.25 3.25
Never hinged 14.50
On cover 6.50
22 A2 7kr ultra 11.00 12.00
Never hinged 17.50
On cover 27.50
23 A2 18kr bister 150.00 *1,750.*
Never hinged 250.00
On cover *6,000.*
On cover, single franking *8,000.*
Pair on cover *10,500.*
Nos. 13-23 (11) 266.00 1,921.

Counterfeit cancels exist on No. 23.

1869
24 A3 (½s) dull violet brown 4.75 8.75
Never hinged 8.00
On cover 32.50
a. ½s dark red brown 9.25 *19.00*
Never hinged 25.00
On cover 60.00
b. ½s dark brown 80.00 55.00
Never hinged 180.00
On cover 125.00

A4

A5

Perf. 14x13½
25 A4 10gr gray 325.00 400.00
Never hinged 550.00
Pen cancellation 65.00
On cover with postmark 2,000.
On cover with pen cancellation 200.00
On cover with pen cancellation and postmark 400.00
26 A5 30gr blue 240.00 *960.00*
Never hinged 450.00
Pen cancellation *140.00*
On cover with postmark *6,000.*
On cover with pen cancellation *475.00*
On cover with pen cancellation and postmark *1,450.*

Counterfeit cancels exist on No. 26.
See Germany designs A2, A3 and A8 for similar stamps.

OFFICIAL STAMPS

O1

1870 Unwmk. Typo. ***Perf. 14½x14***
O1 O1 ¼gr black & buff 27.50 *45.00*
Never hinged 65.00
On cover *140.00*
O2 O1 ⅓gr black & buff 9.50 *20.00*
Never hinged 20.00
On cover *80.00*
O3 O1 ½gr black & buff 2.75 *4.00*
Never hinged 5.50
On cover *15.00*
O4 O1 1gr black & buff 2.75 2.00
Never hinged 5.50
On cover 4.00
O5 O1 2gr black & buff 7.25 4.75
Never hinged 13.00
On cover 15.00
O6 O1 1kr black & gray 32.50 *250.00*
Never hinged 65.00
On cover *700.00*
O7 O1 2kr black & gray 80.00 *875.00*
Never hinged 160.00
On cover *2,400.*
O8 O1 3kr black & gray 25.00 *47.50*
Never hinged 57.50
On cover *200.00*
O9 O1 7kr black & gray 45.00 *275.00*
Never hinged 80.00
On cover *700.00*
Nos. O1-O9 (9) 232.25 1,523.

Counterfeit cancels exist on Nos. O6-O9.
The stamps of the North German Confederation were replaced by those of the German Empire on Jan. 1, 1872.

GERMANY

'jər-mə-nē

LOCATION — In northern Europe bordering on the Baltic and North Seas
AREA — 182,104 sq. mi. (until 1945)
POP. — 67,032,242 (1946)
CAPITAL — Berlin

30 Silbergroschen or Groschen = 1 Thaler
60 Kreuzer = 1 Gulden
100 Pfennigs = 1 Mark (1875)

Watermarks

Wmk. 48 — Diagonal Zigzag Lines

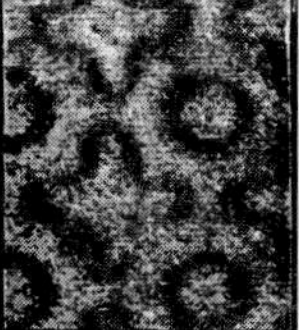

Wmk. 116 — Crosses and Circles

Wmk. 125 — Lozenges

Wmk. 126 — Network

Wmk. 127 — Quatrefoils

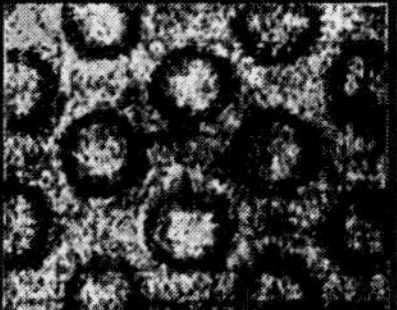

Wmk. 192 — Circles

Wmk. 223 — Eagle

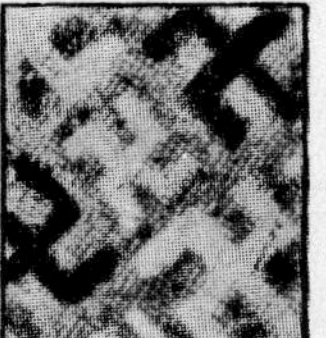

Wmk. 237 — Swastikas

Wmk. 241 — Cross

Empire

Values for unused stamps are for examples with original gum as defined in the catalogue introduction. Any exceptions are specifically mentioned.

Imperial Eagle — A1

Typographed, Center Embossed

1872 Unwmk. ***Perf. 13½x14½***

Eagle with small shield

No.	Design	Description	Unused	Used
1	A1	¼gr violet	200.00	85.00
		Never hinged	1,200.	
		No gum	85.00	
		On cover		360.00
2	A1	⅓gr green	475.00	36.00
		Never hinged	3,600.	
		No gum	175.00	
		On cover		60.00
a.		Imperf.		—
b.		⅓gr dk gray grn	1,150.	120.00
		Never hinged	*11,000.*	
		No gum	325.00	
		On cover		250.00
3	A1	½gr red orange	950.00	40.00
		Never hinged	5,400.	
		No gum	350.00	
		On cover		60.00
a.		½gr orange yellow	1,100.	47.50
		Never hinged	11,000.	
		No gum	425.00	
		On cover		57.50
4	A1	1gr rose	290.00	7.25
		Never hinged	2,300.	
		No gum	100.00	
		On cover		14.50
a.		Imperf.		—
b.		Half used as ½gr on cover		*50,000.*
5	A1	2gr ultra	1,500.	13.50
		Never hinged	10,000.	
		No gum	590.00	
		On cover		30.00
a.		Imperf.		*8,500.*
6	A1	5gr bister	825.00	85.00
		No gum	300.00	
		Never hinged	6,500.	
		On cover		225.00
a.		Imperf.		*10,000.*
7	A1	1kr green	650.00	50.00
		Never hinged	4,750.	
		No gum	190.00	
		On cover		100.00
8	A1	2kr orange	35.00	*160.00*
		Never hinged	130.00	
		No gum	15.00	
		On cover		290.00
a.		2kr red orange	590.00	285.00
		Never hinged	4,750.	
		No gum	175.00	
		On cover		360.00
9	A1	3kr rose	1,700.	14.50
		Never hinged	11,750.	
		No gum	490.00	
		On cover		21.50
10	A1	7kr ultra	2,350.	85.00
		Never hinged	13,000.	
		No gum	700.00	
		On cover		130.00
11	A1	18kr bister	475.00	360.00
		Never hinged	3,150.	
		No gum	175.00	
		On cover		1,650.

Values for imperforates are for stamps postmarked at Leipzig (⅓gr), Coblenz (1gr), Hoengen (2gr) and Leutersdorf (5gr).

Values for Pairs

No.	Design	Description	Unused	Used
1	A1	¼gr violet	450.00	190.00
		On cover		325.00
2	A1	⅓gr green	1,100.	80.00
		On cover		150.00
b.		⅓gr dk gray grn	275.00	
		On cover		425.00
3	A1	½gr red orange	2,000.	100.00
		On cover		120.00
a.		½gr orange yellow	100.00	
		On cover		120.00
4	A1	1gr rose	650.00	40.00
		On cover		45.00
5	A1	2gr ultramarine	85.00	
		On cover		95.00
6	A1	5gr bister	1,950.	200.00
		On cover		325.00
7	A1	1kr green	1,400.	125.00
		On cover		175.00
8	A1	2kr orange	80.00	575.00
		On cover		775.00
a.		2kr red orange	1,300.	775.00
		On cover		1,100.
9	A1	3kr rose	45.00	
		On cover		200.00
10	A1	7kr ultramarine	215.00	
		On cover		425.00
11	A1	18kr ultramarine	215.00	
		On cover		*1,750.*

Values for Strips of 3

No.	Design	Description	Unused	Used
1	A1	¼gr violet		325.00
		On cover		500.00
2	A1	⅓gr green		125.00
		On cover		250.00
b.		⅓gr dk gray grn		450.00
		On cover		650.00
3	A1	½gr red orange		250.00
		On cover		400.00
a.		½gr orange yellow		325.00
		On cover		500.00
4	A1	1gr rose		90.00
		On cover		125.00
5	A1	2gr ultramarine		200.00
		On cover		275.00
6	A1	5gr bister		300.00
		On cover		400.00
7	A1	1kr green		200.00
		On cover		250.00
8	A1	2kr orange		1,800.
		On cover		*2,250.*
a.		2kr red orange		2,600.
		On cover		*3,200.*
9	A1	3kr rose		165.00
		On cover		275.00
10	A1	7kr ultramarine		575.00
		On cover		825.00
11	A1	18kr ultramarine		1,750.
		On cover		*3,000.*

Values for Strips of 4 or Blocks of 4

No.	Design	Description	Unused	Used
1	A1	¼gr violet	1,100.	525.00
		On cover		775.00
2	A1	⅓gr green	3,250.	1,600.
		On cover		2,000.
3	A1	½gr red orange	5,600.	575.00
		On cover		850.00
a.		½gr orange yellow	7,000.	725.00
		On cover		900.00
4	A1	1gr rose	2,000.	300.00
		On cover		400.00
5	A1	2gr ultramarine	7,500.	1,150.
		On cover		1,800.
6	A1	5gr bister	3,750.	500.00
		On cover		700.00
7	A1	1kr green	3,750.	1,800.
		On cover		2,250.
8	A1	2kr orange	180.00	*4,250.*
		On cover		—
a.		2kr red orange	3,750.	—
		On cover		—
9	A1	3kr rose	8,750.	1,000.
		On cover		*1,500.*
10	A1	7kr ultramarine	*10,000.*	*4,000.*
		On cover		5,000.
11	A1	18kr ultramarine	2,650.	3,250.
		On cover		—

A2

A3

1872 Typo. ***Perf. 14½x13½***

No.	Design	Description	Unused	Used
12	A2	10gr gray	50.00	*1,300.*
		Never hinged	120.00	
		No gum	16.50	
		Pen cancellation		160.00
		Pen cancellation and postmark		200.00
		On cover with postmark		3,600.
		On cover with pen cancellation		475.00
		On cover with pen cancellation and postmark		590.00
13	A3	30gr blue	90.00	*2,500.*
		Never hinged	200.00	
		No gum	25.00	
		Pen cancellation		*540.00*
		Pen cancellation and postmark		800.00
		On cover with postmark		10,000.
		On cover with pen cancellation		1,150.
		On cover with pen cancellation and postmark		1,350.

For similar designs see A8, North German Confederation A4, A5.

Values for Pairs

No.	Design	Description	Unused	Used
12	A2	10gr gray	100.00	2,750.
		Pen cancellation		340.00
		On cover with pen cancellation		575.00
13	A3	30gr blue	200.00	5,000.
		Pen cancellation		1,200.
		On cover with pen cancellation		1,400.

Values for Strips of 3

No.	Design	Description	Unused	Used
12	A2	10gr gray	160.00	4,250.
		Pen cancellation		500.00
		On cover with pen cancellation		725.00
13	A3	30gr blue	300.00	—
		Pen cancellation		*1,800.*
		On cover with pen cancellation		*2,100.*

Values for Strips of 4 or Blocks of 4

No.	Design	Description	Unused	Used
12	A2	10gr gray	240.00	—
		Pen cancellation		800.00
		On cover with pen cancellation		1,250.
13	A3	30gr blue	400.00	—
		Pen cancellation		*2,250.*
		On cover with pen cancellation		*2,750.*

A4

Center Embossed

1872 ***Perf. 13½x14½***

Eagle with large shield

No.	Design	Description	Unused	Used
14	A4	¼gr violet	70.00	120.00
		Never hinged	200.00	
		No gum	8.25	
		On cover		340.00
15	A4	⅓gr yellow green	32.50	13.50
		Never hinged	125.00	
		No gum	8.00	
		On cover		34.00
a.		⅓gr blue green	120.00	110.00
		Never hinged	400.00	
		No gum	35.00	
		On cover		275.00
16	A4	½gr orange	34.00	9.00
		Never hinged	125.00	
		No gum	8.00	
		On cover		13.50
17	A4	1gr rose	67.50	5.50
		Never hinged	200.00	
		No gum	19.00	
		On cover		11.00
a.		Imperf.		*15,000.*
		On cover		*67,500.*
b.		Half used as ½gr on cover		*60,000.*
18	A4	2gr ultra	20.00	6.25
		Never hinged	67.50	
		No gum	6.50	
		On cover		13.50
19	A4	2½gr orange brn	1,800.	67.50
		Never hinged	17,000.	
		No gum	625.00	
		On cover		190.00
a.		2½gr lilac brown	*4,750.*	540.00
		Never hinged	*20,500.*	
		No gum	2,000.	
		On cover		810.00
20	A4	5gr bister	27.50	27.50
		Never hinged	125.00	
		No gum	8.00	
		On cover		125.00
a.		Imperf.		*7,500.*
		On cover		*135,000.*
21	A4	1kr yel grn	34.00	32.50
		Never hinged	125.00	
		No gum	8.00	
		On cover		55.00
a.		1kr blue green	325.00	475.00
		Never hinged	1,250.	
		No gum	75.00	
		On cover		810.00
22	A4	2kr orange	450.00	*2,250.*
		Never hinged	2,750.	
		No gum	140.00	
		On cover		*3,150.*
23	A4	3kr rose	20.00	6.25
		Never hinged	80.00	
		No gum	7.00	
		On cover		13.50

24 A4 7kr ultra 30.00 *60.00*
Never hinged 125.00
No gum 8.00
On cover *110.00*
25 A4 9kr red brown 410.00 375.00
Never hinged 1,750.
No gum 125.00
On cover 525.00
a. 9kr lilac brown 1,350. 400.00
Never hinged 10,500.
No gum 475.00
On cover 825.00
26 A4 18kr bister 32.50 *1,900.*
Never hinged 100.00
No gum 8.00
On cover *11,750.*

Values for Pairs

14 A4 ¼gr violet 150.00 190.00
On cover 350.00
15 A4 ⅓gr yellow green 70.00 40.00
On cover 100.00
a. ⅓ blue green 250.00 275.00
On cover 475.00
16 A4 ½gr orange 75.00 20.00
On cover 40.00
17 A4 1gr rose 140.00 17.50
On cover 27.50
18 A4 2gr ultramarine 45.00 20.00
On cover 52.50
19 A4 2½gr orange brown 160.00
On cover 375.00
a. 2½gr lilac brown *1,200.*
On cover *1,900.*
20 A4 5gr bister 65.00 100.00
On cover 160.00
21 A4 1kr yellow green 80.00 75.00
On cover 100.00
a. 1kr blue green 750.00 *1,100.*
On cover *1,400.*
22 A4 2kr orange 1,000. 75.00
On cover *5,250.*
23 A4 3kr rose 45.00 24.00
On cover 65.00
24 A4 7kr ultramarine 70.00 180.00
On cover 350.00
25 A4 9kr red brown 900.00 900.00
On cover 1,300.
a. 9kr lilac brown 1,175.
On cover 1,600.
26 A4 18kr bister 70.00 5,500.
On cover 1,300.

Values for Strips of 3

14 A4 ¼gr violet 225.00 325.00
On cover 500.00
15 A4 ⅓gr yellow green 105.00 100.00
On cover 575.00
a. ⅓ blue green 400.00 475.00
On cover 575.00
16 A4 ½gr orange 115.00 80.00
On cover 160.00
17 A4 1gr rose 220.00 25.00
On cover 55.00
18 A4 2gr ultramarine 70.00 100.00
On cover 180.00
19 A4 2½gr orange brown — 350.00
On cover 575.00
a. 2½gr lilac brown — *1,800.*
On cover —
20 A4 5gr bister 100.00 160.00
On cover 275.00
21 A4 1kr yellow green 125.00 150.00
On cover 200.00
a. 1kr blue green 1,150. *1,500.*
On cover *1,800.*
22 A4 2kr orange 1,600. —
On cover —
23 A4 3kr rose 75.00 125.00
On cover 275.00
24 A4 7kr ultramarine 110.00 650.00
On cover 1,000.
25 A4 9kr red brown 1,450. *1,500.*
On cover —
a. 9kr lilac brown — 2,000.
On cover —
26 A4 18kr bister — *7,750.*
On cover —

Values for Strips of 4 and Blocks of 4

14 A4 ¼gr violet 300.00 575.00
On cover 1,450.
15 A4 ⅓gr yellow green 175.00 900.00
On cover 2,000.
a. ⅓ blue green 600.00 3,000.
On cover —
16 A4 ½gr orange 175.00 250.00
On cover 600.00
17 A4 1gr rose 300.00 150.00
On cover 375.00
18 A4 2gr ultramarine 110.00 550.00
On cover 1,350.
19 A4 2½gr orange brown 13,500. *1,250.*
On cover 2,500.
a. 2½gr lilac brown *3,000.*
On cover —
20 A4 5gr bister 150.00 375.00
On cover 800.00
21 A4 1kr yellow green 170.00 2,000.
On cover *3,750.*
a. 1kr blue green 1,600. —
On cover —
22 A4 2kr orange 2,250. *15,000.*
On cover —
23 A4 3kr rose 110.00 1,500.
On cover —
24 A4 7kr ultramarine 160.00 3,250.
On cover —
25 A4 9kr red brown 2,000. *2,400.*
On cover —
a. 9kr lilac brown *10,000.* *4,000.*
On cover —
26 A4 18kr bister 165.00 *12,500.*
On cover —

Values for Nos. 17a and 20a are for stamps postmarked at Potsdam (1gr), Damgarten or Anklam (5gr).

Nos. 14-26 with embossing inverted are fraudulent.

A5

1874 Brown Surcharge

27 A5 2½gr on 2½gr brn 37.50 42.50
Never hinged 92.50
On cover 170.00
28 A5 9kr on 9kr brown 82.50 *450.00*
Never hinged 170.00
On cover *825.00*

A6

A7

"Pfennige"

1875-77 Typo.

29 A6 3pf blue green 57.50 5.25
Never hinged 450.00
On cover 10.00
a. yellow green 100.00 9.25
Never hinged 875.00
On cover 19.00
30 A6 5pf violet 97.50 3.75
Never hinged 925.00
On cover 5.75

Center Embossed

31 A7 10pf rose 42.50 1.50
Never hinged 300.00
On cover 4.00
a. reddish brown ('75) *1,350.* 190.00
Never hinged —
On cover 260.00
32 A7 20pf ultra 450.00 1.90
Never hinged 2,700.
On cover 7.50
a. blue 525.00 30.00
Never hinged 3,850.
On cover 45.00
33 A7 25pf red brown 500.00 18.00
Never hinged 4,500.
On cover 60.00
On cover, single franking 550.00
a. yellow brown 2,300. 100.00
Never hinged *19,000.*
On cover 210.00
b. deep brown ('78) 2,750. 225.00
Never hinged 21,500.
On cover 300.00
On cover, single franking 750.00
34 A7 50pf gray 1,650. 11.00
Never hinged 7,500.
On cover 57.50
On cover, single franking 85.00
a. gray black 3,400. 340.00
Never hinged —
On cover 450.00
On cover, single franking 600.00
35 A7 50pf ol gray ('77) 1,900. 14.00
Never hinged 11,500.
On cover 70.00
a. dk ol green 3,750. 325.00
Never hinged *17,500.*
On cover 450.00
Nos. 29-35 (7) 4,698. 55.40

See Nos. 37-42. For surcharges see Offices in Turkey Nos. 1-6.

Values for used blocks of 4

29 A6 3pf blue green 425.00
a. 3pf yellow green 450.00
30 A6 5pf violet 30.00
31 A7 10pf rose 22.50
a. 10pf reddish brown —
32 A7 20pf ultramarine 190.00
a. 20pf blue 300.00
33 A7 25pf red brown 350.00
a. 25pf yellow brown 800.00
b. 25pf deep brown —
34 A7 50pf gray 150.00
a. 50pf gray black 1,500.
35 A7 50pf olive gray 190.00
a. 50pf dark olive green 1,100.

A8

1875-90 Typo. *Perf. 14½x13½*

36 A8 2m brnsh pur ('90) 75.00 6.00
Never hinged 250.00
On cover 60.00
a. 2m purple ('75) 1,900. 340.00
On cover 275.00
b. 2m dull vio pur ('89) 1,500. 60.00
c. 2m pur lilac ('80) *3,000.* 50.00
On cover 300.00
d. 2m rose lilac ('84) 1,250. 37.50
On cover 160.00
e. 2m carmine lilac ('99) 110.00 42.50
Never hinged 360.00
On cover 210.00

No. 36a used is valued as a stamp with cds cancel dated between Jan. 1875 and November 17, 1884.

Values for Nos. 36a, 36c, 36d on cover are for pencanceled stamps.

Values for used pairs

36 A8 2m brownish pur 15.00
a. 2m pur violet *1,000.*
b. 2m dull vio pur 140.00
c. 2m pur lilac 150.00
d. 2m rose lilac 42.50
e. 2m carmine lilac 125.00

Value for used strips of 3

36 A8 2m brownish pur 22.50
a. 2m pur violet *1,750.*
b. 2m dull vio pur 210.00
c. 2m pur lilac 250.00
d. 2m rose lilac 65.00
e. 2m carmine lilac 190.00

Values for used strips of 4

36 A8 2m brownish pur 30.00
a. 2m pur violet *2,500.*
b. 2m dull vio pur 300.00
c. 2m pur lilac 410.00
d. 2m rose lilac 125.00
e. 2m carmine lilac 300.00

Values for used blocks of 4

36 A8 2m brownish pur 37.50
a. 2m pur violet —
b. 2m dull vio pur 410.00
c. 2m pur lilac 500.00
d. 2m rose lilac 150.00
e. 2m carmine lilac 325.00

Values for postmarked stamps on parcel post receipt cards

36 A8 2m brownish pur 32.50
a. 2m pur violet 250.00
b. 2m dull vio pur 190.00
c. 2m pur lilac 160.00
d. 2m rose lilac 65.00
e. 2m carmine lilac 160.00

Values for postmarked stamps on registered, insured covers

36 A8 2m brownish pur 65.00
a. 2m pur violet 500.00
b. 2m dull vio pur 390.00
c. 2m pur lilac 325.00
d. 2m rose lilac 140.00
e. 2m carmine lilac 325.00

On cover values are for covers with cancellations falling within the following dates: No. 36 ('90-'99), No. 36a ('75-'80, '93-'94), No. 36b ('89-'90), No. 36c ('80-Nov. '84), No. 36d ('84-'89), No. 36e ('99-'00).

Types of 1875-77, "Pfennig" without final "e"

1880-83 *Perf. 13½x14½*

37 A6 3pf yel green 3.00 1.50
Never hinged 13.50
On cover 2.75
a. Imperf. —
b. 3pf green (shades) 6.25 1.00
Never hinged 32.50
On cover 3.25
38 A6 5pf violet 2.25 2.00
Never hinged 9.75
On cover 2.50

Center Embossed

39 A7 10pf red 13.00 2.00
Never hinged 37.50
On cover 2.00
a. Imperf. *325.00*
Never hinged *575.00*
b. 10pf rose 20.00 2.00
Never hinged 72.50
On cover 2.50
40 A7 20pf brt ultra 6.00 1.50
Never hinged 19.00
On cover 2.25
a. 20pf grayish ultra 110.00 3.25
Never hinged 575.00
On cover 5.25
b. 20pf blue 72.50 7.25
Never hinged 250.00
On cover 13.50
41 A7 25pf dull rose brn 19.00 5.25
Never hinged 75.00
On cover 42.50
a. 25pf red brown, thick paper 200.00 6.00
Never hinged 700.00
On cover 32.50
b. 25pf orange brown 150.00 5.25
Never hinged 550.00
On cover 32.50
c. 25pf brown ocher 225.00 26.00
Never hinged 950.00
On cover 82.50
42 A7 50pf dp grayish ol grn 15.00 1.50
Never hinged 75.00
On cover 12.50
a. 50pf olive green 210.00 1.50
Never hinged 1,800.
On cover 15.00
b. 50pf yellowish ol grn 230.00 30.00
Never hinged 1,150.
On cover 65.00
c. 50pf dk green 190.00 27.50
Never hinged 2,100.
On cover 75.00
Nos. 37-42 (6) 58.25 13.75

Values for Nos. 37-42 are for stamps on thin paper. Those on thick paper sell for considerably more.

On cover values are for covers canceled within the following dates: Nos. 37-37a ('80-'89), No. 39 ('87-'89), No. 39b ('80-'89), No. 40 ('86-'89), No. 40a ('80-'84), No. 40b ('82-'85), No. 41 ('87-'89), Nos. 41a-41b ('83), No. 41c ('80-'83), No. 42 ('85-'91), No. 42a ('80-'86), No. 42b ('87-'89), No. 42c ('89).

Values for used blocks of 4

37 A6 3pf yel green 120.00
b. 3pf green (shades) 120.00
38 A6 5pf violet 19.00
39 A7 10pf red 19.00
b. 10pf rose 15.00
40 A7 20pf br ultra 15.00
a. 20pf greyish ultra 32.50
b. 20pf blue 75.00
41 A7 25pf dull rose brn 19.00
a. 25pf red brn, thick paper 67.50
b. 25pf org brn 45.00
c. 25pf brn ocher 180.00
42 A7 50pf grayish ol grn 19.00
a. 50pf ol grn 19.00
b. 50pf yellowish ol grn 190.00
c. 50pf dk grn 125.00

A9

A10

1889-1900 *Perf. 13½x14½*

45 A9 2pf gray ('00) .90 *.90*
Never hinged 2.25
On cover 3.75
a. "REIGHSPOST" 60.00 *140.00*
Never hinged 190.00
On cover 250.00
46 A9 3pf brown 3.00 1.40
Never hinged 11.50
On cover 1.90
a. 3pf yellow brown 9.00 1.40
Never hinged 75.00
On cover 2.25
b. Imperf. 600.00 —
Never hinged 1,800.
c. 3pf reddish brown 52.50 8.25
Never hinged 390.00
On cover 30.00
d. 3pf dark brown 600.00 62.50
Never hinged 2,250.
On cover 125.00
e. 3pf olive brown 7.50 3.50
Never hinged 50.00
On cover 6.50
f. 3pf ocher brown 15.25 5.25
On cover 12.50

On cover values are for covers canceled within the normal period of use: No. 46 ('91-'97), Nos. 46a, 46c ('97-'00), No. 46d ('89-'90), Nos. 46e-46f ('99-'00).

47 A9 5pf blue green 3.00 1.40
Never hinged 15.00
On cover 1.90
a. 5pf yellow green 115.00 3.75
Never hinged 600.00
On cover 7.50
b. 5pf gray green 150.00 3.75
Never hinged 675.00
On cover 7.50

On cover values are for covers canceled within the following dates: No. 47 ('91-'00), No. 47a ('90-'92), No. 47b ('89-'92).

48 A10 10pf carmine 4.50 1.50
Never hinged 15.00
On cover 2.25
a. Imperf. 225.00
Never hinged 675.00
b. 10pf brownish rose 11.50 1.50
Never hinged 90.00
On cover 2.25
c. 10pf dark carmine 45.00 9.75
Never hinged 300.00
On cover 35.00
d. 10pf brownish red 75.00 8.25
Never hinged 600.00
On cover 30.00
e. 10pf rose carmine 210.00 9.75
Never hinged 900.00
On cover 30.00

On cover values are for covers canceled within the following dates: No. 48 ('93-'00), No. 48b ('90-'95), No. 48c, ('99-'00), No. 48d ('94-'00), No. 48e ('89-'90).

49 A10 20pf ultra 7.50 1.40
Never hinged 52.50
On cover 1.90
a. 20pf Prus blue 2,250. 115.00
Never hinged 9,000.
On cover 190.00
b. 20pf grayish ultra 67.50 4.50
Never hinged 300.00
On cover 7.75
c. 20pf blue (shades) 60.00 1.40
Never hinged 410.00
On cover 3.75

On cover values are for covers canceled within the following dates: No. 49a ('81-'93), No. 49b ('92-'94), No. 49c ('91-'95).

50 A10 25pf orange ('90) 30.00 2.00
Never hinged 130.00
On cover 15.00
On cover, single franking 125.00
a. Imperf. 260.00
Never hinged 750.00
b. 25pf yellow orange 180.00 7.50
Never hinged 1,350.
On cover 45.00
On cover, single franking 350.00

On cover values are for covers canceled within the following dates: v50 ('91-'00), No. 51b ('89-'96).

51 A10 50pf chocolate 30.00 1.40
Never hinged 115.00
On cover 4.00
a. 50pf copper brown 375.00 9.75
Never hinged 1,500.
On cover 35.00
b. Imperf. 450.00
Never hinged 1,350.
c. 50pf brownish red 1,500. 210.00
Never hinged 11,000.
On cover 600.00

d. 50pf reddish brown 1,000. 22.50
Never hinged 6,000.
On cover 45.00
e. 50pf dull rose brown 90.00 3.75
Never hinged 1,100.
On cover 15.00
Nos. 45-51 (7) 78.90 10.00
Set, never hinged 320.00

On cover values are for covers canceled within the following dates: No. 51 ('90-'00), Nos. 51a, 51d ('89-'91), No. 51c ('89-'90), No. 51e, ('93-'94).

For surcharges and overprints see Offices in China Nos. 1-6, 16, Offices in Morocco 1-6, Offices in Turkey 8-12.

Values for used blocks of 4

45 A9 2pf gray 37.50
46 A9 3pf brown 110.00
a. 3pf yellow brown 135.00
c. 3pf reddish brown 300.00
e. 3pf olive brown 75.00
f. 3pf ocher brown 210.00
47 A9 5pf blue green 37.50
a. 5pf yellow green 75.00
b. 5pf gray green 750.00
48 A10 10pf carmine 11.50
b. 10pf brownish rose 13.50
c. 10pf dark carmine 160.00
d. 10pf brownish red 160.00
e. 10pf rose carmine 190.00
49 A10 20pf ultra 15.00
a. 20pf Prussian blue 750.00
b. 20pf grayish ultra 110.00
c. 20pf blue (shades) 40.00
50 A10 25pf reddish orange 67.50
b. 25pf yellow orange 190.00
51 A10 50pf chocolate 22.50
a. 50pf copper brown —
c. 50pf brownish red —
d. 50pf reddish brown —
e. 50pf dull rose brown 75.00

Germania — A11

1900, Jan. 1 ***Perf. 14***

52 A11 2pf gray .85 .60
Never hinged 2.60
On cover 4.00
On cover, single franking 6.00
a. Imperf. 400.00
Never hinged 1,600.
53 A11 3pf brown .85 1.00
Never hinged 2.40
On cover 2.25
On cover, single franking 2.75
a. Imperf. 400.00
Never hinged 1,600.
54 A11 5pf green 1.60 .90
Never hinged 9.50
On cover 2.40
On cover, single franking 3.00
55 A11 10pf carmine 2.40 .75
Never hinged 12.00
On cover 2.40
On cover, single franking 2.90
a. Imperf. 60.00
Never hinged 160.00
56 A11 20pf ultra 11.00 .90
Never hinged 55.00
On cover 4.00
On cover, single franking 8.50
57 A11 25pf org & blk, *yel* 15.00 4.50
Never hinged 72.50
On cover 19.00
On cover, single franking 120.00
58 A11 30pf org & blk, *sal* 22.50 .90
Never hinged 140.00
On cover 18.00
On cover, single franking 47.50
59 A11 40pf lake & black 26.00 1.50
Never hinged 150.00
On cover 19.00
On cover, single franking 65.00
60 A11 50pf pur & blk, *sal* 27.50 1.20
Never hinged 150.00
On cover 19.00
On cover, single franking 65.00
61 A11 80pf lake & blk, *rose* 37.50 2.25
Never hinged 210.00
On cover 45.00
On cover, single franking 100.00
Nos. 52-61 (10) 145.20 14.50
Set, never hinged 800.00

Early printings of Nos. 57-61 had "REICHSPOST" in taller and thicker letters than on the ordinary stamps.

For surcharges see Nos. 65B, Offices in China 17-32, Offices in Morocco 7-15, 32A, Offices in Turkey 13-20, 25-27.

"REICHSPOST" Larger

57a A11 25pf *1,900.* *7,200.*
Never hinged *4,400.*
58a A11 30pf *1,900.* *4,800.*
Never hinged *4,400.*
59a A11 40pf *1,900.* *4,800.*
Never hinged *4,400.*
60a A11 50pf *1,900.* *4,800.*
Never hinged *4,400.*
61a A11 80pf *1,900.* *4,800.*
Never hinged *4,400.*

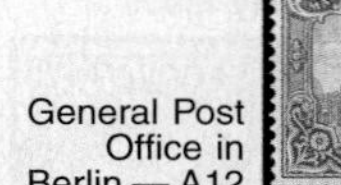
General Post Office in Berlin — A12

"Union of North and South Germany" A13

Unveiling Kaiser Wilhelm I Memorial, Berlin — A14

Wilhelm II Speaking at Empire's 25th Anniversary Celebration A15

Type I

Type II

Two types of 5m:
I — "5" is thick; "M" has slight serifs.
II — "5" thinner; "M" has distinct serifs.

Engr. ***Perf. 14½x14***

62 A12 1m carmine rose 110.00 3.25
Never hinged 450.00
On cover 340.00
On cover, single franking 400.00
a. Imperf. *2,800.*
63 A13 2m gray blue 110.00 8.00
Never hinged 475.00
On cover 160.00
On cover, single franking 600.00
64 A14 3m black violet 120.00 50.00
Never hinged 650.00
On cover 1,450.
On cover, single franking 2,300.
65 A15 5m slate & car, I 1,350. 2,250.
Never hinged 5,250.
On cover 4,800.
On cover, single franking, hand painted —
d. Red and white retouched 375.00 *400.00*
Never hinged 1,450.
On cover *2,000.*
e. White only retouched 640.00 *640.00*
Never hinged 1,750.
On cover *2,400.*
65A A15 5m slate & car, II 375.00 *400.00*
Never hinged 1,450.
On cover 2,000.
On cover, single franking 3,800.

Nos. 62-65 exist perf. 11½.

The vignette and frame of No. 65 usually did not align perfectly during printing. Red paint was used to retouch the vignette and/or white paint was used to retouch the inner frame.

No. 62a is without gum.

For surcharges see Offices in China Nos. 33-36A, Offices in Morocco 16-19A, Offices in Turkey 21-24B, 28-30.

Half of No. 54 Handstamp Surcharged in Violet

3PF

1901 ***Perf. 14***

65B A11 3pf on half of 5pf *9,750.* *7,500.*
Never hinged *26,500.*
On newsprint wrapper *16,500.*

This provisional was produced aboard the German cruiser Vineta. The purser, with the ship commander's approval, surcharged and bisected 300 5pf stamps so the ship's post office could meet the need for a 3pf (printed matter rate). The crew wanted to send home U.S. newspapers reporting celebrations of the Kaiser's birthday.

Forgeries exist and improper usages as well.

A16

1902 **Typo.**

65C A16 2pf gray 1.50 .60
Never hinged 6.75
On cover 2.50
66 A16 3pf brown .75 *1.00*
Never hinged 2.60
On cover 3.00
a. "DFUTSCHES" 9.75 *42.50*
Never hinged 30.00
On cover *145.00*
b. 3pf yellow brown 240.00 45.00
Never hinged 675.00
On cover 75.00
67 A16 5pf green 4.00 1.00
Never hinged 15.00
On cover 2.25
a. 5pf deep blue green 325.00 9.50
Never hinged 950.00
On cover 24.00
68 A16 10pf carmine 9.00 1.00
Never hinged 37.50
On cover 2.25
69 A16 20pf ultra 30.00 1.00
Never hinged 120.00
On cover 4.50
a. 20pf violet blue 600.00 75.00
Never hinged 2,250.
On cover 160.00
b. 20pf gray blue 900.00 *1,150.*
Never hinged 6,750.
On cover —
70 A16 25pf org & blk, *yel* 45.00 2.10
Never hinged 180.00
On cover 19.00
71 A16 30pf org & blk, *sal* 60.00 .60
Never hinged 225.00
On cover 19.00
72 A16 40pf lake & blk 90.00 1.00
Never hinged 300.00
On cover 19.00
73 A16 50pf pur & blk, *buff* 70.00 1.10
Never hinged 275.00
On cover 27.50
74 A16 80pf lake & blk, *rose* 200.00 3.00
Never hinged 800.00
On cover 47.50
Nos. 65C-74 (10) 510.25 12.40
Set, never hinged 1,965.

Nos. 65C-74 exist imperf. Value, set: unused $1,600; never hinged $3,750.

See Nos. 80-91, 118-119, 121-132, 169, 174, 210. For surcharges see Nos. 133-136, B1, Offices in China 37-47, 47-52, Offices in Morocco 20-28, 33-41, 45-53, Offices in Turkey 31-38, 43-50, 55-59. For overprints, see Bavaria Nos. 177-178, 180, 182-183, 185-187. Poland Nos. 15, 17-19, 21, 24-26.

A17

A18

A19

A20

Perf. 14¼-14½ (26x17 holes)
Engr.

75 A17 1m car rose 240.00 2.75
Never hinged 1,400.
On parcel post receipt card 27.50
On registered letter 52.50
a. Imperf. 900.00 *11,500.*
Never hinged 3,000.
76 A18 2m gray blue 82.50 *97.50*
Never hinged 260.00
On parcel post receipt card 300.00
On registered letter 600.00
77 A19 3m black violet 225.00 19.00
Never hinged 1,350.
On parcel post receipt card 315.00
On registered letter 625.00
a. Imperf. 900.00 *11,500.*
Never hinged 3,000.
78 A20 5m slate & car 210.00 19.00
Never hinged 675.00
On parcel post receipt card 325.00
On registered letter 650.00
a. Imperf. 900.00 *11,500.*
Never hinged 2,750.

See Nos. 92, 94-95, 102, 111-113. For surcharges see Nos. 115-116, Offices in China 43, 45-46, 53, 55-56, Offices in Morocco 29, 31-32, 42, 44, 54, 56-57, Offices in Turkey 39, 41-42, 51, 53-54. For overprints, see Bavaria Nos. 188, 190-191.

A21

79 A21 2m gray blue 120.00 5.00
Never hinged 375.00
On parcel post receipt card 110.00
On registered letter 225.00
a. Imperf. 900.00 *11,500.*
Never hinged 2,600.
Nos. 75-79 (5) 877.50 143.25
Set, never hinged 3,125.

See Nos. 93, 114. For surcharges see Nos. 117, Offices in China 44, 54, Offices in Morocco 30, 43, 55, Offices in Turkey 40, 52. For overprint, see Bavaria No. 189.

Perf. 14 (25x16 holes)

75b A17 1m carmine red 600.00 26.00
Never hinged 1,900.
On parcel post receipt card 125.00
On registered letter 250.00
77b A19 3m black violet 75.00 26.00
Never hinged 275.00
On parcel post receipt card 450.00
On registered letter 900.00
78b A20 5m slate & car *26,000.* *4,500.*
Never hinged *37,500.*
On parcel post receipt card *6,750.*
On registered letter *13,500.*
79b A18 2m gray blue 975.00 30.00
Never hinged 2,800.
On parcel post receipt card 210.00
On registered letter 425.00

1905-19 Typo. Wmk. 125 ***Perf. 14***
Wartime Printing
Stamps with dark colors, indistinct impressions, yellow gum

81 A16 3pf brown ('15) .60 *1.50*
Never hinged 1.40
On cover *1.90*
a. 3pf dark brown 22.50 *105.00*
Never hinged 52.50
On cover *135.00*
82 A16 5pf grn (shades) .60 *1.50*
Never hinged 1.40
On cover 1.90
b. Bklt. pane of 5 + label ('11) 250.00 500.00
Never hinged 500.00
c. Bklt. pane of 4 + 2 labels ('10) 400.00 800.00
Never hinged 800.00
d. Bklt. pane of 2 + 4 labels ('12) 250.00 500.00
Never hinged 500.00
e. Bklt. pane, #82 + 5 #83 ('17) 75.00 190.00
Never hinged 190.00
f. Bklt. pane, 2 #82 + 4 #83 ('20) 21.00 50.00
Never hinged 50.00
g. Bklt. pane, 4 #82 + 2 #83 ('19) 21.00 50.00
Never hinged 50.00
83 A16 10pf red .60 *1.50*
Never hinged 1.40
On cover *1.90*
b. Bklt. pane of 5 + label ('10) 325.00 650.00
Never hinged 650.00
c. Bklt. pane of 4 + 2 labels ('12) 300.00 625.00
Never hinged 625.00
d. 10pf carmine red 2.00 1.50
Never hinged 5.25
On cover 2.25
e. 10pf orange red 75.00 *160.00*
Never hinged 225.00
On cover *230.00*
f. 10pf lilac red 260.00 82.50
Never hinged 900.00
On cover 150.00
84 A16 20pf bl vio ('18) .75 *1.50*
Never hinged 2.10
On cover *1.50*
a. 20pf light blue 13.00 3.75
Never hinged 52.50
On cover 8.25
b. 20pf ultramarine 8.00 1.50
Never hinged 42.50

On cover 2.25
c. Imperf. 625.00 2,750.
Never hinged 1,750.
d. Half used as 10pf on cover 700.00

No. 84d was used at Field Post Office No. 107 in 1915, and at Field Post Office No. 766 during 1917.

85 A16 25pf org & blk, *yel* .60 1.50
Never hinged 1.40
On cover 1.90
86 A16 30pf org & blk, *buff* .75 1.50
Never hinged 1.40
On cover 1.90
a. 30pf org & blk, *cr* 26.00 90.00
Never hinged 82.50
On cover 150.00
87 A16 40pf lake & black 1.10 1.50
Never hinged 3.25
On cover 1.90
88 A16 50pf pur & blk, *buff* .75 1.50
Never hinged 1.40
On cover 1.90
a. 50pf pur & blk, *yel org* 19.00 75.00
Never hinged 47.50
On cover 110.00
89 A16 60pf magenta 1.50 1.50
Never hinged 4.50
On cover 1.90
a. 60pf red violet 22.50 13.50
Never hinged 67.50
On cover 60.00
90 A16 75pf grn & blk ('19) .25 2.25
Never hinged .75
On cover 3.75
a. 75pf dk bluish grn & greenish blk 1.10 3.00
Never hinged 3.75
On cover 4.50
91 A16 80pf lake & blk, *rose* 1.10 1.90
Never hinged 3.25
On cover 5.00

Perf. 14½ (25x17 holes)

Engr.

92 A17 1m car rose 2.60 2.25
Never hinged 7.50
On cover 3.75
93 A21 2m brt blue 5.25 4.75
Never hinged 14.00
On cover 9.75
a. 2m gray blue ('16) 42.50 52.50
Never hinged 140.00
On cover 90.00
94 A19 3m violet gray 3.00 4.25
Never hinged 9.00
On cover 19.00
b. 3m blk violet 11.50 26.00
Never hinged 26.00
On cover 55.00
95 A20 5m slate & car 3.00 4.75
Never hinged 7.50
On cover 27.50
a. Center inverted 45,000. 65,000.
On cover 67,500.
Nos. 80-95 (15) 22.45 33.65
Set, Never Hinged 67.00

Perf. 14¼-14¾ (26x17 holes)

92a A17 1m car red 140.00 110.00
Never hinged 500.00
On cover 150.00
93b A21 2m bright blue 105.00 47.50
Never hinged 325.00
On cover 82.50
94c A19 3m violet gray 225.00 500.00
Never hinged 675.00
On cover 975.00
95b A20 5m slate & car 65.00 97.50
Never hinged 150.00
On cover 375.00
Nos. 92a-95b (4) 535.00 755.00

Labels in No. 82c contain an "X." The version with advertising is worth 3 times as much. No. 82f has three 10pf stamps in the top row. The version with 3 on the bottom row is worth 4 times as much.

Pre-War Printing

Stamps with bright colors, sharp impressions, high quality (often surfaced) paper, white gum

80 A16 2pf gray ('05) 1.60 2.60
Never hinged 4.50
On cover 9.00
81b A16 3pf dk yellowish brn ('05) 2.25 1.50
Never hinged 5.25
On cover 1.90
82h A16 5pf dk bluish grn 1.60 1.40
Never hinged 6.00
On cover 1.90
82i A16 5pf yel grn ('05) 35.00 14.00
Never hinged 140.00
On cover 37.50
83g A16 10pf red 3.00 1.40
Never hinged 10.50
On cover 1.90
83h A16 10pf rose red ('05) 10.50 1.40
Never hinged 45.00
On cover 1.90
83i A16 10pf carmine 225.00 150.00
Never hinged 900.00
On cover 375.00
83j A16 10pf orange red 180.00 3,750.
Never hinged 525.00
On cover (late '13-14) 5,250.
84e A16 20pf ultra 11.50 1.50
Never hinged 57.50
On cover 2.25
84f A16 20pf light bl ('06) 250.00 4.50
Never hinged 900.00
On cover 11.50
84g A16 20pf vio bl ('06) 190.00 5.25
Never hinged 750.00
On cover 11.50

85a A16 25pf org & blk, *yel* ('06) 37.50 2.75
Never hinged 145.00
On cover 7.50
86b A16 30pf org & blk, *pale yel* ('05) 35.00 1.75
Never hinged 135.00
On cover 6.50
86c A16 30pf org & blk, *yel org* 750.00 82.50
Never hinged 2,500.
On cover 180.00
87a A16 40pf lake & blk ('06) 37.50 2.10
Never hinged 150.00
On cover 11.50
88b A16 50pf pur & blk, *pale yel* ('06) 60.00 2.10
Never hinged 180.00
On cover 11.50
88c A16 50pf pur & blk, *yel org* 900.00 75.00
Never hinged 3,600.
On cover 150.00
89b A16 60pf magenta ('11) 190.00 13.50
Never hinged 675.00
On cover 75.00
89c A16 60pf violet — 900.00
Never hinged —
On cover —
91a A16 80pf lake & blk, *rose* ('06) 19.00 3.00
Never hinged 75.00
On cover 11.50

Engr.

Perf. 14¼-14¾ (26x17 holes)

92b A17 1m car red ('06) 67.50 2.25
Never hinged 315.00
On cover 22.50
93c A21 2m brt blue ('06) 65.00 3.00
Never hinged 275.00
On cover 22.50
94a A19 3m brnsh vio ('11) 52.50 26.00
Never hinged 190.00
On cover 110.00
95c A20 5m slate & car ('06) 45.00 21.00
Never hinged 90.00
On cover 135.00

Surcharged and overprinted stamps of designs A16-A22 are listed under Allenstein, Belgium, Danzig, France, Latvia, Lithuania, Marienwerder, Memel, Poland, Romania, Saar, Upper Silesia and German States-Bavaria.

A22

1916-19 **Typo.**

96 A22 2pf lt gray ('18) .30 3.75
Never hinged .75
On cover 7.75
97 A22 2½pf lt gray .25 1.90
Never hinged .60
On cover 2.50
98 A22 7½pf red orange .50 2.25
Never hinged 1.75
On cover 2.60
b. Bklt. pane, 4 #98 + 2 #100 110.00 275.00
Never hinged 275.00
c. Bklt. pane, 2 #98 + 4 #99 125.00 300.00
Never hinged 300.00
d. Bklt. pane, 2 #98 + 4 #100 110.00 275.00
Never hinged 275.00
e. Bklt. pane, 2 #82 + 4 #98 37.50 90.00
Never hinged 90.00
f. 7½pf yellow orange 3.50 2.25
Never hinged 13.50
On cover 3.00
99 A22 15pf yellow brown 3.00 2.25
Never hinged 13.50
On cover 3.50
a. 15pf olive brown 19.00 21.00
Never hinged 60.00
On cover 42.50
100 A22 15pf dk violet ('17) .25 1.90
Never hinged 1.00
On cover 2.25
a. 15pf blue violet 75.00 75.00
Never hinged 190.00
On cover 190.00
b. Bklt. pane, 4 #82 + 2 #100 110.00 275.00
Never hinged 275.00
c. Bklt. pane, 2 #83 + 4 #100 82.50 210.00
Never hinged 210.00
d. 15pf blackish violet 3.00 3.50
Never hinged 9.00
On cover 4.50
101 A22 35pf red brn ('19) .30 2.25
Never hinged .75
On cover 3.75
a. 35pf dk lake brown 21.00 18.00
Never hinged 60.00
On cover 52.50
Nos. 96-101 (6) 4.60 14.30
Set, never hinged 17.00

See No. 120. For surcharge see No. B2. For overprints, see Bavaria Nos. 176, 179, 184. Poland Nos. 16, 20, 23.

Nos. 98e and 100c have the 2 stamps first in the bottom row.

Type of 1902

1920 Engr. Wmk. 192 *Perf. 14½*

102 A19 3m black violet 1,875. 3,750.
Never hinged 4,500.

Republic

National Assembly Issue

A23

A24

Rebuilding Germany — A25

Designs: A23, Live Stump of Tree Symbolizing that Germany will Survive her Difficulties. A24, New Shoots from Oak Stump Symbolical of New Government.

Perf. 13x13½

1919-20 Unwmk. Typo.

105 A23 10pf carmine rose .25 1.50
Never hinged .75
On cover 2.60
106 A24 15pf choc & blue .25 1.50
Never hinged .75
On cover 2.60
107 A25 25pf green & red .25 1.50
Never hinged .75
On cover 2.60
a. "1019" instead of "1919" 97.50 300.00
Never hinged 225.00
On cover 425.00
108 A25 30pf red vio & red ('20) .25 2.25
Never hinged 1.25
On cover 2.60
a. A25 30pf pale lilac & brownish red 4.50 15.00
Never hinged 19.00
On cover 27.50
b. "1019" instead of "1919" 45.00 150.00
Never hinged 105.00
On cover 225.00
Nos. 105-108 (4) 1.00 6.75
Set, never hinged 3.50

Types of 1902

Perf. 15x14½

1920 Wmk. 125 Offset

111 A17 1m red 3.75 2.40
Never hinged 15.00
On cover 3.25
a. Double impression 120.00 600.00
Never hinged 350.00
b. 1m brown lilac 35.00 27.50
Never hinged 100.00
On cover 47.50
c. As "b," double impression 800.00
112 A17 1.25m green 3.75 1.90
Never hinged 7.50
On cover 2.50
a. Double impression 900.00
113 A17 1.50m yellow brown .50 1.90
Never hinged 1.25
On cover 2.50
a. 1.50m dark brown 15.00 90.00
Never hinged 45.00
On cover 190.00
b. 1.50m red brown 19.00 15.00
Never hinged 80.00
On cover 25.00
c. As "a," double impression 100.00 725.00
Never hinged 275.00
d. As "b," double impression 875.00
114 A21 2.50m lilac rose .50 2.50
Never hinged 1.50
On cover 3.00
a. 2.50m magenta 1.50 2.25
Never hinged 6.00
On cover 3.75
b. 2.50m brown lilac .75 2.75
Never hinged 1.90
On cover 3.75
c. Double impression 100.00 725.00
Never hinged 275.00
d. As "a," double impression 650.00
e. As "b," double impression 650.00
Nos. 111-114 (4) 8.50 8.70
Set, never hinged 25.00

Nos. 111, 112 and 113 differ from the illustration in many minor respects. The numerals of Nos. 75 and 92 are outlined, with shaded background. Those of No. 111 are plain, with solid background and flags have been added to the top of the building, at right and left.

Types of 1902 Surcharged

1920 Engr. *Perf. 14½*

115 A17 1.25m on 1m green .40 6.00
Never hinged 1.50
On cover 13.00
116 A17 1.50m on 1m org brn .40 7.25
Never hinged 1.50
On cover 13.50
117 A21 2.50m on 2m lilac rose 8.75 200.00
Never hinged 26.00
On cover 300.00
Nos. 115-117 (3) 9.55 213.25
Set, never hinged 29.00

Germania Types of 1902-16

1920 Typo. *Perf. 14, 14½*

118 A16 5pf brown .25 2.00
Never hinged .70
On cover 2.60
a. 5pf dark brown 1.60 6.00
Never hinged 4.25
On cover 11.50
119 A16 10pf orange .25 1.50
Never hinged .55
On cover 1.90
a. Tête bêche pair 1.75 7.00
Never hinged 3.00
d. Bklt. pane, 4 #119 + 2 #123 8.25 13.50
Never hinged 13.50
120 A22 15pf violet brn .25 1.90
Never hinged .70
On cover 2.60
a. Imperf. 67.50
Never hinged 190.00
b. 15pf pale lake brn 1.50 6.00
Never hinged 4.25
On cover 10.50
c. Bklt. pane, 4 #84 + 2 #120 22.50 30.00
Never hinged 40.00
121 A16 20pf green .25 2.25
Never hinged .90
On cover 2.60
a. Imperf. 1,200.
b. 20pf yellow green 1.10 3.00
Never hinged 3.00
On cover 7.50
c. 20pf blue green 37.50 100.00
Never hinged 120.00
On cover 140.00
123 A16 30pf dull blue .25 1.50
Never hinged .60
On cover 1.90
a. Tête bêche pair 3.50 13.50
Never hinged 6.00
d. Bklt. pane, 2 #123 + 4 #124 8.25 15.00
Never hinged 15.00
124 A16 40pf carmine rose .25 1.90
Never hinged .60
On cover 2.25
a. Tête bêche pair 1.90 7.00
Never hinged 3.00
b. Imperf. 150.00 900.00
Never hinged 375.00
d. Bklt. pane, 2 #124 + 4 #126 12.00 75.00
Never hinged 20.00
125 A16 50pf red lilac .60 2.25
Never hinged 1.60
On cover 3.00
126 A16 60pf olive green .25 1.60
Never hinged .55
On cover 1.90
a. Tête bêche pair 2.75 20.00
Never hinged 4.50
c. Imperf. 160.00
Never hinged 425.00
127 A16 75pf red violet .60 1.90
Never hinged 1.90
On cover 3.00
128 A16 80pf blue violet .25 2.25
Never hinged .75
On cover 3.00
a. Imperf. 190.00
Never hinged 450.00
b. 80pf grayish ultra 22.50 75.00
Never hinged 75.00
On cover 105.00
129 A16 1m violet & grn .25 2.25
Never hinged .55
On cover 3.00
a. Imperf. 77.50
Never hinged 190.00
130 A16 1¼m ver & mag .25 1.90
Never hinged .55
On cover 2.25
131 A16 2m carmine & bl .60 1.50
Never hinged 2.25
On cover 3.00
132 A16 4m black & rose .25 2.25
Never hinged .55
On cover 3.75
Nos. 118-132 (14) 4.55 26.95
Set, never hinged 12.50

Stamps of 1920 Surcharged

No. 133

No. 135

Nos. 134, 136

1921, Aug.
133 A16 1.60m on 5pf .25 2.25
Never hinged 1.00
On cover 3.00
a. On #118a 75.00 425.00
Never hinged 190.00
On cover 500.00
134 A16 3m on 1¼m .25 2.60
Never hinged 1.00
On cover 3.50
135 A16 5m on 75pf (G) .25 2.25
Never hinged 1.15
On cover 3.00
136 A16 10m on 75pf .40 2.25
Never hinged 1.35
On cover 3.50
Nos. 133-136 (4) 1.15 *9.35*
Set, never hinged 4.50

In 1920 the current stamps of Bavaria were overprinted "Deutsches Reich". These stamps were available for postage throughout Germany, but because they were used almost exclusively in Bavaria, they are listed among the issues of that state.

A26

Iron Workers
A27

Miners
A28

Farmers
A29

Post Horn
A30

Numeral of Value — A31

Plowing
A32

Wmk. Lozenges (125)

1921 Typo. *Perf. 14*
137 A26 5pf claret .25 2.00
Never hinged .45
On cover 4.50
138 A26 10pf olive green .25 2.00
Never hinged .75
On cover 2.60
a. Tête bêche pair 5.50 37.50
Never hinged 9.00
b. Bklt. pane, 5 #138 + 1 #141 12.00 —
Never hinged 20.00
c. 10pf blackish olive 52.50 275.00
Never hinged 150.00
On cover 375.00
139 A26 15pf grnsh blue .25 1.60
Never hinged .45
On cover 3.00
140 A26 25pf dark brown .25 1.60
Never hinged .45
On cover 2.25
141 A26 30pf blue green .25 1.60
Never hinged .45
On cover 2.25
a. Tête bêche pair 5.50 37.50
Never hinged 9.00
b. Bklt. pane, 2 #124 + 4 #141 12.00 75.00
Never hinged 20.00
142 A26 40pf red orange .25 1.60
Never hinged .45
On cover 1.90
143 A26 50pf violet .30 1.60
Never hinged 1.15
On cover 2.60
144 A27 60pf red violet .25 1.60
Never hinged .45
On cover 1.90
145 A27 80pf carmine rose .25 5.25
Never hinged .45
On cover 15.00
146 A28 100pf yellow grn .30 2.00
Never hinged 1.05
On cover 5.75
147 A28 120pf ultra .25 1.60
Never hinged .45
On cover 3.75
148 A29 150pf orange .25 2.00
Never hinged .90
On cover 3.75
149 A29 160pf slate grn .25 8.50
Never hinged .45
On cover 19.00
150 A30 2m dp vio & rose .40 3.50
Never hinged 1.50
On cover 7.50
151 A30 3m red & yel .40 15.00
Never hinged 1.50
On cover 30.00
152 A30 4m dp grn & yel grn .25 3.50
Never hinged 1.00
On cover 6.00

Engr.
153 A31 5m orange .30 2.25
Never hinged 1.00
On cover 3.25
a. 5m brown orange 15.00 25.00
Never hinged 55.00
On cover 45.00
b. 5m red orange 75.00 200.00
Never hinged 200.00
On cover 260.00
154 A31 10m carmine rose .50 3.00
Never hinged 1.90
On cover 5.25
155 A32 20m indigo & grn 3.00 2.75
Never hinged 7.50
On cover 5.25
a. Green background inverted 190.00 1,050.
Never hinged 675.00
On cover 1,150.
b. 20m blk bl & dull grn 30.00 72.50
Never hinged 75.00
On cover 130.00
Nos. 137-155 (19) 8.20 *62.95*
Set, never hinged 20.00

See Nos. 156-209, 211, 222-223, 225, 227.
For surcharges and overprints see Nos. 241-245, 247-248, 261-262, 273-276, B6-B7, O24.

1922 Litho. *Perf. 14½x14*
156 A31 100m brown vio, *buff* .25 1.40
Never hinged .75
On cover 3.00
157 A31 200m rose, *buff* .25 1.40
Never hinged .55
On cover 3.00
158 A31 300m green, *buff* .25 1.40
Never hinged .55
On cover 2.25
159 A31 400m bis brn, *buff* .55 2.25
Never hinged 1.50
On cover 7.50
a. 400m ol brn, *buff* 7.50 90.00
Never hinged 22.50
On cover 190.00
b. 400m red brn, *buff* 15.00 140.00
Never hinged 50.00
On cover 190.00
c. 400m pale brn, *buff* 26.00 225.00
Never hinged 72.50
On cover 300.00
160 A31 500m orange, *buff* .25 1.40
Never hinged .35
On cover 3.00
Nos. 156-160 (5) 1.55 *7.85*
Set, never hinged 3.70

Postally Used vs. CTO

Values quoted for canceled stamps of the 1921-1923 issues are for postally used stamps. These bring higher prices than the plentiful canceled-to-order stamps made by applying genuine handstamps to remainders. C.T.O. examples sell for about the same price as unused stamps. Certification of postal usage by competent authorities is necessary.

Perf. 14, 14½
1921-22 Typo. Wmk. 126
161 A26 5pf claret .75 200.00
Never hinged 2.25
On cover 375.00
162 A26 10pf olive grn 7.00 190.00
Never hinged 22.50
On cover 350.00
163 A26 15pf grnsh blue .55 225.00
Never hinged 1.50
On cover 375.00
164 A26 25pf dark brown .25 3.75
Never hinged .45
On cover 9.00
165 A26 30pf blue green .85 325.00
Never hinged 2.60
On cover 675.00
166 A26 40pf red orange .25 3.75
Never hinged .45
On cover 9.00
167 A26 50pf violet ('21) .25 1.50
Never hinged 1.00
On cover 2.25
168 A27 60pf red violet .25 20.00
Never hinged .45
On cover 34.00
169 A16 75pf red violet .40 2.75
Never hinged 1.35
On cover 6.00
a. 75pf rose lilac 115.00 135.00
Never hinged 360.00
On cover 200.00
170 A26 75pf deep ultra .25 3.00
Never hinged .45
On cover 7.50
171 A27 80pf car rose .40 57.50
Never hinged 1.20
On cover 90.00
172 A28 100pf olive green .25 1.50
Never hinged 1.00
On cover 2.25
a. Imperf. 60.00 1,500.
Never hinged 150.00
b. 100pf bluish green 6.00 30.00
Never hinged 16.50
On cover 52.50
c. 100pf blackish green 7.50 22.50
Never hinged 22.50
On cover 30.00
173 A28 120pf ultra .70 110.00
Never hinged 2.00
On cover 190.00
174 A16 1¼m ver & mag .25 1.50
Never hinged .60
On cover 3.00
175 A29 150pf orange .25 1.50
Never hinged .45
On cover 1.90
a. Imperf. 37.50
Never hinged 110.00
176 A29 160pf slate green .70 175.00
Never hinged 2.00
On cover 260.00
177 A30 2m violet & rose .25 1.50
Never hinged .45
On cover 1.90
178 A30 3m red & yel ('21) .25 1.50
Never hinged .45
On cover 2.25
a. Imperf. 37.50 375.00
Never hinged 110.00
179 A30 4m dp grn & yel grn .25 1.50
Never hinged .45
On cover 2.60
180 A30 5m org & yel .30 2.00
Never hinged 1.15
On cover 2.60
a. Imperf. 130.00
Never hinged 300.00 3,000.
181 A30 10m car & pale rose .30 2.25
Never hinged 1.10
On cover 4.50
a. Pale rose (background) omitted 45.00 975.00
Never hinged 150.00
182 A30 20m violet & org .25 3.00
Never hinged .55
On cover 5.50
183 A30 30m brown & yel .25 1.50
Never hinged .65
On cover 1.90
184 A30 50m dk grn & vio .25 1.50
Never hinged .65
On cover 2.60
Nos. 161-184 (24) 15.45 *1,337.*
Set, never hinged 37.50

1922-23

SIX MARKS:

Type I — Numerals upright.

Type II — Numerals leaning toward the right and slightly thinner.

EIGHT MARKS:

Type I — Numerals 2½mm wide with thick strokes.

Type II — Numerals 2mm wide with thinner strokes.

185 A30 2m blue violet .25 1.50
Never hinged .75
On cover 1.90
a. Imperf. 100.00
Never hinged 190.00
b. 2m deep reddish vio 2.25 6.75
Never hinged 6.50
On cover 15.00
c. 2m deep violet 19.00 82.50
Never hinged 45.00
On cover 135.00
186 A30 3m red .25 1.50
Never hinged .55
On cover 1.90
187 A30 4m dark green .25 1.50
Never hinged .75
On cover 1.90
a. Imperf. 30.00
Never hinged 75.00
b. 4m deep blue green 1.50 5.25
Never hinged 4.00
On cover 9.00
188 A30 5m orange .25 1.50
Never hinged .75
On cover 1.90
a. Imperf. 80.00
Never hinged 160.00
189 A30 6m dark blue (II) .25 1.50
Never hinged .75
On cover 1.90
a. Type I .25 1.90
Never hinged 1.10
On cover 2.60
b. Imperf. 80.00
Never hinged 160.00
190 A30 8m olive green (I) .25 1.50
Never hinged .75
On cover 2.60
a. Type II .40 37.50
Never hinged 1.20
On cover 50.00
191 A30 20m dk violet ('23) .25 1.50
Never hinged .75
On cover 2.25
192 A30 30m pur brn ('23) .25 7.50
Never hinged .75
On cover 13.50
a. 30m deep brown 1.25 35.00
Never hinged 4.25
On cover 65.00
193 A30 40m lt green .25 2.25
Never hinged .90
On cover 3.00

Engr.
194 A31 5m orange .25 1.50
Never hinged 1.10
On cover 2.60
a. Imperf. 140.00 2,100.
Never hinged 225.00
b. 5m red orange 26.00 67.50
Never hinged 75.00
On cover 97.50
c. 5m brown orange 75.00 27.50
Never hinged 375.00
On cover 55.00
195 A31 10m carmine rose .55 2.25
Never hinged 1.50
On cover 4.50
196 A32 20m indigo & grn .25 3.50
Never hinged .65
On cover 5.50
a. Imperf. 175.00 2,100.
Never hinged 225.00
b. Green background inverted 32.50 675.00
Never hinged 75.00
c. Green background double 750.00 3,750.
Never hinged 2,600.
Nos. 185-196 (12) 3.30 *27.50*
Set, never hinged 8.85

1922-23 Litho. *Perf. 14½x14*
198 A31 50m indigo .25 1.50
Never hinged .75
On cover 2.60
199 A31 100m brn vio, *buff* ('23) .25 1.40
Never hinged .55
On cover 2.60
200 A31 200m rose, *buff* ('23) .25 1.90
Never hinged .75
On cover 2.60
a. 200m pale red, *buff* 3.00 26.00
Never hinged 10.00
On cover 40.00
b. 200m reddish lilac, *buff* 22.50 75.00
Never hinged 72.50
On cover 110.00
201 A31 300m grn, *buff* ('23) .25 1.50
Never hinged .40
On cover 1.90
202 A31 400m bis brn, *buff* ('23) .25 1.50
Never hinged .40
On cover 1.90
203 A31 500m org, *buff* ('23) .25 1.50
Never hinged .40
On cover 1.90
204 A31 1000m gray ('23) .25 1.50
Never hinged .40
On cover 1.90
205 A31 2000m bl ('23) .35 1.90
Never hinged .50
On cover 1.90
a. 2000m dark blue .75 6.00
Never hinged 2.60
On cover 12.50
206 A31 3000m brn ('23) .25 2.75
Never hinged .75
On cover 3.75
a. 3000m deep yel brn .75 3.25
Never hinged 2.60
On cover 5.25
b. 3000m dk gray brn .85 4.75
Never hinged 2.75
On cover 9.00
c. 3000m blk brn 67.50 300.00
Never hinged 160.00
On cover 450.00
207 A31 4000m vio ('23) .25 1.50
Never hinged .55
On cover 3.75
a. Imperf. 37.50 190.00
Never hinged 110.00
208 A31 5000m gray grn ('23) .30 1.50
Never hinged 1.00
On cover 4.50
a. Imperf. 52.50 225.00
Never hinged 150.00
b. 5000m dp bl grn 1.40 37.50
Never hinged 4.00
On cover 60.00
c. 5000m blk grn 6.75 150.00
Never hinged 25.00
On cover 260.00
209 A31 100,000m ver ('23) .25 1.40
Never hinged .55
On cover 3.00
a. Imperf. 52.50 225.00
Never hinged 150.00
Nos. 198-209 (12) 3.15 *19.85*
Set, never hinged 6.50

1920-22 Wmk. 127 Typo.
210 A16 1¼m ver & mag 450.00 975.00
Never hinged 1,350.
On cover 1,350.
211 A30 50m grn & vio ('22) 2.25 825.00
Never hinged 5.25
On cover 1,500.

Wmk. 127 was intended for use only in printing revenue stamps.

Arms of Munich — A33

Wmk. Network (126)

1922, Apr. 22 Typo. *Perf. 13x13½*

212 A33 1¼m claret .25 *1.90*
Never hinged .75
On cover 3.00
a. 1¼m brn car 2.60 *7.50*
Never hinged 7.50
On cover *15.00*
b. 1¼m pale lilac rose 30.00 *300.00*
Never hinged 82.50
On cover *450.00*
213 A33 2m dark violet .25 *1.90*
Never hinged .75
On cover 3.00
a. 2m dk red vio 20.00 *130.00*
Never hinged 65.00
On cover *165.00*
214 A33 3m vermilion .25 *1.90*
Never hinged .55
On cover 3.00
215 A33 4m deep blue .25 *1.90*
Never hinged .55
On cover 3.00

Wmk. Lozenges (125)

216 A33 10m brown, *buff* .60 *2.75*
Never hinged 2.40
On cover 7.50
a. 10m vio brn, *buff* 26.00 *90.00*
Never hinged 97.50
On cover *120.00*
217 A33 20m lilac rose, *pink* 3.75 *11.50*
Never hinged 12.00
On cover 26.00
a. 20m red, *pink* 12.00 *52.50*
Never hinged 37.50
On cover *90.00*
Nos. 212-217 (6) 5.35 *21.85*
Set, never hinged 17.00

Munich Industrial Fair.

Type of 1921 and

Miners — A34

A35

1922-23 Wmk. 126 *Perf. 14*

221 A34 5m orange .25 *13.00*
Never hinged .30
On cover *30.00*
222 A29 10m dull blue ('22) .25 *1.50*
Never hinged .30
On cover 1.90
223 A29 12m vermilion ('22) .25 *1.50*
Never hinged .30
On cover 3.75
224 A34 20m red lilac .25 *1.50*
Never hinged .55
On cover 1.90
a. Wmk. sideways .75 *60.00*
Never hinged 2.60
On cover *115.00*
225 A29 25m olive brown .25 *1.50*
Never hinged .30
On cover 2.75
226 A34 30m olive green .25 *2.25*
Never hinged .65
On cover *7.50*
a. 30m blk ol grn .75 *37.50*
Never hinged 2.25
On cover *67.50*
227 A29 40m green .25 *1.50*
Never hinged .90
On cover 2.25
228 A34 50m grnsh blue .40 *125.00*
Never hinged 1.20
On cover *190.00*
229 A35 100m violet .25 *1.50*
Never hinged .75
On cover 2.60
a. 100m purple violet .30 *1.50*
Never hinged .75
On cover 3.00
230 A35 200m carmine rose .25 *1.50*
Never hinged .45
On cover 3.75
231 A35 300m green .25 *1.40*
Never hinged .35
On cover 3.00
232 A35 400m dark brown .25 *5.75*
Never hinged .35
On cover *11.00*
233 A35 500m red orange .25 *6.50*
Never hinged .35
On cover *11.00*
234 A35 1000m slate .25 *1.40*
Never hinged .35
On cover 3.75
Nos. 221-234 (14) 3.65 *165.80*
Set, never hinged 7.00

The 50m was issued only in vertical coils.
Nos. 222-223 exist imperf.
For surcharges and overprints see Nos. 246, 249-260, 263-271, 277, 310, B5, O22-O23, O25-O28.

Wartburg Castle — A36

Cathedral of Cologne — A37

1923 Engr.

237 A36 5000m deep blue .30 *3.25*
Never hinged .90
On cover *5.75*
a. Imperf. 300.00 *1,200.*
Never hinged 750.00
b. 5000m dk grn bl 6.00 *75.00*
Never hinged 16.50
On cover *115.00*
238 A37 10,000m brn ol .30 *4.00*
Never hinged 1.10
On cover *11.50*
a. 10,000m ol grn .75 *12.00*
Never hinged 2.50
On cover *19.00*
Set, never hinged 2.00

Abbreviations:
Th = (Tausend) Thousand
Mil = (Million) Million
Mlrd = (Milliarde) Billion

A38

1923 Typo.

238A A38 5th m grnsh blue .25 *17.00*
Never hinged .40
On cover *37.50*
b. Imperf. 90.00
Never hinged 240.00
239 A38 50th m bister .25 *1.50*
Never hinged .40
On cover 2.25
a. Imperf. 22.50 *3,750.*
Never hinged 60.00
240 A38 75th m dark violet .25 *11.00*
Never hinged .40
On cover *19.00*
Nos. 238A-240 (3) .75 29.50
Set, never hinged 1.20

For surcharges see Nos. 272, 278.

Stamps and Types of 1922-23 Surcharged in Black, Blue, Green or Brown

No. 241

No. 243

No. 246

No. 253

No. 269

Wmk. Lozenges (125)

1923 *Perf. 14*

241 A26 8th m on 30pf .25 *1.75*
Never hinged .40
On cover *2.60*
a. "8" inverted 21.00 *325.00*
Never hinged 60.00

Wmk. Network (126)

242 A26 5th m on 40pf .25 *1.60*
Never hinged .40
On cover *2.60*
242A A26 8th m on 30pf 24.00 *6,000.*
Never hinged 60.00
On cover *9,000.*
243 A29 15th m on 40m .25 *2.00*
Never hinged .75
On cover 2.25
244 A29 20th m on 12m .25 *1.50*
Never hinged .40
On cover *3.00*
a. Inverted surcharge 120.00 *1,100.*
245 A29 20th m on 25m .25 *2.25*
Never hinged .40
On cover 4.25
246 A35 20th m on 200m .25 *2.25*
Never hinged .75
On cover 2.25
a. Inverted surcharge 57.50 750.00
Never hinged 150.00
247 A29 25th m on 25m .25 *14.50*
Never hinged .40
On cover *35.00*
248 A29 30th m on 10m dp bl .25 *1.50*
Never hinged .40
On cover 3.00
a. Inverted surcharge 70.00
Never hinged 180.00
249 A35 30th m on 200m pale bl (Bl) .25 *1.50*
Never hinged .40
On cover 3.00
a. Without surcharge 115.00
Never hinged 225.00
250 A35 75th m on 300m yel grn .25 *14.50*
Never hinged .40
On cover *32.50*
a. Imperf. 45.00
Never hinged 125.00
251 A35 75th m on 400m yel grn .25 *1.50*
Never hinged .75
On cover 2.25
252 A35 75th m on 1000m yel grn .25 *1.90*
Never hinged .75
On cover 2.60
a. Without surcharge 115.00
Never hinged 225.00
253 A35 100th m on 100m .25 *2.25*
Never hinged .75
On cover *3.75*
a. Double surcharge 37.50 *450.00*
Never hinged 97.50
b. Inverted surcharge 14.50
Never hinged 37.50 *600.00*
254 A35 100th m on 400m bluish grn (G) .25 *1.50*
Never hinged .40
On cover 1.90
a. Imperf. 50.00 750.00
Never hinged 115.00
b. Without surcharge 115.00
Never hinged 225.00
255 A35 125th m on 1000m sal .25 *1.90*
Never hinged .60
On cover 3.00
256 A35 250th m on 200m .25 *5.25*
Never hinged .40
On cover *13.00*
a. Inverted surcharge 35.00
Never hinged 90.00
b. Double surcharge 52.50
Never hinged 140.00
257 A35 250th m on 300m dp grn .25 *17.00*
Never hinged .40
On cover *30.00*
a. Inverted surcharge 35.00
Never hinged 90.00
258 A35 250th m on 400m .25 *19.00*
Never hinged .40
On cover *30.00*
a. Inverted surcharge 26.00
Never hinged 75.00
259 A35 250th m on 500m pink .25 *1.50*
Never hinged .40
On cover 1.90
a. Imperf. 52.50 *675.00*
Never hinged 125.00
260 A35 250th m on 500m red org .25 *19.00*
Never hinged .40
On cover *30.00*
a. Double surcharge 30.00 *975.00*
Never hinged 75.00
b. Inverted surcharge 30.00
Never hinged 82.50
261 A26 800th m on 5pf lt grn (G) .25 *4.25*
Never hinged .40
On cover *9.00*
a. Imperf. 35.00 *150.00*
Never hinged 90.00
262 A26 800th m on 10pf lt grn (G) .25 *5.00*
Never hinged .40
On cover *9.00*
a. Imperf. 30.00
Never hinged 90.00
263 A35 800th m on 200m .25 *75.00*
Never hinged .55
On cover *190.00*
a. Double surcharge 75.00 *975.00*
Never hinged 190.00
b. Inverted surcharge 37.50
Never hinged 110.00
264 A35 800th m on 300m lt grn (G) .25 *5.00*
Never hinged .40
On cover *7.50*
a. Black surcharge 47.50
Never hinged 75.00
265 A35 800th m on 400m dk brn .25 *14.50*
Never hinged .40
On cover *40.00*
a. Inverted surcharge 42.50
Never hinged 110.00
b. Double surcharge 75.00
Never hinged 190.00
266 A35 800th m on 400m lt grn (G) .25 *3.75*
Never hinged .40
On cover *7.50*
267 A35 800th m on 500m lt grn (G) .25 *1,500.*
Never hinged .40
On cover *1,900.*
a. 800th m on 500m red org (Bk) 37.50
Never hinged 67.50
268 A35 800th m on 1000m lt grn (G) .25 *1.50*
Never hinged .70
On cover 3.00
269 A35 2mil m on 200m rose red .25 *2.25*
Never hinged .75
On cover 4.50
b. 2mil m on 200m car rose (#230) *1,500.*
Never hinged 3,400.
c. As "b," wmk sideways 3.00 *325.00*
Never hinged 7.50
On cover 525.00
270 A35 2mil m on 300m dp grn .25 *2.25*
Never hinged .50
On cover *3.75*
a. Inverted surcharge 42.50
Never hinged 110.00
b. Double surcharge 75.00
Never hinged 190.00
271 A35 2mil m on 500m dl rose .25 *6.50*
Never hinged .40
On cover *11.50*
272 A38 2mil m on 5th m dl rose .25 *1.50*
Never hinged .90
On cover 2.25
b. Imperf. 42.50 *125.00*
Never hinged 85.00

Nos. 264a, 267a were not put in use.

Serrate Roulette 13½

273 A26 400th m on 15pf bis (Br) .25 *4.50*
Never hinged .40
On cover *7.50*
a. Imperf. 52.50 275.00
Never hinged 125.00
274 A26 400th m on 25pf bis (Br) .25 *4.50*
Never hinged .40
On cover *7.50*
a. Imperf. 90.00 *275.00*
Never hinged 225.00
275 A26 400th m on 30pf bis (Br) .25 *4.50*
Never hinged .40
On cover *7.50*
a. Imperf. 45.00
Never hinged 110.00
b. Double surcharge 90.00
Never hinged 175.00
276 A26 400th m on 40pf bis (Br) .25 *4.50*
Never hinged .40
On cover *7.50*
a. Imperf. 45.00 —
Never hinged 110.00
b. Double surcharge 90.00
Never hinged 175.00
277 A35 2mil m on 200m rose red .45 *150.00*
Never hinged .65
On cover *210.00*
278 A38 2mil m on 5th m dull rose .25 *9.00*
Never hinged .40
On cover *16.50*
Nos. 241-278 (39) 33.70 *7,913.*
Set, never hinged 51.00

Surcharge Omitted

272c A38 2mil m on 5th m 150.00
Never hinged 375.00
273b A26 400th m on 15pf 150.00
Never hinged 375.00
274b A26 400th m on 25pf 150.00
Never hinged 375.00

275c A26 400th m on 30pf 150.00
Never hinged 375.00
276c A26 400th m on 40pf 150.00
Never hinged 375.00

A39

A39a

The stamps of types A39 and A39a usually have the value darker than the rest of the design.

1923 Wmk. 126 *Perf. 14*

280 A39 500th m brown .25 *2.75*
Never hinged .40
On cover *7.50*
281 A39 1mil m grnsh bl .25 *1.60*
Never hinged .70
On cover 2.25
a. Imperf. 52.50 *1,500.*
Never hinged 115.00
b. 1mil m grnsh bl (rotary press) .25 2.10
282 A39 2mil m dull vio .25 *20.00*
Never hinged .75
On cover *37.50*
a. 2mil m deep pur 22.50 *7,500.*
Never hinged 75.00
On cover *9,000.*
284 A39 4mil m yel grn .25 *1.50*
Never hinged .75
On cover 2.60
a. Value double 57.50
Never hinged 140.00
b. Imperf. 42.50
Never hinged 97.50
c. 4mil m yel grn (rotary press) .55 *34.00*
285 A39 5mil m rose .25 *1.50*
Never hinged .70
On cover 1.90
a. 5mil m rose (rotary press) .25 2.60
286 A39 10mil m red .25 *1.50*
Never hinged .40
On cover 1.90
a. Value double 50.00 *3,750.*
Never hinged 125.00
287 A39 20mil m ultra .25 *1.90*
Never hinged .65
On cover 2.60
a. 20mil m blk bl (rotary press) 12.00 *1,500.*
Never hinged 30.00
On cover *2,100.*
288 A39 30mil m red brn .25 *9.25*
Never hinged .40
On cover *19.00*
289 A39 50mil m dull ol grn .25 *1.90*
Never hinged .75
On cover 2.75
a. Imperf. 52.50 *350.00*
Never hinged 125.00
b. Value inverted 45.00
Never hinged 120.00
c. 50mil m bl grn (rotary press) 1.90 *50.00*
Never hinged 5.00
On cover *115.00*
290 A39 100mil m gray .25 *1.50*
Never hinged .40
On cover 2.60
291 A39 200mil m bis brn .25 *1.50*
Never hinged .65
On cover 2.60
a. Imperf. 42.50
Never hinged 97.50
b. 200mil m bis brn (rotary press) .30 1.10
293 A39 500mil m ol grn .25 *1.40*
Never hinged .65
On cover 2.25
294 A39a 1mlrd m choc .30 *1.90*
Never hinged .90
On cover 2.60
a. 1mird m blk brn (flat press) *500.00* *6,750.*
Never hinged *1,200.*
On cover *11,000.*
b. 1mird m blk brn (rotary press) 7.75 *90.00*
Never hinged 24.00
On cover *120.00*
295 A39a 2mlrd m pale brn & grn .25 *1.90*
Never hinged .70
On cover 2.60
a. 2mlrd m pale brn & grn (rotary press) .45 1.60
296 A39a 5mlrd m yellow & brn .25 *1.50*
Never hinged .70
On cover 2.60
a. 5mlrd m yellow & brn (rotary press) .25 1.50
297 A39a 10mlrd m ap grn & grn .25 *1.50*
Never hinged .70
On cover 3.00
a. Imperf. 45.00 *275.00*
Never hinged 115.00
b. 10mlrd m ap grn & grn (rotary press) .30 1.10
298 A39a 20mlrd m bluish grn & brn .25 *1.90*
Never hinged .70
On cover 3.00
a. 20mlrd m bluish grn & brn (rotary press) .30 1.50
299 A39a 50mlrd m bl & dp bl .25 *35.00*
Never hinged .90
On cover *75.00*
Nos. 280-299 (18) 4.55 *90.00*
Set, never hinged 11.50

Nos. 294, 294a are 21.5x17.7mm. Nos. 287a, 289c, 294b are 22x18mm. Nos. 287, 289 exist from both flat and rotary press printings.

See Nos. 301-309. For surcharges and overprints see Nos. 311-321, O40-O46.

Value Omitted

280a A39 500th m 92.50 *360.00*
Never hinged 190.00
281b A39 1mil m 55.00
Never hinged 150.00
284c A39 4mil m 72.50
Never hinged 150.00
285a A39 5mil m 72.50 *375.00*
Never hinged 150.00
286b A39 10mil m 100.00 *375.00*
Never hinged 190.00
287b A39 20mil m 37.50
Never hinged 75.00
290a A39 100mil m 50.00
Never hinged 97.50
291b A39 200mil m 72.50
Never hinged 120.00
293a A39 500mil m 50.00
Never hinged 97.50
294c A39 1mird m 50.00 *150.00*
Never hinged 97.50
296a A39 5mird m 50.00
Never hinged 97.50
298a A39 20mird m 62.50
Never hinged 125.00
299a A39 50mird m 62.50
Never hinged 125.00

Serrate Roulette 13½

301 A39 10mil m red .55 *45.00*
Never hinged 1.60
On cover *75.00*
302 A39 20mil m ultra .55 *300.00*
Never hinged 1.50
On cover *425.00*
303 A39 50mil m dull grn .55 *6.00*
Never hinged 1.50
On cover *13.00*
304 A39 200mil m bis brn .55 *11.50*
Never hinged 1.50
On cover *19.00*
305 A39a 1mlrd m choc .55 *7.50*
Never hinged 1.50
On cover *12.50*
306 A39a 2mlrd m pale brn & grn .55 *3.50*
Never hinged 1.50
On cover 7.50
307 A39a 5mlrd m yel & brn .75 *2.25*
Never hinged 1.90
On cover *6.75*
308 A39a 20mlrd m bluish grn & brn .75 *11.50*
Never hinged 2.10
On cover *19.00*
309 A39a 50mlrd m bl & dp bl 1.90 *675.00*
Never hinged 5.25
On cover *1,500.*
Nos. 301-309 (9) 6.70 *1,062.*
Set, never hinged 18.50

Stamps and Types of 1923 Surcharged with New Values

1923 *Perf. 14*

Design Type A35

310 1mlrd m on 100m vio .25 *29.00*
Never hinged 1.25
On cover *57.50*
a. Inverted surcharge 115.00
Never hinged 300.00
b. Deep reddish purple 60.00 *3,600.*
Never hinged 150.00
On cover (Munich) *5,250.*

Design Type A39

311 5mlrd m on 2mil m .25 *140.00*
Never hinged .90
On cover *190.00*
a. Inverted surcharge 19.00
Never hinged 57.50
b. Double surcharge 45.00
Never hinged 110.00
c. Deep purple 52.50 *9,750.*
Never hinged 150.00
312 5mlrd m on 4mil m .25 *22.50*
Never hinged .65
On cover *37.50*
a. Inverted surcharge 37.50 *1,200.*
Never hinged 110.00
b. Double surcharge 37.50
Never hinged 97.50
313 5mlrd m on 10mil m .25 *2.75*
Never hinged .55
On cover *5.50*
a. Inverted surcharge 19.00 *1,100.*
Never hinged 57.50
b. Double surcharge 37.50
Never hinged 97.50
314 10mlrd m on 20mil m .25 *4.50*
Never hinged .75
On cover *6.75*
a. Double surcharge 45.00
Never hinged 125.00
b. Inverted surcharge 26.00
Never hinged 75.00
c. Triple surcharge 525.00
d. On #287a 32.50 *1,650.*
Never hinged 92.50
On cover *2,750.*
315 10mlrd m on 50mil m .25 *4.50*
Never hinged .65
On cover *7.50*
a. Inverted surcharge 19.00 *900.00*
Never hinged 57.50
b. Double surcharge 45.00
Never hinged 125.00
c. On #289c 135.00 *1,500.*
Never hinged 400.00
On cover *2,750.*
316 10mlrd m on 100mil m .25 *7.50*
Never hinged .55
On cover *13.00*
a. Inverted surcharge 26.00 *1,500.*
Never hinged 75.00
b. Double surcharge 45.00
Never hinged 125.00
Nos. 310-316 (7) 1.75 *210.75*
Set, never hinged 5.25

No. 310b was issued in Bavaria only and is known as the Hitler provisional. Excellent forgeries exist.

Serrate Roulette 13½

Design Type A39

319 5mlrd m on 10mil m 1.90 *190.00*
Never hinged 6.00
On cover *325.00*
a. Inverted surcharge 26.00 *1,100.*
Never hinged 67.50
b. Double surcharge 45.00
Never hinged 110.00
320 10mlrd m on 20mil m 5.00 *110.00*
Never hinged 10.50
On cover *160.00*
321 10mlrd m on 50mil m 1.90 *37.50*
Never hinged 6.00
On cover *105.00*
a. Inverted surcharge 26.00 *1,100.*
Never hinged 67.50
Nos. 319-321 (3) 8.80 *337.50*
Set, never hinged 22.50

A40

1923 *Perf. 14*

323 A40 3pf brown .40 .25
Never hinged 2.25
On cover .85
324 A40 5pf dark green .40 .25
Never hinged 2.25
On cover .85
325 A40 10pf carmine .40 .25
Never hinged 2.25
On cover .85
326 A40 20pf deep ultra 1.20 .40
Never hinged 5.25
On cover 1.10
327 A40 50pf orange 2.75 1.00
Never hinged 19.00
On cover 5.25
328 A40 100pf brn vio 8.50 1.20
Never hinged 52.50
On cover 11.00
Nos. 323-328 (6) 13.65 3.35
Set, never hinged 85.00

For overprints see Nos. O47-O52.

Imperf

323a A40 3pf 125.00 *275.00*
Never hinged 300.00
324a A40 5pf 110.00 —
Never hinged 260.00
325a A40 10pf 140.00 260.00
Never hinged 350.00
326a A40 20pf 140.00 *260.00*
Never hinged 350.00
327a A40 50pf 800.00 —
Never hinged 2,250.
328a A40 100pf 175.00 —
Never hinged 525.00
Nos. 323a-328a (6) 1,490. *795.00*
Set, never hinged 3,650.

Value Omitted

323b A40 3pf 180.00 *300.00*
Never hinged 525.00
324b A40 5pf 160.00 *300.00*
Never hinged 375.00
325b A40 10pf 160.00 *300.00*
Never hinged 450.00
326b A40 20pf 165.00 *300.00*
Never hinged 525.00
327b A40 50pf 160.00
Never hinged 375.00
328b A40 100pf 160.00
Never hinged 375.00
Nos. 323b-328b (6) 985.00
Set, never hinged 2,475.

German Eagle — A41

1924 Wmk. 126

330 A41 3pf lt brown .30 .40
Never hinged 1.50
On cover 1.10
331 A41 5pf lt green .30 .40
Never hinged 2.00
On cover .75
332 A41 10pf vermilion .40 .40
Never hinged 2.60
On cover .75
333 A41 20pf dull blue 1.90 .40
Never hinged 26.00
On cover 2.25
334 A41 30pf rose lilac 1.90 .45
Never hinged 26.00
On cover 3.75
335 A41 40pf olive green 13.00 .75
Never hinged 90.00
On cover 5.75
336 A41 50pf orange 15.00 1.15
Never hinged 130.00
On cover 6.00
Nos. 330-336 (7) 32.80 3.95
Set, never hinged 277.50

The values above 5pf have "Pf" in the upper right corner.

For overprints see Nos. O53-O61.

Imperf.

330a A41 3pf 140.00 *375.00*
Never hinged 350.00
331a A41 5pf 175.00 *375.00*
Never hinged 425.00
332a A41 10pf 225.00
Never hinged 525.00
333a A41 20pf 160.00
Never hinged 375.00
334a A41 30pf 160.00
Never hinged 375.00
335a A41 40pf 190.00
Never hinged 450.00
Nos. 330a-335a (6) 1,050.
Set, never hinged 2,500.

Watermark Sideways

330b A41 3pf 125.00 37.50
Never hinged 300.00
331b A41 5pf — *5,000.*
Never hinged *10,000.*
332b A41 10pf 25.00 12.00
Never hinged 90.00

Rheinstein Castle — A43

View of Cologne A44

Marienburg Castle — A45

1924 Engr. Wmk. 126

337 A43 1m green 13.00 3.50
Never hinged 40.00
On cover 9.00
a. Watermark sideways ('27) 35.00 12.00
Never hinged 97.50
On cover 42.50
338 A44 2m blue 18.00 3.50
Never hinged 50.00
On cover 30.00
339 A45 3m claret 25.00 6.50
Never hinged 70.00
On cover 60.00
Nos. 337-339 (3) 56.00 13.50
Set, never hinged 160.00

See No. 387.

Dr. Heinrich von Stephan
A46 A47

1924-28 Typo.

340 A46 10pf dark green .55 .30
Never hinged 1.90
On cover 1.50
a. Imperf *325.00*
341 A46 20pf dark blue 1.50 .75
Never hinged 5.75
On cover 2.25
342 A47 60pf red brown 3.75 .75
Never hinged 19.00
On cover 6.00
a. Chalky paper ('28) 22.50 13.50
Never hinged 105.00
On cover 45.00
343 A47 80pf slate 10.00 1.50
Never hinged 52.50
On cover 35.00
Nos. 340-343 (4) 15.80 3.30
Set, never hinged 79.00

Universal Postal Union, 50th anniversary.

Traffic Wheel — A48

1925, May 30 *Perf. 13½x13*

No.	Type	Description	Unused	Used
345	A48	5pf deep green	4.25	5.50
		Never hinged	21.00	
		On cover		19.00
346	A48	10pf vermilion	4.25	10.50
		Never hinged	21.00	
		On cover		22.50
		Set, never hinged	42.00	

German Traffic Exhibition, Munich, May 30-Oct. 11, 1925.

German Eagle Watching Rhine Valley — A49

1925 *Perf. 14*

No.	Type	Description	Unused	Used
347	A49	5pf green	.45	.40
		Never hinged	2.25	
		On cover		.75
348	A49	10pf vermilion	.70	.40
		Never hinged	3.75	
		On cover		.75
349	A49	20pf deep blue	5.25	1.10
		Never hinged	29.00	
		On cover		4.25
		Nos. 347-349 (3)	6.40	1.90
		Set, never hinged	35.00	

1000 years' union of the Rhineland with Germany.

Speyer Cathedral A50

1925, Sept. 11 **Engr.**

No.	Type	Description	Unused	Used
350	A50	5m dull green	37.50	16.00
		Never hinged	135.00	
		On cover		65.00

Johann Wolfgang von Goethe — A51

Designs: 3pf, 25pf, Goethe. 5pf, Friedrich von Schiller. 8pf, 20pf, Ludwig van Beethoven. 10pf, Frederick the Great. 15pf, Immanuel Kant. 30pf, Gotthold Ephraim Lessing. 40pf, Gottfried Wilhelm Leibnitz. 50pf, Johann Sebastian Bach. 80pf, Albrecht Durer.

1926-27 **Typo.** *Perf. 14*

No.	Type	Description	Unused	Used
351	A51	3pf olive brown	1.25	.40
		Never hinged	4.75	
		On cover		1.10
352	A51	3pf bister ('27)	1.25	.40
		Never hinged	8.00	
		On cover		1.10
353	A51	5pf dark green	1.25	.40
		Never hinged	9.50	
		On cover		.75
b.		5pf light green ('27)	1.50	.40
		Never hinged	8.00	
		On cover		1.25
354	A51	8pf blue grn ('27)	1.60	.40
		Never hinged	8.75	
		On cover		1.25
355	A51	10pf carmine	1.60	.40
		Never hinged	8.75	
		On cover		1.10
356	A51	15pf vermilion	2.40	.40
		Never hinged	13.50	
		On cover		.75
a.		Booklet pane of 8 + 2 labels	1,100.	
		Never hinged	1,800.	
357	A51	20pf myrtle grn	11.00	1.20
		Never hinged	125.00	
		On cover		5.50
a.		Wmk. sideways	2,250.	375.00
		Never hinged	11,250.	
358	A51	25pf blue	3.50	.90
		Never hinged	29.50	
		On cover		5.50
359	A51	30pf olive grn	6.50	.65
		Never hinged	45.00	
		On cover		4.00
360	A51	40pf dp violet	12.00	.65
		Never hinged	120.00	
		On cover		6.50
361	A51	50pf brown	15.00	8.00
		Never hinged	120.00	
		On cover		27.50
362	A51	80pf chocolate	30.00	5.00
		Never hinged	375.00	
		On cover		57.50
		Nos. 351-362 (12)	87.35	18.80
		Set, never hinged	875.00	

Imperf

No.	Type	Description	Value
351a	A51	3pf Never hinged	525.
352a	A51	3pf Never hinged	525.
353a	A51	5pf Never hinged	525.
354a	A51	8pf Never hinged	525.
356b	A51	15pf Never hinged	525.
357b	A51	20pf Never hinged	2,000.

Nos. 354, 356 and 358 Overprinted

1927, Oct. 10

No.	Type	Description	Unused	Used
363	A51	8pf blue green	17.50	*67.50*
		Never hinged	62.50	
		On cover		110.00
364	A51	15pf vermilion	17.50	*67.50*
		Never hinged	62.50	
		On cover		110.00
365	A51	25pf blue	17.50	*67.50*
		Never hinged	62.50	
		On cover		140.00
		Nos. 363-365 (3)	52.50	*202.50*
		Set, never hinged	187.50	

"I.A.A." stands for "Internationales Arbeitsamt," (Intl. Labor Bureau), an agency of the League of Nations. Issued in connection with a meeting of the I.A.A. in Berlin, Oct. 10-15, 1927, they were on sale to the public.

Pres. Friedrich Ebert A60

Pres. Paul von Hindenburg A61

1928-32 **Typo.** *Perf. 14*

No.	Type	Description	Unused	Used
366	A60	3pf bister	.25	.65
		Never hinged	2.25	
		On cover		1.10
367	A61	4pf lt blue ('31)	.90	1.25
		Never hinged	4.75	
		On cover		1.50
a.		Tête bêche pair	22.50	40.00
		Never hinged	37.50	
b.		Bklt. pane of 9 + label	100.00	190.00
		Never hinged	165.00	
368	A61	5pf lt green	.40	.65
		Never hinged	1.60	
		On cover		1.00
a.		Tête bêche pair	18.00	30.00
		Never hinged	30.00	
b.		Imperf.	125.00	
		Never hinged	250.00	
c.		Bklt. pane of 6 + 4 labels	82.50	120.00
		Never hinged	140.00	
d.		Bklt. pane, 4 #368 + 6 #369	100.00	180.00
		Never hinged	165.00	
369	A60	6pf lt olive grn ('32)	.75	.70
		Never hinged	4.75	
		On cover		1.00
a.		Bklt. pane, 2 #369 + 8 #373	100.00	180.00
		Never hinged	165.00	
370	A60	8pf dark green	.25	.65
		Never hinged	1.60	
		On cover		1.00
a.		Tête bêche pair	18.00	30.00
		Never hinged	30.00	
b.		Watermark sideways	65.00	*145.00*
		Never hinged	160.00	
		On cover		—
371	A60	10pf vermilion	2.00	2.40
		Never hinged	13.50	
		On cover		5.50
372	A60	10pf red violet ('30)	.85	.80
		Never hinged	8.00	
		On cover		1.25
373	A61	12pf orange ('32)	1.60	.70
		Never hinged	9.50	
		On cover		1.00
a.		Tête bêche pair	22.50	37.50
		Never hinged	37.50	
374	A61	15pf car rose	.65	.65
		Never hinged	3.50	
		On cover		1.00
a.		Tête bêche pair	18.00	30.00
		Never hinged	30.00	
b.		Bklt. pane 6 + 4 labels	82.50	120.00
		Never hinged	140.00	
c.		Imperf	350.00	
375	A60	20pf Prus green	6.25	4.75
		Never hinged	40.00	
		On cover		7.25
a.		Imperf.	300.00	
		Never hinged	650.00	
376	A60	20pf gray ('30)	6.25	.80
		Never hinged	47.50	
		On cover		2.50
377	A61	25pf blue	8.00	.95
		Never hinged	47.50	
		On cover		2.00
378	A60	30pf olive green	5.50	.95
		Never hinged	35.00	
		On cover		2.00
379	A61	40pf violet	16.00	.95
		Never hinged	175.00	
		On cover		4.00
380	A60	45pf orange	9.50	3.25
		Never hinged	72.50	
		On cover		6.50
381	A61	50pf brown	10.50	2.75
		Never hinged	115.00	
		On cover		8.00
382	A60	60pf orange brn	12.00	3.25
		Never hinged	115.00	
		On cover		8.00
383	A61	80pf chocolate	24.00	7.25
		Never hinged	275.00	
		On cover		40.00
384	A61	80pf yel bis ('30)	9.25	2.40
		Never hinged	70.00	
		On cover		32.50
		Nos. 366-384 (19)	114.90	35.75
		Set, never hinged	1,025.	

Stamps of 1928 Overprinted

1930, June 30

No.	Type	Description	Unused	Used
385	A60	8pf dark green	1.60	.95
		Never hinged	7.00	
		On cover		1.40
386	A61	15pf carmine rose	2.00	.95
		Never hinged	9.00	
		On cover		1.40
		Set, never hinged	16.00	

Issued in commemoration of the final evacuation of the Rhineland by the Allied forces.

View of Cologne A63

1930 **Engr.** **Wmk. 126**

Inscribed: "Reichsmark"

No.	Type	Description	Unused	Used
387	A63	2m dark blue	27.50	15.00
		Never hinged	110.00	
		On cover		95.00

A type of design A43 in green exists with "Reichsmark" instead of "Mark." It was not issued, though some examples are known in private hands. Value $15,000.

Pres. von Hindenburg — A64

1932, Oct. 1 **Typo.** **Wmk. 126**

No.	Type	Description	Unused	Used
391	A64	4pf blue	.55	.60
		Never hinged	2.00	
		On cover		2.50
392	A64	5pf brt green	.90	.60
		Never hinged	3.25	
		On cover		2.75
393	A64	12pf dp orange	5.00	.60
		Never hinged	18.50	
		On cover		2.50
394	A64	15pf dk red	3.00	*10.00*
		Never hinged	11.00	
		On cover		55.00
395	A64	25pf ultra	2.50	.75
		Never hinged	9.00	
		On cover		8.00
396	A64	40pf violet	21.00	1.60
		Never hinged	77.50	
		On cover		20.00
397	A64	50pf dk brown	4.00	*11.00*
		Never hinged	14.00	
		On cover		55.00
		Nos. 391-397 (7)	36.95	25.15
		Set, never hinged	135.00	

85th birthday of von Hindenburg.

See Nos. 401-431, 436-441. For surcharges and overprints see France N27-N58, Luxembourg N1-N16 and Poland N17-N29.

Frederick the Great — A65

1933, Apr. 12 **Photo.**

No.	Type	Description	Unused	Used
398	A65	6pf dk green	.80	.95
		Never hinged	4.75	
		On cover		1.90
a.		Tête bêche pair	18.00	30.00
		Never hinged	30.00	
399	A65	12pf carmine	1.20	.95
		Never hinged	7.25	
		On cover		1.90
a.		Tête bêche pair	18.00	30.00
		Never hinged	30.00	
b.		Bklt. pane of 5 + label	75.00	65.00
		Never hinged	120.00	
400	A65	25pf ultra	42.50	22.50
		Never hinged	250.00	
		On cover		37.50
		Nos. 398-400 (3)	44.50	24.40
		Set, never hinged	260.00	

Celebration of Potsdam Day.

Hindenburg Type of 1932

1933 **Typo.**

No.	Type	Description	Unused	Used
401	A64	3pf olive bister	17.50	.80
		Never hinged	95.00	
		On cover		2.75
402	A64	4pf dull blue	4.00	.80
		Never hinged	17.50	
		On cover		1.50
403	A64	6pf dk green	2.00	.80
		Never hinged	7.50	
		On cover		2.40
404	A64	8pf dp orange	6.50	.80
		Never hinged	15.00	
		On cover		2.40
a.		Bklt. pane, 3 #404 + 5 #406	110.00	*180.00*
		Never hinged	190.00	
b.		Open "D"	20.00	4.00
		Never hinged	52.50	
405	A64	10pf chocolate	4.00	.80
		Never hinged	22.50	
		On cover		8.00
406	A64	12pf dp carmine	2.40	.80
		Never hinged	15.00	
		On cover		2.40
a.		Bklt. pane, 4 #392 + 4 #406	82.50	*150.00*
		Never hinged	140.00	
407	A64	15pf maroon	5.50	*27.50*
		Never hinged	22.50	
		On cover		55.00
408	A64	20pf brt blue	7.25	1.60
		Never hinged	55.00	
		On cover		20.00
409	A64	30pf olive grn	7.25	1.40
		Never hinged	19.00	
		On cover		20.00
410	A64	40pf red violet	29.00	2.75
		Never hinged	220.00	
		On cover		35.00
411	A64	50pf dk grn & blk	16.00	2.40
		Never hinged	110.00	
		On cover		65.00
412	A64	60pf claret & blk	29.00	1.00
		Never hinged	200.00	
		On cover		60.00
413	A64	80pf dk blue & blk	9.50	1.20
		Never hinged	24.00	
		On cover		87.50
414	A64	100pf orange & blk	25.00	13.50
		Never hinged	140.00	
		On cover		120.00
		Nos. 401-414 (14)	164.90	*56.15*
		Set, never hinged	950.00	

Hindenburg Type of 1932

1933-36 **Wmk. 237** *Perf. 14*

No.	Type	Description	Unused	Used
415	A64	1pf black	.25	.40
		Never hinged	.40	
		On cover		.65
a.		Bklt. pane, 4 #415, 3 #417, label	15.00	*17.00*
		Never hinged	26.00	
b.		Bklt. pane, 3 #415, 3 #416 + 2 #418	21.00	*37.50*
		Never hinged	35.00	
c.		Bklt. pane, 2 #415, 5 #420, label	22.50	*42.50*
		Never hinged	37.50	
d.		Bklt. pane, 4 #415 + 4 #422	21.00	*37.50*
		Never hinged	35.00	
416	A64	3pf olive bis ('34)	.25	.40
		Never hinged	.40	
		On cover		.65
a.		Bklt. pane, 4 #416 + 4 #418	22.50	*42.50*
		Never hinged	37.50	
b.		Bklt. pane, 4 #416 + 4 #419	21.00	*37.50*
		Never hinged	35.00	
c.		Bklt. pane, 6 #416, 1 #422, label	12.00	*17.00*
		Never hinged	19.00	
417	A64	4pf dull blue ('34)	.25	.40
		Never hinged	.40	
		On cover		.65
a.		Bklt. pane, 3 #417, 4 #422, label	21.00	*37.50*
		Never hinged	35.00	
418	A64	5pf brt green ('34)	.25	.40
		Never hinged	.40	
		On cover		.65
a.		Bklt. pane, 2 #418, 5 #419, label	15.00	*17.00*
		Never hinged	19.00	
b.		Bklt. pane, 2 #418, 3 #419 + 3 #420	21.00	*37.50*
		Never hinged	35.00	
c.		Bklt. pane, 4 #418 + 4 #420	40.00	*75.00*
		Never hinged	67.50	
419	A64	6pf dk green ('34)	.25	.40
		Never hinged	.40	
		On cover		.65
b.		Bklt. pane of 7 + label	9.00	*17.00*
		Never hinged	15.00	
c.		Bklt. pane, 1 #419, 6 #422, label	67.50	*105.00*
		Never hinged	120.00	
420	A64	8pf dp orange ('34)	.25	.40
		Never hinged	.40	
		On cover		.65
a.		Bklt. pane, 3 #420, 4 #422, label	15.00	*17.00*
		Never hinged	27.50	
b.		Open "D"	4.50	4.50
		Never hinged	13.00	

421 A64 10pf choc ('34) .25 .40
Never hinged .75
On cover .75
422 A64 12pf dp car ('34) .25 .40
Never hinged .40
On cover .55
a. Bklt. pane of 7 + label 22.50 *42.50*
Never hinged 37.50
423 A64 15pf maroon ('34) .30 .40
Never hinged 1.60
On cover .75
424 A64 20pf brt blue ('34) .45 .40
Never hinged 3.50
On cover .75
425 A64 25pf ultra ('34) .45 .40
Never hinged 3.50
On cover .75
426 A64 30pf olive grn ('34) .75 .40
Never hinged 7.25
On cover .75
427 A64 40pf red violet ('34) 1.60 .40
Never hinged 10.50
On cover 1.60
428 A64 50pf dk grn & blk ('34) 3.25 .40
Never hinged 15.00
On cover 1.90
429 A64 60pf claret & blk ('34) .75 .40
Never hinged 6.50
On cover 1.90
430 A64 80pf dk bl & blk ('36) 2.40 1.25
Never hinged 6.75
On cover 3.75
431 A64 100pf org & blk ('34) 3.25 1.20
Never hinged 8.75
On cover 5.50
Nos. 415-431 (17) 15.20 8.45
Set, never hinged 65.00

Karl Peters — A66

Designs: 3pf, Franz Adolf E. Lüderitz. 6pf, Dr. Gustav Nachtigal. 12pf, Karl Peters. 25pf, Hermann von Wissmann.

1934, June 30 ***Perf. 13x13½***
432 A66 3pf brown & choc 2.50 *6.50*
Never hinged 25.00
On cover 20.00
433 A66 6pf dk grn & choc .95 1.60
Never hinged 9.00
On cover 4.75
434 A66 12pf dk car & choc 2.75 1.60
Never hinged 27.50
On cover 4.75
435 A66 25pf brt blue & choc 9.50 *20.00*
Never hinged 92.50
On cover 47.50
Nos. 432-435 (4) 15.70 29.70
Set, never hinged 154.00

Issued in remembrance of the lost colonies of Germany.

Hindenburg Memorial Issue
Type of 1932
With Black Border

1934, Sept. 4 ***Perf. 14***
436 A64 3pf olive bister .50 .45
Never hinged 4.00
On cover 1.60
437 A64 5pf brt green .50 .55
Never hinged 4.00
On cover 2.00
438 A64 6pf dk green 1.00 .45
Never hinged 9.00
On cover 1.00
439 A64 8pf vermilion 2.40 .45
Never hinged 20.00
On cover 1.60
440 A64 12pf deep carmine 3.00 .45
Never hinged 25.00
On cover 1.00
441 A64 25pf ultra 7.50 *8.75*
Never hinged 65.00
On cover 20.00
Nos. 436-441 (6) 14.90 11.10
Set, never hinged 127.00

Swastika, Sun and Nuremberg Castle — A70

1934, Sept. 1 **Photo.**
442 A70 6pf dark green 3.00 .60
Never hinged 28.00
On cover 1.50
a. Imperf, never hinged *750.00*
443 A70 12pf dark carmine 4.00 .60
Never hinged 40.00
On cover 1.50
a. Imperf, never hinged *750.00*
Set, never hinged 68.00

Nazi Congress at Nuremberg.

Allegory "Saar Belongs to Germany" A71

German Eagle A72

1934, Aug. 26 **Typo.** **Wmk. 237**
444 A71 6pf dark green 3.25 .60
Never hinged 32.50
On cover 1.25
445 A72 12pf dark carmine 4.00 .60
Never hinged 40.00
On cover 1.25
Set, never hinged 72.50

Issued to mark the Saar Plebiscite.

Friedrich von Schiller — A73

1934, Nov. 5
446 A73 6pf green 2.25 .60
Never hinged 27.50
On cover 1.00
447 A73 12pf carmine 5.00 .60
Never hinged 60.00
On cover 1.00
Set, never hinged 87.50

175th anniv. of the birth of von Schiller.

Germania Welcoming Home the Saar — A74

1935, Jan. 16 **Photo.**
448 A74 3pf brown .25 1.20
Never hinged 3.25
On cover 2.40
449 A74 6pf dark green .25 .75
Never hinged 3.25
On cover .80
450 A74 12pf lake 2.00 .75
Never hinged 20.00
On cover 1.00
451 A74 25pf dark blue 7.25 8.50
Never hinged 70.00
On cover 20.00
Nos. 448-451 (4) 9.75 11.20
Set, never hinged 96.50

Return of the Saar to Germany.

German Soldier — A75

1935, Mar. 15
452 A75 6pf dark green 1.60 1.60
Never hinged 8.00
On cover 2.75
453 A75 12pf copper red 1.75 1.60
Never hinged 9.00
On cover 2.75
Set, never hinged 17.00

Issued to commemorate War Heroes' Day.

Wreath and Swastika — A76

1935, Apr. 26 **Unwmk.**
454 A76 6pf dark green 1.10 1.40
Never hinged 8.00
On cover 3.50
455 A76 12pf crimson 1.75 1.40
Never hinged 12.00
On cover 3.50
Set, never hinged 20.00

Young Workers' Professional Competitions.

Heinrich Schütz — A77

Wmk. Swastikas (237)

1935, June 21 **Engr.** ***Perf. 14***
456 A77 6pf shown .85 .80
Never hinged 5.50
On cover 1.60
457 A77 12pf Bach 1.20 .80
Never hinged 8.00
On cover 1.60
458 A77 25pf Handel 1.75 .90
Never hinged 12.00
On cover 5.50
Nos. 456-458 (3) 3.80 2.50
Set, never hinged 25.50

Schutz-Bach-Handel celebration.

"The Eagle" — A80

Designs: 12pf, Modern express train. 25pf, "The Hamburg Flyer." 40pf, Streamlined locomotive.

1935, July 10 ***Perf. 14***
459 A80 6pf dark green .95 .80
Never hinged 6.50
On cover 3.25
a. Imperf 475.00
460 A80 12pf copper red .95 .80
Never hinged 6.50
On cover 3.25
a. Imperf 475.00
461 A80 25pf ultra 5.50 1.90
Never hinged 35.00
On cover 22.50
a. Imperf 475.00
462 A80 40pf red violet 9.00 1.90
Never hinged 60.00
On cover 24.00
a. Imperf 475.00
Nos. 459-462 (4) 16.40 5.40
Set, never hinged 108.00

Centenary of railroad in Germany.

Values for never hinged examples of Nos. 459a-462a are 3x the hinged values.

Bugler of Hitler Youth Movement — A84

1935, July 25 **Photo.**
463 A84 6pf deep green 1.25 2.40
Never hinged 7.25
On cover 5.50
464 A84 15pf brown lake 2.50 3.25
Never hinged 16.00
On cover 7.25
Set, never hinged 23.00

Hitler Youth Meeting.

Eagle and Swastika over Nuremberg — A85

1935, Aug. 30 **Engr.**
465 A85 6pf gray green 1.25 .55
Never hinged 5.50
On cover 1.25
466 A85 12pf dark carmine 2.25 .55
Never hinged 10.50
On cover 1.25
Set, never hinged 16.00

1935 Nazi Congress at Nuremberg.

Nazi Flag Bearer and Feldherrnhalle at Munich — A86

1935, Nov. 5 **Photo.** ***Perf. 13½***
467 A86 3pf brown .25 .70
Never hinged 3.25
On cover 1.25
468 A86 12pf dark carmine .60 .70
Never hinged 9.50
On cover 1.25
Set, never hinged 12.75

12th anniv. of the 1st Hitler "Putsch" at Munich, Nov. 9, 1923.

Airplane — A87

1936, Jan. 6
469 A87 40pf sapphire 6.40 3.25
Never hinged 45.00
On cover 16.00

10th anniv. of the Lufthansa air service.

Gottlieb Daimler — A88

Carl Benz — A89

1936, Feb. 15 ***Perf. 14***
470 A88 6pf dark green .70 1.00
Never hinged 5.50
On cover 1.00
471 A89 12pf copper red .90 1.00
Never hinged 7.25
On cover 1.25
Set, never hinged 12.75

The 50th anniv. of the automobile; Intl. Automobile and Motorcycle Show, Berlin.

Otto von Guericke — A90

1936, May 4
472 A90 6pf dark green .30 1.25
Never hinged 1.30
On cover .80

250th anniv. of the death of the German inventor, Otto von Guericke, May 11, 1686.

Symbolical of Municipalities A91

1936, June 3
473 A91 3pf dark brown .50 .30
Never hinged 2.00
On cover 1.60
474 A91 5pf deep green .70 .30
Never hinged 2.75
On cover 1.60
475 A91 12pf lake .90 .60
Never hinged 3.75
On cover 1.60
476 A91 25pf dark ultra 1.90 1.10
Never hinged 7.50
On cover 6.00
Nos. 473-476 (4) 4.00 2.30
Set, never hinged 16.00

6th Intl. Cong. of Municipalities, June 7-13.

Allegory of Recreation Congress — A92

1936, June 30
477 A92 6pf dark green .65 .55
Never hinged 4.75
On cover 2.50

478 A92 15pf deep claret 1.25 1.00
Never hinged 9.50
On cover 3.25
Set, never hinged 14.25

World Congress for Vacation and Recreation held at Hamburg.

Salute to Swastika — A93

1936, Sept. 3 *Perf. 14*

479 A93 6pf deep green .60 .60
Never hinged 4.50
On cover 1.40
480 A93 12pf copper red 1.00 .60
Never hinged 6.75
On cover 1.40
Set, never hinged 11.25

The 1936 Nazi Congress.

Shield Bearer — A94

1937, Mar. 3 **Engr.** **Unwmk.**

481 A94 3pf brown .50 .40
Never hinged 2.40
On cover .80
482 A94 6pf green .65 .40
Never hinged 3.25
On cover .80
483 A94 12pf carmine 1.25 .75
Never hinged 6.50
On cover 1.25
Nos. 481-483 (3) 2.40 1.55
Set, never hinged 12.00

The Reich's Air Protection League.

German and Austrian Carrying Nazi Flag — A95

Wmk. Swastikas (237)

1938, Apr. 8 **Photo.** *Perf. 14x13½*

Size: 23x28mm

484 A95 6pf dark green .80 .65
Never hinged 2.00
On cover .80

Unwmk. *Perf. 12½*

Size: 21½x26mm

485 A95 6pf deep green .80 1.40
Never hinged 2.00
On cover 1.60

Union of Austria and Germany.

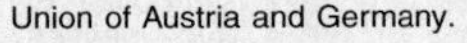

Cathedral Island A96

Hermann Goering Stadium A97

Town Hall, Breslau — A98

Centennial Hall, Breslau — A99

1938, June 21 **Engr.** *Perf. 14*

486 A96 3pf dark brown .30 .55
Never hinged 1.25
On cover 2.00
487 A97 6pf deep green .30 .55
Never hinged 1.25
On cover 1.40
488 A98 12pf copper red .75 .55
Never hinged 3.25
On cover 1.40
489 A99 15pf violet brown 1.75 .80
Never hinged 7.25
On cover 4.00
Nos. 486-489 (4) 3.10 2.45
Set, never hinged 13.00

16th German Gymnastic and Sports Festival held at Breslau, July 23-31, 1938.

Nazi Emblem — A100

1939, Apr. 4 **Photo.** **Wmk. 237**

490 A100 6pf dark green 1.90 4.00
Never hinged 9.00
On cover 7.25
491 A100 12pf deep carmine 2.50 4.00
Never hinged 11.00
On cover 7.25
Set, never hinged 20.00

Young Workers' Professional Competitions.

St. Mary's Church — A101

The Krantor, Danzig — A102

1939, Sept. 18

492 A101 6pf dark green .45 .80
Never hinged 1.60
On cover 1.60
493 A102 12pf orange red .65 .80
Never hinged 2.40
On cover 1.60
Set, never hinged 4.00

Unification of Danzig with the Reich.

Johannes Gutenberg and Library at Leipzig — A103

Designs: 6pf, "High House," Leipzig. 12pf, Old Town Hall, Leipzig. 25pf, View of Leipzig Fair.

Inscribed "Leipziger Messe"

Perf. 10½

1940, Mar. 3 **Photo.** **Unwmk.**

494 A103 3pf dark brown .45 .50
Never hinged 1.60
On cover 1.60
495 A103 6pf dk gray green .45 .50
Never hinged 1.60
On cover 1.25
496 A103 12pf henna brown .45 .50
Never hinged 1.60
On cover 1.25
497 A103 25pf ultra 1.10 1.25
Never hinged 3.25
On cover 4.75
Nos. 494-497 (4) 2.45 2.75
Set, never hinged 8.00

Leipzig Fair.

SEMI-POSTAL STAMPS

Issues of the Republic

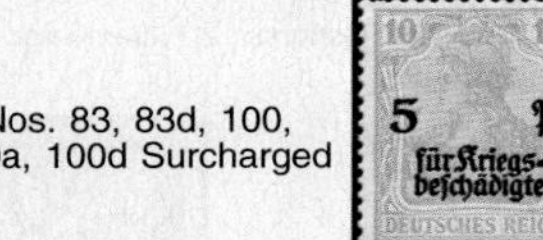
Nos. 83, 83d, 100, 100a, 100d Surcharged

1919, May 1 **Wmk. 125** *Perf. 14*

B1 A16 10pf + 5pf on #83d .45 4.50
Never hinged 1.60
On cover 9.00
a. On #83 5.25 140.00
Never hinged 14.50
On cover 240.00
B2 A22 15pf + 5pf on #100 .45 4.75
Never hinged 1.60
On cover 9.00
a. On #100a 12.00 250.00
Never hinged 32.50
On cover 275.00
b. On #100d 15.00 350.00
Never hinged 47.50
On cover 650.00
Set, never hinged 3.25

The surtax was for the war wounded.

"Planting Charity" — SP1

1922, Dec. 11 **Litho.** **Wmk. 126**

B3 SP1 6m + 4m ultra & brn .25 24.00
Never hinged 1.00
On cover 40.00
B4 SP1 12m + 8m red org & bl gray .25 24.00
Never hinged 1.00
On cover 40.00
Set, never hinged 2.00

Nos. 221, 225 and 196 Surcharged

1923, Feb. 19

B5 A34 5m + 100m .25 9.00
Never hinged .65
On cover 20.00
B6 A29 25m + 500m .25 22.50
Never hinged .65
On cover 47.50
a. Inverted surcharge 75.00
Never hinged 200.00
B7 A32 20m + 1000m 2.10 87.50
Never hinged 4.50
On cover 150.00
a. Inverted surcharge 1,000. 3,750.
Never hinged 2,200.
b. Green background inverted 325.00 1,750.
Never hinged 800.00
Nos. B5-B7 (3) 2.60 119.00
Set, never hinged 6.50

Note following No. 160 applies to Nos. B1-B7.

Feeding the Hungry — SP2

Designs: 10pf+30pf, Giving drink to the thirsty. 20pf+60pf, Clothing the naked. 50pf+1.50m, Healing the sick.

1924, Feb. 25 **Typo.** *Perf. 14½x15*

B8 SP2 5pf + 15pf dk grn 1.75 3.50
Never hinged 6.50
On cover 9.50
B9 SP2 10pf + 30pf ver 1.75 3.50
Never hinged 6.50
On cover 12.00
B10 SP2 20pf + 60pf dk blue 5.50 8.50
Never hinged 22.00
On cover 24.00
B11 SP2 50pf + 1.50m red brn 20.00 67.50
Never hinged 95.00
On cover 120.00
Nos. B8-B11 (4) 29.00 83.00
Set, never hinged 130.00

The surtax was used for emergency aid. See No. B58.

Prussia — SP6

1925, Dec. 15 *Perf. 14*

Inscribed: "1925"

B12 SP6 5pf + 5pf shown .60 2.00
Never hinged 1.75
On cover 8.00
B13 SP6 10pf + 10pf Bavaria 1.75 5.50
Never hinged 5.50
On cover 12.00
B14 SP6 20pf + 20pf Saxony 8.00 12.00
Never hinged 28.00
On cover 35.00
a. Bklt. pane of 2 + 2 labels 375.00 1,100.
Never hinged 600.00
Nos. B12-B14 (3) 10.35 19.50
Set, never hinged 35.00

1926, Dec. 1 **Inscribed: "1926"**

B15 SP6 5pf + 5pf Wurttemberg 1.00 2.25
Never hinged 3.25
On cover 4.75
B16 SP6 10pf + 10pf Baden 1.75 3.00
Never hinged 5.25
On cover 6.00
a. Bklt. pane of 6 + 2 labels 275.00 675.00
Never hinged 450.00
B17 SP6 25pf + 25pf Thuringia 9.00 18.00
Never hinged 27.50
On cover 42.50
B18 SP6 50pf + 50pf Hesse 42.50 90.00
Never hinged 135.00
On cover 140.00
Nos. B15-B18 (4) 54.25 113.25
Set, never hinged 170.00

Nos. B15-B16 are usually found with sideways watermarks. Both exist with an upright watermark, which is very scarce. No. B18 is usually found with an upright watermark. Examples of No. B18 with a sideways watermark are scarce.

See Nos. B23-B32.

Pres. Paul von Hindenburg — SP13

1927, Sept. 26 **Photo.**

B19 SP13 8pf dark green .75 1.50
Never hinged 3.00
On cover 6.00
a. Bklt. pane, 4 #B19, 3 #B20 + label 110.00 190.00
Never hinged 175.00
B20 SP13 15pf scarlet 1.25 2.40
Never hinged 4.50
On cover 8.00
B21 SP13 25pf deep blue 9.00 21.00
Never hinged 32.50
On cover 45.00
B22 SP13 50pf bister brown 11.00 22.50
Never hinged 40.00
On cover 50.00
Nos. B19-B22 (4) 22.00 47.40
Set, never hinged 80.00

80th birthday of Pres. Hindenburg. The stamps were sold at double face value. The surtax was given to a fund for War Invalids.

Arms Type of 1925

Design: 8pf+7pf, Mecklenburg-Schwerin.

1928, Nov. 15 **Typo.**

Design Type SP6

Inscribed: "1928"

B23 5pf + 5pf Hamburg .60 3.75
Never hinged 2.00
On cover 6.00
B24 8pf + 7pf multi .50 3.75
Never hinged 1.75
On cover 6.00
a. Bklt. pane, 4 #B24, 3 #B25 + label 225.00 450.00
Never hinged 400.00
B25 15pf + 15pf Oldenburg .75 3.75
Never hinged 2.50
On cover 8.00
B26 25pf + 25pf Brunswick 16.00 45.00
Never hinged 52.50
On cover 80.00
B27 50pf + 50pf Anhalt 37.50 90.00
Never hinged 135.00
On cover 130.00
Nos. B23-B27 (5) 55.35 146.25
Set, never hinged 194.00

Nos. B23-B26 are valued with sideways watermark. All exist with upright watermark, which is scarce to very rare.

1929, Nov. 4 **Inscribed: "1929"**

Coats of Arms: 8pf+4pf, Lippe-Detmold. 25pf+10pf, Mecklenburg-Strelitz. 50pf+40pf, Schaumburg-Lippe.

B28 SP6 5pf + 2pf Bremen .75 *2.00*
Never hinged 2.25
On cover 4.00
a. Bklt. pane of 6 + 2 labels 90.00 140.00
Never hinged 150.00
B29 SP6 8pf + 4pf multi .85 *2.00*
Never hinged 2.75
On cover 4.00
a. Bklt. pane, 4 #B29, 3 #B30 + label 120.00 140.00
Never hinged 190.00
B30 SP6 15pf + 5pf Lubeck 1.20 1.50
Never hinged 3.75
On cover 5.50
B31 SP6 25pf + 10pf multi 15.00 *45.00*
Never hinged 52.50
On cover 55.00
B32 SP6 50pf + 40pf choc, ocher & red 40.00 *85.00*
Never hinged 120.00
On cover 120.00
a. "PE" for "PF" 150.00 400.00
Never hinged 475.00
Nos. B28-B32 (5) 57.80 *135.50*
Set, never hinged 180.00

Cathedral of Aachen — SP24

Brandenburg Gate, Berlin — SP25

Castle of Marienwerder SP26

Statue of St. Kilian and Marienburg Fortress at Würzburg SP27

Souvenir Sheet

Wmk. 223

1930, Sept. 12 **Engr.** ***Perf. 14***

B33 Sheet of 4 385.00 *1,250.*
Never hinged 1,100.
On cover *1,800.*
a. SP24 8pf + 4pf dark green 28.00 *87.50*
Never hinged 77.50
b. SP25 15pf + 5pf carmine 28.00 *87.50*
Never hinged 77.50
c. SP26 25pf + 10p dark blue 28.00 *87.50*
Never hinged 77.50
d. SP27 50pf + 40pf dark brown 28.00 *87.50*
Never hinged 77.50
Any single, never hinged 50.00
Any single, on cover 200.00

Intl. Phil. Exhib., Berlin, Sept. 12-21, 1930.

No. B33 is watermarked Eagle on each stamp and "IPOSTA"-"1930" in the margins. Size: approximately 105x150. Each holder of an admission ticket was entitled to purchase one sheet. The ticket cost 1m and the sheet 1.70m (face value 98pf, charity 59pf, special paper 13pf).

The margin of the souvenir sheet is ungummed.

Types of International Philatelic Exhibition Issue

1930, Nov. 1 **Wmk. 126**

B34 SP24 8 + 4pf dp green .50 .95
Never hinged 3.00
On cover 4.00
a. Bklt. pane of 7 + label 90.00 175.00
Never hinged 150.00
b. Bklt. pane, 3 #B34, 4 #B35 + label 120.00 190.00
Never hinged 190.00
B35 SP25 15 + 5pf car .60 *1.25*
Never hinged 4.00
On cover 6.50
B36 SP26 25 + 10pf dk blue 8.00 *20.00*
Never hinged 28.00
On cover 35.00
B37 SP27 50 + 40pf dp brn 22.50 *77.50*
Never hinged 75.00
On cover 120.00
Nos. B34-B37 (4) 31.60 *99.70*
Set, never hinged 110.00

The surtax was for charity.

The Zwinger at Dresden SP28

Breslau City Hall SP29

Heidelberg Castle SP30

Holsten Gate, Lübeck SP31

1931, Nov. 1

B38 SP28 8 + 4pf dk grn .45 *1.20*
Never hinged 2.75
On cover 5.50
a. Bklt. pane of 7 + label 90.00 175.00
Never hinged 150.00
b. Bklt. pane, 3 #B38, 4 #B39 + label 100.00 190.00
Never hinged 175.00
B39 SP29 15 + 5pf carmine .45 *1.20*
Never hinged 2.75
On cover 6.50
B40 SP30 25 + 10pf dk blue 12.50 *30.00*
Never hinged 45.00
On cover 47.50
B41 SP31 50 + 40pf dp brown 35.00 *70.00*
Never hinged 130.00
On cover 120.00
Nos. B38-B41 (4) 48.40 *102.40*
Set, never hinged 180.00

The surtax was for charity.

Nos. B38-B39 Surcharged

1932, Feb. 2

B42 SP28 6 + 4pf on 8+4pf 4.50 *9.75*
Never hinged 20.00
On cover 16.00
B43 SP29 12 + 3pf on 15+5pf 5.25 *12.00*
Never hinged 25.00
On cover 24.00
Set, never hinged 45.00

Wartburg Castle — SP32

Stolzenfels Castle — SP33

Nuremberg Castle — SP34

Lichtenstein Castle — SP35

Marburg Castle — SP36

1932, Nov. 1 **Engr.**

B44 SP32 4 + 2pf lt blue .60 1.20
Never hinged 3.00
On cover 5.50
a. Bklt. pane, 5 #B44, 5 #B45 45.00 85.00
Never hinged 75.00
B45 SP33 6 + 4pf olive grn .90 1.20
Never hinged 4.00
On cover 4.75
B46 SP34 12 + 3pf lt red .60 1.20
Never hinged 3.50
On cover 6.50
b. Bklt. pane of 8 + 2 labels 45.00 85.00
Never hinged 75.00
B47 SP35 25 + 10pf dp blue 9.50 *19.00*
Never hinged 32.50
On cover 32.50
B48 SP36 40 + 40pf brn vio 32.50 *65.00*
Never hinged 110.00
On cover 95.00
Nos. B44-B48 (5) 44.10 *87.60*
Set, never hinged 153.00

The surtax was for charity.

"Tannhäuser" SP37

Designs: 4pf+2pf, "Der Fliegende Hollander." 5pf+2pf, "Das Rheingold." 6pf+4pf, "Die Meistersinger." 8pf+4pf, "Die Walkure." 12pf+3pf, "Siegfried." 20pf+10pf, "Tristan und Isolde." 25pf+15pf, "Lohengrin." 40pf+35pf, "Parsifal."

Wmk. Swastikas (237)

1933, Nov. 1 ***Perf. 13½x13***

B49 SP37 3 + 2pf bis brn 4.25 *6.00*
Never hinged 25.00
On cover 9.50
B50 SP37 4 + 2pf dk blue 2.75 *2.40*
Never hinged 15.00
On cover 4.00
b. Bklt. pane, 5 #B50, 5 #B52 140.00 260.00
Never hinged 225.00
B51 SP37 5 + 2pf brt grn 6.75 *7.25*
Never hinged 40.00
On cover 13.00
B52 SP37 6 + 4pf gray grn 2.75 *2.40*
Never hinged 15.00
On cover 4.00
B53 SP37 8 + 4pf dp org 4.00 4.00
Never hinged 22.50
On cover 8.00
b. Bklt. pane, 5 #B53, 4 #B54 + label 140.00 260.00
Never hinged 225.00
B54 SP37 12 + 3pf brn red 4.00 2.75
Never hinged 22.50
On cover 4.75
B55 SP37 20 + 10pf blue 200.00 *200.00*
Never hinged 1,200.
On cover 360.00
B56 SP37 25 + 15pf ultra 47.50 *40.00*
Never hinged 270.00
On cover 72.50
B57 SP37 40 + 35pf mag 125.00 *125.00*
Never hinged 750.00
On cover 200.00
Nos. B49-B57 (9) 397.00 389.80
Set, never hinged 2,360.

Perf. 13½x14

B50a SP37 4 + 2pf dark blue 2.75 *3.00*
Never hinged 16.00
On cover 4.50
B52a SP37 6 + 4pf gray grn 2.75 *4.75*
Never hinged 16.00
On cover 8.00
B53a SP37 8 + 4pf dp org 3.50 *4.50*
Never hinged 20.00
On cover 8.00
B54a SP37 12 + 3pf brn red 3.50 *6.75*
Never hinged 20.00
On cover 10.50
B55a SP37 20 + 10pf blue 125.00 100.00
Never hinged 750.00
On cover 150.00
Nos. B50a-B55a (5) 137.50 119.00
Set, never hinged 822.00

Types of Semi-Postal Stamps of 1924 Issue Overprinted

Souvenir Sheet

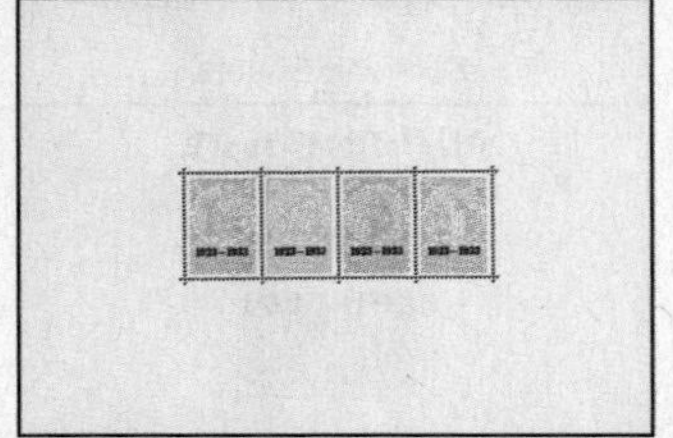

1933, Nov. 29 **Typo.** ***Perf. 14½***

B58 Sheet of 4 1,450. *10,500.*
Never hinged 5,600.
On cover *12,000.*
a. SP2 5 + 15pf dark green 90.00 *400.00*
b. SP2 10 + 30pf vermilion 90.00 *400.00*
c. SP2 20 + 60pf dark blue 90.00 *400.00*
d. SP2 50pf + 1.50m dk brown 90.00 *400.00*
Any single, never hinged 240.00
Any single, on cover 650.00

The Swastika watermark covers the four stamps and above them appears a further watermark "10 Jahre Deutsche Nothilfe" and "1923-1933" below. Sheet size: 208x148mm.

The margin of the souvenir sheet is ungummed.

Businessman SP46

Judge SP54

Designs: 4pf+2pf, Blacksmith. 5pf+2pf, Mason. 6pf+4f, Miner. 8pf+4pf, Architect. 12pf+3pf, Farmer. 20pf+10pf, Agricultural Chemist. 25pf+15pf, Sculptor.

1934, Nov. 5 **Engr.** ***Perf. 13x13½***

B59 SP46 3 + 2pf brown 1.25 *1.50*
Never hinged 7.25
On cover 4.50
B60 SP46 4 + 2pf black .90 *1.50*
Never hinged 4.75
On cover 4.00
a. Bklt. pane, 5 #B60, 5 #B62 52.50 105.00
Never hinged 90.00
B61 SP46 5 + 2pf green 6.50 *8.00*
Never hinged 35.00
On cover 20.00
B62 SP46 6 + 4pf dull grn .75 *.65*
Never hinged 4.00
On cover 4.00
B63 SP46 8 + 4pf org brn 1.25 *2.00*
Never hinged 7.25
On cover 4.50
a. Bklt. pane, 5 #B63, 4 #B64 + label 82.50 150.00
Never hinged 140.00
B64 SP46 12 + 3pf hn brn .55 *.65*
Never hinged 3.25
On cover 4.00
B65 SP46 20 + 10pf Prus bl 16.00 *22.50*
Never hinged 90.00
On cover 40.00
B66 SP46 25 + 15pf ultra 17.50 *22.50*
Never hinged 95.00
On cover 40.00
B67 SP54 40 + 35pf plum 37.50 *70.00*
Never hinged 200.00
On cover 110.00
Nos. B59-B67 (9) 82.20 *129.30*
Set, never hinged 450.00

Souvenir Sheet

SP55

1935, June 23 **Wmk. 241** ***Perf. 14***

B68 SP55 Sheet of 4 875.00 700.00
On cover 800.00
a. 3pf red brown 35.00 40.00
b. 6pf dark green 35.00 40.00
c. 12pf dark carmine 35.00 40.00
d. 25pf dark blue 35.00 40.00
Any single, on cover 110.00

Watermarked cross on each stamp and "OSTROPA 1935" in the margins of the sheet. Size: 148x104mm. 1.70m was the price of a ticket of admission to the Intl. Exhib., Königsberg, June 23-July 3, 1935.

Because the gum on No. B68 contains sulphuric acid and tends to damage the sheet, most collectors prefer to remove it. **Catalogue unused values are for sheet and singles without gum.**

East Prussia — SP59

Designs (Costumes of Various Sections of Germany): 4pf+3pf, Silesia. 5pf+3pf, Rhineland. 6pf+4pf, Lower Saxony. 8pf+4pf, Brandenburg. 12pf+6pf, Black Forest. 15pf+10pf, Hesse. 25pf+15pf, Upper Bavaria. 30pf+20pf, Friesland. 40pf+35pf, Franconia.

Wmk. Swastikas (237)

1935, Oct. 4 ***Perf. 14x13½***

B69 SP59 3 + 2pf dk brown .30 *.40*
Never hinged 1.60
On cover 2.25
a. Bklt. pane, 4 #B69, 5 #B74 + label 40.00 75.00
Never hinged 70.00

B70 SP59 4 + 3pf gray 1.20 *1.50*
Never hinged 6.50
On cover 3.00

B71 SP59 5 + 3pf emerald .30 *1.00*
Never hinged 1.60
On cover 2.00

a. Bklt. pane, 5 #B71, 5 #B72 27.50 50.00
Never hinged 45.00

B72 SP59 6 + 4pf dk green .25 *.40*
Never hinged .80
On cover 1.60

B73 SP59 8 + 4pf yel brn 1.90 1.50
Never hinged 9.50
On cover 5.50

B74 SP59 12 + 6pf dk car .25 *.40*
Never hinged 1.10
On cover 1.00

B75 SP59 15 + 10pf red brn 4.50 *6.00*
Never hinged 22.50
On cover 21.00

B76 SP59 25 + 15pf ultra 8.00 6.50
Never hinged 40.00
On cover 20.00

B77 SP59 30 + 20pf olive brn 9.50 *20.00*
Never hinged 47.50
On cover 32.50

B78 SP59 40 + 35p plum 8.50 *14.00*
Never hinged 45.00
On cover 32.50

Nos. B69-B78 (10) 34.70 *51.70*
Set, never hinged 160.00

Skating — SP69

12+6pf, Ski jump. 25+15pf, Bobsledding.

1935, Nov. 25 ***Perf. 13½***

B79 SP69 6 + 4pf green .95 *1.40*
Never hinged 5.00
On cover 3.25

B80 SP69 12 + 6pf carmine 1.90 1.20
Never hinged 10.00
On cover 4.75

B81 SP69 25 + 15pf ultra 8.00 *8.00*
Never hinged 40.00
On cover 16.00

Nos. B79-B81 (3) 10.85 10.60
Set, never hinged 55.00

Winter Olympic Games held in Bavaria, Feb. 6-16, 1936.

1936, May 8

Designs: 3pf+2pf, Horizontal bar. 4pf+3pf, Diving. 6pf+4pf, Soccer. 8pf+4pf, Throwing javelin. 12pf+6pf, Torch runner. 15pf+10pf, Fencing. 25pf+15pf, Sculling. 40pf+35pf, Equestrian.

B82 SP69 3 + 2pf brown .30 *.45*
Never hinged 2.00
On cover 1.60

a. Bklt. pane, 5 #B82, 5 #B86 27.50 50.00
Never hinged 45.00

B83 SP69 4 + 3pf indigo .25 *.75*
Never hinged 1.80
On cover 2.25

a. Bklt. pane, 5 #B83, 5 #B84 27.50 50.00
Never hinged 45.00

B84 SP69 6 + 4pf green .25 *.45*
Never hinged 1.60
On cover 2.00

B85 SP69 8 + 4pf red org 3.00 1.25
Never hinged 20.00
On cover 3.00

B86 SP69 12 + 6pf carmine .35 *.45*
Never hinged 2.25
On cover 1.60

B87 SP69 15 + 10pf brn vio 5.50 3.00
Never hinged 35.00
On cover 12.00

B88 SP69 25 + 15pf ultra 3.00 *4.00*
Never hinged 20.00
On cover 12.00

B89 SP69 40 + 35pf violet 5.50 *8.00*
Never hinged 35.00
On cover 17.50

Nos. B82-B89 (8) 18.15 *18.35*
Set, never hinged 110.00

Summer Olympic Games, Berlin, 8/1-16/36.
See Nos. B91-B92.

Souvenir Sheet

Horse Race — SP80

1936, June 22 Wmk. 237 ***Perf. 14***

B90 SP80 42pf brown 12.50 *14.50*
Never hinged 25.00
On cover 40.00

A surtax of 1.08m was to provide a 100,000m sweepstakes prize. Wmk. 237 appears on the stamp, with "Munchen Riem 1936" watermarked on sheet margin.
For overprint see No. B105.

Types of 1936
Souvenir Sheets

1936, Aug. 1 ***Perf. 14x13½***

B91 SP69 Sheet of 4 40.00 *50.00*
Never hinged 110.00
On cover *200.00*

B92 SP69 Sheet of 4 40.00 *50.00*
Never hinged 110.00
On cover *200.00*

Set, never hinged 220.00

11th Olympic Games, Berlin. No. B91 contains Nos. B82-B84, B89. No. B92 contains Nos. B85-B88.
Wmk. 237 appears on each stamp with "XI Olympische Spiele-Berlin 1936" watermarked on sheet margin. Sold for 1m each.

Frontier Highway, Munich — SP81

Designs: 4pf+3pf, Ministry of Aviation. 5pf+3pf, Nuremberg Memorial. 6pf+4pf, Bridge over the Saale, Saxony. 8pf+4pf, Germany Hall, Berlin. 12pf+6pf, German Alpine highway. 15pf+10pf, Fuhrer House, Munich. 25pf+15pf, Bridge over the Mangfall. 40pf+35pf, Museum of German Art, Munich.

Perf. 13½x14

1936, Sept. 21 **Unwmk.**

B93 SP81 3pf + 2pf blk brn .25 *.40*
Never hinged 1.00
On cover 1.20

a. Bklt. pane, 4 #B93 + 5 #B98 + label 27.50 55.00
Never hinged 45.00

B94 SP81 4pf + 3pf black .25 *.50*
Never hinged 1.20
On cover 2.00

B95 SP81 5pf + 3pf brt grn .25 *.40*
Never hinged 1.00
On cover 1.20

a. Bklt. pane, 5 #B95, 5 #B96) 14.00 26.00
Never hinged 22.50

B96 SP81 6pf + 4pf dk grn .25 *.40*
Never hinged 1.00
On cover .80

B97 SP81 8pf + 4pf brown .95 *1.40*
Never hinged 5.50
On cover 2.40

B98 SP81 12pf + 6pf brn car .25 *.40*
Never hinged 1.00
On cover 1.40

B99 SP81 15pf + 10pf vio brn 3.50 *3.50*
Never hinged 20.00
On cover 7.50

B100 SP81 25pf + 15pf indigo 2.40 *7.00*
Never hinged 13.50
On cover 12.00

B101 SP81 40pf + 35pf rose vio 4.00 *6.00*
Never hinged 22.50
On cover 16.00

Nos. B93-B101 (9) 12.10 *20.00*
Set, never hinged 66.00

Souvenir Sheets

Adolf Hitler — SP90

Wmk. 237

1937, Apr. 5 Photo. ***Perf. 14***

B102 SP90 Sheet of 4 19.00 12.50
Never hinged 55.00
On cover *75.00*

a. 6pf dark green 1.20 *1.60*
Never hinged 4.50
On cover 5.50

48th birthday of Adolf Hitler. Sold for 1m.
See Nos. B103-B104. For overprint see No. B106.

1937, Apr. 16 ***Imperf.***

B103 SP90 Sheet of 4 40.00 24.00
Never hinged 175.00
On cover 50.00

a. 6pf dark green 4.00 3.00
Never hinged 12.50
On cover 12.00

German Natl. Phil. Exhib., Berlin, June 16-18, 1937 and the Phil. Exhib. of the Stamp Collectors Group of the Strength Through Joy Organization at Hamburg, Apr. 17-20, 1937.
Sold at the Exhib. post offices for 1.50m.

No. B102 with Marginal Inscriptions
Perf. 14 and Rouletted

1937, June 10 **Wmk. 237**

B104 SP90 Sheet of 4 40.00 *70.00*
Never hinged 250.00
On cover 200.00

a. 6pf dark grn + 25pf label 4.00 7.00
Never hinged 16.00
On cover 20.00

No. B104 inscribed in the margin beside each stamp "25 Rpf. einschliesslich Kulturspende" in three lines.
The sheets were rouletted to allow for separation of each stamp with its component label. Sold at the post office as individual stamps with labels attached or in complete sheets.

Souvenir Sheet No. B90 Overprinted in Red

1937, Aug. 1 ***Perf. 14***

B105 SP80 42pf brown 65.00 *105.00*
Never hinged 150.00
On cover 550.00

a. Inverted overprint *14,500.* *27,500.*

4th running of the "Brown Ribbon" horse race at the Munich-Riem Race Course, Aug. 1, 1937.

Souvenir Sheet No. B104 Overprinted in Black on Each Stamp

Perf. 14 and Rouletted

1937, Sept. 3 **Wmk. 237**

B106 SP90 Sheet of 4 75.00 45.00
Never hinged 260.00
On cover 80.00

a. 6pf dark grn + 25pf label 4.50 6.00
Never hinged 14.00
On cover 19.00

1937 Nazi Congress at Nuremburg.

Lifeboat — SP91

Designs: 4pf+3pf, Lightship "Elbe I." 5pf+3pf, Fishing smacks. 6pf+4pf, Steamer. 8pf+4pf, Sailing vessel. 12pf+6pf, The "Tannenberg." 15pf+10pf, Sea-Train "Schwerin." 25pf+15pf, S. S. Hamburg. 40pf+35pf, S. S. Bremen.

Perf. 13½

1937, Nov. 4 Engr. **Unwmk.**

B107 SP91 3pf + 2pf dk brwn .25 .40
Never hinged .40
On cover 1.25

a. Bklt. pane, 4 #B107 + 5 #B112 + label 27.50 *50.00*
Never hinged 47.50

B108 SP91 4pf + 3pf black 1.00 *1.20*
Never hinged 8.00
On cover 2.75

B109 SP91 5pf + 3pf yel grn .25 *.40*
Never hinged .40
On cover 1.75

a. Bklt. pane, 5 #B109, 5 #B110 14.00 *27.50*
Never hinged 24.00

B110 SP91 6pf + 4pf bl grn .25 *.40*
Never hinged .40
On cover 1.25

B111 SP91 8pf + 4pf orange .60 *1.25*
Never hinged 4.75
On cover 2.75

B112 SP91 12pf + 6pf car lake .25 .40
Never hinged .80
On cover 1.25

B113 SP91 15pf + 10pf vio brn 1.25 *4.00*
Never hinged 10.00
On cover 12.00

B114 SP91 25pf + 15pf ultra 3.00 *4.00*
Never hinged 24.00
On cover 9.50

B115 SP91 40pf + 35pf red vio 5.00 *8.00*
Never hinged 40.00
On cover 20.00

Nos. B107-B115 (9) 11.85 *20.05*
Set, never hinged 88.75

No. B115 actually pictures the S.S. Europa.

Youth Carrying Torch and Laurel — SP100

Wmk. 237

1938, Jan. 28 Photo. ***Perf. 14***

B116 SP100 6 + 4pf dk green 1.20 *2.00*
Never hinged 8.00
On cover 3.25

B117 SP100 12 + 8pf brt car 1.20 *2.00*
Never hinged 8.00
On cover 4.00

Set, never hinged 16.00

Assumption of power by the Nazis, 5th anniv.

Adolf Hitler — SP101

1938, Apr. 13 Engr. **Unwmk.**

B118 SP101 12 + 38pf copper red 2.00 *2.75*
Never hinged 10.00
On cover 5.50

Hitler's 49th birthday.

Horsewoman SP102

1938, July 20

B119 SP102 42 + 108pf dp brn 22.50 *45.00*
Never hinged 125.00
On cover 67.50

5th "Brown Ribbon" at Munich.

Adolf Hitler — SP103

1938, Sept. 1

B120 SP103 6 + 19pf deep grn 2.25 *4.00*
Never hinged 16.00
On cover 6.50

1938 Nazi Congress at Nuremberg. The surtax was for Hitler's National Culture Fund.

Theater at Saarbrücken SP104

1938, Oct. 9 Photo. **Wmk. 237**

B121 SP104 6 + 4pf blue grn 1.50 *2.00*
Never hinged 9.50
On cover 5.50

B122 SP104 12 + 8pf dk car 1.90 *2.75*
Never hinged 12.00
On cover 8.00
Set, never hinged 21.50

Inauguration of the theater of the District of Saarpfalz at Saarbrücken. The surtax was for Hitler's National Culture Fund.

Castle of Forchtenstein SP105

Designs (scenes in Austria and various flowers): 4pf+3pf, Flexenstrasse in Vorarlberg. 5pf+3pf, Zell am See, Salzburg. 6pf+4pf, Grossglockner. 8pf+4pf, Ruins of Aggstein. 12pf+6pf, Prince Eugene Monument, Vienna. 15pf+10pf, Erzberg. 25pf+15pf, Hall, Tyrol. 40pf+35pf, Braunau.

Unwmk.
1938, Nov. 18 Engr. *Perf. 14*

B123 SP105 3 + 2pf ol brn .25 *.45*
Never hinged .65
On cover 1.60
a. Bklt. pane, 4 #B123, 5 #B128 + label 27.50 50.00
Never hinged 47.50
B124 SP105 4 + 3pf indigo 1.75 1.25
Never hinged 8.75
On cover 3.25
B125 SP105 5 + 3pf emer .25 *.45*
Never hinged .50
On cover 2.00
a. Bklt. pane, 5 #B125, 5 #B126 12.50 27.50
Never hinged 24.00
B126 SP105 6 + 4pf dk grn .25 .40
Never hinged .50
On cover 1.25
B127 SP105 8 + 4pf red org 1.75 1.25
Never hinged 8.75
On cover 3.25
B128 SP105 12 + 6pf dk car .25 *.45*
Never hinged .55
On cover 1.25
B129 SP105 15 + 10pf dp cl 3.00 *4.50*
Never hinged 16.00
On cover 12.00
B130 SP105 25 + 15pf dk bl 2.75 *4.50*
Never hinged 13.50
On cover 8.00
B131 SP105 40 + 35pf plum 6.25 *8.00*
Never hinged 32.50
On cover 16.00
Nos. B123-B131 (9) 16.50 *21.25*
Set, never hinged 81.00

The surtax was for "Winter Help."

Sudeten Couple — SP114

1938, Dec. 2 Photo. Wmk. 237

B132 SP114 6 + 4pf blue grn 1.60 *3.25*
Never hinged 13.50
On cover 6.50
B133 SP114 12 + 8pf dk car 2.40 *3.25*
Never hinged 19.00
On cover 8.00
Set, never hinged 32.50

Annexation of the Sudeten Territory. The surtax was for Hitler's National Culture Fund.

Early Types of Automobiles SP115

Designs: 12pf+8pf, Racing cars. 25pf+10pf, Modern automobile.

1939

B134 SP115 6 + 4pf dk grn 3.75 3.50
Never hinged 24.00
On cover 8.00
B135 SP115 12 + 8pf brt car 3.75 3.50
Never hinged 24.00
On cover 9.50
B136 SP115 25 + 10pf dp blue 6.25 *6.50*
Never hinged 40.00
On cover 14.50
Nos. B134-B136 (3) 13.75 13.50
Set, never hinged 88.00

Berlin Automobile and Motorcycle Exhibition. The surtax was for Hitler's National Culture Fund. For overprints see Nos. B141-B143.

Adolf Hitler — SP118

Unwmk.
1939, Apr. 13 Engr. *Perf. 14*

B137 SP118 12 + 38pf carmine 1.50 *4.50*
Never hinged 9.00
On cover 9.50

Hitler's 50th birthday. The surtax was for Hitler's National Culture Fund.

Exhibition Building — SP119

1939, Apr. 22 Photo. *Perf. 12½*

B138 SP119 6 + 4pf dk green 1.25 *3.00*
Never hinged 6.50
On cover 7.25
B139 SP119 15 + 5pf dp plum 1.90 *4.00*
Never hinged 9.50
On cover 8.00
Set, never hinged 16.00

Horticultural Exhib. held at Stuttgart. Surtax for Hitler's National Culture Fund.

Adolf Hitler — SP120

Perf. 14x13½
1939, Apr. 28 Wmk. 237

B140 SP120 6 + 19pf black brn 4.00 *5.00*
Never hinged 12.50
On cover 9.50

Day of National Labor. The surtax was for Hitler's National Culture Fund.
See No. B147.

Nos. B134-B136 Overprinted in Black

1939, May 18 *Perf. 14*

B141 SP115 6 + 4pf dk grn 19.00 *27.50*
Never hinged 75.00
On cover 60.00
B142 SP115 12 + 8pf brt car 19.00 *27.50*
Never hinged 75.00
On cover 60.00
B143 SP115 25 + 10pf dp bl 19.00 *27.50*
Never hinged 75.00
On cover 60.00
Nos. B141-B143 (3) 57.00 *82.50*
Set, never hinged 225.00

Nurburgring Auto Races, 5/21, 7/23/39.

Racehorse "Investment" and Jockey SP121

1939, June 18 Engr. Unwmk.

B144 SP121 25 + 50pf ultra 15.00 15.00
Never hinged 65.00
On cover 28.00

70th anniv. of the German Derby. The surtax was divided between Hitler's National Culture Fund and the race promoters.

Man Holding Rearing Horse — SP122

1939, July 12

B145 SP122 42 + 108pf dp brn 15.00 *24.00*
Never hinged 62.50
On cover 40.00

6th "Brown Ribbon" at Munich.

"Venetian Woman" by Albrecht Dürer — SP123

1939, July 12 Photo. Wmk. 237

B146 SP123 6 + 19pf dk grn 5.25 *10.00*
Never hinged 27.50
On cover 16.00

Day of German Art. The surtax was used for Hitler's National Culture Fund.

Hitler Type of 1939
Inscribed "Reichsparteitag 1939"

1939, Aug. 25 *Perf. 14x13½*

B147 SP120 6 + 19pf blk brn 4.50 *9.50*
Never hinged 19.00
On cover 14.50

1939 Nazi Congress at Nuremberg.

Meeting in German Hall, Berlin SP124

Designs: 4pf+3pf, Meeting of postal and telegraph employees. 5pf+3pf, Professional competitions. 6pf+4pf, 6pf+9pf, Professional camp. 8pf+4pf, 8pf+12pf, Gold flag competitions. 10pf+5pf, Awarding prizes. 12&f+6pf, 12pf+18pf, Automobile race. 15pf+10pf, Sports. 16pf+10pf, 16pf+24pf, Postal police. 20pf+10pf, 20pf+30pf, Glider workshops. 24pf+10pf, 24pf+36pf, Mail coach. 25pf+15pf, Convalescent home, Konigstein.

Perf. 13½x14
1939-41 Unwmk. Photo.

B148 3 + 2pf bister brn 2.25 *5.25*
Never hinged 13.00
On cover 13.50
B149 4 + 3pf slate blue 2.00 *5.25*
Never hinged 11.00
On cover 12.00
B150 5 + 3pf brt bl grn .60 *1.50*
Never hinged 3.25
On cover 4.75
B151 6 + 4pf myrtle grn .75 *1.50*
Never hinged 4.00
On cover 4.00
B151A 6 + 9pf dk grn ('41) .75 *2.25*
Never hinged 4.00
On cover 3.25
B152 8 + 4pf dp org .75 *1.50*
Never hinged 4.00
On cover 4.00
B152A 8 + 12pf hn brn ('41) .90 *1.50*
Never hinged 6.00
On cover 4.00
B153 10 + 5pf dk brown .75 *2.00*
Never hinged 4.00
On cover 4.00
B154 12 + 6pf rose brown .90 *2.00*
Never hinged 4.75
On cover 4.00
B154A 12 + 18pf dk car rose ('41) 1.10 *2.00*
Never hinged 6.00
On cover 2.75
B155 15 + 10pf dp red lilac .75 *2.25*
Never hinged 4.00
On cover 8.00
B156 16 + 10pf slate grn .75 *2.25*
Never hinged 4.00
On cover 9.50
B156A 16 + 24pf black ('41) 1.10 *4.00*
Never hinged 6.00
On cover 8.75
B157 20 + 10pf ultra .75 *2.25*
Never hinged 4.00
On cover 12.00
B157A 20 + 30pf ultra ('41) 1.50 *4.00*
Never hinged 8.00
On cover 12.00
B158 24 + 10pf ol grn 2.00 *4.00*
Never hinged 10.00
On cover 12.00
B158A 24 + 36pf pur ('41) 3.75 *12.00*
Never hinged 20.00
On cover 20.00
B159 25 + 15pf dk blue 1.90 *3.25*
Never hinged 10.00
On cover 13.50
Nos. B148-B159 (18) 23.25 *58.75*
Set, never hinged 125.00

The surtax was used for Hitler's National Culture Fund and the Postal Employees' Fund.
See Nos. B273, B275-B277 in Scott Standard catalogue, Vol. 3.

Elbogen Castle — SP136

Buildings: 4pf+3pf, Drachenfels on the Rhine. 5pf+3pf, Kaiserpfalz at Goslar. 6pf+4pf, Clocktower at Graz. 8pf+4pf, Town Hall, Frankfurt. 12pf+6pf, Guild House, Klagenfurt. 15pf+10pf, Ruins of Schreckenstein Castle. 25pf+15pf, Fortress of Salzburg. 40pf+35pf, Castle of Hohentwiel.

1939 Unwmk. Engr. *Perf. 14*

B160 SP136 3 + 2pf dk brn .25 *.45*
Never hinged 1.00
On cover 1.40
a. Bklt. pane, 4 #B160, 5 #B165 + label 27.50 50.00
Never hinged 47.50
B161 SP136 4 + 3pf gray blk 1.60 *2.00*
Never hinged 7.25
On cover 4.00
B162 SP136 5 + 3pf emerald .35 *.55*
Never hinged 1.60
On cover 1.25
a. Bklt. pane, 5 #B162, 5 #B163 13.00 26.00
Never hinged 24.00
B163 SP136 6 + 4pf slate grn .25 *.40*
Never hinged 1.00
On cover 1.25
B164 SP136 8 + 4pf red org 1.60 *1.75*
Never hinged 7.25
On cover 2.75
B165 SP136 12 + 6pf dk car .35 *.80*
Never hinged 3.25
On cover 2.25
B166 SP136 15 + 10pf brn vio 2.40 *4.75*
Never hinged 11.00
On cover 9.50
B167 SP136 25 + 15pf ultra 1.90 *4.75*
Never hinged 8.75
On cover 9.50
B168 SP136 40 + 35pf rose vio 2.50 *6.50*
Never hinged 12.00
On cover 12.50
Nos. B160-B168 (9) 11.20 *21.95*
Set, never hinged 53.00

Hall of Honor at Chancellery, Berlin — SP145

1940, Mar. 28

B169 SP145 24 + 76pf dk grn 6.00 *17.00*
Never hinged 28.00
On cover 24.00

2nd National Stamp Exposition, Berlin.

Child Greeting Hitler — SP146

Perf. 14x13½
1940, Apr. 10 Photo. Wmk. 237

B170 SP146 12 + 38pf cop red 1.50 *6.00*
Never hinged 14.00
On cover 12.00

51st birthday of Adolf Hitler.

Armed Warrior — SP147

1940, Apr. 30 Unwmk. *Perf. 14*

B171 SP147 6 + 4pf sl grn & lt grn .30 *1.25*
Never hinged 1.40
On cover 2.75

Issued to commemorate May Day.

Horseman SP148

Perf. 14x13½

1940, June 22 Wmk. 237

B172 SP148 25 + 100pf dp ultra 4.25 *11.00*
Never hinged 21.00
On cover 16.00

Blue Ribbon race, Hamburg, June 30, 1940. Surtax for Hitler's National Culture Fund.

Chariot SP149

Unwmk.

1940, July 20 Engr. *Perf. 14*

B173 SP149 42 + 108pf brown 22.50 *26.00*
Never hinged 90.00
On cover 40.00

7th "Brown Ribbon" at Munich.

The surtax was for Hitler's National Culture Fund and the promoters of the race.

View of Malmedy SP150

Design: 12pf+8pf, View of Eupen.

Perf. 14x13½

1940, July 25 Photo. Wmk. 237

B174 SP150 6 + 4pf dk green 1.20 *3.00*
Never hinged 5.00
On cover 4.00

B175 SP150 12 + 8pf org red 1.20 *3.00*
Never hinged 5.00
On cover 4.00

Set, never hinged 10.00

Issued on the occasion of the reunion of Eupen-Malmedy with the Reich.

Rocky Cliffs of Heligoland SP152

1940, Aug. 9 Unwmk.

B176 SP152 6 + 94pf brt bl grn & red org 6.00 *12.00*
Never hinged 24.00
On cover 16.00

Heligoland's 50th year as part of Germany.

Artushof in Danzig — SP153

Buildings: 4pf+3pf, Town Hall, Thorn. 5pf+3pf, Castle at Kaub. 6pf+4pf, City Theater, Poznan. 8pf+4pf, Castle at Heidelberg. 12pf+6pf, Porta Nigra Trier. 15pf+10pf, New German Theater, Prague. 25pf+15pf, Town Hall, Bremen. 40pf+35pf, Town Hall, Munster.

1940, Nov. 5 Engr. *Perf. 14*

B177 SP153 3 + 2pf dk brn .30 *.45*
Never hinged 1.00
On cover 2.00
a. Bklt. pane, 4 #B177 + 5 #B182 + label 27.50 47.50
Never hinged 45.00

B178 SP153 4 + 3pf bluish blk 1.00 *.80*
Never hinged 3.25
On cover 3.25

B179 SP153 5 + 3pf yel grn .30 *.45*
Never hinged 1.00
On cover 1.40
a. Bklt. pane, 5 #B179, 5 #B180 14.00 27.50
Never hinged 24.00

B180 SP153 6 + 4pf dk grn .35 *.45*
Never hinged 1.10
On cover 1.00

B181 SP153 8 + 4pf dp org 1.50 .85
Never hinged 4.75
On cover 3.25

B182 SP153 12 + 6pf carmine .35 *.45*
Never hinged 1.25
On cover 1.45

B183 SP153 15 + 10pf dk vio brn 1.50 *2.75*
Never hinged 5.25
On cover 5.50

B184 SP153 25 + 15pf dp ultra 2.00 *2.75*
Never hinged 6.75
On cover 6.00

B185 SP153 40 + 35pf red lil 4.00 *6.50*
Never hinged 13.50
On cover 12.00

Nos. B177-B185 (9) 11.30 *15.45*
Set, never hinged 37.50

von Behring — SP162

1940, Nov. 26 Photo.

B186 SP162 6 + 4pf dp green 1.25 *2.25*
Never hinged 4.75
On cover 3.25

B187 SP162 25 + 10pf brt ultra 1.90 *2.25*
Never hinged 7.25
On cover 4.00

Set, never hinged 12.00

Dr. Emil von Behring (1854-1917), bacteriologist.

AIR POST STAMPS

Issues of the Republic

Post Horn with Wings — AP1

Biplane AP2

Perf. 15x14½

1919, Nov. 10 Typo. Unwmk.

C1 AP1 10pf orange .25 *2.75*
Never hinged .70
On cover 8.00

C2 AP2 40pf dark green .25 *3.25*
Never hinged .70
On cover 8.00
a. Imperf. 2,000.

Set, never hinged 1.40

No. C2a is ungummed.

Carrier Pigeon — AP3

1922-23 Wmk. 126 *Perf. 14, 14½*

Size: 19x23mm

C3 AP3 25(pf) chocolate .45 *18.00*
Never hinged 2.00
On cover 32.50

C4 AP3 40(pf) orange .35 *24.00*
Never hinged 2.00
On cover 40.00

C5 AP3 50(pf) violet .25 *8.25*
Never hinged .75
On cover 20.00

C6 AP3 60(pf) carmine .50 *20.00*
Never hinged 2.00
On cover 30.00

C7 AP3 80(pf) blue grn .35 *20.00*
Never hinged 1.50
On cover 30.00

Perf. 13x13½

Size: 22x28mm

C8 AP3 1m dk grn & pale grn .25 *3.75*
Never hinged .50
On cover 9.00

C9 AP3 2m lake & gray .25 *3.75*
Never hinged .50
On cover 9.00

C10 AP3 3m dk blue & gray .25 *4.50*
Never hinged .80
On cover 9.00

C11 AP3 5m red org & yel .25 *3.75*
Never hinged .50
On cover 9.00

C12 AP3 10m vio & rose ('23) .25 *10.50*
Never hinged .50
On cover 19.00

C13 AP3 25m brn & yel ('23) .25 *8.50*
Never hinged .50
On cover 16.50

C14 AP3 100m ol grn & rose ('23) .25 *7.25*
Never hinged .50
On cover 16.50

Nos. C3-C14 (12) 3.65 *132.25*
Set, never hinged 11.50

1923

C15 AP3 5m vermilion .25 *45.00*
Never hinged .45
On cover 75.00

C16 AP3 10m violet .25 *10.50*
Never hinged .45
On cover 21.00

C17 AP3 25m dark brown .25 *10.50*
Never hinged .40
On cover 19.00

C18 AP3 100m olive grn .25 *11.00*
Never hinged .40
On cover 16.50

C19 AP3 200m deep blue .25 *32.50*
Never hinged .40
On cover 67.50
a. Imperf. 60.00
Never hinged 150.00

Nos. C15-C19 (5) 1.25 109.50
Set, never hinged 2.25

Issued: Nos. C15-C18, 6/1. No. C19, 7/25.

Note following No. 160 applies to Nos. C1-C19.

1924, Jan. 11 *Perf. 14*

Size: 19x23mm

C20 AP3 5(pf) yellow grn 1.25 *2.25*
Never hinged 4.25
On cover 4.50

C21 AP3 10(pf) carmine 1.25 *1.90*
Never hinged 4.25
On cover 6.00

C22 AP3 20(pf) violet blue 6.75 5.25
Never hinged 21.00
On cover 10.00

C23 AP3 50(pf) orange 11.00 *24.00*
Never hinged 110.00
On cover 37.50

C24 AP3 100(pf) dull violet 30.00 *55.00*
Never hinged 200.00
On cover 75.00

C25 AP3 200(pf) grnsh bl 55.00 *75.00*
Never hinged 260.00
On cover 300.00

C26 AP3 300(pf) gray 97.50 100.00
Never hinged 575.00
On cover 450.00
a. Imperf. *900.00*
Never hinged 1,650.

Nos. C20-C26 (7) 202.75 *263.40*
Set, never hinged 1,130.

German Eagle — AP4

1926-27

C27 AP4 5pf green 1.20 *1.20*
Never hinged 3.00
On cover 2.25

C28 AP4 10pf rose red 2.00 *1.20*
Never hinged 5.50
On cover 2.00
b. Tête bêche pair 160.00 275.00
Never hinged 275.00
d. Bklt. pane 10 (6 No. C28 + 4 No. C29) 225.00 350.00
Never hinged 375.00

C29 AP4 15pf lil rose ('27) 2.00 2.00
Never hinged 17.00
On cover 3.75
a. Double impression *1,375.*

C30 AP4 20pf dull blue 2.00 *2.00*
Never hinged 17.00
On cover 4.50
a. Tête bêche pair 160.00 275.00
Never hinged 275.00
b. Bklt. pane 4 (4 No. C30 + 6 labels) 225.00 350.00
Never hinged 375.00
c. Bklt. pane 5 (5 No. C30 + 5 labels) 450.00 1,000.
Never hinged 900.00

C31 AP4 50pf brown org 18.00 5.25
Never hinged 225.00
On cover 17.50

C32 AP4 1m blk & sal 18.00 6.00
Never hinged 115.00
On cover 20.00

C33 AP4 2m black & blue 18.00 *22.50*
Never hinged 160.00
On cover 47.50

C34 AP4 3m blk & ol grn 55.00 *95.00*
Never hinged 425.00
On cover 160.00

Nos. C27-C34 (8) 116.20 *135.15*
Set, never hinged 967.50

"Graf Zeppelin" Crossing Ocean — AP5

1928-31 Photo.

C35 AP5 1m carmine ('31) 25.00 *35.00*
Never hinged 80.00
On cover 65.00

C36 AP5 2m ultra 45.00 *52.50*
Never hinged 240.00
On cover 100.00

C37 AP5 4m black brown 27.50 *35.00*
Never hinged 100.00
On cover 100.00

Nos. C35-C37 (3) 97.50 *122.50*
Set, never hinged 420.00

Issued: 2m, 4m, Sept. 20. 1m, May 8.

For overprints see Nos. C40-C45.

AP6

1930, Apr. 19 Wmk. 126

C38 AP6 2m ultra 250.00 *400.00*
Never hinged 1,350.
On cover 425.00

C39 AP6 4m black brown 250.00 *400.00*
Never hinged 1,400.
On cover 425.00

Set, never hinged 2,750.

First flight of Graf Zeppelin to South America. No. C38 is value with horizontal watermark. No. C39 is valued with vertical watermark. No. C38 with vertical watermark and No. C39 with horizontal watermark are worth 10%-20% more.

Counterfeits exist of Nos. C38-C45.

Nos. C35-C37 Overprinted in Brown

1931, July 15

C40 AP5 1m carmine 120.00 110.00
Never hinged 450.00
On cover 200.00
a. Hyphen in ovpt. omitted 475.00 *1,200.*
Never hinged 2,000.
On cover 1,750.

C41 AP5 2m ultra 175.00 *200.00*
Never hinged 1,000.
On cover 350.00
a. Hyphen in ovpt. omitted 525.00 *1,200.*
Never hinged 2,200.
On cover 1,750.

C42 AP5 4m black brown 450.00 *675.00*
Never hinged 1,750.
On cover 875.00
a. Hyphen in ovpt. omitted *12,000.*
Nos. C40-C42 (3) 745.00 *985.00*
Set, never hinged 3,200.

Polar flight of Graf Zeppelin.

Nos. C35-C37 Overprinted

1933, Sept. 25

C43 AP5 1m carmine 800.00 *400.00*
Never hinged 2,700.
On cover *450.00*
C44 AP5 2m ultra 75.00 *200.00*
Never hinged 250.00
On cover *275.00*
C45 AP5 4m black brown 75.00 *200.00*
Never hinged 250.00
On cover *650.00*
Nos. C43-C45 (3) 950.00 *800.00*
Set, never hinged 3,200.

Graf Zeppelin flight to Century of Progress International Exhibition, Chicago.

Swastika Sun, Globe and Eagle — AP7

Otto Lilienthal — AP8

Design: 3m, Count Ferdinand von Zeppelin.

Perf. 14, 13½x13

1934, Jan. 21 Typo. Wmk. 237

C46 AP7 5(pf) brt green 1.10 .90
Never hinged 4.75
On cover 2.00
C47 AP7 10(pf) brt carmine 1.10 .90
Never hinged 4.75
On cover 2.40
C48 AP7 15(pf) ultra 1.90 1.25
Never hinged 6.50
On cover 2.40
C49 AP7 20(pf) dull blue 3.50 1.75
Never hinged 12.50
On cover 3.25
C50 AP7 25(pf) brown 4.75 2.00
Never hinged 40.00
On cover 3.25
C51 AP7 40(pf) red violet 7.00 1.20
Never hinged 65.00
On cover 3.25
C52 AP7 50(pf) dk green 12.50 .90
Never hinged 95.00
On cover 6.00
C53 AP7 80(pf) orange yel 4.00 4.00
Never hinged 50.00
On cover 27.50
C54 AP7 100(pf) black 8.00 2.75
Never hinged 65.00
On cover 27.50
C55 AP8 2m green & blk 17.50 *20.00*
Never hinged 100.00
On cover 60.00
C56 AP8 3m blue & blk 32.50 *45.00*
Never hinged 160.00
On cover 80.00
Nos. C46-C56 (11) 93.85 80.65
Set, never hinged 600.00

"Hindenburg" — AP10

Perf. 14, 14½x14

1936, Mar. 16 Engr.

C57 AP10 50pf dark blue 19.00 1.00
On cover 8.00
C58 AP10 75pf dull green 20.00 1.25
On cover 10.00

The note concerning gum after No. B68 also applies to Nos. C57-C58.

Unused values are for stamps without gum.

Count Zeppelin — AP11

Airship Gondola — AP12

1938, July 5 Unwmk. *Perf. 13½*

C59 AP11 25pf dull blue 2.90 1.50
Never hinged 17.50
On cover 9.50
C60 AP12 50pf green 4.50 1.50
Never hinged 27.50
On cover 9.50
Set, never hinged 45.00

Count Ferdinand von Zeppelin (1838-1917), airship inventor and builder.

AIR POST SEMI-OFFICIAL STAMPS

Pigeon holding letter — CL1

Perf. 11½

1912, June 10 Typo. Unwmk.

CL1 APL1 10pf dp red org, *pale gray* 6.50 24.00
Never hinged 24.00
On cover 35.00
CL2 APL1 20pf dp red org, *pale gray* 16.00 65.00
Never hinged 55.00
On cover 80.00
CL3 APL1 30pf dp grn, *pale gray* 35.00 95.00
Never hinged 100.00
On cover 325.00

Nos. CL1-CL3 were issued for the first Rhine-Main airmail flights in Germany. The flights raised money for charities under the patronage of the Grand Duke of Hesse, in conujunction with postal authorities who authorized the stamps. Mail was carried between Darmstadt and Frankfurt am Main by the airship "Schwaben" or the airplane "Gelber Hund". Postage was prepared with regularly issued stamps in addition to the semi-official air post stamps.

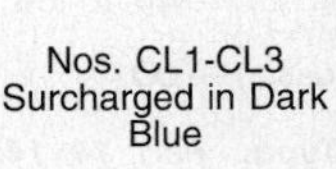

Nos. CL1-CL3 Surcharged in Dark Blue

1912, June 10

CL4 APL1 1m on 10pf dp red org, *pale gray* 500.00 160.00
Never hinged 2,000.
On cover 225.00
a. Inverted overprint 5,500. *14,500.*
Never hinged 12,000.
On cover 16,000.
b. "Huna" instead of "Hund" 1,200. 290.00
Never hinged 4,000.
On cover 400.00

Approximately 10,000 semi-official air post stamps on covers were surcharged and carried as souvenirs on the airplane "Gelber Hund".

Nos. CL1, CL2 Overprinted

1912, June 22

CL5 APL1 10pf dp red org, *pale gray* 725.00 *2,400.*
Never hinged 1,750.
On cover 2,750.
CL6 APL1 20pf dp red org, *pale gray* 100.00 *1,400.*
Never hinged 350.00
On cover 1,750.

OFFICIAL STAMPS

Issues of the Republic

In 1920 the Official Stamps of Bavaria and Wurttemberg then current were overprinted "Deutsches Reich" and made available for official use in all parts of Germany. They were, however, used almost exclusively in the two states where they originated and we have listed them among the issues of those states.

O1

O2

O3 O4

O5 O6

O7 O8

O9 O10

O11

O12

1920-21 Typo. Wmk. 125 *Perf. 14*

O1 O1 5pf deep green .90 *14.00*
Never hinged 4.00
On cover *20.00*
O2 O2 10pf car rose .25 1.75
Never hinged .50
On cover 2.25
O3 O2 10pf orange ('21) .60 *450.00*
Never hinged 2.50
On cover *600.00*
O4 O3 15pf violet brn .25 2.25
Never hinged .50
On cover 3.00
a. Imperf. ('21) *750.00 750.00*
O5 O4 20pf deep ultra .25 2.00
Never hinged .50
On cover 2.25
O6 O5 30pf org, *buff* .25 2.00
Never hinged .50
On cover 2.25
O7 O6 40pf carmine .25 2.00
Never hinged .50
On cover 2.25
O8 O7 50pf violet, *buff* .25 2.00
Never hinged .50
On cover 2.25
O9 O8 60pf red brn ('21) .25 2.00
Never hinged 1.20
On cover 2.00
O10 O9 1m red, *buff* .25 2.00
Never hinged .50
On cover 2.25
O11 O10 1.25m dk bl, *yel* .25 2.25
Never hinged .50
On cover 4.75
O12 O11 2m dark blue 4.25 4.00
Never hinged 24.00
On cover 8.00
O13 O12 5m brown, *yel* .25 3.00
Never hinged 1.25
On cover 3.75
Nos. O1-O13 (13) 8.25 *489.25*
Set, never hinged 36.50

The value of No. O4a is for a stamp postmarked at Bautzen.

See No. O15. For surcharges see Nos. O29-O33, O35-O36, O38. For overprints see Upper Silesia Nos. O39-O51.

Postally Used vs. CTO
Values quoted for canceled examples of Nos. O1-O46 are for postally used stamps. See note after No. 160.

O13

O14

O15

Wmk. 126, 125 (#O16-O17)

1922-23

O14 O13 75pf dark blue .25 *8.00*
Never hinged .80
On cover *16.00*
O15 O11 2m dark blue .25 *1.50*
Never hinged .50
On cover 2.00
a. Imperf. 97.50
Never hinged 300.00
O16 O14 3m brown, *rose* .25 *1.50*
Never hinged .50
On cover 4.00
O17 O15 10m dk grn, *rose* .25 *1.50*
Never hinged .80
On cover 2.00
O18 O15 10m dk grn, *rose* .25 *9.00*
Never hinged .80
On cover *16.00*
O19 O15 20m dk bl, *rose* .25 *1.50*
Never hinged .50
On cover 2.00
O20 O15 50m vio, *rose* .25 *1.50*
Never hinged .50
On cover 2.00
a. Imperf 100.00
Never hinged 325.00
O21 O15 100m rose red, *rose* .25 *1.50*
Never hinged .60
On cover 2.00
a. Imperf 110.00 *775.00*
Never hinged 325.00
Nos. O14-O21 (8) 2.00 *26.00*
Set, never hinged 5.00

Issue date: Nos. O18-O21, 1923.
Nos. O20-O21 exist imperf.
For surcharges see Nos. O34, O37, O39.

Regular Issue of 1923 Overprinted — a

1923

O22 A34 20m red lilac .30 *7.50*
Never hinged 1.10
On cover *16.00*
O23 A34 30m olive grn .25 *35.00*
Never hinged .50
On cover *55.00*
O24 A29 40m green .25 *3.00*
Never hinged 1.10
On cover *6.25*
O25 A35 200m car rose .25 *1.50*
Never hinged .50
On cover *2.00*
O26 A35 300m green .25 *1.50*
Never hinged .50
On cover *2.00*
O27 A35 400m dk brn .25 *1.50*
Never hinged .50
On cover *2.00*
O28 A35 500m red orange .25 *1.50*
Never hinged .50
On cover *2.00*
Nos. O22-O28 (7) 1.80 *51.50*
Set, never hinged 4.50

Official Stamps of 1920-23 Surcharged with New Values

Abbreviations:
Th=(Tausend) Thousand
Mil=(Million) Million
Mlrd=(Milliarde) Billion

1923 **Wmk. 125**

O29 O12 5th m on 5m .25 *3.00*
Never hinged .30
On cover *8.00*
a. Inverted surcharge 50.00
Never hinged 115.00
O30 O5 20th m on 30pf .25 *3.00*
Never hinged .30
On cover *8.00*
a. Inverted surcharge 55.00
Never hinged 130.00
b. Imperf. 60.00
Never hinged 150.00
O31 O3 100th m on 15pf .25 *3.00*
Never hinged .30
On cover *8.00*
a. Imperf. 60.00
Never hinged 150.00
b. Inverted surcharge 50.00
Never hinged 115.00
O32 O2 250th m on 10pf car rose .25 *3.00*
Never hinged .30
On cover *8.00*
a. Double surcharge 50.00
Never hinged 115.00
O33 O5 800th m on 30pf .60 *300.00*
Never hinged 1.60
On cover *400.00*

Official Stamps and Types of 1920-23 Surcharged with New Values

Wmk. 126

O34 O15 75th m on 50m .25 *3.00*
Never hinged .30
On cover *8.00*
a. Inverted surcharge 50.00
Never hinged 115.00
O35 O3 400th m on 15pf brn .25 *27.50*
Never hinged .30
On cover *45.00*
O36 O5 800th m on 30pf org, *buff* .30 *4.50*
Never hinged 1.10
On cover *12.00*
O37 O13 1 mil m on 75pf .25 *37.50*
Never hinged .30
On cover *95.00*
O38 O2 2 mil m on 10pf car rose .30 *3.75*
Never hinged 1.10
On cover *8.00*
a. Imperf. 95.00
Never hinged 225.00
O39 O15 5 mil m on 100m .25 *5.75*
Never hinged .30
On cover *12.50*
Nos. O29-O39 (11) 3.20 *394.00*
Set, never hinged 6.00

The 10, 15 and 30 pfennig are not known with this watermark and without surcharge.

Nos. 290-291, 295-299 Overprinted Type "a"

1923

O40 A39 100 mil m .25 *150.00*
Never hinged .60
On cover *350.00*
O41 A39 200 mil m .30 *150.00*
Never hinged 1.10
On cover *350.00*
O42 A39a 2 mlrd m .25 *115.00*
Never hinged .90
On cover *350.00*
O43 A39a 5 mlrd m .25 *90.00*
Never hinged 1.50
On cover *350.00*
O44 A39a 10 mlrd m 3.75 *140.00*
Never hinged 10.00
On cover *350.00*
O45 A39a 20 mlrd m 3.75 *150.00*
Never hinged 13.50
On cover *350.00*
O46 A39a 50 mlrd m 2.00 *200.00*
Never hinged 5.75
On cover *425.00*
Nos. O40-O46 (7) 10.55 *995.00*
Set, never hinged 34.50

Same Overprint on Nos. 323-328, Values in Rentenpfennig

1923

O47 A40 3pf brown .25 *.75*
Never hinged 1.50
On cover 2.25
O48 A40 5pf dk green .25 *.75*
Never hinged 1.50
On cover 1.50
a. Inverted overprint 115.00 300.00
Never hinged 300.00
O49 A40 10pf carmine .25 *.75*
Never hinged 1.50
On cover 1.50
a. Inverted overprint 80.00 175.00
Never hinged 150.00
b. Imperf. 60.00
Never hinged 150.00
O50 A40 20pf dp ultra .60 *1.10*
Never hinged 2.75
On cover 2.00
O51 A40 50pf orange .60 *1.50*
Never hinged 3.50
On cover 15.00
O52 A40 100pf brown vio 3.75 *7.50*
Never hinged 15.00
On cover 125.00
Nos. O47-O52 (6) 5.70 *12.35*
Set, never hinged 25.75

Same Overprint On Issues of 1924

1924

O53 A41 3pf lt brown .35 *2.25*
Never hinged 2.25
On cover 3.50
a. Inverted overprint 60.00 300.00
Never hinged 300.00
O54 A41 5pf lt green .25 *.75*
Never hinged 1.50
On cover 1.10
a. Imperf. 75.00
Never hinged 225.00
b. Inverted overprint 110.00
Never hinged 300.00
O55 A41 10pf vermilion .25 *.75*
Never hinged 1.00
On cover 1.10
O56 A41 20pf blue .25 *.75*
Never hinged 1.10
On cover 2.75
O57 A41 30pf rose lilac .75 *.75*
Never hinged 4.00
On cover 2.75
O58 A41 40pf olive green .75 *.75*
Never hinged 4.00
On cover 6.00
O59 A41 50pf orange 6.75 3.75
Never hinged 20.00
On cover 10.00
O60 A47 60pf red brown 1.50 *3.75*
Never hinged 8.00
On cover 24.00
O61 A47 80pf slate 6.75 *35.00*
Never hinged 21.00
On cover *350.00*
Nos. O53-O61 (9) 17.60 *48.50*
Set, never hinged 62.50

O16

1927-33 ***Perf. 14***

O62 O16 3pf bister .30 *.75*
Never hinged 1.15
On cover 1.50
O63 O16 4pf lt bl ('31) .50 *.90*
Never hinged 1.50
On cover 2.25
O64 O16 4pf blue ('33) 6.75 *13.50*
Never hinged 57.50
On cover 26.00
O65 O16 5pf green .25 *.75*
Never hinged .60
On cover 1.50
O66 O16 6pf pale ol grn ('32) .75 *.90*
Never hinged 2.60
On cover 2.25
O67 O16 8pf dk grn .30 *.75*
Never hinged 1.10
On cover 1.50
O68 O16 10pf carmine 7.50 6.00
Never hinged 27.00
On cover 22.50
O69 O16 10pf ver ('29), wmk. upright 15.00 *19.00*
Never hinged 70.00
On cover 67.50
a. Wmk. sideways 15.00 *20.00*
Never hinged 60.00
On cover *45.00*
O70 O16 10pf red vio ('30) .45 *.90*
Never hinged 1.50
On cover 1.90
a. Imperf. 150.00
Never hinged 400.00
O71 O16 10pf choc ('33) 3.00 *9.00*
Never hinged 27.50
On cover 15.00
O72 O16 12pf org ('32) .50 *.90*
Never hinged 1.50
On cover 2.25
O73 O16 15pf vermilion 1.75 .90
Never hinged 6.00
On cover 3.00
O74 O16 15pf car ('29) .45 *.90*
Never hinged 1.40
On cover 2.25
O75 O16 20pf Prus grn, wmk. upright 7.50 3.00
Never hinged 26.00
On cover 9.00
a. Wmk. sideways 20.00 *75.00*
Never hinged 85.00
On cover *120.00*
O76 O16 20pf gray ('30), wmk. upright 2.25 1.10
Never hinged 6.75
On cover 1.90
a. Wmk. sideways *675.00* *450.00*
Never hinged *5,000.*
On cover *650.00*
O77 O16 30pf olive grn .90 .90
Never hinged 3.25
On cover 1.50
O78 O16 40pf violet, wmk upright .75 *.90*
Never hinged 3.75
On cover 3.25
a. Wmk sideways 8.25 *30.00*
Never hinged 32.50
On cover 80.00
O79 O16 60pf red brn ('28) 1.10 *1.90*
Never hinged 5.00
On cover 8.00
Nos. O62-O79 (18) 50.00 62.95
Set, never hinged 275.00

Swastika — O17

1934, Jan. 18 **Wmk. 237**

O80 O17 3pf bister .75 *1.10*
Never hinged 3.25
On cover 2.40
O81 O17 4pf dull blue .30 *.90*
Never hinged 1.00
On cover 2.00
O82 O17 5pf brt green .25 *1.10*
Never hinged .60
On cover 9.50
O83 O17 6pf dk green .25 *.90*
Never hinged .60
On cover 1.60
a. Imperf. 150.00
Never hinged 400.00
O84 O17 8pf vermilion 2.25 .90
Never hinged 7.25
On cover 2.00
O85 O17 10pf chocolate .30 *7.50*
Never hinged 1.40
On cover 12.00
O86 O17 12pf brt carmine 2.25 1.50
Never hinged 12.00
On cover 2.25
a. Unwmkd. 5.00 *7.00*
Never hinged 12.00
O87 O17 15pf claret .90 *9.00*
Never hinged 4.75
On cover *16.00*
O88 O17 20pf light blue .45 *1.50*
Never hinged 1.60
On cover 2.25
O89 O17 30pf olive grn .90 *1.50*
Never hinged 2.75
On cover 3.75
O90 O17 40pf red violet .90 *1.50*
Never hinged 2.75
On cover 8.00
O91 O17 50pf orange yel 1.40 *3.75*
Never hinged 4.75
On cover 17.50
Nos. O80-O91 (12) 10.90 *31.15*
Set, never hinged 42.50

LOCAL OFFICIAL STAMPS

For Use in Prussia

("Nr. 21" refers to the district of Prussia) — LO1

1903 **Unwmk.** **Typo.** ***Perf. 14, 14½***

OL1 LO1 2pf slate 1.20 *4.50*
Never hinged 2.25
On cover 24.00
OL2 LO1 3pf bister brn 1.20 *4.50*
Never hinged 2.25
On cover 21.00
OL3 LO1 5pf green .30 *.50*
Never hinged .80
On cover 13.50
OL4 LO1 10pf carmine .30 *.50*
Never hinged .80
On cover 8.00
OL5 LO1 20pf ultra .30 *.50*
Never hinged .80
On cover 8.00
OL6 LO1 25pf org & blk, *yel* .75 *1.75*
Never hinged 1.50
On cover 21.00
OL7 LO1 40pf lake & blk .75 *2.00*
Never hinged 1.50
On cover 27.50
OL8 LO1 50pf pur & blk, *sal* .90 *2.00*
Never hinged 2.00
On cover 40.00
Nos. OL1-OL8 (8) 5.70 *16.25*
Set, never hinged 11.90

LO2

LO3

LO4

LO5

LO6

LO7

LO8

1920 **Typo.** **Wmk. 125** ***Perf. 14***

OL9 LO2 5pf green .25 *3.00*
Never hinged 1.10
On cover 6.00
OL10 LO3 10pf carmine .70 *1.50*
Never hinged 3.25
On cover 3.25
OL11 LO4 15pf vio brn .25 *1.50*
Never hinged .55
On cover 2.75
OL12 LO5 20pf dp ultra .25 *1.40*
Never hinged .50
On cover 2.75
OL13 LO6 30pf org, *buff* .25 *1.40*
Never hinged .50
On cover 2.75
OL14 LO7 50pf brn lil, *buff* .30 *1.50*
Never hinged 1.60
On cover 2.75
OL15 LO8 1m red, *buff* 8.25 *3.75*
Never hinged 32.50
On cover 12.00
Nos. OL9-OL15 (7) 10.25 *14.05*
Set, never hinged 40.00

For overprints see Upper Silesia Nos. O32-O38.

For Use in Baden

LO9

1905 **Unwmk.** **Typo.** ***Perf. 14, 14½***

OL16 LO9 2pf gray blue 52.50 *75.00*
Never hinged 600.00
On cover 145.00
OL17 LO9 3pf brown 6.00 *10.50*
Never hinged 27.50
On cover 40.00
OL18 LO9 5pf green 4.25 *7.50*
Never hinged 19.00
On cover 20.00
OL19 LO9 10pf rose .75 *2.10*
Never hinged 3.25
On cover 17.50
OL20 LO9 20pf blue 1.50 *3.00*
Never hinged 12.00
On cover 20.00
OL21 LO9 25pf org & blk, *yel* 35.00 *52.50*
Never hinged 240.00
On cover 130.00
Nos. OL16-OL21 (6) 100.00 *150.60*
Set, never hinged 900.00

NEWSPAPER STAMPS

Newsboy and Globe — N1

Wmk. Swastikas (237)

1939, Nov. 1 **Photo.** ***Perf. 14***

P1 N1 5pf green .60 *5.25*
Never hinged 2.50
On wrapper or address label *200.00*
P2 N1 10pf red brown .60 *5.25*
Never hinged 2.50
On wrapper or address label *200.00*
Set, never hinged 5.00

FRANCHISE STAMPS

For use by the National Socialist German Workers' Party

Party Emblem — F1

1938 Typo. Wmk. 237 *Perf. 14*
S1 F1 1pf black .70 *3.00*
Never hinged 6.00
On cover 8.00
S2 F1 3pf bister .70 *1.90*
Never hinged 6.00
On cover 6.50
S3 F1 4pf dull blue .70 *1.50*
Never hinged 7.25
On cover 4.00
S4 F1 5pf brt green .40 *1.50*
Never hinged 2.75
On cover 8.00
S5 F1 6pf dk green .40 *1.50*
Never hinged 2.75
On cover 4.00
S6 F1 8pf vermilion 2.75 1.50
Never hinged 24.00
On cover 4.00
S7 F1 12pf brt car 4.50 1.50
Never hinged 42.50
On cover 4.00
S8 F1 16pf gray .65 *9.00*
Never hinged 6.00
On cover 32.50
S9 F1 24pf citron 1.00 *4.75*
Never hinged 11.00
On cover 24.00
S10 F1 30pf olive 1.00 *7.50*
Never hinged 8.75
On cover 24.00
S11 F1 40pf red violet 1.00 *11.00*
Never hinged 10.00
On cover 32.50
Nos. S1-S11 (11) 13.80 *44.65*
Set, never hinged 127.00

GERMAN OCCUPATION STAMPS

100 Centimes = 1 Franc
100 Pfennig = 1 Mark
Issued under Belgian Occupation

Belgian Stamps of 1915-1920 Overprinted

Perf. 11½, 14, 14½
1919-21 Unwmk.
1N1 A46 1c orange .30 *.60*
Never hinged 1.10
On parcel post receipt card 67.50
1N2 A46 2c chocolate .30 *.60*
Never hinged 1.10
On parcel post receipt card 67.50
1N3 A46 3c gray blk ('21) .30 *2.25*
Never hinged 1.50
On parcel post receipt card 100.00
1N4 A46 5c green .60 *1.10*
Never hinged 1.50
On parcel post receipt card 67.50
1N5 A46 10c carmine 1.10 *2.25*
Never hinged 5.25
On parcel post receipt card 67.50
1N6 A46 15c purple .60 *1.10*
Never hinged 2.25
On parcel post receipt card 67.50
1N7 A46 20c red violet .90 *1.10*
Never hinged 3.00
On parcel post receipt card 67.50
1N8 A46 25c blue 1.10 *1.90*
Never hinged 4.50
On parcel post receipt card 67.50
1N9 A54 25c dp blue ('21) 3.75 *11.00*
Never hinged 12.50
On parcel post receipt card 100.00

Belgian Stamps of 1915-1920 Overprinted

1N10 A47 35c brn org & blk 1.10 *1.10*
Never hinged 4.50
On parcel post receipt card 85.00
1N11 A48 40c green & blk 1.10 *2.25*
Never hinged 5.25
On parcel post receipt card 85.00
1N12 A49 50c car rose & blk 6.00 *10.50*
Never hinged 19.00
On parcel post ereceipt card 85.00
1N13 A56 65c cl & blk ('21) 3.00 *11.00*
Never hinged 9.00
On cover —
1N14 A50 1fr violet 21.00 19.00
Never hinged 60.00
On cover —
1N15 A51 2fr slate 35.00 *45.00*
Never hinged 135.00
On cover —
1N16 A52 5fr deep blue 8.25 *11.00*
Never hinged 34.00
On cover —
1N17 A53 10fr brown 45.00 60.00
Never hinged 150.00
On cover —
Nos. 1N1-1N17 (17) 129.40 *181.75*
Set, never hinged 450.00

Nos. 1N1-1N17 were valid for postage until April 30, 1931, nearly one year after the Belgians and other occupation forces evacuated the Rhineland. Mixed frankings with Belgian stamps were permitted. The values for used stamps are for stamps with cancels from the Belgian military post offices in occupied Germany.

Nos. 1N14-1N17 exist with two overprint types: spacing between "Allemagne" and "Duitshland" 2mm (1919) and 1mm (1920).

Belgian Stamps of 1915 Surcharged

Nos. 1N18-1N22

Nos. 1N23-1N24

1920 Black Surcharge
1N18 A46 5pf on 5c grn .30 1.00
Never hinged 1.10
On cover 14.00
On cover, single franking 45.00
1N19 A46 10pf on 10c car .30 1.10
Never hinged 1.40
On cover 14.00
On cover, single franking 37.50
1N20 A46 15pf on 15c pur .50 1.50
Never hinged 1.90
On cover 14.00
1N21 A46 20pf on 20c red vio .50 *1.90*
Never hinged 2.25
On cover 14.00
On cover, single franking 37.50
1N22 A46 30pf on 25c blue .75 *1.90*
Never hinged 2.60
On cover 14.00
On cover, single franking 37.50

Red Surcharge
1N23 A49 75pf on 50c car rose & blk 15.00 19.00
Never hinged 55.00
On cover 65.00
1N24 A50 1m25pf on 1fr vio 21.00 20.00
Never hinged 70.00
On cover —
Nos. 1N18-1N24 (7) 38.35 *46.40*
Set, never hinged 135.00

EUPEN ISSUE
Belgian Stamps of 1915-20 Overprinted

Nos. 1N25-1N36

Nos. 1N37-1N41

1920-21 *Perf. 11½, 14, 14½*
1N25 A46 1c orange .35 *.90*
Never hinged .85
On cover 8.75
1N26 A46 2c chocolate .35 *.90*
Never hinged .85
On cover 8.75
1N27 A46 3c gray blk ('21) .60 *3.75*
Never hinged 1.10
On cover 50.00
1N28 A46 5c green .60 *.90*
Never hinged 1.10
On cover 8.75
On cover, single franking 45.00
1N29 A46 10c carmine .95 *1.25*
Never hinged 1.75
On cover 8.75
On cover, single franking 32.50
1N30 A46 15c purple 1.25 *1.25*
Never hinged 2.40
On cover 8.75
1N31 A46 20c red violet 1.50 *1.50*
Never hinged 3.00
On cover 8.75
On cover, single franking 50.00
1N32 A46 25c blue 1.25 *1.90*
Never hinged 2.60
On cover 10.00
On cover, single franking 27.50
1N33 A54 25c dp blue ('21) 4.50 *16.00*
Never hinged 9.00
On cover 45.00
On cover, single franking 50.00
1N34 A47 35c brn org & blk 1.90 *1.90*
Never hinged 3.75
On cover 32.50
1N35 A48 40c green & blk 2.25 *2.25*
Never hinged 4.50
On cover 32.50
1N36 49 50c car rose & blk 6.00 *7.50*
Never hinged 12.50
On cover 32.50
On cover, single franking 110.00
1N37 A56 65c cl & blk ('21) 3.25 *21.00*
Never hinged 6.75
On cover 65.00
1N38 A50 1fr violet 24.00 19.00
Never hinged 47.50
On cover 65.00
1N39 A51 2fr slate 40.00 30.00
Never hinged 82.50
On cover 120.00
1N40 A52 5fr deep blue 13.00 *11.00*
Never hinged 26.00
On cover —
1N41 A53 10fr brown 60.00 *50.00*
Never hinged 115.00
On cover —
Nos. 1N25-1N41 (17) 161.75 *171.00*
Set, never hinged 320.00

MALMEDY ISSUE
Belgian Stamps of 1915-20 Overprinted

Nos. 1N42-1N50

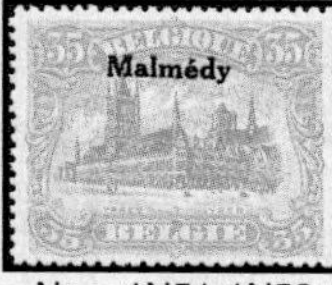

Nos. 1N51-1N53

Nos. 1N54-1N58

1920-21
1N42 A46 1c orange .45 *.90*
Never hinged .90
On cover 8.75
1N43 A46 2c chocolate .45 *.90*
Never hinged .90
On cover 8.75
1N44 A46 3c gray blk ('21) .45 *3.75*
Never hinged .90
On cover 50.00
1N45 A46 5c green .65 *.90*
Never hinged 1.25
On cover 8.75
On cover, single franking 45.00
1N46 A46 10c carmine .95 *1.25*
Never hinged 1.90
On cover 8.75
1N47 A46 15c purple 1.50 *1.50*
Never hinged 3.00
On cover 8.75
1N48 A46 20c red violet 1.90 *1.90*
Never hinged 3.75
On cover 8.75
On cover, single franking 50.00
1N49 A46 25c blue 1.50 *1.90*
Never hinged 3.00
On cover 11.00
On cover, single franking 27.50
1N50 A54 25c dp blue ('21) 4.50 *16.00*
Never hinged 9.00
On cover 45.00
On cover, single franking 50.00
1N51 A47 35c brn org & blk 1.90 *1.90*
Never hinged 3.75
On cover 32.50
1N52 A48 40c green & blk 1.90 2.25
Never hinged 3.75
On cover 32.50
1N53 A49 50c car rose & blk 7.50 *7.50*
Never hinged 15.00
On cover 30.00
On cover, single franking 35.00
1N54 A56 65c cl & blk ('21) 3.25 *21.00*
Never hinged 6.75
On cover 65.00
1N55 A50 1fr violet 24.00 18.00
Never hinged 47.50
On cover 65.00
On cover, single franking 100.00
1N56 A51 2fr slate 40.00 30.00
Never hinged 80.00
On cover 125.00
On cover, single franking 325.00
1N57 A52 5fr deep blue 13.00 *16.00*
Never hinged 26.00
On cover —
1N58 A53 10fr brown 60.00 *55.00*
Never hinged 110.00
On cover —
Nos. 1N42-1N58 (17) 163.90 *180.65*
Set, never hinged 325.00

OCCUPATION POSTAGE DUE STAMPS

Belgian Postage Due Stamps of 1919-20, Overprinted

1920 Unwmk. *Perf. 14½*
1NJ1 D3 5c green .95 *1.10*
Never hinged 1.90
On cover 50.00
On cover, single franking 65.00
1NJ2 D3 10c carmine 1.90 *1.90*
Never hinged 3.75
On cover 50.00
1NJ3 D3 20c gray green 3.75 *4.50*
Never hinged 7.50
On cover 65.00
1NJ4 D3 30c bright blue 3.75 *4.50*
Never hinged 7.50
On cover 65.00
On cover, single franking 100.00
1NJ5 D3 50c gray 18.00 *15.00*
Never hinged 37.50
Nos. 1NJ1-1NJ5 (5) 28.35 *27.00*
Set, never hinged 57.50

Belgian Postage Due Stamps of 1919-20, Overprinted

Unwmk.
1NJ6 D3 5c green 1.90 1.10
Never hinged 3.75
On cover 65.00
On cover, single franking 100.00
1NJ7 D3 10c carmine 3.75 1.90
Never hinged 7.50
On cover 65.00
a. Inverted overprint —
1NJ8 D3 20c gray green 13.00 *11.00*
Never hinged 26.00
On cover 82.50
1NJ9 D3 30c bright blue 7.50 *8.00*
Never hinged 15.00
On cover 100.00
1NJ10 D3 50c gray 15.00 11.00
Never hinged 30.00
On cover 140.00
Nos. 1NJ6-1NJ10 (5) 41.15 *33.00*
Set, never hinged 82.50

Nos. 1NJ1-1NJ10 were valid for postage until April 30, 1931, nearly one year after the Belgians and other occupation forces evacuated the Rhineland. Mixed frankings with Belgian stamps were permitted. The values for used stamps are for stamps with cancels from the Belgian military post offices in occupied Germany.

GERMANY OFFICES ABROAD

OFFICES IN CHINA

100 Pfennings = 1 Mark
100 Cents = 1 Dollar (1905)

Stamps of Germany, 1889-90, Overprinted in Black at 56 degree Angle

1898 Unwmk. Perf. 13½x14½

1 A9 3pf dark brown 5.75 6.00
Never hinged 20.00
On cover 27.50
a. 3pf yellow brown 12.00 12.00
Never hinged 42.50
On cover 92.50
b. 3pf reddish ocher 37.50 125.00
Never hinged 190.00
On cover 300.00
2 A9 5pf green 3.25 3.25
Never hinged 12.00
On cover 19.00
3 A10 10pf carmine 5.75 6.25
Never hinged 19.00
On cover 17.00
4 A10 20pf ultramarine 17.00 16.50
Never hinged 42.50
On cover 37.50
5 A10 25pf orange 32.50 30.00
Never hinged 75.00
On cover 92.50
6 A10 50pf red brown 16.00 13.50
On cover 52.50
Never hinged 37.50
Nos. 1-6 (6) 80.25 75.50

Overprinted at 45 degree Angle

1c A9 3pf yellow brown 135.00 23,000.
Never hinged 400.00
On cover 37,500.
1d A9 3pf reddish ocher 375.00
Never hinged 1,000.
e. 3pf gray brown 1,850. 23,000.
Never hinged 3,000.
2a A9 5pf green 11.50 13.00
Never hinged 30.00
On cover 35.00
3a A10 10pf carmine 32.50 10.50
Never hinged 100.00
On cover 27.50
4a A10 20pf ultramarine 14.50 10.50
Never hinged 40.00
On cover 27.50
5a A10 25pf orange 50.00 65.00
Never hinged 190.00
On cover 160.00
6a A10 50pf red brown 21.00 17.50
Never hinged 80.00
On cover 57.50

Value for No. 1c used is for a stamp with small 1898 Shanghai cancel. Examples with other cancellations or later Shanghai cancels sell for about half the value quoted.

Covers: Values for Nos. 6, 6a are for overfranked complete covers, usually philatelic.

Foochow Issue

Nos. 3 and 3a Handstamp Surcharged

1900

16 A10 5pf on 10pf, #3 550.00 800.00
Never hinged 1,100.
On cover 2,000.
a. On No. 3a 650.00 950.00
Never hinged 1,400.
On cover 2,000.

For similar 5pf surcharges on 10pf carmine, see Tsingtau Issue, Kiauchau.

Tientsin Issue

German Stamps of 1900 Issue Handstamped

1900

17 A11 3pf brown 600.00 800.00
Never hinged 2,250.
On cover 1,350.
a. Double overprint 3,000.
Never hinged 4,000.
18 A11 5pf green 400.00 360.00
Never hinged 1,500.
On cover 1,500.
a. Double overprint 2,000.
Never hinged 2,500.
19 A11 10pf carmine 950.00 875.00
Never hinged 4,500.
On cover 2,250.
a. Double overprint 4,250.
Never hinged 6,500.
20 A11 20pf ultra 800.00 950.00
Never hinged 4,000.
On cover 2,600.
a. Double overprint 3,800.
Never hinged 6,000.
21 A11 30pf org & blk, sal 4,750. 4,750.
Never hinged 14,500.
On cover 11,500.
a. Double overprint 12,500.
Never hinged 15,000.
22 A11 50pf pur & blk, sal 16,000. 13,500.
Never hinged 45,000.
On cover 27,500.
a. Double overprint —
Never hinged —
23 A11 80pf lake & blk, rose 4,750. 4,750.
Never hinged 15,000.
On cover 11,500.
a. Double overprint 12,500.
Never hinged 15,000.

This handstamp is known inverted and double on most values.

Excellent faked handstamps are plentiful.

Unissued denominations include 25pf black and orange, yellow (value unused, $37,500); 40pf carmine and black (value unused, $37,500); 2m deep blue; and 3m violet black. Used examples are favor canceled.

Used values for Nos. 16-23 are for postally used items, CTO on philatelic usage is about half.

Covers: Values for Nos. 22-23 are for overfranked complete covers, usually philatelic.

Regular Issue

Germany No. 53 Overprinted

Germany No. 64 Ovptd.

Germany No. 65A Ovptd.

1901 Perf. 14, 14½

Overprinted Horizontally in Black

24 A11 3pf brown 1.50 2.10
Never hinged 5.25
On cover 75.00
a. 3pf light red brown 105.00 45.00
Never hinged 375.00
On cover 190.00
25 A11 5pf green 1.50 1.60
Never hinged 5.25
On cover 15.00
26 A11 10pf carmine 2.40 1.25
Never hinged 7.25
On cover 15.00
27 A11 20pf ultra 3.25 1.60
Never hinged 10.50
On cover 15.00
28 A11 25pf org & blk, yel 9.50 16.00
Never hinged 29.00
On cover 35.00
29 A11 30pf org & blk, sal 9.50 13.00
Never hinged 29.00
On cover 27.50
30 A11 40pf lake & blk 9.50 9.50
Never hinged 29.00
On cover 27.50
31 A11 50pf pur & blk, sal 9.50 9.50
Never hinged 29.00
On cover 19.00
32 A11 80pf lake & blk, rose 11.00 11.00
Never hinged 32.50
On cover 27.50

Overprinted in Black or Red

33 A12 1m car rose 27.50 32.50
Never hinged 97.50
On cover 70.00
34 A13 2m gray blue 27.50 29.00
Never hinged 87.50
On cover 67.50
35 A14 3m blk vio (R) 47.50 65.00
Never hinged 160.00
On cover 130.00
36 A15 5m slate & car, I 1,350. 2,400.
Never hinged 2,900.
On cover —
b. Red and/or white retouched 210.00 300.00
Never hinged 550.00
On cover 600.00
36A A15 5m slate & car, II 210.00 325.00
Never hinged 550.00
On cover 600.00
Nos. 24-36A (14) 1,720. 2,917.

See note after Germany No. 65A for information on retouches on No. 36. For description of the 5m Type I and Type II, see note above Germany No. 62.

Surcharged on German Stamps of 1902 in Black or Red

a

b

c

1905 Unwmk.

37 A16(a) 1c on 3pf 3.00 3.50
Never hinged 8.00
On cover 22.50
38 A16(a) 2c on 5pf 3.00 1.60
Never hinged 13.00
On cover 15.00
39 A16(a) 4c on 10pf 5.50 1.60
Never hinged 23.00
On cover 15.00
40 A16(a) 10c on 20pf 3.00 1.75
Never hinged 12.00
On cover 15.00
41 A16(a) 20c on 40pf 19.00 7.25
Never hinged 65.00
On cover 30.00
42 A16(a) 40c on 80pf 30.00 13.50
Never hinged 115.00
On cover 30.00
43 A17(b) ½d on 1m (26x17 perf. holes) 16.00 20.00
Never hinged 72.50
On cover 45.00
a. ½d on 1m, 25x16 perf. holes 67.50 65.00
Never hinged 210.00
On cover 175.00
44 A21(b) 1d on 2m 16.00 22.50
Never hinged 65.00
On cover 45.00
45 A19(c) 1½d on 3m (R) (26x17 perf. holes) 255.00 115.00
Never hinged 900.00
On cover 150.00
a. 1½d on 3m, 25x16 perf. holes 17.00 47.50
Never hinged 57.50
On cover 85.00
46 A20(b) 2½d on 5m 100.00 300.00
Never hinged 340.00
On cover 650.00
Nos. 37-46 (10) 450.50 486.70

Surcharged on German Stamps of 1905 in Black or Red

1906-13 Wmk. 125

47 A16(a) 1c on 3pf .65 1.25
Never hinged 1.60
On cover 15.00
48 A16(a) 2c on 5pf .45 1.25
Never hinged .75
On cover 15.00
49 A16(a) 4c on 10pf .80 1.60
Never hinged 2.00
On cover 15.00
50 A16(a) 10c on 20pf .80 7.00
Never hinged 2.00
On cover 15.00
51 A16(a) 20c on 40pf 1.60 3.50
Never hinged 3.50
On cover 9.00
52 A16(a) 40c on 80pf 1.60 52.50
Never hinged 3.50
On cover 150.00
53 A17(b) ½d on 1m 6.50 40.00
Never hinged 19.00
On cover 110.00
54 A21(b) 1d on 2m 10.50 40.00
Never hinged 52.50
On cover 85.00
55 A19(c) 1½d on 3m (R) 8.00 120.00
Never hinged 57.50
On cover 240.00
56 A20(b) 2½d on 5m (26x17 perf. holes) 29.00 80.00
Never hinged 115.00
On cover 190.00
a. 2½d on 5m, 25x17 perf. holes 30.00
Never hinged 150.00
Nos. 47-56 (10) 59.90 347.10

Forged cancellations exist.

OFFICES IN MOROCCO

100 Centimos = 1 Peseta

Stamps of Germany Surcharged in Black

1899 Unwmk. Perf. 13½x14½

1 A9 3c on 3pf dk brn 3.25 2.10
Never hinged 7.50
On cover 30.00
2 A9 5c on 5pf green 3.25 2.40
Never hinged 7.50
On cover 22.50
3 A10 10c on 10pf car 9.00 9.00
Never hinged 19.00
On cover 35.00
4 A10 25c on 20pf ultra 18.00 13.50
Never hinged 37.50
On cover 60.00
5 A10 30c on 25pf orange 27.50 32.50
Never hinged 75.00
On cover 140.00
6 A10 60c on 50pf red brn 22.50 37.50
Never hinged 65.00
On cover 92.50
Nos. 1-6 (6) 83.50 97.00

Covers: Value for No. 6 is for overfranked complete covers, usually philatelic.

Before Nos. 1-6 were issued, the same six basic stamps of Germany's 1889-1900 issue were overprinted "Marocco" diagonally without the currency-changing surcharge line, but were not issued. Value set, $775 hinged, $1,800. never hinged.

German Stamps of 1900 Surcharged in Black or Red

Germany No. 55 Srchd.

Germany No. 62 Srchd.

Germany No. 63 Srchd.

Germany No. 64 Srchd.

Germany No. 65A Srchd.

1900 Perf. 14, 14½

7 A11 3c on 3pf brn 1.25 2.25
Never hinged 2.75
On cover 11.50
8 A11 5c on 5pf grn 1.50 1.50
Never hinged 5.00
On cover 15.00
9 A11 10c on 10pf car 2.25 1.50
Never hinged 7.00
On cover 15.00
10 A11 25c on 20pf ultra 3.00 2.75
Never hinged 9.00
On cover 27.50

11 A11 30c on 25pf org & blk, *yel* 9.00 *15.00*
Never hinged 35.00
On cover 35.00
12 A11 35c on 30pf org & blk, *sal* 6.75 6.00
Never hinged 22.50
On cover 30.00
13 A11 50c on 40pf lake & blk 6.75 6.00
Never hinged 22.50
On cover 30.00
14 A11 60c on 50pf pur & blk, *sal* 13.50 *29.00*
Never hinged 50.00
On cover 60.00
15 A11 1p on 80pf lake & blk, *rose* 12.00 10.50
Never hinged 42.50
On cover 45.00
16 A12 1p25c on 1m car rose 30.00 *45.00*
Never hinged 100.00
On cover 100.00
17 A13 2p50c on 2m gray bl 37.50 *57.50*
Never hinged 100.00
On cover 110.00
18 A14 3p75c on 3m blk vio (R) 45.00 *65.00*
Never hinged 170.00
On cover 150.00
19 A15 6p25c on 5m sl & car, type I 975.00 *1,325.*
Never hinged 1,950.
On cover —
b. Red and/or white retouched 165.00 *300.00*
Never hinged 550.00
On cover 600.00
c. White only retouched 200.00 *325.00*
Never hinged 525.00
On cover 900.00
19A A15 6p25c on 5m sl & car, type II 1,500. —
Never hinged 3,000.
On cover —
Nos. 7-19A (14) 2,644. *1,567.*

See note after Germany No. 65A for information on retouches on No. 19. For description of the 5m Type I and Type II, see note above Germany No. 62.

1903 New Surcharge Plates

8D A11 5c on 5pf grn 70.00 11.00
Never hinged 190.00
On cover 75.00
16D A12 1p25c on 1m car rose 350.00 180.00
Never hinged 1,050.
On cover 450.00
17D A13 2p50c on 2m gray bl 500.00 110.00
never hinged 2,100.
On cover 300.00
18D A14 3p75c on 3m blk vio (R) 1,300. 240.00
Never hinged 4,500.
On cover 575.00
19D A15 6p25c on 5m sl & car, type II 200.00 260.00
Never hinged 475.00
On cover 750.00

The 1903 printing Nos. 8D, 16D-18D, 19D differs from Nos. 8, 16-18 and 19A in the "M" and "t" of the surcharge.

German Stamps of 1902 Surcharged in Black or Red

a

b

c

1905 Unwmk.

20 A16(a) 3c on 3pf 2.60 3.50
Never hinged 6.75
On cover 22.50
21 A16(a) 5c on 5pf 4.50 1.10
Never hinged 11.00
On cover 15.00
22 A16(a) 10c on 10pf 8.25 1.10
Never hinged 27.50
On cover 15.00
23 A16(a) 25c on 20pf 18.00 3.25
Never hinged 45.00
On cover 27.50
24 A16(a) 30c on 25pf 6.00 6.00
Never hinged 19.00
On cover 45.00
25 A16(a) 35c on 30pf 9.00 5.50
Never hinged 30.00
On cover 45.00
26 A16(a) 50c on 40pf 9.00 7.50
Never hinged 27.50
On cover 45.00
27 A16(a) 60c on 50pf 20.00 *22.50*
Never hinged 52.50
On cover 50.00
28 A16(a) 1p on 80pf 20.00 18.00
Never hinged 52.50
On cover 45.00
29 A17(b) 1p25c on 1m 50.00 35.00
Never hinged 200.00
On cover 67.50
30 A21(b) 2p50c on 2m 95.00 *135.00*
Never hinged 270.00
On cover 260.00
31 A19(c) 3p75c on 3m (R) 42.50 *52.50*
Never hinged 110.00
On cover 120.00
32 A20(b) 6p25c on 5m 150.00 *200.00*
Never hinged 325.00
On cover 370.00
Nos. 20-32 (13) 434.85 *490.95*

Surcharged on Germany No. 54

32A A11(a) 5c on 5pf 7.50 *24.00*
Never hinged 18.00
On cover 1,900.

German Stamps of 1905 Surcharged

1906-11 Wmk. 125

33 A16(a) 3c on 3pf 8.25 2.00
Never hinged 18.00
On cover 22.50
34 A16(a) 5c on 5pf 6.50 1.10
Never hinged 13.50
On cover 15.00
35 A16(a) 10c on 10pf 6.50 1.10
Never hinged 13.50
On cover 15.00
36 A16(a) 25c on 20pf 19.00 7.50
Never hinged 45.00
On cover 30.00
37 A16(a) 30c on 25pf 19.00 15.00
Never hinged 45.00
On cover 45.00
38 A16(a) 35c on 30pf 15.00 9.75
Never hinged 32.50
On cover 45.00
39 A16(a) 50c on 40pf 30.00 *135.00*
Never hinged 70.00
On cover 275.00
40 A16(a) 60c on 50pf 22.50 17.00
Never hinged 65.00
On cover 35.00
41 A16(a) 1p on 80pf *110.00* *260.00*
Never hinged 325.00
On cover 525.00
42 A17(b) 1p25c on 1m 60.00 *165.00*
Never hinged 160.00
On cover 300.00
43 A21(b) 2p50c on 2m 60.00 *165.00*
Never hinged 160.00
On cover 300.00
44 A20(b) 6p25c on 5m 110.00 *300.00*
Never hinged 325.00
On cover 600.00
Nos. 33-44 (12) 466.75 *1,078.*

Excellent forgeries exist of No. 41.

Surcharge Spelled "Marokko" in Black or Red

1911

45 A16(a) 3c on 3pf .55 *.75*
Never hinged 1.00
On cover 19.00
46 A16(a) 5c on 5pf .55 *1.00*
Never hinged 1.00
On cover 15.00
47 A16(a) 10c on 10pf .55 *1.10*
Never hinged 1.10
On cover 15.00
48 A16(a) 25c on 20pf .65 *1.40*
Never hinged 1.10
On cover 22.50
49 A16(a) 30c on 25pf 1.50 *16.00*
Never hinged 3.50
On cover 45.00
50 A16(a) 35c on 30pf 1.50 *8.75*
Never hinged 3.50
On cover 35.00
51 A16(a) 50c on 40pf *1.25* *5.25*
Never hinged 2.75
On cover 22.50
52 A16(a) 60c on 50pf *2.40* *37.50*
Never hinged 5.50
On cover 75.00
53 A16(a) 1p on 80pf 1.60 *24.00*
Never hinged 4.50
On cover 57.50
54 A17(b) 1p25c on 1m *4.50* *65.00*
Never hinged 11.50
On cover 110.00
55 A21(b) 2p50c on 2m *6.00* *47.50*
Never hinged 13.50
On cover 100.00
56 A19(c) 3p75c on 3m (R) 10.50 *225.00*
Never hinged 24.00
On cover 425.00
57 A20(b) 6p25c on 5m 19.00 *325.00*
Never hinged 45.00
On cover 575.00
Nos. 45-57 (13) 50.55 *758.25*

Forged cancellations exist.

OFFICES IN THE TURKISH EMPIRE

Unused values for Nos. 1-6 are for stamps with original gum. Stamps without gum sell for about one-third of the figures quoted.

40 Paras = 1 Piaster

German Stamps of 1880-83 Surcharged in Black or Blue

Germany No. 30 Surcharged

Germany No. 31 Surcharged

1884 Unwmk. *Perf. 13½x14½*

1 A6 10pa on 5pf dull vio 52.50 30.00
Never hinged 700.00
On cover 375.00
2 A7 20pa on 10pf rose 75.00 75.00
Never hinged 1,050.
On cover 300.00
3 A7 1pi on 20pf ultra (Bk) 60.00 7.50
Never hinged 300.00
On cover 92.50
4 A7 1pi on 20pf ultra (Bl) 2,250. 72.50
Never hinged 6,750.
On cover 375.00
5 A7 1¼pi on 25pf brn 120.00 *260.00*
Never hinged 1,100.
On cover 825.00
a. 1¼ on 25pf choc brn ('91) 175.00 *225.00*
Never hinged 1,650.
6 A7 2½pi on 50pf gray grn 120.00 140.00
Never hinged 1,100.
On cover 925.00
a. 2½pi on 50pf deep olive grn 275.00 210.00
Never hinged 2,300.
On cover 1,100.
Nos. 1-6 (6) 2,678. 585.00

There are two types of the surcharge on the 1¼pi and 2½pi stamps, the difference being in the spacing between the figures and the word "PIASTER."

Covers: Values for Nos. 6, 6a are for overfranked complete covers, usually philatelic.

There are re-issues of these stamps which vary only slightly from the originals in overprint measurements.

German Stamps of 1880-1900 Surcharged in Black

Germany No. 47 Surcharged

Germany No. 48 Surcharged

Germany No. 50 Surcharged

1889

8 A9 10pa on 5pf grn 3.50 3.75
Never hinged 23.00
On cover 27.50
9 A10 20pa on 10pf car 9.00 3.25
Never hinged 50.00
On cover 23.00
10 A10 1pi on 20pf ultra 6.00 2.25
Never hinged 35.00
On cover 27.50
11 A10 1¼pi on 25pf org 22.50 20.00
Never hinged 120.00
On cover 100.00
12 A10 2½pi on 50pf choc 35.00 22.50
Never hinged 260.00
On cover 150.00
a. 2½pi on 50pf copper brown 190.00 110.00
Never hinged 1,450.
On cover 450.00
Nos. 8-12 (5) 76.00 51.75

Covers: Values for Nos. 12, 12a are for overfranked complete covers, usually philatelic.

German Stamps of 1900 Surcharged

Germany No. 55 Surcharged

Germany No. 62 Srchd.

Germany No. 63 Srchd.

Germany No. 64 Srchd.

Germany No. 65A Srchd.

1900 *Perf. 14, 14½*

Black or Red Surcharge

13 A11 10pa on 5pf grn 1.75 1.75
Never hinged 5.25
On cover 15.00
14 A11 20pa on 10pf car 2.75 2.25
Never hinged 6.00
On cover 15.00
15 A11 1pi on 20pf ultra 4.50 1.75
Never hinged 11.50
On cover 15.00
16 A11 1¼pi on 25pf org & blk, *yel* 6.00 4.50
Never hinged 22.50
On cover 19.00
17 A11 1½pi on 30pf org & blk, *sal* 6.00 4.50
Never hinged 22.50
On cover 19.00
18 A11 2pi on 40pf lake & blk 6.00 4.50
Never hinged 22.50
On cover 19.00
19 A11 2½pi on 50pf pur & blk, *sal* 12.00 *13.00*
Never hinged 35.00
On cover 35.00
20 A11 4pi on 80pf lake & blk, *rose* 13.50 13.00
Never hinged 45.00
On cover 35.00
21 A12 5pi on 1m car rose 35.00 37.50
Never hinged 105.00
On cover 100.00
22 A13 10pi on 2m gray bl 30.00 *42.50*
Never hinged 105.00
On cover 92.50
23 A14 15pi on 3m blk vio (R) 45.00 *110.00*
Never hinged 160.00
On cover 275.00
24 A15 25pi on 5m sl & car, type I 640.00 *1,250.*
Never hinged 1,800.
On cover —
a. Double surcharge *9,000.*
d. Red and/or white retouched 175.00 *250.00*
Never hinged 500.00
On cover 675.00
e. White only retouched 290.00 500.00
Never hinged 700.00
On cover 200.00
24B A15 25pi on 5m sl & car, type II 290.00 *500.00*
Never hinged 700.00
On cover 750.00

c. Double surcharge 9,750. —
Never hinged 9,800.
Nos. 13-24B (13) 1,093. 1,985.

See note after Germany No. 65A for information on retouches on No. 24. For description of the 5m Type I and Type II, see note above Germany No. 62.

Covers: Values for Nos. 19-24B are for overfranked complete covers, usually philatelic.

German Stamps of 1900 Surcharged in Black

1903-05

25 A11 10pa on 5pf green 9.00 *13.50*
Never hinged 32.50
On cover 75.00
26 A11 20pa on 10pf car 30.00 19.00
Never hinged 75.00
On cover 100.00
27 A11 1pi on 20pf ultra 8.25 7.25
Never hinged 30.00
On cover 60.00

German Stamps of 1900, 1905 Surcharged in Black

28 A12 5pi on 1m car rose 140.00 95.00
Never hinged 375.00
On cover 290.00
29 A13 10pi on 2m bl ('05) 150.00 *260.00*
Never hinged 450.00
On cover 525.00
30 A15 25pi on 5m sl & car 190.00 *525.00*
Never hinged 650.00
On cover 850.00
a. Double surcharge *4,500.*
Never hinged 9,000.
Nos. 25-30 (6) 527.25 *919.75*

The 1903-05 surcharges may be easily distinguished from those of 1900 by the added bar at the top of the letter "A."

German Stamps of 1902 Surcharged in Black or Red

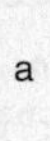
a

b

1905 **Unwmk.**

31 A16(a) 10pa on 5pf 3.50 2.50
Never hinged 5.75
On cover 15.00
32 A16(a) 20pa on 10pf 9.00 3.25
Never hinged 19.00
On cover 15.00
33 A16(a) 1pi on 20pf 19.00 2.00
Never hinged 50.00
On cover 15.00
34 A16(a) 1¼pi on 25pf 9.00 7.50
Never hinged 22.50
On cover 26.00
35 A16(a) 1½pi on 30pf 13.50 15.00
Never hinged 70.00
On cover 45.00
36 A16(a) 2pi on 40pf 22.50 15.00
Never hinged 57.50
On cover 45.00
37 A16(a) 2½pi on 50pf 9.00 *22.50*
Never hinged 15.00
On cover 57.50
38 A16(a) 4pi on 80pf 27.50 17.50
Never hinged 70.00
On cover 42.50
39 A17(b) 5pi on 1m 45.00 45.00
Never hinged 140.00
On cover 75.00
40 A21(b) 10pi on 2m 37.50 *45.00*
Never hinged 82.50
On cover 110.00
41 A19(b) 15pi on 3m (R) 45.00 *52.50*
Never hinged 170.00
On cover 130.00
42 A20(b) 25pi on 5m 225.00 *525.00*
Never hinged 500.00
On cover 1,000.
Nos. 31-42 (12) 465.50 *752.75*

German Stamps of 1905 Surcharged in Black or Red

1906-12 **Wmk. 125**

43 A16(a) 10pa on 5pf 2.25 .90
Never hinged 5.25
On cover 15.00
44 A16(a) 20pa on 10pf 4.50 .90
Never hinged 5.75
On cover 15.00
45 A16(a) 1pi on 20pf 6.00 .90
Never hinged 19.00
On cover 15.00
46 A16(a) 1¼pi on 25pf 12.00 12.00
Never hinged 42.50
On cover 37.50
47 A16(a) 1½pi on 30pf 12.00 10.00
Never hinged 42.50
On cover 27.50
48 A16(a) 2pi on 40pf 6.00 1.75
Never hinged 17.00
On cover 19.00
49 A16(a) 2½pi on 50pf 9.00 *16.50*
Never hinged 37.50
On cover 30.00
50 A16(a) 4pi on 80pf 15.00 *22.50*
Never hinged 52.50
On cover 42.50
51 A17(b) 5pi on 1m 35.00 30.00
Never hinged 100.00
On cover 85.00
52 A21(b) 10pi on 2m 35.00 *45.00*
Never hinged 110.00
On cover 110.00
53 A19(b) 15pi on 3m (R) 60.00 *450.00*
Never hinged 290.00
On cover 1,500.
54 A20(b) 25pi on 5m 30.00 *75.00*
Never hinged 75.00
On cover 240.00
Nos. 43-54 (12) 226.75 665.45

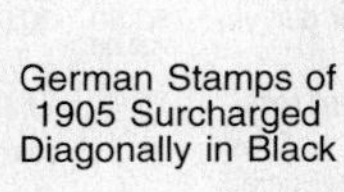
German Stamps of 1905 Surcharged Diagonally in Black

1908

55 A16 5c on 5pf 1.90 *2.75*
Never hinged 3.75
On cover 15.00
56 A16 10c on 10pf 2.75 *4.50*
Never hinged 6.00
On cover 22.50
57 A16 25c on 20pf 6.00 *22.50*
Never hinged 17.00
On cover 75.00
58 A16 50c on 40pf 30.00 *55.00*
Never hinged 82.50
On cover 150.00
59 A16 100c on 80pf 52.50 *60.00*
Never hinged 140.00
On cover 210.00
Nos. 55-59 (5) 93.15 *144.75*

Forged cancellations exist on Nos. 37, 53-54, 57-59.

GIBRALTAR

jə-ˈbrol-tər

LOCATION — A fortified promontory, including the Rock, extending from Spain's southeast coast at the entrance to the Mediterranean Sea
GOVT. — British Crown Colony
AREA — 2.5 sq. mi.
POP. — 31,183 (1982)
CAPITAL — Gibraltar

12 Pence = 1 Shilling
20 Shillings = 1 Pound
100 Centimos = 1 Peseta (1889-95)

Catalogue values for unused stamps in this country are for Never Hinged items, beginning with Scott 119 in the regular postage section.

STAMPS OF GREAT BRITAIN USED IN GIBRALTAR

British Post Office opened Jan. 1, 1857. Transferred to Colonial authority Jan. 1, 1886.

Values are for clear cancellations on sound, fault-free stamps, with average to fine centering. In many cases, very fine examples are rare or non-existent.

Canceled with barred "G" obliterator

1857-59

A1 1p red brn, Die I (#8) 425.00
A2 1p red brn, Die II (#9) 800.00
A3 1p red brn, Die II (#12) 375.00
A4 1p red brn, Die II (#16) 100.00
A5 1p rose red (#20) 25.00
A6 2p blue (#13) 500.00
A7 2p blue (#19) 400.00
A8 2p blue (#17) 80.00
A9 2p blue, Plate 7 (#29) 350.00
A10 4p rose (#26) 65.00
a. Thick glazed paper —
A11 6p lilac (#27) 45.00
a. Blued paper (#27c) 900.00
A12 1sh green (#28) 140.00
a. Thick paper (#28d) —
b. Blued paper (#28c) 1,600.

Canceled with barred oval "A26" obliterator

1859-85

A13 ½p rose red, plates 4-6, 8, 10-15, 19, 20 (#58), *value from* 42.50
A14 1p red brn (#3), *value from* *2,500.*
A15 1p red brn, Die II (#16) 275.00
A16 1p rose red (#20) 15.00
A17 1p rose red, plates 71-74, 76, 78-125, 127, 129-225 (#33) 26.00
A18 1½p lake red, plates 1, 3 (#32), *value from* 800.00
A19 2p blue (#17) 160.00
A20 2p blue, plates 7, 8, 9, 12 (#29), *value from* 26.00
A21 2p blue, plates 13, 14, 15 (#30), *value from* 26.00
A22 2½p claret, plates 1, 2, 3 (#66), *value from* 35.00
a. Bluish paper, plates 1, 2 (#66a), *value from* 110.00
b. Lettered "LH-FL" (#66b) *3,500.*
A23 2½p claret, plates 3-17 (#67), *value from* 22.50
A24 2½p blue plates 17-20 (#68), *value from* 14.50
A25 2½p blue plates 21-23 (#82), *value from* 12.00
A26 3p rose (#37) 375.00
A27 3p rose (#44) 95.00
A28 3p rose, plates 4-10 (#49), *value from* 52.50
A29 3p rose, plates 11, 12, 14-20 (#61), *value from* 70.00
A30 3p rose, plates 20, 21 (#83) —
A31 3p on 3d violet (#94) *225.00*
A32 4p rose (#26) 120.00
a. Thick glazed paper (#26b) —
A33 4p ver, plate 3 (#34) 52.50
a. Hair lines (#34c) 60.00
A34 4p ver, plates 7-14 (#43), *value from* 32.50
A35 4p ver, plate 15 (#69) 325.00
A36 4p pale ol grn, plate 15 (#70) 175.00
Plate 16 (#70) 160.00
A37 4p gray brn, plate 17 (#71) 450.00
A38 4p gray brn, plates 17, 18 (#84), *value from* 80.00
A39 6p lilac (#27) 45.00
A40 6p lilac, plate 3 (#39) 42.50
a. Hairlines, plate 4 (#39d) 100.00
A41 6p lilac, plate 5 (#45) 45.00
Plate 6 (#45) 100.00
A42 6p dull vio, plate 6 (#50) 50.00
A43 6p violet, plates 6, 8, 9 (#51) 35.00
A44 6p brn, plate 11 (#59) 40.00
a. 6p pale buff, plate 11 (#59b) 160.00
Plate 12 (#59b) 175.00
A45 6p gray, plate 12 (#60) 110.00
A46 6p gray, plates 13-17 (#62), *value from* 42.50
A47 6p gray, plates 17, 18 (#86), *value from* 400.00
A48 6p on 6p violet (#95) 140.00
A49 8p orange (#73) 800.00
A50 9p straw (#40) 950.00
a. 9p bister (#40a) 400.00
A51 9p straw (#46) 900.00
A52 9p bister (#52) *350.00*
A53 10p red brown (#53) 160.00
A54 1sh green (#28) 125.00
A55 1sh green (#42) 80.00
A56 1sh green (#48) 65.00
A57 1sh green, plates 4-7 (#54), *value from* 42.50
A58 1sh green, plates 8-13 (#64), *value from* 100.00
A59 1sh salmon, plate 13 (#65) 500.00
A60 1sh sal, plates 13, 14 (#87), *value from* 140.00
A61 2sh blue (#55) 375.00
A62 5sh rose, plate 1 (#57) *1,100.*

1880

A63 ½p deep green (#78) 32.50
a. ½p green (#78c) 32.50
A64 1p red brown (#79) 32.50
A65 1½p red brown (#80) 425.00
A66 2p lilac rose (#81) 80.00
a. 2p deep lilac rose (#81a) 80.00
A67 5p indigo (#85) 175.00

1881

A68 1p lilac, 14 dots (#88) 45.00
A69 1p lilac, 16 dots (#89) 12.50

1883-84

A70 ½p slate blue (#98) 35.00
A71 2p lilac (#100) 140.00
A72 2½p lilac (#101) 20.00
A73 3p lilac (#102) —
A74 4p dull green (#103) 225.00
A75 6p dull green (#105) —

POSTAL FISCAL STAMPS
Canceled with barred oval "A26" obliterator

1878-81

AAR1 1p purple, wmk. 28 ('78) *750.00*
AAR2 1p purple, wmk. 29 ('81) *1,200.*

Types of Bermuda Overprinted in Black

1886, Jan. 1 **Wmk. 2** ***Perf. 14***

1 A6 ½p green 24.00 13.00
2 A1 1p rose 92.50 6.50
3 A2 2p violet brown 155.00 92.50
4 A8 2½p ultra 220.00 4.25
5 A7 4p orange brn 210.00 120.00
6 A4 6p violet 330.00 250.00
7 A5 1sh bister brn 500.00 400.00
Nos. 1-7 (7) 1,532. 886.25

Forged overprints of No. 7 are plentiful.

Victoria
A6 A7

A8

A9

1886-98 **Typo.**

8 A6 ½p dull green ('87) 18.50 4.50
9 A6 ½p gray grn ('98) 14.50 2.00
10 A7 1p rose ('87) 52.50 5.00
11 A7 1p car rose ('98) 14.50 .55
12 A8 2p brn violet 35.00 36.00
13 A8 2p brn vio & ultra ('98) 30.00 2.25
14 A9 2½p brt ultra ('98) 47.50 .80
a. 2½p ultramarine 95.00 3.25
16 A8 4p orange brn 90.00 90.00
17 A8 4p org brn & grn ('98) 21.00 7.50
18 A8 6p violet 145.00 145.00
19 A8 6p vio & car rose ('98) 47.50 25.00
20 A8 1sh bister 275.00 250.00

21 A8 1sh bis & car rose ('98) 47.50 12.00
Nos. 8-14,16-21 (13) 838.50 580.60

Stamps of 1886 Issue Surcharged in Black

1889, July

22 A6 5c on ½p green 13.00 *32.50*
23 A7 10c on 1p rose 15.00 *20.00*
24 A8 25c on 2p brn vio 6.00 *11.50*
a. Small "I" in "CENTIMOS" 140.00 *190.00*
b. Broken "N" 140.00 *190.00*
25 A9 25c on 2½p ultra 30.00 2.75
a. Small "I" in "CENTIMOS" 400.00 125.00
b. Broken "N" 400.00 125.00
26 A8 40c on 4p org brn 62.50 *87.50*
27 A8 50c on 6p violet 67.50 *87.50*
28 A8 75c on 1sh bister 67.50 *82.50*
Nos. 22-28 (7) 261.50 *324.25*
Set, ovptd. "SPECIMEN" 375.00

There are two varieties of the figure "5" in the 5c, 25c, 50c and 75c.

A11

1889-95

29 A11 5c green 7.00 1.25
30 A11 10c rose 5.50 .60
a. Value omitted 7,000.
31 A11 20c ol green ('95) 19.00 *100.00*
31A A11 20c ol grn & brn ('95) 40.00 25.00
32 A11 25c ultra 27.50 .90
a. 25c deep ultramarine 35.00 .90
33 A11 40c orange brn 4.75 4.75
34 A11 50c violet 4.25 2.50
35 A11 75c olive green 42.50 42.50
36 A11 1p bister 92.50 25.00
36A A11 1p bis & bl ('95) 6.00 *8.50*
37 A11 2p blk & car rose ('95) 13.00 *37.50*
38 A11 5p steel blue 52.50 *125.00*
Nos. 29-38 (12) 314.50 *373.50*

A12

A13

King Edward VII

1903, May 1

39 A12 ½p grn & bl grn 14.50 11.00
40 A12 1p violet, *red* 37.50 .70
41 A12 2p grn & car rose 30.00 *45.00*
42 A12 2½p vio & blk, *bl* 8.75 .70
43 A12 6p violet & pur 40.00 26.00
44 A12 1sh blk & car rose 32.50 *42.50*
45 A13 2sh green & ultra 200.00 *275.00*
46 A13 4sh vio & green 150.00 *225.00*
47 A13 8sh vio & blk, *bl* 170.00 *200.00*
48 A13 £1 vio & blk, *red* 650.00 *750.00*
Nos. 39-48 (10) 1,333. *1,576.*
Set, ovptd. "SPECIMEN" 575.00

1904-12 Wmk. 3 Ordinary Paper

49A A12 ½p dull grn & br grn 24.00 4.50
50 A12 1p violet, *red* 30.00 .60
a. Bisected, used as ½p on card 1,800.
51 A12 1p car ('07) 6.50 .70
52 A12 2p grn & car rose ('05) 30.00 14.00
53 A12 2p gray ('10) 10.00 *13.00*
55 A12 2½p ultra ('07) 9.00 1.90
56 A12 6p vio & pur ('06) 52.50 40.00
a. 6p vio & red violet ('12) 160.00 *450.00*
57 A12 1sh blk & car rose ('05) 67.50 22.50
59 A13 2sh grn & ultra ('05) 120.00 *150.00*

Chalky Paper

49 A12 ½p blue grn ('07) 16.00 2.00
49Ab A12 ½p dull grn & br grn ('04) 14.00 9.00
50b A12 1p violet, *red* ('05) 8.50 1.00
52a A12 2p grn & car rose ('07) 10.00 *15.00*
54 A12 2½p vio & blk, *bl* ('07) 45.00 *110.00*
56b A12 6p vio & pur ('08) 35.00 22.50
57a A12 1sh blk & car rose ('06) 57.50 25.00
58 A12 1sh blk, *grn* ('10) 27.50 25.00
59a A13 2sh grn & ultra ('07) 120.00 *150.00*
60 A13 2sh vio & bl, *bl* ('10) 67.50 *57.50*
61 A13 4sh vio & grn 350.00 425.00
62 A13 4sh blk & red ('10) 170.00 *190.00*
63 A13 8sh vio & grn ('11) 250.00 *250.00*
64 A12 £1 vio & blk, *red* 650.00 *700.00*
Nos. 49-64 (14) 1,821. 1,982.

No. 56a, used, must have a 1912 cancellation. Stamps used later sell for about the same as unused.

A14

King George V — A15

1912, July 17 Ordinary Paper

66 A14 ½p green 4.00 .80
a. ½p yellow green ('17) 7.50 2.25
67 A14 1p carmine 4.75 .90
a. 1p scarlet ('16) 10.00 1.60
68 A14 2p gray 20.00 1.75
69 A14 2½p ultra 11.00 3.00
a. 2½p pale ultramarine ('17) 11.00 2.75

Chalky Paper

70 A14 6p dl vio & red vio 11.00 *19.00*
71 A14 1sh black, *green* 18.00 4.25
a. 1sh black, *emerald* ('24) 32.50 *110.00*
b. 1sh blk, *bl grn, ol back* ('19) 29.00 *30.00*
c. 1sh blk, *emer, ol back* ('23) 32.50 *82.50*
72 A15 2sh vio & ultra, *bl* 30.00 4.50
73 A15 4sh black & scar 40.00 *65.00*
74 A15 8sh vio & green 110.00 *130.00*
75 A15 £1 vio & blk, *red* 160.00 *275.00*
Nos. 66-75 (10) 408.75 *504.20*
Set, ovptd. "SPECIMEN" 575.00

1921-32 Ordinary Paper Wmk. 4

76 A14 ½p grn ('26) 1.60 *1.90*
77 A14 1p rose red 2.25 1.40
78 A14 1½p red brn ('22) 2.25 .60
a. 1½p pale red brown ('24) 2.25 .60
79 A14 2p gray 1.60 1.60
80 A14 2½p ultra 22.50 *60.00*
81 A14 3p ultra 2.75 1.75
a. 3p br blue ('22) 3.50 4.75

Chalky Paper

82 A14 6p dl vio & red vio ('26) 1.75 *4.00*
a. 6p gray lilac & red violet ('23) 7.00 6.50
83 A14 1sh blk, *emer* 12.00 *26.00*
84 A14 1sh ol grn & blk 17.50 *42.50*
a. 1sh brn olive & black ('32) 17.50 *21.00*
85 A15 2sh gray vio & ultra, *blue* 21.00 *80.00*
a. 2sh red vio & ultra, *blue* ('25) 8.25 47.50
86 A15 2sh red brn & black 11.00 *40.00*
87 A15 2sh6p grn & blk 11.00 *30.00*
88 A15 4sh blk & scar 75.00 *130.00*
89 A15 5sh car & blk 19.00 *75.00*
90 A15 8sh vio & grn 325.00 *550.00*
91 A15 10sh ultra & blk 37.50 *80.00*
92 A15 £1 org & blk 190.00 *300.00*
93 A15 £5 dl vio & blk 1,750. *6,000.*
Ovptd. "SPECIMEN" 800.00
Nos. 76-92 (17) 753.70 *1,425.*
Nos. 76-92, ovptd. "SPECIMEN" 1,200.

Years issued: Nos. 83, 85, 4sh, 8sh, 1924. 2sh6p, 5sh, 10sh, £5, 1925. £1, 1927. Nos. 84, 86, 1929.

No. 81 is inscribed "3 PENCE".

No. 81

THREE PENCE
No. 94

1930, Apr. 12 Ordinary Paper

94 A14 3p ultramarine 9.50 2.25
Perf "SPECIMEN" 80.00

No. 94 is inscribed "THREE PENCE".

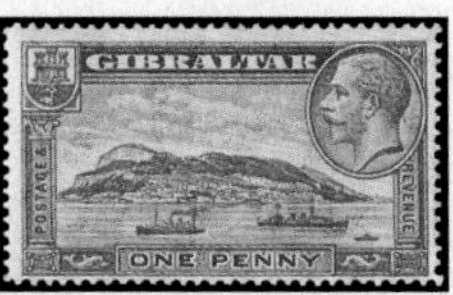

Rock of Gibraltar A16

1931-33 Engr. *Perf. 14*

96 A16 1p red 2.75 *3.00*
a. Perf. 13½x14 22.50 8.50
97 A16 1½p red brown 2.75 *3.00*
a. Perf. 13½x14 18.00 5.00
98 A16 2p gray ('32) 8.75 2.00
a. Perf. 13½x14 21.00 4.25
99 A16 3p dk blue ('33) 10.00 3.50
a. Perf. 13½x14 45.00 *42.50*
Nos. 96-99 (4) 24.25 11.50
Set, never hinged 47.50
Set, perf "SPECIMEN" 225.00
Nos. 96a-99a (4) 106.50 60.25
Set, never hinged 185.00

Common Design Types pictured following the introduction.

Silver Jubilee Issue
Common Design Type

1935, May 6 *Perf. 11x12*

100 CD301 2p black & ultra 1.50 *2.25*
101 CD301 3p ultra & brown 3.25 4.50
102 CD301 6p indigo & grn 11.00 *16.00*
103 CD301 1sh brn vio & ind 13.00 *20.00*
Nos. 100-103 (4) 28.75 42.75
Set, never hinged 57.50
Set, perf "SPECIMEN" 225.00

Coronation Issue
Common Design Type

1937, May 12 *Perf. 11x11½*

104 CD302 ½p deep green .25 *.45*
105 CD302 2p gray black .75 *3.00*
106 CD302 3p deep ultra 1.25 *3.00*
Nos. 104-106 (3) 2.25 6.45
Set, never hinged 4.50
Set, perf "SPECIMEN" 200.00

George VI — A17

Rock of Gibraltar A18

Designs: 2p, Rock from north side. 3p, 5p, Europa Point. 6p, Moorish Castle. 1sh, Southport Gate. 2sh, Eliott Memorial. 5sh, Government House. 10sh, Catalan Bay.

Perf. 13, 13½x14 (½p, No. 118), 14 (1½p)

1938-49 Engr. Wmk. 4

107 A17 ½p gray green .25 *.40*
108 A18 1p red brn ('42) .80 .60
a. 1p chestnut, perf. 14 *20.00* 2.75
b. 1p chestnut, perf. 13½ 20.00 2.50
c. Perf. 13½, wmk. sideways ('40) *4.50* *7.75*
109 A18 1½p car rose 20.00 .90
b. Perf. 13½ 190.00 30.00
109A A18 1½p gray vio ('43) .45 *1.60*
110 A18 2p dk gray ('43) 1.40 1.50
a. Perf. 14 22.00 .55
c. Perf. 13½ 4.00 .45
d. Perf. 13½, wmk. sideways ('41) 500.00 52.50
110B A18 2p car rose ('44) 1.00 .55
111 A18 3p blue ('42) 2.00 .35
a. Perf. 14 100.00 6.00
b. Perf. 13½ 22.50 1.10
112 A18 5p red org ('47) 1.00 1.25
113 A18 6p dl vio & car rose 6.00 1.90
a. Perf. 14 90.00 1.60
b. Perf. 13½ 30.00 4.00
114 A18 1sh grn & blk ('42) 2.25 *4.50*
a. Perf. 14 30.00 27.50
b. Perf. 13½ 45.00 8.25
115 A18 2sh org brn & blk ('42) 6.00 6.50
a. Perf. 14 40.00 30.00
b. Perf. 13½ 90.00 55.00
116 A18 5sh dk car & blk ('44) 12.50 *14.00*
a. Perf 14 ('38) 60.00 *175.00*
b. Perf. 13½ 35.00 16.00
117 A18 10sh bl & blk ('43) 22.50 22.50
a. Perf. 14 45.00 *150.00*
118 A17 £1 orange 30.00 *55.00*
Nos. 107-118 (14) 106.15 111.55
Set, never hinged 200.00
Set, perf "SPECIMEN" 900.00

Nos. 108c and 110d were issued in coils.

No. 108 (1p, perf. 13) exists with watermark both normal and sideways. Nos. 110 and 110B (both 2p, perf. 13) have watermark sideways.

For overprints see Nos. 127-130.

Catalogue values for unused stamps in this section, from this point to the end of the section, are for Never Hinged items.

Peace Issue
Common Design Type

1946, Oct. 12 *Perf. 13½x14*

119 CD303 ½p bright green .30 *.50*
120 CD303 3p bright ultra .45 *.50*
Set, perf "SPECIMEN" 175.00

Silver Wedding Issue
Common Design Types

1948, Dec. 1 Photo. *Perf. 14x14½*

121 CD304 ½p dark green 1.00 *3.00*

Engr.; Name Typo.
Perf. 11½x11

122 CD305 £1 brown orange 60.00 *75.00*
Set, hinged 40.00

UPU Issue
Common Design Types
Engr.; Name Typo. on 3p, 6p
Perf. 13½, 11x11½

1949, Oct. 10 Wmk. 4

123 CD306 2p rose carmine 1.25 1.25
124 CD307 3p indigo 2.00 1.50
125 CD308 6p rose violet 1.40 *2.00*
126 CD309 1sh blue green 1.25 *4.00*
Nos. 123-126 (4) 5.90 *8.75*

Nos. 110B, 111, 113-114 overprinted in Black or Carmine

1950, Aug. 1 *Perf. 13x12½*

127 A18 2p carmine rose .40 *1.50*
128 A18 3p blue .85 *1.25*
129 A18 6p dl vio & car rose 1.00 *2.00*
a. Double overprint 1,000. *1,300.*
130 A18 1sh grn & blk (C) 1.25 *2.00*
Nos. 127-130 (4) 3.50 *6.75*

Adoption of Constitution of 1950.

WAR TAX STAMP

No. 66 Overprinted

1918, Apr. Wmk. 3 *Perf. 14*

MR1 A14 ½p green 1.75 *2.40*

a. Double overprint 900.00

GILBERT & ELLICE ISLANDS

'gil-bərt ən,d, 'e-ləs 'ī-lənds

LOCATION — Groups of islands in the Pacific Ocean northeast of Australia
GOVT. — British Crown Colony
AREA — 375 sq. mi.
POP. — 57,816 (est. 1973)
CAPITAL — Tarawa

The Gilbert group of which Butaritari, Tarawa and Tamana are the more important, is on the Equator. Ellice Islands, Phoenix Islands, Line Islands (Fanning, Washington and Christmas), and Ocean Island are included in the Colony. The islands were annexed by Great Britain in 1892 and formed into the Gilbert and Ellice Islands Colony in 1915 on request of the native governments.

The colony divided into the Gilbert Islands and Tuvalu, Jan. 1, 1976.

12 Pence = 1 Shilling
20 Shillings = 1 Pound

Catalogue values for unused stamps in this country are for Never Hinged items, beginning with Scott 52.

Stamps and Type of Fiji Overprinted in Black or Red

1911, Jan. 1 Wmk. 3 *Perf. 14*

Ordinary Paper

1 A22 ½p green 7.50 *50.00*
2 A22 1p carmine 50.00 30.00
a. Pair, one without overprint
3 A22 2p gray 22.50 *17.50*
4 A22 2½p ultramarine 18.00 *50.00*

Chalky Paper

5 A22 5p violet & ol grn 65.00 *95.00*
6 A22 6p violet 25.00 *50.00*
7 A22 1sh black, *green* 26.00 *70.00*
Nos. 1-7 (7) 214.00 *362.50*
Set, ovptd. "SPECIMEN" 350.00

Nos. 1-7 are known with a forged Ocean Island postmark dated "JY 15 11."

Pandanus — A2

1911, Mar. Engr. Ordinary Paper

8 A2 ½p green 5.00 *24.00*
9 A2 1p carmine 2.75 *12.00*
10 A2 2p gray 1.75 *7.50*
11 A2 2½p ultramarine 13.00 *17.50*
Nos. 8-11 (4) 22.50 *61.00*
Set, ovptd. "SPECIMEN" 190.00

King George V — A3

For description of Dies I and II, see front section of the Catalogue.

1912-24 Die I Typo.

14 A3 ½p deep green .60 *6.00*
a. ½p yellow green ('14) 5.00 *13.00*
15 A3 1p carmine 2.50 *14.00*
a. 1p scarlet ('15) 4.25 *15.00*
16 A3 2p gray ('16) 16.00 *26.00*
17 A3 2½p ultra ('16) 3.25 *11.00*

Chalky Paper

18 A3 3p vio, *yel* ('19) 2.75 *13.50*
19 A3 4p blk & red, *yel* .90 *6.50*
20 A3 5p vio & ol grn 2.00 *6.25*
21 A3 6p vio & red vio 1.50 *6.75*
22 A3 1sh black, *green* 1.50 *5.25*
23 A3 2sh vio & ultra, *bl* 15.00 *36.00*
24 A3 2sh6p blk & red, *bl* 23.00 *25.00*
25 A3 5sh grn & red, *yel* 37.50 *65.00*

Die II

26 A3 £1 vio & blk, *red* ('24) 600.00 *1,600.*
Nos. 14-26 (13) 706.50 *1,821.*
Set, ovptd. "SPECIMEN" 700.00

Die II

1921-27 Wmk. 4 Ordinary Paper

27 A3 ½p green 3.75 *3.25*
28 A3 1p deep vio ('27) 5.00 *8.00*
29 A3 1½p scarlet ('24) 8.50 *3.50*
30 A3 2p gray 8.00 *45.00*

Chalky Paper

31 A3 10sh green & red, *emer* ('24) 160.00 *375.00*
Nos. 27-31 (5) 185.25 *434.75*
Set, ovptd. "SPECIMEN" 300.00

Most of Nos. 14-31 are known with the forged cancellation described in the note following Nos. 1-7.

Common Design Types pictured following the introduction.

Silver Jubilee Issue
Common Design Type

1935, May 6 Engr. *Perf. 11x12*

33 CD301 1p black & ultra 2.25 *10.00*
34 CD301 1½p car & blue 1.75 *3.50*
35 CD301 3p ultra & brn 5.00 *19.00*
36 CD301 1sh brn vio & indigo 22.50 *17.50*
Nos. 33-36 (4) 31.50 *50.00*
Set, never hinged 62.50
Set, perf "SPECIMEN" 225.00

Coronation Issue
Common Design Type

1937, May 12 *Perf. 13½x14*

37 CD302 1p dark purple .25 .65
38 CD302 1½p carmine .25 .65
39 CD302 3p bright ultra .35 .70
Nos. 37-39 (3) .85 2.00
Set, never hinged 1.10
Set, perf "SPECIMEN" 175.00

Great Frigate Bird — A4

Pandanus — A5

Designs: 1½p, Canoe crossing reef. 2p, Canoe and boat house. 2½p, Islander's house. 3p, Seascape. 5p, Ellice Islands canoe. 6p, Coconut trees. 1sh, Phosphate loading jetty, Ocean Island. 2sh, Cutter "Nimanoa." 2sh6p, Gilbert Islands canoe. 5sh, Coat of arms of colony.

Perf. 11½x11 (Nos. 40, 43, 50), 12½ (Type A5), 13½ (Nos. 42, 44, 45, 48)

1939, Jan. 14 Engr. Wmk. 4

40 A4 ½p dk grn & sl bl .40 *1.00*
41 A5 1p dk vio & brt bl green .25 *1.50*
42 A4 1½p car & black .25 *1.25*
43 A4 2p black & brn .70 *1.00*
44 A4 2½p dp olive & blk .60 *1.00*
a. 2½ olive grn & black ('43) 6.00 *7.50*
45 A4 3p ultra & black .40 *1.00*
a. Perf. 12 ('55) .60 *2.75*
46 A5 5p dk brn & dp ultra 3.50 2.75
a. 5p dp brn & ultra ('43) 12.00 *20.00*
b. 5p blackish brn & ultra ('44) 7.00 *8.50*
47 A5 6p dl vio & olive .45 *.60*
48 A4 1sh gray bl & blk 9.00 3.50
a. 1sh turq blue & blk ('43) 20.00 5.00
b. Perf. 12 ('51) 2.00 *16.00*
49 A5 2sh red org & ultra 5.25 10.00
50 A4 2sh6p brt bl grn & bl 5.25 *11.00*
51 A5 5sh dp blue & red 7.25 *16.00*
Nos. 40-51 (12) 33.30 *50.60*
Set, never hinged 65.00
Set, perf "SPECIMEN" 625.00

Catalogue values for unused stamps in this section, from this point to the end of the section, are for Never Hinged items.

Peace Issue
Common Design Type

1946, Dec. 16 *Perf. 13½x14*

52 CD303 1p deep magenta .25 .25
53 CD303 3p deep blue .25 .25
Set, perf "SPECIMEN" 150.00

Silver Wedding Issue
Common Design Types

1949, Aug. 29 Photo. *Perf. 14x14½*

54 CD304 1p violet .25 .25

Engraved; Name Typographed
Perf. 11½x11

55 CD305 £1 red 14.00 *22.50*

UPU Issue
Common Design Types

Engr.; Name Typo. on 2p, 3p

1949, Oct. 1 *Perf. 13½, 11x11½*

56 CD306 1p rose violet .75 *1.10*
57 CD307 2p gray black 2.25 *2.50*
58 CD308 3p indigo .90 *2.50*
59 CD309 1sh blue .80 *1.75*
Nos. 56-59 (4) 4.70 *7.85*

POSTAGE DUE STAMPS

D1

1940, Aug. Typo. Wmk. 4 *Perf. 12*

J1 D1 1p emerald 5.50 *22.50*
J2 D1 2p dark red 6.00 *22.50*
J3 D1 3p chocolate 8.25 *24.00*
J4 D1 4p deep blue 10.00 *32.50*
J5 D1 5p deep green 12.00 *32.50*
J6 D1 6p brt red vio 12.00 *32.50*
J7 D1 1sh dull violet 20.00 *45.00*
J8 D1 1sh6p turq green 30.00 *80.00*
Nos. J1-J8 (8) 103.75 *291.50*
Set, never hinged 175.00
Set, perf "SPECIMEN" 250.00

WAR TAX STAMP

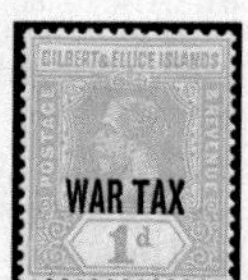

No. 15a Overprinted

1918 Wmk. 3 *Perf. 14*

MR1 A3 1p scarlet .70 *6.50*
Overprinted "SPECIMEN" 75.00

GOLD COAST

'gōld 'kōst

LOCATION — West Africa between Dahomey and Ivory Coast
GOVT. — Former British Crown Colony
AREA — 91,843 sq. mi.
POP. — 3,089,000 (1952)
CAPITAL — Accra

Attached to the colony were Ashanti and Northern Territories (protectorate). Togoland, under British mandate, was also included for administrative purposes.

12 Pence = 1 Shilling
20 Shillings = 1 Pound

Catalogue values for unused stamps in this country are for Never Hinged items, beginning with Scott 128.

Queen Victoria — A1

Perf. 12½

1875, July Typo. Wmk. 1

1 A1 1p blue 550.00 100.00
2 A1 4p red violet 525.00 150.00
3 A1 6p orange 825.00 82.50
Nos. 1-3 (3) 1,900. 332.50

1876-79 *Perf. 14*

4 A1 ½p bister ('79) 100.00 42.50
5 A1 1p blue 40.00 8.00
a. Half used as ½p on cover *4,500.*
6 A1 2p green ('79) 150.00 11.50
a. Half used as 1p on cover *4,250.*
b. Quarter used as ½p on cover *7,500.*
7 A1 4p red violet 275.00 7.25
a. Quarter used as 1p on cover *10,000.*
b. Half used as 2p on cover *8,000.*
8 A1 6p orange 325.00 27.50
a. One sixth used as 1p on cover *13,000.*
b. Half used as 3p on cover *10,000.*
Nos. 4-8 (5) 890.00 96.75

Handstamp Surcharged "1D" in Black

1883, May

9 A1 1p on 4p red violet

Some experts question the status of No. 9. One canceled example is in the British Museum. Another example is supposed to exist (Ferrari).

1883-91 Wmk. 2

10 A1 ½p bister ('83) 275.00 85.00
11 A1 ½p green ('84) 5.00 1.50
a. ½p dull green 4.25 1.10
12 A1 1p blue ('83) 1,000. 85.00
13 A1 1p rose ('84) 6.25 .60
a. Half used as ½p on cover *5,000.*
b. 1p carmine 4.75 .60
14 A1 2p gray ('84) 50.00 7.00
a. 2p slate 15.00 .60
b. Half used as 1p on cover *5,000.*
15 A1 2½p bl & org ('91) 14.00 .85
16 A1 3p ol green ('89) 27.50 14.00
a. 3p olive bister 27.50 12.00
17 A1 4p dull vio ('84) 29.00 4.25
a. 4p claret 32.50 7.50
b. Half used as 2p on cover —
18 A1 6p orange ('89) 27.50 6.50
a. One sixth used as 1p on cover —
b. 6p orange brown 17.00 6.00
19 A1 1sh purple ('88) 16.00 3.25
a. 1sh violet 50.00 15.00
20 A1 2sh brown ('84) 60.00 17.50
a. 2sh yellow brown ('88) 115.00 45.00

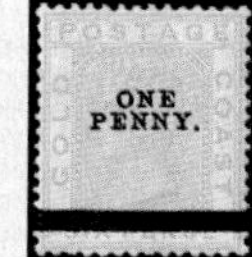

No. 18 Surcharged in Black

1889, Mar.

21 A1 1p on 6p orange 150.00 60.00
a. Double surcharge *4,750.*

The surcharge exists in two spacings between "PENNY" and bar: 7mm (normal) and 8mm.

No. 21a does not exist unused.

Queen Victoria — A3

1889
22 A3 5sh lilac & ultra 82.50 30.00
23 A3 10sh lilac & red 145.00 17.50
a. 10sh lilac & carmine 800.00 290.00
24 A3 20sh green & red 3,500.

1894
25 A3 20sh vio & blk, *red* 190.00 40.00
Nos. 22-25, ovptd. "SPECIMEN" 450.00

1898-1902
26 A3 ½p lilac & green 7.50 1.75
27 A3 1p lil & car rose 8.00 .60
28 A3 2p lil & red ('02) 60.00 *175.00*
29 A3 2½p lilac & ultra 11.00 12.50
30 A3 3p lilac & yel 11.00 4.50
31 A3 6p lilac & purple 14.00 3.75
32 A3 1sh gray grn & blk 20.00 *45.00*
33 A3 2sh gray grn & car rose 37.50 *45.00*
34 A3 5sh grn & lil ('00) 110.00 65.00
35 A3 10sh grn & brn ('00) 225.00 72.50
Nos. 26-35 (10) 504.00 *425.60*
Set, ovptd. "SPECIMEN" 325.00

Numerals of 2p, 3p and 6p of type A3 are in color on colorless tablet.

Nos. 29 and 31 Surcharged in Black

1901, Oct. 6
36 A3 1p on 2½p lil & ultra 11.00 7.50
a. "ONE" omitted 1,200.
37 A3 1p on 6p lilac & pur 11.00 5.00
a. "ONE" omitted 325.00 *650.00*

Beware of copies offered as No. 37a that have part of "ONE" showing.

King Edward VII — A5

1902 **Wmk. 2**
38 A5 ½p violet & green 1.75 .50
39 A5 1p vio & car rose 1.75 .25
40 A5 2p vio & red org 47.50 8.50
41 A5 2½p vio & ultra 5.50 *11.00*
42 A5 3p vio & orange 6.00 2.75
43 A5 6p violet & pur 7.50 3.00
44 A5 1sh green & blk 24.00 4.50
45 A5 2sh grn & car rose 24.00 *40.00*
46 A5 5sh green & violet 67.50 *120.00*
47 A5 10sh green & brn 87.50 *160.00*
48 A5 20sh vio & blk, *red* 200.00 *240.00*
Nos. 38-48 (11) 473.00 *590.50*
Set, ovptd. "SPECIMEN" 275.00

Numerals of 2p, 3p, 6p and 2sh6p of type A5 are in color on colorless tablet.

1904-07 **Wmk. 3**

Chalky or Ordinary Paper

49 A5 ½p vio & grn ('07) 3.00 *8.50*
50 A5 1p vio & car rose 17.50 2.50
a. Chalky paper ('06) 30.00 3.00
51 A5 2p vio & red org 16.00 2.50
a. Chalky paper ('06) 30.00 3.00
52 A5 2½p vio & ultra ('06) 65.00 *80.00*
53 A5 3p vio & org ('05) 70.00 7.00
a. Chalky paper ('06) 29.00 1.25
54 A5 6p vio & pur ('06) 90.00 8.00
a. Chalky paper ('06) 45.00 2.00
55 A5 2sh6p grn & yel ('06), chalky paper 35.00 *140.00*
Ovptd. "SPECIMEN" 50.00
Nos. 49-55 (7) 296.50 *248.50*

1907-13 **Ordinary Paper**
56 A5 ½p green 12.00 .40
a. ½p blue green ('09) 20.00 2.25
57 A5 1p carmine 17.50 .50
58 A5 2p gray ('09) 3.00 1.00
59 A5 2½p ultramarine 22.50 5.25

Chalky Paper

60 A5 3p vio, *yel* ('09) 9.50 1.00
61 A5 6p dull vio ('08) 40.00 2.25
a. 6p dull violet & red violet 8.50 8.00
62 A5 1sh blk, *grn* ('09) 28.00 1.25
63 A5 2sh vio & bl, *bl* ('10) 18.00 16.00
a. Ordinary paper 9.50 *19.00*
64 A5 2sh6p blk & red, *blue* ('11) 42.50 *105.00*
65 A5 5sh grn & red, *yel* ('13) 65.00 *250.00*
Nos. 56-65 (10) 258.00 *382.65*
Set, ovptd. "SPECIMEN" 425.00

No. 63 is on both ordinary and chalky paper.

King Edward VII — A6

1908, Nov. **Ordinary Paper**
66 A6 1p carmine 9.50 .25
Ovptd. "SPECIMEN" 60.00

King George V
A7 A8

For description of Dies I and II, see front section of the Catalogue.

Die I

1913-21 **Ordinary Paper**
69 A7 ½p green 3.00 2.25
70 A8 1p carmine 2.25 .25
a. 1p scarlet 4.25 .60
71 A7 2p gray 12.50 3.00
72 A7 2½p ultramarine 16.00 2.75

Chalky Paper

73 A7 3p vio, *yel* ('15) 4.50 1.00
a. Die II ('19) 65.00 6.75
74 A7 6p dull vio & red vio 14.00 3.25
75 A7 1sh black, *green* 6.75 2.75
a. 1sh black, *emerald* 4.00 2.50
b. 1sh black, *bl grn*, ol back 18.00 .95
c. Die II ('21) 3.25 .60
76 A7 2sh vio & bl, *bl* 14.00 5.25
a. Die II ('21) 190.00 77.50
77 A7 2sh6p blk & red, *bl* 14.50 *16.00*
a. Die II ('21) 45.00 *50.00*
78 A7 5sh grn & red, *yel* 30.00 *70.00*
a. Die II ('21) 52.50 *180.00*
79 A7 10sh grn & red, *grn* ('16) 70.00 *120.00*
a. 10sh grn & red, *emer* 50.00 *200.00*
b. 10sh grn & red, *bl grn*, ol back 42.50 *100.00*
80 A7 20sh vio & blk, *red* ('16) 160.00 120.00

Surface-colored Paper

81 A7 3p violet, *yel* 2.10 1.00
82 A7 5sh grn & red, *yel* 30.00 *72.50*
Nos. 69-82 (14) 379.60 *420.00*

Numerals of 2p, 3p, 6p and 2sh6p of type A7 are in color on plain tablet.

Die II

1921-25 **Ordinary Paper** **Wmk. 4**
83 A7 ½p green ('22) 1.25 .75
84 A8 1p brown ('22) 1.00 .25
85 A7 1½p carmine ('22) 2.60 .25
86 A7 2p gray 2.60 .40
87 A7 2½p orange ('23) 3.25 *16.00*
88 A7 3p ultra ('22) 2.10 1.25

Chalky Paper

89 A7 6p dl vio & red vio ('22) 4.75 *3.50*
90 A7 1sh blk, *emer* ('25) 11.00 4.00
91 A7 2sh vio & bl, *bl* ('24) 4.50 *4.00*
92 A7 2sh6p blk & red, *bl* ('25) 14.00 *42.50*
93 A7 5sh grn & red, *yel* ('25) 28.00 *85.00*

Die I

94 A7 15sh dl vio & grn ('21) 200.00 *550.00*
a. Die II ('25) 140.00 *550.00*
95 A7 £2 grn & org 550.00 *1,600.*
Nos. 83-95 (13) 825.05 *2,308.*
Set, ovptd. "SPECIMEN" 500.00

Christiansborg Castle — A9

1928, Aug. 1 **Photo.** ***Perf. 13½x14½***
98 A9 ½p green 1.25 .50
99 A9 1p red brown 1.00 .25
100 A9 1½p scarlet 4.50 1.60
101 A9 2p slate 4.50 .25
102 A9 2½p yellow 4.75 *3.50*
103 A9 3p ultramarine 4.50 .50
104 A9 6p dull vio & blk 5.25 .50
105 A9 1sh red org & blk 7.75 1.90
106 A9 2sh purple & black 36.00 7.25
107 A9 5sh ol green & car 72.50 55.00
Nos. 98-107 (10) 142.00 71.25
Set, ovptd. "SPECIMEN" 300.00

Common Design Types pictured following the introduction.

Silver Jubilee Issue

Common Design Type

1935, May 6 **Engr.** ***Perf. 11x12***
108 CD301 1p black & ultra 1.00 .60
109 CD301 3p ultra & brown 3.25 *7.25*
110 CD301 6p indigo & grn 17.00 *22.50*
111 CD301 1sh brn vio & indigo 5.00 *32.50*
Nos. 108-111 (4) 26.25 *62.85*
Set, never hinged 42.50
Set, perf "SPECIMEN" 125.00

Coronation Issue

Common Design Type

1937, May 12 ***Perf. 11x11½***
112 CD302 1p brown .85 *2.50*
113 CD302 2p dark gray 1.00 *4.75*
114 CD302 3p deep ultra 1.25 *2.75*
Nos. 112-114 (3) 3.10 *10.00*
Set, never hinged 6.00
Set, perf "SPECIMEN" 125.00

A10

George VI and Christiansborg Castle — A11

Perf. 12, 11½x12 (#124, 127)

1938-41 **Wmk. 4**
115 A10 ½p green .35 *.50*
116 A10 1p red brown .35 .25
117 A10 1½p rose red .35 *.50*
118 A10 2p gray black .35 .25
119 A10 3p ultramarine .35 .35
120 A10 4p rose lilac .70 *1.25*
121 A10 6p rose violet .70 .25
122 A10 9p red orange 1.10 .55
123 A11 1sh gray grn & blk 1.40 .65
124 A11 1sh3p turq grn & red brown 1.75 .50
125 A11 2sh dk vio & dp bl 4.00 *19.00*
126 A11 5sh rose car & ol green 7.50 *22.00*
127 A11 10sh pur & blk 7.50 *29.00*
Nos. 115-127 (13) 26.40 *75.05*
Set, never hinged 40.00
Set, perf "SPECIMEN" 425.00

Issued: 10sh, July, 1940; 1sh3p, Apr. 12, 1941; others, Apr. 1.

Perf. 12x11½

115a A10 ½p green 7.50 4.00
116a A10 1p red brown 12.00 .30
117a A10 1½p rose red 12.50 6.00
118a A10 2p gray black 10.00 2.00
119a A10 3p ultramarine 6.50 1.25
120a A10 4p rose lilac 6.50 4.50
121a A10 6p rose violet 15.00 1.75
122a A10 9p red orange 6.50 3.00
123a A10 1sh gray grn & blk 17.50 2.25
125a A10 2sh dk vio & dp blue 45.00 27.50
126a A10 5sh rose car & ol grn 65.00 32.50
Nos. 115a-126a (11) 204.00 85.05

Catalogue values for unused stamps in this section, from this point to the end of the section, are for Never Hinged items.

Peace Issue

Common Design Type

1946, Oct. 14 ***Perf. 13½***
128 CD303 2p purple .25 .25
a. Perf. 13½x14 19.00 3.00
129 CD303 4p deep red violet 1.60 *3.50*
a. Perf. 13½x14 3.50 3.75
Set, perf "SPECIMEN" 110.00

A12

A13

½p, Mounted Constable. 1p, Christiansborg Castle. 1½p, Emblem of Joint Provincial Council. 2p, Talking Drums. 2½p, Map. 3p, Manganese mine. 4p, Lake Bosumtwi. 6p, Cacao farmer. 1sh, Breaking cacao pods. 2sh, Trooping the colors. 5sh, Surfboats. 10sh, Forest.

1948, July 1 **Engr.** ***Perf. 12***
130 A12 ½p emerald .25 *.40*
131 A13 1p deep blue .25 .25
132 A13 1½p red 1.50 1.50
133 A12 2p chocolate .65 .25
134 A13 2½p lt brown & red 2.50 *4.50*
135 A13 3p blue 5.00 1.00
136 A13 4p dk car rose 4.25 4.00
137 A12 6p org & black 1.00 .40
138 A13 1sh red org & blk 2.25 .40
139 A13 2sh rose car & ol brn 10.00 4.75
140 A13 5sh gray & red vio 35.00 11.00
141 A12 10sh ol grn & black 20.00 15.00
Nos. 130-141 (12) 82.65 43.45
Set, perf "SPECIMEN" 425.00

Silver Wedding Issue

Common Design Types

1948, Dec. 20 **Photo.** ***Perf. 14x14½***
142 CD304 1½p scarlet .25 .25

Engraved; Name Typographed

Perf. 11½x11

143 CD305 10sh dk brn olive 35.00 *37.50*

UPU Issue

Common Design Types

Engr.; Name Typo. on 2½p and 3p

1949, Oct. 10 ***Perf. 13½, 11x11½***
144 CD306 2p red brown .25 .25
145 CD307 2½p deep orange 1.90 *4.50*
146 CD308 3p indigo .45 *1.75*
147 CD309 1sh blue green .45 .45
Nos. 144-147 (4) 3.05 *6.95*

POSTAGE DUE STAMPS

D1

1923 **Typo.** **Wmk. 4** ***Perf. 14***

Yellowish Toned Paper

J1 D1 ½p black 19.00 *125.00*
J2 D1 1p black .95 *1.50*
J3 D1 2p black 13.00 *3.50*
J4 D1 3p black 22.50 *3.00*
Nos. J1-J4 (4) 55.45 *133.00*
Set, ovptd. "SPECIMEN" 95.00

1951-52 **Typo.** **Wmk. 4** ***Perf. 14***

Chalk-Surfaced Paper

J5 D1 2p black 4.00 *32.50*
a. Wmk. 4a (error) 750.00
b. Wmk. 4, crown missing (error) 1,500.
J6 D1 3p black 4.50 *30.00*
a. Wmk. 4a (error) 700.00
b. Wmk. 4, crown missing (error) 1,400.
J7 D1 6p black ('52) 2.10 *17.50*
a. Wmk. 4a (error) 1,300.
b. Wmk. 4, crown missing (error) 2,000.
J8 D1 1sh black ('52) 2.10 *80.00*
a. Wmk. 4a (error) 1,600.
Nos. J5-J8 (4) 12.70 *160.00*

Issued: Nos. J7-J8, 10/1.

WAR TAX STAMP

Regular Issue of 1913 Surcharged

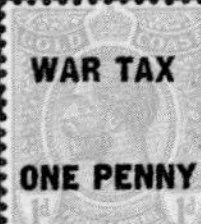

1918, June **Wmk. 3** ***Perf. 14***

MR1 A8 1p on 1p scarlet 4.00 1.00
Ovpted. "SPECIMEN" 70.00

GRAND COMORO

ˈgrand ˈkä-mə-ˌrō

LOCATION — One of the Comoro Islands in the Mozambique Channel between Madagascar and Mozambique.
GOVT. — French Colony
AREA — 385 sq. mi. (approx.)
POP. — 50,000 (approx.)
CAPITAL — Moroni

See Comoro Islands

100 Centimes = 1 Franc

Navigation and Commerce — A1

Perf. 14x13½

1897-1907 **Typo.** **Unwmk.**

Name of Colony in Blue or Carmine

1 A1 1c blk, *lil bl* 1.25 1.25
Never hinged 2.00
On cover 310.00
2 A1 2c brn, *buff* 2.00 2.00
Never hinged 3.10
On cover 350.00
3 A1 4c claret, *lav* 2.50 2.50
Never hinged 3.75
On cover 375.00
4 A1 5c grn, *grnsh* 4.50 4.50
Never hinged 7.25
On cover 250.00
5 A1 10c blk, *lavender* 10.00 6.50
Never hinged 18.00
On cover 290.00
6 A1 10c red ('00) 11.00 11.00
Never hinged 17.50
On cover 225.00
7 A1 15c blue, quadrille paper 22.00 14.50
Never hinged 45.00
On cover 275.00
8 A1 15c gray, *lt gray* ('00) 11.00 11.00
Never hinged 18.00
On cover 225.00
9 A1 20c red, *grn* 12.50 12.50
Never hinged 24.00
On cover 310.00
On cover, single franking 425.00
10 A1 25c blk, *rose* 18.50 17.00
Never hinged 32.50
On cover 340.00
On cover, single franking 500.00
11 A1 25c blue ('00) 22.00 21.50
Never hinged 45.00
On cover 250.00
On cover, single franking 440.00
12 A1 30c brn, *bister* 23.00 20.00
Never hinged 45.00
On cover 275.00
On cover, single franking 500.00
13 A1 35c blk, *yel* ('06) 22.00 20.00
Never hinged 45.00
On cover 275.00
On cover, single franking 500.00
14 A1 40c red, *straw* 23.00 20.00
Never hinged 45.00
On cover 310.00
On cover, single franking 425.00
15 A1 45c blk, *gray grn* ('07) 85.00 70.00
Never hinged 170.00
On cover 625.00
On cover, single franking 875.00
16 A1 50c car, *rose* 45.00 24.00
Never hinged 87.50
On cover 425.00
On cover, single franking 550.00
17 A1 50c brn, *bluish* ('00) 47.50 45.00
Never hinged 100.00
On cover 375.00
On cover, single franking 550.00
18 A1 75c dp vio, *org* 60.00 40.00
Never hinged 120.00
On cover 500.00
On cover, single franking 625.00
19 A1 1fr brnz grn, *straw* 42.50 36.00
Never hinged 92.50
On cover 550.00
On cover, single franking 625.00
Nos. 1-19 (19) 465.25 379.25

Perf. 13½x14 stamps are counterfeits.

Issues of 1897-1907 Surcharged in Black or Carmine

Spacing between figures of surcharge 1.5mm (5c), 2mm (10c)

1912

20 A1 5c on 2c brn, *buff* 1.50 1.50
Never hinged 2.50
On cover 77.50
a. Inverted surcharge 260.00
b. Pair, one without surcharge 1,700.
e. As "a," one without surcharge 2,400.
21 A1 5c on 4c cl, *lav* (C) 1.60 1.60
Never hinged 2.75
On cover 72.50
a. Pair, one without surcharge 1,000.
22 A1 5c on 15c blue (C) 1.50 1.50
Never hinged 2.50
On cover 77.50
23 A1 5c on 20c red, *grn* 1.75 1.75
Never hinged 2.90
On cover 100.00
24 A1 5c on 25c blk, *rose* (C) 1.60 1.60
Never hinged 2.75
On cover 87.50
25 A1 5c on 30c brn, *bis* (C) 1.75 1.75
Never hinged 3.10
On cover 87.50
26 A1 10c on 40c red, *straw* 2.00 2.00
Never hinged 3.50
On cover 100.00
27 A1 10c on 45c blk, *gray grn* (C) 2.75 2.75
Never hinged 5.00
On cover 92.50
28 A1 10c on 50c car, *rose* 2.50 2.50
Never hinged 4.25
On cover 92.50
29 A1 10c on 75c dp vio, *org* 3.00 3.00
Never hinged 6.00
On cover 140.00
Nos. 20-29 (10) 19.95 19.95

Spacing between figures of surcharge 2.25mm (5c), 2.75mm (10c)

20c A1 5c on 2c brn, *buff* 7.50 7.50
Never hinged 14.00
21b A1 5c on 4c cl, *lav* (C) 8.50 8.50
Never hinged 18.00
22a A1 5c on 15c blue (C) 11.00 11.00
Never hinged 21.00
23a A1 5c on 20c red, *grn* 12.50 12.50
Never hinged 25.00
24a A1 5c on 25c blk, *rose* (C) 12.00 12.00
Never hinged 21.00
25a A1 5c on 30c brn, *bis* (C) 13.50 13.50
Never hinged 25.00
26a A1 10c on 40c red, *straw* 92.50 92.50
Never hinged 190.00
27a A1 10c on 45c blk, *gray grn* (C) 92.50 92.50
Never hinged 190.00
28a A1 10c on 50c car, *rose* 92.50 92.50
Never hinged 190.00
29a A1 10 on 75c dp vio, *org* 150.00 150.00
Never hinged 240.00
Nos. 20c-29a (10) 492.50 492.50

Se-tenant Pairs, Both Ovpt. Settings

20d A1 5c on 2c, #20 + #20c 10.00 10.00
Never hinged 19.00
21c A1 5c on 4c, #21 + #21b 9.50 9.50
Never hinged 18.00
22b A1 5c on 15c, #22 + #22a 12.00 12.00
Never hinged 21.00
23b A1 5c on 20c, #23 + #23a 14.00 14.00
Never hinged 25.00
24b A1 5c on 25c, #24 + #24a 12.00 12.00
Never hinged 21.00
25b A1 5c on 30c, #25 + #25a 14.00 14.00
Never hinged 25.00
26b A1 10c on 40c, #26 + #26a 95.00 95.00
Never hinged 190.00
27b A1 10c on 45c, #27 + #27a 100.00 100.00
Never hinged 190.00
28b A1 10c on 50c, #28 + #28a 100.00 100.00
Never hinged 190.00
29b A1 10c on 75c, #29 + #29a 160.00 160.00
Never hinged 240.00
Nos. 20d-29b (10) 526.50 526.50

Nos. 20-29 were available for use in Madagascar and the entire Comoro archipelago.

Stamps of Grand Comoro were superseded by those of Madagascar, and in 1950 by those of Comoro Islands.

GREAT BRITAIN

ˈgrāt ˈbri-tᵊn

(United Kingdom)

LOCATION — Northwest of the continent of Europe and separated from it by the English Channel
GOVT. — Constitutional monarchy
AREA — 94,511 sq. mi.
POP. — 55,767,387 (1981)
CAPITAL — London

12 Pence = 1 Shilling
20 Shillings = 1 Pound

The letters in the corners of the early postage issues indicate position in the horizontal and vertical rows in which that particular specimen was placed.

In the case of illustration A1, this stamp came from the first horizontal row (A) and was the 11th stamp (K) from the left in that row. The left corner refers to the horizontal row and the right corner to the vertical row. Thus no two stamps on the plate bore the same combination of letters.

When four corner letters are used (starting in 1858), the lower ones indicate the stamp's position in the sheet and the top ones are the same letters reversed.

Catalogue values for unused stamps in this country are for Never Hinged items, beginning with Scott 264 in the regular postage section, Scott J34 in the postage due section, Scott 10 in British Offices — East Africa Forces, and Scott 93, Scott 246 and Scott 523 in British Offices in Morocco. All of the listings in British Offices — for Use in Eritrea and for Use in Tripolitania are valued as never-hinged.

Watermarks

Wmk. 18 — Small Crown

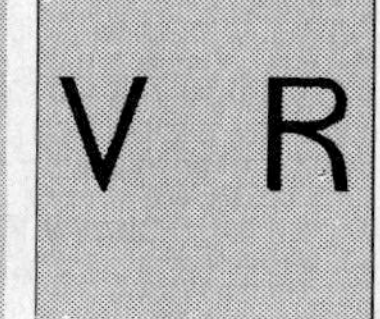

Wmk. 19 — V R

Wmk. 20 — Large Crown

Wmk. 21 — Small Garter

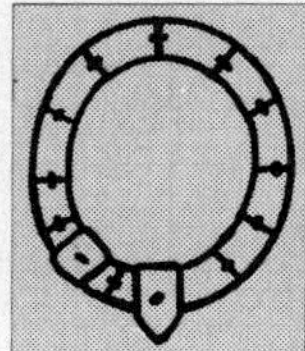

Wmk. 22 — Medium Garter

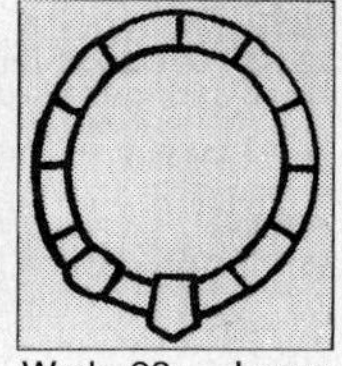

Wmk. 23 — Large Garter

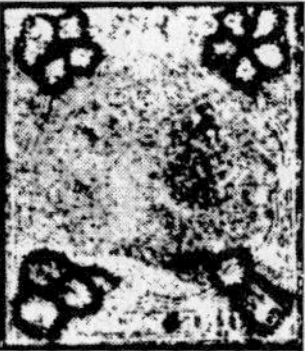

Wmk. 24 — Heraldic Emblems

Wmk. 25 — Spray of Rose

Wmk. 26 — Maltese Cross

Wmk. 27 — "Half Penny" in Script

Wmk. 28 — Anchor

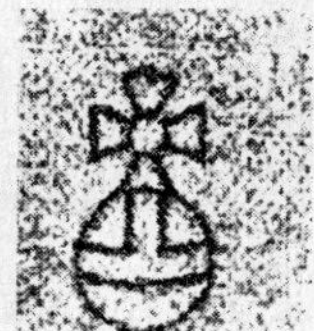

Wmk. 29 — Orb

Wmk. 30 — Imperial Crown

Wmk. 31 — Anchor

Wmk. 32 — Crown and GvR Multiple

Wmk. 33 — Crown and GvR

Wmk. 33 — In the normal watermark (sometimes termed the "repeated" watermark) the letters "GvR" are extended. The royal cyphers are placed one above the other and usually two appear on each stamp. In the multiple watermark the letters "GvR" are condensed, the cyphers are smaller and are so placed that those in each succeeding row are below the spaces between the cyphers in the row above.

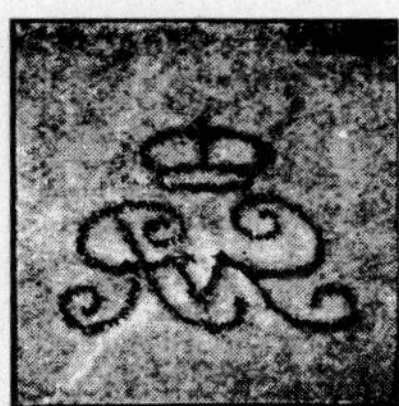

Wmk. 34 — Large Crown and GvR

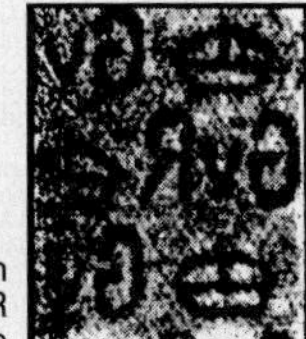

Wmk. 35 — Crown and Block GvR Multiple

Wmk. 219 — Large Crown and GvR

Wmk. 250 — Crown and E8R Multiple

Wmk. 251 — Crown and GviR Multiple

Wmk. 259 — Crown and Large G VI R

Values for mint stamps of Great Britain are for stamps with original gum as defined in the catalogue introduction.

Values for unused and used stamps in this country are for examples with fresh color and all the attributes of fine-to-very fine condition (unless specified otherwise) through 1900 (Scott 126). All other stamps are for examples in the condition of very fine. Expect perforations to touch the design on one or two sides on all engraved stamps (Scott Nos. 8-21, 29-33 and 58) and early small format typographed stamps (Nos. 22-28, 34-56, 59-73, 78-89 and 94-95) because of the very narrow spacing between the stamps in the setting of the plates. Examples with margins clear of the design on all four sides range from scarce to very rare and command substantial premiums.

Cancellations on stamps from the 1847 issue to the 1900 issues, and in many cases beyond, are usually heavy. Values quoted are for stamps with better than average cancellations. **Poorly centered stamps and heavily canceled stamps may sell for 10 to 20 percent of the values listed here.**

Stamps with circular datestamps (especially those with a steel cds) range from scarce to very rare and command much higher prices. Premiums to be applied for fresh mint stamps with original gum and for used stamps that have both fine to very fine centering and circular datestamps can be found in footnotes for stamps from Scott 8 through Scott 126, including Official stamps for this period. For stamps that have both fine to very fine centering and circular datestamps, add the premiums together. Apply these premiums to covers, taking into account the overall condition of the cover and the stamps.

Queen Victoria — A1

1840, May Wmk. 18 Engr. *Imperf.*

White Paper

1	A1 1p black	11,000.	320.00
	On cover		640.00
a.	1p intense black	15,000.	325.00
	On cover		600.00
b.	1p gray black (worn plate)	14,000.	360.00
	On cover		500.00
c.	Watermark inverted	*45,000.*	*2,500.*
d.	On blued paper (Plates 1-8), *from*	*65,000.*	*675.00*
2	A1 2p blue	35,000.	700.00
	On cover		2,250.
a.	2p pale blue	45,000.	900.00
	On cover		2,350.
b.	2p deep bright blue	42,500.	1,000.
	On cover		2,350.
c.	Watermark inverted	*82,500.*	*6,000.*

Full margins = ½mm.

No. 1 was printed from 11 plates; No. 2 from 2 plates. The 1p plates 1, 2, 5, 6, 8 and 9 can be found in two or more states. Stamp and on cover values are for the most common plates.

Issue dates: 1p, May 6; 2p, May 7.

See Nos. 3, 8-9, 11-12, 14, 16, 18, 20, O1.

Compare designs A1-A2 with A8, A10.

Values for pairs

1	A1 1p black, *from*	55,000.	1,250.
	On cover, *from*		*1,500.*
2	A1 2p blue, *from*	110,000.	2,100.
	On cover, *from*		2,500.

Values for strips of 3

1	A1 1p black	*75,000.*	1,875.
	On cover		—
2	A1 2p blue	*150,000.*	3,250.
	On cover		—

Values for blocks of 4

1	A1 1p black	*145,000.*	*25,000.*
	On cover		—
2	A1 2p blue	*275,000.*	*40,000.*
	On cover		—

Values for Certified Plated Examples

Stamps from each plate used for Nos. 1-2 can be plated with certainty by experts. Certificates are recommended. Values are for the most common shades of each plate.

1	1p black		
	Plate 1, 1st state	18,500.	350.
	Plate 1, 2nd state	12,500.	325.
	Plate 2	12,500.	325.
	Plate 3	20,000.	425.
	Plate 4	12,500.	325.
	Plate 5	12,500.	325.
	Plate 6	13,500.	325.
	Plate 7	13,500.	350.
	Plate 8	16,500.	475.
	Plate 9	20,000.	625.
	Plate 10	25,000.	850.
	Plate 11	22,500.	4,500.
2	2p blue		
	Plate 1	35,000.	750.
	Plate 2	45,000.	1,000.

Values for cancellations

No. 1, Left Column

No. 2, Right Column

Maltese Cross, red	390.	925.
Maltese Cross, black	360.	875.
Maltese Cross, blue	12,500.	15,000.
Maltese Cross, magenta	3,100.	12,500.
Maltese Cross, yellow	—	—
"Penny Post" straight line, black	5,500.	15,000.
Town postmark, black, *from*	17,000.	9,000.
Town postmark, red, *from*	18,500.	—
Town postmark, yellow, *from*	*60,000.*	
Numeral postmark, 1844 onwards, *from*	1,800.	2,500.

Maltese Crosses with Numerals in Center, black

No. 1	17,500.	17,500.
No. 2	17,500.	17,500.
No. 3	17,500.	17,500.
No. 4	17,500.	17,500.
No. 5	17,500.	17,500.
No. 6	17,500.	17,500.
No. 7	17,500.	17,500.
No. 8	17,500.	17,500.
No. 9	17,500.	17,500.
No. 10	17,500.	17,500.
No. 11	17,500.	17,500.
No. 12	17,500.	17,500.

Early Dates on Cover

May 6	*165,000.*	—
May 7	20,500.	—
May 8	9,250.	*16,500.*
May 9	5,000.	*75,000.*
May 10 (Sunday)	*65,000.*	180,000.
May 11-16	3,600.	18,000.
May 17 (Sunday)	*15,500.*	*52,000.*
May 18-23	2,900.	18,000.
May 24 (Sunday)	*14,500.*	*52,000.*
May 25-30	2,050.	18,000.
May 31 (Sunday)	*13,500.*	*52,000.*

Used in Combination with Mulready Envelopes & Letter Sheets

1d black on U1	15,500.
1p black on U2	*39,000.*
1p black on U3	15,500.
1p black on U4	*39,500.*
2p blue on U1	*50,000.*
2p blue on U2	*43,500.*
2p blue on U3	*50,000.*
2p blue on U4	*43,500.*

A1a

A2

1841 Bluish Paper

3	A1a 1p red brown	625.00	9.00
	On cover		27.50
a.	1p orange brown	1,350.	55.00
	On cover		125.00
b.	1p lake red	5,500.	825.00
	On cover		*1,650.*
c.	Rouletted 12	*26,000.*	
d.	"A" missing in lower right corner (position BA, P77)	—	*25,000.*
e.	Watermark inverted	4,000.	360.00
f.	On deep blue paper	725.00	24.00
4	A2 2p blue	4,500.	50.00
	On cover		190.00
a.	2p pale blue	6,000.	50.00
	On cover		190.00
b.	2p deep bright blue	5,000.	55.00
	On cover		165.00
c.	2p violet blue	*15,000.*	1,000.
	On cover		—
d.	Watermark inverted	6,750.	100.00
e.	"Ivory Head"	6,500.	90.00

Full margins = ½mm.

No. 3 exists on silk thread paper, but was not regularly issued.

No. 4 was printed from two plates.

See Nos. 10, 13, 15, 17, 19, 21.

Values for pairs

3	A1a 1p red brown	1,200.	52.50
	On cover		65.00
4	A2 2p blue	15,000.	275.00
	On cover		625.00

Values for strips of 3

3	A1a 1p red brown	2,000.	92.50
	On cover		*300.00*
4	A2 2p blue	*15,000.*	275.00
	On cover		925.00

Values for blocks of 4

3	A1a 1p red brown	3,250.	350.00
	On cover		*1,100.*
	With Maltese Cross postmarks		900.00
	On cover		*1,350.*
4	A2 2p blue	*42,500.*	*1,750.*
	On cover		—
	With Maltese Cross postmarks		*6,250.*

Values for cancellations

No. 3, Left Column

No. 4, Right Column

Maltese Cross, red	5,250.	*22,750.*
Maltese Cross, black	57.50	275.00
Maltese Cross, blue	675.00	5,250.
"Penny Post" straight line, black	1,150.	—
Town postmark, black (from)	825.00	3,650.
Town postmark, red (from)	15,500.	—
Town postmark, yellow (from)	—	—
Town postmark, blue (from)	2,600.	4,650.
Town postmark, green (from)	5,250.	—
Numeral postmark, black (from)	24.00	85.00
Numeral postmark, blue (from)	250.00	1,000.
Numeral postmark, red (from)	10,000.	*29,500.*
Numeral postmark, green (from)	3,100.	8,250.
Numeral postmark, violet (from)	4,250.	—

Maltese Crosses with Numerals in Center, black

No. 1	185.00	725.00
No. 2	185.00	725.00
No. 3	235.00	725.00
No. 4	625.00	725.00
No. 5	185.00	785.00
No. 6	165.00	725.00
No. 7	165.00	1,250.
No. 8	165.00	1,050.
No. 9	185.00	1,250.
No. 10	325.00	1,550.
No. 11	350.00	875.00
No. 12	350.00	575.00

Used in Combination with Mulready Envelopes & Letter Sheets

1d red brown on U1 15,000.
1p red brown on U2 *42,500.*
1p red brown on U3 15,000.
1p red brown on U4 *47,500.*
2p blue on U1 *42,500.*
2p blue on U2 *47,500.*
2p blue on U3 *42,500.*
2p blue on U4 *42,500.*

During the reigns of Victoria and Edward VII, many color trials were produced on perfed, gummed and watermarked papers.

Nos. 5-7 were printed one stamp at a time on the sheet. Space between the stamps usually is very small. Impressions that touch, or even overlap, are numerous.

Stamps with margins ½mm beyond the outer frame are considered as having full margins. Values for mint or used single embossed stamps are for full-margin examples.

Cover values are for average stamps with complete design but clear, white margins on one or two sides only. On-cover examples with four full margins sell for much more.

A3

With Vertical Silk Threads

1847 Embossed Unwmk.

5 A3 1sh pale green 20,000. 900.00
Block of 4 *145,000.*
On cover 1,275.
Pair on cover 2,400.
Cut to shape 15.00
a. 1sh green 20,000. 925.00
On cover 1,350.
Pair on cover 2,400.
Cut to shape 15.00
b. 1sh deep green 25,000. 1,050.
On cover 1,400.
Pair on cover 2,500.
Cut to shape 22.50

Die numbers (on base of bust): 1 and 2.

A3a

1848

6 A3a 10p red brown 11,500. 1,500.
Block of 4 *92,500.* *14,500.*
On cover 3,000.
Pair on cover *4,500.*
Cut to shape *500.00* 20.00

Die numbers (on base of bust): 1, 2, 3, 4; also without die number.

A4

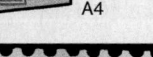

"Thick"

"Thin"

1854 Wmk. 19

7 A4 6p red violet 18,000. 1,000.
Block of 4 *145,000.*
On cover 1,900.
Pair on cover 3,250.
a. 6p dull violet 18,000. 1,000.
On cover 1,900.
Pair on cover 32,500.
b. 6p deep violet *26,000.* 4,250.
On cover —
c. 6p mauve 18,500. 1,000.
On cover 2,000.
Pair on cover 3,250.
Cut to shape 10.00
d. Watermark inverted 18,000. 1,000.
e. Watermark inverted and reversed 1,000.
f. Watermark upright 1,900.

The normal watermark 19 appears reversed when viewed from the front and as 'VR' when viewed from the back. This should be taken into consideration when determing whether the watermark is inverted or reversed.

1854-55 Wmk. 18 Engr. *Perf. 16*
Bluish Paper

8 A1 1p red brown 325.00 30.00
Block of 4 *2,500.* *400.00*
On cover 57.50
Pair on cover 100.00
a. 1p yellow brown 375.00 45.00
On cover 85.00
9 A1 1p red brn, re-engraved ('55) 425.00 60.00
Block of 4 *3,600.* *625.00*
On cover 115.00
Pair on cover 225.00
a. Imperf. —
b. Watermark inverted 1,250. 250.00
10 A2 2p blue 4,000. 90.00
Block of 4 *20,000.* *1,850.*
On cover 200.00
a. 2p pale blue 4,500. 100.00
On cover 200.00
b. 2p blue, plate 5 8,000. 300.00
On cover 500.00

In the re-engraved 1p stamps, the lines of the features are deeper and stronger, the fillet behind the ear more distinct, the shading about the eye heavier, the line of the nostril is turned downward at right and an indentation of color appears between lower lip and chin.

Perf. 14

11 A1 1p red brown ('55) 625.00 80.00
Block of 4 *5,250.* *725.00*
On cover 145.00
a. Imperf. —
b. Watermark inverted 300.00
12 A1 1p red brn, re-engraved ('55) 600.00 67.50
Block of 4 *4,400* *675.00*
On cover 115.00
Pair on cover *195.00*
a. 1p org brn, re-engraved 1,700. 150.00
On cover 250.00
b. As #12, watermark inverted 1,675. 350.00
13 A2 2p blue ('55) 10,000. 210.00
Block of 4 *2,500.*
On cover 375.00
Plate 5 10,500. 375.00
Block of 4 *3,250.*
On cover 500.00
a. Imperf. (P5) *10,000.*
b. Watermark inverted 575.00
As "b," Plate 5 —

Wmk. 20 exists in two types. The first includes two vertical prongs, rising from the top of the crown's headband and extending into each of the two balancing midsections. The second type (illustrated), introduced in 1861, omits these prongs.

1855 Wmk. 20 *Perf. 16*
Bluish Paper

14 A1 1p red brn, re-engraved 2,000. 110.00
Block of 4 9,250. 1,200.
On cover 225.00
Pair on cover *400.00*
a. Watermark inverted 425.00
15 A2 2p blue 14,000. 450.00
Block of 4 *3,600.*
On cover 575.00
a. Imperf. (P5) *11,000.*
b. Watermark inverted 1,000.

Some specialists regard No. 15a as a proof.

1855 Bluish Paper *Perf. 14*

16 A1 1p red brn, re-engraved 225.00 21.00
Block of 4 2,000. 300.00
On cover 40.00
Pair on cover 70.00
a. 1p orange brn, re-engraved 650.00 62.50
On cover 95.00
b. 1p brown rose, re-engraved 325.00 50.00
On cover 90.00
c. Imperf. 4,000. 3,500.
17 A2 2p blue 2,500. 72.50
Block of 4 *16,500.* 1,000.
On cover 180.00
a. Watermark inverted 325.00

Nos. 19, 21 With Lines Above and Below Head Thinner

1856-58 White Paper *Perf. 16*

18 A1 1p rose red, re-engraved ('57) 2,400. 72.50
Block of 4 12,500. 575.00
On cover 160.00
Pair on cover *320.00*
a. Watermark inverted 475.00
19 A2 2p blue, thin lines ('58) 12,500. 375.00
Block of 4 *3,250.*
On cover 550.00
a. Watermark inverted 1,000.

Perf. 14

20 A1 1p rose red, re-engraved ('57) 55.00 11.50
Block of 4 325.00 100.00
On cover 22.50
a. Imperf. 4,500. 3,500.
b. 1p red brown, re-engraved 2,000. 375.00
On cover 1,100.
c. As #20, watermark inverted 150.00 75.00
d. Double perf. 500.00 90.00
21 A2 2p blue, thin lines ('57) 3,000. 70.00
Block of 4 *17,500.* 1,150.
On cover 180.00
a. Imperf. — *11,000.*
b. Vertical pair, imperf horiz. 20,000.
c. Watermark inverted 325.00
d. Double perf. 180.00

For examples of Nos. 8-21 with margins clear of the design on all four sides, add a 50 percent premium to the value listed. For stamps with clear circular datestamps, apply a 75 percent premium. Add the two premiums together for covers with stamps having these attributes.

Nos. 18, 20-21, 24-29, etc., used abroad.

See Antigua, Argentina, Bahamas, Bolivia, Brazil, British Guiana, British Honduras, Chile, Colombia, Cuba, Cyprus, Danish West Indies, Dominica, Dominican Republic, Ecuador, Egypt, Gibraltar, Grenada, Haiti, Jamaica, Malta, Mexico, Montserrat, Nevis, Nicaragua, Offices in the Turkish Empire, Peru, Puerto Rico, St. Christopher, St. Lucia, St. Vincent, Tobago, Uruguay, Venezuela, and Virgin Islands for listings of numeral cancels numbered A01-A15, A18, A26-A37, A39-A49, A51-A62, A64-A78, B01-B02, B32, C, C28, C30, C35-C43, C51, C56, C57-C63, C65, C81-C83, C86-C88, D22, D74, D87, E53, E88, F69, F83-F85, F87-F88, G, S, G06, 124, 582, 942, 969, 974, 975, 981, 982.

See Ascension for local cancellations used on Great Britain stamps.

Queen Victoria — A5

1855 Typo. Wmk. 21

22 A5 4p rose, *bluish* 8,750. 440.00
Block of 4 *62,500.* —
On cover 775.00
a. Watermark inverted 1,250.
23 A5 4p rose, *white* — 1,150.
On cover —

Compare design A5 with A11, A16, A31.

1856 Wmk. 22

24 A5 4p rose, *bluish* *11,250.* 540.
Block of 4 *62,500.* 3,600.
On cover 775.
a. Watermark inverted 1,250.
b. White glazed paper *9,250.*
25 A5 4p rose, *white* 8,800. 400.
Block of 4 *55,000.*
On cover 675.

1857 Wmk. 23

26 A5 4p rose, *white* 1,750. 125.00
Block of 4 *12,500.* 800.00
On cover 215.00
a. 4p carmine rose, *white* 2,000. 125.00
On cover 215.00
b. Thick glazed paper 6,750. 360.00
On cover —
c. Watermark inverted (as #26) 360.00

A6

A7

1856 Wmk. 24

27 A6 6p lilac 1,400. 100.00
Block of four 8,000. 725.00
On cover 200.00
a. 6p deep lilac 1,850. 140.00
On cover 225.00
b. Wmk. 3 roses and shamrock — —
c. 6p lilac, blued paper 8,250. 950.00
d. 6p lilac, thick paper 4,200. 400.00
e. Watermark inverted 3,150. 360.00
f. Watermark inverted & reversed 5,200.
28 A7 1sh green 3,000. 300.00
Block of four 16,000. 2,100.
On cover 425.00
a. 1sh pale green 3,000. 300.00
On cover 425.00
b. 1sh deep green 5,750. 450.00
On cover 575.00
c. 1sh green, blued paper 2,000.
d. 1sh green, thick paper 365.00
e. Imperf —
f. Watermark inverted 625.00
f. Watermark inverted & reversed 1,350.

Compare design A6 with A13, A18, A22. Compare A7 with A15, A21, A29.

For examples of Nos. 22-28 with margins clear of the design on all four sides, add a 50 percent premium to the value listed. For stamps with clear circular datestamps, apply a 75 percent premium. Add the two premiums together for covers with stamps having these attributes.

Forgeries of No. 27c and 28c exist.

A8

1858-69 Engr. Wmk. 20 *Perf. 14*

29 A8 2p deep blue (P9) 350.00 12.50
On cover 50.00
a. 2p blue 350.00 12.50
Plate 7 1,600. 55.00
Block of four *10,000.* 1,150.
On cover 200.00
Watermark inverted 750.00
Plate 8 1,450. 40.00
Block of four *9,250.* 775.00
On cover 160.00
Watermark inverted 275.00
Plate 9 350.00 12.50
Block of four *2,150.* 155.00
On cover 50.00
Watermark inverted 235.00
Plate 12 3,000. 135.00
Block of four *14,000.* 875.00
On cover 300.00
Watermark inverted 440.00
b. Imperf. (P9) *12,500.*
c. Watermark inverted 235.00

Plate numbers are contained in the scroll work at the sides of the stamp.

Lines Above and Below Head Thinner

30 A8 2p blue ('69) (P13) 350.00 32.50
Block of four 2,500. 300.00
On cover 75.00
Plate 14 475.00 35.00
Block of four 3,150. 400.00
On cover 70.00
Watermark inverted 335.00
Plate 15 500.00 35.00
Block of four 3,400. 525.00
Watermark inverted 475.00
On cover 70.00
a. Imperf. (P13) *10,500.*
b. Watermark inverted, *from* 310.00

A9

1860-70

31 A9 1½p lil rose, *bluish* (P1) ('60) 8,750. *11,000.*
32 A9 1½p dull rose ('70) (P3) 500.00 65.00
Block of four 2,500. 600.00
On cover 275.00
a. 1½p lake red 600.00 65.00
On cover, #32 or 32a 275.00
Plate 1 725.00 90.00
On cover 325.00
c. Imperf (P13) *9,500.*

d.	Lettered "OP-PC"	—	
e.	Watermark inverted (P3)		450.00
f.	Imperf (P3)	9,250.	

The 1½p stamps from Plate 1 carry no plate number. The Plate 3 number is in the border at each side above the lower corner letters.

No. 31 was prepared but not issued.

Queen Victoria — A10

1864

33	A10 1p rose red	25.00	2.75
a.	1p brick red	25.00	2.75
b.	1p lake red	25.00	2.75
	Block of four, *from*	125.00	30.00
	On cover, #33, 33a or 33b		8.50
c.	Imperf. (P116, see footnote)	*8,750.*	*4,500.*

Plate numbers are contained in the scroll work at the sides of the stamp.

No. 33 was printed from 1864 to 1879.

Thirty-nine plate numbers besides Plate 116 (No. 33c) are also known imperforate and used. Values for used examples start at $450.

Stamps from plate 177 have been altered and offered as plate 77.

For examples of Nos. 29-33 with margins clear of the design on all four sides, add a 50 percent premium to the value listed. For stamps with clear circular datestamps, apply a 75 percent premium. Add the two premiums together for covers with stamps having these attributes.

Plate Numbers

Plate 71	52.50	4.00
On cover		5.75
Plate 72	57.50	5.00
Plate 73	57.50	4.00
Plate 74	57.50	3.00
Plate 76	52.50	3.00
Plate 77	—	*500,000.*
Plate 78	125.00	3.00
Plate 79	45.00	3.00
Plate 80	62.50	3.00
Plate 81	62.50	3.00
Plate 82	125.00	5.00
Plate 83	150.00	9.00
Plate 84	77.50	3.00
Plate 85	57.50	4.00
Plate 86	67.50	5.00
Plate 87	45.00	3.00
Plate 88	180.00	10.00
Plate 89	57.50	3.00
Plate 90	57.50	3.00
Plate 91	72.50	7.25
Plate 92	52.50	3.00
Plate 93	67.50	3.00
Plate 94	62.50	6.00
Plate 95	57.50	3.00
Plate 96	62.50	3.00
Plate 97	57.50	4.50
Plate 98	67.50	7.00
Plate 99	72.50	6.00
Plate 100	77.50	3.00
Plate 101	77.50	11.50
Plate 102	62.50	3.00
Plate 103	67.50	5.00
Plate 104	100.00	6.25
Plate 105	125.00	9.50
Plate 106	72.50	3.00
Plate 107	77.50	9.00
Plate 108	105.00	3.00
Plate 109	115.00	4.50
Plate 110	77.50	11.50
Plate 111	67.50	3.00
Plate 112	87.50	3.00
Plate 113	67.50	16.00
Plate 114	325.00	16.00
Plate 115	125.00	3.00
Plate 116	100.00	11.50
Plate 117	62.50	3.00
Plate 118	67.50	3.00
Plate 119	62.50	3.00
Plate 120	26.00	3.00
Plate 121	57.50	11.50
Plate 122	26.00	3.00
Plate 123	57.50	3.00
Plate 124	42.50	3.00
Plate 125	57.50	3.00
Plate 127	72.50	3.00
Plate 129	57.50	11.00
Plate 130	72.50	3.00
Plate 131	82.50	21.00
Plate 132	180.00	28.00
Plate 133	155.00	11.50
Plate 134	26.00	3.00
Plate 135	125.00	30.00
Plate 136	125.00	25.00
Plate 137	42.50	3.00
Plate 138	32.50	3.00
Plate 139	77.50	21.00
Plate 140	32.50	3.00
Plate 141	155.00	11.50
Plate 142	92.50	30.00
Plate 143	77.50	17.50
Plate 144	125.00	26.00
Plate 145	47.50	3.00
Plate 146	57.50	7.00
Plate 147	67.50	4.00
Plate 148	57.50	4.00
Plate 149	57.50	7.00
Plate 150	26.00	3.00
Plate 151	77.50	11.50
Plate 152	77.50	7.50
Plate 153	135.00	11.50
Plate 154	67.50	3.00
Plate 155	67.50	3.00
Plate 156	62.50	3.00
Plate 157	67.50	3.00
Plate 158	47.50	3.00
Plate 159	47.50	3.00
Plate 160	47.50	3.00
Plate 161	77.50	9.00
Plate 162	67.50	9.00
Plate 163	67.50	9.00
Plate 164	67.50	9.00
Plate 165	62.50	3.00
Plate 166	62.50	7.25
Plate 167	62.50	3.00
Plate 168	67.50	11.00
Plate 169	77.50	9.25
Plate 170	52.50	3.00
Plate 171	26.00	3.00
Plate 172	47.50	3.00
Plate 173	92.50	11.50
Plate 174	47.50	3.00
Plate 175	77.50	4.50
Plate 176	77.50	3.00
Plate 177	57.50	3.00
Plate 178	77.50	4.50
Plate 179	67.50	3.00
Plate 180	77.50	6.75
Plate 181	62.50	3.00
Plate 182	125.00	6.75
Plate 183	72.50	4.00
Plate 184	47.50	3.00
Plate 185	67.50	4.00
Plate 186	87.50	3.00
Plate 187	67.50	3.00
Plate 188	92.50	12.50
Plate 189	92.50	12.50
Plate 190	67.50	7.50
Plate 191	47.50	9.25
Plate 192	67.50	3.00
Plate 193	47.50	3.00
Plates 194-195	67.50	11.00
Plate 196	67.50	11.00
Plate 197	67.50	11.50
Plate 198	57.50	7.25
Plate 199	72.50	7.25
Plate 200	77.50	3.00
Plate 201	47.50	6.25
Plate 202	77.50	11.00
Plate 203	47.50	21.00
Plate 204	72.50	3.00
Plate 205	72.50	4.00
Plate 206	72.50	11.50
Plate 207	77.50	11.50
Plate 208	72.50	18.50
Plate 209	62.50	10.50
Plate 210	87.50	16.00
Plate 211	92.50	26.00
Plate 212	77.50	13.50
Plate 213	77.50	13.50
Plate 214	87.50	24.00
Plate 215	87.50	24.00
Plate 216	92.50	24.00
Plate 217	92.50	9.25
Plate 218	87.50	11.00
Plate 219	125.00	87.50
Plate 220	57.50	9.25
Plate 221	92.50	21.00
Plate 222	105.00	52.50
Plate 223	125.00	77.50
Plate 224	155.00	57.50
Plate 225	3,300.	825.00

Plate Numbers On Cover

Plate 71	8.50
Plate 72	10.00
Plate 73	8.50
Plates 73-76, 78-81	8.50
Plate 77	—
Plate 82	24.00
Plate 83	35.00
Plate 84	8.00
Plate 85	12.00
Plate 86	9.50
Plate 87	8.50
Plate 88	47.50
Plate 89	8.50
Plate 90	12.00
Plate 91	14.00
Plate 92	8.50
Plate 93	8.50
Plate 94	12.00
Plates 95-96	8.50
Plate 97	8.50
Plate 98	15.00
Plate 99	12.00
Plate 100	35.00
Plate 101	23.00
Plate 102	8.50
Plate 103	12.00
Plate 104	35.00
Plate 105	27.50
Plate 106	8.50
Plate 107	18.00
Plate 108	27.50
Plate 109	24.00
Plate 110	24.00
Plate 111	8.50
Plate 112	20.00
Plate 113	30.00
Plate 114	30.00
Plate 115	24.00
Plate 116	24.00
Plates 117-120	8.50
Plate 121	24.00
Plates 122-125, 127	8.50
Plate 129	21.00
Plate 130	8.50
Plate 131	42.50
Plate 132	57.50
Plate 133	47.50
Plate 134	8.50
Plate 135	60.00
Plate 136	50.00
Plates 137, 138	8.50
Plate 139	42.50
Plate 140	8.50
Plate 141	35.00
Plate 142	60.00
Plate 143	35.00
Plate 144	52.50
Plate 145	8.50
Plate 146	14.00
Plate 147	10.00
Plate 148	8.50
Plate 149	14.00
Plate 150	8.50
Plate 151	24.00
Plate 152	15.00
Plate 153	60.00
Plates 154-160	8.50
Plate 161	27.50
Plate 162	17.50
Plate 163	9.00
Plate 164	14.00
Plate 165	8.50
Plate 166	15.00
Plate 167	8.50
Plate 168	21.00
Plate 169	24.00
Plates 170-172	8.50
Plate 173	24.00
Plate 174	8.50
Plates 175-176	14.00
Plate 177	8.50
Plate 178	24.00
Plate 179	9.00
Plate 180	35.00
Plate 181	8.50
Plate 182	32.50
Plate 183	9.00
Plate 184	20.00
Plate 185	24.00
Plate 186	20.00
Plate 187	9.00
Plate 188	25.00
Plates 189-190	32.50
Plate 191	20.00
Plate 192	8.50
Plate 193	14.00
Plate 194-195	21.00
Plate 196	14.00
Plate 197	24.00
Plates 198-199	15.00
Plate 200	20.00
Plate 201	13.00
Plate 202	24.00
Plate 203	30.00
Plate 204	24.00
Plates 205-207	32.50
Plate 208	37.50
Plate 209	37.50
Plate 210	32.50
Plate 211	120.00
Plates 212-217	72.50
Plate 218	120.00
Plate 219	180.00
Plate 220	72.50
Plate 221	100.00
Plate 222	120.00
Plate 223	155.00
Plate 224	130.00
Plate 225	1,600.

A11

1862 Typo. Wmk. 23

34	A11 4p vermilion	1,900.	75.00
	Block of four	*11,000.*	750.00
	On cover		140.00
a.	4p bright red	2,100.	92.50
	On cover		160.00
b.	Hair lines (P4)	2,150.	65.00
	On cover		165.00
c.	As "a," hair lines (P4)	2,150.	75.00
	On cover		175.00
d.	Imperf. (P4)	3,800.	
e.	Watermark inverted		315.00

Hair lines on No. 34b, 34c and 34d are fine colorless lines drawn diagonally across the corners of the stamp.

A12

A13

A14

A15

1862 Wmk. 24

37	A12 3p pale rose	2,500.	300.00
	Block of four	*14,000.*	3,250.
	On cover		550.00
a.	3p deep rose	5,000.	525.00
	On cover		800.00
b.	With white dots under side ornaments	*40,000.*	*16,000.*
d.	As "b," imperf.	6,750.	
e.	Thick paper		465.00
39	A13 6p lilac (P3)	2,250.	105.00
	Block of four	*12,500.*	750.00
	On cover		210.00
a.	6p lilac, blued paper	—	1,400.
b.	6p lilac, thick paper	—	375.00
c.	6p lilac, wmk. 3 roses & thistle	—	*8,000.*
d.	6p lilac, hair lines (P4) ('64)	2,900.	210.00
	On cover		240.00
e.	As "d," imperf.	4,500.	
f.	As "d," thick paper	4,000.	260.00
g.	Wmk. missing shamrock		
h.	6p deep lilac (P3)	2,600.	120.00
	On cover		275.00
40	A14 9p straw (p2)	3,900.	400.00
	Block of four	*24,000.*	
	On cover		900.00
a.	9p straw, blued paper		
b.	9p straw, thick paper	6,000.	525.00
c.	9p straw, wmk. 3 roses & thistle		—
d.	9p bister (P2)	5,500.	525.00
	On cover		925.00
e.	9p bister, hair lines (P3)	*35,000.*	*14,000.*
42	A15 1sh green	3,100.	260.00
	Block of four	16,500.	1,500.
	On cover		450.00
a.	1sh deep green (P1)	4,750.	450.00
	On cover		600.00
c.	1sh deep green, with hair lines (P2)	*35,000.*	
d.	Thick paper		340.00
e.	As "c.," imperf	*7,500.*	

Hair lines on Nos. 39d, 39e, 39f, 39g, 40e and 42c are fine colorless lines drawn diagonally across the corners of the stamp.

Compare design A14 with A19.

For examples of Nos. 34-42 with margins clear of the design on all four sides, add a 50 percent premium to the value listed. For stamps with clear circular datestamps, apply a 75 percent premium. Add the two premiums together for covers with stamps having these attributes.

Forgeries exist of Nos. 39a and 40a.

Stamps from plate 2 are unissued.

A16

1865 Wmk. 23

43	A16 4p vermilion (P12)	600.00	62.50
	Block of four	3,500.	650.00
	On cover		145.00
	Plate 9	625.00	72.50
	Plate 10	850.00	150.00
	On cover		225.00
	Plate 11	650.00	72.50
	On cover		175.00
	Plate 13	375.00	47.50
	Plate 14	800.00	92.50
	On cover		200.00
a.	4p dull vermilion (P8)	550.00	90.00
	Block of four	3,300.	550.00
	On cover		200.00
	Plate 7	600.00	100.00
	Block of four	3,300.	550.00
	On cover		200.00
	Plate 8	625.00	72.50
	Block of four	3,300.	550.00
	On cover		200.00
	Plates 9	625.00	72.50
	Block of four	3,300.	550.00
	On cover		175.00
	Plate 10	850.00	150.00
	Block of four	4,250.	725.00
	On cover		225.00
	Plate 11	650.00	72.50
	Block of four	3,300.	550.00
	On cover		175.00
	Plate 12	600.00	62.50
	Block of four	3,250.	525.00
	On cover		175.00
	Plate 14	800.00	92.50
	Block of four	3,900.	625.00
	On cover		200.00
	Plate 13	375.00	47.50
	Block of four	3,600.	550.00
	On cover		175.00
b.	Imperf. (P11,12)	7,750.	

A17

(Hyphen after SIX) — A18

A19

A20

A21

1865 Wmk. 24

44	A17 3p rose (P4)	2,350.	215.00
	Block of four	12,500.	1,600.
	On cover		400.00
a.	Wmk. error, 3 roses & shamrock	6,250.	1,250.
b.	Thick paper	3,500.	260.00
c.	Watermark inverted		*500.00*
45	A18 6p lilac (P5)	1,125.	100.00
	Block of four	6,250.	650.00
	On cover		190.00
a.	6p deep lilac	1,875.	180.00
	On cover		190.00
	Plate 6	3,700.	190.00
	On cover		350.00
b.	Double impression (P6)		*16,500.*
c.	Wmk. error, 3 roses & shamrock (P5)		*1,400.*
	As "c," Plate 6		*2,400.*
d.	Thick paper	1,500.	140.00
e.	Watermark inverted	1,875.	215.00

f. Watermark inverted (P6) 6,250. 450.00
46 A19 9p straw (P4) 4,500. 575.00
On cover 1,150.
Plate 5 *20,000.*
a. Wmk. error, 3 roses & shamrock (P4) — *2,250.*
b. Thick paper (P4) *5,250.* 800.00
c. Watermark inverted *1,150.*
47 A20 10p red brn (P1) *55,000.*
48 A21 1sh grn (P4) 2,500. 225.00
Block of four *14,000.* 1,350.
On cover 400.00
a. Thick paper 3,250. 350.00
b. Wmk. error, 3 roses & shamrock 1,500.
c. Vert. pair, imperf. btwn. *16,500.*
d. Watermark inverted 625.00

No. 46, plate 5 is from a proof sheet.

See Nos.49-50, 52-54. Compare design A17 with A27.

For examples of Nos. 43-48 with margins clear of the design on all four sides, add a 40 percent premium to the value listed. For stamps with clear circular datestamps, apply a 60 percent premium. Add the two premiums together for covers with stamps having these attributes.

(No hyphen after SIX) — A22

A23

1867-80 **Wmk. 25**

49 A17 3p rose (P5) 525.00 62.50
On cover 110.00
a. 3p deep rose 825.00 92.50
On cover 120.00
Plate 4 1,850. 300.00
On cover 425.00
Plate 6 550.00 62.50
On cover 95.00
Plate 7 400.00 67.50
On cover 105.00
Plate 8 600.00 62.50
On cover 100.00
Plate 9 600.00 67.50
On cover 110.00
Plate 10 900.00 145.00
On cover 225.00
b. Imperf. (P5,6,8,9) 10,000.
50 A18 6p dl vio (P6) 1,850. 92.50
On cover 175.00
a. 6p bright violet (P6) 1,750. 100.00
On cover 175.00
b. Imperf. (P6) *5,000.*
51 A22 6p red vio ('69) (P9) 650.00 90.00
On cover 145.00
a. 6p violet (P9) 675.00 92.50
On cover 155.00
Plate 8 675.00 135.00
On cover 200.00
Plate 10 *35,000.*
b. Imperf. (P8, 9) 10,000. 4,500.
52 A19 9p bis (P4) ('67) 2,400. 300.00
On cover 525.00
a. Imperf. (P4) 15,000.
53 A20 10p red brn (P1) 3,500. 350.00
On cover 800.00
Plate 2 *50,000.* *15,000.*
a. 10p deep red brown 5,000. 600.00
On cover 900.00
b. Imperf. (P1) 12,000.
54 A21 1sh grn (P4) 1,200. 40.00
On cover 100.00
Plate 5 825.00 40.00
On cover 92.50
Plate 6 1,200. 40.00
On cover 80.00
Plate 7 1,400. 82.50
On cover 135.00
a. 1sh deep green 1,250. 70.00
On cover 95.00
b. Imperf. (P4) *8,750.* *5,500.*
55 A23 2sh blue (P1) 3,750. 200.00
On cover 750.00
a. 2sh pale blue 4,750. 240.00
On cover 800.00
Plate 3 *14,000.*
b. Imperf. (P1) 20,000.
c. 2sh cobalt blue (P1) 22,000. 2,900.
d. 2sh milky blue (P1) 20,000. 1,850.
56 A23 2sh pale brn (P1) ('80) *27,500.* 3,750.
On cover *9,250.*
a. Imperf. *27,500.*

No. 51, plate 10 and No. 53, plate 2, are from proof sheets.

For examples of Nos. 49-56 with margins clear of the design on all four sides, add a 35 percent premium to the value listed. For stamps with clear circular datestamps, apply a 40 percent premium. Add the two premiums together for covers with stamps having these attributes.

A24

1867 **Wmk. 26** ***Perf. 15½x15***

57 A24 5sh rose (P1) 11,000. 600.00
Plate 2 17,500. 1,200.
a. 5sh pale rose 11,000. 600.00
Plate 2 17,500. 1,200.
b. Imperf. (P1) *19,000.* *19,000.*

See No. 90. Compare design A24 with A51.

For examples of No. 57 with margins clear of the design on all four sides, add a 50 percent premium to the value listed. For stamps with clear circular datestamps, apply a 50 percent premium. Add the two premiums together for covers with stamps having these attributes.

A25

1870 **Engr.** **Wmk. 27** ***Perf. 14***

58 A25 ½p rose (P5) 110.00 22.00
Block of four *575.00* 210.00
On cover 65.00
Plate 1 325.00 90.00
Block of four 1,500. 800.00
On cover 240.00
Plate 3 225.00 50.00
Block of four 1,000. 800.00
On cover 130.00
Plate 4 150.00 37.50
Block of four 750.00 375.00
On cover 95.00
Plate 5 110.00 22.50
Block of four 575.00 210.00
On cover 40.00
Plate 6 125.00 22.00
Block of four 575.00 210.00
On cover 65.00
Plate 8 575.00 210.00
Block of four
On cover 300.00
Plate 9 6,000. 850.00
Block of four *25,000.* *7,500.*
On cover *1,650.*
Plate 10 125.00 22.00
Block of four 575.00 210.00
On cover 72.50
Plate 11, 13 125.00 22.00
Block of four 575.00 210.00
On cover 72.50
Plate 12, 14 125.00 22.00
Block of four 600.00 210.00
On cover 72.50
Plate 15 180.00 40.00
Block of four 900.00 400.00
On cover 130.00
Plate 19 300.00 60.00
Block of four 1,500. 600.00
On cover 160.00
Plate 20 350.00 80.00
Block of four 1,750. 800.00
On cover 240.00
a. Imperf (see footnote) — —
b. Watermark inverted & reversed 310.00 100.00

Plates 1, 4-6, 8, 13 and 14 are known imperf. Values: from $3,750 unused, $3,250 used.

For examples of No. 58 with margins clear of the design on all four sides, add a 125 percent premium to the value listed. For stamps with clear circular datestamps, apply a 75 percent premium. Add the two premiums together for covers with stamps having these attributes.

A26

1872-73 **Wmk. 25** **Typo.**

59 A26 6p brown (P11) 800.00 55.00
On cover 140.00
Plate 12 *4,000.*
a. 6p deep brown (P11) 1,300. 110.00
On cover 210.00
Plate 12 *3,500.*
b. 6p pale buff (P11) 1,000. 100.00
On cover 275.00
Plate 12 3,300. 300.00
On cover 525.00
60 A26 6p gray (P12) ('73) 1,900. 250.00
On cover 325.00
a. Imperf. *10,000.*

For examples of Nos. 59-60 with margins clear of the design on all four sides, add a 25 percent premium to the value listed. For stamps with clear circular datestamps, apply a 25 percent premium. Add the two premiums together for covers with stamps having these attributes.

A27

A28

A29

Type A28 has a lined background.

1873-80

61 A27 3p rose (shades) (P11) 400.00 50.00
On cover 70.00
Plates 12 500.00 50.00
On cover 70.00
Plate 14 525.00 50.00
On cover 70.00
Plates 15-16 400.00 50.00
On cover 70.00
Plates 17-18 500.00 50.00
On cover 70.00
Plate 19 425.00 50.00
On cover 70.00
Plate 20 800.00 110.00
On cover 130.00
62 A28 6p gray (P13-16) 500.00 70.00
On cover 115.00
Plate 17 1,000. 165.00
On cover 250.00
63 A28 6p buff (P13) *25,000.*
64 A29 1sh pale green (P12, 13) 600.00 120.00
On cover 240.00
Plate 10 750.00 160.00
On cover 275.00
Plate 11 750.00 140.00
On cover 260.00
Plate 14 *40,000.*
a. 1sh deep green (P8, 9) 1,000. 180.00
On cover 290.00
65 A29 1sh sal (P13) ('80) 4,750. 700.00
On cover 1,500.

No. 63, plate 13, and No. 64, plate 14, are from proof sheets.

See Nos. 83, 86-87. For surcharges see Nos. 94-95. For overprints see Nos. O6, O30.

For examples of Nos. 61-65 with margins clear of the design on all four sides, add a 40 percent premium to the value listed. For stamps with clear circular datestamps, apply a 60 percent premium. Add the two premiums together for covers with stamps having these attributes.

A30

1875 **Wmk. 28**

66 A30 2½p claret (P1, 2) 600.00 90.00
On cover 160.00
Plate 3 900.00 135.00
On cover 195.00
a. Bluish paper (P1) 900.00 140.00
On cover 205.00
Plate 2 *8,250.* 1,500.
On cover 2,000.
Plate 3 *5,500.*
On cover *7,750.*
b. Lettered "LH-FL" *29,000.* 2,500.
On cover —

Forgeries exist of 66a.

1876-80 **Wmk. 29**

67 A30 2½p claret (P4-9, 11-16) 500.00 60.00
On cover 105.00
Plate 3 1,300. 125.00
On cover 100.00
Plate 10 550.00 75.00
On cover 115.00
Plate 17 1,750. 275.00
On cover 525.00
68 A30 2½p ultra ('80) (P19, 20) 550.00 65.00
On cover 110.00
Plate 17 550.00 65.00
On cover 110.00
Plate 18 550.00 45.00
On cover 75.00

See No. 82.

A31

A32

1876-80 **Wmk. 23**

69 A31 4p vermilion (P15) 2,750. 500.00
On cover 1,000.
Plate 16 *35,000.*
70 A31 4p pale ol grn ('77) (P16) 1,350. 325.00
On cover 575.00
Plate 15 1,350. 325.00
On cover 650.00
Plate 17 *20,000.*
a. Imperf (P15) *1,400.*
71 A31 4p gray brn (P17) ('80) 2,750. 500.00
On cover 1,500.
72 A32 8p brn lilac (P1) ('76) 11,750.
73 A32 8p org (P1) ('76) 1,750. 350.00
On cover 600.00

Some specialists consider No. 70a a proof.

No. 72 was never placed in use.

No. 69, plate 16, is from proof sheets.

See No. 84.

For examples of Nos. 66-73 with margins clear of the design on all four sides, add a 50 percent premium to the value listed. For stamps with clear circular datestamps, apply a 50 percent premium. Add the two premiums together for covers with stamps having these attributes.

A33

A34

1878 **Wmk. 26** ***Perf. 15½x15***

74 A33 10sh slate (P1) 60,000. 3,250.
75 A34 £1 brn lilac (P1) 90,000. 4,500.

See Nos. 91-92. Compare design A34 with A52.

For examples of Nos. 74-75 with margins clear of the design on all four sides, add a 40 percent premium to the value listed. For stamps with clear circular datestamps, apply a 60 percent premium. Add the two premiums together for covers with stamps having these attributes.

A35

A36

A37

A38

A39

1880-81 **Wmk. 30** ***Perf. 14***

78 A35 ½p deep green 50.00 13.50
On cover 27.50
a. Imperf. 4,400.
b. No watermark *9,000.*
c. ½p green *50.00* 20.00
On cover 37.50
79 A36 1p red brown 27.50 12.50
On cover 30.00
a. Imperf. 5,000.
b. Wmk. 29, error 25,000.
80 A37 1½p red brown 240.00 50.00
On cover 150.00
81 A38 2p lilac rose 300.00 100.00
On cover 275.00
a. 2p deep rose 350.00 100.00
82 A30 2½p ultra ('81) (P23) 425.00 32.50
On cover 55.00
Plate 21 475.00 40.00
On cover 55.00
Plate 22 425.00 40.00
On cover 55.00
a. Imperf. (P23) *750.00*
83 A27 3p rose ('81) (P21) 500.00 90.00
On cover 175.00
Plate 20 900.00 155.00
On cover 225.00

84 A31 4p gray brown (P17, 18) 440.00 67.50
On cover 180.00
85 A39 5p dp indigo ('81) 725.00 125.00
On cover 275.00
a. Imperf. *6,750.* *4,500.*
86 A28 6p gray (P18) 375.00 72.50
On cover 125.00
Plate 17 440.00 72.50
On cover 125.00
87 A29 1sh salmon (P14) ('81) 700.00 165.00
On cover 525.00
Plate 13 700.00 165.00
On cover 525.00
Nos. 78-87 (10) 3,783. 728.50

Some specialists consider No. 82a a proof.

The 1sh in purple was not issued. Value, unused, $8,750.

See No. 98. For overprints, see Nos. O2-O3.

Compare design A35 with A54.

For examples of Nos. 78-87 with margins clear of the design on all four sides, add a 50 percent premium to the value listed. For stamps with clear circular datestamps, apply a 25 percent premium. Add the two premiums together for covers with stamps having these attributes.

A40

Die I

Die II

1881

88 A40 1p lilac (14 dots in each angle) 225.00 32.50
On cover 52.50
89 A40 1p lilac (16 dots in each angle) 2.75 2.00
On cover 4.00
a. Printed on both sides 900.
b. Imperf., pair 7,250.
c. Unwmkd. 7,750.
d. Bluish paper 4,750.
e. Printed on the gummed side 925.
f. As "a," reverse impression inverted 1,000.

For overprints, see Nos. O4, O37, O45 and O55.

For examples of Nos. 88-89 with margins clear of the design on all four sides, add a 25 percent premium to the value listed. For stamps with clear circular datestamps, apply a 25 percent premium. Add the two premiums together for covers with stamps having these attributes.

1882-83 Wmk. 31

90 A24 5sh rose, *bluish* (P4) 35,000. 5,000.
a. White paper 32,500. 5,000.
91 A33 10sh slate, *bluish* (P1) 135,000. 5,500.
a. White paper 155,000. 4,750.
92 A34 £1 brown lilac, *bluish* (P1) 155,000. 10,000.
a. White paper 180,000. 9,250.

A41

1882 Wmk. Two Anchors (31)

93 A41 £5 brt org (P1) 14,000. 5,000.
a. £5 pale dull org, *bluish* *72,500.* *15,500.*
b. £5 bright org, *bluish* *72,500.* *15,500.*

The paper of No. 93b is less bluish than that of No. 93a, and it is a later printing.

For examples of Nos. 90-93 with margins clear of the design on all four sides, add a 25 percent premium to the value listed. For stamps with clear circular datestamps, apply a 50 percent premium. Add the two premiums together for covers with stamps having these attributes.

Types of 1873-80 Surcharged in Carmine

1883 Wmk. 30

94 A27 3p on 3p violet 625.00 150.00
On cover 440.00
95 A28 6p on 6p violet 675.00 150.00
On cover 440.00
a. Double surcharge *12,500.*

For examples of Nos. 94-95 with margins clear of the design on all four sides, add a 40 percent premium to the value listed. For stamps with clear circular datestamps, apply a 50 percent premium. Add the two premiums together for covers with stamps having these attributes.

A44

1883 Wmk. 31

96 A44 2sh6p lilac 625.00 165.00
a. Bluish paper *9,250.* *3,750.*

For examples of No. 96 with margins clear of the design on all four sides, add a 25 percent premium to the value listed. For stamps with clear circular datestamps, apply a 25 percent premium. Add the two premiums together for covers with stamps having these attributes.

See British Offices Abroad for overprints on types A44-A133. These overprints include "M.E.F.," "B.A.," "B.M.A.," "E.A.F.," "CHINA," "Morocco Agencies," "TANGIER," "LEVANT," "PARAS," and "PIASTRE(S)."

A45

A46

A47

A48

A49

A50

1883-84 Wmk. 30

98 A35 ½p slate bl ('84) 29.00 9.00
On cover 18.50
99 A45 1½p lilac ('84) 120.00 42.50
On cover 125.00
100 A46 2p lilac ('84) 225.00 77.50
On cover 155.00
101 A47 2½p lilac ('84) 90.00 18.00
On cover 30.00
102 A48 3p lilac ('84) 275.00 100.00
On cover 190.00
103 A49 4p green ('84) 575.00 210.00
On cover 360.00
104 A45 5p green ('84) 575.00 210.00
On cover 360.00
105 A46 6p green ('84) 600.00 240.00
On cover 400.00
106 A50 9p green 1,250. 475.00
On cover *2,500.*
107 A48 1sh green ('84) 1,450. 300.00
On cover 625.00
Nos. 98-107 (10) 5,189. 1,682.

For examples of Nos. 98-107 with margins clear of the design on all four sides, add a 50 percent premium to the value listed. For stamps with clear circular datestamps, apply a 50 percent premium. Add the two premiums together for covers with stamps having these attributes.

Imperforate Singles

98a A35 ½p 3,750.
99a A45 1½p 3,750.
100a A46 2p 4,750.
101a A47 2½p 4,750.
102a A48 3p 4,750.
103a A49 4p 4,750.
104a A45 5p 5,500.
105a A46 6p 5,500.
107a A48 1sh 8,250.

Nos. 99-107 were printed by De La Rue in a newly invented doubly fugitive ink that was only available in lilac and green. The stamps were unpopular with the public and postal clerks because they were unattractive and the different denominations were difficult to distinguish from one another.

Values are for stamps of good color. Faded stamps sell for much less. Soaking stamps will cause the color to run.

No. 104 with line instead of period under "d" was not regularly issued. Value, $27,500.

For overprints see Nos. O5, O7, O27-O29.

A51

A52

1884 Wmk. 31

108 A51 5sh car rose 1,100. 250.00
a. Bluish paper 18,750. 4,000.
b. 5sh deep crimson 1,000. 250.00
109 A52 10sh ultra 2,250. 550.00
a. 10sh cobalt *40,000.* 8,500.
b. Bluish paper *40,000.* *8,500.*
c. As "a," bluish paper *65,000.* *14,000.*

For overprints see Nos. O8-O9.

For examples of Nos. 108-109 with margins clear of the design on all four sides, add a 25 percent premium to the value listed. For stamps with clear circular datestamps, apply a 25 percent premium. Add the two premiums together for covers with stamps having these attributes.

A53

1884 Wmk. 30

110 A53 £1 brn violet 32,500. 3,000.
a. Frame broken, position JC or TA 62,500. 5,250.

See Nos. 123-124. For overprints see Nos. O10, O13, O15.

For examples of No. 110 with margins clear of the design on all four sides, add a 25 percent premium to the value listed. For stamps with clear circular datestamps, apply a 25 percent premium. Add the two premiums together for covers with stamps having these attributes.

Queen Victoria Jubilee Issue

A54

A55

A56

A57

A58 A59

A60

A61

A62

A63

A64

A65

Two types of 5p:
I — Squarish dots beside "d."
II — Tiny vertical dashes beside "d."

1887-92 Wmk. 30

111 A54 ½p vermilion 1.80 1.10
On cover 7.00
a. Printed on both sides
b. Double impression *29,000.*
c. Imperf. 4,400.
d. Printed on gummed side 3,300. —
112 A55 1½p violet & grn 18.00 8.25
On cover 25.00
a. Double impression of violet 9,250.
113 A56 2p grn & car rose 35.00 13.50
On cover 27.50
a. 2p green & vermilion 440.00 250.00
On cover 750.00
114 A57 2½p violet, *blue* 25.00 3.50
On cover 8.00
a. Imperf. 10,500.
b. Printed on gummed side 13,500.
115 A58 3p violet, *yel* 25.00 3.50
On cover 37.50
a. 3p violet, *orange* 825.00 175.00
On cover 750.00
b. Imperf. 10,500.
116 A59 4p brn & grn 40.00 15.00
On cover 42.50
117 A60 4½p car rose & grn ('92) 11.00 45.00
On cover 92.50
118 A61 5p lilac & bl, II 42.50 12.50
On cover 50.00
a. Type I 825.00 125.00
On cover 215.00
119 A62 6p violet, *rose* 40.00 12.50
On cover 90.00
120 A63 9p blue & lilac 77.50 45.00
On cover 250.00
121 A64 10p car rose & lilac ('90) 62.50 42.50
On cover 275.00
a. Imperf. *16,500.* —
b. 10p scarlet & lilac 97.50 62.50
On cover 265.00
c. 10p dp carmine & red lilac 625.00 250.00
122 A65 1sh green 275.00 72.50
On cover 195.00
Nos. 111-122 (12) 653.30 274.85

The unpopular green and lilac issue (Nos. 98-107) were replaced by these stamps in colored inks and papers that made it easier to distinguish the different denominations.

Soaking these stamps will cause the color to run.

See Nos. 125-126. For overprints see Nos. O11-O12, O14, O16-O18, O31-O36, O38, O44, O46-O48, O54, O56-O58, O65-O66.

1888 Wmk. Three Orbs (29)

123 A53 £1 brown violet 75,000. 4,400.
a. Frame broken, position JC or TA *135,000.* 9,250.

1891 Wmk. 30

124 A53 £1 green 4,000. 800.00
a. Frame broken, position JC or TA 8,750. 2,000.

1900 Wmk. 30

125 A54 ½p blue green 2.00 *2.25*
On cover 6.50
a. Imperf *7,250.*
b. Printed on gum side —
126 A65 1sh car rose & grn 67.50 *145.00*
On cover 1,000.

No. 125 in bright blue is a color changeling.

For examples of Nos. 111-126 with margins clear of the design on all four sides, add a 25 percent premium to the value listed. For stamps with clear circular datestamps, apply a 25 percent premium. Add the two premiums together for covers with stamps having these attributes.

King Edward VII

A66 A67

A68 A69

A70 A71

A72 A73

A74 A75

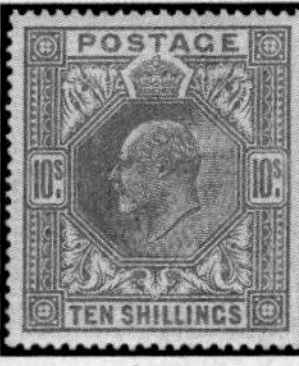

A76 A77

A78

The stamps of King Edward VII were printed by three printers. De La Rue (DLR) held the contract from Jan. 1, 1902, through Dec. 31, 1910. De La Rue was replaced by Harrison & Sons (H) on Jan. 1, 1911. From July, 1911, the bi-colored issues were produced by Somerset House (S), while Harrison continued to produce most of the monocolor stamps.

De La Rue printings were made on both ordinary and chalky papers and tend to be more finely printed than those of either of its successors. Soaking the green De La Rue stamps will cause the color to run.

The Harrison printings are only on ordinary paper. The stamps perforated 15x14 were only printed by Harrison & Sons and can serve as a comparison to identify printings.

The Somerset House printings are all on ordinary paper, except the 6p dull purple on Dickinson Coated paper (#135f) and the 6p bright magenta on chalky paper (#135j).

1902-11 Wmk. 30 *Perf. 14*

Ordinary Paper

127 A66 ½p gray grn (DLR) 2.00 1.75
Never hinged 3.25
On cover 2.90
a. ½p blue green (DLR) 2.00 1.75
Never hinged 3.25
On cover 2.90
b. ½p deep bluish green '11 (H) 12.50 6.50
Never hinged 18.00
On cover 7.50
c. ½p very pale bluish grn ('11) (H) 45.00 45.00
Never hinged 70.00
On cover 65.00
d. ½p bright green (fine impression; '11) (H) 275.00 175.00
Never hinged 425.00
On cover —

128 A66 1p scarlet (DLR) 2.25 1.60
Never hinged 3.25
On cover 2.90
a. 1p rose red ('11) (H) 9.25 *14.00*
Never hinged 13.50
On cover 20.00
b. 1p rose carmine ('11) (H) 62.50 35.00
Never hinged 95.00
On cover 50.00
c. 1p aniline rose ('11) (H) 225.00 145.00
Never hinged 325.00
On cover —
d. 1p aniline pink ('11) (H) 650.00 360.00
Never hinged 1,000.
On cover —
e. Booklet pane of 6 110.00
f. No watermark ('11) (H) 47.50 *90.00*
Never hinged 65.00
g. Imperf., pair (DLR) *29,000.*
h. 1p rose carmine (02) (DLR) 30.00 20.00
Never hinged 42.50

129 A67 1½p vio & grn (DLR) 45.00 22.50
Never hinged 65.00
On cover 35.00
a. 1½p slate purple & green 50.00 22.50
Never hinged 75.00
On cover 35.00
b. 1½p reddish pur & bright grn ('11) (S) 50.00 40.00
Never hinged 80.00
On cover 57.50
c. 1½p dull purple & green ('12) (S) 35.00 *32.50*
Never hinged 50.00
On cover 60.00

130 A68 2p yel grn & car (DLR) 52.50 22.50
Never hinged 82.50
On cover 35.00
a. 2p gray grn & car red '04 (DLR) 60.00 32.50
Never hinged 85.00
On cover 40.00
b. 2p deep grn & red ('11) (S) 27.50 20.00
Never hinged 47.50
On cover 55.00
c. 2p deep grn & car ('11-'12) (S) 30.00 22.50
Never hinged 45.00
On cover 55.00

131 A66 2½p ultra (DLR) 22.50 11.50
Never hinged 32.50
On cover 22.50
a. 2½p pale ultra (DLR) 22.50 11.50
Never hinged 32.50
On cover 22.50
b. 2½p bright blue ('11) (H) 62.50 35.00
Never hinged 110.00
On cover 57.50

132 A69 3p dull pur, *org yel* (DLR) 45.00 19.00
Never hinged 80.00
On cover 35.00
a. 3p deep pur, *org yel* (DLR) 45.00 19.00
Never hinged 80.00
On cover 35.00
b. 3p purple, *lemon* ('11) (H) 92.50 *235.00*
Never hinged 150.00
On cover 625.00
c. 3p gray, *lemon* ('11) (H) *4,500.*
Never hinged *6,750.*

133 A70 4p gray brn & grn (DLR) 57.50 35.00
Never hinged 110.00
On cover 50.00
a. 4p choc brn & green (DLR) 57.50 35.00
Never hinged 100.00
On cover 45.00

134 A71 5p dull pur & ultra (DLR) 67.50 22.50
Never hinged 87.50
On cover 57.50
a. 5p dull reddish pur & brt blue ('11) (S) 35.00 22.50
Never hinged 55.00
On cover 75.00
b. 5p deep reddish pur & brt blue ('11) (S) 35.00 22.50
Never hinged 55.00
On cover 75.00

135 A66 6p pale dull vio (DLR) 45.00 22.50
Never hinged 55.00
On cover 55.00
a. 6p slate purple (DLR) 45.00 22.50
Never hinged 55.00
On cover 55.00
b. 6p red violet ('11) (S) 45.00 26.00
Never hinged 62.50
On cover 60.00
c. 6p dark violet ('12) (S) 45.00 30.00
Never hinged 62.50
On cover 65.00
d. 6p deep plum ('13) (S) 32.50 *80.00*
Never hinged 45.00
On cover 140.00
e. 6p royal purple ('11) (S) 57.50 *100.00*
Never hinged 95.00
On cover 195.00
f. 6p dull purple, "Dickinson" coated paper ('13) (S) 250.00 190.00
Never hinged *500.00*
On cover —
g. No cross on crown (S), *from* 1,000.
Never hinged 1,500.

136 A72 9p ultra & dull vio (DLR) 100.00 70.00
Never hinged 190.00
On cover 210.00
a. 9p ultra & slate vio (DLR) 100.00 70.00
Never hinged 190.00
On cover 210.00
b. 9p lt bl & reddish pur ('11) (S) 92.50 85.00
Never hinged 160.00
On cover 210.00
c. 9p deep brt bl & deep dull reddish pur (S) 92.50 85.00
Never hinged 160.00
On cover 200.00
d. 9p blue & dull reddish pur ('11) (S) 70.00 70.00
Never hinged 125.00
On cover 200.00
e. 9p blue & deep plum ('13) (S) 70.00 70.00
Never hinged 125.00
On cover 200.00
f. 9p cobalt bl & slate vio ('11) (S) 140.00 115.00
Never hinged 210.00
On cover 200.00

137 A73 10p car & dull pur (DLR) 100.00 70.00
Never hinged 175.00
On cover 240.00
a. 10p scarlet & dull pur (S) 92.50 85.00
Never hinged 125.00
On cover 240.00
b. 10p aniline pink & dull reddish pur ('11) (S) 290.00 260.00
Never hinged 450.00
On cover 375.00
c. 10p car & dull reddish pur ('12) (S) 92.50 70.00
Never hinged 150.00
On cover 260.00
d. As No. 137, no cross on crown, *from* 400.00 260.00
Never hinged 600.00

138 A74 1sh car & dull grn (DLR) 92.50 40.00
Never hinged 150.00
On cover 155.00
a. 1sh scar & dark green ('11) (S) 125.00 70.00
Never hinged 190.00
On cover 160.00
b. 1sh scar & deep dark grn ('11) (S) 80.00 40.00
Never hinged 120.00
On cover 125.00
c. 1sh car & lt green ('12) (S) 62.50 40.00
Never hinged 100.00
On cover 180.00

Wmk. 31

139 A75 2sh6p lilac (DLR) 260.00 150.00
Never hinged 575.00
On cover 800.00
a. 2sh6p dark violet ('11) (S) 300.00 200.00
Never hinged 600.00
On cover 600.00
b. 2sh6p dull grayish pur ('11) (S) 850.00 475.00
Never hinged 1,500.
On cover —
c. 2sh6p dull reddish pur ('11) (S) 275.00 190.00
Never hinged 625.00
On cover 1,100.

140 A76 5sh car rose (DLR) 400.00 225.00
Never hinged 600.00
On cover 1,000.
a. 5sh deep brt carmine (DLR) 400.00 225.00
Never hinged 600.00
On cover 1,000.
b. 5sh carmine (S) 425.00 225.00
Never hinged 650.00
On cover 1,100.

141 A77 10sh ultra (DLR) 875.00 525.00
Never hinged 1,600.
On cover —
a. 10sh bright blue ('12) (S) 1,000. 625.00
Never hinged 1,750.
On cover —

Wmk. Three Imperial Crowns (30)

142 A78 £1 blue grn (DLR) 2,000. 825.00
Never hinged 3,250.
On cover —
b. £1 deep green ('11) (S) 2,000. 800.00
Never hinged 3,250.
On cover —
Nos. 127-138 (12) 631.75 338.85

CHALKY PAPER

129d A67 1½p pale pur & green ('05) (DLR) 45.00 22.50
Never hinged 65.00
On cover 32.50
e. 1½p slate pur & bl grn (DLR) 45.00 20.00
Never hinged 65.00
On cover 35.00
130d A68 2p pale gray grn & car red ('06) (DLR) 55.00 32.50
Never hinged 80.00
On cover 54.00
e. 2p pale gray grn & scar ('09) (DLR) 45.00 30.00
Never hinged 90.00
On cover 50.00
f. 2p dull bl grn & car ('07) (DLR) 80.00 57.50
Never hinged 160.00
On cover 110.00
132d A69 3p dull pur, *org yel* ('06) (DLR) 200.00 80.00
Never hinged 300.00
On cover 100.00
e. 3p pale reddish pur, *org yel* ('06) (DLR) 200.00 80.00
Never hinged 300.00
On cover 100.00
f. 3p dull reddish pur, *yel, lemon back* (DLR) 200.00 *92.50*
Never hinged 300.00
On cover —
g. 3p pale pur, *lemon* (DLR) *45.00* 20.00
Never hinged *65.00*
On cover 40.00
h. 3p purple, *lemon* (DLR) *45.00* 20.00
Never hinged *65.00*
On cover 40.00
133b A70 4p choc brn & grn (DLR) 57.50 35.00
Never hinged 85.00
On cover 85.00
c. 4p choc brn & deep green ('06) (DLR) 45.00 21.00
Never hinged 65.00
On cover 45.00
134c A71 5p dull pur & ultra ('06) (DLR) 62.50 22.50
Never hinged 92.50
On cover 55.00
d. 5p slate pur & ultra ('06) (DLR) 57.50 22.50
Never hinged 85.00
On cover 52.50
135h A66 6p pale dull pur ('06) (DLR) 45.00 22.50
Never hinged 60.00
On cover 55.00
i. 6p dull purple ('06) (DLR) 45.00 22.50
Never hinged 60.00
On cover 55.00
j. 6p bright magenta ('11) (S) *12,500.*
Never hinged *17,500.*
136g A72 9p ultra & dull vio ('05) (DLR) 100.00 70.00
Never hinged 190.00
On cover 200.00
h. 9p ultra & slate vio ('05) (DLR) 100.00 70.00
Never hinged 190.00
On cover 210.00

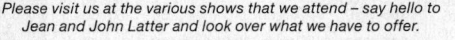

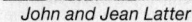

No.	Description	Unused	Used
137e	A73 10p car & dull pur ('06) (DLR)	100.00	70.00
	Never hinged	175.00	
	On cover		210.00
f.	10p car & slate vio ('06) (DLR)	100.00	70.00
	Never hinged	175.00	
	On cover		210.00
g.	10p scar & dull pur ('10) (DLR)	110.00	70.00
	Never hinged	175.00	
	On cover		210.00
h.	Chalky paper, no cross on crown (DLR), *from*	450.00	275.00
	Never hinged	750.00	
138d	A74 1sh car & dull grn ('05) (DLR)	92.50	40.00
	Never hinged	150.00	
	On cover		140.00
e.	1sh scar & dull green ('10) (DLR)	92.50	57.50
	Never hinged	150.00	
	On cover		140.00

Wmk. 31

No.	Description	Unused	Used
139d	A75 2sh6p pale dull pur ('05) (DLR)	290.00	175.00
	Never hinged	525.00	
	On cover		925.00
e.	2sh6p deep dull pur (DLR)	260.00	175.00
	Never hinged	500.00	
	On cover		925.00

See Nos. 143, 144, 146-150. For overprints see Nos. O19-O26, O39-O43, O49-O53, O59-O64, O67-O83.

See British Offices Abroad for overprints on types A44-A133. These overprints include "M.E.F.," "B.A.," "B.M.A.," "E.A.F.," "CHINA," "Morocco Agencies," "TANGIER," "LEVANT," "PARAS," and "PIASTRE(S)."

Type of 1902-11 Issue

1904 Wmk. 30

No.	Description	Unused	Used
143	A66 ½p pale yel grn (DLR)	2.00	1.75
	Never hinged	3.00	
	On cover		3.00
a.	½p yellow green (DLR)	2.00	1.75
	Never hinged	3.00	
	On cover		3.00
b.	Booklet pane of 5 + label (DLR, H)	525.00	
c.	Booklet pane of 6 (DLR, H)	190.00	
d.	Double impression (DLR)	*29,000.*	
e.	Imperf., pair (H)	*37,500.*	

Edward VII — A79

1909-10

No.	Description	Unused	Used
144	A70 4p pale org (DLR)	20.00	16.00
	Never hinged	30.00	
	On cover		40.00
a.	4p orange red (DLR)	22.50	17.50
	Never hinged	32.50	
	On cover		40.00
b.	4p brown orange (DLR)	190.00	150.00
	Never hinged	250.00	
	On cover		—
c.	4p bright orange ('11) (H)	100.00	62.50
	Never hinged	175.00	
	On cover		190.00
145	A79 7p gray ('10) (DLR)	42.50	*22.50*
	Never hinged	80.00	
	On cover		225.00
a.	7p deep gray blk ('10) (DLR)	125.00	110.00
	Never hinged	160.00	
	On cover		300.00
b.	7p slate gray ('12) (S)	17.50	*25.00*
	Never hinged	25.00	
	On cover		200.00

Type of 1902-11 Issue

1911 ***Perf. 15x14***

No.	Description	Unused	Used
146	A66 ½p dl yel grn (H)	45.00	*50.00*
	Never hinged	65.00	
	On cover		110.00
a.	½p deep dull green (H)	45.00	*50.00*
	Never hinged	65.00	
	On cover		110.00
147	A66 1p car rose (H)	17.50	17.50
	Never hinged	30.00	
	On cover		35.00
a.	1p pale car rose (H)	25.00	17.50
	Never hinged	37.50	
	On cover		35.00
b.	1p rose red (H)	47.50	30.00
	Never hinged	70.00	
	On cover		47.50
148	A66 2½p brt ultra (H)	25.00	17.50
	Never hinged	55.00	
	On cover		37.50
a.	2½p dull blue (H)	25.00	*17.50*
	Never hinged	55.00	
	On cover		32.50
149	A69 3p vio, *lem* (H)	52.50	17.50
	Never hinged	85.00	
	On cover		45.00
a.	3p gray, *lemon* (H)	*3,400.*	
	Never hinged	*5,000.*	
150	A70 4p orange (H)	35.00	17.50
	Never hinged	55.00	
	On cover		75.00
	Nos. 146-150 (5)	175.00	120.00

King George V
A80 A81

Original Die, Type 1

½p: on the right-hand dolphin, the three uppermost scales form a complete triangle.

1p: the ribbon on the wreath at the right of the crown is crossed by two complete lines from top to bottom.

Perf. 15x14

1911, June 22 Wmk. 30

No.	Description	Unused	Used
151	A80 ½p yellow green	5.75	4.50
	Never hinged	8.25	
a.	Booklet pane of 6	175.00	
b.	Perf. 14 (error)	*18,500.*	1,050.
	Never hinged	—	
c.	½p bluish green	400.00	210.00
	Never hinged	550.00	
152	A81 1p carmine	5.25	3.00
	Never hinged	7.50	
a.	Booklet pane of 6	175.00	
b.	Perf. 14 (error)	—	—
	Never hinged	—	
c.	1p pale carmine	16.00	3.50
	Never hinged	25.00	
d.	As "c," booklet pane of 6	*125.00*	
e.	As "c," no cross on crown	875.00	525.00
	Never hinged	1,275.	

Original Die, Type 2

½p: on the right-hand dolphin, the three uppermost scales do not complete the triangle, with the line on the left side of the top scale missing entirely.

1p: the ribbon on the wreath at the right of the crown is crossed by one complete line from top to bottom, the other being interrupted.

No.	Description	Unused	Used
151d	A80 ½p bright green	9.00	1.75
	Never hinged	17.50	
f.	½p yellow green	13.50	1.75
	Never hinged	27.50	
g.	½p bluish green	190.00	110.00
	Never hinged	300.00	
152g	A81 1p carmine	10.00	3.50
	Never hinged	16.50	
h.	1p pale carmine	11.50	4.50
	Never hinged	18.00	
i.	As "h," no cross on crown	825.00	525.00
	Never hinged	—	
j.	1p rose pink	140.00	50.00
	Never hinged	200.00	
k.	1p scarlet	50.00	21.00
	Never hinged	100.00	
l.	1p aniline scarlet	235.00	125.00
	Never hinged	390.00	

1912, Jan. 1 Re-engraved

No.	Description	Unused	Used
153	A80 ½p yellow green	10.00	4.50
	Never hinged	15.00	
a.	No cross on crown	110.00	57.50
	Never hinged	175.00	
b.	½p green	10.00	4.50
	Never hinged	15.00	
c.	½p deep green	17.50	9.25
	Never hinged	21.00	
154	A81 1p scarlet	7.50	3.50
	Never hinged	11.00	
a.	No cross on crown	92.50	57.50
	Never hinged	150.00	
b.	1p aniline scarlet	180.00	100.00
	Never hinged	250.00	
c.	As "b," no cross on crown	1,450.	

In the re-engraved stamps the lines of the hair and beard are clearer. The re-engraved ½p has 3 lines of shading instead of 4 between the point of neck and frame; in the 1p the body of the lion is nearly covered by lines of shading.

1912, Aug. Wmk. 33 ***Perf. 15x14***

Die I (Before Re-engraving)

No.	Description	Unused	Used
155	A80 ½p yellow green	45.00	45.00
	Never hinged	90.00	
a.	Booklet pane of 6	270.00	
	Never hinged	525.00	
156	A81 1p scarlet	30.00	30.00
	Never hinged	50.00	
a.	Booklet pane of 6	210.00	
	Never hinged	375.00	

Die II (Re-engraved)

No.	Description	Unused	Used
157	A80 ½p yellow green	8.00	3.50
	Never hinged	17.50	
a.	No cross on crown	210.00	130.00
	Never hinged	325.00	
158	A81 1p scarlet	9.25	4.75
	Never hinged	15.00	
a.	No cross on crown	110.00	57.50
	Never hinged	160.00	

1912, Sept.-Oct. Wmk. 32

No.	Description	Unused	Used
158A	A80 ½p yellow green	15.50	9.25
	Never hinged	25.00	
d.	½p green	14.00	9.25
	Never hinged	21.00	
e.	Imperf., pair	300.00	
	Never hinged	400.00	
f.	No cross on crown	180.00	130.00
	Never hinged	290.00	
158B	A81 1p scarlet	20.00	11.50
	Never hinged	30.00	
e.	Imperf., pair	300.00	
	Never hinged	400.00	
f.	No cross on crown	155.00	62.50
	Never hinged	225.00	

A82

A83

A84

A85

A86

A87

A88

A89

King George V — A90

TWO PENCE:

Die I — Four horizontal lines above the head. Heavy colored lines above and below the bottom tablet. The inner frame line is closer to the central design than it is to the outer frame line.

Die II — Three lines above the head. Thinner lines above and below the bottom tablet. The inner frame line is midway between the central design and the outer frame line.

1912-13 Wmk. 33 ***Perf. 15x14***

No.	Description	Unused	Used
159	A82 ½p green ('13)	1.10	1.10
	Never hinged	1.60	
a.	Double impression	*26,000.*	
b.	Booklet pane of 6	90.00	
	Never hinged	135.00	
c.	½p deep green	5.50	2.25
	Never hinged	9.00	
d.	½p yellow green	6.50	3.50
	Never hinged	10.00	
e.	½p blue green	45.00	29.00
	Never hinged	57.50	
f.	½p very yellow green ('14)	*8,500.*	
	Never hinged	*12,750.*	
160	A83 1p scarlet	1.10	1.10
	Never hinged	1.90	
a.	Booklet pane of 6	100.00	
	Never hinged	140.00	
b.	Tete beche pair	*77,500.*	
c.	1p vermilion	5.75	2.90
	Never hinged	8.50	
d.	1p pale rose red	21.00	5.25
	Never hinged	24.00	
e.	1p carmine red	12.50	5.75
	Never hinged	20.00	
f.	1p scarlet vermilion	140.00	57.50
	Never hinged	175.00	
161	A84 1½p red brown	4.50	1.75
	Never hinged	7.00	
a.	"PENCF"	350.00	260.00
	Never hinged	325.00	
b.	1½p orange brown	21.00	17.50
	Never hinged	32.50	
c.	1½p chestnut	5.75	1.10
	Never hinged	9.75	
d.	As "c," "PENCF"	130.00	115.00
	Never hinged	190.00	
e.	1½p chocolate brown	11.50	2.25
	Never hinged	17.50	
f.	As "e," Unwmkd.	235.00	235.00
	Never hinged	350.00	
g.	Booklet pane of 6	125.00	
	Never hinged	275.00	
h.	Booklet pane of 4 + 2 labels	675.00	
162	A85 2p deep org (I)	5.00	3.50
	Never hinged	6.50	
a.	2p deep orange (II) ('21)	5.75	4.25
	Never hinged	9.50	
b.	Booklet pane of 6 (I)	200.00	
	Never hinged	300.00	
c.	Booklet pane of 6 (II)	350.00	
	Never hinged	475.00	
d.	2p bright orange (I)	5.75	3.50
	Never hinged	9.50	
e.	2p orange yellow (I)	9.00	3.50
	Never hinged	15.00	
163	A86 2½p ultramarine	14.00	4.50
	Never hinged	24.00	
a.	2½ cobalt blue	14.00	4.50
	Never hinged	24.00	
b.	2½ bright blue ('14)	14.00	4.50
	Never hinged	24.00	
c.	2½ indigo blue ('20)	3,650.	2,600.
	Never hinged	*5,000.*	
d.	2½ Prussian blue	1,050.	825.00
	Never hinged	1,550.	
164	A87 3p bluish vio ('13)	9.25	3.25
	Never hinged	15.00	
a.	3p violet	8.50	3.50
	Never hinged	15.00	
b.	3p reddish violet	14.00	3.25
	Never hinged	21.00	
165	A88 4p slate green	17.50	2.25
	Never hinged	26.00	
a.	4p pale gray green	29.00	5.75
	Never hinged	40.00	
b.	4p deep gray green ('13)	45.00	26.00
	Never hinged	67.50	
166	A89 5p yellow brown	17.50	5.75
	Never hinged	26.00	
a.	Unwmkd.	1,250.	
	Never hinged	*1,750.*	
b.	5p brown ('13)	17.50	5.75
	Never hinged	26.00	
c.	5p bister brown	145.00	67.50
	Never hinged	215.00	
167	A89 6p rose lilac	17.50	8.00
	Never hinged	30.00	
a.	6p dull violet ('13)	30.00	11.50
	Never hinged	35.00	
b.	Perf. 14	92.50	*115.00*
	Never hinged	130.00	
c.	6p reddish purple	30.00	5.75
d.	6p dp reddish purple	40.00	7.00
	Never hinged	60.00	
168	A89 7p ol grn ('13)	22.50	10.50
	Never hinged	32.50	
a.	7p bronze green ('15)	72.50	29.00
	Never hinged	115.00	
b.	7p sage green ('17)	72.50	19.00
	Never hinged	115.00	
169	A89 8p blk, *yel* ('13)	37.50	12.50
	Never hinged	65.00	
a.	8p black, *buff*, granite ('17)	45.00	17.50
	Never hinged	62.50	
170	A90 9p blk brn ('13)	22.50	6.75
	Never hinged	32.50	
171	A90 10p light blue ('13)	25.00	22.50
	Never hinged	42.50	
a.	10p bright blue	92.50	32.50
	Never hinged	145.00	
172	A90 1sh bister ('13)	24.00	4.50
	Never hinged	35.00	
a.	1sh bister brown	40.00	14.00
	Never hinged	65.00	
	Nos. 159-172 (14)	218.95	87.95

No. 167 is on chalky paper.

The distinctive yellow green ink used in printing No. 159f, also called "Cyprus" green, is fluorescent under UV light, unlike the inks used in printing other ½p varieties.

See Nos. 177-178, 183, 187-200, 210, 212-220.

For overprints see Ireland Nos. 1-11, 15-35, 39-55, 59-62.

Compare design A82 with A97.

See British Offices Abroad for overprints on types A44-A133. These overprints include "M.E.F.," "B.A.," "B.M.A.," "E.A.F.," "CHINA," "Morocco Agencies," "TANGIER," "LEVANT," "PARAS," and "PIASTRE(S)."

Waterlow Brothers & Layton Printing (1913)

"Britannia Rule the Waves" A91

Measure 22mm vertically. Perforation holes are larger and evenly spaced.

1913 Engr. Wmk. 34 ***Perf. 11x12***

No.	Description	Unused	Used
173	A91 2sh6p dk brn	275.00	180.00
	Never hinged	390.00	
b.	2sh6p black brown	290.00	190.00
	Never hinged	425.00	
174	A91 5sh rose car	525.00	375.00
	Never hinged	1,050.	
175	A91 10sh indigo blue	1,000.	475.00
	Never hinged	2,000.	
176	A91 £1 green	3,250.	1,550.
	Never hinged	4,900.	
a.	£1 dull blue green	3,250.	1,800.
	Never hinged	5,000.	
	Nos. 173-176 (4)	5,050.	2,580.

De La Rue & Co. Printing (1915)

Measure 22mm vertically. Gum tends to be yellowish and patchy. The top right and top left perf teeth are wider than the others. Perforation holes are smaller.

1915 Engr. Wmk. 34 *Perf. 11x12*

173a A91 2sh6p lt brn (worn plate) 360.00 290.00
Never hinged 600.00
173c A91 2sh6p dp yel brn 350.00 250.00
Never hinged 600.00
173d A91 2sh6p yel brn 300.00 225.00
Never hinged 525.00
173e A91 2sh6p sepia brn 290.00 260.00
Never hinged 450.00
174a A91 5sh br car 475.00 375.00
Never hinged 575.00
174b A91 5sh carmine 450.00 360.00
Never hinged 625.00
174c A91 5sh pale car (worn plate) 625.00 460.00
Never hinged 900.00
175a A91 10sh light blue 3,000. 825.00
Never hinged 4,500.
175b A91 10sh blue 2,600. 825.00
Never hinged 3,900.
175c A91 10sh deep blue 3,150. 1,000.
Never hinged 4,750.

See Nos. 179-181, 222-224.

For overprints see Ireland Nos. 12-14, 36-38, 56-58, 77-79.

1913 Wmk. 32 Typo. *Perf. 15x14*
Coil Stamps

177 A82 ½p green 175.00 *210.00*
Never hinged 250.00
178 A83 1p scarlet 260.00 *260.00*
Never hinged 375.00

Bradbury, Wilkinson & Co. Printing (1918-19)

Seahorses Types of 1913-15 Retouched

Measure 22.5-23mm vertically. Most examples have a small dot of color at top center, outside of frameline. Perforation holes are larger and usually are evenly spaced.

1919 Engr. Wmk. 34 *Perf. 11x12*

179 A91 2sh6p olive brown 125.00 75.00
Never hinged 225.00
a. 2sh6p gray brown 125.00 75.00
Never hinged 225.00
b. 2sh6p chocolate brown 140.00 80.00
Never hinged 260.00
c. 2sh6p reddish brown 140.00 80.00
Never hinged 260.00
180 A91 5sh car rose 300.00 125.00
Never hinged 325.00
181 A91 10sh blue 425.00 160.00
Never hinged 500.00
Nos. 179-181 (3) 850.00 360.00

Type of 1912-13

1922 Typo. Wmk. 33 *Perf. 15x14*

183 A90 9p olive green 120.00 35.00
Never hinged 250.00

British Empire Exhibition Issue

British Lion and George V
A92

Wmk. 35

1924, Apr. 23 Engr. *Perf. 14*

185 A92 1p vermilion 11.50 12.50
Never hinged 17.50
186 A92 1½p dark brown 17.50 17.50
Never hinged 26.00

See Nos. 203-204.

Types of 1912-13 Issue

1924 Typo. *Perf. 15x14*

187 A82 ½p green 1.10 1.10
Never hinged 1.50
a. Wmk. sideways 10.00 4.00
Never hinged 20.00
b. Booklet pane of 6 90.00
Never hinged 140.00
c. Double impression *11,500.*
188 A83 1p scarlet 1.10 1.10
Never hinged 1.40
a. Wmk. sideways 22.50 17.50
Never hinged 45.00
b. Booklet pane of 6 90.00
Never hinged 140.00
189 A84 1½p red brown 1.10 1.10
Never hinged 1.40
a. Tête bêche pair 550.00 *875.00*
Never hinged 775.00
b. Wmk. sideways 20.00 4.00
Never hinged 40.00
c. Booklet pane of 6 50.00
Never hinged 75.00
d. Bklt. pane of 4 + 2 labels 235.00
Never hinged 375.00
e. Double impression *19,000.*
190 A85 2p dp org (II) 2.90 2.90
Never hinged 3.75
a. Wmk. sideways 110.00 *110.00*
Never hinged 200.00
b. Unwatermarked 1,000.
Never hinged 1,500.
191 A86 2½p ultra 5.75 3.50
Never hinged 10.00
a. Unwatermarked 2,100.
Never hinged 3,250.
192 A87 3p violet 11.50 2.75
Never hinged 19.00
193 A88 4p slate green 15.00 2.75
Never hinged 29.00
a. Printed on gummed side 3,900.
194 A89 5p yel brown 22.50 4.00
Never hinged 47.50
195 A89 6p dull violet 3.50 1.75
Never hinged 5.00
a. 6p purple, chalky paper 14.00 2.90
Never hinged 25.00
198 A90 9p olive green 13.50 4.00
Never hinged 27.50
199 A90 10p dull blue 45.00 45.00
Never hinged 110.00
200 A90 1sh bister 25.00 3.50
Never hinged 55.00
Nos. 187-200 (12) 147.95 73.45

Nos. 187a, 188a, 189b, 190a issued in coils.

Inverted watermarks on the three lowest values are usually from booklet panes.

Nos. 188-189 were issued also on experimental paper with variety of Wmk. 35: closer spacing; letters shorter, rounder.

British Empire Exhibition Issue

Type of 1924, Dated "1925"

1925, May 9 Engr. *Perf. 14*

203 A92 1p vermilion 17.00 *32.50*
Never hinged 25.00
204 A92 1½p brown 45.00 *80.00*
Never hinged 67.50

A93

A94

A95

1929, May 10 Typo. *Perf. 15x14*

205 A93 ½p green 2.50 2.50
Never hinged 3.75
a. Wmk. sideways 45.00 45.00
Never hinged 120.00
b. Booklet pane of 6 150.00
206 A94 1p scarlet 2.50 2.50
Never hinged 3.75
a. Wmk. sideways 82.50 82.50
Never hinged 120.00
b. Booklet pane of 6 150.00
207 A94 1½p dark brown 2.50 2.00
Never hinged 4.00
a. Wmk. sideways 45.00 45.00
Never hinged 90.00
b. Booklet pane of 6 60.00
c. Booklet pane of 4 + 2 labels 400.00
208 A95 2½p deep blue 11.50 11.50
Never hinged 24.00
Nos. 205-208 (4) 19.00 18.50
Set, never hinged 35.00

Inverted watermarks on the three lowest values are usually from booklet panes.

Nos. 205a, 206a and 207a were issued in coils.

St. George Slaying the Dragon
A96

Wmk. 219

1929, May 10 Engr. *Perf. 12*

209 A96 £1 black 800.00 800.00
Never hinged 1,500.

Universal Postal Union, 9th Congress.

A97

Type A97 designs are re-engraved versions of the types of the 1912-13 issue, with the most obvious difference being the solid appearance of the central field. The backgrounds appear to be solid, although the photoengraving screen can be seen under magnification.

Perf. 14½x14

1934-36 Photo. Wmk. 35

210 A97 ½p dark green .45 .45
Never hinged .90
a. Wmk. sideways 8.00 3.25
Never hinged 17.50
b. Booklet pane of 6 85.00
211 A97 1p carmine .45 .45
Never hinged .90
a. Wmk. sideways 15.00 15.00
Never hinged 40.00
b. Booklet pane of 6 85.00
c. Imperf., pair *5,000.*
d. Pair, imperf. btwn. 7,000.
e. Printed on gummed side *575.00*
212 A97 1½p red brown .45 .45
Never hinged .90
a. Imperf., pair 1,100.
b. Wmk. sideways 6.00 2.00
Never hinged 18.00
c. Booklet pane of 6 30.00
d. Booklet pane of 4 + 2 labels 160.00
213 A97 2p red org ('35) .55 .55
Never hinged 1.60
a. Imperf., pair *5,000.*
b. Wmk. sideways 90.00 70.00
Never hinged 275.00
214 A97 2½p ultra ('35) .90 .75
Never hinged 3.00
215 A97 3p dk violet ('35) .90 1.00
Never hinged 3.00
216 A97 4p dk sl grn ('35) 1.75 1.00
Never hinged 4.00
217 A97 5p yel brown ('36) 6.00 1.50
Never hinged 19.00
218 A97 9p dk ol grn ('35) 9.00 2.75
Never hinged 19.00
219 A97 10p Prus blue ('36) 15.00 11.00
Never hinged 32.50
220 A97 1sh bister brn ('36) 15.00 1.25
Never hinged 40.00
Nos. 210-220 (11) 50.45 21.15
Set, never hinged 120.00

The designs in this set are slightly smaller than the 1912-13 issue.

Inverted watermarks on the three lowest values are usually from booklet panes.

Nos. 210a, 211a, 212b and 213b were issued in coils.

Britannia Type of 1913-19 Reengraved

1934 Engr. Wmk. 34 *Perf. 11x12*

222 A91 2sh6p brown 80.00 25.00
Never hinged 150.00
223 A91 5sh carmine 175.00 60.00
Never hinged 375.00
224 A91 10sh dark blue 375.00 65.00
Never hinged 750.00
Nos. 222-224 (3) 630.00 150.00

Printed by Waterlow & Sons. Can be distinguished by the crossed lines in background of portrait. Previous issues have horizontal lines only.

For overprints see Ireland Nos. 93-95.

Silver Jubilee Issue

A98

Perf. 14½x14

1935, May 7 Photo. Wmk. 35

226 A98 ½p dark green 1.00 .60
Never hinged 1.40
a. Booklet pane of 4 40.00
227 A98 1p carmine 1.25 *1.75*
Never hinged 2.00
a. Booklet pane of 4 40.00
228 A98 1½p red brown 1.00 .60
Never hinged 1.40
a. Booklet pane of 4 17.50
229 A98 2½p ultra 4.00 *4.50*
Never hinged 6.50
a. 2½p Prussian blue *9,500.* *11,000.*
Never hinged *11,000.*
Nos. 226-229 (4) 7.25 *7.45*
Set, never hinged 11.00

25th anniv. of the reign of George V. Device at right differs on 1½p and 2½p.

Inverted watermarks on the three lowest values are usually from booklet panes.

Edward VIII — A99

1936 Wmk. 250

230 A99 ½p dark green .25 .25
Never hinged .40
a. Booklet pane of 6 25.00
Never hinged 30.00
231 A99 1p crimson .50 .50
Never hinged .70
a. Booklet pane of 6 17.50
Never hinged 25.00
232 A99 1½p red brown .25 *.35*
Never hinged .40
a. Booklet pane of 6 11.00
Never hinged 15.00
b. Booklet pane of 4 + 2 labels 62.50
Never hinged 85.00
c. Booklet pane of 2 20.00
Never hinged 30.00
233 A99 2½p bright ultra .25 *1.00*
Never hinged .40
Nos. 230-233 (4) 1.25 *2.10*
Set, never hinged 1.75

Inverted watermarks on the three lowest values are usually from booklet panes.

King George VI and Queen Elizabeth
A100

Perf. 14½x14

1937, May 13 Wmk. 251

234 A100 1½p purple brown .25 .25
Never hinged .35

Coronation of George VI and Elizabeth.

See British Offices Abroad for overprints on types A44-A133.
These overprints include "M.E.F.," "B.A.," "B.M.A.," "E.A.F.," "CHINA," "Morocco Agencies," "TANGIER," "LEVANT," "PARAS," and "PIASTRE(S)."

A101

A102

King George VI — A103

Nos. 235-240 show face and neck highlighted, background solid.

1937-39

235 A101 ½p deep green .25 .25
Never hinged .30
a. Wmk. sideways .40 .45
Never hinged .55
b. Booklet pane of 6 32.50
Never hinged 45.00
c. Booklet pane of 4 60.00 32.50
Never hinged 85.00
d. Booklet pane of 2 70.00
Never hinged 100.00
236 A101 1p scarlet .25 .25
Never hinged .30
a. Wmk. sideways 8.50 7.50
Never hinged 22.50
b. Booklet pane of 6 40.00
Never hinged 55.00
c. Booklet pane of 4 100.00 *100.00*
Never hinged 150.00
d. Booklet pane of 2 70.00
Never hinged 100.00
237 A101 1½p red brown .25 .25
Never hinged .40
a. Wmk. sideways .65 *1.25*
Never hinged 1.40
b. Booklet pane of 6 35.00
Never hinged 50.00
c. Booklet pane of 4 + 2 labels 85.00
Never hinged 120.00
d. Booklet pane of 2 20.00
Never hinged 30.00
238 A101 2p org ('38) .60 .50
Never hinged 1.00
a. Wmk. sideways 30.00 32.50
Never hinged 80.00
b. Booklet pane of 6 100.00
Never hinged 150.00
239 A101 2½p bright ultra .25 .25
Never hinged .35
a. Wmk. sideways 45.00 32.50
Never hinged 90.00
b. Booklet pane of 6 85.00
Never hinged 120.00
c. Tête bêche pair *22,000.*
240 A101 3p dk pur ('38) 3.00 .95
Never hinged 5.00

241 A102 4p gray grn ('38) .45 .75
Never hinged .70
a. Imperf., pair *7,000.*
Never hinged *8,500.*
b. Horiz. pair, imperf. on 3 sides *7,500.*
Never hinged *9,000.*
242 A102 5p lt brn ('38) 1.10 .80
Never hinged 3.00
a. Imperf., pair *6,500.*
Never hinged *8,000.*
b. Horiz. pair, imperf. on 3 sides *7,000.*
Never hinged *8,500.*
243 A102 6p rose lil ('39) .80 .60
Never hinged 1.50
244 A103 7p emer ('39) 2.00 .60
Never hinged 6.00
a. Horiz. pair, imperf. on 3 sides *6,500.*
Never hinged *8,500.*
245 A103 8p brt rose ('39) 3.25 .80
Never hinged 7.00
246 A103 9p dp ol grn ('39) 3.25 .80
Never hinged 6.50
247 A103 10p royal bl ('39) 3.25 .80
Never hinged 6.50
a. Imperf., pair 5,700.
Never hinged 7,000.
248 A103 1sh brown ('39) 3.25 1.00
Never hinged 9.00
Nos. 235-248 (14) 21.95 8.60
Set, never hinged 47.00

Nos. 235a, 236a, 237a, 238a and 239a were issued in coils.

Nos. 235c and 236c are watermarked sideways.

The ½p, 1p, 1½p, 2p and 2½p with watermark inverted are from booklet panes.

No. 238 bisects were used in Guernsey from 12/27/40 to 2/24/41. Value, on cover $32.50.

See Nos. 258-263, 266, 280-285.

Oman Surcharges

Various definitive and commemorative stamps between Nos. 243 and 372 were surcharged in annas (a), new paisa (np) and rupees (r) for use in Oman. The surcharges do not indicate where the stamps were used.

King George VI and Royal Arms — A104

King George VI — A105

1939-42 Engr. Wmk. 259 *Perf. 14*

249 A104 2sh6p chestnut 40.00 5.00
Never hinged 110.00
249A A104 2sh6p yel grn ('42) 7.50 1.50
Never hinged 14.00
250 A104 5sh dull red 10.00 1.75
Never hinged 22.50
251 A105 10sh indigo 140.00 22.50
Never hinged 300.00
251A A105 10sh ultra ('42) 16.00 4.00
Never hinged 40.00
Nos. 249-251A (5) 213.50 34.75
Set, never hinged 485.00

See No. 275.

Victoria and George VI A106

Perf. 14½x14

1940, May 6 Photo. Wmk. 251

252 A106 ½p deep green .25 .25
Never hinged .30
253 A106 1p scarlet 1.00 .40
Never hinged 1.10
254 A106 1½p red brown .25 *.75*
Never hinged .55
255 A106 2p orange .50 .75
Never hinged 1.00
256 A106 2½p brt ultra 1.00 .55
Never hinged 2.25
257 A106 3p dark purple 1.75 *3.50*
Never hinged 3.00
Nos. 252-257 (6) 4.75 6.20
Set, never hinged 8.00

Centenary of the postage stamp.

No. 255 bisects were used in Guernsey from 12/27/40 to 2/24/41. Value, on cover, $40.

Type of 1937-39, with Background Lightened

1941-42

258 A101 ½p green .25 .25
Never hinged .30
a. Booklet pane of 6 14.00
Never hinged 20.00
b. Booklet pane of 2 7.00
Never hinged 10.00
c. Imperf., pair *6,500.*
Never hinged *8,500.*
d. Tete beche pair *8,000.*
Never hinged *17,500.*
e. Booklet pane of 4
259 A101 1p vermilion .25 .25
Never hinged .30
a. Wmk. sideways ('42) 3.00 5.75
Never hinged 5.00
b. Booklet pane of 2 35.00
Never hinged 50.00
c. Imperf., pair *6,000.*
Never hinged *8,000.*
d. Booklet pane of 4
e. Horiz. pair, imperf on 3 sides *6,000.*
Never hinged *8,500.*
260 A101 1½p lt red brn ('42) .30 .85
Never hinged .60
a. Booklet pane of 2 7.00
Never hinged 10.00
b. Booklet pane of 4
261 A101 2p light orange .25 .50
Never hinged .50
a. Wmk. sideways ('42) 16.50 *21.00*
Never hinged 32.50
b. Booklet pane of 6 17.50
Never hinged 25.00
c. Imperf., pair *5,500.*
Never hinged *7,500.*
d. Tete beche pair *11,500.*
Never hinged *17,500.*
262 A101 2½p ultra .25 .40
Never hinged .35
a. Wmk. sideways ('42) 9.00 *11.00*
Never hinged 17.50
b. Booklet pane of 6 11.00
Never hinged 15.00
c. Imperf., pair *3,350.*
Never hinged *4,750.*
d. Tete beche pair *11,500.*
Never hinged *17,500.*
263 A101 3p violet .75 1.10
Never hinged 2.00
Nos. 258-263 (6) 2.05 3.35
Set, never hinged 4.00

The ½p, 2p and 2 ½p with inverted watermarks are from booklets.

Nos. 259a, 261a and 262a were issued in coils.

Nos. 258b, 258e, 259b, 259d, 260a-260b are made from sheets.

Catalogue values for unused stamps in this section, from this point to the end of the section, are for Never Hinged items.

Peace Issue

A107

King George VI and Symbols of Peace and Industry A108

Perf. 14½x14

1946, June 11 Photo. Wmk. 251

264 A107 2½p bright ultra .25 .25
265 A108 3p violet .25 .45

Return to peace at the close of WW II.

George VI Type of 1939

1947, Dec. 29

266 A103 11p violet brown 2.50 2.00

A109

King George VI and Queen Elizabeth A110

1948, Apr. 26 *Perf. 14½x14, 14x14½*

267 A109 2½p brt ultra .40 .25
268 A110 £1 dp chalky blue 40.00 40.00

25th anniv. of the marriage of King George VI and Queen Elizabeth.

A111

Vraicking (Gathering Seaweed) A112

1948, May 10 *Perf. 14½x14*

269 A111 1p red .25 .25
270 A112 2½p bright ultra .25 .25

3rd anniversary of the liberation of the Channel Islands from German occupation.

Sold at post offices in the Channel Islands and at major philatelic windows in the United Kingdom, and valid for postage throughout Great Britain.

A113

A114

A115

A116

1948, July 29

271 A113 2½p bright ultra .40 .25
272 A114 3p deep violet .50 .50
273 A115 6p red violet 2.50 .75
274 A116 1sh dark brown 4.00 1.50
Nos. 271-274 (4) 7.40 3.00

1948 Olympic Games held at Wembley during July and August.

George VI Type of 1939
Wmk. 259

1948, Oct. 1 Engr. *Perf. 14*

275 A105 £1 red brown 25.00 20.00

A117

A118

A119

A120

Perf. 14½x14

1949, Oct. 10 Photo. Wmk. 251

276 A117 2½p bright ultra .25 .25
277 A118 3p brt violet .25 *.40*
278 A119 6p red violet .35 *.45*
279 A120 1sh brown .50 *1.00*
Nos. 276-279 (4) 1.35 *2.10*

UPU, 75th anniversary.

Types of 1937

1950-51 Wmk. 251 *Perf. 14½x14*

280 A101 ½p light orange .25 .25
a. Booklet pane of 2 10.00
b. Booklet pane of 4 15.00
c. Booklet pane of 6 10.00
d. Imperf., pair *6,000.*
e. Tete beche pair *18,000.*
281 A101 1p ultramarine .25 .25
a. Wmk. sideways .50 .90
b. Booklet pane of 2 10.00
c. Booklet pane of 4 20.00
d. Booklet pane of 6 35.00
e. Booklet pane of 3 + 3 labels 20.00
f. Imperf., pair *5,000.*
g. Horiz. pair, imperf on 3 sides *6,500.*
282 A101 1½p green .50 .50
a. Wmk. sideways 2.00 *3.00*
b. Booklet pane of 2 10.00
c. Booklet pane of 4 15.00
d. Booklet pane of 6 25.00
283 A101 2p lt red brown .60 .45
a. Wmk. sideways 1.50 *1.25*
b. Booklet pane of 6 25.00
c. Tete beche pair *18,000.*
d. Horiz. pair, imperf on 3 sides *8,000.*
284 A101 2½p vermilion .50 .45
a. Wmk. sideways 1.00 1.00
b. Booklet pane of 6 8.00
c. Tete beche pair
285 A102 4p ultra ('50) 1.50 1.50
a. Double impression *8,250.*
Nos. 280-285 (6) 3.60 3.40

Inverted watermarks on Nos. 280-284 are usually from booklets.

Nos. 281a, 282a, 283a and 284a were issued in coils.

H.M.S. Victory A121

St. George Slaying the Dragon A122

Royal Arms A123

Design: 5sh, White Cliffs, Dover.

Perf. 11x12

1951, May 3 Engr. Wmk. 259
286 A121 2sh6p green 9.00 1.00
287 A121 5sh dull red 25.00 1.75
288 A122 10sh ultra 27.50 5.00
289 A123 £1 lt red brown 32.50 16.00
Nos. 286-289 (4) 94.00 23.75

Britannia, Symbols of Commerce and Prosperity, King George VI — A124

Festival Symbol A125

Perf. 14½x14

1951, May 3 Photo. Wmk. 251
290 A124 2½p scarlet .25 .25
291 A125 4p bright ultra .35 .75

Festival of Britain, 1951.

Complete Booklets can be found following the Letter Sheets section.

POSTAGE DUE STAMPS

The watermarks on Nos. J1-J67 are sideways.

D1

Perf. 14x14½

1914-24 Typo. Wmk. 33
J1 D1 ½p emerald .50 .30
Never hinged 2.00
J2 D1 1p rose .50 .30
Never hinged 2.00
a. 1p pale carmine .85 .55
Never hinged 1.75
b. 1p carmine, thick chalky paper ('24) 2.60 *4.00*
Never hinged 4.90
J3 D1 1½p red brown ('22) 47.50 20.00
Never hinged 160.00
J4 D1 2p brown black .50 .30
Never hinged 2.00
J5 D1 3p violet ('18) 6.50 .85
Never hinged 30.00
a. 3p bluish violet ('18) 7.00 3.00
Never hinged 12.50
J6 D1 4p gray green ('21) 47.50 5.75
Never hinged 150.00
J7 D1 5p org brown 8.00 4.00
Never hinged 22.50
J8 D1 1sh blue ('15) 45.00 5.50
Never hinged 170.00
a. 1sh deep bright blue 45.00 5.75
Never hinged 150.00
Nos. J1-J8 (8) 156.00 37.00

Values for No. J6 are for stamps with sideways inverted watermark. No. J6 also exists on paper with sideways watermark. Values thus: $150 unused, $50 used.

From the front of the stamp the sideways watermark reads up in normal type. From the back, the watermark still reads up, but the letters are reversed. The sideways inverted watermark reads down.

D2

1924-30 Wmk. 35
J9 D1 ½p emerald 1.10 .85
Never hinged 3.00
J10 D1 1p car rose .65 .30
Never hinged 3.00
J11 D1 1½p red brown 52.50 22.50
Never hinged 175.00
J12 D1 2p black brown 1.60 .30
Never hinged 10.50
J13 D1 3p violet 2.25 .30
Never hinged 11.50
a. Experimental wmk. 75.00 55.00
Never hinged 110.00
b. Printed on the gummed side 125.00
Never hinged 160.00
J14 D1 4p deep green 17.50 4.00
Never hinged 67.50
J15 D1 5p org brown ('30) 65.00 45.00
Never hinged 165.00
J16 D1 1sh blue 11.50 1.10
Never hinged 45.00
J17 D2 2sh6p brown, *yellow* 85.00 2.25
Never hinged 250.00
Nos. J9-J17 (9) 237.10 76.60

The experimental watermark of No. J13a resembles Wmk. 35 but is spaced more closely, with letters short and rounded, crown with flat arch and sides high, lines thicker.

1936-37 Wmk. 250
J18 D1 ½p emerald ('37) 7.50 *10.00*
Never hinged 13.50
J19 D1 1p car rose ('37) 1.50 *1.75*
Never hinged 2.50
J20 D1 2p blk brn ('37) 10.00 *12.50*
Never hinged 17.50
J21 D1 3p violet ('37) 1.50 *2.00*
Never hinged 2.25
J22 D1 4p slate green 24.00 *32.50*
Never hinged 50.00
J23 D1 5p bister ('37) 20.00 *26.00*
Never hinged 30.00
a. 5p orange brown 35.00 *30.00*
Never hinged 75.00
J24 D1 1sh blue ('36) 7.50 *8.50*
Never hinged 16.00
J25 D2 2sh6p brn, *yel* ('37) 140.00 12.50
Never hinged 350.00
Nos. J18-J25 (8) 212.00 *105.75*

1938-39 Wmk. 251
J26 D1 ½p emerald 8.50 5.75
Never hinged 13.00
J27 D1 1p carmine rose 1.40 .85
Never hinged 3.50
J28 D1 2p black brown 1.50 .85
Never hinged 3.00
J29 D1 3p violet 7.00 1.10
Never hinged 14.00
J30 D1 4p slate green 40.00 10.00
Never hinged 110.00
J31 D1 5p bister ('39) 6.75 .85
Never hinged 16.00
J32 D1 1sh blue 25.00 2.25
Never hinged 80.00
J33 D2 2sh6p brown, *yel* ('39) 40.00 3.00
Never hinged 95.00
Nos. J26-J33 (8) 130.15 24.65

Catalogue values for unused stamps in this section, from this point to the end of the section, are for Never Hinged items.

1951-52
J34 D1 ½p orange 3.50 3.50
J35 D1 1p violet blue 1.50 .75
J36 D1 1½p green ('52) 2.00 *2.50*
J37 D1 4p bright blue 50.00 24.00
J38 D1 1sh olive bister 32.50 10.00
Nos. J34-J38 (5) 89.50 40.75

OFFICIAL STAMPS

Type of Regular Issue of 1840 "V R" in Upper Corners

O1

1840 Wmk. 18 *Imperf.*
O1 O1 1p black *35,000. 35,000.*
On cover —

No. O1 was never placed in use but examples are known used and on covers that passed through the mails by oversight. The stamp also was used experimentally to test cancellations.

Postage stamps perforated with a crown and initials "H.M.O.W.," "O.W.," "B.T." or "S.O.," or with only the initials "H.M.S.O." or "D.S.I.R.," were used for official purposes.

Counterfeits exist of Nos. O2-O83.

Inland Revenue

Regular Issues Overprinted in Black

a

b

Type "a" is overprinted on the stamps of ½ penny to 1 shilling inclusive, type "b" on the higher values.

1882-85 Wmk. 30 *Perf. 14*
O2 A35 ½p pale green 135.00 52.50
On cover 115.00
a. ½p green 110.00 37.50
O3 A35 ½p slate bl ('85) 87.50 30.00
On cover 140.00
O4 A40 1p lilac 7.75 5.25
On cover 30.00
a. "OFFICIAL" omitted *10,000.*
b. Ovpt. lines transposed
O5 A47 2½p lilac ('85) 520.00 190.00
On cover 1,500.
O6 A28 6p gray 600.00 140.00
On cover —
O7 A48 1sh green ('85) *6,250.* 1,900.
On cover —

Wmk. 31
O8 A51 5sh car rose ('85) 10,000. 2,500.
a. Bluish paper ('85) *17,500.* 6,250.
b. Raised period after "R" *10,500.* 3,150.
O9 A52 10sh ultra *11,500.* 3,600.
a. 10sh cobalt *37,500.* 10,000.
b. Bluish paper *24,000.* 7,250.
c. Raised period after "R" *12,500.* 4,500.

Wmk. Three Imperial Crowns (30)
O10 A53 £1 brown vio *80,000. 31,500.*
a. Frame broken (JC or TA) *90,000.*

1888-89 Wmk. 30
O11 A54 ½p vermilion 12.50 5.25
On cover 100.00
a. "I.R." omitted *5,750.*
O12 A65 1sh green ('89) 950.00 350.00
On cover 3,650.

1890 Wmk. Three Orbs (29)
O13 A53 £1 brown vio *100,000. 42,500.*
a. Frame broken (JC or TA) *125,000.*

1891 Wmk. 30
O14 A57 2½p violet, *blue* 150.00 21.00
On cover 450.00

Wmk. Three Imperial Crowns (30)

1892
O15 A53 £1 green *12,500.* 2,600.
a. No period after "R" — *4,250.*
b. Frame broken (JC or TA) *21,000. 5,500.*

For examples of Nos. O2-O15 with margins clear of the design on all four sides, add a 20 percent premium to the value listed. For stamps with clear circular datestamps, apply a 20 percent premium. Add the two premiums together for covers with stamps having these attributes.

1901 Wmk. 30
O16 A54 ½p blue green 19.00 12.50
On cover 350.00
O17 A62 6p violet, *rose* 400.00 115.00
On cover —
O18 A65 1sh car rose & green 4,400. 1,900.
On cover —

1902-04
O19 A66 ½p gray grn 32.50 3.25
On cover 125.00
O20 A66 1p carmine 21.00 2.50
On cover 82.50
O21 A66 2½p ultra 950.00 260.00
On cover —
O22 A66 6p dull vio ('04) *400,000. 190,000.*
O23 A74 1sh car rose & grn 3,750. 725.00
On cover —

Wmk. 31
O24 A76 5sh car rose *36,500. 10,500.*
a. Raised period after "R" *42,500. 12,500.*
O25 A77 10sh ultra *110,000. 47,500.*
a. Raised period after "R" *125,000. 47,500.*

Wmk. Three Imperial Crowns (30)
O26 A78 £1 green *62,500. 25,000.*

Nos. O4, O8, O9 and O13 also exist with overprint in blue black.

Government Parcels

Overprinted

1883-86 Wmk. 30
O27 A45 1½p lilac ('86) 400.00 92.50
O28 A46 6p green ('86) 3,150. 1,250.
O29 A50 9p green 2,600. 1,050.
O30 A29 1sh sal (P13) 1,675. 290.00
Plate 14 3,500. 525.00
Nos. O27-O30 (4) 7,825. 2,683.

1887-92
O31 A55 1½p vio & grn 145.00 18.50
O32 A56 2p grn & car rose ('91) 235.00 40.00
O33 A60 4½p car rose & grn ('92) 375.00 260.00
O34 A62 6p violet, *rose* 260.00 62.50
O35 A63 9p blue & lil ('88) 400.00 92.50
O36 A65 1sh green 675.00 260.00
Nos. O31-O36 (6) 2,090. 733.50

1897
O37 A40 1p lilac 92.50 22.50
a. Inverted overprint 7,250. 3,400.

1900
O38 A65 1sh car rose & grn 625.00 260.00
a. Inverted overprint *17,500.*

For examples of Nos. O27-38 with margins clear of the design on all four sides, add a 25 percent premium to the value listed. For stamps with clear circular datestamps, apply a 100 percent premium. Add the two premiums together for covers with stamps having these attributes.

1902
O39 A66 1p carmine 32.50 14.00
O40 A68 2p green & car 160.00 40.00
O41 A66 6p dull violet 260.00 40.00
a. Double overprint, one albino *7,500.*
O42 A72 9p ultra & violet 625.00 175.00
O43 A74 1sh car rose & grn 1,350. 300.00
Nos. O39-O43 (5) 2,428. 569.00

Office of Works

Overprinted

1896
O44 A54 ½p vermilion 300.00 135.00
On cover 800.00
O45 A40 1p lilac 500.00 135.00
On cover 950.00

For examples of Nos. O44-O45 with margins clear of the design on all four sides, add a 20 percent premium to the value listed. For stamps with clear circular datestamps, apply a 15 percent premium. Add the two premiums together for covers with stamps having these attributes.

1901-02
O46 A54 ½p blue green 450.00 200.00
On cover —
O47 A61 5p lilac & ultra 3,650. 1,250.
On cover —
O48 A64 10p car rose & lil 6,250. 2,100.
On cover —

1902
O49 A66 ½p gray grn 575.00 160.00
On cover 1,900.

O50 A66 1p carmine 575.00 160.00
On cover 425.00
O51 A68 2p grn & car 2,000. 425.00
On cover 3,250.
O52 A66 2½p ultra 3,400. 625.00
On cover 4,250.
O53 A73 10p car rose & vio *40,000.* 7,000.
On cover —

Army

Overprinted

a

b

1896

O54 A54(a) ½p vermilion 6.25 2.75
On cover 62.50
a. "OFFICIAI" 290.00 125.00
b. Lines of ovpt. transposed 4,500.
O55 A40(a) 1p lilac 6.25 6.00
On cover 100.00
a. "OFFICIAI" 225.00 140.00
O56 A57(b) 2½p violet, *blue* 45.00 30.00
On cover 725.00
Nos. O54-O56 (3) 57.50 38.75

1900

O57 A54(a) ½p blue green 6.25 *12.50*
On cover *125.00*

For examples of Nos. O54-O57 with margins clear of the design on all four sides, add a 20 percent premium to the value listed. For stamps with clear circular datestamps, apply a 15 percent premium. Add the two premiums together for covers with stamps having these attributes.

1901

O58 A62(b) 6p violet, *rose* 100.00 52.50
On cover 1,650.

1902

O59 A66(a) ½p gray green 6.00 2.40
On cover 110.00
O60 A66(a) 1p carmine 6.00 2.40
On cover 110.00
a. "ARMY" omitted —
O61 A66(a) 6p dull violet 175.00 80.00
On cover —
Nos. O59-O61 (3) 187.00 84.80

Overprinted

1903

O62 A66 6p dull violet 3,250. 1,550.

Royal Household

Overprinted

1902

O63 A66 ½p gray green 400.00 220.00
On cover 1,200.
O64 A66 1p carmine 350.00 190.00
On cover 1,100.

Board of Education

Overprinted

1902

O65 A61 5p lilac & ultra 4,650. 1,150.
O66 A65 1sh car rose & grn 10,500. 5,750.

1902-04

O67 A66 ½p gray green 160.00 40.00
On cover 400.00
O68 A66 1p carmine 160.00 40.00
On cover 425.00
O69 A66 2½p ultramarine 5,000. 410.00
On cover —
O70 A71 5p lilac & ultra ('04) 31,500. 10,000.
On cover —
O71 A74 1sh car rose & grn *180,000.* —

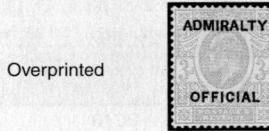

Admiralty

Overprinted

1903

O72 A66 ½p gray green 28.00 13.50
On cover —
O73 A66 1p carmine 17.00 6.75
On cover 325.00
O74 A67 1½p vio & green 310.00 145.00
On cover —
O75 A68 2p green & car 340.00 160.00
On cover —
O76 A66 2½p ultra 475.00 145.00
On cover —
O77 A69 3p violet, *yel* 425.00 160.00
On cover —
Nos. O72-O77 (6) 1,595. 630.25

Overprinted

1903

O78 A66 ½p gray green 57.50 22.50
On cover 525.00
O79 A66 1p carmine 57.50 22.50
On cover 145.00
O80 A67 1½p vio & grn 1,150. 625.00
On cover —
O81 A68 2p grn & car 2,750. 840.00
On cover —
O82 A66 2½p ultramarine 2,850. 890.00
On cover —
O83 A69 3p violet, *yel* 2,500. 375.00
On cover —

The two types of the "Admiralty Official" overprint differ principally in the shape of the letter "M."

ENVELOPES

Britannia Sending Letters to World (William Mulready, Designer) — E1

1840

U1 E1 1p black 360.00 *525.00*
U2 E1 2p blue 450.00 *2,000.*

LETTER SHEETS

U3 E1 1p black 335.00 *500.00*
U4 E1 2p blue 440.00 *2,000.*

BOOKLETS

Booklets are listed in denomination sequence by reign. Numbers in parenthesis following each listing reflect the number of cover varieties or edition numbers that apply to each cover style.

Values shown for complete booklets are for examples containing most panes having full perforations on two edges of the pane only. Booklets containing most or all panes with very fine, full perforations on all sides are scarce and will sell for more. Also, in booklets where most of the value is contained in only one pane of several, it is assumed that this pane has full perforations on two sides only. If this pane is very fine, the booklet will be worth a considerable premium over the value given.

Sterling Currency

BC1

1904

BK1 BC1 2sh½p *red,* 4 #128e 450.00

1906-11

BK2 BC1 2sh *red,* 2 #128e, 3 #143c, #143b 1,350.
BK3 BC1 2sh *red,* 3 #128e, 1 each #143b-143c (4) 1,150.

Cover inscription on Nos. BK2-BK3 revised to reflect changed contents.

1911

BK4 BC1 2sh *red,* 2#151a, 3 #152a 900.00

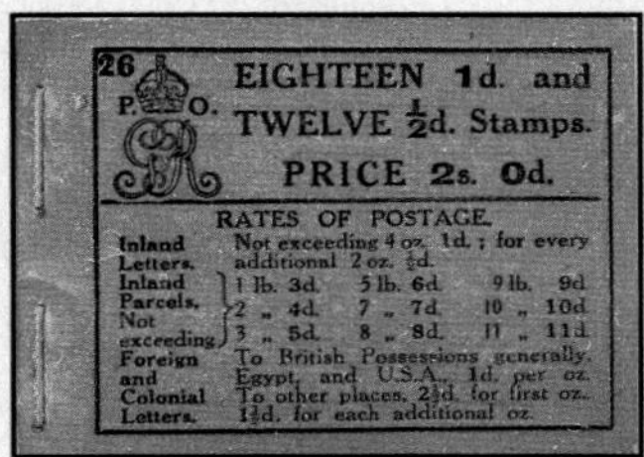

BC2

1912-13

BK5 BC2 2sh *red,* 2 #151a, 3 #152a 1,050.
BK6 BC2 2sh *red,* 2 #155a, 3 #156a (4) 1,250.

Cover inscription on Nos. BK5-BK6 shows only Inland Postage Rates.

1913

BK7 BC2 2sh *red,* 2 #159b, 3 #160a (35) 500.00
BK8 BC2 2sh *org,* 2 #159b,3 #160a (20) 525.00

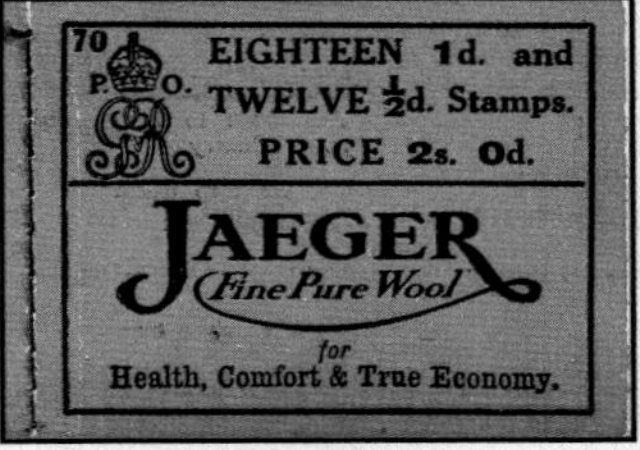

BC3

1917

BK9 BC3 2sh *org,* 2 #159b, 3 #160a (17) 500.00

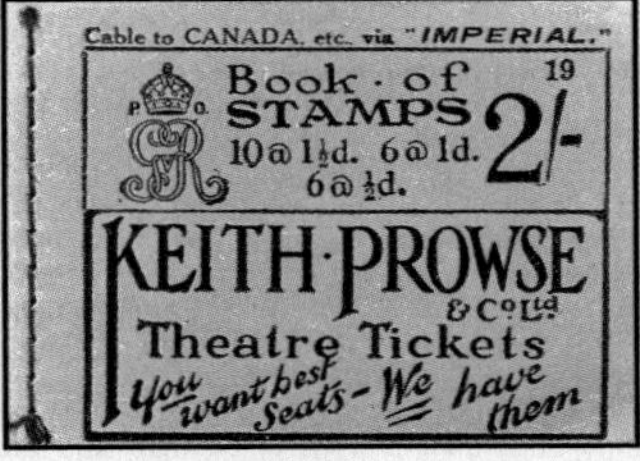

BC4

1924-34

BK10 BC4 2sh *blue,* #159b, 160a, 161g-161h (2) 1,250.
BK11 BC4 2sh *blue,* #187b, 188b, 189c-189d (277) 750.00

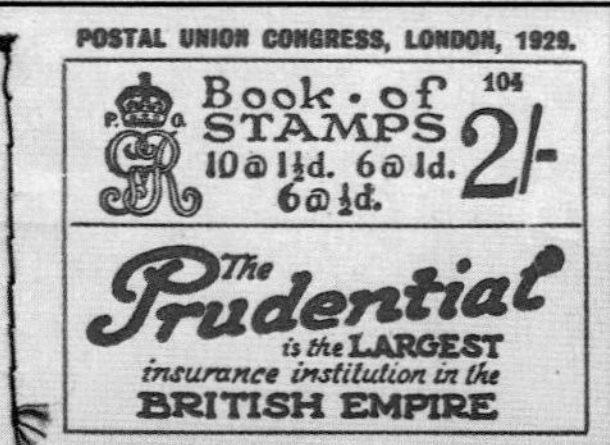

BC5

1929

BK12 BC5 2sh blue, *buff,* #205b-207b, 207c 775.00

1935

BK13 BC4 2sh *blue,* #210b-211b, 212c-212d (58) 550.00

BC6

1935

BK14 BC6 2sh blue, *buff,* #226a-227a, 3 #228a 140.00

1918-19

BK15 BC4 3sh *org,* 2 each #159b, 160a, 161g (11) 650.00
BK16 BC4 3sh *org,* #159b, 160a, 3 #161g (15) 650.00

Cover used for Nos. BK15-BK16 does not have inscription above top line.

1921

BK17 BC4 3sh *blue,* 3 #162b (3) 850.00
BK18 BC4 3sh *blue,* 3 #162c (3) 1,100.

1922

BK19 BC4 3sh *scar,* #159b, 160a, 3 #161g (33) 850.00
BK20 BC4 3sh *blue,* 4 #161g (2) 900.00

1924-34

BK21 BC4 3sh *scar,* #187b-188b, 3 #189c (237) 525.00

1929

BK22 BC5 3sh blue, *buff,* #205b-206b, 3 #207b (5) 500.00

1935

BK23 BC4 3sh *scar,* #210b-211b, 3 #212c (27) 375.00
BK24 BC6 3sh red, *buff,* #226a-227a, 5 #228a (4) 140.00

1920

BK25 BC4 3sh6p *org,* #160a, 3 #162b (6) 850.00

Cover used for No. BK25 does not have inscription above top line.

1921

BK26 BC4 3sh6p *org red,* #159b, 160a, 161g, 2 #162b (7) 900.00
BK27 BC4 3sh6p *org red,* #159b, 160a, 161g, 2 #162c (13) 1,050.

1931-35

BK28 BC4 5sh *grn,* #187b-188b, 189d, 5 #189c 4,000.

BK29 BC4 5sh *buff,* #187b-188b, 189d, 5 #189c (7) 1,250.

BK30 BC4 5sh *buff,* #210b-211b, 212d, 5 #212c (7) 500.00

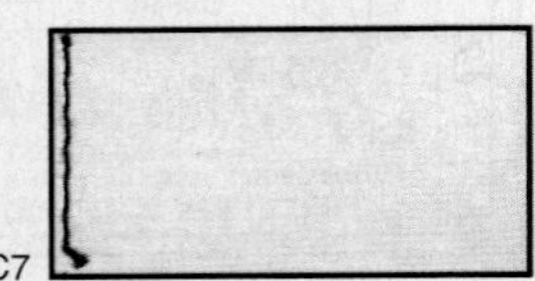

BC7

1936

BK31 BC7 6p *buff,* 2 #232c 70.00

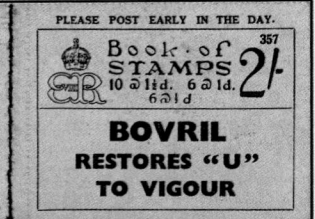

BC8

BK32 BC8 2sh *blue,* #230a-231a, #232a-232b (31) 140.00

BK33 BC8 3sh *scar,* #230a-231a, 3 #232a (12) 110.00

BK34 BC8 5sh *buff,* #230a-231a, 6 #232a (2) 250.00

1938-40

BK35 BC7 6p *buff,* 2 #237d 70.00

BK36 BC7 6p *pink,* #235d-237d 325.00

BK37 BC7 6p *pale grn,* #235c-236c 150.00

No. BK37 is 53x41mm.

1947-51

BK38 BC7 1sh *buff,* 2 each #258b-259b, 260a 27.50

BK39 BC7 1sh *buff,* 2 each #280a, 281b-282b 27.50

BK40 BC7 1sh *buff,* #258e, 259d, 260b 6,000.

BK41 BC7 1sh *buff,* #280b-282b 37.50

Nos. BK40-BK41 are 53x41mm.

Round GPO Emblem — BC9

1952-53

BK42 BC9 1sh *buff,* #280b, 281c-282c 22.50

a. Inland postage rate corrected in ink on inside booklet cover 25.00

Oval GPO Emblem — BC10

1954

BK43 BC10 1sh *buff,* #280b, 281c-282c 32.50

1937

BK44 BC8 2sh *blue,* #235b-236b, #237b-237c (26) 450.00

BC11

1938

BK45 BC11 2sh *blue,* #235b-236b, #237b-237c (95) 450.00

1940-42 **2sh6p Booklets**

BK46 BC11 *scar,* #235b, #238b-239b (7) 1,050.

BK47 BC11 *blue,* #235b, #238b-239b (6) 1,050.

Denomination part of cover of Nos. BK46-BK47 is printed in white on black background.

BK48 BC11 *grn,* #235b, #238b-239b (80) 550.00

BK49 BC11 *grn,* #258a, #261b-262b (120) 550.00

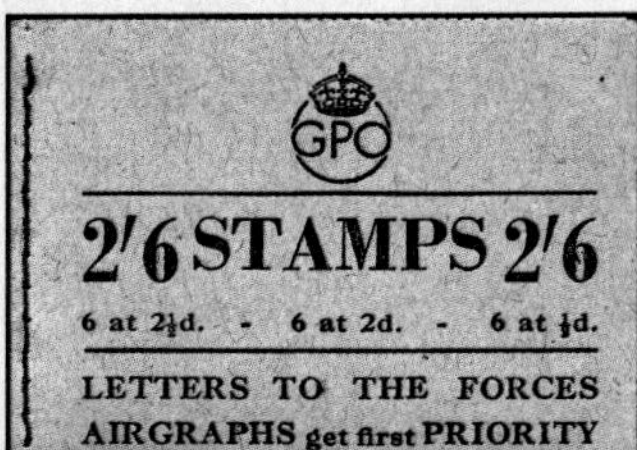

BC12

1943

BK50 BC12 *grn,* #258a, #261b-262b (90) 65.00

With booklets issued in August and September 1943, commercial advertising on British booklets was discontinued. Covers and interleaving were used for Post Office slogans. Booklets were no longer numbered, but carried the month and year of issue.

1951-52

BK51 BC12 *grn,* #280c, #283b-284b (10) 45.00

BK52 BC12 *grn,* #280c, 281e, #282d, 284b (15) 50.00

1937-38 **3sh Booklets**

BK53 BC8 *scar,* #235b-236b, 3 #237b (10) 850.00

BK54 BC11 *scar,* #235b-236b, 3 #237b (34) 850.00

1937-43 **5sh Booklets**

BK55 BC8 *buff,* #235b-236b, 237c, 5 #237b (3) 1,000.

BK56 BC11 *buff,* #235b-236b, 237c, 5 #237b (9) 950.00

BK57 BC11 *buff,* #235b, 238b, 3 #239b (16) 975.00

BK58 BC11 *buff,* #258a, 261b, 3 #262b (20) 950.00

1943-53

BK59 BC12 *tan,* #258a, 261b, 3 #262b (49) 110.00

BK60 BC12 *tan,* #258a, 261b, 3 #262b (20) 1,250.

Cover on No. BK60 has thick horizontal lines separating the GPO emblem and the various inscriptions.

BK61 BC12 *tan,* #280a, 283b, 3 #284b (5) 85.00

BK62 BC12 *tan,* #280c, 281e, 282d, 3 #284b (5) 62.50

BK63 BC12 *tan,* #280c, 281d-282d, 283b, 2 #284b (2) 62.50

BC13

1953-54 **2sh6p Booklets**

BK64 BC12 *grn,* #280c, 281e, 294c, #296a (6) 40.00

BK65 BC13 *grn,* #280c, 281e, 294c, 296a (7) 40.00

BK66 BC13 *grn,* #281e, 292c, 294c, 296a 500.00

5sh Booklets

BK67 BC12 *brn,* #280c, 281d, 283b, 294c, 2 #296a (3) 50.00

BK68 BC13 *brn,* #280c, 281d, 283b, 294c, 2 #296a (2) 70.00

BK69 BC13 *brn,* #281d, 283b, 292c, 294c, 2 #296a 300.00

BK70 BC13 *brn,* #283b, 292c-294c, 2 #296a 160.00

GUERNSEY OCCUPATION STAMPS

Issued Under German Occupation

Bisects of Great Britain Nos. 238 and 255 were used in Guernsey from 12/27/40 to 2./24/41. Values, on cover or postcard: No. 238, $45; No. 255, $40.

OS1

Rouletted 14x7

1941-44 **Typo.** **Unwmk.**

N1	OS1 ½p light green	3.50	3.50
	Never hinged	6.00	
a.	½p dull green	2.50	2.00
	Never hinged	4.00	
b.	½p pale yellow green	2.50	3.00
	Never hinged	4.00	
c.	½p emerald green	3.50	2.00
	Never hinged	6.00	
d.	½p bluish green	20.00	13.00
	Never hinged	32.00	
e.	½p bright green	13.00	10.00
	Never hinged	22.00	
f.	½p olive green	27.50	25.00
	Never hinged	45.00	
g.	Imperf, pair	140.00	
	Never hinged	225.00	
h.	Horiz. pair, imperf between	450.00	
	Never hinged	750.00	
i.	Vert. pair, imperf between	525.00	
	Never hinged	875.00	
N2	OS1 1p red	3.00	2.00
	Never hinged	3.50	
a.	Printed double	65.00	
	Never hinged	110.00	
b.	1p pale vermilion	3.00	*2.00*
	Never hinged	5.00	
c.	1p carmine red	2.10	*2.00*
	Never hinged	3.50	
d.	Imperf, pair	125.00	90.00
	Never hinged	175.00	
e.	Horiz. pair, imperf between	550.00	
	Never hinged	800.00	
f.	Vert. pair, imperf between	750.00	
	Never hinged	950.00	
N3	OS1 2½p ultramarine	8.00	12.00
	Never hinged	13.00	
a.	2½p pale ultramarine	6.00	*7.00*
	Never hinged	10.00	
	Nos. N1-N3 (3)	14.50	17.50

Issued: No. N1b, 4/7/41; No. N1c, 6/41; No. N1d, 11/41; No. N1e, 2/42; No. N1a, 9/42; No. N1f, 2/43; No. N1, from 7/43; No. N2, 2/18/41; No. N2a, 7/43; No. N2b, 1943; No. N3, 4/12/44; No. N3a, 7/44.

Additional shades and papers exist. The rouletting is very crude and may not be measurable. This is not a defect.

Bluish French Bank Note Paper

Wmk. 396 Chain Link Fence

1942 *Rouletted 14x7*

N4	OS1 ½p green	22.50	22.50
	Never hinged	30.00	
N5	OS1 1p red	14.50	*21.00*
	Never hinged	16.00	

Issue dates: ½p, Mar. 11; 1p, Apr. 9.
Nos. N1-N5 remained valid until 4/13/46.

JERSEY OCCUPATION STAMPS

Issued Under German Occupation

OS1

1941-42 **Typo.** **Unwmk.** *Perf. 11*

N1	OS1 ½p bright green	7.00	6.00
	Never hinged	8.00	
a.	Imperf, pair	500.00	
	Never hinged	850.00	
b.	Vert. pair, imperf between	450.00	
	Never hinged	750.00	
c.	Horiz. pair, imperf between	600.00	
	Never hinged	800.00	
d.	On grayish paper	7.25	12.00
	Never hinged	12.00	
N2	OS1 1p vermilion	7.00	5.00
	Never hinged	8.00	
a.	Imperf, pair	240.00	
	Never hinged	325.00	
b.	Vert. pair, imperf between	765.00	
	Never hinged	850.00	
c.	Horiz. pair, imperf between	675.00	
	Never hinged	750.00	
d.	On chalk-surfaced paper	32.50	50.00
	Never hinged	55.00	
e.	On grayish paper	8.50	*14.00*
	Never hinged	14.00	

Issue dates: No. N1, 1/29/42; No. N1d, 1/43; No. N2, 4/1/41; No. N2e, 1/43.

Jersey Views — OS2

Designs: ½p, Old Jersey farm; 1p, Portelet Bay; 1½p, Corbiere Lighthouse; 2p, Elizabeth Castle; 2½, Mont Orgueil Castle; 3p, Gathering seaweed.

1943-44 *Perf. 13½*

N3	OS2 ½p dark green	7.25	12.00
	Never hinged	12.00	
a.	On rough, gray paper	9.00	14.00
	Never hinged	15.00	
N4	OS2 1p scarlet	1.75	.80
	Never hinged	3.00	
a.	On newsprint	2.10	1.50
	Never hinged	3.50	
N5	OS2 1½p brown	7.25	5.75
	Never hinged	8.00	
N6	OS2 2p orange	6.75	2.00
	Never hinged	7.50	
N7	OS2 2½p blue	2.00	1.40
	Never hinged	3.00	
a.	On newsprint	.90	1.75
	Never hinged	1.25	
b.	On pelure paper	160.00	
	Never hinged	275.00	
N8	OS2 3p red violet	2.00	2.75
	Never hinged	3.00	
	Nos. N3-N8 (6)	27.00	24.70

Issued: ½p, 1p, 6/1/43; 1½p, 2p, 6/8/43; 2½p, 3p, 6/29/43; No. N4a, 2/28/44; No. N7a, 2/25/44.

Nos. N1-N8 remained valid until 4/13/46.

GREAT BRITAIN OFFICES ABROAD

OFFICES IN AFRICA

Catalogue values for unused stamps in this section are for Never Hinged items, except for Nos. 1a-5c, which are for hinged stamps with original gum, except as noted.

MIDDLE EAST FORCES

For use in Ethiopia, Cyrenaica, Eritrea, the Dodecanese and Somalia

Stamps of Great Britain, 1937-42 Overprinted in Black or Blue Black

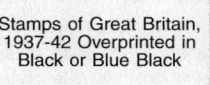

London Printing — ovpt. 14mm long, square dots

1942-43 Wmk. 251 *Perf. 14½x14*

1 A101 1p scarlet 3.50 *4.75*
2 A101 2p orange 3.00 *6.00*
3 A101 2½p bright ultra 3.00 *2.00*
4 A101 3p dark purple 2.75 .35
a. Double overprint *6,400.*
5 A102 5p lt brn (Blk) 2.75 1.00
a. Blue black overprint ('43) 4.25 .25
6 A102 6p rose lilac ('43) .65 .25
7 A103 9p dp olive grn ('43) 1.00 .25
8 A103 1sh brown ('43) .55 .25

Wmk. 259

Perf. 14

9 A104 2sh6p yel green ('43) 8.00 1.10
Nos. 1-9 (9) 25.20 15.95

Cairo Printing — ovpt. 13.5mm long, square dots

1a A101 1p scarlet 40.00 25.00
Never hinged 62.50
2a A101 2p orange 65.00 *155.00*
Never hinged 87.50
3a A101 2½p bright ultra 47.50 11.00
Never hinged 70.00
4b A101 3p dark purple 105.00 60.00
Never hinged 140.00
5b A101 5p light brown 350.00 125.00
Never hinged 500.00

Cairo Printing — ovpt. 13.5mm long, round dots

1b A101 1p scarlet 32.50 17.50
Never hinged 50.00
2b A101 2p orange 50.00 *135.00*
Never hinged 80.00
3b A101 2½p bright ultra 42.50 9.00
Never hinged 65.00
4c A101 3p dark purple 85.00 45.00
Never hinged 130.00
5c A101 5p light brown 255.00 110.00
Never hinged 440.00

Vertical pairs, square and round dots

1c A101 1p #1a + #1b 150.00 160.00
Never hinged 225.00
2c A101 2p #2a + #2b 300.00 *700.00*
Never hinged 450.00
3c A101 2½p #3a + 3b 200.00 80.00
Never hinged 325.00
4d A101 3p #4b + #4c 400.00 350.00
Never hinged 650.00
5d A101 5p #5b + #5c 1,200. *975.00*
Never hinged 1,825.

The Cairo printing was made on panes of 60 (6x10), with rows 2, 3 and 7 overprinted with square dots, and the other seven rows printed with rounds dots.

Same Overprint in Blue Black on Nos. 259, 261, 262 and 263

1943, Jan. 1 Wmk. 251

10 A101 1p vermilion 1.75 .25
11 A101 2p light orange 1.75 1.40
12 A101 2½p ultramarine .55 .25
13 A101 3p violet 1.75 .25
Nos. 10-13 (4) 5.80 2.15

There were two printings of Nos. 1-5, both issued Mar. 2, 1942, and both black. Nos. 5a and 6-13 compose a third printing, also made in London. On these stamps, issued Jan. 1, 1943, the overprint is 13½mm wide. The 2sh6p overprint is black, the others blue black.

Same Ovpt. in Black on #250, 251A

1947 Wmk. 259 *Perf. 14*

14 A104 5sh dull red 15.00 *20.00*
15 A105 10sh ultramarine 17.50 11.50

In 1950 Nos. 1-15 were declared valid for use in Great Britain. Used values are for stamps postmarked in territory of issue. Others sell for about 25 percent less.

POSTAGE DUE STAMPS

Catalogue values for unused stamps in this section are for Never Hinged items.

Postage Due Stamps of Great Britain Overprinted in Blue

1942 Wmk. 251 *Perf. 14x14½*

J1 D1 ½p emerald .40 *14.00*
J2 D1 1p carmine rose .40 *2.00*
J3 D1 2p black brown 3.00 1.40
J4 D1 3p violet .55 *4.75*
J5 D1 1sh blue 4.25 *14.00*
Nos. J1-J5 (5) 8.60 *36.15*

No. J1-J5 were used in Eritrea.

FOR USE IN ERITREA

Catalogue values for unused stamps in this section are for Never Hinged items.

100 Cents = 1 Shilling

Stamps of Great Britain 1937-42 Surcharged — a

Perf. 14½x14

1948, June -49 Wmk. 251

1 A101 5c on ½p green (II) 2.75 .75
On commercial cover 75.00
2 A101 10c on 1p vermilion (II) 2.00 *2.75*
On commercial cover 75.00
3 A101 20c on 2p light org (II) 3.00 *2.50*
On commercial cover 75.00
4 A101 25c on 2½p ultra (II) 2.00 .70
On commercial cover 75.00
5 A101 30c on 3p violet (II) 2.50 *5.00*
On commercial cover 75.00
6 A101 40c on 5p light brn 2.75 *4.75*
On commercial cover 75.00
7 A101 50c on 6p rose lilac 2.25 *1.10*
On commercial cover 150.00
8 A103 75c on 9p dp ol grn 3.75 *.85*
On commercial cover 75.00
9 A103 1sh on 1sh brown 2.50 .55
On commercial cover 375.00

Great Britain Nos. 249A, 250 and 251A Surcharged

Wmk. 259

Perf. 14

10 A104 2sh50c on 2sh6p yel grn 13.00 *11.50*
On commercial cover *950.00*
11 A104 5sh on 5sh dl red 14.00 *25.00*
On commercial cover *7,500.*
12 A105 10sh on 10sh ultra 30.00 25.00
On commercial cover *11,500.*

Great Britain No. 245 Surcharged Type "a"

Wmk. 251

Perf. 14½x14

13 A103 65c on 8p brt rose ('49) 8.00 2.25
Nos. 1-13 (13) 88.50 *82.70*

"B. M. A." stands for British Military Administration.

Stamps of Great Britain 1937-42 Surcharged — c

1950, Feb. 6

14 A101 5c on ½p green (II) 1.50 *9.25*
On commercial cover 150.00
15 A101 10c on 1p ver (II) .45 *3.50*
On commercial cover 75.00
16 A101 20c on 2p lt org (II) 1.50 *.90*
On commercial cover 1,250.
17 A101 25c on 2½p ultra (II) 1.00 .70
On commercial cover 325.00
18 A101 30c on 3p violet (II) .45 *2.50*
On commercial cover 75.00
19 A102 40c on 5p light brown 3.00 *2.00*
On commercial cover 225.00
20 A102 50c on 6p rose lilac .45 .25
On commercial cover 75.00
21 A103 65c on 8p bright rose 6.50 1.75
On commercial cover 75.00
22 A103 75c on 9p dp ol grn 2.00 .30
On commercial cover 125.00
23 A103 1sh on 1sh brown .45 .25
On commercial cover 75.00

Great Britain Nos. 249A, 250, 251A Surcharged

Wmk. 259 *Perf. 14*

24 A104 2sh50c on 2sh6p yel grn 9.75 5.50
On commercial cover 1,100.
On parcel post receipt 1,100.
On telegram form 600.00
25 A104 5sh on 5sh dl red 9.75 *14.00*
On commercial cover 4,500.
On parcel post receipt 2,250.
On telegram form 750.00
26 A105 10sh on 10sh ultra 80.00 70.00
On commercial cover *7,500.*
On parcel post receipt *15,000.*
On telegram form 850.00
Nos. 14-26 (13) 116.80 110.90

Great Britain Nos. 280, 281, 283 and 284 Surcharged Type "c"

Perf. 14½x14

1951, May 3 Wmk. 251

27 A101 5c on ½p lt orange 3.25 *4.25*
28 A101 10c on 1p ultra 2.75 *.85*
29 A101 20c on 2p lt red brown 3.25 .35
30 A101 25c on 2½p vermilion 3.25 .35

Great Britain Nos. 286-288 Surcharged

Perf. 11x12

1951, May 31 Wmk. 259

31 A121 2sh50c on 2sh6p grn 21.00 *30.00*
32 A121 5sh on 5sh dl red 24.00 *35.00*
33 A122 10sh on 10sh ultra 30.00 *35.00*
Nos. 27-33 (7) 87.50 *105.80*

Surcharge arranged to fit the design on No. 33.

POSTAGE DUE STAMPS

Catalogue values for unused stamps in this section are for Never Hinged items.

Great Britain Nos. J26-J29, J32 Surcharged

1948 Wmk. 251 *Perf. 14x14½*

J1 D1 5c on ½p emer 11.00 *25.00*
J2 D1 10c on 1p car rose 11.00 *27.50*
J3 D1 20c on 2p blk brn 16.50 *18.00*
J4 D1 30c on 3p violet 13.00 *16.50*
J5 D1 1sh on 1sh blue 20.00 *35.00*
Nos. J1-J5 (5) 71.50 *122.00*

Great Britain Nos. J26 to J29 and J32 Surcharged

1950, Feb. 6

J6 D1 5c on ½p emer 15.50 *65.00*
J7 D1 10c on 1p car rose 15.50 *21.00*
a. "C" of CENTS omitted *5,000.*
Lightly hinged *3,000.*
J8 D1 20c on 2p blk brn 16.00 *17.50*
J9 D1 30c on 3p violet 19.50 *26.00*
J10 D1 1sh on 1sh blue 21.00 *26.00*
a. Period after "A" omitted *650.00*
Lightly hinged *425.00*
Nos. J6-J10 (5) 87.50 *155.50*

EAST AFRICAN FORCES

FOR USE IN SOMALIA (ITALIAN SOMALILAND)

Catalogue values for unused stamps in this section are for Never Hinged items.

12 Pence = 1 Shilling
100 Cents = 1 Shilling

Stamps of Great Britain 1938-42 Overprinted in Blue

Perf. 14½x14

1943, Jan. 15 Wmk. 251

1 A101 1p vermilion .80 .65
2 A101 2p light orange 1.75 1.35
3 A101 2½p ultramarine .80 *3.75*
4 A101 3p violet 1.10 .25
5 A101 5p light brown 1.90 .45
6 A101 6p rose lilac 1.10 *1.40*
7 A103 9p dp olive green 1.60 *2.40*
8 A103 1sh brown 2.75 .25

On Great Britain No. 249A

1946 Wmk. 259 *Perf. 14*

9 A104 2sh6p yellow green 16.00 8.00
Nos. 1-9 (9) 27.80 *18.50*

Stamps of Great Britain, 1937-42 Surcharged

Perf. 14½x14

1948, May 27 Wmk. 251

10 A101 5c on ½p grn (II) 1.40 *2.15*
11 A101 15c on 1½p lt red brn (II) 2.00 *17.50*
12 A101 20c on 2p lt org (II) 3.50 *6.50*
13 A101 25c on 2½p ultra (II) 2.50 *5.00*
14 A101 30c on 3p vio (II) 2.50 *10.50*
15 A102 40c on 5p lt brown 1.40 .25
16 A102 50c on 6p rose lilac .55 *2.25*
17 A103 75c on 9p dp ol grn 2.25 *27.50*
18 A103 1sh on 1sh brown 1.40 .25

Great Britain Nos. 249A and 250 Surcharged

Wmk. 259 ***Perf. 14***

19 A104 2sh50c on 2sh6p yel grn 9.75 *29.00*
20 A104 5sh on 5sh dl red 21.00 *65.00*
Nos. 10-20 (11) 48.25 *165.90*

Stamps of Great Britain 1937-42 Surcharged

Perf. 14½x14

1950, Jan. 2 **Wmk. 251**

21 A101 5c on ½p grn (II) .25 *3.50*
22 A101 15c on 1½p lt red brn (II) .85 *19.00*
23 A101 20c on 2p lt org (II) .85 *8.50*
24 A101 25c on 2½p ultra (II) .55 *13.50*
25 A101 30c on 3p violet (II) 1.40 *9.75*
26 A102 40c on 5p light brn .65 *2.50*
27 A102 50c on 6p rose lilac .55 *1.10*
28 A103 75c on 9p deep ol grn 2.25 *13.00*
29 A103 1sh on 1sh brown .70 *1.75*

Great Britain Nos. 249A and 250 Surcharged

Wmk. 259 ***Perf. 14***

30 A104 2sh50c on 2sh 6p yel grn 8.50 *37.50*
31 A104 5sh on 5sh dull red 22.00 *55.00*
Nos. 21-31 (11) 38.55 *165.10*

FOR USE IN TRIPOLITANIA

Catalogue values for unused stamps in this section are for Never Hinged items.

Stamps of Great Britain, 1937-42, Surcharged

M.A.L. = Military Authority Lire

Perf. 14½x14

1948, July 1 **Wmk. 251**

1 A101 1 l on ½p green (II) 1.00 *4.50*
2 A101 2 l on 1p ver (II) .50 .25
3 A101 3 l on 1½p lt red brn (II) .50 *.50*
4 A101 4 l on 2p lt org (II) .50 *.75*
5 A101 5 l on 2½p ultra (II) .50 .25
6 A101 6 l on 3p violet (II) .50 *.45*
7 A102 10 l on 5p lt brown .50 .25
8 A102 12 l on 6p rose lilac .50 .25
9 A103 18 l on 9p dp ol grn 1.50 *1.75*
10 A103 24 l on 1sh brown 2.50 *3.00*

Great Britain Nos. 249A, 250 and 251A Surcharged

Wmk. 259 ***Perf. 14***

11 A104 60 l on 2sh6p yel grn 9.25 *16.50*
12 A104 120 l on 5sh dl red 28.00 *30.00*
13 A105 240 l on 10sh ultra 32.50 *150.00*
Nos. 1-13 (13) 78.25 *208.45*

Stamps of Great Britain 1937-42 Surcharged

Perf. 14½x14

1950, Feb. 6 **Wmk. 251**

14 A101 1 l on ½p green (II) 6.00 *13.00*
15 A101 2 l on 1p ver (II) 5.00 *.45*
16 A101 3 l on 1½p lt red brn (II) 4.00 *13.00*
17 A101 4 l on 2p lt org (II) 4.25 *4.40*
18 A101 5 l on 2½p ultra (II) 2.25 *.75*
19 A101 6 l on 3p violet (II) 3.75 *3.25*
20 A102 10 l on 5p lt brown 3.75 *4.00*
21 A102 12 l on 6p rose lilac 5.00 .50
22 A103 18 l on 9p dp ol grn 7.75 *2.75*
23 A103 24 l on 1sh brown 7.25 *3.75*

Great Britain Nos. 249A, 250 and 251A Surcharged

Wmk. 259 ***Perf. 14***

24 A104 60 l on 2sh6p yel grn 18.50 *40.00*
25 A104 120 l on 5sh dl red 40.00 *87.50*
26 A105 240 l on 10sh ultra 55.00 *165.00*
Nos. 14-26 (13) 162.50 *338.35*

Great Britain Nos. 280-284 Surcharged like Nos. 14-23

Perf. 14½x14

1951, May 3 **Wmk. 251**

27 A101 1 l on ½p lt org .55 *10.00*
28 A101 2 l on 1p ultra .55 *1.10*
29 A101 3 l on 1½p green .55 *9.25*
30 A101 4 l on 2p lt red brown .55 *1.40*
31 A101 5 l on 2½p ver .65 *8.50*

Great Britain Nos. 286-288 Surcharged

1951, May 3 **Wmk. 259** ***Perf. 11x12***

32 A121 60 l on 2sh6p grn 20.00 *40.00*
33 A121 120 l on 5sh dl red 20.00 *40.00*
34 A122 240 l on 10sh ultra 50.00 *82.50*
Nos. 27-34 (8) 92.85 *192.75*

Surcharge arranged to fit the design on No. 34.

POSTAGE DUE STAMPS

Catalogue values for unused stamps in this section are for Never Hinged items.

Great Britain Nos. J26-J29, J32 Surcharged

1948 **Wmk. 251** ***Perf. 14x14½***

J1 D1 1 l on ½p emer 7.50 *65.00*
J2 D1 2 l on 1p car rose 2.50 *57.50*
J3 D1 4 l on 2p blk brn 13.50 *52.50*
J4 D1 6 l on 3p violet 8.00 *30.00*
J5 D1 24 l on 1sh blue 30.00 *115.00*
Nos. J1-J5 (5) 61.50 *320.00*

Great Britain Nos. J26-J29, J32 Surcharged

1950, Feb. 6

J6 D1 1 l on ½p emer 15.00 *115.00*
J7 D1 2 l on 1p car rose 10.00 *35.00*
J8 D1 4 l on 2p blk brn 12.00 *50.00*
J9 D1 6 l on 3p violet 20.00 *80.00*
J10 D1 24 l on 1sh blue 57.50 *185.00*
Nos. J6-J10 (5) 114.50 *465.00*

CHINA

100 Cents = 1 Dollar

Stamps of Hong Kong, 1912-14, Overprinted

1917 **Wmk. 3** ***Perf. 14***

Ordinary Paper

1 A11 1c brown 4.50 3.00
2 A11 2c deep green 8.00 .35
3 A12 4c scarlet 6.25 .35
4 A13 6c orange 6.25 .70
5 A12 8c gray 14.00 1.40
6 A11 10c ultramarine 14.00 .35

Chalky Paper

7 A14 12c violet, *yel* 12.50 5.00
8 A14 20c olive grn & vio 14.00 .70
9 A15 25c red vio & dl vio (on #117) 9.25 *17.50*
10 A13 30c orange & violet 40.00 6.25
11 A14 50c black, *emerald* 40.00 6.50
a. 50c blk, *blue green,* ol back 75.00 1.75
b. 50c blk, *emerald,* ol back 50.00 9.75
12 A11 $1 blue & vio, *bl* 80.00 2.90
13 A14 $2 black & red 260.00 62.50
14 A13 $3 violet & grn 625.00 210.00
15 A14 $5 red & grn, *bl grn,* ol back 400.00 290.00
16 A13 $10 blk & vio, *red* 1,000. 550.00
Nos. 1-16 (16) 2,534. 1,158.

Stamps of Hong Kong, 1921-26, Overprinted

1922-27 **Ordinary Paper** **Wmk. 4**

17 A11 1c brown 2.60 *4.25*
18 A11 2c green 4.00 2.60
19 A12 4c scarlet 7.00 2.60
20 A13 6c orange 5.00 4.75
21 A12 8c gray 9.25 *17.50*
22 A11 10c ultramarine 10.00 4.00

Chalky Paper

23 A14 20c ol grn & vio 16.00 5.75
24 A15 25c red violet & dull vio 26.00 *80.00*
25 A14 50c blk, *emerald* ('27) 70.00 *210.00*
26 A11 $1 ultra & vio, *bl* 85.00 *70.00*
27 A14 $2 black & red 225.00 *290.00*
Nos. 17-27 (11) 459.85 *691.45*

MOROCCO

100 Centimos = 1 Peseta
12 Pence = 1 Shilling
20 Shillings = 1 Pound
100 Centimes = 1 Franc

These stamps were issued for various purposes:

a — For general use at the British Post Offices throughout Morocco.

b — For use in the Spanish Zone of Northern Morocco.

c — For use in the French Zone of Southern Morocco.

d — For use in the International Zone of Tangier.

For convenience these stamps are listed in four groups according to the coinage expressed or surcharged on the stamps, namely:

1 — Value expressed in Spanish currency.
2 — Value in British currency.
3 — Value in French currency.
4 — Stamps overprinted "Tangier."

Spanish Currency

Gibraltar Stamps of 1889-95 Overprinted

1898 **Wmk. 2** ***Perf. 14***

Black Overprint

1 A11 5c green 3.00 *3.00*
On cover 25.00
2 A11 10c carmine rose 5.00 .85
On cover 50.00
b. Double overprint 625.00
3 A11 20c olive green 11.00 6.25
On cover 400.00
4 A11 25c ultramarine 4.50 .70
On cover 300.00
5 A11 40c orange brown 7.00 3.75
On cover 500.00
6 A11 50c violet 20.00 *26.00*
On cover 500.00
7 A11 1pe bister & blue 20.00 *30.00*
On cover 300.00
8 A11 2pe blk & car rose 25.00 *30.00*
On cover 300.00
Nos. 1-8 (8) 95.50 *100.55*

Covers: Values for Nos. 1-6 are for covers bearing stamps paying thr correct rates. Values for Nos. 7-8 are for overfranked covers, usually philatelic.

Dark Blue Overprint

9 A11 40c orange brown *50.00* *35.00*
On cover 500.00
10 A11 50c violet 14.00 14.00
On cover 500.00
11 A11 1pe bister & blue *175.00* *210.00*
On cover

Inverted "V" for "A"

1a A11 5c 40.00 *50.00*
2a A11 10c 260.00 310.00
3a A11 20c 85.00 *95.00*
4a A11 25c 140.00 *150.00*
5a A11 40c 190.00 210.00
6a A11 50c 290.00 *375.00*
7a A11 1pe 275.00 *400.00*
8a A11 2pe 350.00 *400.00*

Overprinted in Black

(Narrower "M," ear of "g" horiz.)

1899

12 A11 5c green .55 *1.10*
On cover 15.00
13 A11 10c carmine rose 2.90 .35
On cover 25.00
14 A11 20c olive green 8.00 .80
On cover 150.00
15 A11 25c ultramarine 12.50 1.00
On cover 100.00
16 A11 40c orange brown 47.50 35.00
On cover 350.00
17 A11 50c violet 11.00 4.00
On cover 350.00
18 A11 1pe bister & blue 32.50 *50.00*
On cover 250.00
19 A11 2pe blk & car rose 62.50 *55.00*
On cover 300.00
Nos. 12-19 (8) 177.45 *147.25*

Covers: Values for Nos. 18-19 are for overfranked covers, usually philatelic.

"M" with long serif

12a A11 5c 10.00 *15.00*
13a A11 10c 11.50 *13.50*
14a A11 20c 40.00 *42.50*
15a A11 25c 50.00 *55.00*
16a A11 40c 260.00 *290.00*
17a A11 50c 125.00 *140.00*
18a A11 1pe *175.00* *290.00*
19a A11 2pe 375.00 *400.00*

Type of Gibraltar, 1903, with Value in Spanish Currency, Overprinted

1903-05

20 A12 5c gray grn & bl grn 11.00 4.00
21 A12 10c violet, *red* 9.75 .45
22 A12 20c gray grn & car rose ('04) 20.00 *52.50*
23 A12 25c vio & blk, *bl* 9.25 .35
24 A12 50c violet 100.00 *190.00*
25 A12 1pe blk & car rose 47.50 *175.00*
26 A12 2pe black & ultra 57.50 *140.00*
Nos. 20-26 (7) 255.00 *562.30*

"M" with long serif

20a A12 5c 57.50 *62.50*
21a A12 10c 50.00 45.00
22a A12 20c 110.00 *210.00*
23a A12 25c 57.50 50.00
24a A12 50c 400.00 *700.00*
25a A12 1pe 260.00 *575.00*
26a A12 2pe 300.00 *550.00*

1905-06 Wmk. 3 Chalky Paper

No.	Type	Description	Unused	Used
27	A12	5c gray grn & bl grn	11.00	*3.50*
28	A12	10c violet, *red*	12.50	2.25
29	A12	20c gray grn & car rose ('06)	6.25	*35.00*
30	A12	25c vio & blk, *bl* ('06)	45.00	9.75
31	A12	50c violet	8.50	*50.00*
32	A12	1pe blk & car rose	32.50	*92.50*
33	A12	2pe black & ultra	18.00	*40.00*
		Nos. 27-33 (7)	133.75	*233.00*

No. 29 is on ordinary paper. Nos. 27 and 28 are on both ordinary and chalky paper.

"M" with long serif

No.	Type	Description	Unused	Used
27a	A12	5c	62.50	50.00
28a	A12	10c	62.50	42.50
29a	A12	20c	57.50	175.00
30a	A12	25c	350.00	175.00
31a	A12	50c	175.00	290.00
32a	A12	1pe	225.00	375.00
33a	A12	2pe	210.00	290.00

Numerous other minor overprint varieties exist of Nos. 1-33.

British Stamps of 1902-10 Surcharged in Spanish Currency

a

b

1907-10 Wmk. 30

No.	Type	Description	Unused	Used
34(a)	A66	5c on ½p pale grn	9.25	.25
35(a)	A66	10c on 1p car	13.50	.25
36(a)	A67	15c on 1½p vio & grn	3.50	.25
a.		"1" of "15" omitted	5,400.	
37(a)	A68	20c on 2p grn & car	3.00	.25
38(a)	A66	25c on 2½p ultra	2.00	.25
39(a)	A70	40c on 4p brn & grn	1.40	*3.50*
40(a)	A70	40c on 4p org ('10)	1.10	.70
41(a)	A71	50c on 5p lil & ultra	2.25	*3.75*
42(a)	A73	1pe on 10p car rose & vio	25.00	*14.00*
		Wmk. 31		
43(b)	A75	3pe on 2sh6p vio	24.00	*29.00*
44(b)	A76	6pe on 5sh car rose	40.00	*52.50*
45(b)	A77	12pe on 10sh ultra	85.00	85.00
		Nos. 34-45 (12)	210.00	*189.70*

Nos. 36-37, 39-43 are on chalky paper.

Great Britain Nos. 153, 154 and 148 Surcharged

1912 Wmk. 30 *Perf. 15x14*

No.	Type	Description	Unused	Used
46(a)	A80	5c on ½p yel grn	3.50	.25
47(a)	A81	10c on 1p scarlet	1.10	.25
48(a)	A66	25c on 2½p ultra	42.50	30.00
		Nos. 46-48 (3)	47.10	30.50

British Stamps of 1912-18 Surcharged in Black or Carmine

c

d

e

1914-18 Wmk. 33

No.	Type	Description	Unused	Used
49	A82(a)	5c on ½p grn	.85	.25
50	A83(d)	10c on 1p scar	1.75	.25
51	A84(c)	15c on 1½p red brn ('15)	1.10	.25
52	A85(d)	20c on 2p org (I)	1.10	.25
53	A86(d)	25c on 2½p ultra	2.00	.25
54	A90(d)	1pe on 10p lt bl	4.00	*8.00*

Wmk. 34

Perf. 11x12

No.	Type	Description	Unused	Used
55	A91(e)	3pe on 2sh6p lt brn	35.00	*160.00*
a.		3pe on 2sh6p dark brown	45.00	*125.00*
56	A91(e)	6pe on 5sh car	32.50	*55.00*
a.		6pe on 5sh light carmine	150.00	*210.00*
57	A91(e)	12pe on 10sh dk bl (C)	110.00	*190.00*
a.		12pe on 10sh blue	100.00	*190.00*
		Nos. 49-57 (9)	188.30	*414.25*

Great Britain Nos. 159, 165 Surcharged in Spanish Currency

f

g

1917-23 Wmk. 33 *Perf. 15x14*

No.	Type	Description	Unused	Used
58	A82(f)	3c on ½p green	1.40	*5.00*
59	A88(g)	40c on 4p sl green	3.50	*4.50*

Great Britain Nos. 189, 191, 179 Surcharged in Spanish Currency

1926 Wmk. 35

No.	Type	Description	Unused	Used
60	A84(c)	15c on 1½p red brn	8.50	*26.00*
61	A86(d)	25c on 2½p ultra	2.90	*2.90*
		Wmk. 34		
		Perf. 11x12		
62	A91(e)	3pe on 2sh6p brn	26.00	*85.00*
		Nos. 60-62 (3)	37.40	*113.90*

British Stamps of 1924 Surcharged in Spanish Currency

1929-31 Wmk. 35 *Perf. 15x14*

No.	Type	Description	Unused	Used
63	A82(a)	5c on ½p grn ('31)	3.00	*17.50*
64	A83(d)	10c on 1p scar	21.00	*30.00*
65	A85(d)	20c on 2p org (II) ('31)	3.50	*10.00*
66	A88(g)	40c on 4p sl grn ('30)	2.90	2.90
		Nos. 63-66 (4)	30.40	*60.40*

Silver Jubilee Issue

Great Britain Nos. 226-229 Srchd. in Blue or Red

1935, May 8 *Perf. 14½x14*

No.	Type	Description	Unused	Used
67	A98	5c on ½p dk grn	1.10	1.10
68	A98	10c on 1p car	3.00	2.50
a.		Pair, one reading "CEN-TIMES"	1,600.	1,800.
69	A98	15c on 1½p red brn	6.25	*20.00*
70	A98	25c on 2½p ultra (R)	4.00	2.50
		Nos. 67-70 (4)	14.35	*26.10*

25th anniv. of the reign of King George V.

Catalogue values for unused stamps in this section, from this point to the end of the section, are for Never Hinged items.

Great Britain Nos. 210-214, 216, 219 Surcharged in Spanish Currency

1935-37 Photo.

No.	Type	Description	Unused	Used
71	A97(a)	5c on ½p dk grn ('36)	1.25	*21.00*
72	A97(d)	10c on 1p car	3.25	*11.00*
73	A97(c)	15c on 1½p red brn	7.00	3.75
74	A97(d)	20c on 2p red org ('36)	.75	.30
75	A97(d)	25c on 2½p ultra ('36)	1.75	*5.00*
76	A97(d)	40c on 4p dk sl grn ('37)	.75	*3.50*
77	A97(d)	1pe on 10p Prus bl ('37)	7.00	.35
		Nos. 71-77 (7)	21.75	*44.90*

Great Britain Nos. 230-233 Surcharged

"MOROCCO" 14mm

1936 Wmk. 250

No.	Type	Description	Unused	Used
78	A99	5c on ½p dk green	.25	.25
79	A99	10c on 1p crimson	.55	*2.25*
a.		"Morocco" 15mm long	4.00	*16.00*
80	A99	15c on 1½p red brown	.25	.25
81	A99	25c on 2½p brt ultra	.25	.25
		Nos. 78-81 (4)	1.30	*3.00*

Great Britain #234 Surcharged in Blue

Perf. 14½x14

1937, May 13 Wmk. 251

No.	Type	Description	Unused	Used
82	A100	15c on 1½p purple brn	.80	.80

Coronation of George VI and Elizabeth.

Great Britain Nos. 235-237, 239, 241, 244 Surcharged in Blue or Black

h

1937-40

No.	Type	Description	Unused	Used
83	A101	5c on ½p dp grn (Bl)	1.40	.35
84	A101	10c on 1p scarlet	1.10	.25
85	A101	15c on 1½p red brown (Bl)	1.40	.30
86	A101	25c on 2½p brt ultra	2.25	1.40
87	A102	40c on 4p gray grn ('40)	35.00	15.00
88	A103	70c on 7p emer ('40)	2.00	*16.00*
		Nos. 83-88 (6)	43.15	*33.30*

Great Britain Nos. 252-254, 256 Surcharged in Blue or Black

1940, May 6

No.	Type	Description	Unused	Used
89	A106	5c on ½p dp grn (Bl)	.35	*3.00*
90	A106	10c on 1p scarlet	4.25	*2.90*
91	A106	15c on 1½p red brn (Bl)	.80	*2.90*
92	A106	25c on 2½p brt ultra	.90	*1.10*
		Nos. 89-92 (4)	6.30	*9.90*

Centenary of the postage stamp.

Great Britain Nos. 267 and 268 Surcharged in Black

i

j

Perf. 14½x14, 14x14½

1948, Apr. 26 Wmk. 251

No.	Type	Description	Unused	Used
93	A109(i)	25c on 2½p	1.10	.35
94	A110(j)	45pe on £1	19.00	*25.00*

25th anniv. of the marriage of King George VI and Queen Elizabeth.

Great Britain Nos. 271-274 Surcharged "MOROCCO AGENCIES" and New Value

1948, July 29 *Perf. 14½x14*

No.	Type	Description	Unused	Used
95	A113	25c on 2½p brt ultra	.55	*1.40*
96	A114	30c on 3p dp vio	.55	*1.40*
97	A115	60c on 6p red vio	.55	*1.40*
98	A116	1.20pe on 1sh dk brn	.70	*1.40*
a.		Double surcharge	925.00	
		Nos. 95-98 (4)	2.35	*5.60*

1948 Olympic Games, Wembley, July-Aug.

A square of dots obliterates the original denomination on No. 98.

Great Britain Nos. 280-282, 284-285, 247 Surcharged Type "h"

1951-52 Wmk. 251 *Perf. 14½x14*

No.	Type	Description	Unused	Used
99	A101	5c on ½p lt org	2.25	*5.00*
100	A101	10c on 1p ultra	3.75	*8.50*
101	A101	15c on 1½p green	2.00	*19.00*
102	A101	25c on 2½p ver	2.00	*11.00*
103	A102	40c on 4p ultra ('52)	.70	*11.50*
104	A103	1pe on 10p ryl bl ('52)	2.50	*4.00*
		Nos. 99-104 (6)	13.20	*59.00*

BRITISH CURRENCY

Stamps of Morocco Agencies were accepted for postage in Great Britain, starting in mid-1950. Examples with contemporaneous Morocco cancellations sell for more.

British Stamps of 1902-11 Overprinted

a

b

Overprint "a" 14½mm long

1907-12 Wmk. 30 *Perf. 14*

Ordinary Paper

No.	Type	Description	Unused	Used
201	A66	½p pale yel grn	2.50	*9.75*
202	A66	1p carmine	11.00	6.25
		Chalky Paper		
203	A68	2p green & car	11.50	6.25
204	A70	4p brown & grn	4.25	*4.50*
205	A70	4p orange ('12)	11.50	*12.50*
a.		Perf. 15x14	25.00	*27.50*
206	A66	6p dull vio	17.00	*21.00*
207	A74	1sh car rose & grn	30.00	*19.00*
		Overprinted Type "b"		
		Wmk. 31		
208	A75	2sh6p violet	92.50	*140.00*
		Nos. 201-208 (8)	180.25	*219.25*

British Stamps of 1912-18 Overprinted Type "a"

Perf. 14½x14, 15x14

1914-21 Wmk. 33

No.	Type	Description	Unused	Used
209	A82	½p green ('18)	4.00	.55
210	A83	1p scarlet ('17)	1.00	.25
211	A84	1½p red brn ('21)	3.75	*14.00*
212	A85	2p orange ('18)	4.50	.70
213	A87	3p violet ('21)	1.40	.40
214	A88	4p slate grn ('21)	3.75	1.40
215	A89	6p dull vio ('21)	5.50	*17.50*
216	A90	1sh bister ('17)	6.25	1.40

c

Wmk. 34 *Perf. 11x12*

No.	Type	Description	Unused	Used
217	A91	2sh6p lt brown	42.50	*57.50*
a.		2sh6p brown	55.00	35.00
b.		2sh6p black brown	52.50	*62.50*
c.		Double overprint	1,900.	1,350.
		Nos. 209-217 (9)	72.65	*93.70*

Same Overprint on Great Britain Nos. 179-180

1925-31
218 A91 2sh6p gray brown 42.50 29.00
219 A91 5sh car rose ('31) 62.50 100.00

British Stamps of 1924 Overprinted Type "a" (14½mm long)

1925-31 Wmk. 35 *Perf. 15x14*
220 A82 ½p green 2.25 .55
221 A84 1½p red brn ('31) 13.50 15.00
222 A85 2p dp org (Die II) 2.50 1.10
223 A86 2½p ultra 2.50 5.75
224 A89 6p red vio ('31) 2.25 9.50
225 A90 1sh bister 19.00 5.75
Nos. 220-225 (6) 42.00 37.65

Silver Jubilee Issue

Great Britain Nos. 226-229 Overprinted in Blue or Red

1935, May 8 *Perf. 14½x14*
226 A98 ½p dark green (Bl) 1.40 7.50
227 A98 1p carmine (Bl) 1.40 7.50
228 A98 1½p red brown (Bl) 2.50 11.00
229 A98 2½p ultramarine (R) 2.90 2.90
Nos. 226-229 (4) 8.20 28.90

25th anniversary of the reign of King George V.

British Stamps of 1924 Overprinted Type "a" (15½mm long)

1935-36
230 A82 ½p green 9.50 45.00
231 A86 2½p ultra 110.00 35.00
232 A88 4p slate green 8.00 40.00
233 A89 6p red violet 1.10 .70
234 A90 1sh bister 62.50 57.50
Nos. 230-234 (5) 191.10 178.20

British Stamps of 1934-36 Overprinted "MOROCCO AGENCIES"

1935-36
235 A97 1p carmine 3.50 16.00
236 A97 1½p red brn ('36) 3.50 19.00
237 A97 2p red org ('36) 1.40 9.00
238 A97 2½p ultra ('36) 2.00 4.75
239 A97 3p dk vio ('36) .55 .35
240 A97 4p dk sl grn ('36) .55 .35
241 A97 1sh bis brn ('36) .90 4.00

Overprinted Type "c"

Wmk. 34
Perf. 11x12
242 A91 2sh6p brown 45.00 70.00
243 A91 5sh car ('37) 27.50 110.00
Nos. 235-243 (9) 84.90 233.45

Catalogue values for unused stamps in this section, from this point to the end of the section, are for Never Hinged items.

Great Britain Nos. 231, 233 Overprinted

"MOROCCO" 14mm

1936 Wmk. 250 *Perf. 14½x14*
244 A99 1p crimson .25 .25
a. "Morocco" 15mm long 7.00 19.00
245 A99 2½p bright ultra .25 .25
a. "Morocco" 15mm long 1.10 4.75

Great Britain Nos. 258-263, 241-248, 266, 249A-250 Overprinted "MOROCCO AGENCIES" (14½mm long)

1949, Aug. 16 Wmk. 251
246 A101 ½p green 2.00 8.00
247 A101 1p vermilion 3.00 10.00
248 A101 1½p lt red brown 3.00 9.50
249 A101 2p lt orange 3.50 10.00
250 A101 2½p ultra 3.75 11.50
251 A101 3p violet 1.75 2.00
252 A102 4p gray green .55 1.40
253 A102 5p lt brown 3.50 17.00
254 A102 6p rose lilac 1.75 1.75
255 A103 7p emerald .55 18.00
256 A103 8p brt rose 3.50 7.50
257 A103 9p dp olive grn .55 12.50
258 A103 10p royal blue .55 7.50
259 A103 11p violet brn .80 8.50
260 A103 1sh brown 3.00 7.00

"MOROCCO AGENCIES" 17½mm long

Wmk. 259
Perf. 14
261 A104 2sh6p yellow grn 18.00 40.00
262 A104 5sh dull red 32.50 70.00
Nos. 246-262 (17) 82.25 242.15

Great Britain Nos. 280-284, 286-287 Overprinted "MOROCCO AGENCIES" (14½mm long)

Perf. 14½x14
1951, May 3 Wmk. 251
263 A101 ½p lt orange 2.25 1.10
264 A101 1p ultra 2.25 1.60
265 A101 1½p green 2.25 3.00
266 A101 2p lt red brown 2.50 4.50
267 A101 2½p vermilion 2.25 4.75

"MOROCCO AGENCIES" 17½mm long

Wmk. 259
Perf. 11x12
268 A121 2sh6p green 15.00 24.00
269 A121 5sh dull red 15.00 26.00
Nos. 263-269 (7) 41.50 64.95

French Currency

British Stamps of 1912-22 Surcharged in French Currency in Red or Black

h

i

Perf. 14½x14, 15x14
1917-24 Wmk. 33
401 A82(h) 3c on ½p grn (R) 1.10 2.90
402 A82(h) 5c on ½p green .45 1.75
403 A83(h) 10c on 1p scarlet 3.75 .45
404 A84(h) 15c on 1½p red brn 2.90 .25
405 A86(h) 25c on 2½p ultra 2.25 .25
406 A88(h) 40c on 4p slate grn 2.90 1.75
407 A89(h) 50c on 5p yel brn ('23) .90 3.00
408 A90(h) 75c on 9p ol grn ('24) 1.10 .85
409 A90(i) 1fr on 10p lt blue 8.00 3.50
Nos. 401-409 (9) 23.35 14.70

Great Britain No. 179 Surcharged

k

1924 Wmk. 34 *Perf. 11x12*
410 A91(k) 3fr on 2sh6p brn 8.50 1.75

British Stamps of 1924 Surcharged in French Currency as in 1917-24

1925-26 Wmk. 35 *Perf. 15x14*
411 A82(h) 5c on ½p green .35 7.50
412 A83(h) 10c on 1p scarlet .35 2.25
413 A84(h) 15c on 1½p red brn 1.10 2.00
414 A86(h) 25c on 2½p ultra 1.75 .55
415 A88(h) 40c on 4p sl green .70 .90
416 A89(h) 50c on 5p yel brn 1.75 .25
417 A90(h) 75c on 9p ol green 4.00 .25
418 A90(i) 1fr on 10p dl blue 1.40 .25
Nos. 411-418 (8) 11.40 13.95

Great Britain Nos. 180, 198 and 200 Surcharged type "k"

1932 Wmk. 34 *Perf. 11x12*
419 A91 6fr on 5sh car rose 42.50 47.50

1934 Wmk. 35 *Perf. 14½x14*
420 A90 90c on 9p ol green 18.00 8.50
421 A90 1.50fr on 1sh bister 11.50 2.50

Silver Jubilee Issue

Great Britain Nos. 226-229 Surcharged in Blue or Red

1935, May 8 *Perf. 14½x14*
422 A98 5c on ½p dk green .25 .25
423 A98 10c on 1p carmine 3.00 .85
424 A98 15c on 1½p red brn .40 .55
425 A98 25c on 2½p ultra (R) .25 .35
Nos. 422-425 (4) 3.90 2.00

25th anniv. of the reign of King George V.

British Stamps of 1934-36 Surcharged Types "h" or "k"

Perf. 14½x14
1935-37 Photo. Wmk. 35
426 A97(h) 5c on ½p dk grn .55 5.75
427 A97(h) 10c on 1p car ('36) .40 .35
428 A97(h) 15c on 1½p red brn 5.50 6.25
429 A97(h) 25c on 2½p ultra .35 .25
430 A97(h) 40c on 4p dk sl grn .35 .25
431 A97(h) 50c on 5p yel brn .35 .25
432 A97(h) 90c on 9p dk ol grn .40 2.00
433 A97(k) 1fr on 10p Prus bl .35 .35
434 A97(h) 1.50fr on 1sh bister brn ('37) .85 3.75

Waterlow Printing

Wmk. 34 *Perf. 11x12*
435 A91(k) 3fr on 2sh6p brn 5.50 14.00
436 A91(k) 6fr on 5sh car ('36) 7.00 24.00
Nos. 426-436 (11) 21.60 57.20

Great Britain Nos. 230, 232 Surcharged

1936 Wmk. 250 *Perf. 14½x14*
437 A99 5c on ½p dark green .25 .25
438 A99 15c on 1½p red brown .25 .25

Great Britain No. 234 Surcharged in Blue

1937, May 13 Wmk. 251
439 A100 15c on 1½p pur brn .35 .25

Coronation of George VI and Elizabeth.

Great Britain No. 235 Surcharged in Blue

1937
440 A101 5c on ½p deep green 2.50 2.90

For Use in the International Zone of Tangier

Great Britain Nos. 187-190 Overprinted in Black — a

1927 Wmk. 35 *Perf. 15x14*
501 A82 ½p green 3.50 .25
502 A83 1p scarlet 3.50 .30
503 A84 1½p red brown 7.00 4.25
504 A85 2p orange (II) 3.75 .25
Nos. 501-504 (4) 17.75 5.05

Same Overprint on Great Britain Nos. 210-212

1934-35 Photo. *Perf. 14½x14*
505 A97 ½p dark green 1.40 1.75
506 A97 1p carmine 4.75 2.75
507 A97 1½p red brown .55 .25
Nos. 505-507 (3) 6.70 4.75

Silver Jubilee Issue

Great Britain Nos. 226-228 Overprinted in Blue

b

1935, May 8
508 A98 ½p dark green 1.40 5.75
509 A98 1p carmine 16.00 17.00
510 A98 1½p red brown 1.40 1.10
Nos. 508-510 (3) 18.80 23.85

25th anniv. of the reign of King George V.

Great Britain Nos. 230-232 Overprinted Type "a"

1936 Wmk. 250
511 A99 ½p dark green .25 .25
512 A99 1p crimson .25 .25
513 A99 1½p red brown .25 .25
Nos. 511-513 (3) .75 .75

Great Britain No. 234 Overprinted Type "b" in Blue

1937, May 13 Wmk. 251
514 A100 1½p purple brown .55 .55

Coronation of George VI and Elizabeth.

Great Britain Nos. 235-237 Overprinted in Blue or Black — c

1937 *Perf. 14½x14*
515 A101 ½p deep green (Bl) 2.75 1.75
516 A101 1p scarlet (Bk) 8.00 1.75
517 A101 1½p red brown (Bl) 2.75 .30
Nos. 515-517 (3) 13.50 3.80

Great Britain Nos. 252-254 Ovptd. Type "a" in Blue or Black

1940, May 6
518 A106 ½p deep green (Bl) .35 5.50
519 A106 1p scarlet (Bk) .50 .60
520 A106 1½p red brown (Bl) 2.25 5.75
Nos. 518-520 (3) 3.10 11.85

Centenary of the postage stamp.

Great Britain Nos. 258 and 259 Overprinted Type "c" in Blue or Black

1944-45
521 A101 ½p green (Bl) 12.50 5.00
522 A101 1p ver (Bk) ('45) 12.50 3.50

Catalogue values for unused stamps in this section, from this point to the end of the section, are for Never Hinged items.

Great Britain Nos. 264-265 Overprinted

d

e

1946, June 11

523 A107(d) 2½p bright ultra .75 .75
524 A108(e) 3p violet .75 *2.25*

Return to peace at close of World War II.

Great Britain Nos. 267 and 268 Overprinted Type "a"

1948, Apr. 26 ***Perf. 14½x14, 14x14½***

525 A109 2½p bright ultra .60 .25
a. Pair, one without overprint *5,400.*
526 A110 £1 dp chalky bl 22.50 29.00

25th anniv. of the marriage of King George VI and Queen Elizabeth.

Great Britain Nos. 271 to 274 Overprinted Type "a"

1948, July 29 ***Perf. 14½x14***

527 A113 2½p bright ultra 1.10 *2.25*
528 A114 3p deep violet 1.10 *2.25*
529 A115 6p red violet 1.10 *2.25*
530 A116 1sh dark brown 1.10 *1.40*
Nos. 527-530 (4) 4.40 *8.15*

1948 Olympic Games, Wembley, July-Aug.

Stamps of Great Britain, 1937-47, and Nos. 249A, 250 and 251A Overprinted Type "c"

1949, Jan. 1

531 A101 2p lt org (II) 5.75 *7.00*
532 A101 2½p ultra (II) 2.00 *7.00*
533 A101 3p violet (II) .80 *1.40*
534 A102 4p gray green 12.50 11.50
535 A102 5p light brown 4.25 *22.50*
536 A102 6p rose lilac .80 .35
537 A103 7p emerald 1.40 *15.00*
538 A103 8p bright rose 4.25 *12.50*
539 A103 9p deep ol grn 1.40 *13.50*
540 A103 10p royal blue 1.40 *15.00*
541 A103 11p violet brn 1.75 *12.50*
542 A103 1sh brown 1.40 *3.00*

Wmk. 259

Perf. 14

543 A104 2sh6p yellow grn 5.00 *13.50*
544 A104 5sh dull red 15.00 *42.50*
545 A105 10sh ultra 50.00 *110.00*
Nos. 531-545 (15) 107.70 *287.25*

Great Britain Nos. 276 to 279 Overprinted Type "a"

Perf. 14½x14

1949, Oct. 10 **Wmk. 251**

546 A117 2½p bright ultra .80 *3.00*
547 A118 3p bright violet .80 *2.00*
548 A119 6p red violet .80 *1.40*
549 A120 1sh brown .80 *3.75*
Nos. 546-549 (4) 3.20 *10.15*

Great Britain Nos. 280-288 Overprinted Type "c" or "a" (Shilling Values)

1950-51

550 A101 ½p lt orange 1.00 *1.75*
551 A101 1p ultra 1.10 *3.50*
552 A101 1½p green 1.10 *16.00*
553 A101 2p lt red brn 1.10 *2.90*
554 A101 2½p vermilion 1.10 *5.75*
555 A102 4p ultra ('50) 3.50 3.50

Wmk. 259

Perf. 11x12

556 A121 2sh6p green 11.00 5.75
557 A121 5sh dull red 17.50 *19.00*
558 A122 10sh ultra 22.50 19.00
Nos. 550-558 (9) 59.90 *77.15*

TURKISH EMPIRE

STAMPS OF GREAT BRITAIN USED IN THE TURKISH EMPIRE

Values are for clear cancellations on sound, fault-free stamps, with average to fine centering. In many cases, very fine stamps are rare or non-existent.

BEIRUT

British P.O. opened 1873; closed Sept. 30, 1914

No. A22

Stamps of Great Britain, Canceled with barred oval "G06" or circular date stamp "BEYROUT"

1873-80

A1 ½p rose red (#58, P 12-14) 52.50
Plate 19 110.00
Plate 20 150.00
A2 1p rose red (#33, P107, 118, 130, 140, 145, 148, 155, 157, 162, 167, 177, 179, 180, 184-187, 195, 198, 200, 203, 204, 211, 213, 215, 218, 220, 222) *value from* 22.50
A3 1½p lake red (#32, P 3) 350.00
A4 2p blue (#30, P 13-15), *value from* 30.00
A5 2½p claret (#66, P 1-3), *value from* 37.50
a. Bluish paper (#66a, P 1) 87.50
A6 2½p claret (#67, P 3-17), *value from* 30.00
A7 2½p blue (#68, P 17-20), *value from* 19.00
A8 2½p blue (#82, P 21-23), *value from* 13.50
On cover, *value from* *75.00*
A9 3p rose (#49, P 10) —
A10 3p rose (#61, P 12, 15, 16, 18-20), *value from* 52.50
A11 3p rose (#83, P 20, 21) —
A12 4p vermilion (#43, P 11-14), *value from* 45.00
A13 4p vermilion (#69, P 15) 375.00
A14 4p pale ol grn (#70, P 15) 250.00
Plate 16 225.00
A15 4p gray brown (#71, P 17) —
A16 4p gray brown (#84, P17, 18), *value from* 60.00
A17 6p violet (#52, P 8, 9) —
A18 6p brown (#59, P 11) 50.00
a. 6p pale buff (#59b, P 11) 100.00
Plate 12 250.00
A19 6p gray (#60, P 12) —
A20 6p gray (#62, P 13-17), *value from* 35.00
A21 8p orange (#73) 500.00
A22 10p red brown (#53) 325.00
A23 1sh green (#54, P 6, 7), *value from* 37.50
A24 1sh green (#64, P 8-10, 12, 13), *value from* 52.50
A25 1sh salmon (#65, P 13) —
A26 1sh salmon (#87, P 13, 14) 80.00
A27 2sh blue (#55) 175.00
A28 5sh rose (#57, P 1) 775.00
Plate 2 925.00

1880

A29 ½p deep green (#78) 13.50
a. ½p green (#78c) 14.50
A30 1p red brown (#79) 19.00
A31 1½p red brown (#80) 210.00
A32 2p lilac rose (#81) 72.50
a. 2p deep lilac rose (#81a) 72.50
A33 5p indigo (#85) 110.00

1881

A34 1p lilac, 14 dots (#88) —
A35 1p lilac, 16 dots (#88) 8.00

1883-84

A36 ½p slate blue (#98) 21.00
A37 1½p lilac (#99) 105.00
A38 2p lilac (#100) 87.50
A39 2½p lilac (#101) 13.50
On cover *75.00*
A41 4p dull green (#103) 225.00
A42 5p dull green (#104) 130.00
A45 1sh dull green (#107) 375.00

1887-92

A46 ½p vermilion 10.00
A53 6p violet, *rose* 27.50
A56 1sh dull green 175.00

1900

A57 ½p blue green 13.50
A58 1sh car rose & grn 210.00

1902-04

A59 ½p blue green 5.75
A60 ½p yellow green 6.00
A61 1p scarlet 5.50
A65 1sh car & dull grn 37.50

CONSTANTINOPLE

British P.O. opened Sept. 1, 1857; closed Sept. 30, 1914; reopened Feb. 4, 1919; closed Sept. 27, 1923

No. A122

Stamps of Great Britain, Canceled with barred oval "C" or circular date stamp "CONSTANTINOPLE"

1857-83

A75 ½p rose red (#58, P 5, 6, 10-15, 20), *value from* 30.00
A76 1p red brown (#8) —
A77 1p red brown (#12) —
A78 1p red brown (#16) 22.50
A79 1p rose red (#20) 8.50
A80 1p rose red (#33, P 71-74, 76, 78-81, 83, 85, 87, 89, 90, 92-97, 99, 101, 102, 105, 106, 108-110, 113, 116, 118-125, 127, 129-131, 134-138, 140, 141, 143-152, 155-167, 170-184, 186-198, 200, 201, 203-208, 210, 212, 214-216, 220, 222, 224) *value from* 10.00
A81 1½p lake red (#32a, P 1) 250.00
A82 2p blue (#17) —
A83 2p blue (#29, P 7) 65.00
Plate 8 55.00
Plate 9 14.00
Plate 12 *200.00*
Plate 13 27.50
Plate 14 37.50
Plate 15 37.50
A84 2½p claret (#66, P 1-3), *value from* 35.00
a. Bluish paper (#66a, P 1, 2) 65.00
b. Lettered "LH-FL" (#66b) —
A85 2½p claret (#67, P 3-17), *value from* 27.50
A86 2½p blue (#68, P 17-20), *value from* 13.50
A87 2½p blue (#82, P 21-23), *value from* 9.00
A88 3p rose (#37) 160.00
A89 3p rose (#44) 87.50
A90 3p rose (#49, P 4-10), *value from* 82.50
A91 3p rose (#61, P 11, 12, 15-18, 19), *value from* 30.00
A92 3p rose (#83, P 21) —
A93 3p on 3p violet (#94) —
A94 4p rose (#26) 55.00
a. 4p carmine rose (#26a) —
A95 4p vermilion (#34, P 3) 45.00
a. Hairlines (#34c) 60.00
A96 4p ver (#43, P 7-14), *value from* 30.00
A97 4p vermilion (#69, P 15) 375.00
A98 4p pale ol grn (#70, P 15) 250.00
Plate 16 225.00
A99 4p gray brn (#71, P 17) —
A100 4p gray brn (#84, P17, 18), *value from* 47.50
A101 6p lilac (#27) 70.00
A102 6p lilac (#39, P 3) 75.00
a. 6p lilac, thick paper (#39b, P 4) *200.00*
A103 6p lilac (#45, P 5) 42.50
Plate 6 *175.00*
A104 6p dull violet (#50, P 6) 50.00
A105 6p violet (#51, 6, 8, 9), *value from* 37.50
A106 6p brown (#59, P 11) 35.00
a. 6p pale buff (#59b, P 11) 80.00
Plate 12 225.00
A107 6p gray (#60, P 12) 90.00
A108 6p gray (#62, P 13-16), *value from* 30.00
A109 6p gray (#86, P 17, 18), *value from* 30.00
A110 6p on 6p violet (#95) 100.00
A111 8p orange (#73) 375.00
A112 10p red brown (#47) *32,500.*
A113 10p red brown (#53) 190.00
A114 1sh green (#28) 275.00
a. 1sh green, thick paper (#28d) *275.00*
A115 1sh green (#42) 70.00
A116 1sh green (#48, P 4) 75.00
A117 1sh green (#54, P 4-7), *value from* 20.00
A118 1sh green (#64, P 8-13), *value from* 32.50
A119 1sh salmon (#65, P 13) *240.00*
A120 1sh salmon (#87, P 13, 14), *value from* 55.00
A121 2sh blue (#55) 150.00
A122 5sh rose (#57, P 1) 575.00
Plate 2 850.00
A123 5sh rose, *blue* (#90) *1,600.*
a. White paper (#90a) *1,000.*

1880

A124 ½p deep green (#78) 9.00
a. ½p green (#78c) 11.00
A125 1p red brown (#79) 12.50
A126 2p lilac rose (#81) 50.00
a. 2p deep rose (#81a) 50.00
A127 5p indigo (#85) —

1881

A128 1p lilac, 14 dots (#88) —
A129 1p lilac, 16 dots (#88) 4.00

1883-84

A130 ½p slate blue (#98) 9.00
A131 1½p lilac (#99) —
A132 2p lilac (#100) 75.00
A133 2½p lilac (#101) 10.00
A134 3p lilac (#102) —
A135 4p dull green (#103) —
A136 5p dull green (#104) 130.00
A137 6p dull green (#105) —
A138 9p dull green (#106) —
A139 1sh dull green (#107) 300.00
A140 2sh6p lilac, *bluish* (#90) 775.00
a. White paper (#90a) 100.00
A141 5sh rose (#108) —
a. Bluish paper (#108a)

1887-92

A142 ½p vermilion 4.00
A150 6p violet, *rose* 13.50
A153 1sh dull green 100.00

1900

A154 ½p blue green 6.50
A155 1sh car rose & grn 175.00

1902-04

A156 ½p blue green 4.50
A157 ½p yellow green 5.00
A158 1p scarlet 4.00
A165 6p purple 13.00
A168 1sh car & dull grn 27.50
A169 2sh6p lilac —
A170 5sh carmine —

Postal Fiscal stamps of Great Britain are found used in Constantinople. They are rare.

SALONICA

British P.O. opened May 1, 1900; closed October, 1914

Stamps of Great Britain, Canceled with circular date stamp "SALONICA," with single or double circle

1887-92

A197 ½p vermilion 22.50
A198 1p lilac 25.00
A199 6p violet, *rose* 35.00
A200 5sh rose (#90a) 1,050.

1900

A201 ½p blue green 25.00
A202 1sh car rose & grn 225.00

1902-04

A203 ½p blue green 27.50
A204 ½p yellow green 22.50
A205 1p scarlet 22.50
A206 6p purple
A207 1sh car & dull grn 60.00

SMYRNA

British P.O. opened 1872; closed Sept. 30, 1914; reopened Mar. 1, 1919; closed Sept., 1922

Stamps of Great Britain, Canceled with barred numeral "F87" or with circular date stamps (various types)

1872-83

A229 ½p rose red (#58, P 11-15), *value from* 35.00
A230 1p rose red (#33, P 120, 124, 134, 137-140, 142, 143, 145, 146, 148-153, 155-164, 166-178, 183-188, 193, 195, 196, 198, 200, 201, 204, 210, 212, 215, 217, 218), *value from* 16.00
A231 1½p lake red (#32a, P 1, 3), *value from* 275.00
A232 2p blue (#15) —
A233 2p blue (#30, P 13-15), *value from* 19.00
A234 2½p claret (#66, P 1-3), *value from* 32.50
a. Bluish paper (#66a, P 1, 2) 70.00
b. Lettered "LH-FL" (#66b) —
A235 2½p claret (#67, P 3-17), *value from* 26.00
A236 2½p blue (#68, P 17-20), *value from* 22.50
A237 2½p blue (#82, P 21-23), *value from* 11.00
A238 3p rose (#49, P 5, 7, 9, 10), *value from* 47.50
A239 3p rose (#61, P 14, 15) —
A240 4p ver (#43, P 12-14), *value from* 30.00
A241 4p vermilion (#69, P 15) 375.00
A242 4p pale ol grn (#70, P 15) 250.00
Plate 16 225.00
A243 4p gray brown (#71, P 17) —
A244 4p gray brown (#84, P17, 18), *value from* 42.50
A245 6p brown (#59, P 11), *value from* —
a. 6p pale buff (#59b, P 11) 100.00
Plate 12 225.00
A246 6p gray (#60, P 12) 95.00
A247 6p gray (#62, P 13-17), *value from* 30.00

A248 6p gray (#86, P 17, 18), *value from* 60.00
A249 6p on 6p violet (#95) 125.00
A250 8p orange (#73) —
A251 9p bister (#52) *400.00*
A252 10p red brown (#53) *275.00*
A253 1sh green (#54, P 6, 7), *value from* —
A254 1sh green (#64, P 8-13), *value from* 35.00
A255 1sh salmon (#65, P 13) *250.00*
A256 1sh salmon (#87, P 13, 14), *value from* 60.00
A257 5sh rose (#57, P 2) —

1880
A258 ½p deep green (#78) 10.00
a. ½p green (#78c) 10.00
A259 1p red brown (#79) 15.00
A260 1½p red brown (#80) 140.00
A261 2p lilac rose (#81) 52.50
a. 2p deep rose (#81a) 52.50
A262 5p indigo (#85) 82.50

1881
A263 1p lilac, 16 dots (#88) 6.00

1883-84
A264 ½p slate blue (#98) 17.50
A266 2p lilac (#100) 82.50
A267 2½p lilac (#101) 12.00
A269 4p dull green (#103) —
A270 5p dull green (#104) 140.00
A273 1sh dull green (#107) 350.00

1887-92
A275 ½p vermilion 6.00
A282 6p violet, *rose* 22.50
A283 1sh dull green 140.00

1900
A285 ½p blue green 8.75
A286 1sh car rose & grn —

1902-04
A287 ½p blue green 5.50
A288 ½p yellow green 6.00
A289 1p scarlet 5.50
A296 6p purple 16.00
A299 1sh car & dull grn 30.00
A300 2sh6p lilac —
A301 5sh carmine —

STAMBOUL

British P.O. opened Apr. 1, 1884; closed Aug. 25, 1896; reopened Feb. 10, 1908; closed Sept. 30, 1914

Stamps of Great Britain, Canceled with barred "S" or circular date stamps "BRITISH POST OFFICE CONSTANTINOPLE S" or "BRITISH POST OFFICE STAMBOUL"

1883-84
A323 ½p slate blue (#98) 27.50
A324 2p lilac (#99) 13.50
A325 2p lilac (#100) —
A326 2½p lilac (#101) 16.00
A327 5p dull green (#104) 160.00

1887-92
A330 ½p vermilion 16.00
A338 6p violet, *rose* 37.50
A341 1sh dull green —

BRITISH STAMPS OVERPRINTED

40 Paras = 1 Piaster
12 Pence = 1 Shilling (1905)

a

b

c

Surcharged on Great Britain Nos. 101, 104, 96

1885, Apr. 1 Wmk. 30 *Perf. 14*
1 A47(a) 40pa on 2½p lil 110.00 1.50
On cover 10.00
2 A45(b) 80pa on 5p grn 210.00 12.50
On cover 80.00

Wmk. 31
3 A44(c) 12pi on 2sh6p lil 52.50 27.50
On cover 250.00
a. Bluish paper 400.00 260.00
On cover 1,600.
Nos. 1-3 (3) 372.50 41.50

Great Britain Nos. 114, 118 Surcharged

1887 Wmk. 30
4 A57(a) 40pa on 2½p vio, *bl* 4.75 .25
On cover 5.00
a. Double surcharge *2,250.* *2,900.*
5 A61(b) 80pa on 5p lil & bl 17.50 .35
On cover 5.00
a. Small "0" in "80" 225.00 100.00
On cover 375.00

Great Britain No. 111 Handstamp Surcharged — d

1893, Feb. 25
6 A54(d) 40pa on ½p ver *500.00* *125.00*
On cover 375.00

No. 6 was a provisional, made and used at Constantinople for five days. Excellent forgeries are known.

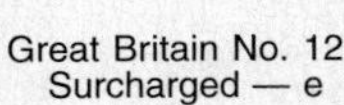

Great Britain No. 121 Surcharged — e

1896
7 A64(e) 4pi on 10p car rose & lil 47.50 9.25
On cover 50.00

British Stamps of 1902 Surcharged

1902-05 Wmk. 30
8 A66(a) 40pa on 2½p ultra 17.50 .25
9 A71(b) 80pa on 5p lil & bl 9.00 2.90
a. Small "0" in "80" 250.00 210.00
10 A73(e) 4pi on 10p car rose & vio 13.50 4.50

Wmk. 31
11 A75(c) 12pi on 2sh6p vio ('03) 40.00 40.00
12 A76(c) 24pi on 5sh car rose ('05) 35.00 47.50
Nos. 8-12 (5) 115.00 *95.15*

Great Britain Nos. 131, 134 Surcharged — f

1906 Wmk. 30
13 A66(f) 1pi on 2½p ultra 17.50 .25
14 A71(f) 2pi on 5p lil & ultra 32.50 2.75

Nos. 10, 11, 14 are on both ordinary and chalky paper.

Great Britain Nos. 127-135, 138 Overprinted — g

1905
15 A66 ½p pale green 10.00 .25
16 A66 1p carmine 9.50 .25
17 A67 1½p violet & grn 6.25 2.00
18 A68 2p green & car 3.50 *8.00*
19 A66 2½p ultra 10.00 *22.50*
20 A69 3p violet, *yel* 7.25 *13.50*
21 A70 4p brown & grn 10.00 *50.00*
22 A71 5p lilac & ultra 19.00 *32.50*
23 A66 6p dull violet 15.00 *29.00*
24 A74 1sh car rose & grn 42.50 *57.50*
Nos. 15-24 (10) 133.00 *215.50*

Nos. 17, 18 and 24 are on both ordinary and chalky paper.

No. 18 Surcharged

1906, July 2
25 A68 1pi on 2p grn & car 1,500. 700.00

British Stamps of 1902-09 Surcharged

j

k

1909
26 A67 30pa on 1½p vio & grn 11.50 1.40
27 A69 1pi10pa on 3p vio, *yel* 13.50 *40.00*
28 A70 1pi30pa on 4p brn & grn 5.75 *19.00*
29 A70 1pi30pa on 4p org 20.00 *70.00*
30 A66 2pi20pa on 6p dl vio 22.50 *70.00*
31 A74 5pi on 1sh car rose & grn 5.00 *11.00*
Nos. 26-31 (6) 78.25 *211.40*

No. 29 is on ordinary paper, the others are on chalky paper.

Great Britain Nos. 132, 144, 135 Surcharged

m

n

1910
32 A69(m) 1¼pi on 3p vio, *yel* .60 *1.25*
33 A70(m) 1¾pi on 4p orange .60 *.75*
34 A66(n) 2½pi on 6p dl vio 1.60 .80
Nos. 32-34 (3) 2.80 2.80

There are three different varieties of "4" in the fraction of the 1¾ piastre.

Great Britain Nos. 151-154 Overprinted Type g

1911-12 *Perf. 15x14*
35 A80 ½p yellow green 2.25 1.75
36 A81 1p carmine .55 *7.00*

Re-engraved
37 A80 ½p yel grn ('12) .90 .25
38 A81 1p scarlet ('12) .90 *1.75*

Great Britain No. 148 Surcharged — o

39 A66(o) 1pi on 2½p ultra 15.00 3.00
Nos. 35-39 (5) 19.60 13.75

The surcharge on No. 39 exists in two types with the letters 2½ and 3mm high respectively. The stamp also differs from No. 13 in the perforation.

British Stamps of 1912-13 Surcharged with New Values

1913-14 Wmk. 33
40 A84(j) 30pa on 1½p red brn 4.00 *16.00*
41 A86(o) 1pi on 2½p ultra 8.50 .25
42 A87(m) 1¼pi on 3p vio 5.50 4.75
43 A88(m) 1¾pi on 4p sl grn 3.50 *7.00*
44 A90(o) 4pi on 10p lt bl 9.00 *22.50*
45 A90(o) 5pi on 1sh bis 45.00 *70.00*
Nos. 40-45 (6) *75.50* 120.50

British Stamps of 1912-19 Overprinted Type "g"

1913-21
46 A82 ½p green .45 *1.40*
47 A83 1p scarlet .35 *5.75*
48 A85 2p orange ('21) 1.40 *32.50*
49 A87 3p violet ('21) 8.50 *11.50*
50 A88 4p sl grn ('21) 5.75 *16.00*
51 A89 5p yel brn ('21) 13.50 *32.50*
52 A89 6p dl vio ('21) 30.00 *10.00*
53 A90 1sh bister ('21) 15.00 *10.00*

Wmk. 34
Perf. 11x12
54 A91 2sh6p brn ('21) 42.50 *100.00*
Nos. 46-54 (9) 117.45 *219.65*

British Stamps of 1912-19 Surcharged as in 1909-10 and

p

q

1921 Wmk. 33 *Perf. 14½x14*
55 A82(j) 30pa on ½p grn .90 *13.50*
a. Inverted surcharge 100.00
56 A83(p) 1½pi on 1p scar 1.75 1.40
57 A86(p) 3¾pi on 2½p ultra 1.50 .35
58 A87(p) 4½pi on 3p vio 2.25 *4.25*
59 A89(p) 7½pi on 5p yel brn .60 .25
60 A90(p) 15pi on 10p lt bl .85 .25
61 A90(p) 18¾pi on 1sh bis 5.00 *5.00*

Wmk. 34
Perf. 11x12
62 A91(q) 45pi on 2sh6p brown 22.50 *52.50*
63 A91(q) 90pi on 5sh car rose 30.00 *35.00*
64 A91(q) 180pi on 10sh blue 52.50 45.00
Nos. 55-64 (10) 117.85 *157.50*

GREECE

'grēs

(Hellas)

LOCATION — Southern part of the Balkan Peninsula in southeastern Europe, bordering on the Ionian, Aegean and Mediterranean Seas
GOVT. — Republic
AREA — 50,949 sq. mi.
POP. — 9,740,417 (1981)
CAPITAL — Athens

In 1923 the reigning king was forced to abdicate and the following year Greece was declared a republic. In 1935, the king was recalled by a "plebiscite" of the people. Greece became a republic in June 1973. The country today includes the Aegean Islands of Chios, Mytilene (Lesbos), Samos, Icaria (Nicaria) and Lemnos, the Ionian Islands (Corfu, etc.) Crete, Macedonia, Western Thrace and part of Eastern Thrace, the Mount Athos District, Epirus and the Dodecanese Islands.

100 Lepta = 1 Drachma

Values for unused stamps are for examples with original gum as defined in the catalogue introduction. Any exceptions will be noted.

Values for Large Hermes Head stamps with double control numbers on the back, Nos. 20e, 21c, 27a, et al, are for examples with two distinct and separate impressions, not for blurred or "slide doubles" caused by paper slippage on the press.

Watermarks

Wmk. 129 — Crown and ET

Wmk. 252 — Crowns

Paris Print

Hermes (Mercury) — A1

Paris Print, Fine Impression

The enlarged illustrations show the head in various states of the plates. The differences are best seen in the shading lines on the cheek and neck.

1861 Unwmk. Typo. *Imperf.*

Without Figures on Back

1 A1 1 l choc, *brnish* 600.00 550.00
No gum 200.00
On cover, single franking 1,150.
Single franking on newspaper *1,350.*
a. 1 l red brown, *brnish* 725.00 600.00
No gum 240.00
On cover, single franking 1,200.
Single franking on newspaper *1,350.*
b. 1 l brown 575.00 475.00
No gum 200.00
On cover, single franking 1,150.
Single franking on newspaper *1,350.*
2 A1 2 l ol bis, *straw* 67.50 87.50
No gum 40.00
On cover, with other stamps *2,000.*
On cover, single franking *2,250.*
a. 2 l brown buff, *buff* 55.00 75.00
No gum 40.00
On cover, with other stamps *2,000.*
On cover, single franking *2,250.*
b. 2 l yellowish bister 55.00 75.00
No gum 22.50
On cover, single franking *2,000.*
3 A1 5 l yel grn, *grnsh* 700.00 150.00
No gum 240.00
On cover 475.00
a. 5 l emerald green 875.00 175.00
No gum 180.00
On cover 325.00
4 A1 20 l bl, *bluish* 1,150. 95.00
No gum 275.00
On cover 240.00
a. 20 l deep blue, *bluish* 1,100. 340.00
No gum 475.00
On cover —
b. On pelure paper 1,350. *275.00*
On cover —
5 A1 40 l vio, *bl* 325.00 130.00
On cover 600.00
6 A1 80 l rose, *pink* 250.00 120.00
No gum 110.00
On cover 550.00
a. 80 l carmine, *pink* 250.00 120.00
No gum 110.00
On cover 550.00

Large Figures, 8mm high, on Back

7 A1 10 l red org, *bl* 1,040. 500.00
No gum 450.00
On cover 1,650.
a. "10" on back inverted — —
c. "0" of "10" invtd. on back — *1,850.*
d. "1" of "10" invtd. on back — *2,750.*

Full margins = ¾mm.

No. 7 without "10" on back is a proof.

Trial impressions of Paris prints exist in many shades, some being close to those of the issued stamps. The gum used was thin and smooth instead of thick, brownish and crackly as on the issued stamps.

See Nos. 8-58. For surcharges see Nos. 130, 132-133, 137-139, 141-143, 147-149, 153-154, 157-158.

Values for stamps in pairs

1 A1 1 l choc, *brnish* 1,375. *1,650.*
a. 1 l red brown, *brnish* 1,500. *1,850.*
2 A1 2 l ol bis, *straw* 110.00 *300.00*
a. 2 l brown buff, *buff* 165.00 *300.00*
3 A1 5 l yel grn, *grnsh* 1,500. 450.00
4 A1 20 l bl, *bluish* 2,400. 290.00
a. 20 l deep blue, *bluish* 1,000.
5 A1 40 l vio, *bl* 620.00 *650.00*
6 A1 80 l rose, *pink* 550.00 *615.00*
a. 80 l carmine, *pink* 675.00 410.00
7 A1 10 l red org, *bl* 2,000. 1,550.

Values for stamps in strips of 3

1 A1 1 l choc, *brnish* 3,000. 600.00
2 A1 2 l ol bis, *straw* 180.00 600.00
3 A1 5 l yel grn, *grnsh* — 900.00
4 A1 20 l bl, *bluish* — 800.00
5 A1 40 l vio, *bl* 1,600. —
6 A1 80 l rose, *pink* 1,100. 1,250.
7 A1 10 l red org, *bl* — *3,250.*

Values for stamps in blocks of 4

1 A1 1 l choc, *brnish* *13,500.* *12,750.*
No gum *3,000.*
2 A1 2 l ol bis, *straw* *400.00* *1,000.*
No gum *275.00*
3 A1 5 l yel grn, *grnsh* *9,250.* —
No gum *3,500.*
4 A1 20 l bl, *bluish* *10,500.*
No gum *3,500.*
5 A1 40 l vio, *bl* *4,250.*
No gum *2,000.*
6 A1 80 l rose, *pink* *1,750.*
No gum *1,000.*
7 A1 10 l red org, *bl* *13,000.*
No gum *4,500.*

Faint quadrille, horizontal or vertical lines are visible in the background of some Athens print large Hermes head stamps.

Nos. 16, 16a, 16b are the only 1 l stamps that have these lines.

Athens Prints

Athens Print, Typical Fine Impression

Athens Print, Typical Coarse Impression

Figures on Back

5 l:

#11

#18-45

Fine Printing (F)

Fine Printing (F, '62) see footnote

Coarse Printing (C)

1861-62 Without Figures on Back

8 A1 1 l choc, *brnish* (F, '62) 490.00 *490.00*
No gum 350.00
On cover 2,750.
a. 1 l dk chocolate, *brnish* (F) 1,300. 1,325.
No gum 700.00
On cover 4,250.
b. 1 l chocolate, *brnish* (F) 590.00 590.00
No gum 460.00
On cover 2,750.
9 A1 2 l bis brn, *bister* (F) 75.00 *110.00*
No gum 40.00
On cover 1,500.
a. 2 l dark brown, *straw,* (C) *6,750.* —
On cover —
b. 2 l bister brown, *bister* (C) 90.00 *135.00*
On cover 1,750.
c. 2 l bister brown, *bister* (F, '62) 90.00 *135.00*
On cover 1,750.
10 A1 20 l dk bl, *bluish* (C) *15,000.*
On cover *75,000.*

With Figures on Back

11 A1 5 l grn, *grnsh* (F) 300.00 135.00
No gum 175.00
On cover 1,500.
a. 5 l green, *greenish* (C) 375.00 190.00
On cover —
b. As "a," double "5" on back (F, C) *2,850.*
c. 5 l green, *greenish,* bl grn figures on back (F, '62) 350.00 135.00
On cover —
12 A1 10 l org, *grnsh* (F, '62) 600.00 90.00
No gum 325.00
On cover —
a. 10 l orange, *greenish* (C) 1,950. 300.00
On cover —
c. 10 l orange, *greenish* (F) 600.00 135.00
On cover —
13 A1 20 l blue, *bluish* (F, '62) *475.00* 57.50
On cover 125.00
a. 20 l dull blue, *bluish* (C) *6,750.* 245.00
On cover 625.00
b. 20 l dark blue, *bluish,* (F) *3,500.* 110.00
On cover 490.00
14 A1 40 l red vio, *pale bl* (F, '62) *5,250.* 475.00
On cover 1,250.
a. 40 l red violet, *blue* (C) *10,000.* 600.00
On cover 1,500.
b. 40 l red violet, *blue,* (F) *5,250.* 475.00
On cover 1,250.
15 A1 80 l car, *pink* (F, '62) 1,200. 165.00
On cover 475.00
a. 80 l carmine, *pink* (F) 1,200. 165.00
On cover 475.00
b. 80 l dl rose, *pink* (F) 1,200. 165.00
On cover 475.00

Full margins = ¾mm.

Nos. 8-15 are known as the "Athens Provisionals." The first printings were not very successful, producing the "coarse printings." Later printings used an altered printing method that gave better results (the "fine printings"). All these were issued in the normal manner by the Post Office.

Nos. 8, 9c, 11c, 12, 13, 14, 15 have uninterrupted and even shading lines that do not taper off at the ends. They were produced in May 1862 (F, '62). Other fine printing stamps were produced in Feb.-Apr. 1862 (F).

The numerals on the back are strongly shaded in the right lines with the corresponding left lines being quite thin. The colors of the numerals are generally strong and often show clumps of ink.

Nos. 15a and 15b have vermilion figures on the back, while those of all later printings are carmine.

Athens Print, Consecutive Print

With Figures on Back

Except 1 l, 2 l

1862-67

16 A1 1 l brn, *brnish* (poor print) 60.00 60.00
No gum 35.00
On cover 350.00
a. 1 l red brn, *brnish* (poor print) 150.00 150.00
No gum 85.00
On cover 850.00
b. 1 l choc, *brnish* 67.50 67.50
No gum 35.00
On cover 350.00
17 A1 2 l bister, *bister* 55.00 *60.00*
No gum 30.00
On cover 825.00
a. 2 l brnsh bis, *bister* 13.00 *24.00*
No gum 7.50
On cover 550.00
18 A1 5 l grn, *grnsh* 250.00 24.00
No gum 125.00
On cover 80.00
a. 5 l yellowish green, *grnsh* 250.00 12.00
No gum 125.00
On cover 80.00
19 A1 10 l org, *blue* ('64) 400.00 47.50
No gum 225.00
On cover 95.00
a. 10 l yel org, *bluish* 650.00 60.00
No gum 350.00
On cover 150.00
b. As "a," "10" inverted on front of stamp *23,500.*
c. 10 l red org, *bl* (Dec. '65) *650.00* 27.50
No gum 350.00
On cover 75.00
d. "01" on back *9,000.* *175.00*
20 A1 20 l bl, *bluish* 250.00 24.00
No gum 115.00
On cover 17.50
a. 20 l lt bl, *bluish* (fine print) 375.00 24.00
No gum 200.00
On cover 275.00
b. 20 l dark blue, *bluish* 2,000. 67.50
No gum 1,200.
On cover, single franking 275.00
c. 20 l blue, *greenish* *1,700.* 37.50
No gum 950.00
On cover, single franking 275.00
d. "80" on back *2,450.*
e. Double "20" on back *1,500.*
f. Without "20" on back *5,500.*
21 A1 40 l lilac, *bl* 550.00 37.50
No gum 300.00
On cover 275.00
a. 40 l grayish lilac, *blue* 1,750. 37.50
On cover 275.00
b. 40 l lilac brown, *lil gray* *1,500.* 47.50
On cover 275.00
c. Double "40" on back 1,600.
22 A1 80 l car, *pale rose* 80.00 24.00
No gum 37.50
On cover 325.00
a. 80 l rose, *pale rose* 80.00 24.00
No gum 37.50
On cover 325.00
b. "8" on back inverted — 550.00
c. "80" on back inverted —
d. "8" only on back 700.00
e. "0" only on back 700.00

Nos. 16-22 represent a series of printings for each value, from 1862 through 1867, until a major cleaning of the plates was done in 1868. Impressions range from very fine and clear to coarse and blotchy.

Some printings of Nos. 16, 16a, 16b show faint vertical, horizontal or quadrilled lines in the background. Later 1 l stamps do not show these lines.

Many stamps of this and succeeding issues which are normally imperforate are known privately rouletted, pin-perforated, percé en scie, etc.

With Figures on Back, Except 1 l, 2 l

1868 From Cleaned Plates

23 A1 1 l gray brn, *brnish* 67.50 75.00
No gum 37.50
On cover, single franking 475.00
a. 1 l brown, *brownish* 67.50 82.50
No gum 37.50
On cover, single franking 475.00
b. 1 l chocolate brown 67.50 82.50
No gum 37.50
On cover, single franking 150.00
c. 1 l chocolate brown 67.50 82.50
No gum 37.50
On cover, single franking 150.00
24 A1 2 l gray bis, *bister* 32.50 *47.50*
No gum 19.00
On cover, single franking 550.00
25 A1 5 l grn, *grnsh* *6,500.* 150.00
No gum 3,750.
On cover, with other stamps *300.00*
On cover, single franking —
a. 5 l yellow green, *grnsh* 6,500. 50.00
No gum 3,750.
On cover, with other stamps *300.00*
On cover, single franking —
26 A1 10 l pale org, *bluish* *1,650.* 40.00
No gum 900.00
On cover, with other stamps *80.00*
On cover, single franking —
a. "01" on back — —
b. 10 l red orange, *bluish* 1,650. 40.00
No gum 900.00
On cover, with other stamps *80.00*
On cover, single franking —
c. 10 l red orange, *very blue* — 175.00
d. 10 l salmon, *bluish* — *650.00*
27 A1 20 l pale bl, *bluish* *1,500.* 24.00
No gum 825.00
On cover 47.50
a. Double "20" on back — *1,450.*
28 A1 40 l rose vio, *bl* 325.00 37.50
On cover 275.00
a. "20" on back, corrected to "40" — *2,750.*
29 A1 80 l rose car, *pale rose* 190.00 250.00
On cover 750.00

The "0" on the back of No. 29 is printed more heavily than the "8."

With Figures on Back, Except 1 l

1870

30 A1 1 l dp reddish brn, *brnish* 175.00 *200.00*
On cover, single franking 900.00
a. 1 l redsh brn, *brnish* 200.00 *240.00*
On cover, single franking 950.00
31 A1 20 l lt bl, *bluish* *1,900.* 24.00
On cover 67.50
a. 20 l blue, *bluish* *2,000.* 35.00
On cover 75.00
b. "02" on back 1,225.
c. "20" on back inverted 675.00

Nos. 30 and 30a have short lines of shading on cheek. The spandrels of No. 31 are very pale with the lines often broken or missing.
This was an Athens Printing made under supervision of German workmen.

Medium to Thin Paper
With Figures on Back, Except 1 l, 2 l

1870 Without Mesh

32 A1 1 l brn, *brnish* 325.00 325.00
On cover *500.00*
a. 1 l purple brown, *brnish* 325.00 325.00
On cover *500.00*
33 A1 2 l sal bis, *bister* 19.00 *45.00*
On cover 475.00
34 A1 5 l grn, *grnsh* *6,000.* 120.00
On cover 250.00
35 A1 10 l lt red org, *grnsh* — 240.00
On cover *500.00*
a. "01" on back — —
b. "10" on back inverted — —
36 A1 20 l bl, *bluish* *1,400.* 24.00
On cover 60.00
a. "02" on back — 600.00
b. Double "20" on back — 1,375.
37 A1 40 l sal, *grnsh* 825.00 82.50
On cover 400.00
a. 40 l lilac, *greenish* *75,000.*

The stamps of this issue have rather coarse figures on back.
No. 37a is printed in the exact shade of the numerals on the back of No. 37.

Thin Transparent Paper
With Figures on Back, Except 1 l

1872 Showing Mesh

38 A1 1 l grayish brn, *straw* 55.00 *75.00*
On cover *150.00*
a. 1 l red brn, *yelsh* 82.50 *115.00*
On cover *225.00*
39 A1 5 l grn, *greenish* 675.00 30.00
On cover *60.00*
a. 5 l dark green, *grnsh* 725.00 40.00
On cover *60.00*
b. Double "5" on back 225.00
40 A1 10 l red org, *grnsh* *1,050.* 37.50
On cover 80.00
a. 10 l red orange, *pale lilac* *7,750.* 150.00
On cover 300.00
b. As #40, "10" on back inverted — 90.00
c. Double "10" on back — 1,125.
d. "0" on back — 525.00
e. "01" on back — *2,100.*
41 A1 20 l dp bl, *bluish* 1,375. 30.00
On cover 67.50
a. 20 l blue, *bluish* 1,375. 32.50
On cover 67.50
b. 20 l dark blue, *blue* 2,500. 55.00
On cover 140.00
42 A1 40 l brn, *bl* 45.00 *67.50*
On cover 200.00
a. 40 l olive brown, *blue* 45.00 *70.00*
On cover 200.00
b. 40 l red violet, *blue* 1,000. 95.00
On cover 300.00
c. 40 l gray violet, *blue* 825.00 75.00
On cover 240.00
d. Figures on back bister (#42b, 42c) 1,100. 95.00

The mesh is not apparent on Nos. 38, 38a.

On Cream Paper Unless Otherwise Stated
With Figures on Back, Except 1 l, 2 l

1875

43 A1 1 l gray brn 15.00 12.00
On cover 40.00
a. 1 l Deep red brown 35.00 20.00
On cover 100.00
b. 1 l black brown, *yellowish* 175.00 *160.00*
On cover —
c. 1 l red brown 45.00 *60.00*
On cover 82.50
d. 1 l dark red brown 75.00 *87.50*
On cover 110.00
e. 1 l purple brown 75.00 *87.50*
On cover 110.00
44 A1 2 l bister 30.00 *32.50*
On cover 72.50
45 A1 5 l pale yel grn 200.00 30.00
On cover 45.00
a. 5 l dk yel grn 275.00 40.00
On cover 45.00
46 A1 10 l orange 425.00 45.00
On cover 65.00
a. 10 l orange, *yellow* 240.00 25.00
On cover 50.00
c. "00" on back 925.00 200.00
d. "1" on back — 260.00
e. "0" on back — 225.00
f. "01" on back — 535.00
g. Double "10" on back — 800.00
On cover —
47 A1 20 l ultra 160.00 24.00
On cover 67.50
a. 20 l blue 290.00 24.00
On cover 67.50
b. 20 l deep Prussian blue 1,600. 60.00
On cover 200.00
c. "02" on back — 475.00
d. "20" on back inverted — *11,000.*
e. "2" instead of "20," inverted — *3,000.*
f. Double "20" on back — 1,350.
g. "20" inverted, on front of stamp 210,000.
48 A1 40 l salmon 30.00 *90.00*
On cover 1,000.

The back figures are found in many varieties, including "1" and "0" inverted in "10."
Value for No. 47e is for example with "2" of "02" broken (deformed). Also known with unbroken "2"; value used about $600.

Paris Print, Clear Impression

1876 Without Figures on Back

49 A1 30 l ol brn, *yelsh* 290.00 60.00
On cover 525.00
a. 30 l brown, *yellowish* 500.00 135.00
On cover 950.00
50 A1 60 l grn, *grnsh* 40.00 *115.00*
On cover 3,000.

Athens Print, Coarse Impression, Yellowish Paper

51 A1 30 l dark brown 75.00 13.50
On cover 40.00
a. 30 l black brown 75.00 13.50
On cover 40.00
52 A1 60 l green 625.00 67.50
On cover 3,000.

Without Figures on Back

1880-82 Cream Paper

53 A1 5 l green 30.00 9.50
On cover, single franking 275.00
54 A1 10 l orange 27.50 9.50
On cover 140.00
a. 10 l yellow 27.50 9.50
On cover, single franking 140.00
b. 10 l red orange *8,250.* 75.00
On cover —
55 A1 20 l ultra 450.00 190.00
On cover, single franking 550.00
56 A1 20 l pale rose (aniline ink) ('82) 8.25 8.25
On cover, single franking 35.00
a. 20 l rose (aniline ink) ('82) 8.25 8.25
On cover, single franking 35.00
b. 20 l deep carmine *275.00* 17.50
On cover, single franking 160.00
57 A1 30 l ultra ('82) 225.00 17.50
On cover, single franking 175.00
a. 30 l slate blue 230.00 17.50
On cover, single franking 175.00
58 A1 40 l lilac 67.50 15.00
On cover, single franking 375.00
a. 40 l violet 67.50 24.00
On cover, single franking 375.00

Stamps of type A1 were not regularly issued with perf. 11½ but were freely used on mail.

Hermes — A2

Lepta denominations have white numeral tablets.

Belgian Print, Clear Impression

1886-88 ***Imperf.***

64 A2 1 l brown ('88) 4.00 4.00
65 A2 2 l bister ('88) 9.50 *225.00*
66 A2 5 l yel grn ('88) 12.00 2.75
67 A2 10 l yellow ('88) 16.00 2.40
68 A2 20 l car rose ('88) 45.00 4.00
69 A2 25 l blue 160.00 2.75
70 A2 40 l violet ('88) 105.00 30.00
71 A2 50 l gray grn 8.25 2.75
72 A2 1d gray 120.00 4.00
Nos. 64-72 (9) 479.75 277.65

See Nos. 81-116. For surcharges see Nos. 129, 134, 140, 144, 150, 151-152, 155-156.

1891 ***Perf. 11½***

81 A2 1 l brown 8.25 3.50
82 A2 2 l bister 13.50 —
83 A2 5 l yel grn 27.50 13.00
84 A2 10 l yellow 40.00 13.00
85 A2 20 l car rose 55.00 18.00
86 A2 25 l blue 275.00 25.00
87 A2 40 l violet 190.00 190.00
88 A2 50 l gray grn 22.50 6.50
89 A2 1d gray 200.00 8.25
Nos. 81-89 (9) 831.75 277.25

The Belgian Printings perf. 13½ and most of the values perf. 11½ (Nos. 82-86) were perforated on request of philatelists at the main post office in Athens. While not regularly issued they were freely used for postage.

Athens Print, Poor Impression
Wmk. Greek Words in Some Sheets

1889-95 ***Imperf.***

90 A2 1 l black brn 6.75 2.75
a. 1 l brown 6.75 4.00
91 A2 2 l pale bister 1.75 1.60
a. 2 l buff 2.75 *2.75*
92 A2 5 l green 11.00 1.60
a. Double impression *200.00*
b. 5 l deep green 40.00 9.50
93 A2 10 l yellow 125.00 5.50
a. 10 l orange 47.50 4.00
b. 10 l dull yellow 125.00 5.50
94 A2 20 l carmine 11.00 8.25
a. 20 l rose 75.00 40.00
95 A2 25 l dull blue 125.00 9.50
a. 25 l indigo 150.00 6.75
b. 25 l ultra 125.00 6.75
c. 25 l brt blue 135.00 9.50
96 A2 25 l lilac 13.50 2.75
a. 25 l red vio ('93) 20.00 4.00
97 A2 40 l red vio ('91) 125.00 27.50
98 A2 40 l blue ('93) 9.50 2.75
99 A2 1d gray ('95) 475.00 8.25

Perf. 13½

100 A2 1 l brown 80.00 —
101 A2 2 l buff 2.00 1.60
104 A2 20 l carmine 67.50 5.25
a. 20 l rose 80.00 6.25
105 A2 40 l red violet 130.00 47.50

Other denominations of type A2 were not officially issued with perf. 13½.

Perf. 11½

107 A2 1 l brown 3.00 1.60
a. 1 l black brown 7.25 5.75
108 A2 2 l pale bister 2.50 2.00
a. 2 l buff 2.75 2.75
109 A2 5 l pale green 13.50 2.00
a. 5 l deep green 55.00 3.00
110 A2 10 l yellow 95.00 1.25
a. 10 l dull yellow 165.00 2.50
b. 10 l orange 300.00 5.75
111 A2 20 l carmine 55.00 .75
a. 20 l rose 160.00 1.60
112 A2 25 l dull blue 110.00 3.75
a. 25 l indigo 300.00 21.00
b. 25 l ultra 110.00 52.50
c. 25 l bright blue 160.00 9.00
113 A2 25 l lilac 6.75 1.60
a. 25 l red violet 20.00 2.75
114 A2 40 l red violet 160.00 37.50
115 A2 40 l blue 16.50 2.75
116 A2 1d gray 600.00 10.00

Partly-perforated varieties sell for about twice as much as normal stamps.
The watermark on Nos. 90-116 consists of three Greek words meaning Paper for Public Service. It is in double-lined capitals, measures 270x35mm, and extends across three panes.

Boxers — A3

Discobolus by Myron — A4

Vase Depicting Pallas Athene (Minerva) — A5

Chariot Driving A6

Stadium and Acropolis A7

Statue of Hermes by Praxiteles — A8

Statue of Victory by Paeonius — A9

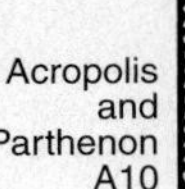

Acropolis and Parthenon A10

Perf. 14x13½, 13½x14

1896 Unwmk.

117 A3 1 l ocher 4.00 3.00
118 A3 2 l rose 3.00 3.00
a. Without engraver's name 30.00 21.00
119 A4 5 l lilac 12.50 5.25
120 A4 10 l slate gray 12.50 7.25
121 A5 20 l red brn 25.00 8.25
122 A6 25 l red 30.00 10.50
123 A5 40 l violet 14.50 9.50
124 A6 60 l black 42.50 21.00
125 A7 1d blue 115.00 26.00
126 A8 2d bister 325.00 105.00
a. Horiz. pair, imperf. btwn. —
127 A9 5d green 575.00 500.00
128 A10 10d brown 625.00 550.00
Nos. 117-128 (12) 1,784. 1,249.

1st intl. Olympic Games of the modern era, held at Athens. Counterfeits of Nos. 123-124 and 126-128 exist.
For surcharges see Nos. 159-164.

Preceding Issues Surcharged

1900 ***Imperf.***

129 A2 20 l on 25 l dl bl, #95c 3.00 1.60
a. 20 l on 25 l indigo, #95a 67.50 47.50
b. 20 l on 25 l ultra, #95b 70.00 55.00
c. Double surcharge 57.50 57.50
d. Triple surcharge 85.00 85.00
e. Inverted surcharge 60.00 57.50
f. "20" above word 110.00 105.00
g. Pair, one without surcharge 250.00 250.00
h. "20" without word 165.00 165.00

130 A1 30 l on 40 l vio, *cr*, #58a 6.50 6.25
a. 30 l on 40 l lilac, #58 15.50 15.50
b. Broad "0" in "30" 10.50 8.25
c. First letter of word is "A" 135.00 135.00
d. Double surcharge *625.00* *625.00*
132 A1 40 l on 2 l bis, *cr*, #44 8.50 8.25
a. Broad "0" in "40" 12.50 12.50
b. First letter of word is "A" 165.00 165.00
133 A1 50 l on 40 l sal, *cr*, #48 6.25 6.25
a. Broad "0" in "50" 10.00 8.25
b. First letter of word is "A" 135.00 135.00
c. "50" without word 200.00 175.00
d. "50" above word 200.00 175.00
134 A2 1d on 40 l red vio (No. 97) 15.50 6.25
137 A1 3d on 10 l org, *cr*, #54 52.50 52.50
a. 3d on 10 l yellow, #54a 52.50 52.50
138 A1 5d on 40 l red vio, *bl*, #21 150.00 150.00
a. 5d on 40 l red vio, *bl*, #28 190.00 *190.00*
b. "20" on back corrected to "40" *1,400.*
139 A1 5d on 40 l red vio, *bl*, #42b 575.00

Perf. 11½

140 A2 20 l on 25 l dl bl, #112 3.25 3.25
a. 20 l on 25 l indigo, #112a 100.00 90.00
b. 20 l on 25 l ultra, #112b 80.00 77.50
c. Double surcharge 67.50 70.00
d. Triple surcharge 95.00 95.00
e. Inverted surcharge 67.50 67.50
f. "20" above word 150.00 150.00
141 A1 30 l on 40 l vio, *cr*, #58a 10.50 10.50
a. 30 l on 40 l lilac, #58 17.50 17.50
b. Broad "0" in "30" 12.50 12.50
c. First letter of word is "A" 150.00 150.00
d. Double surcharge
142 A1 40 l on 2 l bis, *cr*, #44 15.50 15.50
a. Broad "0" in "40" 15.50 15.50
b. First letter of word is "A" 165.00 165.00
143 A1 50 l on 40 l sal, *cr*, #48 10.50 10.50
a. Broad "0" in "50" 12.50 12.50
b. First letter of word is "A" 135.00 135.00
c. "50" without word 200.00 175.00
144 A2 1d on 40 l red vio, #114 145.00 160.00
147 A1 3d on 10 l yel, *cream*, #54a 57.50 57.50
a. 3d on 10 l org, *cr*, #54 60.00 *65.00*
148 A1 5d on 40 l red vio, *bl*, #21 150.00 175.00
a. 5d on 40 l red vio, *bl*, #28 175.00 *225.00*
149 A1 5d on 40 l red vio, *bl*, #42b 625.00

Perf. 13½

150 A2 2d on 40 l red vio, #105 12.00 12.50

The 1d on 40 l perf. 13½ and the 2d on 40 l, both imperf. and perf. 13½, were not officially issued.

Surcharge Including "A M"

"A M" = "Axia Metalliki" or "Value in Metal (gold)."

1900 ***Imperf.***

151 A2 25 l on 40 l vio, #70 6.00 10.50
152 A2 50 l on 25 l bl, #69 26.50 24.00
153 A1 1d on 40 l brn, *bl*, #42b 125.00 *150.00*
154 A1 2d on 5 l grn, *cr*, #53 16.00 *21.00*

Perf. 11½

155 A2 25 l on 40 l vio, #87 12.00 15.50
156 A2 50 l on 25 l bl, #86 52.50 62.50
157 A1 1d on 40 l brn, *bl*, #42b 160.00 160.00
158 A1 2d on 5 l grn, *cr*, #53 20.00 26.00
Nos. 151-158 (8) 418.00 469.50

Partly-perforated varieties of Nos. 129-158 sell for about two to three times as much as normal stamps.

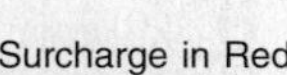

Surcharge in Red

1900-01 ***Perf. 14x13½***

159 A7 5 l on 1d blue 15.00 9.50
a. Wrong font "M" with serifs 75.00 *80.00*
b. Double surcharge 225.00 200.00
160 A5 25 l on 40 l vio 70.00 67.50
a. Double surcharge 900.00
161 A8 50 l on 2d bister 80.00 62.50
a. Broad "0" in "50" 80.00 62.50
162 A9 1d on 5d grn ('01) 250.00 200.00
a. Greek "Δ" instead of "A" as 3rd letter 650.00 700.00
163 A10 2d on 10d brn ('01) 70.00 *100.00*
a. Greek "Δ" instead of "A" as 3rd letter 275.00 250.00
Nos. 159-163 (5) 485.00 439.50

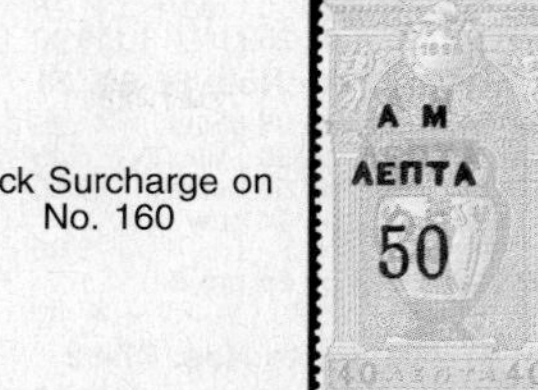

Black Surcharge on No. 160

164 A5 50 l on 25 l on 40 l vio (R + Bk) 500.00 475.00
a. Broad "0" in "50" 475.00 *575.00*

Nos. 151-164 and 179-183, gold currency stamps, were generally used for parcel post and foreign money orders. They were also available for use on letters, but cost about 20 per cent more than the regular stamps of the same denomination.

Counterfeit surcharges exist of Nos. 159-164.

Giovanni da Bologna's Hermes
A11 A12

A13

Type I

Type II

FIVE LEPTA.

Type I — Letters of "ΕΛΛΑΣ" not outlined at top and left. Only a few faint horizontal lines between the outer vertical lines at sides.

Type II — Letters of "ΕΛΛΑΣ" fully outlined. Heavy horizontal lines between the vertical frame lines.

Perf. 11½, 12½, 13½

1901 **Engr.** **Wmk. 129**

165 A11 1 l yellow brn .40 .25
166 A11 2 l gray .60 .25
167 A11 3 l orange .65 .30
168 A12 5 l grn, type I .80 .25
a. 5 l yellow green, type I .60 .25
b. 5 l yellow green, type II .60 .25
169 A12 10 l rose 3.25 .25
170 A11 20 l red lilac 6.50 .25
171 A12 25 l ultra 6.50 .25
172 A11 30 l dl vio 12.00 2.00
173 A11 40 l dk brn 25.00 3.00
174 A11 50 l brn lake 20.00 1.50

Perf. 12½, 14 and Compound

175 A13 1d black 47.50 3.00
a. Horiz. pair, imperf. btwn. 325.00
c. Horiz. pair, imperf. vert. 300.00
d. Vert. pair, imperf. horiz. 300.00

Litho.

Perf. 12½

176 A13 2d bronze 11.00 8.00
177 A13 3d silver 11.00 *12.00*
178 A13 5d gold 13.00 *15.00*
Nos. 165-178 (14) 158.20 46.30
Set, never hinged 325.00

All values 1 l through 1d issued on both thick and thin paper. Nos. 173-174 are values for thin paper — values for thick paper are higher.

For overprints and surcharges see Nos. RA3-RA13, N16, N109.

Imperf., Pairs

165a	A11	1 l	12.00
166a	A11	2 l	15.00
167a	A11	3 l	15.00
168c	A12	5 l	12.00
169a	A12	10 l	19.00
170a	A11	20 l	15.00
171a	A12	25 l	15.00
172a	A11	30 l	250.00
173a	A11	40 l	300.00
174a	A11	50 l	70.00
175b	A13	1d	250.00

Nos. 165a-175a were issued on both thick and thin paper. Values are for the less expensive thin paper.

Hermes — A14

1902, Jan. 1 **Engr.** ***Perf. 13½***

179 A14 5 l deep orange 2.00 1.10
a. Imperf., pair 82.50
180 A14 25 l emerald 30.00 3.00
181 A14 50 l ultra 30.00 3.75
a. Imperf., pair 550.00
182 A14 1d rose red 30.00 8.25
183 A14 2d orange brn 52.50 50.00
Nos. 179-183 (5) 144.50 66.10
Set, never hinged 375.00

See note after No. 164. In 1913 remainders of Nos. 179-183 were used as postage dues.

Apollo Throwing Discus
A15

Jumper, with Jumping Weights
A16

Victory — A17

Atlas and Hercules
A18

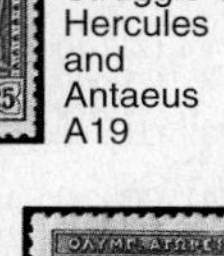
Struggle of Hercules and Antaeus
A19

Wrestlers
A20

Daemon of the Games
A21

Foot Race
A22

Nike, Priest and Athletes in Pre-Games Offering to Zeus
A23

Wmk. Crown and ET (129)

1906, Mar. **Engr.** ***Perf. 13½, 14***

184 A15 1 l brown .55 .40
a. Imperf., pair *300.00*
185 A15 2 l gray .55 .40
a. Imperf., pair *300.00*
186 A16 3 l orange .55 .40
a. Imperf., pair 300.00
187 A16 5 l green 1.25 .40
a. Imperf., pair 110.00
188 A17 10 l rose red 3.00 .60
a. Imperf., pair *300.00*
189 A18 20 l magenta 5.00 .60
a. Imperf., pair *575.00*
190 A19 25 l ultra 6.00 .85
a. Imperf., pair *575.00*
191 A20 30 l dl pur 5.00 2.75
a. Double impression *1,100.*
192 A21 40 l dk brown 5.00 2.75
193 A18 50 l brn lake 10.00 3.25
194 A22 1d gray blk 65.00 13.00
a. Imperf., pair *1,100.*
195 A22 2d rose 100.00 35.00
196 A22 3d olive yel 155.00 125.00
197 A23 5d dull blue 160.00 140.00
Nos. 184-197 (14) 516.90 325.40
Set, never hinged 1,500.

Greek Special Olympic Games of 1906 at Athens, celebrating the 10th anniv. of the modern Olympic Games.

Surcharged stamps of this issue are revenues.

A24

Iris Holding Caduceus
A25

Hermes Donning Sandals
A26

Hermes Carrying Infant Arcas — A27

Hermes, from Old Cretan Coin — A28

Designs A24 to A28 are from Cretan and Arcadian coins of the 4th Century, B.C.

Serrate Roulette 13½

1911-21 **Engr.** **Unwmk.**

198 A24 1 l green .65 .30
199 A25 2 l car rose .65 .30
200 A24 3 l vermilion .95 .30
201 A26 5 l green 2.00 .30
202 A24 10 l car rose 9.50 .30
203 A25 20 l gray lilac 3.00 .80
204 A25 25 l ultra 15.00 .80
a. Rouletted in black 190.00 140.00
205 A26 30 l car rose 4.50 1.60
206 A25 40 l deep blue 10.00 4.00
207 A26 50 l dl vio 15.00 3.00
208 A27 1d ultra 20.00 .80
209 A27 2d vermilion 27.50 .95
210 A27 3d car rose 27.50 1.40
a. Size 20¼x25½mm ('21) 100.00 50.00
211 A27 5d ultra 35.00 4.00
a. Size 20¼x25½mm ('21) 200.00 25.00

212 A27 10d dp bl ('21) 140.00 70.00
a. Size 20x26½mm ('11) 300.00 125.00
213 A28 25d deep blue 87.50 55.00
Nos. 198-213 (16) 398.75 143.85
Set, never hinged 750.00

The 1921 reissues of the 3d, 5d and 10d measure 20¼x25½mm instead of 20x26½mm.

See Nos. 214-231. For overprints see Nos. 233-248B, N1, N10-N15, N17-N52A, N110-N148, Thrace 22-30, N26-N75.

Imperf., Pairs

198a A24 1 l 90.00 90.00
200a A24 3 l 240.00 240.00
201a A26 5 l 30.00 30.00
202a A24 10 l 52.50 52.50
203a A25 20 l 225.00 225.00
204b A25 25 l 300.00 300.00
206a A25 40 l 350.00
207a A26 50 l 350.00
208a A27 1d 350.00
209a A27 2d 350.00
210b A27 3d 350.00
211b A27 5d 240.00
212b A27 10d As "a" *1,600.*
213a A28 25d *2,250.*

Serrate Roulette 10½x13½, 13½

1913-23 **Litho.**

214 A24 1 l green .25 .25
a. Without period after "ΕΛ-ΛΑΣ" 77.50 —
215 A25 2 l rose .25 .25
216 A24 3 l vermilion .25 .25
217 A26 5 l green .25 .25
218 A24 10 l carmine .25 .25
219 A25 15 l dl bl ('18) .35 .25
220 A25 20 l slate .35 .25
221 A25 25 l ultra 4.00 .50
a. 25 l blue .25 .25
c. Double impression —
222 A26 30 l rose ('14) .95 .40
223 A25 40 l indigo ('14) 2.10 .70
224 A26 50 l vio brn ('14) 4.25 .35
225 A26 80 l vio brn ('23) 5.25 1.40
226 A27 1d ultra ('19) 7.00 .70
227 A27 2d ver ('19) 6.50 .70
228 A27 3d car rose ('20) 8.50 .80
229 A27 5d ultra ('22) 12.00 1.00
230 A27 10d dp bl ('22) 12.00 1.25
231 A28 25d indigo ('22) 16.00 4.75
Nos. 214-231 (18) 80.50 14.30
Set, never hinged 225.00

Nos. 221, 223 and 226 were re-issued in 1926, printed in Vienna from new plates. There are slight differences in minor details.

The 10 lepta brown, on thick paper, type A28, is not a postage stamp. It was issued in 1922 to replace coins of this denomination during a shortage of copper.

Imperf., Pairs

214b A24 1 l 65.00
215a A25 2 l 110.00
216a A24 3 l 175.00
217a A26 5 l 65.00
218a A24 10 l 82.50
220a A25 20 l 82.50
221b A25 25 l 175.00
222a A26 30 l 175.00
223a A25 40 l 175.00
224a A26 50 l 300.00
225b A26 80 l 92.50
226a A27 1d 250.00
227a A27 2d 100.00
228b A27 3d 300.00
229a A27 5d 360.00

Raising Greek Flag at Suda Bay, Crete A29

1913, Dec. 1 **Engr.** ***Perf. 14½***

232 A29 25 l blue & black 8.00 5.00
Never hinged 16.00
a. Imperf., pair *1,400.*

Union of Crete with Greece. Used only in Crete.

Stamps of 1911-14 Overprinted in Red or Black

Serrate Roulette 13½

1916, Nov. 1 **Litho.**

233 A24 1 l green (R) .25 .25
234 A25 2 l rose .25 .25
235 A24 3 l vermilion .25 .25
236 A26 5 l green (R) .50 .40
237 A24 10 l carmine .75 .40
238 A25 20 l slate (R) 1.50 .40
239 A25 25 l blue (R) 1.50 .40
a. 25 l ultra 140.00 26.00
240 A26 30 l rose 1.50 .90
a. Pair, one without ovpt.
241 A25 40 l indigo (R) 11.00 3.00
242 A26 50 l vio brn (R) 37.50 2.50

Engr.

243 A24 3 l vermilion .50 .50
244 A26 30 l car rose 1.25 1.25
245 A27 1d ultra (R) 40.00 .80
a. Rouletted in black 325.00 225.00
246 A27 2d vermilion 24.00 3.50
247 A27 3d car rose 14.00 3.50
248 A27 5d ultra (R) 95.00 15.00
248B A27 10d dp bl (R) 24.00 22.50
Nos. 233-248B (17) 253.75 55.80
Set, never hinged 500.00

Most of Nos. 233-248B exist with overprint double, inverted, etc. Minimum value of errors $18. Excellent counterfeits of the overprint varieties exist.

Issued by the Venizelist Provisional Government

Iris — A32

1917, Feb. 5 **Litho.** ***Perf. 14***

249 A32 1 l dp green .40 .25
250 A32 5 l yel grn .40 .25
251 A32 10 l rose .80 .35
252 A32 25 l lt blue 1.10 .35
253 A32 50 l gray vio 9.00 2.50
254 A32 1d ultra 2.25 .75
255 A32 2d lt red 4.50 1.50
256 A32 3d claret 25.00 7.75
257 A32 5d gray bl 5.75 3.00
258 A32 10d dk blue 70.00 20.00
259 A32 25d slate 125.00 *160.00*
Nos. 249-259 (11) 244.20 196.70
Set, never hinged 400.00

The 4d was used only as a revenue stamp.

Imperf., Pairs

249a A32 1 l 9.50
250a A32 5 l 9.50
251a A32 10 l 9.50
252a A32 25 l 17.50
253a A32 50 l 25.00
254a A32 1d 22.50
255a A32 2d 30.00
256a A32 3d 65.00
257a A32 5d 65.00
258a A32 10d 110.00
259a A32 25d 125.00

Stamps of 1917 Surcharged

1923

260 A32 5 l on 10 l rose .25 .25
a. Inverted surcharge 24.00 *35.00*
261 A32 50 l on 50 l gray vio .25 .25
262 A32 1d on 1d ultra .25 .25
a. 1d on 1d gray .25 .25
263 A32 2d on 2d lt red .55 .55
264 A32 3d on 3d claret 1.60 1.60
265 A32 5d on 5d dk bl 2.00 2.00
266 A32 25d on 25d slate 27.50 27.50
Nos. 260-266 (7) 32.40 32.40
Set, never hinged 125.00

Same Surcharge on Occupation of Turkey Stamps, 1913

Perf. 13½

267 O2 5 l on 3 l org .25 .25
a. Inverted surcharge 19.00
268 O1 10 l on 20 l vio 1.50 1.50
a. Inverted surcharge 82.50
269 O2 10 l on 25 l pale bl .25 .25
a. Inverted surcharge 60.00 35.00
270 O1 10 l on 30 l gray grn .25 .25
271 O2 10 l on 40 l ind 1.25 1.25
272 O1 50 l on 50 l dk bl .25 .25
a. Inverted surcharge 72.50 37.50
273 O1 2d on 2d gray brn 60.00 60.00
274 O2 3d on 3d dl bl 4.50 *6.00*
a. Imperf., pair 500.00
275 O1 5d on 5d gray 4.00 *7.00*
276 O2 10d on 1d vio brn 15.00 *22.50*
276A O2 10d on 10d car 800.00
Never hinged 1,200.
Nos. 267-276 (10) 87.25 99.25
Set, never hinged 150.00

Dangerous counterfeits of No. 276A exist.

Same Surcharge on Stamps of Crete

Perf. 14

On Crete Nos. 50, 52, 59

276B A6 5 l on 1 l red brn 27.50 27.50
277 A8 10 l on 10 l red .25 .25
277B A8 10 l on 25 l bl 110.00 110.00

On Crete Nos. 66-69, 71

278 A8 10 l on 25 l blue .25 .25
279 A6 50 l on 50 l lilac .45 *.70*
279A A6 50 l on 50 l ultra 8.50 *14.00*
280 A9 50 l on 1d gray vio 3.00 *4.00*
280A A11 50 l on 5d grn & blk 27.50 27.50

On Crete Nos. 77-82

281 A15 10 l on 20 l bl grn 125.00 125.00
282 A16 10 l on 25 l ultra .45 .45
a. Double surcharge 50.00 50.00
283 A17 50 l on 50 l yel brn .25 .35
284 A18 50 l on 1d rose car & brn 2.00 1.75
a. Imperf., pair 425.00
285 A19 3d on 3d org & blk 14.00 14.00
286 A20 5d on 5d ol grn & blk 9.00 9.00

On Crete Nos. 83-84

287 A21 10 l on 25 l bl & blk 3.25 1.75
a. Imperf., pair
287B A22 50 l on 1d grn & blk 8.00 4.50

On Crete No. 96

288 A23 10 l on 10 l brn red .25 .25
a. Inverted surcharge 45.00 40.00

On Crete No. 91

288B A17 50 l on 50 l yel brn *800.00*

Dangerous counterfeits of the overprint on No. 288B are plentiful.

On Crete No. 109

289 A19 3d on 3d org & blk 17.50 17.50

On Crete Nos. 111, 113-120

290 A6 5 l on 1 l vio brn .25 .25
a. Inverted surcharge 25.00
291 A13 5 l on 5 l grn .25 .25
a. Inverted surcharge 47.50
292 A23 10 l on 10 l brn red .25 .25
a. Inverted surcharge 47.50
293 A15 10 l on 20 l bl grn .30 .30
a. Inverted surcharge 47.50
294 A16 10 l on 25 l ultra .35 .35
a. Inverted surcharge 47.50
295 A17 50 l on 50 l yel brn .40 .40
296 A18 50 l on 1d rose car & brn 5.25 5.25
a. Inverted surcharge
b. Double surcharge 225.00
c. Double surch., one invtd.
d. Imperf., pair
297 A19 3d on 3d org & blk 16.00 16.00
298 A20 5d on 5d ol grn & blk 200.00 200.00

Dangerous counterfeits of No. 298 exist.

Crete Nos. J2-J9

299 D1 5 l on 5 l red .25 .25
a. Inverted surcharge 45.00 6.75
300 D1 5 l on 10 l red .30 .30
301 D1 10 l on 20 l red 12.00 12.00
a. Inverted surcharge
302 D1 10 l on 40 l red .30 .30
303 D1 50 l on 50 l red .30 *.55*
304 D1 50 l on 1d red .30 .50
a. Double surcharge
305 D1 50 l on 1d on 1d red 9.50 9.50
306 D1 2d on 2d red 1.25 1.25

On Crete Nos. J11-J13

307 D1 5 l on 5 l red 6.00 6.00
308 D1 5 l on 10 l red 1.50 1.50
a. "ΕΛΛΑΣ" inverted 6.50
309 D1 10 l on 20 l red 55.00 55.00

On Crete Nos. J20-J22, J24-J26

310 D1 5 l on 5 l red .25 .25
311 D1 5 l on 10 l red .25 .25
a. Inverted surcharge 12.00
312 D1 10 l on 20 l red .25 .25
313 D1 50 l on 50 l red .55 .55
314 D1 50 l on 1d red 4.00 4.00
315 D1 2d on 2d red 7.00 7.00

These surcharged Postage Due stamps were intended for the payment of ordinary postage.

Nos. 260 to 315 were surcharged in commemoration of the revolution of 1922.

Nos. 59, 91, 109, 111, 113-120, J11-J13, J20-J22, J24-J26 are on stamps previously overprinted by Crete.

Issues of the Republic

Lord Byron — A33

Byron at Missolonghi — A34

1924, Apr. 16 **Engr.** ***Perf. 12***

316 A33 80 l dark blue .55 .25
317 A34 2d dk vio & blk 1.25 .65
Set, never hinged 3.25

Death of Lord Byron (1788-1824) at Missolonghi.

Tomb of Markos Botsaris — A35

Serrate Roulette 13½

1926, Apr. 24 **Litho.**

318 A35 25 l lilac .85 .50
Never hinged 1.75

Centenary of the defense of Missolonghi against the Turks.

Corinth Canal A36

Macedonian Costume A38

Dodecanese Costume A37

Monastery of Simon Peter on Mt. Athos A39

White Tower of Salonika A40

Temple of Hephaestus A41

The Acropolis — A42

Cruiser "Georgios Averoff" — A43

Academy of Sciences, Athens — A44

Temple of Hephaestus A45

Acropolis A46

Perf. 12½x13, 13, 13x12½, 13½, 13½x13

1927, Apr. 1 **Engr.**

No.	Type	Description	Unused	Used
321	A36	5 l dark green	.25	.25
a.		Vert. pair, imperf. horiz.	140.00	92.50
322	A37	10 l orange red	.30	.25
a.		Horiz. pair, imperf. between	140.00	92.50
c.		Double impression	77.50	
323	A38	20 l violet	.30	.25
324	A39	25 l slate blue	.50	.25
a.		Imperf., pair	140.00	140.00
b.		Vert. pair, imperf. between	150.00	110.00
325	A40	40 l slate blue	.50	.25
326	A36	50 l violet	1.10	.25
327	A36	80 l dk bl & blk	.95	.25
a.		Imperf., pair	825.00	
328	A41	1d dk bl & bis brn (I)	1.10	.25
a.		Imperf., pair	150.00	125.00
b.		Center inverted		*6,500.*
c.		Double impression of center	325.00	225.00
d.		Double impression of frame	325.00	225.00
329	A42	2d dk grn & blk	6.50	.30
a.		Imperf., pair	600.00	*800.00*
330	A43	3d dp vio & blk	6.00	.30
a.		Double impression of center	225.00	*275.00*
b.		Center inverted		*8,000.*
331	A44	5d yel & blk	15.00	2.00
a.		Imperf., pair	925.00	925.00
b.		Center inverted	10,000.	*4,500.*
c.		5d yellow & green	110.00	37.50
332	A45	10d brn car & blk	45.00	11.00
333	A44	15d brt yel grn & blk	57.50	16.00
334	A46	25d green & blk	110.00	18.00
a.		Double impression of center		—
		Nos. 321-334 (14)	245.00	49.60
		Set, never hinged	700.00	

See Nos. 364-371 and notes preceding No. 364. For overprints see Nos. RA55, RA57, RA60; and RA66, RA70-RA71 in Scott Standard catalogue, Vol. 3.

This series as prepared, included a 1 lepton dark brown, type A37, but that value was never issued. Most stamps were burned. Value $300.

Gen. Charles N. Fabvier and Acropolis A47

1927, Aug. 1 *Perf. 12*

No.	Type	Description	Unused	Used
335	A47	1d red	.30	.25
336	A47	3d dark blue	2.00	.60
337	A47	6d green	12.00	9.00
		Nos. 335-337 (3)	14.30	9.85
		Set, never hinged	42.50	

Cent. of the liberation of Athens from the Turks in 1826.

For surcharges see Nos. 376-377.

Bay of Navarino and Pylos A48

Battle of Navarino A49

"Edward" omitted — A50

"Edward" added — A51

Admiral de Rigny — A52

Admiral van der Heyden — A53

Designs: Nos. 340-341, Sir Edward Codrington.

Perf. 13½x12½, 12½x13½, 13x12½, 12½x13

1927-28 **Litho.**

No.	Type	Description	Unused	Used
338	A48	1.50d gray green	1.60	.35
a.		Imperf., pair	275.00	
b.		Horiz. pair, imperf. btwn.	875.00	
c.		Horiz. pair, imperf. vert.	250.00	
339	A49	4d dk gray bl ('28)	7.00	1.50
340	A50	5d dk brn & gray	5.50	*4.75*
a.		5d blk brn & blk ('28)	13.00	6.50
341	A51	5d dk brn & blk ('28)	35.00	12.00
342	A52	5d vio bl & blk ('28)	35.00	12.00
343	A53	5d lake & blk ('28)	20.00	9.50
		Nos. 338-343 (6)	104.10	40.10
		Set, never hinged	275.00	

Centenary of the naval battle of Navarino.

For surcharges see Nos. 372-375.

Admiral Lascarina Bouboulina A54

Athanasios Diakos A55

Map of Greece in 1830 and 1930 — A56

Sortie from Missolonghi A58

Patriots Declaring Independence — A57

Portraits: 10 l, Constantine Rhigas Ferreos. 20 l, Gregorios V. 40 l, Prince Alexandros Ypsilantis. No. 345, Bouboulina. No. 355, Diakos. No. 346, Theodoros Kolokotronis. No. 356, Konstantinos Kanaris. No.347, Georgios Karaiskakis. No. 357, Markos Botsaris. 2d, Andreas Miaoulis. 3d, Lazaros Koundouriotis. 5d, Count John Capo d'Istria (Capodistria), statesman and doctor. 10d, Petros Mavromichalis. 15d, Dionysios Solomos. 20d, Adamantios Korais.

Various Frames

1930, Apr. 1 **Engr.** ***Perf. 13½, 14***

Imprint of Perkins, Bacon & Co.

No.	Type	Description	Unused	Used
344	A55	10 l brown	.25	.25
345	A54	50 l red	.25	.25
346	A54	1d car rose	.30	.30
347	A55	1.50d lt blue	.40	.40
348	A55	2d orange	.45	.45
349	A55	5d purple	1.50	1.50
350	A54	10d gray blk	6.50	6.50
351	A54	15d yellow grn	12.00	12.00
352	A55	20d blue blk	17.50	17.50

Imprint of Bradbury, Wilkinson & Co.

Perf. 12

No.	Type	Description	Unused	Used
353	A55	20 l black	.25	.25
354	A55	40 l blue grn	.25	.25
355	A55	50 l brt blue	.25	.25
356	A55	1d brown org	.30	.30
357	A55	1.50d dk red	.40	.40
358	A55	3d dk brown	.65	.65
359	A56	4d dk blue	3.00	3.00
360	A57	25d black	17.50	17.50
361	A58	50d red brn	45.00	45.00
		Nos. 344-361 (18)	106.75	106.75
		Set, never hinged	275.00	

Greek independence, cent. Some exist imperf.

Arcadi Monastery and Abbot Gabriel (Mt. Ida in Background) A60

1930, Nov. 8 *Perf. 12*

No.	Type	Description	Unused	Used
363	A60	8d deep violet	13.00	1.10
		Never hinged	55.00	

Issue of 1927 Re-engraved

Type I

Type II

1d. Type I — Greek letters "Λ," "A," "Δ" have sharp pointed tops; numerals "1" are 1½mm wide at the foot, and have a straight slanting serif at top.

1d. Type II — Greek letters "Λ," "A," "Δ" have flat tops; numerals "1" are 2mm wide at foot and the serif at top is slightly curved. Perf. 14.

There are many minor differences in the lines of the two designs.

1d. Type III — The "1" in lower left corner has no serif at left of foot. Lines of temple have been deepened, so details stand out more clearly.

2d. On 1927 stamp the Parthenon is indistinct and blurred. On 1933 stamp it is strongly outlined and clear. Between the two pillars at lower right are four blocks of marble. These blocks are clear and distinct on the 1933 stamp but run together on the 1927 issue.

3d. Design is clearer, especially vertical lines of shading in smoke stacks and reflections in the water. Two or more sides perf. 11½.

10d. Background and shading of entire stamp have been lightened. Detail of frame is clearer and more distinct.

15d. Many more lines of shading in sky and foreground. Engraving is sharp and clear, particularly in frame. Two or more sides perf. 11½.

25d. Background has been lightened and foreground reduced until base of larger upright column is removed and fallen column appears nearly submerged.

50 l, Design is clearer, especially "50" and the 10 letters.

Sizes in millimeters:

50 l, 1927, 18x24¾. 1933, 18½x24½.

1d, 1927, 24¾x17¾. 1931, 24¾x17¼. 1933, 24½x18¼.

2d, 1927, 24½x17¾. 1933, 24½x18½.

Perf. 11½, 11½x12½, 12½x10, 13, 13x12½, 14

1931-35

No.	Type	Description	Unused	Used
364	A36	50 l dk vio ('33)	4.00	1.00
365	A41	1d dk bl & org brn, type II	10.00	1.00
366	A41	1d dk bl & org brn, type III ('33)	5.75	.25
367	A42	2d dk grn & blk ('33)	2.75	.50
368	A43	3d red vio & blk ('34)	3.25	.25
a.		Imperf., pair		
369	A45	10d brn car & blk ('35)	47.50	1.50
370	A44	15d pale yel grn & blk ('34)	82.50	17.50
a.		Imperf., pair		*1,100.*
371	A46	25d dk grn & blk ('35)	25.00	17.00
		Nos. 364-371 (8)	180.75	39.00
		Set, never hinged	600.00	

Nos. 336-337, 340-343 Surcharged in Red

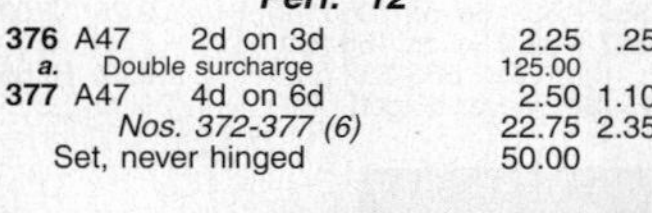

1932 *Perf. 12½x13½, 12½x13*

No.	Type	Description	Unused	Used
372	A52	1.50d on 5d	2.00	.25
373	A53	1.50d on 5d	2.00	.25
a.		Double surcharge	110.00	
374	A50	2d on 5d	5.00	.25
375	A51	2d on 5d	9.00	.25

Perf. 12

No.	Type	Description	Unused	Used
376	A47	2d on 3d	2.25	.25
a.		Double surcharge	125.00	
377	A47	4d on 6d	2.50	1.10
		Nos. 372-377 (6)	22.75	2.35
		Set, never hinged	50.00	

Adm. Pavlos Koundouriotis and Cruiser "Averoff" — A61

Pallas Athene — A62

Youth of Marathon — A63

1933 *Perf. 13½x13, 13x13½*

No.	Type	Description	Unused	Used
378	A61	50d black & ind	50.00	1.60
a.		Imperf., pair	*2,250.*	
379	A62	75d blk & vio brn	110.00	*175.00*
a.		Imperf., pair	825.00	
		Never hinged	1,700.	
380	A63	100d brn & dull grn	625.00	29.00
a.		Imperf., pair	2,750.	
		Nos. 378-380 (3)	785.00	*205.60*
		Set, never hinged	1,800.	

The imperf pairs are without gum.

For surcharges see Nos. 386-387.

Approach to Athens Stadium A64

Perf. 11½, 11½x10, 13x11½

1934, Dec. 10

No.	Type	Description	Unused	Used
381	A64	8d blue	65.00	2.25
		Never hinged	200.00	

Perforations on No. 381 range from 10½ to 13, including compounds.

Church of Pantanassa, Mistra — A65

1935, Nov. 1 *Perf. 13x12½*
382 A65 4d brown 17.00 1.60
Never hinged 47.50
a. Horiz. pair, imperf. between 725.00
b. Imperf., pair 725.00

Issues of the Monarchy

J71, J76, J82, 380, 379 Surcharged in Red or Blue

Nos. 383-385

Nos. 386-387

Serrate Roulette 13½
1935, Nov. 24 **Litho.**
383 D3 50 l on 40 l indigo (R) .25 .25
a. Double surcharge 27.50
384 D3 3d on 3d car (Bl) .55 .40

Perf. 13
385 D3 3d on 3d rose red (Bl) 2.75 2.00

Perf. 13x13½
386 A63 5d on 100d (R) 2.25 2.00
387 A62 15d on 75d (Bl) 6.50 6.00
Nos. 383-387 (5) 12.30 10.65
Set, never hinged 30.00

King Constantine — A66

Center Engr., Frame Litho.
Perf. 12x13½
1936, Nov. 18 **Wmk. 252**
389 A66 3d black & brown .55 .40
a. Pair, printer's name in Greek 22.50
b. Pair, printer's name in English 22.50
390 A66 8d black & blue 1.10 .90
a. Pair, printer's name in Greek 22.50
b. Pair, printer's name in English 22.50
Set, never hinged 3.25

Re-burial of the remains of King Constantine and Queen Sophia.

Two printings exist, the first containing varieties "a" and "b" with gray border; second with black border.

King George II — A67

1937, Jan. 24 **Engr.** *Perf. 12½x12*
391 A67 1d green .25 .25
392 A67 3d red brown .25 .25
393 A67 8d dp blue .90 .40
394 A67 100d carmine lake 12.00 12.00
Nos. 391-394 (4) 13.40 12.90
Set, never hinged 30.00

For surcharges see Nos. 484-487, 498-500, RA86-RA87, N241-N242 in Scott Standard catalogue, Vol. 3.

Pallas Athene — A68

1937, Apr. 17 **Unwmk.** *Perf. 11½*
395 A68 3d yellow brown .55 .25
Never hinged 1.10

Centenary of the University of Athens.

Contest with Bull — A69

Lady of Tiryns — A70

Zeus of Dodona — A71

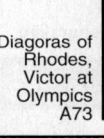

Coin of Amphictyonic League A72

Diagoras of Rhodes, Victor at Olympics A73

Venus of Melos — A74

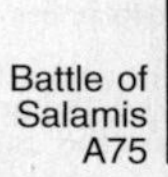

Battle of Salamis A75

Chariot of Panathenaic Festival A76

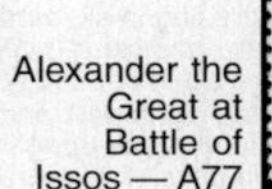

Alexander the Great at Battle of Issos — A77

St. Paul Preaching to Athenians A78

St. Demetrius' Church at Salonika A79

Leo III Victory over Arabs — A80

Allegorical Figure of Glory — A81

Perf. 13½x12, 12x13½
1937, Nov. 1 **Litho.** **Wmk. 252**
396 A69 5 l brn red & bl .25 .25
a. Double impression of frame 60.00
397 A70 10 l bl & brn red .25 .25
a. Double impression of frame 60.00
398 A71 20 l black & grn .25 .25
399 A72 40 l green & blk .25 .25
a. Green impression doubled 60.00
400 A73 50 l brown & blk .25 .25
401 A74 80 l ind & yel brn .25 .25

Engr.
402 A75 2d ultra .25 .25
403 A76 5d red .25 .25
a. Printer's name omitted 5.50
404 A77 6d olive brn .25 .25
405 A78 7d dk brown .55 .50
406 A79 10d red brown .25 .25
407 A80 15d green .25 .25
408 A81 25d dk blue .25 .25
Nos. 396-408 (13) 3.55 3.50
Set, never hinged 4.00

See Nos. 413, 459-466. For overprints and surcharges see Nos. 455-458, 476-477, RA75-RA78, RA83-RA85, N202-N217, N246-N247. Post 1940 issues in Scott Standard catalogue, Vol. 3.

Cerigo, Paxos, Lefkas

Greek stamps with Italian overprints for the islands of Cerigo (Kithyra), Paxos and Lefkas (Santa Maura) are fraudulent.

Royal Wedding Issue

Princess Frederika-Louise and Crown Prince Paul — A82

1938 **Wmk. 252** *Perf. 13½x12*
409 A82 1d green .25 .25
410 A82 3d orange brn .30 .25
411 A82 8d dark blue .55 .65
Nos. 409-411 (3) 1.10 1.15
Set, never hinged 2.75

Arms of Greece, Romania, Yugoslavia and Turkey — A83

Perf. 12x12½
1938, Feb. 8 **Litho.** **Unwmk.**
412 A83 6d blue 5.50 1.75
Never hinged 14.00

Balkan Entente.

Tiryns Lady Type of 1937 Corrected Inscription

1938 **Wmk. 252** *Perf. 12x13½*
413 A70 10 l blue & brn red .50 *.70*
Never hinged .85

The first four letters of the third word of the inscription read "TIPY" instead of "TYPI."

Statue of King Constantine — A84

Perf. 12x13½
1938, Oct. 8 **Engr.** **Unwmk.**
414 A84 1.50d green .45 .25
415 A84 30d orange brn 2.25 *3.25*
Set, never hinged 5.50

For overprint see No. N218.

Coats of Arms of Ionian Islands — A85

Fort at Corfu — A86

King George I of Greece and Queen Victoria of England A87

Perf. 12½x12, 13½x12
1939, May 21 **Engr.** **Unwmk.**
416 A85 1d dk blue .85 .25
417 A86 4d green 2.90 1.00
418 A87 20d yellow org 17.00 17.00
419 A87 20d dull blue 17.00 17.00
420 A87 20d car lake 17.00 17.00
Nos. 416-420 (5) 54.75 52.25
Set, never hinged 125.00

75th anniv. of the union of the Ionian Islands with Greece.

Runner with Shield — A88

10th Pan-Balkan Games: 3d, Javelin thrower. 6d, Discus thrower. 8d, Jumper.

Perf. 12x13½
1939, Oct. 1 **Litho.** **Unwmk.**
421 A88 50 l slate grn & grn .25 .25
422 A88 3d hen brn & dl rose 1.25 .55
423 A88 6d cop brn & dl org 3.00 2.25
424 A88 8d ultra & gray 3.00 2.50
Nos. 421-424 (4) 7.50 5.55
Set, never hinged 18.00

Arms of Greece, Romania, Turkey and Yugoslavia — A92

Perf. 13x12½

1940, May 27 **Wmk. 252**

425 A92 6d blue 10.00 2.25
426 A92 8d blue gray 7.00 2.25
Set, never hinged 45.00

Balkan Entente.

Emblem of Youth Organization A93

Boy Member — A94

Designs: 3d, 100d, Emblem of Greek Youth Organization. 10d, Girl member. 15d, Javelin Thrower. 20d, Column of members. 25d, Flag bearers and buglers. 30d, Three youths. 50d, Line formation. 75d, Coat of arms.

Perf. 12½, 13½x12½

1940, Aug. 3 **Litho.** **Wmk. 252**

427 A93 3d sil, dp ultra & red .85 *1.25*
428 A94 5d dk bl & blk 6.50 *7.50*
429 A94 10d red org & blk 7.50 *10.00*
430 A94 15d dk grn & blk 30.00 *32.50*
431 A94 20d lake & blk 25.00 25.00
432 A94 25d dk bl & blk 25.00 25.00
433 A94 30d rose vio & blk 25.00 25.00
434 A94 50d lake & blk 30.00 30.00
435 A94 75d dk bl, brn & gold 30.00 32.50
436 A93 100d sil, dp ultra & red 50.00 *37.50*
Nos. 427-436,C38-C47 (20) 555.70 529.00
Set, never hinged 1,000.

4th anniv. of the founding of the Greek Youth Organization. The stamps were good for postal duty Aug. 3-5, 1940, only. They remained on sale until Feb. 3, 1941.

For overprints see Nos. N219-N238.

AIR POST STAMPS

Italy-Greece-Turkey-Rhodes Service

Flying Boat off Phaleron Bay — AP1

Flying Boat over Acropolis — AP2

Flying Boat over Map of Southern Europe — AP3

Flying Boat Seen through Colonnade — AP4

Perf. 11½

1926, Oct. 20 **Unwmk.** **Litho.**

C1 AP1 2d multicolored 1.60 1.25
a. Horiz. pair, imperf. vert. 725.00
C2 AP2 3d multicolored 12.00 11.00
C3 AP3 5d multicolored 1.60 1.25
C4 AP4 10d multicolored 12.00 12.00
Nos. C1-C4 (4) 27.20 25.50
Set, never hinged 80.00

Graf Zeppelin Issue

Zeppelin over Acropolis AP5

1933, May 2 *Perf. 13½x12½*

C5 AP5 30d rose red 13.00 13.00
C6 AP5 100d deep blue 52.50 52.50
C7 AP5 120d dark brown 52.50 52.50
Nos. C5-C7 (3) 118.00 118.00
Set, never hinged 325.00

Propeller and Pilot's Head AP6

Temple of Apollo, Corinth AP7

Plane over Hermoupolis, Syros — AP8

Allegory of Flight
AP9 AP12

Map of Italy-Greece-Turkey-Rhodes Airmail Route — AP10

Head of Hermes and Airplane — AP11

1933, Oct. 10 **Engr.** *Perf. 12*

C8 AP6 50 l green & org .25 .25
C9 AP7 1d bl & brn org .30 .25
C10 AP8 3d dk vio & org brn .50 .50
C11 AP9 5d brn org & dk bl 7.25 4.50
C12 AP10 10d dp red & blk 1.50 1.40
C13 AP11 20d black & grn 7.25 4.00
C14 AP12 50d dp brn & dp bl 50.00 *55.00*
Nos. C8-C14 (7) 67.05 *65.90*
Set, never hinged 200.00

By error the 1d stamp is inscribed in the plural "ΔΡΑΧΜΑΙ" instead of the singular "ΔΡΑΧΜΗ." This stamp exists bisected, used as a 50 lepta denomination.

All values of this set exist imperforate but were not regularly issued.

For General Air Post Service

Airplane over Map of Greece — AP13

Airplane over Map of Icarian Sea — AP14

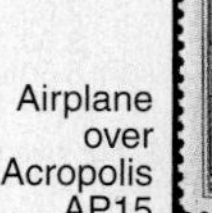
Airplane over Acropolis AP15

Perf. 13x13½, 13x12½, 13½x13, 12½x13

1933, Nov. 2

C15 AP13 50 l green .25 .25
C16 AP13 1d red brown .30 *.55*
C17 AP14 2d lt violet .60 *.85*
C18 AP15 5d ultra 3.50 3.50
a. Imperf., pair 650.00 550.00
b. Horiz. pair, imperf. vert. 650.00
C19 AP14 10d car rose 6.50 *7.75*
C20 AP13 25d dark blue 30.00 20.00
C21 AP15 50d dark brown 30.00 *42.50*
a. Imperf., pair 775.00 650.00
Nos. C15-C21 (7) 71.15 75.40
Set, never hinged 225.00

Helios Driving the Sun Chariot AP16

Iris — AP17

Daedalus Preparing Icarus for Flying — AP18

Pallas Athene Holding Pegasus — AP19

Hermes AP20

Zeus Carrying off Ganymede AP21

Triptolemos, King of Eleusis AP22

Bellerophon and Pegasus — AP23

Phrixos and Helle on the Ram Flying over the Hellespont AP24

Perf. 13x12½, 12½x13

1935, Nov. 10 **Engr.**

Grayish Paper

Size: 34x23½mm, 23½x34mm

C22 AP16 1d deep red 1.50 1.50
C23 AP17 2d dull blue 1.50 1.50
C24 AP18 5d dk violet 17.50 4.00
C25 AP19 7d blue violet 25.00 7.25
C26 AP20 10d bister brown 5.00 5.00
C27 AP21 25d rose 6.00 5.75
C28 AP22 30d dark green 2.00 2.00
C29 AP23 50d violet 8.00 6.00
C30 AP24 100d brown 2.50 2.25
Nos. C22-C30 (9) 69.00 35.25
Set, never hinged 150.00

Re-engraved

Size: 34¼x24mm, 24x34¼mm

1937-39 **White Paper**

C31 AP16 1d red .30 .25
C32 AP17 2d gray blue .30 .25
C33 AP18 5d violet .30 .25
C34 AP19 7d dp ultra .30 .25
C35 AP20 10d brn org 2.40 *3.50*
Nos. C31-C35 (5) 3.60 *4.50*
Set, never hinged 7.00

Issued: #C35, 3/1/39; others 8/3/37.

Postage Due Stamp, 1913, Overprinted in Red

Serrate Roulette 13½

1938, Aug. 8		Litho.	Unwmk.	
C36	D3	50 l violet brown	.25	.25
		Never hinged	.25	
a.		"O" for "P" in word at foot	30.00	30.00

Same Overprint on No. J79 in Red

1939, June 26		*Perf. 13½x12½*		
C37	D3	50 l dark brown	.25	.25
		Never hinged	.25	

Meteora Monasteries, near Trikkala — AP25

Designs: 4d, Simon Peter Monastery. 6d, View of Santorin. 8d, Church of Pantanassa. 16d, Santorin view. 32d, Ponticonissi, Corfu. 45d, Acropolis, Athens. 55d, Erechtheum. 65d, Temple of Nike Apteros. 100d, Temple of the Olympian Zeus, Athens.

Wmk. Crowns (252)

1940, Aug. 3		Litho.	*Perf. 12½*	
C38	AP25	2d red org & blk	.85	*1.25*
C39	AP25	4d dk grn & blk	4.00	3.50
C40	AP25	6d lake & blk	7.25	6.50
C41	AP25	8d dk bl & blk	18.75	16.50
C42	AP25	16d rose vio & blk	30.00	25.00
C43	AP25	32d red org & blk	40.00	*47.50*
C44	AP25	45d dk grn & blk	52.50	47.50
C45	AP25	55d lake & blk	52.50	47.50
C46	AP25	65d dk bl & blk	52.50	47.50
C47	AP25	100d rose vio & blk	67.50	60.00
		Nos. C38-C47 (10)	325.85	302.75
		Set, never hinged	800.00	

4th anniv. of the founding of the Greek Youth Organization. The stamps were good for postal duty on Aug. 3-5, 1940, only. They remained on sale until Feb. 3, 1941.

For overprints see Nos. N229-N238.

POSTAGE DUE STAMPS

D1

Perf. 9, 9½, and 10, 10½ and Compound

1875		Litho.	Unwmk.	
J1	D1	1 l green & black	1.50	1.50
J2	D1	2 l green & black	1.50	1.50
J3	D1	5 l green & black	1.75	1.25
J4	D1	10 l green & black	1.75	1.25
J5	D1	20 l green & black	42.50	30.00
J6	D1	40 l green & black	8.25	5.50
J7	D1	60 l green & black	42.50	30.00
J8	D1	70 l green & black	8.25	5.50
J9	D1	80 l green & black	17.50	14.50
J10	D1	90 l green & black	11.00	11.00
J11	D1	1d green & black	12.00	11.00
J12	D1	2d green & black	13.00	11.00
		Nos. J1-J12 (12)	161.50	124.00

Imperforate and part perforated, double and inverted center varieties of Nos. J1-J12 are believed to be printers' waste.

Perf. 12, 13 and 10½x13

J13	D1	1 l green & black	1.60	1.60
J14	D1	2 l green & black	22.50	22.50
J15	D1	5 l green & black	2.75	2.75
J16	D1	10 l green & black	3.25	3.25
J17	D1	20 l green & black	40.00	27.50
J18	D1	40 l green & black	10.00	7.75
J19	D1	60 l green & black	42.50	27.50
J20	D1	70 l green & black	7.75	7.75
J21	D1	80 l green & black	12.00	12.00
J22	D1	90 l green & black	17.50	12.00
J23	D1	1d green & black	27.50	17.50
J24	D1	2d green & black	22.50	17.50
		Nos. J13-J24 (12)	209.85	159.60

D2

Redrawn
"Lepton" or "Lepta" in Larger Greek Letters

1876		*Perf. 9, 9½, and 10, 10½*		
J25	D2	1 l green & black	4.50	4.50
J26	D2	2 l dk grn & blk	6.00	5.75
J27	D2	5 l dk grn & blk	360.00	275.00
J28	D2	10 l green & black	3.00	2.10
J29	D2	20 l green & black	4.00	3.00
J30	D2	40 l green & black	32.50	25.00
J31	D2	60 l green & black	27.50	15.00
J32	D2	70 l green & black	22.50	25.00
J33	D2	80 l green & black	17.50	15.00
J34	D2	90 l green & black	17.50	16.00
J35	D2	100 l green & black	22.50	15.00
J36	D2	200 l green & black	22.50	15.00
		Nos. J25-J36 (12)	540.00	416.35

Perf. 11½ to 13

J37	D2	1 l yel grn & blk	1.75	.95
J38	D2	2 l yel grn & blk	1.75	.95
J39	D2	5 l yel grn & blk	4.75	1.25
J40	D2	10 l yel grn & blk	2.75	2.00
a.		Perf. 10-10½x11½-13	4.00	
J41	D2	20 l yel grn & blk	2.75	2.00
J42	D2	40 l yel grn & blk	15.00	11.00
J43	D2	60 l yel grn & blk	9.50	9.50
J47	D2	100 l yel grn & blk	12.00	12.00
J48	D2	200 l yel grn & blk	13.50	11.00
		Nos. J37-J48 (9)	63.75	50.65

Footnote below No. J12 applies also to Nos. J25-J48.

D3

1902		Engr. Wmk. 129	*Perf. 13½*	
J49	D3	1 l chocolate	.30	.25
J50	D3	2 l gray	.30	.25
J51	D3	3 l orange	.30	.25
J52	D3	5 l yel grn	.30	.25
J53	D3	10 l scarlet	.30	.25
J54	D3	20 l lilac	.45	.25
J55	D3	25 l ultra	8.00	4.00
J56	D3	30 l dp vio	.50	.30
J57	D3	40 l dk brn	.60	.50
J58	D3	50 l red brn	.60	.40
J59	D3	1d black	1.50	.90

Litho.

J60	D3	2d bronze	2.00	1.25
J61	D3	3d silver	3.00	3.00
J62	D3	5d gold	6.50	*9.00*
		Nos. J49-J62 (14)	24.65	20.85

See Nos. J63-J88, J90-J93. For overprints and surcharges see Nos. 383-385, J89, RA56, RA58-RA59, NJ1-NJ31. Post 1940 issues in Scott Standard catalogue, Vol. 3.

Imperf., Pairs

J50a	D3	2 l	90.00
J51a	D3	3 l	90.00
J52a	D3	5 l	90.00
J55a	D3	25 l	150.00
J56a	D3	30 l	150.00
J58a	D3	50 l	150.00
J59a	D3	1d	150.00

Serrate Roulette 13½

1913-26			Unwmk.	
J63	D3	1 l green	.25	.25
J64	D3	2 l carmine	.25	.25
J65	D3	3 l vermilion	.25	.25
J66	D3	5 l green	.25	.25
a.		Imperf., pair	150.00	
b.		Double impression	60.00	
c.		"o" for "p" in lowest word	5.00	5.00
J67	D3	10 l carmine	.25	.25
J68	D3	20 l slate	.25	.25
J69	D3	25 l ultra	.25	.25
J70	D3	30 l carmine	.25	.25
J71	D3	40 l indigo	.25	.25
J72	D3	50 l vio brn	.30	.25
a.		"o" for "p" in lowest word	25.00	20.00
J73	D3	80 l lil brn ('24)	.40	.25
J74	D3	1d blue	8.00	1.25
a.		1d ultramarine	12.00	5.00
J75	D3	2d vermilion	8.00	1.50
J76	D3	3d carmine	8.00	1.50
J77	D3	5d ultra	30.00	12.00
J78	D3	5d gray bl ('26)	8.00	4.00
		Nos. J63-J78 (16)	64.95	23.00

In 1922-23 and 1941-42 some postage due stamps were used for ordinary postage.

In 1916 Nos. J52, and J63 to J75 were surcharged for the Mount Athos District (see note after No. N166) but were never issued there. By error some of them were put in use as ordinary postage due stamps in Dec., 1924. In 1932 the balance of them was burned.

Type of 1902 Issue

Perf. 13, 13½x12½, 13½x13

1930			Litho.	
J79	D3	50 l dk brown	.30	.30
J80	D3	1d lt blue	.30	.30
J81	D3	2d lt red	.30	.30
J82	D3	3d rose red	27.50	25.00
J83	D3	5d gray blue	.30	.30
J84	D3	10d gray green	.30	.30
J85	D3	15d red brown	.30	.30
J86	D3	25d light red	.70	.65
		Nos. J79-J86 (8)	30.00	27.45

Type of 1902 Issue

1935		Engr.	*Perf. 12½x13*	
J87	D3	50d orange	.30	.30
J88	D3	100d slate green	.30	.30

POSTAL TAX STAMPS

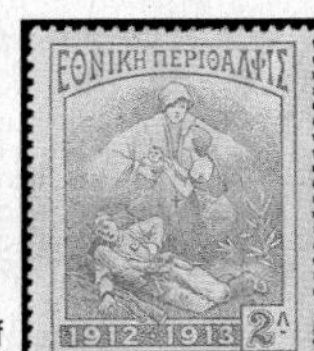

"The Tragedy of War" — PT1

Serrate Roulette 13½

1914		Litho.	Unwmk.	
RA1	PT1	2 l red ('18)	.30	.25
a.		2 l carmine	.45	.25
b.		Imperf., pair	265.00	
RA2	PT1	5 l blue	.50	*.50*
a.		Imperf., pair	375.00	

Red Cross, Nurses, Wounded and Bearers — PT1a

1915		*Serrate Roulette 13*		
RA2B	PT1a	(5 l) dk bl & red	12.00	2.00

The tax was for the Red Cross.

Women's Patriotic League Badge — PT1b

1915, Nov.			*Perf. 11½*	
RA2C	PT1b	(5 l) dk bl & car	1.25	1.25
d.		Horiz. pair, imperf. btwn.	55.00	
e.		Imperf., pair	55.00	

The tax was for the Greek Women's Patriotic League.

Nos. 165, 167, 170, 172-175 Surcharged in Black or Brown

a

b

In type "b" the letters, especially those in the first line, are thinner than in type "a," making them appear taller.

Perf. 11½, 12½, 13½ and Compound

1917		Engr.	Wmk. 129	
RA3	A11(a)	1 l on 1 l	1.50	1.50
a.		Double surcharge	8.50	
b.		Inverted surcharge	10.00	
c.		Dbl. surch., one invtd.	10.00	
RA4	A11(a)	1 l on 1 l (Br)	24.00	*30.00*
RA5	A11(a)	1 l on 3 l	.30	.30
RA6	A11(b)	1 l on 3 l	.30	.30
a.		Triple surcharge	12.00	
b.		Dbl. surch., one invtd.	6.00	
c.		"K.M." for "K.П."	20.00	
d.		Inverted surcharge	7.00	
e.		Double surcharge	7.00	
RA7	A11(a)	5 l on 1 l	2.00	2.00
a.		Double surcharge	12.00	
b.		Dbl. surch., one invtd.	12.00	
c.		Inverted surcharge	13.50	
RA8	A11(a)	5 l on 20 l	.65	.65
a.		Double surcharge	13.50	
b.		Dbl. surch., one invtd.	13.50	
c.		Inverted surcharge	15.00	
RA9	A11(b)	5 l on 40 l	.65	.65
a.		Imperf.	*200.00*	*250.00*
b.		Double surcharge	13.50	
c.		Dbl. surch., one invtd.	13.50	
d.		Triple surcharge	47.50	
RA10	A11(b)	5 l on 50 l	.65	.65
a.		Double surcharge	25.00	
b.		Dbl. surch., one invtd.	25.00	
c.		Inverted surcharge	15.00	
d.		Triple surcharge	24.00	
e.		Triple surch., two invtd.	30.00	
f.		Pair, imperf.	*225.00*	*185.00*
RA11	A13(b)	5 l on 1d	2.25	2.25
a.		Imperf.	*200.00*	
b.		Inverted surcharge	55.00	
c.		Double surcharge	35.00	
d.		Dbl. surch., one invtd.	55.00	
e.		Triple surcharge	55.00	
f.		Horiz. pair, imperf. vert.	—	
g.		Vert. pair, imperf. horiz.	—	
RA12	A11(a)	10 l on 30 l	.80	.80
a.		Imperf.		
b.		Double surcharge	18.00	
c.		Dbl. surch., one invtd.	18.00	
d.		Inverted surcharge	35.00	
RA13	A11(a)	30 l on 30 l	.90	.90
a.		Double surcharge	20.00	
b.		Dbl. surch., one invtd.	24.00	
c.		Triple surch., one invtd.	24.00	
d.		Inverted surcharge	17.00	
		Nos. RA3-RA13 (11)	34.00	40.00

Same Surcharge On Occupation Stamps of 1912

Serrate Roulette 13½

1917		Litho.	Unwmk.	
RA14	O2 (b)	5 l on 25 l pale bl	.45	.45
a.		Triple surch., one invtd.	15.00	
b.		Double surcharge	12.00	
c.		Dbl. surch., one invtd.	13.50	
d.		Dbl. surch., both invtd.	13.50	
e.		Inverted surcharge	15.50	
RA15	O2 (b)	5 l on 40 l indigo	.35	.35
a.		Dbl. surch., one invtd.	10.00	
b.		Double surcharge	10.00	
c.		Dbl. surch., both invtd.	13.50	
d.		Inverted surcharge	13.50	
e.		Triple surcharge	13.50	
f.		Triple surch., one invtd.	20.00	
RA16	O1 (b)	5 l on 50 l dk bl	.25	.25
a.		Double surcharge	12.00	
b.		Inverted surcharge	12.00	
c.		Dbl. surch., one invtd.	13.50	
d.		Triple surcharge	27.00	
e.		Triple surch., two invtd.	27.00	
		Nos. RA14-RA16 (3)	1.05	1.05

There are many wrong font, omitted and misplaced letters and punctuation marks and similar varieties in the surcharges on Nos. RA3 to RA16.

Revenue Stamps Surcharged in Brown

"Victory"

1917				
RA17	R1	1 l on 10 l blue	.70	*1.00*
RA18	R1	1 l on 80 l blue	.70	*1.00*
RA19	R1	5 l on 10 l blue	18.00	*27.50*
RA20	R1	5 l on 60 l blue	6.00	*7.25*
a.		Perf. vert. through middle	9.50	*15.00*
b.		As "a," inverted surcharge		
RA21	R1	5 l on 80 l blue	3.25	*4.50*
a.		Perf. vert. through middle	9.50	*15.00*
b.		Inverted surcharge		
RA22	R1	10 l on 70 l blue	18.00	*25.00*
a.		Perf. vert. through middle	7.25	*10.00*
RA23	R1	10 l on 90 l blue	13.50	37.50
a.		Perf. vert. through middle	22.50	*45.00*
RA24	R1	20 l on 20 l blue	*6,500.*	*3,600.*
RA25	R1	20 l on 30 l blue	12.00	9.50
RA26	R1	20 l on 40 l blue	14.50	*21.00*
RA27	R1	20 l on 50 l blue	12.00	12.00
RA28	R1	20 l on 60 l blue	500.00	375.00
RA29	R1	20 l on 80 l blue	60.00	*72.50*

RA30 R1 20 l on 90 l blue 5.00 *9.75*
a. Inverted surcharge *100.00*
b. Double surcharge
Nos. RA17-RA30 (14) 7,164. 4,204.

No. RA19 is known only with vertical perforation through the middle.

Counterfeits exist of Nos. RA17-RA43, used.

Surcharged in Brown or Black

RA31 R1 1 l on 50 l vio (Bk) .85 *1.40*
RA32 R1 5 l on 10 l bl (Br) .85 *1.40*
a. Inverted surcharge 85.00
b. Left "5" invert. 97.50
RA33 R1 5 l on 10 l vio (Br) .85 *1.40*
RA34 R1 10 l on 50 l vio (Br) 6.00 *12.00*
RA35 R1 10 l on 50 l vio (Bk) 25.00 *32.50*
a. Double surcharge *85.00*
RA36 R1 20 l on 2d bl (Bk) 9.75 9.75
a. Surcharged "20 lept. 30" 80.00 *120.00*
b. Horiz. pair, imperf. btwn.
Nos. RA31-RA36 (6) 43.30 58.45

The "T," fourth Greek letter of the denomination in the surcharge ("ΛΕΠΤ."), is normally omitted on Nos. RA31, RA34-RA36.

Corfu Issue

Surcharged in Black

1917
RA37 R1 1 l on 10 l blue 2.50 2.50
RA38 R1 5 l on 50 l blue 60.00 *80.00*
RA39 R1 10 l on 50 l blue 725.00 725.00
RA40 R1 20 l on 50 l blue 2,850. 1,075.

Surcharged in Black

RA41 R1 10 l on 50 l blue 13.50 *14.50*
RA42 R1 20 l on 50 l blue 30.00 30.00
RA43 R1 30 l on 50 l blue 18.00 18.00

Surcharged in Black

Without serifs

With serifs

RA44 R1 5 l on 10 l vio & red 9.75 *13.50*
a. "K" with serifs 13.50 *25.00*

Counterfeits exist of Nos. RA17-RA44.

Similar stamps with denominations higher than 30 lepta were for revenue use.

Wounded Soldier — PT2

1918 ***Serrate Roulette 13½, 11½***
RA45 PT2 5 l bl, yel & red 8.50 2.00

Overprinted

RA46 PT2 5 l blue, yel & red 11.00 2.00
e. Double overprint 290.00

The letters are the initials of Greek words equivalent to "Patriotic Relief Institution." The proceeds were given to the Patriotic League, for the aid of disabled soldiers.

Counterfeits exist of Nos. RA45-RA46.

PT3

Surcharge in Red

1922 **Litho.** ***Perf. 11½***
Dark Blue & Red

RA46A PT3 5 l on 10 l *325.00* 16.00
f. Double surcharge *410.00 410.00*
RA46B PT3 5 l on 20 l 97.50 57.50
RA46C PT3 5 l on 50 l 325.00 275.00
RA46D PT3 5 l on 1d 12.00 *60.00*

Counterfeit surcharges exist. Examples of Nos. RA46A-RA46C without surcharge, each 50 cents.

Value for No. RA46Af unused is for example without gum.

Red Cross Help to Soldier and Family — PT3a

1924 ***Perf. 13½ x 12½***
RA47 PT3a 10 l blue, buff & red .85 .25

Proceeds were given to the Red Cross.

1926 ***Perf. 11½***
RA47C PT3a 10 l blue, buff & red .30 .25
a. Imperf., pair 40.00
b. Horiz. pair, imperf. btwn. 40.00
d. Horiz. pair, imperf. vert. 45.00
e. Vert. pair, imperf. horiz. 50.00

St. Demetrius — PT4

1934 ***Perf. 11½***
RA48 PT4 20 l brown .35 .25
a. Horizontal pair, imperf. between 10.00
b. Vertical pair, imperf. between 16.00
c. Imperf., pair 18.00
d. Horiz. pair, imperf. vert. 16.00
e. Vert. pair, imperf. horiz. 16.00
f. Double impression *60.00*

No. RA48 was obligatory as a tax on all interior mail, including air post, mailed from Salonika.

For surcharge see No. RA69 in Scott Standard catalogue, Vol. 3.

"Health" — PT5

1934, Dec. 28 ***Perf. 13, 13x13½***
RA49 PT5 10 l bl grn, org & buff .25 .25
a. Vert. pair, imperf. horiz.
RA50 PT5 20 l ultra, org & buff .25 .25
RA51 PT5 50 l grn, org & buff 2.00 .70
Nos. RA49-RA51 (3) 2.50 1.20

For surcharge see No. RA67 in Scott Standard catalogue, Vol. 3.

"Health" — PT6

1935
RA52 PT6 10 l yel grn, org & buff .25 .25
RA53 PT6 20 l ultra, org & buff .30 .25
RA54 PT6 50 l grn, org & buff .70 .70
Nos. RA52-RA54 (3) 1.25 1.20

The use of #RA49-RA54 was obligatory on all mail during 4 weeks each year including Christmas, the New Year and Easter, and on parcel post packages at all times. For the benefit of the tubercular clerks and officials of the Post, Telephone and Telegraph Service.

See No. RA64. For surcharge see No. RA68 in Scott Standard catalogue, Vol. 3.

No. 364 Overprinted in Red

1937, Jan. 20 **Engr.** ***Perf. 13x12½***
RA55 A36 50 l violet 1.40 .25
a. Inverted overprint .75 .25

No. RA55a first appeared as an error, then was issued deliberately in quantity to avoid speculation.

Same Overprint in Blue on No. J67
Litho.
Serrate Roulette 13½

RA56 D3 10 l carmine .80 .25
a. Inverted overprint 50.00
b. Without accent mark on "O" .90 .50

No. RA56 has accent mark on "O." No. RA56 with blue overprint double exists only with additional black overprint of Ionian Islands No. NRA1a.

Same Overprint in Green on No. 364

1937 **Engr.** ***Perf. 13x12½***
RA57 A36 50 l violet .30 .25

Nos. J66, J68 and 323 Surcharged in Blue or Black

Serrate Roulette 13½

1938 **Litho.** **Unwmk.**
RA58 D3 50 l on 5 l grn 1.50 .80
a. Accent mark on "O" 7.50 1.00
b. "O" for "P" in lowest word 30.00 25.00
c. As No. RA58, vert. pair, imperf. horiz. 65.00 120.00
RA59 D3 50 l on 20 l slate 1.50 .80
a. Accent mark on "O" 240.00 47.50

Nos. RA58 and RA59 have no accent mark on "O."

Engr. ***Perf. 13x12½***
RA60 A38 50 l on 20 l vio (Bk) .40 .25
Nos. RA58-RA60 (3) 3.40 1.85

Surcharge on No. RA60 is 14½x16½mm.

Queens Olga and Sophia PT7

1939, Feb. 1 **Litho.** ***Perf. 13½x12***
RA61 PT7 10 l brt rose, *pale rose* .25 .25
RA62 PT7 50 l gray grn, *pale grn* .25 .25
a. Double impression 120.00
b. Imperf., pair
RA63 PT7 1d dl bl, *lt bl* .25 .25
Nos. RA61-RA63 (3) .75 .75

For overprints and surcharges see Nos. RA65, RA79-RA81A (in Scott Standard catalogue, Vol. 3), NRA1-NRA3.

"Health" Type of 1935

1939 ***Perf. 12½***
RA64 PT6 50 l brn & buff .40 .30

No. RA62 Overprinted in Red

1940 ***Perf. 13½x12***
RA65 PT7 50 l gray grn, *pale grn* .25 .25
a. Inverted overprint 27.50
b. Pair, one without overprint 80.00
c. Double impression 120.00

Proceeds of Nos. RA64-RA65 were used for the benefit of tubercular clerks and officials of the Post, Telephone and Telegraph Service. No. RA65 was used in Albania during the Greek occupation, 1940-41 without additional overprint.

OCCUPATION AND ANNEXATION STAMPS

During the Balkan wars, 1912-13, Greece occupied certain of the Aegean Islands and part of Western Turkey. She subsequently acquired these territories and they were known as the New Greece.

Most of the special issues for the Aegean Islands were made by order of the military commanders.

For Use in the Aegean Islands Occupied by Greece

CHIOS

Greece No. 221 Overprinted in Red

Serrate Roulette 13½

1913 **Litho.** **Unwmk.**
N1 A25 25 l ultramarine 60.00 *85.00*
Never hinged 120.00
a. Inverted overprint 200.00 *225.00*
Never hinged 440.00
b. "Λ" for "Δ" in overprint 225.00 *250.00*
Never hinged 475.00
c. As "b," overprint inverted 475.00 *525.00*
Never hinged 950.00

ICARIA (NICARIA)

Penelope — I1

1912 Unwmk. Litho. *Perf. 11½*

N2 I1 2 l orange 1.25 2.50
Never hinged 3.25
N3 I1 5 l blue green 1.25 2.50
Never hinged 3.25
N4 I1 10 l rose 1.25 2.50
Never hinged 3.25
N5 I1 25 l ultra 1.25 2.50
Never hinged 3.25
a. Pair, imperf. between 80.00 80.00
N6 I1 50 l gray lilac 1.50 3.50
Never hinged 4.75
a. Pair, imperf. between 80.00 80.00
N7 I1 1d dark brown 2.50 *9.00*
Never hinged 6.50
N8 I1 2d claret 3.50 *15.00*
Never hinged 8.00
N9 I1 5d slate 5.00 *22.50*
Never hinged 11.00
Nos. N2-N9 (8) 17.50 *60.00*

Counterfeits of Nos. N1-N15 are plentiful.

Stamps of Greece, 1911-23, Overprinted Reading Up

1913 On Issue of 1911-21 Engr.

N10 A25 2 l car rose 40.00 30.00
Never hinged 55.00
N11 A24 3 l vermilion 40.00 30.00
Never hinged 55.00

Litho.

On Issue of 1912-23

N12 A24 1 l green 40.00 30.00
Never hinged 55.00
N12A A25 2 l car rose 40.00 30.00
Never hinged 55.00
N13 A24 3 l vermilion 40.00 30.00
Never hinged 55.00
N14 A26 5 l green 40.00 30.00
Never hinged 55.00
N15 A24 10 l carmine 40.00 30.00
Never hinged 55.00
Nos. N10-N15 (6) 240.00 180.00

LEMNOS

Regular Issues of Greece Overprinted in Black

On Issue of 1901

1912 Wmk. 129 Engr. *Perf. 13½*

N16 A11 20 l red lilac 2.00 2.00
Never hinged 3.00
a. Inverted overprint 22.50
Never hinged 35.00
b. Double overprint 22.50
Never hinged 35.00

On Issue of 1911-21

Unwmk.

Serrate Roulette 13½

N17 A24 1 l green .60 .60
Never hinged .90
a. Inverted overprint 15.00
Never hinged 22.50
b. Double overprint 15.00
Never hinged 22.50
c. Double ovpt., one inverted 30.00
Never hinged 60.00
N18 A25 2 l carmine rose .70 .70
Never hinged 1.00
a. Inverted overprint 15.00
Never hinged 22.50
b. Double overprint 15.00
Never hinged 22.50
N19 A24 3 l vermilion .70 .70
Never hinged 1.00
a. Inverted overprint 15.00
Never hinged 22.50
b. Double overprint 15.00
Never hinged 22.50
c. Double ovpt., one inverted 20.00
Never hinged 30.00
d. Triple overprint 72.50
Never hinged 120.00
e. Triple ovpt., one inverted 72.50
Never hinged 120.00
f. Inverted ovpt. on face, upright ovpt. on reverse 120.00
Never hinged 160.00
N20 A26 5 l green .70 .70
Never hinged 1.00
a. Inverted overprint 15.00
Never hinged 22.50
b. Double overprint 15.00
Never hinged 22.50
N21 A24 10 l car rose 1.00 1.00
Never hinged 1.35
a. Inverted overprint 15.00
Never hinged 22.50
b. Double overprint 15.00
Never hinged 22.50
c. Double ovpt., one inverted 30.00
Never hinged 60.00
N22 A25 20 l gray lilac 1.50 1.75
Never hinged 2.50
a. Inverted overprint 15.00
Never hinged 22.50
b. Double overprint 27.00
Never hinged 40.00
N23 A25 25 l ultra 1.50 1.75
Never hinged 2.25
a. Inverted overprint 22.50
Never hinged 32.50
b. Double overprint 22.50
Never hinged 32.50
N24 A26 30 l car rose 3.00 3.00
Never hinged 4.75
a. Inverted overprint 50.00
Never hinged 70.00
b. Double overprint 50.00
Never hinged 70.00
N25 A25 40 l deep blue 4.75 *5.50*
Never hinged 7.25
a. Inverted overprint 55.00
Never hinged 80.00
N26 A26 50 l dl violet 5.00 *5.50*
Never hinged 6.75
N27 A27 1d ultra 6.00 6.00
Never hinged 9.00
a. Inverted overprint 60.00
Never hinged 90.00
b. Double overprint 60.00
Never hinged 90.00
N28 A27 2d vermilion 20.00 20.00
Never hinged 35.00
N29 A27 3d car rose 22.50 22.50
Never hinged 37.50
N30 A27 5d ultra 26.00 26.00
Never hinged 45.00
a. Double overprint 80.00
Never hinged 120.00
N31 A27 10d deep blue 80.00 *97.50*
Never hinged 150.00
N32 A28 25d deep blue 150.00 150.00
Never hinged 200.00
Nos. N17-N32 (16) 323.95 343.20

"Λ" for "Λ" in "ΛΗΜΝΟΣ"

N17g A24 1 l green 6.00 6.00
Never hinged 9.00
N18g A25 2 l carmine rose 6.00 6.00
Never hinged 9.00
N19g A24 3 l vermilion 6.00 6.00
Never hinged 9.00
N20g A26 5 l green 10.00 10.00
Never hinged 15.00
N21g A24 10 l carmine rose 10.00 10.00
Never hinged 15.00
N22g A25 20 l gray lilac 10.00 10.00
Never hinged 15.00
N23g A25 25 l ultramarine 10.00 10.00
Never hinged 15.00
N24g A26 30 l carmine rose 12.00 12.00
Never hinged 18.00
N25g A25 40 l deep blue 15.00 15.00
Never hinged 22.50
N26g A26 50 l dull violet 15.00 15.00
Never hinged 22.50
N27g A27 1d ultramarine 20.00 20.00
Never hinged 30.00
N28g A27 2d vermilion 120.00 120.00
Never hinged 180.00
N29g A27 3d carmine rose 120.00 120.00
Never hinged 180.00
N30g A27 5d ultramarine 150.00 150.00
Never hinged 225.00
N31g A27 10d deep blue 600.00 600.00
Never hinged 900.00

Large "Σ" for "Λ" in "ΛΗΜΝΟΣ"

N17h A24 1 l green 6.00 6.00
Never hinged 9.00
N18h A25 2 l carmine rose 6.00 6.00
Never hinged 9.00
N19h A24 3 l vermilion 6.00 6.00
Never hinged 9.00
N20h A26 5 l green 10.00 10.00
Never hinged 15.00
N21h A24 10 l carmine rose 10.00 10.00
Never hinged 15.00
N22h A25 20 l gray lilac 10.00 10.00
Never hinged 15.00
N23h A25 25 l ultramarine 10.00 10.00
Never hinged 15.00
N24h A26 30 l carmine rose 12.00 12.00
Never hinged 18.00
N25h A25 40 l deep blue 15.00 15.00
Never hinged 22.50
N26h A26 50 l dull violet 15.00 15.00
Never hinged 22.50
N27h A27 1d ultramarine 20.00 20.00
Never hinged 30.00
N28h A27 2d vermilion 120.00 120.00
Never hinged 180.00
N29h A27 3d carmine rose 120.00 120.00
Never hinged 180.00
N30h A27 5d ultramarine 150.00 150.00
Never hinged 225.00
N31h A27 10d deep blue 600.00 600.00
Never hinged 900.00

Round "O" for "Λ" in "ΛΗΜΝΟΣ"

N17i A24 1 l green 4.00 4.00
Never hinged 6.00
N18i A25 2 l carmine rose 4.00 4.00
Never hinged 6.00
N19i A24 3 l vermilion 4.00 4.00
Never hinged 6.00
N20i A26 5 l green 6.00 6.00
Never hinged 9.00
N21i A24 10 l carmine rose 6.00 6.00
Never hinged 9.00
N22i A25 20 l gray lilac 6.00 6.00
Never hinged 9.00
N23i A25 25 l ultramarine 7.00 7.00
Never hinged 10.50
N24i A26 30 l carmine rose 8.00 8.00
Never hinged 12.00
N25i A25 40 l deep blue 9.00 9.00
Never hinged 13.50
N26i A26 50 l dull violet 9.00 9.00
Never hinged 13.50
N27i A27 1d ultramarine 16.00 16.00
Never hinged 24.00
N28i A27 2d vermilion 75.00 75.00
Never hinged 110.00
N29i A27 3d carmine rose 75.00 75.00
Never hinged 110.00
N30i A27 5d ultramarine 110.00 110.00
Never hinged 160.00
N31i A27 10d deep blue 390.00 390.00
Never hinged 575.00
N32i A28 25d deep blue 700.00 700.00
Never hinged 1,050.

"Δ" for "Λ" in "ΛΗΜΝΟΣ"

N17j A24 1 l green 4.00 4.00
Never hinged 6.00
N18j A25 2 l carmine rose 4.00 4.00
Never hinged 6.00
N19j A24 3 l vermilion 4.00 4.00
Never hinged 6.00
N20j A26 5 l green 6.00 6.00
Never hinged 9.00
N21j A24 10 l carmine rose 6.00 6.00
Never hinged 9.00
N22j A25 20 l gray lilac 6.00 6.00
Never hinged 9.00
N23j A25 25 l ultramarine 6.00 6.00
Never hinged 9.00
N24j A26 30 l carmine rose 8.00 8.00
Never hinged 12.00
N25j A25 40 l deep blue 8.00 8.00
Never hinged 12.00
N26j A26 50 l dull violet 9.00 9.00
Never hinged 13.50
N27j A27 1d ultramarine 16.00 16.00
Never hinged 24.00
N28j A27 2d vermilion 75.00 75.00
Never hinged 110.00
N29j A27 3d carmine rose 75.00 75.00
Never hinged 110.00
N30j A27 5d ultramarine 95.00 95.00
Never hinged 150.00
N31j A27 10d deep blue 350.00 350.00
Never hinged 525.00

On Issue of 1912-23

Litho.

N33 A24 1 l green .60 .60
Never hinged .75
a. Inverted overprint 15.00
Never hinged 22.50
b. Double overprint 15.00
Never hinged 22.50
c. Double overprint, one inverted 22.50
Never hinged 32.50
d. Double overprint, both inverted 22.50
Never hinged 32.50
e. Inverted overprint on face, upright overprint on reverse 40.00
Never hinged 60.00
f. Without period after "ΕΛ-ΛΑΣ" (on #214a) 275.00 275.00
Never hinged 400.00
g. Triple ovpt, one inverted 40.00
Never hinged 60.00
N34 A26 5 l green .70 .70
Never hinged 1.00
a. Inverted overprint 12.00
Never hinged 18.00
b. Double overprint 12.00
Never hinged 18.00
N35 A24 10 l carmine .70 .70
a. Inverted overprint 120.00
b. Double overprint 13.50
Never hinged 20.00
N36 A25 25 l ultra 3.00 3.00
Never hinged 5.50
a. Inverted overprint 22.50
Never hinged 34.00
b. Double overprint 15.00
Never hinged 22.50
Nos. N33-N36 (4) 5.00 5.00

Red Overprint

On Issue of 1911-23

Engr.

N37 A25 40 l deep blue 2.00 2.00
Never hinged 3.00
N38 A26 50 l dull violet 2.00 2.00
Never hinged 3.00
N39 A27 1d ultramarine 3.00 3.00
Never hinged 5.00
N40 A27 3d car rose 15.00 15.00
Never hinged 30.00
N41 A27 5d gray blue 400.00 300.00
Never hinged 600.00
N42 A27 10d deep blue 120.00 120.00
Never hinged 180.00
N43 A28 25d deep blue 150.00 150.00
Never hinged 300.00
a. Round "O" in "ΛΗΜΝΟΣ" 650.00
Never hinged 975.00

Litho.

N44 A24 5 l green .60 .60
Never hinged 15.00
a. Inverted oveprint —
Never hinged —
b. Double overprint —
Never hinged —
N45 A25 25 l ultramarine 2.00 2.00
Never hinged 3.50
a. Double overprint, one oblique *30.00*
Nos. N37-N45 (9) 694.60 594.60

"Δ" for "Λ" in "ΛΗΜΝΟΣ"

N37d A25 40 l deep blue 22.50 22.50
Never hinged 32.50
N38d A26 50 l dull violet 22.50 22.50
Never hinged 32.50
N39d A27 1d ultramarine 22.50 22.50
Never hinged 32.50
N40d A27 3d carmine rose 75.00 75.00
Never hinged 110.00
N41d A27 5d ultramarine 425.00 425.00
Never hinged 625.00

Carmine Overprint

Engr.

N46 A25 2 l carmine 3.00 3.00
Never hinged 4.50
a. Double overprint 30.00
Never hinged 60.00
b. Triple overprint 60.00
Never hinged 120.00
N47 A24 3 l vermilion 3.00 3.00
Never hinged 4.50
N48 A25 20 l gray blue 12.00 12.00
Never hinged 20.00
N49 A26 30 l carmine rose 6.00 6.00
Never hinged 10.00
a. Inverted overprint 30.00
Never hinged 60.00
b. Double overprint 30.00
Never hinged 60.00
N50 A27 2d vermilion 360.00 300.00
Never hinged 725.00
a. Inverted overprint —
Never hinged —
b. Double overprint —
Never hinged —
c. Double ovpt., both inverted —
Never hinged —
N51 A27 3d car rose 120.00 90.00
Never hinged 240.00
N51A A27 5d ultramarine 60.00 60.00
Never hinged 130.00
b. Double overprint 120.00
Never hinged —
N51B A28 25d deep blue 1,200. 475.00
Never hinged 2,400.

Litho.

N51C A24 1 l green 2.00 2.00
Never hinged 3.00
a. Without period after "ΕΛ-ΛΑΣ" (on #214a) 175.00 185.00
Never hinged 375.00
b. As "a.," double overprint — —
e. As N51C, double ovpt. 15.00
Never hinged 30.00
N52 A24 10 l carmine 4.00 4.00
Never hinged 6.00
g. Double overprint 24.00
Never hinged 47.50
Nos. N46-N52 (10) 1,770. 955.00

"Δ" for "Λ" in "ΛΗΜΝΟΣ"

N46d A25 2 l carmine rose 10.00 10.00
Never hinged 15.00
N47d A24 3 l vermilion 15.00 15.00
Never hinged 22.50
N48d A25 20 l gray blue 50.00 50.00
Never hinged 75.00
N49d A26 30 l carmine rose 15.00 15.00
Never hinged 22.50
N50d A27 2d vermilion 500.00 500.00
Never hinged 750.00
N51d A27 3d carmine rose 225.00 225.00
Never hinged 325.00
N51Ad A27 5d ultramarine 200.00 200.00
Never hinged 300.00
N51Cd A24 1 l green 10.00 10.00
Never hinged 15.00

No. N33 with Added "Greek Administration" Overprint, as on Nos. N109-N148, in Black

1913

N52A A24 1 l green 25.00 25.00
Never hinged 50.00
b. Period omitted after "ΕΛ-ΛΑΣ" (on #N33f) 360.00
Never hinged 600.00
c. Inverted "ΛΗΜΝΟΣ" overprint (on No. N33a) 90.00
Never hinged 120.00
d. Double"ΛΗΜΝΟΣ" overprint (on No. N33a) 90.00
Never hinged 120.00
e. As "b," double"ΛΗΜΝΟΣ" overprint (on No. N33f) —
Never hinged —
f. As "b," inverted"ΛΗΜΝΟΣ" overprint (on No. N33f) —
Never hinged —

Counterfeits of Nos. N16-N52A are plentiful.

MYTILENE (LESBOS)

Turkey Nos. 162, 158 Overprinted in Blue

Perf. 12, 13½ and Compound

1912 Typo. Unwmk.

N53 A21 20pa rose 22.50 22.50
Never hinged 45.00
N54 A21 10pi dull red 125.00 *135.00*
Never hinged 200.00

On Turkey Nos. P68, 151-155, 137, 157-158 in Black

N55 A21 2pa olive green 2.00 2.00
Never hinged 3.00

N56 A21 5pa ocher 2.00 2.00
Never hinged 3.00
N57 A21 10pa blue green 2.00 2.00
Never hinged 3.00
N58 A21 20pa rose 2.00 2.00
Never hinged 3.00
N59 A21 1pi ultra 4.00 4.00
Never hinged 6.00
N60 A21 2pi blue black 25.00 25.00
Never hinged 35.00
N61 A19 2½pi dk brown 12.00 12.00
Never hinged 18.00
N62 A21 5pi dk violet 26.00 26.00
Never hinged 35.00
N63 A21 10pi dull red 125.00 *135.00*
Never hinged 200.00
Nos. N55-N63 (9) 200.00 210.00

On Turkey Nos. 161-163, 145 in Black

N64 A21 10pa blue green 7.25 7.25
Never hinged 12.00
a. Double overprint 47.50 47.50
Never hinged 80.00
N65 A21 20pa rose 7.25 7.25
Never hinged 12.00
a. Blue overprint 40.00 40.00
Never hinged 65.00
N66 A21 1pi ultra 7.25 7.25
Never hinged 12.00
N67 A19 2pi blue black 65.00 65.00
Never hinged 120.00

Nos. N55, N58, N65, N59 Surcharged in Blue or Black

N68 A21 25 l on 2pa 12.00 12.00
Never hinged 18.00
a. New value inverted 45.00 *50.00*
Never hinged 85.00
b. 25 "ΛΕΠΤΑ" 35.00 35.00
Never hinged 52.50
N68C A21 25 l on 20pa 30.00 30.00
Never hinged 65.00
N68D A21 50 l on 2pa 30.00 30.00
Never hinged 65.00
N69 A21 50 l on 20pa 12.00 12.00
Never hinged 18.00
b. New value inverted 50.00 *55.00*
Never hinged 85.00
N70 A21 1d on 20pa (N65) (Bk) 40.00 40.00
Never hinged 60.00
a. New value inverted 72.50 72.50
Never hinged 110.00
b. "ΔΙΔΡΑΧΜΗ" for "ΔΡΑΧΜΗ" 120.00
Never hinged 180.00
c. Blue surcharge 37.50 40.00
Never hinged 80.00
d. As "c," new value inverted 120.00 120.00
Never hinged 200.00
N71 A21 2d on 1pi (Bk) 24.00 27.50
Never hinged 55.00
a. New value inverted
b. "ΔΙΔΡΑΧΜΗ" instead of "ΔΙΔΡΑΧΜΟΝ" 120.00
Never hinged 180.00

Same Overprint on Turkey No. J49

N72 A19 1pi blk, *dp rose* 60.00 72.50
Never hinged 100.00

The overprint is found on all values reading up or down with inverted "i" in the first word and inverted "e" in the third word.
No. N72 was only used for postage.
Counterfeits of Nos. N53-N72 are plentiful.

SAMOS

Issues of the Provisional Government

Map of Samos OS1

1912 Unwmk. Typo. *Imperf.*

N73 OS1 5 l gray green 24.00 10.00
Never hinged 37.50
a. 5 l red (error) 240.00 —
Never hinged 480.00
b. 5 l blue (error) 240.00 —
Never hinged 480.00
c. Tête bêche pair 450.00 —
Never hinged 600.00
N74 OS1 10 l red 20.00 10.00
Never hinged 37.50
a. 10 l pale green (error) 240.00 —
Never hinged 480.00
b. 10 l blue (error) 240.00 —
Never hinged 480.00
c. Tête bêche pair 440.00 —
Never hinged 600.00
N75 OS1 25 l blue 55.00 20.00
Never hinged 120.00
a. 25 l pale green (error) *500.00* *600.00*
Never hinged 900.00
b. 25 l red (error) 500.00 —
Never hinged 900.00
c. 25 l violet (error) *4,000.*
d. Tête bêche pair 2,400. —
Never hinged 4,800.
Nos. N73-N75 (3) 99.00 40.00

Only one example of No. N75c is known.
Counterfeits exist of Nos. N73 to N75.

Hermes — OS2

1912 Litho. *Perf. 11½*

Without Overprint

N76 OS2 1 l gray 2.00 1.50
Never hinged 3.50
N77 OS2 5 l lt green 2.00 1.50
Never hinged 3.50
N78 OS2 10 l rose 3.50 1.80
Never hinged 5.00
b. Half used as 5 l on cover *240.00*
N79 OS2 25 l lt blue 8.50 2.25
Never hinged 13.50
N80 OS2 50 l violet brn 15.00 6.00
Never hinged 24.00

With Overprint

N81 OS2 1 l gray 1.00 1.20
Never hinged 2.00
b. Pair, imperf. between 120.00
Never hinged 180.00
N82 OS2 5 l blue grn 1.00 1.20
Never hinged 2.00
b. Pair, imperf. between 120.00
Never hinged 180.00
N83 OS2 10 l rose 1.00 1.20
Never hinged 2.00
b. Half used as 5 l on cover *240.00*
N84 OS2 25 l blue 2.00 1.50
Never hinged 3.50
N85 OS2 50 l violet brn 12.00 7.25
Never hinged 18.00
N86 OS2 1d orange 15.00 13.50
Never hinged 27.50
Nos. N76-N86 (11) 63.00 38.90

For overprints and surcharge see Nos. N92-N103.

Imperf., Pairs
Without Overprint

N76a OS2 1 l 37.50 30.00
Never hinged 72.50
N77a OS2 5 l 37.50 30.00
Never hinged 72.50
N78a OS2 10 l 37.50 30.00
Never hinged 72.50
N79a OS2 25 l 37.50 30.00
Never hinged 72.50
N80a OS2 50 l 37.50 30.00
Never hinged 72.50

With Overprint

N81a OS2 1 l 85.00 40.00
Never hinged 150.00
N82a OS2 5 l 85.00 40.00
Never hinged 150.00
N83a OS2 10 l 85.00 40.00
Never hinged 150.00
N84a OS2 25 l 85.00 40.00
Never hinged 150.00
N85a OS2 50 l 85.00 40.00
Never hinged 150.00

Church in Savior's Name and Fort Ruins OS3

Manuscript Initials in Red or Black

1913

N87 OS3 1d brown (R) 18.00 15.00
Never hinged 37.50
a. Without initials 23.00 *42.50*
Never hinged 50.00
N88 OS3 2d deep blue (R) 18.00 15.00
Never hinged 37.50
a. Without initials 23.00 *42.50*
Never hinged 50.00
N89 OS3 5d gray grn (R) 37.50 30.00
Never hinged 80.00
a. Without initials 80.00 *120.00*
Never hinged 140.00
N90 OS3 10d yellow grn (R) 100.00 95.00
Never hinged 180.00
a. Without initials 180.00 *250.00*
Never hinged 300.00
c. Horiz. pair, imperf. vert. 800.00
Never hinged 1,325.
N91 OS3 25d red (Bk) 100.00 85.00
Never hinged 240.00
a. Without initials 180.00 *225.00*
Never hinged 300.00
c. Horiz. pair, imperf. vert. 800.00
Never hinged 1,325.
d. Initials in red
Nos. N87-N91 (5) 273.50 240.00

Victory of the Greek fleet in 1824 and the union with Greece of Samos in 1912. The manuscript initials are those of Pres. Themistokles Sofulis.
Exist imperf. Counterfeits of Nos. N87-N91 are plentiful.
For overprints see Nos. N104-N108.

Imperf., Pairs
Without Initials

N87b OS3 1 d 150.00
Never hinged 300.00
N88b OS3 2 d 150.00
Never hinged 300.00
N89b OS3 5 d 200.00
Never hinged 400.00
N90b OS3 10 d 800.00
Never hinged 1,400.
N91b OS3 25 d 800.00
Never hinged 1,400.

Nos. N76 to N80 Overprinted

1914

N92 OS2 1 l gray 7.25 6.00
Never hinged 12.00
a. Inverted overprint 200.00 160.00
Never hinged 400.00
b. Imperf., pair 90.00
Never hinged 180.00
N93 OS2 5 l lt green 7.25 6.00
Never hinged 12.00
a. Inverted overprint 200.00 160.00
Never hinged 400.00
b. Imperf., pair 90.00
Never hinged 180.00
N94 OS2 10 l rose 7.25 6.00
Never hinged 12.00
a. Double overprint 60.00
Never hinged 120.00
b. Inverted overprint 230.00 175.00
Never hinged 450.00
c. Imperf., pair 90.00
Never hinged 180.00
N95 OS2 25 l lt blue 12.00 12.00
Never hinged 18.00
b. Inverted overprint 230.00 175.00
Never hinged 450.00
c. Imperf., pair 90.00
Never hinged 180.00
N96 OS2 50 l violet brn 9.00 9.00
Never hinged 18.00
a. Double overprint 90.00 *100.00*
Never hinged 260.00
b. Inverted overprint 170.00 135.00
Never hinged 340.00
c. Imperf., pair 90.00
Never hinged 180.00
Nos. N92-N96 (5) 42.75 39.00

Charity Issues of Greek Administration

Nos. N81 to N86 Overprinted in Red or Black

1915

N97 OS2 1 l gray (R) 18.00 22.00
Never hinged 35.00
a. Black overprint 145.00 160.00
Never hinged 240.00
b. As N97, double overprint 180.00
Never hinged 325.00
c. Embossed control mark omitted 80.00
Never hinged 150.00
N98 OS2 5 l blue grn (Bk) 1.50 *2.00*
Never hinged 3.50
a. Red overprint 135.00 *150.00*
Never hinged 240.00
b. As N98, double overprint 145.00 *220.00*
Never hinged 250.00
c. Double embossed control mark 80.00
Never hinged 140.00
N99 OS2 10 l rose (Bk) 1.50 *2.00*
Never hinged 3.50
a. Red overprint 135.00 *160.00*
Never hinged 240.00
b. As N99, inverted overprint 125.00 *150.00*
Never hinged 225.00
N100 OS2 25 l blue (Bk) 1.50 *2.00*
Never hinged 3.50
a. Red overprint 135.00 *160.00*
Never hinged 240.00
b. Embossed control mark omitted 80.00
Never hinged 140.00
N101 OS2 50 l violet brn (Bk) 1.50 *2.00*
Never hinged 4.00
a. Red overprint 135.00 *160.00*
Never hinged 325.00
b. Embossed control mark omitted 80.00
Never hinged 140.00
c. Double embossed control mark 80.00
Never hinged 140.00
N102 OS2 1d orange (R) 3.50 *4.00*
Never hinged 7.25
a. Inverted overprint 135.00 *220.00*
Never hinged 240.00
b. Black overprint 120.00 *190.00*
Never hinged 180.00
c. As "b," double overprint 160.00 *220.00*
Never hinged 240.00

No. N102 With Additional Surcharge in Black

N103 OS2 1 l on 1d orange 20.00 20.00
Never hinged 40.00
a. Black surcharge double 180.00 *325.00*
Never hinged 650.00
b. Black surcharge inverted 180.00
Nos. N97-N103 (7) 47.50 54.00

Issue of 1913 Overprinted in Red or Black

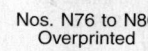

Without Sofoulis' Initials Above Overprint

1915

N104 OS3 1d brown (R) 28.00 17.00
Never hinged 60.00
a. With initials 40.00 25.00
Never hinged 60.00
N105 OS3 2d dp blue (R) 28.00 23.00
Never hinged 60.00
a. With initials 47.50 37.50
Never hinged 110.00
b. As "a," double overprint
N106 OS3 5d gray grn (R) 45.00 28.00
Never hinged 85.00
a. With initials 40.00 25.00
Never hinged 95.00
b. As "a," black overprint 1,500.
Never hinged 2,400.
N107 OS3 10d yellow grn (Bk) 85.00 72.50
Never hinged 145.00
a. Inverted overprint 1,600.
Never hinged 2,650.
N108 OS3 25d red (Bk) *600.00* *650.00*
Never hinged 1,050.
a. With initials 750.00 750.00
Never hinged 1,500.
Nos. N104-N108 (5) 786.00 790.50

Nos. N97 to N108 inclusive have an embossed control mark, consisting of a cross encircled by a Greek inscription.
Counterfeits of Nos. N104-N108 are plentiful.

FOR USE IN PARTS OF TURKEY OCCUPIED BY GREECE (NEW GREECE)

Regular Issues of Greece Overprinted

Black Overprint Meaning "Greek Administration" On Issue of 1901 Overprint Reading Up

1912 Wmk. 129 Engr. *Perf. 13½*

N109 A11 20 l red lilac 3.25 2.75
Never hinged 7.25
a. Double overprint 45.00 45.00
Never hinged 120.00

On Issue of 1911-21
Unwmk.
Serrate Roulette 13½

N110 A24 1 l green 1.00 1.00
Never hinged 1.50
a. Double overprint 22.50 22.00
Never hinged 45.00
N111 A25 2 l car rose 1.00 1.00
Never hinged 1.50
a. Double overprint 6.75 *8.00*
Never hinged 12.00
b. Double ovpt., one inverted 70.00
Never hinged *140.00*
N112 A24 3 l vermilion 1.00 1.00
Never hinged 1.50
a. Double overprint 6.75 *8.00*
Never hinged 12.00
N113 A26 5 l green 1.00 1.00
Never hinged 1.50
a. Double overprint 10.00 10.00
Never hinged 20.00

N114 A24 10 l car rose 1.50 2.00
Never hinged 3.00
a. Double overprint 10.00 10.00
Never hinged 20.00
N115 A25 20 l gray lilac 2.75 2.75
Never hinged 5.00
a. Double overprint 22.50 22.50
Never hinged 45.00
b. Double ovpt., one inverted 60.00 60.00
Never hinged 125.00
c. Triple overprint 85.00 —
Never hinged 175.00
g. Imperf., pair 1,200.
Never hinged 2,400.
N116 A25 25 l ultra 2.75 2.75
Never hinged 5.00
a. Double overprint 22.50 18.50
Never hinged 45.00
N117 A26 30 l car rose 2.75 *3.00*
Never hinged 5.50
a. Double overprint 25.00 25.00
Never hinged 55.00
N118 A25 40 l deep blue 3.75 *4.50*
Never hinged 9.00
a. Double overprint 27.50 24.00
Never hinged 55.00
N119 A26 50 l dl violet 4.50 *5.00*
Never hinged 11.00
a. Double overprint 30.00 *30.00*
Never hinged 90.00
N120 A27 1d ultra 11.00 3.50
Never hinged 22.00
a. 1d gray ultramarine (on #208a) 100.00 80.00
Never hinged 240.00
b. Double overprint 90.00 90.00
Never hinged 180.00
c. Double ovpt., one inverted *2,500.*
N121 A27 2d vermilion 55.00 25.00
Never hinged 110.00
a. Double overprint 120.00 120.00
Never hinged 240.00
N122 A27 3d car rose 55.00 32.50
Never hinged 110.00
N123 A27 5d ultra 25.00 32.50
Never hinged 50.00
a. Double overprint 45.00 45.00
Never hinged 100.00
b. 5d deep gray blue 35.00 35.00
Never hinged 65.00
N124 A27 10d deep blue 265.00 265.00
Never hinged 500.00
a. Double overprint *850.00 850.00*
Never hinged *1,900.*
N125 A28 25d dp bl, ovpt. horiz. 325.00 325.00
Never hinged 650.00
a. Last "Σ" of "ΔΙΟΙΚΗΣΙΣ" inverted 2,750.

On Issue of 1913-23
Litho.

N126 A24 1 l green 1.00 1.00
Never hinged 1.50
a. Double overprint 5.50 *7.00*
Never hinged 11.00
b. Double ovpt., one inverted 55.00 55.00
Never hinged 110.00
c. Period omitted after "ΕΛ-ΛΑΣ" (on #214a) 145.00 75.00
Never hinged 225.00
f. As "c," double overprint
g. As "c," double ovpt., one inverted
N127 A26 5 l green 1.00 1.00
Never hinged 1.50
a. Double overprint 7.00 *8.00*
Never hinged 13.50
b. Imperf., pair
N128 A24 10 l carmine 4.00 3.00
Never hinged 6.00
a. Double overprint 7.00 *8.00*
Never hinged 14.00
b. Double overprint, one inverted 140.00 140.00
Never hinged 275.00
N129 A25 25 l blue 6.00 6.00
Never hinged 10.00
a. Double overprint 22.50 22.50
Never hinged 45.00
b. Triple overprint 225.00
Never hinged 450.00
Nos. N109-N129 (21) 773.25 721.25

Overprinted Reading Down (Inverted)

N109d A11 20 l red lilac 10.00 10.00
Never hinged 20.00
N110d A24 1 l green 50.00 50.00
Never hinged 100.00
N111d A25 2 l carmine rose 2.00 2.00
Never hinged 3.50
e. Double overprint 90.00
Never hinged 180.00
N112d A24 3 l carmine rose 3.00 3.00
Never hinged 5.00
N113d A26 5 l green 4.50 4.00
Never hinged 6.50
e. Double overprint 140.00
Never hinged 280.00
N114d A24 10 l carmine rose 150.00 160.00
Never hinged 375.00
N115d A25 20 l gray lilac 6.50 6.50
Never hinged 17.00
e. Double overprint 180.00
Never hinged 360.00
f. Pair, one without ovpt. 180.00
Never hinged 360.00
N116d A25 25 l ultramarine 145.00 120.00
Never hinged 300.00
N117d A26 30 l carmine rose 400.00 400.00
Never hinged 1,000.
N118d A26 40 l deep blue 250.00 200.00
Never hinged 750.00
N119d A26 40 l dull violet 375.00 375.00
Never hinged 900.00
e. Double overprint 950.00
Never hinged 1,800.
N120d A27 1d ultra 95.00 80.00
Never hinged 250.00
e. 1d gray ultra (on #208a) 80.00 72.50
Never hinged 190.00
N121d A27 2d vermilion 140.00 125.00
Never hinged 325.00
N122d A27 3d carmine rose 125.00 125.00
Never hinged 300.00
N123d A27 5d ultramarine 600.00 600.00
Never hinged 1,750.
e. 5d deep gray blue 650.00 650.00
Never hinged 1,950.
N126d A24 1 l green 10.00 10.00
Never hinged 19.00
e. Double overprint 75.00
Never hinged 180.00
N127d A26 5 l green 4.00 4.00
Never hinged 6.00
e. Double overprint 150.00
Never hinged 300.00
N128d A24 10 l carmine 5.00 5.00
Never hinged 8.00
N129d A25 25 l carmine 75.00 75.00
Never hinged 190.00
e. Double overprint 80.00
Never hinged 190.00

Red Overprint, Reading Up On Issues of 1911-21
Engr.

N130 A24 1 l green 1.00 1.00
Never hinged 2.00
N131 A26 5 l green 1.00 1.00
Never hinged 2.00
a. Double overprint
N132 A25 20 l gray lilac 5.50 5.00
Never hinged 13.00
a. Inverted overprint (reading down) *3,000. 1,800.*
Never hinged *6,500.*
N133 A25 40 l deep blue 2.75 2.75
Never hinged 5.50
a. Double overprint 275.00 275.00
Never hinged 500.00
b. Pair, one stamp without overprint 125.00
Never hinged 250.00
N134 A26 50 l dull violet 3.25 3.25
Never hinged 6.00
a. Double overprint, one black, one red 1,250.
Never hinged 2,500.
N135 A27 1d ultramarine 20.00 15.00
Never hinged 37.50
N136 A27 2d vermilion 90.00 *100.00*
Never hinged 180.00
N137 A27 3d carmine rose 32.50 *45.00*
Never hinged 65.00
N138 A27 5d ultramarine 550.00 400.00
Never hinged 1,250.
N139 A27 10d deep blue 40.00 *55.00*
Never hinged 80.00
a. Double overprint 725.00
Never hinged 1,250.
b. Double ovpt., one inverted 725.00
Never hinged 1,450.
c. Double ovpt., one black, one red 950.00
Never hinged 1,900.
N140 A28 25d dp bl, ovpt. horiz. 75.00 100.00
Never hinged 180.00
a. Double overprint 1,800.
Never hinged 5,400.
b. Inverted overprint (reading down) 550.00 550.00
Never hinged 1,100
c. Inverted overprint (reading up) 650.00 650.00
Never hinged 1,600.

Litho.

N141 A26 5 l green 1.60 1.75
Never hinged 2.80
a. Inverted overprint (reading down) 1,900.
N142 A25 25 l ultra, ovpt. vert. (reading up) 2.75 1.75
Never hinged 5.50
a. Inverted overprint (reading down) 225.00
Never hinged 475.00
Nos. N130-N142 (13) 825.35 731.50

Nos. N140b and N140c were the only horizontal or vertical overprints placed into normal circulation.

Engr.
Carmine Overprint, Reading Up

N143 A25 2 l carmine rose 12.00 *13.00*
Never hinged 25.00
a. Double overprint 40.00
Never hinged 80.00
b. Inverted overprint (reading down) — —
N144 A24 3 l vermilion 12.00 *13.00*
Never hinged 25.00
N145 A25 20 l gray lilac 50.00 *80.00*
Never hinged 100.00
a. Double overprint 75.00
Never hinged 180.00
N146 A25 25 l ultramarine 90.00 90.00
Never hinged 180.00
N147 A26 30 l carmine rose 110.00 110.00
Never hinged 225.00
a. Double overprint 290.00
Never hinged 575.00
N148 A27 2d vermilion 200.00 165.00
Never hinged 425.00
a. Double overprint 300.00
Never hinged 600.00
N149 A27 5d ultramarine *.550.00* 400.00
Never hinged 1,150.
a. Double overprint 625.00
Never hinged 1,250.

Litho.

N150 A24 1 l green 11.00 12.50
Never hinged 17.00
b. Period omitted after "ΕΛ-ΛΑΣ" (on #214a) *450.00*
Never hinged 875.00
e. Ovpt. reading down *1,575.*
Never hinged *2,500.*
f. As "e," period omitted after "ΕΛΛΑΣ" (on #214a)
N151 A24 10 l carmine rose 65.00 65.00
Never hinged 150.00
Nos. N143-N151 (9) 1,100. 948.50

There are numerous broken, missing and wrong font letters with a Greek "Λ" instead of "Δ" as the first letter of the second word.

Counterfeits exist of Nos. N109-N151.

Cross of Constantine O1

Eagle of Zeus O2

1912 **Litho.**

N150A O1 1 l brn, *grayish* .30 .30
Never hinged .75
c. 1 l brown, *yellowish* 5.50 5.50
Never hinged 11.00
d. As "c," imperf., pair 550.00
Never hinged 1,200.
N152 O2 2 l red, *yelwsh* .30 .30
Never hinged .75
a. 2 l rose 1.25 .85
Never hinged 2.00
N153 O2 3 l org, *grayish* .30 .30
Never hinged .75
a. 3 l orange, *yellowish* 5.50 5.50
Never hinged 11.00
N154 O1 5 l grn, *grayish* .30 .30
Never hinged .75
a. 5 l green, *yellowish* 6.50 6.50
Never hinged 13.00
N155 O1 10 l rose red, *grayish* .30 .30
Never hinged .75
a. 10 l rose red, *yellowish* 11.00 3.25
Never hinged 24.00
N156 O1 20 l vio, *grayish* 22.50 4.00
Never hinged 45.00
N157 O2 25 l pale bl, *yelwsh* 3.00 1.00
Never hinged 10.00
N158 O1 30 l gray grn, *yelwsh* 70.00 3.00
Never hinged 210.00
N159 O2 40 l indigo, *grayish* 11.00 5.00
Never hinged 25.00
a. 40 l indigo, *yellowish* 17.50 8.50
Never hinged 35.00
c. Double impression —
N160 O1 50 l dk bl, *yelwsh* 5.00 3.00
Never hinged 13.50
N161 O2 1d vio brn, *grayish* 15.00 4.50
Never hinged 32.50
a. 1d violet brn, *yellowish*
N162 O1 2d gray brn, *grayish* 55.00 9.00
Never hinged 125.00
a. 2d violet brn
N163 O2 3d dl bl, *yelwsh* 225.00 32.50
Never hinged 1,300.
a. 3d dull blue, *grayish* *700.00* 110.00
Never hinged *3,500.*
N164 O1 5d gray, *yelwsh* 200.00 32.50
Never hinged *1,500.*
N165 O2 10d car, *grayish* *225.00 325.00*
Never hinged *550.00*
N166 O1 25d gray blk, *yelwsh* *225.00 350.00*
Never hinged *550.00*
Nos. N150A-N166 (16) 1,058. 771.00

Occupation of Macedonia, Epirus and some of the Aegean Islands.

Sold only in New Greece.

Dangerous forgeries of Nos. N165-N166 exist.

In 1916 some stamps of this issue were overprinted in Greek: "I (era) Koinotis Ag (iou) Orous" for the Mount Athos Monastery District. They were never placed in use and most of them were destroyed.

For surcharges and overprints see Nos. 267-276A, RA14-RA16, Thrace 31-33.

Imperf., Pairs
Without Overprint

N150d O1 1 l (as #N150Ac) 500.00
Never hinged 900.00
N151b O2 2 l 600.00
Never hinged 900.00
N152b O2 2 l 500.00
Never hinged *1,200.*
N153b O2 3 l (as #153a) 450.00
Never hinged 1,000.
N154b O1 5 l (as #154a) 200.00
Never hinged 350.00
N155b O1 10 l (as #155a) 200.00
Never hinged 350.00
N156b O1 20 l 1,800.
Never hinged 2,800.
N157b O2 25 l 1,800.
Never hinged 3,000.
N158b O1 30 l 1,800.
Never hinged 3,000.
N159b O2 40 l 1,800.
Never hinged 3,000.
N160b O1 50 l 2,000.
Never hinged 3,600.
N161b O2 1d 2,000.
Never hinged 3,950.
N162b O1 2d 2,800.
Never hinged 3,600.
N163b O2 3d *2,800.*
Never hinged 3,600.
N163c O2 3d (As #N163a)
N164a O1 5d *2,800.*
Never hinged *5,500.*
N165a O2 10d *2,800.*
Never hinged *5,500.*

CAVALLA

Bulgaria Nos. 89-97 Surcharged in Red

1913 **Unwmk.** **Engr.** ***Perf. 12***

N167 A20 5 l on 1s myr grn *30.00 30.00*
Never hinged *55.00*
N168 A25 10 l on 10s red & blk *550.00 450.00*
Never hinged *850.00*
N169 A25 10 l on 15s brn bis *70.00 70.00*
Never hinged *125.00*
N170 A26 10 l on 25s ultra & blk *35.00 35.00*
Never hinged *70.00*
N171 A21 15 l on 2s car & blk *70.00 70.00*
Never hinged *125.00*
N172 A22 20 l on 3s lake & blk *70.00 70.00*
Never hinged *125.00*
N173 A23 25 l on 5s grn & blk *25.00 15.00*
Never hinged *45.00*
N174 A24 50 l on 10s red & blk *45.00 35.00*
Never hinged *80.00*
N175 A25 1d on 15s brn bis *300.00 250.00*
Never hinged *600.00*
N176 A27 1d on 30s bl & blk *120.00 120.00*
Never hinged *240.00*
N177 A28 1d on 50s ocher & blk *165.00 165.00*
Never hinged *350.00*

Blue Surcharge

N178 A24 50 l on 10s red & blk *25.00 25.00*
Never hinged *47.50*
Nos. N167-N178 (11) *955.00 885.00*

The counterfeits and reprints of Nos. N167-N178 are difficult to distinguish from originals. Many overprint varieties exist.

Some specialists question the status of Nos. N167-N178.

DEDEAGATCH

(Alexandroupolis)

D1-(10 lepta)

Control Mark in Red

1913 **Unwmk.** **Typeset** ***Perf. 11½***

N179 D1 5 l black 40.00 30.00
N180 D1 10 l black 5.50 4.00
N181 D1 25 l black 6.50 5.00
a. Sheet of 8 135.00 110.00
Nos. N179-N181 (3) 52.00 39.00

Nos. N179-N181 issued without gum in sheets of 8, consisting of one 5 l, three 10 l normal, one 10 l inverted, three 25 l and one blank. The sheet yields se-tenant pairs of 5 l & 10 l, 10 l & 25 l; tete beche pairs of 5 l & 10 l, 10 l & 25 l and 10 l & 10 l.

Also issued imperf., value $200 unused, $160 canceled.

The 5 l reads "PENTE LEPTA" in Greek letters; the 10 l is illustrated; the 25 l carries the numeral "25."

Bulgaria Nos. 89-90, 92-93, 95 Surcharged

1913 Red Surcharge *Perf. 12*

N182 A20 5 l on 1s myr grn 65.00 45.00
Never hinged 150.00
a. "ΔΕΔΕΑΓΤΕ" instead of "ΔΕΔΕΑΓΤΕ" 150.00 110.00
N183 A26 1d on 25s ultra & blk 100.00 60.00
Never hinged 250.00
a. "ΔΕΔΕΑΓΤΕ" instead of "ΔΕΔΕΑΓΤΕ" 180.00 125.00

Blue Surcharge

N184 A24 10 l on 10s red & blk 32.50 25.00
Never hinged 65.00
a. "ΔΕΔΕΑΓΤΕ" instead of "ΔΕΔΕΑΓΤΕ" 190.00 140.00
b. Double surcharge 1,650.
c. As "b," "ΔΕΔΕΑΓΤΕ" instead of "ΔΕΔΕΑΓΤΕ" 4,400.
N185 A23 25 l on 5s grn & blk 35.00 27.50
Never hinged 70.00
a. "ΔΕΔΕΑΓΤΕ" instead of "ΔΕΔΕΑΓΤΕ" 190.00 140.00
N187 A21 50 l on 2s car & blk 65.00 45.00
Never hinged 145.00
a. "ΔΕΔΕΑΓΤΕ" instead of "ΔΕΔΕΑΓΤΕ" 200.00 150.00
Nos. N182-N185,N187 (5) 297.50 202.50

The surcharges on Nos. N182 to N187 are printed from a setting of eight, which was used for all, with the necessary changes of value. No. 6 in the setting has a Greek "L" instead of "D" for the third letter of the third word of the surcharge.

The 25 l surcharge also exists on 8 examples of the 25s, Bulgaria No. 95.

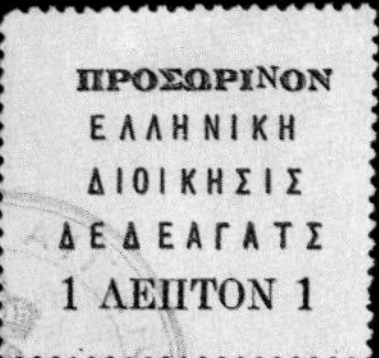

D2

1913, Sept. 15 Typeset *Perf. 11½*

Control Mark in Blue

N188 D2 1 l blue *200.00* 65.00
N189 D2 2 l blue *200.00* 65.00
N190 D2 3 l blue *200.00* 65.00
N191 D2 5 l blue *200.00* 65.00
N192 D2 10 l blue *200.00* 65.00
N193 D2 25 l blue *200.00* 65.00
N194 D2 40 l blue *200.00* 65.00
N195 D2 50 l blue *200.00* 65.00
a. Sheet of 8 *2,200.* *1,000.*
Nos. N188-N195 (8) 1,600. 520.00

Issued without gum in sheets of 8 containing all values.

Counterfeits of Nos. N188-N195 exist.

D3

1913, Sept. 25 Typeset

Control Mark in Blue

N196 D3 1 l blue, *gray blue* *175.00* 55.00
N197 D3 5 l blue, *gray blue* *175.00* 55.00
N198 D3 10 l blue, *gray blue* *175.00* 55.00
N199 D3 25 l blue, *gray blue* *175.00* 55.00
N200 D3 30 l blue, *gray blue* *175.00* 55.00
N201 D3 50 l blue, *gray blue* *175.00* 55.00
a. Sheet of 6 *1,350.* *500.00*
Nos. N196-N201 (6) 1,050. 330.00

Nos. N196 to N201 were issued without gum in sheets of six containing all values.

Counterfeits of Nos. N182-N201 are plentiful.

FOR USE IN NORTH EPIRUS (ALBANIA)

Greek Stamps of 1937-38 Overprinted in Black

Perf. 13½x12, 12x13½

1940 Litho. Wmk. 252

N202 A69 5 l brn red & bl .25 .30
Never hinged .30
a. Inverted overprint 55.00
Never hinged 65.00
b. Double impression of frame
N203 A70 10 l bl & brn red (No. 413) .25 .30
Never hinged .30
a. Double impression of frame *150.00*
b. Double overprint
N204 A71 20 l blk & grn .25 .30
Never hinged .30
a. Inverted overprint 55.00
b. Double impression of grn
N205 A72 40 l grn & blk .25 .30
Never hinged .30
a. Inverted overprint 55.00
Never hinged 65.00
b. Double impression of grn
N206 A73 50 l brn & blk .25 .30
Never hinged .30
N207 A74 80 l ind & yel brn .35 .35
Never hinged .60
a. Double impression of frame 55.00
N208 A67 1d green .35 .35
Never hinged .60
a. Inverted overprint *90.00*
b. "ΛΙΟΙΚΗΕΙΕ" instead of "ΔΙΟΙΚΗΕΙΕ" 24.00
Never hinged 45.00
c. Double overprint 200.00
N209 A75 2d ultra .35 .40
Never hinged .45
N210 A67 3d red brn .75 .80
Never hinged .80
a. "ΛΙΟΙΚΗΕΙΕ" instead of "ΔΙΟΙΚΗΕΙΕ" 24.00
Never hinged 37.50
N211 A76 5d red .75 .80
Never hinged .85
N212 A77 6d ol brn .85 .95
Never hinged 1.25
N213 A78 7d dk brn .95 1.00
Never hinged 1.25
N214 A67 8d deep blue .95 1.00
Never hinged 1.75
a. "ΛΙΟΙΚΗΕΙΕ" instead of "ΔΙΟΙΚΗΕΙΕ" 24.00
Never hinged 37.50
N215 A79 10d red brn 2.00 2.00
Never hinged 3.00
N216 A80 15d green 2.00 2.00
Never hinged 3.00
N217 A81 25d dark blue 5.00 *6.25*
Never hinged 10.00
a. Inverted overprint *100.00*
Never hinged 125.00

Engr. Unwmk.

N218 A84 30d org brn 8.00 *15.00*
Never hinged 12.00
a. Double overprint
Nos. N202-N218 (17) 23.55 32.40

Same Overprinted in Carmine on National Youth Issue

1941 Litho. *Perf. 12½, 13½x12½*

N219 A93 3d sil, dp ultra & red 1.00 *1.00*
Never hinged 1.25
N220 A94 5d dk bl & blk 3.00 *4.50*
Never hinged 4.25
N221 A94 10d red org & blk 4.50 *6.75*
Never hinged 7.00
N222 A94 15d dk grn & blk 18.50 *20.00*
Never hinged 30.00
N223 A94 20d lake & blk 13.50 *15.00*
Never hinged 18.00
N224 A94 25d dk bl & blk 13.50 *15.00*
Never hinged 18.00
N225 A94 30d rose vio & blk 13.50 *15.00*
Never hinged 18.00
N226 A94 50d lake & blk 13.50 *15.00*
Never hinged 18.00
N227 A94 75d dk bl, brn & gold 15.00 15.00
Never hinged 23.00
N228 A93 100d sil, dp ultra & red 22.50 *20.00*
Never hinged 30.00
a. Inverted overprint *475.00*
Never hinged 750.00
Nos. N219-N228 (10) 118.50 127.25

Same Overprint in Carmine on National Youth Air Post Stamps

N229 AP25 2d red org & blk 1.00 *1.00*
Never hinged 1.20
a. Inverted overprint *165.00*
Never hinged 210.00
N230 AP25 4d dk grn & blk 3.50 *4.50*
Never hinged 5.00
a. Inverted overprint *165.00*
Never hinged 210.00
N231 AP25 6d lake & blk 6.50 *7.00*
Never hinged 8.00
a. Inverted overprint *165.00*
Never hinged 210.00
N232 AP25 8d dk bl & blk 6.50 *7.00*
Never hinged 8.50
N233 AP25 16d rose vio & blk 11.00 9.00
Never hinged 14.00
N234 AP25 32d red org & blk 15.00 15.00
Never hinged 20.00
N235 AP25 45d dk grn & blk 16.00 14.00
Never hinged 20.00
N236 AP25 55d lake & blk 16.00 14.00
Never hinged 20.00
N237 AP25 65d dk bl & blk 16.00 14.00
Never hinged 20.00
N238 AP25 100d rose vio & blk 25.00 *30.00*
Never hinged 37.50
a. Inverted overprint *850.00*
Never hinged 1,200.
Nos. N229-N238 (10) 116.50 115.50

Some specialists have questioned the status of Nos. N230a and N231a.

For other stamps issued by Greece for use in occupied parts of Epirus and Thrace, see the catalogue listings of those countries.

POSTAGE DUE STAMPS

FOR USE IN PARTS OF TURKEY OCCUPIED BY GREECE (NEW GREECE)

1902 Postage Due Stamps of Greece Overprinted

1912 Wmk. 129 Engr. *Perf. 13½*

Black Overprint, Reading Up

NJ1 D3 1 l chocolate .55 .65
Never hinged 1.10
a. Double overprint 22.00
Never hinged 45.00
b. Double overprint, one inverted 47.50
Never hinged 85.00
c. Double overprint, one on reverse 75.00
Never hinged 150.00
d. Inverted overprint (reading down) 47.50 47.50
Never hinged 95.00
NJ2 D3 2 l gray .55 .65
Never hinged 1.10
a. Double overprint 15.50
Never hinged 32.50
b. Double overprint, one inverted 25.00
Never hinged 50.00
c. Double overprint, one on reverse reading down 350.00
Never hinged 700.00
d. Inverted overprint (reading down) 37.50 *65.00*
Never hinged 75.00
NJ3 D3 3 l orange .55 .65
Never hinged 1.10
a. Double overprint 15.50 *20.00*
Never hinged 32.50
b. Double overprint, one inverted 47.50 60.00
Never hinged 100.00
c. Double overprint, both inverted 100.00
Never hinged 150.00
d. Pair, one without ovpt. —
e. Pair, one with ovpt. reading down —
NJ4 D3 5 l yel grn .95 1.10
Never hinged 2.00
a. Double overprint 20.00
Never hinged 40.00
NJ5 D3 10 l scarlet 1.45 1.60
Never hinged 2.90
a. Double overprint 20.00
Never hinged 40.00
NJ6 D3 20 l lilac 1.45 1.60
Never hinged 3.00
NJ7 D3 30 l dp vio 3.00 3.50
Never hinged 6.00
a. Double overprint 75.00
Never hinged 150.00
b. Double overprint, one on reverse 190.00
Never hinged 375.00
NJ8 D3 40 l dk brn 6.50 *7.00*
Never hinged 8.50
a. Double overprint 122.50
Never hinged 250.00
NJ9 D3 50 l red brn 9.50 10.00
Never hinged 18.00
NJ10 D3 1d black 45.00 *47.50*
Never hinged 90.00
NJ11 D3 2d bronze (overprint reading down) 72.50 82.50
Never hinged 145.00
NJ12 D3 3d silver (overprint reading down) 142.50 120.00
Never hinged 285.00
NJ13 D3 5d gold (overprint reading down) 225.00 250.00
Never hinged 500.00
Nos. NJ1-NJ13 (13) 509.50 526.75

Red Overprint, Reading Up

NJ14 D3 1 l chocolate 1.00 1.00
Never hinged 1.90
NJ15 D3 2 l gray 1.00 1.00
Never hinged 1.90
a. Double overprint 80.00
Never hinged 160.00
b. Inverted overprint (reading down)
NJ16 D3 5 l yellow green 1.00 1.00
Never hinged 1.90
a. Inverted overprint (reading down)
NJ17 D3 20 l lilac 1.00 1.00
Never hinged 1.90
NJ18 D3 30 l deep violet 5.00 5.00
Never hinged 10.00
a. Inverted overprint (reading down) 30.00 45.00
Never hinged 60.00
NJ19 D3 40 l dark brown 1.45 1.60
Never hinged 3.00
NJ20 D3 50 l red brown 1.45 1.60
Never hinged 3.00
NJ21 D3 1d black 10.00 10.50
Never hinged 18.00
NJ22 D3 2d bronze 20.00 *21.00*
Never hinged 37.50
NJ23 D3 3d silver 24.50 *27.00*
Never hinged 50.00
a. Inverted overprint (reading down)
NJ24 D3 5d gold 60.00 *62.50*
Never hinged 120.00
Nos. NJ14-NJ24 (11) 126.40 133.20

Carmine Overprint, Reading Up

NJ25 D3 2 l gray 10.00 11.00
Never hinged 20.00
NJ26 D3 3 l orange 147.50 *170.00*
Never hinged 295.00
NJ27 D3 1d black 82.50 *110.00*
Never hinged 165.00
a. Double overprint, one inverted 245.00
Never hinged 500.00
NJ28 D3 2d bronze 500.00
Never hinged 1,250.
NJ29 D3 3d silver *2,000.*
Nos. NJ25-NJ29 (5) 740.00 2,291.

Carmine Overprint, Reading Down

NJ30 D3 2 l gray 4.00 4.00
Never hinged 8.00
NJ31 D3 3 l orange 10.00 11.00
Never hinged 20.00
NJ32 D3 5 l yellow green 9.00 9.00
Never hinged 18.00
NJ33 D3 10 l scarlet 15.00 15.00
Never hinged 30.00
NJ34 D3 1d black 55.00 55.00
Never hinged 120.00
a. Double overprint 275.00
Never hinged 550.00
NJ35 D3 2d bronze 85.00 *90.00*
Never hinged 175.00
NJ36 D3 3d silver 385.00 *400.00*
Never hinged 850.00
NJ37 D3 5d gold 750.00 *775.00*
Never hinged 1,900.
Nos. NJ30-NJ37 (8) 1,313. 1,359.

Some of the varieties of lettering that occur on the postage stamps are also found on the postage due stamps.

FOR USE IN NORTH EPIRUS (ALBANIA)

Postage Due Stamps of Greece, 1930, Surcharged or Overprinted in Black:

a

b

Perf. 13, 13x12½

1940 Litho. Unwmk.

NJ38 D3(a) 50 l on 25d lt red .45 .90
Never hinged .60
NJ39 D3(b) 2d light red 1.10 *1.75*
Never hinged 1.40
a. Inverted overprint 67.50
Never hinged 85.00
NJ40 D3(b) 5d blue gray .55 *1.45*
Never hinged .90
NJ41 D3(b) 10d green 1.10 *1.90*
Never hinged 1.50
NJ42 D3(b) 15d red brown 1.10 *1.90*
Never hinged 1.50
Nos. NJ38-NJ42 (5) 4.30 7.90

POSTAL TAX STAMPS

FOR USE IN NORTH EPIRUS (ALBANIA)

Postal Tax Stamps of Greece, Nos. RA61-RA63, Overprinted Type "b" in Black

1940 Unwmk. Litho.	*Perf. 13½x12*	
NRA1 PT7 10 l	.25	.35
Never hinged	.30	
NRA2 PT7 50 l	.35	.55
Never hinged	.50	
a. Inverted overprint	65.00	
Never hinged	90.00	
b. Double overprint	65.00	
Never hinged	90.00	
NRA3 PT7 1d	.95	*1.75*
Never hinged	1.20	
Nos. NRA1-NRA3 (3)	1.55	2.65

GREENLAND

'grēn-lənd

LOCATION — North Atlantic Ocean
GOVT. — Danish
AREA — 840,000 sq. mi.
POP. — 52,347 (1984)
CAPITAL — Nuuk (Godthaab)

100 Ore = 1 Krone

Christian X — A1

Polar Bear — A2

Perf. 13x12½

1938-46 Unwmk.		Engr.
1 A1 1o olive black	.30	*.30*
Never hinged	.55	
2 A1 5o rose lake	2.10	1.25
Never hinged	5.25	
On cover		55.00
3 A1 7o yellow green	3.75	*4.00*
Never hinged	6.00	
On cover		70.00
4 A1 10o dk violet	1.00	1.00
Never hinged	1.95	
On cover		62.50
a. 10o light violet ('45)	2.10	1.60
Never hinged	4.00	
On cover		70.00
5 A1 15o red	1.00	1.00
Never hinged	2.50	
On cover		42.50
6 A1 20o red ('46)	1.10	*1.25*
Never hinged	3.00	
On cover		27.50
7 A2 30o blue	4.50	*7.50*
Never hinged	13.50	
On cover		125.00
8 A2 40o blue ('46)	21.00	11.50
Never hinged	82.50	
On cover		110.00
9 A2 1k light brown	5.25	*10.00*
Never hinged	19.00	
On cover		140.00
Nos. 1-9 (9)	40.00	*37.80*
Set, never hinged	100.00	

Issued: Nov. 1, 1938; Aug. 1, 1946.

Nos. 1 and 2 exist in two engraving types.

For surcharges see Nos. 39-40 in Scott Standard catalogue, Vol. 3.

PARCEL POST STAMPS

Arms of Greenland PP1

1905-10 Unwmk. Typo.	*Perf. 12¼*	
Q1a 1o ol grn ('05)	600.00	650.00
Never hinged	1,400.	
Q3a 5o brown ('05-'10)	600.00	*650.00*
Never hinged	1,400.	
Q4a 10o blue ('05-'10)	750.00	550.00
Never hinged	1,575.	
Set of 3	1,750.	1,625.

1915-28		
Q1 PP1 1o ol grn ('15-'26)	47.50	*52.50*
Never hinged	125.00	
Q2 PP1 2o yel ('15-'24)	300.00	110.00
Never hinged	400.00	
Q3 PP1 5o brn ('18-'28)	140.00	140.00
Never hinged	280.00	
Q4b PP1 10o blue ('18)	45.00	*55.00*
Never hinged	100.00	
Q5 PP1 15o vio ('15-'28)	240.00	240.00
Never hinged	950.00	
Q6 PP1 20o red ('15-'33)	10.00	12.00
Never hinged	20.00	
Nos. Q1-Q6 (6)	782.50	*609.50*

1930		
Q7a PP1 70o violet	225.00	200.00
Never hinged	800.00	
Q8a PP1 1k yellow	40.00	*55.00*
Never hinged	85.00	
Q9 PP1 3k brown	110.00	*160.00*
Never hinged	270.00	
Nos. Q7a-Q9 (3)	375.00	*415.00*
Nos. Q1-Q9, never hinged	3,000.	

1937 Litho.		*Perf. 10¾*
Q10 PP1 70o pale violet	27.50	*140.00*
Never hinged	65.00	
Q11 PP1 1k yellow	30.00	*90.00*
Never hinged	65.00	
Nos. Q10-Q11, never hinged	150.00	

1937		Typo.
Q4 PP1 10o blue ('37)	30.00	*60.00*
Q6a PP1 20o red	42.50	*60.00*
Never hinged	90.00	
Q7 PP1 70o violet ('37)	27.50	*140.00*
Never hinged	65.00	
Q8 PP1 1k yellow ('37)	32.50	*100.00*
Never hinged	65.00	
Nos. Q4-Q8 (4)	132.50	*360.00*

On lithographed stamps, PAKKE-PORTO is slightly larger, hyphen has rounded ends and lines in shield are fine, straight and evenly spaced.

On typographed stamps, hyphen has squared ends and shield lines are coarse, uneven and inclined to be slightly wavy.

Used values are for stamps postally used from Denmark. Numeral cancels indicate use as postal savings stamps and are usually worth as much or more than postally used examples. Greenland village cancels on Nos. Q6, Q6a and Q8a often relfect postal savings use. These are often worth as much or more than postally used examples. Parcel post stamps not regularly used for postal savings that have village cancellations are often worth much more.

Sheets of 25. Certain printings of Nos. Q1-Q2, Q3a, Q4a and Q5-Q6 were issued without sheet margins. Stamps from the outer rows are straight edged. Some of these sheets had the outer straight edges officially perforated in 1918. Stamps with falsified reperforations exist.

GRENADA

grə-'nā-də

LOCATION — Windward Islands, West Indies
GOVT. — Independent nation in the British Commonwealth
AREA — 133 sq. mi.
POP. — 115,000 (est. 1981)
CAPITAL — St. George's

Grenada consists of Grenada Island and the southern Grenadines, including Carriacou. This colony was granted associated statehood with Great Britain in 1967 and became an independent state Feb. 7, 1974.

12 Pence = 1 Shilling
100 Cents = 1 Dollar (1949)

Catalogue values for unused stamps in this country are for Never Hinged items, beginning with Scott 143 in the regular postage section, Scott J15 in the postage due section.

Watermarks

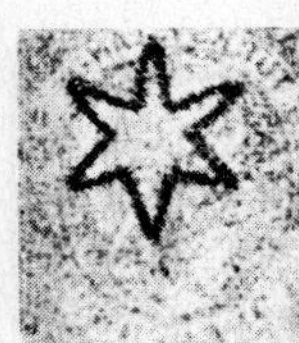
Wmk. 5 — Small Star

Wmk. 6 — Large Star

Wmk. 7 — Large Star with Broad Points

PRE-STAMP POSTAL MARKINGS

Crowned Circle handstamp type I is pictured in the Crowned Circle Handstamps and Great Britain Used Abroad section.

St. George's

1850-58		
A2 I "Grenada" crowned circle handstamp in red, on cover		2,250.

In 1846 a Crowned Circle handstamp was issued inscribed "Carriacou." No examples are known.

STAMPS OF GREAT BRITAIN USED IN GRENADA

Numeral cancellation type A is pictured in the Crowned Circle Handstamps and Great Britain Used Abroad section.

1858-60	(St. George's)
A3 A15 1p rose red (#20)	500.00
A4 A15 2p blue (#29, P7)	1,200.
A5 A15 4p rose (#26)	325.00
A6 A15 6p lilac (#27)	150.00
A7 A15 1sh green (#28)	1,500.

Values for unused stamps are for examples with original gum as defined in the catalogue introduction. Very fine examples of Nos. 1-19, 27-29, and 31-38 will have perforations touching the design on at least one side due to the narrow spacing of the stamps on the plates. Stamps with perfs clear of the design on all four sides are scarce and will command higher prices.

Queen Victoria — A1

Rough Perf. 14 to 16

1861 Engr.		Unwmk.
1 A1 1p green	57.50	55.00
a. 1p blue green	5,250.	350.00
b. As No. 1, horiz. pair, imperf. btwn.		
2 A1 6p rose	1,050.	110.00
b. 6p lake red, perf. 11-12½	1,000.	

No. 2b was not issued. No. 2 imperf is a proof.

1863-71		Wmk. 5
3 A1 1p green ('64)	120.00	17.50
a. 1p yellow green	145.00	30.00
4 A1 6p rose	775.00	20.00
5 A1 6p vermilion ('71)	875.00	20.00
a. 6p dull red	4,000.	275.00
g. Double impression		2,350.
i. 6p orange red ('66)	750.00	14.00

No. 5a always has sideways watermark. Other colors sometimes have sideways watermark.

1873-78	*Clean-Cut Perf. about 15*	
5B A1 1p deep green	140.00	55.00
j. Pair, imperf between		*14,000.*
c. 1p blue green ('78)	275.00	45.00
h. Half used as ½p on cover		11,000.
5D A1 6p vermilion ('75)	925.00	55.00
e. 6p dull red	950.00	40.00
f. Double impression		2,350.

1873		Wmk. 6
6 A1 1p blue green	110.00	26.00
a. Diagonal half used as ½p on cover		11,000.
7 A1 6p vermilion	775.00	35.00

1875		*Perf. 14*
7A A1 1p yellow green	95.00	9.00
b. Half used as ½p on cover		16,000.
c. Perf. 15	10,000.	*2,600.*

A2

A2a

Revenue Designs Surcharged in Black

Perf. 14, 14½

1875-81		
8 A2 ½p purple ('81)	17.50	7.50
a. "OSTAGE"	225.00	150.00
b. Imperf., pair	350.00	
c. "ALF"	*4,000.*	
e. No hyphen between "HALF" and "PENNY"	225.00	150.00
f. Double surcharge	350.00	350.00
9 A2a 2½p lake ('81)	75.00	10.00
a. Imperf., pair	650.00	
b. Imperf. vertically, pair	6,500.	
c. "PENCF"	525.00	225.00
d. No period after "PENNY"	290.00	90.00
10 A2 4p blue ('81)	150.00	10.00

Revenue Designs Surcharged in Dark Blue

11 A2 1sh purple	775.00	20.00
a. "SHLLIING"	*6,500.*	800.00
b. "NE SHILLING"		*3,250.*
c. "OSTAGE"	7,250.	*3,000.*
d. Invtd. "S" in "POSTAGE"	*4,500.*	*750.00*

See Nos. 27-35.

1881		Wmk. 7
12 A2 2½p lake	200.00	57.50
a. 2½p claret	550.00	200.00
b. As No. 12, "PENCF"	875.00	325.00
c. As No. 12, No period after "PENNY"	650.00	230.00
d. As "a," "PENCF"	1,850.	825.00
e. As "a," no period after "PENNY"	1,275.	575.00
13 A2 4p blue	350.00	210.00

Revenue Stamp Overprinted "POSTAGE" in Black

A3

A4

A5

Revenue Stamp Handstamped "POSTAGE" in Manuscript

A6

1883		Wmk. 5
Denomination & Crown in 2nd Color		
14 A3 ½p orange & grn	900.00	275.00
a. Unsevered pair	*5,000.*	*1,500.*
b. "POSTAGE" inverted		1,500.
15 A4 ½p orange & grn	325.00	150.00
a. Unsevered pair	*2,000.*	*525.00*
16 A5 1p orange & grn	*400.00*	65.00
a. Inverted overprint	3,500.	2,600.
b. Double overprint	1,625.	1,275.
c. Inverted "S" in "Postage"	1,150.	700.00

d. Diagonal half used as ½p on cover 3,500.

"Postage" in Manuscript, Red or Black

18 A6 1p org & grn (R) 21,000.
19 A6 1p org & grn — 15,000.

On Nos. 14-19 the words "ONE PENNY" measure from 10-11¼mm in length.
On No. 15, the lower "POSTAGE" is always inverted.
It has been claimed that although Nos. 18 and 19 were used, they were not officially authorized by Grenada's postmaster.

A8

1883 Wmk. 2 Perf. 14

20 A8 ½p green 2.75 1.25
a. Tete beche pair 5.50 21.00
21 A8 1p rose 90.00 4.00
a. Tete beche pair 325.00 375.00
22 A8 2½p ultra 9.00 1.25
a. Tete beche pair 30.00 60.00
23 A8 4p slate 12.00 2.25
a. Tete beche pair 30.00 65.00
24 A8 6p red lilac 6.00 6.50
a. Tete beche pair 21.00 65.00
25 A8 8p bister 10.50 14.00
a. Tete beche pair 40.00 90.00
26 A8 1sh violet 160.00 65.00
a. Tete beche pair 2,000. 2,250.
Nos. 20-26 (7) 290.25 94.25

Stamps of types A8, A10 and D2 were printed with alternate horizontal rows inverted.
For surcharges see Nos. 36-38, J4-J7.

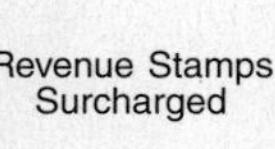
Revenue Stamps Surcharged

1886 Wmk. 6

27 A2 1p on 1½ org & grn 60.00 50.00
a. Inverted surcharge 350.00 350.00
b. Diagonal half used as ½ on cover 2,250.
c. Double surcharge 600.00 350.00
d. "HALH" instead of "HALF" 300.00 275.00
e. "F" for first "E" in "THREE" 300.00 225.00
f. "PFNCE" for "PENCE" 300.00 225.00
28 A2 1p on 1sh org & grn 50.00 45.00
a. "SHILLNG" instead of "SHILLING" 525.00 450.00
b. No period after "POSTAGE" 500.00
c. Half used as ½p on cover 2,350.

Wmk. 5

29 A2 1p on 4p org & grn 190.00 110.00

A10

1887 Wmk. 2

30 A10 1p rose 5.00 1.75
a. Tete beche pair 11.00 30.00

Revenue Stamps Surcharged

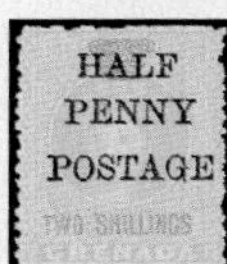

h

i

j

k

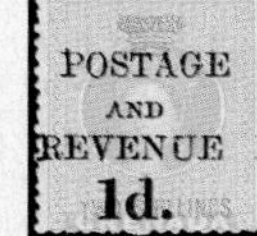

l

1888-91 Wmk. 5 Perf. 14½

31 A2 (h) ½p on 2sh org & grn ('89) 17.50 32.50
a. Double surcharge 350.00 375.00
b. First "S" in "SHILLINGS" inverted 325.00 350.00
32 A2 (i) 4p on 2sh org & grn 50.00 22.50
a. "4d" and "POSTAGE" 5mm apart 80.00 37.50
b. "S" inverted, as in #31b 550.00 400.00
c. As "a," inverted "S," as in #31b 750.00 650.00

"d" Vertical instead of Slanting

33 A2 (j) 4p on 2sh org & grn 875.00 475.00
34 A2 (k) 1p on 2sh org & grn ('90) 92.50 87.50
a. Inverted surcharge 875.00 —
b. "S" inverted 825.00 750.00
35 A2 (l) 1p on 2sh org & grn ('91) 75.00 70.00
b. No period after "d" 450.00 —
c. "S" inverted 575.00 575.00

No. 25 Surcharged in Black

Wmk. 2

36 A8 1p on 8p bister 12.00 20.00
a. Tete beche pair 50.00 70.00
b. Inverted surcharge 375.00 325.00
c. No period after "d" 300.00 300.00

"2" of "½" Upright

37 A8 2½p on 8p bister 11.00 14.00
a. Tete beche pair 50.00 70.00
c. Double surcharge 1,000. 925.00
d. Triple surcharge 1,100.
e. Double surcharge, one inverted 650.00 575.00

"2" of "½" Italic

38 A8 2½p on 8p bister 22.00 13.00
Ovptd. "SPECIMEN" 75.00
a. Tete beche pair 50.00 70.00
b. Tete beche pair, #37, 38 125.00
c. Inverted surcharge
d. Double surcharge 875.00 925.00
e. Triple surcharge 1,050.
f. Triple surch., two inverted 1,000.
g. Double surcharge, one inverted 625.00 575.00

Queen Victoria — A17

1895-99 Wmk. 2 Typo. Perf. 14

39 A17 ½p lilac & green 4.25 2.00
40 A17 1p lil & car rose 5.75 .90
41 A17 2p lilac & brown 47.50 37.50
42 A17 2½p lilac & ultra 11.50 1.75
43 A17 3p lilac & orange 8.00 18.00
44 A17 6p lilac & green 20.00 65.00
45 A17 8p lilac & black 15.00 52.50
46 A17 1sh green & org 22.50 65.00
Nos. 39-46 (8) 134.50 242.65
Set, ovptd. "SPECIMEN" 190.00

Numerals of ½p, 3p, 8p and 1sh of type A17 are in color on colorless tablet.
Issue dates: 1p, May, 1896; ½p, 2p, Sept. 1899; others, Sept. 5, 1895.

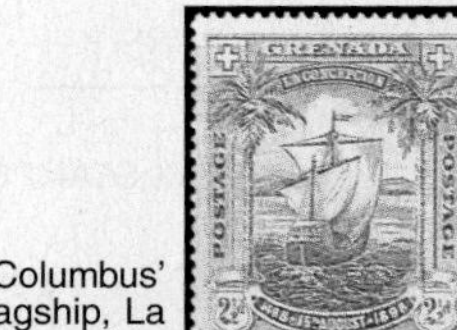
Columbus' Flagship, La Concepcion — A18

1898, Aug. 15 Engr. Wmk. 1

47 A18 2½p ultra 22.50 8.00
Ovptd. "SPECIMEN" 100.00
a. Bluish paper 40.00 47.50

Discovery of the island by Columbus, Aug. 15th, 1498.

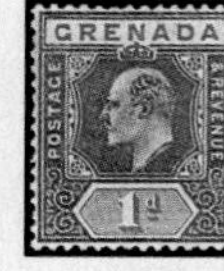

King Edward VII — A19

1902 Wmk. 2 Typo.

48 A19 ½p violet & grn 4.50 1.50
49 A19 1p vio & car rose 9.00 .35
50 A19 2p vio & brown 5.50 11.50
51 A19 2½p vio & ultra 7.00 3.25
52 A19 3p vio & org 7.00 10.50
53 A19 6p vio & green 9.00 20.00
54 A19 1sh green & org 11.00 40.00
55 A19 2sh grn & ultra 40.00 65.00
56 A19 5sh grn & car rose 47.50 85.00
57 A19 10sh green & vio 160.00 300.00
Nos. 48-57 (10) 300.50 537.10
Set, ovptd. "SPECIMEN" 225.00

Numerals of ½p, 3p, 1sh, 2sh and 10sh of type A19 are in color on colorless tablet.

1904-06 Wmk. 3 Perf. 14

Ordinary Paper

58 A19 ½p vio & green 22.50 47.50
59 A19 1p vio & car rose 22.50 3.00
60 A19 2p vio & brown 65.00 130.00
61 A19 2½p vio & ultra 65.00 75.00
62 A19 3p vio & org 5.00 12.00
a. Chalky paper 6.00 9.00
63 A19 6p vio & green 14.00 30.00
a. Chalky paper 15.00 40.00
64 A19 1sh green & org 7.00 40.00
65 A19 2sh grn & ultra 60.00 85.00
a. Chalky paper 50.00 80.00
66 A19 5sh grn & car rose 80.00 120.00
67 A19 10sh green & vio 190.00 300.00
Nos. 58-67 (10) 531.00 842.50

Issued: Nos. 58, 60-62, 64, 1905; Nos. 63, 65-67, 1906.

Seal of Colony — A20

1906-11 Engr.

68 A20 ½p green 5.25 .35
69 A20 1p carmine 9.00 .25
70 A20 2p yellow 4.75 3.50
71 A20 2½p blue 7.00 2.00
a. 2½p ultramarine 11.00 3.75

Typo.

Chalky Paper

Numerals white on dark ground

72 A20 3p vio, *yel* ('08) 7.50 1.90
73 A20 6p violet ('08) 22.50 25.00
74 A20 1sh blk, *grn* ('11) 8.00 5.00
75 A20 2sh vio & blue, *blue* ('08) 35.00 14.00
76 A20 5sh red & grn, *yel* ('08) 80.00 95.00
Nos. 68-76 (9) 179.00 147.00

1908 Wmk. 2

77 A20 1sh black, *green* 50.00 80.00
78 A20 10sh red & grn, *grn* 160.00 300.00

King George V — A21

1913 Ordinary Paper Wmk. 3

79 A21 ½p green 1.25 1.60
80 A21 1p carmine 2.50 .35
a. 1p scarlet ('16) 14.00 2.00
81 A21 2p orange 1.90 .35
82 A21 2½p ultra 2.00 2.00

Chalky Paper

83 A21 3p violet, *yel* .75 1.00
84 A21 6p dl vio & red vio 1.75 10.00
85 A21 1sh black, *green* 1.10 11.50
a. 1sh black, *emerald* 1.75 20.00
b. 1sh blk, *bl grn*, olive back 52.50 90.00
c. As "a," olive back 1.75 15.00
86 A21 2sh vio & ultra, *bl* 7.25 14.00
87 A21 5sh grn & red, *yel* 20.00 67.50
88 A21 10sh grn & red, *grn* 70.00 130.00
a. 10sh grn & red, *emer* 70.00 190.00
Nos. 79-88 (10) 108.50 238.30
Set, ovptd "SPECIMEN" 225.00

1914 Surface-colored Paper

89 A21 3p violet, *yel* .70 1.60
90 A21 1sh black, *green* 1.40 8.50

1921-29 Ordinary Paper Wmk. 4

91 A21 ½p green 1.40 .35
92 A21 1p rose red .90 .85
93 A21 1p brown ('23) 1.75 .35
94 A21 1½p rose red ('22) 1.75 1.75
95 A21 2p orange 1.40 .35
96 A21 2p gray ('26) 2.75 3.00
97 A21 2½p ultramarine 7.50 10.00
98 A21 2½p gray ('22) 1.10 10.00
99 A21 3p ultra ('22) 1.75 12.50

Chalky Paper

100 A21 3p vio, *yel* ('26) 3.50 5.75
101 A21 4p blk & red, *yel* ('26) 1.10 4.25
102 A21 5p gray vio & ol grn ('22) 1.75 4.75
103 A21 6p dl vio & red vio 1.50 29.00
104 A21 6p blk & red ('26) 2.50 2.75
105 A21 9p gray vio & blk ('22) 2.50 11.00
106 A21 1sh blk, *emer* ('23) 3.00 60.00
107 A21 1sh org brn ('26) 4.50 11.00
108 A21 2sh vio & ultra, *bl* ('22) 7.00 19.00
109 A21 2sh6p blk & red, *bl* ('29) 10.00 24.00
110 A21 3sh grn & vio ('22) 12.00 30.00
111 A21 5sh grn & red, *yel* ('23) 14.00 40.00
112 A21 10sh grn & red, *emer* ('23) 57.50 150.00
Nos. 91-112 (22) 141.15 430.65

Grand Anse Beach — A22

Seal of the Colony — A23

View of Grand Etang — A24

View of St. George's — A25

1934, Oct. 23 Engr. Perf. 12½

114 A22 ½p green .25 1.25
a. Perf. 12½x13 ('36) 11.00 70.00

Perf. 13½x12½

115 A23 1p blk brn & blk .65 .35
a. Perf 12½ 2.00 3.50

Perf. 12½x13½

116 A24 1½p car & black 1.25 .45
a. Perf 12½ ('36) 9.00 6.50

Perf. 12½

117 A23 2p org & black 1.10 .80
118 A25 2½p deep blue .55 .55
119 A23 3p ol grn & blk 1.10 3.25
120 A23 6p claret & blk 3.00 2.00
121 A23 1sh brown & blk 3.50 4.50
122 A23 2sh6p ultra & blk 9.00 30.00
123 A23 5sh vio & black 50.00 55.00
Nos. 114-123 (10) 70.40 98.15
Set, never hinged 130.00
Set, perf. "SPECIMEN" 200.00

Common Design Types pictured following the introduction.

Silver Jubilee Issue
Common Design Type

1935, May 6 ***Perf. 11x12***

124 CD301 ½p green & blk 1.00 *1.35*
125 CD301 1p black & ultra 1.10 *2.00*
126 CD301 1½p car & blue 1.10 *3.25*
127 CD301 1sh brn vio & ind 13.50 *34.00*
Nos. 124-127 (4) 16.70 *40.60*
Set, never hinged 29.00
Set, perf. "SPECIMEN" 110.00

Coronation Issue
Common Design Type

1937, May 12 Wmk. 4 ***Perf. 11x11½***

128 CD302 1p dark purple .25 .25
129 CD302 1½p dark carmine .25 .25
130 CD302 2½p deep ultra .50 .35
Nos. 128-130 (3) 1.00 .85
Set, never hinged 1.60
Set, perf. "SPECIMEN" 110.00

George VI — A26

Chalky Paper

1937, July 12 Photo. ***Perf. 14½x14***

131 A26 ¼p chestnut 3.25 *.25*
a. Ordinary paper ('42) .65 3.00
b. chocolate, ordinary paper ('45) .80 3.00
c. As "b," chalky paper ('50) 2.75 7.50

Grand Anse Beach — A27

Seal of the Colony — A28

View of Grand Etang — A29

View of St. George's — A30

Seal of the Colony — A31

1938, Mar. 16 Engr. ***Perf. 12½***

132 A27 ½p green .70 *1.40*
133 A28 1p blk brn & blk .50 .55
134 A29 1½p scarlet & blk .25 *.95*
135 A28 2p orange & blk .25 *.55*
136 A30 2½p ultramarine .25 *.35*
137 A28 3p ol grn & blk .25 *2.10*
138 A28 6p red vio & blk 2.10 .45
139 A28 1sh org brn & blk 3.00 .45
140 A28 2sh ultra & black 21.00 2.00
141 A28 5sh purple & blk 4.25 *2.75*

Perf. 14

142 A31 10sh rose car & gray blue 19.00 13.00
a. 10sh deep car & gray blue, perf. 12 ('43) 500.00 *1,900.*
b. Perf. 12x13 36.00 12.00
Nos. 131-142 (12) 54.80 24.80
Set, never hinged 72.50

1938-42 ***Perf. 12½x13½, 13½x12½***

132a A27 ½p 3.00 .90
133a A28 1p .30 .25
134a A29 1½p car & blk 1.10 .40
135a A28 2p 1.25 .75
136a A30 2½p *7,500.* *200.00*
137a A28 3p 2.10 *1.00*
138a A28 6p ('42) 1.10 .35
139a A28 1sh ('42) 2.50 2.50
140a A28 2sh ('41) 21.00 2.00
141a A28 5sh ('47) 3.50 *4.50*

Catalogue values for unused stamps in this section, from this point to the end of the section, are for Never Hinged items.

Peace Issue
Common Design Type

1946, Sept. 25 ***Perf. 13½x14***

143 CD303 1½p carmine .25 .25
144 CD303 3½p deep blue .25 *.70*
Set, perf. "SPECIMEN" 90.00

Silver Wedding Issue
Common Design Types

1948, Oct. 27 Photo. ***Perf. 14x14½***

145 CD304 1½p scarlet .25 .25

Engr.; Name Typo.

Perf. 11½x11

146 CD305 10sh gray green 21.50 21.50

UPU Issue
Common Design Types

Engr.; Name Typo. on 6c, 12c

Perf. 13½, 11x11½

1949, Oct. 10 **Wmk. 4**

147 CD306 5c ultra .25 .25
148 CD307 6c deep olive 1.35 *2.25*
149 CD308 12c red lilac .30 *.50*
150 CD309 24c red brown .25 *.55*
Nos. 147-150 (4) 2.15 3.55

A32

A33

A34

1951, Jan. 8 Engr. ***Perf. 11½***

Center in Black

151 A32 ½c chestnut .25 *1.30*
152 A32 1c blue green .25 *.55*
153 A32 2c dark brown .25 .25
154 A32 3c carmine .25 .25
155 A32 4c deep orange .40 .25
156 A32 5c purple .50 .30
157 A32 6c olive .50 .60
158 A32 7c blue 2.00 .30
159 A32 12c red violet 2.25 .70

Perf. 11½x12½

160 A33 25c dark brown 2.50 .85
161 A33 50c ultra 6.50 .55
162 A33 $1.50 orange 8.25 8.00

Perf. 11½x13

Center in Gray Blue

163 A34 $2.50 deep carmine 9.50 5.50
Nos. 151-163 (13) 33.40 19.40

See Nos. 180-183, 202 in Scott Standard catalogue, Vol. 3. For overprints see Nos. 166-169.

University Issue
Common Design Types

1951, Feb. 16 ***Perf. 14x14½***

164 CD310 3c dp car & gray blk .55 *1.00*
165 CD311 6c olive & black .65 .60

Nos. 154-156 and 159 Overprinted in Black or Carmine

1951, Sept. 21 ***Perf. 11½***

166 A32 3c carmine & black .25 *.40*
167 A32 4c dp orange & black .25 *.40*
168 A32 5c purple & black (C) .30 *.65*
169 A32 12c red violet & black .30 *.90*
Nos. 166-169 (4) 1.10 *2.35*

Adoption of a new constitution for the Windward Islands.

POSTAGE DUE STAMPS

D1

1892 Typo. Wmk. 2 ***Perf. 14***

J1 D1 1p black 30.00 2.75
J2 D1 2p black 225.00 3.25
J3 D1 3p black 200.00 4.00
Nos. J1-J3 (3) 455.00 10.00

Nos. 24 & 25 Surcharged in Black

J4 A8 1p on 6p red lilac 110.00 2.25
a. Tete beche pair 2,750. *1,800.*
b. Double surcharge 225.00
c. Same as "b," tete beche pair
J5 A8 1p on 8p bister 1,600. 6.00
a. Tete beche pair *8,500.* *2,500.*
J6 A8 2p on 6p red lilac 190.00 4.50
a. Tete beche pair *3,500.* 1,800.
J7 A8 2p on 8p bister 3,200. 12.00
a. Tete beche pair *7,500.* 5,000.
Nos. J4-J7 (4) 5,100. 24.75

Nos. J4-J7 were printed with alternate horizontal rows inverted.

1906-11 **Wmk. 3**

J8 D1 1p black ('11) 3.75 *7.50*
J9 D1 2p black 12.50 3.75
J10 D1 3p black 15.00 6.50
Nos. J8-J10 (3) 31.25 17.75

D3

1921-22 **Wmk. 4**

J11 D3 1p black 2.00 *1.40*
J12 D3 1½p black 10.00 *25.00*
J13 D3 2p black 3.00 *4.50*
J14 D3 3p black 3.00 *4.75*
Nos. J11-J14 (4) 18.00 *35.65*
Set, ovpt. "SPECIMEN" 80,00

Issued: 1½p, Dec. 15, 1922, others, Dec. 1921.

Catalogue values for unused stamps in this section, from this point to the end of the section, are for Never Hinged items.

1952, Mar. 1

J15 D3 2c black .50 *9.00*
a. Wmk. 4a (error) 55.00
J16 D3 4c black .50 *17.00*
a. Wmk. 4a (error) 60.00
J17 D3 6c black .65 *13.00*
a. Wmk. 4a (error) 100.00
J18 D3 8c black .75 *14.00*
a. Wmk. 4a (error) 200.00
Nos. J15-J18 (4) 2.40 *53.00*

WAR TAX STAMPS

Nos. 80a, 80 Overprinted

1916 Wmk. 3 ***Perf. 14***

MR1 A21 1p carmine 2.50 2.00
a. 1p scarlet 3.00 3.00
b. Double overprint 325.00
c. Inverted overprint 325.00
Handstamped "SPECIMEN" 50.00

No. 80 Overprinted

MR2 A21 1p scarlet .30 .25
Ovptd. "SPECIMEN" 45.00

GRIQUALAND WEST

'gri-kwə-ˌland 'west

LOCATION — In South Africa west of the Orange Free State and north of the Orange River
GOVT. — Former British Crown Colony
AREA — 15,197 sq. mi.
POP. — 83,375 (1891)
CAPITAL — Kimberley

Originally a territorial division of the Cape of Good Hope Colony, Griqualand West was declared a British Crown Colony in 1873 and together with Griqualand East was annexed to the Cape Colony in 1880.

12 Pence = 1 Shilling

Beware of forgeries.

Stamps of Cape of Good Hope 1864-65 (Type I, 4p, 6p, 1sh) and 1871-76 (Type II, ½p, 1p, 4p, 5sh) Surcharged or Overprinted

Cape of Good Hope No. 17 Surcharged

Type I — With frame line around stamp.
Type II — Without frame line.

Manuscript Surcharge in Dark Red

1874 Wmk. 1 *Perf. 14*
1 A3 1p on 4p blue (type I) 1,900. *2,600.*

Overprinted

1877 Black Overprint
2 1p rose 800.00 115.00
a. Double overprint *3,250.*

Red Overprint
3 4p blue (type II) 425.00 85.00

Overprinted In Black on the One Penny, in Red on the Other Values

a b c d

G G G
e f g

4 (a) ½p gray black 45.00 *47.50*
5 (a) 1p rose 45.00 30.00
6 (a) 4p blue (type I) 475.00 75.00
7 (a) 4p blue (type II) 425.00 50.00
8 (a) 6p dull violet 325.00 57.50
9 (a) 1sh green 375.00 47.50
a. Inverted overprint 1,000.
10 (a) 5sh orange 1,150. 57.50
11 (b) ½p gray black 105.00 125.00
12 (b) 1p rose 115.00 67.50
13 (b) 4p blue (type I) 1,150. 190.00
14 (b) 4p blue (type II) 900.00 145.00
15 (b) 6p dull violet 625.00 155.00
16 (b) 1sh green 800.00 115.00
17 (b) 5sh orange 1,900. 135.00
18 (c) ½p gray black 800.00 *850.00*
19 (c) 1p rose 115.00 52.50
20 (c) 4p blue (type I) *3,750.* 1,000.
21 (c) 4p blue (type II) *3,400.* 800.00
22 (c) 6p dull violet *3,250.* 950.00
23 (c) 1sh green *4,250.* 950.00
24 (c) 5sh orange *4,750.* 1,050.
25 (d) ½p gray black 62.50 *75.00*
26 (d) 1p rose 62.50 42.50
27 (d) 4p blue (type I) 800.00 105.00
28 (d) 4p blue (type II) 575.00 75.00
29 (d) 6p dull violet 425.00 80.00
30 (d) 1sh green 575.00 62.50
31 (d) 5sh orange 1,575. 80.00
32 (e) ½p gray black 105.00 *125.00*
33 (e) 1p rose 115.00 67.50
34 (e) 4p blue (type I) 1,150. 190.00
35 (e) 4p blue (type II) 900.00 145.00
36 (e) 6p dull violet 625.00 155.00
37 (e) 1sh green 800.00 115.00
a. Inverted overprint 1,600.
38 (e) 5sh orange 1,900. 135.00
39 (f) ½p gray black 115.00 *135.00*
40 (f) 1p rose 125.00 85.00
41 (f) 4p blue (type I) 1,250. 235.00
42 (f) 4p blue (type II) 950.00 165.00
43 (f) 6p dull violet 750.00 175.00
44 (f) 1sh green 900.00 145.00
45 (f) 5sh orange 2,900. 165.00
46 (g) ½p gray black 57.50 67.50
47 (g) 1p rose 45.00 30.00
48 (g) 4p blue (type I) 575.00 95.00
49 (g) 4p blue (type II) 525.00 62.50
50 (g) 6p dull violet 400.00 77.50
51 (g) 1sh green 525.00 57.50
a. Inverted overprint — 1,150.
52 (g) 5sh orange 1,475. 67.50

There are minor varieties of types e and f.

Overprinted in Black

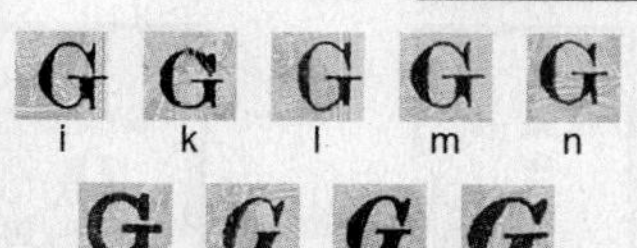

i k l m n
o p q r

1878
54 (g) 4p blue (type II) 625.00 100.00
55 (g) 6p dull violet 900.00 145.00
56 (i) 1p rose 57.50 35.00
57 (i) 4p blue (type II) 325.00 47.50
58 (i) 6p dull violet 525.00 95.00
a. Double overprint *1,600.*
59 (k) 1p rose 115.00 52.50
60 (k) 4p blue (type II) 575.00 90.00
61 (k) 6p dull violet 850.00 135.00
62 (l) 1p rose 50.00 32.50
63 (l) 4p blue (type II) 290.00 47.50
64 (l) 6p dull violet 475.00 85.00
a. Double overprint *1,100.*
65 (m) 1p rose 80.00 70.00
66 (m) 4p blue (type II) 400.00 82.50
67 (m) 6p dull violet 550.00 150.00
68 (n) 1p rose 145.00 95.00
69 (n) 4p blue (type II) 750.00 125.00
70 (n) 6p dull violet 1,000. 190.00
a. Double overprint *1,750.*
71 (o) 1p rose 125.00 75.00
72 (o) 4p blue (type II) 625.00 105.00
73 (o) 6p dull violet 900.00 175.00
74 (p) 1p rose 200.00 135.00
75 (p) 4p blue (type II) 1,000. 190.00
76 (p) 6p dull violet 1,375. 300.00
77 (q) 1p rose 125.00 85.00
78 (q) 4p blue (type II) 625.00 105.00
79 (q) 6p dull violet 900.00 175.00
80 (r) 1p rose 625.00 425.00
81 (r) 4p blue (type II) *3,000.* 625.00
82 (r) 6p dull violet *3,750.* 950.00

There are two minor varieties of type i and one of type p.

s

G
t

1878 Overprinted in Red
83 (s) ½p gray black 28.00 30.00
a. Double overprint 85.00 *100.00*
b. Inverted overprint 30.00 30.00
c. Double overprint, inverted 165.00 *190.00*
84 (s) 4p blue (type II) 625.00 165.00
a. Inverted overprint 700.00 135.00
85 (t) ½p gray black 30.00 30.00
a. Double overprint 135.00 135.00
b. Inverted overprint 30.00 *30.00*
86 (t) 4p blue (type II) — 150.00
a. Inverted overprint 625.00 150.00

Black Overprint
87 (s) ½p gray black 375.00 190.00
a. Inverted overprint 400.00 *400.00*
b. With 2nd ovpt. *(s)* in red, invtd. 625.00
c. With 2nd ovpt. *(t)* in red, invtd. 350.00
88 (s) 1p rose 30.00 20.00
a. Double overprint 375.00 90.00
b. Inverted overprint 30.00 30.00
c. Double overprint, both inverted 375.00 115.00
d. With second overprint *(s)* in red, both inverted 70.00 75.00
89 (s) 4p blue (type I) 300.00
90 (s) 4p blue (type II) 265.00 50.00
a. Double overprint — 400.00
b. Inverted overprint 425.00 150.00
c. Double overprint, both inverted — 475.00
91 (s) 6p dull violet 290.00 50.00
92 (t) ½p gray black 85.00 85.00
a. Inverted overprint 180.00 125.00
b. With 2nd ovpt. inverted 350.00
93 (t) 1p rose 30.00 22.50
a. Double overprint — 160.00
b. Inverted overprint 145.00 50.00
c. Double overprint, both inverted — 190.00
d. With 2nd ovpt. *(t)* in red, both invtd. 150.00 150.00
94 (t) 4p blue (type I) 300.00
95 (t) 4p blue (type II) 300.00 27.50
a. Double overprint — 375.00
b. Inverted overprint 450.00 50.00
c. Double overprint, both inverted — 200.00
96 (t) 6p dull violet 50.00

Overprinted in Black

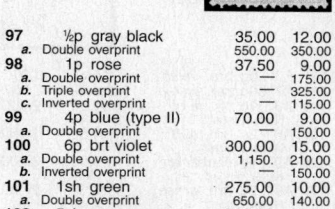

97 ½p gray black 35.00 12.00
a. Double overprint 550.00 350.00
98 1p rose 37.50 9.00
a. Double overprint — 175.00
b. Triple overprint — 325.00
c. Inverted overprint — 115.00
99 4p blue (type II) 70.00 9.00
a. Double overprint — 150.00
100 6p brt violet 300.00 15.00
a. Double overprint 1,150. 210.00
b. Inverted overprint — 150.00
101 1sh green 275.00 10.00
a. Double overprint 650.00 140.00
102 5sh orange 850.00 27.50
a. Double overprint 1,050. 140.00
b. Triple overprint — 425.00

These stamps were declared obsolete in 1880 and the remainders were used in Cape of Good Hope offices as ordinary stamps. Prices for used stamps are for examples with such cancels.

GUADELOUPE

'gwä-dᵊl-ˌüp

LOCATION — In the West Indies lying between Montserrat and Dominica
GOVT. — French colony
AREA — 688 sq. mi.
POP. — 271,262 (1946)
CAPITAL — Basse-Terre

Guadeloupe consists of two large islands, Guadeloupe proper and Grande-Terre, together with five smaller dependencies.

100 Centimes = 1 Franc

FORERUNNERS

Crowned Circle handstamp types are pictured in the Crowned Circle Handstamps and Great Britain Used Abroad section.

BRITISH POST OFFICES IN GUADELOUPE

Guadeloupe

British P.O. opened Oct. 1, 1848; closed 1874

Pre-Stamp Postal Markings

1841
A1 Crowned Circle handstamp Type I, on cover, inscribed "GUADELOUPE", *from* *2,500.*

Earliest known use Mar. 9, 1849.

Issues under French Administration

Stamps of French Colonies Surcharged

1884 Unwmk. *Imperf.*
1 A8 20c on 30c brn, *bis* 72.50 60.00
Never hinged 140.00
On cover 375.00
On cover, single franking 1,000.
a. Large "2" 325.00 260.00
b. Pair, #1 and #1a 425.00 375.00
2 A8 25c on 35c blk, *org* 60.00 60.00
Never hinged 120.00
On cover 375.00
On cover, single franking 625.00
a. Large "2" 325.00 260.00
b. Large "5" 160.00 125.00
c. Pair, #2 and #2a 425.00 375.00
d. Pair, #2 and #2b 240.00 225.00

The 5c on 4c (French Colonies No. 40) was not regularly issued. Three examples exist. Value $42,500.

The 5c on 4c also exists as an essay, surcharge similar to the issued values. Value $1,000.

c

d

1889 *Perf. 14x13½*

Surcharged Type c
3 A9 3c on 20c red, *grn* 5.25 5.25
Never hinged 10.50
On cover 200.00
On cover, single franking 400.00
4 A9 15c on 20c red, *grn* 32.50 27.50
Never hinged 65.00
On cover 225.00
On cover, single franking 400.00
5 A9 25c on 20c red, *grn* 32.50 27.50
Never hinged 65.00
On cover 225.00
On cover, single franking 400.00
Nos. 3-5 (3) 70.25 60.25

Surcharged Type d
6 A9 5c on 1c blk, *lil bl* 14.50 13.50
Never hinged 25.00
On cover 175.00
On cover, single franking 450.00
a. Inverted surcharge *1,400.*
b. Double surcharge *450.00* *450.00*
7 A9 10c on 40c red, *straw* 40.00 35.00
Never hinged 80.00
On cover 300.00
On cover, single franking 450.00
a. Double surcharge 475.00 475.00
8 A9 15c on 20c red, *grn* 32.50 30.00
Never hinged 72.50
On cover 325.00
On cover, single franking 450.00
a. Double surcharge 475.00 475.00
9 A9 25c on 30c brn, *bis* 52.50 45.00
Never hinged 100.00
On cover 350.00
On cover, single franking 450.00
a. Double surcharge 475.00 475.00
Nos. 6-9 (4) 139.50 123.50

The word "centimes" in surcharges "b" and "c" varies from 10 to 12½mm.

Issue dates: No. 6, June 25; others, Mar. 22.

Stamps of French Colonies Surcharged

1891
10 A9 5c on 10c blk, *lav* 16.00 12.00
Never hinged 32.50
On cover 175.00
On cover, single franking 450.00
11 A9 5c on 1fr brnz grn, *straw* 17.00 12.50
Never hinged 30.00
On cover 175.00
On cover, single franking 450.00

Stamps of French Colonies Overprinted in Black

1891 ***Imperf.***
12 A7 30c brn, *yelsh* 350.00 *375.00*
a. Double overprint 725.00 725.00
13 A7 80c car, *pnksh* 1,100. *1,300.*

Perf. 14x13½
14 A9 1c blk, *lil bl* 1.75 1.60
Never hinged 3.25
On cover 160.00
a. Double overprint 40.00 40.00
b. Inverted overprint 150.00 150.00
15 A9 2c brn, *buff* 2.60 2.00
Never hinged 4.50
On cover 160.00
a. Double overprint 45.00 40.00
16 A9 4c claret, *lav* 6.00 5.25
Never hinged 10.50
On cover 160.00
17 A9 5c grn, *grnsh* 8.75 7.25
Never hinged 16.00
On cover 85.00
a. Double overprint 45.00 40.00
b. Inverted overprint 160.00 160.00
18 A9 10c blk, *lavender* 17.00 13.50
Never hinged 30.00
On cover 100.00
19 A9 15c blue 52.50 6.00
Never hinged 110.00
On cover 55.00
a. Double overprint 110.00
20 A9 20c red, *grn* 45.00 30.00
Never hinged 95.00
On cover 250.00
a. Double overprint 240.00 240.00
21 A9 25c blk, *rose* 47.50 5.25
Never hinged 105.00
On cover 72.50
a. Double overprint 240.00 240.00
b. Inverted overprint 225.00 225.00
22 A9 30c brn, *bister* 45.00 30.00
Never hinged 95.00
On cover 210.00
a. Double overprint 240.00 240.00
23 A9 35c dp vio, *org* 87.50 72.50
Never hinged 200.00
On cover 425.00
a. Double overprint 675.00 675.00
24 A9 40c red, *straw* 65.00 52.50
Never hinged 130.00
On cover 275.00
a. Double overprint 675.00 675.00
25 A9 75c car, *rose* 130.00 125.00
On cover 625.00
26 A9 1fr brnz grn, *straw* 92.50 72.50
Never hinged 200.00
On cover 450.00
Nos. 14-26 (13) 601.10 423.35

Overprinted "GNADELOUPE"

12c A7 30c brn, *yelsh* 1,050. *1,050.*
13c A7 80c car, *pnksh* 5,750. *5,750.*
14c A9 1c blk, *lil bl* 10.50 10.50
Never hinged 21.00
15c A9 2c brn, *buff* 11.00 11.00
Never hinged 22.50
16c A9 4c claret, *lav* 16.50 16.50
Never hinged 32.50
17c A9 5c grn, *grnsh* 18.00 18.00
Never hinged 45.00
18c A9 10c blk, *lavender* 47.50 47.50
Never hinged 100.00
19c A9 15c blue 95.00 95.00
Never hinged 190.00
20c A9 20c red, *grn* 110.00 110.00
Never hinged 225.00
21c A9 25c blk, *rose* 95.00 95.00
Never hinged 190.00
22c A9 30c brn, *bister* 175.00 175.00
23c A9 35c dp vio, *org* 500.00 500.00
24c A9 40c red, *straw* 275.00 275.00
25c A9 75c car, *rose* 450.00 450.00
26c A9 1fr brnz grn, *straw* 300.00 300.00

Overprinted "GUADBLOUPE"

12d A7 30c brn, *yelsh* 2,500. *2,500.*
13d A7 80c car, *pnksh* 10,750. *10,750.*
14d A9 1c blk, *lil bl* 10.50 10.50
Never hinged 21.00
15d A9 2c brn, *buff* 11.00 11.00
Never hinged 22.50
16d A9 4c claret, *lav* 16.50 16.50
Never hinged 32.50
17d A9 5c grn, *grnsh* 18.00 18.00
Never hinged 45.00
18d A9 10c blk, *lavender* 47.50 47.50
Never hinged 100.00
19d A9 15c blue 95.00 95.00
Never hinged 190.00
20d A9 20c red, *grn* 110.00 110.00
Never hinged 225.00
21d A9 25c blk, *rose* 130.00 130.00
22d A9 30c brn, *bister* 160.00 160.00
23d A9 35c dp vio, *org* 525.00 525.00
24d A9 40c red, *straw* 525.00 525.00
25d A9 75c car, *rose* 675.00 675.00
26d A9 1fr brnz grn, *straw* 300.00 300.00

Overprinted "GUADELONPE"

12e A7 30c brn, *yelsh* 2,500. *2,500.*
13e A7 80c car, *pnksh* *10,750.* *10,750.*
14e A9 1c blk, *lil bl* 10.50 10.50
Never hinged 21.00
15e A9 2c brn, *buff* 11.00 11.00
Never hinged 22.50
16e A9 4c claret, *lav* 20.00 20.00
Never hinged 40.00
17e A9 5c grn, *grnsh* 25.00 25.00
Never hinged 52.50
18e A9 10c blk, *lavender* 52.50 52.50
Never hinged 105.00
19e A9 15c blue 105.00 105.00
Never hinged 200.00
20e A9 20c red, *grn* 120.00 120.00
Never hinged 240.00
21e A9 25c blk, *rose* 130.00 130.00
22e A9 30c brn, *bister* 160.00 160.00
23e A9 35c dp vio, *org* 550.00 550.00
24e A9 40c red, *straw* 540.00 540.00
25e A9 75c car, *rose* 700.00 700.00
26e A9 1fr brnz grn, *straw* 350.00 350.00

Overprinted "GUADELOUEP"

12f A7 30c brn, *yelsh* *3,000.* *3,000.*
13f A7 80c car, *pnksh* *12,500.* *12,500.*
14f A9 1c blk, *lil bl* 24.00 24.00
Never hinged 47.50
15f A9 2c brn, *buff* 14.50 14.50
Never hinged 29.00
16f A9 4c claret, *lav* 25.00 25.00
Never hinged 50.00
17f A9 5c grn, *grnsh* 27.50 27.50
Never hinged 55.00
18f A9 10c blk, *lavender* 65.00 65.00
Never hinged 130.00
19f A9 15c blue 110.00 110.00
Never hinged 225.00
20f A9 20c red, *grn* 135.00 135.00
21f A9 25c blk, *rose* 160.00 160.00
22f A9 30c brn, *bister* 200.00 200.00
23f A9 35c dp vio, *org* 725.00 725.00
24f A9 40c red, *straw* 650.00 650.00
25f A9 75c car, *rose* 775.00 775.00
26f A9 1fr brnz grn, *straw* — —

Navigation and Commerce — A7

Perf. 14x13½
1892-1901 Typo. Unwmk.
Colony Name in Blue or Carmine
27 A7 1c blk, *lil bl* 1.40 1.40
Never hinged 1.60
On cover 100.00
a. 1c blk, *gray* 1.50 1.50
b. 1c blk, *blue* 2.00 2.00
c. 1c blk, *yellowish* 1.50 1.50
28 A7 2c brn, *buff* 1.50 1.40
Never hinged 1.60
On cover 100.00
29 A7 4c claret, *lav* 1.75 1.50
Never hinged 2.75
On cover 97.50
30 A7 5c grn, *grnsh* 3.50 1.50
Never hinged 6.00
On cover 40.00
31 A7 5c yel grn ('01) 6.00 1.60
Never hinged 9.50
On cover 13.00
32 A7 10c blk, *lavender* 10.00 3.25
Never hinged 17.50
On cover 25.00
a. 10c blk, *rose* 10.00 3.00
33 A7 10c red ('00) 8.75 2.40
Never hinged 14.50
On cover 15.00
a. Imperf. 120.00
b. As "a," country name omitted 150.00
34 A7 15c blue, quadrille paper 18.00 1.75
Never hinged 32.50
On cover 30.00
35 A7 15c gray, *lt gray* ('00) 13.00 1.60
Never hinged 24.00
On cover 14.50
36 A7 20c red, *grn* 11.00 6.50
Never hinged 19.00
On cover 65.00
On cover, single franking 120.00
37 A7 25c blk, *rose* 11.00 3.00
Never hinged 19.00
On cover 37.50
On cover, single franking 80.00
38 A7 25c blue ('00) 100.00 100.00
Never hinged 200.00
On cover 300.00
On cover, single franking 450.00
39 A7 30c brn, *bister* 24.00 15.00
Never hinged 42.50
On cover 110.00
On cover, single franking 240.00
40 A7 40c red, *straw* 24.00 15.00
Never hinged 45.00
On cover 175.00
On cover, single franking 450.00
41 A7 50c car, *rose* 30.00 16.00
Never hinged 65.00
On cover 225.00
On cover, single franking 600.00
42 A7 50c brn, *az* ('00) 45.00 42.50
Never hinged 80.00
On cover 340.00
On cover, single franking 600.00
43 A7 75c dp vio, *org* 32.50 22.50
Never hinged 65.00
On cover 300.00
On cover, single franking 675.00
44 A7 1fr brnz grn, *straw* 32.50 30.00
Never hinged 65.00
On cover 300.00
On cover, single franking 675.00
Nos. 27-44 (18) 373.90 266.90

Perf. 13½x14 stamps are counterfeits.
For surcharges see Nos. 45-53, 83-85.

Nos. 39-41, 43-44 Surcharged in Black

f g h

1903
45 A7 (f) 5c on 30c 4.00 4.00
Never hinged 7.25
On cover 85.00
a. "C" instead of "G" 32.50 32.50
Never hinged 60.00
b. Inverted surcharge 45.00 45.00
Never hinged 80.00
c. Double surcharge 140.00 140.00
d. Double surch., inverted 160.00
46 A7 (g) 10c on 40c 9.50 9.50
Never hinged 14.50
On cover 100.00
a. "C" instead of "G" 40.00 40.00
Never hinged 60.00
b. "1" inverted 60.00 60.00
Never hinged 120.00
c. Inverted surcharge 55.00 55.00
Never hinged 95.00
d. Double surcharge 200.00 200.00
47 A7 (f) 15c on 50c 13.00 13.00
Never hinged 25.00
On cover 100.00
a. "C" instead of "G" 40.00 40.00
Never hinged 75.00
b. Inverted surcharge 110.00 110.00
c. "15" inverted 375.00 375.00
d. Pair, tête-bêche surcharge 375.00
e. Double surcharge 200.00 200.00
48 A7 (g) 40c on 1fr 13.00 13.00
Never hinged 25.00
On cover 115.00
a. "C" instead of "G" 52.50 52.50
Never hinged 100.00
b. "4" inverted 120.00 120.00
Never hinged 225.00
c. Inverted surcharge 110.00 110.00
d. Double surcharge 240.00 240.00
e. Double triple 450.00 *500.00*
49 A7 (h) 1fr on 75c 42.50 42.50
Never hinged 80.00
On cover 350.00
a. "C" instead of "G" 160.00 160.00
Never hinged 275.00
b. "1" inverted 160.00 160.00
Never hinged 275.00
c. Value above "G & D" 300.00 300.00
Never hinged 450.00
d. Inverted surcharge 125.00 125.00
Nos. 45-49 (5) 82.00 82.00

Letters and figures from several fonts were used for these surcharges, resulting in numerous minor varieties.

Nos. 48-49 With Additional Overprint "1903" in a Frame

1904, Mar. Red Overprint
50 A7 (g) 40c on 1fr 75.00 85.00
Never hinged 120.00
On cover 340.00
a. "C" instead of "G" 175.00 *200.00*
Never hinged 275.00
b. Inverted surcharge 600.00 650.00
Never hinged 1,000.
c. Double surcharge 1,250. 1,250.
Never hinged 2,000.
51 A7 (h) 1fr on 75c 92.50 100.00
Never hinged 160.00
On cover 340.00
a. Double surcharge 950.00 950.00
b. Inverted surcharge 1,000. 800.00

Overprinted in Blue

52 A7 (g) 40c on 1fr 60.00 65.00
Never hinged 120.00
On cover 275.00
a. Double surcharge 1,150. *1,200.*
b. Double surcharge, one inverted 1,150. *1,150.*
53 A7 (h) 1fr on 75c 87.50 95.00
Never hinged 160.00
On cover 375.00
a. Double surcharge 750.00 800.00
Never hinged 1,500.
Nos. 50-53 (4) 315.00 345.00

The date "1903" may be found in 19 different positions and type faces within the frame. These stamps may also be found with the minor varieties of Nos. 48-49.

The 40c exists with black overprint. Value, $500 unused or used.

Harbor at Basse-Terre — A8

View of La Soufrière A9

Pointe-à-Pitre, Grand-Terre — A10

1905-27 Typo. *Perf. 14x13½*
54 A8 1c blk, *bluish* .30 .30
Never hinged .55
On cover 40.00
55 A8 2c vio brn, *straw* .30 .30
Never hinged .55
On cover 40.00
56 A8 4c bis brn, *az* .30 .30
Never hinged .55
On cover 35.00
57 A8 5c green 2.40 .65
Never hinged 3.50
On cover 12.00
58 A8 5c dp blue ('22) .25 .25
Never hinged .40
On cover 16.00
On cover, single franking 40.00
59 A8 10c rose 2.25 .65
Never hinged 2.90
On cover 8.50
60 A8 10c green ('22) 1.40 1.25
Never hinged 2.25
On cover 9.00
61 A8 10c red, *bluish* ('25) .25 .25
Never hinged .40
On cover 5.50
62 A8 15c violet .55 .50
Never hinged .85
On cover 6.50
63 A9 20c red, *grn* .55 .40
Never hinged .85
On cover 9.50
64 A9 20c bl grn ('25) .65 .65
Never hinged 1.20
On cover 6.50
65 A9 25c blue .95 .55
Never hinged 1.40
On cover 20.00
On cover, single franking 67.50
66 A9 25c ol grn ('22) .65 .65
Never hinged 1.00
On cover 4.00
67 A9 30c black 5.00 3.25
Never hinged 8.00
On cover 16.00
On cover, single franking 80.00
68 A9 30c rose ('22) .70 .70
Never hinged 1.10
On cover 12.00
On cover, single franking 47.50

69 A9 30c brn ol, *lav* ('25) .55 .55
Never hinged .85
On cover 4.00
70 A9 35c blk, *yel* ('06) .80 .80
Never hinged 1.25
On cover 20.00
On cover, single franking 80.00
71 A9 40c red, *straw* .80 .80
Never hinged 1.20
On cover 20.00
On cover, single franking 47.50
72 A9 45c ol gray, *lil* ('07) 1.40 .80
Never hinged 2.10
On cover 24.00
On cover, single franking 60.00
73 A9 45c rose ('25) .80 .80
Never hinged 1.25
On cover 16.00
On cover, single franking 60.00
74 A9 50c gray grn, *straw* 5.50 4.00
Never hinged 8.50
On cover 40.00
On cover, single franking 80.00
75 A9 50c dp bl ('22) 1.25 1.10
Never hinged 2.10
On cover 16.00
On cover, single franking 55.00
76 A9 50c violet ('25) .70 .70
Never hinged 1.10
On cover 14.50
On cover, single franking 47.50
77 A9 65c blue ('27) .70 .70
Never hinged 1.10
On cover 17.50
On cover, single franking 65.00
78 A9 75c car, *bl* .90 .80
Never hinged 1.40
On cover 32.50
On cover, single franking 67.50
79 A10 1fr blk, *green* 1.75 1.50
Never hinged 2.40
On cover 35.00
On cover, single franking 67.50
80 A10 1fr lt bl ('25) 1.00 .95
Never hinged 1.90
On cover 40.00
On cover, single franking 67.50
81 A10 2fr car, *org* 2.25 2.00
Never hinged 3.25
On cover 32.50
On cover, single franking 52.50
82 A10 5fr dp bl, *org* 7.50 7.50
Never hinged 12.00
On cover 72.50
On cover, single franking 120.00
Nos. 54-82 (29) 42.40 33.65

Nos. 57, 59 and 82 exist imperf. Value, Nos. 57 and 59 each $60, No. 82 $140.

For surcharges see Nos. 86-95, 167 (in Scott Standard catalogue, Vol. 3), B1-B2.

Nos. 29, 39 and 40 Surcharged in Carmine or Black

Spacing between figures of surcharge 1.5mm (5c), 2mm (10c)

1912, Nov.

83 A7 5c on 4c claret, *lav* (C) 1.50 1.50
Never hinged 2.60
On cover 40.00
84 A7 5c on 30c brn, *bis* (C) 2.00 2.00
Never hinged 3.40
On cover 47.50
85 A7 10c on 40c red, *straw* 2.25 2.25
Never hinged 3.75
On cover 55.00
Nos. 83-85 (3) 5.75 5.75

Spacing between figures of surcharge 2.25mm (5c), 2.75mm (10c)

83a A7 5c on 4c claret, *lav* (C) 170.00 170.00
Never hinged 240.00
84a A7 5c on 30c brn, *bis* (C) 225.00 225.00
Never hinged 325.00
85a A7 10c on 40c red, *straw* 165.00 165.00
Never hinged 260.00
Nos. 83a-85a (3) 560.00 560.00

Se-tenant Pairs, Both Ovpt. Settings

83b A7 5c on 4c claret, *lav* (C), #83 + #83a 190.00
Never hinged 275.00
84b A7 5c on 30c brn, *bis* (C), #84 + #84a 250.00
Never hinged 325.00
85b A7 10c on 40c red, *straw*, #85 + 85a 190.00

Stamps & Types of 1905-27 Surcharged

No. 89

No. 94

1924-27

86 A10 25c on 5fr dp bl, *org* .75 .70
Never hinged 1.10
On cover 6.50
87 A10 65c on 1fr gray grn 1.40 1.25
Never hinged 2.00
On cover 17.50
On cover, single franking 32.50
88 A10 85c on 1fr gray grn 1.50 1.40
Never hinged 2.25
On cover 20.00
On cover, single franking 40.00
89 A9 90c on 75c dl red 1.40 1.25
Never hinged 2.25
On cover 20.00
On cover, single franking 67.50
90 A10 1.05fr on 2fr ver (Bl) 1.00 .85
Never hinged 1.75
On cover 20.00
On cover, single franking 72.50
91 A10 1.25fr on 1fr lt bl (R) .65 .65
Never hinged 1.00
On cover 20.00
On cover, single franking 80.00
92 A10 1.50fr on 1fr dk bl 1.25 1.25
Never hinged 2.00
On cover 24.00
On cover, single franking 85.00
93 A10 3fr on 5fr org brn 1.50 1.50
Never hinged 2.40
On cover 32.50
On cover, single franking 90.00
94 A10 10fr on 5fr vio rose, *org* 11.00 11.00
Never hinged 16.00
On cover 47.50
On cover, single franking 110.00
95 A10 20fr on 5fr rose lil, *pnksh* 14.00 13.00
Never hinged 22.50
On cover 60.00
On cover, single franking 130.00
Nos. 86-95 (10) 34.45 32.85

Years issued: Nos. 87-88, 1925. Nos. 90-91, 1926. Nos. 89, 92-95, 1927.

Sugar Mill — A11

Saints Roadstead A12

Harbor Scene A13

Perf. 14x13½

1928-40 **Unwmk.** **Typo.**

96 A11 1c yel & vio .25 .25
Never hinged .30
On cover 27.50
97 A11 2c blk & lt red .25 .25
Never hinged .30
On cover 27.50
98 A11 3c yel & red vio ('40) .30 .30
Never hinged .450
On cover 32.50
99 A11 4c yel grn & org brn .25 .25
Never hinged .30
On cover 24.00
100 A11 5c ver & grn .25 .25
Never hinged .30
On cover 20.00
101 A11 10c bis brn & dp bl .25 .25
Never hinged .30
On cover 16.00
102 A11 15c brn red & blk .30 .30
Never hinged .45
On cover 16.00
103 A11 20c lil & ol brn .50 .50
Never hinged .65
On cover 12.00
104 A12 25c grnsh bl & olvn .55 .55
Never hinged .80
On cover 6.50
105 A12 30c gray grn & yel grn .40 .40
Never hinged .65
On cover 8.00
106 A12 35c bl grn ('38) .40 .40
Never hinged .55
On cover 9.50
107 A12 40c yel & vio .40 .40
Never hinged .65
On cover 4.00
108 A12 45c vio brn & slate .95 .80
Never hinged 1.30
On cover 6.50
109 A12 45c bl grn & dl grn ('40) 1.10 1.00
Never hinged 1.50
On cover 27.50
110 A12 50c dl grn & org .30 .30
Never hinged .45
On cover 4.00
111 A12 55c ultra & car ('38) 1.40 1.25
Never hinged 2.00
On cover 8.00
112 A12 60c ultra & car ('40) .65 .65
Never hinged .80
On cover 20.00
113 A12 65c gray blk & ver .55 .55
Never hinged .80
On cover 5.50
114 A12 70c gray blk & ver ('40) .70 .70
Never hinged .95
On cover 8.00
115 A12 75c dl red & bl grn .70 .70
Never hinged .95
On cover 5.50
116 A12 80c car & brn ('38) .85 .65
Never hinged 1.20
On cover 10.50
117 A12 90c dl red & dl rose 2.00 1.75
Never hinged 2.75
On cover 16.00
On cover, single franking 50.00
118 A12 90c rose red & bl ('39) 1.25 1.10
Never hinged 1.50
On cover 9.50
119 A13 1fr lt rose & lt bl 5.25 3.75
Never hinged 7.50
On cover 40.00
On cover, single franking 65.00
120 A13 1fr rose red & org ('38) 1.75 1.50
Never hinged 2.75
On cover 12.00
On cover, single franking 20.00
121 A13 1fr bl gray & blk brn ('40) .70 .70
Never hinged .95
On cover 5.50
122 A13 1.05fr lt bl & rose 1.25 1.10
Never hinged 1.75
On cover 12.00
On cover, single franking 27.50
123 A13 1.10fr lt red & grn 4.00 2.75
Never hinged 6.75
On cover 47.50
On cover, single franking 100.00
124 A13 1.25fr bl gray & blk brn ('33) .65 .65
Never hinged .80
On cover 9.50
On cover, single franking 16.00
125 A13 1.25fr brt rose & red org ('39) .95 .95
Never hinged 1.25
On cover 47.50
On cover, single franking 80.00
126 A13 1.40fr lt bl & lil rose ('40) .70 .70
Never hinged .95
On cover 32.50
On cover, single franking 60.00
127 A13 1.50fr dl bl & bl .40 .40
Never hinged .65
On cover 10.50
On cover, single franking 20.00
128 A13 1.60fr lil rose & yel brn ('40) .70 .70
Never hinged .95
On cover 32.50
On cover, single franking 65.00
129 A13 1.75fr lil rose & yel brn ('33) 5.75 3.25
Never hinged 8.25
On cover 32.50
On cover, single franking 95.00
130 A13 1.75fr vio bl ('38) 6.00 4.00
Never hinged 8.50
On cover 35.00
On cover, single franking 110.00
131 A13 2fr bl grn & dk brn .40 .40
Never hinged .65
On cover 21.00
On cover, single franking 32.50
132 A13 2.25fr vio bl ('39) 1.25 1.25
Never hinged 1.50
On cover 45.00
On cover, single franking 80.00
133 A13 2.50fr pale org & grn ('40) 1.25 1.25
Never hinged 1.50
On cover 35.00
On cover, single franking 60.00
134 A13 3fr org brn & sl .65 .65
Never hinged .85
On cover 26.00
On cover, single franking 45.00
135 A13 5fr dl bl & org 1.25 1.00
Never hinged 1.60
On cover 35.00
On cover, single franking 60.00
136 A13 10fr vio & ol brn 1.25 1.00
Never hinged 1.60
On cover 45.00
On cover, single franking 67.50
137 A13 20fr green & mag 1.50 1.40
Never hinged 2.00
On cover 52.50
On cover, single franking 80.00
Nos. 96-137 (42) 50.20 40.95

Nos. 96-103, 110, 119, 123, 134, 137 exist imperf. Values each $30-$60.

For surcharges see Nos. 161-166 in Scott Standard catalogue, Vol. 3.

For 10c, type A11, without "RF," see No. 163A in Scott Standard catalogue, Vol. 3.

Common Design Types pictured following the introduction.

Colonial Exposition Issue
Common Design Types

1931, Apr. 13 **Engr.** ***Perf. 12½***

Name of Country in Black

138 CD70 40c deep green 4.75 4.75
Never hinged 6.50
On cover 40.00
139 CD71 50c violet 4.75 4.75
Never hinged 6.50
On cover 32.50
140 CD72 90c red orange 4.75 4.75
Never hinged 7.25
On cover 60.00
On cover, single franking 85.00
141 CD73 1.50fr dull blue 4.75 4.75
Never hinged 7.25
On cover 52.50
On cover, single franking 80.00
Nos. 138-141 (4) 19.00 19.00

Cardinal Richelieu Establishing French Antilles Co., 1635 — A14

Victor Hugues and his Corsairs — A15

1935 ***Perf. 13***

142 A14 40c gray brown 10.00 10.00
Never hinged 14.50
On cover 45.00
143 A14 50c dull red 10.00 10.00
Never hinged 14.50
On cover 35.00
144 A14 1.50fr dull blue 10.00 10.00
Never hinged 14.50
On cover 60.00
On cover, single franking 90.00
145 A15 1.75fr lilac rose 10.00 10.00
Never hinged 14.50
On cover 50.00
On cover, single franking 80.00
146 A15 5fr dark brown 10.00 10.00
Never hinged 14.50
On cover 50.00
On cover, single franking 80.00
147 A15 10fr blue green 10.00 10.00
Never hinged 14.50
On cover 67.50
On cover, single franking 120.00
Nos. 142-147 (6) 60.00 60.00

Tercentenary of the establishment of the French colonies in the West Indies.

Paris International Exposition Issue
Common Design Types

1937 ***Perf. 13***

148 CD74 20c deep violet 1.90 1.90
Never hinged 2.60
On cover 52.50
149 CD75 30c dark green 1.75 1.75
Never hinged 2.10
On cover 45.00
150 CD76 40c car rose 1.50 1.50
Never hinged 2.10
On cover 40.00
151 CD77 50c dk brn & blk 1.50 1.50
Never hinged 1.80
On cover 32.50
152 CD78 90c red 1.50 1.50
Never hinged 2.10
On cover 55.00
On cover, single franking 100.00
153 CD79 1.50fr ultra 1.90 1.90
Never hinged 2.60
On cover 47.50
On cover, single franking 85.00
Nos. 148-153 (6) 10.05 10.05

Colonial Arts Exhibition Issue
Souvenir Sheet
Common Design Type

1937 *Imperf.*
154 CD75 3fr dark blue 9.50 *11.00*
Never hinged 12.50
On cover 100.00
On cover, single franking 125.00

New York World's Fair Issue
Common Design Type

1939 Engr. *Perf. 12½x12*
155 CD82 1.25fr car lake 1.25 1.25
Never hinged 1.60
On cover 40.00
On cover, single franking 85.00
156 CD82 2.25fr ultra 1.25 1.25
Never hinged 1.60
On cover 40.00
On cover, single franking 80.00

For surcharges see Nos. 159-160 in Scott Standard catalogue, Vol. 3.

SEMI-POSTAL STAMPS

Nos. 59 and 62 Surcharged in Red

1915-17 Unwmk. *Perf. 14 x 13½*
B1 A8 10c + 5c rose 5.25 3.50
Never hinged 8.75
On cover 35.00
B2 A8 15c + 5c violet 5.25 3.50
Never hinged 8.75
On cover 35.00
a. Double surcharge 225.00 225.00
b. Triple surcharge 240.00 240.00
c. Inverted surcharge 240.00 240.00
d. In pair with unovptd. stamp 275.00

Curie Issue
Common Design Type

1938, Oct. 24 *Perf. 13*
B3 CD80 1.75fr + 50c brt ultra 11.00 10.50
Never hinged 15.00
On cover 60.00
On cover, single franking 100.00

French Revolution Issue
Common Design Type
Name and Value Typo. in Black

1939, July 5 Photo. *Perf. 13*
B4 CD83 45c + 25c green 10.00 10.00
Never hinged 15.00
On cover 80.00
B5 CD83 70c + 30c brown 10.00 10.00
Never hinged 15.00
On cover 60.00
B6 CD83 90c + 35c red org 10.00 10.00
Never hinged 15.00
On cover 55.00
B7 CD83 1.25fr + 1fr rose pink 10.00 10.00
Never hinged 15.00
On cover 80.00
On cover, single franking 130.00
B8 CD83 2.25fr + 2fr blue 10.00 10.00
Never hinged 15.00
On cover 72.50
On cover, single franking 120.00
Nos. B4-B8 (5) 50.00 50.00

POSTAGE DUE STAMPS

D1 D2 D3

1876 Unwmk. Typeset *Imperf.*
J1 D1 25c black 1,350. 925.
On cover 4,500.
J2 D2 40c black, *blue* *37,500.*
On cover *60,000.*
J3 D3 40c black 1,500. 1,200.
On cover 4,500.

Twenty varieties of each.
Nos. J1 and J3 have been reprinted on thinner and whiter paper than the originals.

D4

1879
J4 D4 15c black, *blue* 55.00 52.50
Never hinged 110.00
On cover 4,500.
a. Period after "c" omitted 175.00 175.00
b. "c" of denomination omitted 200.00 200.00
c. "i" of "percevoir" omitted 200.00 200.00
d. Accent over "a" of "á percevoir" omitted 175.00 175.00
e. 15c black, *deep blue* 75.00 65.00
J5 D4 30c black 110.00 87.50
On cover 2,500.
a. Period after "c" omitted 240.00 225.00
b. "c" of denomination omitted 300.00 260.00
c. "i" of "percevoir" omitted 300.00 260.00

Twenty varieties of each.

D5

1884
J6 D5 5c black 35.00 35.00
Never hinged 67.50
On cover 3,000.
a. Double impression 100.00 100.00
J7 D5 10c black, *blue* 75.00 65.00
Never hinged 135.00
On cover 3,250.
a. Double impression 150.00 150.00
J8 D5 15c black, *violet* 110.00 87.50
On cover *3,500.*
a. Double impression 225.00 225.00
J9 D5 20c black, *rose* 160.00 100.00
On cover *3,500.*
a. Italic "2" in "20" 1,000. 950.00
J10 D5 30c black, *yellow* 160.00 160.00
On cover 3,750.
a. Double impression 450.00 450.00
J11 D5 35c black, *gray* 60.00 52.50
On cover 3,250.
a. Double impression 225.00 225.00
J12 D5 50c black, *green* 32.50 27.50
Never hinged 67.50
On cover 3,000.
a. Double impression 200.00 200.00
Nos. J6-J12 (7) 632.50 527.50

There are ten varieties of the 35c, and fifteen of each of the other values, also numerous wrong font and missing letters.

Postage Due Stamps of French Colonies Surcharged in Black

Two surcharge types: I, wide font, "3" with rounded top; II, narrow font, "3" with flat top.

1903 **Type I**
J13 D1 30c on 60c brn, *cr* 325.00 325.00
a. Inverted surcharge 1,100. 1,100.
b. Bee corner ornament turned 1,150. 1,150.
c. As "b," inverted surcharge 1,700.
d. "G" omitted 800.00 800.00
e. As "d," inverted surcharge 1,250.
f. Corrected surcharge, "30" over "33" 10,500. 10,500.
J14 D1 30c on 1fr rose, *cr* 400.00 400.00
a. Inverted surcharge 1,150. 1,150.
b. "30" sideways 10,000. 10,000.
c. As "b," inverted surcharge 10,000. 10,000.

Type II
J13A D1 30c on 60c brn, *cr* 1,000. 1,000.
a. Inverted surcharge 1,900. 1,900.
b. Bee corner ornament turned 1,600. 1,600.
c. As "b," inverted surcharge 2,200.
d. "G" omitted 1,000 1,000.
e. As "d," inverted surcharge 1,500.
f. Corrected surcharge, "30" over "33" 10,500. 10,500.
J14A D1 30c on 1fr rose, *cr* 400.00 400.00
a. Inverted surcharge 1,200. 1,200.
b. "30" sideways 10,500. 10,500.
c. As "b," inverted surcharge 10,500. 10,500.

Gustavia Bay — D6

1905-06 Typo. *Perf. 14x13½*
J15 D6 5c blue .55 .55
Never hinged .70
On cover 150.00
J16 D6 10c brown .55 .55
Never hinged .70
On cover 150.00
J17 D6 15c green 1.00 1.00
Never hinged 1.40
On cover 150.00
J18 D6 20c black, *yel* ('06) 1.00 1.00
Never hinged 1.40
On cover 150.00
J19 D6 30c rose 1.25 1.25
Never hinged 1.60
On cover 150.00
J20 D6 50c black 3.25 3.25
Never hinged 4.50
On cover *175.00*
J21 D6 60c brown orange 1.75 1.75
Never hinged 2.40
On cover *175.00*
J22 D6 1fr violet 3.25 3.25
Never hinged 4.50
On cover *225.00*
Nos. J15-J22 (8) 12.60 12.60

Type of 1905-06 Issue Surcharged

1926-27
J23 D6 2fr on 1fr gray 2.00 2.00
Never hinged 3.25
On cover 120.00
J24 D6 3fr on 1fr ultra ('27) 2.75 2.75
Never hinged 4.00
On cover *140.00*

Avenue of Royal Palms — D7

1928, June 18
J25 D7 2c olive brn & lil .25 .25
Never hinged .30
On cover *60.00*
J26 D7 4c bl & org brn .25 .25
Never hinged .30
On cover *60.00*
J27 D7 5c gray grn & dk brn .25 .25
Never hinged .30
On cover *45.00*
J28 D7 10c dl vio & yel .30 .30
Never hinged .45
On cover *45.00*
J29 D7 15c rose & olive grn .30 .30
Never hinged .45
On cover *50.00*
J30 D7 20c brn org & ol grn .50 .50
Never hinged .65
On cover *50.00*
J31 D7 25c brn red & bl grn .50 .50
Never hinged .65
On cover *50.00*
J32 D7 30c slate & olivine .80 .80
Never hinged .95
On cover *55.00*
J33 D7 50c ol brn & lt red .80 .80
Never hinged .95
On cover *60.00*
J34 D7 60c dp bl & blk .80 .80
Never hinged .95
On cover *60.00*
J35 D7 1fr green & orange 3.00 2.60
Never hinged 3.75
On cover *80.00*
J36 D7 2fr bis brn & lt red 2.25 1.90
Never hinged 2.75
On cover *80.00*
J37 D7 3fr vio & bl blk 1.25 1.10
Never hinged 1.60
On cover *90.00*
Nos. J25-J37 (13) 11.25 10.35

GUATEMALA

ˌgwä-lə-ˈmä-lə

LOCATION — Central America, bordering on Atlantic and Pacific Oceans
GOVT. — Republic
AREA — 42,042 sq. mi.
POP. — 6,577,000 (est. 1984)
CAPITAL — Guatemala City

100 Centavos = 8 Reales = 1 Peso
100 Centavos de Quetzal = 1 Quetzal (1927)

Coat of Arms — A1

Two types of 10c:
Type I — Both zeros in "10" are wide.
Type II — Left zero narrow.

Perf. 14x13½

1871, Mar. 1 Typo. Unwmk.
1 A1 1c ocher 2.00 *50.00*
a. Imperf., pair 10.00
b. Printed on both sides, imperf. 135.00
On cover, *from* *3,000.*
2 A1 5c lt bister brn 9.00 *22.50*
On cover, *from* *3,000.*
On cover, single franking, *from* *3,000.*
a. Imperf. pair 50.00
b. Tête bêche pair 350.00
c. Tête bêche pair, imperf. *3,500.*
3 A1 10c blue (I) 11.00 *25.00*
On cover, *from* *3,000.*
Half used as 5c on cover *5,000.*
a. Imperf., pair (I) 75.00
b. Type II 25.00 *50.00*
c. Imperf. pair (II) 110.00
4 A1 20c rose 9.00 *24.00*
On cover, *from* *5,000.*
a. Imperf., pair 75.00
b. 20c blue (error) 350.00 *125.00*
On cover, *from* *60,000.*
c. As "b," imperf. *1,750.*
Nos. 1-4 (4) 31.00 *121.50*

Forgeries exist. Forged cancellations abound. See No. C458 in Scott Standard catalogue, Vol. 3.
Only one on-cover example of No. 4b is known to exist.

Coat of Arms — A2

1873 Litho. *Perf. 12*
5 A2 4r dull red vio 675.00 175.00
On cover, *from* *7,500.*
On cover, pair *15,000.*
6 A2 1p dull yellow 350.00 215.00
On cover, *from* *12,500.*

Forgeries exist. Only one pair of No. 5 is known on cover.

Liberty
A3 A4

A5 A6

1875, Apr. 15 **Engr.**
7 A3 ¼r black 42.50 *22.00*
No gum 3.50
On cover, *from* *4,500.*
8 A4 ½r blue green 42.50 *14.00*
No gum 3.50
On cover, *from* *3,000.*
9 A5 1r blue 42.50 *14.00*
No gum 3.50
On cover, *from* *7,500.*
a. Half used as ½r on cover *4,000.*
10 A6 2r dull red 42.50 *14.00*
No gum 3.50
On cover, *from* *2,500.*
Nos. 7-10 (4) 170.00 *64.00*

Nos. 7-10 normally lack gum. Unused values are for examples without gum.
Forgeries and forged cancellations exist.

Indian Woman — A7

Typographed on Tinted Paper

1878, Jan. 10 *Perf. 13*

11 A7 ½r yellow grn 2.75 *6.75*
On cover, *from* *1,750.*
12 A7 2r carmine rose 4.25 *13.00*
On cover, pair, *from* *1,500.*
On cover, single franking, *from* *2,000.*
13 A7 4r violet 4.25 *14.50*
On cover, single franking, *from* *2,500.*
14 A7 1p yellow 5.00 *35.00*
On cover, *from* *3,750.*
On cover, pair *6,000.*
c. Half used as 4r on cover *6,000.*
Nos. 11-14 (4) 16.25 *69.25*

Some sheets of Nos. 11-14 have papermaker's watermark, "LACROIX FRERES," in double-lined capitals appearing on six stamps.

Part perforate pairs of Nos. 11, 12 and 14 exist. Value for each, about $100.

Forgeries of Nos. 11-14 are plentiful. Forged cancellations exist.

For surcharges see Nos. 18, 20.

One pair of No. 14 is known to exist on cover.

Imperf., Pairs

11a A7 ½r yellow green 215.00
Vert. pair, imperf. between 250.00
Horiz. pair, imperf. vert. 250.00
12a A7 2r carmine rose 215.00
13a A7 4r violet 215.00
14a A7 1p yellow 215.00

Quetzal — A8

1879 **Engr.** *Perf. 12*

15 A8 ¼r brown & green 16.00 *20.00*
On cover, *from* *1,250.*
On cover, single franking, *from* *1,500.*
16 A8 1r black & green 24.00 *30.00*
On cover, *from* *1,250.*

For similar types see A11, A72, A103, A121, A146. For surcharges see Nos. 17, 19.

Nos. 11, 12, 15, 16 Surcharged in Black

1881 *Perf. 12 and 13*

17 A8 1c on ¼r brn & grn 25.00 *35.00*
On cover, *from* *1,250.*
a. "ecntavo," 87.50 *100.00*
b. Pair, one without surcharge 425.00
c. Period omitted 87.50 *100.00*
18 A7 5c on ½r yel grn 19.00 *30.00*
On cover, *from* *1,250.*
On cover, single franking, *from* *2,000.*
a. "ecntavos," 80.00 *110.00*
b. "5" omitted 215.00
c. Double surcharge 200.00 *260.00*
19 A8 10c on 1r blk & grn 40.00 *50.00*
On cover, *from* *1,250.*
a. "s" of "centavos" missing 115.00 135.00
b. "ecntavos" 145.00 *190.00*
20 A7 20c on 2r car rose 100.00 *145.00*
On cover, *from* —
a. Horiz. pair, imperf. between 750.00
b. Period omitted 125.00 *175.00*
c. Comma for period 200.00 *260.00*
Nos. 17-20 (4) 184.00 *260.00*

The 5c had three settings.

Surcharge varieties found on Nos. 17-20 include: Period omitted; comma instead of period; "ecntavo." or "ecntavos."; "s" omitted; spaced "centavos."; wider "0" in "20."

Counterfeits of Nos. 17-20 are plentiful.

Quetzal — A11

1881, Nov. 7 **Engr.** *Perf. 12*

21 A11 1c black & grn 6.00 4.25
On cover, *from* *650.00*
22 A11 2c brown & grn 6.00 4.50
On cover, *from* *650.00*
a. Center inverted *725.00* *550.00*
No gum 450.00
23 A11 5c red & grn 13.00 5.50
On cover, *from* *750.00*
a. Center inverted *7,000.* *2,500.*
No gum *3,500.*
24 A11 10c gray vio & grn 6.00 4.50
On cover, *from* *650.00*
25 A11 20c yellow & grn 6.00 5.25
On cover, *from* *1,000.*
a. Center inverted *825.00* *575.00*
No gum 550.00
Nos. 21-25 (5) 37.00 24.00

Surcharged in Black

Gen. Justo Rufino Barrios — A12

A12a

A12b

1886, Mar. 6

26 A12 25c on 1p ver 1.00 1.00
a. "centovos" 20.00 20.00
b. "centanos" 20.00 20.00
c. "255" instead of "25" 150.00 225.00
d. Inverted "S" in "Nacionales" 20.00 22.50
f. "cen avos" 40.00
h. "Corre cionales" 25.00
i. Inverted surcharge *100.00*
27 A12 50c on 1p ver 1.00 1.00
a. "centovos" 10.00 10.00
b. "centanos" 10.00 10.00
c. "Carreos" 10.00 10.00
d. Inverted surcharge 100.00 100.00
e. Double surcharge 110.00
f. Inverted "S" in "Nacionales" 110.00
g. "centavo" 22.50
h. "cen avos" 40.00
28 A12 75c on 1p ver 1.00 1.00
a. "centovos" 10.00 10.00
b. "centanos" 10.00 10.00
c. "Carreos" 10.00 10.00
d. "50" for "75" at upper right 10.00 10.00
e. Inverted "S" in "Nacionales" 10.00 10.00
f. Double surcharge 100.00
g. "ales" inverted 100.00
29 A12a 100c on 1p ver 2.00 3.00
a. "110" at upper left and "á" at lower left, instead of "100" 17.50 25.00
b. Inverted surcharge 100.00 *100.00*
c. "Guatemala" bolder; 23mm instead of 18½mm wide 9.00 *10.00*
d. Double surcharge, one diagonal 100.00
30 A12b 150c on 1p ver 2.00 3.50
a. Inverted "G" 7.50 7.50
b. "Guatemala" and italic "5" in upper 4 numerals 10.00 10.00
d. Inverted surcharge 125.00
e. Pair, one without surcharge 150.00
f. Double surcharge 130.00
Nos. 26-30 (5) 7.00 9.50

There are many other minor varieties, such as wrong font letters, etc.

Used values of Nos. 26-30 are for canceled to order stamps. Postally used sell for much more.

National Emblem — A13

1886, July 1 **Litho.** *Perf. 12*

31 A13 1c dull blue 7.50 3.00
On cover, *from* *50.00*
32 A13 2c brown 8.50 4.50
On cover *40.00*
33 A13 5c purple 55.00 1.50
On cover, *from* *50.00*
34 A13 10c red 25.00 1.50
On cover *80.00*
On cover, single franking *80.00*
35 A13 20c emerald 25.00 2.00
36 A13 25c orange 27.50 2.00
37 A13 50c olive green 15.00 4.50
38 A13 75c carmine rose 17.50 4.50
39 A13 100c red brown 17.50 10.00
40 A13 150c dark blue 20.00 12.50
41 A13 200c orange yellow 25.00 12.50
Nos. 31-41 (11) 243.50 58.50

Used values of Nos. 38-41 are for canceled to order stamps. Postally used sell for more.

See Nos. 43-50, 99-107. For surcharges see Nos. 42, 51-59, 75-85, 97-98, 108-110, 124-130.

No. 32 Surcharged in Black

Two settings:
I — "1886" (no period).
II — "1886." (period).

1886, Nov. 12

42 A13 1c on 2c brown, I 5.50 *10.00*
On cover, *from* *75.00*
a. Date inverted, I 125.00
b. Date double, I 125.00
c. Date omitted, I 125.00
d. Date double, one invtd., I 135.00
e. Date triple, one inverted, I *135.00*
f. Setting II 3.50 2.00
g. Inverted surcharge, II 10.00
h. Double surcharge, II 125.00

Forgeries exist.

Type I

Type II

Two types of 5c:
I — Thin "5"
II — Larger, thick "5"

1886-95 **Engr.** *Perf. 12*

43 A13 1c blue 1.50 .50
On cover, *from* *40.00*
44 A13 2c yellow brn 3.50 .50
On cover *25.00*
a. Half used as 1c on cover 125.00
45 A13 5c purple (I) 200.00 5.00
On cover *125.00*
46 A13 5c vio (II) ('88) 4.50 .75
On cover, *from* *40.00*
47 A13 6c lilac ('95) 4.50 .50
On cover *90.00*
48 A13 10c red ('90) 4.50 .50
On cover, single franking *100.00*
On cover, *from* *40.00*
49 A13 20c green ('93) 7.50 1.00
On cover *150.00*
50 A13 25c red org ('93) 12.50 2.00
On cover *125.00*
Nos. 43-44,46-50 (7) 38.50 5.75

The impression of the engraved stamps is sharper than that of the lithographed. On the engraved stamps the top four lines at left are heavier than those below them. (This is also true of the 1c litho., which is distinguished from the engraved only by a slight color difference and the impression.)

The "2" and "5" (I) are more open than the litho. numerals. The "10" of the engraved is wider. The 20c and 25c of the engraved have a vertical line at right end of the "centavos" ribbon.

No. 38 Surcharged in Blue Black

"1894" 14½mm wide

1894, Apr. 25

51 A13 10c on 75c car rose 9.00 7.50
a. Double surcharge 175.00
b. Inverted surcharge 90.00

Same on Nos. 38-41 in Blue or Red "1894" 14mm wide

1894, June 13

52 A13 2c on 100c 7.50 6.00
53 A13 6c on 150c (R) 8.00 5.50
54 A13 10c on 75c 1,000. 900.00
a. Thick "1" in "10" 1,100. 1,100.
55 A13 10c on 200c 10.00 5.00
c. Inverted surcharge 125.00
d. "207" (position 29) 50.00
e. Thick "1" in "10" 12.50 7.50

Nos. 54-55 exist with thick or thin "1" in new value.

Same on Nos. 39-41 in Black or Red "1894" 12mm wide

1894, July 14

52a A13 2c on 100c red brn (Bk) 12.50 6.50
b. Vert. pair, one without surcharge *250.00*
53a A13 6c on 150c dk bl (R) 12.50 6.50
55a A13 10c on 200c org yel (Bk) 12.50 6.50
d. Inverted surcharge 110.00
e. Vert. pair, one without surcharge 160.00
f. "207" (position 29) *250.00*

Nos. 44 and 46 Surcharged in Black, Blue Black, or Red

b

c

d

e

1894-96

56 A13 (b) 1c on 2c (Bk) .75 .30
- *a.* "Centav" 5.00 5.00
- *b.* Double surcharge 75.00
- *c.* As "a," dbl. surcharge 150.00
- *d.* Blue black surcharge 20.00 20.00
- *e.* Dbl. surch., one inverted 150.00

57 A13 (c) 1c on 5c (R) ('95) .50 .25
- *a.* Inverted surcharge 3.00 3.00
- *b.* "1894" instead of "1895" 3.50 3.00
- *c.* Double surcharge 50.00

58 A13 (d) 1c on 5c (R) ('95) .75 .25
- *a.* Inverted surcharge 50.00 50.00
- *b.* Double surcharge 50.00

59 A13 (e) 1c on 5c (R) ('96) 1.25 .40
- *a.* Inverted surcharge 50.00 50.00
- *b.* Double surcharge 50.00

Nos. 56-59 (4) 3.25 1.20

Nos. 56-58 may be found with thick or thin "1" in the new value.

National Arms and President J. M. Reyna Barrios A21

1897, Jan. 1 Engr. Unwmk.

No.	Type	Denomination	Unused	Used
60	A21	1c blk, *gray*	.55	.55
61	A21	2c blk, *grnsh gray*	.55	.55
62	A21	6c blk, *brn org*	.55	.55
63	A21	10c blk, *dl bl*	.55	.55
64	A21	12c blk, *rose red*	.55	.55
65	A21	18c blk, *grysh white*	9.50	9.50
66	A21	20c blk, *scarlet*	1.00	1.00
67	A21	25c blk, *bis brn*	1.60	1.00
68	A21	50c blk, *redsh brn*	1.00	1.00
69	A21	75c blk, *gray*	52.50	52.50
70	A21	100c blk, *bl grn*	1.00	1.00
71	A21	150c blk, *dl rose*	105.00	*135.00*
72	A21	200c blk, *magenta*	1.00	1.00
73	A21	500c blk, *yel grn*	1.00	1.00
		Nos. 60-73 (14)	176.35	*205.75*

Issued for Central American Exposition.

Stamps often sold as Nos. 65, 69 and 71 are examples with telegraph overprint removed.

Used values for Nos. 60-73 are for canceled-to-order stamps. Postally used examples are worth more.

The paper of Nos. 64 and 66 was originally colored on one side only, but has "bled through" on some examples.

No. 64 Surcharged in Violet

1897, Nov.

74 A21 1c on 12c *rose red* 1.00 1.00
- *a.* Inverted surcharge 30.00 30.00
- *b.* Pair, one without surcharge 75.00
- *c.* Dbl. surch., one invtd. 100.00

Stamps of 1886-93 Surcharged in Red

f

g

1898

75 (f) 1c on 5c violet 1.00 1.00
- *a.* Inverted surcharge 75.00

76 (f) 1c on 50c ol grn 1.50 1.25
- *a.* Inverted surcharge 100.00 100.00

77 (f) 6c on 5c violet 4.50 1.50

78 (f) 6c on 150c dk bl 4.50 3.25

79 (g) 10c on 20c emerald 5.00 4.00
- *a.* Double surch., one inverted 125.00 125.00

Nos. 75-79 (5) 16.50 11.00

Black Surcharge

80 (f) 1c on 25c red org 2.00 2.00

81 (f) 1c on 75c car rose 1.50 1.50
- *a.* Double surcharge 100.00

82 (f) 6c on 10c red 10.00 9.00

83 (f) 6c on 20c emer 5.00 4.00

84 (f) 6c on 100c red brn 5.00 4.00

85 (f) 6c on 200c org yel 5.00 4.00
- *a.* Inverted surcharge 50.00 50.00

Nos. 80-85 (6) 28.50 24.50

Information indicates that No. 77 inverted and double surcharges are counterfeits.

National Emblem — A24

Revenue Stamp Overprinted or Surcharged in Carmine

Perf. 12, 12x14, 14x12

1898, Oct. 8 Litho.

86 A24 1c dark blue 1.40 1.40
- *a.* Inverted overprint 12.50 12.50

87 A24 2c on 1c dk bl 2.25 2.25
- *a.* Inverted surcharge 12.50 12.50

Counterfeits exist.

See type A26.

National Emblem — A25

Revenue Stamps Surcharged in Carmine

1898 Engr. *Perf. 12½ to 16*

88 A25 1c on 10c bl gray .75 .75
- *a.* "ENTAVO" 5.00 5.00

89 A25 2c on 5c pur 1.25 1.00

90 A25 2c on 10c bl gray 6.50 *7.00*
- *a.* Double surch., car & blk 100.00 75.00

91 A25 2c on 50c dp bl 9.25 *9.25*
- *a.* Double surch., car & blk 100.00 100.00

Nos. 88-91 (4) 17.75 *18.00*

Black Surcharge

92 A25 2c on 1c lil rose 3.50 2.00

93 A25 2c on 25c red 7.50 8.00

94 A25 6c on 1p purple 4.00 4.50

95 A25 6c on 5p gray vio 7.50 7.50

96 A25 6c on 10p emer 7.50 7.50

Nos. 92-96 (5) 30.00 29.50

Nos. 88 and 90 are found in shades ranging from Prussian blue to slate blue.

Varieties other than those listed are bogus.

Counterfeits exist of No. 92.

Soaking in water causes marked fading.

See type A27.

No. 46 Surcharged in Red

1899, Sept. *Perf. 12*

97 A13 1c on 5c violet .40 .25
- *a.* Inverted surcharge 7.50 7.50
- *b.* Double surcharge 15.00 15.00
- *c.* Double surcharge, one inverted 15.00 15.00

No. 48 Surcharged in Black

1900, Jan.

98 A13 1c on 10c red .65 .50
- *a.* Inverted surcharge 10.00 10.00
- *b.* Double surcharge 75.00 75.00

Quetzal Type of 1886

1900-02 Engr.

No.	Type	Denomination	Unused	Used
99	A13	1c dark green	.60	.25
100	A13	2c carmine	.60	.25
101	A13	5c blue (II)	2.25	1.25
102	A13	6c lt green	.75	.25
103	A13	10c bister brown	7.50	1.00
104	A13	20c purple	7.50	7.50
105	A13	20c bister brn ('02)	7.50	7.50
106	A13	25c yellow	7.50	7.50
107	A13	25c blue green ('02)	7.50	7.50
		Nos. 99-107 (9)	41.70	33.00

No. 49 Surcharged in Black

1901, May

108 A13 1c on 20c green .50 .50
- *a.* Inverted surcharge 22.50 22.50
- *b.* Double surch., one diagonal 50.00

109 A13 2c on 20c green 1.50 1.50

No. 50 Surcharged in Black

1901, Apr.

110 A13 1c on 25c red org .60 .60
- *a.* Inverted surcharge 25.00 25.00
- *b.* Double surcharge 50.00 50.00

A26

A27

Revenue Stamps Surcharged in Carmine or Black

1902, July *Perf. 12, 14x12, 12x14*

111 A26 1c on 1c dk blue 1.10 1.10
- *a.* Double surcharge 20.00
- *b.* Inverted surcharge 20.00

112 A26 2c on 1c dk blue 1.10 1.10
- *a.* Double surcharge 90.00
- *b.* Inverted surcharge 25.00

Perf. 14, 15

113 A27 6c on 25c red (Bk) 2.50 2.50
- *a.* Double surch., one invtd. 75.00 75.00

Nos. 111-113 (3) 4.70 4.70

National Emblem — A28

Statue of Justo Rufino Barrios — A29

"La Reforma" Palace — A30

Temple of Minerva — A31

Lake Amatitlán — A32

Cathedral in Guatemala — A33

Columbus Theater — A34

Artillery Barracks — A35

Monument to Columbus — A36

School for Indians — A37

1902 Engr. *Perf. 12 to 16*

114 A28 1c grn & claret .25 .25
- *a.* Horiz. pair, imperf. vert. 100.00

115 A29 2c lake & blk .25 .25
- *a.* Horiz. or vert. pair, imperf. btwn. 150.00

116 A30 5c blue & blk .30 .25
- *a.* 5c ultra & blk .75 .40
- *b.* Imperf., pair 100.00 100.00
- *c.* Horiz. pair, imperf. vert. 100.00

117 A31 6c bister & grn .30 .25
- *a.* Horiz. pair, imperf. btwn. 150.00

118 A32 10c orange & bl .40 .40
- *a.* Horiz. pair, imperf. vert. 100.00

119 A33 20c rose lil & blk .60 .40
- *a.* Horiz. pair, imperf. vert. 100.00

120 A34 50c red brn & bl .45 .40
- *a.* Vert. pair, imperf. btwn. 350.00

121 A35 75c gray lil & blk .55 .40
- *a.* Horiz. pair, imperf. btwn. 150.00
- *b.* Horiz. pair, imperf. vert. 100.00

122 A36 1p brown & blk .85 .40
- *a.* Horiz. pair, imperf. btwn. 150.00

123 A37 2p ver & blk 1.00 .85

Nos. 114-123 (10) 4.95 3.85

See Nos. 210, 212-214, 219, 223, 239-241, 243. For overprints and surcharges see Nos. 133, 135-139, 144-157, 168, 170-171, 178, 192-194, 298-299, 301 (in Scott Standard catalogue, Vol. 3), C19, C27, C123.

Issues of 1886-1900 Surcharged in Black or Carmine

1903, Apr. 18 *Perf. 12*

124	A13 25c on 1c dk grn	1.25	.55
a.	Inverted surcharge	50.00	50.00
125	A13 25c on 2c carmine	1.50	.55
126	A13 25c on 6c lt grn	2.50	1.75
a.	Inverted surcharge	40.00	40.00
127	A13 25c on 10c bis brn	7.50	7.00
128	A13 25c on 75c rose	10.00	10.00
129	A13 25c on 150c dk bl (C)	9.00	9.00
130	A13 25c on 200c yellow	10.00	10.00
	Nos. 124-130 (7)	41.75	38.85

Forgeries and bogus varieties exist.

Declaration of Independence A38

1907, Jan. 1 *Perf. 13½ to 15*

132	A38 12½c ultra & blk	.45	.45
a.	Horiz. pair, imperf. btwn.	150.00	

For surcharge see No. 134.

Nos. 118, 119 and 132 Surcharged in Black or Red

1908, May

133	A32 1c on 10c org & bl	.30	.30
a.	Double surcharge	25.00	
b.	Inverted surcharge	15.00	15.00
c.	Pair, one without surcharge	50.00	
134	A38 2c on 12½c ultra & blk (R)	.25	.25
a.	Horiz. or vert. pair, imperf. btwn.	100.00	
b.	Inverted surcharge	15.00	10.00
c.	Double surcharge	30.00	
135	A33 6c on 20c rose lil & blk	.45	.25
a.	Inverted surcharge	20.00	20.00
	Nos. 133-135 (3)	1.00	.80

Similar Surcharge, Dated 1909, in Red or Black on Nos. 121 and 120

1909, Apr.

136	A35 2c on 75c (R)	.55	.55
137	A34 6c on 50c (R)	62.50	62.50
a.	Double surcharge	125.00	125.00
138	A34 6c on 50c (Bk)	.30	.30
	Nos. 136-138 (3)	63.35	63.35

Counterfeits exist of Nos. 137, 137a.

No. 123 Surcharged in Black

139	A37 12½c on 2p ver & blk	.30	.30
a.	Inverted surcharge	25.00	25.00
b.	Period omitted after "1909"	12.50	12.50

Counterfeits exist.

Gen. Miguel García Granados, Birth Cent. (in 1909) — A39

1910, Feb. 11 *Perf. 14*

140	A39 6c bis & indigo	.55	.40
a.	Imperf., pair	55.00	

Some sheets used for this issue contained a two-line watermark, "SPECIAL POSTAGE PAPER / LONDON." For surcharge see No. 143.

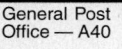

General Post Office — A40

Pres. Manuel Estrada Cabrera — A41

1911, June *Perf. 12*

141	A40 25c bl & blk	.55	.25
a.	Center inverted	*1,750.*	900.00
142	A41 5p red & blk	.65	.65
a.	Center inverted	30.00	27.50

Nos. 116, 118 and 140 Surcharged in Black or Red

h

i

j

1911 *Perf. 14*

143	A39 (h) 1c on 6c	25.00	9.75
a.	Double surcharge	75.00	75.00
144	A30 (i) 2c on 5c (R)	1.60	.85
145	A32 (j) 6c on 10c	1.25	1.25
a.	Double surcharge	50.00	
	Nos. 143-145 (3)	27.85	11.85

See watermark note after No. 140. Forgeries exist.

Nos. 119-121 Surcharged in Black

k

l

m

1912, Sept.

147	A33 (k) 1c on 20c	.40	.40
a.	Inverted surcharge	12.50	12.50
b.	Double surcharge	15.00	15.00
148	A34 (l) 2c on 50c	.40	.40
a.	Inverted surcharge	12.50	12.50
b.	Double surcharge	12.50	
c.	Double inverted surcharge	25.00	
149	A35 (m) 5c on 75c	.80	.80
a.	"191" for "1912"	7.50	7.50
b.	Double surcharge	15.00	15.00
c.	Inverted surcharge	10.00	
	Nos. 147-149 (3)	1.60	1.60

Forgeries exist.

Nos. 120, 122 and 123 Surcharged in Blue, Green or Black

n

o

p

1913, July

151	A34 (n) 1c on 50c (Bl)	.25	.25
a.	Inverted surcharge	10.00	
b.	Double surcharge	17.50	
c.	Horiz. pair, imperf. btwn.	100.00	
152	A36 (o) 6c on 1p (G)	.30	.30
153	A37 (p) 12½c on 2p (Bk)	.30	.30
a.	Inverted surcharge	15.00	15.00
b.	Double surcharge	40.00	
c.	Horiz. pair, imperf. btwn.	100.00	
	Nos. 151-153 (3)	.85	.85

Forgeries exist.

Nos. 114 and 115 Surcharged in Black

q

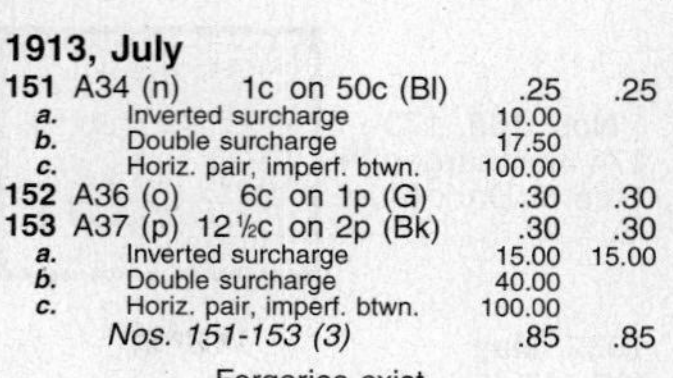

r

s

t

1916-17

154	A28 (q) 2c on 1c ('17)	.25	.25
155	A28 (r) 6c on 1c	.25	.25
156	A28 (s) 12½c on 1c	.25	.25
157	A29 (t) 25c on 2c	.25	.25
	Nos. 154-157 (4)	1.00	1.00

Numerous errors of value and color, inverted and double surcharges and similar varieties are in the market. They were not regularly issued, but were surreptitiously made and sold.

Counterfeit surcharges abound.

"Liberty" and President Estrada Cabrera — A51

1917, Mar. 15 *Perf. 14, 15*

158	A51 25c dp blue & brown	.25	.25

Re-election of President Estrada Cabrera.

Estrada Cabrera and Quetzal — A52

1918 *Perf. 12*

161	A52 1.50p dark blue	.30	.25

Radio Station — A54

"Joaquina" Maternity Hospital — A55

"Estrada Cabrera" Vocational School — A56

National Emblem — A57

1919, May 3 *Perf. 14, 15*

162	A54 30c red & blk	2.75	.75
163	A55 60c ol grn & blk	.80	.50
164	A56 90c red brn & blk	.80	.75
165	A57 3p dp grn & blk	1.75	.50
	Nos. 162-165 (4)	6.10	2.50

See Nos. 215, 227. For surcharges see Nos. 166-167, 179-185, 188, 195-198, 245-246, C8-C11, C21-C22.

No. 162 Ovptd. in Blue & Srchd. in Black

1920, Jan. **Unwmk.**

166	A54 2c on 30c red & blk	.30	.25
a.	Inverted surcharge	12.50	12.50
b.	"1920" double	10.00	10.00
c.	"1920" omitted	15.00	15.00
d.	"2 centavos" omitted	20.00	
e.	Imperf, pair	100.00	
f.	Pair, imperf. btwn.	100.00	

Nos. 123 and 163 Surcharged

u

v

1920

167	A55 2c on 60c (Bk & R)	.25	.25
a.	Inverted surcharge	10.00	10.00
b.	"1920" inverted	7.50	7.50
c.	"1920" omitted	10.00	10.00
d.	"1920" only	10.00	
e.	Double surcharge	25.00	
168	A37 25c on 2p (Bk)	.30	.25
a.	"35" for "25"	10.00	10.00
b.	Large "5" in "25"	10.00	10.00
c.	Inverted surcharge	15.00	15.00
d.	Double surcharge	25.00	

A61

1920

169	A61 25c green	.25	.25
a.	Double overprint		50.00
b.	Double overprint, inverted	75.00	

See types A65-A66.

No. 119 Surcharged

1921, Apr.

170	A33 12½c on 20c	.25	.25
a.	Double surcharge	15.00	
b.	Inverted surcharge	15.00	

No. 121 Surcharged

1921, Apr.

171 A35 50c on 75c lil & blk .50 .30
a. Double surcharge 22.50
b. Inverted surcharge 25.00 25.00

Mayan Stele at Quiriguá — A62

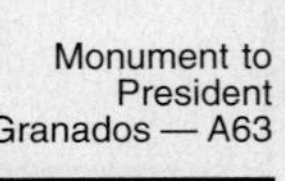

Monument to President Granados — A63

"La Penitenciaria" Bridge — A64

1921, Sept. 1 ***Perf. 13½, 14, 15***

172 A62 1.50p blue & org .85 .25
173 A63 5p brown & grn 2.75 1.25
174 A64 15p black & ver 22.50 12.50
Nos. 172-174 (3) 26.10 14.00

See Nos. 216, 228, 229. For surcharges see Nos. 186-187, 189-191, 199-201, 207, 231, 247-251, C1-C5, C12, C23-C24.

Telegraph Stamps Overprinted or Surcharged in Black or Red

A65

A66

1921 ***Perf. 14***

175 A65 25c green .25 .25
176 A66 12½c on 25c grn (R) .25 .25
177 A66 12½c on 25c grn 15.00 15.00
Nos. 175-177 (3) 15.50 15.50

Nos. 119, 163 and 164 Surcharged in Black or Red

w

x

1922, Mar.

178 A33(w) 12½c on 20c .25 .25
a. Inverted surcharge 10.00
179 A55(w) 12½c on 60c (R) .50 .50
a. Inverted surcharge 25.00
180 A56(w) 12½c on 90c .50 .50
a. Inverted surcharge 25.00
181 A55(x) 25c on 60c 1.00 1.00
a. Inverted surcharge 20.00
182 A55(x) 25c on 60c (R) 125.00 125.00
183 A56(x) 25c on 90c 1.00 1.00
a. Inverted surcharge 25.00
184 A56(x) 25c on 90c (R) 4.00 4.00
Nos. 178-181,183-184 (6) 7.25 7.25

Counterfeits exist.

Nos. 165, 173-174 Surcharged in Red or Dark Blue

1922, May

185 A57 12½c on 3p grn & blk (R) .25 .25
186 A63 12½c on 5p brn & grn .50 .45
187 A64 12½c on 15p blk & ver .50 .45
Nos. 185-187 (3) 1.25 1.15

Nos. 165, 173-174 Surcharged in Red or Black

Type I

Type II

Type III

Type IV

1922

188 A57 25c on 3p (I) (R) .25 .25
a. Type II .60 .60
b. Type III .60 .60
c. Type IV .30 .30
d. Inverted surcharge 40.00
e. Horiz. or vert. pair, imperf. btwn. (I) 125.00
189 A63 25c on 5p (I) 1.00 *2.00*
a. Type II 2.00 *3.00*
b. Type III 2.00 *3.00*
c. Type IV 1.00 *2.00*
190 A64 25c on 15p (I) 1.00 *1.50*
a. Type II 2.00 *3.00*
b. Type III 2.00 *3.00*
c. Type IV 1.00 *1.50*
191 A64 25c on 15p (I) (R) 22.50 *30.00*
a. Type II 40.00 *45.00*
b. Type III 45.00 45.00
c. Type IV 30.00 *35.00*
Nos. 188-191 (4) 24.75 *33.75*

Stamps of 1902-21 Surcharged in Dark Blue or Red

Type V

Type VI

Type VII

Type VIII

Type IX

1922, Aug. **On Nos. 121-123**

192 A35 25c on 75c (V) .40 .40
a. Type VI .40 .40
b. Type VII 1.75 1.75
c. Type VIII 5.50 4.75
d. Type IX 6.50 6.00
193 A36 25c on 1p (V) .30 .30
a. Type VI .30 .30
b. Type VII 1.25 1.25
c. Type VIII 2.50 2.50
d. Type IX 4.00 3.50
e. Inverted surcharge 40.00
194 A37 25c on 2p (V) .45 .45
a. Type VI .45 .45
b. Type VII 1.25 1.25
c. Type VIII 4.00 4.00
d. Type IX 6.50 6.50

On Nos. 162-165

195 A54 25c on 30c (V) .45 .45
a. Type VI .45 .45
b. Type VII 1.25 1.25
c. Type VIII 5.50 5.50
d. Type IX 6.50 6.50
196 A55 25c on 60c (V) 1.00 *1.50*
a. Type VI 1.25 *1.50*
b. Type VII 6.25 *7.75*
c. Type VIII 8.50 *9.50*
d. Type IX 10.00 *11.00*
197 A56 25c on 90c (V) 1.00 *1.50*
a. Type VI 1.50 *2.00*
b. Type VII 6.00 *6.75*
c. Type VIII 8.50 *9.50*
d. Type IX 10.00 *11.00*
198 A57 25c on 3p (R) (V) .40 .40
a. Type VI .40 .40
b. Type VII 1.25 1.00
c. Type VIII 6.00 4.50
d. Type IX 6.50 6.00
e. Inverted surcharge 50.00

On Nos. 172-174

199 A62 25c on 1.50p (V) .30 .30
a. Type VI .30 .30
b. Type VII 1.25 1.00
c. Type VIII 3.00 3.00
d. Type IX 4.50 4.50
e. Inverted surcharge 40.00
200 A63 25c on 5p (V) .75 *.90*
a. Type VI .80 *1.00*
b. Type VII 3.00 *3.50*
c. Type VIII 5.50 *6.00*
d. Type IX 8.00 *8.50*
201 A64 25c on 15p (V) .85 *.90*
a. Type VI 1.50 1.50
b. Type VII 5.00 *5.50*
c. Type VIII 6.50 6.50
d. Type IX 12.00 12.00
Nos. 192-201 (10) 5.90 7.10

Centenary Palace — A69

National Palace at Antigua — A70

Printed by Waterlow & Sons

1922 ***Perf. 14, 14½***

202 A69 12½c green .30 .25
a. Horiz. or vert. pair, imperf. btwn. 100.00
203 A70 25c brown .30 .25

See Nos. 211, 221, 234.

Columbus Theater A71

Quetzal A72

Granados Monument — A73

Litho. by Castillo Bros.

1924, Feb. ***Perf. 12***

204 A71 50c rose .50 .25
a. Imperf., pair 7.50
b. Horiz. or vert. pair, imperf. btwn. 25.00
205 A72 1p dark green 2.25 .25
a. Imperf. vertically 15.00
b. Vert. pair, imperf. btwn. 20.00
c. Imperf., pair 7.50
206 A73 5p orange 1.25 .50
a. Imperf., pair 8.50
b. Horiz. pair, imperf. btwn. 20.00
Nos. 204-206 (3) 4.00 1.00

For surcharges see Nos. 208-209.

Nos. 172 and 206 Surcharged

1924, July

207 A62 1p on 1.50p bl & org .30 .25
208 A73 1.25p on 5p orange .50 .50
a. "UN PESO 25 Cents." omitted 40.00
b. Horiz. pair, imperf. btwn. 25.00

No. 208 Overprinted

1924

209 A73 1p on 5p orange .50 .50

Types of 1902-22 Issues Engr. by Perkins Bacon & Co.

1924, Aug. **Re-engraved** ***Perf. 14***

210 A31 6c bister .25 .25
211 A70 25c brown .25 .25
212 A34 50c red .25 .25
213 A36 1p orange brn .25 .25
214 A37 2p orange .35 .25
215 A57 3p deep green 2.00 .50
216 A64 15p black 5.00 2.75
Nos. 210-216 (7) 8.35 4.50

The designs of the stamps of 1924 differ from those of the 1902-22 issues in many details which are too minute to illustrate. The re-engraved issue may be readily distinguished by the imprint "Perkins Bacon & Co. Ld. Londres."

Pres. Justo Rufino Barrios A74

Lorenzo Montúfar A75

1924, Aug.

217 A74 1.25p ultra .25 .25
218 A75 2.50p dk violet 1.00 .25

See Nos. 224, 226. For surcharges see Nos. 232, C6, C20.

Aurora Park — A76

National Post Office — A77

National Observatory A78

Types of 1921-24 Re-engraved and New Designs Dated 1926

Engraved by Waterlow & Sons, Ltd.

1926, July-Aug. ***Perf. 12½***

219 A31 6c ocher .25 .25
220 A76 12½c green .25 .25
221 A70 25c brown .25 .25

222 A77 50c red .25 .25
223 A36 1p orange brn .25 .25
224 A74 1.50p dk blue .25 .25
225 A78 2p orange 1.25 1.00
226 A75 2.50p dk violet 1.50 1.25
227 A57 3p dark green .45 .25
228 A63 5p brown vio 1.00 .40
229 A64 15p black 6.00 2.75
Nos. 219-229 (11) 11.70 7.15

These stamps may be distinguished from those of the same designs in preceding issues by the imprint "Waterlow & Sons, Limited, Londres," the date, "1926," and the perforation.

See Nos. 233, 242. For surcharge see No. 230.

Nos. 225-226, 228 Surcharged in Various Colors

1928

230 A78 ½c on 2p (Bl) .65 .50
a. Inverted surcharge 12.50
231 A63 ½c on 5p (Bk) .35 .25
a. Inverted surcharge 10.00 10.00
b. Double surcharge 50.00
c. Blue surcharge 45.00 45.00
d. Blue and black surcharge 50.00 50.00
232 A75 1c on 2.50p (R) .35 .25
b. Double surcharge 50.00
Nos. 230-232 (3) 1.35 1.00

Barrios — A79

Montúfar — A80

Granados A81

General Orellana A82

Coat of Arms of Guatemala City — A83

Engraved by T. De la Rue & Co.

1929, Jan. ***Perf. 14***

233 A78 ½c yellow grn .75 .25
234 A70 1c dark brown .25 .25
235 A79 2c deep blue .25 .25
236 A80 3c dark violet .25 .25
237 A81 4c orange .25 .25
238 A82 5c dk carmine .50 .25
239 A31 10c brown .40 .25
240 A36 15c ultra .50 .25
241 A29 25c brown org 1.00 .25
242 A76 30c green .90 .30
243 A32 50c pale rose 2.00 .60
244 A83 1q black 3.00 .40
Nos. 233-244 (12) 10.05 3.55

Nos. 233, 234 and 239 to 243 differ from the illustrations in many minor details, particularly in the borders.

See No. 300 in Scott Standard catalogue (Vol. 3) for bisect of No. 235. For overprints and surcharges see Nos. 297, C13, C17-C18, C25-C26, C28, E1, RA17-RA18 (in Scott Standard catalogue, Vol. 3).

No. 227 Surcharged in Black or Red

1929, Dec. 28 ***Perf. 12½, 13***

245 A57 3c on 3p dk grn (Blk) 1.25 *1.90*
a. Inverted surcharge 15.00 15.00
246 A57 5c on 3p dk grn (R) 1.25 *1.90*
a. Inverted surcharge 15.00 15.00

Inauguration of the Eastern Railroad connecting Guatemala and El Salvador.

No. 229 Surcharged in Red

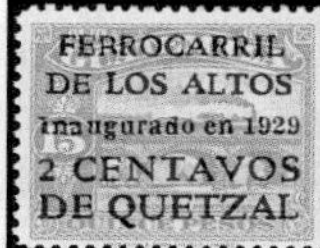

1930, Mar. 30 **Unwmk.**

247 A64 1c on 15p black 1.25 *1.40*
248 A64 2c on 15p black 1.25 *1.40*
249 A64 3c on 15p black 1.25 *1.40*
250 A64 5c on 15p black 1.25 *1.40*
251 A64 15c on 15p black 1.25 1.40
Nos. 247-251 (5) 6.25 *7.00*

Opening of Los Altos electric railway.

Hydroelectric Dam — A85

Los Altos Railway A86

Railroad Station A87

1930, Mar. 30 **Typo.** ***Perf. 12***

252 A85 2c brn vio & blk 1.40 *1.90*
a. Horiz. pair, imperf. btwn. 125.00
253 A86 3c dp red & blk 2.75 *2.75*
a. Vert. pair, imperf. btwn. 125.00
254 A87 5c buff & dk bl 2.75 *2.75*
Nos. 252-254 (3) 6.90 *7.40*

Opening of Los Altos electric railway. Exist imperf.

Mayan Stele at Quiriguá — A91

1932, Apr. 8 **Engr.**

258 A91 3c carmine rose 1.90 .40

See Nos. 302-303 in Scott Standard catalogue, Vol. 3.

Flag of the Race, Columbus and Tecum Uman A92

1933, Aug. 3 **Litho.** ***Perf. 12½***

259 A92 ½c dark green .75 .75
260 A92 1c dull brown 1.25 1.10
261 A92 2c deep blue 1.25 1.10
262 A92 3c dull violet 1.25 .75
263 A92 5c rose 1.25 1.10
Nos. 259-263 (5) 5.75 *4.80*

Day of the Race and 441st anniv. of the sailing of Columbus from Palos, Spain, Aug. 3, 1492, on his 1st voyage to the New World.

The 3c and 5c exist imperf.

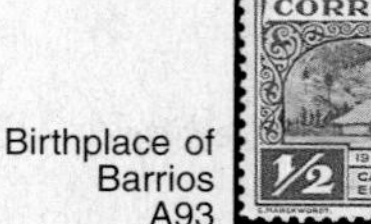

Birthplace of Barrios A93

View of San Lorenzo A94

Justo Rufino Barrios A95

National Emblem and Locomotive A96

General Post Office — A97

Telegraph Building and Barrios A98

Military Academy A99

National Police Headquarters — A100

Jorge Ubico and J. R. Barrios A101

1935, July 19 **Photo.**

264 A93 ½c yel grn & mag .40 *.45*
265 A94 1c org red & pck bl .40 *.45*
266 A95 2c orange & blk .40 *.55*
267 A96 3c car rose & pck bl 4.50 2.25
268 A97 4c pck bl & org red 4.50 *10.00*
269 A98 5c bl grn & brn 3.25 *4.25*
270 A99 10c slate grn & rose lake 4.50 *5.50*
271 A100 15c ol grn & org brn 4.50 *4.75*
272 A101 25c scarlet & bl 4.50 *4.75*
Nos. 264-272 (9) 26.95 *32.95*

General Barrios. See Nos. C29-C31.

Lake Atitlán A102

Quetzal A103

Legislative Building — A104

1935, Oct. 10

273 A102 1c brown & crim .25 .25
274 A103 3c rose car & pck grn .70 .25
275 A103 3c red org & pck grn .70 .25
276 A104 4c brt bl & dp rose .35 .25
Nos. 273-276 (4) 2.00 1.00

See No. 277. For surcharges see Nos. B1-B3.

No. 273 perforated diagonally through the center

1936, June ***Perf. 12½x12***

277 A102 (½c) brown & crimson .25 .25
a. Unsevered pair .50 .60

Bureau of Printing — A105

Map of Guatemala A106

1936, Sept. 24 ***Perf. 12½***

278 A105 ½c green & pur .25 .25
279 A106 5c blue & dk brn .90 .25

For surcharge see No. B4.

Quetzal A107

Union Park, Quezaltenango A108

Gen. Jorge Ubico on Horseback A109

1c, Tower of the Reformer. 3c, National Post Office. 4c, Government Building, Retalhuleu. 5c, Legislative Palace entrance. 10c, Custom House. 15c, Aurora Airport Custom House. 25c, National Fair. 50c, Residence of Presidential Guard. 1.50q, General Ubico, portrait standing, no cap.

1937, May 20

280	A107	½c pck bl & car rose	.70	*.45*
281	A107	1c ol gray & red brn	.70	.35
282	A108	2c vio & car rose	.60	.35
283	A108	3c brn vio & brt bl	.50	.25
284	A108	4c yel & dl ol grn	3.00	*3.00*
285	A107	5c crim & brt vio	3.00	3.00
286	A107	10c mag & brn blk	4.00	*4.00*
287	A108	15c ultra & cop red	3.00	*3.00*
288	A108	25c red org & vio	4.00	*4.00*
289	A108	50c dk grn & org red	6.00	*6.00*
290	A109	1q mag & blk	*50.00*	*50.00*
291	A109	1.50q red brn & blk	*50.00*	*50.00*
		Nos. 280-291 (12)	125.50	124.40

Second term of President Ubico.

Mayan Calendar A119

Natl. Flower (White Nun Orchid) A120

Quetzal — A121

Map of Guatemala A122

1939, Sept. 7 ***Perf. 13x12, 12½***

292	A119	½c grn & red brn	*.85*	.25
293	A120	2c bl & gray blk	*5.00*	1.00
294	A121	3c red org & turq grn	*6.50*	1.75
295	A121	3c ol bis & turq grn	*6.50*	1.75
296	A122	5c blue & red	*5.75*	5.75
		Nos. 292-296 (5)	24.60	10.50

For overprints see Nos. 324, C157 in Scott Standard catalogue, Vol. 3.

No. 235 Surcharged in Red

1939, Sept. ***Perf. 14***

297 A79 1c on 2c deep blue .25 .25

Stamps of 1929 Surcharged in Blue

y

z

1940, June

298	A29 (y)	1c on 25c brn org	.25	.25
299	A32 (z)	5c on 50c pale rose (bar 10x¾mm)	.25	.25
a.		Bar 12½x2mm	.30	.25
b.		Bar 12½x1mm	50.00	5.00

SEMI-POSTAL STAMPS

Regular Issues of 1935-36 Surcharged in Blue or Red similar to illustration

1937, Mar. 15 **Unwmk.** ***Perf. 12½***

B1	A102	1c + 1c brn & crim	.75	*1.00*
B2	A103	3c + 1c rose car & pck grn	.75	*1.00*
B3	A103	3c + 1c red org & pck grn	.75	*1.00*
B4	A106	5c + 1c bl & dk brn (R)	.75	*1.00*
		Nos. B1-B4 (4)	3.00	*4.00*

1st Phil. Exhib. held in Guatemala, Mar. 15-20.

AIR POST STAMPS

No. 229 Surcharged in Red

1929, May 20 **Unwmk.** ***Perf. 12½***

C1	A64	3c on 15p blk	1.10	*1.40*
C2	A64	5c on 15p blk	.55	.45
C3	A64	15c on 15p blk	1.50	.45
a.		Double surcharge (G & R)	100.00	
C4	A64	20c on 15p blk	2.25	2.25
a.		Inverted surcharge	100.00	
b.		Double surcharge	100.00	

No. 216 Surcharged in Red

1929, May 20 ***Perf. 14***

C5	A64	5c on 15p black	3.25	2.25
		Nos. C1-C5 (5)	8.65	6.80

No. 218 Surcharged in Black

1929, Oct. 9

C6 A75 3c on 2.50p dk vio 1.00 1.00

Airplane and Mt. Agua AP3

1930, June 4 **Litho.** ***Perf. 12½***

C7	AP3	6c rose red	*5.00*	*5.00*
a.		Double impression	25.00	25.00
b.		Imperf., pair	350.00	

For overprint see No. C14.

Nos. 227, 229 Surcharged in Black or Red

1930, Dec. 9 ***Perf. 12½***

C8	A57	1c on 3p grn (Bk)	.40	.40
a.		Double surcharge	100.00	
C9	A57	2c on 3p grn (Bk)	1.10	*1.50*
C10	A57	3c on 3p grn (R)	1.10	*1.50*
C11	A57	4c on 3p grn (R)	1.10	*1.50*
C12	A64	10c on 15p blk (R)	5.00	*5.00*
a.		Double surcharge	125.00	
		Nos. C8-C12 (5)	8.70	*9.90*

No. 237 Overprinted

1931, May 19 ***Perf. 14***

C13	A81	4c orange	.40	.30
a.		Double overprint	40.00	*50.00*

No. C7 Overprinted

Perf. 12½

C14	AP3	6c rose red	*2.00*	*2.00*
a.		On No. C7a	30.00	30.00
b.		Inverted overprint	7.00	*7.00*

Nos. 240, 242 Overprinted in Red

1931, Oct. 21 ***Perf. 14***

C15	A36	15c ultra	2.00	.25
a.		Double overprint	125.00	125.00
C16	A76	30c green	3.00	.95
a.		Double overprint	75.00	75.00

Nos. 235-236 Overprinted in Red or Green

1931, Dec. 5

C17	A79	2c dp bl (R)	2.50	*3.00*
C18	A80	3c dk vio (G)	2.50	*3.00*

No. 240 Overprinted in Red

C19 A36 15c ultra 2.75 *3.00*

Nos. C17-C19 were issued in connection with the 1st postal flight from Barrios to Miami.

No. 224 Surcharged in Red

1932-33 ***Perf. 12½***

C20 A74 2c on 1.50p dk bl .80 .55

Nos. 227, 229 Surcharged in Violet, Red or Blue

C21	A57	3c on 3p grn (V)	.80	.25
a.		Inverted surcharge	45.00	45.00
b.		Vert. pair, imperf. horiz.	900.00	
C22	A57	3c on 3p grn (R)	.80	.25
C23	A64	10c on 15p blk (R)	7.75	6.25
b.		First "I" of "Interior" missing	10.00	10.00
C24	A64	15c on 15p blk (Bl)	9.00	8.50
a.		First "I" of "Interior" missing	15.00	15.00
		Nos. C20-C24 (5)	19.15	15.80

Issued: No. C22, 1/1/33; others, 2/11/32.

No. 237 Overprinted in Green

1933, Jan. 1 ***Perf. 14***

C25	A81	4c orange	.40	.35
a.		Double overprint	40.00	40.00

Nos. 235, 238 and 240 Overprinted in Red or Black

1934, Aug. 7

C26	A82	5c dk car (Bk)	1.50	.25
C27	A36	15c ultra (R)	1.50	.25

Overprinted in Red

C28 A79 2c deep blue .55 .25

View of Port Barrios — AP7

Designs: 15c, Tomb of Barrios. 30c, Equestrian Statue of Barrios.

1935, July 19 **Photo.** ***Perf. 12½***

C29	AP7	10c yel brn & pck grn	6.00	4.50
C30	AP7	15c gray & brn	1.50	*1.75*
C31	AP7	30c car rose & bl vio	1.50	1.25
		Nos. C29-C31 (3)	9.00	7.50

Birth cent. of Gen. Justo Rufino Barrios.

Lake Amatitlán AP10

Designs: Nos. C36, C37, C45, C46. Different views of Lake Amatitlan. 3c, Port Barrios. No. C34, C35, Ruins of Fort San Felipe. 10c, Port Livingston. No. C39, C40, Port San Jose. No. C41, C42, View of Atitlan. No. C43, C44, Aurora Airport.

Overprinted with Quetzal in Green

1935-37 **Size: 37x17mm**

C32	AP10	2c org brn	.25	.25
C33	AP10	3c blue	.25	.25
C34	AP10	4c black	.25	.25
C35	AP10	4c ultra ('37)	.25	.25
C36	AP10	6c yel grn	.25	.25
C37	AP10	6c blk vio ('37)	4.00	.25
C38	AP10	10c claret	.50	.25

C39 AP10 15c red org .65 .40
C40 AP10 15c yel grn ('37) .65 .65
C41 AP10 30c olive grn 6.00 6.50
C42 AP10 30c ol bis ('37) .75 .50
C43 AP10 50c rose vio 17.50 15.00
C44 AP10 50c Prus bl ('36) 4.00 3.00
C45 AP10 1q scarlet 17.50 20.00
C46 AP10 1q car ('36) 4.50 3.00
Nos. C32-C46 (15) 57.30 50.80

Issue dates follow No. C69.

For overprints and surcharges see Nos. C70-C79, CB1-CB2.

Central Park, Antigua
AP11

Designs: 1c, Guatemala City. 2c, Central Park, Guatemala City. 3c, Monastery. Nos. C50-C51, Mouth of Dulce River. Nos. C52-C53, Plaza Barrios. Nos. C54-C55, Los Proceres Monument. No. C56, Central Park, Antigua. No. C57, Dulce River. Nos. C58-C59, Quezaltenango. Nos. C60-C61, Ruins at Antigua. Nos. C62-C63, Dock at Port Barrios. Nos. C64-C65, Port San Jose. Nos. C66-C67, Aurora Airport. 2.50q, Island off Atlantic Coast. 5q, Atlantic Coast view.

Overprinted with Quetzal in Green

Size: 34x15mm

C47 AP11 1c yel brn .25 .25
C48 AP11 2c vermilion .25 .25
C49 AP11 3c magenta .50 .25
C50 AP11 4c org yel ('36) 1.75 1.40
C51 AP11 4c car lake ('37) 1.00 .75
C52 AP11 5c dl bl .25 .25
C53 AP11 5c org ('37) .25 .25
C54 AP11 10c red brn .50 .35
C55 AP11 10c ol grn ('37) .50 .30
C56 AP11 15c rose red .25 .25
C57 AP11 15c ver ('37) .25 .25
C58 AP11 20c ultra 2.50 *3.00*
C59 AP11 20c dp cl ('37) .50 .25
C60 AP11 25c gray blk 3.00 *3.50*
C61 AP11 25c bl grn ('37) .45 .25
a. Quetzal omitted *1,100.*
C62 AP11 30c yel grn 1.50 1.50
C63 AP11 30c rose red ('37) 1.00 .25
C64 AP11 50c car rose 7.00 *8.00*
C65 AP11 50c pur ('36) 6.50 *7.50*
C66 AP11 1q dk bl 22.50 *25.00*
C67 AP11 1q dk grn ('36) 7.50 7.50

Size: 46x20mm

C68 AP11 2.50q rose red & ol grn ('36) 5.00 3.00
C69 AP11 5q org & ind ('36) 7.00 4.00
a. Quetzal omitted 1,500. 1,250.
Nos. C47-C69 (23) 70.20 *68.30*

Issued: Nos. C32-C34, C36, C38-C39, C41, C43, C45, C47-C49, C52, C54, C56, C58, C60, C62, 11/1/35; Nos. C44, C50, C67-C69, 10/1/36; Nos. C35, C37, C40, C42, C51, C53, C55, C57, C59, C61, C63, 1/1/37.

Value for No. C61a is for a sound stamp.

For overprints and surcharges see Nos. C80-C91, CB3-CB4.

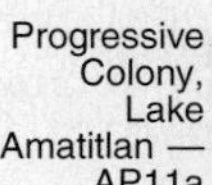

Progressive Colony, Lake Amatitlan — AP11a

2c, Quezaltenango. 3c, Lake Atitian. 6c, Carmen Hill. 10c, Relief map. 15c, National University. 30c, Espana Plaza. 50c, Police Station, Aurora Airport. 75c, Amphitheater, Aurora Airport. 1q, Aurora Airport.

Center in Brown Black

1937, May 18

Overprinted with Airplane in Blue

Size: 34x15mm

C70 AP11a 2c carmine .25 .25
C71 AP11a 3c blue 1.00 *1.25*
C72 AP11a 4c citron .25 .25
C73 AP11a 6c yel grn .35 .25
C74 AP11a 10c red vio 2.00 *2.25*
C75 AP11a 15c orange 1.50 1.00
C76 AP11a 30c ol grn 3.75 3.00
C77 AP11a 50c pck bl 5.00 4.25
C78 AP11a 75c dk vio 10.00 *11.00*
C79 AP11a 1q dp rose 11.00 *12.00*
Nos. C70-C79 (10) 35.10 *35.50*

7th Ave., Guatemala City — AP11b

2c, Los Proceres Monument. 3c, Natl. Printing Office. 5c, Natl. Museum. 10c, Central Park. 15c, Escuintla. 20c, Motorcycle Police. 25c, Slaughterhouse, Escuintla. 30c, Exhibition Hall. 50c, Barrios Plaza. 1q, Polytechnic School. 1.50q, Aurora Airport.

Overprinted with Airplane in Black

Size: 33x15mm

C80 AP11b 1c yel brn & brt bl .25 .25
C81 AP11b 2c crim & dp vio .25 .25
C82 AP11b 3c red vio & red brn .50 .50
C83 AP11b 5c pck grn & cop red 4.00 3.00
C84 AP11b 10c car & grn 1.25 1.00
C85 AP11b 15c rose & dl ol grn .50 .25
C86 AP11b 20c ultra & blk 3.00 1.75
C87 AP11b 25c dk gray & scar 2.50 2.50
C88 AP11b 30c grn & dp vio 1.25 1.25
C89 AP11b 50c mag & ultra 10.00 *12.00*

Size: 42x19mm

C90 AP11b 1q ol grn & red vio 10.00 *12.00*
C91 AP11b 1.50q scar & ol brn 10.00 *12.00*
Nos. C80-C91 (12) 43.50 *46.75*

Second term of President Ubico.

Souvenir Sheet

AP12

1938, Jan. 10 ***Perf. 12½***

C92 AP12 Sheet of 4 8.00 8.00
a. 15c George Washington 1.50 1.50
b. 4c Franklin D. Roosevelt 1.50 1.50
c. 4c Map of the Americas 1.50 1.50
d. 15c Pan American Union Building, Washington, DC .75 .75

150th anniv. of US Constitution.

President Arosemena, Panama
AP13

Flags of Central American Countries — AP19

Designs: 2c, Pres. Cortés Castro, Costa Rica. 3c, Pres. Somoza, Nicaragua. 4c, Pres. Carias Andino, Honduras. 5c, Pres. Martinez, El Salvador. 10c, Pres. Ubico, Guatemala.

1938, Nov. 20 **Unwmk.**

C93 AP13 1c org & ol brn .25 .25
C94 AP13 2c scar, pale pink & sl grn .30 .25
C95 AP13 3c grn, buff & ol brn .40 .30
C96 AP13 4c dk cl, pale lil & brn .55 .35
C97 AP13 5c bis, pale grn & ol brn .50 *.60*
C98 AP13 10c ultra, pale bl & brn 1.00 *1.25*
Nos. C93-C98 (6) 3.00 *3.00*

Souvenir Sheet

C99 AP19 Sheet of 6 8.00 8.00
a. 1c Guatemala .80 .80
b. 2c El Salvador .80 .80
c. 3c Honduras 1.10 1.10
d. 4c Nicaragua 1.40 1.40
e. 5c Costa Rica 1.40 1.40
f. 10c Panama 2.40 2.40

1st Central American Phil. Exhib., Guatemala City, Nov. 20-27.

For overprints see Nos. CO1-CO7.

La Merced Church, Antigua
AP20

Designs: 2c, Ruins of Christ School, Antigua. 3c, Aurora Airport. 4c, Drill ground, Guatemala City. 5c, Cavalry barracks. 6c, Palace of Justice. 10c, Customhouse, San José. 15c, Communications Building, Retalhuleu. 30c, Municipal Theater, Quezaltenango. 50c, Customhouse, Retalhuleu. 1q, Departmental Building.

Inscribed "Aéreo Interior"

Overprinted with Quetzal in Green

1939, Feb. 14

C100 AP20 1c ol bis & chnt .25 .25
C101 AP20 2c rose red & sl grn .25 .25
C102 AP20 3c dl bl & bis .25 .25
C103 AP20 4c rose pink & yel grn .25 .25
C104 AP20 5c brn lake & brt ultra .30 .25
C105 AP20 6c org & gray brn .35 .25
C106 AP20 10c bis brn & gray blk .50 .25
C107 AP20 15c dl vio & blk .75 .25
C108 AP20 30c dp bl & dk car 1.10 .25
C109 AP20 50c org & brt vio 1.50 .40
a. Quetzal omitted *1,750.*
C110 AP20 1q yel grn & brt ultra 2.50 1.25
Nos. C100-C110 (11) 8.00 3.90

See Nos. C111-C122. For overprint and surcharge see No. C124, C132 in Scott Standard catalogue, Vol. 3.

View of Antigua — AP20a

Inscribed "Aéreo Internacional" or "Aérea Exterior"

Designs: 1c, Mayan Altar, Aurora Park. 2c, Sanitation Building. 3c, Lake Amatitlan. 4c, Lake Atitlan. 5c, Tamazulapa River bridge. 10c, Los proceres Monument. 15c, Palace of Captains General. 20c, Church on Carmen Hill. 25c, Barrios Park. 30c, Mayan Altar. 50c, Charles III fountain.

Overprinted with Quetzal in Green

1939, Feb. 14

C111 AP20a 1c ol grn & gldn brn .25 .25
C112 AP20a 2c lt grn & blk .30 .25
C113 AP20a 3c ultra & cob bl .25 .25
C114 AP20a 4c org brn & yel grn .25 .25
C115 AP20a 5c sage grn & red org .35 .25
C116 AP20a 10c lake & sl blk 1.75 .25
C117 AP20a 15c ultra & brt rose 1.75 .25
C118 AP20a 20c yel grn & ap grn .60 .25
C119 AP20a 25c dl vio & lt ol grn .60 .25
C120 AP20a 30c dl rose & blk .80 .25
C121 AP20a 50c scar & brt yel 1.50 .25
C122 AP20a 1q org & yel grn 2.50 .35
Nos. C111-C122 (12) 10.90 3.10

No. 240 Overprinted in Carmine

1940, Apr. 14 ***Perf. 14***

C123 A36 15c ultra .60 .25

Pan American Union, 50th anniversary.

AIR POST SEMI-POSTAL STAMPS

Air Post Stamps of 1937 Surcharged in Red or Blue

1937, Mar. 15 **Unwmk.** ***Perf. 12½***

CB1 AP10 4c + 1c ultra (R) .90 *1.25*
CB2 AP10 6c + 1c blk vio (R) .90 *1.25*
CB3 AP11 10c + 1c ol grn (Bl) .90 *1.25*
CB4 AP11 15c + 1c ver (Bl) .90 *1.25*
Nos. CB1-CB4 (4) 3.60 *5.00*

1st Phil. Exhib. held in Guatemala, Mar. 15-20.

AIR POST OFFICIAL STAMPS

Nos. C93-C98 Overprinted in Black

1939, Apr. 29 **Unwmk.** ***Perf. 12½***

CO1 AP13 1c org & ol brn 1.60 1.60
CO2 AP13 2c multi 1.60 1.60
CO3 AP13 3c multi 1.60 1.60
CO4 AP13 4c multi 1.60 1.60
CO5 AP13 5c multi 1.60 1.60
CO6 AP13 10c multi 1.60 1.60
Nos. CO1-CO6 (6) 9.60 9.60

No. C99 Overprinted in Black

1939

CO7 AP19 Sheet of 6 5.00 5.00
a. 1c yel org, blue & blk .75 .75
b. 2c lake, org, blue & blk .75 .75
c. 3c olive, blue & orange .75 .75
d. 4c dk claret, bl, org & blk .75 .75
e. 5c grnsh bl, bl, red, org & blk .75 .75
f. 10c olive bister, red & org .75 .75

SPECIAL DELIVERY STAMPS

No. 237 Overprinted in Red

1940, June **Unwmk.** ***Perf. 14***

E1 A81 4c orange 1.50 .35

No. E1 paid for express service by motorcycle messenger between Guatemala City and Coban.

OFFICIAL STAMPS

O1

1902, Dec. 18 **Typeset** ***Perf. 12***

O1	O1	1c green	9.00	5.50
O2	O1	2c carmine	9.00	5.50
O3	O1	5c ultra	9.00	4.50
O4	O1	10c brown violet	12.00	4.50
O5	O1	25c orange	12.00	4.50
a.		Horiz. pair, imperf. between	125.00	
		Nos. O1-O5 (5)	51.00	24.50

Nos. O1-O5 printed on thin paper with sheet watermark "AMERICAN LINEN BOND." Nos. O1-O3 also printed on thick paper with sheet watermark "ROYAL BANK BOND." Values are for copies that do not show the watermark. Counterfeits of Nos. O1-O5 exist.

During the years 1912 to 1926 the Post Office Department perforated the word "OFICIAL" on limited quantities of the following stamps: Nos. 114-123, 132, 141-149, 151-153, 158, 202, 210-229 and RA2. The perforating was done in blocks of four stamps at a time and was of two types.

A rubber handstamp "OFICIAL" was also used during the same period and was applied in violet, red, blue or black to stamps No. 117-118, 121-123, 163-165, 172 and 202-218.

Both perforating and handstamping were done in the post office at Guatemala City and use of the stamps was limited to that city.

National Emblem — O2

1929, Jan. **Engr.** ***Perf. 14***

O6	O2	1c pale grnsh bl	.30	.30
O7	O2	2c dark brown	.30	.30
O8	O2	3c green	.30	.30
O9	O2	4c deep violet	.40	.35
O10	O2	5c brown car	.40	.35
O11	O2	10c brown orange	.70	.70
O12	O2	25c dark blue	1.40	1.10
		Nos. O6-O12 (7)	3.80	3.40

POSTAL TAX STAMPS

National Emblem — PT1

Perf. 13½, 14, 15

1919, May 3 **Engr.** **Unwmk.**

RA1 PT1 12½c carmine .30 .25

Tax for rebuilding post offices.

G. P. O. and Telegraph Building — PT2

1927, Nov. 10 **Typo.** ***Perf. 14***

RA2 PT2 1c olive green .55 .25

Tax to provide a fund for building a post office in Guatemala City.

No. RA2 Overprinted in Green

1936, June 30

RA3 PT2 1c olive green *5.75* *4.00*

Liberal revolution, 65th anniversary.

No. RA2 Overprinted in Blue

1936, Sept. 15

RA4 PT2 1c olive green .55 .55

115th anniv. of the Independence of Guatemala.

No. RA2 Overprinted in Red Brown

1936, Nov. 15

RA5 PT2 1c olive green .55 .45

National Fair.

No. RA2 Overprinted in Red

1937, Mar. 15

RA6 PT2 1c olive green .55 .55

No. RA2 Overprinted in Blue

1938, Jan. 10 ***Perf. 14x14½***

RA7 PT2 1c olive green .30 .25
a. "1937-1939" omitted 110.00

150th anniv. of the US Constitution.

No. RA2 Overprinted in Blue or Red

1938 ***Perf. 14***

RA8 PT2 1c olive green (Bl) .40 .30
RA9 PT2 1c olive green (R) .40 .30

No. RA2 Overprinted in Violet

1938, Nov. 20

RA10 PT2 1c olive green .40 .25

1st Central American Philatelic Exposition.

No. RA2 Overprinted in Green or Black

1939

RA11 PT2 1c olive green (G) .40 .25
RA12 PT2 1c olive green (Bk) .40 .25

No. RA2 Overprinted in Violet or Brown

1940

RA13 PT2 1c olive green (V) .40 .25
RA14 PT2 1c olive green (Br) .40 .25

No. RA2 Overprinted in Red

1940, Apr. 14

RA15 PT2 1c olive green .40 .25

Pan American Union, 50th anniversary.

HAITI

'hā-tē

LOCATION — Western part of Hispaniola
GOVT. — Republic
AREA — 10,700 sq. mi.
POP. — 5,198,000 (est. 1984)
CAPITAL — Port-au-Prince

100 Centimes = 1 Piaster (1906)
100 Centimes = 1 Gourde

GREAT BRITAIN POST OFFICES IN HAITI

British postal agencies were opened in Jacmel in 1830 and in Port-au-Prince in 1842 and operated until June 30, 1881. During this period, British postal agencies also operated in Aux Cayes (1848-63), Cap Haitien (1842-63), Gonaives (1849-57), St. Marc (1854-61) and, possibly, Le Mole (ca. 1841). British stamps were used at the Jacmel agency from 1865 and at the Port-au-Prince agency from 1869.

Values are for clear cancellations on sound, fault-free stamps, with average to fine centering. In many cases, very fine examples are rare or non-existent.

JACMEL
Pre-Stamp Postmark

1843

Crowned Circle Handstamp Type II

A1 Inscribed "PAID AT JACMEL" in red, on cover *1,100.*

Earliest known use 6/29/43.

Stamps of Great Britain Canceled with barred oval "C59" obliterator

No. A31

1859-85

A2	½p rose red, plates 4-6, 10-12, 14, 15 (#58), *value from*	65.00
A3	1p rose red, plates 74, 81, 84, 87, 95, 106, 107, 109, 122, 136, 137, 139, 146, 148, 150-152, 156, 157, 159, 160, 162, 164, 166, 167, 170, 171, 179, 181, 183, 186, 187, 189, 192, 194, 198, 200, 204, 206, 215, 219 (#33), *value from*	50.00
A4	1½p lake red, plate 3 (#32)	70.00
A5	2p blue, plate 9 (#29)	45.00
A6	2p blue, plates 13, 14, 15 (#30), *value from*	45.00
A7	2½p claret, plate 4 (#67)	—
A8	3p rose, plates 5-10 (#49), *value from*	52.50
A9	3p rose, plates 11, 12, 14, 16-19 (#61), *value from*	55.00
A10	4p vermilion, hair lines (#34c)	130.00
A11	4p vermilion, plates 7-13 (#43), *value from*	52.50
A12	4p vermilion, plate 15 (#69)	325.00
A13	4p pale olive green, plate 15 (#70)	225.00
	Plate 16 (#70)	210.00
A14	4p gray brown, plate 17 (#71)	350.00
A15	4p gray brown, plate 17 (#84)	60.00
A16	6p dull violet, plate 6 (#50)	85.00
A17	6p violet, plates 8, 9 (#51)	80.00
A18	6p brown plate 11 (#59)	—
a.	6p pale buff, plate 11 (#59b)	90.00
	Plate 12 (#59b)	100.00
A19	6p gray, plate 12 (#60)	—
A20	6p gray, plates 13-17 (#62), *value from*	60.00
A21	8p orange (#73)	350.00
A22	9p straw (#40)	300.00
A23	9p straw (#46)	225.00
A24	10p red brown (#53)	325.00
A25	1sh green, plate 4 (#48)	150.00
A26	1sh green, plates 4-7 (#54), *value from*	50.00
A27	1sh green, plates 8-13 (#64), *value from*	75.00
A28	1sh salmon, plate 13 (#65)	425.00
A29	2sh blue (#55)	150.00
A30	2sh brown (#56)	*2,750.*
A31	5sh rose, plate 1 (#57)	*550.00*
	Plate 2 (#57)	*675.00*

1880

A32	½p deep green (#78)	85.00
A33	1p red brown (#79)	85.00
A34	1½p red brown (#80)	120.00
A35	2p lilac rose (#81)	160.00

PORT-AU-PRINCE
Pre-Stamp Postmark

1843

Crowned Circle Handstamp Type II

A40 Inscribed "PAID AT PORT-AU-PRINCE" in red, on cover *3,000.*

Earliest known use 6/29/43.

Stamps of Great Britain Canceled with barred oval "E53" obliterator

1865-81

A45	½p rose red, plates 5,6, 10-14 (#58), *value from*	65.00
A46	1p rose red, plates 87, 134, 154, 159, 167, 171, 173, 174, 177, 181, 183, 187, 189, 192, 193, 199-202, 206, 210, 218, 219 (#33), *value from*	50.00
A47	1½p lake red, plate 3 (#32)	85.00
A48	2p blue, plate 9 (#29)	55.00
A49	2p blue, plates 14, 15 (#30), *value from*	55.00
A50	2½p claret, plates 3, 9 (#67), *value from*	165.00
A51	3p rose, plates 6, 7 (#49)	—
A52	3p rose, plates 17, 18, 20 (#61), *value from*	55.00
A53	4p vermilion, plates 11-14 (#43), *value from*	55.00

A54 4p vermilion, plate 15 (#69) 325.00
A55 4p pale olive green, plate 15 (#70) 225.00
Plate 16 (#70) 210.00
A56 4p gray brown, plate 17 (#71) 350.00
A57 4p gray brown, plate 17 (#84) 60.00
A58 6p gray, plates 15, 16 (#62) —
A59 8p orange (#73) 350.00
A60 1sh green, plates 4-7 (#54), *value from* 50.00
A61 1sh green, plates 8-13 (#64), *value from* 75.00
A62 1sh salmon, plate 13 (#65) 425.00
A63 1sh salmon, plates 13, 14 (#87) 140.00
A64 2sh blue (#55) 175.00
A65 2sh brown (#56) *2,500.*
A66 5sh rose, plate 1 (#57) *500.00*
Plate 2 (#57) *675.00*
A67 10sh slate (#74) *4,000.*

1880

A68 ½p deep green (#78) 85.00
A69 1p red brown (#79) 85.00
A70 1½p red brown (#80) 120.00
A71 2p lilac rose (#81) 160.00

ISSUES OF THE REPUBLIC

Watermark

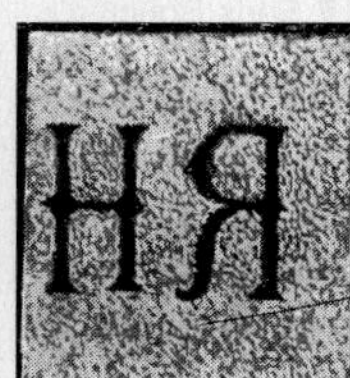

Wmk. 131 — RH

Liberty Head — A1

On A3 (Nos. 18, 19) there are crossed lines of dots on face. On A4 the "5" is 3mm wide, on A1 2½mm wide.

1881 Unwmk. Typo. *Imperf.*
Surface-colored Paper

1 A1 1c vermilion, *yelsh* 10.00 5.50
Never hinged 22.50
a. 1c carmine, *yelsh* 10.00 5.50
Never hinged 22.50
b. 1c rose red, *cream* 13.00 8.00
Never hinged 26.00
c. Vert. pair, tête-beche 3,000.
d. Paper colored on back only — 125.00
2 A1 2c violet, *pale lil* 12.00 5.50
Never hinged 24.00
a. 2c purple, *pale lil* 13.50 10.00
Never hinged 26.00
b. 2c purple, *white* 17.50
Never hinged 35.00
c. Vert. pair, tête-beche 1,250.
d. Paper colored on back only — 80.00
3 A1 3c gray bister, *pale bis* 22.50 8.00
Never hinged 42.50
a. 3c olive bister, *cream* 22.50 10.00
Never hinged 42.50
4 A1 5c yel green, *grnsh* 35.00 16.00
Never hinged 67.50
a. 5c blue green, *grnsh* 35.00 16.00
Never hinged 67.50
5 A1 7c deep blue, *grysh* 24.00 4.00
Never hinged 47.50
a. 7c pale blue, *grysh* 24.00 4.00
Never hinged 47.50
6 A1 20c red brown, *yelsh* 85.00 30.00
Never hinged 180.00
a. 20c brown, *cream* 87.50 32.50
Never hinged 180.00
Nos. 1-6 (6) 188.50 69.00

Nos. 1-6 were printed from plate I, Nos. 7-13 from plates II and III.

1882 *Perf. 13½*

7 A1 1c dp ver, *dp yelsh* ('83) 6.25 2.10
Never hinged 13.50
a. Vert. pair imperf. btwn. 200.00 *250.00*
Never hinged 300.00
b. 1c pale ver, *pale yelsh* ('84) 6.25 2.25
Never hinged 13.50
c. As "b," vert. pair, imperf between 200.00 *250.00*
8 A1 2c dp purple, *pale lil* ('83) 12.00 3.25
Never hinged 27.50
a. 2c dark violet, *white* ('84) 13.00 6.50
Never hinged 32.50
b. As "a," vert. pair, imperf between 175.00 *250.00*
c. As "a," horiz. pair, imperf between 175.00 *250.00*

d. 2c red violet, *pale lilac* ('85) 8.00 2.60
Never hinged 16.50
e. As "d," vert. pair, imperf between 175.00 *275.00*
Never hinged 300.00
f. As "d," horiz. pair, imperf between 175.00 *275.00*
Never hinged 300.00
9 A1 3c gray bister, *pale bis* 12.50 3.25
Never hinged 27.50
a. 3c olive bister, *bister* ('85) 12.50 3.25
Never hinged 27.50
b. As "a," horiz. pair, imperf between 125.00 *225.00*
10 A1 5c blue grn, *grnsh* 9.00 1.60
Never hinged 19.00
a. 5c yellow green, *greenish* ('85) 8.50 1.40
Never hinged 32.50
b. 5c deep green, *greenish* ('85) 8.50 1.40
Never hinged 32.50
c. As "b," horiz. pair, imperf between 190.00 *275.00*
Never hinged 300.00
11 A1 7c deep blue, *grysh* ('85) 11.50 2.10
Never hinged 26.50
a. Horiz. pair, imperf. between 150.00 *250.00*
Never hinged 300.00
12 A1 7c ultra, *grysh* ('85) 17.50 3.25
Never hinged 37.50
a. Vert. pair, imperf. between 150.00 *250.00*
Never hinged 300.00
13 A1 20c pale brn, *yelsh* ('86) 17.50 4.50
Never hinged 37.50
a. Vert. pair, imperf between 175.00 *275.00*
Never hinged 300.00
b. 20c red brown, *yellowish* ('84) 21.00 8.00
Never hinged 47.50
c. As "b," vert. pair, imperf between 150.00 *300.00*
Never hinged 300.00
d. As "b," horiz. pair, imperf between 150.00 *300.00*
Never hinged 300.00
Nos. 7-13 (7) 86.25 20.05

Stamps perf. 14, 16 are postal forgeries.

A3

A4

1886-87 *Perf. 13½*

18 A3 1c vermilion, *yelsh* 5.75 2.00
Never hinged 12.00
a. Horiz. pair, imperf. vert. 175.00 175.00
Never hinged 350.00
b. Horiz. pair, imperf. between 200.00 190.00
Never hinged 350.00
19 A3 2c dk violet, *lilac* 42.50 7.00
Never hinged 85.00
20 A4 5c green ('87) 20.00 2.75
Never hinged 40.00
Nos. 18-20 (3) 68.25 11.75

General Louis Etienne Félicité Salomon — A5

1887 Engr. *Perf. 14*

21 A5 1c lake .40 .30
Never hinged .75
22 A5 2c violet 1.00 .70
Never hinged 2.00
23 A5 3c blue .70 .45
Never hinged 1.25
24 A5 5c green 50.00 .55
Never hinged 85.00
a. Double impression *2,250.*
Nos. 21-24 (4) 52.10 2.00

Imperfs. of Nos. 21-24 are plate proofs. Value per pair, $50.

Nos. 21-22 are known overprinted "R:S:" and postally used. Neither is known unused. Overprint is of a provisional or revolutionary government.

No. 23 Handstamp Surcharged in Red

1890

25 A5 2c on 3c blue 3.50 3.00
Never hinged 15.00
a. Inverted surcharge 30.00 *40.00*
b. Double surcharge 20.00 *27.50*
Never hinged 30.00
c. Double surcharge, one inverted — *37.50*
d. Pair, one without surcharge *100.00*

Missing letters are frequently found. This applies to succeeding surcharged issues.

Coat of Arms — A7

1891 *Perf. 13*

26 A7 1c violet 1.00 .30
Never hinged 2.75
27 A7 2c blue 1.50 .30
Never hinged 4.50
28 A7 3c gray lilac 2.00 .45
Never hinged 5.50
a. 3c slate 1.75 .55
Never hinged 5.00
29 A7 5c orange 5.50 .50
Never hinged 15.00
30 A7 7c red 20.00 2.75
Never hinged 52.50
Nos. 26-30 (5) 30.00 4.30
Set, never hinged 81.00

Nos. 26-30 exist imperf. Value of unused pairs, each $50.

The 2c, 3c and 7c exist imperf. vertically. Value, each $50 and up.

No. 28 Surcharged Like No. 25 in Red

1892

31 A7 2c on 3c gray lilac 3.00 2.00
Never hinged 10.00
a. 2c on 3c slate 3.50 2.25
Never hinged 10.00
b. Inverted surcharge 24.00
Never hinged 35.00
c. Double surcharge 32.50
Never hinged 45.00
d. Pair, one without surcharge 32.50
Never hinged 100.00

Coat of Arms (Leaves Drooping) — A9

1892-95 Engr., Litho. (20c) *Perf. 14*

32 A9 1c lilac .40 .25
Never hinged 1.00
b. Double impression *500.00*
33 A9 2c deep blue .50 .25
Never hinged 1.25
34 A9 3c gray .70 .45
Never hinged 1.75
35 A9 5c orange 2.75 .50
Never hinged 7.00
36 A9 7c red .50 .25
Never hinged 1.25
a. Imperf., pair 30.00
Never hinged 50.00
37 A9 20c brown 1.40 1.00
Never hinged 3.50
Nos. 32-37 (6) 6.25 2.70
Set, never hinged 15.75

Nos. 32, 33, 35 exist in horiz. pairs, imperf. vert., Nos. 33, 35, in vert. pairs, imperf. horiz. No. 32 exists imperf. It is a proof.

1896 Engr. *Perf. 13½*

38 A9 1c light blue .55 *.70*
Never hinged 3.25
39 A9 2c red brown .65 *1.20*
Never hinged 4.00
40 A9 3c lilac brown .55 *1.20*
Never hinged 3.25
41 A9 5c slate green .65 *1.20*
Never hinged 4.00
42 A9 7c dark gray .90 *1.75*
Never hinged 5.50
43 A9 20c orange 1.10 *2.25*
Never hinged 7.50
Nos. 38-43 (6) 4.40 8.30
Set, never hinged 27.50

Nos. 32-37 are 23¾mm high, Nos. 38-43 23¼mm to 23½mm. The "C" is closed on Nos. 32-37, open on Nos. 38-43. Other differences exist. The stamps of the two issues may be readily distinguished by their colors and perfs.

Nos. 38-43 exist imperf. and in horiz. pairs, imperf. vert. The 1c, 3c, 5c, 7c exist in vert. pairs, imperf. horiz. or imperf. between. The 5c, 7c exist in horiz. pairs, imperf. between. Value of unused pairs, $9 and up.

Nos. 37, 43 Surcharged Like No. 25 in Red

1898

44 A9 2c on 20c brown 3.00 *6.00*
Never hinged 10.00
a. Inverted surcharge 27.50
Never hinged 40.00
b. Double surcharge 32.50
Never hinged 45.00
45 A9 2c on 20c orange 1.75 1.40
Never hinged 6.00
a. Inverted surcharge 18.00
Never hinged 25.00
b. Double surcharge 27.50
Never hinged 40.00
c. Double surcharge, one inverted 35.00
Never hinged 50.00

No. 45 exists in various part perf. varieties.

Coat of Arms — A11

1898 Wmk. 131 *Perf. 11*

46 A11 1c ultra 2.50 *5.00*
Never hinged 5.00
47 A11 2c brown carmine .55 .40
Never hinged 1.00
48 A11 3c dull violet 2.50 *5.00*
Never hinged 5.00
49 A11 5c dark green .55 .40
Never hinged 1.00
a. Double impression *600.00*
50 A11 7c gray 5.00 *10.00*
Never hinged 10.00
51 A11 20c orange 10.00 *20.00*
Never hinged 20.00
Nos. 46-51 (6) 21.10 *40.80*
Set, never hinged 42.00

Nos. 46-51 exist imperforate. They are plate proofs. Value, pair $30-$40 each.

Pres. T. Augustin Simon Sam — A12

Coat of Arms — A13

1898-99 Unwmk. *Perf. 12*

52 A12 1c ultra .25 .25
Never hinged .75
53 A13 1c yel green ('99) .25 .25
Never hinged .75
54 A12 2c deep orange .25 .25
Never hinged .75
55 A13 2c car lake ('99) .25 .25
Never hinged .75
56 A12 3c green .25 .25
Never hinged .75
57 A13 4c red .25 .25
Never hinged .75
58 A12 5c red brown .25 .25
Never hinged .75
59 A13 5c pale blue ('99) .25 .25
Never hinged .75
60 A12 7c gray .25 .25
Never hinged .75
61 A13 8c carmine .25 .25
Never hinged .75
62 A13 10c orange red .25 .25
Never hinged .75
63 A13 15c olive green .60 .45
Never hinged 1.75
64 A12 20c black .60 .45
Never hinged 1.75
65 A12 50c rose brown 1.00 .50
Never hinged 3.00
66 A12 1g red violet 2.25 2.00
Never hinged 7.00
Nos. 52-66 (15) 7.20 6.15
Set, never hinged 21.66

For overprints see Nos. 67-81, 110-124, 169, 247-248.

Stamps of 1898-99 Handstamped in Black

1902

67 A12 1c ultra .60 *1.50*
Never hinged 1.50
a. Inverted overprint 3.50
Never hinged 20.00
b. Pair, one without overprint *40.00*
Never hinged 80.00
68 A13 1c yellow green .45 .30
Never hinged 1.10
a. Inverted overprint 3.50
Never hinged 10.00
b. Double overprint 30.00
Never hinged 10.00

c. Pair, one without overprint 50.00
Never hinged 60.00
69 A12 2c deep orange .80 *1.50*
Never hinged 2.00
a. Inverted overprint 4.50
Never hinged 30.00
b. Double overprint 6.00
Never hinged 30.00
c. Pair, one without overprint *50.00*
Never hinged 80.00
70 A13 2c carmine lake .45 .30
Never hinged 1.10
a. Inverted overprint 4.00
Never hinged 10.00
b. Double overprint 6.00
Never hinged 30.00
71 A12 3c green .45 .45
Never hinged 1.10
a. Inverted overprint 3.50
Never hinged 20.00
72 A13 4c red .60 *.90*
Never hinged 1.50
a. Inverted overprint 3.50
Never hinged 15.00
b. Double overprint 6.00
Never hinged 30.00
c. Pair, one without overprint 50.00
73 A12 5c red brown 1.25 *6.00*
Never hinged 3.00
a. Inverted overprint 6.00
Never hinged 50.00
74 A13 5c pale blue .45 .45
Never hinged 1.10
a. Inverted overprint 3.75
Never hinged 20.00
b. Double overprint 20.00
Never hinged 30.00
75 A12 7c gray .95 .95
Never hinged 2.50
a. Inverted overprint 4.00
Never hinged 40.00
b. Double overprint 6.00
Never hinged 90.00
76 A13 8c carmine .95 *8.50*
Never hinged 2.50
a. Inverted overprint 5.00
Never hinged 55.00
b. Double overprint 6.00
Never hinged 85.00
77 A13 10c orange red .95 *1.50*
Never hinged 2.50
a. Inverted overprint 6.00
Never hinged 80.00
b. Double overprint 6.00
Never hinged 80.00
78 A13 15c olive green 5.00 *7.00*
Never hinged 12.50
a. Inverted overprint 18.00
Never hinged 100.00
b. Double overprint 10.00
Never hinged 140.00
79 A12 20c black 5.00 *6.00*
Never hinged 12.50
a. Inverted overprint 14.00
Never hinged 130.00
b. Double overprint 16.00
Never hinged 90.00
80 A12 50c rose brown 17.50 *37.50*
Never hinged 42.50
a. Inverted overprint 45.00
Never hinged 200.00
81 A12 1g red violet 25.00 *60.00*
Never hinged 60.00
a. Inverted overprint 120.00
Never hinged 300.00
b. Pair, one without overprint 150.00
Never hinged 400.00
Nos. 67-81 (15) 60.40 132.85

Many forgeries exist of this overprint.
Specialists have called into question the existence of the double-overprint errors listed for this set except Nos. 68b and 74b. The editors would like to see documented evidence of the existence of Nos. 69b, 70b, 72b, 75b, 76b, 77b, 78b, 79b and 81b.

Centenary of Independence Issues

Coat of Arms — A14

Francois-Dominique Toussaint L'Ouverture — A15

Emperor Jean Jacques Dessalines A16

Pres. Alexandre Sabes Pétion A17

1903, Dec. 31 Engr. *Perf. 13¼, 14*
82 A14 1c green .35 .35
Never hinged 1.00

Center Engr., Frame Litho.

83 A15 2c rose & blk 1.25 *3.00*
Never hinged 5.50
84 A15 5c dull blue & blk 1.25 *3.00*
Never hinged 5.50
85 A16 7c plum & blk 1.25 *3.00*
Never hinged 5.50
86 A16 10c yellow & blk 1.25 *3.00*
Never hinged 5.50
87 A17 20c slate & blk 1.25 *3.00*
Never hinged 5.50
88 A17 50c olive & blk 1.25 *3.00*
Never hinged 5.50
Nos. 82-88 (7) 7.85 18.35

Nos. 82 to 88 exist imperforate.
Nos. 83-88 exist with centers inverted. Some are known with head omitted.
Forgeries exist both perforated and imperf and constitute the great majority of Nos. 83-88 offered in the marketplace. Stamps perforated 13½ are forgeries. Many forgeries exist with heads lithographed instead of engraved.

Same Handstamped in Blue

1904
89 A14 1c green .50 1.50
Never hinged 5.00
90 A15 2c rose & blk .50 1.50
Never hinged 5.00
91 A15 5c dull blue & blk .50 1.50
Never hinged 5.00
92 A16 7c plum & blk .50 1.50
Never hinged 5.00
93 A16 10c yellow & blk .50 1.50
Never hinged 5.00
94 A17 20c slate & blk .50 1.50
Never hinged 5.00
95 A17 50c olive & blk .50 1.50
Never hinged 5.00
Nos. 89-95 (7) 3.50 10.50

Two dies were used for the handstamped overprint on Nos. 89-95. Letters and figures are larger on one than on the other. All values exist imperforate.

Pres. Pierre Nord-Alexis — A18

1904 Engr. *Perf. 13¼, 14*
96 A18 1c green .35 .35
Never hinged 2.75
97 A18 2c carmine .35 .35
Never hinged 2.75
98 A18 5c dark blue .35 .35
Never hinged 2.75
99 A18 10c orange brown .35 .35
Never hinged 2.75
100 A18 20c orange .35 .35
Never hinged 2.75
101 A18 50c claret .35 .35
Never hinged 2.75
a. Tête bêche pair *500.00*
Never hinged 1,000.
Nos. 96-101 (6) 2.10 2.10

Used values are for c-t-o's. Postally used examples are worth considerably more.
Nos. 96-101 exist imperforate. Value, set $10.
This issue, and the overprints and surcharges, exist in horiz. pairs, imperf. vert., and in vert. pairs, imperf. horiz.
For overprints and surcharges see Nos. 102-109, 150-161, 170-176, 217-218, 235-238, 240-242, 302-303.
Forgeries of Nos. 96, 101, 101a exist.
Some specialists believe No. 101a is a proof. Research is ongoing.
Reprints or very accurate imitations of this issue exist, including No. 101a. Some are printed in very bright colors on very white paper and are found both perforated and imperforate. The original stamps are perf. 13¼ or 14, the reprints (forgeries) perf 13½, as well as numerous other perforations, including compound perfs.

Same Handstamped in Blue like Nos. 89-95

1904
102 A18 1c green .60 1.50
Never hinged 5.00
103 A18 2c carmine .60 1.50
Never hinged 5.00
104 A18 5c dark blue .60 1.50
Never hinged 5.00
105 A18 10c orange brown .60 1.50
Never hinged 5.00
106 A18 20c orange .60 1.50
Never hinged 5.00
107 A18 50c claret .60 1.50
Never hinged 5.00
Nos. 102-107 (6) 3.60 9.00

The note after No. 95 applies also to Nos. 102-107. All values exist imperf.
Forgeries exist.

Regular Issue of 1904 Handstamp Surcharged in Black

1906, Feb. 20
108 A18 1c on 20c orange .35 .25
Never hinged 5.00
a. 1c on 50c claret *950.00*
Never hinged 1,500.
109 A18 2c on 50c claret .35 .25
Never hinged 5.00

No. 108a is known only with inverted surcharge.
Forgeries exist.

Nos. 52-66 Handstamped in Red

1906
110 A12 1c ultra 1.40 .95
Never hinged 5.00
a. Inverted overprint 3.00
Never hinged 10.00
111 A13 1c yellow green .75 .75
Never hinged 2.50
a. Inverted overprint —
112 A12 2c deep orange 2.50 2.25
Never hinged 8.50
a. Inverted overprint 3.00 *25.00*
Never hinged 10.00
113 A13 2c carmine lake 1.50 1.25
Never hinged 5.00
a. Inverted overprint 3.00
Never hinged 10.00
114 A12 3c green 1.50 1.25
Never hinged 5.00
a. Inverted overprint 3.00 *10.00*
Never hinged 10.00
115 A13 4c red 5.75 4.50
Never hinged 20.00
a. Pair, one without overprint *200.00*
116 A12 5c red brown 7.00 5.50
Never hinged 25.00
a. Inverted overprint 10.00
Never hinged 35.00
117 A13 5c pale blue 1.10 .60
Never hinged 3.75
a. Inverted overprint 3.75
Never hinged 13.00
118 A12 7c gray 5.00 4.50
Never hinged 17.50
a. Inverted overprint 20.00
Never hinged 70.00
119 A13 8c carmine 1.10 1.00
Never hinged 3.75
a. Inverted overprint 5.00
b. Double overprint 60.00
c. Pair, one without overprint *100.00*
120 A13 10c orange red 2.00 1.25
Never hinged 7.00
a. Inverted overprint 6.00
b. Pair, one without overprint *100.00* *150.00*
121 A13 15c olive green 2.50 1.25
Never hinged 8.50
a. Inverted overprint 18.00
Never hinged 60.00
122 A12 20c black 5.75 4.50
Never hinged 20.00
a. Sideways overprint —
123 A12 50c rose brown 5.50 3.50
Never hinged 19.00
a. Inverted overprint 45.00
Never hinged 150.00
124 A12 1g red violet 15.00 10.00
Never hinged 50.00
a. Inverted overprint 120.00
Nos. 110-124 (15) 58.35 43.05

The ink used in this overprint is fugitive and will bleed in water.
Forgeries of this overprint are plentiful.

Coat of Arms — A19

President Nord-Alexis A20

Market at Port-au-Prince A21

Sans Souci Palace — A22

Independence Palace at Gonaives — A23

Entrance to Catholic College at Port-au-Prince A24

Monastery and Church at Port-au-Prince A25

Seat of Government at Port-au-Prince A26

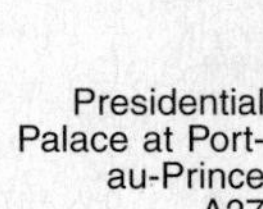

Presidential Palace at Port-au-Prince A27

For Foreign Postage (centimes de piastre)

1906-13 *Perf. 12*
125 A19 1c de p green .35 .25
Never hinged .75
126 A20 2c de p ver .45 .25
Never hinged 1.00
127 A21 3c de p brown .60 .25
Never hinged 1.25
128 A21 3c de p org yel ('11) 6.00 6.00
Never hinged 12.00
129 A22 4c de p car lake .60 .35
Never hinged 1.25
130 A22 4c de p lt ol grn ('13) 25.00 25.00
Never hinged 50.00
131 A20 5c de p dk blue 2.50 .30
Never hinged 5.00
132 A23 7c de p gray 1.75 .85
Never hinged 3.50
133 A23 7c de p org red ('13) 65.00 65.00
Never hinged 125.00
134 A24 8c de p car rose 1.75 .80
Never hinged 3.50
135 A24 8c de p ol grn ('13) 55.00 42.50
Never hinged 110.00
136 A25 10c de p org red 1.25 .30
Never hinged 2.50

137 A25 10c de p red brn ('13) 27.50 22.50
Never hinged 55.00
138 A26 15c de p sl grn 2.25 .90
Never hinged 5.00
139 A26 15c dp p yel ('13) 20.00 12.00
Never hinged 40.00
140 A20 20c de p blue grn 2.25 .90
Never hinged 4.50
141 A19 50c de p red 3.25 2.25
Never hinged 6.50
142 A19 50c de p org yel ('13) 20.00 12.00
Never hinged 40.00
143 A27 1p claret 7.25 4.50
Never hinged 15.00
144 A27 1p red ('13) 13.00 11.00
Never hinged 25.00
Nos. 125-144 (20) 255.75 207.90

All 1906 values exist imperf. These are plate proofs.

For overprints and surcharges see Nos. 177-195, 213-216, 239, 245, 249-260, 263, 265-277, 279-284, 286-301, 304.

Nord-Alexis A28

Coat of Arms — A29

For Domestic Postage (centimes de gourde)

1906-10

145 A28 1c de g blue .35 .25
Never hinged 2.00
146 A29 2c de g org yel .45 .25
Never hinged 3.00
147 A29 2c de g lemon ('10) .65 .25
Never hinged 4.50
148 A28 3c de g slate .40 .25
Never hinged 2.75
149 A29 7c de g green 1.25 .45
Never hinged 8.50
Nos. 145-149 (5) 3.10 1.45

For overprints see Nos. 196-197.

Regular Issue of 1904 Handstamp Surcharged in Red like Nos. 108-109

1907

150 A18 1c on 5c dk bl .40 .35
Never hinged 7.50
151 A18 1c on 20c org .40 .25
Never hinged 7.50
152 A18 2c on 10c org brn .40 .40
Never hinged 7.50
153 A18 2c on 50c claret .50 .40
Never hinged 7.50

Black Surcharge

154 A18 1c on 5c dk bl .50 .40
Never hinged 10.00
155 A18 1c on 10c org brn .50 .25
Never hinged 10.00
156 A18 2c on 20c org .40 .40
Never hinged 10.00

Brown Surcharge

157 A18 1c on 5c dk bl 1.50 1.25
Never hinged 5.00
158 A18 1c on 10c org brn 1.50 1.25
Never hinged 5.00
159 A18 2c on 20c org 5.00 4.00
Never hinged 15.00
160 A18 2c on 50c claret 27.50 22.50
Never hinged 125.00

Violet Surcharge

161 A18 1c on 20c org 150.00
Never hinged 400.00

The handstamps are found sideways, diagonal, inverted and double.

Forgeries exist.

A30

President Antoine T. Simon — A31

1910 For Foreign Postage

162 A30 2c de p rose red & blk .65 .50
Never hinged 15.00
163 A30 5c de p bl & blk 13.00 1.00
Never hinged 30.00
164 A30 20c de p yel grn & blk 12.50 12.50
Never hinged 30.00

For Domestic Postage

165 A31 1c de g lake & blk .30 .25
Never hinged .75
Nos. 162-165 (4) 26.45 14.25

For overprint and surcharges see Nos. 198, 262, 278, 285.

A32

A33

Pres. Cincinnatus Leconte — A34

1912

166 A32 1c de g car lake .40 .40
Never hinged 4.00
167 A33 2c de g dp org .50 .40
Never hinged 5.00

For Foreign Postage

168 A34 5c de p dp blue .90 .40
Never hinged 9.00
Nos. 166-168 (3) 1.80 1.20

For overprints see Nos. 199-201.

Stamps of Preceding Issues Handstamped Vertically

1914 On No. 61

169 A13 8c carmine 20.00 13.00
Never hinged 60.00

On Nos. 96-101

170 A18 1c green 47.50 35.00
Never hinged 140.00
171 A18 2c carmine 47.50 35.00
Never hinged 140.00
172 A18 5c dk blue .75 .50
Never hinged 2.25
173 A18 10c orange brn .75 .50
Never hinged 2.25
174 A18 20c orange 1.25 .60
Never hinged 3.75
175 A18 50c claret 3.00 1.50
Never hinged 7.50
Nos. 170-175 (6) 100.75 73.10

Perforation varieties of Nos. 172-175 exist.

No. 175 overprinted "T. M." is a revenue stamp. The letters are the initials of "Timbre Mobile."

On No. 107

176 A18 50c claret *10,000. 13,000.*

Horizontally on Stamps of 1906-13

177 A19 1c de p green .55 .45
Never hinged 2.25
178 A20 2c de p ver .75 .45
Never hinged 3.00
179 A21 3c de p brown 1.25 .65
Never hinged 5.00
180 A21 3c de p org yel .55 .45
Never hinged 2.25
181 A22 4c de p car lake 1.25 .65
Never hinged 5.00
182 A22 4c de p lt ol grn 3.00 1.60
Never hinged 12.00
183 A23 7c de p gray 2.75 2.75
Never hinged 11.00
184 A23 7c de p org red 7.25 6.75
Never hinged 30.00
185 A24 8c de p car rose 5.00 4.50
Never hinged 20.00
186 A24 8c de p ol grn 9.25 9.00
Never hinged 35.00
187 A25 10c de p org red 1.50 .65
Never hinged 6.00
188 A25 10c de p red brn 4.00 2.50
Never hinged 16.00
189 A26 15c de p sl grn 4.25 3.75
Never hinged 17.50
190 A26 15c de p yellow 3.00 1.60
Never hinged 12.00
191 A20 20c de p bl grn 3.75 1.40
Never hinged 15.00
192 A19 50c de p red 6.50 6.00
Never hinged 27.50
193 A19 50c de p org yel 11.00 10.00
Never hinged 40.00
194 A27 1p claret 6.50 6.00
Never hinged 27.50
195 A27 1p red 12.00 11.00
Never hinged 47.50
196 A29 2c de g lemon .55 .45
Never hinged 2.25
197 A28 3c de g slate .55 .45
Never hinged 2.25
Nos. 177-197 (21) 85.20 71.05

On No. 164

198 A30 20c de p yel grn & blk 3.75 3.50
Never hinged 25.00

Vertically on Nos. 166-168

199 A32 1c de g car lake .50 .40
Never hinged 7.00
200 A33 2c de g dp org .65 .50
Never hinged 8.00
201 A34 5c de p dp blue 1.10 .40
Never hinged 15.00
Nos. 199-201 (3) 2.25 1.30

Two handstamps were used for the overprints on Nos. 169-201. They may be distinguished by the short and long foot of the "L" of "GL" and the position of the first "1" in "1914" with regard to the period above it. Both handstamps are found on all but Nos. 176, 294, 295, 306, 308.

Handstamp Surcharged

On Nos. 141 and 143

213 A19 1c de p on 50c de p red .50 .40
Never hinged 8.00
214 A27 1c de p on 1p claret .65 .50
Never hinged 8.00

On Nos. 142 and 144

215 A19 1c de p on 50c de p org yel .65 .50
Never hinged 8.00
216 A27 1c de p on 1p red .65 .50
Never hinged 8.00

Handstamp Surcharged

On Nos. 100 and 101

217 A18 7c on 20c orange .50 .25
Never hinged 8.00
218 A18 7c on 50c claret .45 .25
Never hinged 8.00

The initials on the preceding handstamps are those of Gen. Oreste Zamor; the date is that of his triumphal entry into Port-au-Prince.

Pres. Oreste Zamor

Coat of Arms

Pres. Tancrède Auguste

Owing to the theft of a large quantity of this 1914 issue, while in transit from the printers, the stamps were never placed on sale at post offices. A few stamps have been canceled through carelessness of favor. Value, set of 10, $8.50.

Preceding Issues Handstamp Surcharged in Carmine or Blue

1915-16 On Nos. 98-101

235 A18 1c on 5c dk bl (C) 2.00 2.25
Never hinged 7.00
236 A18 1c on 10c org brn .60 .75
Never hinged 2.00
237 A18 1c on 20c orange .60 .75
Never hinged 2.00
238 A18 1c on 50c claret .60 .75
Never hinged 2.00

On No. 132

239 A23 1c on 7c de p gray (C) .60 .75
Never hinged 2.00

On Nos. 106-107

240 A18 1c on 20c orange 1.50 1.50
Never hinged 5.00
241 A18 1c on 50c claret 3.50 1.50
Never hinged 12.00
242 A18 1c on 50c cl (C) *125.00 150.00*
Never hinged 400.00
Nos. 235-242 (8) 134.40 158.25

Nos. 240-242 are known with two types of the "Post Paye" overprint. No. 237 with red surcharge and any stamps with violet surcharge are unofficial.

> Values for Nos. 245-308 are for examples with the boxed "Gourde" surcharge partially on the stamp. Examples upon which this surcharge is fully present on the stamp command substantial premiums.

No. 143 Handstamp Surcharged in Red

1917-19

245 A27 2c on 1p claret .50 .50
Never hinged 7.00

Stamps of 1906-14 Handstamp Surcharged in Various Colors

1c, 5c

On Nos. 123-124

247 A12 1c on 50c (R) 90.00 40.00
248 A12 1c on 1g (R) 90.00 40.00

On #127, 129, 134, 136, 138, 140-141

249 A22 1c on 4c de p (Br) .65 *.75*
Never hinged 5.00
250 A25 1c on 10c de p (Bl) .65 *.75*
Never hinged 5.00
252 A20 1c on 20c de p (R) .65 *.75*
Never hinged 5.00
253 A20 1c on 20c de p (Bk) .65 *.75*
Never hinged 5.00
254 A19 1c on 50c de p (R) .65 *.75*
Never hinged 5.00
255 A19 1c on 50c de p (Bk) .65 *.75*
Never hinged 5.00
256 A21 2c on 3c de p (R) .65 *.75*
Never hinged 5.00
257 A24 2c on 8c de p (R) .65 *.75*
Never hinged 5.00
258 A24 2c on 8c de p (Bk) .65 *.75*
Never hinged 5.00
259 A26 2c on 15c de p (R) .65 *.75*
Never hinged 5.00
260 A20 2c on 20c de p (R) .65 *.75*
Never hinged 5.00
Nos. 249-260 (11) 7.15 8.25

The 1c on 10c de p stamp in black is actually a blue ink which bled into the stamps.

On Nos. 164, 128

262 A30 1c on 20c de p (Bk) 3.75 3.50
Never hinged 15.00
263 A21 2c on 3c de p (R) .60 .75
Never hinged 2.50

On #130, 133, 135, 137, 139, 142, 144

265 A22 1c on 4c de p (R) .70 *.85*
Never hinged 3.50
266 A23 1c on 7c de p (Br) .70 *.85*
Never hinged 3.50
267 A26 1c on 15c de p (R) .70 *.85*
Never hinged 3.50
268 A19 1c on 50c de p (Bk) 2.25 *2.75*
Never hinged 12.00
269 A27 1c on 1p (Bk) 2.25 *2.75*
Never hinged 12.00
270 A24 2c on 8c de p (R) .70 *.85*
Never hinged 3.50
271 A25 2c on 10c de p (Br) .70 *.85*
Never hinged 3.50
272 A26 2c on 15c de p (R) .70 *.85*
Never hinged 3.50
274 A25 5c on 10c de p (Bk) .70 *.85*
Never hinged 3.50
275 A26 5c on 15c de p (R) 5.50 *6.75*
Never hinged 25.00
Nos. 265-275 (10) 14.90 *18.20*

"O. Z." Stamps of 1914 Handstamp Surcharged in Red or Brown

276 A26 1c on 15c de p sl grn .70 *.85*
Never hinged 2.25
277 A20 1c on 20c de p bl grn .70 *.85*
Never hinged 2.25
278 A30 1c on 20c de p yel grn & blk .70 *.85*
Never hinged 2.25
279 A27 1c on 1p claret (Br) .70 *.85*
Never hinged 2.25
280 A27 1c on 1p claret 2.25 *2.75*
Never hinged 6.50
281 A27 5c on 1p red (Br) .70 *.85*
Never hinged 2.25
Nos. 276-281 (6) 5.75 *7.00*

Srchd. in Violet, Green, Red, Magenta or Black 1 ct and 2 cts as in 1917-19 and

1919-20

282 A22 2c on 4c de p car lake (V) .70 *.85*
Never hinged 4.00
283 A24 2c on 8c de p car rose (G) .70 *.85*
Never hinged 4.00
284 A24 2c on 8c de p ol grn (R) .70 *.85*
Never hinged 4.00
285 A30 2c on 20c de p yel grn & blk (R) .85 *1.10*
Never hinged 4.50
286 A19 2c on 50c de p red (G) .70 *.85*
Never hinged 4.00
288 A19 2c on 50c de p red (R) .70 *.85*
Never hinged 4.00
289 A19 2c on 50c de p org yel (R) .70 *.85*
Never hinged 4.00
290 A27 2c on 1p claret (R) 3.50 *4.00*
Never hinged 20.00
291 A27 2c on 1p red (R) 2.25 *2.75*
Never hinged 15.00
292 A21 3c on 3c de p brn (R) .70 *.85*
Never hinged 4.00
293 A23 3c on 7c de p org red (R) .70 *.85*
Never hinged 4.00
294 A21 5c on 3c de p brn (R) .70 *.85*
Never hinged 4.00
295 A21 5c on 3c de p org yel (R) 2.25 *2.75*
Never hinged 15.00
296 A22 5c on 4c de p car lake (R) .70 *.85*
Never hinged 4.00
297 A22 5c on 4c de p ol grn (R) .70 *.85*
Never hinged 4.00
298 A23 5c on 7c de p gray (V) .70 *.85*
Never hinged 4.00
299 A23 5c on 7c de p org red (V) .70 *.85*
Never hinged 4.00
300 A25 5c on 10c de p org red (V) .70 *.85*
Never hinged 4.00
301 A26 5c on 15c de p yel (M) .70 *.85*
Never hinged 4.00
Nos. 282-301 (19) 19.35 *23.35*

Nos. 217 and 218 Handstamp Surcharged with New Value in Magenta

302 A18 5c on 7c on 20c orange .60 .75
Never hinged 3.00
303 A18 5c on 7c on 50c claret 3.50 4.00
Never hinged 15.00

No. 187 Handstamp Surcharged in Magenta

304 A25 5c de p on 10c de p .60 .75
Never hinged 8.00

Postage Due Stamps of 1906-14 Handstamp Surcharged in Black or Magenta (#308)

On Stamp of 1906

305 D2 5c on 50c ol gray 15.00 15.00
Never hinged 75.00

On Stamp of 1914

306 D2 5c on 10c violet .60 .75
Never hinged 3.00
307 D2 5c on 50c olive gray .60 .75
Never hinged 3.00
308 D2 5c on 50c ol gray (M) 2.50 2.00
Never hinged 12.00
Nos. 305-308 (4) 18.70 18.50

Nos. 299 with red surcharge and 306-307 with violet are trial colors or essays.

Allegory of Agriculture A40

Allegory of Commerce A41

1920, Apr. Engr. *Perf. 12*

310 A40 3c deep orange .40 .40
Never hinged 3.00
311 A40 5c green .40 .40
Never hinged 3.00
312 A41 10c vermilion .50 .40
Never hinged 4.00
313 A41 15c violet .50 .40
Never hinged 4.00
314 A41 25c deep blue .65 .50
Never hinged 4.50
Nos. 310-314 (5) 2.45 2.10
Set, never hinged 18.50

Nos. 311-313 overprinted "T. M." are revenue stamps. The letters are the initials of "Timbre Mobile."

President Louis J. Borno — A42

Christophe's Citadel — A43

Old Map of West Indies — A44

Borno — A45

National Capitol — A46

1924, Sept. 3

315 A42 5c deep green .40 .25
Never hinged 2.50
316 A43 10c carmine .40 .25
Never hinged 2.50
317 A44 20c violet blue .90 .40
Never hinged 5.00
318 A45 50c orange & blk .90 .40
Never hinged 5.00
319 A46 1g olive green 1.60 .50
Never hinged 10.00
Nos. 315-319 (5) 4.20 1.80
Set, never hinged 25.00

For surcharges see Nos. 359 (in Scott Standard catalogue, Vol.3), C4A.

Coffee Beans and Flowers — A47

1928, Feb. 6

320 A47 35c deep green 3.75 .60
Never hinged 8.00

For surcharge see No. 337.

Pres. Louis Borno — A48

1929, Nov. 4

321 A48 10c carmine rose .50 .40
Never hinged 5.00

Signing of the "Frontier" treaty between Haiti and the Dominican Republic.

Presidents Salomon and Vincent — A49

Pres. Sténio Vincent — A50

1931, Oct. 16

322 A49 5c deep green 1.30 .50
Never hinged 4.00
323 A50 10c carmine rose 1.30 .50
Never hinged 4.00

50th anniv. of Haiti's joining the UPU.

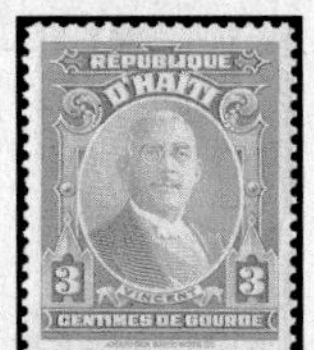

President Vincent — A52

Aqueduct at Port-au-Prince A53

Fort National — A54

Palace of Sans Souci — A55

Christophe's Chapel at Milot — A56

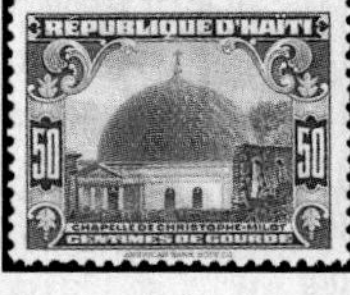

King's Gallery Citadel — A57

Vallières Battery — A58

1933-40

325 A52 3c orange .30 .25
Never hinged 1.50
326 A52 3c dp ol grn ('39) .30 .25
Never hinged 1.50
327 A53 5c green .30 .25
Never hinged 1.50
a. 5c emerald ('38) .30 .25
Never hinged 1.50
b. 5c bright green ('39) .30 .25
Never hinged 1.50
c. 5c brown olive ('40) .50 .25
Never hinged 2.50

329 A54 10c rose car .50 .25
Never hinged 2.50
a. 10c vermilion .65 .25
Never hinged 3.00
330 A54 10c red brn ('40) .50 .25
Never hinged 2.50
331 A55 25c blue .90 .25
Never hinged 4.50
332 A56 50c brown 2.50 .55
Never hinged 12.50
333 A57 1g dark green 2.50 .55
Never hinged 12.50
334 A58 2.50g olive bister 4.50 .90
Never hinged 22.50
Nos. 325-334 (9) 12.30 3.50
Set, never hinged 70.00

For surcharges see Nos. 357-358, 360 in Scott Standard catalogue, Vol. 3.

Alexandre Dumas, His Father and Son — A59

1935, Dec. 29 Litho. *Perf. 11½*
335 A59 10c rose pink & choc .90 .40
Never hinged 3.50
336 A59 25c blue & chocolate 1.60 .50
Never hinged 8.00
Nos. 335-336,C10 (3) 7.00 3.40
Set, never hinged 70.00

Visit of a delegation from France to Haiti.
No. 335 exists imperf and in horiz. pair, imperf. between. No. 336 exists as pair, imperf horiz.

No. 320 Surcharged in Red

1939, Jan. 24 *Perf. 12*
337 A47 25c on 35c dp grn .90 .40
Never hinged 5.00

SEMI-POSTAL STAMPS

Pierre de Coubertin SP1

Engraved & Litho (flag)
1939, Oct. 3 Unwmk. *Perf. 12*
B1 SP1 10c + 10c multi 27.50 27.50
Never hinged 50.00
Nos. B1,CB1-CB2 (3) 77.50 77.50

Pierre de Coubertin, organizer of the modern Olympic Games. The surtax was used to build a Sports Stadium at Port-au-Prince.

AIR POST STAMPS

Plane over Port-au-Prince — AP1

1929-30 Unwmk. Engr. *Perf. 12*
C1 AP1 25c dp grn ('30) .50 .40
Never hinged 2.00
C2 AP1 50c dp vio .65 .40
Never hinged 2.50
C3 AP1 75c red brn ('30) 1.75 1.25
Never hinged 2.00
C4 AP1 1g dp ultra 1.90 1.60
Never hinged 2.50
Nos. C1-C4 (4) 4.80 3.65

No. 317 Surcharged in Red

1933, July 6
C4A A44 60c on 20c vio blue 75.00 80.00
Never hinged 150.00

Non-stop flight of Capt. J. Errol Boyd and Robert G. Lyon from New York to Port-au-Prince.

Plane over Christophe's Citadel — AP2

1933-40
C5 AP2 50c org brn 5.25 1.00
Never hinged 22.50
C6 AP2 50c ol grn ('35) 4.00 1.00
Never hinged 16.00
C7 AP2 50c car rose ('37) 3.50 2.00
Never hinged 15.00
C8 AP2 50c blk ('38) 2.00 1.00
Never hinged 8.00
C8A AP2 60c choc ('40) 1.10 .50
Never hinged 4.50
C9 AP2 1g ultra 1.75 .50
Never hinged 7.00
Nos. C5-C9 (6) 17.60 6.00

For surcharge see No. C24 in Scott Standard catalogue, Vol. 3.

Dumas Type of Regular Issue

1935, Dec. 29 Litho. *Perf. 11½*
C10 A59 60c brt vio & choc 4.50 2.50
Never hinged 10.00

Visit of delegation from France to Haiti.

Arms of Haiti and Portrait of George Washington — AP4

1938, Aug. 29 Engr. *Perf. 12*
C11 AP4 60c deep blue .70 .40
Never hinged 5.00

150th anniv. of the US Constitution.

AIR POST SEMI-POSTAL STAMPS

Coubertin Semipostal Type of 1939

Unwmk.
1939, Oct. 3 Engr. *Perf. 12*
CB1 SP1 60c + 40c multi 25.00 25.00
Never hinged 50.00
CB2 SP1 1.25g + 60c multi 25.00 25.00
Never hinged 50.00

POSTAGE DUE STAMPS

D1

1898, Aug. Unwmk. Engr. *Perf. 12*
J1 D1 2c black 1.00 .75
Never hinged 4.00
J2 D1 5c red brown 1.50 1.00
Never hinged 6.00
J3 D1 10c brown orange 2.00 1.50
Never hinged 8.00
J4 D1 50c slate 3.00 2.50
Never hinged 12.00
Nos. J1-J4 (4) 7.50 5.75

For overprints see Nos. J5-J9, J14-J16.

Stamps of 1898 Handstamped like Nos. 67-81

1902 Black Overprint
J5 D1 2c black 2.50 1.50
Never hinged 7.75
J6 D1 5c red brown 2.50 1.50
Never hinged 7.75
J7 D1 10c brown orange 2.50 1.50
Never hinged 7.75
J8 D1 50c slate 12.00 7.00
Never hinged 105.00

Red Overprint
J9 D1 2c black 3.50 3.50
Never hinged 32.50
Nos. J5-J9 (5) 23.00 15.00

D2

1906
J10 D2 2c dull red 1.50 1.00
Never hinged 5.00
J11 D2 5c ultra 2.75 2.50
Never hinged 8.00
J12 D2 10c violet 2.75 2.50
Never hinged 8.00
J13 D2 50c olive gray 11.50 7.50
Never hinged 32.50
Nos. J10-J13 (4) 18.50 13.50

For surcharges and overprints see Nos. 305-308, J17-J20.

Preceding Issues Handstamped like Nos. 169-201

1914 On Stamps of 1898
J14 D1 5c red brown 1.50 1.10
Never hinged 7.50
J15 D1 10c brown orange 1.50 1.10
Never hinged 7.50
J16 D1 50c slate 6.00 5.50
Never hinged 30.00
Nos. J14-J16 (3) 9.00 7.70

On Stamps of 1906
J17 D2 2c dull red 1.25 1.00
Never hinged 3.00
J18 D2 5c ultra 2.25 2.25
Never hinged 6.50
J19 D2 10c violet 7.50 5.50
Never hinged 22.50
J20 D2 50c olive gray 45.00 45.00
Never hinged 125.00
Nos. J17-J20 (4) 56.00 53.75

The note after No. 201 applies to Nos. J14-J20 also.

HATAY

hä-'tī

LOCATION — Northwest of Syria, bordering on Mediterranean Sea.
GOVT. — Former semi-independent republic
AREA — 10,000 sq. mi. (approx.)
POP. — 273,350 (1939)
CAPITAL — Antioch

Alexandretta, a semi-autonomous district of Syria under French mandate, was renamed Hatay in 1938 and transferred to Turkey in 1939.

100 Santims = 1 Kurush
40 Paras = 1 Kurush (1939)

Stamps of Turkey, 1931-38, Surcharged in Black

On A77

On A78

1939 Unwmk. *Perf. 11½x12*
1 A77 10s on 20pa dp org 1.75 .35
Never hinged 3.50
a. "Sent" instead of "Sant" 135.00 22.50
Never hinged 300.00
2 A78 25s on 1ku dk sl grn 2.00 .35
Never hinged 4.00
a. Small "25" 13.50 1.50
Never hinged 28.00
3 A78 50s on 2ku dk vio 2.00 .35
Never hinged 4.00
a. Small "50" 6.00 2.00
Never hinged 14.00
4 A77 75s on 2½ku green 1.75 .40
Never hinged 3.50
5 A78 1ku on 4ku slate 10.00 4.25
Never hinged 20.00
6 A78 1ku on 5ku rose red 5.50 1.40
Never hinged 11.00
7 A78 1½ku on 3ku brn org 3.50 1.25
Never hinged 6.00
8 A78 2½ku on 4ku slate 4.00 1.00
Never hinged 8.50
9 A78 5ku on 8ku brt blue 6.00 1.25
Never hinged 12.00
10 A77 12½ku on 20ku ol grn 7.00 2.00
Never hinged 14.00
11 A77 20ku on 25ku Prus bl 13.00 7.00
Never hinged 30.00
Nos. 1-11 (11) 56.50 19.60
Set, never hinged 115.00

Map of Hatay — A1

Lions of Antioch A2

Flag of Hatay A3

Post Office A4

1939 Unwmk. Typo. *Perf. 12*
12 A1 10p orange & aqua 2.50 .75
Never hinged 5.00
13 A1 30p lt vio & aqua 2.50 .75
Never hinged 5.00
14 A1 1½ku olive & aqua 2.50 .75
Never hinged 5.00
15 A2 2½ku turq grn 3.00 1.00
Never hinged 6.00
16 A2 3ku light blue 3.00 1.00
Never hinged 6.00
17 A2 5ku chocolate 3.00 1.00
Never hinged 6.00
18 A3 6ku brt blue & car 3.75 1.25
Never hinged 7.50
19 A3 7½ku dp grn & car 4.25 1.40
Never hinged 8.50
20 A3 12ku violet & car 5.00 1.40
Never hinged 10.00
21 A3 12½ku dk blue & car 4.50 1.50
Never hinged 8.00

22 A4 17½ku brown car 8.00 3.00
Never hinged 16.00
23 A4 25ku olive brn 9.00 3.50
Never hinged 18.00
24 A4 50ku slate blue 18.00 8.50
Never hinged 45.00
Nos. 12-24 (13) 69.00 25.80
Set, never hinged 146.00

Stamps of 1939 Overprinted in Black

1939

25 A1 10p orange & aqua 1.75 .75
Never hinged 3.50
a. Overprint reading up 30.00
Never hinged 45.00
26 A1 30p lt vio & aqua 1.75 .75
Never hinged 3.50
27 A1 1½ku ol & aqua 2.50 .80
Never hinged 5.00
28 A2 2½ku turq grn 2.50 .80
Never hinged 5.00 5.00
29 A2 3ku light blue 2.75 .80
Never hinged 5.50
30 A2 5ku chocolate 3.50 1.25
Never hinged 7.00
a. Overprint inverted 30.00
Never hinged 45.00
31 A3 6ku brt bl & car 3.75 1.25
Never hinged 7.50
32 A3 7½ku dp grn & car 4.25 2.00
Never hinged 8.50
33 A3 12ku vio & car 4.00 1.25
Never hinged 8.00
34 A3 12½ku dk bl & car 4.50 1.25
Never hinged 9.00
35 A4 17½ku brn car 5.50 2.25
Never hinged 11.00
a. Overprint inverted 30.00
Never hinged 45.00
36 A4 25ku olive brn 9.00 4.25
Never hinged 22.00
37 A4 50ku slate blue 19.00 10.00
Never hinged 50.00
Nos. 25-37 (13) 64.75 27.40
Set, never hinged 145.00

The overprint reads "Date of annexation to the Turkish Republic, June 30, 1939."

On Nos. 25-27, the overprint reads down. On Nos. 28-37, it is horizontal.

POSTAGE DUE STAMPS

Postage Due Stamps of Turkey, 1936, Surcharged or Overprinted in Black

1939 Unwmk. *Perf. 11½*

J1 D6 1ku on 2ku lt bl 4.00 .95
Never hinged 7.50
J2 D6 3ku bright violet 4.50 1.50
Never hinged 8.50
J3 D6 4ku on 5ku Prus bl 4.75 1.75
Never hinged 8.50
J4 D6 5ku on 12ku brt rose 5.25 1.75
Never hinged 12.00
J5 D6 12ku bright rose 57.50 40.00
Never hinged 125.00
Nos. J1-J5 (5) 76.00 45.95
Set, never hinged 162.00

Castle at Antioch
D1

1939 Typo. *Perf. 12*

J6 D1 1ku red orange 4.75 1.75
Never hinged 9.00
J7 D1 3ku dk olive brown 5.50 2.00
Never hinged 10.00
J8 D1 4ku turqoise green 6.00 2.25
Never hinged 11.00
J9 D1 5ku slate black 7.00 2.75
Never hinged 13.00
Nos. J6-J9 (4) 23.25 8.75
Set, never hinged 43.00

Nos. J6-J9 Overprinted in Black like Nos. 25-37

1939

J10 D1 1ku red orange 4.50 1.75
Never hinged 8.50
J11 D1 3ku dk olive brown 5.50 2.00
Never hinged 10.00
J12 D1 4ku turqoise green 5.75 2.25
Never hinged 10.00
J13 D1 5ku slate black 8.00 3.00
Never hinged 15.00
a. Overprint inverted 42.50
Never hinged 60.00
Nos. J10-J13 (4) 23.75 9.00
Set, never hinged 44.00

HELIGOLAND

'he-lə-gō-ˌland

LOCATION — An island in the North Sea near the northern coast of Germany
GOVT. — British Possession
AREA — ¼ sq. mi.
POP. — 2,307 (1900)

Great Britain ceded Heligoland to Germany in 1890. It became part of Schleswig-Holstein province. Stamps of Heligoland were superseded by those of the German Empire.

16 Schillings = 1 Mark
100 Pfennig = 1 Mark = 1 Schilling (1875)

REPRINTS

Most Heligoland issues were extensively reprinted between 1875 and 1895, and these comprise the great majority of Heligoland stamps in the marketplace. Such reprints sell for much less than the originals, usually for $1-$2 each. All stamps on surfaced paper with glossy white gum, and small hole perforations are reprints from Leipzig. All stamps perforated 14 are reprints from Hamburg. Reprints from Berlin are discussed after each listing. Expertization of Heligoland issues is strongly recommended by the editors.

Some Heligoland issues were officially reprinted for the Philatelic Archive in Bonn. A few have become available to the public and are exceedingly scarce.

Queen Victoria
A1 A2

A2a

A3

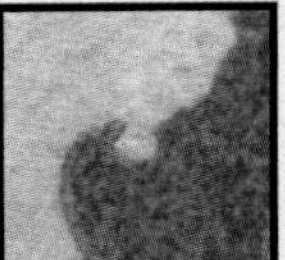
Type I

Type II

Type III

Type I: Curl below chignon is rounded
Type II: Curl resembles an upsidedown question mark
Type III: Curl is hooked
All stamps with a different head type from the listing are reprints.

Typo., Head Embossed

1867-68 Unwmk. *Rouletted 10*

1 A1 ½sch bl grn & rose, I 350.00 *1,000.*
On cover *7,250.*
1A A2 ½sch bl grn & rose, II 800.00 *1,700.*
On cover *9,500.*
2 A1 1sch rose & dp grn, I 190.00 *200.00*
On cover *2,600.*
3 A3 2sch rose & pale grn, I 20.00 *65.00*
On cover *1,300.*
4 A3 6sch gray grn & rose, I 20.00 *475.00*
On cover *8,750.*

All genuine stamps have a ridge that appears as a very faint gray line near the rouletting, best viewed under angled light. The ridge must be visible on at least one margin. Reprints lack the ridge. The 2sch and 6sch perforated exist only as reprints.

1869-71 *Perf. 13½x14¼*

Thick Soft Paper

5 A2 ½sch ol grn & car rose, II 125.00 *160.00*
On cover *1,300.*
a. ½sch blue green & carmine 240.00 *250.00*
On cover *1,400.*
b. ½sch yellow green & rose 475.00 *450.00*
On cover *1,400.*
c. ½sch yellow green & carmine 550.00 525.00
On cover *1,750.*
6 A2a 1sch red & yel grn, III 175.00 *300.00*
On cover *1,500.*
a. 1sch rose carmine & dark green 2,000. 1,000.
On cover *2,500.*

Berlin reprints have comparatively poor printing quality. The thin frame line inside the text is broken and often merges with the thick frame line.

A4

1873 Thick Quadrille Paper

7 A4 ¼sch pale rose & pale grn, I 35.00 *2,250.*
On cover *6,000.*
a. ¼sch dp carmine & pale yel grn *325.00* *2,250.*
On cover *6,000.*
8 A4 ¾sch yel grn & rose, I 135.00 *3,600.*
On cover *10,500.*
9 A2 ½sch brt grn & rose, II 125.00 *210.00*
On cover *1,100.*
10 A4 ¾sch gray grn & pale rose, I 50.00 *2,250.*
On cover *5,250.*
11 A2a 1sch rose & yel grn, III 210.00 *425.00*
On cover *1,400.*
a. rose & pale yel grn (porous printing) 210.00 450.00
On cover *1,400.*
12 A4 1½sch yel grn & rose, I 95.00 *325.00*
On cover *875.00*

Reprints are never on quadrille paper.

1874 Thin Wove Paper

13 A4 ¼sch rose & yel grn, I 17.50

Berlin reprints are head type 2.

A5

A6

A7

1875 Wove Paper

14 A5 1pf dk rose & dk grn, II 20.00 *600.00*
On cover *1,650.*
15 A5 2pf yel grn & dk rose, II 21.00 *875.00*
On cover *1,900.*
16 A6 5pf dk rose & dk grn, II 23.00 *21.00*
On cover *60.00*
17 A6 10pf blue grn & red, II 17.00 *37.50*
On cover *110.00*
a. 10pf yel green & dark rose 110.00 *27.50*
On cover *82.50*
b. 10pf lt green & pink red 140.00 *25.00*
On cover *82.50*
18 A7 25pf rose & dk grn, II 24.00 *30.00*
On cover *87.50*
a. 25pf dk rose & dk green 24.00 *30.00*
On cover *87.50*
19 A7 50pf grn & brick red, II 26.00 *85.00*
On cover *190.00*
a. 50pf dl grn & dk rose 65.00 *37.50*
On cover *110.00*

Under UV the red in Berlin reprints glows orange. Originals remain dull.

There are no reprints of Nos. 16-19.

Coat of Arms — A8

1876-88 Typo.

20 A8 3pf dp grn & dl red 275.00 *1,600.*
On cover *2,700.*
On cover, single franking *8,250.*
a. 3pf green & bright red ('77) 175.00 *1,000.*
On cover *2,000.*
On cover, single franking *8,250.*
21 A8 20pf ver & brt yel grn ('88) 15.00 *32.50*
On cover *92.50*
a. 20pf ver & yel grn ('87) 425.00 *47.50*
On cover *140.00*
b. 20pf lila rose & grn ('82) 240.00 *125.00*
On cover *360.00*
c. 20pf salmon & yel grn ('85) 425.00 *65.00*
On cover *160.00*
d. 20pf vio car & yel grn ('76) 240.00 *125.00*
On cover *410.00*
e. 20pf lila rose & dk grn ('80) 240.00 *125.00*
On cover *360.00*
f. 20pf rose red & grn ('84) 350.00 80.00
On cover *175.00*
g. 20pf brn org & yel grn ('90) 15.00 80.00
On cover *160.00*

The coat-of-arms on Nos. 20, 21 and subvarieties is printed in three colors: varying shades of yellow, red and green.

The 3pf has been reprinted. Reprints usually have a paler red. However some Berlin reprints are the same shade as the originals. Expertizing is strongly recommended.

A9

A10

1879 Typo.

22 A9 1m dp grn & car 225.00 *225.00*
On cover *650.00*
a. 1m blue green & salmon 225.00 *240.00*
On cover *650.00*
b. 1m dark green & ver 80.00

23 A10 5m blue grn & sal 225.00 *1,200.*
On cover *2,250.*

Perf. 11½

24 A9 1m dp grn & car 1,500. —
25 A10 5m bl grn & rose red 1,500. —
a. Horiz. pair, imperf. vert. *6,000.*

Nos. 13, 22b, 24 and 25 were never placed in use. Forged cancellations of Nos. 1-23 are plentiful.

Covers: Values for Nos. 22, 22a, 23 are for overfranked complete covers, usually philatelic.

Nos. 22-25 were not reprinted.

Heligoland stamps were replaced by those of the German Empire in 1890.

HONDURAS

hän-'dur-əs

LOCATION — Central America, between Guatemala on the north and Nicaragua on the south
GOVT. — Republic
AREA — 43,277 sq. mi.
POP. — 4,092,174 (est. 1983)
CAPITAL — Tegucigalpa

8 Reales = 1 Peso
100 Centavos = 1 Peso (1878)
100 Centavos = 1 Lempira (1933)

Values for unused stamps are for examples with original gum as defined in the catalogue introduction. Very fine examples of the locally printed Nos. 95-110, 127, 140, 151-210C, and 218-279 will have margins clear of the perforations but will be noticeably off center.

Watermark

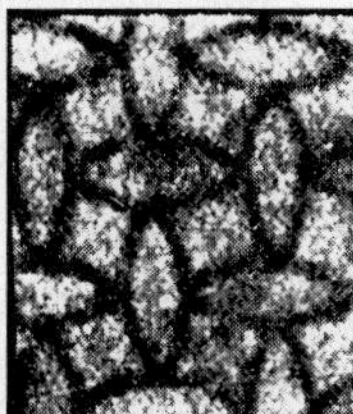

Wmk. 209 — Multiple Ovals

Coat of Arms — A1

1865, Dec. Unwmk. Litho. *Imperf.*

1 A1 2r black, *green* .65 *250.00*
2 A1 2r black, *pink* .65 *250.00*

Nos. 1 and 2, although inscribed "DOS," were sold for one real.

Most used examples are pen cancelled with cross. Pre-philatelic handstamp cancellations command a premium.

One in 12 stamps has "LOS" for "DOS," and one stamp in each pane of 120 is inscribed "DGS" or "CORRFOS."

No covers are known bearing No. 1. Two covers bearing No. 2 are known.

Comayagua

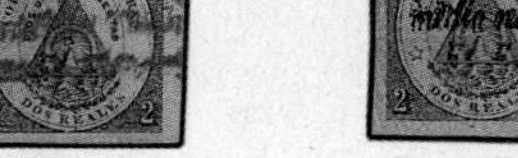

Tegucigalpa

Medio real = ½ real
Un real = 1 real
Dos reales = 2 reales

Comayagua Issue

1877, May Red Surcharge

3 A1 ½r on 2r blk, *grn* 70.00

Blue Surcharge

5 A1 2r on 2r blk, *grn* 150.00 —
6 A1 2r on 2r blk, *pink* *475.00* —

Black Surcharge

7 A1 1r on 2r blk, *grn* 150.00
8 A1 2r on 2r blk, *grn* *800.00*
9 A1 2r on 2r blk, *pink* 500.00

No. 5 may exist only as the base for No. 13a.

Tegucigalpa Issue

1877, July Black Surcharge

13 A1 1r on 2r blk, *grn* 15.00 *35.00*
a. Surcharged on #5 *1000.*
14 A1 1r on 2r blk, *pink* *80.00*
16 A1 2r on 2r blk, *pink* —

Blue Surcharge

18 A1 ½r on 2r blk, *grn* *80.00*
19 A1 ½r on 2r blk, *pink* *25.00*
20 A1 1r on 2r blk, *pink* *35.00*
23 A1 2r on 2r blk, *pink* 15.00 *25.00*

Red Surcharge

24 A1 ½r on 2r blk, *grn* 15.00 *35.00*
25 A1 ½r on 2r blk, *pink* 60.00

Only the stamps valued or dashed used are known to have been postally used. Nos. 3 and 7 may have been postally used, but to date no examples are recorded used. The other listed stamps were sold as remainders. No covers bearing Nos. 3 to 25 are known.

The blue surcharges range from light blue to violet black. The black surcharge has no tinge of blue. The red surcharges range from light to dark carmine. Some exist double or inverted, but genuine errors are rare. Normal cancel is a blue or black 7-bar killer. Target cancels on Nos. 1-24 are forgeries. Surcharges and cancels have been extensively forged.

Regular Issue

President Francisco Morazán — A4

Printed by National Bank Note Co. of N.Y.
Thin, hard paper, colorless gum
Various Frames

1878, July Engr. *Perf. 12*

30 A4 1c violet .50 .50
On cover *1,000.*
31 A4 2c brown .50 .50
On cover *1,500.*
32 A4 ½r black 5.00 .50
On cover *350.00*
33 A4 1r green 25.00 .50
On cover *450.00*
34 A4 2r deep blue 3.00 *5.00*
On cover *3,500.*
35 A4 4r vermilion 5.00 *10.00*
36 A4 1p orange 6.00 *25.00*
Nos. 30-36 (7) 45.00 *42.00*

Nos. 35 and 36 are not known on cover.

Various counterfeit cancellations exist on Nos. 30-36. Most used examples of Nos. 35-36 offered are actually 35a-36a with fake or favor cancels.

Printed by American Bank Note Co. of N.Y.
Re-Issue Soft paper, yellowish gum
Various Frames

1889

30a A4 1c deep violet *10.00*
31a A4 2c red brown .25
32a A4 ½r black .25
33a A4 1r blue green .25
34a A4 2r ultramarine *5.00*
35a A4 4r scarlet vermilion .25
36a A4 1p orange yellow .25
Nos. 30a-36a (7) 16.25

Although Nos. 30a-36a were not intended for postal use, they were valid, and genuine cancels are known on Nos. 31a-34a.

Arms of Honduras — A5

1890, Jan. 6

40 A5 1c yellow green .30 .30
41 A5 2c red .30 .30
42 A5 5c blue .30 .30
43 A5 10c orange .35 *.40*
44 A5 20c ocher .35 *.40*
45 A5 25c rose red .35 *.40*
46 A5 30c purple .50 *.60*
47 A5 40c dark blue .50 *.80*
48 A5 50c brown .55 *.80*
49 A5 75c blue green .55 *2.00*
50 A5 1p carmine .70 *2.25*
Nos. 40-50 (11) 4.75 *8.55*

The tablets and numerals of Nos. 40 to 50 differ for each denomination.

For overprints see Nos. O1-O11.

Used values of Nos. 1-110 are for stamps with genuine cancellations applied while the stamps were valid. Various counterfeit cancellations exist.

A6

President Luis Bográn — A7

1891, July 31

51 A6 1c dark blue .30 .30
52 A6 2c yellow brown .30 .30
53 A6 5c blue green .30 .30
54 A6 10c vermilion .30 .30
55 A6 20c brown red .30 .30
56 A6 25c magenta .40 *.55*
57 A6 30c slate .40 *.55*
58 A6 40c blue green .40 *.55*
59 A6 50c black brown .50 *.80*
60 A6 75c purple .50 *1.25*
61 A6 1p brown .75 *1.60*
62 A7 2p brn & black 2.25 *5.00*
a. Head inverted 225.00
63 A7 5p pur & black 2.00 *5.75*
a. Head inverted 60.00
64 A7 10p green & blk 2.00 *5.75*
a. Head inverted 75.00
Nos. 51-64 (14) 10.70 *23.30*

Nos. 62, 64 exist with papermakers watermark.

For overprints see Nos. O12-O22.

Columbus Sighting Honduran Coast — A8

1892, July 31

65 A8 1c slate .40 *.45*
66 A8 2c deep blue .40 *.45*
67 A8 5c yellow green .40 *.45*
68 A8 10c blue green .40 *.45*
69 A8 20c red .40 *.45*
70 A8 25c orange brown .50 *.55*
71 A8 30c ultramarine .50 *.60*
72 A8 40c orange .50 *.90*
73 A8 50c brown .65 *.85*
74 A8 75c lake .75 *1.25*
75 A8 1p purple .75 *1.40*
Nos. 65-75 (11) 5.65 *7.80*

Discovery of America by Christopher Columbus, 400th anniv.

General Trinidad Cabanas — A9

1893, Aug.

76 A9 1c green .25 *1.50*
77 A9 2c scarlet .25 *1.50*
78 A9 5c dark blue .25 *1.50*
79 A9 10c orange brn .25 *1.50*
80 A9 20c brown red .25 *1.50*
81 A9 25c dark blue .30 *1.50*
82 A9 30c red orange .50 *1.50*
83 A9 40c black .50 *1.50*
84 A9 50c olive brn .50 *1.50*
85 A9 75c purple .75 *1.50*
86 A9 1p deep magenta .75 *1.75*
Nos. 76-86 (11) 4.55 *16.75*

"Justice" — A10

1895, Feb. 15

87 A10 1c vermilion .30 .30
88 A10 2c deep blue .30 .30
89 A10 5c slate .35 *.50*
90 A10 10c brown rose .45 *.50*
91 A10 20c violet .45 *.50*
92 A10 30c deep violet .45 *.85*
93 A10 50c olive brown .55 *1.25*
94 A10 1p dark green .60 *1.60*
Nos. 87-94 (8) 3.45 *5.80*

The tablets and numerals of Nos. 76-94 differ for each denomination.

President Celio Arias — A11

1896, Jan. 1 Litho. *Perf. 11½*

95 A11 1c dark blue .30 *.35*
96 A11 2c yellow brn .30 *.35*
97 A11 5c purple 1.10 .30
a. 5c red violet .60 *1.10*
98 A11 10c vermilion .40 .40
a. 10c red 4.50 *4.50*
99 A11 20c emerald .75 .50
a. 20c deep green
100 A11 30c ultramarine .65 *.70*
101 A11 50c rose .90 *1.00*
102 A11 1p black brown 1.25 *1.50*
Nos. 95-102 (8) 5.65 *5.10*

Counterfeits are plentiful. Nos. 95-102 exist imperf. between horiz. or vertically.

Originals of Nos. 95 to 102 are on both thin, semi-transparent paper and opaque paper; reprints are on thicker, opaque paper and usually have a black cancellation "HONDURAS" between horizontal bars.

Railroad Train — A12

1898, Aug. 1

103 A12 1c brown .50 .25
104 A12 2c rose .50 .25
105 A12 5c dull ultra 1.00 .25
b. 5c red violet (error) 1.50 .70
106 A12 6c red violet .90 .25
b. 6c dull rose (error)
107 A12 10c dark blue 1.00 .30
108 A12 20c dull orange 1.25 .75
109 A12 50c orange red 2.00 1.25
110 A12 1p blue green 4.00 3.00
Nos. 103-110 (8) 11.15 6.30

Excellent counterfeits of Nos. 103-110 exist.

For overprints see Nos. O23-O27.

Laid Paper

103a A12 1c 1.00 .70
104a A12 2c 1.25 .70
105a A12 5c 1.60 .70
106a A12 6c 1.60 .75
107a A12 10c 1.60 1.00
Nos. 103a-107a (5) 7.05 3.85

General Santos Guardiola — A13

1903, Jan. 1 Engr. *Perf. 12*

111 A13 1c yellow grn .35 .25
112 A13 2c carmine rose .35 .30
113 A13 5c blue .35 .30
114 A13 6c dk violet .35 .30

115 A13 10c brown .40 .30
116 A13 20c dull ultra .45 .40
117 A13 50c vermilion 1.25 1.10
118 A13 1p orange 1.25 1.10
Nos. 111-118 (8) 4.75 4.05

"PERMITASE" handstamped on stamps of 1896-1903 was applied as a control mark by the isolated Pacific Coast post office of Amapala to prevent use of stolen stamps.

President José Medina — A14

1907, Jan. 1 ***Perf. 14***
119 A14 1c dark green .25 .25
120 A14 2c scarlet .25 .25
120A A14 2c carmine 9.00 5.50
121 A14 5c blue .30 .30
122 A14 6c purple .35 .30
a. 6c dark violet .80 .60
123 A14 10c gray brown .40 .35
124 A14 20c ultra .90 .85
a. 20c blue violet 110.00 110.00
125 A14 50c deep lake 1.10 1.10
126 A14 1p orange 1.50 1.50
a. 1p orange yellow —
Nos. 119-126 (9) 14.05 10.40

All values of the above set exist imperforate, imperforate horizontally and in horizontal pairs, imperforate between. No. 124a imperf is worth only 10% of the listed perforated variety.
For surcharges see Nos. 128-130.

1909 **Typo.** ***Perf. 11½***
127 A14 1c green 1.25 1.00
a. Imperf., pair 4.00 4.00
b. Printed on both sides 7.50 10.00

The 1909 issue is roughly typographed in imitation of the 1907 design. It exists pin perf. 8, 13, etc.

No. 124 Handstamp Surcharged in Black, Green or Red

1910, Nov. ***Perf. 14***
128 A14 1c on 20c ultra 8.50 6.00
129 A14 5c on 20c ultra (G) 8.50 6.00
130 A14 10c on 20c ultra (R) 8.50 6.00
Nos. 128-130 (3) 25.50 18.00

As is usual with handstamped surcharges inverts and double exist.

Honduran Scene — A15

1911, Jan. **Litho.** ***Perf. 14, 12 (1p)***
131 A15 1c violet .35 .25
132 A15 2c green .35 .25
a. Perf. 12 5.00 1.25
133 A15 5c carmine .40 .25
a. Perf. 12 8.00 3.50
134 A15 6c ultramarine .50 .30
135 A15 10c blue .60 .40
136 A15 20c yellow .60 .50
137 A15 50c brown 2.00 1.75
138 A15 1p olive green 2.50 2.00
Nos. 131-138 (8) 7.30 5.70

For overprints and surcharges see Nos. 139, 141-147, O28-O47.

No. 132a Overprinted in Red

1911, Sept. 19 ***Perf. 12***
139 A15 2c green 20.00 18.00
a. Inverted overprint 24.00 22.50

90th anniversary of Independence.
Counterfeit overprints on perf. 14 stamps exist.

President Manuel Bonilla — A16

1912, Feb. 1 **Typo.** ***Perf. 11½***
140 A16 1c orange red 12.00 12.00

Election of Pres. Manuel Bonilla.

Stamps of 1911 Surcharged in Black, Red or Blue

a

b

1913 **Litho.** ***Perf. 14***
141 A15(a) 2c on 1c violet 1.25 .75
a. Double surcharge 3.25
b. Inverted surcharge 4.50
c. Double surch., one invtd. 6.75
d. Red surcharge 40.00 40.00
142 A15(b) 2c on 1c violet 7.00 5.75
a. Inverted surcharge 14.00
143 A15(b) 2c on 10c blue 2.75 2.25
a. Double surcharge 5.75 5.75
b. Inverted surcharge
144 A15(b) 2c on 20c yellow 7.00 6.75
145 A15(b) 5c on 1c violet 2.50 .75
146 A15(b) 5c on 10c bl (Bl) 2.75 1.50
147 A15(b) 6c on 1c violet 2.75 2.25
Nos. 141-147 (7) 26.00 20.00

Counterfeit surcharges exist.

Terencio Sierra — A17

Bonilla — A18

ONE CENTAVO:
Type I — Solid border at sides below numerals.
Type II — Border of light and dark stripes.

1913-14 **Typo.** ***Perf. 11½***
151 A17 1c dark brn, I .25 .25
a. 1c brown, type II .75 .45
152 A17 2c carmine .25 .25
153 A18 5c blue .40 .25
154 A18 5c ultra ('14) .40 .25
155 A18 6c gray vio .50 .25
156 A18 6c purple ('14) .40 .25
a. 6c red lilac .60 .35
157 A17 10c blue .75 .75
158 A17 10c brown ('14) 1.25 .50
159 A17 20c brown 1.00 .75
160 A18 50c rose 2.00 2.00
161 A18 1p gray green 2.25 2.25
Nos. 151-161 (11) 9.45 7.75

For overprints and surcharges see Nos. 162-173, O48-O57.

Surcharged in Black or Carmine

1914
162 A17 1c on 2c carmine .75 .75
163 A17 5c on 2c carmine 1.25 .90
164 A18 5c on 6c gray vio 2.00 2.00
165 A17 10c on 2c carmine 2.00 2.00
166 A18 10c on 6c gray vio 2.00 2.00
a. Double surcharge 10.00
167 A18 10c on 6c gray vio (C) 2.00 2.00
168 A18 10c on 50c rose 6.50 5.00
Nos. 162-168 (7) 16.50 14.65

No. 158 Surcharged

1915
173 A17 5c on 10c brown 2.50 1.75

Ulua Bridge — A19

Bonilla Theater — A20

1915-16 **Typo.**
174 A19 1c chocolate .25 .25
175 A19 2c carmine .25 .25
a. Tête bêche pair 1.00 1.00
176 A20 5c bright blue .25 .25
177 A20 6c deep purple .35 .25
178 A19 10c dull blue .75 .25
179 A19 20c red brown 1.25 1.00
a. Tête bêche pair 4.00 4.00
180 A20 50c red 1.50 1.50
181 A20 1p yellow grn 2.50 2.50
Nos. 174-181 (8) 7.10 6.25

For overprints & surcharges see Nos. 183, 231-232, 237, 239-240, 285, 292, C1-C13, C25, C28, C31, C36, C57, CO21, CO30-CO32, CO42, O58-O65.

Imperf., Pairs

174a	A19	1c	2.00	2.00
175b	A19	2c	2.00	2.00
176a	A20	5c	3.50	
178a	A19	10c	3.50	
179b	A19	20c	5.25	
180b	A20	50c	7.00	
181a	A20	1p	8.75	8.75

Francisco Bertrand — A21

1916, Feb. 1
182 A21 1c orange 2.00 2.00

Election of Pres. Francisco Bertrand.
Unauthorized reprints exist.

Official Stamp No. O60 Overprinted

1918
183 A20 5c bright blue 2.00 1.50
a. Inverted overprint 5.00 5.00

Statue to Francisco Morazán — A22

1919 **Typo.**
184 A22 1c brown .25 .25
a. Printed on both sides 2.00
b. Imperf., pair .70
185 A22 2c carmine .25 .25
186 A22 5c lilac rose .25 .25
187 A22 6c brt purple .25 .25
188 A22 10c dull blue .25 .25
189 A22 15c light blue .75 .25
190 A22 15c dark violet .60 .25
191 A22 20c orange brn 1.00 .30
a. 20c gray brown 10.00 .30
b. Imperf., pair 2.75
192 A22 50c light brown 4.00 2.50
a. Imperf. pair 15.00
193 A22 1p yellow green 7.50 *20.00*
a. Imperf., pair 20.00
b. Printed on both sides 9.00
c. Tête bêche pair 15.00
Nos. 184-193 (10) 15.10 24.55

See note on handstamp following No. 217.
Unauthorized reprints exist.
For overprints and surcharges see Nos. 201-210C, 230, 233, 235-236, 238, 241-243, 287, 289, C58, C61, CO23, CO25, CO33, CO36-CO38, CO39, CO40, O66-O74.

"Dawn of Peace" — A23

1920, Feb. 1 **Size: 27x21mm**
194 A23 2c rose 2.50 2.50
a. Tête bêche pair 15.00 12.50
b. Imperf., pair 15.00 12.50

Size: 51x40mm
195 A23 2c gold 10.00 10.00
196 A23 2c silver 10.00 10.00
197 A23 2c bronze 10.00 10.00
198 A23 2c red 12.00 12.00
Nos. 194-198 (5) 44.50 44.50

Assumption of power by Gen. Rafael Lopez Gutierrez.
Nos. 195-198 exist imperf.
Unauthorized reprints of Nos. 195-198 exist.

Type of 1919, Dated "1920"

1921
201 A22 6c dark violet 10.00 *5.00*
a. Tête bêche pair 15.00
b. Imperf., pair 15.00

Unauthorized reprints exist.

No. 185 Surcharged in Antique Letters

1922
202 A22 6c on 2c carmine .40 .40
a. "ALE" for "VALE" 2.00 2.00
b. Comma after "CTS" 2.00 2.00
c. Without period after "CTS" 2.00 2.00
d. "CT" for "CTS" 2.00 2.00
e. Double surcharge 4.25
f. Inverted surcharge 4.25

Stamps of 1919 Surcharged in Roman Figures and Antique Letters in Green

1923
203 A22 10c on 1c brown 1.50 1.50
204 A22 50c on 2c carmine 2.00 2.00
a. Inverted surcharge 10.00 10.00
b. "HABILTADO" 6.00 6.00

Surcharged in Black or Violet Blue

205 A22 1p on 5c lil rose (Bk) 3.50 3.50
a. "PSEO" 20.00 20.00
b. Inverted surcharge 20.00 20.00
206 A22 1p on 5c lil rose (VB) 20.00 20.00
a. "PSEO" 70.00

On Nos. 205-206, "Habilitado Vale" is in Antique letters, "Un Peso" in Roman.

No. 185 Surcharged in Roman Letters in Green

207 A22 6c on 2c carmine 3.50 2.75

Nos. 184-185 Surcharged in Roman Letters in Green

208 A22 10c on 1c brown 1.75 1.25
a. "DIES" 6.00
b. "DEIZ" 6.00
c. "DEIZ CAS" 6.00
d. "TTS" for "CTS" 6.00
e. "HABILTADO" 6.00
f. "HABILITAD" 6.00
g. "HABILITA" 6.00
h. Inverted surcharge 30.00
209 A22 50c on 2c carmine 3.75 2.75
a. "CAT" for "CTA" 10.00
b. "TCA" for "CTA" 10.00
c. "TTS" for "CTS" 10.00
d. "CAS" for "CTS" 10.00
e. "HABILTADO" 10.00

Surcharge on No. 209 is found in two spacings between value and HABILITADO: 5mm (illustrated) and 1½mm.

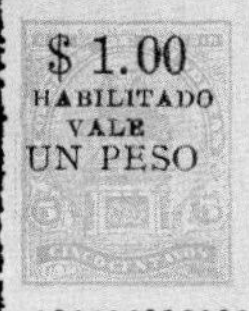

No. 186 Surcharged in Antique Letters in Black

210 A22 1p on 5c lil rose 25.00 *25.00*
a. "PFSO" 75.00

In the surcharges on Nos. 202 to 210 there are various wrong font, inverted and omitted letters.

No. 184 Surcharged in Large Antique Letters in Green

210C A22 10c on 1c brown 15.00 15.00
d. "DIFZ" 55.00 55.00

Dionisio de Herrera — A24

1924, June Litho. *Perf. 11, 11½*
211 A24 1c olive green .30 .25
212 A24 2c deep rose .35 .25
213 A24 6c red violet .40 .25
214 A24 10c blue .40 .25
215 A24 20c yellow brn .80 .35
216 A24 50c vermilion 1.75 1.10
217 A24 1p emerald 4.00 2.75
Nos. 211-217 (7) 8.00 5.20

In 1924 a facsimile of the signatures of Santiago Herrera and Francisco Caceres, covering four stamps, was handstamped in violet to prevent the use of stamps that had been stolen during a revolution.

Imperfs exist.

For overprints and surcharges see Nos. 280-281, 290-291, C14-C24, C26-C27, C29-C30, C32-C35, C56, C60, C73-C76, CO1-CO5, CO22, CO24, CO28-CO29, CO34-CO35, CO38A, CO39A, CO41, CO43, O75-O81.

Pres. Miguel Paz Baraona — A25

1925, Feb. 1 Typo. *Perf. 11½*
218 A25 1c dull blue 2.00 2.00
a. 1c dark blue 2.00 2.00
219 A25 1c car rose 5.00 5.00
a. 1c brown carmine 5.00 5.00
220 A25 1c olive brn 14.00 14.00
a. 1c orange brown 14.00 14.00
b. 1c dark brown 14.00 14.00
c. 1c black brown 14.00 14.00
221 A25 1c buff 12.00 12.00
222 A25 1c red 60.00 60.00
223 A25 1c green 40.00 40.00
Nos. 218-223 (6) 133.00 133.00

Imperf
225 A25 1c dull blue 5.50 5.50
a. 1c dark blue 5.50 5.50
226 A25 1c car rose 8.75 8.75
a. 1c brown carmine 8.75 8.75
227 A25 1c olive brn 8.75 8.75
a. 1c orange brown 8.75 8.75
b. 1c deep brown 8.75 8.75
c. 1c black brown 8.75 8.75
228 A25 1c buff 8.75 8.75
229 A25 1c red 60.00 60.00
229A A25 1c green 27.50 27.50
Nos. 225-229A (6) 119.25 119.25

Inauguration of President Baraona. Counterfeits and unauthorized reprints exist.

No. 187 Overprinted in Black and Red

1926, June *Perf. 11½*
230 A22 6c brt purple 1.50 1.25

Many varieties of this two-part overprint exist: one or both inverted or double, and various combinations. Value, each $10.

Nos. 177 and 187 Overprinted in Black or Red

1926
231 A20 6c deep pur (Bk) 2.00 2.00
a. Inverted overprint 5.50 5.50
b. Double overprint 5.50 5.50
232 A20 6c deep pur (R) 2.50 2.50
a. Double overprint 5.00 5.00
233 A22 6c lilac (Bk) .60 .60
a. 6c violet .75 .75
b. Inverted overprint 5.00 5.00
c. Double overprint 5.00 5.00
d. Double ovpt., one inverted 5.00 5.00
e. "192" 7.50 7.50
f. Double ovpt., both inverted 7.50 7.50

No. 230 Overprinted

235 A22 6c violet 20.00 20.00
a. "1926" inverted 20.00 20.00
b. "Habilitado" triple, one invtd. 20.00 20.00

No. 188 Surcharged in Red or Black

236 A22 6c on 10c blue (R) .50 .25
c. Double surcharge 5.00 4.00
d. Without bar
e. Inverted surcharge 4.00 3.50
f. "Vale" omitted
g. "6cts" omitted
h. "cts" omitted
k. Black surcharge *55.00 55.00*

Nos. 175 and 185 Overprinted in Green

237 A19 2c carmine .25 .25
a. Tête bêche pair 4.00 4.00
b. Double overprint 2.00 1.40
c. "HARILITADO" 2.00 1.40
d. "1926" only 2.75 2.75
e. Double overprint, one inverted 2.75 2.75
f. "1926" omitted 3.50 3.50
g. Triple overprint, two inverted 5.25 5.25
h. Double on face, one on back 5.25 5.25
238 A22 2c carmine .25 .25
a. "HARILITADO" .90 .90
b. Double overprint 1.40 1.40
c. Inverted overprint 2.00 2.00

No. 177 Overprinted in Red

1927 Large Numerals, 12x5mm
239 A20 6c deep purple 25.00 25.00
a. "1926" over "1927" 35.00 35.00
b. Invtd. ovpt. on face of stamp, normal ovpt. on back 30.00

No. 179 Surcharged

1927
240 A19 6c on 20c brown .75 .75
a. Tête bêche pair 2.75 2.75
c. Interted surcharge 2.50 2.50
d. Double surcharge 8.50 8.50

Nos. 8 and 10 in the setting have no period after "cts" and No. 50 has the "t" of "cts" inverted.

Nos. 189-191 Surcharged

241 A22 6c on 15c blue 27.50 27.50
a. "c" of "cts" omitted
242 A22 6c on 15c vio .70 .70
a. Double surcharge 1.75 1.75
b. Double surch., one invtd. 2.00 2.00
c. "L" of "Vale" omitted
243 A22 6c on 20c yel brn .60 .60
a. 6c on 20c deep brown
b. "6" omitted 1.75 1.75
c. "Vale" and "cts" omitted 3.50 3.50
Nos. 240-243 (4) 29.55 29.55

On Nos. 242 and 243 stamps Nos. 12, 16 and 43 in the setting have no period after "cts" and No. 34 often lacks the "s." On No. 243 the "c" of "cts" is missing on stamp No. 38. On No. 241 occur the varieties "ct" or "ts" for "cts." and no period.

Southern Highway — A26

Ruins of Copán — A27

Pine Tree — A28

Presidential Palace — A29

Ponciano Leiva — A30

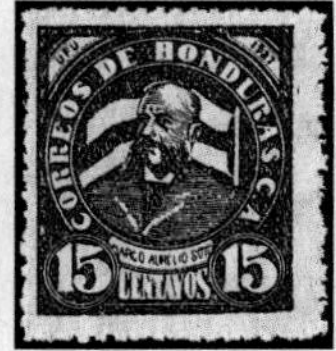

Pres. M.A. Soto — A31

Lempira — A32

Map of Honduras — A33

President Juan Lindo — A34

Statue of Columbus — A35

1927-29 Typo. Wmk. 209
244 A26 1c ultramarine .30 .25
a. 1c blue .30 .25
245 A27 2c carmine .30 .25
246 A28 5c dull violet .30 .25
247 A28 5c bl gray ('29) 25.00 7.00
248 A29 6c blue black .75 .50
a. 6c gray black .75 .50
249 A29 6c dark bl ('29) .40 .25
a. 6c light blue .40 .25
250 A30 10c blue .70 .25
251 A31 15c deep blue 1.00 .50
252 A32 20c dark blue 1.25 .60
253 A33 30c dark brown 1.50 1.00
254 A34 50c light blue 2.50 1.50
255 A35 1p red 5.00 2.50
Nos. 244-255 (12) 39.00 14.85

In 1929 a quantity of imperforate sheets of No. 249 were stolen from the Litografia Nacional. Some of them were perforated by sewing machine and a few copies were passed through the post. To prevent the use of stolen stamps of the 1927-29 issues they were declared invalid and the stock on hand was overprinted "1929 a 1930."

For overprints and surcharges see Nos. 259-278, CO19-CO20B.

Pres. Vicente Mejia Colindres and Vice-Pres. Rafael Diaz Chávez — A36

President Mejia Colindres — A37

1929, Feb. 25

256 A36 1c dk carmine 3.00 3.00
257 A37 2c emerald 3.00 3.00

Installation of Pres. Vicente Mejia Colindres. Printed in sheets of ten.

Nos. 256 and 257 were surreptitiously printed in transposed colors. They were not regularly issued.

Stamps of 1927-29 Overprinted in Various Colors

1929, Oct.

259 A26 1c blue (R) .25 .25
a. 1c ultramarine (R) .50 .25
b. Double overprint 2.50 1.75
c. As "a", double overprint 2.50 1.75
260 A26 1c blue (Bk) 6.50 6.50
a. 1c ultramarine (Bk)
261 A27 2c car (R Br) 3.50 3.50
a. Double overprint
262 A27 2c car (Bl Gr) 1.00 1.00
a. Double overprint
263 A27 2c car (Bk) 1.00 .50
264 A27 2c car (V) .50 .25
a. Double overprint
b. Double ovpt., one inverted
265 A27 2c org red (V) 1.50
266 A28 5c dl vio (R) .40 .30
a. Double overprint (R+V)
267 A28 5c bl gray (R) 1.00 .75
a. Double overprint (R+Bk)
269 A29 6c gray blk (R) 2.50 2.00
a. Double overprint 6.00 6.00
272 A29 6c dk blue (R) .40 .25
a. 6c light blue (R) .40 .25
b. Double overprint 2.00 2.00
c. Double overprint (R+V)
273 A30 10c blue (R) .40 .25
a. Double overprint 2.50 1.75
274 A31 15c dp blue (R) .50 .25
a. Double overprint 3.50 2.50
275 A32 20c dark bl (R) .50 .35
276 A33 30c dark brn (R) .75 .60
a. Double overprint 3.50 2.50
277 A34 50c light bl (R) 2.00 1.00
278 A35 1p red (V) 5.00 2.50
Nos. 259-278 (17) 27.70 20.25

Nos. 259-278 exist in numerous shades. There are also various shades of the red and violet overprints. The overprint may be found reading upwards, downwards, inverted, double, triple, tête bêche or combinations.

Status of both 6c stamps with overprint in black is questioned.

A38

1929, Dec. 10

279 A38 1c on 6c lilac rose .70 .70
a. "1992" for "1929"
b. "9192" for "1929"
c. Surcharge reading down 8.00
d. Dbl. surch., one reading down

Varieties include "1992" reading down and pairs with one surcharge reading down, double or with "1992."

No. 214 Surcharged in Red

Perf. 11, 11½

1930, Mar. 26 **Unwmk.**

280 A24 1c on 10c blue .35 .30
a. "1093" for "1930" 1.40
b. "tsc" for "cts" 1.40
281 A24 2c on 10c blue .35 .30
a. "tsc" for "cts" 2.00
b. "Vale 2" omitted

Official Stamps of 1929 Overprinted in Red or Violet

1930, Mar. **Wmk. 209** ***Perf. 11½***

282 O1 1c blue (R) .50 .50
a. Double overprint 2.00 2.00
284 O1 2c carmine (V) .90 .90

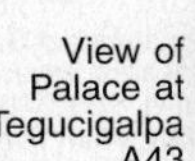

Stamps of 1915-26 Overprinted in Blue

On No. 174

1930, July 19 **Unwmk.**

285 A19 1c chocolate .30 .25
a. Double overprint 1.00 1.00
b. Inverted overprint 1.40 1.40
c. Dbl. ovpt., one inverted 1.40 1.40

On No. 184

287 A22 1c brown 15.00 15.00
a. Double overprint
c. Inverted overprint

On No. 204

289 A22 50c on 2c carmine 100.00 90.00
b. Inverted surcharge

On Nos. 211 and 212

290 A24 1c olive green .25 .25
a. Double overprint 1.75 1.75
b. Inverted overprint 1.75 1.75
d. On No. O75 12.00
291 A24 2c carmine rose .25 .25
a. Double overprint 1.75 1.75
b. Inverted overprint 1.75 1.75

On No. 237

292 A19 2c car (G & Bl) 100.00 100.00

From Title Page of Government Gazette, First Issue — A39

1930, Aug. 11 **Typo.** **Wmk. 209**

295 A39 2c orange 2.00 2.00
296 A39 2c ultramarine 2.00 2.00
297 A39 2c red 2.00 2.00
Nos. 295-297 (3) 6.00 6.00

Publication of the 1st newspaper in Honduras, cent. The stamps were on sale and available for postage on Aug. 11th, 1930, only. Not more than 5 examples of each color could be purchased by an applicant.

Nos. 295-297 exist imperf. and part-perforate. Unauthorized reprints exist.

For surcharges see Nos. CO15-CO18A.

Paz Baraona — A40

Manuel Bonilla — A41

Lake Yojoa — A42

View of Palace at Tegucigalpa A43

City of Amapala A44

Mayan Stele at Copán A45

Christopher Columbus A46

Discovery of America A47

Loarque Bridge A48

Unwmk.

1931, Jan. 2 **Engr.** ***Perf. 12***

298 A40 1c black brown .75 .25
299 A41 2c carmine rose .75 .25
300 A42 5c dull violet 1.00 .25
301 A43 6c deep green 1.00 .25
302 A44 10c brown 1.50 .25
303 A45 15c dark blue 2.00 .30
304 A46 20c black 3.50 .40
305 A47 50c olive green 4.50 1.50
306 A48 1p slate black 9.00 2.50
Nos. 298-306 (9) 24.00 5.95

Regular Issue of 1931 Overprinted in Black or Various Colors

1931

307 A40 1c black brown .40 .30
308 A41 2c carmine rose .60 .30
309 A45 15c dark blue 1.00 .30
310 A46 20c black 2.50 .40

Overprinted

311 A42 5c dull violet .50 .30
312 A43 6c deep green .50 .30
315 A44 10c brown 1.50 .35
316 A47 50c olive green 8.00 5.00
317 A48 1p slate black 10.00 7.50
Nos. 307-317 (9) 25.00 14.75
Nos. 307-317,C51-C55 (14) 50.00 35.75

The overprint is a control mark. It stands for "Tribunal Superior de Cuentas" (Superior Tribunal of Accounts).

Overprint varieties include: inverted; double; double, one or both inverted; on back; pair, one without overprint; differing colors (6c exists with overprint in orange, yellow and red).

President Carías and Vice-President Williams — A49

1933, Apr. 29

318 A49 2c carmine rose .50 .35
319 A49 6c deep green .75 .40
320 A49 10c deep blue 1.00 .50
321 A49 15c red orange 1.25 .75
Nos. 318-321 (4) 3.50 2.00

Inauguration of Pres. Tiburcio Carias Andino and Vice-Pres. Abraham Williams, Feb. 1, 1933.

Columbus' Fleet and Flag of the Race — A50

Wmk. 209

1933, Aug. 3 **Typo.** ***Perf. 11½***

322 A50 2c ultramarine 1.00 .65
323 A50 6c yellow 1.00 .65
324 A50 10c lemon 1.40 .85

Perf. 12

325 A50 15c violet 2.00 1.50
326 A50 50c red 4.00 3.50
327 A50 1 l emerald 7.00 7.00
Nos. 322-327 (6) 16.40 14.15

"Day of the Race," an annual holiday throughout Spanish-American countries. Also for the 441st anniv. of the sailing of Columbus to the New World, Aug. 3, 1492.

Masonic Temple, Tegucigalpa — A51

Designs: 2c, President Carias. 5c, Flag. 6c, Tomás Estrada Palma.

Unwmk.

1935, Jan. 12 **Engr.** ***Perf. 12***

328 A51 1c green .40 .25
329 A51 2c carmine .40 .25
330 A51 5c dark blue .40 .25
331 A51 6c black brown .40 .25
a. Vert. pair, imperf. btwn. 20.00 20.00
Nos. 328-331 (4) 1.60 1.00
Nos. 328-331,C77-C83 (11) 15.20 6.60

Gen. Carías Bridge — A55

1937, June 4

332 A55 6c car & ol green .90 .40
333 A55 21c grn & violet 1.50 .65
334 A55 46c orange & brn 2.10 1.50
335 A55 55c ultra & black 3.00 2.40
Nos. 332-335 (4) 7.50 4.95

Prolongation of the Presidential term to Jan. 19, 1943.

Seal of Honduras A56

Central District Palace — A57

Designs: 3c, Map of Honduras. 5c, Bridge of Choluteca. 8c, Flag.

1939, Mar. 1 ***Perf. 12½***

No.	Description	Unused	Used
336	A56 1c orange yellow	.25	.25
337	A57 2c red orange	.25	.25
338	A57 3c carmine	.30	.25
339	A57 5c orange	.30	.25
340	A56 8c dark blue	.50	.25
	Nos. 336-340 (5)	1.60	1.25
	Nos. 336-340,C89-C98 (15)	15.45	8.90

Nos. 336-340 exist imperf.
For overprints see Nos. 342-343.

AIR POST STAMPS

Regular Issue of 1915-16 Overprinted in Black, Blue or Red

1925 **Unwmk.** ***Perf. 11½***

No.	Description	Unused	Used
C1	A20 5c lt blue (Bk)	87.50	87.50
C2	A20 5c lt blue (Bl)	300.00	300.00
a.	Inverted overprint	*400.00*	
b.	Vertical overprint	*600.00*	
c.	Double overprint	*800.00*	
C3	A20 5c lt blue (R)	*7,250.*	

Value for No. C3 is for an example without gum.

No.	Description	Unused	Used
C4	A19 10c dk blue (R)	175.00	
a.	Inverted overprint	325.00	
b.	Overprint tête bêche, pair	*800.00*	
C5	A19 10c dk blue (Bk)	*1,100.*	
C6	A19 20c red brn (Bk)	175.00	175.00
a.	Inverted overprint	250.00	
b.	Tête bêche pair	400.00	
c.	Overprint tête bêche, pair	*725.00*	
d.	"AFRO"	*1,400.*	
e.	Double overprint	*600.00*	
C7	A19 20c red brn (Bl)	175.00	175.00
a.	Inverted overprint	*700.00*	
b.	Tête bêche pair	*1,000*	
c.	Vertical overprint	900.00	
C8	A20 50c red (Bk)	450.00	300.00
a.	Inverted overprint	*550.00*	
b.	Overprint tête bêche, pair	*900.00*	
C9	A20 1p yel grn (Bk)	600.00	600.00

Surcharged in Black or Blue

No.	Description	Unused	Used
C10	A19 25c on 1c choc	125.00	125.00
a.	Inverted surcharge	700.00	
C11	A20 25c on 5c lt bl (Bl)	225.00	225.00
a.	Inverted surcharge	700.00	
b.	Double inverted surcharge	*675.00*	
C12	A19 25c on 10c dk bl	*125,000.*	
C13	A19 25c on 20c brn (Bl)	200.00	200.00
a.	Inverted surcharge	325.00	
b.	Tête bêche pair	450.00	

Counterfeits of Nos. C1-C13 are plentiful.

Monoplane and Lisandro Garay AP1

1929, June 5 **Engr.** ***Perf. 12***

No.	Description	Unused	Used
C13C	AP1 50c carmine	2.25	1.75

No. 216 Surcharged in Blue

1929 ***Perf. 11, 11½***

No.	Description	Unused	Used
C14	A24 25c on 50c ver	5.00	3.50

In the surcharges on Nos. C14 to C40 there are various wrong font and defective letters and numerals, also periods omitted.

Nos. 215-217 Surcharged in Green, Black or Red

1929, Oct.

No.	Description	Unused	Used
C15	A24 5c on 20c yel brn (G)	1.40	1.40
a.	Double surcharge (R+G)	45.00	
C16	A24 10c on 50c ver (Bk)	2.25	1.90
C17	A24 15c on 1p emer (R)	3.50	3.50
	Nos. C15-C17 (3)	7.15	6.80

Nos. 214 and 216 Surcharged Vertically in Red or Black

a

b

1929, Dec. 10

No.	Description	Unused	Used
C18	A24(a) 5c on 10c bl (R)	.60	.60
C19	A24(b) 20c on 50c ver	1.00	1.00
a.	"1299" for "1929"	190.00	
b.	"cts. cts." for "cts. oro."	190.00	
c.	"r" of "Aereo" omitted	2.00	
d.	Horiz. pair, imperf. btwn.	20.00	

Nos. 214, 215 and 180 Surcharged in Various Colors

1930, Feb.

No.	Description	Unused	Used
C20	A24 5c on 10c (R)	.50	.50
a.	"1930" reading down	3.50	
b.	"1903" for "1930"	3.50	
c.	Surcharge reading down	10.00	
d.	Double surcharge	14.00	
e.	Dbl. surch., one downward	14.00	
C21	A24 5c on 10c (Y)	*450.00*	*450.00*
C22	A24 5c on 20c (Bl)	125.00	125.00
C23	A24 10c on 20c (Bk)	.75	.75
a.	"0" for "10"	3.50	
b.	Double surcharge	8.75	
c.	Dbl. surch., one downward	12.00	
d.	Horiz. pair, imperf. btwn.	70.00	
C24	A24 10c on 20c (V)	*750.00*	*750.00*
a.	"0" for "10"	*1,600.*	
C25	A20 25c on 50c (Bk)	.95	.95
a.	"Internaoicnal"	3.50	
b.	"o" for "oro"	3.50	
c.	Inverted surcharge	17.50	
d.	As "a," invtd. surch.	*175.00*	
e.	As "b," invtd. surch.	*175.00*	

Surcharge on Nos. C20-C24 are vertical.

Nos. 214, 215 and 180 Surcharged

1930, Apr. 1

No.	Description	Unused	Used
C26	A24 5c on 10c blue	.50	.50
a.	Double surcharge	9.50	
b.	"Servicioa"	3.50	
C27	A24 15c on 20c yel brn	.55	.55
a.	Double surcharge	7.00	
C28	A20 20c on 50c red, surch. reading down	.95	.95
a.	Surcharge reading up	7.00	
	Nos. C26-C28 (3)	2.00	2.00

Nos. C22 and C23 Surcharged Vertically in Red

1930

No.	Description	Unused	Used
C29	A24 10c on 5c on 20c (Bl+R)	.90	.90
a.	"1930" reading down	9.00	9.00
b.	"1903" for "1930"	9.00	9.00
c.	Red surcharge, reading down	14.00	
C30	A24 10c on 10c on 20c (Bk+R)	87.50	87.50
a.	"0" for "10"	190.00	

No. 181 Surcharged as No. C25 and Resurcharged

No.	Description	Unused	Used
C31	A20 50c on 25c on 1p grn	4.25	4.25
a.	"Internaoicnal"	7.00	
b.	"o" for "oro"	7.00	
c.	25c surcharge inverted	17.50	17.50
d.	50c surcharge inverted	17.50	17.50
e.	As "a" and "c"		
f.	As "a" and "d"		
g.	As "b" and "c"		
h.	As "b" and "d"		
	Nos. C29-C31 (3)	92.65	92.65

No. 215 Surcharged in Dark Blue

1930, May 22

No.	Description	Unused	Used
C32	A24 5c on 20c yel brn	1.25	1.00
a.	Double surcharge	5.25	5.25
b.	Horiz. pair, imperf. btwn.	60.00	60.00
c.	Vertical pair, imperf. between	20.00	20.00

Nos. O78-O80 Surcharged in Various Colors

1930

No.	Description	Unused	Used
C33	A24 5c on 10c (R)	450.00	350.00
a.	"1930" reading down	*1,500.*	
b.	"1903" for "1930"	*1,500.*	
C34	A24 5c on 20c (Bl)	400.00	400.00
C35	A24 25c on 50c (Bk)	225.00	225.00
a.	55c on 50c vermilion	325.00	325.00

No. C35 exists with inverted surcharge.

No. O64 Surcharged like No. C28

No.	Description	Unused	Used
C36	A20 20c on 50c red, surcharge reading down	*350.00*	*350.00*
a.	Surcharge reading up	*350.00*	*350.00*
b.	Dbl. surch., reading down	*350.00*	*350.00*
c.	Dbl. surch., reading up	*350.00*	*350.00*

No. O87 Overprinted

1930, Feb. 21 **Wmk. 209** ***Perf. 11½***

No.	Description	Unused	Used
C37	O1 50c yel, grn & blue	1.40	1.25
a.	"Internacional"	5.25	
b.	"luternacional"	5.25	
c.	Double overprint	5.25	

Nos. O86-O88 Overprinted in Various Colors

1930, May 23

No.	Description	Unused	Used
C38	O1 20c dark blue (R)	1.10	.85
a.	Double overprint	8.75	
b.	Triple overprint	12.00	
C39	O1 50c org, grn & bl (Bk)	1.10	.90
C40	O1 1p buff (Bl)	1.40	1.25
a.	Double overprint	10.50	
	Nos. C38-C40 (3)	3.60	3.00

National Palace AP3

Unwmk.

1930, Oct. 1 **Engr.** ***Perf. 12***

No.	Description	Unused	Used
C41	AP3 5c yel orange	.50	.30
C42	AP3 10c carmine	.75	.60
C43	AP3 15c green	1.00	.75
C44	AP3 20c dull violet	1.25	.60
C45	AP3 1p light brown	4.00	4.00
	Nos. C41-C45 (5)	7.50	6.25

Overprinted in Various Colors

1931 ***Perf. 12***

No.	Description	Unused	Used
C51	AP3 5c yel orange (R)	*2.00*	*1.50*
C52	AP3 10c carmine (Bk)	*3.00*	*2.50*
C53	AP3 15c green (Br)	*5.00*	*4.00*
C54	AP3 20c dull vio (O)	*5.00*	*4.25*
C55	AP3 1p lt brown (G)	*10.00*	*8.75*
	Nos. C51-C55 (5)	*25.00*	*21.00*

See note after No. 317.

Stamps of Various Issues Surcharged in Blue or Black (#C59)

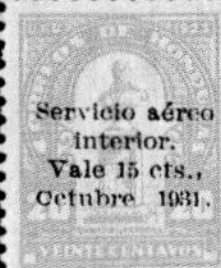

1931, Oct. **On No. 215** ***Perf. 11½***

No.	Description	Unused	Used
C56	A24 15c on 20c yel brn	3.50	2.75
a.	Horiz. pair, imperf. btwn.	42.50	
b.	Green surcharge	20.00	20.00

On No. O64

No.	Description	Unused	Used
C57	A20 15c on 50c red	4.25	3.50
a.	Inverted surcharge	10.50	10.50

On No. O72

No.	Description	Unused	Used
C58	A22 15c on 20c brn	4.25	4.25
a.	Vert. pair, imperf. between	12.00	

On Nos. C57 and C58 the word "OFICIAL" is canceled by two bars.

On No. O88

Wmk. 209

No.	Description	Unused	Used
C59	O1 15c on 1p buff	4.25	4.25
a.	Vert. pair, imperf. horiz.	25.00	
b.	"Sevricio"	14.00	14.00

The varieties "Vaie" for "Vale," "aereo" with circumflex accent on the first "e" and "Interior" with initial capital "I" are found on Nos. C56, C58-C59. No. C57 is known with initial capital in "Interior."

A similar surcharge, in slightly larger letters and with many minor varieties, exists on Nos. 215, O63, O64 and O73. The authenticity of this surcharge is questioned.

Nos. 215, O73, O87-O88 Surcharged in Green, Red or Black

1931, Nov. **Unwmk.**

No.	Description	Unused	Used
C60	A24 15c on 20c (G)	3.50	2.75
a.	Inverted surcharge	6.25	
b.	"XI" omitted	6.25	
c.	"X" for "XI"	6.25	
d.	"PI" for "XI"	6.25	
C61	A22 15c on 50c (R)	3.50	2.75
a.	"XI" omitted	6.75	
b.	"PI" for "XI"	6.75	
c.	Double surcharge	20.00	20.00

On No. C61 the word "OFICIAL" is not barred out.

Wmk. 209

No.	Description	Unused	Used
C62	O1 15c on 50c (Bk)	2.75	2.50
a.	"1391" for "1931"	10.50	10.50
b.	Double surcharge	8.75	8.75
C63	O1 15c on 1p (Bk)	2.50	2.25
a.	"1391" for "1931"	12.50	
b.	Surcharged on both sides	7.00	

Nos. O76-O78 Surcharged in Black or Red

1932 Unwmk. *Perf. 11, 11½*

C73 A24 15c on 2c .80 .80
- *a.* Double surcharge 5.50
- *b.* Inverted surcharge 4.25
- *c.* "Ae" of "Aero" omitted 1.00
- *d.* On No. 212 (no "Official")

C74 A24 15c on 6c .80 .80
- *a.* Double surcharge 3.50
- *b.* Horiz. pair, imperf. btwn. 17.50
- *c.* "Aer" omitted
- *d.* "A" omitted 1.00
- *e.* Inverted surcharge 3.50

C75 A24 15c on 10c (R) .80 .80
- *a.* Double surcharge 5.50
- *b.* Inverted surcharge 3.50
- *c.* "r" of "Aereo" omitted 1.00

Same Surcharge on No. 214 in Red

C76 A24 15c on 10c dp bl *150.00 100.00*

There are various broken and missing letters in the setting.

A similar surcharge with slightly larger letters exists.

Post Office and National Palace AP4

View of Tegucigalpa — AP5

Designs: 15c, Map of Honduras. 20c, Mayol Bridge. 40c, View of Tegucigalpa. 50c, Owl. 1 l, Coat of Arms.

1935, Jan. 10 *Perf. 12*

C77 AP4 8c blue .25 .25
C78 AP5 10c gray .25 .25
C79 AP5 15c olive gray .40 .25
C80 AP5 20c dull green .50 .25
C81 AP5 40c brown .70 .25
C82 AP4 50c yellow 8.25 1.60
C83 AP4 1 l green 3.25 2.75
Nos. C77-C83 (7) 13.55 5.35

Flags of US and Honduras — AP11

Engr. & Litho.

1937, Sept. 17 Unwmk.

C84 AP11 46c multicolored 2.75 1.40

US Constitution, 150th anniv.

Comayagua Cathedral AP12

Founding of Comayagua AP13

Alonzo Cáceres and Pres. Carías — AP14

Lintel of Royal Palace AP15

1937, Dec. 7 Engr.

C85 AP12 2c copper red .25 .25
C86 AP13 8c dark blue .35 .25
C87 AP14 15c slate black .70 .70
C88 AP15 50c dark brown 4.25 2.75
Nos. C85-C88 (4) 5.55 3.95

City of Comayagua founding, 400th anniv.

For surcharges see Nos. C144-C146 in Scott Standard catalogue, Vol. 3.

Mayan Stele at Copán AP16

Mayan Temple, Copán AP17

Designs: 15c, President Carias. 30c, José C. de Valle. 40c, Presidential House. 46c, Lempira. 55c, Church of Our Lady of Suyapa. 66c, J. T. Reyes. 1 l, Hospital at Choluteca. 2 l, Ramón Rosa.

1939, Mar. 1 *Perf. 12½*

C89 AP16 10c orange brn .25 .25
C90 AP16 15c grnsh blue .30 .25
C91 AP17 21c gray .50 .25
C92 AP16 30c dk blue grn .55 .25
C93 AP17 40c dull violet 1.00 .25
C94 AP16 46c dk gray brn 1.00 .65
C95 AP16 55c green 1.25 1.00
- *a.* Imperf., pair 22.50

C96 AP16 66c black 1.75 1.25
C97 AP16 1 l olive grn 3.00 1.00
C98 AP16 2 l henna red 4.25 2.50
Nos. C89-C98 (10) 13.80 7.45

For surcharges see Nos. C118-C119, C147-C152 in Scott Standard catalogue, Vol. 3.

Souvenir Sheets

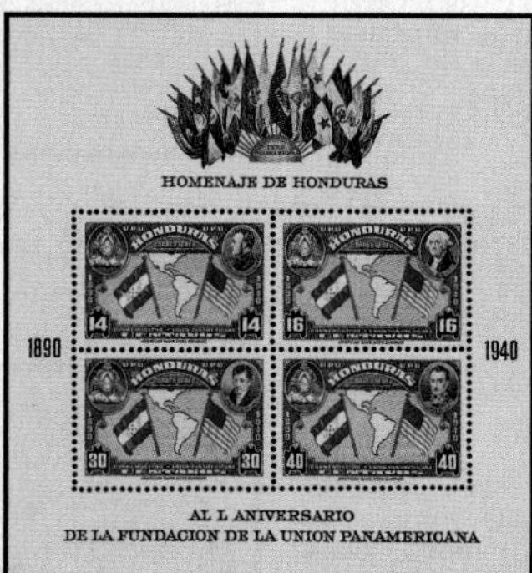

AP26

14c, Francisco Morazan. 16c, George Washington. 30c, J. C. de Valle. 40c, Simon Bolivar.

1940, Apr. 13 Engr. *Perf. 12*

Centers of Stamps Lithographed

C99 AP26 Sheet of 4 10.00 10.00
- *a.* 14c black, yellow, ultra & rose 1.40 1.40
- *b.* 16c black, yellow, ultra & rose 1.75 1.75
- *c.* 30c black, yellow, ultra & rose 2.40 2.40
- *d.* 40c black, yellow, ultra & rose 2.75 2.75

Imperf

C100 AP26 Sheet of 4 16.00 16.00
- *a.* 14c black, yellow, ultra & rose 2.25 2.25
- *b.* 16c black, yellow, ultra & rose 2.75 2.75
- *c.* 30c black, yellow, ultra & rose 4.00 4.00
- *d.* 40c black, yellow, ultra & rose 4.50 4.50

Pan American Union, 50th anniv.

For overprints see Nos. C153-C154, C187 in Scott Standard catalogue, Vol. 3.

Air Post Official Stamps of 1939 Overprinted in Red

1940, Oct. 12 *Perf. 12½*

C101 OA2 2c dp bl & green .25 .25
C102 OA2 5c dp blue & org .25 .25
C103 OA2 8c deep bl & brn .30 .30
C104 OA2 15c dp blue & car .50 .50
C105 OA2 46c dp bl & ol grn .80 .80
C106 OA2 50c dp bl & vio .90 .90
C107 OA2 1 l dp bl & red brn 3.75 3.75
C108 OA2 2 l dp bl & red org 7.50 7.50
Nos. C101-C108 (8) 14.25 14.25

Erection and dedication of the Columbus Memorial Lighthouse.

AIR POST SEMI-POSTAL STAMPS

No. C13C Surcharged in Black

Unwmk.

1929, June 5 Engr. *Perf. 12*

CB1 AP1 50c + 5c carmine .65 .30
CB2 AP1 50c + 10c carmine .70 .35
CB3 AP1 50c + 15c carmine .95 .55
CB4 AP1 50c + 20c carmine 1.40 .75
Nos. CB1-CB4 (4) 3.70 1.95

AIR POST OFFICIAL STAMPS

Official Stamps Nos. O78 to O81 Overprinted in Red, Green or Black

1930 *Perf. 11, 11½*

CO1 A24 10c deep blue (R) 1.25 1.25
CO2 A24 20c yellow brown 1.25 1.25
- *a.* Vert. pair, imperf. btwn. 14.00

CO3 A24 50c vermilion (Bk) 1.40 1.40
CO4 A24 1p emerald (R) 1.25 1.25
Nos. CO1-CO4 (4) 5.15 5.15

OA1

Green Surcharge

CO5 OA1 5c on 6c red vio 1.00 1.00
- *a.* "1910" for "1930" 2.75 2.75
- *b.* "1920" for "1930" 2.75 2.75

The overprint exists in other colors and on other denominations but the status of these is questioned.

Official Stamps of 1931 Overprinted

1931 Unwmk. *Perf. 12*

CO6 O2 1c ultra .35 .35
CO7 O2 2c black brown .85 .85
CO8 O2 5c olive gray 1.00 1.00
CO9 O2 6c orange red 1.00 1.00
- *a.* Inverted overprint 24.00 24.00

CO10 O2 10c dark green 1.25 1.25
CO11 O2 15c olive brown 2.00 1.75
- *a.* Inverted overprint 20.00 20.00

CO12 O2 20c red brown 2.00 1.75
CO13 O2 50c gray violet 1.40 1.40
CO14 O2 1p deep orange 2.00 1.75
Nos. CO6-CO14 (9) 11.85 11.10

In the setting of the overprint there are numerous errors in the spelling and punctuation, letters omitted and similar varieties.

This set is known with blue overprint. A similar overprint is known in larger type, but its status has not been fully determined.

Postage Stamps of 1918-30 Surcharged Type "a" or Type "b" (#CO22-CO23) in Green, Black, Red and Blue

a

b

1933 Wmk. 209, Unwmk.

CO15 A39 20c on 2c #295 (G) 3.25 3.25
CO16 A39 20c on 2c #296 (G) 3.25 3.25
CO17 A39 20c on 2c #297 (G) 3.25 3.25
CO17A A39 40c on 2c #295 2.00 2.00
CO18 A39 40c on 2c #297 (G) 7.00 7.00
CO18A A39 40c on 2c #297 4.25 4.25
CO19 A28 40c on 5c #246 4.25 4.25
CO19A A28 40c on 5c #247 7.00 7.00
CO20 A28 40c on 5c #266 15.00 15.00
CO20A A28 40c on 5c #267 9.00 9.00
CO20B A28 40c on 5c #267 (R) 14.00 14.00
CO21 A20 70c on 5c #183 3.00 3.00
CO22 A24 70c on 10c #214 (R) 3.25 3.25
CO23 A22 1 l on 20c #191 (Bl) 3.25 3.25
CO24 A24 1 l on 50c #216 (Bl) 14.00 14.00
CO25 A22 1.20 l on 1p #193 (Bl) 1.00 1.00
Nos. CO15-CO25 (16) 96.75 96.75

Official Stamps of 1915-29 Surcharged Type "a" or Type "b" (#CO28-CO29, CO33-CO41, CO43) in Black, Red, Green, Orange, Carmine or Blue

CO26 O1 40c on 5c #O84 (Bk) 1.00 1.00
CO27 O1 40c on 5c #O84 (R) 25.00 25.00
CO28 A24 60c on 6c #O77 (Bk) .70 .70
CO29 A24 60c on 6c #O77 (G) 25.00 25.00
CO30 A20 70c on 5c #O60 (Bk) 5.25 5.25
CO31 A19 70c on 10c #O62 (R) 9.00 9.00
CO32 A19 70c on 10c #O62 (Bk) 7.75 7.75
CO33 A22 70c on 10c #O70 (R) 4.50 4.00
CO34 A24 70c on 10c #O78 (O) 3.50 3.50
CO35 A24 70c on 10c #O78 (C) 4.50 4.50
CO36 A22 70c on 15c #O71 (R) 87.50 87.50
CO37 A22 90c on 10c #O70 (R) 5.25 5.25
CO38 A22 90c on 15c #O71 (R) 8.00 8.00
CO38A A24 1 l on 2c #O76 1.40 1.40
CO39 A22 1 l on 20c #O72 2.50 2.50
CO39A A24 1 l on 20c #O79 3.75 3.75
CO40 A22 1 l on 50c #O73 1.90 1.90

CO41 A24 1 l on 50c #O80 4.25 4.25
CO42 A20 1.20 l on 1p #O65 9.00 7.00
CO43 A24 1.20 l on 1p #O81 3.00 3.00
Nos. CO26-CO43 (20) 212.75 210.25

Varieties of foregoing surcharges exist.

Merchant Flag and Seal of Honduras
OA2

1939, Feb. 27 Unwmk. *Perf. 12½*

CO44 OA2 2c dp blue & grn .25 .25
CO45 OA2 5c dp blue & org .25 .25
CO46 OA2 8c dp blue & brn .25 .25
CO47 OA2 15c dp blue & car .30 .25
CO48 OA2 46c dp blue & ol grn .40 .30
CO49 OA2 50c dp blue & vio .50 .30
CO50 OA2 1 l dp blue & red brn 1.75 1.25
CO51 OA2 2 l dp blue & red org 3.75 2.25
Nos. CO44-CO51 (8) 7.45 5.10

For overprints and surcharges see Nos. C101-C117.

OFFICIAL STAMPS

Type of Regular Issue of 1890 Overprinted in Red

1890 Unwmk. *Perf. 12*

O1 A5 1c pale yellow .25
O2 A5 2c pale yellow .25
O3 A5 5c pale yellow .25
O4 A5 10c pale yellow .25
O5 A5 20c pale yellow .25
O6 A5 25c pale yellow .25
O7 A5 30c pale yellow .25
O8 A5 40c pale yellow .25
O9 A5 50c pale yellow .25
O10 A5 75c pale yellow .25
O11 A5 1p pale yellow .25
Nos. O1-O11 (11) 2.75

Type of Regular Issue of 1891 Overprinted in Red

1891

O12 A6 1c yellow .25
O13 A6 2c yellow .25
O14 A6 5c yellow .25
O15 A6 10c yellow .25
O16 A6 20c yellow .25
O17 A6 25c yellow .25
O18 A6 30c yellow .25
O19 A6 40c yellow .25
O20 A6 50c yellow .25
O21 A6 75c yellow .25
O22 A6 1p yellow .25
Nos. O12-O22 (11) 2.75

Nos. O1 to O22 were never placed in use. Cancellations were applied to remainders. They exist with overprint inverted, double, triple and omitted; also, imperf. and part perf.

Regular Issue of 1898 Overprinted

1898-99 *Perf. 11½*

O23 A12 5c dl ultra .40
O24 A12 10c dark bl .80
O25 A12 20c dull org 1.25
O26 A12 50c org red 2.40
O27 A12 1p blue grn 3.00
Nos. O23-O27 (5) 7.85

Counterfeits of basic stamps and of overprint exist.

Regular Issue of 1911 Overprinted

1911-15 *Perf. 12, 14*

Carmine Overprint

O28 A15 1c violet 1.50 .65
 a. Inverted overprint 2.40 2.40
 b. Double overprint 2.00
O29 A15 6c ultra 2.50 2.00
 a. Inverted overprint 2.75 2.75
O30 A15 10c blue 1.50 1.25
 a. "OFICAIL" 2.50
 b. Double overprint 3.50
O31 A15 20c yellow 15.00 12.00
O32 A15 50c brown 8.00 7.00
O33 A15 1p ol grn 12.00 10.00
Nos. O28-O33 (6) 40.50 32.90

Black Overprint

O34 A15 2c green 1.00 .70
 a. "CIFICAL" 5.00
O35 A15 5c carmine 1.50 1.00
 a. Perf. 12 7.50 5.00
O36 A15 6c ultra 4.50 4.50
O37 A15 10c blue 4.00 4.00
O38 A15 20c yellow 5.00 5.00
O39 A15 50c brown 5.50 4.00
Nos. O34-O39 (6) 21.50 19.20

Counterfeits of overprint of Nos. O28-O39 exist.

With Additional Surcharge

1913-14

O40 A15 1c on 5c car 1.75 1.50
O41 A15 2c on 5c car 2.00 1.50
O42 A15 10c on 1c vio 4.00 3.50
 a. "OFICIAL" inverted 7.50
O43 A15 20c on 1c vio 3.00 2.50
Nos. O40-O43 (4) 10.75 9.00

On No. O40 the surcharge reads "1 cent." Nos. O40-O43 exist with double surcharge.

No. O43 Surcharged Vertically in Black, Yellow or Maroon

1914

O44 A15 10c on 20c on 1c 20.00 20.00
 a. Maroon surcharge 20.00 20.00
O45 A15 10c on 20c on 1c (Y) 40.00 40.00

No. O35 Surcharged

1915

O46 A15 10c on 5c car *20.00 20.00*

No. O39 Surcharged

O47 A15 20c on 50c brn 5.00 5.00

Regular Issues of 1913-14 Overprinted in Red or Black

1915 *Perf. 11½*

O48 A17 1c brn (R) .40 .40
 a. "OFICAIL" 5.00
O49 A17 2c car (Bk) .40 .40
 a. "OFICAIL" 5.00
 b. Double overprint 4.00
O50 A18 5c ultra (Bk) .45 .45
 a. "OFIC" 4.00
O51 A18 5c ultra (R) 1.00 1.00
 a. "OFIC"
 b. "OFICAIL" 5.00
O52 A18 6c pur (Bk) 1.50 1.50
 a. 6c red lil (Bk)
O53 A17 10c brn (Bk) 1.25 1.25
O54 A17 20c brn (Bk) 3.00 3.00
O55 A17 20c brn (R) 3.00 3.00
 a. Double overprint (R+Bk) 10.00
 b. "OFICAIL" 5.00
O56 A18 50c rose (Bk) 6.00 6.00
Nos. O48-O56 (9) 17.00 17.00

The 10c blue has the overprint "OFICIAL" in different type from the other stamps of the series. It is stated that forty stamps were overprinted for the Postmaster General but the stamp was never put in use or on sale at the post office.

No. 152 Surcharged

O57 A17 1c on 2c car 2.00 2.00
 a. "0.10" for "0.01" 4.25 4.25
 b. "0.20" for "0.01" 4.25 4.25
 c. Double surcharge 8.50 8.50
 d. As "a," double surcharge 77.50
 e. As "b," double surcharge 77.50

Regular Issue of 1915-16 Overprinted in Black or Red

1915-16

O58 A19 1c choc (Bk) .25 .25
O59 A19 2c car (Bk) .25 .25
 a. Tête bêche pair 1.25 1.25
 b. Double overprint 2.00
 c. Double overprint, one inverted 2.00
 d. "b" and "c" in tête bêche pair
O60 A20 5c brt blue (R) .30 .30
 a. Inverted overprint 3.00
O61 A20 6c deep pur (R) .40 .40
 a. Black overprint 3.00
 b. Inverted overprint 2.00 2.00
O62 A19 10c dl bl (R) .40 .40
O63 A19 20c red brn (Bk) .60 .60
 a. Tête bêche pair 2.50
O64 A20 50c red (Bk) 1.75 1.75
O65 A20 1p yel grn (C) 3.75 3.75
Nos. O58-O65 (8) 7.70 7.70

The 6c, 10c and 1p exist imperf.

Regular Issue of 1919 Overprinted

1921

O66 A22 1c brown *2.25 2.25*
 a. Inverted overprint 3.00 3.00
O67 A22 2c carmine *6.50 6.50*
 a. Inverted overprint 3.00 3.00
O68 A22 5c lilac rose *6.50 6.50*
 a. Inverted overprint 3.00
O69 A22 6c brt vio .50 .50
 a. Inverted overprint
O70 A22 10c dull blue .60 .60
 a. Double overprint
O71 A22 15c light blue .70 .70
 a. Inverted overprint 2.00
 b. Double ovpt., one inverted 4.00
O72 A22 20c brown 1.00 1.00
O73 A22 50c light brown 1.50 1.50
O74 A22 1p yellow green 3.00 3.00
Nos. O66-O74 (9) 22.55 22.55

Regular Issue of 1924 Overprinted

1924 *Perf. 11, 11½*

O75 A24 1c olive brn .25 .25
O76 A24 2c deep rose .25 .25
O77 A24 6c red vio .30 .30
O78 A24 10c deep bl .45 .45
O79 A24 20c yel brn .60 .60
O80 A24 50c vermilion 1.25 1.25
O81 A24 1p emerald 2.00 2.00
Nos. O75-O81 (7) 5.10 5.10

J. C. del Valle — O1

Designs: 2c, J. R. Molina. 5c, Coffee tree. 10c, J. T. Reyes. 20c, Tegucigalpa Cathedral. 50c, San Lorenzo Creek. 1p, Radio station.

1929 Litho. Wmk. 209 *Perf. 11½*

O82 O1 1c blue .25 .25
O83 O1 2c carmine .25 .25
 a. 2c rose .25 .25
O84 O1 5c purple .35 .35
O85 O1 10c emerald .50 .35
O86 O1 20c dk bl .60 .60
O87 O1 50c org, grn & bl 1.00 1.00
O88 O1 1p buff 1.75 1.75
Nos. O82-O88 (7) 4.70 4.55

Nos. O82-O88 exist imperf.

For overprints and surcharges see Nos. 282, 284, C37-C40, C59, C62-C63, CO26-CO27.

View of Tegucigalpa
O2

1931 Unwmk. Engr. *Perf. 12*

O89 O2 1c ultra .30 .25
O90 O2 2c black brn .30 .25
O91 O2 5c olive gray .35 .25
O92 O2 6c orange red .40 .30
O93 O2 10c dark green .50 .35
O94 O2 15c olive brn .65 .40
O95 O2 20c red brown .75 .50
O96 O2 50c gray vio 1.00 .65
O97 O2 1p dp orange 1.75 1.75
Nos. O89-O97 (9) 6.00 4.70

For overprints see Nos. CO6-CO14, O98-O105.

Official Stamps of 1931 Overprinted in Black

1936-37

O98 O2 1c ultra .25 .25
O99 O2 2c black brn .25 .25
 a. Inverted overprint 10.00
O100 O2 5c olive gray .30 .30
O101 O2 6c red orange .40 .40
O102 O2 10c dark green .40 .40
O103 O2 15c olive brown .50 .50
 a. Inverted overprint 5.00
O104 O2 20c red brown 1.00 1.00
 a. "1938-1935"
O105 O2 50c gray violet 4.00 3.00
Nos. O98-O105 (8) 7.10 6.10

Double overprints exist on 1c and 2c. No. O97 with this overprint is fraudulent.

HONG KONG

'häŋ-,käŋ

LOCATION — A peninsula and island in southeast China at the mouth of the Canton River
GOVT. — British Crown Colony
AREA — 426 sq. mi.
POP. — 5,313,000 (est. 1983)
CAPITAL — Victoria

100 Cents = 1 Dollar

Catalogue values for unused stamps in this country are for Never Hinged items, beginning with Scott 174 in the regular postage section.

Pre-Stamp Postal Markings

1843-52

A1 Crowned Circle handstamp Type II, on cover, inscribed "PAID AT HONG KONG" in red *1,100.*
A2 Crowned Circle handstamp Type I, on cover, inscribed "PAID AT HONG KONG" in red *900.*
A3 Crowned Circle handstamp Type IV, on cover, inscribed "PAID AT HONG KONG" in red *550.*

Earliest known uses: A1, 10/17/43; A2, 8/21/44; A3, 6/16/52.

Values for unused stamps are for examples with original gum as defined in the catalogue introduction. Very fine examples of Nos. 1-25, 29-48, 61-66d and 69-70a will have perforations touching the design on at least one side due to the narrow spacing of the stamps on the plates. Stamps with perfs clear of the design on all four sides are scarce and will command higher prices.

Queen Victoria — A1

Unwmk.

1862, Dec. 8 Typo. *Perf. 14*

1 A1 2c pale brown 525.00 110.00
On cover 650.00
a. 2c deep brown 725.00 160.00
On cover 800.00
2 A1 8c buff 725.00 80.00
On cover 500.00
3 A1 12c blue 625.00 55.00
On cover 425.00
4 A1 18c lilac 625.00 50.00
On cover 475.00
5 A1 24c green 1,150. 110.00
On cover 800.00
6 A1 48c rose 2,600. 325.00
On cover 3,000.
7 A1 96c gray 3,500. 400.00
On cover —

1863-80 Wmk. 1

8 A1 2c brn ('65) 120.00 7.75
On cover 50.00
a. 2c deep brown ('64) 325.00 32.50
On cover 165.00
b. 2c pale yellowish brown 180.00 14.00
On cover 75.00
9 A1 2c dull rose ('80) 250.00 37.50
On cover 210.00
a. 2c rose 275.00 32.50
Never hinged 210.00
10 A1 4c slate 110.00 8.75
On cover 50.00
a. 4c greenish grey 325.00 45.00
On cover 325.00
b. 4c bluish slate 450.00 25.00
On cover 135.00
11 A1 5c ultra ('80) 775.00 52.50
On cover 135.00
12 A1 6c lilac 425.00 17.50
On cover 175.00
a. 6c violet 625.00 18.00
On cover 175.00
13 A1 8c org buff ('65) 575.00 12.50
On cover 170.00
a. 8c bright orange 450.00 15.00
On cover 150.00
b. 8c brownish orange 475.00 15.00
On cover 150.00
14 A1 10c violet ('80) 775.00 17.00
On cover 130.00
15 A1 12c light blue 30.00 8.00
On cover 55.00
a. 12c light greenish blue 1,100. 37.50
On cover 350.00
b. 12c deep blue 275.00 13.00
On cover 145.00
16 A1 16c yel ('77) 1,900. 62.50
On cover 525.00
17 A1 18c lilac ('66) 6,750. 300.00
On cover 3,250.
18 A1 24c grn ('65) 625.00 11.00
On cover 110.00
a. 24c deep green 1,250. 32.50
On cover 140.00
b. 24c pale green 875.00 17.50
On cover 180.00
19 A1 30c vermilion 1,050. 14.50
On cover 180.00
a. 30c orange vermilion 925.00 17.50
On cover 180.00
20 A1 30c violet ('71) 250.00 5.00
On cover 110.00
21 A1 48c rose car 900.00 30.00
On cover 275.00
a. 48c pale rose 1,400. 65.00
On cover 300.00
22 A1 48c brn ('80) 1,400. 100.00
On cover —
23 A1 96c bis ('65) *77,500.* 700.00
On cover *45,000.*
24 A1 96c gray ('66) 1,400. 62.50
On cover *8,250.*
a. 96c brownish black 2,100. 62.50
On cover —

Imperfs. are plate proofs.

1874 *Perf. 12½*

25 A1 4c slate 11,000. 250.00
On cover 3,000.

See Nos. 36-49. For surcharges or overprints on stamps of type A1 see Nos. 29-35B, 51-56, 61-66, 69-70.

A2

A3

A4

1874 Engr. Wmk. 1 *Perf. 15½x15*

26 A2 $2 sage green 400.00 67.50
On cover —
a. $2 Thin transluscent paper 425.00 67.50
27 A3 $3 violet 375.00 52.50
On cover —
a. $2 Thin transluscent paper 400.00 42.50
28 A4 $10 rose 8,250. 725.00
On cover —

Nos. 26-28 are revenues which were used postally. Used values are for postally canceled examples. Black "Paid All" cancels are fiscal usage.

See Nos. 57-59. For surcharges see Nos. 50, 67. For type surcharged see No. 60.

Nos. 17 and 20 Surcharged in Black

1876 *Perf. 14*

29 A1 16c on 18c lilac 2,100. 140.00
On cover 2,750.
a. Wide space btwn. "n" & "t" 8,250. 1,000.
b. Wide space btwn. "s" & period 8,250. 1,000.
c. Broken "1" in "16" *4,000.* *475.00*
30 A1 28c on 30c violet 1,400. 47.50
On cover 1,450.

Stamps of 1863-80 Surcharged in Black

1879-80

31 A1 5c on 8c org ('80) 1,000. 100.00
On cover 1,450.
a. Inverted surcharge *20,000.*
b. Double surcharge *20,000.*
32 A1 5c on 18c lilac 900.00 62.50
On cover 2,500.
33 A1 10c on 12c pale blue 1,100. 50.00
On cover 825.00
a. 10c on 12c blue 1,600. 100.00
b. Double surcharge *47,500.*
34 A1 10c on 16c yellow 4,000. 140.00
On cover 2,500.
a. Inverted surcharge *90,000.*
b. Double surcharge *72,500.*
35 A1 10c on 24c grn ('80) 1,400. 95.00
On cover 1,650.

Most examples of No. 31a are damaged.

Nos. 16-17 Surcharged in Black

No. 35B Surcharged in Black

1879

35A A5 3c on 16c on card *325.* *2,200.*
Stamp off card 475.
d. White card, red printing 475.
e. Yellow card, black printing 525.
f. As No. 35A, short "T" in "CENTS" 575.
35B A5 5c on 18c on card *350.* *2,600.*
Stamp off card 475.
g. White card, red printing 475.
h. Blue card, white printing 525.
i. As No. 35B, short "T" in "CENTS" 575.
35C A6 3c on 5c on 18c on card *8,500.* *9,500.*
Stamp off card *8,000.* *8,250.*
j. Short "T" in "CENTS" *9,000.*

Nos. 35A-35C were sold affixed to postal cards. Most used examples are found off card so values are given for these.

Type of 1862

1882-1902 Wmk. 2 *Perf. 14*

36 A1 2c rose lake 290.00 35.00
On cover 45.00
a. 2c rose pink 235.00 35.00
On cover 50.00
b. 2c carmine ('84) 50.00 2.75
On cover 25.00
c. 2c aniline carmine ('84) 57.50 2.75
On cover 25.00
37 A1 2c green ('00) 27.50 1.00
On cover 25.00
38 A1 4c slate ('96) 28.00 2.75
On cover 42.50
39 A1 4c car rose ('00) 20.00 1.00
On cover 25.00
40 A1 5c ultramarine 45.00 1.00
On cover 32.50
41 A1 5c yellow ('00) 26.00 8.00
On cover 82.50
42 A1 10c lilac 975.00 21.00
On cover 80.00
43 A1 10c green 175.00 2.00
On cover 25.00
a. 10c blue green 1,700. 37.50
On cover 1,225.
44 A1 10c vio, *red* ('91) 42.50 1.75
On cover 25.00
45 A1 10c ultra ('00) 50.00 2.25
On cover 30.00
46 A1 12c blue ('02) 46.00 *67.50*
On cover 775.00
47 A1 30c gray grn ('91) 100.00 26.00
On cover 165.00
a. 30c yellow green 135.00 42.50
On cover 275.00
48 A1 30c brown ('01) 57.50 26.00
On cover 275.00
a. Pair, imperf. *2,000.*
Nos. 36-48 (13) 1,883. 195.25

No. 47 has fugitive ink. Both colors will turn dull green upon soaking.

The 2c rose, perf 12, is a proof.

No. 28 Surcharged in Black

1880 Wmk. 1 *Perf. 15½x15*

50 A4 12c on $10 rose 925.00 325.00
On cover —

Surcharged in Black

1885-91 Wmk. 2 *Perf. 14*

51 A1 20c on 30c ver 185.00 6.75
On cover 250.00
a. Double surcharge — —
52 A1 20c on 30c gray grn ('91) 100.00 *140.00*
On cover 1,250.
a. 20c on 30c yellow green 170.00 160.00
53 A1 50c on 48c brown 375.00 42.50
On cover 400.00
54 A1 50c on 48c lil ('91) 275.00 *300.00*
On cover 1,650.
55 A1 $1 on 96c ol gray 725.00 82.50
On cover 1,000.
56 A1 $1 on 96c vio, *red* ('91) 750.00 325.00
On cover *900.00*

For overprints see Nos. 61-63.

Types of 1874 and

A7

1890-1902 Wmk. 2 *Perf. 14*

56A A7 2c dull purple 175.00 40.00
On cover 125.00

Wmk. 1

57 A2 $2 gray green 425.00 250.00
On cover —
58 A3 $3 lilac ('02) 625.00 525.00
On cover —
a. Bluish paper 2,100.
On cover —
59 A4 $10 gray grn ('92) *11,500. 10,500.*
Fiscal cancellation *500.00*
On cover —

Due to a shortage of 2c postage stamps, No. 56A was authorized for postal use December 24-30, 1890.

Fake postmarks are known on No. 59. Beware also of fiscal cancels altered to resemble postal cancels.

For surcharge see No. 68.

Type of 1874 Surcharged in Black

1891, Jan. 1 Wmk. 2

60 A4 $5 on $10 vio, *red* 375.00 110.00
On cover —

Nos. 36b, 44 Overprinted

a

b

1891, Jan. 1

60A A1 2c carmine (a) 925.00 350.00
60B A1 2c carmine (b) 400.00 190.00
a. Inverted overprint *9,000.*
60C A1 10c vio, *red* (a) *1,600.* 425.00

Nos. 60A-60C were overprinted for use as fiscal stamps, "S.O." denoting "Stamp Office" and "S.D." denoting "Stamp Duty." They were authorized for postal use Jan. 1, 1891-1893. Examples of No. 60A with "O" changed to "D" in manuscript are known.

Forged overprints are often encountered. Expertization is required.

Nos. 52, 54 and 56 Handstamped with Chinese characters

g

h

i

61 A1 (g) 20c on 30c yellow green 52.50 12.50
On cover 165.00
a. 20c on 30c dull green 42.50 11.00
On cover 130.00
b. "20 CENTS" double *24,000. 24,000.*
62 A1 (h) 50c on 48c 75.00 5.00
On cover 575.00
63 A1 (i) $1 on 96c 425.00 21.00
On cover 825.00
a. Chinese inscriptions both sides *750.00*

No. 61 may be found with Chinese character 2mm, 2 ½mm or 3mm high.

The handstamped Chinese surcharges on Nos. 61-63 exist in several varieties including inverted, double, triple, misplaced, omitted and (on No. 63) on both front and back.

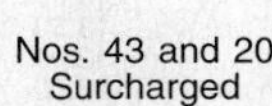

Nos. 43 and 20 Surcharged

1891

64 A1 7c on 10c green 90.00 9.50
On cover 300.00
a. Double surcharge *6,250. 1,250.*
On cover —
b. Antique "t" in "cents" 675.00 150.00
c. Small "t" in "cents" 650.00 145.00
On cover —

Wmk. 1

65 A1 14c on 30c violet 190.00 77.50
On cover 725.00
a. Antique "t" in "cents" 2,900. 1,000.
On cover *3,500.*
b. Small "t" in "cents" 1,400. 500.00
On cover *2,250.*

Beware of faked varieties.

No. 36 Overprinted in Black

1891, Jan. 22 Wmk. 2

66 A1 2c rose *450.00* 130.00
Never hinged *1,250.*
On cover *3,250.*
a. Double overprint *17,500. 13,500.*
b. "U" of "JUBILEE" shorter *775.00* 200.00
c. "J" of "JUBILEE" shorter *775.00* 200.00
d. Tall "K" in "KONG" *1,250.* 450.00
e. Wide space btwn. "o" & "n" 1,800. 800.00
f. Broken "1" in "1891" 1,000. 325.00
g. "1841" omitted *7,500.*

50th anniversary of the colony.

Beware of faked varieties. Value for 66a are for doubling clearly seperated & visible. Overprint nearly over each other are valued much less. No. 66g is from a shift of a single row or 12 of the overprint.

No. 26 Surcharged (Chinese Handstamped)

1897, Sept. Wmk. 1 *Perf. 15½x15*

67 A2 $1 on $2 sage green 225.00 125.00
On cover —
a. Without Chinese surcharges 4,000. 3,750.
On cover —
b. Diagonal Chinese surcharge omitted *29,500.*

On No. 57
Perf. 14

68 A2 $1 on $2 gray green 250.00 140.00
On cover —
a. Without Chinese surcharges 1,900. *1,700.*
On cover —
b. Diagonal Chinese surcharge omitted *22,000.*
c. Vertical Chinese surcharge omitted —
Handstamped "SPECIMEN" 150.00

Handstamp Surcharged in Black

1898 Wmk. 2

69 A1 10c on 30c gray grn 72.50 *87.50*
On cover 500.00
a. Large Chinese surcharge *1,400. 1,400.*
b. Without Chinese surcharge 600.00 *1,200.*
On cover —
c. As #69, 1 ½mm between "1" & "0" 800.00 *1,000.*
d. As #69b, 1 ½mm between "1" & "0" *8,000.*

70 A1 $1 on 96c black 240.00 32.50
On cover 1,000.
a. Without Chinese surcharge 3,000. *4,000.*
Overprinted "SPECIMEN" 625.00

The Chinese surcharge is added separately.

See notes below Nos. 61-63. The small Chinese surcharge is illustrated.

King Edward VII — A10

1903 Wmk. 2

71 A10 1c brown & lilac 2.25 .55
72 A10 2c gray green 20.00 2.10
73 A10 4c violet, *red* 23.00 .45
74 A10 5c org & gray grn 22.00 9.50
75 A10 8c vio & blk 14.50 1.75
76 A10 10c ultra & lil, *bl* 62.50 1.40
77 A10 12c red vio & gray grn, *yel* 11.50 5.75
78 A10 20c org brn & blk 62.50 4.75
79 A10 30c blk & gray grn 62.50 24.00
80 A10 50c red vio & gray grn 65.00 62.50
81 A10 $1 ol grn & lil 125.00 26.00
82 A10 $2 scar & black 350.00 350.00
83 A10 $3 dp bl & blk 425.00 *400.00*
84 A10 $5 blue grn & lil 625.00 575.00
85 A10 $10 org & blk, *bl* 1,300. 450.00
Nos. 71-85 (15) 3,171. 1,914.

1904-11 Wmk. 3

Ordinary or Chalky Paper

86 A10 1c brown ('10) 9.00 1.00
a. Booklet pane of 4
87 A10 2c gray green 22.50 2.75
88 A10 2c deep green 42.00 1.50
a. Booklet pane of 4
b. Booklet pane of 12
89 A10 4c violet, *red* 34.00 .50
90 A10 4c carmine 18.00 .40
a. Booklet pane of 4
b. Booklet pane of 12
91 A10 5c org & gray grn 62.50 17.50
a. Chalky paper ('06) 22.50 6.50
92 A10 6c red vio & org ('07) 34.00 8.25
93 A10 8c vio & blk ('07) 18.00 1.75
94 A10 10c ultra & lil, *bl* 32.00 1.25
95 A10 10c ultramarine 57.50 .50
96 A10 12c red vio & gray grn, *yel* ('07) 22.00 7.75
97 A10 20c org brn & blk 67.50 4.00
a. Chalky paper ('06) 62.50 3.50
98 A10 20c ol grn & vio ('11) 50.00 50.00
99 A10 30c blk & gray grn 62.50 32.50
a. Chalky paper ('06) 62.50 22.50
100 A10 30c org & vio ('11) 62.50 42.50
101 A10 50c red vio & gray green 105.00 15.50
a. Chalky paper ('06) 90.00
102 A10 50c blk, *grn* ('11) 52.50 19.00
103 A10 $1 ol grn & lil 190.00 42.00
a. Chalky paper ('06) 160.00
104 A10 $2 scar & black 440.00 160.00
a. Chalky paper ('06) 325.00 125.00
105 A10 $2 blk & car ('10) 400.00 440.00
106 A10 $3 dp bl & blk 340.00 325.00
107 A10 $5 bl grn & lil 475.00 450.00
108 A10 $10 org & blk, *bl* 1,800. 1,450.
a. Chalky paper ('06) 1,900. 1,100.
Nos. 86-108 (23) 4,397. 3,074.

Nos. 86, 88, 90, 94 and 95 are on ordinary paper only. Nos. 92, 93, 96, 98, 100, 102, 105, 106 and 107 are on chalky paper and the others of the issue are on both papers.

The 4c, 5c, 8c, 12c 20c, 50c, $2 and $5 denominations of type A10 are expressed in colored letters or numerals and letters on a colorless background.

King George V
A11 A12

A13

A14

A15

Type I Type II

Two Types of 25c:

I: A short vertical stroke crosses the bottom of the top Chinese character in the left label.

II: The vertical stroke is absent from the character.

1912-14 Ordinary Paper

109 A11 1c brown 4.50 .60
a. Booklet pane of 12
110 A11 2c deep green 12.00 .40
a. Booklet pane of 12
111 A12 4c carmine 6.50 .40
a. Booklet pane of 12
b. Booklet pane of 4
112 A13 6c orange 6.00 2.25
113 A12 8c gray 27.50 8.00
114 A11 10c ultramarine 27.50 .35

Chalky Paper

115 A14 12c vio, *yel* 9.00 *10.00*
116 A14 20c ol grn & vio 12.00 1.50
117 A15 25c red vio & dl vio (I) ('14) 32.50 *32.50*
118 A13 30c org & violet 29.00 8.50
119 A14 50c black, *bl grn, white back* 25.00 2.00
a. 50c black, *emerald* 27.50 10.00
b. 50c black, *bl grn,* ol back 1,250. 27.50
c. 50c black, *emer,* ol back 32.50 10.00
120 A11 $1 blue & vio, *bl* 55.00 5.75
121 A14 $2 black & red 180.00 70.00
122 A13 $3 vio & green 275.00 100.00
123 A14 $5 red & grn, *grn* 675.00 400.00
a. $5 red & grn, *bl grn,* ol back 1,150. 375.00
124 A13 $10 blk & vio, *red* 575.00 95.00
Nos. 109-124 (16) 1,952. 737.25

For overprints see British Offices in China Nos. 1-27.

1914, May Surface-colored Paper

125 A14 12c violet, *yel* 10.00 *18.00*
126 A14 50c black, *green* 30.00 4.00
127 A14 $5 red & grn, *grn* 575.00 350.00
Nos. 125-127 (3) 615.00 372.00

Stamp of 1912-14 Redrawn (Type II)

1919, Aug. Chalky Paper

128 A15 25c red vio & dl vio 250.00 80.00

Types of 1912-14 Issue

1921-37 Ordinary Paper Wmk. 4

129 A11 1c brown 1.25 .50
130 A11 2c deep green 4.00 .75
131 A11 2c gray ('37) 22.50 8.00
132 A12 3c gray ('31) 10.00 1.50
133 A12 4c rose red 5.50 1.00
134 A12 5c violet ('31) 18.00 .40
135 A12 8c gray 21.00 *37.50*
136 A12 8c orange 5.75 2.00
137 A11 10c ultramarine 7.50 .45

Chalky Paper

138 A14 12c vio, *yel* ('33) 20.00 4.00
139 A14 20c ol grn & dl vio 8.50 .40
140 A15 25c red vio & dl vio, redrawn 7.50 1.50
141 A13 30c yel & violet 12.00 1.75
142 A14 50c blk, *emerald* 24.00 .45
143 A11 $1 ultra & vio, *bl* 45.00 .60
144 A14 $2 black & red 135.00 7.50
145 A13 $3 dl vio & grn ('26) 190.00 67.50
146 A14 $5 red & grn, *emer* ('25) 475.00 77.50
Nos. 129-146 (18) 1,013. 213.30

Common Design Types pictured following the introduction.

Silver Jubilee Issue
Common Design Type

1935, May 6 Engr. *Perf. 11x12*

147 CD301 3c black & ultra 3.50 3.00
148 CD301 5c indigo & grn 9.00 3.50
149 CD301 10c ultra & brn 18.00 4.00
150 CD301 20c brn vio & ind 28.50 8.25
Nos. 147-150 (4) 59.00 18.75
Set, never hinged 125.00

Coronation Issue
Common Design Type

1937, May 12 *Perf. 11x11½*

151 CD302 4c deep green 3.50 5.75
152 CD302 15c dark carmine 8.50 2.75
153 CD302 25c deep ultra 11.00 4.00
Nos. 151-153 (3) 23.00 12.50
Set, never hinged 32.50

King George VI — A16

1938-52 Typo. *Perf. 14*

Ordinary Paper

154 A16 1c brown 1.00 *2.00*
a. Double printed *7,500.*
b. pale brown ('52) 2.00 *6.50*
155 A16 2c gray 1.00 .25
156 A16 4c orange 5.00 4.00
157 A16 5c green .60 .25
157B A16 8c brn red ('41) 1.00 *1.75*
c. Imperf., pair 60,000. —
d. Period after cents
158 A16 10c violet 4.00 .60
159 A16 15c carmine 1.00 .30
159A A16 20c gray ('46) .60 .30
159B A16 20c rose red ('48) 7.00 .45
160 A16 25c ultramarine 14.50 2.75
160A A16 25c gray ol ('46) 4.25 *2.75*
161 A16 30c olive bister 75.00 1.90
161B A16 30c lt ultra ('46) 3.50 .25

Chalky Paper

162 A16 50c red violet 6.00 .40
b. Ordinary paper 8.50 .75
162C A16 80c lilac rose ('48) 3.25 .70
163 A16 $1 lilac & ultra 4.25 2.50
a. Ordinary paper 11.00 *16.00*
163B A16 $1 dp org & grn ('46) 26.00 1.00
c. Ordinary paper 13.50 .30
164 A16 $2 dp org & grn 40.00 20.00
164A A16 $2 vio & red ('46) 27.50 .60
b. Ordinary paper 25.00 6.75
165 A16 $5 lilac & red 35.00 *30.00*
165A A16 $5 grn & vio ('46) 60.00 3.50
b. Ordinary paper 25.00 17.00
166 A16 $10 grn & vio 350.00 97.50
166A A16 $10 vio & ultra ('46) 100.00 12.50
b. Ordinary paper 70.00 32.50
Nos. 154-166A (23) 770.45 186.25
Set, never hinged 1,200.

Coarse Impressions
Ordinary Rough-Surfaced Paper

1941-46 *Perf. 14½x14*

155a A16 2c gray .90 *4.25*
156a A16 4c orange ('46) 2.50 2.00
157a A16 5c green 1.75 *3.00*
158a A16 10c violet 4.75 .25
161a A16 30c dull olive bister 14.00 6.75
162a A16 50c red lilac 15.00 .75
Nos. 155a-162a (6) 38.90 17.00
Set, never hinged 80.00

A17

1938, Jan. 11 Wmk. 4

167 A17 5c green 60.00 15.00
Never hinged 110.00

No. 167 is a revenue stamp officially authorized to be sold and used for postal purposes. Used Jan. 11-20, 1938. The used price is for the stamp on cover. CTO covers exist.

Street Scene — A18

Hong Kong Bank — A22

Liner and Junk — A19

University of Hong Kong — A20

Harbor — A21

China Clipper and Seaplane A23

Perf. 13½x13, 13x13½

1941, Feb. 26 Engr. Wmk. 4

168 A18 2c sepia & org 4.00 1.75
169 A19 4c rose car & vio 4.75 3.50
170 A20 5c yel grn & blk 1.75 .35
171 A21 15c red & black 4.75 2.75
172 A22 25c dp blue & dk brn 9.50 6.50
173 A23 $1 brn org & brt bl 25.00 9.25
Nos. 168-173 (6) 49.75 24.10
Set, never hinged 80.00

Centenary of British rule.

Catalogue values for unused stamps in this section, from this point to the end of the section, are for Never Hinged items.

Peace Issue

Phoenix Rising from Flames A24

1946, Aug. 29 *Perf. 13x12½*

174 A24 30c car & dp blue 3.00 2.40
175 A24 $1 car & brown 3.75 .75
Set, hinged 4.00

Return to peace after WWII.

Silver Wedding Issue
Common Design Types

Perf. 14x14½

1948, Dec. 22 Photo. Wmk. 4

178 CD304 10c purple 3.50 1.50

Engr.; Name Typo.

Perf. 11½x11

179 CD305 $10 rose car 300.00 95.00
Set, hinged 225.00

UPU Issue
Common Design Types

Engr.; Name Typo. on 20c & 30c

1949, Oct. 10 *Perf. 13½, 11x11½*

180 CD306 10c violet 3.75 1.00
181 CD307 20c deep car 13.50 4.75
182 CD308 30c indigo 12.00 5.00
183 CD309 80c red violet 28.00 7.50
Nos. 180-183 (4) 57.25 18.25
Set, hinged 23.00

POSTAGE DUE STAMPS

Scales Showing Letter Overweight — D1

1923, Dec. Typo. Wmk. 4 *Perf. 14*

J1 D1 1c brown 2.75 .70
a. Chalky paper, wmkd. sideways 1.60 *3.50*
J2 D1 2c green 40.00 9.50
J3 D1 4c red 52.50 7.25
J4 D1 6c orange 34.00 13.50
J5 D1 10c ultramarine 28.00 9.00
Nos. J1-J5 (5) 157.25 39.95
Set, never hinged 300.00

No. J1a issued Mar. 21, 1956.

1938-47 *Perf. 14*

J6 D1 2c gray 6.75 *9.50*
J7 D1 4c orange yellow 10.00 *5.25*
J8 D1 6c carmine 3.50 5.75
J9 D1 8c fawn ('46) 3.00 *34.00*
J10 D1 10c violet 19.00 .55
J11 D1 20c black ('46) 3.75 2.50
J12 D1 50c blue ('47) 40.00 13.50
Nos. J6-J12 (7) 86.00 71.05
Set, never hinged 190.00

Nos. J6-J7 and J10 exist on both ordinary and chalky paper.

OCCUPATION STAMPS

Issued under Japanese Occupation

Japan No. 325 Surcharged in Black

Japan No. 259 Surcharged in Black

Japan No. 261 Surcharged in Black

Wmk. 257

1945, Apr. Typo. *Perf. 13*

N1 A144 1½y on 1s org brn 37.50 32.00
N2 A84 3y on 2s ver 12.50 *27.50*
N3 A86 5y on 5s brn lake 1,000. 160.00
Nos. N1-N3 (3) 1,050. 219.50

No. N1 has eleven characters.

TREATY PORTS

AMOY

Values for stamps of Hong Kong used at AMOY with "AMOY PAID" c.d.s., "A1", "D27", or "AMOY" c.d.s.

1862 Unwmk. *Perf. 14*

On Nos. 1-7

LAM1 A1 2c pale brown 285.00
a. deep brown 300.00
LAM2 A1 8c buff 235.00
LAM3 A1 12c blue 210.00
LAM4 A1 18c lilac 160.00
LAM5 A1 24c green 260.00
LAM6 A1 48c rose 1,450.
LAM7 A1 96c gray 1,150.

1863-80 Wmk. 1 *Perf. 14*

On Nos. 8-25

LAM8 A1 2c brown 40.00
LAM9 A1 2c dull rose 57.50
LAM10 A1 4c slate 45.00
LAM11 A1 5c ultra 100.00
LAM12 A1 6c lilac 72.50
LAM13 A1 8c orange buff 52.50
LAM14 A1 10c violet 75.00
LAM15 A1 12c lt blue 25.00
LAM16 A1 16c yellow 150.00
LAM17 A1 18c lilac 110.00
LAM18 A1 24c green 67.50
LAM19 A1 30c vermilion 150.00
LAM20 A1 30c violet 22.50
LAM21 A1 48c rose carmine 85.00
LAM22 A1 48c brown 325.00
LAM23 A1 96c bister 3,750.
LAM24 A1 96c gray 400.00

Perf. 12½

LAM25 A1 4c slate —

1874 Wmk. 1 *Perf. 15½x15*

On Nos. 26-27

LAM26 A2 $2 sage green 225.00
LAM27 A3 $3 dull violet 225.00

1876-77 On Nos. 29-30

LAM28 A1 16c on 18c lilac 375.00
LAM29 A1 28c on 30c violet 160.00

1879-80 On Nos. 31-35

LAM30 A1 5c on 8c orange 150.00
LAM31 A1 5c on 18c lilac 110.00
LAM32 A1 10c on 12c blue 110.00
LAM33 A1 10c on 16c yellow 250.00
LAM34 A1 10c on 24c green 150.00

1879 Wmk. 1 *Perf. 14*

On Nos. 35A-35B

LAM35 A5 3c on 16c yel on card 1,100.
LAM36 A5 5c on 18c lilac on card 1,100.

See note after No. 35C.

1882-1902 Wmk. 2 *Perf. 14*

On Nos. 36-48

LAM37 A1 2c rose lake 62.50
a. carmine 5.50
LAM38 A1 2c green 5.50
LAM39 A1 4c slate 15.00
LAM40 A1 4c carmine rose 4.00
LAM41 A1 5c ultramarine 5.00
LAM42 A1 5c yellow 24.00
LAM43 A1 10c lilac 50.00
LAM44 A1 10c green 6.00
LAM45 A1 10c vio, *red* 6.00
LAM46 A1 10c ultra 6.50
LAM47 A1 12c blue 225.00
LAM48 A1 30c gray green 50.00
LAM49 A1 30c brown 90.00

1885-91 Wmk. 2 *Perf. 14*

On Nos. 51-56

LAM50 A1 20c on 30c vermilion 20.00
LAM51 A1 20c on 30c green 20.00
LAM52 A1 50c on 48c brown 90.00
LAM53 A1 50c on 48c lilac 20.00
LAM54 A1 $1 on 96c olive gray 150.00
LAM55 A1 $1 on 96c vio, *red* 57.50

1891 Wmk. 2 *Perf. 14*

On Nos. 60, 64-65

LAM56 A4 $5 on $10 vio, *red* 350.00
LAM57 A1 7c on 10c green 27.50

Wmk. 1

LAM58 A1 14c on 30c violet 140.00

1891 Wmk. 2 *Perf. 14*

On No. 66

LAM59 A1 2c carmine *1,100.*

50th anniv. of the colony.

1897 Wmk. 1 *Perf. 15½x15*
On Nos. 67-68

LAM60 A2 $1 on $2 sage grn —

Perf. 14

LAM61 A2 $1 on $2 gray grn 450.00

1898 Wmk. 2 *Perf. 14*
On Nos. 69-70

LAM62 A1 10c on 30c gray green 275.00
LAM63 A1 $1 on 96c black 75.00

1903 Wmk. 2 *Perf. 14*
On Nos. 71-83

LAM64 A10 1c brown & lilac 5.50
LAM65 A10 2c gray green 5.50
LAM66 A10 4c violet, *red* 3.50
LAM67 A10 5c org & gray green 25.00
LAM68 A10 8c vio & blk 8.50
LAM69 A10 10c ultra & lilac, *blue* 5.00
LAM70 A10 12c red vio & gray grn, *yel* 18.00
LAM71 A10 20c org brn & blk 14.00
LAM72 A10 30c blk & gray grn 67.50
LAM73 A10 50c red vio & gray grn 115.00
LAM74 A10 $2 scarlet & blk 550.00
LAM75 A10 $3 dull blue & blk 900.00

1904-11 Wmk. 3 *Perf. 14*
On Nos. 86-107

LAM76 A10 1c brown 5.50
LAM77 A10 2c gray green 5.50
LAM78 A10 2c deep green 5.00
LAM79 A10 4c violet, *red* 3.50
LAM80 A10 4c carmine 3.50
LAM81 A10 5c org & gray grn 20.00
LAM82 A10 6c red vio & org 20.00
LAM83 A10 8c vio & blk 12.00
LAM84 A10 10c ultra & lil, *blue* 5.00
LAM85 A10 10c ultra 4.50
LAM86 A10 12c red vio & gray grn, *yel* 22.50
LAM87 A10 20c org brn & blk 14.00
LAM88 A10 20c olive grn & vio 80.00
LAM89 A10 30c blk & gray grn 45.00
LAM90 A10 30c org & vio 85.00
LAM91 A10 50c red vio & gray grn 45.00
LAM92 A10 50c blk, *grn* 85.00
LAM93 A10 $1 ol grn & lil 110.00
LAM94 A10 $2 scarlet & blk 450.00
LAM95 A10 $5 bl grn & lil 800.00

1912-15 Wmk. 3 *Perf. 14*
On Nos. 109-122

LAM96 A11 1c brown 7.00
LAM97 A11 2c deep green 6.50
LAM98 A12 4c carmine 3.50
LAM99 A13 6c orange 8.00
LAM100 A12 8c gray 25.00
LAM101 A11 10c ultramarine 5.00
LAM102 A14 12c vio, *yel* 35.00
LAM103 A14 20c ol grn & vio 8.50
LAM104 A15 25c red vio & dl vio 100.00
LAM105 A13 30c org & vio 30.00
LAM106 A14 50c blk, *blue grn*, white back 17.00
LAM107 A11 $1 blk & vio, *blue* 32.50
LAM108 A13 $3 vio & grn 250.00

ANPING

Values for stamps of Hong Kong used at ANPING

1882-91 Wmk. 2 *Perf. 14*
On Nos. 36b-44

LAP1 A1 2c carmine *1,100.*
LAP2 A1 5c ultramarine *900.00*
LAP3 A1 10c green *1,000.*
LAP4 A1 10c vio, *red* *1,150.*

1885-91 Wmk. 2 *Perf. 14*
On Nos. 51, 53

LAP5 A1 20c on 30c vermilion *1,100.*
LAP6 A1 50c on 48c brown *1,900.*

CANTON

Values for stamps of Hong Kong used at CANTON with "C1" or c.d.s.

1862 Unwmk. *Perf. 14*
On No. 4

LCA1 A1 18c lilac 200.00

1863-80 Wmk. 1 *Perf. 14*
On Nos. 8-24

LCA2 A1 2c brown 42.50
LCA3 A1 2c dull rose 57.50
LCA4 A1 4c slate 45.00
LCA5 A1 5c ultra 90.00
LCA6 A1 6c lilac 72.50
LCA7 A1 8c orange buff 52.50
LCA8 A1 10c violet 65.00
LCA9 A1 12c lt blue 25.00
LCA10 A1 16c yellow 190.00
LCA11 A1 24c green 80.00
LCA12 A1 30c vermilion —
LCA13 A1 30c violet 25.00
LCA14 A1 48c rose carmine 135.00
LCA15 A1 96c gray 325.00

1874 Wmk. 1 *Perf. 15½x15*
On No. 26

LCA16 A2 $2 sage green 225.00

1876-77 On Nos. 29-30

LCA17 A1 16c on 18c lilac 350.00
LCA18 A1 28c on 30c violet 150.00

1879-80 On Nos. 31-35

LCA19 A1 5c on 8c orange 190.00
LCA20 A1 5c on 18c lilac 145.00
LCA21 A1 10c on 12c blue 135.00
LCA22 A1 10c on 16c yellow 300.00
LCA23 A1 10c on 24c green 175.00

1879 Wmk. 1 *Perf. 14*
On Nos. 35A-35B

LCA24 A5 3c on 16c yel on card 850.00
LCA25 A5 5c on 18c lilac on card 1,000.

See note after No. 35C.

1882-1902 Wmk. 2 *Perf. 14*
On Nos. 36-48

LCA26 A1 2c rose lake 45.00
a. carmine 4.00
LCA27 A1 2c green 5.00
LCA28 A1 4c slate 16.00
LCA29 A1 4c carmine rose 4.50
LCA30 A1 5c ultramarine 6.00
LCA31 A1 5c yellow 37.50
LCA32 A1 10c lilac 45.00
LCA33 A1 10c green 11.00
LCA34 A1 10c vio, *red* 5.50
LCA35 A1 10c ultra 5.00
LCA36 A1 12c blue 160.00
LCA37 A1 30c gray green 50.00
LCA38 A1 30c brown 80.00

1885-91 Wmk. 2 *Perf. 14*
On Nos. 51-56

LCA39 A1 20c on 30c vermilion 18.00
LCA40 A1 20c on 30c yel green 325.00
LCA41 A1 50c on 48c brown 90.00
LCA42 A1 50c on 48c lilac 25.00
LCA43 A1 $1 on 96c olive gray 160.00
LCA44 A1 $1 on 96c vio, *red* 75.00

1891 Wmk. 2 *Perf. 14*
On Nos. 60, 61a, 64-65

LCA45 A4 $5 on $10 vio, *red* 475.00
LCA46 A1(g) 20c on 30c dull grn 22.50
LCA47 A1 7c on 10c green 27.50

Wmk. 1

LCA48 A1 14c on 30c violet 150.00

1891 Wmk. 2 *Perf. 14*
On No. 66

LCA49 A1 2c carmine *1,100.*

50th anniv. of the colony.

1897 Wmk. 1 *Perf. 15½x15*
On No. 67

LCA50 A2 $1 on $2 sage grn —

1898 Wmk. 2 *Perf. 14*
On Nos. 69-70

LCA51 A1 10c on 30c gray green 200.00
LCA52 A1 $1 on 96c black 175.00

1903 Wmk. 2 *Perf. 14*
On Nos. 71-80

LCA53 A10 1c brown & lilac 5.00
LCA54 A10 2c gray green 5.50
LCA55 A10 4c violet, *red* 4.00
LCA56 A10 5c org & gray green 25.00
LCA57 A10 8c vio & blk 10.00
LCA58 A10 10c ultra & lilac, *blue* 5.00
LCA59 A10 12c red vio & gray grn, *yel* 20.00
LCA60 A10 20c org brn & blk 12.00
LCA61 A10 30c blk & gray grn 62.50
LCA62 A10 50c red vio & gray green 100.00

1904-11 Wmk. 3 *Perf. 14*
On Nos. 86-108

LCA63 A10 1c brown 5.00
LCA64 A10 2c gray green 5.00
LCA65 A10 2c deep green 5.00
LCA66 A10 4c violet, *red* 4.00
LCA67 A10 4c carmine 4.00
LCA68 A10 5c org & gray grn 24.00
LCA69 A10 6c red vio & org 24.00
LCA70 A10 8c vio & blk 16.00
LCA71 A10 10c ultra & lil, *blue* 5.00
LCA72 A10 10c ultra 5.00
LCA73 A10 12c red vio & gray grn, *yel* 26.00
LCA74 A10 20c org brn & blk 15.00
LCA75 A10 20c olive grn & vio 85.00
LCA76 A10 30c blk & gray grn 45.00
LCA77 A10 30c org & vio 72.50
LCA78 A10 50c red vio & gray grn 50.00
LCA79 A10 50c blk, *grn* 52.50
LCA80 A10 $1 ol grn & lil 90.00
LCA81 A10 $2 scarlet & blk 575.00
LCA82 A10 $2 carmine & blk 675.00
LCA83 A10 $3 dp blue & blk 750.00
LCA84 A10 $10 org & blk, *blue* 2,000.

1912-14 Wmk. 3 *Perf. 14*
On Nos. 109-124

LCA85 A11 1c brown 5.00
LCA86 A11 2c deep green 4.50
LCA87 A12 4c carmine 3.50
LCA88 A13 6c orange 7.50
LCA89 A12 8c gray 24.00
LCA90 A11 10c ultramarine 5.00
LCA91 A14 12c vio, *yel* 24.00
LCA92 A14 20c ol grn & vio 7.50
LCA93 A15 25c red vio & dl vio 100.00
LCA94 A13 30c org & vio 25.00
LCA95 A14 50c blk, *blue grn* 9.00
LCA96 A11 $1 blk & vio, *blue* 45.00
LCA97 A14 $2 blk & red 150.00
LCA98 A13 $3 vio & grn 275.00
LCA99 A13 $10 blk & vio, *red* 450.00

CHEFOO

Values for stamps of Hong Kong used at CHEFOO with c.d.s.

1882-1902 Wmk. 2 *Perf. 14*
On Nos. 37-48

LCH1 A1 2c green 30.00
LCH2 A1 4c carmine rose 30.00
LCH3 A1 5c ultramarine 42.50
LCH4 A1 5c yellow 80.00
LCH5 A1 10c ultra 30.00
LCH6 A1 30c brown 180.00

1891 Wmk. 2 *Perf. 14*
On No. 52

LCH7 A1 20c on 30c gray green 62.50

1898 Wmk. 2 *Perf. 14*
On No. 70

LCH8 A1 $1 on 96c black 150.00

1903 Wmk. 2 *Perf. 14*
On Nos. 71-81

LCH9 A10 1c brown & lilac 12.50
LCH10 A10 2c gray green 11.00
LCH11 A10 4c violet, *red* 10.00
LCH12 A10 5c org & gray green 30.00
LCH13 A10 8c vio & blk 22.50
LCH14 A10 10c ultra & lilac, *blue* 14.00
LCH15 A10 12c red vio & gray grn, *yel* 40.00
LCH16 A10 20c org brn & blk 45.00
LCH17 A10 50c red vio & gray green 150.00
LCH18 A10 $1 ol grn & lilac 160.00

1904-11 Wmk. 3 *Perf. 14*
On Nos. 86-107

LCH19 A10 1c brown 12.50
LCH20 A10 2c gray green 11.00
LCH21 A10 2c deep green 11.50
LCH22 A10 4c violet, *red* 9.00
LCH23 A10 4c carmine 10.00
LCH24 A10 5c org & gray grn 22.50
LCH25 A10 6c red vio & org 40.00
LCH26 A10 8c vio & blk 20.00
LCH27 A10 10c ultra & lil, *blue* 11.00
LCH28 A10 10c ultra 11.00
LCH29 A10 12c red vio & gray grn, *yel* 35.00
LCH30 A10 20c org brn & blk 25.00
LCH31 A10 20c olive grn & vio 115.00
LCH32 A10 30c blk & gray grn 75.00
LCH33 A10 30c org & vio 90.00
LCH34 A10 50c red vio & gray grn 75.00
LCH35 A10 50c blk, *grn* 75.00
LCH36 A10 $1 ol grn & lil 125.00
LCH37 A10 $2 scarlet & blk 350.00
LCH38 A10 $2 carmine & blk 750.00
LCH39 A10 $3 dp blue & blk 675.00
LCH40 A10 $5 bl grn & lil 1,000.

1912-14 Wmk. 3 *Perf. 14*
On Nos. 109-124

LCH41 A11 1c brown 10.00
LCH42 A11 2c deep green 10.00
LCH43 A12 4c carmine 8.00
LCH44 A13 6c orange 20.00
LCH45 A12 8c gray 42.50
LCH46 A11 10c ultramarine 10.00
LCH47 A14 12c vio, *yel* 45.00
LCH48 A14 20c ol grn & vio 15.00
LCH49 A13 30c org & vio 27.50
LCH50 A14 50c blk, *blue grn* 15.00
LCH51 A11 $1 blk & vio, *blue* 25.00
LCH52 A14 $2 blk & red 125.00
LCH53 A13 $3 vio & grn 190.00
LCH54 A14 $5 red & grn, *grn* 675.00
LCH55 A13 $10 blk & vio, *red* 450.00

FOOCHOW

Values for stamps of Hong Kong used at FOOCHOW with "F1" or "FOOCHOWFOO" c.d.s.

1862 Unwmk. *Perf. 14*
On No. 4

LFO1 A1 18c lilac 225.00

1863-80 Wmk. 1 *Perf. 14*
On Nos. 8-24

LFO2 A1 2c brown 37.50
LFO3 A1 2c dull rose 50.00
LFO4 A1 4c slate 37.50
LFO5 A1 5c ultra 95.00
LFO6 A1 6c lilac 57.50
LFO7 A1 8c orange buff 52.50
LFO8 A1 10c violet 55.00
LFO9 A1 12c lt blue 22.50
LFO10 A1 16c yellow 175.00
LFO11 A1 18c lilac 1,050.
LFO12 A1 24c green 80.00
LFO13 A1 30c vermilion 250.00
LFO14 A1 30c violet 20.00
LFO15 A1 48c rose carmine 135.00
LFO16 A1 48c brpwn 300.00
LFO17 A1 96c gray 450.00

1874 Wmk. 1 *Perf. 15½x15*
On Nos. 26-27

LFO18 A2 $2 sage green 190.00
LFO19 A3 $3 violet 175.00

1876-77 On Nos. 29-30

LFO20 A1 16c on 18c lilac 375.00
LFO21 A1 28c on 30c violet 175.00

1879-80 On Nos. 31-35

LFO22 A1 5c on 8c orange 375.00
LFO23 A1 5c on 18c lilac 135.00
LFO24 A1 10c on 12c blue 135.00
LFO25 A1 10c on 16c yellow —
LFO26 A1 10c on 24c green 180.00

1879 Wmk. 1 *Perf. 14*
On No. 35A

LFO27 A5 3c on 16c yel on card 1,100.

See note after No. 35C.

1882-1902 Wmk. 2 *Perf. 14*
On Nos. 36b-48

LFO28 A1 2c rose lake 42.50
a. carmine 3.25
LFO29 A1 2c green 5.00
LFO30 A1 4c slate 9.50
LFO31 A1 4c carmine rose 5.50
LFO32 A1 5c ultramarine 4.00
LFO33 A1 5c yellow 25.00
LFO34 A1 10c lilac 47.50
LFO35 A1 10c green 11.50
LFO36 A1 10c vio, *red* 4.75
LFO37 A1 10c ultra 5.00
LFO38 A1 30c gray green 52.50
LFO39 A1 30c brown 100.00

1885-91 Wmk. 2 *Perf. 14*
On Nos. 51-56

LFO40 A1 20c on 30c vermilion 20.00
LFO41 A1 20c on 30c yel green 300.00
LFO42 A1 50c on 48c brown 90.00
LFO43 A1 50c on 48c lilac 30.00
LFO44 A1 $1 on 96c olive gray 150.00
LFO45 A1 $1 on 96c vio, *red* 75.00

1891 Wmk. 2 *Perf. 14*
On Nos. 61a, 64-65

LFO46 A1(g) 20c on 30c dull grn 25.00
LFO47 A1 7c on 10c green 70.00

Wmk. 1

LFO48 A1 14c on 30c violet 125.00

1898 Wmk. 2 *Perf. 14*
On Nos. 69-70

LFO49 A1 10c on 30c gray green 250.00
LFO50 A1 $1 on 96c black 110.00

1903 Wmk. 2 *Perf. 14*
On Nos. 71-81

LFO51 A10 1c brown & lilac 6.00
LFO52 A10 2c gray green 5.00
LFO53 A10 4c violet, *red* 3.50
LFO54 A10 5c org & gray green 24.00
LFO55 A10 8c vio & blk 14.00
LFO56 A10 10c ultra & lilac, *blue* 5.00
LFO57 A10 12c red vio & gray grn, *yel* 24.00

LFO58 A10 20c org brn & blk 15.00
LFO59 A10 30c blk & gray grn 57.50
LFO60 A10 50c red vio & gray green 95.00
LFO61 A10 $1 ol grn & lilac 85.00

1904-11 Wmk. 3 *Perf. 14*
On Nos. 86-103

LFO62 A10 1c brown 4.50
LFO63 A10 2c gray green 5.00
LFO64 A10 2c deep green 4.50
LFO65 A10 4c violet, *red* 3.50
LFO66 A10 4c carmine 3.50
LFO67 A10 5c org & gray grn 18.00
LFO68 A10 6c red vio & org 22.50
LFO69 A10 8c vio & blk 12.00
LFO70 A10 10c ultra & lil, *blue* 5.00
LFO71 A10 10c ultra 4.50
LFO72 A10 12c red vio & gray grn, *yel* 26.00
LFO73 A10 20c org brn & blk 12.50
LFO74 A10 20c olive grn & vio 85.00
LFO75 A10 30c blk & gray grn 52.50
LFO76 A10 30c org & vio 72.50
LFO77 A10 50c red vio & gray grn 45.00
LFO78 A10 50c blk, *grn* 52.50
LFO79 A10 $1 ol grn & lil 90.00

1912-14 Wmk. 3 *Perf. 14*
On Nos. 109-119

LFO80 A11 1c brown 6.00
LFO81 A11 2c deep green 4.75
LFO82 A12 4c carmine 3.50
LFO83 A13 6c orange 15.00
LFO84 A12 8c gray 27.50
LFO85 A11 10c ultramarine 5.00
LFO86 A14 12c vio, *yel* 37.50
LFO87 A14 20c ol grn & vio 8.00
LFO88 A15 25c red vio & dl vio 100.00
LFO89 A13 30c org & vio 27.50
LFO90 A14 50c blk, *blue grn* 25.00

HANKOW

Values for stamps of Hong Kong used at HANKOW with "D29" or c.d.s.

1862 Unwmk. *Perf. 14*
On No. 4

LHA1 A1 18c lilac 450.00

1863-80 Wmk. 1 *Perf. 14*
On Nos. 8-24

LHA2 A1 2c brown 135.00
LHA3 A1 2c dull rose 110.00
LHA4 A1 4c slate 135.00
LHA5 A1 5c ultra 125.00
LHA6 A1 6c lilac 180.00
LHA7 A1 8c orange buff 175.00
LHA8 A1 10c violet 135.00
LHA9 A1 12c lt blue 55.00
LHA10 A1 16c yellow *800.00*
LHA11 A1 18c lilac 1,250.
LHA12 A1 24c green 275.00
LHA13 A1 30c violet 135.00
LHA14 A1 48c rose carmine 375.00
LHA15 A1 48c brown 500.00
LHA16 A1 96c gray —

1874 Wmk. 1 *Perf. 15½x15*
On No. 26

LHA17 A2 $2 sage green 325.00

1876-77 On Nos. 29-30

LHA18 A1 16c on 18c lilac 550.00
LHA19 A1 28c on 30c violet 350.00

1879-80 On Nos. 31-35

LHA20 A1 5c on 8c orange 350.00
LHA21 A1 5c on 18c lilac 250.00
LHA22 A1 10c on 12c blue 275.00
LHA23 A1 10c on 16c yellow 525.00
LHA24 A1 10c on 24c green 325.00

1879 Wmk. 1 *Perf. 14*
On No. 35A

LHA25 A5 3c on 16c yel on card *1,750.*

See note after No. 35C.

1882-1902 Wmk. 2 *Perf. 14*
On Nos. 36b-48

LHA26 A1 2c carmine 10.00
LHA27 A1 2c green 7.00
LHA28 A1 4c slate 22.50
LHA29 A1 4c carmine rose 7.50
LHA30 A1 5c ultramarine 11.00
LHA31 A1 5c yellow 37.50
LHA32 A1 10c lilac 110.00
LHA33 A1 10c green 14.00
LHA34 A1 10c vio, *red* 12.00
LHA35 A1 10c ultra 9.00
LHA36 A1 12c blue 200.00
LHA37 A1 30c gray green 80.00
LHA38 A1 30c brown 110.00

1885-91 Wmk. 2 *Perf. 14*
On Nos. 51-56

LHA39 A1 20c on 30c vermilion 45.00
LHA40 A1 20c on 30c yel green 30.00
LHA41 A1 50c on 48c brown 110.00
LHA42 A1 50c on 48c lilac 32.50
LHA43 A1 $1 on 96c olive gray 225.00
LHA44 A1 $1 on 96c vio, *red* 100.00

1890 Wmk. 1 *Perf. 14*
On No. 57

LHA45 A2 $2 gray green 550.00

1891 Wmk. 2 *Perf. 14*
On Nos. 64-65

LHA46 A1 7c on 10c green 45.00

Wmk. 1

LHA47 A1 14c on 30c violet 175.00

1897 Wmk. 1 *Perf. 15½x15*
On No. 67

LHA48 A2 $1 on $2 sage grn 800.00

1898 Wmk. 2 *Perf. 14*
On Nos. 69-70

LHA49 A1 10c on 30c gray green 325.00
LHA50 A1 $1 on 96c black 125.00

1903 Wmk. 2 *Perf. 14*
On Nos. 71-81

LHA51 A10 1c brown & lilac 7.50
LHA52 A10 2c gray green 7.00
LHA53 A10 4c violet, *red* 6.00
LHA54 A10 5c org & gray green 27.50
LHA55 A10 8c vio & blk 22.50
LHA56 A10 10c ultra & lilac, *blue* 6.50
LHA57 A10 12c red vio & gray grn, *yel* 27.50
LHA58 A10 20c org brn & blk 20.00
LHA59 A10 30c blk & gray grn 65.00
LHA60 A10 50c red vio & gray green 110.00
LHA61 A10 $1 ol grn & lilac 90.00

1904-11 Wmk. 3 *Perf. 14*
On Nos. 86-108

LHA62 A10 1c brown 7.00
LHA63 A10 2c gray green 6.50
LHA64 A10 2c deep green 6.00
LHA65 A10 4c violet, *red* 5.50
LHA66 A10 4c carmine 4.50
LHA67 A10 5c org & gray grn 25.00
LHA68 A10 6c red vio & org 27.50
LHA69 A10 8c vio & blk 12.50
LHA70 A10 10c ultra & lil, *blue* 6.50
LHA71 A10 10c ultra 6.50
LHA72 A10 12c red vio & gray grn, *yel* 30.00
LHA73 A10 20c org brn & blk 20.00
LHA74 A10 20c olive grn & vio 110.00
LHA75 A10 30c blk & gray grn 55.00
LHA76 A10 30c org & vio 100.00
LHA77 A10 50c red vio & gray grn 45.00
LHA78 A10 $1 ol grn & lil 90.00
LHA79 A10 $2 scarlet & blk 525.00
LHA80 A10 $5 bl grn & lilac 1,000.
LHA81 A10 $10 org & blk, *blue* *2,400.*

1912-14 Wmk. 3 *Perf. 14*
On Nos. 109-123

LHA82 A11 1c brown 8.00
LHA83 A11 2c deep green 7.00
LHA84 A12 4c carmine 5.50
LHA85 A13 6c orange 16.00
LHA86 A11 10c ultramarine 6.50
LHA87 A14 20c ol grn & vio 16.00
LHA88 A13 30c org & vio 35.00
LHA89 A14 50c blk, *blue grn* 20.00
LHA90 A11 $1 blk & vio, *blue* 80.00
LHA91 A14 $5 red & grn, *grn* 900.00

KIUNGCHOW (HOIHAO)

Values for stamps of Hong Kong used at KIUNGCHOW (HOIHAO) with "D28", c.d.s. inscribed "KIUNG-CHOW" or c.d.s. inscribed "Hoi-Hao"

1863-80 Wmk. 1 *Perf. 14*
On Nos. 8-24

LKC1 A1 2c brown *1,100.*
LKC2 A1 4c slate *900.00*
LKC3 A1 5c ultra *900.00*
LKC4 A1 6c lilac *1,800.*
LKC5 A1 8c orange buff *1,850.*
LKC6 A1 10c violet *1,050.*
LKC7 A1 12c lt blue *600.00*
LKC8 A1 16c yellow *3,000.*
LKC9 A1 24c green *1,800.*
LKC10 A1 30c vermilion —
LKC11 A1 30c violet 325.00
LKC12 A1 48c rose carmine *2,750.*
LKC13 A1 96c gray *2,750.*

1874 Wmk. 1 *Perf. 15½x15*
On No. 26

LKC14 A2 $2 sage green 525.00

1876-77
On Nos. 29-30

LKC15 A1 16c on 18c lilac *1,900.*
LKC16 A1 28c on 30c violet *1,600.*

1879-80
On Nos. 31-35

LKC17 A1 5c on 8c orange *1,250.*
LKC18 A1 5c on 18c lilac *1,100.*
LKC19 A1 10c on 12c blue *1,100.*
LKC20 A1 10c on 16c yellow *2,250.*
LKC21 A1 10c on 24c green —

1882-1902 Wmk. 2 *Perf. 14*
On Nos. 36b-48

LKC22 A1 2c carmine 65.00
LKC23 A1 2c green 85.00
LKC24 A1 4c slate 90.00
LKC25 A1 4c carmine rose 42.50
LKC26 A1 5c ultramarine 65.00
LKC27 A1 5c yellow 110.00
LKC28 A1 10c lilac 850.00
LKC29 A1 10c green 90.00
LKC30 A1 10c vio, *red* 75.00
LKC31 A1 10c ultra 47.50
LKC32 A1 30c gray green 150.00
LKC33 A1 30c brown 210.00

1885-91 Wmk. 2 *Perf. 14*
On Nos. 51-56

LKC34 A1 20c on 30c vermilion 175.00
LKC35 A1 20c on 30c yel green 75.00
LKC36 A1 50c on 48c brown 190.00
LKC37 A1 50c on 48c lilac 100.00
LKC38 A1 $1 on 96c olive gray 350.00
LKC39 A1 $1 on 96c vio, *red* 210.00

1890 Wmk. 1 *Perf. 14*
On No. 57

LKC40 A2 $2 gray green 775.00

1891 Wmk. 2 *Perf. 14*
On No. 64

LKC41 A1 7c on 10c green 225.00

1891 Wmk. 2 *Perf. 14*
On No. 66

LKC42 A1 2c carmine *3,250.*

50th anniv. of the colony.

1897 Wmk. 1 *Perf. 15½x15*
On No. 67

LKC43 A2 $1 on $2 sage grn 575.00

1898 Wmk. 2 *Perf. 14*
On Nos. 69-70

LKC44 A1 10c on 30c gray green 575.00
LKC45 A1 $1 on 96c black 400.00

1903 Wmk. 2 *Perf. 14*
On Nos. 71-82

LKC46 A10 1c brown & lilac 30.00
LKC47 A10 2c gray green 30.00
LKC48 A10 4c violet, *red* 21.00
LKC49 A10 5c org & gray green 62.50
LKC50 A10 8c vio & blk 52.50
LKC51 A10 10c ultra & lilac, *blue* 26.00
LKC52 A10 12c red vio & gray grn, *yel* 67.50
LKC53 A10 20c org brn & blk 80.00
LKC54 A10 30c blk & gray grn 145.00
LKC55 A10 50c red vio & gray green 225.00
LKC56 A10 $1 ol grn & lilac 350.00
LKC57 A10 $2 scar & blk 1,050.

1904-11 Wmk. 3 *Perf. 14*
On Nos. 86-103

LKC58 A10 1c brown 27.50
LKC59 A10 2c gray green 27.50
LKC60 A10 2c deep green 26.00
LKC61 A10 4c violet, *red* 21.00
LKC62 A10 4c carmine 21.00
LKC63 A10 5c org & gray grn 62.50
LKC64 A10 6c red vio & org 67.50
LKC65 A10 8c vio & blk 37.50
LKC66 A10 10c ultra & lil, *blue* 24.00
LKC67 A10 10c ultra 24.00
LKC68 A10 12c red vio & gray grn, *yel* 67.50
LKC69 A10 20c org brn & blk 80.00
LKC70 A10 20c olive grn & vio 115.00
LKC71 A10 30c blk & gray grn 100.00
LKC72 A10 30c org & vio 100.00
LKC72 A10 $1 ol grn & lil 550.00

1912-14 Wmk. 3 *Perf. 14*
On Nos. 109-120

LKC74 A11 1c brown 25.00
LKC75 A11 2c deep green 24.00
LKC76 A12 4c carmine 21.00
LKC77 A13 6c orange 40.00
LKC78 A12 8c gray 100.00
LKC79 A11 10c ultramarine 21.00
LKC80 A14 12c vio, *yel* 72.50
LKC81 A14 20c ol grn & vio 47.50
LKC82 A15 25c red vio & dl vio 135.00
LKC83 A13 30c org & vio 110.00
LKC84 A14 50c blk, *blue grn,* 85.00
LKC85 A11 $1 blk & vio, *blue* 90.00

NINGPO

Values for stamps of Hong Kong used at LINGPO with "N1" or c.d.s.

1862 Unwmk. *Perf. 14*
On No. 4

LNG1 A1 18c lilac *1,350.*

1863-80 Wmk. 1 *Perf. 14*
On Nos. 8-25

LNG2 A1 2c brown 500.00
LNG3 A1 4c slate 500.00
LNG4 A1 5c ultra 250.00
LNG5 A1 6c lilac 550.00
LNG6 A1 8c orange buff 550.00
LNG7 A1 10c violet 250.00
LNG8 A1 12c lt blue 180.00
LNG9 A1 16c yellow 675.00
LNG10 A1 18c lilac —
LNG11 A1 24c green 550.00
LNG12 A1 30c vermilion 650.00
LNG13 A1 30c violet 160.00
LNG14 A1 48c rose carmine 950.00
LNG15 A1 48c brown 1,100.
LNG16 A1 96c gray 1.100.

Perf. 12½

LNG17 A1 4c slate —

1874 Wmk. 1 *Perf. 15½x15*
On No. 26

LNG19 A2 $2 sage green 500.00

1876-77 On Nos. 29-30

LNG20 A1 16c on 18c lilac 800.00
LNG21 A1 28c on 30c violet 500.00

1879-80 On Nos. 31-35

LNG22 A1 5c on 8c orange 550.00
LNG23 A1 5c on 18c lilac 475.00
LNG24 A1 10c on 12c blue 500.00
LNG25 A1 10c on 24c green 550.00

1879 Wmk. 1 *Perf. 14*
On No. 35A

LNG26 A5 3c on 16c yellow on card *2,000.*

See note after No. 35C.

1882-1902 Wmk. 2 *Perf. 14*
On Nos. 36b-47

LNG27 A1 2c carmine 52.50
LNG28 A1 2c green 35.00
LNG29 A1 4c slate 90.00
LNG30 A1 4c carmine rose 35.00
LNG31 A1 5c ultramarine 52.50
LNG32 A1 10c lilac 250.00
LNG33 A1 10c green 67.50
LNG34 A1 10c vio, *red* 57.50
LNG35 A1 10c ultra 35.00
LNG36 A1 30c gray green 160.00

1890 Wmk. 1 *Perf. 15½x15*
On No. 50

LNG37 A4 12c on $10 rose —

1885-91 Wmk. 2 *Perf. 14*
On Nos. 52-56

LNG38 A1 20c on 30c yel green 60.00
LNG39 A1 50c on 48c brown 200.00
LNG40 A1 50c on 48c lilac 100.00
LNG41 A1 $1 on 96c vio, *red* 190.00

1891 Wmk. 2 *Perf. 14*
On Nos. 64-65

LNG42 A1 7c on 10c green 90.00

Wmk. 1

LNG43 A1 14c on 30c violet 325.00

1897 Wmk. 1 *Perf. 15½x15*
On No. 67

LNG44 A2 $1 on $2 sage grn —

1898 Wmk. 2 *Perf. 14*
On Nos. 69-70
LNG45 A1 10c on 30c gray green 400.00
LNG46 A1 $1 on 96c black 225.00

1903 Wmk. 2 *Perf. 14*
On Nos. 71-80
LNG47 A10 1c brown & lilac 35.00
LNG48 A10 2c gray green 35.00
LNG49 A10 4c violet, *red* 25.00
LNG50 A10 5c org & gray green 75.00
LNG51 A10 8c vio & blk 42.50
LNG52 A10 10c ultra & lilac, *blue* 27.50
LNG53 A10 12c red vio & gray grn, *yel* 85.00
LNG54 A10 50c red vio & gray green 160.00

1904-11 Wmk. 3 *Perf. 14*
On Nos. 86-103
LNG55 A10 1c brown 25.00
LNG56 A10 2c gray green 30.00
LNG57 A10 2c deep green 25.00
LNG58 A10 4c violet, *red* 25.00
LNG59 A10 4c carmine 25.00
LNG60 A10 8c vio & blk 57.50
LNG61 A10 10c ultra 25.00
LNG62 A10 12c red vio & gray grn, *yel* 80.00
LNG63 A10 20c org brn & blk 75.00
LNG64 A10 20c olive grn & vio 135.00
LNG65 A10 30c blk & gray grn 110.00
LNG66 A10 30c org & vio 125.00
LNG67 A10 50c red vio & gray grn 100.00
LNG68 A10 $1 ol grn & lil 150.00

1912-14 Wmk. 3 *Perf. 14*
On Nos. 109-120
LNG69 A11 1c brown 27.50
LNG70 A11 2c deep green 25.00
LNG71 A12 4c carmine 25.00
LNG72 A12 8c gray 85.00
LNG73 A11 10c ultramarine 25.00
LNG74 A14 20c ol grn & vio 65.00
LNG75 A13 30c org & vio 100.00
LNG76 A11 $1 blk & vio, *blue* 90.00

SHANGHAI

Values for stamps of Hong Kong used at SHANGHAI with "S1", "SHANGHAE" or "SHANGHAF" c.d.s.

The popular "Sunburst" cancellation was also applied at Shanghai in 1864-65. It is scarce and commands premiums starting at $350 for the least rare values. It can be found together with the "B62" canceller of Hong Kong, and in that combination has a premium of about $300 for the least rare values. These values assume clear and reasonably complete strikes.

1862 Unwmk. *Perf. 14*
On Nos. 1-7
LSH1 A1 2c pale brown 175.00
a. deep brown 190.00
LSH2 A1 8c buff 200.00
LSH3 A1 12c blue 150.00
LSH4 A1 18c lilac 125.00
LSH5 A1 24c green 240.00
LSH6 A1 48c rose 650.00
LSH7 A1 96c gray 850.00

1863-80 Wmk. 1 *Perf. 14*
On Nos. 8-25
LSH8 A1 2c brown 12.50
LSH9 A1 2c dull rose 42.50
LSH10 A1 4c slate 12.00
LSH11 A1 5c ultra 72.50
LSH12 A1 6c lilac 25.00
LSH13 A1 8c orange buff 20.00
LSH14 A1 10c violet 24.00
LSH15 A1 12c lt blue 12.00
LSH16 A1 16c yellow 85.00
LSH17 A1 18c lilac 400.00
LSH18 A1 24c green 18.00
LSH19 A1 30c vermilion 27.50
LSH20 A1 30c violet 9.00
LSH21 A1 48c rose carmine 45.00
LSH22 A1 48c brown 160.00
LSH23 A1 96c bister *1,500.*
LSH24 A1 96c gray 70.00
Perf. 12½
LSH25 A1 4c slate 300.00

1874 Wmk. 1 *Perf. 15½x15*
On Nos. 26-28
LSH26 A2 $2 sage green 80.00
LSH27 A3 $3 dull violet 55.00
LSH28 A4 $10 rose 825.00

1876-77 **On Nos. 29-30**
LSH29 A1 16c on 18c lilac 200.00
LSH30 A1 28c on 30c violet 60.00

1879-80 **On Nos. 31-35**
LSH31 A1 5c on 8c orange 115.00
LSH32 A1 5c on 18c lilac 75.00
LSH33 A1 10c on 12c blue 60.00
LSH34 A1 10c on 16c yellow 190.00
LSH35 A1 10c on 24c green 115.00

1879 Wmk. 1 *Perf. 14*
On Nos. 35A-35B
LSH36 A5 3c on 16c yel on card 575.00
LSH37 A5 5c on 18c lilac on card 700.00

See note after No. 35C.

1882-1902 Wmk. 2 *Perf. 14*
On Nos. 36-48
LSH38 A1 2c rose lake 40.00
a. carmine 3.50
LSH39 A1 2c green 1.50
LSH40 A1 4c slate 3.75
LSH41 A1 4c carmine rose 1.50
LSH42 A1 5c ultramarine 2.00
LSH43 A1 5c yellow 10.00
LSH44 A1 10c lilac 27.50
LSH45 A1 10c green 2.50
LSH46 A1 10c vio, *red* 2.00
LSH47 A1 10c ultra 3.00
LSH48 A1 12c blue 110.00
LSH49 A1 30c gray green 42.50
LSH50 A1 30c brown 42.50

1890 Wmk. 1 *Perf. 15½x15*
On No. 50
LSH51 A4 12c on $10 rose 375.00

1885-91 Wmk. 2 *Perf. 14*
On Nos. 51-56
LSH52 A1 20c on 30c vermilion 10.00
LSH53 A1 20c on 30c green —
LSH54 A1 50c on 48c brown 75.00
LSH55 A1 50c on 48c lilac 350.00
LSH56 A1 $1 on 96c olive gray 125.00
LSH57 A1 $1 on 96c vio, *red* 450.00

1890 Wmk. 1 *Perf. 14*
On Nos. 57-58, 60
LSH58 A2 $2 gray green 300.00
LSH59 A3 $3 lilac 600.00
Wmk. 2
LSH60 A4 $5 on $10 vio, *red* 200.00

1891 Wmk. 2 *Perf. 14*
On Nos. 61-65
LSH61 A1(g) 20c on 30c gray grn 11.00
LSH62 A1(h) 50c on 48c lilac 8.50
LSH63 A1(i) $1 on 96c vio, *red* 32.50
LSH64 A1 7c on 10c green 17.00
Wmk. 1
LSH65 A1 14c on 30c violet 100.00

1897 Wmk. 1 *Perf. 15½x15*
On Nos. 67-68
LSH66 A2 $1 on $2 sage grn 240.00
Perf. 14
LSH67 A2 $1 on $2 gray grn 325.00

1898 Wmk. 2 *Perf. 14*
On Nos. 69-70
LSH68 A1 10c on 30c gray green 125.00
LSH69 A1 $1 on 96c black 50.00

1903 Wmk. 2 *Perf. 14*
On Nos. 71-85
LSH70 A10 1c brown & lilac 1.10
LSH71 A10 2c gray green 2.75
LSH72 A10 4c violet, *red* 1.00
LSH73 A10 5c org & gray green 16.00
LSH74 A10 8c vio & blk 3.25
LSH75 A10 10c ultra & lilac, *blue* 2.25
LSH76 A10 12c red vio & gray grn, *yel* 9.00
LSH77 A10 20c org brn & blk 6.25
LSH78 A10 30c blk & gray grn 40.00
LSH79 A10 50c red vio & gray green 80.00
LSH80 A10 $1 ol grn & lil 42.50
LSH81 A10 $2 scarlet & blk 500.00
LSH82 A10 $3 dull blue & blk 700.00
LSH83 A10 $5 bl grn & lil 800.00
LSH84 A10 $10 org & blk, *blue* 900.00

1904-11 Wmk. 3 *Perf. 14*
On Nos. 86-108
LSH85 A10 1c brown 2.00
LSH86 A10 2c gray green 3.25
LSH87 A10 2c deep green 2.25
LSH88 A10 4c violet, *red* 1.00
LSH89 A10 4c carmine 1.00
LSH90 A10 5c org & gray grn 10.00
LSH91 A10 6c red vio & org 10.00
LSH92 A10 8c vio & blk 4.00
LSH93 A10 10c ultra & lil, *blue* 2.00
LSH94 A10 10c ultra 1.00
LSH95 A10 12c red vio & gray grn, *yel* 11.00
LSH96 A10 20c org brn & blk 5.00
LSH97 A10 20c olive grn & vio 62.50
LSH98 A10 30c blk & gray grn 32.50
LSH99 A10 30c org & vio 47.50
LSH100 A10 50c red vio & gray grn 21.00
LSH101 A10 50c blk, *grn* 30.00
LSH102 A10 $1 ol grn & lil 47.50
LSH103 A10 $2 scarlet & blk 225.00
LSH104 A10 $2 blk & carmine 575.00
LSH105 A10 $3 dp blue & blk 500.00
LSH106 A10 $5 bl grn & lil 725.00
LSH107 A10 $10 org & blk, *blue* *1,850.*

1912-15 Wmk. 3 *Perf. 14*
On Nos. 109-120
LSH108 A11 1c brown 1.50
LSH109 A11 2c deep green 1.00
LSH110 A12 4c carmine 1.00
LSH111 A13 6c orange 3.75
LSH112 A12 8c gray 11.50
LSH113 A11 10c ultramarine 1.00
LSH114 A14 12c vio, *yel* 17.00
LSH115 A14 20c ol grn & vio 2.50
LSH116 A13 30c org & vio 16.00
LSH117 A14 50c blk, *emerald* 6.25
LSH118 A11 $1 blk & vio, *blue* 10.00

SWATOW

Values for stamps of Hong Kong used at SWATOW with "S2" or c.d.s.

1862 Unwmk. *Perf. 14*
On No. 4
LSW1 A1 18c lilac 500.00

1863-80 Wmk. 1 *Perf. 14*
On Nos. 8-25
LSW2 A1 2c brown 170.00
LSW3 A1 2c dull rose 150.00
LSW4 A1 4c slate 160.00
LSW5 A1 5c ultra 175.00
LSW6 A1 6c lilac 625.00
LSW7 A1 8c orange buff 160.00
LSW8 A1 10c violet 180.00
LSW9 A1 12c lt blue 57.50
LSW10 A1 16c yellow 575.00
LSW11 A1 18c lilac 1,250.
LSW12 A1 24c green 200.00
LSW13 A1 30c vermilion
LSW14 A1 30c violet 57.50
LSW15 A1 48c rose carmine 325.00
LSW16 A1 96c gray 1,150.
Perf. 12½
LSW17 A1 4c slate

1874 Wmk. 1 *Perf. 15½x15*
On Nos. 26-27
LSW18 A2 $2 sage green 190.00
LSW19 A3 $3 violet 175.00

1876-77 **On Nos. 29-30**
LSW20 A1 16c on 18c lilac 575.00
LSW21 A1 28c on 30c violet 325.00

1879-80 **On Nos. 31-35**
LSW22 A1 5c on 8c orange 375.00
LSW23 A1 5c on 18c lilac 300.00
LSW24 A1 10c on 12c blue 325.00
LSW25 A1 10c on 16c yellow 325.00
LSW26 A1 10c on 24c green 425.00

1879 Wmk. 1 *Perf. 14*
On No. 35A
LSW27 A5 3c on 16c yel on card *1,500.*

See note after No. 35C.

1882-1902 Wmk. 2 *Perf. 14*
On Nos. 36b-48
LSW28 A1 2c carmine 8.50
LSW29 A1 2c green 10.00
LSW20 A1 4c slate 26.00
LSW31 A1 4c carmine rose 8.00
LSW32 A1 5c ultramarine 10.00
LSW33 A1 5c yellow 30.00
LSW34 A1 10c lilac 135.00
LSW35 A1 10c green 12.50
LSW36 A1 10c vio, *red* 8.50
LSW37 A1 10c ultra 8.00
LSW38 A1 12c blue 225.00
LSW39 A1 30c gray green 72.50
LSW40 A1 30c brown 80.00

1885-91 Wmk. 2 *Perf. 14*
On Nos. 51-56
LSW41 A1 20c on 30c ver 24.00
LSW42 A1 20c on 30c yel green 35.00
LSW43 A1 50c on 48c lilac 475.00
LSW44 A1 $1 on 96c ol gray 225.00
LSW45 A1 $1 on 96c vio, *red* 700.00

1890 Wmk. 1 *Perf. 14*
On No. 57
LSW46 A2 $2 sage green 575.00

1891 Wmk. 2 *Perf. 14*
On Nos. 62-65
LSW47 A1(h) 50c on 48c lilac 35.00
LSW48 A1(i) $1 on 96c vio, *red* 80.00
LSW49 A1 7c on 10c green 45.00
Wmk. 1
LSW50 A1 14c on 30c violet 175.00

1891 Wmk. 2 *Perf. 14*
On No. 66
LSW51 A1 2c carmine *1,500.*

50th anniv. of the colony.

1898 Wmk. 2 *Perf. 14*
On Nos. 69-70
LSW52 A1 10c on 30c gray green 325.00
LSW53 A1 $1 on 96c black 110.00

1903 Wmk. 2 *Perf. 14*
On Nos. 71-81
LSW54 A10 1c brown & lilac 8.00
LSW55 A10 2c gray green 8.00
LSW56 A10 4c violet, *red* 7.00
LSW57 A10 5c org & gray green 24.00
LSW58 A10 8c vio & blk 16.00
LSW59 A10 10c ultra & lilac, *blue* 8.00
LSW60 A10 12c red vio & gray grn, *yel* 22.50
LSW61 A10 20c org brn & blk 11.50
LSW62 A10 30c blk & gray grn 65.00
LSW63 A10 50c red vio & gray green 115.00
LSW64 A10 $1 ol grn & lil 100.00

1904-11 Wmk. 3 *Perf. 14*
On Nos. 86-108
LSW65 A10 1c brown 10.00
LSW66 A10 2c gray green 8.00
LSW67 A10 2c deep green 10.00
LSW68 A10 4c violet, *red* 7.50
LSW69 A10 4c carmine 6.50
LSW70 A10 5c org & gray grn 24.00
LSW71 A10 6c red vio & org 20.00
LSW72 A10 8c vio & blk 15.00
LSW73 A10 10c ultra & lil, *bl* 8.00
LSW74 A10 10c ultra 7.50
LSW75 A10 12c red vio & gray grn, *yel* 25.00
LSW76 A10 20c org brn & blk 15.00
LSW77 A10 20c olive grn & vio 110.00
LSW78 A10 30c blk & gray grn 57.50
LSW79 A10 30c org & vio 90.00
LSW80 A10 50c red vio & gray grn 40.00
LSW81 A10 50c blk, *grn* 52.50
LSW82 A10 $1 ol grn & lil 100.00
LSW83 A10 $2 scar & blk 375.00
LSW84 A10 $10 org & blk, *bl* *2,250.*

1912-14 Wmk. 3 *Perf. 14*
On Nos. 109-120
LSW85 A11 1c brown 7.50
LSW86 A11 2c deep green 6.00
LSW87 A12 4c carmine 5.00
LSW88 A13 6c orange 11.00
LSW89 A12 8c gray 30.00
LSW90 A11 10c ultramarine 5.00
LSW91 A14 12c vio, *yel* 24.00
LSW92 A14 20c ol grn & vio 8.00
LSW93 A15 25c red vio & dl vio 75.00
LSW94 A13 30c org & vio 35.00
LSW95 A14 50c blk, *emerald* 17.50
LSW96 A11 $1 blk & vio, *blue* 30.00

TIENTSIN

Values for stamps of Hong Kong used at TIENTSIN with c.d.s.

1903 Wmk. 2 *Perf. 14*
On Nos. 71-77
LTS1 A10 1c brown & lilac 17.50
LTS2 A10 4c violet, *red* 22.50
LTS3 A10 5c org & gray green 40.00
LTS4 A10 8c vio & blk 17.50
LTS5 A10 12c red vio & gray grn, *yel* 55.00

1904-11 Wmk. 3 *Perf. 14*
On Nos. 86-108
LTS6 A10 1c brown 8.00
LTS7 A10 2c gray green 7.50
LTS8 A10 2c deep green 6.00
LTS9 A10 4c violet, *red* 5.50
LTS10 A10 4c carmine 5.00
LTS11 A10 5c org & gray grn 22.50
LTS12 A10 6c red vio & org 25.00
LTS13 A10 8c vio & blk 17.50
LTS14 A10 10c ultra & lil, *bl* 7.50
LTS15 A10 10c ultra 6.00
LTS16 A10 12c red vio & gray grn, *yel* 27.50

LTS17 A10 20c org brn & blk 17.50
LTS18 A10 20c olive grn & vio 110.00
LTS19 A10 30c blk & gray grn 55.00
LTS20 A10 30c org & vio 100.00
LTS21 A10 50c red vio & gray grn 45.00
LTS22 A10 50c blk, *grn* 75.00
LTS23 A10 $1 ol grn & lil 80.00
LTS24 A10 $2 scar & blk 350.00
LTS25 A10 $2 blk & car 800.00
LTS26 A10 $3 dp bl & blk 875.00
LTS27 A10 $5 bl grn & lil 1,200.
LTS28 A10 $10 org & blk, *bl* *2,400.*

1912-14 Wmk. 3 *Perf. 14*
On Nos. 109-123

LTS29 A11 1c brown 7.50
LTS30 A11 2c deep green 7.00
LTS31 A12 4c carmine 5.00
LTS32 A13 6c orange 10.00
LTS33 A12 8c gray 40.00
LTS34 A11 10c ultramarine 7.00
LTS35 A14 12c vio, *yel* 42.50
LTS36 A14 20c ol grn & vio 11.00
LTS37 A13 30c org & vio 24.00
LTS38 A14 50c blk, *emerald* 14.00
LTS39 A11 $1 blk & vio, *blue* 20.00
LTS40 A13 $3 vio & grn 250.00
LTS41 A14 $5 red & grn, *grn* 800.00

WEI HAI WEI (Liu Kung Tau)

Values for stamps of Hong Kong cancelled with "LIU KUNG TAU *POST OFFICE*" double oval.

1862 Unwmk. *Perf. 14*
On No. 3

LWH1 A1 12c blue —

1874 Wmk. 1 *Perf. 15½x15*
On No. 26

LWH2 A2 $2 sage green 1,150.

1882-1902 Wmk. 2 *Perf. 14*
On Nos. 36b-48

LWH3 A1 2c carmine 85.00
LWH4 A1 2c green 12.50
LWH5 A1 4c slate 100.00
LWH6 A1 4c carmine rose 12.50
LWH7 A1 5c ultramarine 85.00
LWH8 A1 5c yellow 37.50
LWH9 A1 10c vio, *red* 55.00
LWH10 A1 10c ultra 12.50
LWH11 A1 12c blue 180.00
LWH12 A1 30c gray green 100.00
LWH13 A1 30c brown 110.00

1885-91 Wmk. 2 *Perf. 14*
On Nos. 51, 54

LWH14 A1 20c on 30c yel green 67.50
LWH15 A1 50c on 48c lilac 72.50

1898 Wmk. 2 *Perf. 14*
On No. 70

LWH16 A1 $1 on 96c black 150.00

1903 Wmk. 2 *Perf. 14*
On Nos. 71-81

LWH17 A10 1c brown & lilac 10.00
LWH18 A10 2c gray green 10.00
LWH19 A10 4c violet, *red* 8.00
LWH20 A10 5c org & gray green 27.50
LWH21 A10 8c vio & blk 20.00
LWH22 A10 10c ultra & lilac, *blue* 12.50
LWH23 A10 12c red vio & gray grn, *yel* 42.50
LWH24 A10 20c org brn & blk 22.50
LWH25 A10 30c blk & gray grn 75.00
LWH26 A10 50c red vio & gray green 125.00
LWH27 A10 $1 ol grn & lil 110.00

1904-11 Wmk. 3 *Perf. 14*
On Nos. 86-102

LWH28 A10 1c brown 11.00
LWH29 A10 2c gray green 10.00
LWH30 A10 2c deep green 11.00
LWH31 A10 4c violet, *red* 10.00
LWH32 A10 4c carmine 8.00
LWH33 A10 8c vio & blk 18.00
LWH34 A10 10c ultra 9.00
LWH35 A10 20c org brn & blk 37.50
LWH36 A10 20c olive grn & vio 125.00
LWH37 A10 30c blk & gray grn 110.00
LWH38 A10 30c org & vio 110.00
LWH39 A10 50c red vio & gray grn 85.00
LWH40 A10 50c blk, *grn* 90.00

1912-14 Wmk. 3 *Perf. 14*
On Nos. 109-120

LWH41 A11 1c brown 12.50
LWH42 A11 2c deep green 10.00
LWH43 A12 4c carmine 8.00
LWH44 A13 6c orange 18.00
LWH45 A12 8c gray 42.50
LWH46 A11 10c ultramarine 10.00
LWH47 A11 $1 blk & vio, *blue* 42.50

Values for stamps of Hong Kong cancelled with "PORT EDWARD" rectangular or c.d.s.

1882-1902 Wmk. 2 *Perf. 14*
On Nos. 37, 45

LPE1 A1 2c green 100.00
LPE2 A1 10c ultra 125.00

1903 Wmk. 2 *Perf. 14*
On Nos. 71-81

LPE3 A10 1c brown & lilac 40.0
LPE4 A10 2c gray green 40.00
LPE5 A10 4c violet, *red* 35.00
LPE6 A10 5c org & gray green 55.00
LPE7 A10 8c vio & blk 55.00
LPE8 A10 10c ultra & lilac, *blue* 45.00
LPE9 A10 12c red vio & gray grn, *yel* 80.00
LPE10 A10 20c org brn & blk 110.00
LPE11 A10 30c blk & gray grn 110.00
LPE12 A10 50c red vio & gray green 145.00
LPE13 A10 $1 ol grn & lil 115.00

1904-11 Wmk. 3 *Perf. 14*
On Nos. 86-102

LPE14 A10 1c brown 22.50
LPE15 A10 2c gray green 22.50
LPE16 A10 2c deep green 22.50
LPE17 A10 4c violet, *red* 20.00
LPE18 A10 4c carmine 15.00
LPE19 A10 5c org & gray grn 35.00
LPE20 A10 6c red vio & org 45.00
LPE21 A10 8c vio & blk 27.50
LPE22 A10 10c ultra 17.50
LPE23 A10 20c org brn & blk 100.00
LPE24 A10 20c olive grn & vio 125.00
LPE25 A10 30c blk & gray grn 100.00
LPE26 A10 50c red vio & gray grn 100.00
LPE27 A10 50c blk, *grn* 75.00

1912-14 Wmk. 3 *Perf. 14*
On Nos. 109-120

LPE28 A11 1c brown 20.00
LPE29 A11 2c deep green 14.00
LPE30 A12 4c carmine 9.00
LPE31 A12 8c gray 40.00
LPE32 A11 10c ultramarine 10.00
LPE34 A10 50c blk, *grn* 35.00
LPE35 A11 $1 blk & vio, *blue* 35.00

BRITISH OFFICES IN JAPAN

HIOGO (KOBE)

Values for stamps of Hong Kong used at HIOGO (Kobe) with "D30" or c.d.s.

1863-71 Wmk. 1 *Perf. 14*
On Nos. 8-24

LHG1 A1 2c brown *6,750.*
LHG2 A1 4c slate *5,000.*
LHG3 A1 6c lilac *6,250.*
LHG4 A1 8c orange buff *6,250.*
LHG5 A1 12c lt blue *6,750.*
LHG6 A1 16c yellow *8,000.*
LHG7 A1 18c lilac —
LHG8 A1 24c green *5,250.*
LHG9 A1 30c vermilion —
LHG10 A1 30c violet *6,750.*
LHG11 A1 48c rose carmine *10,500.*
LHG12 A1 96c bister —
LHG13 A1 96c gray *10,500.*

1876 On No. 29

LHG14 A1 16c on 18c lilac —

NAGASAKI

Values for stamps of Hong Kong used at NAGASAKI with "N2" or c.d.s.

1862 Unwmk. *Perf. 14*
On No. 4

LNA1 A1 18c lilac *4,250.*

1863-77 Wmk. 1 *Perf. 14*
On Nos. 8-24

LNA2 A1 2c brown *2,750.*
LNA3 A1 4c slate *2,400.*
LNA4 A1 6c lilac *2,400.*
LNA5 A1 8c orange buff *2,400.*
LNA6 A1 12c lt blue *2,400.*
LNA7 A1 16c yellow *3,750.*
LNA8 A1 18c lilac *5,000.*
LNA9 A1 24c green *4,250.*
LNA10 A1 30c vermilion —
LAN11 A1 30c violet *3,750.*
LNA12 A1 48c rose carmine *4,750.*
LNA13 A1 96c bister —
LNA14 A1 96c gray —

1876 On Nos. 29-30

LNA15 A1 16c on 18c lilac *3,750.*
LNA16 A1 28c on 30c violet *2,750.*

YOKOHAMA

Values for stamps of Hong Kong used at YOKOHAMA with "Y1" or c.d.s.

Two types of "Y1" canceller:
Type I: Tall, thin "Y".
Type II: Short, stubby "Y".

1862 Unwmk. *Perf. 14*
On Nos. 2, 4

LYO1 A1 8c buff 475.00
LYO2 A1 18c lilac 150.00

1863-77 Wmk. 1 *Perf. 14*
On Nos. 8-25
Type II "Y1" canceller

LYO3 A1 2c brown 22.50
LYO4 A1 4c slate 24.00
LYO5 A1 6c lilac 30.00
LYO6 A1 8c orange buff 30.00
LYO7 A1 12c lt blue 22.50
LYO8 A1 16c yellow 135.00
LYO9 A1 18c lilac 725.00
LYO10 A1 24c green 27.50
LYO11 A1 30c vermilion 72.50
LYO12 A1 30c violet 22.50
LYO13 A1 48c rose carmine 62.50
LYO14 A1 96c bister *6,000.*
LYO15 A1 96c gray *85.00*

Perf. 12½

LYO16 A1 4c slate 575.00

Type I "Y1" canceller

LYO3a brown 27.50
LYO4a slate 27.50
LYO5a lilac 35.00
LYO6a orange buff 37.50
LYO7a lt blue 25.00
LYO8a yellow 150.00
LYO9a lilac 800.00
LYO10a green 32.50
LYO11a vermilion 80.00
LYO12a violet 27.50
LYO13a rose carmine 75.00
LYO15a gray 100.00

1874 Wmk. 1 *Perf. 15½x15*
On Nos. 26-28

LYO17 A2 $2 sage green 175.00
LYO18 A3 $3 dull violet 160.00
LYO19 A4 $10 rose 2,250.

1876 On Nos. 29-30
Type II "Y1" cancel

LYO20 A1 16c on 18c lilac 325.00
LYO21 A1 28c on 30c violet 100.00

Type I "Y1" cancel

LYO20a on 18c lilac 400.00
LYO21a on 30c violet 125.00

HORTA

'hor-tə

LOCATION — An administrative district of the Azores, consisting of the islands of Pico, Fayal, Flores and Corvo

GOVT. — A district of the Republic of Portugal

AREA — 305 sq. mi.

POP. — 49,000 (approx.)

CAPITAL — Horta

1000 Reis = 1 Milreis

STAMPS OF PORTUGAL USED IN HORTA

Barred Numeral "49"

1853 Queen Maria II

A1 5r org brn (#1) 1,200.
A2 25r blue (#2) 60.
A3 50r dp yel grn (#3) 1,100.
a. 50r blue green (#3a) 1,500.
A4 100r lilac (#4) 2,250.

1855 King Pedro V (Straight Hair)

A5 5r red brn (#5) 1,200.
A6 25r blue, type II (#6) 57.50
a. Type I (#6a) 60.00
A7 50r green (#7) 95.00
A8 100r lilac (#8) 110.00

1856-58
King Pedro V (Curled Hair)

A9 5r red brn (#9) 110.00
A10 25r blue, type II (#10) 70.00
a. Type I (#10a) 67.50
A11 25r rose, type II (#11; '58) 19.00

1862-64 King Luiz

A12 5r brown (#12) 60.00
A13 10r orange (#13) 67.50
A14 25r rose (#14) 13.50
A15 50r yel green (#15) 90.00
A16 100r lilac (#16; '64) 110.00

1866-67 King Luiz
Imperf.

A17 5r black (#17) 90.00
A18 10r yellow (#18) 140.00
A19 20r bister (#19) 140.00
A20 25r rose (#20; '67) 45.00
A21 50r green (#21) 125.00
A22 80r orange (#22) 125.00
A23 100r dk lilac (#23; '67) 150.00
A24 120r blue (#24) 125.00

Perf. 12½

A28 25r rose (#28) 125.00

Issued under Portuguese Administration

King Carlos — A1

Chalk-surfaced Paper

Perf. 11½, 12½, 13½

1892-93 Typo. Unwmk.

1 A1 5r yellow 2.00 1.50
2 A1 10r reddish violet 2.00 1.75
3 A1 15r chocolate 2.00 2.00
4 A1 20r lavender 6.00 3.00
5 A1 25r dp grn, perf. 11½ 5.00 1.00
a. Perf. 13½ 5.75 3.75
6 A1 50r blue 7.00 3.00
a. Perf. 13½ 9.00 5.25
7 A1 75r carmine 8.00 4.00
8 A1 80r yellow green 9.00 6.00
9 A1 100r brn, *yel* ('93) 35.00 10.00
a. Perf. 12½ 125.00 90.00
10 A1 150r car, *rose* ('93) 55.00 32.50
11 A1 200r dk bl, *bl* ('93) 60.00 32.50
12 A1 300r dk bl, *sal* ('93) 70.00 35.00
Nos. 1-12 (12) 261.00 132.25

Bisects of No. 1 were used in Aug. 1894. Value, on newsprint, $16.

The reprints have shiny white gum and clean-cut perforation 13½. The white paper is thinner than that of the originals. Value unused, $12 each.

King Carlos — A2

1897-1905 *Perf. 11½*
Name and Value in Black Except 500r

13 A2 2½r gray .50 .30
14 A2 5r orange .50 .30
15 A2 10r lt green .50 .30
16 A2 15r brown 4.00 2.50
17 A2 15r gray grn ('99) 1.25 .80
18 A2 20r gray violet 1.75 .85
19 A2 25r sea green 2.25 .45
20 A2 25r car rose ('99) .90 .50
21 A2 50r blue 3.00 .70
22 A2 50r ultra ('05) 18.00 7.00
23 A2 65r slate blue ('98) .70 .55
24 A2 75r rose 2.00 .95
25 A2 75r brn, *yel* ('05) 20.00 10.00
26 A2 80r violet 1.25 1.10
27 A2 100r dk blue, *bl* 1.75 .95
28 A2 115r org brn, *pink* ('98) 4.00 1.50
29 A2 130r gray brn, *buff* ('98) 4.00 1.50
30 A2 150r lt brn, *buff* 4.00 1.50
31 A2 180r sl, *pnksh* ('98) 4.00 1.75
32 A2 200r red vio, *pale lil* 12.00 4.00
33 A2 300r dk blue, *rose* 18.00 7.00
34 A2 500r blk & red, *bl* 20.00 8.50
Nos. 13-34 (22) 124.35 53.00

Stamps of Portugal replaced those of Horta.

HUNGARY

'hәŋ-gә-ˌrē

LOCATION — Central Europe
GOVT. — Republic
AREA — 35,911 sq. mi.
POP. — 10,679,000 (est. 1984)
CAPITAL — Budapest

Prior to World War I, Hungary together with Austria comprised the Austro-Hungarian Empire. The Hungarian post became independent on May 1, 1867. During 1850-1871 stamps listed under Austria were also used in Hungary. Copies showing clear Hungarian cancels sell for substantially more.

100 Krajczár (Kreuzer) = 1 Forint
100 Fillér = 1 Korona (1900)
100 Fillér = 1 Pengö (1926)

Catalogue values for unused stamps in this country are for Never Hinged items, beginning with Scott 503 in the regular postage section, Scott B92 in the semi-postal section, Scott C35 in the airpost section, and Scott J130 in the postage due section.

Watermarks

Wmk. 91 — "ZEITUNGS-MARKEN" in Double-lined Capitals across the Sheet

Wmk. 106 — Multiple Star

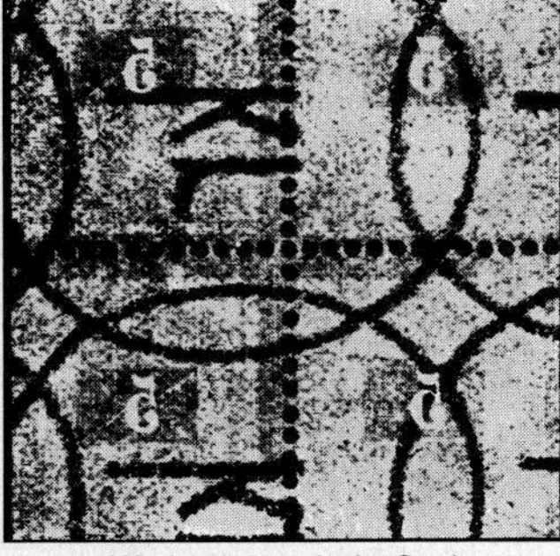

Wmk. 132 — kr in Oval

Wmk. 133 — Four Double Crosses

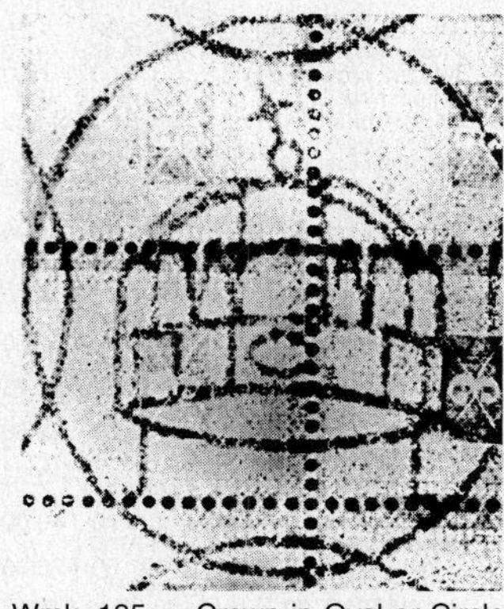

Wmk. 135 — Crown in Oval or Circle, Sideways

Wmk. 136

Wmk. 136a

Wmk. 137 — Double Cross

Wmk. 210 — Double Cross on Pyramid

Watermarks 132, 135, 136 and 136a can be found normal, reversed, inverted, or reversed and inverted.

Values for unused stamps are for examples with original gum as defined in the catalogue introduction. Very fine examples of Nos. 1-12 will have perforations touching the framelines on one or two sides due to imperfect perforating methods. Stamps with perfs clear on all four sides are very scarce and will command substantial premiums.

Issues of the Monarchy

Franz Josef I — A1

1871 Unwmk. Litho. *Perf. 9½*

1	A1	2k orange	325.00	100.00
a.		2k yellow	1,200.	250.00
2	A1	3k lt green	1,000.	600.00
3	A1	5k rose	450.00	25.00
a.		5k brick red	900.00	75.00
4	A1	10k blue	1,250.	100.00
a.		10k pale blue	1,400.	150.00
5	A1	15k yellow brn	1,250.	125.00
6	A1	25k violet	1,000.	200.00
a.		25k bright violet	1,500.	300.00

The first printing of No. 1, in dark yellow, was not issued because of spots on the King's face. A few stamps were used at Pest in 1873. Value, $2,500.

1871-72 Engr.

7	A1	2k orange	40.00	7.50
a.		2k yellow	175.00	20.00
b.		Bisect on cover		—
8	A1	3k green	125.00	25.00
a.		3k blue green	150.00	30.00
9	A1	5k rose	110.00	1.75
a.		5k brick red	200.00	8.00
10	A1	10k deep blue	300.00	10.00
11	A1	15k brown	475.00	15.00
a.		15k copper brown	—	1,500.
b.		15k black brown	875.00	85.00
12	A1	25k lilac	200.00	40.00
		Nos. 7-12 (6)	1,250.	99.25

Reprints are perf. 11½ and watermarked "kr" in oval. Value, set $225.

Crown of St. Stephen — A2

1874-76 *Perf. 13*

13	A2	2k red violet	30.00	2.00
		Never hinged	60.00	
a.		2k violet	35.00	2.50
		Never hinged	70.00	
14	A2	3k yellow green	30.00	2.00
		Never hinged	60.00	
a.		3k blue green	37.50	2.50
		Never hinged	75.00	
15	A2	5k red	10.00	.50
		Never hinged	20.00	
a.		5k brick red	45.00	1.50
		Never hinged	90.00	
b.		5k lilac red	15.00	.75
		Never hinged	30.00	
c.		5k rose	10.00	.40
		Never hinged	20.00	
16	A2	10k blue	35.00	.75
		Never hinged	70.00	
17	A2	20k grnsh gray	700.00	9.00
		Never hinged	1,400.	
a.		20k gray	750.00	10.00
		Never hinged	1,500.	
		Nos. 13-17 (5)	805.00	14.25

Perf. 11½

13b	A2	2k red violet	45.00	5.00
		Never hinged	90.00	
c.		2k violet	—	6.00
d.		2k rose lilac	75.00	4.50
		Never hinged	150.00	
e.		2k gray blue	60.00	3.75
		Never hinged	120.00	
14b	A2	3k yellow green	50.00	4.00
		Never hinged	100.00	
c.		3k blue green	60.00	5.00
		Never hinged	120.00	
15d	A2	5k red	60.00	1.00
		Never hinged	120.00	
e.		5k rose	50.00	.75
		Never hinged	100.00	
16a	A2	10k blue	75.00	5.00
		Never hinged	150.00	
17b	A2	20k gray	700.00	45.00
		Never hinged	1,400.	

Perf. 13x11½

13f	A2	2k red violet	180.00	30.00
		Never hinged	360.00	
g.		2k rose lilac	200.00	30.00
		Never hinged	400.00	
14d	A2	3k yellow green	125.00	4.50
		Never hinged	250.00	
15f	A2	5k lilac red	250.00	12.00
		Never hinged	500.00	
g.		5k rose	300.00	15.00
		Never hinged	600.00	
16b	A2	10k blue	250.00	6.00
		Never hinged	500.00	
17c	A2	20k gray	800.00	50.00
		Never hinged	1,600.	

Perf. 11½x13

13h	A2	2k red violet	60.00	5.00
		Never hinged	120.00	
i.		2k rose lilac	100.00	4.00
		Never hinged	200.00	
j.		2k gray blue	75.00	3.75
		Never hinged	150.00	
15h	A2	5k red	75.00	1.00
		Never hinged	150.00	
17d	A2	20k gray	—	100.00

Perf. 9½

14e	A2	3k green	*7,500.*	*2,500.*

All examples of the 5k perf 9½ are counterfeit.

1881 Wmk. 132 *Perf. 11½*

18	A2	2k lilac	3.50	.40
		Never hinged	6.25	
a.		2k violet	3.50	.40
		Never hinged	6.25	
b.		2k gray blue	4.50	.50
		Never hinged	8.00	
19	A2	3k blue green	3.50	.40
		Never hinged	6.25	
a.		3k yellow green	4.50	.60
		Never hinged	8.00	
20	A2	5k rose	2.50	.25
		Never hinged	4.50	
21	A2	10k blue	6.00	.40
		Never hinged	11.00	
a.		10k pale blue	7.00	.60
		Never hinged	12.50	
22	A2	20k gray	4.50	.65
		Never hinged	8.00	
a.		20k greenish gray	5.00	.75
		Never hinged	9.00	
		Nos. 18-22 (5)	20.00	2.10

Perf. 13

18c	A2	2k violet	150.00	20.00
		Never hinged	275.00	
d.		2k gray blue	120.00	10.00
		Never hinged	225.00	
19b	A2	3k blue green	90.00	4.00
		Never hinged	175.00	
c.		3k yellow green	100.00	5.50
		Never hinged	175.00	
20a	A2	5k rose	120.00	4.00
		Never hinged	225.00	
21b	A2	10k blue	75.00	5.00
		Never hinged	130.00	
22b	A2	20k gray	350.00	15.00
		Never hinged	625.00	

Perf. 13x11½

18e	A2	2k violet	—	40.00
19d	A2	3k blue green	160.00	6.00
		Never hinged	275.00	
e.		3k yellow green	—	8.00
20b	A2	5k rose	—	15.00
21c	A2	10k blue	—	8.00
22c	A2	20k gray	—	12.50

Perf. 11½x13

18f	A2	2k violet	200.00	9.00
		Never hinged	350.00	
g.		2k gray blue	180.00	6.00
		Never hinged	325.00	

19f A2 3k blue green — 60.00
g. 3k yellow green — 75.00
20c A2 5k rose 150.00 1.00
Never hinged 250.00
21d A2 10k blue — 1.75
22d A2 20k gray — 40.00

Perf. 12x11½

18h A2 2k lilac 1.00 .25
Never hinged 1.75
i. 2k violet 15.00 1.20
Never hinged 25.00
19h A2 3k blue green 1.00 .25
Never hinged 1.75
20d A2 5k rose 2.50 .25
Never hinged 4.00
21e A2 10k blue 3.00 .25
Never hinged 5.00
22e A2 20k gray 300.00 7.50
Never hinged 500.00

Crown of St. Stephen — A3

Design A3 has an overall burelage of colored vertical lines. Compare with design N3.

1888-98 Typo. *Perf. 12x11¾*

Numerals in Black

22A A3 1k black, one plate 1.25 .30
Never hinged 2.50
c. "1" printed separately 15.00 3.00
Never hinged 30.00
23 A3 2k red violet 1.50 .50
Never hinged 3.00
24 A3 3k green 1.75 .40
Never hinged 3.50
25 A3 5k rose 2.00 .25
Never hinged 4.00
26 A3 8k orange 6.00 .60
Never hinged 12.00
a. "8" double 150.00
27 A3 10k blue 5.00 1.25
Never hinged 10.00
28 A3 12k brown & green 12.50 1.00
Never hinged 25.00
29 A3 15k claret & blue 10.00 .40
Never hinged 20.00
30 A3 20k gray 7.50 2.00
Never hinged 15.00
31 A3 24k brn vio & red 22.50 1.25
Never hinged 45.00
32 A3 30k ol grn & brn 25.00 .35
Never hinged 50.00
33 A3 50k red & org 40.00 1.50
Never hinged 80.00

Numerals in Red

34 A3 1fo gray bl & sil 175.00 2.25
Never hinged 350.00
Nos. 22A-34 (13) 310.00 12.05

Perf. 11½

Numerals in Black

22i A3 1k black, one plate 1.00 .40
Never hinged 2.00
j. "1" printed separately 500.00 125.00
Never hinged 1,000.
23i A3 2k red violet 600.00 50.00
Never hinged 1,200.
24i A3 3k green 60.00 20.00
Never hinged 120.00
25i A3 5k rose 60.00 20.00
Never hinged 120.00
26i A3 8k orange 10.00 .75
Never hinged 20.00
27i A3 10k blue 1,750. 750.00
28i A3 12k brown & green 12.50 2.00
Never hinged 25.00
29i A3 15k claret & green 14.00 .40
Never hinged 27.50
30i A3 20k gray 2,000. 900.00
31i A3 24k brn vio & red 25.00 2.00
Never hinged 50.00
32i A3 30k ol grn & brn 275.00 .50
Never hinged 550.00
33i A3 50k red & org 40.00 3.00
Never hinged 80.00

Numerals in Red

34i A3 1fo gray blue & sil 190.00 3.00
Never hinged 375.00
35 A3 3fo lilac brn & gold 25.00 12.00
Never hinged 50.00

1898-99 *Perf. 12x11½*

Numerals in Black

Wmk. 135 (Oval)

35A A3 1k black 1.50 .50
Never hinged 3.00
36 A3 2k violet 6.00 .50
Never hinged 12.00
37 A3 3k green 4.00 .60
Never hinged 8.00
38 A3 5k rose 5.00 .40
Never hinged 10.00
39 A3 8k orange 17.50 4.00
Never hinged 35.00
40 A3 10k blue 5.00 1.00
Never hinged 10.00
41 A3 12k red brn & grn 75.00 9.00
Never hinged 150.00
42 A3 15k rose & blue 5.00 .75
Never hinged 10.00
43 A3 20k gray 35.00 2.00
Never hinged 70.00
44 A3 24k vio brn & red 6.00 4.75
Never hinged 12.00
45 A3 30k ol grn & brn 40.00 1.50
Never hinged 80.00

46 A3 50k dull red & org 100.00 15.00
Never hinged 200.00
Nos. 35A-46 (12) 300.00 40.00

Perf. 11½

35Ab A3 1k black 40.00 7.50
Never hinged 80.00
36a A3 2k violet 125.00 20.00
Never hinged 250.00
37a A3 3k green 100.00 15.00
Never hinged 200.00
38a A3 5k rose 140.00 15.00
Never hinged 275.00
39a A3 8k orange 250.00 120.00
Never hinged 500.00
40a A3 10k blue 150.00 60.00
Never hinged 300.00
41a A3 12k red brn & grn 375.00 100.00
Never hinged 750.00
42a A3 15k rose & blue 250.00 60.00
Never hinged 500.00
43a A3 20k gray 375.00 75.00
Never hinged 750.00
44a A3 24k vio brn & red 450.00 200.00
Never hinged 900.00
45a A3 30k ol grn & brn 250.00 60.00
Never hinged 500.00
46a A3 50k dull red & org 500.00 250.00
Never hinged 1,000.

Wmk. 135 (Circle)

Perf. 12x11½

35Ac A3 1k black 14.00 2.50
Never hinged 27.50
36b A3 2k violet 7.50 1.50
Never hinged 15.00
37b A3 3k green 8.50 2.00
Never hinged 17.00
38b A3 5k rose 10.00 1.00
Never hinged 20.00
39b A3 8k orange 50.00 25.00
Never hinged 100.00
40b A3 10k blue 75.00 4.00
Never hinged 150.00
41b A3 12k red brn & grn 60.00 30.00
Never hinged 120.00
42b A3 15k rose & blue 250.00 4.00
Never hinged 500.00
43b A3 20k gray 5.00 6.00
Never hinged 10.00
44b A3 24k vio brn & red 1,250. 45.00
Never hinged 2,500.
45b A3 30k ol grn & brn 5.00 4.00
Never hinged 10.00
46b A3 50k dull red & org 15.00 35.00
Never hinged 30.00

Perf. 11½

35Ad A3 1k black 50.00 15.00
Never hinged 100.00
36c A3 2k violet 200.00 25.00
Never hinged 400.00
37c A3 3k green 200.00 40.00
Never hinged 400.00
38c A3 5k rose 100.00 15.00
Never hinged 200.00
39c A3 8k orange 80.00 12.50
Never hinged 160.00
40c A3 10k blue 450.00 80.00
Never hinged 900.00
41c A3 12k red brn & grn 750.00 300.00
Never hinged 1,500.
42c A3 15k rose & blue 450.00 200.00
Never hinged 950.00
43c A3 20k gray 1,500. 350.00
Never hinged 3,000.
44c A3 24k vio brn & red 2,250. 600.00
Never hinged 4,500.
45c A3 30k ol grn & brn 750.00 150.00
Never hinged 1,500.
46c A3 50k dull red & org 500.00 400.00
Never hinged 1,000.

In the watermark with circles, a four-pointed star and "VI" appear four times in the sheet in the large spaces between the intersecting circles. The paper with the circular watermark is often yellowish and thinner than that with the oval watermark.

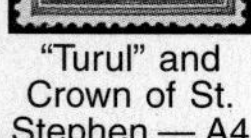

"Turul" and Crown of St. Stephen — A4

Franz Josef I Wearing Hungarian Crown — A5

1900-04 Wmk. 135 *Perf. 12x11½*

Numerals in Black

47 A4 1f gray .75 .30
Never hinged 1.50
a. 1f dull lilac .75 .30
Never hinged 1.50
48 A4 2f olive yel 1.00 .75
Never hinged 2.00
49 A4 3f orange .75 .25
Never hinged 1.50
50 A4 4f violet 1.00 .25
Never hinged 2.00
a. Booklet pane of 6 60.00
51 A4 5f emerald 2.50 .25
Never hinged 5.00
a. Booklet pane of 6 35.00
52 A4 6f claret 1.50 .60
Never hinged 3.00
a. 6f violet brown 2.50 .50
Never hinged 5.00
53 A4 6f bister ('01) 20.00 1.20
Never hinged 40.00
54 A4 6f olive grn ('02) 7.50 .50
Never hinged 15.00
55 A4 10f carmine 4.00 .25
Never hinged 8.00
a. Booklet pane of 6 35.00
56 A4 12f violet ('04) 2.00 1.25
Never hinged 4.00
57 A4 20f brown ('01) 4.00 .60
Never hinged 8.00
58 A4 25f blue 5.00 .60
Never hinged 10.00
a. Booklet pane of 6 60.00
59 A4 30f orange brn 24.00 .25
Never hinged 47.50
60 A4 35f red vio ('01) 14.00 1.00
Never hinged 27.50
a. Booklet pane of 6 100.00
61 A4 50f lake 12.00 1.00
Never hinged 24.00
62 A4 60f green 45.00 .30
Never hinged 90.00
63 A5 1k brown red 37.50 .75
Never hinged 75.00
64 A5 2k gray blue ('01) 600.00 22.50
Never hinged 1,200.
65 A5 3k sea green 90.00 3.75
Never hinged 175.00
66 A5 5k vio brown ('01) 125.00 40.00
Never hinged 175.00
Nos. 47-66 (20) 997.50 76.35

The watermark on Nos. 47 to 66 is always the circular form of Wmk. 135 described in the note following No. 46.

Pairs imperf between of Nos. 47-49, 51 were favor prints made for an influential Budapest collector. Value, $90 each.

For overprints & surcharges see Nos. B35-B52, 2N1-2N3, 6N1-6N6, 6NB127N1-7N6, 7NB1, 10N1.

Perf. 11½

47b A4 1f gray 350.00 80.00
Never hinged 700.00
48a A4 2f olive yel 350.00 60.00
Never hinged 700.00
49a A4 3f orange 100.00 20.00
Never hinged 200.00
50b A4 4f violet 225.00 12.50
Never hinged 450.00
51b A4 5f emerald 50.00 3.75
Never hinged 100.00
52b A4 6f claret — 60.00
Never hinged —
53a A4 6f bister ('01) — 110.00
Never hinged —
54a A4 6f olive grn ('02) — 300.00
Never hinged —
55b A4 10f carmine 400.00 25.00
Never hinged 800.00
56a A4 12f violet ('04) 250.00 80.00
Never hinged 500.00
57a A4 20f brown ('01) — 150.00
Never hinged —
58b A4 25f blue — 75.00
Never hinged —
59a A4 30f orange brn — 125.00
Never hinged —
60b A4 35f red vio ('01) — 275.00
Never hinged —
61a A4 50f lake 400.00 75.00
Never hinged 800.00
62a A4 60f green 600.00 150.00
Never hinged 1,200.
63a A5 1k brown red 175.00 15.00
Never hinged 350.00
64a A5 2k gray blue ('01) — 600.00
Never hinged —
65a A5 3k sea green — *4,000.*
Never hinged —
66a A5 5k vio brown ('01) — 1,000.
Never hinged —

1908-13 Wmk. 136 *Perf. 15*

67 A4 1f slate .30 .25
Never hinged .60
68 A4 2f olive yellow .25 .25
Never hinged .50
69 A4 3f orange .30 .25
Never hinged .60
70 A4 5f emerald .30 .25
Never hinged .60
c. Booklet pane of 6 100.00
71 A4 6f olive green .30 .25
Never hinged .60
72 A4 10f carmine .40 .25
Never hinged .80
c. Booklet pane of 6 100.00
73 A4 12f violet .40 .25
Never hinged .80
74 A4 16f gray green ('13) .50 .50
Never hinged 1.00
75 A4 20f dark brown 7.50 .25
Never hinged 15.00
76 A4 25f blue 6.25 .25
Never hinged 12.50
77 A4 30f orange brown 7.50 .25
Never hinged 15.00
78 A4 35f red violet 10.00 .25
Never hinged 20.00
79 A4 50f lake 3.00 .30
Never hinged 6.00
80 A4 60f green 9.00 .25
Never hinged 17.50
81 A5 1k brown red 12.50 .25
Never hinged 25.00
82 A5 2k gray blue 90.00 .40
Never hinged 175.00
83 A5 5k violet brown 125.00 9.00
Never hinged 250.00
Nos. 67-83 (17) 273.50 13.45

Nos. 67-73, 75-83 exist imperf. Value, set $1,000.

1904-05 Wmk. 136a *Perf. 12x11½*

67a A4 1f slate 2.50 *2.50*
Never hinged 5.00
68a A4 2f olive yellow 5.00 .30
Never hinged 10.00
69a A4 3f orange 2.00 .40
Never hinged 4.00
70a A4 5f emerald 4.00 .25
Never hinged 8.00
71a A4 6f olive green 2.50 .40
Never hinged 5.00
72a A4 10f carmine 7.50 .25
Never hinged 15.00
73a A4 12f violet 4.00 3.00
Never hinged 8.00
75a A4 20f dark brown 20.00 1.00
Never hinged 40.00
76a A4 25f blue 40.00 1.00
Never hinged 80.00
77a A4 30f orange brown 9.00 .40
Never hinged 17.50
78a A4 35f red violet 22.50 .40
Never hinged 45.00
79a A4 50f lake 15.00 4.00
Never hinged 30.00
c. 50f magenta 1.00 *10.00*
Never hinged 2.00
80a A4 60f green 250.00 .40
Never hinged 500.00
81a A5 1k brown red 250.00 .75
Never hinged 500.00
82a A5 2k gray blue *900.00* 50.00
Never hinged 1,750.
c. Perf. 11½ *2,000.* 150.00
83a A5 5k violet brown 240.00 75.00
Nos. 67a-83a (16) *1,774.* 140.05

1906 *Perf. 15*

67b A4 1f slate 2.50 .50
Never hinged 5.00
68b A4 2f olive yellow 1.75 .25
Never hinged 3.50
69b A4 3f orange 2.25 .25
Never hinged 4.50
70b A4 5f emerald 2.00 .25
Never hinged 4.00
71b A4 6f olive green 2.00 .25
Never hinged 4.00
72b A4 10f carmine 2.50 .25
Never hinged 5.00
73b A4 12f violet 4.00 .25
Never hinged 8.00
75b A4 20f dark brown 10.00 .30
Never hinged 20.00
76b A4 25f blue 8.00 .30
Never hinged 16.00
77b A4 30f orange brown 10.00 .25
Never hinged 20.00
78b A4 35f red violet 50.00 .25
Never hinged 100.00
79b A4 50f lake 5.00 1.00
Never hinged 10.00
80b A4 60f green 62.50 .25
Never hinged 125.00
81b A5 1k brown red 60.00 .60
Never hinged 120.00
82b A5 2k gray blue 225.00 8.00
Never hinged 450.00
Nos. 67b-82b (15) 447.50 12.95

1913-16 Wmk. 137 Vert. *Perf. 15*

84 A4 1f slate .25 .25
Never hinged .50
85 A4 2f olive yellow .25 .25
Never hinged .50
86 A4 3f orange .25 .25
Never hinged .50
87 A4 5f emerald .50 .25
Never hinged 1.00
88 A4 6f olive green .25 .25
Never hinged .50
89 A4 10f carmine .25 .25
Never hinged .50
90 A4 12f violet, *yel* .30 .25
Never hinged .60
91 A4 16f gray green .35 .90
Never hinged .70
92 A4 20f dark brown 1.00 .25
Never hinged 2.00
93 A4 25f ultra 1.20 .25
Never hinged 2.50
94 A4 30f orange brown .90 .25
Never hinged 1.75
95 A4 35f red violet .90 .25
Never hinged 1.75
96 A4 50f lake, *blue* .30 .25
Never hinged .60
a. Cliché of 35f in plate of 50f 325.00 —
97 A4 60f green 5.75 2.00
Never hinged 11.50
98 A4 60f green, *salmon* .80 .30
Never hinged 1.60
99 A4 70f red brn, *grn* ('16) .25 .25
Never hinged .50
100 A4 80f dull violet ('16) .25 .25
Never hinged .50
101 A5 1k dull red 2.50 .25
Never hinged 5.00
102 A5 2k dull blue 4.25 .25
Never hinged 8.50
103 A5 5k violet brown 20.00 5.00
Never hinged 40.00
Nos. 84-103 (20) 40.50 12.20

Nos. 89-97, 99-103 exist imperf. Value, set $1,200.

For overprints and surcharges see Nos. 2N1-2N3, 6N1-6N6, 6NB12, 7N1-7N6, 7NB1, 10N1.

Wmk. 137 Horiz.

84a A4 1f slate .75 .60
Never hinged 1.50
85a A4 2f olive yellow 2.00 .40
Never hinged 4.00
87a A4 5f emerald .50 .25
Never hinged 1.00
88a A4 6f olive green 1.00 .25
Never hinged 2.00
89b A4 10f carmine 1.00 .25
Never hinged 2.00
90a A4 12f violet, *yellow* 2.00 .25
Never hinged 4.00
92a A4 20f dark brown 6.25 .25
Never hinged 12.50
94a A4 30f orange brown 50.00 .25
Never hinged 100.00
95a A4 35f red violet 200.00 .25
Never hinged 400.00
96b A4 50f lake, *blue* 15.00 6.25
Never hinged 30.00
97a A4 60f green 4.25 1.75
Never hinged 8.50

98a A4 60f green, *salmon* 1.50 .25
Never hinged 3.00
101a A5 1k dull red 16.00 .25
Never hinged 32.50
102a A5 2k dull blue 100.00 1.00
Never hinged 200.00
Nos. 84a-102a (14) 400.25 12.25

A5a

Wmk. 137 Vert.

1916, July 1 ***Perf. 15***
103A A5a 10f violet brown .25 .25

Although issued as a postal savings stamp, No. 103A was also valid for postage. Used value is for postal usage.
Exists imperf. Value $10.
For overprints and surcharges see Nos. 2N59, 5N23, 6N50, 8N13, 10N42.

Queen Zita — A6
Charles IV — A7

1916, Dec. 30
104 A6 10f violet 1.25 1.25
Never hinged 2.00
105 A7 15f red 1.25 1.25
Never hinged 2.00

Coronation of King Charles IV and Queen Zita on Dec. 30, 1916.
Exist imperf. Value, set $20.

During 1921-24 the two center rows of panes of various stamps then current were punched with three holes forming a triangle. These were sold at post offices. Collectors and dealers who wanted the stamps unpunched would have to purchase them through the philatelic agency at a 10% advance over face value.

Harvesting (White Numerals) — A8

1916
106 A8 10f rose .75 .25
Never hinged 1.25
107 A8 15f violet .75 .25
Never hinged 1.25

Exist imperf. Value, set $20.
For overprints and surcharges see Nos. B56-B57, 2N4-2N5, 5N1.

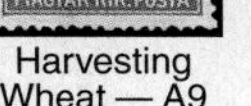
Harvesting Wheat — A9
Parliament Building at Budapest — A10

1916-18 **Wmk. 137 Vert.** ***Perf. 15***
108 A9 2f brown orange .25 .25
Never hinged .30
109 A9 3f red lilac .25 .25
Never hinged .30
110 A9 4f slate gray ('18) .25 .25
Never hinged .30
111 A9 5f green .25 .25
Never hinged .30
112 A9 6f grnsh blue .25 .25
Never hinged .30
113 A9 10f rose red 1.40 .25
Never hinged 3.50
114 A9 15f violet .25 .25
Never hinged .30
115 A9 20f gray brown .25 .25
Never hinged .30
116 A9 25f dull blue .30 .25
Never hinged .75
117 A9 35f brown .25 .25
Never hinged .30
118 A9 40f olive green .25 .25
Never hinged .30

Perf. 14
Wmk. 137 Horiz.
119 A10 50f red vio & lil .25 .25
Never hinged .35
120 A10 75f brt bl & pale bl .25 .25
Never hinged .35
121 A10 80f grn & pale grn .25 .25
Never hinged .35
122 A10 1k red brn & claret .25 .25
Never hinged .35
123 A10 2k ol brn & bister .25 .25
Never hinged .50
124 A10 3k dk vio & indigo .60 .25
Never hinged 1.75
125 A10 5k dk brn & lt brn .60 .25
Never hinged 1.75
126 A10 10k vio brn & vio 1.20 .25
Never hinged 3.00
Nos. 108-126 (19) 7.60 4.75

Three-Hole Punch
115a A9 20f gray brown .25 *.40*
Never hinged .50
118a A9 40f olive green .25 *.40*
Never hinged .50
122a A10 1k red brn & claret .25 .25
Never hinged .65
123a A10 2k ol brn & bister .50 .25
Never hinged 1.25
124a A10 3k dk vio & indigo 2.10 .25
Never hinged 5.25
125a A10 5k dk brn & lt brn 2.25 .25
Never hinged 5.50
126a A10 10k vio brn & vio 4.25 .40
Never hinged 10.50
Nos. 115a-126a (7) 9.85 2.20

Nos. 108-126 exist imperf. Value, set $100.
See Nos. 335-377, 388-396. For overprints and surcharges see Nos. 153-167, C1-C5, J76-J99, 1N1-1N21, 1N26-1N30, 1N33, 1N36-1N39, 2N6-2N27, 2N33-2N38, 2N41, 2N43-2N48, 4N1-4N4, 5N2-5N17, 6N7-6N24, 6N29-6N39, 7N7-7N30, 7N38, 7N41-7N42, 8N1-8N4, 9N1-9N2, 9N4, 10N2-10N16, 10N25-10N29, 10N31, 10N33-10N41, 11N1-15, 11N20-24, 11N27, 11N30, 11N32-33.

Charles IV — A11

Queen Zita — A12

1918 **Wmk. 137 Vert.** ***Perf. 15***
127 A11 10f scarlet .55 .35
Never hinged 1.00
128 A11 15f deep violet .55 .35
Never hinged 1.00
129 A11 20f dark brown .55 .35
Never hinged 1.00
130 A11 25f brt blue .55 .35
Never hinged 1.00
131 A12 40f olive green .55 .35
Never hinged 1.00
132 A12 50f lilac .55 .35
Never hinged 1.00
Nos. 127-132 (6) 3.30 2.10

Exist imperf. Value, set $35.
For overprints see Nos. 168-173, 1N32, 1N34-1N35, 2N28-2N32, 2N39-2N40, 2N42, 2N49-2N51, 5N18-5N22, 6N25-6N28, 6N40-6N43, 7N31-7N37, 7N39-7N40, 8N5, 9N3, 10N17-10N21, 10N30, 10N32, 11N16-19, 11N25-26, 11N28-29, 11N31.

Issues of the Republic

Hungarian Stamps of 1916-18 Overprinted in Black

1918-19 **Wmk. 137** ***Perf. 15, 14***
On Stamps of 1916-18
153 A9 2f brown orange .25 .25
Never hinged .30
154 A9 3f red lilac .25 .25
Never hinged .30
155 A9 4f slate gray .25 .25
Never hinged .30
156 A9 5f green .25 .25
Never hinged .30
157 A9 6f grnsh blue .25 .25
Never hinged .30
158 A9 10f rose red .25 .25
Never hinged .30
159 A9 20f gray brown .25 .25
Never hinged .30
162 A9 40f olive green .25 .25
Never hinged .30
163 A10 1k red brn & claret .25 .25
Never hinged .30
164 A10 2k ol brn & bis .25 .25
Never hinged .45
165 A10 3k dk violet & ind .40 1.00
Never hinged .60
166 A10 5k dk brn & lt brn 2.00 5.00
Never hinged 4.00
167 A10 10k vio brn & vio .65 1.50
Never hinged .90

On Stamps of 1918
168 A11 10f scarlet .25 .25
Never hinged .30
169 A11 15f deep violet .25 .25
Never hinged .30
170 A11 20f dark brown .25 .25
Never hinged .30
171 A11 25f brt blue .25 .25
Never hinged .30
172 A12 40f olive green .30 .60
Never hinged .40
173 A12 50f lilac .25 .30
Never hinged .30
Nos. 153-173 (19) 7.10 11.90

Nos. 153-164 exist imperf. Value, set $90.
Nos. 153-162, 168-173 exist with overprint inverted. Value, each $6.

A13

A14

1919-20 ***Perf. 15***
174 A13 2f brown orange .25 .25
Never hinged .30
176 A13 4f slate gray .25 .25
Never hinged .30
177 A13 5f yellow grn .25 .25
Never hinged .30
178 A13 6f grnsh blue .25 .25
Never hinged .30
179 A13 10f red .25 .25
Never hinged .30
180 A13 15f violet .25 .25
Never hinged .30
181 A13 20f dark brown .25 .25
Never hinged .30
182 A13 20f green ('20) .25 .25
Never hinged .30
183 A13 25f dull blue .25 .25
Never hinged .30
184 A13 40f olive green .25 .25
Never hinged .30
185 A13 40f rose red ('20) .25 .25
Never hinged .30
186 A13 45f orange .25 .25
Never hinged .30

Perf. 14
187 A14 50f brn vio & pale vio .25 .25
Never hinged .30
188 A14 60f brown & bl ('20) .25 .25
Never hinged .30
189 A14 95f dk bl & bl .25 .25
Never hinged .30
190 A14 1k red brn .25 .25
Never hinged .30
191 A14 1k dk bl & dull bl ('20) .25 .25
Never hinged .30
192 A14 1.20k dk grn & grn .25 .25
Never hinged .30
193 A14 1.40k yellow green .25 .25
Never hinged .30
194 A14 2k ol brn & bis .25 .25
Never hinged .30
195 A14 3k dk vio & ind .25 .25
Never hinged .30
196 A14 5k dk brn & brn .25 .85
Never hinged .30
197 A14 10k vio brn & red vio .50 .75
Never hinged .95
Nos. 174-197 (23) 6.00 6.85

The 3f red lilac, type A13, was never regularly issued without overprint (Nos. 204 and 312). In 1923 a small quantity was sold by the Government at public auction. Value $3.
For overprints see Nos. 203-222, 306-330, 1N40, 2N52-2N58, 6N44-6N49, 8N6-8N12, 10N22-10N24, 11N34-35.
Nos. 174, 177-179, 181-197 exist imperf. Value set $60.

Issues of the Soviet Republic

Karl Marx — A15

Sándor Petőfi — A16

Ignác Martinovics — A17

György Dózsa — A18

Friedrich Engels — A19

Wmk. 137 Horiz.

1919, June 12 **Litho.** ***Perf. 12½x12***
198 A15 20f rose & brown .50 *1.00*
Never hinged 1.00
199 A16 45f brn org & dk grn .50 *1.00*
Never hinged 1.00
200 A17 60f blue gray & brn 4.00 *4.00*
Never hinged 7.00
201 A18 75f claret & vio brn 4.00 *4.00*
Never hinged 7.00
202 A19 80f olive db & blk brn 4.00 *4.00*
Never hinged 7.00
Nos. 198-202 (5) 13.00 *14.00*

Used values are for favor cancels.
Exist imperf. Value, Set $150.

Wmk. Vertical
198a A15 20f 7.50 *10.00*
Never hinged 13.00
199a A16 45f 7.50 *10.00*
Never hinged 13.00
200a A17 60f 7.50 *10.00*
Never hinged 13.00
201a A18 75f 7.50 *10.00*
Never hinged 13.00
202a A19 80f 25.00 25.00
Never hinged 25.00
Nos. 198a-202a (5) 55.00

Nos. 198a-202a were not used postally. Used examples are favor canceled.

Stamps of 1919 Overprinted in Red

1919, July 21 **Typo.** ***Perf. 15***
203 A13 2f brown orange .25 .25
Never hinged .30
204 A13 3f red lilac .25 .25
Never hinged .30
205 A13 4f slate gray .25 .25
Never hinged .30

206 A13 5f yellow green .25 .25
Never hinged .30
207 A13 6f grnsh blue .25 .25
Never hinged .30
208 A13 10f red .25 .25
Never hinged .30
209 A13 15f violet .25 .25
Never hinged .30
210 A13 20f dark brown .25 .25
Never hinged .30
211 A13 25f dull blue .25 .25
Never hinged .30
212 A13 40f olive green .25 .25
Never hinged .35
213 A13 45f orange .25 .25
Never hinged .35

Overprinted in Red

Perf. 14

214 A14 50f brn vio & pale vio .25 .30
Never hinged .30
215 A14 95f dk blue & blue .25 .30
Never hinged .30
216 A14 1k red brown .25 .30
Never hinged .30
217 A14 1.20k dk grn & grn .25 .40
Never hinged .40
218 A14 1.40k yellow green .25 .40
Never hinged .40
219 A14 2k ol brn & bister .40 1.25
Never hinged .80
220 A14 3k dk vio & ind .65 1.00
Never hinged 1.00
221 A14 5k dk brn & brn .50 .80
Never hinged .80
222 A14 10k vio brn & red vio .75 1.75
Never hinged 1.50
Nos. 203-222 (20) 6.30 9.25

"Magyar Tanacsköztarsasag" on Nos. 198 to 222 means "Hungarian Soviet Republic."

Nos. 203-218, 221-222 exist imperf. Value, set $125.

Issues of the Kingdom

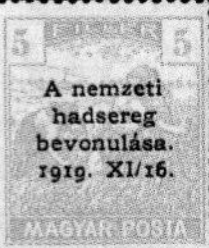

Stamps of 1919 Overprinted in Black

1919, Nov. 16

306 A13 5f green .65 1.00
Never hinged 1.00
307 A13 10f rose red .65 1.00
Never hinged 1.00
308 A13 15f violet .65 1.00
Never hinged 1.00
309 A13 20f gray brown .65 1.00
Never hinged 1.00
310 A13 25f dull blue .65 1.00
Never hinged 1.00
Nos. 306-310 (5) 3.25 5.00

Issued to commemorate the Romanian evacuation. The overprint reads: "Entry of the National Army-November 16, 1919."

Forged overprints exist.

Nos. 203 to 213 Overprinted in Black

1920, Jan. 26 *Perf. 15*

311 A13 2f brown orange 1.25 1.60
Never hinged 1.60
312 A13 3f red lilac .25 .30
Never hinged .30
313 A13 4f slate gray 1.25 1.60
Never hinged 1.60
314 A13 5f yellow green .25 .25
Never hinged .30
315 A13 6f blue green .25 .40
Never hinged .40
316 A13 10f red .25 .25
Never hinged .30
317 A13 15f violet .25 .25
Never hinged .30
318 A13 20f dark brown .25 .25
Never hinged .30
319 A13 25f dull blue .25 .30
Never hinged .30
320 A13 40f olive green 1.50 2.00
Never hinged 1.75
321 A13 45f orange 1.50 2.00
Never hinged 1.75

Nos. 214 to 222 Overprinted in Black

Perf. 14

322 A14 50f brn vio & pale vio 1.50 2.00
Never hinged 1.75
323 A14 95f dk bl & bl 1.50 2.00
Never hinged 1.75
324 A14 1k red brown 1.50 2.00
Never hinged 1.75
325 A14 1.20k dk grn & grn 1.50 2.50
Never hinged 1.75
326 A14 1.40k yellow green 1.50 2.50
Never hinged 1.75
327 A14 2k ol brn & bis 8.50 17.50
Never hinged 14.00
328 A14 3k dk vio & ind 8.50 17.50
Never hinged 11.00
329 A14 5k dk brn & brn .25 .50
Never hinged .35
330 A14 10k vio brn & red vio 8.50 17.50
Never hinged 11.00
Nos. 311-330 (20) 40.50 73.20

Counterfeit overprints exist.

Types of 1916-18 Issue
Denomination Tablets Without Inner Frame on Nos. 350 to 363

1920-24 Wmk. 137 *Perf. 15*

335 A9 5f brown orange .25 .25
Never hinged .30
336 A9 10f red violet .25 .25
Never hinged .35
337 A9 40f rose red .25 .25
Never hinged .30
338 A9 50f yellow green .25 .25
Never hinged .30
339 A9 50f blue vio ('22) .25 .25
Never hinged .30
340 A9 60f black .25 .25
Never hinged .30
341 A9 1k green ('22) .25 .25
Never hinged .35
342 A9 1½k brown vio ('22) .25 .25
Never hinged .30
343 A9 2k grnsh blue ('22) .25 .25
Never hinged .30
344 A9 2½k dp green ('22) .25 .25
Never hinged .30
345 A9 3k brown org ('22) .25 .25
Never hinged .40
346 A9 4k lt red ('22) .25 .25
Never hinged .40
347 A9 4½k dull violet ('22) .25 .25
Never hinged .40
348 A9 5k dp brn ('22) .25 .25
Never hinged .40
349 A9 6k dark blue ('22) .25 .25
Never hinged .40
350 A9 10k brown ('23) .25 .25
Never hinged .40
351 A9 15k slate ('23) .25 .25
Never hinged .50
352 A9 20k red vio ('23) .25 .25
Never hinged .50
353 A9 25k orange ('23) .25 .25
Never hinged .50
354 A9 40k gray grn ('23) .25 .25
Never hinged .50
355 A9 50k dark blue ('23) .25 .25
Never hinged .50
356 A9 100k claret ('23) .25 .25
Never hinged .60
357 A9 150k dk grn ('23) .30 .25
Never hinged .55
358 A9 200k green ('23) .30 .25
Never hinged .55
359 A9 300k rose red ('24) .80 .30
Never hinged 1.00
360 A9 350k violet ('23) 1.50 .30
Never hinged 4.00
361 A9 500k dark gray ('24) 2.50 .30
Never hinged 5.75
362 A9 600k olive bis ('24) 2.50 .30
Never hinged 5.75
363 A9 800k org yel ('24) 2.50 .30
Never hinged 5.50

Perf. 14

364 A10 2.50k bl & gray bl .25 .25
Never hinged .30
365 A10 3.50k gray .25 .25
Never hinged .35
366 A10 10k brown ('22) .50 .25
Never hinged 1.00
367 A10 15k dk gray ('22) .25 .25
Never hinged .30
368 A10 20k red vio ('22) .25 .25
Never hinged .30
369 A10 25k orange ('22) .25 .25
Never hinged .35
370 A10 30k claret ('22) .75 .25
Never hinged .35
371 A10 40k gray grn ('22) .75 .25
Never hinged .40
372 A10 50k dp blue ('22) .75 .25
Never hinged .40
373 A10 100k yel brn ('22) .75 .25
Never hinged .50
374 A10 400k turq bl ('23) .75 .30
Never hinged 1.50
375 A10 500k brt vio ('23) 1.10 .25
Never hinged 1.25
376 A10 1000k lilac ('24) 1.50 .25
Never hinged 3.00
377 A10 2000k car ('24) 2.00 .60
Never hinged 4.00
Nos. 335-377 (43) 26.00 11.40

Three-Hole Punch

335a A9 5f brown orange .50 1.25
Never hinged 1.00
336a A9 10f red violet .40 1.00
Never hinged .75
338a A9 50f yellow green .25 .25
Never hinged .40
339a A9 50f blue vio ('22) .25 .25
Never hinged .40
340a A9 60f black .25 .25
Never hinged .40
341a A9 1k green ('22) .25 .25
Never hinged .45
342a A9 1½k brown vio ('22) .25 .45
Never hinged .45
343a A9 2k grnsh blue ('22) .25 .40
Never hinged .40
344a A9 2½k dp green ('22) .25 .40
Never hinged .40
345a A9 3k brown org ('22) .25 .60
Never hinged .45
346a A9 4k lt red ('22) .25 .60
Never hinged .45
347a A9 4½k dull violet ('22) .25 .50
Never hinged .40
348a A9 5k deep brown ('22) .25 .40
Never hinged .50
349a A9 6k dark blue ('22) .25 .50
Never hinged .40
350a A9 10k brown ('23) .25 .40
Never hinged .40
351a A9 15k slate ('23) .25 .50
Never hinged .45
352a A9 20k red vio ('23) .25 .35
Never hinged .45
353a A9 25k orange ('23) .25 .35
Never hinged .45
354a A9 40k gray grn ('23) .25 .35
Never hinged .50
355a A9 50k dark blue ('23) .25 .40
Never hinged .40
356a A9 100k claret ('23) .40 .50
Never hinged .75
357a A9 150k dark green ('23) .50 .40
Never hinged 1.00
358a A9 200k green ('23) .50 .40
Never hinged 1.00
360a A9 350k violet ('23) 2.00 1.75
Never hinged 3.75
364a A10 2.50k bl & gray bl .30 .30
Never hinged .50
365a A10 3.50k gray .30 .30
Never hinged .50
366a A10 10k brown ('22) .75 .35
Never hinged 1.00
367a A10 15k dk gray ('22) .30 .40
Never hinged .50
368a A10 20k red vio ('22) .30 .40
Never hinged .50
369a A10 25k orange ('22) .35 .30
Never hinged .60
370a A10 30k claret ('22) .35 .30
Never hinged .60
371a A10 40k gray grn ('22) .35 .30
Never hinged .60
372a A10 50k dp blue ('22) .35 .30
Never hinged .60
373a A10 100k yel brn ('22) .35 .30
Never hinged .60
374a A10 400k turq bl ('23) 1.25 .50
Never hinged 2.50
375a A10 500k brt vio ('23) 1.25 .50
Never hinged 2.50
Nos. 335a-375a (36) 15.00 16.75

Nos. 372 to 377 have colored numerals.

Nos. 335-338, 340, 350-365, 368, 370, 372-377 exist imperf. Value, set $200.

Madonna and Child — A23

1921-25 Typo. *Perf. 12*

378 A23 50k dk brn & bl .25 .25
Never hinged .50
379 A23 100k ol bis & yel brn .40 .35
Never hinged .75

Wmk. 133

380 A23 200k dk bl & ultra .40 .25
Never hinged .75
381 A23 500k vio brn & vio .75 .40
Never hinged 1.50
382 A23 1000k vio & red vio 1.00 .35
Never hinged 2.00
383 A23 2000k grnsh bl & vio 1.75 .50
Never hinged 3.00
384 A23 2500k ol brn & buff 2.00 .25
Never hinged 4.00
385 A23 3000k brn red & vio 2.00 .25
Never hinged 4.00
386 A23 5000k dk grn & yel grn 2.00 .25
Never hinged 4.00
a. Center inverted *20,000.* *16,000.*
Never hinged *25,000.*
387 A23 10000k gray vio & pale bl 2.00 .25
Never hinged 4.00
Nos. 378-387 (10) 12.55 3.10

Three-Hole Punch

378a A23 50k dk brn & bl .55 .40
Never hinged 1.00
379a A23 100k ol bis & yel brn .85 .60
Never hinged 1.50
380a A23 200k dk bl & ultra .85 .50
Never hinged 1.50
381a A23 500k vio brn & vio 1.40 .75
Never hinged 2.50
382a A23 1000k vio & red vio 2.25 1.25
Never hinged 4.00
383a A23 2000k grnsh bl & vio 2.50 2.50
Never hinged 4.50
Nos. 378a-383a (6) 8.40 6.00

Nos. 380-387 exist imperf. Value, set of 8 $175.

Issue dates: 50k, 100k, Feb. 27, 1921; 2500k, 10,000k, 1925; others, 1923.

Types of 1916-18
Denomination Tablets Without Inner Frame on Nos. 388-394

1924 Wmk. 133 *Perf. 15*

388 A9 100k claret .40 .25
Never hinged .80
389 A9 200k yellow grn .25 .25
Never hinged .50
390 A9 300k rose red .30 .35
Never hinged .60
391 A9 400k deep blue .30 .35
Never hinged .60
392 A9 500k dark gray .40 .25
Never hinged .75
393 A9 600k olive bister .45 .25
Never hinged .90
a. "800" in upper right corner 110.00 260.00
Never hinged 150.00
394 A9 800k org yel .50 .25
Never hinged 1.00

Perf. 14½x14

395 A10 1000k lilac 1.50 .25
Never hinged 3.00
396 A10 2000k carmine 2.00 .25
Never hinged 4.00
Nos. 388-396 (9) 6.10 2.45

Nos. 395 and 396 have colored numerals. Exist imperf. Value, set $37.50.

Maurus Jókai (1825-1904), Novelist A24

1925, Feb. 1 Unwmk. *Perf. 12*

400 A24 1000k dp grn & blk brn 1.75 3.25
Never hinged 3.00
401 A24 2000k lt brn & blk brn .80 1.00
Never hinged 1.00
402 A24 2500k dk bl & blk brn 1.75 3.25
Never hinged 3.00
Nos. 400-402 (3) 4.30 7.50

Exist imperf. Value, set $90.

Crown of St. Stephen A25

Matthias Cathedral A26

Palace at Budapest — A27

1926-27 Wmk. 133 Litho. *Perf. 15*

403 A25 1f dk gray .45 .25
Never hinged .60
404 A25 2f lt blue .55 .25
Never hinged .80
405 A25 3f orange .55 .25
Never hinged .80
406 A25 4f violet .65 .25
Never hinged .90
407 A25 6f lt green .90 .25
Never hinged 1.25
408 A25 8f lilac rose 1.60 .25
Never hinged 2.25

Typo.

409 A26 10f deep blue 2.75 .25
Never hinged 4.00
410 A26 16f dark violet 2.25 .25
Never hinged 3.25
411 A26 20f carmine 2.75 .25
Never hinged 4.00
412 A26 25f lt brown 2.75 .25
Never hinged 4.00

Perf. 14¼x14

413 A27 32f dp vio & brt vio 4.25 .25
Never hinged 6.00

414 A27 40f dk blue & blue 5.00 .25
Never hinged 8.00
Nos. 403-414 (12) 24.45 3.00

Perf. 14x14¼

403a A25 1f dk gray .85 .25
Never hinged 1.50
404a A25 2f lt blue 14.00 2.50
Never hinged 25.00
405a A25 3f orange 1.00 .25
Never hinged 1.75
406a A25 4f violet 1.00 .25
Never hinged 1.75
407a A25 6f lt green 1.40 .30
Never hinged 2.50
408a A25 8f lilac rose 2.75 .25
Never hinged 5.00

Typo.

409a A26 10f deep blue 1.00 .25
Never hinged 1.75
410a A26 16f dark violet .85 .25
Never hinged 1.50
411a A26 20f carmine 1.10 .25
Never hinged 2.00
412a A26 25f lt brown 1.10 .25
Never hinged 2.00

See Nos. 428-436. For surcharges see Nos. 450-456, 466-467.

Nos. 403-414, 418-421 exist imperf. Value, set $250.

Madonna and Child — A28

1926-27 Engr. Perf. 14
415 A28 1p violet 15.00 .65
Never hinged 30.00
416 A28 2p red 17.50 .85
Never hinged 30.00
417 A28 5p blue ('27) 17.50 4.00
Never hinged 30.00
Nos. 415-417 (3) 50.00 5.50

Exist imperf. Value, set $400.

Palace at Budapest A29

1926-27 Typo. Perf. 14x14¼
418 A29 30f blue grn ('27) 4.00 .25
Never hinged 6.00
419 A29 46f ultra ('27) 5.25 .30
Never hinged 6.50
420 A29 50f brown blk ('27) 6.00 .25
Never hinged 7.50
421 A29 70f scarlet 9.75 .25
Never hinged 12.50
Nos. 418-421 (4) 25.00 1.05

For surcharge see No. 480.

St. Stephen — A30

1928-29 Engr. Perf. 15
422 A30 8f yellow grn .65 .30
Never hinged 1.10
423 A30 8f rose lake ('29) .65 .30
Never hinged 1.10
424 A30 16f orange red .85 .30
Never hinged 1.10
425 A30 16f violet ('29) .85 .30
Never hinged 1.10
426 A30 32f ultra 2.50 4.00
Never hinged 4.50
427 A30 32f bister ('29) 2.50 4.00
Never hinged 4.50
Nos. 422-427 (6) 8.00 9.20

890th death anniversary of St. Stephen, the first king of Hungary.

Exist imperf. Value, set $300.

Types of 1926-27 Issue

1928-30 Typo. Wmk. 210 Perf. 15
428 A25 1f black .25 .25
Never hinged .50
429 A25 2f blue .35 .25
Never hinged .60
430 A25 3f orange .35 .25
Never hinged .60
431 A25 4f violet .45 .25
Never hinged .75
432 A25 6f blue grn .60 .25
Never hinged 1.00
433 A25 8f lilac rose 1.25 .25
Never hinged 1.75
434 A26 10f dp blue ('30) 4.50 .25
Never hinged 6.00
435 A26 16f violet 1.50 .25
Never hinged 3.00
436 A26 20f dull red 1.25 .25
Never hinged 2.50
Nos. 428-436 (9) 10.50 2.25

Perf. 14x14¼

429a A25 2f blue 5.00 1.50
Never hinged 9.00
433a A25 8f lilac rose 3.00 .50
Never hinged 5.50
435a A26 16f violet 3.00 .70
Never hinged 4.50

On Nos. 428-433 the numerals have thicker strokes than on the same values of the 1926-27 issue.

Exist imperf. Value, set $110.

Palace at Budapest — A31

Type A31 resembles A27 but the steamer is nearer the right of the design. A31, A29 & A27 are similar but the frame borders are different.

1928-31 Perf. 14¼x14
437 A31 30f emerald ('31) 4.00 .25
Never hinged 6.00
438 A31 32f red violet 4.00 .25
Never hinged 6.00
439 A31 40f deep blue 5.00 .25
Never hinged 8.00
440 A31 46f apple green 4.50 .25
Never hinged 6.75
441 A31 50f ocher ('31) 4.50 .25
Never hinged 6.75
Nos. 437-441 (5) 22.00 1.25

Exist imperf. Value, set $110.

Admiral Nicholas Horthy — A32

1930, Mar. 1 Litho. Perf. 15
445 A32 8f myrtle green .75 .25
Never hinged 1.50
446 A32 16f purple 1.00 .25
Never hinged 2.00
447 A32 20f carmine 6.00 1.10
Never hinged 12.00
448 A32 32f olive brown 4.00 1.25
Never hinged 8.00
449 A32 40f dull blue 7.00 .50
Never hinged 14.00
Nos. 445-449 (5) 18.75 3.35

10th anniv. of the election of Adm. Nicholas Horthy as Regent, Mar. 1, 1920.

Exist imperf. Value, set, $200.

Stamps of 1926-28 Surcharged

1931, Jan. 1 Perf. 14¼, 15
450 A25 2f on 3f orange .50 *.40*
Never hinged 1.00
451 A25 6f on 8f magenta .50 .25
Never hinged 1.00
a. Perf. 14x14¼ 30.00 *30.00*
Never hinged 42.50
452 A26 10f on 16f violet .50 .25
Never hinged 1.00

Wmk. 133

453 A25 2f on 3f orange 2.50 5.00
Never hinged 5.00
a. Perf. 14x14¼ 3.00 *6.00*
Never hinged 6.00
454 A25 6f on 8f magenta 2.00 4.00
Never hinged 4.00
a. Perf. 14x14¼ 50.00 100.00
Never hinged 100.00
455 A26 10f on 16f dk vio 1.75 3.50
Never hinged 3.50
a. Perf. 14x14¼ 2.00 *4.00*
Never hinged 4.00
456 A26 20f on 25f lt brn 1.25 2.50
Never hinged 3.00
a. Perf. 14x14¼ 1.25 2.25
Never hinged 3.00
Nos. 450-456 (7) 9.00 15.90

For surcharges see Nos. 466-467.

St. Elizabeth A33

Ministering to Children A34

Wmk. 210

1932, Apr. 21 Photo. Perf. 15
458 A33 10f ultra .75 .25
Never hinged 1.50
459 A33 20f scarlet .75 .25
Never hinged 1.50

Perf. 14

460 A34 32f deep violet 1.50 2.50
Never hinged 3.00
461 A34 40f deep blue 2.00 1.00
Never hinged 4.00
Nos. 458-461 (4) 5.00 4.00

700th anniv. of the death of St. Elizabeth of Hungary.

Exist imperf. Value, set $100.

Madonna, Patroness of Hungary — A35

1932, June 1 Perf. 12
462 A35 1p yellow grn 30.00 .25
Never hinged 60.00
463 A35 2p carmine 30.00 .40
Never hinged 60.00
464 A35 5p deep blue 42.50 3.00
Never hinged 90.00
465 A35 10p olive bister 42.50 22.50
Never hinged 90.00
Nos. 462-465 (4) 145.00 26.15

Exist imperf. Value, set $1,000.

Nos. 451 and 454 Surcharged

1932, June 14 Wmk. 210 Perf. 15
466 A25 2f on 6f on 8f mag .25 .25
Never hinged .50

Wmk. 133

467 A25 2f on 6f on 8f mag 50.00 100.00
Never hinged 100.00

Imre Madách — A36

Designs: 2f, Janos Arany. 4f, Dr. Ignaz Semmelweis. 6f, Baron Lorand Eotvos. 10f, Count Stephen Szechenyi. 16f, Ferenc Deak. 20f, Franz Liszt. 30f, Louis Kossuth. 32f, Stephen Tisza. 40f, Mihaly Munkacsy. 50f, Alexander Csoma. 70f, Farkas Bolyai.

1932 Wmk. 210 Perf. 15
468 A36 1f slate violet .25 .25
Never hinged .30
469 A36 2f orange .25 .25
Never hinged .30
470 A36 4f ultra .25 .25
Never hinged .30
471 A36 6f yellow grn .25 .25
Never hinged .30
472 A36 10f Prus green .35 .25
Never hinged .75
473 A36 16f dull violet .35 .25
Never hinged .75
474 A36 20f deep rose .30 .25
Never hinged .60
475 A36 30f brown .50 .25
Never hinged 1.00
476 A36 32f brown vio .70 .25
Never hinged 1.20
477 A36 40f dull blue .85 .25
Never hinged 1.60
478 A36 50f deep green 1.10 .25
Never hinged 2.25
479 A36 70f cerise 1.50 .25
Never hinged 2.50
Nos. 468-479 (12) 6.65 3.00
Set, never hinged 11.50

Issued in honor of famous Hungarians.

Exist imperf. Value, set $125.

See Nos. 509-510.

No. 421 Surcharged

1933, Apr. 15 Wmk. 133 Perf. 14
480 A29 10f on 70f scarlet 3.00 .40
Never hinged 6.00

Leaping Stag and Double Cross — A47

Wmk. 210

1933, July 10 Photo. Perf. 15
481 A47 10f dk green .75 .80
Never hinged 1.50
482 A47 16f violet brn 2.00 *2.50*
Never hinged 4.00
483 A47 20f car lake 1.50 1.25
Never hinged 3.00
484 A47 32f yellow 5.00 *6.00*
Never hinged 8.50
485 A47 40f deep blue 5.00 4.00
Never hinged 10.50
Nos. 481-485 (5) 14.25 14.55
Set, never hinged 27.50

Boy Scout Jamboree at Gödöllö, Hungary, July 20 - Aug. 20, 1933.

Exists imperf. Value, set $150.

Souvenir Sheet

Franz Liszt — A48

1934, May 6 Perf. 15
486 A48 20f lake 70.00 90.00
Never hinged 140.00

2nd Hungarian Phil. Exhib., Budapest, and Jubilee of the 1st Hungarian Phil. Soc. Sold for 90f, including entrance fee. Size: 64x76mm.

Exists imperf. Value $2,500.

Francis II Rákóczy (1676-1735), Prince of Transylvania A49

1935, Apr. 8 Perf. 12
487 A49 10f yellow green .90 .50
Never hinged 1.50
488 A49 16f brt violet 5.00 3.75
Never hinged 6.25
489 A49 20f dark carmine 2.00 1.50
Never hinged 5.00
490 A49 32f brown lake 7.00 7.25
Never hinged 8.50
491 A49 40f blue 8.50 8.50
Never hinged 13.50
Nos. 487-491 (5) 23.40 21.50
Set, never hinged 42.50

Exists imperf. Value, set $400.

Cardinal Pázmány — A50

Signing the Charter — A51

1935, Sept. 25

No.	Type	Denomination	Unused	Used
492	A50	6f dull green	1.10	1.00
		Never hinged	2.00	
493	A51	10f dark green	.25	.25
		Never hinged	.50	
494	A50	16f slate violet	1.50	1.60
		Never hinged	3.00	
495	A50	20f magenta	.25	.40
		Never hinged	.50	
496	A51	32f deep claret	2.50	3.25
		Never hinged	5.00	
497	A51	40f dark blue	2.00	3.25
		Never hinged	4.00	
		Nos. 492-497 (6)	7.60	9.75
		Set, never hinged	15.00	

Tercentenary of the founding of the University of Budapest by Peter Cardinal Pázmány.
Exists imperf. Value, set $400.

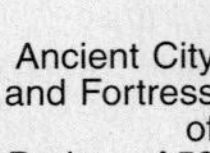

Ancient City and Fortress of Buda — A52

Guardian Angel over Buda — A53

Shield of Buda, Cannon and Massed Flags — A54

First Hungarian Soldier to Enter Buda — A55

1936, Sept. 2 — ***Perf. 11½x12½***

No.	Type	Denomination	Unused	Used
498	A52	10f dark green	.40	.25
		Never hinged	.75	
499	A53	16f deep violet	2.50	*3.50*
		Never hinged	4.50	
500	A54	20f car lake	.40	.25
		Never hinged	.75	
501	A55	32f dark brown	2.50	*3.25*
		Never hinged	5.00	
502	A52	40f deep blue	2.50	*3.25*
		Never hinged	5.00	
		Nos. 498-502 (5)	8.30	10.50
		Set, never hinged	16.00	

250th anniv. of the recapture of Budapest from the Turks.
Exists imperf. Value, set $400.

Catalogue values for unused stamps in this section, from this point to the end of the section, are for Never Hinged items.

Budapest International Fair — A56

1937, Feb. 22 — ***Perf. 12***

No.	Type	Denomination	Unused	Used
503	A56	2f deep orange	.25	.25
504	A56	6f yellow green	.40	.25
505	A56	10f myrtle green	.55	.25
506	A56	20f deep cerise	1.25	.40
507	A56	32f dark violet	2.00	.55
508	A56	40f ultra	1.60	.80
		Nos. 503-508 (6)	6.05	2.50

Exist imperf. Value, set $250.

Portrait Type of 1932

5f, Ferenc Kolcsey. 25f, Mihaly Vorosmarty.

1937, May 5 — ***Perf. 15***

No.	Type	Denomination	Unused	Used
509	A36	5f brown orange	.80	.25
510	A36	25f olive green	1.60	.25

Exist imperf. Value, set $400.

Pope Sylvester II, Archbishop Astrik — A59

Designs: 2f, 16f, Stephen the Church builder. 4f, 20f, St. Stephen enthroned. 5f, 25f, Sts. Gerhardt, Emerich, Stephen. 6f, 30f, St. Stephen offering holy crown to Virgin Mary. 10f, same as 1f. 32f, 50f, Portrait of St. Stephen. 40f, Madonna and Child. 70f, Crown of St. Stephen.

See designs A75-A77 for smaller stamps of designs similar to Nos. 521-524, but with slanted "MAGYAR KIR POSTA."

1938, Jan. 1 — ***Perf. 12***

No.	Type	Denomination	Unused	Used
511	A59	1f deep violet	.40	.25
512	A59	2f olive brown	.40	.25
513	A59	4f brt blue	.80	.25
514	A59	5f magenta	1.25	.25
515	A59	6f dp yel grn	1.60	.25
516	A59	10f red orange	1.25	.25
517	A59	16f gray violet	2.00	.55
518	A59	20f car lake	1.25	.25
519	A59	25f dark green	1.60	.80
520	A59	30f olive bister	2.50	.25
521	A59	32f dp claret, *buff*	2.50	2.00
522	A59	40f Prus green	2.50	.25
523	A59	50f rose vio, *grnsh*	2.75	.25
524	A59	70f ol grn, *bluish*	4.50	.55
		Nos. 511-524 (14)	25.30	6.40

900th anniv. of the death of St. Stephen.
Exists imperf. Value, set $400.
For overprints see Nos. 535-536.

Admiral Horthy — A67

1938, Jan. 1 — ***Perf. 12½x12***

No.	Type	Denomination	Unused	Used
525	A67	1p peacock green	2.75	.25
526	A67	2p brown	3.25	.35
527	A67	5p sapphire blue	4.00	1.90
		Nos. 525-527 (3)	10.00	2.50

Exist imperf. Value, set $475.

Souvenir Sheet

St. Stephen — A68

1938, May 22 — **Wmk. 210** — ***Perf. 12***

No.	Type	Denomination	Unused	Used
528	A68	20f carmine lake	32.50	25.00

3rd Hungarian Phil. Exhib., Budapest. Sheet sold only at exhibition with 1p ticket.
Exists imperf. Value $4,500.

College of Debrecen A69

Three Students — A71

George Marothy — A73

10f, 18th cent. view of College. 20f, 19th cent. view of College. 40f, Stephen Hatvani.

Perf. 12x12½, 12½x12

1938, Sept. 24 — **Wmk. 210**

No.	Type	Denomination	Unused	Used
529	A69	6f deep green	.40	.25
530	A69	10f brown	.40	.25
531	A71	16f brown car	.40	.30
532	A69	20f crimson	.40	.25
533	A73	32f slate green	1.10	.75
534	A73	40f brt blue	1.10	.60
		Nos. 529-534 (6)	3.80	2.40

Founding of Debrecen College, 400th anniv.
Exists imperf. Value $300.

Types of 1938 Overprinted in Blue (#535) or Carmine (#536)

a

b

1938 — ***Perf. 12***

No.	Type	Denomination	Unused	Used
535	A59(a)	20f sal pink	2.00	1.60
536	A59(b)	70f brn, *grnsh*	2.00	1.60
a.		Overprint omitted	*12,500.*	*7,500.*

Restoration of the territory ceded by Czechoslovakia.
Exists imperf. Value $135.
Forgeries exist of No. 536a.

Crown of St. Stephen A75

St. Stephen A76

Madonna, Patroness of Hungary A77

Coronation Church, Budapest A78

Reformed Church, Debrecen A79

Cathedral, Esztergom A80

Deak Square Evangelical Church, Budapest — A81

Cathedral of Kassa — A82

Wmk. 210

1939, June 1 — **Photo.** — ***Perf. 15***

No.	Type	Denomination	Unused	Used
537	A75	1f brown car	.25	.25
538	A75	2f Prus green	.25	.25
539	A75	4f ocher	.25	.25
540	A75	5f brown violet	.25	.25
541	A75	6f yellow green	.25	.25
542	A75	10f bister brn	.25	.25
543	A75	16f rose violet	.25	.25
544	A76	20f rose red	.25	.25
545	A77	25f blue gray	.25	.25
		Perf. 12		
546	A78	30f red violet	.40	.25
547	A79	32f brown	.25	.25
548	A80	40f greenish blue	.40	.25
549	A81	50f olive	.50	.25
550	A82	70f henna brown	.50	.25
		Nos. 537-550 (14)	4.30	3.50

See Nos. 521-524, 578-596. For overprints see Nos. 559-560 in Scott. Post 1940 issues in Scott Standard catalogue, Vol. 3.
Exists imperf. Value, set $250.

Girl Scout Sign and Olive Branch — A83

6f, Scout lily, Hungary's shield, Crown of St. Stephen. 10f, Girls in Scout hat & national headdress. 20f, Dove & Scout emblems.

1939, July 20 — **Photo.** — ***Perf. 12***

No.	Type	Denomination	Unused	Used
551	A83	2f brown orange	.50	.35
552	A83	6f green	.50	.35
553	A83	10f brown	.80	.45
554	A83	20f lilac rose	1.25	.80
		Nos. 551-554 (4)	3.05	1.95

Girl Scout Jamboree at Gödöllö.
Exists imperf. Value, set $300.

Admiral Horthy at Szeged, 1919 — A87

Admiral Nicholas Horthy A88

Cathedral of Kassa and Angel Ringing "Bell of Liberty" A89

1940, Mar. 1

No.	Type	Description	Unused	Used
555	A87	6f green	.25	.25
556	A88	10f ol blk & ol bis	.25	.25
557	A89	20f brt rose brown	.80	.55
		Nos. 555-557 (3)	1.30	1.05

20th anniversary of the election of Admiral Horthy as Regent of Hungary.

Exists imperf. Value, set $100.

Crown of St. Stephen A90

1940, Sept. 5

No.	Type	Description	Unused	Used
558	A90	10f dk green & yellow	.40	.40

Issued in commemoration of the recovery of northeastern Transylvania from Romania.

Exists imperf. Value $25.

SEMI-POSTAL STAMPS

Issues of the Monarchy

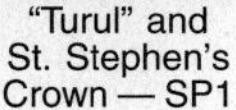

"Turul" and St. Stephen's Crown — SP1

Franz Josef I Wearing Hungarian Crown — SP2

Wmk. Double Cross (137)

1913, Nov. 20 Typo. *Perf. 14*

No.	Type	Description	Unused	Used
B1	SP1	1f slate	.40	.25
		Never hinged	.80	
B2	SP1	2f olive yellow	.40	.25
		Never hinged	.80	
B3	SP1	3f orange	.40	.25
		Never hinged	.80	
B4	SP1	5f emerald	.40	.25
		Never hinged	.80	
B5	SP1	6f olive green	.40	.25
		Never hinged	.80	
B6	SP1	10f carmine	.60	.25
		Never hinged	1.25	
B7	SP1	12f violet, *yellow*	.50	.25
		Never hinged	1.00	
B8	SP1	16f gray green	.75	.25
		Never hinged	1.50	
B9	SP1	20f dark brown	3.00	.40
		Never hinged	6.00	
B10	SP1	25f ultra	1.75	.25
		Never hinged	3.50	
B11	SP1	30f org brn	2.00	.25
		Never hinged	4.00	
B12	SP1	35f red violet	2.00	.25
		Never hinged	4.00	
B13	SP1	50f lake, *blue*	3.75	.60
		Never hinged	7.50	
B14	SP1	60f grn, *sal*	3.75	.50
		Never hinged	7.50	
B15	SP2	1k dull red	25.00	2.00
		Never hinged	50.00	
B16	SP2	2k dull blue	75.00	40.00
		Never hinged	150.00	
B17	SP2	5k violet brown	30.00	30.00
		Never hinged	60.00	
		Nos. B1-B17 (17)	150.10	76.25

Nos. B1-B17 were sold at an advance of 2f over face value, as indicated by the label at bottom. The surtax was to aid flood victims.

For overprints see Nos. 5NB1-5NB10, 6NB1-6NB11.

Exist imperf. Value, set $1,000.

Semi-Postal Stamps of 1913 Surcharged in Red, Green or Brown

a

b

1914

No.	Type	Description	Unused	Used
B18	SP1(a)	1f slate	.25	.25
		Never hinged	.50	
B19	SP1(a)	2f olive yel	.25	.25
		Never hinged	.50	
B20	SP1(a)	3f orange	.25	.25
		Never hinged	.50	
B21	SP1(a)	5f emerald	.25	.25
		Never hinged	.50	
B22	SP1(a)	6f olive green	.25	.25
		Never hinged	.50	
B23	SP1(a)	10f carmine (G)	.35	.25
		Never hinged	.70	
B24	SP1(a)	12f violet, *yel*	.25	.25
		Never hinged	.50	
B25	SP1(a)	16f gray green	.30	.25
		Never hinged	.60	
B26	SP1(a)	20f dark brown	.90	.25
		Never hinged	2.00	
B27	SP1(a)	25f ultra	.90	.25
		Never hinged	2.00	
B28	SP1(a)	30f orange brn	1.10	.25
		Never hinged	2.75	
B29	SP1(a)	35f red violet	1.90	.25
		Never hinged	4.50	
B30	SP1(a)	50f lake, *bl*	1.50	.50
		Never hinged	3.00	
B31	SP1(a)	60f grn, *sal*	2.00	.55
		Never hinged	4.00	
B32	SP2(b)	1k dull red (Br)	60.00	25.00
		Never hinged	125.00	
B33	SP2(b)	2k dull blue	37.50	26.00
		Never hinged	75.00	
B34	SP2(b)	5k violet brn	30.00	21.00
		Never hinged	60.00	
		Nos. B18-B34 (17)	137.95	76.05

Exist imperf. Value, set $800.

Regular Issue of 1913 Surcharged in Red or Green

c

d

1915, Jan. 1

No.	Type	Description	Unused	Used
B35	A4(c)	1f slate	.25	.25
		Never hinged	.50	
B36	A4(c)	2f olive yel	.25	.25
		Never hinged	.50	
B37	A4(c)	3f orange	.25	.25
		Never hinged	.50	
B38	A4(c)	5f emerald	.25	.25
		Never hinged	.50	
B39	A4(c)	6f olive grn	.25	.25
		Never hinged	.50	
B40	A4(c)	10f carmine (G)	.25	.25
		Never hinged	.50	
B41	A4(c)	12f violet, *yel*	.25	.25
		Never hinged	.50	
B42	A4(c)	16f gray green	.25	.25
		Never hinged	.50	
B43	A4(c)	20f dark brown	.25	.25
		Never hinged	.50	
B44	A4(c)	25f ultra	.25	.25
		Never hinged	.50	
B45	A4(c)	30f orange brn	.40	.25
		Never hinged	.80	
B46	A4(c)	35f red violet	.45	.25
		Never hinged	.90	
B47	A4(c)	50f lake, *bl*	.65	.25
		Never hinged	1.25	
a.		On No. 96a	*5,000.*	
B48	A4(c)	60f green, *salmon*	.80	.30
		Never hinged	1.60	
B49	A5(d)	1k dull red	1.10	3.00
		Never hinged	2.25	
B50	A5(d)	2k dull blue	3.00	7.50
		Never hinged	6.00	
B51	A5(d)	5k violet brown	9.50	17.50
		Never hinged	18.50	

Surcharged as Type "c" but in Smaller Letters

No.	Type	Description	Unused	Used
B52	A4	60f green, *salmon*	2.25	1.25
		Never hinged	9.50	
		Nos. B35-B52 (18)	20.65	32.80

Nos. B18-B52 were sold at an advance of 2f over face value. The surtax to aid war widows and orphans.

Exist imperf. Value, set $200.

Soldiers Fighting SP3 SP4

Eagle with Sword — SP5

1916-17 *Perf. 15*

No.	Type	Description	Unused	Used
B53	SP3	10f + 2f rose red	.25	.30
		Never hinged	.50	
B54	SP4	15f + 2f dull violet	.25	.30
		Never hinged	.50	
B55	SP5	40f + 2f brn car ('17)	.25	.40
		Never hinged	.50	
		Nos. B53-B55 (3)	.75	1.00

Exist imperf. Value, set $15.

For overprints and surcharge see Nos. B58-B60. 1NB1-1NB3, 2NB1-2NB6, 4NJ1, 5NB11-5NB13, 6NB13-6NB15, 7NB2-7NB3, 9NB1, 10NB1-10NB4, 11NB1-B4.

Nos. 106-107 Surcharged in Red

1917, Sept. 15

No.	Type	Description	Unused	Used
B56	A8	10f + 1k rose	.60	*1.00*
		Never hinged	1.00	
B57	A8	15f + 1k violet	.60	*1.00*
		Never hinged	1.00	

Nos. B56 and B57 were issued in connection with the War Exhibition of Archduke Josef.

Issues of the Republic

Semi-Postal Stamps of 1916-17 Overprinted in Black

1918

No.	Type	Description	Unused	Used
B58	SP3	10f + 2f rose red	.25	.25
		Never hinged	.50	
B59	SP4	15f + 2f dull violet	.25	.25
		Never hinged	.50	
B60	SP5	40f + 2f brown car	.25	.25
		Never hinged	.50	
		Nos. B58-B60 (3)	.75	.75

Nos. B58-B60 exist with inverted overprint.

Exist imperf. Value, set $12.50.

Postally used examples of Nos. B69-B130 sell for more.

Issues of the Kingdom

Released Prisoner Walking Home — SP7

Prisoners of War — SP8

Homecoming of Soldier — SP9

Wmk. 137 Vertical

1920, Mar. 10 *Perf. 12*

No.	Type	Description	Unused	Used
B69	SP7	40f + 1k dull red	5.00	10.00
		Never hinged	10.00	
B70	SP8	60f + 2k gray brown	3.50	3.50
		Never hinged	7.00	
B71	SP9	1k + 5k dk blue	1.75	3.50
		Never hinged	3.50	
		Nos. B69-B71 (3)	10.25	17.00
		Nos. B69a-B71 (1)	1.75	3.50
		Set, never hinged	20.00	

Wmk. 137 Horizontal

No.	Type	Description	Unused	Used
B69a	SP7	40f + 1k dull red	1.75	3.50
		Never hinged	3.50	
B70a	SP8	60f + 2k gray brown	3.00	6.00
		Never hinged	6.00	
B71a	SP9	1k + 5k dk blue	3.50	3.50
		Never hinged	7.00	
		Nos. B69a-B71a (1)	3.50	3.50
		Set, never hinged	18.50	

The surtax was used to help prisoners of war return home from Siberia.

Exist imperf. Value, set $100.

Statue of Petőfi — SP10

Griffin — SP11

Sándor Petőfi — SP12

Petőfi Dying — SP13

Petőfi Addressing People — SP14

1923, Jan. 23 *Perf. 14 (10k, 40k), 12*

No.	Type	Description	Unused	Used
B72	SP10	10k slate green	.50	*1.00*
		Never hinged	1.00	
B73	SP11	15k dull blue	1.00	*2.75*
		Never hinged	2.00	
B74	SP12	25k gray brown	.50	*1.00*
		Never hinged	1.00	
B75	SP13	40k brown violet	1.50	3.00
		Never hinged	3.00	
B76	SP14	50k violet brown	1.50	3.00
		Never hinged	3.00	
		Nos. B72-B76 (5)	5.00	10.75
		Set, never hinged	10.00	

Birth centenary of the Hungarian poet Sándor Petőfi. The stamps were on sale at double face value, for a limited time and in restricted quantities, after which the remainders were given to a charitable organization.

Exist imperf. Value, set $100.

Child with Symbols of Peace — SP15

Mother and Infant — SP16

Instruction in Archery — SP17

Wmk. 133

1924, Apr. 8 Engr. *Perf. 12*

B77	SP15 300k dark blue	1.50	*4.00*
	Never hinged	4.00	
a.	Perf. 11½	35.00	30.00
B78	SP16 500k black brown	1.50	*4.00*
	Never hinged	4.00	
B79	SP17 1000k black green	1.50	*4.00*
	Never hinged	4.00	
	Nos. B77-B79 (3)	4.50	*12.00*
	Set, never hinged	12.00	

Each stamp has on the back an inscription stating that it was sold at a premium of 100 per cent over the face value.

Exist imperf. Value, set $90.

Parade of Athletes SP18

Skiing — SP19

Skating — SP20

Diving — SP21

Fencing SP22

Scouts Camping — SP23

Soccer SP24

Hurdling — SP25

Perf. 12, 12½ and Compound

1925 Typo. Unwmk.

B80	SP18 100k bl grn & brn	2.25	*2.00*
	Never hinged	4.50	
B81	SP19 200k lt brn & myr grn	2.90	*2.50*
	Never hinged	5.50	
B82	SP20 300k dark blue	3.50	*3.50*
	Never hinged	6.50	
B83	SP21 400k dp bl & dp grn	3.80	*3.50*
	Never hinged	7.50	
B84	SP22 500k pur brn	7.50	*10.00*
	Never hinged	10.50	
B85	SP23 1000k red brown	6.25	*7.00*
	Never hinged	12.00	
B86	SP24 2000k brown violet	7.50	*7.50*
	Never hinged	13.50	
B87	SP25 2500k olive brown	7.50	*9.00*
	Never hinged	15.00	
	Nos. B80-B87 (8)	41.20	*45.00*
	Set, never hinged	75.00	

These stamps were sold at double face value, plus a premium of 10 per cent on orders sent by mail. They did not serve any postal need and were issued solely to raise funds to aid athletic associations. An inscription regarding the 100 per cent premium is printed on the back of each stamp.

Exist imperf. Value, set $450.

St. Emerich SP26

Sts. Stephen and Gisela SP27

St. Ladislaus SP28

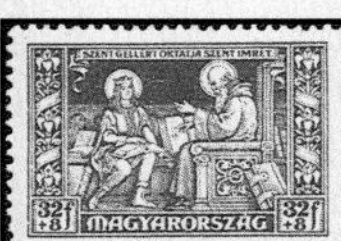

Sts. Gerhardt and Emerich SP29

1930, May 15 Wmk. 210 *Perf. 14*

B88	SP26 8f + 2f deep green	.45	.40
	Never hinged	1.00	
B89	SP27 16f + 4f brt violet	.65	*.60*
	Never hinged	1.10	
B90	SP28 20f + 4f deep rose	1.90	*2.00*
	Never hinged	3.75	
B91	SP29 32f + 8f ultra	2.50	*4.50*
	Never hinged	5.50	
	Nos. B88-B91 (4)	5.50	*7.50*
	Set, never hinged	11.00	

900th anniv. of the death of St. Emerich, son of Stephen I, king, saint and martyr.

Exist imperf. Value, set $150.

Catalogue values for unused stamps in this section, from this point to the end of the section, are for Never Hinged items.

St. Ladislaus — SP30

Holy Sacrament SP31

SP32

1938 May 16 Photo. *Perf. 12*

B92	SP30 16f + 16f dull slate bl	3.00	3.00
B93	SP31 20f + 20f dk car	3.00	3.00

Souvenir Sheet

B94	SP32 Sheet of 7	50.00	32.50
a.	6f + 6f St. Stephen	4.00	3.00
b.	10f + 10f St. Emerich	4.00	3.00
c.	16f + 16f slate blue (B92)	4.00	3.00
d.	20f + 20f dark carmine (B93)	4.00	3.00
e.	32f + 32f St. Elizabeth	4.00	3.00
f.	40f + 40f St. Maurice	4.00	3.00
g.	50f + 50f St. Margaret	4.00	3.00

Printed in sheets measuring 136½x155mm. Nos. B94c and B94d are slightly smaller than B92 and B93.

Eucharistic Cong. in Budapest, May, 1938.

Exist imperf. Value: set $125; souvenir sheet $3,750.

St. Stephen, Victorious Warrior SP33

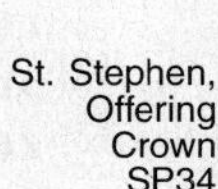

St. Stephen, Offering Crown SP34

SP35

1938, Aug. 12 *Perf. 12*

B95	SP33 10f + 10f violet brn	3.00	3.00
B96	SP34 20f + 20f red org	3.00	3.00

Souvenir Sheet

B97	SP35 Sheet of 7	32.50	20.00
a.	6f + 6f St. Stephen the Missionary	3.25	2.00
b.	10f + 10f violet brown (B95)	3.25	2.00
c.	16f + 16f Seated Upon Throne	3.25	2.00
d.	20f + 20f red orange (B96)	3.25	2.00
e.	32f + 32f Receives Bishops and Monks	3.25	2.00
f.	40f + 40f St. Gisela, St. Stephen and St. Emerich	3.25	2.00
g.	50f + 50f St. Stephen on Bier	3.25	2.00

Death of St. Stephen, 900th anniversary.

No. B97 is on brownish paper, Nos. B95-B96 on white.

Nos. B95-B97 exist imperf. Values: Nos. B95-B96 $150; No. B97 $4,500.

Statue Symbolizing Recovered Territories SP36

Castle of Munkács SP37

Admiral Horthy Entering Komárom SP38

Cathedral of Kassa SP39

Girl Offering Flowers to Soldier — SP40

1939, Jan. 16

B98	SP36 6f + 3f myrtle grn	1.00	.65
B99	SP37 10f + 5f olive grn	.65	.45
B100	SP38 20f + 10f dark red	.65	.45
B101	SP39 30f + 15f grnsh blue	1.25	.80
B102	SP40 40f + 20f dk bl gray	1.75	.80
	Nos. B98-B102 (5)	5.30	3.15

The surtax was for the aid of "Hungary for Hungarians" patriotic movement.

Exist imperf. Value, set $175.

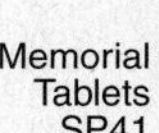

Memorial Tablets SP41

Gáspár Károlyi, Translator of the Bible into Hungarian SP42

Albert Molnár de Szenci, Translator of the Psalms SP43

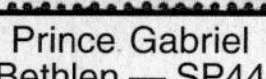

Prince Gabriel Bethlen — SP44 Susanna Lórántffy — SP45

Perf. 12x12½, 12½x12

1939 Photo. Wmk. 210

B103 SP41 6f + 3f green .70 .70
B104 SP42 10f + 5f claret 1.00 1.00
B105 SP43 20f + 10f cop red 1.00 1.00
B106 SP44 32f + 16f bister 1.00 1.00
B107 SP45 40f + 20f chalky blue 1.00 1.00
Nos. B103-B107 (5) 4.70 4.70

Souvenir Sheets

Perf. 12

B108 SP44 32f olive & vio brn 30.00 15.00

Imperf

B109 SP44 32f bl grn, cop red & gold 30.00 15.00

National Protestant Day. The surtax was used to erect an Intl. Protestant Institute.
The souvenir sheets sold for 1.32p each.
Nos. B103-B108 exist imperf. Values: Nos. B103-B107 $350; No. B108 $4,000.
Issue dates: Nos. B103-B107, Oct. 2. Nos. B108-B109, Oct. 27.

Boy Scout Flying Kite — SP47 Allegory of Flight — SP48

Archangel Gabriel from Millennium Monument, Budapest, and Planes — SP49

1940, Jan. 1 ***Perf. 12½x12***

B110 SP47 6f + 6f yellow grn .75 1.00
B111 SP48 10f + 10f chocolate .95 1.25
B112 SP49 20f + 20f copper red 1.40 1.25
Nos. B110-B112 (3) 3.10 3.50

The surtax was used for the Horthy National Aviation Fund.
Exist imperf. Value, set $150.

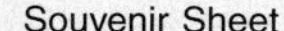

Souvenir Sheet

SP50

Wmk. 210

1940, May 6 Photo. ***Perf. 12***

B113 SP50 20f + 1p dk blue grn 6.00 6.00

Exist imperf. Value $4,500.

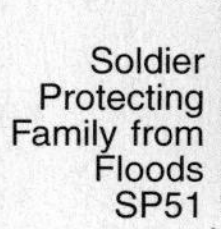

Soldier Protecting Family from Floods SP51

1940, May

B114 SP51 10f + 2f gray brown .40 .25
B115 SP51 20f + 4f orange red .40 .25
B116 SP51 20f + 50f red brown 1.25 1.25
Nos. B114-B116 (3) 2.05 1.75

The surtax on Nos. B113-B116 was used to aid flood victims.
Exist imperf. Value, set $200.

Hunyadi Coat of Arms SP52 King Matthias SP54

Hunyadi Castle SP53

Equestrian Statue of King Matthias SP55

Corvin Codex — SP56

Equestrian Statue of King Matthias — SP57

1940 ***Perf. 12½x12, 12x12½***

B117 SP52 6f + 3f blue grn .60 .60
B118 SP53 10f + 5f gldn brn .60 .60
B119 SP54 16f + 8f dk ol bis .80 .80
B120 SP55 20f + 10f brick red .80 .80
B121 SP56 32f + 16f dk gray 1.25 1.10
Nos. B117-B121 (5) 4.05 3.90

Souvenir Sheet

B122 SP57 20f + 1p dk bl grn & pale grn 6.00 6.00

King Matthias (1440-1490) at Kolozsvar, Transylvania. The surtax was used for war relief.
Nos. B117-B122 exist imperf. Values: Nos. B117-B121 $250; No. B122 $4,500.
Issued: Nos. B117-B121, July 1. No. B122. Nov. 7.

Hungarian Soldier — SP58

20f+50f, Virgin Mary and Szekley, symbolizing the return of transylvania. 32f+50f, Szekley Mother Offering Infant Son to the Fatherland.

1940, Dec. 2 Photo. ***Perf. 12½x12***

B123 SP58 10f + 50f dk blue grn 1.25 1.25
B124 SP58 20f + 50f brown car 1.40 1.40
B125 SP58 32f + 50f yellow brn 1.60 1.60
Nos. B123-B125 (3) 4.25 4.25

Occupation of Transylvania. The surtax was for the Pro-Transylvania movement.
Exist imperf. Value, set $225.

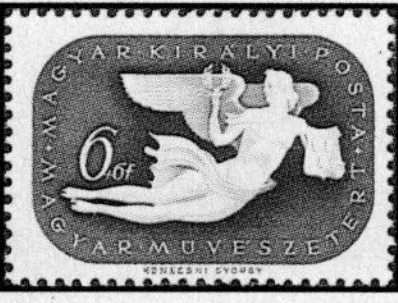

Symbol for Drama SP61

Symbol for Sculpture — SP62

Symbols: 16f+16f, Art. 20f+20f, Literature.

1940, Dec. 15 ***Perf. 12x12½, 12½x12***

B126 SP61 6f + 6f dark green 1.40 1.25
B127 SP62 10f + 10f olive bis 1.40 1.25
B128 SP62 16f + 16f dk violet 1.40 1.25
B129 SP61 20f + 20f fawn 1.40 1.25
Nos. B126-B129 (4) 5.60 5.00

AIR POST STAMPS

Issues of the Monarchy

Nos. 120, 123 Surcharged in Red or Blue

Wmk. 137

1918, July 4 Typo. ***Perf. 14***

C1 A10 1k 50f on 75f (R) 25.00 *27.50*
Never hinged 37.50
C2 A10 4k 50f on 2k (Bl) 25.00 *27.50*
Never hinged 37.50

Counterfeits exist.
Exist imperf. Value, set $350.

No. 126 Surcharged

1920, Nov. 7

C3 A10 3k on 10k (G) 1.40 *2.25*
Never hinged 2.50
On cover 40.00
C4 A10 8k on 10k (R) 1.40 *2.25*
Never hinged 2.50
On cover 7.50
C5 A10 12k on 10k (Bl) 1.40 *2.25*
Never hinged 2.50
On cover 7.50
Nos. C3-C5 (3) 4.20 6.75
Set, never hinged 7.50

Icarus — AP3

1924-25 ***Perf. 14***

C6 AP3 100k red brn & red 1.25 *2.50*
Never hinged 2.75
C7 AP3 500k bl grn & yel grn 1.25 *2.50*
Never hinged 2.75
C8 AP3 1000k bis brn & brn 1.25 *2.50*
Never hinged 2.75
C9 AP3 2000k dk bl & lt bl 1.25 *2.50*
Never hinged 2.75

Wmk. 133

C10 AP3 5000k dl vio & brt vio 2.00 *2.50*
Never hinged 3.50
C11 AP3 10000k red & dl vio 2.00 *4.00*
Never hinged 5.50
Nos. C6-C11 (6) 9.00 16.50
Set, never hinged 20.00

Issue dates: 100k-2000k, 4/11/24. Others, 4/20/25.
Exist imperf. Value, set $100.
Forgeries exist.
For surcharges see Nos. J112-J116.

Mythical "Turul" AP4 "Turul" Carrying Messenger AP5

1927-30 Engr. ***Perf. 14***

C12 AP4 4f orange ('30) .25 *.40*
Never hinged .50
C13 AP4 12f deep green .45 *.40*
Never hinged .50
C14 AP4 16f red brown .45 *.40*
Never hinged .50
C15 AP4 20f carmine .45 *.40*
Never hinged .50
C16 AP4 32f brown vio 1.75 1.20
Never hinged 3.50
C17 AP4 40f dp ultra 1.40 .80
Never hinged 3.50
C18 AP5 50f claret 1.40 .80
Never hinged 3.50
C19 AP5 72f olive grn 1.90 1.20
Never hinged 3.50
C20 AP5 80f dp violet 1.90 1.20
Never hinged 4.00
C21 AP5 1p emerald ('30) 2.25 .50
Never hinged 6.50

C22 AP5 2p red ('30) 4.50 3.00
Never hinged 8.50
C23 AP5 5p dk blue ('30) 16.50 27.50
Never hinged 20.00
Nos. C12-C23 (12) 33.20 37.80
Set, never hinged 55.00

Exist imperf. Value, set $250.

"Turul" Carrying Messenger — AP6

1931, Mar. 27 **Overprinted**
C24 AP6 1p orange (Bk) 40.00 65.00
Never hinged 80.00
C25 AP6 2p dull vio (G) 40.00 65.00
Never hinged 80.00
Set, never hinged 160.00

Exist imperf. Value, set $375.

Monoplane over Danube Valley — AP7

Worker Welcoming Plane, Double Cross and Sun Rays — AP8

Spirit of Flight on Plane Wing AP9

"Flight" Holding Propeller AP10

Wmk. 210
1933, June 20 **Photo.** ***Perf. 15***
C26 AP7 10f blue green 2.00 .40
Never hinged 4.75
C27 AP7 16f purple 2.00 .40
Never hinged 3.25

Perf. 12½x12
C28 AP8 20f carmine 4.50 .75
Never hinged 8.00
C29 AP8 40f blue 4.00 1.25
Never hinged 7.50
C30 AP9 48f gray black 9.50 2.00
Never hinged 17.50
C31 AP9 72f bister brn 20.00 3.00
Never hinged 37.50
C32 AP10 1p yellow grn 25.00 3.00
Never hinged 45.00
C33 AP10 2p violet brn 47.50 18.00
Never hinged 135.00
C34 AP10 5p dk gray 85.00 150.00
Never hinged 135.00
Nos. C26-C34 (9) 199.50 178.80
Set, never hinged 375.00

Exist imperf. Value, set $2,600.

Catalogue values for unused stamps in this section, from this point to the end of the section, are for Never Hinged items.

Fokker F VII over Mail Coach AP11

Plane over Parliament AP12

Airplane AP13

1936, May 8 ***Perf. 12x12½***
C35 AP11 10f brt green .80 .40
C36 AP11 20f crimson .80 .40
C37 AP11 36f brown .90 .40
C38 AP12 40f brt blue .90 .40
C39 AP12 52f red org 3.25 .85
C40 AP12 60f brt violet 20.00 2.00
C41 AP12 80f dk sl grn 4.00 .60
C42 AP13 1p dk yel grn 4.75 .55
C43 AP13 2p brown car 7.50 2.00
C44 AP13 5p dark blue 24.00 19.50
Nos. C35-C44 (10) 66.90 27.10
Set, hinged 27.50

Exist imperf. Value, set $675.

SPECIAL DELIVERY STAMPS

Issue of the Monarchy

SD1

1916 **Typo.** **Wmk. 137** ***Perf. 15***
E1 SD1 2f gray green & red .25 .25
Never hinged .30

Exists imperf. Value $7.50.
For overprints and surcharges see Nos. 1NE1, 2NE1, 4N5, 5NE1, 6NE1, 7NE1, 8NE1, 10NE1, 11NE1, 11NJ7-J8.

Issues of the Republic

Special Delivery Stamp of 1916 Overprinted

1919
E2 SD1 2f gray green & red .25 .75
Never hinged .30

Exists imperf. Value $12.50.

General Issue

SD2

1919
E3 SD2 2f gray green & red .25 .75
Never hinged .30

Exists imperf. Value $10.

POSTAGE DUE STAMPS

Issues of the Monarchy

D1

Perf. 11¾x12
1903 **Typo.** **Wmk. 135**
J1 D1 1f green & blk .50 .50
Never hinged 1.00
J2 D1 2f green & blk 3.00 1.50
Never hinged 6.00
J3 D1 5f green & blk 15.00 6.50
Never hinged 30.00
J4 D1 6f green & blk 12.00 6.00
Never hinged 24.00
J5 D1 10f green & blk 80.00 3.00
Never hinged 160.00
J6 D1 12f green & blk 2.50 2.50
Never hinged 5.00
J7 D1 20f green & blk 20.00 1.50
Never hinged 40.00
J8 D1 50f green & blk 16.00 12.50
Never hinged 32.50
J9 D1 100f green & blk 1.00 1.00
Never hinged 2.00
Nos. J1-J9 (9) 150.00 35.00

Perf. 11½
J1a D1 1f green & blk 1.00 1.00
Never hinged 2.00
J2a D1 2f green & blk 15.00 7.50
Never hinged 30.00
J3a D1 5f green & blk 14.00 6.00
Never hinged 27.50
J4a D1 6f green & blk 15.00 9.00
Never hinged 30.00
J5a D1 10f green & blk 90.00 10.00
Never hinged 175.00
J6a D1 12f green & blk 225.00 150.00
Never hinged 450.00
J7a D1 20f green & blk 300.00 60.00
Never hinged 600.00
J8a D1 50f green & blk 400.00 450.00
Never hinged 800.00

See Nos. J10-J26, J28-J43. For overprints and surcharges see Nos. J27, J44-J50, 1NJ1-1NJ5, 2NJ1-2NJ16, 4NJ2-4NJ3, 5NJ1-5NJ8, 6NJ1-6NJ9, 7NJ1-7NJ4, 9NJ1-9NJ3, 10NJ1-10NJ6, 11NJ1-J6.

1908-09 **Wmk. 136** ***Perf. 15***
J10 D1 1f green & black .75 .50
Never hinged 1.50
J11 D1 2f green & black 1.00 .50
Never hinged 2.00
J12 D1 5f green & black 2.50 .75
Never hinged 5.00
J13 D1 6f green & black 1.50 .50
Never hinged 3.00
J14 D1 10f green & black 1.50 .50
Never hinged 3.00
J15 D1 12f green & black 1.25 .50
Never hinged 2.50
J16 D1 20f green & black 10.00 .50
Never hinged 20.00
c. Center inverted 9,000. 9,000.
J17 D1 50f green & black 1.75 .75
Never hinged 3.50
Nos. J10-J17 (8) 20.25 4.50

1905 **Wmk. 136a** ***Perf. 11½x12***
J12a D1 5f green & black 175.00 70.00
Never hinged 350.00
J13a D1 6f green & black 14.00 7.50
Never hinged 27.50
J14a D1 10f green & black 175.00 5.00
Never hinged 350.00
J15a D1 12f green & black 25.00 16.00
Never hinged 50.00
J17a D1 50f green & black 6.00 2.50
Never hinged 12.00
J18 D1 100f green & black 5.00
Never hinged 10.00

1906 ***Perf. 15***
J11b D1 2f green & black 3.50 3.50
Never hinged 7.00
J12b D1 5f green & black 2.50 2.00
Never hinged 5.00
J13b D1 6f green & black 2.50 2.00
Never hinged 5.00
J14b D1 10f green & black 15.00 .60
Never hinged 30.00
J15b D1 12f green & black .75 .60
Never hinged 1.50
J16b D1 20f green & black 25.00 .60
Never hinged 50.00
d. Center inverted 9,000. 9,000.
J17b D1 50f green & black 1.00 1.00
Never hinged 2.00
Nos. J11b-J17b (7) 50.25 10.30

1914 **Wmk. 137 Horiz.** ***Perf. 15***
J19 D1 1f green & black .35 .25
Never hinged .50
J20 D1 2f green & black .25 .25
Never hinged .35
J21 D1 5f green & black .40 .40
Never hinged .60
J22 D1 6f green & black .80 .60
Never hinged 1.20
J23 D1 10f green & black .90 .70
Never hinged 1.40
J24 D1 12f green & black .40 .25
Never hinged .60
J25 D1 20f green & black .35 .25
Never hinged .50
J26 D1 50f green & black .70 .25
Never hinged 2.00
Nos. J19-J26 (8) 4.15 2.95

1914 **Wmk. 137 Vert.**
J20a D1 2f green & black 57.50 57.50
Never hinged 85.00
J21a D1 5f green & black 4.50 4.50
Never hinged 6.50
J22a D1 6f green & black 9.00 7.50
Never hinged 13.50
J25a D1 20f green & black 2,250. 900.00
Never hinged 3,250.
J26a D1 50f green & black 2.50 2.50
Never hinged 3.75

During 1921-24, a number of Postage Due stamps were punched with three holes prior to sale. See note following No. 105 in the Regular Postage section.

No. J9 Surcharged in Red

1915 **Wmk. 135**
J27 D1 20f on 100f grn & blk .50 2.00
Never hinged 1.00
a. On No. J18, Wmk. 136a 15.00 37.50
Never hinged 30.00

1915-22 **Wmk. 137**
J28 D1 1f green & red .25 .25
Never hinged .30
J29 D1 2f green & red .25 .25
Never hinged .30
J30 D1 5f green & red .35 .25
Never hinged .75
J31 D1 6f green & red .25 .25
Never hinged .30
J32 D1 10f green & red .25 .25
Never hinged .30
J33 D1 12f green & red .25 .25
Never hinged .30
J34 D1 15f green & red .35 .50
Never hinged .60
J35 D1 20f green & red .25 .25
Never hinged .30
J36 D1 30f green & red .25 .25
Never hinged .30
J37 D1 40f green & red ('20) .25 .25
Never hinged .30
J38 D1 50f green & red ('20) .25 .25
Never hinged .30
a. Center inverted 60.00
J39 D1 120f green & red ('20) .25 .25
Never hinged .30
J40 D1 200f green & red ('20) .25 .25
Never hinged .30
J41 D1 2k green & red ('22) .25 .90
Never hinged .60
J42 D1 5k green & red ('22) .25 .25
Never hinged .30
J43 D1 50k green & red ('22) .50 .30
Never hinged 1.00
Nos. J28-J43 (16) 4.45 4.95

Three-Hole Punch
J32a D1 10f green & red .25 .40
Never hinged .40
J35a D1 20f green & red .25 .35
Never hinged .40
J37a D1 40f green & red ('20) .25 .40
Never hinged .40
J38a D1 50f green & red ('20) .25 .40
Never hinged .40
J39a D1 120f green & red ('20) .25 .25
Never hinged .40
J40a D1 200f green & red ('20) .25 .25
Never hinged .40
J41a D1 2k green & red ('22) .45 1.10
Never hinged .90
J42a D1 5k green & red ('22) .25 .40
Never hinged .40
J43a D1 50k green & red ('22) .25 .40
Never hinged .40
Nos. J32a-J43a (9) 2.45 3.95

Issues of the Republic

Postage Due Stamps of 1914-18 Overprinted in Black

1918-19 **On Issue of 1914**
J44 D1 50f green & black 3.00 5.50
Never hinged 6.00

On Stamps and Type of 1915-18
J45 D1 2f green & red .25 .75
Never hinged .40
J46 D1 3f green & red .25 .75
Never hinged .40
a. "KOZTARSASAG" omitted 650.00
J47 D1 10f green & red .25 .75
Never hinged .40
J48 D1 20f green & red .25 .75
Never hinged .40
J49 D1 40f green & red .25 .75
Never hinged .40
a. Inverted overprint 60.00 60.00
J50 D1 50f green & red .25 .75
Never hinged .40
a. Center and overprint inverted 75.00 75.00
Nos. J44-J50 (7) 4.50 10.00

Issues of the Kingdom

D3

1919-20 **Typo.**
J65 D3 2f green & black .25 .50
Never hinged .30
a. Inverted center 2,100.
Never hinged 3,000.
J66 D3 3f green & black .25 .50
Never hinged .30
J67 D3 20f green & black .25 .50
Never hinged .30
J68 D3 40f green & black .25 .50
Never hinged .30

J69 D3 50f green & black .25 .50
Never hinged .30
Nos. J65-J69 (5) 1.25 2.50

Postage Due Stamps of this type have been overprinted "Magyar Tancskztarsasag" but have not been reported as having been issued without the additional overprint "heads of wheat."

For overprints see Nos. J70-J75.

Additional Overprint in Black

1920

J70 D3 2f green & black .85 1.50
Never hinged 1.50
J71 D3 3f green & black .85 1.50
Never hinged 1.50
J72 D3 10f green & black 1.40 2.50
Never hinged 2.50
J73 D3 20f green & black .85 1.50
Never hinged 1.50
J74 D3 40f green & black .85 1.50
Never hinged 1.50
J75 D3 50f green & black .85 1.50
Never hinged 1.50
Nos. J70-J75 (6) 5.65 10.00

Postage Issues Surcharged

a

b

c

1921-25 Red Surcharge

J76 A9(a) 100f on 15f violet .25 .25
Never hinged .30
J77 A9(a) 500f on 15f violet .25 .25
Never hinged .30
J78 A9(b) 2½k on 10f red vio .25 .25
Never hinged .30
J79 A9(b) 3k on 15f violet .25 .25
Never hinged .30
J80 A9(c) 6k on 1½k violet .25 *1.50*
Never hinged .30
J81 A9(b) 9k on 40f ol grn .25 .25
Never hinged .30
J82 A9(c) 10k on 2½k green .25 *1.25*
Never hinged .30
J83 A9(b) 12k on 60f blk brn .25 .25
Never hinged .30
J84 A9(c) 15k on 1½k vio .25 .25
Never hinged .30
J85 A9(c) 20k on 2½k grn .25 *1.10*
Never hinged .30
J86 A9(c) 25k on 1½k vio .25 .25
Never hinged .30
J87 A9(c) 30k on 1½k vio .25 .25
Never hinged .30
J88 A9(c) 40k on 2½k grn .25 *1.25*
Never hinged .30
J89 A9(c) 50k on 1½k vio .25 .25
Never hinged .30
J90 A9(c) 100k on 4½k dl vio .25 .25
Never hinged .30
J91 A9(c) 200k on 4½k dl vio .25 .25
Never hinged .35
J92 A9(c) 300k on 4½k dl vio .25 .25
Never hinged .35
J93 A9(c) 500k on 2k grnsh bl .60 .25
Never hinged 1.00
J94 A9(c) 500k on 3k org brn 2.10 .30
Never hinged 3.50
J95 A9(c) 1000k on 2k grnsh bl 1.20 .25
Never hinged 2.00
J96 A9(c) 1000k on 3k org brn 1.75 .25
Never hinged 3.00
J97 A9(c) 2000k on 2k grnsh bl 1.20 .40
Never hinged 2.00
J98 A9(c) 2000k on 3k org brn 2.10 .35
Never hinged 3.50
J99 A9(c) 5000k on 5k brown .90 *1.75*
Never hinged 1.50
Nos. J76-J99 (24) 14.10 11.90

Three-Hole Punch

J78a A9 2½k on 10f red vio .25 *.30*
Never hinged .40
J80a A9 6k on 1½k violet .25 *1.50*
Never hinged .40
J81a A9 9k on 40f ol grn .25 *.30*
Never hinged .40
J82a A9 10k on 2½k green .25 *2.00*
Never hinged .40
J83a A9 12k on 60f blk brn .25 *.30*
Never hinged .40
J84a A9 15k on 1½k vio .25 *.30*
Never hinged .40
J85a A9 20k on 2½k grn .25 *2.00*
Never hinged .40
J86a A9 25k on 1½k vio .25 *.30*
Never hinged .40
J87a A9 30k on 1½k vio .25 *.30*
Never hinged .40
J88a A9 40k on 2½k grn .25 *2.00*
Never hinged .40
J89a A9 50k on 1½k vio .25 *.30*
Never hinged .40
J90a A9 100k on 4½k dl vio .25 .25
Never hinged .40
J91a A9 200k on 4½k dl vio .30 .25
Never hinged .50
J92a A9 300k on 4½k dl vio .30 .25
Never hinged .50
J93a A9 500k on 2k grnsh bl 1.25 .50
Never hinged 2.10
J94a A9 500k on 3k org brn 4.25 .60
Never hinged 7.00
J95a A9 1000k on 2k grnsh bl 2.50 .50
Never hinged 4.00
J96a A9 1000k on 3k org brn 3.50 .25
Never hinged 5.75
J97a A9 2000k on 2k grnsh bl 2.50 .80
Never hinged 4.00
J98a A9 2000k on 3k org brn 4.25 .70
Never hinged 7.00
J99a A9 5000k on 5k brown 1.75 *3.50*
Never hinged 3.00
Nos. J78a-J99a (21) 23.60 17.20

Year of issue: 6k, 15k, 25k, 30k, 50k, 1922. 10k, 20k, 40k, 100k - No. J93, Nos. J95, J97, 1923. 5,000k, 1924. Nos. J94, J96, J98, 1925. Others, 1921.

D6

1926 Wmk. 133 Litho. *Perf. 15*

J100 D6 1f rose red .25 .25
Never hinged .30
J101 D6 2f rose red .25 .25
Never hinged .30
J102 D6 3f rose red .30 .60
Never hinged .60
J103 D6 4f rose red .25 .25
Never hinged .30
J104 D6 5f rose red 1.75 *2.50*
Never hinged 3.50
J105 D6 8f rose red .25 .25
Never hinged .40
J106 D6 10f rose red 1.25 .25
Never hinged 2.50
J107 D6 16f rose red .30 .25
Never hinged .60
J108 D6 32f rose red .50 .25
Never hinged 1.00
J109 D6 40f rose red .75 .25
Never hinged 1.25
J110 D6 50f rose red .90 .40
Never hinged 1.40
J111 D6 80f rose red 1.25 .65
Never hinged 2.50
Nos. J100-J111 (12) 8.00 6.15

Perf. 14x14½

J103a D6 4f rose red .25 .25
Never hinged .30
J104a D6 5f rose red 1.25 *2.50*
Never hinged 2.50
J105a D6 8f rose red .25 .25
Never hinged .30
J106a D6 10f rose red .25 .25
Never hinged .30
J107a D6 16f rose red .25 .25
Never hinged .30

Exist imperf. Value, set $100.

See Nos. J117-J123. For surcharges see Nos. J124-J129.

Nos. C7-C11 Surcharged in Red or Green

1926 Wmk. 137 *Perf. 14*

J112 AP3 1f on 500k (R) .25 .30
Never hinged .30
J113 AP3 2f on 1000k (G) .25 .30
Never hinged .30
J114 AP3 3f on 2000k (R) .25 .30
Never hinged .30

Wmk. 133

J115 AP3 5f on 5000k (G) .65 *1.50*
Never hinged 1.00
J116 AP3 10f on 10000k (G) .50 *1.10*
Never hinged .90
Nos. J112-J116 (5) 1.90 *3.50*

Type of 1926 Issue

1928-32 Wmk. 210 *Perf. 15*

J117 D6 2f rose red .25 .25
Never hinged .30
J118 D6 4f rose red ('32) .25 .25
Never hinged .30
J119 D6 8f rose red .25 .25
Never hinged .40
J120 D6 10f rose red .25 .25
Never hinged .40
J121 D6 16f rose red .35 .25
Never hinged .60
J122 D6 20f rose red .60 .25
Never hinged 1.00
J123 D6 40f rose red .50 .25
Never hinged .80
Nos. J117-J123 (7) 2.45 1.75

Exist imperf. Value, set $60.

Postage Due Stamps of 1926 Surcharged in Black

1931-33 Wmk. 133

J124 D6 4f on 5f rose red .25 .25
Never hinged .30
J125 D6 10f on 16f rose red 1.50 *3.75*
Never hinged 2.50
J126 D6 10f on 80f rose red ('33) .30 .25
Never hinged .50
J127 D6 12f on 50f rose red ('33) .35 .25
Never hinged .60
J128 D6 20f on 32f rose red .35 .30
Never hinged .60
Nos. J124-J128 (5) 2.75 *4.80*

Perf. 14x14½

J124a D6 4f on 5f rose red .45 .45
Never hinged .75
J125a D6 10f on 16f rose red 2.25 *3.75*
Never hinged 3.75

Surcharged on No. J121

1931 Wmk. 210 *Perf. 15*

J129 D6 10f on 16f rose red .85 *1.25*
Never hinged 1.50

Catalogue values for unused stamps in this section, from this point to the end of the section, are for Never Hinged items.

Figure of Value — D7

1934 Photo. Wmk. 210

J130 D7 2f ultra .25 .25
J131 D7 4f ultra .25 .25
J132 D7 6f ultra .25 .25
J133 D7 8f ultra .25 .25
J134 D7 10f ultra .25 .25
J135 D7 12f ultra .25 .25
J136 D7 16f ultra .25 .25
J137 D7 20f ultra .40 .25
J138 D7 40f ultra .60 .25
J139 D7 80f ultra 2.00 .50
Nos. J130-J139 (10) 4.75 2.75

Exist imperf. Value, set $60.

OFFICIAL STAMPS

During 1921-24, a number of Official stamps were punched with three holes prior to sale. See note following No. 105 in the Regular Postage section.

O1

1921-23 Wmk. 137 Typo. *Perf. 15*

O1 O1 10f brn vio & blk .25 .25
Never hinged .30
O2 O1 20f ol brn & blk .25 .25
Never hinged .30
a. "HIVATALOS" inverted *10,000.*
O3 O1 60f blk brn & blk .25 .25
Never hinged .30
O4 O1 100f dl rose & blk .25 .25
Never hinged .30
O5 O1 250f bl & blk .25 .25
Never hinged .30
O6 O1 350f gray & blk .25 .25
Never hinged .30
O7 O1 500f lt brn & blk .25 .25
Never hinged .30
O8 O1 1000f lil brn & blk .25 .25
Never hinged .30
O9 O1 5k brn ('23) .25 .25
Never hinged .30
O10 O1 10k choc ('23) .25 .25
Never hinged .30
O11 O1 15k gray blk ('23) .25 .25
Never hinged .30
O12 O1 25k org ('23) .25 .25
Never hinged .30
O13 O1 50k brn & red ('22) .25 .25
Never hinged .30
O14 O1 100k bis & red ('22) .25 .25
Never hinged .30
O15 O1 150k grn & red ('23) .25 .25
Never hinged .30
O16 O1 300k dl red & red ('23) .25 .25
Never hinged .30
O17 O1 350k vio & red ('23) .30 .25
Never hinged .50
O18 O1 500k org & red ('22) .30 .25
Never hinged .50
O19 O1 600k ol bis & red ('23) .80 .60
Never hinged 1.25
O20 O1 1000k bl & red ('22) 1.20 .25
Never hinged 1.75
Nos. O1-O20 (20) 6.60 5.35

Three-Hole Punch

O1a O1 10f brn vio & blk .25 .50
Never hinged .30
O2b O1 20f ol brn & blk .25 .25
Never hinged .30
O3a O1 60f blk brn & blk .25 .40
Never hinged .35
O4a O1 100f dl rose & blk .25 .25
Never hinged .35
O5a O1 250f bl & blk .25 .25
Never hinged .40
O6a O1 350f gray & blk .35 .25
Never hinged .45
O7a O1 500f lt brn & blk .35 .25
Never hinged .45
O8a O1 1000f lil brn & blk .35 .50
Never hinged .50
O9a O1 5k brn ('23) .30 .25
Never hinged .40
O10a O1 10k choc ('23) .30 .25
Never hinged .40
O11a O1 15k gray blk ('23) .35 .25
Never hinged .50
O12a O1 25k org ('23) .35 .25
Never hinged .50
O13a O1 50k brn & red ('22) .35 .25
Never hinged .50
O14a O1 100k bis & red ('22) .35 .25
Never hinged .50
Nos. O1a-O14a (14) 4.30 4.15

Counterfeits of No. O2a exist.

Stamps of 1921 Surcharged in Red

1922

O21 O1 15k on 20f ol brn & blk .25 .25
Never hinged .30
O22 O1 25k on 60f blk brn & blk .25 .25
Never hinged .30

Three-Hole Punch

O21a O1 15k on 20f ol brn & blk .30 .25
Never hinged .50
O22a O1 25k on 60f blk brn & blk .30 .25
Never hinged .50

Stamps of 1921 Overprinted in Red

1923

O23 O1 350k gray & blk .25 .25
Never hinged .50

With Additional Surcharge of New Value in Red

O24 O1 150k on 100f dl rose & blk .30 .25
Never hinged .50
O25 O1 2000k on 250f bl & blk 1.50 .40
Never hinged 2.50
Nos. O23-O25 (3) 2.05 .90

Three-Hole Punch

O23a O1 350k gray & blk .60 .40
Never hinged 1.00
O24a O1 150k on 100f dl rose & blk .60 .40
Never hinged 1.00
O25a O1 2000k on 250f bl & blk 2.40 2.00
Never hinged 4.00

1923-24

Paper with Gray Moiré on Face

O26 O1 500k org & red ('23) 2.10 .25
Never hinged 3.50
O27 O1 1000k bl & red ('23) 2.10 .25
Never hinged 3.50
O28 O1 3000k vio & red ('24) 2.10 1.25
Never hinged 3.50
O29 O1 5000k bl & red ('24) 2.40 1.50
Never hinged 4.00
Nos. O26-O29 (4) 8.70 3.25

Three-Hole Punch

O26a O1 500k org & red ('23) 3.00 .50
Never hinged 5.00
O27a O1 1000k bl & red ('23) 3.00 .50
Never hinged 5.00

1924 Wmk. 133
O30 O1 500k orange & red 1.40 1.00
Never hinged 2.25
O31 O1 1000k blue & red 1.40 1.00
Never hinged 2.25

NEWSPAPER STAMPS

Issues of the Monarchy

St. Stephen's Crown and Post Horn
N1 N2

Litho. (#P1), Typo. (#P2)
1871-72 Unwmk. *Imperf.*
P1 N1 (1k) ver red 50.00 20.00
P2 N2 (1k) rose red ('72) 20.00 6.00
a. (1k) vermilion 10.00 2.00
b. Printed on both sides

Reprints of No. P2 are watermarked. Value, $450.

Letter with Crown and Post Horn — N3

1874
P3 N3 1k orange 3.75 .35

1881 Wmk. "kr" in Oval (132)
P4 N3 1k orange 1.25 .25
a. 1k lemon yellow 16.00 3.50
b. Printed on both sides

1898 Wmk. 135
P5 N3 1k orange 1.25 .25

See watermark note after No. 46.

N5

1900 Wmk. Crown in Circle (135)
P6 N5 (2f) red orange .75 .25
Never hinged 1.50

1905 Wmk. Crown (136a)
P7 N5 (2f) red orange 1.00 .25
Never hinged 2.00
a. Wmk. 136 ('08) 1.00 .25
Never hinged 2.00

1914-22 Wmk. Double Cross (137)
P8 N5 (2f) orange .25 .25
Never hinged .30
a. Wmk. horiz. 4.50 3.75
Never hinged 9.00
P9 N5 (10f) deep blue ('20) .25 .25
Never hinged .30
P10 N5 (20f) lilac ('22) .25 .25
Never hinged .300
Nos. P8-P10 (3) .75 .75

For overprints and surcharges see Nos. 1NJ6-1NJ10, 1NP1, 2NP1, 5NP1, 6NP1, 8NP1, 10NP1, 11NP1.

NEWSPAPER TAX STAMPS

Issues of the Monarchy

NT1

NT2

Wmk. 91; Unwmk. from 1871
1868 Typo. *Imperf.*
PR1 NT1 1k blue 4.00 1.00
a. Pair, one sideways
PR2 NT2 2k brown 20.00 10.00
a. 2k red brown 275.00 47.50

NT3

1868
PR2B NT3 1k blue *15,000. 11,000.*

No. PR2B was issued for the Military Border District only. All used stamps are precanceled (newspaper text printed on the stamp). A similar 2k was not issued.

1889-90 Wmk. "kr" in Oval (132)
PR3 NT1 1k blue 2.00 .80
PR4 NT2 2k brown 5.50 5.00

1898 Wmk. Crown in Oval (135)
PR5 NT1 1k blue 6.00 7.50

These stamps did not pay postage, but represented a fiscal tax collected by the postal authorities on newspapers.

Nos. PR3 and PR5 have a tall "k" in "kr."

OCCUPATION STAMPS

Issued under French Occupation

ARAD ISSUE

The overprints on this issue have been extensively forged. Even the inexpensive values are difficult to find with genuine overprints. Values are for genuine overprints. Collectors should be aware that stamps sold "as is" are likely to be forgeries, and unexpertized collections should be assumed to consist of mostly forged stamps. Education plus working with knowledgeable dealers is mandatory in this collecting area. More valuable stamps should be expertized.

Stamps of Hungary Overprinted in Red or Blue

On Issue of 1916-18
1919 Wmk. 137 *Perf. 15, 14*
1N1 A9 2f brn org (R) 1.60 1.60
1N2 A9 3f red lil (R) .75 .75
1N3 A9 5f green (R) 20.00 20.00
1N4 A9 6f grnsh bl (R) 1.90 1.90
a. Inverted overprint 30.00 30.00
1N5 A9 10f rose red 4.00 4.00
1N6 A9 15f violet (R) 1.75 1.75
a. Double overprint 50.00 50.00
1N7 A9 20f gray brn (R) 50.00 50.00
1N8 A9 35f brown (R) 65.00 65.00
1N9 A9 40f ol grn (R) 37.50 37.50
1N10 A10 50f red vio & lil 6.00 6.00
1N11 A10 75f brt bl & pale bl 2.00 2.00
1N12 A10 80f grn & pale grn 2.75 2.75
1N13 A10 1k red brn & cl 15.00 15.00
1N14 A10 2k ol brn & bis 3.00 3.00
a. Inverted overprint 50.00 50.00
1N15 A10 3k dk vio & ind 17.50 17.50
1N16 A10 5k dk brn & lt brn 13.50 13.50
1N17 A10 10k vio brn & vio 70.00 70.00
Nos. 1N1-1N17 (17) 312.25 312.25

With Additional Surcharges

a

b

c

d

1N18 A9 (a) 45f on 2f brn org 8.00 8.00
1N19 A9 (b) 45f on 2f brn org 8.00 8.00
1N20 A9 (c) 50f on 3f red lil 8.00 8.00
1N21 A9 (d) 50f on 3f red lil 8.00 8.00
Nos. 1N18-1N21 (4) 32.00 32.00

Overprinted On Issue of 1918
1N22 A11 10f scarlet (Bl) 60.00 60.00
1N23 A11 20f dk brn .90 .90
1N24 A11 25f brt bl 2.40 2.40
a. Inverted overprint 30.00 30.00
1N25 A12 40f ol grn 3.25 3.25
Nos. 1N22-1N25 (4) 66.55 66.55

Ovptd. On Issue of 1918-19, Overprinted "Koztarsasag"
1N26 A9 2f brn org 2.00 2.00
a. Inverted overprint 50.00 50.00
1N27 A9 4f slate gray 2.00 2.00
1N28 A9 5f green .60 .60
1N29 A9 6f grnsh bl 12.00 12.00
a. Inverted overprint 30.00 30.00
1N30 A9 10f rose red (Bl) 60.00 60.00
1N31 A9 20f gray brn 15.00 15.00
1N32 A11 25f brt bl 2.75 2.75
a. Inverted overprint 30.00 30.00
1N33 A9 40f ol grn 2.00 2.00
1N34 A12 40f ol grn 60.00 60.00
a. Inverted overprint 125.00 125.00
1N35 A12 50f lilac 8.00 8.00
1N36 A10 1k red brn & cl (Bl) 3.25 3.25
1N37 A10 3k dk vio & ind (Bl) 15.00 15.00
Nos. 1N26-1N37 (12) 182.60 182.60

No. 1N36 With Additional Surcharge

e

f

1N38 A10 (e) 10k on 1k 13.50 13.50
1N39 A10 (f) 10k on 1k 13.50 13.50

On Issue of 1919
Inscribed "MAGYAR POSTA"
1N40 A13 5f red (R) 55.00 55.00
1N41 A13 10f red (Bl) 6.50 6.50

SEMI-POSTAL STAMPS

Hungarian Semi-Postal Stamps of 1916-17 Overprinted "Occupation francaise" in Blue or Red

1919 Wmk. 137 *Perf. 15*
1NB1 SP3 10f + 2f rose red 65.00 65.00
1NB2 SP4 15f + 2f dl vio (R) 9.50 9.50
1NB3 SP5 40f + 2f brn car 12.50 12.50
Nos. 1NB1-1NB3 (3) 87.00 87.00

SPECIAL DELIVERY STAMP

Hungarian Special Delivery Stamp of 1916 Overprinted "Occupation francaise"

1919 Wmk. 137 *Perf. 15*
1NE1 SD1 2f gray green & red .60 .60

POSTAGE DUE STAMPS

Hungarian Postage Due Stamps of 1915 Overprinted "Occupation francaise"

1919 Wmk. 137 *Perf. 15*
1NJ1 D1 2f green & red 7.50 7.50
1NJ2 D1 10f green & red 4.00 4.00
1NJ3 D1 12f green & red 32.50 32.50
1NJ4 D1 15f green & red 42.50 42.50
1NJ5 D1 20f green & red 3.00 3.00

Hungarian Newspaper Stamp of 1914 Surcharged

Occupation française
12 Porto 12

1NJ6 N5 12f on 2f orange 8.00 8.00
1NJ7 N5 15f on 2f orange 8.00 8.00
1NJ8 N5 30f on 2f orange 8.00 8.00
a. Double surcharge 50.00 50.00
1NJ9 N5 50f on 2f orange 8.00 8.00
1NJ10 N5 100f on 2f orange 8.00 8.00
Nos. 1NJ1-1NJ10 (10) 129.50 129.50

NEWSPAPER STAMP

Hungarian Newspaper Stamp of 1914 Overprinted "Occupation francaise"

1919 Wmk. 137 *Imperf.*
1NP1 N5 (2f) orange 1.25 1.25

ISSUED UNDER ROMANIAN OCCUPATION

FIRST DEBRECEN ISSUE

The overprints on this issue have been extensively forged. Even the inexpensive values are difficult to find with genuine overprints. The more extensive note before No. 1N1 also applies to Nos. 2N1-2NP16.

Hungarian Stamps of 1913-19 Overprinted in Blue, Red or Black

1919 Wmk. 137 *Perf. 15, 14½x14*
On Stamps of 1913
2N1 A4 2f ol yel *90.00 90.00*
2N2 A4 3f orange *125.00 125.00*
2N3 A4 6f ol grn (R) 50.00 50.00

On Stamps of 1916
2N4 A8 10f rose 75.00 75.00
2N5 A8 15f violet (Bk) 65.00 65.00

On Stamps of 1916-18
2N6 A9 2f brown org 1.50 1.50
2N7 A9 3f red lilac .70 .70
2N8 A9 5f green 4.75 4.75
2N9 A9 6f grnsh bl (R) 1.60 1.60
2N10 A9 15f violet (Bk) .80 .80
a. Red overprint 75.00 75.00
2N11 A9 20f gray brn *125.00 125.00*
2N12 A9 25f dull bl (Bk) 4.50 4.50
2N13 A9 35f brown 60.00 60.00
2N14 A9 40f olive grn 3.75 3.75
2N15 A10 50f red vio & lil 8.25 8.25
2N16 A10 75f brt bl & pale bl (Bk) 2.00 2.00
2N17 A10 80f grn & pale grn (R) 3.50 3.50
2N18 A10 1k red brn & cl 4.75 4.75
2N19 A10 2k ol brn & bis (Bk) 1.75 1.75
2N20 A10 3k dk vio & ind (R) 30.00 30.00
a. Blue overprint *65.00 65.00*
b. Black overprint *250.00 250.00*
2N21 A10 5k dk brn & lt brn (Bk) 27.50 27.50
2N22 A10 10k vio brn & vio *160.00 160.00*

With New Value Added
2N23 A9 35f on 3f red lil 2.00 2.00
2N24 A9 45f on 2f brn org 2.00 2.00
2N25 A10 3k on 75f brt bl & pale bl (Bk) 4.00 4.00
2N26 A10 5k on 75f brt bl & pale bl (Bk) 3.75 3.75

2N27 A10 10k on 80f grn & pale grn (R) 3.50 3.50

On Stamps of 1918

2N28 A11 10f scarlet 60.00 60.00
2N28A A11 15f violet (R) 75.00 75.00
b. Black overprint 125.00 125.00
2N29 A11 20f dk brn (R) 6.25 6.25
a. Black overprint 30.00 30.00
b. Blue overprint 75.00 75.00
2N30 A11 25f brt blue (R) 7.00 7.00
a. Black overprint 75.00 75.00
2N31 A12 40f ol grn 3.00 3.00
2N32 A12 50f lilac 50.00 50.00

On Stamps of 1918-19, Overprinted "Koztarsasag"

2N33 A9 2f brn org 3.00 3.00
2N34 A9 3f red lilac 65.00 65.00
2N35 A9 4f sl gray (R) 1.75 1.75
2N36 A9 5f green .65 .65
2N37 A9 6f grnsh bl (R) 30.00 30.00
2N38 A9 10f rose red 37.50 37.50
2N39 A11 10f scarlet 25.00 25.00
2N40 A11 15f dp vio (Bk) 45.00 45.00
a. Red overprint 125.00 125.00
2N41 A9 20f gray brn 3.25 3.25
2N42 A11 20f dk brn (Bk) 37.50 37.50
b. Red overprint 50.00 50.00
2N43 A9 40f olive grn 1.75 1.75
2N44 A10 1k red brn & cl 2.75 2.75
2N45 A10 2k ol brn & bis (Bk) 60.00 60.00
a. Blue overprint 125.00 125.00
2N46 A10 3k dk vio & ind (R) 9.75 9.75
a. Blue overprint 60.00 60.00
b. Black overprint *200.00 200.00*
2N47 A10 5k dk & lt brn (Bk) *225.00 225.00*
2N48 A10 10k vio brn & vio *500.00 500.00*
2N49 A11 25f brt bl (R) 3.25 3.25
a. Black overprint 25.00 25.00
2N50 A12 40f olive grn *125.00 125.00*
2N51 A12 50f lilac 2.25 2.25

On Stamps of 1919

2N52 A13 5f green .50 .50
2N53 A13 6f grnsh bl (Bk) 22.50 22.50
2N54 A13 10f red .25 .25
2N55 A13 20f dk brown .25 .25
2N56 A13 25f dl bl (Bk) 1.25 1.25
2N56A A13 40f ol grn 125.00 125.00
2N57 A13 45f orange 15.00 15.00
2N57A A14 95f dk bl & bl 125.00 125.00
2N57B A14 1.20k dk grn & grn 125.00 125.00
2N57C A14 1.40k yel grn 125.00 125.00

No. 2N58

2N58 A14 5k dk brn & brn 3,000. 3,000.

#2N58 is handstamped. Counterfeits exist. Expertization is required.

On No. 103A

2N59 A5a 10f violet brn (R) 50.00 50.00

On No. 208

2N60 A13 10f red 75.00 75.00
Nos. 2N1-2N57,2N59-2N60 (61) 2,530. 2,530.

SEMI-POSTAL STAMPS

Hungary Nos. B36, B37 Overprinted like Regular Issues in Blue

1919 Wmk. 137 *Perf. 14*

2NB1 A4(c) 2f olive yellow 125.00 125.00
2NB1A A4(c) 3f orange 125.00 125.00

Same Overprint in Blue or Black on Hungary Nos. B53--B55

1919 Wmk. 137 *Perf. 15*

2NB1B SP3 10f + 2f rose red 4.00 4.00
2NB2 SP4 15f + 2f dl vio (Bk) 17.00 17.00
2NB3 SP5 40f + 2f brn car 11.00 11.00
Nos. 2NB1B-2NB3 (3) 32.00 32.00

Same Overprint on Hungary Nos. B58-B60 (with "Köztarsasag")

1919

2NB4 SP3 10f + 2f rose red 42.50 42.50
2NB5 SP4 15f + 2f dl vio (Bk) 75.00 75.00
2NB6 SP5 40f + 2f brn car 32.50 32.50
Nos. 2NB4-2NB6 (3) 150.00 150.00

SPECIAL DELIVERY STAMP

Hungarian Special Delivery Stamp of 1916 Overprinted like Regular Issues

1919 Wmk. 137 *Perf. 15*

2NE1 SD1 2f gray grn & red (Bl) 3.00 3.00

POSTAGE DUE STAMPS

Hungarian Postage Due Stamps of 1914-19 Overprinted in Black like Regular Issues

1919 Wmk. 137 *Perf. 15*

On Stamp of 1914

2NJ1 D1 50f grn & blk *125.00 125.00*

On Stamps of 1915

2NJ2 D1 1f green & red 62.50 62.50
2NJ3 D1 2f green & red 2.00 2.00
2NJ4 D1 5f green & red *225.00 225.00*
2NJ5 D1 6f green & red *125.00 125.00*
2NJ6 D1 10f green & red .80 .80
2NJ7 D1 12f green & red *125.00 125.00*
2NJ8 D1 15f green & red 20.00 20.00
2NJ9 D1 20f green & red 4.50 4.50
2NJ10 D1 30f green & red 13.50 13.50

On Stamps of 1918-19, Overprinted "Koztarsasag"

2NJ11 D1 2f green & red 25.00 25.00
2NJ12 D1 3f green & red 30.00 30.00
2NJ13 D1 10f green & red 30.00 30.00
2NJ14 D1 20f green & red 30.00 30.00
2NJ15 D1 40f green & red 30.00 30.00
2NJ16 D1 50f green & red 30.00 30.00
Nos. 2NJ1-2NJ16 (16) 878.30 878.30

NEWSPAPER STAMP

Hungarian Newspaper Stamp of 1914 Overprinted like Regular Issues

1919 Wmk. 137 *Imperf.*

2NP1 N5 (2f) orange (Bl) .55 .55
a. Inverted overprint 50.00 50.00
b. Double overprint 125.00 125.00

SECOND DEBRECEN ISSUE

Complete forgeries exist of this issue and are often found in large multiples or even complete sheets. Values are for genuine stamps.

Mythical "Turul" — OS5

Throwing Lariat OS6

Hungarian Peasant OS7

1920 Unwmk. Typo. *Perf. 11½*

3N1 OS5 2f lt brown 2.25 2.25
3N2 OS5 3f red brown 2.25 2.25
3N3 OS5 4f gray 2.25 2.25
3N4 OS5 5f lt green .50 .50
3N5 OS5 6f slate 2.25 2.25
3N6 OS5 10f scarlet .50 .50
3N7 OS5 15f dk violet 3.00 3.00
3N8 OS5 20f dk brown .60 .60
3N9 OS6 25f ultra 1.25 1.25
3N10 OS6 30f buff .65 .65
3N11 OS6 35f claret 1.25 1.25
3N12 OS6 40f olive grn .75 .75
3N13 OS6 45f salmon 1.00 1.00
3N14 OS6 50f pale vio .75 .75
3N15 OS6 60f yellow grn .90 .90
3N16 OS6 75f Prus blue .75 .75
3N17 OS7 80f gray grn .85 .85
3N18 OS7 1k brown red 3.00 3.00
3N19 OS7 2k chocolate 3.00 3.00
3N20 OS7 3k brown vio 2.25 2.25
3N21 OS7 5k bister brn 2.25 2.25
3N22 OS7 10k dull vio 2.25 2.25
Nos. 3N1-3N22 (22) 34.50 34.50

Thick, Glazed Paper

3N23 OS5 2f lt brown 3.00 3.00
3N24 OS5 3f red brown 3.00 3.00
3N25 OS5 4f gray 3.00 3.00
3N26 OS5 5f lt green 3.00 3.00
3N27 OS5 6f slate 3.00 3.00
3N28 OS5 10f scarlet .75 .75
3N29 OS5 15f dk vio 3.00 3.00
3N30 OS5 20f dk brown 1.00 1.00
3N31 OS7 80f gray grn 1.50 1.50
3N32 OS7 1k brown red 4.00 4.00
3N33 OS7 1.20k orange 8.00 8.00
3N34 OS7 2k chocolate 4.50 4.50
Nos. 3N23-3N34 (12) 37.75 37.75

SEMI-POSTAL STAMPS

Carrying Wounded — SP1

1920 Unwmk. Typo. *Perf. 11½*

3NB1 SP1 20f green 1.25 1.25
3NB2 SP1 50f gray brn 2.25 2.25
3NB3 SP1 1k blue green 2.25 2.25
3NB4 SP1 2k dk green 2.25 2.25

Colored Paper

3NB5 SP1 20f green, *bl* 3.00 3.00
3NB6 SP1 50f brn, *rose* 3.00 3.00
3NB7 SP1 1k dk grn, *grn* 3.00 3.00
Nos. 3NB1-3NB7 (7) 17.00 17.00

POSTAGE DUE STAMPS

D1

1920 Typo. *Perf. 15*

3NJ1 D1 5f blue green 1.50 1.50
3NJ2 D1 10f blue green 1.50 1.50
3NJ3 D1 20f blue green .75 .75
3NJ4 D1 30f blue green .75 .75
3NJ5 D1 40f blue green 1.25 1.25
Nos. 3NJ1-3NJ5 (5) 5.75 5.75

TEMESVAR ISSUE

Issued under Romanian Occupation

Forgeries exist of the inverted and color error surcharges.

Hungary Nos. 108, 155, 109, 111, E1 Surcharged

1919 Wmk. 137 *Perf. 15*

4N1 A9 30f on 2f brn org (Bl) .40 .40
a. Red surcharge 2.00 2.00
b. Inverted surcharge (R) 25.00 25.00
4N2 A9 1k on 4f sl gray (R) .30 .30
4N3 A9 150f on 3f red lil (Bk) .25 .25
4N4 A9 150f on 5f grn (Bk) .40 .40
4N5 SD1 3k on 2f gray grn & red (Bk) 2.00 2.00
a. Blue surcharge .80 .80
Nos. 4N1-4N5 (5) 3.35 3.35

POSTAGE DUE STAMPS

D1

D2

1919 Wmk. 137 *Perf. 15*

4NJ1 D1 40f on 15f + 2f vio (Bk) .50 .50
a. Red surcharge 2.00 2.00
4NJ2 D2 60f on 2f grn & red (Bk) 2.50 2.50
a. Red surcharge 8.00 8.00
4NJ3 D2 60f on 10f grn & red (Bk) 1.25 1.25
a. Red surcharge 4.00 4.00
Nos. 4NJ1-4NJ3 (3) 4.25 4.25

FIRST TRANSYLVANIA ISSUE

Issued under Romanian Occupation

The scarcer values of this issue have been extensively forged. Genuine common values are more easily found.

Issued in Kolozsvar (Cluj)

Hungarian Stamps of 1916-18 Overprinted

1919 Wmk. 137 *Perf. 15, 14*

On Stamp of 1916, White Numerals

5N1 A8 15b violet 4.75 4.75

On Stamps of 1916-18

5N2 A9 2b brown org .25 .25
5N3 A9 3b red lilac .25 .25
5N4 A9 5b green .25 .25
5N5 A9 6b grnsh blue .40 .40
5N5A A9 10b rose red 60.00 60.00
5N6 A9 15b violet .25 .25
5N7 A9 25b dull blue .25 .25
5N8 A9 35b brown .25 .25
5N9 A9 40b olive grn .50 .50
5N10 A10 50b red vio & lil 1.00 1.00
5N11 A10 75b brt bl & pale bl .30 .30
5N12 A10 80b grn & pale grn .25 .25
5N13 A10 1 l red brn & cl .25 .25
5N14 A10 2 l ol brn & bis .60 .60
5N15 A10 3 l dk vio & ind 3.50 3.50
5N16 A10 5 l dk brn & lt brn 2.50 2.50
5N17 A10 10 l vio brn & vio 3.00 3.00

On Stamps of 1918

5N18 A11 10b scarlet 40.00 40.00
5N19 A11 15b dp violet 20.00 20.00
5N20 A11 20b dk brown .25 .25
a. Gold overprint 75.00 75.00
b. Silver overprint 75.00 75.00
5N21 A11 25b brt blue .65 .65
5N22 A12 40b olive grn .30 .30

On No. 103A

5N23 A5a 10b violet brn .35 .35
Nos. 5N1-5N23 (24) 140.10 140.10

SEMI-POSTAL STAMPS

Hungarian Semi-Postal Stamps of 1913-17 Overprinted like Regular Issues

On Issue of 1913

1919 Wmk. 137 *Perf. 14*

5NB1 SP1 1 l on 1f slate 27.50 27.50
5NB2 SP1 1 l on 2f ol yel 70.00 70.00
5NB3 SP1 1 l on 3f org 37.50 37.50
5NB4 SP1 1 l on 5f emer 3.25 3.25
5NB5 SP1 1 l on 10f car 4.50 4.50
5NB6 SP1 1 l on 12f vio,*yel* 16.00 16.00
5NB7 SP1 1 l on 16f gray grn 6.25 6.25
5NB8 SP1 1 l on 25f ultra 60.00 60.00
5NB9 SP1 1 l on 35f red vio 10.00 10.00
5NB10 SP2 1 l on 1k dl red 60.00 60.00

On Issue of 1916-17

Perf. 15

5NB11 SP3 10b + 2b rose red .25 .25
5NB12 SP4 15b + 2b dull vio .25 .25
5NB13 SP5 40b + 2b brn car .25 .25
Nos. 5NB1-5NB13 (13) 295.75 295.75

SPECIAL DELIVERY STAMP

Hungarian Special Delivery Stamp of 1916 Overprinted like Regular Issues

1919 Wmk. 137 *Perf. 15*

5NE1 SD1 2b gray grn & red .30 .30

POSTAGE DUE STAMPS

Hungarian Postage Due Stamps of 1914-18 Overprinted like Regular Issues

On Stamp of 1914

1919 Wmk. 137 *Perf. 15*

5NJ1 D1 50b green & blk 13.00 13.00

On Stamps of 1915

5NJ2 D1 1b green & red *350.00 350.00*
5NJ3 D1 2b green & red .70 .70
5NJ4 D1 5b green & red 60.00 60.00
5NJ5 D1 10b green & red .45 .45
5NJ6 D1 15b green & red 20.00 20.00
5NJ7 D1 20b green & red .40 .40
5NJ8 D1 30b green & red 30.00 30.00
Nos. 5NJ1-5NJ8 (8) 474.55 474.55

NEWSPAPER STAMP

Hungarian Newspaper Stamp of 1914 Overprinted like Regular Issues

1919 Wmk. 137 *Imperf.*

5NP1 N5 2b orange 3.75 3.75

SECOND TRANSYLVANIA ISSUE

The scarcer values of this issue have been extensively forged. Genuine common values are more easily found.

Issued in Nagyvarad (Oradea)

Hungarian Stamps of 1916-19 Overprinted

1919 Wmk. 137 *Perf. 15, 14*

On Stamps of 1913-16

6N1 A4 2b olive yel 7.00 7.00
6N2 A4 3b orange 13.00 13.00
6N3 A4 6b olive grn 1.75 1.75
6N4 A4 16b gray grn 37.50 37.50
6N5 A4 50b lake, *bl* 1.75 1.75
6N6 A4 70b red brn & grn 26.00 26.00

On Stamp of 1916 (White Numerals)

6N6A A8 15b violet 125.00 125.00

On Stamps of 1916-18

6N7 A9 2b brown org .25 .25
6N8 A9 3b red lilac .25 .25
6N9 A9 5b green .30 .30
6N10 A9 6b grnsh blue 1.60 1.60
6N11 A9 10b rose red 2.10 2.10
6N12 A9 15b violet .25 .25
6N13 A9 20b gray brn 20.00 20.00
6N14 A9 25b dull blue .30 .30
6N15 A9 35b brown .45 .45
6N16 A9 40b olive grn .30 .30
6N17 A10 50b red vio & lil .60 .60
6N18 A10 75b brt bl & pale bl .25 .25
6N19 A10 80b grn & pale grn .30 .30
6N20 A10 1 l red brn & cl .75 .75
6N21 A10 2 l ol brn & bis .25 .25
6N22 A10 3 l dk vio & ind 6.50 6.50
6N23 A10 5 l dk brn & lt brn 3.25 3.25
6N24 A10 10 l vio brn & vio 1.50 1.50

On Stamps of 1918

6N25 A11 10b scarlet 3.25 3.25
6N26 A11 20b dk brown .25 .25
6N27 A11 25b brt blue .75 .75
6N28 A12 40b olive grn 1.10 1.10

On Stamps of 1918-19, Overprinted "Koztarsasag"

6N29 A9 2b brown org 4.00 4.00
6N30 A9 3b red lilac .25 .25
6N31 A9 4b slate gray .25 .25
6N32 A9 5b green .50 .50
6N33 A9 6b grnsh bl 3.00 3.00
6N34 A9 10b rose red 17.50 17.50
6N35 A9 20b gray brn 2.50 2.50
6N36 A9 40b olive grn .50 .50
6N37 A10 1 l red brn & cl .25 .25
6N38 A10 3 l dk vio & ind .75 .75
6N39 A10 5 l dk brn & lt brn 4.50 4.50
6N40 A11 10b scarlet *75.00 75.00*
6N41 A11 20b dk brown 4.50 4.50
6N42 A11 25b brt blue 1.25 1.25
6N43 A12 50b lilac .25 .25

On Stamps of 1919

Inscribed "MAGYAR POSTA"

6N44 A13 5b yellow grn .25 .25
6N45 A13 10b red .25 .25
6N46 A13 20b dk brown .40 .40
6N47 A13 25b dull blue 2.00 2.00
6N48 A13 40b olive grn .65 .65
6N49 A14 5 l dk brn & brn 6.50 6.50

On No. 103A

6N50 A5a 10b violet brn .85 .85
Nos. 6N1-6N50 (51) 382.45 382.45

SEMI-POSTAL STAMPS

Hungarian Semi-Postal Stamps of 1913-17 Overprinted like Regular Issues

On Stamps of 1913

1919 Wmk. 137 *Perf. 14*

6NB1 SP1 1 l on 1f slate 2.25 2.25
6NB2 SP1 1 l on 2f olive yel 8.50 8.50
6NB3 SP1 1 l on 3f orange 2.75 2.75
6NB4 SP1 1 l on 5f emerald .25 .25
6NB5 SP1 1 l on 6f olive grn 2.25 2.25
6NB6 SP1 1 l on 10f carmine .30 .30
6NB7 SP1 1 l on 12f vio, *yel* 60.00 60.00
6NB8 SP1 1 l on 16f gray grn 2.50 2.50
6NB9 SP1 1 l on 20f dk brn 11.00 11.00
6NB10 SP1 1 l on 25f ultra 7.50 7.50
6NB11 SP1 1 l on 35f red vio 7.75 7.75

On Stamp of 1915

Wmk. 135 *Perf. 11½*

6NB12 A4 5b emerald 20.00 20.00

On Stamps of 1916-17

Wmk. 137 *Perf. 15*

6NB13 SP3 10b + 2b rose red 1.25 1.25
6NB14 SP4 15b + 2b dull vio .45 .45
6NB15 SP5 40b + 2b brn car .25 .25
Nos. 6NB1-6NB15 (15) 127.00 127.00

SPECIAL DELIVERY STAMP

Hungarian Special Delivery Stamp of 1916 Overprinted like Regular Issues

1919 Wmk. 137 *Perf. 15*

6NE1 SD1 2b gray grn & red .40 .40

POSTAGE DUE STAMPS

Hungarian Postage Due Stamps of 1915 Overprinted like Regular Issues

1919 Wmk. 137 *Perf. 15*

6NJ1 D1 1b green & red 30.00 30.00
6NJ2 D1 2b green & red .25 .25
6NJ3 D1 5b green & red 9.75 9.75
6NJ4 D1 6b green & red 6.75 6.75
6NJ5 D1 10b green & red .25 .25
6NJ6 D1 12b green & red 1.50 1.50
6NJ7 D1 15b green & red 1.50 1.50
6NJ8 D1 20b green & red .25 .25
6NJ9 D1 30b green & red 1.60 1.60
Nos. 6NJ1-6NJ9 (9) 51.85 51.85

On Hungary No. J27

Perf. 11½x12

Wmk. 135

6NJ10 D1 20b on 100b grn & blk 350.00 350.00

NEWSPAPER STAMP

Hungarian Newspaper Stamp of 1914 Overprinted like Regular Issues

1919 Wmk. 137 *Imperf.*

6NP1 N5 2b orange .45 .45

FIRST BARANYA ISSUE

Issued under Serbian Occupation

The scarcer values of this issue have been extensively forged. Genuine common values are more easily found.

Hungarian Stamps of 1913-18 Overprinted in Black or Red

On A4, A9, A11, A12

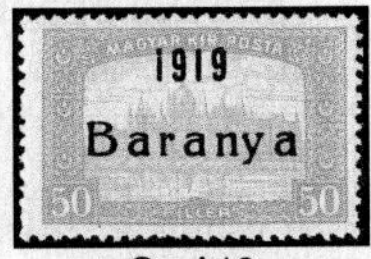

On A10

1919 Wmk. 137 *Perf. 15*

On Issue of 1913-16

7N1 A4 6f olive grn (R) .90 .90
7N2 A4 50f lake, *bl* .25 .25
7N3 A4 60f grn, *salmon* .75 .75
7N4 A4 70f red brn & grn (R) 2.00 2.00
7N5 A4 70f red brn & grn (Bk) .25 .25
7N6 A4 80f dl vio (R) 3.25 3.25

On Issue of 1916-18

7N7 A9 2f brown org (Bk) 4.25 4.25
7N8 A9 2f brown org (R) .25 .25
7N9 A9 3f red lilac (Bk) .25 .25
7N10 A9 3f red lilac (R) .80 .80
7N11 A9 5f green (Bk) .80 .80
7N12 A9 5f green (R) .25 .25
7N13 A9 6f grnsh bl (Bk) 1.75 1.75
7N14 A9 6f grnsh bl (R) 2.00 2.00
7N15 A9 15f violet .35 .35
7N16 A9 20f gray brn 20.00 20.00
7N17 A9 25f dull blue 3.50 3.50
7N18 A9 35f brown 5.75 5.75
7N19 A9 40f olive grn 20.00 20.00
7N20 A10 50f red vio & lil 2.00 2.00
7N21 A10 75f brt bl & pale bl .40 .40
7N22 A10 80f grn & pale grn .65 .65
7N23 A10 1k red brn & cl .55 .55
7N24 A10 2k ol brn & bis .65 .65
7N25 A10 3k dk vio & ind .65 .65
7N26 A10 5k dk brn & lt brn 1.25 1.25
7N27 A10 10k vio brn & vio 4.00 *4.00*

7N28 A9 45f on 2f brn org .35 .35
7N29 A9 45f on 5f green .25 .25
7N30 A9 45f on 15f violet .25 .25

On Issue of 1918

7N31 A11 10f scarlet (Bk) .25 .25
7N32 A11 20f dk brn (Bk) .25 .25
7N34 A11 25f dp blue (Bk) 1.90 1.90
7N35 A11 25f dp blue (R) 1.10 1.10
7N36 A12 40f olive grn (Bk) 4.50 4.50
7N37 A12 40f olive grn (R) 30.00 30.00

On Issue of 1918-19 (Koztarsasag)

7N38 A9 2f brown org (Bk) 3.50 3.50
7N39 A12 40f ol grn (Bk) *125.00 125.00*
7N40 A12 40f olive grn (R) 20.00 20.00

With New Value Added

7N41 A9 45f on 2f brn org (Bk) 2.00 2.00
7N42 A9 45f on 2f brn org (R) .45 .45

The overprints were set in groups of 25. In each group two stamps have the figures "1" of "1919" with serifs.

SEMI-POSTAL STAMPS

Hungarian Semi-Postal Stamps Overprinted Regular Issue First Type On Stamp of 1915

1919 Wmk. 137 *Perf. 15*

7NB1 A4 50f + 2f lake, *bl* 16.00 16.00

On Stamps of 1916

7NB2 SP3 10f + 2f rose red .30 .30
7NB3 SP4 15f + 2f dull vio .40 .40
Nos. 7NB1-7NB3 (3) 16.70 16.70

SPECIAL DELIVERY STAMP

SD1

1919 Wmk. 137 *Perf. 15*

7NE1 SD1 105f on 2f gray grn & red 1.25 1.25

POSTAGE DUE STAMPS

Overprinted or Surcharged on Hungary Nos. J29, J32, J35

1919 Wmk. 137 *Perf. 15*

7NJ1 D1 2f green & red 3.75 3.75
7NJ2 D1 10f green & red 1.25 1.25
7NJ3 D1 20f green & red 1.60 1.60

With New Value Added

7NJ4 D1 40f on 2f grn & red 1.50 1.50
Nos. 7NJ1-7NJ4 (4) 8.10 8.10

SECOND BARANYA ISSUE

The scarcer values of this issue have been extensively forged. Genuine common values are more easily found.

Hungarian Stamps of 1916-19 Surcharged in Black and Red

1919 On Stamps of 1916-18

8N1 A9 20f on 2f brn org 4.25 4.25
8N2 A9 50f on 5f green 2.00 2.00
8N3 A9 150f on 15f violet 2.00 2.00
8N4 A10 200f on 75f brt bl & pale bl .75 .75

On Stamp of 1918-19, Overprinted "Koztarsasag"

8N5 A11 150f on 15f dp vio .50 .50

On Stamps of 1919

8N6 A13 20f on 2f brn org .35 .35
8N7 A13 30f on 6f grnsh bl .70 .70
8N8 A13 50f on 5f yel grn .25 .25
8N9 A13 100f on 25f dull bl .25 .25
8N10 A13 100f on 40f ol grn .25 .25
8N11 A13 100f on 45f orange 1.10 1.10
8N12 A13 150f on 20f dk brn 1.40 1.40

On No. 103A

8N13 A5a 10f on 10f vio brn .75 .75
Nos. 8N1-8N13 (13) 14.55 14.55

SPECIAL DELIVERY STAMP

Hungarian Special Delivery Stamp of 1916 Surcharged like Regular Issues

1919 Wmk. 137 *Perf. 15*

8NE1 SD1 10f on 2f gray grn & red .65 .65

NEWSPAPER STAMP

Hungarian Newspaper Stamp of 1914 Surcharged like Regular Issues

1919 Wmk. 137 *Imperf.*

8NP1 N5 10f on 2f orange .80 .80

TEMESVAR ISSUES

Issued under Serbian Occupation

Forgeries exist of the inverted and color error surcharges.

Hungarian Stamps of 1916-18 Surcharged in Black, Blue or Brown

a

b

1919

9N1 A9(a) 10f on 2f brn org (Bl) .25 .25
a. Black surcharge 15.00 15.00
9N2 A9(b) 30f on 2f brn org .25 .25
a. Inverted surcharge 75.00 75.00
9N3 A11(b) 50f on 20f dk brn (Bl) .25 .25
a. Inverted surcharge
9N4 A9(b) 1k 50f on 15f vio .30 .30
a. Brown surcharge .75 .75
b. Double surcharge (Bk) 50.00 50.00
Nos. 9N1-9N4 (4) 1.05 1.05

SEMI-POSTAL STAMP

Hungarian Semi-Postal Stamp of 1916 Surcharged in Blue

1919 Wmk. 137 *Perf. 15*

9NB1 SP3 45f on 10f + 2f rose red .25 .25

POSTAGE DUE STAMPS

Hungarian Postage Due Stamps of 1915 Surcharged

1919 Wmk. 137 *Perf. 15*

9NJ1 D1 40f on 2f grn & red .80 .80
9NJ2 D1 60f on 2f grn & red .80 .80
9NJ3 D1 100f on 2f grn & red .80 .80
Nos. 9NJ1-9NJ3 (3) 2.40 2.40

BANAT, BACSKA ISSUE

Issued under Serbian Occupation

Postal authorities at Temesvar applied these overprints. The stamps were available for postage, but were chiefly used to pay postal employees' salaries.

The overprints on this issue have been extensively forged. Even the inexpensive values are difficult to find with genuine overprints. The more extensive note before 1N1 also applies to Nos. 10N1-10NP1.

Hungarian Stamps of 1913-19 Overprinted in Black or Red

a

b

1919

Type "a" on Stamp of 1913

10N1 A4 50f lake, *blue* 4.00 4.00

Type "a" on Stamps of 1916-18

10N2 A9 2f brown org 4.00 4.00
10N3 A9 3f red lilac 4.00 4.00
10N4 A9 5f green 4.00 4.00
10N5 A9 6f grnsh blue 4.00 4.00
10N6 A9 15f violet 4.00 4.00
10N7 A9 35f brown 35.00 35.00

Type "b"

10N8 A10 50f red vio & lil (R) 30.00 30.00
10N9 A10 75f brt bl & pale bl 4.00 4.00
10N10 A10 80f grn & pale grn 4.00 4.00
a. Red overprint 37.50 37.50
10N11 A10 1k red brn & cl 4.00 4.00
10N12 A10 2k ol brn & bis 4.00 4.00
a. Red overprint 37.50 37.50
10N14 A10 3k dk vio & ind 65.00 65.00
10N15 A10 5k dk brn & lt brn 4.00 4.00
10N16 A10 10k vio brn & vio 4.00 4.00

Type "a" on Stamps of 1918

10N17 A11 10f scarlet 4.00 4.00
10N18 A11 20f dk brown 4.00 4.00
10N19 A11 25f brt blue 4.00 4.00
10N20 A12 40f olive grn 4.00 4.00
10N21 A12 50f lilac 4.00 4.00

Type "a" on Stamps of 1919 Inscribed "Magyar Posta"

10N22 A13 10f red *30.00 30.00*
10N23 A13 20f dk brown *30.00 30.00*
10N24 A13 25f dull blue *37.50 37.50*

Type "a" on Stamps of 1918-19 Overprinted "Koztarsasag"

10N25 A9 4f slate gray 3.50 3.50
10N26 A9 4f sl gray (R) 42.50 42.50
10N27 A9 5f green 4.00 4.00
10N28 A9 6f grnsh blue 4.00 4.00
10N29 A9 10f rose red 30.00 30.00
10N30 A11 15f dp violet 30.00 30.00
10N31 A9 20f gray brn 30.00 30.00
10N32 A11 25f brt blue 30.00 30.00
10N33 A9 40f olive grn 3.50 3.50
10N34 A9 40f ol grn (R) 32.50 32.50

Type "b"

10N35 A10 1k red brn & cl 4.00 4.00
10N36 A10 2k ol brn & bis 30.00 30.00
10N37 A10 3k dk vio & ind 30.00 30.00
10N38 A10 5k dk brn & lt brn 30.00 30.00
10N39 A10 10k vio brn & vio 30.00 30.00

Type "a" on Temesvár Issue

10N40 A9 10f on 2f brn org (Bl & Bk) 4.00 4.00
10N41 A9 1k50f on 15f vio 4.00 4.00

10N42 A5a 50f on 10f vio brn 4.00 4.00
a. Red overprint 75.00 75.00
Nos. 10N1-10N42 (41) 641.50 641.50

SEMI-POSTAL STAMPS

Semi-Postal Stamps of 1916-17 Overprinted Type "a" in Black

1919

10NB1 SP3 10f + 2f rose red 4.00 4.00
10NB2 SP4 15f + 2f dull vio 4.00 4.00
10NB3 SP5 40f + 2f brn car 4.00 4.00

Same Overprint on Temesvar Issue

10NB4 SP3 45f on 10f + 2f rose red (Bl & Bk) 4.00 4.00
Nos. 10NB1-10NB4 (4) 16.00 16.00

SPECIAL DELIVERY STAMP

Hungary No. E1 Surcharged in Black

1919

10NE1 SD1 30f on 2f gray grn & red 4.00 4.00
a. Red overprint 75.00 75.00

POSTAGE DUE STAMPS

Postage Due Stamps of 1914-15 Overprinted Type "a" in Black

1919

10NJ1 D1 2f green & red 4.00 4.00
10NJ2 D1 10f green & red 4.00 4.00
10NJ3 D1 15f green & red 32.50 32.50
10NJ4 D1 20f green & red 4.00 4.00
10NJ5 D1 30f green & red 30.00 30.00
10NJ6 D1 50f green & blk 30.00 30.00
Nos. 10NJ1-10NJ6 (6) 104.50 104.50

NEWSPAPER STAMP

Stamp of 1914 Overprinted Type "a" in Black

1919

10NP1 N5 (2f) orange 4.00 4.00

SZEGED ISSUE

The "Hungarian National Government, Szeged, 1919," as the overprint reads, was an anti-Bolshevist government which opposed the Soviet Republic then in control at Budapest.

The overprints on this issue have been extensively forged. Even the inexpensive stamps are difficult to find with genuine overprints. The more extensive note before No. 1N1 also applies to Szeged Nos. 11N1-11NP1.

Hungary Stamps of 1916-19 Overprinted in Green, Red and Blue

On Stamps of 1916-18

1919 *Perf. 15, 14*

11N1 A9 2f brn org (G) 2.25 2.25
11N2 A9 3f red lilac (G) .75 .75
11N3 A9 5f green 2.75 2.75
11N4 A9 6f grnsh blue 32.50 32.50
11N5 A9 15f violet 3.50 3.50
11N6 A10 50f red vio & lil 19.00 19.00
11N7 A10 75f brt bl & pale bl 4.25 4.25
11N8 A10 80f grn & pale grn 18.00 18.00
11N9 A10 1k red brn & cl (G) 2.25 2.25
11N10 A10 2k ol brn & bis 4.75 4.75
11N11 A10 3k dk vio & ind 7.25 7.25
11N12 A10 5k dk brn & lt brn 60.00 60.00
11N13 A10 10k vio brn & vio 60.00 60.00

With New Value Added

11N14 A9 45f on 3f red lil (R & G) .80 .80
11N15 A10 10k on 1k red brn & cl (Bl & G) 8.00 8.00

On Stamps of 1918

11N16 A11 10f scarlet (G) 2.50 2.50
11N17 A11 20f dk brown .60 .60
11N18 A11 25f brt blue 22.50 22.50
11N19 A12 40f olive grn 11.00 11.00

On Stamps of 1918-19 Overprinted "Koztarsasag"

11N20 A9 3f red lil (G) 42.50 42.50
11N21 A9 4f slate gray 11.00 11.00
11N22 A9 5f green 25.00 25.00
11N23 A9 6f grnsh blue 15.00 15.00
11N24 A9 10f rose red (G) 32.50 32.50
11N25 A11 10f scarlet) 30.00 30.00
11N26 A11 15f dp violet 10.00 10.00
11N27 A9 20f gray brown 50.00 50.00
11N28 A11 20f dk brown 65.00 65.00
11N29 A11 25f brt blue 20.00 20.00
11N30 A9 40f olive 2.25 2.25
11N31 A12 50f lilac 1.75 1.75
11N32 A10 3k dk vio & ind 37.50 37.50

With New Value Added

11N33 A9 20f on 2f brn org (R & G) .80 .80

On Stamps of 1919 Inscribed "Magyar Posta"

11N34 A13 20f dk brown 60.00 60.00
11N35 A13 25f dull blue 1.75 1.75
Nos. 11N1-11N35 (35) 667.70 667.70

SEMI-POSTAL STAMPS

Szeged Overprint on Semi-Postal Stamps of 1916-17 in Green or Red

1919

11NB1 SP3 10f + 2f rose red (G) .85 .85
11NB2 SP4 15f + 2f dl vio (R) 3.75 3.75
11NB3 SP5 40f + 2f brn car (G) 10.00 10.00

With Additional Overprint "Koztarsasag"

11NB4 SP5 40f + 2f brn car (Bk & G) 15.00 15.00
Nos. 11NB1-11NB4 (4) 29.60 29.60

SPECIAL DELIVERY STAMP

Szeged Overprint on Special Delivery Stamp of 1916 in Red

1919

11NE1 SD1 2f gray grn & red 11.00 11.00

POSTAGE DUE STAMPS

Szeged Overprint on Stamps of 1915-18 in Red

1919

11NJ1	D1	2f green & red	3.00	3.00
11NJ2	D1	6f green & red	9.75	9.75
11NJ3	D1	10f green & red	3.75	3.75
11NJ4	D1	12f green & red	4.75	4.75
11NJ5	D1	20f green & red	6.00	6.00
11NJ6	D1	30f green & red	9.00	9.00

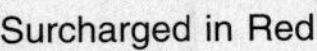

Surcharged in Red

11NJ7	SD1	50f on 2f gray grn & red	2.75	2.75
11NJ8	SD1	100f on 2f gray grn & red	2.75	2.75
		Nos. 11NJ1-11NJ8 (8)	41.75	41.75

NEWSPAPER STAMP

Szeged Overprint on Stamp of 1914 in Green

1919 **Wmk. 137** ***Imperf.***

11NP1	N5	(2f) orange	.85	.85

WESTERN HUNGARY

Following World War I, under the terms of the Trianon Treaty of 1920, four districts of western Hungary were transferred to Austrian administration. Three of these districts were German-speaking and joined Austria as the province of Burgenland. In the fourth district, which included the city of Sopron, Hungarian militia resisted incorporation into Austria, and in a plebiscite held Dec. 14-16, 1921, the area's citizens, although mostly German-speaking, overwhelmingly voted for the district to remain a part of Hungary.

During Sept.-Dec., the following stamps were issued by the local authorities and were sold at post offices within the area controlled by the Hungarian partisans.

Overprinted on Hungarian Stamps of 1916-20

1921, Sept. 4

1	A9	10f red violet	12.50	12.50
2	A9	20f gray brown	.65	.65
a.		Inverted overprint	50.00	50.00
3	A9	25f dull blue	75.00	75.00
a.		Inverted overprint	125.00	125.00
4	A9	40f olive green	1.40	1.40
a.		Inverted overprint	50.00	50.00
5	A9	50f yellow green	1.00	1.00
a.		Inverted overprint	50.00	50.00
6	A9	60f black	.90	.90
7	A10	1k red brn & cl	1.60	1.60
a.		Inverted overprint	50.00	50.00
8	A10	2k ol brn & bis	25.00	25.00
a.		Inverted overprint	75.00	75.00
9	A10	2.50k bl & gray bl	60.00	60.00
10	A10	3k dk vio & ind	25.00	25.00
a.		Inverted overprint	125.00	125.00
		Nos. 1-10 (10)	203.05	203.05

This overprint was also applied to 21 other contemporaneous Hungarian stamps, including 5 postage due stamps, but these were not issued. Value, each $10.

Nos. 1-10, and all of the Western Hungary overprints on Hungarian stamps, exist with the three-hole control punch described after Hungary No. 126. Values are for unpunched examples. Stamps with the control punch sell for 20-50 percent more.

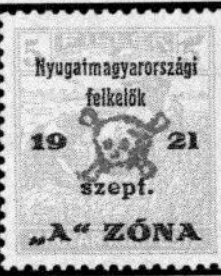

1921, Sept. 19

11	A9	5f brown orange	23.00	23.00
12	A9	10f red violet	30.00	30.00
13	A9	15f violet	75.00	75.00
14	A9	20f gray brown	75.00	75.00
15	A9	40f olive green	75.00	75.00
16	A9	50f yellow green	19.00	19.00
a.		Inverted overprint	125.00	125.00
17	A9	60f black	20.00	20.00
18	A10	1k red brn & cl	20.00	20.00
19	A10	2k ol brn & bister	75.00	75.00
		Nos. 11-19 (9)	412.00	412.00

The text overprinted on Nos. 11-19 was machine-overprinted in black. The skull and crossed bones emblem was separately handstamped in red.

1921, Oct. 5

20	A9	10f red violet	.50	.50
21	A9	15f violet	1.00	1.00
22	A9	20f gray brown	.50	.50
23	A9	40f olive green	.50	.50
24	A9	50f yellow green	1.00	1.00
25	A9	60f black	1.00	1.00
26	A10	1k red brn & cl	1.50	1.50
27	A10	2k ol brn & bis	1.00	1.00
28	A9	2.50k on 2f brn org	50.00	50.00
29	A9	2.50k on 5f brn org	1.00	1.00
30	A10	3k dk vio & ind	2.00	2.00
31	A10	5k dk brn & lt brn	2.00	2.00
32	A10	10k vio brn & vio	2.00	2.00
		Nos. 20-32 (13)	64.00	64.00

1921, Oct. 16

33	A9	5f brown orange	2.00	2.00
34	A9	10f red violet	2.00	2.00
35	A9	15f violet	2.00	2.00
36	A9	20f gray brown	2.00	2.00
37	A9	40f olive green	2.00	2.00
38	A9	50f yellow green	2.00	2.00
39	A9	60f black	2.00	2.00
40	A10	1k red brn & cl	2.00	2.00
41	A10	2k ol brn & bis	3.50	3.50
42	A10	2.50k bl & gray bl	7.50	7.50
43	A10	3.50k gray	5.00	5.00
		Nos. 33-43 (11)	32.00	32.00

1921, Oct. 10

44	A9	5f brown orange	60.00	60.00
45	A9	10f red violet	65.00	65.00
46	A9	15f violet	65.00	65.00
47	A9	20f gray brown	65.00	65.00
48	A9	40f olive green	20.00	20.00
49	A9	50f yellow green	4.00	4.00
a.		Inverted overprint	50.00	50.00
50	A9	60f black	4.00	4.00
a.		Inverted overprint	50.00	50.00
51	A10	1k red brn & cl	4.00	4.00
a.		Inverted overprint	50.00	50.00
a.		Double overprint	50.00	50.00
52	A10	2k ol brn & bis	65.00	65.00
53	A10	2.50k bl & gray bl	20.00	20.00
54	A10	3k dk vio & ind	20.00	20.00
55	A10	3.50k gray	20.00	20.00
56	A10	5k dk brn & lt brn	125.00	125.00
57	A10	10k vio brn & vio	125.00	125.00
58	A23	50k dk brn & bl	125.00	125.00
59	A23	100k ol bis & yel brn	125.00	125.00
		Nos. 44-59 (16)	912.00	912.00

See Nos. J1-J3.

A9a

A9b

1921, Oct. 12

60	A9a	20f on 20f gray brn	.40	.40
61	A9a	50f on 50f yel grn	.40	.40
62	A9b	1k on 10f red vio	.40	.40
63	A9b	2k on 40f ol grn	.40	.40
64	A9b	3k on 60f black	.80	.80
65	A9b	5k on 5f brn org	.80	.80
66	A9b	10k on 15f violet	.80	.80
a.		"01" for "10" in surcharge	40.00	40.00
		Nos. 60-66 (7)	4.00	4.00

The large numerals on korona values are surcharged in red.

Arms — A1

M.M. Pronay — A2

Frakno — A3

Németujvár A4

Városszal A5

Arms — A6

1921, Nov. 11

67	A1	10f violet brown	.45	*.60*
68	A2	20f green	.50	*.75*
69	A3	40f red brown	.50	*.75*
70	A4	50f green	.45	*.60*
71	A3	60f black	.50	*.75*
a.		Tête bêche pair	25.00	25.00
72	A5	1k vermilion	.40	*.60*
73	A1	2.50k blue	.50	*.75*
74	A4	5k dark brown	.50	*.75*
a.		Tête bêche pair	3.50	3.50
75	A2	10k red violet	.50	*.75*
a.		Tête bêche pair	18.00	18.00
76	A5	50k red violet	.50	*.75*
a.		Tête bêche pair	27.50	27.50
77	A6	100k blue	.45	*.60*
a.		Tête bêche pair	12.00	12.00
		Nos. 67-77 (11)	5.25	*7.65*

The 10f-40f, 60f, 1k, 2.50k, 50k and 100k exist imperf. Value, each $2. Tête bêche pairs of the 60f, 10k and 50k also exist imperf. Value, each $50.

Nos. 67-77 in different colors are proofs. Value: 10f-50k, each $5; 100k, $20.

See Nos. J4-J9.

1921, Dec. 14

78	A9	10f red violet	1.00	1.00
a.		Inverted overprint	10.00	10.00
79	A9	20f gray brown	1.00	1.00
a.		Inverted overprint	10.00	10.00
80	A9	40f olive green	1.00	1.00
a.		Inverted overprint	10.00	10.00
81	A9	50f yellow green	.50	.50
a.		Inverted overprint	10.00	10.00
82	A9	60f black	.50	.50
a.		Inverted overprint	10.00	10.00
83	A10	1k red brn & claret	.50	.50
a.		Inverted overprint	10.00	10.00
84	A10	2k ol brn & bis	1.00	1.00
a.		Inverted overprint	10.00	10.00
85	A10	2.50k bl & gray bl	1.00	1.00
a.		Inverted overprint	10.00	10.00
86	A10	3.50k gray	1.00	1.00
a.		Inverted overprint	10.00	10.00
87	A10	5k dk brn & lt brn	1.00	1.00
a.		Inverted overprint	10.00	10.00
88	A10	10k vio brn & vio	1.50	1.50
		Nos. 78-88 (11)	10.00	10.00

Six stamps in this design were prepared in 1921 but not issued. Value, each $40.

POSTAGE DUE STAMPS

1921, Oct. 10

J1	D1	2f green & red	75.00	75.00
J2	D1	120f green & red ('20)	30.00	30.00
a.		Inverted overprint	125.00	125.00
J3	D1	200f green & red ('20)	50.00	50.00

D2

1921, Nov. 11

J4	D2	50f green & black	.35	*.50*
a.		Inverted overprint	75.00	75.00
J5	D2	100f green & black	.35	*.50*
a.		Inverted overprint	75.00	75.00
J6	D2	200f green & black	.35	*.50*
a.		Inverted overprint	75.00	75.00
J7	D2	500f green & black	.35	*.50*
a.		Inverted overprint	75.00	75.00
J8	D2	1000f green & black	.35	*.50*
a.		Inverted overprint	75.00	75.00
		Nos. J4-J8 (5)	1.75	*2.50*

Type D2 exists without denomination. Value $50.

Nos. J4-J8 printed in blue are color proofs. Value, each $35.

No. J6 Surcharged in Red

1921, Nov. 11

J9 D2 50f on 200f grn & blk 30.00 *40.00*

ICELAND

'is-lənd

LOCATION — Island in the North Atlantic Ocean, east of Greenland
AREA — 39,758 sq. mi.
POP. — 238,175 (1983)
CAPITAL — Reykjavik

Iceland became a republic on June 17, 1944. Formerly this country was united with Denmark under the government of King Christian X who, as a ruling sovereign of both countries, was assigned the dual title of king of each. Although the two countries were temporarily united in certain affairs beyond the king's person, both were acknowledged as sovereign states.

96 Skillings = 1 Rigsdaler
100 Aurar (singular "Eyrir") = 1 Krona (1876)

Watermarks

Wmk. 112 — Crown

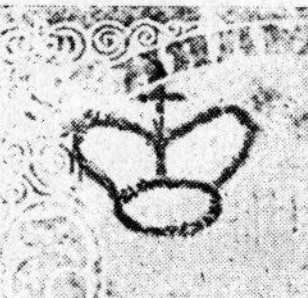
Wmk. 113 — Crown

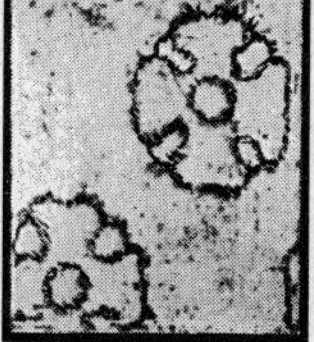
Wmk. 47 — Multiple Rosette

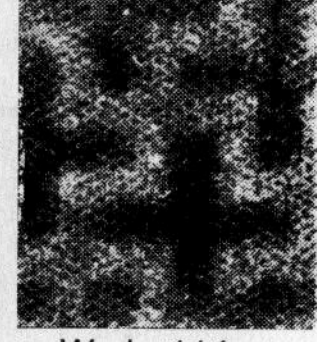
Wmk. 114 — Multiple Crosses

Values for unused stamps are for examples with original gum as defined in the catalogue introduction. Very fine examples of Nos. 1-33A and O1-O12 will have centering with perforations clear of the framelines but with design noticeably off center, and Nos. 1-7 and O1-O3 additionally will have some irregular or shorter perforations. Well centered stamps are quite scarce and will command higher prices.

A1

Perf. 14x13½

1873 Typo. Wmk. 112

1 A1 2s ultra 1,050. *2,150.*
On cover *50,000.*
a. Imperf. 625.
2 A1 4s dark car 175. *900.*
Never hinged 500.
On cover *45,000.*
a. Imperf. 625. —
3 A1 8s brown 325. *1,150.*
Never hinged 900.
On cover *45,000.*
a. Imperf. 350.
4 A1 16s yellow 1,450. *2,500.*
On cover —
a. Imperf. 400.

Perf. 12½

5 A1 3s gray 475. *1,450.*
Never hinged 1,350.
On cover —
a. Imperf. 750.
6 A1 4s carmine 1,400. *2,200.*
On cover —
7 A1 16s yellow 140. *625.*
On cover —

False and favor cancellations are often found on Nos. 1-7. Nos. 1-7 were valid until 7/31/76. Favor cancellations were applied starting in 1882. These cancels have sans-serif letters and dates with lines between the month and day. Values of stamps with favor cancellations range from $75 (Nos. 2, 7) to $575 (No. 4). The imperforate varieties lack gum.

A2

1876

8 A2 5a blue 475.00 *1,000.*
On cover —

Perf. 14x13½

9 A2 5a blue 450.00 *900.00*
Never hinged 1,350.
On cover *9,000.*
a. Imperf. 2,450.
10 A2 6a gray 150.00 35.00
Never hinged 450.00
On cover *1,350.*
11 A2 10a carmine 225.00 8.00
Never hinged 675.00
On cover *900.00*
a. Imperf. 625.00 *750.00*
12 A2 16a brown 140.00 65.00
Never hinged 525.00
On cover *800.00*
13 A2 20a dark violet 35.00 *500.00*
Never hinged 100.00
On cover *3,400.*
a. 20a light violet 1,100. 500.00
14 A2 40a green 100.00 *225.00*
Never hinged 300.00
On cover —

Fake and favor cancellations are almost always found on No. 13, and value is considerably less than that shown.

Beware of unused color-faded examples of No. 13 described as No. 13a. Expertization is recommended.

Small "3" — A3

1882-98

15 A3 3a orange 62.50 30.00
Never hinged 175.00
On cover 550.00
16 A2 5a green 67.50 14.00
Never hinged 200.00
On cover 650.00
17 A2 20a blue 325.00 50.00
Never hinged 950.00
On cover 900.00
a. 20a ultramarine 800.00 275.00
18 A2 40a red violet 70.00 47.50
Never hinged 300.00
a. Perf. 13 ('98) *5,000.*
Never hinged 8,000.
19 A2 50a bl & car ('92) 90.00 *100.00*
Never hinged 275.00
On cover *1,700.*
20 A2 100a brn & vio ('92) 92.50 *140.00*
Never hinged 275.00
On cover *2,100.*
Nos. 15-20 (6) 707.50 381.50

See note after No. 68.

Large "3" — A3a

1896-1901 ***Perf. 13***

21 A3 3a orange ('97) 125.00 12.00
Never hinged 375.00
On cover 550.00
22 A3a 3a yellow ('01) 8.50 *22.50*
Never hinged 26.00
On cover *1,050.*
23 A2 4a rose & gray ('99) 18.00 *20.00*
Never hinged 52.50
On cover 700.00
24 A2 5a green 4.00 3.00
Never hinged 12.00
On cover 550.00
25 A2 6a gray ('97) 17.50 *19.00*
Never hinged 52.50
On cover *1,150.*
26 A2 10a carmine ('97) 17.00 3.00
Never hinged 50.00
On cover 575.00
27 A2 16a brown 75.00 *110.00*
Never hinged 225.00
On cover *1,000.*
28 A2 20a dull blue ('98) 45.00 40.00
Never hinged 140.00
On cover 675.00
a. 20a dull ultramarine 575.00 45.00
Never hinged 1,750.
On cover *1,100.*
29 A2 25a yel brn & bl ('00) 22.50 *32.50*
Never hinged 67.50
On cover *2,900.*
30 A2 50a bl & car ('98) 450.00 *750.00*
Never hinged 1,350.

Value for No. 30 used is for a canceled-to-order example after the stamp was invalidated in 1902. Stamps genuinely used before invalidation are rare and sell for much more.

See note after No. 68.

For surcharges see Nos. 31-33A, 45-68.

Black and Red Surcharge

Large "prir"

1897 ***Perf. 13***

31 A2 3a on 5a green 675. 575.
Never hinged 2,100.
On cover 625.
a. Perf. 14x13½ *2,300.*
b. Inverted surcharge 1,500. *1,250.*
On cover *1,500.*
c. As "a," inverted surcharge *7,500.*

Large "prir" is 6.1mm to 6.3mm wide by 3.5mm tall.

Small "prir"

32 A2 3a on 5a green 700. 575.
Never hinged 2,050.
On cover 625.
a. Inverted surcharge 1,250. 1,050.
On cover *1,400.*
b. Perf. 14x13½ *12,500.* *2,250.*
c. In vert. pair with #31 1,750. 1,500.
d. As "b," in vert. pair with #31a —

All 5 known unused examples of No. 32b lack gum.

Small "prir" is 5.5mm to 5.6mm wide by 3.1mm tall.

Black Surcharge

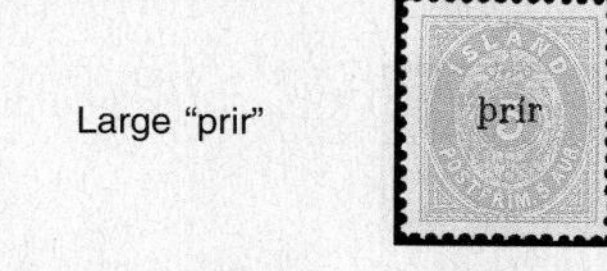
Large "prir"

33 A2 3a on 5a green 1,000. 750.
On cover 800.
b. Inverted surcharge 1,500. 1,250.

Large "prir" is 6.1mm to 6.3mm wide by 3.5mm tall.

Small "prir"

33A A2 3a on 5a green 1,100. 750.
On cover 750.
c. Inverted surcharge 1,800. 1,500.

Excellent counterfeits are known.

Small "prir" is 5.5mm to 5.6mm wide by 3.1mm tall.

King Christian IX — A4

1902-04 Wmk. 113 ***Perf. 13***

34 A4 3a orange 6.25 4.00
Never hinged 15.00
On cover 45.00
35 A4 4a gray & rose 4.00 1.40
Never hinged 10.00
On cover 52.50
36 A4 5a yel green 42.50 1.10
Never hinged 140.00
On cover 30.00
37 A4 6a gray brown 22.50 11.00
Never hinged 62.50
On cover 110.00
38 A4 10a car rose 6.50 1.10
Never hinged 16.00
On cover 47.50
39 A4 16a chocolate 8.50 *11.00*
Never hinged 18.00
On cover 130.00
40 A4 20a deep blue 3.50 *4.50*
Never hinged 7.00
On cover 40.00
a. Inscribed "PJONUSTA" 90.00 *160.00*
Never hinged 175.00
On cover 230.00
41 A4 25a brn & grn 4.00 *7.00*
Never hinged 9.00
On cover 290.00
42 A4 40a violet 4.50 *7.00*
Never hinged 10.50
On cover 400.00
43 A4 50a gray & bl blk 6.25 *25.00*
Never hinged 15.00
On cover 450.00
44 A4 1k sl bl & yel brn 7.50 *10.50*
Never hinged 17.00
On cover *510.00*
44A A4 2k olive brn & brt blue ('04) 29.00 *75.00*
Never hinged 70.00
On cover *975.00*
44B A4 5k org brn & slate blue ('04) 150.00 *230.00*
Never hinged 350.00
On cover 1,400.
Nos. 34-44B (13) 295.00 *388.60*

For surcharge see No. 142.

Stamps of 1882-1901 Overprinted

1902-03 Wmk. 112 ***Perf. 13***

Red Overprint

45 A2 5a green 1.40 *10.50*
Never hinged 2.75
a. Inverted overprint 80.00 *105.00*
b. "I" before Gildi omitted 175.00 250.00
c. '03-'03 750.00
d. 02'-'03 625.00 850.00
e. Pair, one without overprint 175.00
46 A2 6a gray 1.20 *10.50*
a. Double overprint 140.00
b. Inverted overprint 80.00
c. '03-'03 525.00
d. 02'-'03 525.00
e. Pair, one with invtd. ovpt. 400.00
f. Pair, one without overprint 225.00
g. As "f", inverted 400.00
47 A2 20a dull blue 1.20 *12.50*
Never hinged 2.50
a. Inverted overprint 85.00 *110.00*
b. "I" before Gildi omitted 175.00
c. 02'-'03 750.00
48 A2 25a yel brn & bl 1.20 *19.00*
Never hinged 2.50
a. Inverted overprint 75.00 *85.00*
b. '03-'03 450.00
c. 02'-'03 450.00 675.00
d. Double overprint 175.00

Black Overprint

49 A3 3a orange 240.00 *525.00*
Never hinged 625.00
b. Inverted overprint 375.00 850.00
c. "I" before Gildi omitted 575.00
d. '03-'03 625.00
e. 02'-'03 625.00
50 A3a 3a yellow 1.40 *2.50*
Never hinged 2.75
a. Double overprint 400.00
b. Inverted overprint 85.00 *105.00*
c. "I" before Gildi omitted 625.00
d. 02'-'03 750.00
51 A2 4a rose & gray 40.00 *57.50*
Never hinged 105.00
a. Double overprint 525.00
b. Inverted overprint 120.00
c. Dbl. ovpt., one invtd. 400.00
d. "I" before Gildi omitted 290.00
e. '03-'03 525.00 700.00
f. 02'-'03 525.00
g. Pair, one with invtd. ovpt. 400.00
52 A2 5a green 350.00 *925.00*
Never hinged 800.00
a. Inverted overprint 400.00 *975.00*
b. Pair, one without overprint 510.00
c. As "b", inverted 625.00
53 A2 6a gray 750.00 *1,150.*
Never hinged 1,500.
a. Inverted overprint 800.00
b. Pair, one without overprint 800.00
c. Double overprint 1,150.
54 A2 10a carmine 1.40 *12.50*
Never hinged 2.75
a. Inverted overprint 75.00 110.00

b. Pair, one without overprint 210.00
55 A2 16a brown 26.00 *40.00*
Never hinged 70.00
a. Inverted overprint 175.00
b. "I" before Gildi omitted 350.00
c. '03-'03 700.00
d. 02'-'03 625.00
56 A2 20a dull blue *11,000.*
a. Inverted overprint *9,600.*
57 A2 25a yel brn & bl *10,500.*
a. Inverted overprint *14,500.*
58 A2 40a red vio 1.20 *40.00*
Never hinged 2.50
a. Inverted overprint 90.00
59 A2 50a bl & car 3.50 *70.00*
Never hinged 8.00
a. Double overprint 250.00
b. 02'-'03 850.00
c. '03-'03 850.00

Perf. 14x13½

Red Overprint

60 A2 5a green 2,100. —
a. '03-'03 —
b. 02'-'03 *45,500.*
61 A2 6a gray 2,100. —
a. 02'-'03 —
62 A2 20a blue *5,750.* —
b. 02'-'03 —

Black Overprint

63 A3 3a orange 1,350. *2,100.*
a. Inverted overprint 1,750.
b. 02'-'03 2,500.
c. '03-'03 2,750.
64 A2 10a carmine *9,750.* —
65 A2 16a brown 1,500. *2,100.*
a. Inverted overprint 1,900.
b. 02'-'03 2,300.
d. '03-'03 *22,000.*
65C A2 20a dull blue *9,100.* —
a. Inverted overprint *15,500.*
66 A2 40a red vio 21.00 *105.00*
Never hinged 29.00
a. Inverted overprint 250.00 —
b. '03-'03 525.00
c. 02'-'03 525.00
67 A2 50a bl & car 55.00 *140.00*
Never hinged 150.00
a. Inverted overprint 350.00
b. '03-'03 475.00
c. 02'-'03 475.00 800.00
d. As "c," inverted —
68 A2 100a brn & vio 60.00 *80.00*
Never hinged 160.00
a. Inverted overprint 210.00
b. 02'-'03 575.00 800.00
c. '03-'03 850.00

"I GILDI" means "valid."

In 1904 Nos. 20, 22-30, 45-59 (except 49, 52, 53, 56 and 57) and No. 68 were reprinted for the Postal Union. The reprints are perforated 13 and have watermark type 113. Value $120 each. Without overprint, $250 each.

Kings Christian IX and Frederik VIII — A5

Typo., Center Engr.

1907-08 Wmk. 113 *Perf. 13*

71 A5 1e yel grn & red 1.75 1.40
Never hinged 5.25
72 A5 3a yel brn & ocher 4.75 1.75
Never hinged 16.00
73 A5 4a gray & red 3.00 1.75
Never hinged 8.00
74 A5 5a green 95.00 1.40
Never hinged 375.00
75 A5 6a gray & gray brn 60.00 4.00
76 A5 10a scarlet 150.00 1.60
Never hinged 500.00
77 A5 15a red & green 7.50 1.25
Never hinged 29.00
78 A5 16a brown 9.75 *40.00*
Never hinged 35.00
79 A5 20a blue 8.00 5.75
Never hinged 32.50
80 A5 25a bis brn & grn 7.00 *12.00*
Never hinged 29.00
81 A5 40a claret & vio 7.00 *15.00*
Never hinged 29.00
82 A5 50a gray & vio 7.00 *15.00*
Never hinged 29.00
83 A5 1k blue & brn 32.50 *70.00*
Never hinged 70.00
84 A5 2k dk brn & dk grn 37.50 *80.00*
Never hinged 105.00
85 A5 5k brn & slate 175.00 *350.00*
Never hinged 525.00
Nos. 71-85 (15) 605.75 *600.90*

See Nos. 99-107.
For surcharges and overprints see Nos. 130-138, 143, C2, O69.

Jon Sigurdsson — A6

1911 Typo. and Embossed

86 A6 1e olive green 2.50 2.00
Never hinged 7.50
87 A6 3a light brown 5.00 *15.00*
Never hinged 15.00
88 A6 4a ultramarine 1.75 *1.75*
Never hinged 5.25
89 A6 6a gray 14.50 *25.00*
Never hinged 40.00
90 A6 15a violet 15.00 2.00
Never hinged 29.00
91 A6 25a orange 25.00 *50.00*
Never hinged 95.00
Nos. 86-91 (6) 63.75 *95.75*

Sigurdsson (1811-79), statesman and author.
For surcharge see No. 149.

Frederik VIII — A7

1912, Feb. 17

92 A7 5a green 30.00 12.00
Never hinged 85.00
93 A7 10a red 30.00 12.00
Never hinged 85.00
94 A7 20a pale blue 45.00 18.00
Never hinged 110.00
95 A7 50a claret 9.50 *35.00*
Never hinged 19.00
96 A7 1k yellow 30.00 *75.00*
Never hinged 85.00
97 A7 2k rose 30.00 *75.00*
Never hinged 85.00
98 A7 5k brown 160.00 *225.00*
Never hinged 350.00
Nos. 92-98 (7) 334.50 *452.00*

For surcharges and overprints see Nos. 140-141, O50-O51.

Type of 1907-08

Typo., Center Engr.

1915-18 Wmk. 114 *Perf. 14x14½*

99 A5 1e yel grn & red 8.00 *18.00*
Never hinged 32.50
100 A5 3a bister brn 4.00 3.00
Never hinged 17.00
101 A5 4a gray & red 4.00 *9.50*
Never hinged 17.00
102 A5 5a green 100.00 1.40
Never hinged 300.00
103 A5 6a gray & gray brn 22.50 *130.00*
Never hinged 70.00
104 A5 10a scarlet 3.50 1.25
Never hinged 15.00
107 A5 20a blue 225.00 22.50
Never hinged 700.00
Nos. 99-107 (7) 367.00 *185.65*

Revenue cancellations consisting of "TOLLUR" boxed in frame are found on stamps used to pay the tax on parcel post packages entering Iceland.

Christian X — A8

1920-22 Typo.

108 A8 1e yel grn & red 1.25 *1.25*
Never hinged 5.75
Revenue cancellation 9.00
109 A8 3a bister brn 8.50 *17.50*
Never hinged 45.00
Revenue cancellation 9.00
110 A8 4a gray & red 5.75 2.50
Never hinged 30.00
Revenue cancellation 9.00
111 A8 5a green 2.25 5.75
Never hinged 12.00
Revenue cancellation 17.50
112 A8 5a ol green ('22) 5.75 1.75
Never hinged 30.00
Revenue cancellation 6.75
113 A8 6a dark gray 15.00 8.50
Never hinged 75.00
Revenue cancellation 14.00
114 A8 8a dark brown 8.50 2.50
Never hinged 45.00
Revenue cancellation 12.00
115 A8 10a red 3.00 *12.00*
Never hinged 15.00
Revenue cancellation 22.50
116 A8 10a green ('21) 4.00 2.00
Never hinged 20.00
Revenue cancellation 9.00
117 A8 15a violet 40.00 1.40
Never hinged 200.00
Revenue cancellation 9.00
118 A8 20a deep blue 3.50 *19.00*
Never hinged 17.50
Revenue cancellation 22.50
119 A8 20a choc ('22) 65.00 1.75
Never hinged 310.00
Revenue cancellation 9.00
120 A8 25a brown & grn 17.50 2.00
Never hinged 85.00
Revenue cancellation 9.00
121 A8 25a red ('21) 17.00 *57.50*
Never hinged 85.00
Revenue cancellation 4.25
122 A8 30a red & green 52.50 3.50
Never hinged 250.00
Revenue cancellation 9.00
123 A8 40a claret 40.00 3.50
Never hinged 200.00
Revenue cancellation 9.00
124 A8 40a dk bl ('21) 80.00 15.00
Never hinged 400.00
Revenue cancellation 10.50
125 A8 50a dk gray & cl 190.00 12.00
Never hinged 800.00
Revenue cancellation 13.50
126 A8 1k dp bl & dk brn 110.00 1.75
Never hinged 450.00
Revenue cancellation 1.75
127 A8 2k ol brn & myr green 250.00 35.00
Never hinged 1,050.
Revenue cancellation 3.50
128 A8 5k brn & ind 57.50 17.50
Never hinged 275.00
Revenue cancellation 3.50
Nos. 108-128 (21) 977.00 *223.65*

See Nos. 176-187, 202.
For surcharges and overprints see Nos. 139, 150, C1, C9-C14, O52, O70-O71.

A9

A10

A11

1921-25 Wmk. 113 *Perf. 13*

130 A9 5a on 16a brown 4.00 *30.00*
Never hinged 16.00
Revenue cancellation 35.00
131 A11 5a on 16a brown 2.50 *8.50*
Never hinged 10.00
Revenue cancellation 22.50
132 A10 20a on 25a brn & green 8.00 8.50
Never hinged 32.50
a. Double surcharge —
133 A11 20a on 25a bis brn & green 4.50 *8.50*
Never hinged 18.00
134 A9 20a on 40a violet 8.00 *20.00*
Never hinged 32.50
135 A11 20a on 40a cl & vio 15.00 *23.00*
Never hinged 60.00
Revenue cancellation 17.50
137 A9 30a on 50a gray & bl blk ('25) 35.00 *37.50*
Never hinged 110.00
Revenue cancellation 20.00
138 A9 50a on 5k org brn & sl bl ('25) 65.00 52.50
Never hinged 200.00
Revenue cancellation 21.00
Nos. 130-138 (8) 142.00 *188.50*
Set, never hinged 480.00

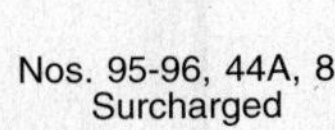

No. 111 Surcharged

1922 Wmk. 114 *Perf. 14x14½*

139 A8 10a on 5a green 8.00 3.50
Never hinged 32.50
Revenue cancellation 35.00

Nos. 95-96, 44A, 85 Surcharged

1924-30 Wmk. 113 *Perf. 13*

140 A7 10k on 50a ('25) 300.00 *450.00*
Never hinged 750.00
Revenue cancellation 35.00
141 A7 10k on 1k 375.00 *625.00*
Never hinged 900.00
Revenue cancellation 75.00
142 A4 10k on 2k ('29) 80.00 32.50
Never hinged 275.00
Revenue cancellation 11.00
143 A5 10k on 5k ('30) 450.00 575.00
Never hinged 1,100.
Revenue cancellation 35.00
Nos. 140-143 (4) 1,205. 1,683.

"Tollur" is a revenue cancellation.

Landing the Mail — A12

Designs: 7a, 50a, Landing the mail. 10a, 35a, View of Reykjavik. 20a, Museum building.

Perf. 14x15

1925, Sept. 12 Typo. Wmk. 114

144 A12 7a yel green 45.00 7.50
Never hinged 125.00
Revenue cancellation 5.75
145 A12 10a dp bl & brn 45.00 .85
Never hinged 125.00
Revenue cancellation 5.75
146 A12 20a vermilion 45.00 .85
Never hinged 125.00
Revenue cancellation 4.50
147 A12 35a deep blue 70.00 9.50
Never hinged 240.00
Revenue cancellation 3.50
148 A12 50a yel grn & brn 70.00 1.75
Never hinged 240.00
Revenue cancellation 1.75
Nos. 144-148 (5) 275.00 20.45

No. 91 Surcharged

1925 Wmk. 113 *Perf. 13*

149 A6 2k on 25a orange 160.00 *140.00*
Never hinged 475.00
Revenue cancellation 17.50

No. 124 Surcharged in Red

1926

150 A8 1k on 40a dark blue 150.00 35.00
Never hinged 600.00
Revenue cancellation 25.00

Parliament Building A15

Designs: 5a, Viking ship in storm. 7a, Parliament meeting place, 1690. 10a, Viking funeral. 15a, Vikings naming land. 20a, The dash for Thing. 25a, Gathering wood. 30a, Thingvalla Lake. 35a, Iceland woman in national costume. 40a, Iceland flag. 50a, First Althing, 930 A.D. 1k, Map of Iceland. 2k, Winter-bound home. 5k, Woman spinning. 10k, Viking Sacrifice to Thor.

Perf. 12½x12

1930, Jan. 1 Litho. Unwmk.

152 A15 3a dull vio & gray vio 3.75 *10.00*
Never hinged 5.00
153 A15 5a dk bl & sl grn 3.75 *10.00*
Never hinged 5.00
154 A15 7a grn & gray grn 3.25 *10.00*
Never hinged 4.50
155 A15 10a dk vio & lilac 10.00 *18.00*
Never hinged 17.50
156 A15 15a dp ultra & bl gray 2.75 *11.00*
Never hinged 3.25
157 A15 20a rose red & sal 45.00 *90.00*
Never hinged 85.00
a. Double impression 350.00
Never hinged 625.00
158 A15 25a dk brn & lt brn 7.50 *15.00*
Never hinged 15.00
159 A15 30a dk grn & sl grn 6.50 *15.00*
Never hinged 13.00
160 A15 35a ultra & bl gray 7.50 *15.00*
Never hinged 13.00
161 A15 40a dk ultra, red & slate grn 6.50 *15.00*
Never hinged 13.00
162 A15 50a red brn & cinn 70.00 *150.00*
Never hinged 160.00
163 A15 1k ol grn & gray green 60.00 *150.00*
Never hinged 140.00
164 A15 2k turq bl & gray green 70.00 *175.00*
Never hinged 160.00
165 A15 5k org & yellow 50.00 *140.00*
Never hinged 110.00

166 A15 10k mag & dl rose 50.00 *140.00*
Never hinged 110.00
Nos. 152-166 (15) 396.50 *964.00*

Millenary of the "Althing," the Icelandic Parliament, oldest in the world.
Imperfs were privately printed.
For overprints see Nos. O53-O67.

Gullfoss (Golden Falls) — A30

1931-32 Unwmk. Engr. *Perf. 14*

170 A30 5a gray 14.00 1.10
Never hinged 42.50
171 A30 20a red 12.00 .25
Never hinged 36.00
172 A30 35a ultramarine 24.00 16.00
Never hinged 36.00
Revenue cancellation 2.25
173 A30 60a red lil ('32) 15.00 1.50
Never hinged 42.50
174 A30 65a red brn ('32) 2.50 1.25
Never hinged 5.00
175 A30 75a grnsh bl ('32) 95.00 32.50
Never hinged 300.00
Revenue cancellation 5.00
Nos. 170-175 (6) 162.50 52.60

Issued: 5a-35a, Dec. 15; 60a-75a, May 30.

Type of 1920 Christian X Issue Redrawn

Perf. 14x14½

1931-33 Typo. Wmk. 114

176 A8 1e yel grn & red 1.00 *1.75*
Never hinged 3.50
Revenue cancellation 3.00
177 A8 3a bister brown 15.00 *15.00*
Never hinged 70.00
Revenue cancellation 8.00
178 A8 4a gray & red 2.50 2.50
Never hinged 12.00
Revenue cancellation 7.00
179 A8 6a dark gray 1.75 *5.00*
Never hinged 8.50
Revenue cancellation 7.00
180 A8 7a yel grn ('33) .65 *1.75*
Never hinged 1.75
Revenue cancellation 9.50
181 A8 10a chocolate 140.00 1.40
Never hinged 575.00
Revenue cancellation 7.00
182 A8 25a brn & green 17.50 4.25
Never hinged 85.00
Revenue cancellation 3.50
183 A8 30a red & green 30.00 7.00
Never hinged 140.00
Revenue cancellation 8.00
184 A8 40a claret 240.00 21.00
Never hinged 1,050.
Revenue cancellation 12.00
185 A8 1k dk bl & lt brn 40.00 7.50
Never hinged 185.00
Revenue cancellation 3.50
186 A8 2k choc & dk grn 240.00 80.00
Never hinged 1,050.
Revenue cancellation 8.00
187 A8 10k yel grn & blk 250.00 210.00
Never hinged 1,100.
Revenue cancellation 17.50
Nos. 176-187 (12) 978.40 357.15

On the redrawn stamps the horizontal lines of the portrait and the oval are closer together than on the 1920 stamps and are crossed by many fine vertical lines.
See No. 202.

Dynjandi Falls — A31

Mount Hekla — A32

Perf. 12½

1935, June 28 Engr. Unwmk.

193 A31 10a blue 24.00 .25
Never hinged 80.00
Revenue cancellation 24.00
194 A32 1k greenish gray 42.50 .25
Never hinged 140.00
Revenue cancellation 5.75

Matthias Jochumsson — A33

1935, Nov. 11

195 A33 3a gray green .75 *4.00*
Never hinged 1.40
Revenue cancellation 4.00
196 A33 5a gray 14.00 1.40
Never hinged 47.50
Revenue cancellation 17.50
197 A33 7a yel green 20.00 2.40
Never hinged 65.00
Revenue cancellation 7.00
198 A33 35a blue .60 *1.40*
Never hinged 1.25
Revenue cancellation 7.00
Nos. 195-198 (4) 35.35 *9.20*

Birth cent. of Matthias Jochumsson, poet.
For surcharges see Nos. 212, 236.

King Christian X — A34

1937, May 14 *Perf. 13x12½*

199 A34 10a green 2.40 *25.00*
Never hinged 4.00
200 A34 30a brown 2.40 *10.50*
Never hinged 4.00
201 A34 40a claret 2.40 *10.50*
Never hinged 4.00
Nos. 199-201 (3) 7.20 *46.00*

Reign of Christian X, 25th anniv.

Christian X Type of 1931-33

1937 Unwmk. Typo. *Perf. 11½*

202 A8 1e yel grn & red .80 *2.50*
Never hinged 2.40

Geyser
A35 A36

1938-47 Engr. *Perf. 14*

203 A35 15a dp rose vio 6.00 *12.00*
Never hinged 15.00
Revenue cancellation 24.00
a. Imperf., pair *1,250.*
Never hinged 1,600.
204 A35 20a rose red 24.00 .25
Never hinged 65.00
Revenue cancellation 17.50
205 A35 35a ultra .70 *1.10*
Never hinged 1.75
Revenue cancellation 22.50
206 A36 40a dk brn ('39) 14.00 *27.50*
Never hinged 32.50
Revenue cancellation 90.00
207 A36 45a brt ultra ('40) .80 *1.10*
Never hinged 2.10
Revenue cancellation 1.75
208 A36 50a dk slate grn 21.00 1.10
Never hinged 57.50
Revenue cancellation 22.50
208A A36 60a brt ultra ('43) 5.75 1.10
Never hinged 15.00
c. Perf. 11½ ('47) 3.00 *12.00*
Never hinged (#208Ac) 7.50
208B A36 1k indigo ('45) 9.50 .50
Never hinged 29.00
d. Perf. 11½ ('47) 3.00 *12.00*
Never hinged (#208Bd) 7.50
Nos. 203-208B (8) 81.75 *44.65*

University of Iceland A37

1938, Dec. 1 *Perf. 13½*

209 A37 25a dark grn 7.50 *16.00*
Never hinged 12.50
210 A37 30a brown 7.50 *16.00*
Never hinged 12.50
211 A37 40a brt red vio 7.50 *16.00*
Never hinged 12.50
Nos. 209-211 (3) 22.50 *48.00*

20th anniversary of independence.

No. 198 Surcharged with New Value

1939, Mar. 17 *Perf. 12½*

212 A33 5a on 35a blue .80 *1.60*
Never hinged 1.40
a. Double surcharge *250.00*
Never hinged 525.00

Trylon and Perisphere A38

Leif Ericsson's Ship and Route to America A39

Statue of Thorfinn Karlsefni — A40

1939 Engr. *Perf. 14*

213 A38 20a crimson 3.50 *7.00*
Never hinged 5.25
214 A39 35a bright ultra 4.00 *8.50*
Never hinged 5.75
215 A40 45a bright green 4.25 *12.00*
Never hinged 6.25
216 A40 2k dark gray 52.50 *150.00*
Never hinged 92.50
Nos. 213-216 (4) 64.25 *177.50*

New York World's Fair.
For overprints see Nos. 232-235.

Codfish — A41

Herring — A42

Flag of Iceland — A43

1939-45 Engr. *Perf. 14, 14x13½*

217 A41 1e Prussian blue .45 *4.50*
Never hinged .90
a. Perf. 14x13½ 1.75 *5.75*
Never hinged 5.25
218 A42 3a dark violet .45 *1.25*
Never hinged .90
a. Perf. 14x13½ 2.40 *8.50*
Never hinged 7.00
219 A41 5a dark brown .45 .45
Never hinged 9.50
c. Perf. 14x13½ 2.75 1.75
Never hinged 8.50
220 A42 7a dark green 4.75 *10.50*
Never hinged 14.00
221 A42 10a green ('40) 35.00 1.25
Never hinged 105.00
b. Perf. 14x13½ 65.00 4.00
Never hinged 210.00
222 A42 10a slate gray ('45) .25 .25
Never hinged .70
223 A42 12a dk grn ('43) .45 .90
Never hinged .70
224 A41 25a brt red ('40) 29.00 .60
Never hinged 85.00
b. Perf. 14x13½ 57.50 3.00
Never hinged (#224b) 190.00
225 A41 25a hn brn ('45) 1.25 .45
Never hinged 4.50
226 A42 35a carmine ('43) .60 .70
Never hinged 1.40
227 A41 50a dk bl grn ('43) .70 .25
Never hinged 1.75

Typo.

228 A43 10a car & ultra 2.50 1.75
Never hinged 5.75
Nos. 217-228 (12) 75.85 *22.85*

Statue of Thorfinn Karlsefni — A44

1939-45 Engr. *Perf. 14*

229 A44 2k dark gray 3.00 .50
Never hinged 6.00
230 A44 5k dk brn ('43) 22.50 .60
Never hinged 57.50
231 A44 10k brn yel ('45) 12.00 2.50
Never hinged 29.00
Nos. 229-231 (3) 37.50 3.60

1947 *Perf. 11½*

229a A44 2k 8.00 1.75
Never hinged 29.00
230a A44 5k 29.00 2.40
Never hinged 110.00
231a A44 10k 12.00 *45.00*
Never hinged 22.50
Nos. 229a-231a (3) 49.00 *49.15*

New York World's Fair Issue of 1939 Overprinted "1940" in Black

1940, May 11 *Perf. 14*

232 A38 20a crimson 8.00 *29.00*
Never hinged 12.00
233 A39 35a bright ultra 8.00 *29.00*
Never hinged 12.00
234 A40 45a bright green 8.00 *29.00*
Never hinged 12.00
235 A40 2k dark gray 100.00 *510.00*
Never hinged 210.00
Nos. 232-235 (4) 124.00 *597.00*

SEMI-POSTAL STAMPS

Shipwreck and Rescue by Breeches Buoy SP1

Children Gathering Rock Plants SP2

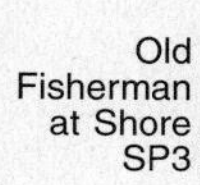

Old Fisherman at Shore SP3

Unwmk.

1933, Apr. 28 Engr. *Perf. 14*

B1 SP1 10a + 10a red brown 1.75 *6.00*
Never hinged 3.50
B2 SP2 20a + 20a org red 1.75 *6.00*
Never hinged 3.50
B3 SP1 35a + 25a ultra 1.75 *6.00*
Never hinged 3.50
B4 SP3 50a + 25a blue grn 1.75 *6.00*
Never hinged 3.50
Nos. B1-B4 (4) 7.00 *24.00*

Receipts from the surtax were devoted to a special fund for use in various charitable works especially those indicated on the stamps: "Slysavarnir" (Rescue work), "Barnahaeli" (Asylum for scrofulous children), "Ellhaeli" (Asylum for the Aged).

Souvenir Sheets

King Christian X — SP4

1937, May 15 Typo.

B5 SP4 Sheet of 3 45.00 *300.00*
Never hinged 85.00
a. 15a violet 10.00 *55.00*
b. 25a red 10.00 *55.00*
c. 50a blue 10.00 *55.00*

Reign of Christian X, 25th anniv. Sheet sold for 2kr.

SP5

Designs: 30a, 40a, Ericsson statue, Reykjavik. 60a, Iceland's position on globe.

1938, Oct. 9 Photo. *Perf. 12*
B6 SP5 Sheet of 3 5.00 *30.00*
Never hinged 10.00
a. 30a scarlet 1.25 *12.00*
b. 40a purple 1.25 *12.00*
c. 60a deep green 1.25 *12.00*

Leif Ericsson Day, Oct. 9, 1938.

AIR POST STAMPS

No. 115 Overprinted

Perf. 14x14½

1928, May 31 Wmk. 114
C1 A8 10a red .85 *12.00*
Never hinged 1.75

Same Overprint on No. 82

1929, June 29 Wmk. 113 *Perf. 13*
C2 A5 50a gray & violet 60.00 *120.00*
Never hinged 200.00

Gyrfalcon AP1

Perf. 12½x12

1930, Jan. 1 Litho. Unwmk.
C3 AP1 10a dp ultra & gray blue 25.00 *75.00*
Never hinged 50.00

Imperfs were privately printed.
For overprint see No. CO1.

Snaefellsjokull, Extinct Volcano — AP2

Parliament Millenary: 20a, Fishing boat. 35a, Iceland pony. 50a, Gullfoss (Golden Falls). 1k, Ingolfour Arnarson Statue.

Wmk. 47

1930, June 1 Typo. *Perf. 14*
C4 AP2 15a org brn & dl bl 30.00 *55.00*
Never hinged 60.00
C5 AP2 20a bis brn & sl bl 30.00 *55.00*
Never hinged 60.00
C6 AP2 35a olive grn & brn 60.00 *120.00*
Never hinged 130.00
C7 AP2 50a dp grn & dp bl 60.00 *120.00*
Never hinged 130.00
C8 AP2 1k olive grn & dk red 60.00 *120.00*
Never hinged 130.00
Nos. C4-C8 (5) 240.00 *470.00*

Regular Issue of 1920 Overprinted

Perf. 14x14½

1931, May 25 Wmk. 114
C9 A8 30a red & green 35.00 *160.00*
Never hinged 70.00
C10 A8 1k dp bl & dk brn 12.00 *120.00*
Never hinged 24.00
C11 A8 2k ol brn & myr grn 50.00 *160.00*
Never hinged 120.00
Nos. C9-C11 (3) 97.00 *440.00*

Nos. 185, 128 and 187 Overprinted in Red

1933, June 16
C12 A8 1k dk bl & lt brn 175. *650.*
Never hinged 475.
C13 A8 5k brn & indigo 600. *1,500.*
Never hinged 1,500.
C14 A8 10k yel grn & blk 1,300. *3,000.*
Never hinged 3,250.

Excellent counterfeit overprints exist.

Visit of the Italian Flying Armada en route from Rome to Chicago; also for the payment of the charges on postal matter sent from Iceland to the US via the Italian seaplanes.

Plane over Thingvalla Lake — AP7

10a-20a, Plane over Thingvalla Lake. 25a-50a, Plane and Aurora Borealis. 1k-2k, Map of Iceland.

Perf. 12½x14

1934, Sept. 1 Engr. Unwmk.
C15 AP7 10a blue 1.75 *3.50*
Never hinged 5.25
Revenue cancellation 17.50
C16 AP7 20a emerald 4.75 *8.00*
Never hinged 15.00
Revenue cancellation 35.00
a. Perf. 14 30.00 21.00
Never hinged 115.00
C17 AP7 25a dk vio, perf. 14 12.00 *19.00*
Never hinged 35.00
Revenue cancellation 50.00
a. Perf. 12½x14 30.00 *35.00*
Never hinged 115.00
C18 AP7 50a red vio, perf. 14 3.50 *8.00*
Never hinged 11.00
Revenue cancellation 24.00
C19 AP7 1k dark brown 17.50 *35.00*
Never hinged 55.00
Revenue cancellation 25.00
C20 AP7 2k red orange 9.00 *15.00*
Never hinged 27.50
Revenue cancellation 24.00
Nos. C15-C20 (6) 48.50 *88.50*

AIR POST OFFICIAL STAMPS

No. C3 Overprinted In Red

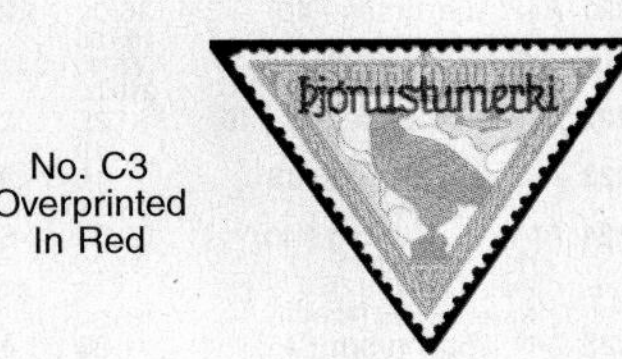

1930, Jan. 1 Unwmk. *Perf. 12½x12*
CO1 AP1 10a dp ultra & gray blue 25.00 *140.00*
Never hinged 50.00

Imperfs were privately printed.

OFFICIAL STAMPS

For Nos. O1-O12, see note on condition before No. 1.

O1

Perf. 14x13½

1873 Typo. Wmk. 112
O1 O1 4s green *8,500.* *9,250.*
a. Imperf. 150.
O2 O1 8s red lilac 650. *700.*
On cover —
a. Imperf. 750.

Perf. 12½

O3 O1 4s green 110. *400.*
Never hinged 350.00
On cover *37,500.*

False and favor cancellations are often found on Nos. O1-O37. Nos. O1-O3 were valid until 7/31/76. Favor cancellations were applied starting in 1882. These cancels have sans-serif letters and dates with lines between the month and day. Values of stamps with favor cancellations range from $140 (#O3) to $2,250 (#O1). The imperforate varieties lack gum.

O2

1876-95 *Perf. 14x13½*
O4 O2 3a yellow 45.00 *60.00*
Never hinged 120.00
On cover *7,000.*
O5 O2 5a brown 9.50 *17.50*
Never hinged 29.00
On cover *5,750.*
a. Imperf. 450.00
O6 O2 10a blue 85.00 16.00
Never hinged 300.00
On cover *5,750.*
a. 10a ultramarine 475.00 85.00
On cover 22,500.
O7 O2 16a carmine 35.00 *60.00*
Never hinged 110.00
On cover —
O8 O2 20a yellow green 35.00 *50.00*
Never hinged 110.00
On cover *5,750.*
O9 O2 50a rose lilac ('95) 90.00 *95.00*
Never hinged 300.00
Nos. O4-O9 (6) 299.50 *298.50*

1898-1902 *Perf. 13*
O10 O2 3a yellow 15.00 *35.00*
Never hinged 50.00
O11 O2 4a gray ('01) 35.00 *50.00*
Never hinged 110.00
On cover —
O12 O2 10a ultra ('02) 65.00 *120.00*
Never hinged 200.00
Nos. O10-O12 (3) 115.00 *205.00*

A 5a brown and 20a yellow green, both perf. 13 with Wmk. 112, exist. They were not regularly issued.

See note after No. O30.
For overprints see Nos. O20-O30.

O3

1902 Wmk. 113 *Perf. 13*
O13 O3 3a buff & black 5.00 3.00
Never hinged 17.50
On cover 500.00
O14 O3 4a dp grn & blk 5.00 2.50
Never hinged 20.00
On cover 500.00
O15 O3 5a org brn & blk 4.00 *5.00*
Never hinged 15.00
On cover 500.00
O16 O3 10a ultra & black 4.00 *5.00*
Never hinged 15.00
On cover 500.00
O17 O3 16a carmine & blk 4.00 *20.00*
Never hinged 15.00
On cover 500.00
O18 O3 20a green & blk 25.00 8.50
Never hinged 95.00
On cover 625.00
O19 O3 50a violet & blk 8.00 *12.50*
Never hinged 25.00
On cover 625.00
Nos. O13-O19 (7) 55.00 *56.50*

Stamps of 1876-1901 Overprinted in Black

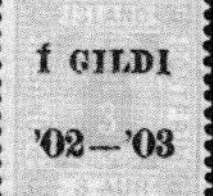

1902-03 Wmk. 112 *Perf. 13*
O20 O2 3a yellow 1.25 *3.00*
Never hinged 2.50
a. "I" before Gildi omitted 175.00
b. Inverted overprint 42.50 *65.00*
c. As "a," invtd. 200.00
d. Pair, one without ovpt. 190.00
e. '03-'03 500.00
f. 02'-'03 500.00
O21 O2 4a gray 1.25 *2.75*
Never hinged 2.50
a. "I" before Gildi omitted 175.00
b. Inverted overprint 60.00 *75.00*
e. '03-'03 525.00
f. 02'-'03 525.00
g. Pair, one without ovpt. 225.00
i. "L" only of "I GILDI" inverted —
O22 O2 5a brown 1.00 *2.75*
Never hinged 2.00
a. Double overprint 225.00
O23 O2 10a ultramarine 1.00 *2.75*
Never hinged 1.50
a. "I" before Gildi omitted 275.00
b. Inverted overprint 55.00 *75.00*
c. '03-'03 425.00
d. 02'-'03 425.00
e. "L" only of "I GILDI" 60.00 90.00
f. As "e," inverted 425.00
g. "IL" only of "I GILDI" 225.00 275.00
O24 O2 20a yel green 1.00 *25.00*
Never hinged 2.00
Nos. O20-O24 (5) 5.50 *36.25*

Perf. 14x13½

O25 O2 3a yellow 325.00 *1,400.*
Never hinged 650.00
a. "02'-'03" 1,100.
b. '03-'03 1,200.
O26 O2 5a brown 8.00 *175.00*
Never hinged 17.50
a. Inverted overprint 90.00
b. '03-'03 425.00
c. 02'-'03 425.00
d. "L" only of "I GILDI" inverted —
O27 O2 10a blue 425.00 *750.00*
Never hinged 950.00
a. "I" before Gildi omitted —
b. Inverted overprint 825.00 *850.00*
c. '03-'03 950.00
d. 02'-'03 950.00
O28 O2 16a carmine 18.00 *75.00*
Never hinged 52.50
a. "I" before Gildi omitted 650.00
c. Dbl. ovpt., one inverted 425.00 —
d. Inverted overprint
e. '03-'03 700.00
f. 02'-'03 700.00
O29 O2 20a yel green 35.00 *95.00*
Never hinged 110.00
a. Inverted overprint 175.00 *190.00*
b. '03-'03 500.00
c. 02'-'03 500.00
O30 O2 50a red lilac 6.00 *60.00*
Never hinged 12.50
a. "I" before Gildi omitted 50.00 110.00
b. Inverted overprint 190.00
Nos. O25-O30 (6) 817.00 *2,555.*

Nos. O10-O12, O20-O24, O28 and O30 were reprinted in 1904. They have the watermark of 1902 (type 113) and are perf. 13. Value $65 each. Without overprint $90 each.

Christian IX, Frederik VIII — O4

Engraved Center

1907-08 Wmk. 113 *Perf. 13*
O31 O4 3a yellow & gray 7.00 *8.00*
Never hinged 28.00
On cover 350.00
O32 O4 4a green & gray 3.50 *9.00*
Never hinged 14.00
On cover 350.00
O33 O4 5a brn org & gray 11.00 4.50
Never hinged 45.00
On cover 350.00
O34 O4 10a deep bl & gray 2.50 *3.25*
Never hinged 10.00
On cover 250.00
O35 O4 15a lt blue & gray 4.75 *9.00*
Never hinged 19.00
On cover 350.00
O36 O4 16a carmine & gray 4.75 *30.00*
Never hinged 19.00
On cover 350.00
O37 O4 20a yel grn & gray 20.00 6.00
Never hinged 80.00
On cover 425.00
O38 O4 50a violet & gray 7.00 *11.00*
Never hinged 28.00
On cover 425.00
Nos. O31-O38 (8) 60.50 *80.75*

1918 Wmk. 114 *Perf. 14x14½*
O39 O4 15a lt bl & gray 15.00 *35.00*
Never hinged 47.50
On cover 350.00

Christian X — O5

1920-30 Typo.
O40 O5 3a yellow & gray 5.00 *4.25*
Never hinged 20.00
Revenue cancellation 30.00
O41 O5 4a dp grn & gray 1.25 *3.75*
Never hinged 5.00

O42 O5 5a orange & gray 1.25 1.75
Never hinged 5.00
Revenue cancellation 30.00
O43 O5 10a dk bl & gray 35.00 1.40
Never hinged 140.00
Revenue cancellation 30.00
O44 O5 15a lt blue & gray .65 *1.25*
Never hinged 2.60
Revenue cancellation 30.00
O45 O5 20a yel grn & gray 50.00 4.50
Never hinged 200.00
O46 O5 50a violet & gray 45.00 2.75
Never hinged 180.00
Revenue cancellation 30.00
O47 O5 1k car & gray 45.00 2.25
Never hinged 180.00
Revenue cancellation 30.00
O48 O5 2k bl & blk ('30) 5.00 *21.00*
Never hinged 20.00
Revenue cancellation 35.00
O49 O5 5k brn & blk ('30) 30.00 *55.00*
Never hinged 120.00
Revenue cancellation 35.00
Nos. O40-O49 (10) 218.15 97.90

See No. O68.

Nos. 97 and 98 Overprinted

1922, May Wmk. 113 *Perf. 13*

O50 A7 2k rose, larger letters, no period 25.00 *60.00*
Never hinged 55.00
a. Smaller letters, with period 95.00 60.00
Never hinged 275.00
O51 A7 5k brown 240.00 *260.00*
Never hinged 600.00

No. 115 Surcharged

1923 Wmk. 114 *Perf. 14x14½*

O52 A8 20a on 10a red 30.00 2.40
Never hinged 115.00

Parliament Millenary Issue

#152-166 Overprinted in Red or Blue

1930, Jan. 1 Unwmk. *Perf. 12½x12*

O53 A15 3a (R) 15.00 *45.00*
Never hinged 25.00
O54 A15 5a (R) 15.00 *45.00*
Never hinged 25.00
O55 A15 7a (R) 15.00 *45.00*
Never hinged 25.00
O56 A15 10a (Bl) 15.00 *45.00*
Never hinged 25.00
O57 A15 15a (R) 15.00 *45.00*
Never hinged 25.00
O58 A15 20a (Bl) 15.00 *45.00*
Never hinged 25.00
O59 A15 25a (Bl) 15.00 *45.00*
Never hinged 25.00
O60 A15 30a (R) 15.00 *45.00*
Never hinged 25.00
O61 A15 35a (R) 15.00 *45.00*
Never hinged 25.00
O62 A15 40a (Bl) 15.00 *45.00*
Never hinged 25.00
O63 A15 50a (Bl) 140.00 *350.00*
Never hinged 400.00
O64 A15 1k (R) 140.00 *350.00*
Never hinged 400.00
O65 A15 2k (R) 175.00 *400.00*
Never hinged 400.00
O66 A15 5k (Bl) 140.00 *350.00*
Never hinged 400.00
O67 A15 10k (Bl) 140.00 *350.00*
Never hinged 400.00
Nos. O53-O67 (15) 885.00 *2,250.*

Type of 1920 Issue Redrawn

1931 Wmk. 114 Typo.

O68 O5 20a yel grn & gray 45.00 3.00
Never hinged 175.00

For differences in redrawing see note after No. 187.

No. 82 Overprinted in Black

Overprint 15mm long

1936, Dec. 7 Wmk. 113 *Perf. 13*

O69 A5 50a gray & vio 25.00 *30.00*
Never hinged 85.00

Same Overprint on Nos. 180 and 115

Perf. 14x14½
Wmk. 114

O70 A8 7a yellow green 2.40 *24.00*
Never hinged 4.75
O71 A8 10a red 15.00 2.25
Never hinged 55.00
Nos. O69-O71 (3) 42.40 *56.25*

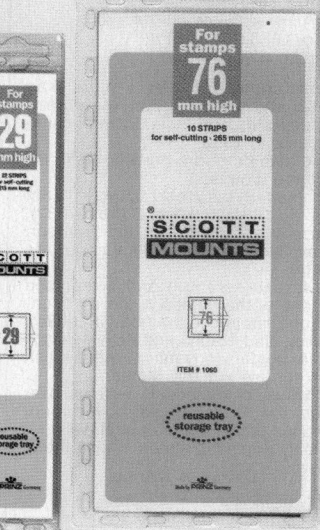

INDIA

'in-dē-ə

LOCATION — Southern, central Asia
GOVT. — Republic
AREA — 1,266,732 sq. mi.
POP. — 683,810,051 (1981)
CAPITAL — New Delhi

On August 15, 1947, India was divided into two self-governing dominions: Pakistan and India. India became a republic in 1950.

The stamps of pre-partition India fall into three groups:

1) Issues inscribed simply "East India" (to 1881) and "India" (from 1882), for use mainly in British India proper, but available and valid throughout the country;

2) Issues as above and overprinted with one of the names of the six "Convention" states (Chamba, Faridkot, Gwalior, Jind, Nabha and Patiala) which had a postal convention with British India, for use in these states.

3) Issues of the feudatory states, over which the British India government exercised little internal control, valid for use only within the states issuing them.

12 Pies = 1 Anna
16 Annas = 1 Rupee

Catalogue values for unused stamps in this country are for Never Hinged items, beginning with Scott 168 in the regular postage section, Scott 51 in Hyderabad regular issues, Scott O54 in Hyderabad officials, Scott 49 in Jaipur regular issues, Scott O30 in Jaipur officials, Scott 39 in Soruth regular issues and Scott O19 in Soruth official

All of the values are for Never Hinged for all of the items in the sections for Jasdan, Rajasthan, and Travancore-Cochin.

Watermarks

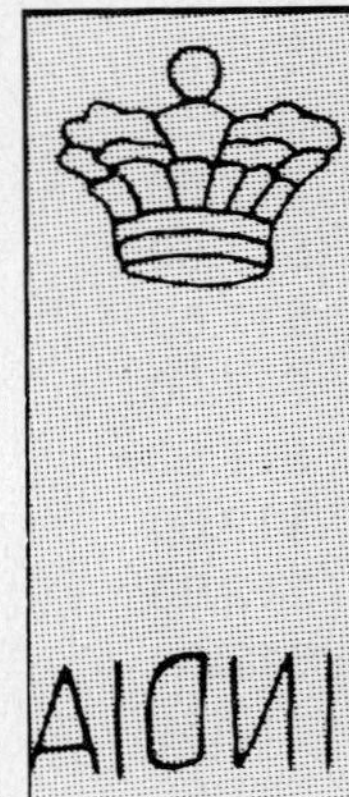

Wmk. 36 — Crown and INDIA

Wmk. 37 — Coat of Arms in Sheet. (Reduced illustration. Watermark covers a large section of the sheet.)

Wmk. 38 — Elephant's Head

Wmk. 39 — Star

Wmk. 40

Wmk. 41 — Small Umbrella

Wmk. 42 — Urdu Characters

Wmk. 43 — Shell

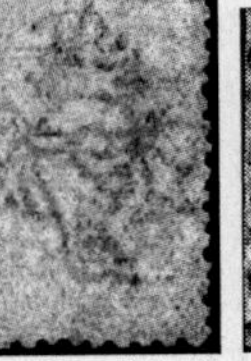

Wmk. 43A — Shell

Wmk. 196 — Multiple Stars

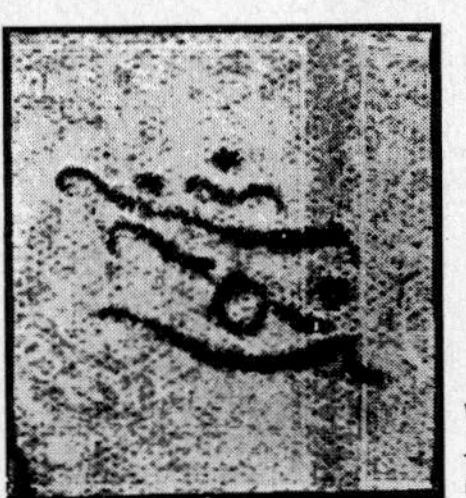

Wmk. 211 — Urdu Characters

Wmk. 294 — Letters and Ornaments in Sheet (size reduced)

SCINDE DISTRICT POST

A1

1852, July 1 Embossed *Imperf.*

A1 A1 ½a *white* 12,000. 2,000.
On cover 12,000.
A2 A1 ½a blue 40,000. 8,000.
On cover 22,500.
A3 A1 ½a *red* 165,000. 26,000.
On cover —

Obsolete October, 1854.

Nos. A1-A3 were issued without gum. No. A3 is embossed on red wafer. It is usually found with cracks and these examples are worth somewhat less than the values given, depending on the degree of cracking.

Two examples of No. 3 are known unused, three on cover or part of cover.

Covers: On cover values are for very fine examples. Average to fine examples sell for approximately 40% of the values given.

GENERAL ISSUES

Unused stamps of India are valued with original gum as defined in the catalogue introduction except for Nos. 1-7 which are valued without gum.

East India Company

A1

A2

A3

A4

A5

Queen Victoria

Litho.; Typo. (#5)

1854 Wmk. 37 *Imperf.*

1 A1 ½a red 1,200.
2 A2 ½a blue 85.00 30.00
On cover 100.00
On cover, pair 250.00
a. ½a deep blue 95.00 35.00
b. Printed on both sides 11,000.
4 A3 1a red 125.00 60.00
On cover 200.00
On cover, pair 500.00
a. 1a scarlet 175.00 70.00
5 A4 2a green 120.00 32.50
On cover 240.00
On cover, pair 600.00
a. Half used as 1a on cover 200,000.
6 A5 4a red & blue 4,500. 500.00
On cover 625.00
On cover, pair 1,500.
a. 4a deep red & blue 4,500. 575.00
Cut to shape 42.50
c. Head inverted 225,000.
As "c," cut to shape 165,000.
e. Double impression of head 25,000.

No. 1 was not placed in use.

Nos. 2, 4, 5 and 6 are known with unofficial perforation.

There are 3 dies of No. 2, and 2 dies of No. 4, showing slight differences.

There are 4 dies of the head and 2 dies of the frame of No. 6.

No. 5 is known with the watermark having the words "One Anna" in place of the lions and shield, with Urdu and Bengali characters. Values: $625 unused; $450 used.

Beware of forgeries.

A6

1855

7 A6 1a red 1,300. 175.00
On cover 525.00

No. 7 was printed from a lithographic transfer made from the original die retouched. The lines of the bust at the lower left are nearly straight and meet in a point.

Beware of forgeries.

Nos. 9-35 are normally found with very heavy cancellations, and values are for stamps so canceled. Lightly canceled stamps are seldom seen. The same holds true for Nos. O1-O26.

Diadem includes Maltese Crosses — A7

1855-64 Unwmk. Typo. *Perf. 14*
Blue Glazed Paper

9 A7 4a black 725.00 22.50
On cover 125.00
a. Imperf., pair 5,500. 5,500.
b. Half used as 2a on cover 12,000.
10 A7 8a rose 650.00 19.00
On cover 175.00
a. Imperf., pair 3,000. —
b. Half used as 4a on cover 80,000.

See Nos. 11-18, 20, 22-25, 31. For overprints see Nos. O1-O5, O7-O9, O16-O19, O22-O24.

1855-64 White Paper

11 A7 ½a blue 95.00 4.50
a. Imperf., pair 475.00 1,750.
12 A7 1a brown 80.00 3.00
a. Imperf., pair 800.00 2,200.
b. Vert. pair, imperf between
c. Half used as ½a on cover 85,000.
13 A7 2a dull rose 750.00 37.50
a. Imperf., pair 2,500. 2,000.
14 A7 2a yellow green 725.00 825.00
a. Imperf., pair 2,000.
15 A7 2a buff 450.00 37.50
a. 2a orange 700.00 45.00
b. Imperf., pair 1,750. 3,250.
16 A7 4a black 450.00 10.00
a. Imperf., pair 2,750. 2,750.
b. Diagonal half used as 2a on cover 35,000.
17 A7 4a green ('64) 1,750. 45.00
18 A7 8a rose 600.00 27.50
a. Half used as 4a on cover 80,000.

No. 14 was not regularly issued. See note after No. 25.

Many stamps of types A7-A90 are overprinted "Service" or "On H. M. S." For these, see listings of Official stamps.

Crown Colony

Queen Victoria — A8

1860-64 Unwmk. *Perf. 14*

19 A8 8p lilac 55.00 6.00
a. Diagonal half used as 4p on cover 85,000.
b. Imperf., pair 4,000. 5,000.
19C A8 8p lilac, *bluish* 275.00 100.00

See No. 21. For overprint see No. O6 and footnote after No. O4.

1865-67 Wmk. 38

20 A7 ½a blue 19.00 1.25
a. Imperf., pair 1,600.
21 A8 8p lilac 10.00 *12.00*
22 A7 1a brown 9.00 1.50

23	A7	2a brnsh org	27.50	2.00
a.		2a yellow	175.00	7.00
b.		Imperf., pair		4,250.
24	A7	4a green	575.00	27.50
25	A7	8a rose	2,000.	85.00

No. 21 was variously surcharged locally, "NINE" or "NINE PIE," to indicate that it was being sold for 9 pies (the soldier's letter rate had been raised from 8 to 9 pies). These surcharges were made without government authorization.

Stamps of types A7 and A9 overprinted with crown and surcharged with new values were for use in Straits Settlements.

A9

A10

Diadem: Rows of pearls & diamonds — A11

Type I

FOUR ANNAS

Type I — Slanting line at corner of mouth extends downward only. Shading about mouth and chin. Pointed chin.

Type II — Line at corner of mouth extends both up and down. Upper lip and chin are defined by a colored line. Rounded chin.

1866-68

26	A9	4a green, type I	95.00	4.25
26B	A9	4a bl grn, type II	30.00	3.50
27	A10	6a8p slate	70.00	27.50
a.		Imperf., pair	3,000.	
28	A11	8a rose ('68)	45.00	7.00
		Nos. 26-28 (4)	240.00	42.25

Type A11 is a redrawing of type A7. Type A7 has Maltese crosses in the diadem, while type A11 has shaded lozenges.

For overprints see Nos. O10, O20-O21, O25-O26.

For designs A9-A85 overprinted CHAMBA, FARIDKOT, GWALIOR, JIND (JHIND, JEEND), NABHA, PATIALA (PUTTIALLA), see the various Convention States.

A12

SIX ANNAS

Type I — "POSTAGE" 3½mm high

Type II — "POSTAGE" 2½mm high

Blue Glazed Paper
Green Overprint
Perf. 14 Vert.

1866, June 28 **Wmk. 36**

29	A12	6a vio, type I	1,000.	140.00
		On cover		700.
a.		Inverted overprint		*14,000.*
30	A12	6a vio, type II	1,850.	175.00
		On cover		1,000.

Nos. 29 and 30 were made from revenue stamps with the labels at top and bottom cut off. Most and sometimes all of the watermark was removed with the labels. Twenty different varieties of this overprint exist.

These stamps are often found with cracked surface or scuffs. Such examples sell for somewhat less.

A13

A14

A15

A16

1873-76 **Wmk. 38** ***Perf. 14***

31	A7	½a blue, redrawn	7.50	1.00
32	A13	9p lilac ('74)	19.00	19.00
33	A14	6a bister ('76)	8.50	2.50
34	A15	12a red brown ('76)	12.00	*27.50*
35	A16	1r slate ('74)	65.00	30.00
		Nos. 31-35 (5)	112.00	80.00
		Set, never hinged	250.00	

In the redrawn ½ anna the lines of the mouth are more deeply cut, making the lips appear fuller and more open, and the nostril is defined by a curved line.

Victorian and Edwardian stamps overprinted "Postal Service" and new denominations were customs fee due stamps, not postage stamps.

Empire

A17

A18

A19

A20

A21

A22

A23

A24

A25

A26

A27

1882-87 **Wmk. 39**

36	A17	½a green	4.50	.25
a.		Double impression	750.00	*1,000.*
37	A18	9p rose	1.10	*2.25*
38	A19	1a maroon	5.25	.35
a.		1a violet brown	5.25	.35
39	A20	1a6p bis brn	1.10	*1.40*
40	A21	2a ultra	4.00	.35
a.		Double impression	1,050.	*1,400.*
41	A22	3a brown org	9.50	1.75
a.		3a orange	14.00	6.25
42	A23	4a olive green	15.00	1.60
43	A24	4a6p green	30.00	5.50
44	A25	8a red violet	27.50	2.25
a.		8a rose lilac	25.00	2.25
45	A26	12a violet, *red*	8.00	3.50
46	A27	1r gray	27.50	6.00
		Nos. 36-46 (11)	133.45	25.20
		Set, never hinged	250.00	

A 6a die essay was prepared, but no stamps were printed.

A postal counterfeit exists of No. 46. Examples are scarce.

No. 40a used value is for copy with postal cancellation.

See Nos. 56-58. For surcharges see Nos. 47, 53 and British East Africa No. 59. For overprints see Nos. M2-M4, M6-M9, Gwalior Nos. O1-O5.

Beginning with the 1882-87 issue, higher denomination stamps exist used for telegrams. The telegraph cancellation has concentric circles. These sell for 10-15% of the postally used values.

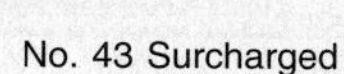
No. 43 Surcharged

1891, Jan. 1

47	A24	2½a on 4a6p green	4.00	.65

A28

A29

1892

48	A28	2a6p green	3.25	.45
49	A29	1r aniline car & grn	17.50	2.00
a.		1r carmine rose & green	20.00	5.00

See No. 59. For overprints see Nos. M5, M10 and Gwalior No. O6.

Queen Victoria — A30

1895, Sept. 1

50	A30	2r yel brn & rose	42.50	10.00
a.		Brn & rose	50.00	10.00
51	A30	3r green & brown	37.50	11.00
52	A30	5r violet & ultra	47.50	30.00
		Nos. 50-52 (3)	127.50	51.00
		Set, never hinged	200.00	

Used high values such as Nos. 50-52, 71-76, 95-98, 124-125, as well as similar high value official issues are for postally used examples. Stamps bearing telegraph or revenue cancellations sell for much lower prices. Most telegraph cancellations on issues of Edward VII and George V can be recognized by the appearance of "T," "TEL" or "GTO" or if they contain the concentric circles of a target.

No. 36 Surcharged

1898

53	A17	¼a on ½a green	.25	*.55*
a.		Double surcharge	250.00	
b.		Double impression of stamp	260.00	

For Nos. 61, 81 with this overprint see Nos. 77, 105.

Queen Victoria — A31

1899

54	A31	3p carmine rose	.45	.25

For overprint see No. M1, Gwalior No. O11.

Type of 1882-1892 Stamps

1900

55	A31	3p gray	.80	*1.40*
56	A17	½a light green	1.75	.50
57	A19	1a carmine rose	2.50	.25
58	A21	2a violet	4.50	2.50
59	A28	2a6p ultramarine	3.75	4.25
		Nos. 55-59 (5)	13.30	8.90

For overprints see Nos. M11, Gwalior O7-O10.

Edward VII — A32
A33
A34
A35
A36
A37
A38
A39
A40
A41
A42
A43

1902-09

No.	Type	Description	Unused	Used
60	A32	3p gray	1.10	.25
61	A33	½a green	1.75	.25
a.		Booklet pane of 6 ('04)	32.50	
62	A34	1a carmine rose	1.60	.25
a.		Booklet pane of 6 ('04)	92.50	
63	A35	2a violet	4.25	.45
64	A36	2a6p ultra	5.00	.65
65	A37	3a brown org	5.00	.65
66	A38	4a olive green	3.25	.65
67	A39	6a bister	12.50	4.75
68	A40	8a red violet	8.75	1.10
69	A41	12a violet, *red*	9.50	2.25
70	A42	1r car rose & grn	6.75	.75
a.		1r rose & green ('11)	40.00	4.50
71	A43	2r brown & rose	47.50	4.50
72	A43	3r grn & brn ('04)	30.00	20.00
73	A43	5r vio & ultra ('04)	72.50	40.00
74	A43	10r car rose & grn ('09)	125.00	30.00
75	A43	15r ol gray & ultra ('09)	175.00	45.00
76	A43	25r ultra & org brn	925.00	925.00
		Never hinged	1,800.	
		Telegraph cancel		300.00
		Nos. 60-75 (16)	509.45	151.50

For overprints see Nos. M12-M20, Gwalior Nos. O12-O18.

No. 61 Surcharged Like No. 53

1905

No.	Type	Description	Unused	Used
77	A33	¼a on ½a green	.60	.25
a.		Inverted surcharge		925.00

A44

A45

1906

No.	Type	Description	Unused	Used
78	A44	½a green	3.25	.25
a.		Booklet pane of 4	17.50	
79	A45	1a carmine rose	1.90	.25
a.		Booklet pane of 4	25.00	

For overprints see Nos. O45-O46, Gwalior Nos. O19-O20.

A46

A47

A48

A49

A50

A51

A52

A53

A54

A55

George V — A56

1911-23 **Wmk. 39**

No.	Type	Description	Unused	Used
80	A46	3p gray	1.50	.25
a.		Booklet pane of 4	25.00	
81	A47	½a green	2.25	.25
a.		Double impression	175.00	
b.		Booklet pane of 4	21.00	
82	A48	1a carmine rose	2.75	.25
a.		Printed on both sides		
b.		Booklet pane of 4	35.00	
83	A48	1a dk brn ('22)	.85	.25
a.		Booklet pane of 4	42.50	
84	A49	2a dull violet	3.50	.40
a.		Booklet pane of 4	42.50	
85	A50	2a6p ultramarine	2.90	*3.25*
86	A51	3a brown org	4.25	.25
87	A51	3a ultra ('23)	13.00	.65
88	A52	4a olive green	8.00	.55
89	A53	6a yel bister	4.25	1.50
90	A53	6a bister ('15)	4.25	1.10
91	A54	8a red violet	6.25	1.25
92	A55	12a claret	6.50	2.40
93	A56	1r grn & red brn	19.00	1.75
94	A56	2r brn & car rose	22.50	1.90
95	A56	5r vio & ultra	55.00	7.00
96	A56	10r car rose & grn	82.50	13.00
97	A56	15r ol grn & ultra	115.00	26.00
98	A56	25r ultra & brn org	190.00	37.50
		Nos. 80-98 (19)	544.25	99.50
		Set, never hinged	800.00	

See Nos. 106-125. For type surcharged see No. 104. For overprints see Nos. M23-M25, M27, M29-M37, M39-M43, Gwalior O21-O27, O29-O32, O35-O39, O44-O45.

Nos. 93-98 also were used to pay for radio licenses, and stamps so used include "WIRELESS" in the cancel. Used values so canceled are worth 10-15% of the values shown, which are for postally used examples.

A57

1913-26

No.	Type	Description	Unused	Used
99	A57	2a6p ultramarine	2.90	.25
100	A57	2a6p brown org ('26)	6.00	6.00

See No. 112. For overprints see Nos. M28, M38.

"One and Half" — A58

1919

No.	Type	Description	Unused	Used
101	A58	1½a chocolate	3.75	.45
a.		Booklet pane of 4	35.00	

For overprint and surcharge see Nos. M26, O75.

"One and a Half" — A59

1921-26

No.	Type	Description	Unused	Used
102	A59	1½a chocolate	3.50	*4.75*
103	A59	1½a rose ('26)	3.25	.35

See No. 109. For surcharge see No. O76.

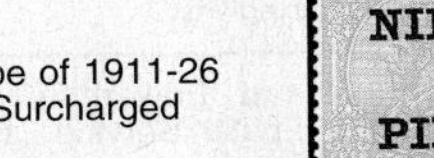

Type of 1911-26 Surcharged

1921

No.	Type	Description	Unused	Used
104	A48	9p on 1a rose	.90	.35
a.		Surcharged "NINE-NINE"	80.00	*150.00*
b.		Surcharged "PIES-PIES"	80.00	*150.00*
c.		Double surcharge	175.00	*210.00*
e.		Booklet pane of 4	27.50	

Forgeries exist of Nos. 104a-104c.

No. 81 Surcharged Like No. 53

1922

No.	Type	Description	Unused	Used
105	A47	¼a on ½a green	.60	.40
a.		Inverted surcharge	10.00	
b.		Pair, one without surcharge	240.00	

Types of 1911-26 Issues

1926-36 **Wmk. 196**

No.	Type	Description	Unused	Used
106	A46	3p slate	.35	.25
107	A47	½a green	1.40	.25
108	A48	1a dark brown	.55	.25
a.		Tete beche pair	1.50	*11.00*
b.		Booklet pane of 4	16.00	
109	A59	1½a car rose ('29)	3.50	.25
110	A49	2a dull violet	2.00	.25
a.		Booklet pane of 4	32.50	
111	A49	2a ver ('34)	4.00	.55
a.		Small die ('36)	5.00	.35
112	A57	2a6p buff	2.50	.25
113	A51	3a ultramarine	11.50	1.25
114	A51	3a blue ('30)	10.00	.25
115	A51	3a car rose ('32)	9.75	.25
116	A52	4a olive green	1.60	.25
117	A53	6a bister ('35)	9.50	2.00
118	A54	8a red violet	4.25	.25
119	A55	12a claret	5.25	.35
120	A56	1r grn & brn	5.50	.50
121	A56	2r brn org & car rose	15.00	.85
122	A56	5r dk vio & ultra	30.00	1.40
123	A56	10r car & grn	62.50	3.50
124	A56	15r ol grn & ultra	28.00	32.50
125	A56	25r blue & ocher	115.00	40.00
		Nos. 106-125 (20)	322.15	85.40
		Set, never hinged	500.00	

No. 111 measures 19x22½mm, while the small die, No. 111a, measures 18½x22mm.

For overprints see Gwalior Nos. O30-O39, O44-O45.

A60

A61

1926-32 **Typo.**

No.	Type	Description	Unused	Used
126	A60	2a dull violet	.55	.25
a.		Tete beche pair	10.00	37.50
b.		2a rose violet	.45	.25
c.		Booklet pane of 4	19.00	
127	A60	2a vermilion ('32)	11.00	7.00
128	A61	4a olive green	6.25	.25
		Nos. 126-128 (3)	17.80	7.50

For overprints see Gwalior Nos. O33-O34.

Fortress of Purana Qila — A62

George V Flanked by Dominion Columns A67

½a, War Memorial Arch. 1a, Council Building. 2a, Viceroy's House. 3a, Parliament Building.

Wmk. 196 Sideways

1931, Feb. 9 **Litho.** ***Perf. 13½x14***

No.	Type	Description	Unused	Used
129	A62	¼a brown & ol grn	3.00	4.50
130	A62	½a green & violet	1.75	.60
131	A62	1a choc & red vio	1.75	.30
132	A62	2a blue & green	2.25	1.50
133	A62	3a car & choc	5.25	3.00
134	A67	1r violet & green	13.50	*30.00*
		Nos. 129-134 (6)	27.50	39.90
		Set, never hinged	66.00	

Change of the seat of Government from Calcutta to New Delhi.

A68

A69

A70

Wmk. 196

1932, Apr. 22 **Litho.** ***Perf. 14***

No.	Type	Description	Unused	Used
135	A68	9p dark green	1.90	.25
136	A69	1a3p violet	.95	.25
137	A70	3a6p deep blue	4.75	.25
		Nos. 135-137 (3)	7.60	.75

No. 135 exists both litho. and typo.

For overprints see Nos. O94, O96, O104 and Gwalior Nos. O41 and O43.

A71

A72

1934 **Typo.**

No.	Type	Description	Unused	Used
138	A71	½a green	5.75	.25
139	A72	1a dark brown	4.00	.25

For overprints see Nos. O93, O95 and Gwalior Nos. O40 and O42.

Silver Jubilee Issue

Gateway of India, Bombay
A73

Designs: 9p, Victoria Memorial, Calcutta. 1a, Rameswaram Temple, Madras. 1¼a, Jain Temple, Calcutta. 2½a, Taj Mahal, Agra. 3½a, Golden Temple, Amritsar. 8a, Pagoda, Mandalay.

Wmk. 196 Sideways

1935 Litho. *Perf. 13½x14*

142	A73	½a	lt green & black	1.50	.55
143	A73	9p	dull green & blk	1.50	.55
144	A73	1a	brown & black	2.25	.55
145	A73	1¼a	violet & black	1.00	.55
146	A73	2½a	brown org & blk	3.25	1.10
147	A73	3½a	blue & black	6.50	2.50
148	A73	8a	rose lilac & blk	7.25	6.00
			Nos. 142-148 (7)	23.25	11.80
			Set, never hinged	50.00	

25th anniv. of the reign of George V.

King George VI
A80 A82

Dak Runner
A81

Mail transport: 2a6p, Dak bullock cart. 3a, Dak tonga. 3a6p, Dak camel. 4a, Mail train. 6a, Mail steamer. 8a, Mail truck. 12a, 14a, Mail plane.

Perf. 13½x14 or 14x13½

1937-40 Typo. Wmk. 196

150	A80	3p	slate	.40	.25
151	A80	½a	brown	1.10	.25
152	A80	9p	green	3.00	.30
153	A80	1a	carmine	.35	.25
a.			Tete beche pair	3.50	2.10
b.			Booklet pane of 4	5.25	
154	A81	2a	scarlet	2.10	.35
155	A81	2a6p	purple	.65	.30
156	A81	3a	yellow green	3.75	.35
157	A81	3a6p	ultramarine	2.50	.60
158	A81	4a	dark brown	10.00	.30
159	A81	6a	pck blue	10.00	.95
160	A81	8a	blue violet	6.00	.60
161	A81	12a	car lake	13.00	1.25
161A	A81	14a	rose vio ('40)	15.00	1.50
162	A82	1r	brn & sl	.90	.25
163	A82	2r	dk brn & dk violet	3.25	.40
164	A82	5r	dp ultra & dk grn	14.00	.70
165	A82	10r	rose car & dk vio	14.00	1.10
166	A82	15r	dk grn & dk brn	70.00	*90.00*
167	A82	25r	dk vio & blue vio	100.00	24.00
			Nos. 150-167 (19)	270.00	*123.70*
			Set, never hinged	580.00	

The King's portrait is larger on No. 161A than on other stamps of type A81.

For overprints see Nos. O97-O103, Gwalior Nos. O46-O51.

Catalogue values for unused stamps in this section, from this point to the end of the section, are for Never Hinged items.

A83

A84

A85

Perf. 13½x14

1941-43 Typo. Wmk. 196

168	A83	3p	slate ('42)	1.00	.25
169	A83	½a	rose vio ('42)	3.50	.25
170	A83	9p	light green	3.50	.25
171	A83	1a	car rose ('43)	3.50	.25
172	A84	1a3p	bister	3.50	.25
172A	A84	1½a	dark pur ('42)	4.00	.25
173	A84	2a	scarlet	5.00	.25
174	A84	3a	violet	10.00	.25
175	A84	3½a	ultramarine	3.50	.65
176	A85	4a	chocolate	2.50	.25
177	A85	6a	peacock blue	11.50	.25
178	A85	8a	blue violet	5.00	.65
179	A85	12a	carmine lake	10.50	1.10
			Nos. 168-179 (13)	67.00	4.90

Early printings of the 1½a and 3a were lithographed.

For surcharge see No. 199.

For stamps with this overprint, or a smaller type, see Oman (Muscat).

Symbols of Victory
A86

1946, Jan. 2 Litho. *Perf. 13*

195	A86	9p	green	.80	1.10
196	A86	1½a	dull purple	.45	.40
197	A86	3½a	ultramarine	1.00	1.00
198	A86	12a	brown lake	2.50	1.10
			Nos. 195-198 (4)	4.75	3.60

Victory of the Allied Nations in WWII.

No. 172 Surcharged With New Value and Bars

1946, Aug. 8 *Perf. 13½x14*

199	A84	3p	on 1a3p bister	.35	.25

Dominion of India

Asoka Pillar — A87

National Flag
A88

Four-Motor Plane
A89

Perf. 14x13½, 13½x14

1947 Litho. Wmk. 196

200	A87	1½a	greenish gray	1.50	.45
201	A88	3½a	multicolored	4.50	*4.75*
202	A89	12a	ultramarine	6.00	*4.75*
			Nos. 200-202 (3)	12.00	9.95

Elevation to dominion status, Aug. 15, 1947.

Mahatma Gandhi — A90

Design: 10r, Gandhi profile.

Perf. 11½

1948, Aug. 15 Unwmk. Photo.

Size: 22x32½mm

203	A90	1½a	brown	*8.25*	1.25
204	A90	3½a	violet	*18.00*	5.00
205	A90	12a	dark gray green	*21.00*	3.00

Size: 22x37mm

206	A90	10r	rose brn & brn	*260.00*	*95.00*
			Nos. 203-206 (4)	307.25	104.25

Mohandas K. Gandhi, 1869-1948.

For overprints see Nos. O112A-O112D.

Ajanta Panel — A91

Konarak Horse — A92

Bodhisattva
A93

Tomb of Muhammad Adil Shah, Bijapur
A95

Sanchi Stupa
A94

Victory Tower, Chittorgarh
A96

Red Fort, Delhi
A97

Satrunjaya Temple, Palitana
A98

9p, Trimurti. 2a, Nataraja. 3½a, Bodh Gaya Temple. 4a, Bhuvanesvara. 8a, Kandarya Mahadeva Temple. 12a, Golden Temple, Amritsar. 5r, Taj Mahal. 10r, Qutb Minar.

Perf. 13½x14, 14x13½

1949, Aug. 15 Typo. Wmk. 196

207	A91	3p	gray violet	.30	.25
208	A92	6p	red brown	.35	.25
209	A93	9p	green	.60	.25
210	A93	1a	turquoise	.85	.25
211	A93	2a	carmine	1.25	.25
212	A94	3a	red orange	3.00	.25
213	A94	3½a	ultramarine	2.50	5.00
214	A94	4a	brown lake	6.00	.35
215	A95	6a	purple	2.75	.90
216	A95	8a	blue green	2.25	.25
217	A95	12a	blue	3.00	.35

Litho.

218	A96	1r	dk green & pur	22.50	.25
219	A97	2r	pur & rose red	20.00	.50
220	A97	5r	brn car & dk grn	45.00	2.00
221	A96	10r	dp bl & brn car	80.00	12.00

Perf. 13½x13

222	A98	15r	dp car & dk brn	32.50	*35.00*
			Nos. 207-222 (16)	222.85	58.10

See Nos. 231, 235-236. For overprints see Nos. M44-M46, M48-M55 and Intl. Commission in Indo-china issues for Cambodia, Nos. 1, 3-5, Laos Nos. 1, 3-5 and Vietnam Nos. 1, 3-5.

Symbols of UPU and Asoka Pillar — A99

1949, Oct. Litho. *Perf. 13½x13*

223	A99	9p	dull green	2.75	1.75
224	A99	2a	carmine rose	2.75	1.75
225	A99	3½a	ultramarine	6.00	3.00
226	A99	12a	red brown	24.00	4.00
			Nos. 223-226 (4)	35.50	10.50

75th anniv. of the formation of the UPU.

AIR POST STAMPS

De Havilland Hercules over Lake
AP1

Wmk. 196 Sideways

1929-30 Typo. *Perf. 14*

C1	AP1	2a	dull green	1.00	.50
C2	AP1	3a	deep blue	1.40	.90
C3	AP1	4a	gray olive	4.00	1.90
a.			4a olive green ('30)	5.00	1.90
C4	AP1	6a	bister	5.00	1.10
C5	AP1	8a	red violet	5.75	5.75
C6	AP1	12a	brown red	17.50	17.50
			Nos. C1-C6 (6)	34.65	27.65
			Set, never hinged	60.00	

Catalogue values for unused stamps in this section, from this point to the end of the section, are for Never Hinged items.

Dominion of India

Lockheed Constellation — AP2

Perf. 13½x14

1948, May 29 Litho. Wmk. 196

C7	AP2	12a	ultra & slate blk	3.25	3.25

Bombay-London flight of June 8, 1948.

MILITARY STAMPS

China Expeditionary Force

Regular Issues of India, 1882-99, Overprinted

1900 Wmk. 39 *Perf. 14*

M1	A31	3p	carmine rose	.70	*2.10*
M2	A17	½a	dark green	1.25	*.45*
M3	A19	1a	maroon	7.00	2.50
M4	A21	2a	ultra	5.25	*15.00*
M5	A28	2a6p	green	4.75	*21.00*
M6	A22	3a	orange	4.75	*27.50*
M7	A23	4a	olive green	4.75	*13.00*

M8 A25 8a red violet 4.75 *30.00*
M9 A26 12a violet, *red* 30.00 *30.00*
M10 A29 1r car rose & grn 37.50 *37.50*
a. Double overprint
Nos. M1-M10 (10) 100.70 *179.05*

The 1a6p of this set was overprinted, but not issued. Value $250.

Overprinted on 1900 Issue of India

1904, Feb. 27

M11 A19 1a carmine rose 55.00 15.00

Overprinted on 1902-09 Issue of India

1904

M12 A32 3p gray 8.00 *10.00*
M13 A34 1a carmine rose 12.00 1.10
M14 A35 2a violet 22.50 3.75
M15 A36 2a6p ultra 5.25 *8.00*
M16 A37 3a brown org 5.75 *6.50*
M17 A38 4a olive green 13.50 *19.00*
M18 A40 8a red violet 13.00 *12.00*
M19 A41 12a violet, *red* 18.00 *30.00*
M20 A42 1r car rose & grn 20.00 *45.00*
Nos. M12-M20 (9) 118.00 *135.35*

Overprinted on 1906 Issue of India

1909

M21 A44 ½a green 1.50 1.00
M22 A45 1a carmine rose 1.50 .40

Overprinted on 1911-19 Issues of India

1913-21

M23 A46 3p gray 8.00 *35.00*
M24 A47 ½a green 6.25 *7.50*
M25 A48 1a car rose 7.25 4.75
M26 A58 1½a chocolate 40.00 *95.00*
M27 A49 2a violet 27.50 *80.00*
M28 A57 2a6p ultra 20.00 *30.00*
M29 A51 3a brn org 40.00 *240.00*
M30 A52 4a ol grn 37.50 *210.00*
M31 A54 8a red violet 40.00 *400.00*
M32 A55 12a claret 37.50 *140.00*
M33 A56 1r grn & red brn 110.00 *375.00*
Nos. M23-M33 (11) 374.00 *1,617.*

Issue dates: No. M23, 1913; others, 1921.

Indian Expeditionary Force

Regular Issues of India, 1911-13, Overprinted

1914 **Wmk. 39** ***Perf. 14***

M34 A46 3p gray .30 .55
a. Double overprint 70.00 55.00
M35 A47 ½a green .80 .55
a. Double overprint 175.00 *300.00*
M36 A48 1a car rose 2.10 .55
M37 A49 2a violet 2.10 .55
M38 A57 2a6p ultra 2.50 4.00
M39 A51 3a brn org 1.75 2.75
M40 A52 4a olive grn 1.75 2.75
M41 A54 8a red violet 2.10 4.25
M42 A55 12a claret 3.75 10.50
a. Double overprint, one albino 65.00
M43 A56 1r grn & red brn 4.50 7.25
a. Double overprint, one albino 115.00
Nos. M34-M43 (10) 21.65 33.70

OFFICIAL STAMPS

Nos. O1-O26 are normally found with very heavy cancellations, and values are for stamps so canceled. Lightly canceled stamps are seldom seen.

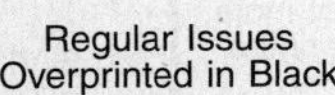
Regular Issues Overprinted in Black

1866, Aug. 1 **Unwmk.** ***Perf. 14***

O1 A7 ½a blue 1,100. 140.00
a. Inverted overprint
O3 A7 1a brown 140.00
O4 A7 8a rose 22.50 50.00

The 8p lilac unwatermarked (No. 19) with "Service" overprint was not officially issued.

Wmk. 38

O5 A7 ½a blue 300.00 12.50
a. Inverted overprint
b. Without period 210.00
O6 A8 8p lilac 20.00 *52.50*
O7 A7 1a brown 300.00 15.00
a. Inverted overprint
O8 A7 2a yellow 300.00 85.00
a. Imperf.
b. Inverted overprint
O9 A7 4a green 200.00 80.00
a. Inverted overprint
O10 A9 4a green (I) 1,000. 250.00

Reprints were made of Nos. O5, O7, O10 (type II).

Revenue Stamps Surcharged or Overprinted

Queen Victoria — O1

Blue Glazed Paper Black Surcharge

1866 **Wmk. 36** ***Perf. 14 Vertically***

O11 O1 2a violet 350.00 250.00

The note after No. 30 will apply here also.

No. O11 is often found with cracked surface or scuffs. Such examples sell for somewhat less.

Reprints of No. O11 are surcharged in either black or green, and have the word "SERVICE" 16½x2½mm, instead of 16½x2¾mm and "TWO ANNAS" 18x3mm, instead of 20x3¼mm.

O2

O3

O4

1866 **Green Overprint**

O12 O2 2a violet 1,000. 325.
O13 O3 4a violet *4,500.* *1,250.*
O14 O4 8a violet *5,000.* *5,000.*

The note after No. 30 will apply here also.

These stamps are often found with cracked surface or scuffs. Such examples sell for somewhat less.

Reprints of No. O12 have the overprint in sans-serif letters 2¼mm high, instead of Roman letters 2½mm high. On the reprints of No. O13 "SERVICE" measures 16½x2¼mm, instead of 20¼x3mm and "POSTAGE" 18x2¼mm, instead of 22x3mm.

On No. O14 "SERVICE" is 20½mm long, instead of 20mm and "POSTAGE" is 23mm long, instead of 22mm. All three overprints are in a darker green than on the original stamps.

O5

Green Overprint

1866 **Wmk. 40** ***Perf. 15½x15***

Lilac Paper

O15 O5 ½a violet 425.00 85.00
a. Double overprint 3,000.

Regular Issues Overprinted in Black

1866-73 **Wmk. 38** ***Perf. 14***

O16 A7 ½a blue 30.00 .35
O17 A7 ½a bl, re-engraved 140.00 67.50
a. Double overprint
O18 A7 1a brown 32.50 .40
O19 A7 2a orange 4.50 2.00
a. 2a yellow 20.00 2.25
O20 A9 4a green (I) 2.75 1.50
O21 A11 8a rose 3.00 1.50
Nos. O16-O21 (6) 212.75 73.25

The 6a8p with this overprint was not issued. Value $25.

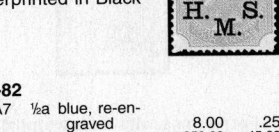

Overprinted in Black

1874-82

O22 A7 ½a blue, re-engraved 8.00 .25
a. Blue overprint 350.00 45.00
O23 A7 1a brown 12.50 .25
a. Blue overprint 550.00 120.00
O24 A7 2a orange 40.00 17.50
O25 A9 4a green (I) 12.50 2.75
O26 A11 8a rose 4.25 4.00
Nos. O22-O26 (5) 77.25 24.75

Same Overprint on Nos. 36, 38, 40, 42, 44, 49

1883-97 **Wmk. 39**

O27 A17 ½a green .40 .25
a. Pair, one without overprint
b. Double overprint 1,150.
O28 A19 1a maroon .75 .25
a. Inverted overprint 350.00 475.00
b. Double overprint 1,150.
c. 1a violet brown 2.25 .35
O29 A21 2a ultramarine 4.50 .50
O30 A23 4a olive green 15.00 .40
O31 A25 8a red violet 7.00 .40
O32 A29 1r car rose & grn 11.00 .40
Nos. O27-O32 (6) 38.65 2.20

Same Overprint on No. 54

1899

O33 A31 3p carmine rose .25 .25

Same Overprint on Nos. 56-58

1900

O34 A17 ½a light green 1.25 .30
O35 A19 1a carmine rose 2.50 .25
a. Double overprint 1,350.
b. Inverted overprint 1,400.
O36 A21 2a violet 27.50 .50
Nos. O34-O36 (3) 31.25 1.05

Same Overprint on Nos. 60-63, 66-68, 70

1902-09

O37 A32 3p gray .85 .25
O38 A33 ½a green 1.00 .25
O39 A34 1a carmine rose .85 .25
O40 A35 2a violet *2.50* .25
O41 A38 4a olive green *4.25* .25
O42 A39 6a bister *2.25* .25
O43 A40 8a red lilac *5.25* .50
O44 A42 1r car rose & green ('05) *4.50* .25
Nos. O37-O44 (8) *21.45* 2.25

Same Overprint on Nos. 78-79

1906-07

O45 A44 ½a green 1.00 .25
O46 A45 1a carmine rose 1.75 .25
a. Pair, one without overprint
b. Overprint on back —

Same Overprint on Nos. 71, 73-76

1909

O47 A43 2r brown & rose *6.50* .90
O48 A43 5r violet & ultra *11.00* 1.00
O49 A43 10r car rose & grn *21.00* 8.50
a. 10r red & green 52.50 6.00
O50 A43 15r ol gray & ultra 52.50 30.00
O51 A43 25r ultra & org brn 130.00 50.00
Nos. O47-O51 (5) 221.00 90.40

For surcharges see Nos. O67-O69.

Regular Issues Overprinted in Black

1912-22

O52 A46 3p gray .25 .25
O53 A47 ½a green .25 .25
a. Double overprint 110.00
O54 A48 1a carmine rose .75 .25
a. Double overprint 950.00
O55 A48 1a dk brn ('22) 1.00 .25
a. Imperf., pair 75.00
O56 A49 2a violet .50 .25
O57 A52 4a olive green .75 .25
O58 A53 6a bister 1.25 *1.75*
O59 A54 8a red violet 1.75 .75

Overprinted in Black

O60 A56 1r green & red brn 2.00 .80
O61 A56 2r yel brn & car rose 2.50 *3.50*
O62 A56 5r violet & ultra 10.50 *13.50*
O63 A56 10r car rose & grn 35.00 32.50
O64 A56 15r ol grn & ultra 80.00 *95.00*
O65 A56 25r ultra & brn org 180.00 150.00
Nos. O52-O65 (14) 316.50 299.30

For surcharge see No. O69b.

O6

1921 **Black Surcharge**

O66 O6 9p on 1a rose .75 .60

For overprint see Gwalior No. O28.

Official Stamps of 1909 Surcharged

1925

O67 A43 1r on 15r ol gray & ultra 4.00 3.00
O68 A43 1r on 25r ultra & org brn 20.00 *60.00*
O69 A43 2r on 10r red & grn 3.50 3.50
a. 2r on 10r car rose & green 210.00 55.00
b. Surcharge on #O63 (error) 4,500.

Official Stamps of 1912-13 Surcharged

O70 A56 1r on 15r ol grn & ultra 19.00 *65.00*
a. Inverted surcharge
O71 A56 1r on 25r ultra & brn org 5.00 *9.00*
a. Inverted surcharge 4,000.
Nos. O67-O71 (5) 51.50 *140.50*

O7

1926 **Black Surcharge**
O73 O7 1a on 6a bister .40 .40

Regular Issues of 1911-26 Surcharged

O74 A48 1a on 1a dk brn (error) 180.00 180.00
O75 A58 1a on 1½a choc .25 .25
O76 A59 1a on 1½a choc 1.75 4.00
b. Double surcharge 30.00
O77 A57 1a on 2a6p ultra .50 .50
Nos. O73-O77 (5) 182.90 185.15

Nos. O74, O75 and O76 have short bars over the numerals in the upper corners.

Regular Issues of 1926-35 Overprinted - a

1926-35 **Wmk. 196**
O78 A46 3p slate ('29) .25 .25
O79 A47 ½a green ('31) 5.00 .40
O80 A48 1a dark brown .25 .25
a. Overprint as on No. O55 100.00 4.75
O81 A49 2a vermilion ('35) 1.00 1.00
a. Small die .85 .25
O82 A60 2a dull violet .25 .25
O83 A60 2a vermilion ('32) .90 2.00
O84 A57 2a6p buff ('32) .25 .25
O85 A52 4a olive green ('35) 1.00 .25
O86 A61 4a olive green .35 .25
O87 A53 6a bister('35) 18.00 9.00
O88 A54 8a red violet .50 .25
O89 A55 12a claret .50 1.75

Nos. 120-121, 123 Overprinted - b

O90 A56 1r grn & brn ('30) 2.25 .90
O91 A56 2r brn org & car rose ('30) 6.00 6.00
O92 A56 10r car & grn ('31) 70.00 50.00
Nos. O78-O92 (15) 106.50 72.80

Nos. 138, 135, 139, 136 Overprinted Type "a"

1932-35
O93 A71 ½a green ('35) .60 .25
O94 A68 9p dark green .25 .25
O95 A72 1a dark brown ('35) 1.90 .25
O96 A69 1a3p violet .25 .25
Nos. O93-O96 (4) 3.00 1.00

Nos. 151-153, 162-165 Overprinted Type "a"

1937-39 ***Perf. 13½x14***
O97 A80 ½a brown ('38) 22.50 .45
O98 A80 9p green 25.00 .60
O99 A80 1a carmine 4.75 .35

Type "b" Overprint
O100 A82 1r brn & slate ('38) .70 .55
O101 A82 2r dk brn & dk vio ('38) 1.90 3.25
O102 A82 5r dp ultra & dk grn ('38) 3.25 7.50
O103 A82 10r rose car & dk violet ('39) 19.00 6.75
Nos. O97-O103 (7) 77.10 19.45

No. 136 Surcharged in Black

1939, May **Wmk. 196** ***Perf. 14***
O104 A69 1a on 1a3p violet 17.00 3.00

King George VI — O8

1939-43 **Typo.** ***Perf. 13½x14***
O105 O8 3p slate .40 .40
O106 O8 ½a brown 8.00 .40
O106A O8 ½a dk rose vio ('43) .40 .40
O107 O8 9p green .40 .40
O108 O8 1a car rose .40 .40
O108A O8 1a3p bister ('41) 7.00 1.25
O108B O8 1½a dull pur ('43) .40 .40
O109 O8 2a scarlet .40 .40
O110 O8 2½a purple .40 .40
O111 O8 4a dark brown .40 .40
O112 O8 8a blue violet .60 .40
Nos. O105-O112 (11) 18.80 5.25

For overprints see Gwalior Nos. O52-O61 and Patiala Nos. O63-O73. Stamps overprinted "Postal Service" or "I. P. N." were not used as postage stamps.

Catalogue values for unused stamps in this section, from this point to the end of the section, are for Never Hinged items.

Nos. 203-206 (Gandhi Issue) Overprinted Type "a"

Perf. 11½

1948, Aug. **Unwmk.** **Photo.**
O112A A90 1½a brown 65.00 45.00
O112B A90 3½a violet 7,500. 750.00
O112C A90 12a dk gray green 8,000. 2,500.
O112D A90 10r rose brn & brn 225,000.

Overprint forgeries exist.

INDIA - CONVENTION STATES

CHAMBA

'chəm-bə

LOCATION — A State of India located in the north Punjab, south of Kashmir.
AREA — 3,127 sq. mi.
POP. — 168,908 (1941)
CAPITAL — Chamba

The varieties with small letters in the overprint are not listed as the letters are merely broken and not from another font of type.

Indian Stamps Overprinted in Black

1887-95 **Wmk. 39** ***Perf. 14***
1 A17 ½a green 1.50 1.75
a. "CHMABA" 600.00 950.00
c. Double overprint 950.00
2 A19 1a vio brn 3.75 3.75
a. "CHMABA" 700.00 950.00
b. 1a plum 4.25 3.75
3 A20 1a6p bis brn ('95) 4.50 21.00
4 A21 2a ultra 2.00 3.25
a. "CHMABA" 2,750. 4,000.
5 A28 2a6p grn ('95) 52.50 150.00
6 A22 3a brn org 4.50 9.00
a. 3a orange 16.00 35.00
b. Inverted overprint
c. "CHMABA" 7,500. 11,000.
7 A23 4a ol grn 8.25 14.00
a. "CHMABA" 2,400. 4,000.
8 A25 8a red violet 13.50 18.00
a. "CHMABA" 6,000. 6,250.
9 A26 12a vio, *red* ('90) 10.50 24.00
a. "CHMABA" 12,500.
b. 1st "T" of "STATE" invtd. 12,500.
10 A27 1r gray 72.50 225.00
a. "CHMABA" 21,000.
11 A29 1r car rose & grn ('95) 14.00 25.00
12 A30 2r brn & rose ('95) 150.00 600.00
13 A30 3r grn & brn ('95) 175.00 525.00
14 A30 5r vio & bl ('95) 190.00 825.00

Wmk. 38
15 A14 6a bis ('90) 8.25 32.50
a. 6a bister brn 21.00 25.00
Nos. 1-15 (15) 710.75 2,477.

1900 **Wmk. 39**
15B A31 3p carmine rose .90 1.40

1902-04
16 A31 3p gray ('04) .90 3.25
a. Inverted overprint 120.00
17 A17 ½a light green 1.00 2.50
18 A19 1a carmine rose 1.00 .60
19 A21 2a violet ('03) 16.00 52.50
Nos. 16-19 (4) 18.90 58.85

1903-05
20 A32 3p gray .35 2.40
21 A33 ½a green 1.20 .90
22 A34 1a carmine rose 2.40 1.40
23 A35 2a violet 2.75 5.25
24 A37 3a brown org ('05) 7.00 9.00
25 A38 4a olive green ('04) 10.50 32.50
26 A39 6a bister ('05) 6.50 35.00
27 A40 8a red violet ('04) 9.00 35.00
28 A41 12a violet, *red* 12.00 47.50
29 A42 1r car rose & grn ('05) 11.00 35.00
Nos. 20-29 (10) 62.70 203.95

1907
30 A44 ½a green 3.75 6.00
31 A45 1a carmine rose 3.75 6.00

1913-24
32 A46 3p gray .60 1.90
33 A47 ½a green 1.50 1.90
34 A48 1a carmine rose 15.00 17.50
35 A48 1a dk brn ('22) 5.25 8.25
36 A49 2a violet 6.00 17.50
37 A51 3a brown orange 7.00 13.00
38 A51 3a ultra ('24) 6.25 35.00
39 A52 4a olive green 6.00 8.25
40 A53 6a bister 6.50 11.00
41 A54 8a red violet 9.00 24.00
42 A55 12a claret 8.25 19.00
43 A56 1r grn & red brn 27.50 47.50
Nos. 32-43 (12) 98.85 204.80

India No. 104 Overprinted

1921
44 A48 9p on 1a rose 1.50 27.50

India Stamps of 1913-26 Overprinted

1922-27
45 A58 1½a chocolate 40.00 190.00
46 A59 1½a chocolate 3.75 9.50
47 A59 1½a rose 1.40 35.00
48 A57 2a6p ultramarine .90 6.50
49 A57 2a6p brown orange 4.00 35.00
Nos. 45-49 (5) 50.05 276.00

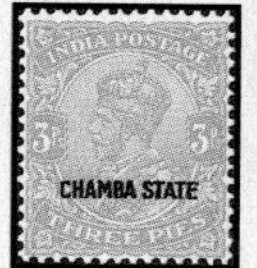

India Stamps of 1926 Overprinted

1927-28 **Wmk. 196**
50 A46 3p slate .30 2.50
51 A47 ½a green .45 3.75
52 A48 1a dark brown 2.50 2.25
53 A60 2a dull violet 3.25 6.00
54 A51 3a ultramarine 1.90 32.50
55 A61 4a olive green 1.90 10.00
57 A54 8a red violet 2.40 17.50
58 A55 12a claret 2.40 24.00

Overprinted

59 A56 1r green & brown 17.50 45.00
Nos. 50-55,57-59 (9) 32.60 143.50

India Stamps of 1926-35 Overprinted

1932-37
60 A71 ½a green 1.60 16.00
61 A68 9p dark green 7.50 32.50
62 A72 1a dark brown 2.50 2.25
63 A69 1a3p violet 2.10 9.50
64 A59 1½a carmine rose 9.50 11.00
65 A49 2a vermilion 1.90 37.50
a. Small die 175.00 210.00
66 A57 2a6p buff 5.00 30.00
67 A51 3a carmine rose 3.25 17.50
68 A52 4a ol grn ('36) 8.25 25.00
69 A53 6a bister ('37) 45.00 250.00
Nos. 60-69 (10) 86.60 431.25

Same Overprint on India Stamps of 1937

1938 **Wmk. 196** ***Perf. 13½x14***
70 A80 3p slate 14.00 32.50
71 A80 ½a brown 2.00 21.00
72 A80 9p green 12.50 57.50
73 A80 1a carmine 2.50 5.50

74 A81 2a scarlet 10.00 24.00
75 A81 2a6p purple 11.00 47.50
76 A81 3a yellow green 11.50 42.50
77 A81 3a6p ultra 11.50 45.00
78 A81 4a dark brown 30.00 45.00
79 A81 6a peacock blue 32.50 100.00
80 A81 8a blue violet 30.00 97.50
81 A81 12a carmine lake 22.50 97.50

Overprinted

82 A82 1r brown & slate 45.00 110.00
83 A82 2r dk brn & dk vio 75.00 525.00
84 A82 5r dp ultra & dk green 120.00 700.00
85 A82 10r rose car & dk vio 190.00 1,100.
86 A82 15r dk grn & dk brown 200.00 1,500.
87 A82 25r dk vio & bl vio 290.00 1,600.
Nos. 70-87 (18) 1,110. 6,151.
Set, never hinged 1,300.

India Nos. 151 and 153 Overprinted

1942
87B A80 ½a brown 62.50 67.50
Never hinged 75.00
88 A80 1a carmine 95.00 90.00
Never hinged 110.00

Same Ovpt. on India Stamps of 1941-42

1942-44
89 A83 3p slate 1.50 8.25
90 A83 ½a rose vio ('43) 1.00 9.50
91 A83 9p lt green ('43) 1.40 30.00
92 A83 1a car rose ('43) 2.50 8.25

93 A84 1½a dk purple ('44) 3.00 *21.00*
94 A84 2a scarlet ('43) 11.00 *24.00*
95 A84 3a violet ('43) 26.00 *72.50*
96 A84 3½a ultra ('43) 14.00 *67.50*
97 A85 4a chocolate ('43) 19.00 75.00
98 A85 6a pck blue ('43) 21.00 *62.50*
99 A85 8a blue vio ('43) 22.50 *75.00*
100 A85 12a car lake ('43) 30.00 *97.50*
Nos. 89-100 (12) 152.90 *551.00*
Set, never hinged 200.00

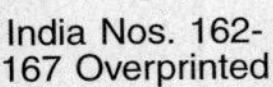

India Nos. 162-167 Overprinted

1943 **Wmk. 196** ***Perf. 13½x14***
101 A82 1r brown & slate 26.00 *97.50*
102 A82 2r dk brn & dk vio 30.00 *400.00*
103 A82 5r dp ultra & dk grn 55.00 *450.00*
104 A82 10r rose car & dk vio 85.00 *700.00*
105 A82 15r dk grn & dk brn 190.00 *1,250.*
106 A82 25r dk vio & bl vio 175.00 *1,250.*
Nos. 101-106 (6) 561.00 *4,148.*
Set, never hinged 850.00

India No. 161A Ovptd.

1947
107 A81 14a rose violet 17.50 4.50

OFFICIAL STAMPS

Indian Stamps Overprinted in Black

1887-98 **Wmk. 39** ***Perf. 14***
O1 A17 ½a green .90 .25
a. "CHMABA" 375.00 375.00
c. "SERV CE"
O2 A19 1a vio brn 3.00 2.25
a. "CHMABA" 600.00 600.00
c. "SERV CE" *5,250.*
d. "SERVICE" double *3,000.* *1,600.*
O3 A21 2a ultra 3.75 3.00
a. "CHMABA" *1,500.* *3,250.*
O4 A22 3a brn org 3.00 *19.00*
a. 3a orange — —
b. "CHMABA" *4,500.* *5,250.*
O5 A23 4a ol grn 4.50 *12.00*
a. "CHMABA" *1,600.* *3,250.*
c. "SERV CE" *6,000.*
O6 A25 8a red violet 4.50 *4.50*
a. "CHMABA" *12,000.* *12,000.*
O7 A26 12a vio, *red* ('90) 12.50 *72.50*
a. "CHMABA" *11,000.*
b. 1st "T" of "STATE" invtd. *10,000.*
O8 A27 1r gray ('90) 19.00 *225.00*
a. "CHMABA" *7,500.*
O9 A29 1r car rose & grn ('98) 9.00 *62.50*

Wmk. 38
O10 A14 6a bister 6.25 *22.50*
Nos. O1-O10 (10) 66.40 423.50

1902-04 **Wmk. 39**
O11 A31 3p gray ('04) .75 *1.20*
O12 A17 ½a light green 1.50 *6.00*
O13 A19 1a carmine rose 1.90 .90
O14 A21 2a violet ('03) 14.50 *52.50*
Nos. O11-O14 (4) 18.65 *60.60*

A 2a value, Scott No. O14, was overprinted in Calcutta but never issued.

1903-05
O15 A32 3p gray .40 .25
O16 A33 ½a green .30 .25
O17 A34 1a carmine rose 1.50 .45
O18 A35 2a violet 1.50 *2.25*
O19 A38 4a olive green ('05) 4.25 *30.00*
O20 A40 8a red violet ('05) 10.00 *30.00*
O21 A42 1r car rose & grn ('05) 2.00 *21.00*
Nos. O15-O21 (7) 19.95 *84.20*

1907
O22 A44 ½a green .85 *1.10*
a. Inverted overprint *6,750.* *8,250.*
O23 A45 1a carmine rose 4.75 *3.75*

1913
O24 A49 2a violet 22.50
O25 A52 4a olive green 20.00

India No. 63 Overprinted

O26 A35 2a violet 60.00

No. O26 was never placed in use.

India Stamps of 1911-29 Overprinted

a

b

1913-25
O27 A46 (a) 3p gray .30 *.60*
O28 A47 (a) ½a green .30 *.90*
O29 A48 (a) 1a carmine rose .30 *.25*
O30 A48 (a) 1a dk brn ('25) 6.50 1.00
O31 A49 (a) 2a violet ('14) 1.60 *22.50*
O32 A52 (a) 4a olive green 1.60 *30.00*
O33 A54 (a) 8a red violet 2.50 *30.00*
O34 A56 (b) 1r grn & red brn 8.25 *47.50*
Nos. O27-O34 (8) 21.35 132.75

India No. O66 Overprinted

1921
O35 O6 9p on 1a rose .25 *12.50*

India Stamps of 1926-35 Overprinted

1927-39 **Wmk. 196**
O36 A46 3p slate .65 .60
O37 A47 ½a green .40 .25
O38 A68 9p dk grn ('32) 5.00 *16.00*
O39 A48 1a dark brown .25 .25
O40 A69 1a3p violet ('32) 7.50 1.50
O41 A60 2a dull violet 3.25 *.90*
O42 A61 4a olive green 1.90 4.00
O43 A54 8a red violet 10.00 *16.00*
O44 A55 12a claret 6.50 *37.50*

Overprinted

O45 A56 1r grn & brn 19.00 *72.50*
O45A A56 2r brn org & car rose ('39) 30.00 *375.00*
O45B A56 5r dk vio & ultra ('39) 52.50 *450.00*
O45C A56 10r car & grn ('39) 82.50 *450.00*
Nos. O36-O45C (13) 219.45 1,425.

India Stamps of 1926-35 Overprinted

1935-36
O46 A71 ½a green 7.00 *.75*
O47 A72 1a dark brown 6.75 .65
O48 A49 2a vermilion 7.00 1.90
a. Small die 9.50 *30.00*
O49 A52 4a olive grn ('36) 10.00 9.50
Nos. O46-O49 (4) 30.75 *12.80*

Same Overprint on India Stamps of 1937

1938 ***Perf. 13½x14***
O50 A80 9p green 30.00 *100.00*
Never hinged 37.50
O51 A80 1a carmine 37.50 9.00
Never hinged 45.00

India Stamps of 1937 Overprinted

1940-41
O51A A82 1r brn & sl ('41) 300.00 *1,100.*
O52 A82 2r dk brn & dk vio 52.50 *600.00*
O53 A82 5r dp ultra & dk grn 75.00 *650.00*
O54 A82 10r rose car & dk vio 105.00 *1,200.*
Set, never hinged 625.00

India Official Stamps of 1939-43 Overprinted

1941-46 **Wmk. 196**
O55 O8 3p slate ('44) .85 *1.90*
O56 O8 ½a brown 37.50 5.50
O57 O8 ½a dk rose vio ('44) .85 *5.50*
O58 O8 9p green 8.75 *17.50*
O59 O8 1a carmine rose 1.25 *4.50*
O60 O8 1a3p bister ('46) 105.00 32.50
O61 O8 1½a dull pur ('46) 9.50 *12.50*
O62 O8 2a scarlet ('44) 9.50 *12.50*
O63 O8 2½a purple ('44) 5.50 *35.00*
O64 O8 4a dk brn ('44) 9.50 *27.50*
O65 O8 8a blue vio ('41) 21.00 *100.00*
Nos. O55-O65 (11) 209.20 *254.90*
Set, never hinged 250.00

India Nos. 162-165 Overprinted

1944
O66 A82 1r brown & slate 27.50 *325.00*
O67 A82 2r dk brn & dk vio 42.50 *450.00*
O68 A82 5r dp ultra & dk grn 80.00 *650.00*
O69 A82 10r rose car & dk vio 95.00 *1,100.*
Nos. O66-O69 (4) 245.00 *2,525.*
Set, never hinged 295.00

FARIDKOT

fe-'rēd-,kōt

LOCATION — A State of India lying northeast of Nabha in the central Punjab.
AREA — 638 sq. mi.
POP. — 164,364
CAPITAL — Faridkot

Previous stamp issues are listed under Feudatory States. Stamps of Faridkot were superseded by those of India in 1901.

The varieties with small letters in the overprint are not listed as the letters are merely broken and not from another font.

India Stamps Overprinted in Black

1887-93 **Wmk. 39** ***Perf. 14***
4 A17 ½a green 3.75 2.50
a. "ARIDKOT" — —
b. "FAR DKOT" *2,500.*
5 A19 1a violet brown 2.25 *3.75*
6 A21 2a ultramarine 4.75 *10.50*
7 A22 3a orange 5.50 *9.00*
8 A23 4a olive green 12.50 *27.50*
a. "ARIDKOT" 2,100.
9 A25 8a red violet 22.50 *67.50*
a. "ARIDKOT" 4,500.
10 A27 1r gray 67.50 *550.00*
a. "ARIDKOT" *5,250.*
11 A29 1r car rose & grn ('93) 60.00 *175.00*

Wmk. 38
12 A14 6a bister 3.00 *27.50*
a. "ARIDKOT" 2,750.
Nos. 4-12 (9) 181.75 *873.25*

1900 **Wmk. Star. (39)**
13 A31 3p car rose 2.25 *67.50*
14 A26 12a violet, *red* 67.50 *625.00*

OFFICIAL STAMPS

India Stamps Overprinted in Black

1886 **Wmk. 39** ***Perf. 14***
O1 A17 ½a green .90 *1.10*
a. "SERV CE" 3,750.
b. "FAR DKOT" 3,500.
c. "ESRVICE" 3,500.
O2 A19 1a violet brown 1.50 *3.00*
a. "SERV CE" 5,500.
O3 A21 2a ultramarine 3.00 *16.00*
a. "SERV CE" 5,500.
O4 A22 3a orange 6.00 *57.50*
O5 A23 4a olive green 7.00 *45.00*
a. "SERV CE" 4,750.
O6 A25 8a red lilac 15.00 *45.00*
a. "SERV CE" 4,500.
O7 A27 1r gray 82.50 *400.00*

Wmk. 38
O8 A14 6a bister 37.50 *42.50*
a. "ARIDKOT" 2,100.
b. "SERVIC" 4,500.
Nos. O1-O8 (8) 153.40 *610.10*

1896 **Wmk. 39**
O9 A29 1r car rose & grn 140.00 *1,000.*

Obsolete March 31, 1901.

GWALIOR

'gwäl-ē-,o,ə,r

LOCATION — One of the Central Provinces of India
AREA — 26,008 sq. mi.
POP. — 4,006,159 (1941)
CAPITAL — Lashkar

The varieties with small letters in the overprint are not listed as the letters are merely broken and not from another font.

India Stamps Overprinted in Black

Lines Spaced 16-17mm

1885 **Wmk. 39** ***Perf. 14***
1 A17 ½a green 90.00
2 A19 1a violet brown 97.50
3 A20 1a6p bister brown 125.00
4 A21 2a ultramarine 100.00
5 A25 8a red lilac 110.00
6 A27 1r gray 110.00

Wmk. 38

7 A9 4a green 140.00
8 A14 6a bister 140.00
Nos. 1-8 (8) 912.50

The Hindi overprint measures 13½-14x2mm and 15-15½x2½mm.

The two sizes are found in the same sheet in the proportion of one of the smaller to three of the larger.

The ½a, 1a, 2a, also exist with lines 13mm apart and the short Hindi overprint.

Reprints of the ½a and 1a have the 13mm spacing, the short Hindi overprint and usually carry the overprint "Specimen."

India Stamps Overprinted

Red Overprint

1885 Wmk. 39

9 A17 ½a green 1.90 .25
10 A21 2a ultramarine 35.00 *27.50*
11 A27 1r gray 12.50 *37.50*

Wmk. 38

12 A9 4a green 42.50 24.00
Nos. 9-12 (4) 91.90 89.25

Nos. 9-12 have been reprinted. They have the short Hindi overprint. Most stamps bear the word "Reprint." Those without it cannot be distinguished from the originals.

1885-91 Black Overprint Wmk. 39

13 A17 ½a green .75 .25
a. "GWALICR" 125.00 *150.00*
b. Double overprint 1,400.
c. Small raised "R" 100.00
14 A18 9p rose 47.50 *82.50*
15 A19 1a violet brown 3.00 .25
c. Small raised "R" 110.00
16 A20 1a6p bister brown 3.25 2.00
17 A21 2a ultramarine 4.00 .25
c. Small raised "R" 240.00
18 A22 3a orange 7.00 .25
c. Small raised "R" 1,300.
19 A23 4a olive green 8.50 2.00
c. Small raised "R" 600.00
20 A25 8a red violet 9.00 2.00
21 A26 12a violet, *red* 5.00 1.00
22 A27 1r gray 6.50 5.25

Wmk. 38

23 A14 6a bister 7.50 18.00
Nos. 13-23 (11) 102.00 *113.75*

The Hindi overprint measures 13½-14x2mm and 15-15½x2½mm as in the preceding issue.

1896 Wmk. 39

24 A28 2a6p green 14.00 *30.00*
a. "GWALICR" 1,000.
25 A29 1r car rose & grn 12.00 8.50
a. "GWALICR" 1,350 *2,400.*
26 A30 2r bis brn & rose 8.25 4.50
c. Small raised "R" 540.00 300.00
27 A30 3r grn & brn 11.00 5.25
c. Small raised "R" 650.00 325.00
28 A30 5r vio & blue 21.00 9.50
c. Small raised "R" 700.00 400.00
Nos. 24-28 (5) 66.25 57.75

The Hindi inscription varies from 13 to 15½mm long.

1899

29 A31 3p carmine rose .75 .25
a. Inverted overprint 1,650. 825.00

1901-04

30 A31 3p gray ('04) 11.00 *90.00*
31 A17 ½a light green 2.10 *2.40*
32 A19 1a carmine rose 1.90 .50
33 A21 2a violet 4.00 8.25
34 A28 2a6p ultra ('03) 2.25 9.50
Nos. 30-34 (5) 21.25 *110.65*

1903-08

35 A32 3p gray 2.10 .25
36 A33 ½a green 2.25 .45
37 A34 1a carmine rose 2.25 .45
38 A35 2a violet 3.00 1.50
39 A36 2a6p ultra ('05) 37.50 *120.00*
40 A37 3a brn org ('04) 3.00 .50
41 A38 4a olive green 3.75 .60
42 A39 6a bister ('06) 9.00 2.10
43 A40 8a red violet 7.50 2.40
44 A41 12a vio, *red* ('05) 4.50 *30.00*
45 A42 1r car rose & grn ('05) 4.50 2.50
46 A43 2r brown & rose 13.50 *16.50*
47 A43 3r grn & brn ('08) 42.50 *75.00*
48 A43 5r vio & bl ('08) 27.50 *40.00*
Nos. 35-48 (14) 162.85 *292.25*

There are two settings of the overprint on Nos. 35, 37-46. In the first (1903), "GWALIOR" is 14mm long and lines are spaced 1¾mm. In the second (1908), "GWALIOR" is 13mm long and lines are 2¾mm apart. No. 36 exists only with first overprint, Nos. 47-48 only with second.

1907

49 A44 ½a green .30 *1.00*
50 A45 1a carmine rose 2.25 .25

No. 49 exists with both settings of overprint. See note below No. 48.

1912-23

51 A46 3p gray .30 .25
52 A47 ½a green .30 .25
a. Inverted overprint *600.00*
53 A48 1a car rose .35 .25
a. Double overprint 37.50
54 A48 1a dk brown ('23) 1.60 .25
55 A49 2a violet 1.20 .25
56 A51 3a brown orange 1.00 .25
57 A52 4a olive grn ('13) .90 .90
58 A53 6a bister 1.90 2.10
59 A54 8a red vio ('13) 3.25 1.20
60 A55 12a claret ('14) 2.10 *6.00*
61 A56 1r green & red brn 13.50 .65
62 A56 2r brn & car rose 7.50 6.50
63 A56 5r violet & ultra 35.00 9.50
Nos. 51-63 (13) 68.90 28.35

India No. 104 Overprinted

1921

64 A48 9p on 1a rose 1.00 .75
a. Inverted overprint — —

India Stamps of 1911-26 Overprinted

Hindi Overprint 15mm Long

1923-27

66 A59 1½a choc ('25) 3.25 .75
67 A59 1½a rose ('27) .30 .25
a. Inverted overprint — —
68 A57 2a6p ultra ('25) 3.25 2.50
69 A57 2a6p brown org ('27) .50 *.75*
70 A51 3a ultra ('24) 3.75 .90
Nos. 66-70 (5) 11.05 5.15

Similar Ovpt. on India Stamps of 1926-35
Hindi Overprint 13½mm Long

1928-32 Wmk. 196

71 A46 3p slate ('32) 1.25 .25
72 A47 ½a green ('30) 1.90 .25
73 A48 1a dark brown 1.10 .25
74 A60 2a dull violet .70 .45
75 A51 3a ultramarine 1.25 .60
76 A61 4a olive green 1.60 1.50
77 A54 8a red violet 1.60 1.60
78 A55 12a claret 2.75 *5.25*

Overprinted

79 A56 1r green & brown 3.75 *6.00*
80 A56 2r brn org & car rose 6.75 6.50
81 A56 5r dk vio & ultra ('29) 24.00 *37.50*
82 A56 10r car & grn ('30) 82.50 62.50
83 A56 15r ol grn & ultra ('30) 130.00 100.00
84 A56 25r bl & ocher ('30) 275.00 250.00
Nos. 71-84 (14) 534.15 472.65

India Stamps of 1932-35 Overprinted in Black

Hindi Overprint 13½mm Long

1933-36

85 A71 ½a green ('36) .65 .25
86 A68 9p dk green ('33) 3.75 .45
87 A72 1a dk brown ('36) .30 .25
88 A69 1a3p violet ('36) .65 .25
89 A49 2a vermilion ('36) 3.75 5.25
Nos. 85-89 (5) 9.10 6.45

Same Ovpt. on India Stamps of 1937

1938-40 *Perf. 13½x14*

90 A80 3p slate ('40) 10.00 .25
91 A80 ½a brown 11.00 .25
92 A80 9p green ('40) 60.00 6.00
93 A80 1a carmine 10.00 .25
94 A81 3a yel green ('39) 35.00 7.50
95 A81 4a dk brown 55.00 5.25
96 A81 6a pck blue ('39) 5.00 *16.50*
Nos. 90-96 (7) 186.00 36.00
Set, never hinged 225.00

Same Overprinted on India Stamps of 1941-43

1942-49

100 A83 3p slate ('44) .55 .25
101 A83 ½a rose vio ('46) 1.25 .25
102 A83 9p light green .55 .25
103 A83 1a car rose ('44) 1.25 .25
104 A84 1½a dk purple ('44) 8.75 .25
105 A84 2a scarlet ('44) 1.90 .25
106 A84 3a violet ('44) 20.00 2.50
108 A85 4a choc ('44) 4.00 .25
109 A85 6a pck blue ('48) 17.50 *40.00*
110 A85 8a blue violet 4.75 *4.00*
111 A85 12a carmine lake 7.00 *35.00*

India Nos. 162-167 Overprinted

Perf. 13½x14

112 A82 1r brn & sl ('45) 15.00 2.50
113 A82 2r dk brn & dk vio ('49) 62.50 14.00
114 A82 5r dp ultra & dk grn ('49) 40.00 60.00
115 A82 10r rose car & dk vio ('49) 40.00 *62.50*
116 A82 15r dk grn & dk brn ('48) 110.00 *250.00*
117 A82 25r dk vio & blue vio ('48) 110.00 *190.00*
Nos. 100-106,108-117 (17) 445.00 662.25
Set, never hinged 525.00

India Stamps of 1941-43 Overprinted

1949

118 A83 3p slate 2.50 .75
119 A83 ½a rose violet 2.50 .75
120 A83 1a carmine rose 2.25 .90
121 A84 2a scarlet 32.50 3.25
122 A84 3a violet 80.00 45.00
123 A85 4a chocolate 9.25 5.00
124 A85 6a pck blue 67.50 *97.50*
125 A85 8a blue violet 140.00 82.50
126 A85 12a carmine lake 525.00 225.00
Nos. 118-126 (9) 861.50 460.65
Set, never hinged 1,050.

OFFICIAL STAMPS

India Stamps Overprinted in Black

1895 Wmk. 39 *Perf. 14*

O1 A17 ½a green .75 .25
a. Double overprint 1,400.
O2 A19 1a maroon 18.00 2.10
O3 A21 2a ultramarine 5.00 .60
O4 A23 4a olive green 5.25 2.25
O5 A25 8a red violet 6.50 5.00
O6 A29 1r car rose & grn 12.50 4.50
Nos. O1-O6 (6) 48.00 14.70

Nos. O1 to O6 inclusive are known with the last two characters of the lower word transposed.

1901-04

O7 A31 3p gray ('04) 3.75 *5.25*
O8 A17 ½a light green 1.10 .25
O9 A19 1a carmine rose 9.00 .25
O10 A21 2a violet ('03) 2.50 2.25
Nos. O7-O10 (4) 16.35 8.00

1902

O11 A31 3p carmine rose 1.90 .35

1903-05

O12 A32 3p gray .90 .25
O13 A33 ½a green 4.00 .25
O14 A34 1a carmine rose 1.40 .25
O15 A35 2a violet 2.25 .45
O16 A38 4a olive grn ('05) 22.50 2.50
O17 A40 8a red violet 9.50 1.00
O18 A42 1r car rose & grn ('05) 3.50 3.00
Nos. O12-O18 (7) 44.05 7.70

1907

O19 A44 ½a green 2.50 .25
O20 A45 1a carmine rose 10.00 .25

Two spacings of the overprint lines, 10mm and 8mm, are found on Nos. O12-O20.

No. O13 with 10mm spacing is known with the two overprint lines transposed. This is due to a shift in the positioning of the overprint, rathern than an actual transposition of the overprint.

1913

O21 A46 3p gray .35 .25
O22 A47 ½a green .30 .25
O23 A48 1a carmine rose .45 .25
a. Double overprint 97.50
O24 A49 2a violet 2.25 .25
O25 A52 4a olive green .90 *2.25*
O26 A54 8a red violet 1.90 1.50
O27 A56 1r grn & red brn 40.00 35.00
Nos. O21-O27 (7) 46.15 39.75

India No. O66 Overprinted

1921

O28 O6 9p on 1a rose .25 *.45*

India No. 83 Overprinted

1923

O29 A48 1a dark brown 5.50 .25

Similar Ovpt. on India Stamps of 1926-35

1927-35 Wmk. 196

O30 A46 3p slate .30 .25
O31 A47 ½a green .30 .25
O32 A48 1a dark brown .30 .25
O33 A60 2a dull violet .30 .25
O34 A61 4a olive green 1.00 .45
O35 A54 8a red violet .90 *1.60*

Overprinted

O36 A56 1r green & brown 1.50 *2.50*
O37 A56 2r brn org & car rose ('35) 29.00 *30.00*
O38 A56 5r dk vio & ultra ('32) 35.00 *250.00*
O39 A56 10r car & grn ('32) 240.00 *650.00*
Nos. O30-O39 (10) 308.60 *935.55*

India Stamps of 1926-35 Overprinted

1933-37 *Perf. 13½x14, 14*

O40 A71 ½a green ('36) .35 .25
O41 A68 9p dk green ('35) .30 .25
O42 A72 1a dk brown ('36) .30 .25
O43 A69 1a3p violet ('33) .75 .25
O44 A49 2a ver ('36) .30 *.60*
a. Small die ('36) 3.75 1.90
O45 A52 4a olive green ('37) .90 *1.10*
Nos. O40-O45 (6) 2.90 2.70

For surcharge see No. O62.

Same Overprint on India Stamps

1938 *Perf. 13½x14*

O46 A80 ½a brown 8.00 .45
Never hinged 9.50
O47 A80 1a carmine 2.00 .25
Never hinged 2.25

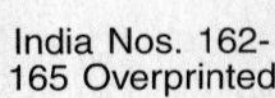

India Nos. 162-165 Overprinted

1945-48 **Wmk. 196** *Perf. 13½x14*

O48 A82 1r brown & slate 12.50 *32.50.*
O49 A82 2r dk brn & dk vio 22.50 *140.00*
O50 A82 5r dp ultra & dk grn ('46) 37.50 *825.00*
O51 A82 10r rose car & dk vio ('48) 100.00 *1,650.*
Nos. O48-O51 (4) 172.50 *2,648.*
Set, never hinged 200.00

India Official Stamps of 1939-43 Overprinted

1940-44 **Wmk. 196** *Perf. 13½x14*

O52 O8 3p slate .65 .25
O53 O8 ½a brown 5.50 .35
O54 O8 ½a dk rose vio ('43) .75 .25
O55 O8 9p green ('43) .85 *1.00*
O56 O8 1a car rose ('41) 2.75 .25
O57 O8 1a3p bister ('42) 55.00 2.50
O58 O8 1½a dl pur ('43) 1.50 .45
O59 O8 2a scarlet ('41) 1.50 .45
O60 O8 4a dk brn ('44) 1.50 *5.00*
O61 O8 8a blue vio ('44) 6.00 *14.00*
Nos. O52-O61 (10) 76.00 24.50
Set, never hinged 95.00

Gwalior No. O43 with Additional Surcharge in Black

1942

O62 A69 1a on 1a3p violet 30.00 4.50
Never hinged 37.50

JIND

'jind

(Jhind)

LOCATION — A State of India in the north Punjab.
AREA — 1,299 sq. mi.
POP. — 361,812 (1941)
CAPITAL — Sangrur

Previous stamp issues are listed under Feudatory States.

The varieties with small letters are not listed as the letters are merely broken and not from another font.

India Stamps Overprinted in Black

1885 **Wmk. 39** *Perf. 14*

33 A17 ½a green 7.00 *8.25*
a. Overprint reading down 140.00 *160.00*
34 A19 1a violet brown 62.50 *90.00*
a. Overprint reading down 1,400. *1,500.*
35 A21 2a ultra 29.00 *32.50*
a. Overprint reading down 1,000. *1,200.*
36 A25 8a red lilac 625.00
a. Overprint reading down *18,000.*
37 A27 1r gray 700.00
a. Overprint reading down *21,000.*

Wmk. 38

38 A9 4a green 97.50 *140.00*
Nos. 33-38 (6) 1,521. *270.75*

On the reprints of Nos. 33 to 38 "Jhind" measures 8mm instead of 9mm and "State" 9mm instead of 9½mm.

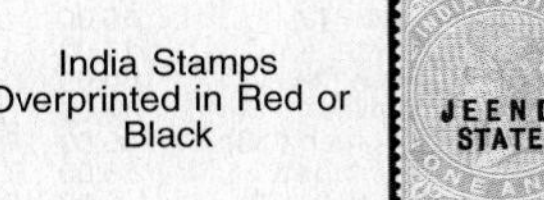

India Stamps Overprinted in Red or Black

1885 **Wmk. 39**

39 A17 ½a green (R) 210.00
40 A19 1a violet brown 210.00
41 A21 2a ultra (R) 210.00
42 A25 8a red lilac 290.00
43 A27 1r gray (R) 290.00

Wmk. 38

44 A9 4a green (R) 290.00
Nos. 39-44 (6) 1,500.

India Stamps Overprinted

1886 **Wmk. 39** **Red Overprint**

45 A17 ½a green 52.50
a. "JEIND" 1,800.
46 A21 2a ultramarine 57.50
a. "JEIND" 1,800.
47 A27 1r gray 90.00
a. "JEIND" 2,750.

Wmk. 38

48 A9 4a green 90.00
Nos. 45-48 (4) 290.00

Nos. 46, 47 and 48 were not placed in use.

1886-98 **Wmk. 39** **Black Overprint**

49 A17 ½a green ('88) 1.20 .25
a. Inverted overprint 300.00
50 A19 1a vio brn 3.75 .25
a. "JEIND" 750.00
51 A20 1a6p bis brn ('97) 3.75 *5.50*
52 A21 2a ultra 3.75 .60
53 A22 3a orange 5.00 1.00
54 A23 4a olive green 6.00 3.25
55 A25 8a red violet 12.50 *30.00*
a. "JEIND" 2,400.
56 A26 12a vio, *red* ('97) 10.00 *37.50*
57 A27 1r gray ('91) 17.50 *82.50*
58 A29 1r car rose & grn ('98) 16.50 *90.00*
59 A30 2r brn & rose ('97) 525.00 *1,500.*
60 A30 3r grn & brn ('97) 750.00 *1,350.*
61 A30 5r vio & bl ('97) 750.00 *1,250.*

Wmk. 38

62 A14 6a bister 6.50 *21.00*
Nos. 49-62 (14) 2,111. *4,372.*

1900 **Wmk. 39**

63 A31 3p carmine rose 1.60 *2.50*

1902-04

64 A31 3p gray ('04) .60 *6.00*
65 A17 ½a light green 7.00 *10.00*
66 A19 1a carmine rose 1.90 *10.00*
Nos. 64-66 (3) 9.50 *26.00*

1903-09

67 A32 3p gray .35 .25
68 A33 ½a green 2.50 *2.50*
69 A34 1a car rose ('09) 2.75 2.40
70 A35 2a violet ('06) 4.25 3.25
70A A36 2a6p ultra ('09) .85 *10.00*
71 A37 3a brown orange 3.25 .60
a. Double overprint 175.00 *325.00*
72 A38 4a olive green 11.50 *14.00*
73 A39 6a bister ('05) 9.25 *32.50*
74 A40 8a red violet 4.00 *32.50*
75 A41 12a vio, *red* ('05) 4.25 *17.50*
76 A42 1r car rose & grn ('05) 4.75 *32.50*
Nos. 67-76 (11) 47.70 *148.00*

1907

77 A44 ½a green .60 .25
78 A45 1a carmine rose 2.25 1.00

1913

80 A46 3p gray .30 3.50
81 A47 ½a green .30 1.10
82 A48 1a carmine rose .30 .65
83 A49 2a violet .30 6.25
84 A51 3a brown orange 2.25 *21.00*
85 A53 6a bister 12.50 *42.50*
Nos. 80-85 (6) 15.95 *75.00*

India Stamps of 1911-26 Overprinted

1913-14

88 A46 3p gray 1.50 .25
89 A47 ½a green 3.75 .25
90 A48 1a carmine rose 2.40 .25
91 A49 2a violet 6.50 1.90
92 A51 3a brown orange .75 *6.00*
93 A52 4a olive green 3.00 *14.00*
94 A53 6a bister 6.00 *24.00*
95 A54 8a red violet 8.25 *24.00*
96 A55 12a claret 7.50 *30.00*
97 A56 1r grn & red brn 17.50 *35.00*
Nos. 88-97 (10) 57.15 *135.65*

India No. 104 Overprinted

1921

98 A48 9p on 1a rose 1.90 *22.50*

India Stamps of 1913-19 Overprinted

1922

99 A58 1½a chocolate 5.00 *9.00*
100 A57 2a6p ultramarine .75 *7.00*

Same Overprint on India Stamps of 1911-26

1924

101 A48 1a dark brown 9.00 4.50
102 A59 1½a chocolate .75 *2.25*

Same Overprint on India No. 87

1925

103 A51 3a ultramarine 3.00 *7.50*

Same Overprint on India Stamps of 1911-26

1927

104 A59 1½a rose .30 *2.25*
105 A57 2a6p brown orange 1.90 12.00
106 A56 2r yel brn & car rose 9.50 *225.00*
107 A56 5r violet & ultra 67.50 *450.00*
Nos. 104-107 (4) 79.20 *689.25*

India Stamps of 1926-35 Overprinted

1927-32 **Wmk. 196**

108 A46 3p slate .30 .25
109 A47 ½a green .30 *.50*
110 A68 9p dk grn ('32) 2.75 .60
111 A48 1a dark brown .30 .25
112 A69 1a3p violet ('32) .35 *.45*
113 A59 1½a carmine rose .75 *5.50*
114 A60 2a dull violet 4.25 .60
115 A57 2a6p buff 2.00 *16.00*
116 A51 3a ultramarine 8.00 *27.50*
117 A61 4a olive green 2.00 *5.25*
118 A54 8a red violet 7.50 3.25
119 A55 12a claret 12.00 *32.50*

Indian Stamps of 1911-23 Overprinted

120 A56 1r grn & brn 6.50 *9.00*
121 A56 2r buff & car rose 55.00 *225.00*
122 A56 5r dk vio & ultra 16.00 *62.50*
123 A56 10r car rose & grn 19.00 *27.50*
124 A56 15r ol grn & blue 120.00 *1,050.*
125 A56 25r blue & ocher 190.00 *1,250.*
Nos. 108-125 (18) 447.00 *2,717.*

India Stamps of 1926-35 Overprinted

1934-37

126 A71 ½a green .45 .35
127 A72 1a dark brown 2.50 .45
128 A49 2a vermilion 4.75 .90
129 A51 3a carmine rose 4.25 .60
130 A70 3a6p deep blue ('37) 3.25 *30.00*
131 A52 4a olive green 4.25 2.25
132 A53 6a bister ('37) .85 *32.50*
Nos. 126-132 (7) 20.30 *67.05*

Same Overprint on India Stamps of 1937

1937-38 **Wmk. 196** *Perf. 13½x14*

133 A80 3p slate ('38) 11.00 3.75
134 A80 ½a brown ('38) .80 *7.50*
135 A80 9p green .80 *6.00*
136 A80 1a carmine .80 .90
137 A81 2a scarlet ('38) 1.75 *27.50*
138 A81 2a6p purple ('38) 1.40 *35.00*
139 A81 3a yel grn ('38) 6.75 *30.00*
140 A81 3a6p ultra ('38) 4.25 *35.00*
141 A81 4a dk brown ('38) 10.00 *27.50*
142 A81 6a pck blue ('38) 6.50 *42.50*
143 A81 8a blue vio ('38) 5.25 *35.00*
144 A81 12a car lake ('38) 3.00 *45.00*

Indian Stamps of 1937-40 Overprinted

1938

145 A82 1r brn & slate 13.00 *62.50*
146 A82 2r dk brn & dk vio 16.00 *190.00*
147 A82 5r dp ultra & dk grn 25.00 *125.00*
148 A82 10r rose car & dk violet 50.00 *120.00*
149 A82 15r dk grn & dk brown 110.00 *1,200.*
150 A82 25r dk vio & bl vio 575.00 *1,400.*
Nos. 133-150 (18) 841.30 *3,393.*
Set, never hinged 1,200.

India Stamps of 1937 Overprinted

1942-43 **Wmk. 196** *Perf. 13½x14*

155 A80 3p slate 17.50 *32.50*
156 A80 ½a brown 1.25 *3.75*
157 A80 9p green 16.00 *30.00*
158 A80 1a carmine 1.25 *9.00*
159 A82 1r brn & slate 11.00 *40.00*
160 A82 2r dk brn & dk violet 22.50 *52.50*
161 A82 5r dp ultra & dk green 50.00 *140.00*
162 A82 10r rose car & dk vio ('43) 75.00 *140.00*
163 A82 15r dk grn & dk brn ('43) 160.00 *250.00*
164 A82 25r dk vio & bl vio 75.00 *525.00*
Nos. 155-164 (10) 429.50 *1,223.*
Set, never hinged 510.00

Same Overprint on India Stamps of 1941-43

165 A83 3p slate .60 *2.10*
166 A83 ½a rose vio ('43) .60 *3.25*
167 A83 9p light green .95 *6.50*
168 A83 1a car rose ('43) 1.25 *2.25*
169 A84 1a3p bister ('43) 1.25 *7.50*
170 A84 1½a dark purple 10.00 7.50
171 A84 2a scarlet 2.25 *7.50*
172 A84 3a violet ('43) 30.00 9.00
173 A84 3½a ultramarine 11.00 *17.50*
174 A85 4a chocolate 7.50 *9.00*
175 A85 6a pck blue 8.00 *25.00*
176 A85 8a blue violet 5.25 *22.50*
177 A85 12a carmine lake 17.50 *27.50*
Nos. 165-177 (13) 96.15 *147.10*
Set, never hinged 115.00

OFFICIAL STAMPS

India Stamps Overprinted in Black

1885 Wmk. 39 ***Perf. 14***

O1 A17 ½a green 3.00 .60
a. "JHIND STATE" reading down 150.00 90.00
O2 A19 1a violet brown 1.00 .25
a. "JHIND STATE" reading down 17.50 11.00
O3 A21 2a ultra 60.00 *72.50*
a. "JHIND STATE" reading down *1,500.* *1,750.*
Nos. O1-O3 (3) 64.00 73.35

The reprints may be distinguished by the same measurements as the reprints of the corresponding regular issue.

India Stamps Overprinted in Red or Black

1885

O4 A17 ½a green (R) 150.00
O5 A19 1a violet brown 125.00
O6 A21 2a ultra (R) 140.00
Nos. O4-O6 (3) 415.00

India Stamps Overprinted

1886 Red Overprint

O7 A17 ½a green 42.50
a. "JEIND" *1,050.*
b. "ERVICE" 6,000.
O8 A21 2a ultramarine 47.50
a. "JEIND" *1,750.*
b. "ERVICE" 3,750.

No. O8 was not placed in use.

1886-96 Black Overprint

O9 A17 ½a green ('88) 2.50 .25
O10 A19 1a violet brown 16.00 2.25
a. "JEIND" *750.00*
b. "ERVICE"
O11 A21 2a ultramarine 4.25 1.50
O12 A23 4a olive green 4.50 3.00
O13 A25 8a red violet 7.00 *12.50*
O14 A29 1r car rose & grn ('96) 8.00 *75.00*
Nos. O9-O14 (6) 42.25 *94.50*

1902

O15 A17 ½a light green 3.75 .45

1903-06

O16 A32 3p gray .85 .25
O17 A33 ½a green 4.50 .25
a. "HIND" 4,500. 450.00
O18 A34 1a carmine rose 3.75 .25
a. "HIND" 5,250. 400.00
O19 A35 2a violet 2.50 .25
O20 A38 4a olive green 2.10 .65
O21 A40 8a red violet 7.50 2.25
O22 A42 1r car rose & grn ('06) 3.25 3.25
Nos. O16-O22 (7) 24.45 7.15

1907

O23 A44 ½a green 1.50 .25
O24 A45 1a carmine rose 2.50 .25

Indian Stamps of 1911-26 Overprinted

a

b

1914-27

O25 A46(a) 3p gray .30 .25
O26 A47(a) ½a green .40 .25
O27 A48(a) 1a car rose 1.00 .25
O28 A49(a) 2a violet .35 *.45*
O29 A52(a) 4a olive green 1.90 .25
O30 A54(a) 8a red violet 1.00 1.50
O31 A56(b) 1r grn & red brn 3.75 2.50
O32 A56(b) 2r yel brn & car rose ('27) 27.50 *100.00*
O33 A56(b) 5r vio & ultra ('27) 35.00 *375.00*
Nos. O25-O33 (9) 71.20 *480.45*

India Nos. 83 and 89 Overprinted Type "a"

1924-27

O34 A48 1a dark brown .90 .25
O35 A53 6a bister ('27) 2.50 *3.25*

India Stamps of 1926-35 Overprinted — c

1927-32

O36 A46 3p slate .25 .25
O37 A47 ½a green .25 *1.50*
O38 A68 9p dark green ('32) .90 .25
O39 A48 1a dark brown .25 .25
O40 A69 1a3p violet ('32) .60 .25
O41 A60 2a dull violet .35 .25
O42 A61 4a olive green .50 .35
O43 A54 8a red violet .90 *2.50*
O44 A55 12a claret 3.25 *27.50*

Indian Stamps of 1911-23 Overprinted — d

O45 A56 1r green & brown 7.50 *8.25*
O46 A56 2r buff & car rose 75.00 62.50
O47 A56 5r dk vio & ultra 19.00 *400.00*
O48 A56 10r car rose & grn 57.50 *225.00*
Nos. O36-O48 (13) 166.25 *728.85*

India Stamps of 1926-35 Overprinted Type "c"

1934-37

O49 A71 ½a green .30 .25
O50 A72 1a dark brown .30 .25
O51 A49 2a vermilion .45 .25
O52 A57 2a6p buff ('37) 1.90 *30.00*
O53 A52 4a olive green 9.00 .45
O54 A53 6a bister ('37) 5.50 25.00
Nos. O49-O54 (6) 17.45 56.20

India Nos. 151-153 Overprinted Type "c"

1937-42 ***Perf. 13½x14***

O55 A80 ½a brown ('42) 67.50 .45
O56 A80 9p green 2.50 *24.00*
O57 A80 1a carmine 1.90 .45

India Nos. 162-165 Overprinted Type "d"

O58 A82 1r brn & sl ('40) 45.00 *67.50*
O59 A82 2r dk brn & dk vio ('40) 47.50 *375.00*
O60 A82 5r dp ultra & dk grn ('40) 100.00 *600.00*
O61 A82 10r rose car & dk vio ('40) 450.00 *1,500.*
Nos. O55-O61 (7) 714.40 *2,567.*
Set, never hinged 875.00

India Official Stamps of 1939-43 Overprinted

1940-43

O62 O8 3p slate .65 *3.00*
O63 O8 ½a brown 2.10 1.90
O64 O8 ½a dk rose vio ('43) .65 .45
O65 O8 9p green 3.25 19.00
O66 O8 1a car rose 3.75 .25
O67 O8 1½a dull pur ('43) 9.25 2.40
O68 O8 2a scarlet 8.50 .45
O69 O8 2½a purple 5.25 *14.00*
O70 O8 4a dark brown 9.50 7.00
O71 O8 8a blue violet 9.50 *12.00*

India Nos. 162-165 Overprinted

1942 Wmk. 196 ***Perf. 13½x14***

O72 A82 1r brown & slate 19.00 *82.50*
O73 A82 2r dk brn & dk vio 45.00 *250.00*
O74 A82 5r dp ultra & dk green 75.00 *625.00*
O75 A82 10r rose car & dk violet 150.00 *825.00*
Nos. O62-O75 (14) 341.40 *1,843.*
Set, never hinged 500.00

NABHA

'näb-hə

LOCATION — A State of India in the eastern and southeastern Punjab
AREA — 966 sq. mi.
POP. — 340,044 (1941)
CAPITAL — Nabha

The varieties with small letters in the overprint are not listed as the letters are merely broken and not from another font.

Indian Stamps Overprinted in Black

1885 Wmk. 39 ***Perf. 14***

1 A17 ½a green 6.25 *9.00*
2 A19 1a violet brown 82.50 *290.00*
3 A21 2a ultramarine 37.50 *97.50*
4 A25 8a red lilac 475.00
5 A27 1r gray 550.00

Wmk. 38

6 A9 4a green 125.00 *375.00*

On the reprints "Nabha" and "State" each measure 9½mm. On the originals they measure 11 and 10mm respectively.

Indian Stamps Overprinted

1885 Wmk. 39 Red Overprint

7 A17 ½a green 1.90 1.50
8 A21 2a ultramarine 3.75 3.25
9 A27 1r gray 190.00 *450.00*

Wmk. 38

10 A9 4a green 67.50 *325.00*

1885-97 Wmk. 39 Black Overprint

11 A17 ½a green .90 .25
12 A18 9p rose ('92) .30 *5.25*
13 A19 1a violet brown 4.50 1.50
14 A20 1a6p bister brn 2.50 *6.00*
a. "ABHA" 450.00
15 A21 2a ultramarine 4.50 3.00
16 A22 3a orange 16.00 *32.50*
17 A23 4a olive green 9.00 5.00
18 A25 8a red lilac 6.00 5.25
19 A26 12a vio, *red* ('89) 7.00 *8.25*
20 A27 1r gray 22.50 *90.00*
21 A29 1r car rose & grn ('93) 21.00 10.50
a. "N BHA" —
22 A30 2r brn & rose ('97) 210.00 *450.00*
23 A30 3r grn & brn ('97) 210.00 *550.00*
24 A30 5r vio & blk ('97) 225.00 *825.00*

Wmk. 38

25 A14 6a bister ('89) 5.50 *6.50*
Nos. 11-25 (15) 744.70 *1,999.*

Nos. 7, 8, 9, 10, 13, and 18 have been reprinted. They usually bear the overprint "Specimen."

1900 Wmk. 39

26 A31 3p carmine rose .45 .25

1903-09

27 A32 3p gray .95 .25
28 A33 ½a green 1.40 1.00
a. "NABH" 1,650.
29 A34 1a car rose 2.10 2.25
30 A35 2a violet 3.25 *5.25*
30A A36 2a6p ultra 24.50 *130.00*
31 A37 3a brn org 2.00 .60
32 A38 4a olive green 6.00 2.50
33 A39 6a bister 5.00 *30.00*
34 A40 8a red violet 13.00 *40.00*
35 A41 12a violet, *red* 5.50 *40.00*
36 A42 1r car rose & grn 12.00 *27.50*
Nos. 27-36 (11) 75.70 *279.35*

1907

37 A44 ½a green 2.25 1.90
38 A45 1a carmine rose 2.25 1.00

1913

40 A46 3p gray .75 .75
41 A47 ½a green .75 .45
42 A48 1a carmine rose 1.60 .25
43 A49 2a violet 1.50 1.50
44 A51 3a brown orange .75 .45
45 A52 4a olive green 1.00 *3.00*
46 A53 6a bister 1.90 *9.50*
47 A54 8a red violet 9.50 9.00
48 A55 12a claret 4.50 *35.00*
49 A56 1r green & red brn 15.00 11.00
Nos. 40-49 (10) 37.25 *70.90*

1924

50 A48 1a dark brown 10.00 6.00

India Stamps of 1926-35 Overprinted

1927-32 Wmk. 196

51 A46 3p slate ('32) 2.50 .25
52 A47 ½a green 1.50 .45
53 A48 1a dark brown 2.25 .25
54 A60 2a dull violet ('32) 3.75 .50
55 A57 2a6p buff ('32) 1.75 *14.00*
56 A51 3a blue ('30) 4.50 2.10
57 A61 4a olive green ('32) 6.75 3.75

Indian Stamps of 1937-40 Overprinted

58 A56 2r brn org & car rose ('32) 47.50 *210.00*
59 A56 5r dk vio & ultra ('32) 110.00 *600.00*
Nos. 51-59 (9) 180.50 *831.30*

India Stamps of 1926-35 Overprinted

1936-37

63 A71 ½a green .75 .60
64 A68 9p dark green ('37) 3.00 1.60
65 A72 1a dark brown .75 .45
66 A69 1a3p violet ('37) 3.50 *11.00*
67 A51 3a car rose ('37) 5.00 *25.00*
68 A52 4a olive green ('37) 7.50 7.50
Nos. 63-68 (6) 20.50 *46.15*
Set, never hinged 25.00

Same Overprint in Black on 1937 Stamps of India

1938-39 ***Perf. 13½x14***

69 A80 3p slate 9.50 2.25
70 A80 ½a brown 7.50 2.50
71 A80 9p green 21.00 7.50
72 A80 1a carmine 3.25 1.50
73 A81 2a scarlet 1.25 *12.00*

74 A81 2a6p purple 1.25 *17.50*
75 A81 3a yel green 1.50 *9.00*
76 A81 3a6p ultramarine 1.75 *37.50*
77 A81 4a dark brown 8.00 *10.50*
78 A81 6a peacock blue 3.50 *40.00*
79 A81 8a blue violet 2.25 *37.50*
80 A81 12a car lake 3.00 *37.50*

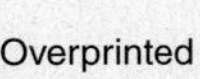
Overprinted

81 A82 1r brown & slate 13.00 *52.50*
82 A82 2r dk brn & dk vio 32.50 *175.00*
83 A82 5r dp ultra & dk green 42.50 *300.00*
84 A82 10r rose car & dk vio ('39) 65.00 *600.00*
85 A82 15r dk grn & dk brn ('39) 200.00 *1,250.*
86 A82 25r dk vio & blue vio ('39) 150.00 *1,250.*
Nos. 69-86 (18) 566.75 *3,843.*
Set, never hinged 1,200.

India Stamps of 1937 Overprinted in Black

1942 ***Perf. 13½x14***
87 A80 3p slate 50.00 9.00
88 A80 ½a brown 100.00 10.50
89 A80 9p green 14.00 24.00
90 A80 1a carmine 15.00 6.50
Nos. 87-90 (4) 179.00 50.00
Set, never hinged 210.00

Same on India Nos. 168-179

1942-46 **Wmk. 196**
100 A83 3p slate 1.25 1.25
101 A83 ½a rose vio ('43) 3.25 2.50
102 A83 9p lt green ('43) 2.50 2.50
103 A83 1a car rose ('46) 1.10 *6.50*
104 A84 1a3p bister ('44) 1.10 *5.50*
105 A84 1½a dark pur ('43) 2.50 *4.50*
106 A84 2a scarlet ('44) 1.20 *6.50*
107 A84 3a violet ('44) 7.00 7.00
108 A84 3½a ultramarine 18.00 *100.00*
109 A85 4a choc ('43) 1.90 1.50
110 A85 6a pck blue ('44) 15.00 *82.50*
111 A85 8a blue vio ('44) 13.50 62.50
112 A85 12a car lake ('44) 12.00 *100.00*
Nos. 100-112 (13) 80.30 *382.75*
Set, never hinged 110.00

OFFICIAL STAMPS

Indian Stamps Overprinted in Black

1885 **Wmk. 39** ***Perf. 14***
O1 A17 ½a green 7.50 2.25
O2 A19 1a violet brown 1.00 .30
O3 A21 2a ultra 125.00 *250.00*
Nos. O1-O3 (3) 133.50 *252.55*

The reprints have the same measurements as the reprints of the regular issue of the same date.

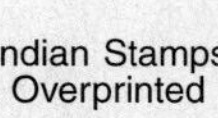
Indian Stamps Overprinted

1885 **Red Overprint**
O4 A17 ½a green 11.00 8.25
O5 A21 2a ultramarine 2.40 *.80*

1885-97 **Black Overprint**
O6 A17 ½a green .60 .25
a. Period after "SERVICE" 190.00 3.25
O7 A19 1a violet brown 3.00 .35
a. "NABHA STATE" double 2,750. *375.00*
b. Period after "SERVICE" 13.50 1.10
O8 A21 2a ultra 5.00 2.50
O9 A22 3a orange 37.50 *140.00*
O10 A23 4a olive green 5.25 2.25
O11 A25 8a red vio ('89) 4.00 2.25
O12 A26 12a vio, *red* ('89) 9.50 *32.50*
O13 A27 1r gray ('89) 62.50 *525.00*
O14 A29 1r car rose & grn ('97) 24.00 *35.00*

Wmk. 38
O15 A14 6a bister ('89) 32.50 *52.50*
Nos. O6-O15 (10) 183.85 *792.60*

Nos. O4, O5, and O7 have been reprinted. They usually bear the overprint "Specimen."

1903-06 **Wmk. 39**
O16 A32 3p gray ('06) 3.75 25.00
O17 A33 ½a green 1.20 .50
O18 A34 1a carmine rose 1.20 .25
O19 A35 2a violet 5.00 2.10
O20 A38 4a olive green 2.40 .75
O21 A40 8a red violet 2.50 2.25
O22 A42 1r car rose & grn 2.50 *3.75*
Nos. O16-O22 (7) 18.55 34.60

1907
O23 A44 ½a green 2.50 .75
O24 A45 1a carmine rose 1.00 .40

1913
O25 A52 4a olive green 17.50 *100.00*
O26 A56 1r grn & red brn 92.50 *750.00*

Indian Stamps of 1911-26 Overprinted

a

b

1913
O27 A46(a) 3p gray 1.40 *15.00*
O28 A47(a) ½a green .85 .25
O29 A48(a) 1a carmine rose .75 .25
O30 A49(a) 2a violet 1.60 .25
O31 A52(a) 4a olive green 1.25 .90
O32 A54(a) 8a red violet 2.10 *3.00*
O33 A56(b) 1r grn & red brn 8.50 6.50
Nos. O27-O33 (7) 16.45 *26.15*

India Stamps of 1926-35 Overprinted

Perf. 13½x14, 14

1932-45 **Wmk. 196**
O34 A46 3p slate .30 .25
O35 A72 1a dk brn ('35) .30 .25
O36 A52 4a ol grn ('45) 35.00 3.75
O37 A54 8a red violet ('37) 1.50 *4.00*
Nos. O34-O37 (4) 37.10 8.25

Same Overprint in Black on India Stamps of 1937

1938
O38 A80 9p green 6.00 6.00
Never hinged 7.00
O39 A80 1a carmine 22.50 1.60
Never hinged 27.50

Official Stamps of India 1939-43 Overprinted in Black

1942-44 ***Perf. 13½x14***
O40 O8 3p slate 1.25 *3.00*
O41 O8 ½a brown ('43) 1.20 .45
O42 O8 ½a dk rose vio ('44) 4.75 2.25
O43 O8 9p green ('43) 1.25 .45
O44 O8 1a car rose ('43) .65 .25
O45 O8 1½a dull purple ('43) .70 .60
O46 O8 2a scarlet ('43) 2.25 2.25
O47 O8 4a dark brown ('43) 3.50 *5.25*
O48 O8 8a blue violet ('43) 6.75 *30.00*

India Nos. 162-164 Overprinted in Black

O49 A82 1r brown & slate 9.00 *62.50*
O50 A82 2r dk brn & dk vio 32.50 *275.00*
O51 A82 5r dp ultra & dk green 175.00 *825.00*
Nos. O40-O51 (12) 238.80 *1,207.*
Set, never hinged 300.00

PATIALA

ˌpət-ē-ˈäl-ə

LOCATION — A State of India in the central Punjab
AREA — 5,942 sq. mi.
POP. — 1,936,259 (1941)
CAPITAL — Patiala

The varieties with small letters in the overprint are not listed as the letters are merely broken and not from another font.

Indian Stamps Overprinted in Red

1884 **Wmk. 39** ***Perf. 14***
1 A17 ½a green 6.00 *7.00*
a. Double ovpt., one horiz. 4,750. 1,200.
2 A19 1a violet brown 75.00 *110.00*
a. Double overprint
b. Double ovpt., one in black 1,050.
c. Pair, one as "b," one without overprint
3 A21 2a ultra 19.00 *24.00*
4 A25 8a red lilac 650.00 *1,600.*
a. Double ovpt., one in black 190.00 *650.00*
c. Overprint reversed
d. Pair like "a," one with overprint reversed
5 A27 1r gray 225.00 *950.00*

Wmk. 38
6 A9 4a green 140.00 150.00
Nos. 1-6 (6) 1,115. *2,841.*

Indian Stamps Overprinted in Red

1885 **Wmk. 39**
7 A17 ½a green 3.25 .45
a. "AUTTIALLA" 24.00 *52.50*
c. "STATE" only
8 A21 2a ultra 9.00 2.50
a. "AUTTIALLA" 62.50
9 A27 1r gray 24.00 *125.00*
a. "AUTTIALLA" 650.00

Wmk. 38
10 A9 4a green 6.00 *6.25*
a. Double overprint, one in black 375.00
b. Pair, one as "a," one with black overprint

Same, Overprinted in Black

Wmk. 39
11 A19 1a violet brown .90 .45
a. "AUTTIALLA" 100.00
c. Double overprint, one in red 17.50 *140.00*
d. Pair, one as "c," one without overprint
12 A25 8a red lilac 35.00 *82.50*
a. "AUTTIALLA" 550.00
Nos. 7-12 (6) 78.15 *217.15*

Nos. 7-12 have been reprinted. Most of them bear the word "Reprint." The few stamps that escaped the overprint cannot be distinguished from the originals.

The error "AUTTIALLA" has been reprinted in entire sheets, in red on the ½, 2, 4a and 1r and in black on the ½, 1, 2, 4, 8a and 1r. "STATE" is 7¾mm long, instead of 8½mm. Most stamps are overprinted "Reprint."

Same, Overprinted in Black

1891-96
13 A17 ½a green .75 .25
14 A18 9p rose 1.50 3.25
15 A19 1a violet brown 2.10 .45
a. "STATE" only 300.00 *625.00*
16 A20 1a6p bister brown 2.10 *3.00*
17 A21 2a ultra 3.25 1.50
18 A22 3a orange 3.75 1.10
19 A23 4a ol grn ('96) 3.75 1.10
a. "STATE" only 750.00 375.00
20 A25 8a red vio ('96) 5.50 *24.00*
21 A26 12a violet, *red* 3.75 *24.00*
22 A29 1r car rose & grn ('96) 6.50 *82.50*
23 A30 2r brn & rose ('95) 210.00 *1,250.*
24 A30 3r grn & brn ('95) 290.00 *1,350.*
25 A30 5r vio & bl ('95) 325.00 *1,400.*

Wmk. 38
26 A14 6a bister 3.75 *22.50*
Nos. 13-26 (14) 861.70 4,164.

1899 **Wmk. 39**
27 A31 3p carmine rose .45 .25
a. Pair, one without overprint 6,000.

1902
28 A17 ½a light green 1.50 .90
29 A19 1a carmine rose 3.75 2.50

1903-06
31 A32 3p gray .50 .25
32 A33 ½a green 1.40 .25
33 A34 1a carmine rose 1.75 .25
a. Pair, one without overprint *1,500.*
34 A35 2a violet 2.00 1.00
35 A37 3a brown orange 2.00 .50
36 A38 4a olive green ('06) 3.50 2.25
37 A39 6a bister ('05) 4.25 *15.00*
38 A40 8a red violet ('06) 4.75 4.50
39 A41 12a vio, *red* ('06) 9.25 *40.00*
40 A42 1r car rose & grn ('05) 5.50 *9.00*
Nos. 31-40 (10) 34.90 *73.00*

1908
41 A44 ½a green .60 .35
42 A45 1a carmine rose 2.50 1.50

1912-14
43 A46 3p gray .35 .25
44 A47 ½a green .85 .25
45 A48 1a carmine rose 2.00 .25
46 A49 2a violet 1.90 2.25
47 A51 3a brown orange 3.25 2.50
48 A52 4a olive green 4.50 5.25
49 A53 6a bister 2.50 *6.50*
50 A54 8a red violet 3.75 3.75
51 A55 12a claret 4.75 *15.00*
52 A56 1r green & red brn 12.00 *22.50*
Nos. 43-52 (10) 35.85 *58.50*

1922-26
53 A48 1a dk brown ('23) 3.50 .75
54 A58 1½a chocolate .35 *.85*
55 A51 3a ultra ('26) 4.25 *14.00*
56 A56 2r yel brn & car rose ('26) 18.00 *225.00*
57 A56 5r vio & ultra ('26) 45.00 *300.00*
Nos. 53-57 (5) 71.10 *540.60*

India Stamps of 1926-35 Overprinted

1928-34 **Wmk. 196**
60 A46 3p slate 2.50 .25
61 A47 ½a green .35 .25
62 A68 9p dark green 2.75 1.50
63 A48 1a dark brown .95 .35
64 A69 1a3p violet 3.75 .25
65 A60 2a dull violet 2.10 .60
66 A57 2a6p buff 6.00 4.00
67 A51 3a blue 3.75 4.00
68 A61 4a olive green 6.50 3.00
69 A54 8a red violet 10.50 6.00

Indian Stamps of 1911-23 Overprinted

70 A56 1r green & brown 9.00 *15.00*
71 A56 2r buff & car rose 13.50 *82.50*
Nos. 60-71 (12) 61.65 117.70

India Stamps of 1926-35 Overprinted Like Nos. 60-69

1935-37 ***Perf. 14***
75 A71 ½a green ('37) 1.00 .45
76 A72 1a dk brown ('36) 1.40 .25
77 A49 2a ver ('36) .50 *2.25*
78 A51 3a car rose ('37) 7.00 *8.00*
79 A52 4a olive green 2.25 3.50
Nos. 75-79 (5) 12.15 *14.45*
Set, never hinged 29.00

Same Overprint in Black on Stamps of India, 1937

1937-38 ***Perf. 13½x14***
80 A80 3p slate ('38) 21.00 .50
81 A80 ½a brown ('38) 8.50 .75
82 A80 9p green 5.25 1.50
83 A80 1a carmine 3.00 .25
84 A81 2a scarlet ('38) 1.60 *14.00*
85 A81 2a6p purple ('38) 6.00 *30.00*
86 A81 3a yel green ('38) 6.50 *13.50*
87 A81 3a6p ultra ('38) 6.75 *37.50*
88 A81 4a dk brn ('38) 24.00 25.00
89 A81 6a pck blue ('38) 25.00 *90.00*
90 A81 8a blue violet ('38) 27.50 *62.50*
91 A81 12a car lake ('38) 25.00 *105.00*

Overprinted Like Nos. 70-71

1938
92 A82 1r brown & slate 30.00 *62.50*
93 A82 2r dk brn & dk vio 30.00 *160.00*
94 A82 5r dp ultra & dk green 40.00 *375.00*
95 A82 10r rose car & dk vio 52.50 *600.00*
96 A82 15r dk grn & dk brn 130.00 *950.00*
97 A82 25r dk vio & bl vio 150.00 *950.00*
Nos. 80-97 (18) 592.60 *3,478.*
Set, never hinged 850.00

India Nos. 150-153 Overprinted in Black

1942-43 ***Perf. 13½x14***
98 A80 3p slate 11.50 4.00
99 A80 ½a brown ('43) 6.75 3.25
100 A80 9p green ('43) 320.00 12.00
101 A80 1a carmine 25.00 3.75
Nos. 98-101 (4) 363.25 23.00
Set, never hinged 515.00

India Stamps of 1941-43 with same Overprint in Black

1942-47 ***Perf. 13½x14***
102 A83 3p slate 4.25 .25
103 A83 ½a rose vio ('43) 4.25 .25
104 A83 9p lt grn ('43) 1.60 .25
a. Pair, one without overprint *4,750.*
105 A83 1a car rose ('46) 1.10 .25
106 A84 1a3p bister ('43) 1.75 *5.25*
107 A84 1½a dk pur ('43) 13.50 5.50
108 A84 2a scar ('46) 9.50 .75
109 A84 3a violet ('46) 8.50 3.75
110 A84 3½a ultra ('46) 20.00 *57.50*
111 A85 4a choc ('46) 9.25 6.50
112 A85 6a pck blue ('46) 3.50 *45.00*
113 A85 8a blue vio ('46) 3.25 *22.50*
114 A85 12a car lake ('45) 30.00 *125.00*

No. 102 India No. 162 Overprinted in Black

115 A82 1r brn & slate ('47) 16.00 *120.00*
Nos. 102-115 (14) 126.45 *392.75*
Set, never hinged 170.00

OFFICIAL STAMPS

Indian Stamps Overprinted in Black and Red

1884 **Wmk. 39** ***Perf. 14***
O1 A17 ½a green 27.50 .60
O2 A19 1a vio brown 1.50 .25
a. "SERVICE" double 3,000. 950.00
b. "SERVICE" inverted 2,500.
c. "PUTTIALLA STATE" dbl. 175.00
d. "PUTTIALLA STATE" invtd. 3,000. 400.00
O3 A21 2a ultra *7,500.* 175.00

Overprinted in Red or Black

a b

1885-90
O4 A17(a) ½a grn (R & Bk) 2.25 .35
a. "AUTTIALLA" 80.00 25.00
d. "SERVICE" double 1,050.
O5 A17(b) ½a green (Bk) 2.25 .25
O6 A19(a) 1a vio brn (Bk) 2.25 .25
a. "AUTTILLA" 1,050. 72.50
c. "SERVICE" dble., one invtd. 900.00
d. "SERVICE" double 3,000.
O7 A21(b) 2a ultra (R) 1.10 .60
c. "SERVICE" dbl., one invtd. 45.00 *290.00*
Nos. O4-O7 (4) 7.85 1.45

There are reprints of Nos. O4, O6 and O7. That of No. O4 has "SERVICE" overprinted in red in large letters and that of No. O6 has the same overprint in black. The originals have the word in small black letters. The reprints of No. O7, except those overprinted "Reprint," cannot be distinguished from the originals. These three reprints also exist with the error "AUTTIALLA."

Same, Overprinted in Black

1891-1900
O8 A17 ½a green ('95) .75 .25
b. "SERVICE" inverted 90.00
O9 A19 1a vio brn ('00) 9.00 .25
a. "SERVICE" inverted 90.00
O10 A21 2a ultramarine 5.00 3.25
a. "SERVICE" inverted 90.00 *300.00*
O11 A22 3a orange 3.75 5.00
O12 A23 4a olive green 3.00 .45
O13 A25 8a red violet 5.25 2.50
O14 A26 12a violet, *red* 3.50 .80
O15 A27 1r gray 3.75 1.00

Wmk. 38
O16 A14 6a bister 2.40 .50
Nos. O8-O16 (9) 36.40 14.00

1902 **Wmk. 39**
O17 A19 1a carmine rose 1.40 .25

1903
O18 A29 1r car rose & green 9.00 15.00

1903-09
O19 A32 3p gray .60 .25
O20 A33 ½a green 1.50 .25
O21 A34 1a carmine rose .90 .25
O22 A35 2a violet 1.20 .25
O23 A37 3a brown orange 6.00 5.25
O24 A38 4a olive green ('05) 4.00 .25
O25 A40 8a red violet 2.50 1.10
O26 A42 1r car rose & grn ('06) 3.00 1.20
Nos. O19-O26 (8) 19.70 8.80

1907
O27 A44 ½a green .75 .25
O28 A45 1a carmine rose .90 .25

India Stamps of 1911-26 Overprinted

a b

1913-26
O29 A46(a) 3p gray .30 .25
O30 A47(a) ½a green .25 .25
O31 A48(a) 1a car rose .25 .25
O32 A49(a) 2a violet 1.20 1.10
O33 A52(a) 4a olive green .75 .50
O34 A54(a) 8a red violet .80 *1.00*
O35 A56(b) 1r grn & red brn 1.75 2.10
O36 A56(b) 2r yel brn & car rose ('26) 24.00 *75.00*
O37 A56(b) 5r vio & ultra ('26) 15.00 *35.00*
Nos. O29-O37 (9) 44.30 *115.45*

Same Overprint on India Nos. 83 and 89

1925-26
O38 A48(a) 1a dark brown 9.50 1.50
O39 A53(a) 6a bister ('26) 2.10 *3.75*

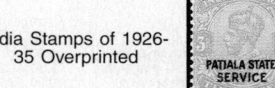

India Stamps of 1926-35 Overprinted

1927-36 **Wmk. 196**
O40 A46 3p slate .25 .25
O41 A47 ½a green 1.25 .80
O42 A48 1a dark brown .25 .25
O43 A69 1a3p violet .60 .25
O44 A60 2a dull violet .25 *.45*
O45 A60 2a vermilion .45 .50
O46 A57 2a6p buff 3.75 .50
O47 A61 4a olive green .75 .45
O48 A54 8a red violet 1.60 1.00

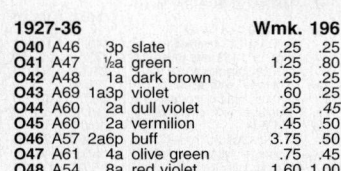

Indian Stamps of 1911-23 Overprinted

O49 A56 1r green & brown 6.50 5.00
O50 A56 2r brn org & car rose ('36) 20.00 *62.50*
Nos. O40-O50 (11) 35.65 *71.95*

India Stamps of 1926-34 Overprinted

1935-36
O51 A71 ½a green ('36) .25 .25
O52 A72 1a dark brown ('36) .45 .45
O53 A49 2a vermilion .30 *.45*
a. Small die 21.00 7.50
O54 A52 4a olive green ('36) 3.50 2.50
Nos. O51-O54 (4) 4.50 *3.65*
Set, never hinged 5.00

Same Overprint on India Nos. 151-153

1938-39 ***Perf. 13½x14***
O55 A80 ½a brown ('39) .95 .30
O56 A80 9p green ('39) 16.00 *95.00*
O57 A80 1a carmine .95 .60
Nos. O55-O57 (3) 17.90 *95.90*
Set, never hinged 22.00

India No. 136 Surcharged in Black

1939 ***Perf. 14***
O58 A69 1a on 1a3p violet 15.00 5.25
Never hinged 18.00

"SERVICE" measures 9¼mm.

No. 64 Surcharged in Black

1940
O59 A69 1a on 1a3p violet 12.50 5.00
Never hinged 15.00

"SERVICE" measures 8½mm.

India Nos. 162-164 Overprinted

Perf. 13½x14
O60 A82 1r brown & slate 1.25 *10.50*
O61 A82 2r dk brn & dk vio 7.50 7.50
O62 A82 5r dp ultra & dk grn 21.00 95.00
Set, never hinged 36.00

India Official Stamps of 1939-43 Overprinted

1940-45
O63 O8 3p slate ('41) 1.90 .25
O64 O8 ½a brown 5.25 .25
O65 O8 ½a dk rose vio ('43) 1.10 .25
O66 O8 9p green 1.10 .75
O67 O8 1a carmine rose 3.50 .25
O68 O8 1a3p bister ('41) 1.25 .35
O69 O8 1½a dull purple ('45) 6.75 1.90
O70 O8 2a scarlet ('41) 11.00 .50
O71 O8 2½a purple ('41) 4.00 1.50
O72 O8 4a dk brown ('45) 1.90 *3.75*
O73 O8 8a blue violet ('45) 5.25 *9.00*

India Nos. 162-164 Overprinted in Black

O74 A82 1r brn & slate ('43) 5.25 *16.00*
O75 A82 2r dk brn & dk vio ('45) 13.50 *95.00*
O76 A82 5r dp ultra & dk grn ('45) 22.00 *125.00*
Nos. O63-O76 (14) 83.75 *254.75*
Set, never hinged 145.00

INDIA - FEUDATORY STATES

ALWAR

'əl-wər

LOCATION — A Feudatory State of India, lying southwest of Delhi in the Jaipur Residency.
AREA — 3,158 sq. mi.
POP. — 749,751.
CAPITAL — Alwar

Katar (Indian Dagger) — A1

1877 Unwmk. Litho. *Rouletted*

1 A1 ¼a ultramarine 7.00 1.60
 a. ¼a blue 7.00 1.60
2 A1 1a brown 5.25 1.90
 a. 1a yellow brown 16.00 8.25
 b. 1a red brown 5.00 2.25

Redrawn

1899-1901 *Pin-perf. 12*

3 A1 ¼a sl blue, wide margins 12.50 4.50
 a. Horiz. pair, imperf. between 600.00 *750.00*
 b. Vert. pair, imperf. between 1,200. *1,250.*
4 A1 ¼a yel grn, narrow margins ('01) 11.00 4.00
 a. Horiz. pair, imperf. between 950.00
 b. Imperf, pair 950.00
 c. ¼a emer, wide margins ('99) 600.00
 d. ¼a emer, narrow margins 5.25 4.75
 e. As "d," imperf, pair 550.00
 f. As "d," vert. pair, imperf horiz. 500.00
 g. As "d," horiz. pair, imperf vert. 450.00 *525.00*
 h. As "d," vert. pair, imperf horiz. 450.00 *525.00*

Nos. 3 and 4b are printed farther apart in the sheet.

On Nos. 3 and 4, the shading of the left border line is missing.

Nos. 1 to 4 occasionally show portions of the papermaker's watermark, W. T. & Co.

Alwar stamps became obsolete in 1902.

BAMRA

'bäm-rə

LOCATION — A Feudatory State in the Eastern States, Orissa States Agency, Bengal.
AREA — 1,988 sq. mi.
POP. — 151,259
CAPITAL — Deogarh

Stamps of Bamra were issued without gum.

A1

1888 Unwmk. Typeset *Imperf.*

1 A1 ¼a black, *yellow* 700.00
 a. "g" inverted *7,000.*
2 A1 ½a black, *rose* 125.00
 a. "g" inverted *2,400.*
3 A1 1a black, *blue* 100.00
 a. "g" inverted *2,100.*
4 A1 2a black, *green* 140.00 *550.00*
 a. "postge" *2,400.*
5 A1 4a black, *yellow* 120.00 *550.00*
 a. "postge" *2,250.*
6 A1 8a black, *rose* 72.50
 a. "postge" *1,900.*
 Nos. 1-6 (6) 1,258.

All values may be found with the scroll inverted, and with the long end of the scroll pointing to the right or left.

On No. 5 the last character on the 3rd line is a vertical line. On No. 1 it is not vertical.

On No. 2 the last character on the 3rd line looks like a backwards "R" with a bent leg. On No. 6 it looks like an apostrophe.

Nos. 1 and 2 have been reprinted in blocks of 8 and Nos. 1-6 in blocks of 20. In the reprints the 4th character of the native inscription often has the curved upper line broken at the left, but in many instances comparison with photographic reproductions of the original settings is the only certain test.

A2

1890

7 A2 ¼a blk, *rose lil* 7.00 *9.00*
 a. "Quatrer" 32.50 *57.50*
 b. "e" of "Postage" inverted 32.50 *57.50*
 c. "Eeudatory" 32.50 *57.50*
8 A2 ½a black, *green* 5.25 5.25
 a. "Eeudatory" 90.00 *110.00*
 b. "postage" with small "p" 5.25 5.25
9 A2 1a black, *yellow* 6.50 5.00
 a. "Eeudatory" 195.00 *225.00*
 b. "postage" with small "p" 6.50 5.00
 c. "annas" 300.00 *325.00*
10 A2 2a blk, *rose lil* 30.00 *57.50*
 a. "Eeudatory" 275.00 *550.00*
11 A2 4a blk, *brt rose* 9.50 *12.50*
 a. "Eeudatory" 6,750.
12 A2 8a blk, *rose lil* 40.00 *100.00*
 a. "BAMBA" 375.00 *550.00*
 b. "Foudatory" & "Postage" 375.00 *550.00*
 c. "postage" with small "p" 40.00 *100.00*
13 A2 1r blk, *rose lil* 100.00 *160.00*
 a. "BAMBA" 650.00 *825.00*
 b. "Eeudatory" 825.00 *1,050.*
 c. "postage" with small "p" 100.00 160.00
 Nos. 7-13 (7) 198.25 *349.25*

1893

14 A2 ¼a black, *rose* 3.00 *4.50*
 a. "postage" with small "p" 3.00 *4.50*
15 A2 ¼a black, *magenta* 3.00 *4.00*
 a. "postage" with small "p" 3.00 *4.00*
 b. "AM" of "BAMRA" invtd.
 c. "M" OF "BAMRA" invtd.
 d. "AMRA" of "BAMRA" inverted 100.00 100.00
 e. "M" and 2nd "A" of "BAMRA" inverted 140.00 140.00
 f. First "a" of "anna" inverted 72.50 82.50
16 A2 2a black, *rose* 21.00 12.00
 a. "postage" with small "p" 21.00 12.00
17 A2 4a black, *rose* 16.00 12.00
 a. "postage" with small "p" 16.00 12.00
 b. "BAMBA" 1,600. *1,800.*
18 A2 8a black, *rose* 42.50 29.00
 a. "postage" with small "p" 42.50 29.00
19 A2 1r black, *rose* 35.00 35.00
 a. "postage" with small "p" 35.00 35.00
 Nos. 14-19 (6) 120.50 96.50

The central ornament varies in size and may be found in various positions.

Bamra stamps became obsolete Dec. 31, 1894.

BARWANI

bər-'wän-ē

LOCATION — A Feudatory State of Central India, in the Malwa Agency.
AREA — 1,178 sq. mi.
POP. — 141,110
CAPITAL — Barwani

The stamps of Barwani were all typographed and normally issued in booklets containing panes of four. Exceptions are noted (Nos. 14-15, 20-25). The majority were completely perforated, but some of the earlier printings were perforated only between the stamps, leaving one or two sides imperf. Nos. 1-25 were issued without gum. Many shades exist.

Rana Ranjit Singh — A1

1921, April (?) Unwmk. *Pin-Perf 7*
Toned Medium Wove Paper
Clear Impression

1 A1 ¼a dull Prus green 225.00 *625.00*
2 A1 ½a dull blue 500.00 *950.00*

1921 *Coarse Perf. 7 x Imperf.*
White Thin Wove Paper
Blurred Impression

3 A1 ¼a dull green 37.50 *190.00*
4 A1 ½a pale blue 25.00 *275.00*

1921 Toned Laid Paper *Imperf.*

5 A1 ¼a light green 30.00 *125.00*
6 A1 ½a light green 8.25
 a. Perf. 11, top or bottom only 7.00

1921 *Coarse Perf. 7, 7 x Imperf.*
Thick Wove Paper
Very Blurred Impression

7 A1 ¼a dull blue 25.00
8 A1 ½a dull green 22.50

In 1927 Nos. 7-8 were printed on thin hard paper.

Rana Ranjit Singh — A2

1922 *Perf. 7 x Imperf.*
Thick Glazed Paper

9 A1 ¼a dull ultra 160.00

Rough Perf. 11 x Imperf.

10 A2 1a vermilion 3.75 *30.00*
11 A2 2a violet 3.25 *37.50*
 a. Double impression *450.00*
 Nos. 9-11 (3) 167.00 67.50

Shades of No. 11 include purple. No. 11 was also printed on thick dark toned paper.

1923-26 Wove, Laid Paper *Perf.*

12 A1 ¼a grayish ultra, perf. 8½ 2.40 *72.50*
13 A1 ¼a black, perf. 7 x imperf. 110.00 *550.00*
14 A1 ¼a dull rose, perf. 11½-12 3.75 *21.00*
15 A1 ¼a dk bl, perf. 11 ('26) 2.25 *16.00*
16 A1 ½a grn, perf. 11 x imperf. 1.90 *30.00*
 Nos. 12-16 (5) 120.30 *689.50*

No. 12 was also printed on pale gray thin toned paper.

No. 14 was printed on horizontally laid paper in horizontal sheets of 12 containing three panes of 4.

No. 15 was printed on vertically laid paper in horizontal sheets of 8.

Rana Ranjit Singh — A3

1927-28 Thin Wove Paper *Perf. 7*

17 A3 4a dull orange 200.00 *675.00*

No. 17 was also printed in light brown on thick paper, pin-perf. 6, and in orange brown on thick paper, rough perf. 7.

1928 *Coarse Perf. 7*
Thick Glazed Paper

18 A1 ¼a bright blue 16.00
19 A1 ½a bright yel green 37.50

1928, Nov. *Rough Perf. 10½*

20 A1 ¼a deep ultra 9.50
 a. Tête bêche pair 19.00
21 A1 ½a yellow green 7.00
 a. Tête bêche pair 14.00

1929-31 *Perf. 11*

22 A1 ¼a blue 3.25 *21.00*
 a. ¼a ultramarine 3.00 *21.00*
23 A1 ½a emerald green 4.00 *24.00*
24 A2 1a car pink ('31) 24.00 *67.50*
25 A3 4a salmon 120.00 *325.00*
 Nos. 22-25 (4) 151.25 437.50

Nos. 20-25 were printed in sheets of 8 (4x2).

No. 22 had five printings in various shades (bright to deep blue) in horizontal or vertical format.

No. 23 also printed in dark myrtle green.

Rana Devi Singh — A4

1932-48 Glazed Paper *Perf. 11, 12*

26 A4 ¼a dark gray 3.75 *35.00*
27 A4 ½a blue green 6.00 *35.00*
28 A4 1a brown 6.00 *32.50*
 a. 1a chocolate, perf. 8½ ('48) 21.00 75.00
29 A4 2a deep red violet 5.50 *62.50*
 a. Perf. 12x11
 b. 2a red lilac 12.50
30 A4 4a olive green 9.00 *62.50*
 Nos. 26-30 (5) 30.25 *227.50*

Types of 1921-27

1934-48 *Perf. 11*

31 A1 ¼a slate gray 6.00 *47.50*
32 A1 ½a green 6.50 *60.00*
33 A2 1a dark brown 16.00 *29.00*
 a. 1a brown, perf. 8½ ('48) 15.00 *75.00*
34 A2 2a brt purple ('38) 125.00 *490.00*
35 A2 2a rose car ('46) 35.00 *190.00*
36 A3 4a olive green 20.00 *67.50*
 Nos. 31-36 (6) 208.50 884.00

In the nine printings of Nos. 26-36, several plate settings spaced the cliches from 2 to 9mm apart. Hence the stamps come in different overall sizes. Not all values were in each printing. Values are for the commonest varieties.

No. 36 was also printed in pale sage green.

Rana Devi Singh — A5

1938

37 A5 1a dark brown 50.00 *110.00*
 a. Booklet pane of 4 —

Stamps of type A5 in red are revenues.

Barwani stamps became obsolete July 1, 1948.

BHOPAL

bō-'päl

LOCATION — A Feudatory State of Central India, in the Bhopal Agency.
AREA — 6,924 sq. mi.
POP. — 995,745
CAPITAL — Bhopal

Inscription in Urdu in an octagon embossed on Nos. 1-83, in a circle embossed on Nos. 84-90. On designs A1-A3, A7, A11-A12, A14-A15, A19-A21 the embossing makes up the central part of the design.

The embossing may be found inverted or sideways.

Expect irregular perfs on the perforated stamps, Nos. 19-77, due to a combination of imperfect perforating methods and the fragility of the papers.

Nos. 1-90 issued without gum.

A1

Double Lined Frame

1876 Unwmk. Litho. *Imperf.*

1 A1 ¼a black 950.00 700.00
 a. "EGAM" 2,750. 2,400.
 b. "BFGAM" 2,750. 2,400.
 c. "BEGAN" 1,500. 1,250.
2 A1 ½a red 30.00 *72.50*
 a. "EGAM" 110.00 *250.00*
 b. "BFGAM" 110.00 *250.00*
 c. "BEGAN" 72.50 *160.00*

A2

1877 Single Lined Frame
3 A2 ¼a black 9,000.
4 A2 ½a red 52.50 110.00
a. "NWAB" 250.00 490.00

A3

1878
5 A3 ¼a black 12.00 24.00
a. "J" diagonal, plate II 13.50 27.50

All stamps of type A3 are lettered "EEGAM" for "BEGAM."

A4

1878
6 A4 ½a pale red 10.50 24.00
a. ½a brown red 42.50 67.50
b. "NWAB" 35.00
c. "JAHN" 57.50
d. "EECAM" 57.50

A5

1879-80
7 A5 ¼a green 21.00 40.00
8 A5 ½a red 27.50 35.00

Perf.
9 A5 ¼a green 16.00 27.50
10 A5 ½a red 160.00
Nos. 7-10 (4) 224.50 102.50

Nos. 7 and 9 have the value in parenthesis; Nos. 8 and 10 are without parenthesis.

A6

1881 Imperf.
11 A6 ¼a green 13.50
a. "NAWA" 42.50
b. "CHAH" 120.00

Perf.
12 A6 ¼a green 18.00
a. "NAWA" 67.50
b. "CHAH" 160.00

A7

1881-89 Imperf.
13 A7 ¼a black 9.00 35.00
a. "NWAB" 22.50
14 A7 ½a red 7.50 25.00
a. "NWAB" 18.00
15 A7 1a brown 6.50 29.00
a. "NWAB" 14.00
16 A7 2a blue 5.00 29.00
a. "NWAB" 9.50
17 A7 4a yellow 30.00 100.00
a. "NWAB" 82.50
Nos. 13-17 (5) 58.00 218.00

A8 A9

1884 Perf.
19 A8 ¼a green 225.00 275.00
a. "JAN" 225.00 275.00
b. "BEGM" 450.00 625.00
c. "NWAB" 950.00
d. "SHAHAN" 950.00
f. "JAHA" 450.00
20 A9 ¼a green 8.25 27.50

On type A9 there is a dash at the left of "JA" of "JAHAN" instead of a character like a comma as on types A5 and A6.

Imitations of No. 19 were printed about 1904 in black on wove paper and in red on laid paper, both imperf. and pin-perf.

A10

1884 Laid Paper Imperf.
21 A10 ¼a blue green 240.00 275.00
a. "NWAB" 675.00
b. "NAWAJANAN" 675.00
c. "SAH" 675.00
22 A10 ½a black 3.25 3.75
a. "NWAB" 15.00 18.00
b. "NAWAJANAN" 15.00 18.00
c. "SAH" 15.00 18.00

Perf.
23 A10 ¼a blue green 1.50 6.00
a. "NWAB" 6.00
b. "NAWAJANAN" 6.00
c. "SAH" 6.00
24 A10 ½a black 1.40 5.00
a. "NWAB" 5.50 12.50
b. "NAWAJANAN" 5.50 12.50
c. "SAH" 5.50 12.50
Nos. 21-24 (4) 246.15 289.75

Type Redrawn
1886 Wove Paper Imperf.
25 A10 ¼a grayish green .80 5.00
a. ¼a green .80 5.00
b. "NWAB" 4.50 13.50
c. "NAWA" 3.00 10.50
d. "NAWAA" 4.50 13.50
e. "NAWABABEGAAM" 4.50 13.50
f. "NWABA" 4.50 13.50
26 A10 ½a red 1.00 2.50
a. "SAH" 6.00 9.50
b. "NAWABA" 4.50 7.50

Perf.
27 A10 ¼a green 3.75 6.00
a. "NWAB" 20.00
b. "NAWA" 12.00
c. "NAWAA" 20.00
d. "NAWABABEGAAM" 20.00
e. "NWABA" 20.00
28 A10 ½a red 1.20 3.00
a. "SAH" 9.00
b. "NAWABA" 12.00
Nos. 25-28 (4) 6.75 16.50

On Nos. 25-28 the inscriptions are closer to the value than on Nos. 21-24.

A11

A12

1886 Imperf.
29 A11 ½a red 4.00 15.00
a. "BEGAM" 18.00 47.50
b. "NWAB" 18.00

Laid Paper
30 A12 4a yellow 18.00 57.50
a. "EEGAM" 24.00
b. Wove paper 1,500.
c. As "a," wove paper 1,900.

Perf.
31 A12 4a yellow 6.50 30.00
a. "EEGAM" 9.50 42.50
Nos. 29-31 (3) 28.50

A13 A14

1889 Wove Paper Imperf.
32 A13 ¼a green 1.50 3.00
a. "SAH" 6.50 10.50
b. "NAWA" 6.50 10.50
33 A14 ¼a black 3.25 8.25
a. "EEGAN" 27.50 47.50

Perf.
34 A13 ¼a green 3.00 4.00
a. "SAH" 11.00 13.50
b. "NAWA" 11.00 13.50
c. Vert. pair, imperf between 325.00
35 A14 ¼a black 2.50 8.25
a. "EEGAN" 22.50 47.50
b. Horiz. pair, imperf. between 400.00
Nos. 32-35 (4) 10.25 23.50

Type A13 has smaller letters in the upper corners than Type A10.

A15

A16

1890 Imperf.
36 A15 ¼a black 3.25 3.00
37 A15 1a brown 3.25 7.00
a. "EEGAM" 21.00 40.00
b. "BBGAM" 21.00 40.00
38 A7 2a greenish blue 3.00 3.25
a. "BBEGAM" 12.50 21.00
b. "NAWAH" 12.50 21.00
39 A7 4a yellow 3.75 5.50
40 A16 8a blue 100.00 180.00
a. "HAH" 110.00 190.00
b. "JABAN" 120.00
Nos. 36-40 (5) 113.25 198.75

An imperf. imitation of Nos. 36 and 41 was printed about 1904 in black on wove paper.

Perf.
41 A15 ¼a black 4.50 6.25
a. Pair, imperf. between 500.00
42 A15 1a brown 6.50 11.00
a. "EECAM" 37.50 52.50
b. "BBGAM" 37.50 52.50
43 A7 2a greenish blue 3.75 5.50
a. "BBEGAM" 14.00 27.50
b. "NAWAH" 14.00 27.50
44 A7 4a yellow 4.50 12.00
45 A16 8a blue 100.00 180.00
a. "HAH" 110.00
b. "JABAN" 120.00
Nos. 41-45 (5) 119.25 214.75

Nos. 40 and 45 have a frame line around each stamp.

Imperf
46 A12 ½a red (BECAM) 3.00 5.50
47 A13 ½a red (NWAB) 3.00 2.25
a. Inverted "N"
b. "SAH" 9.00

Perf.
48 A12 ½a red (BECAM) 2.50 7.00
a. Without embossing
49 A13 ½a red (NWAB) 1.20 3.00
a. Inverted "N"
b. "SAH" 7.50
Nos. 46-49 (4) 9.70 17.75

1891-93 Laid Paper Imperf.
50 A16 8a deep green 110.00 225.00
a. "HAH" 125.00
b. "JABAN" 150.00

Perf.
51 A16 8a deep green 110.00 225.00
a. "HAH" 125.00
b. "JABAN" 140.00

For overprint, see No. 83.

1894 Redrawn Imperf.
53 A10 ¼a green 2.25 2.50
a. "NAWAH" 11.00 12.00
54 A11 ½a brick red 3.25 3.25
55 A16 8a blue black 32.50 32.50
a. Laid paper 300.00 450.00

Perf.
56 A10 ¼a green 4.50 3.25
a. "NAWAH" 19.00 16.00
57 A11 ½a brick red 1.20 3.00
58 A16 8a blue black 45.00 60.00
Nos. 53-58 (6) 88.70 104.50

The ¼a redrawn has letters in corners larger; value in very small characters.

The 8a redrawn has no frame to each stamp but a frame to the sheet.

1898 Imperf.
60 A16 8a black 62.50 82.50
b. "E" of "BEGAM" inverted 140.00 150.00

A17 A18

A19

A20

A21

1895 Laid Paper
61 A17 ¼a green 2.25 2.50
62 A18 ¼a red 10.50 5.00
63 A19 ¼a black 5.25 4.50
a. "A" inserted in "NAW B" 12.50 10.00
64 A20 ½a black 2.25 2.50
65 A21 ½a red 3.25 3.25

Perf.
66 A17 ¼a green 4.50 3.25
67 A18 ¼a red 1,250.
Nos. 61-67 (7) 28.00 1,271.

On No. 63a, the second "A" in "NAWAB" has been inserted by hand and varies somewhat in size.

Imperf. imitations of No. 65 were printed about 1904 in deep red on laid paper and in black on wove paper.

Stamps of types A16 and A19-A21 with a circular embossed seal and perforated, were prepared but not issued.

A22

A23

1898 Imperf.
72 A22 ¼a black .75 .75
a. "SHAN" 5.00 5.00
73 A22 ¼a green 1.10 1.20
a. "SHAN" 5.25 5.25
74 A23 ¼a black 2.10 2.10
Nos. 72-74 (3) 3.95 4.05

1899
75 A13 ½a black ("NWAB") 6.50 9.50
b. "NWASBAHJAHNJ" 32.50 42.50
d. "SBAH" 15.00 22.50
e. "SBAN" 32.50 42.50
f. "NWIB" 32.50 42.50
g. "BEIAM" 32.50 42.50

A24

1902

76 A24 ¼a red 5.50 *9.00*
77 A24 ½a black 6.00 *10.00*
a. Printed on both sides 1,100.
78 A24 1a brown 10.00 *25.00*
79 A24 2a blue 12.50 *22.50*
80 A24 4a orange 110.00 *160.00*
81 A24 8a violet 150.00 *290.00*
82 A24 1r rose 400.00 *600.00*
Nos. 76-82 (7) 694.00 *1,117.*

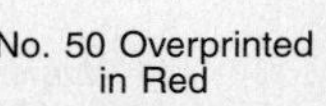
No. 50 Overprinted in Red

1903

83 A16 8a deep green 210.00 225.00
a. Inverted overprint 550.00 *600.00*

There are two types of the overprint which is the Arabic S, initial of the Begum.

Inscription in Circle Embossed on Each Stamp

1903 **Wove Paper**

84 A24 ¼a red 2.25 *7.50*
85 A24 ½a black 1.90 *7.50*
86 A24 1a brown 4.50 *11.00*
87 A24 2a blue 10.00 *37.50*
88 A24 4a orange 27.50 *75.00*
89 A24 8a violet 82.50 *190.00*
90 A24 1r rose 125.00 *290.00*
Nos. 84-90 (7) 253.65 *618.50*

Laid Paper

84a A24 ¼a red 1.50 *12.00*
85a A24 ½a black 1.50 *12.50*
86a A24 1a brown 10.00
87a A24 2a blue 250.00 *325.00*
88a A24 4a orange 500.00 500.00
89a A24 8a violet 2,400.
90a A24 1r rose 1,900.
Nos. 84a-90a (7) 5,063. *849.50*

The embossing in a circle, which was first used in 1903, has been applied to many early stamps and impressions from redrawn plates of early issues. So far as is now known, these should be classed as reprints.

Coat of Arms — A25

1908 **Engr.** ***Perf. 13½***

99 A25 1a yellow green 5.50 *6.75*
a. Printed on both sides 180.00

OFFICIAL STAMPS

O1

Overprinted

Size: 20½x25mm

1908 **Unwmk.** **Engr.** ***Perf. 13½***

O1 O1 ½a yellow green 3.25 .25
a. Pair, one without ovpt. 950.00
b. Inverted overprint 275.00 225.00
c. Double ovpt., one invtd. 160.00
O2 O1 1a carmine 6.25 .60
a. Inverted overprint 180.00 150.00
O3 O1 2a blue 36.00 .25
O4 O1 4a red brown 21.00 .80
Nos. O1-O4 (4) 66.50 1.90

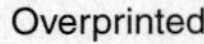
Overprinted

O5 O1 ½a yellow green 11.00 1.90
O6 O1 1a carmine 14.00 1.40
O7 O1 2a blue 6.00 .90
a. Inverted overprint 37.50
O8 O1 4a red brown 120.00 2.25
a. Inverted overprint 30.00 *100.00*
Nos. O5-O8 (4) 151.00 6.45

The difference in the two overprints is in the shape of the letters, most noticeable in the "R."

Type of 1908 Issue

Overprinted

Size: 25½x30½mm

1930-31 **Litho.** ***Perf. 14***

O9 O1 ½a gray green ('31) 18.00 2.50
O10 O1 1a carmine 16.00 .25
O11 O1 2a blue 14.00 .65
O12 O1 4a brown 15.00 1.40
Nos. O9-O12 (4) 63.00 4.80

½a, 2a, 4a are inscribed "POSTAGE" on the left side; 1a "POSTAGE AND REVENUE."

Similar to Type O1
Size: 21x25mm
"POSTAGE" at left
"BHOPAL STATE" at right

1932-33 ***Perf. 11½, 13, 13½, 14***

O13 O1 ¼a orange yellow 3.75 .75
a. Pair, one without overprint 180.00
b. Perf. 13½ 16.00 .45
c. Perf. 14 18.00 .45

"BHOPAL GOVT." at right
Perf. 13½

O14 O1 ½a yellow green 11.00 .25
a. Perf 14 ('34) 24.00 .60
O15 O1 1a brown red 16.00 .25
O16 O1 2a blue 16.00 .65
O17 O1 4a brown 16.00 1.50
a. Perf 14 ('34) 24.00 16.00
Nos. O13-O17 (5) 62.75 3.40

No. O14, O16-O17 Surcharged in Red, Violet, Black or Blue

a

b

c

1935-36 ***Perf. 13½***

O18 O1(a) ¼a on ½a (R) 47.50 21.00
a. Inverted surcharge 300.00 125.00
O19 O1(b) 3p on ½a (R) 5.50 5.25
O20 O1(a) ¼a on 2a (R) 42.50 30.00
a. Inverted surcharge 300.00 110.00
O21 O1(b) 3p on 2a (R) 6.75 6.75
a. Inverted surcharge 120.00 60.00
O22 O1(a) ¼a on 4a (R) 1,500. 500.00
O23 O1(a) ¼a on 4a (Bk) ('36) 120.00 40.00
O24 O1(b) 3p on 4a (R) 210.00 100.00
O25 O1(b) 3p on 4a (Bk) ('36) 3.75 *5.00*
O26 O1(c) 1a on ½a (V) 7.50 2.25
a. Inverted surcharge 100.00 67.50
O27 O1(c) 1a on 2a (R) 3.25 3.00
a. Inverted surcharge 140.00 140.00
O28 O1(c) 1a on 2a (Bk) ('36) 1.00 *3.75*
O29 O1(c) 1a on 4a (Bl) 10.50 *7.50*
Nos. O18-O29 (12) 1,958. 724.50

Nos. O18-O25 are arranged in composite sheets of 100. The 2 top horizontal rows of each value are surcharged "a" and the next 5 rows as "b." The next 3 rows as "b" but in a narrower setting.

Various errors of spelling or inverted letters are found on Nos. O18-O29.

Arms of Bhopal — O2

1935 **Litho.**

O30 O2 1a3p claret & blue 5.25 2.25

Inscribed: "Bhopal State Postage" Ovptd. "SERVICE" 11mm long

1937 ***Perf. 12***

O31 O2 1a6p dk clar & bl 3.75 1.50
a. Overprint omitted 275.00 210.00
b. Double overprint, one inverted 750.00 750.00
c. Blue printing double 250.00
d. Imperf, pair 275.00
e. Pair, imperf between 300.00 *325.00*

See Nos. O42, O45.

Arms of Bhopal — O3

Brown or Black Overprint

1936-38 **Typo.**

O32 O3 ¼a orange (Br) 1.40 .90
a. Inverted overprint 525.00 400.00
b. Vert. pair, imperf between 250.00
c. Horiz. pair, imperf between 450.00
d. Black overprint 12.50 1.10
e. As "d," inverted ovpt. 600.00
f. As "d," double ovpt. 450.00
O32G O3 ¼a yel (Br) ('38) 5.25 2.25
O33 O3 1a carmine 1.90 .25
a. Horiz. pair, imperf vert. 250.00
b. Vert. pair, imperf between 490.00
c. Horiz. pair, imperf between 200.00 *225.00*
d. Block of 4, imperf between 625.00 625.00
Nos. O32-O33 (3) 8.55 3.40

Moti Mahal O4

Overprinted in Black

1936 ***Perf. 11½***

O34 O4 ½a grn & choc .85 *1.20*
a. Double impression of stamp 150.00 22.50
b. Double overprint 350.00 250.00
c. Vert. pair, imperf between 325.00
d. Horiz. pair, imperf between 325.00

Moti Masjid — O5

4a, Taj Mahal and Be-Nazir Palaces.

Overprinted in Black

1937 ***Perf. 11½***

O35 O5 2a dk blue & brown 2.50 1.40
a. Inverted overprint 375.00 *550.00*
b. Vert. pair, imperf between 525.00
c. Horiz. pair, imperf between 375.00
O36 O5 4a bister brn & blue 4.50 .75
a. Double overprint 240.00
b. Center double 600.00
c. Horiz. pair, imperf between 1,000.
d. Overprint omitted 490.00

Types of 1937
Overprinted "SERVICE" in Black or Brown

Designs: 4a, Taj Mahal. 8a, Ahmadabad Palace. 1r, Rait-Ghat.

1938-44

O37 O4 ½a dp grn & brn .90 .60
O38 O5 2a vio & dp grn 15.00 .45
O39 O5 4a red brn & brt bl 4.25 .80
a. Frame double 450.00
O40 O5 8a red vio & blue 7.00 3.25
a. "SERAICE" 550.00 *825.00*
b. Overprint omitted 250.00
c. Double overprint 240.00
d. Vert. pair, imperf between 625.00
e. "1" for "I" in "SERVICE" 550.00 *825.00*
O41 O5 1r bl & red vio (Br) 27.50 12.50
a. Black overprint ('44) 21.00 6.50
b. "SREVICE" 160.00 *375.00*
c. Overprint omitted 1,100.
d. Vert. pair, imperf horiz. 2,250.
Nos. O37-O41 (5) 54.65 17.60

No. O39 measures 36½x22½mm, No. O40 39x24mm, No. O41 45½x27¾mm.

Type of 1935

1939 ***Perf. 12***

O42 O2 1a6p dark claret 7.50 2.50
a. Overprint omitted 625.00
b. Double overprint 625.00
c. Double overprint, one inverted 625.00
d. Pair, imperf between 250.00 *325.00*

Tiger — O6

Design: 1a, Deer.

1940 **Typo.** ***Perf. 11½***

O43 O6 ¼a ultramarine 6.00 2.50
O44 O6 1a red violet 35.00 4.50

Type of 1935
Inscribed: "Bhopal State Postage"

1941

O45 O2 1a3p emerald 2.50 3.25
a. Pair, imperf between 550.00 *700.00*

Moti Palace — O7

Coat of Arms — O8

2a, Moti Mosque. 4a, Be-Nazir Palaces.

Perf. 11½, 12

1944-46 **Unwmk.** **Typo.**

O46 O8 3p ultramarine 1.25 1.25
O47 O7 ½a light green 1.10 *1.50*
O48 O8 9p org brn ('46) 12.00 5.00
a. Imperf., pair 290.00
O49 O8 1a brt red vio ('45) 6.25 2.60
O50 O8 1½a deep plum 1.90 1.90
O51 O7 2a red violet ('45) 13.50 6.00
O52 O8 3a yellow ('46) 16.00 *21.00*
a. Imperf., pair 290.00
O53 O7 4a brown ('45) 8.75 3.25
O54 O8 6a brt rose ('46) 24.00 *75.00*
a. Imperf., pair 400.00
Nos. O46-O54 (9) 84.75 *117.50*

For surcharges see Nos. O58-O59.

1946-47 **Unwmk.** ***Perf. 11½***

O55 O8 1a violet 11.00 4.75
O56 O7 2a violet ('47) 13.50 22.50
O57 O8 3a deep orange 125.00 *160.00*
a. Imperf., pair — 275.00
Nos. O55-O57 (3) 149.50 187.25

No. O50 Surcharged "2 As." and Bars

1949 ***Perf. 12***

O58 O8 2a on 1½a dp plum 3.00 *11.00*
c. Imperf., pair 300.00 *450.00*

Same Surcharged "2 As." and Rosettes

1949 ***Imperf.***

O59 O8 2a on 1½a dp plum 1,250. 1,500.
a. Perf 12 1,350. *1,600.*

Three or more types of "2" in surcharge. Bhopal stamps became obsolete in 1950.

BHOR

'bō͵ə͵r

LOCATION — A Feudatory State in the Kolhapur Residency and Deccan States Agency.
AREA — 910 sq. mi.
POP. — 141,546
CAPITAL — Bhor

A1

A2

Handstamped

1879 Unwmk. *Imperf.*
Without Gum

1	A1	½a carmine	5.50	*7.50*
2	A2	1a carmine	8.25	*12.00*

Pant Sachiv Shankarrao — A3

1901 Without Gum Typo.

3	A3	½a red	24.00	*60.00*

BIJAWAR

bi-'jä-wər

LOCATION — A Feudatory State in the Bundelkhand Agency of Central India.
AREA — 973 sq. mi.
POP. — 115,852
CAPITAL — Bijawar

Maharaja Sir Sawant Singh — A1

1935-36 Typo. Unwmk. *Perf. 10½*

1	A1	3p brown	11.00	8.25
a.		Imperf., pair	13.50	
b.		Rouletted 7 ('36)	9.00	*9.00*
2	A1	6p carmine	9.50	8.25
a.		Rouletted 7 ('36)	12.00	*32.50*
3	A1	9p purple	12.50	7.50
a.		Rouletted 7 ('36)	9.00	*160.00*
4	A1	1a dark blue	14.00	8.25
a.		Rouletted 7 ('36)	15.00	*180.00*
5	A1	2a slate green	13.50	7.50
a.		Rouletted 7 ('36)	19.00	*190.00*

Maharaja Sir Sawant Singh — A2

1937 *Perf. 9*

6	A2	4a red orange	22.50	*140.00*
7	A2	6a yellow	22.50	*140.00*
8	A2	8a emerald	24.00	*180.00*
9	A2	12a turquoise blue	24.00	*200.00*
10	A2	1r purple	62.50	*250.00*
a.		"1Rs" instead of "1R"	75.00	*500.00*
		Nos. 1-10 (10)	216.00	*949.75*

Bijawar stamps became obsolete in 1939.

BUNDI

'bün-dē

LOCATION — A Feudatory State in the Rajputana Agency of India.
AREA — 2,220 sq. mi.
POP. — 216,722
CAPITAL — Bundi

Katar (Indian Dagger) — A1

Laid Paper
Without Gum
Gutters between Stamps

1894 Unwmk. Litho. *Imperf.*

1	A1	½a slate	19,000.	*3,250.*

Redrawn; Blade Does Not Touch Oval
No Gutters between Stamps
Wove Paper

1A	A1	½a slate	67.50	*72.50*
b.		Value above, name below	400.00	*525.00*
c.		Top right ornament omitted	3,750.	*4,000.*

On No. 1A, the dagger is thinner and its point does not touch the oval inner frame.

A2

Without Gum

1896 Laid Paper

2	A2	½a slate	9.00	14.00

A3

1897-98 Without Gum

3	A3	1a red	18.00	*27.50*
4	A3	2a yellow green	21.00	*40.00*
5	A3	4a yellow green	100.00	*140.00*
6	A3	8a red	160.00	*450.00*
7	A3	1r yellow, *blue*	500.00	*825.00*
		Nos. 3-7 (5)	799.00	*1,483.*

A4

A5

Redrawn; Blade Wider and Diamond-shaped

1898-1900 Without Gum

8	A3	½a slate	7.00	7.00
9	A3	1a red	5.50	5.50
10	A3	2a emerald	19.00	25.00
a.		1st 2 characters of value omitted	3,000.	3,000.
11	A3	4a yel grn	42.50	*100.00*
12	A4	8a red	21.00	*27.50*
13	A5	1r yellow, *blue*	47.50	*82.50*
a.		Wove paper	24.00	*40.00*
		Nos. 8-13 (6)	142.50	*247.50*

On Nos. 9-10, the blade is wider and nearly diamond-shaped.

Point of Dagger to Left

14	A3	4a green	5.00	5.00

Maharao Rajah with Symbols of Spiritual and Temporal Power — A6

Rouletted 11 to 13 in Color

1915 Typo. Without Gum

"Bundi" in 3 Characters (word at top right)

No.	Type	Value	Color	Unused	Used
15	A6	¼a	blue	2.90	*6.25*
a.			Laid paper	6.75	*35.00*
16	A6	½a	black	4.00	*9.00*
17	A6	1a	vermilion	5.50	*18.00*
a.			Laid paper	15.00	*45.00*
18	A6	2a	emerald	11.00	*35.00*
19	A6	2½a	yellow	11.00	*40.00*
20	A6	3a	brown	12.50	*67.50*
21	A6	4a	yel green	5.25	*62.50*
23	A6	6a	ultramarine	21.00	*160.00*
a.			6a deep blue	11.00	*180.00*
24	A6	8a	orange	11.00	*160.00*
25	A6	10a	olive	24.00	*150.00*
26	A6	12a	dark green	19.00	*140.00*
27	A6	1r	violet	40.00	*250.00*
28	A6	2r	car brn & blk	125.00	*325.00*
29	A6	3r	blue & brown	210.00	*450.00*
30	A6	4r	pale grn & red brn	400.00	*550.00*
31	A6	5r	ver & pale grn	400.00	*550.00*
			Nos. 15-31 (16)	1,302.	*2,973.*

Minor differences in lettering in top and bottom panels may be divided into 8 types, but not all values come in each type. In one subtype the top appears as one word. Nos. 30-31 have an ornamental frame around the design.

For overprints see Nos. O1-O39.

1941 ***Perf. 11***

"Bundi" in 4 Characters (word at top right)

No.	Type	Value	Color	Unused	Used
32	A6	¼a	light blue	2.25	62.50
33	A6	½a	black	40.00	47.50
34	A6	1a	carmine	15.00	*75.00*
35	A6	2a	yellow green	20.00	110.00
			Nos. 32-35 (4)	77.25	295.00

The 4-character spelling of "Bundi" is found also on stamps rouletted in color: on ½a and 4a in small characters, and on ¼a, ½a, 1a, 4a, 4r and 5r in large characters like those on Nos. 32-35.

For overprints see Nos. O41-O48.

Arms of Bundi — A7

1941-45 Typo. ***Perf. 11***

No.	Type	Value	Color	Unused	Used
36	A7	3p	bright ultra	3.50	*7.50*
37	A7	6p	indigo	5.25	*12.50*
38	A7	1a	red orange	8.00	*15.00*
39	A7	2a	fawn	10.50	*27.50*
a.			2a brown ('45)	19.00	*30.00*
40	A7	4a	brt yel green	19.00	*82.50*
41	A7	8a	dull green	25.00	*300.00*
42	A7	1r	royal blue	52.50	*450.00*
			Nos. 36-42 (7)	123.75	*895.00*

The 1st printing of Nos. 36-42 was gummed. All later printings were without gum. **Values are for stamps without gum.**

For overprints see Nos. O49-O55.

A8

Maj. Maharao Rajah Bahadur Singh — A9

View of Bundi — A10

1947 ***Perf. 11***

No.	Type	Value	Color	Unused	Used
43	A8	¼a	deep green	2.75	*57.50*
44	A8	½a	purple	2.50	*47.50*
45	A8	1a	yellow green	2.50	*47.50*
46	A9	2a	red	2.40	*97.50*
47	A9	4a	deep orange	2.75	*140.00*
48	A10	8a	violet blue	3.75	
49	A10	1r	chocolate	19.00	
			Nos. 43-49 (7)	35.65	

For overprints see Rajasthan Nos. 1-14.

OFFICIAL STAMPS

Regular Issue of 1915 Handstamped in Black, Red or Green

a

Rouletted 11 to 13 in Color

1918 Unwmk. Without Gum

No.	Type	Value	Color	Unused	Used
O1	A6	¼a	dark blue	1.90	
O2	A6	½a	black	1.10	
O3	A6	1a	vermilion	1.90	
O4	A6	2a	emerald	9.50	
O5	A6	2½a	yellow	6.00	
O6	A6	3a	brown	5.50	
O7	A6	4a	yel green	18.00	
O8	A6	6a	blue	22.50	
O9	A6	8a	orange	22.50	
O10	A6	10a	olive green	75.00	
O11	A6	12a	dark green	75.00	
O12	A6	1r	violet	90.00	
O13	A6	2r	car brn & blk	600.00	
O14	A6	3r	blue & brown	525.00	
O15	A6	4r	pale grn & red brn	450.00	
O16	A6	5r	ver & pale grn	490.00	
			Nos. O1-O16 (16)	2,394.	

All values come with black handstamp and most exist in red. The overprint is found in various positions, double, inverted, etc.

Several denominations exist in two or more types. See notes following Nos. 31 and 35.

Regular Issue of 1915 Handstamped in Black, Red or Green

b

1919 Without Gum

No.	Type	Value	Color	Unused	Used
O17	A6	¼a	dark blue	2.60	
O18	A6	½a	black	4.50	
O19	A6	1a	vermilion	16.00	
O20	A6	2a	emerald	29.00	
O21	A6	2½a	yellow	30.00	
O22	A6	3a	brown	35.00	
O23	A6	4a	yel green	120.00	
O24	A6	6a	blue	45.00	
O25	A6	8a	orange	52.50	
O26	A6	10a	olive green	140.00	
O27	A6	12a	dark green	120.00	
O28	A6	1r	violet	82.50	
O29	A6	2r	car brn & blk	275.00	
O30	A6	3r	blue & brown	325.00	
O31	A6	4r	pale grn & red brn	450.00	
O32	A6	5r	ver & pale grn	490.00	
			Nos. O17-O32 (16)	2,217.	

Note following No. O16 applies to this issue.

Regular Issue of 1915 Handstamped in Carmine or Black

c

1919 ***Rouletted in Color***

Without Gum

No.	Type	Value	Color	Unused	Used
O33	A6	¼a	blue	11.00	
O34	A6	½a	black	18.00	
O35	A6	1a	vermilion	35.00	
O36	A6	2a	yel green	140.00	
O37	A6	8a	orange	450.00	
O38	A6	10a	olive	700.00	
O39	A6	12a	dark green	900.00	
			Nos. O33-O39 (7)	2,254.	

Nos. 33 and 35 Handstamped Type "a" in Black or Carmine

1941 ***Perf. 11***

No.	Type	Value	Color	Unused	Used
O41	A6	½a	black	24.00	
O42	A6	2a	yellow green	825.00	

Nos. 32 and 35 Handstamped Type "b" in Black or Carmine

No.	Type	Value	Color	Unused	Used
O43	A6	¼a	light blue	90.00	
O44	A6	2a	yellow green	210.00	

Nos. 32-35 Handstamped Type "c" in Black or Carmine

1941

No.	Type	Value	Color	Unused	Used
O45	A6	¼a	light blue	190.00	
O46	A6	½a	black	375.00	
O47	A6	1a	carmine	700.00	
O48	A6	2a	yellow green	625.00	
			Nos. O45-O48 (4)	1,890.	

Nos. 36 to 42 Overprinted in Black or Carmine

1941 ***Perf. 11***

No.	Type	Value	Color	Unused	Used
O49	A7	3p	brt ultra (C)	7.50	*24.00*
O50	A7	6p	indigo (C)	20.00	*24.00*
O51	A7	1a	red orange	19.00	*16.00*
O52	A7	2a	fawn	20.00	*19.00*
O53	A7	4a	brt yel green	72.50	*160.00*
O54	A7	8a	dull green	225.00	*950.00*
O55	A7	1r	royal blue (C)	310.00	*950.00*
			Nos. O49-O55 (7)	674.00	*2,143.*

BUSSAHIR

ˈbus-ə-ˌhi̦ə̦r

(Bashahr)

LOCATION — A Feudatory State in the Punjab Hill States Agency
AREA — 3,439 sq. mi.
POP. — 100,192
CAPITAL — Bashahr

A1 Tiger A2

A3 A4

A5

A6

A7 A8

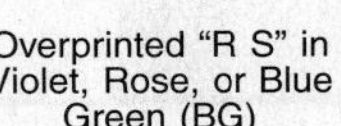

Overprinted "R S" in Violet, Rose, or Blue Green (BG)

Laid Paper

1895 Unwmk. Litho. ***Imperf.***

No.	Type	Value	Color	Unused	Used
1	A1	¼a	pink (V)	3,750.	
2	A2	½a	slate (R)	750.00	*1,000.*
3	A3	1a	red (V)	300.00	
4	A4	2a	yellow (V,R)	110.00	*300.00*
5	A5	4a	violet (V,R)	190.00	
6	A6	8a	brown (V,BG)	210.00	*375.00*
a.			Without overprint	400.00	
7	A7	12a	green (R)	450.00	
8	A8	1r	ultra (R)	190.00	
			Nos. 1-8 (8)	5,950.	

Perf. 7 to 14

No.	Type	Value	Color	Unused	Used
9	A1	¼a	pink (V,BG)	100.00	*150.00*
10	A2	½a	slate (R)	35.00	*210.00*
11	A3	1a	red (V)	35.00	*140.00*
a.			Pin-perf.	275.00	*300.00*
12	A4	2a	yel (V,R,BG)	47.50	*140.00*
a.			Pin-perf. (V,R)	100.00	*240.00*
13	A5	4a	vio (V,R,BG)	37.50	*140.00*
a.			Pin-perf. (R)	450.00	
14	A6	8a	brown (V,BG)	35.00	*160.00*
15	A7	12a	green (V,R)	120.00	*200.00*
a.			Pin-perf. (R)	650.00	*825.00*
b.			Without overprint	325.00	
16	A8	1r	ultra (V,R)	65.00	*180.00*
a.			Pin-perf. (R)	700.00	
			Nos. 9-16 (8)	475.00	*1,320.*

"R. S." are the initials of Tika Raghunath Singh, son of the Raja.

Overprinted "R S" Like Nos. 1-16

A9

A10

A11 A12

A13

A14

Wove Paper

1896 Engr. ***Pin-perf.***

No.	Type	Value	Color	Unused	Used
17	A9	¼a	dk gray vio (R)	—	1,500.
18	A10	½a	blue gray (R)	1,200.	450.00

1900 Litho. ***Imperf.***

No.	Type	Value	Color	Unused	Used
19	A9	¼a	red (V,BG)	7.50	*16.00*
20	A9	¼a	violet (V,R)	12.50	
21	A10	½a	blue (V,R)	15.00	*40.00*
22	A11	1a	olive (R)	27.50	*65.00*
23	A11	1a	red (V,BG)	7.00	*24.00*
24	A12	2a	yellow (V)	75.00	
a.			2a ocher (R)	75.00	
25	A13	2a	yellow (V)	90.00	
26	A14	4a	brn vio (V,R,BG)	82.50	*180.00*
			Nos. 19-26 (8)	317.00	

Pin-perf.

27	A9	¼a red (V,BG)	6.25	*16.00*
28	A9	¼a violet (R)	30.00	27.50
29	A10	½a blue (V,R)	90.00	140.00
30	A11	1a olive (V,R)	40.00	
31	A11	1a red (V)	—	300.00
32	A11	1a vermilion (BG)	11.00	*22.50*
33	A12	2a yellow (BG)	1,250.	*1,300.*
34	A13	2a yellow (V,R)	75.00	*120.00*
a.		2a ocher (V)	100.00	
35	A14	4a brn vio (V,R,BG)	120.00	
		Nos. 27-35 (9)	1,622.	

Obsolete March 31, 1901.

Stamps overprinted with the monogram above (RNS) or with the monogram "PS" were never issued for postal purposes. They are either reprints or remainders to which this overprint has been applied. Many other varieties have appeared since the stamps became obsolete. It is probable that all or nearly all of them are reprints.

CHARKHARI

chər-'kär-ē

LOCATION — A Feudatory State in the Bundelkhand Agency in Central India.
AREA — 880 sq. mi.
POP. — 120,351
CAPITAL — Maharajnagar

A1

Thin White or Blue Wove Paper
Value in the Plural
Without Gum

1894		**Unwmk.**	**Typo.**	***Imperf.***
1	A1	1a green	2,750.	*3,750.*
2	A1	2a green	3,250.	
3	A1	4a green	2,250.	

Value in the Singular

1897			**Without Gum**	
3A	A1	¼a rose	1,800.	1,100.
4	A1	¼a purple	5.50	5.50
5	A1	½a purple	3.75	*4.50*
6	A1	1a green	6.50	*9.50*
7	A1	2a green	11.00	*12.50*
8	A1	4a green	17.50	*27.50*
		Nos. 4-8 (5)	44.25	*59.50*

In a later printing, the numerals of Nos. 4-8 are smaller or of different shape.

Proofs are known on paper of various colors.

A2

Size: 19½x23mm

1909		**Litho.**		***Perf. 11***
9	A2	1p red brown	7.00	*57.50*
10	A2	1p pale blue	.90	.65
11	A2	½a scarlet	1.50	*1.90*
12	A2	1a light green	3.75	2.40
13	A2	2a ultra	4.50	*5.25*
14	A2	4a deep green	6.25	*8.25*
15	A2	8a brick red	11.00	*30.00*
16	A2	1r red brown	19.00	*62.50*
		Nos. 9-16 (8)	53.90	*168.45*

See Nos. 22-27, 39-43. For surcharges see Nos. 37-38A.

A3

1912-17		**Handstamped Without Gum**		***Imperf.***
21	A3	1p violet ('17)	10.50	7.50
c.		Double frameline	1,050.	125.00

The 1p black, type A3, is a proof.

A3a

Wove Paper
Handstamped

1922		**Without Gum**		***Imperf.***
21A	A3a	1a violet	120.00	*125.00*
b.		Perf. 11, laid paper	110.00	*210.00*

Type of 1909 Issue Redrawn
Size: 20x23½mm

1930-40		**Without Gum**		**Typo.**
22	A2	1p dark blue	.90	*21.00*
23	A2	½a olive green	3.75	*21.00*
23A	A2	½a cop brown ('40)	9.00	*37.50*
24	A2	1a light green	3.75	*24.00*
25	A2	1a chocolate	19.00	*40.00*
25A	A2	1a dull red ('40)	190.00	100.00
26	A2	2a light blue	1.90	*25.00*
a.		Tête bêche pair	14.00	
27	A2	4a carmine	4.50	*30.00*
a.		Tête bêche pair	21.00	
		Nos. 22-27 (8)	232.80	*298.50*

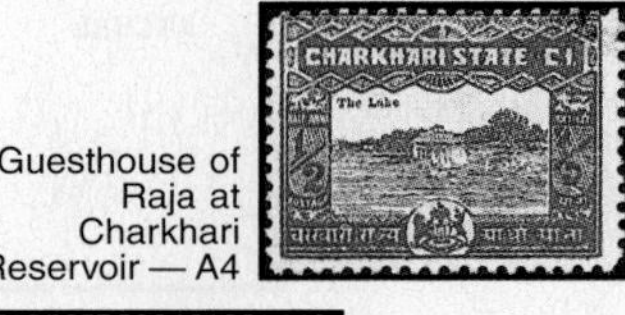

Guesthouse of Raja at Charkhari Reservoir — A4

Imlia Palace — A5

Industrial School — A6

View of City — A7

Maharajnagar Fort, Charkhari City — A8

Guesthouse A9

Palace Gate — A10

Temples at Rampur — A11

Govordhan Temple — A12

1931				***Perf. 11, 11½, 12***
28	A4	½a dull green	3.25	.25
29	A5	1a black brown	2.40	.25
30	A6	2a purple	2.50	.25
31	A7	4a olive green	2.25	.25
32	A8	8a magenta	3.00	.25
33	A9	1r rose & green	4.00	.30
34	A10	2r brown & red	6.00	.35
35	A11	3r bl grn & choc	22.50	.60
36	A12	5r violet & blue	14.00	.75
		Nos. 28-36 (9)	59.90	3.25

Size range of A4-A12: 30-31x19½-24mm.
Many errors of perforation and printing exist.
Used values are for canceled to order stamps.

Nos. 15-16 Surcharged in Black

1940				***Perf. 11***
37	A2	½a on 8a brick red	52.50	*200.00*
a.		Surcharge inverted	450.00	600.00
b.		"1" of "½" inverted	400.00	
38	A2	1a on 1r red brown	175.00	*625.00*
b.		Surcharge inverted	490.00	
38A	A2	"1 ANNA" on 1r red brown	400.00	*450.00*

Type of 1930

1943		**Unwmk.**	**Typo.**	***Imperf.***
		Size: 20x23½mm		
39	A2	1p violet	32.50	*240.00*
a.		Tête bêche pair	82.50	
40	A2	1p apple green	90.00	*325.00*
41	A2	½a orange red	30.00	*62.50*
42	A2	½a black	90.00	*290.00*
43	A2	2a grayish green	140.00	*290.00*
a.		Tête bêche pair	180.00	
		Nos. 39-43 (5)	382.50	*1,208.*

COCHIN

kō-'chin

LOCATION — A Feudatory State in the Madras States Agency in Southern India.
AREA — 1,480 sq. mi.
POP. — 1,422,875 (1941)
CAPITAL — Ernakulam

See the United State of Travancore and Cochin.

6 Puttans = 5 Annas
12 Pies = 1 Anna
16 Annas = 1 Rupee

A1

State Seal

1892		**Unwmk.**	**Typo.**	***Perf. 12***
1	A1	½p yellow	3.75	4.50
a.		Imperf., pair	—	—
b.		Laid paper	800.00	200.00
c.		½p orange buff	4.25	3.00
d.		½p orange buff, laid paper	700.00	200.00
e.		½p buff	3.00	3.50
f.		½p orange, laid paper	775.00	200.00
2	A1	1p red violet	4.50	4.00
a.		Vert. pair, imperf. between		*4,000.*
b.		1p purple (error)	175.00	125.00
3	A1	2p purple	3.00	*3.25*
a.		Imperf.		
		Nos. 1-3 (3)	11.25	11.75

Nos. 1 to 3 sometimes have watermark large umbrella in the sheet.

A1a

Wmk. Coat of Arms and Inscription in Sheet

1896				
4	A1a	1p violet	145.00	*160.00*
		Wmk. 43		
4A	A1a	1p violet	27.50	*47.50*

Originally intended for revenue use, Nos. 4-4A were later authorized for postal use. Beware of fraudulently removed fiscal markings.

1894		**Wmk. 41**		**Thin Paper**
5	A1	½p orange	4.00	2.25
a.		Imperf., pair		
b.		½p buff	11.00	5.50
c.		½p yellow	7.75	2.25
6	A1	1p magenta	12.00	10.50
7	A1	2p purple	9.00	5.00
a.		Imperf., pair	—	—
b.		Double impression		*2,000.*
c.		Printed on both sides	*2,500.*	
d.		Tete beche pair	*6,250.*	
		Nos. 5-7 (3)	25.00	17.75

A2

A3

A4

A5

1898				**Thin Paper**
8	A2	3p ultra	2.10	1.60
a.		Double impression	950.00	
b.		Horiz. pair, imperf. between	800.00	
c.		Vert. pair, imperf. between	900.00	
9	A3	½p gray green	2.50	2.25
a.		Pair, one sideways		3,750.
b.		Horiz. pair, imperf. between	*1,750.*	*1,700.*
10	A4	1p rose	5.50	2.50
a.		Laid paper		2,400.
b.		Tete beche pair	5,250.	3,250.
c.		As "a," tete beche pair		*12,000.*
11	A5	2p purple	5.00	3.25
a.		Vert. pair, imperf. between	850.00	
b.		Vert. strip of 3, imperf. between	1,000.	
		Nos. 8-11 (4)	15.10	9.60

1903 **Thick Paper**

12 A2 3p ultra 1.80 .25
 d. Horiz. pair, imperf. between *1,350.*
 i. Double impression 450.00
12A A3 ½p gray green 1.90 .60
 e. Double impression 450.00
 f. Pair, one sideways 1,350. 1,350.
 j. Horiz. pair, imperf. between *1,750.*
12B A4 1p rose 2.50 .25
 g. Tete beche pair 5,250.
12C A5 2p purple 3.75 .75
 h. Double impression 1,250. 450.00
 Nos. 12-12C (4) 9.95 1.85

Beware of fake overprint surcharge varieties, such as double, inverted, etc. This applies also to early Official varieties. Such varieties require expertization.

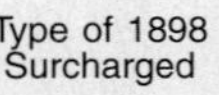
Type of 1898 Surcharged

1909

13 A2 2p on 3p red violet .25 *.75*
 a. Inverted surcharge 160.00 160.00
 b. Pair, stamps tete beche 250.00 *300.00*
 c. Pair, stamps & surch. tete beche 300.00 *400.00*

The surcharge is also known in a thin "2" measuring 5½x7mm, with curving foot. Values: unused $1,200; used $600.

Sri Rama Varma I — A6

1911-13 **Engr.** ***Perf. 14***

14 A6 2p brown .55 .25
 a. Imperf., pair
15 A6 3p blue 3.00 .25
 a. Perf. 14x12½ 40.00 3.00
16 A6 4p yel green 3.25 .25
16A A6 4p apple green 4.00 .75
17 A6 9p car rose 2.75 .25
18 A6 1a orange buff 4.50 .25
19 A6 1½a lilac 11.00 .65
20 A6 2a gray 11.00 .60
21 A6 3a vermilion 57.50 57.50
 Nos. 14-21 (8) 93.55 60.00

For surcharge and overprints see Nos. 34, O2-O9, O23-O24, O27.

Sri Rama Varma II
A7 A8

1918-23 **Engr.** ***Perf. 14***

23 A7 2p brown 12.00 .25
 a. Imperf., pair *750.00*
24 A7 4p green 1.50 .25
25 A7 6p red brown ('22) 3.75 .25
26 A7 8p black brown ('23) 2.50 .25
27 A7 9p carmine rose 32.50 .50
28 A7 10p deep blue 9.00 .25
29 A8 1a brown orange 27.50 5.00
30 A7 1½a red violet ('21) 5.50 .30
31 A7 2a gray 6.25 .25
32 A7 2¼a yel green ('22) 10.50 4.75
33 A7 3a vermilion 17.50 .50
 Nos. 23-33 (11) 128.50 12.55

The 2p and 1a are found in two types, the difference lying in the first of the three characters directly above the maharaja's head.

For surcharges and overprints see Nos. 36-40, 52-53, O10-O22, O25-O26, O28-O36, O71A.

No. 15 Surcharged

Type I — Numeral 8mm high. Curved foot. Top begins with a ball. (As illustrated.)
Type II — Numeral 9mm high. Curved foot. Top begins with a curved line.
Type III — Numeral 6mm high. Straight foot. "Two pies" 15mm wide.
Type IV — "2" as in type III. Capital "P" in "Pies." "Two Pies" 13mm wide.
Type V — Heavy gothic numeral. Capital "P" in "Pies."

1922-29

34 A6 2p on 3p blue (Type I) .60 .45
 a. Type II 5.00 1.25
 b. Type III 10.50 .50
 c. Type IV 17.50 20.00
 d. Type V 120.00 *225.00*
 e. Double surcharge, I 500.00 500.00
 f. Double surcharge II 1,100.
 g. As "b," perf. 14x12½ 17.50 20.00

Types II and III exist with a capital "P" in "Pies." It occurs once in each sheet of the second and third settings. There are four settings.

Type V is the first stamp, fourth row, of the fourth setting.

No. 32 Surcharged

1928

36 A7 1a on 2¼a yel green 9.00 *18.00*
 a. Double surcharge
 b. "REVENUF" for "REVENUE" 85.00 125.00

Nos. 24, 26 and 28 Surcharged in Black

1932-33

38 A7 3p on 4p green 1.90 *2.10*
 a. "r" in "Three" inverted *575.00*
39 A7 3p on 8p black brown 3.25 *4.00*
40 A7 9p on 10p deep blue 2.25 *5.00*
 Nos. 38-40 (3) 7.40 11.10

Sri Rama Varma III
A9 A10

1933-38 **Engr.** ***Perf. 13x13½***

41 A9 2p brown ('36) 1.50 .75
42 A9 4p green .90 .25
43 A9 6p red brown 1.00 .25
44 A10 1a brown org ('34) 2.00 .30
45 A9 1a8p rose red 4.50 *9.50*
46 A9 2a gray black ('38) 9.00 2.40
47 A9 2¼a yellow green 2.50 .45
48 A9 3a red org ('38) 8.25 2.40
49 A9 3a4p violet 2.50 2.10
50 A9 6a8p black brown 2.50 22.50
51 A9 10a deep blue 4.50 25.00
 Nos. 41-51 (11) 39.15 65.90

See Nos. 55-58. For overprints and surcharges see Nos. 54, 59-62, 73A-74, 76-77, 89, O37-O57, O70-O71, O72-O77A, O89.

Nos. 26 and 28 Surcharged in Red

1934 ***Perf. 13½***

52 A7 6p on 8p black brown 1.10 .90
53 A7 6p on 10p dark blue 2.50 *3.00*

No. 44 Overprinted in Black — a

1939 **Engr.**

54 A10 1a brown orange 10.00 2.50

Types of 1933-38

1938-41 **Litho.** ***Perf. 11***

55 A9 2p dull brown 1.25 .60
56 A9 4p dl grn ('41) 1.25 .50
57 A9 6p red brown 4.50 .25
57A A10 1a brn org 95.00 *140.00*
58 A10 2¼a yellow green 7.50 .35
 Nos. 55-58 (5) 109.50 *141.70*

Perf. 13x13½

55B A9 2p dull brown 11.00 1.00
56B A9 4p dl grn ('41) 10.00 20.00
57C A9 6p red brown 5,250.
57D A10 1a brn org 160.00 *200.00*
58B A10 2¼a yellow green 22.50 8.00

Type of 1934 Overprinted in Black Type "a" or — b

1941-42 ***Perf. 11 (#59), 13 (#60)***

59 A10(a) 1a brown org 525.00 2.50
 a. Perf. 13 525.00
60 A10(b) 1a brn org ('42) 20.00 1.00
 a. Perf. 11 1.25 2.50

No. 45 Surcharged in Black — c

1943-44 **Engr.** ***Perf. 13x13½***

61 A9 3p on 1a8p rose red ('44) 12.50 *25.00*
62 A9 1a3p on 1a8p rose red 1.25 .75

Maharaja Sri Kerala Varma
A11 A12

1943 **Litho.** **Wmk. 294** ***Perf. 11, 13***

63 A11 2p dull gray brn, wmk. 41 8.00 *9.00*
 a. Wmk. 294 42.50 6.25
 b. #63, Perf. 11 *3,500.*
 c. As 'a,', perf. 11 *4,500.*
64 A11 4p gray green, wmk. 294 8.00 25.00
 a. Wmk. 41 1,750. *625.00*
 b. #64, perf. 11 4.75 *6.25*
65 A11 6p red brown 7.50 .25
 a. Perf. 11 10.00 2.00
66 A11 9p ultramarine 75.00 1.90
 a. Horiz. pair, imperf. between 3,500.
67 A12 1a brn org, wmk. 294 27.50 85.00
 a. Wmk. 41 150.00 *175.00*
 b. Perf. 13x13½ *225.00* *275.00*
68 A11 2¼a lt ol green 35.00 10.00
 a. Perf. 13x13½ 40.00 6.00
 Nos. 63-68 (6) 161.00 131.15

For surcharges and overprints see Nos. 69-73, 75, 78, 78B, O58-O69.

No. 64 Surcharged Type "c"

69 A11 3p on 4p gray green 9.50 .25
 a. Wmk. 41 140.00 35.00

Nos. 64, 64a and 65 Surcharged in Black — d

1944-48 **Wmk. 294**

70 A11 2p on 6p red brown .95 *6.00*
 a. Perf. 11 1.20 3.50
71 A11 3p on 4p gray green 12.50 .25
72 A11 3p on 6p red brown 1.00 1.00
 a. Perf. 13x13½ 2.50 .25
73 A11 4p on 6p red brown 8.50 *18.00*
 Nos. 70-73 (4) 22.95 25.25

Nos. 57A, 67a Surcharged in Black

1944 **Litho.** **Wmk. 41**

73A A10 6p on 1a brn org *250.00* 100.00
 b. Perf. 11 450.00 275.00
74 A10 9p on 1a brn org 550.00 60.00
75 A12 9p on 1a brn org 12.00 6.25
 Nos. 73A-75 (3) *812.00* 166.25

No. 56 Surcharged Type "c" in Black

76 A9 3p on 4p dull green 8.75 6.00
 a. Perf. 13x13½ 25.00 5.00

Nos. 57A, 67a Surcharged in Black

1944

77 A10 9p on 1a brown orange 45.00 12.50
78 A12 9p on 1a brown orange 14.00 5.00

No. 67a Surcharged Type "c"

1944 **Wmk. 41**

78B A12 1a3p on 1a brn org 7,750.

Maharaja Ravi Varma — A13

1944-46 **Wmk. 294** ***Perf. 13***

79 A13 9p ultra ('46) 32.50 27.50
 a. Perf. 11 27.50 8.00
 b. Perf. 13x13½ 62.50 7.00
80 A13 1a3p magenta 12.50 12.50
 a. Perf. 13x13½ *500.00* 110.00
81 A13 1a9p ultra ('46) 12.00 24.00
 Nos. 79-81 (3) 57.00 64.00

For overprints and surcharges see Nos. O78-O80, Travancore-Cochin Nos. 12, 14, O10.

Maharaja Ravi Varma — A15

1946-50 Litho. *Perf. 13*

82 A15 2p dull brown 4.00 .25
a. Perf. 11 10.00 .90
b. Perf. 11x13 *550.00* 210.00
c. Vert. pair, imperf. horiz. *4,250.* *4,250.*
83 A15 3p carmine rose .60 .45
83A A15 4p gray grn ('50) *4,000.* 120.00
84 A15 6p red brn ('47) 30.00 11.00
a. Perf. 11 250.00 8.25
85 A15 9p ultramarine 3.50 .25
a. Horiz. pair, imperf. between *4,000.*
86 A15 1a dp org ('47) 11.00 *47.50*
a. Perf. 11 750.00
87 A15 2a gray ('47) 175.00 12.50
a. Perf. 11 225.00 10.00
88 A15 3a vermilion 110.00 4.00
Nos. 82-83,84-88 (7) 334.10 75.95

For surcharges and overprints see Nos. 98-99, O81-O88, Travancore-Cochin Nos. 8, 13, 15-15A, O11.

No. 45 Surcharged Type "d"

Perf. 13x13½

1947-48 Wmk. 41 Engr.

89 A9 6p on 1a8p rose red 6.00 30.00

Maharaja Sri Kerala Varma II — A16

Die I Die II

Two dies on 2p:
Die I, back of headdress almost touches value tablet.
Die II, back of headdress farther away from value tablet.

Die I

Die II

Two dies on 3a4p:
Die I, white frame line around head is continuous, and two white lines beneath value inscriptions at bottom.
Die II, white frame line around head broken by value tablets at the sides, and single white line beneath value inscriptions at bottom. Die II comes from the first two stamps of the bottom row of the sheet.

1948-49 Wmk. 294 *Perf. 11*

90 A16 2p olive brown 2.25 .25
a. Die II 190.00 4.50
b. #90, horiz. pair, imperf. vert. *4,000.*
91 A16 3p car ('49) 4.00 .25
a. #90, vert. pair, imperf. between *2,900.*
92 A16 4p gray green 21.00 6.25
a. Horiz. pair, imperf. vert. 375.00 500.00
93 A16 6p red brown 27.50 .35
94 A16 9p ultra ('49) 3.00 .90
95 A16 2a black 90.00 3.75
96 A16 3a ver ('49) 100.00 1.50
97 A16 3a4p violet ('49) 87.50 525.00
a. Die II 350.00
Nos. 90-97 (8) 335.25 538.25

For overprints see Nos. O90-O97, Travancore-Cochin Nos. 9-11, O8-O9, O24.

No. 86 Surcharged Type "d" in Black

1949

98 A15 6p on 1a dp orange 90.00 *225.00*
99 A15 9p on 1a dp orange 150.00 *225.00*

A17

Design: 2a, Chinese fishing net. 2¼a, Dutch Palace.

1949 Unwmk. *Perf. 11*

100 A17 2a gray black 9.00 *15.00*
a. Imperf. vert., horiz. pair 750.00
101 A17 2¼a dull green 3.50 *15.00*
a. Imperf. vert., horiz. pair 750.00 600.00

See Travancore-Cochin for succeeding issues.

OFFICIAL STAMPS

See note above No. 13.

Stamps and Type of 1911-14 Overprinted — h

1913-14 Wmk. 41 Engr. *Perf. 14*

O2 A6 4p yel green 15.00 .25
a. Inverted overprint — 450.00
O3 A6 9p car rose 25.00 .25
O4 A6 1½a red violet 72.50 .25
a. Double overprint — 1,100.
O5 A6 2a gray 19.00 .25
O6 A6 3a vermilion 82.50 .65
O7 A6 6a violet 90.00 3.00
O8 A6 12a blue 60.00 10.00
O9 A6 1½r deep green 52.50 *110.00*
Nos. O2-O9 (8) 416.50 124.65

Values for Nos. O2 and O3 are for the cheaper varieties with watermark sideways.

Stamps and Type of 1918-23 Overprinted — i

1918-34

O10 A7 4p green 6.25 .25
a. Double overprint — 825.00
O11 A7 6p red brn ('22) 22.50 .25
a. Double overprint — 750.00
O12 A7 8p blk brn ('26) 16.00 .25
O13 A7 9p carmine rose 97.50 .25
O14 A7 10p dp blue ('23) 22.50 .25
O16 A7 1½a red vio ('21) 8.25 .25
a. Double overprint 1,100.
O17 A7 2a gray 62.50 .45
O18 A7 2¼a yel grn ('22) 20.00 .25
b. Double overprint 750.00
O19 A7 3a ver ('22) 27.50 .35
a. Double overprint 750.00
O20 A7 6a violet ('22) 57.50 .75
O21 A7 12a blue ('29) 25.00 7.50
O22 A7 1½r dk green ('34) 37.50 *175.00*
Nos. O10-O22 (12) 403.00 *185.80*

On Nos. O2-O22, width of overprint varies from 14¾mm to 16½mm.

No. 15 Overprinted in Red — j

1921

O23 A6 3p blue 175.00 .25
a. Overprint in black *1,900.*
b. Double overprint (R) 750.00
c. Inverted "S" (R) 75.00

Nos. O3 and O13 Surcharged with New Values

1923-29

O24 A6 8p on 9p car rose 525.00 2.50
a. Double surcharge 500.00
b. Uppercase "P" in "pies" 1,600. 75.00
O25 A7 8p on 9p car rose 150.00 .25
a. Double surcharge 400.00
b. Uppercase "P" in "pies" 250.00 15.00
O26 A7 10p on 9p car rose ('25) 120.00 1.50
a. Double surcharge 450.00
b. Surcharge measures 25mm 450.00
c. As "b," double surcharge 500.00
O27 A6 10p on 9p car rose ('29) 2,200. 27.50
a. Double surcharge 900.00
Nos. O24-O27 (4) 2,995. 31.75

Surcharge measures 27½ mm.

Regular Issue of 1918-23 Overprinted — k

1929-31

O28 A7 4p green ('31) 32.50 3.00
O29 A7 6p red brown ('30) 21.00 .25
O30 A7 8p black brown ('30) 10.00 .25
O31 A7 10p deep blue 9.00 .25
O32 A7 2a gray ('30) 60.00 .35
O33 A7 3a vermilion ('30) 12.50 .30
O34 A7 6a dk violet ('30) 150.00 4.50
Nos. O28-O34 (7) 295.00 8.90

Inverted "S" in Overprint

O28a A7 4p green ('31) 325.00 25.00
O29a A7 6p red brown ('30) 175.00 5.50
O30a A7 8p black brown ('30) 85.00 6.00
O31a A7 10p deep blue 85.00 6.00
O32a A7 2a gray ('30) 400.00 15.00
O33a A7 3a vermilion ('30) 150.00 10.00
O34a A7 6a dk violet ('30) 950.00 125.00
Nos. O28a-O34a (7) 2,170. 192.50

Same with Additional Surcharge on Type of Regular Issue of 1918-23 in Red

1933

O35 A7 6p on 8p black brown 3.75 .25
a. Inverted "S" 32.50 6.00
O36 A7 6p on 10p dk blue 6.00 .25
a. Inverted "S" 60.00 5.00

Regular Issue of 1933 Overprinted Type "k" in Black as in 1933-34

1933-35 *Perf. 13x13½*

O37 A9 4p green 8.50 .25
O38 A9 6p red brown 7.50 .25
O39 A10 1a brown orange 27.50 .25
O40 A9 1a8p rose red 2.25 .45
O41 A9 2a gray 35.00 .25
O42 A9 2¼a yellow green 12.50 .25
O43 A9 3a vermilion 67.50 .25
O44 A9 3a4p violet 2.25 .25
O45 A9 6a8p black brown 2.25 .30
O46 A9 10a deep blue 2.25 2.00
Nos. O37-O46 (10) 167.50 4.50

Regular Stamps of 1934-38 Overprinted in Black — m

1937-38 *Perf. 11, 13x13½*

O47 A10 1a brown orange 50.00 .90
O48 A9 2a gray black 27.50 3.00
O49 A9 3a red orange 13.50 3.75
Nos. O47-O49 (3) 91.00 7.65

Similar Overprint on Types of 1933-36

Perf. 11, 13x13½

1938-44 Litho. Wmk. 294

O50 A9 4p dl grn, perf. 13x13½ 3.00 1.00
a. Perf. 11 ('42) 110.00 24.00

Wmk. 41

O51 A9 6p red brown ('41) 18.00 7.00
a. Wmk. 294 25.00 1.50
b. As "a," perf. 11 250.00 12.50
c. Printed both sides *250.00*
O52 A10 1a brown orange 1.25 .25
a. Wmk. 294 3.00 *6.50*
b. As "a," perf. 11 15.00 6.00
c. Printed both sides *250.00*
O53 A9 3a orange ('40) 3.75 3.25
b. Wmk. 294 30.00 12.50
Nos. O50-O53 (4) 26.00 11.50

Similar Overprint in Narrow Serifed Capitals on No. 57

Wmk. 41 *Perf. 11*

O53A A9 6p red brown 1,250. 600.00

Type of 1933-36 Overprinted in Black — o

Perf. 10½, 11, 13x13½

O54 A9 4p dl grn, perf. 13x13½ ('41) 27.50 3.25
a. Perf. 11 40.00 4.00
b. Inverted "S" 55.00 4.00
O55 A9 6p red brown ('41) 40.00 .60
a. Inverted "S" 50.00 3.00
O56 A9 2a gray black 25.00 1.50
a. Inverted "S" 27.50 2.00
Nos. O54-O56 (3) 92.50 5.35

Type of 1934 Overprinted in Black — p

1941 *Perf. 11*

O57 A10 1a brown orange 425.00 3.75

Stamps and Types of 1944 Overprinted in Black — q

Perf. 11, 13x13½

1944-48 Wmk. 294

O58 A11 4p gray green 75.00 12.50
a. Perf. 11 200.00 8.25
b. Perf. 13 750.00 90.00
O59 A11 6p red brn, perf. 11 3.50 .25
a. Perf. 13x13½ 5.50 .25
b. Perf. 13 10.00 3.50
c. As "a," double overprint 175.00 8.25
d. As "b," double overprint *120.00*
O59E A11 1a brn org, perf. 13x13½ 17,000. 85.00
O60 A11 2a gray black 8.75 1.50
O61 A11 2¼a dl yel grn 5.25 1.60
a. Additional ovpt. on reverse 200.00
O62 A11 3a red org, perf. 13x13½ 13.50 3.75
a. Perf. 11 16.00 .50
Nos. O58-O62 (5) 106.00 19.60

Same Overprint with Additional Surcharge

O63 A11 3p on 4p gray grn, perf. 13x13½ 5.50 .25
a. Perf. 11 12.50 .75
b. As "a," additional overprint on reverse 210.00
O64 A12 3p on 1a brn org 40.00 12.50
O65 A11 9p on 6p red brn 17.00 6.00
a. Additional overprint on reverse 750.00
O66 A12 1a3p on 1a brn org 26.00 5.00
Nos. O63-O66 (4) 88.50 23.75

Same Overprint in Black on Types of 1944 Surcharged Type "c"

O67 A11 3p on 4p gray grn, perf. 13½x13 8.00 .80
a. Perf. 11 600.00 225.00
O68 A11 9p on 6p red brn 7.50 1.00
O69 A12 1a3p on 1a brn org 5.50 .25
Nos. O67-O69 (3) 21.00 2.05

Nos. O52 and O16 Surcharged Type "d"

1944 Wmk. 41 ***Perf. 11, 13x13½, 14***
O70 A10 3p on 1a brn org 5.00 *5.00*
O71 A10 9p on 1a brn org 475.00 87.50

Engr.

O71A A7 9p on 1½a red vio 1,000. 40.00

No. O52 Surcharged Type "c"

O72 A10 1a3p on 1a brn org 500.00 150.00

No. 76 Overprinted in Black

Perf. 13x13½
O72A A9 3p on 4p dl grn 250.00 90.00

No. 45 Overprinted Type "k" and Surcharged Type "d"

1944-48 Wmk. 41 ***Perf. 13x13½***
O73 A9 9p on 1a8p rose red 200.00 50.00
O74 A9 1a9p on 1a8p rose red 5.00 4.00

No. 45 Overprinted Type "k" and Surcharged Type "c"

O75 A9 3p on 1a8p rose red 8.00 4.50
O76 A9 1a9p on 1a8p rose red 3.50 .60

Type of 1939-41 Overprinted in Black

1946 Wmk. 294 ***Perf. 11***
O77 A9 2a gray 110.00 1.20
b. Overprint omitted 2,000.
O77A A9 2¼a yellow green 2,900. 12.00

Same Overprint in Black on Nos. 79-81

1946 Litho. ***Perf. 13***
O78 A13 9p ultramarine 4.00 .25
a. Perf. 13x13½ 7.50 .25
b. Additional overprint on reverse 900.00
O79 A13 1a3p magenta 2.00 .25
a. Double overprint 25.00 18.00
b. Additional overprint on reverse 200.00
c. As "b," overprint doubled and inverted 110.00 100.00
O80 A13 1a9p ultramarine .50 *1.50*
a. Double overprint
b. Pair, one without overprint 2,750.
Nos. O78-O80 (3) 6.50 2.00

Types and Stamps of 1946-48 Overprinted Type "h"

1946-48
O81 A15 3p car rose 2.75 .25
a. Additional overprint on reverse *950.00*
O82 A15 4p gray green 40.00 10.00
O83 A15 6p red brown 25.00 4.00
O84 A15 9p ultra 1.00 .25
a. Additional overprint on reverse, inverted
O85 A15 1a3p magenta 7.50 2.10
O86 A15 1a9p ultra 8.50 .60
O87 A15 2a gray black 19.00 4.50
O88 A15 2¼a olive green 35.00 10.00
Nos. O81-O88 (8) 138.75 31.70

No. 56 Overprinted Type "q" and Surcharged Type "d"

1947 Wmk. 41 Engr. ***Perf. 13x13½***
O89 A9 3p on 4p dull green 50.00 17.50
a. Double surcharge 650.00 300.00

Stamps and Type of 1948-49 Overprinted Type "o"

1948-49 Wmk. 294 Litho. ***Perf. 11***
O90 A16 3p car ('49) 1.50 .25
O91 A16 4p gray green 3.00 .60
b. Additional overprint on reverse 120.00 120.00
c. Horizontal pair, imperf. between 2,500.
d. Vertical pair, imperf. between 2,500.
O92 A16 6p red brown 5.00 .45
b. Vertical pair, imperf. between 3,250.
O93 A16 9p ultramarine 6.00 .25
O94 A16 2a black ('49) 4.50 .25
O95 A16 2¼a lt ol grn ('49) 6.00 *9.50*
O96 A16 3a ver ('49) 1.50 *1.75*
O97 A16 3a4p dp pur ('49) 75.00 70.00
Nos. O90-O97 (8) 102.50 83.05

See Travancore-Cochin for succeeding issues.

"C" for "G" in Overprint

O90a A16 3p carmine 25.00 5.00
O91a A16 4p gray green 27.50 7.00
O92a A16 6p red brown 45.00 5.00
O93a A16 9p ultramarine 50.00 5.00
O94a A16 2a black ('49) 42.50 5.25
O95a A16 2¼a lt ol grn ('49) 50.00 *85.00*
O96a A16 3a vermilion ('49) 30.00 17.50
O97a A16 3a4p dp pur ('49) 425.00 *450.00*
Nos. O90a-O97a (8) 695.00 579.75

DHAR

'där

LOCATION — A Feudatory State in the Malwa Agency in Central India.
AREA — 1,800 sq. mi.
POP. — 243,521
CAPITAL — Dhar

Arms of Dhar — A1

The stamps of type A1 have an oval control mark handstamped in black.

1897-1900 Unwmk. Typeset Without Gum ***Imperf.***
1 A1 ½p black, *red* 4.50 *5.00*
a. Characters for "pice" transposed 100.00
b. Four characters in first word 4.00 *6.00*
c. Without control mark 500.00
2 A1 ¼a blk, *org red* ('00) 5.50 *7.50*
a. Without control mark 375.00
3 A1 ½a black, *lil rose* 6.75 *8.25*
4 A1 1a black, *bl grn* 12.50 *25.00*
5 A1 2a black, *yel* ('00) 42.50 *75.00*
Nos. 1-5 (5) 71.75 *120.75*

Arms of Dhar — A2

1898-1900 Typo. ***Perf. 11½***
6 A2 ½a red 7.00 *9.50*
7 A2 ½a rose ('00) 6.25 *9.00*
a. Imperf., pair 60.00
8 A2 1a maroon 6.25 *12.00*
9 A2 1a violet ('00) 6.25 *22.50*
10 A2 1a claret ('00) 6.25 *12.00*
11 A2 2a dark green ('00) 11.00 *37.50*
Nos. 6-11 (6) 43.00 *102.50*

Obsolete Mar. 31, 1901.

DUNGARPUR

'dəŋ-gˌə-ˌpər

LOCATION — A princely state in Rajasthan, in northwestern India.
AREA — 1,447 sq. mi.
POP. — 100,103 (1901)
CAPITAL — Dungarpur

Arms of Dungarpur — A1

1933-1947 Unwmk. Litho. ***Perf. 11***
1 A1 ¼a bister yellow 2,000. 400.00
On cover 1,000.
a. ¼a lemon yellow ('34) 2,500. 500.00
On cover 1,250.
2 A1 ¼a salmon ('35) 5,000. 1,000.
On cover 2,500.
a. ¼a red brown ('36) 3,750. 750.00
On cover 1,900.
b. ¼a orange red ('38) 6,250. 1,250.
On cover 3,100.
3 A1 1a pale turq bl 1,500. 300.00
On cover 750.00
a. 1a turquoise blue 2,000. 400.00
On cover 1,000.
4 A1 1a3p dp red vio ('35) 3,000. 600.00
On cover 2,400.
5 A1 2a dp dl grn ('47) 3,750. 750.00
On cover 3,000.
6 A1 4a dull rose red 6,250. 1,250.
On cover 5,000.
a. 4a rose red ('34) 7,000. 1,400.
On cover 5,500.

A2

A3

A4

A5

Maharawal Lakshman Singh

1934-38 Typo. ***Perf. 12***
7 A2 ¼a org buff ('36) 1,750. 200.00
On cover 450.00
8 A3 ½a vermilion, Die I 500.00 125.00
On cover 350.00
9 A4 1a blue
a. Perf 11½ ('38) 750.00 125.00
On cover 350.00
10 A5 4a gray brown 2,000. 650.00
On cover 2,000.

There are three dies of the ½ anna: Die I measures 21x25½mm, and width of turban is 7½mm; Die II measures 20x20½mm; Die III measures 21x25½mm, and width of turban is 6½mm. There are 4 distinct cliches of Die III, printed in a block of 4, differing in the space between the top of the turban and the frame: Pos. 1 = 2mm; Pos. 2 = 2.5mm; Pos. 3 = 1mm; Pos. 4 = 1.5mm.

Maharawal Lakshman Singh — A6

1940-41 ***Perf. 11, 11½ (#15)***
11 A2 ¼a dull org('41) 1,500. 150.00
On cover 300.00
12 A3 ½a carmine, Die I 500.00 150.00
On cover 450.00
13 A4 1a blue 500.00 100.00
On cover 250.00
14 A6 2a bright green 2,500. 900.00
On cover 2,500.
15 A5 4a gray brown 1,800. 450.00
On cover 1,350.

1943 ***Pin-Perf 11½***
16 A6 2a bright green 2,500. 900.00
On cover 2,500.

A7

A8

Maharawal Lakshman Singh

1943-44 ***Perf. 10½***
17 A2 ¼a dull org('44) 1,500. 150.00
On cover 300.00
18 A3 ½a ver, Die I ('44) 600.00 175.00
On cover 550.00
19 A7 ½a ver, Die II ('44) 600.00 175.00
On cover 550.00
a. Horiz. pair, #18 + #19 1,300. 450.
On cover 1,000.
b. Vert. pair, imperf between 5,000.
20 A4 1a blue ('44) 500.00 100.00
On cover 250.00
21 A8 1a3p mauve 2,000. 450.00
On cover 1,500.
22 A5 4a pale brown ('44) 2,400. 650.00
On cover 2,000.

A9

A10

Maharawal Lakshman Singh

1945 ***Perf. 10***
23 A2 ¼a orange 2,000. 150.00
On cover 300.00
24 A9 ½a ver, Die III ('44) 800.00 100.00
On cover 250.00
25 A4 1a blue 500.00 100.00
On cover 250.00
26 A8 1a3p bright mauve 2,000. 450.00
On cover 1,500.
27 A10 1½a deep violet 2,000. 450.00
On cover 1,350.
28 A5 4a brown 1,600. 400.00
On cover 1,000.

The stamps of Dungarpur became obsolete in Sept. 1949.

DUTTIA

'dət-ē-ə

(Datia)

LOCATION — A Feudatory State in the Bundelkhand Agency in Central India.
AREA — 912 sq. mi.
POP. — 158,834
CAPITAL — Datia

Ganesh, Elephant-headed God

A1 A2

All Duttia stamps have a circular control mark, about 23mm in diameter, handstamped in blue or black. All were issued without gum.

1893 Typeset Unwmk. *Imperf.*

1 A1 ¼a blk, *org red* 6,250.
2 A1 ½a blk, *grysh grn* 24,000.
3 A2 1a black, *red* 4,750. *7,500.*
4 A1 2a blk, *yel* 5,250.
5 A1 4a black, *rose* 1,900.

Type A2 with Frameline around God, Rosettes in Lower Corners

1896 (?)

5A A2 ½ black, *green* *15,000.*
5C A2 2a dk blue, *lemon* *3,750.*

A 1a in this revised type has been reported.

1897

6 A2 ½a black, *green* 100.00 *675.00*
7 A2 1a black 150.00 *525.00*
a. Laid paper 32.50
8 A2 2a black, *yellow* 42.50 *500.00*
9 A2 4a black, *rose* 40.00 *325.00*
Nos. 6-9 (4) 332.50 *2,025.*

A3

10 A3 ½a black, *green* 150.00 *825.00*
11 A3 1a black 290.00
12 A3 2a black, *yellow* 175.00 *825.00*
13 A3 4a black, *rose* 175.00 *825.00*
Nos. 10-13 (4) 790.00 2,475.

A4

Rouletted in Colored Lines on 2 or 3 Sides

1899-1900

14 A4 ¼a red (shades) 5.00 *32.50*
b. Tete beche pair *4,900.*
15 A4 ½a black, *green* 4.00 *30.00*
16 A4 1a black 4.50 *30.00*
17 A4 2a black, *yellow* 5.25 *35.00*
18 A4 4a black, *rose red* 5.00 *32.50*
a. Tete beche pair
Nos. 14-18 (5) 23.75 160.00

1904 ***Imperf.***

22 A4 ¼a carmine 5.50 *47.50*
23 A4 ½a black, *green* 27.50
24 A4 1a black 21.00 *75.00*
Nos. 22-24 (3) 54.00 122.50

1911 ***Perf. 13½***

25 A4 ¼a carmine 9.50 *75.00*

1916 ***Imperf.***

26 A4 ¼a dull blue 8.25 *40.00*
27 A4 ½a green 8.25 *40.00*
28 A4 1a violet 10.00 *42.50*
a. Tete beche pair 35.00
29 A4 2a brown 22.50 *52.50*
29A A4 4a brick red 110.00
Nos. 26-29A (5) 159.00 175.00

1918

31 A4 ½a ultramarine 5.25 *27.50*
32 A4 1a rose 5.25 *27.50*
33 A4 2a violet 11.00 *40.00*

Perf. 12

34 A4 ¼a black 7.50 *37.50*
Nos. 31-34 (4) 29.00 *132.50*

1920 ***Rouletted***

35 A4 ¼a blue 4.00 *21.00*
36 A4 ½a rose 5.25 *24.00*

Perf. 7

37 A4 ½a dull red 24.00 *62.50*
Nos. 35-37 (3) 33.25 *107.50*

Duttia stamps became obsolete in 1921.

FARIDKOT

fe-ˈrēd-ˌkōt

LOCATION — A Feudatory State in the Punjab Agency of India.
AREA — 638 sq. mi.
POP. — 164,364
CAPITAL — Faridkot

4 Folus or Paisas = 1 Anna

A1

A2

A3

Handstamped

1879-86 Unwmk. *Imperf.*
Without Gum

1 A1 1f ultramarine 4.00 *6.00*
a. Laid paper 21.00 *24.00*
b. Tete beche pair 400.00
2 A2 1p ultramarine 7.50 *16.00*
a. Laid paper 125.00 *150.00*
3 A3 1p ultramarine 2.25
a. Tete beche pair 340.00
Nos. 1-3 (3) 13.75 22.00

Several other varieties exist, but it is believed that only the stamps listed here were issued for postal use. They became obsolete Dec. 31, 1886. See Faridkot under Convention States for issues of 1887-1900.

HYDERABAD (DECCAN)

ˈhīd-ə-ˌrə-ˌbad

LOCATION — Central India
AREA — 82,313 sq. mi.
POP. — 16,338,534 (1941)
CAPITAL — Hyderabad

This independent princely state was occupied and annexed by India in 1948.

Catalogue values for unused stamps in this State are for Never Hinged items, beginning with Scott 51 in the regular postage section, and Scott O54 in the officials section.

Expect irregular perfs on the Nos. 1-14 and O1-O20 due to the nature of the paper.

A1

A2

1869-71 Engr. Unwmk. *Perf. 11½*

1 A1 ½a brown ('71) 6.00 *6.50*
2 A2 1a olive green 27.50 11.00
a. Imperf. horiz., pair 900.00 175.00
3 A1 2a green ('71) 90.00 72.50
Nos. 1-3 (3) 123.50 90.00

For overprints see Nos. O1-O3, O11-O13.
The reprints are perforated 12½.

A3

Wove Paper

1871-1909 ***Perf. 12½***

4 A3 ½a org brn 4.00 .25
a. ½a red brown 4.00 .25
b. ½a magenta (error) 75.00 12.00
c. Perf. 11½ 27.50 *30.00*
d. ½a rose 4.00 .30
e. ½a bright vermilion 4.00 .25
5 A3 1a dark brown 1.90 .25
a. Imperf., pair 550.00
b. Horiz. pair, imperf. vert. 1,350.
c. Vert. pair, imperf. horiz. 1,350.
d. Perf. 11½ 180.00 *200.00*
6 A3 1a black ('09) 3.50 .25
7 A3 2a green 5.50 .25
a. 2a olive green ('09) 5.50 .50
b. Perf. 11½ 1,900.
8 A3 3a yellow brown 4.50 2.25
a. Perf. 11½ 60.00 *82.50*
9 A3 4a slate 11.00 5.25
a. Imperf. horiz., pair 1,350. 1,350.
b. Perf. 11½ 225.00 225.00
10 A3 4a deep green 8.25 5.00
a. 4a olive green 9.00 3.75
11 A3 8a bister brown 5.25 *6.50*
a. Perf. 11½
12 A3 12a blue 7.00 *12.00*
a. Perf. 11½ 500.00
b. 12a slate green 7.50 7.50
Nos. 4-12 (9) 50.90 32.00

For overprints see Nos. 13, O4-O10, O14-O20, O25-O26.

Surcharged

1900

13 A3 ¼a on ½a brt ver .75 *1.25*
a. Inverted surcharge 57.50 35.00

A4

1900, Sept. 20

14 A4 ¼a blue 8.25 5.25

Seal of the Nizam — A5

Engraved by A. G. Wyon

1905 Wmk. 42

17 A5 ¼a blue 3.75 .90
18 A5 ½a red 6.00 .35
19 A5 ½a orange 9.00 .50
Nos. 17-19 (3) 18.75 1.75

For overprints see Nos. O21-O23.

Perf. 11, 11½, 12½, 13½ and Compound

1908-11

20 A5 ¼a gray 1.50 .25
21 A5 ½a green 7.00 .25
22 A5 1a carmine 5.25 .25
23 A5 2a lilac 2.40 .25
24 A5 3a brn orange ('09) 4.00 1.50
25 A5 4a olive green ('09) 4.50 1.90
26 A5 8a violet ('11) 1.90 1.20
27 A5 12a blue green ('11) 10.50 6.00
Nos. 20-27 (8) 37.05 11.60

For overprints see Nos. O24, O27-O38.

Engr. by Bradbury, Wilkinson & Co.

1912

28 A5 ¼a brown violet 1.20 .25
29 A5 ½a deep green 2.50 .25
a. Imperf., pair 550.00

The frame of type A5 differs slightly in each denomination.
Nos. 20-21 measure 19½x20½mm.
Nos. 28-29 measure 20x21½mm.
For overprints see Nos 37, O39-O40, O44.

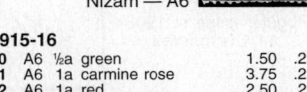

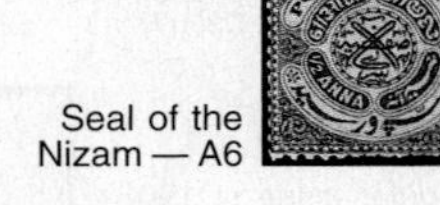
Seal of the Nizam — A6

1915-16

30 A6 ½a green 1.50 .25
31 A6 1a carmine rose 3.75 .25
32 A6 1a red 2.50 .25
Nos. 30-32 (3) 7.75 .75

Unless used, imperf. stamps of types A5 and A6 are from plate proof sheets.

See No. 58. For overprints see Nos. 38, O41-O43, O45.

A7

1927 Wmk. 211 *Perf. 13½*

36 A7 1r yellow 13.50 *18.00*

Stamps of 1912-16 Surcharged in Red

(4 pies)

(8 pies)

1930

37 A5 4p on ¼a brn vio .45 .25
a. Perf. 11 675.00
b. Double surcharge 350.00
38 A6 8p on ½a green .60 .25
a. Perf. 11 400.00 210.00

For overprints see Nos. O44-O45.

Seal of Nizam — A8

Char Minar — A9

High Court of Justice A10

Reservoir for City of Hyderabad A11

Bidar College — A13

Entrance to Ajanta Caves A12

Victory Tower at Daulatabad A14

Wmk. 211

1931-48 Engr. *Perf. 13½*

39 A8 4p black .45 .25
a. Laid paper ('47) 3.75 *8.25*
39B A8 6p car lake ('48) 15.00 12.50
40 A8 8p green .75 .25
a. 8p yel grn, laid paper ('47) 4.50 *6.75*
b. Imperf., pair 90.00 *180.00*
41 A9 1a dark brown .75 .25
42 A10 2a dark violet 4.50 .25
a. Imperf., pair 195.00 *400.00*
43 A11 4a ultramarine 2.40 1.00
a. Imperf., pair 210.00 *500.00*

44 A12 8a deep orange 10.50 6.00
45 A13 12a scarlet 11.00 *18.00*
46 A14 1r yellow 7.50 7.00
Nos. 39-46 (9) 52.85 45.50

On No. 39B, "POSTAGE" has been moved to ribbon at bottom of design.

Nos. 39a and 40a are printed from worn plates. The background of the design is unshaded.

See No. 59. For overprints see Nos. O46-O53, O56.

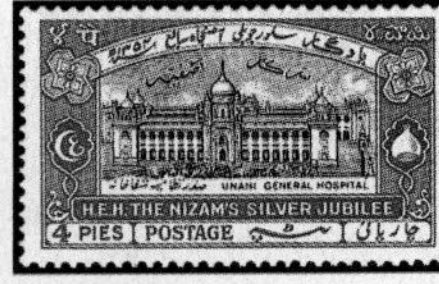

Unani General Hospital A15

Osmania General Hospital A16

Osmania University A17

Osmania Jubilee Hall — A18

Perf. 13½x14

1937, Feb. 13 Litho. Unwmk.

47 A15 4p violet & black .75 *3.25*
48 A16 8p brown & black 1.25 *3.25*
49 A17 1a dull orange & gray 1.75 *2.10*
50 A18 2a dull green & gray 2.25 *6.75*
Nos. 47-50 (4) 6.00 *15.35*

The Nizam's Silver Jubilee.

Catalogue values for unused stamps in this section, from this point to the end of the section, are for Never Hinged items.

Returning Soldier — A19

1946 Typo. *Perf. 13½*

51 A19 1a dark blue .25 .25

Wmk. 211

52 A19 1a blue .25 .25

Wmk. Nizam's Seal in Sheet

Laid Paper

53 A19 1a dark blue 1.00 *1.20*
Nos. 51-53 (3) 1.50 1.70

Victory of the Allied Nations in WW II.

Town Hall, Hyderabad A20

1947, Feb. 17 Litho. Wove Paper

54 A20 1a black 2.00 *2.90*

Inauguration of the Reformed Legislature, Feb. 17th, 1947.

Power House, Hyderabad A21

Designs: 3a, Kaktyai Arch, Warangal Fort. 6a, Golkunda Fort.

Perf. 13½x14

1947-49 Typo. Wmk. 211

55 A21 1a4p dark green 1.50 *3.25*
56 A21 3a blue 2.50 *6.50*
57 A21 6a olive brown 5.50 *27.50*
a. 6a red brown ('49) 25.00 *47.50*
b. Imperf., pair 190.00
Nos. 55-57 (3) 9.50 37.25

Seal Type of 1915

1947 Engr. *Perf. 13½*

58 A6 ½a rose lake 3.75 1.10

For overprint see No. O54.

Seal Type of 1931

1949 Litho.

59 A8 2p brown 3.00 3.50

For overprint see No. O55.

OFFICIAL STAMPS

Regular Issues of 1869-71 Overprinted

1873 Unwmk. *Perf. 11½, 12½*

Red Overprint

O1 A1 ½a brown 195.00 125.00
O2 A2 1a olive green 35.00 35.00
O3 A1 2a green 72.50 57.50
O4 A3 ½a red brown 27.50 9.00
O5 A3 1a dark brown 195.00 125.00
O6 A3 2a green 72.50 57.50
O7 A3 3a yel brown 250.00 250.00
O8 A3 4a slate 120.00 72.50
O9 A3 8a bister 125.00 *225.00*
O10 A3 12a blue 195.00 *240.00*

Black Overprint

O11 A1 ½a brown 52.50
O12 A2 1a olive green 4.50 3.75
O13 A1 2a green 7.50 *9.00*
O14 A3 ½a red brown 16.00 5.25
O15 A3 1a dark brown — 52.50
O16 A3 2a green 7.50 *9.00*
O17 A3 3a yel brown 62.50 52.50
O18 A3 4a slate 32.50 30.00
O19 A3 8a bister 75.00 62.50
O20 A3 12a blue 90.00 *120.00*

The above official stamps became obsolete in August, 1878. Since that date the "Official" overprint has been applied to the reprints and probably to original stamps. Two new varieties of the overprint have also appeared, both on the reprints and on the current stamps. These are overprinted in various colors, positions and combinations.

Same Ovpt. On Regular Issues of 1905-11

1908 Wmk. 42

O21 A5 ½a green 30.00 .25
O22 A5 1a carmine 97.50 .25
O23 A5 2a lilac 97.50 .25
Nos. O21-O23 (3) 225.00 .75

Perf. 11, 11½, 12½, 13½ and Compound

1909-11

O24 A5 ½a red 210.00 .25
O25 A3 1a black 140.00 .75
O26 A3 2a olive green 150.00 1.50
O27 A5 3a brown orange 11.00 5.00
O28 A5 4a olive green ('11) 45.00 1.90
O29 A5 8a violet ('11) 19.00 5.25
O30 A5 12a blue green ('11) 15.00 5.00
Nos. O24-O30 (7) 590.00 19.65

Regular Issue of 1908-11 Overprinted

1911-12

O31 A5 ¼a gray 6.75 1.10
O32 A5 ½a green 5.25 .25
O33 A5 1a carmine 3.00 .25
O34 A5 2a lilac 2.50 1.90
O35 A5 3a brown orange 27.50 1.10
O36 A5 4a olive green 7.00 .25
O37 A5 8a violet 11.00 .30
O38 A5 12a blue green 36.00 3.75
Nos. O31-O38 (8) 99.00 8.90

Same Overprint on Regular Issue of 1912

1912

O39 A5 ¼a brown violet 5.50 .25
a. ¼a gray violet 5.50 .25
O40 A5 ½a deep green 5.25 .25

Same Ovpt. On Regular Issue of 1915-16

1917

O41 A6 ½a green 5.25 .25
O42 A6 1a carmine rose 7.00 .25
O43 A6 1a red 4.00 .25
Nos. O41-O43 (3) 16.25 .75

Same Overprint on Nos. 37 and 38

1930

O44 A5 4p on ¼a brown violet 3.25 .25
O45 A6 8p on ½a green 2.25 .25

Same Overprint on Regular Issue of 1931

1934-47 Wmk. 211 *Perf. 13½*

O46 A8 4p black 4.00 .25
a. Laid paper ('47) 7.50
b. Imperf., pair 120.00
O47 A8 8p green 1.90 .25
a. 8p yel grn, laid paper ('47) 10.00 7.50
b. Inverted overprint 240.00
O48 A9 1a dark brown 3.00 .25
O49 A10 2a dark violet 11.00 .25
O50 A11 4a ultramarine 6.00 .35
O51 A12 8a deep orange 21.00 .90
O52 A13 12a scarlet 19.00 2.50
O53 A14 1r yellow 30.00 3.75
Nos. O46-O53 (8) 95.90 8.50

Catalogue values for unused stamps in this section, from this point to the end of the section, are for Never Hinged items.

Same Overprint on Nos. 58-59, 39B

1947-50 *Perf. 13½*

O54 A6 ½a rose lake 9.00 *10.50*
O55 A8 2p brown ('49) 9.00 *15.00*
O56 A8 6p car lake ('50) 11.00 *35.00*
Nos. O54-O56 (3) 29.00 *60.50*

IDAR

'ē-dər

LOCATION — A Feudatory State in the Western India States Agency.
AREA — 1,669 sq. mi.
POP. — 262,660
CAPITAL — Himmatnagar

Stamps of Idar are in booklet panes of four. All stamps have one or two straight edges.

Maharaja Shri Himatsinhji — A1

1939 Unwmk. Typo. *Perf. 11*

1 A1 ½a light green 21.00 *37.50*

1941 Same Redrawn

2 A1 ½a green 17.50 *40.00*

The panels containing denomination and name of state are shaded.

Maharaja Shri Himatsinhji — A2

1944 Unwmk. *Perf. 12*

3 A2 ½a green 4.00 *110.00*
4 A2 1a purple 4.00 *100.00*
a. Imperf., pair 250.00
5 A2 2a blue 4.50 *150.00*
6 A2 4a red 4.75 *160.00*
Nos. 3-6 (4) 17.25

INDORE

in-'dō(ə)r

(Holkar)

LOCATION — A Feudatory State in the Indore Agency in Central India.
AREA — 9,902 sq. mi.
POP. — 1,513,966
CAPITAL — Indore

Maharaja Tukoji Rao II — A1

A2

1886 Unwmk. Litho. *Perf. 15*

1 A1 ½a lilac 5.50 3.25

1889 Handstamped *Imperf.*

3 A2 ¼a black, *rose* 5.25 *5.50*

No. 3 exists in two types.

The originals of this stamp are printed in water color. The reprints are in oil color and on paper of a deeper shade of rose.

Maharaja Shivaji Rao — A3

1889-92 Engr. *Perf. 15*

4 A3 ¼a orange 2.25 1.20
5 A3 ½a brown violet 3.75 .25
6 A3 1a green 4.50 1.90
7 A3 2a vermilion 10.50 3.00
Nos. 4-7 (4) 21.00 6.35

For overprint see No. 14.

Maharaja Tukoji Rao III
A4 A5

1904-08 *Perf. 13½, 14*

8 A4 ¼a orange .90 .25
9 A5 ½a lake ('08) 13.50 .25
a. Imperf., pair 35.00
10 A5 1a green ('07) 3.75 .25
a. Imperf., pair 175.00
11 A5 2a brown ('05) 22.50 1.50
a. Imperf., pair 120.00
12 A5 3a violet 35.00 10.50
13 A5 4a ultramarine 7.50 2.10
Nos. 8-13 (6) 83.15 14.85

For overprints see Nos. O1-O7.

No. 5 Surcharged

1905 *Perf. 15*

14 A3 ¼a on ½a brown violet 9.00 *30.00*

Maharaja Yeshwant Rao II
A6 A7

1928-38 **Engr.** *Perf. 13½*

15 A6 ¼a orange .90 .30
16 A6 ½a claret 3.25 .25
17 A6 1a green 4.00 .25
18 A6 1¼a green ('33) 6.00 1.25
19 A6 2a dark brown 19.00 3.25
20 A6 2a Prus blue ('36) 19.00 3.25
a. Imperf., pair 37.50 *275.00*
21 A6 3a dull violet 3.00 *14.00*
22 A6 3½a dull violet ('34) 10.50 *15.00*
a. Imperf, pair 100.00 *650.00*
23 A6 4a ultramarine 10.50 7.50
24 A6 4a bister ('38) 52.50 2.50
a. Imperf, pair 45.00 *500.00*
25 A6 8a gray 9.50 6.50
26 A6 8a red orange ('38) 40.00 35.00
27 A6 12a rose red ('34) 7.50 *15.00*

Perf. 14

28 A7 1r lt blue & black 12.50 *22.50*
29 A7 2r car lake & black 82.50 *90.00*
30 A7 5r org brn & black 140.00 140.00
Nos. 15-30 (16) 420.65 *356.55*

Imperforates of types A6 and A7 were used with official sanction at Indore City during a stamp shortage in 1938. They were from sheets placed by the printers (Perkins, Bacon) on top of packets of 100 perforated sheets as identification.

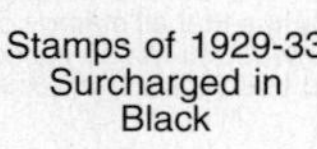

Stamps of 1929-33 Surcharged in Black

1940 *Perf. 13, 14*

31 A7 ¼a on 5r org brn & blk 19.00 2.50
a. Dbl. surch., black over green 700.00
32 A7 ½a on 2r car lake & blk 32.50 5.00
33 A6 1a on 1¼a green 32.50 1.20
a. Inverted surcharge 110.00
Nos. 31-33 (3) 84.00 8.70

Stamps with green surcharge only are proofs.

A8

1941-47 **Typo.** *Perf. 11*

34 A8 ¼a orange 2.50 .25
35 A8 ½a rose lilac 4.75 .25
36 A8 1a dk olive green 12.50 .25
37 A8 1¼a yellow green 20.00 20.00
a. Imperf., pair 275.00
38 A8 2a turquoise blue 14.00 1.75
39 A8 4a bister ('47) 20.00 20.00

Size: 23x28¼mm

40 A8 2r car lake & blk ('47) 16.00 *250.00*
41 A8 5r brn org & blk 15.00 *325.00*
Nos. 34-41 (8) 104.75 *617.50*

OFFICIAL STAMPS

Stamps and Type of 1904-08 Overprinted

1904-06 *Perf. 13½, 14*

O1 A5 ½a lake 1.10 *1.90*
a. Inverted overprint 35.00 *62.50*
b. Double overprint 35.00
c. Imperf., pair 110.00
O2 A5 1a green .25 .25
O3 A5 2a brown ('05) .45 .45
O4 A5 3a violet ('06) 2.50 *5.50*
a. Imperf., pair 425.00
O5 A5 4a ultra ('05) 7.50 2.25
Nos. O1-O5 (5) 11.80 10.35

No. O1-O5 has an "R" that has a curved foot that is wholly underneath the curve of the "R"

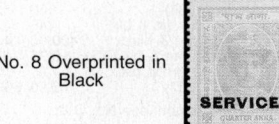

No. 8 Overprinted in Black

1907

O6 A4 ¼a orange 1.10 *1.90*

No. 9 Overprinted

O7 A5 ½a lake .25 1.75

No. O7 "SERVICE" in slightly thinner letters and the letter "R" has a straight foot which projects at a distinct angle beyond the curve of the "R" than No. O1.

JAIPUR

'jī-ˌpu̇ə̦r

LOCATION — A Feudatory State in the Jaipur Residency of India.
AREA — 15,610 sq. mi.
POP. — 3,040,876
CAPITAL — Jaipur

Catalogue values for unused stamps in this State are for Never Hinged items, beginning with Scott 49 in the regular postage section, and Scott O30 in the officials section.

A1

A1a

Chariot of Surya, Sun God

Pin-perf. 14x14½

1904 **Typo.** **Unwmk.**

1 A1 ½a ultramarine 290.00 275.00
a. ½a pale blue 210.00 *275.00*
b. ½a gray blue 3,250. 300.00
c. As "b," imperf. 525.00 *900.00*
1D A1a ½a blue 5.00 *10.00*
e. ½a ultramarine 5.50 *10.00*
f. Imperf. 5.50 *10.00*
2 A1 1a dull red 8.25 *21.00*
a. 1a chestnut 8.25 *21.00*
3 A1 2a pale green 8.25 *21.00*
a. 2a emerald 9.00
Nos. 1-3 (4) 311.50 *327.00*

No. 1 has 36 varieties (on 2 plates), differing in minor details. Nos. 1b and 1c are from plate II. No. 1D has 24 varieties (one plate).

Chariot of Surya — A2

Perf. 12½x12 and 13½

1904-06 **Engr.**

4 A2 ¼a olive green ('06) 1.25 *1.60*
5 A2 ½a deep blue 2.75 .75
6 A2 1a carmine 3.75 *6.75*
7 A2 2a dark green 5.25 2.25
8 A2 4a red brown 11.00 3.25
9 A2 8a violet 6.00 4.00
10 A2 1r yellow 35.00 24.00
Nos. 4-10 (7) 65.00 42.60

For overprints see Nos. 21-22.

A3

Without Gum

1911 **Typo.** *Imperf.*

11 A3 ¼a yellow green 3.75 *5.00*
a. ¼a olive green 3.75 *5.00*
b. "¼" inverted 9.00
12 A3 ¼a olive yellow .45 *1.50*
b. ¼a blue (error) —
13 A3 ½a ultramarine .45 *1.50*
a. ½a dull blue 4.00 4.00
b. "⅓" for "½" 7.00
14 A3 1a carmine .75 *1.50*
15 A3 2a deep green 3.00 *9.50*
a. 2a gray green 4.00 *8.25*
Nos. 11-15 (5) 8.40 *19.00*

There are six types for each value and several settings of the ¼a and ½a in the 1911 issue.

A4

Wmk. "Dorling & Co., London" in Sheet

1913-18 *Perf. 11*

16 A4 ¼a olive bister 1.00 *2.25*
a. Vert. pair, imperf. between 300.00 300.00
b. Horiz. pair, imperf. between — 240.00
17 A4 ½a ultramarine 2.25 1.90
18 A4 1a carmine ('18) 8.25 8.25
a. 1a scarlet 6.00 5.50
b. Vert. pair, imperf. btwn. 1,250. 1,250.
c. Vert. pair, imperf. horiz. 1,250.
19 A4 2a green ('18) 6.00 7.50
20 A4 4a red brown 10.50 *15.00*
Nos. 16-20 (5) 28.00 *34.90*

For overprints see Nos. O1-O6, O9-O10.

Stamps of 1904-06 Surcharged

1926 **Unwmk.** **Engr.** *Perf. 13½*

21 A2 3a on 8a violet 3.00 *5.25*
a. Inverted surcharge 275.00 210.00
22 A2 3a on 1r yellow 4.00 *9.50*
a. Inverted surcharge 825.00 275.00

Wmk. "Overland Bank" in Sheet

1928 **Typo.** *Perf. 12*

17a A4 ½a ultramarine 4.75 *6.00*
18d A4 1a rose red 40.00 25.00
18e A4 1a scarlet 62.50 17.50
19a A4 2a green 140.00 45.00
20a A4 4a pale brown
23 A4 1r red orange 600.00 *825.00*

Durbar Commemorative Issue

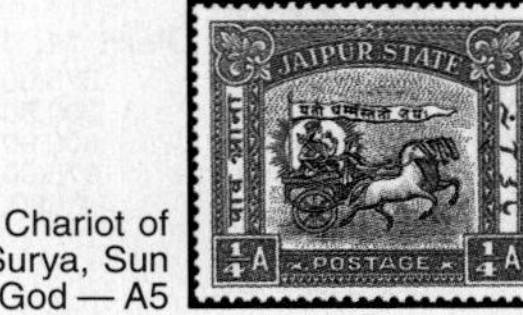

Chariot of Surya, Sun God — A5

Maharaja Man Singh II — A6

Elephant with Standard — A7

Sowar in Armor — A8

Blue Peafowl — A9

Royal Bullock Carriage — A10

Royal Elephant Carriage — A11

Albert Museum — A12

Sireh-Deorhi Gate — A13

Chandra Palace — A14

Amber Palace — A15

Rajas Jai Singh II and Man Singh II — A16

Perf. 13½x14, 14, 14x13½

1931, Mar. 14 Typo. Unwmk.
24 A5 ¼a red brn & blk 4.50 4.00
25 A6 ½a dull vio & blk .75 .30
26 A7 1a blue & black 13.50 *14.00*
27 A8 2a ocher & black 13.50 *14.00*
28 A9 2½a rose & black 47.50 *90.00*
29 A10 3a dk green & blk 27.50 *67.50*
30 A11 4a dull grn & blk 27.50 *82.50*
31 A12 6a dk blue & blk 9.00 *82.50*
32 A13 8a brown & black 30.00 *140.00*
33 A14 1r olive & black 60.00 *500.00*
34 A15 2r lt green & blk 62.50 *550.00*
35 A16 5r violet & black 82.50 *600.00*
Nos. 24-35 (12) 378.75 *2,145.*

Investiture of the Maharaja Man Singh II with full ruling powers.

Eighteen sets of this issue were overprinted in red "INVESTITURE—MARCH 14, 1931" for presentation to distinguished personages.

For surcharges see Nos. 47, 48, 58. For overprints see Nos. O12-O16, O22-O32, Rajasthan 16.

Man Singh II Type of 1931 and

Raja Man Singh II — A18

1932-46 ***Perf. 14***
36 A6 ¼a red brn & blk .75 .75
36A A6 ¾a brn org & blk ('43) 12.00 6.25
37 A18 1a blue & black 5.00 2.50
37A A6 1a blue & black 14.00 6.75
38 A18 2a ocher & black 6.75 4.00
38A A6 2a ocher & blk ('45) 19.00 7.50
39 A6 2½a dk car & blk 6.75 5.00
40 A6 3a green & black 6.00 1.00
41 A18 4a gray grn & blk 6.75 *17.50*
41A A6 4a gray grn & blk ('45) 72.50 2.40
42 A6 6a blue & black 9.00 *45.00*
43 A18 8a choc & black 9.00 *22.50*
43A A6 8a choc & blk ('45) 42.50 *190.00*
44 A18 1r bis & gray blk 40.00 *175.00*
44A A6 1r bis & gray blk ('46) 30.00 *240.00*
45 A18 2r yel grn & blk 140.00 *700.00*
Nos. 36-45 (16) 420.00 *1,426.*

For overprints see Nos. O17-O30, Rajasthan Nos. 15, 17-25.

Stamps of 1931-32 Surcharged in Red or Black

1936 ***Perf. 14x13½, 13½x14***
46 A18 1r on 2r yel grn & blk (R) 15.00 *160.00*
47 A16 1r on 5r violet & blk 15.00 *125.00*

No. 25 Surcharged in Red

1938 ***Perf. 14x13½***
48 A6 ¼a on ½a dl vio & blk 17.50 *25.00*

Catalogue values for unused stamps in this section, from this point to the end of the section, are for Never Hinged items.

Amber Palace A19

Designs: ¼a, Palace gate. ¾a, Map of Jaipur. 1a, Observatory. 2a, Palace of the Winds. 3a, Arms of the Raja. 4a, Gate of Amber Fort. 8a, Chariot of the Sun. 1r, Raja Man Singh II.

1947-48 Unwmk. Engr. ***Perf. 14***
49 A19 ¼a dk grn & red brn ('48) 2.25 *7.50*
50 A19 ½a blue vio & dp grn .75 *6.75*
51 A19 ¾a dk car & blk ('48) 2.25 *9.00*
52 A19 1a dp ultra & choc 1.50 *7.00*
53 A19 2a car & blue vio 1.50 *7.50*
54 A19 3a dk gray & grn ('48) 2.50 *9.50*
55 A19 4a choc & dp ultra 1.50 *7.50*
56 A19 8a dk brown & red 1.50 *9.00*
57 A19 1r dk red vio & bl grn ('48) 4.00 *67.50*
Nos. 49-57 (9) 17.75 *131.25*

25th anniv. of the enthronement of Raja Man Singh II.

No. 25 Surcharged in Carmine with New Value and Bars

1947
58 A6 3p on ½a 25.00 40.00
a. "3 PIE" 75.00 *160.00*
b. Inverted surcharge 72.50 62.50
c. Double surch., one inverted 110.00 82.50
d. As "a," inverted surcharge 375.00 325.00

For overprint see No. O31.

OFFICIAL STAMPS

Regular Issue of 1913-22 Overprinted in Black or Red

1929 Unwmk. ***Perf. 12½x12, 11***
O1 A4 ¼a olive green 3.75 *4.00*
O2 A4 ½a ultramarine 1.90 .30
a. Inverted overprint 675.00
O3 A4 ½a ultra (R) 4.00 .45
O4 A4 1a red 2.25 .45
O5 A4 2a green 2.25 .60
O6 A4 4a red brown 3.00 2.50
O7 A4 8a purple (R) 25.00 *82.50*
O8 A4 1r red orange 57.50 *550.00*
Nos. O1-O8 (8) 99.65 *640.80*

The 8a and 1r not issued without overprint.
For overprint see No. O11.

Regular Issue of 1913-22 Overprinted in Black or Red — b

1931 ***Perf. 11, 12½x12***
O9 A4 ½a ultra 575.00 .25
O10 A4 ½a ultra (R) 300.00 .25
O10A A4 8a purple 800.00 300.00
O10B A4 1r red orange 975.00 400.00
Nos. O9-O10B (4) 2,650. 700.50

No. O5 Surcharged

1932
O11 A4 ½a on 2a green 225.00 3.00

Regular Issue of 1931 Overprinted in Red

1931-37 ***Perf. 13½x14, 14***
O12 A6 ¼a red brn & blk ('36) .60 .25
O13 A6 ½a dull vio & blk .45 .25
O14 A7 1a blue & black 400.00 4.50
O15 A8 2a ocher & blk ('36) 6.75 *8.25*
O16 A11 4a dl grn & blk ('37) 72.50 60.00

For overprint see No. O32.

Same on Regular Issue of 1932 in Red

1932-37 ***Perf. 14***
O17 A18 1a blue & black 6.75 .30
O18 A18 2a ocher & black 8.25 .30
O19 A18 4a gray grn & blk ('37) *550.00* *16.00*
O20 A18 8a choc & black 17.50 1.60
O21 A18 1r bister & gray blk 45.00 40.00
Nos. O17-O21 (5) *627.50* *58.20*

No. 36 Overprinted Type "b" in Black

1939 ***Perf. 14***
O22 A6 ¼a red brown & blk 140.00 110.00

Nos. 36A, 38A, 39, 41A, 43A, 44A and Type of 1931 Overprinted in Carmine

1941-46 Unwmk. ***Perf. 13½, 14***
O23 A6 ¾a brn org & blk ('43) 2.25 .75
O24 A6 1a blue & blk ('41) 6.75 .45
O25 A6 2a ocher & black 6.00 5.00
O26 A6 2½a dk car & blk ('46) 16.00 *160.00*
O27 A6 4a gray grn & blk ('46) 9.00 *11.00*
O28 A6 8a choc & black 6.00 12.50
O29 A6 1r bis & gray blk *60.00*
Nos. O23-O28 (6) 46.00 *189.70*

Catalogue values for unused stamps in this section, from this point to the end of the section, are for Never Hinged items.

No. O24 Surcharged with New Value and Bars in Carmine

1947 ***Perf. 13½***
O30 A6 9p on 1a blue & blk 5.50 5.50

No. 58 Overprinted in Red "SERVICE"

Perf. 14
O31 A6 3p on ½a 9.00 *21.00*
a. Inverted surcharge — 2,250.
b. Double surch., one inverted 72.50 72.50
c. "3 PIE" 400.00 *450.00*

No. O13 Surcharged "Three-quarter Anna" in Devanagari, similar to surcharge on No. 48, and Bars in Carmine

1949 ***Perf. 14x13½***
O32 A6 ¾a on ½a dl vio & blk 27.50 *30.00*

For later issues see Rajasthan.

JAMMU AND KASHMIR

ˈjəm-ə-ˌü and ˈkash-ˌmi(ə)r

LOCATION — A Feudatory State in the Kashmir Residency in the extreme north of India.
AREA — 82,258 sq. mi.
POP. — 4,021,616 (1941)
CAPITAL — Srinagar

All stamps of Jammu and Kashmir were issued without gum.

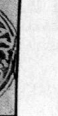

½ Anna — A1

1 Anna — A2

4 Annas (¼ Rupee) — A3

Native Grayish Laid Paper

Handstamped

1866-67 Unwmk. ***Imperf.***

Printed in Water Colors

1 A1 ½a gray black 375.00 150.00
Cut to shape 75.00 30.00
2 A2 1a dull blue 900.00 180.00
a. 1a ultramarine 900.00 180.00
b. 1a royal blue — 750.00
Cut to shape — 150.00
3 A2 1a gray black 2,400. 2,100.
Cut to shape 475.00 425.00
4 A3 4a dull blue *4,500.* *4,500.*
a. 4a ultramarine *4,500.* *4,500.*
b. 4a indigo *4,500.* *4,500.*
Cut to shape 900.00 900.00
5 A3 4a gray black 3,000.
Cut to shape 1,600. —
Nos. 1-5 (5) 11,175. 6,930.

It has now been proved by the leading authorities on Indian stamps that all stamps of ½ anna and 1 anna printed from the so-called Die A are forgeries and that no such die was ever in use.

See Nos. 24-59.

JAMMU

A part of the Feudatory State of Jammu & Kashmir, both being ruled by the same sovereign.

½ Anna — A4

1 Anna — A5

Printed in blocks of four, three types of the ½a and one of the 1a.

Native Grayish Laid Paper

Printed in Water Colors

1867-77 Unwmk. ***Imperf.***
6 A4 ½a black 1,800. 625.00
7 A4 ½a indigo 625.00 490.00
a. ½a deep ultramarine 490.00 290.00
b. ½a deep violet blue 325.00 160.00
8 A4 ½a red 12.50 6.75
a. ½a orange red 375.00 120.00
b. ½a orange 195.00 *225.00*
9 A5 1a black 3,750. 2,600.
10 A5 1a indigo 1,350 625.00
a. 1a deep ultramarine 1,200. 625.00
b. 1a deep violet blue 1,200. 625.00
11 A5 1a red 30.00 19.00
a. 1a orange red 1,250. 525.00
b. 1a orange 4,750. 2,750.

1876
12 A4 ½a emerald 3,750. 1,900.
13 A4 ½a bright blue 2,400. 550.00
14 A5 1a emerald 5,250. 3,000.
15 A5 1a bright blue 700.00 *750.00*

Native Grayish Laid Paper

1877 Printed in Oil Colors

No.	Type	Denomination	Unused	Used
16	A4	½a red	18.00	13.50
a.		½a brown red	—	67.50
17	A4	½a black		1,800.
18	A5	1a red	57.50	40.00
a.		1a brown red	—	225.00
19	A5	1a black	*3,750.*	*2,750.*

The formerly listed ½a dark blue, ½a dark green, 1a dark blue and 1a dark green are believed to be reprints.

European White Laid Paper

No.	Type	Denomination	Unused	Used
20	A4	½a red	—	*1,600.*
a.		Thin laid bâtonné paper		*2,750.*
21	A5	1a red	—	
a.		Thin laid bâtonné paper	*6,750.*	

European White Wove Paper

No.	Type	Denomination	Unused	Used
22	A4	½a red		*675.00*
23	A5	1a red		

RE-ISSUES
For Jammu Only
Native Grayish Laid Paper
Printed in Water Colors

1869-76 *Imperf.*

No.	Type	Denomination	Unused	Used
24	A1	½a deep black	*500.00*	
25	A1	½a bright blue	550.00	*675.00*
26	A1	½a orange red	1,000.	1,100.
a.		½a orange to salmon	400.00	
b.		½a red	150.00	*525.00*
27	A1	½a emerald	175.00	*450.00*
28	A1	½a yellow	1,100.	*1,400.*
29	A2	1a deep black	500.00	
30	A2	1a bright blue	195.00	*550.00*
31	A2	1a orange red	1,000.	*1,100.*
b.		1a red	300.00	*500.00*
32	A2	1a emerald	195.00	450.00
33	A2	1a yellow	1,400.	
34	A3	4a deep black	450.00	—
35	A3	4a bright blue	325.00	
a.		4a indigo	—	—
36	A3	4a orange red	325.00	*425.00*
a.		4a orange		—
b.		4a red	325.00	*425.00*
37	A3	4a emerald	450.00	*1,000.*
38	A3	4a yellow	900.00	

Native Grayish Laid Paper

1877 Printed in Oil Colors

No.	Type	Denomination	Unused	Used
39	A1	½a red	52.50	*90.00*
40	A1	½a black	57.50	*97.50*
41	A1	½a slate blue	240.00	*400.00*
42	A1	½a sage green	210.00	
43	A2	1a red	72.50	*290.00*
45	A2	1a slate blue	57.50	*450.00*
46	A2	1a sage green	225.00	
47	A3	4a red	475.00	*825.00*
50	A3	4a sage green	225.00	

European White Laid Paper

No.	Type	Denomination	Unused	Used
51	A1	½a red		1,800.
52	A1	½a black	47.50	*97.50*
53	A1	½a slate blue	82.50	*450.00*
54	A1	½a yellow	*240.00*	
56	A2	1a slate blue	90.00	*600.00*
57	A3	4a red	650.00	*750.00*
58	A3	4a sage green	*2,250.*	

European Brownish Wove Paper

No.	Type	Denomination	Unused	Used
59	A1	½a red		*1,400.*

It is probable that the issues of 1876, 1877 and the re-issues of the circular stamps were made to supply the demands of philatelists more than for postal needs. They were, however, available for postage.

There exist also reprints, printed in a variety of colors, on native and European thin wove paper. Collectors are warned against official imitations, which are very numerous. They are printed on several kinds of paper and in a great variety of colors.

A5a

Handstamped in Oil Color

1877, Nov.

No.	Type	Denomination	Unused	Used
60	A5a (½a)	red		*1,900.*

This provisional, made with a canceling device, was used only in Nov. 1877, at Jammu city.

KASHMIR

A part of the Feudatory State of Jammu & Kashmir, both being ruled by the same sovereign.

½ Anna — A6

Printed in Water Colors
Native Grayish Laid Paper
Printed from a Single Die

1866 Unwmk. *Imperf.*

No.	Type	Denomination	Unused	Used
62	A6	½a black	*5,250.*	675.00

¼ Anna — A7

½ Anna — A8

1 Anna A9

2 Annas A10

4 Annas — A11

8 Annas — A12

The ¼a, 1a and 2a are printed in strips of five varieties, the ½a in sheets of twenty varieties and the 4a and 8a from single dies.

1866-70

No.	Type	Denomination	Unused	Used
63	A7	¼a black	6.75	*7.00*
64	A8	½a black	*2,250.*	*300.00*
65	A8	½a ultra	7.50	2.50
a.		½a blue	13.50	6.75
66	A9	1a black	4,000.	750.00
67	A9	1a red orange	22.50	17.50
68	A9	1a Venetian red	27.50	19.00
69	A9	1a orange brown	22.50	17.50
70	A9	1a ultra	*6,500.*	*2,500.*
71	A10	2a olive yellow	30.00	*32.50*
72	A11	4a emerald	75.00	72.50
73	A12	8a red	75.00	72.50

All the stamps printed in oil colors are reprints.

As in Jammu, official imitations are numerous and are found in many colors and on various papers.

JAMMU & KASHMIR

¼ Anna — A13

½ Anna — A14

1 Anna — A15

Laid Paper
Printed in Oil Colors

1878 *Rough Perf. 10-14*

No.	Type	Denomination	Unused	Used
74	A13	¼a red	—	—
75	A14	½a red	21.00	*25.00*
a.		Wove paper		*500.00*
76	A14	½a slate blue	110.00	110.00
77	A15	1a red		1,900.
78	A15	1a bright violet	—	—

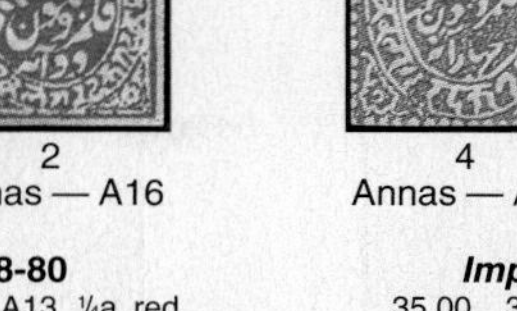

2 Annas — A16 4 Annas — A17

1878-80 *Imperf.*

No.	Type	Denomination	Unused	Used
79	A13	¼a red	35.00	30.00
80	A14	½a red	15.00	*16.00*
81	A14	½a slate	27.50	24.00
82	A15	1a red	14.00	17.50
83	A15	1a violet	40.00	42.50
a.		1a dull purple	67.50	62.50
84	A16	2a red	140.00	140.00
85	A16	2a bright violet	60.00	57.50
86	A16	2a dull ultra	*175.00*	175.00
87	A17	4a red	340.00	290.00

Thick Wove Paper

No.	Type	Denomination	Unused	Used
88	A14	½a red	47.50	*90.00*
89	A15	1a red	75.00	37.50
90	A16	2a red	32.50	40.00

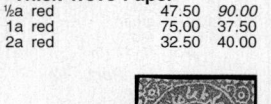

8 Annas — A18

1879-80 Thin Toned Wove Paper

No.	Type	Denomination	Unused	Used
91	A13	¼a red	5.50	*6.75*
92	A14	½a red	1.50	1.50
93	A15	1a red	3.75	*5.25*
94	A16	2a red	5.00	*7.00*
95	A17	4a red	16.00	16.00
96	A18	8a red	17.50	20.00
		Nos. 91-96 (6)	49.25	56.50

Thin Laid Bâtonné Paper

1880 Printed in Water Color

No.	Type	Denomination	Unused	Used
97	A13	¼a ultramarine	1,350.	900.00

Thin Toned Wove Paper

1881 Printed in Oil Colors

No.	Type	Denomination	Unused	Used
98	A13	¼a orange	17.50	*24.00*
99	A14	½a orange	35.00	25.00
100	A15	1a orange	37.50	21.00
101	A16	2a orange	27.50	21.00
102	A17	4a orange	67.50	*82.50*
103	A18	8a orange	110.00	*120.00*
		Nos. 98-103 (6)	295.00	293.50

⅛ Anna — A19

Thin White or Yellowish Wove Paper

1883-94

No.	Type	Denomination	Unused	Used
104	A19	⅛a yellow brown	2.25	*3.00*
a.		⅛a yellow	2.25	*3.00*
105	A13	¼a brown	1.90	1.50
a.		Double impression	1,800.	
106	A14	½a red	1.90	1.25
a.		½a rose	2.40	1.50
106B	A19	⅛a bright blue	82.50	
c.		⅛a dull blue	12.00	
107	A15	1a bronze green	1.50	1.50
108	A15	1a yel green	1.50	1.50
109	A15	1a blue green	3.00	
110	A15	1a bister	—	
111	A17	4a green	6.50	6.00
112	A17	4a olive green	6.00	*7.00*
113	A18	8a deep blue	19.00	*22.50*
114	A18	8a dark ultra	18.00	*21.00*
115	A18	8a gray violet	15.00	*32.50*

Printed in Water Color

No.	Type	Denomination	Unused	Used
116	A18	8a gray blue	225.00	225.00

Printed in Oil Colors
Yellow Pelure Paper

No.	Type	Denomination	Unused	Used
117	A16	2a red	4.00	1.90

Yellow Green Pelure Paper

No.	Type	Denomination	Unused	Used
118	A16	2a red	5.50	*6.00*

Deep Green Pelure Paper

No.	Type	Denomination	Unused	Used
119	A16	2a red	27.50	27.50

Coarse Green Pelure Paper

No.	Type	Denomination	Unused	Used
120	A16	2a red	4.00	1.90
		Nos. 104-120 (18)	425.05	360.05

Thin Creamy Laid Paper

1886-94

No.	Type	Denomination	Unused	Used
121	A19	⅛a yellow	90.00	*100.00*
122	A13	¼a brown	13.50	*10.00*
123	A14	½a vermilion	15.00	9.50
124	A14	½a rose red		110.00
125	A15	1a green	150.00	150.00
126	A17	4a green	—	—

Printed in Water Color

No.	Type	Denomination	Unused	Used
127	A18	8a gray blue	160.00	150.00
		Nos. 121-127 (7)	428.50	529.50

Impressions of types A13 to A19 in colors other than the issued stamps are proofs. Forgeries to defraud the post exist, and some are common.

A fugitive pigment in No. 104 often leaves the stamp a dull yellowish brown.

1/4 Anna

Stamps of the above type, printed in red or black, were never placed in use.

OFFICIAL STAMPS
Same Types as Regular Issues
White Laid Paper

1878 Unwmk. *Rough Perf. 10-14*

No.	Type	Denomination	Unused	Used
O1	A14	½a black		*3,000.*

Imperf

No.	Type	Denomination	Unused	Used
O3	A14	½a black	150.00	140.00
O4	A15	1a black	100.00	100.00
O5	A16	2a black	82.50	*90.00*
		Nos. O3-O5 (3)	332.50	330.00

Thin White or Yellowish Wove Paper

1880

No.	Type	Denomination	Unused	Used
O6	A13	¼a black	2.50	*3.00*
O7	A14	½a black	.25	*1.10*
O8	A15	1a black	3.00	*1.50*
O9	A16	2a black	.45	*.65*
O10	A17	4a black	1.90	*2.50*
O11	A18	8a black	3.75	1.60
		Nos. O6-O11 (6)	11.85	10.35

Thin Creamy Laid Paper

1890-91

No.	Type	Denomination	Unused	Used
O12	A13	¼a black	12.50	*13.50*
O13	A14	½a black	7.00	*7.00*
O14	A15	1a black	4.00	*5.25*
O15	A16	2a black	22.50	
O16	A17	4a black	82.50	*97.50*
O17	A18	8a black	42.50	*75.00*
		Nos. O12-O17 (6)	171.00	

Obsolete October 31, 1894.

JASDAN

jas-dən

LOCATION — A Feudatory State in the Kathiawar Agency in Western India.
AREA — 296 sq. mi.
POP. — 34,056 (1931)
CAPITAL — Jasdan

In 1948 Jasdan was incorporated in the United State of Saurashtra (see Soruth).

Catalogue values for all unused stamps in this state are for Never Hinged items.

Sun — A1

Perf. 8½ to 10½

1942 Unwmk. Typo.

No.	Type	Denomination	Unused	Used
1	A1	1a green	30.00	240.00

Issued in booklet panes of 4 and 8.

The 1a carmine is a revenue stamp.

Jasdan's stamp became obsolete Feb. 15, 1948.

JHALAWAR

'jäl-ə-ˌwär

LOCATION — A Feudatory State in the Rajputana Agency of India.
AREA — 813 sq. mi.
POP. — 107,890
CAPITAL — Jhalrapatan

Apsaras, Hindu Nymph
A1 A2

Laid Paper

1887-90 Unwmk. *Imperf.*
Without Gum

No.	Type	Description	Unused	Used
1	A1	1p yellow green	7.00	*22.50*
2	A2	¼a green	1.90	*3.75*

Obsolete October 31, 1900.

JIND

'jind

(Jhind)

LOCATION — A State of India in the north Punjab.
AREA — 1,299 sq. mi.
POP. — 361,812 (1941)
CAPITAL — Sangrur

A1

A2

A3

A4

A5

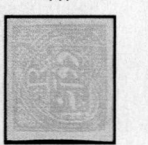

1874 Unwmk. Litho. *Imperf.*
Without Gum
Thin White Wove Paper

No.	Type	Description	Unused	Used
1	A1	½a blue	10.00	6.25
2	A2	1a lilac	10.00	9.50
3	A3	2a yellow	1.50	6.75
4	A4	4a green	37.50	9.00
5	A5	8a dark violet	340.00	140.00
		Nos. 1-5 (5)	399.00	171.50

Thick Blue Laid Paper

1875 Without Gum

No.	Type	Description	Unused	Used
6	A1	½a blue	1.50	*7.00*
7	A2	1a red violet	4.00	*16.00*
8	A3	2a brown orange	6.50	*22.50*
9	A4	4a green	5.50	*22.50*
10	A5	8a purple	13.50	*32.50*
		Nos. 6-10 (5)	31.00	*100.50*

Nos. 3 and 6 were perforated 12 in 1885 for use as fiscal stamps.

A6

A7

A8

A9

A10

A11

1882-84 Without Gum *Imperf.*
Thin Yellowish Wove Paper

No.	Type	Description	Unused	Used
12	A6	¼a buff	.45	*2.25*
a.		Double impression	75.00	
13	A7	½a yellow	3.75	2.50
14	A8	1a brown	2.50	*5.00*
15	A9	2a blue	3.00	*13.50*
16	A10	4a green	2.25	1.50
17	A11	8a red	9.50	6.75
		Nos. 12-17 (6)	21.45	*31.50*

Perf. 12

No.	Type	Description	Unused	Used
18	A6	¼a buff	1.50	*4.00*
19	A7	½a yellow	240.00	240.00
20	A8	1a brown	3.75	*8.25*
21	A9	2a blue	5.50	*15.00*
22	A10	4a green	7.50	16.00
23	A11	8a red	18.00	
a.		Thick white paper	15.00	
		Nos. 18-23 (6)	276.25	*283.25*

Laid Paper
Imperf

No.	Type	Description	Unused	Used
24	A6	¼a buff	1.90	
25	A7	½a yellow	1.90	
26	A8	1a brown	1.90	*3.75*
27	A9	2a blue	27.50	*30.00*
28	A11	8a red	3.75	*16.00*
		Nos. 24-28 (5)	36.95	*49.75*

Perf. 12

No.	Type	Description	Unused	Used
29	A6	¼a buff	12.50	
30	A7	½a yellow	190.00	40.00
31	A8	1a brown	2.25	
32	A11	8a red	3.75	*15.00*
		Nos. 29-32 (4)	208.50	55.00

As postage stamps these issues became obsolete in July, 1885, but some possibly remained in use as revenue stamps.

For later issues see Jind under Convention States.

KISHANGARH

'kish-ən-ˌgär

LOCATION — A Feudatory State in the Jaipur Residency of India.
AREA — 858 sq. mi.
POP. — 85,744
CAPITAL — Kishangarh

Kishangarh was incorporated in Rajasthan in 1947-49.

Stamps were issued without gum except Nos. 27-35.

Coat of Arms — A1

1899-1900 Unwmk. Typo. *Imperf.*
Soft Porous Paper

No.	Type	Description	Unused	Used
1	A1	1a green	32.50	*90.00*
2	A1	1a blue ('00)	*600.00*	

Pin-perf

No.	Type	Description	Unused	Used
3	A1	1a green	110.00	

A2 A3

Coat of Arms — A4

Maharaja Sardul Singh — A5

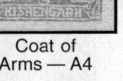

A6

A7

Coat of Arms — A9
A8

Thin Wove Paper

1899-1900 Handstamped *Imperf.*

No.	Type	Description	Unused	Used
4	A2	¼a rose pink	1.90	*4.00*
a.		¼a carmine	12.50	
5	A2	¼a green	825.00	1,200.
6	A3	½a light blue	1.90	*2.50*
7	A3	½a green	57.50	*62.50*
8	A3	½a carmine	3,750.	*1,900.*
9	A3	½a violet	240.00	*490.00*
10	A4	1a gray violet	1.60	1.50
a.		1a gray	7.50	7.50
11	A4	1a rose	110.00	*300.00*
11A	A5	2a orange	7.50	6.75
12	A6	4a chocolate	9.00	*15.00*
a.		Laid paper	125.00	125.00
13	A7	1r dull green	35.00	*52.50*
13A	A7	1r light brown	30.00	*37.50*
14	A8	2r brown red	125.00	*190.00*
a.		Laid paper	100.00	
15	A9	5r violet	120.00	150.00
a.		Laid paper	120.00	

Pin-perf

No.	Type	Description	Unused	Used
16	A2	¼a magenta	7.50	*10.00*
a.		¼a rose	.35	*.60*
17	A2	¼a green	*400.00*	*700.00*
a.		Imperf. vertically, pair	1,900.	
18	A3	½a blue	1.50	.75
a.		½a dark blue	3.75	*5.00*
19	A3	½a green	27.50	*40.00*
a.		Imperf. vert., pair	275.00	
20	A4	1a gray violet	1.10	*1.50*
a.		1a gray	8.25	5.25
b.		1a red lilac	2.25	3.00
d.		As "b," laid paper	62.50	19.00
20E	A4	1a rose	125.00	*375.00*
21	A5	2a orange	6.00	*7.50*
21B	A6	4a pale red brn	5.25	*9.00*
c.		4a chocolate	3.50	*9.00*
22	A7	1r dull green	16.00	*22.50*
b.		Laid paper	140.00	
23	A8	2r brown red	52.50	82.50
b.		Laid paper	67.50	
24	A9	5r red violet	52.50	82.50
d.		Laid paper	110.00	

Nos. 4-24 exist tête bêche and sell for a slight premium.

For overprints see Nos. O1-O11, Rajasthan Nos. 26-28, 30-32.

A9a

A9b

1901 Soft Porous Paper Typo.

No.	Type	Description	Unused	Used
24A	A9a	½a rose	12.00	9.00
24B	A9b	1a dull violet	72.50	40.00

For overprint see No. O12.

A10

1903 Stout Hard Paper *Imperf.*

No.	Type	Description	Unused	Used
25	A10	½a pink	20.00	5.25
a.		Printed on both sides		*2,100.*

A11

1904 Thin Wove Paper *Pin-perf.*

No.	Type	Description	Unused	Used
25B	A11	8a gray	7.50	*11.00*
c.		tête bêche pair	40.00	

For overprints see Nos. O13, O33, Rajasthan No. 29.

A11a

No.	Type	Description	Unused	Used
25D	A11a	1r green	27.50	27.50

For overprint see No. O13A.

Maharaja Sardul Singh — A12

1903 Stout Hard Paper *Imperf.*

No.	Type	Description	Unused	Used
26	A12	2a yellow	4.50	9.00

For overprints see Nos. O14, O34.

Maharaja Madan Singh — A13

1904-05 Engr. *Perf. 12½, 13½*

No.	Type	Description	Unused	Used
27	A13	¼a carmine	.65	*1.10*
28	A13	½a chestnut	1.90	.45
29	A13	1a deep blue	3.75	*4.00*
30	A13	2a orange	22.50	10.00
31	A13	4a dark brown	22.50	*25.00*
32	A13	8a purple ('05)	19.00	*37.50*
33	A13	1r dark green	42.50	*67.50*
34	A13	2r lemon yellow	42.50	*250.00*
35	A13	5r purple brown	35.00	*300.00*
		Nos. 27-35 (9)	190.30	*695.55*

For overprints see Nos. O15-O22, O35-O38, Rajasthan Nos. 33-39.

Maharaja Madan Singh — A14

Thin Wove Paper

1913 Typo. *Rouletted 9½*

No.	Type	Description	Unused	Used
37	A14	2 "ANNA" violet	8.25	*13.50*
a.		tête bêche pair	18.00	*60.00*

See Nos. 40-50. For overprint see Rajasthan No. 43.

Maharaja Madan Singh
A15 A16

Thick, Chalk-surfaced Paper

1913 *Rouletted 6½, 12*

38 A15 ¼a pale blue .45 *1.40*
 a. "Kishangahr" 7.50 *10.00*
 b. Imperf., pair 11.00
39 A16 2a purple 12.50 *27.50*
 a. "Kishangahr" 75.00 *140.00*

For overprint see No. O23.

1913-16 *Rouletted 12, 14½*

40 A14 ¼a pale blue .30 *.65*
41 A14 ½a green ('15) .30 *1.50*
 a. Printed on both sides 350.00
42 A14 1a carmine 1.90 3.75
43 A14 2 "ANNAS" pur 9.00 *12.00*
44 A14 4a ultramarine 9.00 *12.00*
45 A14 8a brown 10.00 *60.00*
46 A14 1r rose lilac 24.00 *190.00*
47 A14 2r dark green 150.00 *525.00*
48 A14 5r brown 60.00 *675.00*
 Nos. 40-48 (9) 264.50 *1,480.*

On Nos. 40-48 the halftone screen covers the entire design.

Nos. 41-48 have ornaments on both sides of value in top panel.

For overprints see Nos. O24-O30, O39-O43, Rajasthan Nos. 40-42, 44-48.

Type of 1913-16 Redrawn

1918 *Rouletted*

50 A14 1a rose red 2.25 *8.25*

The redrawn stamp is 24¾mm wide instead of 26mm. There is a white oval around the portrait with only traces of the red line. There is less shading outside the wreath.

For overprint see No. O44.

Maharaja Jagjanarajan Singh
A17 A18

Thick Glazed Paper

1928-29 *Pin-perf. 14½ to 16*

52 A17 ¼a light blue 1.90 *3.00*
53 A17 ½a lt yellow green 6.00 3.50
 a. Imperf., pair 180.00 180.00
54 A18 1a carmine rose 1.10 *2.25*
55 A18 2a red violet 5.00 *12.50*
56 A17 4a yellow brown 2.50 2.50
57 A17 8a purple 8.25 *42.50*
58 A17 1r green 30.00 *95.00*
59 A17 2r lemon 42.50 *340.00*
60 A17 5r red brown 67.50 *400.00*
 a. Imperf., pair 190.00
 Nos. 52-60 (9) 164.75 *901.25*

1945-47

Thick Soft Unglazed Paper

52a A17 ¼a gray blue 6.25 *19.00*
 b. ¼a greenish blue ('47) 4.00 *15.00*
53b A17 ½a deep green 2.25 *4.00*
54a A18 1a dull carmine 12.50 6.50
55a A18 2a deep red violet 16.00 *19.00*
 b. 2a violet brown, imperf. 125.00 30.00
56a A17 4a brown 35.00 *30.00*
57a A17 8a violet 60.00 *240.00*
58a A17 1r deep green 75.00 *250.00*
59a A17 2r lemon —
60b A17 5r red brown 875.00 *1,100.*

For overprints see Rajasthan Nos. 49-58.
For later issues see Rajasthan.

OFFICIAL STAMPS

Used values are for CTO stamps.

Regular Issues of 1899-1916 Handstamped in Black

On Issue of 1899-1900

1918 **Unwmk.** *Imperf.*

O1 A2 ¼a carmine 12.00
O2 A4 1a gray violet 82.50 8.25
O3 A6 4a chocolate — 190.00

Pin-perf

O4 A2 ¼a carmine 3.25 .90
O4A A2 ¼a green — 175.00
O4B A3 ½a blue 640.00 67.50
O6 A4 1a gray violet 67.50 2.25
O7 A5 2a orange — 225.00
O8 A6 4a chocolate 100.00 24.00
O9 A7 1r dull green 250.00 180.00
O10 A8 2r brown red — 1,400.
O11 A9 5r red violet — 3,000.

See tete beche note after No. 24.

On Issue of 1901

O12 A9b 1a dull violet 75.00 2.25

On Issue of 1904

O13 A11 8a gray 140.00 35.00
O13A A11a 1r green *1,350.*

Imperf.

O14 A12 2a yellow 125.00 7.50

On Issue of 1904-05

Perf. 12½, 13

O15 A13 ¼a carmine *450.00*
O16 A13 ½a chestnut 1.50 .50
O17 A13 1a deep blue 16.00 6.00
O18 A13 2a orange — 1,500.
O19 A13 4a dk brn 90.00 27.50
O20 A13 8a purple 600.00 375.00
O21 A13 1r dk grn 1,200. 1,100.
O22 A13 5r purple brn

On Issue of 1913

Rouletted

O23 A15 ¼a pale blue 11.00

On Issue of 1913-16

O24 A14 ¼a pale blue .90 .75
O25 A14 ½a green 1.50 1.10
O26 A14 1a carmine 24.00 13.50
O27 A14 2a purple 12.50 6.00
O28 A14 4a ultra 42.50 22.50
O29 A14 8a brown 190.00 67.50
O30 A14 1r rose lilac 525.00 500.00
O31 A14 2r dk grn
O32 A14 5r brown 2,750.

Red Handstamp

On Issue of 1904

Pin-perf

O33 A11 8a gray — 450.00

Imperf

O34 A12 2a yellow 675.00 400.00

On Issue of 1904-05

Perf. 12½, 13

O35 A13 1a deep blue 35.00 10.00
O36 A13 4a dk brn 140.00 62.50
O37 A13 8a purple — *400.00*
O38 A13 1r dk grn — *1,000.*

On Issue of 1913-16

Rouletted

O39 A14 ¼a pale blue 3.00 2.50
O40 A14 ½a green 6.50 2.40
O41 A14 2a purple 210.00 100.00
O42 A14 4a ultra — 52.50
O43 A14 8a brown — 140.00

On Issue of 1918

Redrawn

O44 A14 1a rose red

The overprint on Nos. O1 to O44 is handstamped and, as usual with that style of overprint, is found inverted, double, etc. In this instance there is evidence that many of the varieties were deliberately made.

KOTAH

kō-tə

LOCATION — A Feudatory State in the Rajputana Agency of India.
AREA — 5714 sq. mi.
POP. — 526,827 (1880)
CAPITAL — Kotah City

All Kotah stamps are only known on cover, including the uncanceled stamps. Values are for covers bearing a single stamp.

A1

A2

A3

Wove Paper

Handstamped

1883 **Unwmk.** *Imperf.*

1 A1 2p green, *yellow* 20,000. 8,500.
 a. Double impression —
2 A2 2p black, *yellow* *20,000.*
3 A3 2p indigo, *pink* *20,000.*

A4

1886 **Wove Paper**

4 A4 1p green, *yellow* —

The stamps of Kotah became obsolete in 1886.

LAS BELA

ləs 'bāl-ə

LOCATION — A Feudatory State in the Baluchistan District.
AREA — 7,132 sq. mi.
POP. — 63,008
CAPITAL — Bela

A1

1897-98 **Unwmk.** **Typo.** *Perf. 12*

1 A1 ½a black, *white* 45.00 25.00
2 A1 ½a black, *gray* 25.00 16.00
3 A1 ½a black, *blue* ('98) 30.00 16.00
 Nos. 1-3 (3) 100.00 57.00

A2

1901

4 A2 1a black, *red orange* 40.00 *75.00*

1904 *Pin-perf*

5 A1 ½a black, *lt blue* 24.00 13.50

Granite Paper

6 A1 ½a black, *greenish gray* 24.00 13.50

Las Bela stamps became obsolete in Mar. 1907.

MORVI

'mor-vē

LOCATION — A Feudatory State in the Kathiawar Agency, Western India.
AREA — 822 sq. mi.
POP. — 113,023
CAPITAL — Morvi

In 1948 Morvi was incorporated in the United State of Saurashtra (see Soruth).

Sir Lakhdhirji Waghji The Thakur Sahib of Morvi — A1

Size: 21½x26½mm

1931 **Unwmk.** **Typo.** *Perf. 12*

1 A1 3p red 4.50 *22.50*
 a. 3p deep blue (error) 6.50 *35.00*
2 A1 ½a deep blue 40.00 67.50
3 A1 1a red brown 5.00 *25.00*
4 A1 2a yellow brown 6.00 *60.00*
 Nos. 1-4 (4) 55.50 *175.00*

Nos. 1-4 and 1a were printed in two blocks of four, with stamps 5½mm apart, and perforated on four sides. Nos. 1 and 2 were also printed in blocks of four, with stamps 10mm apart, and perforated on two or three sides.

A2

1932 **Size: 21x25½mm** *Perf. 11*

5 A2 3p rose 7.50 *21.00*
6 A2 6p gray green 12.00 *25.00*
7 A2 6p emerald 9.50 *21.00*
8 A2 1a ultramarine 6.50 *21.00*
9 A2 2a violet 16.00 *60.00*
 Nos. 5-9 (5) 51.50 *148.00*

A3

1934-48 *Perf. 14, Rough Perf. 11*

10 A3 3p carmine rose 3.75 *5.25*
 a. 3p red 2.50 *6.50*
11 A3 6p emerald 2.50 *10.00*
 a. 6p green 10.00 *25.00*
12 A3 1a red brown 2.75 *21.00*
 a. 1a brown 15.00 *25.00*
13 A3 2a violet 3.75 *30.00*
 Nos. 10-13 (4) 12.75 *66.25*

The 1934 London printing of Nos. 10-13 is perf. 14; the later Morvi Press printing is rough perf. 11.

Morvi stamps became obsolete Feb. 15, 1948.

NANDGAON

'nän͵d-͵gaun

LOCATION — A Feudatory State in the Chhattisgarh States Agency in Central India.
AREA — 871 sq. mi.
POP. — 182,380
CAPITAL — Rajnandgaon

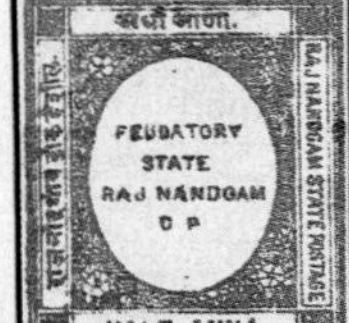

A1

White Paper

1892, Feb. Unwmk. Typo. *Imperf.*
Without Gum

1 A1 ½a blue 10.00 *275.00*
2 A1 2a rose 40.00 *825.00*

Some authorities claim that No. 2 was a revenue stamp.

For overprints see Nos. O1-O2.

A2

1893 Without Gum

4 A2 ½a green 19.00 *140.00*
5 A2 2a rose 19.00 *140.00*

For overprint see No. O5.

Same Redrawn

1894 Without Gum

6 A2 ½a yellow green 37.50 *140.00*
7 A2 1a rose 82.50 *175.00*
a. Laid paper 375.00

The redrawn stamps have smaller value characters and wavy lines between the stamps.

For overprints see Nos. O3-O4.

OFFICIAL STAMPS

Regular Issues Handstamped in Violet

1893-94 Unwmk. *Imperf.*
Without Gum

O1 A1 ½a blue *550.00*
O2 A1 2a red *1,350.*
O3 A2 ½a yellow green 9.50 17.50
O4 A2 1a rose 16.00 *37.50*
a. Laid paper 16.00 *125.00*
O5 A2 2a rose 3.00 3.00

Some authorities believe that this handstamp was used as a control mark, rather than to indicate a stamp for official mail.

The 1 anna has been reprinted in brown and in blue.

Nandgaon stamps became obsolete in July, 1895.

NOWANUGGUR

ˌnau-ə-ˈnəg-ər

(Navanagar)

LOCATION — A Feudatory State in the Kathiawar Agency, Western India.
AREA — 3,791 sq. mi.
POP. — 402,192
CAPITAL — Navanagar

Stamps of Nowanuggur were superseded by those of India.

6 Dokra = 1 Anna
16 Annas = 1 Rupee

Kandjar (Indian Dagger) — A1

Without Gum
Laid Paper

1877 Unwmk. Typo. *Imperf.*

1 A1 1d dull blue 1.00 *37.50*
a. 1d ultramarine 1.00 *37.50*
b. Tete beche pair 1,900.

Perf. 12½

2 A1 1d slate 120.00 175.00
a. Tete beche pair 2,400.

No. 2 on wove paper is of private origin.

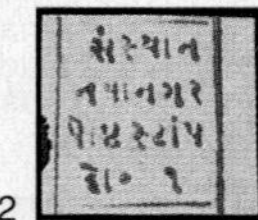
A2

Wove Paper

1877-88 Without Gum *Imperf.*

3 A2 1d black, *red violet* 5.25 *16.00*
a. 1d black, *rose* 5.25
b. Characters at beginning of 3rd line read "4102" instead of "418"
4 A2 2d black, *green* 8.25 *21.00*
a. 2d black, *blue green* 12.50
b. "4102" instead of "418"
5 A2 3d black, *yellow* 9.00 *30.00*
a. 3d black, *orange yellow* 19.00
b. "4102" instead of "418"
c. Laid paper 160.00
d. 2d black, *yellow* (error in sheet of 3d) 600.00
Nos. 3-5 (3) 22.50 *67.00*

Nos. 3-5 range in width from 14 to 19mm.

Seal of the State — A3

Without Gum

1893 Thick Paper *Imperf.*

6 A3 1d black 450.00

Perf. 12

7 A3 1d black 6.50
8 A3 3d orange 7.50

Imperf
Thin Paper

9 A3 1d black 350.00
10 A3 2d dark green 450.00
11 A3 3d orange 400.00
Nos. 9-11 (3) 1,200.

Perf. 12

12 A3 1d black 2.50 *9.00*
13 A3 2d green 3.40 *12.00*
14 A3 3d orange 3.40 *17.50*
a. Imperf. vert., pair
Nos. 12-14 (3) 9.30 38.50

Obsolete at end of 1895.

ORCHHA

ˈor-chə

(Orcha)

LOCATION — A Feudatory State in the Bundelkhand Agency in Central India.
AREA — 2,080 sq. mi.
POP. — 314,661
CAPITAL — Tikamgarh

Seal of Orchha — A1

Without Gum

1913-17 Unwmk. Litho. *Imperf.*

1 A1 ¼a ultra ('15) 3.00 *7.50*
2 A1 ½a emerald ('14) .85 *9.50*
a. Background of arms unshaded 52.50 *150.00*
3 A1 1a carmine ('14) 3.75 *10.00*
a. Background of arms unshaded 30.00 *275.00*
4 A1 2a brown ('17) 6.75 *35.00*
5 A1 4a orange ('14) 12.00 *57.50*
Nos. 1-5 (5) 26.35 *119.50*

Essays similar to Nos. 2-5 are in different colors.

A2

Maharaja Singh Dev — A3

1939-40 *Perf. 13½, 13½x14*

6 A2 ¼a chocolate 5.00 *12.00*
7 A2 ½a yellow green 4.50 *100.00*
8 A2 ¾a ultramarine 7.00 *150.00*
9 A2 1a rose red 4.50 *30.00*
10 A2 1¼a deep blue 5.50 *150.00*
11 A2 1½a lilac 6.00 *190.00*
12 A2 2a vermilion 4.50 *120.00*
13 A2 2½a turq green 7.50 *340.00*
14 A2 3a dull violet 8.00 *180.00*
15 A2 4a blue gray 9.00 *42.50*
16 A2 8a rose lilac 15.00 *340.00*
17 A3 1r sage green 26.00 *750.00*
18 A3 2r lt violet ('40) 60.00 *1,000.*
19 A3 5r yel org ('40) 200.00 *2,750.*
20 A3 10r blue 700.00 *4,500.*
Nos. 6-20 (15) 1,063. *10,655.*

POONCH

ˈpünch

LOCATION — A Feudatory State in the Kashmir Residency in India.
AREA — 1,627 sq. mi.
POP. — 287,000 (estimated)
CAPITAL — Poonch

Poonch was feudatory to Jammu and Kashmir. Cancellations of Jammu and Kashmir are found on Poonch stamps, which became obsolete in 1894. The stamps are all printed in watercolor and handstamped from single dies. They may be found on various papers, including wove, laid, wove batonne, laid batonne and ribbed, in various colors and tones. Nearly all Poonch stamps exist tete beche and impressed sideways. Issued without gum.

A1

White Paper

Handstamped
1876 Unwmk. *Imperf.*
Size: 22x21mm

1 A1 6p red 18,000. 240.

1877 Size: 19x17mm

1A A1 ½a red 22,500. *7,500.*

1879 Size: 21x19mm

1B A1 ½a red — 7,500.

A2

A3

A4

A5

A6

1880-88 White Paper

2 A2 1p red ('84) 40.00 40.00
3 A3 ½a red 4.00 *5.25*
4 A4 1a red 6.75
5 A5 2a red 16.00 *19.00*
6 A6 4a red 25.00

Yellow Paper

7 A2 1p red 5.50 5.50
8 A3 ½a red 9.50 9.50
9 A4 1a red 82.50
10 A5 2a red 15.00 *17.50*
11 A6 4a red 7.50 7.50

Blue Paper

12 A2 1p red 4.00 3.75
13 A4 1a red 600.00 *625.00*

Orange Paper

14 A2 1p red 5.50 5.50
15 A3 ½a red 42.50
16 A5 2a red 150.00
17 A6 4a red 37.50

Green Paper

18 A3 ½a red 67.50
19 A4 1a red 5.00 *7.50*
20 A5 2a red 67.50
21 A6 4a red 100.00

Lavender Paper

22 A2 1p red 75.00 *82.50*
23 A4 1a red 125.00 *160.00*
24 A5 2a red 5.00 *5.50*

OFFICIAL STAMPS
White Paper
Handstamped

1888 Unwmk. *Imperf.*

O1 A2 1p black 4.00 *4.50*
O2 A3 ½a black 4.50 *6.00*
O3 A4 1a black 4.00 *4.50*
O4 A5 2a black 7.50 7.50
O5 A6 4a black 12.00 *16.00*
Nos. O1-O5 (5) 32.00 *38.50*

1890 Yellowish Paper

O6 A2 1p black 3.75
O7 A3 ½a black 4.50 *5.25*
O8 A4 1a black 22.50 21.00
O9 A5 2a black 9.50 9.50
O10 A6 4a black 15.00
Nos. O6-O10 (5) 55.25 35.75

Obsolete since 1894.

RAJASTHAN

ˈrä-jə-ˌstän

(Greater Rajasthan Union)

AREA — 128,424 sq. miles
POP. — 13,085,000

The Rajasthan Union was formed in 1947-49 by 14 Indian States, including the stamp-issuing States of Bundi, Dungarpur, Jaipur and Kishangarh.

Catalogue values for all unused stamps in this state are for Never Hinged items.

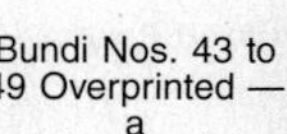

Bundi Nos. 43 to 49 Overprinted — a

1948 Unwmk. *Perf. 11*
Handstamped in Black

1 A8 ¼a dp grn 8.25 *50.00*
a. Pair, one without overprint 550.00
2 A8 ½a purple 8.25 *50.00*
a. Pair, one without overprint 600.00
3 A8 1a yel green 7.00 *42.50*
4 A9 2a red 21.00 *125.00*
5 A9 4a dp orange 72.50 *450.00*
6 A10 8a vio blue 13.50 *80.00*
Nos. 1-6 (6) 130.50 *797.50*

Handstamped in Violet

1b A8 ¼a dp grn 9.00 *55.00*
2b A8 ½a purple 9.00 *55.00*
c. Pair, one without overprint 550.00
3a A8 1a yel green 24.00 *140.00*
b. Pair, one without overprint 550.00

4a A9 2a red 47.50 *275.00*
5a A9 4a dp orange 47.50 *275.00*
6a A10 8a vio blue 14.00 *80.00*
7 A10 1r chocolate 400.00 2,400.
Nos. 1b-7 (7) 551.00 *3,280.*

Handstamped in Blue

1c A8 ¼a dp grn 52.50 *300.00*
2d A8 ½a purple 72.50 *450.00*
3c A8 1a yel green 67.50 *400.00*
5b A9 4a dp orange 190.00 *1,100.*
6b A10 8a vio blue 120.00 *725.00*
7a A10 1r chocolate 140.00 825.00
Nos. 1c-7a (6) 642.50 *3,800.*

Typo. in Black

11 A9 2a red 15.00 *100.00*
a. Inverted overprint 450.00
12 A9 4a deep orange 6.00 *100.00*
a. Double overprint 400.00
13 A10 8a violet blue 27.50
a. Inverted overprint 950.00
b. Double overprint 600.00
14 A10 1r chocolate 11.00
Nos. 11-14 (4) 59.50

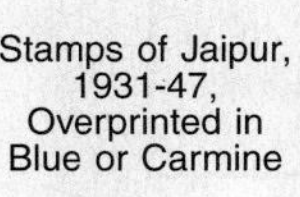

Stamps of Jaipur, 1931-47, Overprinted in Blue or Carmine

1949 **Center in Black** ***Perf. 14***
15 A6 ¼a red brown (Bl) 12.00 *32.50*
16 A6 ½a dull violet 9.50 *35.00*
17 A6 ¾a brown org (Bl) 15.00 *40.00*
18 A6 1a blue 11.00 *72.50*
19 A6 2a ocher 12.50 *100.00*
20 A6 2½a rose (Bl) 13.50 *45.00*
21 A6 3a green 16.00 *110.00*
22 A6 4a gray green 14.00 *125.00*
23 A6 6a blue 14.00 *180.00*
24 A6 8a chocolate 24.00 *250.00*
25 A6 1r bister 35.00 *375.00*
Nos. 15-25 (11) 176.50 *1,365.*

Kishangarh Stamps and Types of 1899-1904 Handstamped Type "a" in Rose

1949 ***Pin-perf., Rouletted***
26 A3 ½a blue (#18) 900.00
27 A4 1a dull lilac (#20) 21.00 *62.50*
28 A6 4a pale red brn (#21B) 125.00 *160.00*
29 A11 8a gray (#25B) 160.00 *275.00*
30 A7 1r dull green (#22) 450.00 *500.00*
31 A8 2r brown red (#23) 550.00
32 A9 5r red violet (#24) 525.00 525.00
Nos. 26-32 (7) 2,731.

Kishangarh Nos. 28, 31-36 Handstamped Type "a" in Rose or Green

1949 **Engr.** ***Perf. 13½, 12½***
33 A13 ½a chestnut (R) 300.00
34 A13 4a dark brown (G) 375.00
35 A13 4a dark brown (R) 20.00
36 A13 8a purple (R) 16.00
37 A13 1r dark green (R) 21.00
38 A13 2r lemon yellow (R) 27.50
39 A13 5r purple brown (R) 47.50

Kishangarh Nos. 40-42, 37, 43, 46-48 Handstamped Type "a" in Rose

1949 **Typo.** ***Rouletted***
40 A14 ¼a pale blue 8.00 8.00
41 A14 ½a green 675.00 375.00
42 A14 1a carmine — 450.00
43 A14 2 "anna" violet 825.00
44 A14 2 "annas" purple 4.50 12.50
45 A14 8a brown 7.50
46 A14 1r rose lilac 15.00
47 A14 2r dark green 15.00
48 A14 5r brown 675.00
Nos. 40-48 (9) 2,225.

Kishangarh Stamps and Types of 1928-29 Handstamped Type "a" in Rose

1949 ***Pin-perf***
49 A17 ¼a greenish blue 75.00 75.00
50 A17 ½a yel green 60.00 60.00
51 A18 1a car rose 110.00 110.00
52 A18 2a red violet 325.00 325.00
53 A17 4a yel brown 4.00 *12.50*
54 A17 8a purple 21.00 *90.00*
55 A17 1r deep green 10.00
56 A17 2r lemon 140.00
57 A17 5r red brown 75.00
Nos. 49-57 (9) 820.00

Type of Kishangarh 1928-29, Handstamped Type "a" in Rose

1949 ***Pin-perf***
58 A18 1a dark violet blue 140.00

No. 58 exists imperf.

Rajasthan stamps became obsolete Apr. 1, 1950.

RAJPEEPLA

räj-ˈpē-plə

(Rajpipla)

LOCATION — A Feudatory State near Bombay in the Gujarat States Agency in India.
AREA — 1,517 sq. mi.
POP. — 206,086
CAPITAL — Nandod

4 Paisas = 1 Anna

Kandjar (Indian Daggers) — A1

A2

A3

Without Gum

1880 **Unwmk.** **Litho.** ***Perf. 11, 12½***
1 A1 1pa ultramarine 5.25 *57.50*
2 A2 2a green 45.00 *160.00*
a. Horiz. pair, imperf. btwn. 900.00 900.00
3 A3 4a red 24.00 *100.00*
Nos. 1-3 (3) 74.25 *317.50*

The stamps of Rajpeepla have been obsolete since 1886.

SIRMOOR

sir-ˈmu̇ə̦r

(Sirmur)

LOCATION — A Feudatory State in the Punjab District of India.
AREA — 1,046 sq. mi.
POP. — 148,568
CAPITAL — Nahan

A1

Wove Paper

1879 **Unwmk.** ***Perf. 11½***
1 A1 1p green 24.00 *500.00*
a. Imperf., pair

Laid Paper

2 A1 1p blue 6.75 *250.00*
a. Imperf., pair

Raja Sir Shamsher Prakash — A2

1885-88 **Litho.** ***Perf. 14 and 14½.***
3 A2 3p brown 1.00 .60
4 A2 3p orange 2.50 .45
5 A2 6p green 6.50 6.00
6 A2 1a blue 4.00 *5.50*
7 A2 2a carmine 6.25 *21.00*
Nos. 3-7 (5) 20.25 *33.55*

There are several printings, dies and minor variations of this issue.

For overprints see Nos. O1-O16.

A3

1893 ***Perf. 11½***
9 A3 1p yellow green 1.60 1.60
a. 1pa dark blue green 1.10 1.10
10 A3 1p ultramarine 1.90 1.20
b. Imperf., pair 110.00

Nos. 9 and 10 are re-issues, which were available for postage.

The printed perforation, which is a part of the design, is in addition to the regular perforation.

Elephant — A4

1895-99 **Engr.** ***Perf. 14***
11 A4 3p orange 5.45 .45
12 A4 6p green 1.10 .45
a. Vert. pair, imperf between 15,000.
13 A4 1a dull blue 6.50 5.25
14 A4 2a dull red 5.25 2.25
15 A4 3a yellow green 35.00 *67.50*
16 A4 4a dark green 24.00 *35.00*
17 A4 8a deep blue 27.50 *42.50*
18 A4 1r vermilion 57.50 *110.00*
Nos. 11-18 (8) 162.30 *263.40*

No. 12a is unique.

Sir Surendar Bikram Prakash — A5

1899
19 A5 3a yellow green 6.25 *32.50*
20 A5 4a dark green 8.25 *35.00*
21 A5 8a blue 11.00 *30.00*
22 A5 1r vermilion 18.00 *75.00*
Nos. 19-22 (4) 43.50 *172.50*

OFFICIAL STAMPS

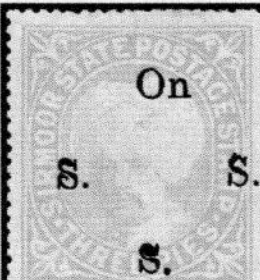

Regular Stamps Overprinted in Black

1890-91 **Unwmk.** ***Perf. 14, 14½***
O1 A2 3p orange 4.50 *52.50*
O2 A2 6p green 2.25 2.25
a. Double overprint 275.00
b. Double ovpt., one in red 1,250.
O3 A2 1a blue 600.00 *700.00*
O4 A2 2a carmine 27.50 *100.00*
Nos. O1-O4 (4) 634.25

1890-92 **Red Overprint**
O5 A2 6p green 42.50 3.50
O6 A2 1a blue 37.50 *47.50*

O7 A2 6p green 8.25 .75
b. Inverted overprint 210.00 150.00
O8 A2 1a blue 27.50 6.25
a. Inverted overprint 500.00 300.00
b. Double overprint 500.00

1892 **Black Overprint**
O9 A2 3p orange .90 .75
a. Inverted overprint 375.00
O10 A2 6p green 12.00 3.25
O11 A2 1a blue 18.00 1.50
a. Double overprint 600.00
O12 A2 2a carmine 10.00 10.00
a. Inverted overprint 1,350. 1,350.
Nos. O9-O12 (4) 40.90 15.50

Black Overprint

O13 A2 3p orange 19.00 1.90
a. Inverted overprint
b. Double overprint 1,000.
O14 A2 6p green 8.25 .90
O15 A2 1a blue 11.00 1.90
O16 A2 2a carmine 25.00 21.00
Nos. O13-O16 (4) 63.25 25.70

There are several settings of some of these overprints, differing in the sizes and shapes of the letters, the presence or absence of the periods, etc.

The overprints on Nos. O1-O16 are press printed. In addition, nine varieties of handstamped overprints were applied in 1894-96. Most of the handstamps are very similar to the press printed overprints.

Obsolete Mar. 31, 1901.

SORUTH

(Sorath)

(Junagarh)

(Saurashtra)

LOCATION — A Feudatory State near Bombay in the Western India States Agency in India.
AREA — 3,337 sq. mi.
POP. — 670,719
CAPITAL — Junagarh

The United State of Saurashtra (area 31,885 sq. mi.; population 2,900,000) was formed in 1948 by 217 States, including the stamp-issuing States of Jasdan, Morvi, Nowanuggur and Wadhwan.

Nos. 1-27 were issued without gum.

Catalogue values for unused stamps in this State are for Never Hinged items, beginning with Scott 39 in the regular postage section, and Scott O19 in the officials section.

Junagarh

A1

Handstamped in Watercolor

1864 **Unwmk.** ***Imperf.***

Laid Paper

1 A1 (1a) black, *bluish* 950.00 125.00
a. Wove paper 275.00
1B A1 (1a) black, *gray* 950.00 125.00

Wove Paper

2 A1 (1a) black, *cream* 1,500.

A2

1868 Typo. *Imperf.*

Wove Paper

3 A2 1a black, *yellowish* 37,500.
4 A2 1a red, *green* 16,000.
5 A2 1a red, *blue* 12,500.
6 A2 1a black, *pink* 825.00 110.00
7 A2 2a black, *yellow* 16,000.

Laid Paper

8 A2 1a black, *blue* 140.00 13.50
a. Left character, 3rd line, omitted
9 A2 1a red 32.50 37.50
a. Left character, 3rd line, omitted
10 A2 4a black 400.00 *675.00*
a. Left character, 3rd line, omitted

A 1a black on white laid paper exists in type A2. Value, used $9,500.

In 1890 official imitations of 1a and 4a stamps, type A2, were printed in sheets of 16 and 4. Original sheets have 20 stamps. Four of these imitations are perf. 12, six are imperf.

A3

A4

1877-86 Laid Paper *Imperf.*

11 A3 1a green 1.50 .75
a. Printed on both sides 750.00 *825.00*
12 A4 4a vermilion 4.00 2.50
a. Printed on both sides 950.00
13 A4 4a scarlet, *bluish* 5.50 5.00
Nos. 11-13 (3) 11.00 8.25

Perf. 12

14 A3 1a green .60 .25
a. 1a blue (error) 900.00 900.00
c. Wove paper 5.25 2.25
d. Imperf., pair 120.00 160.00
e. As "a," wove paper — 900.00
f. As "c," vert. pair, imperf horiz. 240.00
15 A3 1a green, *bluish* 5.25 *6.75*
a. Vert. pair, imperf horiz. 525.00
b. Horiz. pair, imperf vert. 210.00 —
16 A4 4a red 4.00 1.90
a. 4a carmine 6.50 5.25
c. Wove paper 7.50 18.00
d. As "c," imperf., pair 340.00 450.00
17 A4 4a scarlet, *bluish* 16.00 *25.00*
Nos. 14-17 (4) 25.85 *33.90*

Nos. 14d and 16c Surcharged

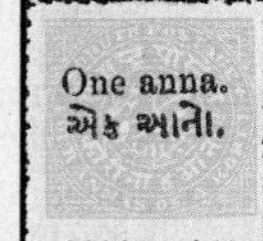

1913-14 *Perf. 12*

18 A3 3p on 1a green .25 .45
a. Laid paper 110.00 45.00
b. Inverted surcharge 52.50 30.00
c. Imperf., pair 52.50
19 A4 1a on 4a red 3.75 10.00
a. Laid paper 11.00 *82.50*
b. Imperf., pair 950.00
c. Double surcharge 1,000.

A5

A6

1914 *Perf. 12*

20 A5 3p green 2.10 .50
a. Imperf., pair 12.50 *40.00*
21 A6 1a rose carmine 2.25 *3.25*
a. Imperf., pair 30.00 140.00
b. Laid paper 375.00 160.00

Nawab Mahabat Khan III
A7 A8

1923-29 Wove Paper *Perf. 12*

22 A7 3p violet .50 .65
a. Imperf., pair 450.00
b. Laid paper ('29) 7.50 6.50
c. As "b," imperf, pair ('29) 5.25 *52.50*
d. As "b," horiz. pair, imperf btwn. 4.50 *37.50*
23 A8 1a red 4.50 *14.00*
b. Laid paper 4.50 14.00

Single examples of Nos. 23 and 23b cannot usually be distinguished.

Surcharged with New Value

27 A8 3p on 1a red 7.50 10.00

Two types of surcharge.

Junagarh City and The Girnar A9

Gir Lion — A10

Nawab Mahabat Khan III — A11

Kathi Horse A12

1929 *Perf. 14*

30 A9 3p dk green & blk 1.50 .25
31 A10 ½a dk blue & blk 9.00 .25
32 A11 1a claret & blk 7.50 1.50
33 A12 2a org buff & blk 19.00 3.00
34 A9 3a car rose & blk 9.00 *19.00*
35 A10 4a dull vio & blk 19.00 *42.50*
36 A12 8a apple grn & blk 25.00 *35.00*
37 A11 1r dull blue & blk 21.00 *45.00*
Nos. 30-37 (8) 111.00 *146.50*

For surcharges see Nos. 40-42, O20-O25. For overprints see Nos. O1-O14.

Type of 1929

Inscribed "Postage and Revenue"

1937

38 A11 1a claret & black 15.00 1.50

For overprint see No. O15.

Catalogue values for unused stamps in this section, from this point to the end of the section, are for Never Hinged items.

United State of Saurashtra

A13

Bhavnagar Court Fee Stamp Overprinted in Black "U.S.S. Revenue & Postage Saurashtra"

1949 Unwmk. Typo. *Perf. 11*

39 A13 1a deep claret 16.00 15.00
a. "POSTAGE" omitted 525.00 375.00
b. Double overprint 525.00 *600.00*

Nos. 30, 31 Surcharged in Black or Carmine "POSTAGE & REVENUE ONE ANNA"

1949-50 *Perf. 14*

40 A9 1a on 3p dk grn & blk (bl) ('50) 60.00 *82.50*
a. "OSTAGE" 750.00 *900.00*
41 A10 1a on ½a dk bl & blk (C) 14.00 7.50
a. Double surcharge 825.00

For overprint see No. O19.

No. 33 Surcharged in Green "Postage & Revenue ONE ANNA"

1949

42 A12 1a on 2a org buff & blk 24.00 *40.00*
a. "EVENUE" omitted 1,100.

For overprint see No. O26.

OFFICIAL STAMPS

Regular Issue of 1929 Overprinted in Red

a

1929 Unwmk. *Perf. 14*

O1 A9 3p dk green & black 2.50 .25
O2 A10 ½a dk blue & black 6.00 .25
O3 A11 1a claret & black 6.00 .25
O4 A12 2a org buff & black 3.75 .90
O5 A9 3a car rose & black 1.10 .75
O6 A10 4a dull violet & blk 6.25 .65
O7 A12 8a apple green & blk 5.50 4.50
O8 A11 1r dull blue & blk 5.50 *35.00*
Nos. O1-O8 (8) 36.60 42.55

For surcharges see Nos. O20-O24.

Regular Issue of 1929 Overprinted in Red

b

1933-49

O9 A9 3p dk grn & blk ('49) 375.00 25.00
O10 A10 ½a dk bl & blk ('49) 900.00 22.50
O11 A9 3a car rose & blk 32.50 27.50
O12 A10 4a dull vio & blk 42.50 24.00
O13 A12 8a apple grn & blk 47.50 27.50
O14 A11 1r dull blue & blk 52.50 140.00

The 3p is also known with ms. "SARKARI" overprint in carmine.

For surcharge see No. O25.

No. 38 Overprinted Type "a" in Red

1938

O15 A11 1a claret & black 21.00 2.25

Catalogue values for unused stamps in this section, from this point to the end of the section, are for Never Hinged items.

United State of Saurashtra No. 41 with Manuscript "Service" in Carmine

1949

O19 A10 1a on ½a dk bl & blk (C) 225.00

Used value for No. O19 is for an example used on piece, cancelled at Gadhda or Una between June and December, 1949.

No. 42 is also known with carmine ms. "Service" overprint in English or Gujarati.

Nos. O4-O8 and O14 Surcharged "ONE ANNA" in Blue or Black

1949 Surcharge 2¼mm high

O20 A12 1a on 2a (Bl) 21,000. 40.00
O21 A9 1a on 3a 5,250. 100.00
O22 A10 1a on 4a 600.00 100.00
O23 A12 1a on 8a 525.00 72.50

Surcharge 4mm High, Handstamped

O24 A11 1a on 1r (#O8) 3,250. 72.50
O25 A11 1a on 1r (#O14) 1,350. 75.00
Nos. O20-O25 (6) 31,975. 460.00

No. 42 Overprinted Type "b" in Carmine

1949 Unwmk. *Perf. 14*

O26 A12 1a on 2a 125.00 35.00

TONK

'tänk

LOCATION — A Feudatory State in the Rajputana Agency of India.
AREA — 2509 sq. mi.
POP. — 307,528 (1900)
CAPITAL — Nimbahera

Three examples of Tonk No. 1 are known. All are on covers dated 1906.

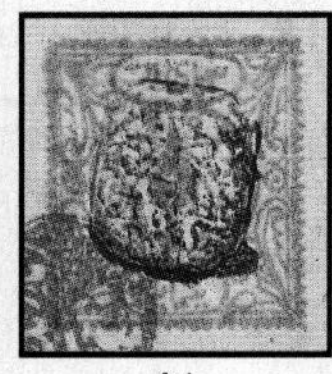

A1

Handstamped with black octagonal control seal

1906 Unwmk. Litho. *Imperf.*

Wove Paper

1 A1 ¼a yellow brown —

The stamps of Tonk became obsolete in 1907.

TRAVANCORE

'trav-ən-ˌkō̜ə̜r

LOCATION — A Feudatory State in the Madras States Agency, on the extreme southwest coast of India.
AREA — 7,662 sq. mi.
POP. — 6,070,018 (1941)
CAPITAL — Trivandrum

16 Cash = 1 Chuckram
2 Chuckrams = 1 Anna

Conch Shell (State Seal) — A1

1888 Unwmk. Typo. *Perf. 12*

Laid Paper

1 A1 1ch ultramarine 5.00 5.000
2 A1 2ch orange red 8.00 *12.00*
3 A1 4ch green 25.00 18.00
Nos. 1-3 (3) 38.00 35.00

The frame and details of the central medallion differ slightly on each denomination of type A1.

Laid paper printings of Nos. 1-3, 5-7 in completely different colors are essays.

1889-99 Wmk. 43 Wove Paper

4 A1 ½ch violet .90 .35
a. Vert. pair, imperf. between 450.00 450.00
b. Double impression 450.00
c. ½ch slate lilac ('94) 3.25 .75
d. As "c," double impression 450.00
e. ½ch purple ('99) 1.50 .35
f. As "e," double impression 450.00
g. ½ch dull purple ('04) 1.75 .35
5 A1 1ch ultramarine 2.25 .25
a. Vert. pair, imperf. between 675.00
b. Horiz. pair, imperf. between 675.00
c. Double impression 600.00
d. Tete beche pair 5,750. 5,000.

e. 1ch pale ultra ('92) 3.25 .35
f. 1ch violet blue ('01) 5.00 .50
6 A1 2ch scarlet 5.00 1.25
a. Horiz. pair, imperf. between 550.00 550.00
b. Vert. pair, imperf. between 250.00
c. Double impression 300.00
d. 2ch rose ('91) 4.00 .50
e. As "d," imperf. pair *750.00*
f. 2ch red ('04) 4.00 .50
7 A1 4ch dark green 5.00 1.00
a. Double impression *650.00*
b. 4ch yellow green ('01) 3.00 1.00
c. 4ch dull green ('04) 8.00 1.50
Nos. 4-7 (4) 13.15 2.85

Shades exist for each denomination.

For surcharges see Nos. 10-11. For type surcharged see No. 20. For overprints see Nos. O1-O2, O4, O6, O18, O24-O25, O27B, O32-O33, O42.

Conch Shell (State Seal) — A2

1901-32 Handmade Wove Paper

8 A2 ¾ch black 3.00 1.50
9 A2 ¾ch brt violet ('32) .50 .25
a. Horizontal pair, imperf. between *275.00*
b. ¾ch mauve, perf 12½ ('37) 17.50 1.00
c. As "b," horiz. pair, imperf. between 225.00
d. Perf. compound 12x12½ 25.00 10.00
e. As "d," horiz. pair, imperf. between 325.00

Machine-made Paper

Wmk. 43A

8A A2 ¾ch black ('32) 11.50 .75

For overprints see Nos. O26-O27, O44, O52.

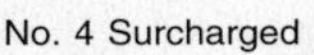

No. 4 Surcharged

1906 Wmk. 43

10 A1 ¼ch on ½ch violet 1.10 .25
a. Inverted surcharge 100.00 55.00
b. ¼ on ½ch reddish lilac 1.10 .45
c. ¼ on ½ch lilac 2.00 .45
11 A1 ⅜ch on ½ch violet .60 .50
a. Pair, one without surcharge —
b. Inverted surcharge 90.00
c. Double surcharge
d. Figure "8" omitted in fraction 60.00
e. ⅜ch on ½ch reddish lilac .60 .50
f. ⅜ch on ½ch lilac 1.25 .50

A3

A4

1908-11

12 A3 4ca rose .45 .25
a. Vertical pair, imperf. between 450.00 425.00
13 A1 6ca red brown ('10) .45 .25
a. Printed on both sides 75.00
b. Horizontal pair, imperf. between *425.00*
14 A4 3ch purple ('11) 4.00 .30
a. Vertical pair, imperf. between 450.00 *425.00*
b. Vertical strip of 3, imperf. between *500.00*
Nos. 12-14 (3) 4.90 .80

For surcharge & overprints see Nos. 19, O3, O5, O8, O13, O15, O20, O22, O30-O31, O53.

A5

A6

1916

15 A5 7ch red violet 3.50 1.00
a. 7ch carmine-red (error) 60.00

16 A6 14ch orange 4.00 3.75
a. Horizontal strip of 3, imperf. vertically 625.00

For overprints see Nos. O11-O12, O34-O35.

A7

1920-33

17 A7 1¼ch claret .80 .80
a. Horiz. pair, imperf. between 500.00 *475.00*
18 A7 1½ch light red ('33) 4.00 .25
a. Horizontal strip of 3, imperf. between 325.00
b. Perf. 12½ 25.00 3.25
c. Perf. compound 12x12½ 60.00

For surcharges see Nos. 27-28. For overprints see Nos. O7, O17, O28-O29, O38, O56.

No. 12 and Type of 1888 Surcharged

1921

19 A3 1ca on 4ca rose .25 .25
a. Inverted surcharge 37.50 25.00
20 A1 5ca on 1ch dull bl (R) 1.50 .25
a. Inverted surcharge 19.00 12.50
b. Double surcharge 100.00 75.00
c. Vertical pair, imperf. between *425.00*

A8

1921-32

21 A8 5ca bister 1.20 .25
a. Horizontal pair, imperf. between 75.00 75.00
22 A8 5ca brown ('32) 4.00 .35
a. Horizontal pair, imperf. between 55.00
b. Vertical pair, imperf. between 300.00
23 A8 10ca rose .60 .25
Nos. 21-23 (3) 5.80 .85

For surcharges & overprints see Nos. 29-30, O9-O10, O14, O16, O19, O21, O23, O36-O37.

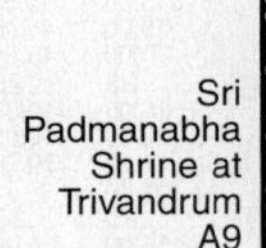

Sri Padmanabha Shrine at Trivandrum A9

State Chariot — A10

Maharaja Sir Bala Rama Varma — A11

1931, Nov. 6

24 A9 6ca emer & blk 2.40 2.40
a. Horizontal pair, imperf. between 225.00 225.00
25 A10 10ca ultra & black 1.90 1.00
a. Vertical pair, imperf. between *750.00*
26 A11 3ch violet & black 4.00 4.50
Nos. 24-26 (3) 8.30 7.90

Investiture of Sir Bala Rama Varma with full ruling powers.

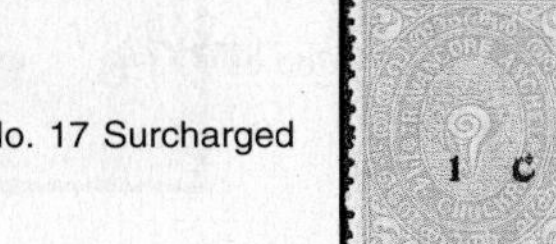

No. 17 Surcharged

1932, Jan. 14

27 A7 1ca on 1¼ch claret .25 *.75*
a. Inverted surcharge 6.50 *10.00*
b. Double surcharge 50.00 47.50
c. Horizontal pair, imperf. between 190.00
d. Pair, one without surcharge 175.00 190.00
e. Letter "c" omitted 55.00 55.00
28 A7 2ca on 1¼ch claret .25 .25
a. Inverted surcharge 6.50 *10.00*
b. Double surcharge 42.50
c. Pair, one without surcharge 180.00 190.00
d. Double surcharge, one inverted 80.00
e. Triple surcharge 100.00
f. Triple surcharge, one inverted 85.00 85.00
g. Numeral "2" omitted 55.00 55.00
h. Letter "c" omitted 55.00 55.00
i. Horizontal pair, imperf. between 180.00
j. Vertical pair, imperf. between 190.00

Type of 1932 and No. 23 Surcharged like Nos. 19-20

1932, Mar. 5

29 A8 1ca on 5ca chocolate .25 .25
a. Inverted surcharge 11.00 *15.00*
b. Double surcharge
c. Pair, one without surcharge 180.00
d. Horizontal pair, imperf. between 190.00
e. Surcharge inverted on reverse only 115.00
f. Numeral "1" omitted 50.00
g. Letter "c" omitted 45.00
30 A8 2ca on 10ca rose .25 .25
a. Inverted surcharge 7.50 *12.00*
b. Double surcharge 32.50 *35.00*
c. Horizontal pair, imperf. between 200.00
d. Double surcharge, one inverted 115.00 110.00
e. Double surcharge, both inverted 65.00
31 A8 1ca on 5ca slate pur 2.25 .50
a. Inverted surcharge 450.00
b. Numeral "1" inverted 125.00 *110.00*

Untouchables Entering Temple and Maharaja — A12

Designs: Different temples and frames.

1937, Mar. 29 Litho. *Perf. 11½*

32 A12 6ca carmine 4.25 1.50
b. Horizontal strip of 3, imperf. between 750.00
33 A12 12ca ultramarine 5.25 .90
d. Vertical pair, imperf. between 750.00
34 A12 1½ch light green 2.25 *3.50*
b. Vertical pair, imperf. between 525.00
35 A12 3ch purple 6.50 3.50
Nos. 32-35 (4) 18.25 9.40

Temple Entry Bill.

Perf. 12½

32A A12 6ca carmine 3.75 3.00
c. Compound perf. 75.00 82.50
33A A12 12ca ultramarine 7.00 1.25
b. Vertical pair, imperf. between 700.00
c. Compound perf. 110.00
34A A12 1½ch light green 40.00 11.50
c. Compound perf. 175.00
35A A12 3ch purple 6.50 5.50
Nos. 32A-35A (4) 57.25 21.25

Lake Ashtamudi A13

A14

A15

Sir Bala Rama Varma — A16

Sri Padmanabha Shrine — A17

View of Cape Comerin A18

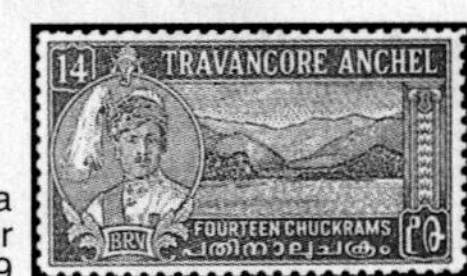

Pachipara Reservoir A19

1939, May 9 Litho. *Perf. 12½*

36 A13 1ch yellow green 12.00 .25
37 A14 1½ch carmine 7.00 *7.00*
d. Perf. 13½ 27.50 *100.00*
38 A15 2ch orange 12.00 4.00
39 A16 3ch chocolate 11.00 .25
40 A17 4ch henna brown 14.00 .60
41 A18 7ch light blue 17.50 *30.00*
42 A19 14ch turq green 10.00 *100.00*
Nos. 36-42 (7) 83.50 142.10

Perf. 11

36A A13 1ch yellow green 17.50 .25
d. Vert. pair, imperf. between —
e. Vertical strip of 3, imperf. between —
37A A14 1½ch carmine 8.00 37.50
38A A15 2ch orange 27.50 2.75
39A A16 3ch chocolate 30.00 .50
40A A17 4ch henna brown 62.50 .75
41A A18 7ch light blue 150.00 62.50
42A A19 14ch turq green 18.00 *180.00*

Perf. 12

36B A13 1ch yellow green 37.50 3.75
d. Vert. pair, imperf. between —
e. Vertical strip of 3, imperf. between —
37B A14 1½ch carmine 62.50 9.00
38B A15 2ch orange 175.00 10.00
39B A16 3ch chocolate 65.00 7.50
40B A17 4ch henna brown 55.00 14.00

Perf. Compound 11, 12, 12½

36C A13 1ch yellow green 45.00 5.00
d. Vert. pair, imperf. between —
37C A14 1½ch carmine 85.00 15.00
38C A15 2ch orange 175.00 10.00
39C A16 3ch chocolate 75.00 1.50
40C A17 4ch henna brown 275.00 200.00
41C A17 7ch light blue 175.00 75.00

27th birthday of Maharaja Sir Bala Rama Varma.

For surcharges and overprints see Nos. 45, O45-O51, Travancore-Cochin 3-7, O3-O7.

Maharaja Sir Bala Rama Varma and Aruvikara Falls A20

Maharaja and Marthanda Varma Bridge, Alwaye A21

1941, Oct. 20 Typo. *Perf. 12½*

43 A20 6ca violet black 11.00 .25
- *a.* Perf. 11 9.00 .25
- *b.* As "a," vertical pair, imperf. between 35.00
- *c.* As "a," vertical pair, imperf. horiz. 80.00 100.00
- *d.* Perf. 12 80.00 100.00
- *e.* As "d," horiz. pair, imperf. between 37.50
- *f.* As "d," vert. pair, imperf. between 90.00
- *g.* As "d," vert. strip of 3, imperf. between 40.00
- *h.* Compound perf. 14.50 3.00

44 A21 ¾ch dull brown 12.50 .35
- *a.* Vertical pair, imperf. between *750.00*
- *b.* Perf. 11 12.00 .25
- *c.* As "b," horizontal pair, imperf. between *350.00*
- *d.* As "b," vert. pair, imperf. between 37.50 85.00
- *e.* As "b," vert. strip of 3, imperf. between 45.00
- *f.* As "b," block of 4, imperf. between horiz. & vert. 400.00
- *g.* Perf. 12 80.00 16.00
- *h.* Compound perf. 22.50 1.25

29th birthday of the Maharaja, Oct. 20, 1941.

For overprints & surcharges see Nos. 46-47, 49, O54-O55, O58-O59, Travancore-Cochin Nos. 1, O1.

Stamps and Types of 1939-41 Surcharged in Black

Perf. 11, 12½

1943, Sept. 17 Wmk. 43

45 A14 2ca on 1½ch car 2.25 1.90
- *a.* Vertical pair, imperf. between 80.00
- *b.* "2" omitted in surcharge 500.00 475.00
- *c.* "CA" omitted in surcharge 900.00
- *d.* "ASH" omitted in surcharge 900.00
- *e.* Perf. 11 .50 .50
- *f.* As "e," "CA" omitted in surcharge 900.00
- *g.* As "e," horizontal pair, imperf. between *400.00*
- *h.* Compound perf. 1.15 2.40
- *i.* As "h," vertical pair, imperf. between 240.00
- *j.* As "h," numeral "2" omitted in surcharge 550.00

46 A21 4ca on ¾ch dl brn 6.00 .45
- *a.* Perf. 11 8.00 1.00
- *b.* Perf. 12 *225.00*
- *c.* Compound perf. 10.00 2.00

47 A20 8ca on 6ca red 7.00 .25
- *a.* Perf. 11 7.00 .25
- *b.* As "a," horiz. pair, imperf. between 60.00
- *c.* Perf. 12 125.00
- *d.* Compound perf. 25.00 13.50

Nos. 45-47 (3) 15.25 2.60

For overprints see Nos. O57-O59.

Maharaja Sir Bala Rama Varma — A22

1946, Oct. 24 Typo. *Perf. 11*

48 A22 8ca rose red 3.50 3.00
- *a.* Perf. 12½ 3.50 3.00
- *b.* Perf. 12 50.00 7.00
- *c.* As "b," horizontal pair, imperf. between *100.00* 100.00
- *d.* As "b," horizontal strip of 3, imperf. between *100.00*
- *e.* Compound perf.

For overprint see No. O60. For surcharges see Travancore-Cochin Nos. 2, O2.

No. O54 Overprinted "SPECIAL" Vertically in Orange

1946 *Perf. 12½*

49 A20 6ca violet black 9.50 5.00
- *a.* Perf. 11 55.00 9.00
- *b.* Compound perf. 10.00 9.00

OFFICIAL STAMPS

Nos. O1-O60 were issued without gum.

Regular Issues of 1889-1911 Overprinted in Red or Black

Perf. 12, 12½

1911, Aug. 16 Wmk. 43

O1 A1 1ch indigo (R) 1.65 .25
- *a.* Inverted overprint 10.00 6.50
- *b.* "nO" for "On" 120.00 120.00
- *c.* Double overprint 100.00 75.00
- *d.* Vertical pair, imperf. between *275.00*
- *e.* "O" inverted 15.00 3.00
- *f.* Left "S" inverted 15.00 2.50
- *g.* Right "S" inverted 15.00 2.75
- *h.* "SS" inverted — 80.00

O2 A1 2ch scarlet .50 .25
- *a.* Inverted overprint 12.00 12.00
- *b.* Blue overprint 180.00
- *c.* "O" inverted 15.00 1.50
- *d.* Left "S" inverted 15.00 1.50
- *e.* Right "S" inverted 15.00 2.75

O3 A4 3ch purple .50 .25
- *a.* Inverted overprint 15.00 15.00
- *b.* Double overprint 120.00 100.00
- *c.* Vertical pair, imperf. between 325.00 *300.00*
- *d.* Horizontal pair, imperf. vertically 225.00
- *e.* Blue overprint 225.00 110.00
- *f.* Right "S" inverted 6.50 1.00
- *g.* Right "S" omitted 225.00 160.00
- *h.* Left "S" omitted 225.00 160.00

O4 A1 4ch dark green .80 .25
- *a.* Inverted overprint 82.50 19.00
- *b.* Double overprint 190.00 140.00
- *c.* Horizontal pair, imperf. between *400.00*
- *d.* "O" inverted 18.00 3.00
- *e.* Left "S" inverted 20.00 5.00
- *f.* Right "S" inverted 22.50 6.00
- *g.* Left "S" omitted 225.00 160.00

Nos. O1-O4 (4) 3.45 1.00

Same Ovpt. on Regular Issues of 1889-1920

1918-20

O5 A3 4ca rose .25 .25
- *a.* Imperf., pair 450.00 450.00
- *b.* Inverted overprint 120.00
- *c.* Double overprint 180.00 140.00
- *d.* Double impression *425.00*
- *e.* "SS" inverted 60.00 30.00
- *f.* Left "S" inverted — 27.50
- *g.* "O" inverted — 40.00

O6 A1 ½ch violet (R) 3.75 .50
- *a.* Inverted overprint 19.00 6.00
- *b.* "chucrram" 18.50 6.50
- *c.* Double overprint, both inverted 240.00
- *d.* "On" omitted *210.00*
- *e.* Double impression 75.00
- *f.* Horizontal pair, imperf. between 240.00 210.00
- *g.* Vertical pair, imperf. between 100.00 100.00
- *h.* Right "S" inverted — 50.00
- *i.* Right "S" omitted — 250.00

O7 A7 1¼ch claret .60 .25
- *a.* Inverted overprint 14.00 12.00
- *b.* Double overprint 67.50
- *d.* Double impression *475.00*
- *e.* A7 1¼ch carmine (error of color) 60.00
- *f.* "O" inverted 20.00 2.25
- *g.* Left "S" inverted 25.00 4.50
- *h.* Right "S" inverted 25.00 6.00

Nos. O5-O7 (3) 4.60 1.00

Same Ovpt. on Regular Issues of 1909-21

1921

O8 A1 6ca red brown .45 .25
- *a.* Inverted overprint 200.00 18.00
- *b.* Double overprint 200.00 180.00
- *c.* Vertical pair, imperf. between *350.00*
- *d.* "O" inverted 6.50 3.00
- *e.* Left "S" inverted 12.00 3.50
- *f.* Right "S" inverted 13.00 3.50

O9 A8 10ca rose 2.00 .25
- *a.* Inverted overprint 27.50
- *b.* Double overprint 100.00 100.00
- *c.* Horizontal pair, imperf. between *225.00*
- *d.* 10ca scarlet ('25) 18.00
- *e.* "O" inverted 16.00 4.50
- *f.* Left "S" inverted 15.00 3.50
- *g.* Right "S" inverted 16.00 4.50

Same Overprint on Regular Issue of 1921

1922

O10 A8 5ca bister 2.50 .25
- *a.* Inverted overprint 21.00 13.50
- *b.* "O" inverted 12.00 3.50
- *c.* Left "S" inverted 14.00 3.50
- *d.* Right "S" inverted 14.00 3.50

For surcharge see No. O39B.

Same Overprint on Regular Issue of 1916

1925

O11 A5 7ch plum 2.50 .45
- *a.* 7ch carmine red 75.00
- *b.* "O" inverted 27.50 4.50
- *c.* Left "S" inverted 22.50 4.00
- *d.* Right "S" inverted 27.50 4.50

O12 A6 14ch orange 3.25 .60
- *a.* "O" inverted 25.00 5.00
- *b.* Left "S" inverted 15.00 3.50
- *c.* Right "S" inverted 25.00 5.00

Same Overprint in Blue on Regular Issues of 1889-1921

O13 A3 4ca rose 80.00 *1.00*
- *a.* "O" inverted — 35.00

O14 A8 5ca bister .90 .25
- *a.* Horizontal pair, imperf. between 375.00 *375.00*
- *b.* Inverted overprint 40.00 22.50
- *c.* "O" inverted 10.00 5.50
- *d.* Left "S" inverted 7.50 4.50
- *e.* Right "S" inverted 10.00 5.50

O15 A1 6ca red brown 22.00 2.50
- *a.* Inverted overprint 225.00 175.00
- *b.* "O" inverted 90.00 22.50
- *c.* Left "S" inverted 90.00 22.50
- *d.* Right "S" inverted 90.00 22.50

O16 A8 10ca rose 120.00 32.50
- *a.* Inverted overprint *115.00*
- *b.* "O" inverted — 100.00

O17 A7 1¼ch claret — 120.00
- *a.* "O" inverted — 350.00
- *b.* Left "S" inverted — 350.00
- *c.* Right "S" inverted — 350.00

O18 A1 4ch dark green — *150.00*
- *a.* "O" inverted — 300.00
- *b.* Left "S" inverted — 300.00
- *c.* Right "S" inverted — 300.00

Some authorities question the authenticity of No. O14.

1930 Black Overprint

O19 A8 5ca brown .35 *.90*
- *a.* Inverted overprint 27.50
- *b.* Vertical pair, imperf. between *425.00*
- *c.* "O" inverted 6.50 8.00
- *d.* Left "S" inverted 6.50 8.00

Regular Issues of 1889-1932 Overprinted in Black or Red

1930-34

O20 A3 4ca rose 30.00 *95.00*

O21 A8 5ca brown 45.00 14.00
- *a.* Inverted overprint 100.00 110.00

O22 A1 6ca org brown .25 .25
- *a.* Inverted overprint 30.00
- *b.* Double overprint 100.00
- *c.* "nO" for "On" 200.00 200.00
- *d.* Vertical pair, imperf. between 100.00 100.00
- *e.* Right "S" inverted 45.00 30.00
- *f.* Right "S" omitted 150.00
- *g.* Perf. 12½ — 25.00
- *h.* Compound perf. (12x12½) — 45.00

O23 A8 10ca rose 6.50 4.50
- *a.* Horizontal pair, imperf. between 20.00 *35.00*
- *b.* Vertical pair, imperf. between 15.00 *32.50*
- *c.* "O" inverted 70.00 45.00
- *d.* Right "S" inverted 70.00 45.00

O24 A1 ½ch violet ('34) .85 .25
- *a.* "chucrram" 15.00 10.00
- *b.* "Ou" for "On" 120.00 110.00
- *c.* Left "S" omitted — 250.00
- *d.* "O" of "On" inverted 350.00

O25 A1 ½ch purple (R) .25 .25
- *a.* "chucrram" 15.00 10.00
- *b.* Vertical pair, imperf. between 180.00 *175.00*
- *c.* Left "S" inverted 45.00 40.00

O26 A2 ¾ch blk (R) ('32) .60 .25
- *a.* Inverted overprint *375.00*
- *b.* "N" omitted in overprint 160.00 *155.00*

O27 A2 ¾ch brt vio ('33) .45 .25
- *a.* Double overprint 200.00
- *c.* Vertical pair, imperf. between 240.00
- *d.* Compound perf. (12x12½) 50.00 32.50
- *e.* "Ou" for "On" 110.00 90.00
- *f.* "O" inverted 40.00 30.00
- *g.* Right "S" inverted — 37.50

O27B A1 1ch gray blue (R) ('33) 1.50 .35
- *e.* Horizontal pair, imperf. between 200.00 200.00
- *f.* Vertical pair, imperf. between 32.50 *47.50*
- *g.* Perf. 12½ 15.00 8.50
- *h.* Compound perf. (12x12½) 37.50 17.50
- *i.* As "h," vertical pair, imperf. between *325.00*
- *j.* Left "S" inverted — 70.00

O28 A7 1¼ch claret 2.10 *2.00*

O29 A7 1½ch dl red ('32) .60 .25
- *a.* Double overprint 80.00 80.00
- *b.* Perf. 12½ 70.00 18.00
- *c.* Compound perf. (12x12½) 45.00
- *d.* As "c," double impression 350.00
- *e.* Vertical pair, imperf. between *250.00*
- *f.* "O" inverted 8.00 4.50
- *g.* Left "S" inverted — 45.00

O30 A4 3ch purple ('33) 1.90 .90
- *a.* Double overprint 150.00
- *b.* "O" inverted 40.00 17.50

O31 A4 3ch purple (R) 1.20 .25
- *a.* Inverted overprint 80.00
- *b.* Horizontal pair, imperf. between 150.00 75.00
- *c.* Vertical pair, imperf. between 110.00 65.00
- *d.* Perf. 12½ 5.00
- *e.* As "d," vertical pair, imperf. between *325.00*
- *f.* Compound perf. (12x12½) — 20.00
- *g.* As "f", horiz. pair, imperf. between 350.00
- *h.* "O" inverted 37.50 20.00
- *i.* "Ou" for "On" — 130.00

O32 A1 4ch dp grn (R) 3.00 .25

O33 A1 4ch deep green 2.75 *7.50*

O34 A5 7ch maroon 1.90 .45
- *a.* Vertical pair, imperf. between 65.00 65.00
- *b.* Perf. 12½ 20.00
- *c.* Compound perf. (12x12½) 75.00 16.00
- *d.* As "c", vertical pair, imperf. between 190.00
- *e.* As "c," vertical strip of 3, imperf. between 250.00 *250.00*
- *f.* "O" inverted 60.00 22.50
- *g.* Left "S" inverted 80.00 37.50

O35 A6 14ch orange ('31) 2.50 .60
- *a.* Inverted overprint 500.00 425.00
- *b.* Horizontal pair, imperf. between 60.00 *85.00*
- *c.* Vertical pair, imperf. between 300.00

Nos. O20-O35 (17) 101.35 127.30

The overprint on Nos. O22, O26 and O28 is smaller than the illustration. There are three sizes of the overprint on No. O27.

For surcharges see Nos. O39, O40-O41.

Type of 1921-32 and No. 17 Surcharged and Overprinted

1932

O36 A8 6ca on 5ca dk brn .50 *.50*
- *b.* Inverted surcharge 12.00 12.50
- *c.* Double surcharge 150.00
- *d.* Double surcharge, one inverted 130.00
- *e.* Pair, one without surcharge 500.00
- *f.* "O" inverted 6.00 6.50
- *g.* Left "S" inverted 8.00 8.00

O36A A8 6ca on 5ca bister 2.50 *3.00*
- *f.* Inverted surcharge 110.00
- *g.* Left "S" inverted 22.50 16.00
- *h.* Right "S" inverted 22.50 16.00
- *i.* "6" omitted — 160.00

O37 A8 12ca on 10a rose .25 .25
- *a.* New value inverted 9.00 *11.00*
- *b.* Overprint and surcharge inverted 55.00 50.00
- *c.* Double surcharge 160.00
- *d.* Inverted overprint 11.00 11.00
- *e.* "O" inverted 27.50 27.50
- *f.* Right "S" inverted 30.00 30.00
- *g.* "On" omitted — 200.00
- *h.* "n" omitted — 200.00
- *i.* "c" omitted 65.00 65.00
- *j.* Double overprint 120.00
- *k.* Surcharge on front and back 300.00

O38 A7 1ch8ca on 1¼ch cl .50 .30
- *a.* Inverted surcharge *200.00*
- *b.* Double surcharge 75.00
- *c.* Vertical pair, imperf. between 500.00
- *d.* "O" inverted 5.50 4.50
- *e.* Wrong font "1c" 27.50 22.50
- *f.* "1ch" omitted 140.00

Nos. O36-O38 (4) 3.75 *4.05*

Nos. O21, O10, O23 and O28 Surcharged in Black

O39 A8 6ca on 5ca dk brown .30 .45
- *a.* New value inverted 16.00 *19.00*
- *c.* Pair, one without surcharge 325.00

O39B A8 6ca on 5ca bis *50.00* *20.00*

O40 A8 12ca on 10ca rose 3.00 2.25
- *a.* New value inverted 10.00 10.00
- *b.* "On S S" inverted 24.00 27.50
- *c.* Ovpt. & surch. inverted 60.00 *70.00*
- *d.* Ovpt. & surch. inverted 60.00 *62.50*

O41 A7 1ch8ca on 1¼ch cl 4.50 1.90
- *a.* New value inverted 160.00
- *b.* "O" inverted 20.00 8.00

c. Left "S" inverted 20.00 8.00
d. Right "S" inverted 20.00 8.00
Nos. O39-O41 (4) 57.80 24.60

No. O39B can be distinguished from O36A by the letters "S" in the overprint, which are closer together on No. O39B.

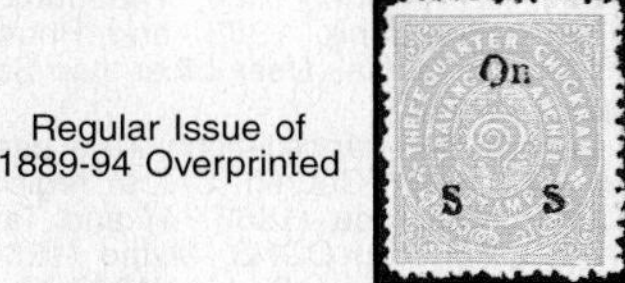

Regular Issue of 1889-94 Overprinted

1933

O42 A1 ¾ch violet 5.50 .25
a. Horizontal pair, imperf. between 130.00 100.00
b. Horizontal strip of 3, imperf. between *250.00*
c. Vertical pair, imperf. between *200.00*
d. Double impression *325.00*

Regular Issue of 1901 Overprinted in Red

1933

O44 A2 ¾ch black .50 .40
a. Left "S" omitted 145.00 135.00
b. Right "S" omitted 145.00

No. O44 can be distinguished from No. O26 by its overprint, which is significantly smaller than No. O26.

Regular Issue of 1939 Overprinted in Black

a

"SERVICE" 13mm wide, letter "R" with curved tail

1939 First Overprint *Perf. 12½*

O45 A13 1ch yellow green 11.00 .50
O46 A14 1½ch carmine 20.00 2.50
a. "SESVICE" 200.00 45.00
b. Perf. 12 110.00 27.50
c. As "b," "SESVICE" *325.00*
d. As "b," horizontal pair, imperf. between *450.00*
e. Compound perf. (12x12½) 37.50 *5.50*
O47 A15 2ch orange 11.00 11.00
a. "SESVICE" 190.00 *210.00*
b. Compound perf. (12x12½) 200.00 200.00
O48 A16 3ch chocolate 9.50 .30
a. "SESVICE" 150.00 30.00
b. Perf. 12 50.00 .75
c. As "b," "SESVICE" 450.00 65.00
d. Compound perf. (12x12½) 22.50 7.00
O49 A17 4ch henna brown 24.00 8.50
O50 A18 7ch light blue 25.00 6.50
O51 A19 14ch turq green 42.50 12.50
Nos. O45-O51 (7) 143.00 41.80

27th birthday of Maharaja Sir Bala Rama Varma.

Overprinted "SERVICE" 13½mm wide, letter "R" with straight tail

1941-42 *Perf. 12½*

Second Overprint

O45F A13 1ch yel grn 2.00 .25
a. Inverted overprint 60.00
b. Double overprint 30.00
c. Vertical pair, imperf. between 85.00 85.00
O46F A14 1½ch scarlet 6.50 .25
a. Horizontal pair, imperf. between 100.00
O47F A15 2ch orange 5.50 .35
O48F A16 3ch chocolate 4.00 .25
a. Vertical pair, imperf. between *1,000.*
O49F A17 4ch hen brn 5.50 1.25
O50F A18 7ch light blue 11.00 .45
O51F A19 14ch turq green 19.00 .85

Perf. 11

O45G A13 1ch yel grn 1.25 .25
a. Double overprint 225.00 210.00
b. Vertical pair, imperf. between 65.00
O46G A14 1½ch scarlet 5.00 .25
a. Vertical pair, imperf. between 240.00 225.00
b. Vertical strip of 3, imperf. between 175.00
c. Horizontal pair, imperf. between 225.00

O47G A15 2ch orange 20.00 4.00
a. Vertical pair, imperf. between *1,000.*
O48G A16 3ch chocolate 4.25 .25
O49G A17 4ch hen brn 6.50 .65
O50G A18 7ch light blue 11.00 .45
a. 7ch blue 22.50 11.50
O51G A19 14ch turq green 24.00 1.75

Perf. 12

O45H A13 1ch yel grn 5.00 .60
a. Inverted overprint *210.00*
b. Double overprint 27.50 42.50
c. Double impression 180.00
d. Vertical pair, imperf. between 140.00 135.00
O46H A14 1½ch scarlet 11.00 1.25
a. Vertical strip of 3, imperf. between 350.00
O47H A15 2ch orange 225.00 200.00
a. Vertical pair, imperf. between 1,100. *1,000.*
O48H A16 3ch chocolate 10.00 4.00
a. Vertical pair, imperf. between 1,000. *900.00*
O49H A17 4ch hen brn 32.50 9.00
O50H A18 7ch light blue 37.50 15.00
a. 7ch blue 13.00 10.00
O51H A19 14ch turq green 17.50 3.00

Perf. Compound (12x12½)

O45I A13 1ch yel grn 10.00 3.00
O46I A14 1½ch scarlet 5.00 .50
O47I A15 2ch orange 200.00 *200.00*
O48I A16 3ch chocolate 32.50 1.00
O49I A17 4ch hen brn 80.00 32.50
O50I A18 7ch light blue 25.00 6.00
O51I A19 14ch turq green 125.00 20.00

"SERVICE" Overprint 13mm

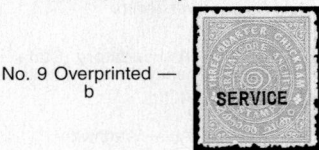

No. 9 Overprinted — b

1939 Wmk. 43 *Perf. 12.*

O52 A2 ¾ch violet 42.50 2.50
a. Perf. 12½ 260.00 125.00
b. Compound perf. (12x12½) 240.00 120.00

"SERVICE" 13½mm

1941 *Perf. 12½*

O52F A2 ¾ch violet 25.00 .25
a. Horizontal pair, imperf. between 220.00 220.00
b. Perf. 11 100.00 1.25
c. Perf. 12 30.00 .25
d. Compound perf. (12x12½) 55.00 1.00

No. 13 Overprinted Type "b"

1941

O53 A1 6ca red brown 1.25 .50
a. Perf. 11 2.00 .90
b. Perf. 12 1.00 .40
c. Compound perf. (12x12½) 1.00 1.25

Nos. 43-44 Overprinted Type "a"

1941 *Perf. 12½*

O54 A20 6ca violet black .90 .75
a. Perf. 11 1.00 .25
b. Perf. 12 110.00 17.50
c. Compound perf. (12x12½) 1.75 1.75
O55 A21 ¾ch dull brown 9.50 .25
a. Vertical pair, imperf. between *750.00*
b. Perf. 11 10.00 .25
c. Perf. 12 110.00 5.00
d. Compound perf. (12x12½) 12.50 1.00

29th birthday of the Maharaja, Oct. 20, 1941.
For overprint see No. 49.

No. 18 Overprinted Type "b"

1944 *Perf. 12*

O56 A7 1½ch light red 6.50 1.25
a. Perf. 12½ ('44) 21.00 12.00
b. Compound perf. (12x12½) 28.50 17.50

Nos. 45-48 Overprinted Type "a"

1945-49 *Perf. 11, 12*

O57 A14 2ca on 1½ch car .90 *1.50*
a. Pair, one without surcharge 500.00
b. Perf. 12½ .75 1.20
c. Compound perf. (12x12½) 1.00 1.50
d. As "c," "2" omitted in surcharge 750.00 750.00
e. Perf. 12
O58 A21 4ca on ¾ch dl brn 6.00 .60
a. Perf. 12½ ('45) 8.00 .75
b. Compound perf. (12x12½) 4.50 1.75
O59 A20 8ca on 6ca red 2.00 .25
a. Inverted surcharge *2,250.*
b. Perf. 12½ 4.00 .40
c. Compound perf. (12x12½) 10.00 1.50
O60 A22 8ca rose red ('49) 5.00 1.75
a. Double impression of stamp 47.50
b. Horizontal pair, imperf. between 65.00
c. Vertical pair, imperf. between *375.00*
d. Perf. 12½ .75 1.20
e. As "d," double impression 50.00

f. Perf. 12 4.50 1.75
g. As "f," double impression 75.00
Nos. O57-O60 (4) 13.90 4.10

Travancore stamps became obsolete June 30, 1949.

TRAVANCORE-COCHIN

ˈtrav-ən-ˌkō̜ə̜r kō-ˈchin

LOCATION — Southern India
AREA — 9,155 sq. mi.
POP. — 7,492,000

The United State of Travancore-Cochin was established July 1, 1949.

Catalogue values for all unused stamps in this state are for Never Hinged items.

Travancore Stamps of 1939-47 Surcharged in Red or Black

a

1949, July 1 Wmk. 43 *Perf. 12*

1 A20 2p on 6ca vio blk (R) .95 .30
a. Horiz. pair, imperf. between 110.00 —
b. Vert. pair, imperf. between 10.00 26.00
c. Inverted surcharge 200.00 —
d. Vert. strip of 3, imperf. between 47.50 —
e. Horiz. strip of 3, imperf. between 110.00 —
f. Block of 4, imperf. between (horiz. & vert.) 100.00 —
2 A22 4p on 8ca rose red 1.85 .40
a. Vert. pair, imperf. between 30.00 —
b. Inverted surcharge 250.00 —
c. Pair, one without surcharge 325.00 —
d. "FOUP" 225.00 125.00
e. "S" inverted 150.00
3 A13 ½a on 1ch yel grn 1.25 .50
a. Horiz. pair, imperf. between 110.00 110.00
b. Vert. pair, imperf. between 8.00 22.50
c. Inverted surcharge 6.25
d. "NANA" 400.00 200.00
e. Block of 4, imperf. between (horiz. & vert.) 80.00 —
4 A15 1a on 2ch orange 6.25 .65
a. Horiz. pair, imperf. between 17.50 —
b. Vert. pair, imperf. between 10.00 25.00
c. Block of 4, imperf. between (horiz. & vert.) 80.00
5 A17 2a on 4ch hen brn 6.25 .70
a. "O" inverted 85.00 27.50
6 A18 3a on 7ch lt blue 16.00 5.00
7 A19 6a on 14ch turq grn 35.00 *55.00*
a. Accent omitted from Malayalam surcharge *600.00* *675.00*
Nos. 1-7 (7) 67.55 62.55

For overprints see Nos. O1-O7, O12-O17.
For types overprinted see Nos. O18-O23.

Perf. 11

1g A20 2p on 6ca vio blk (R) 2.75 .50
h. Vert. pair, imperf. between 375.00 375.00
i. Pair, one without surcharge 190.00 —
2g A22 4p on 8ca rose red 3.50 .40
h. Vert. pair, imperf. between 325.00 325.00
i. Pair, one without surcharge 325.00 —
j. Inverted surcharge 200.00 —
k. "FOUP" 310.00 160.00
l. "S" inverted 150.00 62.50
3g A13 ½a on 1ch yel grn 4.25 .25
h. Vert. pair, imperf. between 55.00 —
i. Inverted surcharge — 450.00
j. "NANA" 400.00 185.00
k. Inverted "H" in "HALF" — 175.00
4g A15 1a on 2ch orange 1.85 .40
h. Double surcharge 67.50
5g A17 2a on 4ch hen brn 5.25 .75
h. "O" inverted — 27.50
6g A18 3a on 2ch lt blue 8.00 5.50
h. Blue 100.00 6.25
i. "3" omitted — *1,500.*
7g A19 6a on 14ch turq grn 30.00 50.00
h. Accent omitted from Malayalam surcharge *550.00* *650.00*
Nos. 1g-7g (7) 55.60 57.80

Perf. 12½

1m A20 2p on 6ca vio blk (R) 4.25 2.25
n. Inverted surcharge 62.50 —
2m A22 4p on 8ca rose red 2.25 .50
n. Inverted surcharge 92.50 —
o. "S" inverted 150.00 62.50
3m A13 ½a on 1ch yel grn 5.25 .40
n. Vert. pair, imperf. between — 325.00
o. "NANA" 350.00 135.00
p. Inverted "H" in "HALF" — 175.00
4m A15 1a on 2ch orange 5.50 .40
5m A17 2a on 4ch hen brn 6.25 .75
n. Inverted surcharge — 475.00
o. "O" inverted 75.00 25.00
6m A18 3a on 2ch lt blue 16.00 9.00
7m A19 6a on 14ch turq grn 35.00 67.50
n. Accent omitted from Malayalam surcharge *550.00* *625.00*
Nos. 1m-7m (7) 74.50 80.80

Perf. 14

1q A20 2p on 6ca vio blk (R) — 800.00
3q A13 ½a on 1ch yel grn — 775.00

Perf. 13½

2r A22 4p on 8ca rose red — *1,100.*
4r A15 1a on 2ch orange 275.00 2.50

Compound Perforation

1s A20 2p on 6ca vio blk (R) — 62.50
2s A22 4p on 8ca rose red — 67.50
3s A13 ½a on 1ch yel grn — 67.50
4s A15 1a on 2ch orange 75.00 30.00
5s A17 2a on 4ch hen brn 85.00 52.50
6s A18 3a on 7ch lt blue — 125.00
t. Blue — 175.00
7s A19 6a on 14ch turq grn 92.50 110.00
t. Accent omitted from Malayalam surcharge *875.00*
Nos. 1s-7s (7) 252.50 515.00

Imperforate Pairs

1u A20 2p on 6ca vio blk (R) 12.00 —
2u A22 4p on 8ca rose red 110.00 —
3u A13 ½a on 1ch yel grn 12.50 30.00
4u A15 1a on 2ch orange 15.00 —
7u A19 6a on 14ch turq grn — —
Nos. 1u-7u (5) 149.50 30.00

Cochin Nos. 80, 91 and Types of 1944-46 Surcharged in Black or Carmine — b

1949-50 Wmk. 294 *Perf. 11, 13*

8 A15 3p on 9p ultra 15.00 *32.50*
9 A16 3p on 9p ultra 5.75 3.50
a. Vert. pair, imperf. between *4,000.*
b. Double surcharge 975.00
c. Surcharged on both sides 725.00
10 A16 3p on 9p ultra (C) 11.00 *3.50*
11 A16 6p on 9p ultra (C) 2.75 .60
12 A13 6p on 1a3p mag ('50) 11.50 *8.50*
13 A15 6p on 1a3p magenta 25.00 *23.00*
a. Double surcharge *1,100.*
14 A13 1a on 1a9p ultra (C) 3.00 *1.90*
15 A15 1a on 1a9p ultra (C) 7.25 3.25
b. Black surcharge *5,500.*
c. Hindi characters 7.5mm long *7,500.*
Nos. 8-15 (8) 81.25 76.75

The surcharge exists with line of Hindi characters varying from 16½ to 23mm wide.
For overprints see Nos. O10-O11, O24.

Cochin No. 86 Overprinted

1949

15A A15 1a deep orange 11.00 *125.00*
d. No period after "S" 110.00 —
e. Raised period after "T" 110.00 —

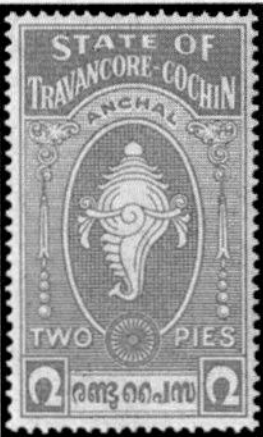

Conch Shell — A23

View of River — A24

Wmk. 196

1950, Oct. Litho. *Perf. 14*

16 A23 2p rose red 4.50 *5.50*
17 A24 4p ultramarine 5.50 *22.00*

Cochin No. 86 and Type of 1948-50 Overprinted in Black

1950, Apr. 1 Wmk. 294 *Perf. 13, 11*

18 A15 1a deep orange 11.00 *110.00*
- *a.* No period after "T" 80.00 *450.00*
- *b.* Inverted overprint 375.00
- *c.* As No. 18b, raised period after "T" *2,450.*

No. 18 Surcharged in Black

20 A15 6p on 1a dp org 6.75 *90.00*
- *a.* Surcharge on No. 15A 18.00
- *b.* As No. 20a, no period after "S" 275.00
- *c.* As No. 20a, raised period after "T" 275.00

21 A15 9p on 1a dp org 5.50 *90.00*
- *a.* Surcharge on No. 15A 275.00
- *b.* As No. 21a, no period after "S" 1,150.
- *c.* As No. 21a, raised period after "T" 1,150.

OFFICIAL STAMPS

Travancore Stamps of 1939-46 Surcharged Type "a" in Red or Black and Overprinted

c

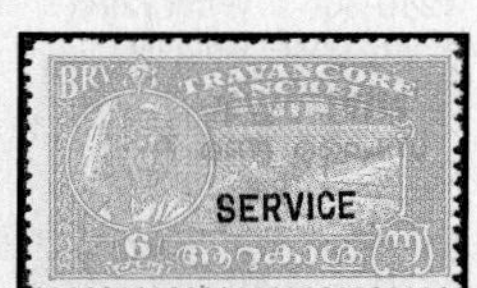

1949 Wmk. 43 *Perf. 12*

O1 A20 2p on 6ca vio blk (R) 1.80 .75
- *a.* Horiz. pair, imperf. between 15.00 35.00
- *b.* Vert. pair, imperf. between 8.00
- *c.* Block of 4, imperf. between (horiz. & vert.) 35.00

O2 A22 4p on 8ca rose red 7.25 1.25
- *a.* "FOUB" 200.00 72.50
- *b.* Pair, one without 4p surcharge 1,350.

O3 A13 ½a on 1ch yel grn 24.50 3.50
- *a.* "NANA" 800.00 300.00
- *b.* Pair, one without surcharge 220.00
- *c.* Inverted surcharge on back only 600.00

O4 A15 1a on 2ch orange — —

O5 A17 2a on 4ch hen brn 12.00 6.75
- *a.* Pair, one without surcharge 1,050.

O6 A18 3a on 7ch lt blue 6.00 9.75
- *a.* Horiz. pair, imperf. between 30.00
- *b.* Vert. pair, imperf. between 11.00
- *c.* Block of 4, imperf. between (horiz. & vert.) 60.00
- *d.* blue 100.00 6.75
- *e.* As "d," horiz. pair, imperf. between 1,000.

O7 A19 6a on 14ch turq grn 80.00 *13.50*
- *a.* Horiz. pair, imperf. between 40.00
- *b.* Vert. pair, imperf. between 50.00
- *c.* Block of 4, imperf. between (horiz. & vert.) 85.00

Nos. O1-O7 (7) 97.50 6.10

Perf. 11

O1f A20 2p on 6ca vio blk (R) 1.50 .25
- *g.* Vert. pair, imperf. between 375.00 375.00

O2f A22 4p on 8ca rose red 6.00 .35
- *g.* "FOUB" 160.00 40.00

O3f A13 ½a on 1ch yel grn 3.75 .30
- *g.* Inverted surcharge 110.00 —
- *h.* "NANA" 500.00 160.00
- *i.* Pair, one without surcharge 300.00

O4f A15 1a on 2ch orange 19.50 9.00
- *g.* Pair, one without surcharge 1,150.

O5f A17 2a on 4ch hen brn 8.50 .75
- *g.* Inverted surcharge 1,700.

O6f A18 3a on 2ch lt blue 6.75 1.25
- *g.* blue 100.00 22.00

O7f A19 6a on 14ch turq grn 19.50 14.50

Nos. O1f-O7f (7) 65.50 26.40

Perf. 12½

O1j A20 2p on 6ca vio blk (R) 2.50 1.00
- *k.* Vert. pair, imperf. between 375.00 375.00
- *l.* Pair, one without surcharge 325.00

O2j A22 4p on 8ca rose red 8.50 1.50
- *k.* "FOUB" 400.00 145.00

O3J A13 ½a on 1ch yel grn 2.75 .30
- *k.* "NANA" 500.00 135.00
- *l* Pair, one without surcharge 175.00
- *m.* Inverted surcharge 50.00

O4j A15 1a on 2ch orange 22.00 9.75
- *k.* Pair, one without surcharge 1,050.
- *l.* Inverted surcharge 125.00

O5j A17 2a on 4ch hen brn 4.50 1.25

O6j A18 3a on 2ch lt blue 8.50 4.00
- *k.* Vert. pair, imperf. between 30.00

O7j A19 6a on 14ch turq grn 24.50 16.00
- *k* Vert. pair, imperf. between 50.00

Nos. O1j-O7j (7) 73.25 33.80

Compound Perforation

O1n A20 2p on 6ca vio blk (R) 100.00 —
O2n A22 4p on 8ca rose red 35.00 30.00
O3n A13 ½a on 1ch yel grn 50.00
O5n A17 2a on 4ch hen brn 67.50

Nos. O1n-O5n (4) 135.00 147.50

Imperforate Pairs

O1o A20 2p on 6ca vio blk (R) 10.00 35.00
O5o A17 2a on 4ch hen brn 17.00
O6o A18 3a on 7ch lt blue 16.00 —
O7o A19 6a on 14ch turq grn 20.00 —

Nos. O1o-O7o (4) 63.00 35.00

Cochin Nos. O90-O91 Surcharged Type "b" in Black

1950 Wmk. 294 *Perf. 11*

O8 A16 6p on 3p carmine 1.90 1.10
- *a.* Double surcharge — 525.00
- *b.* Vert. pair, imperf. between — 2,300.
- *c.* "C" in place of "G" 24.50 12.25

O9 A16 9p on 4p gray grn 1.60 *4.00*
- *a.* Horiz. pair, imperf. between 1,250. 1,350.
- *b.* Hindi characters 22mm long 1.35 1.55
- *c.* As "b," horiz. pair, imperf. between 1,175. 1,175.
- *d.* "C" in place of "G" 32.50 37.50

Hindi characters in surcharge on No. O9 are 18mm long.

Travancore-Cochin Nos. 14-15 Overprinted "ON C G S"
Perf. 13

O10 A13 1a on 1a9p ultra .90 1.00
O11 A15 1a on 1a9p ultra 37.50 25.00

Nos. 2-7 Overprinted in Black — d

1949-51 Wmk. 43 *Perf. 12*

O12 A22 4p on 8ca rose red .35 .25
O13 A13 ½a on 1ch yel green 1.50 .25
- *a.* "AANA" 170.00 80.00

O14 A15 1a on 2ch orange .60 .25
O15 A17 2a on 4ch hen brn 18.00 1.35
O16 A18 3a on 7ch lt blue 6.00 2.50
O17 A19 6a on 14ch turq grn 60.00 *8.00*

Nos. O12-O17 (6) 86.45 12.60

Perf. 11

O12b A22 4p on 8ca rose red .60 .25
O13b A13 ½a on 1ch yel green .60 .25
- *c.* "AANA" 110.00 50.00

O14b A15 1a on 2ch orange 4.50 .60
O15b A17 2a on 4ch hen brn 1.85 1.35
O16b A18 3a on 7ch lt blue 1.85 1.35
O17b A19 6a on 14ch turq grn 17.00 8.00

Nos. O12b-O17b (6) 26.40 11.80

Perf. 12½

O12d A22 4p on 8ca rose red 1.25 .25
O13d A13 ½a on 1ch yel green 2.75 .25
- *e.* "AANA" 400.00 90.00

O14d A15 1a on 2ch orange .50 .35
O15d A17 2a on 4ch hen brn 5.25 1.00
O16d A18 3a on 7ch lt blue 10.50 1.35
O17d A19 6a on 14ch turq grn 1.85 *5.50*

Nos. O12d-O17d (6) 22.10 8.70

Compound Perforation

O12f A22 4p on 8ca rose red 14.50 14.50
O13f A13 ½a on 1ch yel green 57.50 32.00
- *g.* "AANA" — 425.00

O14f A15 1a on 2ch orange 36.50 32.00
O15f A17 2a on 4ch hen brn 36.50 24.50
O16f A18 3a on 7ch lt blue — 100.00
O17f A19 6a on 14ch turq grn 170.00 *170.00*

Nos. O12f-O17f (6) 315.00 373.00

Imperforate Pairs

O12h A22 4p on 8ca rose red 10.00 —
O13h A13 ½a on 1ch yel green 11.00 30.00
O14h A15 1a on 2ch orange 29.00 —
O16h A18 3a on 7ch lt blue 67.50 —

Nos. O12h-O16h (4) 117.50 30.00

Types of 1949 Overprinted Type "d"

1951 Wmk. 294

O18 A13 ½a on 1ch yel grn, perf. 12½ 5.50 .80
- *a.* Perf. 11 .50 .50
- *b.* Perf. 12 28.00 19.50
- *c.* Compound perf. 21.00 3.75

O19 A15 1a on 2ch org, perf. 12½ 2.75 1.25
- *a.* Perf. 11 .60 .50
- *b.* Perf. 12 16.00 5.00
- *c.* Perf. 13½ 2.50 1.25
- *d.* Compound perf. 8.50 3.75

Type of 1949 Overprinted Type "c" Unwmk.

O20 A22 4p on 8ca rose red 1.40 1.10

No. O20 is not from an unwatermarked part of sheet with wmk. 294 but is printed on paper entirely without watermark.

Nos. 1, 3 and 5 Overprinted Type "c"

Wmk. 294

O21 A13 ½a on 1ch yel grn 1.10 .50
O22 A20 2p on 6ca vio blk, perf. 12½ .50 *2.75*
- *a.* "SERVICE" double 22.00 —
- *b.* Perf. 11 .60 2.75
- *c.* Perf. 12 1.50 2.10

O23 A17 2a on 4ch hen brn, perf. 12½ 4.00 3.25
- *a.* Perf. 11 1.85 1.35
- *b.* Vert. pair, imperf. between 525.00 *525.00*
- *c.* Perf. 12 — 115.00
- *d.* Compound perf. 90.00 55.00

Nos. O21-O23 (3) 5.60 6.50

No. 9 Overprinted in Black

1951

O24 A16 3p on 9p ultra .90 *1.20*
- *a.* Horiz. pair, imperf. between *3,500.*

WADHWAN

wə-'dwän

LOCATION — A Feudatory State in Kathiawar Agency, Western India.
AREA — 242 sq. mi.
POP. — 44,259
CAPITAL — Wadhwan

Coat of Arms — A1

1888 Litho. Unwmk. *Pin-perf.*
Thin Paper

1 A1 ½p black 160.00

Perf. 12½

2 A1 ½p black 30.00 *100.00*

1889 *Perf. 12 and 12½*
Thick Paper

3 A1 ½p black 12.50 *14.00*

Nos. 1-3 (3) 202.50

INDO-CHINA

ˌin-ˌdō-'chī-nə

LOCATION — French possessions on the Cambodian Peninsula in southeastern Asia, bordering on the South China Sea and the Gulf of Siam
GOVT. — Former French Colony and Protectorate
AREA — 280,849 sq. mi.
POP. — 27,030,000 (estimated 1949)
CAPITAL — Hanoi

100 Centimes = 1 Franc
100 Cents = 1 Piaster (1918)

For French and French Colonies General Issue stamps used in Indo-China, values in the first column are for stamps with clear Indo-Chinese postmarks; values in the second column are for examples on cover. The numbers in parentheses are the catalogue numbers of the basic French or French Colonies stamp.

The Lozenge cancellations inscribed "CCH" were used in various post offices in Cochin China: Saigon, 1864-76; Bentre, 1872-73; Cholen, 1876; Go-Cong, 1872-73; Hatien, 1874-76; Mocai, 1870; Mytho, 1873-74; Sadec, 1875; Tan-an, 1868-75; Tayninh, 1874; Thaudumot, 1868; Vinh-Long, 1868; and Pnum-Penh (Cambodia). Uses other than Saigon are rare.

The "CCN" cancellations were used in the North Cochin China region: CCN2, Bien-Hoa (1863-74) and Tay-Ninh (1866-79); CCN3, Mytho (1864-70' 1872-75) and Sadec (1867-70s); CCN4, Baria (1864-75) and Cho-Len (1864-76); CCN5, Go-Cong (1864-73); CCN6, Tay-Ninh (1866-67) and Travinh (1868-72); CCN7, Tong-Keou (1864-76) and Chau-Doc (1867-76); and CCN8, Trang-Bang (1865-68(?)) and Tanan (1865-?).

STAMPS OF FRANCE USED IN INDO-CHINA

Canceled "CCH" or "CCN2" in Lozenge of Dots

1851

1A1 A3 10c bistre (#14)
- canceled "CCH" 325.00 3,500.

1A2 A3 20c blue (#15)
- canceled "CCH" 175.00 3,250.
- canceled "CCN2" 450.00

1A3 A3 40c orange (#18)
- canceled "CCH" 325.00

1A4 A3 80c rose (#19)
- canceled "CCH" 400.00

STAMPS OF FRENCH COLONIES GENERAL ISSUES USED IN INDO-CHINA

Eagle and Crown Issue
Canceled "CCH" or "CCN" and number in Lozenge of Dots

1859-65

2A1 A1 1c olive green, *pale blue* (#1)
- canceled "CCH" 90.00
- c.d.s. Saigon —

2A2 A1 5c yellow green, *greenish* (#2)
- canceled "CCH" 35.00 525.00
- canceled "CCN3" 325.00
- canceled "CCN7" 440.00

2A3 A1 10c bister, *yellow* (#3)
- canceled "CCH" 25.00 500.00
- canceled "CCN2" 130.00
- canceled "CCN3" 210.00
- canceled "CCN4" 325.00
- canceled "CCN5" 525.00
- canceled "CCN6" 350.00
- canceled "CCN7" 360.00
- canceled "CCN8" 440.00

2A4 A1 20c blue, *bluish* (#4)
- canceled "CCH" 25.00 350.00
- canceled "CCN2" 120.00
- canceled "CCN3" 175.00
- canceled "CCN4" 275.00
- canceled "CCN6" 300.00
- canceled "CCN7" 300.00
- canceled "CCN8" 400.00

2A5 A1 40c orange, *yel* (#5)
- canceled "CCH" 35.00 600.00
- canceled "CCN2" 175.00
- canceled "CCN3" 260.00
- canceled "CCN4" 360.00

2A6 A1 80c car rose, *pnksh* (#6)
- canceled "CCH" 90.00 1,300.

Values for stamps on cover are for covers paying ordinary rates.

Ceres and Napoleon III Types

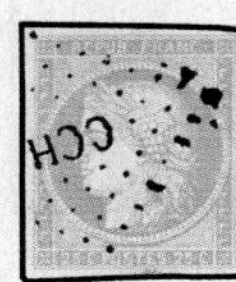

CCH in Lozenge of Dots

1871-72

2A7 A2 1c ol grn, *pale bl* (#7)
Lozenge "CCH" 90.00
2A8 A3 5c yel grn, *grnsh* (#8)
Lozenge "CCH" 400.00
Lozenge "CCN3" 475.00
Lozenge "CCN4" 525.00
Lozenge "CCN5" 640.00
2A9 A4 10c bis, *yelsh (#9)*
Lozenge "CCH" 175.00
Lozenge "CCN4" 275.00
2A10 A4 15c bis, *yelsh (#10)*
Lozenge "CCH" 47.50
c.d.s. Bien-Hoa 110.00
c.d.s. Ha-Noi 175.00
c.d.s. Hai-Phong 225.00
c.d.s. Hue 175.00
c.d.s. Quin-Hon 260.00
Military datestamp Saigon 90.00
Military datestamp Ha-Noi 175.00
Military datestamp Hai-Phong 225.00
Military datestamp Hue 160.00
Military datestamp dated January 1879 225.00
Military datestamp Quin-Hon 260.00
Military datestamp Tong-Keou 300.00
Military datestamp Vinh-Long 300.00
2A11 A4 20c blue, *bluish* (#11)
Lozenge "CCH" 160.00
Lozenge "CCN2" 225.00
Lozenge "CCN6" 525.00
Lozenge "CCN7" 400.00
2A12 A4 25c blue, *bluish* (#12)
Lozenge "CCH" 55.00
Lozenge "CCN6" 225.00
c.d.s. Bien-Hoa 100.00
c.d.s. Chaudoc 225.00
c.d.s. Ha-Noi 130.00
c.d.s. Hai-Phong 160.00
c.d.s. Hue 130.00
c.d.s. Pnum-Penh (Cambodia) 130.00
c.d.s. Quin-Hon 175.00
c.d.s. Vinh-Long 225.00
Military datestamp Cho-Len 260.00
Military datestamp Hue 120.00
Military datestamp Long-Xuyen 440.00
Military datestamp Quin-Hon 130.00
Military datestamp Tong-Keou 260.00
Military datestamp Traon 375.00
Military datestamp Vinh-Long 260.00
2A13 A5 30c brn, *yelsh (#13)*
Lozenge "CCH" 100.00
c.d.s. Ha-Noi 300.00
c.d.s. Hai-Phong 360.00
c.d.s. Hue 340.00
c.d.s. Pnum-Penh (Cambodia) 440.00
c.d.s. Soctrang 300.00
2A14 A4 40c org, *yel* (#14)
Lozenge "CCH" 67.50
Lozenge "CCN4" 260.00
Lozenge "CCN6" 275.00
Military datestamp Vinh-Long 240.00
2A15 A5 80c rose, *pnksh* (#15)
canceled "CCH" 130.00

Ceres Types

Saigon c.d.s.

1872-77

2A16 A6 1c ol grn, *pale bl* (#16)
Lozenge "CCH" 120.00
With c.d.s. of Indo-China —
2A17 A6 2c red brn, *yelsh* (#17)
Lozenge "CCH" 875.00 *18,500.*
c.d.s. Saigon *800.00*
c.d.s. Pnum-Penh (Cambodia) *1,600.*
2A18 A6 4c gray (#18)
Lozenge "CCH" 525.00 *12,000.*
c.d.s. Saigon *650.00*
With other c.d.s. of Indo-China —
2A19 A6 5c grn, pale bl (#19)
Lozenge "CCH" 35.00
c.d.s. Ha-Noi 160.00
c.d.s. Hai-Phong 190.00
c.d.s. Hue 175.00
c.d.s. Pnum-Penh (Cambodia) 160.00
c.d.s. Quin-Hon 260.00
Military datestamp Saigon 120.00
Military datestamp Cap St.-Jacques 150.00
Military datestamp Ha-Noi 175.00
Military datestamp Quin-Hon 260.00
Military datestamp Tay-Ninh 240.00
2A20 A7 10c bis, rose (#20)
Lozenge "CCH" 35.00
c.d.s. Ha-Noi 160.00
c.d.s. Hai-Phong 190.00
c.d.s. Hue 225.00
c.d.s. Quin-Hon 260.00
c.d.s. Soctrang 260.00
c.d.s. Traon 175.00
Military datestamp Saigon 110.00
Military datestamp Chaudoc 225.00
Military datestamp My-Tho 175.00
Military datestamp Quin-Hon 275.00
Military datestamp Tay-Ninh 225.00
2A22 A7 30c brn, yelsh (#22)
Lozenge "CCH" 60.00
2A23 A7 80c rose, pnksh (#23)
Lozenge "CCH" 175.00
Military datestamp Saigon 325.00

No. 2A17 was used only in Cochin-China and Pnum-Penh (Cambodia).
Beware of dangerous forgeries of Nos. 2A17 and 2A18.

Peace and Commerce Types Canceled with Circular Date Stamps

1877-78 **Type I**

2A24 A8 1c green, *grnsh* (#24)
c.d.s. Saigon 90.00
c.d.s. Ha-Noi 110.00
c.d.s. Hai-Phong 125.00
Military datestamp Ha-Noi 225.00
2A25 A8 4c green, *grnsh* (#25)
c.d.s. Saigon 45.00
Military datestamp Ha-Noi 260.00
2A26 A8 30c brown, *yelsh* (#26)
c.d.s. Saigon 120.00
c.d.s. Ha-Noi 130.00
c.d.s. Hai-Phong 160.00
2A27 A8 40c ver, *straw* (#27)
c.d.s. Saigon 87.50
c.d.s. Ha-Noi 110.00
c.d.s. Hai-Phong 125.00
c.d.s. Soctrang 225.00
2A28 A8 75c rose, *rose* (#28)
c.d.s. Saigon 225.00
a. 75c carmine, *rose* (#28a)
c.d.s. Saigon 225.00
2A29 A8 1fr bronze grn, *straw* (#29)
c.d.s. Saigon 240.00
Military datestamp Hai-Phong 260.00

Type II

2A30 A8 2c green, *grnsh* (#30)
c.d.s. Saigon 67.50
c.d.s. Ha-Noi 130.00
c.d.s. Hai-Phong 160.00
2A31 A8 5c green, *grnsh* (#31)
c.d.s. Saigon 20.00
c.d.s. Ha-Noi 87.50
c.d.s. Hai-Phong 110.00
c.d.s. Hue 120.00
c.d.s. Pnum-Penh (Cambodia) 110.00
Military datestamp Saigon 67.50
Military datestamp Nien-Hoa 130.00
Military datestamp Chaudoc 175.00
Military datestamp My-Tho 130.00
2A32 A8 10c green, *grnsh* (#32)
c.d.s. Saigon 72.50
Military datestamp Saigon 90.00
2A33 A8 15c gray, *grnsh* (#33)
c.d.s. Saigon 140.00
c.d.s. Hue 225.00
Military datestamp Saigon 200.00
Military datestamp Hue 240.00
2A34 A8 20c red brn, *straw* (#34)
c.d.s. Saigon 45.00
c.d.s. Ha-Noi 90.00
c.d.s. Hai-Phong 110.00
c.d.s. Hue 160.00
2A35 A8 25c ultra, *bluish* (#35)
c.d.s. Saigon 35.00
c.d.s. Ha-Noi 87.50
c.d.s. Hai-Phong 110.00
c.d.s. Pnum-Penh (Cambodia) 87.50
Military datestamp Soctrang 350.00
Telegraph office, Poulocondor 140.00
a. 25c blue, *bluish* (#35a)
c.d.s. Saigon 35.00
c.d.s. Ha-Noi 87.50
c.d.s. Hai-Phong 110.00
c.d.s. Pnum-Penh (Cambodia) 87.50
Military datestamp Soctrang 350.00
2A36 A8 35c vio blk, *org* (#36)
c.d.s. Saigon 90.00

1878-80 **Type II**

2A38 A8 1c blk, *lil blue* (#38)
c.d.s. Saigon 67.50
2A41 A8 10c blk, *lav* (#41)
c.d.s. Saigon 60.00
2A42 A8 15c blue (#42)
c.d.s. Saigon 45.00
c.d.s. Ha-Noi 87.50
c.d.s. Hai-Phong 110.00
c.d.s. Hue 175.00
c.d.s. Traon 160.00
Military datestamp Saigon 90.00
Military datestamp Baria 175.00
Military datestamp Hanoi 90.00
Military datestamp Hai-Phong 130.00
Military datestamp Hue 130.00
Military datestamp My-Tho 110.00
Military datestamp Pnum-Pehn (Cambodia) 360.00
Military datestamp Tai-Ninh 200.00
Military datestamp Tong-Keou 240.00

Commerce Type

1881-86

2A46 A9 1c blk, *lil bl* (#46)
c.d.s. Saigon 24.00
c.d.s. Hanoi 27.50
c.d.s. Hai-Phong 35.00
c.d.s. Hue 110.00
c.d.s. Pnum-Pehn (Cambodia) 52.50
2A47 A9 2c brn, *buff* (#47)
c.d.s. Saigon 24.00
c.d.s. Hanoi 27.50
c.d.s. Hai-Phong 35.00
c.d.s. Hue 110.00
c.d.s. Pnum-Pehn (Cambodia) 52.50
2A48 A9 4c claret, *lav* (#48)
c.d.s. Saigon 24.00
c.d.s. Hanoi 27.50
c.d.s. Hai-Phong 35.00
c.d.s. Hue 110.00
c.d.s. Pnum-Pehn (Cambodia) 52.50
2A49 A9 5c grn, *grnsh* (#49)
c.d.s. Saigon 20.00
c.d.s. Hanoi 24.00
c.d.s. Hai-Phong 27.50
c.d.s. Hue 87.50
c.d.s. Pnum-Pehn (Cambodia) 45.00
c.d.s. Vinh-Long 160.00
Military datestamp Poulocondore 140.00
Steamship c.d.s. 130.00
2A50 A9 10c blk, *lav* (#50)
c.d.s. Saigon 14.50
c.d.s. Hanoi 24.00
c.d.s. Hai-Phong 27.50
c.d.s. Hue 87.50
c.d.s. Pnum-Pehn (Cambodia) 45.00
Military datestamp Poulocondore 140.00
2A51 A9 15c blue (#51)
c.d.s. Saigon 13.50
Chaudoc 120.00
Tonkin Expeditionary Force datestamp 65.00
c.d.s. Hanoi 24.00
c.d.s. Hai-Phong (2 types) 27.50
c.d.s. Hue 87.50
c.d.s. Pnum-Pehn (Cambodia) 45.00
c.d.s. Rach-Gia 67.50
c.d.s. Soctrang 225.00
c.d.s. Traon 90.00
Military datestamp Saigon 52.50
Military datestamp Hai-Phong 87.50
Military datestamp Hatien 210.00
Military datestamp Poulocondore 140.00
Military datestamp Rach-Gia 130.00
Military datestamp Sadec 225.00
Military datestamp Tai-Ninh 120.00
Military datestamp Vinh Long 120.00
Steamship #2 datestamp (scalloped) 175.00
Telegraph office, Krochmar (Cambodia) 260.00
Telegraph office, Rocacon 240.00
Telegraph office, Takeo 275.00
2A52 A9 20c red, *yel grn* (#52)
c.d.s. Saigon 24.00
c.d.s. Hanoi 27.50
c.d.s. Hai-Phong 35.00
c.d.s. Hue 110.00
c.d.s. Pnum-Pehn (Cambodia) 52.50
2A53 A9 25c yel, *yel grn* (#53)
c.d.s. Saigon 20.00
Tonkin Expeditionary Force datestamp 87.50
c.d.s. Dong-Dang 225.00
c.d.s. Hue 87.50
c.d.s. Lang-son 92.50
c.d.s. Pnum-Pehn (Cambodia) 45.00
Military datestamp Ha-Noi 67.50
Military datestamp Hai-Phong 110.00
2A54 A9 25c blk, *rose* (#54)
c.d.s. Saigon 12.00
c.d.s. Ha-Noi 16.00
c.d.s. Hai-Phong 20.00
c.d.s. Hue 60.00
c.d.s. Pnum-Pehn (Cambodia) 27.50
Telegraph office, Poulocondore 110.00
Steamship #2 datestamp (scalloped) 175.00
2A55 A9 30c brn, *bis* (#55)
c.d.s. Saigon 45.00
c.d.s. Hanoi 65.00
c.d.s. Hai-Phong 80.00
c.d.s. Hue 100.00
c.d.s. Pnum-Pehn (Cambodia) 72.50
2A56 A9 35c vio blk, *yel org* (#56)
c.d.s. Saigon 92.50
c.d.s. Hanoi 120.00
c.d.s. Hai-Phong 150.00
2A57 A9 40c ver, *straw* (#57)
c.d.s. Saigon 45.00
c.d.s. Hanoi 65.00
c.d.s. Hai-Duong 65.00
c.d.s. Hai-Phong 80.00
c.d.s. Hue 110.00
c.d.s. Pnum-Pehn (Cambodia) 72.50
2A58 A9 75c car, *rose* (#58)
c.d.s. Saigon 110.00
c.d.s. Hanoi 160.00
c.d.s. Hai-Phong 190.00
c.d.s. Pnum-Pehn (Cambodia) 150.00
2A59 A9 1fr brnz grn, *straw* (#59)
c.d.s. Saigon 90.00
c.d.s. Hanoi 120.00
c.d.s. Hai-Phong 150.00
c.d.s. Pnum-Pehn (Cambodia) 110.00

Stamps of French Colonies Surcharged in Black or Red

a

b

1889 **Unwmk.** ***Perf. 14x13½***

1 A9(a) 5c on 35c dp vio, *org* 14.00 *12.00*
On cover *1,000.*
a. "89" omitted 275.00 250.00
b. Pair, #1 and #1a 425.00 425.00
c. "86" instead of "89" *22,500.*
2 A9(b) 5c on 35c dp vio, *org* (R) 110.00 100.00
On cover *1,200.*
a. Date in smaller type 275.00 260.00
b. Inverted surcharge, #2 2,000. 2,000.
c. Inverted surcharge, #2a 3,000. 3,000.
d. Pair, #2 and #2a 575.00 575.00

Issue dates: No. 1, Jan. 8; No. 2, Jan. 10.
"R" is is the Colonial Governor, P. Richaud, "D" is the Saigon P.M. General P. Demars.

For other overprints on designs A3-A27a see various issues of French Offices in China.

Navigation & Commerce — A3

Name of Colony in Blue or Carmine

1892-1900 **Typo.** ***Perf. 14x13½***

3 A3 1c blk, *lil bl* 1.25 1.25
Never hinged 2.00
On cover 45.00
a. "INDO-CHINE" double *9,000.*
4 A3 2c brn, *buff* 1.75 1.75
Never hinged 2.40
On cover 45.00
5 A3 4c claret, *lav* 1.75 1.75
Never hinged 2.40
On cover 45.00
6 A3 5c grn, *grnsh* 2.50 2.50
Never hinged 3.50
On cover 21.00
7 A3 5c yel grn ('00) 2.10 1.25
Never hinged 3.25
On cover 17.00
8 A3 10c blk, *lavender* 8.00 2.00
Never hinged 12.50
On cover 17.00
9 A3 10c red ('00) 3.75 2.25
Never hinged 5.50
On cover 12.50
10 A3 15c blue, quadrille paper 42.50 2.25
Never hinged 70.00
On cover 17.00
11 A3 15c gray ('00) 9.00 2.40
Never hinged 15.00
On cover 12.50
12 A3 20c red, *grn* 12.00 7.25
Never hinged 18.00
On cover 42.50
On cover, single franking 75.00
13 A3 25c blk, *rose* 20.00 4.25
Never hinged 35.00
On cover 35.00
On cover, single franking 62.50
a. "INDO-CHINE" omitted *7,500.* *7,500.*

14 A3 25c blue ('00) 24.00 5.00
Never hinged 32.50
On cover 35.00
On cover, single franking 62.50
15 A3 30c brn, *bis* 29.00 8.00
Never hinged 47.50
On cover 35.00
On cover, single franking 50.00
16 A3 40c red, *straw* 29.00 15.00
Never hinged 47.50
On cover 37.50
On cover, single franking 60.00
17 A3 50c car, *rose* 45.00 16.00
Never hinged 75.00
On cover 72.50
On cover, single franking 115.00
18 A3 50c brn, *az* ('00) 30.00 9.50
Never hinged 55.00
On cover 55.00
On cover, single franking 85.00
19 A3 75c dp vio, *org* 24.00 19.00
Never hinged 42.50
On cover 115.00
On cover, single franking 175.00
a. "INDO-CHINE" inverted *7,750.* *7,750.*
b. As "a", in pair with normal *10,000.*
20 A3 1fr brnz grn, *straw* 60.00 40.00
Never hinged 110.00
On cover 150.00
On cover, single franking 250.00
a. "INDO-CHINE" double 1,200. *1,400.*
21 A3 5fr red lil, *lav* ('96) 145.00 120.00
Never hinged 250.00
On cover 300.00
On cover, single franking 500.00
Nos. 3-21 (19) 490.60 261.40

Perf. 13½x14 stamps are counterfeits.

For surcharges and overprints see Nos. 22-23, Q2-Q4.

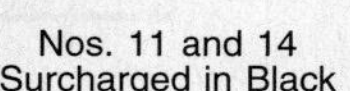
Nos. 11 and 14 Surcharged in Black

1903

22 A3 5c on 15c gray 2.00 1.25
Never hinged 3.25
On cover 12.50
23 A3 15c on 25c blue 2.50 1.60
Never hinged 4.00
On cover 10.50

Issue dates: No. 22, Dec. 4; No. 23, Aug. 8.

France — A4

1904-06

24 A4 1c olive grn .80 .80
Never hinged 1.20
On cover 37.50
25 A4 2c vio brn, *buff* 1.25 .80
Never hinged 1.60
On cover 37.50
26 A4 4c claret, *bluish* .80 .80
Never hinged 1.20
On cover 37.50
27 A4 5c deep green 1.25 .50
Never hinged 1.60
On cover 12.50
a. Double impression *450.00* *450.00*
b. Imperf. *450.00*
28 A4 10c carmine 1.60 .75
Never hinged 2.40
On cover 8.50
29 A4 15c org brn, *bl* 1.60 1.00
Never hinged 2.40
On cover 8.50
a. Imperf. *45.00*
30 A4 20c red, *grn* 3.50 1.60
Never hinged 5.50
On cover 30.00
On cover, single franking 50.00
31 A4 25c deep blue 15.00 1.60
Never hinged 25.00
On cover 21.00
On cover, single franking 37.50
32 A4 30c pale brn 6.00 3.00
Never hinged 10.00
On cover 21.00
On cover, single franking 30.00
a. Imperf. *270.00*
33 A4 35c blk, *yel* ('06) 22.00 3.25
Never hinged 42.50
On cover 35.00
On cover, single franking 47.50
34 A4 40c blk, *bluish* 5.75 1.60
Never hinged 9.50
On cover 25.00
On cover, single franking 37.50
a. Imperf. *270.00*
35 A4 50c bister brn 11.00 3.00
Never hinged 16.00
On cover 42.50
On cover, single franking 72.50
36 A4 75c red, *org* 45.00 30.00
Never hinged 80.00
On cover 85.00
On cover, single franking 140.00
37 A4 1fr pale grn 22.50 8.50
Never hinged 35.00
On cover 105.00
On cover, single franking 175.00

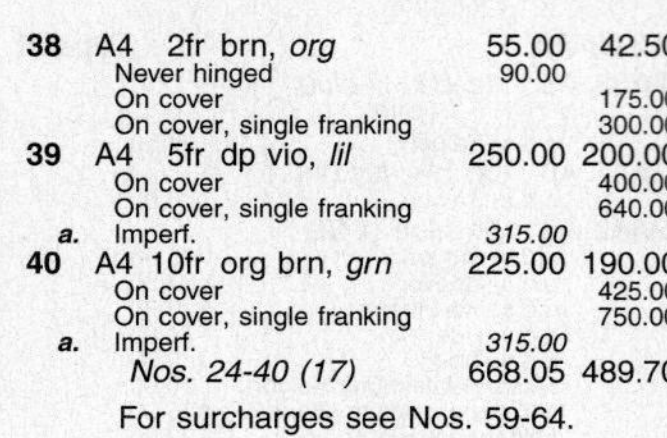

38 A4 2fr brn, *org* 55.00 42.50
Never hinged 90.00
On cover 175.00
On cover, single franking 300.00
39 A4 5fr dp vio, *lil* 250.00 200.00
On cover 400.00
On cover, single franking 640.00
a. Imperf. *315.00*
40 A4 10fr org brn, *grn* 225.00 190.00
On cover 425.00
On cover, single franking 750.00
a. Imperf. *315.00*
Nos. 24-40 (17) 668.05 489.70

For surcharges see Nos. 59-64.

Annamite Girl — A5

Cambodian Girl — A6

Cambodian Woman — A7

Annamite Women — A8

Hmong Woman — A9

Laotian Woman — A10

Cambodian Woman — A11

1907 ***Perf. 14x13½***

41 A5 1c ol brn & blk .40 .40
Never hinged .55
On cover 17.00
42 A5 2c yel brn & blk .40 .40
Never hinged .55
On cover 17.00
43 A5 4c blue & blk 1.25 1.25
Never hinged 1.90
On cover 17.00
44 A5 5c grn & blk 1.60 .80
Never hinged 2.40
On cover 10.00
45 A5 10c red & blk 1.60 .55
Never hinged 2.40
On cover 6.75
46 A5 15c vio & blk 1.40 1.25
Never hinged 2.10
On cover 6.75
47 A6 20c vio & blk 3.75 1.60
Never hinged 5.25
On cover 10.00
48 A6 25c bl & blk 8.50 1.25
Never hinged 12.50
On cover 17.00
On cover, single franking 30.00
49 A6 30c brn & blk 13.00 7.50
Never hinged 19.00
On cover 35.00
On cover, single franking 55.00
50 A6 35c ol grn & blk 2.75 2.25
Never hinged 4.75
On cover 21.00
On cover, single franking 35.00
51 A6 40c yel brn & blk 4.50 2.00
Never hinged 7.25
On cover 35.00
On cover, single franking 72.50
52 A6 45c org & blk 11.00 7.00
Never hinged 16.00
On cover 42.50
On cover, single franking 62.50
53 A6 50c car & blk 16.00 6.00
Never hinged 24.00
On cover 37.50

On cover, single franking 60.00

Perf. 13½x14

54 A7 75c ver & blk 14.00 9.00
Never hinged 22.00
On cover 42.50
On cover, single franking 75.00
55 A8 1fr car & blk 62.50 22.50
Never hinged 95.00
On cover 85.00
On cover, single franking 175.00
56 A9 2fr grn & blk 18.00 17.50
Never hinged 27.50
On cover 97.50
On cover, single franking 190.00
57 A10 5fr blue & blk 47.50 *55.00*
Never hinged 72.50
On cover 125.00
On cover, single franking 250.00
58 A11 10fr pur & blk 100.00 *110.00*
Never hinged 160.00
On cover 225.00
On cover, single franking 425.00
Nos. 41-58 (18) 308.15 246.25

For surcharges see Nos. 65-93, B1-B7. Nos. 41, 47-51, 54-55 exist imperf.

Stamps of 1904-06 Surcharged in Black or Carmine

There are two settings of surcharge. Type 1: 2½mm between numerals. Type II: 3mm between numerals.

1912, Nov. ***Perf. 14x13½***

Spacing between figures of surcharge 1.5mm (5c), 2mm (10c)

59 A4 5c on 4c cl, *bluish* 6.00 6.00
Never hinged 10.00
On cover 62.50
60 A4 5c on 15c org brn, *bl* (C) 1.25 1.25
Never hinged 1.75
On cover 21.00
61 A4 5c on 30c pale brn 1.60 1.60
Never hinged 2.50
On cover 42.50
62 A4 10c on 40c blk, *bluish* (C) 1.60 1.60
Never hinged 2.50
On cover 42.50
63 A4 10c on 50c bis brn (C) 2.00 2.00
Never hinged 3.50
On cover 45.00
64 A4 10c on 75c red, *org* 5.25 5.25
Never hinged 8.50
On cover 55.00
Nos. 59-64 (6) 17.70 17.70

Spacing between figures of surcharge 2.25mm (5c), 2.75mm (10c)

59a A4 5c on 4c cl, *bluish* 875.00 875.00
Never hinged 1,450.
60a A4 5c on 15c org brn, *bl* (C) 35.00 35.00
Never hinged 55.00
61a A4 5c on 30c pale brn 85.00 85.00
Never hinged 140.00
62a A4 10c on 40c blk, *bluish* (C) 67.50 67.50
Never hinged 120.00
63a A4 10c on 50c bis brn (C) 75.00 75.00
Never hinged 125.00
64a A4 10c on 75c red, *org* 120.00 120.00
Never hinged 190.00
Nos. 59a-64a (6) 1,258. 1,258.

Se-tenant Pairs, Both Ovpt. Settings

59b A4 5c on 4c, #59 + #59a 1,050. 1,050.
Never hinged 1,600.
60b A4 5c on 15c, #60 + #60a 42.50 42.50
Never hinged 72.50
61b A4 5c on 30c, #61 + #61a 100.00 100.00
Never hinged 160.00
62b A4 10c on 40c, #62 + #62a 77.50 77.50
Never hinged 125.00
63b A4 10c on 50c, #63 + #63a 85.00 85.00
Never hinged 140.00
64b A4 10c on 75c, #64 + #64a 140.00 140.00
Never hinged 225.00
Nos. 59b-64b (6) 1,495. 1,495.

Nos. 41-58 Surcharged in Cents or Piasters in Black, Red or Blue

1919, Jan.

65 A5 ⅖c on 1c .85 .55
Never hinged 1.20
On cover 21.00
66 A5 ⅘c on 2c 1.40 .90
Never hinged 2.00
On cover 21.00
67 A5 1⅗c on 4c (R) 2.00 .80
Never hinged 3.25
On cover 20.00
68 A5 2c on 5c 1.75 .30
Never hinged 2.40
On cover 12.50
a. Inverted surcharge 160.00
Never hinged 240.00
69 A5 4c on 10c (Bl) 1.60 .55
Never hinged 2.40
On cover 8.50
a. Closed "4" 32.50 3.25
Never hinged 50.00
On cover 21.00
b. Double surcharge 160.00
Never hinged 250.00
c. As "a," double surcharge 225.00
Never hinged 325.00
70 A5 6c on 15c 6.75 1.25
Never hinged 10.00
On cover 8.50
a. Inverted surcharge 160.00
Never hinged 200.00
71 A6 8c on 20c 5.50 1.90
Never hinged 8.75
On cover 12.50
72 A6 10c on 25c 5.25 1.00
Never hinged 8.00
On cover 14.50
a. Pair, one without surcharge *675.00*
73 A6 12c on 30c 7.00 1.10
Never hinged 11.00
On cover 21.00
74 A6 14c on 35c 3.50 .75
Never hinged 4.75
On cover 17.00
a. Closed "4" 12.00 5.75
Never hinged 19.00
On cover 37.50
75 A6 16c on 40c 6.75 2.00
Never hinged 10.00
On cover 25.00
76 A6 18c on 45c 8.50 2.75
Never hinged 12.50
On cover 30.00
77 A6 20c on 50c (Bl) 13.00 1.25
Never hinged 18.00
On cover 25.00
78 A7 30c on 75c (Bl) 16.00 2.75
Never hinged 24.00
On cover 30.00
79 A8 40c on 1fr (Bl) 25.00 2.75
Never hinged 40.00
On cover 30.00
80 A9 80c on 2fr (R) 29.00 8.50
Never hinged 47.50
On cover 47.50
a. Double surcharge 400.00 300.00
81 A10 2pi on 5fr (R) 110.00 110.00
Never hinged 210.00
On cover 250.00
82 A11 4pi on 10fr (R) 150.00 150.00
Never hinged 250.00
On cover 340.00
Nos. 65-82 (18) 393.85 289.10

Types of 1907 Issue Surcharged with New Values in Black or Red

Nos. 88-92

No. 93

1922

88 A5 1c on 5c ocher & blk 1.60
Never hinged 2.40
89 A5 2c on 10c gray grn & blk 2.40
Never hinged 4.00
90 A6 6c on 30c lt red & blk 2.75
Never hinged 4.75
91 A6 10c on 50c lt bl & blk 2.75
Never hinged 4.75
92 A6 11c on 55c vio & blk, *bluish* 3.00
Never hinged 4.75
93 A6 12c on 60c lt bl & blk, *pnksh* (R) 3.00
Never hinged 4.75
Nos. 88-93 (6) 15.50

Nos. 88-93 were sold officially in Paris but were never placed in use in the colony.

Nos. 88-93 exist without surcharge but were not regularly issued in that condition. Value, Nos. 88-89, each $190; Nos. 90-91, each $140; Nos. 92-93, each $100.

A12

A13

Type 1

Type 2

Type 1

Type 2

Two types of "CENTS" for the 4c, 5c, 10c-12c values: Type 1, thin font (April 1922); type 2, thicker font (Oct. 1922 and later printings). All other denominations are type 2.

"CENTS" below Numerals

1922-23 ***Perf. 14x13½***

No.	Type	Description		
94	A12	1/10c blk & sal ('23)	.25	.25
		Never hinged	.40	
		On cover		17.00
a.		Double impression of frame		
95	A12	1/5c blue & blk	.25	.25
		Never hinged	.40	
		On cover		17.00
96	A12	2/5c ol brn & blk	.25	.25
		Never hinged	.40	
		On cover		17.00
a.		Head and value doubled	260.00	260.00
		Never hinged	400.00	
97	A12	4/5c rose & blk, *lav*	.40	.35
		Never hinged	.50	
		On cover		10.00
98	A12	1c yel brn & blk	.25	.25
		Never hinged	.40	
		On cover		6.75
99	A12	2c gray grn & blk	.75	.55
		Never hinged	1.10	
		On cover		6.75
100	A12	3c vio & blk	.35	.35
		Never hinged	.50	
		On cover		4.25
101	A12	4c org & blk, type 2	.35	.35
		Never hinged	.45	
		On cover		4.00
a.		Type 1	.55	.55
		Never hinged	.85	
		On cover		6.50
b.		Head and value doubled	175.00	175.00
		Never hinged	250.00	
102	A12	5c car & blk, type 2	.35	.35
		Never hinged	.45	
		On cover		4.00
a.		Type 1	.65	.65
		Never hinged	.95	
		On cover		6.50
b.		Head and value doubled	290.00	290.00
		Never hinged	250.00	
		Never hinged	425.00	
103	A13	6c dl red & blk	.50	.30
		Never hinged	.65	
		On cover		4.25
104	A13	7c grn & blk	.75	.65
		Never hinged	1.10	
		On cover		6.00
105	A13	8c blk, *lav*	2.00	1.25
		Never hinged	2.50	
		On cover		8.50
106	A13	9c ocher & blk, *grnsh*	1.50	.90
		Never hinged	1.90	
		On cover		8.50
107	A13	10c bl & blk, type 2	.80	.75
		Never hinged	1.20	
		On cover		8.50
a.		Type 1	.80	.75
		Never hinged	1.20	
		On cover		8.50
108	A13	11c vio & blk, type 2	.75	.75
		Never hinged	1.10	
		On cover		10.00
a.		Type 1	.75	.75
		Never hinged	1.10	
		On cover		10.00
109	A13	12c brn & blk, type 2	.55	.55
		Never hinged	.70	
		On cover		13.50
a.		Type 1	.55	.55
		Never hinged	.70	
		On cover		13.50
b.		Head and value double (11c+12c)	450.00	450.00
		Never hinged	625.00	
110	A13	15c org & blk	1.10	.80
		Never hinged	1.60	
		On cover		17.00
111	A13	20c bl & blk, *straw*	1.75	.80
		Never hinged	2.40	
		On cover		20.00
112	A13	40c ver & blk, *bluish*	2.75	1.40
		Never hinged	4.00	
		On cover		21.00
113	A13	1pi bl grn & blk, *grnsh*	5.25	5.25
		Never hinged	8.75	
		On cover		35.00
114	A13	2pi vio brn & blk, *pnksh*	13.00	13.00
		Never hinged	21.00	
		On cover		45.00
		Nos. 94-114 (21)	33.90	29.35

For overprints see Nos. O17-O32.

Plowing near Tower of Confucius A14

Ha Long Bay A15

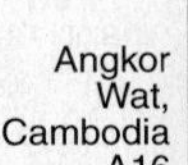

Angkor Wat, Cambodia A16

Carving Wood A17

That Luang Temple, Laos A18

Founding of Saigon A19

1927, Sept. 26

No.	Type	Description		
115	A14	1/10c lt olive grn	.25	.25
		Never hinged	.40	
		On cover		17.00
116	A14	1/5c yellow	.25	.25
		Never hinged	.40	
		On cover		17.00
117	A14	2/5c light blue	.25	.25
		Never hinged	.40	
		On cover		17.00
118	A14	4/5c dp brn	.55	.55
		Never hinged	.80	
		On cover		10.00
119	A14	1c orange	.65	.30
		Never hinged	.85	
		On cover		6.75
120	A14	2c blue grn	1.10	.50
		Never hinged	1.60	
		On cover		6.75
121	A14	3c indigo	.70	.30
		Never hinged	.95	
		On cover		4.25
122	A14	4c lil rose	1.60	1.25
		Never hinged	2.00	
		On cover		5.00
123	A14	5c dp vio	.80	.30
		Never hinged	1.10	
		On cover		4.25
a.		Booklet pane of 10	*200.00*	
124	A15	6c deep red	2.25	.80
		Never hinged	3.25	
		On cover		4.25
a.		Booklet pane of 10	*200.00*	
125	A15	7c lt brn	1.50	.80
		Never hinged	2.00	
		On cover		6.00
126	A15	8c gray green	2.10	1.00
		Never hinged	3.25	
		On cover		8.50
127	A15	9c red vio	1.50	1.00
		Never hinged	2.00	
		On cover		8.50
128	A15	10c light blue	2.00	1.25
		Never hinged	2.75	
		On cover		8.50
129	A15	11c orange	2.00	1.25
		Never hinged	2.75	
		On cover		10.00
130	A15	12c myrtle grn	1.50	1.00
		Never hinged	2.00	
		On cover		12.50
131	A16	15c dl rose & ol brn	8.00	7.50
		Never hinged	12.00	
		On cover		30.00
132	A16	20c vio & slate	4.00	2.40
		Never hinged	6.50	
		On cover		17.00
133	A17	25c org brn & lil rose	8.50	6.50
		Never hinged	12.50	
		On cover		30.00
134	A17	30c dp bl & ol gray	5.00	4.00
		Never hinged	8.00	
		On cover		21.00
135	A18	40c ver & lt bl	7.75	3.25
		Never hinged	12.00	
		On cover		21.00
136	A18	50c lt grn & slate	10.00	3.25
		Never hinged	14.50	
		On cover		21.00
137	A19	1pi dk bl, blk & yel	22.50	9.50
		Never hinged	32.50	
		On cover		42.50
a.		Yellow omitted	275.00	
		Never hinged	425.00	
138	A19	2pi red, dp bl & org	30.00	16.50
		Never hinged	47.50	
		On cover		55.00
		Nos. 115-138 (24)	114.75	63.95

Common Design Types pictured following the introduction.

Colonial Exposition Issue

Common Design Types Surcharged

No. 140

No. 141

No. 142

1931, Apr. 13 Engr. *Perf. 12½*

Name of Country in Black

No.	Type	Description		
140	CD71	4c on 50c violet	3.50	3.50
		Never hinged	5.25	
		On cover		30.00
141	CD72	6c on 90c red org	3.50	3.50
		Never hinged	5.25	
		On cover		42.50
142	CD73	10c on 1.50fr dl bl	4.50	4.50
		Never hinged	7.00	
		On cover		42.50
		Nos. 140-142 (3)	11.50	11.50
		Set, never hinged	18.50	

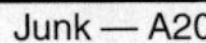

Junk — A20

Tower at Ruins of Angkor Thom — A21

Planting Rice — A22

Apsaras, Celestial Dancer A23

1931-41 Photo. *Perf. 13½x13*

No.	Type	Description		
143	A20	1/10c Prus blue	.25	.25
		Never hinged	.40	
		On cover		12.50
144	A20	1/5c lake	.25	.25
		Never hinged	.40	
		On cover		12.50
145	A20	2/5c org red	.25	.25
		Never hinged	.40	
		On cover		12.50
146	A20	1/2c red brn	.25	.25
		Never hinged	.40	
		On cover		12.50
147	A20	4/5c dk vio	.25	.25
		Never hinged	.40	
		On cover		10.00
148	A20	1c blk brn	.25	.25
		Never hinged	.40	
		On cover		6.75
149	A20	2c dk grn	.25	.25
		Never hinged	.40	
		On cover		6.00
150	A21	3c dp brn	.25	.25
		Never hinged	.40	
		On cover		4.25
151	A21	3c dk grn ('34)	6.00	1.60
		Never hinged	8.00	
		On cover		8.50
152	A21	4c dk bl	1.25	.50
		Never hinged	1.75	
		On cover		4.25
153	A21	4c dk grn ('38)	.80	.55
		Never hinged	1.10	
		On cover		5.00
153A	A21	4c yel org ('40)	.40	.40
		Never hinged	.50	
		On cover		8.50
154	A21	5c dp vio	.30	.30
		Never hinged	.50	
		On cover		4.25
154A	A21	5c dp grn ('41)	.40	.40
		Never hinged	.60	
		On cover		6.75
155	A21	6c org red	.25	.25
		Never hinged	.40	
		On cover		4.25
a.		Bklt. pane 5 + 1 label	100.00	
156	A21	7c blk ('38)	.30	.30
		Never hinged	.50	
		On cover		4.25
157	A21	8c rose lake ('38)	.40	.40
		Never hinged	.65	
		On cover		4.25
157A	A21	9c blk, *yel* ('41)	.75	.75
		Never hinged	1.00	
		On cover		6.75
158	A22	10c dark blue	.65	.50
		Never hinged	.85	
		On cover		4.25
158A	A22	10c ultra, *pink* ('41)	.55	.55
		Never hinged	.85	
		On cover		6.75
159	A22	15c dk brn	5.75	1.40
		Never hinged	8.00	
		On cover		5.00
160	A22	15c dk bl ('33)	.25	.25
		Never hinged	.40	
		On cover		4.25
161	A22	18c blue ('38)	.75	.50
		Never hinged	.95	
		On cover		5.00
162	A22	20c rose	.30	.25
		Never hinged	.50	
		On cover		8.50
163	A22	21c olive grn	.30	.30
		Never hinged	.50	
		On cover		10.00
164	A22	22c dk grn ('38)	.55	.55
		Never hinged	.65	
		On cover		5.00
165	A22	25c dp vio	3.50	1.60
		Never hinged	4.75	
		On cover		12.50
165A	A22	25c dk bl ('41)	.55	.55
		Never hinged	.85	
		On cover		12.50
166	A22	30c org brn ('32)	.50	.30
		Never hinged	.65	
		On cover		12.50

Perf. 13½

No.	Type	Description		
167	A23	50c dk brn	.75	.25
		Never hinged	1.00	
		On cover		12.50
168	A23	60c dl vio ('32)	.90	.65
		Never hinged	1.00	
		On cover		17.00
168A	A23	70c lt bl ('41)	.55	.55
		Never hinged	.95	
		On cover		17.00
169	A23	1pi yel grn	.90	.65
		Never hinged	1.25	
		On cover		17.00
170	A23	2pi red	1.10	.75
		Never hinged	1.40	
		On cover		25.00
		Nos. 143-170 (34)	30.70	17.05

Nos. 166, 167, 169 and 170 were issued without the letters "RF" in 1943, by the Vichy Government.

For surcharge & overprints see Nos. 214A (in Scott Standard catalogue, Vol. 3), O1-O16, Viet Nam, Democratic Republic No. 1L14 (in Scott Standard catalogue, Vol. 6).

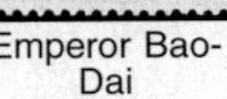

Emperor Bao-Dai A24

King Sisowath Monivong A25

For Use in Annam

1936, Nov. 20 Engr. *Perf. 13*

No.	Type	Description		
171	A24	1c brown	1.00	1.00
		Never hinged	1.25	
		On cover		10.00

172 A24 2c green 1.00 1.00
Never hinged 1.25
On cover 8.50
173 A24 4c violet 1.00 1.00
Never hinged 1.25
On cover 6.50
174 A24 5c red brn 1.50 1.50
Never hinged 1.90
On cover 6.00
175 A24 10c lil rose 2.00 2.00
Never hinged 2.60
On cover 6.00
176 A24 15c ultra 2.75 2.75
Never hinged 4.00
On cover 8.50
177 A24 20c scarlet 2.75 2.75
Never hinged 4.00
On cover 10.00
178 A24 30c plum 3.50 3.50
Never hinged 5.50
On cover 17.00
179 A24 50c slate grn 3.50 3.50
Never hinged 5.50
On cover 21.00
180 A24 1pi rose vio 4.75 4.75
Never hinged 6.50
On cover 30.00
181 A24 2pi black 5.75 5.75
Never hinged 7.25
On cover 35.00
Nos. 171-181 (11) 29.50 29.50

For Use in Cambodia

182 A25 1c brown 1.00 1.00
Never hinged 1.25
On cover 10.00
183 A25 2c green 1.00 1.00
Never hinged 1.25
On cover 8.50
184 A25 4c violet 1.10 1.10
Never hinged 1.40
On cover 6.75
185 A25 5c red brn 1.10 1.10
Never hinged 1.40
On cover 6.00
186 A25 10c lil rose 2.40 2.40
Never hinged 3.25
On cover 6.75
187 A25 15c ultra 3.25 3.25
Never hinged 4.75
On cover 8.50
188 A25 20c scarlet 2.75 2.75
Never hinged 4.00
On cover 10.00
189 A25 30c plum 3.25 3.25
Never hinged 4.75
On cover 16.00
190 A25 50c slate grn 3.25 3.25
Never hinged 4.75
On cover 19.00
191 A25 1pi rose vio 4.25 4.25
Never hinged 6.50
On cover 25.00
192 A25 2pi black 5.75 5.75
Never hinged 7.25
On cover 30.00
Nos. 182-192 (11) 29.10 29.10

Paris International Exposition Issue
Common Design Types

1937, Apr. 15
193 CD74 2c dp vio 1.60 1.60
Never hinged 2.50
On cover 30.00
194 CD75 3c dk grn 1.10 1.10
Never hinged 1.75
On cover 12.50
195 CD76 4c car rose 1.10 1.10
Never hinged 1.75
On cover 6.75
196 CD77 6c dk brn 1.10 1.10
Never hinged 1.75
On cover 12.50
197 CD78 9c red 1.40 1.40
Never hinged 1.75
On cover 12.50
198 CD79 15c ultra 1.40 1.40
Never hinged 2.00
On cover 12.50
Nos. 193-198 (6) 7.70 7.70
Set, never hinged 14.00

Colonial Arts Exhibition Issue
Souvenir Sheet
Common Design Type

1937, Apr. 15 *Imperf.*
199 CD79 30c dull violet 10.00 *12.00*
Never hinged 16.50
On cover 62.50
On cover, single franking 92.50

Governor-General Paul Doumer — A26

1938, June 8 Photo. ***Perf. 13½x13***
200 A26 5c rose car 1.00 .65
Never hinged 2.00
On cover 4.25
201 A26 6c brown 1.10 1.10
Never hinged 2.00
On cover 4.25
202 A26 18c brt bl 1.10 1.10
Never hinged 2.00
On cover 6.75
Nos. 200-202,C18 (4) 3.95 3.10
Set, never hinged 6.50

Trans-Indo-Chinese Railway, 35th anniv.

New York World's Fair Issue
Common Design Type

1939, May 10 Engr. ***Perf. 12½x12***
203 CD82 13c car lake .80 .80
Never hinged 1.40
On cover 35.00
204 CD82 23c ultra 1.25 1.25
Never hinged 2.25
On cover 35.00

Mot Cot Pagoda, Hanoi — A27

1939, June 12 ***Perf. 13***
205 A27 6c blk brn 1.10 1.10
Never hinged 1.60
On cover 8.50
206 A27 9c vermilion 1.10 1.10
Never hinged 1.60
On cover 4.25
207 A27 23c ultra 1.10 1.10
Never hinged 1.60
On cover 6.75
208 A27 39c rose vio 1.50 1.50
Never hinged 2.40
On cover 8.50
Nos. 205-208 (4) 4.80 4.80

Golden Gate International Exposition.

SEMI-POSTAL STAMPS

No. 45 Surcharged

Perf. 14x13½

1914, Oct. 28 **Unwmk.**
B1 A5 10c +5c red & blk 1.60 1.60
Never hinged 2.40
On cover 12.50

Nos. 44-46 Surcharged

1915-17
B2 A5 5c + 5c grn & blk ('17) 1.60 1.60
Never hinged 2.40
On cover 12.50
a. Double surcharge 220.00 210.00
Never hinged 325.00
B3 A5 10c + 5c red & blk 2.50 2.00
Never hinged 4.00
On cover 12.50
B4 A5 15c + 5c vio & blk ('17) 2.50 2.00
Never hinged 4.00
On cover 14.50
a. Triple surcharge 200.00
Never hinged 300.00
b. Quadruple surcharge 200.00
Never hinged 300.00
Nos. B2-B4 (3) 6.60 5.60

Nos. B2-B4 Surcharged with New Values in Blue or Black

1918-19
B5 A5 4c on 5c + 5c (Bl) 4.25 4.25
Never hinged 6.50
On cover 30.00
a. Closed "4" 220.00
Never hinged 325.00
B6 A5 6c on 10c + 5c 3.75 *4.00*
Never hinged 6.25
On cover 30.00
B7 A5 8c on 15c + 5c ('19) 15.00 15.00
Never hinged 18.50
On cover 62.50
a. Double surcharge 225.00
Never hinged 325.00
Nos. B5-B7 (3) 23.00 23.25

France Nos. B5-B10 Surcharged

1919 (?)
B8 SP5 10c on 15c + 10c 1.60 1.60
Never hinged 3.00
On cover 17.00
a. "10 CENTS" double 525.00 525.00
B9 SP5 16c on 25c + 15c 4.00 4.00
Never hinged 7.50
On cover 21.00
B10 SP6 24c on 35c + 25c 7.25 7.25
Never hinged 11.50
On cover 42.50
a. Double surcharge 800.00 800.00
b. CENTS" double 950.00
B11 SP7 40c on 50c + 50c 12.50 12.50
Never hinged 20.00
On cover 72.50
B12 SP8 80c on 1fr + 1fr 27.50 27.50
Never hinged 50.00
On cover 85.00
B13 SP8 4pi on 5fr + 5fr 225.00 225.00
Never hinged 450.00
On cover 425.00
a. PIASTRES" double 6,250. 5,400.
Nos. B8-B13 (6) 277.85 277.85

Curie Issue
Common Design Type
Inscription and Date in Upper Margin

1938, Oct. 24 Engr. ***Perf. 13***
B14 CD80 18c + 5c brt ultra 12.00 12.00
Never hinged 20.00
On cover 42.50
On cover, single franking 72.50

French Revolution Issue
Common Design Type
Name and Value Typo. in Black

1939, July 5 **Photo.**
B15 CD83 6c + 2c green 12.00 12.00
Never hinged 22.50
On cover 75.00
B16 CD83 7c + 3c brown 12.00 12.00
Never hinged 22.50
On cover 55.00
B17 CD83 9c + 4c red org 12.00 12.00
Never hinged 22.50
On cover 45.00
B18 CD83 13c + 10c rose pink 12.00 12.00
Never hinged 22.50
On cover 75.00
On cover, single franking 115.00
B19 CD83 23c + 20c blue 12.00 12.00
Never hinged 22.50
On cover 75.00
On cover, single franking 115.00
Nos. B15-B19 (5) 60.00 60.00
Set, never hinged 112.50

AIR POST STAMPS

Airplane AP1

1933-41 Unwmk. Photo. ***Perf. 13½***
C1 AP1 1c ol brn .25 .25
Never hinged .60
On cover 6.00
C2 AP1 2c dk grn .30 .25
Never hinged .75
On cover 6.00
C3 AP1 5c yel grn .30 .25
Never hinged .75
On cover 4.25
C4 AP1 10c red brn .65 .30
Never hinged 1.25
On cover 4.25
C5 AP1 11c rose car ('38) .80 .30
Never hinged 1.60
On cover 4.25
C6 AP1 15c dp bl .70 .25
Never hinged 1.50
On cover 4.25
C6A AP1 16c brt pink ('41) .35 .35
Never hinged .75
On cover 12.50
C7 AP1 20c grnsh gray .50 .50
Never hinged .95
On cover 5.00
C8 AP1 30c org brn .30 .25
Never hinged .75
On cover 5.00
C9 AP1 36c car rose 1.90 .35
Never hinged 3.75
On cover 6.75
C10 AP1 37c ol grn ('38) .80 .30
Never hinged 1.60
On cover 6.00
C10A AP1 39c dk ol grn ('41) .35 .35
Never hinged .75
On cover 17.00
C11 AP1 60c dk vio 1.90 .35
Never hinged 3.75
On cover 8.50
C12 AP1 66c olive grn .55 .25
Never hinged 1.25
On cover 8.50
C13 AP1 67c brt bl ('38) 1.20 1.00
Never hinged 2.60
On cover 8.50
C13A AP1 69c brt ultra ('41) .65 .65
Never hinged 1.25
On cover 21.00
C14 AP1 1pi black .70 .25
Never hinged 1.25
On cover 12.50
C15 AP1 2pi yel org 1.00 .35
Never hinged 1.90
On cover 14.50
C16 AP1 5pi purple 1.90 .50
Never hinged 3.75
On cover 17.00
C17 AP1 10pi deep red 3.75 .90
Never hinged 7.50
On cover 21.00
Nos. C1-C17 (20) 18.85 7.95

See Nos. C27-C28 in Scott Standard catalogue, Vol. 3.

Issue dates: 11c, 37c, June 8; 67c, Oct. 5; 16c, 39c, 69c, Feb. 5; others, June 1, 1933.

Stamps of type AP1 without "RF" monogram were issued in 1942 and 1943 by the Vichy Government. On the Vichy stamps, the figure of value has been moved to the lower left corner of the vignette.

Trans-Indo-Chinese Railway Type

1938, June 8
C18 A26 37c red orange .75 .25
Never hinged .95
On cover 7.50

AIR POST SEMI-POSTAL STAMP

French Revolution Issue
Common Design Type
Unwmk.

1939, July 5 Photo. ***Perf. 13***
Name and Value Typo. in Orange
CB1 CD83 39c + 40c brn blk 25.00 25.00
Never hinged 45.00
On cover 100.00
On cover, single franking 160.00

POSTAGE DUE STAMPS

Cover values are for examples bearing stamps used to pay correct postage due rates.

French Colonies No. J21 Surcharged

1904, June 26 Unwmk. ***Imperf.***
J1 D1 5c on 60c brn, *buff* 14.50 14.50
On cover 800.00

French Colonies Nos. J10-J11 Surcharged in Carmine

1905, July 22
J2 D1 5c on 40c black 32.00 16.00
On cover 500.00
J3 D1 10c on 60c black 32.00 20.00
On cover 500.00
J4 D1 30c on 60c black 32.00 20.00
On cover 500.00
Nos. J2-J4 (3) 96.00 56.00

Dragon from Steps of Angkor Wat — D1

1908 Typo. ***Perf. 14x13½***
J5 D1 2c black 1.40 1.00
Never hinged 2.00
On cover 35.00
J6 D1 4c dp bl 1.40 1.00
Never hinged 2.00
On cover 35.00
J7 D1 5c bl grn 1.75 1.10
Never hinged 2.40
On cover 17.00
J8 D1 10c carmine 3.00 1.10
Never hinged 4.25
On cover 12.50
J9 D1 15c violet 3.75 2.75
Never hinged 5.50
On cover 21.00
J10 D1 20c chocolate 1.90 1.40
Never hinged 2.75
On cover 17.00
J11 D1 30c ol grn 1.90 1.40
Never hinged 2.75
On cover 25.00

No.	Type	Description	Unused	Used
J12	D1	40c claret	8.50	7.25
		Never hinged	13.00	
		On cover		62.50
J13	D1	50c grnsh bl	7.25	1.60
		Never hinged	11.00	
		On cover		50.00
		On cover		80.00
J14	D1	60c orange	12.00	11.00
		Never hinged	17.50	
		On cover		72.50
J15	D1	1fr gray	24.00	18.50
		Never hinged	40.00	
		On cover		100.00
J16	D1	2fr yel brn	24.00	18.50
		Never hinged	40.00	
		On cover		100.00
J17	D1	5fr red	40.00	37.50
		Never hinged	65.00	
		On cover		175.00
		Nos. J5-J17 (13)	130.85	104.10

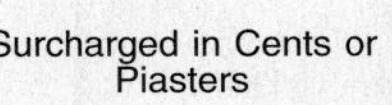

Surcharged in Cents or Piasters

1919

No.	Type	Description	Unused	Used
J18	D1	⅘c on 2c blk	1.75	1.25
		Never hinged	2.40	
		On cover		37.50
J19	D1	1⅗c on 4c dp bl	1.75	1.25
		Never hinged	2.40	
		On cover		37.50
J20	D1	2c on 5c bl grn	3.00	1.60
		Never hinged	4.25	
		On cover		21.00
J21	D1	4c on 10c car	4.25	1.25
		Never hinged	6.50	
		On cover		18.00
J22	D1	6c on 15c vio	9.50	3.00
		Never hinged	14.00	
		On cover		25.00
J23	D1	8c on 20c choc	6.75	2.40
		Never hinged	10.00	
		On cover		25.00
J24	D1	12c on 30c ol grn	9.50	2.40
		Never hinged	14.00	
		On cover		25.00
J25	D1	16c on 40c cl	9.50	2.00
		Never hinged	14.00	
		On cover		35.00
J26	D1	20c on 50c grnsh bl	12.50	6.50
		Never hinged	18.00	
		On cover		72.50
J27	D1	24c on 60c org	3.25	2.00
		Never hinged	4.75	
		On cover		55.00
	a.	Closed "4"	20.00	16.00
		Never hinged	35.00	
		On cover		85.00
J28	D1	40c on 1fr gray	5.50	1.60
		Never hinged	8.00	
		On cover		55.00
	a.	Closed "4"	20.00	16.00
		Never hinged	32.50	
		On cover		85.00
J29	D1	80c on 2fr yel brn	42.50	20.00
		Never hinged	67.50	
		On cover		110.00
J30	D1	2pi on 5fr red	62.50	42.50
		Never hinged	100.00	
		On cover		190.00
	a.	Double surcharge	240.00	190.00
		Never hinged	350.00	
	b.	Triple surcharge	225.00	180.00
		Never hinged	350.00	
		Nos. J18-J30 (13)	172.25	87.75

Dragon from Steps of Angkor Wat — D2

"CENT" below Numerals

1922, Oct.

No.	Type	Description	Unused	Used
J31	D2	⅖c black	.25	.25
		Never hinged	.40	
		On cover		25.00
J32	D2	⅘c red	.30	.30
		Never hinged	.50	
		On cover		14.00
J33	D2	1c buff	.50	.40
		Never hinged	.65	
		On cover		12.50
J34	D2	2c gray grn	.65	.50
		Never hinged	.95	
		On cover		12.50
J35	D2	3c violet	.75	.75
		Never hinged	1.00	
		On cover		12.50
J36	D2	4c orange	.75	.40
		Never hinged	1.00	
		On cover		8.50
	a.	"4 CENTS" omitted	700.00	
	b.	"4 CENTS" double	105.00	105.00
		Never hinged	175.00	
J37	D2	6c ol grn	1.60	.65
		Never hinged	2.40	
		On cover		12.50
J38	D2	8c blk, *lav*	1.25	.65
		Never hinged	1.60	
		On cover		12.50
J39	D2	10c dp bl	2.00	.65
		Never hinged	2.75	
		On cover		12.50
J40	D2	12c ocher, *grnsh*	1.60	1.25
		Never hinged	2.40	
		On cover		12.50
J41	D2	20c dp bl, *straw*	2.00	.90
		Never hinged	2.60	
		On cover		21.00
J42	D2	40c red, *bluish*	2.00	1.10
		Never hinged	2.75	
		On cover		30.00
J43	D2	1pi brn vio, *pnksh*	6.75	3.75
		Never hinged	11.00	
		On cover		45.00
		Nos. J31-J43 (13)	20.40	11.55

Pagoda of Mot Cot, Hanoi — D3

Dragon of Annam — D4

Perf. 14x13½, 13½x14

1927, Sept. 26

No.	Type	Description	Unused	Used
J44	D3	⅖c vio brn & org	.25	.25
		Never hinged	.40	
		On cover		25.00
J45	D3	⅘c vio & blk	.25	.25
		Never hinged	.40	
		On cover		14.50
J46	D3	1c brn red & sl	.90	.90
		Never hinged	1.25	
		On cover		12.50
J47	D3	2c grn & brn ol	1.00	1.00
		Never hinged	1.40	
		On cover		12.50
J48	D3	3c red brn & bl	1.60	1.60
		Never hinged	2.40	
		On cover		12.50
J49	D3	4c ind & brn	1.60	1.60
		Never hinged	2.40	
		On cover		12.50
J50	D3	6c dp red & ver	2.00	1.60
		Never hinged	2.75	
		On cover		14.50
J51	D3	8c ol brn & vio	1.60	1.25
		Never hinged	2.40	
		On cover		14.50
J52	D4	10c dp bl	2.50	1.25
		Never hinged	4.00	
		On cover		14.50
J53	D4	12c olive	5.75	4.75
		Never hinged	8.75	
		On cover		25.00
J54	D4	20c rose	4.00	2.00
		Never hinged	5.50	
		On cover		25.00
J55	D4	40c bl grn	4.00	3.50
		Never hinged	5.50	
		On cover		35.00
J56	D4	1pi red org	20.00	20.00
		Never hinged	26.00	
		On cover		85.00
		Nos. J44-J56 (13)	45.45	39.95

Surcharged in Black or Blue — D5

1931-41 ***Perf. 13***

No.	Type	Description	Unused	Used
J57	D5	⅕c red, *org* ('38)	.25	.25
		Never hinged	.40	
		On cover		17.00
J58	D5	⅖c red, *org*	.25	.25
		Never hinged	.40	
		On cover		17.00
J59	D5	⅘c red, *org*	.25	.25
		Never hinged	.40	
		On cover		8.50
J60	D5	1c red, *org*	.25	.25
		Never hinged	.40	
		On cover		8.50
J61	D5	2c red, *org*	.25	.25
		Never hinged	.40	
		On cover		8.50
J62	D5	2.5c red, *org* ('40)	.25	.25
		Never hinged	.40	
		On cover		10.00
J63	D5	3c red, *org* ('38)	.40	.25
		Never hinged	.55	
		On cover		8.50
J64	D5	4c red, *org*	.30	.30
		Never hinged	.50	
		On cover		8.50
J65	D5	5c red, *org* ('38)	.40	.30
		Never hinged	.65	
		On cover		8.50
J66	D5	6c red, *org*	.30	.30
		Never hinged	.50	
		On cover		8.50
J67	D5	10c red, *org*	.30	.30
		Never hinged	.50	
		On cover		8.50
J68	D5	12c red, *org*	.50	.30
		Never hinged	.65	
		On cover		10.00
J69	D5	14c red, *org* ('38)	.50	.30
		Never hinged	.80	
		On cover		8.50
J70	D5	18c red, *org* ('41)	.50	.50
		Never hinged	.65	
		On cover		12.50
J71	D5	20c red, *org*	.50	.50
		Never hinged	.65	
		On cover		12.50
J72	D5	50c red, *org*	.75	.50
		Never hinged	1.00	
		On cover		17.00
J72A	D5	1pi red, *org*	10.00	9.50
		Never hinged	13.50	
		On cover		42.50
J73	D5	1pi red, *org* (Bl)	2.25	1.25
		Never hinged	2.90	
		On cover		25.00
		Nos. J57-J73 (18)	18.20	15.80

OFFICIAL STAMPS

Regular Issues of 1931-32 Overprinted in Blue or Red

Perf. 13, 13½

1933, Feb. 27 **Unwmk.**

No.	Type	Description	Unused	Used
O1	A20	1c black brown (Bl)	.80	.75
		Never hinged	1.10	
		On cover		10.00
O2	A20	2c dark green (Bl)	.90	.50
		Never hinged	1.20	
		On cover		8.50

Regular Issues of 1931-32 Overprinted in Blue or Red

No.	Type	Description	Unused	Used
O3	A21	3c deep brown (Bl)	1.25	.65
		Never hinged	1.60	
		On cover		6.00
	a.	Inverted overprint	160.00	
		Never hinged	210.00	
O4	A21	4c dark blue (R)	1.50	.90
		Never hinged	2.00	
		On cover		60.00
	a.	Inverted overprint	160.00	
		Never hinged	210.00	
O5	A21	5c deep violet (Bl)	2.40	.90
		Never hinged	3.25	
		On cover		6.00
O6	A21	6c orange red (Bl)	2.40	1.25
		Never hinged	3.25	
		On cover		6.00

Regular Issues of 1931-32 Overprinted in Blue or Red

No.	Type	Description	Unused	Used
O7	A22	10c dk blue (R)	1.25	1.00
		Never hinged	1.60	
		On cover		6.00
O8	A22	15c dk brown (Bl)	3.00	1.75
		Never hinged	3.50	
		On cover		7.50
O9	A22	20c rose (Bl)	3.25	.85
		Never hinged	4.00	
		On cover		12.50
O10	A22	21c olive grn (Bl)	3.00	1.75
		Never hinged	3.50	
		On cover		15.00
O11	A22	25c dp violet (Bl)	1.60	.50
		Never hinged	2.40	
		On cover		18.50
O12	A22	30c orange brn (Bl)	3.25	.85
		Never hinged	4.50	
		On cover		18.50

Regular Issues of 1931-32 Overprinted in Blue or Red

No.	Type	Description	Unused	Used
O13	A23	50c dark brown (Bl)	12.50	3.50
		Never hinged	18.00	
		On cover		21.00
O14	A23	60c dull violet (Bl)	2.75	2.40
		Never hinged	4.00	
		On cover		25.00
O15	A23	1pi yellow green (Bl)	30.00	11.00
		Never hinged	40.00	
		On cover		35.00
O16	A23	2pi red (Bl)	11.50	9.50
		Never hinged	16.00	
		On cover		37.50
		Nos. O1-O16 (16)	81.35	38.05

Type of 1922-23 Issue Overprinted diagonally in Black or Red

1934, Oct. 4 ***Perf. 14x13***

No.	Type	Description	Unused	Used
O17	A13	1c olive green	1.25	.75
		Never hinged	1.25	
		On cover		10.00
O18	A13	2c brown orange	1.25	.75
		Never hinged	1.25	
		On cover		10.00
O19	A13	3c yellow green	1.40	.65
		Never hinged	1.75	
		On cover		6.00
O20	A13	4c cerise	2.50	1.30
		Never hinged	3.00	
		On cover		12.00
O21	A13	5c yellow	1.40	.75
		Never hinged	1.75	
		On cover		6.00
O22	A13	6c orange red	6.00	5.25
		Never hinged	8.50	
		On cover		30.00
O23	A13	10c gray grn (R)	3.50	2.25
		Never hinged	4.50	
		On cover		15.00
O24	A13	15c ultra	2.10	1.50
		Never hinged	2.90	
		On cover		12.50
O25	A13	20c gray black (R)	2.00	1.50
		Never hinged	2.50	
		On cover		14.50
O26	A13	21c light violet	11.00	9.25
		Never hinged	15.00	
		On cover		45.00
O27	A13	25c rose lake	13.00	11.00
		Never hinged	19.00	
		On cover		55.00
O28	A13	30c lilac gray	1.75	1.30
		Never hinged	2.10	
		On cover		17.00
O29	A13	50c brt violet	8.00	6.75
		Never hinged	12.00	
		On cover		35.00
O30	A13	60c gray	15.00	11.00
		Never hinged	22.00	
		On cover		55.00
O31	A13	1pi blue (R)	30.00	24.50
		Never hinged	42.50	
		On cover		67.50
O32	A13	2pi deep red	47.50	37.50
		Never hinged	67.50	
		On cover		100.00
		Nos. O17-O32 (16)	147.65	116.00

The value tablet has colorless numeral and letters on solid background.

PARCEL POST STAMPS

French Colonies No. 50 Overprinted

1891 **Unwmk.** ***Perf. 14x13½***

No.	Type	Description	Unused	Used
Q1	A9	10c black, *lavender*	24.00	10.50
		Never hinged	55.00	
		On parcel post receipt card		400.00

The overprint on No. Q1 was also handstamped in shiny ink. Value unused, $750.

Indo-China No. 8 Overprinted

1898

No.	Type	Description	Unused	Used
Q2	A3	10c black, *lavender*	29.00	29.00
		Never hinged	65.00	
		On parcel post receipt card		400.00

Nos. 8 and 9 Overprinted

1902

No.	Type	Description	Unused	Used
Q3	A3	10c black, *lavender*	55.00	35.00
		Never hinged	120.00	
		On parcel post receipt card		400.00
	a.	Inverted overprint	115.00	50.00
Q4	A3	10c red	55.00	24.00
		Never hinged	120.00	
		On parcel post receipt card		400.00
	a.	Inverted overprint	85.00	50.00
	b.	Double overprint	85.00	50.00

INHAMBANE

ˌin-yəm-ˈban-ə

LOCATION — East Africa
GOVT. — A district of Mozambique, former Portuguese colony
AREA — 21,000 sq. mi. (approx.)
POP. — 248,000 (approx.)
CAPITAL — Inhambane

1000 Reis = 1 Milreis
100 Centavos = 1 Escudo (1913)

Stamps of Mozambique Overprinted

On 1886 Issue

1895, July 1 Unwmk. *Perf. 12½*
Without Gum

No.	Type	Description	Unused	Used
1	A2	5r black	37.50	30.00
2	A2	10r green	50.00	25.00
a.		Perf. 13½	80.00	75.00
3	A2	20r rose	60.00	30.00
4	A2	25r lilac	*1,000.*	*250.00*
5	A2	40r chocolate	60.00	40.00
6	A2	50r blue	60.00	32.50
a.		Perf. 13½	50.00	50.00
7	A2	100r yellow brown	*1,000.*	*400.00*
8	A2	200r gray violet	75.00	40.00
9	A2	300r orange	75.00	40.00
		Nos. 1-9 (9)	*2,418.*	*887.50*

On 1894 Issue

Perf. 11½

No.	Type	Description	Unused	Used
10	A3	50r lt blue	42.50	35.00
a.		Perf. 12½	55.00	42.50
11	A3	75r rose	55.00	40.00
12	A3	80r yellow green	45.00	37.50
13	A3	100r brown, *buff*	200.00	60.00
14	A3	150r carmine, *rose*	50.00	45.00
		Nos. 10-14 (5)	392.50	217.50

700th anniv. of the birth of St. Anthony of Padua.

The status of Nos. 4 and 7 is questionable. No. 3 is always discolored.

Forged overprints exist. Genuine overprints are 21mm high.

King Carlos — A1

1903, Jan. 1 Typo. *Perf. 11½*
Name and Value in Black except 500r

No.	Type	Description	Unused	Used
15	A1	2½r gray	.30	.30
16	A1	5r orange	.30	.30
17	A1	10r lt green	.60	.40
18	A1	15r gray green	1.00	.75
19	A1	20r gray violet	.85	.55
20	A1	25r carmine	.70	.55
21	A1	50r brown	1.75	1.25
22	A1	65r dull blue	25.00	15.00
23	A1	75r lilac	2.00	1.40
24	A1	100r dk blue, *blue*	2.75	1.25
25	A1	115r org brn, *pink*	5.00	5.00
26	A1	130r brown, *straw*	5.00	5.00
27	A1	200r red vio, *pink*	5.00	4.25
28	A1	400r dull bl, *straw*	8.25	7.50
29	A1	500r blk & red, *bl*	18.00	12.00
30	A1	700r gray blk, *straw*	20.00	13.00
		Nos. 15-30 (16)	96.50	68.50

For surcharge & overprints see Nos. 31-47, 88-101.

No. 22 Surcharged in Black

1905

No.	Type	Description	Unused	Used
31	A1	50r on 65r dull blue	3.00	2.00

Nos. 15-21, 23-30 Overprinted in Carmine or Green

1911

No.	Type	Description	Unused	Used
32	A1	2½r gray	.25	.25
33	A1	5r orange	.25	.25
34	A1	10r lt green	.25	.25
35	A1	15r gray green	.30	.30
36	A1	20r gray violet	.30	.30
37	A1	25r carmine (G)	.70	.50
38	A1	50r brown	.50	.50
39	A1	75r lilac	.50	.50
40	A1	100r dk blue, *bl*	.50	.50
41	A1	115r org brn, *pink*	1.00	.95
42	A1	130r brown, *straw*	1.00	.95
43	A1	200r red vio, *pink*	1.00	.95
44	A1	400r dull bl, *straw*	1.25	1.00
45	A1	500r blk & red, *bl*	1.50	1.00
46	A1	700r gray blk, *straw*	1.75	1.50
		Nos. 32-46 (15)	11.05	9.70

No. 31 Overprinted in Red

1914

No.	Type	Description	Unused	Used
47	A1	50r on 65r dull blue	1.75	1.25
a.		"Republica" inverted	25.00	25.00

Vasco da Gama Issue of Various Portuguese Colonies

Common Design Types CD20-CD27 Surcharged

1913 On Stamps of Macao

No.	Type	Description	Unused	Used
48	CD20	¼c on ½a bl grn	1.25	1.25
49	CD21	½c on 1a red	1.25	1.25
50	CD22	1c on 2a red vio	1.25	1.25
a.		Inverted surcharge	35.00	35.00
51	CD23	2½c on 4a yel grn	1.25	1.25
52	CD24	5c on 8a dk bl	1.25	1.25
53	CD25	7½c on 12a vio brn	2.25	2.25
54	CD26	10c on 16a bis brn	1.75	1.75
55	CD27	15c on 24a bis	1.75	1.75
		Nos. 48-55 (8)	12.00	12.00

On Stamps of Portuguese Africa

No.	Type	Description	Unused	Used
56	CD20	¼c on 2½r bl grn	1.25	1.00
57	CD21	½c on 5r red	1.25	1.00
58	CD22	1c on 10r red vio	1.25	1.00
59	CD23	2½c on 25r yel grn	1.25	1.00
60	CD24	5c on 50r dk bl	1.25	1.00
61	CD25	7½c on 75r vio brn	2.00	2.00
62	CD26	10c on 100r bis brn	1.50	1.50
63	CD27	15c on 150r bis	1.50	1.50
		Nos. 56-63 (8)	11.25	10.00

On Stamps of Timor

No.	Type	Description	Unused	Used
64	CD20	¼c on ½a bl grn	1.25	1.25
a.		Inverted surcharge	35.00	35.00
65	CD21	½c on 1a red	1.25	1.25
66	CD22	1c on 2a red vio	1.25	1.25
67	CD23	2½c on 4a yel grn	1.25	1.25
68	CD24	5c on 8a dk bl	1.25	1.25
69	CD25	7½c on 12a vio brn	2.50	2.50
70	CD26	10c on 16a bis brn	1.75	1.75
71	CD27	15c on 24a bis	1.75	1.75
		Nos. 64-71 (8)	12.25	12.25
		Nos. 48-71 (24)	35.50	34.25

Ceres — A2

Name and Value in Black
Chalky Paper

1914 Typo. *Perf. 15x14*

No.	Type	Description	Unused	Used
72	A2	¼c olive brown	.50	.50
		Never hinged	.80	
73	A2	½c black	.50	.50
		Never hinged	.80	
a.		Imperf.		
74	A2	1c blue green	.50	.50
		Never hinged	.80	
75	A2	1½c lilac brown	.50	.50
		Never hinged	.80	
76	A2	2c carmine	.50	.50
		Never hinged	.80	
77	A2	2½c lt violet	.35	.35
		Never hinged	.55	
78	A2	5c deep blue	.80	.80
		Never hinged	1.25	
79	A2	7½c yellow brown	1.25	1.25
		Never hinged	2.00	
80	A2	8c slate	1.25	1.25
		Never hinged	2.00	
81	A2	10c orange brown	1.10	1.10
		Never hinged	1.75	
82	A2	15c plum	3.00	1.60
		Never hinged	3.25	
83	A2	20c yellow green	3.00	1.60
		Never hinged	3.25	
84	A2	30c brown, *grn*	4.00	2.50
		Never hinged	4.75	
85	A2	40c brown, *pink*	5.00	3.00
		Never hinged	6.00	
86	A2	50c orange, *sal*	6.00	5.00
		Never hinged	9.25	
87	A2	1e green, *blue*	8.00	6.00
		Never hinged	12.50	
		Nos. 72-87 (16)	36.25	26.95

No. 31 Overprinted in Carmine

1915 *Perf. 11½*

No.	Type	Description	Unused	Used
88	A1	50c on 65r dull blue	9.00	6.00

Nos. 15-21, 23-30 Overprinted Locally

1917

No.	Type	Description	Unused	Used
89	A1	2½r gray	25.00	25.00
90	A1	5r orange	25.00	25.00
91	A1	15r gray green	4.00	2.50
92	A1	20r gray violet	4.00	2.00
93	A1	50r brown	3.00	2.00
94	A1	75r lilac	3.00	2.00
95	A1	100r blue, *blue*	4.00	2.50
96	A1	115r org brn, *pink*	4.00	2.50
97	A1	130r brn, *straw*	4.00	2.50
98	A1	200r red vio, *pink*	4.00	2.50
99	A1	400r dull bl, *straw*	6.00	3.00
100	A1	500r blk & red, *bl*	7.00	3.00
101	A1	700r gray blk, *straw*	14.00	8.00
		Nos. 89-101 (13)	107.00	82.50

The stamps of Inhambane have been superseded by those of Mozambique.

ININI

ˌē-ni-ˈnē

LOCATION — In northeastern South America, adjoining French Guiana
GOVT. — Former territory of French Guiana
AREA — 30,301 sq. mi.
POP. — 5,024 (1946)
CAPITAL — St. Elie

Inini was separated from French Guiana in 1930 and reunited with it in when the colony became an integral part of the Republic, acquiring the same status as the departments of Metropolitan France, under a law effective Jan. 1, 1947.

100 Centimes = 1 Franc

Used values are for canceled-to-order stamps.

Stamps of French Guiana, 1929-40, Overprinted in Black, Red or Blue

Nos. 1-9

Nos. 10-26

Nos. 27-40

1932-40 Unwmk. *Perf. 13½x14*

No.	Type	Description	Unused	Used
1	A16	1c gray lil & grnsh bl	.40	*.55*
		Never hinged	.60	
		On cover, *from*		300.00
2	A16	2c dk red & bl grn	.40	*.55*
		Never hinged	.60	
		On cover, *from*		300.00
3	A16	3c gray lil & grnsh bl ('40)	.55	*.70*
		Never hinged	.75	
		On cover, *from*		340.00
4	A16	4c ol brn & red vio ('38)	.55	*.80*
		Never hinged	.85	
		On cover, *from*		300.00
5	A16	5c Prus bl & red org	.55	*.80*
		Never hinged	.85	
		On cover, *from*		290.00
6	A16	10c magenta & brn	.40	*.55*
		Never hinged	.60	
		On cover, *from*		275.00
7	A16	15c yel brn & red org	.40	*.55*
		Never hinged	.60	
		On cover, *from*		275.00
8	A16	20c dk bl & ol grn	.40	*.55*
		Never hinged	.60	
		On cover, *from*		250.00
9	A16	25c dk red & dk brn	.90	*1.25*
		Never hinged	1.20	
		On cover, *from*		250.00

Perf. 14x13½

No.	Type	Description	Unused	Used
10	A17	30c dl grn & lt grn	2.40	*2.40*
		Never hinged	3.25	
		On cover, *from*		250.00
11	A17	30c grn & brn ('40)	.60	*.90*
		Never hinged	.90	
		On cover, *from*		290.00
12	A17	35c Prus grn & ol ('38)	1.20	*1.40*
		Never hinged	1.50	
		On cover, *from*		290.00
13	A17	40c org brn & ol gray	.80	*1.20*
		Never hinged	1.20	
		On cover, *from*		250.00
14	A17	45c ol grn & lt grn ('40)	1.40	*1.50*
		Never hinged	2.75	
		On cover, *from*		250.00
15	A17	50c dk bl & ol gray	.70	*1.05*
		Never hinged	.95	
		On cover, *from*		290.00
16	A17	55c vio bl & car ('38)	5.50	*6.50*
		Never hinged	7.00	
		On cover, *from*		250.00
17	A17	60c sal & grn ('40)	.70	*1.05*
		Never hinged	.95	
		On cover, *from*		250.00
18	A17	65c sal & grn ('38)	2.10	*2.25*
		Never hinged	3.00	
		On cover, *from*		250.00
19	A17	70c ind & sl bl ('40)	1.00	*1.10*
		Never hinged	1.50	
		On cover, *from*		250.00
20	A17	75c ind & sl bl (Bl)	4.25	*3.50*
		Never hinged	4.75	
		On cover, *from*		250.00
21	A17	80c blk & vio bl (R) ('38)	1.25	*1.25*
		Never hinged	1.60	
		On cover, *from*		250.00
22	A17	90c dk red & ver	3.50	*2.25*
		Never hinged	4.75	
		On cover, *from*		310.00
		On cover, single franking, *from*		500.00
23	A17	90c red vio & brn ('39)	1.75	*1.40*
		Never hinged	2.40	
		On cover, *from*		250.00

24 A17 1fr lt vio & brn 22.50 *24.00*
Never hinged 32.50
On cover, *from* *500.00*
On cover, single franking, *from* 700.00
25 A17 1fr car & lt red ('38) 2.75 *1.75*
Never hinged 3.75
On cover, *from* 310.00
On cover, single franking, *from* 550.00
26 A17 1fr blk & vio bl ('40) 1.00 *1.40*
Never hinged 1.25
On cover, *from* 250.00
27 A18 1.25fr blk brn & bl grn ('33) 2.25 *1.60*
Never hinged 2.75
On cover, *from* 250.00
On cover, single franking, *from* 400.00
28 A18 1.25fr rose & lt red ('39) 1.40 *1.40*
Never hinged 2.00
On cover, *from* 250.00
On cover, single franking, *from* 475.00
29 A18 1.40fr ol brn & red vio ('40) 1.25 *1.40*
Never hinged 1.75
On cover, *from* 310.00
On cover, single franking, *from* 475.00
30 A18 1.50fr dk bl & lt bl 1.05 *1.50*
Never hinged 1.40
On cover, *from* 300.00
On cover, single franking, *from* 425.00
31 A18 1.60fr ol brn & bl grn ('40) 1.00 *1.40*
Never hinged 1.25
On cover, *from* 250.00
On cover, single franking, *from* 475.00
32 A18 1.75fr brn, red & blk brn ('33) 30.00 27.50
Never hinged 40.00
On cover, *from* *500.00*
On cover, single franking, *from* 700.00
33 A18 1.75fr vio bl ('38) 1.75 *2.40*
Never hinged 2.50
On cover, *from* 250.00
On cover, single franking, *from* 425.00
34 A18 2fr dk grn & rose red 1.25 *1.75*
Never hinged 1.60
On cover, *from* 250.00
On cover, single franking, *from* 425.00
35 A18 2.25fr vio bl ('39) 1.10 *1.40*
Never hinged 1.50
On cover, *from* 250.00
On cover, single franking, *from* 400.00
36 A18 2.50fr cop red & brn ('40) 1.00 *1.40*
Never hinged 1.25
On cover, *from* 250.00
On cover, single franking, *from* 400.00
37 A18 3fr brn red & red vio 1.50 *1.75*
Never hinged 2.10
On cover, *from* 275.00
On cover, single franking, *from* 500.00
38 A18 5fr dl vio & yel grn 1.25 *1.75*
Never hinged 1.60
On cover, *from* 300.00
On cover, single franking, *from* 500.00
39 A18 10fr ol gray & dp ultra (R) 1.75 *2.10*
Never hinged 2.40
On cover, *from* 325.00
On cover, single franking, *from* 550.00
40 A18 20fr indigo & ver 1.75 *2.10*
Never hinged 2.40
On cover, *from* *450.00*
On cover, single franking, *from* 750.00
Nos. 1-40 (40) 106.25 *110.65*

Cover values are for examples bearing stamps used to pay correct postage rates.

Common Design Types pictured following the introduction.

Colonial Arts Exhibition Issue

Souvenir Sheet
Common Design Type

1937 ***Imperf.***
41 CD75 3fr red brown 19.00 *22.50*
Never hinged 28.00
On cover 275.00
On cover, single franking 375.00

New York World's Fair Issue

Common Design Type

1939, May 10 Engr. *Perf. 12½x12*
42 CD82 1.25fr car lake 3.75 *4.50*
Never hinged 5.75
On cover 250.00
On cover, single franking 340.00
43 CD82 2.25fr ultra 3.75 *4.50*
Never hinged 5.75
On cover 250.00
On cover, single franking 325.00

SEMI-POSTAL STAMPS

French Revolution Issue

Common Design Type

Photo.; Name & Value Typo. in Black

1939, July 5 Unwmk. *Perf. 13*
B1 CD83 45c + 25c green 15.00 *17.50*
Never hinged 23.00
On cover 190.00
B2 CD83 70c + 30c brown 15.00 *17.50*
Never hinged 23.00
On cover 160.00
B3 CD83 90c + 35c red org 15.00 *17.50*
Never hinged 23.00
On cover 140.00
B4 CD83 1.25fr + 1fr rose pink 15.00 *17.50*
Never hinged 23.00
On cover 225.00
On cover, single franking 310.00
B5 CD83 2.25fr + 2fr blue 15.00 *17.50*
Never hinged 23.00
On cover 210.00
On cover, single franking 275.00
Nos. B1-B5 (5) 75.00 87.50

POSTAGE DUE STAMPS

Cover values are for examples bearing stamps used to pay correct postage due rates.

Postage Due Stamps of French Guiana, 1929, Overprinted in Black

1932, Apr. 7 Unwmk. *Perf. 13½x14*
J1 D3 5c indigo & Prus bl .25 *.40*
Never hinged .40
On cover *1,250.*
J2 D3 10c bis brn & Prus grn .65 *1.00*
Never hinged .95
On cover *1,250.*
J3 D3 20c grn & rose red .65 *1.00*
Never hinged .95
On cover *1,250.*
J4 D3 30c ol brn & rose red .65 *1.00*
Never hinged .95
On cover *1,250.*
J5 D3 50c vio & ol brn 1.00 *1.50*
Never hinged 1.40
On cover *1,250.*
J6 D3 60c brn red & ol brn 1.10 *1.50*
Never hinged 1.40
On cover *1,250.*

Overprinted in Black or Red

J7 D4 1fr dp bl & org brn 1.75 *1.75*
Never hinged 2.50
On cover *1,250.*
J8 D4 2fr brn red & bluish grn 2.50 *2.50*
Never hinged 3.50
On cover *1,250.*
J9 D4 3fr vio & blk (R) 7.50 7.50
Never hinged 14.00
On cover *1,250.*
J10 D4 3fr vio & blk 4.25 *5.00*
Never hinged 6.00
On cover *1,250.*
Nos. J1-J10 (10) 20.30 *23.15*

IONIAN ISLANDS

ī-ˈō-nē-ən ˈī-lənds

LOCATION — A group of seven islands, of which six-Corfu, Paxos Lefkas (Santa Maura), Cephalonia, Ithaca and Zante-are in the Ionian Sea west of Greece, and a seventh-Kythera (Cerigo)-is in the Mediterranean south of Greece.
GOVT. — British Protectorate
AREA — 752 sq. mi.
POP. — 251,000 (approx.)

These islands were acquired by Great Britain in 1815 but in 1864 were ceded to Greece on request of the inhabitants.

10 Oboli = 1 Penny
12 Pence = 1 Shilling

Watermarks

Wmk. 138 — "2"

Wmk. 139 — "1"

PRE-STAMP POSTAL MARKINGS

No. A2

Cephalonia

1844
A1 Crowned Circle handstamp Type I, on cover, inscribed "PAID AT CEPHALONIA" in black *2,000.*

Corfu

A2 Crowned Circle handstamp Type I, on cover, inscribed "PAID AT CORFU" in black *675.00*
A3 Crowned Circle handstamp Type I, on cover, inscribed "PAID AT CORFU" in green or blue —

Zante

A4 Crowned Circle handstamp Type I, on cover, inscribed "PAID AT ZANTE" in black *1,500.*

Earliest known uses: A1, 4/19/44; A2, 4/19/44; A3, 1844; A4, 4/19/44.

ISSUES OF THE BRITISH PROTECTORATE

Queen Victoria — A1

1859 Unwmk. Engr. *Imperf.*
1 A1 (½p) orange 140.00 *750.00*

Wmk. 138

2 A1 (1p) blue 35.00 *300.00*

Wmk. 139

3 A1 (2p) lake 28.00 *300.00*
Nos. 1-3 (3) 203.00 *1,350.*

Full margins = ¼mm at sides, ¾mm at top and bottom.

Forged cancellations are plentiful.

IRAN

i-ˈrän

(Persia)

LOCATION — Western Asia, bordering on the Persian Gulf and the Gulf of Oman
GOVT. — Islamic republic
AREA — 636,000 sq. mi.
POP. — 43,830,000 (est. 1984)
CAPITAL — Tehran

20 Shahis (or Chahis) = 1 Kran
10 Krans = 1 Toman
100 Centimes = 1 Franc = 1 Kran (1881)
100 Dinars = 1 Rial (1933)
100 Rials = 1 Pahlavi

Beware of forgeries and/or reprints of most Iran stamps between the years 1870-1925. Scott values are for genuine stamps. Collectors should be aware that forgeries of many issues outnumber genuine examples by factors of 10 or 20 to one. Failing specialized knowledge on the part of the collector, these stamps should be examined or authenticated by acknowledged experts before purchase.

Watermark

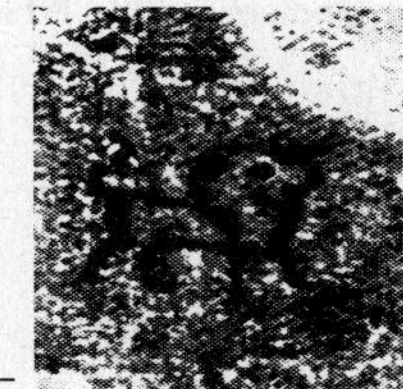

Wmk. 161 — Lion

Many issues have handstamped surcharges. As usual with such surcharges there are numerous inverted, double and similar varieties.

Values of early stamps vary according to condition. Quotations for Nos. 1-20, 33-40 are for fine stamps. Very fine to superb examples sell at much higher prices, and inferior or poor examples sell at reduced prices, depending on the condition of the individual stamp.

Cracked gum on unused stamps does not detract from the value.

Coat of Arms — A1

Design A2 has value numeral below lion.

1870 Unwmk. Typo. *Imperf.*
1 A1 1s dull violet 325.00
2 A1 2s green 275.00
3 A1 4s greenish blue 225.00
On cover, internal use 2,500.
4 A1 8s red 275.00
Nos. 1-4 (4) 1,100.

Values for used examples of Nos. 1-4 are omitted, since this issue was only pen canceled. After 1875, postmarked remainders were sold to collectors. Values same as unused.

Printed in blocks of 4. Many shades exist. Forgeries exist.

Printed on Both Sides

1a A1 1s 20,000.
2a A1 2s 40,000.
3a A1 4s
4a A1 8s 18,000.

Coat of Arms — A2

Vertically Rouletted 10½ on 1 or 2 Sides

1875 Thick Wove Paper

No.	Design	Description	Unused	Used
11	A2	1s black	225.00	75.00
		On cover with #13, internal use		7,500.
a.		Imperf.	*3,500.*	*5,000.*
12	A2	2s blue	225.00	75.00
a.		Tête bêche pair	*30,000.*	
b.		Imperf.	—	—
13	A2	4s vermilion	300.00	100.00
		On cover with #11, internal use		7,500.
a.		Imperf.	—	—
b.		4s bright red, thin paper, imperf.	750.00	*750.00*
14	A2	8s yellow green	200.00	175.00
b.		Tête bêche pair	*15,000.*	*10,000.*
c.		Imperf.	*2,000.*	*1,250.*
		Nos. 11-14 (4)	950.00	425.00

Four varieties of each.

Nos. 11-14 were printed in horizontal strips of 4 with 3-10mm spacing between stamps. The strips were then cut very close all around (generally touching or cutting the outer framelines). Then they were hand-rouletted between the stamps. Values are for stamps with rouletting on both sides and margins clear at top and bottom. Stamps showing the rouletting on only one side sell for considerably less.

Nos. 11 to 14 also exist pin-perforated and percé en scie.

No. 13b has spacing of 2-3mm.

See Nos. 15-20, 33-40.

Medium to Thin White or Grayish Paper

1876 ***Imperf.***

No.	Design	Description	Unused	Used
14A	A2	1s black	400.00	*600.00*
15	A2	1s gray black	50.00	*175.00*
		On cover, internal use		9,750.
a.		Printed on both sides	*1,500.*	
b.		Laid paper	1,000.	1,500.
16	A2	2s gray blue	600.00	*750.00*
a.		Printed on both sides	*7,000.*	
b.		Half used as 1s on cover		*100,000.*
17	A2	2s black	1,000.	
		Pair	7,500.	
a.		Tête bêche pair	*6,000.*	
18	A2	4s vermilion	500.00	150.00
a.		Printed on both sides	5,000.	5,000.
19	A2	1k rose	1,500.	100.00
a.		Printed on both sides		4,000.
b.		Laid paper	*6,000.*	1,200.
c.		1k yellow (error)	*35,000.*	15,000.
d.		Tête bêche pair		*120,000.*
20	A2	4k yellow	3,000.	300.00
a.		Printed on both sides		*5,000.*
b.		Laid paper	*5,000.*	300.00
c.		Tête bêche pair		*18,000.*

Nos. 15-16, 18-20 were printed in blocks of 4, and Nos. 14A and 17 in vertical strips of 4, with spacing of 2mm or less.

Nos. 14A and 17 are on medium to thick grayish wove paper. Forgeries exist.

Official reprints of the 1s and 4s are on thick coarse white paper without gum. Value, each $350.

1875 and 1876 issues

Various forgeries exist including forgeries printed from the replica cliches of the genuine issues in Paris by the order of Fabius Boital, a French engineer who was a concession-hunter, living in Iran during the 1870s through 1890s. There also are modern forgeries made by laser printers.

Nasser-eddin Shah Qajar — A3

Perf. 10½, 11, 12, 13, and Compounds

1876 Litho.

No.	Design	Description	Unused	Used
27	A3	1s lilac & blk	30.00	6.00
28	A3	2s green & blk	35.00	7.50
29	A3	5s rose & blk	30.00	4.00
		On cover, internal use		175.00
		On cover, international use		2,200.
30	A3	10s blue & blk	45.00	8.00
		On cover		200.00
		Nos. 27-30 (4)	140.00	25.50

Bisects of the 5s and 1s, the latter used with 2s stamps, were used to make up the 2½ shahis postcard rate. Bisects of the 10s were used in the absence of 5s stamps to make up the letter rate.

The 10s was bisected and surcharged "5 Shahi" or "5 Shahy" for local use in Azerbaijan province and Khoy in 1877.

"Imperfs" of the 5s are envelope cutouts.

Forgeries and official reprints exist.

Very fine examples will have perforations cutting the background net on one side. Genuine stamps withs perfs clear of net on all four sides are very scarce.

1878 Typo. ***Imperf.***

No.	Design	Description	Unused	Used
33	A2	1k car rose	950.00	175.00
34	A2	1k red, *yellow*	*5,000.*	175.00
a.		Tête bêche pair		*10,000.*
35	A2	4k ultramarine	450.00	175.00
a.		Printed on both sides		*4,000.*
36	A2	5k violet	1,500.	350.00
37	A2	5k gold	*8,500.*	750.00
38	A2	5k red bronze	*35,000.*	2,500.
39	A2	5k vio bronze	*65,000.*	4,000.
a.		A2 5k slate-green bronze	—	—
40	A2	1t bronze, *bl*	*75,000.*	*8,000.*

Four varieties of each except for 4k which has 3.

Nos. 33 and 34 are printed from redrawn clichés. They have wide colorless circles around the corner numerals.

Nasser-eddin Shah Qajar — A6

Perf. 10½, 12, 13, and Compounds

1879 Litho.

No.	Design	Description	Unused	Used
41	A6	1k brown & blk	450.00	7.00
a.		Pair, imperf between		—
b.		Inverted center		*5,000.*
42	A6	5k blue & blk	400.00	5.00
a.		Imperf., pair	3,000.	*600.00*
b.		Inverted center		2,500.
c.		Inverted center, imperf		2,500.

1880

No.	Design	Description	Unused	Used
43	A6	1s red & black	50.00	15.00
b.		Pair, imperf between	*4,500.*	
44	A6	2s yellow & blk	85.00	10.00
a.		Imperf., pair		*2,500.*
45	A6	5s green & blk	350.00	2.00
46	A6	10s violet & blk	700.00	30.00
		Nos. 43-46 (4)	1,185.	57.00

Forgeries and official reprints exist.

Imperf examples of No. 46 are proofs on thin yellow paper or thick white card with a cancellation line.

The 2, 5 and 10sh of this issue and the 1 and 5kr of the 1879 issue have been reprinted from a new die which resembles the 5 shahi envelope. The aigrette is shorter than on the original stamps and touches the circle above it.

Sun — A7

1881 Litho. ***Perf. 12, 13, 12x13***

No.	Design	Description	Unused	Used
47	A7	5c dull violet	50.00	25.00
		On cover, single franking		125.00
48	A7	10c rose	50.00	25.00
49	A7	25c green	6,750.	100.00
		On cover, internal use		1,200.
		On cover, international use		2,750.
		Nos. 47-49 (3)	6,850.	150.00

1882 Engr., Border Litho.

No.	Design	Description	Unused	Used
50	A7	5c blue vio & vio	50.00	60.00
51	A7	10c dp pink & rose	50.00	60.00
52	A7	25c deep grn & grn	1,400.	40.00
		On cover, internal use		125.00
		On cover, international use		325.00
		Nos. 50-52 (3)	1,500.	160.00

Very fine examples of Nos. 50-52 will have perforations cutting the outer colored border but clear of the inner framelines.

Counterfeits of Nos. 50-52, 53, 53a are plentiful and have been used to create forgeries of Nos. 66, 66a, 70 and 70a. They usually have a strong, complete inner frameline at right. On genuine stamps that line is weak or missing.

A8

Type I

Type II (error)

Shah Nasr-ed-Din

A9 A10

A11

Type I: Three dots at right end of scroll.
Type II: Two dots at right end of scroll.

1882-84 Engr.

No.	Design	Description	Unused	Used
53	A8	5s green, type I	50.00	1.50
		On cover, internal use		75.00
a.		5s green, type II	100.00	10.00
54	A9	10s buff, org & blk	85.00	10.00
55	A10	50c buff, org & blk	700.00	80.00
56	A10	50c gray & blk ('84)	150.00	70.00
57	A10	1fr blue & black	150.00	20.00
58	A10	5fr rose red & blk	140.00	20.00
59	A11	10fr buff, red & blk	150.00	30.00
		Nos. 53-59 (7)	1,425.	231.50

Crude forgeries of Nos. 58-59 exist. Halves of the 10s, 50c and 1fr surcharged with Farsi characters in red or black are frauds. The 50c and 1fr surcharged with a large "5" surrounded by rays are also frauds.

No. 59 used is valued for c-t-o.

For overprints and surcharges see Nos 66-72.

Very fine examples of Nos. 53-59 will have perforations cutting the outer colored border but clear of the inner framelines.

A12

Perf. 12-12½, 13

1885, March-May Litho.

No.	Design	Description	Unused	Used
59A	A12	5c blue	1,500.	50.00
a.		5c violet blue	1,500.	75.00
b.		5c ultramarine	1,500.	75.00
c.		5c dp reddish lilac	2,500.	300.00
d.		As "a," imperf	7,500.	

No. 59A was issued because of an urgent need for 5c stamps, pending the arrival of No. 62 in July. No. 59A has 88 sunrays instead of the 124 sunrays on the typographed stamp, No. 62.

A13

1885-86 Typo.

No.	Design	Description	Unused	Used
60	A12	1c green	25.00	2.00
61	A12	2c rose	25.00	2.00
62	A12	5c dull blue	200.00	1.00
		On cover, internal use		45.00
63	A13	10c brown	40.00	2.00
64	A13	1k slate	100.00	3.00
65	A13	5k dull vio ('86)	800.00	40.00
		Nos. 60-65 (6)	1,190.	50.00

Nos. 53, 54, 56 and 58 Surcharged in Black

a

b

c

d

e

f

1885

No.	Surch.	Description	Unused	Used
66	(a)	6c on 5s grn, type I	150.00	30.00
		On cover, international use		4,500.
a.		6c on 5s green, type II	*275.00*	*100.00*
67	(b)	12c on 50c gray & blk	150.00	30.00
68	(c)	18c on 10s buff, org & black	150.00	30.00
69	(d)	1t on 5fr rose red & black	150.00	50.00
		Nos. 66-69 (4)	600.00	140.00

1887

No.	Surch.	Description	Unused	Used
70	(e)	3c on 5s grn, type I	150.00	30.00
a.		3c on 5s green, type II	*275.00*	*100.00*
71	(a)	6c on 10s buff, org & blk	150.00	30.00
		On cover, international use		4,500.

72	(f)	8c on 50c gray & blk	150.00	30.00
		Nos. 70-72 (3)	450.00	90.00

The word "OFFICIEL" indicated that the surcharged stamps were officially authorized.

Surcharges on the same basic stamps of values other than those listed are believed to be bogus.

Counterfeits of Nos. 66-72 abound.

Very fine examples of Nos. 66-72 will have perforations cutting the outer colored border but clear of the inner framelines.

Beware of forgeries and/or reprints of most Iran stamps between the years 1870-1925. Scott values are for genuine stamps. Collectors should be aware that forgeries of many issues outnumber genuine examples by factors of 10 or 20 to one. Failing specialized knowledge on the part of the collector, these stamps should be examined or authenticated by acknowledged experts before purchase.

A14

A15

1889 Typo. *Perf. 11, 13½, 11x13½*

73	A14	1c pale rose	2.50	.75
74	A14	2c pale blue	2.50	.75
75	A14	5c lilac	1.50	.50
		On cover, internal use		40.00
76	A14	7c brown	7.50	1.50
		On cover, international use		1,500.
77	A15	10c black	2.50	.75
78	A15	1k red orange	4.50	.75
79	A15	2k rose	40.00	6.00
80	A15	5k green	25.00	6.00
		Nos. 73-80 (8)	86.00	17.00

All values exist imperforate.

Canceled to order stamps of No. 76 abound.

For surcharges see Nos. 622-625.

Nos. 73-80 with average centering, faded colors and/or toned paper sell for much less.

A16

A17

1891 *Perf. 10½, 11½*

81	A16	1c black	2.50	1.00
82	A16	2c brown	2.50	1.00
83	A16	5c deep blue	2.50	.25
		On cover, internal use		45.00
84	A16	7c gray	350.00	12.00
		On cover, international use		550.00
85	A16	10c rose	2.50	.50
86	A16	14c orange	2.50	1.50
87	A17	1k green	30.00	2.00
88	A17	2k orange	700.00	25.00
89	A17	5k ocher yellow	8.00	*30.00*
		Nos. 81-89 (9)	1,101.	73.25

For surcharges see Nos. 626-629.

A18

Nasser-eddin Shah Qajar — A19

1894 *Perf. 12½*

90	A18	1c lilac	1.00	.25
91	A18	2c blue green	1.00	.25
92	A18	5c ultramarine	1.00	.25
		On cover, internal use		30.00
93	A18	8c brown	1.00	.25
		Perf. 11½x11		
94	A19	10c orange	1.25	.75
		On cover, international use		350.00
95	A19	16c rose	25.00	*75.00*
96	A19	1k red & yellow	3.00	.75
97	A19	2k brn org & pale bl	4.00	1.00
98	A19	5k violet & silver	10.00	1.50
99	A19	10k red & gold	20.00	10.00
100	A19	50k green & gold	50.00	15.00
		Nos. 90-100 (11)	117.25	105.00

Canceled to order stamps sell for one-third of listed values.

Reprints exist. They are hard to distinguish from the originals. Value, set $15.

See Nos. 104-112, 136-144. For overprints see Nos. 120-128, 152-167, 173-181. For surcharges see Nos. 101-103, 168, 206, 211.

Nos. 93, 98 With Violet or Magenta Surcharge

a

b

1897 *Perf. 12½, 11½x11*

101	A18(a)	5c on 8c brn (V)	30.00	5.00
a.		Inverted surcharge	*150.00*	*25.00*
102	A19(b)	1k on 5k vio & sil (V)	40.00	20.00
103	A19(b)	2k on 5k vio & sil (M)	60.00	35.00
		Nos. 101-103 (3)	130.00	60.00

Forgeries exist.

Lion Type of 1894 and

Mozaffar-eddin Shah Qajar — A22

1898 Typo. *Perf. 12½*

104	A18	1c gray	5.00	.35
105	A18	2c pale brown	5.00	.35
106	A18	3c dull violet	10.00	3.00
107	A18	4c vermilion	10.00	3.00
108	A18	5c yellow	5.00	.25
		On cover, internal use		30.00
109	A18	8c orange	20.00	7.00
110	A18	10c light blue	5.00	.50
111	A18	12c rose	15.00	1.00
		On cover, international use		100.00
112	A18	16c green	20.00	7.00
113	A22	1k ultramarine	10.00	1.00
114	A22	2k pink	10.00	2.00
115	A22	3k yellow	10.00	3.00
116	A22	4k gray	10.00	5.00
117	A22	5k emerald	10.00	6.00
118	A22	10k orange	40.00	15.00
119	A22	50k bright vio	60.00	25.00
		Nos. 104-119 (16)	245.00	79.45

Unauthorized reprints of Nos. 104-119 were made from original clichés. Paper shows a vertical mesh. These abound unused and canceled to order. Value set, unused, hinged, $20.

See Nos. 145-151. For overprints see Nos. 129-135, 182-188. For surcharges see Nos. 169, 171, 207, 209, 211.

Reprints have been used to make counterfeits of Nos. 120-135, 152-167.

Stamps of 1898 Handstamped in Violet

a

b

c

d

e

f

g

h

1899

120	(a)	1c gray	5.00	5.00
121	(b)	2c pale brown	5.00	*8.00*
122	(b)	3c dull violet	12.00	*15.00*
123	(c)	4c vermilion	18.00	*30.00*
124	(c)	5c yellow	10.00	3.00
		On cover, internal use		65.00
125	(d)	8c orange	15.00	*40.00*
126	(d)	10c light blue	6.50	*10.00*
a.		Type "b" handstamp	*500.00*	*500.00*
127	(d)	12c rose	15.00	8.00
		On cover, international use		175.00
128	(d)	16c green	25.00	*30.00*
129	(e)	1k ultramarine	25.00	10.00
130	(f)	2k pink	30.00	25.00
131	(f)	3k yellow	80.00	*250.00*
132	(g)	4k gray	100.00	*250.00*
133	(g)	5k emerald	30.00	*40.00*
134	(h)	10k orange	60.00	60.00
135	(h)	50k brt violet	120.00	*150.00*
		Nos. 120-135 (16)	556.50	934.00

The handstamped control marks on Nos. 120-135 exist sideways, inverted and double. Counterfeits are plentiful.

Types of 1894-98

1899 Typo. *Perf. 12½*

136	A18	1c gray, *green*	7.50	.75
137	A18	2c brown, *green*	7.50	.75
138	A18	3c violet, *green*	20.00	5.00
139	A18	4c red, *green*	12.00	5.00
140	A18	5c yellow, *green*	5.00	.30
		On cover, internal use		30.00
141	A18	8c orange, *green*	15.00	5.00
142	A18	10c pale blue, *grn*	5.00	.50
143	A18	12c lake, *green*	15.00	1.25
		On cover, international use		45.00
144	A18	16c green, *green*	25.00	5.00
145	A22	1k red	30.00	1.25
146	A22	2k deep green	35.00	8.50
147	A22	3k lilac brown	35.00	17.00
148	A22	4k orange red	35.00	17.00
149	A22	5k gray brown	40.00	17.00
150	A22	10k deep blue	400.00	100.00
151	A22	50k brown	75.00	30.00
		Nos. 136-151 (16)	762.00	214.30

Canceled to order stamps abound.

Unauthorized reprints of Nos. 136-151 were made from original clichés. Paper is chalky and has white gum. The design can be seen through the back of the reprints. Value unused, hinged, set, $30.

For surcharges and overprints see Nos. 171, 173-188, 206-207, 209, 211.

Nos. 104-111 Handstamped in Violet

(Struck once on every two stamps.)

1900

152	A18	1c gray	50.00	20.00
153	A18	2c pale brown	60.00	25.00
154	A18	3c dull violet	150.00	70.00
155	A18	4c vermilion	150.00	70.00
156	A18	5c yellow	25.00	10.00
		On cover, internal use		85.00
158	A18	10c light blue	*2,500.*	*2,500.*
159	A18	12c rose	100.00	50.00
		On cover, international use		375.00
		Nos. 152-159 (7)	3,035.	2,745.

Values are for single authenticated stamps. Pairs sell for much more.

This control mark, in genuine state, was not applied to the 8c orange (Nos. 109, 125).

Same Overprint Handstamped on Nos. 120-127 in Violet

(Struck once on each block of 4.)

160	A18	1c gray	100.00	50.00
163	A18	4c vermilion	300.00	140.00
164	A18	5c yellow	50.00	20.00
		On cover, internal use		225.00
166	A18	10c light blue	1,250.	600.00
a.		Type "b" handstamp	500.00	250.00
167	A18	12c rose	150.00	50.00
		On cover, international use		425.00
		Nos. 160-167 (5)		860.00

Values are for single authenticated stamps. Blocks are rare and worth much more.

Counterfeits exist of Nos. 152-167.

No. 93 Surcharged in Violet

1900

168	A18	5c on 8c brown	50.00	2.50
a.		Inverted surcharge	*250.00*	*25.00*

No. 145 Surcharged in Violet

1901

169	A22	12c on 1k red	100.00	100.00
a.		Blue surcharge	125.00	125.00

Counterfeits exist.

Some specialists state that No. 169 with black surcharge was made for collectors.

A23

1902 Violet Surcharge

171	A23	5k on 50k brown	200.00	80.00
a.		Blue surcharge	200.00	90.00

Counterfeits exist. See No. 207.

Nos. 136-151 Overprinted in Black

1902

173	A18	1c gray, *green*	50.00	20.00
174	A18	2c brown, *green*	50.00	20.00
175	A18	3c violet, *green*	300.00	300.00
176	A18	4c red, *green*	400.00	*400.00*
177	A18	5c yellow, *green*	20.00	5.00
178	A18	8c orange, *green*	400.00	*400.00*
179	A18	10c pale blue, *grn*	50.00	15.00
180	A18	12c lake, *green*	125.00	50.00
181	A18	16c green, *green*	500.00	400.00
182	A22	1k red	100.00	45.00
183	A22	2k deep green	250.00	100.00
188	A22	50k brown	600.00	250.00

Overprinted on No. 168

206	A18	5c on 8c brown	200.00	100.00

Overprinted on Nos. 171 and 171a

207	A23	5k on 50k brown	200.00	100.00
a.		On #171a	250.00	100.00

Overprinted on Nos. 169 and 169a

209	A22	12c on 1k red	100.00	50.00
a.		On #169a	100.00	50.00

Counterfeits of the overprint of Nos. 173-183, 188, 206-207, 209 are plentiful. Practically all examples with overprint sideways, inverted, double and double with one inverted are frauds.

Nos. 142 Surcharged in Violet

1902

211 A18 5c on 10c pale bl, *grn* 60.00 20.00

Surcharges in different colors were made for collectors.

Initials of Victor Castaigne, Postmaster of Meshed — A24

1902 **Typo.** ***Imperf.***

222 A24 1c black 1,500. *450.00*
a. Inverted frame —
b. Inverted center — *3,000.*
223 A24 2c black 1,250. *450.00*
a. Inverted frame —
b. "2" in right upper corner *3,000.* *1,750.*
224 A24 3c black 3,250. *1,750.*
225 A24 5c violet 750.00 *200.00*
a. "5" in right upper corner —
b. Frame printed on both sides *2,250.* *1,000.*
c. Inverted center —
226 A24 5c black 900.00 *350.00*
a. Persian "5" in lower left corner —
b. Inverted center —
227 A24 12c dull blue 4,000. *1,500.*
a. Inverted frame —
b. Inverted center —
228 A24 1k rose 30,000. *3,500.*

Used values for Nos. 222-228 canceled to order are about ⅓ to ½ the values shown, which are for postally used stamps.

The design of No. 228, shown, differs slightly from the design of Nos. 222-227.

Nos. 222-228 were printed in three operations. Inverted centers have frames and numerals upright. Inverted frames have centers and numerals upright.

Pin-perforated

234 A24 12c dull blue 4,000. *1,500.*

Monsieur Victor Castaigne, the Belgian director of post and customs in the northwestern province of Khorassan, on his own intiiative, prepared a set of provisional stamps to meet the shortage of low-denomination stamps. These stamps were printed individually from two cliches, one for the frame and one for the vignette, reading V.C. (Castaigne's initials taken from his ring). Printed stamps were initialed by the director in red in for the shahis (ch) denominations and in violet ink for the 1k. Remainders exist posthumously canceled wtih fake MECHED postmarks. Various forgeries exist, including examples printed by two cliches for the frame and vignette, as well as one cliche for both. Values quoted are for examples accompanied by certificates of authenticity.

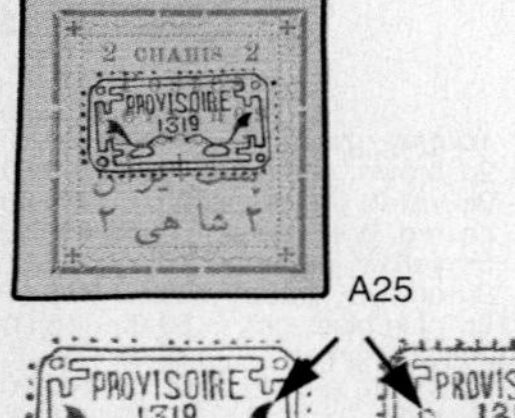

A25

Black Serpents Head — Hollow Serpents Head

TWO TYPES:

Type I — "CHAHI" or "KRANS" are in capital letters.

Type II — Only "C" of "Chahi" or "K" of "Krans" is a capital. The handstamp appears only on type I stamps and comes in two varieties: black serpent's head and hollow serpent's head.

The 3c and 5c sometimes have a tall narrow figure in the upper left corner. The 5c is also found with the cross at the upper left broken or missing. These varieties are known with many of the overprints.

Stamps of Design A25 have a faint fancy background in the color of the stamp. All issued stamps have handstamped controls as listed.

Type I
Handstamp Overprinted in Black

1902 **Typeset** ***Imperf.***

235 A25 1c gray & buff *300.00* 150.00
236 A25 2c brown & buff *400.00* 150.00
237 A25 3c green & buff *400.00* 150.00
238 A25 5c red & buff *300.00* 100.00
239 A25 12c ultra & buff *500.00* 150.00
Nos. 235-239 (5) *1,900.* 700.00

Counterfeits abound. Type II stamps with this overprint are forgeries.

The 3c with violet overprint is believed not to have been regularly issued.

Handstamp Overprinted in Rose

1902 **Type I**

247 A25 1c gray & buff 25.00 2.00
a. With Persian numerals "2" 100.00
248 A25 2c brown & buff 25.00 2.00
249 A25 3c dp grn & buff 25.00 2.00
250 A25 5c red & buff 25.00 .75
251 A25 10c ol yel & buff 50.00 3.00
252 A25 12c ultra & buff 75.00 5.00
253 A25 1k violet & bl 60.00 6.00
254 A25 2k ol grn & bl 100.00 12.50
256 A25 10k dk bl & bl 150.00 30.00
257 A25 50k red & blue 1,500. 800.00
Nos. 247-257 (10) 2,035. 863.25

A 5k exists but its status is doubtful. Value *$500.*

Stamps with handstamps other than bright red are either fake or were not regularly issued.

Type II

280 A25 1c gray & yellow 250.00 200.00
281 A25 2c brown & yel 200.00 200.00
282 A25 3c dk grn & yel *2,000.* *750.00*
a. "Persans" — —
283 A25 5c red & yellow 50.00 *15.00*
284 A25 10c ol yel & yel 100.00 15.00
285 A25 12c blue & yel 150.00 25.00
290 A25 50k org red & bl 1,250. 600.00

The 3c, inscribed "Persans," was never issued.

Denominations with handstamps other than bright red are either fake or not regularly issued.

Remainders exist with fake control handstamps.

Type II stamps with high denominations of 10t (100k), 20t, 25t, 50t and 100t with blue rosette 1319 handstamps and black control numbers on the front were used on postal money orders. Denominations with control numbers in colors other than black are forgeries.

> Beware of forgeries and/or reprints of most Iran stamps between the years 1870-1925. Scott values are for genuine stamps. Collectors should be aware that forgeries of many issues outnumber genuine examples by factors of 10 or 20 to one. Lacking specialized knowledge on the part of the collector, these stamps should be examined or authenticated by acknowledged experts before purchase.

Handstamp Surcharged in Black

1902 **Type I**

308 A25 5k on 5k ocher & bl *200.00* *50.00*

Counterfeits of No. 308 abound.

This surcharge in rose, violet, blue or green is considered bogus.

This surcharge on 50k orange red and blue, and on 5k ocher and blue, type II, is considered bogus.

Handstamp Overprinted Diagonally in Black

1902 **Type I**

315 A25 2c brown & buff 250.00 125.00
a. Rose overprint *500.00* *500.00*

Type II

316 A25 2c brown & yel — —
a. Rose overprint — —

"P. L." stands for "Poste Locale."

Counterfeits of Nos. 315-316 exist.

Some specialists believe that Type II stamps were not used officially for this overprint.

Handstamp Overprinted in Black or Rose

1902 **Type II**

317 A25 2c brn & yellow 250.00 125.00
318 A25 2c brown & yel (R) *500.00* *500.00*

Counterfeits of Nos. 317-318 exist.

Overprinted in Blue

1903 **Type I**

321 A25 1k violet & blue 125.00 125.00

Type II

336 A25 1c gray & yellow 60.00 60.00
337 A25 2c brown & yellow 60.00 60.00
338 A25 5c red & yellow 40.00 40.00
339 A25 10c olive yel & yel 75.00 75.00
340 A25 12c blue & yellow 90.00 90.00
Nos. 321-340 (6) 450.00 450.00

A 3c Type I exists but was not regularly issued. Value $250.

The overprint also exists in violet and black, but it is doubtful whether such items were regularly issued.

Forgeries of Nos. 321, 336-340 abound. Genuine unused examples are seldom found.

Arms of Persia — A26

Mozaffar-eddin Shah Qajar — A27

1902 (Dec.)-1904 **Typo.** ***Perf. 12½***

351 A26 1c violet 2.00 .25
352 A26 2c gray 2.00 .25
353 A26 3c green 2.00 .25
354 A26 5c rose 2.00 .25
355 A26 10c yellow brn 3.00 1.50
356 A26 12c blue 4.00 .50

Engr.

Perf. 11½x11

357 A27 1k violet 15.00 .50
358 A27 2k ultramarine 25.00 1.25
359 A27 5k orange brn 40.00 2.00
360 A27 10k rose red 50.00 4.00
361 A27 20k orange ('04) 45.00 5.00
362 A27 30k green ('04) 70.00 12.50
363 A27 50k green 550.00 100.00
Nos. 351-363 (13) 810.00 128.25

No. 355 exists with blue diagonal surcharge "1 CHAHI"; its status is questioned.

A government decree in November, 1903, required that all picture postcards be censored by the Central Post Office, which would apply a control mark on each card to show that the 2c tax for this service had been paid. No. 352 was overprinted "Controle" in several styles, for this purpose. Value: unused $100; used, from $25.

See Nos. 428-433. For surcharges and overprints see #364-420, 446-447, 464-469, O8-O28, P1.

No. 353 Surcharged in Violet or Blue

1903

364 A26 1c on 3c green (V) 75.00 25.00
365 A26 2c on 3c green (Bl) 75.00 25.00

A 2c surcharge on No. 354 exists, but its status is dubious.

No. 360 Surcharged in Blue

366 A27 12c on 10k rose red 75.00 40.00
a. Black surcharge 150.00 70.00
b. Violet surcharge 150.00 70.00
Nos. 364-366 (3) 225.00 90.00

Nos. 366, 366a and 366b used are valued canceled to order.

No. 363 Surcharged in Blue or Black

1903

368 A27 2t on 50k grn (Bl) 200.00 60.00
a. Rose surcharge 225.00 100.00
b. Black surcharge 225.00 100.00
370 A27 3t on 50k grn (Bk) 200.00 60.00
a. Violet surcharge 225.00 60.00
b. Rose surcharge 250.00 125.00

No. 363 Surcharged in Blue or Black

1904

372 A27 2t on 50k grn (Bl) 200.00 60.00
375 A27 3t on 50k grn (Bk) 200.00 60.00

The 2t on 50k also exists with surcharge in rose, violet, black and magenta; the 3t on 50k in rose, violet and blue. Values about the same unused; about 50 percent higher used.

No. 352 Overprinted in Violet

1904 ***Perf. 12½***

393 A26 2c gray 100.00 25.00
a. Black overprint 150.00 50.00
b. Rose overprint 135.00 35.00

This overprint also exists in blue, violet blue, maroon and gray, but these were not regularly issued.

Stamps of 1903 Surcharged in Black

a

b

c

1904
400 A26(a) 3c on 5c rose 40.00 .75
401 A26(b) 6c on 10c brown 75.00 .75
402 A27(c) 9c on 1k violet 50.00 3.50
Nos. 400-402 (3) 165.00 5.00

Stamps of 1903 Surcharged in Black, Magenta or Violet

1905-06
404 A26 1c on 3c green ('06) 75.00 25.00
405 A27 1c on 1k violet 35.00 15.00
406 A27 2c on 5k orange brn 40.00 25.00
407 A26 1c on 3c grn (M) ('06) 15.00 5.00
408 A27 1c on 1k violet (M) 20.00 10.00
409 A27 2c on 5k org brn (V) 30.00 15.00
Nos. 404-409 (6) 215.00 95.00

Nos. 355 and 358 Surcharged in Violet

1906
419 A26 1c on 10c brown *150.00* —
420 A27 2c on 2k ultra *250.00* —

These stamps were prepared on the initiative of the Tabriz postmaster. Tabriz is the capital of the northeastern province of Azerbaijan.

Forgeries of Nos. 419-420 are common. Forgeries of No. 420, especially, are hard to distinguish since the original handstamp was used. Genuine used stamps may, in some cases, be identified by the cancellation.

A28

Typeset; "Provisoire" Overprint Handstamped in Black

1906 ***Imperf.***
422 A28 1c violet 25.00 1.00
a. Irregular pin perf. or perf. 10½ 75.00 25.00
423 A28 2c gray 150.00 10.00
424 A28 3c green 25.00 1.00
425 A28 6c red 25.00 .75
426 A28 10c brown 70.00 *40.00*
427 A28 13c blue 50.00 10.00
Nos. 422-427 (6) 345.00 62.75

Stamps of type A28 have a faint background pattern of tiny squares within squares, an ornamental frame and open rectangles for the value corners.

The 3c and 6c also exist perforated.

Nos. 422-427 are known without overprint but were probably not issued in that condition. Nearly all values are known with overprint inverted and double.

Forgeries are plentiful.

Lion Type of 1903 and

Mohammed-Ali Shah Qajar
A29 A30

1907-09 **Typo.** ***Perf. 12½***
428 A26 1c vio, *blue* 5.00 .25
429 A26 2c gray, *blue* 5.00 .25
430 A26 3c green, *blue* 5.00 .25
431 A26 6c rose, *blue* 5.00 .25
432 A26 9c org, *blue* 5.00 .30
433 A26 10c brown, *blue* 6.00 1.00

Engr.
Perf. 11, 11½
434 A29 13c dark blue 10.00 2.00
435 A29 1k red 10.00 1.50
436 A29 26c red brown 10.00 2.00
437 A29 2k deep grn 30.00 1.50
438 A29 3k pale blue 30.00 1.00
439 A29 4k brt yellow 500.00 17.50
440 A29 4k bister 30.00 3.00
441 A29 5k dark brown 35.00 3.00
442 A29 10k pink 40.00 3.00
443 A29 20k gray black 40.00 10.00
444 A29 30k dark violet 45.00 15.00
445 A30 50k gold, ver & black ('09) 165.00 30.00
Nos. 428-445 (18) 976.00 91.80

Frame of No. 445 lithographed. Nos. 434-444 were issued in 1908.

Remainders canceled to order abound. Used values for Nos. 437-445 are for c-t-os.

Nos. 428-429 Overprinted in Black

1909 ***Perf. 12½***
446 A26 1c violet, *blue* 90.00 40.00
447 A26 2c gray, *blue* 80.00 30.00

Counterfeits of Nos. 446-447 exist.

Coat of Arms — A31

1909 **Typo.** ***Perf. 12½x12***
448 A31 1c org & maroon *.50* .35
449 A31 2c vio & maroon *.50* .35
450 A31 3c yel grn & mar *.50* .35
451 A31 6c red & maroon *.50* .25
452 A31 9c gray & maroon *.50* .35
453 A31 10c red vio & mar *.50* .35
454 A31 13c dk blue & mar *.50* *2.00*
455 A31 1k sil, vio & bis brn *1.00* *2.00*
456 A31 26c dk grn & mar *1.00* *3.00*
457 A31 2k sil, dk grn & bis brown *1.00* *2.00*
458 A31 3k sil, gray & bis brn *1.00* *3.50*
459 A31 4k sil, by & bis brn *1.00* *3.50*
460 A31 5k gold, brn & bis brn *2.50* *3.50*
461 A31 10k gold, org & bis brn *5.00* *10.00*
462 A31 20k gold, ol grn & bis brn *7.00* 20.00
463 A31 30k gold, car & bis brn *12.00* *20.00*
Nos. 448-463 (16) 35.00 71.50

Unauthorized reprints of Nos. 448-463 abound. Originals have clean, bright colors, centers stand out clearly, and paper is much thinner. Nos. 460-463 originals have gleaming gold margins; reprint margins appear as blackish yellow. Centers of reprints of Nos. 448-454, 456 are brown.

Values above are for unused reprints and for authenticated used stamps. Original unused stamps sell for much higher prices.

For surcharges & overprints see Nos. 516-519, 541-549. 582-585, 588-594, 597, 601-606, 707-722, C1-C16, O31-O40.

In 1909 two sets of 16 stamps were prepared for the coronation of Ahmad Shad Qajar. The first set with lion and sun high values and gold borders was for postal use, while the second set with city gate high values and silver borders was inscribed "SERVICE". While neither set was placed in use, both were sold to collectors at a later date.

Nos. 428-444, Imperf., Surcharged in Red or Black

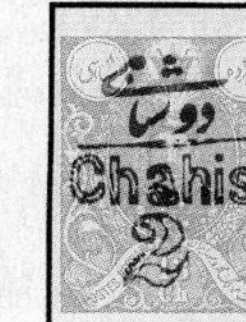

1910 **Blue Paper** ***Imperf.***
464 A26 1c on 1c violet 200.00 140.00
465 A26 1c on 2c gray 200.00 140.00
466 A26 1c on 3c green 200.00 140.00
467 A26 1c on 6c rose (Bk) 200.00 140.00
468 A26 1c on 9c orange 200.00 140.00
469 A26 1c on 10c brown 200.00 140.00

White Paper
470 A29 2c on 13c dp bl 200.00 140.00
471 A29 2c on 26c red brn (Bk) 200.00 140.00
472 A29 2c on 1k red (Bk) 200.00 140.00
473 A29 2c on 2k dp grn 200.00 140.00
474 A29 2c on 3k pale bl 200.00 140.00
475 A29 2c on 4k brt yel 200.00 140.00
476 A29 2c on 4k bister 200.00 140.00
477 A29 2c on 5k dk brn 200.00 140.00
478 A29 2c on 10k pink (Bk) 200.00 140.00
479 A29 2c on 20k gray blk 200.00 140.00
480 A29 2c on 30k dk vio 200.00 140.00
Nos. 464-480 (17) 3,400. 2,380.

Nos. 464-480 were prepared for use on newspapers, but nearly the entire printing was sold to stamp dealers. The issue is generally considered speculative. Counterfeit surcharges exist on trimmed stamps.

Used values are for c-t-o.

Early printings of Nos. 481-500 were made by wet printing, while later issues were mostly produced by dry printing. As a result, there are two heights of the central (engraved) vignette, 23mm (dry printing) and 22½ (wet printing), caused by the shrinkage of the paper as it dried after printing.

Ahmad Shah Qajar — A32

Engr. center, Typo. frame

1911-21

Tall Portrait (23mm)

Perf. 11½
481 A32 1c green & org .50 1.00
482 A32 2c red & sepia .50 1.00
483 A32 3c gray brn & grn .50 1.00
483B A32 3c 3c bister brown & green .50 1.00
484 A32 5c brn & car ('13) .50
485 A32 6c gray & car .50 .30
486 A32 6c grn & red brn ('13) .50 .40
487 A32 9c yel brn & vio .75 2.00
488 A32 10c red & org brn .75 35.00
489 A32 12c grn & ultra ('13) .50 .50
490 A32 13c violet & ultra 1.00 2.00
491 A32 1k ultra & car 1.00 4.00
492 A32 24c vio & grn ('13) .50 .50
493 A32 26c ultra & green 1.00 5.00
494 A32 2k grn & red vio 2.00 2.00
495 A32 3k violet & blk 2.00 4.00
496 A32 4k ultra & gray ('13) —
497 A32 5k red & ultra 3.00 4.00
498 A32 10k ol bis & cl 5.00 5.00
499 A32 20k vio brn & bis 5.00 5.00
500 A32 30k red & green 7.00 5.00
Nos. 481-500 (21) 33.00 78.70

Values for Nos. 481-500 unused are for reprints, which cannot be distinguished from the late printings of the stamps.

The reprints include inverted centers for some denominations. Values, each $30-$50.

For surcharges and overprints see Nos. 501-515, 520-540, 586-587, 595, 596, 598, 600, 607-609, 630-634, 646-666.

Perf. 11½x11
481a A32 1c green & org 10.00 .25
Never hinged 20.00
482a A32 2c red & sepia 20.00 .25
Never hinged 30.00
483a A32 3c gray brn & grn 25.00 .25
Never hinged 35.00
483Ba A32 3c bister brn & grn ('21) 60.00 3.00
Never hinged 80.00
484a A32 5c brn & car ('13) 35.00 .40
Never hinged 50.00
485a A32 6c gray & car 30.00 .30
Never hinged 40.00
486a A32 6c grn & red brown ('13) 35.00 .40
Never hinged 45.00
487a A32 9c yel brn & violet 40.00 .25
Never hinged 50.00
488a A32 10c red & org brn 55.00 .25
Never hinged 75.00
489a A32 12c grn & ultra ('13) 45.00 .50
Never hinged 60.00
490a A32 13c violet & ultra 60.00 2.00
Never hinged 75.00
491a A32 1k ultra & carmine 200.00 1.00
Never hinged 300.00
492a A32 24c ultra & carmine 60.00 .50
Never hinged 75.00
494a A32 2k green & red vio 115.00 1,00
Never hinged 140.00
495a A32 3k violet & black 170.00 4.00
Never hinged 200.00
497a A32 5k red & ultra 150.00 4.00
Never hinged 200.00
498a A32 10k ol bis & claret 500.00 5.00
Never hinged 650.00
499a A32 20k vio brn & bister 500.00 5.00
Never hinged 650.00
500a A32 30k red & green 500.00 5.00
Never hinged 650.00
Nos. 481a-500a (18) 2,410. 31.45

Perf. 11½x12
488b A32 10c red & org brn 75.00 25.00
Never hinged 100.00
490b A32 13c violet & ultra 75.00 2.00
Never hinged 100.00
493b A32 26c ultra & green 250.00 75.00
Never hinged 350.00
496b A32 4k ultra & gray ('13) 450.00 100.00
Never hinged 600.00
497b A32 5k red & ultra 300.00 50.00
Never hinged 350.00
Nos. 488b-497b (5) 1,150. 252.00

No. 496b with inverted center is a reprint. Value, $50.

Short Portrait (22½mm)

Perf. 11½
481c A32 1c green & org 50.00 20.00
Never hinged 85.00
482c A32 2c red & sepia 85.00 20.00
Never hinged 100.00
483c A32 3c gray brn & grn 70.00 10.00
Never hinged 95.00
484c A32 5c brn & car ('13) — —
485c A32 6c gray & car 35.00 5.00
Never hinged 50.00
487c A32 9c yel brn & violet 30.00 5.00
Never hinged 40.00
491c A32 1k ultra & carmine —
493c A32 26c ultra & green 135.00 15.00
Never hinged 175.00
494c A32 2k green & red vio 300.00
Never hinged 400.00
495c A32 3k violet & black 65.00
Never hinged 100.00
496c A32 4k violet & black ('13) —
500c A32 30k red & green 800.00 75.00
Never hinged 950.00
Nos. 481c-500c (12) 1,570. 150.00

No. 491c is known only with the "Controlle 1922" overprint. Nos. 494c and 495c were apparently never used.

Perf. 11½x11
481d A32 1c green & org 35.00 1.00
Never hinged 50.00
482d A32 2c red & sepia 85.00 10.00
Never hinged 100.00
483d A32 3c gray brn & grn 70.00 10.00
Never hinged 95.00
485d A32 6c gray & car 60.00 3.00
Never hinged 75.00
488d A32 10c red & org brn 95.00 30.00
Never hinged 110.00
490d A32 13c violet & ultra 75.00 2.00
Never hinged 100.00
491d A32 1k ultra & carmine 125.00 2.00
Never hinged 175.00
493d A32 26c ultra & green 70.00 15.00
Never hinged 85.00
494d A32 2k green & red vio 150.00 2.00
Never hinged 200.00
495d A32 3k violet & black 300.00 10.00
Never hinged 400.00
497d A32 5k red & ultra 350.00 20.00
Never hinged 400.00

498d A32 10k ol bis & claret 650.00 75.00
Never hinged 750.00
Nos. 481d-498d (12) 2,065. 180.00

Perf. 11½x12

493e A32 26c ultra & green 500.00 100.00
Never hinged 600.00
494e A32 2k green & red vio 400.00 30.00
Never hinged 600.00
495e A32 3k violet & black 400.00 35.00
Never hinged 600.00
496e A32 4k violet & black ('13) 600.00 150.00
Never hinged 750.00
498e A32 10k ol bis & claret 700.00 50.00
Never hinged 800.00
499e A32 20k vio brn & bister 800.00 75.00
Never hinged 950.00
Nos. 493e-499e (6) 3,400. 440.00

Stamps of 1911 Overprinted in Black

1911 "Officiel" Overprint
On Nos. 481/500

1911 Tall Portrait *Perf. 11½*

503 A32 3c gray brn & grn 50.00 8.00
Never hinged 100.00
504 A32 6c gray & car 50.00 8.00
Never hinged 100.00
507 A32 13c vio & ultra 125.00 12.00
Never hinged 200.00
509 A32 26c ultra & green 175.00 15.00
Never hinged 300.00
513 A32 10k ol bis & claret 1,350. 75.00
Never hinged 2,250.
Nos. 503-513 (5) 1,750. 118.00

On Nos. 481a/500a

Perf. 11½x11

501 A32 1c green & org 50.00 8.00
Never hinged 100.00
502 A32 2c red & sepia 50.00 8.00
Never hinged 100.00
503a A32 3c gray brn & grn 50.00 8.00
Never hinged 100.00
504a A32 6c gray & carmine 20.00
506 A32 10c red & org brn 85.00 12.00
Never hinged 170.00
508 A32 1k ultra & car *195.00 15.00*
Never hinged *350.00*
510 A32 2k grn & red vio 225.00 17.00
Never hinged 400.00
511 A32 3k vio & black 300.00 25.00
Never hinged 500.00
512 A32 5k red & ultra 350.00 50.00
Never hinged 650.00
513a A32 10k ol bis & claret 1,350. 75.00
Never hinged 2,250.
514 A32 20k vio brn & bis 1,150. 85.00
Never hinged 2,250.
515 A32 30k red & green 1,350. 90.00
Never hinged 2,300.
Nos. 501-515 (12) 5,155. 413.00

Short Portrait
On Nos. 481c/500c

Perf. 11½

501c A32 1c green & org 20.00
502c A32 2c red & sepia 20.00
503c A32 3c gray brn & grn 20.00
504c A32 6c gray & carmine 70.00 12.00
Never hinged 150.00
505 A32 9c yel brn & vio 70.00 12.00
Never hinged 150.00
515c A32 30k red & green 1,500. 100.00
Never hinged 3,000.
Nos. 501c-515c (6) 1,640. 184.00

On Nos. 481d/514d

Perf. 11½x11

501d A32 1c green & org 70.00 12.00
Never hinged 150.00
502d A32 2c red & sepia 70.00 12.00
Never hinged 150.00
503d A32 3c gray brn & grn 70.00 12.00
Never hinged 150.00
504d A32 6c gray & carmine 70.00 12.00
Never hinged 150.00
506d A32 10c red & org brn 85.00 12.00
Never hinged 170.00
507d A32 13c violet & ultra 125.00 12.00
Never hinged 200.00
508d A32 1k ultra & carmine 95.00
509d A32 26c ultra & grn 175.00 15.00
Never hinged 300.00
510d A32 2k grn & red violet 225.00 17.00
Never hinged 400.00
511d A32 3k violet & black 300.00 25.00
Never hinged 500.00
512d A32 5k red & ultra 350.00 50.00
Never hinged 650.00
513d A32 10k olive bister & claret 1,500. 85.00
Never hinged 3,000.
514d A32 20k vio brn & bis 1,250. 90.00
Never hinged 2,250.
Nos. 501d-514d (13) 4,290. 449.00

The "Officiel" overprint does not signify that the stamps were intended for use on official correspondence but that they were issued by authority. It was applied to the stocks in Tabriz and all post offices in the Tabriz region after a large quantity of stamps had been stolen during the Russian occupation of Tabriz.

The "Officiel" overprint has been counterfeited.

Stamps of 1909-11 Overprinted in Black

1911, Oct. On #449-451, 454

516 A31 2c vio & maroon 300.00 150.00
517 A31 3c yel grn & mar 300.00 150.00
518 A31 6c red & maroon 300.00 150.00
519 A31 13c dk blue & mar 300.00 150.00
Nos. 516-519 (4) 1,200. 600.00

On Nos. 482a/490s

520 A32 2c red & sepia (on #482a) 300.00 150.00
b. On #482c — —
c. On #482d — —
521 A32 3c gray brn & grn (on #483d) — —
a. On #483a 300.00 150.00
522 A32 6c gray & car (on #485) 125.00 75.00
a. On #485a — —
b. On #485c — —
c. On #485d — —
523 A32 13c violet & ultra (on #490) 200.00 125.00
a. On #490a — —
b. On #490d — —
Nos. 520-523 (4) 625.00 350.00

Stamps were sold at a 10% discount to stagecoach station keepers on the Tehran-Recht route. To prevent speculation, these stamps were overprinted "Stagecoach Stations" in French and Farsi.

Forgeries exist, usually overprinted on reprints of the 1909 issue and used examples of the 1911 issue. Values are for authenticated stamps.

In 1912 this overprint, reading 'Sultan Mohammad Ali Shah Qajar,' was hand-stamped on outgoing mail in the Persian Kurdistan region occupied by the forces of the former Shah Mohammad Ali. It was applied after the stamps were on cover and is found on 8 of the Shah Ahmed stamps of 1911 (1c, 2c, 3c, 6c, 9c, 13c, 1k and 26c). Two covers are known with 10c stamp.

Nos. 490 and 493 Surcharged

a

b

1914

535 A32(a) 1c on 13c (on #490) 30.00 2.00
Never hinged 60.00
a. On #490a 30.00 2.00
Never hinged 60.00
b. On #490b) 30.00 2.00
Never hinged 60.00
c. On #490d 30.00 2.00
Never hinged 60.00
536 A32(b) 3c on 26c (on #493) 30.00 4.00
Never hinged 60.00
a. On #493b 30.00 2.00
Never hinged 60.00
b. On #493c 30.00 2.00
Never hinged 60.00
c. on 26c (on #493d) 30.00 2.00
Never hinged 60.00
d. On #493e 30.00 2.00
Never hinged 60.00

In 1914 a set of 19 stamps was prepared as a coronation issue. The 10 lower values each carry a different portrait; the 9 higher values show buildings and scenes. Value $2,500 each set. The same set printed with black centers was overprinted in red "SERVICE."

Nos. 484 and 489 Surcharged in Black or Violet

c

d

1915

537 A32(c) 1c on 5c (on #484a) 20.00 2.00
Never hinged 40.00
538 A32(c) 2c on 5c (on #484a) 200.00 40.00
Never hinged 300.00
539 A32(c) 2c on 5c (V) (on #484a) 20.00 2.00
Never hinged 40.00
540 A32(d) 6c on 12c (on #489a) 30.00 2.00
Never hinged 60.00
Nos. 537-540 (4) 270.00 46.00

Nos. 455, 454 Surcharged

e

f

1915 *Perf. 12½x12*

541 A31(e) 5c on 1k multi 75.00 5.00
542 A31(f) 12c on 13c multi 110.00 7.00

Counterfeit surcharges on reprints abound.

Nos. 448-453, 455 Overprinted

1915

543 A31 1c org & maroon 70.00 5.00
544 A31 2c vio & maroon 50.00 5.00
545 A31 3c grn & maroon 60.00 5.00
546 A31 6c red & maroon 60.00 5.00
547 A31 9c gray & maroon 100.00 7.00
548 A31 10c red vio & mar 150.00 10.00
549 A31 1k sil, vio & bis brn 250.00 10.00
Nos. 543-549 (7) 740.00 47.00

This overprint ("1333") also exists on the 2k, 10k, 20k and 30k, but they were not issued.

Counterfeit overprints, usually on reprints, abound.

Beware of forgeries and/or reprints of most Iran stamps between the years 1870-1925. Scott values are for genuine stamps. Collectors should be aware that forgeries of many issues outnumber genuine examples by factors of 10 or 20 to one. Failing specialized knowledge on the part of the collector, these stamps should be examined or authenticated by acknowledged experts before purchase.

Imperial Crown — A33

King Darius, Farvahar overhead — A34

Ruins of Persepolis — A35

Perf. 11½ or Compound 11x11½
Engr., Typo.

1915, Mar. Wmk. 161

560 A33 1c car & indigo .25 *2.00*
561 A33 2c bl & carmine .25 *2.00*
562 A33 3c dark green .25 *2.00*
a. Inverted center —
564 A33 5c red .25 *2.50*
565 A33 6c olive grn & car .25 *2.00*
a. Inverted center —
566 A33 9c yel brn & vio .25 *2.00*
567 A33 10c bl grn & yel brn .25 *2.00*
568 A33 12c ultramarine .25 *2.00*
569 A34 1k sil, yel brn & gray .65 *5.00*
570 A33 24c yel brn & dk brn .25 *5.00*
571 A34 2k silver, bl & rose .65 *5.00*
572 A34 3k sil, vio & brn .65 *5.00*
573 A34 5k sil, brn & green .65 *7.00*
574 A35 1t gold, pur & blk .65 *10.00*
575 A35 2t gold, grn & brn 1.00 *10.00*
576 A35 3t gold, cl & red brn 1.00 *10.00*
577 A35 5t gold, blue & ind 1.00 *10.00*
Nos. 560-577 (17) 8.50 *83.50*

Coronation of Shah Ahmed.

Nos. 560-568, 570 are engraved. Nos. 569, 571-573 are engraved except for silver margins. Nos. 574-577 have centers engraved, frames typographed.

The 3c and 6c with inverted centers are considered genuine errors. Unauthorized reprints exist of these varieties and of other denominations with inverted centers. **Values unused for Nos. 560-577 are for reprints.**

For surcharges and overprints see Nos. 610-616, 635-646, O41-O57, Q19-Q35.

Nos. 455, 461-463 Overprinted

1915 Unwmk. Typo. *Perf. 12½x12*

582 A31 1k sil, vio & bis brn *2.00 20.00*
583 A31 10k multicolored *5.00 30.00*
584 A31 20k multicolored *10.00 100.00*
585 A31 30k multicolored *12.00 60.00*
Nos. 582-585 (4) *29.00 210.00*

Genuine unused examples are rare. Most unused stamps offered in the marketplace are reprints, and the unused values above are for reprints. Used values for authenticated stamps.

Forgeries abound of Nos. 582-585.

In May 1917, 17 contemporaneous Russian stamps overprinted "Occupation Azerbayedjan" appeared on the philatelic market. These were a bogus production, purportedly prepared by Anglo-Russian forces in occupation of the province of Azerbaijan in Iran. While

British and Russian troops were indeed in the province at that time, they were there strictly to support Persian forces against the Turks, and were in no sense occupiers. Covers canceled with the consular handstamp of Tabriz were privately created to lend credence to the issue. Later, other covers were created using a forged October 1917 datestamp of Baku, causing subsequent catalogs to attribute them to the Russian province of Azerbaijan. The issue has been extensively forged.

No. 491 Surcharged

1917 ***Perf. 11½***

586 A32 12c on 1k multi (on #491a) *2,500.* *3,500.*
Never hinged 3,500.
587 A32 24c on 1k multi (on #491a) *1,500.* *1,750.*
Never hinged 2,500.

Issued during the Turkish occupation of Kermanshah. Forgeries exist.
Values for unused stamps are for reprints.

No. 448 Overprinted "1335" in Persian Numerals

1917 ***Perf. 12½x12***

588 A31 1c org & maroon *350.00* 250.00

Overprint on No. 588 is similar to date in "k" and "l" surcharges. Forgeries exist.

Nos. 449, 452-453, 456 Surcharged

k

l

1917

589 A31(k) 1c on 2c 30.00 3.00
590 A31(k) 1c on 9c 40.00 4.00
591 A31(k) 1c on 10c 30.00 3.00
592 A31(l) 3c on 9c 50.00 4.00
593 A31(l) 3c on 10c 40.00 3.00
594 A31(l) 3c on 26c 40.00 5.00

Same Surcharge on No. 488

595 A32(k) 1c on 10c (on #488) 75.00 2.00
Never hinged 125.00
a. On #488a 75.00 2.00
Never hinged 125.00
b. On #488d 75.00 2.00
Never hinged 125.00
596 A32(l) 3c on 10c (on #488) 75.00 2.00
Never hinged 125.00
a. On #488a 75.00 2.00
Never hinged 125.00
b. On #488d 100.00 2.00
Never hinged 150.00

Nos. 454 & 491 Surcharged Type "e"

597 A31 5c on 13c 50.00 5.00
598 A32 5c on 1k (on #489a) 75.00 2.00
Never hinged 125.00

Counterfeit surcharges on "canceled" reprints of Nos. 449, 452-454, 456 abound.

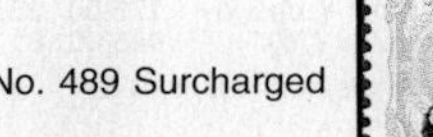
No. 489 Surcharged

600 A32 6c on 12c grn & ultra (on #489a) 125.00 20.00
Never hinged 220.00

No. 457 Overprinted

1918

601 A31 2k multi 175.00 25.00

Nos. 459-460 Surcharged

1918

602 A31 24c on 4k multi 150.00 25.00
603 A31 10k on 5k multi 175.00 25.00

The surcharges of Nos. 602-603 have been counterfeited.

Nos. 457-463 Overprinted

1918

603A A31 2k multicolored *3.00* *65.00*
604 A31 3k multicolored *3.00* *15.00*
604A A31 4k multicolored *5.00* *150.00*
604B A31 5k multicolored *5.00* *75.00*
605 A31 10k multicolored *8.00* *50.00*
605A A31 20k multicolored *20.00* *200.00*
606 A31 30k multicolored *15.00* *100.00*
Nos. 603A-606 (7) *59.00* *655.00*

Genuine unused examples are rare. Most unused stamps offered in the marketplace are reprints, and the unused values above are for reprints. Used values for authenticated stamps.
Forgeries abound of Nos. 603A-606.

Nos. 489, 488 and 491 Surcharged

m

n

607 A32(m) 3c on 12c (on #489a) 75.00 2.00
Never hinged 125.00
608 A32(n) 6c on 10c (on #489a) 100.00 2.00
Never hinged 200.00
609 A32(m) 6c on 1k (on #491) 75.00 2.00
Never hinged 125.00
a. On #491a 75.00 2.00
Never hinged 125.00
Nos. 607-609 (3) 250.00 6.00

Nos. 571-577 Overprinted in Black or Red

1918 **Wmk. 161**

610 A34 2k sil, blue & rose 15.00 15.00
611 A34 3k sil, vio & brn (R) 15.00 15.00
612 A34 5k sil, brn & grn (R) 15.00 15.00
613 A35 1t gold, pur & black (R) 20.00 20.00
614 A35 2t gold, grn & brn 20.00 20.00
615 A35 3t gold, cl & red brn 20.00 20.00
616 A35 5t gold, bl & ind (R) 25.00 25.00
Nos. 610-616 (7) 130.00 130.00

The overprint commemorates the end of World War I. Counterfeits of this overprint are plentiful.

A36

Color Litho., Black Typo.

1919 **Unwmk.** ***Perf. 11½***

617 A36 1c yel & black 25.00 2.00
618 A36 3c green & black 25.00 2.00
619 A36 5c rose & black 65.00 5.00
620 A36 6c vio & black 45.00 2.00
621 A36 12c blue & black 150.00 15.00
Nos. 617-621 (5) 310.00 26.00

Nos. 617-621 exist imperf.
This issue has been extensively counterfeited, and most examples in the marketplace are forgeries.
Counterfeits having double line over "POSTES" abound.

Nos. 75, 85-86 Surcharged in Various Colors

1919 ***Perf. 10½, 11, 11½, 13½***

622 A14 2k on 5c lilac (Bk) 15.00 15.00
623 A14 3k on 5c lilac (Br) 15.00 15.00
624 A14 4k on 5c lilac (G) 15.00 15.00
625 A14 5k on 5c lilac (V) 15.00 15.00
626 A16 10k on 10c rose (Bl) 25.00 25.00
627 A16 20k on 10c rose (G) 25.00 25.00
628 A16 30k on 10c rose (Br) 25.00 25.00
629 A16 50k on 14c org (V) 30.00 30.00
Nos. 622-629 (8) 165.00 165.00

Nos. 622-629 exist with inverted and double surcharge. Some specialists consider these fraudulent. Forgeries exist.

Nos. 486, 489 Handstamp Surcharged

1921 ***Perf. 11½, 11½x11***

630 A32 10c on 6c (on #486) 100.00 25.00
No gum 50.00
Never hinged 150.00
a. On #486a 100.00 25.00
No gum 50.00
Never hinged 150.00
631 A32 1k on 12c (on #489) 100.00 25.00
No gum 50.00
Never hinged 150.00
a. On #489a 100.00 25.00
No gum 50.00
Never hinged 150.00

Counterfeits exist.

No. 489 Surcharged

632 A32 6c on 12c (on #489) 650.00 20.00
No gum 250.00
Never hinged 800.00
a. On #489a 650.00 20.00
No gum 250.00
Never hinged 800.00

Surcharged in Black or Violet

1921

633 A32 10c on 6c (V) (on #486) *200.00* *50.00*
No gum *100.00*
Never hinged *300.00*
a. Surcharge handstamped in black 400.00 350.00
No gum 200.00
Never hinged 550.00
634 A32 1k on 12c (V) (on #489) 200.00 50.00
No gum 100.00
Never hinged 300.00
a. On #489 200.00 50.00
No gum 100.00
Never hinged 300.00
b. As "a," black surcharge 400.00 50.00
No gum 200.00
Never hinged 550.00

Counterfeits exist.

Coronation Issue of 1915 Overprinted

1921, May **Wmk. 161** ***Perf. 11, 11½***

635 A33 3c dark grn 15.00
a. Center and overprint inverted —
636 A33 5c red 15.00
637 A33 6c olive grn & car 15.00
638 A33 10c bl grn & yel brn 15.00
639 A33 12c ultramarine 15.00
640 A34 1k sil, yel brn & gray 20.00
641 A34 2k sil, blue & rose 20.00
642 A34 5k sil, brn & green 20.00
643 A35 2t gold, grn & brn 25.00
644 A35 3t gold, cl & red brn 30.00
645 A35 5t gold, blue & ind 30.00
Nos. 635-645 (11) 220.00

Counterfeits of this Feb. 21, 1921, overprint are plentiful. Inverted overprints exist on all values; some specialists consider them fraudulent.

Stamps of 1911-13 Overprinted

1922 **Unwmk.** ***Perf. 11½, 11½x11***

646 A32 1c grn & orange (on #481) 10.00 .35
Never hinged 20.00
a. Inverted overprint *300.00*
b. On #481a 10.00 .35
Never hinged 20.00
c. As "b," pair, one without 300.00 —
Never hinged —
d. On #481c 200.00 .50
Never hinged 350.00
647 A32 2c red & sepia (on #482) 10.00 .35
Never hinged 20.00
a. On #482a 15.00 .35
Never hinged 30.00
648 A32 3c brn & green (on #483) *15.00* .35
Never hinged 30.00
a. On #483a 15.00 .35
Never hinged 30.00
648C A32 3c brn & green (on #483B) 15.00 1.00
Never hinged 30.00
a. On #483Ba 15.00 1.00
Never hinged 30.00
649 A32 5c brown & car (on #484a) 150.00 50.00
Never hinged 300.00
a. On #484c 150.00 50.00
Never hinged 300.00
650 A32 6c grn & red brn (on #486) 10.00 .35
Never hinged 20.00
a. On #486a 10.00 .35
Never hinged 20.00

651 A32 9c yel brn & vio (on #487) 12.00 .35
  Never hinged 25.00
  a. On #487a 12.00 .35
  Never hinged 25.00
652 A32 10c red & org brn (on #488) 20.00 .50
  Never hinged 40.00
  a. Double ovpt., one inverted *500.00*
  b. On #488c 20.00 .50
  Never hinged 40.00
  c. On #488a 30.00 1.00
  Never hinged 60.00
653 A32 12c green & ultra (on #489) 30.00 .75
  Never hinged 60.00
  a. Double overprint 500.00
  b. On #487a 30.00 .75
  Never hinged 60.00
654 A32 1k ultra & car (on #491) 35.00 1.00
  Never hinged 70.00
  a. On #491a 35.00 1.00
  Never hinged 70.00
  b. On #491c 40.00 1.00
  Never hinged 85.00
655 A32 24c vio & green (on #492) 30.00 1.00
  Never hinged 60.00
  a. On #492a 30.00 1.00
  Never hinged 60.00
656 A32 2k grn & red vio (on #494) 95.00 1.00
  Never hinged 200.00
  a. On #494a 95.00 1.00
  Never hinged 200.00
657 A32 3k vio & black (on #495) 100.00 2.00
  Never hinged 200.00
  a. On #495a 100.00 2.00
  Never hinged 200.00
658 A32 4k ultra & gray (on #496b) 250.00 45.00
  Never hinged 500.00
  a. On #496c 75.00
  b. On #496e 350.00 60.00
  Never hinged 600.00
659 A32 5k red & ultra (on #497) 250.00 3.00
  Never hinged 450.00
660 A32 10k ol bis & cl (on #498) *1,000.* 7.00
  Never hinged 1,800.
  a. On #498a 1,000. 7.00
  Never hinged 1,800.
661 A32 20k vio brn & bis (on #499) *1,000.* 8.00
  Never hinged 1,800.
  a. On #499a 1,000. 8.00
  Never hinged 2,000.
  b. On #499c 1,000. 30.00
  Never hinged 2,500.
662 A32 30k red & green (on #500) *1,000.* 15.00
  Never hinged 1,800.
  Nos. 646-662 (18) *4,032.* 137.00

The status of inverted overprints on 5c and 12c is dubious. Unlisted inverts on other denominations are generally considered fraudulent. Counterfeits of this overprint exist.

Nos. 653, 655 Surcharged

1922

663 A32 3c on 12c (on #489) 100.00 2.00
  No gum 50.00
  Never hinged 200.00
  a. On #489a 150.00 2.00
  No gum 50.00
  Never hinged 250.00
664 A32 6c on 24c (on #492) 150.00 3.00
  No gum 75.00
  Never hinged 300.00
  a. On #492a 250.00 3.00
  No gum 75.00
  Never hinged 400.00

Nos. 661-662 Surcharged

Type I Type II

1923

665 A32 10c on 20k (on #499) 175.00 15.00
  No gum 65.00
  Never hinged 350.00
666 A32 1k on 30k (on #500), Ty I *200.00* *20.00*
  No gum *80.00*
  Never hinged *400.00*
  a. 1k on 30k, Ty 2 250.00 25.00
  Never hinged 500.00

There are two types of 'K' in 'Kran' — Type I: No. 666, one with straight serifs. Type II: No. 666a with a curved serif on the top right bar. Values are the same for either type.

Forgeries exist, generally made by handstamps applied to mint reprints or postally used original stamps.

Ahmed Shah Qajar — A37

Perf. 11½, 11x11½, 11½x11

1924-25 **Engr.**

667 A37 1c orange 2.50 .25
668 A37 2c magenta 2.50 .25
  a. Imperf. btwn., pair *3,000.*
669 A37 3c org brn 2.50 .25
670 A37 6c blk brn 2.50 .25
671 A37 9c dark green 2.00 5.00
672 A37 10c dark violet 2.00 .30
673 A37 12c red 2.00 .30
674 A37 1k dark blue 2.00 .35
675 A37 2k indigo & red 5.00 5.00
  a. Center inverted 45,000. *7,500.*
676 A37 3k dk vio & red brn 17.00 2.00
677 A37 5k red & brn 20.00 *30.00*
678 A37 10k choc & lilac 25.00 25.00
679 A37 20k dk grn & brn 30.00 30.00
680 A37 30k org & blk brn 40.00 40.00
  Nos. 667-680 (14) 155.00 138.95

For overprints see Nos. 703-706.

A38

SIX CHAHIS

Type I Type II

Dated 1924
Color Litho., Black Typo.

1924 ***Perf. 11***

681 A38 1c yel brn & blk 20.00 1.00
682 A38 2c gray & blk 20.00 1.00
683 A38 3c dp rose & blk 20.00 1.00
684 A38 6c orange & blk (I) 30.00 1.50
  a. 6c orange & blk (II) 35.00 2.00
  Nos. 681-684 (4) 90.00 4.50

The 1c was surcharged "Chahis" by error. Later the "s" was blocked out in black.

Counterfeits having double line over "POSTES" are plentiful.

1925 **Dated 1925**

686 A38 2c yel grn & blk 10.00 1.00
687 A38 3c red & blk 10.00 1.00
689 A38 6c chalky bl & blk 10.00 1.00

690 A38 9c lt brn & blk 30.00 2.00
691 A38 10c gray & blk 75.00 5.00
694 A38 1k emer & blk 65.00 10.00
695 A38 2k lilac & blk 175.00 40.00
  Nos. 686-695 (7) 375.00 60.00

Counterfeits having double line over "POSTES" are plentiful.

A39

Gold Overprint on Treasury Department Stamps

1925

697 A39 1c red 20.00 6.00
698 A39 2c yellow 20.00 6.00
699 A39 3c yellow green 20.00 6.00
700 A39 5c dark gray 75.00 30.00
701 A39 10c deep orange 45.00 10.00
702 A39 1k ultramarine 50.00 15.00
  Nos. 697-702 (6) 230.00 73.00

Deposition of Ahmad Shah Qajar and establishment of provisional government of Reza Shah Pahlavi.

Nos. 697-702 have same center (Persian lion in sunburst) with 6 different frames. Overprint reads: "Post / Provisional Government / of Pahlavi / 9th Abanmah / 1304 / 1925."

Nos. 667-670 Overprinted

1926 ***Perf. 11½, 11x11½, 11½x11***

703 A37 1c orange 5.00 3.00
704 A37 2c magenta 5.00 5.00
705 A37 3c orange brown 5.00 3.00
706 A37 6c black brown 125.00 85.00
  Nos. 703-706 (4) 140.00 96.00

Overprinted to commemorate the Pahlavi dynasty, dated 16 December 1925. Counterfeits exist.

Nos. 448-463 Overprinted

1926 ***Perf. 11½, 12½x12***

707 A31 1c org & maroon 20.00 .25
  a. Inverted overprint 2,000.
708 A31 2c vio & maroon 20.00 .25
709 A31 3c yel grn & mar 20.00 .25
  a. Inverted overprint 2,000.
710 A31 6c red & maroon 20.00 .25
711 A31 9c gray & mar 20.00 .25
712 A31 10c red vio & mar 25.00 .35
713 A31 13c dk bl & mar 30.00 .35
714 A31 1k multi 65.00 .35
715 A31 26c dk grn & mar 30.00 .35
716 A31 2k multi 75.00 1.00
717 A31 3k multi 175.00 2.00
718 A31 4k sil, bl & bis brn 550.00 35.00
719 A31 5k multi 250.00 10.00
720 A31 10k multi 800.00 15.00
721 A31 20k multi 850.00 15.00
722 A31 30k multi 900.00 20.00
  Nos. 707-722 (16) 3,850. 100.65

Overprinted to commemorate the Pahlavi government in 1926.

Values for Nos. 707-722 are for stamps perf. 11½, on thick paper. Stamps perf. 12½x12 on thin paper are worth substantially more.

Forgeries exist perf. 12½x12, with either machine overprints or handstamps. Most of these fakes can be identified by the absence of the top serif of the "1" in "1926."

A40

Reza Shah Pahlavi — A41

1926-29 **Typo.** ***Perf. 11***

723 A40 1c yellow green 6.00 .25
724 A40 2c gray violet 6.00 .25
725 A40 3c emerald 6.00 .25
727 A40 6c magenta 6.00 .25
728 A40 9c rose 12.00 .50
729 A40 10c bister brown 30.00 5.00
730 A40 12c deep orange 30.00 3.00
731 A40 15c pale ultra 35.00 2.00
733 A41 1k dull bl ('27) 60.00 15.00
734 A41 2k brt vio ('29) 180.00 75.00
  Nos. 723-734 (10) 371.00 101.50

1928 **Redrawn**

740 A40 1c yellow green 30.00 .25
741 A40 2c gray violet 30.00 .25
742 A40 3c emerald 30.00 .25
743 A40 6c rose 30.00 .50
  Nos. 740-743 (4) 120.00 1.25

On the redrawn stamps much of the shading of the face, throat, collar, etc., has been removed.

The letters of "Postes Persanes" and those in the circle at upper right are smaller. The redrawn stamps measure 20¼x25¾mm instead of 19¾x25¼mm.

A42

Reza Shah Pahlavi — A43

Perf. 11½, 12, 12½, Compound

1929 **Photo.**

744 A42 1c yel grn & cer 3.50 .25
745 A42 2c scar & brt blue 3.50 .25
  a. Center inverted *45,000.* *7,500.*
746 A42 3c mag & myr grn 3.50 .25
747 A42 6c yel brn & ol grn 3.50 .25
748 A42 9c Prus bl & ver 5.00 .25
749 A42 10c bl grn & choc 6.00 .25
750 A42 12c gray blk & pur 8.00 .30
751 A42 15c citron & ultra 10.00 .30
752 A42 1k dull bl & blk 15.00 .50
753 A42 24c ol grn & red brn 12.00 .50

Engr.
Perf. 11½

754 A42 2k brn org & dk vio 125.00 3.00
755 A42 3k dark grn & dp rose 150.00 5.00
756 A42 5k red brn & dp green 100.00 5.00
757 A42 1t ultra & dp rose 125.00 10.00
758 A42 2t carmine & blk 200.00 20.00

Engr. and Typo.

759 A43 3t gold & dp vio 175.00 35.00
  Nos. 744-759 (16) 945.00 81.10

For overprints see Nos. 810-817.

Reza Shah Pahlavi — A44

1931-32 Litho. *Perf. 11*

No.	Type	Description	Unused	Used
760	A44	1c ol brn & ultra	6.00	.25
761	A44	2c red brn & blk	6.00	.25
762	A44	3c lilac rose & ol	6.00	.25
763	A44	6c red org & vio	6.00	.25
764	A44	9c ultra & red org	12.00	.40
765	A44	10c ver & gray	40.00	1.00
766	A44	11c bl & dull red	37.50	35.00
767	A44	12c turq blue & lil rose	45.00	.70
768	A44	16c black & red	50.00	1.75
769	A44	1k car & turq bl	85.00	1.75
770	A44	27c dk gray & dl bl	90.00	1.75
		Nos. 760-770 (11)	383.50	43.35

For overprints see Nos. 818-826.

A45

Reza Shah Pahlavi — A46

1933-34

No.	Type	Description	Unused	Used
771	A45	5d olive brown	3.00	.25
772	A45	10d blue	3.00	.25
773	A45	15d gray	3.00	.25
774	A45	30d emerald	3.00	.25
775	A45	45d turq blue	3.00	.50
776	A45	50d magenta	4.00	.50
777	A45	60d green	5.00	.50
778	A45	75d brown	8.00	1.50
779	A45	90d red	10.00	2.50
780	A46	1r dk rose & blk	25.00	2.00
781	A46	1.20r gray blk & rose	30.00	2.00
782	A46	1.50 citron & bl	35.00	2.00
783	A46	2r lt bl & choc	45.00	2.00
784	A46	3r mag & green	60.00	4.00
785	A46	5r dk brn & red org	225.00	50.00
		Nos. 771-785 (15)	462.00	68.50

For overprints see Nos. 795-809.

"Justice" A47

"Education" A49

Ruins of Persepolis A48

Tehran Airport A50

Sanatorium at Sakhtessar — A51

Cement Factory, Chah-Abdul-Azim — A52

Gunboat "Palang" A53

Railway Bridge over Karun River A54

Post Office and Customs Building, Tehran A55

1935, Feb. 21 Photo. *Perf. 12½*

No.	Type	Description	Unused	Used
786	A47	5d red brn & grn	1.00	.75
787	A48	10d red org & gray black	1.00	.75
788	A49	15d mag & Prus bl	1.50	.75
789	A50	30d black & green	1.50	.75
790	A51	45d ol grn & red brn	2.00	.75
791	A52	75d grn & dark brn	6.00	1.25
792	A53	90d blue & car rose	20.00	5.00
793	A54	1r red brn & pur	60.00	30.00
794	A55	1½r violet & ultra	25.00	10.00
		Nos. 786-794 (9)	118.00	50.00

Reign of Reza Shah Pahlavi, 10th anniv.

Stamps of 1933-34 Overprinted in Black

1935 *Perf. 11*

No.	Type	Description	Unused	Used
795	A45	5d olive brown	3.00	.50
796	A45	10d blue	3.00	.50
797	A45	15d gray	3.00	.50
798	A45	30d emerald	3.00	.50
799	A45	45d turq blue	10.00	3.00
800	A45	50d magenta	6.00	.50
801	A45	60d green	6.00	.50
802	A45	75d brown	10.00	10.00
803	A45	90d red	35.00	40.00
804	A46	1r dk rose & blk	125.00	*200.00*
805	A46	1.20r gray blk & rose	15.00	2.00
806	A46	1.50r citron & bl	15.00	2.00
807	A46	2r lt bl & choc	40.00	2.00
808	A46	3r mag & green	75.00	10.00
809	A46	5r dk brn & red org	300.00	*500.00*
		Nos. 795-809 (15)	649.00	772.00

Same Overprint on Stamps of 1929

1935 *Perf. 12, 12x12½*

No.	Type	Description	Unused	Used
810	A42	1c yel grn & cerise	500.00	*600.00*
811	A42	2c scar & brt blue	300.00	*400.00*
812	A42	3c mag & myr grn	200.00	*200.00*
813	A42	6c yel brn & ol grn	140.00	*150.00*
814	A42	9c Prus bl & ver	85.00	*100.00*
		Perf. 11½		
815	A42	1t ultra & dp rose	50.00	*75.00*
816	A42	2t carmine & blk	50.00	40.00
817	A43	3t gold & dp vio	70.00	50.00
		Nos. 810-817 (8)	1,395.	1,615.

No. 817 is overprinted vertically.
Forged overprints exist.

Same Ovpt. on Stamps of 1931-32

1935 *Perf. 11*

No.	Type	Description	Unused	Used
818	A44	1c ol brn & ultra	400.00	400.00
819	A44	2c red brn & blk	150.00	150.00
820	A44	3c lil rose & ol	100.00	125.00
821	A44	6c red org & vio	200.00	200.00
822	A44	9c ultra & red org	200.00	*225.00*
823	A44	11c blue & dull red	12.50	3.50
824	A44	12c turq bl & lil rose	600.00	*900.00*
825	A44	16c black & red	15.00	5.00
826	A44	27c dk gray & dull bl	19.00	5.00
		Nos. 818-826 (9)	1,697.	2,014.

Forged overprints exist.

Reza Shah Pahlavi — A56

1935 Photo. *Perf. 11*

Size: 19x27mm

No.	Type	Description	Unused	Used
827	A56	5d violet	3.00	.25
828	A56	10d lilac rose	3.00	.25
829	A56	15d turquoise bl	3.00	.25
830	A56	30d emerald	3.00	.25
831	A56	45d orange	3.00	.25
832	A56	50d dull lt brn	4.00	.30
833	A56	60d ultramarine	15.00	.65
834	A56	75d red orange	15.00	.75
835	A56	90d rose	15.00	.75
		Size: 21½x31mm		
836	A56	1r dull lilac	30.00	.50
837	A56	1.50r blue	45.00	2.00
838	A56	2r dk olive grn	45.00	.75
839	A56	3r dark brown	50.00	2.00
840	A56	5r slate black	275.00	15.00
		Nos. 827-840 (14)	509.00	23.95

Reza Shah Pahlavi — A57

1936-37 Litho. *Perf. 11*

Size: 20x27mm

No.	Type	Description	Unused	Used
841	A57	5d bright vio	4.00	.25
842	A57	10d magenta	4.00	.25
843	A57	15d bright ultra	6.00	.25
844	A57	30d yellow green	25.00	.25
845	A57	45d vermilion	25.00	.25
846	A57	50d blk brn ('37)	30.00	.25
847	A57	60d brown orange	25.00	.25
848	A57	75d rose lake	15.00	.25
849	A57	90d rose red	20.00	.35
		Size: 23x31mm		
850	A57	1r turq green	20.00	.25
851	A57	1.50r deep blue	20.00	.35
852	A57	2r bright blue	35.00	.35
853	A57	3r violet brown	45.00	.80
854	A57	5r slate green	45.00	1.25
855	A57	10r dk brn & ultra ('37)	225.00	25.00
		Nos. 841-855 (15)	544.00	30.35

Reza Shah Pahlavi — A58

1938-39 Size: 20x27mm *Perf. 11*

No.	Type	Description	Unused	Used
856	A58	5d light violet	2.00	.25
857	A58	10d magenta	2.00	.25
858	A58	15d violet blue	2.00	.25
859	A58	30d bright green	2.00	.25
860	A58	45d vermilion	3.00	.25
861	A58	50d black brown	3.00	.25
862	A58	60d brown orange	3.00	.25
863	A58	75d rose lake	3.00	.25
864	A58	90d rose red ('39)	5.00	.25
		Size: 22½x30mm		
865	A58	1r turq green	10.00	.25
866	A58	1.50r deep blue	15.00	.30
867	A58	2r lt blue ('39)	30.00	.30
868	A58	3r violet brown	30.00	.70
869	A58	5r gray grn ('39)	50.00	1.25
870	A58	10r dk brn & ultra ('39)	175.00	10.00
		Nos. 856-870 (15)	335.00	15.05

Reza Shah Pahlavi — A58a

1939, Mar. 15 *Perf. 13*

No.	Type	Description	Unused	Used
870A	A58a	5d gray blue	3.00	3.00
870B	A58a	10d brown	3.00	3.00
870C	A58a	30d green	3.00	3.00
870D	A58a	60d dk brn	3.00	3.00
870E	A58a	90d red	5.00	5.00
870F	A58a	1.50r blue	15.00	10.00
870G	A58a	5r lilac	35.00	30.00
870H	A58a	10r carmine	50.00	50.00
		Nos. 870A-870H (8)	117.00	107.00

60th birthday of Reza Shah Pahlavi. Printed in sheets of 4, perf. 13 and imperf. The 1r violet and 2r orange were not available to the public. Value, perf. 13 unused $35 each, imperf, 35% more. Value of sheets (including 1r and 2r), perf. 13 $1,100, imperf. $1,500.

Crown Prince and Princess Fawziya A59

1939, Apr. 25 Photo. *Perf. 11½*

No.	Type	Description	Unused	Used
871	A59	5d red brown	.50	.50
872	A59	10d bright violet	.50	.50
873	A59	30d emerald	1.50	.50
874	A59	90d red	12.00	2.00
875	A59	1.50r bright blue	20.00	4.00
		Nos. 871-875 (5)	34.50	7.50

Wedding of Crown Prince Mohammad Reza Pahlavi to Princess Fawziya of Egypt.

AIR POST STAMPS

Type of 1909 Overprinted

1927 Unwmk. Typo. *Perf. 11½*

No.	Type	Description	Unused	Used
C1	A31	1c org & maroon	3.50	1.50
C2	A31	2c vio & maroon	3.50	1.50
C3	A31	3c grn & maroon	3.50	1.50
C4	A31	6c red & maroon	3.50	1.50
C5	A31	9c gray & maroon	5.00	2.00
C6	A31	10c red vio & mar	7.00	2.50
C7	A31	13c dk bl & mar	8.00	3.00
C8	A31	1k sil, vio & bis brn	8.00	3.00
C9	A31	26c dk grn & mar	8.00	4.00
C10	A31	2k sil, dk grn & bis brown	15.00	5.00
C11	A31	3k sil, gray & bis brn	25.00	7.50
C12	A31	4k sil, bl & bis brn	45.00	17.50
C13	A31	5k gold, brn & bis brown	45.00	15.00
C14	A31	10k gold, org & bis brown	275.00	300.00
C15	A31	20k gold, ol grn & bis brn	275.00	300.00
C16	A31	30k gold, car & bis brown	275.00	300.00
		Nos. C1-C16 (16)	1,005.	965.50

Counterfeit overprints are plentiful. They are found on Nos. 448-463, perf. 12½x12 instead of 11½.

Exist without overprint. Value, set $4,000.

AP1

AP2

AP3

AP4

AP5

Airplane, Value and "Poste aérièn" Surcharged on Revenue Stamps

1928			*Perf. 11*	
C17	AP1	3k yellow brn	125.00	40.00
C18	AP2	5k dark brown	30.00	20.00
C19	AP3	1t gray vio	40.00	30.00
C20	AP4	2t olive bister	40.00	30.00
C21	AP5	3t deep green	55.00	40.00
		Nos. C17-C21 (5)	290.00	160.00

AP6

AP7

1928-29		"Poste aerienne"		
C22	AP6	1c emerald	2.50	.50
a.		1c yellow green	2.50	.50
b.		Double overprint	35.00	
C23	AP6	2c light blue	2.50	.25
a.		Rosette in place of "2"	*150.00*	*100.00*
C24	AP6	3c bright rose	2.50	.25
C25	AP6	5c olive brn	1.25	.25
a.		"5" omitted	3,000.	*2,250.*
b.		Horiz. pair, imperf. btwn.	*300.00*	
C26	AP6	10c dark green	2.00	.25
a.		"10" omitted	40.00	
b.		"1" inverted	75.00	
C27	AP7	1k dull vio	3.00	1.00
a.		"1" inverted	100.00	
C28	AP7	2k orange	10.00	3.50
a.		"S" for "s" in "Krs"	300.00	*175.00*
		Nos. C22-C28 (7)	23.75	6.00

Counterfeits exist.

Revenue Stamps Similar to Nos. C17 to C21, Overprinted like Nos. C22 to C28: "Poste aerienne"

1929				
C29	AP1	3k yellow brn	100.00	25.00
C30	AP2	5k dark brn	25.00	10.00
C31	AP3	10k violet	40.00	30.00
C32	AP4	20k olive grn	45.00	35.00
C33	AP5	30k deep grn	55.00	45.00
a.		"80" instead of "30"		*4,000.*
		Nos. C29-C33 (5)	265.00	145.00

Reza Shah Pahlavi and Eagle — AP8

1930, July 6	Photo.	*Perf. 12½x11½*		
C34	AP8	1c ol bis & brt bl	1.00	1.00
C35	AP8	2c bl & gray blk	1.00	1.00
C36	AP8	3c ol grn & dk vio	1.00	1.00
C37	AP8	4c dk vio & pck bl	1.00	1.00
C38	AP8	5c lt grn & mag	1.00	1.00
C39	AP8	6c mag & bl grn	1.00	1.00
C40	AP8	8c dk gray & dp vio	1.00	1.00
C41	AP8	10c dp ultra & ver	1.00	1.00
C42	AP8	12c slate & org	1.00	1.00
C43	AP8	15c org brn & ol grn	1.00	1.00
C44	AP8	1k Prus bl & scar	8.00	4.00
		Engr.		
C45	AP8	2k black & ultra	10.00	5.00
C46	AP8	3k dk brn & gray grn	20.00	6.00
C47	AP8	5k dp red & gray black	15.00	5.00
C48	AP8	1t orange & vio	52.00	12.00
C49	AP8	2t dk grn & red brown	50.00	40.00
C50	AP8	3t brn vio & sl bl	250.00	85.00
		Nos. C34-C50 (17)	415.00	167.00

Nos. C34-C50 Overprinted in Black

1935			Photo.	
C51	AP8	1c ol bis & brt bl	1.00	1.00
C52	AP8	2c blue & gray blk	1.00	1.00
C53	AP8	3c ol grn & dk vio	1.00	1.00
C54	AP8	4c dk vio & pck bl	1.00	1.00
C55	AP8	5c lt grn & mag	1.00	1.00
C56	AP8	6c mag & bl grn	1.00	1.00
C57	AP8	8c dk gray & dp violet	1.00	1.00
C58	AP8	10c dp ultra & ver	1.00	1.00
C59	AP8	12c slate & org	1.00	1.00
C60	AP8	15c org brn & ol green	1.00	1.00
C61	AP8	1k Prus bl & scar	75.00	*100.00*
		Engr.		
C62	AP8	2k blk & ultra	50.00	*65.00*
C63	AP8	3k dk brn & gray green	25.00	15.00
C64	AP8	5k dp red & gray black	10.00	10.00
C65	AP8	1t orange & vio	225.00	175.00
C66	AP8	2t dk grn & red brown	45.00	40.00
C67	AP8	3t brn vio & sl bl	75.00	50.00
		Nos. C51-C67 (17)	515.00	465.00

OFFICIAL STAMPS

Four bicolored stamps of this design (1s, 2s, 5s, 10s), with centers embossed, exist, but were never issued or used in Iran. Value $40. They are known imperforate and in many trial colors.

Shah Muzaffar-ed-Din O1

No. 145 Surcharged in Black

1902			*Perf. 12½*	
O5	O1	5c on 1k red	30.00	30.00
O6	O1	10c on 1k red	30.00	30.00
O7	O1	12c on 1k red	40.00	40.00
		Nos. O5-O7 (3)	100.00	100.00

Nos. 351-363 Overprinted in Black

1903-06				
O8	A26	1c violet	5.00	.75
O9	A26	2c gray	5.00	.75
O10	A26	3c green	5.00	.75
O11	A26	5c rose	5.00	.75
O12	A26	10c yel brown	8.00	.75
O13	A26	12c blue	12.00	.75
		Perf. 11½x11		
O14	A27	1k violet	14.00	7.50
O15	A27	2k ultra	25.00	12.50
a.		Violet overprint	75.00	
O16	A27	5k org brown	40.00	20.00
O17	A27	10k rose red	50.00	19.00
a.		Violet overprint		75.00
O18	A27	20k orange ('06)	200.00	40.00
O19	A27	30k green ('06)	250.00	90.00
O20	A27	50k green	250.00	125.00
		Nos. O8-O20 (13)	869.00	318.50

Two types of genuine handstamps exist. Type 2 was not regularly issued, and values are for stamps with type 2 handstamps. Values for stamps with type 1 handstamp are considerably higher.

Overprinted on Nos. 368, 370a

O21	A27	2t on 50k grn (Bl)	175.00	75.00
O22	A27	3t on 50k grn (V)	175.00	75.00

Overprinted on Nos. 372, 375, New Value Surcharged in Blue or Black

1905				
O23	A27	2t on 50k grn (Bl)	200.00	75.00
O28	A27	3t on 50k grn (Bk)	200.00	75.00

The 2t on 50k also exists with surcharge in black and magenta; the 3t on 50k in violet and magenta. Values about the same.

Regular Issue of 1909 Overprinted

There is a space between the word "Service" and the Persian characters.

1911			*Perf. 12½x12*	
O31	A31	1c org & maroon	15.00	7.50
O32	A31	2c vio & maroon	15.00	7.50
O33	A31	3c yel grn & mar	15.00	7.50
O34	A31	6c red & maroon	15.00	7.50
O35	A31	9c gray & maroon	25.00	13.00
O36	A31	10c multicolored	30.00	13.00
O38	A31	1k multicolored	60.00	45.00
O40	A31	2k multicolored	150.00	90.00
		Nos. O31-O40 (8)	325.00	191.00

The 13c, 26c and 3k to 30k denominations were not regularly issued with this overprint.

Dangerous counterfeits exist, usually on reprints.

Regular Issue of 1915 Overprinted

1915	Wmk. 161		*Perf. 11, 11½*	
O41	A33	1c car & indigo	2.50	*4.00*
O42	A33	2c bl & carmine	2.50	*4.00*
O43	A33	3c dark green	2.50	*4.00*
O44	A33	5c red	2.50	*4.00*
O45	A33	6c ol grn & car	2.50	*4.00*
O46	A33	9c yel brn & vio	2.50	*4.00*
O47	A33	10c multicolored	2.50	*4.50*
O48	A33	12c ultramarine	3.00	*5.00*
O49	A34	1k multicolored	7.00	*10.00*
O50	A33	24c multicolored	3.50	*10.00*
O51	A34	2k sil, bl & rose	7.00	*15.00*
O52	A34	3k sil, vio & brn	7.00	*15.00*
O53	A34	5k multicolored	7.50	*15.00*
O54	A35	1t gold, pur & blk	10.00	*20.00*
O55	A35	2t gold, grn & brn	10.00	*27.50*
O56	A35	3t multicolored	12.50	*27.50*
O57	A35	5t gold, bl & ind	15.00	*30.00*
		Nos. O41-O57 (17)	100.00	*203.50*

Coronation of Shah Ahmed.

Reprints have dull rather than shiny overprint. **Value, set, $17.50.**

NEWSPAPER STAMP

No. 429 Overprinted

1909	Typo.	Unwmk.	*Perf. 12½*	
P1	A26	2c gray, *blue*	60.00	30.00

PARCEL POST STAMPS

Regular issues of 1907-08 (types A26, A29) with the handstamp above in blue, black or green are of questionable status as issued stamps. The handstamp probably is a cancellation.

No. 436 Overprinted in Black

1909	Engr.		*Perf. 11½*	
Q18	A29	26c red brown	20.00	15.00

The overprint is printed.

Regular Issue of 1915 Overprinted in Black

1915	Wmk. 161		*Perf. 11, 11½*	
Q19	A33	1c car & indigo	*2.50*	*3.50*
Q20	A33	2c bl & carmine	*2.50*	*3.50*
Q21	A33	3c dark green	*2.50*	*3.50*
Q22	A33	5c red	*2.50*	*3.50*
Q23	A33	6c ol green & car	*2.50*	*3.50*
Q24	A33	9c yel brn & vio	*2.50*	*3.50*
Q25	A33	10c bl grn & yel brn	*2.50*	*3.50*
Q26	A33	12c ultramarine	*3.00*	*5.00*
Q27	A34	1k multicolored	*7.00*	*9.00*
Q28	A33	24c multicolored	*3.50*	*5.00*
Q29	A34	2k multicolored	*7.00*	*9.00*
Q30	A34	3k multicolored	*7.00*	*10.00*
Q31	A34	5k multicolored	*7.50*	*10.00*
Q32	A35	1t multicolored	*10.00*	*15.00*
Q33	A35	2t gold, grn & brn	*10.00*	*15.00*
Q34	A35	3t multicolored	*12.50*	*17.50*
Q35	A35	5t multicolored	*15.00*	*20.00*
		Nos. Q19-Q35 (17)	*100.00*	*140.00*

Coronation of Shah Ahmed.

Reprints have dull rather than shiny overprint.Value, set, $16.

IRAQ

i-räk

LOCATION — In western Asia, bounded on the north by Syria and Turkey, on the east by Iran, on the south by Saudi Arabia, and on the west by Jordan
GOVT. — Republic
AREA — 167,925 sq. mi.
POP. — 12,029,700 (est. 1982)
CAPITAL — Baghdad

Iraq, formerly Mesopotamia, a province of Turkey, was mandated to Great Britain in 1920. The mandate was terminated in 1932. For earlier issues, see Mesopotamia.

16 Annas = 1 Rupee.
1000 Fils = 1 Dinar (1932)

Issues under British Mandate

Sunni Mosque — A1

Gufas on the Tigris — A2

Assyrian Winged Bull — A4

Ctesiphon Arch — A5

Motif of Assyrian Origin — A3

Colors of the Dulaim Camel Corps — A6

Golden Shiah Mosque of Kadhimain — A7

Conventionalized Date Palm or "Tree of Life" — A8

1923-25 Engr. Wmk. 4 Perf. 12

1 A1 ½a olive grn 1.00 .25
Never hinged 2.00
2 A2 1a brown 1.75 .25
Never hinged 3.50
3 A3 1½a car lake 1.00 .25
Never hinged 2.00
4 A4 2a brown org 1.00 .25
Never hinged 2.00
5 A5 3a dp blue 2.00 .25
Never hinged 4.00
6 A6 4a dull vio 4.50 .35
Never hinged 7.00
7 A7 6a blue grn 2.75 .35
Never hinged 5.50
8 A6 8a olive bis 4.00 .75
Never hinged 8.00
9 A8 1r grn & brn 6.50 .90
Never hinged 12.00
10 A1 2r black 22.50 8.50
Never hinged 42.50
11 A1 2r bister ('25) 60.00 4.00
Never hinged 115.00
12 A6 5r orange 55.00 17.50
Never hinged 105.00
13 A7 10r carmine 67.50 25.00
Never hinged 135.00
Nos. 1-13 (13) 229.50 58.60

For overprints see Nos. O1-O24, O42, O47, O51-O53.

King Faisal I — A9

1927

14 A9 1r red brown 15.00 2.00
Never hinged 20.00

See No. 27. For overprint and surcharges see Nos. 43, O25, O54.

King Faisal I
A10 A11

1931

15 A10 ½a green 1.00 .30
Never hinged 1.50
16 A10 1a chestnut 1.00 .30
Never hinged 1.50
17 A10 1½a carmine 1.50 .45
Never hinged 2.25
18 A10 2a orange 1.25 .25
Never hinged 1.90
19 A10 3a light blue 1.50 .25
Never hinged 2.25
20 A10 4a pur brown 2.00 *1.75*
Never hinged 3.00
21 A10 6a Prus blue 2.50 .80
Never hinged 3.75
22 A10 8a dark green 3.00 2.00
Never hinged 4.50
23 A11 1r dark brown 5.50 1.75
Never hinged 8.25
24 A11 2r yel brown 7.75 5.00
Never hinged 12.00
25 A11 5r dp orange 27.50 *35.00*
Never hinged 42.50
26 A11 10r red 82.50 *85.00*
Never hinged 125.00
27 A9 25r violet 700.00 *800.00*
Never hinged 1,050.
Nos. 15-27 (13) 837.00 *932.85*

See Nos. 44-60. For overprints see Nos. O26-O41, O43-O46, O48-O50, O54-O71.

Issues of the Kingdom

Nos. 6, 15-27 Surcharged in "Fils" or "Dinars" in Red, Black or Green

a

b

c

d

1932, Apr. 1

28 A10(a) 2f on ½a (R) .50 .25
29 A10(a) 3f on ½a .50 .25
a. Double surcharge *160.00*
b. Inverted surcharge *160.00*
30 A10(a) 4f on 1a (G) 1.75 .35
31 A10(a) 5f on 1a .65 .25
a. Double surcharge 275.00
b. Inverted Arabic "5" *35.00 40.00*
32 A10(a) 8f on 1½a .75 .50
a. Inverted surcharge *160.00*
33 A10(a) 10f on 2a .80 .25
34 A10(a) 15f on 3a 1.75 1.50
35 A10(a) 20f on 4a 2.75 1.50
36 A6(b) 25f on 4a 4.50 3.75
a. "Flis" for "Fils" *350.00 425.00*
b. Inverted Arabic "5" *425.00 550.00*
37 A10(a) 30f on 6a 5.00 .75
38 A10(a) 40f on 8a 4.25 2.75
39 A11(c) 75f on 1r 4.50 4.50
40 A11(c) 100f on 2r 10.00 4.75
41 A11(c) 200f on 5r 42.50 *42.50*
42 A11(d) ½d on 10r 125.00 95.00
a. Bar in "½" omitted *1,200. 1,200.*
43 A9(d) 1d on 25r 250.00 250.00
Nos. 28-43 (16) 455.20 *408.85*

King Faisal I
A12 A13

A14

Values in "Fils" and "Dinars"

1932, May 9 Engr.

44 A12 2f ultra .50 .25
45 A12 3f green .50 .25
46 A12 4f vio brown .50 .25
47 A12 5f gray green .60 .25
48 A12 8f deep red 2.00 .25
49 A12 10f yellow 1.75 .25
50 A12 15f deep blue 1.90 .25
51 A12 20f orange 3.10 .55
52 A12 25f rose lilac 1.75 .55
53 A12 30f olive grn 5.00 .25
54 A12 40f dark violet 2.25 1.00
55 A13 50f deep brown 3.00 .30
56 A13 75f lt ultra 4.00 2.00
57 A13 100f deep green 10.00 1.25
58 A13 200f dark red 25.00 7.00
59 A14 ½d gray blue 90.00 40.00
60 A14 1d claret 175.00 *100.00*
Nos. 44-60 (17) 326.85 154.65

For overprints see Nos. O55-O71.

A15

A16

King Ghazi — A17

1934-38 Unwmk.

61 A15 1f purple ('38) .75 .25
62 A15 2f ultra .45 .25
63 A15 3f green .45 .25
64 A15 4f pur brown .45 .25
65 A15 5f gray green .45 .25
66 A15 8f deep red .75 .25
67 A15 10f yellow .95 .25
68 A15 15f deep blue .95 .25
69 A15 20f orange .95 .25
70 A15 25f brown vio 1.75 .35
71 A15 30f olive grn 1.50 .25
72 A15 40f dark vio 1.75 .25
73 A16 50f deep brown 3.50 .25
74 A16 75f ultra 4.00 .40
75 A16 100f deep green 5.00 .50
76 A16 200f dark red 7.50 3.00
77 A17 ½d gray blue 27.50 20.00
78 A17 1d claret 85.00 30.00
Nos. 61-78 (18) 143.65 57.25

For overprints see Nos. 226 (in Scott Standard catalogue, Vol. 3), O72-O89.

OFFICIAL STAMPS

British Mandate

Regular Issue of 1923 Overprinted

k

l

1923 Wmk. 4 Perf. 12

O1 A1(k) ½a olive grn 1.25 .50
Never hinged 1.60
O2 A2(k) 1a brown 1.50 .25
Never hinged 1.75
O3 A3(l) 1½a car lake 3.25 .75
Never hinged 4.50
O4 A4(k) 2a brown org 2.25 .30
Never hinged 3.00
O5 A5(k) 3a deep blue 4.00 .75
Never hinged 6.00
O6 A6(l) 4a dull violet 4.25 .50
Never hinged 7.00
O7 A7(k) 6a blue green 6.00 1.40
Never hinged 9.00
O8 A6(l) 8a olive bister 6.50 1.30
Never hinged 11.00
O9 A8(l) 1r grn & brn 7.50 1.40
Never hinged 12.00
O10 A1(k) 2r black (R) 22.50 9.00
Never hinged 37.50
O11 A6(l) 5r orange 65.00 27.50
Never hinged 105.00
O12 A7(k) 10r carmine 95.00 60.00
Never hinged 160.00
Nos. O1-O12 (12) 219.00 103.65

Regular Issue of 1923-25 Overprinted

m

n

1924-25

O13 A1(m) ½a olive green 1.75 .30
Never hinged 2.25
O14 A2(m) 1a brown 1.50 .30
Never hinged 7.00
O15 A3(n) 1½a car lake 1.50 .30
Never hinged 1.90
O16 A4(m) 2a brown org 2.25 .30
Never hinged 3.00
O17 A5(m) 3a deep blue 2.75 .30
Never hinged 3.75
O18 A6(n) 4a dull violet 5.75 .30
Never hinged 7.75
O19 A7(m) 6a blue green 2.75 .30
Never hinged 3.75
O20 A6(n) 8a olive bister 5.75 .40
Never hinged 7.75
O21 A8(n) 1r grn & brn 13.00 1.00
Never hinged 18.00
O22 A1(m) 2r bister ('25) 42.50 4.50
Never hinged 70.00
O23 A6(n) 5r orange 70.00 50.00
Never hinged 110.00
O24 A7(m) 10r brown red 100.00 52.50
Never hinged 150.00
Nos. O13-O24 (12) 249.50 110.50

For overprint see Nos. O42, O47, O51-O53.

No. 14 Overprinted Type "n"

1927

O25 A9 1r red brown 10.00 2.00
Never hinged 13.50

Regular Issue of 1931 Overprinted Vertically

o

1931

O26 A10 ½a green .35 *3.00*
Never hinged .35
O27 A10 1a chestnut .35 .25
Never hinged .35
O28 A10 1½a carmine 8.75 *16.00*
Never hinged 12.00
O29 A10 2a orange .85 .25
Never hinged 1.10
O30 A10 3a light blue 1.50 .70
Never hinged 2.10
O31 A10 4a purple brown 1.75 .90
Never hinged 2.25
O32 A10 6a Pruss blue 5.75 *12.50*
Never hinged 7.75
O33 A10 8a dark green 5.75 12.50
Never hinged 7.75

Overprinted Horizontally

p

O34 A11 1r dark brown 11.00 *12.50*
Never hinged 15.00
O35 A11 2r yellow brown 22.50 *45.00*
Never hinged 32.50
O36 A11 5r deep orange 52.50 *85.00*
Never hinged 75.00
O37 A11 10r red 95.00 *140.00*
Never hinged 140.00
Nos. O26-O37 (12) 206.05 328.60

Overprinted Vertically Reading Up

O38 A9(p) 25r violet 925.00 *1,200.*

For overprints see Nos. O39-O41, O43-O46, O48-O50, O54.

Kingdom

Nos. O15, O19, O22-O24, O26-O31, O33-O35, O38 Surcharged with New Values in Fils and Dinars, like Nos. 28-43

1932, Apr. 1

O39 A10 3f on ½a 4.25 4.00
O40 A10 4f on 1a (G) 3.00 .25
O41 A10 5f on 1a 3.00 .25
a. Inverted Arabic "5" *52.50 35.00*
O42 A3 8f on 1½a 6.75 .60
O43 A10 10f on 2a 4.00 .25
O44 A10 15f on 3a 5.25 2.75
O45 A10 20f on 4a 5.25 2.75
O46 A10 25f on 4a 5.50 2.25
O47 A7 30f on 6a 5.75 2.00
O48 A10 40f on 8a 5.00 4.00
a. "Flis" for "Fils" *300.00 450.00*
O49 A11 50f on 1r 6.75 4.00
O50 A11 75f on 1r 7.50 7.00
O51 A1 100f on 2r 22.00 4.00
O52 A6 200f on 5r 29.00 26.00
O53 A7 ½d on 10r 8.00 *100.00*
a. Bar in "½" omitted *850.00 975.00*
O54 A9 1d on 25r 150.00 *210.00*
Nos. O39-O54 (16) 271.00 370.10

Regular Issue of 1932 Overprinted Vertically like Nos. O26-O33

1932, May 9

O55 A12 2f ultramarine 1.10 .30
O56 A12 3f green 1.10 .30
O57 A12 4f violet brn 1.40 .30
O58 A12 5f gray 1.40 .30
O59 A12 8f deep red 1.40 .30
O60 A12 10f yellow 2.50 .30
O61 A12 15f deep blue 3.00 .30
O62 A12 20f orange 3.00 .30
O63 A12 25f rose lilac 3.00 .45
O64 A12 30f olive grn 4.25 .45
O65 A12 40f dark violet 6.50 .45

Overprinted Horizontally Like Nos. O34 to O37

O66 A13 50f deep brown 4.00 .55
O67 A13 75f lt ultra 3.00 1.10
O68 A13 100f deep green 13.50 1.75
O69 A13 200f dark red 25.00 10.00

Overprinted Vertically like No. O38

O70 A14 ½d gray blue 17.50 25.00
O71 A14 1d claret 80.00 *125.00*
Nos. O55-O71 (17) 171.65 *167.15*

Regular Issue of 1934-38 Overprinted Type "o" Vertically Reading up in Black

1934-38 **Unwmk.**

O72 A15 1f purple ('38) 1.25 .75
O73 A15 2f ultramarine 1.25 .30
O74 A15 3f green .75 .30
O75 A15 4f purple brn 1.25 .30
O76 A15 5f gray green 1.10 .30
O77 A15 8f deep red 5.00 .30
O78 A15 10f yellow .55 .30
O79 A15 15f deep blue 11.00 2.00
O80 A15 20f orange 1.25 .30
O81 A15 25f brown violet 22.50 7.00
O82 A15 30f olive green 5.25 .30
O83 A15 40f dark violet 6.25 .45

Overprinted Type "p"

O84 A16 50f deep brown 1.25 .75
O85 A16 75f ultramarine 7.25 1.10
O86 A16 100f deep green 2.00 1.25
O87 A16 200f dark red 5.00 3.50

Overprinted Type "p" Vertically Reading Up

O88 A17 ½d gray blue 12.50 *20.00*
O89 A17 1d claret 50.00 *60.00*
Nos. O72-O89 (18) 135.40 99.20

IRELAND

'ir-lənd

(Eire)

LOCATION — Comprises the entire island of Ireland, except 5,237 square miles at the extreme north
GOVT. — Republic
AREA — 27,136 sq. mi.
POP. — 3,443,405 (1981)
CAPITAL — Dublin

12 Pence = 1 Shilling

Catalogue values for unused stamps in this country are for Never Hinged items, beginning with Scott 99 in the regular postage section, and Scott J5 in the postage due section.

Watermarks

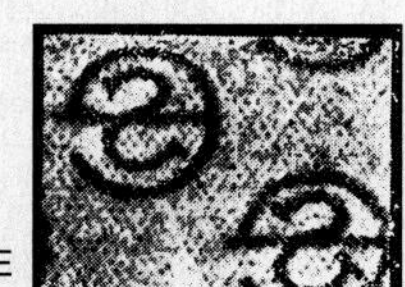

Wmk. 44 — SE in Monogram

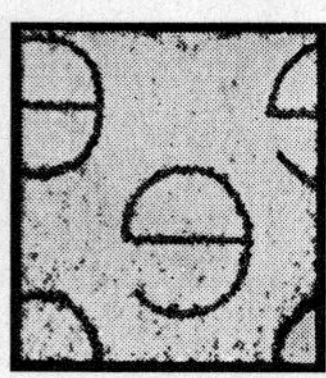

Wmk. 262 — Multiple "e"

Overprinted by Dollard, Ltd.

Great Britain Nos. 159-167, 170-172, 179-181 Overprinted

Overprint means "Provisional Government of Ireland."

Overprint measures 15x17½mm Black or Gray Black Overprint

1922, Feb. 17 **Wmk. 33** ***Perf. 15x14***

1 A82 ½p green 2.00 1.35
Never hinged 3.40
a. Inverted overprint 450.00 *625.00*
Never hinged *750.00*
b. Date omitted 110.00 *90.00*
2 A83 1p scarlet 3.40 1.35
Never hinged 5.00
a. Inverted overprint 300.00 *500.00*
Never hinged *450.00*
b. Double overprint *1,600.*
c. Double overprint, one albino 600.00 —
3 A86 2½p ultra 3.40 *14.50*
Never hinged 13.50
a. Double overprint, one albino 400.00 —
4 A87 3p violet 9.00 *12.00*
Never hinged 16.00
5 A88 4p slate green 9.00 *22.50*
Never hinged 15.00
a. Double overprint, one albino *500.00*
Never hinged *800.00*
6 A89 5p yel brown 9.00 *20.00*
Never hinged 16.00
7 A90 9p black brown 26.00 *40.00*
Never hinged 47.50
a. Double overprint, one albino 600.00
Never hinged *900.00*
8 A90 10p light blue 16.00 *32.50*
Never hinged 27.00
Nos. 1-8 (8) 77.80 *144.20*

The ½p with red overprint is a proof. Value, $150.

Red or Carmine Overprint

1922, Apr.-July

9 A86 2½p ultra 2.75 *8.50*
Never hinged 5.50
10 A88 4p sl grn (R) 16.00 *27.00*
Never hinged 32.50
10A A88 4p sl grn (C) 80.00 *130.00*
Never hinged 135.00
11 A90 9p blk brn (R) 32.50 *35.00*
Never hinged 55.00
11A A90 9p blk brn (C) 135.00 *160.00*
Never hinged 200.00
Nos. 9-11A (5) 266.25 *360.50*

Overprinted in Black

There is a variation that is 21x14mm.
The "h" and "é" are 1mm apart.
See Nos. 36-38.

Overprint measures 21½x14mm

1922, Feb. 17 **Wmk. 34** ***Perf. 11x12***

12 A91 2sh6p brown 55.00 *100.00*
Never hinged 145.00
a. Double overprint, one albino 1,200. —
13 A91 5sh car rose 90.00 *190.00*
Never hinged 210.00
a. Double overprint, one albino 1,200. —
14 A91 10sh gray blue 225.00 *400.00*
Never hinged 450.00
Nos. 12-14 (3) 370.00 *690.00*

Overprinted by Alex. Thom & Co.

Overprinted in Black

TWO PENCE
Die I — Four horizontal lines above the head. Heavy colored lines above and below the bottom tablet. The inner frame line is closer to the central design than it is to the outer frame line.
Die II — Three lines above the head. Thinner lines above and below the bottom tablet. The inner frame line is midway between the central design and the outer frame line.

Overprint measures 14½x16mm

1922, Feb. 17 **Wmk. 33** ***Perf. 15x14***

15 A84 1½p red brown 3.25 *2.75*
Never hinged 4.50
a. "PENCF" 540.00 *475.00*
16 A85 2p orange (II) 5.50 2.00
Never hinged 6.50
a. Inverted overprint (II) 375.00 *450.00*
b. 2p orange (I) 5.00 1.75
As "b," never hinged 6.50
c. Inverted overprint (I) 200.00 *300.00*
17 A89 6p red violet 20.00 *27.50*
Never hinged 27.50
18 A90 1sh bister 22.50 20.00
Never hinged 42.50
Nos. 15-18 (4) 51.25 52.25

Important: see Nos. 25-26, 31, 35.

Overprinted by Harrison & Sons

Overprinted in Black in Glossy Black Ink

Overprint measures 15¼x17mm

1922, June **Coil Stamps**

19 A82 ½p green 5.50 *22.50*
Never hinged 7.00
20 A83 1p scarlet 4.50 *18.00*
Never hinged 6.75
21 A84 1½p red brown 7.25 *52.50*
Never hinged 11.00
22 A85 2p orange (I) 27.00 *45.00*
Never hinged 42.50
a. 2p orange (II) 27.00 *42.50*
Never hinged 45.00
Nos. 19-22 (4) 44.25 *138.00*

In Harrison overprint, "i" of "Rialtas" extends below the base of the other letters.

The Harrison stamps were issued in coils, either horizontal or vertical. The paper is double where the ends of the strips were overlapped. Mint pairs with the overlap sell for about three times the price of a single. The perforations are often clipped.

Overprinted by Alex. Thom & Co.

Stamps of Great Britain, 1912-22 Overprinted as Nos. 15 to 18, in Shiny to Dull Blue Black, or Red

Note: The blue black overprints can best be distinguished from the black by use of 50-power magnification with a light source behind the stamp.

Overprint measures 14½x16mm

1922, July-Nov. ***Perf. 15x14***

23 A82 ½p green 3.50 1.80
Never hinged 5.00
24 A83 1p scarlet 3.00 2.00
Never hinged 3.50
25 A84 1½p red brown 6.00 *9.00*
Never hinged 13.50
26 A85 2p orange (II) 5.50 2.00
Never hinged 6.50
a. Inverted overprint (II) 375.00 *500.00*
b. 2p orange (I) 32.50 3.75
Never hinged 45.00
27 A86 2½p ultra (R) 9.00 *32.50*
Never hinged 18.00
28 A87 3p violet 10.00 *6.50*
Never hinged 12.50
29 A88 4p sl grn (R) 4.50 *11.00*
Never hinged 11.00
30 A89 5p yellow brown 9.00 *16.00*
Never hinged 18.00
31 A89 6p red violet 15.00 6.75
Never hinged 18.00
32 A90 9p blk brn (R) 20.00 *26.00*
Never hinged 35.00
33 A90 9p ol grn (R) 11.00 *45.00*
Never hinged 20.00
34 A90 10p light blue 27.50 *67.50*
Never hinged 60.00
35 A90 1sh bister 15.00 *15.00*
Never hinged 32.50
Nos. 23-35 (13) 139.00 *241.05*

Nos. 23, 24, 28, 34 overprinted in dull black, rather than the normal blue-black, are believed to be proofs, pressed into use when supplies of the issued values ran low.

Overprinted as Nos. 12 to 14 in Blue Black (Shiny to Dull)

The "h" and "é" are ½mm apart.

Overprint measures 21x13½mm

1922 **Wmk. 34** ***Perf. 11x12***

36 A91 2sh6p gray brn 290. *400.*
Never hinged 500.
37 A91 5sh car rose 300. *450.*
Never hinged 525.
38 A91 10sh gray blue 1,700. *2,000.*
Never hinged 2,400.
Nos. 36-38 (3) 2,290. *2,850.*

Overprinted in Blue Black

Overprint measures 15¾x16mm

1922, Dec. Wmk. 33 *Perf. 15x14*

No.	Type	Description	Unused	Used
39	A82	½p green	1.35	2.50
		Never hinged	2.50	
40	A83	1p scarlet	5.50	4.50
		Never hinged	8.00	
41	A84	1½p red brown	3.25	16.00
		Never hinged	7.25	
42	A85	2p orange (II)	13.50	13.50
		Never hinged	22.50	
43	A90	1sh bister	45.00	72.50
		Never hinged	60.00	
		Nos. 39-43 (5)	68.60	109.00

Stamps of Great Britain, 1912-22, Overprinted in Shiny to Dull Blue Black or Red

This overprint means "Irish Free State"

The inner loop of the "9" is an upright oval.

The measurement of "1922" is made across the bottom of the numerals and does not include the serif at the top of the "1."

There were 5 plates for printing the overprint on Nos. 44-55. In the impressions from plate I the 12th stamp in the 15th row has no accent on the 2nd "A" of "SAORSTAT." To correct this an accent was inserted by hand, sometimes this was in a reversed position.

On Nos. 56-58 the accent was omitted on the 2nd stamp in the 3rd and 8th rows. Damage to the plate makes the accent look reversed on the 4th stamp in the 7th row. The top of the "t" slants down in a line with the so-called accent.

Overprint measures 15x8½mm "1922" is 6¼mm long

1922-23 Wmk. 33 *Perf. 15x14*

No.	Type	Description	Unused	Used
44	A82	½p green	1.80	1.35
		Never hinged	2.50	
a.		Accent omitted	1,275.	900.00
b.		Accent added	115.00	135.00
45	A83	1p scarlet	2.25	1.35
		Never hinged	2.50	
a.		Accent omitted	15,250.	9,000.
b.		Accent added	145.00	165.00
c.		Accent and final "t" omitted	13,500.	7,250.
d.		Accent and final "t" added	225.00	270.00
46	A84	1½p red brn	3.25	16.00
		Never hinged	9.00	
47	A85	2p org (II)	2.75	4.50
		Never hinged	7.50	
48	A86	2½p ultra (R)	6.75	13.00
		Never hinged	9.00	
a.		Accent omitted	145.00	180.00
49	A87	3p violet	9.00	11.50
		Never hinged	20.00	
a.		Accent omitted	300.00	390.00
50	A88	4p sl grn (R)	5.50	12.50
		Never hinged	10.00	
a.		Accent omitted	200.00	270.00
51	A89	5p yel brn	5.25	5.25
		Never hinged	9.50	
52	A89	6p dull vio	3.50	2.75
		Never hinged	6.50	
a.		Accent added	825.00	825.00
53	A90	9p ol grn (R)	10.00	11.00
		Never hinged	12.50	
a.		Accent omitted	250.00	315.00
54	A90	10p lt blue	18.00	52.50
		Never hinged	45.00	
55	A90	1sh bister	13.50	13.50
		Never hinged	35.00	
a.		Accent omitted	11,000.	11,000.
b.		Accent added	750.00	825.00

Perf. 11x12

Wmk. 34

No.	Type	Description	Unused	Used
56	A91	2sh6p lt brown	57.50	90.00
		Never hinged	125.00	
a.		Accent omitted	410.00	540.00
57	A91	5sh car rose	90.00	180.00
		Never hinged	225.00	
a.		Accent omitted	550.00	825.00
58	A91	10sh gray blue	200.00	450.00
		Never hinged	500.00	
a.		Accent omitted	2,750.	3,600.
		Nos. 44-58 (15)	429.05	865.20

Overprinted by Harrison & Sons

Coil Stamps

Same Ovpt. in Black or Blue Black

1923 Wmk. 33 *Perf. 15x14*

No.	Type	Description	Unused	Used
59	A82	½p green	3.00	13.50
		Never hinged	6.50	
a.		Tall "1"	18.00	50.00
		Never hinged	27.50	
60	A83	1p scarlet	7.75	21.00
		Never hinged	15.00	
a.		Tall "1"	72.50	145.00
		Never hinged	95.00	
61	A84	1½p red brown	7.75	50.00
		Never hinged	22.50	
a.		Tall "1"	90.00	225.00
		Never hinged	170.00	
62	A85	2p orange (II)	11.00	18.00
		Never hinged	17.00	
a.		Tall "1"	32.50	55.00
		Never hinged	40.00	
		Nos. 59-62 (4)	29.50	102.50

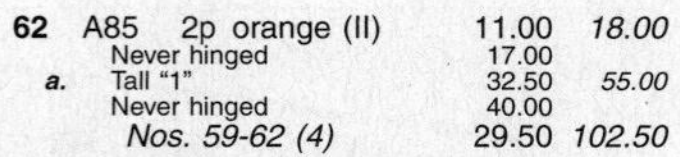

These stamps were issued in coils, made by joining horizontal or vertical strips of the stamps. See 2nd paragraph after No. 22. In some strips there were two stamps with the "1" of "1922" 2½mm high and with serif at foot.

In this setting the middle "e" of "eireann" is a trifle above the line of the other letters, making the word appear slightly curved. The lower end of the "1" of "1922" is rounded on Nos. 59-62 instead of flat as on Nos. 44-47.

The inner loop of the "9" is round.

See Nos. 77b, 78b and 79b.

Booklet Panes

For very fine, the perforation holes at top or bottom of the pane should be visible, though not necessarily perfect half circles.

"Sword of Light" — A1

Map of Ireland — A2

Coat of Arms — A3

Celtic Cross — A4

Perf. 15x14

1922-23 Typo. Wmk. 44

No.	Type	Description	Unused	Used
65	A1	½p emerald	2.75	1.50
		Never hinged	4.50	
a.		Booklet pane of 6	350.00	
66	A2	1p car rose	2.25	1.50
		Never hinged	4.50	
a.		Booklet pane of 6	350.00	
b.		Booklet pane of 3 + 3 labels	400.00	
67	A2	1½p claret	3.75	3.00
		Never hinged	8.50	
68	A2	2p deep green	2.25	.75
		Never hinged	3.50	
a.		Booklet pane of 6	350.00	
b.		Perf. 15 horiz. ('35)	12,500.	2,000.

No. 68b is valued in the grade of fine.

No.	Type	Description	Unused	Used
69	A3	2½p chocolate	5.50	8.50
		Never hinged	11.00	
70	A4	3p ultra	3.50	3.00
		Never hinged	7.25	
71	A3	4p slate	6.25	6.25
		Never hinged	12.50	
72	A1	5p deep violet	22.50	15.00
		Never hinged	57.50	
73	A1	6p red violet	7.25	5.75
		Never hinged	14.50	
74	A3	9p violet	35.00	25.00
		Never hinged	125.00	
75	A4	10p brown	17.00	35.00
		Never hinged	57.50	
76	A1	1sh light blue	35.00	17.00
		Never hinged	110.00	
		Nos. 65-76 (12)	143.00	122.25

The 2p was issued in 1922; other denominations in 1923.

No. 68b is a vertical coil stamp.

See Nos. 87, 91-92, 105-117, 137-138, 225-226, 326. For types overprinted see Nos. 118-119. Post 1940 issues in Scott Standard catalogue, Vol. 3.

Overprinted by the Government Printing Office, Dublin Castle and British Board of Inland Revenue at Somerset House, London

Great Britain Nos. 179-181 Ovptd. in Black or Gray Black

The measurement of "1922" is made across the bottom of the numerals and does not include the serif at the top of the "1."

"1922" is 5½mm long

1925 Wmk. 34 *Perf. 11x12*

No.	Type	Description	Unused	Used
77	A91	2sh6p gray brown	70.00	175.00
		Never hinged	125.00	
78	A91	5sh rose red	95.00	275.00
		Never hinged	160.00	
79	A91	10sh gray blue	225.00	575.00
		Never hinged	425.00	
		Nos. 77-79 (3)	390.00	1,025.

In 1927 the 2sh6p, 5sh and 10sh stamps were overprinted from a plate in which the Thom and Castle clichés were combined, thus including wide and narrow "1922" in the same setting.

Overprinted by British Board of Inland Revenue at Somerset House, London

Pair with "1922" Wide and Narrow

1927

No.	Type	Description	Unused	Used
77a	A91	2sh6p	400.	
		Never hinged	775.	
78a	A91	5sh	700.	
		Never hinged	1,350.	
79a	A91	10sh	1,700.	
		Never hinged	3,750.	
		Nos. 77a-79a (3)	2,800.	

Wide "1922" "1922" is 6¼mm long

1927-28

No.	Type	Description	Unused	Used
77b	A91	2sh6p	60.00	60.00
		Never hinged	110.00	
78b	A91	5sh ('28)	90.00	140.00
		Never hinged	225.00	
79b	A91	10sh ('28)	250.00	425.00
		Never hinged	550.00	
		Nos. 77b-79b (3)	400.00	625.00

Daniel O'Connell — A5

Perf. 15x14

1929, June 22 Wmk. 44

No.	Type	Description	Unused	Used
80	A5	2p dark green	.75	.55
		Never hinged	1.25	
81	A5	3p dark blue	4.25	14.00
		Never hinged	15.00	
82	A5	9p dark violet	4.75	13.50
		Never hinged	16.00	
		Nos. 80-82 (3)	9.75	28.05

Catholic Emancipation in Ireland, centenary.

Shannon River Hydroelectric Station — A6

1930, Oct. 15

No.	Type	Description	Unused	Used
83	A6	2p black brown	1.25	2.75
		Never hinged	4.25	

Opening of the hydroelectric development of the River Shannon.

Farmer with Scythe — A7

1931, June 12

No.	Type	Description	Unused	Used
84	A7	2p pale blue	1.00	1.50
		Never hinged	2.50	

Bicentenary of Royal Dublin Society.

Cross of Cong and Chalice — A8

1932, May 12

No.	Type	Description	Unused	Used
85	A8	2p dark green	2.50	.85
		Never hinged	3.50	
86	A8	3p bright blue	4.50	8.00
		Never hinged	7.00	

International Eucharistic Congress.

Type of 1922-23 Issue Coil Stamp

1933-34 *Perf. 15 Horizontally*

No.	Type	Description	Unused	Used
87	A2	1p rose ('34)	27.50	60.00
		Never hinged	45.00	
a.		1p carmine rose	125.00	300.00
		Never hinged	200.00	

No. 87a has a single perforation at each side near the top, while No. 87 is perforated top and bottom only.

See No. 68b.

Adoration of the Cross — A9

1933, Sept. 18 *Perf. 15x14*

No.	Type	Description	Unused	Used
88	A9	2p slate green	1.25	.55
		Never hinged	2.50	
89	A9	3p deep blue	3.00	6.00
		Never hinged	8.75	

Holy Year.

Hurling — A10

1934, July 27

No.	Type	Description	Unused	Used
90	A10	2p green	1.00	1.50
		Never hinged	2.50	

50th anniv. of the Gaelic Athletic Assoc.

Types of 1922-23 Coil Stamps

Wmk. 44 Sideways

1934 *Perf. 14 Vertically*

No.	Type	Description	Unused	Used
91	A1	½p green	30.00	75.00
		Never hinged	45.00	
92	A2	2p gray green	50.00	125.00
		Never hinged	85.00	

Overprinted by Harrison & Sons

Great Britain Nos. 222-224 Overprinted in Black

1935 Wmk. 34 *Perf. 11x12*

No.	Type	Description	Unused	Used
93	A91	2sh6p brown	52.50	70.00
		Never hinged	100.00	
94	A91	5sh carmine	200.00	225.00
		Never hinged	350.00	
95	A91	10sh dark blue	400.00	650.00
		Never hinged	1,100.	
		Nos. 93-95 (3)	652.50	945.00

Waterlow printing can be distinguished by the crossed lines in the background of portrait. Previous issues have horizontal lines only.

St. Patrick and Paschal Fire — A11

1937, Sept. 8 Wmk. 44 *Perf. 14x15*

No.	Type	Description	Unused	Used
96	A11	2sh6p bright green	90.00	90.00
		Never hinged	225.00	
97	A11	5sh brown violet	110.00	110.00
		Never hinged	250.00	

98 A11 10sh dark blue 90.00 90.00
Never hinged 225.00
Nos. 96-98 (3) 290.00 290.00

See Nos. 121-123 in Scott Standard catalogue, Vol. 3.

Catalogue values for unused stamps in this section, from this point to the end of the section, are for Never Hinged items.

Allegory of Ireland and Constitution
A12

1937, Dec. 29 ***Perf. 15x14***
99 A12 2p plum 2.00 .30
100 A12 3p deep blue 7.00 7.00

Constitution Day.

See Nos. 169-170 in Scott Standard catalogue, Vol. 3.

Father Theobald Mathew
A13

1938, July 1
101 A13 2p black brown 2.00 .45
102 A13 3p ultramarine 9.00 9.00

Temperance Crusade by Father Mathew, centenary.

Washington, US Eagle and Harp — A14

1939, Mar. 1
103 A14 2p bright carmine 1.50 .50
104 A14 3p deep blue 13.00 12.00

US Constitution, 150th anniv.

Type of 1922-23
Coil Stamp

1940-46 Wmk. 262 ***Perf. 15 Horiz.***
105 A2 1p car rose ('46) 40.00 32.50
a. Perf. 14 horiz. 60.00 60.00

Types of 1922-23

1940-42 ***Perf. 15x14***

Size: 18x22mm

106 A1 ½p emerald ('41) 2.75 1.40
a. Booklet pane of 6 *350.00*
107 A2 1p car rose ('41) 2.00 1.40
a. Booklet pane of 6 6.00
b. Bklt. pane of 3 + 3 labels *3,500.*
108 A2 1½p claret ('41) 17.00 1.40
a. Booklet pane of 6 140.00
109 A2 2p deep green 2.50 1.40
a. Booklet pane of 6 12.50
110 A3 2½p choc ('41) 17.00 3.50
a. Booklet pane of 6 95.00
111 A4 3p dull blue ('41) 2.75 1.40
a. Booklet pane of 6 40.00
112 A3 4p slate 2.75 1.40
a. Booklet pane of 6 65.00
113 A1 5p deep violet 2.75 1.40
114 A1 6p red violet ('42) 2.75 1.40
115 A3 9p violet 2.75 1.40
116 A4 10p olive brown 2.75 1.40
117 A1 1sh blue 175.00 42.50
Nos. 106-117 (12) 232.75 60.00

POSTAGE DUE STAMPS

D1

1925 Typo. Wmk. 44 ***Perf. 14x15***
J1 D1 ½p emerald 27.50 42.50
Never hinged 140.00
J2 D1 1p carmine 17.00 12.50
Never hinged 60.00
J3 D1 2p dark green 32.50 15.00
Never hinged 125.00
J4 D1 6p plum 10.50 14.00
Never hinged 45.00
Nos. J1-J4 (4) 87.50 84.00

Catalogue values for unused stamps in this section, from this point to the end of the section, are for Never Hinged items.

1940-70 **Wmk. 262**
J5 D1 ½p emerald ('43) 27.50 22.50
J6 D1 1p brt carmine ('41) 1.10 .50
J7 D1 1½p vermilion ('52) 2.25 *5.00*
J8 D1 2p dark green 1.25 .55
J9 D1 3p blue ('52) 2.25 2.00
J10 D1 5p royal purple ('43) 3.50 *7.50*
J11 D1 6p plum ('60) 4.00 1.75
J12 D1 8p orange ('62) 7.50 7.50
J13 D1 10p red lilac ('65) 8.50 7.00
J14 D1 1sh lt yel grn ('69) 25.00 9.00
Nos. J5-J14 (10) 82.85 63.30

ITALIAN COLONIES

ə-'tal-yən 'kä-lə-nēz

General Issues for all Colonies

100 Centesimi = 1 Lira

Used values in italics are for postaly used stamps. CTO's or stamps with fake cancels sell for about the same as unused, hinged stamps.

Type of Italy, Dante Alighieri Society Issue, in New Colors

Overprinted in Red or Black

1932, July 11 Wmk. 140 *Perf. 14*

No.	Type	Description	Unused	Used
1	A126	10c gray blk	1.45	3.50
		Never hinged	3.50	
		On cover		100.00
2	A126	15c olive brn	1.45	3.50
		Never hinged	3.50	
		On cover		125.00
3	A126	20c slate grn	1.45	2.00
		Never hinged	3.50	
		On cover		100.00
4	A126	25c dk grn	1.45	2.00
		Never hinged	3.50	
		On cover		100.00
5	A126	30c red brn (Bk)	1.45	2.00
		Never hinged	3.50	
		On cover		175.00
6	A126	50c bl blk	1.45	1.35
		Never hinged	3.50	
		On cover		80.00
7	A126	75c car rose (Bk)	1.90	5.75
		Never hinged	4.50	
		On cover		125.00
8	A126	1.25 l dk bl	1.90	8.00
		Never hinged	4.50	
		On cover		240.00
9	A126	1.75 l violet	1.90	13.00
		Never hinged	4.50	
		On cover		525.00
10	A126	2.75 l org (Bk)	1.90	22.00
		Never hinged	4.50	
		On cover		600.00
11	A126	5 l + 2 l ol grn	1.90	25.00
		Never hinged	4.50	
		On cover		—
12	A126	10 l + 2.50 l dp bl	1.90	40.00
		Never hinged	4.50	
		On cover		—
		Nos. 1-12,C1-C6 (18)	41.10	234.10
		Nos. 1-12, set on overfranked philatelic cover		300.00

Types of Italy, Garibaldi Issue, in New Colors and Inscribed: "POSTE COLONIALI ITALIANE"

1932, July 1 Photo.

No.	Type	Description	Unused	Used
13	A138	10c green	4.25	15.00
		Never hinged	11.00	
		On cover		190.00
14	A138	20c car rose	4.25	10.00
		Never hinged	11.00	
		On cover		145.00
15	A138	25c green	4.25	10.00
		Never hinged	11.00	
		On cover		145.00
16	A138	30c green	4.25	16.00
		Never hinged	11.00	
		On cover		190.00
17	A138	50c car rose	4.25	10.00
		Never hinged	11.00	
		On cover		110.00
18	A141	75c car rose	4.25	17.00
		Never hinged	11.00	
		On cover		215.00
19	A141	1.25 l deep blue	4.25	17.00
		Never hinged	11.00	
		On cover		270.00
20	A141	1.75 l + 25c dp bl	8.50	22.50
		Never hinged	22.00	
		On cover		540.00
21	A144	2.55 l + 50c ol brn	8.50	40.00
		Never hinged	22.00	
		On cover		—
22	A145	5 l + 1 l dp bl	8.50	50.00
		Never hinged	22.00	
		On cover		—
		Nos. 13-22,C8-C12 (15)	89.25	322.50
		Nos. 13-22, set on overfranked philatelic cover		500.00

See Nos. CE1-CE2.

Plowing with Oxen — A1

Pack Camel — A2

Lioness — A3

1933, Mar. 27 Wmk. 140

No.	Type	Description	Unused	Used
23	A1	10c ol brn	14.50	20.00
		Never hinged	35.00	
		On cover		125.00
24	A2	20c dl vio	14.50	20.00
		Never hinged	35.00	
		On cover		110.00
25	A3	25c green	14.50	20.00
		Never hinged	35.00	
		On cover		160.00
26	A1	50c purple	14.50	20.00
		Never hinged	35.00	
		On cover		110.00
27	A2	75c carmine	14.50	24.00
		Never hinged	35.00	
		On cover		200.00
28	A3	1.25 l blue	14.50	24.00
		Never hinged	35.00	
		On cover		270.00
29	A1	2.75 l red orange	24.00	42.50
		Never hinged	55.00	
		On cover		575.00
30	A2	5 l + 2 l gray grn	32.00	85.00
		Never hinged	75.00	
		On cover		—
31	A3	10 l + 2.50 l org brn	32.00	130.00
		Never hinged	75.00	
		On cover		—
		Nos. 23-31,C13-C19 (16)	347.00	775.50
		Nos. 23-31, set on overfranked philatelic cover		725.00

Annexation of Eritrea by Italy, 50th anniv.

Agricultural Implements A4

Arab and Camel — A5

"Eager with New Life" — A7

Steam Roller — A6

1933 Photo. *Perf. 14*

No.	Type	Description	Unused	Used
32	A4	5c orange	8.50	12.50
		Never hinged	20.00	
		On cover		145.00
33	A5	25c green	8.50	12.50
		Never hinged	20.00	
		On cover		160.00
34	A6	50c purple	8.50	11.00
		Never hinged	20.00	
		On cover		110.00
35	A4	75c carmine	8.50	22.00
		Never hinged	20.00	
		On cover		170.00
36	A5	1.25 l deep blue	8.50	22.00
		Never hinged	20.00	
		On cover		225.00
37	A6	1.75 l rose red	8.50	22.00
		Never hinged	20.00	
		On cover		290.00
38	A4	2.75 l dark blue	8.50	32.00
		Never hinged	20.00	
		On cover		400.00
39	A5	5 l brnsh blk	17.00	42.50
		Never hinged	37.50	
		On cover		—
40	A6	10 l bluish blk	17.00	55.00
		Never hinged	50.00	
		On cover		—
41	A7	25 l gray black	20.00	85.00
		Never hinged	55.00	
		On cover		—
		Nos. 32-41,C20-C27 (18)	229.50	631.00
		Nos. 32-41, set on overfranked philatelic cover		725.00

10th anniversary of Fascism. Each denomination bears a different inscription.

Issue dates: 25 l, Dec. 26; others, Oct. 5.

Scoring a Goal — A9

Soccer Kickoff — A10

Mercury and Fasces — A8

1934, Apr. 18

No.	Type	Description	Unused	Used
42	A8	20c red orange	2.50	7.25
		Never hinged	5.50	
		On cover		110.00
43	A8	30c slate green	2.50	7.25
		Never hinged	5.50	
		On cover		160.00
44	A8	50c indigo	2.50	7.25
		Never hinged	5.50	
		On cover		160.00
45	A8	1.25 l blue	2.50	14.50
		Never hinged	5.50	
		On cover		315.00
		Nos. 42-45 (4)	10.00	36.25
		Nos. 42-45, set on overfranked philatelic cover		160.00

15th annual Trade Fair, Milan.

1934, June 5

No.	Type	Description	Unused	Used
46	A9	10c olive green	27.00	47.50
		Never hinged	60.00	
		On cover		400.00
47	A9	50c purple	57.50	32.00
		Never hinged	120.00	
		On cover		360.00
48	A9	1.25 l blue	57.50	110.00
		Never hinged	120.00	
		On cover		600.00
49	A10	5 l brown	80.00	360.00
		Never hinged	190.00	
		On cover		—
50	A10	10 l gray blue	80.00	360.00
		Never hinged	190.00	
		On cover		—
		Nos. 46-50,C29-C35 (12)	662.00	1,925.
		Nos. 46-50, set on overfranked philatelic cover		2,150.

2nd World Soccer Championship.

SEMI-POSTAL STAMPS

Many issues of Italy and Italian Colonies include one or more semi-postal denominations. To avoid splitting sets, these issues are generally listed as regular postage, airmail, etc., unless all values carry a surtax.

AIR POST STAMPS

Italian Air Post Stamps for Dante Alighieri Society Issue in New Colors and Overprinted in Red or Black Like #1-12

1932, July 11 Wmk. 140 *Perf. 14*

No.	Type	Description	Unused	Used
C1	AP10	50c gray blk (R)	3.00	7.25
		Never hinged	6.25	
		On cover		85.00
C2	AP11	1 l indigo (R)	3.00	7.25
		Never hinged	6.25	
		On cover		110.00
C3	AP11	3 l gray (R)	3.75	11.00
		Never hinged	7.75	
		On cover		475.00
C4	AP11	5 l ol brn (R)	3.75	16.00
		Never hinged	7.75	
		On cover		550.00
C5	AP10	7.70 l + 2 l car rose	3.75	22.00
		Never hinged	7.75	
		On cover		—
C6	AP11	10 l + 2.50 l org	3.75	42.50
		Never hinged	7.75	
		On cover		—
		Nos. C1-C6 (6)	21.00	106.00
		Nos. C1-C6, set on flown cover		290.00

Leonardo da Vinci — AP1

1932, Sept. 7 Photo. *Perf. 14½*

No.	Type	Description	Unused	Used
C7	AP1	100 l dp grn & brn	14.50	125.00
		Never hinged	37.50	
		On cover		650.00

Types of Italian Air Post Stamps, Garibaldi Issue, in New Colors and Inscribed: "POSTE AEREA COLONIALE ITALIANA"

1932, July 1

No.	Type	Description	Unused	Used
C8	AP13	50c car rose	4.25	17.00
		Never hinged	11.00	
		On cover		140.00
C9	AP14	80c green	4.25	17.00
		Never hinged	11.00	
		On cover		215.00
C10	AP13	1 l + 25c ol brn	8.50	27.00
		Never hinged	22.00	
		On cover		400.00
C11	AP13	2 l + 50c ol brn	8.50	27.00
		Never hinged	22.00	
		On cover		—
C12	AP14	5 l + 1 l ol brn	8.50	27.00
		Never hinged	22.00	
		On cover		—
		Nos. C8-C12 (5)	34.00	115.00
		Nos. C8-C12, set on flown cover		500.00

Eagle AP2

Savoia Marchetti 55 — AP3

Savoia Marchetti 55 Over Map of Eritrea AP4

1933 *Perf. 14*

No.	Type	Description	Unused	Used
C13	AP2	50c org brn	13.00	20.00
		Never hinged	25.00	
		On cover		160.00
C14	AP2	1 l blk vio	13.00	20.00
		Never hinged	32.50	
		On cover		170.00
C15	AP3	3 l carmine	25.00	40.00
		Never hinged	67.50	
		On cover		425.00
C16	AP3	5 l olive brn	25.00	40.00
		Never hinged	67.50	
		On cover		500.00
C17	AP2	7.70 l + 2 l slate	32.00	90.00
		Never hinged	77.50	
		On cover		—

C18 AP3 10 l + 2.50 l dp bl 32.00 *90.00*
Never hinged 77.50
On cover —
C19 AP4 50 l dk vio 32.00 *90.00*
Never hinged 70.00
On cover —
Nos. C13-C19 (7) 172.00 *390.00*
Nos. C13-C19, set on flown cover 725.00

50th anniv. of Italian Government of Eritrea. Issue dates: 50 l, June 1; others, Mar. 27.

Macchi-Costoldi Seaplane — AP5

Savoia S73 — AP6

Winding Propeller AP7

"More Efficient Machinery" AP8

1933-34
C20 AP5 50c org brn 11.50 19.00
Never hinged 27.00
On cover 160.00
C21 AP6 75c red vio 11.50 19.00
Never hinged 27.00
On cover 170.00
C22 AP5 1 l bis brn 11.50 19.00
Never hinged 27.00
On cover 225.00
C23 AP6 3 l olive gray 11.50 *37.50*
Never hinged 27.00
On cover 360.00
C24 AP5 10 l dp vio 11.50 *37.50*
Never hinged 27.00
On cover —
C25 AP6 12 l bl grn 11.50 *57.50*
Never hinged 27.00
On cover —
C26 AP7 20 l gray blk 17.00 *65.00*
Never hinged 37.50
On cover —
C27 AP8 50 l blue ('34) 30.00 *60.00*
Never hinged 70.00
On cover —
On cover, single franking 150.00
Nos. C20-C27 (8) 116.00 *314.50*
Nos. C20-C27, set on flown cover 725.00

Tenth anniversary of Fascism. Issue dates: 50 1, Dec. 26; others, Oct. 5.

Natives Hailing Dornier Wal — AP9

1934, Apr. 24
C28 AP9 25 l brown olive 24.00 *215.00*
Never hinged 57.50
On flown cover 425.00
On flown cover, single franking 425.00

Issued in honor of Luigi Amadeo, Duke of the Abruzzi (1873-1933).

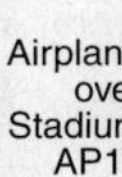
Airplane over Stadium AP10

Goalkeeper Leaping — AP11

Seaplane and Soccer Ball AP12

1934, June
C29 AP10 50c yel brn 16.00 *47.50*
Never hinged 35.00
On cover 360.00
C30 AP10 75c dp vio 16.00 *47.50*
Never hinged 35.00
On cover 475.00
C31 AP11 5 l brn blk 60.00 *110.00*
Never hinged 125.00
On cover 850.00
C32 AP11 10 l red org 60.00 *110.00*
Never hinged 125.00
On cover —
C33 AP10 15 l car rose 60.00 *110.00*
Never hinged 125.00
On cover —
C34 AP11 25 l green 60.00 250.00
Never hinged 125.00
On cover —
C35 AP12 50 l bl grn 60.00 250.00
Never hinged 125.00
On flown cover, single franking 375.00
Nos. C29-C35 (7) 332.00 *925.00*
Nos. C29-C35, set on flown cover 2,200.

World Soccer Championship Games, Rome. Issued: 50 l, June 21; others, June 5.

AIR POST SPECIAL DELIVERY STAMPS

Garibaldi Type of Italy
Wmk. 140
1932, Oct. 6 Photo. *Perf. 14*
CE1 APSD1 2.25 l + 1 l dk vio & sl 10.00 *27.00*
Never hinged 25.00
On cover —
CE2 APSD1 4.50 l + 1.50 l dk brn & grn 10.00 *42.50*
Never hinged 25.00
On cover —
Nos. CE1-CE2, set on flown cover 400.00

ITALIAN EAST AFRICA

ə-ˈtal-yən ˈēst ˈa-fri-kə

LOCATION — In eastern Africa, bordering on the Red Sea and Indian Ocean
GOVT. — Italian Colony
AREA — 665,977 sq. mi. (estimated)
POP. — 12,100,000 (estimated)
CAPITAL — Asmara

This colony was formed in 1936 and included Ethiopia and the former colonies of Eritrea and Italian Somaliland. For previous issues see listings under these headings.

100 Centesimi = 1 Lira

Used values in italics are for postaly used stamps. CTO's or stamps with fake cancels sell for about the same as unused, hinged stamps.

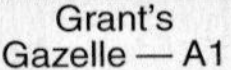
Grant's Gazelle — A1

Eagle and Lion — A2

Victor Emmanuel III — A3

Fascist Legionary — A5

Statue of the Nile — A4

Desert Road — A6

Wmk. 140
1938, Feb. 7 Photo. *Perf. 14*
1 A1 2c red orange 2.25 *1.00*
Never hinged 4.50
On cover 35.00
2 A2 5c brown 2.25 .25
Never hinged 4.50
On cover 24.00
3 A3 7½c dk violet 3.00 *4.25*
Never hinged 6.00
On cover 225.00
4 A4 10c olive brown 3.00 .25
Never hinged 6.00
On cover 9.50
5 A5 15c slate green 2.25 .35
Never hinged 4.50
On cover 35.00
6 A3 20c crimson 2.25 .25
Never hinged 4.50
On cover 24.00
7 A6 25c green 3.00 .25
Never hinged 6.00
On cover 9.50
8 A1 30c olive brown 2.25 .70
Never hinged 4.50
On cover 24.00
9 A2 35c sapphire 3.00 *11.00*
Never hinged 6.25
On cover 225.00
10 A3 50c purple 2.25 .25
Never hinged 4.50
On cover 5.50

Engr.
11 A5 75c carmine lake 3.00 .35
Never hinged 6.25
On cover 65.00
12 A6 1 l olive green 1.90 .25
Never hinged 4.50
On cover 5.50
13 A3 1.25 l deep blue 3.00 .35
Never hinged 6.25
On cover 24.00
14 A4 1.75 l orange 15.50 .25
Never hinged 42.50
On cover 5.50
15 A2 2 l cerise 3.00 .35
Never hinged 6.25
On cover 27.50
16 A6 2.55 l dark brown 18.00 *29.00*
Never hinged 50.00
On cover 450.00
17 A1 3.70 l purple 57.50 *85.00*
Never hinged 145.00
On cover 675.00
18 A5 5 l blue 18.00 4.25
Never hinged 37.50
On cover 400.00
19 A2 10 l henna brown 25.00 18.00
Never hinged 55.00
On cover 550.00
20 A4 20 l dull green 36.00 *42.50*
Never hinged 77.50
On cover —
Nos. 1-20,C1-C11,CE1-CE2 (33) 415.20 343.30
Nos. 1-20, set on over-franked philatelic cover 1,000.

Augustus Caesar (Octavianus) A7

Goddess Abundantia A8

1938, Apr. 25 Photo. *Perf. 14*
21 A7 5c bister brn .75 *1.80*
Never hinged 2.10
On cover 180.00
22 A8 10c copper red .75 1.20
Never hinged 2.10
On cover 60.00
23 A7 25c deep green 1.45 1.10
Never hinged 3.25
On cover 95.00
24 A8 50c purple 1.45 .75
Never hinged 3.75
On cover 52.50
25 A7 75c crimson 1.45 2.75
Never hinged 3.75
On cover 210.00
26 A8 1.25 l deep blue 1.45 7.75
Never hinged 3.75
On cover 325.00
Nos. 21-26,C12-C13 (8) 8.70 *22.60*
Nos. 21-26, set on over-franked philatelic cover 200.00

Bimillenary of the birth of Augustus Caesar (Octavianus), first Roman emperor.

Rome-Berlin Axis.
Four stamps of type AP8, without "Posta Aerea," were prepared in 1941, but not issued. Value, each $2,400.

Native Boat — A9

Native Soldier — A10

Statue Suggesting Italy's Conquest of Ethiopia — A11

1940, May 11 Wmk. 140
27 A9 5c olive brown .75 *1.10*
Never hinged 2.10
On cover 125.00
28 A10 10c red orange .75 *1.10*
Never hinged 2.10
On cover 72.50
29 A11 25c green 2.25 1.80
Never hinged 4.50
On cover 95.00
30 A9 50c purple 2.25 1.10
Never hinged 4.50
On cover 72.50
31 A10 75c rose red 2.25 *7.00*
Never hinged 4.50
On cover 300.00
32 A11 1.25 l dark blue 2.25 5.50
Never hinged 4.50
On cover 340.00
33 A10 2 l + 75c carmine 2.25 *20.00*
Never hinged 4.50
On cover —
Nos. 27-33,C14-C17 (11) 23.25 52.10
Nos. 27-33, set on over-franked philatelic cover 325.00

Issued in connection with the first Triennial Overseas Exposition held at Naples.

SEMI-POSTAL STAMPS

Many issues of Italy and Italian Colonies include one or more semi-postal denominations. To avoid splitting sets, these issues are generally listed as regular postage, airmail, etc., unless all values carry a surtax.

AIR POST STAMPS

Plane Flying over Mountains AP1

Mussolini Carved in Stone Cliff — AP2

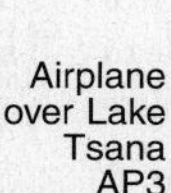

Airplane over Lake Tsana AP3

Bataleur Eagle — AP4

Wmk. Crowns (140)

1938, Feb. 7 Photo. *Perf. 14*

C1 AP1 25c slate green 3.00 *4.25*
Never hinged 7.25
On cover 67.50
C2 AP2 50c olive brown 70.00 .25
Never hinged 150.00
On cover 4.75
C3 AP3 60c red orange 3.00 *13.00*
Never hinged 6.75
On cover 225.00
C4 AP1 75c orange brn 3.75 2.25
Never hinged 8.50
On cover 27.50
C5 AP4 1 l slate blue 1.10 .25
Never hinged 2.75
On cover 4.25

Engr.

C6 AP2 1.50 l violet 1.60 .35
Never hinged 3.75
On cover 27.50
C7 AP3 2 l slate blue 1.60 1.60
Never hinged 3.75
On cover 60.00
C8 AP1 3 l carmine lake 2.25 6.00
Never hinged 5.75
On cover 140.00
C9 AP4 5 l red brown 70.00 42.50
Never hinged 150.00
On cover 450.00
C10 AP2 10 l violet brn 11.00 13.00
Never hinged 27.50
On cover 600.00
C11 AP1 25 l slate blue 29.00 32.00
Never hinged 52.50
On cover —
Nos. C1-C11 (11) 196.30 115.45
Nos. C1-C11, set on overfranked philatelic flown cover 500.00

Eagle Attacking Serpent — AP5

1938, Apr. 25 Photo.

C12 AP5 50c bister brown .70 2.50
Never hinged 2.75
On cover 55.00
C13 AP5 1 l purple .70 *4.75*
Never hinged 2.75
On cover 100.00
Nos. C12-C13, set on overfranked philatelic flown cover 80.00

Bimillenary of the birth of Augustus Caesar (Octavianus), first Roman emperor.

Triennial Overseas Exposition Type

#C14, C16, Tractor. #C15, C17, Plane over city.

1940, May 11

C14 A10 50c olive gray 2.25 *7.25*
Never hinged 5.50
On cover 225.00
C15 A9 1 l purple 2.25 *7.25*
Never hinged 5.50
On cover 200.00
C16 A10 2 l + 75c gray blue 3.00 —
Never hinged 7.25
On cover —
C17 A9 5 l + 2.50 l red brn 3.00 —
Never hinged 7.25
On cover —
Nos. C14-C17 (4) 10.50 *14.50*
Nos. C14-C17, set on overfranked philatelic flown cover 200.00

AIR POST SPECIAL DELIVERY STAMPS

Plow and Airplane — APSD1

Wmk. 140

1938, Feb. 7 Engr. *Perf. 14*

CE1 APSD1 2 l slate blue 7.00 *11.00*
Never hinged 17.50
On cover 900.00
CE2 APSD1 2.50 l dk brn 5.50 *18.00*
Never hinged 13.50
On cover —

SPECIAL DELIVERY STAMPS

Victor Emmanuel III — SD1

Wmk. 140

1938, Apr. 16 Engr. *Perf. 14*

E1 SD1 1.25 l dark green 11.00 11.00
Never hinged 25.00
On cover 290.00
E2 SD1 2.50 l dark carmine 11.00 *32.00*
Never hinged 25.00
On cover —

ITALIAN STATES

ə-'tal-yən 'stāts

Watermarks

Wmk. 157 — Large Letter "A"

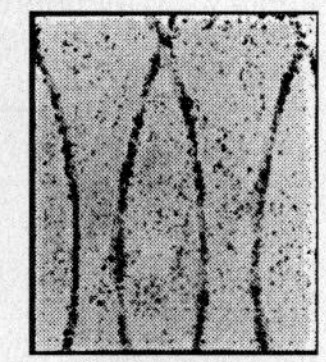

Wmk. 184 — Interlaced Wavy Lines

Wmk. 184 has double lined letters diagonally across the sheet readiing: "II R R POSTE TOSCANE."

Wmk. 185 — Crowns in the sheet

The watermark consists of twelve crowns, arranged in four rows of three, with horizontal and vertical lines between them. Only parts of the watermark appear on each stamp.
(Reduced illustration.)

Wmk. 186 — Fleurs-de-Lis in Sheet

MODENA

LOCATION — In northern Italy
GOVT. — Duchy
AREA — 1,003 sq. mi.
POP. — 448,000 (approx.)
CAPITAL — Modena

In 1852, when the first postage stamps were issued, Modena was under the rule of Duke Francis V of the House of Este-Lorraine. In June, 1859, he was overthrown and the Duchy was annexed to the Kingdom of Sardinia which on March 17, 1861, became the Kingdom of Italy.

100 Centesimi = 1 Lira

Values of Modena stamps vary tremendously according to condition. Values are for very fine examples, and values for unused stamps are for examples with original gum as defined in the catalogue introduction. Extremely fine or superb examples sell at much higher prices, and fine or poor examples sell at greatly reduced prices.

Coat of Arms — A1

1852-57 Unwmk. Typo. *Imperf.*

Without Period After Figures of Value

1 A1 5c blk, *green* 2,300. 115.00
No gum 575.00
On cover 460.00
a. Pair, Nos. 1, 6 2,875. 1,850.
No gum 725.00
On cover 7,500.
2 A1 10c blk, *rose* 690.00 72.50
No gum 170.00
On cover 275.00
a. "EENT. 10" *9,500.* *2,875.*
No gum 2,150.
On cover *14,250.*
b. "1" of "10" inverted *9,500.* *2,875.*
No gum 2,150.
On cover *14,250.*
c. "CNET" *1,575.* *1,600.*
No gum 360.00
On cover *7,900.*
d. No period after "CENT" *2,150.* 750.00
No gum 500.00
On cover *3,750.*
e. Pair, Nos. 2, 7 1,250. 2,250.
No gum 315.00
On cover *9,200.*
f. Frame below figure of value omitted 9,500. 1,600.
On cover *8,000.*
3 A1 15c blk, *yellow* 70.00 29.00
No gum 17.00
On cover 145.00
a. "CETN 15." *9,500.* *950.00*
No gum 2,375.
On cover *4,750.*
b. No period after "CENT" 345.00 *500.00*
No gum 85.00
On cover *2,500.*
4 A1 25c blk, *buff* 145.00 42.50
No gum 29.00
On cover 215.00
a. No period after "CENT" 690.00 *950.00*
No gum 170.00
On cover *4,750.*
b. "ENT.25" omitted *1,000.* —
No gum 260.00
c. 25c black, *green* (error) 4,400. 2,875.
d. "N" of "CENT" omitted 750.00 1,575.
No gum 170.00
On cover *8,000.*
e. Raised period after "CENT" 1,600. —
5 A1 40c blk, *blue* 460.00 100.00
No gum 115.00
On cover 500.00
a. 40c black, *pale blue* *20,000.* 2,000.
On cover 10,000.
b. No period after "CENT" *2,000.* *1,600.*
No gum 500.00
On cover *8,000.*
c. As "a," no period after "CENT" — —
d. Pair, Nos. 5, 8 *630.00* *2,150.*
No gum 230.00
On cover *8,650.*

Full margins = 1mm.
There are dividing lines between stamps.

Unused examples of No. 5a lack gum.
Used examples of No. 4c have a green administrative cancellation.
See Nos. PR3-PR4.

Values for pairs

1 A1 5c black, *green* 4,600. 260.00
On cover 1,100.
2 A1 10c black, *rose* 1,375. 260.00
On cover 1,300.
3 A1 15c black, *yellow* 140.00 *200.00*
On cover 1,000.
4 A1 25c black, *buff* 290.00 *400.00*
On cover 2,000.
5 A1 40c black, *blue* 925.00 400.00
On cover 2,000.
5a A1 40c black, *pale blue* — *20,000.*

With Period After Figures of Value

6 A1 5c blk, *green* 40.00 *40.00*
No gum 10.00
On cover 160.00
Single franking, on newspaper 2,150.
a. 5c black, *olive green* ('55) 525.00 160.00
No gum 32.50
On cover 525.00
b. "ENT" — *2,850.*
On cover *14,250.*
c. "CNET" *4,350.* *3,500.*
No gum 1,300.
On cover *17,250.*
d. As "a," "CNET" *2,300.* *1,850.*
No gum 800.00
On cover *9,250.*
e. "E" of "CENT" sideways — *5,150.*
No gum —
On cover *26,000.*
f. As "a," "CEN1" *2,875.* *2,150.*
No gum 725.00
On cover *10,500.*
g. As "a," no period after "5" 750.00 475.00
No gum 190.00
On cover *2,450.*
h. Double impression, no gum *1,275.* —
i. As "a," double impression *1,275.* —
No gum 260.00
j. Pair, #6a, 6g 1,275. *2,300.*
No gum 525.00
On cover 9,250.
k. No space between "T" and "5" 12,750. 5,150.
On cover *26,000.*
7 A1 10c blk, *rose* ('57) 475.00 340.00
No gum 115.00
On cover 1,000.
On cover, single franking 4,000.
a. "CENE" 1,600. *1,575.*
No gum 525.00
On cover *7,900.*
b. "CNET" 700.00 *750.00*
No gum 190.00
On cover 3,750.
c. "CE6T" 1,600. *1,600.*
No gum 475.00
On cover *7,900.*
d. "N" of "CENT" sideways *12,750.* *4,300.*
No gum 3,150.
On cover *21,500.*
e. Double impression 1,275. *1,275.*
No gum 425.00

f. Raised period after "10" 1,600. 1,600.
No gum 525.00
On cover *8,000.*
g. Pair, one with no period after value, on cover *2,300.*
No gum

8 A1 40c blk, *blue* ('54) 52.50 *100.00*
No gum 11.50
On cover 500.00
a. "CNET" 290.00 *750.00*
No gum 100.00
On cover 3,750.
b. "CENE" 700.00 *1,600.*
No gum 215.00
On cover *7,900.*
c. "CE6T" 700.00 *1,600.*
No gum 215.00
On cover *7,900.*
d. "49" 290.00 *750.00*
No gum 95.00
On cover 3,750.
e. "4C" 700.00 *1,600.*
No gum 145.00
On cover *7,900.*
f. "CEN.T" *37,500.* —
No gum *20,000.*
g. Space between "T" and period 290.00 *750.00*
No gum 95.00
On cover *3,750.*
h. Pair, one with no period after value, on cover *2,300.*
No gum

Values for pairs

6	A1	5c black, *green*	80.00	*115.00*
		On cover		460.00
6a	A1	5c black, *olive green*	1,050.	290.00
		On cover		1,150.
7	A1	10c black, *rose*	925.00	775.00
		On cover		2,300.
8	A1	40c black, *blue*	105.00	*400.00*
		On cover		2,000.
9	A1	1L black	105.00	*9,250.*
		On cover		*40,000.*

Wmk. 157

9 A1 1 l black ('53) 52.50 *2,450.*
No gum 13.50
On cover *9,750.*
On cover, single franking *47,500.*
a. With period after "LIRA" 135.00 *4,600.*
No gum 45.00
On cover *23,000.*
b. No period after "1" 130.00 *4,000.*
No gum 42.50
On cover *20,000.*
c. Very large dot after "1" 75.00 *2,875.*
No gum 22.50
On cover *14,500.*

Full margins = 1mm.
There are dividing lines between stamps.

Provisional Government

Coat of Arms — A2

1859 **Unwmk.**

10 A2 5c green 1,375. *630.00*
No gum 350.00
On cover 3,150.
On cover, single franking *42,500.*
a. 5c emerald 1,425. *690.00*
No gum 375.00
On cover 3,450.
b. 5c dark green 1,425. 690.00
No gum 400.00
On cover 3,450.

11 A2 15c brown 2,175. *3,700.*
No gum 540.00
On cover *26,000.*
a. 15c gray brown 350.00
No gum 80.00
b. 15c black brown 2,450. 5,175.
No gum 630.00
On cover *36,000.*
c. No period after "15" *3,450.* *4,600.*
No gum 875.00
d. Period before "CENT" *4,300.* *6,900.*
No gum 1,000.
e. Double impression (#11a) *1,725.*
No gum 575.00
f. As #11a, no period after "15" 400.00
No gum 100.00
g As #11a, period before "CENT" 750.00
No gum 210.00
h. As #11, figure "5" malformed as "6" *5,750.* *5,750.*
No gum 1,000.
i. As #11a, figure "5" malformed as "6" 460.00 175.00
No gum 1,000.

12 A2 20c lilac 87.50 *1,300.*
No gum 21.00
On cover 5,175.
a. 20c violet 3,750. 190.00
No gum 960.00
On cover 1,150.
b. 20c blue violet 2,575. 190.00
No gum 650.00
On cover 1,150.
c. As #12, no period after "20" 100.00 *1,425.*
No gum 25.00
On cover 7,150.
d. As #12, "ECNT" 230.00 *3,150.*
No gum 57.50
On cover *15,750.*
e. As #12, "N" inverted 190.00 *2,150.*
No gum 50.00
On cover 10,500.
f. Double impression (#12b) *6,900.*
No gum —
g. As #12b, no period after "20" 3,450. 800.00

13 A2 40c carmine 170.00 *1,300.*
No gum 42.50
On cover *9,000.*
On cover, single franking *31,500.*
a. 40c brown rose 175.00 *1,300.*
No gum 42.50
On cover *9,000.*
b. No period after "40" 350.00 *2,150.*
No gum 100.00
On cover —
c. Period before "CENT" 345.00 *2,150.*
No gum 100.00
On cover —
d. Inverted "5" before the "C", no gum *40,000.* *48,000.*
e. Large period after "40" 345.00 *2,150.*
No gum 92.50
On cover 10,500.

14 A2 80c buff 175.00 *20,000.*
No gum 42.50
On cover *160,000.*
On cover, single franking *200,000.*
a. 80c brown orange 175.00 *20,000.*
No gum 42.50
On cover *160,000.*
b. "CENT 8" 345.00 —
No gum 100.00
c. "CENT 0" 1,250. —
No gum 360.00
d. No period after "80" 345.00 —
No gum 100.00
e. "N" inverted 345.00 —
No gum 100.00

Full margins = 1mm.
There are dividing lines between stamps.

Values for pairs

10	A2	5c green	2,750.	1,375.
		On cover		*6,300.*
11	A2	15c brown	4,300.	*11,500.*
		On cover		—
11a	A2	15c gray brown	700.00	—
12	A2	20c lilac	175.00	*5,750.*
		On cover		*34,500.*
12b	A2	20c blue violet	5,175.	*2,000.*
		On cover		*12,000.*
13	A2	40c carmine	345.00	*12,500.*
		On cover		*100,000.*
14	A2	80c buff	345.00	—
		On cover		

Values for blocks of 4

10	A2	5c green	6,325.	*45,000.*
11	A2	15c brown	9,500.	
11a	A2	15c gray brown	1,500.	
12	A2	20c lilac	375.00	*5,750.*
12b	A2	20c blue violet	11,500.	
13	A2	40c carmine	775.00	
14	A2	80c buff	775.00	

The reprints of the 1859 issue have the word "CENT" and the figures of value in different type from the originals. There is no frame line at the bottom of the small square in the lower right corner.

NEWSPAPER TAX STAMPS

NT1

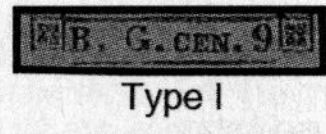

Type I

Type II

1853 **Unwmk.** **Typo.** ***Imperf.***

PR1 NT1 9c blk, *violet* (I) — *2,875.*
No gum *17,250.*
On newspaper *10,000.*
PR2 NT1 9c blk, *violet* (II) 690.00 70.00
No gum 175.00
On newspaper 175.00
a. No period after "9" 1,000. 215.00
No gum 275.00
On newspaper 850.00

Full margins = 1mm.
There are dividing lines between stamps.

All known unused examples of #PR1 lack gum.

1855-57

PR3 A1 9c blk, *violet* 3.00
No gum .75
a. No period after "9" 5.75
No gum 1.45
b. No period after "CENT" 8.75
No gum 2.25
c. Large period after "9" 7.00
No gum 2.40

PR4 A1 10c blk, *gray vio* ('57) 70.00 *230.00*
No gum 17.00
On newspaper 1,375.
On newspaper, uncanceled 37.50
a. "CEN1" 290.00 *1,150.*
No gum 87.50
On newspaper 4,600.
b. Frameline under value tablet missing 400.00 *1,425.*
No gum 100.00

Full margins = 1mm.
There are dividing lines between stamps.

No. PR3 was never placed in use.

NT2

1859

PR5 NT2 10c black 1,000. *1,875.*
No gum 250.00
On newspaper 7,500.
On newspaper, uncancelled 575.00
a. Double impression *15,000.* *18,750.*
b. Vert. guidelines between stamps 1,000.
No gum 250.00
c. Blurred and shifted impression 1,425. *2,875.*
On newspaper 11,500.

Full margins = 1 ½mm.

No. PR5 has horizontal guide lines between stamps. No. PR5b is a second printing, which was not issued.

Values for unused pairs

PR5	NT2	10c black	2,150.
PR5b	NT2	10c black	—

Values for unused blocks

PR5	NT2	10c black	*7,200.*

These stamps did not pay postage, but were a fiscal tax collected by the postal authorities on newspapers arriving from foreign countries.

The stamps of Modena were superseded by those of Sardinia in February, 1860.

PARMA

LOCATION — Comprising the present provinces of Parma and Piacenza in northern Italy.
GOVT. — Independent Duchy
AREA — 2,750 sq. mi. (1860)
POP. — 500,000 (1860)
CAPITAL — Parma

Parma was annexed to Sardinia in 1860.

100 Centesimi = 1 Lira

Values of Parma stamps vary tremendously according to condition. Values are for very fine examples, and values for unused stamps are for examples with original gum as defined in the catalogue introduction except for No. 8 which is known only without gum. Extremely fine or superb copies sell at much higher prices, and fine or poor stamps sell at greatly reduced prices. In addition, very fine unused stamps without gum sell for about 20% of the values shown.

Crown and Fleur-de-lis — A1

1852 **Unwmk.** **Typo.** ***Imperf.***

1 A1 5c blk, *yellow* 125.00 *135.00*
No gum 30.00
On cover 375.00
On cover, single franking 4,350.
a. 5c black, pale greenish yellow 1,200. 210.00
No gum 350.00
On cover 435.00

2 A1 10c blk, *white* 120.00 *120.00*
No gum 30.00
On cover 375.00
On cover, single franking *10,500.*

3 A1 15c blk, *pink* 5,250. 75.00
No gum 1,325.
On cover 200.00
a. Tête bêche pair, horiz. *85,000.*
On cover *175,000.*
Tête bêche pair, vert., on cover *225,000.*
b. Double impression *4,100.*

4 A1 25c blk, *violet* *18,000.* 195.00
No gum 4,500.
On cover 575.00

5 A1 40c blk, *blue* 3,850. 440.00
No gum 950.00
On cover 1,675.
a. 40c black, *pale blue* *6,750.* 650.00
No gum 4,500.
On cover 2,650.

Full margins = ½mm.
Covers dated June 1, 1852, *from* $95,000.

Values for pairs

1	A1	5c black, *yellow*	250.00	*260.00*
		On cover		725.00
2	A1	10c black	260.00	*170.00*
		On cover		1,100.
3	A1	15c black, *pink*	11,500.	200.00
		On cover		775.00
4	A1	25c black, *violet*	*38,000.*	*8,000.*
		On cover		*24,000.*
5	A1	40c black, *blue*	8,500.	1,325.
		On cover		6,500.
5a	A1	40c black, *pale blue*	*14,500.*	1,925.
		On cover		7,700.

Values for strips of 3

1	A1	5c black, *yellow*		*550.00*
		On cover		1,650.
2	A1	10c black		*675.00*
		On cover		2,750.
3	A1	15c black, *pink*		15,000.
4	A1	25c black, *violet*		*30,000.*

1854-55

6 A1 5c org yel *11,500.* 625.00
No gum 2,900.
On cover 1,575.
On cover or newspaper, single franking *21,500.*
a. 5c lemon yellow *13,250.* 800.00
No gum 2,900.
On cover 1,925.
b. Double impression *15,750.*

7 A1 15c red *13,250.* 240.00
No gum 3,300.
On cover 370.00

8 A1 25c red brn ('55) *12,000.* *365.00*
On cover 1,100.
a. Double impression *32,000.*

Full margins = ½mm.

No. 8 unused is without gum.

Values for pairs

6	A1	5c orange yellow	—	1,275.
		On cover		3,250.
6a	A1	5c lemon yellow		—
		On cover		—
7	A1	15c red	*28,000.*	525.00
		On cover		1,325.
8	A1	25c red brown		*16,000.*
		On cover		*47,500.*

Values for strips of 3

6	A1	5c orange yellow		2,400.
		On cover		6,000.
7	A1	15c red		18,000.
		On cover		55,000.

Crown and Fleur-de-lis — A2

1857-59

9 A2 15c red ('59) 350.00 300.00
No gum 85.00
On cover 900.00

10 A2 25c red brown 650.00 175.00
No gum 170.00
On cover 425.00

11 A2 40c bl, wide "0" ('58) 72.50 *440.00*
No gum 18.00
On cover 1,750.
a. Narrow "0" in "40" 77.50 *550.00*
No gum 18.00
On cover 2,200.
b. Pair, #11, 11a 300.00 *1,800.*
No gum 100.00
On cover 8,000.

Full margins = 1mm.

Values for pairs

9	A2	15c red	775.00	*650.00*
		On cover		2,000.
10	A2	25c red brown	2,250.	*4,000.*
		On cover		*16,500.*
11	A2	40c blue	350.00	*1,000.*
		On cover		4,000.
11a	A2	40c blue	500.00	2,400.
		On cover		9,500.

Values for strips of 3

9	A2	15c red		*7,500.*
		On cover		22,000.
10	A2	25c red brown		*12,500.*
		On cover		*50,000.*
11	A2	40c blue		*6,500.*
		On cover		25,000.

Provisional Government

A3

1859

12 A3 5c yel grn 500.00 *29,000.*
No gum 125.00
On cover —
a. 5c blue green 2,900. *4,250.*
No gum 725.00
On cover *27,500.*
13 A3 10c brown 1,000. *525.00*
No gum 240.00
On cover 2,650.
a. 10c deep brown 1,000. *525.00*
No gum 240.00
On cover 2,650.
b. "1" of "10" inverted 2,000. *4,250.*
No gum 550.00
On cover 28,000.
c. Thick "0" in "10" 1,450. *675.00*
No gum 350.00
On cover 32,000.
14 A3 20c pale blue 1,000. 215.00
No gum 240.00
On cover 1,100.
a. 20c deep blue 1,000. 240.00
No gum 240.00
On cover 1,225.
b. Thick "0" in "20" 1,450. 240.00
No gum 375.00
On cover 1,225.
15 A3 40c red 525.00 *8,000.*
No gum 135.00
On cover *40,000.*
a. 40c brown red *22,000.* *12,500.*
No gum 7,250.
On cover *37,500.*
b. Thick "0" in "40" (#15) 775.00 *10,000.*
No gum 210.00
On cover *47,500.*
c. Thick "0" in "40," (#15a) *24,000.* *13,750.*
No gum 8,000.
On cover *40,000.*
16 A3 80c ol yel 7,250. *200,000.*
No gum 2,400.
a. 80c orange yellow 10,000. —
No gum 3,150.
b. 80c bister 8,000.
No gum 2,400.
c. 80c orange bister 8,750.
No gum 2,400.
d. Thick "0" in "80" (#16) 8,000.
No gum 2,500.
e. Thick "0" in "80," (#16a) 10,000.
No gum 3,600.

Full margins = 1 ¼mm.

Nos. 12-16 exist in two other varieties: with spelling "CFNTESIMI" and with small "A" in "STATI." These are valued about 50 per cent more than normal stamps.

See Nos. PR1-PR2.

Values for pairs

12 A3 5c yellow green 1,250. 60,000.
On cover 100,000.
12a A3 5c blue green 6,000. 8,750.
On cover 52,500.
13 A3 10c brown 2,600. 1,100.
On cover 5,500.
14 A3 20c pale blue 2,600. 4,500.
On cover 27,500.
15 A3 40c red 1,450.
15a A3 40c brown red 50,000.
16 A3 80c org yel 17,500.
16a A3 80c olive yellow 25,000.

NEWSPAPER TAX STAMPS

Type of 1859
Normal Paper ('53)

1853-57 Unwmk. Typo. *Imperf.*

PR1 A3 6c blk, *dp rose* 2,400. 300.00
No gum 600.00
On newspaper *14,500.*
On newspaper, uncanceled 600.00
PR2 A3 9c black, *blue* 875.00 *5,000.*
No gum 225.00
On newspaper *10,000.*
On newspaper, uncanceled 325.00

Full margins = 1 ¼mm.

Thin, Semitransparent Paper ('57)

PR1a A3 6c black, *rose* ('57) 135.00
No gum 35.00
PR2a A3 9c black, *blue* 77.50
No gum 20.00

These stamps belong to the same class as the Newspaper Tax Stamps of Modena, Austria, etc.

Note following #16 also applies to #PR1-PR2.

Nos. PR1a-PR2a were not issued.

The stamps of Parma were superseded by those of Sardinia in 1860.

ROMAGNA

LOCATION — Comprised the present Italian provinces of Forli, Ravenna, Ferrara and Bologna.
GOVT. — One of the Roman States
AREA — 5,626 sq. mi.
POP. — 1,341,091 (1853)
CAPITAL — Ravenna

Postage stamps were issued when a provisional government was formed pending the unification of Italy. In 1860 Romagna was annexed to Sardinia and since 1862 the postage stamps of Italy have been used.

100 Bajocchi = 1 Scudo

Values of Romagna stamps vary tremendously according to condition. Values are for very fine examples, and values for unused stamps are for examples with original gum as defined in the catalogue introduction. Extremely fine or superb stamps sell at much higher prices, and fine or poor stamps sell at greatly reduced prices. In addition, very fine unused stamps without gum sell for about 20% of the values shown.

A1

1859 Unwmk. Typo. *Imperf.*

1 A1 ½b blk, *straw* 42.50 *360.00*
No gum 10.50
On cover 1,825.
On newspaper, single franking *20,000.*
On printed circular *16,500.*
a. Half used as ¼b on cover *16,250.*
As "a," single franking *150,000.*
2 A1 1b blk, *drab* 42.50 *180.00*
No gum 10.50
On cover 900.00
3 A1 2b blk, *buff* 55.00 *210.00*
No gum 13.50
On cover 1,050.
a. Half used as 1b on cover 6,250.
4 A1 3b blk, *dk grn* 60.00 *360.00*
No gum 15.00
On cover 2,550.
5 A1 4b blk, *fawn* 650.00 165.00
No gum 165.00
On cover 850.00
a. Half used as 2b on cover *30,000.*
6 A1 5b blk, *gray vio* 72.50 *400.00*
No gum 18.00
On cover 4,000.
7 A1 6b blk, *yel grn* 500.00 *9,000.*
No gum 125.00
On cover *90,000.*
a. Half used as 3b on cover *150,000.*
8 A1 8b blk, *rose* 210.00 *1,800.*
No gum 52.50
On cover *18,000.*
a. Half used as 4b on cover *150,000.*
9 A1 20b blk, *gray grn* 200.00 *2,400.*
No gum 50.00
On cover *24,000.*

Full margins = 1mm.
There are dividing lines between stamps.

Forged cancellations are plentiful.
Bisects used Oct. 12, 1859 to Mar. 1, 1860.

Values for pairs

1 A1 ½b black, *straw* 80.00 *725.00*
On cover 3,650.
2 A1 1b black, *drab* 80.00 *650.00*
On cover 3,000.
3 A1 2b black, *buff* 110.00 *550.00*
On cover 2,700.
4 A1 3b blk, *dk grn* 125.00 *2,000.*
On cover 12,500.
5 A1 4b black, *fawn* 1,550. *2,700.*
On cover 13,500.
6 A1 5b blk, *gray vio* 165.00
7 A1 6b blk, *yel grn* 1,000.
8 A1 8b black, *rose* 475.00
9 A1 20b blk, *gray grn* 475.00

Values for blocks of 4

1 A1 ½b black, *straw* 200.00 —
2 A1 1b black, *drab* 200.00
3 A1 2b black, *buff* 240.00
4 A1 3b black, *dark green* 270.00
5 A1 4b black, *fawn* 3,250.
6 A1 5b black, *gray vio* 325.00
7 A1 6b blk, *yel grn* 2,250.
8 A1 8b black, *rose* 975.00
9 A1 20b blk, *gray grn* 975.00

These stamps have been reprinted several times. The reprints usually resemble the originals in the color of the paper but there are impressions on incorrect colors and also in colors on white paper. They often show broken letters and other injuries. The Y shaped ornaments between the small circles in the corners are broken and blurred and the dots outside the circles are often missing or joined to the circles.

The stamps of Romagna were superseded by those of Sardinia in February, 1860.

ROMAN STATES

LOCATION — Comprised most of the central Italian Peninsula, bounded by the former Kingdom of Lombardy-Venetia and Modena on the north, Tuscany on the west, and the Kingdom of Naples on the southeast.
GOVT. — Under the direct government of the See of Rome.
AREA — 16,000 sq. mi.
POP. — 3,124,758 (1853)
CAPITAL — Rome

Upon the formation of the Kingdom of Italy, the area of the Roman States was greatly reduced and in 1870 they disappeared from the political map of Europe. Postage stamps of Italy have been used since that time.

100 Bajocchi = 1 Scudo
100 Centesimi = 1 Lira (1867)

Values of Roman States stamps vary tremendously according to condition. Values are for very fine examples, and values for unused stamps are for examples with original gum as defined in the catalogue introduction. Extremely fine or superb stamps sell at much higher prices, and fine or poor stamps sell at greatly reduced prices. In addition, very fine unused stamps without gum sell for about 20% of the values shown.

Papal Arms
A1 A2

A3

A4

A5

A6

A7

A8

A9

A10

A11

1852 Unwmk. Typo. *Imperf.*

1 A1 ½b blk, *dl vio* 55.00 *135.00*
No gum 13.50
On cover 550.00
On cover, single franking 1,100.
a. ½b black, *gray blue* 675.00 90.00
No gum 170.00
On cover 270.00
On cover, single franking 540.00
b. ½b black, *gray lilac* 675.00 360.00
No gum 170.00
On cover 1,100.
On cover, single franking 2,250.
c. ½b black, *gray* 675.00 90.00
No gum 170.00
On cover 275.00
On cover, single franking 550.00
d. ½b black, *reddish vio* 3,500. 2,700.
No gum 900.00
On cover *8,000.*
e. ½b black, *dark violet* 295.00 315.00
No gum 67.50
On cover 1,300.
f. Vertical pair, tête bêche — *30,000.*
On cover *87,500.*
g. Horizontal pair, tête bêche — *45,000.*
On cover *130,000.*
h. As "a," half used as ¼b on wrapper *54,000.*
As "h," pen canceled *9,000.*
i. As #1, double impression — *6,000.*
j. Impression on both sides — *13,000.*
k. As #1a, double impression *5,750.*
l. ½b black, *grayish violet* ('64) 67.50 150.00
No gum 17.50
On cover 600.00
2 A2 1b blk, *gray grn* 390.00 9.00
No gum 100.00
On cover 24.00
a. 1b black, *blue green* 800.00 50.00
No gum 120.00
On cover 160.00
b. As "a," half used as ½b on cover 425.00
c. Grayish oily ink 1,100. 27.50
No gum 550.00
On cover 90.00
d. Double impression *5,750.*
On cover *27,500.*
e. Impression on both sides — *12,750.*
f. 1b black, deep green, machine paper 120.00 72.50
No gum 24.00
On cover 200.00
3 A3 2b blk, *grnsh white* 16.00 *65.00*
No gum 4.00
On cover 190.00
a. 2b black, *yel grn* 240.00 16.00
No gum 60.00
On cover 50.00
b. As #3, half used as 1b on cover *5,400.*
c. As "a," half used as 1b on cover 360.00
d. Grayish oily ink 1,275. 32.50
No gum 650.00
On cover 100.00
e. No period after "BAJ" 145.00 32.50
No gum 40.00
On cover 100.00
f. As "a" and "e" 500.00 32.50
No gum 125.00
On cover 100.00
g. Double impression *5,750.*
4 A4 3b blk, *brn* 275.00 55.00
No gum 75.00
On cover 135.00
a. 3b black, *light brown* 5,250. 160.00
No gum 1,250.
On cover 475.00
b. 3b black, *yel brn* 2,500. 40.00
No gum 625.00
On cover 120.00
c. 3b black, *yellow buff* 2,500. *40.00*
No gum 625.00
On cover 120.00
d. 3b black, *chrome yel* 42.50 *160.00*
No gum 11.00
On cover 500.00
e. One-third used as 1b on circular *3,250.*
f. Two-thirds used as 2b on circular *10,500.*
g. Grayish oily ink 7,000. 210.00
No gum *3,500.*
On cover 650.00
h. Impression on both sides — *11,000.*
i. Double impression — *6,000.*
j. Half used as 1½b on cover *11,500.*
5 A5 4b blk, *lem* 240.00 70.00
No gum 60.00
On cover 190.00
a. 4b black, *yellow* 240.00 72.50
No gum 60.00
On cover 190.00
b. 4b black, *rose brown* 13,500. 120.00
No gum 3,000.
On cover 360.00
c. 4b black, *gray brown* 11,500. 72.50
No gum 3,000.
On cover 190.00
d. Half used as 2b on cover 2,250.
e. One-quarter used as 1b on cover *20,000.*
f. Impression on both sides — *11,000.*
g. Ribbed paper 325.00 90.00
No gum 80.00
On cover 250.00
h. Grayish oily ink 23,500. 325.00
No gum 11,750.
On cover 1,000.
i. As "a," half used as 2b on cover 3,750.
j. As "a," one-quarter used as 1b on cover *21,500.*

6 A6 5b black, *rose* 225.00 14.00
No gum 55.00
On cover 45.00
a. 5b black, *pale rose* 225.00 16.00
No gum 55.00
On cover 50.00
c. Impression on both sides *11,000.*
d. Double impression *5,500.*
On cover *30,000.*
e. Grayish oily ink 1,400. 32.50
No gum 725.00
On cover 110.00
f. Half used as 2½b on cover *54,000.*
7 A7 6b blk, *grnsh gray* 975.00 67.50
No gum 240.00
On cover 190.00
a. 6b black, *gray* 1,500. 72.50
No gum 375.00
On cover 210.00
b. 6b black, *grayish lil* 1,700. 210.00
No gum 425.00
On cover 850.00
c. Grayish oily ink 3,750. 250.00
No gum 1,700.
On cover 800.00
d. Double impression — *6,000.*
On cover *30,000.*
e. Half used as 3b on cover 4,250.
f. One-third used as 2b on cover *16,000.*
8 A8 7b black, *blue* 1,425. 72.50
No gum 375.00
On cover 275.00
On cover, single franking 4,500.
a. Half used as 3¼b on cover *30,000.*
b. Double impression — 5,750.
On cover —
c. Grayish oily ink 5,000. 135.00
No gum 2,500.
On cover 540.00
9 A9 8b black 550.00 40.00
No gum 140.00
On cover 125.00
a. Half used as 4b on cover 8,000.
b. Quarter used as 2b on cover *80,000.*
c. Double impression —
d. Grayish oily ink 2,250. 210.00
No gum 1,000.
On cover 575.00
10 A10 50b dull blue *15,000.* 1,650.
No gum 3,750.
On cover 6,750.
On cover, single franking 32,500.
a. 50b deep blue (worn impression) *21,500.* 2,950.
No gum 5,375.
On cover (from an 1864 printing) 45,000.
11 A11 1sc rose *4,000.* *3,250.*
No gum 950.00
On cover, with grill cancellation 50,000.
On cover, single franking, with c.d.s. 85,000.

Values for strips of 3

1 A1 ½b black, *dull vio* ('64) 575.00
On cover 2,250.
1c A1 ½b black, *gray* 400.00
On cover 1,550.
2a A2 1b black, *gray green* 70.00
On cover 280.00
3 A3 2b black, *greenish white* 425.00
On cover 1,675.
3a A3 2b black, *yellow green* 145.00
On cover 560.00
4 A4 3b black, *brown* ('63) 400.00
On cover 1,175.
4c A4 3b black, *yellow buff* 335.00
On cover 1,000.
4d A4 3b black, *chrome yellow* 1,250.
On cover 3,750.
5a A5 4b black, *yellow* 700.00
On cover 2,800.
5c A5 4b black, *gray brn* 700.00
On cover 2,800.
6 A6 5b black, *rose* 85.00
On cover 250.00
6a A6 5b black, *pale rose* 92.50
On cover 280.00
7 A7 6b black, *greenish gray* 425.00
On cover 1,675.
7b A7 6b black, *grayish lilac* 1,125.
On cover 4,500.
8 A8 7b black, *blue* 400.00
On cover 1,550.
9 A9 8b black 170.00
On cover 675.00
10 A10 50b dull blue —
On cover —
11 A11 1sc rose —
On cover —

Full margins: Nos. 1-2, 4-5, 10-11 = ½mm; Nos. 3, 6-8 = ¾mm; No. 9 = 1¼mm. There are double dividing lines between stamps on Nos. 1-2, 4-5, 9.

Counterfeits exist of Nos. 10-11. Fraudulent cancellations are found on No. 11.

Covers: Values for Nos. 1-2, 4-5, 9 are for covers bearing stamps with at least one frameline complete on each side; for Nos. 3, 6-8, 10-11, stamps are cut square clear of the design. Covers bearing stamps with framelines missing are worth much less; covers with stamps showing all 8 framelines intact are worth much more.

Nos. 1, 8, 10-11 single frankings are worth much more. Nos. 10-11 with circular datestamps are worth 10-50% more.

Grayish oily ink stamps are from specific 1854 printings. Covers usually are dated 1854.

A12

A13

A14

A15

A16

A17

A18

1867 Glazed Paper *Imperf.*

12 A12 2c blk, *grn* 90.00 *315.00*
No gum 22.00
On cover 1,000.
On cover, single franking 1,950.
a. No period after "Cent" 110.00 *350.00*
No gum 27.50
On cover 1,100.
13 A13 3c blk, *gray* 1,300. *8,000.*
No gum 240.00
On cover *95,000.*
a. 3c black, *lilac gray* 3,250. 2,150.
No gum 800.00
On cover 17,000.
14 A14 5c blk, *lt bl* 190.00 *215.00*
No gum 47.50
On cover 425.00
On cover, single franking 1,350.
a. No period after "5" 375.00 *450.00*
No gum 95.00
On cover 900.00
15 A15 10c blk, *ver* 1,900. 95.00
No gum 475.00
On cover 190.00
a. Double impression 5,750.
On cover *27,500.*
16 A16 20c blk, *cop red (unglazed)* 190.00 120.00
No gum 47.50
On cover 235.00
a. No period after "20" 540.00 360.00
No gum 135.00
On cover 725.00
b. No period after "CENT" 540.00 360.00
No gum 135.00
On cover 725.00
17 A17 40c blk, *yel* 200.00 *160.00*
No gum 52.50
On cover 500.00
a. No period after "40" 260.00 200.00
No gum 55.00
On cover 600.00
18 A18 80c blk, *lil rose* 180.00 *450.00*
No gum 45.00
On cover 1,900.
On cover, single franking 3,600.
a. No period after "80" 250.00 *675.00*
No gum 62.50
On cover 2,750.
b. 80c black, bright lilac rose 210.00 950.00
No gum 50.00
On cover *3,250.*
On cover *6,500.*

Values for stamps in pairs

12 A12 2c black, *green* 175.00 625.00
On cover 1,850.
13 A13 3c black, *gray* 2,700. 18,500.
On cover —
13a A13 3c blk, *lil gray* 7,500. 7,000.
On cover —
14 A14 5c blk, *lt blue* 375.00 425.00
On cover 800.00
15 A15 10c blk, *ver* 4,000. 300.00
On cover 1,100.
16 A16 20c black, *copper red* (unglazed) 400.00 575.00
On cover 2,200.
17 A17 40c black, *yellow* 425.00 *700.00*
On cover 3,000.
18 A18 80c blk, *lil rose* 400.00 *1,100.*
On cover 4,250.

Values for strips of 3

12 A12 2c blk, *grn* 1,350.
4,000.
13 A13 3c blk, *gray* —
On cover —
13a A13 3c black, *lilac gray* —
On cover —
14 A14 5c blk, *lt bl* 2,750.
On cover 8,000.
15 A15 10c blk, *ver* 1,350.
On cover 5,400.
16 A16 20c blk, *cop red* (unglazed) 2,700.
On cover *11,000.*
17 A17 40c blk, *yel* *2,700.*
On cover *11,000.*
18 A18 80c blk, *lil rose* *2,700.*
On cover *11,000.*

Full margins: No. 12 = 2mm; Nos. 13, 17 = 1¼mm; Nos. 14, 18 = 1½mm at sides, 1mm at top and bottom;

No. 15 = 2½mm at sides, 1mm at top and bottom; No. 16 = 1½mm at sides, ¼mm at top and bottom.

There are double dividing lines between stamps.

Imperforate stamps on unglazed paper, or in colors other than listed, are unfinished remainders of the 1868 issue.

Fraudulent cancellations are found on Nos. 13, 14, 17, 18.

Covers: Values for Nos. 12-18 are for covers bearing stamps with at least one frameline complete on each side.

Covers bearing stamps with framelines missing are worth much less; covers with stamps showing all 8 framelines intact are worth much more.

1868 Glazed Paper *Perf. 13*

19 A12 2c blk, *grn* 9.00 *90.00*
No gum 2.25
On cover 225.00
On newspaper, single franking 450.00
a. No period after "CENT" 11.00 *110.00*
No gum 2.75
On cover 265.00
b. Figure "2" omitted *37,500.* *16,500.*
20 A13 3c blk, *gray* 55.00 *3,250.*
No gum 13.50
On cover *27,000.*
a. 3c black, *lilac gray* *10,000.* *18,000.*
No gum 2,500.
On cover *215,000.*
21 A14 5c blk, *lt blue* 60.00 *60.00*
No gum 15.00
On cover 150.00
On cover, single franking 1,350.
a. No period after "5" 75.00 *72.50*
No gum 15.00
On cover 150.00
b. No period after "Cent" 150.00 *350.00*
No gum 37.50
On cover 900.00
c. 5c black, *lt bl* (unglazed, imperf., without gum) 120.00 —
22 A15 10c blk, *org ver* 3.00 *15.00*
No gum .75
On cover 30.00
a. 10c black, *vermilion* 60.00 15.00
No gum 15.00
On cover 30.00
b. 10c black, *ver* (unglazed) 1.25 —
No gum —
c. 10c black, *ver* (unglazed, imperf., without gum) 1.25 —
23 A16 20c blk, *dp crim* 4.75 *30.00*
No gum 1.25
On cover 75.00
a. 20c black, *magenta* 6.00 *42.50*
No gum 1.50
On cover 105.00
b. 20c blk, *mag* (unglazed) 300.00 *35.00*
No gum 75.00
On cover 100.00
c. 20c blk, *mag* (imperf., without gum) 2.50 —
d. 20c blk, *cop red* (unglazed) 1,950. 42.50
No gum 500.00
On cover 100.00
e. 20c blk, *dp crim* (imperf., without gum) 2.50 —
f. No period after "20" *(copper red)* *2,800.* 350.00
No gum 600.00
On cover 900.00
g. No period after "20" *(mag)* 24.00 *180.00*
No gum 6.00
On cover 450.00
h. No period after "20" *(deep crimson)* 25.00 *180.00*
No gum 6.25
On cover 450.00
i. No period after "CENT" *(cop red)* *2,800.* 375.00
No gum 540.00
On cover 900.00
j. No period after "CENT" *(mag)* 24.00 *180.00*
No gum 6.00
On cover 450.00
k. No period after "CENT" *(dp crim)* 24.00 *180.00*
No gum 6.00
On cover 450.00
24 A17 40c blk, *grnsh yel* 11.00 *125.00*
No gum 2.75
On cover 375.00
a. 40c black, *yellow* 210.00 *75.00*
No gum 55.00
On cover 225.00
b. 40c black, *org yel* 90.00 *750.00*
No gum 22.50
On cover 2,250.
c. No period after "40" 15.00 *95.00*
No gum 3.75
On cover 290.00
25 A18 80c blk, *rose lil* 210.00 *415.00*
No gum 52.50
On cover 1,650.
On cover, single franking 3,250.
a. 80c blk, *brt rose* *6,250.* *60,000.*
No gum 850.00
On cover *240,000.*
b. 80c black, *rose* (unglazed) 65.00 —
No gum 16.50
c. No period after "80" *(rose lilac)* 110.00 —
No gum 27.50
On cover —
d. 80c black, *pale rose lilac* (unglazed) 77.50 —
e. 80c black, *pale rose* 55.00 425.00
No gum 13.50
On cover 1,725.
f. As "e," no period after "80" 65.00 650.00
No gum 16.50
On cover 2,800.
g. As "a," no period after "80" 7,000. —
No gum 1,750.
h. As "e," double impression — —
Nos. 19-25 (7) 352.75 3,985.

Values for stamps in pairs

19 A12 2c blk, *grn* 22.50 *155.00*
On cover 425.00
20 A13 3c black, *gray* 90.00 *8,250.*
On cover *65,000.*
20a A13 3c blk, *lil gray* *20,000.*
21 A14 5c blk, *lt blue* 65.00 *125.00*
On cover 260.00
22 A15 10c blk, *org ver* 8.25 *32.50*
On cover 100.00
23 A16 20c blk, *dp crim* 11.50 *290.00*
On cover 1,150.
23d A16 20c blk, *cop red* (unglazed) *4,000.* 290.00
On cover 1,150.
24 A17 40c blk, *grnsh yel* 22.00 *325.00*
On cover 1,350.
25a A18 80c blk, *brt rose* *13,000.*
25b A18 80c blk, *rose lil* (unglazed) 135.00
25c A18 80c blk, *pale rose* 90.00 *900.00*
On cover 3,600.

Values for strips of 3

19 A12 2c blk, *grn* 475.00
On cover 1,425.
20 A13 3c black, *gray* —
20a A13 3c blk, *lil gray* —
21 A14 5c blk, *lt blue* 525.00
On cover 1,625.
22 A15 10c blk, *org ver* 175.00
On cover 700.00
23 A16 20c blk, *dp crim* 1,200.
On cover 4,750.
23d A16 20c blk, *cop red* (unglazed) 1,200.
On cover 4,750.
24 A17 40c blk, *grnsh yel* 1,325.
On cover 5,400.
25a A18 80c blk, *brt rose* —
25b A18 80c blk, *rose lil* (unglazed) —
25e A18 80c blk, *pale rose* (glazed) 1,625.
On cover 6,500.

Vertical pairs, imperf. horizontally

19c A12 2c blk, *grn* 425.00 —
22d A15 10c As 22 360.00 —
22e A15 10c As 22a 500.00 —
24d A17 40c blk, *grnsh yel* 400.00 —
25i A18 80c As 25e 400.00 —
25j A18 80c As 25 1,100. —
25k A18 80c As 25b 500.00 —

Horizontal pairs, imperf. vertically

19d A12 2c blk, *grn* 425.00 —
21d A14 5c blk, *lt blue* 425.00 —
22f A15 10c As 22 275.00 —
22g A15 10c As 22a 400.00 —
23l A16 20c blk, *dp crim* 275.00 —
24e A17 40c blk, *grnsh yel* 400.00 —
25l A18 80c As 25b 575.00 —
25m A18 80c As 25e 425.00 —

Vertical pair, imperf. between

22j A15 10c As 22a 1,100. *5,000.*
23o A16 20c As 23 550.00
23p A16 20c As 23d —
25o A18 80c As 25 1,450.
25p A18 80c As 25e 1,000.

Horizontal pairs, imperf. between

19e	A12	2c blk, *grn*	800.00	—
21e	A14	5c blk, *lt blue*	800.00	*4,250.*
22i	A15	10c As 22a	900.00	*4,750.*
22h	A15	10c As 22	425.00	—
23m	A16	20c As 23	425.00	
23n	A16	20c As 23d	5,000.	*9,500.*
25n	A18	80c As 25b	—	—

Double perforations on one side

19f	A12	2c blk, *grn*	57.50	650.00
20b	A13	3c black, *gray*	92.50	—
21f	A14	5c blk, *lt blue*	110.00	—
22k	A15	10c As 22a	145.00	250.00
22m	A15	10c As 22	42.50	250.00
23q	A16	20c As 23d		725.00
23r	A16	20c As 23a		1,000.
24f	A17	40c blk, *grnsh yel*	115.00	—
25q	A18	80c As 25e	130.00	—
25r	A18	80c As 25b	200.00	—

Double impressions are known of the 5c, 10c, 20c (all three colors), 40c and 80c.

Covers: Nos. 21, 25 single frankings are worth much more.

Fraudulent cancellations are found on Nos. 20, 24 and 25.

The stamps of the 1867 and 1868 issues have been privately reprinted; many of these reprints are well executed and it is difficult to distinguish them from the originals. Most reprints show more or less pronounced defects of the design. On the originals the horizontal lines between stamps are unbroken, while on most of the reprints these lines are broken. Most of the perforated reprints gauge 11½.

Roman States stamps were replaced by those of Italy in 1870.

SARDINIA

LOCATION — An island in the Mediterranean Sea off the west coast of Italy and a large area in northwestern Italy, including the cities of Genoa, Turin and Nice.

GOVT. — Kingdom

As a result of war and revolution, most of the former independent Italian States were joined to the Kingdom of Sardinia in 1859 and 1860. On March 17, 1861, the name was changed to the Kingdom of Italy.

100 Centesimi = 1 Lira

Values of Sardinia stamps vary tremendously according to condition. Values are for very fine examples, and values for unused stamps are for examples with original gum as defined in the catalogue introduction. Extremely fine or superb stamps sell at much higher prices, and fine or poor stamps sell at greatly reduced prices.

King Victor Emmanuel II — A1

1851 Unwmk. Litho. *Imperf.*

1	A1	5c gray black	13,000.	2,000.
		No gum	3,250.	
		On cover		5,750.
		On cover, single franking		16,500.
a.		5c black	13,000.	2,000.
		No gum	3,250.	
		On cover		*5,750.*
		On cover, single franking		*16,500.*
2	A1	20c blue	9,500.	235.00
		No gum	2,350.	
		On cover		700.00
a.		20c deep blue	9,500.	235.00
		No gum	2,350.	
		On cover		700.00
b.		20c pale blue	9,500.	235.00
		No gum	2,350.	
		On cover		875.00
c.		20c deep sky blue	17,500.	1,600.
		No gum	3,600.	
		On cover		4,250.
3	A1	40c rose	17,750.	*4,000.*
		No gum	4,500.	
		On cover		14,500.
a.		40c violet rose	17,750.	*5,250.*
		No gum	4,500.	
		On cover		*20,000.*
		On cover, single franking		*22,500.*
b.		40c bright carmine rose	20,500.	5,850.
		No gum	4,500.	
		On cover		*20,000.*
		On cover, single franking		22,500.
c.		40c lilac rose	28,500.	23,500.
		No gum	4,750.	
		On cover		*24,000.*

Full margins = ½mm.

Values for pairs

1a	A1	5c black	*37,500.*	*4,650.*
		On cover		*14,500.*
2	A1	20c blue	*20,000.*	*1,200.*
		On cover		*4,750.*
3	A1	40c rose	*42,500.*	*11,000.*
		On cover		*42,500.*

Values for blocks of 4

1a	A1	5c black	*80,000.*
2	A1	20c blue	*80,000.*
3	A1	40c rose	*120,000.*

King Victor Emmanuel II — A2

Vignette & Inscriptions Embossed

1853

4	A2	5c *blue green*	*17,500.*	1,100.
		No gum	4,250.	
		On cover		3,150.
		On cover, single franking		7,750.
a.		Double embossing		*3,000.*
		On cover		*8,750.*
5	A2	20c *dull blue*	*18,500.*	200.00
		No gum	4,500.	
		On cover		525.00
a.		Double embossing		*1,250.*
		On cover		*3,750.*
6	A2	40c *pale rose*	*11,250.*	800.00
		No gum	2,850.	
		On cover		3,250.
a.		40c *rose*	*17,500.*	1,750.
		No gum	3,750.	
		On cover		5,750.
b.		Double embossing		*2,250.*
		On cover		*8,750.*

Full margins = ¾mm.

Values for pairs

4	A2	5c *blue green*	*37,500.*	2,500.
		On cover		*7,000.*
5	A2	20c *dull blue*	*40,000.*	1,000.
		On cover		3,000.
6	A2	40c *pale rose*	*25,000.*	2,700.
		On cover		*10,750.*

Values for blocks of 4

4	A2	5c *blue green*		67,500.
5	A2	20c *dull blue*		
6	A2	40c *pale rose*	*60,000.*	55,000.

King Victor Emmanuel II — A3

Lithographed Frame in Color, Colorless Embossed Vignette

1854

7	A3	5c yellow green	30,000.	575.00
		No gum	11,250.	
		On cover		2,500.
		On cover, single franking		6,000.
a.		Double embossing		1,250.
		On cover		4,750.
b.		5c grayish green	3,600.	
		No gum	900.00	
c.		5c deep green	3,600.	
8	A3	20c blue	16,000.	175.00
		No gum	6,250.	
		On cover		500.00
a.		Double embossing		525.00
		On cover		1,600.
b.		20c indigo	700.00	
		No gum	165.00	
9	A3	40c rose	*82,500.*	2,750.
		No gum	*37,500.*	
		On cover		*8,750.*
a.		Double embossing		5,500.
		On cover		16,500.
b.		40c brown rose	180.00	—
		No gum	40.00	

Full margins = ¾mm.

Values for pairs

7	A3	5c yellow green		1,275.
		On cover		5,250.
b.		5c grayish green	*7,500.*	
8	A3	20c blue		950.00
		On cover		2,850.
b.		20c indigo	2,150.	
9	A3	40c rose		*9,250.*
		On cover		*24,000.*
b.		40c brown rose	500.00	

Values for blocks of 4

7	A3	5c yellow green		*100,000.*
b.		5c grayish green	22,500.	
8	A3	20c blue		—
b.		20c indigo	3,600.	
9	A3	40c rose		—
b.		40c brown rose	900.00	

Nos. 7b, 8b and 9b, differing in shade from the original stamps, were prepared but not issued.

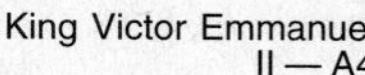

King Victor Emmanuel II — A4

Stamps of this issue vary greatly in color, paper and sharpness of embossing as between the early (1855-59) printings and the later (1860-63) ones. Year dates after each color name indicate whether the stamp falls into the Early or Late printing group.

As a rule, early printings are on smooth thick paper with sharp embossing, while later printings are usually on paper varying from thick to thin and of inferior quality with embossing less distinct and printing blurred. The outer frame shows a distinct design on the early printings, while this design is more or less blurred or even a solid line on the later printings.

Typographed Frame in Color, Colorless Embossed Vignette

1855-63 Unwmk. *Imperf.*

10	A4	5c grn ('62-63)	4.50	*11.00*
		No gum	1.15	
		On cover		35.00
		On cover, single franking		75.00
a.		5c yel grn ('62-63)	95.00	17.00
		No gum	18.00	
		On cover		67.50
		On cover, single franking		115.00
b.		5c olive green ('60-61)	435.00	67.50
		No gum	85.00	
		On cover		270.00
		On cover, single franking		360.00
c.		5c yel grn ('55-59)	900.00	160.00
		No gum	225.00	
		On cover		630.00
		On cover, single franking		800.00
d.		5c myrtle green ('57)	7,500.	475.00
		No gum	1,750.	
		On cover		1,800.
		On cover, single franking		2,200.
e.		5c emerald ('55-57)	3,900.	375.00
		No gum	975.00	
		On cover		1,425.
		On cover, single franking		1,900.
f.		Head inverted	—	3,700.
		On cover		*35,000.*
g.		Double head, one inverted	—	*3,500.*
		On cover		—
11	A4	10c bister ('63)	4.50	*24.00*
		No gum	1.15	
		On cover		70.00
a.		10c ocher ('62)	90.00	22.00
		No gum	22.50	
		On cover		65.00
b.		10c olive bister ('62)	190.00	22.00
		No gum	47.50	
		On cover		67.50
c.		10c olive brown ('61)	190.00	29.00
		No gum	50.00	
		On cover		90.00
d.		10c reddish brn ('61)	1,800.	160.00
		No gum	450.00	
		On cover		475.00
e.		10c gray brown ('61)	150.00	40.00
		No gum	37.50	
		On cover		100.00
f.		10c olive gray ('60-61)	370.00	55.00
		No gum	90.00	
		On cover		170.00
g.		10c gray ('60)	1,350.	180.00
		No gum	375.00	
		On cover		540.00
h.		10c grayish brown ('59)	130.00	210.00
		No gum	35.00	
		On cover		650.00
i.		10c violet brown ('59)	525.00	300.00
		No gum	150.00	
		On cover		900.00
j.		10c dark brown ('58)	*775.00*	360.00
		No gum	190.00	
		On cover		1,100.
k.		Head inverted	—	4,000.
		On cover		*40,000.*
l.		Double head, one inverted	—	4,000.
		On cover		*40,000.*
m.		Pair, one without embossing	*2,000.*	—
n.		Half used as 5c on cover (15c rate)		*125,000.*
o.		Half used as 5c on cover (5c rate)		*210,000.*
12	A4	20c indigo ('62)	85.00	40.00
		No gum	22.00	
		On cover		115.00
a.		20c blue ('61)	165.00	16.00
		No gum	42.50	
		On cover		47.50
b.		20c light blue ('60-61)	165.00	16.00
		No gum	42.50	
		On cover		47.50
c.		20c Prus bl ('59-60)	775.00	27.50
		No gum	200.00	
		On cover		80.00
d.		20c indigo ('57-58)	460.00	40.00
		No gum	115.00	
		On cover		115.00
e.		20c sky blue ('55-56)	7,100.	170.00
		No gum	2,000.	
		On cover		525.00
f.		20c cobalt ('55)	3,600.	100.00
		No gum	900.00	
		On cover		300.00
g.		Head inverted	3,100.	1,600.
		No gum	1,550.	
		On cover		*16,000.*
h.		Double head, one inverted	—	—
i.		Pair, one without embossing	1,100.	—
		No gum	550.00	
j.		Half used as 10c on cover		*160,000.*
k.		As "c", one without embossing	1,250.	—
		No gum	600.00	
13	A4	40c red ('63)	17.00	*40.00*
		No gum	4.25	
		On cover		120.00
a.		40c rose ('61-62)	135.00	60.00
		No gum	35.00	
		On cover		170.00
b.		40c carmine ('60)	775.00	350.00
		No gum	170.00	
		On cover		1,100.
c.		40c light red ('57)	3,800.	110.00
		No gum	950.00	
		On cover		350.00
d.		40c vermilion ('55-57)	7,250.	325.00
		No gum	1,650.	
		On cover		1,300.
e.		Head inverted	—	6,250.
		On cover		*50,000.*
f.		Double head, one inverted	—	*6,250.*
g.		Pair, one without embossing	1,625.	—
		No gum	825.00	
h.		Half used as 20c on cover		*67,500.*
14	A4	80c org yel ('62)	22.00	*390.00*
		No gum	5.50	
		On cover		2,500.
a.		80c yellow ('60-61)	25.00	*360.00*
		No gum	6.75	
		On cover		2,150.
b.		80c yellow ocher ('59)	900.00	690.00
		No gum	225.00	
		On cover		4,750.
c.		80c ocher ('58)	200.00	*540.00*
		No gum	50.00	
		On cover		3,750.
d.		80c brown orange ('58)	220.00	*600.00*
		No gum	55.00	
		On cover		4,250.
e.		Head inverted	—	*22,500.*
		On cover		*110,000.*
f.		Half used as 40c on cover		85,000.
15	A4	3 l bronze, thin paper ('61)	400.00	*3,650.*
		No gum	100.00	
		On cover		*145,000.*
		On cover, single franking		*220,000.*
a.		Thick, opaque paper	525.00	*4,100.*
		No gum	150.00	
		On cover		*145,000.*
		On cover, single franking		*220,000.*
		Nos. 10-15 (6)	533.00	4,155.

Full margins = 1mm.

Values for pairs

10	A4	5c green	11.00	*27.50*
		On cover		130.00
a.		5c yellow green	72.50	40.00
		On cover		170.00
b.		5c olive green	850.00	190.00
		On cover		675.00
c.		5c yellow green	2,000.	475.00
		On cover		1,575.
d.		5c myrtle green	*15,000.*	975.00
		On cover		4,000.
e.		5c emerald	8,500.	775.00
		On cover		4,000.
11	A4	10c bister	11.00	*72.50*
		On cover		215.00
a.		10c ocher	200.00	57.50
		On cover		170.00
b.		10c olive bister	400.00	72.50
		On cover		190.00
c.		10c olive green	475.00	175.00
		On cover		540.00
f.		10c olive gray	800.00	175.00
		On cover		540.00
h.		10c grayish brown	275.00	*425.00*
		On cover		1,425.
j.		10c dark brown	1,600.	1,000.
		On cover		3,100.
12	A4	20c indigo	220.00	130.00
		On cover		450.00
b.		20c light blue	415.00	62.50
		On cover		225.00
c.		20c prussian blue	1,600.	100.00
		On cover		360.00
d.		20c indigo	1,050.	175.00
		On cover		400.00
f.		20c cobalt	7,500.	325.00
		On cover		1,000.
13	A4	40c red	45.00	*135.00*
		On cover		525.00
a.		40c rose	340.00	215.00
		On cover		720.00
b.		40c carmine	1,600.	575.00
		On cover		1,800.
c.		40c light red	8,000.	290.00
		On cover		875.00
d.		40c vermilion	*15,000.*	875.00
		On cover		3,250.
14	A4	80c orange yellow	55.00	*1,100.*
		On cover		6,500.
a.		80c yellow	60.00	*925.00*
		On cover		5,000.
b.		80c yellow ocher	2,000.	1,550.
		On cover		10,000.
c.		80c ocher	450.00	*1,175.*
		On cover		5,000.
d.		80c brown orange	460.00	*1,500.*
		On cover		10,000.
15	A4	3 l bronze, thin paper	900.00	*14,500.*
a.		Thick opaque paper	1,100.	*14,500.*

Forgeries of the inverted and double head varieties have been made by applying a faked head embossing to printer's waste without head. These forgeries are plentiful.

Fraudulent cancellations are found on #13-15.

The 5c, 20c and 40c have been reprinted; the embossing of the reprints is not as sharp as that of the originals, the colors are dull and blurred.

NEWSPAPER STAMPS

N1

Typographed and Embossed

1861 Unwmk. *Imperf.*

P1 N1 1c black 6.75 15.00
No gum 1.75
On newspaper or cover 45.00
a. Numeral "2" 600.00 *2,500.*
No gum 550.00
On newspaper or cover 16,500.
b. Figure of value inverted 2,400. *34,000.*
c. Double impression 2,750. —
No gum 1,800.

P2 N1 2c black 175.00 105.00
No gum 45.00
On newspaper or cover 215.00
a. Numeral "1" *13,000.* *32,500.*
No gum 6,500.
b. Figure of value inverted *2,400.* *34,000.*
No gum 1,200.

Full margins = 1mm.

Values for pairs

P1 N1 1c black 16.00 *30.00*
On newspaper or cover 80.00
P2 N1 2c black 400.00 260.00
On newspaper or cover 525.00

Forgeries of the varieties of the embossed numerals have been made from printer's waste without numerals.

See Italy No. P1 for 2c buff.

The stamps of Sardinia were superseded in 1862 by those of Italy, which were identical with the 1855 issue of Sardinia, but perforated. Until 1863, imperforate and perforated stamps were issued simultaneously.

TUSCANY

LOCATION — In the north central part of the Apennine Peninsula.
GOVT. — Grand Duchy
AREA — 8,890 sq. mi.
POP. — 2,892,000 (approx.)
CAPITAL — Florence

Tuscany was annexed to Sardinia in 1860.

60 Quattrini = 20 Soldi = 12 Crazie = 1 Lira
100 Centesimi = 1 Lira (1860)

Values of Tuscany stamps vary tremendously according to condition. Values are for very fine examples, and values for unused stamps are for examples with original gum as defined in the catalogue introduction. Extremely fine or superb stamps sell at much higher prices, and fine or poor stamps sell at greatly reduced prices. In addition, very fine unused stamps without gum sell for about 20% of the values shown.

Covers: Values are for covers bearing stamps with four margins. Covers with stamps lacking four margins are worth much less.

Dangerous counterfeits exist of #1-PR1c.

Lion of Tuscany — A1

1851-52 Typo. Wmk. 185 *Imperf.*
Blue, Grayish Blue or Gray Paper

1 A1 1q black, *grayish* ('52) 15,000. 2,250.
No gum 3,800.
On cover 5,200.
On newspaper, single franking 12,000.
On circular, single franking 19,250.
a. 1q black, *bluish* ('51) 17,500. 2,000.
No gum 4,500.
On cover *6,400.*
On newspaper, single franking *12,800.*
On circular, single franking *20,000.*

2 A1 1s ocher, *grayish* 17,250. 2,100.
No gum 5,350.
On cover 10,500.
a. 1s orange, *grayish* 19,250. 2,100.
No gum 4,250.
On cover 8,400.
b. 1s yellow, *bluish* 20,750. 2,350.
No gum 5,275.
On cover 9,250.
c. 1s yellow bister, *bluish* 18,750. 2,500.
No gum 5,000.
On cover 9,250.
d. 1s golden yellow, *bluish* 17,250. 2,100.
No gum 7,750.
On cover 9,600.
e. 1s bis org, *grayish* 17,250. 9,600.
No gum 5,500.
On cover 8,400.

3 A1 2s scarlet *57,500.* 9,600.
No gum 14,750.
On cover 24,000.

4 A1 1cr carmine 8,800. 145.00
No gum 2,275.
On cover 425.00
a. 1cr brown carmine 11,600. 145.00
No gum 3,100.
On cover 425.00
b. 1cr lake red, *bluish* 12,000. 400.00
No gum 2,400.
On cover 960.00

5 A1 2cr blue 5,250. 160.00
No gum 1,350.
On cover 625.00
a. 2cr greenish blue 5,600. 160.00
No gum 1,400.
On cover 920.00

6 A1 4cr green 8,800. 125.00
No gum 2,275.
On cover 725.00
a. 4cr bluish green 9,600. 325.00
No gum 2,280.
On cover 1,250.

7 A1 6cr slate blue 9,600. 275.00
No gum 2,600.
On cover 1,125.
a. 6cr blue 8,800. 275.00
No gum 2,275.
On cover 1,125.
b. 6cr indigo 9,600. 300.00
No gum 2,600.
On cover 1,125.

8 A1 9cr gray lilac 21,000. 300.00
No gum 5,275.
On cover 1,125.
a. 9cr deep violet 21,000. 300.00
No gum 5,275.
On cover 1,125.

9 A1 60cr red ('52) *95,000.* *27,500.*
No gum 26,000.
On cover *160,000.*

Values for Pairs

1 A1 1q black, *grayish* ('52) *32,500.* *5,500.*
On cover *15,000.*
2 A1 1s ocher, *grayish* *35,000.* *6,000.*
On cover *25,000.*
3 A1 2s scarlet *20,000.*
On cover *47,500.*
4 A1 1cr carmine *20,000.* 400.00
On cover 1,100.
5 A1 2cr blue 575.00
On cover 2,250.
6 A1 4cr green *20,000.* 800.00
On cover 3,250.
7a A1 6cr blue *22,500.* 850.00
On cover 4,750.
8a A1 9cr deep violet *750.00*
On cover *3,250.*
9 A1 60cr red ('52) *75,000.*

Values for Blocks of 4

1 A1 1q black, *grayish* ('52) *65,000.* *45,000.*
2 A1 1s ocher, *grayish* *85,000.* *55,000.*
4 A1 1cr carmine 8,500.
5 A1 2cr blue *27,500.* *22,500.*
6 A1 4cr green *45,000.* *25,000.*
7a A1 6cr blue *27,500.*
8a A1 9cr deep violet *12,500.*

Full margins = ¼mm.

The first paper was blue, later paper more and more grayish. Stamps on distinctly blue paper sell about 20 percent higher, except Nos. 3 and 9 which were issued on blue paper only. Examples without watermark are proofs.

Reprints of Nos. 3 and 9 have re-engraved value labels, color is too brown and impressions blurred and heavy. Paper same as originals.

No. 14a

1857-59 White Paper Wmk. 184

10 A1 1q black 1,750. 920.00
No gum 600.00
On cover 2,800.
On newspaper, single franking 6,000.
On circular, single franking 12,000.

11 A1 1s yellow *52,000.* 6,250.
No gum 17,500.
On cover 31,000.

12 A1 1cr carmine 11,600. 900.00
No gum 3,100.
On cover 2,600.

13 A1 2cr blue 3,850. 160.00
No gum 1,050.
On cover 625.00
a. 2cr greenish blue 4,750. 195.00
No gum 1,050.
On cover 625.00
b. 2cr yellowish gray green 4,750. 200.00
No gum 1,050.
On cover 625.00

14 A1 4cr green 8,800. 175.00
No gum 2,350.
On cover 725.00
a. Inverted value tablet *1,100,000.*
b. A1 4cr yellow green 12,000. 250.00

15 A1 6cr deep blue *12,500.* 300.00
No gum 3,250.
On cover 1,125.

16 A1 9cr gray lil ('59) *52,000.* *6,250.*
No gum 13,600.
On cover 31,000.

Full margins = ¼mm.

Values for pairs

10 A1 1q black 4,400. 2,200.
On cover 6,600.
11 A1 1s yellow *15,600.*
On cover *80,000.*
12 A1 1cr carmine 31,000. 1,800.
On cover 5,250.
13 A1 2cr blue 9,000. 575.
On cover 2,250.
14 A1 4cr green 22,000. 900.
On cover 3,500.
15 A1 6cr deep blue 48,000. 1,250.
On cover 4,800.
16 A1 9cr gray lilac *16,000.*
On cover *80,000.*

Provisional Government

Coat of Arms — A2

1860

17 A2 1c brn lilac 3,800. 960.00
No gum 960.00
On cover 2,800.
On newspaper or wrapper, single franking 4,200.
On circular, single franking 6,800.
a. 1c red lilac 4,400. 1,075.
No gum 1,800.
On cover 3,200.
On newspaper or wrapper, single franking 4,800.
On circular, single franking 7,600.
b. 1c gray lilac 3,800. 960.00
No gum 960.00
On cover 2,800.
On newspaper or wrapper, single franking 4,600.
On circular, single franking 6,800.

18 A2 5c green 14,000. 260.00
No gum 3,800.
On cover 720.00
On cover, single franking 22,000.
a. 5c olive green 15,200. 275.00
No gum 4,000.
On cover 800.00
b. 5c yellow green 17,600. 360.00
No gum 5,200.
On cover 1,075.

19 A2 10c dp brn 4,800. 62.50
No gum 1,100.
On cover 190.00
a. 10c gray brown 4,800. 62.50
No gum 1,275.
On cover 190.00
b. 10c purple brown 4,125. 62.50
No gum 1,100.
On cover 190.00

20 A2 20c blue 12,400. 180.00
No gum 3,400.
On cover 720.00
a. 20c deep blue 12,400. 220.00
No gum 3,400.
On cover 875.00
b. 20c gray blue 14,000. 220.00
No gum 3,800.
On cover 875.00

21 A2 40c rose 18,000. 350.00
No gum 4,600.
On cover 1,750.
a. 40c carmine 18,000. 350.00
No gum 4,600.
On cover 1,750.
b. Half used as 20c on cover *175,000.*

22 A2 80c pale red brn *32,000.* 1,500.
No gum 8,000.
On cover 7,500.
On cover, single franking 11,250.
a. 80c brown orange *32,000.* 1,525.
No gum 8,000.
On cover 7,500.
On cover, single franking 11,250.

23 A2 3 l ocher *260,000.* *125,000.*
No gum 110,000.

Full margins = ¼mm.

Values for pairs

17b A2 1c gray lilac 8,500. 2,400.
On cover 7,200.
18 A2 5c green *30,000.* 560.00
On cover 1,600.
19a A2 10c deep brown 10,500. 200.00
On cover 600.00
20 A2 20c blue *27,500.* 700.00
On cover 2,700.
21a A2 40c carmine *40,000.* 2,250.
On cover 12,000.
22 A2 80c pale red brn 4,500.
On cover *24,000.*

NEWSPAPER TAX STAMPS

NT1

1854 Unwmk. Typo. *Imperf.*
Yellowish Pelure Paper

PR1 NT1 2s black 80.00
No gum 22.50
On newsprint, uncanceled 240.00
a. Tête bêche pair 750.00
b. As "a," one stamp on back 750.00
c. Double impression 560.00
d. Gummed on the front side 225.00

Full margins = 10mm.

This stamp represented a fiscal tax on newspapers coming from foreign countries. It was not canceled when used.

The stamps of Tuscany were superseded by those of Sardinia in 1861.

TWO SICILIES

LOCATION — Formerly comprised the island of Sicily and the lower half of the Apennine Peninsula.
GOVT. — Independent Kingdom
CAPITAL — Naples

The Kingdom was annexed to Sardinia in 1860.

200 Tornesi = 100 Grana = 1 Ducat

Values of Two Sicilies stamps vary tremendously according to condition. Values are for very fine examples, and values for unused stamps are for examples with original gum as defined in the catalogue introduction. Extremely fine or superb copies sell at much higher prices, and fine or poor copies sell at greatly reduced prices. In addition, very fine unused stamps without gum sell for about 20%-30% of the values shown.

Naples

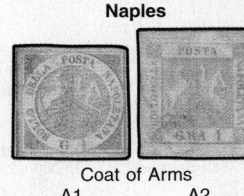

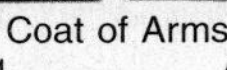
Coat of Arms
A1 A2

A3

A4

A5

A6

A7

1858 Engr. Wmk. 186 *Imperf.*

1 A1 ½g pale lake 2,200. 325.00
No gum 550.00
On cover 550.00
Single franking on newspaper or wrapper 1,450.
Single franking on circular 1,950.
a. ½g rose lake 2,200. 325.00
No gum 550.00
On cover 900.00
Single franking on newspaper or wrapper 1,475.
Single franking on circular 1,950.
b. ½g lake 2,740. 550.00
No gum 675.00
On cover 1,625.
Single franking on newspaper or wrapper 2,450.
Single franking on circular 3,250.
c. ½g carmine lake 3,300. 700.00
No gum 825.00
On cover 2,100.
Single franking on newspaper or wrapper 3,150.
Single franking on circular 4,200.
d. Half used as ¼g on newspaper *225,000.*
2 A2 1g pale lake 950.00 37.50
No gum 240.00
On cover 95.00
a. 1g rose lake 660.00 37.50
No gum 170.00
On cover 95.00
b. 1g brown lake 1,600. 82.50
No gum 400.00
On cover 200.00
c. 1g carmine lake 1,000. 65.00
No gum 250.00
On cover 170.00
d. Printed on both sides 1,750.
e. Printed on both sides, one inverted 900.00
On cover *3,500.*
3 A3 2g pale lake 660.00 14.00
No gum 170.00
On cover 35.00
a. 2g rose lake 660.00 14.00
No gum 170.00
On cover 35.00
b. 2g lake 900.00 22.50
No gum 235.00
On cover 55.00
c. 2g carmine lake 1,100. 22.50
No gum 275.00
On cover 55.00
d. Impression of 1g on reverse *1,650.*
e. Double impression *9,000.*
On cover *27,500.*
f. Printed on both sides 1,775.
4 A4 5g brown lake 3,300. 67.50
No gum 825.00
On cover 200.00
a. 5g rose lake 2,750. 67.50
No gum 675.00
On cover 200.00
b. 5g carmine lake 4,000. 67.50
No gum 1,000.
On cover 200.00
d. Printed on both sides *5,000.*
e. 5g rose carmine 6,000. 165.00
No gum 1,500.
On cover 490.00
f. 5g bright carmine 6,600. 275.00
No gum 1,650.
On cover 550.00
g. 5g dark carmine 7,600. 300.00
No gum 1,900.
On cover 825.00
5 A5 10g rose lake 6,600. 190.00
No gum 1,650.
On cover 540.00
a. 10g lake 7,400. 350.00
No gum 1,900.
On cover 1,100.
b. 10g carmine lake 7,250. 350.00
No gum 1,900.
On cover 1,100.
c. Printed on both sides 15,000.
d. Double impression *15,000.*
On cover *45,000.*
6 A6 20g rose lake 6,000. 675.00
No gum 1,500.
On cover 2,900.
a. 20g lake 6,000. 800.00
No gum 1,500.
On cover 2,900.
b. Double impression *55,000.*
c. 20g pale rose *9,000.* 1,350.
No gum 2,250.
On cover 5,400.
d. 20g pale car rose *9,500.* 1,600.
No gum 2,400.
On cover 6,400.
7 A7 50g rose lake *11,000.* 2,400.
No gum 2,700.
On cover *29,000.*
a. 50g lake *11,000.* 2,400.
No gum 2,700.
On cover *30,000.*

Nos. 1-2, 4-7 have been reprinted in bright rose and Nos. 1, 7 in dull brown. The reprints are on thick unwatermarked paper. Value $8 each.

Values for pairs

1 A1 ½g pale lake 4,400. 700.00
On cover *2,000.*
1b A1 ½g pale lake 5,500. 1,150.
On cover *3,300.*
2 A2 1g pale lake 1,925. 82.50
On cover *200.00*
2a A2 1g rose lake 1,325. 82.50
On cover *200.00*
3 A3 2g pale lake 1,325. 35.00
On cover *85.00*
3a A3 2g rose lake 1,325. 35.00
On cover *85.00*
4a A4 5g rose lake 5,500. 440.00
On cover *1,325.*
4e A4 5g rose carmine *12,000.* 1,100.
On cover *4,400.*
5 A5 10g rose lake *13,250.* 1,650.
On cover *5,000.*
5b A5 10g carmine lake *15,000.* 2,500.
On cover *7,500.*
6 A6 20g rose lake *12,250.* 3,850.
On cover *19,000.*
6c A6 20g pale car rose *18,250.* 7,250.
On cover *35,000.*
7 A7 50g rose lake *22,000.* 8,250.
On cover *100,000.*

Values for strips of 3

1 A1 ½g pale lake 1,100.
On cover *3,300.*
1b A1 ½g pale lake 1,750.
On cover *5,250.*
2 A2 1g pale lake 275.00
On cover *825.00*
2a A2 1g rose lake 275.00
On cover *825.00*
3 A3 2g pale lake 125.00
On cover *500.00*
3a A3 2g rose lake 125.00
On cover *500.00*
4a A4 5g rose lake 1,650.
On cover *8,250.*
4e A4 5g rose carmine 4,125.
On cover *20,000.*
5 A5 10g rose lake 6,000.
On cover *30,000.*
5b A5 10g carmine lake 8,750.
On cover —
6 A6 20g rose lake 16,500.
On cover *82,500.*
6c A6 20g pale car rose 33,000.
On cover —
7 A7 50g rose lake 36,000.
On cover —

Values for blocks of 4

1 A1 ½g pale lake 12,500. 20,000.
1b A1 ½g pale lake 13,750. 35,000.
2 A2 1g pale lake 5,000. 8,500.
2a A2 1g rose lake 3,500. 8,500.
3 A3 2g pale lake 3,500. 2,500.
3a A3 2g rose lake 3,500. 2,500.
4a A4 5g rose lake — *12,750.*
4e A4 5g rose carmine — *22,500.*
5 A5 10g rose lake — *22,500.*
6 A6 20g rose lake *200,000.*
6c A6 20g pale car rose *100,000.*

Full margins = 1mm at sides, 1½mm at top and bottom.

Covers: Single frankings of Nos. 1, 2, 7 on newspapers, wrappers or circulars are worth much more.

Only one example of No. 6b is known.

As a secret mark, the engraver, G. Masini, placed a minute letter of his name just above the lower outer line of each stamp. There were three plates of the 2g, one plate of the 50g, and two plates of each of the other values.

Nos. 1-2, 4-7 have been reprinted in bright rose and Nos. 1, 7 in dull brown. The reprints are on thick unwatermarked paper. Value $8 each.

Provisional Government

A8

A9

1860

8 A8 ½t deep blue 250,000. 11,000.
No gum 82,500.
On newspaper 22,000.
On circular 25,000.
On official document 30,000.
9 A9 ½t blue 50,000. 3,250.
No gum 16,500.
On newspaper 10,500.
On circular 22,000.
On official document 15,500.
a. ½t deep blue 50,000. 3,500.
No gum 16,500.
On newspaper 10,500.
On circular 22,000.
On official document 17,500.

Full margins = 1¼mm at sides, 2mm at top and bottom.

100 varieties of each.

No. 8 was made from the plate of No. 1, which was altered by changing the "G" to "T."

No. 9 was made from the same plate after a second alteration erasing the coat of arms and inserting the Cross of Savoy. Dangerous counterfeits exist of Nos. 8-9.

Covers: Nos. 8-10 on official documents are worth more than on newspapers.

Sicily

Ferdinand II — A10

1859 Unwmk. Engr. *Imperf.*
Soft Porous Paper, Brownish Gum (Naples consignment)

10 A10 ½g orange 1,050. 875.00
No gum 200.00
On cover 4,350.
On circular, single franking 8,750.
On newspaper, single franking 6,600.
a. ½g yellow 11,750. 2,950.
No gum 2,350.
On cover 14,500.
On circular, single franking 29,500.
On newspaper, single franking 22,000.
b. ½g olive yellow — 44,000.
On cover 90,000.
On circular, single franking —
On newspaper, single franking 145,000.
c. Printed on both sides — *44,000.*
d. ½g brownish yellow 27,500. 11,500.
No gum 5,250.
On cover *60,000.*
e. ½g deep orange 2,000. *4,000.*
No gum 375.00
On cover 20,000.
f. ½g reddish orange 29,500.

A newspaper with single franking ½ grana orange, No. 10e, sold for the equivalent of U.S. $14,750 at a Turin auction in 2004.

11 A10 1g dk brn 20,000. 875.00
No gum 5,250.
On cover 4,350.
On cover, single franking 15,000.
a. 1g olive brown (I) 46,500. 1,150.
No gum 10,500.
On cover 5,750.
On cover, single franking 37,500.
12 A10 1g ol grn (III) 2,950. 290.00
No gum 525.00
On cover 875.00
On cover, single franking 19,000.
a. 1g grysh olive grn (II) 6,500. 220.00
No gum 1,450.
On cover 650.00
On cover, single franking 14,000.
b. 1g olive brown (II) 1,750. 175.00
No gum 300.00
On cover 525.00
On cover, single franking 4,500.
c. Double impression 5,250. 4,750.
On cover *32,500.*
13 A10 2g blue 4,350. 120.00
No gum 875.00
On cover 350.00
On cover, single franking 4,000.
a. 2g deep blue *8,000.* 500.00
No gum 1,900.
On cover 1,450.
On cover, single franking 1,100.
b. Printed on both sides — 26,000.
c. 2g greenish blue 1,750. 145.00
No gum 425.00
On cover 375.00
d. 2g ultramarine 14,500. 950.00
No gum 3,000.
On cover 2,950.
e. 2g cobalt 6,500. 190.00
No gum 1,600.
On cover 475.00
f. 2g dark cobalt 14,500. 500.00
No gum 2,900.
On cover 1,400.
14 A10 5g deep rose 950.00 700.00
No gum 240.00
On cover 5,000.
On cover, single franking 8,500.
a. 5g carmine 875.00 700.00
No gum 240.00
On cover 5,000.
On cover, single franking 10,500.
b. 5g brick red 17,500. 6,500.
No gum 4,000.
On cover 32,500.
c. 5g dark carmine 3,800. 1,000.
No gum 1,000.
On cover 13,250.
d. 5g blood red 2,650. 1,100.
No gum 600.00
On cover 7,250.
15 A10 5g vermilion 875.00 *2,350.*
No gum 220.00
On cover 16,000.
On cover, single franking 25,000.
a. 5g orange vermilion 725.00 *2,600.*
No gum 180.00
On cover 18,500.
On cover, single franking 27,500.
b. 5g bright vermilion 725.00 *3,250.*
No gum 180.00
On cover 20,000.
16 A10 10g dark blue 975.00 440.00
No gum 240.00
On cover 3,100.
On cover, single franking 3,100.
a. 10g indigo 975.00 440.00
No gum 240.00
On cover 3,100.
On cover, single franking 3,100.
b. 10g indigo black 5,000. 2,050.
No gum 1,350.
On cover 14,500.
17 A10 20g dk gray vio 975.00 775.00
No gum 240.00
On cover 5,250.
On cover, single franking 16,000.
a. 20g slate black 4,750. 2,100.
No gum 1,175.
On cover 14,500.
b. 20g slate violet 4,750. *3,750.*
No gum 1,250.
On cover 26,000.
18 A10 50g dk brn red 975.00 *5,850.*
No gum 240.00
On cover 115,000.
On cover, single franking —
a. 50g dark purple lake 3,000. 22,500.
No gum 1,000.

Hard White Paper, White Gum (Palermo consignment)

10g A10 ½g orange 700.00 *5,000.*
No gum 175.00
On cover —
10h A10 ½g brt org 700.00 *5,000.*
No gum 175.00
On cover —
12g A10 1g grayish ol (II) 875.00 175.00
No gum 225.00
On cover 525.00
12h A10 1g pale ol grn (III) 275.00 *240.00*
No gum 75.00
On cover 700.00
12i A10 1g ol grn (III) 275.00 240.00
No gum 75.00
On cover 700.00
13g A10 2g blue 200.00 120.00
No gum 60.00
On cover 350.00
13h A10 2g pale blue 200.00 120.00
No gum 60.00
On cover 350.00

Full margins = 1mm.

Covers: Single frankings of Nos. 11, 12, 15, 17 on newspapers or covers are worth more.

Fraudulent cancellations are known on Nos. 10, 15, 15a and 18.

There were three plates each for the 1g and 2g, two each for the ½g and 5g and one plate each for the other values.

Nos. 10a, 10b, 11, 11a, 14, 14a, 14b and 15 are printed from Plate I on which the stamps are 2 to 2½mm apart. On almost all stamps from Plate I, the S and T of POSTA touch.

Nos. 12a, and 15a are from Plate II and No. 12 is from Plate III. On both Plates II and III stamps are spaced 1½mm apart. Most stamps from Plate II have a white line about 1mm long below the beard.

The ½g blue is stated to be a proof of which two examples are known. Both originated on the same cover. One stamp is sound and still on its original partial cover. This item was sold at auction in 2011, where it realized $2.6 million. The second stamp is a faulty, loose single.

Neapolitan Provinces

King Victor Emmanuel II — A11

Lithographed, Center Embossed
1861 Unwmk. *Imperf.*

19 A11 ½t green 14.00 *250.00*
No gum 3.50
On cover 375.00
On newspaper, single franking 375.00
On circular, single franking 625.00
On cover, single franking 4,250.
a. ½t yellow green 425.00 340.00
No gum 105.00
On cover 500.00
On circular, single franking 800.00
b. ½t emerald 7,850. 1,350.
No gum 1,675.
On cover 1,975.
On circular, single franking 2,500.
c. ½t black (error) *135,000.* *160,000.*
No gum *60,000.*
d. Head inverted (green) 200.00
No gum 70.00
e. Head inverted (yel grn) 11,250.
On cover 33,500.
f. Printed on both sides 32,250.
g. ½t olive green 3,100. 550.00
No gum 840.00
On cover 850.00
20 A11 ½g bister 200.00 *225.00*
No gum 50.00
On cover 450.00

No.	Description	Unused	Used
	On cover, single franking		4,250.
a.	½g brown	200.00	310.00
	No gum	50.00	
	On cover		625.00
	On cover, single franking		4,250.
b.	½g gray brown	225.00	225.00
	No gum	55.00	
	On cover		450.00
	On cover, single franking		4,250.
c.	Head inverted	1,950.	—
	No gum	840.00	
21	A11 1g black	310.00	32.50
	No gum	77.50	
	On cover		100.00
	On cover, single franking		925.00
a.	Head inverted		1,675.
	On cover		10,000.
b.	1g silver gray	19,500.	3,000.
	On cover		9,250.
22	A11 2g blue	125.00	14.00
	No gum	35.00	
	On cover		35.00
a.	2g deep blue	125.00	14.00
	No gum	35.00	
	On cover		37.50
b.	Head inverted	400.00	1,000.
	No gum	100.00	
	On cover		6,250.
c.	2g black (error)		160,000.
d.	2g sky blue	2,650.	22.50
	No gum	700.00	
	On cover		55.00
e.	2g slate blue	5,600.	170.00
	No gum	1,550.	
	On cover		425.00
f.	2g indigo	—	450.00
	No gum	—	
	On cover		1,125.
23	A11 5g car rose	225.00	125.00
	No gum	55.00	
	On cover		470.00
a.	5g vermilion	225.00	160.00
	No gum	55.00	
	On cover		470.00
b.	5g lilac rose	250.00	250.00
	No gum	62.50	
	On cover		750.00
c.	Head inverted	1,250.	8,400.
	No gum	500.00	
e.	Printed on both sides		21,000.
f.	5g lilac	300.00	370.00
	No gum	85.00	
	On cover		1,100.
g.	5g dark lilac	675.00	500.00
	No gum	170.00	
	On cover		1,550.
25	A11 10g orange	100.00	275.00
	No gum	25.00	
	On cover		840.00
a.	10g ocher	1,250.	625.00
	No gum	340.00	
	On cover		1,825.
b.	10g bister	110.00	275.00
	No gum	27.50	
	On cover		850.00
c.	10g olive bister	550.00	1,000.
	No gum	125.00	
	On cover		2,400.
26	A11 20g yellow	425.00	3,350.
	No gum	100.00	
	On cover		13,500.
a.	Head inverted		42,000.
b.	20g orange yellow	450.00	3,500.
	No gum	110.00	
	On cover		14,000.
27	A11 50g gray	32.50	8,500.
	No gum	11.50	
	On cover		135,000.
	On cover, single franking		165,000.
a.	50g slate	40.00	8,500.
	No gum	11.50	
	On cover		135,000.
b.	50g slate blue	45.00	11,250.
	No gum	11.50	
	On cover		180,000.
c.	50g blackish gray	125.00	
	No gum	30.00	
	Nos. 19-27 (8)	1,432.	12,772.

Full margins = 1mm.

Counterfeits of the inverted head varieties of this issue are plentiful. See note on forgeries after Sardinia No. 15.

Values for pairs

19	A11 ½t green	32.50	675.00
	On cover		1,675.
20	A11 ½t bister	435.00	475.00
	On cover		1,000.
21	A11 1g black	675.00	72.50
	On cover		200.00
22	A11 2g blue	295.00	57.50
	On cover		225.00
23	A11 5g carmine rose	500.00	450.00
	On cover		1,850.
25	A11 10g orange	225.00	1,825.
	On cover		7,250.
26	A11 20g yellow	925.00	8,500.
	On cover		34,000.
27	A11 50g gray	85.00	27,500.

Values for blocks of 4

19	A11 ½t green	62.50	28,000.
	On cover		100,000.
20	A11 ½t bister	875.00	34,000.
	On cover		110,000.
21	A11 1g black	1,375.	15,500.
	On cover		53,500.
22	A11 2g blue	575.00	16,750.
	On cover		56,000.
23	A11 5g carmine rose	1,000.	—
25	A11 10g orange	440.00	—
26	A11 20g yellow	1,850.	—
27	A11 50g gray	150.00	

Fraudulent cancellations are found on Nos. 19-20, 23-27.

Stamps similar to those of Sardinia 1855-61, type A4 but with inscriptions in larger, clearer lettering, were prepared in 1861 for the Neapolitan Provinces. They were not officially issued although a few are known postally used. Denominations: 5c, 10c, 20c, 40c and 80c.

Stamps of Two Sicilies were replaced by those of Italy in 1862.

ITALY

'i-tᵊl-ē

LOCATION — Southern Europe
GOVT. — Republic
AREA — 119,764 sq. mi.
POP. — 56,929,101 (est. 1983)
CAPITAL — Rome

Kingdom

100 Centesimi = 1 Lira

Watermarks

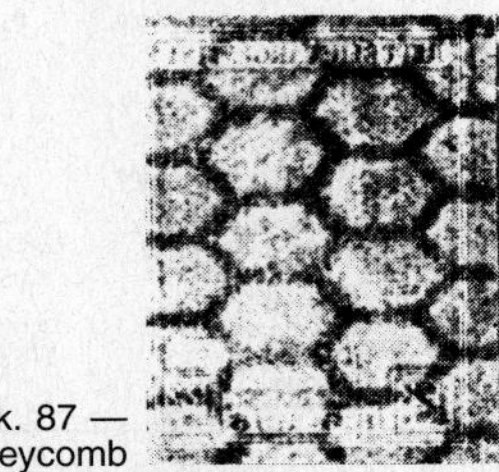

Wmk. 87 — Honeycomb

Wmk. 140 — Crown

Values of Italy stamps vary tremendously according to condition. Quotations are for very fine examples, and values for unused stamps are for examples with original gum as defined in the catalogue introduction. Extremely fine or superb examples sell at much higher prices, and fine or poor examples sell at greatly reduced prices.

Very fine examples of Nos. 17-21, 24-75, J2-J27, O1-O8 and Q1-Q6 will have perforations barely clear of the frameline or design due to the narrow spacing of the stamps on the plates.

Values for never hinged stamps are for examples centered clear of perfs. Premiums do not apply to stamps with perforations cutting the design.

King Victor Emmanuel II — A4

Typographed; Head Embossed

1862 Unwmk. *Perf. 11½x12*

No.	Description	Unused	Used
17	A4 10c bister	8,000.	325.00
	No gum	2,200.	
	Never hinged	12,000.	
	On cover		800.00
a.	10c yellow brown	8,250.	350.00
	No gum	2,400.	
	On cover		975.00
b.	10c brown	16,500.	475.00
	No gum	8,250.	
	On cover		1,175.
c.	10c dk olive brn	13,500.	1,200.
	No gum	11,750.	
	On cover		3,000.
d.	10c dark brown	32,500.	1,300.
	No gum	16,500.	
	On cover		3,250.
e.	10c olive bister	21,500.	500.00
	No gum	10,500.	
	On cover		1,200.
f.	10c reddish org	23,000.	1,300.
	No gum	11,750.	
	On cover		3,250.
g.	Vert. half used as 5c on cover		125,000.
19	A4 20c dark blue	20.00	32.50
	No gum	12.00	
	Never hinged	50.00	
	On cover		125.00
a.	20c blue	1,800.	1,300.
	No gum	950.00	
	On cover		5,250.
b.	20c pale blue	14,500.	4,500.
	No gum	7,500.	
	On cover		17,500.
c.	20c pale milky blue	22,500.	8,000.
	No gum	10,750.	
	On cover		32,500.
d.	20c gray blue	700.00	875.00
	No gum	350.00	
	On cover		3,500.
e.	20c dp dk blue	14,000.	4,500.
	No gum	7,500.	
	On cover		17,500.
f.	Vert. half used as 10c on cover		170,000.
20	A4 40c red	250.00	175.00
	No gum	125.00	
	Never hinged	625.00	
	On cover		350.00
a.	40c pale rose	600.00	525.00
	No gum	275.00	
	On cover		1,000.
b.	40c brt car red	300.00	210.00
	No gum	135.00	
	On cover		425.00
c.	40c deep car red	300.00	210.00
	No gum	135.00	
	On cover		425.00
21	A4 80c orange	50.00	1,900.
	No gum	35.00	
	Never hinged	125.00	
	On cover		7,750.
a.	80c bright yellow	50.00	1,900.
	No gum	35.00	
	On cover		7,750.
b.	80c dark yellow	50.00	1,900.
	No gum	35.00	
	On cover		7,750.
c.	80c olive yellow	8,000.	
	No gum	3,500.	
	On cover		—

The outer frame shows a distinct design on the early printings, while this design is more or less blurred, or even a solid line, on the later printings.

The 20c and 40c exist perf. 11½. These are remainders of Sardinia with forged perforations.

Counterfeit cancellations are often found on No. 21.

Values for pairs

17	A4 10c bister	16,500.	700.00
	On cover		1,750.
19	A4 20c dark blue	50.00	90.00
	On cover		300.00
20	A4 40c red	700.00	700.00
	On cover		2,800.
21	A4 80c orange	160.00	5,750.
	On cover		35,000.

Values for strips of 3

17	A4 10c bister	—	1,900.
	On cover		9,500.
19	A4 20c dark blue	75.00	350.00
	On cover		1,600.
20	A4 40c red	1,100.	3,500.
	On cover		28,000.
21	A4 80c orange	250.00	—
	On cover		—

Values for strips of 4

17	A4 10c bister	—	7,600.
	On cover		38,000.
19	A4 20c dark blue	105.00	3,250.
	On cover		16,000.
20	A4 40c red	—	—
	On cover		—
21	A4 80c orange	—	—
	On cover		—

Values for blocks of 4

17	A4 10c bister	21,000.	—
	On cover		—
19	A4 20c dark blue	87.50	17,500.
	On cover		—
20	A4 40c red	900.00	—
	On cover		—
21	A4 80c orange	175.00	—
	On cover		—

Values for strips of 5

17	A4 10c bister	—	—
	On cover		—
19	A4 20c dark blue	—	8,000.
	On cover		40,000.
20	A4 40c red	—	—
	On cover		—
21	A4 80c orange	—	—
	On cover		—

Lithographed; Head Embossed

1863 *Imperf.*

No.	Description	Unused	Used
22	A4 15c blue	57.50	45.00
	No gum	27.50	
	Never hinged	145.00	
	On cover		115.00
a.	Head inverted		70,000.
	On cover		175,000.
b.	Double head	115.00	70.00
	No gum	57.50	
	Never hinged	235.00	
	On cover		175.00
c.	Head omitted	575.00	40,000.
	On cover		100,000.
d.	15c deep blue	57.50	47.50
	No gum	32.50	
	Never hinged	115.00	
	On cover		115.00
e.	15c pale blue	57.50	47.50
	No gum	32.50	
	Never hinged	115.00	
	On cover		115.00
f.	15c milky blue	175.00	1,175.
	No gum	87.50	
	On cover		3,500.
g.	15c sky blue	500.00	825.00
	No gum	235.00	
	Never hinged	1,000.	
	On cover		2,500.
h.	15c violet indigo	175.00	235.00
	No gum	80.00	
	Never hinged	350.00	
	On cover		700.00
i.	15c gray blue	2,050.	1,450.
	No gum	1,300.	
	On cover		1,750.
j.	Triple head	265.00	475.00
	No gum	115.00	
	On cover		1,175.

See note after Sardinia No. 15.

No. 22c is valued with original gum only.

Values for a pair of stamps

22	A4 15c blue	120.00	150.00
	On cover		450.00

Values for used strip of 3

22	A4 15c blue	650.00
	On cover	2,600.

Values for used strip of 4

22	A4 15c blue	5,250.
	On cover	26,500.

Values for block of 4

22	A4 15c blue	450.00	22,000.
	On cover		87,500.

King Victor Emmanuel II — A5

Type I — First "C" in bottom line nearly closed.

Type II — "C" open. Line broken below "Q."

1863 Litho.

No.	Description	Unused	Used
23	A5 15c blue, Type II	7.00	11.50
	No gum	3.25	
	Never hinged	17.50	
	On cover		32.50
a.	Type I	300.00	24.00
	No gum	35.00	
	Never hinged	725.00	
	On cover		57.50
b.	15c slate blue (II)	11.00	65.00
	No gum	4.00	
	Never hinged	26.00	
	On cover		160.00
c.	As "a," double impression		3,800.
	On cover		14,500.
d.	15c pale blue (I)	300.00	24.50
	No gum	45.00	
	On cover		57.50
e.	15c pale blue (II)	7.00	13.00
	No gum	3.00	
	Never hinged	17.50	
	On cover		32.50
f.	As "a," printed on both sides		17,500.

One example of No. 23f is known used, cancelled "Milano, 25-VII-1863." Unused examples always lack gum and are from printer's waste. They are of little value.

Values for pairs

23	A5 15c blue (II)	14.50	27.00
	On cover		65.00
a.	Type I	525.00	55.00
	On cover		140.00

Values for used strips of 3

23	A5 15c blue (II)	105.00
	On cover	425.00
a.	Type I	155.00
	On cover	625.00

Values for used strips of 4

23	A5 15c blue (II)	440.00
	On cover	1,750.
a.	Type I	750.00
	On cover	3,000.

Values for blocks of 4

23	A5 15c blue (II)	52.50	19,000.
	On cover		46,000.
a.	Type I	2,200.	13,500.
	On cover		52,500.

Values for used strips of 5

23	A5 15c blue (II)	1,750.
	On cover	10,500.
a.	Type I	3,800.
	On cover	23,000.

Values for Nos. 24-33 are for well-centered stamps with perforations clear of frameline. Values for used stamps are for stamps canceled with legible circular date stamps. Examples with numeral and other cancellations sell for somewhat less.

Values for never hinged mint stamps are for examples with very fine centering. Never hinged premiums over hinged original gum values do not apply to stamps with perforations cutting into the design. This applies to all 19th century issues.

A6

A7

A8

A13

1863-77 Typo. Wmk. 140 *Perf. 14*

Turin Printing

24	A6 1c gray grn	6.00	3.00
	No gum	1.50	
	Never hinged	15.00	
	On cover		6.00
25	A7 2c org brn ('65)	24.00	2.00
	No gum	4.25	
	Never hinged	60.00	
	On cover		4.00
a.	Imperf., pair	210.00	*300.00*
	Imperf single, on cover		440.00
26	A8 5c slate grn	1,825.	3.25
	No gum	225.00	
	Never hinged	3,650.	
	On cover		6.50
27	A8 10c buff	3,100.	4.25
	No gum	340.00	
	Never hinged	6,250.	
	On cover		8.25
28	A8 10c blue ('77)	5,850.	4.75
	No gum	700.00	
	Never hinged	11,750.	
	On cover		12.00
29	A8 15c blue	2,350.	3.00
	No gum	250.00	
	Never hinged	4,650.	
	On cover		12.00
30	A8 30c brown	9.00	9.00
	No gum	1.75	
	Never hinged	22.00	
	On cover		35.00
a.	Imperf., single		—
	Imperf., single, on cover		—
31	A8 40c carmine	6,500.	5.75
	No gum	750.00	
	Never hinged	13,000.	
a.	40c rose	8,750.	8.00
	No gum	1,050.	
	Never hinged	14,500.	
	On cover, #31 or 31a		24.00
32	A8 60c lilac	9.00	*14.00*
	No gum	1.75	
	Never hinged	22.50	
	On cover		55.00
33	A13 2 l vermilion	24.00	*90.00*
	No gum	9.00	
	Never hinged	60.00	
	On cover		2,350.
	On cover, single franking		4,750.

Nos. 26 to 32 have the head of type A8 but with different corner designs for each value.

Early printings of Nos. 24-27, 29-33 were made in London by De La Rue, later printings in Turin. Used examples can be determined by cancellation date. Unused singles cannot be distinguished.

For overprints see Italian Offices Abroad Nos. 1-5, 8-11.

De La Rue Printing

Stamps from De La Rue printing are distinguished by legible datestamps with dates between Dec. 1863 and Dec. 1865.

24	A6 1c	18.00
	On cover	35.00
	On cover, single franking	215.00
a.	Imperf., pair	*20,500.*
	On cover	*62,500.*
25	A7 2c	90.00
	On cover	175.00
26	A8 5c	18.00
	On cover	35.00
27	A8 10c	18.00
a.	10c orange brown	18.00
	On cover, #27 or 27a	35.00
	On cover, single franking, #27 or 27a	275.00
29	A8 15c	3.00
	On cover	12.00
a.	Imperf, single	*5,750.*
	On cover	*42,000.*
30	A8 30c	75.00
	On cover	225.00
31	A8 40c	20.00
	On cover	60.00
32	A8 60c	35.00
	On cover	140.00
33	A13 2 l	475.00
	On cover	*10,500.*
	On cover, single franking	*13,000.*

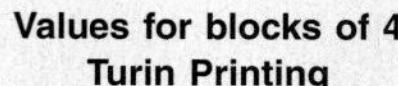

Values for blocks of 4

Turin Printing

24	A6 1c	50.00	18.00
	On cover		70.00
25	A7 2c	260.00	22.50
	On cover		100.00
26	A8 5c	10,000.	45.00
	On cover		275.00
27	A8 10c	17,500.	100.00
	On cover		750.00
28	A8 10c	35,000.	350.00
	On cover		2,150.
30	A8 30c	75.00	*450.00*
	On cover		3,500.
31	A8 40c	34,500.	450.00
a.	40c	47,500.	775.00
	On cover, #31 or 31a		3,500.
32	A8 60c	75.00	*1,500.*
	On cover		10,000.
33	A13 2 l	175.00	*3,800.*

Values for blocks of 4

De La Rue Printing

24	A6 1c	2,000.	150.00
	On cover		900.00
25	A7 2c	11,000.	4,650.
26	A8 5c	9,000.	150.00
	On cover		900.00
27	A8 10c	16,000.	350.00
	On cover		2,500.
29	A8 15c	13,250.	2,200.
	On cover		13,000.
30	A8 30c	22,500.	*6,500.*
	On cover		26,000.
31	A8 40c	29,000.	2,100.
	On cover		16,000.

Watermark Inverted

De La Rue Printing

24b	A6 1c	130.00
	On cover	525.00
25b	A7 2c	875.00
	On cover	—
27b	A8 10c	275.00
	On cover	—
29b	A8 15c	130.00
	On cover	525.00

Turin Printing

24c	A6 1c	40.00	25.00
	On cover		120.00
25c	A7 2c	115.00	87.50
	On cover		425.00
26a	A8 5c	—	100.00
	On cover		475.00
27b	A8 10c	—	87.50
	On cover		425.00
28a	A8 10c	—	75.00
	On cover		350.00
30b	A8 30c	80.00	325.00
	On cover		—
31b	A8 40c	—	200.00
	On cover		1,000.
32a	A8 60c	—	300.00
	On cover		1,500.
33a	A13 2 l	—	650.00
	On cover		—

No. 29 Surcharged in Brown

Type I — Dots flanking stars in oval, and dot in eight check-mark ornaments in corners.
Type II — Dots in oval, none in corners.
Type III — No dots.

1865

34	A8 20c on 15c bl (I)	645.00	4.00
	No gum	90.00	
	Never hinged	1,300.	
	On cover		10.00
a.	Type II	8,750.	15.00
	No gum	1,200.	
	Never hinged	17,500.	
	On cover		37.50
b.	Type III	1,750.	6.00
	No gum	325.00	
	Never hinged	3,500.	
	On cover		15.00
c.	Inverted surcharge (I)		*65,000.*
d.	Double surcharge, on cover (I)		*60,000.*
e.	Double surcharge (III)		*25,000.*
	On cover		*60,000.*

Values for blocks of 4

34	A8 20c on 15c blue (I)	1,850.	2,750.
	On cover		14,000.
a.	Type II	24,000.	4,750.
	On cover		24,000.
b.	Type III	5,000.	4,000.
	On cover		20,000.

A15

1867-77 Typo.

35	A15 20c sky blue (London)	1,600.	3.00
	No gum	190.00	
	Never hinged	3,250.	
	On cover		11.50
a.	20c blue (Torino)	575.00	1.25
	No gum	100.00	
	Never hinged	1,200.	
	On cover		2.50
36	A15 20c orange ('77)	4,400.	3.00
	No gum	500.00	
	Never hinged	8,750.	
	On cover		9.00

Values for blocks of 4

35	A15 20c sky blue (London)	5,000.	4,000.
	On cover		5,000.
a.	20c blue (Torina)	1,900.	2,500.
	On cover		1,100.
36	A15 20c orange	12,000.	975.00
	On cover		9,750.

For overprints see Italian Offices Abroad Nos. 9-10.

Official Stamps Surcharged in Blue

1878

37	O1 2c on 2c lake	180.00	25.00
	No gum	17.50	
	Never hinged	375.00	
	On cover		50.00
38	O1 2c on 5c lake	225.00	30.00
	No gum	35.00	
	Never hinged	450.00	
	On cover		60.00
39	O1 2c on 20c lake	800.00	3.50
	No gum	130.00	
	Never hinged	1,650.	
	On cover		7.00
40	O1 2c on 30c lake	700.00	12.50
	No gum	65.00	
	Never hinged	1,475.	
	On cover		24.00
41	O1 2c on 1 l lake	550.00	4.00
	No gum	70.00	
	Never hinged	1,200.	
	On cover		8.00
42	O1 2c on 2 l lake	550.00	10.00
	No gum	70.00	
	Never hinged	1,225.	
	On cover		19.00
43	O1 2c on 5 l lake	800.00	13.00
	No gum	90.00	
	Never hinged	1,600.	
	On cover		26.00
44	O1 2c on 10 l lake	550.00	16.50
	No gum	70.00	
	Never hinged	1,225.	
	On cover		32.50
	Nos. 37-44 (8)	4,355.	114.50

Inverted Surcharge

37a	O1 2c on 2c		1,625.
	On cover		*16,250.*
38a	O1 2c on 5c		1,300.
	On cover		*13,000.*
39a	O1 2c on 20c	*38,000.*	875.
	On cover		*8,750.*
40a	O1 2c on 30c		1,300.
	On cover		*13,000.*
41a	O1 2c on 1 l	*44,000.*	1,200.
	On cover		*12,000.*
42a	O1 2c on 2 l	*44,000.*	1,300.
	On cover		*13,000.*
43a	O1 2c on 5 l		1,300.
	On cover		*13,000.*
44a	O1 2c on 10 l		1,300.
	On cover		*13,000.*

Values for blocks of 4

37	O1 2c on 2c lake	550.00	180.00
	On cover		*1,000.*
38	O1 2c on 5c lake	650.00	225.00
	On cover		*1,275.*
39	O1 2c on 20c lake	2,250.	65.00
	On cover		*325.00*
40	O1 2c on 30c lake	2,100.	100.00
	On cover		*550.00*
41	O1 2c on 1 l lake	1,750.	65.00
	On cover		*325.00*
42	O1 2c on 2 l lake	1,700.	135.00
	On cover		*725.00*
43	O1 2c on 5 l lake	2,250.	165.00
	On cover		*900.00*
44	O1 2c on 10 l lake	1,750.	200.00
	On cover		*1,100.*

Values for Nos. 37-44 in blocks of 4 are for examples with perforations cutting into design. Fine-to-very fine blocks, with perforations clear on all stamps, are worth 2 to 2.5 times the value above.

King Humbert I — A17

1879 Typo. *Perf. 14*

45	A17 5c blue green	8.00	1.45
	No gum	2.00	
	Never hinged	20.00	
	On cover		3.50
46	A17 10c claret	450.00	1.50
	No gum	75.00	
	Never hinged	900.00	
	On cover		4.00
47	A17 20c orange	425.00	1.45
	No gum	65.00	
	Never hinged	850.00	
	On cover		4.40
48	A17 25c blue	800.00	7.25
	No gum	110.00	
	Never hinged	1,600.	
	On cover		22.00
49	A17 30c brown	150.00	*2,650.*
	No gum	100.00	
	Never hinged	325.00	
	On cover		*19,000.*
50	A17 50c violet	20.00	22.00
	No gum	5.50	
	Never hinged	50.00	
	On cover		65.00
51	A17 2 l vermilion	52.50	*350.00*
	No gum	30.00	
	Never hinged	130.00	
	On cover		*105,000.*

Values for blocks of 4

45	A17 5c blue green	30.00	50.00
	On cover		180.00
46	A17 10c claret	1,500.	80.00
	On cover		360.00
47	A17 20c orange	1,350.	180.00
	On cover		1,475.
48	A17 25c blue	2,500.	650.00
	On cover		6,500.
49	A17 30c brown	675.00	
50	A17 50c violet	75.00	*1,650.*
	On cover		14,000.
51	A17 2 l vermilion	200.00	*25,000.*

Nos. 45-51 have the head of type A17 with different corner designs for each value.

Beware of forged cancellations on No. 49, on or off cover.

No. 51 on complete commercial covers is very rare. On large pieces or cover fronts, it is worth $1,500-$15,000, depending on the usage and on the individual piece.

Values for Nos. 45-51 in blocks of 4 are for examples with perforations cutting into design. Fine-to-very fine blocks, with perforations clear on all stamps, are worth 2 to 2.5 times the value above.

For surcharges and overprints see Nos. 64-66, Italian Offices Abroad 12-17.

Arms of Savoy — A24

Humbert I — A25

A26

A27

A28

A29

1889

52 A24 5c dark green 775.00 3.00
No gum 87.50
Never hinged 1,800.
On cover 7.25
53 A25 40c brown 13.00 17.50
No gum 5.75
Never hinged 32.50
On cover 87.50
a. Horiz. pair, imperf. between 17,500.
54 A26 45c gray green 2,350. 8.50
No gum 450.00
Never hinged 6,000.
On cover 26.00
55 A27 60c violet 17.00 *42.50*
No gum 7.25
Never hinged 42.50
On cover 525.00
On cover, single franking 2,600.
56 A28 1 l brown & yel 17.00 22.00
No gum 7.25
Never hinged 42.50
On cover 170.00
On cover, single franking 1,450.
a. 1 l brown & orange 19.00 27.00
No gum 7.50
Never hinged 45.00
On cover 215.00
On cover, single franking 1,600.
57 A29 5 l grn & claret 35.00 *1,075.*
No gum 17.50
Never hinged 87.50
On cover *160,000.*

Values for blocks of 4

52	A24	5c dark green	2,250.	72.50
		On cover		315.00
53	A25	40c brown	50.00	*1,150.*
		On cover		10,750.
54	A26	45c gray green	9,500.	1,625.
		On cover		14,500.
55	A27	60c violet	55.00	*3,250.*
		On cover		29,000.
56	A28	1 l brown & yel	55.00	*1,450.*
		On cover		7,200.
57	A29	5 l grn & claret	95.00	

Forged cancellations exist on Nos. 51, 57.

No. 57 on complete commercial covers is very rare. On large pieces or cover fronts, it is worth $2,850-$20,000, depending on the usage and on the individual piece.

Values for Nos. 52-57 in blocks of 4 are for examples with perforations cutting into design. Fine-to-very fine blocks, with perforations clear on all stamps, are worth 2 to 2.5 times the value above.

Parcel Post Stamps of 1884-86 Surcharged in Black

1890

58 PP1 2c on 10c ol gray 5.40 *7.00*
No gum 3.25
Never hinged 22.00
On cover 29.00
a. Inverted surcharge 500.00 *3,250.*
59 PP1 2c on 20c blue 5.40 *7.00*
No gum 3.25
Never hinged 22.00
On cover 29.00
60 PP1 2c on 50c claret 57.50 42.50
No gum 23.50
Never hinged 225.00
On cover 125.00
a. Inverted surcharge *45,000.*
61 PP1 2c on 75c blue grn 5.40 *7.00*
No gum 3.25
Never hinged 22.00
On cover 29.00
62 PP1 2c on 1.25 l org 50.00 37.50
No gum 20.00
Never hinged 200.00
On cover 110.00
a. Inverted surcharge *85,000.* *42,500.*
63 PP1 2c on 1.75 l brn 22.00 *55.00*
No gum 12.50
Never hinged 85.00
On cover 160.00
Nos. 58-63 (6) 145.70 156.00

Values for blocks of 4

58	PP1	2c on 10c ol gray	25.00	65.00
		On cover		315.00
59	PP1	2c on 20c blue	25.00	65.00
		On cover		315.00
60	PP1	2c on 50c claret	275.00	290.00
		On cover		1,125.
61	PP1	2c on 75c blue grn	25.00	65.00
		On cover		315.00
62	PP1	2c on 1.25 l org	225.00	250.00
		On cover		1,000.
63	PP1	2c on 1.75 l brn	100.00	*315.00*
		On cover		1,250.

Covers: Single frankings of Nos. 58-63 on newspapers or circulars are worth more.

Values for Nos. 58-63 in blocks of 4 are for examples with perforations cutting into design. Fine-to-very fine blocks, with perforations clear on all stamps, are worth 2 to 2.5 times the value above.

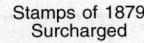

Stamps of 1879 Surcharged

1890-91

64 A17 2c on 5c bl grn ('91) 20.00 50.00
No gum 6.00
Never hinged 50.00
On cover 110.00
a. "2" with thin tail 125.00 290.00
On cover 1,125.
65 A17 20c on 30c brn 425.00 11.00
No gum 72.50
Never hinged 950.00
On cover 27.00
66 A17 20c on 50c violet 500.00 42.50
No gum 80.00
Never hinged 1,050.
On cover 150.00
Nos. 64-66 (3) 945.00 103.50

Values for blocks of 4

64	A17	2c on 5c bl grn ('91)	65.00	*250.00*
		On cover		600.00
65	A17	20c on 30c brown	1,100.	4,750.
		On cover		19,000.
66	A17	20c on 50c violet	1,400.	*4,000.*
		On cover		16,000.

Values for Nos. 64-66 in blocks of 4 are for examples with perforations cutting into design. Fine-to-very fine blocks, with perforations clear on all stamps, are worth 2 to 2.5 times the value above.

On Nos. 65-66 the period is omitted in the surcharge.

Arms of Savoy — A33

Humbert I — A34

A35

A36

A37

A38

1891-96 **Typo.**

67 A33 5c green 500.00 2.25
No gum 67.50
Never hinged 1,000.
On cover 6.50
68 A34 10c claret ('96) 8.50 2.25
No gum 2.25
Never hinged 21.50
On cover 4.25
69 A35 20c orange ('95) 8.50 2.25
No gum 2.25
Never hinged 21.50
On cover 4.25
70 A36 25c blue 8.50 9.00
No gum 2.25
Never hinged 21.50
On cover 36.00
71 A37 45c ol grn ('95) 8.50 9.00
No gum 2.25
Never hinged 21.50
On cover 36.00
72 A38 5 l blue & rose 85.00 *230.00*
No gum 36.00
Never hinged 200.00
On cover *21,500.*

Values for blocks of 4

67	A33	5c green	3,600.	35.00
		On cover		240.00
68	A34	10c claret ('96)	72.50	40.00
		On cover		250.00
69	A35	20c orange ('95)	72.50	*175.00*
		On cover		1,750.
70	A36	25c blue	72.50	*325.00*
		On cover		3,250.
71	A37	45c ol grn ('95)	72.50	*600.00*
		On cover		6,000.
72	A38	5 l blue & rose	650.00	*2,800.*

Value of No. 72 on cover is for a complete cover. Stamps on piece or cover fronts are more common and worth much less.

Arms of Savoy — A39

A40

A41

1896-97

73 A39 1c brown 9.00 7.00
No gum 3.00
Never hinged 25.00
On cover 14.50
a. Half used as ½c on cover *1,450.*
74 A40 2c orange brown 10.00 1.80
No gum 2.25
Never hinged 25.00
On cover 3.60
75 A41 5c green ('97) 36.00 1.80
No gum 7.25
Never hinged 90.00
On cover 3.60
Nos. 73-75 (3) 55.00 10.60

Values for blocks of 4

73	A39	1c brown	85.00	40.00
		On cover		120.00
74	A40	2c orange brown	85.00	20.00
		On cover		120.00
75	A41	5c green ('97)	300.00	32.50
		On cover		190.00

A42

Coat of Arms

A43 A44

Victor Emmanuel III

A45 A46

1901-26

76 A42 1c brown 1.45 .35
Never hinged 3.60
On cover 1.10
a. Imperf, single 400.00 *650.00*
b. Vert. pair, lower stamp imperf. *3,000.*
77 A43 2c org brn 1.45 .35
Never hinged 3.60
On cover 1.10
a. Double impression 110.00 *200.00*
Never hinged 185.00
b. Imperf, single 115.00 *160.00*
78 A44 5c blue grn 80.00 .55
Never hinged 180.00
On cover 1.45
a. Imperf, single 1,800.
79 A45 10c claret 110.00 1.10
Never hinged 270.00
On cover 4.40
a. Imperf, single — *10,000.*
80 A45 20c orange 22.00 1.10
Never hinged 55.00
On cover 4.40
81 A45 25c ultra 250.00 3.75
Never hinged 540.00
On cover 36.00
a. 25c dp blue 250.00 3.60
Never hinged 540.00
On cover 36.00
82 A46 25c grn & pale grn ('26) 1.45 .30
Never hinged 3.60
On cover 1.25
a. Frame & vignette double 75.00 3.60
b. Floral design double 42.50 50.00
c. Floral design omitted 12.00 6.00
d. "POSTE ITALIANE" omitted 1,150.
e. Imperf., single 75.00 75.00
Never hinged 200.00
f. Vert. pair, lower stamp imperf. 1,900.
83 A45 40c brown 720.00 8.75
Never hinged 1,800.
On cover 50.00
84 A45 45c olive grn 11.00 .35
Never hinged 27.00
On cover 10.00
a. Imperf, single 145.00 *190.00*
85 A45 50c violet 850.00 16.00
Never hinged 1,800.
On cover 180.00
86 A46 75c dk red & rose ('26) 4.25 .30
Never hinged 11.00
On cover 200.00
a. Floral design omitted 115.00
b. Imperf., single 100.00 100.00
Never hinged 250.00
87 A46 1 l brn & grn 4.25 .35
Never hinged 11.00
On cover 3.60
a. Imperf, single 72.50 *110.00*
b. Floral design (green) omitted 145.00
c. Double impression of vignette (brown) 72.50 *100.00*
d. "POSTE ITALIANE" omitted 550.00
88 A46 1.25 l bl & ultra ('26) 11.00 .30
Never hinged 32.50
On cover 1.80
a. Floral design double 175.00
b. Floral design omitted 35.00 10.00
c. Imperf, single 145.00 145.00
Never hinged 375.00
89 A46 2 l dk grn & org ('23) 22.00 7.25
Never hinged 55.00
On cover 57.50
90 A46 2.50 l dk grn & org ('26) 57.50 7.25
Never hinged 135.00
On cover 62.50
91 A46 5 l blue & rose 30.00 5.75
Never hinged 72.50
On cover 220.00
Nos. 76-91 (16) 2,176. 53.80

Values for Blocks of 4

76	A42	1c brown	11.00	2.40
77	A43	2c org brn	11.00	2.25
78	A44	5c blue grn	560.00	9.75
79	A45	10c claret	775.00	12.00
80	A45	20c orange	170.00	14.50
81	A45	25c ultra	1,600.	72.50
81a	A45	25c deep blue	1,600.	72.50
82	A46	25c grn & pale grn ('26)	6.00	6.00
		Never hinged	12.50	
83	A45	40c brown	5,000.	340.00
84	A45	45c olive grn	85.00	18.00
85	A45	50c violet	6,200.	500.00
86	A46	75c dk red & rose ('26)	19.00	6.00
		Never hinged	45.00	
87	A46	1 l brown & grn	36.00	2.50
88	A46	1.25 bl & ultra l ('26)	40.00	6.00
		Never hinged	100.00	
89	A46	2 l dk grn & org ('23)	125.00	100.00
		Never hinged	200.00	
90	A46	2.50 dk grn & org l ('26)	225.00	30.00
		Never hinged	550.00	
91	A46	5 l blue & rose	225.00	72.50

Nos. 83, 85, unused, are valued in fine condition.

The borders of Nos. 79-81, 83-85, 87, 89 and 91 differ slightly for each denomination.

On Nos. 82, 86, 88 and 90, the value is expressed as "Cent. 25," etc.

See No. 87d in set following No. 174G.

For surcharges and overprints see Nos. 148-149, 152, 158, 174F-174G, B16; Austria N20-N21, N27, N30, N52-N53, N58, N60, N64-N65, N71, N74; Dalmatia 1, 6-7.

Overprints & Surcharges
See Castellorizo, Italian Offices in China, Crete, Africa, Turkish Empire (Albania to Valona) and Aegean Islands for types A36-A58 overprinted or surcharged.

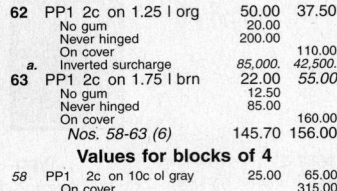

No. 80 Surcharged in Black

1905

92 A45 15c on 20c org 70.00 1.80
Never hinged 180.00
Block of 4 325.00 100.00
Never hinged 800.00
On cover 8.50
a. Double surcharge *5,000.*

A47

No. 93

No. 111

No. 123

1906 Unwmk. Engr. *Perf. 12*

93 A47 15c slate 70.00 .90
Never hinged 180.00
Block of 4 325.00 24.00
Never hinged 800.00
On cover 5.50
a. Vert. pair, imperf horiz. 180.00 180.00
b. Horiz. pair, imperf vert. 180.00 180.00
c. Booklet pane of 6 *3,300.*
Complete bklt., 4 #93c *14,500.*
d. On thin paper 92.50 3.00
Never hinged 185.00

A48

1906-19 Wmk. 140 Typo. *Perf. 14*

94 A48 5c green 1.45 .35
Never hinged 4.25
Block of 4 8.75 1.50
Never hinged 16.00
On cover .70
a. Imperf, single 36.00 36.00
b. Printed on both sides 225.00
Never hinged 400.00
95 A48 10c claret 3.00 .30
Never hinged 8.00
Block of 4 15.00 1.50
Never hinged 30.00
On cover .75
a. Imperf, single 32.50 37.50
b. Printed on both sides 225.00
Never hinged 400.00
96 A48 15c slate ('19) 2.90 .30
Never hinged 7.00
Block of 4 13.00
Never hinged 40.00
On cover 1.45
a. Imperf, single 125.00 *200.00*
Nos. 94-96 (3) 7.35 .95

The frame of No. 95 differs in several details.
See Nos. 96b-96d following No. 174G.
For overprints and surcharge see Nos. 142A-142B, 150, 174A, B5, B9-B10; Austria N22-N23, N31, N54-N55, N61-N62, N66-N67; Dalmatia 2-5.

A49

1908-27

97 A49 20c brn org ('25) 1.45 .90
Never hinged 3.60
On cover 4.25
98 A49 20c green ('25) .35 .75
Never hinged .80
On cover 3.50
99 A49 20c lil brn ('26) 2.75 .30
Never hinged 7.25
On cover 1.10
100 A49 25c blue 2.25 .30
Never hinged 5.40
On cover .90
a. Imperf., pair 105.00 105.00
Never hinged 210.00
b. Printed on both sides 200.00 *325.00*
Never hinged 325.00
101 A49 25c lt grn ('27) 7.25 *18.00*
Never hinged 18.00
On cover 55.00
102 A49 30c org brn ('22) 3.00 .70
Never hinged 7.25
On cover 4.25
a. Imperf, single 240.00 —
103 A49 30c gray ('25) 4.25 .25
Never hinged 11.00
On cover 2.90
a. Imperf., single 115.00 145.00
Never hinged 240.00
104 A49 40c brown 3.75 .30
Never hinged 9.00
On cover .90
a. Imperf., pair 160.00 175.00
Never hinged 325.00
105 A49 50c violet 1.45 .30
Never hinged 3.60
On cover .90
a. Imperf., pair 150.00 150.00
Never hinged 300.00
106 A49 55c dl vio ('20) 17.00 *37.50*
Never hinged 42.50
On cover 180.00
107 A49 60c car ('17) 2.25 .35
Never hinged 5.50
On cover 2.25
108 A49 60c blue ('23) 8.50 *80.00*
Never hinged 22.50
On cover 290.00
On foreign postcard 200.00
109 A49 60c brn org ('26) 11.50 .55
Never hinged 29.00
On cover 7.25
110 A49 85c red brn ('20) 22.00 30.00
Never hinged 55.00
On cover 115.00
Nos. 97-110 (14) 87.75 *170.20*

Values for Mint Never Hinged and Used Blocks of 4

97	A49	20c	brn org ('25)	22.00	
98	A49	20c	green ('25)	4.25	
99	A49	20c	lil brn ('26)	42.50	
100	A49	25c	blue	26.00	
101	A49	25c	lt grn ('27)	87.50	*200.00*
102	A49	30c	org brn ('22)	35.00	12.50
103	A49	30c	gray ('25)	52.50	
104	A49	40c	brown	45.00	
105	A49	50c	violet	17.50	
106	A49	55c	dl vio ('20)	210.00	
107	A49	60c	car ('17)	32.50	
108	A49	60c	blue ('23)	100.00	*550.00*
109	A49	60c	brn org ('26)	140.00	
110	A49	85c	red brn ('20)	260.00	

Hinged blocks of Nos. 97-110 do not command a premium above the value of the single stamps that comprise them. Similarly, used blocks not valued above are worth the combined value of 4 singles.

The upper panels of Nos. 104 and 105 are in solid color with white letters. A body of water has been added to the background.
See Nos. 100c-105j following No. 174G.
For overprints & surcharges see Nos. 142C-142D,147, 151, 153-157, 174B-174E, B7-B8, B12-B15A; Austria N25-N26, N28-N29, N57, N59, N69-N70, N72-N73.

A50

Redrawn

Perf. 13x13½, 13½x14

1909-17 Typo. Unwmk.

111 A50 15c slate black 270.00 2.25
Never hinged 675.00
Block of 4 1,150. 60.00
Never hinged 3,000.
On cover 8.00
112 A50 20c brn org ('16) 57.50 4.25
Never hinged 145.00
Block of 4 275.00 160.00
Never hinged 625.00
On cover 14.50

No. 111 is similar to No. 93, but the design has been redrawn and the stamp is 23mm high instead of 25mm. There is a star at each side of the coat collar, but one is not distinct. See illustrations next to A47.
For overprints and surcharges see Nos. B6, B11; Austria N24, N32, N56, N63, N68.

Wmk. 140 *Perf. 14*

113 A50 20c brn org ('17) 7.25 .35
Never hinged 18.00
Block of 4 80.00
Never hinged
On cover 1.45
a. Imperf., pair 50.00
Never hinged 60.00

Stamps overprinted "Prestito Nazionale, 1917," or later dates, are Thrift or Postal Savings Stamps.

A51

1910, Nov. 1

114 A51 10 l gray grn & red 72.50 32.00
Never hinged 180.00
Block of 4 325.00 220.00
Never hinged 800.00
On cover 1,600.
On cover, single franking *4,900.*
a. Red inverted *6,600.*

For surcharge see Dalmatia No. 8.

A52

Perf. 14x13½

1910, Apr. 15 Unwmk.

115 A52 5c green 29.00 25.00
Never hinged 115.00
Block of 4 125.00
Never hinged 500.00
On cover 125.00
116 A52 15c claret 50.00 50.00
Never hinged 200.00
Block of 4 220.00
Never hinged 900.00
On cover 250.00

50th anniversary of freedom of Sicily.

Giuseppe Garibaldi — A53

1910, Dec. 1

117 A53 5c claret 125.00 125.00
Never hinged 500.00
Block of 4 540.00
Never hinged 2,250.
On cover 600.00
118 A53 15c green 225.00 180.00
Never hinged 900.00
Block of 4 1,000.
Never hinged 4,000.
On cover 1,000.
Nos. 115-118, set of 2 commem covers 1,100.

50th anniversary of the plebiscite of the southern Italian provinces in 1860.
Nos. 115-118 sold for 5c above face value to benefit the anniversary committee. The stamps were valid only on mail to addresses within the Kingdom of Italy. Nos. 115-116 were valid to June 30, 1910; Nos. 117-118 were valid to Jan. 31, 1911.

Used values in italics are for postally used stamps. CTO's sell for about the same as unused, hinged stamps.

Symbols of Rome and Turin — A54

Symbol of Valor — A55

Genius of Italy — A56

Glory of Rome — A57

1911, May 1 Engr. *Perf. 14x13½*

119 A54 2c brown 2.90 *5.75*
Never hinged 7.25
Block of 4 17.00 30.00
Never hinged 31.50
On cover 30.00
a. Vert. pair, imperf horiz. 85.00 87.50
b. Horiz. pair, imperf vert. 85.00 87.50
c. Perf. 13½ 42.50 42.50
120 A55 5c deep green 40.00 36.00
Never hinged 100.00
Block of 4 180.00 175.00
Never hinged 450.00
On cover 110.00
a. Perf. 13½ 145.00 85.00
121 A56 10c carmine 29.00 *55.00*
Never hinged 72.50
Block of 4 175.00 325.00
Never hinged 315.00
On cover 160.00
a. Vert. pair, imperf horiz. — —
b. Horiz. pair, imperf vert. 180.00 180.00
c. Perf 13½ — —
122 A57 15c slate 37.50 *72.50*
Never hinged 85.00
Block of 4 215.00 440.00
Never hinged 425.00
On cover 175.00
Nos. 119-122 (4) 109.40 *169.25*
Set on commem cover 340.00

50th anniv. of the union of Italian States to form the Kingdom of Italy.
Nos. 119 to 122 were sold at a premium over their face value to benefit the anniversary committee. They were valid to Dec. 31, 1911. The stamps were valid only for mail to addresses within the Kingdom of Italy. They were used by military post offices in Libya. After 1913, No. 119 was sold without the premium.
For surcharges see Nos. 126-128.

Victor Emmanuel III — A58

1911, Oct. Re-engraved *Perf. 13½*

123 A58 15c slate 29.00 1.10
Never hinged 72.50
Block of 4 125.00 20.00
Never hinged 315.00
On cover 2.90
a. Imperf., single 87.50 *110.00*

b. Printed on both sides 360.00 *475.00*
c. Bklt. pane of 6 *1,500.*
Cplt. bklt., 4 #123c *3,250.*

The re-engraved stamp is 24mm high. The stars at each side of the coat collar show plainly and the "C" of "Cent" is nearer the frame than in No. 93. See illustrations next to A47.

For surcharge see No. 129.

Campanile, Venice — A59

1912, Apr. 25 ***Perf. 14x13½***

124 A59 5c indigo 8.50 *13.00*
Never hinged 22.00
Block of 4 36.00 65.00
Never hinged 90.00
On cover 40.00
125 A59 15c dk brn 47.50 *60.00*
Never hinged 125.00
Block of 4 200.00 360.00
Never hinged 390.00
On cover 160.00
Set on commem cover 145.00

Re-erection of the Campanile at Venice.

Nos. 124-125 were sold only in Venice and were valid to Dec. 31, 1912. The stamps were valid only for mail within Italy.

Nos. 120-121 Surcharged in Black

1913, Mar. 1

126 A55 2c on 5c dp grn 2.25 *6.00*
Never hinged 5.50
Block of 4 13.00 25.00
Never hinged 23.50
On cover 40.00
a. On #120a 36.00 *54.00*
127 A56 2c on 10c car 2.25 *6.00*
Never hinged 5.50
Block of 4 13.00 25.00
Never hinged 23.50
On cover 40.00

No. 122 Surcharged in Violet

128 A57 2c on 15c slate 2.25 *6.00*
Never hinged 5.50
Block of 4 13.00 26.00
Never hinged 23.50
On cover 40.00
Nos. 126-128 (3) 6.75 *18.00*
Set, never hinged 16.50
Set on commem cover 80.00

No. 123 Surcharged

1916, Jan. 8

129 A58 20c on 15c slate 16.00 1.10
Never hinged 40.00
Block of 4 67.50 18.00
Never hinged 170.00
On cover 2.90
a. Bklt. pane of 6 *675.00*
Cplt. bklt., 4 #129a *2,700.*
b. Inverted surcharge 315.00 315.00
Never hinged 525.00
c. Double surcharge 200.00 200.00
Never hinged 290.00
d. Surcharge on reverse 200.00
Never hinged 325.00
e. Vert. pair, one without surcharge 1,600.
Never hinged 2,000.
f. Horiz. strip of 3, 2 without surcharge 1,800.
Never hinged 2,750.
g. Imperf, single 145.00 *180.00*
Never hinged 225.00
h. Pair, one stamp with albino surcharge 500.00
Never hinged 825.00

Old Seal of Republic of Trieste — A60

Wmk. 140

1921, June 5 **Litho.** ***Perf. 14***

130 A60 15c blk & rose 6.50 *50.00*
Never hinged 16.50
Block of 4 37.50
Never hinged 70.00
On cover 600.00
a. Horiz. pair, imperf btwn. 850.00
Never hinged 1,750.
131 A60 25c bl & rose 6.50 *50.00*
Never hinged 16.50
Block of 4 39.00
Never hinged 70.00
On cover 600.00
132 A60 40c brn & rose 6.50 *50.00*
Never hinged 16.50
Block of 4 40.00
Never hinged 70.00
On cover 600.00
Nos. 130-132 (3) 19.50 *150.00*
Set, never hinged 50.00
Set on commem cover 425.00

Reunion of Venezia Giulia with Italy.

Allegory of Dante's Divine Comedy — A61

Italy Holding Laurels for Dante — A62

Dante Alighieri — A63

1921, Sept. 28 **Typo.**

133 A61 15c vio brn 6.50 *32.00*
Never hinged 16.00
Block of 4 27.00
Never hinged 70.00
On cover 160.00
a. Imperf, single 36.00 36.00
b. Imperf, pair 80.00
Never hinged 130.00
134 A62 25c gray grn 6.50 *32.00*
Never hinged 16.00
Block of 4 27.00
Never hinged 70.00
On cover 160.00
a. Imperf, single 36.00 36.00
Imperf, pair 80.00
Never hinged 130.00
135 A63 40c brown 6.50 *32.00*
Never hinged 16.00
Block of 4 27.00
Never hinged 70.00
On cover 160.00
a. Imperf, single 36.00 36.00
Imperf, pair 80.00
Never hinged 130.00
Nos. 133-135 (3) 19.50 *96.00*
Set, never hinged 48.00
Set on commem cover 170.00

600th anniversary of the death of Dante.

A 15c gray was not issued. Value: hinged $145, never hinged $360, canceled $425; block of 4, hinged $600, never hinged $1,275; imperf., single, hinged $400, canceled $6,100. A 15c gray violet, never issued: hinged $700, never hinged $1,400.

Nos. 133-135 exist in part perforate pairs.

"Victory" — A64

1921, Nov. 1 **Engr.** ***Perf. 14***

136 A64 5c olive green 1.45 *1.80*
Never hinged 3.60
Block of 4 6.25
Never hinged 16.00
On cover 12.50
137 A64 10c red 2.10 2.25
Never hinged 5.40
Block of 4 9.00
Never hinged 22.50
On cover 25.00
138 A64 15c slate green 3.75 *8.50*
Never hinged 9.00
Block of 4 16.00
Never hinged 37.50
On cover 42.50
139 A64 25c ultra 2.10 *5.75*
Never hinged 5.40
Block of 4 9.00
Never hinged 22.50
On cover 29.00
Nos. 136-139 (4) 9.40 *18.30*
Set, never hinged 23.50
Set on commem cover 54.00

3rd anniv. of the victory on the Piave.

For surcharges see Nos. 171-174.

Perf. 14x13¼

136a A64 5c 2.25 *2.90*
Never hinged 5.50
137a A64 10c 2.90 *3.60*
Never hinged 7.25
138a A64 15c 7.25 *13.00*
Never hinged 18.00
139a A64 25c 2.90 *7.25*
Never hinged 7.25

Perf. 13½

137b A64 10c 110.00 *160.00*
139b A64 25c 160.00 *200.00*

Imperf Singles

136b A64 5c 225.00 250.00
Never hinged *375.00*
137c A64 10c 225.00 *475.00*
Never hinged *375.00*
139c A64 25c 145.00 145.00
Never hinged *250.00*
d. Double impression 500.00 —
Never hinged 900.00

Unwmk.

136c A64 5c 4.75 *8.75*
Never hinged 11.50
137d A64 10c 11.00 *18.00*
Never hinged 27.00
138b A64 15c 25.00 *40.00*
Never hinged 60.00
139e A64 25c 11.00 *18.00*
Never hinged 27.00

Wmk. Small Cross

136d A64 5c 18.00 *29.00*
Never hinged 45.00
137e A64 10c 36.00 *65.00*
Never hinged 90.00
138c A64 15c 90.00 *145.00*
Never hinged 225.00
139f A64 25c 36.00 *65.00*
Never hinged 90.00

Flame of Patriotism Tempering Sword of Justice — A65

Giuseppe Mazzini — A66

Mazzini's Tomb A67

1922, Sept. 20 **Typo.** ***Perf. 14***

140 A65 25c maroon 11.50 *32.00*
Never hinged 29.00
Block of 4 72.50
Never hinged 125.00
On cover 270.00
141 A66 40c vio brn 22.50 *40.00*
Never hinged 57.50
Block of 4 145.00
Never hinged 250.00
On cover 290.00
142 A67 80c dk bl 11.50 *50.00*
Never hinged 29.00
Block of 4 72.50
Never hinged 125.00
On cover 425.00
Nos. 140-142 (3) 45.50 *122.00*
Set, never hinged 145.00
Set on commem cover 250.00

Mazzini (1805-1872), patriot and writer.

Nos. 95, 96, 100 and 104 Overprinted in Black

1922, June 4 **Wmk. 140** ***Perf. 14***

142A A48 10c claret 425.00 425.00
Never hinged 1,100.
On cover 1,150.
142B A48 15c slate 225.00 225.00
Never hinged 575.00
On cover 1,100.
142C A49 25c blue 225.00 225.00
Never hinged 550.00
On cover 1,100.
142D A49 40c brown 360.00 360.00
Never hinged 900.00
On cover 1,150.
Nos. 142A-142D (4) 1,235. 1,235.
Set, never hinged 3,125.
Set on commem postal card 1,350.
Set on commem cover 1,600.

9th Italian Philatelic Congress, Trieste. Nos. 142A-142D were on sale to Sept. 30, 1922. Counterfeits exist.

Values for mint never hinged and used blocks of 4

142A A48 10c claret 5,000. 2,800.
142B A48 15c slate 2,600. 1,425.
142C A49 25c blue 2,600. 1,425.
142D A49 40c brown 4,000. 2,350.

Christ Preaching The Gospel — A68

Portrait at upper right and badge at lower right differ on each value. Portrait at upper left is of Pope Gregory XV. Others: 20c, St. Theresa. 30c, St. Dominic. 50c, St. Francis of Assisi. 1 l, St. Francis Xavier.

1923, June 11

143 A68 20c ol grn & brn org 5.75 *175.00*
Never hinged 14.50
Block of 4 25.00
Never hinged 62.50
On cover 1,000.
On cover, single franking *1,500.*
144 A68 30c clar & brn org 5.75 *175.00*
Never hinged 14.50
Block of 4 25.00
Never hinged 62.50
On cover 1,000.
On cover, single franking *1,500.*
145 A68 50c vio & brn org 5.75 *175.00*
Never hinged 14.50
Block of 4 25.00
Never hinged 62.50
On cover 1,000.
On cover, single franking *1,500.*
146 A68 1 l bl & brn org 5.75 *175.00*
Never hinged 14.50
Block of 4 25.00
Never hinged 62.50
On cover 1,000.
On cover, single franking *1,500.*
Nos. 143-146 (4) 23.00 *700.00*
Set, never hinged 58.00
Set on commem cover 1,000.

300th anniv. of the Propagation of the Faith. Practically the entire issue was delivered to speculators.

Forged cancellations exist on Nos. 143-146.

Imperf Singles

143a A68 20c 500.00 *650.00*
144a A68 30c 500.00 *650.00*
145a A68 50c 500.00 *650.00*
146a A68 1 l 500.00 *650.00*

Perf. 14 Horiz., Singles

144b A68 30c 110.00 *315.00*
Never hinged 200.00
145b A68 50c 110.00 *315.00*
Never hinged 200.00
146b A68 1 l 110.00 *315.00*
Never hinged 200.00

Horiz. Pairs, Imperf Between

144c A68 30c 1,100. *1,500.*
Never hinged 1,600.
145c A68 50c 1,750. *2,150.*
Never hinged 2,750.

No.	Description	Unused	Used
146c	A68 1 l	1,100.	1,500.
	Never hinged	1,750.	

Vert. Pairs, Imperf Between

No.	Description	Unused	Used
143b	A68 20c	1,100.	1,500.
	Never hinged	1,750.	
144d	A68 30c	1,100.	1,500.
	Never hinged	1,750.	
145d	A68 50c	1,100.	1,500.
	Never hinged	1,750.	
146d	A68 1 l	1,100.	1,500.
	Never hinged	1,750.	

Stamps of Previous Issues, Surcharged

a

b

c

d

e

Type I

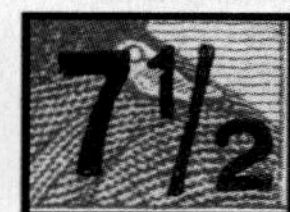
Type II

Type I

Type II

Two types of 7½c surcharge:
Type I: Base of "1" level with top of "2."
Type II: Base of "1" higher than top of "2," fraction bar longer and thinner.

Two types of 25c on 60c surcharge:
Type I: Bars of obliterator long and widely spaced. Bars measure 3.5mm to 3.75mm wide, and the space between the bars measure 10.5mm to 11mm
Type II: Bars shorter and narrowly spaced. Bars measure 3mm wide, and the space between the bars measures 11.5mm.

1923-25

No.	Description	Unused	Used
147	A49(a) 7½c on 85c (I)	.35	1.20
	Never hinged	.90	
	On cover		22.00
	On cover, single franking		32.50
a.	Double surcharge	—	1,450.
b.	Type II	17.50	80.00
	Never hinged	44.00	
	On cover		250.00
	On cover, single franking		525.00
c.	As "b," double surcharge	400.00	—
148	A42(b) 10c on 1c	.35	.35
	Never hinged	.90	
	On cover		2.90
a.	Inverted surcharge	22.00	36.00
	Never hinged	42.50	
149	A43(b) 10c on 2c	.35	.30
	Never hinged	.90	
	On cover		2.90
a.	Inverted surcharge	55.00	85.00
	Never hinged	100.00	
b.	Vert. pair, one without surcharge	1,100.	—
150	A48(c) 10c on 15c	.35	.30
	Never hinged	.90	
	On cover		3.60
a.	Vert. pair, one without surcharge	1,000.	—
b.	Surcharge on reverse only	200.00	
151	A49(a) 20c on 25c	.35	.30
	Never hinged	.90	
	On cover		3.60
152	A45(d) 25c on 45c	1.45	14.50
	Never hinged	3.60	
	On cover		110.00
a.	Vert. pair, one without surcharge	1,000.	—
153	A49(a) 25c on 60c (I)	3.00	.90
	Never hinged	7.25	
	On cover		22.00
a.	Vert. pair, one without surcharge	1,000.	
b.	Type II	29.00	145.00
	Never hinged	72.50	
	On cover		475.00
	On cover, single franking		725.00
c.	As "a," Type II	1,000.	

Single franked covers bearing No. 153b were canceled between 2/15/25 and 3/16/25.

No.	Description	Unused	Used
154	A49(a) 30c on 50c	.35	.30
	Never hinged	.90	
	On cover		18.00
	On cover, single franking		60.00
155	A49(a) 30c on 55c	1.45	.30
	Never hinged	3.60	
	On cover		42.50
	On cover, single franking		100.00
156	A49(a) 50c on 40c	4.00	.35
	Never hinged	14.50	
	On cover		4.25
a.	Inverted surcharge	215.00	325.00
	Never hinged	400.00	
b.	Double surcharge	115.00	135.00
	Never hinged	200.00	
157	A49(a) 50c on 55c	20.00	14.50
	Never hinged	50.00	
	On cover		36.00
a.	Inverted surcharge	1,100.	2,000.
	Never hinged	1,750.	
158	A51(e) 1.75 l on 10 l	14.50	32.00
	Never hinged	36.00	
	On cover		425.00
	On cover, single franking		1,450.
a.	Vert. pair, one without surcharge	1,600.	
	Never hinged	1,800.	
	Nos. 147-158 (12)	46.50	65.30
	Set, never hinged	120.00	

Years of issue: Nos. 148-149, 156-157, 1923; Nos. 147, 152-153, 1924; others, 1925.

Values for mint never hinged blocks of 4

147	A49(a)	7½c on 85c (I)	3.75
147b	A49(a)	7½c on 85c (II)	220.00
148	A42(b)	10c on 1c	3.75
149	A43(b)	10c on 2c	3.75
150	A48(c)	10c on 15c	3.75
151	A49(a)	20c on 25c	3.75
152	A45(d)	25c on 45c	15.00
153	A49(a)	25c on 60c (I)	32.50
153b	A49(a)	25c on 60c (II)	300.00
154	A49(a)	30c on 50c	3.75
155	A49(a)	30c on 55c	15.50
156	A49(a)	50c on 40c	62.50
157	A49(a)	50c on 55c	220.00
158	A51(e)	1.75 l on 10 l	155.00

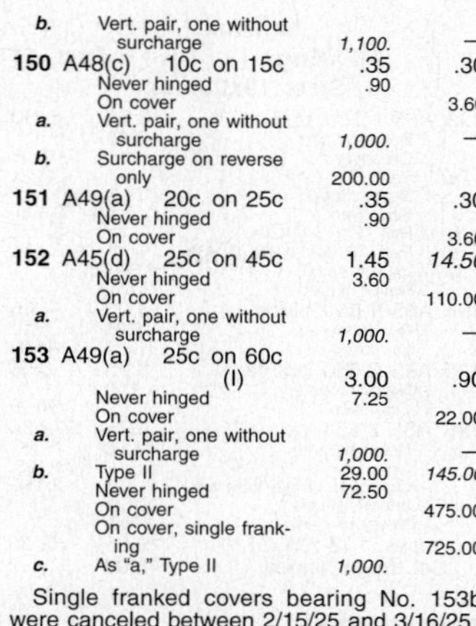

Emblem of the New Government A69

Wreath of Victory, Eagle and Fasces A70

Symbolical of Fascism and Italy — A71

Unwmk.

1923, Oct. 24 **Engr.** ***Perf. 14***

No.	Description	Unused	Used
159	A69 10c dark green	4.25	10.00
	Never hinged	11.00	
	On cover		50.00
a.	Imperf, single	725.00	850.00
	Never hinged	1,100.	
160	A69 30c dark violet	4.25	10.00
	Never hinged	11.00	
	On cover		50.00
161	A69 50c brn car	8.50	18.00
	Never hinged	21.50	
	On cover		110.00

Wmk. 140 **Typo.**

No.	Description	Unused	Used
162	A70 1 l blue	14.50	18.00
	Never hinged	36.00	
	On cover		160.00
163	A70 2 l brown	17.00	22.00
	Never hinged	42.50	
	On cover		250.00
164	A71 5 l blk & bl	29.00	57.50
	Never hinged	72.50	
	On cover		500.00
a.	Imperf, single	290.00	—
	Never hinged	475.00	
	Nos. 159-164 (6)	77.50	135.50
	Set, never hinged	195.00	
	Set on commem cover		540.00

Anniv. of the March of the Fascisti on Rome.

Values for mint never hinged blocks of 4

159	A69	10c dark green	47.50
160	A69	30c dark violet	47.50
161	A69	50c brown carmine	95.00
162	A70	1 l blue	160.00
163	A70	2 l brown	190.00
164	A71	5 l blk & bl	315.00

Fishing Scene A72

Designs: 15c, Mt. Resegone. 30c, Fugitives bidding farewell to native mountains. 50c, Part of Lake Como. 1 l, Manzoni's home, Milan. 5 l, Alessandro Manzoni. The first four designs show scenes from Manzoni's work "I Promessi Sposi."

1923, Dec. 29 ***Perf. 14***

No.	Description	Unused	Used
165	A72 10c brn red & blk	22.00	180.00
	Never hinged	54.00	
	On cover		700.00
166	A72 15c bl grn & blk	22.00	180.00
	Never hinged	54.00	
	On cover		700.00
167	A72 30c blk & slate	22.00	180.00
	Never hinged	54.00	
	On cover		700.00
a.	Imperf, single	2,700.	
	Never hinged	5,250.	
	Imperf, pair	—	
168	A72 50c org brn & blk	22.00	180.00
	Never hinged	54.00	
	On cover		700.00
a.	Imperf, single	3,600.	
169	A72 1 l blue & blk	145.00	700.00
	Never hinged	360.00	
	On cover		2,500.
a.	Imperf, single, no gum	290.00	—
	As "a," with gum	575.00	
170	A72 5 l vio & blk	725.00	3,950.
	Never hinged	1,800.	
	On cover		—
a.	Imperf, single	850.00	
	Never hinged	2,150.	
	Imperf, pair	—	
	Nos. 165-170 (6)	958.00	5,370.
	Set, never hinged	2,375.	
	Set on commem cover		13,500.

50th anniv. of the death of Alessandro Manzoni.
Values are for stamps with perforations clear of the design. Very fine centered examples command a 50% premium.

Values for mint never hinged blocks of 4

165	A72	10c brn red & blk	250.00
166	A72	15c bl grn & blk	250.00
167	A72	30c blk & slate	250.00
168	A72	50c org brn & blk	250.00
169	A72	1 l blue & blk	1,750.
170	A72	5 l vio & blk	8,750.

Nos. 136-139 Surcharged

1924, Feb. ***Perf. 14***

No.	Description	Unused	Used
171	A64 1 l on 5c ol grn	22.50	225.00
	Never hinged	55.00	
	On cover		1,400.
172	A64 1 l on 10c red	14.50	225.00
	Never hinged	36.00	
	On cover		1,400.
173	A64 1 l on 15c slate grn	22.50	225.00
	Never hinged	55.00	
	On cover		1,400.
174	A64 1 l on 25c ultra	14.50	225.00
	Never hinged	36.00	
	On cover		1,400.
	Nos. 171-174 (4)	74.00	900.00
	Set, never hinged	180.00	
	Set on commem cover		4,250.

Surcharge forgeries exist.

Perf. 14x13½

No.	Description	Unused	Used
171a	A64 1 l on 5c	32.00	300.00
	Never hinged	62.50	
172a	A64 1 l on 10c	18.00	300.00
	Never hinged	36.00	
173a	A64 1 l on 15c	32.00	300.00
	Never hinged	62.50	
174h	A64 1 l on 25c	18.00	300.00
	Never hinged	36.00	
	Nos. 171a-174h (4)	100.00	1,200.
	Set, never hinged	195.00	

Perf. 13½

No.	Description	Unused	Used
171b	A64 1 l on 5c	160.00	900.00
	Never hinged	315.00	
172c	A64 1 l on 10c	315.00	
174i	A64 1 l on 25c	160.00	—
	Never hinged	315.00	

Unwmk.

No.	Description	Unused	Used
171c	A64 1 l on 5c	72.50	—
	Never hinged	125.00	
172b	A64 1 l on 10c	47.50	—
	Never hinged	100.00	
173b	A64 1 l on 15c	72.50	—
	Never hinged	125.00	
174j	A64 1 l on 25c	47.50	—
	Never hinged	100.00	

Nos. 95, 102, 105, 108, 110, 87 and 89 Overprinted in Black or Red

1924, Feb. 16

No.	Description	Unused	Used
174A	A48 10c claret	2.25	42.50
	Never hinged	5.40	
	On cover		215.00
174B	A49 30c org brn	2.25	42.50
	Never hinged	5.40	
	On cover		215.00
174C	A49 50c violet	2.25	42.50
	Never hinged	5.40	
	On cover		215.00
174D	A49 60c bl (R)	14.50	125.00
	Never hinged	36.00	
	On cover		425.00
174E	A49 85c choc (R)	7.25	125.00
	Never hinged	18.00	
	On cover		425.00
174F	A46 1 l brn & grn	42.50	425.00
	Never hinged	110.00	
	On cover		2,150.
174G	A46 2 l dk grn & org	32.00	425.00
	Never hinged	80.00	
	On cover		2,900.
	Nos. 174A-174G (7)	103.00	1,228.
	Set, never hinged	260.00	
	Set on commem cover		3,750.

Values for mint never hinged blocks of 4

174A	A48	10c claret	24.00
174B	A49	30c org brn	24.00
174C	A49	50c violet	24.00
174D	A49	60c bl (R)	160.00
174E	A49	85c choc (R)	80.00
174F	A46	1 l brn & grn	475.00
174G	A46	2 l dk grn & org	360.00

These stamps were sold on an Italian merchant ship which made a cruise to South American ports in 1924.
Overprint forgeries exist of Nos. 174D-174G.

Stamps of 1901-22 with Advertising Labels Attached

Perf. 14 all around, Imperf. between

1924-25

No.	Description	Unused	Used
96b	A48 15c + Bitter Campari	3.75	25.00
	Never hinged	9.00	
	On cover		110.00
96c	A48 15c + Cordial Campari	3.75	22.00
	Never hinged	9.00	
	On cover		90.00
96d	A48 15c + Columbia	57.50	50.00
	Never hinged	145.00	
	On cover		240.00
100c	A49 25c + Abrador	100.00	125.00
	Never hinged	200.00	
	On cover		825.00
100d	A49 25c + Coen	215.00	65.00
	Never hinged	540.00	
	On cover		400.00
100e	A49 25c + Piperno	1,450.	1,100.
	Never hinged	2,900.	
	On cover		3,600.
100f	A49 25c + Reinach	100.00	85.00
	Never hinged	200.00	
	On cover		550.00
100g	A49 25c + Tagliacozzo	850.00	1,150.
	Never hinged	1,700.	
	On cover		3,600.
102b	A49 30c + Columbia	29.00	40.00
	Never hinged	72.50	
	On cover		180.00
105b	A49 50c + Coen	1,450.	85.00
	Never hinged	2,900.	
	On cover		400.00
105c	A49 50c + Columbia	22.00	16.00
	Never hinged	54.00	
	On cover		72.50
105d	A49 50c + De Montel	3.75	16.00
	Never hinged	9.00	
	On cover		215.00

105e A49 50c + Piperno 2,000. 315.00
Never hinged 4,000.
On cover 1,100.
105f A49 50c + Reinach 215.00 65.00
Never hinged 540.00
On cover 290.00
105g A49 50c + Siero Casali 22.00 *47.50*
Never hinged 54.00
On cover 215.00
105h A49 50c + Singer 3.75 *11.00*
Never hinged 9.00
On cover 42.50
105i A49 50c + Tagliacozzo *2,175.* 600.00
Never hinged 4,250.
On cover 2,250.
105j A49 50c + Tantal 360.00 200.00
Never hinged 900.00
On cover 700.00
87d A46 1 l + Columbia 850.00 950.00
Never hinged 1,700.
On cover 4,250.
Nos. 96b-87d (19) 9,911. 4,968.
Set, never hinged 20,000.

No. 97 with Columbia label and No. E3 with Cioccolato Perugina label were prepared but not issued. Values: Columbia, unused $50, never hinged $125; Cioccolato, unused $18, never hinged $42.50.

King Victor Emmanuel III — A78

1925-26 Engr. Unwmk. *Perf. 11*

175 A78 60c brn car 1.45 .70
Never hinged 3.60
On cover 4.25
a. Perf. 13½ 7.25 2.25
Never hinged 18.00
On cover 5.75
b. Imperf., pair 235.00 260.00
Never hinged 360.00
c. Perf. 11x13½ 575.00 360.00
Never hinged 1,050.
d. Perf. 13½x11 575.00 360.00
Never hinged 1,050.
176 A78 1 l dk bl 1.45 .70
Never hinged 3.60
On cover 2.50
a. Perf. 13½ 14.50 14.50
Never hinged 36.00
On cover 42.50
b. Imperf., pair 235.00 —
Never hinged 375.00
c. Perf. 11x13½ 500.00 250.00
Never hinged 925.00
d. Perf. 13½x11 500.00 250.00
Never hinged 925.00

Perf. 13½

177 A78 1.25 l dk bl ('26) 4.25 2.25
Never hinged 11.00
On cover 22.00
a. Perf. 11 100.00 125.00
Never hinged 250.00
On cover 375.00
b. Imperf., pair 550.00 —
Never hinged 1,100.
c. Perf. 11x13½ 850.00 400.00
Never hinged 1,500.
d. Perf. 13½x11 850.00 400.00
Never hinged 1,500.
Nos. 175-177 (3) 7.15 3.65
Set, never hinged 18.00

25th year of the reign of Victor Emmanuel III.

Nos. 175 to 177 exist with sideways watermark of fragments of letters or a crown, which are normally on the sheet margin.

St. Francis and His Vision A79

Monastery of St. Damien A80

Assisi Monastery A81

St. Francis' Death A82

St. Francis — A83

1926, Jan. 30 Wmk. 140 *Perf. 14*

178 A79 20c gray grn .70 *.90*
Never hinged 1.80
On cover 4.00
a. Imperf single 1,100. 1,100.
Never hinged 1,850.
179 A80 40c dk vio .70 *.90*
Never hinged 1.80
On cover 4.00
180 A81 60c red brn .90 *.90*
Never hinged 1.80
On cover 4.00
a. Imperf single 500.00 500.00
Never hinged 875.00

Unwmk. *Perf. 11*

181 A83 30c slate blk .75 *.90*
Never hinged 1.80
On cover 4.00
a. Perf. 13½ 11.00 *20.00*
Never hinged 27.00
On cover 40.00
b. Perf. 13½x11 450.00
c. Perf. 11x13½ 450.00 350.00
182 A82 1.25 l dark blue 3.75 .90
Never hinged 9.00
On cover 8.50
a. Perf. 13½ 425.00 40.00
Never hinged 1,100.
On cover 110.00

Perf. 13½

183 A83 5 l + 2.50 l dk brn 10.00 *125.00*
Never hinged 25.00
On cover —
Nos. 178-183 (6) 16.80 *129.50*
Set, never hinged 40.00

700th anniv. of the death of St. Francis of Assisi.

Alessandro Volta — A84

1927 Wmk. 140 Typo. *Perf. 14*

188 A84 20c dk car 3.00 1.10
Never hinged 7.25
On cover 11.00
189 A84 50c grnsh blk 3.00 .75
Never hinged 7.25
On cover 10.00
a. Vert. pair, imperf. between 2,750.
190 A84 60c chocolate 4.25 4.50
Never hinged 11.00
On cover 47.50
a. Horiz. pair, imperf. between 1,250.
Never hinged 2,750.
191 A84 1.25 l ultra 14.50 7.25
Never hinged 26.00
On cover 72.50
Nos. 188-191 (4) 24.75 13.60
Set, never hinged 50.00

Cent. of the death of Alessandro Volta. The 20c in purple is Cyrenaica No. 25a.

A85

1927-29 Size: 17½x22mm *Perf. 14*

192 A85 50c brn & slate 3.00 .35
Never hinged 7.25
On cover 1.25
a. Imperf, pair — —
As "a," single 215.00 290.00
Never hinged 350.00
b. Double frame 400.00 325.00
Never hinged *850.00*
c. Double vignette 750.00 650.00
Never hinged *1,600.*

Unwmk.
Engr. *Perf. 11*
Size: 19x23mm

193 A85 1.75 l dp brn 3.75 .30
Never hinged 9.00
On cover 1.25
a. Perf. 13½ ('29) *37,500.* *3,150.*
Never hinged *57,500.*
On cover 9,500.
b. Perf. 11x13½ ('29) — 3,150.
c. Perf. 13½x11 ('29) — 3,150.
d. Imperf, single *4,750.*
Never hinged 7,000.
194 A85 1.85 l black 3.00 .65
Never hinged 5.25
On cover 40.00
195 A85 2.55 l brn car 3.75 *8.50*
Never hinged 9.00
On cover 180.00
196 A85 2.65 l dp vio 5.75 *72.50*
Never hinged 14.50
On cover 1,125.
On cover, single franking 2,150.
a. Imperf, single 3,150.
Never hinged 4,250.
Nos. 192-196 (5) 19.25 *82.30*
Set, never hinged 45.00

A86

1928-29 Wmk. 140 Typo. *Perf. 14*

197 A86 7½c lt brown 3.00 *11.00*
Never hinged 7.25
On cover 29.00
On cover, single franking 180.00
198 A86 15c brn org ('29) 3.00 .30
Never hinged 7.25
On cover 5.75
199 A86 35c gray blk ('29) 8.00 14.50
Never hinged 20.00
On cover 60.00
On cover, single franking 600.00
200 A86 50c dull violet 17.00 .30
Never hinged 42.50
On cover .90
a. Imperf single 225.00
Never hinged 375.00
Nos. 197-200 (4) 31.00 *26.10*
Set, never hinged 75.00

Emmanuel Philibert, Duke of Savoy — A87

Statue of Philibert, Turin — A88

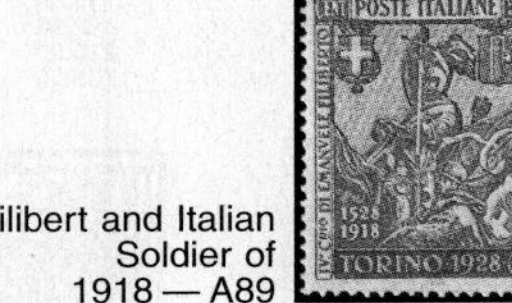
Philibert and Italian Soldier of 1918 — A89

1928 *Perf. 11*

201 A87 20c red brn & ultra 9.50 *16.00*
Never hinged 25.00
On cover 45.00
a. Perf. 13½ 240.00 240.00
Never hinged 500.00
On cover 600.00
202 A87 25c dp red & bl grn 9.50 *16.00*
Never hinged 20.00
On cover 45.00
a. Perf. 13½ 47.50 *52.50*
Never hinged 160.00
On cover 160.00
203 A87 30c bl grn & red brn 16.00 *32.00*
Never hinged 40.00
On cover 87.50
a. Center inverted *67,500.* *9,200.*
No gum *75,000.*
b. Perf. 13½ 35.00 35.00
Never hinged 80.00
On cover 110.00

Perf. 14

204 A89 50c org brn & bl 4.00 1.25
Never hinged 10.00
On cover 5.50
205 A89 75c dp red 4.75 4.00
Never hinged 12.00
On cover 20.00
206 A88 1.25 l bl & blk 4.75 4.00
Never hinged 12.00
On cover 22.50
207 A89 1.75 l bl grn 32.50 *40.00*
Never hinged 80.00
On cover 110.00
208 A87 5 l vio & bl grn (Perf. 11) 29.00 *110.00*
Never hinged 72.50
On cover 550.00
209 A89 10 l blk & pink 35.00 *225.00*
Never hinged 87.50
On cover *9,200.*
210 A88 20 l vio & blk 70.00 *725.00*
Never hinged 175.00
On cover 15,000.
Nos. 201-210 (10) 215.00 *1,173.*
Set, never hinged 535.00

400th anniv. of the birth of Emmanuel Philibert, Duke of Savoy; 10th anniv. of the victory of 1918; Turin Exhibition.

She-wolf Suckling Romulus and Remus
A90 A95a

Julius Caesar A91

Augustus Caesar A92

"Italia" — A93

A94

A95

1929-42 Wmk. 140 Photo. *Perf. 14*

213 A90 5c olive brn .25 .25
Never hinged .50
On cover .40
214 A91 7½c deep vio 1.60 .25
Never hinged 4.00
On cover 20.00
215 A92 10c dk brn .25 .25
Never hinged .50
On cover .40
216 A93 15c slate grn .25 .25
Never hinged .50
On cover .40
217 A91 20c rose red .25 .25
Never hinged .50
On cover .40
218 A94 25c dp green .25 .25
Never hinged .50
On cover .40
219 A95 30c olive brn .25 .25
Never hinged .50
On cover .40
a. Imperf., pair 1,100.
Never hinged 2,250.
220 A93 35c dp blue .25 .25
Never hinged .50
On cover 32.50
221 A95 50c purple .25 .25
Never hinged .50
On cover .40
a. Imperf., pair 725.00 *875.00*
Never hinged 1,450.
222 A94 75c rose red .25 .25
Never hinged .50
On cover .40
222A A91 1 l dk pur ('42) .25 .25
Never hinged .50
On cover 20.00
223 A94 1.25 l dp blue .25 .25
Never hinged .50
On cover .40
224 A92 1.75 l red org .25 .25
Never hinged .50
On cover .40
225 A93 2 l car lake .25 .25
Never hinged .50
On cover .40
226 A95a 2.55 l slate grn .25 .80
Never hinged .50
On cover 32.50
226A A95a 3.70 l pur ('30) .25 .80
Never hinged .50
On cover 60.00
227 A95a 5 l rose red .25 .25
Never hinged .50
On cover 20.00

228 A93 10 l purple 4.00 4.00
Never hinged 10.00
On cover 72.50
229 A91 20 l lt green 4.75 *12.00*
Never hinged 12.00
On cover 325.00
230 A92 25 l bluish sl 11.00 *35.00*
Never hinged 27.50
On cover 2,400.
231 A94 50 l dp violet 13.00 *40.00*
Never hinged 32.50
On cover 2,400.
Nos. 213-231 (21) 38.35 *96.35*
Set, never hinged 94.00

Stamps of the 1929-42 issue overprinted "G.N.R." are 1943 local issues of the Guardia Nazionale Republicana.

See Nos. 427-438, 441-459 in Scott Standard catalogue, Vol. 3.

For surcharge and overprints see Nos. 460, M1-M13, 1N10-1N13, 1LN1-1LN1A, 1LN10, Italian Social Republic 1-5A, and Ionian Islands Nos. N18-N25 in Scott Standard catalogue, Vol. 3; Yugoslavia-Ljubljana N36-N54 in Scott Standard catalogue, Vol. 6.

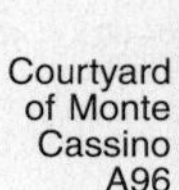

Courtyard of Monte Cassino A96

Monks Laying Cornerstone — A98

St. Benedict of Nursia — A100

Designs: 25c, Fresco, "Death of St. Benedict." 75c+15c, 5 l+1 l, Monte Cassino Abbey.

1929, Aug. 1 Photo. Wmk. 140

232 A96 20c red orange 1.60 1.60
Never hinged 4.00
On cover 8.00
233 A96 25c dk green 1.60 1.60
Never hinged 4.00
On cover 8.00
234 A98 50c + 10c ol brn 4.00 *30.00*
Never hinged 10.00
On cover 87.50
235 A98 75c + 15c crim 4.75 *40.00*
Never hinged 12.00
On cover 110.00
236 A96 1.25 l + 25c saph 6.50 *45.00*
Never hinged 16.00
On cover 125.00
237 A98 5 l + 1 l dk vio 9.50 *175.00*
Never hinged 23.00
On cover 475.00

Unwmk.
Engr.

238 A100 10 l + 2 l slate grn 14.50 *325.00*
Never hinged 35.00
On cover 2,750.
Nos. 232-238 (7) 42.45 *618.20*
Set, never hinged 105.00
Set on overfranked philatelic cover 1,200.

14th cent. of the founding of the Abbey of Monte Cassino by St. Benedict in 529 A.D. The premium on some of the stamps was given to the committee for the celebration of the centenary.

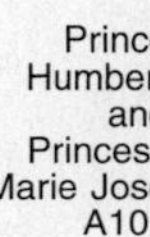

Prince Humbert and Princess Marie José A101

1930, Jan. 8 Photo. Wmk. 140

239 A101 20c orange red .80 .60
Never hinged 2.00
On cover 4.00
240 A101 50c + 10c ol brn 2.40 *4.00*
Never hinged 6.00
On cover 9.50
241 A101 1.25 l + 25c dp bl 5.50 *13.00*
Never hinged 14.00
On cover 32.50
Nos. 239-241 (3) 8.70 *17.60*
Set, never hinged 22.00
Set on overfranked philatelic cover 35.00

Marriage of Prince Humbert of Savoy with Princess Marie José of Belgium.

The surtax on Nos. 240 and 241 was for the benefit of the Italian Red Cross Society.

The 20c in green is Cyrenaica No. 35a.

Ferrucci Leading His Army A102

Fabrizio Maramaldo Killing Ferrucci A103

Francesco Ferrucci — A104

1930, July 10

242 A102 20c rose red .80 .80
Never hinged 2.00
On cover 9.50
243 A103 25c deep green 1.40 .80
Never hinged 3.50
On cover 9.50
244 A103 50c purple .80 .40
Never hinged 2.00
On cover 4.75
245 A103 1.25 l deep blue 11.00 4.75
Never hinged 27.50
On cover 60.00
246 A104 5 l + 2 l org red 22.50 *140.00*
Never hinged 55.00
On cover 600.00
Nos. 242-246 (5) 36.50 *146.75*
Set, never hinged 90.00
Set on overfranked philatelic cover 550.00
Nos. 242-246,C20-C22 (8) 60.50 *314.75*
Set, never hinged 150.00

4th cent. of the death of Francesco Ferrucci, Tuscan warrior.

Overprints

See Castellorizo and Aegean Islands for types A103-A145 Overprinted.

Helenus and Aeneas A106

Designs: 20c, Anchises and Aeneas watch passing of Roman Legions. 25c, Aeneas feasting in shade of Albunea. 30c, Ceres and her children with fruits of Earth. 50c, Harvesters at work. 75c, Woman at loom, children and calf. 1.25 l, Anchises and his sailors in sight of Italy. 5 l+1.50 l, Shepherd piping by fireside. 10 l+2.50 l, Aeneas leading his army.

1930, Oct. 21 Photo. *Perf. 14*

248 A106 15c olive brn 2.40 2.40
Never hinged 6.00
On cover 16.00
249 A106 20c orange 2.40 1.60
Never hinged 6.00
On cover 8.00
250 A106 25c green 3.20 1.60
Never hinged 8.00
On cover 8.00
251 A106 30c dull vio 9.50 4.00
Never hinged 24.00
On cover 20.00
252 A106 50c violet 16.00 .80
Never hinged 40.00
On cover 4.00
253 A106 75c rose red 4.00 *12.00*
Never hinged 10.00
On cover 52.50
254 A106 1.25 l blue 4.00 *12.00*
Never hinged 10.00
On cover 65.00

Unwmk. Engr.

255 A106 5 l +1.50 l red brn 60.00 *525.00*
Never hinged 150.00
On cover 1,200.
256 A106 10 l +2.50 l gray grn 60.00 *725.00*
Never hinged 150.00
On cover *4,000.*
Nos. 248-256 (9) 161.50 *1,284.*
Set, never hinged 405.00
Set on overfranked philatelic cover 3,250.
Nos. 248-256,C23-C26 (13) 332.00 *2,019.*
Set, never hinged 835.00

Bimillenary of the birth of Virgil. Surtax on Nos. 255-256 was for the National Institute Figli del Littorio.

Arms of Italy (Fascist Emblems Support House of Savoy Arms) — A115

1930, Dec. 16 Photo. Wmk. 140

257 A115 2c deep orange 1.60 .25
Never hinged 4.00
On cover 12.00

St. Anthony being Installed as a Franciscan A116

Olivares Hermitage, Portugal A118

St. Anthony Freeing Prisoners A120

St. Anthony's Death A121

St. Anthony Succoring the Poor — A122

Designs: 25c, St. Anthony preaching to the fishes. 50c, Basilica of St. Anthony, Padua.

Wmk. 140

1931, Mar. 9 Photo. *Perf. 14*

258 A116 20c dull violet 4.00 1.25
Never hinged 10.00
On cover 4.75
259 A116 25c gray green 2.40 1.25
Never hinged 6.00
On cover 4.75
260 A118 30c brown 6.50 2.40
Never hinged 16.00
On cover 12.00
261 A118 50c violet 2.00 .80
Never hinged 5.00
On cover 3.50
262 A120 1.25 l blue 20.00 9.50
Never hinged 50.00
On cover 45.00

Unwmk. Engr.

263 A121 75c brown red 9.50 *16.00*
Never hinged 24.00
On cover 67.50
a. Perf. 12 100.00 *375.00*
Never hinged 240.00
On cover 750.00
264 A122 5 l + 2.50 l ol grn 40.00 *325.00*
Never hinged 100.00
On cover 725.00
Nos. 258-264 (7) 84.40 *356.20*
Set, never hinged 210.00
Set on overfranked philatelic cover 525.00

7th centenary of the death of Saint Anthony of Padua.

Tower of Meloria — A123

Training Ship "Amerigo Vespucci" A124

Cruiser "Trento" A125

1931, Nov. 29 Photo. Wmk. 140

265 A123 20c rose red 8.75 2.00
Never hinged 35.00
On cover 9.50
266 A124 50c purple 8.75 1.60
Never hinged 35.00
On cover 8.00
267 A125 1.25 l dk bl 24.00 4.75
Never hinged 95.00
On cover 40.00
Nos. 265-267 (3) 41.50 8.35
Set, never hinged 165.00
Set on overfranked philatelic cover 45.00

Royal Naval Academy at Leghorn (Livorno), 50th anniv.

Giovanni Boccaccio A126

Designs: 15c, Niccolo Machiavelli. 20c, Paolo Sarpi. 25c, Count Vittorio Alfieri. 30c, Ugo Foscolo. 50c, Count Giacomo Leopardi. 75c, Giosue Carducci. 1.25 l, Carlo Giuseppe Botta. 1.75 l, Torquato Tasso. 2.75 l, Francesco Petrarca. 5 l+2 l, Ludovico Ariosto. 10 l+2.50 l, Dante Alighieri.

1932, Mar. 14 *Perf. 14*

268 A126 10c olive brn 3.25 1.60
Never hinged 8.00
On cover 14.00
269 A126 15c slate grn 3.25 2.00
Never hinged 8.00
On cover 32.50
270 A126 20c rose red 3.25 1.60
Never hinged 8.00
On cover 8.00
271 A126 25c dp green 3.25 1.25
Never hinged 8.00
On cover 6.50
272 A126 30c olive brn 4.00 1.60
Never hinged 10.00
On cover 20.00
273 A126 50c violet 2.40 .80
Never hinged 6.00
On cover 3.50
274 A126 75c car rose 16.00 8.00
Never hinged 40.00
On cover 40.00
275 A126 1.25 l dp blue 4.75 4.00
Never hinged 12.00
On cover 32.50
276 A126 1.75 l orange 12.00 8.00
Never hinged 30.00
On cover 47.50
277 A126 2.75 l gray 24.00 *40.00*
Never hinged 60.00
On cover 175.00
278 A126 5 l + 2 l car rose 29.00 *300.00*
Never hinged 72.50
On cover 1,100.
279 A126 10 l + 2.50 l ol grn 35.00 *450.00*
Never hinged 87.50
On cover *2,750.*
Nos. 268-279 (12) 140.15 *818.85*

Set, never hinged 350.00
Set on overfranked philatelic cover 2,000.
Nos. 268-279,C28-C33,C34 (19) 237.90 *2,427.*
Set, never hinged 600.00

Dante Alighieri Society, a natl. literary association founded to promote development of the Italian language and culture. The surtax was added to the Society funds to help in its work.

View of Caprera A138

Garibaldi Carrying His Dying Wife A141

Garibaldi Memorial A144

Giuseppe Garibaldi A145

Designs: 20c, 30c, Garibaldi meeting Victor Emmanuel II. 25c, 50c, Garibaldi at Battle of Calatafimi. 1.25 l, Garibaldi's tomb. 1.75 l+25c, Rock of Quarto.

1932, Apr. 6

280 A138 10c gray blk 2.40 1.60
Never hinged 6.00
On cover 14.50
281 A138 20c olive brn 2.40 1.25
Never hinged 6.00
On cover 11.00
282 A138 25c dull grn 3.25 1.60
Never hinged 8.00
On cover 8.00
283 A138 30c orange 3.25 2.40
Never hinged 8.00
On cover 35.00
284 A138 50c violet 1.60 .40
Never hinged 4.00
On cover 3.25
285 A141 75c rose red 16.00 9.50
Never hinged 40.00
On cover 45.00
286 A141 1.25 l dp blue 32.50 4.00
Never hinged 80.00
On cover 40.00
287 A141 1.75 l + 25c bl gray 40.00 *87.50*
Never hinged 100.00
On cover 450.00
288 A144 2.55 l + 50c red brn 32.50 *125.00*
Never hinged 80.00
On cover 500.00
289 A145 5 l + 1 l cop red 32.50 *130.00*
Never hinged 80.00
On cover 675.00
Nos. 280-289 (10) 166.40 *363.25*
Set, never hinged 410.00
Set on overfranked philatelic cover 950.00
Nos. 280-289,C35-C39,CE1-CE2 (17) 242.40 *619.25*
Set, never hinged 600.00

50th anniv. of the death of Giuseppe Garibaldi, patriot.

Plowing with Oxen and Tractor A146

10c, Soldier guarding mountain pass. 15c, Marine, battleship & seaplane. 20c, Head of Fascist youth. 25c, Hands of workers & tools. 30c, Flags, Bible & altar. 35c, "New roads for the new Legions." 50c, Mussolini statue, Bologna. 60c, Hands with spades. 75c, Excavating ruins. 1 l, Steamers & galleons. 1.25 l, Italian flag, map & points of compass. 1.75 l, Flag, athlete & stadium. 2.55 l, Mother & child. 2.75 l, Emblems of drama, music, art & sport. 5 l+2.50 l, Roman emperor.

1932, Oct. 27 **Photo.**

290 A146 5c dk brown 2.40 1.25
Never hinged 6.00
On cover 27.50
291 A146 10c dk brown 2.40 .80
Never hinged 6.00
On cover 9.50
292 A146 15c dk gray grn 2.40 1.25
Never hinged 6.00
On cover 16.00
293 A146 20c car rose 2.40 .60
Never hinged 6.00
On cover 3.25
294 A146 25c dp green 2.40 .40
Never hinged 6.00
On cover 3.25
295 A146 30c dk brown 3.25 2.40
Never hinged 8.00
On cover 20.00
296 A146 35c dk blue 8.00 *9.50*
Never hinged 20.00
On cover 87.50
297 A146 50c purple 1.60 .40
Never hinged 4.00
On cover 2.00
298 A146 60c orange brn 12.00 8.00
Never hinged 30.00
On cover 55.00
299 A146 75c car rose 4.00 4.00
Never hinged 10.00
On cover 20.00
300 A146 1 l black vio 16.00 6.50
Never hinged 40.00
On cover 52.50
301 A146 1.25 l dp blue 4.00 1.60
Never hinged 10.00
On cover 20.00
302 A146 1.75 l orange 24.00 2.00
Never hinged 60.00
On cover 20.00
303 A146 2.55 l dk gray 29.00 *40.00*
Never hinged 72.50
On cover 160.00
304 A146 2.75 l slate grn 29.00 *40.00*
Never hinged 72.50
On cover 200.00
305 A146 5 l + 2.50 l car rose 40.00 *450.00*
Never hinged 100.00
On cover *1,900.*
Nos. 290-305 (16) 182.85 *568.70*
Set, never hinged 455.00
Set on overfranked philatelic cover 1,650.
Nos. 290-305,C40-C41,E16-E17 (20) 202.75 *769.80*
Set, never hinged 520.00

10th anniv. of the Fascist government and the March on Rome.

Statue of Athlete — A162

1933, Aug. 16 ***Perf. 14***

306 A162 10c dk brown .80 .80
Never hinged 2.00
On cover 8.00
307 A162 20c rose red .80 .80
Never hinged 2.00
On cover *9.50*
308 A162 50c purple .80 .40
Never hinged 2.00
On cover *4.75*
309 A162 1.25 l blue 4.75 *6.50*
Never hinged 12.00
On cover *47.50*
Nos. 306-309 (4) 7.15 8.50
Set, never hinged 18.00
Set on overfranked philatelic cover 52.50

Intl. University Games at Turin, Sept., 1933.

Cross in Halo, St. Peter's Dome — A163

Designs: 25c, 50c, Angel with cross. 1.25 l, as 20c. 2.55 l, + 2.50 l, Cross with doves.

1933, Oct. 23

310 A163 20c rose red 4.75 1.25
Never hinged 12.00
On cover *8.00*
311 A163 25c green 12.00 1.60
Never hinged 30.00
On cover *8.00*
312 A163 50c purple 4.75 .40
Never hinged 12.00
On cover *3.25*
313 A163 1.25 l dp blue 12.00 4.75
Never hinged 30.00
On cover *40.00*
314 A163 2.55 l + 2.50 l blk 8.00 *240.00*
Never hinged 20.00
On cover *725.00*
Nos. 310-314 (5) 41.50 *248.00*
Set, never hinged 105.00
Set on overfranked philatelic cover 725.00
Nos. 310-314,CB1-CB2 (7) 47.90 *435.50*
Set, never hinged 121.00

Issued at the solicitation of the Order of the Holy Sepulchre of Jerusalem to mark the Holy Year.

Anchor of the "Emanuele Filiberto" — A166

Designs: 20c, Anchor. 50c, Gabriele d'Annunzio. 1.25 l, St. Vito's Tower. 1.75 l, Symbolizing Fiume's annexation. 2.55 l+2 l, Victor Emmanuel III arriving aboard "Brindisi." 2.75 l+2.50 l, Galley, gondola and battleship.

1934, Mar. 12

315 A166 10c dk brown 8.00 4.00
Never hinged 20.00
On cover *32.50*
316 A166 20c rose red 1.60 1.60
Never hinged 4.00
On cover *17.50*
317 A166 50c purple 1.60 1.60
Never hinged 4.00
On cover *16.00*
318 A166 1.25 l blue 1.60 *6.50*
Never hinged 4.00
On cover *60.00*
319 A166 1.75 l + 1 l indigo 1.60 *35.00*
Never hinged 4.00
On cover *475.00*
320 A166 2.55 l + 2 l dull vio 1.60 *55.00*
Never hinged 4.00
On cover *600.00*
321 A166 2.75 l + 2.50 l ol grn 1.60 *55.00*
Never hinged 4.00
On cover *650.00*
Nos. 315-321 (7) 17.60 *158.70*
Set, never hinged 44.00
Set on overfranked philatelic cover 950.00
Nos. 315-321,C56-C61,CE5-CE7 (16) 29.95 *308.60*
Set, never hinged 66.50

10th anniversary of annexation of Fiume.

Antonio Pacinotti — A172

1934, May 23

322 A172 50c purple .80 .40
Never hinged 2.00
On cover *4.00*
323 A172 1.25 l sapphire 1.25 *2.75*
Never hinged 3.00
On cover *35.00*
Set, never hinged 5.00
Set on overfranked philatelic cover 35.00

75th anniv. of invention of the dynamo by Antonio Pacinotti (1841-1912), scientist.

Guarding the Goal — A173

Players — A175

Soccer Players A174

1934, May 23

324 A173 20c red orange 6.50 *8.00*
Never hinged 16.00
On cover 80.00
325 A174 25c green 6.50 2.40
Never hinged 16.00
On cover 52.50
326 A174 50c purple 6.50 1.25
Never hinged 16.00
On cover 40.00
327 A174 1.25 l blue 16.00 16.00
Never hinged 40.00
On cover 240.00
328 A175 5 l + 2.50 l brn 95.00 *700.00*
Never hinged 240.00
On cover *4,000.*
Nos. 324-328 (5) 130.50 *727.65*
Set, never hinged 330.00
Set on overfranked philatelic cover *3,750.*
Nos. 324-328,C62-C65 (9) 264.00 *1,465.*
Set, never hinged 625.00

2nd World Soccer Championship.

For overprints see Aegean Islands Nos. 31-35.

Luigi Galvani — A176

1934, Aug. 16

329 A176 30c brown, *buff* 1.00 .80
Never hinged 2.50
On cover 8.00
330 A176 75c carmine, *rose* 1.40 3.25
Never hinged 3.50
On cover 35.00
Set, never hinged 6.00
Set on overfranked philatelic cover 40.00

Intl. Congress of Electro-Radio-Biology.

Carabinieri Emblem — A177

Cutting Barbed Wire A178

Designs: 20c, Sardinian Grenadier and soldier throwing grenade. 25c, Alpine Infantry. 30c, Military courage. 75c, Artillery. 1.25 l, Acclaiming the Service. 1.75 l+1 l, Cavalry. 2.55 l+2 l, Sapping Detail. 2.75 l+2 l, First aid.

1934, Sept. 6 **Photo.** **Wmk. 140**

331 A177 10c dk brown 2.40 2.40
Never hinged 6.00
On cover 17.50
332 A178 15c olive grn 2.40 *4.00*
Never hinged 6.00
On cover 24.00
333 A178 20c rose red 2.40 1.60
Never hinged 6.00
On cover 12.00
334 A177 25c green 4.00 1.60
Never hinged 10.00
On cover 12.00
335 A178 30c dk brown 4.00 *8.00*
Never hinged 10.00
On cover 35.00
336 A178 50c purple 2.40 .80
Never hinged 6.00
On cover 4.00
337 A178 75c car rose 40.00 12.00
Never hinged 100.00
On cover 52.50
338 A178 1.25 l dk blue 40.00 8.00
Never hinged 100.00
On cover 40.00

339 A177 1.75 l + 1 l red org 17.50 *60.00*
Never hinged 42.50
On cover 550.00
340 A178 2.55 l + 2 l dp cl 17.50 *80.00*
Never hinged 42.50
On cover 675.00
341 A178 2.75 l + 2 l vio 21.00 *80.00*
Never hinged 52.50
On cover 950.00
Nos. 331-341 (11) 153.60 *258.40*
Set, never hinged 385.00
Set on overfranked philatelic cover 1,300.
Nos. 331-341,C66-C72 (18) 202.10 *421.40*
Set, never hinged 505.00

Centenary of Military Medal of Valor.
For overprints see Aegean Islands Nos. 36-46.

Man Holding Fasces A187

Standard Bearer, Bayonet Attack A188

Design: 30c, Eagle and soldier.

1935, Apr. 23 ***Perf. 14***
342 A187 20c rose red .80 .80
Never hinged 2.00
On cover 8.00
343 A187 30c dk brown 6.50 16.00
Never hinged 16.00
On cover 65.00
344 A188 50c purple .80 .40
Never hinged 2.00
On cover 6.50
Nos. 342-344 (3) 8.10 17.20
Set, never hinged 20.00
Set on overfranked philatelic cover 65.00

Issued in honor of the University Contests.

Fascist Flight Symbolism A190

Leonardo da Vinci — A191

1935, Oct. 1
345 A190 20c rose red 20.00 2.00
Never hinged 80.00
On cover 25.00
346 A190 30c brown 35.00 6.50
Never hinged 140.00
On cover 87.50
347 A191 50c purple 72.50 1.25
Never hinged 290.00
On cover 17.50
348 A191 1.25 l dk blue 80.00 7.25
Never hinged 320.00
On cover 110.00
Nos. 345-348 (4) 207.50 17.00
Set, never hinged 830.00
Set on overfranked philatelic cover 200.00

International Aeronautical Salon, Milan.

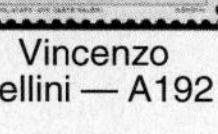

Vincenzo Bellini — A192

Bellini's Villa — A194

Bellini's Piano A193

1935, Oct. 15
349 A192 20c rose red 16.00 4.00
Never hinged 40.00
On cover 24.00
350 A192 30c brown 24.00 14.50
Never hinged 60.00
On cover 40.00
351 A192 50c violet 24.00 1.60
Never hinged 60.00
On cover 16.00
352 A192 1.25 l dk blue 40.00 20.00
Never hinged 100.00
On cover 110.00
353 A193 1.75 l + 1 l red org 35.00 *325.00*
Never hinged 90.00
On cover 725.00
354 A194 2.75 l + 2 l ol blk 65.00 *340.00*
Never hinged 160.00
On cover 1,000.
Nos. 349-354 (6) 204.00 *705.10*
Set, never hinged 510.00
Set on overfranked philatelic cover 1,350.
Nos. 349-354,C79-C83 (11) 287.00 *1,022.*
Set, never hinged 710.00

Bellini (1801-35), operatic composer.

Map of Italian Industries A195

Designs: 20c, 1.25 l, Map of Italian Industries. 30c, 50c, Cogwheel and plow.

1936, Mar. 23
355 A195 20c red .80 .40
Never hinged 2.00
On cover 4.75
356 A195 30c brown .80 1.25
Never hinged 2.00
On cover 12.00
357 A195 50c purple .80 .35
Never hinged 2.00
On cover 3.25
358 A195 1.25 l blue 4.75 3.25
Never hinged 12.00
On cover 20.00
Nos. 355-358 (4) 7.15 5.25
Set, never hinged 18.00
Set on overfranked philatelic cover 24.00

The 17th Milan Trade Fair.

Flock of Sheep A197

Ajax Defying the Lightning A199

Bust of Horace A200

Designs: 20c, 1.25 l+1 l, Countryside in Spring. 75c, Capitol. 1.75 l+1 l, Pan piping. 2.55 l+1 l, Dying warrior.

Wmk. Crowns (140)

1936, July 1 **Photo.** ***Perf. 14***
359 A197 10c dp green 6.50 1.25
Never hinged 16.00
On cover 9.50
360 A197 20c rose red 4.75 .80
Never hinged 12.00
On cover 8.00
361 A199 30c olive brn 6.50 2.40
Never hinged 16.00
On cover 20.00
362 A200 50c purple 6.50 .40
Never hinged 16.00
On cover 4.75
363 A197 75c rose red 16.00 12.00
Never hinged 40.00
On cover 45.00

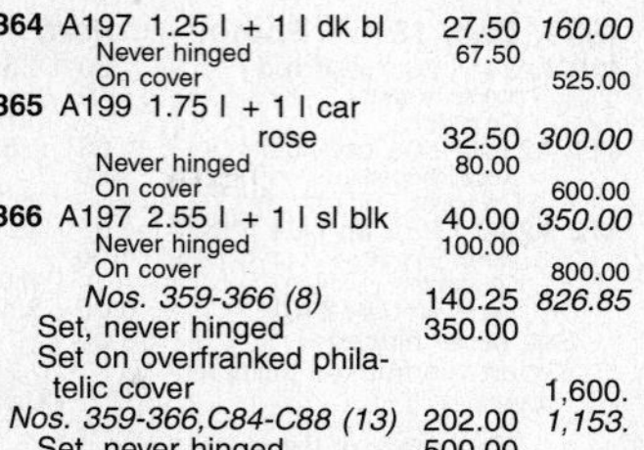

364 A197 1.25 l + 1 l dk bl 27.50 *160.00*
Never hinged 67.50
On cover 525.00
365 A199 1.75 l + 1 l car rose 32.50 *300.00*
Never hinged 80.00
On cover 600.00
366 A197 2.55 l + 1 l sl blk 40.00 *350.00*
Never hinged 100.00
On cover 800.00
Nos. 359-366 (8) 140.25 *826.85*
Set, never hinged 350.00
Set on overfranked philatelic cover 1,600.
Nos. 359-366,C84-C88 (13) 202.00 *1,153.*
Set, never hinged 500.00

2000th anniv. of the birth of Quintus Horatius Flaccus (Horace), Roman poet.

Child Holding Wheat — A204

Child Giving Salute — A205

Child and Fasces — A206

"Il Bambino" by della Robbia — A207

1937, June 28
367 A204 10c yellow brn 3.25 1.60
Never hinged 8.00
On cover 20.00
368 A205 20c car rose 3.25 1.25
Never hinged 8.00
On cover 6.50
369 A204 25c green 3.25 2.00
Never hinged 8.00
On cover 24.00
370 A206 30c dk brown 4.75 4.00
Never hinged 12.00
On cover 30.00
371 A205 50c purple 3.25 .40
Never hinged 8.00
On cover 4.00
372 A207 75c rose red 16.00 *17.50*
Never hinged 40.00
On cover 80.00
373 A205 1.25 l dk blue 20.00 17.50
Never hinged 50.00
On cover 72.50
374 A206 1.75 l + 75c org 40.00 *250.00*
Never hinged 100.00
On cover 800.00
375 A207 2.75 l + 1.25 l dk bl grn 32.50 *275.00*
Never hinged 80.00
On cover 1,000.
376 A205 5 l + 3 l bl gray 40.00 *375.00*
Never hinged 100.00
On cover 2,200.
Nos. 367-376 (10) 166.25 *944.25*
Set, never hinged 415.00
Set on overfranked philatelic cover 2,750.
Nos. 367-376,C89-C94 (16) 262.25 *1,378.*
Set, never hinged 655.00

Summer Exhibition for Child Welfare. The surtax on Nos. 374-376 was used to support summer camps for children.

Rostral Column — A208

15c, Army Trophies. 20c, Augustus Caesar (Octavianus) offering sacrifice. 25c, Cross Roman Standards. 30c, Julius Caesar and Julian Star. 50c, Augustus receiving acclaim. 75c, Augustus Caesar. 1.25 l, Symbolizing maritime glory of Rome. 1.75 l+1 l, Sacrificial Altar. 2.55 l+2 l, Capitol.

1937, Sept. 23
377 A208 10c myrtle grn 3.25 .80
Never hinged 8.00
On cover 6.50
378 A208 15c olive grn 3.25 1.25
Never hinged 8.00
On cover 16.00
379 A208 20c red 3.25 .60
Never hinged 8.00
On cover 4.75
380 A208 25c green 3.25 .60
Never hinged 8.00
On cover 4.75
381 A208 30c olive bis 4.00 .80
Never hinged 10.00
On cover 12.00
382 A208 50c purple 3.25 .35
Never hinged 8.00
On cover 3.50
383 A208 75c scarlet 3.25 4.75
Never hinged 8.00
On cover 24.00
384 A208 1.25 l dk blue 8.00 5.50
Never hinged 20.00
On cover 27.50
385 A208 1.75 l + 1 l plum 40.00 *225.00*
Never hinged 100.00
On cover 550.00
386 A208 2.55 l + 2 l sl blk 52.50 *300.00*
Never hinged 130.00
On cover 725.00
Nos. 377-386 (10) 124.00 *539.65*
Set, never hinged 300.00
Set on overfranked philatelic cover 1,000.
Nos. 377-386,C95-C99 (15) 259.00 *812.65*
Set, never hinged 625.00

Bimillenary of the birth of Emperor Augustus Caesar (Octavianus) on the occasion of the exhibition opened in Rome by Mussolini, Sept. 22, 1937.
For overprints see Aegean Islands Nos. 47-56.

Gasparo Luigi Pacifico Spontini A218

Antonius Stradivarius A219

Count Giacomo Leopardi A220

Giovanni Battista Pergolesi A221

Giotto di Bondone — A222

1937, Oct. 25
387 A218 10c dk brown 1.60 .80
Never hinged 4.00
On cover 6.50
388 A219 20c rose red 1.60 .80
Never hinged 4.00
On cover 4.75
389 A220 25c dk green 1.60 .80
Never hinged 4.00
On cover 4.75
390 A221 30c dk brown 1.60 1.60
Never hinged 4.00
On cover 16.00
391 A220 50c purple 1.60 .80
Never hinged 4.00
On cover 3.25
392 A221 75c crimson 2.25 *4.75*
Never hinged 5.50
On cover 35.00
393 A222 1.25 l dp blue 3.25 *4.75*
Never hinged 8.00
On cover 35.00
394 A218 1.75 l dp orange 3.25 *4.75*
Never hinged 8.00
On cover 35.00

395 A219 2.55 l + 2 l gray grn 16.00 *260.00*
Never hinged 40.00
On cover 675.00
396 A222 2.75 l + 2 l red brn 16.00 *300.00*
Never hinged 40.00
On cover 725.00
Nos. 387-396 (10) 48.75 *579.05*
Set, never hinged 125.00
Set on overfranked philatelic cover 1,100.

Centennials of Spontini, Stradivarius, Leopardi, Pergolesi and Giotto.

For overprints see Aegean Islands Nos. 57-58.

Guglielmo Marconi — A223

1938, Jan. 24

397 A223 20c rose pink 3.25 .80
Never hinged 8.00
On cover 6.50
398 A223 50c purple .80 .40
Never hinged 2.00
On cover 4.75
399 A223 1.25 l blue 3.25 6.75
Never hinged 8.00
On cover 45.00
Nos. 397-399 (3) 7.30 7.95
Set, never hinged 18.00
Set on overfranked philatelic cover 40.00

Guglielmo Marconi (1874-1937), electrical engineer, inventor of wireless telegraphy.

Augustus Caesar (Octavianus) A224

10c, Romulus Plowing. 25c, Dante. 30c, Columbus. 50c, Leonardo da Vinci. 75c, Victor Emmanuel II and Garibaldi. 1.25 l, Tomb of Unknown Soldier, Rome. 1.75 l, Blackshirts' March on Rome, 1922. 2.75 l, Map of Italian East Africa and Iron Crown of Monza. 5 l, Victor Emmanuel III.

1938, Oct. 28

400 A224 10c brown 2.40 .80
Never hinged 6.00
On cover 8.00
401 A224 20c car rose 2.40 .80
Never hinged 6.00
On cover 8.00
402 A224 25c dk green 2.40 .80
Never hinged 6.00
On cover 8.00
403 A224 30c olive brn 2.40 2.00
Never hinged 6.00
On cover 14.50
404 A224 50c lt violet 2.40 .80
Never hinged 6.00
On cover 3.50
405 A224 75c rose red 3.25 3.25
Never hinged 8.00
On cover 35.00
406 A224 1.25 l dp blue 6.50 3.25
Never hinged 16.00
On cover 35.00
407 A224 1.75 l vio blk 8.00 4.00
Never hinged 20.00
On cover 47.50
408 A224 2.75 l slate grn 27.50 *47.50*
Never hinged 67.50
On cover 240.00
409 A224 5 l lt red brn 32.50 *52.50*
Never hinged 82.50
On cover 400.00
Nos. 400-409 (10) 89.75 *115.70*
Set, never hinged 220.00
Set on overfranked philatelic cover 600.00
Nos. 400-409,C100-C105 (16) 143.25 *284.20*
Set, never hinged 350.00

Proclamation of the Empire.

Wood-burning Engine and Streamlined Electric Engine — A234

1939, Dec. 15 Photo. *Perf. 14*

410 A234 20c rose red .80 .60
Never hinged 2.00
On cover 9.50
411 A234 50c brt violet 1.60 .80
Never hinged 4.00
On cover 8.00
412 A234 1.25 l dp blue 4.00 4.00
Never hinged 10.00
On cover 40.00
Nos. 410-412 (3) 6.40 5.40
Set, never hinged 16.00
Set on overfranked philatelic cover 40.00

Centenary of Italian railroads.

SEMI-POSTAL STAMPS

Many issues of Italy and Italian Colonies include one or more semi-postal denominations. To avoid splitting sets, these issues are generally listed as regular postage, airmail, etc., unless all values carry a surtax.

Italian Flag — SP1

Italian Eagle Bearing Arms of Savoy — SP2

1915-16 Typo. *Perf. 14*

B1 SP1 10c + 5c rose 8.50 12.00
Never hinged 21.00
On cover 47.50
B2 SP2 15c + 5c slate 6.75 9.50
Never hinged 17.00
On cover 47.50
On cover, single franking 275.00
B3 SP2 20c + 5c orange 32.50 65.00
Never hinged 85.00
On cover 175.00
Nos. B1-B3 (3) 47.75 *86.50*
Set, never hinged 125.00

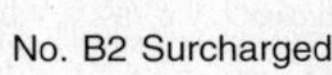

No. B2 Surcharged

1916

B4 SP2 20c on 15c + 5c 20.00 55.00
Never hinged 50.00
On cover 240.00
a. Double overprint 800.00 —
Never hinged —
b. Inverted overprint 800.00 1,400.
Never hinged —
c. Pair, one without surcharge 1,800.
Never hinged 2,600.

Regular Issues of 1906-16 Overprinted in Blue or Red

1921

B5 A48 10c claret (Bl) 900.00 1,450.
No gum 425.00
Never hinged 1,800.
On BLP envelope 475.00 *5,000.*
a. Double overprint 1,300.
Never hinged 2,050.
B6 A50 20c brn org (Bl) 1,250. 425.00
No gum 525.00
Never hinged 2,500.
On BLP envelope 575.00 1,100.
B7 A49 25c blue (R) 220.00 180.00
No gum 90.00
Never hinged 540.00
On BLP envelope 100.00 *500.00*
a. Double overprint 360.00
Never hinged 525.00
B8 A49 40c brn (Bl) 85.00 18.00
No gum 32.50
Never hinged 215.00
On BLP envelope 36.00 *57.50*
a. Inverted overprint 425.00 700.00
b. Violet ovpt. 145.00 *25.00*
No gum 42.50
Never hinged 360.00
On BLP envelope 37.50 82.50
c. Maroon ovpt. 100.00 22.00
No gum 40.00
Never hinged 250.00
On BLP envelope 42.50 85.00
d. Blue black ovpt. 215.00 65.00
No gum 72.50
Never hinged 540.00
On BLP envelope 82.50 250.00
Nos. B5-B8 (4) 2,455. 2,073.
Set, never hinged 5,000.

Regular Issues of 1901-22 Overprinted in Black, Blue, Brown or Red

1922-23 Typographed Ovpt.

B9 A48 10c cl ('23) (Bk) 110.00 100.00
No gum 42.50
Never hinged 290.00
On BLP envelope 47.50 *650.00*
a. Blue ovpt. 85.00 80.00
No gum 36.00
Never hinged 215.00
On BLP envelope 40.00 *950.00*
b. Brown ovpt. 85.00 80.00
No gum 36.00
Never hinged 215.00
On BLP envelope 40.00 1,450.
d. Blk ovpt. double 160.00
Never hinged 250.00
e. As "b," ovpt. double 160.00
Never hinged 250.00
B10 A48 15c slate (Org) 290.00 *475.00*
No gum 125.00
Never hinged 725.00
On BLP envelope 145.00 *6,500.*
b. Red overprint 360.00 575.00
No gum 190.00
Never hinged 900.00
On BLP envelope 215.00 *8,000.*
B11 A50 20c brn org (Bk) 360.00 *475.00*
No gum 145.00
Never hinged 900.00
On BLP envelope 160.00 *2,200.*
B12b A49 25c Red overprint *200.00* 475.00
No gum 140.00
Never hinged 725.00
On BLP envelope 160.00 —
B12c A49 25c Orange overprint *325.00* 540.00
No gum 140.00
Never hinged 800.00
On BLP envelope 160.00 —
B12A A49 30c org brn (Bk) 220.00 200.00
No gum 90.00
Never hinged 540.00
On BLP envelope 100.00 *3,400.*
B15A A49 85c choc (Bk) 290.00 *475.00*
No gum 125.00
Never hinged 725.00
On BLP envelope 145.00 *12,500.*

Litho. Ovpt.

B9c A48 10c Blk ovpt. 110.00 80.00
No gum 42.50
Never hinged 290.00
On BLP envelope 47.50 *240.00*
B10a A48 15c Blue ovpt. 900.00 725.00
No gum 400.00
Never hinged 1,900.
On BLP envelope 425.00 *5,750.*
c. Blk ovpt. 3,600. —
Never hinged 7,250.
B11a A50 20c Blue ovpt. 800.00 325.00
No gum 290.00
Never hinged 1,575.
On BLP envelope 315.00 *1,000.*
b. Blk ovpt. 800.00 550.00
No gum 290.00
Never hinged 1,575.
On BLP envelope 315.00 *1,200.*
B12 A49 25c blue (Bk) ('23) 100.00 87.50
No gum 42.50
Never hinged 250.00
On BLP envelope 50.00 *725.00*
B13 A49 40c brn (Bl) 170.00 87.50
No gum 65.00
Never hinged 425.00
On BLP envelope 72.50 *725.00*
a. Black ovpt. 190.00 87.50
No gum 65.00
Never hinged 425.00
On BLP envelope 72.50 *725.00*
b. As "a," invtd. ovpt. 210.00 —
B14 A49 50c vio ('23) (Bk) 725.00 500.00
No gum 250.00
Never hinged 1,450.
On BLP envelope 290.00 1,825.
a. Blue overprint
B15 A49 60c car (Bk) 2,200. 1,900.
No gum 950.00
Never hinged 4,000.
On BLP envelope 1,100. 6,500.
B16 A46 1 l brn & grn ('23) (Bk) 3,250. 2,200.
No gum 1,600.
Never hinged 6,500.
On BLP envelope 1,750. *4,350.*
a. Inverted overprint *5,000.*
Never hinged *6,250.*
b. Overprint on reverse 3,100.
Never hinged *6,250.*
Nos. B9-B16 (10) 7,715. 6,500.
Set, never hinged 21,060.
Set, #B9-B16, B12A, B15A, never hinged 17,625.

The stamps overprinted "B. L. P." were sold by the Government below face value to the National Federation for Assisting War Invalids. Most of them were affixed to special envelopes (Buste Lettere Postali) which bore advertisements. The Federation was permitted to sell these envelopes at a reduction of 5c from the face value of each stamp. The profits for the war invalids were derived from the advertisements.

Values of Nos. B5-B16 unused are for stamps with original gum. Most copies without gum or with part gum sell for about a quarter of values quoted. Uncanceled stamps affixed to the special envelopes usually sell for about half value.

The overprint on Nos. B9-B16 is wider (13½mm) than that on Nos. B5-B8 (11mm). The 1922-23 overprint exists both typo. and litho. on 10c, 15c, 20c and 25c; only litho. on 40c, 50c, 60c and 1 l; and only typo. on 30c and 85c.

Counterfeits of the B.L.P. overprints exist.

Administering Fascist Oath — SP3

1923, Oct. 29 *Perf. 14x14½*

B17 SP3 30c + 30c brown 32.50 *160.00*
Never hinged 85.00
On cover 550.00
B18 SP3 50c + 50c violet 32.50 *160.00*
Never hinged 85.00
On cover 550.00
a. Horiz. pair, imperf between 1,900.
B19 SP3 1 l + 1 l gray 32.50 *160.00*
Never hinged 85.00
On cover 550.00
Nos. B17-B19 (3) 97.50 *480.00*
Set, never hinged 250.00
Set on commem cover 925.00

The surtax was given to the Benevolent Fund of the Black Shirts (the Italian National Militia).

Anniv. of the March of the Fascisti on Rome.

St. Maria Maggiore SP4

Pope Opening Holy Door SP8

Designs: 30c+15c, St. John Lateran. 50c+25c, St. Paul's Church. 60c+30c, St. Peter's Basilica. 5 l+2.50 l, Pope closing Holy Door.

1924, Dec. 24 *Perf. 12*

B20 SP4 20c + 10c dk grn & brn 4.50 *12.50*
Never hinged 10.50
On cover 47.50
B21 SP4 30c + 15c dk brn & brn 4.50 *12.50*
Never hinged 10.50
On cover 47.50
B22 SP4 50c + 25c vio & brn 4.50 *12.50*
Never hinged 10.50
On cover 55.00
B23 SP4 60c + 30c dp rose & brn 4.50 *40.00*
Never hinged 10.50
On cover 95.00
B24 SP8 1 l + 50c dp bl & vio 7.50 *40.00*
Never hinged 17.00
On cover 175.00
B25 SP8 5 l + 2.50 l org brn & vio 9.50 *80.00*
Never hinged 23.00
On cover 400.00
Nos. B20-B25 (6) 35.00 *197.50*
Set, never hinged 82.00
Set on commem cover 350.00

The surtax was contributed toward the Holy Year expenses.

Castle of St. Angelo SP10

Designs: 50c+20c, 60c+30c, Aqueduct of Claudius. 1.25 l+50c, 1.25 l+60c, Capitol, Roman Forum. 5 l+2 l, 5 l+2.50 l, People's Gate.

Unwmk.

1926, Oct. 26 Engr. *Perf. 11*

B26 SP10 40c + 20c dk brn & blk 3.25 *24.00*
Never hinged 8.00
On cover 100.00
B27 SP10 60c + 30c brn red & ol brn 3.25 *24.00*
Never hinged 8.00
On cover 100.00
B28 SP10 1.25 l + 60c bl grn & blk 3.25 *72.50*
Never hinged 8.00
On cover 225.00
B29 SP10 5 l + 2.50 l dk bl & blk 6.50 *225.00*
Never hinged 16.00
On cover 675.00
Nos. B26-B29 (4) 16.25 *345.50*
Set, never hinged 40.00
Set on commem cover 650.00

Stamps inscribed "Poste Italiane" and "Fiere Campionaria di Tripoli" are listed in Libya.

1928, Mar. 1

B30 SP10 30c + 10c dl vio & blk 12.50 *65.00*
Never hinged 30.00
On cover 125.00
B31 SP10 50c + 20c ol grn & sl 21.00 *65.00*
Never hinged 52.50
On cover 125.00
B32 SP10 1.25 l + 50c dp bl & blk 25.00 *140.00*
Never hinged 62.50
On cover 275.00
B33 SP10 5 l + 2 l brn red & blk 55.00 *450.00*
Never hinged 140.00
On cover 875.00
Nos. B30-B33 (4) 113.50 *720.00*
Set, never hinged 275.00
Set on commem cover 1,350.

The tax on Nos. B26 to B33 was devoted to the charitable work of the Voluntary Militia for National Defense.

See Nos. B35-B38.

Victor Emmanuel II — SP14

1929, Jan. 4 Photo. *Perf. 14*

B34 SP14 50c + 10c ol grn 4.75 *12.00*
Never hinged 12.00
On cover 60.00

50th anniv. of the death of King Victor Emmanuel II. The surtax was for veterans.

Type of 1926 Issue

Designs in same order.

1930, July 1 Engr.

B35 SP10 30c + 10c dk grn & vio 2.40 *40.00*
Never hinged 6.00
On cover 120.00
B36 SP10 50c + 10c dk grn & bl grn 3.25 *30.00*
Never hinged 8.00
On cover 67.50
B37 SP10 1.25 l + 30c ind & grn 8.00 *95.00*
Never hinged 20.00
On cover 240.00
B38 SP10 5 l + 1.50 l blk brn & ol brn 16.00 *450.00*
Never hinged 40.00
On cover 1,250.
Nos. B35-B38 (4) 29.65 *615.00*
Set, never hinged 74.00
Set on commem cover 1,200.

The surtax was for the charitable work of the Voluntary Militia for National Defense.

Militiamen at Ceremonial Fire with Quotation from Leonardo da Vinci — SP15

Symbolical of Pride for Militia — SP16

Symbolical of Militia Guarding Immortality of Italy SP17

Militia Passing Through Arch of Constantine SP18

1935, July 1 Photo. Wmk. 140

B39 SP15 20c + 10c rose red 9.50 *12.50*
Never hinged 24.00
On cover 95.00
B40 SP16 25c + 15c grn 9.50 *20.00*
Never hinged 24.00
On cover 95.00
B41 SP17 50c + 30c pur 9.50 *28.00*
Never hinged 24.00
On cover 325.00
B42 SP18 1.25 l + 75c blue 9.50 *42.50*
Never hinged 24.00
On cover 500.00
Nos. B39-B42 (4) 38.00 *103.00*
Set, never hinged 96.00
Set on commemorative cover 400.00
Nos. B39-B42,CB3 (5) 47.50 *143.00*
Set, never hinged 117.50

The surtax was for the Militia.

AIR POST STAMPS

Used values for Nos. C1-C105 are for postally used stamps with legible cancellations. Forged cancels on these issues abound, and expertization is srongly recommended.

Special Delivery No. E1 Ovptd.

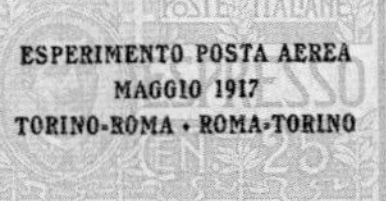

1917, May Wmk. 140 *Perf. 14*

C1 SD1 25c rose red 24.00 *40.00*
Never hinged 60.00
On flown colored postcard 100.00
On flown white postcard *1,300.*

Type of SD3 Surcharged in Black

1917, June 27

C2 SD3 25c on 40c violet 24.00 *47.50*
Never hinged 60.00
On flown cover or postcard 105.00

Type SD3 was not issued without surcharge.

AP2

1926-28 Typo.

C3 AP2 50c rose red ('28) 19.00 12.00
Never hinged 47.50
On commercial cover 40.00
C4 AP2 60c gray 4.75 *12.00*
Never hinged 12.00
On commercial cover 40.00
C5 AP2 80c brn vio & brn ('28) 35.00 *120.00*
Never hinged 87.50
On commercial cover 400.00
C6 AP2 1 l blue 12.00 *12.00*
Never hinged 30.00
On commercial cover 40.00
C7 AP2 1.20 l brn ('27) 24.00 *120.00*
Never hinged 60.00
On commercial cover 260.00
C8 AP2 1.50 l buff 19.00 32.50
Never hinged 47.50
On commercial cover 100.00
C9 AP2 5 l gray grn 40.00 *105.00*
Never hinged 100.00
On commercial cover 325.00
Nos. C3-C9 (7) 153.75 *413.50*
Set, never hinged 385.00
Nos. C4, C6, C8, C9 on overfranked philatelic cover (Mar. 1926) 550.00

Nos. C4 and C6 Surcharged

1927, Sept. 16

C10 AP2 50c on 60c gray 24.00 *95.00*
Never hinged 50.00
On commercial cover 190.00
a. Pair, one without surcharge 2,250.
Never hinged 3,250.
C11 AP2 80c on 1 l blue 60.00 *450.00*
Never hinged 150.00
On commercial cover 875.00
Set, never hinged 200.00
On overfranked commem. cover 950.00

Pegasus AP3

Wings AP4

Spirit of Flight — AP5

Arrows AP6

1930-32 Photo. Wmk. 140

C12 AP4 25c dk grn ('32) .25 .25
Never hinged .50
On commercial cover 14.50
C13 AP3 50c olive brn .25 .25
Never hinged .50
On commercial cover 1.60
C14 AP5 75c org brn ('32) .40 .25
Never hinged 1.00
On commercial cover 24.00
C15 AP4 80c org red .25 *.70*
Never hinged .50
On commercial cover 60.00
C16 AP5 1 l purple .25 .25
Never hinged .50
On commercial cover 1.60
C17 AP6 2 l deep blue .40 .25
Never hinged 1.00
On commercial cover 27.50
C18 AP3 5 l dk green .80 *1.60*
Never hinged 2.00
On commercial cover 52.50
C19 AP3 10 l dp car 1.60 *6.50*
Never hinged 4.00
On commercial cover 95.00
Nos. C12-C19 (8) 4.20 10.05
Set, never hinged 10.00

The 50c, 1 l and 2 l were reprinted in 1942 with labels similar to those of Nos. 427-438, but were not issued. Value, set of 3: unused $550; never hinged $1,400.

For overprints see Nos. MC1-MC5 in Scott Standard catalogue, Vol. 3. For overprints and surcharges on design AP6 see Nos. C52-C55; Yugoslavia-Ljubljana NB9-NB20, NC11-NC17 (in Scott Standard catalogue, Vol. 6).

Ferrucci Type of Postage

Statue of Ferrucci.

1930, July 10

C20 A104 50c purple 4.00 *17.50*
Never hinged 10.00
On commercial cover 95.00
C21 A104 1 l orange brn 4.00 *20.00*
Never hinged 10.00
On commercial cover 130.00
C22 A104 5 l + 2 l brn vio 16.00 *130.00*
Never hinged 40.00
On commercial cover 650.00
Nos. C20-C22 (3) 24.00 *167.50*
Set, never hinged 60.00
Set, on flown overfranked commem. cover 450.00

For overprinted types see Aegean Islands Nos. C1-C3.

Virgil Type of Postage

Jupiter sending forth his eagle.

1930, Oct. 21 Photo. Wmk. 140

C23 A106 50c lt brown 24.00 *40.00*
Never hinged 60.00
On commercial cover 87.50
C24 A106 1 l orange 24.00 *45.00*
Never hinged 60.00
On commercial cover 160.00

Engr.

Unwmk.

C25 A106 7.70 l + 1.30 l vio brn 55.00 *520.00*
Never hinged 140.00
On commercial cover 2,200.
C26 A106 9 l + 2 l indigo 65.00 *600.00*
Never hinged 160.00
On commercial cover 3,000.
Nos. C23-C26 (4) 168.00 *1,205.*
Set, never hinged 430.00
Set, on flown overfranked commem. cover 2,300.

The surtax on Nos. C25-C26 was for the National Institute Figli del Littorio.

For overprinted types see Aegean Islands Nos. C4-C7.

Trans-Atlantic Squadron — AP9

1930, Dec. 15 Photo. Wmk. 140

C27 AP9 7.70 l Prus bl & gray 450.00 *1,600.*
Never hinged 900.00
On flown cover *2,000.*
a. Seven stars instead of six 2,000. —
Never hinged 4,000.
On flown cover *36,000.*

Flight by Italian aviators from Rome to Rio de Janeiro, Dec. 1930-Jan. 12, 1931.

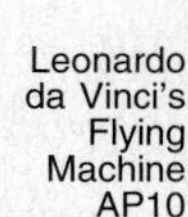

Leonardo da Vinci's Flying Machine AP10

Leonardo da Vinci AP11

Leonardo da Vinci — AP12

1932

C28 AP10 50c olive brn 4.75 *14.50*
Never hinged 12.00
On commercial cover 55.00
C29 AP11 1 l violet 6.50 *16.00*
Never hinged 16.00
On commercial cover 95.00
C30 AP11 3 l brown red 8.00 *40.00*
Never hinged 20.00
On commercial cover 160.00
C31 AP11 5 l dp green 13.00 *47.50*
Never hinged 32.50
On commercial cover 240.00
C32 AP10 7.70 l + 2 l dk bl 9.50 *200.00*
Never hinged 24.00
On commercial cover *2,000.*
C33 AP11 10 l + 2.50 l blk brn 11.00 *340.00*
Never hinged 27.50
On commercial cover *2,600.*
Nos. C28-C33 (6) 52.75 *658.00*
Set, never hinged 132.00
Set, on flown overfranked commem. cover 1,600.

Engr.
Unwmk.

C34 AP12 100 l brt bl & grnsh blk 45.00 *950.00*
Never hinged 110.00
On flown cover *2,750.*
a. Thin paper 260.00 *1,800.*
Never hinged 525.00

Dante Alighieri Soc. and especially Leonardo da Vinci, to whom the invention of a flying machine has been attributed. Surtax was for the benefit of the Society.

Inscription on No. C34: "Man with his large wings by beating against the air will be able to dominate it and lift himself above it."

Issued: Nos. C28-C33, 3/14; No. C34, 8/6.

For overprinted types see Aegean Islands Nos. C8-C13.

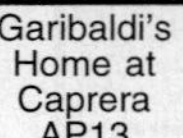
Garibaldi's Home at Caprera AP13

Farmhouse where Anita Garibaldi Died AP14

50c, 1 l+25c, Garibaldi's home, Caprera. 2 l+50c, Anita Garibaldi. 5 l+1 l, Giuseppe Garibaldi.

1932, Apr. 6 Photo. Wmk. 140

C35 AP13 50c copper red 4.75 *8.00*
Never hinged 12.00
On commercial cover 55.00
C36 AP14 80c deep green 5.00 *13.00*
Never hinged 12.50
On commercial cover 125.00
C37 AP13 1 l + 25c red brn 8.00 *32.50*
Never hinged 20.00
On commercial cover 175.00
C38 AP13 2 l + 50c dp bl 13.00 *45.00*
Never hinged 32.50
On commercial cover 240.00
C39 AP14 5 l + 1 l dp grn 13.00 *52.50*
Never hinged 32.50
On commercial cover 650.00
Nos. C35-C39 (5) 43.75 *151.00*
Set, never hinged 110.00
Set, on flown overfranked commem. cover 475.00

50th anniv. of the death of Giuseppe Garibaldi, patriot. The surtax was for the benefit of the Garibaldi Volunteers.

For overprinted types see Aegean Islands Nos. C15-C19.

March on Rome Type of Postage

50c, Eagle sculpture and airplane. 75c, Italian buildings from the air.

1932, Oct. 27 ***Perf. 14***

C40 A146 50c dark brown 3.25 *9.50*
Never hinged 8.00
On cover 40.00
C41 A146 75c orange brn 9.50 *32.50*
Never hinged 24.00
On cover 100.00
Set, never hinged 32.00
Set, on flown overfranked commem. cover 130.00

Graf Zeppelin Issue

Zeppelin over Pyramid of Caius Cestius AP19

5 l, Tomb of Cecilia Metlella. 10 l, Stadium of Mussolini. 12 l, St. Angelo Castle and Bridge. 15 l, Roman Forum. 20 l, Imperial Avenue.

1933, Apr. 24

C42 AP19 3 l blk & grn 22.50 *125.00*
Never hinged 55.00
On flown cover 300.00
C43 AP19 5 l grn & brn 22.50 *140.00*
Never hinged 55.00
On flown cover 425.00
C44 AP19 10 l car & dl bl 22.50 *325.00*
Never hinged 55.00
On flown cover 950.00
C45 AP19 12 l dk bl & red org 22.50 *575.00*
Never hinged 55.00
On flown cover 1,250.
C46 AP19 15 l dk brn & gray 22.50 *725.00*
Never hinged 55.00
On flown cover 1,800.
C47 AP19 20 l org brn & bl 22.50 *800.00*
Never hinged 55.00
On flown cover 2,000.
a. Vertical pair, imperf. between 10,000.
Never hinged 15,000.
Nos. C42-C47 (6) 135.00 *2,690.*
Set, never hinged 330.00
Set, on flown overfranked commem. cover 6,750.

Balbo's Trans-Atlantic Flight Issue

Italian Flag

King Victor Emmanuel III

Allegory "Flight" — AP25

No. C49, Colosseum at Rome, Chicago skyline. Nos. C48-C49 consist of 3 parts; Italian flag, Victor Emmanuel III, & scene arranged horizontally.

1933, May 20

C48 AP25 5.25 l + 19.75 l red, grn & ultra 125.00 *2,000.*
Never hinged 250.00
On flown cover 3,000.
a. Left stamp without ovpt. *37,500.*
Never hinged *57,500.*
C49 AP25 5.25 l + 44.75 l grn, red & ultra 160.00 *2,000.*
Never hinged 325.00
On flown cover 3,000.

Transatlantic Flight, Rome-Chicago, of 24-seaplane squadron led by Gen. Italo Balbo. Center and right sections paid postage. At left is registered air express label overprinted "APPARECCHIO" and abbreviated pilot's name. Twenty triptychs of each value differ in name overprint.

No. C49 overprinted "VOLO DI RITORNO/ NEW YORK-ROMA" was not issued; flight canceled. Value: unused $36,000; never hinged $54,000.

Nos. C48-C49 exist imperf. at bottom. Value, set $112,000.

For overprints see Nos. CO1, Aegean Islands C26-C27.

Type of Air Post Stamp of 1930 Surcharged in Black

1934, Jan. 18

C52 AP6 2 l on 2 l yel 10.50 *95.00*
Never hinged 26.00
On flight cover 160.00
C53 AP6 3 l on 2 l yel grn 10.50 *140.00*
Never hinged 26.00
On flight cover 190.00
C54 AP6 5 l on 2 l rose 10.50 *275.00*
Never hinged 26.00
On flight cover 600.00
C55 AP6 10 l on 2 l vio 10.50 *400.00*
Never hinged 26.00
On flight cover 875.00
Nos. C52-C55 (4) 42.00 *910.00*
Set, never hinged 104.00
Set, on overfranked flown cover 1,600.

For use on mail carried on a special flight from Rome to Buenos Aires.

Annexation of Fiume Type

25c, 75c, View of Fiume Harbor. 50c, 1 l+50c, Monument to the Dead. 2 l+1.50 l, Venetian Lions. 3 l+2 l, Julian wall.

1934, Mar. 12

C56 A166 25c green .95 *4.00*
Never hinged 2.40
On cover 67.50
C57 A166 50c brown .95 *2.40*
Never hinged 2.40
On cover 52.50
C58 A166 75c org brn .95 *9.50*
Never hinged 2.40
On cover 180.00
C59 A166 1 l + 50c dl vio .95 *16.00*
Never hinged 2.40
On cover 240.00
C60 A166 2 l + 1.50 l dl bl .95 *21.00*
Never hinged 2.40
On cover 400.00
C61 A166 3 l + 2 l blk brn .95 *23.00*
Never hinged 2.40
On cover 550.00
Nos. C56-C61 (6) 4.80 *76.40*
Set, never hinged 14.40
Nos. C56-C61, CE6-CE7 on overfranked commem. cover 875.00
No. CE5 on commem. cover (July 1934) 875.00

Airplane and View of Stadium AP32

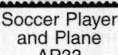

Soccer Player and Plane AP33

Airplane and Stadium Entrance AP35

Airplane over Stadium AP34

1934, May 24

C62 AP32 50c car rose 11.00 *52.50*
Never hinged 27.50
On cover 225.00
C63 AP33 75c gray blue 17.50 *65.00*
Never hinged 45.00
On cover 300.00
C64 AP34 5 l + 2.50 l ol grn 52.50 *425.00*
Never hinged 130.00
On cover *1,900.*
C65 AP35 10 l + 5 l brn blk 52.50 *650.00*
Never hinged 130.00
On cover *3,500.*
Nos. C62-C65 (4) 133.50 *1,193.*
Set, never hinged 332.50
Set, on overfranked commem. cover 3,750.

2nd World Soccer Championships.

For overprinted types see Aegean Islands Nos. C28-C31.

Zeppelin under Fire AP36

Air Force Memorial — AP40

Designs: 25c, 80c, Zeppelin under fire. 50c, 75c, Motorboat patrol. 1 l+50c, Desert infantry. 2 l+1 l, Plane attacking troops.

1934, Apr. 24

C66 AP36 25c dk green 3.25 *8.00*
Never hinged 8.00
On cover 60.00
C67 AP36 50c gray 3.25 *9.50*
Never hinged 8.00
On cover 52.50
C68 AP36 75c dk brown 3.25 *11.00*
Never hinged 8.00
On cover 160.00
C69 AP36 80c slate blue 3.25 *14.50*
Never hinged 8.00
On cover 225.00
C70 AP36 1 l + 50c red brn 8.00 *32.50*
Never hinged 20.00
On cover 325.00
C71 AP36 2 l + 1 l brt bl 11.50 *40.00*
Never hinged 29.00
On cover 550.00
C72 AP40 3 l + 2 l brn blk 16.00 *47.50*
Never hinged 40.00
On cover 600.00
Nos. C66-C72 (7) 48.50 *149.00*
Set, never hinged 120.00
Nos. C66-C72, CE8-CE9 on overfranked commem. cover 1,200.

Cent. of the institution of the Military Medal of Valor.

For overprinted types see Aegean Islands Nos. C32-C38.

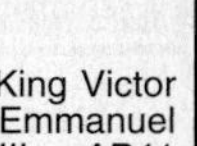

King Victor Emmanuel III — AP41

1934, Nov. 5

C73 AP41 1 l purple 3.25 *95.00*
Never hinged 8.00
On cover 210.00
C74 AP41 2 l brt blue 3.25 *105.00*
Never hinged 8.00
On cover 240.00
C75 AP41 4 l red brown 7.50 *325.00*
Never hinged 19.00
On cover 550.00
C76 AP41 5 l dull green 7.50 *425.00*
Never hinged 19.00
On cover 725.00
C77 AP41 8 l rose red 23.00 *525.00*
Never hinged 57.50
On cover 1,200.
C78 AP41 10 l brown 25.00 *800.00*
Never hinged 62.50
On cover 1,450.
Nos. C73-C78 (6) 69.50 *2,275.*
Set, never hinged 160.00
Set, on overfranked commem. cover 3,250.

65th birthday of King Victor Emmanuel III and the nonstop flight from Rome to Mogadiscio.

For overprint see No. CO2.

Muse Playing Harp AP42

Angelic Dirge for Bellini AP43

Scene from Bellini Opera, La Sonnambula — AP44

1935, Sept. 24

C79 AP42 25c dull yellow 4.75 *13.00*
Never hinged 12.00
On cover 52.50
C80 AP42 50c brown 4.75 *11.00*
Never hinged 12.00
On cover 52.50
C81 AP42 60c rose carmine 16.00 *32.50*
Never hinged 40.00
On cover 110.00
C82 AP43 1 l + 1 l purple 24.00 *240.00*
Never hinged 60.00
On cover 550.00
C83 AP44 5 l + 2 l green 32.50 *325.00*
Never hinged 80.00
On cover 800.00
Nos. C79-C83 (5) 82.00 *621.50*
Set, never hinged 204.00
Set, on overfranked commem. cover 1,200.

Vincenzo Bellini, (1801-35), operatic composer.

Quintus Horatius Flaccus Type

25c, Seaplane in Flight. 50c, 1 l+1 l, Monoplane over valley. 60c, Oak and eagle. 5 l+2 l, Ruins of ancient Rome.

1936, July 1

C84 A197 25c dp green 3.25 *12.00*
Never hinged 8.00
On cover 52.50
C85 A197 50c dk brown 5.00 *12.00*
Never hinged 12.50
On cover 52.50
C86 A197 60c scarlet 8.50 *20.00*
Never hinged 21.00
On cover 120.00
C87 A197 1 l + 1 l vio 19.00 *240.00*
Never hinged 47.50
On cover 600.00
C88 A197 5 l + 2 l slate bl 24.00 *350.00*
Never hinged 60.00
On cover 1,200.
Nos. C84-C88 (5) 59.75 *634.00*
Set, never hinged 150.00
Set, on overfranked commem. cover 1,250.

Child of the Balilla AP49

Heads of Children AP50

1937, June 28

C89 AP49 25c dk bl grn 8.00 *27.50*
Never hinged 20.00
On cover 110.00
C90 AP50 50c brown 16.00 17.50
Never hinged 40.00
On cover 87.50
C91 AP49 1 l purple 12.00 *35.00*
Never hinged 30.00
On cover 110.00
C92 AP50 2 l + 1 l dk bl 16.00 *200.00*
Never hinged 40.00
On cover 600.00
C93 AP49 3 l + 2 l org 20.00 *275.00*
Never hinged 50.00
On cover 1,050.
C94 AP50 5 l + 3 l rose lake 24.00 *340.00*
Never hinged 60.00
On cover 2,000.
Nos. C89-C94 (6) 96.00 *895.00*
Set, never hinged 240.00
Set, on overfranked commem. cover 2,600.

Summer Exhibition for Child Welfare. The surtax on Nos. C92-C94 was used to support summer camps for poor children.

Prosperous Italy AP51

50c, Prolific Italy. 80c, Apollo's steeds. 1 l+1 l, Map & Roman Standard. 5 l+1 l, Augustus Caesar.

1937, Sept. 23

C95 AP51 25c red vio 8.00 *16.00*
Never hinged 20.00
On cover 47.50
C96 AP51 50c olive brn 8.00 *12.00*
Never hinged 20.00
On cover 47.50
C97 AP51 80c orange brn 24.00 *22.50*
Never hinged 60.00
On cover 87.50
C98 AP51 1 l + 1 l dk bl 30.00 *175.00*
Never hinged 75.00
On cover 450.00
C99 AP51 5 l + 1 l dl vio 65.00 *340.00*
Never hinged 160.00
On cover 725.00
Nos. C95-C99 (5) 135.00 *565.50*
Set, never hinged 335.00
Set, on overfranked commem. cover 1,100.

Bimillenary of the birth of Augustus Caesar (Octavianus) on the occasion of the exhibition opened in Rome by Mussolini on Sept. 22nd, 1937.

For overprinted types see Aegean Islands Nos. C39-C43.

King Victor Emmanuel III — AP56

25c, 3 l, King Victor Emmanuel III. 50c, 1 l, Dante Alighieri. 2 l, 5 l, Leonardo da Vinci.

1938, Oct. 28

C100 AP56 25c dull green 4.75 6.50
Never hinged 12.00
On cover 40.00
C101 AP56 50c dk yel brn 4.75 6.50
Never hinged 12.00
On cover 32.50
C102 AP56 1 l violet 8.00 *9.50*
Never hinged 20.00
On cover 40.00
C103 AP56 2 l royal blue 8.00 *36.00*
Never hinged 20.00
On cover 95.00
C104 AP56 3 l brown car 13.00 *45.00*
Never hinged 32.50
On cover 200.00
C105 AP56 5 l dp green 15.00 *65.00*
Never hinged 37.50
On cover 275.00
Nos. C100-C105 (6) 54.00 *170.50*
Set, never hinged 134.00
Set, on overfranked commem. cover 525.00

Proclamation of the Empire.

AIR POST SEMI-POSTAL STAMPS

Holy Year Type of Postage

Dome of St. Peter's, dove with olive branch, Church of the Holy Sepulcher.

Wmk. 140
1933, Oct. 23 Photo. *Perf. 14*

CB1 A163 50c + 25c org brn 2.40 *27.50*
Never hinged 6.00
On cover 72.50
CB2 A163 75c + 50c brn vio 4.00 *160.00*
Never hinged 10.00
On cover 275.00
Set, never hinged 16.00

Symbolical of Military Air Force — SPAP2

1935, July 1

CB3 SPAP2 50c + 50c brown 9.50 *40.00*
Never hinged 24.00
On cover 240.00

The surtax was for the Militia.

AIR POST SPECIAL DELIVERY STAMPS

Garibaldi, Anita Garibaldi, Plane APSD1

Wmk. 140
1932, June 2 Photo. *Perf. 14*

CE1 APSD1 2.25 l + 1 l 16.00 *52.50*
Never hinged 40.00
On cover 475.00
CE2 APSD1 4.50 l + 1.50 l 16.00 *52.50*
Never hinged 40.00
On cover 600.00
Set, never hinged 80.00

Death of Giuseppe Garibaldi, 50th anniv.

For overprinted types see Aegean Islands Nos. CE1-CE2.

Airplane and Sunburst APSD2

1933-34

CE3 APSD2 2 l gray blk ('34) .25 *3.25*
Never hinged .50
On cover 40.00
CE4 APSD2 2.25 l gray blk 4.75 *200.00*
Never hinged 12.00
On cover 875.00
Set, never hinged 12.50

For overprint and surcharge see Nos. MCE1 in Scott Standard catalogue, Vol. 3; Yugoslavia-Ljubljana NCE1 in Scott Standard catalogue, Vol. 6.

Annexation of Fiume Type

Flag raising before Fascist headquarters.

1934, Mar. 12

CE5 A166 2 l + 1.25 l 4.75 *27.50*
Never hinged 12.00
On cover 875.00
CE6 A166 2.25 l + 1.25 l .95 *22.50*
Never hinged 2.50
On cover 650.00
CE7 A166 4.50 l + 2 l .95 *24.00*
Never hinged 2.50
On cover 725.00
Nos. CE5-CE7 (3) 5.60 *77.00*
Set, never hinged 17.00

Triumphal Arch in Rome APSD4

1934, Aug. 31

CE8 APSD4 2 l + 1.25 l brown 16.00 *45.00*
Never hinged 40.00
On cover 725.00
CE9 APSD4 4.50 l + 2 l cop red 20.00 *45.00*
Never hinged 50.00
On cover 725.00
Set, never hinged 90.00

Centenary of the institution of the Military Medal of Valor.

For overprinted types see Aegean Islands Nos. CE3-CE4.

AIR POST OFFICIAL STAMPS

Balbo Flight Type of Air Post Stamp of 1933 Overprinted

1933 Wmk. 140 *Perf. 14*

CO1 AP25 5.25 l + 44.75 l red, grn & red vio 3,300. *14,000.*
Never hinged 5,000.
On cover 21,000.

Air Post Stamp of 1934 Overprinted in Gold

1934

CO2 AP41 10 l blue blk 875.00 *14,000.*
Never hinged 1,750.
On cover 27,500.

65th birthday of King Victor Emmanuel III and the non-stop flight from Rome to Mogadiscio.

PNEUMATIC POST STAMPS

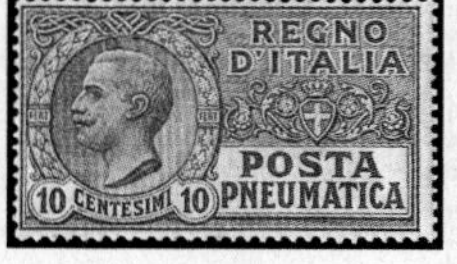

PN1

1913-28 Wmk. 140 Typo. *Perf. 14*

D1 PN1 10c brown 2.40 *32.50*
Never hinged 6.00
On cover 140.00
D2 PN1 15c brn vio ('28) 3.25 *16.00*
Never hinged 8.00
On cover 65.00
a. 15c dull violet ('21) 3.25 *45.00*
Never hinged 8.00
On cover 200.00
D3 PN1 15c rose red ('28) 16.00 *40.00*
Never hinged 40.00
On cover 160.00
D4 PN1 15c claret ('28) 4.75 *16.00*
Never hinged 12.00
On cover 65.00
D5 PN1 20c brn vio ('25) 24.00 *65.00*
Never hinged 60.00
On cover 260.00
D6 PN1 30c blue ('23) 8.00 *225.00*
Never hinged 20.00
On cover 875.00
D7 PN1 35c rose red ('27) 25.00 *475.00*
Never hinged 62.50
On cover 1,900.
D8 PN1 40c dp red ('26) 27.50 *450.00*
Never hinged 67.50
On cover 1,900.
Nos. D1-D8 (8) 110.90 *1,320.*

Nos. D1, D2a, D5-D6, D8 Surcharged Like Nos. C10-C11

1924-27

D9 PN1 15c on 10c 4.75 *40.00*
Never hinged 12.00
On cover 160.00
D10 PN1 15c on 20c ('27) 9.50 *72.50*
Never hinged 23.00
On cover 275.00
D11 PN1 20c on 10c ('25) 9.50 *80.00*
Never hinged 23.00
On cover 325.00
D12 PN1 20c on 15c ('25) 12.50 *47.50*
Never hinged 30.00
On cover 200.00
D13 PN1 35c on 40c ('27) 21.00 *400.00*
Never hinged 52.50
On cover 1,600.
D14 PN1 40c on 30c ('25) 12.50 *425.00*
Never hinged 30.00
On cover 1,050.
Nos. D9-D14 (6) 69.75 *1,065.*

Dante Alighieri PN2

Galileo Galilei PN3

1933, Mar. 29 **Photo.**
D15 PN2 15c dark violet .45 *1.60*
Never hinged .75
On cover 40.00
D16 PN3 35c rose red .45 *7.25*
Never hinged .75
On cover 375.00

SPECIAL DELIVERY STAMPS

Victor Emmanuel III — SD1

1903-26 **Typo.** **Wmk. 140** ***Perf. 14***
E1 SD1 25c rose red 47.50 1.20
Never hinged 120.00
On cover 9.50
a. Imperf., pair 475.00 600.00
E2 SD1 50c dl red ('20) 4.75 1.60
Never hinged 12.00
On cover 14.00
E3 SD1 60c dl red ('22) 9.50 1.20
Never hinged 24.00
On cover 12.00
E4 SD1 70c dl red ('25) 1.60 .35
Never hinged 4.00
On cover 6.50
E5 SD1 1.25 l dp bl ('26) .80 .25
Never hinged 2.00
On cover 1.60
Nos. E1-E5 (5) 64.15 4.60

No. E1 is almost always found poorly centered, and it is valued thus.

For overprints and surcharges see Nos. C1, E11, E13, Austria NE1-NE2, Dalmatia E1, Offices in Crete, Offices in Africa, Offices in Turkish Empire.

Victor Emmanuel III — SD2

1908-26
E6 SD2 30c blue & rose 2.25 *4.00*
Never hinged 5.50
On cover 27.50
E7 SD2 2 l bl & red ('25) 8.00 *160.00*
Never hinged 20.00
On cover 800.00
E8 SD2 2.50 l bl & red ('26) 3.25 *10.50*
Never hinged 8.00
On cover 100.00
Nos. E6-E8 (3) 13.50 *174.50*

The 1.20 lire blue and red (see No. E12) was prepared in 1922, but not issued. Value: unused $200; never hinged $400.

For surcharges and overprints see Nos. E10, E12, Austria NE3, Dalmatia E2, Offices in China, Offices in Africa, Offices in Turkish Empire.

SD3

1917, Nov.
E9 SD3 25c on 40c violet 40.00 *125.00*
Never hinged 100.00
On cover 450.00

Type SD3 not issued without surcharge. For surcharge see No. C2.

No. E6 Surcharged

1921, Oct.
E10 SD2 1.20 l on 30c 2.40 *27.50*
Never hinged 6.00
On cover 160.00
a. Comma in value omitted 12.50 *55.00*
b. Double surcharge 350.00

No. E2 Surcharged

1922, Jan. 9
E11 SD1 60c on 50c dull red 47.50 1.60
Never hinged 120.00
On cover 16.00
a. Inverted surcharge 275.00 275.00
b. Double surcharge 2,000.
c. Imperf., pair 475.00 *600.00*

Type of 1908 Surcharged

1924, May
E12 SD2 1.60 l on 1.20 l bl & red 3.25 *135.00*
Never hinged 8.00
On cover 800.00
a. Double surch., one inverted 350.00

No. E3 Surcharged like No. E11

1925, Apr. 11
E13 SD1 70c on 60c dull red 1.60 1.20
Never hinged 4.00
On cover 12.00
a. Inverted surcharge 340.00 *400.00*

Victor Emmanuel III — SD4

1932-33 **Photo.**
E14 SD4 1.25 l green .30 .25
Never hinged .30
On cover .60
E15 SD4 2.50 l dp org ('33) .30 *6.50*
Never hinged .40
On cover 47.50

For overprints and surcharges see Italian Social Republic Nos. E1-E2; Yugoslavia-Ljubljana NB5-NB8, NE1 (in Scott Standard catalogue, Vol. 6).

March on Rome Type of Postage

1.25 l Ancient Pillars and Entrenchments. 2.50 l, Head of Mussolini, trophies of flags, etc.

1932, Oct. 27
E16 A146 1.25 l deep green 2.40 1.60
Never hinged 6.00
On cover 20.00
E17 A146 2.50 l deep orange 8.00 *160.00*
Never hinged 20.00
On cover 675.00
Set, never hinged 26.00

AUTHORIZED DELIVERY STAMPS

For the payment of a special tax for the authorized delivery of correspondence privately instead of through the post office.

AD1

1928 **Wmk. 140** **Typo.** ***Perf. 14***
EY1 AD1 10c dull blue 9.50 .60
Never hinged 24.00
On cover 6.00
a. Perf. 11 37.50 4.75
Never hinged 95.00
On cover 45.00

Coat of Arms — AD2

1930 **Photo.** ***Perf. 14***
EY2 AD2 10c dark brown .25 .25
Never hinged .25
On cover 1.60

For surcharge and overprint see Nos. EY3, Italian Social Republic EY1 in Scott Standard catalogue, Vol. 3.

POSTAGE DUE STAMPS

Unused values for Postage Due stamps are for examples with full original gum. Stamps with part gum or privately gummed sell for much less.

D1

1863 **Unwmk.** **Litho.** ***Imperf.***
J1 D1 10c yellow 2,000. 240.00
No gum 80.00
Never hinged 3,000.
On cover 725.00
On cover, uncanceled 100.00
a. 10c yellow orange 2,250. 260.00
No gum 90.00
Never hinged 3,000.
On cover 775.00
On cover, uncanceled 100.00

D2

1869 **Wmk. 140** **Typo.** ***Perf. 14***
J2 D2 10c buff 9,000. 80.00
No gum 950.00
Never hinged 18,000.
On cover 240.00

D3

1870-1925
J3 D3 1c buff & mag 4.00 12.00
No gum 1.60
Never hinged 10.00
On cover 120.00
J4 D3 2c buff & mag 8.00 24.00
No gum 4.00
Never hinged 20.00
On cover 190.00
J5 D3 5c buff & mag .80 .80
No gum .40
Never hinged 2.00
On cover 6.50
J6 D3 10c buff & mag ('71) .80 .80
No gum .40
Never hinged 2.00
On cover 6.50
b. Imperf, single *2,200.*
J7 D3 20c buff & mag ('94) 8.00 .80
No gum 40.00
Never hinged 20.00
On cover 6.50
a. Imperf., pair 240.00 *240.00*
J8 D3 30c buff & mag 2.40 1.20
No gum 1.20
Never hinged 6.00
On cover 12.00
b. Imperf, pair *6,000.* 3,600.
J9 D3 40c buff & mag 2.40 2.40
No gum 1.20
Never hinged 6.00
On cover 47.50
J10 D3 50c buff & mag 2.40 1.20
No gum 1.20
Never hinged 6.00
On cover 12.00
b. Imperf, single *2,000.*
J11 D3 60c buff & mag 120.00 4.75
No gum 32.50
Never hinged 300.00
On cover 95.00
J12 D3 60c buff & brn ('25) 40.00 16.00
Never hinged 100.00
On cover 65.00
J13 D3 1 l lt bl & brn 8,000. 20.00
No gum 1,100.
Never hinged 16,000.
On cover 140.00
J14 D3 1 l bl & mag ('94) 45.00 1.25
No gum 4.75
Never hinged 110.00
On cover 12.00
a. Imperf., pair 400.00 350.00
J15 D3 2 l lt bl & brn 7,250. 32.50
No gum 1,050.
Never hinged 14,500.
On cover 950.00
J16 D3 2 l bl & mag ('03) 65.00 9.50
Never hinged 160.00
On cover 340.00
J17 D3 5 l bl & brn ('74) 500.00 35.00
No gum 105.00
Never hinged 1,250.
On cover *40,000.*
J18 D3 5 l bl & mag ('03) 250.00 55.00
Never hinged 625.00
On cover 1,400.
J19 D3 10 l bl & brn ('74) *9,500.* 35.00
No gum 1,900.
Never hinged 19,000.
On cover —
J20 D3 10 l bl & mag ('94) 225.00 8.00
No gum 27.50
Never hinged 550.00
On cover 9,500.

Early printings of 5c, 10c, 30c, 40c, 50c and 60c were in buff and magenta, later ones (1890-94) in stronger shades. The earlier, paler shades and their inverted-numeral varieties sell for considerably more than those of the later shades. Values are for the later shades.

Covers: Covers bearing Nos. J5-J6, J8-J11 dated between Jan. 1870 and Dec. 1889 have stamps from early printings and are worth more.

For surcharges and overprints see Nos. J25-J27, Offices in China, Offices in Turkish Empire; Austria NJ1-NJ16.

Numeral Inverted

J3a	D3	1c	4,750.	3,000.
J4a	D3	2c	*12,000.*	4,500.
		On cover		*45,000.*
J5a	D3	5c	6.50	12.00
		On cover		350.00
J6a	D3	10c	8.00	16.00
		On cover		*475.00*
J7b	D3	20c	65.00	60.00
		On cover		1,800.
J8a	D3	30c	12.00	*24.00*
		On cover		*725.00*
J9a	D3	40c	550.00	*650.00*
		On cover		19,000.
J10a	D3	50c	60.00	80.00
		On cover		2,400.
J11a	D3	60c	550.00	400.00
		On cover		12,000.
J13a	D3	1 l		—
J14b	D3	1 l	5,200.	4,500.
		On cover		*18,000.*
J15a	D3	2 l		*3,000.*
J16a	D3	2 l	*4,500.*	*4,500.*
		On cover		13,000.
J17a	D3	5 l		1,400.
J19a	D3	10 l		450.00

D4

1884-1903
J21 D4 50 l green 87.50 95.00
No gum 45.00
Never hinged 225.00
J22 D4 50 l yellow ('03) 95.00 47.50
Never hinged 240.00
J23 D4 100 l claret 87.50 47.50
No gum 22.50
Never hinged 225.00
J24 D4 100 l blue ('03) 72.50 20.00
Never hinged 175.00
Nos. J21-J24 (4) 342.50 210.00

Nos. J21-J24 were used for Post Office internal accounting purposes and are not known used on cover.

Nos. J3 & J4 Surcharged in Black

1890-91
J25 D3 10c on 2c 130.00 35.00
No gum 27.50
Never hinged 250.00
On cover 225.00

J26 D3 20c on 1c 525.00 27.50
No gum 80.00
Never hinged 1,000.
On cover 160.00
a. Inverted surcharge *10,000.*
J27 D3 30c on 2c 2,000. 12.00
No gum 275.00
Never hinged 4,000.
On cover 120.00
a. Inverted surcharge *2,750.*
Nos. J25-J27 (3) 2,655. 74.50

Coat of Arms
D6 D7

1934 **Photo.**

J28 D6 5c brown .80 .40
Never hinged 2.00
On cover 5.50
J29 D6 10c blue .80 .40
Never hinged 2.00
On cover 4.75
J30 D6 20c rose red .80 .40
Never hinged 2.00
On cover 3.25
J31 D6 25c green .80 .40
Never hinged 2.00
On cover 3.25
J32 D6 30c red org .80 .40
Never hinged 2.00
On cover 5.50
J33 D6 40c blk brn .80 *4.75*
Never hinged 2.00
On cover 12.00
J34 D6 50c violet .80 .40
Never hinged 2.00
On cover 2.40
J35 D6 60c slate blk .80 *14.00*
Never hinged 2.00
On cover 27.50
J36 D7 1 l red org .80 .40
Never hinged 2.00
On cover 2.40
J37 D7 2 l green .80 .40
Never hinged 2.00
On cover 9.50
J38 D7 5 l violet 1.60 .80
Never hinged 4.00
On cover 24.00
J39 D7 10 l blue 6.50 *12.00*
Never hinged 16.00
On cover 65.00
J40 D7 20 l car rose 12.50 *40.00*
Never hinged 30.00
Nos. J28-J40 (13) 28.60 74.75

For overprints and surcharges see Italian Social Republic #J1-J13 in Scott Standard catalogue, Vol. 3; Yugoslavia-Ljubljana NJ14-NJ22 in Scott Standard catalogue, Vol. 6.

OFFICIAL STAMPS

O1

1875 **Wmk. 140** **Typo.** ***Perf. 14***

O1 O1 2c lake 3.25 *4.75*
No gum .80
Never hinged 8.00
On cover 9.50
O2 O1 5c lake 3.25 *4.75*
No gum .80
Never hinged 8.00
On cover 14.50
O3 O1 20c lake 1.60 *1.60*
No gum .40
Never hinged 4.00
On cover 3.25
O4 O1 30c lake 1.60 *3.25*
No gum .40
Never hinged 4.00
On cover 6.50
O5 O1 1 l lake 4.75 *20.00*
No gum 1.20
Never hinged 12.00
On cover 200.00
O6 O1 2 l lake 12.50 *60.00*
No gum 3.25
Never hinged 32.50
On cover 600.00
O7 O1 5 l lake 55.00 *225.00*
No gum 14.00
Never hinged 140.00
On cover 4,750.
O8 O1 10 l lake 95.00 160.00
No gum 24.00
Never hinged 240.00
On cover 12,000.
Nos. O1-O8 (8) 176.95 *479.35*

Covers: Values for Nos. O7-O8 are for over-franked covers.

For surcharges see Nos. 37-44.

Stamps inscribed "Servizio Commissioni" were used in connection with the postal service but not for the payment of postage.

NEWSPAPER STAMP

N1

Typographed, Numeral Embossed
1862 **Unwmk.** ***Imperf.***

P1 N1 2c buff 52.50 *110.00*
No gum 27.50
Never hinged 110.00
On newspaper or cover 275.00
a. Numeral double 475.00 *1,650.*
On newspaper or cover *6,750.*
b. Printed on gummed side 500.00

Black 1c and 2c stamps of similar type are listed under Sardinia.

PARCEL POST STAMPS

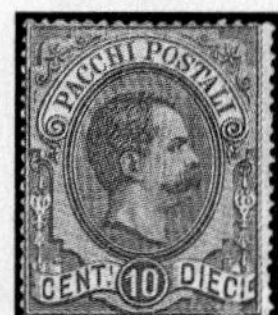

King Humbert I — PP1

1884-86 **Wmk. 140** **Typo.** ***Perf. 14***
Various Frames

Q1 PP1 10c olive gray 125.00 120.00
No gum 32.50
Never hinged 525.00
On parcel post receipt card *1,500.*
Q2 PP1 20c blue 260.00 175.00
No gum 65.00
Never hinged 1,000.
On parcel post receipt card *4,250.*
Q3 PP1 50c claret 9.50 14.50
No gum 3.25
Never hinged 40.00
On parcel post receipt card *2,200.*
Q4 PP1 75c blue grn 9.50 14.50
No gum 3.25
Never hinged 40.00
On parcel post receipt card *2,200.*
Q5 PP1 1.25 l orange 20.00 32.50
No gum 8.00
Never hinged 80.00
On parcel post receipt card *3,000.*
Q6 PP1 1.75 l brown 24.00 *120.00*
No gum 14.50
Never hinged 95.00
On parcel post receipt card —
Nos. Q1-Q6 (6) 448.00 476.50

For surcharges see Nos. 58-63.

Parcel Post stamps from No. Q7 onward were used by affixing them to the waybill so that one half remained on it following the parcel, the other half staying on the receipt given the sender. Most used halves are right halves. Complete stamps were and are obtainable canceled, probably to order.

Both unused and used values are for complete stamps.

PP2

1914-22 **Wmk. 140** ***Perf. 13***

Q7 PP2 5c brown 4.75 *20.00*
Q8 PP2 10c deep blue 4.75 *20.00*
Q9 PP2 20c black ('17) 17.50 *20.00*
Q10 PP2 25c red 24.00 *20.00*
Q11 PP2 50c orange 35.00 *40.00*
Q12 PP2 1 l violet 40.00 16.00
Q13 PP2 2 l green 40.00 20.00
Q14 PP2 3 l bister 47.50 55.00
Q15 PP2 4 l slate 60.00 72.50
Q16 PP2 10 l lilac ('22) 95.00 72.50
a. 10 l brn lilac 95.00 72.50
b. 10 l rose brn 95.00 80.00
Q17 PP2 12 l red brn ('22) 160.00 *450.00*
Q18 PP2 15 l ol grn ('22) 140.00 *450.00*
Q19 PP2 20 l brn vio ('22) 120.00 *450.00*
Nos. Q7-Q19 (13) 788.50 *1,706.*

Halves Used

Q7-Q14, each .40
Q15 .80
Q16 1.60
Q17 4.00
Q18 4.00
Q19 6.50

Imperfs exist. Value per pair: 20c, 25c, 50c, 2 l, 3l, 4 l: $50 each; 10l $225.

No. Q7 Surcharged

Q20 PP2 30c on 5c brown 1.60 *24.00*
Half stamp 3.25
Q21 PP2 60c on 5c brown 1.60 *24.00*
Half stamp 3.25
Q22 PP2 1.50 l on 5c brown 6.50 *190.00*
Half stamp 6.50
a. Double surcharge 250.00

No. Q16 Surcharged

Q23 PP2 3 l on 10 l rose lil 6.50 *80.00*
Half stamp 3.25
Nos. Q20-Q23 (4) 16.20 *318.00*

PP3

1927-39 **Wmk. 140**

Q24 PP3 5c brn ('38) .80 *3.25*
Q25 PP3 10c dp bl ('39) .80 *3.25*
Q26 PP3 25c red ('32) .80 *3.25*
Q27 PP3 30c ultra .80 *4.00*
Q28 PP3 50c org ('32) .80 *3.25*
Q29 PP3 60c red .80 *4.00*
Q30 PP3 1 l lilac ('31) .80 *3.25*
Q31 PP3 1 l brn vio ('36) 24.00 87.50
Q32 PP3 2 l grn ('32) .80 *4.00*
Q33 PP3 3 l yel bister .80 *9.50*
a. Printed on both sides 65.00
Q34 PP3 4 l gray .80 *9.50*
Q35 PP3 10 l rose lil ('34) 2.40 *55.00*
Q36 PP3 20 l lil brn ('33) 3.25 *80.00*
Nos. Q24-Q36 (13) 37.65 *269.75*

Value of used halves: Nos. Q24-Q34, each 40c; Q35 80c; Q36 $4.

For overprints see Italian Social Republic Nos. Q1-Q12 in Scott Standard catalogue, Vol. 3.

OCCUPATION STAMPS

Issued under Austrian Occupation

Austria Nos. M49-M64 Surcharged in Black

Austria Nos. M65-M67 Surcharged in Black

1918 **Unwmk.** ***Perf. 12½***

N1 M3 2c on 1h grnsh bl .25 *.45*
Never hinged .80
On cover 32.50
N2 M3 3c on 2h red org .25 *.40*
Never hinged .80
On cover 32.50
N3 M3 4c on 3h ol gray .25 *.45*
Never hinged .80
On cover 32.50
N4 M3 6c on 5h ol grn .25 *.40*
Never hinged .80
On cover 27.50
N5 M3 7c on 6h vio .25 *.45*
Never hinged .80
On cover 32.50
a. Perf. 12½x11½ 16.00 *95.00*
Never hinged 47.50
On cover —
N6 M3 11c on 10h org brn .25 *.45*
Never hinged .80
On cover 27.50
N7 M3 13c on 12h blue .25 *.45*
Never hinged .80
On cover 32.50
N8 M3 16c on 15h brt rose .25 *.40*
Never hinged .80
On cover 32.50
N9 M3 22c on 20h red brn .25 *.45*
Never hinged .80
On cover 32.50
a. Perf. 11½ 24.00 *80.00*
Never hinged 55.00
N10 M3 27c on 25h ultra .65 *1.60*
Never hinged 2.40
On cover 75.00
N11 M3 32c on 30h slate .65 *1.60*
Never hinged 2.40
On cover 60.00
N12 M3 43c on 40h ol bis .65 *1.60*
Never hinged 2.40
On cover 45.00
a. Perf. 11½ 16.00 *72.50*
Never hinged 47.50
N13 M3 53c on 50h dp grn .65 *1.60*
Never hinged 2.40
On cover 60.00
N14 M3 64c on 60h rose .65 *1.60*
Never hinged 2.40
On cover 95.00
N15 M3 85c on 80h dl bl .65 *1.20*
Never hinged .80
On cover 80.00
N16 M3 95c on 90h dk vio .65 *1.20*
Never hinged 2.40
On cover 95.00
N17 M4 2 l 11c on 2k rose, *straw* .65 2.40
Never hinged 3.25
On cover 200.00
N18 M4 3 l 16c on 3k grn, *bl* 1.20 3.25
Never hinged 4.00
N19 M4 4 l 22c on 4k rose, *grn* 2.40 5.50
Never hinged 5.50
Nos. N1-N19 (19) 11.05 *25.45*

Exist imperf. Values: unused, $160; never hinged, $325. See No. N33.

Austria Nos. M69-M82 Surcharged in Black

1918

N20 M5 2c on 1h grnsh bl 6.00
Never hinged 20.00
N21 M5 3c on 2h orange 6.00
Never hinged 20.00
N22 M5 4c on 3h ol gray 6.00
Never hinged 20.00
N23 M5 6c on 5h yel grn 6.00
Never hinged 20.00
N24 M5 11c on 10h dk brn 6.00
Never hinged 20.00
N25 M5 22c on 20h red 6.00
Never hinged 20.00
N26 M5 27c on 25h blue 6.00
Never hinged 20.00
N27 M5 32c on 30h bister 6.00
Never hinged 20.00
N28 M5 48c on 45h dk sl 6.00
Never hinged 20.00
N29 M5 53c on 50h dp grn 6.00
Never hinged 20.00
N30 M5 64c on 60h violet 6.00
Never hinged 20.00
N31 M5 85c on 80h rose 6.00
Never hinged 20.00
N32 M5 95c on 90h brn vio 6.00
Never hinged 20.00
N33 M4 1 l 6c on 1k ol bister, *blue* 6.00
Never hinged 20.00
Nos. N20-N33 (14) 84.00

Nos. N20 to N33 inclusive were never placed in use in the occupied territory. They were, however, on sale at the Post Office in Vienna for a few days before the Armistice.

Exist imperf. Values unused, $325; never hinged, $800.

OCCUPATION SPECIAL DELIVERY STAMPS

Bosnia Nos. QE1-QE2 Surcharged

1918 **Unwmk.** ***Perf. 12½***

NE1 SH1 3c on 2h ver 12.00 *24.00*
Never hinged 47.50
NE2 SH1 6c on 5h dp grn 12.00 *24.00*
Never hinged 47.50

Nos. NE1-NE2 are on yellowish paper. Reprints on white paper sell for about $1.25 a set.

OCCUPATION POSTAGE DUE STAMPS

Bosnia Nos. J16, J18-J19, J21-J24 Surcharged Like Nos. NE1-NE2

1918 Unwmk. *Perf. 12½*

NJ1 D2 6c on 5h red 3.25 *6.50*
Never hinged 6.50
a. Perf. 11½ 8.00 *12.00*
Never hinged 20.00
NJ2 D2 11c on 10h red 2.40 *8.00*
Never hinged 9.50
a. Perf. 11½ 8.00 *12.00*
Never hinged 20.00
NJ3 D2 16c on 15h red .80 *3.25*
Never hinged 3.25
NJ4 D2 27c on 25h red .80 *3.25*
Never hinged 3.25
NJ5 D2 32c on 30h red .80 *4.00*
Never hinged 3.25
NJ6 D2 43c on 40h red .80 *4.00*
Never hinged 3.25
NJ7 D2 53c on 50h red .80 *4.00*
Never hinged 3.25
Nos. NJ1-NJ7 (7) 9.65 *33.00*

OCCUPATION NEWSPAPER STAMPS

Austrian Nos. MP1-MP4 Surcharged

1918 Unwmk. *Perf. 12½*

NP1 MN1 3c on 2h blue .80 *1.20*
Never hinged 2.40
a. Perf. 11½ 12.00 *40.00*
Never hinged 40.00
NP2 MN1 7c on 6h org 1.10 *2.40*
Never hinged 3.25
NP3 MN1 11c on 10h car 1.10 *2.40*
Never hinged 3.25
NP4 MN1 22c on 20h brn 1.10 *2.75*
Never hinged 3.25
a. Perf. 11½ 125.00 *250.00*
Never hinged 250.00
Nos. NP1-NP4 (4) 4.10 *8.75*

ITALY OFFICES ABROAD

Stamps listed under this heading were issued for use in the Italian Post Offices which, for various reasons, were maintained from time to time in foreign countries.

100 Centesimi = 1 Lira

GENERAL ISSUE

Values of Italian Offices Abroad stamps vary tremendously according to condition. Quotations are for very fine examples, and values for unused stamps are for examples with original gum as defined in the catalogue introduction. Extremely fine or superb examples sell at much higher prices, and fine or poor examples sell at greatly reduced prices. In addition, unused examples without gum are discounted severely.

Very fine examples of Nos. 1-17 will have perforations barely clear of the frameline or design due to the narrow spacing of the stamps on the plates.

Italian Stamps with Corner Designs Slightly Altered and Overprinted

1874-78 Wmk. 140 *Perf. 14*

1 A6 1c ol grn 47.50 *47.50*
No gum 9.50
Never hinged 120.00
On cover *725.00*
On newspaper, single franking 2,600.
a. Inverted overprint *40,000.*
c. 2 dots in lower right corner 87.50 *275.00*
d. Three dots in upper right corner 400.00 *1,750.*
e. Without overprint 75,000.
f. 1c gray green 95.00
On cover *725.00*
2 A7 2c org brn 52.50 *55.00*
No gum 12.50
Never hinged 130.00
On cover *800.00*
a. Without overprint 75,000.
3 A8 5c slate grn 1,200. 55.00
No gum 240.00
Never hinged 2,400.
On cover *550.00*
On newspaper, single franking 1,600.
a. Lower right corner not altered *24,000.* 2,600.
4 A8 10c buff 3,600. 120.00
No gum 550.00
Never hinged 7,250.
On cover *600.00*
On newspaper, single franking 8,750.
a. Upper left corner not altered *30,000.* 1,800.
b. None of the corners altered — *75,000.*
c. Lower corners not altered *12,000.*
5 A8 10c blue ('78) 725.00 35.00
No gum 140.00
Never hinged 1,400.
On cover *540.00*
6 A15 20c blue 2,800. 55.00
No gum 525.00
Never hinged 5,500.
On cover *275.00*
On newspaper, single franking *2,000.*
7 A15 20c org ('78) 13,000. 32.50
No gum 2,600.
Never hinged *19,500.*
On cover *475.00*
8 A8 30c brown 8.00 *32.50*
No gum 2.40
Never hinged 20.00
On cover *260.00*
a. None of the corners altered *55,000.*
b. Right lower corner not altered — —
c. Double overprint —
9 A8 40c rose 8.00 *32.50*
No gum 2.40
Never hinged 20.00
On cover *200.00*
10 A8 60c lilac 27.50 *350.00*
No gum 9.50
Never hinged 70.00
On cover *3,750.*
a. 60c pale lilac 240.00 *350.00*
On cover *3,800.*
11 A13 2 l vermilion 350.00 *1,100.*
No gum 95.00
Never hinged 725.00
On cover *27,500.*

Values for pairs

1 A6 1c olive green 95.00 *110.00*
On cover *1,600.*
2 A7 2c org brn 105.00 *120.00*
On cover *1,800.*
3 A8 5c slate grn 2,400. 120.00
On cover *1,200.*
4 A8 10c buff 7,200. 260.00
On cover *1,600.*
5 A8 10c blue 1,450. 80.00
On cover *1,200.*
6 A15 20c blue 5,600. 120.00
On cover *600.00*
7 A15 20c orange 26,000. 160.00
On cover *3,250.*
8 A8 30c brown 16.00 *240.00*
On cover *1,900.*
9 A8 40c rose 16.00 *72.50*
On cover *2,200.*
10 A8 60c lilac 55.00 *800.00*
On cover *9,500.*
11 A13 2 l vermilion 700.00 *2,800.*
On cover —

1881

12 A17 5c green 47.50 20.00
No gum 8.00
Never hinged 120.00
On cover 300.00
On cover, single franking 1,400.
13 A17 10c claret 9.50 *16.00*
No gum 2.40
Never hinged 24.00
On cover *400.00*
14 A17 20c orange 9.50 *9.50*
No gum 2.40
Never hinged 24.00
On cover *190.00*
a. Double overprint, on piece —
15 A17 25c blue 9.50 *24.00*
No gum 2.40
Never hinged 24.00
On cover *1,200.*
16 A17 50c violet 24.00 *80.00*
No gum 4.75
Never hinged 60.00
On cover *2,750.*
17 A17 2 l vermilion 47.50 —
No gum 8.00
Never hinged 120.00
Nos. 12-17 (6) 147.50
Nos. 12-16 (5) 149.50

Values for Pairs

12 A17 5c green 95.00 *45.00*
On cover 650.00
13 A17 10c claret 19.00 *35.00*
On cover 900.00
14 A17 20c orange 19.00 *47.50*
On cover 950.00
15 A17 25c blue 19.00 *72.50*
On cover *3,500.*
16 A17 50c violet 48.00 *200.00*
On cover *6,500.*
17 A17 2 l vermilion 95.00 —

The "Estero" stamps were used in various parts of the world, South America, Africa, Turkey, etc.

Forged cancellations exist on Nos. 1-2, 9-11, 16.

OFFICES IN CHINA

100 Cents = 1 Dollar

PEKING

Italian Stamps of 1901-16 Handstamped

Wmk. 140, Unwmk.

1917 *Perf. 12, 13½, 14*

1 A48 2c on 5c green 450.00 300.00
Never hinged 875.00
On cover 600.00
a. Inverted surcharge 400.00 275.00
Never hinged 800.00
b. Double surcharge, one inverted 1,100. 875.00
c. 4c on 5c green *9,500.*
Never hinged 14,000.
d. 8c on 5c green —
e. Pair, one with "PECHINO", one "TIENTSIN" 8,750.
Never hinged 12,500.
3 A48 4c on 10c claret (No. 95) 800.00 475.00
Never hinged 1,600.
On cover 950.00
a. Inverted surcharge 725.00 450.00
Never hinged 1,400.
b. Double surcharge, one inverted 1,750. 1,200.
c. 4c on 10c claret (No. 79) —
5 A58 6c on 15c slate 1,600. 1,100.
Never hinged 3,250.
On cover 2,250.
b. 8c on 15c slate 5,500. 5,200.
Never hinged 11,000.
c. Pair, one without surcharge —
d. Pair, one with "PECHINO", one "TIENTSIN" 17,500.
Never hinged —
7 A58 8c on 20c on 15c slate 6,000. 4,500.
Never hinged 12,000.
On cover 4,500.
a. Inverted surcharge 5,500. 4,000.
Never hinged 11,000.
8 A50 8c on 20c brn org (No. 112) *12,000.* 4,500.
Never hinged *17,500.*
On cover 4,500.
a. Inverted surcharge *10,500.* *4,200.*
Never hinged 16,000.
9 A49 20c on 50c vio *40,000.* *30,000.*
Never hinged *90,000.*
On cover —
a. Inverted surcharge *52,000.* *34,000.*
Never hinged *77,500.*
b. 40c on 50c violet *24,000.* *24,000.*
Never hinged 36,000.
c. As "b," inverted surcharge *22,000.* *22,000.*
Never hinged *32,000.*
11 A46 40c on 1 l brn & grn *350,000.* *60,000.*
Never hinged 440,000.
On cover —
a. Inverted surcharge 300,000. 52,000.

Excellent forgeries exist of the higher valued stamps of Offices in China.

Italian Stamps of 1901-16 Overprinted

1917-18

12 A42 1c brown 40.00 *80.00*
Never hinged 90.00
On cover 650.00
13 A43 2c orange brown 40.00 *80.00*
Never hinged 90.00
On cover 650.00
a. Double overprint 450.00 —
14 A48 5c green 12.00 *27.50*
Never hinged 26.00
On cover 350.00
a. Double overprint 275.00 —
Never hinged 400.00
15 A48 10c claret 12.00 *27.50*
Never hinged 26.00
On cover 350.00
16 A50 20c brn org (No. 112) 300.00 *350.00*
Never hinged 650.00
On cover —
17 A49 25c blue 12.00 *35.00*
Never hinged 26.00
On cover 350.00
18 A49 50c violet 12.00 *35.00*
Never hinged 26.00
On cover 600.00
19 A46 1 l brown & grn 27.50 *72.50*
Never hinged 60.00
On cover 875.00
20 A46 5 l blue & rose 55.00 *120.00*
Never hinged 120.00
On cover —
21 A51 10 l gray grn & red 400.00 *675.00*
Never hinged 875.00
On cover —
Nos. 12-21 (10) 910.50 *1,503.*

Italy No. 113, the watermarked 20c brown orange, was also overprinted "Pechino," but not issued. Value: hinged $32.50; never hinged $80.

Italian Stamps of 1901-16 Surcharged

Type I

Type II

TWO DOLLARS:
Type I — Surcharged "2 dollari Pechino"
Type II — Surcharged "2 DOLLARI."
Type III — Surcharged "2 dollari." "Pechino" measures 11½mm wide, instead of 13mm.

1918-19 *Perf. 14*

22 A42 ½c on 1c brown 350.00 *350.00*
Never hinged 875.00
On cover —
a. Surcharged "1 cents" 1,100. 1,200.
Never hinged 2,200.
23 A43 1c on 2c org brn 12.00 *24.00*
Never hinged 30.00
On cover 400.00
a. Surcharged "1 cents" 550.00 650.00
Never hinged 1,100.
24 A48 2c on 5c green 12.00 *24.00*
Never hinged 30.00
On cover 325.00
25 A48 4c on 10c clar 12.00 *24.00*
Never hinged 30.00
On cover 325.00
26 A50 8c on 20c brn org (No. 112) 65.00 *47.50*
Never hinged 160.00
On cover 525.00
a. "8 CENTS" doubled 525.00 525.00
Never hinged 800.00
27 A49 10c on 25c blue 24.00 *47.50*
Never hinged 60.00
On cover 525.00
a. "10 CENTS" doubled 525.00 525.00
Never hinged 800.00
28 A49 20c on 50c vio 32.50 *47.50*
Never hinged 80.00
On cover 675.00
29 A46 40c on 1 l brn & grn 350.00 *450.00*
Never hinged 875.00
On cover —
30 A46 $2 on 5 l bl & rose (type I) 650.00 *1,050.*
Never hinged 1,600.
On cover —
a. Type II *100,000.* *90,000.*
Never hinged *185,000.*
b. Type III *20,000.* *16,000.*
Never hinged *30,000.*
On cover —
Nos. 22-30 (9) 1,508. *2,065.*

Italy No. 100 Surcharged

1919

32 A49 10c on 25c blue 11.00 *27.50*
Never hinged 27.50
On cover 275.00

Imperf. examples of No. 32 are proofs.

PEKING SPECIAL DELIVERY STAMPS

Italian Special Delivery Stamp 1908 Ovptd.

1917 Wmk. 140 *Perf. 14*

E1 SD2 30c blue & rose 16.00 *60.00*
Never hinged 40.00
On cover 1,200.

No. E1 Surcharged

1918

E2 SD2 12c on 30c bl & rose 125.00 *450.00*
Never hinged 325.00
On cover 2,200.

PEKING POSTAGE DUE STAMPS

Italian Postage Due Stamps Overprinted Like Nos. 12-21

1917 Wmk. 140 *Perf. 14*

J1 D3 10c buff & magenta 5.50 *14.00*
Never hinged 13.50
a. Double overprint 400.00
J2 D3 20c buff & magenta 5.50 *14.00*
Never hinged 13.50
J3 D3 30c buff & magenta 5.50 *14.00*
Never hinged 13.50
J4 D3 40c buff & magenta 11.00 *14.00*
Never hinged 27.50
Nos. J1-J4 (4) 27.50 *56.00*

Nos. J1-J4 Surcharged Like No. E2

1918

J5 D3 4c on 10c *125,000. 100,000.*
Never hinged *160,000.*
J6 D3 8c on 20c 55.00 *110.00*
Never hinged 140.00
a. Pair, one without surcharge 2,000.
Never hinged 3,000.
J7 D3 12c on 30c 125.00 *275.00*
Never hinged 300.00
J8 D3 16c on 40c 550.00 *950.00*
Never hinged 1,350.

In 1919, the same new values were surcharged on Italy Nos. J6-J9 in a different style: four lines to cancel the denomination, and "-PECHINO- 4 CENTS." These were not issued. Value $17.50 each, never hinged $42.50 each.

TIENTSIN

Italian Stamps of 1906 Handstamped

Wmk. 140, Unwmk.

1917 *Perf. 12, 13½, 14*

1 A48 2c on 5c green 650.00 650.00
Never hinged 1,300.
On cover 1,250.
a. Surcharge inverted 600.00 600.00
Never hinged 1,200.
b. Double surcharge 1,200. 875.00
Never hinged 1,750.
c. 4c on 5c green *16,000.* —
Never hinged
d. Double surcharge, one inverted 1,250. 950.00
Never hinged *1,900.*
2 A48 4c on 10c claret 1,200. 1,000.
Never hinged 2,400.
On cover 2,000.
a. Surcharge inverted 1,100. 950.00
Never hinged *2,200.*
b. Double surcharge 1,900. 1,100.
Never hinged *2,800.*
c. Double surcharge, one inverted 2,000. 1,200.
Never hinged *3,000.*
4 A58 6c on 15c slate 2,600. 2,000.
Never hinged 5,200.
On cover 3,000.
a. Surcharge inverted 2,400. 1,900.
Never hinged 4,000.
b. 4c on 15c slate 8,750. 8,000.
Never hinged 13,000.
Nos. 1-4 (3) 4,450. 3,650.

Italian Stamps of 1901-16 Overprinted

1917-18

5 A42 1c brown 40.00 *80.00*
Never hinged 100.00
On cover 650.00
a. Inverted overprint 525.00 525.00
Never hinged *1,050.*
6 A43 2c orange brn 40.00 *80.00*
Never hinged 100.00
On cover 650.00
7 A48 5c green 12.00 *27.50*
Never hinged 30.00
On cover 350.00
8 A48 10c claret 12.00 *27.50*
Never hinged 30.00
On cover 350.00
a. Double overprint 550.00
Never hinged *1,100.*
9 A50 20c brn org (#112) 300.00 *350.00*
Never hinged 750.00
On cover —
10 A49 25c blue 12.00 *35.00*
Never hinged 30.00
On cover 350.00
11 A49 50c violet 12.00 *35.00*
Never hinged 30.00
On cover 600.00
12 A46 1 l brown & grn 27.50 *72.50*
Never hinged 67.50
On cover 875.00
13 A46 5 l blue & rose 55.00 *120.00*
Never hinged 140.00
On cover —
14 A51 10 l gray grn & red 400.00 *675.00*
Never hinged 1,000.
On cover —
Nos. 5-14 (10) 910.50 *1,503.*

Italy No. 113, the watermarked 20c brown orange was also overprinted "Tientsin," but not issued. Value: hinged $32.50; never hinged $80.

Italian Stamps of 1901-16 Surcharged

Type I

TWO DOLLARS:
Type I — Surcharged "2 Dollari Tientsin"
Type II — Surcharged "2 dollari."
Type III — Surcharged "2 Dollari." "Tientsin" measures 10mm wide instead of 13mm.

1918-21 *Perf. 14*

15 A42 ½c on 1c brn 350.00 *350.00*
Never hinged 875.00
On cover —
a. Inverted surcharge 650.00 650.00
Never hinged 1,300.
b. Surcharged "1 cents" 1,100. 1,200.
Never hinged 2,100.
c. Vertical fraction bar 800.00
Never hinged 1,600.
16 A43 1c on 2c org brn 12.00 *24.00*
Never hinged 30.00
On cover 400.00
a. Surcharged "1 cents" 550.00 650.00
Never hinged 1,100.
b. Inverted surcharge 650.00 650.00
Never hinged 1,300.
17 A48 2c on 5c grn 12.00 *24.00*
Never hinged 30.00
On cover 325.00
18 A48 4c on 10c clar 12.00 *24.00*
Never hinged 30.00
On cover 325.00
19 A50 8c on 20c brn org (#112) 65.00 55.00
Never hinged 160.00
On cover 525.00
20 A49 10c on 25c blue 24.00 *47.50*
Never hinged 60.00
On cover 525.00
21 A49 20c on 50c vio 32.50 *47.50*
Never hinged 80.00
On cover 675.00
22 A46 40c on 1 l brn & grn 350.00 *450.00*
Never hinged 875.00
On cover —
23 A46 $2 on 5 l bl & rose (type I) 650.00 *1,050.*
Never hinged 1,600.
On cover —
a. Type II *20,000. 20,000.*
Never hinged *30,000.*
On cover —
b. Type III ('21) *17,500. 16,000.*
Never hinged *26,000.*
On cover —
Nos. 15-23 (9) 1,508. *2,072.*

SPECIAL DELIVERY STAMPS

Italian Special Delivery Stamp of 1908 Overprinted

1917 Wmk. 140 *Perf. 14*

E1 SD2 30c blue & rose 16.00 *60.00*
Never hinged 40.00
On cover 1,200.

No. E1 Surcharged

1918

E2 SD2 12c on 30c bl & rose 125.00 *450.00*
Never hinged 325.00
On cover 2,200.

POSTAGE DUE STAMPS

Italian Postage Due Stamps Overprinted

1917 Wmk. 140 *Perf. 14*

J1 D3 10c buff & magenta 5.50 *14.00*
Never hinged 13.50
a. Double overprint 400.00
Never hinged 800.00
J2 D3 20c buff & magenta 5.50 *14.00*
Never hinged 13.50
J3 D3 30c buff & magenta 5.50 *14.00*
Never hinged 13.50
a. Double overprint 400.00
Never hinged 800.00
J4 D3 40c buff & magenta 11.00 *14.00*
Never hinged 27.50
Nos. J1-J4 (4) 27.50 *56.00*

Nos. J1-J4 Surcharged

1918

J5 D3 4c on 10c *9,500. 9,500.*
Never hinged *14,000.*
a. "4 CENTS" handstamped *16,000. 17,500.*
Never hinged *20,000.*
J6 D3 8c on 20c 55.00 *110.00*
Never hinged 140.00
a. "8 CENTS" double 2,750.
Never hinged 5,500.
J7 D3 12c on 30c 120.00 *275.00*
Never hinged 300.00
J8 D3 16c on 40c 550.00 *950.00*
Never hinged 1,350.

In 1919, the same new values were surcharged on Italy Nos. J6-J9 in a different style: four lines to cancel the denomination, and "-TIENTSIN- 4 CENTS." These were not issued. Value $17 each, never hinged $42.50 each.

OFFICES IN CRETE

40 Paras = 1 Piaster
100 Centesimi = 1 Lira (1906)

Italy Nos. 70 and 81 Surcharged in Red or Black

a

b

1900-01 Wmk. 140 *Perf. 14*

1 A36(a) 1pi on 25c blue 8.00 *80.00*
Never hinged 47.50
No gum 6.50
On cover 2,200.
2 A45(b) 1pi on 25c dp bl (Bk) ('01) 4.50 *10.00*
Never hinged 12.00
On cover 475.00

Values for pairs

1 A36(a) 1pi on 25c blue 38.00 *225.00*
2 A45(b) 1pi on 25c dp bl (Bk) ('01) 9.50

Italian Stamps Overprinted

1906

On Nos. 76-79, 92, 81, 83-85, 87, 91

3 A42 1c brown 2.75 *6.00*
Never hinged 8.00
On cover 325.00
a. Pair, one without ovpt. *1,325.*
b. Double overprint 375.00
4 A43 2c org brn 2.75 *6.00*
Never hinged 8.00
On cover 300.00
a. Imperf., pair *2,400.*
b. Double overprint 375.00
5 A44 5c bl grn 5.00 *7.00*
Never hinged 16.00
On cover 175.00
6 A45 10c claret 300.00 250.00
Never hinged 1,100.
On cover —
7 A45 15c on 20c org 5.00 *7.00*
Never hinged 16.00
On cover 325.00
8 A45 25c blue 11.50 *23.00*
Never hinged 60.00
On cover 525.00
9 A45 40c brown 11.50 *23.00*
Never hinged 60.00
On cover 875.00
10 A45 45c ol grn 11.50 *23.00*
Never hinged 40.00
On cover 1,100.
11 A45 50c violet 11.50 *23.00*
Never hinged 60.00
On cover 1,400.
12 A46 1 l brn & grn 45.00 *85.00*
Never hinged 225.00
On cover —
13 A46 5 l bl & rose 375.00 *500.00*
Never hinged 1,350.
On cover —
Nos. 3-13 (11) 781.50 *953.00*
Set on overfranked philatelic cover 2,500.

Values for blocks of four

6 A45 10c claret 4,250. —
13 A46 5 l bl & rose 4,300. *3,250.*

On Nos. 94-95, 100, 104-105

1907-10

14 A48 5c green 1.90 2.00
Never hinged 8.00
On cover 125.00
a. Inverted overprint 300.00
Never hinged 750.00
15 A48 10c claret 1.90 2.00
Never hinged 8.00
On cover 200.00
a. Double overprint
16 A49 25c blue 2.75 *14.50*
Never hinged 11.50
On cover 240.00
17 A49 40c brown 30.00 *45.00*
Never hinged 100.00
On cover 475.00
18 A49 50c violet 2.75 *14.50*
Never hinged 11.50
On cover 550.00
Nos. 14-18 (5) 39.30 *78.00*

On No. 111 in Violet

1912 Unwmk. *Perf. 13x13½*

19 A50 15c slate black 3.00 *4.00*
Never hinged 11.00
On cover 240.00
Nos. 14-19 on overfranked philatelic cover 275.00

SPECIAL DELIVERY STAMPS

Special Delivery Stamp of Italy Overprinted

1906 Wmk. 140 *Perf. 14*

E1 SD1 25c rose red 12.00 *24.00*
Never hinged 32.50
On cover 725.00

Some sheets from the first printing have a second, albino overprint.

OFFICES IN AFRICA

40 Paras = 1 Piaster
100 Centesimi = 1 Lira (1910)

BENGASI

Italy No. 81 Surcharged in Black

1901 Wmk. 140 *Perf. 14*

1 A45 1pi on 25c dp bl 65.00 *160.00*
Never hinged 160.00
On cover 475.00

Same Surcharge on Italy No. 100

1911

1A A49 1pi on 25c blue 65.00 *160.00*
Never hinged 160.00
On cover 475.00

TRIPOLI

Italian Stamps of 1901-09 Overprinted in Black or Violet

1909 Wmk. 140

2 A42 1c brown 4.75 3.25
Never hinged 12.00
On cover 250.00
a. Inverted overprint 275.00
Never hinged 550.00
3 A43 2c orange brn 2.40 *3.25*
Never hinged 6.00
On cover 200.00
4 A48 5c green 175.00 9.50
Never hinged 425.00
On cover 80.00
a. Double overprint 325.00
Never hinged 600.00
5 A48 10c claret 3.25 3.25
Never hinged 8.00
On cover 87.50
a. Double overprint 225.00 *225.00*
Never hinged 450.00
6 A49 25c blue 2.40 *3.25*
Never hinged 6.00
On cover 175.00
7 A49 40c brown 8.00 8.00
Never hinged 20.00
On cover 450.00
8 A49 50c violet 9.50 9.50
Never hinged 24.00
On cover 525.00

Perf. 13½x14
Unwmk.

9 A50 15c slate blk (V) 4.75 4.75
Never hinged 12.00
On cover 240.00
Nos. 2-9 (8) 210.05 *44.75*

Italian Stamps of 1901 Overprinted

1909 Wmk. 140 *Perf. 14*

10 A46 1 l brown & grn 140.00 100.00
Never hinged 350.00
On cover 1,000.
11 A46 5 l blue & rose 47.50 300.00
Never hinged 120.00
On cover —
Set of 10 on overfranked, philatelic cover 650.00

Same Overprint on Italy Nos. 76-77

1915

12 A42 1c brown 3.50
Never hinged 8.75
13 A43 2c orange brown 3.50
Never hinged 8.75

Nos. 12-13 were prepared but not issued. No. 12 exists as a pair, one without overprint, value $2,400 hinged, $3,600 never hinged. No. 12 also exists with inverted overprint. Value, $1,600.

SPECIAL DELIVERY STAMPS

Italy Nos. E1, E6 Ovptd. Like Nos. 10-11

1909 Wmk. 140 *Perf. 14*

E1 SD1 25c rose red 19.00 12.00
Never hinged 47.50
On cover 325.00
E2 SD2 30c blue & rose 6.50 *16.00*
Never hinged 16.00
On cover 800.00

Tripoli was ceded by Turkey to Italy in Oct., 1912, and became known as the Colony of Libia. Later issues will be found under Libya.

OFFICES IN TURKISH EMPIRE

40 Paras = 1 Piaster

Various powers maintained post offices in the Turkish Empire before World War I by authority of treaties which ended with the signing of the Treaty of Lausanne in 1923. The foreign post offices were closed Oct. 27, 1923.

GENERAL ISSUE

Italian Stamps of 1906-08 Surcharged

Printed at Turin

1908 Wmk. 140

1 A48 10pa on 5c green 8.00 4.75
Never hinged 20.00
On cover 110.00
2 A48 20pa on 10c claret 8.00 4.75
Never hinged 20.00
On cover 140.00
3 A49 40pa on 25c blue 3.25 3.25
Never hinged 8.00
On cover *80.00*
4 A49 80pa on 50c violet 6.50 4.75
Never hinged 16.00
On cover 140.00

See Janina Nos. 1-4.

Surcharged in Violet

Unwmk.

5 A47 30pa on 15c slate 2.40 2.40
Never hinged 6.00
On cover 65.00
Nos. 1-5 (5) 28.15 19.90

Nos. 1, 2, 3 and 5 were first issued in Janina, Albania, and subsequently for general use. They can only be distinguished by the cancellations.

Italian Stamps of 1901-08 Surcharged

Nos. 6-8

No. 9

Nos. 10-12

Printed at Constantinople

1908 First Printing

6 A48 10pa on 5c grn 400.00 475.
Never hinged 800.00
On cover 725.00
a. Vert. pair, one without surcharge 4,000.
Never hinged *7,500.*
7 A48 20pa on 10c claret 400.00 475.
Never hinged 800.00
On cover 725.00
8 A47 30pa on 15c slate 1,200. *1,400.*
Never hinged 2,400.
On cover 2,100.
9 A49 1pi on 25c blue 1,200. *1,400.*
Never hinged 2,400.
On cover 2,900.
a. "PIASTRE" 2,000. 2,000.
10 A49 2pi on 50c vio 3,250. *4,000.*
Never hinged 6,500.
On cover 8,000.
11 A46 4pi on 1 l brn & grn *17,500.* *12,000.*
Never hinged *26,000.*
On cover 17,500.
12 A46 20pi on 5 l bl & rose *40,000.* *35,000.*
Never hinged *60,000.*
On cover 54,000.

On Nos. 8, 9 and 10 the surcharge is at the top of the stamp. No. 11 has the "4" closed at the top. No. 12 has the "20" wide.

Second Printing

Italian Stamps of 1901-08 Surcharged

Nos. 13-15

No. 16

Nos. 17-19

13 A48 10pa on 5c green 40.00 *52.50*
Never hinged 100.00
On cover 450.00
14 A48 20pa on 10c claret 40.00 *52.50*
Never hinged 100.00
On cover 450.00
15 A47 30pa on 15c slate 160.00 *120.00*
Never hinged 400.00
On cover 650.00
a. Double surcharge 350.00 350.00
b. Triple surcharge 800.00 800.00
16 A49 1pi on 25c blue 40.00 *52.50*
Never hinged 100.00
On cover 675.00
a. "PIPSTRA" 250.00 250.00
b. "1" omitted 250.00 250.00
17 A49 2pi on 50c violet 240.00 240.00
Never hinged 600.00
On cover 2,200.
a. Surcharged "20 PIASTRE" 2,400. 2,400.
Never hinged 3,600.
b. "20" with "0" scratched out 800.00 800.00
c. "2" 5mm from "PIASTRE" 650.00 650.00
18 A46 4pi on 1 l brn & grn 1,600. 1,600.
Never hinged 3,200.
On cover 4,000.
19 A46 20pi on 5 l bl & rose 9,500. 5,200.
Never hinged 14,500.
On cover 16,000.
Nos. 13-19 (7) 11,620. 7,318.

On No. 18 the "4" is open at the top.

Third Printing

Surcharged in Red

20 A47 30pa on 15c slate 9.50 *9.50*
Never hinged 24.00
On cover 140.00
a. Double surcharge 240.00 240.00

Fourth Printing

20B A46 4pi on 1 l brn & grn 65.00 95.00
Never hinged 160.00
On cover —
c. Inverted "S" 200.00 200.00
20D A46 20pi on 5 l bl & rose 210.00 *240.00*
Never hinged 525.00
On cover —
i. Inverted "S" 550.00 550.00

Fifth Printing

20E A46 4pi on 1 l brn & grn 55.00 72.50
Never hinged 140.00
On cover —
f. Surch. "20 PIASTRE" 2,750.
Never hinged 3,250.
20G A46 20pi on 5 l bl & rose 55.00 72.50
Never hinged 140.00
On cover —
h. Double surcharge 1,600. 1,600.
Never hinged 2,400.

Italian Stamps of 1906-19 Surcharged

1921

21 A48 1pi on 5c green 350.00 *475.00*
Never hinged 875.00
On cover —
22 A48 2pi on 15c slate 8.00 *12.00*
Never hinged 20.00
On cover 275.00
23 A50 4pi on 20c brn org (No. 113) 80.00 *95.00*
Never hinged 200.00
On cover —
24 A49 5pi on 25c blue 80.00 *95.00*
Never hinged 200.00
On cover —
a. Double surcharge 350.00
25 A49 10pi on 60c carmine 4.75 *8.00*
Never hinged 12.00
On cover —
Nos. 21-25 (5) 522.75 *685.00*
Set of 5 on overfranked philatelic cover 1,000.

No. 21 is almost always found poorly centered, and it is valued thus.

On No. 25 the "10" is placed above "PIASTRE."

Italian Stamps of 1901-19 Surcharged

n

o

1922

26 A42(n) 10pa on 1c brn 2.40 *2.75*
Never hinged 6.00
On cover —

27 A43(n) 20pa on 2c org brn 2.40 *2.75*
Never hinged 6.00
On cover —
28 A48(n) 30pa on 5c grn 6.50 *6.50*
Never hinged 16.00
On cover 300.00
29 A48(o) 1pi20pa on 15c slate 7.25 *2.75*
Never hinged 18.00
On cover 175.00
30 A50(n) 3pi on 20c brn org (#113) 9.50 *17.50*
Never hinged 24.00
On cover 200.00
31 A49(o) 3pi30pa on 25c blue 4.75 *2.75*
Never hinged 12.00
On cover 160.00
32 A49(o) 7pi20pa on 60c carmine 9.50 *6.50*
Never hinged 24.00
On cover 240.00
33 A46(n) 15pi on 1 l brn & grn 27.50 *47.50*
Never hinged 67.50
On cover —
Nos. 26-33 (8) 69.80 *89.00*
Set of 5 on overfranked philatelic cover 175.00

On No. 32, the distance between the two lines is 2mm. See note after No. 58A.

Italy No. 100 Surcharged

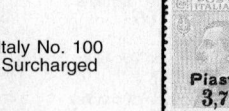

34 A49 3.75pi on 25c blue 2.40 2.75
Never hinged 6.00
On cover 95.00

Italian Stamps of 1901-20 Surcharged

q

r

1922

35 A48 30pi on 5c grn 4.00 *17.50*
Never hinged 10.00
On cover 275.00
36 A49 1.50pi on 25c blue 2.40 *9.50*
Never hinged 6.00
On cover 80.00
37 A49 3.75pi on 40c brn 3.25 *11.00*
Never hinged 8.00
On cover 72.50
a. Double surcharge 325.00
38 A49 4.50pi on 50c vio 8.00 *24.00*
Never hinged 20.00
On cover 80.00
39 A49 7.50pi on 60c car 6.50 *17.50*
Never hinged 16.00
On cover 95.00
a. Double surcharge 400.00
b. Pair, one without surcharge 1,750.
40 A49 15pi on 85c red brn 12.00 *40.00*
Never hinged 30.00
On cover 120.00
41 A46 18.75pi on 1 l brn & grn 5.50 *32.50*
Never hinged 14.00
On cover 240.00

On No. 40 the numerals of the surcharge are above "PIASTRE."

Italian Stamps of 1901-20 Surcharged

42 A46 45pi on 5 l bl & rose 450.00 *725.00*
Never hinged 1,100.
On cover —
43 A51 90pi on 10 l gray grn & red 475.00 *875.00*
Never hinged 1,200.
On cover —

On No. 42 the figure "4" is open at top. See note after No. 61.

On No. 43 the figure "9" has a curved or arched bottom. See note after No. 62.

Italian Stamps of 1901-17 Surcharged Type "q" or:

44 A43 30pa on 2c org brn 2.40 *6.50*
Never hinged 6.00
On cover 200.00
45 A50 1.50pi on 20c brn org (#113) 2.40 *6.50*
Never hinged 6.00
On cover 95.00
Nos. 35-45 (11) 971.45 *1,765.*
Nos. 36-45, set of 10 on overfranked philatelic cover 2,600.

Italian Stamps of 1901-20 Surcharged in Black or Red

46 A48 30pa on 5c green 2.40 *4.00*
Never hinged 6.00
On cover 275.00
a. "RARA" instead of "PARA" 20.00 20.00
47 A48 1½pi on 10c claret 2.40 *4.00*
Never hinged 6.00
On cover 175.00
48 A49 3pi on 25c blue 20.00 8.00
Never hinged 50.00
On cover 225.00
49 A49 3¾pi on 40c brown 4.00 *4.00*
Never hinged 10.00
On cover 250.00
50 A49 4½pi on 50c violet 47.50 45.00
Never hinged 120.00
On cover 325.00
51 A49 7½pi on 85c red brn 9.50 *12.00*
Never hinged 24.00
On cover 160.00
a. "PIASIRE" 47.50 *47.50*
52 A46 7½pi on 1 l brn & grn (R) 12.00 *14.00*
Never hinged 27.50
On cover 225.00
a. Double surcharge 175.00
b. "PIASIRE" 55.00 *55.00*
53 A46 15pi on 1 l brn & grn 72.50 *175.00*
Never hinged 175.00
On cover —
54 A46 45pi on 5 l blue & rose 110.00 *110.00*
Never hinged 275.00
On cover —
55 A51 90pi on 10 l gray grn & red 87.50 *200.00*
Never hinged 210.00
Nos. 46-55 (10) 367.80 *576.00*
Set of 10 on overfranked philatelic cover 825.00

Italian Stamps of 1901-20 Surcharged Type "o" or

No. 58

No. 59

Nos. 61-62

1923

56 A49 1pi20pa on 25c blue 14.00
Never hinged 35.00
57 A49 3pi30pa on 40c brn 14.00
Never hinged 35.00
58 A49 4pi20pa on 50c vio 14.00
Never hinged 35.00
58A A49 7pi20pa on 60c car 40.00
Never hinged 100.00
59 A49 15pi on 85c red brn 14.00
Never hinged 35.00
60 A46 18pi30pa on 1 l brn & grn 14.00
Never hinged 35.00
a. Double surcharge *325.00*
61 A46 45pi on 5 l bl & rose 40.00
Never hinged 100.00
62 A51 90pi on 10 l gray grn & red 35.00
Never hinged 87.50
Nos. 56-62 (8) 185.00

On No. 58A the distance between the lines is 1.5mm. On No. 61 the figure "4" is closed at top. On No. 62 the figure "9" is nearly rectilinear at bottom.

Nos. 56-62 were not issued.

SPECIAL DELIVERY STAMPS

Italian Special Delivery Stamps Surcharged

1908 **Wmk. 140** ***Perf. 14***

E1 SD1 1pi on 25c rose red 3.25 *4.75*
Never hinged 8.00
On cover 550.00

Surcharged

1910

E2 SD2 60pa on 30c blue & rose 6.50 *8.00*
Never hinged 16.00
On cover *2,000.*
Nos. E1 and E2, set of two on overfranked philatelic cover 650.00

Surcharged

1922

E3 SD2 15pi on 1.20 l on 30c bl & rose 35.00 *87.50*
Never hinged 87.50
On cover 875.00
a. Missing comma between "1" and "20" (position 13) 175.00 240.00

On No. E3, lines obliterate the first two denominations.

Surcharged

1922

E4 SD2 15pi on 30c bl & rose 525.00 *1,050.*
Never hinged 1,300.
On cover —

Surcharged

1923

E5 SD2 15pi on 1.20 l blue & red 16.00
Never hinged 40.00

No. E5 was not regularly issued.

ALBANIA

Stamps of Italy Surcharged in Black

1902 **Wmk. 140** ***Perf. 14***

1 A44 10pa on 5c green 4.75 2.40
Never hinged 12.00
On cover 175.00
2 A45 35pa on 20c orange 7.25 8.00
Never hinged 18.00
On cover 350.00
3 A45 40pa on 25c blue 14.00 8.00
Never hinged 35.00
On cover 325.00
Nos. 1-3 (3) 26.00 18.40
Set of 3 on overfranked philatelic cover 95.00

Nos. 1-3 with red surcharges are proofs.

1907

4 A48 10pa on 5c green 55.00 *65.00*
Never hinged 140.00
On cover 325.00
5 A48 20pa on 10c claret 35.00 *27.50*
Never hinged 87.50
On cover 275.00
6 A45 80pa on 50c violet 35.00 *27.50*
Never hinged 87.50
On cover 675.00
Nos. 4-6 (3) 125.00 *120.00*
Set of 3 on overfranked philatelic cover 275.00

No. 5 is almost always found poorly centered, and it is valued thus.

CONSTANTINOPLE

Stamps of Italy Surcharged in Black or Violet

Wmk. 140, Unwmk. (#3)

1909-11 ***Perf. 14, 12***

1 A48 10pa on 5c green 2.40 *2.40*
Never hinged 6.00
On cover 87.50
2 A48 20pa on 10c claret 2.40 *2.40*
Never hinged 6.00
On cover 87.50
3 A47 30pa on 15c slate (V) 2.40 *2.40*
Never hinged 6.00
On cover 125.00
4 A49 1pi on 25c blue 2.40 *2.40*
Never hinged 6.00
On cover 125.00
a. Double surcharge 210.00 *210.00*
5 A49 2pi on 50c violet 4.75 *3.25*
Never hinged 12.00
On cover 200.00

Surcharged

6 A46 4pi on 1 l brn & grn 4.75 4.00
Never hinged 12.00
On cover —
7 A46 20pi on 5 l bl & rose 72.50 72.50
Never hinged 175.00
8 A51 40pi on 10 l gray grn & red 8.00 *32.50*
Never hinged 20.00
On cover —
Nos. 1-8 (8) 99.60 *121.85*
Set of 8 on overfranked philatelic cover 240.00

Italian Stamps of 1901-19 Surcharged

Nos. 10, 12-13

Nos. 9, 11

1922

9 A48 20pa on 5c green 20.00 *32.50*
Never hinged 50.00
On cover 875.00
10 A48 1pi20pa on 15c slate 2.40 2.40
Never hinged 6.00
On cover 240.00
11 A49 3pi on 30c org brn 2.40 2.40
Never hinged 6.00
On cover 87.50
12 A49 3pi30pa on 40c brown 2.40 2.40
Never hinged 6.00
On cover 200.00
13 A46 7pi20pa on 1 l brn & grn 2.40 2.40
Never hinged 6.00
On cover 225.00
Nos. 9-13 (5) 29.60 42.10
Set of 8 on overfranked philatelic cover 160.00

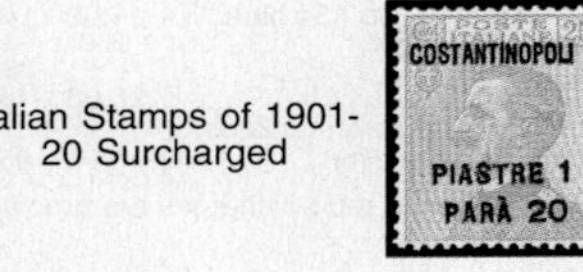

Italian Stamps of 1901-20 Surcharged

1923

14 A48 30pa on 5c grn 3.25 2.40
Never hinged 8.00
On cover 450.00
15 A49 1pi20pa on 25c blue 3.25 2.40
Never hinged 8.00
On cover 125.00
16 A49 3pi30pa on 40c brn 3.25 2.00
Never hinged 8.00
On cover 125.00
17 A49 4pi20pa on 50c vio 3.25 2.00
Never hinged 8.00
On cover 100.00
18 A49 7pi20pa on 60c car 3.25 2.00
Never hinged 8.00
On cover 160.00
19 A49 15pi on 85c red brn 3.25 3.25
Never hinged 8.00
On cover 275.00
20 A46 18pi30pa on 1 l brn & grn 3.25 3.25
Never hinged 8.00
On cover 450.00
21 A46 45pi on 5 l bl & rose 3.25 *7.25*
Never hinged 8.00
On cover —
22 A51 90pi on 10 l gray grn & red 3.25 *8.00*
Never hinged 7.00
On cover —
Nos. 14-22 (9) 29.25 32.55
Set of 9 on overfranked philatelic cover 125.00

CONSTANTINOPLE SPECIAL DELIVERY STAMP

Unissued Italian Special Delivery Stamp of 1922 Surcharged in Black

1923 Wmk. 140 *Perf. 14*

E1 SD2 15pi on 1.20 l bl & red 8.00 *45.00*
Never hinged 20.00
On cover *875.00*

CONSTANTINOPLE POSTAGE DUE STAMPS

Italian Postage Due Stamps of 1870-1903 Overprinted

1922 Wmk. 140 *Perf. 14*

J1 D3 10c buff & mag 80.00 *110.00*
Never hinged 160.00
J2 D3 30c buff & mag 80.00 *110.00*
Never hinged 160.00
J3 D3 60c buff & mag 80.00 *110.00*
Never hinged 160.00
J4 D3 1 l blue & mag 80.00 *110.00*
Never hinged 160.00
J5 D3 2 l blue & mag 1,900. *3,400.*
Never hinged 3,800.
J6 D3 5 l blue & mag 875.00 *1,200.*
Never hinged 1,750.
Nos. J1-J6 (6) 3,095. *5,040.*

A circular control mark with the inscription "Poste Italiane Constantinopoli" and with the arms of the Kingdom of Italy (Savoy Cross) in the center was applied to each block of four of these stamps in black. Value, set of 6 blocks of four with control marks: unused $20,000; used $28,000.

Without Control Mark

J1a D3 10c buff & mag 1,900.
Never hinged 2,900.
J2a D3 30c buff & mag 1,900.
Never hinged 2,900.
J3a D3 60c buff & mag 1,900.
Never hinged 2,900.
J4a D3 1 l blue & mag 1,900.
Never hinged 2,900.
J5a D3 2 l blue & mag —
Never hinged —
J6a D3 5 l blue & mag —
Never hinged —
Nos. J1a-J4a (4) 7,600.

DURAZZO

Stamps of Italy Surcharged in Black or Violet

Wmk. 140, Unwmk. (#3)

1909-11 *Perf. 14, 12*

1 A48 10pa on 5c green 1.60 *3.25*
Never hinged 4.00
On cover 87.50
2 A48 20pa on 10c claret 1.60 *3.25*
Never hinged 4.00
On cover 87.50
3 A47 30pa on 15c slate (V) 80.00 4.00
Never hinged 200.00
On cover 175.00
4 A49 1pi on 25c blue 2.40 *4.00*
Never hinged 6.00
On cover 175.00
5 A49 2pi on 50c violet 2.40 *4.00*
Never hinged 6.00
On cover 350.00

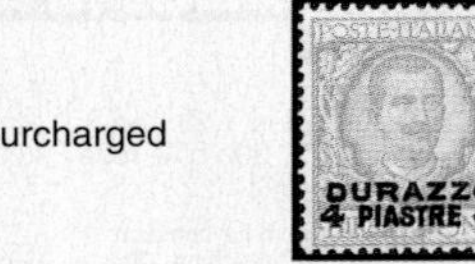

Surcharged

6 A46 4pi on 1 l brn & grn 4.00 *4.75*
Never hinged 10.00
On cover 475.00
7 A46 20pi on 5 l bl & rose 325.00 275.00
Never hinged 800.00
8 A51 40pi on 10 l gray grn & red 20.00 *140.00*
Never hinged 50.00
Nos. 1-8 (8) 437.00 438.25
Set of 8 stamps on overfranked philatelic cover 650.00

No. 3 Surcharged

1916 Unwmk. *Perf. 12*

9 A47 20c on 30pa on 15c slate 4.75 *20.00*
Never hinged 12.00
On cover 120.00

JANINA

Stamps of Italy Surcharged

1902-07 Wmk. 140 *Perf. 14*

1 A44 10pa on 5c green 9.50 3.75
Never hinged 27.50
On cover 110.00
2 A45 35pa on 20c orange 7.00 *4.00*
Never hinged 20.00
On cover 225.00
3 A45 40pa on 25c blue 35.00 11.50
Never hinged 100.00
On cover 325.00
4 A45 80pa on 50c vio ('07) 62.50 *47.50*
Never hinged 160.00
On cover 475.00
Nos. 1-4 (4) 114.00 *66.75*
Nos. 1-3 on overfranked philatelic cover 140.00

Surcharged in Black or Violet

Wmk. 140, Unwmk. (#7)

1909-11 *Perf. 14, 12*

5 A48 10pa on 5c green 1.25 *2.50*
Never hinged 4.00
On cover 95.00
6 A48 20pa on 10c claret 1.25 *2.50*
Never hinged 4.00
On cover 95.00
7 A47 30pa on 15c slate (V) 1.25 *2.50*
Never hinged 4.00
On cover 175.00
8 A49 1pi on 25c blue 1.25 *2.50*
Never hinged 4.00
On cover 175.00
9 A49 2pi on 50c violet 1.25 *3.25*
Never hinged 4.00
On cover 350.00

Surcharged

10 A46 4pi on 1 l brn & grn 4.00 *4.75*
Never hinged 10.00
On cover 525.00
11 A46 20pi on 5 l bl & rose *275.00 350.00*
Never hinged 940.00
12 A51 40pi on 10 l gray grn & red 17.50 *100.00*
Never hinged 50.00
Nos. 5-12 (8) 302.75 468.00
Set of 8 on overfranked philatelic cover 825.00

JERUSALEM

Stamps of Italy Surcharged in Black or Violet

Wmk. 140, Unwmk. (#3)

1909-11 *Perf. 14, 12*

1 A48 10pa on 5c green 8.00 *20.00*
Never hinged 20.00
On cover 525.00
2 A48 20pa on 10c claret 8.00 *20.00*
Never hinged 20.00
On cover 525.00
3 A47 30pa on 15c slate (V) 8.00 *27.50*
Never hinged 20.00
On cover 875.00
4 A49 1pi on 25c blue 8.00 *20.00*
Never hinged 20.00
On cover 1,200.
5 A49 2pi on 50c violet 27.50 *65.00*
Never hinged 67.50
On cover 1,800.

Surcharged

6 A46 4pi on 1 l brn & grn 35.00 *87.50*
Never hinged 87.50
On cover 4,750.
7 A46 20pi on 5 l bl & rose 1,250. *1,400.*
Never hinged 3,100.
8 A51 40pi on 10 l gray grn & red 47.50 *600.00*
Never hinged 120.00
Nos. 1-8 (8) 1,392. *2,240.*
Set of 8 on overfranked philatelic cover 8,750.

Forged cancellations exist on Nos. 1-8.

SALONIKA

Stamps of Italy Surcharged in Black or Violet

Wmk. 140, Unwmk. (#3)

1909-11 *Perf. 14, 12*

1 A48 10pa on 5c green 1.50 *3.25*
Never hinged 4.00
On cover 87.50
2 A48 20pa on 10c claret 1.50 *3.25*
Never hinged 4.00
On cover 87.50
3 A47 30pa on 15c slate (V) 1.75 *3.50*
Never hinged 6.00
On cover 160.00
4 A49 1pi on 25c blue 1.75 *3.50*
Never hinged 6.00
On cover 120.00
5 A49 2pi on 50c violet 2.40 *4.25*
Never hinged 6.00
On cover 250.00

Surcharged

6 A46 4pi on 1 l brn & grn 3.50 *4.75*
Never hinged 10.00
On cover 475.00
7 A46 20pi on 5 l bl & rose *475.00 600.00*
Never hinged 1,350.
8 A51 40pi on 10 l gray grn & red 16.50 *95.00*
Never hinged 50.00
Nos. 1-8 (8) 503.90 717.50
Set of 8 on overfranked philatelic cover 1,100.

SCUTARI

Stamps of Italy Surcharged in Black or Violet

Wmk. 140, Unwmk. (#3)

1909-11 *Perf. 14, 12*

1 A48 10pa on 5c green 1.60 *3.25*
Never hinged 4.00
On cover 87.50
2 A48 20pa on 10c claret 1.60 *3.25*
Never hinged 4.00
On cover 87.50
3 A47 30pa on 15c slate (V) 27.50 6.50
Never hinged 67.50
On cover 200.00
4 A49 1pi on 25c blue 1.60 *3.25*
Never hinged 4.00
On cover 125.00
5 A49 2pi on 50c violet 1.60 *4.75*
Never hinged 4.00
On cover 525.00

Surcharged

6 A46 4pi on 1 l brn & grn 3.25 *4.75*
Never hinged 8.00
On cover 725.00
7 A46 20pi on 5 l bl & rose 35.00 *55.00*
Never hinged 87.50

8 A51 40pi on 10 l gray grn & red 75.00 *175.00*
Never hinged 190.00
On cover —
Nos. 1-8 (8) 147.15 *255.75*
Set of 8 on overfranked philatelic cover 350.00

Surcharged like Nos. 1-5

1915
9 A43 4pa on 2c org brn 2.40 *5.50*
Never hinged 6.00
On cover 110.00

No. 3 Surcharged

1916 Unwmk. *Perf. 12*
10 A47 20c on 30pa on 15c slate 6.50 *27.50*
Never hinged 16.00
On cover 275.00

SMYRNA

Stamps of Italy Surcharged in Black or Violet

Wmk. 140, Unwmk. (#3)
1909-11 *Perf. 14, 12*
1 A48 10pa on 5c green 1.60 1.60
Never hinged 4.00
On cover 87.50
2 A48 20pa on 10c claret 1.60 1.60
Never hinged 4.00
On cover 87.50
3 A47 30pa on 15c slate (V) 3.25 *4.75*
Never hinged 8.00
On cover 200.00
4 A49 1pi on 25c blue 3.25 *4.75*
Never hinged 8.00
On cover 125.00
5 A49 2pi on 50c violet 4.00 *6.50*
Never hinged 10.00
On cover 450.00

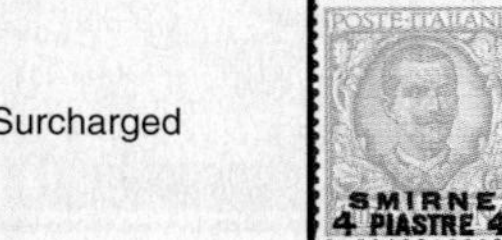

Surcharged

6 A46 4pi on 1 l brn & grn 4.75 *8.00*
Never hinged 12.00
On cover 525.00
7 A46 20pi on 5 l bl & rose 190.00 240.00
Never hinged 475.00
8 A51 40pi on 10 l gray grn & red 20.00 *120.00*
Never hinged 50.00
Nos. 1-8 (8) 228.45 *387.20*
Set of 8 on overfranked philatelic cover 570.00

Italian Stamps of 1901-22 Surcharged

Nos. 10, 12-13

Nos. 9, 11

1922
9 A48 20pa on 5c green 32.50
Never hinged 80.00
10 A48 1pi20pa on 15c slate 1.60
Never hinged 4.00
11 A49 3pi on 30c org brn 1.60
Never hinged 4.00
12 A49 3pi30pa on 40c brn 4.00
Never hinged 10.00
13 A46 7pi20pa on 1 l brn & grn 4.00
Never hinged 10.00
Nos. 9-13 (5) 43.70

Nos. 9-13 were not issued.

VALONA

Stamps of Italy Surcharged in Black or Violet

Wmk. 140, Unwmk. (#3)
1909-11 *Perf. 14, 12*
1 A48 10pa on 5c green 1.60 *3.25*
Never hinged 4.00
On cover 87.50
2 A48 20pa on 10c claret 1.60 *3.25*
Never hinged 4.00
On cover 87.50
3 A47 30pa on 15c slate (V) 20.00 6.50
Never hinged 50.00
On cover 175.00
4 A49 1pi on 25c blue 2.40 *3.25*
Never hinged 6.00
On cover 140.00
5 A49 2pi on 50c violet 2.40 *4.00*
Never hinged 6.00
On cover 400.00

Surcharged

6 A46 4pi on 1 l brn & grn 2.40 *4.00*
Never hinged 6.00
On cover 600.00
7 A46 20pi on 5 l bl & rose 55.00 65.00
Never hinged 140.00
8 A51 40pi on 10 l gray grn & red 65.00 *175.00*
Never hinged 160.00
Nos. 1-8 (8) 150.40 *264.25*
Set of 8 on overfranked philatelic cover 390.00

Italy No. 123 Surcharged in Violet or Red Violet

1916
9 A58 30pa on 15c slate (V) 4.75 *14.00*
Never hinged 12.00
On cover 200.00
a. Red violet surcharge 11.00 *32.50*
Never hinged 27.50

No. 9 Surcharged

10 A58 20c on 30pa on 15c slate 2.40 *20.00*
Never hinged 6.00
On cover 175.00

AEGEAN ISLANDS

(Dodecanese)

A group of islands in the Aegean Sea off the coast of Turkey. They were occupied by Italy during the Tripoli War and were ceded to Italy by Turkey in 1924 by the Treaty of Lausanne. Stamps of Italy overprinted with the name of the island were in use at the post offices maintained in the various islands.

Rhodes, on the island of the same name, was capital of the entire group.

100 Centesimi = 1 Lira

GENERAL ISSUE

Italian Stamps of 1907-08 Overprinted

1912 Wmk. 140 *Perf. 14*
1 A49 25c blue 55.00 *35.00*
Never hinged 140.00
On cover 110.00
a. Inverted overprint 300.00 *300.00*
2 A49 50c violet 55.00 *35.00*
Never hinged 140.00
On cover 125.00
a. Inverted overprint 300.00 *300.00*
Set on overfranked philatelic cover 140.00

Virgil Issue

Italian Stamps of 1930 Ovptd. in Red or Blue

1930 Photo. Wmk. 140 *Perf. 14*
3 A106 15c vio blk 1.60 *21.00*
Never hinged 4.00
On cover 125.00
4 A106 20c org brn 1.60 *21.00*
Never hinged 4.00
On cover 120.00
5 A106 25c dk green 1.60 *9.50*
Never hinged 4.00
On cover 100.00
6 A106 30c lt brown 1.60 *9.50*
Never hinged 4.00
On cover 120.00
7 A106 50c dull vio 1.60 *9.50*
Never hinged 4.00
On cover 100.00
8 A106 75c rose red 1.60 *21.00*
Never hinged 4.00
On cover 225.00
9 A106 1.25 l gray bl 1.60 *27.50*
Never hinged 4.00
On cover 300.00

Engr.
Unwmk.
10 A106 5 l + 1.50 l dk vio 4.75 *52.50*
Never hinged 12.00
On cover —
11 A106 10 l + 2.50 l ol brn 4.75 *52.50*
Never hinged 12.00
On cover —
Nos. 3-11,C4-C7 (13) *35.00* 436.50
Set on overfranked philatelic cover 500.00

St. Anthony of Padua Issue

Italian Stamps of 1931 Ovptd. in Blue or Red

1932 Photo. Wmk. 140 *Perf. 14*
12 A116 20c black brn 32.50 27.50
Never hinged 80.00
On cover 200.00
13 A116 25c dull grn 32.50 27.50
Never hinged 80.00
On cover 180.00
14 A118 30c brown org 32.50 32.50
Never hinged 80.00
On cover 200.00
15 A118 50c dull vio 32.50 24.00
Never hinged 80.00
On cover 160.00
16 A120 1.25 l gray bl 32.50 47.50
Never hinged 80.00
On cover 450.00

Engr.
Unwmk.
17 A121 75c lt red 32.50 *35.00*
Never hinged 80.00
On cover 300.00
18 A122 5 l + 2.50 l dp org 32.50 *175.00*
Never hinged 80.00
On cover —
Nos. 12-18 (7) 227.50 *369.00*
Set on overfranked philatelic cover 675.00

Dante Alighieri Society Issue

Italian Stamps of 1932 Overprinted

1932 Photo. Wmk. 140
19 A126 10c grnsh gray 1.60 *8.00*
Never hinged 4.00
On cover 95.00
20 A126 15c black vio 1.60 *8.00*
Never hinged 4.00
On cover 120.00
21 A126 20c brown org 1.60 *8.00*
Never hinged 4.00
On cover 120.00
22 A126 25c dp green 1.60 8.00
Never hinged 4.00
On cover 80.00
23 A126 30c dp org 1.60 *8.00*
Never hinged 4.00
On cover 120.00
24 A126 50c dull vio 1.60 4.00
Never hinged 4.00
On cover 80.00
25 A126 75c rose red 1.60 *11.00*
Never hinged 4.00
On cover 160.00
26 A126 1.25 l blue 1.60 *9.50*
Never hinged 4.00
On cover 175.00
27 A126 1.75 l ol brn 3.25 *11.00*
Never hinged 8.00
On cover 325.00
28 A126 2.75 l car rose 3.25 *11.00*
Never hinged 8.00
On cover 375.00
29 A126 5 l + 2 l dp vio 3.25 *25.00*
Never hinged 8.00
On cover —
30 A126 10 l + 2.50 l dk brn 3.25 *45.00*
Never hinged 8.00
On cover —
Nos. 19-30 (12) 25.80 *156.50*
Set of on overfranked philatelic cover 450.00

See Nos. C8-C14.

Soccer Issue

Types of Italy, "Soccer" Issue, Overprinted in Black or Red

1934
31 A173 20c brn rose (Bk) 87.50 100.00
Never hinged 220.00
On cover 675.00
32 A174 25c green (R) 87.50 100.00
Never hinged 220.00
On cover 550.00
33 A174 50c violet (R) 340.00 80.00
Never hinged 850.00
On cover 450.00
34 A174 1.25 l gray bl (R) 87.50 *190.00*
Never hinged 220.00
On cover 875.00
35 A175 5 l +2.50 l bl (R) 87.50 *450.00*
Never hinged 220.00
On cover —
Nos. 31-35 (5) 690.00 *920.00*
Set on overfranked philatelic cover 2,200.

See Nos. C28-C31.

Same Overprint on Types of Medal of Valor Issue of Italy, in Red or Black

1935
36 A177 10c sl gray (R) 47.50 *95.00*
Never hinged 120.00
On cover 275.00
37 A178 15c brn (Bk) 47.50 *95.00*
Never hinged 120.00
On cover 275.00
38 A178 20c red org (Bk) 47.50 *95.00*
Never hinged 120.00
On cover 275.00
39 A177 25c dp grn (R) 47.50 *95.00*
Never hinged 120.00
On cover 275.00
40 A178 30c lake (Bk) 47.50 *95.00*
Never hinged 120.00
On cover 275.00
41 A178 50c ol grn (Bk) 47.50 *95.00*
Never hinged 120.00
On cover 275.00
42 A178 75c rose red (Bk) 47.50 *95.00*
Never hinged 120.00
On cover 450.00
43 A178 1.25 l dp bl (R) 47.50 *95.00*
Never hinged 120.00
On cover 550.00
44 A177 1.75 l + 1 l pur (R) 47.50 *95.00*
Never hinged 120.00
On cover —

45 A178 2.55 l + 2 l dk car (Bk) 47.50 *95.00*
Never hinged 120.00
On cover —
46 A178 2.75 l + 2 l org brn (Bk) 47.50 *95.00*
Never hinged 120.00
On cover —
Nos. 36-46 (11) 522.50 *1,045.*
Set on overfranked philatelic cover 2,400.

See Nos. C32-C38, CE3-CE4.

Types of Italy, 1937, Overprinted in Blue or Red

1938 **Wmk. 140** ***Perf. 14***
47 A208 10c dk brn (Bl) 4.00 9.50
Never hinged 10.00
On cover 200.00
48 A208 15c pur (R) 4.00 9.50
Never hinged 10.00
On cover 190.00
49 A208 20c chestnut (Bl) 4.00 9.50
Never hinged 10.00
On cover 140.00
50 A208 25c myr grn (R) 4.00 9.50
Never hinged 10.00
On cover 175.00
51 A208 30c dp cl (Bl) 4.00 9.50
Never hinged 10.00
On cover 200.00
52 A208 50c sl grn (R) 4.00 16.00
Never hinged 10.00
On cover 140.00
53 A208 75c rose red (Bl) 4.00 16.00
Never hinged 10.00
On cover 250.00
54 A208 1.25 l dk bl (R) 4.00 16.00
Never hinged 10.00
On cover 425.00
55 A208 1.75 l + 1 l dp org (Bl) 6.50 *30.00*
Never hinged 16.00
On cover —
56 A208 2.55 l + 2 l ol brn (R) 6.50 *30.00*
Never hinged 16.00
On cover —
Nos. 47-56 (10) 45.00 155.50
Set on overfranked philatelic cover 550.00

Bimillenary of birth of Augustus Caesar (Octavianus), first Roman emperor.
See Nos. C39-C43.

Same Overprint of Type of Italy, 1937, in Red

1938
57 A222 1.25 l deep blue 1.60 *2.40*
Never hinged 4.00
On cover 110.00
58 A222 2.75 l + 2 l brown 1.75 *9.50*
Never hinged 4.25
On cover 450.00
Set on overfranked philatelic cover 65.00

600th anniversary of the death of Giotto di Bondone, Italian painter.

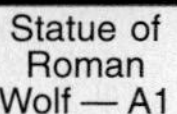

Statue of Roman Wolf — A1

Arms of Rhodes — A2

Dante's House, Rhodes A3

1940 **Photo.**
59 A1 5c lt brown .80 1.20
Never hinged 2.00
On cover 160.00
60 A2 10c pale org .80 1.20
Never hinged 2.00
On cover 120.00
61 A3 25c blue grn 1.60 2.00
Never hinged 4.00
On cover 100.00
62 A1 50c rose vio 1.60 2.00
Never hinged 4.00
On cover 100.00
63 A2 75c dull ver 1.60 4.00
Never hinged 4.00
On cover 240.00
64 A3 1.25 l dull blue 1.60 4.00
Never hinged 4.00
On cover 325.00
65 A2 2 l + 75c rose 1.60 27.50
Never hinged 4.00
Nos. 59-65,C44-C47 (11) 18.60 81.40
Nos. 59-65 on overfranked philatelic cover 120.00

Triennial Overseas Exposition, Naples.

AIR POST STAMPS

Ferrucci Issue

Types of Italian Air Post Stamps of 1930 Overprinted in Blue or Red Like Nos. 12-18

1930 **Wmk. 140** ***Perf. 14***
C1 A104 50c brn vio (Bl) 11.00 *24.00*
Never hinged 27.50
On cover 175.00
C2 A104 1 l dk bl (R) 11.00 *24.00*
Never hinged 27.50
On cover 300.00
C3 A104 5 l + 2 l dp car (Bl) 21.00 *67.50*
Never hinged 52.50
On cover —
Nos. C1-C3 (3) 43.00 *115.50*
Set on overfranked philatelic flown cover 340.00

Nos. C1-C3 were sold at Rhodes only.

Virgil Issue

Types of Italian Air Post Stamps of 1930 Overprinted in Red or Blue Like Nos. 3-11

1930 **Photo.**
C4 A106 50c dp grn (R) 2.40 *40.00*
Never hinged 6.00
On cover 190.00
C5 A106 1 l rose red (Bl) 2.40 *40.00*
Never hinged 6.00
On cover 325.00

Engr.
Unwmk.
C6 A106 7.70 l + 1.30 l dk brn (R) 4.75 *52.50*
Never hinged 12.00
On cover —
C7 A106 9 l + 2 l gray (R) 4.75 *80.00*
Never hinged 12.00
On cover —
Nos. C4-C7 (4) 14.30 *212.50*
Set on overfranked philatelic flown cover 500.00

Dante Alighieri Society Issue

Types of Italian Air Post Stamps of 1932 Overprinted Like Nos. 19-30

1932 **Wmk. 140**
C8 AP10 50c car rose 1.60 *6.50*
Never hinged 4.00
On cover 160.00
C9 AP11 1 l dp grn 1.60 *6.50*
Never hinged 4.00
On cover 175.00
C10 AP11 3 l dl vio 1.60 *9.50*
Never hinged 4.00
On cover 325.00
C11 AP11 5 l dp org 1.60 *9.50*
Never hinged 4.00
On cover 400.00
C12 AP10 7.70 l + 2 l ol brn 4.75 *22.50*
Never hinged 12.00
On cover —
C13 AP11 10 l + 2.50 l dk bl 4.75 *30.00*
Never hinged 12.00
On cover —
Nos. C8-C13 (6) 15.90 *84.50*
Set on overfranked philatelic flown cover 325.00

Leonardo da Vinci — AP12

1932 **Photo.** ***Perf. 14½***
C14 AP12 100 l dp bl & grnsh gray 21.00 *140.00*
Never hinged 52.50
On flown cover *575.00*

Garibaldi Types of Italian Air Post Stamps of 1932 Overprinted in Red or Blue

1932
C15 AP13 50c deep green 60.00 *140.00*
Never hinged 150.00
On cover 300.00
C16 AP14 80c copper red 60.00 *140.00*
Never hinged 150.00
On cover 400.00
C17 AP13 1 l + 25c dl bl 60.00 *140.00*
Never hinged 150.00
On cover 525.00
C18 AP13 2 l + 50c red brn 60.00 *140.00*
Never hinged 150.00
On cover 650.00
C19 AP14 5 l + 1 l bluish sl 60.00 *140.00*
Never hinged 150.00
On cover —
Nos. C15-C19 (5) 300.00 *700.00*
Set on overfranked philatelic flown cover 1,400.

See Nos. CE1-CE2.

Graf Zeppelin over Rhodes AP17

1933 ***Perf. 14***
C20 AP17 3 l olive brn 95.00 *240.00*
Never hinged 240.00
On cover 475.00
C21 AP17 5 l dp vio 95.00 *275.00*
Never hinged 240.00
On cover 675.00
C22 AP17 10 l dk green 95.00 *450.00*
Never hinged 240.00
On cover 950.00
C23 AP17 12 l dk blue 95.00 *500.00*
Never hinged 240.00
On cover 1,200.
C24 AP17 15 l car rose 95.00 *500.00*
Never hinged 240.00
On cover 1,200.
C25 AP17 20 l gray blk 95.00 *500.00*
Never hinged 240.00
On cover 1,200.
Nos. C20-C25 (6) 570.00 *2,465.*
Set on overfranked philatelic flown cover 4,750.
Set of 6 flown covers 5,700.

Balbo Flight Issue

Italian Air Post Stamps of 1933 Ovptd.

1933 **Wmk. 140** ***Perf. 14***
C26 AP25 5.25 l + 19.75 l grn, red & bl gray 60.00 *165.00*
Never hinged 150.00
On cover 4,200.
C27 AP25 5.25 l + 44.75 l red, grn & bl gray 60.00 *165.00*
Never hinged 190.00
On cover 4,200.
Set on overfranked philatelic flown cover 8,250.

Soccer Issue

Types of Italian Air Post Stamps of 1934 Overprinted in Black or Red Like #31-35

1934
C28 AP32 50c brown (R) 20.00 *80.00*
Never hinged 50.00
On cover 600.00
C29 AP33 75c rose red) 20.00 *80.00*
Never hinged 50.00
On cover 550.00
C30 AP34 5 l + 2.50 l red org 32.50 *160.00*
Never hinged 80.00
On cover —
C31 AP35 10 l + 5 l grn (R) 32.50 *190.00*
Never hinged 80.00
On cover —
Nos. C28-C31 (4) 105.00 *510.00*
Set on overfranked philatelic flown cover 2,050.

Types of Medal of Valor Issue of Italy Overprinted in Red or Black Like Nos. 31-35

1935
C32 AP36 25c dp grn 67.50 *110.00*
Never hinged 170.00
On cover 400.00
C33 AP36 50c blk brn (R) 67.50 *110.00*
Never hinged 170.00
On cover 350.00
C34 AP36 75c rose 67.50 *110.00*
Never hinged 170.00
On cover 400.00
C35 AP36 80c dk brn 67.50 *110.00*
Never hinged 170.00
On cover 525.00
C36 AP36 1 l + 50c ol grn 47.50 *110.00*
Never hinged 120.00
On cover —
C37 AP36 2 l + 1 l dp bl (R) 47.50 *110.00*
Never hinged 120.00
On cover —
C38 AP40 3 l + 2 l vio (R) 47.50 *110.00*
Never hinged 120.00
On cover —
Nos. C32-C38 (7) 412.50 *770.00*
Nos. C32-C38, CE3-CE4 on overfranked philatelic flown cover 2,400.

Types of Italy Air Post Stamps, 1937, Overprinted in Blue or Red Like Nos. 47-56

1938 **Wmk. 140** ***Perf. 14***
C39 AP51 25c dl gray vio (R) 4.75 9.50
Never hinged 12.00
On cover 250.00
C40 AP51 50c grn (R) 4.75 9.50
Never hinged 12.00
On cover 175.00
C41 AP51 80c brt bl (R) 4.75 30.00
Never hinged 12.00
On cover 275.00
C42 AP51 1 l + 1 l rose lake 9.50 30.00
Never hinged 24.00
On cover —
C43 AP51 5 l + 1 l rose red 12.50 *60.00*
Never hinged 30.00
On cover —
Nos. C39-C43 (5) 36.25 139.00
Set on overfranked philatelic flown cover 600.00

Bimillenary of the birth of Augustus Caesar (Octavianus).

Statues of Stag and Roman Wolf AP18

Plane over Government Palace, Rhodes — AP19

1940 **Photo.**
C44 AP18 50c olive blk 2.40 4.00
Never hinged 6.00
On cover 240.00
C45 AP19 1 l dk vio 2.40 4.00
Never hinged 6.00
On cover 250.00
C46 AP18 2 l + 75c dk bl 2.40 12.00
Never hinged 6.00
On cover —
C47 AP19 5 l + 2.50 l cop brn 2.40 22.50
Never hinged 6.00
On cover —
Nos. C44-C47 (4) 9.60 42.50
Set on overfranked philatelic flown cover 200.00

Triennial Overseas Exposition, Naples.

AIR POST SPECIAL DELIVERY STAMPS

Type of Italian Garibaldi Air Post Special Delivery Stamps Overprinted in Blue or Ocher Like Nos. 12-18

1932 **Wmk. 140** ***Perf. 14***
CE1 APSD1 2.25 l + 1 l bl & rose & (Bl) 95.00 *260.00*
Never hinged 240.00
On cover —

CE2 APSD1 4.50 l + 1.50 l ocher & gray (O) 95.00 *260.00*
Never hinged 240.00
On cover —
Set on overfranked philatelic flown cover 1,050.

Type of Medal of Valor Issue of Italy, Ovptd. in Black

1935
CE3 APSD4 2 l + 1.25 l dp bl 47.50 *110.00*
Never hinged 120.00
CE4 APSD4 4.50 l + 2 l grn 47.50 *110.00*
Never hinged 120.00

ISSUES FOR THE INDIVIDUAL ISLANDS

Italian Stamps of 1901-20 Overprinted with Names of Various Islands as

a

b

c

The 1912-22 issues of each island have type "a" overprint in black on all values except 15c (type A58) and 20c on 15c, which have type "b" overprint in violet.

The 1930-32 Ferrucci and Garibaldi issues are types of the Italian issues overprinted type "c." Stamps with type "c" overprints are also listed in Castellorizo.

CALCHI

Overprinted "Karki" in Black or Violet

1912-22 Wmk. 140 *Perf. 13½, 14*
1 A43 2c orange brn 8.00 9.50
Never hinged 20.00
On cover 110.00
a. Double overprint 400.00 *600.00*
2 A48 5c green 4.75 *9.50*
Never hinged 12.00
On cover 65.00
3 A48 10c claret 1.60 *9.50*
Never hinged 4.00
On cover 65.00
4 A48 15c slate ('22) 4.75 *47.50*
Never hinged 12.00
On cover 475.00
a. Double overprint 400.00
5 A50 20c brn org ('21) 4.75 *45.00*
Never hinged 12.00
On cover 450.00
6 A49 25c blue 1.60 *9.50*
Never hinged 4.00
On cover 110.00
7 A49 40c brown 1.60 *9.50*
Never hinged 4.00
On cover 240.00
8 A49 50c violet 1.60 *19.00*
Never hinged 4.00
On cover 275.00

Unwmk.
9 A58 15c slate (V) 47.50 19.00
Never hinged 120.00
On cover 180.00
10 A50 20c brn org ('17) 140.00 *175.00*
Never hinged 350.00
On cover 875.00
Nos. 1-10 (10) 216.15 *353.00*
Nos. 1-3, 6-9 on overfranked philatelic cover 160.00

No. 9 Surcharged

1916 *Perf. 13½*
11 A58 20c on 15c slate 2.40 *27.50*
Never hinged 6.00
On cover 140.00

Ferrucci Issue
Types of Italy
Overprinted in Red or Blue

1930 Wmk. 140 *Perf. 14*
12 A102 20c vio (R) 4.00 *9.50*
Never hinged 10.00
On cover 140.00
13 A103 25c dk grn (R) 4.00 *9.50*
Never hinged 10.00
On cover 190.00
14 A103 50c blk (R) 4.75 *16.00*
Never hinged 12.00
On cover 125.00
15 A103 1.25 l dp bl (R) 4.75 *16.00*
Never hinged 12.00
On cover 300.00
16 A104 5 l + 2 l dp car (Bl) 11.00 *27.50*
Never hinged 27.50
On cover —
Nos. 12-16 (5) 28.50 *78.50*
Set on overfranked philatelic cover 140.00

Garibaldi Issue
Types of Italy
Overprinted "CARCHI" in Red or Blue

1932
17 A138 10c brown 19.00 *36.00*
Never hinged 47.50
On cover 250.00
18 A138 20c red brn (Bl) 19.00 *36.00*
Never hinged 47.50
On cover 160.00
19 A138 25c dp grn 19.00 *36.00*
Never hinged 47.50
On cover 160.00
20 A138 30c bluish sl 19.00 *36.00*
Never hinged 47.50
On cover 240.00
21 A138 50c red vio (Bl) 19.00 *36.00*
Never hinged 47.50
On cover 125.00
22 A141 75c cop red (Bl) 19.00 *36.00*
Never hinged 47.50
On cover 350.00
23 A141 1.25 l dl bl 19.00 *36.00*
Never hinged 47.50
On cover 550.00
24 A141 1.75 l + 25c brn 19.00 *36.00*
Never hinged 47.50
On cover —
25 A144 2.55 l + 50c org (Bl) 19.00 *36.00*
Never hinged 47.50
On cover —
26 A145 5 l + 1 l dl vio 19.00 *36.00*
Never hinged 47.50
On cover —
Nos. 17-26 (10) 190.00 *360.00*
Set on overfranked philatelic cover 650.00

CALINO

Overprinted "Calimno" in Black or Violet

1912-21 Wmk. 140 *Perf. 13½, 14*
1 A43 2c orange brn 9.50 9.50
Never hinged 24.00
On cover 110.00
2 A48 5c green 3.25 *9.50*
Never hinged 8.00
On cover 65.00
3 A48 10c claret 1.60 *9.50*
Never hinged 4.00
On cover 65.00
4 A48 15c slate ('21) 4.75 *55.00*
Never hinged 12.00
On cover 550.00
5 A50 20c brn org ('21) 4.75 *55.00*
Never hinged 12.00
On cover 400.00
6 A49 25c blue 9.50 *9.50*
Never hinged 24.00
On cover 110.00
7 A49 40c brown 1.60 *9.50*
Never hinged 4.00
On cover 240.00
8 A49 50c violet 1.60 *19.00*
Never hinged 4.00
On cover 275.00

Unwmk.
9 A58 15c slate (V) 40.00 19.00
Never hinged 100.00
On cover 180.00
10 A50 20c brn org ('17) 95.00 *225.00*
Never hinged 240.00
On cover 400.00
Nos. 1-10 (10) 171.55 *420.50*
Nos. 1-3, 6-9 on overfranked philatelic cover 160.00

No. 9 Surcharged Like Calchi No. 11

1916 *Perf. 13½*
11 A58 20c on 15c slate 17.50 *40.00*
Never hinged 42.50
On cover 200.00

Ferrucci Issue
Types of Italy
Overprinted in Red or Blue

1930 Wmk. 140 *Perf. 14*
12 A102 20c violet (R) 4.00 *9.50*
Never hinged 10.00
On cover 140.00
13 A103 25c dk grn (R) 4.00 *9.50*
Never hinged 10.00
On cover 190.00
14 A103 50c black (R) 4.75 *16.00*
Never hinged 12.00
On cover 125.00
15 A103 1.25 l dp bl (R) 4.75 *16.00*
Never hinged 12.00
On cover 300.00
16 A104 5 l + 2 l dp car (Bl) 11.00 *27.50*
Never hinged 27.50
On cover —
Nos. 12-16 (5) 28.50 *78.50*
Set on overfranked philatelic cover 140.00

Garibaldi Issue
Types of Italy
Overprinted in Red or Blue

1932
17 A138 10c brown 19.00 *35.00*
Never hinged 47.50
On cover 250.00
18 A138 20c red brn (Bl) 19.00 *35.00*
Never hinged 47.50
On cover 160.00
19 A138 25c dp grn 19.00 *35.00*
Never hinged 47.50
On cover 160.00
20 A138 30c bluish sl 19.00 *35.00*
Never hinged 47.50
On cover 240.00
21 A138 50c red vio (Bl) 19.00 *35.00*
Never hinged 47.50
On cover 120.00
22 A141 75c cop red (Bl) 19.00 *35.00*
Never hinged 47.50
On cover 350.00
23 A141 1.25 l dull blue 19.00 *35.00*
Never hinged 47.50
On cover 550.00
24 A141 1.75 l + 25c brn 19.00 *35.00*
Never hinged 47.50
On cover —
25 A144 2.55 l + 50c org (Bl) 19.00 *35.00*
Never hinged 47.50
On cover —
26 A145 5 l + 1 l dl vio 19.00 *35.00*
Never hinged 47.50
On cover —
Nos. 17-26 (10) 190.00 *350.00*
Set on overfranked philatelic cover 650.00

CASO

Overprinted "Caso" in Black or Violet

1912-21 Wmk. 140 *Perf. 13½, 14*
1 A43 2c orange brn 8.00 9.50
Never hinged 20.00
On cover 110.00
2 A48 5c green 4.75 *9.50*
Never hinged 12.00
On cover 65.00
3 A48 10c claret 1.60 *9.50*
Never hinged 4.00
On cover 65.00
4 A48 15c slate ('21) 4.75 *47.50*
Never hinged 12.00
On cover 475.00
5 A50 20c brn org ('20) 4.00 *35.00*
Never hinged 10.00
On cover 350.00
6 A49 25c blue 1.60 *9.50*
Never hinged 4.00
On cover 110.00
7 A49 40c brown 1.60 *9.50*
Never hinged 4.00
On cover 240.00
8 A49 50c violet 1.60 *19.00*
Never hinged 4.00
On cover 275.00

Unwmk.
9 A58 15c slate (V) 47.50 *19.00*
Never hinged 120.00
On cover 180.00
10 A50 20c brn org ('17) 140.00 *225.00*
Never hinged 350.00
On cover 650.00
Nos. 1-10 (10) 215.40 *393.00*
Nos. 1-3, 6-9 on overfranked philatelic cover 160.00

No. 9 Surcharged Like Calchi No. 11

1916 *Perf. 13½*
11 A58 20c on 15c slate 1.60 *40.00*
Never hinged 4.00
On cover 200.00

Ferrucci Issue
Types of Italy
Overprinted in Red or Blue

1930 Wmk. 140 *Perf. 14*
12 A102 20c violet (R) 4.00 *9.50*
Never hinged 10.00
On cover 140.00
13 A103 25c dk green (R) 4.00 *9.50*
Never hinged 10.00
On cover 190.00
14 A103 50c black (R) 4.00 *16.00*
Never hinged 10.00
On cover 125.00
15 A103 1.25 l dp bl (R) 4.00 *16.00*
Never hinged 10.00
On cover 300.00
16 A104 5 l + 2 l dp car (Bl) 11.00 *27.50*
Never hinged 27.50
On cover —
Nos. 12-16 (5) 27.00 *78.50*
Set on overfranked philatelic cover 140.00

Garibaldi Issue
Types of Italy
Overprinted in Red or Blue

1932
17 A138 10c brown 19.00 *35.00*
Never hinged 47.50
On cover 250.00
18 A138 20c red brn (Bl) 19.00 *35.00*
Never hinged 47.50
On cover 160.00
19 A138 25c dp grn 19.00 *35.00*
Never hinged 47.50
On cover 160.00
20 A138 30c bluish sl 19.00 *35.00*
Never hinged 47.50
On cover 240.00
21 A138 50c red vio (Bl) 19.00 *35.00*
Never hinged 47.50
On cover 125.00
22 A141 75c cop red (Bl) 19.00 *35.00*
Never hinged 47.50
On cover 350.00
23 A141 1.25 l dull blue 19.00 *35.00*
Never hinged 47.50
On cover 550.00
24 A141 1.75 l + 25c brn 19.00 *35.00*
Never hinged 47.50
On cover —
25 A144 2.55 l + 50c org (Bl) 19.00 *35.00*
Never hinged 47.50
On cover —
26 A145 5 l + 1 l dl vio 19.00 *35.00*
Never hinged 47.50
On cover —
Nos. 17-26 (10) 190.00 *350.00*
Set on overfranked philatelic cover 650.00

COO

(Cos, Kos)

Overprinted "Cos" in Black or Violet

1912-22 Wmk. 140 *Perf. 13½, 14*
1 A43 2c orange brn 8.00 9.50
Never hinged 20.00
On cover 110.00
2 A48 5c green 100.00 9.50
Never hinged 250.00
On cover 65.00
3 A48 10c claret 4.75 *9.50*
Never hinged 12.00
On cover 65.00
4 A48 15c slate ('22) 4.75 *55.00*
Never hinged 12.00
On cover 550.00
5 A50 20c brn org ('21) 4.00 *35.00*
Never hinged 10.00
On cover 350.00
6 A49 25c blue 40.00 9.50
Never hinged 100.00
On cover 110.00
7 A49 40c brown 1.60 *9.50*
Never hinged 4.00
On cover 240.00
8 A49 50c violet 1.60 *19.00*
Never hinged 4.00
On cover 275.00

Unwmk.
9 A58 15c slate (V) 60.00 19.00
Never hinged 150.00
On cover 180.00
10 A50 20c brn org ('17) 65.00 *225.00*
Never hinged 160.00
On cover 650.00
Nos. 1-10 (10) 289.70 *400.50*
Nos. 1-3, 6-9 on overfranked philatelic cover 160.00

No. 9 Surcharged Like Calchi No. 11

1916 *Perf. 13½*
11 A58 20c on 15c slate 19.00 *40.00*
Never hinged 47.50
On cover 200.00

Ferrucci Issue
Types of Italy
Overprinted in Red or Blue

1930 Wmk. 140 *Perf. 14*
12 A102 20c violet (R) 4.00 *9.50*
Never hinged 10.00
On cover 140.00

13 A103 25c dk green (R) 4.00 9.50
Never hinged 10.00
On cover 190.00
14 A103 50c black (R) 4.00 16.00
Never hinged 10.00
On cover 125.00
15 A103 1.25 l dp bl (R) 4.00 16.00
Never hinged 10.00
On cover 300.00
16 A104 5 l + 2 l dp car (Bl) 11.00 27.50
Never hinged 27.50
On cover —
Nos. 12-16 (5) 27.00 78.50
Set on overfranked philatelic cover 140.00

Garibaldi Issue
Types of Italy
Overprinted in Red or Blue

1932
17 A138 10c brown 19.00 35.00
Never hinged 47.50
On cover 250.00
18 A138 20c red brn (Bl) 19.00 35.00
Never hinged 47.50
On cover 160.00
19 A138 25c dp grn 19.00 35.00
Never hinged 47.50
On cover 160.00
20 A138 30c bluish sl 19.00 35.00
Never hinged 47.50
On cover 240.00
21 A138 50c red vio (Bl) 19.00 35.00
Never hinged 47.50
On cover 125.00
22 A141 75c cop red (Bl) 19.00 35.00
Never hinged 47.50
On cover 350.00
23 A141 1.25 l dull blue 19.00 35.00
Never hinged 47.50
On cover 550.00
24 A141 1.75 l + 25c brn 19.00 35.00
Never hinged 47.50
On cover —
25 A144 2.55 l + 50c org (Bl) 19.00 35.00
Never hinged 47.50
On cover —
26 A145 5 l + 1 l dl vio 19.00 35.00
Never hinged 47.50
On cover —
Nos. 17-26 (10) 190.00 350.00
Set on overfranked philatelic cover 650.00

LERO

Overprinted "Leros" in Black or Violet

1912-22 Wmk. 140 Perf. 13½, 14
1 A43 2c orange brn 9.50 9.50
Never hinged 24.00
On cover 110.00
2 A48 5c green 8.00 9.50
Never hinged 24.00
On cover 65.00
3 A48 10c claret 3.25 9.50
Never hinged 8.00
On cover 65.00
4 A48 15c slate ('22) 4.75 40.00
Never hinged 12.00
On cover 400.00
5 A50 20c brn org ('21) 175.00 125.00
Never hinged 425.00
On cover 525.00
6 A49 25c blue 72.50 9.50
Never hinged 180.00
On cover 110.00
7 A49 40c brown 4.75 9.50
Never hinged 12.00
On cover 240.00
8 A49 50c violet 1.60 19.00
Never hinged 4.00
On cover 275.00

Unwmk.
9 A58 15c slate (V) 87.50 19.00
Never hinged 220.00
On cover 180.00
10 A50 20c brn org ('17) 65.00 225.00
Never hinged 160.00
On cover 650.00
Nos. 1-10 (10) 431.85 475.50
Nos. 1-3, 6-9 on overfranked philatelic cover 160.00

No. 9 Surcharged Like Calchi No. 11

1916 Perf. 13½
11 A58 20c on 15c slate 19.00 40.00
Never hinged 47.50
On cover 200.00

Ferrucci Issue
Types of Italy
Overprinted in Red or Blue

1930 Perf. 14
12 A102 20c violet (R) 4.00 9.50
Never hinged 10.00
On cover 140.00
13 A103 25c dk green (R) 4.00 9.50
Never hinged 10.00
On cover 190.00
14 A103 50c black (R) 4.00 16.00
Never hinged 10.00
On cover 125.00
15 A103 1.25 l dp bl (R) 4.00 16.00
Never hinged 10.00
On cover 300.00
16 A104 5 l + 2 l dp car (Bl) 11.00 27.50
Never hinged 27.50
On cover —
Nos. 12-16 (5) 27.00 78.50
Set on overfranked philatelic cover 140.00

Garibaldi Issue
Types of Italy
Overprinted in Red or Blue

1932
17 A138 10c brown 19.00 35.00
Never hinged 47.50
On cover 250.00
18 A138 20c red brn (Bl) 19.00 35.00
Never hinged 47.50
On cover 160.00
19 A138 25c dp grn 19.00 35.00
Never hinged 47.50
On cover 160.00
20 A138 30c bluish sl 19.00 35.00
Never hinged 47.50
On cover 240.00
21 A138 50c red vio (Bl) 19.00 35.00
Never hinged 47.50
On cover 125.00
22 A141 75c cop red (Bl) 19.00 35.00
Never hinged 47.50
On cover 350.00
23 A141 1.25 l dull blue 19.00 35.00
Never hinged 47.50
On cover 550.00
24 A141 1.75 l + 25c brn 19.00 35.00
Never hinged 47.50
On cover —
25 A144 2.55 l + 50c org (Bl) 19.00 35.00
Never hinged 47.50
On cover —
26 A145 5 l + 1 l dl vio 19.00 35.00
Never hinged 47.50
On cover —
Nos. 17-26 (10) 190.00 350.00
Set on overfranked philatelic cover 650.00

LISSO

Overprinted "Lipso" in Black or Violet

1912-22 Wmk. 140 Perf. 13½, 14
1 A43 2c orange brn 8.00 9.50
Never hinged 20.00
On cover 110.00
2 A48 5c green 4.75 9.50
Never hinged 12.00
On cover 65.00
3 A48 10c claret 3.25 9.50
Never hinged 8.00
On cover 65.00
4 A48 15c slate ('22) 4.75 40.00
Never hinged 12.00
On cover 400.00
5 A50 20c brn org ('21) 4.75 47.50
Never hinged 12.00
On cover 475.00
6 A49 25c blue 1.60 9.50
Never hinged 4.00
On cover 110.00
7 A49 40c brown 3.25 9.50
Never hinged 8.00
On cover 240.00
8 A49 50c violet 1.60 19.00
Never hinged 4.00
On cover 275.00

Unwmk.
9 A58 15c slate (V) 47.50 19.00
Never hinged 120.00
On cover 180.00
10 A50 20c brn org ('17) 95.00 225.00
Never hinged 240.00
On cover 650.00
Nos. 1-10 (10) 174.45 398.00
Nos. 1-3, 6-9 on overfranked philatelic cover 160.00

No. 9 Surcharged Like Calchi No. 11

1916 Perf. 13½
11 A58 20c on 15c slate 1.60 40.00
Never hinged 4.00
On cover 200.00

Ferrucci Issue
Types of Italy
Overprinted in Red or Blue

1930 Wmk. 140 Perf. 14
12 A102 20c violet (R) 4.00 9.50
Never hinged 10.00
On cover 140.00
13 A103 25c dk green (R) 4.00 9.50
Never hinged 10.00
On cover 190.00
14 A103 50c black (R) 4.00 16.00
Never hinged 10.00
On cover 125.00
15 A103 1.25 l dp bl (R) 4.00 16.00
Never hinged 10.00
On cover 300.00
16 A104 5 l + 2 l dp car (Bl) 11.00 29.00
Never hinged 27.50
On cover —
Nos. 12-16 (5) 27.00 80.00
Set on overfranked philatelic cover 140.00

Garibaldi Issue
Types of Italy
Overprinted "LIPSO" in Red or Blue

1932
17 A138 10c brown 19.00 35.00
Never hinged 47.50
On cover 250.00
18 A138 20c red brn (Bl) 19.00 35.00
Never hinged 47.50
On cover 160.00
19 A138 25c dp grn 19.00 35.00
Never hinged 47.50
On cover 160.00
20 A138 30c bluish sl 19.00 35.00
Never hinged 47.50
On cover 240.00
21 A138 50c red vio (Bl) 19.00 35.00
Never hinged 47.50
On cover 125.00
22 A141 75c cop red (Bl) 19.00 35.00
Never hinged 47.50
On cover 350.00
23 A141 1.25 l dull blue 19.00 35.00
Never hinged 47.50
On cover 550.00
24 A141 1.75 l + 25c brn 19.00 35.00
Never hinged 47.50
On cover —
25 A144 2.55 l + 50c org (Bl) 19.00 35.00
Never hinged 47.50
On cover —
26 A145 5 l + 1 l dl vio 19.00 35.00
Never hinged 47.50
On cover —
Nos. 17-26 (10) 190.00 350.00
Set on overfranked philatelic cover 650.00

NISIRO

Overprinted "Nisiros" in Black or Violet

1912-22 Wmk. 140 Perf. 13½, 14
1 A43 2c orange brn 8.00 9.50
Never hinged 20.00
On cover 110.00
2 A48 5c green 4.75 9.50
Never hinged 12.00
On cover 65.00
3 A48 10c claret 1.60 9.50
Never hinged 4.00
On cover 65.00
4 A48 15c slate ('22) 32.50 55.00
Never hinged 80.00
On cover 400.00
5 A50 20c brn org ('21) 110.00 125.00
Never hinged 275.00
On cover 650.00
6 A49 25c blue 3.25 9.50
Never hinged 8.00
On cover 110.00
7 A49 40c brown 1.60 9.50
Never hinged 4.00
On cover 240.00
8 A49 50c violet 4.00 19.00
Never hinged 10.00
On cover 275.00

Unwmk.
9 A58 15c slate (V) 47.50 19.00
Never hinged 120.00
On cover 180.00
10 A50 20c brn org ('17) 140.00 225.00
Never hinged 350.00
On cover 650.00
Nos. 1-10 (10) 353.20 490.50
Nos. 1-3, 6-9 on overfranked philatelic cover 160.00

No. 9 Surcharged Like Calchi No. 11

1916 Perf. 13½
11 A58 20c on 15c slate 1.60 40.00
Never hinged 4.00
On cover 200.00

Ferrucci Issue
Types of Italy
Overprinted in Red or Blue

1930 Wmk. 140 Perf. 14
12 A102 20c violet (R) 4.00 9.50
Never hinged 10.00
On cover 140.00
13 A103 25c dk grn (R) 4.00 9.50
Never hinged 10.00
On cover 190.00
14 A103 50c black (R) 4.00 16.00
Never hinged 10.00
On cover 125.00
15 A103 1.25 l dp bl (R) 4.00 16.00
Never hinged 10.00
On cover 300.00
16 A104 5 l + 2 l dp car (Bl) 11.00 27.50
Never hinged 27.50
On cover —
Nos. 12-16 (5) 27.00 78.50
Set on overfranked philatelic cover 140.00

Garibaldi Issue
Types of Italy
Overprinted in Red or Blue

1932
17 A138 10c brown 19.00 35.00
Never hinged 47.50
On cover 250.00
18 A138 20c red brn (Bl) 19.00 35.00
Never hinged 47.50
On cover 160.00
19 A138 25c dp grn 19.00 35.00
Never hinged 47.50
On cover 160.00
20 A138 30c bluish sl 19.00 35.00
Never hinged 47.50
On cover 240.00
21 A138 50c red vio (Bl) 19.00 35.00
Never hinged 47.50
On cover 125.00
22 A141 75c cop red (Bl) 19.00 35.00
Never hinged 47.50
On cover 350.00
23 A141 1.25 l dull blue 19.00 35.00
Never hinged 47.50
On cover 550.00
24 A141 1.75 l + 25c brn 19.00 35.00
Never hinged 47.50
On cover —
25 A144 2.55 l + 50c org (Bl) 19.00 35.00
Never hinged 47.50
On cover —
26 A145 5 l + 1 l dl vio 19.00 35.00
Never hinged 47.50
On cover —
Nos. 17-26 (10) 190.00 350.00
Set on overfranked philatelic cover 650.00

PATMO

Overprinted "Patmos" in Black or Violet

1912-22 Wmk. 140 Perf. 13½, 14
1 A43 2c orange brn 8.00 9.50
Never hinged 20.00
On cover 110.00
2 A48 5c green 4.75 9.50
Never hinged 12.00
On cover 65.00
3 A48 10c claret 3.25 9.50
Never hinged 8.00
On cover 65.00
4 A48 15c slate ('22) 4.75 52.50
Never hinged 12.00
On cover 350.00
5 A50 20c brn org ('21) 175.00 225.00
Never hinged 450.00
On cover 650.00
6 A49 25c blue 1.60 9.50
Never hinged 4.00
On cover 110.00
7 A49 40c brown 4.00 9.50
Never hinged 10.00
On cover 240.00
8 A49 50c violet 1.60 19.00
Never hinged 4.00
On cover 275.00

Unwmk.
9 A58 15c slate (V) 47.50 19.00
Never hinged 120.00
On cover 180.00
10 A50 20c brn org ('17) 95.00 225.00
Never hinged 240.00
On cover 650.00
Nos. 1-10 (10) 345.45 588.00
Nos. 1-3, 6-9 on overfranked philatelic cover 140.00

No. 9 Surcharged Like Calchi No. 11

1916 Perf. 13½
11 A58 20c on 15c slate 19.00 40.00
Never hinged 47.50
On cover 200.00

Ferrucci Issue
Types of Italy
Overprinted in Red or Blue

1930 Wmk. 140 Perf. 14
12 A102 20c violet (R) 4.00 9.50
Never hinged 10.00
On cover 140.00
13 A103 25c dk green (R) 4.00 9.50
Never hinged 10.00
On cover 190.00
14 A103 50c black (R) 4.00 16.00
Never hinged 10.00
On cover 125.00
15 A103 1.25 l dp bl (R) 4.00 16.00
Never hinged 10.00
On cover 300.00
16 A104 5 l + 2 l dp car (Bl) 11.00 29.00
Never hinged 27.50
On cover —
Nos. 12-16 (5) 27.00 80.00
Set on overfranked philatelic cover 140.00

Garibaldi Issue
Types of Italy
Overprinted in Red or Blue

1932
17 A138 10c brown 19.00 35.00
Never hinged 47.50
On cover 250.00
18 A138 20c red brn (Bl) 19.00 35.00
Never hinged 47.50
On cover 160.00
19 A138 25c dp grn 19.00 35.00
Never hinged 47.50
On cover 160.00
20 A138 30c bluish sl 19.00 35.00
Never hinged 47.50
On cover 240.00

21 A138 50c red vio (Bl) 19.00 *35.00*
Never hinged 47.50
On cover 125.00
22 A141 75c cop red (Bl) 19.00 *35.00*
Never hinged 47.50
On cover 350.00
23 A141 1.25 l dull blue 19.00 *35.00*
Never hinged 47.50
On cover 550.00
24 A141 1.75 l + 25c brn 19.00 *35.00*
Never hinged 47.50
On cover —
25 A144 2.55 l + 50c org (Bl) 19.00 *35.00*
Never hinged 47.50
On cover —
26 A145 5 l + 1 l dl vio 19.00 *35.00*
Never hinged 47.50
On cover —
Nos. 17-26 (10) 190.00 *350.00*
Set on overfranked philatelic cover 650.00

PISCOPI

Overprinted "Piscopi" in Black or Violet

1912-21 Wmk. 140 *Perf. 13½, 14*
1 A43 2c orange brn 8.00 9.50
Never hinged 20.00
On cover 110.00
2 A48 5c green 4.75 *9.50*
Never hinged 12.00
On cover 65.00
3 A48 10c claret 1.60 *9.50*
Never hinged 4.00
On cover 180.00
4 A48 15c slate ('21) 19.00 *52.50*
Never hinged 47.50
On cover 350.00
5 A50 20c brn org ('21) 65.00 *72.50*
Never hinged 160.00
On cover 575.00
6 A49 25c blue 1.60 *9.50*
Never hinged 4.00
On cover 110.00
7 A49 40c brown 1.60 *9.50*
Never hinged 4.00
On cover 240.00
8 A49 50c violet 1.60 *19.00*
Never hinged 4.00
On cover 275.00

Unwmk.
9 A58 15c slate (V) 47.50 19.00
Never hinged 120.00
On cover 180.00
10 A50 20c brn org ('17) 95.00 *225.00*
Never hinged 240.00
On cover 650.00
Nos. 1-10 (10) 245.65 *435.50*
Nos. 1-3, 6-9 on overfranked philatelic cover 160.00

No. 9 Surcharged Like Calchi No. 11

1916 *Perf. 13½*
11 A58 20c on 15c slate 1.60 *40.00*
Never hinged 4.00
On cover 200.00

Ferrucci Issue
Types of Italy
Overprinted in Red or Blue

1930 Wmk. 140 *Perf. 14*
12 A102 20c violet (R) 4.00 *9.50*
Never hinged 10.00
On cover 140.00
13 A103 25c dk green (R) 4.00 *9.50*
Never hinged 10.00
On cover 190.00
14 A103 50c black (R) 4.00 *16.00*
Never hinged 10.00
On cover 125.00
15 A103 1.25 l dp bl (R) 4.00 *16.00*
Never hinged 10.00
On cover 300.00
16 A104 5 l + 2 l dp car (Bl) 11.00 *29.00*
Never hinged 27.50
On cover —
Nos. 12-16 (5) 27.00 *80.00*
Set on overfranked philatelic cover 140.00

Garibaldi Issue
Types of Italy
Overprinted in Red or Blue

1932
17 A138 10c brown 19.00 *35.00*
Never hinged 47.50
On cover 250.00
18 A138 20c red brn (Bl) 19.00 *35.00*
Never hinged 47.50
On cover 160.00
19 A138 25c dp grn 19.00 *35.00*
Never hinged 47.50
On cover 160.00
20 A138 30c bluish sl 19.00 *35.00*
Never hinged 47.50
On cover 240.00
21 A138 50c red vio (Bl) 19.00 *35.00*
Never hinged 47.50
On cover 125.00
22 A141 75c cop red (Bl) 19.00 *35.00*
Never hinged 47.50
On cover 350.00
23 A141 1.25 l dull blue 19.00 *35.00*
Never hinged 47.50
On cover 550.00
24 A141 1.75 l + 25c brn 19.00 *35.00*
Never hinged 47.50
On cover —
25 A144 2.55 l + 50c org (Bl) 19.00 *35.00*
Never hinged 47.50
On cover —
26 A145 5 l + 1 l dl vio 19.00 *35.00*
Never hinged 47.50
On cover —
Nos. 17-26 (10) 190.00 *350.00*
Set on overfranked philatelic cover 650.00

RHODES

(Rodi)
Overprinted "Rodi" in Black or Violet

1912-24 Wmk. 140 *Perf. 13½, 14*
1 A43 2c org brn 1.60 *9.50*
Never hinged 4.00
On cover 87.50
2 A48 5c green 4.75 *9.50*
Never hinged 12.00
On cover 52.50
a. Double overprint 400.00 *600.00*
3 A48 10c claret 1.60 *9.50*
Never hinged 4.00
On cover 52.50
4 A48 15c slate ('21) 175.00 72.50
Never hinged 450.00
On cover 500.00
5 A45 20c org ('16) 3.25 *8.00*
Never hinged 8.00
On cover 160.00
6 A50 20c brn org ('19) 6.50 *20.00*
Never hinged 16.00
On cover 240.00
a. Double overprint 87.50
7 A49 25c blue 4.75 *9.50*
Never hinged 12.00
On cover 110.00
8 A49 40c brown 6.50 *9.50*
Never hinged 16.00
On cover 240.00
9 A49 50c violet 1.60 *19.00*
Never hinged 4.00
On cover 275.00
10 A49 85c red brn ('22) 87.50 *125.00*
Never hinged 225.00
On cover 375.00
11 A46 1 l brn & grn ('24) 3.25
Never hinged 8.00

No. 11 was not regularly issued.

Unwmk.
12 A58 15c slate (V) 47.50 19.00
Never hinged 120.00
On cover 180.00
13 A50 20c brn org ('17) 240.00 225.00
Never hinged 600.00
On cover 650.00
Nos. 1-13 (13) 583.80 536.00
Nos. 1-3, 7-9, 12 on overfranked philatelic cover *160.00*

No. 12 Surcharged Like Calchi No. 11

1916 *Perf. 13½*
14 A58 20c on 15c slate 140.00 *175.00*
Never hinged 350.00
On cover 350.00

Windmill, Rhodes — A1

Medieval Galley — A2

Christian Knight — A3

Crusader Kneeling in Prayer — A4

Crusader's Tomb — A5

No Imprint

1929 Unwmk. Litho. *Perf. 11*
15 A1 5c magenta 11.00 2.40
Never hinged 27.50
On cover 52.50
16 A2 10c olive brn 11.00 1.60
Never hinged 27.50
On cover 20.00
17 A3 20c rose red 11.00 .80
Never hinged 27.50
On cover 14.00
18 A3 25c green 11.00 .80
Never hinged 27.50
On cover 14.00
19 A4 30c dk blue 72.50 2.40
Never hinged 180.00
On cover 40.00
20 A5 50c dk brown 11.00 .80
Never hinged 27.50
On cover 9.50
21 A5 1.25 l dk blue 11.00 2.40
Never hinged 27.50
On cover 60.00
22 A4 5 l magenta 80.00 *140.00*
Never hinged 200.00
On cover 1,400.
23 A4 10 l olive brn 240.00 *340.00*
Never hinged 600.00
On cover 4,200.
Nos. 15-23 (9) 458.50 *491.20*
Set on overfranked philatelic cover *1,900.*

Visit of the King and Queen of Italy to the Aegean Islands. The stamps are inscribed "Rodi" but were available for use in all the Aegean Islands.

Nos. 15-23 and C1-C4 were used in eastern Crete in 1941-42 with Greek postmarks.

See Nos. 55-63. For surcharges and overprints see Nos. 29-44, B1-B18, E3-E4.

Ferrucci Issue
Overprinted in Red or Blue

1930 Wmk. 140 *Perf. 14*
24 A102 20c violet (R) 4.00 *9.50*
Never hinged 10.00
On cover 140.00
25 A103 25c dk green (R) 4.00 *9.50*
Never hinged 10.00
On cover 190.00
26 A103 50c black (R) 4.00 *16.00*
Never hinged 10.00
On cover 125.00
27 A103 1.25 l dp blue (R) 4.00 *16.00*
Never hinged 10.00
On cover 300.00
28 A104 5 l + 2 l dp car (Bl) 11.00 *29.00*
Never hinged 27.50
On cover —
Nos. 24-28 (5) 27.00 *80.00*
Set on overfranked philatelic cover *140.00*

Hydrological Congress Issue

Rhodes Issue of 1929 Overprinted

1930 Unwmk. *Perf. 11*
29 A1 5c magenta 65.00 55.00
Never hinged 160.00
On cover 525.00
30 A2 10c olive brn 65.00 55.00
Never hinged 160.00
On cover 450.00
31 A3 20c rose red 72.50 55.00
Never hinged 180.00
On cover 450.00
32 A3 25c green 80.00 55.00
Never hinged 200.00
On cover 525.00
33 A4 30c dk blue 65.00 55.00
Never hinged 160.00
On cover 525.00
34 A5 50c dk brown 600.00 95.00
Never hinged 1,500.
On cover 400.00
35 A5 1.25 l dk blue 450.00 140.00
Never hinged 1,100.
On cover 725.00
36 A4 5 l magenta 400.00 *600.00*
Never hinged 1,000.
On cover —
37 A4 10 l olive grn 400.00 *650.00*
Never hinged 1,000.
On cover —
Nos. 29-37 (9) 2,198. *1,760.*
Set on overfranked philatelic cover *3,250.*

Rhodes Issue of 1929 Overprinted in Blue or Red

1931
38 A1 5c mag (Bl) 9.50 *22.50*
Never hinged 24.00
On cover 260.00
39 A2 10c ol brn (R) 9.50 *22.50*
Never hinged 24.00
On cover 225.00
40 A3 20c rose red (Bl) 9.50 *37.50*
Never hinged 24.00
On cover 225.00
41 A3 25c green (R) 9.50 *37.50*
Never hinged 24.00
On cover 260.00
42 A4 30c dk blue (R) 9.50 *37.50*
Never hinged 24.00
On cover 325.00
43 A5 50c dk brown (R) 65.00 *87.50*
Never hinged 160.00
On cover 340.00
44 A5 1.25 l dk bl (R) 55.00 *125.00*
Never hinged 140.00
On cover 600.00
Nos. 38-44 (7) 167.50 370.00
Set on overfranked philatelic cover 725.00

Italian Eucharistic Congress, 1931.

Garibaldi Issue
Types of Italy
Overprinted in Red or Blue

1932 Wmk. 140 *Perf. 14*
45 A138 10c brown 19.00 *35.00*
Never hinged 47.50
On cover 250.00
46 A138 20c red brn (Bl) 19.00 *35.00*
Never hinged 47.50
On cover 240.00
47 A138 25c dp grn 19.00 *35.00*
Never hinged 47.50
On cover 160.00
48 A138 30c bluish sl 19.00 *35.00*
Never hinged 47.50
On cover 240.00
49 A138 50c red vio (Bl) 19.00 *35.00*
Never hinged 47.50
On cover 125.00
50 A141 75c cop red (Bl) 19.00 *35.00*
Never hinged 47.50
On cover 350.00
51 A141 1.25 l dl bl 19.00 *35.00*
Never hinged 47.50
On cover 550.00
52 A141 1.75 l + 25c brn 19.00 *35.00*
Never hinged 47.50
On cover —
53 A144 2.55 l + 50c org (Bl) 19.00 *35.00*
Never hinged 47.50
On cover —
54 A145 5 l + 1 l dl vio 19.00 *35.00*
Never hinged 47.50
On cover —
Nos. 45-54 (10) 190.00 *350.00*
Set on overfranked philatelic cover 650.00

Types of Rhodes Issue of 1929
Imprint: "Officina Carte-Valori Roma"

1932
55 A1 5c rose lake 1.60 .25
Never hinged 4.00
On cover 16.00
56 A2 10c dk brn 1.60 .25
Never hinged 4.00
On cover 6.00
57 A3 20c red 1.60 .25
Never hinged 4.00
On cover 4.00
58 A3 25c dl grn 1.60 .25
Never hinged 4.00
On cover 4.00
59 A4 30c dl bl 1.60 .25
Never hinged 4.00
On cover 4.00
60 A5 50c blk brn 1.60 .25
Never hinged 4.00
On cover 2.00
61 A5 1.25 l dp bl 1.60 .25
Never hinged 4.00
On cover 6.00
62 A4 5 l rose lake 1.60 2.25
Never hinged 2.40
On cover 600.00
63 A4 10 l ol brn 4.00 *4.75*
Never hinged 10.00
On cover 1,800.
Nos. 55-63 (9) 16.80 8.75

Aerial View of Rhodes A6

Map of Rhodes — A7

1932 Wmk. 140 Litho. *Perf. 11*

Shield in Red

64 A6 5c blk & grn 9.50 *24.00*
Never hinged 24.00
On cover 350.00
65 A6 10c blk & vio bl 9.50 *20.00*
Never hinged 24.00
On cover 225.00
66 A6 20c blk & dl yel 9.50 *20.00*
Never hinged 24.00
On cover 225.00
67 A6 25c lil & blk 9.50 *20.00*
Never hinged 24.00
On cover 260.00
68 A6 30c blk & pink 9.50 *20.00*
Never hinged 24.00
On cover 300.00

Shield and Map Dots in Red

69 A7 50c blk & gray 9.50 *20.00*
Never hinged 24.00
On cover 225.00
70 A7 1.25 l red brn & gray 9.50 *40.00*
Never hinged 24.00
On cover 450.00
71 A7 5 l dk bl & gray 24.00 *100.00*
Never hinged 60.00
On cover —
72 A7 10 l dk grn & gray 65.00 *180.00*
Never hinged 160.00
On cover —
73 A7 25 l choc & gray 250.00 *1,200.*
Never hinged 625.00
On cover —
Nos. 64-73 (10) 405.50 *1,644.*
Set on overfranked philatelic cover *3,250.*

20th anniv. of the Italian occupation and 10th anniv. of Fascist rule.

Deer and Palm — A8

1935, Apr. Photo. Wmk. 140

74 A8 5c orange 27.50 *35.00*
Never hinged 67.50
On cover 450.00
75 A8 10c brown 27.50 *35.00*
Never hinged 67.50
On cover 250.00
76 A8 20c car rose 27.50 *45.00*
Never hinged 67.50
On cover 275.00
77 A8 25c green 27.50 *45.00*
Never hinged 67.50
On cover 300.00
78 A8 30c purple 27.50 *52.50*
Never hinged 67.50
On cover 325.00
79 A8 50c red brn 27.50 *52.50*
Never hinged 67.50
On cover 250.00
80 A8 1.25l blue 27.50 *120.00*
Never hinged 67.50
On cover 475.00
81 A8 5 l yellow 240.00 *450.00*
Never hinged 600.00
On cover —
Nos. 74-81 (8) 432.50 *835.00*
Set on overfranked philatelic cover 1,200.

Holy Year.

RHODES AIR POST STAMPS

Symbolical of Flight — AP18

Wmk. 140 Upright

1934 Typo. *Perf. 14¼*

C1 AP18 50c blk & yel .80 .40
Never hinged 2.00
On cover 2.40
C2 AP18 80c blk & mag 3.25 *4.00*
Never hinged 8.00
On cover 87.50
C3 AP18 1 l blk & grn 1.60 .40
Never hinged 4.00
On cover 4.00
C4 AP18 5 l blk & red vio 19.00 *9.50*
Never hinged 47.50
On cover 350.00
Nos. C1-C4 (4) 24.65 *14.30*

Wmk. 140 Sideways

1937-38 Typo. *Perf. 14*

C1a AP18 50c blk & yel — .40
Never hinged —
On cover 2.40
C2a AP18 80c blk & mag .80 *2.40*
Never hinged 2.00
On cover 80.00
C3a AP18 1 l blk & grn .80 .40
Never hinged 2.00
On cover 4.00
C4a AP18 5 l blk & red vio 1.60 *4.75*
Never hinged 4.00
On cover 350.00
Nos. C1a-C4a (4) 3.20 *7.95*

RHODES SPECIAL DELIVERY STAMPS

Stag — SD1

1936 Photo. Wmk. 140 *Perf. 14*

E1 SD1 1.25 l green 4.75 4.75
Never hinged 12.00
On cover 200.00
E2 SD1 2.50 l vermilion 8.00 8.00
Never hinged 20.00
On cover 650.00

RHODES POSTAGE DUE STAMPS

Maltese Cross PD1

Immortelle PD2

1934 Photo. Wmk. 140 *Perf. 13*

J1 PD1 5c vermilion 4.75 8.00
Never hinged 12.00
On cover *475.00*
J2 PD1 10c carmine 4.75 8.00
Never hinged 12.00
On cover 300.00
J3 PD1 20c dk grn 4.75 6.50
Never hinged 12.00
On cover 300.00
J4 PD1 30c purple 4.75 6.50
Never hinged 12.00
On cover 300.00
J5 PD1 40c dk bl 4.75 12.50
Never hinged 12.00
On cover *475.00*
J6 PD2 50c vermilion 4.75 6.50
Never hinged 12.00
On cover 210.00
J7 PD2 60c carmine 4.75 24.00
Never hinged 12.00
On cover *475.00*
J8 PD2 1 l dk grn 4.75 24.00
Never hinged 12.00
On cover *400.00*
J9 PD2 2 l purple 4.75 12.50
Never hinged 12.00
On cover *525.00*
Nos. J1-J9 (9) 42.75 108.50

RHODES PARCEL POST STAMPS

Both unused and used values are for complete stamps.

PP1

PP2

1934 Photo. Wmk. 140 *Perf. 13*

Q1 PP1 5c vermilion 6.50 12.00
Never hinged 16.00
Q2 PP1 10c carmine 6.50 12.00
Never hinged 16.00
Q3 PP1 20c dk green 6.50 12.00
Never hinged 16.00
Q4 PP1 25c purple 6.50 12.00
Never hinged 16.00
Q5 PP1 50c dk blue 6.50 12.00
Never hinged 16.00
Q6 PP1 60c black 6.50 12.00
Never hinged 16.00
Q7 PP2 1 l vermilion 6.50 12.00
Never hinged 16.00
Q8 PP2 2 l carmine 6.50 12.00
Never hinged 16.00
Q9 PP2 3 l dk green 6.50 12.00
Never hinged 16.00
Q10 PP2 4 l purple 6.50 12.00
Never hinged 16.00
Q11 PP2 10 l dk blue 6.50 12.00
Never hinged 16.00
Nos. Q1-Q11 (11) 71.50 132.00

Value of used halves, Nos. Q1-Q11, each 80 cents.

See note preceding No. Q7 of Italy.

SCARPANTO

Overprinted "Scarpanto" in Black or Violet

1912-22 Wmk. 140 *Perf. 13½, 14*

1 A43 2c org brn 9.50 9.50
Never hinged 24.00
On cover 110.00
2 A48 5c green 3.25 *9.50*
Never hinged 8.00
On cover 65.00
3 A48 10c claret 1.60 *9.50*
Never hinged 4.00
On cover 65.00
4 A48 15c slate ('22) 19.00 *40.00*
Never hinged 47.50
On cover 400.00
5 A50 20c brn org ('21) 65.00 65.00
Never hinged 160.00
On cover 450.00
6 A49 25c blue 9.50 9.50
Never hinged 24.00
On cover 110.00
7 A49 40c brown 1.60 *9.50*
Never hinged 4.00
On cover 240.00
8 A49 50c violet 3.25 *19.00*
Never hinged 8.00
On cover 275.00

Unwmk.

9 A58 15c slate (V) 40.00 19.00
Never hinged 100.00
On cover 180.00
10 A50 20c brn org ('17) 140.00 *225.00*
Never hinged 350.00
On cover 650.00
Nos. 1-10 (10) 292.70 *415.50*
Nos. 1-3, 6-9 on overfranked philatelic cover 160.00

No 9 Surcharged Like Calchi No. 11

1916 *Perf. 13½*

11 A58 20c on 15c slate 1.60 *40.00*
Never hinged 4.00
On cover 200.00

Ferrucci Issue

Types of Italy

Overprinted in Red or Blue

1930 Wmk. 140 *Perf. 14*

12 A102 20c violet (R) 4.00 *9.50*
Never hinged 10.00
On cover 140.00
13 A103 25c dk green (R) 4.00 *9.50*
Never hinged 10.00
On cover 190.00
14 A103 50c black (R) 4.00 *16.00*
Never hinged 10.00
On cover 120.00
15 A103 1.25 l dp bl (R) 4.00 *16.00*
Never hinged 10.00
On cover 300.00
16 A104 5 l + 2 l dp car (Bl) 11.00 *27.50*
Never hinged 27.50
On cover —
Nos. 12-16 (5) 27.00 *78.50*
Set on overfranked philatelic cover 140.00

Garibaldi Issue

Types of Italy

Overprinted in Red or Blue

1932

17 A138 10c brown 19.00 *35.00*
Never hinged 47.50
On cover 250.00
18 A138 20c red brn (Bl) 19.00 *35.00*
Never hinged 47.50
On cover 160.00
19 A138 25c dp grn 19.00 *35.00*
Never hinged 47.50
On cover 160.00
20 A138 30c bluish sl 19.00 *35.00*
Never hinged 47.50
On cover 240.00
21 A138 50c red vio (Bl) 19.00 *35.00*
Never hinged 47.50
On cover 125.00
22 A141 75c cop red (Bl) 19.00 *35.00*
Never hinged 47.50
On cover 350.00
23 A141 1.25 l dull blue 19.00 *35.00*
Never hinged 47.50
On cover 550.00
24 A141 1.75 l + 25c brn 19.00 *35.00*
Never hinged 47.50
On cover —
25 A144 2.55 l + 50c org (Bl) 19.00 *35.00*
Never hinged 47.50
On cover —
26 A145 5 l + 1 l dl vio 19.00 *35.00*
Never hinged 47.50
On cover —
Nos. 17-26 (10) 190.00 *350.00*
Set on overfranked philatelic cover 650.00

SIMI

Overprinted "Simi" in Black or Violet

1912-21 Wmk. 140 *Perf. 13½, 14*

1 A43 2c org brn 16.00 9.50
Never hinged 40.00
On cover 110.00
2 A48 5c green 40.00 9.50
Never hinged 100.00
On cover 65.00
3 A48 10c claret 1.60 *9.50*
Never hinged 4.00
On cover 65.00
4 A48 15c slate ('21) 140.00 72.50
Never hinged 350.00
On cover 450.00
5 A50 20c brn org ('21) 72.50 40.00
Never hinged 180.00
On cover 400.00
6 A49 25c blue 9.50 *9.50*
Never hinged 24.00
On cover 110.00
7 A49 40c brown 1.60 *9.50*
Never hinged 4.00
On cover 240.00
8 A49 50c violet 1.60 *19.00*
Never hinged 4.00
On cover 275.00

Unwmk.

9 A58 15c slate (V) 72.00 19.00
Never hinged 180.00
On cover 180.00
10 A50 20c brn org ('17) 72.50 *125.00*
Never hinged 180.00
On cover 525.00
Nos. 1-10 (10) 427.30 *323.00*
Nos. 1-3, 6-9 on overfranked philatelic cover 160.00

No. 9 Surcharged Like Calchi No. 11

1916 *Perf. 13½*

11 A58 20c on 15c slate 9.50 *40.00*
Never hinged 24.00
On cover 200.00

Ferrucci Issue

Types of Italy

Overprinted in Red or Blue

1930 Wmk. 140 *Perf. 14*

12 A102 20c violet (R) 4.75 *9.50*
Never hinged 12.00
On cover 140.00
13 A103 25c dk green (R) 4.75 *9.50*
Never hinged 12.00
On cover 190.00
14 A103 50c black (R) 4.75 *16.00*
Never hinged 12.00
On cover 125.00
15 A103 1.25 l dp bl (R) 4.75 *16.00*
Never hinged 12.00
On cover 300.00
16 A104 5 l + 2 l dp car (Bl) 11.00 *27.50*
Never hinged 27.50
On cover —
Nos. 12-16 (5) 30.00 *78.50*
Set on overfranked philatelic cover 140.00

Garibaldi Issue

Types of Italy

Overprinted in Red or Blue

1932

17 A138 10c brown 19.00 *35.00*
Never hinged 47.50
On cover 250.00
18 A138 20c red brn (Bl) 19.00 *35.00*
Never hinged 47.50
On cover 160.00
19 A138 25c dp grn 19.00 *35.00*
Never hinged 47.50
On cover 160.00
20 A138 30c bluish sl 19.00 *35.00*
Never hinged 47.50
On cover 240.00
21 A138 50c red vio (Bl) 19.00 *35.00*
Never hinged 47.50
On cover 125.00
22 A141 75c cop red (Bl) 19.00 *35.00*
Never hinged 47.50
On cover 350.00
23 A141 1.25 l dull blue 19.00 *35.00*
Never hinged 47.50
On cover 550.00
24 A141 1.75 l + 25c brn 19.00 *35.00*
Never hinged 47.50
On cover —
25 A144 2.55 l + 50c org (Bl) 19.00 *35.00*
Never hinged 47.50
On cover —

26 A145 5 l + 1 l dl vio 19.00 35.00
Never hinged 47.50
On cover —
Nos. 17-26 (10) 190.00 350.00
Set on overfranked philatelic cover 650.00

STAMPALIA

Overprinted "Stampalia" in Black or Violet

1912-21 Wmk. 140 *Perf. 13½, 14*

1 A43 2c org brn 9.50 9.50
Never hinged 24.00
On cover 110.00
2 A48 5c green 1.60 9.50
Never hinged 4.00
On cover 65.00
3 A48 10c claret 1.60 9.50
Never hinged 4.00
On cover 65.00
4 A48 15c slate ('21) 11.00 40.00
Never hinged 27.50
On cover 400.00
5 A50 20c brn org ('21) 55.00 72.50
Never hinged 140.00
On cover 500.00
6 A49 25c blue 1.60 9.50
Never hinged 4.00
On cover 110.00
7 A49 40c brown 4.75 9.50
Never hinged 12.00
On cover 240.00
8 A49 50c violet 1.60 19.00
Never hinged 4.00
On cover 275.00

Unwmk.

9 A58 15c slate (V) 47.50 19.00
Never hinged 120.00
On cover 180.00
10 A50 20c brn org ('17) 95.00 125.00
Never hinged 240.00
On cover 525.00
Nos. 1-10 (10) 229.15 323.00
Nos. 1-3, 6-9 on overfranked philatelic cover 140.00

No. 9 Surcharged Like Calchi No. 11

1916 *Perf. 13½*

11 A58 20c on 15c slate 1.60 40.00
Never hinged 4.00
On cover 200.00

Ferrucci Issue

Types of Italy
Overprinted in Red or Blue

1930 Wmk. 140 *Perf. 14*

12 A102 20c violet (R) 4.00 9.50
Never hinged 10.00
On cover 140.00
13 A103 25c dk green (R) 4.00 9.50
Never hinged 10.00
On cover 190.00
14 A103 50c black (R) 4.00 16.00
Never hinged 10.00
On cover 125.00
15 A103 1.25 l dp bl (R) 4.00 16.00
Never hinged 10.00
On cover 300.00
16 A104 5 l + 2 l dp car (Bl) 11.00 27.50
Never hinged 27.50
On cover —
Nos. 12-16 (5) 27.00 78.50
Set on overfranked philatelic cover 140.00

Garibaldi Issue

Types of Italy
Overprinted in Red or Blue

1932

17 A138 10c brown 19.00 35.00
Never hinged 47.50
On cover 250.00
18 A138 20c red brn (Bl) 19.00 35.00
Never hinged 47.50
On cover 160.00
19 A138 25c dp grn 19.00 35.00
Never hinged 47.50
On cover 160.00
20 A138 30c bluish sl 19.00 35.00
Never hinged 47.50
On cover 240.00
21 A138 50c red vio (Bl) 19.00 35.00
Never hinged 47.50
On cover 125.00
22 A141 75c cop red (Bl) 19.00 35.00
Never hinged 47.50
On cover 350.00
23 A141 1.25 l dull blue 19.00 35.00
Never hinged 47.50
On cover 550.00
24 A141 1.75 l + 25c brn 19.00 35.00
Never hinged 47.50
On cover —
25 A144 2.55 l + 50c org (Bl) 19.00 35.00
Never hinged 47.50
On cover —
26 A145 5 l + 1 l dl vio 19.00 35.00
Never hinged 47.50
On cover —
Nos. 17-26 (10) 190.00 350.00
Set on overfranked philatelic cover 650.00

IVORY COAST

'iv-rē 'kōst

LOCATION — West coast of Africa, bordering on Gulf of Guinea
GOVT. — French Colony
AREA — 127,520 sq. mi.
POP. — 13,107,000 (est. 1991)
CAPITAL — Yamoussoukro

100 Centimes = 1 Franc

Navigation and Commerce — A1

Perf. 14x13½

1892-1900 Typo. Unwmk.

Colony Name in Blue or Carmine

1 A1 1c black, *lil bl* 2.25 2.25
Never hinged 3.25
On cover 105.00
2 A1 2c brown, *buff* 3.75 3.00
Never hinged 5.00
On cover 105.00
3 A1 4c claret, *lav* 5.25 4.50
Never hinged 8.25
On cover 105.00
4 A1 5c green, *grnsh* 15.00 11.00
Never hinged 22.50
On cover 55.00
5 A1 10c black, *lavender* 20.00 15.00
Never hinged 35.00
On cover 50.00
6 A1 10c red ('00) 130.00 110.00
Never hinged 225.00
On cover 425.00
7 A1 15c blue, quadrille paper 32.50 13.50
Never hinged 60.00
On cover 55.00
8 A1 15c gray ('00) 20.00 5.75
Never hinged 35.00
On cover 42.50
9 A1 20c red, *green* 21.00 16.00
Never hinged 40.00
On cover 92.50
On cover, single franking 160.00
10 A1 25c black, *rose* 24.00 7.50
Never hinged 45.00
On cover 42.50
11 A1 25c blue ('00) 40.00 37.50
Never hinged 75.00
On cover 190.00
12 A1 30c brown, *bister* 35.00 27.50
Never hinged 72.50
On cover 92.50
On cover, single franking 140.00
13 A1 40c red, *straw* 30.00 16.00
Never hinged 50.00
On cover 87.50
On cover, single franking 125.00
14 A1 50c car, *rose* 75.00 65.00
Never hinged 150.00
On cover 210.00
On cover, single franking 275.00
15 A1 50c brn, *azure* ('00) 37.50 32.50
Never hinged 75.00
On cover 300.00
On cover, single franking 400.00
16 A1 75c deep vio, *org* 32.50 32.50
Never hinged 65.00
On cover 340.00
On cover, single franking 500.00
17 A1 1fr brnz grn, *straw* 52.50 45.00
Never hinged 105.00
On cover 350.00
On cover, single franking 550.00
Nos. 1-17 (17) 576.25 444.50

Perf. 13½x14 stamps are counterfeits.
For surcharges see Nos. 18-20, 37-41.

Nos. 12, 16-17 Surcharged in Black

1904

18 A1 0,05c on 30c brn, *bis* 87.50 87.50
Never hinged 175.00
On cover 500.00
19 A1 0,10c on 75c vio, *org* 18.00 18.00
Never hinged 32.50
On cover 210.00
20 A1 0,15c on 1fr brnz grn, *straw* 26.00 26.00
Never hinged 45.00
On cover 225.00
Nos. 18-20 (3) 131.50 131.50

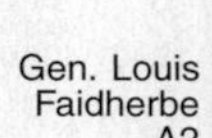

Gen. Louis Faidherbe A2

Oil Palm — A3

Dr. N. Eugène Ballay A4

1906-07

Name of Colony in Red or Blue

21 A2 1c slate 2.00 2.00
Never hinged 3.25
On cover 67.50
a. "CÔTE D'IVOIRE" omitted 160.00 160.00
22 A2 2c chocolate 2.00 2.00
Never hinged 3.25
On cover 67.50
23 A2 4c choc, *gray bl* 2.40 2.40
Never hinged 3.75
On cover 67.50
a. "CÔTE D'IVOIRE" double 225.00
b. "CÔTE D'IVOIRE" omitted 190.00
24 A2 5c green 4.00 2.75
Never hinged 8.00
On cover 42.50
a. "CÔTE D'IVOIRE" omitted 110.00 92.50
25 A2 10c carmine (B) 9.50 6.50
Never hinged 19.00
On cover 27.50
a. "CÔTE D'IVOIRE" double 210.00 400.00
b. "CÔTE D'IVOIRE" omitted 400.00
26 A3 20c black, *azure* 11.00 9.50
Never hinged 20.00
On cover 42.50
27 A3 25c bl, *pinkish* 9.50 6.00
Never hinged 20.00
On cover 42.50
28 A3 30c choc, *pnksh* 15.00 8.75
Never hinged 25.00
On cover 42.50
On cover, single franking 75.00
30 A3 35c black, *yel* 15.00 5.75
Never hinged 25.00
On cover 42.50
On cover, single franking 62.50
a. "CÔTE D'IVOIRE" omitted 225.00
31 A3 45c choc, *grnsh* 18.00 12.50
Never hinged 35.00
On cover 92.50
On cover, single franking 125.00
32 A3 50c deep violet 16.00 12.50
Never hinged 35.00
On cover 67.50
On cover, single franking 110.00
33 A3 75c blue, *org* 16.00 12.50
Never hinged 35.00
On cover 100.00
On cover, single franking 225.00
34 A4 1fr black, *azure* 40.00 35.00
Never hinged 80.00
On cover 150.00
On cover, single franking 300.00
35 A4 2fr blue, *pink* 52.50 50.00
Never hinged 110.00
On cover 200.00
On cover, single franking 350.00
36 A4 5fr car, *straw* (B) 100.00 95.00
Never hinged 190.00
On cover 275.00
On cover, single franking 425.00
Nos. 21-36 (15) 312.90 263.15

Stamps of 1892-1900 Surcharged in Carmine or Black

1912

Spacing between figures of surcharge 1.5mm (5c), 2mm (10c)

37 A1 5c on 15c gray (C) 1.60 1.60
Never hinged 2.50
On cover 55.00
38 A1 5c on 30c brn, *bis* (C) 2.40 2.75
Never hinged 3.75
On cover 75.00
39 A1 10c on 40c red, *straw* 2.40 2.75
Never hinged 3.75
On cover 75.00
a. Pair, one without surcharge 75.00 75.00
40 A1 10c on 50c brn, *az* (C) 4.00 4.75
Never hinged 6.75
On cover 95.00
41 A1 10c on 75c dp vio, *org* 9.00 10.00
Never hinged 15.00
On cover 145.00
Nos. 37-41 (5) 19.40 21.85

Spacing between figures of surcharge 2.25mm (5c), 2.75mm (10c)

37a A1 5c on 15c gray (C) 13.50 13.50
Never hinged 22.50
38a A1 5c on 30c brn, *bis* (C) 19.00 19.00
Never hinged 30.00
39b A1 10c on 40c red, *straw* 60.00 60.00
Never hinged 125.00
40a A1 10c on 50c brn, *az* (C) 110.00 110.00
Never hinged 210.00
41a A1 10c on 75c dp vio, *org* 225.00 225.00
Never hinged —
Nos. 37a-41a (5) 427.50 427.50

River Scene A5

1913-35

42 A5 1c vio brn & vio .25 .25
Never hinged .75
On cover 55.00
43 A5 2c brown & blk .30 .25
Never hinged .75
On cover 55.00
44 A5 4c vio & vio brn .35 .30
Never hinged .75
On cover 55.00
45 A5 5c yel grn & bl grn 1.10 .50
Never hinged 1.60
On cover 22.50
a. Chalky paper 2.25 1.25
Never hinged 3.75
46 A5 5c choc & ol brn ('22) .35 .35
Never hinged .75
On cover 25.00
47 A5 10c red org & rose 2.00 .95
Never hinged 3.00
On cover 14.00
a. Chalky paper 2.50 1.60
Never hinged 4.50
48 A5 10c yel grn & bl grn ('22) .70 .70
Never hinged 1.40
On cover 42.50
49 A5 10c car rose, *bluish* ('26) .35 .35
Never hinged .75
On cover 42.50
50 A5 15c org & rose ('17) 1.10 .75
Never hinged 1.90
On cover 14.00
a. Chalky paper 1.50 .75
Never hinged 2.25
On cover 15.00
51 A5 20c black & gray .80 .55
Never hinged 1.50
On cover 25.00
52 A5 25c ultra & bl 11.00 6.50
Never hinged 19.00
On cover 37.50
On cover, single franking 67.50
a. Chalky paper 11.00 6.50
Never hinged 19.00
On cover 37.50
53 A5 25c blk & vio ('22) .75 .75
Never hinged 1.50
On cover 7.50
54 A5 30c choc & brn 2.40 2.00
Never hinged 3.50
On cover 30.00
On cover, single franking 75.00
55 A5 30c red org & rose ('22) 2.75 2.75
Never hinged 4.50
On cover 30.00
On cover, single franking 55.00
56 A5 30c lt bl & rose red ('26) .40 .40
Never hinged .75
On cover 10.00
a. Chalky paper 1.50 1.50
Never hinged 2.25
On cover 14.00
57 A5 30c dl grn & grn ('27) .80 .80
Never hinged 1.25
On cover 25.00
58 A5 35c vio & org 1.10 .80
Never hinged 1.50
On cover 37.50
On cover, single franking 75.00
a. Chalky paper 1.10 .90
Never hinged 1.90
On cover 37.50
59 A5 40c gray & bl grn 1.60 .80
Never hinged 2.40
On cover 42.50
On cover, single franking 92.50

No.	Type	Description	Unused	Used
60	A5	45c red org & choc	1.10	.80
		Never hinged	1.50	
		On cover		50.00
		On cover, single franking		110.00
61	A5	45c dp rose & mar ('34)	5.25	4.50
		Never hinged	11.00	
		On cover		55.00
62	A5	50c black & vio	5.00	3.50
		Never hinged	7.50	
		On cover		62.50
		On cover, single franking		125.00
63	A5	50c ultra & bl ('22)	2.25	2.25
		Never hinged	3.00	
		On cover		25.00
		On cover, single franking		55.00
64	A5	50c ol grn & bl ('25)	.80	.80
		Never hinged	1.10	
		On cover		7.50
65	A5	60c vio, *pnksh* ('25)	.80	.80
		Never hinged	1.10	
		On cover		25.00
		On cover, single franking		62.50
66	A5	65c car rose & ol grn ('26)	1.60	1.60
		Never hinged	2.40	
		On cover		14.00
		On cover, single franking		22.50
67	A5	75c brn & rose	1.10	.80
		Never hinged	1.50	
		On cover		42.50
		On cover, single franking		105.00
68	A5	75c ind & ultra ('34)	3.75	3.75
		Never hinged	6.00	
		On cover		32.50
69	A5	85c red vio & blk ('26)	1.60	1.60
		Never hinged	2.40	
		On cover		35.00
		On cover, single franking		92.50
70	A5	90c brn red & rose ('30)	11.00	11.00
		Never hinged	19.00	
		On cover		67.50
		On cover, single franking		165.00
71	A5	1fr org & black	1.10	1.00
		Never hinged	1.60	
		On cover		55.00
		On cover, single franking		140.00
72	A5	1.10fr dl grn & dk brn ('28)	7.50	7.50
		Never hinged	11.00	
		On cover		110.00
		On cover, single franking		275.00
73	A5	1.50fr lt bl & dp bl ('30)	7.50	7.50
		Never hinged	11.00	
		On cover		50.00
		On cover, single franking		140.00
74	A5	1.75fr lt ultra & mag ('35)	15.00	9.00
		Never hinged	22.50	
		On cover		62.50
		On cover, single franking		87.50
75	A5	2fr brn & blue	5.25	2.60
		Never hinged	9.75	
		On cover		67.50
		On cover, single franking		140.00
76	A5	3fr red vio ('30)	7.50	7.50
		Never hinged	11.00	
		On cover		87.50
		On cover, single franking		190.00
77	A5	5fr dk bl & choc	7.50	5.25
		Never hinged	15.00	
		On cover		87.50
		On cover, single franking		165.00
		Nos. 42-77 (36)	113.70	91.50

For surcharges see Nos. 78-91, B1.

Nos. 45, 47 and 52, pasted on cardboard and overprinted "Valeur d'echange" and value of basic stamp, were used as emergency currency in 1920.

Stamps and Type of 1913-34 Srchd.

1922-34

No.	Type	Description	Unused	Used
78	A5	50c on 45c dp rose & mar ('34)	4.00	2.75
		Never hinged	7.50	
		On cover		16.00
79	A5	50c on 75c indigo & ultra ('34)	3.00	2.00
		Never hinged	5.25	
		On cover		14.00
80	A5	50c on 90c brn red & rose ('34)	3.00	2.25
		Never hinged	5.25	
		On cover		14.00
81	A5	60c on 75c vio, *pnksh*	.75	.75
		Never hinged	1.00	
		On cover		16.00
		On cover, single franking		275.00
a.		Surcharge omitted	160.00	*175.00*
		Never hinged	225.00	
82	A5	65c on 15c org & rose ('25)	1.25	1.25
		Never hinged	1.75	
		On cover		55.00
		On cover, single franking		125.00
a.		Chalky paper (on #50a)	2.25	2.10
		Never hinged	3.75	
83	A5	85c on 75c brn & rose ('25)	1.40	1.10
		Never hinged	1.90	
		On cover		42.50
		On cover, single franking		80.00
		Nos. 78-83 (6)	13.40	10.10

Stamps and Type of 1913 Surcharged with New Value and Bars

1924-27

No.	Type	Description	Unused	Used
84	A5	25c on 2fr (R)	.35	1.00
		Never hinged	1.10	
		On cover		7.50
85	A5	25c on 5fr	.35	1.00
		Never hinged	1.10	
		On cover		7.50
86	A5	90c on 75c brn red & cer ('27)	2.00	1.60
		Never hinged	3.00	
		On cover		42.50
		On cover, single franking		80.00
a.		Surcharge omitted	240.00	
		Never hinged	325.00	
87	A5	1.25fr on 1fr dk bl & ultra (R) ('26)	1.25	1.25
		Never hinged	1.75	
		On cover		50.00
		On cover, single franking		92.50
88	A5	1.50fr on 1fr lt bl & dk blue ('27)	1.90	1.90
		Never hinged	2.25	
		On cover		37.50
		On cover, single franking		62.50
89	A5	3fr on 5fr brn red & bl grn ('27)	6.00	6.00
		Never hinged	9.00	
		On cover		67.50
		On cover, single franking		140.00
a.		Double surcharge	160.00	
90	A5	10fr on 5fr dl red & rose lil ('27)	19.00	16.00
		Never hinged	26.00	
		On cover		92.50
		On cover, single franking		190.00
91	A5	20fr on 5fr bl grn & ver ('27)	19.00	18.00
		Never hinged	30.00	
		On cover		105.00
		On cover, single franking		225.00
		Nos. 84-91 (8)	49.85	46.75

Common Design Types pictured following the introduction.

Colonial Exposition Issue

Common Design Types
Name of Country in Black

1931 **Engr.** ***Perf. 12½***

No.	Type	Description	Unused	Used
92	CD70	40c deep green	4.50	4.50
		Never hinged	6.75	
		On cover		87.50
93	CD71	50c violet	6.00	6.00
		Never hinged	9.00	
		On cover		75.00
94	CD72	90c red orange	6.00	6.00
		Never hinged	9.00	
		On cover		125.00
		On cover, single franking		190.00
95	CD73	1.50fr dull blue	6.00	6.00
		Never hinged	9.00	
		On cover		110.00
		On cover, single franking		165.00
		Nos. 92-95 (4)	22.50	22.50

Stamps of Upper Volta 1928, Overprinted

1933 ***Perf. 13½x14***

No.	Type	Description	Unused	Used
96	A5	2c brown & lilac	.25	.25
		Never hinged	.40	
		On cover		42.50
a.		Inverted overprint	27.50	
		Never hinged	40.00	
b.		Double overprint	40.00	47.50
		Never hinged	50.00	
		On cover		67.50
97	A5	4c blk & yellow	.25	.30
		Never hinged	.35	
		On cover		42.50
a.		Inverted overprint	100.00	
		Never hinged	150.00	
b.		Double overprint	65.00	72.50
		Never hinged	100.00	
		On cover		100.00
98	A5	5c ind & gray bl	.35	.45
		Never hinged	.75	
		On cover		37.50
a.		Inverted overprint	47.50	
		Never hinged	100.00	
b.		Double overprint	65.00	
		Never hinged	100.00	
99	A5	10c indigo & pink	.35	.45
		Never hinged	.75	
		On cover		30.00
100	A5	15c brown & blue	1.10	.90
		Never hinged	1.50	
		On cover		37.50
a.		Double overprint	65.00	
		Never hinged	90.00	
101	A5	20c brown & green	1.10	.90
		Never hinged	1.50	
		On cover		17.50
102	A6	25c brn & yellow	2.25	1.90
		Never hinged	3.75	
		On cover		42.50
103	A6	30c dp grn & grn	2.75	1.75
		Never hinged	3.75	
		On cover		50.00
a.		Double overprint	75.00	
		Never hinged	110.00	
104	A6	45c brown & blue	8.25	6.00
		Never hinged	11.00	
		On cover		62.50
a.		Inverted overprint	80.00	
		Never hinged	110.00	
b.		Double overprint	120.00	
		Never hinged	175.00	
105	A6	65c indigo & bl	3.00	2.60
		Never hinged	4.50	
		On cover		75.00
a.		Double overprint	95.00	
		Never hinged	150.00	
106	A6	75c black & lilac	3.75	2.25
		Never hinged	5.25	
		On cover		40.00
a.		Double overprint	95.00	
		Never hinged	150.00	
107	A6	90c brn red & lil	3.00	2.60
		Never hinged	4.50	
		On cover		75.00
		On cover, single franking		140.00

Burkina Faso Nos. 58 & 60 Ovptd.

No.	Type	Description	Unused	Used
108	A7	1fr brn & grn	3.75	3.00
		Never hinged	5.25	
		On cover		50.00
		On cover, single franking		67.50
a.		Inverted overprint	150.00	160.00
		Never hinged	200.00	
		On cover		260.00
109	A7	1.50fr ultra & grysh	3.75	3.00
		Never hinged	5.25	
		On cover		50.00
		On cover, single franking		110.00
a.		Inverted overprint	150.00	
		Never hinged	225.00	
b.		Double overprint	95.00	
		Never hinged	140.00	

Burkina Faso Nos. 52 & 54 Surcharged

No.	Type	Description	Unused	Used
110	A6	1.25fr on 40c blk & pink	2.25	2.25
		Never hinged	3.75	
		On cover		27.50
		On cover, single franking		67.50
a.		Double overprint	100.00	
		Never hinged	150.00	
111	A6	1.75fr on 50c blk & green	3.75	3.00
		Never hinged	6.00	
		On cover		27.50
		On cover, single franking		42.50
a.		Double overprint	100.00	
		Never hinged	150.00	
		Nos. 96-111 (16)	39.90	31.60

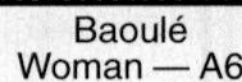

Baoulé Woman — A6

Rapids on Comoe River — A9

Mosque at Bobo-Dioulasso — A7

Coastal Scene A8

1936-44 ***Perf. 13***

No.	Type	Description	Unused	Used
112	A6	1c carmine rose	.25	.25
		Never hinged	.40	
		On cover		25.00
113	A6	2c ultramarine	.25	.25
		Never hinged	.40	
		On cover		25.00
114	A6	3c dp grn ('40)	.25	.25
		Never hinged	.40	
		On cover		25.00
115	A6	4c chocolate	.25	.25
		Never hinged	.40	
		On cover		25.00
116	A6	5c violet	.25	.25
		Never hinged	.40	
		On cover		21.00
117	A6	10c Prussian bl	.25	.25
		Never hinged	.40	
		On cover		19.00
118	A6	15c copper red	.25	.25
		Never hinged	.40	
		On cover		12.50
119	A7	20c ultramarine	.25	.25
		Never hinged	.40	
		On cover		12.50
120	A7	25c copper red	.25	.25
		Never hinged	.40	
		On cover		8.75
121	A7	30c blue green	.25	.25
		Never hinged	.40	
		On cover		19.00
122	A7	30c brown ('40)	.25	.25
		Never hinged	.40	
		On cover		7.50
123	A6	35c dp grn ('38)	.75	.75
		Never hinged	1.10	
		On cover		27.50
124	A7	40c carmine rose	.25	.25
		Never hinged	.75	
		On cover		7.50
125	A7	45c brown	.35	.35
		Never hinged	.75	
		On cover		25.00
126	A7	45c blue grn ('40)	.25	.25
		Never hinged	.40	
		On cover		19.00
127	A7	50c plum	.35	.35
		Never hinged	.75	
		On cover		6.25
128	A7	55c dark vio ('38)	.40	.75
		Never hinged	.75	
		On cover		8.75
129	A8	60c car rose ('40)	.25	.25
		Never hinged	.75	
		On cover		19.00
130	A8	65c red brown	.40	.40
		Never hinged	.75	
		On cover		45.00
131	A8	70c red brn ('40)	.40	.25
		Never hinged	.75	
		On cover		21.00
132	A8	75c dark violet	1.10	.75
		Never hinged	1.50	
		On cover		10.00
133	A8	80c blk brn ('38)	1.20	.75
		Never hinged	1.50	
		On cover		50.00
		On cover, single franking		87.50
134	A8	90c carmine rose	8.25	5.25
		Never hinged	11.00	
		On cover		30.00
		On cover, single franking		55.00
135	A8	90c dk grn ('39)	.75	.75
		Never hinged	1.10	
		On cover		35.00
		On cover, single franking		67.50
136	A8	1fr dark green	3.75	2.75
		Never hinged	5.25	
		On cover		15.00
		On cover, single franking		25.00
137	A8	1fr car rose ('38)	1.50	.75
		Never hinged	1.90	
		On cover		37.50
		On cover, single franking		67.50
138	A8	1fr dk vio ('40)	.35	.35
		Never hinged	.75	
		On cover		6.25
139	A8	1.25fr copper red	.35	.35
		Never hinged	.75	
		On cover		25.00
		On cover, single franking		37.50
140	A8	1.40fr ultra ('40)	.35	.35
		Never hinged	.75	
		On cover		30.00
		On cover, single franking		67.50
141	A8	1.50fr ultramarine	.35	.35
		Never hinged	.75	
		On cover		19.00
		On cover, single franking		32.50
141A	A8	1.50fr grnsh blk ('42)	1.90	1.50
		Never hinged	2.25	
		On cover		9.25
142	A8	1.60fr blk brn ('40)	.75	.75
		Never hinged	1.50	
		On cover		30.00
		On cover, single franking		80.00
143	A9	1.75fr carmine rose	.35	.35
		Never hinged	.75	
		On cover		10.00
		On cover, single franking		19.00
144	A9	1.75fr dull bl ('38)	1.50	.75
		Never hinged	2.25	
		On cover		37.50
		On cover, single franking		100.00
145	A9	2fr ultramarine	.75	.75
		Never hinged	1.10	
		On cover		19.00
		On cover, single franking		22.50
146	A9	2.25fr dark bl ('39)	1.10	1.10
		Never hinged	1.90	
		On cover		50.00
		On cover, single franking		92.50

147 A9 2.50fr rose red ('40) 1.10 1.10
Never hinged 1.90
On cover 27.50
On cover, single franking 50.00
148 A9 3fr green .75 .75
Never hinged 1.10
On cover 30.00
On cover, single franking 55.00
149 A9 5fr chocolate .75 .75
Never hinged 1.10
On cover 37.50
On cover, single franking 67.50
150 A9 10fr violet 1.10 1.10
Never hinged 1.50
On cover 42.50
On cover, single franking 80.00
151 A9 20fr copper red 1.50 1.50
Never hinged 2.25
On cover 55.00
On cover, single franking 92.50
Nos. 112-151 (41) 35.65 29.15

Stamps of types A7-A9 without "RF" were issued in 1944 and are listed Nos.166A-166D in Vol. 3 of the *Scott Standard Postage Stamp Catalogue*.

For surcharges see Nos. B8-B11 in the same volume.

Paris International Exposition Issue
Common Design Types

1937 ***Perf. 13***
152 CD74 20c deep violet 2.00 2.00
Never hinged 3.00
On cover 95.00
153 CD75 30c dark green 2.00 2.00
Never hinged 3.00
On cover 80.00
154 CD76 40c car rose 2.00 2.00
Never hinged 3.00
On cover 62.50
155 CD77 50c dk brn & bl 1.60 1.60
Never hinged 2.75
On cover 55.00
156 CD78 90c red 1.60 1.60
Never hinged 2.75
On cover 100.00
On cover, single franking 190.00
157 CD79 1.50fr ultra 2.00 2.00
Never hinged 3.75
On cover 87.50
On cover, single franking 165.00
Nos. 152-157 (6) 11.20 11.20

Colonial Arts Exhibition Issue
Souvenir Sheet
Common Design Type

1937 ***Imperf.***
158 CD76 3fr sepia 11.00 *15.00*
Never hinged 15.00
On cover 125.00
On cover, single franking 190.00

Louis Gustave Binger A10

1937 ***Perf. 13***
159 A10 65c red brown .35 .35
Never hinged .75
On cover 6.25

Death of Governor General Binger; 50th anniv. of his exploration of the Niger.

Caillie Issue
Common Design Type

1939 **Engr.** ***Perf. 12½x12***
160 CD81 90c org brn & org .35 .75
Never hinged .75
On cover 6.25
161 CD81 2fr bright violet .35 .90
Never hinged .75
On cover 22.50
On cover, single franking 45.00
162 CD81 2.25fr ultra & dk bl .35 .90
Never hinged .75
On cover 26.00
On cover, single franking 50.00
Nos. 160-162 (3) 1.05 2.55

New York World's Fair Issue
Common Design Type

1939
163 CD82 1.25fr carmine lake .75 1.50
Never hinged 1.10
On cover 67.50
On cover, single franking 140.00
164 CD82 2.25fr ultramarine .75 1.50
Never hinged 1.10
On cover 67.50
On cover, single franking 125.00

SEMI-POSTAL STAMPS

No. 47 Surcharged in Red

1915 **Unwmk.** ***Perf. 14x13½***
B1 A5 10c + 5c 1.60 1.60
Never hinged 2.40
On cover 37.50
a. Double surcharge 80.00 80.00
Never hinged 125.00
b. Chalky paper (on #47a) 1.75 1.75
Never hinged 2.75

Curie Issue
Common Design Type

1938 ***Perf. 13***
B2 CD80 1.75fr + 50c brt ultra 11.00 7.50
Never hinged 19.00
On cover 95.00
On cover, single franking 165.00

French Revolution Issue
Common Design Type

1939 **Photo.**
Name and Value Typo. in Black
B3 CD83 45c + 25c grn 8.75 8.75
Never hinged 14.00
On cover 140.00
B4 CD83 70c + 30c brn 8.75 8.75
Never hinged 14.00
On cover 100.00
B5 CD83 90c + 35c red org 8.75 8.75
Never hinged 14.00
On cover 87.50
B6 CD83 1.25fr + 1fr rose pink 8.75 8.75
Never hinged 14.00
On cover 150.00
On cover, single franking 225.00
B7 CD83 2.25fr + 2fr blue 8.75 8.75
Never hinged 17.50
On cover 140.00
On cover, single franking 200.00
Nos. B3-B7 (5) 43.75 43.75

AIR POST STAMPS

Common Design Type

1940 **Unwmk.** **Engr.** ***Perf. 12½x12***
C1 CD85 1.90fr ultramarine .40 .40
Never hinged .75
On cover 35.00
C2 CD85 2.90fr dark red .40 .40
Never hinged .75
On cover 35.00
C3 CD85 4.50fr dk gray grn .75 .75
Never hinged 1.10
On cover 40.00
C4 CD85 4.90fr yel bister .75 .75
Never hinged 1.10
On cover 45.00
C5 CD85 6.90fr deep orange 1.50 1.50
Never hinged 1.90
On cover 62.50
Nos. C1-C5 (5) 3.80 3.80

POSTAGE DUE STAMPS

Natives — D1

Perf. 14x13½
1906-07 **Unwmk.** **Typo.**
J1 D1 5c grn, *greenish* 4.00 4.00
Never hinged 7.25
On cover 95.00
J2 D1 10c red brown 4.00 4.00
Never hinged 7.25
On cover 87.50
J3 D1 15c dark blue 6.50 6.50
Never hinged 13.50
On cover 100.00
J4 D1 20c blk, *yellow* 9.50 9.50
Never hinged 20.00
On cover 105.00
J5 D1 30c red, *straw* 9.50 9.50
Never hinged 20.00
On cover 110.00
J6 D1 50c violet 7.25 7.25
Never hinged 14.50
On cover 80.00
J7 D1 60c black, *buff* 32.50 32.50
Never hinged 67.50
On cover 160.00
J8 D1 1fr blk, *pinkish* 35.00 35.00
Never hinged 75.00
On cover 190.00
Nos. J1-J8 (8) 108.25 108.25

D2

1914
J9 D2 5c green .25 .25
Never hinged .40
On cover 50.00
J10 D2 10c rose .30 .30
Never hinged .55
On cover 50.00
J11 D2 15c gray .30 .30
Never hinged .55
On cover 50.00
J12 D2 20c brown .55 .55
Never hinged .80
On cover 55.00
J13 D2 30c blue .55 .55
Never hinged .80
On cover 55.00
J14 D2 50c black .90 .90
Never hinged 1.20
On cover 62.50
J15 D2 60c orange 1.25 1.25
Never hinged 1.60
On cover 70.00
J16 D2 1fr violet 1.50 1.50
Never hinged 2.10
On cover 80.00
Nos. J9-J16 (8) 5.60 5.60

Type of 1914 Issue Surcharged

1927
J17 D2 2fr on 1fr lilac rose 2.75 2.75
Never hinged 3.75
On cover 95.00
J18 D2 3fr on 1fr org brown 2.75 2.75
Never hinged 3.75
On cover 100.00

PARCEL POST STAMPS

Postage Due Stamps of French Colonies Overprinted

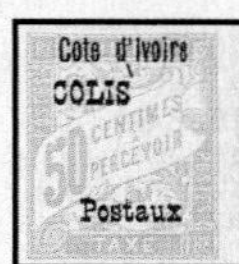

Overprinted In Black

1903 **Unwmk.** ***Imperf.***
Q1 D1 50c lilac 42.50 40.00
Never hinged 60.00
Q2 D1 1fr rose, *buff* 42.50 40.00
Never hinged 60.00

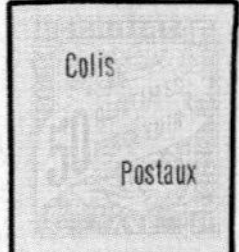

Overprinted In Black

Q3 D1 50c lilac *3,300.* *3,400.*
Q4 D1 1fr rose, *buff* *3,300.* *3,400.*

Accents on "O" of "COTE"

Nos. Q7-Q8, Q11-Q12, Q15, Q17-Q18, Q21-Q22, Q24-Q25 exist with or without accent.

Overprinted In Red and Black

Red Overprint

Q5 D1 50c lilac 120.00 120.00
Never hinged 160.00
a. Inverted overprint 425.00 425.00

Blue Black Overprint

Q6 D1 1fr rose, *buff* 87.50 87.50
Never hinged 100.00
a. Inverted overprint 350.00 350.00

Surcharged in Black

a

b

c

d

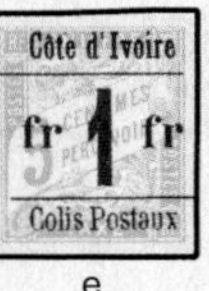

e

f

g

h

1903
Q7 D1 50c on 15c pale grn 16.00 16.00
Never hinged 24.00
a. Inverted surcharge 225.00 225.00
Q8 D1 50c on 60c brn, *buff* 35.00 35.00
Never hinged 52.50
a. Inverted surcharge 225.00 225.00
Q9 (a) 1fr on 5c blue *4,400.* *3,600.*
Q10 (b) 1fr on 5c blue *4,400.* *2,800.*
Q11 (c) 1fr on 5c blue 18.00 16.00
Never hinged 25.00
a. Inverted surcharge 950.00 950.00
Q12 (d) 1fr on 5c blue 27.50 24.00
Never hinged 45.00
Q13 (e) 1fr on 5c blue *4,800.* *4,000.*
Q14 (f) 1fr on 5c blue *12,000.* *9,500.*
Q15 (g) 1fr on 5c blue 110.00 110.00
Never hinged 150.00
Q16 (h) 1fr on 5c blue *3,750.* *3,850.*
Q17 (c) 1fr on 10c gray brn 27.50 24.00
Never hinged 32.50
a. Inverted surcharge 325.00 325.00
Q18 (d) 1fr on 10c gray brn 47.50 45.00
Never hinged 72.50
a. Inverted surcharge 475.00 475.00
Q19 (g) 1fr on 10c gray brn *4,000.* *3,850.*
Q20 (h) 1fr on 10c gray brn *46,000.*

Some authorities regard Nos. Q9 and Q10 as essays. A sub-type of type "a" has smaller, bold "XX" without serifs.

Surcharged in Black

j

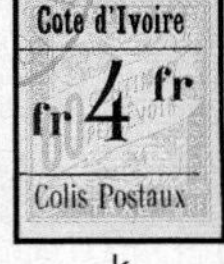

k

l

Q21 (j) 4fr on 60c brn, *buff* 140.00 140.00
Never hinged 175.00
a. Double surcharge 5,600.
Q22 (k) 4fr on 60c brn, *buff* 375.00 375.00
Never hinged 525.00
Q23 (l) 4fr on 60c brn, *buff* 1,200. 1,000.

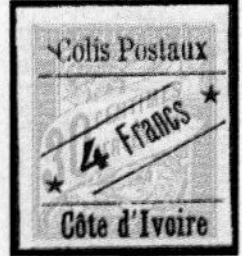

Surcharged in Black

Q24 D1 4fr on 15c green 130.00 130.00
Never hinged 175.00
a. One large star 525.00 525.00
b. Two large stars 300.00 300.00
Q25 D1 4fr on 30c rose 130.00 130.00
Never hinged 175.00
a. One large star 525.00 525.00
b. Two large stars 300.00 300.00

Overprinted in Black

1904

Q26 D1 50c lilac 45.00 45.00
Never hinged 50.00
a. Inverted overprint
Q27 D1 1fr rose, *buff* 45.00 45.00
Never hinged 50.00
a. Inverted overprint

Overprinted in Black

Q28 D1 50c lilac 42.50 42.50
Never hinged 50.00
a. Inverted overprint 225.00 225.00
Q29 D1 1fr rose, *buff* 42.50 42.50
Never hinged 50.00
a. Inverted overprint 225.00 225.00

Surcharged in Black

Q30 D1 4fr on 5c blue 240.00 240.00
Never hinged 310.00
Q31 D1 8fr on 15c green 240.00 240.00
Never hinged 310.00

Overprinted in Black

1905

Q32 D1 50c lilac 92.50 92.50
Never hinged 125.00
Q33 D1 1fr rose, *buff* 92.50 92.50
Never hinged 125.00

Surcharged in Black

Q34 D1 2fr on 1fr rose, *buff* 240.00 240.00
Never hinged 350.00
Q35 D1 4fr on 1fr rose, *buff* 240.00 240.00
Never hinged 350.00
a. Italic "4" 2,200. 2,200.
Q36 D1 8fr on 1fr rose, *buff* 700.00 700.00

JAMAICA

jə-ˈmā-kə

LOCATION — Caribbean Sea, about 90 miles south of Cuba
GOVT. — Independent state in the British Commonwealth
AREA — 4,411 sq. mi.
POP. — 2,230,000 (est. 1982)
CAPITAL — Kingston

Jamaica administered two dependencies: Cayman Islands and Turks and Caicos Islands.

12 Pence = 1 Shilling
20 Shillings = 1 Pound

Catalogue values for unused stamps in this country are for Never Hinged items, beginning with Scott 129 in the regular postage section.

Watermark

Wmk. 45 — Pineapple

STAMPS OF GREAT BRITAIN USED IN JAMAICA

For information on these cancels, see the Crowned Circle Handstamps and Great Britain Used Abroad section.

A01 (Kingston)

Type A Cancel

Short letter and numbers.

1858-60

A1 A 1p rose red, perf. 16 (#18) *900.00*
A2 A 1p rose red, perf. 14 (#20) 120.00
A3 A 4p rose (#26) 85.00
A4 A 6p lilac (#27) 90.00
A5 A 1sh green (#28) 450.00

See note after No. A13.

Duplex cancel

Tall letter and numbers.

1859-60

A6 1p rose red (#20) 425.00
A7 4p rose (#26) 87.50
A8 6p lilac (#27) 95.00
A9 1sh green (#28) 850.00

Double Numeral cancel

As type A but bolder letter and numbers.

A10 1p rose red (#20) 625.00
A11 4p rose (#26) 350.00
a. Thick glazed paper (#26b) 700.00
A12 6p lilac (#27) 375.00
A13 1sh green (#28) —

Single examples of Nos. A10-A12 can be difficult to distinguish from Nos. A2-A4.

A27 (Alexandria)

A14 A 1p rose red (#20) *1,150.*
A15 A 2p blue (#21) 1,950.
A16 A 4p rose (#26) 400.00
A17 A 6p lilac (#27) 800.00

A28 (Anotto Bay)

A18 A 1p rose red (#20) 575.00
A19 A 4p rose (#26) 225.00
A20 A 6p lilac (#27) 475.00

A29 (Bath)

A21 A 1p rose red (#20) 425.00
A22 A 4p rose (#26) 225.00
A23 A 6p lilac (#27) 700.00

A30 (Black River)

A24 A 1p rose red (#20) 425.00
A25 A 4p rose (#26) 165.00
A26 A 6p lilac (#27) 350.00

A31 (Brown's Town)

A27 A 1p rose red (#20) 525.00
A28 A 4p rose (#26) 400.00
A29 A 6p lilac (#27) 425.00

A32 (Buff Bay)

A30 A 1p rose red (#20) 475.00
A31 A 4p rose (#26) 325.00
A32 A 6p lilac (#27) 325.00

A33 (Chapelton)

A33 A 1p rose red (#20) 475.00
A34 A 4p rose (#26) 275.00
A35 A 6p lilac (#27) 400.00

A34 (Claremont)

A36 A 1p rose red (#20) 800.00
A37 A 4p rose (#26) 350.00
A38 A 6p lilac (#27) 425.00

A35 (Clarendon)

A39 A 1p rose red (#20) 525.00
A40 A 4p rose (#26) 300.00
A41 A 6p lilac (#27) 425.00

A36 (Dry Harbour)

A42 A 1p rose red (#20) 800.00
A43 A 4p rose (#26) 525.00
A44 A 6p lilac (#27) 475.00

A37 (Duncans)

A45 A 1p rose red (#20) 950.00
A46 A 4p rose (#26) 650.00
A47 A 6p lilac (#27) 550.00

A39 (Falmouth)

A48 A 1p rose red (#20) 325.00
A49 A 4p rose (#26) 150.00
A50 A 6p lilac (#27) 170.00
A51 A 1sh green (#28) *1,450.*

A40 (Flint River)

A52 A 1p rose red (#20) 475.00
A53 A 4p rose (#26) 300.00
A54 A 6p lilac (#27) 375.00
A55 A 1sh green (#28) 1,450.

A41 (Gayle)

A56 A 1p rose red (#20) 800.00
A57 A 4p rose (#26) 250.00
A58 A 6p lilac (#27) 350.00
A59 A 1sh green (#28) 1,100.

A42 (Golden Spring)

A60 A 1p rose red (#20) 575.00
A61 A 4p rose (#26) 425.00
A62 A 6p lilac (#27) 750.00
A63 A 1sh green (#28) 1,300.

A43 (Gordon Town)

A64 A 1p rose red (#20) —
A65 A 4p rose (#26) —
A66 A 6p lilac (#27) *1,000.*

A44 (Goshen)

A67 A 1p rose red (#20) 375.00
A68 A 4p rose (#26) 275.00
A69 A 6p lilac (#27) 170.00

A45 (Grange Hill)

A70 A 1p rose red (#20) 400.00
A71 A 4p rose (#26) 140.00
A72 A 6p lilac (#27) 180.00
A73 A 1sh green (#28) *1,350.*

A46 (Green Island)

A74 A 1p rose red (#20) 525.00
A77 A 4p rose (#26) 325.00
A76 A 6p lilac (#27) 475.00
A77 A 1sh green (#28) *1,350.*

A47 (Highgate)

A78 A 1p rose red (#20) 425.00
A79 A 4p rose (#26) 250.00
A80 A 6p lilac (#27) 500.00

A48 (Hope Bay)

A81 A 1p rose red (#20) 800.00
A82 A 4p rose (#26) 350.00
A83 A 6p lilac (#27) 800.00

A49 (Lilliput)

A84 A 1p rose red (#20) 375.00
A85 A 4p rose (#26) 350.00
A86 A 6p lilac (#27) 225.00

A51 (Lucea)

A87 A 1p rose red (#20) 525.00
A88 A 4p rose (#26) 200.00
A89 A 6p lilac (#27) 400.00

A52 (Manchioneal)

A90 A 1p rose red (#20) 675.00
A91 A 4p rose (#26) 350.00
A92 A 6p lilac (#27) 700.00

A53 (Mandeville)

A93 A 1p rose red (#20) 400.00
A94 A 4p rose (#26) 150.00
A95 A 6p lilac (#27) 350.00

A54 (May Hill)

A96 A 1p rose red (#20) 300.00
A97 A 4p rose (#26) 225.00
A98 A 6p lilac (#27) 160.00
A98A A 1sh green (#28) *2,100.*

A55 (Mile Gulley)

A99 A 1p rose red (#20) 500.00
A100 A 4p rose (#26) 375.00
A101 A 6p lilac (#27) 400.00

A56 (Moneague)

A102 A 1p rose red (#20) 475.00
A103 A 4p rose (#26) 400.00
A104 A 6p lilac (#27) 800.00

A57 (Montego Bay)

A105 A 1p rose red (#20) 400.00
A106 A 4p rose (#26) 140.00
A107 A 6p lilac (#27) 150.00
A108 A 1sh green (#28) *1,500.*

A58 (Montpelier)

A109 A 1p rose red (#20) —
A110 A 4p rose (#26) —
A111 A 6p lilac (#27) *1,400.*

A59 (Morant Bay)

A112 A 1p rose red (#20) 625.00
A113 A 4p rose (#26) 150.00
A114 A 6p lilac (#27) 180.00

A60 (Ocho Rios)

A115 A 1p rose red (#20) *1,250.*
A116 A 4p rose (#26) 190.00
A117 A 6p lilac (#27) 425.00

A61 (Old Harbour)

A118 A 1p rose red (#20) 425.00
A119 A 4p rose (#26) 250.00
A120 A 6p lilac (#27) 325.00

A62 (Plantain Garden River)

A121 A 1p rose red (#20) 350.00
A122 A 4p rose (#26) 210.00
A123 A 6p lilac (#27) 325.00

A64 (Port Antonio)

A124 A 1p rose red (#20) 675.00
A125 A 4p rose (#26) 425.00
A126 A 6p lilac (#27) 450.00

A65 (Port Morant)

A127 A 1p rose red (#20) 475.00
A128 A 4p rose (#26) 225.00
A129 A 6p lilac (#27) 450.00

A66 (Port Maria)

A130 A 1p rose red (#20) 475.00
A131 A 4p rose (#26) 175.00
A132 A 6p lilac (#27) 450.00

A67 (Port Royal)

A133 A 1p rose red (#20) 725.00
A134 A 2p blue (#27, P9) *2,875.*
A135 A 4p rose (#26) 725.00
A136 A 6p lilac (#27) 750.00

A68 (Porus)

A137 A 1p rose red (#20) 475.00
A138 A 4p rose (#26) 225.00
A139 A 6p lilac (#27) 650.00

A69 (Ramble)

A140 A 1p rose red (#20) 400.00
A141 A 4p rose (#26) 325.00
a. Thick glazed paper (#26b) *750.00*
A142 A 6p lilac (#27) 475.00

A70 (Rio Bueno)

A143 A 1p rose red (#20) 475.00
A144 A 4p rose (#26) 325.00
A145 A 6p lilac (#27) 275.00

A71 (Rodney Hall)

A146 A 1p rose red (#20) 375.00
A147 A 4p rose (#26) 225.00
A148 A 6p lilac (#27) 275.00

A72 (St. David's)

A149 A 1p rose red (#20) 475.00
A150 A 4p rose (#26) 600.00
A151 A 6p lilac (#27) —

A73 (St. Ann's Bay)

A152 A 1p rose red (#20) 400.00
A153 A 4p rose (#26) 200.00
A154 A 6p lilac (#27) 325.00
A154A A 1sh green (#28) *2,000.*

A74 (Salt Gut)

A155 A 1p rose red (#20) 475.00
A156 A 4p rose (#26) 300.00
A157 A 6p lilac (#27) 400.00

A75 (Savannah-la-Mar)

A158 A 1p rose red (#20) 225.00
A159 A 4p rose (#26) 160.00
A160 A 6p lilac (#27) 350.00
A161 A 1sh green (#28) 1,500.

A76 (Spanish Town)

A162 A 1p rose red (#20) 275.00
A163 A 4p rose (#26) 140.00
A164 A 6p lilac (#27) 180.00
A165 A 1sh green (#28) 1,200.

A77 (Stewart Town)

A166 A 1p rose red (#20) 725.00
A167 A 4p rose (#26) 500.00
A168 A 6p lilac (#27) 400.00

A78 (Vere)

A169 A 1p rose red (#20) 575.00
A170 A 4p rose (#26) 225.00
A171 A 6p lilac (#27) 160.00
A172 A 1sh green (#28) *1,700.*

Cancels A38 (Ewarton) and A50 (Little River) were received after the post offices were closed. The numbers were reallocated in 1862 to Falmouth and Malvern, respectively. Cancel A63 (Pear Tree Grove) has not been found canceling stamps of Great Britain, even though its allocation is well documented.

Issued under British Administration

Values for unused stamps are for examples with original gum as defined in the catalogue introduction. Very fine examples of Nos. 1-12 will have perforations touching the design on at least one side due to the narrow spacing of the stamps on the plates. Stamps with perfs clear on all four sides are scarce and will command higher prices.

Queen Victoria
A1 A2

A3

A4

A5 A6

1860-63 Typo. Wmk. 45 *Perf. 14*

1 A1 1p blue 72.50 16.00
a. Diagonal half used as ½p on cover 825.00
b. 1p deep blue 145.00 37.50
c. 1p pale blue 77.50 20.00
d. 1p pale greenish blue 115.00 24.00
2 A2 2p rose 225.00 60.00
a. 2p deep rose 220.00 60.00
3 A3 3p green ('63) 170.00 32.50
4 A4 4p brown org 275.00 62.50
a. 4p orange 250.00 25.00
5 A5 6p lilac 240.00 25.00
a. 6p deep lilac 1,050. 60.00
b. 6p gray lilac 350.00 40.00
6 A6 1sh brown 230.00 35.00
a. 1sh lilac brown 650.00 30.00
b. 1sh yellow brown 575.00 32.50
c. "$" for "S" in "SHILLING" *3,000.* 775.00

All except No. 3 exist imperforate.

1870-71 Wmk. 1

7 A1 1p blue 100.00 .90
a. 1p deep blue 85.00 1.75
8 A2 2p rose 110.00 .85
a. 2p brownish rose 120.00 1.10
9 A3 3p green 155.00 10.00
10 A4 4p brown org ('72) 350.00 13.50
a. 4p red orange 450.00 6.50
11 A5 6p lilac ('71) 100.00 6.00
12 A6 1sh brown ('73) 27.50 9.50
a. "$" for "S" in "SHILLING" 1,400. 675.00
Nos. 7-12 (6) 842.50 40.75

The 1p and 4p exist imperf.
See Nos. 17-23, 28, 40, 43, 47-53.

A7

1872, Oct. 29

13 A7 ½p claret 22.00 4.00
a. ½p deep claret 29.00 6.00

Exists imperf. See No. 16.

A8

A9

1875, Aug. 27 *Perf. 12½*

14 A8 2sh red brown 50.00 37.50
15 A9 5sh violet 125.00 *175.00*

Exist imperf.
See Nos. 29-30, 44, 54.

1883-90 Wmk. 2 *Perf. 14*

16 A7 ½p blue green ('85) 11.00 1.75
a. ½p gray green 3.25 .25
17 A1 1p blue ('84) 350.00 7.75
18 A1 1p carmine ('85) 72.50 1.10
a. 1p rose 87.50 2.50
19 A2 2p rose ('84) 240.00 5.75
20 A2 2p slate ('85) 115.00 .70
a. 2p gray 160.00 9.00
21 A3 3p ol green ('86) 2.75 2.25
a. 3p sage green ('86) 4.00 1.00
22 A4 4p red brown 2.25 .40
a. 4p orange brown 475.00 25.00
23 A5 6p orange yel ('90) 6.00 5.00
a. 6p yellow 40.00 8.75
Nos. 16-23 (8) 799.50 24.70
Nos. 16, 18a, 20a, 21a, 22a, 23a overprinted "SPECIMEN" 750.00

Nos. 18 and 20 exist imperf. Perf. 12 stamps are considered to be proofs.
For surcharge, see No. 27.

Nos. 16-26, O1-O4 used in Cayman Islands.
See Cayman Islands for stamps with Grand Cayman and Cayman Brac cancellations.

A10

1889-91

24 A10 1p lilac & red vio 12.00 .25
25 A10 2p deep green 22.50 8.00
a. 2p green 40.00 7.50
26 A10 2½p lilac & ultra ('91) 9.50 .75
Nos. 24-26 (3) 44.00 *9.00*

Unused examples of No. 25 may be distinguished from No. 25a by their brown gum.

No. 22 Surcharged in Black

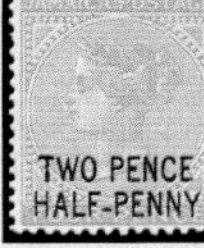

1890, June

27 A4 2½p on 4p red brn 40.00 17.50
a. 1.5mm btw lines of surcharge 45.00 20.00
b. Double surcharge 350.00 250.00
d. "PFNNY" 100.00 70.00
f. As "d," double surcharge —

Three settings of surcharge.

1897

28 A6 1sh brown 10.00 6.50
a. "$" for "S" in "SHILLING" 875.00 550.00
29 A8 2sh red brown 35.00 35.00
30 A9 5sh violet 70.00 *100.00*
Nos. 28-30 (3) 115.00 *141.50*

The 2sh exists imperf.

Llandovery Falls — A12

1900, May 1 Engr. Wmk. 1

31 A12 1p red 13.50 .25

1901, Sept. 25

32 A12 1p red & black 12.00 .25
a. Pair, imperf. horiz. 25,000.
b. Bluish paper 120.00 110.00
Set, overprinted "SPECIMEN" 140.00

Arms of Jamaica — A13

1903-04 Typo. Wmk. 2

33 A13 ½p grn & blk 2.25 .40
b. "SERv ET" for "SERVIET" 45.00 *50.00*
34 A13 1p car & blk ('04) 4.75 .25
b. "SERv ET" for "SERVIET" 35.00 40.00
35 A13 2½p ultra & black 9.50 .45
a. "SERv ET" for "SERVIET" 72.50 *85.00*
36 A13 5p yel & blk ('04) 17.50 *26.00*
a. "SERv ET" for "SERVIET" 875.00 *1,100.*
Nos. 33-36 (4) 34.00 *27.10*
Set, overprinted "SPECIMEN" 90.00

1905-11 Chalky Paper Wmk. 3

37 A13 ½p grn & blk 4.50 .25
b. "SERv ET" for "SERVIET" 32.50 *45.00*
38 A13 1p car & black 20.00 2.00
39 A13 2½p ultra & blk ('07) 6.75 *8.75*
39A A3 3p vio, *yel* ('10) 2.25 1.60
40 A4 4p blk, *yel* ('10) 16.00 *60.00*
Overprinted "SPECIMEN" 50.00
41 A13 5p yel & blk ('07) 67.50 *82.50*
a. "SERv ET" for "SERVIET" 1,425. *1,600.*
42 A13 6p red vio & vio ('11) 15.50 *21.00*
Overprinted "SPECIMEN" 50.00
42A A5 6p purple ('10) 11.50 *32.50*
43 A6 1sh blk, *grn* ('10) 12.00 *10.00*
Overprinted "SPECIMEN" 50.00
a. "$" for "S" in "SHILLING" 1,000. *1,300.*
44 A8 2sh vio, *blue* ('10) 14.00 7.50
Overprinted "SPECIMEN" 50.00
45 A13 5sh vio & black 57.50 57.50
Overprinted "SPECIMEN" 40.00
Nos. 37-45 (11) 227.50 283.60

1905-11 Ordinary Paper

46 A13 2½p ultra ('10) 5.25 1.40
a. 2½p deep ultramarine 2.75 1.90
Overprinted "SPECIMEN" 50.00
47 A3 3p sage grn ('07) 8.00 3.25
a. 3p olive green ('05) 12.00 4.75
48 A3 3p pale pur, *yel* ('10) 9.50 3.75
Overprinted "SPECIMEN" 50.00
49 A4 4p red brn ('08) 77.50 *82.50*
50 A4 4p red, *yel* ('11) 1.75 *7.50*
Overprinted "SPECIMEN" 45.00
51 A5 6p dull vio ('09) 35.00 *62.50*
Overprinted "SPECIMEN" 45.00
52 A5 6p org yel ('09) 40.00 *67.50*
a. 6p orange ('06) 17.00 27.50
53 A6 1sh brown ('06) 27.50 *52.50*
a. 1sh deep brown 40.00 *62.50*
b. "$" for "S" in "SHILLING" 1,500. *1,600.*
54 A8 2sh red brn ('08) 160.00 *170.00*
Nos. 46-54 (9) 364.50 *450.90*

A14

A15

1906

58 A14 ½p green 4.00 .25
a. Booklet pane of 6 —
b. ½p yellow green 10.00 .55
Overprinted "SPECIMEN" 37.50
c. ½p deep green 5.00 .25
59 A15 1p carmine 1.60 .25
a. Booklet pane of 6 —
Overprinted "SPECIMEN" 47.50

For overprints see Nos. MR1, MR4, MR7, MR10.

Edward VII — A16

1911, Feb. 3

60 A16 2p gray 9.00 *15.00*
Overprinted "SPECIMEN" 52.50

George V — A17

1912-20

61 A17 1p scarlet ('16) 9.00 .80
a. 1p carmine ('12) 1.75 .25
b. Booklet pane of 6 —
62 A17 1½p brn org ('16) 2.00 .70
a. 1½p yellow orange 18.50 1.25
63 A17 2p gray 2.50 *2.00*
a. 2p slate gray 2.50 3.00
64 A17 2½p dp br blue .90 *1.25*
a. 2½p ultra ('13) 2.00 .25

Chalky Paper

65 A17 3p violet, *yel* .60 .50
a. 3p violet, *lemon* ('16) 4.25 1.75
As "a," overprinted "SPECIMEN" 32.50
66 A17 4p scar & blk, *yel* ('13) .60 *4.00*
a. 4p scar & blk, *lemon* ('16) 26.00 21.00
As "a," overprinted "SPECIMEN" 32.50
b. 4p scar & blk, *pale yel* ('19) 24.00 17.00
67 A17 6p red vio & dl vio 1.90 2.00
a. 6p dull purple & bright purple ('12) 4.50 *10.50*
b. 6p dull purple & bright magenta ('20) 5.25 2.50
68 A17 1sh black, *green* 2.60 2.25
a. 1sh blk, *bl grn,* olive back ('20) 4.25 *11.00*
69 A17 2sh ultra & vio, *blue* ('19) 26.00 *35.00*
70 A17 5sh scar & grn, *yel* ('19) 82.50 *105.00*
a. 5sh scarlet & green, *pale yellow* ('20) 95.00 *115.00*
b. 5sh scarlet & green, *orange buff* ('20) 160.00 *200.00*

Surface-colored Paper

71 A17 3p violet, *yel* ('13) .60 .45
72 A17 4p scar & blk, *yel* ('14) .85 *4.25*
73 A17 1sh blk, *grn* ('15) 6.00 *5.00*
Nos. 61-73 (13) 136.05 *163.20*
Nos. 61-70 overprinted "SPECIMEN" 235.00

See Nos. 101-102. For overprints see Nos. MR2-MR3, MR5-MR6, MR8-MR9, MR11.

Exhibition Buildings of 1891 — A18

Arawak Woman Preparing Cassava — A19

World War I Contingent Embarking for Overseas Duty — A20

King's House, Spanish Town — A21

Return of Overseas Contingent, 1919 — A22

Columbus Landing in Jamaica — A23

Cathedral in Spanish Town — A24

Statue of Queen Victoria — A26

Memorial to Admiral Rodney — A27

Monument to Sir Charles Metcalfe — A28

Woodland Scene — A29

King George V — A30

1919-21 Typo. Wmk. 3 *Perf. 14*

Chalky Paper

75 A18 ½p ol grn & dk grn ('20) 1.10 1.10
76 A19 1p org & car ('21) 2.00 1.90

Engr.

Ordinary Paper

77 A20 1½p green .45 1.10
78 A21 2p grn & bl ('21) 1.25 *4.50*
79 A22 2½p blue blk & blue 2.25 2.00
a. 2½p blue & dark blue ('21) 15.00 3.50
b. "C" of "CA" missing from watermark *350.00* *300.00*
c. "A" of "CA" missing from watermark *350.00*
80 A23 3p blue & grn ('21) 6.50 *2.75*
81 A24 4p grn & dk brn ('21) 2.75 *10.00*
83 A26 1sh brt org & org ('20) 4.25 *5.75*
a. Frame inverted *40,000.* *25,000.*
As "a," revenue cancel *2,500.*
b. "C" of "CA" missing from watermark *1,100.*
c. "A" of "CA" missing from watermark *1,200.* *1,000.*
84 A27 2sh brn & bl ('20) 12.50 *37.50*
b. "C" of "CA" missing from watermark *800.00*
c. "A" of "CA" missing from watermark
85 A28 3sh org & vio ('20) 27.50 *135.00*
86 A29 5sh ocher & blue ('21) 55.00 *82.50*
87 A30 10sh dk myr grn ('20) 85.00 *160.00*
Nos. 75-87 (12) 200.55 *444.10*

See note after No. 100. Watermark varieties exist and sell for much higher values.

A 6p stamp depicting the abolition of slavery was sent to the Colony but was not issued. "Specimen" examples exist with wmk. 3 or 4. Value $875 each.

Without "Specimen," values: wmk. 3, $60,000; wmk. 4, $40,000.

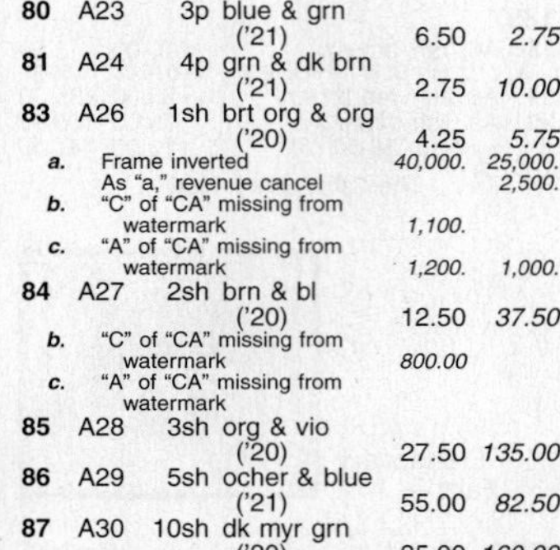

Port Royal in 1853 A31

1921-23 Typo. Wmk. 4 *Perf. 14*

Chalky Paper

88 A18 ½p ol grn & dk grn ('22) .60 .60
a. Booklet pane of 4 150.00
89 A19 1p org & car ('22) 1.75 .25
a. Booklet pane of 6 225.00

Engr.

Ordinary Paper

90 A20 1½p green 3.50 .55
91 A21 2p grn & blue 8.50 .90
92 A22 2½p bl & dk bl 6.50 2.00
a. 2½p blue & dull blue 7.00 .70
93 A23 3p bl & grn ('22) 6.50 .80
a. 3p pale blue & green 4.00 .25
94 A24 4p grn & dk brn 1.40 .40
95 A31 6p bl & blk ('22) 16.00 2.25
96 A26 1sh brn org & dl org 2.50 .90
97 A27 2sh brn & bl ('22) 3.75 .75
98 A28 3sh org & violet 20.00 11.00
99 A29 5sh ocher & bl ('23) 35.00 29.00
a. 5sh orange & blue 82.50 *82.50*
100 A30 10sh dk myr grn ('22) 60.00 80.00
Nos. 88-100 (13) 166.00 129.40
Set, never hinged 380.00

No. 89 differs from No. 76 in having the words "Postage and Revenue" at the bottom.

On No. 79 the horizontal bar of the flag at the left has a broad white line below the colored line. On No. 92 this has been corrected and the broad white line placed above the colored line.

Watermark is sideways on Nos. 76-77, 87, 89-90. Watermark varieties other than these and normal are scarce and sell for much higher values.

Type of 1912-19 Issue

1921-27 Typo. Wmk. 4

101 A17 ½p green ('27) 4.00 .25
a. Booklet pane of 6
102 A17 6p red vio & dl vio 18.50 5.00

No. 102 is on chalky paper.

A32

Type I

Type II

Type II — Cross shading beneath "Jamaica."

1929-32 Engr. *Perf. 13½x14, 14*

103 A32 1p red, type I 16.50 .25
a. 1p red, type II ('32) 16.50 .25
b. Booklet pane of 6, type II
104 A32 1½p brown 10.00 .25
105 A32 9p violet brown 10.00 1.25
Nos. 103-105 (3) 36.50 1.75
Set, never hinged 42.50
Set, overprinted "SPECIMEN" 145.00

The frames on Nos. 103 to 105 differ.

Coco Palms at Columbus Cove — A33

Scene near Castleton, St. Andrew — A34

Priestman's River, Portland Parish — A35

1932 *Perf. 12½*

106 A33 2p grn & gray blk 40.00 4.50
a. Vertical pair, imperf. between *15,000.*
107 A34 2½p ultra & sl bl 6.75 1.75
a. Vertical pair, imperf. between *25,000.* *25,000.*
108 A35 6p red vio & gray blk 37.50 6.00
Nos. 106-108 (3) 84.25 12.25
Set, never hinged 125.00
Set, overprinted "SPECIMEN" 125.00

Common Design Types pictured following the introduction.

Silver Jubilee Issue

Common Design Type

1935, May 6 *Perf. 11x12*

109 CD301 1p car & blue .45 .25
a. Booklet pane of 6 175.00
110 CD301 1½p black & ultra .55 *1.75*
111 CD301 6p indigo & grn 10.00 *18.50*
112 CD301 1sh brn vio & ind 6.00 *18.50*
Nos. 109-112 (4) 17.00 39.00
Set, never hinged 32.50
Set, perforated "SPECIMEN" 115.00

Coronation Issue

Common Design Type

1937, May 12 *Perf. 13½x14*

113 CD302 1p carmine .25 .25
114 CD302 1½p gray black .40 .30
115 CD302 2½p bright ultra .60 *.70*
Nos. 113-115 (3) 1.25 1.25
Set, never hinged 1.75
Set, perforated "SPECIMEN" 105.00

King George VI — A36

Coco Palms at Columbus Cove — A37

Scene near Castleton, St. Andrew — A38

Bananas A39

Citrus Grove A40

Priestman's River, Portland Parish — A41

Kingston Harbor A42

Sugar Industry A43

Bamboo Walk — A44

Woodland Scene — A45

King George VI — A46

1938-51 *Perf. 13½x14*

116 A36 ½p dk blue grn 1.10 .25
a. Booklet pane of 6 8.00
b. Wmkd. sideways — 8,500.
117 A36 1p carmine .85 .25
a. Booklet pane of 6 12.00
118 A36 1½p brown .85 .25

Perf. 12½, 13x13½, 13½x13, 12½x13

119 A37 2p grn & gray blk, perf. 12½ .85 .85
a. Perf. 13x13½ ('39) 1.90 .50
b. Perf. 12½x13 ('51) .85 .25
120 A38 2½p ultra & sl bl 4.25 *1.75*
121 A39 3p grn & lt ultra .75 *1.40*
122 A40 4p grn & yel brn .55 .25
123 A41 6p red vio & gray blk, perf. 13½x13 ('50) 1.60 .25
a. Perf. 12½ 4.50 .30
b. As "a," double impression of gray blk —
124 A42 9p rose lake .55 .45
125 A43 1sh dk brn & brt grn 6.50 .25
126 A44 2sh brn & brt bl 17.50 1.00

Perf. 13, 14

127 A45 5sh ocher & bl, perf. 13 ('50) 4.75 3.50
a. Bluish paper, perf. 13 ('49) 4.75 2.75
b. Perf. 14 6.25 3.25

128 A46 10sh dk myr grn, perf. 14 5.75 *8.50*
a. Perf. 13 ('50) 10.00 *6.50*
Nos. 116-128 (13) 45.85 18.95
Set, never hinged 90.00

See Nos. 140, 148, 149, 152.

Catalogue values for unused stamps in this section, from this point to the end of the section, are for Never Hinged items.

Courthouse, Falmouth
A47

Kings Charles II and George VI
A48

House of Assembly, 1762-1869
A50

Institute of Jamaica — A49

Allegory of Labor and Learning — A51

Constitution and Flag of Jamaica
A52

Perf. 12½
1945, Aug. 20 Engr. Wmk. 4
129 A47 1½p brown .30 .30
a. Booklet pane of 4 37.50
b. Perf. 12½x13½ ('46) 11.00 1.75
130 A48 2p dp grn, perf. 12½x13½ .30 *.50*
a. Perf. 12½ 14.00 1.10
131 A49 3p bright ultra .25 *.50*
a. Perf. 13 ('46) 3.00 *2.50*
132 A50 4½p slate black 1.10 .35
a. Perf. 13 ('46) 4.50 *4.75*
133 A51 2sh chocolate 1.25 .50
134 A52 5sh deep blue 3.00 1.10
135 A49 10sh green 2.75 *2.00*
Nos. 129-135 (7) 8.95 *5.25*

Granting of a new Constitution in 1944.

Peace Issue
Common Design Type
1946, Oct. 14 Wmk. 4 *Perf. 13½*
136 CD303 1½p black brown .30 *4.50*
a. Perf. 13½x14 2.50 .25

Perf. 13½x14
137 CD303 3p deep blue .50 8.00
a. Perf. 13½ 6.50 *2.75*

Silver Wedding Issue
Common Design Types
1948, Dec. 1 Photo. *Perf. 14x14½*
138 CD304 1½p red brown .35 .25

Engr.; Name Typo.
Perf. 11½x11
139 CD305 £1 red 27.50 *60.00*

Type of 1938 and

Tobacco Industry
A53

1949, Aug. 15 Engr. *Perf. 12½*
140 A39 3p ultra & slate blue 3.25 1.00
141 A53 £1 purple & brown 45.00 32.50

UPU Issue
Common Design Types
Perf. 13½, 11x11½
1949, Oct. 10 Wmk. 4
142 CD306 1½p red brown .25 .25
143 CD307 2p dark green 1.10 1.00
144 CD308 3p indigo .40 *.50*
145 CD309 6p rose violet .50 *.70*
Nos. 142-145 (4) 2.25 2.45

University Issue
Common Design Types
1951, Feb. 16 *Perf. 14x14½*
146 CD310 2p brown & gray blk .35 .40
147 CD311 6p rose lil & gray blk .55 .30

George VI Type of 1938
1951, Oct. 25 *Perf. 13½x14*
148 A36 ½p orange 2.25 .30
a. Booklet pane of 6 16.00
149 A36 1p blue green 3.00 .25
a. Booklet pane of 6 21.00

Boy Scout Emblem with Map — A54

Map and Emblem
A55

Perf. 13½x13, 13x13½
1952, Mar. 5 Typo. Wmk. 4
150 A54 2p blk, yel grn & blue .30 .25
151 A55 6p blk, yel grn & dk red .70 .60

1st Caribbean Boy Scout Jamboree, 1952.

Banana Type of 1938
1952, July 1 Engr. *Perf. 12½*
152 A39 3p rose red & green 3.75 .30

SEMI-POSTAL STAMPS

Native Girl — SP1

Native Boy — SP2

Native Boy and Girl — SP3

1923, Nov. 1 Engr. *Perf. 12*
B1 SP1 ½p green & black 1.25 *5.00*
B2 SP2 1p car & black 3.25 *10.00*
B3 SP3 2½p blue & black 14.00 *13.00*
Nos. B1-B3 (3) 18.50 *28.00*
Set, overprinted "SPECIMEN" 125.00

Each stamp was sold for ½p over face value. The surtax benefited the Child Saving League of Jamaica.

WAR TAX STAMPS

Regular Issues of 1906-19 Overprinted

1916 Wmk. 3 *Perf. 14*
MR1 A14 ½p green .25 .40
a. Without period 17.50 *27.50*
b. Double overprint 140.00 *160.00*
c. Inverted overprint 130.00 *150.00*
d. As "c," without period 350.00
MR2 A17 3p violet, *yel* 2.25 *24.00*
a. Without period 42.50 *100.00*

Surface-colored Paper
MR3 A17 3p violet, *yel* 34.00 *52.50*
Nos. MR1-MR3 (3) 36.50 *76.90*

Regular Issues of 1906-18 Overprinted

MR4 A14 ½p green .25 .30
a. Without period 20.00 *52.50*
b. Pair, one without ovpt. 6,500. 5,250.
c. "R" inserted by hand 1,800. 1,500.
d. "WAR" only 125.00
MR5 A17 1½p orange .25 .25
a. Without period 5.75 *8.50*
b. "TAMP" 210.00 *240.00*
c. "S" inserted by hand 450.00
d. "R" omitted 3,600. 3,100.
e. "R" inserted by hand 1,550. 1,250.
MR6 A17 3p violet, *yel* 5.00 .90
a. Without period 70.00 *75.00*
b. "TAMP" 1,000. 1,000.
c. "S" inserted by hand 225.00 225.00
d. Inverted overprint 350.00 190.00
e. As "a," inverted
Nos. MR4-MR6 (3) 5.50 1.45

Regular Issues of 1906-19 Overprinted

1917, Mar.
MR7 A14 ½p green 2.00 .35
a. Without period 18.50 *30.00*
b. Overprinted on back instead of face 290.00
c. Inverted overprint 27.50 57.50
MR8 A17 1½p orange .25 .25
a. Without period 4.00 *20.00*
b. Double overprint 92.50 *100.00*
c. Inverted overprint 92.50 85.00
d. As "a," inverted *400.00*
MR9 A17 3p violet, *yel* 2.25 *1.30*
a. Without period 27.50 *52.50*
b. Vertical overprint 425.00 425.00
c. Inverted overprint 160.00 190.00
d. As "a," inverted *450.00*
e. Pair, overprint omitted on one 4,250.
Nos. MR7-MR9 (3) 4.50 1.90

There are many minor varieties of Nos. MR1-MR9.

Regular Issues of 1906-19 Overprinted in Red

1919, Oct. 4
MR10 A14 ½p green .25 .25
MR11 A17 3p violet, *yel* 15.00 3.75
a. 3p pale pur, *buff* 4.75 1.25
Set, overprinted "SPECIMEN" 95.00

OFFICIAL STAMPS

No. 16 Overprinted in Black

Type I — Word 15 to 16mm long.
Type II — Word 17 to 17½mm long.

1890 Wmk. 2 *Perf. 14*
O1 A7 ½p green (II) 18.50 2.50
a. Type I 47.50 30.00
b. Inverted overprint (II) 110.00 *120.00*
c. Double overprint (II) 110.00 *120.00*
d. Dbl. ovpt., one invtd. (II) 575.00 575.00
e. Dbl. ovpt., one vert. (II) 1,100.
f. Double overprint (I) 825.00
g. Missing "O" 700.00
h. Missing "L" 800.00 800.00
i. Missing both "I"s 850.00 850.00
j. Missing one "I"

No. 16 and Type of 1889 Overprinted

1890-91
O2 A7 ½p green 9.50 1.80
O3 A10 1p carmine rose 8.50 1.40
O4 A10 2p slate 29.00 1.40
Nos. O2-O4 (3) 47.00 4.60
Set, overprinted "SPECIMEN" 160.00

JAPAN

jə-ˈpan

LOCATION — North Pacific Ocean, east of China
GOVT. — Constitutional monarchy
AREA — 142,726 sq. mi.
POP. — 120,020,000 (est. 1984)
CAPITAL — Tokyo

1000 Mon = 10 Sen
100 Sen = 1 Yen (or En)
10 Rin = 1 Sen

Watermarks

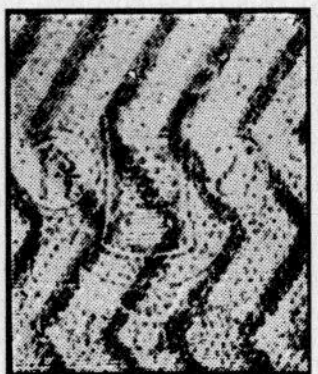
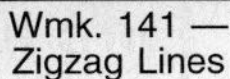
Wmk. 141 — Zigzag Lines

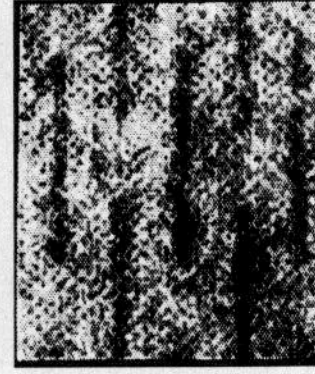
Wmk. 142 — Parallel Lines

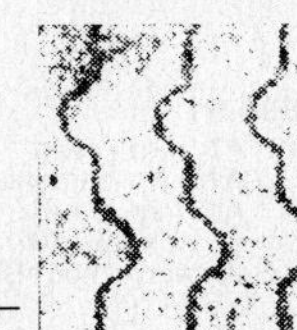
Wmk. 257 — Curved Wavy Lines

Counterfeits of Nos. 1-71 are plentiful. Some are excellent and deceive many collectors.

Nos. 1-54A were printed from plates of 40 with individually engraved subjects. Each stamp in the sheet is slightly different.

Pair of Dragons Facing Characters of Value — A1

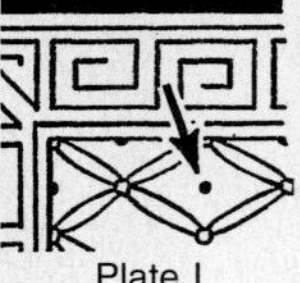
Plate I

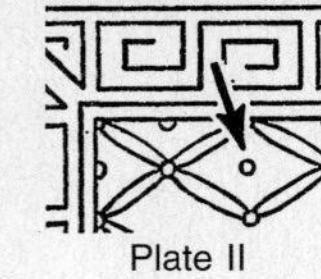
Plate II

48 mon:
Plate I — Solid dots in inner border.
Plate II — Tiny circles replace dots.

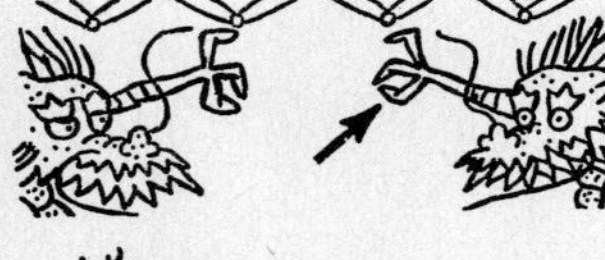
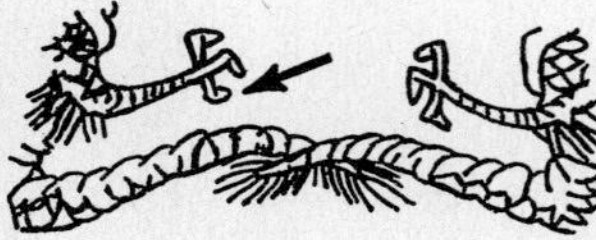
Plate I

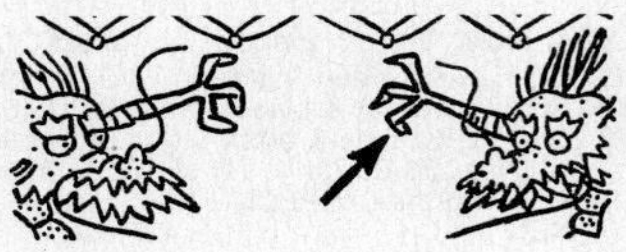
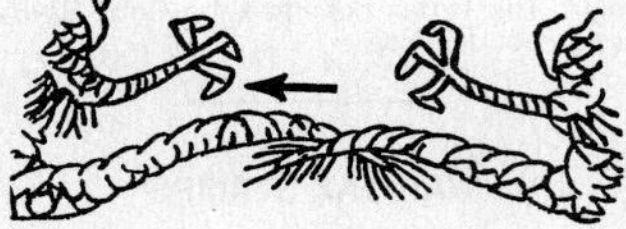
Plate II

100 mon:
Plate I — Lowest dragon claw at upper right and at lower left point upward.
Plate II — Same two claws point downward.

Plate I

Plate II

200 mon:
Plate I — Dot in upper left corner.
Plate II — No dot. (Some Plate I copies show dot faintly; these can be mistaken for Plate II.)

Plate I

Plate II

500 mon:
Plate I — Lower right corner of Greek-type border incomplete
Plate II — Short horizontal line completes corner border pattern.

Unwmk.

1871, Apr. 20 Engr. ***Imperf.***

Native Laid Paper Without Gum
Denomination in Black

No.		Description	Unused	Used
1	A1	48m brown (I)	250.	250.
a.		48m red brown (I)	375.	375.
b.		Wove paper (I)	300.	300.
c.		48m brown (II)	325.	325.
d.		Wove paper (II)	400.	400.
2	A1	100m blue (I)	250.	250.
a.		Wove paper (I)	350.	350.
b.		Plate II	550.	550.
c.		Wove paper (II)	800.	800.
3	A1	200m ver (I)	425.	400.
a.		Wove paper (I)	525.	450.
b.		Plate II	2,500.	2,000.
c.		Wove paper (II)		*4,000.*
4	A1	500m bl grn (I)	650.	650.
a.		500m greenish blue (I)	700.	675.
b.		500m green (I)	2,000.	1,400.
c.		500m yellow green (I)	3,500.	1,500.
d.		Wove paper (I)	750.	650.
e.		500m blue green (II)	775.	*4,000.*
f.		500m greenish blue (II)	775.	*4,000.*
g.		Wove paper (II)	2,750.	*5,000.*
h.		Denomination inverted (I)		*175,000.*

Perforations, Nos. 5-8

Perforations on Nos. 5-8 generally are rough and irregular due to the perforating equipment used and the quality of the paper. Values are for stamps with rough perfs that touch the frameline on one or more sides.

Dragons and Denomination — A1a

½ sen:
Plate I — Same as 48m Plate II. Measures not less than 19.8x19.8mm. Some subjects on this plate measure 20.3x20.2mm.
Plate II — Same as 48m Plate II. Measures not more than 19.7x19.3mm. Some subjects measure 19.3x18.7mm.

Plate I & II

Plate III

1 sen:
Plate I — Same as 100m Plate I. Narrow space between frameline and Greek-type border.
Plate II — Same as 100m Plate II. Same narrow space between frameline and border.
Plate III — Space between frameline and border is much wider. Frameline thinner. Shading on dragon heads heavier than on Plates I and II.

Native Laid Paper
With or Without Gum

1872 ***Perf. 9-12 & compound***

Denomination in Black

No.		Description	Unused	Used
5	A1a	½s brown (II)	120.00	120.00
a.		½s red brown (II)	130.00	130.00
b.		½s gray brown (II)	130.00	130.00
c.		Wove paper (II)	725.00	675.00
d.		½s brown (I)	200.00	200.00
e.		½s red brown (I)	200.00	200.00
f.		½s gray brown (I)	200.00	200.00
g.		Wove paper (I)	275.00	275.00
6	A1a	1s blue (II)	425.00	425.00
a.		Wove paper (II)	675.00	675.00
b.		Plate I	1,400.	*3,000.*
c.		Wove paper (I)	*7,000.*	
d.		Plate III	*15,000.*	2,500.
e.		Wove paper (III)		*7,500.*
7	A1a	2s vermilion	575.00	575.00
a.		Wove paper	625.00	625.00
8	A1a	5s blue green	825.00	825.00
a.		5s yellow green	875.00	875.00
b.		Wove paper	900.00	900.00

In 1896 the government made imperforate imitations of Nos. 6-7 to include in a presentation book.

Beginning with No. 9, Japanese stamps intended for distribution outside the Postal Ministry were overprinted with three characters, as shown above, reading "Mihon" (specimen). These specimens were included in ministry announcements detailing forthcoming issues and were in presentation booklets given to government officials, foreign governments, etc.

Expect perforations on Nos. 9-71 to be rough and irregular.

Imperial Crest and Branches of Kiri Tree — A2

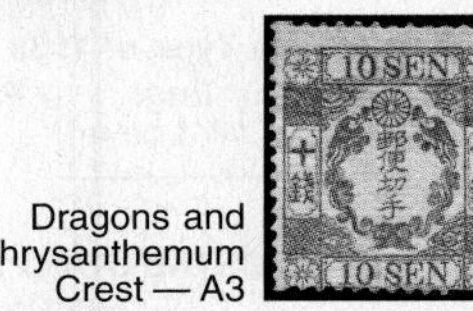
Dragons and Chrysanthemum Crest — A3

Imperial Chrysanthemum Crest — A4

Imperial Crest and Branches of Kiri Tree — A5

Perf. 9 to 13 and Compound

1872-73

Native Wove or Laid Paper of Varying Thickness

No.		Description	Unused	Used
9	A2	½s brn, *hard wove*	25.00	20.00
a.		Upper character in left label has 2 diagonal top strokes missing	2,100.	1,250.
b.		Laid paper	80.00	—
c.		As "a," laid paper	2,200.	—
d.		½s gray brown, *soft porous native wove*	80.00	—

Nos. 9, 9a are on stiff, brittle wove paper. Nos. 9b, 9c and 9d on a soft, fibrous paper. Nos. 9b, 9c and 9d probably were never put in use, though genuine used examples do exist.

No.		Description	Unused	Used
10	A2	1s blue, *wove*	50.00	26.00
a.		Laid paper	52.50	29.00
11	A2	2s ver, *wove*	100.00	50.00
12	A2	2s dull rose, *laid*	75.00	35.00
a.		Wove paper	100.00	50.00
13	A2	2s yel, *laid* ('73)	75.00	21.00
a.		Wove paper ('73)	175.00	26.00
14	A2	4s rose, *laid* ('73)	67.50	26.00
a.		Wove paper ('73)	210.00	32.00
15	A3	10s blue grn, *wove*	250.00	160.00
16	A3	10s yel grn, *laid*	475.00	325.00
a.		Wove paper ('73)	1,150.	500.00
17	A4	20s lilac, *wove*	650.00	425.00
a.		20s violet, *wove*	750.00	425.00
b.		20s red violet, *laid*		—
18	A5	30s gray, *wove*	625.00	375.00

See Nos. 24-25, 30-31, 37-39, 51-52.

1874 **Foreign Wove Paper**

No.		Description	Unused	Used
24	A2	4s rose	650.	300.
25	A5	30s gray	*30,000.*	*7,500.*

A6

A7

A8

Design A6 differs from A2 by the addition of a syllabic character in a box covering crossed kiri branches above SEN. Stamps of design A6 differ for each value in border and spandrel designs.

In design A7, the syllabic character appears just below the buckle. In design A8, it appears in an oval frame at bottom center below SE of SEN. Design A3 and A4 have a syllabic character immediately below the central design, above the 'S' of 'SEN'.

With Syllabic Characters

イ	ロ	ハ	ニ	ホ	ヘ	ト	チ
i	ro	ha	ni	ho	he	to	chi
1	2	3	4	5	6	7	8
リ	ヌ	ル	ヲ	ワ	カ	ヨ	タ
ri	nu	ru	wo	wa	ka	yo	ta
9	10	11	12	13	14	15	16
レ	ソ	ツ	子	ナ	ラ	ム	
re	so	tsu	ne	na	ra	mu	
17	18	19	20	21	22	23	

Perf. 9½ to 12½ and Compound

1874 **Native Laid or Wove Paper**

No.		Description	Unused	Used
28	A6	2s yel (Syll. 1)	*27,000.*	400.00
		Syllabic 16	425.00	
29	A7	6s vio brn (Syll. 1)	1,700.	475.00
		Wove paper	1,500.	400.00
		Syllabic 2	1,900.	500.00
		Wove paper	1,750.	500.00
		Syllabic 3	20,000.	1,100.
		Wove paper	20,000.	1,150.
		Syllabic 4	20,000.	600.00
		Wove paper	20,000.	575.00
		Syllabic 5	20,000.	600.00
		Wove paper	20,000.	625.00
		Syllabic 6	20,000.	700.00
		Wove paper	20,000.	775.00
		Syllabic 7	25,000.	550.00
		Wove paper	25,000.	550.00
		Syllabic 8	25,000.	550.00
		Wove paper	25,000.	500.00
		Syllabic 9	20,000.	700.00
		Wove paper	20,000.	675.00
		Syllabic 10		3,500.
		Wove paper		3,000.
		Syllabic 11		3,000.
		Wove paper		3,000.
		Syllabic 12	20,000.	1,900.
		Wove paper	20,000.	1,800.
30	A4	20s red vio (Syll. 3)	*10,000.*	
		Specimen overprint	*10,000.*	
		Syllabic 1	150,000.	

Syllabic 2	*10,000.*	
Specimen overprint	*10,000.*	
31 A5 30s gray (Syll. 1)	3,000.	3,000.
a. Very thin laid paper	3,000.	3,000.

No. 30, syll. 1, comes only with small, eliptical specimen dot (*Sumiten*, "secret mark").

Specimen overprints on No. 30, Syllabics 2 and 3, consist of the three-character *Mihon* overprint.

Perf. 11 to 12½ and Compound

1874 Foreign Wove Paper

32 A6 ½s brn (Syll. 1)	25.00	20.00
Syllabic 2	40.00	40.00
33 A6 1s blue (Syll. 4)	160.00	40.00
Syllabic 1	150.00	35.00
Syllabic 2	225.00	40.00
Syllabic 3	200.00	40.00
Syllabic 5	650.00	150.00
Syllabic 6, 9	150.00	45.00
Syllabic 7	350.00	50.00
Syllabic 8	150.00	40.00
Syllabic 10	225.00	70.00
Syllabic 11	215.00	60.00
Syllabic 12	250.00	65.00
34 A6 2s yel (Syll. 2-4, 15, 17, 20)	175.00	30.00
Syllabic 1	400.00	35.00
Syllabic 5	450.00	30.00
Syllabic 6	2,000.	50.00
Syllabic 7	2,000.	30.00
Syllabic 8	200.00	55.00
Syllabic 9	200.00	35.00
Syllabic 10	*2,750.*	50.00
Syllabic 11	200.00	30.00
Syllabic 12,22	*2,650.*	30.00
Syllabic 13	*2,500.*	30.00
Syllabic 14	*2,650.*	45.00
Syllabic 16	*2,500.*	35.00
Syllabic 18,19	200.00	30.00
Syllabic 21	250.00	30.00
Syllabic 23	265.00	30.00
35 A6 4s rose (Syll. 1)	3,500.	475.00
36 A7 6s vio brn (Syll. 16)	200.00	70.00
Syllabic 10	650.00	650.00
Syllabic 11	500.00	
Syllabic 13	14,000.	*5,000.*
Syllabic 14	300.00	275.00
Syllabic 15	25,000.	*3,000.*
Syllabic 17	240.00	85.00
Syllabic 18	325.00	115.00
37 A3 10s yel grn (Syll. 2)	375.00	100.00
Syllabic 1	525.00	85.00
Syllabic 3	1,000.	300.00
38 A4 20s violet (Syll. 5)	450.00	95.00
Syllabic 4	525.00	100.00
39 A5 30s gray (Syll. 1)	500.00	100.00

1875 *Perf. 9 to 13 and Compound*

40 A6 ½s gray (Syll. 2, 3)	25.00	20.00
Syllabic 4	30.00	1,000.
41 A6 1s brn (Syll. 15)	35.00	22.50
Syllabic 5	375.00	50.00
Syllabic 7	2,250.	275.00
Syllabic 8	*32,500.*	275.00
Syllabic 12	1,300.	225.00
Syllabic 13	50.00	22.50
Syllabic 14	50.00	22.50
Syllabic 16-17	45.00	25.00
42 A6 4s grn (Syll. 1)	130.00	29.00
Syllabic 2	200.00	29.00
Syllabic 3	130.00	29.00
43 A7 6s org (Syll. 16,17)	90.00	25.00
Syllabic 10	175.00	55.00
Syllabic 11	150.00	50.00
Syllabic 13	325.00	45.00
Syllabic 14	160.00	32.50
Syllabic 15		162,500.
44 A8 6s org (Syll. 20)	90.00	25.00
Syllabic 19	125.00	25.00
Syllabic 21	100.00	25.00
Syllabic 22	4,250.	1,750.

Dragons
A9

Wild Goose
A10

Wagtail — A11

Imperial Crest — A11a

Kiri Branches — A11b

Goshawk — A12

45 A9 10s ultra (Syll. 4)	160.00	27.50
Syllabic 5	*4,150.*	350.00
46 A10 12s rose (Syll. 1)	400.00	150.00
Syllabic 2	500.00	175.00
Syllabic 3	*3,500.*	500.00
47 A11 15s lilac (Syll. 1)	300.00	160.00
Syllabic 2	400.00	165.00
Syllabic 3	350.00	175.00
48 A11a 20s rose (Syll. 8)	125.00	25.00
Syllabic 9		—
49 A11b 30s vio (Syll. 2-4)	175.00	70.00
50 A12 45s lake (Syll. 1)	600.00	275.00
Syllabic 2	1,250.	550.00
Syllabic 3	1,200.	425.00

Issued: No. 46, syll. 2, 1882; No. 46, syll. 3, 1883; others, 1875.

The 1s brown on laid paper, type A6, formerly listed as No. 50A, is one of several stamps of the preceding issue which exist on a laid type paper. They are difficult to identify and mainly of interest to specialists.

1875 Without Syllabic Characters

51 A2 1s brown	*6,500.*	725.00
52 A2 4s green	500.00	100.00

Branches of Kiri Tree Tied with Ribbon
A13

Imperial Crest and Kiri Branches
A14

1875-76

53 A13 1s brown	75.00	12.00
54 A13 2s yellow	90.00	20.00
54A A14 5s green ('76)	190.00	100.00
Nos. 53-54A (3)	355.00	132.00

Postal Cancellations

Beta Cancel

Postal Cancel

Telegraph Cancellation

Nos. 58, 61-62, 64-65, 71-84 are found with telegraph or telephone office cancellations. These sell at considerably lower prices than postally used examples. Examples with beta cancels are valued the same as postally used examples.

A15

A16

Imperial Crest, Star and Kiri Branches
A17

Sun, Kikumon and Kiri Branches
A18

Perf. 8 to 14 and Compound

1876-77 Typo.

55 A15 5r slate	25.00	10.00
56 A16 1s black	37.50	4.75
a. Horiz. pair, imperf. btwn.		
57 A16 2s brown ol	52.50	3.00
58 A16 4s blue grn	42.50	5.00
a. 4s green	42.50	5.00
59 A17 5s brown	65.00	25.00
60 A17 6s orange ('77)	160.00	65.00
61 A17 8s vio brn ('77)	67.50	6.00
62 A17 10s blue ('77)	55.00	2.50
63 A17 12s rose ('77)	225.00	150.00
64 A18 15s yel grn ('77)	140.00	2.50
65 A18 20s dk blue ('77)	150.00	12.00
66 A18 30s violet ('77)	225.00	110.00
a. 30s red violet	250.00	110.00
67 A18 45s carmine ('77)	775.00	525.00

1879

68 A16 1s maroon	15.00	1.25
69 A16 2s dk violet	40.00	2.00
70 A16 3s orange	60.00	30.00
71 A18 50s carmine	225.00	15.00
Nos. 68-71 (4)	340.00	48.25

1883

72 A16 1s green	11.50	.80
73 A16 2s car rose	15.00	.25
74 A17 5s ultra	25.00	.60
Nos. 72-74 (3)	51.50	1.65

Imperial Crest and Kiri Branches
A19

Kikumon
A20

1888-92

75 A15 5r gray blk ('89)	5.00	.45
76 A16 3s lilac rose ('92)	14.00	.45
77 A16 4s olive bis	12.00	.45
78 A17 8s blue lilac	18.00	1.60
79 A17 10s brown org	16.00	.45
80 A18 15s purple	55.00	.50
81 A18 20s orange	72.50	1.50
a. 20s yellow	72.50	1.50
82 A19 25s blue green	130.00	1.50
83 A18 50s brown	110.00	3.25
84 A20 1y carmine	160.00	4.25
Nos. 75-84 (10)	592.50	14.40

Stamps of types A16-A18 differ for each value, in backgrounds and ornaments.

Cranes and Imperial Crest — A21

Perf. 11½ to 13 and Compound

1894, Mar. 9

85 A21 2s carmine	21.00	3.00
86 A21 5s ultra	32.50	11.00

25th wedding anniv. of Emperor Meiji (Mutsuhito) and Empress Haru.

Gen. Yoshihisa Kitashirakawa
A22 A23

Field Marshal Akihito Arisugawa
A24 A25

1896, Aug. 1 Engr.

87 A22 2s rose	24.00	3.00
88 A23 5s deep ultra	50.00	3.00
89 A24 2s rose	24.00	3.00
90 A25 5s deep ultra	50.00	3.00
Nos. 87-90 (4)	148.00	12.00

Victory in Chinese-Japanese War (1894-95).

A26

A27

A28

A29

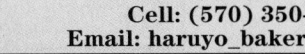

Perf. 11½ to 14 and Compound

1899-1907 **Typo.**

No.	Type	Description	Unused	Used
91	A26	5r gray	5.50	1.00
92	A26	½s gray ('01)	3.00	.25
93	A26	1s lt red brn	3.50	.25
94	A26	1½s ultra ('00)	12.00	.85
95	A26	1½s violet ('06)	9.00	.25
96	A26	2s lt green	9.00	.25
97	A26	3s violet brn	8.50	.25
a.		Double impression		
98	A26	3s rose ('06)	5.00	.25
99	A26	4s rose	6.00	1.25
a.		4s pink ('06)	7.00	1.75
100	A26	5s orange yel	18.00	.25
101	A27	6s maroon ('07)	32.50	3.50
102	A27	8s olive grn	34.00	5.00
103	A27	10s deep blue	11.00	.25
104	A27	15s purple	42.50	2.00
105	A27	20s red orange	21.00	.25
106	A28	25s blue green	67.50	1.00
107	A28	50s red brown	70.00	2.25
108	A29	1y carmine	80.00	3.25
		Nos. 91-108 (18)	438.00	22.35

For overprints see Nos. M1, Offices in China, 1-18, Offices in Korea, 1-14.

Boxes for Rice Cakes and Marriage Certificates — A30

Perf. 11½ to 12½ and Compound

1900, May 10

109 A30 3s carmine 28.00 2.50

Wedding of the Crown Prince Yoshihito and Princess Sadako.

For overprints see Offices in China No. 19, Offices in Korea No. 15.

Symbols of Korea and Japan — A31

1905, July 1

110 A31 3s rose red 80.00 20.00

Issued to commemorate the amalgamation of the postal services of Japan and Korea. Korean stamps were withdrawn from sale June 30, 1905, but remained valid until Aug. 31. No. 110 was used in the Korea and China Offices of Japan, as well as in Japan proper.

Field-piece and Japanese Flag — A32

1906, Apr. 29

111 A32 1½s blue 26.00 4.00
112 A32 3s carmine rose 55.00 16.00

Triumphal military review following the Russo-Japanese War.

Empress Jingo — A33

1908 **Engr.**

113 A33 5y green 850.00 6.00
114 A33 10y dark violet 1,200. 10.00

The frame of No. 114 differs slightly from the illustration.

See Nos. 146-147.

For overprints see Offices in China Nos. 20-21, 48-49.

A34

A35

A36

Perf. 12, 12x13, 13x13½

1913 **Typo.** **Unwmk.**

No.	Type	Description	Unused	Used
115	A34	½s brown	7.00	.85
116	A34	1s orange	14.00	.85
117	A34	1½s lt blue	18.00	1.25
a.		Booklet pane of 6	175.00	
118	A34	2s green	19.00	.85
119	A34	3s rose	26.00	.45
a.		Booklet pane of 6	175.00	
120	A35	4s red	27.50	14.00
121	A35	5s violet	35.00	1.25
122	A35	10s deep blue	100.00	.60
123	A35	20s claret	100.00	1.25
124	A35	25s olive green	100.00	2.75
125	A36	1y yel grn & mar	700.00	45.00
		Nos. 115-125 (11)	1,147.	69.10

1914-25 **Wmk. 141** **Granite Paper**

Size: 19x22½mm ("Old Die")

No.	Type	Description	Unused	Used
127	A34	½s brown	2.10	.25
128	A34	1s orange	2.10	.25
129	A34	1½s blue	2.10	.25
a.		Booklet pane of 6	72.50	
d.		As "a," imperf.		
130	A34	2s green	4.25	.25
a.		Booklet pane of 6	72.50	
131	A34	3s rose	1.60	.25
a.		Booklet pane of 6	60.00	
132	A35	4s red	14.00	1.00
a.		Booklet pane of 6	72.50	
133	A35	5s violet	13.00	.45
134	A35	6s brown ('19)	18.00	2.40
136	A35	8s gray ('19)	15.00	9.00
137	A35	10s deep blue	17.50	.25
a.		Booklet pane of 6	110.00	
138	A35	13s olive brn ('25)	35.00	1.90
139	A35	20s claret	80.00	.60
140	A35	25s olive grn	12.00	.85
141	A36	30s org brn ('19)	18.00	.50
143	A36	50s dk brown ('19)	26.00	1.00
145	A36	1y yel grn & mar	125.00	1.50
b.		Imperf., pair		
146	A33	5y green	400.00	6.00
147	A33	10y violet	600.00	9.50
		Nos. 127-147 (18)	1,386.	36.20

"New Die" Size: 18½x22mm (Flat Plate) or 18½x22½mm (Rotary)

1924-33

No.	Type	Description	Unused	Used
127a	A34	½s brown	1.75	.95
128a	A34	1s orange	1.75	.95
129b	A34	1½s blue	2.75	.30
c.		Bklt. pane of 6 ('30)	19.00	
131b	A34	3s rose	1.10	.25
c.		Bklt. pane of 6 ('28)	45.00	
133a	A35	5s violet	15.00	.25
135	A35	7s red org ('30)	7.75	.25
138a	A35	13s bister brn ('25)	6.00	.25
140a	A35	25s olive green	45.00	.25
142	A36	30s org & grn ('29)	17.00	.30
144	A36	50s yel brn & dk bl ('29)	12.00	.50
145a	A36	1y yel grn & mar	67.50	1.00
		Nos. 127a-145a (11)	177.60	5.25

See Nos. 212-213, 239-241, 243, 245, 249-252, 255. For overprints see Nos. C1-C2, M2-M5, Offices in China, 22-47.

Ceremonial Cap — A37

Imperial Throne — A38

Enthronement Hall, Kyoto — A39

Perf. 12½

1915, Nov. 10 **Typo.** **Unwmk.**

148 A37 1½s red & blk 2.00 .55
149 A38 3s orange & vio 2.50 .80

Engr.

Perf. 12x12½

150 A39 4s carmine rose 12.00 10.00
151 A39 10s ultra 25.00 16.00
Nos. 148-151 (4) 41.50 27.35

Enthronement of Emperor Yoshihito.

Mandarin Duck — A40

Ceremonial Cap — A41

1916, Nov. 3 **Typo.** ***Perf. 12½***

152 A40 1½s grn, red & yel 4.00 1.75
153 A40 3s red & yellow 7.00 2.00
154 A41 10s ultra & dk bl 800.00 275.00

Nomination of the Prince Heir Apparent, later Emperor Hirohito.

A42

Dove and Olive Branch — A43

Perf. 12, 12½, 13½x13

1919, July 1 **Engr.**

155 A42 1½s dark brown 2.00 .60
156 A43 3s gray green 2.50 1.00
157 A42 4s rose 5.50 3.75
158 A43 10s dark blue 23.00 12.00
Nos. 155-158 (4) 33.00 17.35

Restoration of peace after World War I.

Census Officer, A.D. 652 — A44

Perf. 12½

1920, Sept. 25 **Typo.** **Unwmk.**

159 A44 1½s red violet 6.50 2.75
160 A44 3s vermilion 7.00 3.60

Taking of the 1st modern census in Japan. Not available for foreign postage except to China.

Meiji Shrine, Tokyo — A45

1920, Nov. 1 **Engr.**

161 A45 1½s dull violet 2.50 1.10
162 A45 3s rose 2.50 1.10

Dedication of the Meiji Shrine. Not available for foreign postage except to China.

National and Postal Flags — A46

Ministry of Communications Building, Tokyo — A47

Typographed (A46), Engraved (A47)

1921, Apr. 20 ***Perf. 12½, 13x13½***

163 A46 1½s gray grn & red 1.50 .90
164 A47 3s violet brn 2.00 1.00
165 A46 4s rose & red 40.00 18.00
166 A47 10s dark blue 185.00 115.00
Nos. 163-166 (4) 228.50 134.90

50th anniv. of the establishment of postal service and Japanese postage stamps.

Battleships "Katori" and "Kashima" — A48

1921, Sept. 3 **Litho.** ***Perf. 12½***

167 A48 1½s violet 2.00 1.00
168 A48 3s olive green 2.25 1.00
169 A48 4s rose red 32.50 15.00
170 A48 10s deep blue 45.00 18.00
Nos. 167-170 (4) 81.75 35.00

Return of Crown Prince Hirohito from his European visit.

Mount Fuji — A49

Granite Paper

Size: 18½x22mm ("New Die")

Perf. 13x13½

1930-37 **Typo.** **Wmk. 141**

No.	Type	Description	Unused	Used
171	A49	4s green ('37)	2.40	.35
172	A49	4s orange	5.50	.25
174	A49	8s olive green	8.50	.25
175a	A49	20s blue ('37)	19.00	26.00
176	A49	20s brown violet	26.00	.25
		Nos. 171-176 (5)	61.40	27.10

1922-29

Size: 19x22½mm ("Old Die")

No.	Type	Description	Unused	Used
171a	A49	4s green	7.50	2.60
172a	A49	4s orange ('29)	75.00	7.50
173	A49	8s rose	15.00	5.25
174a	A49	8s olive green ('29)	225.00	70.00
175	A49	20s deep blue	17.00	.50
176a	A49	20s brown vio ('29)	75.00	1.25
		Nos. 171a-176a (6)	414.50	87.10

See Nos. 242, 246, 248.

Mt. Niitaka, Taiwan — A50

Perf. 12½

1923, Apr. 16 **Unwmk.** **Engr.**

177 A50 1½s orange 9.50 6.75
178 A50 3s dark violet 14.00 5.75

1st visit of Crown Prince Hirohito to Taiwan. The stamps were sold only in Taiwan, but were valid throughout the empire.

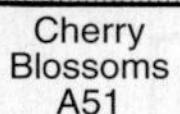

Cherry Blossoms
A51

Sun and Dragonflies
A52

Without Gum; Granite Paper

1923 Wmk. 142 Litho. *Imperf.*

179 A51 ½s gray 4.25 2.25
180 A51 1½s lt blue 4.75 1.00
181 A51 2s red brown 4.25 1.00
182 A51 3s brt rose 3.25 .80
183 A51 4s gray green 37.50 12.00
184 A51 5s dull violet 14.00 1.00
185 A51 8s red orange 60.00 21.00
186 A52 10s deep brown 26.00 1.00
187 A52 20s deep blue 27.50 1.50
Nos. 179-187 (9) 181.50 41.55

Nos. 179-187 exist rouletted and with various perforations. These were made privately.

Empress Jingo — A53

Granite Paper

Perf. 12, 13x13½

1924 Engr. Wmk. 141

188 A53 5y gray green 225.00 3.50
189 A53 10y dull violet 350.00 3.00

See Nos. 253-254.

Cranes — A54

Phoenix — A55

Perf. 10½ to 13½ and Compound

1925, May 10 Litho. Unwmk.

190 A54 1½s gray violet 2.00 1.00
191 A55 3s silver & brn org 2.60 1.50
a. Vert. pair, imperf. btwn. 425.00
192 A54 8s light red 20.00 11.00
193 A55 20s sil & gray grn 45.00 35.00
Nos. 190-193 (4) 69.60 48.50

25th wedding anniv. of the Emperor Yoshihito (Taisho) and Empress Sadako.

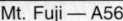

Mt. Fuji — A56

Yomei Gate, Nikko — A57

Nagoya Castle — A58

Granite Paper

Perf. 13½x13

1926-37 Typo. Wmk. 141

194 A56 2s green 1.60 .25
195 A57 6s carmine 6.00 .25
196 A58 10s dark blue 7.00 .25
197 A58 10s carmine ('37) 8.00 7.00
Nos. 194-197 (4) 22.60 7.75

See Nos. 244, 247. For surcharges see People's Republic of China No. 2L5-2L6 in Scott Standard catalogue, Vol. 2.

Baron Hisoka Maeshima — A59

Map of World on Mollweide's Projection — A60

Perf. 12½, 13x13½

1927, June 20 Unwmk.

198 A59 1½s lilac 2.25 1.00
199 A59 3s olive green 2.25 1.00
200 A60 6s carmine rose 50.00 40.00
201 A60 10s blue 62.50 40.00
Nos. 198-201 (4) 117.00 82.00

50th anniv. of Japan's joining the UPU. Baron Maeshima (1835-1919) organized Japan's modern postal system and was postmaster general.

Phoenix — A61

Enthronement Hall, Kyoto — A62

Yellow Paper

1928, Nov. 10 Engr. *Perf. 12½*

202 A61 1½s deep green 1.25 .50
203 A62 3s red violet 1.25 .50
204 A61 6s carmine rose 2.25 1.60
205 A62 10s deep blue 3.00 2.10
Nos. 202-205 (4) 7.75 4.70

Enthronement of Emperor Hirohito.

Great Shrines of Ise — A63

1929, Oct. 2 *Perf. 12½*

206 A63 1½s gray violet 1.00 1.00
207 A63 3s carmine 1.50 1.10

58th rebuilding of the Ise Shrines.

Map of Japanese Empire — A64

1930, Sept. 25 Unwmk.

208 A64 1½s deep violet 2.00 1.25
209 A64 3s deep red 2.25 1.50

2nd census in the Japanese Empire.

Meiji Shrine — A65

1930, Nov. 1 Litho.

210 A65 1½s green 1.50 .85
211 A65 3s brown org 2.00 1.00

10th anniv. of dedication of Meiji Shrine.

Coil Stamps

Wmk. Zigzag Lines (141)

1933 Typo. *Perf. 13 Horiz.*

212 A34 1½s light blue 13.00 17.00
213 A34 3s rose 14.00 21.00

Japanese Red Cross Badge — A66

Red Cross Building, Tokyo — A67

Perf. 12½

1934, Oct. 1 Engr. Unwmk.

214 A66 1½s green & red 1.50 1.00
215 A67 3s dull vio & red 1.75 1.25
216 A66 6s dk car & red 8.00 5.00
217 A67 10s blue & red 12.00 8.00
Nos. 214-217 (4) 23.25 15.25

15th International Red Cross Congress. Sheets of 20 with commemorative marginal inscription. One side of sheet is perf. 13.

White Tower of Liaoyang and Warship "Hiei" — A68

Akasaka Detached Palace, Tokyo — A69

1935, Apr. 2

218 A68 1½s olive green 1.00 .60
219 A69 3s red brown 1.50 1.00
220 A68 6s carmine 6.25 3.00
221 A69 10s blue 9.00 6.00
Nos. 218-221 (4) 17.75 10.60

Visit of Emperor Kang Teh of Manchukuo (Henry Pu-yi) to Tokyo, April 6, 1935. Sheets of 20 with commemorative marginal inscription. One side of sheet is perf. 13.

Mt. Fuji — A70

Granite Paper

1935 Typo. *Perf. 13x13½*

222 A70 1½s rose carmine 10.00 .75
a. Miniature sheet of 20 600.00 450.00

Issued to pay postage on New Year's cards from Dec. 1-31, 1935. After Jan. 1, 1936, used for ordinary letter postage. No. 222 was issued in sheets of 100.

Mt. Fuji
A71

Fuji from Lake Ashi
A72

Fuji from Lake Kawaguchi — A73

Fuji from Mishima
A74

Granite Paper

1936, July 10 Photo. Wmk. 141

223 A71 1½s red brown 3.00 2.00
224 A72 3s dark green 4.50 3.00
225 A73 6s carmine rose 10.00 10.00
226 A74 10s dark blue 12.00 10.00
Nos. 223-226 (4) 29.50 23.00

Fuji-Hakone National Park.

Dove, Map of Manchuria and Kwantung — A75

Shinto Shrine, Port Arthur — A76

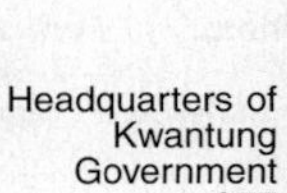

Headquarters of Kwantung Government
A77

Granite Paper

1936, Sept. 1 Litho. *Perf. 12½*

227 A75 1½s gray violet 16.00 10.00
228 A76 3s red brown 12.00 12.00
229 A77 10s dull green 190.00 135.00
Nos. 227-229 (3) 218.00 157.00

30th anniv. of Japanese administration of Kwangtung Leased Territory and the South Manchuria Railway Zone.

Imperial Diet Building
A78

Grand Staircase
A79

1936, Nov. 7 Engr. *Perf. 13*

230 A78 1½s green 2.00 1.00
231 A79 3s brown vio 3.00 1.50
232 A79 6s carmine 6.00 4.00
233 A78 10s blue 10.00 5.75
Nos. 230-233 (4) 21.00 12.25

Opening of the new Diet Building, Tokyo.

"Wedded Rocks," Futamigaura — A80

1936, Dec. 10 **Photo.**
234 A80 1½s rose carmine 3.50 .25

Issued to pay postage on New Year's greeting cards.

Types of 1913-26
Perf. 13½x13, 13x13½

1937 **Typo.** **Wmk. 257**
239 A34 ½s brown 1.75 1.00
240 A34 1s orange yel 2.50 1.25
241 A34 3s rose 1.00 .25
242 A49 4s green 3.50 .25
243 A35 5s violet 4.75 .25
244 A57 6s crimson 7.50 .95
245 A35 7s red org 7.50 .25
246 A49 8s olive bister 8.00 .50
247 A58 10s carmine 6.50 .25
248 A49 20s blue 12.50 .50
249 A35 25s olive grn 37.50 2.00
250 A36 30s org & grn 28.00 .50
251 A36 50s brn org & dk bl 120.00 2.00
252 A36 1y yel grn & mar 57.50 1.50
Nos. 239-252 (14) 298.50 11.45

Engr.
253 A53 5y gray green 275.00 3.25
254 A53 10y dull violet 400.00 3.00

For overprint see People's Republic of China No. 2L6 in Scott Standard catalogue, Vol. 2.

Coil Stamps

1938 **Typo.** ***Perf. 13 Horiz.***
255 A34 3s rose 4.00 4.00

New Year's Decoration — A81

1937, Dec. 15 **Photo.** ***Perf. 13***
256 A81 2s scarlet 6.25 .25

Issued to pay postage on New Year's cards, later for ordinary use.

Trading Ship A82

Harvesting A83

Gen. Maresuke Nogi — A84

Power Plant — A85

Admiral Heihachiro Togo A86

Mount Hodaka A87

Garambi Lighthouse, Taiwan — A88

Diamond Mountains, Korea — A89

Meiji Shrine, Tokyo — A90

Yomei Gate, Nikko — A91

Plane and Map of Japan — A92

Kasuga Shrine, Nara — A93

Mount Fuji and Cherry Blossoms A94

Horyu Temple, Nara A95

Miyajima Torii, Itsukushima Shrine — A96

Golden Pavilion, Kyoto — A97

Great Buddha, Kamakura A98

Kamatari Fujiwara A99

Plum Blossoms — A100

Typographed or Engraved

1937-45 **Wmk. 257** ***Perf. 13***
257 A82 ½s purple .50 .30
258 A83 1s fawn 1.50 .25
259 A84 2s crimson .35 .25
a. Booklet pane of 20 50.00
b. 2s pink, perf. 12 ('45) 1.25 .85
c. 2s vermilion ('44) 2.10 1.60
260 A85 3s green ('39) .35 .25
261 A86 4s dark green .75 .25
a. Booklet pane of 20 13.00
262 A87 5s dark ultra ('39) .75 .25
263 A88 6s orange ('39) 1.50 .60
264 A89 7s deep green ('39) .50 .25
265 A90 8s dk pur & pale vio ('39) .45 .25
266 A91 10s lake ('38) 2.50 .25
267 A92 12s indigo ('39) .50 .30
268 A93 14s rose lake & pale rose ('38) .50 .25
269 A94 20s ultra ('40) .50 .25
270 A95 25s dk brn & pale brn ('38) .50 .25
271 A96 30s pck blue ('39) 1.25 .25
a. Imperf., pair 400.00
272 A97 50s ol & pale ol ('39) .60 .25
a. Pale olive (forest) omitted
273 A98 1y brn & pale brn ('39) 3.50 1.00
274 A99 5y dp gray grn ('39) 25.00 2.50
275 A100 10y dk brn vio ('39) 16.50 2.00
Nos. 257-275 (19) 58.00 9.95

Nos. 257-261, 265, 268, 270, 272- 273 are typographed; the others are engraved.

Coil Stamps

1938-39 **Typo.** ***Perf. 13 Horiz.***
276 A82 ½s purple ('39) 2.50 *4.50*
277 A84 2s crimson 3.00 *4.25*
278 A86 4s dark green 3.50 *4.25*
279 A93 14s rose lake & pale rose 110.00 80.00
Nos. 276-279 (4) 119.00 93.00

See Nos. 329, 331, 333, 341, 351, 360 and 361 in Scott Standard catalogue, Vol. 4. For surcharges see Nos. B4-B5, Burma 2N4-2N27, China-Taiwan 8-9 and People's Republic of China 2L3, 2L7, 2L9-2L10, 2L39 in Scott Vol. 2, Korea 55-56 in Scott Vol. 4. For overprints see Ryukyu Islands (Scott US Specialized catalogue) Nos. 2X1-2X2, 2X4-2X7, 2X10, 2X13-2X14, 2X17, 2X20, 2X23, 2X27, 2X29, 2X33-2X34, 3X2-3X7, 3X10-3X11, 3X14, 3X17, 3X19, 3X21, 3X23, 3X26-3X30, 5X1-5X3, 5X5-5X8, 5X10.

Mount Nantai — A101

Kegon Falls — A102

Sacred Bridge, Nikko A103

Mount Hiuchi A104

Unwmk.

1938, Dec. 25 **Photo.** ***Perf. 13***
280 A101 2s brown orange 1.00 .50
281 A102 4s olive green 1.00 .50
282 A103 10s deep rose 5.75 3.75
283 A104 20s dark blue 5.75 3.75
a. Souvenir sheet of 4, #280-283 45.00 75.00
Never hinged 80.00
Nos. 280-283 (4) 13.50 8.50
Set, never hinged 32.50

Nikko National Park.
No. 283a sold for 50s.

Many souvenir sheets were sold in folders. Values are for sheets without folders.

Mount Daisen A106

Yashima Plateau, Inland Sea A107

Abuto Kwannon Temple A108

Tomo Bay, Inland Sea A109

1939, Apr. 20
285 A106 2s lt brown 1.00 .50
286 A107 4s yellow grn 1.60 1.00
287 A108 10s dull rose 6.50 4.00
288 A109 20s blue 6.50 4.00
a. Souvenir sheet of 4, #285-288 25.00 40.00
Never hinged 50.00
Nos. 285-288 (4) 15.60 9.50
Set, never hinged 32.50

Daisen and Inland Sea National Parks. No. 288a sold for 50s.

View from Kuju Village, Kyushu A111

Mount Naka A112

Crater of Mount Naka A113

Volcanic Cones of Mt. Aso A114

1939, Aug. 15
290 A111 2s olive brown 1.00 .50
291 A112 4s yellow green 3.00 2.00
292 A113 10s carmine 15.00 9.00
293 A114 20s sapphire 22.50 10.00
a. Souvenir sheet of 4, #290-293 85.00 100.00
Never hinged 130.00
Nos. 290-293 (4) 41.50 21.50
Set, never hinged 85.00

Aso National Park. No. 293a sold for 50s.

Globe — A116

Tsunetami Sano — A117

1939, Nov. 15 ***Perf. 12½***
Cross in Carmine
295 A116 2s brown 1.50 .90
296 A117 4s yellow green 1.60 1.00
297 A116 10s crimson 7.00 6.50
298 A117 20s sapphire 7.00 6.50
Nos. 295-298 (4) 17.10 14.90
Set, never hinged 32.50

Intl. Red Cross Society founding, 75th anniv.

Sacred Golden Kite — A118

Mount Takachiho — A119

Five Ayu Fish and Sake Jar — A120

Kashiwara Shrine — A121

1940 Engr. *Perf. 12*

299 A118 2s brown orange .80 .80
300 A119 4s dark green .60 .60
301 A120 10s dark carmine 3.25 3.00
302 A121 20s dark ultra .80 .80
Nos. 299-302 (4) 5.45 5.20
Set, never hinged 7.50

2,600th anniv. of the legendary date of the founding of Japan.

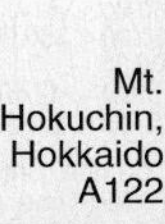

Mt. Hokuchin, Hokkaido A122

Mt. Asahi, Hokkaido A123

Sounkyo Gorge — A124

Tokachi Mountain Range A125

1940, Apr. 20 Photo. *Perf. 13*

303 A122 2s brown 1.00 1.00
304 A123 4s yellow green 2.75 2.00
305 A124 10s carmine 6.00 5.25
306 A125 20s sapphire 6.00 5.50
a. Souvenir sheet of 4, #303-306 175.00 180.00
Never hinged 325.00
Nos. 303-306 (4) 15.75 13.75
Set, never hinged 32.50

Daisetsuzan National Park. No. 306a sold for 50s.

Mt. Karakuni, Kyushu A127

Mt. Takachiho A128

Torii of Kirishima Shrine A129

Lake of the Six Kwannon A130

1940, Aug. 21

308 A127 2s brown 1.00 .75
309 A128 4s green 1.75 1.50
310 A129 10s carmine 6.00 4.75
311 A130 20s deep ultra 7.00 5.75
a. Souvenir sheet of 4, #308-311 155.00 155.00
Never hinged 325.00
Nos. 308-311 (4) 15.75 12.75
Set, never hinged 37.50

Kirishima National Park. No. 311a sold for 50s.

Education Minister with Rescript on Education A132

Characters Signifying Loyalty and Filial Piety A133

1940, Oct. 25 Engr. *Perf. 12½*

313 A132 2s purple .75 .75
314 A133 4s green 1.00 1.00
Set, never hinged 2.25

50th anniv. of the imperial rescript on education, given by Emperor Meiji to clarify Japan's educational policy.

SEMI-POSTAL STAMPS

Douglas Plane over Japan Alps — SP1

Wmk. Zigzag Lines (141)

1937, June 1 Photo. *Perf. 13*

B1 SP1 2s + 2s rose carmine 1.50 .75
B2 SP1 3s + 2s purple 1.50 1.25
B3 SP1 4s + 2s green 2.25 1.00
Nos. B1-B3 (3) 5.25 3.00
Set, never hinged 7.00

The surtax was for the Patriotic Aviation Fund to build civil airports.

AIR POST STAMPS

Regular Issue of 1914 Overprinted in Red or Blue

Wmk. Zigzag Lines (141)

1919, Oct. 3 *Perf. 13x13½*

Granite Paper

C1 A34 1 ½s blue (R) 240.00 67.50
C2 A34 3s rose (Bl) 425.00 185.00

Excellent counterfeits exist.

Passenger Plane over Lake Ashi — AP1

Granite Paper

1929-34 Engr. *Perf. 13½x13*

C3 AP1 8 ½s orange brn 27.50 14.00
C4 AP1 9 ½s rose 9.00 3.75
C5 AP1 16 ½s yellow grn 9.00 4.00
C6 AP1 18s ultra 10.00 3.75
C7 AP1 33s gray 20.00 3.25
Nos. C3-C7 (5) 75.50 28.75
Set, never hinged 170.00

Souvenir Sheet

C8 AP1 Sheet of 4, #C4-C7 1,250. 1,250.
Never hinged 2,000.

Issued: 9 ½s, 3/1/34; No. C8, 4/20/34; others, 10/6/29. No. C8 for Communications Commemoration Day (1st observance of establishment of the postal service and issuance of #1-4). Sold only at Phil. Exhib. p.o., Tokyo, 4/20-27. Size: 110x100mm.

MILITARY STAMPS

Nos. 98, 119, 131 Overprinted

1910-14 Unwmk. *Perf. 11½ to 13½*

M1 A26 3s rose 200.00 35.00
M2 A34 3s rose ('13) 325.00 140.00

Wmk. 141

M3 A34 3s rose ('14) 30.00 16.00
Nos. M1-M3 (3) 555.00 191.00

Nos. M1-M3 overprint type I has 3.85mm between characters; type II, 4-4.5mm (movable type).

1921 On Offices in China No. 37

M4 A34 3s rose *5,750. 4,750.*

No. M4 is a provisional military stamp issued at the Japanese Post Office, Tsingtao, China. The overprint differs from the illustration, being 12mm high with thicker characters. Counterfeits are plentiful.

Overprint 16mm High

1924 On No. 131

M5 A34 3s rose 90.00 72.50
a. 3s rose (#131b) 90.00 75.00

Excellent forgeries exist of Nos. M1-M5.

JAPANESE OFFICES ABROAD

Offices in China

1899-1907 Regular Issues of Japan Overprinted in Red or Black

Perf. 11½, 12, 12½, 13½, 13x13½

1900-06 Unwmk.

1 A26 5r gray (R) 3.25 2.50
2 A26 ½s gray (R) ('01) 2.00 .70
3 A26 1s lt red brn (R) 2.00 .70
4 A26 1 ½s ultra 9.00 2.00
5 A26 1 ½s vio ('06) 5.00 .95
6 A26 2s lt grn (R) 5.00 .70
7 A26 3s violet brn 5.50 .70
8 A26 3s rose ('06) 4.00 .50
9 A26 4s rose 4.50 1.25
10 A26 5s org yel (R) 9.00 1.25
11 A27 6s maroon ('06) 16.00 11.00
12 A27 8s ol grn (R) 9.00 5.50
13 A27 10s deep blue 9.00 1.00
14 A27 15s purple 18.00 1.75
15 A27 20s red org 16.00 1.00
16 A28 25s blue grn (R) 32.50 3.50
17 A28 50s red brown 35.00 2.50
18 A29 1y carmine 55.00 2.50
Nos. 1-18 (18) 239.75 40.00

No. 6 with black overprint is bogus.
Nos. 5, 6, 8, 9 and 13 exist as booklet panes of 6, made from sheet stamps. They are rare.

1900

19 A30 3s carmine 25.00 15.00

Wedding of Crown Prince Yoshihito and Princess Sadako.

Japan Nos. 113 & 114 Overprinted

1908

20 A33 5y green 400.00 47.50
21 A33 10y dark violet 700.00 110.00

On #20-21 the space between characters of the overprint is 6 ½mm instead of 1 ½mm.

Stamps of 1913-33 Issues Overprinted

1913 *Perf. 12, 12x13, 13x13½*

22 A34 ½s brown 14.00 14.00
23 A34 1s orange 15.00 15.00
24 A34 1 ½s lt blue 40.00 18.00
25 A34 2s green 45.00 20.00
26 A34 3s rose 22.50 8.00
27 A35 4s red 62.50 62.50
28 A35 5s violet 62.50 50.00
29 A35 10s deep blue 62.50 21.00
30 A35 20s claret 250.00 140.00
31 A35 25s olive green 90.00 21.00
32 A36 1y yel grn & mar 750.00 500.00
Nos. 22-32 (11) 1,414. 869.50

Nos. 24, 25, 26, 27 and 29 exist in booklet panes of 6, made from sheet stamps. The No. 26 pane is very rare.

Japan Nos. 127-137, 139-147 Overprinted

1914-21 Wmk. 141

Granite Paper

33 A34 ½s brown 3.25 .80
34 A34 1s orange 3.75 .80
35 A34 1 ½s blue 4.25 .80
36 A34 2s green 2.75 .95
37 A34 3s rose 2.40 .80
38 A35 4s red 10.00 4.75
39 A35 5s violet 17.50 1.75
40 A35 6s brown ('20) 30.00 18.00
41 A35 8s gray ('20) 37.50 20.00
42 A35 10s dp blue 12.00 1.25
43 A35 20s claret 42.50 3.25
44 A35 25s olive grn 50.00 3.50
45 A36 30s org brn ('20) 75.00 27.50
46 A36 50s dk brn ('20) 90.00 30.00
47 A36 1y yel grn & mar ('18) 130.00 6.75
48 A33 5y green 1,850. 525.00
49 A33 10y violet ('21) 2,650. 1,600.
Nos. 33-49 (17) 5,011. 2,246.

On Nos. 48-49 the space between characters of overprint is 4 ½mm, instead of 6 ½mm on Nos. 20-21 and 1 ½mm on all lower values. See No. M4.

No. 42 exists as a booklet pane of 6, made from sheet stamps. It is very rare.

Counterfeit overprints exist of Nos. 1-49.

Offices in Korea

Regular Issue of Japan Overprinted in Red or Black

1900 Unwmk. *Perf. 11½, 12, 12½*

No.	Type	Description	Unused	Used
1	A26	5r gray (R)	19.00	8.75
2	A26	1s lt red brn (R)	20.00	5.00
3	A26	1½s ultra	250.00	130.00
4	A26	2s lt green (R)	19.00	10.00
5	A26	3s violet brn	17.00	4.75
6	A26	4s rose	65.00	27.50
7	A26	5s org yel (R)	67.50	27.50
8	A27	8s ol grn (R)	250.00	120.00
9	A27	10s deep blue	35.00	9.00
10	A27	15s purple	62.50	6.00
11	A27	20s red orange	62.50	5.00
12	A28	25s blue grn (R)	220.00	55.00
13	A28	50s red brown	175.00	18.00
14	A29	1y carmine	475.00	14.00
		Nos. 1-14 (14)	1,738.	440.50

1900

No.	Type	Description	Unused	Used
15	A30	3s carmine	125.00	55.00

Wedding of Crown Prince Yoshihito and Princess Sadako.

Counterfeit overprints exist of Nos. 1-15.

JORDAN

ˈjor-dᵊn

Trans-Jordan

LOCATION — In the Near East, separated from the Mediterranean Sea by Israel
GOVT. — Kingdom
AREA — 38,400 sq. mi.
POP. — 3,750,000 (est. 1982)
CAPITAL — Amman

The former Turkish territory was mandated to Great Britain following World War I. It became an independent state in 1946.

10 Milliemes = 1 Piaster
1000 Mils = 1 Palestine Pound (1930)

British Mandate

Stamps and Type of Palestine 1918 Overprinted in Black or Silver

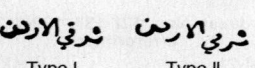

Type I — Type II

1920, Nov. Wmk. 33 *Perf. 15x14*

No.	Type	Description	Unused	Used
1	A1	1m dark brown	3.50	5.00
a.		Inverted overprint	150.00	300.00
2	A1	2m blue green	22.50	25.00
3	A1	3m light brown (I)	3.75	4.25
a.		Overprint type II	1,200.	
4	A1	4m scarlet	4.00	4.00
a.		Arabic "40"	82.50	
5	A1	5m orange	10.00	3.50
6	A1	1pi dark blue (S)	2,200.	
7	A1	2pi olive green (I)	14.00	16.00
a.		Overprint type II	925.00	
8	A1	5pi plum	55.00	82.50
a.		Overprint type II	1,500.	
9	A1	9pi bister	100.00	120.00
		Nos. 1-9 (9)	2,413.	260.25

Perf. 14

No.	Type	Description	Unused	Used
1B	A1	1m dark brown	1.40	5.00
a.		Inverted overprint	180.00	
2B	A1	2m blue green	3.00	4.50
a.		Silver overprint	600.00	650.00
3B	A1	3m light brown	22.50	30.00
4B	A1	4m scarlet	19.00	50.00
a.		Arabic "40"	160.00	
5B	A1	5m orange	2.75	3.50
6B	A1	1pi dark blue (S)	3.75	4.25
7B	A1	2pi olive green	13.00	13.00
8B	A1	5pi plum	7.50	16.00
9B	A1	9pi bister	7.50	55.00
10	A1	10pi ultramarine	20.00	55.00
11	A1	20pi gray	22.50	92.50
		Nos. 1B-11 (11)	122.90	328.75

The overprint reads "Sharqi al-ardan" (East of Jordan).

For overprints see Nos. 12-73, 83A.

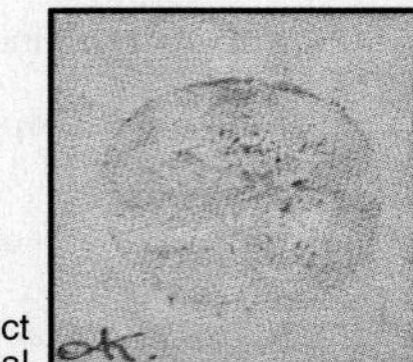

Moab District Seal

1920, Nov. Handstamped *Imperf.*

No.	Type	Description	Unused	Used
12	A2	(1p) pale blue	3,750.	4,250.

No. 12 was issued at Kerak by the political officer for the Moab District and was used until March 1921 pending the arrival of Nos. 1//11.

Stamps of 1920 Issue Handstamp Surcharged "Ashir el qirsh" (tenth of piaster) and numeral in Black, Red or Violet

On Nos. 1-9 (Perf. 15x14)

1922, Nov.

No.	Type	Description	Unused	Used
13	A1	1/10pi on 1m dk brn	32.50	55.00
14	A1	1/10pi on 1m dk brn (R)	77.50	77.50
15	A1	1/10pi on 1m dk brn (V)	77.50	77.50
16	A1	2/10pi on 2m bl grn	37.50	37.50
a.		3/10pi on 2m bl grn (error)	130.00	120.00
17	A1	2/10pi on 2m bl grn (R)	87.50	87.50
18	A1	2/10pi on 2m bl grn (V)	110.00	110.00
19	A1	3/10pi on 3m lt brn	16.00	16.00
a.		Pair, one without surcharge	875.00	
b.		On #3a (type II)	1,300.	1,300.
20	A1	3/10pi on 3m lt brn (V)	160.00	160.00
a.		On #3a (type II)	3,000.	
21	A1	4/10pi on 4m scar	65.00	70.00
22	A1	5/10pi on 5m org	200.00	110.00
23	A1	5/10pi on 5m dp org (V)	275.00	275.00

Handstamp Surcharged "El qirsh" (piaster) and numeral in Black, Red or Violet

No.	Type	Description	Unused	Used
24	A1	2pi on 2pi ol grn	275.00	82.50
a.		On #7a (type II)	1,400.	
25	A1	2pi on 2pi ol grn (R)	350.00	87.50
26	A1	2pi on 2pi ol grn (V)	325.00	100.00
27	A1	5pi on 5pi plum	70.00	87.50
a.		On #8a (type II)	1,750.	
28	A1	9pi on 9pi bister	325.00	375.00
29	A1	9pi on 9pi bister (R)	140.00	150.00

For overprint see No. 83B.

On Nos. 1B-11 (Perf. 14)

No.	Type	Description	Unused	Used
13C	A1	1/10pi on 1m dk brn	27.50	32.50
a.		Pair, one without surcharge	1,600.	
14C	A1	1/10pi on 1m dk brn (R)	65.00	65.00
15C	A1	1/10pi on 1m dk brn (V)	275.00	325.00
16C	A1	2/10pi on 2m bl grn	32.50	32.50
a.		Pair, one without surcharge	1,600.	
b.		3/10pi on 2m bl grn (error)	120.00	120.00
17C	A1	2/10pi on 2m bl grn (R)	87.50	87.50
18C	A1	2/10pi on 2m bl grn (V)	87.50	87.50
22C	A1	5/10pi on 5m org	250.00	110.00
a.		Pair, one without surcharge		2,250.
23C	A1	5/10pi on 5m org (V)	300.00	
23D	A1	1pi on 1pi dk blue (R)	225.00	65.00
a.		Pair, one without surcharge	2,000.	
23E	A1	1pi on 1pi dk blue (V)	450.00	
29C	A1	9pi on 9pi bister	600.00	600.00
31	A1	10pi on 10pi ultra	925.00	1,100.
32	A1	20pi on 20pi gray	700.00	825.00
33	A1	20pi on 20pi gray (V)	1,000.	1,050.

Surcharge in Black on Palestine Nos. 13-14

No.	Type	Description	Unused	Used
34	A1	10pi on 10pi ultra	2,000.	2,750.
35	A1	20pi on 20pi gray	2,750.	3,250.

Nos. 13-35 are handstamped, and the overprints exist double on most values. They have been extensively forged. Values above are for expertized examples.

Stamps of 1920 Handstamped in Violet, Black or Red

1922, Dec. *Perf. 14*

On Nos. 1-5, 7-9 (Perf. 15x14)

No.	Type	Description	Unused	Used
36	A1	1m dk brn (R)	32.50	32.50
37	A1	1m dk brn (V)	32.50	37.50
38	A1	1m dk brn (Blk)	27.50	27.50
39	A1	2m bl grn (R)	30.00	30.00
40	A1	2m bl grn (V)	26.00	26.00
41	A1	2m bl grn (Blk)	25.00	25.00
42	A1	3m lt brn (R)	52.50	52.50
a.		On #3a (type II)	1,750.	
43	A1	3m lt brn (V)	10.00	10.00
a.		Pair, one without surcharge	1,400.	
b.		On #3a (type II)	1,600.	1,600.
44	A1	3m lt brn (Blk)	11.00	11.00
45	A1	4m scar (R)	65.00	70.00
46	A1	4m scar (V)	65.00	70.00
47	A1	4m scar (Blk)	65.00	70.00
48	A1	5m orange (R)	50.00	13.00
49	A1	5m orange (V)	20.00	13.00
50	A1	2pi ol grn (R)	65.00	50.00
a.		On #7a (type II)	1,600.	
52	A1	2pi ol grn (V)	27.50	20.00
a.		On #7a (type II)	1,600.	1,400.
53	A1	2pi ol grn (Blk)	18.00	13.00
54	A1	5pi plum (R)	110.00	130.00
a.		Pair, one without surcharge	1,750.	
55	A1	5pi plum (V)	70.00	90.00
56	A1	9pi bister (R)	450.00	500.00
57	A1	9pi bister (V)	225.00	275.00
a.		Type II overprint	2,500.	
58	A1	9pi bister (Blk)	75.00	90.00

On #1B//11 (Perf. 14)

No.	Type	Description	Unused	Used
36C	A1	1m dk brn (R)	17.50	22.00
a.		Pair, one without ovpt.	1,400.	
37C	A1	1m dk brn (V)	27.50	25.00
38C	A1	1m dk brn (Blk)	25.00	25.00
39C	A1	2m bl grn (R)	35.00	35.00
40C	A1	2m bl grn (V)	11.00	11.00
41C	A1	2m bl grn (Blk)	17.50	17.50
43C	A1	3m lt brn (V)	850.00	375.00
48C	A1	5m orange (R)	325.00	80.00
49C	A1	5m orange (V)	35.00	25.00
51	A1	1pi dark blue (R)	40.00	19.00
51C	A1	1pi dark blue (V)	25.00	12.50
52C	A1	2pi ol grn (V)	85.00	90.00
54C	A1	5pi plum (R)	110.00	120.00
55C	A1	5pi plum (V)	110.00	130.00
57C	A1	9pi bister (V)	1,000.	1,100.
59	A1	10pi ultra (R)	2,000.	2,100.
60	A1	10pi ultra (V)	1,200.	1,750.
61	A1	20pi gray (R)	1,750.	2,200.
62	A1	20pi gray (V)	1,200.	2,000.

The overprint reads "Hukumat al Sharqi al Arabia" (Arab Government of the East) and date, 1923. The surcharges or overprints on Nos. 12 to 61 inclusive are handstamped and, as usual, are found inverted and double.

Ink pads of several colors were in use at the same time and the surcharges and overprints frequently show a mixture of two colors.

For overprints see Nos. 84, 87, 89, 92-93, 95-96.

Stamps of 1920 Overprinted in Gold or Black

1923, Mar. 1 *Perf. 15x14*

No.	Type	Description	Unused	Used
63	A1	1m dark brn (G)	1,600.	1,900.
64	A1	2m blue grn (G)	25.00	27.50
65	A1	3m lt brn (G)	19.00	20.00
a.		Double overprint	550.00	
b.		Inverted overprint	600.00	
c.		Black overprint	82.50	92.50
66	A1	4m scarlet (Blk)	22.50	20.00
67	A1	5m orange (Blk)	65.00	55.00
a.		Original ovpt. albino	1,300.	1,500.
69	A1	2pi ol grn (G)	25.00	22.50
a.		On #7a (type II)	1,300.	1,100.
b.		Black overprint	275.00	275.00
70	A1	5pi plum (G)	80.00	110.00
a.		Inverted overprint	240.00	
b.		On #8a (type II)	2,200.	
c.		As "b," inverted ovpt.	2,750.	
d.		Black overprint inverted	1,600.	

Perf. 14

No.	Type	Description	Unused	Used
63E	A1	1m dark brn (G)	21.00	35.00
a.		Inverted overprint	800.00	
64E	A1	2m blue grn (G)	20.00	22.50
a.		Double overprint	325.00	
b.		Inverted overprint	375.00	375.00
c.		Black overprint	325.00	
d.		As "c," inverted overprint	1,600.	
67E	A1	5m orange (Blk)	15.00	15.00
68	A1	1pi dk blue (G)	15.00	20.00
a.		Double overprint	550.00	600.00
b.		Black overprint	850.00	900.00
71	A1	9pi bister (Blk)	100.00	140.00
a.		Gold overprint	3,250.	
72	A1	10pi ultra (G)	90.00	140.00
73	A1	20pi gray (G)	90.00	140.00
a.		Inverted overprint	400.00	
b.		Double overprint	500.00	
c.		Double ovpt., one inverted	500.00	
d.		Double ovpt., one inverted, one gold, one black, black ovpt. inverted	800.00	
e.		Triple overprint, one inverted	1,200.	
f.		Black overprint	900.00	
g.		As "f," inverted overprint	1,200.	
h.		As "f," double overprint, one inverted	1,400.	

The overprint reads "Hukumat al Sharqi al Arabia, Nissan Sanat 921" (Arab Government of the East, April, 1921).

For overprints see Nos. 85, 99, 100, 102.

Stamps of Hejaz, 1922, Overprinted in Black

Coat of Arms (Hejaz A7)

1923, Apr. Unwmk. *Perf. 11½*

No.	Type	Description	Unused	Used
74A	A7	1/8pi orange brn	5.75	4.50
a.		Double overprint	225.00	
b.		Inverted overprint	120.00	
74B	A7	1/2pi red	5.75	4.50
a.		Inverted overprint	125.00	
74C	A7	1pi dark blue	4.50	1.50
a.		Inverted overprint	140.00	140.00
74D	A7	1½pi violet	4.75	2.75
a.		Double overprint	160.00	
b.		Pair, one without overprint	250.00	
c.		Pair, imperf. between	175.00	
74E	A7	2pi orange	6.00	8.50
74F	A7	3pi olive brn	15.00	20.00
a.		Inverted overprint	250.00	
b.		Double overprint	250.00	250.00
c.		Pair, one without overprint	400.00	
74G	A7	5pi olive green	35.00	47.50
		Nos. 64-70 (7)	76.75	89.25

The overprint is similar to that on the preceding group but is differently arranged. There are numerous varieties in the Arabic letters.

For overprints see Nos. 71-72, 91, J1-J5.

With Additional Surcharge of New Value in Arabic

a

b

No.	Type	Description	Unused	Used
74H	A7(a)	1/4pi on 1/8pi	16.00	11.00
		Never hinged	15.00	
a.		Inverted surcharge	175.00	
b.		Surcharge doubled	—	200.00
74I	A7(b)	10pi on 5pi	37.50	42.50
		Never hinged	45.00	

Independence Issue

Palestine Stamps and Type of 1918 Overprinted Vertically in Black or Gold

1923, May Wmk. 33 *Perf. 15x14*

No.	Type	Description	Unused	Used
74J	A1	1m dark brn (Bk)	24.00	24.00
a.		Double ovpt., one reversed	725.00	650.00
74K	A1	1m dark brn (G)	175.00	175.00
c.		Double ovpt., one reversed	1,000.	
74	A1	2m blue grn	42.50	50.00
75	A1	3m lt brown	14.00	17.50
76	A1	4m scarlet	14.00	17.50
77	A1	5m orange	70.00	80.00
78	A1	1pi dk blue (G)	95.00	110.00
a.		Double overprint	750.00	850.00
79	A1	2pi olive grn	70.00	90.00
80	A1	5pi plum (G)	80.00	90.00
a.		Double overprint (G)	725.00	
b.		Double overprint (Bk)	1,500.	
81	A1	9pi bis, perf. 14	70.00	85.00
82	A1	10pi ultra, perf. 14	80.00	100.00
83	A1	20pi gray	85.00	110.00
		Nos. 73-83 (12)	819.50	949.00

The overprint reads, "Arab Government of the East (abbreviated), Souvenir of Independence, 25th, May, 1923 ('923')."

There were printed 480 complete sets and a larger number of the 1, 2, 3 and 4m. A large number of these sets were distributed to high officials. The overprint was in a setting of twenty-four and the error "933" instead of "923" occurs once in the setting. Value about five times the "923" stamps.

The overprint exists reading downward on all values, as illustrated, and reading upward on all except the 5m and 2pi.
Forged overprints exist.
For overprint see No. 101.

Stamps of Preceding Issues, Handstamp Surcharged

83A A1 2½/10ths pi on 5m dp org 240.00 *240.00*
83B A1 ⁵⁄₁₀pi on 3m (#17) — *120.00*
84 A1 ⁵⁄₁₀pi on 3m (#36) 100.00 60.00
85 A1 ⁵⁄₁₀pi on 3m (#55) 27.50 40.00
86 A1 ⁵⁄₁₀pi on 5pi (#23) 85.00 *100.00*
87 A1 ⁵⁄₁₀pi on 5pi (#48) 10.00 *17.50*
88 A1 1pi on 5pi (#23) 75.00 *140.00*
89 A1 1pi on 5pi (#48) *2,500.* *2,750.*

Same Surcharge on Palestine Stamp of 1918

90 A1 ⁵⁄₁₀pi on 3m lt brn *17,000.*

No. 90 is valued in the grade of fine-very fine. Very fine examples are not known.
As is usual with handstamped surcharges these are found double, inverted, etc.

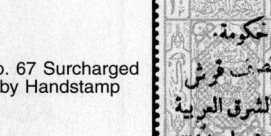

No. 67 Surcharged by Handstamp

Unwmk. ***Perf. 11½***

91 A7 ½pi on 1½pi vio 12.00 *14.00*
Never hinged 24.00
a. Surcharge typographed 55.00 *55.00*
Never hinged 95.00
b. As "a," inverted surcharge 150.00
c. As "a," double surcharge 180.00
d. As "a," pair, one with surcharge 500.00

The surcharge reads: "Nusf el qirsh" (half piastre). See note after No. 90.
Handstamped surcharge exists double; inverted; double, one inverted, etc.

Stamps of Preceding Issues Surcharged by Handstamp

No. 92

Perf. 14, 15x14

1923, Nov. **Wmk. 33**

92 A1 ½pi on 2pi (#45) 70.00 *85.00*
Never hinged 105.00
93 A1 ½pi on 2pi (#47) 110.00 *125.00*
Never hinged 165.00
94 A1 ½pi on 5pi (#23) 75.00 *85.00*
Never hinged 115.00
95 A1 ½pi on 5pi (#48) 3,000. 2,000.
96 A1 ½pi on 5pi (#49) 2,000. *2,750.*
97 A1 ½pi on 9pi (#24) *6,500.*
98 A1 ½pi on 9pi (#25) 95.00 *160.00*
Never hinged 145.00
99 A1 ½pi on 9pi (#61) 200.00 160.00
Never hinged 300.00

Surcharged by Handstamp

No. 102

100 A1 1pi on 10pi (#62) *2,250.* *2,500.*
101 A1 1pi on 10pi (#82) *3,000.* *3,000.*
102 A1 2pi on 20pi (#63) 65.00 *87.50*
Never hinged 100.00

Of the 25 examples of No. 100, a few were handstamped in violet. Value, unused $2,750.

Stamp of Hejaz, 1922, Overprinted by Handstamp

1923, Dec. **Unwmk.** ***Perf. 11½***

103 A7 ½pi red 8.00 *4.25*
Never hinged 16.00

Two settings of No. 103 exist. They differ in the spacing of the characters and the position of the bottom line of the overprint, either to the left or centered.
Nos. 92-103 handstamps exist inverted, doubled, etc.

Stamp of Hejaz, 1922, Overprinted

1924 **Typo.**

104 A7 ½pi red 14.00 *15.00*
Never hinged 20.00

King Hussein Issue

Stamps of Hejaz, 1922, Overprinted

1924 **Gold Overprint**

105 A7 ½pi red 4.00 4.00
Never hinged 8.00
106 A7 1pi dark blue 4.25 3.25
Never hinged 8.50
107 A7 1½pi violet 5.00 *4.50*
Never hinged 10.00
108 A7 2pi orange 12.00 *13.00*
Never hinged 24.00

Black Overprint

109 A7 ½pi red 3.00 3.00
Never hinged 3.75
110 A7 1pi dark blue 3.75 3.75
Never hinged 4.50
111 A7 1½pi violet 5.50 5.50
Never hinged 6.75
112 A7 2pi orange 13.00 13.00
Never hinged 19.50
Nos. 105-112 (8) 50.50 50.00

The overprint reads: "Arab Government of the East. In commemoration of the visit of H. M. the King of the Arabs, 11 Jemad el Than i 1342 (17th Jan. 1924)." The overprint was in a setting of thirty-six and the error "432" instead of "342" occurs once in the setting and is found on all values. Value, $75 each.

Stamps of Hejaz, 1922-24, Overprinted in Black or Red

Coat of Arms (Hejaz A8)

1924

113 A7 ⅛pi red brown 2.00 1.75
Never hinged 2.50
a. Inverted overprint 130.00 —
114 A7 ¼pi yellow green 2.00 1.00
Never hinged 2.50
a. Tête bêche pair 9.00 12.00
b. As "a," one overprint inverted 300.00 —
c. Inverted overprint 85.00 —
115 A7 ½pi red 2.00 .90
Never hinged 2.50
116 A7 1pi dark blue 11.00 1.50
Never hinged 14.00
a. Inverted overprint — —
b. Pair, imperf. between 130.00
117 A7 1½pi violet 7.00 7.00
Never hinged 8.75
118 A7 2pi orange 5.00 3.50
Never hinged 6.75
a. Double overprint — —
119 A7 3pi red brown 5.00 5.00
Never hinged 6.25
a. Double overprint 100.00 —
b. Inverted overprint 100.00 —
120 A7 5pi olive green 7.00 *7.00*
Never hinged 8.75
121 A8 10pi vio & dk brn (R) 15.00 *17.50*
Never hinged 19.00
a. Pair, one without overprint
b. Black overprint 250.00 —
Nos. 113-121 (9) 56.00 45.15

The overprint reads: "Hukumat al Sharqi al Arabia, 1342." (Arab Government of the East, 1924).

Stamps of Hejaz, 1925, Overprinted in Black or Red

(Hejaz A9)

(Hejaz A10)

(Hejaz A11)

1925, Aug.

122 A9 ⅛pi chocolate 1.25 *2.75*
Never hinged 1.60
a. Inverted overprint 70.00 —
b. Pair, imperf. vert. 130.00 *150.00*
123 A9 ¼pi ultramarine 2.25 *4.25*
Never hinged 3.00
a. Inverted overprint 70.00 —
124 A9 ½pi carmine rose 1.75 1.25
Never hinged 2.25
a. Inverted overprint 70.00 —
125 A10 1pi yellow green 1.75 3.00
Never hinged 2.25
126 A10 1½pi orange 4.00 *5.50*
Never hinged 5.00
a. Inverted overprint 70.00 —
127 A10 2pi deep blue 5.00 *7.50*
Never hinged 6.25
a. Triple overprint 160.00 *225.00*
128 A11 3pi dark green (R) 5.50 *11.00*
Never hinged 7.00
a. Inverted overprint 90.00 —
b. Pair, imperf. vert. 130.00 *170.00*
c. 3 pi dark green (Bk) 130.00 *160.00*
129 A11 5pi orange brn 8.00 *18.00*
Never hinged 10.00
a. Inverted overprint 85.00 —
Nos. 122-129 (8) 29.50 *53.25*

The overprint reads: "Hukumat al Sharqi al Arabi. 1343 Sanat." (Arab Government of the East, 1925). Nos. 122-129 exist imperforate, and with overprint double.

Type of Palestine, 1918

1925, Nov. 1 **Wmk. 4** ***Perf. 14***

130 A1 1m dark brown .60 *3.50*
131 A1 2m yellow .85 .65
132 A1 3m Prussian bl 2.75 1.60
133 A1 4m rose 2.75 *3.75*
134 A1 5m orange 3.25 .60
135 A1 6m blue green 2.75 *2.75*
136 A1 7m yel brown 2.75 *2.75*
137 A1 8m red 2.75 1.60
138 A1 1pi gray 2.75 .75
139 A1 13m ultramarine 3.50 *3.50*
140 A1 2pi olive green 4.50 *5.00*
141 A1 5pi plum 9.50 *10.00*
142 A1 9pi bister 14.00 *27.50*
143 A1 10pi light blue 30.00 *40.00*
a. "E.F.F." in bottom panel (error) 800.00 *3,000.*
144 A1 20pi violet 50.00 *90.00*
Nos. 130-144 (15) 132.70 *193.95*

This overprint reads: "Sharqi al-ardan" (East of Jordan).
For overprints see Nos. J12-J23.

Perf. 15x14

142a A1 9pi 950. *1,500.*
143a A1 10pi 100. *110.*
144a A1 20pi 1,100. 1,100.
Nos. 142a-144a (3) 2,150. *2,710.*

Amir Abdullah ibn Hussein
A1 A2

1927-29 **Engr.** ***Perf. 14***

145 A1 2(m) Prus blue 2.50 1.25
146 A1 3(m) rose 3.75 3.00
147 A1 4(m) green 4.50 *6.50*
148 A1 5(m) orange 2.75 .35
149 A1 10(m) red 3.75 *6.50*
150 A1 15(m) ultra 3.50 .50
151 A1 20(m) olive grn 3.75 *4.00*
152 A2 50(m) claret 3.75 *12.00*
153 A2 90(m) bister 9.00 *27.50*
154 A2 100(m) lt blue 10.00 *22.50*
155 A2 200(m) violet 17.50 *45.00*
156 A2 500(m) dp brn ('29) 70.00 *100.00*
157 A2 1000(m) gray ('29) 165.00 *190.00*
Nos. 145-157 (13) 299.75 *419.10*

For overprints see Nos. 158-168, B1-B12, J24-J29.

Stamps of 1927 Overprinted in Black

1928, Sept. 1

158 A1 2(m) Prus blue 3.00 *3.50*
159 A1 3(m) rose 3.50 *4.50*
160 A1 4(m) green 3.50 *5.25*
161 A1 5(m) orange 3.50 *2.50*
162 A1 10(m) red 3.75 *5.75*
163 A1 15(m) ultra 3.75 2.75
164 A1 20(m) olive grn 8.50 *14.00*
165 A2 50(m) claret 12.00 *15.00*
166 A2 90(m) bister 22.50 *45.00*
167 A2 100(m) lt blue 27.50 *65.00*
168 A2 200(m) violet 85.00 *160.00*
Nos. 158-168 (11) 176.50 *323.25*

The overprint is the Arabic word "Dastour," meaning "Constitution." The stamps were in commemoration of the enactment of the law setting forth the Constitution.

A3

"MILS" or "L. P." at lower right and Arabic equivalents at upper left.

1930-36 **Engr.** ***Perf. 14***

Size: 17¼x21mm

169 A3 1m red brn ('34) 2.00 *1.00*
170 A3 2m Prus blue 1.00 *.60*
171 A3 3m rose 1.75 1.00
172 A3 3m green ('34) 2.50 1.25
173 A3 4m green 2.00 *4.00*
174 A3 4m rose ('34) 4.00 1.50
175 A3 5m orange 1.50 .45
a. Perf. 13½x14 (coil) ('36) 34.00 20.00
176 A3 10m red 2.25 .25
177 A3 15m ultra 2.25 .30
a. Perf. 13½x14 (coil) ('36) 32.50 17.50
178 A3 20m olive grn 3.25 .55

Size: 19¼x23½mm

179 A3 50m red violet 4.50 2.25
180 A3 90m bister 4.25 *6.25*
181 A3 100m light blue 5.00 *6.00*
182 A3 200m violet 17.50 *18.00*
183 A3 500m deep brown 32.50 *57.50*
184 A3 £1 gray 77.50 *120.00*
Nos. 169-184 (16) 163.75 *220.90*

See Nos. 199-220, 230-235 in Scott Standard catalogue, Vol. 4. For overprint see No. N15a in Scott Vol. 4.

1939 ***Perf. 13½x13***

Size: 17¼x21mm

169a A3 1m red brown 6.50 4.50
170a A3 2m Prussian blue 16.00 4.00
172a A3 3m green 25.00 7.00
174a A3 4m rose 90.00 29.00
175b A3 5m orange 75.00 4.50
176a A3 10m red 150.00 5.75

177b A3 15m ultramarine 47.50 6.00
178a A3 20m olive green 72.50 17.50
Nos. 169a-178a (8) 482.50 78.25

For overprint see No. N3a in Scott Standard catalogue, Vol. 4.

Mushetta — A4

Nymphaeum, Jerash — A5

Kasr Kharana — A6

Kerak Castle — A7

Temple of Artemis, Jerash — A8

Aijalon Castle — A9

Khazneh, Rock-hewn Temple, Petra — A10

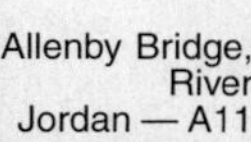

Allenby Bridge, River Jordan — A11

Ancient Threshing Floor — A12

Amir Abdullah ibn Hussein — A13

1933, Feb. 1 ***Perf. 12***

185 A4 1m dk brn & blk 1.75 1.40
Never hinged 1.50
186 A5 2m claret & blk 4.00 1.10
Never hinged 1.60
187 A6 3m blue green 4.25 1.50
Never hinged 1.90
188 A7 4m bister & blk 6.50 3.75
Never hinged 3.00
189 A8 5m orange & blk 4.50 3.75
Never hinged 3.50
190 A9 10m brown red 7.00 3.50
Never hinged 4.25
191 A10 15m dull blue 4.75 1.75
Never hinged 5.75
192 A11 20m ol grn & blk 6.75 5.50
Never hinged 8.25
193 A12 50m brn vio & blk 20.00 17.50
Never hinged 18.00
194 A6 90m yel & black 25.00 *27.50*
Never hinged 26.00
195 A8 100m blue & blk 27.50 *35.00*
Never hinged 30.00
196 A9 200m dk vio & blk 60.00 *80.00*
Never hinged 85.00
197 A10 500m brn & ver 190.00 *275.00*
Never hinged 260.00
198 A13 £1 green & blk 650.00 *950.00*
Never hinged 900.00
Nos. 185-198 (14) 1,012. *1,407.*

Nos. 194-197 are larger than the lower values in the same designs.

SEMI-POSTAL STAMPS

Locust Campaign Issue

Nos. 145-156 Overprinted

1930, Apr. 1 **Wmk. 4** ***Perf. 14***

B1 A1 2(m) Prus blue 2.50 *4.00*
Never hinged 2.40
a. Inverted overprint 200.00
B2 A1 3(m) rose 2.00 *4.00*
Never hinged 2.40
B3 A1 4(m) green 2.75 *5.00*
Never hinged 2.60
B4 A1 5(m) orange 22.50 17.50
Never hinged 27.50
a. Double overprint 300.00
B5 A1 10(m) red 2.25 *3.75*
Never hinged 2.90
B6 A1 15(m) ultra 2.25 *3.50*
Never hinged 2.90
a. Inverted overprint 200.00
B7 A1 20(m) olive grn 2.75 *4.50*
Never hinged 2.90
B8 A2 50(m) claret 5.50 *11.00*
Never hinged 10.00
B9 A2 90(m) bister 16.00 *47.50*
Never hinged 22.50
B10 A2 100(m) lt blue 17.50 *50.00*
Never hinged 27.50
B11 A2 200(m) violet 37.50 *100.00*
Never hinged 65.00
B12 A2 500(m) brown 100.00 *160.00*
Never hinged 190.00
a. "C" of "Locust" omitted 750.00
Nos. B1-B12 (12) 213.50 *410.75*

These stamps were issued to raise funds to help combat a plague of locusts.

POSTAGE DUE STAMPS

Stamps of Regular Issue (Nos. 69, 66-68 Surcharged with New Value like No. 91) Overprinted

This overprint reads: "Mustahaq" (Tax or Due)

Typo. Ovpt. "Mustahaq" 10mm long

1923 **Unwmk.** ***Perf. 11½***

J1 A7 ½pi on 3pi ol brn 57.50 *60.00*
Never hinged 72.50
a. Inverted overprint 200.00 200.00
b. Double overprint 200.00 200.00

Handstamped Overprint 12mm long

J2 A7 ½pi on 3pi ol brn 27.50 *35.00*
Never hinged 20.00
a. Inverted overprint 55.00 —
b. Double overprint 55.00 —
J3 A7 1pi dark blue 18.00 *21.00*
Never hinged 13.50
a. Inverted overprint 50.00 —
b. Double overprint 52.50 —
J4 A7 1½pi violet 21.00 *22.50*
Never hinged 13.50
a. Inverted overprint 50.00 —
b. Double overprint 52.50 —

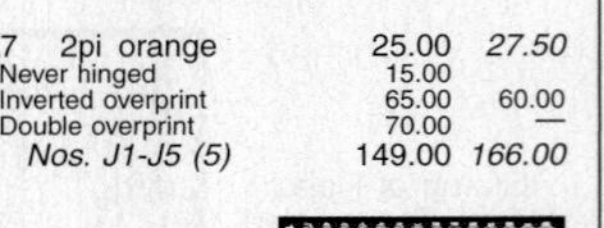

J5 A7 2pi orange 25.00 *27.50*
Never hinged 15.00
a. Inverted overprint 65.00 60.00
b. Double overprint 70.00 —
Nos. J1-J5 (5) 149.00 *166.00*

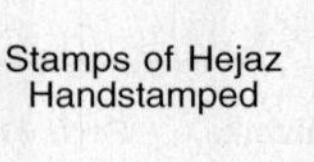

Stamps of Hejaz Handstamped

J6 A7 ½pi red 2.50 *6.00*
Never hinged 2.25
J7 A7 1pi dark blue 6.00 *6.50*
Never hinged 2.50
J8 A7 1½pi violet 5.00 *7.50*
Never hinged 3.00
J9 A7 2pi orange 8.00 *8.00*
Never hinged 3.75
J10 A7 3pi olive brown 12.50 *17.50*
Never hinged 5.25
J11 A7 5pi olive green 15.00 *30.00*
Never hinged 9.00
Nos. J6-J11 (6) 49.00 *75.50*

Type of Palestine, 1918, Overprinted

1925 **Wmk. 4** ***Perf. 14***

J12 A1 1m dark brown 2.50 *6.00*
Never hinged 3.50
J13 A1 2m yellow 4.25 *4.25*
Never hinged 4.50
J14 A1 4m rose 4.75 *6.75*
Never hinged 7.25
J15 A1 8m red 6.50 *12.00*
Never hinged 8.25
J16 A1 13m ultramarine 9.50 *12.00*
Never hinged 11.00
J17 A1 5pi plum 11.00 *19.00*
Never hinged 12.50
a. Perf. 15x14 67.50 *85.00*
Nos. J12-J17 (6) 38.50 *60.00*

The overprint reads: "Mustahaq. Sharqi al'Ardan." (Tax. Eastern Jordan).

Stamps of Palestine, 1918, Surcharged

1926

J18 A1 1m on 1m dk brn 10.00 *12.00*
Never hinged 6.00
J19 A1 2m on 1m dk brn 9.00 *12.00*
Never hinged 6.00
J20 A1 4m on 3m Prus bl 10.00 *15.00*
Never hinged 6.00
J21 A1 8m on 3m Prus bl 10.00 *15.00*
Never hinged 6.25
J22 A1 13m on 13m ultra 13.00 *17.00*
Never hinged 6.25
J23 A1 5pi on 13m ultra 16.00 *25.00*
Never hinged 8.75
Nos. J18-J23 (6) 68.00 *96.00*

The surcharge reads "Tax — Eastern Jordan" and New Value.

Stamps of Regular Issue, 1927, Overprinted

1929

J24 A1 2m Prussian bl 2.50 *6.00*
Never hinged 2.25
J25 A1 10m red 2.50 *6.50*
Never hinged 3.50
J26 A2 50m claret 7.50 *22.50*
Never hinged 13.00
Nos. J24-J26 (3) 12.50 *35.00*

With Additional Surcharge

J27 A1 1(m) on 3(m) rose 1.75 *7.00*
Never hinged 2.25
J28 A1 4(m) on 15(m) ultra 3.00 *8.50*
Never hinged 3.50
a. Inverted surch. and ovpt. 200.00 350.00
J29 A2 20(m) on 100(m) lt bl 7.00 *20.00*
Never hinged 9.50
Nos. J27-J29 (3) 11.75 *35.50*

D1

Size: 17¼x21mm

1929 **Engr.** ***Perf. 14***

J30 D1 1m brown 1.40 *6.50*
Never hinged 1.25
a. Perf. 13½x13 160.00 130.00
J31 D1 2m orange 2.75 *7.00*
Never hinged 1.25
J32 D1 4m green 4.00 *11.00*
Never hinged 1.25
J33 D1 10m carmine 7.00 *10.00*
Never hinged 2.75
J34 D1 20m olive green 13.00 *21.00*
Never hinged 11.00
J35 D1 50m blue 16.00 *32.50*
Never hinged 13.00
Nos. J30-J35 (6) 44.15 *88.00*

See Nos. J39-J43 design with larger type in Scott Standard catalogue, Vol. 4. For surcharge see No. J52 in same volume. For overprints see Nos. NJ1a, NJ3, NJ5a, NJ6-NJ7 in same volume.

OFFICIAL STAMP

Saudi Arabia No. L34 Overprinted

1924, Jan. **Typo.** ***Perf. 11½***

O1 A7 ½pi red *100.00 150.00*
Never hinged 200.00
a. Arabic date "1242" 175.00
Never hinged 400.00

Overprint reads: "(Government) the Arabian East 1342."

KARELIA

kə-'rē-lə-ə

LOCATION — In northwestern Soviet Russia.
GOVT. — An autonomous republic of the Soviet Union.
AREA — 55,198 sq. mi. (approx.).
POP. — 270,000 (approx.).
CAPITAL — Petrozavodsk (Kalininsk).

In 1921 the Karelians rebelled and for a short period a form of sovereignty independent of Russia was maintained.

100 Pennia = 1 Markka

Bear — A1

1922 Unwmk. Litho. *Perf. 11½, 12*

No.	Type	Description	Unused	Used
1	A1	5p dark gray	15.00	*55.00*
2	A1	10p light blue	15.00	*55.00*
3	A1	20p rose red	15.00	*55.00*
4	A1	25p yellow brown	15.00	*55.00*
5	A1	40p magenta	15.00	*55.00*
6	A1	50p gray green	15.00	*55.00*
7	A1	75p orange yellow	25.00	*55.00*
8	A1	1m pink & gray	25.00	*55.00*
9	A1	2m yel grn & gray	27.50	*110.00*
10	A1	3m lt blue & gray	27.50	*140.00*
11	A1	5m red lil & gray	27.50	*175.00*
12	A1	10m lt brn & gray	27.50	*275.00*
13	A1	15m green & car	27.50	*275.00*
14	A1	20m rose & green	27.50	*275.00*
15	A1	25m yellow & blue	30.00	*275.00*
		Nos. 1-15 (15)	335.00	*1,965.*
		Set, never hinged	450.00	

Nos. 1-15 were valid Jan. 31-Feb. 16, 1922. Use probably ended Feb. 3, although cancellations of the 4th and 5th exist.

Nos. 7, 8, 10, 13, 14 and 15 exist imperf. Value, each pair $250 hinged; $500 never hinged. Other denominations may exist imperf.

Counterfeits abound.

KENYA, UGANDA, & TANZANIA

'ke-nyə, ü-'gan-də, ˌtan-zə-'nē-ə

LOCATION — East Africa, bordering on the Indian Ocean
GOVT. — States in British Commonwealth
AREA — 679,802 sq. mi.
POP. — 42,760,000 (est. 1977)
CAPITAL — Nairobi (Kenya), Kampala (Uganda), Dar es Salaam (Tanzania)

Kenya became a crown colony in 1906, including the former East Africa Protectorate leased from the Sultan of Zanzibar and known as the Kenya Protectorate.

The inland Uganda Protectorate, lying west of Kenya Colony, was declared a British Protectorate in 1894.

Tanganyika, a trust territory larger than Kenya or Uganda, was grouped with them postally from 1935 under the East African Posts & Telecommunications Admin.

100 Cents = 1 Rupee
100 Cents = 1 Shilling (1922)
20 Shillings = 1 Pound

Catalogue values for unused stamps in this country are for Never Hinged items, beginning with Scott 90.

East Africa and Uganda Protectorates

King George V
A1 A2

1921 Typo. Wmk. 4 *Perf. 14*

Ordinary Paper

No.	Type	Description	Unused	Used
1	A1	1c black	.90	*1.90*
2	A1	3c green	6.75	*15.00*
3	A1	6c rose red	9.00	*20.00*
4	A1	10c orange	9.75	1.40
5	A1	12c gray	11.00	*140.00*
6	A1	15c ultramarine	12.50	*22.50*

Chalky Paper

No.	Type	Description	Unused	Used
7	A1	50c gray lilac & blk	16.50	*125.00*
8	A2	2r blk & red, *blue*	82.50	*190.00*
9	A2	3r green & violet	150.00	*425.00*
10	A2	5r gray lil & ultra	190.00	*350.00*
11	A2	50r gray grn & red	5,250.	*9,000.*
		Revenue cancel		425.00
		Overprinted "SPECIMEN"	525.00	
		Nos. 1-10 (10)	488.90	*1,291.*

The name of the colony was changed to Kenya in August, 1920, but stamps of the East Africa and Uganda types were continued in use. Stamps of types A1 and A2 watermarked Multiple Crown and C A (3) are listed under East Africa and Uganda Protectorates.

For stamps of Kenya and Uganda overprinted "G. E. A." used in parts of former German East Africa occupied by British forces, see Tanganyika Nos. 1-9.

Kenya and Uganda

King George V
A3 A4

1922-27 Wmk. 4

No.	Type	Description	Unused	Used
18	A3	1c brown	1.10	*4.75*
19	A3	5c violet	6.50	1.00
20	A3	5c grn ('27)	2.40	.55
21	A3	10c green	1.75	.35
22	A3	10c blk ('27)	4.50	.25
23	A3	12c black	14.00	*29.00*
24	A3	15c car rose	1.40	.25
25	A3	20c orange	3.75	.25
26	A3	30c ultra	4.50	.60
27	A3	50c gray	2.75	.25
28	A3	75c ol bister	9.50	*15.00*
29	A4	1sh green	6.50	3.00
30	A4	2sh gray lil	10.00	*19.00*
31	A4	2sh50c brn ('25)	24.00	*125.00*
32	A4	3sh gray blk	20.00	7.50
33	A4	4sh gray ('25)	37.50	*135.00*
34	A4	5sh carmine	27.50	27.50
35	A4	7sh50c org ('25)	140.00	*325.00*
36	A4	10sh ultra	77.50	*77.50*
37	A4	£1 org & blk	230.00	*340.00*
		Revenue cancel		25.00
38	A4	£2 brn vio & grn ('25)	1,150.	*1,950.*
		Revenue cancel		160.00
		Overprinted "SPECIMEN"	300.00	
39	A4	£3 yel & dl vio ('25)	1,850.	—
		Revenue cancel		275.00
		Overprinted "SPECIMEN"	350.00	
40	A4	£4 rose lil & blk ('25)	5,000.	—
		Revenue cancel		300.00
		Overprinted "SPECIMEN"	450.00	
41	A4	£5 blue & blk	5,500.	—
		Revenue cancel		375.00
		Overprinted "SPECIMEN"	500.00	
41A	A4	£10 grn & blk	*15,000.*	
		Revenue cancel		475.00
		Overprinted "SPECIMEN"	775.00	
41B	A4	£20 grn & red ('25)	*34,500.*	
		Revenue cancel		850.00
		Overprinted "SPECIMEN"	1,300.	
41C	A4	£25 red & blk	*43,500.*	
		Revenue cancel		800.00
		Overprinted "SPECIMEN"	1,400.	
41D	A4	£50 brn & blk	*85,000.*	
		Revenue cancel		900.00
		Overprinted "SPECIMEN"	1,750.	
41E	A4	£75 gray & purple	*140,000.*	
		Revenue cancel		3,500.
		Overprinted "SPECIMEN"	3,500.	
41F	A4	£100 blk & red	*160,000.*	
		Revenue cancel		2,250.
		Overprinted "SPECIMEN"	4,000.	
		Nos. 18-37 (20)	625.15	*1,112.*

Nos. 37 and 38 are commonly found with court or fiscal cancellations.

Nos. 39-41F are likely to bear court or fiscal cancels only.

High face value stamps are known with revenue cancellations removed and forged postal cancellations added.

Common Design Types pictured following the introduction.

Kenya, Uganda, Tanganyika Silver Jubilee Issue

Common Design Type

1935, May Engr. *Perf. 13½x14*

No.	Type	Description	Unused	Used
42	CD301	20c ol grn & lt bl	2.00	.25
43	CD301	30c blue & brown	2.75	*3.00*
44	CD301	65c indigo & green	1.75	*2.75*
45	CD301	1sh brt vio & indigo	2.25	*5.00*
		Nos. 42-45 (4)	8.75	*11.00*
		Set, never hinged	20.00	
		Set, perf. "SPECIMEN"	175.00	

Kavirondo Cranes — A5

Dhow on Lake Victoria — A6

Lion — A7

Mount Kilimanjaro — A8

Jinja Bridge by Ripon Falls — A9

Mount Kenya — A10

Lake Naivasha A11

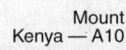

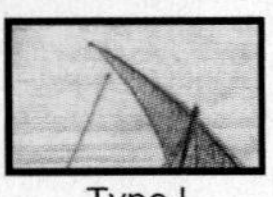
Type I

FIVE CENTS
Type I — Left rope does not touch sail.
Type II — Left rope touches sail.

Perf. 13, 14, 11½x13, 13x11½

Engr.; Typo. (10c, £1)

1935, May 1

No.	Type	Description	Unused	Used
46	A5	1c red brn & blk	1.00	*2.00*
47	A6	5c grn & blk (I)	3.50	.50
a.		Type II	*40.00*	*9.00*
b.		Perf. 13x11½ (I)	*9,750.*	*1,000.*
c.		Perf. 13x11½ (II)	*875.00*	*250.00*
48	A7	10c black & yel	7.50	1.50
49	A8	15c red & black	4.00	.25
50	A5	20c red org & blk	4.00	.25
51	A9	30c dk ultra & blk	5.25	1.25
52	A6	50c blk & red vio (I)	6.00	.25
53	A10	65c yel brn & blk	8.00	*2.25*
54	A11	1sh grn & black	5.25	1.50
a.		Perf. 13x11½ ('36)	*1,600.*	150.00
55	A8	2sh red vio & rose brn	13.00	4.75
56	A11	3sh blk & ultra	18.00	*17.50*
a.		Perf. 13x11½	*2,600.*	
57	A9	5sh car & black	26.00	*35.00*
58	A5	10sh ultra & red vio	110.00	*135.00*
59	A7	£1 blk & scar	325.00	*425.00*
		Nos. 46-59 (14)	536.50	627.00
		Set, never hinged	900.00	
		Set, perf. "SPECIMEN"	550.00	

Coronation Issue

Common Design Type

1937, May 12 Engr. *Perf. 13½x14*

No.	Type	Description	Unused	Used
60	CD302	5c deep green	.25	.25
61	CD302	20c deep orange	.30	.35
62	CD302	30c brt ultra	.45	*1.75*
		Nos. 60-62 (3)	1.00	2.35
		Set, never hinged	1.75	
		Set, perf. "SPECIMEN"	150.00	

Kavirondo Cranes — A12

Dhow on Lake Victoria — A13

Lake Naivasha — A14

Jinja Bridge, Ripon Falls — A16

Mt. Kilimanjaro A15

Lion — A17

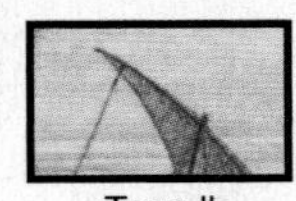
Type II

FIFTY CENTS:
Type I — Left rope does not touch sail.
Type II — Left rope touches sail.

1938-54 Engr. *Perf. 13x13½*

No.	Type	Description	Unused	Used
66	A12	1c vio brn & blk ('42)	.25	*.50*
		Never hinged	.30	
a.		1c red brown & gray black, perf. 13	3.00	.90
		Never hinged	5.00	
b.		"A" of "CA" in wmk. omitted	225.00	

Never hinged 300.00

Perf. 13x11½

67 A13 5c grn & blk 3.25 .55
Never hinged 5.75

68 A13 5c red org & brn ('49) 1.40 *7.50*
Never hinged 2.50
a. Perf. 13x12½ ('50) 2.50 *4.75*
Never hinged 4.25

69 A14 10c org & brn 1.60 .25
Never hinged 2.40
a. Perf. 14 ('41) 95.00 10.00
Never hinged 135.00

70 A14 10c grn & blk ('49) .35 *2.00*
Never hinged .45
a. Perf. 13x12½ ('50) 2.75 .25
Never hinged 4.75

Perf. 13x12½

71 A14 10c gray & red brn ('52) 1.00 .60
Never hinged 1.80

Perf. 13½x13, 13x13½

72 A15 15c car & gray blk ('43) 4.25 2.00
Never hinged 7.25
a. Booklet pane of 4 17.50
Never hinged 30.00
b. Perf. 13 22.50 .60
Never hinged 32.50
c. "A" of "CA" in wmk. omitted 1,500.
Never hinged 1,900.

73 A15 15c grn & blk ('52) 1.90 *6.25*
Never hinged 3.25

74 A12 20c org & gray blk ('42) 5.75 .25
Never hinged 9.50
a. Booklet pane of 4 24.00
Never hinged 40.00
b. Imperf., pair
c. Perf. 13 *35.00* .30
Never hinged 42.50
d. Perf. 14 ('41) *45.00* 3.00
Never hinged 55.00

Perf. 13x12½

75 A13 25c car & blk ('52) 1.25 *2.40*
Never hinged 1.75

Perf. 13x13½

76 A16 30c dp bl & gray blk ('42) 2.00 .35
Never hinged 3.25
a. Perf. 14 ('41) *130.00* 12.50
Never hinged 160.00
b. Perf. 13 *40.00* .45
Never hinged 55.00

77 A16 30c brn & pur ('52) 1.25 .45
Never hinged 1.75

78 A12 40c brt bl & gray blk ('52) 1.50 *5.00*
Never hinged 1.75

Perf. 13x12½

79 A13 50c gray blk & red vio (II) ('49) 7.25 .60
Never hinged 12.50
a. Perf. 13x11½ (II) 14.00 1.10
Never hinged 21.50
b. Perf. 13x11½ (I) 175.00 *250.00*
Never hinged 300.00

Perf. 13x11½

80 A14 1sh yel brn & gray blk 18.00 .30
Never hinged 32.50
a. Perf. 13x12½ ('49) 12.00 .65
Never hinged 21.00
b. 1sh brown & black ('42) 12.00 .30
Never hinged 20.00

Perf. 13½x13

81 A15 2sh red vio & org brn ('44) 30.00 .30
Never hinged 52.50
a. Perf. 13 *110.00* 9.00
Never hinged 135.00
b. Perf. 14 ('41) *62.50* 19.00
Never hinged 80.00

Perf. 13x12½

82 A14 3sh gray blk & ultra ('50) 30.00 9.00
Never hinged 50.00
a. Perf. 13x11½ 50.00 9.00
Never hinged 50.00

Perf. 13x13½

83 A16 5sh car rose & gray blk ('44) 30.00 2.00
Never hinged 50.00
a. Perf. 13 *125.00* 21.00
Never hinged 150.00
b. Perf. 14 ('41) *35.00* 3.25
Never hinged 50.00

84 A12 10sh ultra & red vio ('44) 40.00 8.50
Never hinged 55.00
a. Perf. 13 110.00 30.00
Never hinged 140.00
b. Perf. 14 ('41) 32.50 25.00
Never hinged 50.00

Typo.
Perf. 14

85 A17 £1 blk & scar ('41) 25.00 *27.50*
Never hinged 42.50
a. Perf. 11½x13 300.00 170.00
Never hinged 525.00
b. Perf. 12½ ('54) 12.00 *42.50*
Never hinged 18.00
Nos. 66-85 (20) 206.00 *76.30*

Nos. 85-85b were printed on chalky paper. No. 85 also exists on ordinary paper, from a 1944 printing. Values are the same.
See Nos. 98-99.

South Africa Nos. 48, 57, 60 and 62 Surcharged

Basic stamps of Nos. 86-89 are inscribed alternately in English and Afrikaans.

1941-42 Wmk. 201 Perf. 15x14, 14

86 A6 5c on 1p car & gray, pair 1.10 *3.00*
a. Single, English .25 .25
b. Single, Afrikaans .25 .25

87 A17 10c on 3p ultra, pair 3.50 *10.00*
a. Single, English .30 .35
b. Single, Afrikaans .30 .35

88 A7 20c on 6p org & grn, pair 2.50 *3.75*
a. Single, English .25 .25
b. Single, Afrikaans .25 .25

89 A11 70c on 1sh lt bl & ol brn, pair 15.00 *7.00*
a. Single, English .50 .45
b. Single, Afrikaans .50 .45
Nos. 86-89 (4) 22.10 23.75
Set, never hinged 30.00

Issued: Nos. 86-88, 7/1/41; No. 89, 4/20/42.
Values are for horizontal pairs. Vertical pairs are worth substantially less.

Catalogue values for unused stamps in this section, from this point to the end of the section, are for Never Hinged items.

Peace Issue

Common Design Type
Perf. 13½x14

1946, Nov. 11 Engr. Wmk. 4
90 CD303 20c red orange .25 .25
91 CD303 30c deep blue .40 .40

Silver Wedding Issue

Common Design Types

1948, Dec. 1 Photo. Perf. 14x14½
92 CD304 20c orange .25 .25

Engr.; Name Typo.
Perf. 11½x11
93 CD305 £1 red 50.00 *67.50*

UPU Issue

Common Design Types
Engr.; Typo. on Nos. 95 and 96

1949, Oct. 10 Perf. 13, 11x11½
94 CD306 20c red orange .25 .25
95 CD307 30c indigo 1.75 *2.25*
a. "A" of "CA" in wmk. omitted *1,200.*
96 CD308 50c gray .40 .40
97 CD309 1sh red brown .50 .50
Nos. 94-97 (4) 2.90 3.40

Type of 1949 with Added Inscription: "Royal Visit 1952"

1952, Feb. 1 Engr. Perf. 13x12½
98 A14 10c green & black .30 *1.60*
99 A14 1sh yel brn & gray blk 1.25 *2.25*

Visit of Princess Elizabeth, Duchess of Edinburgh, and the Duke of Edinburgh, 1952.

POSTAGE DUE STAMPS

Kenya and Uganda

D1

Perf. 14½x14

1928-33 Typo. Wmk. 4
J1 D1 5c deep violet 2.25 1.00
J2 D1 10c orange red 2.25 .60
J3 D1 20c yel green 3.50 4.25
J4 D1 30c ol brn ('31) 22.50 20.00
J5 D1 40c dull blue 6.00 *15.00*
J6 D1 1sh grnsh gray ('33) 60.00 *145.00*
Nos. J1-J6 (6) 96.50 *185.85*
Set, never hinged 160.00

Kenya, Uganda, Tanganyika

D2

1935, May 1 Perf. 13½x14
J7 D2 5c violet 2.50 1.75
J8 D2 10c red .35 .45
J9 D2 20c green .50 .45
J10 D2 30c brown 1.50 .45
J11 D2 40c ultramarine 1.60 *3.00*
J12 D2 1sh gray 17.50 17.50
Nos. J7-J12 (6) 23.95 *23.60*
Set, never hinged 40.00

KIAUCHAU

(Kiautschou)

LOCATION — A district of China on the south side of the Shantung peninsula.
GOVT. — A former German colony.
AREA — 200 sq. mi.
POP. — 192,000 (approx. 1914).

The area was seized by Germany in 1897 and through negotiations that followed was leased to Germany by China.

100 Pfennig = 1 Mark
100 Cents = 1 Dollar (1905)

STAMPS OF GERMAN OFFICES IN CHINA USED IN KIAUCHAU

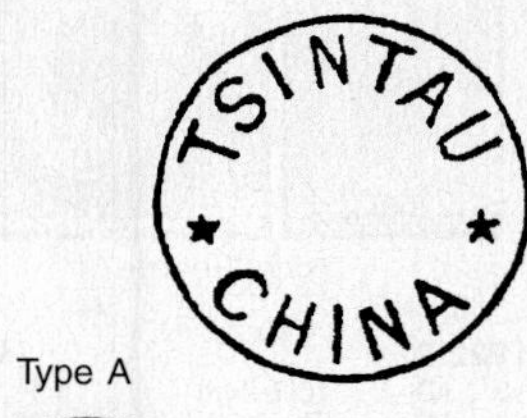

Type A

Type B

Type C

Stamps of Germany canceled Type A, Type B or Type C

1898
A1 A8 2m brownish purple 400.00
On cover 5,000.
a. 2m carmine lilac 575.00
On cover 165.00
On cover —
A2 A9 3pf brown 57.50
On cover 165.00
a. 3pf yellow brown 57.50
On cover 165.00
b. 3pf ocher brown 165.00
On cover 325.00
c. 3pf olive brown 82.50
On cover 250.00
A3 A9 5pf blue green 50.00
On cover 175.00
A4 A10 10pf carmine 20.00
On cover 62.50
a. dark carmine 22.50
On cover 65.00
A5 A10 20pf ultramarine 100.00
On cover 250.00
A6 A10 25pf orange 250.00
On cover 575.00
A7 A9 50 red brown 290.00
On cover 650.00

Stamps of 1898 German Offices in China Canceled Type B or Type C

1898

56 degree Angle

A8 A9 3pf dark brown (#1) 20.00
On cover 40.00
a. 3pf yellow brown (#1a) 16.00
On cover 32.50
b. 3pf reddish brown (#1b) 165.00
On cover 275.00
A9 A9 5pf green (#2) 13.00
On cover 20.00
A10 A10 10pf carmine (#3) 16.00
On cover 25.00
A11 A10 20pf ultramarine (#4) 260.00
On cover 375.00
A12 A10 25pf 25pf orange (#5) 125.00
On cover 250.00
A13 A10 50pf red brown (#6) 90.00
On cover 260.00

Canceled Type A
45 degree Angle

A14 A9 3pf yellow brown (#1c) *12,500.*
On cover —
A15 A9 5pf green (#2a) 20.00
On cover 30.00
A16 A10 10pf carmine (#3a) 16.00
On cover 25.00
A17 A10 20pf ultramarine (#4a) 16.00
On cover 32.50
A18 A10 25pf orange (#5a) 82.50
On cover 165.00
A19 A10 50pf red brown (#6a) 75.00
On cover 225.00

Cancellations other than Types A-C are scarce and command premiums.

TSINGTAU ISSUES

Stamps of Germany, Offices in China 1898, with Additional Surcharge

a

b

c

On Nos. 1-9, a blue or violet line is drawn through "PF. 10 PF." All exist without this line. All examples of Nos. 1b, 2b and 3b lack the colored line.
The three surcharge types can most easily be distinguished by the differences in the lower loop of the "5."

"China" Overprint at 56 degree Angle

1900
1 A10(a) 5pfg on 10pf car 45.00 *52.50*
Never hinged 140.00
On cover 200.00
c. Dbl. surch., one inverted 750.00
Never hinged 1,650.
2 A10(b) 5pfg on 10pf car 45.00 *52.50*
Never hinged 140.00
On cover 200.00
c. Dbl. surch., one inverted 750.00
Never hinged 1,650.
3 A10(c) 5pfg on 10pf car 45.00 *52.50*
Never hinged 140.00
On cover 200.00
c. Dbl. surch., one inverted 750.00
Never hinged 1,650.
Nos. 1-3 (3) 135.00 157.50

"China" Overprint at 45 degree Angle

1a A10(a) 5pfg on 10pf car 145.00 *130.00*
Never hinged 350.00
On cover 325.00
b. Double surcharge 450.00 *575.00*
Never hinged 975.00
2a A10(b) 5pfg on 10pf car 145.00 *130.00*
Never hinged 350.00
On cover 325.00
b. Double surcharge 450.00 *575.00*
Never hinged 975.00
3a A10(c) 5pfg on 10pf car 145.00 *130.00*
Never hinged 350.00
On cover 325.00
b. Double surcharge 450.00 *575.00*
Never hinged 975.00
Nos. 1a-3a (3) 435.00 390.00

Surcharged

d

e

5 Pf.
f

"China" Overprint at 48 degree Angle on Nos. 4-9

4 A10(d) 5pf on 10pf car 3,250. 4,000.
Never hinged 5,000.
On cover *7,500.*
a. Double surcharge *8,250.* *18,000.*
On cover *24,000.*
5 A10(e) 5pf on 10pf car *3,250.* *4,000.*
Never hinged 5,000.
On cover 7,500.
a. Double surcharge *8,250.* *18,000.*
On cover *32,500.*
6 A10(f) 5pf on 10pf car *3,250.* *4,000.*
Never hinged 5,000.
On cover 7,500.
a. Double surcharge *8,250.* *18,000.*
On cover *32,500.*
b. 5fP *18,000.*
On cover —
c. As "b," double surcharge — —

With Add'l Handstamp **5**

7 A10(d) 5pf on 10pf car *40,000.* *50,000.*
Never hinged *57,500.*
On cover *90,000.*
8 A10(f) 5pf on 10pf car *40,000.* *50,000.*
Never hinged *57,500.*
On cover *90,000.*
a. On No. 6b — —

With Additional Handstamp

9 A10(f) 5pf on 10pf car *8,250.* *12,500.*
Never hinged 13,000.
On cover *20,000.*
a. Double surcharge *37,500.*
b. On No. 6a
c. On No. 6b
d. On No. 6c

On Nos. 1-9, a blue or violet line is drawn through "PF. 10 PF." All exist without this line. All examples of Nos. 1b, 2b and 3b lack the colored line.

Kaiser's Yacht "Hohenzollern"
A1 A2

1901, Jan. Unwmk. Typo. *Perf. 14*

10 A1 3pf brown 2.00 2.00
Never hinged 5.00
On cover 40.00
11 A1 5pf green 2.00 1.75
Never hinged 5.00
On cover 16.50
12 A1 10pf carmine 2.50 2.10
Never hinged 6.50
On cover 16.50
13 A1 20pf ultra 7.50 8.50
Never hinged 20.00
On cover 24.00
14 A1 25pf org & blk, *yel* 13.50 *17.00*
Never hinged 32.50
On cover 50.00
15 A1 30pf org & blk, *sal* 13.50 *16.50*
Never hinged 40.00
On cover 52.50
16 A1 40pf lake & blk 16.00 *21.00*
Never hinged 40.00
On cover 52.50
17 A1 50pf pur & blk, *sal* 16.00 *22.50*
Never hinged 40.00
On cover 52.50
18 A1 80pf lake & blk, *rose* 30.00 *52.50*
Never hinged 70.00
On cover 115.00

Engr. *Perf. 14½x14*

19 A2 1m carmine 50.00 *92.50*
Never hinged 135.00
On cover 165.00
20 A2 2m blue 75.00 *110.00*
Never hinged 190.00
On cover 180.00
21 A2 3m blk vio 75.00 *200.00*
Never hinged 190.00
On cover 375.00
22 A2 5m slate & car 210.00 *650.00*
Never hinged 575.00
On cover 1,250.
Nos. 10-22 (13) 513.00 *1,196.*
Set, never hinged 1,350.
Set, ovptd. "SPECIMEN" 1,100.
Set, ovptd. "SPECIMEN," never hinged 2,100.

Covers: Values for Nos. 17-22 are for overfranked complete covers, usually philatelic.

A3

A4

1905 Typo.

23 A3 1c brown 1.25 1.75
Never hinged 4.25
On cover 19.00
24 A3 2c green 2.00 1.75
Never hinged 5.25
On cover 16.50
25 A3 4c carmine 4.50 1.75
Never hinged 11.50
On cover 16.00
26 A3 10c ultra 8.50 5.50
Never hinged 20.00
On cover 24.00
27 A3 20c lake & blk 34.00 20.00
Never hinged 105.00
On cover 52.50
28 A3 40c lake & blk, *rose* 100.00 *100.00*
Never hinged 250.00
On cover 175.00

Engr.

29 A4 $½ carmine 72.50 *85.00*
Never hinged 170.00
On cover 175.00
30 A4 $1 blue, 26x17 holes 190.00 125.00
Never hinged 525.00
On cover 200.00
a. $1 blue, 25x16 holes 150.00 130.00
Never hinged 375.00
On cover 200.00
31 A4 $1½ blk vio, 26x17 holes 1,200. *1,700.*
Never hinged 2,600.
On cover 2,450.
a. blk vio, 25x16 holes *24,000.*
32 A4 $2½ slate & car, 26x17 holes 1,500. *5,000.*
Never hinged 4,300.
On cover 7,500.
a. $2½ slate & car, 25x16 holes 2,100. *3,500.*
Never hinged 4,900.
On cover 5,600.
Nos. 23-32 (10) 3,113. *7,041.*
Set, never hinged 8,000.

Values for Nos. 27-32 on cover are for overfranked, usually philatelic, covers.

1905-16 Wmk. 125 Typo.

33 A3 1c brown ('06) 1.25 1.50
Never hinged 3.25
On cover 32.50
a. 1c yellow brown ('16) .50 —
Never hinged 2.00
34 A3 2c green ('09) 1.10 *1.10*
Never hinged 2.75
On cover 14.50
a. 2c dark green ('14) .50 *1.75*
Never hinged 2.00
On cover 20.00
35 A3 4c carmine ('09) 1.00 *1.10*
Never hinged 2.50
On cover 16.00
36 A3 10c ultra ('09) 1.10 *3.25*
Never hinged 2.50
On cover 22.50
a. 10c blue 12.00 5.00
Never hinged 27.00
On cover 15.00
37 A3 20c lake & blk ('08) 3.00 *16.00*
Never hinged 6.00
On cover 52.50
a. 20c red & black ('18) 1.60
Never hinged 4.00
38 A3 40c lake & blk, *rose* 3.75 *52.50*
Never hinged 9.00
On cover 120.00

Engr.

39 A4 $½ car, 26x17 holes ('07) 9.50 *65.00*
Never hinged 32.50
On cover 140.00
a. $½ pale rose, 25x17 holes ('18) 6.50
Never hinged 22.50
40 A4 $1 blue, 26x17 holes ('06) 12.50 *67.50*
Never hinged 65.00
On cover 150.00
a. $1 bright blue, 25x17 holes ('18) 8.00
Never hinged 29.00
41 A4 $1½ blk violet 11.00 *225.00*
Never hinged 125.00
On cover —
a. $1½ gray violet, 25x17 holes ('18) 20.00
Never hinged 82.50
42 A4 $2½ slate & car 50.00 *475.00*
Never hinged 300.00
On cover 825.00
Nos. 33-42 (10) 94.20 907.95
Set, never hinged 550.00

Nos. 37a, 39a, 40a and 41a were not placed in use.

KIONGA

'kyoŋ-gə

LOCATION — Southeast Africa and northeast Mozambique, on Indian Ocean south of Rovuma River
GOVT. — Part of German East Africa
AREA — 400 sq. mi.

This territory, occupied by Portuguese troops during World War I, was allotted to Portugal by the Treaty of Versailles. Later it became part of Mozambique.

100 Centavos = 1 Escudo

Lourenco Marques No. 149 Surcharged in Red

1916, May 29 Unwmk. *Perf. 11½*

1 A2 ½c on 100r bl, *bl* 30.00 20.00
2 A2 1c on 100r bl, *bl* 25.00 17.00
3 A2 2½c on 100r bl, *bl* 25.00 17.00
4 A2 5c on 100r bl, *bl* 25.00 17.00
Nos. 1-4 (4) 105.00 71.00

Most of the stock of Lourenço Marques No. 149 used for these surcharges lacked gum. Unused examples with original gum are worth approximately 50% more than the values shown.

KOREA

kə-'rē-ə

(Corea)

(Chosen, Tyosen, Tae Han)

LOCATION — Peninsula extending from Manchuria between the Yellow Sea and the Sea of Japan
GOVT. — Republic
AREA — 38,221 sq. mi.
POP. — 39,950,743 (1983)
CAPITAL — Seoul

Korea (or Corea) an independent monarchy for centuries under Chinese influence, came under Japanese influence in 1895. Japanese stamps were used there as early as 1875. Administrative control was assumed by Japan in 1904 and annexation followed in 1910. Postage stamps of Japan were used in Korea from 1905 to early 1946.

100 Mon = 1 Tempo
5 Poon = 1 Cheun
100 Sen = 1 Yen
1000 Re = 100 Cheun = Weun

Stylized Yin Yang
A1 A2

Perf. 8½ to 11½

1884 Typo. Unwmk.

1 A1 5m rose 60.00 6,750.
2 A2 10m blue 50.00 6,750.

Reprints and counterfeits of Nos. 1-2 exist.

These stamps were never placed in use. Values: 25 and 50 mon, each $19; 100 mon $20.
Counterfeits exist.

Yin Yang — A6

Two types of 50p:
I — No period after "50."
II — Period after "50."

Perf. 11½, 12, 12½, 13 and Compound

1895 Litho.

6 A6 5p green 25.00 16.00
a. 5p pale yellow green 75.00 27.50
b. Vert. pair, imperf horiz. 425.00 —
c. Horiz. pair, imperf. vert. 425.00 —
d. Vertical pair, imperf. between 425.00 —
e. Horiz. pair, imperf. btwn. 425.00 —
7 A6 10p deep blue 130.00 40.00
a. Horiz. pair, imperf. between 425.00 —
b. Vert. pair, imperf. horiz. 425.00 —
8 A6 25p maroon 65.00 30.00
a. Horiz. pair, imperf. between 375.00 375.00
b. Vert. pair, imperf. horiz. 375.00 375.00
9 A6 50p purple (II) 22.50 14.00
a. Horiz. pair, imperf. between 400.00 400.00
b. Vert, pair, imperf. horiz. 400.00 400.00
c. Horiz. pair, imperf. vert. 400.00 400.00
d. Type I 75.00 40.00
Nos. 6-9 (4) 242.50 100.00

For overprints and surcharges see Nos. 10-17C, 35-38.
Counterfeits exist of Nos. 6-9 and all surcharges and overprints.

Overprinted "Tae Han" in Korean and Chinese Characters

1897 Red Overprint

10 A6 5p green 90.00 10.00
a. 5p pale yellow green 200.00 150.00
b. Inverted overprint 150.00 150.00
c. Without ovpt. at bottom 150.00 130.00
d. Without overprint at top 150.00 130.00
f. Double overprint at top 140.00 140.00
g. Overprint at bottom in blk 160.00 160.00
h. Pair, one without overprint 450.00 450.00
i. Double overprint at top, inverted at bottom 550.00

11 A6 10p deep blue 100.00 15.00
- *a.* Without ovpt. at bottom 150.00 150.00
- *b.* Without overprint at top 150.00 150.00
- *c.* Double overprint at top 150.00 150.00
- *d.* Bottom overprint inverted 140.00 140.00
- *e.* Top ovpt. dbl., one in blk 210.00 210.00
- *f.* Top overprint omitted, bottom overprint inverted 450.00

12 A6 25p maroon 110.00 17.00
- *a.* Overprint at bottom invtd. 150.00 150.00
- *b.* Overprint at bottom in blk 210.00 210.00
- *c.* Bottom overprint omitted 150.00 150.00
- *e.* Top ovpt. dbl., one in blk 225.00 225.00
- *f.* Top and bottom overprints double, one of each in blk 250.00 250.00
- *g.* Pair, one without overprint 425.00 425.00

13 A6 50p purple 90.00 12.00
- *a.* Without ovpt. at bottom 120.00 110.00
- *b.* Without overprint at top 120.00 110.00
- *c.* Bottom overprint double 120.00 110.00
- *e.* Pair, one without overprint 275.00 275.00

Nos. 10-13 (4) 390.00 54.00

1897 **Black Overprint**

13F A6 5p green 400.00 85.00
13G A6 10p deep blue 400.00 100.00
- *h.* Without ovpt. at bottom 450.00

14 A6 25p maroon 400.00 100.00
- *a.* Without ovpt. at bottom 450.00
- *b.* Without overprint at top 450.00
- *c.* Double overprint at bottom 450.00

15 A6 50p purple 400.00 80.00
- *a.* Without ovpt. at bottom 450.00

Nos. 13F-15 (4) 1,600.

These stamps with black overprint, also No. 16A, are said not to have been officially authorized.

Nos. 6, 6a and 8 Surcharged in Red or Black

1900

15B A6 1p on 5p grn (R) *3,500.* *750.00*
- *c.* Yellow green

16 A6 1p on 25p mar 100.00 60.00

Same Surcharge in Red or Black on Nos. 10, 10a, 12, 12c and 14

16A A6 1p on 5p grn (R) 950.00
- *b.* 1p on 5p pale yellow green 1,000.

17 A6 1p on 25p (#12) 55.00 22.50
- *a.* Figure "1" omitted 100.00
- *b.* On #12c 90.00 70.00

17C A6 1p on 25p (#14) 775.00 175.00

Counterfeit overprints and surcharges of Nos. 10-17C exist. See note after No. 15.

A8 A9

A10 A11

A12 A13

A14 A15

A16 A17

A18 A19

A20 A21

1900-01 **Typo.** ***Perf. 11***

18 A8 2re gray 8.00 3.50
19 A9 1ch yellow grn 11.00 4.25
20B A11 2ch pale blue 26.00 11.00
21 A12 3ch org red 11.00 9.00
- *a.* Vert. pair, imperf. horiz. 200.00 200.00
- *b.* Horiz. pair, imperf. btwn. 500.00
- *c.* 3c brnsh org 12.00 10.00
- *d.* As "c," vert. pair, imperf. btwn. 500.00

22 A13 4ch carmine 37.50 15.00
23 A14 5ch pink 30.00 7.50
24 A15 6ch dp blue 37.50 7.00
25 A16 10ch pur ('01) 45.00 25.00
26 A17 15ch gray vio 67.50 40.00
27 A18 20ch red brown 125.00 42.50
31 A19 50ch ol grn & pink 550.00 200.00
32 A20 1wn rose, blk & bl 1,100. 250.00
33 A21 2wn pur & yel grn 1,100. 550.00

Nos. 18-33 (13) 3,149. 1,165.

Nos. 22, 23, 25, 26, 33 exist imperf.

Some examples of Nos. 18-27 exist with forged Tae Han overprints in red. It is believed that Nos. 18 and 21 exist with genuine Tae Han overprints.

Reprints of No. 24 were made in light blue, perf. 12x13, in 1905 for a souvenir booklet. See note after No. 54.

See Nos. 52-54.

Perf. 10

18a A8 2re 17.50 5.25
19a A9 1ch 17.50 5.50
20 A10 2ch blue 75.00 45.00
- *a.* Horiz. pair, imperf. btwn. *725.00*

20Ba A11 2ch pale blue 50.00 45.00
21e A12 3ch 16.00 9.00
22a A13 4ch 45.00 20.00
23a A14 5ch 40.00 10.00
24a A15 6ch 47.50 12.00
26a A17 15ch 160.00 140.00
27a A18 20ch 225.00 225.00

Nos. 18a-27a (10) 693.50 516.75

Emperor's Crown — A22

1902, Oct. 18 ***Perf. 11½***

34 A22 3ch orange 67.50 35.00

40th year of the reign of Emperor Kojong. An imperf. single was part of the 1905 souvenir booklet. See note following No. 54.

Counterfeits exist.

Nos. 8 and 9 Handstamp Surcharged in Black

1ch 2ch

3ch

Perf. 11½, 12, 12½, 13 and Compound

1902

35 A6 1ch on 25p maroon 25.00 6.00
- *b.* Horiz. pair, imperf. btwn. 275.00
- *c.* Imperf. 90.00
- *d.* Vert. pair, imperf. horiz. 275.00
- *e.* On No. 12 — —

36 A6 2ch on 25p maroon 29.00 7.00
- *b.* Imperf. 75.00
- *d.* On No. 12 90.00 90.00

36E A6 2ch on 50p purple 175.00 175.00
- *f.* Character "cheun" unabbreviated (in two rows instead of one) 250.00 175.00

37 A6 3ch on 50p purple 27.50 8.00
- *b.* With character "cheun" unabbreviated (in two rows instead of one) 2,400. 950.00
- *d.* Horiz. pair, imperf. btwn. 200.00
- *e.* Vert. pair, imperf. btwn. 200.00
- *g.* On No. 13 240.00

38 A6 3ch on 25p maroon 65.00 65.00

Nos. 35-38 (5) 321.50 261.00

There are several sizes of these surcharges. Being handstamped, inverted and double surcharges exist.

Counterfeit surcharges exist.

Falcon — A23

1903 ***Perf. 13½x14***

39 A23 2re slate 10.00 6.25
40 A23 1ch violet brn 11.00 7.50
41 A23 2ch green 15.00 7.50
42 A23 3ch orange 13.00 7.50
43 A23 4ch rose 20.00 9.00
44 A23 5ch yellow brn 20.00 10.00
45 A23 6ch lilac 25.00 11.50
46 A23 10ch blue 30.00 15.00
47 A23 15ch red, *straw* 40.00 20.00
48 A23 20ch vio brn, *straw* 50.00 27.50
49 A23 50ch red, *grn* 175.00 100.00
50 A23 1wn vio, *lav* 450.00 225.00
51 A23 2wn vio, *org* 450.00 225.00

Nos. 39-51 (13) 1,309. 671.75

Values are for stamps with perfs touching the design.

Types of 1901

1903 ***Perf. 12½***

Thin, Semi-Transparent Paper

52 A19 50ch pale ol grn & pale pink *400.00* *160.00*
53 A20 1wn rose, blk & bl *600.00* *200.00*
54 A21 2wn lt vio & lt grn *875.00* *250.00*

Nos. 52-54 (3) *1,875.* 610.00

No. 24, perf. 12x13, No. 34 imperf. and most examples of Nos. 52-54 unused are from souvenir booklets made up in 1905 when the Japanese withdrew all Korean stamps from circulation.

KUWAIT

ku-ˈwāt

LOCATION — Northwestern coast of the Persian Gulf
GOVT. — Sheikdom under British Protection
AREA — 7,000 sq. mi.
POP. — 1,910,856 (est. 1985)
CAPITAL — Kuwait

16 Annas = 1 Rupee

Catalogue values for unused stamps in this country are for Never Hinged items, beginning with Scott 72 in the regular postage section.

There was a first or trial setting of the overprint with the word "Koweit." Twenty-four sets of regular and official stamps were printed with this spelling. Value for set, *$50,000.*.

Catalogue values for Nos. 1-71 used, are for postally used examples. Stamps with telegraph cancellations are worth less.

Iraqi Postal Administration

Stamps of India, 1911-23, Overprinted

a

b

1923-24 **Wmk. 39** ***Perf. 14***

1 A47(a) ½a green 4.75 *15.00*
- Never hinged 7.25
- *a.* Double overprint 375.00
- *b.* Vertical pair, one without overprint *1,900.*

2 A48(a) 1a dk brn 8.00 *5.50*
- Never hinged 12.00
- *a.* Double overprint 525.00
- *b.* Vertical pair, one without overprint *2,100.*

3 A58(a) 1½a choc 6.00 *12.00*
- Never hinged 8.75

4 A49(a) 2a violet 5.00 *9.50*
- Never hinged 7.50
- *a.* 2a reddish purple 14.50
- Never hinged 24.00

5 A57(a) 2a6p ultra 4.25 *8.75*
- Never hinged 6.50

6 A51(a) 3a brn org 5.00 *26.50*
- Never hinged 7.50

7 A51(a) 3a ultra ('24) 12.50 *4.50*
- Never hinged 19.00

8 A52(a) 4a ol green 11.50 *27.00*
- Never hinged 17.00

9 A53(a) 6a bister 13.00 *16.00*
- Never hinged 19.50

10 A54(a) 8a red vio 12.00 *57.50*
- Never hinged 18.00

11 A55(a) 12a claret 16.00 *62.50*
- Never hinged 24.00

12 A56(b) 1r grn & red brn 50.00 *55.00*
- Never hinged 75.00
- *a.* 1r dp turq grn & org brown 62.00 75.00
- Never hinged 95.00

13 A56(b) 2r brn & car rose 67.50 *120.00*
- Never hinged 100.00

14 A56(b) 5r vio & ultra 140.00 *275.00*
- Never hinged 195.00
- *a.* Double ovpt., one albino *750.00*

15 A56(b) 10r car & grn 250.00 *525.00*
- Never hinged 375.00

Nos. 1-15 (15) 605.50 *1,220.*

Overprint "a" on India No. 102 is generally considered unofficial.

Nos. 1-4, 6-7 exist with inverted overprint. None of these are believed to have been sold at the Kuwait post office.

For overprints see Nos. O1-O13.

Stamps of India, 1926-35, Overprinted Type "a"

1929-37 **Wmk. 196**

17 A47 ½a green 6.50 3.00
- Never hinged 10.00

18 A71 ½a green ('34) 11.00 2.00
- Never hinged 17.50

19 A48 1a dark brown 7.75 4.00
- Never hinged 17.50

20 A72 1a dk brown ('34) 16.50 1.25
- Never hinged 25.00

21 A60 2a dk violet 9.50 2.00
- Never hinged 15.00

22 A60 2a vermilion 27.50 *95.00*
- Never hinged 40.00

23 A49 2a ver ('34) 17.50 6.75
- Never hinged 26.00
- *a.* Small die 8.75 3.00
- Never hinged 14.00

24 A51 3a ultramarine 6.00 3.50
- Never hinged 9.00

25 A51 3a car rose ('34) 9.00 4.50
- Never hinged 13.50

No.	Type	Description	Unused	Used
26	A61	4a olive green	40.00	*100.00*
		Never hinged	65.00	
a.		4a sage green	75.00	—
		Never hinged	125.00	
27	A52	4a ol green ('34)	17.50	*14.50*
		Never hinged	26.00	
28	A53	6a bister ('37)	27.50	*70.00*
		Never hinged	42.50	
29	A54	8a red violet	10.00	15.00
		Never hinged	17.50	
30	A55	12a claret	35.00	*50.00*
		Never hinged	60.00	

Overprinted — c

No.	Type	Description	Unused	Used
31	A56	1r grn & brn	27.50	*50.00*
		Never hinged	47.50	
a.		Elongated "T"	1,250.	—
32	A56	2r orange & carmine	25.00	*72.50*
		Never hinged	37.50	
a.		Elongated "T"	775.00	*1,250.*
b.		2r buff & car rose	225.00	230.00
33	A56	5r dk vio & ultra ('37)	145.00	*325.00*
		Never hinged	210.00	
a.		Elongated "T"	1,500.	
34	A56	10r car & grn ('34)	325.00	*550.00*
		Never hinged	500.00	
a.		Elongated "T"	3,100.	
35	A56	15r ol grn & ultra ('37)	975.00	*1,200.*
		Never hinged	1,400.	
a.		Elongated "T"	5,750.	
		Nos. 17-35 (19)	1,739.	*2,569.*

For overprints see Nos. O15-O25.

Stamps of India, 1937, Overprinted Type "a" (A80, A81) or "c" (A82)

1939 Wmk. 196 *Perf. 13½x14*

No.	Type	Description	Unused	Used
45	A80	½a brown	4.25	*3.50*
		Never hinged	7.25	
46	A80	1a carmine	4.25	*3.50*
		Never hinged	7.25	
47	A81	2a scarlet	4.50	*5.00*
		Never hinged	8.75	
48	A81	3a yel green	6.00	3.25
		Never hinged	11.50	
49	A81	4a dark brown	25.00	*30.00*
		Never hinged	42.50	
50	A81	6a peacock blue	16.00	*20.00*
		Never hinged	27.50	
51	A81	8a blue violet	17.50	*35.00*
		Never hinged	30.00	
52	A81	12a car lake	12.00	*85.00*
		Never hinged	20.00	
53	A82	1r brown & slate	16.00	*8.75*
		Never hinged	30.00	
a.		Elongated "T"	650.00	675.00
		Never hinged	20.00	
54	A82	2r dk brn & dk vio	5.00	*27.50*
		Never hinged	20.00	
a.		Elongated "T"	650.00	1,125.
		Never hinged	1,000.	
55	A82	5r dp ultra & dk green	12.00	*30.00*
		Never hinged	20.00	
a.		Elongated "T"	950.00	
		Never hinged	1,350.	
56	A82	10r rose car & dk violet	50.00	*100.00*
		Never hinged	80.00	
a.		Double overprint	500.00	—
		Never hinged	750.00	
b.		Elongated "T"	1,525.	
		Never hinged	2,250.	
57	A82	15r dk grn & dk brn	75.00	*225.00*
		Never hinged	115.00	
a.		Elongated "T"	3,000.	
		Never hinged	4,500.	
		Nos. 45-57 (13)	247.50	*576.50*

The elongated "T" variety was corrected in later printings.

Indian Postal Administration

From May 24, 1941, until August 1947, the Kuwaiti postal service was administered by India, and during 1941-45 unoverprinted Indian stamps were used in Kuwait.

Kuwait postal services were administered by Pakistan from August 1947 through March 1948. Control was transferred to Great Britain on April 1, 1948.

Stamps of India 1940-43, Overprinted in Black

1945 Wmk. 196 *Perf. 13½x14*

No.	Type	Description	Unused	Used
59	A83	3p slate	2.75	*10.00*
		Never hinged	4.00	
60	A83	½a rose violet	1.75	*5.50*
		Never hinged	4.00	
61	A83	9p lt green	2.75	*18.50*
		Never hinged	4.00	
62	A83	1a car rose	2.00	*2.50*
		Never hinged	3.50	
63	A84	1½a dark purple	2.75	*11.00*
		Never hinged	4.25	
64	A84	2a scarlet	3.00	*8.50*
		Never hinged	5.00	
65	A84	3a violet	4.00	*16.00*
		Never hinged	5.50	
66	A84	3½a ultramarine	3.75	*17.50*
		Never hinged	5.50	
67	A85	4a chocolate	4.00	*4.75*
		Never hinged	6.75	
68	A85	6a peacock blue	11.00	22.50
		Never hinged	14.50	
69	A85	8a blue violet	5.75	15.00
		Never hinged	7.25	
70	A85	12a car lake	6.00	9.00
		Never hinged	8.75	
71	A81	14a rose violet	11.00	*24.00*
		Never hinged	15.00	
		Nos. 59-71 (13)	60.50	*164.75*

Catalogue values for unused stamps in this section, from this point to the end of the section, are for Never Hinged items.

British Postal Administration

See Oman (Muscat) for similar stamps with surcharge of new value only.

Great Britain Nos. 258 to 263, 243 and 248 Surcharged in Black

1948-49 Wmk. 251 *Perf. 14½x14*

No.	Type	Description	Unused	Used
72	A101	½a on ½p grn	4.00	*4.25*
73	A101	1a on 1p ver	4.00	2.50
74	A101	1½a on 1½p lt red brown	4.50	2.50
75	A101	2a on 2p lt org	4.00	2.50
76	A101	2½a on 2½p ultra	4.25	1.25
77	A101	3a on 3p violet	4.25	1.10
a.		Pair, one without surcharge	*20,000.*	—
78	A102	6a on 6p rose lil	4.25	1.00
79	A103	1r on 1sh brn	9.00	2.50

Great Britain Nos. 249A, 250 and 251A Surcharged in Black

Wmk. 259 *Perf. 14*

No.	Type	Description	Unused	Used
80	A104	2r on 2sh6p yel grn	9.50	*9.00*
81	A104	5r on 5sh dull red	12.50	9.00
81A	A105	10r on 10sh ultra	62.50	11.50
		Nos. 72-81A (11)	122.75	47.10

Issued: Nos. 72-81, 4/48; 10r, 7/4/49.
Bars of surcharge at bottom on No. 81A.

Silver Wedding Issue

Great Britain Nos. 267 and 268 Surcharged in Black

Perf. 14½x14, 14x14½

1948 Wmk. 251

No.	Type	Description	Unused	Used
82	A109	2½a on 2½p brt ultra	3.00	3.00
83	A110	15r on £1 deep chalky blue	42.50	42.50

Three bars obliterate the original denomination on No. 83.

Olympic Games Issue

Great Britain Nos. 271 to 274 Surcharged "KUWAIT" and New Value in Black

1948 *Perf. 14½x14*

No.	Type	Description	Unused	Used
84	A113	2½a on 2½p brt ultra	1.75	3.25
85	A114	3a on 3p dp violet	2.00	3.50
86	A115	6a on 6p red violet	2.10	4.00
87	A116	1r on 1sh dk brown	2.50	4.50
		Nos. 84-87 (4)	8.35	15.25

A square of dots obliterates the original denomination on No. 87.

UPU Issue

Great Britain Nos. 276 to 279 Surcharged "KUWAIT", New Value and Square of Dots in Black

1949, Oct. 10 Photo.

No.	Type	Description	Unused	Used
89	A117	2½a on 2½p brt ultra	1.25	*2.50*
90	A118	3a on 3p brt vio	1.50	*3.00*
91	A119	6a on 6p red vio	1.60	*3.00*
92	A120	1r on 1sh brown	1.75	1.75
		Nos. 89-92 (4)	6.10	10.25

Great Britain Nos. 280-285 Surcharged Like Nos. 72-79 in Black

1950-51 Wmk. 251 *Perf. 14½x14*

No.	Type	Description	Unused	Used
93	A101	½a on ½p lt org	2.75	1.50
94	A101	1a on 1p ultra	2.75	1.60
95	A101	1½a on 1½p green	2.75	*2.25*
96	A101	2a on 2p lt red brown	2.75	1.50
97	A101	2½a on 2½p ver	2.75	*2.75*
98	A102	4a on 4p ultra ('50)	2.75	1.50

Great Britain Nos. 286-288 Surcharged in Black

Perf. 11x12

Wmk. 259

No.	Type	Description	Unused	Used
99	A121	2r on 2sh6p green	24.00	8.75
100	A121	5r on 5sh dl red	30.00	10.00
101	A122	10r on 10sh ultra	50.00	11.00
		Nos. 93-101 (9)	120.50	40.85

Longer bars, at lower right, on No. 101.
Issued: 4a, 10/2/50; others, 5/3/51.

AIR POST STAMPS

Air Post Stamps of India, 1929-30, Overprinted type "c"

1933-34 Wmk. 196 *Perf. 14*

No.	Type	Description	Unused	Used
C1	AP1	2a dull green	24.00	*27.50*
C2	AP1	3a deep blue	5.00	*3.50*
C3	AP1	4a gray olive	160.00	*225.00*
C4	AP1	6a bister ('34)	8.00	*4.50*
		Nos. C1-C4 (4)	197.00	*260.50*

Counterfeits of Nos. C1-C4 exist.

OFFICIAL STAMPS

Stamps of India, 1911-23, Overprinted

Nos. O1-O9

Nos. O10-O14

1923-24 Wmk. 39 *Perf. 14*

No.	Type	Description	Unused	Used
O1	A47	½a green	6.50	*50.00*
		Never hinged	7.50	
O2	A48	1a brown	5.50	*27.50*
		Never hinged	6.75	
O3	A58	1½a chocolate	5.00	*65.00*
		Never hinged	6.00	
O4	A49	2a violet	11.00	*50.00*
		Never hinged	14.00	
O5	A57	2a6p ultra	7.00	*80.00*
		Never hinged	9.00	
O6	A51	3a brown org	7.50	*75.00*
		Never hinged	9.75	
O7	A51	3a ultra ('24)	7.75	*75.00*
		Never hinged	10.00	
O8	A52	4a olive grn	6.25	*75.00*
		Never hinged	8.00	
O9	A54	8a red violet	9.50	*110.00*
		Never hinged	13.00	
O10	A56	1r grn & brn	35.00	*190.00*
		Never hinged	47.50	
O11	A56	2r brn & car rose	37.50	*275.00*
		Never hinged	45.00	
O12	A56	5r vio & ultra	125.00	*475.00*
		Never hinged	150.00	
O13	A56	10r car & grn	250.00	*440.00*
		Never hinged	325.00	
O14	A56	15r ol grn & ultra	400.00	*675.00*
		Never hinged	525.00	
		Nos. O1-O14 (14)	913.50	*2,663.*

Stamps of India, 1926-30, Overprinted

Nos. O15-O20

Nos. O21-O25

1929-33 Wmk. 196

No.	Type	Description	Unused	Used
O15	A48	1a dk brown	6.50	*42.50*
		Never hinged	10.00	
O16	A60	2a violet	70.00	*250.00*
		Never hinged	105.00	
O17	A51	3a blue	6.00	*55.00*
		Never hinged	9.00	
O18	A61	4a ol green	6.75	*90.00*
		Never hinged	9.00	
O19	A54	8a red violet	9.00	*130.00*
		Never hinged	12.50	
O20	A55	12a claret	45.00	*225.00*
		Never hinged	67.50	
O21	A56	1r green & brn	14.00	*275.00*
		Never hinged	21.00	
O22	A56	2r buff & car rose	18.00	*400.00*
		Never hinged	27.50	
O23	A56	5r dk vio & ultra	50.00	*500.00*
		Never hinged	75.00	
O24	A56	10r car & green	85.00	*850.00*
		Never hinged	125.00	
O25	A56	15r olive grn & ultra	300.00	*1,450.*
		Never hinged	450.00	
		Nos. O15-O25 (11)	610.25	*4,268.*

LABUAN

lə-'bü-ən

LOCATION — An island in the East Indies, about six miles off the northwest coast of Borneo
GOVT. — A British possession, administered as a part of the North Borneo Colony
AREA — 35 sq. mi.
POP. — 8,963 (estimated)
CAPITAL — Victoria

The stamps of Labuan were replaced by those of Straits Settlements in 1906.

100 Cents = 1 Dollar

Covers: There are no known covers bearing Nos. 1-4. Except for Nos. 19, 19a, 29, 29a, covers bearing Nos. 5-32 are very rare. Values for listed covers are for properly franked commercial covers or postal cards. Philatelic covers also exist and sell for much less.

Watermark

Wmk. 46 — C A over Crown

Queen Victoria — A1

On Nos. 1, 2, 3, 4 and 11 the watermark is 32mm high. It is always placed sideways and extends over two stamps.

1879, May Engr. Wmk. 46 *Perf. 14*

1 A1 2c green 1,625. 975.00
2 A1 6c orange 240.00 225.00
a. Missing dot in upper left panel (position 2/4). *625.00* *575.00*
3 A1 12c carmine 1,925. 850.00
a. Missing right foot in second Chinese character (position 2/3). *4,250.* *1,750.*
4 A1 16c blue 77.50 *200.00*
Nos. 1-4 (4) 3,868. 2,250.

Covers: Covers bearing Nos. 1-4 are not known.

See Nos. 5-10, 16-24, 33-39, 42-48. For surcharges see Nos. 12-15, 25, 31, 40-41.

1880-82 Wmk. 1

5 A1 2c green 34.00 *57.50*
6 A1 6c orange 145.00 *160.00*
a. Missing dot in upper left panel (position 2/4). *325.00* *325.00*
7 A1 8c carmine ('82) 135.00 *135.00*
a. Missing dot at lower left 325.00 325.00
8 A1 10c yel brown 205.00 *100.00*
9 A1 12c carmine 330.00 *400.00*
a. Missing right foot in second Chinese character (position 2/3). *625.00* *775.00*
10 A1 16c blue ('81) 100.00 130.00
Nos. 5-10 (6) 949.00 *982.50*

Covers: Covers bearing Nos. 5-10 are very rare.

A2

A3

A3a

A4

1880-83 Wmk. 46

11 A2 6c on 16c blue (with additional "6" across original value) R) 4,200. 1,325.
a. One "6" — —

Wmk. 1

12 A2 8c on 12c car 1,825. 1,000.
a. Original value not obliterated 3,600. 2,000.
b. Additional surcharge "8" across original value 2,300. 1,450.
c. "8" inverted 2,100. 1,200.
d. As "a," "8" inverted *4,200.* —
e. Missing right foot in second Chinese character (position 2/3). *3,900.* *2,000.*
13 A3 8c on 12c car ('81) 475.00 525.00
14 A3a 8c on 12c car ('81) 160.00 170.00
a. "Eighr" *22,500.*
b. Inverted surcharge *16,000.*
c. Double surcharge 2,900. 2,400.
e. Missing right foot in second Chinese character (position 2/3). 350.00 400.00
15 A4 $1 on 16c blue (R) ('83) *4,800.*

Covers: Covers bearing Nos. 11-15 are very rare.

On No. 12 the original value is obliterated by a pen mark in either black or red.

Types of 1879 Issue

1883-86 Wmk. 2

16 A1 2c green 30.00 *55.00*
a. Horiz. pair, imperf. btwn. 18,500.
17 A1 2c rose red ('85) 4.25 *20.00*
a. 2c pale rose red ('86) 4.25 *17.50*
18 A1 8c carmine 325.00 120.00
a. Missing dot at lower left 675.00 250.00
19 A1 8c dk violet ('85) 50.00 9.25
On cover *1,500.*
a. 8c mauve ('86) 45.00 13.50
On cover *1,500.*
b. Missing dot at lower left 105.00 25.00
c. As "a," Missing dot at lower left 95.00 29.00
20 A1 10c yellow brn 62.50 *57.50*
21 A1 10c black brn ('86) 40.00 *72.50*
22 A1 16c blue 115.00 *215.00*
23 A1 16c gray blue ('86) 125.00 *180.00*
24 A1 40c ocher 37.50 *145.00*
Nos. 16-24 (9) 789.25 *874.25*

Covers: Covers bearing Nos. 16-18, 20-24 are very rare.

Nos. 1-10, 16-24 are in sheets of 10.

For surcharges see Nos. 26-30, 32.

A5

A6

A7

1885 Wmk. 1

25 A5 2c on 16c blue 1,150. *1,100.*

Wmk. 2

26 A5 2c on 8c car 275.00 *550.00*
a. Double surcharge —
27 A6 2c on 16c blue 135.00 *200.00*
a. Double surcharge *7,500.*
28 A7 2c on 8c car 80.00 *145.00*
a. Missing dot at lower left 190.00 350.00

Covers: Covers bearing Nos. 25-28 are very rare.

A8

1891 Black or Red Surcharge

29 A8 6c on 8c violet 16.50 17.00
On cover *1,500.*
a. 6c on 8c dark violet 625.00 210.00
On cover *1,750.*
b. Double surcharge 390.00 —
c. As "a," "Cents" omitted 550.00 550.00
d. Inverted surcharge 90.00 *85.00*
e. Dbl. surch., one inverted 1,100. —
f. Dbl. surch., both inverted 1,100. —
g. "6" omitted 625.00
h. Pair, one without surcharge 2,000. 2,000.
i. Invt. surcharge, "Cents" omitted 600.00 —
j. As "d," one without surcharge 2,300. 2,300.
k. As "a," inverted surcharge 300.00 290.00
m. As "a," double surcharge 625.00 —
n. As "a," double surcharge, one inverted 1,200.
p. As "a," pair, one inverted, one omitted 2,100. —
q. As "a," horiz. pair, imperf,. btwn. 15,000. —
30 A8 6c on 8c dk vio (R) 1,550. 825.00
a. Inverted surcharge 1,850. 925.00

Wmk. 46

31 A8 6c on 16c blue 2,800. 2,300.
a. Inverted surcharge 15,500. 8,250.

Wmk. 2

32 A8 6c on 40c ocher 14,000. 5,750.
a. Inverted surcharge 12,000. 9,000.

Covers: Covers bearing Nos. 30-32 are very rare. Values for Nos. 29 and 29a on cover are for properly franked commercial covers or postal cards. Philatelic covers exist and sell for much less.

Types of 1879 Issue

1892 Engr. Unwmk.

33 A1 2c rose 7.25 4.25
On cover *500.00*
34 A1 6c yellow green 14.50 5.75
On cover *550.00*
35 A1 8c violet 13.50 *19.50*
On cover *1,500.*
a. 8c pale violet ('93) 9.50 *18.50*
On cover *1,500.*
36 A1 10c brown 30.00 9.50
On cover *1,000.*
a. 10c dk sepia brown ('93) 25.00 *20.00*
On cover —
37 A1 12c deep ultra 16.00 8.00
On cover *800.00*
38 A1 16c gray 30.00 *45.00*
On cover *1,500.*
39 A1 40c ocher 27.50 *45.00*
On cover —
a. 40c brown buff ('93) 55.00 30.00
On cover —
Nos. 33-39 (7) 138.75 137.00

The 2c, 8c and 10c are in sheets of 30; others in sheets of 10.

Values for covers are for properly franked commercial usages. Philatelic covers exist and sell for lower prices.

Remainders of the 1892 issue were canceled to order, but in most cases cannot be distinguished from postally used examples.

Nos. 39 and 38 Surcharged

1893

40 A1 2c on 40c ocher 200.00 110.00
On cover *1,600.*
a. Inverted surcharge 500.00 *675.00*
41 A1 6c on 16c gray 450.00 180.00
On cover *2,500.*
a. Inverted surcharge 675.00 350.00
b. Surcharge sideways 675.00 375.00
c. "Six" omitted — —
d. "Cents" omitted — —
e. Handstamped "Six Cents" *2,275.*

Surcharges on Nos. 40-41 each exist in 10 types. Counterfeits exist.

No. 41e was handstamped on examples of No. 41 on which the surcharge failed to print or was printed partially or completely albino.

Values for covers are for properly franked commercial usages.

From Jan. 1, 1890, to Jan. 1, 1906, Labuan was administered by the British North Borneo Co. Late in that period, unused remainders of Nos. 42-83, 53a, 63a, 64a, 65a, 66a, 68a, 85-86, 96-118, 103a, 107a, J1-J9, J3a and J6a were canceled to order by bars forming an oval. Values for these stamps used are for those with this form of cancellation, unless described as postally used, which are for stamps with dated town cancellations. Nos. 63b, 64b, 65b, 104a, J6a, and possibly others, only exist c.t.o.

Types of 1879 Issue

1894, Apr. Litho.

42 A1 2c bright rose 2.00 .65
Postally used 18.00
On cover *1,000.*
43 A1 6c yellow green 27.50 .65
Postally used 60.00
On cover *3,000.*
a. Horiz. pair, imperf. btwn. *11,250.*
b. Missing dot in upper left position 50.00 1.50
Postally used 140.00
44 A1 8c bright violet 29.00 .65
Postally used 65.00
On cover *2,750.*
45 A1 10c brown 60.00 .65
Postally used 85.00
On cover *3,750.*
46 A1 12c light ultra 37.50 .80
Postally used 100.00
On cover *4,750.*
a. Missing right foot in second Chinese character 72.50 2.00
Postally used 225.00
47 A1 16c gray 40.00 .65
Postally used 190.00
On cover —
48 A1 40c orange 60.00 .65
Postally used 200.00
On cover —
Nos. 42-48 (7) 256.00 4.70
Set, ovptd. "SPECIMEN" 145.00

Counterfeits exist.

Values for covers are for properly franked commercial usages. Philatelic covers exist and sell for lower prices.

Dyak Chieftain — A9

Malayan Sambar — A10

Sago Palm A11

Argus Pheasant A12

Arms of North Borneo — A13

Dhow — A14

Saltwater Crocodile — A15

Mt. Kinabalu — A16

Arms of North Borneo — A17

Perf. 14 ½-15

1894, May-1896 Engr.

49 A9 1c lilac & black 2.00 .65
Postally used 14.00
On cover *180.00*
a. Vert. pair, imperf. between 1,300. 575.00
50 A10 2c blue & black 3.00 .65
Postally used 14.00
On cover *180.00*
a. Imperf., pair 725.00
51 A11 3c bister & black 4.50 .65
Postally used 25.00
On cover *325.00*
52 A12 5c green & black 38.50 1.10
Postally used 40.00
On cover *425.00*
a. Horiz. pair, imperf. between *1,800.*
53 A13 6c brn red & blk 3.00 .65
Postally used 25.00
On cover *275.00*
a. Imperf., pair 725.00 350.00
54 A14 8c rose & black 10.00 .65
Postally used 32.50
On cover *450.00*
a. 8c red & black 32.50 2.40

Postally used 45.00
On cover 525.00
55 A15 12c orange & black 27.50 .65
Postally used 57.50
On cover —
56 A16 18c ol brn & blk 26.50 .65
Postally used 65.00
On cover —
a. 18c olive bister & black 67.50 .55
Postally used 85.00
On cover —
b. Vert. pair, imperf. between 2,500.
57 A17 24c lilac & blue 20.00 1.30
Postally used 55.00
On cover 900.00
a. 24c mauve & blue 40.00 .55
Postally used 65.00
On cover —
Nos. 49-57 (9) 135.00 6.95
Set, ovptd. "SPECIMEN" 180.00

Perf. 13½-14

49b A9 1c lilac & black 16.50
Postally used 12.00
On cover 200.00
50b A10 2c blue & black 7.00
Postally used 14.50
On cover 200.00
51a A11 3c bister & black 17.50 —
Postally used 11.00
On cover 250.00
52b A12 5c green & black 50.00 —
Postally used 25.00
On cover 275.00
53b A13 6c brn red & blk 3.00
54b A14 8c rose & black 45.00 1.00
Postally used 37.50
On cover 625.00
54c A14 8c red & black 45.00
Postally used 55.00
On cover 750.00
55a A15 12c orange & black 77.50 2.75
Postally used 90.00
On cover —
56c A16 18c ol brn & blk 85.00
56d A16 18c ol bister & blk 32.50
Postally used 77.50
On cover —
57b A17 24c lilac & blue 20.00 1.25
Postally used 55.00
On cover —
57c A17 24c mauve & blue 40.00
Postally used 60.00
On cover —

Perf. 13½-14 compound 14½-15

49c A9 1c lilac & black 40.00
50c A10 2c blue & black 42.50
51b A11 3c bister & black —
53c A13 6c brn red & blk —

Perf. 13½-14 compound 12-13

49d A9 1c lilac & black 40.00 1.10
Postally used 14.50
On cover 275.00
50d A10 2c blue & black —
51c A11 3c bister & black 55.00
52c A12 5c green & black 65.00
53d A13 6c brn red & blk —
55b A15 12c orange & black —
Postally used —
On cover —
56e A16 18c ol bister & blk —

Perf. 12-13

49e A9 1c lilac & black —
50e A10 2c blue & black 190.00
51d A11 3c bister & black —
52d A12 5c green & black 210.00
53e A13 6c brn red & blk 260.00
55c A15 12c orange & black —

Values for covers are for properly franked commercial usages.

For overprints see Nos. 66-71.

A18

1895, June Litho. *Perf. 14*

58 A18 4c on $1 red 4.25 .50
Postally used 4.50
59 A18 10c on $1 red 11.50 .50
Postally used 1.75
60 A18 20c on $1 red 52.50 .50
Postally used 14.50
61 A18 30c on $1 red 57.50 1.50
Postally used 65.00
62 A18 40c on $1 red 57.50 1.50
Postally used 55.00
Nos. 58-62 (5) 183.25 4.50
Set, ovptd. "SPECIMEN" 95.00

A19

A20

A21

1896

63 A19 25c blue green 45.00 .80
Postally used 50.00
a. Imperf, pair 72.50
b. Without overprint 35.00 2.00
c. As "b," imperf, pair 60.00
64 A20 50c claret 42.50 .80
Postally used 50.00
a. Imperf, pair 72.50
b. Without overprint 32.50 2.00
c. As "b," imperf, pair 52.50
65 A21 $1 dark blue 82.50 1.25
Postally used 75.00
a. Imperf, pair 72.50
b. Without overprint 50.00 3.00
c. As "b," imperf, pair 60.00
Nos. 63-65 (3) 170.00 2.85
Set, ovptd. "SPECIMEN" 65.00

For surcharges and overprint see Nos. 93-95, 116-118, 120.

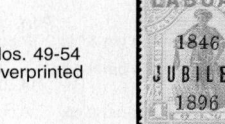

Nos. 49-54 Overprinted

1896 *Perf. 14½-15*

66 A9 1c lilac & black 26.00 1.75
Postally used 27.50
a. "JEBILEE" 1,450. 360.00
Postally used 675.00
b. "JUBILE" 3,000.
c. Orange overprint 325.00 24.00
Postally used 240.00
67 A10 2c blue & black 52.50 1.75
Postally used 35.00
a. Vert. pair, imperf. btwn. 1,525. —
Postally used 1,650.
b. "JEBILEE" 1,850. —
Postally used 1,325.
c. "JUBILE" 3,500. —
Postally used 3,000.
d. Vert. strip of 3, imperf between 8,000.
68 A11 3c bister & black 50.00 1.50
Postally used 27.50
a. "JEBILEE" 2,250. 850.00
Postally used 1,800.
b. "JUBILE" — —
69 A12 5c green & black 72.50 1.50
Postally used 19.50
a. Double overprint 975.00
Postally used 725.00
70 A13 6c brown red & blk 47.50 1.00
Postally used 30.00
a. Double overprint 975.00 —
Postally used 675.00
b. "JUBILE" 3,600. —
71 A14 8c rose & black 57.50 1.00
Postally used 18.50
a. Double overprint — 3,000.
Postally used 3,500.
Nos. 66-71 (6) 306.00 8.50
Set, ovptd. "SPECIMEN" 150.00

Perf. 13½-14

66d A9 1c lilac & black 35.00
Postally used 26.00
e. Double overprint 450.00 —
Postally used 400.00
f. Orange overprint 350.00
Postally used 240.00
67e A10 2c blue & black 52.50
Postally used 24.00
68c A11 3c bister & black 57.50 1.50
Postally used 37.50
d. Triple overprint 1,150.
69b A12 5c green & black 72.50 1.50
Postally used 27.50
70c A13 6c brown red & blk —
Postally used 100.00
71b A14 8c rose & black 52.50 1.00
Postally used 16.00

Perf. 13½-14 compound 14½-15

67f A10 2c blue & black — 50.00
Postally used —

68e A11 3c bister & black —
70d A13 6c brown red & blk —
71c A14 8c rose & black 60.00 22.50
Postally used —

Perf. 13½-14 compound 12-13

66g A9 1c lilac & black 47.50
Postally used 25.00
h. Orange overprint —
Postally used 240.00
67g A10 2c blue & black 57.50
68f A11 3c bister & black 450.00 200.00
Postally used 450.00
g. Double overprint 425.00 195.00
Postally used 450.00
h. Triple overprint 775.00 —
69c A12 5c green & black —

Perf. 12-13

66i A9 1c lilac & black —

Cession of Labuan to Great Britain, 50th anniv.

Dyak Chieftain
A22

Malayan Sambar
A23

Sago Palm
A24

Argus Pheasant
A25

A26

Dhow — A27

Saltwater Crocodile — A28

Mt. Kinabalu "Postal Revenue" — A29

Coat of Arms — A30

1897-1900 Engr. *Perf. 14½-15*

72 A22 1c lilac & black 8.00 .60
Postally used 5.75
72A A22 1c red brn & blk 3.75 .80
73 A23 2c blue & black 32.50 .90
a. Vert. pair, imperf between 1,125.
b. Horiz. pair, imperf between 1,550.
75 A24 3c bister & blk 10.00 .60
Postally used 8.00
a. Vert. pair, imperf between 1,325. 675.00
76 A25 5c green & blk 67.50 .85
Postally used 67.50
78 A26 6c brn red & blk 16.00 .60
Postally used
a. Vert. pair, imperf between 850.00
79 A27 8c red & black 25.00
Postally used 14.50
80 A28 12c red & black 40.00 2.50
Postally used 60.00

82 A30 24c gry lil & bl 14.50 .60
Postally used 60.00
Nos. 72-82 (9) 217.25 7.45
Set (Nos. 72, 73-82), ovptd. "SPECIMEN" 220.00

Perf. 13½-14

72Ab A22 1c red brn & blk 25.00 .80
Postally used 27.50
73c A23 2c blue & black 26.00 .80
Postally used 5.50
74 A23 2c grn & blk ('00) 4.50 .35
Postally used 3.00
a. Horiz. pair, imperf between 3,100. 1,550.
75b A24 3c bister & blk 10.00 .60
Postally used 29.00
76b A25 5c green & blk 67.50 .90
Postally used 67.50
77 A25 5c lt bl & blk ('00) 27.50 .80
Postally used 22.50
78b A26 6c brn red & blk 8.00 .60
Postally used 52.50
79a A27 8c red & black 60.00 1.00
79b A27 8c vermilion & black 14.50 .80
80a A28 12c red & black 140.00 3.00
Postally used 160.00
81 A29 18c ol bis & blk 125.00 2.40
Postally used 125.00
82a A30 24c gry lil & bl 57.50 2.40
Postally used 100.00

Perf. 13½-14 compound 14½-15

72c A22 1c lilac & black —

Perf. 13½-14 compound 12-13

73d A23 2c blue & black 62.50
Postally used 25.00
74b A23 2c grn & blk ('00) —
75c A24 3c bister & blk 25.00 2.00
Postally used 45.00
76c A25 5c green & blk —
Postally used 100.00
77a A25 5c lt bl & blk ('00) —
78c A26 6c brn red & blk 8.25
79c A27 8c red & black 52.50 3.25

Perf. 16

72Ad A22 1c red brn & blk 25.00
Postally used 20.00
73e A23 2c blue & black 8.50
79d A27 8c red & black 7.50
81a A29 18c ol bis & blk 15.00 .60
Postally used 55.00
b. Vert. pair, imperf between 3,750.

For surcharges see Nos. 87-89, 110-112.

"Postage & Revenue" — A31

"Postage & Revenue" — A32

1897, Nov. *Perf. 14½-15*

83 A31 18c bister & black 95.00 2.40
Postally used 72.50
84 A32 24c brn lil & bl 50.00
Postally used 67.50
Overprinted "SPECIMEN" 27.50
a. 24c ocher & blue — 4.75

Perf. 13½-14

83a A31 18c bister & black —
84b A32 24c brn lilac & blue 52.50 *2.40*
Postally used 67.50

Perf. 13½-14 compound 12-13

83c A31 18c bister & black 145.00
84c A32 24c brn lilac & blue —
Postally used 77.50

Perf. 16

83b A31 18c bister & black 10.00
84d A32 24c brn lilac & blue 57.50

No. 84a only exists cto.

For surcharges see Nos. 92, 115.

"Postage & Revenue" — A33

"Postage & Revenue" — A34

1898, Mar. *Perf. 14½-15*

85 A33 12c red & black — 4.00
Postally used —
86 A34 18c bister & black 72.50
Postally used 72.50

Perf. 13½-14

85a A33 12c red & black 50.00
Postally used 60.00
86a A34 18c bister & black 42.50 3.75
Postally used 72.50

Perf. 13½-14 compound 14½-15

85b A33 12c red & black —

Perf. 13½-14 compound 12-13

86b A34 18c bister & black 52.50
Postally used 67.50

Perf. 12-13

86c A34 18c bister & black —

Perf. 16

85c A33 12c red & black 77.50
Postally used 72.50
86d A34 18c bister & black 57.50

For surcharges see Nos. 90-91, 113-114.

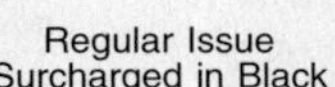

Regular Issue Surcharged in Black

1899 *Perf. 14½-15*

87 A25 4c on 5c grn & blk 55.00 30.00
88 A26 4c on 6c brn red & blk 30.00 22.50
89 A27 4c on 8c red & blk 72.50 52.50
90 A33 4c on 12c red & blk 60.00 42.50
91 A34 4c on 18c bis & blk 40.00 21.50
a. Double surcharge 575.00 *675.00*
92 A32 4c on 24c lil & bl 40.00 *36.00*

Perf. 14

93 A19 4c on 25c blue grn 7.25 *8.00*
94 A20 4c on 50c claret 8.75 *8.00*
95 A21 4c on $1 dk blue 8.75 *8.00*
Nos. 87-95 (9) 322.25 *229.00*
Set, ovptd. "SPECIMEN" 175.00

Perf. 13½-14

88a A26 4c on 6c brn red & blk 45.00 *45.00*
89a A27 4c on 8c red & blk 52.50 *37.50*
90a A33 4c on 12c red & blk 62.50 50.00
92a A32 4c on 24c lil & bl 50.00 *36.00*

Perf. 13½-14 compound 12-13

88b A26 4c on 6c brn red & blk 60.00 *72.50*
89b A27 4c on 8c red & blk 35.00 *45.00*
90b A33 4c on 12c red & blk 72.50 *77.50*
92b A32 4c on 24c lil & bl 50.00 *35.00*

Perf. 12-13

89c A27 4c on 8c red & blk —

Perf. 16

90c A33 4c on 12c red & blk 62.50 47.50
92c A32 4c on 24c lil & bl 55.00 *57.50*

Orangutan A35

Sun Bear A36

Railroad Train — A37

1899-1901 *Perf. 13½-14*

96 A35 4c yel brn & blk 10.00 .75
Postally used 67.50
a. Vert. pair, imperf. btwn. 1,450.
b. Perf 13½-14 compound 12-13 57.50
97 A35 4c car & blk ('00) 22.50 .90
Postally used 3.75
a. Perf 14½-15 6.00 .60
Postally used 16.50
b. Perf 13½-14 compound 12-13 52.50 1.50
Postally used 12.50
c. Perf 16 —
98 A36 10c gray vio & dk brn ('01) 60.00 .75
Postally used 100.00
99 A37 16c org brn & grn (G) ('01) 60.00 3.00
Postally used 140.00
a. Perf 14½-15 190.00
b. Perf 13½-14 compound 12-13 100.00
Postally used 160.00
c. Perf 12-13 440.00
Nos. 96-99 (4) 152.50 5.40
Set, ovptd. "SPECIMEN" 180.00

Crown — A38

1902-03 **Engr.** *Perf. 13½-14*

99A A38 1c vio & black 6.75 .60
Postally used 8.50
100 A38 2c grn & blk 5.00 .35
Postally used 7.25
100A A38 3c sepia & blk 4.00 .35
Postally used 22.50
101 A38 4c car & blk 4.00 .35
Postally used 4.25
102 A38 8c org & blk 15.00 .80
Postally used 11.00
103 A38 10c sl blue & brn 4.00 .35
Postally used 20.00
a. Vert. pair, imperf. between 925.00
104 A38 12c yel & black 16.00 .35
Postally used 24.00
a. Vert. strip of 3, imperf. horiz. *4,000.*
105 A38 16c org brn & grn 5.75 .35
Postally used 37.50
a. Vert. pair, imperf. between — *2,300.*
106 A38 18c bis brn & blk 4.00 .35
Postally used 37.50
107 A38 25c grnsh bl & grn 12.00 .60
Postally used 26.00
a. 25c greenish blue & black 625.00
108 A38 50c gray lil & vio 12.00 2.75
Postally used 55.00
109 A38 $1 org & red brn 10.00 2.75
Postally used 60.00
Nos. 99A-109 (12) 98.50 9.95
Set, ovptd. "SPECIMEN" 230.00

Perf. 14½-15

99Ab A38 1c vio & black 105.00
Postally used 9.00
100b A38 2c green & blk 125.00
Postally used 6.25
101a A38 4c car & black 10.00
Postally used 15.00
102a A38 8c org & black 9.50
103b A38 10c sl blue & brn 9.25 .60
Postally used 20.00
107b A38 25c grnsh bl & grn 18.00 .75
Postally used 52.50
109a A38 $1 org & red brn 12.00 2.40

Perf. 13½-14 compound 12-13

99Ac A38 1c vio & black 92.50
Postally used 60.00
101b A38 4c car & black 82.50
Postally used 60.00
108a A38 50c gray lil & vio 19.50
Postally used 65.00

Perf. 16

104b A38 12c yel & black 14.50
Postally used 25.00

Line Through "B" of "LABUAN"

Perf. 13½-14

99Ad A38 1c vio & black 95.00 11.50
Postally used 125.00
100c A38 2c green & blk 85.00 11.50
Postally used 110.00
100Ac A38 3c sepia & blk 82.50 11.25
Postally used 190.00
101c A38 4c car & black 87.50 11.50
Postally used 92.50
102b A38 8c org & black 140.00 12.50
Postally used 150.00
103c A38 10c sl blue & brn 87.50 11.50
Postally used 195.00
104c A38 12c yel & black 160.00 11.50
Postally used 275.00
105b A38 16c org brn & grn 100.00 11.50
Postally used 340.00
106a A38 18c bis brn & blk 95.00 11.25
Postally used 340.00
107c A38 25c grnsh bl & grn 140.00 12.50
Postally used 325.00
108b A38 50c gray lil & vio 210.00 27.50
Postally used 575.00
109b A38 $1 org & red brn 195.00 27.50
Postally used 575.00
Nos. 99Ad-109b (12) 1,478. 171.50

There are 3 known examples of No. 104a, all cto.

The "line through B" variety is a constant plate flaw in position R5/10.

For overprints and surcharges see Brunei Nos. 1-12.

Regular Issue of 1896-97 Surcharged in Black

1904 *Perf. 14½x15*

110 A25 4c on 5c grn & blk 57.50 17.00
Postally used 52.50
111 A26 4c on 6c brn red & blk 14.50 *17.00*
Postally used 50.00
112 A27 4c on 8c red & blk 30.00 17.00
Postally used 55.00
113 A33 4c on 12c red & blk 45.00 17.00
Postally used 52.50
a. Perf 16 52.50 —
Postally used 52.50
114 A34 4c on 18c bis & blk 30.00 17.00
Postally used 55.00
a. Perf 13½-14, comp. 12-13 42.50
Postally used 55.00
b. Perf 12-13 —
115 A32 4c on 24c brn lil & bl 19.25 17.00
Postally used 60.00
a. Perf 13½-14 42.50
Postally used 45.00
b. Perf 13½-14, comp. 12-13 52.50
Postally used 57.50
c. Perf 16 35.00 17.00
Postally used 50.00

Perf. 14

116 A19 4c on 25c blue grn 10.00 *17.00*
Postally used 37.50
117 A20 4c on 50c clar 10.00 *17.00*
Postally used 37.50
a. Double surcharge 400.00
118 A21 4c on $1 dark blue 14.00 *17.00*
Postally used 37.50
Nos. 110-118 (9) 230.25 153.00

Stamps of North Borneo, 1893, and Labuan No. 65a Overprinted in Black

a

b

c

1905

119 A30(a) 25c slate bl 1,325. 1,100.
120 A21(c) $1 blue 1,050.
121 A33(b) $2 gray grn *4,000.*
Postally used *4,000.*
122 A34(c) $5 red vio *7,250.* *1,850.*
Postally used *8,000.*
a. $5 dull purple 7,000. 1,800.
Postally used *7,750.*
123 A35(c) $10 brown *55,000.* *14,500.*

Nos. 119, 120 and 123 do not exist postally used. No. 120 exists only cto.

POSTAGE DUE STAMPS

Regular Issues Overprinted

1901 **Unwmk.** *Perf. 14*

J1 A23 2c grn & blk 27.50 1.10
Postally used 42.50
a. Double overprint 425.00
J2 A24 3c bis & blk 32.50 1.00
Postally used 135.00
J3 A35 4c car & black 62.50 3.00
a. Double overprint 875.00
J4 A25 5c lt blue & blk 57.50 1.50
Postally used 175.00
J5 A26 6c brn red & blk 50.00 1.10
Postally used 135.00
J6 A27 8c red & black 110.00 3.00
Postally used —
a. Center inverted, ovpt. reading down *12,000.*
d. 8c rose red & blk 100.00
Postally used 155.00
J7 A33 12c red & black 170.00 6.75
a. Overprint reading down *1,125.*
J9 A32 24c brn lil & bl 77.50 7.75
Postally used 175.00
c. 24c ocher & blue 105.00 2.40
Nos. J1-J9 (8) 587.50 25.20

Perf. 14½-15

J3b A35 4c car & black 60.00 .60
Postally used 120.00
J4a A25 5c lt blue & blk 2.00
J5a A26 6c brn red & blk 65.00
Postally used 140.00
J6b A27 8c red & black 100.00 1.00
Postally used 170.00
J6e A27 8c rose red & blk 150.00 9.00
J7b A33 12c red & black 120.00 14.50
Postally used 175.00
J8 A34 18c ol bis & blk 40.00 1.75
Postally used 145.00
J9a A32 24c brn lil & bl 57.50

Perf. 14½-15, Compound 12-13

J1b A23 2c grn & blk 135.00 12.00
Postally used 145.00
J2a A24 3c bis & blk 125.00 4.25
J4b A25 5c lt blue & blk 135.00
Postally used 310.00

Perf. 16

J5b A26 6c brn red & blk 90.00 1.90
J6c A27 8c red & black 110.00
Postally used 130.00
J9d A32 24c ocher & blue 70.00
Postally used 135.00

Perf. 13½-14, Compound 12-13

J9b A32 24c brn lil & bl 115.00

See note after No. 41.

The stamps of Labuan were superseded by those of Straits Settlements in 1906.

LAGOS

ˈlā-ˌgäs

LOCATION — West Africa, bordering on the former Southern Nigeria Colony
GOVT. — British Crown Colony and Protectorate
AREA — 3,460 sq. mi. (approx.)
POP. — 1,500,000 (1901)
CAPITAL — Lagos

This territory was purchased by the British in 1861 and placed under the Governor of Sierra Leone. In 1874 it was detached and formed part of the Gold Coast Colony until 1886 when the Protectorate of Lagos was established. It was chartered to the Royal Niger Company until 1899 when all territories of this Company were surrendered to the Crown of Great Britain and formed into the Northern and Southern Nigeria Protectorates. In 1906 Lagos and Southern Nigeria were united to form the Colony and Protectorate of Southern Nigeria.

12 Pence = 1 Shilling

GREAT BRITAIN POST OFFICES IN LAGOS

British postal agencies were opened in Lagos in April 1852, and a distinctive postal marking was intoduced in 1859.

Pre-Stamp Postmark

1859

Crowned Circle Handstamp Type V

A1 Inscribed "PAID AT LAGOS" in black, on cover *4,250.*

Earliest known use 12/12/71.

Queen Victoria — A1

1874-75 Typo. Wmk. 1 *Perf. 12½*

1 A1 1p lilac 80.00 50.00
2 A1 2p blue 80.00 45.00
3 A1 3p red brown ('75) 130.00 45.00
4 A1 4p rose 150.00 50.00
5 A1 6p blue green 150.00 20.00
6 A1 1sh orange ('75) 425.00 70.00
a. Value 15½mm instead of 16½mm long 700.00 160.00
Nos. 1-6 (6) 1,015. 280.00

1876 *Perf. 14*

7 A1 1p lilac 50.00 21.00
8 A1 2p blue 80.00 15.00
9 A1 3p red brown 120.00 30.00
a. 3p chestnut 125.00 40.00
10 A1 4p rose 225.00 12.50
11 A1 6p green 130.00 7.00
12 A1 1sh orange 950.00 95.00
Nos. 7-12 (6) 1,555. 180.50

The 4p exists with watermark sideways.

#19, 53a

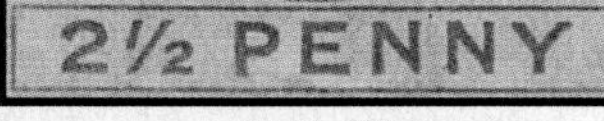

#19b, 53

1882-1902 Wmk. 2

13 A1 ½p green ('86) 2.25 .95
14 A1 1p lilac 37.50 27.50
15 A1 1p car rose 2.25 .95
16 A1 2p blue 200.00 8.50
17 A1 2p gray 100.00 9.50
18 A1 2p lil & bl ('87) 8.50 3.25
19 A1 2½p ultra ('91) 8.00 2.00
a. 2½p blue 90.00 57.50
b. As No. 19, larger letters of value 25.00 19.00
20 A1 3p orange brn 30.00 8.75
21 A1 3p lil & brn org ('91) 3.00 *3.75*
22 A1 4p rose 225.00 14.00
23 A1 4p violet 160.00 11.50
24 A1 4p lil & blk ('87) 2.50 2.00
25 A1 5p lil & grn ('94) 3.00 *12.50*
26 A1 6p olive green 9.00 *55.00*
27 A1 6p lil & red vio ('87) 5.50 3.50
28 A1 6p lilac & car rose ('02) 5.75 *13.50*
29 A1 7½p lilac & car rose ('94) 4.50 *40.00*
30 A1 10p lil & yel ('94) 4.50 *15.00*
31 A1 1sh org ('85) 21.00 *25.00*
32 A1 1sh yel grn & blk ('87) 6.50 *32.50*
a. 1sh blue green & black 5.75 *29.00*
33 A1 2sh6p ol brn ('86) 375.00 325.00
34 A1 2sh6p green & car rose ('87) 27.50 *92.50*
35 A1 5sh blue ('86) 750.00 550.00
36 A1 5sh grn & ultra ('87) 47.50 *175.00*
37 A1 10sh brn vio ('86) 2,750. 2,000.
38 A1 10sh grn & brn ('87) 120.00 *275.00*
Set, ovptd. "SPECIMEN" 775.00

Excellent forgeries exist of Nos. 33, 35 and 37 on paper with genuine watermark.

No. 24 Surcharged in Black

1893

39 A1 ½p on 4p lilac & blk 10.00 3.00
a. Double surcharge 70.00 62.50
b. Triple surcharge 175.00
c. ½p on 2p lilac & blue (#18) — 27,500.

Four settings of surcharge.

Only one used example is known of No. 39c. The two unused examples are in museums.

King Edward VII — A3

#43a

#43

1904, Jan. 22

40 A3 ½p grn & bl grn 3.00 *6.25*
41 A3 1p vio & blk, *red* 1.25 .25
42 A3 2p violet & ultra 6.75 7.00
43 A3 2½p vio & ultra, *bl* 1.50 *1.75*
a. Smaller letters of value 5.00 *9.75*
44 A3 3p vio & org brn 3.25 2.00
45 A3 6p vio & red vio 40.00 11.50
46 A3 1sh green & blk 40.00 *47.50*
47 A3 2sh6p grn & car rose 160.00 *325.00*
48 A3 5sh grn & ultra 150.00 *350.00*
49 A3 10sh green & brn 350.00 *975.00*
Nos. 40-49 (10) 755.75 *1,726.*
Set, ovptd. "SPECIMEN" 225.00

1904-05 Ordinary Paper Wmk. 3

50 A3 ½p grn & bl grn 14.50 3.00
51 A3 1p vio & blk, *red* 8.00 .25
52 A3 2p violet & ultra 5.50 3.50
53 A3 2½p vio & ultra, *bl*, smaller letters of value 62.50 *140.00*
54 A3 3p vio & org brn 4.00 1.50
55 A3 6p vio & red vio 7.50 4.00
56 A3 1sh green & blk 22.50 *30.00*
57 A3 2sh6p grn & car rose 27.50 *75.00*
58 A3 5sh grn & ultra 27.50 *110.00*
59 A3 10sh green & brn 100.00 *275.00*
Nos. 50-59 (10) 279.50 *642.25*

Chalky Paper

50a A3 ½p grn & bl grn 11.50 2.00
51a A3 1p vio & blk, *red* 1.75 .25
52a A3 2p violet & ultra 15.00 11.50
53a A3 2½p vio & ultra, *bl* 2.00 *18.50*
54a A3 3p vio & org brn 17.50 2.00
55a A3 6p vio & red vio 5.00 1.75
56a A3 1sh green & blk 26.00 2.50
57a A3 2sh6p grn & car rose 40.00 67.50
58a A3 5sh grn & ultra 77.50 190.00
59a A3 10sh green & brn 90.00 225.00
Nos. 50a-59a (10) 286.25 *521.00*

The stamps of Lagos were superseded by those of Southern Nigeria.

LATAKIA

ˌla-tə-ˈkē-ə

LOCATION — A division of Syria in Western Asia
GOVT. — French Mandate
AREA — 2,500 sq. mi.
POP. — 278,000 (approx. 1930)
CAPITAL — Latakia

This territory, included in the Syrian Mandate to France under the Versailles Treaty, was formerly known as Alaouites. The name Latakia was adopted in 1930. See Alaouites and Syria.

100 Centimes = 1 Piaster

Stamps of Syria Overprinted in Black or Red

Perf. 12x12½, 13½

1931-33 Unwmk.

1 A6 10c red violet 1.25 1.25
Never hinged 1.60
On cover 37.50
2 A6 10c vio brn ('33) 1.60 1.60
Never hinged 2.40
On cover 37.50
3 A7 20c dk blue (R) 1.25 1.25
Never hinged 1.60
On cover 30.00
4 A7 20c brn org ('33) 1.60 1.60
Never hinged 2.40
On cover 30.00
5 A8 25c gray grn (R) 1.25 1.25
Never hinged 1.60
On cover 30.00
6 A8 25c dk bl gray (R) ('33) 1.60 1.60
Never hinged 2.40
On cover 30.00
7 A9 50c violet 2.00 2.00
Never hinged 2.75
On cover 25.00
8 A15 75c org red ('32) 3.25 3.25
Never hinged 4.75
On cover 25.00
9 A10 1p green (R) 2.40 2.40
Never hinged 3.50
On cover 25.00
10 A11 1.50p bis brn (R) 3.25 3.25
Never hinged 5.25
On cover 30.00
11 A11 1.50p dp grn ('33) 4.00 4.00
Never hinged 6.50
On cover 25.00
12 A12 2p dk vio (R) 4.00 4.00
Never hinged 6.50
On cover 30.00
13 A13 3p yel grn (R) 6.00 6.00
Never hinged 10.00
On cover 42.50
14 A14 4p orange 5.50 5.50
Never hinged 9.00
On cover 55.00
15 A15 4.50p rose car 5.75 5.75
Never hinged 10.00
On cover 62.50
16 A16 6p grnsh blk (R) 5.75 5.75
Never hinged 10.00
On cover 75.00
17 A17 7.50p dl blue (R) 5.50 5.50
Never hinged 8.00
On cover 80.00
a. Inverted overprint 650.00
18 A18 10p dp brown (R) 9.50 9.50
Never hinged 15.00
On cover 105.00
a. Inverted overprint 650.00
19 A19 15p dp green (R) 11.00 11.00
Never hinged 17.50
On cover 125.00
20 A20 25p violet brn 24.00 24.00
Never hinged 40.00
On cover 165.00
21 A21 50p dk brown (R) 22.50 22.50
Never hinged 37.50
On cover 190.00
a. Inverted overprint 650.00
22 A22 100p red orange 55.00 55.00
Never hinged 92.50
On cover 300.00
Nos. 1-22 (22) 177.95 177.95

AIR POST STAMPS

Air Post Stamps of Syria, 1931, Overprinted in Black or Red

1931-33 Unwmk. *Perf. 13½*

C1 AP2 50c ocher 1.25 1.25
Never hinged 1.60
On cover 30.00
a. Inverted overprint 1,200. 1,200.
C2 AP2 50c blk brn (R) ('33) 2.50 2.50
Never hinged 4.25
On cover 25.00
C3 AP2 1p ches brn 2.50 2.50
Never hinged 4.25
On cover 25.00
C4 AP2 2p Prus blue (R) 4.00 4.00
Never hinged 6.25
On cover 37.50
C5 AP2 3p blue grn (R) 5.50 5.50
Never hinged 9.00
On cover 42.50
C6 AP2 5p red violet 7.00 7.00
Never hinged 12.00
On cover 62.50
C7 AP2 10p sl grn (R) 8.75 8.75
Never hinged 13.50
On cover 92.50
C8 AP2 15p orange red 12.50 12.50
Never hinged 20.00
On cover 140.00
C9 AP2 25p orange brn 24.00 24.00
Never hinged 37.50
On cover 200.00
C10 AP2 50p black (R) 40.00 40.00
Never hinged 67.50
On cover 275.00
C11 AP2 100p magenta 42.50 42.50
Never hinged 70.00
On cover 290.00
Nos. C1-C11 (11) 150.50 150.50

POSTAGE DUE STAMPS

Postage Due Stamps of Syria, 1931, Overprinted

1931 Unwmk. *Perf. 13½*

J1 D7 8p blk, *gray bl* (R) 25.00 25.00
Never hinged 42.50
On cover 300.00
J2 D8 15p blk, *dl rose* (R) 25.00 25.00
Never hinged 42.50
On cover 300.00

Stamps of Latakia were superseded in 1937 by those of Syria.

LATVIA

'lat-vē-ə

(Lettonia, Lettland)

LOCATION — Northern Europe, bordering on the Baltic Sea and the Gulf of Riga
GOVT. — Independent Republic
AREA — 25,395 sq. mi.
POP. — 1,994,506 (estimated 1939)
CAPITAL — Riga

Latvia was created a sovereign state following World War I and was admitted to the League of Nations in 1922. In 1940 it became a republic in the Union of Soviet Socialist Republics.

100 Kapeikas = 1 Rublis
100 Santims = 1 Lat (1923)

Watermarks

Wmk. 108 Honeycomb

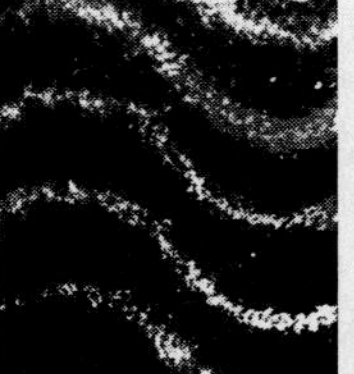

Wmk. 145 — Wavy Lines

Wmk. 181 Wavy Lines

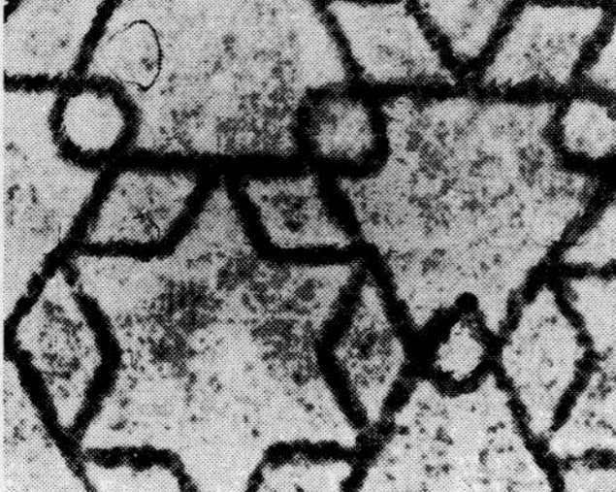

Wmk. 197 — Star and Triangles

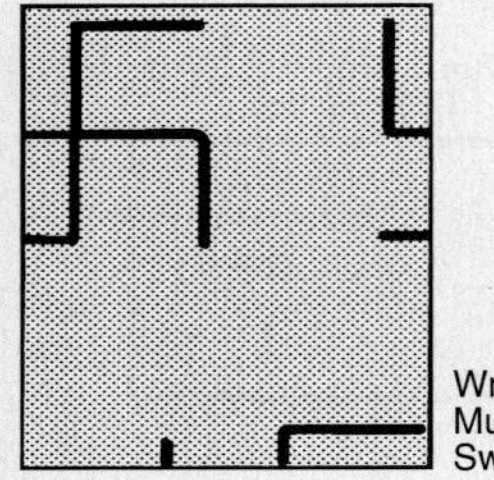

Wmk. 212 Multiple Swastikas

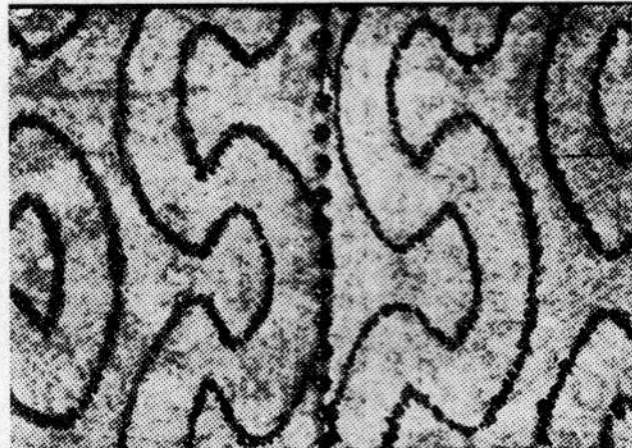

Wmk. 265 — Multiple Waves

Arms — A1

Printed on the Backs of German Military Maps

Unwmk.

1918, Dec. 18 Litho. *Imperf.*

1	A1	5k carmine	1.00	2.00

Perf. 11½

2	A1	5k carmine	1.00	2.00

Values given are for stamps where the map on the back is printed in brown and black. Maps printed only in black are valued at: No. 1 unused $2.00; used $6; No. 2 unused $1.20, used $2.50. Stamps with no map at all valued: No. 1 unused $1.50, used $3.28; No. 2 unused $1.20, used $2.50. Stamps with no printing on the back are from the outer rows of some sheets.

Redrawn

Paper with Ruled Lines

1919 *Imperf.*

3	A1	5k carmine	.25	.25
4	A1	10k dark blue	.25	.25
5	A1	15k green	.50	.50

Perf. 11½

6	A1	5k carmine	2.40	*4.00*
7	A1	10k dark blue	2.40	*4.00*
8	A1	15k deep green	7.25	*9.50*
		Nos. 3-8 (6)	13.05	18.50

In the redrawn design the wheat heads are thicker, the ornament at lower left has five points instead of four, and there are minor changes in other parts of the design.

The sheets of this and subsequent issues were usually divided in half by a single line of perforation gauging 10. Thus stamps are found with this perforation on one side.

1919 Pelure Paper *Imperf.*

9	A1	3k lilac	4.75	4.50
10	A1	5k carmine	.25	.25
11	A1	10k deep blue	.25	.25
12	A1	15k dark green	.25	.25
13	A1	20k orange	.25	.25
13A	A1	25k gray	40.00	40.00
14	A1	35k dark brown	.25	.25
15	A1	50k purple	.25	.25
16	A1	75k emerald	2.50	2.50
		Nos. 9-16 (9)	48.75	48.50

Perf. 11½, 9½

17	A1	3k lilac	35.00	35.00
18	A1	5k carmine	.80	.80
19	A1	10k deep blue	4.00	4.00
20	A1	15k dark green	3.00	3.00
21	A1	20k orange	3.75	3.75
22	A1	35k dark brown	4.50	4.50
23	A1	50k purple	5.50	5.50
24	A1	75k emerald	8.00	8.00
		Nos. 17-24 (8)	64.55	64.55

Values are for perf 11½. Examples Perf 9½ sell for more.

Nos. 17-24 are said to be unofficially perforated varieties of Nos. 9-16.

1919 Wmk. 108 *Imperf.*

25	A1	3k lilac	.30	.25
26	A1	5k carmine	.30	.25
27	A1	10k deep blue	.30	.25
28	A1	15k deep green	.30	.25
29	A1	20k orange	.35	.25
30	A1	25k gray	.40	.35
31	A1	35k dark brown	.35	.25
32	A1	50k purple	.35	.25
33	A1	75k emerald	.35	.25
		Nos. 25-33 (9)	3.00	2.35

The variety "printed on both sides" exists for 3k, 10k, 15k, 20k and 35k. Value, $20 each.

See Nos. 57-58, 76-82. For surcharges and overprints see Nos. 86, 132-133, 2N1-2N8, 2N12-2N19.

Liberation of Riga — A2

1919 Wmk. 108

43	A2	5k carmine	.25	.25
44	A2	15k deep green	.25	.25
45	A2	35k brown	.35	*.80*
		Nos. 43-45 (3)	.85	1.30

Unwmk.

Pelure Paper

49	A2	5k carmine	9.50	*16.00*
50	A2	15k deep green	9.50	*16.00*
51	A2	35k brown	21.00	16.00
		Nos. 49-51 (3)	40.00	48.00

For surcharge and overprints see Nos. 87, 2N9-2N11, 2N20-2N22.

Rising Sun — A4

1919 *Imperf.*

55	A4	10k gray blue	.85	.60

Perf. 11½

56	A4	10k gray blue	1.00	1.50

Type of 1918

1919 Laid Paper *Perf. 11½*

57	A1	3r slate & org	1.00	1.00
58	A1	5r gray brn & org	1.00	1.00

Independence Issue

Allegory of One Year of Independence A5

Wove Paper

Size: 33x45mm

1919, Nov. 18 Unwmk.

59	A5	10k brown & rose	1.75	1.75

Laid Paper

60	A5	10k brown & rose	1.75	1.75

Size: 28x38mm

61	A5	10k brown & rose	.40	.40
a.		Imperf.	50.00	
62	A5	35k indigo & grn	.40	.40
a.		Vert. pair, imperf. btwn.	50.00	45.00

Back of No. 63 Block

Wmk. 197

Thick Wove Paper

Blue Design on Back

63	A5	1r green & red	.55	.55
		Nos. 59-63 (5)	4.85	4.85

There are two types of Nos. 59 and 60. In type I the trunk of the tree is not outlined. In type II it has a distinct white outline.

No. 63 was printed on the backs of unfinished 5r bank notes of the Workers and Soldiers Council, Riga.

For surcharges see Nos. 83-85, 88, 94.

Warrior Slaying Dragon — A6

Wove Paper

64	A6	10k brown & car	.50	.50
a.		Horiz. pair, imperf. btwn.	55.00	45.00
65	A6	25k ind & yel grn	.50	.50
a.		Pair, imperf. btwn.	55.00	45.00
66	A6	35k black & bl ('20)	.50	.50
a.		Horiz. pair, imperf. btwn.	55.00	45.00
67	A6	1r dk grn & brn ('20)	.50	.50
a.		Horiz. pair, imperf. vert.	50.00	40.00
b.		Horiz. pair, imperf. btwn.	50.00	40.00
		Nos. 64-67 (4)	2.00	2.00
		Set, never hinged	5.75	

Issued in honor of the liberation of Kurzeme (Kurland). The paper sometimes shows impressed quadrille lines.

For surcharges see Nos. 91-93.

Latgale Relief Issue

Latvia Welcoming Home Latgale Province — A7

Partial Design of No. 68 Back

Brown and Green Design on Back

1920, Mar.

68	A7	50k dk green & rose	1.00	.50
a.		Horiz. pair, imperf. vert.	50.00	
69	A7	1r slate grn & brn	.50	.50
a.		Horiz. pair, imperf. vert.	50.00	
		Set, never hinged	10.00	

No. 68-69 were printed on the backs of unfinished bank notes of the government of Colonel Bermondt-Avalov and on the so-called German "Ober-Ost" money.

For surcharges see Nos. 95-99.

First National Assembly Issue

Latvia Hears Call to Assemble — A8

1920

70	A8	50k rose	.50	.30
a.		Imperf., pair	5.00	5.00
71	A8	1r blue	.50	.30
a.		Vert. pair, imperf. btwn.	45.00	45.00
b.		Imperf., pair	20.00	15.00
72	A8	3r dk brn & grn	.50	*.75*
73	A8	5r slate & vio brn	.80	.80
		Nos. 70-73 (4)	2.30	2.15
		Set, never hinged	10.00	

For surcharges see Nos. 90, 134.

Type of 1918 Issue

Wove Paper

1920-21 Unwmk. *Perf. 11½*

76	A1	5k carmine	.25	.25
78	A1	20k orange	.25	.25
79	A1	40k lilac ('21)	.30	.25
80	A1	50k violet	.35	.25

81 A1 75k emerald .35 .25
82 A1 5r gray brn & org ('21) 1.50 1.00
Nos. 76-82 (6) 3.00 2.25
Set, never hinged 6.00

No. 63 Surcharged in Black, Brown or Blue

1920, Sept. 1
83 A5 10r on 1r grn & red (Bk) 1.60 1.60
84 A5 20r on 1r grn & red (Br) 4.00 4.00
85 A5 30r on 1r grn & red (Bl) 5.50 4.00
Nos. 83-85 (3) 11.10 9.60
Set, never hinged 20.00

Types of 1919 Surcharged

1920-21 Wmk. 108 *Perf. 11½*
86 A1 2r on 10k dp blue 2.00 *7.25*
87 A2 2r on 35k brown .75 *5.50*
Set, never hinged 5.00

No. 62 Surcharged in Red

Unwmk.
88 A5 2r on 35k ind & grn .40 *.50*
Never hinged .75

No. 70 Surcharged in Blue

1921
90 A8 2r on 50k rose .50 .60
Never hinged 1.00

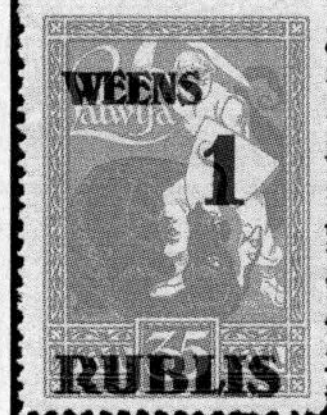

Nos. 64-66 Surcharged in Red or Blue

1920-21
91 A6 1r on 35k blk & bl (R) .35 .35
92 A6 2r on 10k brn & rose (Bl) .70 .75
93 A6 2r on 25k ind & grn (R) .40 .40
a. Imperf. —
Nos. 91-93 (3) 1.45 1.50
Set, never hinged 3.50

On Nos. 92 and 93 the surcharge reads "DIVI 2 RUBLI."

No. 83 with Added Surcharge

1921 Wmk. 197
94 A5 10r on 10r on 1r 1.50 1.00
Never hinged 5.00

Latgale Relief Issue of 1920 Surcharged in Black or Blue

1921, May 31 Unwmk.
95 A7 10r on 50k 1.25 1.00
a. Imperf. —
96 A7 20r on 50k 3.50 4.00
97 A7 30r on 50k 5.00 4.00
98 A7 50r on 50k 7.50 5.00
99 A7 100r on 50k (Bl) 17.50 16.00
Nos. 95-99 (5) 34.75 30.00
Set, never hinged 60.00

Excellent counterfeits exist.

Arms and Stars for Vidzeme, Kurzeme & Latgale — A10

Type I, slanting cipher in value.
Type II, upright cipher in value.

Perf. 10, 11½ and Compound
Wmk. Similar to 181

1921-22 Typo.
101 A10 50k violet (II) .50 .30
102 A10 1r orange yel .50 .50
103 A10 2r deep green .25 .25
104 A10 3r brt green .65 .45
105 A10 5r rose 1.40 .40
106 A10 6r dp claret 2.00 .80
107 A10 9r orange 1.25 .55
108 A10 10r blue (I) 1.25 .25
109 A10 15r ultra 3.25 .50
a. Printed on both sides *50.00*
110 A10 20r dull lilac (II) 20.00 2.00

Coat of Arms — A11

1922, Aug. 21 *Perf. 11½*
111 A11 50r dk brn & pale brn (I) 30.00 4.50
112 A11 100r dk bl & pale bl (I) 35.00 4.50
Nos. 101-112 (12) 96.05 15.00
Set, never hinged 200.00

Nos. 101-131 sometimes show letters and numerals of the paper maker's watermark "PACTIEN LIGAT MILLS 1858." Stamps showing part of the inscription command a 100 percent premium. Pairs with the complete year "1858" command a 300 percent premium.
See Nos. 126-131, 152-154.

A12

2 SANTIMS
Type A, tail of "2" ends in an upstroke.
Type B, tail of "2" is nearly horizontal.

1923-25 *Perf. 10, 11, 11½*
113 A12 1s violet .40 .25
114 A12 2s org yel (A) .60 .35
115 A12 4s dark green .60 .25
a. Horiz. pair, imperf. btwn. 55.00 50.00
116 A12 5s lt green ('25) 2.50 .65
117 A12 6s grn, *yel* ('25) 3.50 .25
118 A12 10s rose red (I) 1.50 .25
a. Horiz. pair, imperf. btwn. 55.00 50.00
119 A12 12s claret .25 .40
120 A12 15s brn, *sal* 3.50 .25
a. Horiz. pair, imperf. btwn. 55.00 50.00
121 A12 20s dp blue (II) 1.50 .25
122 A12 25s ultra ('25) .50 .25
123 A12 30s pink (I) ('25) 5.00 .25
124 A12 40s lilac (I) 2.00 .25
125 A12 50s lil gray (II) 3.75 .35
126 A11 1 l dk brn & pale brn 12.50 1.00
127 A11 2 l dk blue & blue 20.00 1.60
130 A11 5 l dp grn & pale grn 60.00 5.00
131 A11 10 l car rose & pale rose (I) 3.00 6.00
Nos. 113-131 (17) 121.10 17.60
Set, never hinged 250.00

Value in "Santims" (1s); "Santimi" (2s-6s) or "Santimu" (others).
See note after No. 112.
See Nos. 135-151, 155-157. For overprints and surcharges see Nos. 164-167, B21-B23.

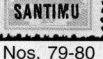

Nos. 79-80 Surcharged

No. 72 Surcharged

1927 Unwmk. *Perf. 11½*
132 A1 15s on 40k lilac .45 .45
133 A1 15s on 50k violet 1.40 *1.60*
134 A8 1 l on 3r brn & grn 11.00 8.00
Nos. 132-134 (3) 12.85 10.05
Set, never hinged 25.00

Types of 1923-25 Issue

1927-33 Wmk. 212 *Perf. 10, 11½*
135 A12 1s dull violet .25 .25
136 A12 2s org yel (A) .35 .25
137 A12 2s org yel (B) ('33) .30 .25
138 A12 3s org red ('31) .25 .25
139 A12 4s dk green ('29) 3.50 2.25
140 A12 5s lt green ('31) .50 .25
141 A12 6s grn, *yel* .25 .25
142 A12 7s dk green ('31) .50 .25
143 A12 10s red (I) 2.50 .70
144 A12 10s grn, *yel* (I) ('32) 10.00 .25
145 A12 15s brn, *sal* 3.50 .45
146 A12 20s pink (I) 5.00 .25
147 A12 20s pink (II) 6.00 .25
148 A12 30s lt blue (I) 1.25 .40
149 A12 35s dk blue ('31) 1.50 .25
150 A12 40s dl lil (I) ('29) 2.25 .25
151 A12 50s gray (II) 2.50 .45
152 A11 1 l dk brn & pale brn 8.00 .30
153 A11 2 l dk bl & bl ('31) 30.00 2.25
154 A11 5 l grn & pale grn ('33) 140.00 30.00
Nos. 135-154 (20) 218.40 39.80
Set, never hinged 400.00

The paper of Nos. 141, 144 and 145 is colored on the surface only.
See note above No. 113 for types A and B, and note above No. 101 for types I and II.

Type of 1927-33 Issue
Paper Colored Through

1931-33 *Perf. 10*
155 A12 6s grn, *yel* .25 .25
156 A12 10s grn, *yel* (I) ('33) 15.00 .25
157 A12 15s brn, *salmon* 3.00 .25
Nos. 155-157 (3) 18.25 .75
Set, never hinged 37.50

View of Rezekne — A13

Designs (Views of Cities): 15s, Jelgava. 20s, Cesis (Wenden). 30s, Liepaja (Libau). 50s, Riga. 1 l, Riga Theater.

1928, Nov. 18 Litho. *Perf. 10, 11½*
158 A13 6s dp grn & vio 1.00 .40
159 A13 15s dk brn & ol grn 1.00 .40
160 A13 20s cerise & bl grn 1.25 .45
161 A13 30s ultra & vio brn 1.50 .40
162 A13 50s dk gray & plum 1.50 1.00
163 A13 1 l blk brn & brn 3.75 1.75
Nos. 158-163 (6) 10.00 4.40
Set, never hinged 20.00

10th anniv. of Latvian Independence.

Riga Exhibition Issue

Stamps of 1927-33 Overprinted

1932, Aug. 30 *Perf. 10, 11*
164 A12 3s orange .95 .50
165 A12 10s green, *yel* .95 .50
166 A12 20s pink (I) 1.90 1.00
167 A12 35s dark blue 4.25 2.00
Nos. 164-167 (4) 8.05 4.00
Set, never hinged 30.00

Riga Castle — A19

Arms and Shield — A20

Allegory of Latvia — A21

Ministry of Foreign Affairs — A22

1934, Dec. 15 Litho. *Perf. 10½, 10*
174 A19 3s red orange .25 .25
175 A20 5s yellow grn .25 .25
176 A20 10s gray grn 1.00 .25
177 A21 20s deep rose 1.00 .25
178 A22 35s dark blue .35 .25
179 A19 40s brown .35 .25
Nos. 174-179 (6) 3.20 1.50
Set, never hinged 6.00

Atis Kronvalds A23

A. Pumpurs A24

Juris Maters A25

Mikus Krogzemis (Auseklis) A26

1936, Jan. 4 Wmk. 212 *Perf. 11½*
180 A23 3s vermilion 3.00 *4.75*
181 A24 10s green 3.00 *4.75*
182 A25 20s rose pink 3.00 *6.00*
183 A26 35s dark blue 3.00 *6.00*
Nos. 180-183 (4) 12.00 21.50
Set, never hinged 40.00

President Karlis Ulmanis — A27

1937, Sept. 4 Litho. *Perf. 10, 11½*

184	A27	3s org red & brn org	.25	.25
185	A27	5s yellow grn	.25	.25
186	A27	10s dk sl grn	.75	.60
187	A27	20s rose lake & brn lake	1.50	.60
188	A27	25s black vio	2.25	1.25
189	A27	30s dark blue	2.25	1.25
190	A27	35s indigo	1.00	1.00
191	A27	40s lt brown	2.00	1.25
192	A27	50s olive blk	2.25	1.50
		Nos. 184-192 (9)	12.50	7.95
		Set, never hinged	25.00	

60th birthday of President Ulmanis.

Independence Monument, Rauna (Ronneburg) A28

Monument Entrance to Cemetery at Riga A29

Independence Monument, Jelgava — A30

War Memorial, Valka — A31

Independence Monument, Iecava — A32

Independence Monument, Riga — A33

Tomb of Col. Kalpaks — A34

Thick Paper

Unwmk.

1937, July 12 Litho. *Perf. 10*

193	A28	3s vermilion	.60	*.90*
194	A29	5s yellow grn	.60	*.90*
195	A30	10s deep grn	.60	*.50*
196	A31	20s carmine	1.50	*1.00*
197	A32	30s lt blue	2.00	2.00

Wmk. 212

Engr. *Perf. 11½*

Thin Paper

198	A33	35s dark blue	2.00	2.00
199	A34	40s brown	3.25	3.00
		Nos. 193-199 (7)	10.55	10.30
		Set, never hinged	22.50	

View of Vidzeme — A35

General J. Balodis A37

President Karlis Ulmanis A38

Views: 5s, Latgale. 30s, Riga waterfront. 35s, Kurzeme. 40s, Zemgale.

1938, Nov. 17 *Perf. 10, 10½x10*

200	A35	3s brown org	.25	.25
a.		Booklet pane of 4	40.00	
201	A35	5s yellow grn	.25	.25
a.		Booklet pane of 4	40.00	
202	A37	10s dk green	.25	.25
a.		Booklet pane of 2	40.00	
203	A38	20s red lilac	.25	.25
a.		Booklet pane of 2	40.00	
204	A35	30s deep blue	.90	.25
205	A35	35s indigo	.90	.25
a.		Booklet pane of 2	40.00	
206	A35	40s rose violet	1.25	.25
		Nos. 200-206 (7)	4.05	1.75
		Set, never hinged	9.00	

The 20th anniversary of the Republic.

School, Riga — A42

Independence Monument, Riga — A45

President Karlis Ulmanis A49

Designs: 5s, Castle of Jelgava. 10s, Riga Castle. 30s, Symbol of Freedom. 35s, Community House Daugavpils. 40s, Powder Tower and War Museum, Riga.

1939, May 13 Photo. *Perf. 10*

207	A42	3s brown orange	.25	.80
208	A42	5s deep green	.50	.80
209	A42	10s dk slate grn	.75	.80
210	A45	20s dk car rose	1.50	1.60
211	A42	30s brt ultra	1.00	.80
212	A42	35s dark blue	1.50	1.60
213	A45	40s brown violet	2.00	1.00
214	A49	50s grnsh black	3.00	1.00
		Nos. 207-214 (8)	10.50	8.40
		Set, never hinged	20.00	

5th anniv. of National Unity Day.

Harvesting Wheat — A50

Apple — A51

1939, Oct. 8

215	A50	10s slate green	.90	.60
216	A51	20s rose lake	.90	.65
		Set, never hinged	3.00	

8th Agricultural Exposition held near Riga.

Arms and Stars for Vidzeme, Kurzeme and Latgale — A52

1940

217	A52	1s dk vio brn	.30	.30
218	A52	2s ocher	.40	.30
219	A52	3s red orange	.25	.25
220	A52	5s dk olive brn	.25	.25
221	A52	7s dk green	.30	.30
222	A52	10s dk blue grn	.75	.25
224	A52	20s rose brown	.75	.25
225	A52	30s dp red brn	1.25	.30
226	A52	35s brt ultra	.25	*.80*
228	A52	50s dk slate grn	1.75	.80
229	A52	1 l olive green	3.50	2.40
		Nos. 217-229 (11)	9.75	6.20
		Set, never hinged	20.00	

SEMI-POSTAL STAMPS

"Mercy" Assisting Wounded Soldier — SP1

Brown and Green Design on Back

1920 Unwmk. Typo. *Perf. 11½*

B1	SP1	20(30)k dk brn & red	.50	*1.00*
B2	SP1	40(55)k dk bl & red	.50	*1.00*
B3	SP1	50(70)k dk grn & red	.50	*1.00*
B4	SP1	1(1.30)r dl sl & red	.50	*1.50*

Wmk. 197

Blue Design on Back

B5	SP1	20(30)k dk brn & red	.70	*1.00*
B6	SP1	40(55)k dk bl & red	.70	*1.00*
a.		Vert. pair, imperf. btwn.	40.00	
B7	SP1	50(70)k dk grn & red	.70	*1.25*
B8	SP1	1(1.30)r dk sl & red	.70	*2.00*

Wmk. Similar to 145

Pink Paper *Imperf.*

Brown, Green and Red Design on Back

B9	SP1	20(30)k dk brn & red	1.00	*2.50*
B10	SP1	40(55)k dk bl & red	1.00	*2.50*
B11	SP1	50(70)k dk grn & red	1.00	*2.50*
B12	SP1	1(1.30)r dk sl & red	2.00	*4.25*
		Nos. B1-B12 (12)	9.80	*21.50*
		Set, never hinged	17.50	

These semi-postal stamps were printed on the backs of unfinished bank notes of the Workers and Soldiers Council, Riga, and the Bermondt-Avalov Army. Blocks of stamps showing complete banknotes on reverse are worth approximately three times the catalogue value of the stamps.

Nos. B1-B8 Surcharged

Brown and Green Design on Back

1921 Unwmk. *Perf. 11½*

B13	SP1	20k + 2r dk brn & red	2.50	*4.00*
B14	SP1	40k + 2r dk bl & red	2.50	*4.00*
B15	SP1	50k + 2r dk grn & red	2.50	*4.00*
B16	SP1	1r + 2r dk sl & red	2.50	*4.00*

Wmk. 197

Blue Design on Back

B17	SP1	20k + 2r dk brn & red	10.00	*40.00*
B18	SP1	40k + 2r dk bl & red	10.00	*40.00*
B19	SP1	50k + 2r dk grn & red	10.00	*40.00*
B20	SP1	1r + 2r dk sl & red	10.00	*40.00*
		Nos. B13-B20 (8)	50.00	*176.00*
		Set, never hinged	140.00	

Regular Issue of 1923-25 Surcharged in Blue

1923 Wmk. Similar to 181 *Perf. 10*

B21	A12	1s + 10s violet	.75	*1.75*
B22	A12	2s + 10s yellow	.75	*1.75*
B23	A12	4s + 10s dk green	.75	*1.75*
		Nos. B21-B23 (3)	2.25	*5.25*
		Set, never hinged	5.00	

The surtax benefited the Latvian War Invalids Society.

Lighthouse and Harbor, Liepaja (Libau) SP2

Church at Liepaja — SP5

Coat of Arms of Liepaja — SP6

Designs: 15s (25s), City Hall, Liepaja. 25s (35s), Public Bathing Pavilion, Liepaja.

1925, July 23 ***Perf. 11½***

B24 SP2	6s (12s) red brn & dp blue	2.50	*5.50*
B25 SP2	15s (25s) dk bl & brn	1.50	*4.00*
B26 SP2	25s (35s) vio & dk grn	2.50	4.00
B27 SP5	30s (40s) dk blue & lake	4.50	*12.00*
B28 SP6	50s (60s) dk grn & vio	6.50	*16.00*
	Nos. B24-B28 (5)	17.50	*41.50*
	Set, never hinged	40.00	

Tercentenary of Liepaja (Libau). The surtax benefited that city. Exist imperf. Value, unused set $500.

President Janis Cakste — SP7

1928, Apr. 18 **Engr.**

B29 SP7	2s (12s) red orange	2.50	*3.25*
B30 SP7	6s (16s) deep green	2.50	*3.25*
B31 SP7	15s (25s) red brown	2.50	*3.25*
B32 SP7	25s (35s) deep blue	2.50	*3.25*
B33 SP7	30s (40s) claret	2.50	*3.25*
	Nos. B29-B33 (5)	12.50	*16.25*
	Set, never hinged	27.50	

The surtax helped erect a monument to Janis Cakste, 1st pres. of the Latvian Republic.

Venta River — SP8

Allegory, "Latvia" — SP9

View of Jelgava SP10

National Theater, Riga — SP11

View of Cesis (Wenden) SP12

Riga Bridge and Trenches SP13

Perf. 11½, Imperf.

1928, Nov. 18 **Wmk. 212** **Litho.**

B34 SP8	6s (16s) green	2.50	*2.75*
B35 SP9	10s (20s) scarlet	2.50	*2.75*
B36 SP10	15s (25s) maroon	2.50	*2.75*
B37 SP11	30s (40s) ultra	2.50	*2.75*
B38 SP12	50s (60s) dk gray	2.50	*2.75*
B39 SP13	1 l (1.10 l) choc	3.75	2.75
	Nos. B34-B39 (6)	16.25	*16.50*
	Set, never hinged	35.00	

The surtax was given to a committee for the erection of a Liberty Memorial.

Z. A. Meierovics SP14

1929, Aug. 22 ***Perf. 11½, Imperf.***

B46 SP14	2s (4s) orange	3.50	2.75
B47 SP14	6s (12s) dp grn	3.50	2.75
B48 SP14	15s (25s) red brown	3.50	2.75
B49 SP14	25s (35s) deep blue	3.50	2.75
B50 SP14	30s (40s) ultra	3.50	2.75
	Nos. B46-B50 (5)	17.50	13.75
	Set, never hinged	35.00	

The surtax was used to erect a monument to Z. A. Meierovics, Latvian statesman.

Tuberculosis Cross — SP15

Allegory of Hope for the Sick — SP16

Gustavs Zemgals — SP17

Riga Castle — SP18

Daisies and Double-barred Cross — SP20

Tuberculosis Sanatorium, near Riga — SP22

Cakste, Kviesis and Zemgals SP23

Designs: No. B61, Janis Cakste, 1st pres. of Latvia. No. B63, Pres. Alberts Kviesis.

1930, Dec. 4 **Typo.** ***Perf. 10, 11½***

B56 SP15	1s (2s) dk vio & red org	.75	.85
B57 SP15	2s (4s) org & red org	.75	.85
a.	Cliché of 1s (2s) in plate of 2s (4s)	*700.00*	*700.00*
B58 SP16	4s (8s) dk grn & red	.75	.85
B59 SP17	5s (10s) brt grn & dk brn	1.50	1.75
B60 SP18	6s (12s) ol grn & bister	1.50	1.75
B61 SP17	10s (20s) dp red & blk	2.20	2.25
B62 SP20	15s (30s) mar & dl green	2.25	2.25
B63 SP17	20s (40s) rose lake & ind	2.25	2.25
B64 SP22	25s (50s) multi	3.00	3.50
B65 SP23	30s (60s) multi	3.50	5.00
	Nos. B56-B65 (10)	18.45	21.30
	Set, never hinged	45.00	

Surtax for the Latvian Anti-Tuberculosis Soc. For surcharges see Nos. B72-B81.

J. Rainis and New Buildings, Riga SP24

Character from Play and Rainis SP25

Characters from Plays — SP26

Rainis and Lyre SP27

Flames, Flag and Rainis SP28

1930, May 23 **Wmk. 212** ***Perf. 11½***

B66 SP24	1s (2s) dull violet	.75	*3.25*
B67 SP25	2s (4s) yellow org	.75	*3.25*
B68 SP26	4s (8s) dp green	.75	*3.25*
B69 SP27	6s (12s) yel grn & red brown	.75	*3.25*
B70 SP28	10s (20s) dark red	22.50	*47.50*
B71 SP27	15s (30s) red brn & yel grn	22.50	*47.50*
	Nos. B66-B71 (6)	48.00	*108.00*
	Set, never hinged	95.00	

Sold at double face value, surtax going to memorial fund for J. Rainis (Jan Plieksans, 1865-1929), writer and politician.

Exist imperf. Value twice that of perf. stamps.

Nos. B56 to B65 Surcharged in Black With Bars

Nos. B56 to B65 Surcharged in Black Without Bars

1931, Aug. 19 ***Perf. 10, 11½***

B72 SP18	9s on 6s (12s)	1.00	2.00
B73 SP15	16s on 1s (2s)	12.50	24.00
B74 SP15	17s on 2s (4s)	1.25	2.00
B75 SP16	19s on 4s (8s)	3.75	*8.50*
B76 SP17	20s on 5s (10s)	2.50	*8.50*
B77 SP20	23s on 15s (30s)	1.00	1.50
B78 SP17	25s on 10s (20s)	2.50	*4.50*
B79 SP17	35s on 20s (40s)	3.75	*7.00*
B80 SP22	45s on 25s (50s)	10.00	*20.00*
B81 SP23	55s on 30s (60s)	12.50	*32.50*
	Nos. B72-B81 (10)	50.75	*110.50*
	Set, never hinged	110.00	

The surcharge replaces the original total price, including surtax.

Nos. B73-B81 have no bars in the surcharge. The surtax aided the Latvian Anti-Tuberculosis Society.

Lacplesis, the Deliverer SP29

Designs: 1s, Kriva telling stories under Holy Oak. 2s, Enslaved Latvians building Riga under knight's supervision. 4s, Death of Black Knight. 5s, Spirit of Lacplesis over freed Riga.

Inscribed: "AIZSARGI" (Army Reserve)

1932, Feb. 10 ***Perf. 10½, Imperf.***

B82 SP29	1s (11s) vio brn & bluish	2.50	2.50
B83 SP29	2s (17s) ocher & ol green	2.50	2.50
B84 SP29	3s (23s) red brn & org brown	2.50	2.50
B85 SP29	4s (34s) dk grn & green	2.50	2.50
B86 SP29	5s (45s) grn & emerald	2.50	2.50
	Nos. B82-B86 (5)	12.50	12.50
	Set, never hinged	22.00	

Surtax aided the Militia Maintenance Fund.

Marching Troops SP30

Infantry in Action SP31

Nurse Binding Soldier's Wound — SP32

Army Soup Kitchen — SP33

Gen. J. Balodis — SP34

1932, May ***Perf. 10½, Imperf.***

B87 SP30 6s (25s) ol brn & red violet 4.50 *6.50*
B88 SP31 7s (35s) dk bl grn & dark blue 4.50 *6.50*
B89 SP32 10s (45s) ol grn & blk brn 4.50 *6.50*
B90 SP33 12s (55s) lake & ol green 4.50 *6.50*
B91 SP34 15s (75s) red org & brn vio 4.50 *6.50*
Nos. B87-B91 (5) 22.50 *32.50*
Set, never hinged 45.00

The surtax aided the Latvian Home Guards.

Symbolical of Unified Latvia — SP35

Symbolical of the Strength of the Latvian Union — SP36

Aid to the Sick SP37

"Charity" SP38

Wmk. 212

1936, Dec. 28 Litho. ***Perf. 11½***

B92 SP35 3s orange red 1.50 *3.50*
B93 SP36 10s green 1.50 *3.50*
B94 SP37 20s rose pink 1.50 *4.50*
B95 SP38 35s blue 1.50 *4.50*
Nos. B92-B95 (4) 6.00 *16.00*
Set, never hinged 12.00

Souvenir Sheets

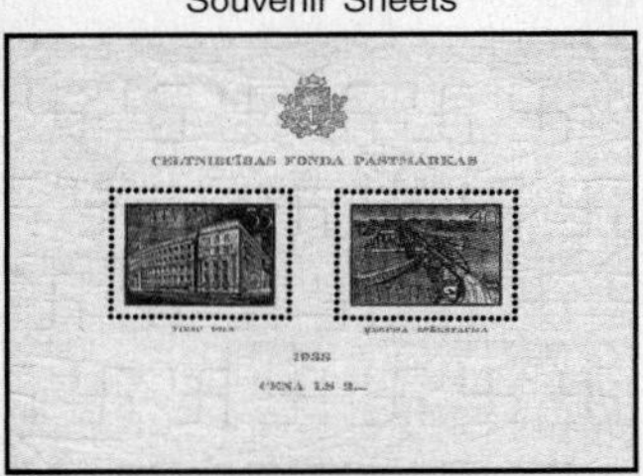

SP39

1938, May 12 Wmk. 212 ***Perf. 11***

B96 SP39 Sheet of 2 12.00 *20.00*
Never hinged 22.50
a. 35s Justice Palace, Riga 2.00 *5.00*
b. 40s Power Station, Kegums 2.00 *5.00*

Sold for 2 l. The surtax of 1.25 l was for the National Reconstruction Fund.

No. B96 exists imperf.

Overprinted in Blue with Dates 1934 1939 and "15" over "V"

1939

B97 SP39 Sheet of 2 15.00 *55.00*
Never hinged 45.00

5th anniv. of Natl. Unity Day. Sold for 2 lats. Surtax for the Natl. Reconstruction Fund.

AIR POST STAMPS

Blériot XI — AP1

Wmk. Wavy Lines Similar to 181

1921, July 30 Litho. ***Perf. 11½***

C1 AP1 10r emerald 3.00 4.50
a. Imperf. 6.00 *35.00*
C2 AP1 20r dark blue 3.00 4.50
a. Imperf. 6.00 *35.00*
Set, perf, never hinged 12.00
Set, imperf, never hinged 25.00

1928, May 1

C3 AP1 10s deep green 4.50 1.60
C4 AP1 15s red 2.00 1.60
C5 AP1 25s ultra 3.75 2.50
a. Pair, imperf. btwn. 35.00
Nos. C3-C5 (3) 10.25 5.70
Set, never hinged 16.00

Nos. C1-C5 sometimes show letters of a paper maker's watermark "PACTIEN LIGAT MILLS."

1931-32 Wmk. 212 ***Perf. 11½***

C6 AP1 10s deep green 1.00 .90
a. Perf. 11 12.00 *14.50*
C7 AP1 15s red 1.50 1.00
a. Perf. 11 120.00 32.50
C8 AP1 25s deep blue ('32) 8.50 1.25
a. Perf. 11 28.00 14.50
Nos. C6-C8 (3) 11.00 3.15
Set, never hinged 22.50

Type of 1921 Overprinted or Surcharged in Black

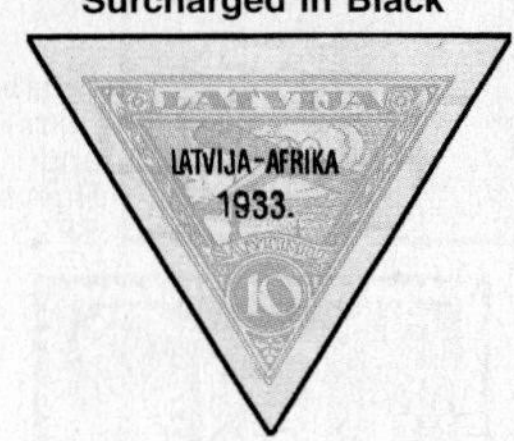

1933, May 26 Wmk. 212 ***Imperf.***

C9 AP1 10s deep green 40.00 *80.00*
C10 AP1 15s red 40.00 *80.00*
C11 AP1 25s deep blue 40.00 *80.00*
C12 AP1 50s on 15s red 200.00 *525.00*
C13 AP1 100s on 25s dp blue 200.00 *525.00*
Nos. C9-C13 (5) 520.00 *1,290.*
Set, never hinged 800.00

Honoring and financing a flight from Riga to Bathurst, Gambia. The plane crashed at Neustettin, Germany.

Counterfeits exist of Nos. C1-C13.

AIR POST SEMI-POSTAL STAMPS

Durbes Castle, Rainis Birthplace — SPAP1

Wmk. 212

1930, May 26 Litho. ***Perf. 11½***

CB1 SPAP1 10s (20s) red & olive green 6.50 *14.50*
CB2 SPAP1 15s (30s) dk yel grn & cop red 6.50 *14.50*
Set, never hinged 25.00

Surtax for the Rainis Memorial Fund.

Imperf.

CB1a SPAP1 10s (20s) 10.00 *27.50*
CB2a SPAP1 15s (30s) 10.00 *27.50*
Set, never hinged 40.00

Nos. C6-C8 Surcharged in Magenta, Blue or Red

1931, Dec. 5

CB3 AP1 10s + 50s dp grn (M) 6.50 *7.50*
CB4 AP1 15s + 1 l red (Bl) 6.50 *7.50*
CB5 AP1 25s + 1.50 l dp blue 6.50 *7.50*
Nos. CB3-CB5 (3) 19.50 *22.50*
Set, never hinged 40.00

Surtax for the Latvian Home Guards.

Imperf.

CB3a AP1 10s + 50s 10.00 *11.00*
CB4a AP1 15s + 1 l 10.00 *11.00*
CB5a AP1 25s + 1.50 l 10.00 *11.00*
Nos. CB3a-CB5a (3) 30.00 *33.00*
Set, never hinged 55.00

SPAP2

1932, June 17 ***Perf. 10½***

CB6 SPAP2 10s (20s) dk sl grn & grn 12.50 *25.00*
CB7 SPAP2 15s (30s) brt red & buff 12.50 *25.00*
CB8 SPAP2 25s (50s) dp bl & gray 12.50 *25.00*
Nos. CB6-CB8 (3) 37.50 *75.00*
Set, never hinged 75.00

Surtax for the Latvian Home Guards.

Imperf.

CB6a SPAP2 10s (20s) 12.50 25.00
CB7a SPAP2 15s (30s) 12.50 25.00
CB8a SPAP2 25s (50s) 12.50 25.00
Nos. CB6a-CB8a (3) 37.50 *75.00*
Set, never hinged 75.00

Icarus — SPAP3

Leonardo da Vinci — SPAP4

Charles Balloon — SPAP5

Wright Brothers Biplane SPAP6

Bleriot Monoplane SPAP7

1932, Dec. ***Perf. 10, 11½***

CB9 SPAP3 5s (25s) ol bis & grn 17.50 *20.00*
CB10 SPAP4 10s (50s) ol brn & gray grn 17.50 *20.00*
CB11 SPAP5 15s (75s) red brn & gray grn 17.50 *20.00*
CB12 SPAP6 20s (1 l) gray grn & lil rose 17.50 *20.00*
CB13 SPAP7 25s (1.25 l) brn & bl 17.50 *20.00*
Nos. CB9-CB13 (5) 87.50 100.00
Set, never hinged 150.00

Issued to honor pioneers of aviation. The surtax of four times the face value was for wounded Latvian aviators.

Imperf.

CB9a SPAP3 5s (25s) 17.50 *20.00*
CB10a SPAP4 10s (50s) 17.50 *20.00*
CB11a SPAP5 15s (75s) 17.50 *20.00*
CB12a SPAP6 20s (1 l) 17.50 *20.00*
CB13a SPAP7 25s (1.25 l) 17.50 *20.00*
Nos. CB9a-CB13a (5) 87.50 100.00
Set, never hinged 150.00

Icarus Falling SPAP8

Monument to Aviators SPAP9

Proposed Tombs for Aviators SPAP10 SPAP11

1933, Mar. 15 ***Perf. 11½***

CB14 SPAP8 2s (52s) blk & ocher 14.00 *20.00*
CB15 SPAP9 3s (53s) blk & red org 14.00 *20.00*
CB16 SPAP10 10s (60s) blk & dk yel green 14.00 *20.00*
CB17 SPAP11 20s (70s) blk & cerise 14.00 *20.00*
Nos. CB14-CB17 (4) 56.00 *80.00*
Set, never hinged 125.00

50s surtax for wounded Latvian aviators.

Imperf.

CB14a SPAP8 2s (52s) 15.00 *21.00*
CB15a SPAP9 3s (53s) 15.00 *21.00*
CB16a SPAP10 10s (60s) 15.00 *21.00*
CB17a SPAP11 20s (70s) 15.00 *21.00*
Nos. CB14a-CB17a (4) 60.00 84.00
Set, never hinged 135.00

Biplane Taking Off SPAP12

Designs: 7s (57s), Biplane under fire at Riga. 35s (1.35 l), Map and planes.

1933, June 15 Wmk. 212 ***Perf. 11½***

CB18 SPAP12 3s (53s) org & sl blue 19.00 *40.00*
CB19 SPAP12 7s (57s) sl bl & dk brn 19.00 *40.00*
CB20 SPAP12 35s (1.35 l) dp ultra & ol blk 19.00 *40.00*
Nos. CB18-CB20 (3) 57.00 *120.00*
Set, never hinged 125.00

Surtax for wounded Latvian aviators. Counterfeits exist.

Imperf.

CB18a SPAP12 3s (53s) 22.50 *42.50*
CB19a SPAP12 7s (57s) 22.50 *42.50*
CB20a SPAP12 35s (1.35 l) 22.50 *42.50*
Nos. CB18a-CB20a (3) 67.50 *127.50*
Set, never hinged 130.00

American Gee-Bee SPAP13

English Seaplane S6B SPAP14

Graf Zeppelin over Riga SPAP15

DO-X SPAP16

1933, Sept. 5 *Perf. 11½*

CB21 SPAP13 8s (68s) brn & gray blk 40.00 *85.00*
CB22 SPAP14 12s (1.12 l) brn car & ol grn 40.00 *85.00*
CB23 SPAP15 30s (1.30 l) bl & gray blk 50.00 *90.00*
CB24 SPAP16 40s (1.90 l) brn vio & indigo 40.00 *85.00*
Nos. CB21-CB24 (4) 170.00 345.00
Set, never hinged 275.00

Surtax for wounded Latvian aviators.

Imperf.

CB21a SPAP13 8s (68s) 40.00 *85.00*
CB22a SPAP14 12s (1.12 l) 40.00 *85.00*
CB23a SPAP15 30s (1.30 l) 50.00 *95.00*
CB24a SPAP16 40s (1.90 l) 40.00 *90.00*
Nos. CB21a-CB24a (4) 170.00 *355.00*
Set, never hinged 275.00

OCCUPATION STAMPS

Issued under German Occupation

German Stamps of 1905-18 Handstamped

Red Overprint

1919 **Wmk. 125** *Perf. 14, 14½*

1N1 A22 2½pf gray 275.00 *325.00*
1N2 A16 5pf green 225.00 100.00
1N3 A22 15pf dk vio 375.00 100.00
1N4 A16 20pf blue vio 135.00 65.00
1N5 A16 25pf org & blk, *yel* 475.00 325.00
1N6 A16 50pf pur & blk, *buff* 475.00 325.00

Violet Blue Overprint

1N7 A22 2½pf gray 275.00 *325.00*
1N8 A16 5pf green 225.00 120.00
1N9 A16 10pf carmine 190.00 47.50
1N10 A22 15pf dk vio 325.00 325.00
1N11 A16 20pf bl vio 135.00 65.00
1N12 A16 25pf org & blk, *yel* 675.00 525.00
1N13 A16 50pf pur & blk, *buff* 675.00 525.00
Nos. 1N1-1N13 (13) 4,460. 3,173.

Inverted and double overprints exist, as well as counterfeit overprints.

Some experts believe that Nos. 1N1-1N7 were not officially issued. All used examples are canceled to order.

ISSUED UNDER RUSSIAN OCCUPATION

Fake overprints/surcharges exist on Nos. 2N1-2N36.

The following stamps were issued at Mitau during the occupation of Kurland by the West Russian Army under Colonel Bermondt-Avalov.

Stamps of Latvia Handstamped

On Stamps of 1919

1919 **Wmk. 108** *Imperf.*

2N1 A1 3k lilac 40.00 *52.50*
2N2 A1 5k carmine 40.00 *52.50*
2N3 A1 10k dp blue 140.00 *240.00*
2N4 A1 20k orange 40.00 *52.50*
2N5 A1 25k gray 40.00 *52.50*
2N6 A1 35k dk brown 40.00 *52.50*
2N7 A1 50k purple 40.00 *52.50*
2N8 A1 75k emerald 40.00 *80.00*

On Riga Liberation Stamps

2N9 A2 5k carmine 40.00 *52.50*
2N10 A2 15k dp green 20.00 *40.00*
2N11 A2 35k brown 20.00 *40.00*

Stamps of Latvia Overprinted

On Stamps of 1919

2N12 A1 3k lilac 6.00 *9.50*
2N13 A1 5k carmine 6.00 *9.50*
2N14 A1 10k dp blue 120.00 *200.00*
2N15 A1 20k orange 12.00 *20.00*
2N16 A1 25k gray 27.50 *60.00*
2N17 A1 35k dk brown 20.00 *27.50*
2N18 A1 50k purple 20.00 *27.50*
2N19 A1 75k emerald 20.00 *27.50*

On Riga Liberation Stamps

2N20 A2 5k carmine 4.00 *8.00*
2N21 A2 15k dp green 4.00 *8.00*
2N22 A2 35k brown 4.00 *8.00*
a. Inverted overprint 200.00
Nos. 2N1-2N22 (22) 743.50 *1,173.*

The letters "Z. A." are the initials of "Zapadnaya Armiya"-i.e. Western Army.

Russian Stamps of 1909-17 Surcharged

On Stamps of 1909-12

Perf. 14, 14½x15

Unwmk.

2N23 A14 10k on 2k grn 6.00 *8.00*
a. Inverted surcharge *30.00*
2N24 A15 30k on 4k car 8.00 *8.00*
2N25 A14 40k on 5k cl 8.00 *9.50*
2N26 A15 50k pn 10k dk bl 6.00 *8.00*
2N27 A11 70k on 15k red brn & bl 6.00 *8.00*
a. Inverted surcharge *200.00*
2N28 A8 90k on 20k bl & car 12.00 *16.00*
2N29 A11 1r on 25k grn & vio 6.00 8.00
2N30 A11 1½r on 35k red brn & grn 47.50 65.00
2N31 A8 2r on 50k vio & grn 12.00 16.00
a. Inverted surcharge *120.00*
2N32 A11 4r on 70k brn & org 20.00 27.50

Perf. 13½

2N33 A9 6r on 1r pale brn, brn & org 27.50 40.00

On Stamps of 1917

Imperf

2N34 A14 20k on 3k red 6.00 *8.00*
2N35 A14 40k on 5k claret 95.00 *100.00*
2N36 A12 10r on 3.50r mar & lt grn 80.00 *80.00*
a. Inverted surcharge *300.00*
Nos. 2N23-2N36 (14) 340.00 *402.00*

Eight typographed stamps of this design were prepared in 1919, but never placed in use. They exist both perforated and imperforate. Value, set, imperf. $1, perf. $2.

Reprints and counterfeits exist.

Catalogue values for unused stamps in this section, from this point to the end of the section, are for Never Hinged items.

Arms of Soviet Latvia — OS1

1940 **Typo.** **Wmk. 265** *Perf. 10*

2N45 OS1 1s dk violet .25 .25
2N46 OS1 2s orange yel .25 .25
2N47 OS1 3s orange ver .25 .25
2N48 OS1 5s dk olive grn .25 .25
2N49 OS1 7s turq green .25 .80
2N50 OS1 10s slate green 2.00 .40
2N51 OS1 20s brown lake 1.20 .25
2N52 OS1 30s light blue 2.40 .40
2N53 OS1 35s brt ultra .25 *.40*
2N54 OS1 40s chocolate 2.00 1.20
2N55 OS1 50s lt gray 2.50 1.20
2N56 OS1 1 l lt brown 3.25 1.50
2N57 OS1 5 l brt green 24.00 13.50
Nos. 2N45-2N57 (13) 38.85 20.65

Used values of Nos. 2N45-2N57 are for CTOs. Commercially used examples are worth three times as much.

LEBANON

'le-bə-nən

(Grand Liban)

LOCATION — Asia Minor, bordering on the Mediterranean Sea
GOVT. — Republic
AREA — 4,036 sq. mi.
POP. — 3,500,000 (est. 1984)
CAPITAL — Beirut

Formerly a part of the Syrian province of Turkey, Lebanon was occupied by French forces after World War I. It was mandated to France after it had been declared a separate state. Limited autonomy was granted in 1927 and full independence achieved in 1941. The French issued two sets of occupation stamps (with T.E.O. overprint) for Lebanon in late 1919. The use of these and later occupation issues (of 1920-24, with overprints "O.M.F." and "Syrie-Grand Liban") was extended to Syria, Cilicia, Alaouites and Alexandretta. By custom, these are all listed under Syria.

100 Centimes = 1 Piaster
100 Piasters = 1 Pound

Issued under French Mandate

Stamps of France 1900-21 Surcharged

Type 1

Type 2

Two types each exist for surcharges on the centime surcharges and on the piastre surcharges on type A18. Centimes: type 1, serif on upper curve of "C"; type 2, serifs on both lower and upper curves of "C." Piastres: type 1, 1.5-2mm space between value and "P," except for 3p (3mm); type 2, 4mm between value and "P."

1924 **Unwmk.** *Perf. 14x13½*

1 A16 10c on 2c vio brn (1) 1.60 1.60
Never hinged 3.25
On cover 16.00
a. Inverted surcharge 45.00 45.00
Never hinged 90.00
b. Type 2 2.40 2.40
Never hinged 4.75
On cover 20.00
c. As "b," double surcharge 45.00 45.00
Never hinged 90.00
d. As "b," in pair with unsurcharged stamp 260.00
2 A22 25c on 5c orange (1) 1.60 1.60
Never hinged 3.25
On cover 13.50
a. Type 2 3.50 3.50
Never hinged 7.00
On cover 24.00
3 A22 50c on 10c green (1) 1.60 1.60
Never hinged 3.25
On cover 12.00
a. "S" of "CENTIEMES" inverted 17.50 17.50
Never hinged 35.00
b. Double surcharge 45.00 45.00
Never hinged 80.00
c. Type 2 3.50 3.50
Never hinged 7.00
On cover 24.00
d. As "c," "R" omitted from "GRAND" 60.00 45.00
Never hinged 120.00
4 A20 75c on 15c sl grn (1) 2.75 2.40
Never hinged 5.50
On cover 12.00
a. Inverted surcharge 45.00 45.00
Never hinged 90.00
b. Type 2 3.50 3.25
Never hinged 7.00
On cover 24.00
5 A22 1p on 20c red brn 1.60 1.60
Never hinged 3.25
On cover 16.00
a. Double surcharge 45.00 45.00
Never hinged 90.00
b. Inverted surcharge 45.00 45.00
Never hinged 90.00
6 A22 1.25p on 25c blue 4.50 2.40
Never hinged 9.00
On cover 16.00
a. Double surcharge 40.00 40.00
Never hinged 80.00
7 A22 1.50p on 30c org 2.75 2.00
Never hinged 5.50
On cover 9.50
8 A22 1.50p on 30c red 2.75 2.40
Never hinged 5.50
On cover 12.00
9 A20 2.50p on 50c dl bl 2.40 2.00
Never hinged 4.75
On cover 16.00
On cover, single franking 24.00
a. Inverted surcharge 35.00 35.00
Never hinged 70.00
b. "0" of "2,50" omitted 35.00 35.00
Never hinged 70.00
c. "2" of "2,50" omitted 65.00 65.00
Never hinged 130.00
d. Comma of "2,50" omitted 13.50 13.50
Never hinged 27.00

Surcharged

10 A18 2p on 40c red & pale bl 5.50 3.75
Never hinged 11.00
a. Inverted surcharge 27.50 27.50
11 A18 3p on 60c vio & ultra 8.00 6.75
Never hinged 16.00
12 A18 5p on 1fr cl & ol grn 10.00 7.50
Never hinged 20.00
13 A18 10p on 2fr org & pale bl 15.00 12.00
Never hinged 30.00
a. Inverted surcharge 50.00 50.00
14 A18 25p on 5fr dk bl & buff 22.50 19.00
Never hinged 45.00
a. Inverted surcharge 85.00 85.00
Nos. 1-14 (14) 82.55 66.60

Broken and missing letters and varieties of spacing are numerous in these surcharges.

For overprints see Nos. C1-C4.

Stamps of France, 1923, (Pasteur) Surcharged "GRAND LIBAN" and New Values

15 A23 50c on 10c green 3.50 1.10
Never hinged 7.00
a. Inverted surcharge 35.00 25.00

16 A23 1.50p on 30c red 4.50 2.25
Never hinged 9.00
17 A23 2.50p on 50c blue 3.75 1.10
Never hinged 7.50
a. Inverted surcharge 30.00 27.50
Nos. 15-17 (3) 11.75 4.45

Commemorative Stamps of France, 1924, (Olympic Games) Surcharged "GRAND LIBAN" and New Values

18 A24 50c on 10c gray grn & yel grn 32.50 *32.50*
Never hinged 65.00
a. Inverted surcharge 350.00
19 A25 1.25p on 25c rose & dk rose 32.50 *32.50*
Never hinged 65.00
a. Inverted surcharge 350.00
20 A26 1.50p on 30c brn red & blk 32.50 *32.50*
Never hinged 65.00
a. Inverted surcharge 350.00
21 A27 2.50p on 50c ultra & dk bl 32.50 *32.50*
Never hinged 65.00
a. Inverted surcharge 350.00
Nos. 18-21 (4) 130.00 130.00

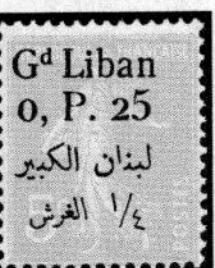

Stamps of France, 1900-24, Surcharged

1924-25

22 A16 10c on 2c vio brn 1.00 .50
Never hinged 1.50
23 A22 25c on 5c orange 1.25 .75
Never hinged 1.75
24 A22 50c on 10c green 2.00 1.40
Never hinged 3.00
25 A20 75c on 15c gray grn 1.75 1.10
Never hinged 2.60
26 A22 1p on 20c red brn 1.50 .95
Never hinged 2.25
27 A22 1.25p on 25c blue 2.25 1.60
Never hinged 3.50
28 A22 1.50p on 30c red 2.00 1.25
Never hinged 3.00
29 A22 1.50p on 30c orange 62.50 57.50
Never hinged 100.00
30 A22 2p on 35c vio ('25) 2.25 1.60
Never hinged 3.50
31 A20 3p on 60c lt vio ('25) 3.00 2.10
Never hinged 4.50
32 A20 4p on 85c ver 3.50 2.50
Never hinged 5.50

Surcharged

33 A18 2p on 40c red & pale bl 2.25 1.60
Never hinged 4.25
a. 2nd line of Arabic reads "2 Piastre" (singular) 2.50 .50
34 A18 2p on 45c grn & bl ('25) 27.50 22.50
Never hinged 42.50
35 A18 3p on 60c vio & ultra 3.50 2.50
Never hinged 6.00
36 A18 5p on 1fr cl & ol grn 4.25 3.25
Never hinged 8.00
37 A18 10p on 2fr org & pale bl 9.75 8.50
Never hinged 17.00
38 A18 25p on 5fr dk bl & buff 15.00 13.50
Never hinged 27.50
Nos. 22-38 (17) 145.25 123.10

Last line of surcharge on No. 33 has four characters, with a 9-like character between the third and fourth in illustration. Last line on No. 33a is as illustrated.

The surcharge may be found inverted on most of Nos. 22-38, and double on some values.

For overprints see Nos. C5-C8.

Stamps of France 1923-24 (Pasteur) Surcharged as Nos. 22-32

39 A23 50c on 10c green 2.00 .85
Never hinged 3.00
a. Inverted surcharge 35.00 25.00
b. Double surcharge 40.00 21.00
40 A23 75c on 15c green 2.25 1.40
Never hinged 3.25
41 A23 1.50p on 30c red 2.75 1.40
Never hinged 4.25
a. Inverted surcharge 35.00 25.00
42 A23 2p on 45c red 5.00 3.50
Never hinged 8.00
a. Inverted surcharge 35.00 21.00
43 A23 2.50p on 50c blue 2.00 .95
Never hinged 3.00
a. Inverted surcharge 35.00 21.00
b. Double surcharge 40.00 21.00
44 A23 4p on 75c blue 5.00 3.50
Never hinged 8.00
Nos. 39-44 (6) 19.00 11.60

France Nos. 198 to 201 (Olympics) Surcharged as Nos. 22-32

45 A24 50c on 10c 32.50 *32.50*
Never hinged 50.00
46 A25 1.25p on 25c 32.50 *32.50*
Never hinged 50.00
47 A26 1.50p on 30c 32.50 *32.50*
Never hinged 50.00
48 A27 2.50p on 50c 32.50 *32.50*
Never hinged 50.00
Nos. 45-48 (4) 130.00 130.00

France No. 219 (Ronsard) Surcharged

49 A28 4p on 75c bl, *bluish* 3.50 3.50
Never hinged 5.00
a. Inverted surcharge 65.00 50.00

Cedar of Lebanon — A1

Crusader Castle, Tripoli — A3

View of Beirut — A2

Designs: 50c, Crusader Castle, Tripoli. 75c, Beit-ed-Din Palace. 1p, Temple of Jupiter, Baalbek. 1.25p, Mouktara Palace. 1.50p, Harbor of Tyre. 2p, View of Zahle. 2.50p, Ruins at Baalbek. 3p, Square at Deir-el-Kamar. 5p, Castle at Sidon. 25p, Square at Beirut.

1925 Litho. *Perf. 12½, 13½*

50 A1 10c dark violet .50 .25
Never hinged .75

Photo.

51 A2 25c olive black .95 .25
Never hinged 1.30
52 A2 50c yellow grn .75 .25
Never hinged 1.25
53 A2 75c brn orange .75 .25
Never hinged 1.25
54 A2 1p magenta 2.00 .80
Never hinged 3.00
55 A2 1.25p deep green 2.25 1.40
Never hinged 3.50
56 A2 1.50p rose red 1.00 .25
Never hinged 1.50
57 A2 2p dark brown 1.25 .25
Never hinged 2.00
58 A2 2.50p peacock bl 2.00 .80
Never hinged 3.00
59 A2 3p orange brn 2.75 1.10
Never hinged 3.75
60 A2 5p violet 3.00 1.40
Never hinged 4.50
61 A3 10p violet brn 7.50 2.10
Never hinged 9.50
62 A2 25p ultramarine 20.00 12.00
Never hinged 30.00
Nos. 50-62 (13) 44.70 21.10

For surcharges and overprints see Nos. 63-107, B1-B12, C9-C38, CB1-CB4.

Stamps of 1925 with Bars and Surcharged

1926

63 A2 3.50p on 75c brn org 1.50 1.50
Never hinged 2.50
64 A2 4p on 25c ol blk 2.50 2.50
Never hinged 4.00
65 A2 6p on 2.50p pck bl 2.00 2.00
Never hinged 3.50
66 A2 12p on 1.25p dp grn 1.40 1.40
Never hinged 2.75
67 A2 20p on 1.25p dp grn 6.75 6.75
Never hinged 9.25

Stamps of 1925 with Bars and Surcharged

68 A2 4.50p on 75c brn org 2.75 2.75
Never hinged 4.50
69 A2 7.50p on 2.50p pck bl 2.75 2.75
Never hinged 4.50
70 A2 15p on 25p ultra 2.75 2.75
Never hinged 4.50
Nos. 63-70 (8) 22.40 22.40

No. 51 with Bars and Surcharged

1927

71 A2 4p on 25c ol blk 2.50 2.50
Never hinged 4.25

Issues of Republic under French Mandate

Stamps of 1925 Issue Overprinted in Black or Red

1927

72 A1 10c dark vio (R) .55 .25
Never hinged 1.00
a. Black overprint 35.00
b. Inverted overprint 35.00
73 A2 50c yellow grn .55 .25
Never hinged 1.00
74 A2 1p magenta .55 .25
Never hinged 1.00
75 A2 1.50p rose red .80 .60
Never hinged 1.50
76 A2 2p dark brown 1.10 .90
Never hinged 2.00
77 A2 3p orange brn .90 .25
Never hinged 1.60
78 A2 5p violet 1.75 1.00
Never hinged 3.00
79 A3 10p violet brn 2.25 1.10
Never hinged 4.00
80 A2 25p ultramarine 19.00 8.00
Never hinged 30.00
Nos. 72-80 (9) 27.45 12.60

On Nos. 72 and 79 the overprint is set in two lines. On all stamps the double bar obliterates GRAND LIBAN.

Same Overprint on Provisional Issues of 1926-27

15 PIASTERS ON 25 PIASTERS

TYPE I — "République Libanaise" at foot of stamp.

TYPE II — "République Libanaise" near top of stamp.

81 A2 4p on 25c ol blk .75 .25
Never hinged 1.25
82 A2 4.50p on 75c brn org .85 .25
Never hinged 1.50
83 A2 7.50p on 2.50p pck bl 1.10 .25
Never hinged 2.00
84 A2 15p on 25p ultra (I) 7.50 5.25
Never hinged 11.00
a. Type II 11.50 8.00
Nos. 81-84 (4) 10.20 6.00

Most of Nos. 72-84 are known with overprint double, inverted or on back as well as face.

Stamps of 1927 Overprinted in Black or Red

1928

86 A1 10c dark vio (R) .80 .60
Never hinged 1.25
a. French overprint omitted, on #50
b. Overprinted on No. 72b
87 A2 50c yel grn (Bk) 2.00 1.50
Never hinged 3.00
a. Arabic overprint inverted 35.00 25.00
88 A2 1p magenta (Bk) 1.00 .70
Never hinged 1.50
a. Inverted overprint 35.00 25.00
89 A2 1.50p rose red (Bk) 2.00 1.50
Never hinged 3.00
90 A2 2p dk brn (R) 2.75 2.10
Never hinged 4.00
90A A2 2p dk brn (Bk+R) 110.00 110.00
91 A2 3p org brn (Bk) 1.90 1.40
Never hinged 3.50
92 A2 5p violet (Bk+R) 3.50 2.75
Never hinged 5.50
93 A2 5p violet (R) 3.00 2.40
Never hinged 4.50
a. French ovpt. below Arabic 30.00 14.00
94 A3 10p vio brn (Bk) 5.00 4.25
Never hinged 8.00
a. Double overprint 100.00 90.00
b. Double overprint inverted
c. Inverted overprint 100.00 70.00
95 A2 25p ultra (Bk+R) 11.50 10.50
Never hinged 17.50
95A A2 25p ultra (R) 13.00 13.00
Never hinged 20.00
Nos. 86-95A (12) 156.45 150.70

On all stamps the double bar with Arabic overprint obliterates Arabic inscription.

Same Overprint on Nos. 81-84

96 A2 4p on 25c (Bk+R) 2.00 1.50
Never hinged 3.00
97 A2 4.50p on 75c (Bk) 2.00 1.50
Never hinged 3.00
98 A2 7.50p on 2.50p (Bk+R) 4.50 3.50
Never hinged 8.00
99 A2 7.50p on 2.50p (R) 7.00 6.00
Never hinged 11.00
100 A2 15p on 25p (II) (Bk+R) 11.00 9.50
Never hinged 17.50
a. Arabic overprint inverted
101 A2 15p on 25p (I) (R) 14.00 12.00
Never hinged 22.50
Nos. 96-101 (6) 40.50 34.00

The new values are surcharged in black. The initials in ( ) refer to the colors of the overprints.

Stamps of 1925 Srchd. in Red or Black

1928-29 *Perf. 13½*

102 A2 50c on 75c brn org (Bk) ('29) 1.50 1.90
Never hinged 2.25
103 A2 2p on 1.25p dp grn 1.50 1.90
Never hinged 2.25
104 A2 4p on 25c ol blk 1.50 1.90
Never hinged 2.25
a. Double surcharge 35.00 25.00
105 A2 7.50p on 2.50p pck bl 2.50 2.75
Never hinged 3.75
a. Double surcharge 40.00 25.00
b. Inverted surcharge 55.00 25.00
106 A2 15p on 25p ultra 22.50 10.00
Never hinged 35.00
Nos. 102-106 (5) 29.50 18.45

On Nos. 103, 104 and 105 the surcharged numerals are 3¼mm high, and have thick strokes.

No. 86 Surcharged in Red

1928

107 A1 5c on 10c dk vio 1.75 .30
Never hinged 3.00

Silkworm, Cocoon and Moth — A4

1930, Feb. 11 Typo. *Perf. 11*

108 A4 4p black brown 15.00 15.00
Never hinged 35.00
109 A4 4½p vermilion 15.00 15.00
Never hinged 35.00
110 A4 7½p dark blue 15.00 15.00
Never hinged 35.00
111 A4 10p dk violet 15.00 15.00
Never hinged 35.00
112 A4 15p dark green 15.00 15.00
Never hinged 35.00

113 A4 25p claret 15.00 15.00
Never hinged 35.00
Nos. 108-113 (6) 90.00 90.00

Sericultural Congress, Beirut. Presentation imperfs exist.

Pigeon Rocks, Ras Beirut — A5

View of Bickfaya A8

Beit-ed-Din Palace A10

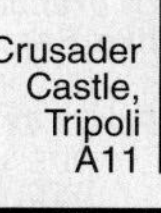

Crusader Castle, Tripoli A11

Ruins of Venus Temple, Baalbek A12

Ancient Bridge, Dog River A13

Belfort Castle A14

Afka Falls — A19

20c, Cedars of Lebanon. 25c, Ruins of Bacchus Temple, Baalbek. 1p, Crusader Castle, Sidon Harbor. 5p, Arcade of Beit-ed-Din Palace. 6p, Tyre Harbor. 7.50p, Ruins of Sun Temple, Baalbek. 10p, View of Hasbeya. 25p, Government House, Beirut. 50p, View of Deir-el-Kamar. 75c, 100p, Ruins at Baalbek.

1930-35 Litho. *Perf. 12½, 13½*

114 A5 10c brn org .60 .25
Never hinged 1.00
115 A5 20c yellow brn .60 .25
Never hinged 1.00
116 A5 25c deep blue .75 .45
Never hinged 1.25

Photo.

117 A8 50c orange brn 3.00 1.50
Never hinged 4.25
118 A11 75c ol brn ('32) 1.50 1.00
Never hinged 2.50
119 A8 1p deep green 1.75 1.25
Never hinged 3.00
120 A8 1p brn vio ('35) 3.00 1.00
Never hinged 4.25
121 A10 1.50p violet brn 3.25 1.90
Never hinged 4.75
122 A10 1.50p dp grn ('32) 3.50 1.50
Never hinged 5.00
123 A11 2p Prussian bl 4.50 1.60
Never hinged 6.50
124 A12 3p black brown 4.50 1.60
Never hinged 6.50
125 A13 4p orange brn 4.75 1.60
Never hinged 7.00
126 A14 4.50p carmine 5.00 1.60
Never hinged 7.50
127 A13 5p greenish blk 3.00 1.50
Never hinged 5.00
128 A13 6p brn violet 5.25 2.75
Never hinged 7.50
129 A10 7.50p deep blue 5.00 1.60
Never hinged 8.00
130 A10 10p dk ol grn 9.00 1.60
Never hinged 13.00
131 A19 15p blk violet 11.50 3.50
Never hinged 15.00
132 A19 25p blue green 20.00 6.00
Never hinged 27.50
133 A8 50p apple grn 60.00 15.00
Never hinged 95.00
134 A11 100p black 65.00 19.00
Never hinged 100.00
Nos. 114-134 (21) 215.45 66.45

See Nos. 135, 144, 152-155. For surcharges see Nos. 147-149; 161, 173-174 in Scott Standard catalogue, Vol 4.

Pigeon Rocks Type of 1930-35 Redrawn

1934 Litho. *Perf. 12½x12*

135 A5 10c dull orange 6.75 4.00

Lines in rocks and water more distinct. Printer's name "Hélio Vaugirard, Paris," in larger letters.

Cedar of Lebanon A23

President Emile Eddé A24

Dog River Panorama A25

1937-40 Typo. *Perf. 14x13½*

137 A23 10c rose car .50 .25
Never hinged .75
137A A23 20c aqua ('40) .50 .25
Never hinged .75
137B A23 25c pale rose lilac ('40) .50 .25
Never hinged .75
138 A23 50c magenta .50 .25
Never hinged .75
138A A23 75c brown ('40) .50 .25
Never hinged .75

Engr.

Perf. 13

139 A24 3p dk violet 4.00 .75
Never hinged 5.00
140 A24 4p black brown .75 .25
Never hinged 1.25
141 A24 4.50p carmine 1.00 .25
Never hinged 1.50
142 A25 10p brn carmine 2.25 .25
Never hinged 3.00
142A A25 12½p dp ultra ('40) 1.00 .25
Never hinged 1.50
143 A25 15p dk grn ('38) 4.00 .75
Never hinged 5.50
143A A25 20p chestnut ('40) 1.00 .25
Never hinged 1.50
143B A25 25p crimson ('40) 1.50 .60
Never hinged 2.25
143C A25 50p dk vio ('40) 5.00 1.60
Never hinged 6.50
143D A25 100p sepia ('40) 3.50 2.25
Never hinged 5.00
Nos. 137-143D (15) 26.50 8.45

Nos. 137A, 137B, 138A, 142A, 143A, 143B, 143C, and 143D exist imperforate.

For surcharges see Nos. 145-146A, 150-151; 160, 162, 175-176 in Scott Standard catalogue, Vol. 4.

View of Bickfaya A26

Type A8 Redrawn

1935 (?) Photo. *Perf. 13½*

144 A26 50c orange brown 17.50 9.75
Never hinged 20.00

Arabic inscriptions more condensed.

Stamps of 1930-37 Surcharged in Black or Red

1937-42 *Perf. 13, 13½*

145 A24 2p on 3p dk vio 1.50 1.50
Never hinged 2.25
146 A24 2½p on 4p blk brn 1.50 1.50
Never hinged 2.25
146A A24 2½p on 4p black brown (R) ('42) 1.50 1.50
Never hinged 2.25
147 A10 6p on 7.50p dp bl (R) 4.00 4.00
Never hinged 6.00

Stamps of 1930-35 and Type of 1937-40 Surcharged in Black or Red

Perf. 13½, 13

148 A8 7.50p on 50p ap grn 2.50 2.50
Never hinged 3.50
149 A11 7.50p on 100p blk (R) 2.50 2.50
Never hinged 3.50
150 A25 12.50p on 7.50p dk bl (R) 5.00 5.00
Never hinged 7.00

Type of 1937-40 Srchd. in Red

1939 Engr. *Perf. 13*

151 A25 12½p on 7.50p dk bl 2.00 2.00
Never hinged 3.00
Nos. 145-151 (8) 20.50 20.50

Type of 1930-35 Redrawn Imprint: "Beiteddine-Imp.-Catholique-Beyrouth-Liban."

1939 Litho. *Perf. 11½*

152 A10 1p dk slate grn 2.25 .25
Never hinged 3.25
153 A10 1.50p brn violet 2.25 .75
Never hinged 3.25
154 A10 7.50p carmine lake 2.25 1.10
Never hinged 3.25
Nos. 152-154 (3) 6.75 2.10

Bridge Type of 1930-35 Imprint: "Degorce" instead of "Hélio Vaugirard"

1940 Engr. *Perf. 13*

155 A13 5p grnsh blue 1.50 .25
Never hinged 2.50

Exists imperforate.

SEMI-POSTAL STAMPS

Stamps of 1925 Srchd. in Red or Black

1926 Unwmk. *Perf. 14x13½*

B1 A2 25c + 25c ol blk 4.25 4.25
Never hinged 6.25
B2 A2 50c + 25c yel grn (B) 4.25 4.25
Never hinged 6.25
B3 A2 75c + 25c brn org (B) 4.25 4.25
Never hinged 6.25
B4 A2 1p + 50c mag 4.25 4.25
Never hinged 6.25
B5 A2 1.25p + 50c dp grn 4.75 4.75
Never hinged 6.75
B6 A2 1.50p + 50c rose red (B) 4.75 4.75
Never hinged 6.75
a. Double surcharge 40.00 30.00
B7 A2 2p + 75c dk brn 4.25 4.25
Never hinged 6.75
B8 A2 2.50p + 75c pck bl 4.75 4.75
Never hinged 6.75
B9 A2 3p + 1p org brn 4.75 4.75
Never hinged 6.75
B10 A2 5p + 1p vio (B) 4.75 4.75
Never hinged 6.75
B11 A3 10p + 2p vio brn (B) 4.75 4.75
Never hinged 6.75
B12 A2 25p + 5p ultra 4.75 4.75
Never hinged 6.75
Nos. B1-B12 (12) 54.50 54.50

On No. B11 the surcharge is set in six lines to fit the shape of the stamp. All values of this series exist with inverted surcharge. Value each, $14.

See Nos. CB1-CB4.

AIR POST STAMPS

Nos. 10-13 with Additional Overprint

1924 Unwmk. *Perf. 14x13½*

C1 A18 2p on 40c 13.00 *13.00*
Never hinged 20.00
a. Double surcharge 52.50 52.50
C2 A18 3p on 60c 13.00 *13.00*
Never hinged 20.00
a. Invtd. surch. and ovpt. 87.50 87.50
C3 A18 5p on 1fr 13.00 *13.00*
Never hinged 20.00
a. Dbl. surch. and ovpt. 72.50 72.50
b. "5" omitted 300.00
C4 A18 10p on 2fr 13.00 *13.00*
Never hinged 20.00
a. Invtd. surch. and ovpt. 110.00 110.00
b. Dbl. surch. and ovpt. 60.00 60.00
Nos. C1-C4 (4) 52.00 *52.00*

Nos. 33, 35-37 Overprinted

C5 A18 2p on 40c 13.00 13.00
Never hinged 20.00
a. Overprint reversed 45.00
C6 A18 3p on 60c 13.00 13.00
Never hinged 20.00
a. Overprint reversed 45.00
C7 A18 5p on 1fr 13.00 13.00
Never hinged 20.00
a. Overprint reversed 45.00
C8 A18 10p on 2fr 13.50 13.50
Never hinged 21.00
a. Overprint reversed 45.00
b. Double surcharge 45.00
Nos. C5-C8 (4) 52.50 52.50

Nos. 57, 59-61 Overprinted in Green

1925

C9 A2 2p dark brown 4.50 4.50
Never hinged 6.75
C10 A2 3p orange brown 4.50 4.50
Never hinged 6.75
C11 A2 5p violet 4.50 4.50
Never hinged 6.75
a. Inverted overprint
C12 A3 10p violet brown 4.50 4.50
Never hinged 6.75
Nos. C9-C12 (4) 18.00 18.00

Nos. 57, 59-61 Ovptd. in Red — c

1926

C13 A2 2p dark brown 4.75 4.75
Never hinged 7.00
C14 A2 3p orange brown 4.75 4.75
Never hinged 7.00
C15 A2 5p violet 4.75 4.75
Never hinged 7.00

C16 A3 10p violet brown 4.75 4.75
Never hinged 7.00
Nos. C13-C16 (4) 19.00 19.00

Airplane pointed down on No. C16.
Exist with inverted overprint. Value, each $45.

Issues of Republic under French Mandate

Nos. C13-C16 Overprinted — d

1927

C17 A2 2p dark brown 5.50 5.50
Never hinged 8.50
C18 A2 3p orange brown 5.50 5.50
Never hinged 8.50
C19 A2 5p violet 5.50 5.50
Never hinged 8.50
C20 A3 10p violet brown 5.50 5.50
Never hinged 8.50
Nos. C17-C20 (4) 22.00 22.00

On No. C19 "Republique Libanaise" is above the bars. Overprint set in two lines on No. C20.

Nos. C17-C20 with Additional Ovpt. — e

1928 **Black Overprint**

C21 A2 2p brown 12.50 10.00
Never hinged 19.00
a. Double overprint 65.00 65.00
b. Inverted overprint 65.00 65.00
C22 A2 3p orange brown 12.50 10.00
Never hinged 19.00
a. Double overprint 65.00 65.00
C23 A2 5p violet 12.50 10.00
Never hinged 19.00
a. Double overprint 65.00 65.00
C24 A3 10p violet brown 12.50 10.00
Never hinged 19.00
a. Double overprint 65.00 65.00
Nos. C21-C24 (4) 50.00 40.00

On Nos. C21-C24 the airplane is always in red.

Nos. 52, 54, 57, 59-62 Ovptd. in Red or Black — f

1928

C25 A2 2p dark brown 4.50 4.50
Never hinged 6.75
C26 A2 3p orange brown 3.00 3.00
Never hinged 4.50
C27 A2 5p violet 4.50 4.50
Never hinged 6.75
C28 A3 10p violet brown 4.50 4.50
Never hinged 6.75

1929

C33 A2 50c yellow green 1.25 1.25
Never hinged 2.00
a. Inverted overprint 45.00 45.00
C34 A2 1p magenta (Bk) 1.00 1.00
Never hinged 1.50
a. Inverted overprint 45.00 45.00
C35 A2 25p ultra 190.00 160.00
Never hinged 390.00
a. Inverted overprint 525.00 525.00
Nos. C25-C34 (6) 18.75 18.75
Nos. C25-C35 (7) 208.75 178.75

On Nos. C25-C28 the airplane is always in red.

On No. C28 the overprinted orientation is horizontal. The bars covering the old country names are at the left.

The red overprint of a silhouetted plane and "Republique Libanaise," as on Nos. C25-C27, was also applied to Nos. C9-C12. These are believed to have been essays, and were not regularly issued.

No. 62 with Surcharge Added in Red

Two types of surcharge:

I — The "5" of "15 P." is italic. The "15" is 4mm high. Arabic characters for "Lebanese Republic" and for "15 P." are on same line in that order.

II — The "5" is in Roman type (upright) and smaller; "15" is 3½mm high. Arabic for "Lebanese Republic" is centered on line by itself, with Arabic for "15 P." below right end of line.

C36 A2 15p on 25p ultra (I) 225.00 175.00
a. Type II (#106) *800.00 800.00*

Nos. 102 Overprinted Type "c" in Blue

C37 A2 50c on 75c 1.00 1.00
Never hinged 1.50
a. Airplane inverted 45.00
b. French and Arabic surch. invtd.
c. "P" omitted
d. Airplane double 50.00

No. 55 Surcharged in Red

1930

C38 A2 2p on 1.25p dp green 1.75 1.25
Never hinged 3.00
a. Inverted surcharge 72.50 45.00

Airplane over Racheya AP2

Designs: 1p, Plane over Broumana. 2p, Baalbek. 3p, Hasroun. 5p, Byblos. 10p, Kadicha River. 15p, Beirut. 25p, Tripoli. 50p, Kabeljas. 100p, Zahle.

1930-31 **Photo.** ***Perf. 13½***

C39 AP2 50c dk violet ('31) .50 .50
Never hinged 1.00
C40 AP2 1p yellow grn ('31) .80 .80
Never hinged 1.60
C41 AP2 2p dp orange ('31) 2.50 2.50
Never hinged 5.00
C42 AP2 3p magenta ('31) 2.50 2.50
Never hinged 5.00
C43 AP2 5p indigo 2.50 2.50
Never hinged 5.00
C44 AP2 10p orange red 3.25 3.25
Never hinged 6.50
C45 AP2 15p orange brn 3.25 3.25
Never hinged 6.50
C46 AP2 25p gray vio ('31) 4.75 4.75
Never hinged 9.50
C47 AP2 50p dp claret 9.00 9.00
Never hinged 18.00
C48 AP2 100p olive brown 12.00 12.00
Never hinged 24.00
Nos. C39-C48 (10) 41.05 41.05

Nos. C39-C48 exist imperforate. Value, set $200.

Tourist Publicity Issue

Skiing in Lebanon AP12

Bay of Jounie AP13

1936, Oct. 12

C49 AP12 50c slate grn 3.00 3.00
Never hinged 6.00
C50 AP13 1p red orange 3.75 3.75
Never hinged 7.50
C51 AP12 2p black violet 3.75 3.75
Never hinged 7.50
C52 AP13 3p yellow grn 4.00 4.00
Never hinged 8.00
C53 AP12 5p brown car 4.00 4.00
Never hinged 8.00
C54 AP13 10p orange brn 4.00 4.00
Never hinged 8.00
C55 AP13 15p dk carmine 37.50 37.50
Never hinged 75.00
C56 AP12 25p green 125.00 125.00
Never hinged 250.00
Nos. C49-C56 (8) 185.00 185.00

Nos. C49-C56 exist imperforate. Value, set $650.

Lebanese Pavilion at Exposition AP14

1937, July 1 ***Perf. 13½***

C57 AP14 50c olive black 1.50 1.50
Never hinged 3.00
C58 AP14 1p yellow green 1.50 1.50
Never hinged 3.00
C59 AP14 2p dk red orange 1.50 1.50
Never hinged 3.00
C60 AP14 3p dk olive grn 1.50 1.50
Never hinged 3.00
C61 AP14 5p deep green 2.00 2.00
Never hinged 4.00
C62 AP14 10p carmine lake 9.00 9.00
Never hinged 18.00
C63 AP14 15p rose lake 10.00 10.00
Never hinged 20.00
C64 AP14 25p orange brn 17.50 17.50
Never hinged 35.00
Nos. C57-C64 (8) 44.50 44.50

Paris International Exposition.

Arcade of Beit-ed-Din Palace AP15

Ruins of Baalbek AP16

1937-40 **Engr.** ***Perf. 13***

C65 AP15 50c ultra ('38) .35 .25
Never hinged .70
C66 AP15 1p hen brn ('40) .35 .25
Never hinged .70
C67 AP15 2p sepia ('40) .35 .25
Never hinged .70
C68 AP15 3p rose ('40) 3.25 1.25
Never hinged 6.50
C69 AP15 5p lt green ('40) .35 .25
Never hinged .70
C70 AP16 10p dull violet .35 .25
Never hinged .70
C71 AP16 15p turq bl ('40) 2.75 1.75
Never hinged 5.50
C72 AP16 25p violet ('40) 6.00 5.00
Never hinged 12.00
C73 AP16 50p yel grn ('40) 11.00 7.00
Never hinged 22.00
C74 AP16 100p brown ('40) 6.00 3.50
Never hinged 12.00
Nos. C65-C74 (10) 30.75 19.75

Nos. C65-C74 exist imperforate.

Medical College of Beirut AP17

1938, May 9 **Photo.** ***Perf. 13***

C75 AP17 2p green 3.00 *3.50*
Never hinged 6.00
C76 AP17 3p orange 3.00 *3.50*
Never hinged 6.00
C77 AP17 5p lilac gray 5.50 *6.50*
Never hinged 11.00
C78 AP17 10p lake 10.50 *12.00*
Never hinged 21.00
Nos. C75-C78 (4) 22.00 *25.50*

Medical Congress.

Maurice Noguès and View of Beirut — AP18

1938, July 15 ***Perf. 11***

C79 AP18 10p brown carmine 4.00 1.50
Never hinged 8.00
a. Souv. sheet of 4, perf. 13½ 35.00 20.00
b. Perf. 13½ 7.50 4.00

10th anniversary of first Marseille-Beirut flight, by Maurice Noguès.

No. C79a has marginal inscriptions in French and Arabic. Exists imperf.; value $250.

AIR POST SEMI-POSTAL STAMPS

Nos. C13-C16 Surcharged Like Nos. B1-B12

1926 ***Perf. 13½***

CB1 A2 2pi + 1pi dk brn 15.00 8.00
CB2 A2 3pi + 2pi org brn 15.00 8.00
CB3 A2 5pi + 3pi violet 15.00 8.00
CB4 A3 10pi + 5pi vio brn 15.00 8.00
Nos. CB1-CB4 (4) 60.00 32.00

These stamps were sold for their combined values, original and surcharged. The latter represented their postal franking value and the former was a contribution to the relief of refugees from the Djebel Druze War.

POSTAGE DUE STAMPS

Postage Due Stamps of France, 1893-1920, Surcharged like Regular Issue

1924 **Unwmk.** ***Perf. 14x13½***

J1 D2 50c on 10c choc 6.75 4.25
J2 D2 1p on 20c ol grn 6.75 4.25
J3 D2 2p on 30c red 6.75 4.25
J4 D2 3p on 50c vio brn 6.75 4.25
J5 D2 5p on 1fr red brn, *straw* 6.75 4.25
Nos. J1-J5 (5) 33.75 21.25

Postage Due Stamps of France, 1893-1920, Surcharged

1924

J6 D2 50c on 10c choc 7.25 4.00
Never hinged 12.00
J7 D2 1p on 20c ol grn 7.25 4.00
Never hinged 12.00
J8 D2 2p on 30c red 7.25 4.00
Never hinged 12.00
J9 D2 3p on 50c vio brn 7.25 4.00
Never hinged 12.00
J10 D2 5p on 1fr red brn, *straw* 7.25 4.00
Never hinged 12.00
Nos. J6-J10 (5) 36.25 20.00

Ancient Bridge across Dog River — D3

Designs: 1p, Village scene. 2p, Pigeon Rocks, near Beirut. 3p, Belfort Castle. 5p, Venus Temple at Baalbek.

1925 **Photo.** ***Perf. 13½***

J11 D3 50c brown, *yellow* .95 .45
J12 D3 1p violet, *rose* 1.35 .65
J13 D3 2p black, *blue* 2.25 .90
J14 D3 3p black, *red org* 3.50 2.00
J15 D3 5p black, *bl grn* 5.75 3.75
Nos. J11-J15 (5) 13.80 7.75
Set, never hinged 42.50

Nos. J11 to J15 Overprinted

1927

J16 D3 50c brown, *yellow* 1.50 .40
J17 D3 1p violet, *rose* 2.50 .85
J18 D3 2p black, *blue* 3.50 1.25
J19 D3 3p black, *red org* 7.25 3.00
J20 D3 5p black, *bl grn* 9.50 4.50
Nos. J16-J20 (5) 24.25 10.00
Set, never hinged 35.00

Nos. J16-J20 with Additional Ovpt.

1928

J21 D3 50c brn, *yel* (Bk+R) 1.75 1.25
Never hinged 3.50
J22 D3 1p vio, *rose* (Bk) 1.75 1.25
Never hinged 3.50
J23 D3 2p blk, *bl* (Bk+R) 3.00 2.00
Never hinged 6.00
J24 D3 3p blk, *red org* (Bk) 6.00 3.50
Never hinged 12.00
J25 D3 5p blk, *bl grn* (Bk+R) 6.75 4.25
Never hinged 13.50
Nos. J21-J25 (5) 19.25 12.25
Set, never hinged 65.00

No. J23 has not the short bars in the upper corners.

Postage Due Stamps of 1925 Overprinted in Red like Nos. J21-J25

1928

J26 D3 50c brn, *yel* (R) 1.00 .50
Never hinged 2.00
J27 D3 2p blk, *bl* (R) 4.25 3.50
Never hinged 8.50
J28 D3 5p blk, *bl grn* (R) 11.50 7.50
Never hinged 23.00
Nos. J26-J28 (3) 16.75 11.50
Set, never hinged 32.50

No. J28 has not the short bars in the upper corners.

D4

Bas-relief of a Ship — D5

D6

D7

D8

Bas-relief from Sarcophagus of King Ahiram — D9

D10

1930-40 Photo.; Engr. (No. J35)

J29 D4 50c black, *rose* .75 .50
Never hinged 1.50
J30 D5 1p blk, *gray bl* 1.25 1.00
Never hinged 2.50
J31 D6 2p blk, *yellow* 1.75 1.25
Never hinged 3.50
J32 D7 3p blk, *bl grn* 1.75 1.25
Never hinged 3.50
J33 D8 5p blk, *orange* 7.25 5.50
Never hinged 14.50
J34 D9 8p blk, *lt rose* 5.00 3.50
Never hinged 10.00
J35 D8 10p dk green ('40) 7.75 4.50
Never hinged 15.50
J36 D10 15p black 6.25 2.75
Never hinged 12.50
Nos. J29-J36 (8) 31.75 20.25
Set, never hinged 65.00

Nos. J29-J36 exist imperf.

LEEWARD ISLANDS

'lē-wərd 'ī-ləndz

LOCATION — A group of islands in the West Indies, southeast of Puerto Rico
GOVT. — British Colony
AREA — 423 sq. mi.
POP. — 108,847 (1946)
CAPITAL — St. John

While stamps inscribed "Leeward Islands" were in use, 1890-1956, the colony consisted of the presidencies (now colonies) of Antigua, Montserrat, St. Christopher (St. Kitts) with Nevis and Anguilla, the British Virgin Islands and Dominica (which became a separate colony in 1940).

Each presidency issued its own stamps, using them along with the Leeward Islands general issues.

12 Pence = 1 Shilling
20 Shillings = 1 Pound

Catalogue values for unused stamps in this country are for Never Hinged items, beginning with Scott 116.

Queen Victoria — A1

1890 Typo. Wmk. 2 *Perf. 14*

1 A1 ½p lilac & green 3.75 1.40
2 A1 1p lilac & car 8.75 .25
3 A1 2½p lilac & ultra 9.50 .30
4 A1 4p lilac & org 12.00 9.50
5 A1 6p lilac & brown 13.50 15.50
6 A1 7p lilac & slate 12.00 *21.00*
7 A1 1sh green & car 24.00 *62.50*
8 A1 5sh green & ultra 145.00 *330.00*
Nos. 1-8 (8) 228.50 *440.45*
Set, ovptd. "SPECIMEN" 275.00

Denomination of Nos. 7-8 are in color on plain tablet: "ONE SHILLING" or "FIVE SHILLINGS."

For overprints and surcharges see Nos. 9-19.

Jubilee Issue

Regular Issue of 1890 Handstamp Overprinted

1897, July 22

9 A1 ½p lilac & green 8.25 *26.00*
10 A1 1p lilac & car 9.25 *26.00*
11 A1 2½p lilac & ultra 9.75 *26.00*
12 A1 4p lilac & org 57.50 *80.00*
13 A1 6p lilac & brown 62.50 *130.00*
14 A1 7p lilac & slate 62.50 *130.00*
15 A1 1sh green & car 130.00 *275.00*
16 A1 5sh green & ultra 525.00 *850.00*
Nos. 9-16 (8) 864.75 *1,543.*

Double Overprints

9a A1 ½p *1,400.*
b. Triple overprint *9,000.*
10a A1 1p *1,150.*
b. Triple overprint *6,250.*
11a A1 2½p *1,350.*
12a A1 4p *1,350.*
13a A1 6p *1,700.* 4,500.
14a A1 7p *1,700.* *2,100.*
15a A1 1sh *2,250.*
16a A1 5sh *6,000.*

60th year of Queen Victoria's reign.
Excellent counterfeits of Nos. 9-16 exist.

Stamps of 1890 Surcharged in Black or Red

b

c

1902, Aug.

17 A1(b) 1p on 4p lilac & org 6.00 *10.00*
a. Tall narrow "O" in "One" 47.50 *77.50*
b. Double surcharge 6,000.
18 A1(b) 1p on 6p lilac & brn 8.00 *19.00*
a. Tall narrow "O" in "One" 67.50 *150.00*
19 A1(c) 1p on 7p lilac & sl 7.00 *15.00*
Nos. 17-19 (3) 21.00 44.00

King Edward VII — A4

Numerals of ¼p, 2p, 3p and 2sh6p of type A4 are in color on plain tablet. The 1sh and 5sh denominations are expressed as "ONE SHILLING" and "FIVE SHILLINGS" on plain tablet.

1902

20 A4 ½p violet & green 6.00 1.10
21 A4 1p vio & car rose 11.00 .25
22 A4 2p violet & bister 3.00 *4.50*
23 A4 2½p violet & ultra 6.75 2.50
24 A4 3p violet & black 10.00 *8.00*
25 A4 6p violet & brown 3.00 *9.00*
26 A4 1sh grn & car rose 10.00 *30.00*
27 A4 2sh6p green & blk 29.00 *80.00*
28 A4 5sh green & ultra 65.00 *95.00*
Nos. 20-28 (9) 143.75 *230.35*
Set, ovptd. "SPECIMEN" 190.00

1905-11 Wmk. 3
Chalky Paper (Ordinary Paper #29, 33)

29 A4 ½p vio & grn ('06) 4.75 2.25
a. Chalky paper ('08) 32.50 23.00
30 A4 1p vio & car rose 11.50 .90
31 A4 2p vio & bis ('08) 14.00 *27.00*
32 A4 2½p vio & ultra 80.00 50.00
33 A4 3p violet & black 25.00 *62.50*
a. Chalky paper ('08) 60.00 100.00
34 A4 3p violet, *yel* ('10) 3.75 *8.00*
35 A4 6p vio & brn ('08) 55.00 *100.00*
36 A4 6p violet & red violet ('11) 10.00 *11.00*
37 A4 1sh grn & car rose ('08) 55.00 *140.00*
38 A4 1sh blk, *grn* ('11) 12.00 *22.50*
39 A4 2sh6p blk & red, *blue* ('11) 45.00 *55.00*
40 A4 5sh grn & red, *yel* ('11) 50.00 *70.00*
Nos. 29-40 (12) 366.00 *549.15*

1907-11 Ordinary Paper

41 A4 ¼p brown ('09) 3.00 1.90
42 A4 ½p green 5.75 1.60
43 A4 1p red 14.50 .85
a. 1p rose carmine 50.00 3.75
44 A4 2p gray ('11) 5.50 *13.50*
45 A4 2½p ultramarine 9.00 4.50
Nos. 41-45 (5) 37.75 *22.35*

King George V — A5

For description of dies I and II, see "Dies of British Colonial Stamps" in Table of Contents.

The ½p, 1p, 2½p and 6p denominations of type A5 show the numeral on horizontally-lined tablet. The 1sh and 5sh denominations are expressed as "ONE SHILLING" and "FIVE SHILLINGS" on plain tablet.

Die I

1912 Ordinary Paper

46 A5 ¼p brown 1.90 1.10
47 A5 ½p green 5.50 2.00
48 A5 1p carmine 5.25 1.10
a. 1p scarlet 15.00 1.10
49 A5 2p gray 4.25 *5.75*
50 A5 2½p ultramarine 3.50 *7.25*

1912-22 Chalky Paper

51 A5 3p violet, *yel* 2.75 *24.00*
52 A5 4p blk & red, *yel* (Die II) ('22) 7.00 *22.50*
53 A5 6p vio & red vio 4.25 *8.50*
54 A5 1sh blk, *bl grn, ol back* 16.50 *8.50*
a. 1sh black, *green* 3.75 *8.50*
55 A5 2sh vio & ultra, *bl* (Die II) ('22) 18.00 *65.00*
56 A5 2sh6p black & red, *blue* ('14) 24.00 *57.50*
57 A5 5sh grn & red, *yel* ('14) 65.00 *120.00*
a. 5sh green & red, *lemon* ('15) 50.00 *85.00*
Nos. 46-57 (12) 157.90 *323.20*
Set, ovptd. "SPECIMEN" 300.00

1913, Nov. Surface-colored Paper

58 A5 3p violet, *yel* 95.00 *180.00*
59 A5 1sh black, *green* 90.00 40.00
60 A5 5sh green & red, *yel* 55.00 *90.00*
Nos. 58-60 (3) 240.00 310.00

King George V — A6

Die II

1921-32 Wmk. 4 Ordinary Paper

61 A5 ¼p dk brn ('22) 2.50 1.10
a. ¼p dark brown (I) ('32) 16.50 *21.00*
62 A5 ½p green 1.25 .80
a. ½p green (I) ('32) 27.50 *65.00*
63 A5 1p carmine 2.50 .60
a. 1p rose red (I) ('32) 45.00 1.00
b. 1p bright scarlet (II) ('29) 15.00 2.50
64 A5 1p dp violet ('22) 2.50 1.10
65 A5 1½p rose red ('26) 8.25 1.50
66 A5 1½p red brn ('29) 2.25 .25
a. 1½p red brown (I) ('32) 4.50 3.00
68 A5 2p gray ('22) 3.25 .85
69 A5 2½p orange ('23) 14.00 *67.50*
70 A5 2½p ultra ('27) 3.75 1.40
a. Die I ('32) 7.50 3.75
71 A5 3p ultra ('23) 17.50 *37.50*
a. 3p deep ultramarine ('25) 65.00 65.00

Chalky Paper

72 A5 3p violet, *yel* *8.50* *6.75*
73 A5 4p blk & red, *yel* ('23) 4.00 *24.00*
74 A5 5p vio & ol grn ('22) 2.75 *4.50*
75 A5 6p vio & red vio ('23) 19.00 *50.00*
a. Die I ('32) 32.50 *100.00*
76 A5 1sh blk, *emer* ('23) 11.00 *8.50*
a. 1sh black, *green* (I) ('32) 60.00 *85.00*
77 A5 2sh vio & ultra, *bl* ('22) 25.00 *45.00*
a. 2sh red purple & blue, *blue* ('26) 14.00 *52.50*
78 A5 2sh6p blk & red, *bl* ('23) 13.00 *27.00*
79 A5 3sh green & vio 12.50 *42.50*
80 A5 4sh black & scar 21.00 *42.50*
81 A5 5sh grn & red, *yel* 50.00 *85.00*
82 A6 10sh red & grn, *emer* ('28) 80.00 *140.00*

Wmk. 3

83 A6 £1 black & vio, *red* ('28) 240.00 325.00
Nos. 61-66,68-83 (22) 544.50 *913.35*

Common Design Types pictured following the introduction.

Silver Jubilee Issue
Common Design Type

Perf. 11x12

1935, May 6 Engr. Wmk. 4

96 CD301 1p car & dk blue 1.75 *3.25*
97 CD301 1½p blk & ultra 2.75 1.60
98 CD301 2½p ultra & brn 4.75 4.75
99 CD301 1sh brn vio & ind 26.50 *40.00*
Nos. 96-99 (4) 35.75 49.60
Set, never hinged 45.00
Set, perf "SPECIMEN" 120.00

Coronation Issue
Common Design Type

1937, May 12 ***Perf. 13½x14***

100 CD302 1p carmine .50 1.00
101 CD302 1½p brown .50 1.50
102 CD302 2½p bright ultra .55 1.50
Nos. 100-102 (3) 1.55 4.00
Set, never hinged 3.00
Set, perf "SPECIMEN" 120.00

A7

King George VI — A8

1938-51 **Typo.** ***Perf. 14***

103 A7 ¼p brown .40 1.50
Never hinged .60
a. ¼p deep brown, chalky paper ('49) .25 *1.75*
Never hinged .30
104 A7 ½p green .75 .75
Never hinged 1.20
105 A7 1p carmine 1.25 1.75
Never hinged 2.25
a. 1p scarlet ('42) 1.40 12.50
Never hinged 2.50
b. 1p red ('48) 3.75 *6.75*
Never hinged 5.75
106 A7 1½p red brown .80 .50
Never hinged 1.00
107 A7 2p gray 2.00 2.25
Never hinged 3.50
a. 2p slate gray ('42) 4.00 3.75
Never hinged 6.25
108 A7 2½p ultramarine .60 *4.00*
Never hinged .80
a. 2½p bright blue 18.00 1.20
Never hinged 32.50
109 A7 3p dl org ('42) .40 *.90*
Never hinged 4.50
a. 3p brown orange 22.50 2.75
Never hinged 35.00
110 A7 6p vio & red vio 6.00 3.50
Never hinged 11.50
a. 6p deep dull purple & bright purple 16.00 7.00
Never hinged 27.50
b. 6p purple & deep magenta ('47) 9.00 5.50
Never hinged 15.50
111 A7 1sh blk, *emer* ('42) 3.50 1.50
Never hinged 4.25
a. 1sh black, *emerald*, chalky paper 10.00 5.50
Never hinged 17.50
112 A7 2sh vio & ultra, *bl* 7.75 2.25
Never hinged 13.50
a. 2sh reddish purple & blue, *blue*, chalky paper 17.00 3.00
Never hinged 30.00
113 A7 5sh grn & red, *yel* 21.00 *18.00*
Never hinged 35.00
a. 5sh green & red, *yel*, chalky paper 30.00 22.50
Never hinged 50.00
114 A8 10sh dp ver & dp grn, *emer*, ordinary paper ('47) 82.50 100.00
Never hinged 130.00
a. 10sh dp red & bluish grn, *green*, chalky paper 125.00 *140.00*
Never hinged 225.00
b. 10sh dull red & pale grn, *green*, ordinary paper ('44) 475.00 375.00
Never hinged 775.00
c. 10sh red & green, *green*, ordinary paper ('45) 100.00 90.00
Never hinged 160.00

Two dies were used for the 1p, differing in thickness of shading line at base of "1."

Wmk. 3 ***Perf. 13***

115 A8 £1 blk & vio, *scar* ('51) 22.50 *37.50*
Never hinged 50.00
a. £1 black & brown purple, *red*, perf. 14 225.00 *375.00*
Never hinged 375.00
b. £1 black & purple, *carmine*, perf. 14 ('41) 55.00 55.00
Never hinged 90.00
c. £1 black & brown purple, *salmon*, perf. 14 ('43) 27.50 29.00
Never hinged 45.00
d. Wmkd. sideways (as #115, perf. 13) *4,000.*
Never hinged 7,000.
Nos. 103-115 (13) 149.45 174.40
Set, never hinged 750.00

The 3p-£1 were issued on chalky paper in 1938 and on ordinary paper in 1942. Values are for the most common varieties.

Issued: #115, 12/13/51; others, 11/25/38.

See Nos. 120-125.

Catalogue values for unused stamps in this section, from this point to the end of the section, are for Never Hinged items.

Peace Issue
Common Design Type
Perf. 13½x14

1946, Nov. 1 **Wmk. 4** **Engr.**

116 CD303 1½p brown .25 .75
117 CD303 3p deep orange .25 .75
Set, perf "SPECIMEN" 100.00

Silver Wedding Issue
Common Design Types

1949, Jan. 2 **Photo.** ***Perf. 14x14½***

118 CD304 2½p bright ultra .25 .25

Perf. 11½x11
Engr.; Name Typographed

119 CD305 5sh green 6.75 8.00

George VI Type of 1938

1949, July 1 **Typo.** ***Perf. 13½x14***

120 A7 ½p gray 2.00 1.50
121 A7 1p green .55 .25
122 A7 1½p orange & black 1.75 .40
123 A7 2p crimson rose 1.40 1.25
124 A7 2½p black & plum 1.00 .25
125 A7 3p ultramarine 1.00 .25
Nos. 120-125 (6) 7.70 3.90

UPU Issue
Common Design Types
Engr.; Name Typo. on 3p and 6p

1949, Oct. 10 ***Perf. 13½, 11x11½***

126 CD306 2½p slate .25 *2.40*
127 CD307 3p indigo 2.00 2.40
128 CD308 6p red lilac .40 *2.40*
129 CD309 1sh blue green .40 *2.40*
Nos. 126-129 (4) 3.05 *9.60*

University Issue
Common Design Types
Perf. 14x14½

1951, Feb. 16 **Engr.** **Wmk. 4**

130 CD310 3c gray black & org .35 *2.00*
131 CD311 12c lilac & rose car 1.00 *2.00*

LIBERIA

lī-ˈbir-ē-ə

LOCATION — West coast of Africa, between Ivory Coast and Sierra Leone
GOVT. — Republic
AREA — 43,000 sq. mi.
POP. — 1,900,000 (est. 1984)
CAPITAL — Monrovia

100 Cents = 1 Dollar

Values for unused stamps are for examples with original gum as defined in the catalogue introduction. Any exceptions will be noted. Very fine examples of Nos. 1-3, 13-21 and 157-159 will have perforations just clear of the design due to the narrow spacing of the stamps on the plates and/or imperfect perforating methods.

Watermarks

Wmk. 116 — Crosses and Circles

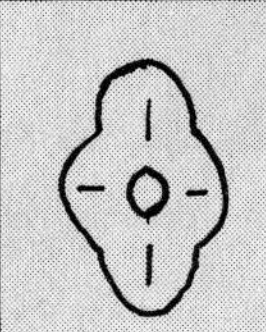
Wmk. 143

"Liberia" — A1

A1a

Thick Paper

1860 **Unwmk.** **Litho.** ***Perf. 12***

1 A1 6c red 400.00 *300.00*
a. Imperf, pair 500.00
2 A1 12c deep blue 25.00 *50.00*
a. Imperf, pair 250.00
3 A1a 24c green 50.00 *50.00*
a. Imperf, pair 300.00
Nos. 1-3 (3) 475.00 *400.00*

Stamps set very close together. Examples of the 12c occasionally show traces of a frame line around the design.

Medium to Thin Paper
With a single-line frame around each stamp, about 1mm from the border

1864 ***Perf. 11, 12***

7 A1 6c red 62.50 *85.00*
a. Imperf, pair 225.00
8 A1 12c blue 80.00 *95.00*
a. Imperf, pair 225.00
9 A1a 24c lt green 87.50 *100.00*
a. Imperf, pair 225.00
Nos. 7-9 (3) 230.00 *280.00*

Stamps set about 5mm apart. Margins large and perforation usually outside the frame line.

1866-69 **Without Frame Line**

13 A1 6c lt red 25.00 *40.00*
14 A1 12c lt blue 25.00 *40.00*
15 A1a 24c lt yellow grn 25.00 *40.00*
Nos. 13-15 (3) 75.00 120.00

Stamps set 2-2½mm apart with small margins. Stamps are usually without frame line but those from one transfer show broken and irregular parts of a frame.

1880 **With Frame Line** ***Perf. 10½***

16 A1 1c ultra 5.00 8.00
17 A1 2c rose 5.00 *5.25*
a. Imperf, pair 175.00
18 A1 6c violet 5.00 5.25
19 A1 12c yellow 5.00 *5.25*
20 A1a 24c rose red 6.00 5.50
Nos. 16-20 (5) 26.00 29.25

Unused values for Nos. 16-20 are for stamps without gum.

For surcharges see Nos. 157-159.

Counterfeits

Counterfeits exist of Nos. 1-28, 32 and 64.

From Arms of Liberia — A2

1881

21 A2 3c black 15.00 10.00

Unused value is for a stamp without gum.

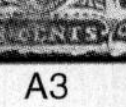
A3

A4

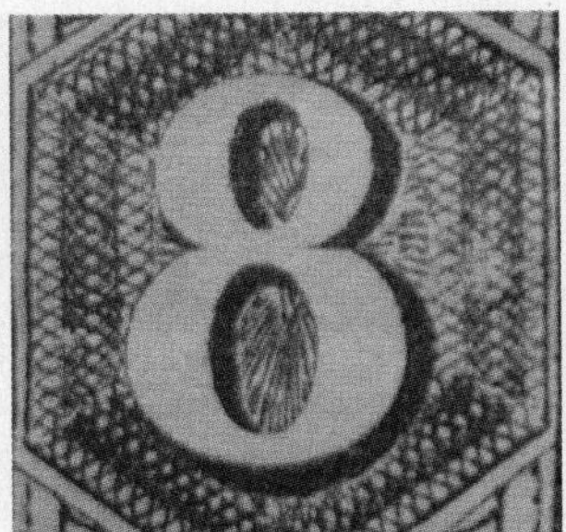
Slanting Lines

Network Lines

On No. 22 the openings in the figure "8" enclose a pattern of slanting lines. Compare with No. 32.

1882 ***Perf. 11½, 12, 14***

22 A3 8c blue 50.00 10.00
23 A4 16c red 8.00 5.00

Canceled to Order

Beginning with the issue of 1885, values in the used column are for "canceled to order" stamps. Postally used examples sell for much more.

A5

A6

From Arms of Liberia — A7

Perf. 10½, 11, 12, 11½x10½, 14, 14½

1885

24 A5 1c carmine 2.00 2.00
a. 1c rose 2.00 2.00
25 A5 2c green 2.00 2.00
26 A5 3c violet 2.00 2.00
27 A5 4c brown 2.00 2.00
28 A5 6c olive gray 2.00 2.00
29 A6 8c bluish gray 4.00 4.00
a. 8c lilac 7.00 7.00
30 A6 16c yellow 15.00 12.00
31 A7 32c deep blue 35.00 29.00
Nos. 24-31 (8) 64.00 55.00

In the 1885 printing, the stamps are spaced 2mm apart and the paper is medium. In the 1892 printing, the stamps are 4½mm apart.

For surcharges see Nos. J1-J2.

Imperf., Pair

24b A5 1c 3.00
25a A5 2c 4.75
26a A5 3c 5.00
27a A5 4c 5.00
28a A5 6c 4.25 4.25
29b A6 8c 12.50
30a A6 16c 30.00
31a A7 32c 50.00

Imperf. pairs with 2mm spacing sell for higher prices.

A8

The openings in the figure "8" are filled with network lines.

1889 ***Perf. 12, 14***

32 A8 8c blue 4.25 4.25
a. Imperf., pair 20.00

See No. 22.

A9

Elephant — A10

Oil Palm — A11

Pres. Hilary R. W. Johnson — A12

Vai Woman in Full Dress — A13

Coat of Arms — A14

Liberian Star — A15

Coat of Arms — A16

Hippopotamus A17

Liberian Star — A18

President Johnson — A19

1892-96 Wmk. 143 Engr. *Perf. 15*

33 A9 1c vermilion .50 .40
a. 1c blue (error) 40.00
34 A9 2c blue .50 .40
a. 2c vermilion (error) 40.00
35 A10 4c green & blk 2.00 1.25
a. Center inverted 225.00
36 A11 6c blue green .70 .50
37 A12 8c brown & blk .95 .95
a. Center inverted 500.00 500.00
b. Center sideways 750.00
38 A12 10c chrome yel & indigo ('96) .95 .65
39 A13 12c rose red .95 .65
40 A13 15c slate ('96) .95 .65

41 A14 16c lilac 3.50 1.75
a. 16c deep greenish blue (error) 110.00
42 A14 20c vermilion ('96) 3.50 1.75
43 A15 24c ol grn, *yel* 2.00 1.10
44 A15 25c yel grn ('96) 2.00 1.40
45 A16 30c steel bl ('96) 6.25 4.50
46 A16 32c grnsh blue 3.50 2.75
a. 32c lilac (error) *110.00*
47 A17 $1 ultra & blk 12.00 9.00
a. $1 blue & black 13.50 11.00
48 A18 $2 brown, *yel* 9.00 8.00
49 A19 $5 carmine & blk 10.00 10.00
a. Center inverted 400.00 400.00
Nos. 33-49 (17) 59.25 45.70

Many imperforates, part-perforated and mis-perforated varieties exist.

The 1c, 2c and 4c were issued in sheets of 60; 6c, sheet of 40; 8c, 10c, sheets of 30; 12c, 15c, 24c, 25c, sheets of 20; 16c, 20c, 30c, sheets of 15; $1, $2, $5, sheets of 10.

For overprints & surcharges see Nos. 50, 64B-64F, 66, 71-77, 79-81, 85-93, 95-100, 160, O1-O13, O15-O25, O37-O41, O44-O45.

No. 36 Surcharged

a

b

1893

50 A11 (a) 5c on 6c blue grn 1.75 1.10
a. "5" with short flag 6.00 6.00
b. Both 5's with short flags 5.00 5.00
c. "i" dot omitted 19.00 19.00
d. Surcharge "b" 30.00 30.00

"Commerce," Globe and Krumen — A22

1894 Unwmk. Engr. *Imperf.*

52 A22 5c carmine & blk 5.00 5.00

Rouletted

53 A22 5c carmine & blk 10.00 7.50

For overprints see Nos. 69, O26-O27.

Oil Palm A23

Hippopotamus A24

Elephant — A25

Liberty — A26

1897-1905 Wmk. 143 *Perf. 14 to 16*

54 A23 1c lilac rose 1.00 .65
a. 1c violet 1.00 .65
55 A23 1c dp grn ('00) 1.25 .95
56 A23 1c lt green ('05) 3.00 1.60
57 A24 2c bister & blk 3.00 1.60
58 A24 2c org red & blk ('00) 6.00 2.10
59 A24 2c rose & blk ('05) 3.00 1.60
60 A25 5c lake & black 3.00 1.60
a. 5c lilac rose & black 3.00 1.60
61 A25 5c gray bl & blk ('00) 6.00 5.00
62 A25 5c ultra & blk ('05) 4.25 2.75
a. Center inverted 1,600.
63 A26 50c red brn & blk 4.00 3.50
Nos. 54-63 (10) 34.50 21.35

For overprints & surcharges see Nos. 65, 66A-68. 70, 78, 82-84, M1, O28-O36, O42, O92.

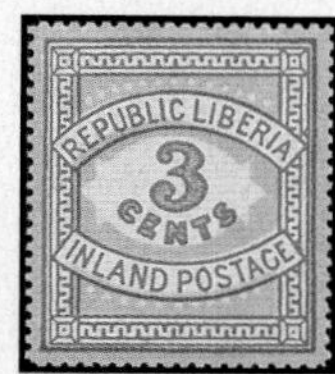
A27

Two types:
I — 13 pearls above "Republic Liberia."
II — 10 pearls.

1897 Unwmk. Litho. *Perf. 14*

64 A27 3c red & green (I) .25 *.60*
a. Type II *20.00* .25

No. 64a is considered a reprint, unissued. "Used" examples are CTO.

For surcharge see No. 128.

Official Stamps Handstamped in Black

1901-02 Wmk. 143

On Nos. O7-O8, O10-O12

64B A14 16c lilac *525.00 525.00*
64C A15 24c ol grn, *yel* *575.00 400.00*
64D A17 $1 blue & blk *3,000. 2,000.*
64E A18 $2 brown, *yel* — —
64F A19 $5 car & blk — —

On Stamps with "O S" Printed

65 A23 1c green *37.50 40.00*
66 A9 2c blue *100.00 100.00*
66A A24 2c bister & blk — *150.00*
67 A24 2c org red & blk *45.00 40.00*
68 A25 5c gray bl & blk *37.50 35.00*
69 A22 5c vio & grn (No. O26) *300.00 300.00*
70 A25 5c lake & blk *275.00 225.00*
71 A12 10c yel & blue blk *37.50 60.00*
a. "O S" omitted —
72 A13 15c slate *40.00 60.00*
73 A14 16c lilac *550.00 350.00*
74 A14 20c vermilion *42.50 50.00*
75 A15 24c ol grn,*yel* *52.50 50.00*
76 A15 25c yellow grn *42.50 50.00*
a. "O S" omitted *750.00*
77 A16 30c steel blue *42.50 40.00*
78 A26 50c red brn & blk *100.00 52.50*
79 A17 $1 ultra & blk *325.00 275.00*
a. "O S" omitted
80 A18 $2 brn, *yel* *2,000. 1,800.*
81 A19 $5 car & blk *2,500. 2,000.*
a. "O S" omitted *3,000. 2,750.*

On Stamps with "O S" Handstamped

82 A23 1c deep green 62.50 —
83 A24 2c org red & blk 75.00 —
84 A25 5c lake & blk 200.00 —
85 A12 10c yel & bl blk 125.00 —
86 A14 20c vermilion 140.00 —
87 A15 24c ol grn, *yel* 140.00 —
88 A15 25c yel grn 160.00 —
89 A16 30c steel blue 525.00 —
90 A16 32c grnsh blue 210.00 —

Varieties of Nos. 65-90 include double and inverted overprints.

Nos. 47, O10, O23a Surcharged in Carmine

1902

91 A17 75c on $1 #47 15.00 13.00
a. Thin "C" and comma 25.00 25.00
b. Inverted surcharge 62.50 62.50
c. As "a," inverted
92 A17 75c on $1 #O10 *2,750.*
a. Thin "C" and comma *4,250.*
93 A17 75c on $1 #O23a *4,000.*
a. Thin "C" and comma *5,250.*

Liberty — A29

1903 Unwmk. Engr. *Perf. 14*

94 A29 3c black .30 .25
a. Printed on both sides 50.00
b. Perf. 12 20.00 6.00

For overprint see No. O43.

Stamps of 1892 Surcharged in Blue

a

b

1903 Wmk. 143

95 A14 (a) 10c on 16c lilac 3.00 5.00
96 A15 (b) 15c on 24c ol grn, *yel* 4.50 6.00
97 A16 (b) 20c on 32c grnsh bl 6.25 8.50
Nos. 95-97 (3) 13.75 19.50

Nos. 50, O3 and 45 Surcharged in Black or Red

1904

98 A11 1c on 5c on 6c bl grn .70 .55
a. "5" with short flag 4.25 4.25
b. Both 5's with short flags 8.75 8.75
c. "i" dot omitted 10.00 10.00
d. Surcharge on #50d 15.00 15.00
e. Inverted surcharge 7.50 7.50
99 A10 2c on 4c grn & blk 2.75 4.00
a. Pair, one without surcharge 35.00
b. Double surcharge *50.00*
c. Double surcharge, red and blk 62.50
d. Surcharged on back also 25.00
e. "Official" overprint missing 35.00
100 A16 2c on 30c stl bl (R) 9.50 15.00
Nos. 98-100 (3) 12.95 19.55

African Elephant — A33

Mercury — A34

Chimpanzee A35

Great Blue Touraco — A36

Agama — A37

Egret — A38

Head of Liberty From Coin — A39

A40

Liberian Flag — A41

Pygmy Hippopotamus A42

Liberty with Star of Liberia on Cap — A43

Mandingos — A44

Executive Mansion and Pres. Arthur Barclay — A45

1906 Unwmk. Engr. *Perf. 14*

101	A33	1c green & blk	1.50	.50
102	A34	2c carmine & blk	.30	.25
103	A35	5c ultra & blk	2.75	.85
104	A36	10c red brn & blk	10.00	.85
105	A37	15c pur & dp grn	14.50	3.00
106	A38	20c orange & blk	8.50	2.50
107	A39	25c dull blue & gray	.85	.25
108	A40	30c deep violet	1.00	.25
109	A41	50c dp grn & blk	1.00	.25
110	A42	75c brown & blk	12.00	2.50
111	A43	$1 rose & gray	3.00	.25

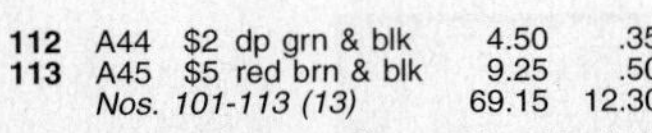

112	A44	$2 dp grn & blk	4.50	.35
113	A45	$5 red brn & blk	9.25	.50
		Nos. 101-113 (13)	69.15	12.30

For surcharges see Nos. 114, 129, 130, 141, 145-149, 161, M2, M5, O72-O73, O82-O85, O96. For overprints see Nos. O46-O58.

Center Inverted

101a	A33	1c	110.00	55.00
102a	A34	2c	120.00	35.00
103a	A35	5c	175.00	175.00
104a	A36	10c	80.00	80.00
105a	A37	15c	175.00	175.00
106b	A38	20c	175.00	175.00
107a	A39	25c	75.00	75.00
109b	A41	50c	75.00	75.00
110b	A42	75c	125.00	125.00
111a	A43	$1	100.00	100.00
112a	A44	$2	95.00	95.00

Imperf., Pairs

101b	A33	1c	13.50	
102b	A34	2c	5.50	
106a	A38	20c	20.00	
107b	A39	25c	55.00	45.00
109a	A41	50c	20.00	
110a	A42	75c	20.00	
113a	A45	$5	27.00	

No. 104 Surcharged in Black

1909

114	A36	3c on 10c red brn & blk	6.00	6.00

Coffee Plantation — A46

Pres. Barclay — A47

S. S. Pres. Daniel E. Howard, former Gunboat Lark — A48

Commerce with Caduceus — A49

Vai Woman Spinning Cotton — A50

Blossom and Fruit of Pepper Plants — A51

Circular House — A52

President Barclay — A53

Men in Canoe — A54

Liberian Village — A55

1909-12 *Perf. 14*

115	A46	1c yel grn & blk	.70	.55
116	A47	2c lake & blk	.70	.55
117	A48	5c ultra & blk	.70	.55
118	A49	10c plum & blk, perf. 12½ ('12)	.70	.55
a.		Imperf., pair	19.00	
b.		Perf 14 ('12)	2.25	2.25
c.		As "b," pair, imperf between	27.50	
d.		Perf 12½x14	2.75	2.25
119	A50	15c indigo & blk	3.50	.60
120	A51	20c rose & grn	4.50	.60
b.		Imperf.		
121	A52	25c dk brn & blk	1.40	.60
a.		Imperf.		
122	A53	30c dark brown	4.50	.60
123	A54	50c green & blk	4.50	.60
124	A55	75c red brn & blk	4.50	.60
		Nos. 115-124 (10)	25.70	5.80

Rouletted

125	A49	10c plum & blk	.75	.45

For surcharges see Nos. 126-127E, 131-133, 136-140, 142-144, 151-156, 162, B1-B2, M3-M4, M6-M7, O70-O1, O74-O81, O86-O91, O97.

For overprints see Nos. O59-O69.

Center Inverted

116a	A47	2c	70.00	60.00
117a	A48	5c	62.50	55.00
119a	A50	15c	100.00	60.00
120a	A51	20c	70.00	55.00
121b	A52	25c	47.50	42.50
123a	A54	50c	95.00	80.00

Stamps and Types of 1909-12 Surcharged in Blue or Red

1910-12 *Rouletted*

126	A49	3c on 10c plum & blk (Bl)	.40	.25
a.		"3" inverted		
126B	A49	3c on 10c blk & ultra (R)	30.00	5.00

No. 126B is roulette 7. It also exists in roulette 13.

Perf. 12½, 14, 12½x14

127	A49	3c on 10c plum & blk (Bl) ('12)	.40	.25
a.		Imperf., pair	22.50	
b.		Double surcharge, one invtd.	22.50	
c.		Double vertical surcharge		
127E	A49	3c on 10c blk & ultra (R) ('12)	17.00	.55
		Nos. 126-127E (4)	47.80	6.05

Nos. 64, 64a Surcharged in Dark Green

1913

128	A27	8c on 3c red & grn (I)	.30	.25
a.		Surcharge on No. 64a	3.00	.25
b.		Double surcharge	6.25	
c.		Imperf., pair	20.00	
d.		Inverted surcharge	25.00	

Stamps of Preceding Issues Surcharged

a

b

1914 On Issue of 1906

129	A39 (a)	2c on 25c dl bl & gray	11.50	3.25
130	A40 (b)	5c on 30c dp vio	11.50	3.25

On Issue of 1909

131	A52 (a)	2c on 25c brn & blk	11.50	3.25
132	A53 (b)	5c on 30c dk brown	11.50	3.25
133	A54 (a)	10c on 50c grn & blk	11.50	3.25
		Nos. 129-133 (5)	57.50	16.25

Liberian House A57

Providence Island, Monrovia Harbor A58

1915 Engr. Wmk. 116 *Perf. 14*

134	A57	2c red	.25	.25
135	A58	3c dull violet	.25	.25

For overprints see Nos. 196-197, O113-O114, O128-O129.

Nos. 109, 111-113, 119-124 Surcharged in Dark Blue, Black or Red

c

d

e

f

g

1915-16 Unwmk.

136	A50 (c)	2c on 15c (R)	.90	.90
137	A52 (d)	2c on 25c (R)	8.50	8.50
138	A51 (e)	5c on 20c (Bk)	1.10	6.25
139	A53 (f)	5c on 30c (R)	4.50	4.50
a.		Double surcharge	15.00	15.00
140	A53 (g)	5c on 30c (R)	40.00	40.00

h

i

141 A41 (h) 10c on 50c (R) 8.00 8.00
- *a.* Double surch., one invtd.

142 A54 (i) 10c on 50c (R) 15.00 15.00
- *a.* Double surcharge red & blk 50.00 35.00
- *b.* Blue surcharge 35.00 35.00

143 A54 (i) 10c on 50c (Bk) 20.00 15.00

j

k

144 A55 (j) 20c on 75c (Bk) 4.00 7.50

145 A43 (k) 25c on $1 (Bk) 42.50 42.50

l m

146 A44 (l) 50c on $2 (R) 12.00 12.00
- *a.* "Ceuts" 30.00 22.50

147 A44 (m) 50c on $2 (R) 800.00 800.00

n

148 A45 $1 on $5 (Bk) 65.00 65.00
- *a.* Double surcharge 90.00 90.00

o

149 A45 $1 on $5 (R) 52.50 52.50

The color of the red surcharge varies from light dull red to almost brown.

Handstamped Surcharge, Type "i"

150 A54 10c on 50c (Dk Bl) 14.00 14.00

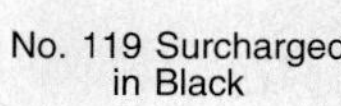

No. 119 Surcharged in Black

151 A50 2c on 15c 650.00 650.00

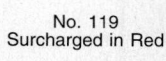

No. 119 Surcharged in Red

152 A50 2c on 15c 45.00 40.00
- *a.* Double surcharge 92.50

Nos. 116-117 Surcharged in Black or Red

a b

c d

e f

g h

i j

k

l

m

n

o

p

q

r

s

t

Types A-J are for No. 153. Types K-T are for No. 154.

153 A47 1c on 2c lake & blk 2.50 2.50
- *a.* Strip of 10 types 35.00

154 A48 2c on 5c ultra & blk (R) 3.50 2.50
- *a.* Black surcharge 14.00 14.00
- *b.* Strip of 10 types (R) 35.00
- *c.* Strip of 10 types (Bk) 175.00

The 10 types of surcharge are repeated in illustrated sequence on 1c on 2c in each horiz. row and on 2c on 5c in each vert. row of sheets of 100 (10x10).

No. 116 and Type of 1909 Surcharged

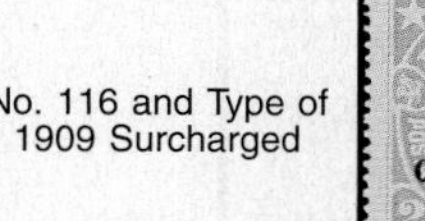

155 A47 1c on 2c lake & blk 190.00 190.00

No. 117 Surcharged

156 A48 2c on 5c turq & blk 140.00 140.00

Nos. 18-20 Surcharged

1916

157 A1 3c on 6c violet 45.00 45.00
- *a.* Inverted surcharge 100.00 75.00

158 A1 5c on 12c yellow 3.00 3.00
- *a.* Inverted surcharge 17.50 17.50
- *b.* Surcharge sideways 17.50

159 A1 10c on 24c rose red 2.75 3.00
- *a.* Inverted surcharge 15.00 15.00
- *b.* Surcharge sideways 20.00

Nos. 157-159 (3) 50.75 51.00

Unused values for Nos. 157-159 are for examples without gum.

Nos. 44 and 108 Surcharged

p

r

1917 **Wmk. 143**

160 A15 (p) 4c on 25c yel grn 12.00 12.00
- *a.* "OUR" 27.50 27.50
- *b.* "FCUR" 27.50 27.50

Unwmk.

161 A40 (r) 5c on 30c dp vio 90.00 90.00

No. 118 Surcharged in Red

1918

162 A49 3c on 10c plum & blk 2.75 4.25
- *a.* "3" inverted 9.25 9.25

Bongo Antelope — A59

Symbols of Liberia — A61

Two-spot Palm Civet A60

A62

Palm-nut Vulture — A66

Oil Palm — A63

Mercury — A64

Traveler's Tree — A65

"Mudskipper" or Bommi Fish — A67

Mandingos A68

"Liberia" A71

Coast Scene A69

Liberia College A70

1918 **Engr.** ***Perf. 12½, 14***

163 A59 1c dp grn & blk .65 .25
164 A60 2c rose & blk .80 .25
165 A61 5c gray bl & blk .25 .25
166 A62 10c dark green .25 .25
167 A63 15c blk & dk grn 3.00 .25
168 A64 20c claret & blk .35 .25
169 A65 25c dk grn & grn 3.25 .25
170 A66 30c red vio & blk 15.00 .80
171 A67 50c ultra & blk 26.50 3.50
172 A68 75c ol bis & blk .90 .25
173 A69 $1 yel brn & bl 7.25 .25
174 A70 $2 lt vio & blk 6.50 .25
175 A71 $5 dark brown 7.00 .40
Nos. 163-175 (13) 71.70 7.20

For surcharges see Nos. 176-177, 228-229, 248-270, B3-B15, O111-O112, O155-O157.
For overprints see Nos. O98-O110.

Nos. 163-164, F10-F14 Surcharged

1920

176 A59 3c on 1c grn & blk 1.10 1.10
a. "CEETS" 17.00 17.00
b. Double surcharge 10.00 10.00
c. Triple surcharge 15.00 15.00
177 A60 4c on 2c rose & blk 1.10 1.10
a. Inverted surcharge 20.00 20.00
b. Double surcharge 10.00 10.00
c. Double surcharge, one invtd. 18.00
d. Triple surcharge, one inverted 25.00 25.00
e. Quadruple surcharge 30.00 30.00
f. Typewritten surcharge
g. Same as "f" but inverted
h. Printed and typewritten surcharges, both inverted
178 R6 5c on 10c bl & blk 2.50 2.75
a. Inverted surcharge 10.00 10.00
b. Double surcharge 10.00 10.00
c. Double surcharge, one invtd. 15.00 15.00
d. Typewritten surcharge ("five") 100.00
e. Printed and typewritten surcharges 100.00
179 R6 5c on 10c org red & blk 2.50 2.75
a. 5c on 10c orange & black 4.00 2.75
b. Inverted surcharge 15.00
c. Double surcharge 15.00
d. Double surcharge, one invtd. 18.00 15.00
e. Typewritten surch. in violet 100.00 100.00
f. Typewritten surch. in black
g. Printed and typewritten surcharges 100.00
180 R6 5c on 10c grn & blk 2.50 2.75
a. Double surcharge 10.00 10.00
b. Double surcharge, one invtd. 18.00 18.00
c. Inverted surcharge 18.00
d. Quadruple surcharge 25.00 25.00
e. Typewritten surcharge 100.00
f. Printed and typewritten surcharges
181 R6 5c on 10c vio & blk (Monrovia) 4.00 5.00
a. Double surcharge, one invtd. 25.00 25.00
182 R6 5c on 10c mag & blk (Robertsport) 2.25 2.40
a. Double surcharge 15.00 15.00
b. Double surcharge, one invtd. 15.00 15.00
c. Double surcharge, both invtd. 25.00
Nos. 176-182 (7) 15.95 17.85

Cape Mesurado A75

Pres. Daniel E. Howard — A76

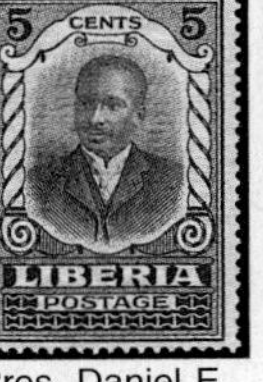

Arms of Liberia — A77

Crocodile A78

Pepper Plant — A79

Leopard A80

Village Scene — A81

Krumen in Dugout A82

Rapids in St. Paul's River — A83

Bongo Antelope A84

Hornbill A85

Elephant A86

1921 **Wmk. 116** ***Perf. 14***

183 A75 1c green .25 .25
184 A76 5c dp bl & blk .25 .25
185 A77 10c red & dl bl .25 .25
186 A78 15c dl vio & grn 6.50 .55
187 A79 20c rose red & grn 2.75 .25
188 A80 25c org & blk 7.50 .55
189 A81 30c grn & dl vio .40 .25
190 A82 50c org & ultra .45 .25
191 A83 75c red & blk brn .80 .25
a. Center inverted 70.00
192 A84 $1 red & blk 20.00 1.75
193 A85 $2 yel & ultra 16.00 1.25
194 A86 $5 car rose & vio 32.50 1.50
Nos. 183-194 (12) 87.65 7.35

For overprints see Nos. 195, 198-208, O115-O127, O130-O140.

Nos. 134-135, 183-194 Ovptd.

195 A75 1c green 22.50 .40
196 A57 2c red 22.50 .40
197 A58 3c dull violet 32.50 .40
198 A76 5c dp bl & blk 3.50 .30
199 A77 10c red & dull bl 50.00 .40
200 A78 15c dull vio & grn 22.50 1.40
201 A79 20c rose red & grn, ovpt. invtd. 7.25 .75
202 A80 25c orange & blk 22.50 1.40
203 A81 30c grn & dull vio 2.50 .30
204 A82 50c orange & ultra 3.50 .30
205 A83 75c red & blk brn 4.75 .30
206 A84 $1 red & blk 62.50 2.10
207 A85 $2 yellow & ultra 22.50 2.10
208 A86 $5 car rose & vio 60.00 2.75
Nos. 195-208 (14) 339.00 13.30

Overprint exists inverted in Nos. 195-208 and normal on No. 201.

First Settlers Landing at Cape Mesurado from U. S. S. Alligator A87

1923 **Litho.**

209 A87 1c lt blue & blk 18.00 .45
210 A87 2c claret & ol gray 26.00 .45
211 A87 5c ol grn & ind 26.00 .45
212 A87 10c bl grn & vio 1.00 .45
213 A87 $1 rose & brn 3.25 .45
Nos. 209-213 (5) 74.25 2.25

Centenary of founding of Liberia.

Memorial to J. J. Roberts, 1st Pres. — A88

Hall of Representatives, Monrovia — A89

Liberian Star — A90

A91

Pres. Charles Dunbar Burgess King — A92

Hippopotamus — A93

Antelope A94

West African Buffalo A95

Grebos Making Dumboy A96

Pineapple A97

Carrying Ivory Tusk A98

Rubber Planter's House — A99

Stockton Lagoon — A100

Grebo Houses — A101

1923 *Perf. 13½x14½, 14½x13½*

White Paper

214	A88	1c yel grn & dp grn	7.50	1.25
215	A89	2c claret & brn	7.50	.25
216	A90	3c lilac & blk	.35	.25
217	A91	5c bl vio & blk	115.00	.25
218	A92	10c slate & brn	.35	.25
219	A93	15c bister & bl	35.00	.50
220	A94	20c bl grn & vio	2.50	.35
221	A95	25c org red & brn	160.00	.60
222	A96	30c dk brn & vio	.60	.25
223	A97	50c dull vio & org	1.25	.25
224	A98	75c gray & bl	1.90	.40
225	A99	$1 dp red & dk vio	30.00	.60
226	A100	$2 orange & blue	7.50	.80
227	A101	$5 dp grn & brn	30.00	.55
		Nos. 214-227 (14)	399.45	6.55

Brownish Paper

222a	A96	30c dk brn & vio	.60	.25
223a	A97	50c dull vio & org	1.00	.25
224a	A98	75c gray & bl	1.90	.45
225a	A99	$1 dp red & dk vio	4.50	.60
226a	A100	$2 orange & blue	5.75	.60
227a	A101	$5 dp grn & brn	8.00	.90

Nos. 222-227 also exist on a light buff paper. Values are the same as for examples on brownish paper.

For overprints see Nos. O141-O154.

No. 163 Surcharged in Black

1926 **Unwmk.** ***Perf. 14***

228 A59 2c on 1c dp grn & blk	3.50	3.50
a. Surcharge with ornamental design as on #O155	17.00	

No. 163 Surcharged in Red

1927

229 A59 2c on 1c dp grn & blk	9.50	9.50
a. "Ceuts"	14.00	
b. "Vwo"	14.00	
c. "Twc"	14.00	
d. Double surcharge	27.50	
e. Wavy lines omitted	17.50	

Palms A102

Map of Africa — A103

President King — A104

1928 **Engr.** ***Perf. 12***

230	A102	1c green	.75	.50
231	A102	2c dark violet	.50	.35
232	A102	3c bister brn	.50	.35
a.		Horiz. pair, imperf vert.		—
233	A103	5c ultra	1.00	.55
234	A104	10c olive gray	1.40	.55
235	A103	15c dull violet	6.25	2.25
236	A103	$1 red brown	77.50	26.50
		Nos. 230-236 (7)	87.90	31.05

For surcharges & overprints see Nos. 288A, 289A, 290A-291, 292A, C1-C3, O158-O165. Post 1940 issues are in Scott Standard catalogue, Vol. 4.

Nos. 164-168, 170-175 Surcharged in Various Colors and Styles

No. 248

No. 250

1936 ***Perf. 12½, 14***

248	A60	1c on 2c (Bl)	.55	*3.50*
249	A61	3c on 5c (Bl)	.25	*2.00*
250	A62	4c on 10c (Br)	.25	*2.00*
251	A63	6c on 15c (Bl)	.55	*3.50*
252	A64	8c on 20c (V)	.25	*2.00*
253	A66	12c on 30c (V)	1.00	*9.75*
254	A67	14c on 50c (Bl)	1.10	*11.00*
255	A68	16c on 75c (Br)	.55	*5.50*
256	A69	18c on $1 (Bk)	.55	*5.50*
a.		22c on $1 yellow brown & blue	7.25	
257	A70	22c on $2 (V)	.75	*7.75*
258	A71	24c on $5 (Bk)	1.00	*9.75*
		Nos. 248-258 (11)	6.80	62.25

Official Stamps, Nos. O99-O110, Srchd. or Ovptd. in Various Colors & Styles

1936

259	A60	1c on 2c (Bl)	.40	*4.00*
260	A61	3c on 5c (Bl)	.40	*4.00*
261	A62	4c on 10c (Bl)	.40	*4.00*
262	A63	6c on 15c (Bl)	.40	*4.00*
263	A64	8c on 20c (V)	.40	*4.00*
264	A66	12c on 30c (V)	1.50	*20.00*
a.		"193" instead of "1936"	19.00	
265	A67	14c on 50c (Bl)	2.00	*21.00*
266	A68	16c on 75c (Bk)	1.00	*12.00*
267	A69	18c on $1 (Bk)	1.00	*12.00*
268	A70	22c on $2 (Bl)	1.25	*15.00*
269	A71	24c on $5 (Bk)	1.50	*17.00*
270	A65	25c (Bk)	2.00	*21.00*
		Nos. 259-270 (12)	12.25	138.00

Hornbill — A106

Designs: 2c, Bushbuck. 3c, West African dwarf buffalo. 4c, Pygmy hippopotamus. 5c, Lesser egret. 6c, Pres. E. J. Barclay.

Perf. Compound of 11½, 12, 12½, 14

1937, Apr. 10 **Engr.** **Unwmk.**

271	A106	1c green & blk	1.50	.45
272	A106	2c carmine & blk	1.50	.45
273	A106	3c violet & blk	1.50	.45
274	A106	4c orange & blk	2.25	.70
275	A106	5c blue & blk	2.25	.65
276	A106	6c green & blk	.80	.25
		Nos. 271-276 (6)	9.80	2.95

Coast Line of Liberia, 1839 A107

Seal of Liberia, Map and Farming Scenes A108

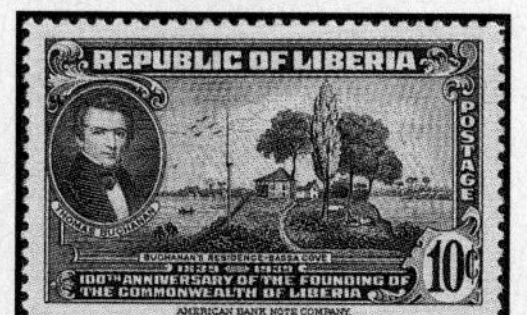

Thomas Buchanan and Residence at Bassa Cove — A109

1940, July 29 **Engr.** ***Perf. 12***

277	A107	3c dark blue	.35	.35
278	A108	5c dull red brn	.35	.35
279	A109	10c dark green	.35	.35
		Nos. 277-279 (3)	1.05	1.05

100th anniv. of the founding of the Commonwealth of Liberia.

For overprints & surcharges see Nos. 280-282, B16-B18, C14-C16, CB1-CB3, CE1, CF1, E1, F35 in the Scott Standard Catalogue, Vol. 4.

SEMI-POSTAL STAMPS

No. 127 Surcharged in Red

1915 **Unwmk.** ***Perf. 14***

B1 A49 2c + 3c on 10c	1.00	*3.50*
a. Double red surcharge		
b. Double blue surcharge		
c. Both surcharges double		
d. Pair, one without "2c"		

Same Surcharge On Official Stamp of 1912

B2 A49 2c + 3c on 10c blk & ultra	1.00	*3.50*
a. Double surcharge		

Regular Issue of 1918 Surcharged in Black and Red

1918 ***Perf. 12½, 14***

B3	A59	1c + 2c dp grn & blk	1.40	*10.50*
B4	A60	2c + 2c rose & blk	1.40	*10.50*
a.		Double surch., one inverted		
b.		Invtd. surch., cross double		
c.		Invtd. surch., cross omitted	17.00	
B5	A61	5c + 2c gray bl & blk	.65	*3.00*
a.		Imperf., pair	19.00	
B6	A62	10c + 2c dk green	1.25	*3.00*
a.		Inverted surcharge	5.75	27.50
B7	A63	15c + 2c blk & dk grn	5.25	10.50
B8	A64	20c + 2c claret & blk	2.10	*8.50*
B9	A65	25c + 2c dk grn & grn	4.25	*15.00*
B10	A66	30c + 2c red vio & blk	10.00	*10.50*
B11	A67	50c + 2c ultra & blk	8.50	*16.00*
B12	A68	75c + 2c ol bis & blk	3.75	*30.00*
B13	A69	$1 + 2c yel brn & bl	6.25	*57.50*
B14	A70	$2 + 2c lt vio & blk	8.50	*80.00*
B15	A71	$5 + 2c dk brown	20.00	*200.00*
		Nos. B3-B15 (13)	73.30	*455.00*

Used values are for postally canceled stamps.

AIR POST STAMPS

Regular Issue of 1928 Srchd. in Black

1936, Feb. 28 **Unwmk.** ***Perf. 12***

C1	A102	6c on 2c violet	250.00	*275.00*
C2	A102	6c on 3c bis brn	250.00	*275.00*

Same Srch. on Official Stamp of 1928

C3	A102	6c on 1c green	250.00	*275.00*
m.		On No. 230 (error)	*750.00*	
		Nos. C1-C3 (3)	750.00	825.00

Values are for stamps with disturbed gum. Many counterfeits exist.

Waco Plane — AP1

1936, Sept. 30 Engr. *Perf. 14*

No.	Type	Description	Unused	Used
C3A	AP1	1c yellow grn & blk	.30	.30
C3B	AP1	2c carmine & blk	.30	.30
C3C	AP1	3c purple & blk	.30	.30
C3D	AP1	4c orange & blk	.30	.30
C3E	AP1	5c blue & blk	.30	.30
C3F	AP1	6c green & blk	.30	.30
		Nos. C3A-C3F (6)	1.80	1.80

Liberia's 1st air mail service of Feb. 28, 1936.

Nos. C3A-C3F exist in pairs imperf. between (value, $50 each) and in pairs imperf. (value $15 each).

Eagle in Flight — AP2

Trimotor Plane AP3

Egrets — AP4

Sikorsky Amphibian — AP5

Designs: 3c, 30c, Albatross.

1938, Sept. 12 Photo. *Perf. 12½*

No.	Type	Description	Unused	Used
C4	AP2	1c green	.25	.25
C5	AP3	2c red orange	.40	.25
C6	AP3	3c olive green	.50	.25
C7	AP4	4c orange	.60	.25
C8	AP4	5c brt blue grn	1.00	.25
C9	AP3	10c violet	1.00	.25
C10	AP5	20c magenta	1.25	.25
C11	AP3	30c gray black	2.25	.25
C12	AP2	50c brown	3.00	.25
C13	AP5	$1 blue	5.25	.25
		Nos. C4-C13 (10)	15.50	2.50

For surcharges see Nos. C17-C36, C45-C46, C47-C48, C49-C50 in Scott Standard catalogue, Vol. 4.

REGISTRATION STAMPS

R1

1893 Unwmk. Litho. *Perf. 14, 15*
Without Value Surcharged

No.	Type	Description	Unused	Used
F1	R1	(10c) blk (Buchanan)	250.	250.
F2	R1	(10c) blk (Greenville)	*2,500.*	—
F3	R1	(10c) blk (Harper)	*2,500.*	—
F4	R1	(10c) blk (Monrovia)	30.	30.
F5	R1	(10c) blk (Robertsport)	1,000.	1,000.

Types of 1893 Surcharged in Black

1894 *Perf. 14*

No.	Type	Description	Unused	Used
F6	R1	10c bl, *pink* (Buchanan)	5.50	5.50
F7	R1	10c grn, *buff* (Harper)	5.50	5.50
F8	R1	10c red, *yel* (Monrovia)	5.50	5.50
F9	R1	10c rose, *blue* (Robertsport)	5.50	5.50
		Nos. F6-F9 (4)	22.00	22.00

Exist imperf or missing one 10. Value, each $10.

President Garretson W. Gibson — R6

1903 Engr. *Perf. 14*

No.	Type	Description	Unused	Used
F10	R6	10c bl & blk (Buchanan)	1.75	.25
a.		Center inverted	100.00	
F11	R6	10c org red & blk ("Grenville")	1.75	
a.		Center inverted	100.00	
b.		10c orange & black	1.90	.25
F12	R6	10c grn & blk (Harper)	1.75	.25
a.		Center inverted	100.00	
F13	R6	10c vio & blk (Monrovia)	1.75	.25
a.		Center inverted	100.00	
b.		10c lilac & black	1.90	
F14	R6	10c magenta & blk (Robertsport)	1.75	.25
a.		Center inverted	100.00	
		Nos. F10-F14 (5)	8.75	
		Nos. F10, F11b, F12-F14		.75

For surcharges see Nos. 178-182.

S.S. Quail on Patrol — R7

1919 Litho. *Serrate Roulette 12*

No.	Type	Description	Unused	Used
F15	R7	10c blk & bl (Buchanan)	1.40	2.75

Serrate Roulette 12, Perf. 14

No.	Type	Description	Unused	Used
F16	R7	10c ocher & blk ("Grenville")	1.40	2.75
F17	R7	10c grn & blk (Harper)	1.40	2.75
F18	R7	10c vio & bl (Monrovia)	1.40	2.75
F19	R7	10c rose & blk (Robertsport)	1.40	2.75
		Nos. F15-F19 (5)	7.00	13.75

Gabon Viper — R8

Wmk. Crosses and Circles (116)
1921 Engr. *Perf. 13x14*

No.	Type	Description	Unused	Used
F20	R8	10c cl & blk (Buchanan)	90.00	3.50
F21	R8	10c red & blk (Greenville)	22.50	3.50
F22	R8	10c ultra & blk (Harper)	22.50	3.50
F23	R8	10c org & blk (Monrovia)	22.50	3.50
a.		Imperf., pair	225.00	
F24	R8	10c grn & blk (Robertsport)	22.50	3.50
a.		Imperf., pair	225.00	
		Nos. F20-F24 (5)	180.00	17.50

Nos. F-20-F24 Overprinted in Black

No.	Type	Description	Unused	Used
F25	R8	10c (Buchanan)	25.00	6.25
F26	R8	10c (Greenville)	25.00	6.25
F27	R8	10c (Harper)	70.00	6.25
F28	R8	10c (Monrovia)	25.00	6.25
F29	R8	10c (Robertsport)	25.00	6.25
		Nos. F25-F29 (5)	170.00	31.25

Nos. F25-F29 exist with "1921" inverted. Value same as normal.

Passengers Going Ashore from Ship — R9

Designs: No. F31, Transporting merchandise, shore to ship (Greenville). No. F32, Sailing ship (Harper). No. F33, Ocean liner (Monrovia). No. F34, Canoe in surf (Robertsport).

1924 Litho. *Perf. 14*

No.	Type	Description	Unused	Used
F30	R9	10c gray & carmine	7.00	.60
F31	R9	10c gray & blue grn	7.00	.60
F32	R9	10c gray & orange	7.00	.60
F33	R9	10c gray & blue	7.00	.60
F34	R9	10c gray & violet	7.00	.60
		Nos. F30-F34 (5)	35.00	3.00

POSTAGE DUE STAMPS

Nos. 26, 28 Surcharged

1892 Unwmk. *Perf. 11*

No.	Type	Description	Unused	Used
J1	A5	3c on 3c violet	6.50	4.25
a.		Imperf., pair	30.00	
b.		Inverted surcharge	45.00	45.00
c.		As "a," inverted surcharge	110.00	

Perf. 12

No.	Type	Description	Unused	Used
J2	A5	6c on 6c olive gray	15.00	13.50
a.		Imperf., pair	40.00	
b.		Inverted surcharge	52.50	35.00

D2

Engr.; Figures of Value Typographed in Black
1893 Wmk. 143 *Perf. 14, 15*

No.	Type	Description	Unused	Used
J3	D2	2c org, *yel*	2.00	1.00
J4	D2	4c rose, *rose*	2.00	1.00
J5	D2	6c brown, *buff*	2.00	1.25
J6	D2	8c blue, *blue*	2.00	1.25
J7	D2	10c grn, *lil rose*	2.25	1.50
J8	D2	20c vio, *gray*	2.25	1.50
a.		Center inverted	110.00	110.00
J9	D2	40c ol brn, *grnsh*	4.50	3.00
		Nos. J3-J9 (7)	17.00	10.50

All values of the above set exist imperforate. Each value also exists with center inverted.

MILITARY STAMPS

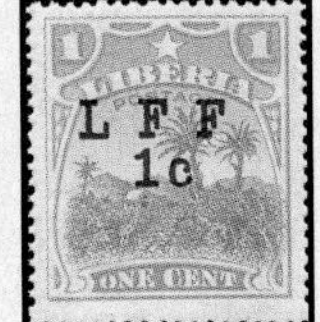

Issues of 1905, 1906 and 1909 Surcharged

1916 Wmk. 143

No.	Type	Description	Unused	Used
M1	A23	1c on 1c lt grn	190.00	190.00
a.		2nd "F" inverted	250.00	250.00
b.		"FLF"	250.00	250.00
c.		Inverted surcharge	250.00	250.00

Unwmk.

No.	Type	Description	Unused	Used
M2	A33	1c on 1c grn & blk	600.00	550.00
a.		2nd "F" inverted	700.00	600.00
b.		"FLF"	700.00	600.00
M3	A46	1c on 1c yel grn & blk	4.00	4.75
a.		2nd "F" inverted	7.50	7.50
b.		"FLF"	7.50	7.50
M4	A47	1c on 2c lake & blk	4.00	4.75
a.		2nd "F" inverted	7.50	7.50
b.		"FLF"	7.50	7.50

Surcharge exists sideways on Nos. M2, M5; double on Nos. M1-M4; inverted on Nos. M2-M4.

Nos. O46, O59-O60 Surcharged

No.	Type	Description	Unused	Used
M5	A33	1c on 1c	500.00	475.00
a.		2nd "F" inverted	700.00	650.00
b.		"FLF"	700.00	650.00
M6	A46	1c on 1c	4.75	5.50
a.		2nd "F" inverted	9.00	9.00
b.		"FLF"	9.00	9.00
c.		"LFF 1c" inverted	12.50	12.50
d.		As "a" and "1c" inverted		15.00
e.		"FLF 1c" inverted		15.00
M7	A47	1c on 2c	3.25	4.00
a.		2nd "F" inverted	6.50	6.50
b.		"FLF"	6.50	6.50
c.		Pair, one without "LFF 1c"		

OFFICIAL STAMPS

Types of Regular Issues Overprinted in Various Colors

Perf. 12½ to 15 and Compound
1892 Wmk. 143

No.	Type	Description	Unused	Used
O1	A9	1c vermilion	.80	.80
O2	A9	2c blue	.80	.80
O3	A10	4c grn & blk	.80	.80
O4	A11	6c bl grn	.80	.80
O5	A12	8c brn & blk	.80	.80
O6	A13	12c rose red	2.00	2.00
O7	A14	16c red lilac	2.00	2.00
O8	A15	24c ol grn, *yel*	2.00	2.00
O9	A16	32c grnsh bl	2.00	2.00
O10	A17	$1 bl & blk	40.00	16.00
O11	A18	$2 brn, *yel*	16.00	11.50
O12	A19	$5 car & blk	24.00	9.00
		Nos. O1-O12 (12)	92.00	48.50

a

"5" With Short Flag

1893

O13 A11 5c on 6c bl grn (a) (No. 50) 1.20 1.20
a. "5" with short flag 6.00 6.00
b. Both 5's with short flags 6.00 6.00
c. "i" dot omitted 20.00 20.00
d. Overprinted on #50d 45.00 45.00

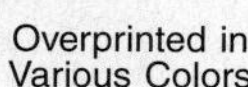
Overprinted in Various Colors

1894

O15 A9 1c vermilion .70 .35
O16 A9 2c blue .85 .40
a. Imperf.
O17 A10 4c grn & blk 1.00 .55
O18 A12 8c brn & blk 1.00 .55
O19 A13 12c rose red 1.40 .60
O20 A14 16c red lilac 1.40 .60
O21 A15 24c ol grn, *yel* 1.40 .70
O22 A16 32c grnsh bl 2.75 .80
O23 A17 $1 bl & blk 27.50 21.00
a. $1 ultra & black 27.50 21.00
O24 A18 $2 brn, *yel* 27.50 21.00
O25 A19 $5 car & blk 125.00 87.50
Nos. O15-O25 (11) 190.50 134.05

Unwmk.

Imperf

O26 A22 5c vio & grn 3.50 2.25

Rouletted

O27 A22 5c vio & grn 3.50 2.25

Regular Issue of 1896-1905 Overprinted in Black or Red

1898-1905 Wmk. 143 *Perf. 14, 15*

O28 A23 1c lil rose .90 .90
O29 A23 1c dp grn ('00) .90 .90
O30 A23 1c lt grn (R) ('05) .90 .90
O31 A24 2c bis & blk 1.75 .60
a. Pair, one without overprint *900.00*
O32 A24 2c org red & blk ('00) 2.75 1.50
O33 A24 2c rose & blk ('05) 4.50 2.75
O34 A25 5c lake & blk 3.00 1.50
O35 A25 5c gray bl & blk ('00) 3.50 1.50
O36 A25 5c ultra & blk (R) ('05) 6.00 3.75
O37 A12 10c chr yel & ind 1.75 1.75
O38 A13 15c slate 1.75 1.75
O39 A14 20c vermilion 3.00 2.10
O40 A15 25c yel grn 1.75 1.75
O41 A16 30c steel blue 4.50 2.75
O42 A26 50c red brn & blk 4.50 2.75
Nos. O28-O42 (15) 41.45 27.15

For surcharge see No. O92.

Official stamps overprinted "ORDINARY" or with a bar with an additional surcharge are listed as Nos. 64B-90, 92-93, 99.

Red Overprint

1903 Unwmk. *Perf. 14*

O43 A29 3c green .25 .25
a. Overprint omitted 5.00
b. Inverted overprint

Two overprint types: I — Thin, sharp, dark red. II — Thick, heavier, orange red. Same value.

No. 50 Surcharged in Black

No. 45 Surcharged in Red

1904 Wmk. 143

O44 A11 1c on 5c on 6c bl grn 1.60 2.00
a. "5" with short flag 4.25
b. Both "5s" with straight flag 8.00 8.00
O45 A16 2c on 30c steel blue 9.50 9.50
a. Double surcharge, red and black
b. Surcharge also on back

Types of Regular Issue Overprinted in Various Colors

a

1906 Unwmk.

O46 A33 1c grn & blk (R) .65 .40
O47 A34 2c car & blk (Bl) .25 .25
a. Center and overprint inverted 30.00 3.00
b. Inverted overprint 6.00
O48 A35 5c ultra & blk (Bk) .65 .40
a. Inverted overprint 15.00 15.00
b. Center and overprint invtd. 50.00
O49 A36 10c dl vio & blk (R) .75 .55
a. Inverted overprint 10.00 10.00
b. Center and overprint invtd. 50.00
O50 A37 15c brn & blk (Bk) 3.00 .55
a. Inverted overprint 4.50
b. Overprint omitted 12.00 6.00
c. Center and overprint invtd. 60.00
O51 A38 20c dp grn & blk (R) .75 .55
a. Overprint omitted 15.00
O52 A39 25c plum & gray (Bl) .50 .25
a. With 2nd ovpt. in blue, invtd. 15.00
O53 A40 30c dk brn (Bk) .55 .25
O54 A41 50c org brn & dp grn (G) .75 .25
a. Inverted overprint 5.00 4.00
O55 A42 75c ultra & blk (Bk) 1.40 .95
a. Inverted overprint 9.50 5.75
b. Overprint omitted 22.50
O56 A43 $1 dp grn & gray (R) .90 .25
a. Inverted overprint
O57 A44 $2 plum & blk (Bl) 2.75 .25
a. Overprint omitted 22.50 15.00
O58 A45 $5 org & blk (Bk) 5.50 .25
a. Overprint omitted 11.00
b. Inverted overprint 12.00 8.00
Nos. O46-O58 (13) 18.40 5.15

Nos. O52, O54, O55, O56 and O58 are known with center inverted.

For surcharges see Nos. O72, O82-O85, O96.

b

1909-12

O59 A46 1c emer & blk (R) .40 .25
O60 A47 2c car rose & brn (Bl) .40 .25
a. Overprint omitted
O61 A48 5c turq & blk (Bk) .45 .25
a. Double overprint, one inverted 7.50
O62 A49 10c blk & ultra (R) ('12) .60 .25
O63 A50 15c cl & blk (Bl) .60 .45
O64 A51 20c bis & grn (Bk) 1.10 .55
O65 A52 25c ultra & grn (Bk) 1.10 .55
a. Double overprint 4.75 4.75
O66 A53 30c dk bl (R) .85 .25
O67 A54 50c brn & grn (Bk) 1.40 .40
a. Center inverted 27.50
b. Inverted overprint 4.00 2.75
O68 A55 75c pur & blk (R) 1.50 .25
Nos. O59-O68 (10) 8.40 3.45

Nos. O63, O64, O67 and O68 are known without overprint and with center inverted.

For surcharges see Nos. O74-O81, O86-O90, O97.

Rouletted

O69 A49 10c blk & ultra (R) 1.00 .95

Nos. 126B and 127E Overprinted type "a" ("OS") in Red

1910-12 *Rouletted*

O70 A49 3c on 10c blk & ultra .70 1.25

Perf. 12½, 14, 12½x14

O71 A49 3c on 10c blk & ultra ('12) .70 .40
a. Pair, one without srch., the other with dbl. srch., one invtd.
b. Double surcharge, one inverted 4.00

Stamps of Preceding Issues Srchd. with New Values like Regular Issue and — c

1914 On Nos. O52 and 110

O72 A39 (a) 2c on 25c plum & gray 30.00 10.50
O73 A42 (c) 20c on 75c brn & blk 8.75 5.25

On Nos. O66 and O68

O74 A53 (b) 5c on 30c dk bl 8.75 5.25
O75 A55 (c) 20c on 75c pur & blk (R) 13.00 5.25
Nos. O72-O75 (4) 60.50 26.25

Official Stamps of 1906-09 Surcharged Like Regular Issues of Same Date

1915-16

O76 A50 (c) 2c on 15c (Bk) .95 .50
O77 A52 (d) 2c on 25c (Bk) 5.25 5.25
O78 A51 (e) 5c on 20c (Bk) .95 .65
O79 A53 (g) 5c on 30c (R) 10.00 8.50
O80 A54 (i) 10c on 50c (Bk) 5.50 3.25
O81 A55 (j) 20c on 75c (R) 2.75 2.75
O82 A43 (k) 25c on $1 (R) 20.00 20.00
a. "25" double 25.00
b. "OS" inverted 25.00
O83 A44 (l) 50c on $2 (Bk) 50.00 50.00
a. "Ceuts" 70.00 70.00
O84 A44 (m) 50c on $2 (Br) 22.50 22.50
O85 A45 (n) $1 on $5 (Bk) 21.00 21.00

Handstamped Surcharge

O86 A54 (i) 10c on 50c (Bk) 11.00 11.00

Nos. O60-O61 Surcharged like Nos. 153-154 in Black or Red

a1, b1

c1, d1

e1, f1

g1, h1

i1, j1

O87 A47 1c on 2c 2.75 2.75
Strip of 10 types 30.00
O88 A48 2c on 5c (R) 2.75 2.75
Strip of 10 types (R) 30.00
a. Black surcharge 10.00 10.00
Strip of 10 types (Bk) 140.00

See note following Nos. 153-154.

Nos. O60-O61 Surcharged

O90 A47 1c on 2c 125.00 125.00
O91 A48 2c on 5c 100.00 100.00

No. O42 Surcharged

O92 A26 10c on 50c (Bk) 11.00 11.00

No. O53 Surcharged

1917

O96 A40 5c on 30c dk brn 21.00 21.00
a. "FIV" 35.00 35.00

The editors consider the 1915-17 issues unnecessary and speculative.

No. O62 Surcharged in Red like No. 162

1918

O97 A49 3c on 10c blk & ultra 2.40 2.40

Types of Regular Issue of 1918 Ovptd. Type "a" in Black, Blue or Red

1918 Unwmk. *Perf. 12½, 14*

O98 A59 1c dp grn & red brn (Bk) .60 .25
O99 A60 2c red & blk (Bl) .60 .25
O100 A61 5c ultra & blk (R) 1.10 .25
O101 A62 10c ultra (R) .60 .25
O102 A63 15c choc & dk grn (Bl) 2.75 .60
O103 A64 20c gray lil & blk (R) .85 .25
O104 A65 25c choc & grn (Bk) 5.25 .65
O105 A66 30c brt vio & blk (R) 6.50 .65
O106 A67 50c mar & blk (Bl) 7.75 .65
a. Overprint omitted 11.00
O107 A68 75c car brn & blk (Bl) 3.00 .25
O108 A69 $1 ol bis & turq bl (Bk) 6.00 .25

O109 A70 $2 ol bis & blk (R) 9.25 .25
O110 A71 $5 yel grn (Bk) 12.00 .40
Nos. O98-O110 (13) 56.25 4.95

For surcharges see Nos. 259-269, O111-O112, O155-O157. For overprint see No. 270.

Official Stamps of 1918 Surcharged like Regular Issue

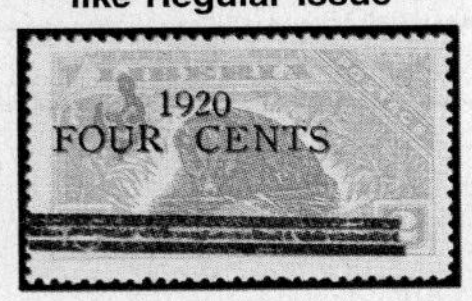

1920
O111 A59 3c on 1c grn & red brn 1.10 .70
a. "CEETS" 15.00 15.00
b. Double surcharge 8.00 8.00
c. Double srch., one invtd. 15.00 15.00
d. Triple surcharge 20.00 20.00
O112 A60 4c on 2c red & blk .70 .70
a. Inverted surcharge 12.00 12.00
b. Double surcharge 12.00 12.00
c. Double srch., one invtd. 10.00 10.00
d. Triple surcharge 15.00 15.00

Types of Regular Issues of 1915-21 Overprinted

1921 **Wmk. 116** ***Perf. 14***
O113 A57 2c rose red 8.25 .25
O114 A58 3c brown 1.75 .25
O115 A79 20c brn & ultra 2.25 .40

Regular Issues of 1921 Overprinted

O116 A75 1c dp grn 1.75 .25
O117 A76 5c dp bl & brn 1.75 .25
O118 A77 10c red vio & blk .85 .25
O119 A78 15c blk & grn 4.75 .60
a. Double overprint
O120 A80 25c org & grn 6.50 .60
O121 A81 30c brn & red 1.75 .25
O122 A82 50c grn & blk 1.75 .25
a. Overprinted "S" only
O123 A83 75c bl & vio 3.25 .25
O124 A84 $1 bl & blk 22.50 .65
O125 A85 $2 grn & org 12.00 .95
O126 A86 $5 grn & bl 13.50 2.10
Nos. O113-O126 (14) 82.60 7.30

Preceding Issues Overprinted

1921
O127 A75 1c dp grn 7.50 .25
O128 A57 2c rose red 7.50 .25
O129 A58 3c brown 7.50 .25
O130 A76 5c dp bl & brn 4.50 .25
O131 A77 10c red vio & blk 7.50 .25
O132 A78 15c blk & grn 8.50 .25
O133 A79 20c brn & ultra 8.50 .40
O134 A80 25c org & grn 8.25 .80
O135 A81 30c brn & red 7.50 .25
O136 A82 50c grn & blk 8.75 .25
O137 A83 75c bl & vio 5.50 .25
O138 A84 $1 bl & blk 15.00 2.00
O139 A85 $2 org & grn 19.00 2.25
O140 A86 $5 grn & bl 15.00 3.25
Nos. O127-O140 (14) 130.50 10.95

Types of Regular Issue of 1923 Ovptd.

1923 ***Perf. 13½x14½, 14½x13½***
White Paper
O141 A88 1c bl grn & blk 8.75 .25
O142 A89 2c dl red & yel brn 8.75 .25
O143 A90 3c gray bl & blk 8.75 .25
O144 A91 5c org & dk grn 8.75 .25
O145 A92 10c ol bis & dk vio 8.75 .25
O146 A93 15c yel grn & bl 1.10 .40
O147 A94 20c vio & ind 1.10 .40
O148 A95 25c brn & red brn 32.50 .40

White, Buff or Brownish Paper
O149 A96 30c dp ultra & brn 1.50 .25
O150 A97 50c dl bis & red brn 1.50 .40
O151 A98 75c gray & grn 2.25 .25
O152 A99 $1 red org & grn 3.00 .45
b. Overprint omitted 11.00
O153 A100 $2 red lil & ver 6.00 .25
O154 A101 $5 bl & brn vio 5.00 1.50
Nos. O141-O154 (14) 97.70 5.55
Nos. O141-O154a (10) 86.70 2.60

Brownish Paper
O149a A96 30c dp ultra & brn 1.10 .30
b. Overprint omitted 2.00
O150a A97 50c dl bis & red brn 2.25 .45
O151a A98 75c gray & grn 1.50 .30
O152a A99 $1 red org & grn 2.25 .65
c. Overprint omitted 11.00
O153a A100 $2 red lil & ver 2.50 1.00
O154a A101 $5 bl & brn vio 4.50 2.25

Nos. O149-O154 also exist on a light buff paper. Values are the same as for stamps on brownish paper.

No. O98 Surcharged in Red Brown

1926 **Unwmk.** ***Perf. 14***
O155 A59 2c on 1c 2.25 2.25
a. "Gents" 15.00
b. Surcharged in black 5.75
c. As "b," "Gents" 15.00

No. O98 Surcharged in Black

1926
O156 A59 2c on 1c 1.00 1.00
a. Inverted surcharge 20.00
b. "Gents" 10.00

No. O98 Surcharged in Red

1927
O157 A59 2c on 1c 35.00 35.00
a. "Ceuts" 55.00
b. "Vwo" 55.00
c. "Twc" 55.00

Regular Issue of 1928 Overprinted in Red or Black

1928 ***Perf. 12***
O158 A102 1c grn (R) 1.10 .55
O159 A102 2c gray vio (R) 3.50 2.10
O160 A102 3c bis brn (Bk) 3.75 4.25
O161 A103 5c ultra (R) 1.10 .55
O162 A104 10c ol gray (R) 3.50 1.75
O163 A103 15c dl vio (R) 3.50 1.00
O164 A103 $1 red brn (Bk) 77.50 22.50
Nos. O158-O164 (7) 93.95 32.70

For surcharges see Nos. C3, O165 (in Scott Standard catalogue, Vol. 4).

LIBYA

'li-bē-ə

(Libia)

LOCATION — North Africa, bordering on the Mediterranean Sea
GOVT. — Republic
AREA — 679,358 sq. mi.
POP. — 3,500,000 (est. 1982)
CAPITAL — Tripoli

In 1939, the four northern provinces of Libya, a former Italian colony, were incorporated in the Italian national territory. Included in the territory is the former Turkish Vilayet of Tripoli, annexed in 1912. See Cyrenaica and Tripolitania.

100 Centesimi = 1 Lira

Watermarks

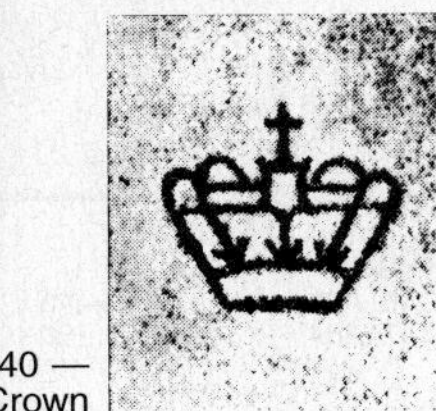

Wmk. 140 — Crown

Used values in italics are for postally used stamps. CTO's sell for about the same as unused, hinged stamps.

Stamps of Italy Overprinted in Black

Libia **Libia**
Type I Type II

Two types of overprint. Type I: bold letters, dots close within letter "i." Type II: thinner letters, dots further away within letter "i."

1912-22 **Wmk. 140** ***Perf. 14***
Type I
1 A42 1c brown ('15) 1.40 .85
Never hinged 3.50
On cover 24.00
a. Double overprint 225.00 225.00
Never hinged 360.00
2 A43 2c orange brn 1.40 .50
Never hinged 3.50
On cover 24.00
3 A48 5c green 1.50 .35
Never hinged 3.50
On cover 8.00
a. Double overprint 85.00 85.00
Never hinged 140.00
b. Imperf., pair 300.00
Never hinged 400.00
c. Inverted overprint —
d. Pair, one without overprint 425.00 425.00
Never hinged 650.00
4 A48 10c claret 14.00 .35
Never hinged 35.00
On cover 8.00
a. Pair, one without overprint 425.00 425.00
Never hinged 650.00
b. Double overprint 160.00 160.00
Never hinged 210.00
5 A48 15c slate ('22) 5.50 *8.50*
Never hinged 14.00
On cover 72.50
6 A45 20c orange ('15) 5.50 .35
Never hinged 13.50
On cover 22.50
a. Double overprint 175.00 *175.00*
Never hinged 300.00
b. Pair, one without overprint 750.00 750.00
Never hinged 1,100.
7 A50 20c brn org ('18) 4.25 *5.50*
Never hinged 10.00
On cover 55.00
a. Double overprint 175.00 —
8 A49 25c blue 5.50 .35
Never hinged 13.50
On cover 55.00
9 A49 40c brown 14.00 1.00
Never hinged 35.00
On cover 200.00
10 A45 45c ol grn ('17) 37.50 30.00
Never hinged 92.50
On cover 125.00
a. Inverted overprint 675.00
Never hinged 925.00
11 A49 50c violet 35.00 1.40
Never hinged 87.50
On cover 275.00
12 A49 60c brn car ('18) 19.00 *25.00*
Never hinged 47.50
On cover 175.00
13 A46 1 l brn & grn ('15) 62.50 1.75
Never hinged 150.00
On cover 110.00
14 A46 5 l bl & rose ('15) 425.00 500.00
Never hinged 1,000.
On cover *4,750.*
15 A51 10 l gray grn & red ('15) 35.00 *190.00*
Never hinged 87.50
Nos. 1-15 (15) 667.05 *765.90*

Type II
1b A42 1c brown ('15) 1.40 1.75
Never hinged 2.75
On cover 95.00
3e A48 5c green 1.40 .70
Never hinged 2.75
On cover 22.50
f. Double overprint 77.50 77.50
Never hinged 110.00
g. Imperf., pair 300.00
Never hinged 400.00
h. Pair, one without overprint 325.00 325.00
Never hinged 425.00
4c A48 10c claret 14.00 .70
Never hinged 35.00
On cover 22.50
d. Pair, one without overprint 325.00 325.00
Never hinged 425.00
e. Double overprint 160.00 160.00
Never hinged 240.00
6c A45 20c orange ('15) 5.50 .70
Never hinged 14.00
On cover 40.00
8a A49 25c blue 5.50 1.40
Never hinged 14.00
On cover 100.00
b. Double overprint, both type II 175.00 —
Never hinged *250.00*
11a A49 50c violet 225.00 1.75
Never hinged 550.00
On cover 475.00
13a A46 1 l brn & grn ('15) 70.00 3.50
Never hinged 175.00
On cover 160.00
14a A46 5 l bl & rose ('15) 420.00 625.00
Never hinged 1,000.
On cover *5,500.*
15a A51 10 l gray grn & red ('15) 4,250.
Never hinged 8,400.

For surcharges see Nos. 37-38.

Overprinted in Violet

1912 **Unwmk.**
16 A58 15c slate 260.00 1.75
Never hinged 650.00
On cover 72.50
a. Blue black overprint *21,000.* 42.50
Never hinged *31,000.*
On cover 140.00

No. 16 Surcharged

1916, Mar. **Unwmk.**
19 A58 20c on 15c slate 55.00 10.00
Never hinged 140.00
On cover 35.00
a. Blue-black surcharge 100.00 24.00
Never hinged 240.00
On cover 85.00

Roman Legionary — A1

Diana of Ephesus — A2

Ancient Galley Leaving Tripoli — A3

"Victory" — A4

1921 Engr. Wmk. 140 *Perf. 14*

20 A1 1c blk & gray brn 2.75 *7.00*
Never hinged 6.75
On cover 95.00
21 A1 2c blk & red brn 2.75 *7.00*
Never hinged 6.75
On cover 95.00
22 A1 5c blk & grn 3.50 .70
Never hinged 8.75
On cover 2.40
a. 5c black & red brown (error) 1,900.
Never hinged 2,600.
b. Center inverted 50.00 77.50
Never hinged 100.00
c. Imperf., pair 525.00 525.00
Never hinged 1,000.
23 A2 10c blk & rose 3.50 .70
Never hinged 8.75
On cover 2.40
a. Center inverted 50.00 77.50
Never hinged 100.00
24 A2 15c blk brn & brn org 85.00 2.75
Never hinged 210.00
On cover 20.00
a. Center inverted 125.00 *240.00*
Never hinged 260.00
25 A2 25c dk bl & bl 3.50 .25
Never hinged 8.75
On cover 2.40
a. Center inverted 17.50 24.50
Never hinged 40.00
b. Imperf., pair 775.00 775.00
Never hinged 1,500.
26 A3 30c blk & blk brn 35.00 .70
Never hinged 87.50
On cover 4.00
a. Center inverted 2,750. 3,000.
Never hinged 3,700.
27 A3 50c blk & ol grn 16.00 .25
Never hinged 40.00
On cover 2.40
a. 50c black & brown (error) 625.00
Never hinged 1,250.
b. Center inverted *4,750.*
28 A3 55c black & vio 16.00 *24.00*
Never hinged 40.00
On cover 525.00
29 A4 1 l dk brn & brn 47.50 .25
Never hinged 120.00
On cover 2.40
30 A4 5 l blk & dk blue 27.50 21.00
Never hinged 67.50
On cover 1,100.
31 A4 10 l dk bl & ol grn 300.00 160.00
Never hinged 750.00
On cover *2,500.*
Nos. 20-31 (12) 543.00 224.60

See No. 47-61. For surcharges see No. 102-121 in Scott Standard catalogue, Vol. 4.

Perf. 14x13¼

20d A1 1c blk & gray brn 5.50 11.00
Never hinged 14.00
21d A1 2c blk & red brn 5.50 11.00
Never hinged 14.00
22d A1 5c blk & red green 7.00 1.40
Never hinged 17.50
23d A2 10c blk & rose 7.00 1.40
Never hinged 17.50
24d A2 15c blk & brn org 160.00 5.50
Never hinged 390.00
25d A2 25c dk bl & bl 7.00 .35
Never hinged 17.50
26d A3 30c blk & blk brn 70.00 1.40
Never hinged 175.00
27d A3 50c blk & ol grn 32.50 .35
Never hinged 80.00
28d A3 55c blk & vio 32.50 55.00
Never hinged 80.00
29d A4 1 l dk brn & brn 95.00 .35
Never hinged 240.00
30d A4 5 l blk & dk blue 55.00 30.00
Never hinged 140.00
31d A4 10 l blk & ol grn 625.00 190.00
Never hinged 1,600.

Italy Nos. 136-139 Overprinted

1922, Apr.

33 A64 5c olive green 1.75 *6.25*
Never hinged 4.25
On cover 125.00
a. Double overprint 450.00 450.00
Never hinged 750.00
34 A64 10c red 1.75 *6.25*
Never hinged 4.25
On cover 240.00
a. Double overprint 450.00 450.00
Never hinged 750.00
b. Inverted overprint 950.00 950.00
Never hinged 1,250.
35 A64 15c slate green 1.75 *9.75*
Never hinged 4.25
On cover 250.00
36 A64 25c ultramarine 1.75 *9.75*
Never hinged 4.25
On cover 300.00
Nos. 33-36 (4) 7.00 *32.00*

3rd anniv. of the victory of the Piave.

Nos. 11, 8 Surcharged

1922, June 1

37 A49 40c on 50c violet 3.50 2.10
Never hinged 8.75
On cover 95.00
a. Type II 3.50 2.10
Never hinged 8.75
On cover 95.00
38 A49 80c on 25c blue 3.50 *8.50*
Never hinged 8.75
On cover 350.00
a. Type II 3.50 8.50
Never hinged 8.75
On cover 350.00

Libyan Sibyl — A6

1924-31 Unwmk. *Perf. 14½x14*

39 A6 20c deep green .70 .25
Never hinged 1.75
On cover 2.00
c. Vert. pair, imperf between and top 1,400.
Never hinged 1,800.
d. Horiz. pair, imperf between and at right 1,400.
Never hinged 1,800.
e. Horiz. pair, imperf between and at left 1,400.
Never hinged 1,800.
40 A6 40c brown 2.10 .70
Never hinged 5.25
On cover 17.50
b. Imperf single 275.00 *425.00*
Never hinged 450.00
41 A6 60c deep blue .70 .25
Never hinged 1.75
On cover 22.50
b. Imperf single 275.00
Never hinged 450.00
42 A6 1.75 l orange ('31) 1.40 .25
Never hinged 3.50
On cover 4.75
43 A6 2 l carmine 4.25 1.00
Never hinged 10.00
On cover 27.50
b. Imperf single 275.00 *425.00*
Never hinged 450.00
44 A6 2.55 l violet ('31) 8.50 17.50
Never hinged 21.00
On cover 240.00
Nos. 39-44 (6) 17.65 19.95

1926-29 *Perf. 11*

39a A6 20c 42.50 .30
Never hinged 100.00
On cover 9.50
40a A6 40c 30.00 2.40
Never hinged 75.00
On cover 22.50
41a A6 60c 30.00 .45
Never hinged 75.00
On cover 45.00
43a A6 2 l ('29) 14.00 5.00
Never hinged 35.00
On cover 52.50
Nos. 39a-43a (4) 116.50 8.15

Type of 1921

1924-40 Unwmk. *Perf. 13½ to 14*

47 A1 1c blk & gray brown 2.75 5.50
Never hinged 6.75
On cover 160.00
48 A1 2c blk & red brn 2.75 5.50
Never hinged 6.75
On cover 160.00
49 A1 5c blk & green 3.50 .70
Never hinged 8.75
On cover 2.40
50 A1 7½c blk & brn ('31) 1.40 14.00
Never hinged 3.50
On cover 110.00
51 A2 10c blk & dl red 2.75 .30
Never hinged 6.75
On cover 2.40
b. 10c blk & carmine 2.75 .30
Never hinged 6.75
On cover 2.40
c. As "b," center inverted 175.00
Never hinged 350.00
52 A2 15c blk brn & org 8.50 1.00
Never hinged 21.00
On cover 20.00
b. Center inverted, perf. 11 *4,500.* *6,500.*
Never hinged *6,750.*
53 A2 25c dk bl & bl 42.50 .50
Never hinged 105.00
On cover 2.40
a. Center inverted 240.00 350.00
Never hinged 360.00
54 A3 30c blk & blk brn 2.75 .50
Never hinged 6.75
On cover 4.00
55 A3 50c blk & ol grn 2.75 .30
Never hinged 6.75
On cover 2.40
b. Center inverted 4,500.
Never hinged 6,750.
56 A3 55c black & vio 625.00 825.00
Never hinged 1,600.
57 A4 75c vio & red ('31) 6.50 .25
Never hinged 16.00
On cover 16.00
58 A4 1 l dk brn & brn 10.00 .35
Never hinged 25.00
On cover 3.25
59 A3 1.25 l indigo & ultra ('31) 1.40 .25
Never hinged 3.50
On cover 12.00
60 A4 5 l blk & dk bl ('40) 150.00 *175.00*
Never hinged 375.00
On cover 1,000.
Nos. 47-60 (14) 862.55 1,029.

Perf. 11

47a A1 1c 375.00
Never hinged 925.00
48a A1 2c 375.00
Never hinged 925.00
49a A1 5c 70.00 17.50
Never hinged 175.00
On cover 60.00
51a A2 10c 35.00 7.00
Never hinged 87.50
On cover 24.00
52a A2 15c 475.00 45.00
Never hinged 1,150.
On cover 160.00
54a A3 30c 140.00 2.10
Never hinged 350.00
On cover 8.00
55a A3 50c 775.00 .25
Never hinged 1,900.
On cover 2.40
58a A4 1 l 350.00 .35
Never hinged 875.00
On cover 14.50
60a A4 5 l ('37) *2,400.* 450.00
Never hinged 4,750.
On cover 1,600.
61 A4 10 l dk bl & ol grn ('37) 625.00 500.00
Never hinged 1,600.
On cover *2,600.*

Nos. 47a and 48a were not sent to the colony. A few philatelically inspired covers exist.

Italy Nos. 197 and 88 Overprinted Like Nos. 1-15

1929 Wmk. 140 *Perf. 14*

62 A86 7½c light brown 10.00 *55.00*
Never hinged 25.00
On cover 350.00
a. Double overprint — —
63 A46 1.25 l blue & ultra 60.00 21.00
Never hinged 150.00
On cover 175.00
a. Inverted overprint 3,750.
Never hinged 4,250.

Italy No. 193 Overprinted Like Nos. 33-36

1929 Unwmk. *Perf. 11*

64 A85 1.75 l deep brown 75.00 2.10
Never hinged 190.00
On cover 67.50
h. Perf 13¾ *12,000.*
On cover *36,000.*

No. 64h is not known unused.

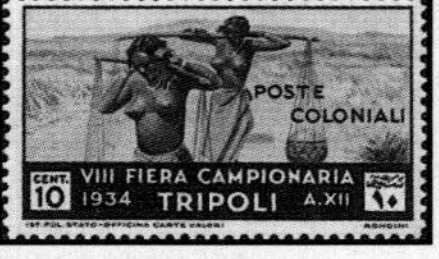
Water Carriers A7

Man of Tripoli — A8

Designs: 25c, Minaret. 30c, 1.25 l, Tomb of Holy Man near Tagiura. 50c, Statue of Emperor Claudius at Leptis. 75c, Ruins of gardens.

1934, Feb. 17 Photo. *Perf. 14*

64A A7 10c brown 4.25 *17.50*
Never hinged 10.50
On cover 190.00
64B A8 20c car rose 4.25 *15.00*
Never hinged 10.50
On cover 210.00
64C A8 25c green 4.25 *15.00*
Never hinged 10.50
On cover 225.00
64D A7 30c dark brown 4.25 *15.00*
Never hinged 10.50
On cover 260.00
64E A8 50c purple 4.25 *15.00*
Never hinged 10.50
On cover 210.00
64F A7 75c rose 4.25 *27.50*
Never hinged 10.50
On cover 325.00
64G A7 1.25 l blue 55.00 *95.00*
Never hinged 140.00
On cover 650.00
Nos. 64A-64G (7) 80.50 *200.00*
Nos. 64A-64G,C14-C18 (12) 508.50 *980.00*
Nos. 64A-64G on overfranked philatelic cover *2,200.*

8th Sample Fair, Tripoli.

Bedouin Woman — A15

1936, May 11 Wmk. 140 *Perf. 14*

65 A15 50c purple 1.75 *2.75*
Never hinged 4.25
On cover 52.50
66 A15 1.25 l deep blue 1.75 *7.75*
Never hinged 4.25
On cover 175.00
Nos. 65-66 on overfranked philatelic cover 55.00

10th Sample Fair, Tripoli.

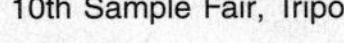

Highway Memorial Arch — A16

1937, Mar. 15

67 A16 50c copper red 2.75 *5.50*
Never hinged 6.75
On cover 190.00
68 A16 1.25 l sapphire 2.75 *12.50*
Never hinged 6.75
On cover 275.00
Nos. 67-68,C28-C29 (4) 11.00 *36.00*

Coastal road to the Egyptian frontier, opening.

Nos. 67-68 Overprinted in Black

1937, Apr. 24

69 A16 50c copper red 14.00 *35.00*
Never hinged 35.00
On cover 210.00
70 A16 1.25 l sapphire 14.00 *35.00*
Never hinged 35.00
On cover 325.00
Nos. 69-70,C30-C31 (4) 56.00 *140.00*

11th Sample Fair, Tripoli.

Roman Wolf and Lion of St. Mark A17

View of Fair Buildings A18

1938, Feb. 20

71 A17 5c brown .30 1.00
Never hinged .75
On cover 87.50
72 A18 10c olive brown .30 .70
Never hinged .75
On cover 47.50
73 A17 25c green .55 1.25
Never hinged 1.25
On cover 87.50
74 A18 50c purple .55 .55
Never hinged 1.25
On cover 40.00
75 A17 75c rose red 1.40 *2.75*
Never hinged 3.50
On cover 190.00
76 A18 1.25 l dark blue 1.40 *7.00*
Never hinged 3.50
On cover 225.00
Nos. 71-76,C32-C33 (8) 7.30 *21.50*
Nos. 71-76 on overfranked philatelic cover 120.00

12th Sample Fair, Tripoli.

Augustus Caesar (Octavianus) A19

Goddess Abundantia A20

1938, Apr. 25

77 A19 5c olive brown .25 1.40
Never hinged .65
On cover 210.00
78 A20 10c brown red .25 1.40
Never hinged .65
On cover 72.50
79 A19 25c dk yel green .50 .70
Never hinged 1.25
On cover 100.00
80 A20 50c dk violet .50 .45
Never hinged 1.25
On cover 60.00
81 A19 75c orange red 1.40 *1.75*
Never hinged 3.50
On cover 225.00
82 A20 1.25 l dull blue 1.40 *2.75*
Never hinged 3.50
On cover 275.00
Nos. 77-82,C34-C35 (8) 5.65 *13.95*
Nos. 77-82 on overfranked philatelic cover 140.00

Birth bimillenary of Augustus Caesar (Octavianus), first Roman emperor.

Desert City — A21

View of Ghadames A22

1939, Apr. 12 **Photo.**

83 A21 5c olive brown .70 1.00
Never hinged 1.75
On cover 67.50
84 A22 20c red brown .70 1.00
Never hinged 1.75
On cover 47.50
85 A21 50c rose violet .70 1.00
Never hinged 1.75
On cover 20.00
86 A22 75c scarlet .70 *3.50*
Never hinged 1.75
On cover 120.00
87 A21 1.25 l gray blue 1.40 *4.25*
Never hinged 3.50
On cover 210.00
Nos. 83-87,C36-C38 (8) 6.60 *17.70*
Nos. 83-87 on overfranked philatelic cover 60.00

13th Sample Fair, Tripoli.

Modern City — A23

Oxen and Plow A24

Mosque — A25

1940, June 3 **Wmk. 140** ***Perf. 14***

88 A23 5c brown .70 1.00
Never hinged 1.75
On cover 95.00
89 A24 10c red orange .70 .70
Never hinged 1.75
On cover 67.50
90 A25 25c dull green .70 *1.00*
Never hinged 1.75
On cover 87.50
91 A23 50c dark violet .70 *.70*
Never hinged 1.75
On cover 45.00
92 A24 75c crimson .70 *3.50*
Never hinged 1.75
On cover 225.00
93 A25 1.25 l ultramarine 1.40 *5.50*
Never hinged 3.50
On cover 325.00
94 A24 2 l + 75c rose lake 1.40 *16.00*
Never hinged 4.00
On cover 600.00
Nos. 88-94,C39-C42 (11) 9.70 *50.50*
Nos. 88-94 on overfranked philatelic cover 200.00

Triennial Overseas Exposition, Naples.

SEMI-POSTAL STAMPS

Many issues of Italy and Italian Colonies include one or more semipostal denominations. To avoid splitting sets, these issues are generally listed as regular postage, semipostals or airmails, etc.

Semi-Postal Stamps of Italy Overprinted

1915-16 **Wmk. 140** ***Perf. 14***

B1 SP1 10c + 5c rose 3.50 *14.00*
Never hinged 8.75
On cover 120.00
a. Double overprint 825.00
Never hinged 1,200.
B2 SP2 15c + 5c slate 30.00 *24.00*
Never hinged 75.00
On cover 225.00
B3 SP2 20c + 5c org ('16) 4.25 *30.00*
Never hinged 10.00
On cover 325.00
a. Double overprint, one albino 500.00
Never hinged 800.00
Nos. B1-B3 (3) 37.75 *68.00*

No. B2 with Additional Surcharge

1916, Mar.

B4 SP2 20c on 15c + 5c slate 30.00 *30.00*
Never hinged 75.00
On cover 240.00
a. Double surcharge 850.00
Never hinged 1,200.
Nos. B1-B4 on overfranked philatelic cover 275.00

View of Port, Tripoli SP1

Designs: B5, B6, View of port, Tripoli. B7, B8, Arch of Marcus Aurelius. B9, B10, View of Tripoli.

1927, Feb. 15 **Litho.**

B5 SP1 20c + 5c brn vio & black 3.50 *15.00*
Never hinged 8.75
On cover 175.00
B6 SP1 25c + 5c bl grn & black 3.50 *15.00*
Never hinged 8.75
On cover 225.00
B7 SP1 40c + 10c blk brn & black 3.50 *15.00*
Never hinged 8.75
On cover 225.00
B8 SP1 60c + 10c org brn & black 3.50 *15.00*
Never hinged 8.75
On cover 250.00
B9 SP1 75c + 20c red & black 3.50 *15.00*
Never hinged 8.75
On cover 325.00
B10 SP1 1.25 l + 20c bl & blk 24.00 *42.50*
Never hinged 60.00
On cover *800.00*
Nos. B5-B10 (6) 41.50 117.50
Set on overfranked philatelic cover 450.00

First Sample Fair, Tripoli. Surtax aided fair. See Nos. EB1-EB2.

View of Tripoli — SP2

Knights of Malta Castle SP3

Designs: 50c+20c, Date palm. 1.25 l+20c, Camel riders. 2.55 l+50c, View of Tripoli. 5 l+1 l, Traction well.

1928, Feb. 20 **Wmk. 140** ***Perf. 14***

B11 SP2 30c + 20c mar & blk 3.50 *15.00*
Never hinged 8.75
On cover 210.00
B12 SP2 50c + 20c bl grn & blk 3.50 *15.00*
Never hinged 8.75
On cover 250.00
B13 SP2 1.25 l + 20c red & blk 3.50 *15.00*
Never hinged 8.75
On cover 325.00
B14 SP3 1.75 l + 20c bl & blk 3.50 *15.00*
Never hinged 8.75
On cover 475.00
B15 SP3 2.55 l + 50c brn & blk 7.00 *22.50*
Never hinged 17.50
On cover 600.00

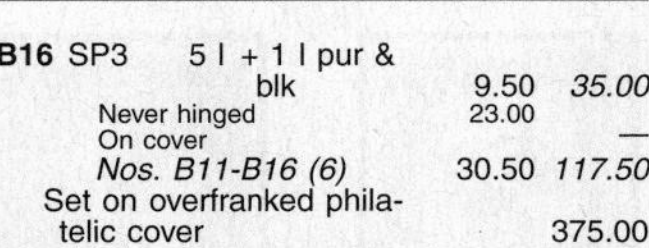

B16 SP3 5 l + 1 l pur & blk 9.50 *35.00*
Never hinged 23.00
On cover —
Nos. B11-B16 (6) 30.50 *117.50*
Set on overfranked philatelic cover 375.00

2nd Sample Fair, Tripoli, 1928. The surtax was for the aid of the Fair.

Olive Tree — SP4

Herding SP5

Designs: 50c+20c, Dorcas gazelle. 1.25 l+20c, Peach blossoms. 2.55 l+50c, Camel caravan. 5 l+1 l, Oasis with date palms.

1929, Apr. 7

B17 SP4 30c + 20c mar & blk 14.00 *27.50*
Never hinged 35.00
On cover 325.00
B18 SP4 50c + 20c bl grn & blk 14.00 *27.50*
Never hinged 35.00
On cover 300.00
B19 SP4 1.25 l + 20c scar & blk 14.00 *27.50*
Never hinged 35.00
On cover 550.00
B20 SP5 1.75 l + 20c bl & blk 14.00 *27.50*
Never hinged 35.00
On cover 800.00
B21 SP5 2.55 l + 50c yel brn & blk 14.00 *27.50*
Never hinged 35.00
On cover 1,100.
B22 SP5 5 l + 1 l pur & blk 125.00 *300.00*
Never hinged 300.00
On cover —
Nos. B17-B22 (6) 195.00 *437.50*
Set on overfranked philatelic cover 1,400.

3rd Sample Fair, Tripoli, 1929. The surtax was for the aid of the Fair.

Harvesting Bananas — SP6

Water Carriers SP7

Designs: 50c, Tobacco plant. 1.25 l, Venus of Cyrene. 2.55 l+45c, Black bucks. 5 l+1 l, Motor and camel transportation. 10 l+2 l, Rome pavilion.

1930, Feb. 20 **Photo.**

B23 SP6 30c dark brown 4.25 *17.50*
Never hinged 10.00
On cover 300.00
B24 SP6 50c violet 4.25 *17.50*
Never hinged 10.00
On cover 260.00
B25 SP6 1.25 l deep blue 4.25 *17.50*
Never hinged 10.00
On cover 400.00
B26 SP7 1.75 l + 20c scar 7.00 *26.00*
Never hinged 10.00
On cover 550.00
B27 SP7 2.55 l + 45c dp grn 16.00 *37.50*
Never hinged 40.00
On cover 800.00
B28 SP7 5 l + 1 l dp org 16.00 *50.00*
Never hinged 40.00
On cover —
B29 SP7 10 l + 2 l dk vio 16.00 *62.50*
Never hinged 40.00
On cover —
Nos. B23-B29 (7) 67.75 *228.50*
Set on overfranked philatelic cover 725.00

4th Sample Fair at Tripoli, 1930. The surtax was for the aid of the Fair.

Statue of Ephebus — SP8

Exhibition Pavilion SP9

Designs: 25c, Arab musician. 50c, View of Zeughet. 1.25 l, Snake charmer. 1.75 l+25c, Windmill. 2.75 l+45c, "Zaptie." 5 l+1 l, Mounted Arab.

1931, Mar. 8

B30 SP8 10c black brown 5.50 *9.75*
Never hinged 13.50
On cover 240.00
B31 SP8 25c green 5.50 *9.75*
Never hinged 13.50
On cover 275.00
B32 SP8 50c purple 5.50 *9.75*
Never hinged 13.50
On cover 240.00
B33 SP8 1.25 l blue 5.50 *14.00*
Never hinged 13.50
On cover 400.00
B34 SP8 1.75 l + 25c car rose 5.50 *16.00*
Never hinged 13.50
On cover —
B35 SP8 2.75 l + 45c org 5.50 *24.00*
Never hinged 13.50
On cover —
B36 SP8 5 l + 1 l dl vio 15.00 *35.00*
Never hinged 37.50
On cover —
B37 SP9 10 l + 2 l brn 50.00 *70.00*
Never hinged 125.00
On cover —
Nos. B30-B37 (8) 98.00 *188.25*
Nos. B30-B37,C3,EB3 (10) 104.90 229.75
Nos. B30-B37 on overfranked philatelic cover 875.00

Fifth Sample Fair, Tripoli. Surtax aided fair.

Papaya Tree SP10

Dorcas Gazelle SP12

Ar Tower, Mogadiscio SP11

Designs: 10c, 50c, Papaya tree. 20c, 30c, Euphorbia abyssinica. 25c, Fig cactus. 75c, Mausoleum, Ghirza. 1.75 l+25c, Lioness. 5 l+1 l, Bedouin with camel.

1932, Mar. 8

B38 SP10 10c olive brn 7.00 *16.00*
Never hinged 17.50
On cover 190.00
B39 SP10 20c brown red 7.00 *16.00*
Never hinged 17.50
On cover 125.00
B40 SP10 25c green 7.00 *16.00*
Never hinged 17.50
On cover 190.00
B41 SP10 30c olive blk 7.00 *16.00*
Never hinged 17.50
On cover 240.00
B42 SP10 50c dk violet 7.00 *16.00*
Never hinged 17.50
On cover 125.00
B43 SP10 75c carmine 8.50 *16.00*
Never hinged 21.00
On cover *375.00*
B44 SP11 1.25 l dk blue 8.50 *24.00*
Never hinged 21.00
On cover *525.00*
B45 SP11 1.75 l + 25c ol brn 27.50 *77.50*
Never hinged 67.50
On cover *675.00*
B46 SP11 5 l + 1 l dp bl 27.50 *190.00*
Never hinged 67.50
On cover —
B47 SP12 10 l + 2 l brn violet 125.00 *350.00*
Never hinged 300.00
On cover —
Nos. B38-B47 (10) 232.00 *737.50*
Nos. B38-B47,C4-C7 (14) 416.00 *1,168.*
Nos. B38-B47 on overfranked philatelic cover *2,500.*

Sixth Sample Fair, Tripoli. Surtax aided fair.

Ostrich — SP13

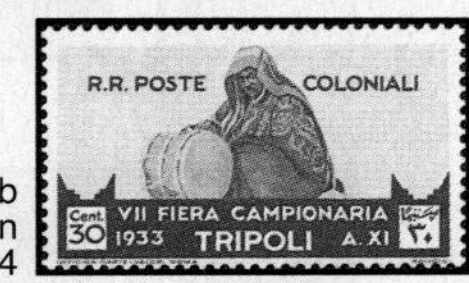

Arab Musician SP14

Designs: 25c, Incense plant. 30c, Arab musician. 50c, Arch of Marcus Aurelius. 1.25 l, African eagle. 5 l+1 l, Leopard. 10 l+2.50 l, Tripoli skyline and fasces.

1933, Mar. 2 Photo. Wmk. 140

B48 SP13 10c dp violet 37.50 42.50
Never hinged 92.50
On cover *275.00*
B49 SP13 25c dp green 21.00 *42.50*
Never hinged 52.50
On cover *225.00*
B50 SP14 30c org brn 21.00 *42.50*
Never hinged 52.50
On cover *275.00*
B51 SP13 50c purple 21.00 *42.50*
Never hinged 52.50
On cover *225.00*
B52 SP13 1.25 l dk blue 50.00 *77.50*
Never hinged 125.00
On cover *650.00*
B53 SP14 5 l + 1 l ol brn 110.00 *175.00*
Never hinged 275.00
On cover —
B54 SP13 10 l + 2.50 l car 110.00 *300.00*
Never hinged 275.00
On cover —
Nos. B48-B54 (7) 370.50 *722.50*
Nos. B48-B54,C8-C13 (13) 481.50 *1,103.*
Nos. B48-B54 on overfranked philatelic cover *2,400.*

Seventh Sample Fair, Tripoli. Surtax aided fair.

Pomegranate Tree — SP15

Designs: 50c+10c, 2 l+50c, Musician. 75c+15c, 1.25 l+25c, Tribesman.

1935, Feb. 16

B55 SP15 10c + 10c brn 1.75 *5.00*
Never hinged 4.25
On cover *210.00*
B56 SP15 20c + 10c rose red 1.75 *5.00*
Never hinged 4.25
On cover *225.00*
B57 SP15 50c + 10c pur 1.75 *5.00*
Never hinged 4.25
On cover *210.00*
B58 SP15 75c + 15c car 1.75 *5.00*
Never hinged 4.25
On cover *275.00*
B59 SP15 1.25 l + 25c dl blue 1.75 *5.00*
Never hinged 4.25
On cover *475.00*
B60 SP15 2 l + 50c ol grn 1.75 *12.50*
Never hinged 4.25
On cover —
Nos. B55-B60 (6) 10.50 *37.50*
Nos. B55-B60,C19-C24 (12) 27.00 *108.00*
Nos. B55-B60 on overfranked philatelic cover 800.00

Ninth Sample Fair, Tripoli. Surtax aided fair.

AIR POST STAMPS

Italy Nos. C3 and C5 Overprinted

1928-29 Wmk. 140 *Perf. 14*

C1 AP2 50c rose red 14.00 *27.50*
Never hinged 35.00
On cover 125.00
C2 AP2 80c brn vio & brn ('29) 55.00 *77.50*
Never hinged 140.00
On cover 475.00

Airplane AP1

1931, Mar. 8 Photo. Wmk. 140

C3 AP1 50c blue 1.40 *14.00*
Never hinged 3.50
On flown cover 180.00

See note after No. B37.

Seaplane over Bedouin Camp AP2

Designs: 50c, 1 l, Seaplane over Bedouin camp. 2 l+1 l, 5 l+2 l, Seaplane over Tripoli.

1932, Mar. 1 *Perf. 14*

C4 AP2 50c dark blue 15.00 *42.50*
Never hinged 37.50
On cover *240.00*
C5 AP2 1 l org brown 15.00 *42.50*
Never hinged 37.50
On cover *275.00*
C6 AP2 2 l + 1 l dk gray 29.00 *120.00*
Never hinged 72.50
On cover —
C7 AP2 5 l + 2 l car 125.00 *225.00*
Never hinged 300.00
On cover —
Nos. C4-C7 (4) 207.50 *495.00*
Set on overfranked philatelic cover 950.00

See note after No. B47.

Seaplane Arriving at Tripoli AP3

Designs: 50c, 2 l+50c, Seaplane arriving at Tripoli. 75c, 10 l+2.50 l, Plane over Tagiura. 1 l, 5 l+1 l, Seaplane leaving Tripoli.

1933, Mar. 1

C8 AP3 50c dp green 11.00 *22.50*
Never hinged 27.50
On cover *240.00*
C9 AP3 75c carmine 11.00 *22.50*
Never hinged 27.50
On cover *300.00*
C10 AP3 1 l dk blue 11.00 *22.50*
Never hinged 27.50
On cover *350.00*
C11 AP3 2 l + 50c pur 18.00 *52.50*
Never hinged 50.00
On cover —
C12 AP3 5 l + 1 l org brn 30.00 *85.00*
Never hinged 75.00
On cover —
C13 AP3 10 l + 2.50 l gray blk 30.00 *175.00*
Never hinged 75.00
On cover —
Nos. C8-C13 (6) 125.00 *390.00*
Set on overfranked philatelic cover 1,000.

See note after No. B54.

Seaplane over Tripoli Harbor AP4

Airplane and Camel — AP5

Designs: 50c, 5 l+1 l, Seaplane over Tripoli harbor. 75c, 10 l+2 l, Plane and minaret.

1934, Feb. 17 Photo. Wmk. 140

C14 AP4 50c slate bl 14.00 *30.00*
Never hinged 35.00
On cover *275.00*
C15 AP4 75c red org 14.00 *30.00*
Never hinged 35.00
On cover *325.00*
C16 AP4 5 l + 1 l dp grn 125.00 *210.00*
Never hinged 300.00
On cover —
C17 AP4 10 l + 2 l dl vio 125.00 *210.00*
Never hinged 300.00
On cover —
C18 AP5 25 l + 3 l org brn 150.00 *300.00*
Never hinged 375.00
On cover —
Nos. C14-C18 (5) 487.00 *900.00*
Set on overfranked philatelic cover 2,100.

Eighth Sample Fair, Tripoli. Surtax aided fair. See Nos. CE1-CE2.

Plane and Ancient Tower — AP6

Camel Train AP7

Designs: 25c+10c, 3 l+1.50 l, Plane and ancient tower. 50c+10c, 2 l+30c, Camel train. 1 l+25c, 10 l+5 l, Arab watching plane.

1935, Apr. 12

C19 AP6 25c + 10c green 1.40 *5.50*
Never hinged 3.50
On cover *250.00*
C20 AP7 50c + 10c slate bl 1.40 *5.50*
Never hinged 3.50
On cover *250.00*
C21 AP7 1 l + 25c blue 1.40 *5.50*
Never hinged 3.50
On cover *325.00*
C22 AP7 2 l + 30c rose red 1.40 *9.50*
Never hinged 3.50
On cover —
C23 AP6 3 l + 1.50 l brn 1.40 *9.50*
Never hinged 3.50
On cover —
C24 AP7 10 l + 5 l dl vio 9.50 *35.00*
Never hinged 23.00
On cover —
Nos. C19-C24 (6) 19.00 *81.50*
Set on overfranked philatelic cover 400.00

See note after No. B60.

Cyrenaica No. C6 Overprinted in Black

1936, Oct.

C25 AP2 50c purple 24.00 .35
Never hinged 60.00
On cover 2.40

Same on Tripolitania Nos. C8 and C12

1937

C26 AP1 50c rose carmine .70 .25
Never hinged 1.75
On cover 2.00
C27 AP2 1 l deep blue 2.10 .85
Never hinged 5.25
On cover 5.50
Set, never hinged 7.00

See Nos. C45-C50 in Scott Standard catalogue, Vol. 4.

Ruins of Odeon Theater, Sabrata AP8

1937, Mar. 15 **Photo.**

C28 AP8 50c dark violet 2.75 *7.00*
Never hinged 6.75
On cover 175.00
C29 AP8 1 l vio black 2.75 *11.00*
Never hinged 6.75
On cover 275.00
Set, never hinged 13.50
Set on overfranked philatelic cover 120.00

Opening of a coastal road to the Egyptian frontier.

Nos. C28-C29 Overprinted "XI FIERA DI TRIPOLI"

1937, Mar. 15

C30 AP8 50c dark violet 14.00 *35.00*
Never hinged 35.00
On cover 120.00
C31 AP8 1 l violet blk 14.00 *35.00*
Never hinged 35.00
On cover 250.00
Set, never hinged 70.00
Set on overfranked philatelic cover 325.00

11th Sample Fair, Tripoli.

View of Tripoli — AP9

1938, Mar. 12 ***Perf. 14***

C32 AP9 50c dk olive grn 1.40 *2.75*
Never hinged 3.50
On cover 65.00
C33 AP9 1 l slate blue 1.40 *5.50*
Never hinged 3.50
On cover 125.00
Set, never hinged 7.00

12th Sample Fair, Tripoli.

Eagle Attacking Serpent — AP10

1938, Apr. 25 **Wmk. 140**

C34 AP10 50c olive brown .35 *1.75*
Never hinged .85
On cover 60.00
C35 AP10 1 l brn violet 1.00 *3.75*
Never hinged 2.50
On cover 120.00
Set, never hinged 3.25

Birth bimillenary Augustus Caesar (Octavianus), first Roman emperor.

Arab and Camel AP11

Design: 50c, Fair entrance.

1939, Apr. 12 **Photo.**

C36 AP11 25c green .70 *2.10*
Never hinged 1.75
On cover 87.50
C37 AP11 50c olive brown .70 *2.10*
Never hinged 1.75
On cover 60.00
C38 AP11 1 l rose violet 1.00 *2.75*
Never hinged 2.50
On cover 175.00
Nos. C36-C38 (3) 1.90 *6.70*
Set, never hinged 6.00

13th Sample Fair, Tripoli.

Plane Over Modern City AP12

Design: 1 l, 5 l+2.50 l, Plane over oasis.

1940, June 3

C39 AP12 50c brn blk .70 *.85*
Never hinged 1.75
On cover 87.50
C40 AP12 1 l brn vio .70 *1.75*
Never hinged 1.75
On cover 125.00
C41 AP12 2 l + 75c indigo 1.00 *7.00*
Never hinged 2.50
On cover —
C42 AP12 5 l + 2.50 l copper brn 1.00 *12.50*
Never hinged 2.50
On cover —
Nos. C39-C42 (4) 4.10 *25.50*
Set, never hinged 8.50
Set on overfranked philatelic cover 160.00

Triennial Overseas Exposition, Naples.

AIR POST SPECIAL DELIVERY STAMPS

APSD1

Wmk. 140

1934, Feb. 17 **Photo.** ***Perf. 14***

CE1 APSD1 2.25 l olive blk 55.00 *70.00*
Never hinged 140.00
On cover 2,000.
CE2 APSD1 4.50 l + 1 l gray blk 55.00 *70.00*
Never hinged 140.00
On cover —
Set, never hinged 280.00
Set, on overfranked flown cover 2,100.

8th Sample Fair at Tripoli. The surtax was for the aid of the Fair.

SPECIAL DELIVERY STAMPS

Special Delivery Stamps of Italy Overprinted

Two types of overprint. See note preceding No. 1 for descriptions.

1915-16. **Wmk. 140** ***Perf. 14***

E1 SD1 25c rose red, ovpt. type I 77.50 30.00
Never hinged 190.00
On cover 240.00
a. Overprinted type II 24.00 17.50
Never hinged 60.00
On cover 125.00
E2 SD2 30c blue & rose, ovpt. type I 7.00 *30.00*
Never hinged 20.00
On cover 450.00
a. Overprinted type II 19.00 30.00
Never hinged 47.50
On cover 450.00
Set, never hinged 217.50

Issued: Nos. E1, E2, Nov. 1915; Nos. E1a, E2a, Dec. 1916.
For surcharges see Nos. E7-E8.

"Italia" SD3

No. E3

No. E4

No. E5

No. E6

Nos. E5-E6 bottom-corner denominations and words are reversed from Nos. E3-E4.

1921-23 **Engr.** ***Perf. 13½***

E3 SD3 30c blue & rose 2.10 *7.00*
Never hinged 5.25
On cover 175.00
E4 SD3 50c rose red & brn 4.25 *10.00*
Never hinged 10.50
On cover 200.00
E5 SD3 60c dk red & brn ('23) 7.00 *15.00*
Never hinged 17.50
On cover 260.00
E6 SD3 2 l dk bl & red ('23) 14.00 *27.50*
Never hinged 35.00
On cover 525.00
Nos. E3-E6 (4) 27.35 *59.50*
Set, never hinged 65.00

30c, 2 l inscribed "EXPRES."
For surcharges see Nos. E9-E12.

Nos. E1-E2 Surcharged

1922, June 1

E7 SD1 60c on 25c rose red 12.50 *17.50*
Never hinged 30.00
On cover 300.00
E8 SD2 1.60 l on 30c bl & rose 15.00 *35.00*
Never hinged 37.50
On cover 675.00
Set, never hinged 67.50

Nos. E5-E6 Surcharged in Blue or Red

No. E9

Nos. E10, E12

No. E11

1926-36

E9 SD3 70c on 60c 7.50 *15.00*
Never hinged 19.00
On cover 225.00
E10 SD3 2.50 l on 2 l (R) 14.00 *27.50*
Never hinged 35.00
On cover 725.00

Perf. 11

E11 SD3 1.25 l on 60c 5.50 1.75
Never hinged 14.00
On cover 20.00
a. Perf. 14 ('36) 21.00 3.50
Never hinged 52.50
On cover 130.00
b. Black surcharge *105,000.* *18,000.*
Never hinged *165,000.*
On cover *47,500.*
E12 SD3 2.50 l on 2 l (R) 240.00 *850.00*
Never hinged 600.00
On cover *3,750.*
Nos. E9-E12 (4) 267.00 *894.25*
Set, never hinged 625.00

Issued: Nos. E9-E10, July 1926; Nos. E11-E12, 1927.

SEMI-POSTAL SPECIAL DELIVERY STAMPS

Camel Caravan SPSD1

Wmk. 140

1927, Feb. 15 **Litho.** ***Perf. 14***

EB1 SPSD1 1.25 l + 30c pur & blk 8.50 42.50
Never hinged 21.00
On cover 325.00
EB2 SPSD1 2.50 l + 1 l yel & blk 8.50 42.50
Never hinged 21.00
On cover —
Set, never hinged 42.00

See note after No. B10.
No. EB2 is inscribed "EXPRES."

War Memorial SPSD2

1931, Mar. 8 **Photo.**

EB3 SPSD2 1.25 l + 20c car rose 5.50 *27.50*
Never hinged 14.00

See note after No. B37.

AUTHORIZED DELIVERY STAMPS

Italy No. EY1 Overprinted in Black

1929, May 11 Wmk. 140 Perf. 14

No.	Type	Description	Unused	Used
EY1	AD1	10c dull blue	30.00	70.00
		Never hinged	77.50	
		On cover		800.00
a.		Perf. 11	125.00	275.00
		Never hinged	300.00	
		On cover		1,600.

POSTAGE DUE STAMPS

Italian Postage Due Stamps, 1870-1903 Overprinted in Black

1915, Nov. Wmk. 140 Perf. 14

No.	Type	Description	Unused	Used
J1	D3	5c buff & mag	2.10	10.00
		Never hinged	4.25	
		On cover		325.00
J2	D3	10c buff & mag	2.10	5.50
		Never hinged	4.25	
		On cover		190.00
J3	D3	20c buff & mag	2.75	8.50
		Never hinged	5.50	
		On cover		190.00
a.		Double overprint	500.00	500.00
		Never hinged	750.00	
b.		Inverted overprint	500.00	
		Never hinged	800.00	
J4	D3	30c buff & mag	7.00	10.00
		Never hinged	14.00	
		On cover		240.00
J5	D3	40c buff & mag	10.00	12.50
		Never hinged	20.00	
		On cover		325.00
a.		"40" in black	4,500.	
		Never hinged	9,000.	
J6	D3	50c buff & mag	7.00	8.50
		Never hinged	14.00	
		On cover		190.00
J7	D3	60c buff & mag	10.00	19.00
		Never hinged	20.00	
		On cover		325.00
J8	D3	1 l blue & mag	7.00	19.00
		Never hinged	14.00	
		On cover		350.00
a.		Double overprint	10,500.	16,000.
J9	D3	2 l blue & mag	55.00	110.00
		Never hinged	110.00	
		On cover		—
J10	D3	5 l blue & mag	77.50	190.00
		Never hinged	155.00	
		On cover		—
		Nos. J1-J10 (10)	180.45	393.00

1926

No.	Type	Description	Unused	Used
J11	D3	60c buff & brown	175.00	325.00
		Never hinged	350.00	
		On cover		650.00

Postage Due Stamps of Italy, 1934, Overprinted in Black

1934

No.	Type	Description	Unused	Used
J12	D6	5c brown	.35	2.75
		Never hinged	.85	
		On cover		260.00
J13	D6	10c blue	.35	2.75
		Never hinged	.85	
		On cover		160.00
J14	D6	20c rose red	1.40	1.40
		Never hinged	3.50	
		On cover		160.00
J15	D6	25c green	1.40	1.40
		Never hinged	3.50	
		On cover		125.00
J16	D6	30c red orange	1.40	5.50
		Never hinged	3.50	
		On cover		240.00
J17	D6	40c black brn	1.40	3.50
		Never hinged	3.50	
		On cover		260.00
J18	D6	50c violet	1.75	.35
		Never hinged	4.25	
		On cover		110.00
J19	D6	60c black	1.75	17.50
		Never hinged	4.25	
		On cover		350.00
J20	D7	1 l red orange	1.40	.35
		Never hinged	3.50	
		On cover		160.00
J21	D7	2 l green	42.50	17.50
		Never hinged	100.00	
		On cover		350.00
J22	D7	5 l violet	95.00	37.50
		Never hinged	240.00	
		On cover		—
J23	D7	10 l blue	12.50	52.50
		Never hinged	30.00	
		On cover		—
J24	D7	20 l carmine	12.50	70.00
		Never hinged	30.00	
		On cover		—
		Nos. J12-J24 (13)	173.70	213.00

PARCEL POST STAMPS

These stamps were used by affixing them to the way bill so that one half remained on it following the parcel, the other half staying on the receipt given the sender. Most used halves are right halves. Complete stamps were obtainable canceled, probably to order. Both unused and used values are for complete stamps.

Italian Parcel Post Stamps, 1914-22, Overprinted

1915-24 Wmk. 140 Perf. 13½

No.	Type	Description	Unused	Used
Q1	PP2	5c brown	7.00	14.00
		Never hinged	14.00	
a.		Double overprint	375.00	
		Never hinged	550.00	
Q2	PP2	10c deep blue	7.00	14.00
		Never hinged	14.00	
Q3	PP2	20c blk ('18)	8.50	14.00
		Never hinged	17.00	
Q4	PP2	25c red	8.50	14.00
		Never hinged	17.00	
Q5	PP2	50c orange	10.00	14.00
		Never hinged	20.00	
Q6	PP2	1 l violet	10.00	21.00
		Never hinged	20.00	
Q7	PP2	2 l green	14.00	21.00
		Never hinged	27.50	
Q8	PP2	3 l bister	21.00	21.00
		Never hinged	42.50	
Q9	PP2	4 l slate	21.00	21.00
		Never hinged	42.50	
Q10	PP2	10 l rose lil ('24)	70.00	125.00
		Never hinged	140.00	
Q11	PP2	12 l red brn ('24)	140.00	260.00
		Never hinged	275.00	
Q12	PP2	15 l ol grn ('24)	140.00	425.00
		Never hinged	275.00	
Q13	PP2	20 l brn vio ('24)	210.00	510.00
		Never hinged	425.00	
		Nos. Q1-Q13 (13)	667.00	1,474.

Halves Used

No.	Value
Q1	1.00
Q2	1.50
Q3	1.50
Q4	1.50
Q5	1.50
Q6	1.50
Q7	1.50
Q8	1.50
Q9	1.50
Q10	10.00
Q11	11.00
Q12	25.00
Q13	65.00

Same Overprint on Parcel Post Stamps of Italy, 1927-36

1927-38

No.	Type	Description	Unused	Used
Q14	PP3	10c dp bl ('36)	7.00	10.00
		Never hinged	14.00	
Q15	PP3	25c red ('36)	7.00	10.00
		Never hinged	14.00	
Q16	PP3	30c ultra ('29)	3.50	7.00
		Never hinged	7.00	
Q17	PP3	50c orange	50.00	350.00
		Never hinged	100.00	
a.		Overprint 8¾x2mm ('31)	87.50	450.00
		Never hinged	175.00	
Q18	PP3	60c red ('29)	3.50	7.00
		Never hinged	7.00	
Q19	PP3	1 l lilac ('36)	37.50	140.00
		Never hinged	75.00	
Q20	PP3	2 l grn ('38)	45.00	140.00
		Never hinged	90.00	
Q21	PP3	3 l bister	4.25	14.00
		Never hinged	8.50	
Q22	PP3	4 l gray	4.25	21.00
		Never hinged	8.50	
Q23	PP3	10 l rose lil ('36)	275.00	625.00
		Never hinged	550.00	
Q24	PP3	20 l brn vio ('36)	300.00	850.00
		Never hinged	600.00	
		Nos. Q14-Q24 (11)	737.00	2,174.

Halves Used

No.	Value
Q14	.50
Q15	.50
Q16	.50
Q17	12.50
Q17a	22.50
Q18	.50
Q19	7.50
Q20	7.50
Q21	1.50
Q22	2.50
Q23	30.00
Q24	35.00

The overprint measures 10x1½mm on No. Q17.

Same Overprint on Italy No. Q24

1939

No.	Type	Description	Unused	Used
Q25	PP3	5c brown	15,000.	
		Never hinged	22,500.	

The overprint was applied to the 5c in error. Few examples exist.

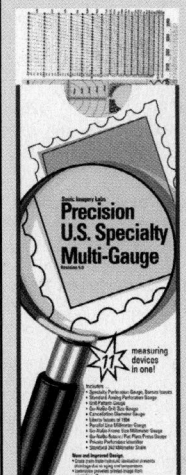

LIECHTENSTEIN

'lik-tən-ˌshtin

LOCATION — Central Europe southeast of Lake Constance, between Austria and Switzerland
GOVT. — Principality
AREA — 61.8 sq. mi.
POP. — 4,896 (est. 1984)
CAPITAL — Vaduz

The Principality of Liechtenstein is a sovereign state consisting of the two counties of Schellenberg and Vaduz. Since 1921 the post office has been administered by Switzerland.

100 Heller = 1 Krone
100 Rappen = 1 Franc (1921)

Watermark

Greek Cross — Wmk. 183

Austrian Administration of the Post Office

Prince Johann II — A1

Perf. 12½x13

1912, Feb. 1 Unwmk. Typo.

Thick Chalky Paper

1 A1 5h yellow green 42.50 17.50
Never hinged 175.00
On cover 32.50
2 A1 10h rose 85.00 17.50
Never hinged 400.00
On cover 32.50
3 A1 25h dark blue 85.00 55.00
Never hinged 325.00
On cover 210.00
Nos. 1-3 (3) 212.50 90.00
Set, never hinged 900.00
First day cover, #1-3 325.00

Nos. 1-3 exist imperf. Value set, $525 unused with original gum, $2,100 never hinged.

Values for blocks of 4 (NH, used)

1 A1 5h yellow green 750.00 105.00
2 A1 10h rose 1,750. 105.00
3 A1 25h dark blue 1,350. 390.00

1915 Thin Unsurfaced Paper

1a A1 5h yellow green 14.00 *21.00*
Never hinged 42.50
On cover 32.50
2a A1 10h rose 85.00 32.50
Never hinged 325.00
On cover 62.50
3a A1 25h dark blue 600.00 200.00
Never hinged 2,450.
On commercial cover, single franking 600.00
b. 25h ultramarine 350.00 425.00
Never hinged 1,550.
On commercial cover, single franking *10,500.*
#1a-3a, never hinged 2,500.

Nos. 1a-3a exist imperf. Value set, $1,150 unused with original gum, $2,000 never hinged.

Values for blocks of 4 (NH, used)

1b A1 5h yellow green 140.00 105.00
2b A1 10h rose 1,050. 175.00
3b A1 25h dark blue 8,800. 1,050.
c. 25h ultramarine 5,200. 2,500.

Coat of Arms — A2

Prince Johann II — A3

1917-18

4 A2 3h violet 2.00 2.00
Never hinged 8.50
On cover 32.50
5 A2 5h yellow green 2.00 2.00
Never hinged 8.50
On cover 25.00
6 A3 10h claret 2.00 2.00
Never hinged 8.50
On cover 37.50
7 A3 15h dull red 2.00 2.00
Never hinged 8.50
On cover 37.50
8 A3 20h dark green 2.00 2.00
Never hinged 8.50
On cover 42.50
9 A3 25h deep blue 2.00 2.00
Never hinged 8.50
On cover 42.50
Nos. 4-9 (6) 12.00 12.00
Set, never hinged 51.00
Nos. 4-7, 9, set of 5 on fdc (6/14/17) 750.00

Exist imperf. Value set unused original gum, $525; never hinged, $1,150.

For surcharges see Nos. 11-16.

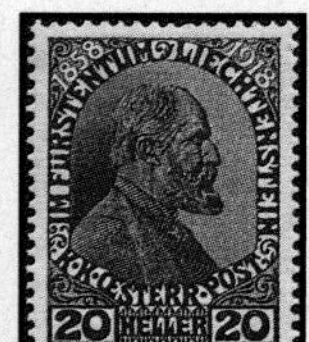

Prince Johann II — A4

Dates in Upper Corners

1918, Nov. 12

10 A4 20h dark green .70 *2.75*
Never hinged 5.50
On cover *37.50*
First day cover 175.00

Accession of Prince Johann II, 60th anniv.

Exists imperf. Value, unused original gum, $225; never hinged, $560.

National Administration of the Post Office

Stamps of 1917-18 Overprinted or Surcharged

a

b

c

1920

11 A2(a) 5h yellow green 2.75 *8.75*
Never hinged 11.00
On cover *625.00*
On cover, overfranked 175.00
a. Inverted overprint 70.00 *175.00*
Never hinged 140.00
b. Double overprint 14.00 *85.00*
Never hinged 35.00
On cover *700.00*
12 A3(a) 10h claret 2.75 *9.50*
Never hinged 12.00
On cover *625.00*
On cover, overfranked 175.00
a. Inverted overprint 70.00 175.00
Never hinged 140.00
b. Double overprint 14.00 *105.00*
Never hinged 35.00
On cover *850.00*
c. Overprint type "c" 14.00 *105.00*
Never hinged 27.50
On cover *625.00*
13 A3(a) 25h deep blue 2.75 *9.50*
Never hinged 14.00
On cover *625.00*
On cover, overfranked 175.00
a. Inverted overprint 70.00 *175.00*
Never hinged 140.00
b. Double overprint 14.00 *105.00*
Never hinged 27.50
On cover *850.00*
14 A2(b) 40h on 3h violet 2.75 *9.50*
Never hinged 11.00
On cover *625.00*
On cover, overfranked 175.00
a. Inverted surcharge 70.00 *175.00*
Never hinged 140.00
15 A3(c) 1k on 15h dull red 2.75 *9.50*
Never hinged 11.00
On cover *625.00*
On cover, overfranked 175.00
a. Inverted surcharge 70.00 *175.00*
Never hinged 140.00
b. Overprint type "a" 87.50 *350.00*
Never hinged 315.00
On cover *1,050.*
16 A3(c) 2½k on 20h dk grn 2.75 *9.50*
Never hinged 12.00
On cover *625.00*
On cover, overfranked 175.00
a. Inverted surcharge 70.00 *175.00*
Never hinged 140.00
Nos. 11-16 (6) 16.50 *56.25*
Set, never hinged 71.00

Coat of Arms A5

Chapel of St. Mamertus A6

Coat of Arms with Supporters A15

Designs: 40h, Gutenberg Castle. 50h, Courtyard, Vaduz Castle. 60h, Red Tower, Vaduz. 80h, Old Roman Tower, Schaan. 1k, Castle at Vaduz. 2k, View of Bendern. 5k, Prince Johann I. 7½k, Prince Johann II.

1920 Engr. *Imperf.*

18 A5 5h olive bister .35 *5.75*
Never hinged .80
On cover 160.00
19 A5 10h deep orange .35 *5.75*
Never hinged .85
On cover 140.00
20 A5 15h dark blue .35 *5.75*
Never hinged .85
On cover 160.00
21 A5 20h deep brown .35 *5.75*
Never hinged 1.00
On cover 105.00
22 A5 25h dark green .35 *5.75*
Never hinged 1.00
On cover 125.00
23 A5 30h gray black .35 *5.75*
Never hinged 1.10
On cover 160.00
24 A5 40h dark red .35 *5.75*
Never hinged 1.50
On cover 105.00
25 A6 1k blue .35 *5.75*
Never hinged 2.75
On cover 160.00
#18-25, set of 8 on fdc (5/5/20) 1,400.

Perf. 12½

32 A5 5h olive bister .35 *.70*
Never hinged .70
On cover *125.00*
33 A5 10h deep orange .35 *.70*
Never hinged .70
On cover *105.00*
34 A5 15h deep blue .35 *.70*
Never hinged .70
On cover *125.00*
35 A5 20h red brown .35 *.70*
Never hinged .70
On cover *90.00*
36 A6 25h olive green .35 *.70*
Never hinged .70
On cover *105.00*
37 A5 30h dark gray .35 *.70*
Never hinged .70
On cover *140.00*
38 A6 40h claret .35 *.70*
Never hinged .70
On cover *125.00*
39 A6 50h yellow green .35 *.70*
Never hinged .70
On cover *125.00*
40 A6 60h red brown .35 *.70*
Never hinged .70
On cover *160.00*
41 A6 80h rose .35 *.70*
Never hinged .70
On cover *77.50*
42 A6 1k dull violet .70 *1.00*
Never hinged 1.40
On cover *125.00*
43 A6 2k light blue .70 *1.25*
Never hinged 2.00
On cover 160.00
44 A6 5k black .70 *1.50*
Never hinged 3.50
On cover *425.00*
45 A6 7½k slate .70 *1.75*
Never hinged 4.25
On cover *525.00*
46 A15 10k ocher .70 *3.00*
Never hinged 14.00
On cover *625.00*
Nos. 18-46 (23) 9.80 *61.50*
Set, never hinged 41.00

No. 25 perf. 12½ was not officially issued. It is known mint, used and on cover.

Used values for Nos. 18-46 are for canceled to order stamps. Value with postal cancels approximately $95.

Many denominations of Nos. 32-46 are found imperforate, imperforate vertically and imperforate horizontally.

For surcharges see Nos. 51-52.

Madonna and Child — A16

1920, Oct. 5

47 A16 50h olive green 1.00 *2.10*
Never hinged 3.50
On cover *210.00*
48 A16 80h brown red 1.00 *2.10*
Never hinged 3.50
On cover *210.00*
49 A16 2k dark blue 1.00 *2.75*
Never hinged 3.50
On cover *210.00*
Nos. 47-49 (3) 3.00 *6.95*
Set, never hinged 10.50
Set of 3 on fdc 160.00
Set of 3 on overfranked cover 25.00

80th birthday of Prince Johann II.

Imperf., Singles

47a A16 50h 7.00 *1,400.*
Never hinged 21.00
48a A16 80h 7.00 *1,400.*
Never hinged 21.00
49a A16 2k 7.00 *1,400.*
Never hinged 21.00
Set, never hinged 63.00
Set of 3 singles on fdc 2,500.

On 1/31/21 the Swiss took over the Post Office administration. Previous issues were demonetized and remainders of Nos. 4-49 were sold.

Swiss Administration of the Post Office

No. 19 Surcharged

No. 51

No. 52

1921 Unwmk. Engr. *Imperf.*

51 A5 2rp on 10h dp org 1.40 *50.00*
Never hinged 7.00
On cover *700.00*
First day cover (2/1/21) *1,500.*
a. Double surcharge 105.00 *140.00*
Never hinged 140.00
On cover *850.00*
b. Inverted surcharge 105.00 *160.00*
Never hinged 140.00
On cover *850.00*
c. Double surch., one inverted 105.00 *175.00*
Never hinged 140.00
On cover *850.00*
d. Comma after "Rp" 70.00 *160.00*
Never hinged 100.00
On cover *850.00*
e. Inverted comma after "Rp" 70.00 *160.00*
Never hinged 100.00
On cover *850.00*
52 A5 2rp on 10h dp org .70 *50.00*
Never hinged 5.50
On cover *450.00*
First day cover (2/27/21) *875.00*
a. Double surcharge 72.50 *160.00*
Never hinged 105.00

On cover 850.00
b. Inverted surcharge 72.50 160.00
Never hinged 105.00
On cover 850.00
c. Double surch., one inverted 87.50 190.00
Never hinged 140.00
On cover 850.00

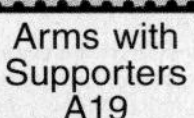
Arms with Supporters
A19

Chapel of St. Mamertus
A20

View of Vaduz
A21

Designs: 25rp, Castle at Vaduz. 30rp, View of Bendern. 35rp, Prince Johann II. 40rp, Old Roman Tower at Schaan. 50rp, Gutenberg Castle. 80rp, Red Tower at Vaduz.

1921 ***Perf. 12½, 9½ (2rp, 10rp, 15rp)***
Surface Tinted Paper (#54-61)

54 A19 2rp lemon 1.40 *14.00*
Never hinged 3.75
On cover *32.50*
55 A19 2½rp black 2.10 *17.50*
Never hinged 7.00
On cover *32.50*
a. Perf. 9½ 1.40 *70.00*
Never hinged 3.50
On cover *75.00*
56 A19 3rp orange 2.10 *17.50*
Never hinged 7.00
On cover *35.00*
a. Perf. 9½ 140.00 *5,000.*
Never hinged 425.00
On cover *6,750.*
57 A19 5rp olive green 14.00 2.10
Never hinged 42.50
On cover 11.00
a. Perf. 9½ 70.00 *27.50*
Never hinged 225.00
On cover *42.50*
58 A19 7½rp dark blue 7.00 *42.50*
Never hinged 25.00
On cover *95.00*
a. Perf. 9½ 275.00 *1,050.*
Never hinged 675.00
On cover *3,500.*
59 A19 10rp yellow green 27.50 17.50
Never hinged 70.00
On cover 27.50
a. Perf. 12½ 27.50 14.00
Never hinged 140.00
On cover 21.00
60 A19 13rp brown 10.50 *90.00*
Never hinged 27.50
On cover *140.00*
a. Perf. 9½ 100.00 *2,450.*
Never hinged 250.00
On cover *5,250.*
b. Perf. 12½x9½ 210.00 —
Never hinged 425.00
61 A19 15rp dark violet 25.00 70.00
Never hinged 40.00
On cover 110.00
a. Perf. 12½ 27.50 *27.50*
Never hinged 50.00
On cover *62.50*
62 A20 20rp dull vio & blk 70.00 2.10
Never hinged 210.00
On cover 11.00
63 A20 25rp rose red & blk 3.50 5.00
Never hinged 11.00
On cover 17.50
64 A20 30rp dp grn & blk 85.00 21.00
Never hinged 275.00
On cover 52.50
65 A20 35rp brn & blk, *straw* 7.00 *17.50*
Never hinged 17.50
On cover *42.50*
66 A20 40rp dk blue & blk 10.50 7.00
Never hinged 30.00
On cover 21.00
67 A20 50rp dk grn & blk 17.50 10.50
Never hinged 42.50
On cover 27.50
68 A20 80rp gray & blk 32.00 *85.00*
Never hinged 70.00
On cover *160.00*
69 A21 1fr dp claret & blk 55.00 55.00
Never hinged 160.00
On cover 140.00
Nos. 54-69 (16) 370.10 *474.20*
Set, never hinged 1,039.

Nos. 54-69 exist imperforate; Nos. 54-61, partly perforated. See Nos. 73, 81. For surcharges see Nos. 70-71.

Nos. 58, 60a Surcharged in Red

1924 ***Perf. 12½, 9½***
70 A19 5rp on 7½rp 1.40 *3.50*
Never hinged 4.25
On cover *42.50*
a. Perf. 9½ 19.00 17.50
Never hinged 50.00
On cover 85.00
71 A19 10rp on 13rp 1.75 *3.50*
Never hinged 5.25
On cover *42.50*
a. Perf. 12½ 20.00 *52.50*
Never hinged 60.00
On cover *260.00*

Type of 1921
Granite Paper

1924 **Wmk. 183** ***Perf. 11½***
73 A19 10rp green 21.00 3.50
Never hinged 85.00
On cover 35.00

Peasant
A28

Government Palace and Church at Vaduz
A30

10rp, 20rp, Courtyard, Vaduz Castle.

1924-28 **Typo.** ***Perf. 11½***
74 A28 2½rp ol grn & red vio ('28) 1.40 *5.50*
Never hinged 4.25
On cover *21.00*
75 A28 5rp brown & blue 2.75 .75
Never hinged 8.50
On cover 5.00
76 A28 7½rp bl grn & brn ('28) 2.10 *5.50*
Never hinged 5.00
On cover *17.50*
77 A28 15rp red brn & bl grn ('28) 10.50 *35.00*
Never hinged 35.00
On cover *70.00*

Engr.

78 A28 10rp yellow grn 11.25 .70
Never hinged 35.00
On cover 5.00
79 A28 20rp deep red 42.50 .70
Never hinged 140.00
On cover 70.00
80 A30 1½fr blue 85.00 *110.00*
Never hinged 275.00
On cover *325.00*
Nos. 74-80 (7) 155.50 *158.15*
Set, never hinged 503.00

Bendern Type of 1921

1925
81 A20 30rp blue & blk 17.50 3.50
Never hinged 55.00
On cover 35.00

Prince Johann II — A31

Prince Johann II as Boy and Man
A32

1928, Nov. 12 **Typo.** **Wmk. 183**
82 A31 10rp lt brn & ol grn 7.00 7.00
Never hinged 12.50
On cover 17.50
83 A31 20rp org red & ol grn 10.50 14.00
Never hinged 22.50
On cover 28.00
84 A31 30rp sl bl & ol grn 35.00 25.00
Never hinged 90.00
On cover 70.00
85 A31 60rp red vio & ol grn 70.00 *70.00*
Never hinged 175.00
On cover *210.00*

Engr.
Unwmk.

86 A32 1.20fr ultra 50.00 *87.50*
Never hinged 110.00
On cover *425.00*
87 A32 1.50fr blk brn 87.50 *210.00*
Never hinged 210.00
On cover *700.00*
88 A32 2fr deep car 87.50 *210.00*
Never hinged 210.00
On cover *700.00*
89 A32 5fr dark green 87.50 *245.00*
Never hinged 210.00
On cover *1,550.*
Nos. 82-89 (8) 435.00 *868.50*
Set, never hinged 1,040.
Set of 8 on fdc 2,800.

70th year of the reign of Prince Johann II.

Prince Francis I, as a Child — A33

Prince Francis I as a Man — A34

Princess Elsa — A35

Prince Francis and Princess Elsa — A36

1929, Dec. 2 **Photo.**
90 A33 10rp olive green .55 *4.25*
Never hinged 1.40
On cover *11.00*
91 A34 20rp carmine .85 *7.00*
Never hinged 2.10
On cover *17.50*
92 A35 30rp ultra 1.40 *17.50*
Never hinged 3.50
On cover *52.50*
93 A36 70rp brown 25.00 *110.00*
Never hinged 70.00
On cover *210.00*
Nos. 90-93 (4) 27.80 *138.75*
Set, never hinged 77.00
Set of 4 on fdc 700.00

Values for used blocks of 4

90 A33 10rp olive green *21.00*
91 A34 20rp carmine *35.00*
92 A35 30rp ultra *105.00*
93 A36 70rp brown *560.00*

Accession of Prince Francis I, Feb. 11, 1929.

Grape Girl — A37

Chamois Hunter — A38

Mountain Cattle — A39

Courtyard, Vaduz Castle — A40

Mt. Naafkopf — A41

Chapel at Steg — A42

Rofenberg Chapel — A43

Chapel of St. Mamertus — A44

Alpine Hotel, Malbun — A45

Gutenberg Castle — A46

Schellenberg Monastery — A47

Castle at Vaduz — A48

Mountain Cottage — A49

Prince Francis and Princess Elsa — A50

1930 ***Perf. 10½***

94 A37 3rp brown lake 1.10 2.80
Never hinged 3.50
On cover *11.00*
95 A38 5rp deep green 2.80 7.00
Never hinged 15.00
On cover 11.00
96 A39 10rp dark violet 2.50 7.00
Never hinged 15.00
On cover 14.00
97 A40 20rp dp rose red 42.50 7.00
Never hinged 105.00
On cover 14.00
98 A41 25rp black 8.50 *45.00*
Never hinged 27.50
On cover *70.00*
99 A42 30rp dp ultra 8.50 10.50
Never hinged 27.50
On cover 21.00
103 A46 60rp olive blk 105.00 42.50
Never hinged 280.00
On cover 70.00
104 A47 90rp violet brn 105.00 *350.00*
Never hinged 350.00
On cover *525.00*
105 A48 1.20fr olive brn 125.00 *375.00*
Never hinged 390.00
On cover *525.00*
106 A49 1.50fr black violet 70.00 77.50
Never hinged 175.00
On cover 210.00
107 A50 2fr gray grn & red brn 85.00 *140.00*
Never hinged 210.00
On cover *210.00*

Perf. 11½

95a A38 5rp dp grn 3.50 2.75
Never hinged 14.00
On cover 7.00
96b A39 10rp dp vio 3.50 2.75
Never hinged 14.00
On cover 7.00
97a A40 20rp dp rose red 27.50 3.50
Never hinged 77.50
On cover 8.50
98a A41 25rp blk 105.00 *350.00*
Never hinged 350.00
On cover *525.00*
99b A42 30rp dp ultra 8.50 5.00
Never hinged 27.50
On cover 17.50
100a A43 35rp dk grn *8,750.* *14,000.*
Never hinged *13,500.*
On cover —
102a A45 50rp blk brn 165.00 *245.00*
Never hinged 600.00
On cover *350.00*
103a A46 60rp olive blk 105.00 35.00
Never hinged 275.00
On cover 70.00
104a A47 90rp vio brn 110.00 140.00
Never hinged 350.00
On cover 275.00
105b A48 1.20fr ol brn 160.00 *275.00*
Never hinged 390.00
On cover *425.00*
106a A49 1.50fr blk vio 55.00 70.00
Never hinged 140.00
On cover 210.00
107b A50 2fr gray grn & red brn 85.00 *140.00*
Never hinged 245.00
On cover *225.00*

Perf. 11½x10½

96a A39 10rp dk violet 11.00 *120.00*
Never hinged 28.00
On cover *160.00*
99a A42 30rp dp ultra *1,050.* *2,500.*
Never hinged 2,175.
On cover *5,750.*
100 A43 35rp dark green 11.00 *21.00*
Never hinged 35.00
On cover *52.50*
101 A44 40rp lt brown 11.00 11.00
Never hinged 35.00
On cover 32.50
102 A45 50rp blk brn 105.00 21.00
Never hinged 300.00
On cover 42.50
105a A48 1.20fr ol brn *8,750.* *14,000.*
Never hinged *13,500.*
107a A50 2fr ol grn & red brn 3,850. *7,750.*
Never hinged *6,750.*
On cover *10,500.*
Nos. 94-107 (11) 555.90 *1,064.*
Set, never hinged 1,600.

For overprints see Nos. O1-O8.

Values for used blocks of 4

Perf. 10½

94	A37	3rp brn lake	14.00
95	A38	5rp dp grn	35.00
96	A39	10rp dk vio	35.00
97	A40	20rp dp rose red	35.00
98	A41	25rp blk	*210.00*
99	A42	30rp dp ultra	50.00
103	A46	60rp ol blk	175.00
104	A47	90rp vio brn	*1,550.*
105	A48	1.20fr ol brn	*1,750.*
106	A49	1.50fr blk vio	390.00
107	A50	2fr ol grn & red brn	*700.00*

Perf. 11½

95a	A38	5rp dp grn	14.00
96b	A39	10rp dk vio	14.00
97a	A40	20rp dp rose red	21.00
98a	A41	25rp blk	*1,750.*
99b	A42	30rp dp ultra	35.00
100a	A43	35rp dk grn	—
102a	A45	50rp blk brn	*1,150.*
103a	A46	60rp ol blk	160.00
104a	A47	90rp vio brn	700.00
105b	A48	1.20fr ol brn	*1,400.*
106a	A49	1.50fr blk vio	350.00
107b	A50	2fr ol grn & red brn	*700.00*

Perf. 11½x10½

96a	A39	10rp dk vio	*500.00*
99a	A42	30rp dp ultra	*11,250.*
100	A43	35rp dk grn	*105.00*
101	A44	40rp lt brn	55.00
102	A45	50rp blk brn	125.00
105a	A48	1.20fr ol brn	—
107a	A50	2fr ol grn & red brn	—

Mt. Naafkopf A51

Gutenberg Castle A52

Vaduz Castle — A53

1933, Jan. 23 ***Perf. 14½***

108 A51 25rp red orange 200.00 87.50
Never hinged 560.00
On cover 125.00
109 A52 90rp dark green 10.50 *105.00*
Never hinged 20.00
On cover *210.00*
110 A53 1.20fr red brown 85.00 *300.00*
Never hinged 260.00
On cover *525.00*
Nos. 108-110 (3) 295.50 *492.50*
Set, never hinged 840.00
Set of 3 on fdc 3,150.

For overprints see Nos. O9-O10.

Values for used blocks of 4

108	A51	25rp red org	450.00
109	A52	90rp dk grn	*525.00*
110	A53	1.20fr red brn	*1,400.*

80th Birthday of Prince Francis I — A54

1933, Aug. 28 ***Perf. 11***

111 A54 10rp purple 21.00 *42.50*
Never hinged 60.00
On cover *70.00*
112 A54 20rp brn car 21.00 *42.50*
Never hinged 60.00
On cover *70.00*
113 A54 30rp dark blue 21.00 *42.50*
Never hinged 60.00
On cover *70.00*
Nos. 111-113 (3) 63.00 *127.50*
Set, never hinged 180.00
Set of 3 on fdc 200.00

Values for used blocks of 4

111	A54	10rp pur	*175.00*
112	A54	20rp brn car	*175.00*
113	A54	30rp dk bl	*175.00*

Prince Francis I — A55

1933, Dec. 15 **Engr.** ***Perf. 12½***

114 A55 3fr violet blue 125.00 *250.00*
Never hinged 250.00
On cover *700.00*
First day cover *3,250.*

See No. 152.

Agricultural Exhibition Issue
Souvenir Sheet

Arms of Liechtenstein — A56

1934, Sept. 29 ***Perf. 12***
Granite Paper

115 A56 5fr brown *1,400.* *2,500.*
Never hinged *2,250.*
On cover *3,500.*
First day cover *3,250.*
Single stamp *1,000.* *1,750.*
Never hinged *1,400.*
On cover *3,500.*
First day cover *4,250.*

See No. 131.

Coat of Arms A57

"Three Sisters" (Landmark) A58

Church of Schaan A59

Bendern A60

Rathaus, Vaduz — A61

Samina Valley — A62

Samina Valley in Winter A63

Ruin at Schellenberg — A64

Government Palace — A65

Vaduz Castle A66

Gutenberg Castle A68

Alpine Hut — A69

Princess Elsa — A70

Coat of Arms — A71

60rp, Vaduz castle, diff. 1.50fr, Valuna.

1934-35 **Photo.** ***Perf. 11½***

116 A57 3rp copper red .35 .70
Never hinged .70
On cover 1.90
117 A58 5rp emerald 5.50 2.10
Never hinged 17.50
On cover 2.75
a. Grilled gum 5.00 11.00
Never hinged 14.00
On cover 14.00
118 A59 10rp deep violet 2.75 1.40
Never hinged 14.00
On cover 2.75
a. Grilled gum .70 8.50
Never hinged 1.75
On cover 14.00
119 A60 15rp red org .35 1.40
Never hinged 1.40
On cover 7.00
120 A61 20rp red .70 1.40
Never hinged 2.10
On cover 3.50
121 A62 25rp brown 28.00 *65.00*
Never hinged 70.00
On cover *90.00*
122 A63 30rp dk blue 5.50 2.10
Never hinged 17.50
On cover 6.25
123 A64 35rp gray grn 2.75 *8.50*
Never hinged 3.50
On cover *17.50*
124 A65 40rp brown 1.75 *7.00*
Never hinged 4.25
On cover *14.00*
125 A66 50rp lt brown 25.00 21.00
Never hinged 85.00
On cover 42.50
126 A66 60rp claret 2.10 *9.00*
Never hinged 7.00
On cover *21.00*
127 A68 90rp deep green 8.50 *32.00*
Never hinged 21.00
On cover *52.50*
128 A69 1.20fr deep blue 3.50 *32.00*
Never hinged 14.00
On cover *52.50*
129 A69 1.50fr brn car 4.25 *35.00*
Never hinged 17.50
On cover *70.00*
Nos. 116-129 (14) 91.00 *218.60*
Set, never hinged 275.00
#125-128 on fdc (6/18/34) 400.00
#116-118 on fdc (12/17/34) 525.00
#120-121 on fdc (1/3/35) 525.00
#119, 122-124, 129 on fdc (12/9/35) 600.00

Engr.
Perf. 12½

130 A70 2fr hen brn ('35) 85.00 *250.00*
Never hinged 140.00
On cover *525.00*

131 A71 5fr dk vio ('35) 425.00 *1,050.*
Never hinged 700.00
On cover *2,800.*

No. 131 has the same design as the 5fr in the souvenir sheet, No. 115. See No. 226 (in Scott Standard catalogue, Vol. 4), B14. For overprints see Nos. O11-O20.

Bridge at Malbun A72

Labor: 20rp, Constructing Road to Triesenberg. 30rp, Binnen Canal. 50rp, Bridge near Planken.

1937, June 30 **Photo.**
132 A72 10rp brt violet 1.75 2.10
Never hinged 5.25
On cover 6.00
133 A72 20rp red 1.75 *2.75*
Never hinged 5.25
On cover *6.00*
134 A72 30rp brt blue 1.75 *3.50*
Never hinged 5.25
On cover *8.00*
135 A72 50rp yellow brown 1.75 *4.25*
Never hinged 5.25
On cover *11.00*
Nos. 132-135 (4) 7.00 12.60
Set, never hinged 21.00
Set of 4 on fdc 165.00

Ruin at Schalun — A76

Peasant in Rhine Valley A77

Ruin at Schellenberg — A78

Knight and Gutenberg Castle A79

Baron von Brandis and Vaduz Castle A80

Designs: 5rp, Chapel at Masescha. 10rp, Knight and Vaduz Castle. 15rp, Upper Valüna Valley. 20rp, Wooden Bridge over Rhine, Bendern. 25rp, Chapel at Steg. 90rp, "The Three Sisters". 1fr, Frontier stone. 1.20fr, Gutenberg Castle and Harpist. 1.50fr, Alpine View of Lawena and Schwartzhorn.

1937-38
136 A76 3rp yellow brown .35 *.70*
Never hinged .70
On cover 2.00

Pale Buff Shading

137 A76 5rp emerald .35 .35
Never hinged .70
On cover 2.00
138 A76 10rp violet .35 .35
Never hinged .70
On cover 2.00
139 A76 15rp dk slate grn .35 *.70*
Never hinged .70
On cover 2.75
140 A76 20rp brn org .35 .70
Never hinged .70
On cover 2.75
141 A76 25rp chestnut .70 *3.50*
Never hinged 2.00
On cover 5.50
142 A77 30rp blue & gray 3.50 1.40
Never hinged 14.50
On cover 4.25
144 A78 40rp dark green 2.10 2.75
Never hinged 7.00
On cover 8.50
145 A79 50rp dark brown 1.40 *7.00*
Never hinged 3.50
On cover *7.00*
146 A80 60rp dp claret ('38) 2.75 *3.50*
Never hinged 7.00
On cover *11.00*
147 A80 90rp gray vio ('38) 7.00 *42.50*
Never hinged 14.00
On cover *42.50*
148 A80 1fr red brown 2.10 *17.50*
Never hinged 7.00
On cover *32.50*
149 A80 1.20fr dp brn ('38) 7.00 *32.00*
Never hinged 27.50
On cover *65.00*
a. Imperf, single *800.00* *3,250.*
Never hinged *1,400.*
On cover *8,750.*
150 A80 1.50fr slate bl ('38) 4.25 *32.50*
Never hinged 11.00
On cover *62.50*
Nos. 136-150 (14) 32.55 145.45
Set, never hinged 97.00

For overprints see Nos. O21-O29.

Souvenir Sheet

Josef Rheinberger — A91

1938, July 30 **Engr.** ***Perf. 12***
151 A91 Sheet of 4 27.50 27.50
Never hinged 70.00
On cover 70.00
On first day cover 90.00
a. 50rp slate gray 3.50 5.25
Never hinged 7.00
On cover 11.00
On first day cover 160.00

Third Philatelic Exhibition of Liechtenstein. Sheet size: 99¾x135mm.
See No. 153.

Francis Type of 1933
Thick Wove Paper

1938, Aug. 15 ***Perf. 12½***
152 A55 3fr black, *buff* 10.50 *100.00*
Never hinged 21.00
On cover 250.00
On first day cover 700.00

Issued in memory of Prince Francis I, who died July 25, 1938. Sheets of 20.

Josef Gabriel Rheinberger (1839-1901), German Composer and Organist — A92

1939, Mar. 31
153 A92 50rp slate green 1.10 *6.25*
Never hinged 2.40
On cover 11.00
On first day cover 140.00

Issued in sheets of 20. See No. 151.

Scene of Homage, 1718 — A93

1939, May 29
154 A93 20rp brown lake 1.40 2.75
Never hinged 5.50
On cover 5.00
155 A93 30rp slate blue 1.40 2.75
Never hinged 4.25
On cover 5.50
156 A93 50rp gray green 1.40 2.75
Never hinged 4.25
On cover 5.00
Nos. 154-156 (3) 4.20 8.25
Set, never hinged 14.00
Set of 3 on fdc 17.50

Honoring Prince Franz Joseph II. Sheets of 20.

Cantonal Coats of Arms — A94

Prince Franz Joseph II — A96

Design: 3fr, Arms of Principality.

1939
157 A94 2fr dk green, *buff* 7.00 *42.50*
Never hinged 17.50
On cover 90.00
158 A94 3fr indigo, *buff* 4.50 *42.50*
Never hinged 10.50
On cover 90.00
159 A96 5fr brown, *buff* 14.00 *27.50*
Never hinged 35.00
On cover 105.00
On first day cover 70.00
a. Sheet of 4 90.00 *140.00*
Never hinged 175.00
Nos. 157-159 (3) 25.50 *112.50*
Set, never hinged 63.00
Set of 3 on fdc 700.00

2fr, 3fr issued in sheets of 12; 5fr in sheets of 4.

Prince Johann as a Child A100

Memorial Tablet A101

Prince Johann II — A102

30rp, Prince Johann and Tower at Vaduz. 50rp, Prince Johann and Gutenberg Castle. 1fr, Prince Johann in 1920 and Vaduz Castle.

1940 **Photo.** ***Perf. 11½.***
160 A100 20rp henna brown .60 *2.25*
Never hinged 1.50
On cover 5.00
161 A100 30rp indigo .60 *3.25*
Never hinged 1.75
On cover 8.50
162 A100 50rp dk slate grn 1.10 *10.50*
Never hinged 3.25
On cover 21.00
163 A100 1fr brown vio 8.25 *70.00*
Never hinged 21.00
On cover 135.00
164 A101 1.50fr violet blk 10.50 *67.50*
Never hinged 27.50
On cover 125.00
165 A102 3fr brown 4.25 *22.50*
Never hinged 11.00
On cover 55.00
On first day cover 52.50
Nos. 160-165 (6) 25.30 *176.00*
Set, never hinged 52.50
Nos. 160-164 on fdc 475.00

Birth centenary of Prince Johann II.
Nos. 160-164 issued in sheets of 25; No. 165 in sheets of 12.
Issue dates: 3fr, Oct. 5; others Aug. 10.

SEMI-POSTAL STAMPS

Prince Johann II — SP1

Wmk. 183

1925, Oct. 5 **Engr.** ***Perf. 11½***
B1 SP1 10rp yellow green 42.50 22.50
Never hinged 120.00
On cover 52.50
B2 SP1 20rp deep red 21.00 22.50
Never hinged 70.00
On cover 52.50
B3 SP1 30rp deep blue 7.00 7.00
Never hinged 20.00
On cover 21.00
Nos. B1-B3 (3) 70.50 52.00
Set, never hinged 210.00
Set of 3 on fdc 625.00

85th birthday of the Prince Regent. Sold at a premium of 5rp each, the excess being devoted to charities.

Coat of Arms — SP2

1927, Oct. 5 **Typo.**
B4 SP2 10rp multicolored 10.50 *25.00*
Never hinged 24.50
On cover 52.50
B5 SP2 20rp multicolored 10.50 *25.00*
Never hinged 24.50
On cover 52.50
B6 SP2 30rp multicolored 5.00 *21.00*
Never hinged 13.00
On cover 52.50
Nos. B4-B6 (3) 26.00 *71.00*
Set, never hinged 62.00
Set of 3 on fdc 525.00

87th birthday of Prince Johann II.
These stamps were sold at premiums of 5, 10 and 20rp respectively. The money thus obtained was devoted to charity.

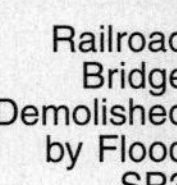

Railroad Bridge Demolished by Flood SP3

Designs: 10rp+10rp, Inundated Village of Ruggel. 20rp+10rp, Austrian soldiers rescuing refugees. 30rp+10rp, Swiss soldiers salvaging personal effects.

1928, Feb. 6 **Litho.** **Unwmk.**
B7 SP3 5rp + 5rp brn vio & brn 17.50 26.00
Never hinged 55.00
On cover 52.50
B8 SP3 10rp + 10rp bl grn & brn 25.00 26.00
Never hinged 55.00
On cover 52.50
B9 SP3 20rp + 10rp dl red & brn 25.00 26.00
Never hinged 55.00
On cover 52.50

B10 SP3 30rp + 10rp dp bl & brn 21.00 26.00
Never hinged 55.00
On cover 52.50
Nos. B7-B10 (4) 88.50 104.00
Set, never hinged 220.00
Set of 4 on fdc 650.00

The surtax on these stamps was used to aid the sufferers from the Rhine floods.

Coat of Arms — SP7

Princess Elsa — SP8

Design: 30rp, Prince Francis I.

1932, Dec. 21 **Photo.**
B11 SP7 10rp (+ 5rp) olive grn 17.50 *25.00*
Never hinged 55.00
On cover 70.00
B12 SP8 20rp (+ 5rp) rose red 17.50 *22.50*
Never hinged 55.00
On cover 70.00
B13 SP8 30rp (+ 10rp) ultra 22.50 *32.50*
Never hinged 62.50
On cover 70.00
Nos. B11-B13 (3) 57.50 *80.00*
Set, never hinged 160.00
Set of 3 on fdc 850.00

The surtax was for the Child Welfare Fund.

Postal Museum Issue
Souvenir Sheet

SP10

1936, Oct. 24 **Litho.** ***Imperf.***
B14 SP10 Sheet of 4 15.00 *35.00*
Never hinged 60.00
On cover 85.00
On first day cover 425.00

Sheet contains 2 each, Nos. 120, 122. Sold for 2fr.

AIR POST STAMPS

Airplane over Snow-capped Mountain Peaks — AP1

Airplane above Vaduz Castle — AP2

Airplane over Rhine Valley — AP3

Perf. 10½, 10½x11½
1930, Aug. 12 **Photo.** **Unwmk.**
Gray Wavy Lines in Background
C1 AP1 15rp dark brown 10.50 *17.50*
Never hinged 28.00
On cover 28.00
C2 AP1 20rp slate 25.00 *25.00*
Never hinged 70.00
On cover 35.00
C3 AP2 25rp olive brown 14.00 *45.00*
Never hinged 42.50
On cover 52.50
C4 AP2 35rp slate blue 21.00 *42.50*
Never hinged 62.50
On cover 52.50
C5 AP3 45rp olive green 50.00 *87.50*
Never hinged 140.00
On cover 105.00
C6 AP3 1fr lake 55.00 *62.50*
Never hinged 175.00
On cover 92.50
Nos. C1-C6 (6) 175.50 *280.00*
Set, never hinged 518.00
Set of 6 on fdc 1,000.

For surcharge see No. C14.

Zeppelin over Naafkopf, Falknis Range AP4

Design: 2fr, Zeppelin over Valüna Valley.

1931, June 1 ***Perf. 11½***
C7 AP4 1fr olive black 70.00 *125.00*
Never hinged 175.00
On cover 140.00
C8 AP4 2fr blue black 140.00 *400.00*
Never hinged 390.00
On cover 425.00
Set, never hinged 565.00

Golden Eagle — AP6

15rp, Golden Eagle in flight, diff. 20rp, Golden Eagle in flight, diff. 30rp, Osprey. 50rp, Eagle.

1934-35
C9 AP6 10rp brt vio ('35) 9.00 *32.50*
Never hinged 70.00
On cover 62.50
C10 AP6 15rp red org ('35) 22.50 *30.00*
Never hinged 77.50
On cover 62.50
C11 AP6 20rp red ('35) 82.50 *30.00*
Never hinged 90.00
On cover 62.50
C12 AP6 30rp brt bl ('35) 22.50 *30.00*
Never hinged 77.50
On cover 62.50
C13 AP6 50rp emerald 15.00 *35.00*
Never hinged 70.00
On cover 65.00
Nos. C9-C13 (5) 151.50 157.50
Set, never hinged 300.00

With Grilled Gum

1936
C9a AP6 10rp brt vio 7.00 *24.50*
Never hinged 21.00
On cover 28.00
C10a AP6 15rp red org 21.00 *55.00*
Never hinged 55.00
On cover 62.50
C11a AP6 20rp red 25.00 *55.00*
Never hinged 70.00
On cover 62.50
C12a AP6 30rp brt bl 25.00 *55.00*
Never hinged 70.00
On cover 62.50
C13a AP6 50rp emerald 21.00 *42.50*
Never hinged 32.50
On cover 42.50
Nos. C9a-C13a (5) 99.00 232.00
Set, never hinged 250.00

No. C6 Surcharged

1935, June 24 ***Perf. 10½x11½***
C14 AP3 60rp on 1fr lake 40.00 42.50
Never hinged 130.00
On cover 55.00
On first day cover 1,750.

Airship "Hindenburg" — AP11

Design: 2fr, Airship "Graf Zeppelin."

1936, May 1 ***Perf. 11½***
C15 AP11 1fr rose carmine 40.00 75.00
Never hinged 125.00
On cover 105.00
C16 AP11 2fr violet 30.00 75.00
Never hinged 35.00
On cover 105.00
Set, never hinged 160.00

AP13

10rp, Barn swallows. 15rp, Black-headed Gulls. 20rp, Gulls. 30rp, Eagle. 50rp, Northern Goshawk. 1fr, Lammergeier. 2fr, Lammergeier.

1939, Apr. 3 **Photo.**
C17 AP13 10rp violet .60 .70
Never hinged 1.40
On cover 2.75
a. Grilled gum 1.40 *1.40*
Never hinged 2.10
On cover 2.75
C18 AP13 15rp red orange .60 2.00
Never hinged 1.40
On cover 6.50
C19 AP13 20rp dark red 2.75 .80
Never hinged 8.50
On cover 3.50
C20 AP13 30rp dull blue 1.20 1.50
Never hinged 3.50
On cover 5.50
C21 AP13 50rp brt green 3.00 3.25
Never hinged 16.00
On cover 10.00
C22 AP13 1fr rose car 2.25 *12.00*
Never hinged 8.75
On cover 32.50
C23 AP13 2fr violet 2.25 *12.00*
Never hinged 8.75
On cover 32.50
Nos. C17-C23 (7) 12.65 *32.25*
Set, never hinged 40.00

POSTAGE DUE STAMPS

National Administration of the Post Office

D1

1920 **Unwmk.** **Engr.** ***Perf. 12½***
J1 D1 5h rose red .35 .40
Never hinged .50
On cover 2,100.
J2 D1 10h rose red .35 .40
Never hinged .50
On cover 2,100.
J3 D1 15h rose red .35 .40
Never hinged .50
On cover 2,300.
J4 D1 20h rose red .35 .55
Never hinged .50
On cover 2,300.
J5 D1 25h rose red .35 .55
Never hinged .70
On cover 2,300.
J6 D1 30h rose red .35 .55
Never hinged .70
On cover 2,300.
J7 D1 40h rose red .35 .55
Never hinged .70
On cover 2,300.
J8 D1 50h rose red .35 .55
Never hinged .70
On cover 2,300.
J9 D1 80h rose red .35 .55
Never hinged .70
On cover 2,300.
J10 D1 1k dull blue .40 1.40
Never hinged 1.75
On cover 2,450.
J11 D1 2k dull blue .40 1.40
Never hinged 1.75
On cover 2,650.
J12 D1 5k dull blue .40 1.75
Never hinged 3.50
On cover —
Nos. J1-J12 (12) 4.35 9.05
Set, never hinged 12.50

Nos. J1-J12 exist imperf. (value, unused, set $260) and part perf. (value, each: unused $2; never hinged $7; used $7).
J3 lacks the outside frame lines.

Swiss Administration of the Post Office

D2

1928 **Litho.** **Wmk. 183** ***Perf. 11½***
Granite Paper
J13 D2 5rp pur & org 1.20 *3.00*
Never hinged 3.50
On cover 21.00
J14 D2 10rp pur & org 1.20 *3.00*
Never hinged 3.50
On cover 21.00
J15 D2 15rp pur & org 1.75 *13.50*
Never hinged 7.00
On cover 50.00
J16 D2 20rp pur & org 1.75 *3.00*
Never hinged 7.00
On cover 21.00
J17 D2 25rp pur & org 1.75 *9.00*
Never hinged 21.00
On cover 32.50
J18 D2 30rp pur & org 6.00 *13.50*
Never hinged 21.00
On cover 52.50
J19 D2 40rp pur & org 7.00 *14.00*
Never hinged 21.00
On cover 85.00
J20 D2 50rp pur & org 9.00 *17.50*
Never hinged 27.50
On cover 140.00
Nos. J13-J20 (8) 29.65 *76.50*
Set, never hinged 65.00

Post Horn — D3

Engraved; Value Typographed in Dark Red
1940 **Unwmk.** ***Perf. 11½***
J21 D3 5rp gray blue 1.25 *2.75*
Never hinged 3.50
On cover 21.00
J22 D3 10rp gray blue .60 *1.40*
Never hinged 1.50
On cover 17.50
J23 D3 15rp gray blue 1.25 *5.00*
Never hinged 2.00
On cover 21.00
J24 D3 20rp gray blue .60 *2.00*
Never hinged 2.50
On cover 17.50
J25 D3 25rp gray blue 1.25 *3.50*
Never hinged 4.50
On cover 21.00
J26 D3 30rp gray blue 2.00 *5.50*
Never hinged 9.00
On cover 32.50
J27 D3 40rp gray blue 2.00 *5.50*
Never hinged 9.00
On cover 52.50
J28 D3 50rp gray blue 3.00 *5.50*
Never hinged 10.00
On cover 70.00
Nos. J21-J28 (8) 11.95 *31.15*
Set, never hinged 35.00

OFFICIAL STAMPS

Regular Issue of 1930 Overprinted in Various Colors

Perf. 11½, 11½x10½ (#O5, O6)
1932 **Unwmk.**
O1 A38 5rp dk grn (Bk) 10.50 15.50
Never hinged 35.00
On cover 32.50
a. Perf 10½ 14.00 *55.00*
Never hinged 55.00
On cover 65.00
O2 A39 10rp dark vio (R) 75.00 15.50
Never hinged 275.00
On cover 28.00
b. Perf 11½x10½ 875.00 *2,000.*
Never hinged 1,400.

On cover 2,500.
c. Perf 10½ 100.00 42.50
Never hinged 275.00
On cover 42.50
O3 A40 20rp dp rose red (Bl) 90.00 15.50
Never hinged 275.00
On cover 28.00
a. Perf. 10½ 250.00 92.50
Never hinged 675.00
On cover 140.00
O4 A42 30rp ultra (R) 17.50 21.00
Never hinged 50.00
On cover 28.00
a. Perf. 10½ 21.00 70.00
Never hinged 70.00
On cover 85.00
O5 A43 35rp dp grn (Bk) (Perf. 11½x10½) 14.00 *35.00*
Never hinged 35.00
On cover 65.00
a. Perf 11½ 8,500. *12,750.*
Never hinged 13,500.
On cover 21,000.
O6 A45 50rp blk brn (Bl) (Perf. 11½x10½) 77.50 *21.00*
Never hinged 210.00
On cover 42.50
a. Perf. 11½ 135.00 *325.00*
Never hinged 550.00
On cover 350.00
O7 A46 60rp olive blk (R) 14.00 *50.00*
Never hinged 42.50
On cover 105.00
a. Perf 10½ 14.00 *50.00*
Never hinged 42.50
On cover 85.00
O8 A48 1.20fr olive brn (G) 150.00 425.00
Never hinged 500.00
On cover 500.00
a. Perf 10½ 150.00 425.00
Never hinged 460.00
On cover 500.00
Nos. O1-O8 (8) 448.50 598.50
Set, never hinged 1,763.

Nos. 108, 110 Overprinted in Black

1933 ***Perf. 14½***
O9 A51 25rp red orange 42.50 45.00
Never hinged 125.00
On cover 75.00
a. Imperf 260.00 *525.00*
Never hinged 525.00
O10 A53 1.20fr red brown 85.00 *275.00*
Never hinged 235.00
On cover 310.00
a. Double overprint 475.00
Set, never hinged 360.00

Regular Issue of 1934-35 Ovptd. in Various Colors

1934-36 ***Perf. 11½***
O11 A58 5rp emerald (R) 2.10 *3.50*
Never hinged 7.00
On cover 5.25
a. Grilled gum 6.00 *12.00*
Never hinged 21.00
On cover 15.00
O12 A59 10rp dp vio (Bk) 4.25 *3.50*
Never hinged 14.00
On cover 5.25
a. Grilled gum 1.40 *62.50*
Never hinged 7.00
On cover 52.50
O13 A60 15rp red org (V) .90 *3.50*
Never hinged 2.10
On cover 5.25
O14 A61 20rp red (Bk) .70 *3.50*
Never hinged 2.75
On cover 5.25
O15 A62 25rp brown (R) 35.00 *115.00*
Never hinged 115.00
On cover 150.00
O16 A62 25rp brown (Bk) 3.50 *15.00*
Never hinged 21.00
On cover 22.50
O17 A63 30rp dark bl (R) 5.00 *10.50*
Never hinged 17.50
On cover 15.00
O18 A66 50rp lt brown (V) 1.40 *17.50*
Never hinged 3.50
On cover 22.50
O19 A68 90rp dp grn (Bk) 7.50 *10.50*
Never hinged 35.00
On cover 60.00
a. Double overprint 150.00
Never hinged 300.00
O20 A69 1.50fr brn car (Bl) 42.50 *280.00*
Never hinged 140.00
On cover 360.00
Nos. O11-O20 (10) 102.85 *462.50*
Set, never hinged 358.00

Regular Issue of 1937-38 Overprinted in Black, Red or Blue

1937-41
O21 A76 5rp emerald (Bk) .40 .75
Never hinged 1.00
On cover 1.50
O22 A76 10rp vio & buff (R) .80 2.00
Never hinged 2.75
On cover 3.00
O23 A76 20rp brn org (Bl) 1.60 2.00
Never hinged 3.25
On cover 3.75
O24 A76 20rp brn org (Bk) ('41) 1.60 2.75
Never hinged 4.25
On cover 3.75
O25 A76 25rp chestnut (Bk) .80 2.75
Never hinged 3.25
On cover 3.75
O26 A77 30rp blue & gray (Bk) 2.75 2.75
Never hinged 8.50
On cover 3.00
O27 A79 50rp dk brn & buff (R) 1.25 2.10
Never hinged 3.50
On cover 3.00
O28 A80 1fr red brown (Bk) 1.25 *12.00*
Never hinged 5.50
On cover 15.00
O29 A80 1.50fr slate bl (Bk) ('38) 5.00 *17.50*
Never hinged 17.50
On cover 19.00
Nos. O21-O29 (9) 15.45 *44.60*
Set, never hinged 49.50

LITHUANIA

ˌli-thə-ˈwā-nē-ə

(Lietuva)

LOCATION — Northern Europe bordering on the Baltic Sea
GOVT. — Independent republic
AREA — 22,959 sq. mi.
POP. — 2,879,070 (1940)
CAPITAL — Vilnius

Lithuania was under Russian rule when it declared its independence in 1918. The League of Nations recognized it in 1922. In 1940 it became a republic in the Union of Soviet Socialist Republics.

100 Skatiku = 1 Auksinas
100 Centai = 1 Litas (1922)

Nos. 1-26 were printed in sheets of 20 (5x4) which were imperf. at the outer sides, so that only 6 stamps in each sheet were fully perforated. Values are for the stamps partly imperf. The stamps fully perforated sell for at least double these values. There was also a printing of Nos. 19-26 in a sheet of 160, composed of blocks of 20 of each stamp. Pairs or blocks with different values se-tenant sell for considerably more than the values for the stamps singly.
Nos. 1-26 are without gum.

Watermarks

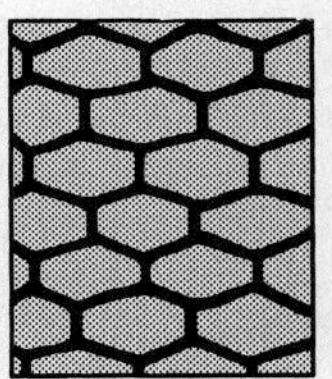
Wmk. 109 — Webbing

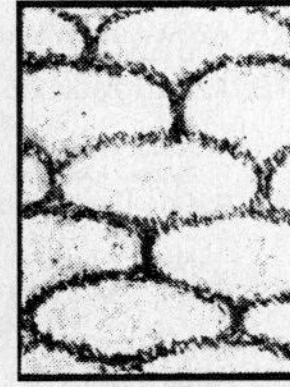
Wmk. 144 — Network

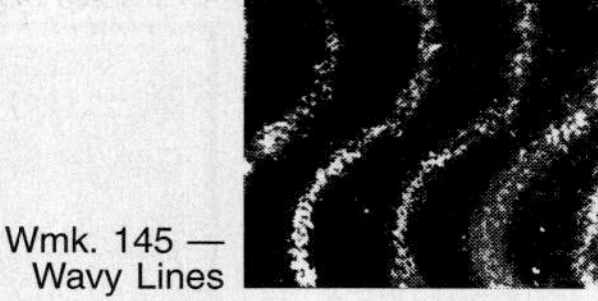
Wmk. 145 — Wavy Lines

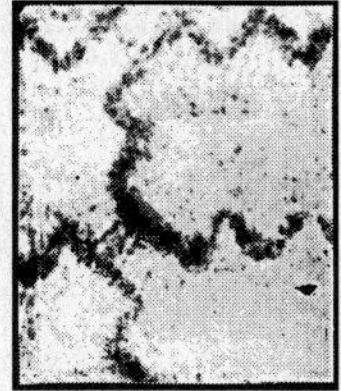
Wmk. 146 — Zigzag Lines Forming Rectangles

Wmk. 147 — Parquetry

Wmk. 198 — Intersecting Diamonds

Wmk. 209 — Multiple Ovals

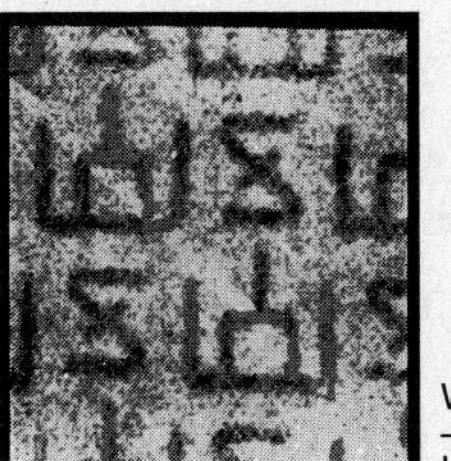
Wmk. 238 — Multiple Letters

First Vilnius Printing

A1

Thin Figures

Perf. 11½

1918, Dec. 27 **Unwmk.** **Typeset**
1 A1 10sk black 150.00 125.00
2 A1 15sk black 150.00 100.00

Second Vilnius Printing

1918, Dec. 31 **Thick Figures**
3 A1 10sk black 70.00 55.00
4 A1 15sk black 70.00 55.00
5 A1 20sk black 30.00 16.00
6 A1 30sk black 35.00 17.50
7 A1 40sk black 50.00 25.00
8 A1 50sk black 40.00 17.50
Nos. 3-8 (6) 295.00 186.00

First Kaunas Issue

A2

1919, Jan. 29
9 A2 10sk black 7.50 3.75
10 A2 15sk black 7.50 3.75
a. "5" for "15" 95.00 72.50
11 A2 20sk black 7.50 3.75
12 A2 30sk black 7.50 3.75
Nos. 9-12 (4) 30.00 15.00

Second Kaunas Issue

A3

1919, Feb. 18
13 A3 10sk black 4.25 2.50
14 A3 15sk black 4.25 2.50
15 A3 20sk black 4.25 2.50
a. "astas" for "pastas" 80.00 75.00
16 A3 30sk black 4.25 2.50
17 A3 40sk black 4.25 2.50
18 A3 50sk black 4.25 2.50
19 A3 60sk black 4.25 2.50
Nos. 13-19 (7) 29.75 17.50

Third Kaunas Issue

A4

1919, Mar. 1
20 A4 10sk black 4.25 1.75
21 A4 15sk black 4.25 1.75
22 A4 20sk black 4.25 1.75
23 A4 30sk black 4.25 1.75
24 A4 40sk black 4.25 1.75
25 A4 50sk black 4.25 1.75
26 A4 60sk black 4.25 1.75
Nos. 20-26 (7) 29.75 12.25

The White Knight "Vytis"
A5 A6

A7

Perf. 10½ to 14 & Compound
1919 **Litho.** **Wmk. 144**
Gray Granite Paper
30 A5 10sk deep rose 1.25 .40
a. Wmk. vert. 17.50 15.00
31 A5 15sk violet 1.25 .40
a. Wmk. vert. 17.50 15.00
32 A5 20sk dark blue 1.60 .40
33 A5 30sk deep orange 1.60 .40
a. Wmk. vert. 17.50 15.00
34 A5 40sk dark brown 1.60 .40
35 A6 50sk blue green 1.60 .50
36 A6 75sk org & dp rose 1.60 .50
37 A7 1auk gray & rose 3.25 .50
38 A7 3auk bis brn & rose 3.25 .50
39 A7 5auk blue grn & rose 3.25 .80
Nos. 30-39 (10) 20.25 4.80

Nos. 30a, 31a and 33a are from the first printing with watermark vertical showing points to left; various perforations.
Nos. 30-39 exist imperf. Value in pairs, $100.
Issued: Nos. 30a, 31a, 33a, 2/17/19; Nos. 30-36, 3/20/19.

Thick White Paper

1919 **Wmk. 145**
40 A5 10sk dull rose .35 .25
41 A5 15sk violet .35 .25
42 A5 20sk dark blue .35 .25
43 A5 30sk orange .35 .25
44 A5 40sk red brown .35 .25
45 A6 50sk pale grayish green .35 .25
46 A6 75sk yel & dp rose .35 .25
47 A7 1auk gray & rose .95 .35

48 A7 3auk yel brn & rose, perf. 12½ .60 .40
49 A7 5auk bl grn & rose 1.00 .40
Nos. 40-49 (10) 5.00 2.90

Nos. 40-49 exist imperf. Value in pairs, $90.

A8

Perf. 10½ to 14 & Compound

1919, May 8 Thin White Paper

50 A5 10sk red .45 .25
51 A5 15sk lilac .45 .25
52 A5 20sk dull blue .45 .25
53 A5 30sk buff .45 .25
54 A5 40sk gray brn .45 .25
55 A6 50sk lt green .45 .25
56 A6 60sk violet & red .45 .25
57 A6 75sk bister & red .45 .25
58 A8 1auk gray & red .45 .25
59 A8 3auk lt brown & red .45 .30
60 A8 5auk blue grn & red .45 .45
Nos. 50-60 (11) 4.95 3.00

Nos. 50-60 exist imperf. Value, pairs $150.
See Nos. 93-96. For surcharges see Nos. 114-115, 120-139, 149-150.

"Lithuania" Receiving Benediction — A9

The Spirit of Lithuania Rises — A10

"Lithuania" with Chains Broken — A11

White Knight — A12

1920, Feb. 16 Wmk. 146 *Perf. 11½*

70 A9 10sk dp rose 3.75 *5.25*
71 A9 15sk lt violet 3.75 *5.25*
72 A9 20sk gray blue 3.75 *5.25*
73 A10 30sk yellow brn 3.75 *5.25*
74 A11 40sk brown & grn 3.75 *5.25*
75 A10 50sk deep rose 3.75 *5.25*
76 A10 60sk lt violet 3.75 *5.25*
77 A11 80sk purple & red 3.75 *5.25*
78 A11 1auk green & red 3.75 *5.25*
79 A12 3auk brown & red 3.75 *5.25*
80 A12 5auk green & red 3.75 *5.25*
a. Right "5" dbl., grn and red 90.00 90.00
Nos. 70-80 (11) 41.25 *57.75*

Anniv. of natl. independence. The stamps were on sale only 3 days in Kaunas. The stamps were available in other cities after that. Only a limited number of stamps was sold at post offices but 40,000 sets were delivered to the bank of Kaunas.
All values exist imperforate.

White Knight — A13

Grand Duke Vytautas — A14

Grand Duke Gediminas A15

Sacred Oak and Altar A16

1920, Aug. 25

81 A13 15sk rose .80 1.60
a. Imperf., pair 40.00
82 A13 15sk dark violet .80 1.60
83 A14 20sk grn & lt grn .80 1.60
84 A13 30sk brown .80 1.60
a. Pair, #82, 84 40.00
85 A15 40sk gray grn & vio .80 1.60
86 A14 50sk brn & brn org 2.00 2.00
87 A14 60sk red & org .80 1.60
88 A15 80sk blk, db & red .80 1.60
89 A16 1auk orange & blk 1.25 1.60
90 A16 3auk green & blk 1.25 1.60
91 A16 5auk gray vio & blk 3.25 2.40
Nos. 81-91 (11) 13.35 18.80

Opening of Lithuanian National Assembly. On sale for three days.

1920

92 A14 20sk green & lilac 125.00
92A A15 40sk gray grn, buff & vio 125.00
92B A14 50sk brown & gray lil 125.00
92C A14 60sk red & green 125.00
92D A15 80sk black, grn & red 125.00
Nos. 92-92D (5) 625.00

Nos. 92 to 92D were trial printings. By order of the Ministry of Posts, 2,000 examples of each were placed on sale at post offices.

Type of 1919 Issue

1920 Unwmk. *Perf. 11½*

93 A5 15sk lilac 6.00 4.50
94 A5 20sk deep blue 6.00 4.50

Wmk. 109

95 A5 20sk deep blue 5.00 5.00
96 A5 40sk gray brown 9.75 8.50
Nos. 93-96 (4) 26.75 22.50
Set, never hinged 40.00

Watermark vertical or horizontal on Nos. 95-96.
No. 96 exists perf. 10½x11½.

Imperf., Pairs

93a	A5	15sk	32.00	32.00
94a	A5	20sk	32.00	32.00
95a	A5	20sk	17.00	17.00
96a	A5	40sk	48.00	48.00

Sower A17

Peasant Sharpening Scythe A18

Prince Kestutis A19

Black Horseman A20

Perf. 11, 11½ and Compound

1921-22

97 A17 10sk brt rose .85 .55
98 A17 15sk violet .35 *.70*
99 A17 20sk ultra .25 .25
100 A18 30sk brown 2.50 *1.10*
101 A19 40sk red .25 .25
102 A18 50sk olive .35 .25
103 A18 60sk grn & vio 2.50 *1.65*
104 A19 80sk brn org & car .35 .25
105 A19 1auk brown & grn .35 .25
106 A19 2auk gray bl & red .35 .25
107 A20 3auk yel brn & dk bl 1.00 .40
108 A17 4auk yel & dk bl ('22) .45 .25
109 A20 5auk gray blk & rose 1.00 *1.50*
110 A17 8auk grn & blk ('22) .45 .25
111 A20 10auk rose & vio 1.00 .55
112 A20 25auk bis brn & grn 1.25 *2.75*
113 A20 100auk dl red & gray blk 12.50 8.00
Nos. 97-113 (17) 25.75 19.20
Set, never hinged 85.00

Imperf., Pairs

97a	A17	10sk	—	
98a	A17	15sk	—	
99a	A17	20sk	—	
100a	A18	30sk	—	
101a	A19	40sk	25.00	
102a	A18	50sk	25.00	
103a	A18	60sk	—	
104a	A19	80sk	—	
105a	A19	1auk	—	
106a	A19	2auk	120.00	
107a	A20	3auk	120.00	
109a	A20	5auk	120.00	
110a	A17	8auk	10.00	10.00
111a	A20	10auk	50.00	
112a	A20	25auk	50.00	
113a	A20	100auk	50.00	

For surcharges see Nos. 140-148, 151-160.

No. 57 Surcharged

Perf. 12½x11½

1922, May Wmk. 145

114 A6 4auk on 75sk bis & red .90 .25
Never hinged 1.50
a. Inverted surcharge 35.00 35.00

Same with Bars over Original Value

115 A6 4auk on 75sk bis & red 4.00 *8.00*
Never hinged 6.50
a. Double surcharge 30.00 30.00

Povilas Luksis — A20a

Justinas Staugaitis, Antanas Smetona, Stasys Silingas — A20b

Portraits: 40s, Lt. Juozapavicius. 50s, Dr. Basanavicius. 60s, Mrs. Petkeviciute. 1auk, Prof. Voldemaras. 2auk, Pranas Dovidaitis. 3auk, Dr. Slezevicius. 4auk, Dr. Galvanauskas. 5auk, Kazys Grinius. 6auk, Dr. Stulginskis. 8auk, Pres. Smetona.

1922 Litho. Unwmk.

116 A20a 20s blk & car rose 1.25 *2.10*
Never hinged 2.00
116A A20a 40s bl grn & vio 1.25 *2.10*
Never hinged 2.00
116B A20a 50s plum & grnsh bl 1.25 *2.10*
Never hinged 2.00
117 A20a 60s pur & org 1.25 *2.10*
Never hinged 2.00
117A A20a 1auk car & lt bl 1.25 *2.10*
Never hinged 2.00
117B A20a 2auk dp bl & yel brn 1.25 *2.10*
Never hinged 2.00
c. Center inverted 100.00 100.00
118 A20a 3auk mar & ultra 1.25 *2.10*
Never hinged 2.00
118A A20a 4auk dk grn & red vio 1.25 *2.10*
Never hinged 2.00
118B A20a 5auk blk brn & dp rose 1.25 *2.10*
Never hinged 2.00
119 A20a 6auk dk bl & grnsh bl 1.25 *2.10*
Never hinged 2.00
a. Cliché of 8auk in sheet of 6auk 175.00 *175.00*
119B A20a 8auk ultra & bis 1.25 *2.10*
Never hinged 2.00
119C A20b 10auk dk vio & bl grn 1.25 *2.10*
Never hinged 2.00
Nos. 116-119C (12) 15.00 25.20

League of Nations' recognition of Lithuania. Sold only on Oct. 1, 1922.
Forty sheets of the 6auk each included eight examples of the 8auk.

Stamps of 1919-22 Surcharged in Black, Carmine or Green On Nos. 37-39

1922 Wmk. 144 *Perf. 11½x12*

Gray Granite Paper

120 A7 3c on 1auk 100.00 *100.00*
Never hinged 175.00
121 A7 3c on 3auk 100.00 *100.00*
Never hinged 175.00
122 A7 3c on 5auk 150.00 *150.00*
Never hinged 200.00
Nos. 120-122 (3) 350.00 350.00

White Paper

Perf. 14, 11½, 12½x11½

Wmk. 145

123 A5 1c on 10sk red .55 1.50
124 A5 1c on 15sk lilac .80 1.50
125 A5 1c on 20sk dull bl .50 1.50
126 A5 1c on 30sk org *250.00 110.00*
Never hinged 350.00
127 A5 1c on 30sk buff .25 .40
128 A5 1c on 40sk gray brn 1.60 1.50
129 A6 2c on 50sk green .70 1.50
130 A6 2c on 60sk vio & red .25 .25
131 A6 2c on 75sk bis & red .40 1.50
132 A8 3c on 1auk gray & red .25 .25
133 A8 3c on 3auk brn & red .25 .25
134 A8 3c on 5auk bl grn & red .25 .25
Nos. 123-125,127-134 (11) 5.80 10.40
Set, never hinged, *Nos. 123-125, 127-134)* 24.00

On Stamps of 1920

1922 Unwmk. *Perf. 11*

136 A5 1c on 20sk dp bl (C) 3.75 2.00

Wmk. Webbing (109)

Perf. 11, 11½

138 A5 1c on 20sk dp bl (C) 3.50 2.00
139 A5 1c on 40sk gray brn (C) 7.50 1.25

Stamps of 1921-22 Surcharged

140 A18 1c on 50sk ol (C) .25 .25
a. Imperf., pair 45.00
b. Inverted surcharge 40.00
c. Double surch., one invtd.
141 A17 3c on 10sk 11.00 8.00
142 A17 3c on 15sk .25 .25
143 A17 3c on 20sk .40 1.50
144 A18 3c on 30sk 18.50 12.00
145 A19 3c on 40sk .40 .40
a. Imperf., pair
146 A18 5c on 50sk .25 .25
147 A18 5c on 60sk 18.50 18.50
148 A19 5c on 80sk .55 .55
a. Imperf., pair 35.00 15.00

Wmk. Wavy Lines (145)

Perf. 12½x11½

149 A6 5c on 4auk on 75sk (No. 114) (G) 1.60 10.00
150 A6 5c on 4auk on 75sk (No. 115) (G) 16.00 17.50

Wmk. Webbing (109)

Perf. 11, 11½

151 A19 10c on 1auk .80 .25
a. Inverted surcharge 55.00
152 A19 10c on 2auk .25 .25
a. Inverted surcharge 50.00
b. Imperf., pair 45.00
153 A17 15c on 4auk .25 .25
a. Inverted surcharge 45.00
154 A20 25c on 3auk 18.50 18.50
155 A20 25c on 5auk 11.00 5.00

156 A20 25c on 10auk 2.25 1.50
a. Imperf., pair 45.00
157 A17 30c on 8auk (C) 1.15 .35
a. Inverted surcharge 45.00 25.00
158 A20 50c on 25auk 3.75 2.50
160 A20 1 l on 100auk 4.00 2.50
Nos. 136-160 (23) 124.40 105.55
Set, never hinged 140.00

A21

Ruin — A22

Seminary Church, Kaunas — A23

1923 Litho. Wmk. 109 *Perf. 11*

165 A21 10c violet 7.00 .25
Never hinged 8.50
166 A21 15c scarlet 2.50 .25
Never hinged 3.00
167 A21 20c olive brown 2.50 .25
Never hinged 3.00
168 A21 25c deep blue 2.50 .25
Never hinged 3.00
169 A22 50c yellow green 2.50 .25
Never hinged 3.00
170 A22 60c red 2.50 .25
Never hinged 3.00
171 A23 1 l orange & grn 10.50 .25
Never hinged 14.50
172 A23 3 l red & gray 15.00 .45
Never hinged 19.00
173 A23 5 l brown & blue 21.00 1.00
Never hinged 28.00
Nos. 165-173 (9) 66.00 3.20
Set, never hinged 125.00

See Nos. 189-209, 281-282. For surcharges see Nos. B1-B42.

Memel Coat of Arms — A24

Lithuanian Coat of Arms — A25

Biruta Chapel — A26

Kaunas, War Memorial A27

Trakai Ruins A28

Memel Lighthouse — A29

Memel Harbor A30

Perf. 11, 11½, 12

1923, Aug. Unwmk.

176 A24 1c rose, grn & blk 1.25 1.60
Never hinged 2.50
177 A25 2c dull vio & blk 1.25 1.60
Never hinged 2.50
178 A26 3c yellow & blk 1.25 1.60
Never hinged 2.50
179 A24 5c bl, buff & blk 2.50 4.50
Never hinged 4.50
180 A27 10c orange & blk 1.90 3.00
Never hinged 3.50
181 A27 15c green & blk 1.90 3.00
Never hinged 3.50
182 A28 25c brt vio & blk 1.90 3.00
Never hinged 3.50
183 A25 30c red vio & blk 4.00 *7.50*
Never hinged 7.50
184 A29 60c ol grn & blk 2.25 *3.00*
Never hinged 4.00
185 A30 1 l bl grn & blk 2.25 *3.00*
Never hinged 4.00
186 A26 2 l red & black 8.25 15.00
Never hinged 15.00
187 A28 3 l blue & black 8.25 15.00
Never hinged 16.00
188 A29 5 l ultra & black 8.25 15.00
Never hinged 16.00
Nos. 176-188 (13) 45.20 76.80
Set, never hinged 100.00

This series was issued ostensibly to commemorate the incorporation of Memel with Lithuania.

Type of 1923

1923 Unwmk. *Perf. 11*

189 A21 5c pale green 3.75 .75
Never hinged 9.00
190 A21 10c violet 5.00 .75
Never hinged 12.00
a. Imperf., pair 50.00
191 A21 15c scarlet 6.00 .75
Never hinged 14.00
a. Imperf., pair 50.00
193 A21 25c blue 10.00 .75
Never hinged 25.00
Nos. 189-193 (4) 24.75 3.00
Set, never hinged 60.00

1923 Wmk. 147

196 A21 2c pale brown 1.50 .45
Never hinged 1.40
197 A21 3c olive bister 2.25 .45
Never hinged 1.60
198 A21 5c pale green 2.25 .45
Never hinged 1.60
199 A21 10c violet 4.50 .45
Never hinged 3.50
202 A21 25c deep blue 11.00 .45
Never hinged 7.00
a. Imperf., pair 40.00
204 A21 36c orange brown 17.50 1.50
Never hinged 11.00
Nos. 196-204 (6) 39.00 3.75
Set, never hinged 70.00

Perf. 11½, 14½, 11½x14½

1923-25 Wmk. 198

207 A21 25c deep blue 750.00 450.00
Never hinged 1,000.
208 A22 50c deep green ('25) *25.00* 1.00
Never hinged 75.00
209 A22 60c carmine ('25) *25.00* .50
Never hinged 75.00

Double-barred Cross — A31

1927, Jan. *Perf. 11½, 14½*

210 A31 2c orange 1.50 .35
Never hinged 2.00
211 A31 3c deep brown 1.50 .35
Never hinged 2.00
212 A31 5c green 2.25 .35
Never hinged 3.50
a. Imperf., pair 25.00
213 A31 10c violet 3.25 .35
Never hinged 4.50
214 A31 15c red 3.25 .35
Never hinged 4.50
a. Imperf., pair 25.00
215 A31 25c blue 3.25 .30
Never hinged 4.50
Nos. 210-215 (6) 15.00 2.05
Set, never hinged 45.00

1926-30 Wmk. 147 *Perf. 14½*

216 A31 5c green 35.00 *150.00*
Never hinged 100.00
217 A31 30c blue ('30) 30.00 10.00
Never hinged 100.00

See Nos. 233-240, 278-280.

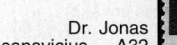

Dr. Jonas Basanavicius — A32

1927 Unwmk. *Perf. 11½, 14½x11½*

219 A32 15c claret & blk 3.00 1.50
Never hinged 4.00
220 A32 25c dull blue & blk 3.00 1.50
Never hinged 4.00
221 A32 50c dk green & blk 3.00 1.50
Never hinged 4.00
222 A32 60c dk violet & blk 9.00 3.00
Never hinged 8.00
Nos. 219-222 (4) 18.00 7.50
Set, never hinged 35.00

Dr. Jonas Basanavicius (1851-1927), patriot and folklorist.

National Arms — A33

1927, Dec. 23 Wmk. 109 *Perf. 14½*

223 A33 1 l blue grn & gray 6.50 .80
Never hinged 3.00
224 A33 3 l vio & pale grn 5.00 .80
Never hinged 8.00
225 A33 5 l brown & gray 6.00 1.40
Never hinged 10.00
Nos. 223-225 (3) 17.50 3.00
Set, never hinged 25.00

Pres. Antanas Smetona — A34

Decade of Independence A35

Dawn of Peace — A36

1928, Feb. Wmk. 109

226 A34 5c org brn & grn 1.00 .75
Never hinged 1.50
227 A34 10c violet & blk 1.25 .75
Never hinged 1.90
228 A34 15c orange & brn 1.25 .75
Never hinged 1.90
229 A34 25c blue & indigo 1.25 .75
Never hinged 1.90
230 A35 50c ultra & dl vio 1.50 .75
Never hinged 2.25
231 A35 60c carmine & blk 1.75 .75
Never hinged 2.50
232 A36 1 l blk brn & drab 2.00 2.25
Never hinged 3.00
Nos. 226-232 (7) 10.00 6.75
Set, never hinged 15.00

10th anniv. of Lithuanian independence.

Type of 1926

1929-31

233 A31 2c orange ('31) 12.00 1.60
Never hinged 18.50
234 A31 5c green 4.00 .35
Never hinged 4.75
235 A31 10c violet ('31) 10.00 2.00
Never hinged 14.00
237 A31 15c red 4.50 .45
Never hinged 5.50
a. Tête bêche pair 45.00 35.00
239 A31 30c dark blue 6.00 .45
Never hinged 8.50

Unwmk.

240 A31 15c red ('30) 10.00 .75
Never hinged 14.00
Nos. 233-240 (6) 46.50 5.60
Set, never hinged 85.00

Grand Duke Vytautas A37

Grand Duke, Mounted A38

1930, Feb. 16 *Perf. 14*

242 A37 2c yel brn & dk brn .30 .25
Never hinged .70
243 A37 3c dk brn & vio .30 .25
Never hinged .70
244 A37 5c yel grn & dp org .30 .25
Never hinged .70
245 A37 10c vio & emer .30 .25
Never hinged .70
246 A37 15c dp rose & vio .30 .25
Never hinged .70
247 A37 30c dk bl & brn vio .50 .25
Never hinged 1.25
248 A37 36c brn vio & ol blk .75 .30
Never hinged 1.90
249 A37 50c dull grn & ultra .50 .35
Never hinged 1.25
250 A37 60c dk blue & rose .50 .40
Never hinged 1.25
251 A38 1 l bl grn, db & red brn 2.10 1.00
Never hinged 5.50
252 A38 3 l dk brn, sal & dk vio 3.25 1.75
Never hinged 8.25
253 A38 5 l ol brn, gray & red 7.50 2.75
Never hinged 19.00
254 A38 10 l multicolored 20.00 16.00
Never hinged 50.00
255 A38 25 l multicolored 42.50 55.00
Never hinged 110.00
Nos. 242-255 (14) 79.10 79.05
Set, never hinged 200.00

5th cent. of the death of the Grand Duke Vytautas.

Kaunas, Railroad Station A39

Cathedral at Vilnius — A39a

Designs: 15c, 25c, Landscape on the Neman River. 50c, Main Post Office, Kaunas.

1932, July 21 Wmk. 238 *Perf. 14*

256 A39 10c dk red brn & ocher .40 *.40*
Never hinged .55
257 A39 15c dk brown & ol .40 *.40*
Never hinged 1.10
258 A39 25c dk blue & ol 1.25 *1.25*
Never hinged 1.60
259 A39 50c gray blk & ol 2.50 2.50
Never hinged 3.50
260 A39a 1 l dk blue & ol 6.50 6.50
Never hinged 9.25
261 A39a 3 l red brn & gray grn 6.50 6.50
Never hinged 9.25

Wmk. 198

262 A39 5c vio bl & ocher .40 *.40*
Never hinged .55
263 A39a 60c grnsh blk & lil 6.50 6.50
Never hinged 9.25
Nos. 256-263 (8) 24.45 24.45
Set, never hinged 60.00

Imperf.

256a A39 10c dk red brn & ocher .35 .35
257a A39 15c dk brown & ol .65 .65
258a A39 25c dk blue & ol 1.00 1.00
259a A39 50c gray blk & ol 2.00 2.00
260a A39a 1 l dk blue & ol 5.25 5.25
261a A39a 3 l red brn & gray grn 5.25 5.25
262a A39 5c violet bl & ocher .35 .35
263a A39a 60c grnsh blk & lil 5.25 5.25

Issued for the benefit of Lithuanian orphans.

In September, 1935, a red overprint was applied to No. 259: "ORO PASTAS / LITUANICA II / 1935 / NEW YORK-KAUNAS." Value, $400.

Vytautas Fleeing from Prison, 1382 A40

Designs: 15c, 25c, Conversion of Ladislas II Jagello and Vytautas (1386). 50c, 60c, Battle at Tannenberg (1410). 1 l, 3 l, Meeting of the Nobles (1429).

1932 Wmk. 209 *Perf. 14*

264 A40 5c red & rose lake .35 *.35*
Never hinged .75
265 A40 10c ol bis & org brn .35 *.35*
Never hinged .85
266 A40 15c rose lil & ol grn .35 *.35*
Never hinged 1.00
267 A40 25c dk vio brn & ocher 1.00 *1.00*
Never hinged 2.25
268 A40 50c dp grn & bis brn 1.00 *1.00*
Never hinged 2.25
269 A40 60c ol grn & brn car 2.40 *2.40*
Never hinged 5.50
270 A40 1 l ultra & ol grn 2.40 *2.40*
Never hinged 6.00
271 A40 3 l dk brn & dk grn 2.40 *2.40*
Never hinged 6.50
Nos. 264-271 (8) 10.25 *10.25*
Set, never hinged 25.00

Imperf.

264a A40 5c red & rose lake .65 .65
265a A40 10c ol bis & org brn .65 .65
266a A40 15c rose lil & ol grn .65 .65
267a A40 25c dk vio brn & ocher 2.00 2.00
268a A40 50c dp grn & bis brn 4.50 4.50
269a A40 60c ol grn & brn car 4.50 4.50
270a A40 1 l ultra & ol grn 4.50 4.50
271a A40 3 l dk brn & dk grn 4.50 4.50

15th anniversary of independence.

A. Visteliauskas A41

Designs: 15c, 25c, Petras Vileisis. 50c, 60c, Dr. John Sliupas. 1 l, 3 l, Jonas Basanavicius.

1933 *Perf. 14*

272 A41 5c yel grn & car .40 .40
Never hinged .60
273 A41 10c ultra & car .40 .40
Never hinged .80
274 A41 15c orange & red .40 .40
Never hinged 1.00
275 A41 25c dk bl & blk brn 1.25 *1.25*
Never hinged 1.50
276 A41 50c ol gray & dk bl 1.25 *1.25*
Never hinged 2.50
277 A41 60c org brn & chnt 5.50 5.50
Never hinged 8.00
277A A41 1 l red & vio brn 5.50 5.50
Never hinged 10.00
277B A41 3 l turq grn & vio brn 5.50 5.50
Never hinged 11.00
Nos. 272-277B (8) 20.20 20.20
Set, never hinged 35.00

Imperf.

272a A41 5c yel grn & car .40 .40
273a A41 10c ultra & car .40 .40
274a A41 15c orange & red .40 .40
275a A41 25c dk bl & blk brn 1.25 1.25
276a A41 50c ol gray & dk bl 1.25 1.25
277a A41 60c org brn & chnt 5.50 5.50
277Aa A41 1 l red & vio brn 5.50 5.50
277Ba A41 3 l turq grn & vio brn 5.50 5.50

50th anniv. of the 1st newspaper, "Ausra," in lithuanian language.

Mother and Child — A42

Designs: 15c, 25c, Boy reading. 50c, 60c, Boy playing with blocks. 1 l, 3 l, Woman and boy at the Spinning Wheel.

1933, Sept. *Perf. 14*

277C A42 5c dp yel grn & org brn .35 .35
Never hinged .50
277D A42 10c rose brn & ultra .35 *.35*
Never hinged .55
277E A42 15c ol grn & plum .35 *.35*
Never hinged .55
277F A42 25c org & gray blk 1.40 *1.40*
Never hinged 1.90
277G A42 50c ol grn & car 1.40 *1.40*
Never hinged 2.50
277H A42 60c blk & yel org 5.75 5.75
Never hinged 8.50
277I A42 1 l dk brn & ultra 5.75 5.75
Never hinged 9.50
277K A42 3 l rose lil & ol grn 5.75 *5.75*
Never hinged 11.00
Nos. 277C-277K (8) 21.10 *21.10*
Set, never hinged 35.00

Imperf.

277Ca A42 5c dp yel grn & org brn .25 .25
277Da A42 10c rose brn & ultra .25 .25
277Ea A42 15c ol grn & plum .25 .25
277Fa A42 25c org & gray blk 1.00 1.00
277Ga A42 50c ol gray & dk bl 1.00 1.00
277Ha A42 60c org brn & chnt 4.25 4.25
277Ia A42 1 l dk brn & ultra 4.25 4.25
277Ka A42 3 l rose lil & ol grn 4.25 4.25

Issued for the benefit of Lithuanian orphans.

Types of 1923-26

1933-34 Wmk. 238 *Perf. 14*

278 A31 2c orange 42.50 6.50
Never hinged 75.00
279 A31 10c dark violet 60.00 9.50
Never hinged 100.00
280 A31 15c red 42.50 4.50
Never hinged 75.00
281 A22 50c green 42.50 9.50
Never hinged 75.00
282 A22 60c red 42.50 9.50
Never hinged 75.00
Nos. 278-282 (5) 230.00 39.50
Set, never hinged 400.00

Pres. Antanas Smetona, 60th Birthday — A43

1934 Engr. Unwmk. *Perf. 11½*

283 A43 15c red 6.50 1.50
Never hinged 11.00
284 A43 30c green 8.25 1.50
Never hinged 8.25
285 A43 60c blue 10.00 2.00
Never hinged 10.00
Nos. 283-285 (3) 24.75 5.00
Set, never hinged 42.50

A44

Arms — A45

Girl with Wheat — A46

A47

Knight A48

Wmk. 198; Wmk. 209 (35c, 10 l)

1934-35 Litho. *Perf. 14*

286 A44 2c rose & dull org 1.50 .25
Never hinged 3.00
287 A44 5c bl grn & grn 1.50 .25
Never hinged 3.00
288 A45 10c chocolate 3.50 .25
Never hinged 7.50
289 A46 25c dk brn & emer 5.50 .25
Never hinged 12.00
290 A45 35c carmine 5.50 .25
Never hinged 12.00
291 A46 50c dk blue & blue 10.00 .25
Never hinged 20.00
292 A47 1 l salmon & mar 92.50 .25
Never hinged 190.00
293 A47 3 l grn & gray grn .45 .25
Never hinged 1.00
294 A48 5 l maroon & gray bl .65 .45
Never hinged 1.25
295 A48 10 l choc & yel 4.50 3.75
Never hinged 10.00
Nos. 286-295 (10) 125.60 6.20
Set, never hinged 275.00

No. 290 exists imperf. Value, pair $65.

For overprint see No. 2N9.

1936-37 Wmk. 238 *Perf. 14*

Size: 17½x23mm

296 A44 2c orange ('37) .40 .30
Never hinged .80
297 A44 5c green .40 .30
Never hinged .80

Pres. Smetona — A49

1936-37 Unwmk.

298 A49 15c carmine 5.50 .35
Never hinged 9.00
299 A49 30c green ('37) 9.00 .35
Never hinged 12.00
300 A49 60c ultra ('37) 10.00 .35
Never hinged 11.00
Nos. 298-300 (3) 24.50 1.05
Set, never hinged 40.00

Arms — A50

No. 304 exists in two types:

I — "50" is fat and broad, with "0" leaning to right.

II — "50" is thinner and narrower, with "0" straight.

Paper with Gray Network

1937-39 Wmk. 238 *Perf. 14*

301 A50 10c green .85 .25
Never hinged 1.90
302 A50 25c magenta .25 .25
Never hinged .25
303 A50 35c red .50 .25
Never hinged 1.00
304 A50 50c brown .30 .25
Never hinged .60
305 A50 1 l dp vio bl ('39) .35 .45
Never hinged .75
Nos. 301-305 (5) 2.25 1.45
Set, never hinged 10.00

For overprint see No. 2N10.

Jonas Basanavicius Reading Act of Independence A51

President Antanas Smetona A52

Perf. 13x13½

1939, Jan. 15 Engr. Unwmk.

306 A51 15c dark red .25 *.30*
Never hinged .50
307 A52 30c deep green .50 .30
Never hinged 1.00
308 A51 35c red lilac .60 .45
Never hinged 1.25
309 A52 60c dark blue .75 .60
Never hinged 1.50
a. Souvenir sheet of 2, #308-309 5.00 10.00
Never hinged 10.00
b. As "a," imperf. 35.00 45.00
Never hinged 72.50
Nos. 306-309 (4) 2.10 1.65
Set, never hinged 5.00

20th anniv. of Independence.
Nos. 309a, 309b sold for 2 l.

Same Overprinted in Blue

1939

310 A51 15c dark red .50 *.90*
Never hinged .85
311 A52 30c deep green .50 *.90*
Never hinged .90
312 A51 35c red lilac 1.25 1.00
Never hinged 2.00
313 A52 60c dark blue 1.25 1.00
Never hinged 2.25
Nos. 310-313 (4) 3.50 3.80
Set, never hinged 7.00

Recovery of Vilnius.

View of Vilnius A53

Gediminas — A54

Trakai Ruins A55

Unwmk.

1940, May 6 Photo. *Perf. 14*

314 A53 15c brn & pale brn .40 .25
Never hinged .75
315 A54 30c dk grn & lt grn .90 .50
Never hinged 1.25
316 A55 60c dk bl & lt bl 2.00 .70
Never hinged 2.25
a. Souv. sheet of 3, #314-316, imperf. 8.00 *16.00*
Never hinged 16.00
Nos. 314-316 (3) 3.30 1.45
Set, never hinged 5.00

Return of Vilnius to Lithuania, Oct. 10, 1939. Exist imperf.
No. 316a has simulated perforations in gold. Sold for 2 l.

White Knight — A56

Angel — A57

Woman Releasing Dove A58

Mother and Children A59

Liberty Bell — A60

Mythical Animal — A61

1940

317 A56 5c brown carmine .40 *.30*
Never hinged .40
318 A57 10c green .40 *.45*
Never hinged 1.25
319 A58 15c dull orange .40 *.30*
Never hinged .40
320 A59 25c light brown .40 *.40*
Never hinged .40
321 A60 30c Prussian green .40 *.30*
Never hinged .45
322 A61 35c red orange .40 *.35*
Never hinged .60
Nos. 317-322 (6) 2.40 *2.10*
Set, never hinged 4.50

Nos. 317-322 exist imperf.
For overprints see Nos. 2N11-2N16.

SEMI-POSTAL STAMPS

Regular Issue of 1923-24 Surcharged in Blue, Violet or Black

On A21

On A22

On A23

1924, Feb. Wmk. 147 *Perf. 11*

B1 A21 2c + 2c pale brn (Bl) .90 *2.25*
B2 A21 3c + 3c ol bis (Bl) .90 *2.25*
B3 A21 5c + 5c pale grn (V) .90 *2.25*
B4 A21 10c + 10c vio (Bk) 2.25 *3.25*
B5 A21 36c + 34c org brn (V) 4.75 *12.00*

Wmk. Webbing (109)

B6 A21 10c + 10c vio (Bk) 7.50 *20.00*
B7 A21 15c + 15c scar (V) 1.10 *2.50*
B8 A21 20c + 20c ol brn (Bl) 2.25 *4.00*
B9 A21 25c + 25c bl (Bk) 21.00 *55.00*
B10 A22 50c + 50c yel grn (V) 5.25 *12.00*
B11 A22 60c + 60c red (V) 5.25 *12.00*
B12 A23 1 l + 1 l org & grn (V) 6.00 *16.00*
B13 A23 3 l + 2 l red & gray (V) 9.00 *32.50*
B14 A23 5 l + 3 l brn & bl (V) 15.00 *40.00*

Unwmk.

B15 A21 25c + 25c dp bl (Bk) 4.75 *12.00*
Nos. B1-B15 (15) 86.80 228.00
Set, never hinged 225.00

For War Invalids

Semi-Postal Stamps of 1924 Surcharged in Gold or Copper

1926, Dec. 3 Wmk. 147

B16 A21 1 + 1c on #B1 1.00 1.25
a. Inverted surcharge 40.00
B17 A21 2 + 2c on #B2 (C) 1.00 1.25
B19 A21 2 + 2c on #B3 1.00 1.25
a. Double surch., one inverted 40.00
B20 A21 5 + 5c on #B4 2.00 2.00
B21 A21 14 + 14c on #B5 6.00 7.00

Wmk. Webbing (109)

B22 A21 5 + 5c on #B6 10.00 10.00
B23 A21 5 + 5c on #B7 2.00 2.00
B24 A21 10 + 10c on #B8 2.00 2.00
B25 A21 10 + 10c on #B9 65.00 65.00

Unwmk.

B26 A21 10 + 10c on #B15 4.00 5.00

Surcharged in Copper or Silver

On A22

On A23

Wmk. Webbing (109)

B27 A22 20 + 20c on #B10 4.00 5.00
B28 A22 25 + 25c on #B11 (S) 6.00 7.00
B29 A23 30 + 30c on #B12 (S) 9.00 11.00
Nos. B16-B29 (13) 113.00 119.75
Set, never hinged 225.00

For War Orphans

Surcharged in Gold

1926, Dec. 3 Wmk. 147

B30 A21 1 + 1c on #B1 .90 .90
B31 A21 2 + 2c on #B2 .90 .90
a. Inverted surcharge 260.00
B32 A21 2 + 2c on #B3 .90 .90
a. Inverted surcharge 30.00
B33 A21 5 + 5c on #B4 2.00 2.25
B34 A21 19 + 19c on #B5 4.00 5.00

Wmk. Webbing (109)

B35 A21 5 + 5c on #B6 10.00 10.00
B36 A21 10 + 10c on #B7 1.75 2.00
B37 A21 15 + 15c on #B8 2.00 2.25
B38 A21 15 + 15c on #B9 65.00 65.00

Unwmk.

B39 A21 15 + 15c on #B15 3.00 3.00

Surcharged in Gold

On A22

On A23

Wmk. 109

B40 A22 25c on #B10 5.00 6.00
B41 A22 30c on #B11 8.00 7.00
B42 A23 50c on #B12 10.00 11.00
Nos. B30-B42 (13) 113.45 116.20
Set, never hinged 225.00

Javelin throwing — SP1

Natl. Olympiad, July 15-20: 5c+5c, Archery. 30c+10c, Diving. 60c+15c, Running.

Unwmk.

1938, July 13 Photo. *Perf. 14*

B43 SP1 5c + 5c grn & dk grn 2.50 2.50
Never hinged 6.50
B44 SP1 15c + 5c org & red org 2.50 2.50
Never hinged 6.50
B45 SP1 30c + 10c bl & dk bl 4.50 4.50
Never hinged 12.00
B46 SP1 60c + 15c tan & brn 5.75 5.75
Never hinged 17.50
Nos. B43-B46 (4) 15.25 15.25
Set, never hinged 45.00

Same Overprinted in Red, Blue or Black

Nos. B47, B50

Nos. B48-B49

1938, July 13

B47 SP1 5c + 5c (R) 5.00 5.00
Never hinged 12.00
B48 SP1 15c + 5c (Bl) 5.00 5.00
Never hinged 12.00
B49 SP1 30c + 10c (R) 5.00 5.00
Never hinged 16.00
B50 SP1 60c + 15c (Bk) 10.00 10.00
Never hinged 20.00
Nos. B47-B50 (4) 25.00 25.00
Set, never hinged 50.00

National Scout Jamboree, July 12-14. Forged cancellations exist.

Basketball Players
SP6 SP7

Flags of Competing Nations and Basketball — SP8

1939 Photo. *Perf. 14*

B52 SP6 15c + 10c copper brn & brn 3.25 *6.50*
Never hinged 6.50
B53 SP7 30c + 15c myrtle grn & grn 3.25 *6.50*
Never hinged 6.50
B54 SP8 60c + 40c blue vio & gray vio 6.00 *12.00*
Never hinged 12.00
Nos. B52-B54 (3) 12.50 *25.00*
Set, never hinged 25.00

3rd European Basketball Championships held at Kaunas. The surtax was used for athletic equipment. Nos. B52-B54 exist imperf. Value, set pairs, $500.

AIR POST STAMPS

Winged Posthorn AP1

Airplane over Neman River — AP2

Air Squadron AP3

Plane over Gediminas Castle — AP4

1921 Litho. Wmk. 109 *Perf. 11½*

C1 AP1 20sk ultra 1.25 .75
Never hinged 3.25
C2 AP1 40sk red orange 1.00 .75
Never hinged 2.50
C3 AP1 60sk green *1.10* .75
Never hinged 2.75
a. Imperf., pair *45.00*
C4 AP1 80sk lt rose 1.50 .75
Never hinged 3.75
a. Horiz. pair, imperf. vert. *50.00* *40.00*
C5 AP2 1auk green & red *1.50* .75
Never hinged 3.75
a. Imperf., pair 90.00 *175.00*
C6 AP3 2auk brown & blue 1.60 .75
Never hinged 4.00
C7 AP4 5auk ol blk & yel 2.00 1.75
Never hinged 5.00
Nos. C1-C7 (7) 9.95 6.25
Set, never hinged 30.00

For surcharges see Nos. C21-C26, C29.

Allegory of Flight — AP5

1921, Nov. 6

C8 AP5 20sk org & gray bl 1.40 *2.00*
Never hinged 2.50
C9 AP5 40sk dl bl & lake 1.40 *2.00*
Never hinged 2.50
C10 AP5 60sk vio bl & ol grn 1.40 *2.00*
Never hinged 2.50
C11 AP5 80sk ocher & dp grn 1.40 *2.00*
Never hinged 2.50
a. Vert. pair, imperf. btwn. 35.00 35.00
C12 AP5 1auk bl grn & bl 1.40 *2.00*
Never hinged 2.50
C13 AP5 2auk gray & brn org 1.40 *2.00*
Never hinged 2.50
C14 AP5 5auk dl lil & Prus bl 1.40 *2.00*
Never hinged 2.50
Nos. C8-C14 (7) 9.80 *14.00*
Set, never hinged 17.50

Opening of airmail service.

Plane over Kaunas — AP6

Black Overprint

1922, July 16 ***Perf. 11, 11½***

C15 AP6 1auk ol brn & red 1.00 *2.75*
Never hinged 3.25
a. Imperf., pair 60.00
C16 AP6 3auk violet & grn 1.00 *2.75*
Never hinged 3.25
C17 AP6 5auk dp blue & yel 1.00 *4.00*
Never hinged 3.25
Nos. C15-C17 (3) 3.00 *9.50*
Set, never hinged 9.75

Nos. C15-C17, without overprint, were to be for the founding of the Air Post service but they were not put in use at that time. Subsequently the word "ZENKLAS" (stamp) was overprinted over "ISTEIGIMAS" (founding) and the date "1921, VI, 25" was obliterated by short vertical lines.

For surcharge see No. C31.

Plane over Gediminas Castle — AP7

1922, July 22

C18 AP7 2auk blue & rose 1.10 .85
Never hinged 1.60
C19 AP7 4auk brown & rose 1.10 .85
Never hinged 1.60
C20 AP7 10auk black & gray bl 1.25 1.40
Never hinged 1.80
Nos. C18-C20 (3) 3.45 3.10
Set, never hinged 11.00

For surcharges see Nos. C27-C28, C30.

Nos. C1-C7, C17-C20 Surcharged like Regular Issues in Black or Carmine

1922

C21 AP1 10c on 20sk 3.25 2.50
Never hinged 5.75
C22 AP1 10c on 40sk 1.75 1.50
Never hinged 3.00
C23 AP1 10c on 60sk 1.75 1.50
Never hinged 3.00
a. Inverted surcharge 45.00
C24 AP1 10c on 80sk 1.75 1.50
Never hinged 3.00
C25 AP2 20c on 1auk 11.00 6.00
Never hinged 20.00
C26 AP3 20c on 2auk 11.00 7.50
Never hinged 20.00
a. Without "CENT" 200.00 140.00
C27 AP7 25c on 2auk 1.00 *1.00*
Never hinged 1.75
a. Inverted surcharge 45.00 40.00
C28 AP7 30c on 4auk (C) 1.00 *1.00*
Never hinged 1.75
a. Double surcharge 50.00 45.00
C29 AP4 50c on 5auk 2.00 1.50
Never hinged 3.50
C30 AP7 50c on 10auk 1.00 *1.00*
Never hinged 1.75
a. Inverted surcharge 50.00 45.00
C31 AP6 1 l on 5auk 16.00 15.00
Never hinged 29.00
a. Double surcharge 50.00
Nos. C21-C31 (11) 51.50 40.00
Set, never hinged 92.50

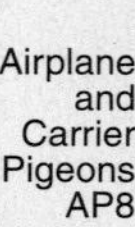

Airplane and Carrier Pigeons AP8

"Flight" AP9

1924, Jan. 28 **Wmk. 147** ***Perf. 11***

C32 AP8 20c yellow 1.15 .75
Never hinged 5.00
C33 AP8 40c emerald 1.15 .75
Never hinged 5.00
a. Horiz. or vert. pair, imperf. between 60.00
C34 AP8 60c rose 1.15 .75
Never hinged 5.00
a. Imperf., pair 75.00
C35 AP9 1 l dk brown 2.50 .75
Never hinged 10.00
Nos. C32-C35 (4) 5.95 3.00
Set, never hinged 25.00

Most stamps, if not all, of the "unwatermarked" varieties show faint traces of watermark, according to experts.

For surcharges see Nos. CB1-CB4.

Swallow — AP10

1926, June 17 **Wmk. 198** ***Perf. 14½***

C37 AP10 20c carmine rose 1.10 .50
Never hinged 1.50
a. Horiz. or vert. pair, imperf. between 55.00
C38 AP10 40c violet & red org 1.10 .50
Never hinged 1.50
a. Horiz. or vert. pair, imperf. between 55.00
C39 AP10 60c blue & black 2.25 .50
Never hinged 3.00
a. Horiz. or vert. pair, imperf. between 55.00
c. Center inverted 250.00 160.00
Nos. C37-C39 (3) 4.45 1.50
Set, never hinged 6.00

Juozas Tubelis — AP11

Vytautas and Airplane over Kaunas AP12

Vytautas and Antanas Smetona AP13

1930, Feb. 16 **Wmk. 109** ***Perf. 14***

C40 AP11 5c blk, bis & brn 1.50 .35
Never hinged 1.75
C41 AP11 10c dk bl, db & blk 1.50 .35
Never hinged 1.75
C42 AP11 15c mar, gray & bl 1.50 .35
Never hinged 1.75
C43 AP12 20c dk brn, org & dl red 1.50 .80
Never hinged 1.75
C44 AP12 40c dk bl, lt bl & vio 4.00 .80
Never hinged 3.25
C45 AP13 60c bl grn, lil & blk 5.00 .85
Never hinged 5.50
C46 AP13 1 l dl red, lil & blk 9.00 1.60
Never hinged 9.50
Nos. C40-C46 (7) 24.00 5.10
Set, never hinged 100.00

5th cent. of the death of the Grand Duke Vytautas.

Map of Lithuania, Klaipeda and Vilnius — AP14

15c, 20c, Airplane over Neman. 40c, 60c, City Hall, Kaunas. 1 l, 2 l, Church of Vytautas, Kaunas.

Wmk. Multiple Letters (238)

1932, July 21 ***Perf. 14***

C47 AP14 5c ver & ol grn .25 *.25*
Never hinged 1.00
C48 AP14 10c dk red brn & ocher .25 *.25*
Never hinged 1.00
C49 AP14 15c dk bl & org yel .25 *.25*
Never hinged 1.00
C50 AP14 20c sl blk & org 1.50 1.50
Never hinged 1.00
C51 AP14 60c ultra & ocher 1.90 *1.90*
Never hinged 7.50
C52 AP14 2 l dk bl & yel 2.00 *2.00*
Never hinged 8.50

Wmk. 198

C53 AP14 40c vio brn & yel 1.60 *1.60*
Never hinged 6.50
C54 AP14 1 l vio brn & grn 2.25 *2.25*
Never hinged 9.00
Nos. C47-C54 (8) 10.00 *10.00*
Set, never hinged 60.00

Imperf.

C47a	AP14	5c ver & ol grn	.25	.35
C48a	AP14	10c dk red brn & ocher	.25	.35
C49a	AP14	15c dk bl & org yel	.25	.35
C50a	AP14	20c sl blk & org	1.50	2.25
C51a	AP14	60c ultra & ocher	1.90	2.75
C52a	AP14	2 l dk bl & yel	2.00	3.00
C53a	AP14	40c vio brn & yel	1.60	2.40
C54a	AP14	1 l vio brn & grn	2.25	3.25

Issued for the benefit of Lithuanian orphans.

Mindaugas in the Battle of Shauyai, 1236 — AP15

15c, 20c, Coronation of Mindaugas (1253). 40c, Grand Duke Gediminas and his followers. 60c, Founding of Vilnius by Gediminas (1332). 1 l, Gediminas capturing the Russian Fortifications. 2 l, Grand Duke Algirdas before Moscow (1368).

1932, Nov. 28 **Wmk. 209** ***Perf. 14***

C55 AP15 5c grn & red lil .45 *.45*
Never hinged .90
C56 AP15 10c emer & rose .45 *.45*
Never hinged .90
C57 AP15 15c rose vio & bis brn .45 *.45*
Never hinged .90
C58 AP15 20c rose red & blk brn 2.25 *2.25*
Never hinged 3.75
C59 AP15 40c choc & dk gray 3.25 *3.25*
Never hinged 5.50
C60 AP15 60c org & gray blk 4.50 *4.50*
Never hinged 7.00
C61 AP15 1 l rose vio & grn 4.50 *4.50*
Never hinged 8.00
C62 AP15 2 l dp bl & brn 4.50 *4.50*
Never hinged 9.00
Nos. C55-C62 (8) 20.35 *20.35*
Set, never hinged 40.00

Imperf.

C55a	AP15	5c grn & red lil	.45	.45
C56a	AP15	10c emer & rose	.45	.45
C57a	AP15	15c rose vio & bis brn	.45	.45
C58a	AP15	20c rose red & blk brn	2.25	2.25
C59a	AP15	40c choc & dk gray	3.25	3.25
C60a	AP15	60c org & gray blk	4.50	4.50
C61a	AP15	1 l rose vio & grn	4.50	4.50
C62a	AP15	2 l dp bl & brn	4.50	4.50

Anniv. of independence.

Nos. C58-C62 exist with overprint "DARIUS-GIRENAS / NEW YORK-1933- KAUNAS" below small plane. The overprint was applied in New York with the approval of the Lithuanian consul general. Lithuanian postal authorities seem not to have been involved in the creation or release of these overprints.

Trakai Castle, Home of the Grand Duke Kestutis — AP16

Designs: 15c, 20c, Meeting of Kestutís and the Hermit Birute. 40c, 60c, Hermit Birute. 1 l, 2 l, Kestutis and his Brother Algirdas.

1933, May 6 ***Perf. 14***

C63 AP16 5c ol gray & dp bl .40 .50
Never hinged .70
C64 AP16 10c gray vio & org brn .40 .50
Never hinged .70
C65 AP16 15c dp blue & lilac .40 .50
Never hinged 1.10
C66 AP16 20c org brn & lilac 2.00 2.50
Never hinged 2.50
C67 AP16 40c lt ultra & lilac 2.00 2.50
Never hinged 5.00
C68 AP16 60c brown & lt ultra 5.25 6.50
Never hinged 7.00
C69 AP16 1 l ol gray & dp bl 5.25 6.50
Never hinged 8.50
C70 AP16 2 l vio gray & yel grn 5.25 *6.50*
Never hinged 9.50
Nos. C63-C70 (8) 20.95 *26.00*
Set, never hinged 30.00

Imperf.

C63a	AP16	5c ol gray & dp bl	.30	.40
C64a	AP16	10c gray vio & org brn	.30	.40
C65a	AP16	15c dp blue & lilac	.30	.40
C66a	AP16	20c org brn & lilac	1.50	2.00
C67a	AP16	40c lt ultra & lilac	1.50	2.00
C68a	AP16	60c brown & lt ultra	4.00	5.25
C69a	AP16	1 l ol gray & dp bl	4.00	5.25
C70a	AP16	2 l vio gray & yel grn	4.00	5.25

Reopening of air service to Berlin-Kaunas-Moscow, and 550th anniv. of the death of Kestutis.

Joseph Maironis — AP17

Joseph Tumas-Vaizgantas — AP17a

Designs: 40c, 60c, Vincas Kudirka. 1 l, 2 l, Julia A. Zemaite.

1933, Sept. 15 ***Perf. 14***

C71 AP17 5c crim & dp bl .25 *.30*
Never hinged 1.10
C72 AP17 10c bl vio & grn .25 *.30*
Never hinged 1.10
C73 AP17a 15c dk grn & choc .25 *.30*
Never hinged 1.10
C74 AP17a 20c brn car & ultra .50 *.60*
Never hinged 1.75
C75 AP17 40c red brn & ol grn 1.50 *2.50*
Never hinged 3.75
C76 AP17 60c dk bl & choc 1.50 *6.00*
Never hinged 4.50
C77 AP17 1 l citron & indigo 2.50 *5.00*
Never hinged 6.75
C78 AP17 2 l dp grn & red brn 3.50 *10.00*
Never hinged 10.00
Nos. C71-C78 (8) 10.25 *25.00*
Set, never hinged 30.00

Imperf.

C71a	AP17	5c crim & dp bl	.25	.25
C72a	AP16	10c bl vio & grn	.25	.25
C73a	AP17a	15c dk grn & choc	.25	.35
C74a	AP17a	20c brn car & ol grn	.50	.50
C75a	AP17	40c red brn & ol grn	1.50	2.00
C76a	AP17	60c dk bl & choc	1.50	5.00
C77a	AP17	1 l citron & indigo	2.50	5.00
C78a	AP17	2 l dp grn & red brn	3.50	8.00

Issued for the benefit of Lithuanian orphans.

Capts. Steponas Darius and Stasys Girenas AP18

Ill-Fated Plane "Lituanica" AP19

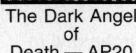

The Dark Angel of Death — AP20

"Lituanica" over Globe — AP21

"Lituanica" and White Knight — AP22

Perf. 11½

1934, May 18 Unwmk. Engr.

C79 AP18 20c scarlet & blk .25 .25
Never hinged .25
C80 AP19 40c dp rose & bl .25 .25
Never hinged .25
C81 AP18 60c dk vio & blk .25 .25
Never hinged .25
C82 AP20 1 l black & rose .35 .25
Never hinged .35
C83 AP21 3 l gray grn & org .45 *.50*
Never hinged .90
C84 AP22 5 l dk brn & bl 1.75 *3.25*
Never hinged 3.50
Nos. C79-C84 (6) 3.30 4.75
Set, never hinged 5.50

Death of Capts. Steponas Darius and Stasys Girenas on their New York-Kaunas flight of 1933.

No. C80 exists with diagonal overprint: "F. VAITKUS / nugalejo Atlanta / 21-22-IX-1935." Value $400.

Felix Waitkus and Map of Transatlantic Flight — AP23

Wmk. 238

1936, Mar. 24 Litho. *Perf. 14*

C85 AP23 15c brown lake 2.25 .85
Never hinged 3.25
C86 AP23 30c dark green 3.25 .85
Never hinged 4.50
C87 AP23 60c blue 4.50 2.50
Never hinged 6.00
Nos. C85-C87 (3) 10.00 4.20
Set, never hinged 13.75

Transatlantic Flight of the Lituanica II, Sept. 21-22, 1935.

AIR POST SEMI-POSTAL STAMPS

Nos. C32-C35 Surcharged like Nos. B1-B9 (No. CB1), Nos. B10-B11 (Nos. CB2-CB3), and Nos. B12-B14 (No. CB4) in Red, Violet or Black

1924 Wmk. 147 *Perf. 11*

CB1 AP8 20c + 20c yellow (R) 12.00 12.00
Never hinged 20.00
CB2 AP8 40c + 40c emerald (V) 12.00 12.00
Never hinged 20.00
CB3 AP8 60c + 60c rose (V) 12.00 12.00
Never hinged 20.00
CB4 AP9 1 l + 1 l dk brown 12.00 12.00
Never hinged 20.00
Nos. CB1-CB4 (4) 48.00 48.00
Set, never hinged 80.00

Surtax for the Red Cross. See note following No. C35.

SOUTH LITHUANIA

GRODNO DISTRICT

Russian Stamps of 1909-12 Surcharged in Black or Red

1919 Unwmk. *Perf. 14, 14½x15*

L1 A14 50sk on 3k red 60.00 57.50
a. Double surcharge *250.00 250.00*
L2 A14 50sk on 5k claret 60.00 57.50
a. Imperf., pair 550.00 475.00
L3 A15 50sk on 10k dk bl (R) 60.00 57.50
L4 A11 50sk on 15k red brn & bl 60.00 57.50
a. Imperf., pair 650.00 550.00
L5 A11 50sk on 25k grn & gray vio (R) 60.00 57.50
L6 A11 50sk on 35k red brn & grn 60.00 57.50
L7 A8 50sk on 50k vio & grn 60.00 57.50
L8 A11 50sk on 70k brn & org 60.00 57.50
Nos. L1-L8 (8) 480.00 460.00

Excellent counterfeits are plentiful.

This surcharge exists on Russia No. 119, the imperf. 1k orange of 1917. Value, unused $90, used $60.

OCCUPATION STAMPS

The issue formerly listed as Lithuania 1N1-1N12 is now listed as Russia N1-N12.

Issued under Russian Occupation

Lithuanian Stamps of 1937-40 Overprinted in Red or Blue

1940 Wmk. 238 *Perf. 14*

2N9 A44 2c orange (Bl) .25 .25
Never hinged .30
2N10 A50 50c brown (Bl) .25 .25
Never hinged .75

Unwmk.

2N11 A56 5c brown car (Bl) .25 .40
Never hinged .30
2N12 A57 10c green (R) 3.75 8.00
Never hinged 10.00
2N13 A58 15c dull orange (Bl) .25 .35
Never hinged .30
2N14 A59 25c lt brown (R) .25 .35
Never hinged .65
2N15 A60 30c Prus green (R) .25 .50
Never hinged .65
2N16 A61 35c red orange (Bl) .35 .50
Never hinged .90
Nos. 2N9-2N16 (8) 5.60 10.60
Set, never hinged 10.00

Values for used stamps are for CTOs. Postally used examples are considerably more.

The Lithuanian Soviet Socialist Republic was proclaimed July 21, 1940.

LOURENCO MARQUES

lə-ˈren,t,-,sō-,mär-ˈkes

LOCATION — In the southern part of Mozambique in Southeast Africa
GOVT. — Part of Portuguese East Africa Colony
AREA — 28,800 sq. mi. (approx.)
POP. — 474,000 (approx.)
CAPITAL — Lourenço Marques

Stamps of Mozambique replaced those of Lourenço Marques in 1920. See Mozambique.

1000 Reis = 1 Milreis
100 Centavos = 1 Escudo (1913)

King Carlos — A1

Perf. 11½, 12½, 13½

1895 Typo. Unwmk.

1 A1 5r yellow 1.00 .25
2 A1 10r redsh violet 1.00 .35
3 A1 15r chocolate 1.50 .50
4 A1 20r lavender 1.50 .50
5 A1 25r blue green 1.50 .30
a. Perf. 11½ 3.50 1.00
6 A1 50r light blue 2.00 1.00
a. Perf. 13½ 15.00 5.00
b. Perf. 11½ — —
7 A1 75r rose 4.00 1.25
8 A1 80r yellow grn 5.00 3.00
9 A1 100r brn, *yel* 3.50 1.00
a. Perf. 12½ 5.00 3.25
10 A1 150r car, *rose* 6.00 3.00
11 A1 200r dk bl, *bl* 7.00 3.00
12 A1 300r dk bl, *sal* 8.00 4.00
Nos. 1-12 (12) 42.00 18.15

For surcharges and overprints see Nos. 29, 58-69, 132-137, 140-143, 156-157, 160.

Saint Anthony of Padua Issue

Regular Issues of Mozambique, 1886 and 1894, Overprinted in Black

On 1886 Issue

1895 Without Gum *Perf. 12½*

13 A2 5r black 22.50 12.00
14 A2 10r green 25.00 12.00
15 A2 20r rose 35.00 14.00
16 A2 25r lilac 40.00 14.00
17 A2 40r chocolate 35.00 15.00
18 A2 50r bl, perf. 13½ 30.00 14.00
a. Perf. 12½ 50.00 27.50
19 A2 100r yellow brn 110.00 90.00
20 A2 200r gray vio 50.00 32.50
21 A2 300r orange 70.00 40.00

On 1894 Issue

Perf. 11½

22 A3 5r yellow 35.00 25.00
23 A3 10r redsh vio 40.00 15.00
24 A3 50r light blue 50.00 32.50
a. Perf. 12½ 275.00 275.00
25 A3 75r rose, perf. 12½ 65.00 50.00
26 A3 80r yellow grn 80.00 65.00
27 A3 100r brown, *buff* 350.00 160.00
28 A3 150r car, *rose*, perf. 12½ 50.00 40.00
Nos. 13-28 (16) 1,088. 631.00

No. 12 Surcharged in Black

1897, Jan. 2

29 A1 50r on 300r 200.00 150.00

Most examples of No. 29 were issued without gum.

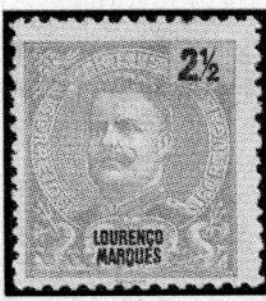

King Carlos — A2

Name, Value in Black except 500r

1898-1903 *Perf. 11½*

30 A2 2½r gray .35 .30
31 A2 5r orange .35 .30
32 A2 10r lt green .35 .30
33 A2 15r brown 1.25 .85
34 A2 15r gray green ('03) .75 .50
a. Imperf.
35 A2 20r gray violet .65 .40
a. Imperf.
36 A2 25r sea green .70 .40
a. Perf. 13½ 25.00 8.50
b. 25r light green (error) *30.00 30.00*
c. Perf. 12½ *40.00* 35.00
37 A2 25r car ('03) .35 .30
a. Imperf.
38 A2 50r blue 2.00 .50
39 A2 50r brown ('03) .90 .75
40 A2 65r dull bl ('03) 30.00 8.50
41 A2 75r rose 2.00 1.50
42 A2 75r lilac ('03) 1.25 .95
a. Imperf.
43 A2 80r violet 2.50 1.25
44 A2 100r dk blue, *blue* 1.75 .65
a. Perf. 13½ 18.00 5.00
45 A2 115r org brn, *pink* ('03) 6.00 5.00
46 A2 130r brn, *straw* ('03) 6.00 5.00
47 A2 150r brn, *straw* 3.00 1.40
48 A2 200r red lil, *pnksh* 3.00 1.25
49 A2 300r dk bl, *rose* 3.25 1.50
50 A2 400r dl bl, *straw* ('03) 10.00 5.00
51 A2 500r blk & red, *bl* ('01) 12.00 3.00
52 A2 700r vio, *yelsh* ('01) 15.00 7.00
Nos. 30-52 (23) 103.40 46.60

For surcharges and overprints see Nos. 57, 71-74, 76-91, 138, 144-155.

Coat of Arms — A3

Surcharged On Upper and Lower Halves of Stamp

1899 *Imperf.*

53 A3 5r on 10r grn & brn 20.00 7.00
54 A3 25r on 10r grn & brn 20.00 7.00
55 A3 50r on 30r grn & brn 30.00 11.00
a. Inverted surcharge 100.00 50.00
56 A3 50r on 800r grn & brn 40.00 20.00
Nos. 53-56 (4) 110.00 45.00

The lower half of No. 55 can be distinguished from that of No. 56 by the background of the label containing the word "REIS." The former is plain, while the latter is formed of white intersecting curved horizontal lines over vertical shading of violet brown.

Values are for undivided stamps. Halves sell for ¼ as much.

Most examples of Nos. 53-56 were issued without gum. Values are for stamps without gum. Values for stamps with gum are two times the values shown.

No. 41 Surcharged in Black

1899 *Perf. 11½*

57 A2 50r on 75r rose 6.00 2.50

Most examples of No. 57 were issued without gum. Values are for stamp without gum.

Surcharged in Black

On Issue of 1895

1902 *Perf. 11½, 12½*

58 A1 65r on 5r yellow 6.00 2.50
59 A1 65r on 15r choc 6.00 2.50
60 A1 65r on 20r lav 7.00 2.50
a. Perf. 12½ 25.00 15.00
61 A1 115r on 10r red vio 7.00 3.00
62 A1 115r on 200r bl, *bl* 7.00 3.00
63 A1 115r on 300r bl, *sal* 7.00 3.00
64 A1 130r on 25r grn, perf. 12½ 4.00 2.00
a. Perf. 11½ 30.00 22.50
65 A1 130r on 80r yel grn 4.00 3.00
66 A1 130r on 150r car, *rose* 5.00 3.00
67 A1 400r on 50r lt bl 8.00 6.00
68 A1 400r on 75r rose 8.00 6.00
69 A1 400r on 100r brn, *buff* 7.00 6.00

On Newspaper Stamp of 1893

70 N1 65r on 2½ brn 5.00 2.00
Nos. 58-70 (13) 81.00 44.50

Surcharge exists inverted on Nos. 61, 70.

Nos. 64, 67 and 68 have been reprinted on thin white paper with shiny white gum and clean-cut perforation 13½. Value $6 each.

For overprints see Nos. 132-137, 140-143, 156-157, 160.

Issue of 1898-1903 Overprinted in Black

1903 ***Perf. 11½***

71 A2 15r brown 2.00 .85
72 A2 25r sea green 1.50 .85
73 A2 50r blue 2.50 .85
74 A2 75r rose 3.00 1.40
a. Inverted overprint 50.00 50.00
Nos. 71-74 (4) 9.00 3.95

Surcharged in Black

1905

76 A2 50r on 65r dull blue 5.00 2.00

Regular Issues Overprinted in Carmine or Green

1911

77 A2 2½r gray .30 .25
78 A2 5r orange .30 .25
a. Double overprint 10.00 10.00
b. Inverted overprint 10.00 10.00
79 A2 10r lt grn .40 .35
80 A2 15r gray grn .40 .35
a. Inverted overprint 10.00 10.00
81 A2 20r dl vio .40 .40
82 A2 25r car (G) .90 .50
83 A2 50r brown .80 .50
84 A2 75r lilac 1.00 .50
85 A2 100r dk bl, *bl* .80 .55
86 A2 115r org brn, *pink* 10.00 3.50
87 A2 130r brn, *straw* .80 .60
88 A2 200r red lil, *pnksh* .85 .60
89 A2 400r dl bl, *straw* 2.00 1.10
90 A2 500r blk & red, *bl* 3.00 1.10
91 A2 700r vio, *yelsh* 4.00 1.25
Nos. 77-91 (15) 25.95 11.80

Vasco da Gama Issue of Various Portuguese Colonies Common Design Types Surcharged

On Stamps of Macao

1913 ***Perf. 12½-16***

92 CD20 ¼c on ½a bl grn 2.50 2.25
93 CD21 ½c on la red 2.50 2.25
94 CD22 1c on 2a red vio 2.50 2.25
95 CD23 2½c on 4a yel grn 2.50 2.25
96 CD24 5c on 8a dk bl 2.50 2.25
97 CD25 7½c on 12a vio brn 4.25 4.25
98 CD26 10c on 16a bis brn 3.50 3.50
a. Inverted surcharge 40.00 40.00
99 CD27 15c on 24a bister 3.75 3.75
Nos. 92-99 (8) 24.00 22.75

On Stamps of Portuguese Africa

100 CD20 ¼c on 2½r bl grn 2.00 1.75
101 CD21 ½c on 5r red 2.00 1.75
102 CD22 1c on 10r red vio 2.00 1.75
103 CD23 2½c on 25r yel grn 2.00 1.75
104 CD24 5c on 50r dk bl 2.00 1.75
105 CD25 7½c on 75r vio brn 4.00 4.00
106 CD26 10c on 100r bis brn 2.75 2.75
107 CD27 15c on 150r bis 2.75 2.75
Nos. 100-107 (8) 19.50 18.25

On Stamps of Timor

108 CD20 ¼c on ½a bl grn 2.00 1.75
109 CD21 ½c on 1a red 2.00 1.75
110 CD22 1c on 2a red vio 2.00 1.75
111 CD23 2½c on 4a yel grn 2.00 1.75
112 CD24 5c on 8a dk bl 2.50 1.75
113 CD25 7½c on 12a vio brn 4.00 4.00
114 CD26 10c on 16a bis brn 2.75 2.75
115 CD27 15c on 24a bister 2.75 2.75
Nos. 108-115 (8) 20.00 18.25
Nos. 92-115 (24) 63.50 59.25

Ceres — A4

Chalky Paper
Name and Value in Black

1914 **Typo.** ***Perf. 15x14***

116 A4 ¼c olive brn .35 .35
Never hinged .60
117 A4 ½c black .35 .35
Never hinged .60
118 A4 1c blue grn .35 .35
Never hinged .60
119 A4 1½c lilac brn .75 .75
Never hinged 1.25
120 A4 2c carmine .75 .75
Never hinged 1.25
121 A4 2½c lt vio .75 .75
Never hinged 1.25
122 A4 5c dp blue .75 .75
Never hinged 1.25
123 A4 7½c yellow brn .95 .75
Never hinged 1.60
124 A4 8c slate .95 .75
Never hinged 1.60
125 A4 10c orange brn 1.50 .85
Never hinged 2.50
126 A4 15c plum 2.00 .70
Never hinged 3.50
127 A4 20c yellow grn 2.50 .90
Never hinged 4.25
128 A4 30c brown, *green* 4.00 1.00
Never hinged 6.00
129 A4 40c brown, *pink* 12.00 4.00
Never hinged 18.00
130 A4 50c orange, *sal* 10.00 3.00
Never hinged 15.00
131 A4 1e green, *blue* 12.00 3.00
Never hinged 17.00
Nos. 116-131 (16) 39.25 16.00

Glazed Paper

131A A4 1c blue grn 1.75 1.45
Never hinged 3.25
131B A4 2½c lt vio 1.75 1.45
Never hinged 3.25

1918 **Ordinary Paper**

131C A4 ¼c olive brn .25 .25
Never hinged .40
131D A4 ½c black .25 .25
Never hinged .40
a. Value omitted 20.00
Never hinged 22.50
131E A4 1c blue grn .25 .25
Never hinged .40
131F A4 1½c lilac brn .25 .25
Never hinged .40
a. Imperf.
131G A4 2c carmine .25 .25
Never hinged .40
131H A4 2½c lt vio .25 .25
Never hinged .40
131I A4 5c dp blue .25 .25
Never hinged .40
131J A4 7½c yellow brn .50 .40
Never hinged .80
131K A4 8c slate .50 .40
Never hinged .80
131L A4 10c orange brn 25.00 18.50
Never hinged 40.00
131M A4 15c plum 2.00 .70
Never hinged 3.25
Nos. 131C-131M (11) 29.75 21.75

For surcharges see Nos. 139, 159, 161-162, B1-B12.

In 1921 Nos. 131D and 131F were surcharged 10c and 30c respectively, for use in Mozambique as Nos. 230 and 231. These same values, surcharged 5c and 10c respectively, with the addition of the word "PORTEADO," were used in Mozambique as postage dues, Nos. J44 and J45.

Provisional Issue of 1902 Overprinted Locally in Carmine

1914 ***Perf. 11½, 12½***

132 A1 115r on 10r red vio 1.50 .45
a. "Republica" inverted 20.00
133 A1 115r on 200r bl, *bl* 1.50 .45
134 A1 115r on 300r bl, *sal* 1.50 .45
a. Double overprint 40.00 40.00
135 A1 130r on 25r grn 2.00 .70
a. Perf. 12½ 3.25 1.60
136 A1 130r on 80r yel grn 1.50 .35
137 A1 130r on 150r car, *rose* 1.50 .35
Nos. 132-137 (6) 9.50 2.75

No. 135a was issued without gum.

Nos. 78 and 117 Perforated Diagonally and Surcharged in Carmine

1915 ***Perf. 11½***

138 A2 ¼c on half of 5r org, pair 5.00 5.00
a. Pair without dividing perfs. 20.00 20.00

Perf. 15x14

139 A4 ¼c on half of ½c blk, pair 9.00 9.00
Never hinged 3.25

The added perforation on Nos. 138-139 runs from lower left to upper right corners, dividing the stamp in two. Values are for pairs, both halves of the stamp.

Provisional Issue of 1902 Overprinted in Carmine

1915 ***Perf. 11½, 12½***

140 A1 115r on 10r red vio .55 .40
141 A1 115r on 200r bl, *bl* .70 .40
142 A1 115r on 300r bl, *sal* .70 .40
143 A1 130r on 150r car, *rose* .75 .40
Nos. 140-143 (4) 2.70 1.60

Nos. 34 and 80 Surcharged

1915 **On Issue of 1903**

144 A2 2c on 15r gray grn 1.00 .80

On Issue of 1911

145 A2 2c on 15r gray grn 1.00 .80
a. New value inverted 22.50

Regular Issues of 1898-1903 Overprinted Locally in Carmine

1916

146 A2 15r gray grn 2.00 1.00
147 A2 50r brown 3.50 2.00
a. Inverted overprint
148 A2 75r lilac 3.50 2.00
149 A2 100r blue, *bl* 3.00 1.00
150 A2 115r org brn, *pink* 3.00 1.00
151 A2 130r brown, *straw* 10.00 5.00
152 A2 200r red lil, *pnksh* 8.00 2.00
153 A2 400r dull bl, *straw* 12.00 4.00
154 A2 500r blk & red, *bl* 8.00 3.00
155 A2 700r vio, *yelsh* 12.00 5.00
Nos. 146-155 (10) 65.00 26.00

Same Overprint on Nos. 67-68

1917

156 A1 400r on 50r lt blue 1.25 .65
a. Perf. 13½ 11.50 9.00
157 A1 400r on 75r rose 2.50 1.00

No. 69 exists with this overprint. It was not officially issued.

Type of 1914 Surcharged in Red

1920 ***Perf. 15x14***

159 A4 4c on 2½c violet 1.00 .30

Stamps of 1914 Surcharged in Green or Black

a

b

1921

160 A1(a) ¼c on 115r on 10r red vio (G) .80 .80
Never hinged 1.25
161 A4(b) 1c on 2½c vio (Bk) .60 .40
Never hinged .95
a. Inverted surcharge 40.00
Never hinged 65.00
162 A4(b) 1½c on 2½c vio (Bk) .80 .60
Never hinged 1.25
Nos. 160-162 (3) 2.20 1.80

Nos. 159-162 were postally valid throughout Mozambique. No. 162 exists on glazed paper. Value the same as No. 162.

SEMI-POSTAL STAMPS

Regular Issue of 1914 Overprinted or Surcharged

a

b

c

1918 ***Perf. 15x14½***

B1 A4(a) ¼c olive brn 3.00 *3.00*
Never hinged 5.00
B2 A4(a) ½c black 3.00 *4.00*
Never hinged 5.00
B3 A4(a) 1c bl grn 3.00 *4.00*
Never hinged 5.00
B4 A4(a) 2½c violet 4.00 4.00
Never hinged 6.75
B5 A4(a) 5c blue 4.00 *6.00*
Never hinged 6.75

Chalky Paper

B5A A4(a) 5c blue 4.00 *6.00*
Never hinged 6.75
B6 A4(a) 10c org brn 5.00 *7.00*
Never hinged 8.50
B7 A4(b) 20c on 1½c lil brn 5.00 *8.00*
Never hinged 8.50
B8 A4(a) 30c brn, *grn* 8.00 *9.00*
Never hinged 11.50
B9 A4(b) 40c on 2c car 8.00 *10.00*
Never hinged 11.50
B10 A4(b) 50c on 7½c bis 12.00 *12.00*
Never hinged 13.50
B11 A4(b) 70c on 8c slate 15.00 *15.00*
Never hinged 19.00
B12 A4(c) $1 on 15c mag 20.00 *15.00*
Never hinged 25.00
Nos. B1-B12 (13) 94.00 *103.00*

Nos. B1-B12 were used in place of ordinary postage stamps on Mar. 9, 1918. Nos. B3 and B4 also exist on glazed paper. The unsurfaced paper on which Nos. B1-B5 were printed show a diamond pattern when held to the light. This pattern is used to determine genuine stamps.

NEWSPAPER STAMPS

Numeral of Value — N1

Perf. 11½

1893, July 28 Typo. Unwmk.
P1 N1 2½r brown .25 .65
a. Perf. 12½ 20.00 17.50

For surcharge see No. 70.

Saint Anthony of Padua Issue

Mozambique No. P6 Overprinted

1895, July 1 ***Perf. 11½, 13½***
P2 N3 2½r brown 20.00 17.50
a. Inverted overprint 30.00 30.00

LUXEMBOURG

'lək-səm-,bərg

LOCATION — Western Europe between southern Belgium, Germany and France
GOVT. — Grand Duchy
AREA — 998 sq. mi.
POP. — 365,800 (est. 1984)
CAPITAL — Luxembourg

12½ Centimes = 1 Silbergroschen
100 Centimes = 1 Franc

Watermarks

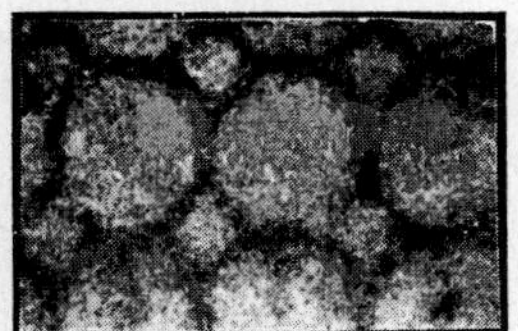

Wmk. 110 — Octagons

Wmk. 149 — W

Wmk. 213 — Double Wavy Lines

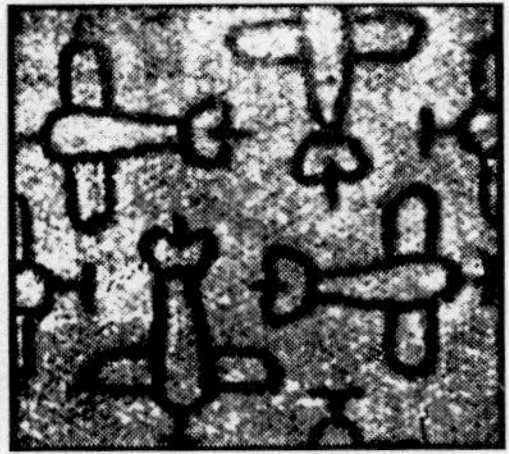

Wmk. 216 — Multiple Airplanes

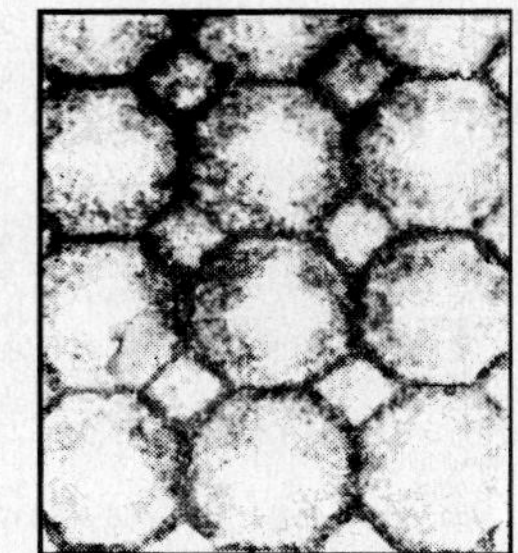

Wmk. 246 — Multiple Cross Enclosed in Octagons

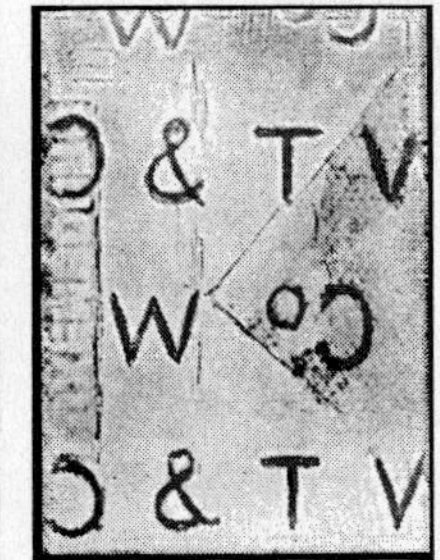

Wmk. 247 — Multiple Letters

Unused values of Nos. 1-47 are for stamps without gum. Though these stamps were issued with gum, most examples offered are without gum. Stamps with original gum sell for more.

Grand Duke William III — A1

Luxembourg Print

Wmk. 149

1852, Sept. 15 Engr. ***Imperf.***
1 A1 10c gray black *2,100.* 55.00
With gum *3,500.*
On cover 465.00
a. 10c greenish black ('53) *2,250.* 55.00
With gum *3,900.*
On cover 525.00
b. 10c intense black ('54) *2,400.* 120.00
With gum —
On cover 1,400.
2 A1 1sg brown red ('53) 1,500. 75.00
With gum —
On cover 900.00
a. 1sg brick red 1,500. 80.00
With gum *2,500.*
On cover 900.00
b. 1sg orange red ('54) 1,300. 87.50
With gum *2,500.*
On cover 1,000.
c. 1sg blood red 2,750. 475.00
With gum —
On cover 1,850.
3 A1 1sg rose ('55) 1,350. 87.50
With gum *2,500.*
On cover 750.00
a. 1sg carmine rose ('56) 1,250. 80.00
With gum *2,500.*
On cover 850.00
b. 1sg dark carmine rose, thin paper ('59) *1,400.* *240.00*
With gum *3,500.*
On cover *2,000.*
Nos. 1-3 (3) 217.50

Full margins = 1mm.

Reprints of both values exist on watermarked paper. Some of the reprints show traces of lines cancelling the plates, but others can be distinguished only by an expert.
See Nos. 278-279, 603 in Scott Standard catalogue, Vol. 4.

Values for pairs

1 A1 10c gray black — 125.00
On cover 1,100.
2b A1 1sg orange red — 275.00
On cover 1,750.
3 A1 1sg rose — 300.00
On cover 1,750.

Values for strips of 3

1 A1 10c gray black — 575.00
On cover 1,600.
2b A1 1sg orange red — —
On cover —
3 A1 1sg rose — 450.00
On cover 2,000.

Values for strips of 4

1 A1 10c gray black — 1,250.
On cover 2,200.
2b A1 1sg orange red — —
On cover —
3 A1 1sg rose — 1,800.
On cover *3,500.*

Values for blocks of 4

1 A1 10c gray black — *6,000.*
On cover *10,000.*
2b A1 1sg orange red — —
On cover —
3 A1 1sg rose — *7,250.*
On cover *12,000.*

Coat of Arms
A2 A3

Frankfurt Print

1859-64 Typo. Unwmk.
4 A2 1c buff ('63) 130.00 *450.00*
With gum 195.00
On cover 2,400.
5 A2 2c black ('60) 95.00 *550.00*
With gum 140.00
On cover 2,900.
6 A2 4c yellow ('64) 175.00 175.00
With gum 260.00
On cover 2,400.
a. 4c orange ('64) 190.00 190.00
With gum 270.00
On cover 2,200.
7 A3 10c blue 175.00 20.00
With gum 260.00
On cover 250.00
a. 10c dark blue 1,700. 40.00
With gum 1,775.
On cover 225.00
8 A3 12½c rose 275.00 160.00
With gum 400.00
On cover 1,100.
9 A3 25c brown 350.00 275.00
With gum 500.00
On cover 2,400.
10 A3 30c rose lilac 290.00 225.00
With gum 405.00
On cover 2,100.
11 A3 37½c green 325.00 200.00
With gum 440.00
On cover 1,400.
12 A3 40c red orange 875.00 240.00
With gum 1,275.
On cover 1,100.

Full margins = ½mm.

Counterfeits of Nos. 1-12 exist.
See Nos. 13-25, 27-38, 40-47. For surcharges and overprints see Nos. 26, 39, O1-O51.

Values for pairs

4 A2 1c buff 360.00 *1,500.*
On cover 9,000.
5 A2 2c black 575.00 *1,700.*
On cover 8,500.
6 A2 4c yellow 650.00 640.00
On cover 7,000.
a. 4c orange 675.00 650.00
On cover *7,000.*
7 A3 10c blue 850.00 225.00
On cover 1,050.
a. 10c dark blue *3,000.* 90.00
On cover —
8 A3 12½c rose 800.00 475.00
On cover 3,350.
9 A3 25c brown 1,400. 1,200.
On cover *4,250.*
10 A3 30c rose lilac 1,150. 725.00
On cover 8,250.
11 A3 37½c green 1,400. 925.00
On cover 6,750.
12 A3 40c red orange 3,200. 750.00
On cover 3,600.

1865-71 ***Rouletted***
13 A2 1c red brown 200.00 240.00
With gum 310.00
On cover 1,600.
14 A2 2c black ('67) 20.00 13.50
With gum 35.00
On cover 540.00
15 A2 4c yellow ('67) 600.00 175.00
With gum 1,025.
On cover 2,350.
16 A2 4c green ('71) 40.00 24.00
With gum 62.50
On cover 290.00
Nos. 13-16 (4) 860.00 452.50

Values for pairs

13 A2 1c red brown 500.00 750.00
On cover 2,500.
14 A2 2c black ('67) 60.00 55.00
On cover 700.00
15 A2 4c yellow ('67) 2,500. 750.00
On cover 2,750.
16 A2 4c green ('71) 115.00 100.00
On cover 625.00

Values for strips of 3

13 A2 1c red brown 750.00 1,450.
On cover 3,600.
14 A2 2c black ('67) 140.00 190.00
On cover 1,200.
15 A2 4c yellow ('67) — 1,750.
On cover —
16 A2 4c green ('71) 250.00 300.00
On cover 1,000.

A4

1865-74 ***Rouletted in Color***
17 A2 1c red brn ('72) 35.00 8.00
With gum 42.50
On cover 140.00
18 A2 1c orange ('69) 40.00 8.00
With gum 50.00
On cover 140.00
a. 1c brown orange ('67) 120.00 35.00
With gum 145.00
On cover —
b. 1c red orange ('69) 1,350. 325.00
With gum 1,725.
On cover —
19 A3 10c rose lilac 120.00 4.00
With gum 180.00
On cover 40.00
a. 10c lilac 100.00 4.00
With gum 115.00
On cover 40.00
b. 10c gray lilac 100.00 4.00
With gum 115.00
On cover 42.50
20 A3 12½c car ('71) 175.00 8.00
With gum 190.00
On cover 140.00
a. 12½c rose 175.00 8.00
With gum 225.00
On cover 140.00
21 A3 20c gray brn ('72) 120.00 8.00
With gum 150.00
On cover 225.00
a. 20c yellow brown ('69) 125.00 8.00
With gum 160.00
On cover 240.00
22 A3 25c blue ('72) 1,100. 11.00
With gum 1,300.
On cover 275.00
22A A3 25c ultra ('65) 1,100. 11.00
With gum 1,300.
On cover 290.00
23 A3 30c lilac rose 1,200. 80.00
With gum 1,400.
On cover 1,800.
24 A3 37½c bister ('66) 750.00 240.00
With gum 930.00
On cover 3,600.
25 A3 40c pale org ('74) 40.00 80.00
With gum 52.50
On cover 1,400.
a. 40c orange red ('66) 1,050. 60.00
With gum 1,250.
On cover 1,300.
26 A4 1fr on 37½c bis ('73) 875.00 80.00
With gum 1,075.
On cover 1,400.
a. Surcharge inverted *3,600.*

Luxembourg Print

1874 Typo. ***Imperf.***
27 A2 4c green 110.00 110.00
With gum 145.00
On cover 925.00

A5

1875-79 Narrow Margins ***Perf. 13***
29 A2 1c red brn ('78) 35.00 8.00
With gum 45.00
On cover 225.00
30 A2 2c black 125.00 27.50
With gum 160.00
On cover 300.00
31 A2 4c green 2.40 *9.50*
With gum 3.25
On cover 425.00
32 A2 5c yellow ('76) 175.00 24.00
With gum 215.00
On cover 145.00
a. 5c orange yellow 600.00 125.00
With gum 725.00
On cover 1,100.
b. Imperf. 925.00 1,100.
With gum 1,100.
33 A3 10c gray lilac 475.00 2.40
With gum 600.00
On cover 30.00
b. 10c lilac 1,350. 29.00
With gum 1,575.
On cover 275.00
c. Imperf. 2,700. *3,250.*
With gum 3,000.
34 A3 12½c lil rose ('77) 600.00 20.00
With gum 750.00
On cover 240.00
35 A3 12½c car rose ('76) 400.00 27.50
With gum 535.00
On cover 250.00
36 A3 25c blue ('77) 800.00 14.00
With gum 1,025.
On cover 550.00
37 A3 30c dull rose ('78) 750.00 450.00
With gum 990.00
On cover 1,900.
38 A3 40c orange ('79) 1.60 *9.50*
With gum 3.25
On cover 1,300.

39 A5 1fr on 37½c bis ('79) 8.00 27.50
With gum 11.00
On cover 1,350.
a. "Pranc" 5,250. 6,400.
With gum 6,000.
b. Without surcharge 475.00
With gum 630.00
c. As "b," imperf. 700.00
With gum 775.00
As "c," pair 1,400.
With gum 1,600.

In the Luxembourg print the perforation is close to the border of the stamp. Excellent forgeries of No. 39a are plentiful, as well as faked cancellations on Nos. 31, 38 and 39.

Nos. 32b and 33c are said to be essays; Nos. 39b and 39c printer's waste.

Haarlem Print

Perf. 12½x12, 13½ (5c, 12½c)

1880-81 Wide Margins

40 A2 1c yel brn ('81) 8.75 6.00
With gum 10.00
On cover 175.00
a. Perf. 11½x12 14.00 11.00
With gum 19.50
b. Perf. 13½ 10.50 6.00
With gum 14.00
On cover 190.00
41 A2 2c black 7.25 1.60
With gum 8.50
On cover 190.00
a. Perf. 11½x12 13.50 8.50
With gum 16.00
b. Perf. 13½ 9.50 1.75
With gum 11.00
On cover 190.00
42 A2 5c yellow ('81) 200.00 95.00
With gum 235.00
On cover 350.00
b. Perf. 12½x12 760.00 390.00
With gum 960.00
On cover —
c. Perf. 11½x12 960.00 575.00
With gum 1,150.
43 A3 10c gray lilac 160.00 1.60
With gum 190.00
On cover 19.00
b. Perf. 11½x12 190.00 5.00
With gum 230.00
c. Perf. 13½ 175.00 2.10
With gum 230.00
On cover 30.00
44 A3 12½c rose ('81) 190.00 190.00
With gum 245.00
On cover 825.00
b. Perf. 12½x12 210.00 190.00
With gum 245.00
On cover 825.00
c. Perf. 11½x12 245.00 210.00
With gum 295.00
45 A3 20c gray brn ('81) 45.00 20.00
With gum 52.50
On cover 250.00
a. Perf. 11½x12 52.50 27.00
With gum 65.00
b. Perf. 13½ 50.00 17.00
With gum 57.50
On cover 300.00
46 A3 25c blue 240.00 4.75
With gum 290.00
On cover 160.00
b. Perf. 11½x12 290.00 20.00
With gum 375.00
c. Perf. 13½ 270.00 5.00
With gum 325.00
On cover 210.00
47 A3 30c dull rose ('81) 8.00 24.00
With gum 4.25
On cover 750.00
a. Perf. 11½x12 8.25 32.50
With gum 10.00

Gray Yellowish Paper

Perf. 12½

42a A2 5c 7.25
With gum 8.75
43a A3 10c 4.00
With gum 5.00
44a A3 12½c 9.50
With gum 11.50
46a A3 25c 5.50
With gum 6.25
Nos. 42a-46a (4) 26.25

Nos. 42a-46a were not regularly issued.

"Industry" and "Commerce" — A6

1882, Dec. 1 Typo. Perf. 12½

48 A6 1c gray lilac .25 .40
Never hinged .50
On cover 6.00
49 A6 2c olive gray .25 .40
Never hinged .40
On cover 5.00
d. 2c olive brown .90 .50
Never hinged 2.50
On cover 11.00
50a A6 4c olive bister .60 2.75
Never hinged 1.50
On cover 8.50
51 A6 5c lt green .80 .40
Never hinged 2.75
On cover 6.00
52 A6 10c rose 8.00 .40
Never hinged 67.50
On cover 5.00
53 A6 12½c slate 1.25 24.00
Never hinged 6.75
On cover 60.00
54 A6 20c orange 3.25 1.60
Never hinged 13.00
On cover 25.00
55 A6 25c ultra 175.00 1.60
Never hinged 925.00
On cover 27.50
57 A6 50c bister brown 1.20 12.00
Never hinged 4.75
On cover 60.00
d. 50c gray brown 25.00 9.50
Never hinged 50.00
On cover 60.00

For overprints see Nos. O52-O64.

Perf. 12½x12

48a A6 1c gray lilac .30 .60
Never hinged .80
49a A6 2c olive gray .45 .80
Never hinged 1.00
50 A6 4c olive bister .25 2.00
Never hinged 1.40
51a A6 5c lt green .85 1.50
Never hinged 2.50
52a A6 10c rose 8.00 1.00
Never hinged 50.00
53a A6 12½c slate 1.75 30.00
Never hinged 5.50
54a A6 20c orange 4.00 5.00
Never hinged 13.00
55a A6 25c ultra 175.00 1.90
Never hinged 1,000.
56a A6 30c gray green 25.00 14.00
Never hinged 90.00
57a A6 50c bister brown 2.40 12.00
Never hinged 9.50
58 A6 1fr pale violet 1.60 24.00
Never hinged 7.50
59a A6 5fr brown orange 37.50 190.00
Never hinged 65.00

Perf. 11½x12

48b A6 1c gray lilac 1.20 6.00
Never hinged 3.00
49b A6 2c olive gray 1.20 6.00
Never hinged 3.00
50b A6 4c olive bister .90 4.00
Never hinged 2.25
51b A6 5c lt green 3.50 7.00
Never hinged 8.50
52b A6 10c rose 10.00 7.00
Never hinged 50.00
53b A6 12½c slate 4.50 40.00
Never hinged 11.50
54b A6 20c orange 6.00 10.00
Never hinged 19.00
55b A6 25c ultra 200.00 6.00
Never hinged 1,150.
56b A6 30c gray green 25.00 35.00
Never hinged 95.00
57b A6 50c bister brown 4.00 12.00
Never hinged 11.50
58b A6 1fr pale violet 2.00 29.00
Never hinged 5.50
59b A6 5fr brown orange 60.00 225.00
Never hinged 100.00

Perf. 13½

48c A6 1c gray lilac 8.00 1.20
Never hinged 16.00
49c A6 2c olive gray 1.20 2.50
Never hinged 2.40
50c A6 4c olive bister .80 2.50
Never hinged 2.00
51c A6 5c lt green 1.50 1.50
Never hinged 4.25
52c A6 10c rose 8.00 4.00
Never hinged 47.50
53c A6 12½c slate 3.50 30.00
Never hinged 9.50
54c A6 20c orange 4.00 6.00
Never hinged 11.50
55c A6 25c ultra 175.00 3.00
Never hinged 1,000.
56 A6 30c gray green 24.00 12.00
Never hinged 105.00
57c A6 50c bister brown 1.90 12.00
Never hinged 7.00
58c A6 1fr pale violet 3.00 30.00
Never hinged 10.00
59 A6 5fr brown orange 37.50 160.00
Never hinged 60.00

Grand Duke Adolphe — A7

Perf. 11, 11½x11, 12½

1891-93 Engr.

60 A7 10c carmine .80 .40
Never hinged 2.25
On cover 5.50
a. Sheet of 25, perf. 11½ 125.00
b. 10c dark carmine 9.50 1.75
Never hinged 19.00
On cover 30.00
61 A7 12½c slate grn ('93) 1.20 .80
Never hinged 6.00
On cover 11.00
62 A7 20c orange ('93) 8.00 .80
Never hinged 35.00
On cover 22.50
a. 20c brown, perf. 11½ 160.00 240.00
Never hinged 275.00
63 A7 25c blue .80 .80
Never hinged 3.50
On cover 8.75
a. Sheet of 25, perf. 11½ 1,000.
Never hinged 1,750.
64 A7 30c olive grn ('93) 1.60 1.25
Never hinged 3.25
On cover 27.50
65 A7 37½c green ('93) 3.25 3.25
Never hinged 7.00
On cover 37.50
66 A7 50c brown ('93) 7.25 4.00
Never hinged 25.00
On cover 37.50
67 A7 1fr dp violet ('93) 14.50 6.50
Never hinged 65.00
On cover 85.00
c. 1fr reddish violet 55.00 11.00
Never hinged 110.00
On cover 150.00
d. 1fr bluish violet 65.00 11.00
Never hinged 130.00
On cover 175.00
68 A7 2½fr black ('93) 1.60 20.00
Never hinged 3.25
On cover 290.00
69 A7 5fr lake ('93) 29.00 72.50
Never hinged 65.00
On cover 850.00
Nos. 60-69 (10) 68.00 110.30

No. 62a was never on sale at any post office, but exists postally used.

Covers: Cover values are for postally used and correctly franked covers. Low denomination stamps on ordinary postcards sell for somewhat less. Overfranked philatelic covers sell for much less.

For overprints see Nos. O65-O74.

Grand Duke Adolphe — A8

1895, May 4 Typo. Perf. 12½

70 A8 1c pearl gray 3.25 .40
Never hinged 19.00
On cover 8.50
71 A8 2c gray brown .40 .25
Never hinged 1.20
On cover 4.00
72 A8 4c olive bister .40 .90
Never hinged 1.75
On cover 8.50
73 A8 5c green 5.50 .25
Never hinged 30.00
On cover 6.00
74 A8 10c carmine 14.50 .25
Never hinged 50.00
On cover 5.00
Nos. 70-74 (5) 24.05 2.05

For overprints see Nos. O75-O79.

Coat of Arms — A9

Grand Duke William IV — A10

1906-26 Typo. Perf. 12½

75 A9 1c gray ('07) .25 .25
Never hinged .30
On cover 2.50
76 A9 2c ol brn ('07) .25 .25
Never hinged .30
On cover 2.50
77 A9 4c bister ('07) .25 .25
Never hinged .40
On cover 3.00
78 A9 5c green ('07) .25 .25
Never hinged 1.20
On cover 2.50
79 A9 5c lilac ('26) .25 .25
Never hinged .30
On cover 2.25
80 A9 6c violet ('07) .25 .25
Never hinged 1.00
On cover 5.00
81 A9 7½c orange ('19) .25 3.25
Never hinged .30
On cover 25.00

Engr.

Perf. 11, 11½x11

82 A10 10c scarlet 1.60 .25
Never hinged 2.75
On cover 11.00
a. Souvenir sheet of 10 450.00 1,200.
Never hinged 700.00
On cover 1,650.
b. Perf. 11 2.40 25.00
Never hinged 13.00
On cover —
83 A10 12½c sl grn ('07) 1.60 .40
Never hinged 9.25
On cover 6.00
84 A10 15c org brn ('07) 1.60 .65
Never hinged 6.50
On cover 9.50
85 A10 20c orange ('07) 2.75 .55
Never hinged 16.00
On cover 9.50
86 A10 25c ultra ('07) 72.50 .40
Never hinged 390.00
On cover 9.50
87 A10 30c ol grn ('08) 1.20 .55
Never hinged 3.00
On cover 9.50
88 A10 37½c green ('07) 1.20 .80
Never hinged 3.50
On cover 16.50
a. Perf. 12½ 16.00 12.00
Never hinged 110.00
On cover 90.00
89 A10 50c brown ('07) 4.00 .80
Never hinged 14.00
On cover 16.50
90 A10 87½c dk blue ('08) 1.60 12.00
Never hinged 5.50
On cover 65.00
91 A10 1fr violet ('08) 4.75 1.60
Never hinged 20.00
On cover 40.00
a. 1fr deep violet 14.00 3.25
Never hinged 60.00
On cover 65.00
92 A10 2½fr ver ('08) 72.50 80.00
Never hinged 210.00
On cover 45.00
93 A10 5fr claret ('08) 12.00 65.00
Never hinged 32.50
On cover 250.00
Nos. 75-93 (19) 179.05 167.75

No. 82a for accession of Grand Duke William IV to the throne.

Set of 12 stamps, imperf on thick paper $1,200.

For surcharges and overprints see Nos. 94-96, 112-117, O80-O98.

Nos. 90, 92-93 Surcharged in Red or Black

1912-15

94 A10 62½c on 87½c (R) 3.25 2.00
Never hinged 6.50
On cover 60.00
95 A10 62½c on 2½fr (Bk) ('15) 3.25 4.00
Never hinged 6.00
On cover 17.50
96 A10 62½c on 5fr (Bk) ('15) 1.60 2.75
Never hinged 2.50
On cover 7.00
Nos. 94-96 (3) 8.10 8.75

Grand Duchess Marie Adelaide — A11

1914-17 Engr. Perf. 11½, 11½x11

97 A11 10c lake .25 .25
Never hinged .30
On cover 1.20
98 A11 12½c dull green .25 .25
Never hinged .30
On cover 1.75
99 A11 15c sepia .25 .25
Never hinged .30
On cover 3.00
100 A11 17½c dp brown ('17) .25 .40
Never hinged .30
On cover 8.50
101 A11 25c ultra .25 .25
Never hinged .30
On cover 1.75
102 A11 30c bister .25 .40
Never hinged .30
On cover 4.00
103 A11 35c dark blue .25 .40
Never hinged .30
On cover 3.00
104 A11 37½c black brn .25 .40
Never hinged .30
On cover 4.00
105 A11 40c orange .25 .40
Never hinged .30
On cover 4.00
106 A11 50c dark gray .25 .40
Never hinged .30
On cover 7.00
107 A11 62½c blue green .40 2.40
Never hinged .50
On cover 25.00
108 A11 87½c orange ('17) .40 2.40
Never hinged .50
On cover 25.00
109 A11 1fr orange brown 2.00 .55
Never hinged 2.40
On cover 25.00
110 A11 2½fr red .40 2.00
Never hinged .50
On cover 90.00
111 A11 5fr dark violet 9.50 47.50
Never hinged 37.50
On cover 190.00
Nos. 97-111 (15) 15.20 58.25
Set, never hinged 42.50

For surcharges and overprints see Nos. 118-124, B7-B10, O99-O113. Nos. 97, 98, 101, 107, 109 and 111 overprinted "Droits de statistique" are revenue stamps.

Stamps of 1906-19 Surcharged with New Value and Bars in Black or Red

1916-24

112 A9 2½c on 5c ('18) .25 .25
Never hinged .40
On cover 1.75
a. Double surcharge 75.00
Never hinged 90.00

113 A9 3c on 2c ('21) .25 *.25*
Never hinged .40
On cover 1.75
114 A9 5c on 1c ('23) .25 *.25*
Never hinged .40
On cover 1.75
115 A9 5c on 4c ('23) .25 *.40*
Never hinged .40
On cover 2.50
116 A9 5c on 7½c ('24) .25 *.25*
Never hinged .40
On cover 2.50
117 A9 6c on 2c (R) ('22) .25 *.25*
Never hinged .50
On cover 2.50
118 A11 7½c on 10c ('18) .25 .25
Never hinged .40
On cover 1.75
119 A11 17½c on 30c .25 *.40*
Never hinged .40
On cover 6.00
120 A11 20c on 17½c ('21) .25 *.25*
Never hinged .40
On cover 2.50
121 A11 25c on 37½c ('23) .25 *.25*
Never hinged .40
On cover 2.50
a. Double surcharge 90.00
Never hinged 120.00
122 A11 75c on 62½c (R) ('22) .25 *.25*
Never hinged .40
On cover 3.50
123 A11 80c on 87½c ('22) .25 *.25*
Never hinged .40
On cover 5.00
124 A11 87½c on 1fr .55 *5.50*
Never hinged 1.60
On cover 30.00
Nos. 112-124 (13) 3.55 *8.80*

Grand Duchess Charlotte — A12

1921, Jan. 6 Engr. *Perf. 11½*
125 A12 15c rose .25 *.25*
Never hinged .40
On cover 3.00
a. Sheet of 5, perf 11 150.00 *250.00*
Never hinged 350.00
Perf. 11, single 6.00 *12.00*
Never hinged 9.50
b. Sheet of 25, perf. 11½, 11x11½, 12x11½ 5.50 *17.00*
Never hinged 7.00

Birth of Prince Jean, first son of Grand Duchess Charlotte, Jan. 5 (No. 125a). No. 125 was printed in sheets of 100.

See Nos. 131-150. For surcharges and overprints see Nos. 154-158, O114-O131, O136.

Vianden Castle — A13

Foundries at Esch — A14

Adolphe Bridge — A15

1921-34 *Perf. 11½*
126 A13 1fr carmine .25 *.40*
Never hinged .50
On cover 15.00
a. Perf. 11x11½ .25 *1.20*
Never hinged .30
On cover 35.00
127 A13 1fr dk blue ('26) .25 *.45*
Never hinged .60
On cover 17.50

Perf. 11½x11; 11½ (#129, 130)
128 A14 2fr indigo .30 *.80*
Never hinged .85
On cover 30.00
129 A14 2fr dk brown ('26) 7.00 2.00
Never hinged 12.00
On cover 60.00
130 A15 5fr dk violet 20.00 9.50
Never hinged 50.00
On cover 150.00
a. Perf. 12½ ('34) 14.00 11.00
Never hinged 70.00
On cover 175.00
b. Perf. 11½x11 12.00 12.00
Never hinged 60.00
On cover 175.00
Nos. 126-130 (5) 27.80 13.15

For overprints see Nos. O132-O135, O137-138, O140.
See No. B85.

Charlotte Type of 1921

1921-26 *Perf. 11½*
131 A12 2c brown .25 .25
Never hinged .30
On cover 3.00
132 A12 3c olive green .25 .25
Never hinged .30
On cover 3.00
a. Sheet of 25 10.00 25.00
Never hinged 25.00
133 A12 6c violet .25 .25
Never hinged .30
On cover 3.00
a. Sheet of 25 10.00 25.00
Never hinged 25.00
134 A12 10c yellow grn .25 .25
Never hinged .30
On cover 3.00
135 A12 10c olive brn ('24) .25 .25
Never hinged .30
On cover 3.00
136 A12 15c brown olive .25 .25
Never hinged .40
On cover 3.00
137 A12 15c pale grn ('24) .25 .25
Never hinged .50
On cover 3.00
138 A12 15c dp orange ('26) .25 .25
Never hinged .40
On cover 3.00
139 A12 20c dp orange .25 .25
Never hinged .40
On cover 3.00
a. Sheet of 25 60.00 *110.00*
Never hinged 95.00
140 A12 20c yellow grn ('26) .25 .25
Never hinged .40
On cover 3.00
141 A12 25c dk green .25 .25
Never hinged .40
On cover 1.75
142 A12 30c carmine rose .25 .25
Never hinged .40
On cover 3.00
143 A12 40c brown orange .25 .25
Never hinged .40
On cover 3.00
144 A12 50c deep blue .40 .45
Never hinged 1.00
On cover 5.50
145 A12 50c red ('24) .25 .25
Never hinged .40
On cover 3.00
146 A12 75c red .25 1.20
Never hinged .60
On cover 12.00
a. Sheet of 25 325.00
Never hinged 450.00
147 A12 75c deep blue ('24) .25 .25
Never hinged .40
On cover 6.00
148 A12 80c black .65 1.25
Never hinged 4.00
On cover 15.00
a. Sheet of 25 325.00
Never hinged 450.00
Nos. 131-148 (18) 5.05 6.65

For surcharges and overprints see Nos. 154-158, O114-O131, O136.

Philatelic Exhibition Issue

1922, Aug. 27 *Imperf.*

Laid Paper
149 A12 25c dark green 2.25 *6.00*
Never hinged 6.75
150 A12 30c carmine rose 2.25 *6.00*
Never hinged 6.75

Nos. 149 and 150 were sold exclusively at the Luxembourg Phil. Exhib., Aug. 1922.

Souvenir Sheet

View of Luxembourg — A16

1923, Jan. 3 *Perf. 11*
151 A16 10fr dp grn, sheet 1,000. *2,400.*
Never hinged 1,600.

Birth of Princess Elisabeth.

1923, Mar. *Perf. 11½*
152 A16 10fr black 9.50 *13.50*
Never hinged 29.00
a. Perf. 12½ ('34) 8.00 *12.00*
Never hinged 17.00

For overprint see No. O141.

The Wolfsschlucht near Echternach — A17

1923-34 *Perf. 11½*
153 A17 3fr dk blue & blue 2.75 .80
Never hinged 13.50
a. Perf. 12½ ('34) 2.75 .80
Never hinged 13.50

For overprint see No. O139.

Stamps of 1921-26 Surcharged with New Values and Bars

1925-28
154 A12 5c on 10c yel grn .25 .30
Never hinged .30
155 A12 15c on 20c yel grn ('28) .25 .25
Never hinged .30
a. Bars omitted
156 A12 35c on 40c brn org ('27) .25 .25
Never hinged .30
157 A12 60c on 75c dp bl ('27) .25 .25
Never hinged .60
158 A12 60c on 80c blk ('28) .40 .35
Never hinged .60
Nos. 154-158 (5) 1.40 1.40

Grand Duchess Charlotte — A18

1926-35 Engr. *Perf. 12*
159 A18 5c dk violet .25 .25
Never hinged .30
160 A18 10c olive grn .25 .25
Never hinged .30
161 A18 15c black ('30) .25 .25
Never hinged .50
162 A18 20c orange .40 .40
Never hinged .50
163 A18 25c yellow grn .40 .40
Never hinged .75
164 A18 25c vio brn ('27) .35 .25
Never hinged .75
165 A18 30c yel grn ('27) .35 .50
Never hinged .75
166 A18 30c gray vio ('30) .30 .25
Never hinged .75
167 A18 35c gray vio ('28) 3.00 .25
Never hinged 3.50
168 A18 35c yel grn ('30) .25 .25
Never hinged .40
169 A18 40c olive gray .25 .30
Never hinged .30
170 A18 50c red brown .25 .30
Never hinged .30
171 A18 60c blue grn ('28) 3.00 .25
Never hinged .50
172 A18 65c black brn .25 1.10
Never hinged .60
173 A18 70c blue vio ('35) .25 .25
Never hinged .30
174 A18 75c rose .25 .65
Never hinged .60
175 A18 75c bis brn ('27) .25 .25
Never hinged .30
176 A18 80c bister brn .35 1.60
Never hinged .60
177 A18 90c rose ('27) 1.50 1.40
Never hinged 4.00
178 A18 1fr black 1.25 .60
Never hinged 3.50
179 A18 1fr rose ('30) .60 .25
Never hinged 1.50
180 A18 1¼fr dk blue .25 .45
Never hinged .40
181 A18 1¼fr yellow ('30) 15.00 1.60
Never hinged 17.50
182 A18 1¼fr blue grn ('31) .45 .25
Never hinged 2.50
183 A18 1¼fr rose car ('34) 22.50 2.00
Never hinged 40.00
184 A18 1½fr dp blue ('27) 3.00 1.40
Never hinged 7.00
185 A18 1¾fr dk blue ('30) .75 .25
Never hinged 1.50
Nos. 159-185 (27) 55.95 15.95
Set, never hinged 90.00

For surcharges and overprints see Nos. 186-193, N17-N29, O142-O178.

Stamps of 1926-35, Surcharged with New Values and Bars

1928-39
186 A18 10(c) on 30c yel grn ('29) .50 .40
Never hinged 1.30
187 A18 15c on 25c yel grn .40 .55
Never hinged 1.50
187A A18 30c on 60c bl grn ('39) .30 1.60
Never hinged .80
188 A18 60c on 65c blk brn .25 .40
Never hinged .65
189 A18 60c on 75c rose .25 .40
Never hinged .65
190 A18 60c on 80c bis brn .35 .65
Never hinged .80
191 A18 70(c) on 75c bis brn ('35) 12.00 .40
Never hinged 23.00
192 A18 75(c) on 90c rose ('29) 2.00 .40
Never hinged 5.25
193 A18 1¾(fr) on 1½fr dp bl ('29) 5.50 1.60
Never hinged 11.50
Nos. 186-193 (9) 21.55 6.40
Set, never hinged 45.00

The surcharge on No. 187A has no bars.

View of Clervaux A19

1928-34 *Perf. 12½*
194 A19 2fr black ('34) 1.75 .80
Never hinged 4.00
a. Perf. 11½ ('28) 2.75 .80
Never hinged 6.00 —

See No. B66. For overprint see No. O179.

Coat of Arms — A20

1930, Dec. 20 Typo. *Perf. 12½*
195 A20 5c claret .85 .40
196 A20 10c olive green 1.10 .25
Set, never hinged 5.50

View of the Lower City of Luxembourg A21

1931, June 20 Engr.
197 A21 20fr deep green 3.50 *17.50*
Never hinged 8.00

For overprint see No. O180.

Gate of "Three Towers" — A22

1934, Aug. 30 *Perf. 14x13½*
198 A22 5fr blue green 3.00 *9.50*
Never hinged 8.50

For surcharge and overprint see Nos. N31, O181.

Castle From Our Valley A23

1935, Nov. 15 *Perf. 12½x12*
199 A23 10fr green 3.00 *14.00*
Never hinged 6.50

For surcharge and overprint see Nos. N32, O182.

Municipal Palace — A24

1936, Aug. 26 Photo. *Perf. 11½*
Granite Paper

200 A24 10c brown .25 .45
201 A24 35c green .35 .90
202 A24 70c red orange .40 *1.40*
203 A24 1fr carmine rose 2.00 *8.50*
204 A24 1.25fr violet 2.50 *12.00*
205 A24 1.75fr brt ultra 1.60 *9.00*
Nos. 200-205 (6) 7.10 *32.25*
Set, never hinged 16.00

11th Cong. of Intl. Federation of Philately.

Arms of Luxembourg A25

William I A26

Designs: 70c, William II. 75c, William III. 1fr, Prince Henry. 1.25fr, Grand Duke Adolphe. 1.75fr, William IV. 3fr, Regent Marie Anne. 5fr, Grand Duchess Marie Adelaide. 10fr, Grand Duchess Charlotte.

1939, May 27 Engr. *Perf. 12½x12*

206 A25 35c brt green .25 .25
207 A25 50c orange .25 .25
208 A26 70c slate green .25 .25
209 A26 75c sepia .65 *.95*
210 A26 1fr red 1.60 *2.00*
211 A26 1.25fr brown violet .25 .25
212 A26 1.75fr dark blue .25 .25
213 A26 3fr lt brown .25 .50
214 A26 5fr gray black .50 *8.00*
215 A26 10fr copper red .75 *10.00*
Nos. 206-215 (10) 5.00 *22.70*
Set, never hinged 8.50

Centenary of Independence.

Allegory of Medicinal Baths — A35

1939, Sept. 18 Photo. *Perf. 11½*

216 A35 2fr brown rose .50 4.00
Never hinged 1.25

Elevation of Mondorf-les-Bains to town status.

See No. B104. For surcharge see No. N30.

Souvenir Sheet

A36

1939, Dec. 20 Engr. *Perf. 14x13*

217 A36 Sheet of 3 45.00 *110.00*
Sheet, never hinged 110.00
a. 2fr vermilion, *buff* 7.00 *22.50*
b. 3fr dark green, *buff* 7.00 *22.50*
c. 5fr blue, *buff* 7.00 *22.50*

20th anniv. of the reign of Grand Duchess Charlotte (Jan. 15, 1919) and her marriage to Prince Felix (Nov. 6, 1919).

See Nos. B98-B103.

SEMI-POSTAL STAMPS

Clervaux Monastery SP1

Designs: 15c+10c, View of Pfaffenthal. 25c+10c, View of Luxembourg.

Engr.; Surcharge Typo. in Red
1921, Aug. 2 Unwmk. *Perf. 11½*

B1 SP1 10c + 5c green .30 *4.50*
B2 SP1 15c + 10c org red .30 *6.00*
B3 SP1 25c + 10c dp grn .30 *4.50*
Nos. B1-B3 (3) .90 *15.00*
Set, never hinged 2.50

The amount received from the surtax on these stamps was added to a fund for the erection of a monument to the soldiers from Luxembourg who died in World War I.

Nos. B1-B3 with Additional Surcharge in Red or Black

1923, May 27

B4 SP1 25c on #B1 (R) 1.10 *14.50*
B5 SP1 25c on #B2 1.25 *20.00*
B6 SP1 25c on #B3 1.10 *14.50*
Nos. B4-B6 (3) 3.45 *49.00*
Set, never hinged 10.00

Unveiling of the monument to the soldiers who died in World War I.

Regular Issue of 1914-15 Surcharged in Black or Red

1924, Apr. 17 *Perf. 11½x11*

B7 A11 12½c + 7½c grn .25 *2.75*
B8 A11 35c + 10c dk bl (R) .25 *2.75*
B9 A11 2½fr + 1fr red 1.75 *27.50*
B10 A11 5fr + 2fr dk vio .55 *17.50*
Nos. B7-B10 (4) 2.80 *50.50*
Set, never hinged 6.25

Nurse and Patient — SP4

1925, Dec. 21 Litho. *Perf. 13*

B11 SP4 5c (+ 5c) dl vio .25 .70
B12 SP4 30c (+ 5c) org .25 3.00
B13 SP4 50c (+ 5c) red brn .25 *5.50*
B14 SP4 1fr (+ 10c) dp bl .40 *14.00*
Nos. B11-B14 (4) 1.15 *23.20*
Set, never hinged 1.75

Prince Jean — SP5

1926, Dec. 15 Photo. *Perf. 12½x12*

B15 SP5 5c (+ 5c) vio & blk .25 .55
B16 SP5 40c (+ 10) grn & blk .25 .90
B17 SP5 50c (+ 15c) lem & blk .25 .95
B18 SP5 75c (+ 20c) lt red & blk .25 *11.00*
B19 SP5 1.50fr (+ 30c) gray bl & blk .35 *12.00*
Nos. B15-B19 (5) 1.35 *25.40*
Set, never hinged 2.50

Grand Duchess Charlotte and Prince Felix — SP6

1927, Sept. 4 Engr. *Perf. 11½*

B20 SP6 25c dp vio 1.10 *10.00*
B21 SP6 50c green 1.50 *16.00*
B22 SP6 75c rose lake 1.10 *10.00*
B23 SP6 1fr gray blk 1.10 *10.00*
B24 SP6 1½fr dp bl 1.10 *10.00*
Nos. B20-B24 (5) 5.90 *56.00*
Set, never hinged 17.00

Introduction of postage stamps in Luxembourg, 75th anniv. These stamps were sold exclusively at the Luxembourg Philatelic Exhibition, September 4-8, 1927, at a premium of 3 francs per set, which was donated to the exhibition funds.

Princess Elisabeth — SP7

1927, Dec. 1 Photo. *Perf. 12½*

B25 SP7 10c (+ 5c) turq bl & blk .25 *.55*
B26 SP7 50c (+ 10c) dk brn & blk .25 *.95*
B27 SP7 75c (+ 20c) org & blk .25 *1.50*
B28 SP7 1fr (+ 30c) brn lake & blk .25 *11.00*
B29 SP7 1½fr (+ 50c) ultra & blk .25 *11.00*
Nos. B25-B29 (5) 1.25 *25.00*
Set, never hinged 4.00

The surtax was for Child Welfare societies.

Princess Marie Adelaide — SP8

1928, Dec. 12 *Perf. 12½x12*

B30 SP8 10c (+ 5c) ol grn & brn vio .25 *1.10*
B31 SP8 60c (+ 10c) brn & ol grn .40 *2.75*
B32 SP8 75c (+ 15c) vio rose & bl grn .70 *7.25*
B33 SP8 1fr (+ 25c) dk grn & brn 1.75 *22.50*
B34 SP8 1½fr (+ 50c) cit & bl 1.75 *22.50*
Nos. B30-B34 (5) 4.85 *56.10*
Set, never hinged 12.00

Princess Marie Gabrielle — SP9

1929, Dec. 14 *Perf. 13*

B35 SP9 10c (+ 10c) mar & dp grn .25 *1.10*
B36 SP9 35c (+ 15c) dk grn & red brn 1.50 *7.25*
B37 SP9 75c (+ 30c) ver & blk 1.75 *9.00*
B38 SP9 1¼fr (+ 50c) mag & bl grn 2.25 *22.50*
B39 SP9 1¾fr (+ 75c) Prus bl & sl 2.75 *27.50*
Nos. B35-B39 (5) 8.50 *67.35*
Set, never hinged 24.00

The surtax was for Child Welfare societies.

Prince Charles — SP10

1930, Dec. 10 *Perf. 12½*

B40 SP10 10c (+ 5c) bl grn & ol brn .25 1.10
B41 SP10 75c (+ 10c) vio brn & bl grn 1.10 *4.75*
B42 SP10 1fr (+ 25c) car rose & vio 2.50 *17.50*
B43 SP10 1¼fr (+ 75c) ol bis & dk brn 4.00 *22.50*
B44 SP10 1¾fr (+ 1.50fr) ultra & red brn 4.50 *22.50*
Nos. B40-B44 (5) 12.35 *68.35*
Set, never hinged 40.00

The surtax was for Child Welfare societies.

Princess Alix — SP11

1931, Dec. 10

B45 SP11 10c (+ 5c) brn org & gray .30 1.10
B46 SP11 75c (+ 10c) clar & bl grn 4.50 *14.50*
B47 SP11 1fr (+ 25c) dp grn & gray 9.00 *29.00*
B48 SP11 1¼fr (+ 75c) dk vio & bl grn 6.00 *29.00*
B49 SP11 1¾fr (+ 1.50fr) bl & gray 16.00 *55.00*
Nos. B45-B49 (5) 35.80 *128.60*
Set, never hinged 110.00

The surtax was for Child Welfare societies.

Countess Ermesinde — SP12

1932, Dec. 8

B50 SP12 10c (+ 5c) ol bis .40 1.10
B51 SP12 75c (+ 10c) dp vio 2.75 *14.50*
B52 SP12 1fr (+ 25c) scar 11.00 *32.50*
B53 SP12 1¼fr (+ 75c) red brn 11.00 *32.50*
B54 SP12 1¾fr (+ 1.50fr) dp bl 11.00 *32.50*
Nos. B50-B54 (5) 36.15 *113.10*
Set, never hinged 92.50

The surtax was for Child Welfare societies.

Count Henry VII — SP13

1933, Dec. 12

B55 SP13 10c (+ 5c) yel brn .40 1.10
B56 SP13 75c (+ 10c) dp vio 4.75 *14.50*
B57 SP13 1fr (+ 25c) car rose 11.00 *35.00*
B58 SP13 1¼fr (+ 75c) org brn 14.50 *47.50*
B59 SP13 1¾fr (+ 1.50fr) brt bl 14.50 *50.00*
Nos. B55-B59 (5) 45.15 *148.10*
Set, never hinged 125.00

John the Blind — SP14

1934, Dec. 5

B60	SP14	10c (+ 5c) dk vio	.25	*1.10*
B61	SP14	35c (+ 10c) dp grn	2.50	*9.00*
B62	SP14	75c (+ 15c) rose lake	2.50	*9.00*
B63	SP14	1fr (+ 25c) dp rose	14.50	*47.50*
B64	SP14	1¼fr (+ 75c) org	14.50	*47.50*
B65	SP14	1¾fr (+ 1.50fr) brt bl	14.50	*47.50*
		Nos. B60-B65 (6)	48.75	*161.60*
		Set, never hinged	125.00	

Teacher SP15

Sculptor and Painter — SP16

Journalist SP17

Engineer SP18

Scientist SP19

Lawyer — SP20

Savings Bank and Adolphe Bridge — SP21

Surgeon SP22

1935, May 1 Unwmk. *Perf. 12½*

B65A	SP15	5c violet	.25	*1.10*
B65B	SP16	10c brn red	.25	*1.10*
B65C	SP17	15c olive	.40	*1.75*
B65D	SP18	20c orange	.55	*3.50*
B65E	SP19	35c yel grn	.70	*3.25*
B65F	SP20	50c gray blk	.95	*4.75*
B65G	SP21	70c dk green	1.40	*5.50*
B65H	SP22	1fr car red	1.75	*7.25*
B65J	SP19	1.25fr turq	7.25	*50.00*
B65K	SP18	1.75fr blue	9.00	*52.50*
B65L	SP16	2fr lt brown	27.50	*110.00*
B65M	SP17	3fr dk brown	37.50	*150.00*
B65N	SP20	5fr lt blue	65.00	*275.00*
B65P	SP15	10fr red vio	160.00	*450.00*
B65Q	SP22	20fr dk green	175.00	*550.00*
		Nos. B65A-B65Q (15)	487.50	*1,666.*
		Set, never hinged	1,250.	

Sold at double face, surtax going to intl. fund to aid professional people.

Philatelic Exhibition Issue

Type of Regular Issue of 1928

Wmk. 246

1935, Aug. 15 Engr. *Imperf.*

B66	A19	2fr (+ 50c) blk	4.75	*16.00*
		Never hinged	13.00	

Philatelic exhibition held at Esch-sur-Alzette.

Charles I — SP23

Perf. 11½

1935, Dec. 2 Photo. Unwmk.

B67	SP23	10c (+ 5c) vio	.25	.40
B68	SP23	35c (+ 10c) grn	.40	*.55*
B69	SP23	70c (+ 20c) dk brn	.95	*1.50*
B70	SP23	1fr (+ 25c) rose lake	14.50	*37.50*
B71	SP23	1.25fr (+ 75c) org brn	14.50	*37.50*
B72	SP23	1.75fr (+ 1.50fr) bl	14.50	*47.50*
		Nos. B67-B72 (6)	45.10	*124.95*
		Set, never hinged	110.00	

Wenceslas I, Duke of Luxembourg — SP24

1936, Dec. 1 *Perf. 11½x13*

B73	SP24	10c + 5(c) blk brn	.25	.25
B74	SP24	35c + 10(c) bl grn	.25	*.55*
B75	SP24	70c + 20(c) blk	.40	*.90*
B76	SP24	1fr + 25(c) rose car	2.50	*14.50*
B77	SP24	1.25fr + 75(c) vio	2.25	*29.00*
B78	SP24	1.75fr + 1.50(fr) saph	1.60	*17.50*
		Nos. B73-B78 (6)	7.25	*62.70*
		Set, never hinged	37.50	

Wenceslas II — SP25

1937, Dec. 1 *Perf. 11½x12½*

B79	SP25	10c + 5c car & blk	.25	.40
B80	SP25	35c + 10c red vio & grn	.25	.55
B81	SP25	70c + 20c ultra & red brn	.25	.55
B82	SP25	1fr + 25c dk grn & scar	1.60	*17.00*
B83	SP25	1.25fr + 75c dk brn & vio	2.25	*17.00*
B84	SP25	1.75fr + 1.50fr blk & ultra	2.75	*17.50*
		Nos. B79-B84 (6)	7.35	*53.00*
		Set, never hinged	23.00	

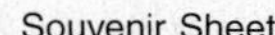

Souvenir Sheet

SP26

Wmk. 110

1937, July 25 Engr. *Perf. 13*

B85	SP26	Sheet of 2	4.00	*11.50*
		Never hinged	11.00	
a.		2fr red brown, single stamp	1.50	*5.50*

National Philatelic Exposition at Dudelange on July 25-26.

Sold for 5fr per sheet, of which 1fr was for the aid of the exposition.

Portrait of St. Willibrord — SP28

St. Willibrord, after a Miniature SP29

Abbey at Echternach — SP30

Designs: No, B87, The Rathaus at Echternach. No. B88, Pavilion in Abbey Park, Echternach. No. B91, Dancing Procession in Honor of St. Willibrord.

Perf. 14x13, 13x14

1938, June 5 Engr. Unwmk.

B86	SP28	35c + 10c dk bl grn	.40	*.55*
B87	SP28	70c + 10c ol gray	.70	*.55*
B88	SP28	1.25fr + 25c brn car	1.50	*2.50*
B89	SP29	1.75fr + 50c sl bl	2.50	*2.75*
B90	SP30	3fr + 2fr vio brn	5.50	*9.00*
B91	SP30	5fr + 5fr dk vio	6.50	*7.25*
		Nos. B86-B91 (6)	17.10	22.60
		Set, never hinged	60.00	

12th centenary of the death of St. Willibrord. The surtax was used for the restoration of the ancient Abbey at Echternach.

Duke Sigismond — SP32

1938, Dec. 1 Photo. *Perf. 11½*

B92	SP32	10c + 5c lil & blk	.25	.40
B93	SP32	35c + 10c grn & blk	.25	.55
B94	SP32	70c + 20c buff & blk	.25	*.55*
B95	SP32	1fr + 25c red org & blk	2.40	*14.50*
B96	SP32	1.25fr + 75c gray bl & blk	2.40	*14.50*
B97	SP32	1.75fr + 1.50fr bl & blk	3.50	*22.50*
		Nos. B92-B97 (6)	9.05	*53.00*
		Set, never hinged	25.00	

Prince Jean — SP33

Designs: Nos. B99, B102, Prince Felix. Nos. B100, B103, Grand Duchess Charlotte.

1939, Dec. 1 Litho. *Perf. 14x13*

B98	SP33	10c + 5c red brn, *buff*	.25	.40
B99	SP33	35c + 10c sl grn, *buff*	.25	1.10
B100	SP33	70c + 20c blk, *buff*	.95	*1.50*
B101	SP33	1fr + 25c red org, *buff*	4.00	*32.50*
B102	SP33	1.25fr + 75c vio brn, *buff*	4.75	*50.00*
B103	SP33	1.75fr + 1.50fr lt bl, *buff*	5.50	*65.00*
		Nos. B98-B103 (6)	15.70	*150.50*
		Set, never hinged	45.00	

See No. 217 (souvenir sheet).

Allegory of Medicinal Baths — SP36

1940, Mar. 1 Photo. *Perf. 11½*

B104	SP36	2fr + 50c gray, blk & slate grn	1.25	*20.00*
		Never hinged	4.50	

For similar stamp see No. 216.

AIR POST STAMPS

Airplane over Luxembourg — AP1

1931-33 Unwmk. Engr. *Perf. 12½*

C1	AP1	50c green ('33)	.55	*1.10*
C2	AP1	75c dark brown	.55	*1.50*
C3	AP1	1fr red	.55	*1.50*
C4	AP1	1¼fr dark violet	.55	*1.50*
C5	AP1	1¾fr dark blue	.55	*1.50*
C6	AP1	3fr gray black ('33)	1.10	*6.00*
		Nos. C1-C6 (6)	3.85	*13.10*
		Set, never hinged	8.25	

POSTAGE DUE STAMPS

Coat of Arms — D1

1907 Unwmk. Typo. *Perf. 12½*

J1 D1 5c green & black .25 *.25*
J2 D1 10c green & black .95 .25
J3 D1 12½c green & black .25 *.80*
J4 D1 20c green & black .55 *.80*
J5 D1 25c green & black 16.00 1.20
J6 D1 50c green & black .45 *3.50*
J7 D1 1fr green & black .25 *3.50*
Nos. J1-J7 (7) 18.70 10.30

See Nos. J10-J22.

Nos. J3, J5 Surcharged

1920

J8 D1 15c on 12½c .50 *7.25*
J9 D1 30c on 25c .60 *9.00*
Set, never hinged 3.50

Arms Type of 1907

1921-35

J10 D1 5c green & red .25 *.40*
J11 D1 10c green & red .25 *.35*
J12 D1 20c green & red .25 *.35*
J13 D1 25c green & red .25 *.35*
J14 D1 30c green & red .55 *.60*
J15 D1 35c green & red ('35) .55 .35
J16 D1 50c green & red .55 *.60*
J17 D1 60c green & red ('28) .45 *.50*
J18 D1 70c green & red ('35) .55 .35
J19 D1 75c green & red ('30) .55 .25
J20 D1 1fr green & red .55 *1.10*
J21 D1 2fr green & red ('30) .55 *6.50*
J22 D1 3fr green & red ('30) 1.60 *18.00*
Nos. J10-J22 (13) 6.90 29.70
Set, never hinged 27.50

OFFICIAL STAMPS

Forged overprints on Nos. O1-O64 abound.

Unused values of Nos. O1-O51 are for stamps without gum. Though these stamps were issued with gum, most examples offered are without gum. Stamps with original gum sell for somewhat more.

Regular Issues Overprinted Reading Diagonally Up or Down

Frankfurt Print

Rouletted in Color except 2c

1875 Unwmk.

O1 A2 1c red brown 27.50 37.50
O2 A2 2c black 27.50 37.50
O3 A3 10c lilac 2,400. 2,400.
O4 A3 12½c rose 475.00 600.00
O5 A3 20c gray brn 37.50 57.50
O6 A3 25c blue 250.00 140.00
O7 A3 25c ultra 2,100. 1,400.
O8 A3 30c lilac rose 32.50 *75.00*
O9 A3 40c pale org 160.00 240.00
a. 40c org red, thick paper 250.00 325.00
c. As "a," thin paper 1,650. 1,400.
O10 A3 1fr on 37½c bis 150.00 22.50

Double overprints exist on Nos. O1-O6, O8-O10.

Overprints reading diagonally down sell for more.

Inverted Overprint

O1a A2 1c 190.00 225.00
O2a A2 2c 190.00 225.00
O3a A3 10c 2,500. 2,500.
O4a A3 12½c 650.00 925.00
O5a A3 20c 55.00 75.00
O6a A3 25c 1,100. 1,300.
O7a A3 25c 2,100. 1,500.
O8a A3 30c 650.00 925.00
O9b A3 40c pale orange 325.00 450.00
O10a A3 1fr on 37½c 175.00 75.00

Luxembourg Print

1875-76 *Perf. 13*

O11 A2 1c red brown 9.50 27.50
O12 A2 2c black 12.00 32.50
O13 A2 4c green 90.00 160.00
O14 A2 5c yellow 65.00 80.00
a. 5c orange yellow 75.00 110.00
O15 A3 10c gray lilac 92.50 120.00
O16 A3 12½c rose 85.00 120.00
O17 A3 12½c lilac rose 225.00 275.00
O18 A3 25c blue 11.00 *32.50*
O19 A3 1fr on 37½c bis 35.00 60.00
Nos. O11-O19 (9) 625.00 907.50

Double overprints exist on Nos. O11-O15.

Inverted Overprint

O11a A2 1c 92.50 *110.00*
O12a A2 2c 150.00 190.00
O13a A2 4c 160.00 190.00
O14b A2 5c 500.00 650.00
O15a A3 10c 500.00 190.00
O16a A3 12½c 400.00 550.00
O17a A3 12½c 450.00 525.00
O18a A3 25c 125.00 175.00
O19a A5 1fr on 37½c 190.00 250.00
Nos. O11a-O19a (9) 2,568. 2,830.

Haarlem Print

1880 *Perf. 11½x12, 12½x12, 13½*

O22 A3 25c blue 2.25 2.75

Overprinted

Frankfurt Print

1878 *Rouletted in Color*

O23 A2 1c red brown 140.00 160.00
O25 A3 20c gray brn 190.00 225.00
O26 A3 30c lilac rose 750.00 575.00
O27 A3 40c orange 325.00 450.00
O28 A3 1fr on 37½c bis 550.00 110.00
Nos. O23-O28 (5) 1,955. 1,520.

Inverted Overprint

O23a A2 1c 225.00 300.00
O25a A3 20c 325.00 400.00
O26a A3 30c 925.00 700.00
O27a A3 40c 875.00 925.00
O28a A3 1fr on 37½c 650.00 200.00

Luxembourg Print

1878-80 *Perf. 13*

O29 A2 1c red brown 750.00 925.00
O30 A2 2c black 190.00 225.00
O31 A2 4c green 190.00 225.00
O32 A2 5c yellow 375.00 450.00
O33 A3 10c gray lilac 375.00 400.00
O34 A3 12½c rose 65.00 110.00
O35 A3 25c blue 525.00 550.00
Nos. O29-O35 (7) 2,470. 2,885.

Inverted Overprint

O29a A2 1c 140.00 160.00
O30a A2 2c 14.50 27.50
O31a A2 4c 150.00 190.00
O32a A2 5c 1,500. 1,500.
O33a A3 10c 92.50 110.00
O34a A3 12½c 525.00 600.00
O35a A3 25c 850.00 1,000.

Overprinted

Frankfurt Print

1881 *Rouletted in Color*

O39 A3 40c orange 37.50 75.00
a. Inverted overprint 210.00 275.00

"S.P." are initials of "Service Public."

Luxembourg Print

Perf. 13

O40 A2 1c red brown 125.00 160.00
O41 A2 4c green 175.00 200.00
a. Inverted overprint 250.00
O42 A2 5c yellow 600.00 750.00
O43 A3 1fr on 37½c bis 32.50 47.50
Nos. O40-O43 (4) 932.50 1,158.

Haarlem Print

Perf. 11½x12, 12½x12, 13½

O44 A2 1c yellow brn 8.50 9.25
O45 A2 2c black 9.25 9.25
O46 A2 5c yellow 160.00 200.00
a. Inverted overprint 225.00
O47 A3 10c gray lilac 160.00 200.00
O48 A3 12½c rose 175.00 240.00
O49 A3 20c gray brown 72.50 92.50
O50 A3 25c blue 72.50 92.50
O51 A3 30c dull rose 75.00 120.00
Nos. O44-O51 (8) 732.75 963.50

Stamps of the 1881 issue with the overprint of the 1882 issue shown below were never issued.

Overprinted

Perf. 11½x12, 12½x12, 12½, 13½

1882

O52 A6 1c gray lilac .25 .40
O53 A6 2c ol gray .25 .40
a. "S" omitted 110.00
O54 A6 4c ol bister .25 .45
O55 A6 5c lt green .25 .55
O56 A6 10c rose 12.00 16.00
O57 A6 12½c slate 1.60 4.75
O58 A6 20c orange 1.60 4.00
O59 A6 25c ultra 19.00 24.00
O60 A6 30c gray grn 4.00 8.75
O61 A6 50c bis brown .95 2.75
O62 A6 1fr pale vio .95 4.00
O63 A6 5fr brown org 16.00 40.00
Nos. O52-O63 (12) 57.10 106.05

Nos. O52-O63 exist without one or both periods, also with varying space between "S" and "P." Nine denominations exist with double overprint, six with inverted overprint.

Overprinted

1883 *Perf. 13½*

O64 A6 5fr brown org *2,200. 2,200.*

Overprinted

1891-93 *Perf. 11, 11½, 11½x11, 12½*

O65 A7 10c carmine .25 .50
a. Sheet of 25 55.00
O66 A7 12½c slate grn 8.00 7.25
O67 A7 20c orange 13.00 8.50
O68 A7 25c blue .25 .45
a. Sheet of 25 65.00
O69 A7 30c olive grn 8.00 8.00
O70 A7 37½c green 8.00 8.00
O71 A7 50c brown 6.00 8.75
O72 A7 1fr dp vio 8.00 9.50
O73 A7 2½fr black 45.00 72.50
O74 A7 5fr lake 40.00 55.00
Nos. O65-O74 (10) 136.50 178.45

1895 *Perf. 12½*

O75 A8 1c pearl gray 1.90 1.90
O76 A8 2c gray brn 1.00 1.60
O77 A8 4c olive bis 1.00 1.60
O78 A8 5c green 4.00 5.00
O79 A8 10c carmine 24.00 35.00
Nos. O75-O79 (5) 31.90 45.10

Nos. O66-O79 exist without overprint and perforated "OFFICIEL" through the stamp. Values for set: unused, $12; used, $45.

Nos. O65a and O68a were issued to commemorate the coronation of Grand Duke Adolphe.

Regular Issue of 1906-26 Overprinted

1908-26 *Perf. 11x11½, 12½*

O80 A9 1c gray .25 .40
a. Inverted overprint 125.00
O81 A9 2c olive brn .25 .40
O82 A9 4c bister .25 .40
a. Double overprint 140.00
O83 A9 5c green .25 .40
O84 A9 5c lilac ('26) .25 .40
O85 A9 6c violet .25 .40
O86 A9 7½c org ('19) .25 .40
O87 A10 10c scarlet .25 .40
O88 A10 12½c slate grn .25 *.55*
O89 A10 15c orange brn .25 *.55*
O90 A10 20c orange .25 *.75*
O91 A10 25c ultra .25 *.75*
O92 A10 30c olive grn 2.75 *6.50*
O93 A10 37½c green .45 .75
O94 A10 50c brown .75 *1.50*
O95 A10 87½c dk blue 2.00 *3.50*
O96 A10 1fr violet 2.75 *4.00*
O97 A10 2½fr vermilion 65.00 65.00
O98 A10 5fr claret 55.00 45.00
Nos. O80-O98 (19) 131.70 132.05

On Regular Issue of 1914-17

1915-17

O99 A11 10c lake .25 *.75*
O100 A11 12½c dull grn .25 *.75*
O101 A11 15c olive blk .25 *.75*
O102 A11 17½c dp brn ('17) .25 .75
O103 A11 25c ultra .25 *.75*
O104 A11 30c bister 1.40 *5.00*
O105 A11 35c dk blue .25 *1.20*
O106 A11 37½c blk brn .25 *1.60*
O107 A11 40c orange .30 *1.20*
O108 A11 50c dk gray .30 *.95*
O109 A11 62½c blue grn .30 *1.60*
O110 A11 87½c org ('17) .30 *1.60*
O111 A11 1fr orange brn .30 *1.60*
O112 A11 2½fr red .30 *2.50*
O113 A11 5fr dk violet .30 *2.75*
Nos. O99-O113 (15) 5.25 23.75

On Regular Issues of 1921-26 in Black

1922-26 *Perf. 11½, 11½x11, 12½*

O114 A12 2c brown .25 .25
O115 A12 3c olive grn .25 .25
O116 A12 6c violet .25 .40
O117 A12 10c yellow grn .25 .40
O118 A12 10c ol grn ('24) .25 .40
O119 A12 15c brown ol .25 .40
O120 A12 15c pale grn ('24) .25 .40
O121 A12 15c dp org ('26) .25 .40
O122 A12 20c dp orange .25 .40
O123 A12 20c yel grn ('26) .25 .40
O124 A12 25c dk green .25 .40
O125 A12 30c car rose .25 .40
O126 A12 40c brown org .25 .40
O127 A12 50c dp blue .25 .45
O128 A12 50c red ('24) .25 .55
O129 A12 75c red .25 .55
O130 A12 75c dp bl ('24) .25 .45
O131 A12 80c black 4.75 8.00
O132 A13 1fr carmine .40 2.00
O133 A14 2fr indigo 3.00 6.00
O134 A14 2fr dk brn ('26) 1.75 5.00
O135 A15 5fr dk vio 17.50 40.00
Nos. O114-O135 (22) 31.65 67.90

On Regular Issues of 1921-26 in Red

1922-34 *Perf. 11, 11½, 11½x11, 12½*

O136 A12 80c blk, perf. 11½ .25 .45
O137 A13 1fr dk bl, perf. 11½ ('26) .25 1.20
O138 A14 2fr ind, perf. 11½x11 .55 2.00
O139 A17 3fr dk bl & bl, perf. 11 2.75 2.75
a. Perf. 11½ .60 1.40
b. Perf. 12½ .50 1.40
O140 A15 5fr dk vio, perf. 11½x11 4.00 9.00
a. Perf. 12½ ('34) 12.00 20.00
O141 A16 10fr blk, perf. 11½ 12.00 24.00
a. Perf. 12½ 12.00 27.50
Nos. O136-O141 (6) 19.80 39.40

On Regular Issue of 1926-35

1926-27 *Perf. 12*

O142 A18 5c dk violet .25 .25
O143 A18 10c olive grn .25 .25
O144 A18 20c orange .25 .25
O145 A18 25c yellow grn .25 .25
O146 A18 25c blk brn ('27) .35 .55
O147 A18 30c yel grn ('27) .65 1.20
O148 A18 40c olive gray .25 .25
O149 A18 50c red brown .25 .25
O150 A18 65c black brn .25 .25
O151 A18 75c rose .25 .25
O152 A18 75c bis brn ('27) .35 .55
O153 A18 80c bister brn .25 .40
O154 A18 90c rose ('27) .35 .55
O155 A18 1fr black .25 .45
O156 A18 1¼fr dk blue .25 .45
O157 A18 1½fr dp blue ('27) .55 1.20
Nos. O142-O157 (16) 5.00 7.35

Type of Regular Issue, 1926-35, Overprinted

1928-35 Wmk. 213

O158 A18 5c dk violet .25 .40
O159 A18 10c olive grn .25 .40
O160 A18 15c black ('30) .25 1.20
O161 A18 20c orange .45 .75
O162 A18 25c violet brn .45 .75
O163 A18 30c yellow grn .50 1.40
O164 A18 30c gray vio ('30) .25 1.20
O165 A18 35c yel grn ('30) .25 1.20
O166 A18 35c gray vio .35 .90
O167 A18 40c olive gray .35 .75
O168 A18 50c red brown .35 .75
O169 A18 60c blue grn .35 .75
O170 A18 70c blue vio ('35) 3.50 7.25

O171 A18 75c bister brn .35 .75
O172 A18 90c rose .35 1.20
O173 A18 1fr black .35 1.20
O174 A18 1fr rose ('30) .45 2.40
O175 A18 1¼fr yel ('30) 4.00 6.50
O176 A18 1¼fr bl grn ('31) 1.50 4.00
O177 A18 1½fr deep blue .35 1.40
O178 A18 1¾fr dk blue ('30) .45 1.60
Nos. O158-O178 (21) 15.35 36.75

Type of Regular Issues of 1928-31 Overprinted Like Nos. O80-O98

1928-31 Wmk. 216 *Perf. 11½*
O179 A19 2fr black .50 1.60

Wmk. 110 *Perf. 12½*
O180 A21 20fr dp green ('31) 2.25 8.00

No. 198 Overprinted Like Nos. O80-O98

1934 Unwmk. *Perf. 14x13½*
O181 A22 5fr blue green 1.50 6.00

Type of Regular Issue of 1935 Overprinted Like Nos. O158-O178 in Red

1935 Wmk. 247 *Perf. 12½x12*
O182 A23 10fr green 1.60 7.00

OCCUPATION STAMPS

Issued under German Occupation

Stamps of Germany, 1933-36, Overprinted in Black

1940, Oct. 1 Wmk. 237 *Perf. 14*
N1 A64 3pf olive bis .25 *.50*
N2 A64 4pf dull blue .25 *.55*
N3 A64 5pf brt grn .25 *.50*
N4 A64 6pf dark green .25 *.50*
N5 A64 8pf vermilion .25 *.50*
N6 A64 10pf chocolate .25 *.50*
N7 A64 12pf deep car .25 *.50*
N8 A64 15pf maroon .35 *.70*
a. Inverted overprint *450.00 1,300.*
N9 A64 20pf bright blue .40 *1.10*
N10 A64 25pf ultra .40 *1.60*
N11 A64 30pf olive green .40 *1.60*
N12 A64 40pf red violet .55 *1.60*
N13 A64 50pf dk grn & blk .95 *3.00*
N14 A64 60pf claret & blk 1.10 *3.00*
N15 A64 80pf dk blue & blk 2.00 *6.50*
N16 A64 100pf org & blk 3.50 *6.50*
Nos. N1-N16 (16) 11.40 *29.15*
Set, never hinged 32.50

Nos. 159-162, 164, 168-171, 173, 175, 179, 182, 216, 198-199 Surcharged in Black

a

b

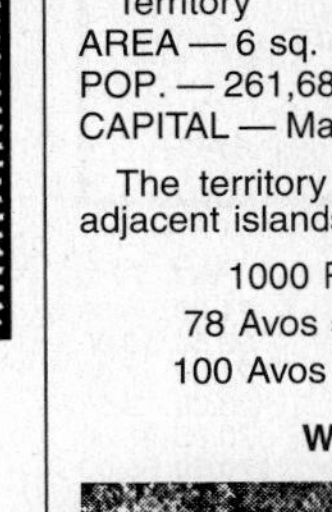

c

d

Perf. 12, 14x13½, 12½x12, 11½

1940, Dec. 5 Unwmk.
N17 A18(a) 3rpf on 15c .25 *.35*
N18 A18(a) 4rpf on 20c .25 *.35*
N19 A18(a) 5rpf on 35c .25 *.35*
N20 A18(a) 6rpf on 10c .25 *.35*
N21 A18(a) 8rpf on 25c .25 *.35*
N22 A18(a) 10rpf on 40c .25 *.35*
N23 A18(a) 12rpf on 60c .25 *.35*
N24 A18(a) 15rpf on 1fr rose .25 *.35*
N25 A18(a) 20rpf on 50c .25 *.60*
N26 A18(a) 25rpf on 5c .25 *1.20*
N27 A18(a) 30rpf on 70c .25 *.60*
N28 A18(a) 40rpf on 75c .30 *1.20*
N29 A18(a) 50rpf on 1¼fr .25 *.60*
N30 A35(b) 60rpf on 2fr 1.40 *9.50*
N31 A22(c) 80rpf on 5fr .40 *2.00*
N32 A23(d) 100rpf on 10fr .65 *2.75*
Nos. N17-N32 (16) 5.75 *21.25*
Set, never hinged 9.00

OCCUPATION SEMI-POSTAL STAMPS

Semi-Postal Stamps of Germany, 1940 Overprinted in Black

1941, Jan. 12 Unwmk. *Perf. 14*
NB1 SP153 3pf + 2pf dk brn .25 *.60*
NB2 SP153 4pf + 3pf bluish blk .25 *.60*
NB3 SP153 5pf + 3pf yel grn .25 *.60*
NB4 SP153 6pf + 4pf dk grn .25 *.60*
NB5 SP153 8pf + 4pf dp org .25 *.60*
NB6 SP153 12pf + 6pf carmine .25 *.60*
NB7 SP153 15pf + 10pf dk vio brn .30 *1.60*
NB8 SP153 25pf + 15pf dp ultra .55 *3.50*
NB9 SP153 40pf + 35pf red lil .85 *6.00*
Nos. NB1-NB9 (9) 3.20 *14.70*
Set, never hinged 8.00

MACAO

mə-'kau

LOCATION — Off the Chinese coast at the mouth of the Canton River
GOVT. — Portuguese Overseas Territory
AREA — 6 sq. mi.
POP. — 261,680 (1981)
CAPITAL — Macao

The territory includes the two small adjacent islands of Coloane and Taipa.

1000 Reis = 1 Milreis
78 Avos = 1 Rupee (1894)
100 Avos = 1 Pataca (1913)

Watermarks

Wmk. 232 — Maltese Cross

PRE-STAMP POSTAL MARKINGS
British Post Office Crowned Paid Postmarks

1844
A1 Crowned double circle handstamp, on cover, inscribed "PAID AT MACAO" in red *35,000.*

1881
A2 Crown and "MACAO" in double circle, with date on two lines, on cover —

Portuguese Crown — A1

1884-85 Typo. Unwmk. *Perf. 13½*
1 A1 5r black 15.00 9.00
2a A1 10r orange 25.00 9.00
3a A1 10r green ('85) 82.50 60.00
4 A1 20r bister 32.50 22.50
5 A1 20r rose ('85) 45.00 18.00
6 A1 25r rose 22.50 5.25
7a A1 25r violet ('85) 140.00 60.00
8 A1 40r blue 115.00 40.00
9a A1 40r yellow ('85) 140.00 60.00
10 A1 50r green 250.00 75.00
11a A1 50r blue ('85) 225.00 70.00
12 A1 80r gray ('85) 57.50 30.00
13 A1 100r red lilac 75.00 24.00
a. 100r lilac 75.00 24.00
14 A1 200r orange 70.00 20.00
15a A1 300r chocolate 250.00 100.00

Perf. 12½
1a A1 5r black 20.00 10.00
2 A1 10r orange 25.00 12.00
3 A1 10r green ('85) 30.00 9.00
4a A1 20r bister 40.00 25.00
6a A1 25r rose 30.00 7.50
7 A1 25r violet ('85) 30.00 13.50
8a A1 40r blue 140.00 45.00
9 A1 40r yellow ('85) 42.50 20.00
10a A1 50r green 450.00 150.00
11 A1 50r blue ('85) 57.50 25.00
12a A1 80r gray ('85) 75.00 40.00
13b A1 100r red lilac 40.00 15.00
c. 100r lilac 40.00 15.00
14a A1 200r orange 125.00 40.00
15 A1 300r chocolate 100.00 25.00

The reprints of the 1885 issue are printed on smooth, white chalky paper, ungummed and on thin white paper with shiny white gum and clean-cut perforation 13½.

For surcharges see Nos. 16-28, 108-109.

Nos. 12, 13a and 14 Surcharged in Black

1884 Without Gum *Perf. 12½*
16 A1 80r on 100r lilac 90.00 45.00
a. Inverted surcharge *200.00 75.00*
b. Without accent on "e" of "reis" 80.00 47.50
c. Perf. 13½ 125.00 55.00
d. As "b," perf. 13½ 140.00 62.50

Nos. 6, 6a, 10, 10a Surcharged in Black, Blue or Red

b

1885 Without Gum
17 A1(b) 5r on 25r rose, perf. 12½ (Bk) 21.00 6.50
a. With accent on "e" of "Reis" 35.00 12.00
b. Double surcharge 225.00 160.00
c. Inverted surcharge 200.00 125.00
d. Perf. 13½ 125.00 100.00
e. As "d," inverted surcharge *200.00 140.00*
f. Thin bar 21.00 6.50
g. As "a," thin bar 22.50 15.00
h. As "c," thin bar *225.00 175.00*
18 A1(b) 10r on 25r rose (Bl) 47.50 18.00
a. Accent on "e" of "Reis" —
b. Pair, one without surcharge —
19 A1(b) 10r on 50r grn, perf. 13½ (Bl) 625.00 225.00
a. Perf. 12½ 625.00 260.00
20 A1(b) 20r on 50r green, perf. 12½ (Bk) 47.50 10.00
a. Double surcharge 160.00
b. Accent on "e" of "Reis" — —
c. Perf. 13½ 50.00 12.50
21 A1(b) 40r on 50r grn, perf. 12½ (R) 175.00 50.00
a. Perf. 13½ 240.00 50.00
Nos. 17-21 (5) 916.00 309.50

c

1885 Without Gum
22 A1(c) 5r on 25r rose (Bk) 32.50 18.00
a. Original value not obliterated
23 A1(c) 10r on 50r green (Bk) 32.50 18.00
a. Inverted surcharge
b. Perf. 12½ 32.50 18.00
c. Thin bar *100.00 100.00*
d. As "b," thin bar *125.00 125.00*

Nos. 12, 12a, 13, 13a, 14, 14a Surcharged in Black

1887 Without Gum *Perf. 13½, 12½*
24 A1 5r on 80r gray 35.00 9.00
a. "R" of "Reis" 4mm high 125.00 50.00
b. Perf. 12½ 150.00 45.00
25 A1 5r on 100r lilac 150.00 90.00
a. Perf. 12½ 95.00 60.00
26 A1 10r on 80r gray 65.00 20.00
a. "R" 4mm high 140.00 47.50
27 A1 10r on 200r orange 160.00 62.50
a. "R" 4mm high, "e" without accent 200.00 80.00
b. Perf. 13½ 140.00 62.50
28 A1 20r on 80r gray 125.00 35.00
a. "R" 4mm high 175.00 47.50
b. Perf. 12½ 100.00 50.00
c. "R" 4mm high, "e" without accent 160.00 47.50
Nos. 24-28 (5) 535.00 216.50

The surcharges with larger "R" (4mm) have accent on "e." Smaller "R" is 3mm high.

Occasionally Nos. 24, 26 and 28 may be found with original gum. Values the same.

Coat of Arms — A6

Red Surcharge Without Gum

1887, Oct. 20 *Perf. 12½*
32 A6 5r green & buff 15.00 7.00
a. With labels, 5r on 10r 77.50 65.00
b. With labels, 5r on 20r 90.00 65.00
c. With labels, 5r on 60r 77.50 65.00
33 A6 10r green & buff 22.50 9.00
a. With labels, 10r on 10r 95.00 75.00
b. With labels, 10r on 60r 110.00 75.00
34 A6 40r green & buff 37.50 *14.00*
a. With labels, 40r on 20r 150.00 *110.00*
Nos. 32-34 (3) 75.00 30.00

Nos. 32-34 were local provisionals, created by perforating contemporary revenue stamps to remove the old value inscriptions and then surcharging the central design portion. The unused portion of the design was normally removed prior to use. For simplicity's sake, we refer to these extraneous portions of the original revenue stamps as "labels."

The 10r also exists with 20r labels, and 40r with 10r labels. Value, $250 each.

King Luiz — A7

Typographed and Embossed

1888, Jan. *Perf. 12½, 13½*

Chalk-surfaced Paper

35 A7 5r black 21.00 4.00
36 A7 10r green 21.00 6.00
a. Perf. 13½ 75.00 37.50
37 A7 20r rose 35.00 13.00
38 A7 25r violet 35.00 13.00
39 A7 40r chocolate 35.00 18.00
a. Perf. 13½ 60.00 26.00
40 A7 50r blue 60.00 13.50
41 A7 80r gray 95.00 22.50
a. Imperf., pair —
42 A7 100r brown 45.00 22.50
43 A7 200r gray lilac 90.00 45.00
44 A7 300r orange 72.50 45.00
Nos. 35-44 (10) 509.50 202.50

Nos. 37-44 were issued without gum.

For surcharges and overprints see Nos. 45, 58-66B, 110-118, 164-170, 239, Timor Nos. P1-P3.

No. 43 Surcharged in Red

1892 **Without Gum** *Perf. 13½*

45 A7 30r on 200r gray lil 80.00 24.00
a. Inverted surcharge 275.00 165.00
b. Perf. 12½ 60.00 20.00

King Carlos — A9

1894, Nov. 15 **Typo.** *Perf. 11½*

46 A9 5r yellow 9.00 3.75
47 A9 10r redsh violet 9.00 3.75
48 A9 15r chocolate 12.50 5.25
49 A9 20r lavender 14.00 6.00
50 A9 25r green 35.00 11.25
51 A9 50r lt blue 37.50 22.50
a. Perf. 13½ *550.00* *400.00*
52 A9 75r carmine 70.00 30.00
53 A9 80r yellow green 37.50 22.50
54 A9 100r brown, *buff* 40.00 22.50
55 A9 150r carmine, *rose* 45.00 22.50
56 A9 200r dk blue, *blue* 62.50 34.00
57 A9 300r dk blue, *sal* 82.50 45.00
Nos. 46-57 (12) 454.50 229.00

Nos. 49-57 were issued without gum, No. 49 with or without gum.

For surcharges and overprints see Nos. 119-130, 171-181, 183-186, 240-251, 257-258.

Stamps of 1888 Surcharged in Red, Green or Black

1894 **Without Gum** *Perf. 12½*

58 A7 1a on 5r black (R) 11.00 4.50
a. Short "1" 11.00 4.50
b. Inverted surcharge 100.00 100.00
c. Double surcharge *400.00*
d. Surch. on back instead of face *200.00* *200.00*
59 A7 3a on 20r car (G) 19.00 4.50
a. Inverted surcharge — —
60 A7 4a on 25r violet (Bk) 21.00 9.00
a. Inverted surcharge 60.00 50.00
61 A7 6a on 40r choc (Bk) 25.00 6.75
a. Perf. 13½ 19.00 12.00
62 A7 8a on 50r blue (R) 55.00 18.00
a. Double surch., one inverted *225.00* *200.00*
b. Inverted surcharge 125.00 60.00
c. Perf. 13½ 62.50 40.00
d. As #62, double surch. 150.00 120.00
63 A7 13a on 80r gray (Bk) 30.00 7.00
a. Double surcharge *150.00* *110.00*
64 A7 16a on 100r brn (Bk) 60.00 18.00
a. Inverted surcharge *200.00* *125.00*
b. Perf. 13½ 115.00 110.00
65 A7 31a on 200r gray lil (Bk) 90.00 25.00
a. Inverted surcharge 150.00 125.00
b. Perf. 13½ 75.00 25.00
66 A7 47a on 300r org (G) 72.50 11.00
a. Double surcharge *160.00* *120.00*
Nos. 58-66 (9) 383.50 103.75

The style of type used for the word "PROVISORIO" on Nos. 58 to 66 differs for each value.

A 2a on 10r green was unofficially surcharged and denounced by the authorities. Value, $500.

On No. 45

66B A7 5a on 30r on 200r 160.00 50.00
c. Perf. 13½ 150.00 50.00

Vasco da Gama Issue

Common Design Types

1898, Apr. 1 **Engr.** *Perf. 12½ to 16*

67 CD20 ½a blue green 7.00 2.25
68 CD21 1a red 7.00 3.75
69 CD22 2a red violet 7.00 5.25
70 CD23 4a yellow green 10.00 7.50
71 CD24 8a dark blue 19.00 12.00
72 CD25 12a violet brown 30.00 22.00
73 CD26 16a bister brown 26.00 22.00
74 CD27 24a bister 30.00 22.00
Nos. 67-74 (8) 136.00 96.75

For overprints and surcharges see Nos. 187-194.

King Carlos — A11

1898-1903 **Typo.** *Perf. 11½*

Name and Value in Black except #103

75 A11 ½a gray 4.50 1.00
a. Perf. 12½ 15.00 7.50
b. As #75, black ("MACAU" and denom.) inverted 100.00 90.00
76 A11 1a orange 4.50 1.00
a. Perf. 12½ 15.00 7.50
b. As #76, black ("MACAU" and denom.) inverted 175.00 150.00
77 A11 2a yellow green 5.75 1.50
a. Black ("MACAU" and denom.) inverted 140.00 110.00
78 A11 2a gray grn ('03) 6.25 1.50
79 A11 2½a red brown 7.50 2.25
80 A11 3a gray violet 7.50 2.25
81 A11 3a slate ('03) 6.25 1.65
82 A11 4a sea green 9.00 5.00
83 A11 4a carmine ('03) 6.25 1.50
84 A11 5a gray brn ('00) 15.00 3.75
85 A11 5a pale yel brn ('03) 9.00 2.25
86 A11 6a red brn ('03) 10.00 2.00
87 A11 8a blue 12.50 3.75
88 A11 8a gray brn ('03) 16.00 4.00
89 A11 10a sl bl ('00) 15.00 3.75
90 A11 12a rose 15.00 6.50
91 A11 12a red lil ('03) 62.50 15.00
92 A11 13a violet 18.00 6.50
93 A11 13a gray lilac ('03) 22.50 6.00
94 A11 15a pale ol grn ('00) 90.00 23.00
95 A11 16a dk blue, *bl* 17.00 7.50
96 A11 18a org brn, *pink* ('03) 32.50 11.50
97 A11 20a brn, *yelsh* ('00) 45.00 11.50
98 A11 24a brown, *buff* 27.50 7.50
99 A11 31a red lilac 27.50 9.00
100 A11 31a red lil, *pink* ('03) 32.50 11.50
101 A11 47a dk blue, *rose* 50.00 11.50
102 A11 47a dull bl, *straw* ('03) 60.00 13.00
103 A11 78a blk & red, *bl* ('00) 85.00 17.50
Nos. 75-103 (29) 720.00 194.65

Issued without gum: Nos. 76a, 77, 79-80, 82, 84, 89, 94, 97 and 103.

For surcharges and overprints see Nos. 104-107, 132-136, 141, 147-157D, 159-161, 182, 195-209, 253-255, 258A.

Nos. 92, 95, 98-99 Surcharged in Black

1900 **Without Gum**

104 A11 5a on 13a violet 20.00 3.50
105 A11 10a on 16a dk bl, *bl* 22.50 5.00
106 A11 15a on 24a brn, *buff* 22.50 8.25
107 A11 20a on 31a red lilac 25.00 13.50
Nos. 104-107 (4) 90.00 30.25

Nos. 106-107 were issued with and without gum.

Regular Issues Surcharged

On Stamps of 1884-85

1902 **Black Surcharge** *Perf. 11½*

108 A1 6a on 10r orange 30.00 9.75
a. Double surcharge *300.00* *175.00*
109 A1 6a on 10r green 21.00 6.00

On Stamps of 1888

Red Surcharge

Perf. 12½, 13½

110 A7 6a on 5r black 10.00 3.50
a. Inverted surcharge 110.00 60.00

Black Surcharge

111 A7 6a on 10r green 8.25 3.50
112 A7 6a on 40r choc 8.25 3.50
a. Double surcharge 125.00 50.00
b. Perf. 13½ 30.00 10.00
113 A7 18a on 20r rose 17.00 4.50
a. Double surcharge 160.00 70.00
b. Inverted surcharge 175.00 —
114 A7 18a on 25r violet 250.00 60.00
115 A7 18a on 80r gray 250.00 67.50
a. Double surcharge 275.00 175.00
116 A7 18a on 100r brown 42.50 26.00
a. Perf. 13½ 90.00 35.00
117 A7 18a on 200r gray lil 250.00 67.50
a. Perf. 12½ 190.00 60.00
118 A7 18a on 300r orange 30.00 10.00
a. Perf. 13½ 57.50 25.00

Issued without gum: Nos. 110-118.

Nos. 109 to 118 inclusive, except No. 111, have been reprinted. The reprints have white gum and clean-cut perforation 13½ and the colors are usually paler than those of the originals.

On Stamps of 1894

1902-10 *Perf. 11½, 13½*

119 A9 6a on 5r yellow 7.75 2.75
a. Inverted surcharge 82.50 65.00
120 A9 6a on 10r red vio 60.00 5.25
121 A9 6a on 15r choc 26.00 5.25
122 A9 6a on 25r green 7.75 2.75
123 A9 6a on 80r yel grn 7.75 2.75
124 A9 6a on 100r brn, *buff* 15.00 6.00
a. Perf. 11½ 26.00 10.00
125 A9 6a on 200r bl, *bl* 10.00 2.75
a. Vert. half used as 3a on cover ('10) *40.00*
126 A9 18a on 20r lavender 21.00 6.75
127 A9 18a on 50r lt blue 26.00 6.75
a. Perf. 13½ 77.50 17.00
128 A9 18a on 75r carmine 21.00 6.75
129 A9 18a on 150r car, *rose* 21.00 7.50
130 A9 18a on 300r bl, *salmon* 26.00 6.75

On Newspaper Stamp of 1893

Perf. 12½

131 N3 18a on 2½r brown 10.00 3.25
a. Perf. 13½ 27.50 9.00
b. Perf. 11½ 45.00 14.00
Nos. 108-131 (24) 1,176. 327.00

Issued without gum: Nos. 122-130, 131b.

Stamps of 1898-1900 Overprinted in Black

1902 *Perf. 11½*

132 A11 2a yellow green 21.00 4.00
133 A11 4a sea green 32.50 10.00
134 A11 8a blue 21.00 7.00
135 A11 10a slate blue 26.00 8.00
136 A11 12a rose 70.00 26.00
Nos. 132-136 (5) 170.50 55.00

Issued without gum: Nos. 133, 135.

Reprints of No. 133 have shiny white gum and clean-cut perforation 13½. Value $1.

No. 91 Surcharged

1905 **Without Gum**

141 A11 10a on 12a red lilac 30.00 12.50

For overprint see No. 182.

Nos. J1-J3 Overprinted

1910, Oct. *Perf. 11½x12*

144 D1 ½a gray green 10.00 6.75
a. Inverted overprint 35.00 30.00
b. Double overprint 40.00 40.00
c. Pair, one without ovpt.
145 D1 1a yellow green 12.00 6.75
a. Inverted overprint 35.00 30.00
146 D1 2a slate 20.00 7.50
a. Inverted overprint *65.00* 45.00
Nos. 144-146 (3) 42.00 21.00

No. 144 issued without gum, Nos. 145-146 with and without gum.

Stamps of 1898-1903 Overprinted in Carmine or Green

Overprint 24½mm long. "A" has flattened top.

Lisbon Overprint

1911, Apr. 2 *Perf. 11½*

147 A11 ½a gray 2.10 .75
a. Inverted overprint 20.00 20.00
147B A11 1a orange 2.00 .75
c. Inverted overprint 20.00 20.00
148 A11 2a gray green 2.00 .75
a. Inverted overprint 12.50 12.50
149 A11 3a slate 6.25 .75
a. Inverted overprint 12.50 12.50
150 A11 4a carmine (G) 6.25 2.00
a. 4a pale yel brn (error) *75.00* *50.00*
b. As No. 150, inverted overprint 50.00 50.00
151 A11 5a pale yel brn 6.25 4.00
152 A11 6a red brown 6.25 4.00
153 A11 8a gray brown 6.25 4.00
154 A11 10a slate blue 6.25 4.00
155 A11 13a gray lilac 10.00 5.00
a. Inverted overprint 60.00 60.00
156 A11 16a dk blue, *bl* 10.00 5.00
a. Inverted overprint 60.00 60.00
157 A11 18a org brn, *pink* 16.00 6.00
157A A11 20a brown, *straw* 16.00 6.00
157B A11 31a red lil, *pink* 30.00 8.00
157C A11 47a dull bl, *straw* 50.00 10.00
157D A11 78a blk & red, *bl* 82.50 12.00
Nos. 147-157D (16) 258.10 73.00

Issued without gum: Nos. 151, 153-157D.

Coat of Arms — A14

Red Surcharge

1911 *Perf. 11½x12*

158 A14 1a on 5r brn & buff 32.50 12.50
a. "1" omitted 80.00 60.00
b. Inverted surcharge 100.00 55.00
c. Larger "1" 52.50 26.50

Stamps of 1900-03 Surcharged

Diagonal Halves

Black Surcharge

1911 **Without Gum** *Perf. 11½*

159 A11 2a on half of 4a car 50.00 32.50
a. "2" omitted 100.00 80.00
b. Inverted surcharge *150.00* 82.50
d. Entire stamp 180.00

159C A11 5a on half of 10a sl bl (#89) 900.00 400.00
e. Entire stamp 8,500. 4,000.

Red Surcharge

160 A11 5a on half of 10a sl bl (#89) 700.00 400.00
a. Inverted surcharge 750.00 500.00
b. Entire stamp 11,000. 5,000.
161 A11 5a on half of 10a sl bl (#135) 150.00 120.00
a. Inverted surcharge 350.00 200.00
b. Entire stamp 500.00

Nos. 159-161 normally were bisected by the government before being placed on sale.

A15

Laid or Wove Paper

1911 *Perf. 12x11½*
162 A15 1a black 525.00 —
a. "Corrieo" 2,000. —
163 A15 2a black 600.00 —
a. "Corrieo" 2,000. —

The vast majority of used stamps were not canceled.

Surcharged Stamps of 1902 Overprinted in Red or Green

Overprint 23mm long. "A" has pointed top.

Local Overprint

1913 **Without Gum** *Perf. 11½*
164 A1 6a on 10r grn (R) 37.50 12.00
a. "REPUBLICA" double 70.00 70.00

Perf. 12½, 13½

165 A7 6a on 5r black (G) 15.00 3.50
166 A7 6a on 10r grn (R) 31.00 8.00
167 A7 6a on 40r choc (R) 10.50 3.00
a. Perf. 13½ 50.00 20.00
168 A7 18a on 20r car (G) 21.00 6.00
169 A7 18a on 100r brn (R) 82.50 40.00
a. Perf. 13½ 100.00 50.00
170 A7 18a on 300r org (R) 32.50 9.00
a. Perf. 13½ 50.00 10.00
Nos. 164-170 (7) 230.00 81.50

"REPUBLICA" Inverted

164b A1 6a on 10r green (R) 65.00 65.00
165a A7 6a on 5r black (G) 65.00 60.00
166a A7 6a on 10r green (R) 65.00 60.00
167b A7 6a on 40r choc (R) 65.00 60.00
168a A7 18a on 20r car (G) 66.00 60.00
169b A7 18a on 100r brown (R) 95.00 60.00
170b A7 18a on 300r org (R) 65.00 60.00

1913 **Without Gum** *Perf. 11½, 13½*
171 A9 6a on 10r red vio (G) 14.50 4.50
172 A9 6a on 10r red vio (R) 300.00 26.00
173 A9 6a on 15r choc (R) 14.50 5.00
174 A9 6a on 25r grn (R) 16.00 5.00
175 A9 6a on 80r yel grn (R) 14.50 5.00
176 A9 6a on 100r brn, *buff* (R) 30.00 7.00
a. Perf. 11½ 32.50 8.00
177 A9 18a on 20r lav (R) 19.00 5.00
178 A9 18a on 50r lt bl (R) 19.00 5.00
a. Perf. 13½ 21.00 6.00
179 A9 18a on 75r car (G) 19.00 5.50
180 A9 18a on 150r car, *rose* (G) 21.00 6.00
181 A9 18a on 300r dk bl, *sal* (R) 32.50 10.00

On No. 141

182 A11 10a on 12a red lil (R) 13.00 4.50
Nos. 171-182 (12) 513.00 88.50

"REPUBLICA" Inverted

171a A9 6a on 10r red vio (G) 65.00 60.00
172a A9 6a on 10r red vio (R) 65.00 60.00
174a A9 6a on 25r green (R) 65.00 60.00
175a A9 6a on 80r yel grn (R) 65.00 60.00
176b A9 6a on 100r brn, *buff*(R) 65.00 60.00
177a A9 18a on 20r lav (R) 65.00 60.00
178b A9 18a on 50r lt bl (R) 65.00 60.00
179a A9 18a on 75r car (G) 65.00 60.00
180a A9 18a on 150r car, *rose* (G) 65.00 60.00
181a A9 18a on 300r dk bl, *buff* (R) 65.00 60.00

Stamps of Preceding Issue Surcharged

1913 **Without Gum** *Perf. 11½*
183 A9 2a on 18a on 20r (R) 15.00 4.00
184 A9 2a on 18a on 50r (R) 15.00 4.00
a. Perf. 13½ 16.00 4.25
185 A9 2a on 18a on 75r (G) 15.00 4.00
186 A9 2a on 18a on 150r (G) 15.00 4.00
Nos. 183-186 (4) 60.00 16.00

"REPUBLICA" Inverted

183b A9 2a on 18a on 20r (R) 20.00 —
184b A9 2a on 18a on 50r (R) 20.00 —
185b A9 2a on 18a on 75r (G) 20.00 —
186b A9 2a on 18a on 150r (G) 20.00 —

"2" Surcharge Inverted

183c A9 2a on 18a on 20r (R) 30.00 32.50
184c A9 2a on 18a on 50r (R) 30.00 32.50
185c A9 2a on 18a on 75r (G) 30.00 32.50
186c A9 2a on 18a on 150r (G) 30.00 32.50

"2" Surcharge Double

183d A9 2a on 18a on 20r (R) 30.00 27.50
184d A9 2a on 18a on 50r (R) 30.00 30.00
185d A9 2a on 18a on 75r (G) 32.50 35.00
186d A9 2a on 18a on 150r (G) 35.00 40.00

Vasco da Gama Issue Overprinted or Surcharged

j

k

187 CD20 (j) ½a blue green 7.75 2.00
188 CD21 (j) 1a red 8.50 2.00
189 CD22 (j) 2a red violet 8.50 2.00
a. Double ovpt., one inverted 100.00
190 CD23 (j) 4a yellow grn 7.75 2.00
191 CD24 (j) 8a dk blue 13.00 2.00
192 CD25 (k) 10a on 12a vio brn 24.00 5.00
193 CD26 (j) 16a bister brn 17.00 4.00
194 CD27 (j) 24a bister 27.50 5.00
Nos. 187-194 (8) 114.00 24.00

Stamps of 1898-1903 Overprinted in Red or Green

1913 **Without Gum** *Perf. 11½*
195 A11 4a carmine (G) 250.00 100.00
a. Double overprint 400.00 175.00
b. Inverted overprint 400.00
196 A11 5a yellow brn 30.00 20.00
a. Inverted overprint 50.00 40.00
197 A11 6a red brown 77.50 40.00
a. Inverted overprint 95.00
198 A11 8a gray brown 625.00 300.00
b. Inverted overprint 1,000. 1,500.
198A A11 10a dull blue 1,000.
199 A11 13a violet 77.50 32.50
a. Inverted overprint 95.00
200 A11 13a gray lilac 40.00 20.00
a. Inverted overprint 95.00
201 A11 16a blue, *bl* 50.00 20.00
202 A11 18a org brn, *pink* 50.00 20.00
a. Inverted overprint 95.00
203 A11 20a brown, *yelsh* 50.00 20.00
204 A11 31a red lil, *pink* 67.50 30.00
a. Inverted overprint 95.00
205 A11 47a dull bl, *straw* 100.00 40.00

Only 20 examples of No. 198A were sold by the Post Office.

Stamps of 1911-13 Surcharged

On Stamps of 1911 With Lisbon "Republica"

1913
206 A11 ½a on 5a yel brn (R) 15.00 3.00
a. "½ Avo" inverted 125.00 70.00
207 A11 4a on 8a gray brn (R) 30.00 4.00
a. "4 Avos" inverted 150.00 70.00

On Stamps of 1913 With Local "Republica"

208 A11 1a on 13a violet (R) 250.00 30.00
209 A11 1a on 13a gray lil (R) 15.00 3.00
a. Surch. on #155 (error) — —
Nos. 206-209 (4) 310.00 40.00

Issued without gum: Nos. 207-209.

"Ceres" — A16

Name and Value in Black

1913 **Chalky Paper** *Perf. 15x14*
210 A16 ½a olive brown 1.75 .25
Never hinged 2.75
211 A16 1a black 1.75 .25
Never hinged 2.75
212 A16 2a blue green 1.75 .25
Never hinged 2.75
213 A16 4a carmine 6.75 1.00
Never hinged 11.00
214 A16 5a lilac brown 7.75 3.00
Never hinged 12.50
215 A16 6a lt violet 7.75 3.00
Never hinged 12.50
216 A16 8a lilac brown 7.75 3.00
Never hinged 12.50
217 A16 10a deep blue 7.75 3.00
Never hinged 12.50
218 A16 12a yellow brn 11.00 3.00
Never hinged 17.50
219 A16 16a slate 20.00 5.00
Never hinged 32.50
220 A16 20a orange brn 20.00 5.00
Never hinged 32.50
221 A16 40a plum 21.00 5.00
Never hinged 35.00
222 A16 58a brown, *grn* 35.00 12.00
Never hinged 55.00
223 A16 76a brown, *pink* 75.00 14.00
Never hinged 80.00
224 A16 1p orange, *sal* 100.00 20.00
Never hinged 110.00
225 A16 3p green, *bl* 200.00 55.00
Never hinged 325.00
Nos. 210-225 (16) 525.00 132.75

Nos. 210, 211 and 212 exist on glazed paper.

1919 **Ordinary Paper** *Perf. 15x14*
226 A16 ½a olive brown 5.50 2.25
Never hinged 8.25
a. Inscriptions inverted 50.00
227 A16 1a black 5.50 2.25
Never hinged 8.25
a. Inscriptions inverted 50.00
b. Inscriptions double 50.00
228 A16 2a blue green 14.50 7.00
Never hinged 22.50
a. Inscriptions inverted 40.00
229 A16 4a carmine 42.50 21.00
Never hinged 65.00
Nos. 226-229 (4) 68.00 32.50

1922-24 *Perf. 12x11½*
230 A16 ½a olive brown 2.75 1.10
Never hinged 4.25
231 A16 1a black 2.75 1.10
Never hinged 4.25
232 A16 1½a yel grn ('24) 1.75 .25
Never hinged 2.75
233 A16 2a blue green 6.00 3.00
Never hinged 9.00
234 A16 3a org brn 10.00 3.00
Never hinged 15.00
235 A16 4a carmine 20.00 5.00
Never hinged 32.50
236 A16 4a lemon ('24) 14.00 5.00
Never hinged 21.00
237 A16 6a gray ('23) 47.50 7.50
Never hinged 72.50
238 A16 8a lilac brown 17.50 5.50
Never hinged 26.00
238A A16 10a pale bl ('23) 27.50 6.00
Never hinged 42.50
238B A16 12a yellow brown 30.00 6.50
Never hinged 45.00
238C A16 14a lilac ('24) 42.50 12.00
Never hinged 65.00
238D A16 16a slate 67.50 20.00
Never hinged 100.00
238E A16 24a sl grn ('23) 25.00 7.00
Never hinged 37.50
238F A16 32a org brn ('24) 25.00 8.00
Never hinged 37.50
238G A16 56a dl rose ('24) 50.00 15.00
Never hinged 75.00
238H A16 72a brown ('23) 67.50 20.00
Never hinged 100.00
238I A16 1p org ('24) 200.00 30.00
Never hinged 300.00

Glazed Paper

238J A16 3p pale turq ('24) 425.00 95.00
Never hinged 725.00
238K A16 5p car rose ('24) 350.00 82.50
Never hinged 600.00
Nos. 230-238K (20) 1,432. 333.45

For surcharges see Nos. 256, 259-267.

Preceding Issues and No. P4 Overprinted in Carmine

On Stamps of 1902

Perf. 11½, 12, 12½, 13½, 11½x12
1915
239 A7 6a on 10r green 14.50 4.00
240 A9 6a on 5r yellow 14.50 4.00
241 A9 6a on 10r red vio 14.50 4.00
242 A9 6a on 15r choc 12.50 3.25
243 A9 6a on 25r green 12.00 4.00
244 A9 6a on 80r yel grn 12.00 4.00
245 A9 6a on 100r brn, *buff* 21.00 4.00
246 A9 6a on 200r bl, *bl* 11.00 6.00
247 A9 18a on 20r lav 21.00 6.00
248 A9 18a on 50r lt bl 45.00 6.75
249 A9 18a on 75r car 40.00 6.75
250 A9 18a on 150r car, *rose* 45.00 8.00
251 A9 18a on 300r bl, *sal* 40.00 10.00
252 N3 18a on 2½r brn 32.50 6.00

With Additional Overprint

253 A11 8a blue 14.50 8.25
254 A11 10a slate blue 14.50 6.00
a. "Provisorio" double 110.00

On Stamp of 1905

255 A11 10a on 12a red lil 19.00 9.75
Nos. 239-255 (17) 383.50 100.75

Issued without gum: Nos. 243-251 and 255.

No. 217 Surcharged

Without Gum

1919-20 *Perf. 15x14*
256 A16 ½a on 5a lilac brn 100.00 32.50
Never hinged 125.00

Nos. 243 and 244 Surcharged

257 A9 2a on 6a on 25r green 500.00 125.00
258 A9 2a on 6a on 80r yel grn 100.00 70.00

No. 152 Surcharged

258A A11 2a on 6a red brown 175.00 70.00
Nos. 256-258A (4) 875.00 297.50

Issued without gum: Nos. 256-258A.

Stamps of 1913-24 Surcharged

1931-33 *Perf. 12x11½*

259 A16 1a on 24a slate grn ('33) 14.50 4.00
Never hinged 26.00
260 A16 2a on 32a org brn ('33) 14.50 4.00
Never hinged 26.00
261 A16 4a on 12a bis brn ('33) 14.50 4.00
Never hinged 26.00
262 A16 5a on 6a lt gray ('33) 57.50 35.00
Never hinged 100.00
264 A16 7a on 8a lil brn 24.00 5.00
Never hinged 45.00
265 A16 12a on 14a lilac 24.00 5.00
Never hinged 45.00
266 A16 15a on 16a dk gray ('33) 24.00 5.00
Never hinged 45.00
267 A16 20a on 56a dull rose ('33) 50.00 11.00
Never hinged 90.00

Chalky Paper
Perf. 15x14

263 A16 5a on 6a lt vio ('33) 30.00 11.00
Never hinged 47.50
Nos. 259-267 (9) 253.00 84.00

"Portugal" and Vasco da Gama's Flagship "San Gabriel" — A17

Wmk. 232

1934, Feb. 1 **Typo.** *Perf. 11½*

268 A17 ½a bister .45 .40
269 A17 1a olive brown .45 .25
270 A17 2a blue green 1.10 .50
271 A17 3a violet 1.40 .50
272 A17 4a black 1.75 .50
273 A17 5a gray 1.75 .80
274 A17 6a brown 1.75 .80
275 A17 7a brt rose 3.25 1.00
276 A17 8a brt blue 3.25 1.00
277 A17 10a red orange 7.25 2.00
278 A17 12a dark blue 7.25 2.00
279 A17 14a olive green 7.25 2.00
280 A17 15a maroon 7.25 2.00
281 A17 20a orange 7.25 2.00
282 A17 30a apple green 14.00 3.50
283 A17 40a violet 14.00 3.50
284 A17 50a olive bister 21.00 5.00
285 A17 1p lt blue 75.00 20.00
286 A17 2p brown org 90.00 27.50
287 A17 3p emerald 150.00 45.00
288 A17 5p dark violet 225.00 67.50
Nos. 268-288 (21) 640.40 187.75

See Nos. 316-323. For overprints and surcharges see Nos. 306-315, C1-C6, J43-J49. Post 1940 listings are in Scott Standard catalogue, Vol. 4.

Common Design Types
Perf. 13½x13

1938, Aug. 1 **Engr.** **Unwmk.**
Name and Value in Black

289 CD34 1a gray green 1.00 .35
290 CD34 2a orange brown 1.25 .55
291 CD34 3a dk vio brn 1.25 .55
292 CD34 4a brt green 1.25 .55
293 CD35 5a dk carmine 1.25 .55
294 CD35 6a slate 1.25 .55
295 CD35 8a rose violet 2.10 2.25
296 CD36 10a brt red vio 2.50 2.25
297 CD36 12a red 3.25 2.60
298 CD36 15a orange 3.25 2.60
299 CD37 20a blue 16.50 2.90
300 CD37 40a gray black 16.50 3.50
301 CD37 50a brown 16.50 3.75
302 CD38 1p brown car 50.00 7.25
303 CD38 2p olive green 85.00 17.50
304 CD38 3p blue violet 115.00 25.00
305 CD38 5p red brown 200.00 37.50
Nos. 289-305 (17) 517.85 110.20

For surcharge see No. 315A in Scott Standard catalogue, Vol. 4.

AIR POST STAMPS

Stamps of 1934 Overprinted or Surcharged in Black

a

b

1936 **Wmk. 232** *Perf. 11½*

C1 A17 (a) 2a blue green 3.00 1.00
C2 A17 (a) 3a violet 4.50 1.50
C3 A17 (b) 5a on 6a brown 4.50 1.90
C4 A17 (a) 7a brt rose 4.50 1.90
C5 A17 (a) 8a brt blue 12.00 5.00
C6 A17 (a) 15a maroon 29.00 11.50
Nos. C1-C6 (6) 57.50 22.80

Common Design Type
Name and Value in Black
Perf. 13½x13

1938, Aug. 1 **Engr.** **Unwmk.**

C7 CD39 1a scarlet .90 .50
C8 CD39 2a purple 1.10 .65
C9 CD39 3a orange 1.60 .90
C10 CD39 5a ultra 3.25 1.25
C11 CD39 10a lilac brn 5.50 1.75
C12 CD39 20a dk green 11.00 3.00
C13 CD39 50a red brown 18.00 4.00
C14 CD39 70a rose car 22.50 5.00
C15 CD39 1p magenta 45.00 18.00
Nos. C7-C15 (9) 108.85 35.05

No. C13 exists with overprint "Exposicao Internacional de Nova York, 1939-1940" and Trylon and Perisphere. Value $325.

POSTAGE DUE STAMPS

Numeral of Value — D1

Name and Value in Black
Perf. 11½x12

1904, July **Typo.** **Unwmk.**

J1 D1 ½a gray green 1.50 1.25
a. Name & value inverted 125.00 60.00
J2 D1 1a yellow grn 2.00 1.25
J3 D1 2a slate 2.00 1.25
J4 D1 4a pale brown 2.75 1.25
J5 D1 5a red orange 3.50 2.00
J6 D1 8a gray brown 4.00 2.00
J7 D1 12a red brown 6.00 2.00
J8 D1 20a dull blue 10.00 4.50
J9 D1 40a carmine 20.00 6.00
J10 D1 50a orange 26.50 12.00
J11 D1 1p gray violet 52.50 25.00
Nos. J1-J11 (11) 130.75 58.50

Issued without gum: Nos. J7-J11. Issued with or without gum: No. J4. Others issued with gum.

For overprints see Nos. 144-146, J12-J32.

Issue of 1904 Overprinted in Carmine or Green

Overprint 24½mm long. "A" has flattened top.

1911 **Lisbon Overprint**

J12 D1 ½a gray green .50 .50
J13 D1 1a yellow green 1.00 1.00
J14 D1 2a slate 1.25 1.40
J15 D1 4a pale brown 1.50 1.50
J16 D1 5a orange 2.00 1.60
J17 D1 8a gray brown 4.00 1.75
J18 D1 12a red brown 7.00 2.00
J19 D1 20a dull blue 9.50 3.00
J20 D1 40a carmine (G) 12.50 6.00
J21 D1 50a orange 16.00 8.50
J22 D1 1p gray violet 30.00 14.00
Nos. J12-J22 (11) 85.25 41.25

Issued without gum: Nos. J19-J22.

Issue of 1904 Overprinted in Red or Green

Overprint 23mm long. "A" has pointed top.

1914 **Local Overprint**

J22A D1 ½a gray green *1,600. 600.00*
J23 D1 1a yellow green 3.00 1.00
J24 D1 2a slate 3.00 1.00
J25 D1 4a pale brown 3.00 1.25
J26 D1 5a orange 4.50 1.25
J27 D1 8a gray brown 5.00 1.50
J28 D1 12a red brown 7.00 2.00
J29 D1 20a dull blue 13.50 5.50
J30 D1 40a car (G) 20.00 7.50
a. Double ovpt., red and green 100.00 27.50
J31 D1 50a orange 27.50 10.00
J32 D1 1p gray violet 45.00 15.00
Nos. J23-J32 (10) 131.50 46.00

Issued without gum: Nos. J28, J30-J32.

WAR TAX STAMPS

Victory WT1

Overprinted in Black or Carmine

1919, Aug. 11 **Unwmk.** *Perf. 15x14*

MR1 WT1 2a green 5.50 4.50
MR2 WT1 11a green (C) 10.00 *14.00*

Nos. MR1-MR2 were also for use in Timor.

A 9a value was issued for revenue use. Value $30.

NEWSPAPER STAMPS

Nos. P1-P2

No. P3

Typographed and Embossed

1892-93 **Unwmk.** *Perf. 12½*
Black Surcharge
Without Gum

P1 A7 2½r on 40r choc 7.00 4.00
a. Inverted surcharge 70.00 65.00
b. Perf. 13½ 8.00 6.00
P2 A7 2½r on 80r gray 9.00 4.00
a. Inverted surcharge 70.00 65.00
b. Double surcharge 70.00 65.00
c. Perf. 13½ 90.00 70.00
P3 A7 2½r on 10r grn ('93) 8.00 4.00
a. Double surcharge — 70.00
b. Perf. 13½ 9.00 9.00
Nos. P1-P3 (3) 24.00 12.00

N3

N4

1893-94 **Typo.** *Perf. 11½*

P4 N3 2½r brown 7.00 4.25
a. Perf. 12½ 6.00 4.00
b. Perf. 13½ 7.00 4.00
P5 N4 ½a on 2½r brn (Bk) ('94) 6.00 4.00
a. Double surcharge

For surcharges see Nos. 131, 252.

POSTAL TAX STAMPS

Pombal Commemorative Issue
Common Design Types
Perf. 12½

1925, Nov. 3 **Engr.** **Unwmk.**

RA1 CD28 2a red org & blk 2.50 1.25
RA2 CD29 2a red org & blk 3.00 1.50
RA3 CD30 2a red org & blk 3.25 1.75
Nos. RA1-RA3 (3) 8.75 4.50

Symbolical of Charity — PT1

1930, Dec. 25 **Litho.** *Perf. 11*

RA4 PT1 5a dk brown, *yel* *37.50 17.50*

POSTAL TAX DUE STAMPS

Pombal Commemorative Issue
Common Design Types

1925 **Unwmk.** *Perf. 12½*

RAJ1 CD28 4a red orange & blk 3.25 2.00
RAJ2 CD29 4a red orange & blk 3.25 2.00
RAJ3 CD30 4a red orange & blk 3.25 2.00
Nos. RAJ1-RAJ3 (3) 9.75 6.00

MADAGASCAR

ˌma-də-ˈgas-kər

LOCATION — Large island off the coast of southeastern Africa
GOVT. — French colony.
AREA — 226,658 sq. mi.
POP. — 3,797,936 (est. 1940)
CAPITAL — Antananarivo

Madagascar became a French protectorate in 1885 and a French colony in 1896 following several years of dispute among France, Great Britain, and the native government. The colony administered the former protectorates of Anjouan, Grand Comoro, Mayotte, Diego-Suarez, Nossi-Be and Sainte-Marie de Madagascar. Previous issues of postage stamps are found under these individual headings.

12 Pence = 1 Shilling
100 Centimes = 1 Franc

British Consular Mail stamps of Madagascar were gummed only in one corner. Unused values are for stamps without gum. Examples having the original corner gum will command higher prices. Most used examples of these stamps have small faults and values are for stamps in this condition. Used stamps without faults are scarce and are worth more. Used stamps are valued with the commonly used crayon or pen cancellations.

"B C M" and Arms — A1

Handstamped "British Vice-Consulate"

Black Seal Handstamped

1884 Unwmk. Typo. *Rouletted*

1 A1 1p violet 550. 450.
 b. Seal omitted 10,000. 10,000.
2 A1 2p violet 375. 325.
3 A1 3p violet 425. 350.
4 A1 4p violet 1 oz. 6,000. 5,250.
 a. "1 oz." corrected to "4 oz." in mss. 1,000. 725.
 b. Seal omitted 9,000. 9,000.
5 A1 6p violet 500. 500.
6 A1 1sh violet 525. 475.
7 A1 1sh6p violet 525. 525.
8 A1 2sh violet 850. 900.
9 A1 1p on 1sh vio
10 A1 4½p on 1sh vio
11 A1 6p red 1,325. 825.

1886 Violet Seal Handstamped

12 A1 4p violet 1,800. —
13 A1 6p violet 2,750. —

Handstamped "British Consular Mail" as on A3

Black Seal Handstamped

14 A1 4p violet 1,850. —

Violet Seal Handstamped

15 A1 4p violet 7,500. —

The 1, 2, 3 and 4 pence are inscribed "POSTAL PACKET," the other values of the series are inscribed "LETTER."

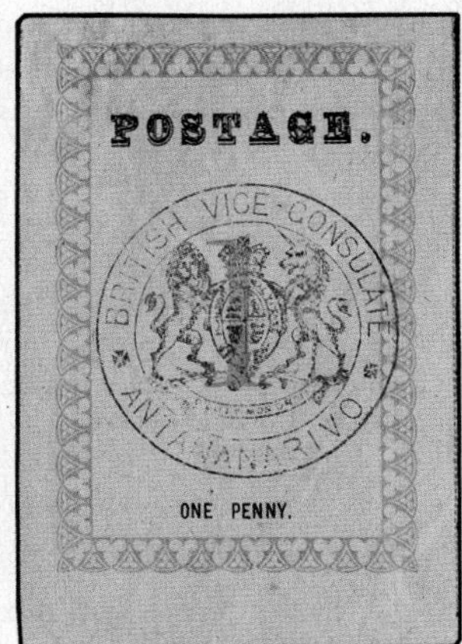

"British Vice-Consulate" — A2

Three types of A2 and A3:
I — "POSTAGE" 29½mm. Periods after "POSTAGE" and value.
II — "POSTAGE" 29½mm. No periods.
III — "POSTAGE" 24½mm. Period after value.

1886 Violet Seal Handstamped

16 A2 1p rose, I 400. —
 a. Type II 1,350. —
17 A2 1½p rose, I 1,500. 875.
 a. Type II 3,000. —
18 A2 2p rose, I 400. —
19 A2 3p rose, I 575. 400.
 a. Type II 1,350. —
20 A2 4p rose, III 500. —
21 A2 4½p rose, I 725. 350.
 a. Type II 2,250. —
22 A2 6p rose, II 1,700. —
23 A2 8p rose, I 2,750. 1,900.
 a. Type III 700. —
24 A2 9p rose 1,350. —
24A A2 1sh rose, III 22,500.
24B A2 1sh6p rose, III 12,500. —
25 A2 2sh rose, III 6,500. —

Black Seal Handstamped

Type I

26 A2 1p rose 145. 275.
27 A2 1½p rose 3,000. 1,300.
28 A2 2p rose 200. —
29 A2 3p rose 4,000. 1,450.
30 A2 4½p rose 3,850. 575.
31 A2 8p rose 5,000. 3,150.
32 A2 9p rose 4,750. 2,900.
32A A2 2sh rose, III — —

"British Consular Mail" — A3

1886 Violet Seal Handstamped

33 A3 1p rose, II 175. —
34 A3 1½p rose, II 275. —
35 A3 2p rose, II 325. —
36 A3 3p rose, II 210. —
37 A3 4p rose, III 475. —
38 A3 4½p rose, II 225. —
39 A3 6p rose, II 500. —
40 A3 8p rose, III 1,450. —
 a. Type I 1,750. —
41 A3 9p rose, I 475. —
42 A3 1sh rose, III 1,750. —
43 A3 1sh6p rose, III 1,750. —
44 A3 2sh rose, III 1,750. —

Black Seal Handstamped

45 A3 1p rose, I 135. —
 a. Type II 135. 210.
46 A3 1½p rose, I 170. 300.
 a. Type II 145. 200.
47 A3 2p rose, I 190. —
 a. Type II 150. 200.
48 A3 3p rose, I 170. 260.
 a. Type II 170. 210.
49 A3 4p rose, III 375. —
50 A3 4½p rose, I 190. 240.
 a. Type II 160. 200.
51 A3 6p rose, II 170. 260.
52 A3 8p rose, I 200. —
 a. Type III 2,250. —
53 A3 9p rose, I 225. 375.
54 A3 1sh rose, III 625. —
55 A3 1sh6p rose, III 775. —
56 A3 2sh rose, III 775. —

Seal Omitted

45b A3 1p rose, II 5,000.
46b A3 1½p rose, II 5,250.
48b A3 3p rose, II 8,000.
49a A3 4p rose, III 6,250.
50b A3 4½p rose, II 8,750.
51a A3 6p rose, II 9,500.
52b A3 8p rose, III 6,250.
53a A3 9p rose, I 8,250.
54a A3 1sh rose, III 8,500.
55a A3 1sh6p rose, III 7,250.
56a A3 2sh rose, III 8,500.

Some students of these issues doubt that the 1886 "seal omitted" varieties were regularly issued.

Red Seal Handstamped

57 A3 3p rose, I 20,000.
58 A3 4½p rose, I 12,750.

FRENCH OFFICES IN MADAGASCAR

The general issues of French Colonies were used in these offices in addition to the stamps listed here.

Stamps of French Colonies Surcharged in Black

a

b

c

Overprint Type "a"

1889 Unwmk. *Perf. 14x13½*

1 A9 05c on 10c blk, *lav* 725. 220.
 a. Inverted surcharge 1,950. 1,300.
 b. Vertical surcharge 1,200. 1,200.
 c. 05c and 25c on 10c blk, lav 2,750. 1,450.
 d. Pair, one without surcharge 2,750.
2 A9 05c on 25c blk, *rose* 725. 220.
 a. Inverted surcharge 1,950. 1,300.
 b. 25c on 10c lav (error) 11,500. 10,000.
 c. Double surcharge 1,400. 1,250.
3 A9 25c on 40c red, *straw* 650. 200.
 On cover 900.
 a. Inverted surcharge 1,700. 1,300.
 b. Double surcharge 1,750. 1,450.
 c. Vertical surcharge 1,400.

Covers: Values are for commercial covers paying correct rates. Philatelic covers sell for less.

1891 Overprint Type "b"

4 A9 05c on 40c red, *straw* 235.00 100.00
 a. Double "5" in surcharge 725.00 700.00
5 A9 15c on 25c blk, *rose* 235.00 110.00
 a. Surcharge vertical 275.00 145.00
 b. Double surcharge 725.00 650.00

Overprint Type "c"

6 A9 5c on 10c blk, *lav* 275.00 125.00
 a. Double surcharge 1,000. 900.00
7 A9 5c on 25c blk, *rose* 275.00 125.00

See Senegal Nos. 4, 8 for similar surcharge on 20c, 30c.

Forgeries of Nos. 1-7 exist.

A4

Without Gum

1891 Type-set *Imperf.*

8 A4 5c blk, *green* 165.00 32.50
9 A4 10c blk, *lt bl* 125.00 40.00
 On cover 575.00
10 A4 15c ultra, *pale bl* 125.00 47.50
 On cover 575.00
11 A4 25c brn, *buff* 30.00 22.50
 On cover 400.00
12 A4 1fr blk, *yellow* 1,300. 300.00
13 A4 5fr vio & blk, *lil* 2,400. 1,275.

Ten varieties of each. Nos. 12-13 have been extensively forged.

Nos. 12 and 13 have a printed network of circles on the colored paper.

Most examples of Nos. 12-13 are defective due to the frail paper. Thinned examples sell for about 25% of the values quoted which are for stamps without damage.

Stamps of France 1876-90, Overprinted in Red or Black

1895 ***Perf. 14x13½***

No.	Type	Description	Unused	Used
14	A15	5c grn, *grnsh* (R)	22.50	11.00
		On cover		175.00
15	A15	10c blk, *lav* (R)	50.00	32.50
		On cover		175.00
16	A15	15c bl (R)	72.50	22.00
		On cover		175.00
17	A15	25c blk, *rose* (R)	100.00	25.00
		On cover		140.00
18	A15	40c red, *straw* (Bk)	95.00	45.00
		On cover		225.00
19	A15	50c rose, *rose* (Bk)	110.00	55.00
		On cover		240.00
20	A15	75c dp vio, *org* (R)	125.00	62.50
		On cover		400.00
21	A15	1fr brnz grn, *straw* (Bk)	135.00	72.50
		On cover		450.00
22	A15	5fr vio, *lav* (Bk)	220.00	100.00
		On cover		*500.00*
		Nos. 14-22 (9)	930.00	425.50

Majunga Issue

Stamps of France, 1876-86, Surcharged with New Value

1895

Manuscript Surcharge in Red

No.	Type	Description	Unused	Used
22A	A15	0,15c on 25c blk, *rose*		*8,000.*
22B	A15	0,15c on 1fr brnz grn, *straw*		*6,000.*

Handstamped in Black

No.	Type	Description	Unused	Used
22C	A15	15c on 25c blk, *rose*		*12,750.*
22D	A15	15c on 1fr brnz grn, *straw*		*11,750.*

On most of No. 22C and all of No. 22D the manuscript surcharge of Nos. 22A-22B was washed off. Three types of "15" were used for No. 22C.

Stamps of France, 1876-84, Surcharged

1896

No.	Type	Description	Unused	Used
23	A15	5c on 1c blk, *bl*	*6,400.*	*2,500.*
		On cover		*6,000.*
24	A15	15c on 2c brn, *buff*	*2,600.*	*1,000.*
		On cover		*3,250.*
25	A15	25c on 3c gray, *grysh*	*3,400.*	*1,100.*
		On cover		*3,250.*
26	A15	25c on 4c cl, *lav*	*6,400.*	*1,950.*
		On cover		*5,500.*
27	A15	25c on 40c red, *straw*	*1,650.*	*875.*
		On cover		*2,750.*

The oval of the 5c and 15c surcharges is smaller than that of the 25c, and it does not extend beyond the edges of the stamp as the 25c surcharge does.

Excellent counterfeits of the surcharges on Nos. 22A to 27 exist.

Issues of the Colony

Navigation and Commerce — A7

1896-1906 **Typo.** ***Perf. 14x13½***

Colony Name in Blue or Carmine

No.	Type	Description	Unused	Used
28	A7	1c blk, *lil bl*	1.50	1.10
		On cover		80.00
a.		Name double	525.00	
29	A7	2c brn, *buff*	2.25	1.50
		On cover		80.00
a.		Name in blue black	4.25	4.50
30	A7	4c claret, *lav*	2.50	1.80
		On cover		65.00
31	A7	5c grn, *grnsh*	8.00	1.50
		On cover		40.00
32	A7	5c yel grn ('01)	1.80	1.10
		On cover		11.00
33	A7	10c blk, *lav*	8.00	2.25
		On cover		30.00
34	A7	10c red ('00)	3.00	1.10
		On cover		11.00
35	A7	15c blue, quadrille paper	14.00	1.50
		On cover		32.50
36	A7	15c gray ('00)	2.50	1.50
		On cover		11.00
37	A7	20c red, *grn*	7.25	2.25
		On cover		55.00
38	A7	25c blk, *rose*	11.00	4.50
		On cover		30.00
39	A7	25c blue ('00)	25.00	32.50
		On cover		*100.00*
40	A7	30c brn, *bis*	8.75	3.75
		On cover		55.00
41	A7	35c blk, *yel* ('06)	45.00	7.25
		On cover		65.00
a.		Name inverted		15,000.
42	A7	40c red, *straw*	11.00	6.00
		On cover		55.00
43	A7	50c car, *rose*	14.50	3.00
		On cover		60.00
44	A7	50c brn, *az* ('00)	32.50	45.00
		On cover		95.00
45	A7	75c dp vio, *org*	6.25	4.50
		On cover		92.50
a.		Thin, transluscent paper	7.50	5.00
46	A7	1fr brnz grn, *straw*	14.50	3.75
		On cover		110.00
a.		Name in blue ('99)	30.00	22.00
47	A7	5fr red lil, *lav* ('99)	37.50	32.50
		On cover		250.00
		Nos. 28-47 (20)	256.80	158.35

Perf. 13½x14 stamps are counterfeits.

For surcharges see Nos. 48-55, 58-60, 115-118, 127-128.

Nos. 32, 43, 44 and 46, affixed to pressboard with animals printed on the back, were used as emergency currency in the Comoro Islands in 1920.

Surcharged in Black

1902

No.	Type	Description	Unused	Used
48	A7	05c on 50c car, *rose*	7.25	6.00
		On cover		45.00
a.		Inverted surcharge	120.00	120.00
49	A7	10c on 5fr red lil, *lav*	25.00	22.00
		On cover		110.00
a.		Inverted surcharge	125.00	125.00
50	A7	15c on 1fr ol grn, *straw*	9.50	8.75
		On cover		45.00
a.		Inverted surcharge	120.00	120.00
b.		Double surcharge	400.00	400.00
		Nos. 48-50 (3)	41.75	36.75

Surcharged in Black

No.	Type	Description	Unused	Used
51	A7	0,01 on 2c brn, *buff*	11.50	11.50
		On cover		72.50
a.		Inverted surcharge	72.50	72.50
b.		"00,1" instead of "0,01"	150.00	155.00
c.		As "b" inverted	—	—
d.		Comma omitted	210.00	210.00
e.		Name in blue black	11.50	11.50
52	A7	0,05 on 30c brn, *bis*	11.50	11.50
		On cover		65.00
a.		Inverted surcharge	72.50	72.50
b.		"00,5" instead of "0,05"	100.00	100.00
c.		As "b" inverted	2,550.	
d.		Comma omitted	210.00	210.00
53	A7	0,10 on 50c car, *rose*	9.50	9.50
		On cover		65.00
a.		Inverted surcharge	72.50	72.50
b.		Comma omitted	210.00	210.00
54	A7	0,15 on 75c vio, *org*	7.25	7.25
		On cover		62.50
a.		Inverted surcharge	72.50	72.50
b.		Comma omitted	210.00	210.00
c.		As "b," inverted	725.00	725.00
55	A7	0,15 on 1fr ol grn, *straw*	14.50	14.50
		On cover		72.50
a.		Inverted surcharge	110.00	110.00
b.		Comma omitted	275.00	275.00
		Nos. 51-55 (5)	54.25	54.25

Surcharged On Stamps of Diego-Suarez

No.	Type	Description	Unused	Used
56	A11	0,05 on 30c brn, *bis*	165.00	145.00
		On cover		400.00
a.		"00,5" instead of "0,05"	1,350.	1,350.
b.		Inverted surcharge	1,450.	1,450.
57	A11	0,10 on 50c car, *rose*	*5,000.*	*5,000.*

Counterfeits of Nos. 56-57 exist with surcharge both normal and inverted.

Surcharged in Black

No.	Type	Description	Unused	Used
58	A7	0,01 on 2c brn, *buff*	11.50	11.50
		On cover		72.50
a.		Inverted surcharge	72.50	72.50
b.		Comma omitted	210.00	210.00
59	A7	0,05 on 30c brn, *bis*	11.50	11.50
		On cover		65.00
a.		Inverted surcharge	72.50	72.50
b.		Comma omitted	210.00	210.00
60	A7	0,10 on 50c car, *rose*	9.50	9.50
		On cover		65.00
a.		Inverted surcharge	72.50	72.50
b.		Comma omitted	210.00	210.00
		Nos. 58-60 (3)	32.50	32.50

Surcharged On Stamps of Diego-Suarez

No.	Type	Description	Unused	Used
61	A11	0,05 on 30c brn, *bis*	165.00	145.00
		On cover		400.00
a.		Inverted surcharge	1,450.	1,450.
62	A11	0,10 on 50c car, *rose*	*5,000.*	*5,000.*

Se-tenant Pairs

No.	Description	Unused	Used
51g	0,01 #51 + #58	25.00	—
52g	0,05 #52 + #59	30.00	—
53g	0,10 #53 + #60	30.00	—
56g	0,05 #56 + #62	550.00	—
57g	0,10 #57 + #63	—	—

BISECTS

During alleged stamp shortages at several Madagascar towns in 1904, it is claimed that bisects were used. After being affixed to letters, these bisects were handstamped "Affranchissement - exceptionnel - (faute de timbres)" and other inscriptions of similar import. The stamps bisected were 10c, 20c, 30c and 50c denominations of Madagascar type A7 and Diego-Suarez type A11. The editors believe these provisionals were unnecessary and speculative.

Zebu, Traveler's Tree and Lemur — A8

1903 **Engr.** ***Perf. 11½***

No.	Type	Description	Unused	Used
63	A8	1c dk violet	.90	.90
a.		On bluish paper	5.00	5.00
64	A8	2c olive brn	.90	.90
65	A8	4c brown	1.20	1.25
66	A8	5c yellow grn	6.00	1.90
67	A8	10c red	11.00	1.25
68	A8	15c carmine	14.00	1.25
a.		On bluish paper	*150.00*	*150.00*
69	A8	20c orange	5.25	2.50
70	A8	25c dull blue	25.00	5.00
71	A8	30c pale red	37.50	13.00
72	A8	40c gray vio	25.00	5.25
73	A8	50c brown org	40.00	25.00
74	A8	75c orange yel	52.50	25.00
75	A8	1fr dp green	52.50	25.00
76	A8	2fr slate	72.50	26.00
77	A8	5fr gray black	82.50	*85.00*
		Nos. 63-77 (15)	426.75	219.20

Nos. 63-77 exist imperf. Value of set, $600.

For surcharges see Nos. 119-124, 129.

Transportation by Sedan Chair — A9

1908-28 **Typo.** ***Perf. 13½x14***

No.	Type	Description	Unused	Used
79	A9	1c violet & ol	.25	.25
80	A9	2c red & ol	.25	.25
81	A9	4c ol brn & brn	.25	.25
82	A9	5c bl grn & ol	1.00	.30
83	A9	5c blk & rose ('22)	.30	.30
84	A9	10c rose & brown	1.00	.30
85	A9	10c bl grn & ol grn ('22)	.60	.40
86	A9	10c org brn & vio ('25)	.35	.35
87	A9	15c dl vio & rose ('16)	.35	.35
88	A9	15c dl grn & lt grn ('27)	.70	.70
89	A9	15c dk bl & rose red ('28)	1.60	1.00
90	A9	20c org & brn	.70	.45
91	A9	25c blue & blk	3.00	1.00
92	A9	25c vio & blk ('22)	.40	.30
93	A9	30c brown & blk	3.00	1.35
94	A9	30c rose red & brn ('22)	.55	.40
95	A9	30c grn & red vio ('25)	.55	.45
96	A9	30c dp grn & yel grn ('27)	1.35	1.00
97	A9	35c red & black	2.00	1.00
98	A9	40c vio brn & blk	1.35	.70
99	A9	45c bl grn & blk	1.00	.70
100	A9	45c red & ver ('25)	.45	.45
101	A9	45c gray lil & mag ('27)	1.25	1.00
102	A9	50c violet & blk	1.00	.70
103	A9	50c blue & blk ('22)	.85	.60
104	A9	50c blk & org ('25)	1.00	.40
105	A9	60c vio, *pnksh* ('25)	.70	.70
106	A9	65c black & bl ('25)	1.00	.75
107	A9	75c rose red & blk	1.00	.70
108	A9	85c grn & ver ('25)	1.35	.85
109	A9	1fr brown & ol	1.00	.70
110	A9	1fr dull blue ('25)	1.00	1.00
111	A9	1fr rose & grn ('28)	5.75	4.50
112	A9	1.10fr bis & bl grn ('28)	2.00	2.00
113	A9	2fr blue & olive	4.00	1.60
114	A9	5fr vio & vio brn	12.50	5.50
		Nos. 79-114 (36)	55.40	33.25

75c violet on pinkish stamps of type A9 are No. 138 without surcharge.

For surcharges and overprints see Nos. 125-126, 130-146, 178-179, B1, 212-214.

Preceding Issues Surcharged in Black or Carmine

1912, Nov. ***Perf. 14x13½***

115 A7 5c on 15c gray (C) 1.00 1.00
a. Wide spacing in surcharge 8.75 1.45
116 A7 5c on 20c red, *grn* 1.35 1.35
a. Inverted surcharge 175.00
b. As #116, wide spacing in surcharge 10.00 10.00
c. As #116a, wide spacing in surcharge 2,200.
117 A7 5c on 30c brn, *bis* (C) 1.00 1.00
a. Wide spacing in surcharge 12.50 12.50
118 A7 10c on 75c vio, *org* 12.50 11.50
a. Double surcharge 310.00
b. As #118, wide spacing in surcharge 210.00 210.00
c. As #118a, wide spacing in surcharge 3,000.
119 A8 5c on 2c ol brn (C) 1.00 1.00
120 A8 5c on 20c org 1.00 1.00
121 A8 5c on 30c pale red 1.75 1.75
122 A8 10c on 40c gray vio (C) 1.75 1.75
123 A8 10c on 50c brn org 3.50 4.50
124 A8 10c on 75c org yel 6.00 7.25
a. Inverted surcharge 230.00
Nos. 115-124 (10) 30.85 32.10

Two spacings between the surcharged numerals are found on Nos. 115 to 118: Narrow spacing between figures of surcharge 1.5mm (5c), 2mm (10c); Wide spacing between figures of surcharge 2.25mm (5c), 2.75mm (10c). Values for Nos. 115-118 are for stamps with narrow spacing.

Stamps of Anjouan, Grand Comoro Island, Mayotte and Mohéli with similar surcharges were also available for use in Madagascar and the entire Comoro archipelago.

Preceding Issues Surcharged in Red or Black

g

h

1921 **On Nos. 98 & 107**

125 A9 (g) 30c on 40c (R) 2.50 2.50
126 A9 (g) 60c on 75c 3.25 3.25

On Nos. 45 & 47

127 A7 (g) 60c on 75c (R) 12.50 12.50
a. Inverted surcharge 220.00 220.00
128 A7 (h) 1fr on 5fr 1.10 1.10

On No. 77

129 A8 (h) 1fr on 5fr (R) 100.00 100.00
Nos. 125-129 (5) 119.35 119.35

Stamps and Type of 1908-16 Surcharged in Black or Red

No. 130

No. 131

130 A9 1c on 15c dl vio & rose 1.10 1.10
131 A9 25c on 35c red & blk 6.50 6.50
132 A9 25c on 35c red & blk (R) 32.50 32.50
133 A9 25c on 40c brn & blk 5.00 5.00
134 A9 25c on 45c grn & blk 4.50 4.50
Nos. 130-134 (5) 49.60 49.60
Nos. 125-134 (10) 168.95 168.95

Stamps and Type of 1908-28 Surcharged with New Value and Bars

1922-27

135 A9 25c on 15c dl vio & rose .35 .35
a. Double surcharge 95.00
136 A9 25c on 2fr bl & ol .50 .50
137 A9 25c on 5fr vio & vio brn .35 .35
138 A9 60c on 75c vio, *pnksh* .60 .60
139 A9 65c on 75c rose red & blk 1.10 1.10
140 A9 85c on 45c bl grn & blk 1.90 1.45
141 A9 90c on 75c dl red & rose red 1.10 1.10
142 A9 1.25fr on 1fr lt bl (R) .75 .50
143 A9 1.50fr on 1fr dp bl & dl bl .75 .60
144 A9 3fr on 5fr grn & vio 2.25 1.45
145 A9 10fr on 5fr org & rose lil 9.50 6.00
146 A9 20fr on 5fr rose & sl bl 10.00 8.00
Nos. 135-146 (12) 29.15 22.00

Years of issue: No. 138, 1922; Nos. 136, 137, 1924; Nos. 135, 139-140, 1925; No. 142, 1926; Nos. 141, 143-146, 1927.

See Nos. 178-179.

Sakalava Chief — A10

Hova Woman — A12

Hova with Oxen A11

Bétsiléo Woman A13

Perf. 13½x14, 14x13½

1930-44 **Typo.**

147 A11 1c dk bl & bl grn ('33) .25 .25
148 A10 2c brn red & dk brn .25 .25
149 A10 4c dk brn & vio .25 .25
150 A11 5c lt grn & red .25 .25
151 A12 10c ver & dp grn .40 .25
152 A13 15c dp red .25 .25
153 A11 20c yel brn & dk bl .25 .25
154 A12 25c vio & dk brn .25 .25
155 A13 30c Prus blue .65 .45
156 A10 40c grn & red .75 .50
157 A13 45c dull violet .90 .55
158 A11 65c brn & vio 1.10 .80
159 A13 75c dk brown .85 .50
160 A11 90c brn red & dk red 1.40 .90
161 A12 1fr yel brn & dk bl 1.75 1.10
162 A12 1fr dk red & car rose ('38) .95 .90
163 A12 1.25fr dp bl & dk brn ('33) 1.60 .90
164 A10 1.50fr dk & dp bl 5.50 1.10
165 A10 1.50fr brn & dk red ('38) .75 .50
165A A10 1.50fr dk red & brn ('44) .50 .50
166 A10 1.75fr dk brn & dk red ('33) 4.25 1.60
167 A10 5fr vio & dk brn 1.25 .70
168 A10 20fr yel brn & dk bl 2.00 1.75
Nos. 147-168 (23) 26.35 14.75

For surcharges and overprints see Nos. 211, 215, 217-218, 222-223, 228-229, 233, 235, 239, 257 and note after No. B10 in Scott Standard catalogue, Vol. 4.

Common Design Types pictured following the introduction.

Colonial Exposition Issue
Common Design Types

1931 **Engr.** ***Perf. 12½***

Name of Country in Black

169 CD70 40c deep green 1.40 1.00
170 CD71 50c violet 2.00 1.25
171 CD72 90c red orange 2.00 1.25
172 CD73 1.50fr dull blue 2.50 1.50
Nos. 169-172 (4) 7.90 5.00

General Joseph Simon Galliéni — A14

Size: 21½x34½mm

1931 **Engr.** ***Perf. 14***

173 A14 1c ultra .50 .45
174 A14 50c orange brn 1.40 .35
175 A14 2fr deep red 5.75 4.25
176 A14 3fr emerald 5.50 3.00
177 A14 10fr dp orange 4.00 3.00
Nos. 173-177 (5) 17.15 11.05

See Nos. 180-190. For overprints and surcharges see Nos. 216, 219, 221, 224, 232, 258 in Scott Standard catalogue, Vol. 4.

Nos. 113 and 109 Surcharged

1932 ***Perf. 13½x14***

178 A9 25c on 2fr bl & ol .75 .50
179 A9 50c on 1fr brn & ol .75 .50

No. 178 has numerals in thick block letters. No. 136 has thin shaded numerals.

Galliéni Type of 1931

1936-40 **Photo.** ***Perf. 13½, 13x13½***

Size: 21x34mm

180 A14 3c sapphire ('40) .25 .25
181 A14 45c brt green ('40) .50 .40
182 A14 50c yellow brown .25 .25
183 A14 60c brt red lil ('40) .40 .25
184 A14 70c brt rose ('40) .60 .40
185 A14 90c copper brn ('39) .50 .40
186 A14 1.40fr org yel ('40) .90 .50
187 A14 1.60fr purple ('40) .90 .60
188 A14 2fr dk carmine .50 .25
189 A14 3fr green 4.50 2.25
190 A14 3fr olive blk ('39) .90 .70
Nos. 180-190 (11) 10.20 6.25

For overprint see note after No. B10 in Scott Standard catalogue, Vol. 4.

Paris International Exposition Issue
Common Design Types

1937, Apr. 15 **Engr.** ***Perf. 13***

191 CD74 20c dp violet 1.60 1.60
192 CD75 30c dk green 1.60 1.60
193 CD76 40c car rose 1.60 1.60
194 CD77 50c dk brn & blk 1.25 1.25
195 CD78 90c red 1.60 1.60
196 CD79 1.50fr ultra 1.60 1.60
Nos. 191-196 (6) 9.25 9.25

Colonial Arts Exhibition Issue
Common Design Type
Souvenir Sheet

1937 ***Imperf.***

197 CD74 3fr orange red 10.00 *12.50*

Jean Laborde A15

1938-40 ***Perf. 13***

198 A15 35c green .60 .35
199 A15 55c dp purple .60 .35
200 A15 65c orange red .80 .35
201 A15 80c violet brn .60 .35
202 A15 1fr rose car .80 .35
203 A15 1.25fr rose car ('39) .35 .25
204 A15 1.75fr dk ultra 1.60 .65
205 A15 2.15fr yel brn 2.25 1.60
206 A15 2.25fr dk ultra ('39) .55 .45
207 A15 2.50fr blk brn ('40) .60 .45
208 A15 10fr dk green ('40) 1.10 .80
Nos. 198-208 (11) 9.85 5.95

Nos. 198-202, 204, 205 commemorate the 60th anniv. of the death of Jean Laborde, explorer.

For overprints and surcharges see Nos. 220, 225-227, 230-231, 234, 236-237 in Scott Standard catalogue, Vol. 4.

New York World's Fair Issue
Common Design Type

1939, May 10 **Engr.** ***Perf. 12½x12***

209 CD82 1.25fr car lake .75 1.25
210 CD82 2.25fr ultra .75 1.25

For surcharge see No. 240 in Scott Standard catalogue, Vol. 4.

SEMI-POSTAL STAMPS

No. 84 Surcharged in Red

1915, Feb. **Unwmk.** ***Perf. 13½x14***

B1 A9 10c + 5c rose & brn 1.50 1.50

Curie Issue
Common Design Type

1938, Oct. 24 ***Perf. 13***

B2 CD80 1.75fr + 50c brt ultra 11.00 11.00

French Revolution Issue
Common Design Type
Name and Value Typographed in Black

1939, July 5 **Photo.**

B3 CD83 45c + 25c grn 9.50 9.50
B4 CD83 70c + 30c brn 9.50 9.50
B5 CD83 90c + 35c red org 9.50 9.50
B6 CD83 1.25fr + 1fr rose pink 9.50 9.50
B7 CD83 2.25fr + 2fr blue 9.50 9.50
Nos. B3-B7 (5) 47.50 47.50

AIR POST STAMPS

Airplane and Map of Madagascar — AP1

Perf. 13x13½

1935-41 **Photo.** **Unwmk.**

Map in Red

C1 AP1 50c yellow green .65 .45
C2 AP1 90c yel grn ('41) .50
C3 AP1 1.25fr claret .50 .50
C4 AP1 1.50fr bright blue .50 .50
C5 AP1 1.60fr br blue ('41) .25 .25
C6 AP1 1.75fr orange 8.75 3.75
C7 AP1 2fr Prus blue .85 .45
C8 AP1 3fr dp org ('41) .25 .25
C9 AP1 3.65fr ol blk ('38) .85 .50
C10 AP1 3.90fr turq grn ('41) .25 .25
C11 AP1 4fr rose 45.00 3.25
C12 AP1 4.50fr black 27.50 2.50
C13 AP1 5.50fr ol blk ('41) .25 .25
C14 AP1 6fr rose lil ('41) .35 .25
C15 AP1 6.90fr dl vio ('41) .25 .25
C16 AP1 8fr rose lilac 1.50 .90
C17 AP1 8.50fr green 1.50 1.10
C18 AP1 9fr ol grn ('41) .35 .35
C19 AP1 12fr violet brown .80 .55
C20 AP1 12.50fr dull violet 1.90 .90
C21 AP1 15fr org yel ('41) .80 .55
C22 AP1 16fr olive green 1.75 1.10
C23 AP1 20fr dark brown 2.50 1.75

C24 AP1 50fr brt ultra ('38) 4.75 4.50
Nos. C1,C3-C24 (23) 102.05 25.10

According to some authorities the 90c was not placed on sale in Madagascar.

AIR POST SEMI-POSTAL STAMPS

French Revolution Issue
Common Design Type
Unwmk.
1939, July 5 Photo. *Perf. 13*
Name and Value in Orange

CB1 CD83 4.50fr + 4fr brn blk 18.00 18.00

POSTAGE DUE STAMPS

Postage Due Stamps of French Colonies Overprinted in Red or Blue — D1

1896 Unwmk. *Imperf.*

J1 D1 5c blue (R) 12.00 9.50
On cover *300.00*
J2 D1 10c brown (R) 11.00 8.00
On cover *300.00*
J3 D1 20c yellow (Bl) 10.00 8.00
On cover *300.00*
J4 D1 30c rose red (Bl) 11.00 8.00
On cover *300.00*
J5 D1 40c lilac (R) 80.00 50.00
On cover *750.00*
J6 D1 50c gray vio (Bl) 14.50 10.00
On cover *400.00*
J7 D1 1fr dk grn (R) 80.00 65.00
On cover —
Nos. J1-J7 (7) 218.50 158.50

Governor's Palace — D2

1908-24 Typo. *Perf. 13½x14*

J8 D2 2c vio brn .25 .25
J9 D2 4c violet .25 .25
J10 D2 5c green .25 .25
J11 D2 10c deep rose .25 .25
J12 D2 20c olive green .40 .40
J13 D2 40c brn, *straw* .45 .45
J14 D2 50c brn, *bl* .60 .60
J15 D2 60c orange ('24) .60 .60
J16 D2 1fr dark blue 1.10 1.10
Nos. J8-J16 (9) 4.15 4.15

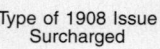

Type of 1908 Issue Surcharged

1924-27

J17 D2 60c on 1fr org 1.90 1.90

Surcharged

J18 D2 2fr on 1fr lil rose ('27) .90 .90
J19 D2 3fr on 1fr ultra ('27) .90 .90

MADEIRA

mə-'dir-ə

LOCATION — A group of islands in the Atlantic Ocean northwest of Africa
GOVT. — Part of the Republic of Portugal
AREA — 314 sq. mi.
POP. — 150,574 (1900)
CAPITAL — Funchal

These islands are considered an integral part of Portugal and since 1898 postage stamps of Portugal have been in use.

1000 Reis = 1 Milreis
100 Centavos = 1 Escudo (1925)

STAMPS OF PORTUGAL USED IN MADEIRA

PRE-STAMP POSTAL MARKINGS
British Post Office Crowned Paid Postmarks

1842

A1 Crowned double circle handstamp, on cover, inscribed "PAID AT MADEIRA" in red *20,000.*
Earliest known use: 2/28/42.

Stamps of Portugal Used in Madeira
Barred Numeral "51"

1853 Queen Maria II

A1 5r org brn (#1) 2,300.
A2 25r blue (#2) 150.
A3 50r dp yel grn (#3) 2,250.
A4 100r lilac (#4) 5,000.

1855 King Pedro V (Straight Hair)

A5 5r red brn (#5) 2,300.
A6 25r blue, type II (#6) 110.00
On cover 500.00
a. Type I (#6a) 120.00
On cover 450.00
A7 50r green (#7) 175.00
On cover 900.00
A8 100r lilac (#8) 190.00

1856-58
King Pedro V (Curled Hair)

A9 5r red brn (#9) 290.00
A10 25r blue, type II (#10) 165.00
On cover 500.00
a. Type I (#10a) 165.00
On cover 475.00
A11 25r rose, type II (#11; '58) 60.00
On cover 300.00

1862-64 King Luiz

A12 5r brown (#12) 175.00
A13 10r orange (#13) 190.00
A14 25r rose (#14) 65.00
On cover 175.00
A15 50r yel green (#15) 180.00
On cover 500.00
A16 100r lilac (#16; '64) 165.00

1866-67 King Luiz
Imperf.

A17 5r black (#17) 190.00
A18 10r yellow (#18) 290.00
A19 20r bister (#19) 290.00
A20 25r rose (#20) 210.00
On cover 375.00
A21 50r green (#21) 290.00
On cover 475.00
A22 80r orange (#22) 290.00
On cover *625.00*
A23 100r dk lilac (#23; '67) 375.00
A24 120r blue (#24) 190.00
On cover *625.00*

Perf. 12½

A28 25r rose (#28) 160.00

Issued under Portuguese Administration

It is recommended that the rare overprinted 1868-81 stamps be purchased accompanied by certificates of authenticity from competent experts.

King Luiz — A1

Stamps of Portugal Overprinted

1868, Jan. 1 Unwmk. *Imperf.*
Black Overprint

2 A1 20r bister 210.00 120.00
a. Inverted overprint —
b. Rouletted —
3 A1 50r green 210.00 120.00
4 A1 80r orange 225.00 125.00
a. Double overprint —
5 A1 100r lilac 225.00 125.00
Nos. 2-5 (4) 870.00 490.00

The 5r black does not exist as a genuinely imperforate original.

Reprints of 1885 are on stout white paper, ungummed. (Also, 5r, 10r and 25r values were overprinted.) Reprints of 1905 are on ordinary white paper with shiny gum and have a wide "D" and "R." Value, $12 each.

Lozenge Perf.

2c A1 20r —
3a A1 50r —
4b A1 80r —
5a A1 100r —

Overprinted in Red or Black

1868-70 *Perf. 12½*

6 A1 5r black (R) 50.00 37.50
8 A1 10r yellow 90.00 80.00
9 A1 20r bister 140.00 110.00
10 A1 25r rose 50.00 12.00
a. Inverted overprint —
11 A1 50r green 200.00 140.00
a. Inverted overprint —
12 A1 80r orange 180.00 140.00
13 A1 100r lilac 190.00 140.00
a. Inverted overprint —
14 A1 120r blue 110.00 80.00
15 A1 240r violet ('70) 700.00 425.00
Nos. 6-15 (9) 1,710. 1,165.

Two types of 5r differ in the position of the "5" at upper right.

The reprints are on stout white paper, ungummed, with rough perforation 13½, and on thin white paper with shiny white gum and clean-cut perforation 13½. The overprint has the wide "D" and "R" and the first reprints included the 5r with both black and red overprint. Value $10 each.

King Luiz — A2

Overprinted in Red or Black

1871-80 *Perf. 12½, 13½*

16 A2 5r black (R) 15.00 8.00
a. Inverted overprint —
b. Double overprint 55.00 55.00
c. Perf. 14 90.00 55.00
18 A2 10r yellow 35.00 22.50
19 A2 10r bl grn ('79) 140.00 110.00
a. Perf. 13½ 160.00 140.00
20 A2 10r yel grn ('80) 65.00 52.50
21 A2 15r brn ('75) 19.00 11.50
22 A2 20r bister 30.00 22.50
23 A2 25r rose 13.50 4.50
a. Inverted overprint 50.00 40.00
b. Double overprint 50.00 40.00
24 A2 50r green ('72) 67.50 30.00
a. Double overprint —
b. Inverted overprint 200.00 200.00
25 A2 50r blue ('80) 125.00 55.00
26 A2 80r orange ('72) 77.50 67.50
27 A2 100r pale lil ('73) 90.00 60.00
a. Perf. 14 200.00 85.00
b. Perf. 13½ 160.00 75.00
28 A2 120r blue 110.00 80.00
29 A2 150r blue ('76) 160.00 140.00
a. Perf. 13½ 175.00 150.00
30 A2 150r yel ('79) 350.00 240.00
31 A2 240r vio ('74) 750.00 500.00
32 A2 300r vio ('76) 75.00 67.50
Nos. 16-32 (16) 2,123. 1,472.

There are two types of the overprint, the second one having a broad "D."

The reprints have the same characteristics as those of the 1868-70 issues.

A3

A4

King Luiz — A5

1880-81

33 A3 5r black 40.00 21.00
34 A4 25r pearl gray 50.00 21.00
a. Inverted overprint 75.00 75.00
35 A5 25r lilac 50.00 11.00
a. 25r purple brown 32.50 11.00
b. 25r gray 35.00 10.00
Nos. 33-35 (3) 140.00 53.00

Nos. 33, 34 and 35 have been reprinted on stout white paper, ungummed, and the last three on thin white paper with shiny white gum. The perforations are as previously described.

Common Design Types pictured following the introduction.

Vasco da Gama Issue
Common Design Types

1898, Apr. 1 Engr. *Perf. 14-15*

37 CD20 2½r blue grn 2.40 1.25
38 CD21 5r red 2.40 1.25
39 CD22 10r red violet 3.00 1.50
40 CD23 25r yel green 2.75 1.25
41 CD24 50r dk blue 6.00 3.25
42 CD25 75r vio brown 8.00 7.00
43 CD26 100r bister brn 8.00 7.00
44 CD27 150r bister 12.00 11.50
Nos. 37-44 (8) 44.55 34.00

Nos. 37-44 with "REPUBLICA" overprint and surcharges are listed as Portugal Nos. 199-206.

Ceres — A6

1928, May 1 Engr. *Perf. 13½*
Value Typographed in Black

45 A6 3c deep violet .40 *.60*
Never hinged .50
46 A6 4c orange .40 *.60*
Never hinged .50
47 A6 5c light blue .40 *.60*
Never hinged .50
48 A6 6c brown .40 *.60*
Never hinged .50
49 A6 10c red .40 *.60*
Never hinged .50
50 A6 15c yel green .40 *.60*
Never hinged .50
51 A6 16c red brown .40 *.60*
Never hinged .55
52 A6 25c violet rose 1.00 .60
Never hinged 1.20
53 A6 32c blue grn 1.00 .60
Never hinged 1.20
54 A6 40c yel brown 1.50 *1.75*
Never hinged 2.40
55 A6 50c slate 1.50 *1.75*
Never hinged 2.40
56 A6 64c Prus blue 1.50 *3.00*
Never hinged 2.40
57 A6 80c dk brown 1.50 *5.00*
Never hinged 2.40
58 A6 96c carmine rose 5.00 *3.00*
Never hinged 8.00
59 A6 1e black 2.00 3.00
Never hinged 3.25
a. Value omitted 42.50 *45.00*
Never hinged 75.00
60 A6 1.20e light rose 2.00 *3.00*
Never hinged 3.25
61 A6 1.60e ultra 2.00 *3.00*
Never hinged 3.25
62 A6 2.40e yellow 3.00 *3.50*
Never hinged 4.25
63 A6 3.36e dull green 4.00 *5.75*
Never hinged 4.75
64 A6 4.50e brown red 5.00 *9.00*
Never hinged 8.00
65 A6 7e dark blue 6.00 *17.50*
Never hinged 9.00
Nos. 45-65 (21) 39.80 *64.65*

It was obligatory to use these stamps in place of those in regular use on May 1, June 5, July 1 and Dec. 31, 1928, Jan. 1 and 31, May 1 and June 5, 1929. The amount obtained from this sale was donated to a fund for building a museum.

Less than very fine examples sell for much less.

NEWSPAPER STAMP

Numeral of Value — N1

Newspaper Stamp of Portugal Overprinted in Black

Perf. 12½, 13½

1876, July 1 **Unwmk.**

P1	N1	2½r olive	9.00	4.25
a.		Inverted overprint	30.00	

The reprints have the same papers, gum, perforations and overprint as the reprints of the regular issues.

POSTAL TAX STAMPS

Pombal Commemorative Issue
Common Design Types

1925 Unwmk. Engr. *Perf. 12½*

RA1	CD28	15c gray & black	.60	.65
RA2	CD29	15c gray & black	.60	.65
RA3	CD30	15c gray & black	.60	.65
		Nos. RA1-RA3 (3)	1.80	1.95

POSTAL TAX DUE STAMPS

Pombal Commemorative Issue
Common Design Types

1925 Unwmk. *Perf. 12½*

RAJ1	CD28	30c gray & black	.85	3.50
RAJ2	CD29	30c gray & black	.85	3.50
RAJ3	CD30	30c gray & black	.85	3.50
		Nos. RAJ1-RAJ3 (3)	2.55	10.50

MALAYA

mə-'lā-ə

Federated Malay States

LOCATION — Malay peninsula
GOVT. — British Protectorate
AREA — 27,585 sq. mi.
CAPITAL — Kuala Lumpur

The Federated Malay States consisted of the sultanates of Negri Sembilan, Pahang, Perak and Selangor.

Stamps of the Federated Malay States replaced those of the individual states and were used until 1935, when individual issues were resumed.

100 Cents = 1 Dollar

Catalogue values for unused stamps in this country are for Never Hinged items, beginning with Scott J20 in the postage due section, Scott 128 in Johore, Scott 55 in Kedah, Scott 44 in Kelantan, Scott 1 in Malacca, Scott 36 in Negri Sembilan, Scott 44 in Pahang, Scott 1 in Penang, Scott 99 in Perak, Scott 1 in Perlis, Scott 74 in Selangor, and Scott 47 in Trengganu.

Watermarks

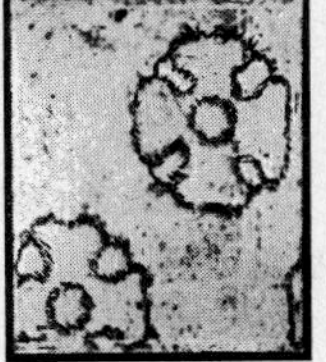

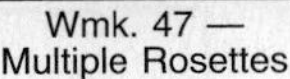

Wmk. 47 — Multiple Rosettes

Wmk. 71 — Rosette

Stamps of Straits Settlements overprinted "BMA MALAYA" are listed in Straits Settlements.

Stamps and Type of Negri Sembilan Overprinted in Black

1900 Wmk. 2 *Perf. 14*

1	A2	1c lilac & green	3.50	*13.50*
2	A2	2c lilac & brown	35.00	*77.50*
3	A2	3c lilac & black	3.25	*7.75*
4	A2	5c lilac & olive	85.00	*200.00*
5	A2	10c lilac & org	17.50	*57.50*
6	A2	20c green & olive	100.00	*135.00*
7	A2	25c grn & car rose	300.00	*425.00*
8	A2	50c green & black	110.00	*175.00*
		Nos. 1-8 (8)	654.25	*1,091.*
		Set, ovptd. "SPECIMEN"	225.00	

Overprinted on Perak Nos. 51, 53, 57-58, 60-61

1900

9	A9	5c lilac & olive	32.50	*77.50*
10	A9	10c lilac & org	90.00	*80.00*

Wmk. 1

11	A10	$1 green & lt grn	210.00	*275.00*
12	A10	$2 green & car rose	200.00	*325.00*
13	A10	$5 green & ultra	575.00	*800.00*
		Revenue cancel		75.00
13A	A10	$25 green & org	*16,000.*	
		Revenue cancel		575.00
		Overprinted "SPECIMEN"	500.00	
		Nos. 9-13 (5)	1,108.	*1,558.*

No. 10 with bar omitted is an essay.

Elephants and Howdah — A3

1900 Typo.

14	A3	$1 green & lt green	200.	*200.*
15	A3	$2 grn & car rose	190.	*210.*
16	A3	$5 green & ultra	475.	500.
a.		$5 green & pale ultramarine	400.	400.
		Revenue cancel		25.
17	A3	$25 grn & orange	4,900.	1,950.
		Revenue cancel		*125.*
		Overprinted "SPECIMEN"	375.	
		Nos. 14-17 (4)	5,765.	2,860.
		Nos. 14-16, ovpted. "SPECIMEN"	190.00	

High values with revenue cancellations are plentiful and inexpensive.

Tiger — A4

Stamps of type A4 are watermarked sideways.

1901 Wmk. 2

18	A4	1c blue grn & blk	20.00	11.00
a.		1c green & gray	6.00	1.25
b.		1c green & gray brown	13.50	.40
19	A4	3c brown & gray	7.25	.45
a.		3c brown & black	25.00	7.50
b.		3c brown & gray brown	11.00	.25
20	A4	4c rose & black	24.00	12.00
a.		4c carmine & gray	12.50	8.25
b.		4c carmine & gray brown	30.00	5.75
21	A4	5c scar & grn, *yel*	3.00	3.75
22	A4	8c ultra & blk	55.00	27.50
a.		8c ultramarine & gray	26.00	9.50
b.		8c ultramarine & gray brown	32.50	4.50
23	A4	10c violet & blk	135.00	57.50
a.		10c violet & gray	90.00	17.50
b.		10c purple & black	170.00	57.50
c.		10c purple & gray	97.50	18.50
d.		10c purple & gray brown	105.00	8.50
24	A4	20c black & gray vio	26.00	17.50
25	A4	50c brn org & black	195.00	155.00
a.		50c brown orange & gray	120.00	60.00
b.		50c brown orange & gray brown	110.00	60.00
		Nos. 18-25 (8)	465.25	284.70
		Set, ovpted. "SPECIMEN"	240.00	

1904-10 Wmk. 3 Sideways

26	A4	1c green & black	85.00	10.00
a.		1c green & gray brown	50.00	.85
27	A4	3c brown & gray	77.50	1.25
a.		3c brn & gray brn ('05)	55.00	2.10
b.		As "a," chalky paper ('05)	50.00	3.25
28	A4	4c rose & black	8.25	1.00
a.		Chalky paper	40.00	4.75
b.		4c scarlet & black	30.00	3.25
c.		4c scarlet & gray brown	52.50	4.00
d.		4c scarlet & gray	62.50	8.50
29	A4	5c scar & grn, *yel*	13.00	3.25
a.		Chalky paper	47.50	8.00
b.		5c carmine & deep green, *yel*	17.00	4.00
c.		5c car & dp grn, *org buff* ('21)	22.50	16.00
d.		5c car & dp grn, *pale yel* ('22)	15.00	12.50
30	A4	8c ultra & black ('05)	85.00	27.50
a.		8c ultra & gr brn ('05)	22.50	5.00
b.		As "a," chalky paper	87.50	17.50
c.		As "b," wmk upright ('07)	11.00	6.25
31	A4	10c violet & black	110.00	6.00
a.		10c claret & gray brown	90.00	11.00
b.		As "a," chalky paper ('05)	135.00	17.50
c.		10c claret & black	42.50	.75
d.		10c purple & gray brown ('05)	85.00	4.00
e.		10c purple & black	42.50	3.50
32	A4	20c blk & gray vio ('05)	24.00	1.50
a.		Chalky paper	18.00	3.50
33	A4	50c brn org & blk ('05)	125.00	30.00
a.		50c orange & gray ('05)	87.50	16.50
b.		50c org brn & gray brn ('06)	72.50	18.00
c.		As "b," chalky paper	67.50	9.00
d.		50c org brn & jet blk ('14)	165.00	35.00
e.		50c orange brown & gray	72.50	15.00

The 1c and 4c are on ordinary paper, the other values on both ordinary and chalky papers.

Chalky Paper

34	A3	$1 green & lt green ('07)	110.00	57.50
35	A3	$2 green & car rose ('06)	120.00	140.00
36	A3	$5 grn & ultra ('06)	325.00	*160.00*
		Revenue cancellation		25.00
37	A3	$25 grn & org ('10)	2,000.	900.00
		Revenue cancellation		75.00
		Nos. 26-36 (11)	1,083.	*438.00*

High values with revenue cancellations are plentiful and inexpensive.

1906-22 Ordinary Paper

Two dies for Nos. 38 and 44:
I — Thick line under "Malay."
II — Thin line under "Malay."

38	A4	1c dull grn, die II	16.00	.25
b.		Die I	27.50	.55
39	A4	1c brown ('19)	3.00	1.25
40	A4	2c green ('19)	2.50	.55
41	A4	3c brown	10.50	.25
42	A4	3c carmine ('09)	5.00	.25
43	A4	3c dp gray ('19)	2.50	.25
44	A4	4c scar, die II	2.25	.25
b.		Die I ('19)	3.75	5.50
45	A4	6c orange ('19)	3.25	*4.00*
46	A4	8c ultra ('09)	16.00	1.40
47	A4	10c ultra ('19)	9.00	2.25
48	A4	35c red, *yellow*	7.50	*17.50*
		Nos. 38-48 (11)	77.50	28.20
		Set, ovptd. "SPECIMEN"	650.00	

1922-32 Wmk. 4 Ordinary Paper

49	A4	1c brown ('22)	2.25	4.75
50	A4	1c black ('23)	.85	.25
51	A4	2c dk brown ('25)	14.00	*15.00*
52	A4	2c green ('26)	3.00	.25
53	A4	3c dp gray ('23)	2.50	*7.50*
54	A4	3c green ('24)	2.75	2.00
55	A4	3c brown ('27)	5.00	.50
56	A4	4c scar (II) ('23)	4.00	.60
57	A4	4c orange ('26)	1.50	.25
c.		Unwatermarked	*475.00*	*300.00*
58	A4	5c vio, *yel* ('22)	1.25	.25
59	A4	5c dk brown ('32)	3.50	.25
60	A4	6c orange ('22)	1.00	.55
61	A4	6c scarlet ('26)	1.50	.25
62	A4	10c ultra ('23)	1.75	*8.50*
63	A4	10c ultra & blk ('23)	2.50	.80
64	A4	10c vio, *yel*, chalky paper ('31)	6.00	.55
65	A4	12c ultra ('22)	1.75	.25

Chalky Paper

66	A4	20c blk & vio ('23)	5.00	2.75
a.		Ordinary paper	72.50	5.25
67	A4	25c red vio & ol vio ('29)	3.50	3.00
68	A4	30c yel & dl vio ('29)	4.00	*5.00*
69	A4	35c red, *yel*, ordinary paper ('28)	6.00	*27.50*
70	A4	35c dk vio & car ('31)	17.00	15.00
71	A4	50c org & blk ('24)	17.00	*20.00*
72	A4	50c blk, *bl grn* ('31)	5.50	2.50
73	A3	$1 gray grn & yel grn ('26)	24.00	*100.00*
a.		$1 green & blue green	24.00	*100.00*
74	A3	$2 grn & car ('26)	42.50	*95.00*
75	A3	$5 grn & ultra ('25)	210.00	*280.00*
76	A3	$25 grn & org ('28)	2,250.	*2,500.*
		Revenue cancel		175.00
		Nos. 49-75 (27)	389.60	*593.25*

1931-34

77	A4	$1 red & blk, *blue*	15.00	5.25
78	A4	$2 car & green, *yel* ('34)	6.50	50.00
79	A4	$5 car & green, *emer* ('34)	350.00	*280.00*
		Nos. 77-79 (3)	371.50	*335.25*
		Set (#49-79), ovptd. "SPECIMEN"	600.00	

POSTAGE DUE STAMPS

D1

Perf. 14½x14

1924-26 Typo. Wmk. 4

J1	D1	1c violet	4.75	*50.00*
J2	D1	2c black	2.25	8.75
J3	D1	4c green ('26)	3.25	*8.00*
J4	D1	8c red	6.00	*47.50*
J5	D1	10c orange	10.00	*17.50*
J6	D1	12c ultramarine	10.00	*27.50*
		Nos. J1-J6 (6)	36.25	*159.25*
		Set, ovptd. "SPECIMEN"	250.00	

The Malayan Postal Union (MPU), established in 1934, linked the postal services of the federated states and Straits Settlements. MPU postage due stamps for common use were issued using the D1 design. Stamps with this design continued to be issued well after the war and were only gradually replaced by postage due stamps issued by Singapore and Malaysia.

D2

1936-38 *Perf. 14½x14*

J7 D2 1c dk violet ('38) 17.50 1.10
J8 D2 4c yellow green 40.00 1.40
J9 D2 8c scarlet 20.00 5.00
J10 D2 10c yel orange 25.00 .50
J11 D2 12c blue violet 40.00 *17.50*
J12 D2 50c black ('38) 30.00 *8.00*
Nos. J7-J12 (6) 172.50 *33.50*

Nos. J7-J12 were also used in Straits Settlements.

For overprints see Nos. NJ1-NJ20, Malacca Nos. NJ1-NJ6.

1945-49

J13 D2 1c reddish violet 5.00 2.25
J14 D2 3c yel green 10.00 6.00
J15 D2 5c org scarlet 6.00 *3.50*
J16 D2 8c yel org ('49) 13.00 *16.00*
J17 D2 9c yel orange 40.00 *50.00*
J18 D2 15c blue vio 110.00 35.00
J19 D2 20c dk blue ('48) 10.00 *10.00*
Nos. J13-J19 (7) 194.00 *122.75*

For surcharge see No. J34.

Catalogue values for unused stamps in this section, from this point to the end of the section, are for Never Hinged items.

1951-54 **Wmk. 4** *Perf. 14*

J20 D2 1c dull violet ('52) .70 1.75
J21 D2 2c dk gray ('53) 1.25 2.25
J22 D2 3c green ('52) 37.50 20.00
J23 D2 4c dk brown ('53) .70 7.00
J24 D2 5c vermilion 50.00 13.00
J25 D2 8c yel orange 2.50 8.00
J26 D2 12c magenta ('54) 1.25 6.50
J27 D2 20c deep blue 8.00 6.75
Nos. J20-J27 (8) 101.90 65.25

Nos. J13-J27 were used throughout the Federation and in Singapore, later in Malaysia.

1957-63 **Ordinary Paper** *Perf. 12½*

J21a D2 2c ('60) 4.50 *24.00*
b. 2c, chalky paper ('62) 1.75 *16.00*
J23a D2 4c ('60) 3.50 *25.00*
b. 4c, chalky paper ('62) 1.00 *20.00*
J26a D2 12c, chalky paper ('62) 5.00 *32.50*
J27a D2 20c 8.00 *25.00*
b. 20c, chalky paper ('63) 10.00 *50.00*
Nos. J21a-J27a (4) 21.00 *106.50*

OCCUPATION STAMPS

Issued Under Japanese Occupation

Malayan Fruit and Fronds OS1

Tin Dredging OS2

Monument to Japanese War Dead — OS3

1943 **Unwmk.** **Litho.** *Perf. 12½*

N30 OS1 2c emerald 1.00 .25
a. Rouletted 2.25 2.25
b. Imperf., pair 6.50 6.50
N31 OS2 4c rose red 3.00 .25
a. Rouletted 2.25 2.25
b. Imperf., pair 6.50 6.50
N32 OS3 8c dull blue .50 .25
Nos. N30-N32 (3) 4.50 .75

Malayan Plowman — OS4

1943, Sept. 1

N33 OS4 8c violet 11.00 3.50
N34 OS4 15c carmine red 8.00 3.50

Publicity for Postal Savings which had reached a $10,000,000 total in Malaya.

Rubber Tapping OS5

Seaside Houses OS6

Japanese Shrine, Singapore OS7

Sago Palms OS8

Johore Bahru and Strait of Johore OS9

Malay Mosque, Kuala Lumpur OS10

1943, Oct. 1

N35 OS5 1c gray green 1.75 .70
N36 OS5 3c olive gray 1.00 .25
N37 OS6 10c red brown 1.25 .25
N38 OS7 15c violet 1.75 *5.00*
N39 OS8 30c olive green 1.50 .50
N40 OS9 50c blue 5.00 5.00
N41 OS10 70c dull blue 27.50 16.00
Nos. N35-N41 (7) 39.75 27.70

Rice Planting and Map of Malaysia — OS11

1944, Feb. 15

N42 OS11 8c carmine 17.50 4.00
N43 OS11 15c violet 5.00 4.00

Issued on the anniversary of the fall of Singapore to commemorate the "Birth of New Malaya".

OCCUPATION POSTAGE DUE STAMPS

Stamps and Type of Postage Due Stamps of 1936-38 Handstamped in Black, Red or Brown

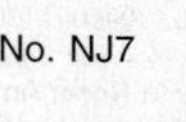

No. NJ7

1942 **Wmk. 4** *Perf. 14½x14*

NJ1 D2 1c violet 14.00 *35.00*
a. Brown overprint 190.00 *225.00*
b. Red overprint 200.00 250.00
NJ2 D2 3c yellow green 87.50 *97.50*
a. Red overprint 450.00 *475.00*
NJ3 D2 4c yellow green 95.00 60.00
a. Brown overprint 220.00 250.00
b. Red overprint 67.50 60.00
NJ4 D2 8c red 190.00 150.00
a. Brown overprint 375.00 375.00
b. Red overprint 275.00 175.00
NJ5 D2 10c yellow orange 40.00 *65.00*
a. Brown overprint 110.00 *140.00*
b. Red overprint 475.00 475.00
NJ6 D2 12c blue violet 27.50 *60.00*
a. Red overprint 475.00 460.00
NJ7 D2 50c black 82.50 *125.00*
a. Red overprint 750.00 *825.00*
Nos. NJ1-NJ7 (7) 536.50 592.50

Overprinted in Black

1942

NJ8 D2 1c violet 3.50 *10.50*
NJ9 D2 3c yel green 27.50 *35.00*
NJ10 D2 4c yel green 25.00 *12.50*
NJ11 D2 8c red 37.50 *27.50*
NJ12 D2 10c yel orange 2.00 *17.00*
NJ13 D2 12c blue violet 2.00 *50.00*
Nos. NJ8-NJ13 (6) 97.50 152.50

The 9c and 15c with this overprint were not regularly issued.

Postage Due Stamps of 1936-45 Overprinted

1943

NJ14 D2 1c reddish vio 2.25 *5.00*
NJ15 D2 3c yel green 2.25 *5.00*
NJ15A D2 4c yel green 70.00 52.50
NJ16 D2 5c scarlet 1.50 *5.00*
NJ17 D2 9c yel orange .90 *8.50*
NJ18 D2 10c yel orange 2.25 *9.00*
NJ19 D2 12c blue violet 2.25 *25.00*
NJ20 D2 15c blue violet 2.25 *10.00*
Nos. NJ14-NJ20 (8) 83.65 120.00

No. NJ15A is said to have been extensively forged.

ISSUED UNDER THAI OCCUPATION

For use in Kedah, Kelantan, Perlis and Trengganu

War Memorial — OS1

Perf. 12½

1943, Dec. **Unwmk.** **Litho.**

2N1 OS1 1c pale yellow 35.00 *37.50*
2N2 OS1 2c buff 14.00 *24.00*
a. Imperf., pair 1,100.
2N3 OS1 3c pale green 22.50 *45.00*
a. Imperf., pair
2N4 OS1 4c dull lilac 16.00 *32.50*
2N5 OS1 8c rose 16.00 *24.00*
2N6 OS1 15c lt blue 45.00 *72.50*
Nos. 2N1-2N6 (6) 148.50 *235.50*

Perf. 12½x11

2N2b OS1 2c buff 20.00 24.00
2N3b OS1 3c pale green 30.00 45.00
2N4b OS1 4c dull lilac 20.00 37.50
2N5b OS1 8c rose 20.00 24.00
2N6b OS1 15c lt blue 45.00 72.50
Nos. 2N2b-2N6b (5) 135.00 203.00

These stamps, in cent denominations, were for use only in the four Malayan states ceded to Thailand by the Japanese. The states reverted to British rule in September 1945.

JOHORE

jə-'hōr

LOCATION — At the extreme south of the Malay Peninsula. Linked to Singapore by a causeway.
AREA — 7,330 sq. mi.
POP. — 1,009,649 (1960)
CAPITAL — Johore Bahru

Stamps of the Straits Settlements Overprinted in Black

Overprinted

1876 **Wmk. 1** *Perf. 14*

1 A2 2c brown *21,500.* 7,000.
b. Double overprint —

Overprinted

Overprint 13 to 14mm Wide

1884-86 **Wmk. 2**

1A A2 2c rose 225.00 *225.00*
c. Double overprint 1,100.

No. 2d

Without Period

Overprint 16¾x2mm ("H" & "E" wide)

2 A2 2c rose 3,200. 800.
a. Double overprint 2,500.
b. "J" raised 3,200. 825.00
c. As "b," double overprint 5,500. 2,500.
d. "H" wide & "E" narrow, ovpt. 16mm 3,750. 1,100.
e. As "d," double overprint —
f. All ovpt. letters narrow *9,000.*

Overprinted

Overprint 11x2½mm

3 A2 2c rose ('86) 130.00 *140.00*

Overprinted

Overprint 17½x2¾mm

4 A2 2c rose ('85) *9,000.* —

Overprinted

Overprint 12½ to 15x2¾mm

5 A2 2c rose 25.00 *22.50*
a. "H" wide ('85) 120.00 110.00

Overprinted

Overprint 9x2½mm

7 A2 2c rose ('86) 80.00 65.00
a. Double overprint 850.00

Overprinted 

Overprint 9x3mm

8 A2 2c rose ('86) 72.50 67.50

Overprinted 

Overprint 14 to 15x3mm

9 A2 2c rose 25.00 12.50
a. 2c bright rose ('90) 22.50 *12.50*

Tall "J" 3½mm high

10 A2 2c rose 300.00 200.00
a. 2c bright rose ('90) 325.00 190.00

Overprinted 

1888 With Period

11 A2 2c rose 225.00 75.00
a. Tall "J" in "Johor" 1,275. 450.00
b. Double overprint 950.00

Overprinted 

Overprint 12½ to 13x2½mm

1890-91

12 A2 2c rose 27.50 27.00

Overprint 12x2¾mm

13 A2 2c rose ('91) *10,500.*

Surcharged in Black

a

b

c

d

1891

14 A3(a) 2c on 24c green 47.50 *62.50*
15 A3(b) 2c on 24c green 150.00 160.00
a. Thin, narrow "J" 625.00 625.00
16 A3(c) 2c on 24c green 30.00 45.00
a. "CENST" 1,000. 525.00
17 A3(d) 2c on 24c green 140.00 150.00
Nos. 14-17 (4) 367.50 417.50

Sultan Abubakar — A5

1891-94 Typo. Unwmk.

18 A5 1c lilac & vio ('94) 1.00 .60
19 A5 2c lilac & yellow .75 *1.75*
20 A5 3c lilac & car rose ('94) .75 .60
21 A5 4c lilac & black 3.25 *22.50*
22 A5 5c lilac & green 8.50 *22.50*
23 A5 6c lilac & blue 9.50 *22.50*
24 A5 $1 green & car rose 90.00 *190.00*
Nos. 18-24 (7) 113.75 *260.45*

For surcharges and overprints see Nos. 26-36.

Stamps of 1892-94 Surcharged in Black 

1894

26 A5 3c on 4c lilac & blk 3.00 .65
a. No period after "Cents" 125.00 85.00
27 A5 3c on 5c lilac & grn 2.40 4.25
a. No period after "Cents" 275.00 175.00
28 A5 3c on 6c lilac & bl 4.00 7.50
a. No period after "Cents" 210.00 240.00
29 A5 3c on $1 green & car 14.50 85.00
a. No period after "Cents" 500.00 900.00
Nos. 26-29 (4) 23.90 97.40

Coronation of Sultan Ibrahim
Stamps of 1892-94 Overprinted

Overprinted "KEMAHKOTAAN"

1896

30 A5 1c lilac & violet .60 1.25
31 A5 2c lilac & yellow .60 1.25
32 A5 3c lilac & car rose .65 1.25
33 A5 4c lilac & black 1.00 3.00
34 A5 5c lilac & green 6.00 8.00
35 A5 6c lilac & blue 4.00 *7.00*
36 A5 $1 green & car rose 70.00 135.00
Nos. 30-36 (7) 82.85 156.75

Overprinted "KETAHKOTAAN"

30a A5 1c 5.00 *6.00*
31a A5 2c 6.50 *8.50*
32a A5 3c 14.50 *20.00*
33a A5 4c 3.50 *21.00*
34a A5 5c 4.25 *8.50*
35a A5 6c 9.00 *20.00*
36a A5 $1 42.50 *190.00*
Nos. 30a-36a (7) 85.25 *274.00*

Sultan Ibrahim — A7

1896-99 Typo. Wmk. 71

37 A7 1c green 1.00 3.50
38 A7 2c green & blue .60 1.40
39 A7 3c green & vio 6.00 3.75
40 A7 4c green & car rose 1.25 3.75
41 A7 4c yel & red ('99) 1.75 2.50
42 A7 5c green & brn 2.40 5.00
43 A7 6c green & yel 2.40 7.50
44 A7 10c green & black 8.50 *55.00*
45 A7 25c green & vio 10.00 *50.00*
46 A7 50c grn & car rose 19.00 *52.50*
47 A7 $1 lilac & green 37.50 *85.00*
48 A7 $2 lilac & car rose 55.00 *100.00*
49 A7 $3 lilac & blue 50.00 *140.00*
50 A7 $4 lilac & brn 52.50 *100.00*
51 A7 $5 lilac & orange 100.00 *150.00*
Nos. 37-51 (15) 347.90 *759.90*

On Nos. 44-46 the numerals are on white tablets. Numerals of Nos. 48-51 are on tablets of solid color.

Stamps of 1896-1926 with revenue cancellations sell for a fraction of those used postally.

For surcharges see Nos. 52-58.

Nos. 40-41 Surcharged in Black 

1903

52 A7 3c on 4c yel & red .80 1.25
a. Without bars 4.00 *27.50*
53 A7 10c on 4c grn & car rose 3.00 14.50
a. Without bars 27.50 *85.00*

Bars on Nos. 52-53 were handruled with pen and ink.

Surcharged 

54 A7 50c on $3 lilac & blue 35.00 *87.50*

Surcharged

One Dollar

55 A7 $1 on $2 lilac & car rose 75.00 *140.00*
a. Inverted "e" in "one" 2,000.

Surcharged 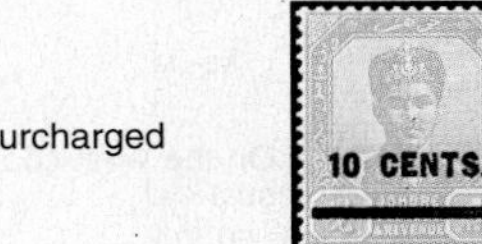

1904

56 A7 10c on 4c yel & red 25.00 42.50
a. Double surcharge *8,750.*
57 A7 10c on 4c grn & car rose 10.50 *72.50*
58 A7 50c on $5 lil & org 80.00 175.00
Nos. 56-58 (3) 115.50 290.00

Sultan Ibrahim — A8

The 10c, 21c, 25c, 50c, and $10 to $500 denominations of type A8 show the numerals on white tablets. The numerals of the 8c, 30c, 40c, and $2 to $5 demoninations are shown on tablets of solid colors.

1904-10 Typo. Wmk. 71
Ordinary Paper

59 A8 1c violet & green 2.00 .40
a. Chalky paper ('09) 18.00 12.50
60 A8 2c violet & brn org 3.00 4.25
a. Chalky paper ('10) 20.00 *22.50*
61 A8 3c violet & black 5.00 .60
62 A8 4c violet & red 9.25 4.50
63 A8 5c violet & ol grn 2.50 3.00
64 A8 8c violet & blue 4.25 *17.50*
65 A8 10c violet & black 52.50 11.50
a. Chalky paper ('10) 120.00 82.50
66 A8 25c violet & green 8.50 *42.50*
67 A8 50c violet & red 47.50 17.50
68 A8 $1 green & vio 19.00 *72.50*
69 A8 $2 green & car 32.50 *62.50*
70 A8 $3 green & blue 45.00 *87.50*
71 A8 $4 green & brn 45.00 *125.00*
72 A8 $5 green & org 65.00 *100.00*
73 A8 $10 green & blk 125.00 *210.00*
74 A8 $50 green & blue *425.00* *575.00*
75 A8 $100 green & scar *625.00* *1,000.*
Revenue cancel 60.00
Nos. 59-73 (15) 466.00 *759.25*

Nos. 74 and 75 were theoretically available for postage but were mostly used for revenue purposes.

For surcharge see No. 86.

1912-19 Wmk. 47 Chalky Paper

76 A8 1c violet & green 1.25 .25
77 A8 2c violet & orange 6.00 1.00
78 A8 3c violet & black 10.00 .70
79 A8 4c violet & red 30.00 1.00
80 A8 5c violet & ol grn 10.00 2.75
81 A8 8c violet & blue 4.50 *14.00*
82 A8 10c violet & black 60.00 3.00
83 A8 25c violet & green 27.50 *55.00*
84 A8 50c violet & red ('19) 77.50 *145.00*
85 A8 $1 green & vio ('18) 120.00 *120.00*
Nos. 76-85 (10) 346.75 *347.70*

No. 64 Surcharged 

1912 Wmk. 71

86 A8 3c on 8c vio & blue 15.00 *11.50*
a. "T" of "CENTS" omitted 1,750.

1918-20 Typo. Wmk. 3
Chalky Paper

87 A8 2c violet & orange 1.00 7.75
88 A8 2c violet & grn ('19) 1.00 5.50
89 A8 4c violet & red 1.75 .70
90 A8 5c vio & olive grn ('20) 2.00 15.00
91 A8 10c violet & blue 2.00 1.75
92 A8 21c violet & orange ('19) 3.00 3.25
93 A8 25c vio & grn ('20) 9.00 45.00
94 A8 50c vio & red ('19) 25.00 67.50
95 A8 $1 grn & red vio 15.00 77.50
96 A8 $2 green & scar 27.50 67.50
97 A8 $3 green & blue 75.00 145.00
98 A8 $4 green & brn 90.00 210.00
99 A8 $5 green & org 145.00 240.00
100 A8 $10 green & blk 450.00 625.00
Nos. 87-100 (14) 847.25 1,511.
Set, ovptd. "SPECIMEN" 750.00

1921-40 Wmk. 4

101 A8 1c violet & black .30 .25
102 A8 2c vio & brn ('24) 1.25 4.25
103 A8 2c green & dk grn ('28) .75 .40
104 A8 3c green ('25) 2.25 6.25
105 A8 3c dull vio & brn ('28) 1.40 1.50
106 A8 4c vio & red 2.50 .25
107 A8 5c vio & ol grn .50 .25
108 A8 6c vio & red brn .50 .50
109 A8 10c vio & blue 20.00 37.50
110 A8 10c vio & yel ('22) .50 .25
111 A8 12c vio & blue 1.25 1.60
111A A8 12c ultra ('40) 57.50 4.00
112 A8 21c dull vio & org ('28) 2.75 3.50
113 A8 25c vio & green 5.50 1.25
114 A8 30c dull vio & org ('36) 9.50 15.00
115 A8 40c dull vio & brn ('36) 10.50 15.00
116 A8 50c violet & red 3.75 1.60
117 A8 $1 grn & red vio 3.75 1.25
118 A8 $2 grn & red 10.00 5.00
119 A8 $3 grn & blue 85.00 105.00
120 A8 $4 grn & brn ('26) 110.00 190.00
121 A8 $5 grn & org 67.50 52.50
122 A8 $10 grn & blk 325.00 450.00
123 A8 $50 grn & ultra 1,450.
Revenue cancel 110.00
124 A8 $100 grn & red 2,000.
Revenue cancel 160.00
125 A8 $500 ultra & org brn ('26) *23,000.*
Revenue cancel 325.00
Nos. 101-122 (23) 721.95 *897.10*

Nos. 123, 124 and 125 were available for postage but were probably used only fiscally.

Sultan Ibrahim, Sultana — A9

1935, May 15 Engr. *Perf. 12½*

126 A9 8c grn & vio 6.75 3.50
Never hinged 10.00

Sultan Ibrahim — A10

1940, Feb. *Perf. 13½*

127 A10 8c blue & blk 26.00 1.35
Never hinged 40.00

Catalogue values for unused stamps in this section, from this point to the end of the section, are for Never Hinged items.

Silver Wedding Issue
Common Design Types
Inscribed: "Malaya Johore"
Perf. 14x14½

1948, Dec. 1 Wmk. 4 Photo.

128	CD304	10c purple	.25	.75

Perf. 11½x11
Engr.; Name Typo.

129	CD305	$5 green	29.00	52.50

Common Design Types
Pictured following the introduction.

Sultan Ibrahim — A11

1949-55 Wmk. 4 Typo. *Perf. 18*

130	A11	1c black	.75	.25
131	A11	2c orange	.40	.30
132	A11	3c green	2.50	1.10
133	A11	4c chocolate	2.00	.25
134	A11	5c rose vio ('52)	3.00	.30
135	A11	6c gray	2.00	.25
a.		Wmk. 4a (error)	3,250.	*2,150.*
136	A11	8c rose red	5.50	1.40
137	A11	8c green ('52)	10.00	2.25
138	A11	10c plum	1.50	.25
a.		Imperf., pair	*5,000.*	
139	A11	12c rose red ('52)	11.00	9.00
140	A11	15c ultra	5.00	.45
141	A11	20c dk grn & blk	3.75	1.25
142	A11	20c ultra ('52)	2.00	.30
143	A11	25c org & rose lil	4.00	.25
144	A11	30c plum & rose red ('55)	3.25	2.75
145	A11	35c dk vio & rose red ('52)	12.00	2.25
146	A11	40c dk vio & rose red	8.50	18.00
147	A11	50c ultra & blk	5.50	.30
148	A11	$1 vio brn & ultra	13.00	2.50
149	A11	$2 rose red & emer	32.50	13.50
150	A11	$5 choc & emer	52.50	17.50
		Nos. 130-150 (21)	180.65	74.40

UPU Issue
Common Design Types
Inscribed: "Malaya-Johore"
Engr.; Name Typo. on 15c, 25c
1949, Oct. 10 *Perf. 13½, 11x11½*

151	CD306	10c rose violet	.30	.40
152	CD307	15c indigo	2.00	1.25
153	CD308	25c orange	.80	3.50
154	CD309	50c slate	1.60	3.75
		Nos. 151-154 (4)	4.70	8.90

POSTAGE DUE STAMPS

D1

Perf. 12½
1938, Jan. 1 Typo. Wmk. 4

J1	D1	1c rose red	22.50	*50.00*
J2	D1	4c green	45.00	*45.00*
J3	D1	8c dull yellow	50.00	*160.00*
J4	D1	10c bister brown	50.00	*57.50*
J5	D1	12c rose violet	60.00	*140.00*
		Nos. J1-J5 (5)	227.50	*452.50*

OCCUPATION POSTAGE DUE STAMPS

Issued under Japanese Occupation

Johore Nos. J1-J5 Overprinted in Black, Brown or Red

1942 Wmk. 4 *Perf. 12½*

NJ1	D1	1c rose red	52.50	85.00
NJ2	D1	4c green	82.50	95.00
NJ3	D1	8c dull yellow	145.00	150.00
NJ4	D1	10c bister brown	52.50	72.50
NJ5	D1	12c rose violet	105.00	115.00
		Nos. NJ1-NJ5 (5)	437.50	517.50

Johore Nos. J1-J5 Overprinted in Black

1943

NJ6	D1	1c rose red	10.00	*35.00*
a.		Second character sideways	375.00	*825.00*
NJ7	D1	4c green	8.00	*40.00*
a.		Second character sideways	400.00	*825.00*
NJ8	D1	8c dull yellow	10.00	*42.50*
a.		Second character sideways	440.00	*850.00*
NJ9	D1	10c bister brown	9.50	*50.00*
a.		Second character sideways	450.00	*950.00*
NJ10	D1	12c rose violet	11.00	*70.00*
a.		Second character sideways	525.00	*1,150.*
		Nos. NJ6-NJ10 (5)	48.50	*237.50*

KEDAH

'ke-də

LOCATION — On the west coast of the Malay Peninsula.
AREA — 3,660 sq. mi.
POP. — 752,706 (1960)
CAPITAL — Alor Star

Sheaf of Rice — A1

Native Plowing — A2

Council Chamber — A3

1912-21 Engr. Wmk. 3 *Perf. 14*

1	A1	1c green & black	.70	.30
2	A1	1c brown ('19)	.75	.60
3	A1	2c green ('19)	.60	.35
4	A1	3c car & black	5.00	.35
5	A1	3c dk violet ('19)	.75	4.00
6	A1	4c slate & car	12.00	.30
7	A1	4c scarlet ('19)	5.50	1.00
8	A1	5c org brown & grn	2.75	*3.50*
9	A1	8c ultra & blk	4.25	*4.00*
10	A2	10c black brn & bl	2.75	1.25
11	A2	20c yel grn & blk	12.50	5.00
12	A2	21c red vio & vio ('19)	6.25	*70.00*
13	A2	25c red vio & bl ('21)	2.10	*37.50*
14	A2	30c car & black	3.50	*12.00*
15	A2	40c lilac & blk	4.00	*22.50*
16	A2	50c dull bl & brn	10.00	*14.00*
17	A3	$1 scar & blk, *yel*	17.50	*24.00*
18	A3	$2 dk brn & dk grn	25.00	*95.00*
19	A3	$3 dk bl & blk, *bl*	135.00	*190.00*
20	A3	$5 car & black	135.00	*200.00*
		Nos. 1-20 (20)	385.90	*685.65*
		Set, ovptd. "SPECIMEN"	550.00	

There are two types of No. 7, one printed from separate plates for frame and center, the other printed from a single plate.

Overprints are listed after No. 45.

Stamps of 1912 Surcharged

1919

21	A3	50c on $2 dk brn & dk grn	80.00	*90.00*
a.		"C" of ovpt. inserted by hand	1,450.	1,650.
22	A3	$1 on $3 dk bl & blk, *blue*	22.50	*110.00*

1921-36 Wmk. 4

Two types of 1c:

I — The 1's have rounded corners, small top serif. Small letters "c."

II — The 1's have square-cut corners, large top serif. Large letters "c."

Two types of 2c:

I — The 2's have oval drops. Letters "c" are fairly thick and rounded.

II — The 2's have round drops. Letters "c" thin and slightly larger.

23	A1	1c brown	1.50	.25
24	A1	1c blk (I) ('22)	1.00	.25
a.		1c black (II) ('39)	170.00	5.00
25	A1	2c green (I)	1.50	.25
a.		2c green (II) ('40)	350.00	8.00
26	A1	3c dk violet	1.00	.80
27	A1	3c green ('22)	2.75	1.00
28	A1	4c carmine	7.50	.25
29	A1	4c dull vio ('26)	1.50	.25
30	A1	5c yellow ('22)	3.00	.25
31	A1	6c scarlet ('26)	2.50	.80
32	A1	8c gray ('36)	22.50	.25
33	A2	10c blk brn & bl	3.25	1.00
34	A2	12c dk ultra & blk ('26)	10.00	5.00
35	A2	20c green & blk	8.00	3.00
36	A2	21c red vio & vio	3.25	*17.50*
37	A2	25c red vio & bl	3.25	*9.00*
38	A2	30c red & blk ('22)	4.00	*11.00*
39	A2	35c claret ('26)	22.50	*45.00*
40	A2	40c red vio & blk	8.00	*65.00*
41	A2	50c dp blue & brn	4.75	*27.50*
42	A3	$1 scar & blk, *yel* ('24)	80.00	85.00
43	A3	$2 brn & green	17.50	*125.00*
44	A3	$3 dk bl & blk, *bl*	80.00	*110.00*
45	A3	$5 car & black	115.00	*200.00*
		Nos. 23-45 (23)	404.25	*708.35*

For overprints see Nos. N1-N6.

Stamps of 1912-21 Overprinted in Black: "MALAYA-BORNEO EXHIBITION." in Three Lines

1922 Wmk. 3

3a	A1	2c green	5.00	*27.50*
12a	A2	21c red vio & vio	45.00	*95.00*
13a	A2	25c red vio & blue	47.50	*110.00*
b.		Inverted overprint	1,625.	
16a	A2	50c dull blue & brn	50.00	*125.00*

Wmk. 4

23a	A1	1c brown	7.50	*30.00*
26a	A1	3c dark violet	5.50	*50.00*
28a	A1	4c carmine	6.00	*25.00*
33a	A2	10c blk brn & blue	14.50	*50.00*
		Nos. 3a-33a (8)	181.00	*512.50*

Industrial fair at Singapore, Mar. 31-Apr. 15, 1922.

On Nos. 12a, 13a and 16a, "BORNEO" exists both 14mm and 15mm wide.

Sultan of Kedah, Sir Abdul Hamid Halim Shah — A4

1937, July Wmk. 4 *Perf. 12½*

46	A4	10c sepia & ultra	4.00	2.25
		Never hinged	8.00	
47	A4	12c gray vio & blk	42.50	*5.50*
		Never hinged	67.50	
48	A4	25c brn vio & ultra	10.00	*5.50*
		Never hinged	16.00	
49	A4	30c dp car & yel grn	10.00	*11.50*
		Never hinged	16.00	
50	A4	40c brn vio & blk	5.00	*16.00*
		Never hinged	8.00	
51	A4	50c dp blue & sepia	10.00	*5.50*
		Never hinged	16.00	
52	A4	$1 dk green & blk	4.00	*11.00*
		Never hinged	6.50	
53	A4	$2 dk brn & yel grn	90.00	*85.00*
		Never hinged	135.00	
54	A4	$5 dp car & black	27.50	*170.00*
		Never hinged	45.00	
		Nos. 46-54 (9)	203.00	*312.25*

For overprints see Nos. N7-N15.

Catalogue values for unused stamps in this section, from this point to the end of the section, are for Never Hinged items.

Silver Wedding Issue
Common Design Types
Inscribed: "Malaya Kedah"

1948, Dec. 1 Photo. *Perf. 14x14½*

55	CD304	10c purple	.25	.25

Perf. 11½x11
Engraved; Name Typographed

56	CD305	$5 rose car	35.00	50.00

UPU Issue
Common Design Types
Inscribed: "Malaya-Kedah"
Engr.; Name Typo. on 15c, 25c
1949, Oct. 10 *Perf. 13½, 11x11½*

57	CD306	10c rose violet	.25	1.25
58	CD307	15c indigo	2.25	1.75
59	CD308	25c orange	.80	3.00
60	CD309	50c slate	1.50	6.00
		Nos. 57-60 (4)	4.80	12.00

Sheaf of Rice A5

Sultan Tungku Badlishah A6

1950-55 Wmk. 4 Typo. *Perf. 18*

61	A5	1c black	.70	.30
62	A5	2c orange	.50	.25
63	A5	3c green	2.00	1.00
64	A5	4c chocolate	.75	.25
65	A5	5c rose vio ('52)	5.50	3.00
66	A5	6c gray	.70	.25
67	A5	8c rose red	3.75	*5.00*
68	A5	8c green ('52)	5.50	3.00
69	A5	10c plum	.70	.25
70	A5	12c rose red ('52)	5.50	3.00
71	A5	15c ultramarine	5.00	.70
72	A5	20c dk green & blk	5.00	3.00
73	A5	20c ultra ('52)	2.50	.35
74	A6	25c org & rose lilac	1.50	.50
75	A6	30c plum & rose red ('55)	6.00	1.50
76	A6	35c dk vio & rose red ('52)	6.25	2.00
77	A6	40c dk vio & rose red	7.50	*10.00*
78	A6	50c ultra & black	6.00	.35
79	A6	$1 vio brown & ultra	7.00	*8.00*
80	A6	$2 rose red & emer	30.00	*45.00*
81	A6	$5 choc & emerald	67.50	*90.00*
		Nos. 61-81 (21)	169.85	*177.70*

OCCUPATION STAMPS

Issued Under Japanese Occupation

Stamps of Kedah 1922-36, Overprinted in Red or Black

1942, May 13 Wmk. 4 *Perf. 14*

N1	A1	1c black (R)	9.50	15.00
N2	A1	2c green (R)	35.00	45.00
N3	A1	4c dull violet (R)	9.50	4.00
N4	A1	5c yellow (R)	5.50	7.50
a.		Black overprint	300.00	325.00
N5	A1	6c scarlet (Bk)	6.00	25.00
N6	A1	8c gray (R)	7.00	5.00

Nos. 46 to 54 Overprinted in Red

Perf. 12½

N7	A4	10c sepia & ultra	18.00	20.00
N8	A4	12c gray vio & blk	42.50	60.00
N9	A4	25c brn vio & ultra	16.00	27.50
a.		Black overprint	450.00	350.00
N10	A4	30c dp car & yel grn	75.00	85.00
N11	A4	40c brn vio & blk	42.50	50.00
N12	A4	50c dp blue & sep	42.50	50.00
N13	A4	$1 dk grn & blk	160.00	160.00
a.		Inverted overprint	875.00	1,000.
N14	A4	$2 dk brn & yel green	210.00	190.00

N15 A4 $5 dp car & blk 90.00 125.00
a. Black overprint 1,600. 1,400.
Nos. N1-N15 (15) 769.00 869.00

KELANTAN

kə-ˈlan-ˌtan

LOCATION — On the eastern coast of the Malay Peninsula.
AREA — 5,750 sq. mi.
POP. — 545,620 (1960)
CAPITAL — Kota Bharu

Symbols of Government — A1

1911-15 Typo. Wmk. 3 *Perf. 14*

Ordinary Paper

1 A1 1c gray green 8.00 1.25
a. 1c green 7.25 .35
2 A1 3c rose red 5.00 .25
3 A1 4c black & red 1.90 .25
4 A1 5c grn & red, *yel* 12.00 1.25
5 A1 8c ultramarine 6.25 1.25
6 A1 10c black & violet 35.00 .90

Chalky Paper

7 A1 30c violet & red 12.50 3.00
a. 30c purple & car 27.50 14.00
8 A1 50c black & org 10.00 3.00
9 A1 $1 green & emer 55.00 45.00
10 A1 $1 grn & brn ('15) 75.00 2.40
11 A1 $2 grn & car rose 1.90 *3.75*
12 A1 $5 green & ultra 4.75 4.00
13 A1 $25 green & org 55.00 *110.00*
Nos. 1-13 (13) 282.30 *176.30*
Set, ovptd. "SPECIMEN" 325.00

For overprints see listings after No. 26. For surcharges see Nos. N20-N22.

1921-28 Wmk. 4

Ordinary Paper

14 A1 1c green 5.00 .75
15 A1 1c black ('23) 1.00 .60
16 A1 2c brown 7.50 4.75
17 A1 2c green ('26) 5.50 .60
18 A1 3c brown ('27) 5.00 1.50
19 A1 4c black & red 3.50 .25
20 A1 5c grn & red, *yel* 1.75 .25
21 A1 6c claret 3.50 2.00
22 A1 6c rose red ('28) 5.00 5.00
23 A1 10c black & violet 3.00 .25

Chalky Paper

24 A1 30c dull vio & red ('26) 5.00 *6.00*
25 A1 50c black & orange 7.25 *52.50*
26 A1 $1 green & brown 35.00 *90.00*
Nos. 14-26 (13) 88.00 *164.45*

Stamps of 1911-21 Overprinted in Black in Three Lines

1922 Wmk. 3

3a A1 4c black & red 7.00 *50.00*
4a A1 5c green & red, *yel* 7.50 *50.00*
7a A1 30c violet & red 8.00 *80.00*
8a A1 50c black & orange 11.00 *90.00*
10a A1 $1 green & brown 35.00 *125.00*
11a A1 $2 green & car rose 95.00 *275.00*
12a A1 $5 green & ultra 275.00 *525.00*

Wmk. 4

14a A1 1c green 4.00 *55.00*
23a A1 10c black & violet 7.50 *75.00*
Nos. 3a-23a (9) 450.00 1,325.

Industrial fair at Singapore. Mar. 31-Apr. 15, 1922.

Sultan Ismail — A2

Size: 21½x30mm

1928-33 Engr. *Perf. 12*

27 A2 $1 ultramarine 17.50 *85.00*

Perf. 14

28 A2 $1 blue ('33) 75.00 *47.50*

Sultan Ismail — A2a

Size: 22½x34½mm

1937-40 *Perf. 12*

29 A2a 1c yel & ol green 1.75 .65
Never hinged 2.75
30 A2a 2c deep green 5.50 .25
Never hinged 8.50
31 A2a 4c brick red 5.50 1.00
Never hinged 8.50
32 A2a 5c red brown 3.00 .25
Never hinged 5.00
33 A2a 6c car lake 16.00 *12.50*
Never hinged 25.00
34 A2a 8c gray green 3.00 .25
Never hinged 5.00
35 A2a 10c dark violet 22.50 3.50
Never hinged 35.00
36 A2a 12c deep blue 5.50 *8.50*
Never hinged 8.50
37 A2a 25c vio & red org 6.00 *4.75*
Never hinged 9.00
38 A2a 30c scar & dk vio 40.00 27.50
Never hinged 60.00
39 A2a 40c blue grn & org 7.00 *45.00*
Never hinged 11.00
40 A2a 50c org & ol grn 55.00 10.00
Never hinged 85.00
41 A2a $1 dp grn & dk violet 40.00 16.00
Never hinged 60.00
42 A2a $2 red & red brn ('40) 250.00 *275.00*
Never hinged 375.00
43 A2a $5 rose lake & org ('40) 550.00 *950.00*
Never hinged 825.00
Nos. 29-43 (15) 1,011. *1,355.*

For overprints see Nos. N1-N19.

Catalogue values for unused stamps in this section, from this point to the end of the section, are for Never Hinged items.

Common Design Types pictured following the introduction.

Silver Wedding Issue

Common Design Types
Inscribed: "Malaya Kelantan"

Perf. 14x14½

1948, Dec. 1 Wmk. 4 Photo.

44 CD304 10c purple .75 *2.75*

Perf. 11½x11

Engraved; Name Typographed

45 CD305 $5 rose car 35.00 *60.00*

UPU Issue

Common Design Types
Inscribed: "Malaya-Kelantan"

Engr.; Name Typo. on 15c, 25c

1949, Oct. 10 *Perf. 13½, 11x11½*

46 CD306 10c rose violet .40 .40
47 CD307 15c indigo 2.25 2.75
48 CD308 25c orange .60 6.50
49 CD309 50c slate 1.00 3.00
Nos. 46-49 (4) 4.25 12.65

Sultan Ibrahim — A3

Perf. 18

1951, July 11 Wmk. 4 Typo.

50 A3 1c black .50 .40
51 A3 2c orange 1.20 .40
52 A3 3c green 6.75 1.75
53 A3 4c chocolate 2.00 .30
54 A3 6c gray .80 .30
55 A3 8c rose red 6.00 4.50
56 A3 10c plum .75 .30
57 A3 15c ultramarine 9.00 .80
58 A3 20c dk green & blk 7.50 15.00
59 A3 25c orange & plum 2.25 .80
60 A3 40c vio brn & rose red 17.50 27.50
61 A3 50c dp ultra & blk 8.00 .60
62 A3 $1 vio brown & ultra 10.00 16.50
63 A3 $2 rose red & emer 47.50 70.00
64 A3 $5 choc & emer 72.50 82.50

1952-55

65 A3 5c rose violet 1.50 .50
66 A3 8c green 7.50 2.25
67 A3 12c rose red 7.50 4.00
68 A3 20c ultramarine 2.00 .25
69 A3 30c plum & rose red ('55) 1.60 6.50
70 A3 35c dk vio & rose red 2.50 1.75
Nos. 50-70 (21) 214.85 236.90

Compare with Pahang A8, Perak A16, Selangor A15, Trengganu A5.

OCCUPATION STAMPS

Issued Under Japanese Occupation

Kelantan No. 35 Handstamped in Black

1942 Wmk. 4 *Perf. 12*

N1 A2a 10c dark violet 400.00 500.00

Some authorities believe No. N1 was not regularly issued.

Kelantan Nos. 29-40 Surcharged in Black or Red and Handstamped with Oval Seal "a" in Red

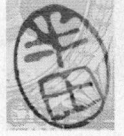

Sunakawa-a Handa-b

1942

N2 1c on 50c org & ol green 225.00 150.00
a. With "b" seal 160.00 200.00
N3 2c on 40c bl grn & orange 300.00 200.00
a. With "b" seal 160.00 200.00
N4 5c on 12c dp bl (R) 200.00 200.00
N5 8c on 5c red brn (R) 175.00 100.00
a. With "b" seal (R) 110.00 175.00
N6 10c on 6c car lake 475.00 500.00
a. With "b" seal 120.00 200.00
N7 12c on 8c gray green (R) 60.00 140.00
N8 30c on 4c brick red 2,500. 2,250.
N9 40c on 2c dp grn (R) 70.00 100.00
N10 50c on 1c yel & ol green 1,800. 1,500.

Kelantan Nos. 29-40, 19-20, 22 Surcharged in Black or Red and Handstamped with Oval Seal "b" in Red

N10A 1c on 50c org & ol green 350.00 200.00
N11 2c on 40c bl grn & orange 900.00 350.00
N11A 4c on 30c scar & dark vio 2,500. 1,400.
N12 5c on 12c dp bl (R) 350.00 200.00
N13 6c on 25c vio & red org 375.00 200.00
N14 8c on 5c red brown (R) 500.00 150.00
N15 10c on 6c car lake 100.00 125.00
N16 12c on 8c gray grn (R) 225.00 375.00
a. Seal omitted 70.00 120.00
N17 25c on 10c dk vio 1,600. 1,500.
N17A 30c on 4c brick red 2,500. 2,250.
N18 40c on 2c dp grn (R) 70.00 100.00
N19 50c on 1c yel & ol green 1,800. 1,500.

Perf. 14

N20 $1 on 4c blk & red (R) 60.00 85.00
N21 $2 on 5c grn & red, *yel* 60.00 85.00
N22 $5 on 6c rose red 60.00 85.00

Examples of Nos. N2-N22 without handstamped seal are from the remainder stocks sent to Singapore after Kelantan was ceded to Thailand. Some authorities believe stamps without seals were used before June 1942.

ISSUED UNDER THAI OCCUPATION

OS1

1943, Nov. 15 *Perf. 11*

2N1 OS1 1c violet & black *240.00 375.00*
2N2 OS1 2c violet & black *300.00 300.00*
a. Violet (arms) omitted *900.00*
2N3 OS1 4c violet & black *300.00 375.00*
a. Violet (arms) omitted *1,000.*
2N4 OS1 8c violet & black *300.00 300.00*
a. Violet (arms) omitted *700.00*
2N5 OS1 10c violet & black *450.00 550.00*
Nos. 2N1-2N5 (5) *1,590. 1,900.*

Stamps with centers in red are revenues.

MALACCA

mə-'la-kə

Melaka

LOCATION — On the west coast of the Malay peninsula.
AREA — 640 sq. mi.
POP. — 318,110 (1960)
CAPITAL — Malacca

Catalogue values for unused stamps in this section are for Never Hinged items.

Common Design Types pictured following the introduction.

Silver Wedding Issue

Common Design Types
Inscribed: "Malaya Malacca"

Perf. 14x14½

1948, Dec. 1 Wmk. 4 Photo.

1	CD304	10c purple	.40	*2.25*

Engraved; Name Typographed

Perf. 11½x11

2	CD305	$5 lt brown	35.00	*47.50*

Type of Straits Settlements, 1937-41, Inscribed "Malacca"

Perf. 18

1949, Mar. 1 Wmk. 4 Typo.

3	A29	1c black	.40	*.85*
4	A29	2c orange	1.00	.60
5	A29	3c green	.40	*2.25*
6	A29	4c chocolate	.40	.25
7	A29	6c gray	.90	*1.10*
8	A29	8c rose red	.90	*7.50*
9	A29	10c plum	.40	.25
10	A29	15c ultramarine	3.50	.85
11	A29	20c dk green & blk	.60	*7.00*
12	A29	25c org & rose lil	.60	.85
13	A29	40c dk vio & rose red	1.50	*13.00*
14	A29	50c ultra & black	1.50	1.50
15	A29	$1 vio brn & ultra	15.00	*26.00*
16	A29	$2 rose red & emer	27.50	27.50
17	A29	$5 choc & emer	60.00	50.00
		Nos. 3-17 (15)	114.60	*139.50*

See Nos. 22-26.

UPU Issue

Common Design Types
Inscribed: "Malaya-Malacca"

Engr.; Name Typo. on 15c, 25c

Perf. 13½, 11x11½

1949, Oct. 10 Wmk. 4

18	CD306	10c rose violet	.35	*.55*
19	CD307	15c indigo	2.40	*2.75*
20	CD308	25c orange	.50	*8.50*
21	CD309	50c slate	1.00	*5.50*
		Nos. 18-21 (4)	4.25	*17.30*

Type of Straits Settlements, 1937-41, Inscribed "Malacca"

1952, Sept. 1 Wmk. 4 *Perf. 18*

22	A29	5c rose violet	1.25	*1.75*
23	A29	8c green	6.00	*5.25*
24	A29	12c rose red	6.00	*9.50*
25	A29	20c ultramarine	7.50	3.00
26	A29	35c dk vio & rose red	6.00	*3.75*
		Nos. 22-26 (5)	26.75	*23.25*

OCCUPATION STAMPS

Issued Under Japanese Occupation

Stamps of Straits Settlements, 1937-41 Handstamped in Carmine

The handstamp covers four stamps. Values are for single stamps. Blocks of four showing complete handstamp sell for six times the price of singles.

1942 Wmk. 4 *Perf. 14*

N1	A29	1c black	125.00	90.00
N2	A29	2c brown orange	75.00	75.00
N3	A29	3c green	80.00	90.00
N4	A29	5c brown	175.00	175.00
N5	A29	8c gray	300.00	150.00
N6	A29	10c dull violet	125.00	125.00
N7	A29	12c ultramarine	140.00	140.00
N8	A29	15c ultramarine	100.00	125.00
N9	A29	30c org & vio	*3,500.*	—
N10	A29	40c dk vio & rose red	700.00	700.00
N11	A29	50c blk, *emerald*	1,100.	1,100.
N12	A29	$1 red & blk, *bl*	1,350.	1,250.
N13	A29	$2 rose red & gray grn	*3,500.*	—
N14	A29	$5 grn & red, *grn*	*3,500.*	—

Some authorities believe Nos. N9, N13, and N14 were not regularly issued.

OCCUPATION POSTAGE DUE STAMPS

Malaya Postage Due Stamps and Type of 1936-38, Handstamped Like Nos. N1-N14 in Carmine

1942 Wmk. 4 *Perf. 14½x14*

NJ1	D2	1c violet	*250.00*	*225.00*
NJ2	D2	4c yel green	*275.00*	*275.00*
NJ3	D2	8c red	*3,500.*	*2,250.*
NJ4	D2	10c yel orange	*550.00*	*525.00*
NJ5	D2	12c blue violet	*800.00*	*725.00*
NJ6	D2	50c black	*3,000.*	*2,000.*
		Nos. NJ1-NJ6 (6)	*8,375.*	*6,000.*

Pricing note above No. N1 also applies to Nos. NJ1-NJ6.

NEGRI SEMBILAN

'ne-grē səm-'bē-lən

LOCATION — South of Selangor on the west coast of the Malay Peninsula, bordering on Pahang on the east and Johore on the south.
AREA — 2,580 sq. mi.
POP. — 401,742 (1960)
CAPITAL — Seremban

Stamps of the Straits Settlements Overprinted in Black

1891 Wmk. 2 *Perf. 14*

Overprint 14½ to 15mm Wide

1	A2	2c rose	3.50	*16.50*

Tiger — A1

1891-94 Typo.

2	A1	1c green ('93)	4.00	1.25
3	A1	2c rose	4.00	*15.00*
4	A1	5c blue ('94)	35.00	*47.50*
		Nos. 2-4 (3)	43.00	*63.75*
		Set, ovptd. "SPECIMEN"	100.00	

Tiger Head — A2

1895-99

5	A2	1c lilac & green	25.00	11.50
6	A2	2c lilac & brown	42.50	*140.00*
7	A2	3c lilac & car rose	18.00	3.00
8	A2	5c lilac & olive	15.00	16.00
9	A2	8c lilac & blue	35.00	22.50
10	A2	10c lilac & orange	32.50	17.00
11	A2	15c green & vio	50.00	*90.00*
12	A2	20c grn & ol ('99)	80.00	*45.00*
13	A2	25c grn & car rose	85.00	*110.00*
14	A2	50c green & black	90.00	80.00
		Nos. 5-14 (10)	473.00	*535.00*
		Set, ovptd. "SPECIMEN"	275.00	

For surcharges see Nos. 15-16, 19-20; Federated Malay States Nos. 1-8.

Stamps of 1891-99 Surcharged

1899 Blue-green Surcharge

15	A2	4c on 8c lil & blue	13.50	5.00
	a.	Double surcharge	3,000.	2,500.
	b.	Pair, one without surcharge	10,000.	5,750.
	c.	Double surcharge, 1 green, 1 red	1,000.	1,100.

Black Surcharge

16	A2	4c on 8c lil & blue	1,400.	*1,500.*

Surcharge on No. 16 is thinner and sharper than on No. 15.

Same Surcharge and Bar in Black

17	A1	4c on 1c green	3.50	*25.00*
18	A1	4c on 5c blue	1.50	*17.00*
19	A2	4c on 3c lil & car rose	6.00	*27.50*
	a.	Double surcharge	2,750.	1,200.
	b.	Pair, one without surcharge	*15,000.*	*7,000.*
	c.	Bar omitted	1,000.	800.00
	d.	Bar double		925.00
	e.	"Four" double (at right)	4,250.	3,750.
	f.	"cents" double (at left)	4,250.	3,750.
	g.	Inverted surcharge	2,500.	1,650.
	h.	As "g," one surcharge albino	—	1,250.

Bar at bottom on Nos. 17-18, at top on No. 19.

No. 11 Surcharged in Black

1900

20	A2	1c on 15c grn & vio	125.00	*350.00*
	a.	Inverted period	500.00	*1,350.*
	b.	Double surcharge, one albino	*500.00*	

Arms of Negri Sembilan — A4

1935-41 Typo. Wmk. 4

21	A4	1c black ('36)	1.40	.25
22	A4	2c dp green ('36)	1.40	.25
22A	A4	2c brown org ('41)	4.00	*75.00*
22B	A4	3c green ('41)	40.00	*11.00*
23	A4	4c brown orange	2.00	.25
24	A4	5c chocolate	2.00	.25
25	A4	6c rose red	17.50	2.75
25A	A4	6c gray ('41)	5.00	*140.00*
26	A4	8c gray	2.00	.40
27	A4	10c dull vio ('36)	1.40	.25
28	A4	12c ultra ('36)	3.25	.75
28A	A4	15c ultra ('41)	11.00	*75.00*
29	A4	25c rose red & dull vio ('36)	2.00	1.00
30	A4	30c org & dull vio ('36)	3.50	2.50
31	A4	40c dull vio & car	3.50	*3.00*
32	A4	50c blk, *emer* ('36)	6.50	2.25
33	A4	$1 red & blk, *bl* ('36)	5.00	7.00
34	A4	$2 rose red & grn ('36)	60.00	22.50
35	A4	$5 brn red & grn, *emer* ('36)	40.00	*135.00*
		Nos. 21-35 (19)	211.45	*479.40*
		Set, never hinged	375.00	

For overprints see Nos. N1-N31.

Catalogue values for unused stamps in this section, from this point to the end of the section, are for Never Hinged items.

Common Design Types pictured following the introduction.

Silver Wedding Issue

Common Design Types
Inscribed: "Malaya Negri Sembilan"

1948, Dec. 1 Photo. *Perf. 14x14½*

36	CD304	10c purple	.60	.70

Perf. 11½x11

Engraved; Name Typographed

37	CD305	$5 green	27.50	37.50

Arms of Negri Sembilan — A5

1949-55 Wmk. 4 Typo. *Perf. 18*

38	A5	1c black	1.25	.25
39	A5	2c orange	1.00	.25
40	A5	3c green	.60	.45
41	A5	4c chocolate	.30	.25
42	A5	5c rose violet	1.00	.45
43	A5	6c gray	2.25	.25
44	A5	8c rose red	.80	.95
45	A5	8c green	5.50	2.25
46	A5	10c plum	.40	.25
47	A5	12c rose red	5.50	3.25
48	A5	15c ultramarine	4.25	.45
49	A5	20c dk green & blk	2.25	2.00
50	A5	20c ultramarine	2.00	.35
51	A5	25c org & rose lilac	1.00	.35
52	A5	30c plum & rose red ('55)	2.00	2.75
53	A5	35c dk vio & rose red	1.50	3.75
54	A5	40c dk vio & rose red	4.75	*6.00*
55	A5	50c ultra & black	5.00	.45
56	A5	$1 vio brn & ultra	6.00	2.25
57	A5	$2 rose red & emer	18.00	*27.50*
58	A5	$5 choc & emerald	60.00	75.00
		Nos. 38-58 (21)	125.35	129.45

UPU Issue

Common Design Types
Inscribed: "Malaya-Negri Sembilan"

Engr.; Name Typo. on 15c, 25c

1949, Oct. 10 *Perf. 13½, 11x11½*

59	CD306	10c rose violet	.25	.25
60	CD307	15c indigo	1.40	3.50
61	CD308	25c orange	.75	3.00
62	CD309	50c slate	1.10	4.00
		Nos. 59-62 (4)	3.50	10.75

OCCUPATION STAMPS

Issued under Japanese Occupation

Stamps and Type of Negri Sembilan, 1935-41, Handstamped in Red, Black, Brown or Violet

1942 Wmk. 4 *Perf. 14*

N1	A4	1c black	25.00	16.00
N2	A4	2c brown org	16.00	17.50
N3	A4	3c green	21.00	21.00
N4	A4	5c chocolate	29.00	27.50
N5	A4	6c rose red	600.00	600.00
N6	A4	6c gray	150.00	150.00
N7	A4	8c gray	87.50	87.50
N8	A4	8c rose red	55.00	47.50
N9	A4	10c dark violet	110.00	110.00
N10	A4	12c ultramarine	900.00	900.00
N11	A4	15c ultramarine	20.00	11.00
N12	A4	25c rose red & dk vio	35.00	40.00

N13	A4	30c org & dk vio	175.00	190.00
N14	A4	40c dk vio & car	750.00	750.00
N15	A4	$1 red & blk, *bl*	140.00	140.00
N16	A4	$5 brn red & grn, *emerald*	325.00	350.00

The 8c rose red is not known to have been issued without overprint.

Some authorities believe Nos. N5 and N7 were not regularly issued.

Stamps of Negri Sembilan, 1935-41, Overprinted in Black

N17	A4	1c black	1.40	1.40
a.		Inverted overprint	17.00	27.50
b.		Dbl. ovpt., one invtd.	47.50	*67.50*
N18	A4	2c brown orange	1.60	1.40
N19	A4	3c green	1.40	1.00
N20	A4	5c chocolate	.90	.90
N21	A4	6c gray	2.00	2.00
a.		Inverted overprint		*1,000.*
N22	A4	8c rose red	2.75	2.75
N23	A4	10c dk violet	5.50	5.50
N24	A4	15c ultramarine	8.00	4.75
N25	A4	25c rose red & dk vio	2.00	*6.75*
N26	A4	30c org & dk vio	4.00	*5.00*
N27	A4	$1 red & blk, *bl*	140.00	175.00
		Nos. N17-N27 (11)	169.55	206.45

The 8c rose red is not known to have been issued without overprint.

Negri Sembilan, Nos. 21, 24 and 29, Overprinted or Surcharged in Black

a

b

c

1943

N28	A4	1c black	.65	.65
a.		Inverted overprint	17.00	24.00
N29	A4	2c on 5c choc	.55	.65
N30	A4	6c on 5c choc	.65	.90
a.		"6 cts." inverted	350.00	*400.00*
N31	A4	25c rose red & dk violet	2.00	2.75
		Nos. N28-N31 (4)	3.85	4.95

The Japanese characters read: "Japanese Postal Service."

PAHANG

pə-'haŋ

LOCATION — On the east coast of the Malay Peninsula, bordering Johore on the south, Parak and Selangor on the west, and Trengganu on the north.

AREA — 13,820 sq. mi.

POP. — 338,210 (1960)

CAPITAL — Kuala Lipis

Stamps of the Straits Settlements Overprinted in Black

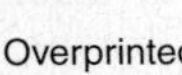
Overprinted

Overprint 16x2¾mm

1889 **Wmk. 2** ***Perf. 14***

1	A2	2c rose	165.00	60.00
2	A3	8c orange	1,800.	2,000.
3	A7	10c slate	225.00	300.00

Overprinted

Overprint 12½x2mm

4	A2	2c rose	15.00	*15.00*
a.		Antique letters	1,000.	
b.		2c pale rose	25.00	*30.00*

Overprinted

1890 **Overprint 15x2½mm**

5	A2	2c rose	12,750.	3,250.

Overprinted

Overprint 16x2¾mm

6	A2	2c rose	135.00	16.00

Surcharged in Black

a

b

c

d

1891

7	A3 (a)	2c on 24c green	1,200.	*1,300.*
8	A3 (b)	2c on 24c green	450.00	*475.00*
9	A3 (c)	2c on 24c green	275.00	*300.00*
10	A3 (d)	2c on 24c green	1,200.	*1,300.*
		Nos. 7-10 (4)	3,125.	3,375.

A5

1892-95 **Typo.**

11	A5	1c green	5.00	4.00
12	A5	2c rose	5.50	4.00
13	A5	5c blue	12.50	*47.50*
		Nos. 11-13 (3)	23.00	*55.50*
		Set, ovptd. "SPECIMEN"	95.00	

For surcharges see Nos. 21-22.

A6

1895-99

14	A6	3c lilac & car rose	10.75	3.75
14A	A6	4c lil & car rose ('99)	20.00	19.50
15	A6	5c lilac & olive	55.00	*25.00*
		Nos. 14-15 (3)	85.75	*48.25*
		Set of 3, ovptd. "SPECIMEN"	90.00	

For surcharge see No. 28.

Stamps of Perak, 1895-99, Overprinted

1898-99

16	A9	10c lilac & orange	27.50	*32.50*
17	A9	25c green & car rose	95.00	*190.00*
18	A9	50c green & black	500.00	*575.00*
18A	A9	50c lilac & black	300.00	425.00

Overprinted

Wmk. 1

19	A10	$1 green & lt grn	425.	700.
20	A10	$5 green & ultra	1,700.	3,250.
		Nos. 16-20 (6)	3,048.	5,173.

No. 13 Cut in Half Diagonally & Srchd. in Red & Initials "JFO" in ms.

1897, Aug. 2 **Wmk. 2**

Red Surcharge

21	A5	2c on half of 5c blue	*1,750.*	*450.*
a.		Black surcharge	*10,750.*	*3,500.*
b.		Bisected horizontally		*2,750.*
22	A5	3c on half of 5c blue	*1,750.*	*450.*
a.		Black surcharge	*10,750.*	*3,500.*
b.		Bisected horizontally	*7,000.*	*2,750.*
c.		Unsevered pair, #21, 22	*14,750.*	*4,800.*
d.		Se-tenant pair, #21, 22	*5,500.*	*1,200.*

Used at Kuala Lipis. No. 22c consists a complete, unsevered, stamp. No. 22d consists of halves of two separate stamps perfed between.

Perak No. 52 Surcharged

1898

25	A9	4c on 8c lilac & blue	4.50	6.50
a.		Double surcharge	875.00	
b.		Inverted surcharge	*3,250.*	1,500.

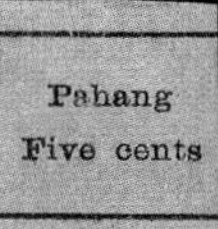

Surcharged on pieces of White Paper

1898 **Without Gum** ***Imperf.***

26		4c black		*5,250.*
27		5c black	*3,250.*	

Pahang No. 15 Surcharged

1899 ***Perf. 14***

28	A6	4c on 5c lilac & olive	25.00	*75.00*

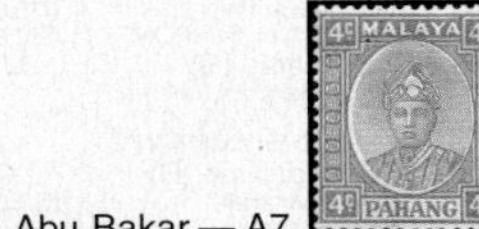

Sultan Abu Bakar — A7

1935-41 **Typo.** **Wmk. 4** ***Perf. 14***

29	A7	1c black ('36)	.25	.25
30	A7	2c dp green ('36)	1.40	.25
30A	A7	3c green ('41)	10.00	*19.00*
31	A7	4c brown orange	.70	.25
32	A7	5c chocolate	.70	.25
33	A7	6c rose red ('36)	12.00	*3.50*
34	A7	8c gray	2.00	.25
34A	A7	8c rose red ('41)	3.00	*60.00*
35	A7	10c dk violet ('36)	1.75	.25
36	A7	12c ultra ('36)	2.10	2.00
36A	A7	15c ultra ('41)	14.00	*65.00*
37	A7	25c rose red & pale vio ('36)	3.00	1.50
38	A7	30c org & dk vio ('36)	1.50	1.25
39	A7	40c dk vio & car	1.25	2.40
40	A7	50c black, *emer* ('36)	2.50	2.00
41	A7	$1 red & blk, *blue* ('36)	2.50	8.00
42	A7	$2 rose red & green ('36)	15.00	*50.00*
43	A7	$5 brn red & grn, *emer* ('36)	6.00	*87.50*
		Nos. 29-43 (18)	79.65	*303.65*

The 3c was printed on both ordinary and chalky paper; the 15c only on ordinary paper; other values only on chalky paper.

Values for Nos. 34A used and 36A used are for stamps with legible postmarks dated in 1941.

A 2c brown orange and 6c gray, type A7, exist, but are not known to have been regularly issued.

For overprints see Nos. N1-N21.

Catalogue values for unused stamps in this section, from this point to the end of the section, are for Never Hinged items.

Common Design Types pictured following the introduction.

Silver Wedding Issue

Common Design Types

Inscribed: "Malaya Pahang"

Perf. 14x14½

1948, Dec. 1 **Photo.** **Wmk. 4**

44	CD304	10c purple	.50	.55

Perf. 11½x11

Engraved; Name Typopgraphed

45	CD305	$5 green	27.50	37.50

UPU Issue

Common Design Types

Inscribed: "Malaya-Pahang"

Engr.; Name Typo. on 15c, 25c

1949, Oct. 10 ***Perf. 13½, 11x11½***

46	CD306	10c rose violet	.30	.25
47	CD307	15c indigo	1.10	1.50
48	CD308	25c orange	.60	*2.50*
49	CD309	50c slate	1.00	3.00
		Nos. 46-49 (4)	3.00	7.25

Sultan Abu Bakar — A8

Perf. 18

1950, June 1 **Wmk. 4** **Typo.**

50	A8	1c black	.30	.30
51	A8	2c orange	.30	.30
52	A8	3c green	.30	.80
53	A8	4c chocolate	2.25	.35
54	A8	6c gray	.50	.35
55	A8	8c rose red	.50	*2.00*
56	A8	10c plum	.30	.30
57	A8	15c ultramarine	.75	.35
58	A8	20c dk green & blk	1.00	*3.00*
59	A8	25c org & rose lilac	.50	.30
60	A8	40c dk vio & rose red	2.25	*8.50*
61	A8	50c dp ultra & black	1.50	.35
62	A8	$1 vio brn & ultra	3.50	3.50
63	A8	$2 rose red & emer	16.00	30.00
64	A8	$5 choc & emer	65.00	*90.00*

1952-55

65	A8	5c rose violet	.50	*.70*
66	A8	8c green	1.25	1.10
67	A8	12c rose red	1.50	1.25
68	A8	20c ultramarine	2.50	.30
69	A8	30c plum & rose red ('55)	2.75	.50
70	A8	35c dk vio & rose red	1.00	.35
		Nos. 50-70 (21)	104.45	*144.60*

OCCUPATION STAMPS

Issued under Japanese Occupation

Stamps of Pahang, 1935-41, Handstamped in Black, Red, Brown or Violet

1942 Wmk. 4 *Perf. 14*

N1 A7 1c black 60.00 55.00
N1A A7 3c green 625.00 350.00
N2 A7 5c chocolate 22.50 14.50
N3 A7 8c rose red 30.00 9.00
N3A A7 8c gray 1,650. 1,100.
N4 A7 10c dk violet 575.00 225.00
N5 A7 12c ultramarine 3,000. 2,900.
N6 A7 15c ultramarine 190.00 130.00
N7 A7 25c rose red & pale vio 29.00 30.00
N8 A7 30c org & dk vio 22.50 35.00
N9 A7 40c dk vio & car 32.50 40.00
N10 A7 50c blk, *emerald* 1,875. 1,900.
N11 A7 $1 red & blk, *bl* 350.00 350.00
N12 A7 $5 brown red & grn, *emer* 875.00 1,000.

Handstamped in Red

N1B A7 1c black 85.00 80.00
N1AB A7 3c green 240.00 300.00
N2B A7 5c chocolate 400.00 140.00
N3B A7 8c rose red 130.00 55.00
N4B A7 10c dark violet 400.00 275.00
N5B A7 12c ultramarine 1,275. 1,275.
N6B A7 15c ultramarine 525.00 275.00
N8B A7 30c org & dk violet 165.00 180.00
N9B A7 40c dk vio & carmine 110.00 11.00
N10B A7 50c black, *emerald* 2,150. 2,175.
N11B A7 $1 red & black, *blue* 185.00 190.00
N12B A7 $5 brn red & grn, *emerald* 1,500. 1,600.

Handstamped in Violet

N1C A7 1c black 450.00 300.00
N1AC A7 3c green 675.00 500.00
N2C A7 5c chocolate 550.00 300.00
N3C A7 8c rose red 110.00 70.00
N3AC A7 8c gray 1,675. 1,100.
N6C A7 15c ultramarine 875.00 550.00

Handstamped in Violet

N1D A7 1c black 350.00 275.00
N2D A7 5c chocolate 325.00 135.00
N3D A7 8c rose red 125.00 80.00
N4D A7 10c dark violet 450.00 300.00
N6D A7 15c ultramarine 750.00 375.00
N9D A7 40c dk vio & carmine 650.00 375.00
N11D A7 $1 red & black, *blue* 800.00 800.00

Some authorities claim the 2c green, 4c brown orange, 6c rose red and $2 rose red and green were not regularly issued with this overprint.

Stamps of Pahang, 1935-41, Overprinted in Black

N13 A7 1c black 3.50 5.00
N14 A7 5c chocolate 2.00 2.00
N15 A7 8c rose red 40.00 3.75
N16 A7 10c violet brown 20.00 11.00
N17 A7 12c ultramarine 4.75 27.50
N18 A7 25c rose red & pale vio 9.50 *42.50*
N19 A7 30c org & dk vio 4.00 *20.00*
Nos. N13-N19 (7) 83.75 *111.75*

Pahang No. 32 Overprinted and Surcharged in Black

e

f

1943

N20 A7(e) 6c on 5c chocolate 1.40 1.40
N21 A7(f) 6c on 5c chocolate 2.50 3.00

The Japanese characters read: "Japanese Postal Service."

PENANG

pə-naŋ

LOCATION — An island off the west coast of the Malay Peninsula, plus a coastal strip called Province Wellesley.
AREA — 400 sq. mi.
POP. — 616,254 (1960)
CAPITAL — Georgetown

Catalogue values for unused stamps in this section are for Never Hinged items.

Common Design Types pictured following the introduction.

Silver Wedding Issue

Common Design Types
Inscribed: "Malaya Penang"

Perf. 14x14½

1948, Dec. 1 Wmk. 4 Photo.

1 CD304 10c purple .50 .30

Perf. 11½x11

Engraved; Name Typographed

2 CD305 $5 lt brown 40.00 37.50

Type of Straits Settlements, 1937-41, Inscribed "Penang"

1949-52 *Perf. 18*

3 A29 1c black 1.50 .30
4 A29 2c orange 1.50 .30
5 A29 3c green .60 1.25
6 A29 4c chocolate .50 .25
7 A29 5c rose vio ('52) 4.25 4.00
8 A29 6c gray 1.50 .30
9 A29 8c rose red 1.25 *5.00*
10 A29 8c green ('52) 4.00 3.00
11 A29 10c plum .50 .25
12 A29 12c rose red ('52) 4.50 9.00
13 A29 15c ultramarine 2.00 .40
14 A29 20c dk grn & blk 2.75 1.50
15 A29 20c ultra ('52) 3.25 1.50
16 A29 25c org & rose lilac 3.00 1.25
17 A29 35c dk vio & rose red ('52) 3.25 1.50
18 A29 40c dk vio & rose red 4.25 *15.00*
19 A29 50c ultra & black 5.50 .30
20 A29 $1 vio brn & ultra 20.00 3.00
21 A29 $2 rose red & emer 26.00 2.50
22 A29 $5 choc & emer 52.50 3.75
Nos. 3-22 (20) 142.60 *54.35*

UPU Issue

Common Design Types
Inscribed: "Malaya-Penang"

Engr.; Name Typo. on 15c, 25c

1949, Oct. 10 *Perf. 13½, 11x11½*

23 CD306 10c rose violet .25 .25
24 CD307 15c indigo 2.50 *3.75*
25 CD308 25c orange .60 *3.75*
26 CD309 50c slate 1.75 *4.00*
Nos. 23-26 (4) 5.10 11.75

OCCUPATION STAMPS

Issued under Japanese Occupation

Stamps of Straits Settlements, 1937-41, Overprinted in Red or Black

1942 Wmk. 4 *Perf. 14*

N1 A29 1c black (R) 10.00 4.00
a. Inverted overprint 725.00 725.00
b. Double overprint 350.00 350.00
N2 A29 2c brown orange 12.00 5.25
a. Inverted overprint 180.00
b. Double overprint 675.00
c. "PE" for "PENANG" 150.00 110.00
N3 A29 3c green (R) 10.00 *10.00*
a. Double overprint, one inverted 475.00
N4 A29 5c brown (R) 4.75 10.00
a. Double overprint 675.00 525.00
b. "N PPON" for "NIPPON" 220.00
N5 A29 8c gray (R) 3.00 1.60
a. Double overprint, one inverted 625.00
b. "N PPON" for "NIPPON" 75.00 70.00
N6 A29 10c dull vio (R) 2.00 2.50
a. Double overprint 500.00 500.00
b. Double overprint, one inverted 450.00 450.00
N7 A29 12c ultra (R) 5.75 *25.00*
a. Double overprint 500.00
b. Double overprint, one inverted 750.00 725.00
c. "N PPON" for "NIPPON" 575.00
N8 A29 15c ultra (R) 2.00 5.00
a. Inverted overprint 450.00 450.00
b. Double overprint 675.00 675.00
c. "N PPON" for "NIPPON" 120.00 150.00
N9 A29 40c dk vio & rose red 9.00 *25.00*
N10 A29 50c black, *emer* (R) 5.25 *42.50*
N11 A29 $1 red & blk, *bl* 14.00 *55.00*
a. Inverted overprint *1,400.*
N12 A29 $2 rose red & gray grn 70.00 *120.00*
N13 A29 $5 grn & red, *grn* 900.00 950.00
Nos. N1-N13 (13) 1,048. 1,256.

Stamps of Straits Settlements Handstamped Okugawa Seal in Red

1942 Wmk. 4 *Perf. 14*

N14 A29 1c black 14.00 18.00
N15 A29 2c brown orange 27.50 30.00
N16 A29 3c green 23.00 30.00
N17 A29 5c brown 35.00 42.50
N18 A29 8c gray 42.50 55.00
N19 A29 10c dull violet 57.50 60.00
N20 A29 12c ultramarine 55.00 60.00
N21 A29 15c ultramarine 65.00 65.00
N22 A29 40c dk vio & rose red 125.00 130.00
N23 A29 50c blk, *emerald* 230.00 260.00
N24 A29 $1 red & blk, *bl* 325.00 350.00
N25 A29 $2 rose red & gray grn 1,000. 850.00
N26 A29 $5 grn & red, *grn* *3,500.* *1,800.*
Nos. N14-N26 (13) 5,500. 3,751.

Uchibori Seal Handstamped in Red

N14a A29 1c 215.00 180.00
N15a A29 2c 215.00 150.00
N16a A29 3c 130.00 130.00
N17a A29 5c *3,750.* *3,750.*
N18a A29 8c 130.00 130.00
N19a A29 10c 240.00 240.00
N20a A29 12c 150.00 165.00
N21a A29 15c 170.00 175.00
Nos. N14a-N21a (8) 5,000. 4,920.

PERAK

'per-ə-ˌak

LOCATION — On the west coast of the Malay Peninsula.
AREA — 7,980 sq. mi.
POP. — 1,327,120 (1960)
CAPITAL — Taiping

Straits Settlements No. 10 Handstamped in Black

1878 Wmk. 1 *Perf. 14*

1 A2 2c brown 2,250. 2,300.

Overprinted

Overprint 17x3½mm Wide

1880-81

2 A2 2c brown 50.00 *90.00*

Overprinted

Overprint 10 to 14½mm Wide

3 A2 2c brown, ovpt. 12-13.5mm ('81) 200.00 *200.00*
a. "R" narrow, "A" wide 215.00 *240.00*
b. "R" narrow, "A" narrow 350.00 *375.00*
c. "P" wide, "K" wide 1,150. 1,150.
d. 2c brown, ovpt. 10.25mm ('80) *2,100.* *950.00*
e. 2c brown, ovpt. 11mm ('80) *3,750.* *900.00*
f. 2c brown, ovpt. 14.5mm ('80) *4,400.* *1,500.*

Same Overprint on Straits Settlements Nos. 40, 41a

1883 Wmk. 2

4 A2 2c brown 26.50 *90.00*
a. Double overprint 750.00
5 A2 2c rose 50.00 *70.00*
a. "A" wide 52.50 *125.00*
b. "E" wide 50.00 *85.00*
c. Double overprint 775.00
d. As "b," double overprint 850.00

Overprinted

Overprint 14 to 15½mm Wide

6 A2 2c rose 5.50 4.00
a. Inverted overprint 475.00 600.00
b. Double overprint 700.00 700.00
c. "E" in overprint narrow 80.00 80.00
d. As "c," inverted overprint 1,800. *1,950.*
e. As "c," double overprint 1,250.

For surcharge, see No. 19E

Overprinted

Overprint 12¾ to 14mm Wide

1886-90

7 A2 2c rose 2.50 *8.00*
a. "FERAK" corrected by pen 450.00 *650.00*
b. 2c pale rose 165.00 45.00

Overprinted

Overprint 10x1¾mm

8 A2 2c rose 30.00 *62.50*

1891

Overprint 13mm long

9 A2 2c bright rose *3,900.*

Overprinted

Overprint 12-12½x2¾mm

10 A2 2c rose 15.50 *57.50*
a. Double overprint 1,650.

Overprinted

Overprint 10½-10¾x2½mm

11 A2 2c rose 225.00 *230.00*

Overprinted

Overprint 13x2¾mm

11A A2 2c rose 3,750.

Straits Settlements Nos. 11, 41a, 42 Surcharged in Black or Blue

q

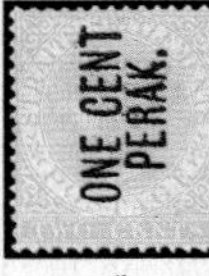

r

s

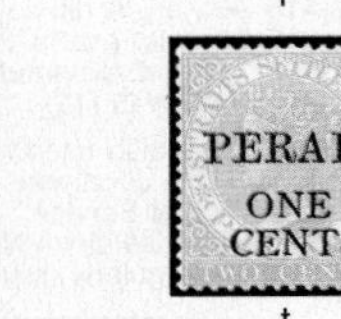

t

12 A2(q) 2c on 4c rose, as #3 ('83) 750.00 350.00
- *a.* 2c on 4c rose, as #5b ('83) 1,250. 525.00
- *b.* 2c on 4c rose, Sts. Setts. #42 (q) 5,000.
- *c.* 2c on 4c rose, Sts. Setts. #11 (q) 10,000.

13 A2(t) 1c on 2c rose 350.00 150.00
- *a.* Without period after "CENT" ('90) — 300.00

14 A2(r) 1c on 2c rose 75.00 92.50
- *a.* Without period after "PERAK" 850.00 850.00
- *b.* Double surcharge 1,250.
- *c.* Both "N"'s wide ('86) 135.00 *155.00*

15 A2(s) 1c on 2c rose (Bl) 75.00 85.00

15A A2(s) 1c on 2c rose (Bk) 2,150. 1,600.

In type "r" PERAK is 11½ to 14mm wide.

No. 12 was first overprinted with the type of No. 3 and then surcharged "TWO CENTS." No. 12a was first overprinted with the type of No. 5c and subsequently surcharged "TWO CENTS." Nos. 12b and 12c were surcharged and overprinted in one operation.

Nos. 13 and 13a were created in two operations, surcharging No. 6.

Nos. 14, 14a, 15 and 15A were overprinted in one operation.

Surcharged in Black

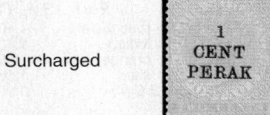

16 A2 1c on 2c rose 210.00 210.00
- *a.* Double surcharge *2,000.* 2,000.

Surcharged

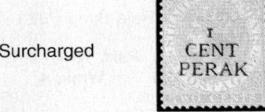

18 A2 1c on 2c rose *3,250.* *3,500.*
- *b.* Double surcharge, one inverted

Surcharged

18A A2 1c on 2c rose 1,750. 1,000.

Surcharged

19 A2 1c on 2c rose 4.25 *20.00*
- *a.* Double surcharge, one inverted
- *b.* Inverted surcharge
- *c.* "One" inverted *3,750.*
- *d.* Double surcharge *1,400.*

No. 6 surcharged "1 CENT" in Italic Serifed Capital Letters

1886

19E A2 1c on 2c rose *4,750.* *3,750.*

Straits Settlements No. 41a Surcharged

u

v

w

x

y

z

h

1889-90

20 A2(u) 1c on 2c rose 4.00 *10.00*
- *a.* Italic Roman "K" in "PERAK" 37.50 *57.50*
- *b.* Double surcharge *1,400.*
- *c.* 2c bright rose 3.25 3.75

21 A2(v) 1c on 2c rose 800.00 *975.00*

23 A2(w) 1c on 2c rose 27.50 *55.00*
- *a.* "PREAK" 900.00 *1,100.*
- *b.* 2c bright rose 27.50 *50.00*
- *c.* As "b," "PREAK" 950.00 *1,250.*

24 A2(x) 1c on 2c rose 150.00 *175.00*

25 A2(y) 1c on 2c rose 17.50 *27.50*
- *a.* 2c bright rose 7.50 *27.50*

26 A2(z) 1c on 2c rose 18.00 *27.50*
- *a.* 2c bright rose 5.50 *27.50*

27 A2(h) 1c on 2c rose 37.50 *57.50*
- *a.* 2c bright rose 20.00 *47.50*

Straits Settlements Nos. 41a, 48, 54 Surcharged in Black

a

b

c

d

e

f

g

1891 **Wmk. 2**

28 A2(a) 1c on 2c rose 2.75 15.00
- *a.* Bar omitted 215.00
- *b.* As #28, narrow "O" in "One" 40.00 *110.00*
- *c.* As #28a, narrow "O" in "One" 3,000.

29 A2(a) 1c on 6c violet 60.00 42.50

30 A3(b) 2c on 24c green 32.50 16.50

31 A2(c) 1c on 2c rose 9.75 52.50
- *a.* Bar omitted *1,000.*

32 A2(d) 1c on 2c rose 2.75 20.00
- *a.* Bar omitted 450.00

33 A2(d) 1c on 6c violet 110.00 95.00

34 A3(d) 2c on 24c green 85.00 42.50

35 A2(e) 1c on 2c rose 9.75 50.00
- *a.* Bar omitted *1,000.*

36 A2(e) 1c on 6c violet 210.00 210.00

37 A3(e) 2c on 24c green 140.00 80.00

38 A2(f) 1c on 6c violet 210.00 200.00

39 A3(f) 2c on 24c green 140.00 95.00

40 A2(g) 1c on 6c violet 210.00 200.00

41 A3(g) 2c on 24c green 140.00 95.00

Nos. 28-41 (14) 1,363. 1,214.

A7

1892-95 **Typo.** ***Perf. 14***

42 A7 1c green 2.40 .45

43 A7 2c rose 1.80 .45

44 A7 2c orange ('95) 1.10 *9.50*

45 A7 5c blue 3.50 8.00

Nos. 42-45 (4) 8.80 *18.40*

Set, ovptd. "SPECIMEN" 125.00

For overprint see No. O10.

Type of 1892 Surcharged in Black

1895

46 A7 3c on 5c rose 4.25 5.50
- Overprinted "SPECIMEN" 37.50

A9

A10

1895-99 **Wmk. 2** ***Perf. 14***

47 A9 1c lilac & green 3.25 .60

48 A9 2c lilac & brown 3.50 .60

49 A9 3c lilac & car rose 4.50 .60

50 A9 4c lil & car rose ('99) 20.00 7.50

51 A9 5c lilac & olive 12.00 .80

52 A9 8c lilac & blue 50.00 .75

53 A9 10c lilac & orange 17.00 .65

54 A9 25c grn & car rose ('96) 225.00 14.00

55 A9 50c lilac & black 52.50 52.50

56 A9 50c grn & blk ('99) 240.00 190.00

Wmk. 1

57 A10 $1 green & lt grn 325.00 225.00

58 A10 $2 grn & car rose ('96) 450.00 375.00

59 A10 $3 green & ol ('96) 650.00 575.00

60 A10 $5 green & ultra 675.00 625.00

61 A10 $25 grn & org ('96) 11,000. 4,500.
- Overprinted "SPECIMEN" 400.00

Nos. 47-57 (11) 952.75 493.00

Nos. 47-60 ovptd. "SPECIMEN" 500.00

For surcharges and overprint see Nos. 62-68, O11, Malaya Nos. 9-13A.

Stamps of 1895-99 Surcharged in Black

i

k

m

n

1900 **Wmk. 2**

62 A9(i) 1c on 2c lilac & brown 1.00 2.75

63 A9(k) 1c on 4c lilac & car rose 1.00 17.50
- *a.* Double surcharge 1,350.

64 A9(i) 1c on 5c lilac & ol 3.25 22.50

65 A9(i) 3c on 8c lilac & blue 13.50 19.00
- *a.* No period after "Cent" 225.00 *325.00*
- *b.* Double surcharge 550.00 625.00

66 A9(i) 3c on 50c green & black 6.00 12.50
- *a.* No period after "Cent" 150.00 *240.00*

Wmk. 1

67 A10(m) 3c on $1 grn & lt green 60.00 *160.00*
- *a.* Double surcharge 1,650.
- *b.* A10(n) Thin "t" in "Cent." 325.00 *550.00*
- *c.* As "b," double surcharge 3,000.

68 A10(m) 3c on $2 grn & car rose 52.50 *90.00*

Nos. 62-68 (7) 137.25 *324.25*

Antique "e" "one"

62c 1c on 2c lilac & brown 65.00 135.00

64c 1c on 5c black & olive 110.00 350.00

Antique "e" "Cent"

62d 1c on 2c lilac & brown 65.00 135.00

64d 1c on 5c black & olive 110.00 350.00

65d 3c on 8c lilac & blue 225.00 350.00

66d 3c on 50c green & black 225.00 350.00

Sultan Iskandar — A14

1935-37 **Typo.** **Wmk. 4**

Chalky Paper

69 A14 1c black ('36) 3.50 .25

70 A14 2c dp green ('36) 3.50 .25

71 A14 4c brown orange 3.50 .25

72 A14 5c chocolate .80 .25

73 A14 6c rose red ('37) 12.50 6.50

74 A14 8c gray 1.00 .25

75 A14 10c dk vio ('36) 1.00 .25

76 A14 12c ultra ('36) 4.75 1.00

77 A14 25c rose red & pale vio ('36) 3.50 1.00

78 A14 30c org & dark vio ('36) 5.00 1.50

79 A14 40c dk vio & car 8.00 8.00

80 A14 50c blk, *emer* ('36) 10.00 1.75

81 A14 $1 red & blk, *bl* ('36) 3.00 1.40

82 A14 $2 rose red & green ('36) 45.00 8.00

83 A14 $5 brn red & grn, *emer* ('36) 175.00 37.50

Nos. 69-83 (15) 280.05 68.15

Set, never hinged 200.00

Set, perf. "SPECIMEN" 500.00

Sultan Iskandar — A15

1938-41

84 A15 1c black ('39) 7.00 .25
Never hinged 20.00
85 A15 2c dp green ('39) 4.50 .25
Never hinged 15.00
85A A15 2c brn org, thin, striated paper ('41) 1.75 *25.00*
Never hinged 4.00
85B A15 3c green ('41) 1.50 18.00
Never hinged 3.50
a. Ordinary paper 5.50 10.50
Never hinged 8.50
86 A15 4c brn org ('39) 20.00 .25
Never hinged 45.00
87 A15 5c choc ('39) 3.50 .25
Never hinged 7.50
88 A15 6c rose red ('39) 14.00 .25
Never hinged 27.50
89 A15 8c gray 16.00 .25
Never hinged 40.00
89A A15 8c rose red, thin, striated paper ('41) .55 *95.00*
Never hinged 1.15
90 A15 10c dk violet 18.00 .25
Never hinged 40.00
91 A15 12c ultra, ordinary paper 13.00 2.00
Never hinged 32.50
91A A15 15c ultra ('41) 2.25 *20.00*
Never hinged 4.50
92 A15 25c rose red & pale vio ('39) 27.50 4.00
Never hinged 62.50
93 A15 30c org & dk vio, chalky paper 5.00 3.00
Never hinged 12.50
a. Thin striated paper ('40) 10.00 37.50
Never hinged 16.00
94 A15 40c dk vio & rose red 27.50 3.00
Never hinged 62.50
95 A15 50c blk, *emerald* 17.50 1.25
Never hinged 35.00
96 A15 $1 red & blk, *bl* ('40) 75.00 32.50
Never hinged 150.00
97 A15 $2 rose red & grn ('40) 100.00 85.00
Never hinged 260.00
98 A15 $5 red, *emer* ('40) 160.00 *525.00*
Never hinged 475.00
Nos. 84-98 (19) 514.55 *815.50*
Set, never hinged 1,325.
Set, perf. "SPECIMEN" 450.00
Never hinged 575.00

For overprints see Nos. N1-N40.

Catalogue values for unused stamps in this section, from this point to the end of the section, are for Never Hinged items.

Common Design Types pictured following the introduction.

Silver Wedding Issue
Common Design Types
Inscribed: "Malaya Perak"

1948, Dec. 1 Photo. *Perf. 14x14½*
99 CD304 10c purple .30 .25

Perf. 11½x11
Engraved; Name Typographed
100 CD305 $5 green 27.50 37.50

UPU Issue
Common Design Types
Inscribed: "Malaya-Perak"
Engr.; Name Typo. on 15c, 25c
Perf. 13½, 11x11½

1949, Oct. 10 Wmk. 4
101 CD306 10c rose violet .25 .25
102 CD307 15c indigo 1.50 2.00
103 CD308 25c orange .40 5.00
104 CD309 50c slate 1.50 3.50
Nos. 101-104 (4) 3.65 10.75

Sultan Yussuf Izuddin Shah — A16

1950, Aug. 17 Typo. *Perf. 18*
105 A16 1c black .25 .40
106 A16 2c orange .25 .40
107 A16 3c green 3.00 1.40
108 A16 4c chocolate .75 .40
109 A16 6c gray .40 .40
110 A16 8c rose red 1.60 2.25
111 A16 10c plum .25 .40
112 A16 15c ultramarine 1.10 .50
113 A16 20c dk grn & blk 1.60 .75
114 A16 25c org & plum .90 .30
115 A16 40c vio brn & rose red 5.00 7.00
116 A16 50c dp ultra & blk 5.00 .30
117 A16 $1 vio brn & ultra 7.00 1.10
118 A16 $2 rose red & emer 17.00 7.50
119 A16 $5 choc & emerald 42.50 22.50

1952-55
120 A16 5c rose violet .50 2.00
121 A16 8c green 1.40 1.25
122 A16 12c rose red 1.40 5.00
123 A16 20c ultramarine 1.10 .30
124 A16 30c plum & rose red ('55) 2.25 .30
125 A16 35c dk vio & rose red 1.40 .40
Nos. 105-125 (21) 94.65 54.85

OFFICIAL STAMPS

Stamps and Types of Straits Settlements Overprinted in Black

1890 Wmk. 1 *Perf. 14*
O1 A3 12c blue 325.00 400.00
O2 A3 24c green 775.00 *900.00*

Wmk. 2
O3 A2 2c rose 10.00 10.00
a. No period after "S" 100.00 125.00
b. Double overprint 1,100. 1,100.
O4 A2 4c brown 37.50 40.00
a. No period after "S" 210.00 *275.00*
O5 A2 6c violet 45.00 60.00
O6 A3 8c orange 55.00 67.50
O7 A7 10c slate 80.00 80.00
O8 A3 12c vio brown 275.00 350.00
O9 A3 24c green 225.00 *240.00*

Wide Spacing Between "G" and "S"
O1a A3 12c blue 1,100.
O2a A3 24c green 2,750.
O3c A2 2c rose 100.00 *125.00*
O4b A2 4c brown 175.00 *200.00*
O5a A2 6c violet 200.00 *240.00*
O6a A3 8c orange 210.00 *300.00*
O7a A7 10c slate 350.00 350.00
O8a A3 12c vio brown 1,050.
O9a A3 24c green 850.00

P.G.S. stands for Perak Government Service.

Perak No. 45 Overprinted

1894
O10 A7 5c blue 140.00 1.25
a. Inverted overprint 1,750. 525.00

Same Overprint on No. 51

1897
O11 A9 5c lilac & olive 3.50 .60
a. Double overprint 750.00 450.00

OCCUPATION STAMPS

Issued under Japanese Occupation

Stamps of Perak, 1938-41, Handstamped in Black, Red, Brown or Violet

1942 Wmk. 4 *Perf. 14*
N1 A15 1c black 75.00 50.00
N2 A15 2c brn orange 40.00 21.00
N3 A15 3c green 35.00 37.50
N4 A15 5c chocolate 12.50 11.00
N5 A15 8c gray 125.00 65.00
N6 A15 8c rose red 50.00 50.00
N7 A15 10c dk violet 27.50 27.50
N8 A15 12c ultramarine 300.00 275.00
N9 A15 15c ultramarine 25.00 35.00
N10 A15 25c rose red & pale vio 27.50 30.00
N11 A15 30c org & dk vio 35.00 40.00
N12 A15 40c dk vio & rose red 900.00 425.00
N13 A15 50c blk, *emer* 60.00 *60.00*
N14 A15 $1 red & blk, *bl* 675.00 450.00
N15 A15 $2 rose red & grn *5,750.* *6,000.*
N16 A15 $5 red, *emer* 650.00

Handstamped in Red
N2a A15 2c brn orange 90.00 40.00
N3a A15 3c green 425.00 275.00
N4a A15 5c chocolate 250.00 210.00
N5a A15 8c gray 675.00 275.00
N7a A15 10c dk violet 575.00 350.00
N9a A15 15c ultramarine 275.00 210.00
N10a A15 25c rose red & pale vio 450.00
N11a A15 30c org & dk vio 45.00 65.00
N13a A15 50c blk, *emerald* 65.00 67.50

Handstamped in Violet
N1b A15 1c black 450.00 175.00
N2b A15 2c brn orange 95.00 75.00
N3b A15 3c green 550.00 350.00
N4b A15 5c chocolate 375.00 225.00
N6b A15 8c rose red 750.00 375.00
N8b A15 12c ultramarine 900.00 375.00

Handstamped in Brown
N1c A15 1c black 135.00 120.00
N2c A15 2c brn orange 85.00 65.00
N3c A15 3c green 250.00 160.00
N4c A15 5c chocolate 60.00 40.00
N5c A15 8c gray 475.00 275.00
N9c A15 15c ultramarine 450.00 275.00
N11c A15 30c org & dk vio 1,250. 675.00
N12c A15 40c dk vio & rose red 675.00 450.00
N13c A15 50c blk, *emerald* 725.00 425.00
N14c A15 $1 red & blk, *bl* 475.00 450.00
N16c A15 $5 red, *emerald* 3,750.

Some authorities claim No. N6 was not regularly issued. This overprint also exists on No. 85

Stamps of Perak, 1938-41, Overprinted in Black

N16A A15 1c black *150.00*
N17 A15 2c brn org 4.50 4.50
a. Inverted overprint 75.00 75.00
N18 A15 3c green 1.50 1.60
a. Inverted overprint 27.50 *30.00*
N18B A15 5c chocolate *135.00*
N19 A15 8c rose red 1.50 .55
a. Inverted overprint 4.50 *10.00*
b. Dbl. ovpt., one invtd. 250.00 *275.00*
c. Pair, one without ovpt. 500.00
N20 A15 10c dk violet 22.50 9.50
N21 A15 15c ultramarine 16.00 6.00
N21A A15 30c org & dk vio *140.00*
N22 A15 50c blk, *emerald* 4.00 *8.00*
N23 A15 $1 red & blk, *bl* 625.00 *675.00*
N24 A15 $5 red, *emerald* 100.00 100.00
a. Inverted overprint 350.00 *425.00*

Some authorities claim Nos. N16A, N18B and N21A were not regularly issued.

Overprinted on Perak No. 87 and Surcharged in Black "2 Cents"
N25 A15 2c on 5c chocolate 2.00 5.00
a. Inverted "s" in "Cents" 75.00

Perak Nos. 84 and 89A Overprinted in Black

N26 A15 1c black 7.00 *11.00*
a. Inverted overprint 20.00 *47.50*
N27 A15 8c rose red 12.50 3.75
a. Inverted overprint 13.50 *27.50*

Overprinted on Perak No. 87 and Surcharged in Black "2 Cents"
N28 A15 2c on 5c chocolate 2.75 *6.50*
a. Inverted overprint 17.50 *50.00*
b. As "a," "2 Cents" omitted 52.50 *75.00*

Stamps of Perak, 1938-41, Overprinted or Surcharged in Black

n

No. N31

No. N32

1943
N29 A15 1c black 1.25 1.75
N30 A15 2c brn orange 35.00 35.00
N31 A15 2c on 5c choc 1.00 1.00
a. "2 Cents" inverted 35.00 40.00
b. Entire surcharge inverted 40.00 45.00
N32 A15 2c on 5c choc 1.40 1.40
a. Vertical characters invtd. 35.00 40.00
b. Entire surcharge inverted 35.00 40.00
N33 A15 3c green 37.50 37.50
N34 A15 5c chocolate 1.00 1.00
a. Inverted overprint 50.00 60.00
N35 A15 8c gray 35.00 35.00
N36 A15 8c rose red 1.25 3.50
a. Inverted overprint 35.00 40.00
N37 A15 10c dk violet 1.25 1.50
N38 A15 30c org & dk vio 5.50 10.00
N39 A15 50c blk, *emerald* 5.50 32.50
N40 A15 $5 red, *emerald* 90.00 175.00
Nos. N29-N40 (12) 215.65 335.15

No. N34 was also used in the Shan States of Burma. The Japanese characters read: "Japanese Postal Service."

Some authorities claim Nos. N30, N33 and N35 were not regularly issued.

PERLIS

'pər-ləs

LOCATION — On the west coast of the Malay peninsula, adjoining Siam and Kedah.
AREA — 310 sq. mi.
POP. — 97,645 (1960)
CAPITAL — Kangar

Catalogue values for unused stamps in this section are for Never Hinged items.

Common Design Types pictured following the introduction.

Silver Wedding Issue
Common Design Types
Inscribed: "Malaya Perlis"
Perf. 14x14½

1948, Dec. 1 Photo. Wmk. 4
1 CD304 10c purple 1.00 *3.00*

Engraved; Name Typographed
Perf. 11½x11
2 CD305 $5 lt brown 32.50 *55.00*

UPU Issue
Common Design Types
Inscribed: "Malaya-Perlis"
Engr.; Name Typo. on 15c, 25c

1949, Oct. 10 *Perf. 13½, 11x11½*
3 CD306 10c rose violet .40 *2.00*
4 CD307 15c indigo 1.40 *4.50*
5 CD308 25c orange .65 *3.50*
6 CD309 50c slate 1.50 *4.25*
Nos. 3-6 (4) 3.95 14.25

Raja Syed Putra — A1

Perf. 18

1951, Mar. 26 Wmk. 4 Typo.
7 A1 1c black .25 *1.00*
8 A1 2c orange .75 .70
9 A1 3c green 1.75 *5.25*
10 A1 4c chocolate 1.75 1.50
11 A1 6c gray 1.50 2.50
12 A1 8c rose red 3.75 7.50
13 A1 10c plum 1.25 .50
14 A1 15c ultramarine 5.00 8.50
15 A1 20c dk green & blk 4.50 11.50
16 A1 25c org & rose lilac 2.25 3.75
17 A1 40c dk vio & rose red 5.00 *29.00*
18 A1 50c ultra & black 4.75 *7.00*
19 A1 $1 vio brn & ultra 10.00 *27.50*
20 A1 $2 rose red & emer 20.00 *60.00*
21 A1 $5 choc & emerald 70.00 *125.00*

1952-55

22 A1 5c rose violet .75 *3.75*
23 A1 8c green 2.75 *4.50*
24 A1 12c rose red 2.00 *6.25*
25 A1 20c ultramarine 1.25 1.75
26 A1 30c plum & rose red ('55) 2.75 *15.00*
27 A1 35c dk vio & rose red 3.00 *8.50*
Nos. 7-27 (21) 145.00 *330.95*

SELANGOR

sə-ˈlaŋ-ər

LOCATION — South of Perak on the west coast of the Malay Peninsula.
AREA — 3,160 sq. mi.
POP. — 1,012,891 (1960)
CAPITAL — Kuala Lumpur

Stamps of the Straits Settlements Overprinted

Handstamped in Black or Red

1878 **Wmk. 1** ***Perf. 14***

1 A2 2c brown (Bk) —

Wmk. 2 ***Perf.***

2 A2 2c brown (R) 600.00

The authenticity of Nos. 1-2 is questioned.

Overprinted in Black

1882

3 A2 2c brown — 3,300.

Overprinted

Overprint 16 to 16¾mm Wide

1881 **Wmk. 1**

5 A2 2c brown 140.00 140.00
a. Double overprint
b. "S" inverted 675.00 *725.00*
c. "S" wide 225.00 *250.00*
d. "N" wide *9,000.* *2,750.*
e. "SE" and "AN" wide ('82) 275.00 *300.00*
f. "SEL" and "N" wide ('82) 275.00 *300.00*
g. "SELAN" wide ('82) 275.00 *300.00*

Overprint 16 to 17mm Wide

1882-83 **Wmk. 2**

"S" wide, all other letters narrow

6 A2 2c brown 200.00 160.00
a. All letters narrow 375.00 160.00
b. "SEL" and "NG" wide 325.00 *375.00*
c. "E" and "ANG" wide 325.00 *375.00*
d. "ELANG" wide 325.00 *375.00*
e. "S" and "L" wide *4,250.*
f. "S" and "A" wide 725.00 600.00
g. "E" wide 500.00 375.00
h. "EL" wide 500.00 375.00
i. "SE" and "N" wide 215.00 210.00
j. "S" and "N" wide 215.00 210.00
7 A2 2c rose 160.00 125.00
a. "N" wide 240.00 210.00
b. "S" and "L" wide 275.00 210.00
c. "E" wide 160.00 135.00
d. "EL" wide 140.00 115.00
e. As "d," double overprint 1,200.
f. As "d," triple overprint
g. "E" and "A" wide 160.00 125.00
h. "A" wide 500.00 215.00
i. "L" wide 600.00 275.00
j. All wide letters, "L" narrow 120.00 110.00
k. All wide letters, "A" narrow 230.00 195.00
l. All wide letters 575.00 275.00

Overprinted

Overprint 14¼x3mm

8 A2 2c rose 11.50 *24.00*
a. Double overprint 975.00 850.00

Overprinted

Overprint 14½ to 15½mm Wide

1886-89

9 A2 2c rose 42.50 *55.00*

Overprinted

Overprint 16½x1¾mm

9A A2 2c rose 67.50 72.50
b. Double overprint 1,000.

Overprinted

Overprint 15½ to 17mm Wide

With Period

10 A2 2c rose 140.00 90.00

Without Period

11 A2 2c rose 14.50 3.25

Same Overprint, but Vertically

12 A2 2c rose 22.50 *37.50*

Overprinted

12A A2 2c rose 150.00 3.75

Overprinted

Overprint 17mm Wide

13 A2 2c rose 1,700. *1,850.*

Overprinted

14 A2 2c rose 400.00 175.00

Overprinted Vertically

1889

15 A2 2c rose 725.00 40.00

Overprinted Vertically

Overprint 19 to 20¾mm Wide

16 A2 2c rose 325.00 95.00

Similar Overprint, but Diagonally

17 A2 2c rose 3,000.

Overprinted Vertically

18 A2 2c rose 90.00 6.75

Same Overprint Horizontally

18A A2 2c rose *4,500.*

Surcharged in Black

a

b

c

d

e

1891

19 A3 (a) 2c on 24c green 40.00 *75.00*
20 A3 (b) 2c on 24c green 225.00 *275.00*
21 A3 (c) 2c on 24c green 225.00 *250.00*
22 A3 (d) 2c on 24c green 125.00 *150.00*
a. Overprinted "SE-LANGCR"
23 A3 (e) 2c on 24c green 225.00 *275.00*
Nos. 19-23 (5) 840.00 1,025.

No. 22a occurred ijn the first printing in one position (R. 8/3) in the sheet.

A6

1891-95 **Typo.** **Wmk. 2**

24 A6 1c green 1.75 .30
25 A6 2c rose 4.00 1.25
26 A6 2c orange ('95) 3.00 1.00
27 A6 5c blue 27.50 5.25
Nos. 24-27 (4) 36.25 7.80
Set, ovptd. "SPECIMEN" 115.00

Type of 1891 Surcharged

1894

28 A6 3c on 5c rose 5.00 .70
Overprinted "SPECIMEN" in black 42.50

A8

A9

1895-99 **Wmk. 2** ***Perf. 14***

29 A8 3c lilac & car rose 7.00 .35
30 A8 5c lilac & olive 8.50 .35
31 A8 8c lilac & blue 55.00 8.50
32 A8 10c lilac & orange 13.50 2.50
33 A8 25c grn & car rose 90.00 60.00
34 A8 50c lilac & black 80.00 29.00
35 A8 50c green & black 475.00 140.00

Wmk. 1

36 A9 $1 green & lt grn 65.00 150.00
37 A9 $2 grn & car rose 250.00 300.00
38 A9 $3 green & olive 600.00 500.00
39 A9 $5 green & ultra 300.00 400.00
40 A9 $10 grn & brn vio 800.00 1,000.
Overprinted "SPECIMEN" 175.00
41 A9 $25 green & org 4,000. 4,000.
Overprinted "SPECIMEN" 325.00
Nos. 29-39, Ovpt. "SPECIMEN" 450.00

High values with revenue cancellations are plentiful and inexpensive.

Surcharged in Black

1900 **Wmk. 2**

42 A8 1c on 5c lilac & olive 75.00 *125.00*
43 A8 1c on 50c grn & blk 3.50 29.00
a. Surcharge reading "cent One cent." 3,500.
44 A8 3c on 50c grn & blk 6.00 *26.00*
a. Antique "t" in "Cents" 160.00 *250.00*
Nos. 42-44 (3) 84.50 *180.00*

Mosque at Klang
A12

Sultan Sulaiman
A13

1935-41 **Typo.** **Wmk. 4** ***Perf. 14***

45 A12 1c black ('36) .30 .25
46 A12 2c dp green ('36) .55 .25
46A A12 2c org brn ('41) 2.25 1.25
46B A12 3c green ('41) 1.25 *8.00*
47 A12 4c orange brown .30 .25
48 A12 5c chocolate .70 .25
49 A12 6c rose red ('37) 4.00 .25
50 A12 8c gray .35 .25
51 A12 10c dk violet ('36) .35 .25
52 A12 12c ultra ('36) .90 .25
52A A12 15c ultra ('41) 7.00 *35.00*
53 A12 25c rose red & pale vio ('36) .60 *.80*
54 A12 30c org & dk vio ('36) .60 *1.10*
55 A12 40c dk vio & car 1.50 1.25
56 A12 50c blk, *emer* ('36) 1.00 .50
57 A13 $1 red & black, *blue* ('36) 6.00 1.10
58 A13 $2 rose red & green ('36) 17.50 9.50
59 A13 $5 brn red & grn, *emer* ('36) 55.00 *30.00*
Nos. 45-59 (18) 100.15 *90.50*
Set, never hinged 170.00

Nos. 46A-46B were printed on both ordinary and chalky paper; 15c only on ordinary paper; other values only on chalky paper.

An 8c rose red was prepared but not issued.

For overprints see Nos. N1-N15, N18A-N24, N26-N39.

Sultan Hisam-ud-Din Alam Shah — A14

1941

72 A14 $1 red & blk, *blue* 11.50 7.00
73 A14 $2 car & green 30.00 *40.00*
Set, never hinged 70.00

A $5 stamp of type A14, issued during the Japanese occupation with different overprints (Nos. N18, N25A, N42), also exists without overprint. The unoverprinted stamp was not issued. Value $125.

For overprints see Nos. N16-N17, N24A, N25, N40-N41.

Catalogue values for unused stamps in this section, from this point to the end of the section, are for Never Hinged items.

Common Design Types pictured following the introduction.

Silver Wedding Issue
Common Design Types
Inscribed: "Malaya Selangor"

Perf. 14x14½

1948, Dec. 1 Photo. Wmk. 4

74 CD304 10c purple .25 *.30*

Perf. 11½x11

Engraved; Name Typographed

75 CD305 $5 green 30.00 25.00

UPU Issue
Common Design Types
Inscribed: "Malaya-Selangor"

Engr.; Name Typo. on Nos. 77 & 78

1949, Oct. 10 *Perf. 13½, 11x11½*

76 CD306 10c rose violet .40 .30
77 CD307 15c indigo 2.50 2.50
78 CD308 25c orange .50 *4.50*
79 CD309 50c slate 1.50 *5.00*
Nos. 76-79 (4) 4.90 12.30

Sultan Hisam-ud-Din Alam Shah — A15

1949, Sept. 12 Typo. *Perf. 18*

80 A15 1c black .25 .60
81 A15 2c orange .30 1.50
82 A15 3c green 4.00 2.00
83 A15 4c chocolate .50 .35
84 A15 6c gray .35 .35
85 A15 8c rose red 2.00 1.25
86 A15 10c plum .25 .25
87 A15 15c ultramarine 8.00 .35
88 A15 20c dk grn & black 5.00 .50
89 A15 25c orange & rose lil 2.00 .35
90 A15 40c dk vio & rose red 11.00 8.00
91 A15 50c ultra & black 3.50 .35
92 A15 $1 vio brn & ultra 4.00 .60
93 A15 $2 rose red & emer 15.00 1.10
94 A15 $5 choc & emerald 55.00 3.00

1952-55

95 A15 5c rose violet 1.00 2.75
96 A15 8c green 1.00 1.75
97 A15 12c rose red 1.25 3.50
98 A15 20c ultramarine 1.25 .35
99 A15 30c plum & rose red ('55) 2.25 2.25
100 A15 35c dk vio & rose red 1.50 1.50
Nos. 80-100 (21) 119.40 32.65

OCCUPATION STAMPS

Issued under Japanese Occupation

Stamps of Selangor 1935-41 Handstamped Vertically or Horizontally in Black, Red, Brown or Violet

1942, Apr. 3 Wmk. 4 *Perf. 14*

N1 A12 1c black 15.00 21.00
N2 A12 2c deep green 2,300. 1,500.
N3 A12 2c orange brown 55.00 55.00
N4 A12 3c green 35.00 17.00
N5 A12 5c chocolate 10.00 10.00
N6 A12 6c rose red 200.00 200.00
N7 A12 8c gray 27.50 27.50
N8 A12 10c dark violet 22.50 27.50
N9 A12 12c ultramarine 47.50 47.50
N10 A12 15c ultramarine 17.00 20.00
N11 A12 25c rose red & pale vio 80.00 95.00
N12 A12 30c org & dk vio 15.00 30.00
N13 A12 40c dk vio & car 100.00 140.00
N14 A12 50c blk, *emerald* 40.00 47.50
N15 A13 $5 brn red & grn, *emer* 275.00 275.00

Some authorities believe No. N15 was not issued regularly.

Handstamped Vertically on Stamps and Type of Selangor 1941 in Black or Red

N16 A14 $1 red & blk, *bl* 67.50 80.00
N17 A14 $2 car & green 80.00 110.00
N18 A14 $5 brn red & grn, *emer* 110.00 110.00

Stamps and Type of Selangor, 1935-41, Overprinted in Black

1942, May

N18A A12 1c black 110.00 110.00
N19 A12 3c green 1.00 1.00
N19A A12 5c chocolate 110.00 110.00
N20 A12 10c dark violet 35.00 35.00
N21 A12 12c ultramarine 2.75 5.00
N22 A12 15c ultramarine 5.50 4.00
N23 A12 30c org & dk vio 35.00 35.00
N24 A12 40c dk vio & car 4.00 4.00
N24A A14 $1 red & blk, *bl* 35.00 35.00
N25 A14 $2 car & green 24.00 30.00
N25A A14 $5 red & grn, *emer* 55.00 55.00
Nos. N18A-N25A (11) 417.25 424.00

Overprint is horizontal on $1, $2, $5.

On Nos. N18A and N19 the overprint is known reading up, instead of down.

Some authorities claim Nos. N18A, N19A, N20, N23, N24A and N25A were not regularly issued.

Selangor No. 46B Overprinted in Black

1942, Dec.

N26 A12 3c green 400.00 400.00

Stamps and Type of Selangor, 1935-41, Ovptd. or Srchd. in Black or Red

i

k

l

m

1943

N27 A12(i) 1c black 1.40 1.40
N28 A12(k) 1c black (R) .90 .90
N29 A12(l) 2c on 5c choc (R) .90 .90
N30 A12(i) 3c green 1.00 1.00
N31 A12(l) 3c on 5c choc .65 1.00
N32 A12(k) 5c choc (R) .65 1.00
N33 A12(l) 6c on 5c choc .25 *.90*
N34 A12(m) 6c on 5c choc .25 *1.00*
N35 A12(i) 12c ultra 1.40 1.60
N36 A12(i) 15c ultra 6.75 10.00
N37 A12(k) 15c ultra 13.50 13.50
N38 A12(m) $1 on 10c dk vio .50 *1.40*
N39 A12(m) $1.50 on 30c org & dk vio .50 *1.40*
N40 A14(i) $1 red & blk, *blue* 6.75 8.50
N41 A14(i) $2 car & grn 24.00 24.00
N42 A14(i) $5 brn red & grn, *emer* 50.00 55.00
Nos. N27-N42 (16) 109.40 123.50

The "i" overprint is vertical on Nos. N40-N42 and is also found reading in the opposite direction on Nos. N30, N35 and N36.

The overprint reads: "Japanese Postal Service."

Singapore is listed following Sierra Leone.

SUNGEI UJONG

ˈsuŋ̩ ü-juŋ

Formerly a nonfederated native state on the Malay Peninsula, which in 1895 was consolidated with the Federated State of Negri Sembilan.

Stamps of the Straits Settlements Overprinted in Black

Overprinted

1878 Wmk. 1 *Perf. 14*

2 A2 2c brown 3,600. 3,900.

Overprinted

4 A2 2c brown 400.00
a. "UJONG" printed twice *2,200.*
b. All letters narrow, evenly spaced 500.00
c. "S" wide, "UJ" close together 1,200.
d. Both "N"s wide 3,600. 3,000.
e. "N" of "SUNGEI" narrow, "N" of "UJONG" wide *5,500. 4,250.*
5 A2 4c rose *1,950.* 2,000.

No. 5 is no longer recognized by some experts.

All Letters Narrow, "UJ" Close Together "SUNGEI" 14mm, "UJONG" approx. 14mm

4F A2 2c brown 275.00
g. "N" and "E" of "SUNGEI" and "U" and "NG" of "UJONG" wide 425.00
h. "SUN" and "E" of "SUNGEI" and "U" and "NG" of "UJONG" wide 450.00
i. "SUN" of "SUNGEI" and "U" and "NG" of "UJONG" wide 425.00
j. "S" of "SUNGEI" wide 400.00
k. As "S" inverted *4,500.*

Overprinted

1882-83 Wmk. 2

6 A2 2c brown 375.00 —
7 A2 4c rose 4,250. 4,800.

This overprint on the 2c brown, wmk. 1, is probably a trial printing.

Overprinted

11 A2 2c brown 325.00 *400.00*

Overprinted

1881-84

14 A2 2c brown 1,200. 750.00
15 A2 2c rose 140.00 140.00
a. "Ujong" printed sideways
b. "Sungei" printed twice
16 A2 4c brown 325.00 425.00
17 A3 8c orange 2,250. 1,700.
18 A7 10c slate 725.00 625.00

Overprinted

19 A2 2c brown 57.50 *160.00*

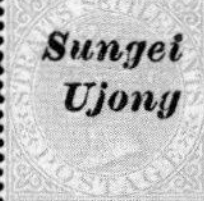

Overprinted

1885-90 Without Period

20 A2 2c rose 45.00 *77.50*

With Period

21 A2 2c rose 125.00 90.00
a. "UNJOG" 5,750. 4,000.

Overprinted

22 A2 2c rose 95.00 110.00
a. Double overprint 775.00 775.00

Overprinted

23 A2 2c rose 125.00 *150.00*

Overprinted

24 A2 2c rose 30.00 *47.50*
a. Double overprint

Overprinted

25 A2 2c rose 110.00 *125.00*

Overprinted

26 A2 2c rose 175.00 175.00
c. Double overprint

Overprint 14-16x3mm

26A A2 2c rose 12.00 16.00

Overprinted

26B A2 2c rose 50.00 21.00

Stamp of 1883-91 Surcharged

a

b

c

d

1891

27 A3 (a) 2c on 24c green 240. 275.
a. Antique "G" in "SUNGEI" 1,300.
b. Antique "G" in "UJONG" 1,300.
28 A3 (b) 2c on 24c green 1,100. *1,200.*
29 A3 (c) 2c on 24c green 425. *500.*
30 A3 (d) 2c on 24c green 1,100. *1,200.*
Nos. 27-30 (4) 2,865. 3,175.

On Nos. 27-28, SUNGEI is 14½mm, UJONG 12¾x2½mm.

A3

1891-94 Typo. *Perf. 14*

31 A3 2c rose 40.00 35.00
32 A3 2c orange ('94) 2.25 5.50
33 A3 5c blue ('93) 6.50 7.75
Nos. 31-33 (3) 48.75 48.25
Set, ovptd. "SPECIMEN" 77.50

Type of 1891 Surcharged in Black

1894

34 A3 1c on 5c green 1.40 .90
35 A3 3c on 5c rose 3.25 *6.00*

A4

1895

36 A4 3c lilac & car rose 15.00 4.75

Stamps of Sungei Ujong were superseded by those of Negri Sembilan in 1895.

TRENGGANU

treŋ'gä-ₒnü

LOCATION — On the eastern coast of the Malay Peninsula.
AREA — 5,050 sq. mi.
POP. — 302,171 (1960)
CAPITAL — Kuala Trengganu

Sultan Zenalabidin
A1 A2

1910-19 Typo. Wmk. 3 *Perf. 14*

Ordinary Paper

1 A1 1c gray green 3.25 1.50
a. 1c blue green 2.10 1.25
2 A1 2c red vio & brn ('15) 1.25 1.10
3 A1 3c rose red 2.75 2.75
4 A1 4c brn orange 4.25 *6.75*
5 A1 4c grn & org brn ('15) 2.50 *5.75*
6 A1 4c scarlet ('19) 1.50 *2.10*
7 A1 5c gray 1.75 *4.50*
8 A1 5c choc & gray ('15) 3.00 2.40
9 A1 8c ultramarine 1.75 11.00
10 A1 10c red & grn, *yel* ('15) 1.75 2.75

Chalky Paper

11 A1 10c violet, *yel* 5.75 15.00
a. 10c violet, *pale yel* 4.00 9.00
12 A1 20c red vio & vio 4.25 *5.75*
13 A1 25c dl vio & grn ('15) 9.75 *42.50*
14 A1 30c blk & dl vio ('15) 8.50 *65.00*
15 A1 50c blk & sep, *grn* 5.75 *11.50*
16 A1 $1 red & blk, *blue* 22.50 *29.00*
17 A1 $3 red & grn, *grn* ('15) 225.00 *500.00*
18 A2 $5 lil & blue grn 225.00 *675.00*
19 A2 $25 green & car 1,800. *2,750.*
Revenue Cancel 300.00
Overprinted "SPECIMEN" 290.00
Nos. 1-18 (18) 530.25 *1,384.*
Nos. 1a-19 (19) 2,330. 4,134.
Nos. 1-18 ovptd. "SPECIMEN" 725.00

On No. 19 the numerals and Arabic inscriptions at top, left and right are in color on a colorless background.

Overprints are listed after No. 41. For surcharges see Nos. B1-B4.

Sultan Badaru'l-alam
A3 A4

1921-38 Wmk. 4 *Perf. 14*

Chalky Paper

20 A3 1c black ('25) 2.75 1.75
21 A3 2c deep green 1.75 2.40
22 A3 3c dp grn ('25) 3.00 1.10
23 A3 3c lt brn ('38) 32.50 *22.50*
24 A3 4c rose red 2.40 2.00
25 A3 5c choc & gray 3.25 8.00
26 A3 5c vio, *yel* ('25) 2.75 2.00
27 A3 6c orange ('24) 6.00 .85
28 A3 8c gray ('38) 42.50 9.50
29 A3 10c ultramarine 3.25 1.50
30 A3 12c ultra ('25) 7.00 *7.25*
31 A3 20c org & dl vio 3.50 *2.40*
32 A3 25c dk vio & grn 3.75 *5.00*
33 A3 30c blk & dl vio 5.50 6.00
34 A3 35c red, *yel* ('25) 7.75 *12.50*
35 A3 50c car & green 11.50 5.25
36 A3 $1 ultra & vio, *bl* ('29) 15.00 6.00
37 A3 $3 red & green, *emer* ('25) 87.50 *240.00*
38 A4 $5 red & grn, *yel* ('38) 500.00 *2,800.*
39 A4 $25 blue & lil 750.00 *1,250.*
Overprinted "SPECIMEN" 160.00
40 A4 $50 org & green 1,850. *3,200.*
Overprinted "SPECIMEN" 350.00
41 A4 $100 red & green 6,500. *9,500.*
Overprinted "SPECIMEN" 625.00
Nos. 20-37 (18) 241.65 *336.00*
Nos. 20-38 ovptd. or perf "SPECIMEN" 800.00

On Nos. 39 to 41 the numerals and Arabic inscriptions at top, left and right are in color on a colorless background.

A 2c orange, 6c gray, 8c rose red and 15c ultramarine, type A3, exist, but are not known to have been regularly issued.

For surcharges and overprints see Nos. 45-46, N1-N60.

Stamps of 1910-21 Overprinted in Black

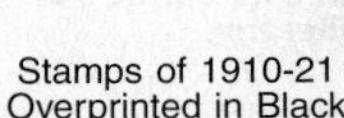

1922, Mar. Wmk. 3

8a A1 5c chocolate & gray 4.75 37.50
10a A1 10c red & green, yel 4.75 37.50
12a A1 20c red vio & violet 4.25 50.00
13a A1 25c dull vio & green 4.25 50.00
14a A1 30c black & dull vio 4.25 50.00
15a A1 50c blk & sepia, grn 4.25 50.00
16a A1 $1 red & blk, blue 20.00 95.00
17a A1 $3 red & grn, green 210.00 575.00
18a A2 $5 lil & blue green 300.00 575.00

Wmk. 4

21a A3 2c deep green 2.75 47.50
24a A3 4c rose red 7.75 47.50
Nos. 8a-24a (11) 567.00 *1,615.*

Industrial fair at Singapore, Mar. 31-Apr. 15.

1921 Wmk. 3 Chalky Paper

42 A3 $1 ultra & vio, *bl* 20.00 *40.00*
43 A3 $3 red & grn, *emer* 140.00 *160.00*
44 A4 $5 red & green, *yel* 140.00 *150.00*
Nos. 42-44 (3) 300.00 *350.00*

Types of 1921-25 Surcharged in Black

1941, May 1 Wmk. 4 *Perf. 13½x14*

45 A3 2c on 5c magenta, *yel* 5.50 *6.50*
46 A3 8c on 10c lt ultra 9.50 *6.50*

For overprints see Nos. N30-N33, N46-N47, N59-N60.

Catalogue values for unused stamps in this section, from this point to the end of the section, are for Never Hinged items.

Common Design Types pictured following the introduction.

Silver Wedding Issue

Common Design Types

Inscribed: "Malaya Trengganu"

1948, Dec. 1 Photo. *Perf. 14x14½*

47 CD304 10c purple .25 .25

Engraved; Name Typographed

Perf. 11½x11

48 CD305 $5 rose car 35.00 62.50

UPU Issue

Common Design Types

Inscribed: "Malaya-Trengganu"

Engr.; Name Typo. on 15c, 25c

Perf. 13½, 11x11½

1949, Oct. 10 Wmk. 4

49 CD306 10c rose violet .65 .65
50 CD307 15c indigo .80 2.10
51 CD308 25c orange 1.40 3.50
52 CD309 50c slate 2.10 3.50
Nos. 49-52 (4) 4.95 9.75

Sultan Ismail Nasiruddin Shah — A5

1949, Dec. 27 Typo. *Perf. 18*

53 A5 1c black .40 .45
54 A5 2c orange .40 .50
55 A5 3c green 1.25 1.50
56 A5 4c chocolate .60 .50
57 A5 6c gray 1.25 1.25
58 A5 8c rose red 1.60 1.90
59 A5 10c plum .60 .50
60 A5 15c ultramarine 1.75 1.60
61 A5 20c dk grn & black 2.40 5.00
62 A5 25c org & rose lilac 2.25 3.25
63 A5 40c dk vio & rose red 4.50 27.50
64 A5 50c dp ultra & black 2.75 2.75
65 A5 $1 vio brn & ultra 5.50 10.00
66 A5 $2 rose red & emer 30.00 24.50
67 A5 $5 choc & emerald 80.00 67.50

1952-55

68 A5 5c rose violet .40 .50
69 A5 8c green 1.60 3.25
70 A5 12c rose red 1.60 *6.75*
71 A5 20c ultramarine 1.60 1.50
72 A5 30c plum & rose red ('55) 3.00 6.75
73 A5 35c dk vio & rose red 3.50 6.75
Nos. 53-73 (21) 146.95 174.20

SEMI-POSTAL STAMPS

Nos. 3, 4 and 9 Surcharged

1917, Oct. Wmk. 3 *Perf. 14*

B1 A1 3c + 2c rose red 1.50 *8.00*
a. "CSOSS" 65.00 *100.00*
b. Comma after "2c" 4.00 *10.50*
c. Pair, one without surcharge 2,900. 2,900.
B2 A1 4c + 2c brn org 2.25 *12.50*
a. "CSOSS" 275.00 *275.00*
b. Comma after "2c" 16.00 *42.50*
B3 A1 8c + 2c ultra 3.50 *24.00*
a. "CSOSS" 175.00 *210.00*
b. Comma after "2c" 13.00 *45.00*
Nos. B1-B3 (3) 7.25 *44.50*

Same Surcharge on No. 5

1918

B4 A1 4c + 2c grn & org brn 4.25 *11.50*
a. Pair, one without surcharge *2,300.*

POSTAGE DUE STAMPS

D1

Perf. 14

1937, Aug. 10 Typo. Wmk. 4

J1 D1 1c rose red 8.25 *65.00*
Never hinged 11.50
J2 D1 4c green 9.00 *72.50*
Never hinged 11.50
J3 D1 8c lemon 47.50 *400.00*
Never hinged 67.50
J4 D1 10c light brown 92.50 *115.00*
Never hinged 125.00
Nos. J1-J4 (4) 157.25 *652.50*
Set, never hinged 275.00
Set, perf "SPECIMEN" 180.00

For overprints see Nos. NJ1-NJ4.

OCCUPATION STAMPS

Issued under Japanese Occupation

No. N6

No. N17A

Stamps of Trengganu, 1921-38, Handstamped in Black or Brown

1942 Wmk. 4 *Perf. 14*

N1 A3 1c black 110.00 110.00
N2 A3 2c deep green 190.00 275.00
N3 A3 3c lt brown 140.00 110.00
N4 A3 4c rose red 275.00 190.00
N5 A3 5c violet, *yel* 17.50 19.00
N6 A3 6c orange 13.50 20.00
N7 A3 8c gray 17.50 25.00
N8 A3 10c ultramarine 13.50 27.50
N9 A3 12c ultramarine 15.00 25.00
N10 A3 20c org & dl vio 15.00 22.50
N11 A3 25c dk vio & grn 13.50 27.50
N12 A3 30c blk & dl vio 13.50 25.00
N13 A3 35c red, *yel* 22.50 27.50
N14 A3 50c car & grn 125.00 95.00
N15 A3 $1 ultra & vio, *blue* 5,750. *5,750.*
N16 A3 $3 red & grn, *emerald* 125.00 140.00
N17 A4 $5 red & grn, *yellow* 240.00 240.00
N17A A4 $25 blue & lil 1,500.
N17B A4 $50 org & grn *8,800.*
N17C A4 $100 red & grn 950.00

Handstamped in Red

N18 A3 1c black 275.00 225.00
N19 A3 2c dp green 140.00 160.00
N20 A3 5c violet, *yel* 35.00 20.00
N21 A3 6c orange 20.00 20.00
N22 A3 8c gray 275.00 240.00
N23 A3 10c ultramarine 275.00 275.00

N24 A3 12c ultramarine 55.00 55.00
N25 A3 20c org & dl vio 35.00 35.00
N26 A3 25c dk vio & grn 40.00 40.00
N27 A3 30c blk & dl vio 35.00 35.00
N28 A3 35c red, *yellow* 35.00 20.00
N29 A3 $3 red & grn, *emerald* 100.00 40.00
N29A A3 $25 blue & lil 500.00 500.00

Handstamped on Nos. 45 and 46 in Black or Red

N30 A3 2c on 5c (Bk) 140.00 140.00
N31 A3 2c on 5c (R) 100.00 100.00
N32 A3 8c on 10c (Bk) 25.00 35.00
N33 A3 8c on 10c (R) 35.00 40.00

Stamps of Trengganu, 1921-38, Overprinted in Black

1942

N34 A3 1c black 15.00 17.00
N35 A3 2c deep green 100.00 *140.00*
N36 A3 3c light brown 16.00 29.00
N37 A3 4c rose red 15.00 20.00
N38 A3 5c violet, *yel* 10.00 20.00
N39 A3 6c orange 10.00 17.00
N40 A3 8c gray 67.50 20.00
N41 A3 12c ultramarine 10.00 13.50
N42 A3 20c org & dl vio 13.50 25.00
N43 A3 25c dk vio & grn 13.50 17.00
N44 A3 30c blk & dl vio 13.50 20.00
N45 A3 $3 red & grn, *emer* 100.00 140.00

Overprinted on Nos. 45 and 46 in Black

N46 A3 2c on 5c mag, *yel* 13.50 17.00
N47 A3 8c on 10c lt ultra 11.50 20.00
Nos. N34-N47 (14) 409.00 *515.50*

Stamps of Trengganu, 1921-38, Overprinted in Black

1943

N48 A3 1c black 13.50 19.00
N49 A3 2c deep green 13.50 27.50
N50 A3 5c violet, *yel* 11.50 27.50
N51 A3 6c orange 15.00 27.50
N52 A3 8c gray 95.00 67.50
N53 A3 10c ultramarine 100.00 175.00
N54 A3 12c ultramarine 19.00 *35.00*
N55 A3 20c org & dl vio 20.00 *35.00*
N56 A3 25c dl vio & grn 19.00 *35.00*
N57 A3 30c blk & dl vio 20.00 *35.00*
N58 A3 35c red, *yellow* 20.00 *40.00*

Overprinted on Nos. 45 and 46 in Black

N59 A3 2c on 5c mag, *yel* 11.00 *35.00*
N60 A3 8c on 10c lt ultra 27.50 *25.00*
Nos. N48-N60 (13) 385.00 *584.00*

The Japanese characters read: "Japanese Postal Service."

OCCUPATION POSTAGE DUE STAMPS

Trengganu Nos. J1-J4 Handstamped in Black or Brown

1942 **Wmk. 4** ***Perf. 14***

NJ1 D1 1c rose red 67.50 *95.00*
NJ2 D1 4c green 125.00 *125.00*
NJ3 D1 8c lemon 25.00 *67.50*
NJ4 D1 10c light brown 25.00 *50.00*
Nos. NJ1-NJ4 (4) 242.50 *337.50*

The handstamp reads: "Seal of Post Office of Malayan Military Department."

MALDIVE ISLANDS

'mol-,dīv 'ī-lǝnds

LOCATION — A group of 2,000 islands in the Indian Ocean about 400 miles southwest of Ceylon.
GOVT. — Republic
AREA — 115 sq. mi.
POP. — 168,000 (est. 1983)
CAPITAL — Male

Maldive Islands was a British Protectorate as a dependency of Ceylon.

100 Cents = 1 Rupee

Catalogue values for unused stamps in this country are for Never Hinged items, beginning with Scott 20.

Watermarks

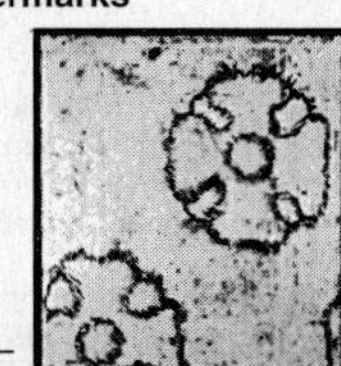

Wmk. 47 — Multiple Rosette

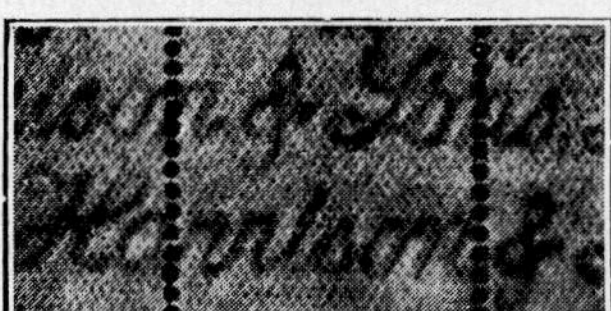

Wmk. 233 — "Harrison & Sons, London" in Script

Stamps of Ceylon, 1904-05, Overprinted

1906, Sept. 9 **Wmk. 3** ***Perf. 14***

1 A36 2c orange brown 17.50 *35.00*
2 A37 3c green 28.00 *40.00*
3 A37 4c yellow & blue 40.00 *62.50*
4 A38 5c dull lilac 4.00 *4.50*
5 A40 15c ultramarine 80.00 *125.00*
6 A40 25c bister 90.00 *160.00*
Nos. 1-6 (6) 259.50 *427.00*

Minaret of Juma Mosque, near Male — A1

1909 **Engr.** **Wmk. 47**

7 A1 2c orange brown 2.25 *4.50*
a. Perf 13½x14 2.50 .90
8 A1 3c green .50 .70
9 A1 5c red violet .50 .35
10 A1 10c carmine 7.50 .80
Nos. 7-10 (4) 10.75 6.35

Type of 1909 Issue Redrawn
Perf. 14½x14

1933 **Photo.** **Wmk. 233**

11 A1 2c gray 2.00 *1.90*
12 A1 3c yellow brown .55 *2.00*
13 A1 5c brown lake 42.50 7.50
14 A1 6c brown red 1.10 *4.25*
15 A1 10c green .65 .40
16 A1 15c gray black 6.50 *21.00*
17 A1 25c red brown 6.50 *21.00*
18 A1 50c red violet 6.50 *26.00*
19 A1 1r blue black 11.00 21.00
Nos. 11-19 (9) 77.30 105.05

On the 6c, 15c, 25c and 50c, the right hand panel carries only the word "CENTS."

Nos. 11-19 exist with watermark vert. or horiz. The 5c with vert. watermark sells for twice the price of the horiz. watermark.

Catalogue values for unused stamps in this section, from this point to the end of the section, are for Never Hinged items.

Palm Tree and Seascape — A2

Unwmk.

1950, Dec. 24 **Engr.** ***Perf. 13***

20 A2 2 l olive green 4.50 *5.50*
21 A2 3 l deep blue 17.00 3.00
22 A2 5 l dp blue green 17.00 3.00
23 A2 6 l red brown 1.25 1.75
24 A2 10 l red 1.25 1.00
25 A2 15 l orange 1.25 1.00
26 A2 25 l rose violet 1.25 *4.00*
27 A2 50 l violet blue 1.50 *6.00*
28 A2 1r dark brown 14.00 *40.00*
Nos. 20-28 (9) 59.00 65.25

Maldive Fish — A3

1952

29 A3 3 l shown 1.75 .75
30 A3 5 l Urns .90 2.00

MALTA

'mol-tǝ

LOCATION — A group of islands in the Mediterranean Sea off the coast of Sicily
GOVT. — Republic within the British Commonwealth
AREA — 122 sq. mi.
POP. — 329,189 (1983)
CAPITAL — Valletta

The former colony includes the islands of Malta, Gozo, and Comino.

4 Farthings = 1 Penny
12 Pence = 1 Shilling
20 Shillings = 1 Pound

Catalogue values for unused stamps in this country are for Never Hinged items, beginning with Scott 206 in the regular postage section.

FORERUNNERS

Values are for clear cancellations on sound, fault-free stamps, with average to fine centering. In many cases, very fine copies are rare or non-existent.

STAMPS OF GREAT BRITAIN USED IN MALTA

Canceled with seven-line wavy obliterator

1855-56

A1 1p red brown, Die I (#8) 950.00
A2 1p red brown, Die II (#12) 925.00
A3 1p red brown, Die II (#14) 950.00
A4 1p red brown, Die II (#16) 925.00
A5 2p blue (#17) —
A6 6p red violet (#7) *4,750.*
A7 1sh green (#5) *5,250.*

Canceled with oval barred "M" obliterator

1857-59

A8 1p red brown (#3) *2,500.*
A9 1p red brown, Die I (#8) 175.00
A10 1p red brown, Die II (#9) 1,050.
A11 1p red brown, Die II (#12) 265.00
A12 1p red brown, Die II (#16) 87.50
A13 1p rose red (#20) 24.00
A14 2p blue (#4) *4,000.*
A15 2p blue (#10) 875.00
A16 2p blue (#17) 70.00
A17 2p blue (#19) 350.00
A18 2p blue, Plate 7 (#29) 67.50
Plate 8 57.50
Plate 9 47.50
A19 4p rose (#26) 50.00
a. Thick glazed paper (#26b) 240.00
A20 6p red violet (#7) *4,250.*
A21 6p lilac (#27) 60.00
a. Thick paper (#27d) 250.00
b. Bluish paper (#27c) 1,000.
A22 1sh green (#28) 140.00
a. Thick paper (#28d) 210.00

Canceled "A25" in barred oval

No. A77

1860-84

A23 ½p rose red, plates 4-6, 8-15, 19 (#58), *value from* 32.50
A24 1p red brown (#3) *3,250.*
A25 1p red brown, Die I (#8) 375.00
A26 1p red brown, Die I (#16) 87.50
A27 1p rose red (#20) 9.00
A28 1p rose red, (#33), plates 71-74, 76, 78-125, 127, 129-224 *value from* 19.00
A29 1½p lake red, plates 1, 3 (#32), *value from* 600.00
A30 2p blue (#4) *4,750.*
A31 2p blue (#17) 82.50
A32 2p blue, plates 7, 8, 9, 12 (#29), *value from* 19.00
A33 2p blue, plates 13, 14, 15 (#30), *value from* 19.00
A34 2½p claret, plates 1, 2, 3 (#66), *value from* 37.50
a. Bluish paper, plates 1, 2 (#66a), *value from* 82.50
b. Lettered "LH-FL" (#66b) *3,500.*
A35 2½p claret, plates 3-17 (#67), *value from* 19.00
A36 2½p blue plates 17-20 (#68), *value from* 22.50
A37 2½p blue plates 21-23 (#82), *value from* 12.50
A38 3p rose (#37) 140.00
A39 3p rose (#44) 87.50
A40 3p rose, plates 4-10 (#49), *value from* 30.00
A41 3p rose, plates 11-20 (#61), *value from* 37.50
A42 3p rose, plates 20, 21 (#83), *value from* 1,050.
A43 3p on 3d violet (#94) 550.00
A44 4p rose (#26) 45.00
a. Thick glazed paper (#26b) 175.00
A45 4p vermilion, plate 3 (#34) 45.00
a. Hair lines (#34c) 55.00
A46 4p vermilion, plates 7-14 (#43), *value from* 27.50
A47 4p vermilion, plate 15 (#69) 225.00
A48 4p pale olive green, plate 15 (#70) 175.00
Plate 16 (#70) 175.00
A49 4p gray brown, plate 17 (#71) 240.00
A50 4p gray brown, plates 17, 18 (#84), *value from* 57.50
A51 6p red violet (#7) *3,750.*
A52 6p lilac (#27) 55.00
a. Thick paper (#27d) —
A53 6p lilac, plate 3 (#39) 45.00
a. Hairlines, plate 4 (#39d) 100.00
A54 6p lilac (#45) 45.00
Plate 6 (#45) 100.00
a. Wmk. 3 (#45c) *1,400.*
Plate 6 (#45c) —
A55 6p dull violet, plate 6 (#50) 50.00
A56 6p violet, plates 6, 8, 9 (#51) 40.00

A57 6p brown plate 11 (#59), *value from* 37.50
a. 6p pale buff, plate 11 (#59b) 120.00
Plate 12 (#59b) 140.00
A58 6p gray, plate 12 (#60) 140.00
A59 6p gray, plates 13-17 (#62), *value from* 37.50
A60 6p gray, plates 17, 18 (#86), *value from* 80.00
A61 6p on 6p violet (#95) 150.00
A62 8p orange (#73) 475.00
A63 9p straw (#40) 700.00
a. 9p bister (#40a) 650.00
A64 9p straw (#46) 650.00
A65 9p bister (#52) 825.00
A66 10p red brown (#53) 190.00
A67 1sh green (#5) *4,000.*
A68 1sh green (#28) 160.00
a. Thick paper (#28d) 325.00
A69 1sh green (#42) 95.00
A70 1sh green (#48) 95.00
A71 1sh green, plates 4-7 (#54), *value from* 32.50
A72 1sh green, plates 8-13 (#64), *value from* 47.50
A73 1sh salmon, plate 13 (#65) 300.00
A74 1sh salmon, plates 13, 14 (#87), *value from* 90.00
A75 2sh blue (#55) 165.00
A76 2sh brown (#56) *3,250.*
A77 5sh rose, plate 1 (#57) 475.00
Plate 2 (#57) 575.00
A78 5sh rose, *bluish* (#90) *2,500.*
a. White paper (#90a) *1,900.*
A79 10sh gray green (#74) *3,500.*

1880

A80 ½p deep green (#78) 16.00
a. ½p green (#78c) 16.00
A81 1p red brown (#79) 15.00
A82 1½p red brown (#80) 500.00
A83 2p lilac rose (#81) 45.00
a. 2p deep lilac rose (#81a) 45.00
A84 5p indigo (#85) 77.50

1881

A85 1p lilac, 14 dots (#88) 35.00
A86 1p lilac, 16 dots (#89) 10.00

1883-84

A87 ½p slate blue (#98) 19.00
A88 1½p lilac (#99) —
A89 2p lilac (#100) 110.00
A90 2½p lilac (#101) 14.00
A91 3p lilac (#102) —
A92 4p dull green (#103) 190.00
A93 5p dull green (#104) 165.00
A94 6p dull green (#105) —
A95 9p dull green (#106) —
A96 1sh dull green (#107) 400.00
A97 5sh rose, white paper (#108) 1,150.
a. Bluish paper (#108a) *2,000.*

Postal Fiscal stamps of Great Britain are found used in Malta. They are rare.

STAMPS OF FRANCE USED IN MALTA

1853-60

A98 5c green (#13) —
On cover —
A99 10c bister (#14) 125.00
On cover *1,400.*
A100 20c blue (#15) 115.00
On cover *1,300.*
A101 40c orange (#18) 92.50
On cover *1,050.*
A102 80c lake, *yellowish* (#19) 145.00
On cover *1,650.*
A103 80c rose, *pinkish* (#20) 145.00
On cover *1,650.*

1862-67

A104 5c green (#23) 57.50
On cover *1,250.*
A105 10c bister (#25) 37.50
On cover *975.00*
A106 20c blue (#26) 92.50
On cover *1,175.*
A107 40c orange (#27) 100.00
On cover *1,300.*
A108 80c rose, *pinkish* (#28) 150.00
On cover *1,550.*
a. 80c carmine rose (#28b) 175.00
On cover *1,600.*

1863-70

A109 10c bister (#32) 80.00
On cover *1,500.*
A110 20c blue (#33) 57.50
On cover *1,350.*
A111 30c brown, *yellowish* (#34) 80.00
On cover *1,650.*
A112 40c orange, *yellowish* (#35) 100.00
On cover *1,500.*
A113 80c rose, *pinkish* (#36) 150.00

Stamps of Italy, and occasionally those of other Mediterranean countries, are found obliterated by the A25 cancellations, usually originating in ship mail.

Issued under British Administration

Values for unused stamps are for examples with original gum as defined in the catalogue introduction. Very fine examples of Nos. 1-7 will have perforations touching the frameline on one or more sides due to the narrow spacing of the stamps on the plate. Stamps with perfs clear of the frameline are scarce and will command higher prices.

Queen Victoria — A1

1860-61 Unwmk. Typo. *Perf. 14*

1 A1 ½p buff ('63) 900.00 425.00
On cover *1,650.*
a. ½p pale buff ('63) 850.00 400.00
On cover *1,650.*
b. ½p brown orange ('61) 1,300. 475.00
On cover *1,750.*
2 A1 ½p buff, *bluish* 1,400. 700.00
On cover *2,400.*
a. Imperf. (single) *12,000.*

1863-80 Wmk. 1

3 A1 ½p yellow buff ('75) 90.00 70.00
a. ½p buff 130.00 80.00
b. ½p brown orange ('67) 450.00 120.00
c. ½p orange yellow ('80) 300.00 130.00
d. ½p bright orange ('64) 800.00 200.00
e. ½p dull orange ('70) 300.00 90.00
f. ½p orange buff ('72) 180.00 80.00
g. ½p pale buff ('77) 190.00 75.00
h. ½p yellow ('81) 130.00 75.00
4 A1 ½p golden yel (aniline) ('74) 350.00 400.00

1865 *Perf. 12½*

5 A1 ½p buff 175.00 120.00
a. ½p yellow buff 425.00 190.00

1878 *Perf. 14x12½*

6 A1 ½p buff 210.00 110.00
a. Perf. 12½x14 —
b. ½p yellow ('79) 225.00 110.00

No. 6a unused is believed to be unique. It has a small fault.

1882 Wmk. 2 *Perf. 14*

7 A1 ½p reddish orange ('84) 21.00 *57.50*
a. ½p orange 42.50 40.00

A2

A3

Queen Victoria — A4

1885, Jan. 1

8 A1 ½p green 6.00 .60
9 A2 1p car rose 14.50 .40
a. 1p rose 100.00 30.00
10 A3 2p gray 11.00 2.25
11 A4 2½p ultramarine 55.00 1.25
a. 2½p bright ultramarine 55.00 1.25
b. 2½p dull blue 70.00 3.25
12 A3 4p brown 13.00 3.50
a. Imperf., pair *6,000.* *6,000.*
13 A3 1sh violet 60.00 22.50
a. 1sh pale dull violet ('90) 70.00 22.50
Nos. 8-13 (6) 159.50 30.50
Set of 6, overprinted "SPECIMEN" *4,250.*

Do not confuse faded examples of No. 13 for No. 13a.

For surcharge see No. 20.

Queen Victoria within Maltese Cross — A5

1886 Wmk. 1

14 A5 5sh rose 125.00 95.00
Overprinted "SPECIMEN" 700.00

Gozo Fishing Boat — A6

Ancient Galley — A7

1899, Feb. 4 Engr. Wmk. 2

15 A6 4½p black brown 28.00 17.50
16 A7 5p brown red 50.00 21.00

See Nos. 42-45.

"Malta" — A8

St. Paul after Shipwreck — A9

1899 Wmk. 1

17 A8 2sh6p olive gray 47.50 17.50
18 A9 10sh blue black 110.00 75.00

See No. 64. For overprint see No. 85.

Valletta Harbor — A10

1901, Jan. 1 Wmk. 2

19 A10 1f red brown 1.75 .55
a. 1f brown 8.00 3.00

See Nos. 28-29.

No. 11 Surcharged in Black

1902, July 4

20 A4 1p on 2½p dull blue 1.75 2.25
a. "Pnney" 35.00 *65.00*
b. Double surcharge *17,500.* *4,500.*
d. 1p on 2½p bright ultra 1.10 *2.00*
e. As "d," "Pnney" 35.00 *65.00*
Overprinted "SPECIMEN" 82.50

King Edward VII — A12

1903-04 Typo.

21 A12 ½p dark green 11.00 1.00
22 A12 1p car & black 17.50 .50
23 A12 2p gray & red vio 32.50 7.00
24 A12 2½p ultra & brn vio 35.00 5.25
25 A12 3p red vio & gray 2.25 .60
26 A12 4p brown & blk ('04) 30.00 21.00
27 A12 1sh violet & gray 32.50 9.50
Nos. 21-27 (7) 160.75 44.85
Set of 7 ovptd "SPECIMEN" 175.00

1904-11 Wmk. 3

28 A10 1f red brown ('05) 10.00 2.75
29 A10 1f dk brown ('10) 9.00 .25
30 A12 ½p green 6.00 .35
31 A12 1p car & blk ('05) 27.50 .25
32 A12 1p carmine ('07) 4.00 .25
33 A12 2p gray & red vio ('05) 16.50 4.00
34 A12 2p gray ('11) 6.00 6.50
35 A12 2½p ultra & brn vio 37.50 .70
36 A12 2½p ultra ('11) 6.50 4.50
37 A12 4p brn & blk ('06) 13.00 9.00
38 A12 4p scar & blk, *yel* ('11) 4.75 5.50
39 A12 1sh violet & gray 57.50 2.40
40 A12 1sh blk, *grn* ('11) 8.75 4.50
41 A12 5sh scar & grn, *yel* ('11) 75.00 87.50

Engr.

42 A6 4½p black brn ('05) 45.00 7.00
43 A6 4½p orange ('11) 5.25 5.00
44 A7 5p red ('04) 45.00 9.00
45 A7 5p ol green ('10) 5.25 4.50
a. 5p deep sage green ('14) 13.00 *16.00*
Nos. 28-45 (18) 382.50 153.95

A13

A15

King George V — A16

1914-21 Ordinary Paper Typo.

49 A13 ¼p brown 1.60 .25
50 A13 ½p green 3.25 .35
51 A13 1p scarlet ('15) 2.75 .45
a. 1p carmine ('14) 1.75 .25
52 A13 2p gray ('15) 16.00 8.25
53 A13 2½p ultramarine 2.75 .70

Chalky Paper

54 A15 3p vio, *yel* 3.00 *22.00*
a. 3p violet, *orange yellow,* 70.00 50.00
58 A13 6p dull vio & red vio 13.00 *23.00*
59 A15 1sh black, *green* 14.00 *47.50*
a. 1sh black, *bl grn, ol back* 22.50 *35.00*
b. 1sh black, *emerald* ('21) 47.50 *97.50*
c. As "b," olive back 13.00 *32.50*
60 A16 2sh ultra & dl vio, *bl* 57.50 40.00
61 A16 5sh scar & grn, *yel* 105.00 *115.00*

Surface-colored Paper

62 A15 1sh blk, *grn* ('14) 17.50 *47.50*
Nos. 49-54,58-62 (11) 236.35 305.00

See Nos. 66-68, 70-72. For overprints see Nos. 77-82, 84.

Valletta Harbor — A17

1915 Ordinary Paper Engr.

63 A17 4p black 17.50 7.75

St. Paul — A18

1919

64 A8 2sh6p olive green 82.50 *95.00*
65 A18 10sh black 3,500. *4,750.*
Revenue cancel 100.00
Overprinted "SPECIMEN" 950.00

For overprint see No. 83.

George V — A19

1921-22 Typo. Wmk. 4

Ordinary Paper

66 A13 ¼p brown 6.50 *45.00*
67 A13 ½p green 7.00 *37.50*
68 A13 1p rose red 7.75 3.00
69 A19 2p gray 11.00 2.00
70 A13 2½p ultramarine 7.75 *52.50*

Chalky Paper

71 A13 6p dull vio & red vio 37.50 *90.00*
72 A16 2sh ultra & dull vio, *bl* 75.00 *240.00*

Engr.

Ordinary Paper

73 A18 10sh black 400.00 *850.00*
Nos. 66-73 (8) 552.50 1,320.

For overprints and surcharge see Nos. 86-93, 97.

Stamps of 1914-19 Overprinted in Red or Black

1922 Ordinary Paper Wmk. 3

Overprint 21mm

77 A13 ½p green 2.50 *4.00*
78 A13 2½p ultra 20.00 *50.00*

Chalky Paper

79 A15 3p violet, *yel* 5.00 *30.00*
80 A13 6p dull lil & red vio 6.50 *40.00*
81 A15 1sh black, *emer* 6.50 *30.00*

Overprint 28mm

82 A16 2sh ultra & dull vio, *bl* (R) 275.00 *525.00*

Ordinary Paper

83 A8 2sh6p olive grn 35.00 *60.00*

Chalky Paper

84 A16 5sh scar & grn, *yel* 65.00 *110.00*
Nos. 77-84 (8) 415.50 *849.00*

Wmk. 1

Ordinary Paper

85 A9 10sh blue black (R) 225.00 *400.00*

Same Overprint on Stamps of 1921

1922 Ordinary Paper Wmk. 4

Overprint 21mm

86 A13 ¼p brown .35 *.80*
87 A13 ½p green 5.50 *14.50*
88 A13 1p rose red 1.10 *.25*
89 A19 2p gray 5.50 *.55*
90 A13 2½p ultramarine 1.25 *2.25*

Chalky Paper

91 A13 6p dull vio & red vio 27.50 *60.00*

Overprint 28mm

92 A16 2sh ultra & dull vio, *bl* (R) 55.00 *100.00*

Ordinary Paper

93 A18 10sh black (R) 160.00 *275.00*
Nos. 86-93 (8) 256.20 *453.35*

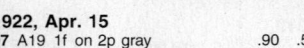

No. 69 Surcharged

1922, Apr. 15

97 A19 1f on 2p gray .90 .50

"Malta" — A20

Britannia and Malta — A21

1922-26 Chalky Paper Typo.

98 A20 ¼p brown 3.00 .70
99 A20 ½p green 3.00 .25
100 A20 1p buff & plum 6.50 .25
101 A20 1p violet ('24) 4.75 .90
102 A20 1½p org brn ('23) 6.00 .25
103 A20 2p ol brn & turq 3.50 1.40
104 A20 2½p ultra ('26) 6.00 *20.00*
105 A20 3p ultramarine 6.50 3.25
 a. 3p blue 8.50 3.75
106 A20 3p blk, *yel* ('26) 5.25 *27.50*
107 A20 4p yel & ultra 3.25 *6.00*
108 A20 6p ol grn & vio 7.00 5.00
109 A21 1sh ol brn & blue 15.00 4.75
110 A21 2sh ultra & ol brn 15.00 *24.00*
111 A21 2sh6p blk & red vio 14.50 *17.50*
112 A21 5sh ultra & org 24.00 *55.00*
113 A21 10sh ol brn & gray 70.00 *175.00*

Engr.

Ordinary Paper

114 A20 £1 car red & blk ('25) 125.00 *500.00*
 a. £1 rose car & blk ('22) 165.00 *375.00*
Nos. 98-114 (17) 318.25 *841.75*

No. 114a has watermark sideways.

For overprints and surcharges see Nos. 115-129.

No. 105 Surcharged

1925, Dec.

115 A20 2½p on 3p ultramarine 2.00 *6.50*

Stamps of 1922-26 Overprinted

1926

116 A20 ¼p brown 1.10 *8.25*
117 A20 ½p green .80 .25
118 A20 1p violet 1.10 .25
119 A20 1½p orange brown 1.40 .70
120 A20 2p ol brn & turq .85 *2.25*
121 A20 2½p ultramarine 1.40 *1.60*
122 A20 3p black, *yel* .85 .90
 a. Inverted overprint 200.00 *550.00*
123 A20 4p yel & ultra 25.00 *42.50*
124 A20 6p ol grn & vio 3.25 *8.25*
125 A21 1sh ol brn & bl 6.25 *25.00*
126 A21 2sh ultra & ol brown 60.00 *160.00*
127 A21 2sh6p blk & red vio 20.00 *55.00*
128 A21 5sh ultra & org 11.00 *55.00*
129 A21 10sh ol brn & gray 8.50 *24.00*
Nos. 116-129 (14) 141.50 383.95

George V — A22

Valletta Harbor — A23

St. Publius — A24

Notabile (Mdina) — A25

Gozo Fishing Boat — A26

Statue of Neptune — A27

Ruins at Mnaidra — A28

St. Paul — A29

1926-27 Typo. *Perf. 14½x14*

131 A22 ¼p brown .90 .25
132 A22 ½p green .70 .25
133 A22 1p red 3.50 1.60
134 A22 1½p orange brn 2.25 .25
135 A22 2p gray 5.25 *18.00*
136 A22 2½p blue 4.50 2.25
137 A22 3p dark violet 5.00 *6.00*
138 A22 4p org red & blk 3.75 *20.00*
139 A22 4½p yel buff & vio 4.00 6.50
140 A22 6p red & violet 5.00 *9.00*

Engr. *Perf. 12½*

Inscribed: "Postage"

141 A23 1sh black 7.50 *12.00*
142 A24 1sh6p green & blk 9.00 *24.00*
143 A25 2sh dp vio & blk 9.50 *30.00*
144 A26 2sh6p ver & black 23.00 *60.00*
145 A27 3sh blue & blk 23.00 *50.00*
146 A28 5sh green & blk 26.00 *82.50*
147 A29 10sh car & blk 70.00 *120.00*
Nos. 131-147 (17) 202.85 *442.60*

See Nos. 167-183. For overprints see Nos. 148-166.

Stamps and Type of 1926-27 Overprinted in Black

1928 *Perf. 14½x14*

148 A22 ¼p brown 1.75 .25
149 A22 ½p green 1.75 .25
150 A22 1p red 2.00 *3.75*
151 A22 1p orange brown 5.25 .25
152 A22 1½p yel brown 2.75 1.00
153 A22 1½p red 5.00 .25
154 A22 2p gray 5.00 *10.50*
155 A22 2½p blue 2.25 .25
156 A22 3p dark violet 2.25 1.00
157 A22 4p org red & blk 2.25 2.00
158 A22 4½p yel & violet 2.50 1.10
159 A22 6p red & violet 2.50 1.75

Overprinted in Red

Perf. 12½

160 A23 1sh black 6.25 3.00
161 A24 1sh6p green & blk 14.50 *12.00*
162 A25 2sh dp vio & blk 30.00 *75.00*
163 A26 2sh6p ver & black 20.00 *26.00*
164 A27 3sh ultra & blk 25.00 *35.00*
165 A28 5sh yel grn & blk 42.50 *75.00*
166 A29 10sh car rose & black 75.00 *110.00*
Nos. 148-166 (19) 248.50 358.35

Issued: Nos. 151, 153, Dec. 5; others, Oct. 1.

Types of 1926-27 Issue

Inscribed: "Postage & Revenue"

1930, Oct. 20 Typo. *Perf. 14½x14*

167 A22 ¼p brown .70 .25
168 A22 ½p green .70 .25
169 A22 1p yel brown .70 .25
170 A22 1½p red .80 .25
171 A22 2p gray 1.40 .60
172 A22 2½p blue 2.25 .25
173 A22 3p dark violet 1.75 .25
174 A22 4p org red & blk 1.40 *7.50*
175 A22 4½p yel & violet 3.75 1.40
176 A22 6p red & violet 3.25 2.50

Engr. *Perf. 12½*

177 A23 1sh black 11.00 *25.00*
178 A24 1sh6p green & blk 9.75 *32.50*
179 A25 2sh dp vio & blk 14.50 *30.00*
180 A26 2sh6p ver & black 20.00 *65.00*
181 A27 3sh ultra & blk 55.00 *65.00*
182 A28 5sh yel grn & blk 60.00 *80.00*
183 A29 10sh car rose & blk 120.00 *200.00*
Nos. 167-183 (17) 306.95 *511.00*

Common Design Types pictured following the introduction.

Silver Jubilee Issue

Common Design Type

1935, May 6 *Perf. 11x12*

184 CD301 ½p green & blk .50 .70
185 CD301 2½p ultra & brn 2.00 *4.00*
186 CD301 6p ol grn & lt bl 5.50 *6.50*
187 CD301 1sh brn vio & ind 14.00 22.50
Nos. 184-187 (4) 22.00 33.70
Set, never hinged 40.00

Coronation Issue

Common Design Type

1937, May 12 Wmk. 4 *Perf. 13½x14*

188 CD302 ½p deep green .25 .25
189 CD302 1½p carmine .50 .60
190 CD302 2½p bright ultra .50 .75
Nos. 188-190 (3) 1.25 1.60
Set, never hinged 2.25

Valletta Harbor — A30

Fort St. Angelo — A31

Verdala Palace — A32

Neolithic Ruins — A33

Victoria and Citadel, Gozo — A34

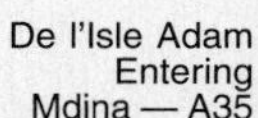

De l'Isle Adam Entering Mdina — A35

St. John's Co-Cathedral A36

Mnaidra Temple — A37

Statue of Antonio Manoel de Vilhena — A38

Woman in Faldetta — A39

St. Publius — A40

Mdina Cathedral A41

Statue of Neptune — A42

Palace Square — A43

St. Paul — A44

1938-43 Wmk. 4 *Perf. 12½*

191	A30	1f brown	.25	.35
192	A31	½p green	2.75	.30
192A	A31	½p chnt ('43)	.35	.30
193	A32	1p chestnut	4.25	.35
193A	A32	1p grn ('43)	.40	.25
194	A33	1½p rose red	2.25	.30
194A	A33	1½p dk gray ('43)	.25	.25
195	A34	2p dark gray	2.25	1.75
195A	A34	2p rose red ('43)	.35	.25
196	A35	2½p blue	4.50	1.25
196A	A35	2½p violet ('43)	.40	.25
197	A36	3p violet	3.00	.80
197A	A36	3p blue ('43)	.30	.25
198	A37	4½p ocher & ol green	.30	.30
199	A38	6p rose red & ol green	1.75	.30
200	A39	1sh black	1.75	.55
201	A40	1sh6p sage grn & black	5.00	4.00
202	A41	2sh dk bl & lt grn	3.25	*7.50*
203	A42	2sh6p rose red & black	5.50	*6.00*
204	A43	5sh bl grn & blk	3.50	*9.00*
205	A44	10sh dp rose & blk	11.50	11.50
		Nos. 191-205 (21)	53.85	45.80
		Set, never hinged	75.00	

See No. 236a. For overprints see Nos. 208-222.

Catalogue values for unused stamps in this section, from this point to the end of the section, are for Never Hinged items.

Peace Issue

Common Design Type

Inscribed: "Malta" and Crosses

Perf. 13½x14

1946, Dec. 3 Engr. Wmk. 4

206	CD303	1p bright green	.25	.25
207	CD303	3p dark ultra	.40	1.75

Stamps of 1938-43 Overprinted in Black or Carmine

a

1948, Nov. 25 *Perf. 12½*

208	A30	1f brown	.30	.25
209	A31	½p chestnut	.30	.25
210	A32	1p green	.30	.25
211	A33	1½p dk gray (C)	1.25	.25
212	A34	2p rose red	1.25	.25
213	A35	2½p violet (C)	.80	.25
214	A36	3p blue (C)	3.00	.25
215	A37	4½p ocher & ol grn	2.75	1.00
216	A38	6p rose red & ol green	3.25	.30
217	A39	1sh black	3.75	.45
218	A40	1sh6p sage grn & blk	2.50	.50
219	A41	2sh dk bl & lt grn (C)	6.00	2.50
220	A42	2sh6p rose red & blk	14.00	2.50
221	A43	5sh bl grn & blk (C)	26.00	3.50
222	A44	10sh dp rose & blk	26.00	25.00
		Nos. 208-222 (15)	91.45	37.50

The overprint is smaller on No. 208. It reads from lower left to upper right on Nos. 209 and 221.

See Nos. 235-240.

Silver Wedding Issue

Common Design Types

Inscribed: "Malta" and Crosses

1949, Jan. 4 Photo. *Perf. 14x14½*

223	CD304	1p dark green	.55	.25

Perf. 11½x11

Engr.

224	CD305	£1 dark blue	40.00	45.00

UPU Issue

Common Design Types

Inscribed: "Malta" and Crosses

Perf. 13½, 11x11½

1949, Oct. 10 Engr. Wmk. 4

225	CD306	2½p violet	.30	.25
226	CD307	3p indigo	3.00	1.10
227	CD308	6p dp carmine	.60	1.00
228	CD309	1sh slate	.60	*2.50*
		Nos. 225-228 (4)	4.50	4.85

Princess Elizabeth — A45

1950, Dec. 1 Engr. *Perf. 12x11½*

229	A45	1p emerald	.25	.25
230	A45	3p bright blue	.25	.25
231	A45	1sh gray black	.90	*2.00*
		Nos. 229-231 (3)	1.40	2.50

Visit of Princess Elizabeth.

Madonna and Child — A46

1951, July 12

232	A46	1p green	.25	.25
233	A46	3p purple	.55	.25
234	A46	1sh slate black	1.60	1.40
		Nos. 232-234 (3)	2.40	1.90

700th anniv. of the presentation of the scapular to St. Simon Stock.

AIR POST STAMPS

No. 140 Overprinted

Perf. 14½x14

1928, Apr. 1 Typo. Wmk. 4

C1	A22	6p red & violet	2.00	1.25
		Never hinged	4.50	

POSTAGE DUE STAMPS

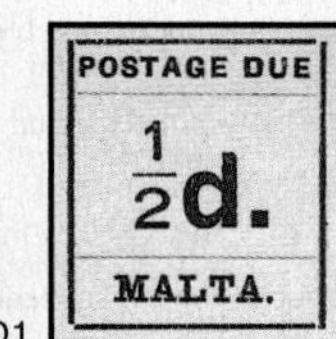

D1

1925 Typeset Unwmk. *Imperf.*

J1	D1	½p black, *white*	1.25	8.00
J2	D1	1p black, *white*	3.00	3.50
J3	D1	1½p black, *white*	2.75	3.50
J4	D1	2p black, *white*	12.00	*21.00*
J5	D1	2½p black, *white*	2.50	2.50
a.		"2" of "½" omitted	1,000.	1,400.
J6	D1	3p black, *gray*	8.50	*15.00*
J7	D1	4p black, *orange*	4.50	*8.50*
J8	D1	6p black, *orange*	4.50	*22.50*
J9	D1	1sh black, *orange*	6.00	*25.00*
J10	D1	1sh6p black, *orange*	16.00	*62.50*
		Nos. J1-J10 (10)	61.00	*172.00*
		Set, never hinged	130.00	

These stamps were typeset in groups of 42. In each sheet there were four impressions of a group, two of them being inverted and making tete-beche pairs. Value set of tete-beche pairs $175.

Forged examples of No. J5a are known.

Maltese Cross — D2

Wmk. 4 Sideways

1925 Typo. *Perf. 12*

J11	D2	½p blue green	1.40	.70
J12	D2	1p violet	1.40	.50
J13	D2	1½p yellow brown	1.75	1.00
J14	D2	2p gray	8.50	1.25
J15	D2	2½p orange	2.25	1.25
J16	D2	3p dark blue	4.50	1.25
J17	D2	4p olive green	12.00	*16.00*
J18	D2	6p claret	3.50	4.75
J19	D2	1sh gray black	7.50	*14.00*
J20	D2	1sh6p deep rose	9.00	*42.50*
		Nos. J11-J20 (10)	51.80	*83.20*
		Set, never hinged	85.00	

In 1953-57 six values (½p-2p, 3p, 4p) were reissued on chalky paper in slightly different colors.

WAR TAX STAMPS

Nos. 50, 25 Overprinted

1918 Wmk. 3 *Perf. 14*

MR1	A13	½p green	2.25	.30

Wmk. 2

MR2	A12	3p red violet & gray	3.00	*15.00*

MANCHUKUO

'man-'chü-'kwō

LOCATION — Covering Manchuria, or China's three northeastern provinces — Fengtien, Kirin and Heilungkiang — plus Jehol province.
GOVT. — Independent state under Japanese influence
AREA — 503,013 sq. mi. (estimated)
POP. — 43,233,954 (est. 1940)
CAPITAL — Hsinking (Changchun)

Manchukuo was formed in 1932 with the assistance of Japan. In 1934 Henry Pu-yi, Chief Executive, was enthroned as Emperor Kang Teh.

100 Fen = 1 Yuan

Watermarks

Wmk. 141 — Horizontal Zigzag Lines

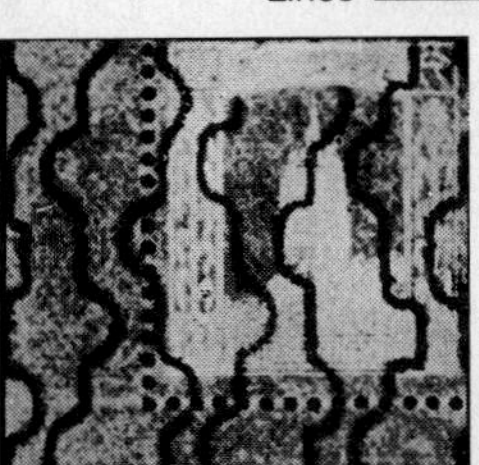

Wmk. 239 — Curved Wavy Lines

Wmk. 242 — Characters

Pagoda at Liaoyang A1

Chief Executive Henry Pu-yi A2

Five characters in top label.
Inscription reads "Manchu State Postal Administration."

Lithographed
Perf. 13x13½

1932, July 26 **Unwmk.**
White Paper

1	A1	½f gray brown	2.00	1.00
2	A1	1f dull red	2.25	1.50
3	A1	1½f lilac	7.00	7.00
4	A1	2f slate	7.00	7.50
5	A1	3f dull brown	9.50	9.50
6	A1	4f olive green	3.50	.70
7	A1	5f green	5.00	1.50
8	A1	6f rose	12.00	5.50
9	A1	7f gray	5.00	3.00
10	A1	8f ocher	20.00	16.00
11	A1	10f orange	7.50	1.50
12	A2	13f dull brown	16.00	10.00
13	A2	15f rose	22.50	5.00
14	A2	16f turquoise grn	32.50	13.00
15	A2	20f gray brown	12.00	4.00
16	A2	30f orange	13.50	5.00
17	A2	50f olive green	27.50	5.00
18	A2	1y violet	45.00	17.50
		Nos. 1-18 (18)	249.75	114.20
		Set, never hinged	300.00	

A local provisional overprint of a horizontal line of four characters in red or black, reading "Chinese Postal Administration," was applied to Nos. 1-18 by followers of Gen. Su Ping-wen, who rebelled against the Manchukuo government in September, 1932. Many counterfeits exist.

See Nos. 23-31. For surcharges see Nos. 36, 59-61.

See note on local handstamps at end of the Manchukuo listings.

Flags, Map and Wreath — A3

Old State Council Building — A4

1933, Mar. 1 ***Perf. 12½***

19	A3	1f orange	8.00	5.50
20	A4	2f dull green	20.00	16.00
21	A3	4f light red	7.00	5.50
22	A4	10f deep blue	40.00	37.50
		Nos. 19-22 (4)	75.00	64.50
		Set, never hinged	110.00	

1st anniv. of the establishing of the State. Nos. 19-22 were printed in sheets of 100 with a special printing in sheets of 20.

Type of 1932
Perf. 13x13½

1934, Feb. **Engr.** **Wmk. 239**
Granite Paper

23	A1	½f dark brown	4.50	2.50
24	A1	1f red brown	5.00	1.25
25	A1	1½f dark violet	8.00	5.00
26	A1	2f slate	10.00	3.50
27	A1	3f brown	5.00	1.10
28	A1	4f olive brown	40.00	7.50
29	A1	10f deep orange	18.00	3.00
30	A2	15f rose	900.00	325.00
31	A2	1y violet	60.00	17.50
		Nos. 23-31 (9)	1,051.	366.35

For surcharge see No. 60.

Emperor's Palace — A5

Phoenix — A6

1934, Mar. 1 ***Perf. 12½***

32	A5	1½f orange brown	7.00	5.50
33	A6	3f carmine	6.50	4.50
34	A5	6f green	20.00	12.50
35	A6	10f dark blue	32.50	20.00
		Nos. 32-35 (4)	66.00	42.50
		Set, never hinged	100.00	

Enthronement of Emperor Kang Teh. Nos. 32-35 were printed in sheets of 100, with a special printing in sheets of 20.

No. 6 Surcharged in Black

Perf. 13x13½

1934 **Unwmk.** **White Paper**

36	A1	1f on 4f olive grn	7.00	5.00
		Never hinged	12.00	
a.		Brown surcharge	47.50	47.50
b.		Upper left character of surcharge omitted		
c.		Inverted surcharge	1,000.	1,000.

Pagoda at Liaoyang A7

Emperor Kang Teh A8

Six characters in top label instead of five as in 1932-34 issues.

Inscription reads "Manchu Empire Postal Administration."

Perf. 13x13½

1934-36 **Wmk. 239** **Engr.**
Granite Paper

37	A7	½f brown	.80	.60
38	A7	1f red brown	1.10	.60
39	A7	1½f dk violet	1.50	1.00
a.		Booklet pane of 6	*200.00*	
41	A7	3f brown ('35)	.90	.70
a.		Booklet pane of 6	*200.00*	
42	A7	5f dk blue ('35)	14.00	4.00
43	A7	5f gray ('36)	6.00	4.00
44	A7	6f rose ('35)	5.00	1.75
45	A7	7f dk gray ('36)	4.00	2.25
47	A7	9f red orange ('35)	3.75	1.75
50	A8	15f ver ('35)	4.00	1.75
51	A8	18f Prus grn ('35)	32.50	8.00
52	A8	20f dk brown ('35)	6.50	2.00
53	A8	30f orange brn ('35)	7.00	2.00
54	A8	50f ol grn ('35)	8.00	3.25
55	A8	1y dk violet ('35)	30.00	9.00
a.		1y violet	32.50	10.00
		Nos. 37-55 (15)	125.05	42.65
		Set, never hinged	155.00	

4f and 8f, type A7, were prepared but not issued. Values $45 and $15, respectively.

1935 **Wmk. 242** ***Perf. 13x13½***

57	A7	10f deep blue	13.00	2.50
58	A8	13f light brown	16.00	8.00
		Set, never hinged	42.00	

Nos. 6 and 28 Surcharged in Black

1935 **White Paper** **Unwmk.**

59	A1	3f on 4f ol grn	70.00	60.00
		Never hinged	100.00	

1935 **Granite Paper** **Wmk. 239**

60	A1	3f on 4f olive brn	10.00	6.00
		Never hinged	17.50	

Similar Surcharge on No. 14

1935 **White Paper** **Unwmk.**

61	A2	3f on 16f turq grn	18.00	12.00
		Never hinged	24.00	
		Nos. 59-61 (3)	98.00	78.00

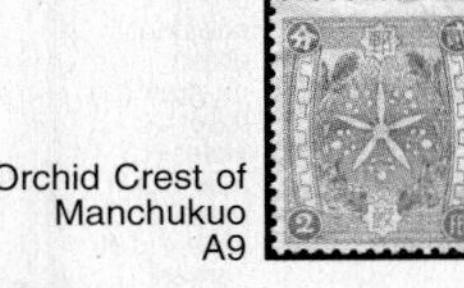

Orchid Crest of Manchukuo A9

Sacred White Mountains and Black Waters A10

1935, Jan. 1 **Litho.** **Wmk. 141**
Granite Paper

62	A9	2f green	6.50	3.50
63	A10	4f dull ol grn	3.25	2.50
64	A9	8f ocher	4.75	3.75
65	A10	12f brown red	16.00	*20.00*
		Nos. 62-65 (4)	30.50	29.75
		Set, never hinged	44.00	

Nos. 62-65 exist imperforate.

1935 **Wmk. 242**

66	A9	2f yellow green	6.00	2.00
68	A9	8f ocher	8.00	8.00
70	A10	12f brown red	15.00	*20.00*
		Nos. 66-70 (3)	29.00	30.00
		Set, never hinged	40.00	

Nos. 62-70 issued primarily to pay postage to China, but valid for any postal use.

See Nos. 75-78, 113, 115, 158 (in Scott Standard catalogue, Vol. 4). For surcharges see Nos. 101, 103-104, 106-109, People's Republic of China No. 2L19 (in Scott Standard catalogue, Vol. 2).

Mt. Fuji — A11

Phoenix — A12

Perf. 11, 12½ and Compound

1935, Apr. 1 **Engr.** **Wmk. 242**

71	A11	1½f dull green	3.75	3.00
72	A12	3f orange	4.00	3.75
a.		3f red orange	7.50	6.00
73	A11	6f dk carmine	8.00	7.00
a.		Horiz. pair, imperf. btwn.	*1,200.*	
b.		Perf. 11x12½	50.00	40.00
74	A12	10f dark blue	10.00	8.50
a.		Perf. 12½x11	85.00	60.00
b.		Perf. 12½	30.00	27.50
		Nos. 71-74 (4)	25.75	22.25
		Set, never hinged	35.00	

Visit of the Emperor of Manchukuo to Tokyo.

Orchid Crest — A13

Types of A9 & A10 Redrawn and Engraved

1936 **Wmk. 242** ***Perf. 13x13½***

75	A13	2f lt green	1.50	1.00
76	A10	4f olive green	4.50	2.50
77	A13	8f ocher	5.00	2.50
78	A10	12f orange brn	47.50	32.50
		Nos. 75-78 (4)	58.50	38.50
		Set, never hinged	80.00	

Unbroken lines of shading in the background of Nos. 76 and 78. Shading has been removed from right and left of the mountains. Nearly all lines have been removed from the lake. There are numerous other alterations in the design.

Issued primarily to pay postage to China, but valid for any postal use.

See No. 112. For surcharges see Nos. 102-106.

Wild Goose over Sea of Japan — A14

Communications Building at Hsinking — A15

Perf. 12x12½, 12½x12

1936, Jan. 26 **Wmk. 242**

79	A14	1½f black brown	4.50	3.00
80	A15	3f rose lilac	4.50	3.00
81	A14	6f carmine rose	9.00	8.00
82	A15	10f blue	14.00	10.00
		Nos. 79-82 (4)	32.00	24.00
		Set, never hinged	50.00	

Postal convention with Japan.

New State Council Building A16

Carting Soybeans A17

North Mausoleum at Mukden A18

Summer Palace at Chengteh A19

1936-37 Wmk. 242 *Perf. 13x13½*

No.	Type	Description	Unused	Used
83	A16	½f brown	.75	.60
84	A16	1f red brown	.75	.50
85	A16	1½f violet	7.00	5.00
a.		Booklet pane of 6	*150.00*	
86	A17	2f lt green ('37)	1.00	.50
a.		Booklet pane of 6	*65.00*	
87	A16	3f chocolate	1.25	.75
a.		Booklet pane of 6	*375.00*	
88	A18	4f lt ol grn ('37)	1.25	.75
a.		Booklet pane of 6	*60.00*	
89	A16	5f gray black	30.00	12.00
90	A17	6f carmine	1.25	.50
91	A18	7f brown blk	1.75	1.00
92	A18	9f red orange	2.25	1.25
93	A19	10f blue	2.50	.60
94	A18	12f dp orange ('37)	2.25	.50
95	A18	13f brown	42.50	37.50
96	A18	15f carmine	3.75	1.00
97	A17	20f dk brown	2.25	.90
98	A19	30f chestnut brn	2.25	.90
99	A17	50f olive green	2.75	1.25
100	A19	1y violet	6.00	1.75
		Nos. 83-100 (18)	111.50	67.25
		Set, never hinged	160.00	

Nos. 83, 84, 86, 88 and 93 are known imperforate but were not regularly issued.

See Nos. 159-163 in Scott Standard catalogue, Vol. 4. For overprints see Nos. 140-141, 148-151 in Scott Vol. 4. For surcharges see People's Republic of China Nos. 2L1-2L2, 2L11-2L18, 2L20-2L37, 2L40-2L52 in Scott Standard catalogue, Vol. 2.

a

b

c

d

1937 Surcharged on No. 66

No.	Type	Description	Unused	Used
101	A9 (a)	2½f on 2f	4.00	3.50

Surcharged on Nos. 75, 76 and 78

No.	Type	Description	Unused	Used
102	A13 (a)	2½f on 2f	4.50	3.50
103	A10 (b)	5f on 4f	5.50	4.50
104	A10 (c)	13f on 12f	14.00	12.00

Surcharged in Black on Nos. 75, 76 and 70

Space between bottom characters of surcharge 4½mm

No.	Type	Description	Unused	Used
105	A13 (d)	2½f on 2f	3.25	3.00
a.		Inverted surcharge	*700.00*	*850.00*
b.		Vert. pair, one without surch.	*200.00*	
106	A10 (b)	5f on 4f	4.50	4.00
107	A10 (c)	13f on 12f	13.50	12.50

Surcharged on No. 70

Space between characters 6½mm

No.	Type	Description	Unused	Used
108	A10 (c)	13f on 12f	225.00	200.00

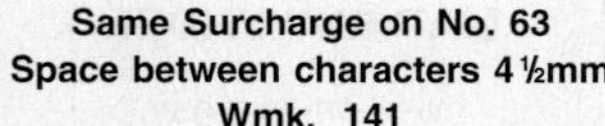

Same Surcharge on No. 63

Space between characters 4½mm

Wmk. 141

No.	Type	Description	Unused	Used
109	A10 (b)	5f on 4f	8.25	7.00
		Nos. 101-109 (9)	282.50	250.00
		Set, never hinged	390.00	

Nos. 101-109 were issued primarily to pay postage to China, but were valid for any postal use.

Rising Sun over Manchurian Plain — A20

Composite Picture of Manchurian City — A21

Perf. 12½

1937, Mar. 1 Litho. Unwmk.

No.	Type	Description	Unused	Used
110	A20	1½f carmine rose	5.00	4.50
111	A21	3f blue green	4.00	3.50
		Set, never hinged	12.00	

5th anniv. of the founding of the State of Manchukuo.

Types of 1936

Perf. 13x13½

1937 Wmk. 242 Engr.

No.	Type	Description	Unused	Used
112	A13	2½f dk violet	1.25	1.00
113	A10	5f black	.65	.65
115	A10	13f dk red brown	2.25	1.00
		Nos. 112-115 (3)	4.15	2.65
		Set, never hinged	7.00	

Issued primarily to pay postage to China, but were valid for any postal use.

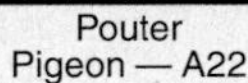

Pouter Pigeon — A22

National Flag and Buildings — A23

Perf. 12x12½

1937, Sept. 16 Unwmk.

No.	Type	Description	Unused	Used
116	A22	2f dark violet	3.25	2.50
117	A23	4f rose carmine	3.50	2.50
118	A22	10f dark green	6.75	5.00
119	A23	20f dark blue	9.00	7.00
		Nos. 116-119 (4)	22.50	17.00
		Set, never hinged	29.00	

Completion of the national capital, Hsinking, under the first Five-Year Construction Plan.

Map — A24

Dept. of Justice Building — A27

Japanese Residents' Association Building — A25

Postal Administration Building — A26

Perf. 12x12½, 13, 12½x13, 13x13½, 13½x13

1937, Dec. 1 Litho. Unwmk.

No.	Type	Description	Unused	Used
121	A24	2f dark carmine	2.00	1.75
122	A25	4f green	3.50	2.50
123	A25	8f orange	6.00	5.00
124	A26	10f blue	6.50	5.00
125	A27	12f lt violet	7.50	7.50
126	A26	20f lilac brown	11.00	8.00
		Nos. 121-126 (6)	36.50	29.75
		Set, never hinged	48.00	

Issued in commemoration of the abolition of extraterritorial rights within Manchukuo.

Perf varieties exist on Nos. 122-126, lowest value listed, others about 25-35% higher.

New Year Greetings — A28

1937, Dec. 15 Engr. *Perf. 12x12½*

No.	Type	Description	Unused	Used
127	A28	2f dk blue & red	3.00	2.00
		Never hinged	4.00	
a.		Double impression of border	*17.50*	

Issued to pay postage on New Year's greeting cards.

Map and Cross — A29

Wmk. 242

1938, Oct. 15 Litho. *Perf. 13*

No.	Type	Description	Unused	Used
128	A29	2f lake & scarlet	2.00	1.50
129	A29	4f slate grn & scar	2.00	1.50
		Set, never hinged	6.00	

Founding of the Red Cross Soc. in Manchukuo.

Network of State Railroads in Manchukuo A30

Express Train "Asia" A31

1939, Oct. 21

No.	Type	Description	Unused	Used
130	A30	2f dk org, blk & dp bl	2.50	1.75
131	A31	4f dp blue & indigo	2.50	1.75
		Set, never hinged	7.00	

Attainment of 10,000 kilometers in the railway mileage in Manchuria.

Stork Flying above Mast of Imperial Flagship — A32

1940 Photo. Unwmk.

No.	Type	Description	Unused	Used
132	A32	2f brt red violet	2.00	1.50
133	A32	4f brt green	2.00	1.50
		Set, never hinged	6.00	

Second visit of Emperor Kang Teh to Emperor Hirohito of Japan.

Census Taker and Map of Manchukuo A33

Census Form A34

1940, Sept. 10 Litho. Wmk. 242

No.	Type	Description	Unused	Used
134	A33	2f vio brn & org	1.50	1.50
135	A34	4f black & green	1.50	1.50
a.		Double impression of green	*100.00*	
		Set, never hinged	4.00	

National census starting Oct. 1.

Message of Congratulation from Premier Chang Ching-hui — A35

Dragon Dance A36

1940, Sept. 18 Engr. *Perf. 13x13½*

No.	Type	Description	Unused	Used
136	A35	2f carmine	1.25	1.25

Perf. 13½x13

No.	Type	Description	Unused	Used
137	A36	4f indigo	1.25	1.25
a.		Imperf., pair	*1,000.*	
		Set, never hinged	3.50	

2600th anniversary of the birth of the Japanese Empire.

Soldier — A37

Perf. 13x13½

1941, May 25 Photo. Unwmk.

No.	Type	Description	Unused	Used
138	A37	2f deep carmine	1.25	1.25
139	A37	4f bright ultra	1.25	1.25
		Set, never hinged	3.50	

Conscription Law, effective June 1, 1941.

AIR POST STAMPS

Sheep Grazing AP1

Railroad Bridge AP2

Wmk. Characters (242)

1936-37 Engr. *Perf. 13x13½*

Granite Paper

No.	Type	Description	Unused	Used
C1	AP1	18f green	16.00	18.00
C2	AP1	19f blue green ('37)	6.00	7.00
C3	AP2	38f blue	17.50	17.50
C4	AP2	39f deep blue ('37)	3.00	4.25
		Nos. C1-C4 (4)	42.50	46.75
		Set, never hinged	54.00	

With the end of World War II and the collapse of Manchukuo, the Northeastern Provinces reverted to China. In many Manchurian towns and cities, the Manchukuo stamps were locally handstamped in ideograms: "Republic of China," "China Postal Service" or "Temporary Use for China." A typical example is shown above. Many of these local issues also were surcharged.

MARIANA ISLANDS

ˌmar-ē-ˈa-nə ˈī-ləndz

LOCATION — A group of 14 islands in the West Pacific Ocean, about 1500 miles east of the Philippines.
GOVT. — Possession of Spain, then of Germany
AREA — 246 sq. mi.
POP. — 44,025 (1935)
CAPITAL — Saipan

Until 1899 this group belonged to Spain but in that year all except Guam were ceded to Germany.

100 Centavos = 1 Peso
100 Pfennig = 1 Mark (1899)

Values for unused stamps are for examples with original gum as defined in the catalogue introduction. Very fine examples of Nos. 1-6 will have perforations touching or just cutting into the design. Stamps with perfs clear on all sides and well centered are rare and sell for substantially more.

Issued under Spanish Dominion

Philippines Stamps Hstmpd. Vert. in Blackish Violet Reading Up or Down

1899, Sept. Unwmk. Perf. 14

1 A39 2c dark blue green 800. 350.
On cover 2,500.
2 A39 3c dark brown 500. 275.
On cover 2,500.
3 A39 5c car rose 800. 275.
On cover 3,000.
4 A39 6c dark blue 5,000. 2,500.
On cover 6,500.
5 A39 8c gray brown 500. 175.
On cover 2,500.
6 A39 15c dull ol grn 1,700. 900.
On cover 5,000.

Overprint forgeries of Nos. 1-6 exist.
No. 4 was issued in a quantity of 50 stamps.

Issued under German Dominion

Values for Nos. 11-16 are for postally used examples in the correct period of use. Favor cancellations exist and are valued at 25 percent to 50 percent of the values shown here if used during the correct period. Expertization is recommended.

Stamps of Germany, 1889-90, Overprinted in Black at 56 degree Angle

1900, May Unwmk. Perf. 13½x14½

11 A9 3pf dark brown 12.00 *30.00*
Never hinged 25.00
On cover *160.00*
12 A9 5pf green 16.00 *32.50*
Never hinged 32.50
On cover *160.00*
13 A10 10pf carmine 20.00 *45.00*
Never hinged 40.00
On cover *95.00*
14 A10 20pf ultra 25.00 *125.00*
Never hinged 60.00
On cover *275.00*
15 A10 25pf orange 62.50 *160.00*
Never hinged 160.00
On cover *475.00*
b. Inverted overprint *2,400.*
Never hinged *3,600.*
16 A10 50pf red brn 65.00 *210.00*
Never hinged 160.00
On cover *475.00*
Nos. 11-16 (6) 200.50 *602.50*

Forged cancellations exist on Nos. 11-16, 17-29.

Covers: Value for No. 16 on cover is for overfranked complete cover, usually philatelic.

Stamps of Germany, 1889-90, Overprinted in Black at 48 degree Angle

1899, Nov. 18

11a A9 3pf light brown *2,000.* *2,000.*
Never hinged 3,600.
On cover *5,600.*
12a A9 5pf green *2,500.* *1,700.*
Never hinged 4,750.
On cover *2,800.*
13a A10 10pf carmine 190.00 *200.00*
Never hinged 550.00
On cover *800.00*
14a A10 20pf ultra 190.00 *200.00*
Never hinged 550.00
On cover *800.00*
15a A10 25pf orange *2,750.* *2,750.*
Never hinged 6,000.
On cover *6,500.*
16a A10 50pf red brown *2,750.* *2,750.*
Never hinged 6,000.
On cover *5,250.*

Covers: Value for No. 16a on cover is for overfranked complete cover, usually philatelic.

Kaiser's Yacht "Hohenzollern"
A4 A5

1901, Jan. Typo. Perf. 14

17 A4 3pf brown 1.10 *1.75*
Never hinged 2.00
On cover *105.00*
18 A4 5pf green 1.10 *1.90*
Never hinged 2.00
On cover *45.00*
19 A4 10pf carmine 1.10 *4.25*
Never hinged 2.00
On cover *52.50*
20 A4 20pf ultra 1.25 *7.25*
Never hinged 2.50
On cover *175.00*
21 A4 25pf org & blk, *yel* 1.75 *12.50*
Never hinged 3.50
On cover *175.00*
22 A4 30pf org & blk, *sal* 1.75 *13.50*
Never hinged 3.50
On cover *175.00*
23 A4 40pf lake & blk 1.75 *13.50*
Never hinged 4.00
On cover *175.00*
24 A4 50pf pur & blk, *sal* 2.00 *15.00*
Never hinged 4.50
On cover *55.00*
25 A4 80pf lake & blk, *rose* 2.50 *25.00*
Never hinged 6.00
On cover *82.50*

Engr.
Perf. 14½x14

26 A5 1m carmine 4.00 *72.50*
Never hinged 20.00
On cover *100.00*
27 A5 2m blue 5.50 *92.50*
Never hinged 24.00
On cover *200.00*
28 A5 3m blk vio 8.00 *140.00*
Never hinged 32.50
On cover *290.00*
29 A5 5m slate & car 140.00 *500.00*
Never hinged 400.00
On cover *725.00*
Nos. 17-29 (13) 171.80 *899.65*

Covers: Values for Nos. 24-29 on cover are for overfranked complete covers, usually philatelic.

Wmk. Lozenges (125)
1916-19 Typo. Perf. 14

30 A4 3pf brown ('19) 1.00
Never hinged 2.00

Engr.
Perf. 14½x14

31 A5 5m slate & carmine, 25x17 holes 30.00
Never hinged 175.00
a. 5m slate & carmine, 26x17 holes 35.00
Never hinged 225.00

Nos. 30 and 31 were never placed in use.

MARIENWERDER

mä-ˈrē-ən-ˌveˌərd-ər

LOCATION — Northeastern Germany, bordering on Poland
GOVT. — District of West Prussia

By the Versailles Treaty the greater portion of West Prussia was ceded to Poland but the district of Marienwerder was allowed a plebiscite which was held in 1920 and resulted in favor of Germany.

100 Pfennig = 1 Mark

Plebiscite Issues

Symbolical of Allied Supervision of the Plebiscite — A1

1920 Unwmk. Litho. Perf. 11½

1 A1 5pf green .75 *2.25*
Never hinged 2.10
On cover 4.00
2 A1 10pf rose red .75 *1.75*
Never hinged 2.10
On cover 4.00
3 A1 15pf gray .75 *2.60*
Never hinged 2.10
On cover 4.00
4 A1 20pf brn org .75 *1.75*
Never hinged 2.10
On cover 4.00
5 A1 25pf deep blue .75 *2.25*
Never hinged 2.10
On cover 8.00
6 A1 30pf orange .95 *2.25*
Never hinged 2.60
On cover 9.50
7 A1 40pf brown .75 *2.75*
Never hinged 2.10
On cover 6.50
8 A1 50pf violet .75 *2.00*
Never hinged 2.10
On cover 6.50
9 A1 60pf red brown 4.25 *3.75*
Never hinged 11.50
On cover 20.00
10 A1 75pf chocolate .95 *2.00*
Never hinged 2.60
On cover 12.00
11 A1 1m brn & grn .75 *2.00*
Never hinged 2.10
On cover 12.00
12 A1 2m dk vio 2.10 *4.50*
Never hinged 5.25
On cover 35.00
13 A1 3m red 5.00 *7.50*
Never hinged 14.00
On cover 40.00
14 A1 5m blue & rose 27.50 22.00
Never hinged 77.50 —
On cover 80.00
a. 5m ultramarine & pale red 22.50 *21.00*
Never hinged 65.00
Nos. 1-14 (14) 46.75 59.35
Set, never hinged 130.00

These stamps occasionally show parts of two papermakers' watermarks, consisting of the letters "O. B. M." with two stars before and after, or "P. & C. M."

Nos. 1-14 exist imperf.; value for set, $700. Nearly all exist part perf.

Stamps of Germany, 1905-19, Overprinted

1920 Wmk. 125 Perf. 14, 14½

24 A16 5pf green 15.00 *30.00*
Never hinged 30.00
On cover 65.00
a. Inverted overprint 125.00
Never hinged 210.00
b. Double overprint, one inverted 450.00 *750.00*
Never hinged 750.00
26 A16 20pf bl vio 7.25 *27.50*
Never hinged 20.00
On cover 40.00
a. Inverted overprint 62.50 *135.00*
Never hinged 125.00
b. Double overprint 85.00
Never hinged 150.00
28 A16 50pf vio & blk, *buff* 375.00 *850.00*
Never hinged 800.00
On cover *1,600.*
a. 50pf vio & blk, *pale yel org* 800.00 *2,750.*
Never hinged *2,750.*
On cover *3,500.*
29 A16 75pf grn & blk 4.75 *8.75*
Never hinged 9.00
On cover 20.00
a. Inverted overprint 62.50 *135.00*
Never hinged 125.00
30 A16 80pf lake & blk, *rose* 75.00 *120.00*
Never hinged 150.00
On cover 300.00
31 A17 1m car rose 85.00 *160.00*
Never hinged 160.00
On cover 400.00
a. Inverted overprint 425.00
Never hinged 850.00
Nos. 24-31 (6) 562.00 *1,196.*
Set, never hinged 1,200.

Trial impressions were made in red, green and lilac, and with 2½mm instead of 3mm space between the lines of the overprint. These were printed on the 75pf and 80pf. The 1 mark was overprinted with the same words in 3 lines of large sans-serif capitals. All these are essays. Some were passed through the post, apparently with speculative intent.

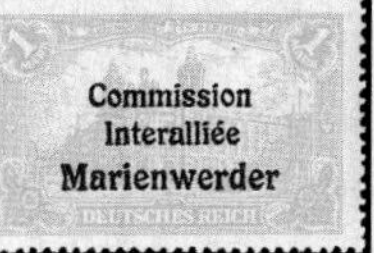

Stamps of Germany, 1905-18, Surcharged

32 A22 1m on 2pf gray 30.00 *45.00*
Never hinged 110.00
On cover 80.00
33 A22 2m on 2½pf gray 15.00 *17.50*
Never hinged 67.50
On cover 80.00
a. Inverted surcharge 55.00 *125.00*
Never hinged 125.00
34 A16 3m on 3pf brown 15.00 *17.50*
Never hinged 67.50
On cover 95.00
a. Double surcharge 55.00 *125.00*
Never hinged 125.00
b. Inverted surcharge 55.00 *120.00*
Never hinged 120.00
35 A22 5m on 7½pf org 15.00 *21.00*
Never hinged 67.50
On cover 120.00
a. Inverted surcharge 55.00 *125.00*
Never hinged 125.00
b. Double surcharge 55.00 *120.00*
Never hinged 125.00
Nos. 32-35 (4) 75.00 *101.00*
Set, never hinged 220.00

There are two types of the letters "M," "C," "i" and "e" and of the numerals "2" and "5" in these surcharges.

Counterfeits exist of Nos. 24-35.

Stamps of Germany, 1920, Overprinted

1920, July Perf. 15x14½

36 A17 1m red 2.50 *7.25*
Never hinged 6.50
On cover 60.00
37 A17 1.25m green 3.25 *9.00*
Never hinged 8.00
On cover 60.00
38 A17 1.50m yellow brown 4.25 *9.75*
Never hinged 10.50
On cover 60.00
39 A21 2.50m lilac rose 2.50 *9.00*
Never hinged 7.50
On cover 80.00
Nos. 36-39 (4) 12.50 *35.00*
Set, never hinged 32.50

A2

1920 Unwmk. Perf. 11½

40 A2 5pf green 4.00 1.60
Never hinged 11.00
On cover 12.00
41 A2 10pf rose red 4.00 1.60
Never hinged 11.00
On cover 16.00
42 A2 15pf gray 15.00 11.00
Never hinged 35.00
On cover 40.00
43 A2 20pf brn org 3.00 *1.60*
Never hinged 7.50
On cover 12.00
44 A2 25pf dp bl 15.00 *14.50*
Never hinged 37.50
On cover 40.00

45 A2 30pf orange 3.00 1.25
Never hinged 7.50
On cover 6.50
46 A2 40pf brown 3.00 *1.25*
Never hinged 7.50
On cover 6.50
47 A2 50pf violet 2.25 1.60
Never hinged 6.00
On cover 8.00
48 A2 60pf red brn 7.50 4.50
Never hinged 19.00
On cover 20.00
49 A2 75pf chocolate 7.50 4.50
Never hinged 22.50
On cover 27.50
50 A2 1m brn & grn 3.00 1.25
Never hinged 7.50
On cover 12.00
51 A2 2m dk vio 3.00 1.25
Never hinged 7.50
On cover 27.50
52 A2 3m light red 3.00 1.60
Never hinged 7.50
On cover 47.50
53 A2 5m blue & rose 4.00 2.25
Never hinged 12.00
On cover 80.00
Nos. 40-53 (14) 77.25 49.75
Set, never hinged 200.00

MARSHALL ISLANDS

ˈmär-shəl ˈī-lәnds

LOCATION — Two chains of islands in the West Pacific Ocean, northwest of the Gilbert and Ellice group
GOVT. — German possession
AREA — 176 sq. mi.
POP. — 15,179 (1913)
CAPITAL — Jaluit

100 Pfennig = 1 Mark

Watermark

Wmk. 125 — Lozenges

Issued under German Dominion

A1

A2

Stamps of Germany Overprinted "Marschall-Inseln" in Black

Two printings of Nos. 1-4: Berlin printing, white, smooth shiny gum; Jaluit printing, yellowish, dull gum.

1897 Unwmk. *Perf. 13½x14½*

1 A1 3pf dark brown (Berlin) 140.00 *725.00*
Never hinged 525.00
On cover 950.00
a. 3pf light yellowish brown (Jaluit) *4,250.* *2,200.*
Never hinged 7,250.
On cover *12,000.*
b. 3pf reddish ochre (Jaluit) 3,600. 2,100.
Never hinged 7,250.
On cover *12,000.*
2 A1 5pf green (Berlin) 120.00 *550.00*
Never hinged 325.00
On cover 875.00
a. 5pf green (Jaluit) 525.00 440.00
Never hinged 1,350.
On cover *950.00*
3 A1 10pf carmine (Berlin) 55.00 *150.00*
Never hinged 150.00
On cover 250.00
a. Vertical half used as 5pf on postcard *27,500.*
b. As "a," on newspaper wrapper *34,000.*
c. 10pf carmine (Jaluit) 60.00 *85.00*
Never hinged 175.00
On cover 240.00
4 A2 20pf ultra (Berlin) 50.00 *150.00*
Never hinged 140.00
On cover 250.00
a. 20pf ultra (Jaluit) 60.00 *95.00*
Never hinged 175.00
On cover 275.00
5 A2 25pf orange (Berlin) 140.00 *925.00*
Never hinged 475.00
On cover *2,400.*
6 A2 50pf red brown (Berlin) 140.00 *925.00*
Never hinged 475.00
On cover *2,000.*
Nos. 1-6 (6) 645.00 3,425.

Nos. 5 and 6 were not placed in use, but canceled stamps and covers exist.

Value for No. 6 on cover is for complete, overfranked covers, usually philatelic.

Forged cancellations are found on almost all Marshall Islands stamps.

Overprinted "Marshall-Inseln"

1899-1900

7 A1 3pf dk brn ('00) 4.50 *5.50*
Never hinged 12.00
On cover 20.00
a. 3pf light brown 275.00 *775.00*
Never hinged 650.00
On cover —
8 A1 5pf green 9.25 *12.50*
Never hinged 24.00
On cover 20.00
9 A2 10pf car ('00) 12.00 *15.00*
Never hinged 40.00
On cover 30.00
a. Half used as 5pf on postcard *8,000.*
10 A2 20pf ultra ('00) 17.00 *25.00*
Never hinged 45.00
On cover 42.50
11 A2 25pf orange 19.00 *42.50*
Never hinged 65.00
On cover 72.50
12 A2 50pf red brown 30.00 *47.50*
Never hinged 110.00
On cover 95.00
a. Half used as 25pf on cover *35,000.*
Nos. 7-12 (6) 91.75 *148.00*

Values for Nos. 9a and 12a are for properly used items, addressed and sent to Germany.

Kaiser's Yacht "Hohenzollern"
A3 A4

1901 Unwmk. Typo. *Perf. 14*

13 A3 3pf brown .65 1.75
Never hinged 1.40
On cover 47.50
14 A3 5pf green .65 1.75
Never hinged 1.40
On cover 20.00
15 A3 10pf carmine .65 *5.00*
Never hinged 1.40
On cover 27.50
16 A3 20pf ultra .95 *9.25*
Never hinged 1.40
On cover 40.00
17 A3 25pf org & blk, *yel* 1.00 *16.00*
Never hinged 2.00
On cover 85.00
18 A3 30pf org & blk, *sal* 1.00 *16.00*
Never hinged 2.00
On cover 80.00
19 A3 40pf lake & blk 1.00 *16.00*
Never hinged 2.00
On cover 80.00
20 A3 50pf pur & blk, *sal* 1.40 *25.00*
Never hinged 4.00
On cover 60.00
21 A3 80pf lake & blk, *rose* 2.50 *35.00*
Never hinged 12.00
On cover 80.00

Engr.
Perf. 14½x14

22 A4 1m carmine 4.00 *85.00*
Never hinged 17.00
On cover *125.00*
23 A4 2m blue 5.50 *120.00*
Never hinged 20.00
On cover *150.00*
24 A4 3m blk vio 8.50 *200.00*
Never hinged 27.50
On cover *240.00*
25 A4 5m slate & car 140.00 *500.00*
Never hinged 490.00
On cover *725.00*
Nos. 13-25 (13) 167.80 1,031.

Covers: Values for Nos. 20-25 on cover are for overfranked complete covers, usually philatelic.

Wmk. Lozenges (125)
1916 Typo. *Perf. 14*

26 A3 3pf brown .85
Never hinged 1.90

Engr.
Perf. 14½x14

27 A4 5m slate & carmine, 25x17 holes 35.00
Never hinged 120.00
a. 5m slate & carmine, 26x17 holes 32.00
Never hinged 140.00

Nos. 26 and 27 were never placed in use.

The stamps of Marshall Islands overprinted "G. R. I." and new values in British currency were all used in New Britain and are listed among the issues for that country.

MARTINIQUE

ˌmär-tᵊn-ˈēk

LOCATION — Island in the West Indies, southeast of Puerto Rico
GOVT. — French Colony
AREA — 385 sq. mi.
POP. — 261,595 (1946)
CAPITAL — Fort-de-France

100 Centimes = 1 Franc

Stamps of French Colonies 1881-86 Surcharged in Black

Nos. 1, 7

No. 2

No. 3

No. 4

Nos. 5-6, 8

Nos. 9-20

1886-91 Unwmk. *Perf. 14x13½*

1 A9 5 on 20c 65.00 55.00
Never hinged 135.00
On cover 375.00
On cover, single franking 625.00
a. Double surcharge *750.00* *750.00*
2 A9 5c on 20c *15,000.* *15,000.*
3 A9 15c on 20c ('87) 275.00 240.00
On cover 1,100.
On cover, single franking 1,900.
a. Inverted surcharge *2,350.* *2,500.*
4 A9 15c on 20c ('87) 100.00 100.00
Never hinged 215.00
On cover 675.00
On cover, single franking 1,100.
a. Inverted surcharge *1,500.* *1,500.*
b. Se-tenant pair, #3-4 475.00 425.00
c. Se-tenant pair, #3a-4a *4,750.* *4,750.*
5 A9 01 on 20c ('88) 20.00 19.00
Never hinged 42.50
On cover 275.00
On cover, single franking 500.00
a. Inverted surcharge *350.00* *350.00*
6 A9 05 on 20c 16.00 13.00
Never hinged 32.50
On cover 150.00
On cover, single franking 500.00
7 A9 15 on 20c ('88) 200.00 180.00
On cover 550.00
On cover, single franking 925.00
c. Inverted surcharge *700.00* *750.00*
8 A9 015 on 20c ('87) 60.00 *65.00*
Never hinged 135.00
On cover 375.00
On cover, single franking 625.00
a. Inverted surcharge *875.00* *825.00*
9 A9 01c on 2c ('88) 4.75 3.25
Never hinged 9.75
On cover 55.00
On cover, single franking 500.00
a. Double surcharge *475.00* *475.00*
b. "MARTINIQUE" below "01" 30.00 30.00
10 A9 01c on 4c ('88) 15.00 4.75
Never hinged 29.00
On cover 75.00
On cover, single franking 375.00
11 A9 05c on 4c ('88) 1,500. 1,375.
12 A9 05c on 10c ('90) 120.00 72.50
On cover 250.00
On cover, single franking 450.00
a. Slanting "5" *300.00* *240.00*
13 A9 05c on 20c ('88) 28.00 20.00
Never hinged 60.00
On cover 150.00
On cover, single franking 375.00
a. Slanting "5" *150.00* *120.00*
On cover 450.00
On cover, single franking 1,050.
b. Inverted surcharge *425.00* *375.00*
14 A9 05c on 30c ('91) 35.00 28.00
Never hinged 72.50
On cover 150.00
On cover, single franking 375.00
a. Slanting "5" *160.00* *150.00*
15 A9 05c on 35c ('91) 20.00 16.00
Never hinged 72.50
On cover 125.00
On cover, single franking 375.00
a. Slanting "5" *160.00* *150.00*
b. Inverted surcharge *325.00* *300.00*
c. "MARTINIQUE" below "05" 60.00 60.00
d. "MARTINIQUE" omitted 60.00 60.00
e. 05c on 35c violet, *yel* ('91) 22.50 18.50
On cover 125.00
On cover, single franking 425.00
16 A9 05c on 40c ('91) 65.00 47.50
Never hinged 135.00
On cover 190.00
On cover, single franking 425.00
a. Slanting "5" *260.00* *165.00*
17 A9 15c on 4c ('88) *12,000.* *11,000.*
On cover —
18 A9 15c on 20c ('87) 150.00 120.00
On cover 550.00
On cover, single franking 950.00
a. Slanting "5" *500.00* *425.00*
b. Double surcharge *700.00* *700.00*
c. "MARTINIQUE" below "15" 350.00 350.00
d. "MARTINIQUE" omitted *2,100.*
19 A9 15c on 25c ('90) 32.50 20.00
Never hinged 65.00
On cover 75.00
On cover, single franking 425.00
a. Slanting "5" *150.00* *130.00*
b. Inverted surcharge *325.00* *275.00*
c. Double surcharge 450.00 450.00
20 A9 15c on 75c ('91) 210.00 175.00
On cover 675.00
On cover, single franking 1,100.
a. Slanting "5" *550.00* *450.00*

French Colonies No. 47 Surcharged

1891

21 A9 01c on 2c brn, *buff* 11.00 11.00
Never hinged 22.50
On cover 150.00
On cover, single franking 375.00
a. No dot after "c" 40.00 40.00

French Colonies Nos. J5-J9 Surcharged

1891-92 Black Surcharge *Imperf.*

22 D1 05c on 5c blk ('92) 17.50 17.00
Never hinged 52.50
On cover 150.00
On cover, single franking 375.00
a. Slanting "5" *72.50* *65.00*
b. #22, "Martinique" omitted 75.00 75.00
23 D1 05c on 15c blk 16.00 16.00
Never hinged 47.50
On cover 120.00
On cover, single franking 375.00
b. Slanting "5" *72.50* *65.00*
c. #23, "Martinique" omitted 130.00 130.00
24 D1 15c on 20c blk 20.00 16.00
Never hinged 60.00
On cover 125.00
On cover, single franking 375.00
a. Inverted surcharge *300.00* *300.00*
b. Double surcharge *300.00* *300.00*
c. #24, "Martinique" omitted 175.00 175.00
25 D1 15c on 30c blk 20.00 16.00
Never hinged 60.00
On cover 125.00
On cover, single franking 375.00
a. Inverted surcharge *300.00* *300.00*
b. Slanting "5" *80.00* *72.50*
c. #25, "Martinique" omitted 175.00 175.00
Nos. 22-25 (4) 73.50 65.00

Red Surcharge

26 D1 05c on 10c blk 14.50 11.00
Never hinged 40.00
On cover 190.00
On cover, single franking 375.00
a. Inverted surcharge *300.00* *300.00*
b. #26, "Martinique" omitted 100.00 100.00
27 D1 05c on 15c blk 16.00 16.00
Never hinged 47.50
On cover 200.00
On cover, single franking 375.00
28 D1 15c on 20c blk 52.50 45.00
Never hinged 135.00
On cover 225.00
On cover, single franking 375.00
a. Inverted surcharge *450.00* *450.00*
Nos. 26-28 (3) 83.00 72.00

French Colonies No. 54 Surcharged in Black

j

k

1892 *Perf. 14x13½*

29 A9 (j) 05c on 25c 65.00 65.00
Never hinged 125.00
On cover 375.00
On cover, single franking 625.00
a. Slanting "5" *300.00* *300.00*
30 A9 (j) 15c on 25c 36.00 36.00
Never hinged 82.50
On cover 210.00

On cover, single franking 325.00
a. Slanting "5" *275.00* *275.00*
31 A9 (k) 05c on 25c 65.00 65.00
Never hinged 135.00
On cover 375.00
On cover, single franking 625.00
a. "1882" instead of "1892" *675.00* *600.00*
b. "95" instead of "05" *850.00* *800.00*
c. Slanting "5" *300.00* *300.00*
32 A9 (k) 15c on 25c 32.50 32.50
Never hinged 70.00
On cover 210.00
On cover, single franking 325.00
a. "1882" instead of "1892" *600.00* *600.00*
On cover 750.00
On cover, single franking 1,250.
b. Slanting "5" *160.00* *160.00*
Nos. 29-32 (4) 198.50 198.50

Navigation and Commerce — A15

1892-1906 Typo. *Perf. 14x13½*
"MARTINIQUE" Colony in Carmine or Blue

33 A15 1c blk, *lil bl* 1.50 1.40
Never hinged 2.25
On cover 75.00
On cover, single franking 125.00
a. "MARTINIQUE" in blue 1,000. 1,000.
b. "MARTINIQUE" omitted 5,500.
34 A15 2c brn, *buff* 1.75 1.40
Never hinged 2.50
On cover 75.00
On cover, business card, printed notice 125.00
35 A15 4c claret, *lav* 2.00 1.50
Never hinged 3.25
On cover 67.50
36 A15 5c grn, *grnsh* 2.40 1.50
Never hinged 4.00
On cover 30.00
On cover, single franking 50.00
On cover, single franking, military letter, *from* 375.00
37 A15 5c yel grn ('99) 3.50 1.10
Never hinged 5.75
On cover 12.00
On cover, single franking 20.00
38 A15 10c blk, *lav* 11.00 2.00
Never hinged 20.00
On cover 22.50
On cover, single franking 37.50
On cover, single franking, military letter, *from* 375.00
39 A15 10c red ('99) 5.25 1.50
Never hinged 9.00
On cover 16.00
On cover, single franking 22.50
40 A15 15c blue, quadrille paper 42.50 8.00
Never hinged 72.50
On cover 27.50
On cover, single franking 45.00
On cover, single franking, military letter, *from* 300.00
41 A15 15c gray ('99) 13.50 2.10
Never hinged 22.50
On cover 16.00
On cover, single franking 37.50
42 A15 20c red, *grn* 20.00 10.00
Never hinged 40.00
On cover 55.00
On cover, single franking 95.00
43 A15 25c blk, *rose* 24.00 3.25
Never hinged 42.50
On cover 60.00
On cover, single franking 115.00
44 A15 25c blue ('99) 16.00 14.50
Never hinged 27.50
On cover 275.00
On cover, single franking 500.00
45 A15 30c brn, *bis* 36.00 19.00
Never hinged 65.00
On cover 175.00
On cover, single franking 310.00
46 A15 35c blk, *yel* ('06) 16.00 9.50
Never hinged 27.50
On cover 125.00
On cover, single franking 700.00
47 A15 40c red, *straw* 36.00 19.00
Never hinged 65.00
On cover 240.00
On cover, single franking 450.00
48 A15 50c car, *rose* 40.00 24.00
Never hinged 70.00
On cover 275.00
On cover, single franking 500.00
49 A15 50c brn, *az* ('99) 42.50 32.50
Never hinged 82.50
On cover 500.00
On cover, single franking 625.00
50 A15 75c dp vio, *org* 32.50 20.00
Never hinged 62.50
On cover 300.00
On cover, single franking 700.00
51 A15 1fr brnz grn, *straw* 32.50 21.00
Never hinged 62.50
On cover 300.00
On cover, single franking 700.00
52 A15 2fr vio, *rose* ('04) 92.50 75.00
Never hinged 190.00
On cover 925.00
On cover, single franking 1,500.
53 A15 5fr lil, *lav* ('03) 110.00 95.00
Never hinged 205.00
On cover 1,050.
On cover, single franking 1,900.
Nos. 33-53 (21) 581.40 363.25

Perf. 13½x14 stamps are counterfeits.

For surcharges see Nos. 54-61, 101-104.

Stamps of 1892-1903 Surcharged in Black

Two types of surcharge: type 1, end of top of "C" round; type 2, end of top of "C" barred serif.

1904

54 A15 10c on 30c brn, *bis* (1) 14.50 14.50
Never hinged 24.00
On cover 75.00
On cover, single franking 125.00
a. Double surcharge 525.00 525.00
b. Inverted surcharge 1,600. 1,600.
c. Type 2 70.00 70.00
Never hinged 135.00
d. Pair, types 1 and 2 110.00 110.00
Never hinged 210.00
55 A15 10c on 5fr lil, *lav* (1) 16.00 16.00
Never hinged 27.50
On cover 125.00
On cover, single franking 130.00
b. Type 2 140.00 140.00
Never hinged 220.00
c. Pair, types 1 and 2 220.00 220.00
Never hinged 325.00

Surcharged

56 A15 10c on 30c brn, *bis* 24.00 24.00
Never hinged 42.50
On cover 115.00
On cover, single franking 190.00
57 A15 10c on 40c red, *straw* 24.00 24.00
Never hinged 42.50
On cover 125.00
On cover, single franking 195.00
a. Double surcharge 600.00 600.00
58 A15 10c on 50c car, *rose* 28.00 28.00
Never hinged 55.00
On cover 195.00
59 A15 10c on 75c dp vio, *org* 20.00 20.00
Never hinged 35.00
On cover 110.00
On cover, single franking 175.00
60 A15 10c on 1fr brnz grn, *straw* 24.00 24.00
Never hinged 42.50
On cover 125.00
On cover, single franking 195.00
a. Double surcharge 350.00 350.00
61 A15 10c on 5fr lil, *lav* 200.00 200.00
On cover *1,000.*
On cover, single franking *1,500.*
Nos. 54-61 (8) 350.50 350.50

Martinique Woman — A16

Girl Bearing Pineapple in Cane Field — A18

View of Fort-de-France — A17

1908-30 Typo.

62 A16 1c red brn & brn .25 .25
Never hinged .30
On cover 40.00
On cover, single franking 62.50
63 A16 2c ol grn & brn .30 .25
Never hinged .45
On cover 40.00
On cover, single franking 62.50
64 A16 4c vio brn & brn .30 .30
Never hinged .45
On cover 40.00
On cover, single franking 55.00
65 A16 5c grn & brn 1.10 .40
Never hinged 1.60
On cover 15.00
On cover, single franking 21.00
a. Perf 11 140.00
Never hinged 190.00
66 A16 5c org & brn ('22) .50 .40
Never hinged .65
On cover 5.00
On cover, single franking 6.25
67 A16 10c car & brn 1.10 .50
Never hinged 1.60
On cover 8.00
On cover, single franking 12.50
68 A16 10c bl grn & grn ('22) .55 .40
Never hinged .80
On cover 30.00
On cover, single franking 45.00
69 A16 10c brn vio & rose ('25) .55 .40
Never hinged .80
On cover 15.00
On cover, single franking 20.00
70 A16 15c brn vio & rose ('17) .65 .40
Never hinged 1.10
On cover 10.00
On cover, single franking 12.50
71 A16 15c bl grn & gray grn ('25) .50 .40
Never hinged .75
On cover 10.00
On cover, single franking 12.50
72 A16 15c dp bl & red org ('28) 1.60 1.60
Never hinged 2.40
On cover 10.00
On cover, single franking 12.50
73 A16 20c vio & brn 1.40 1.10
Never hinged 2.00
On cover 12.50
On cover, single franking 16.00
74 A17 25c bl & brn 2.25 1.10
Never hinged 3.25
On cover 30.00
On cover, single franking 105.00
75 A17 25c org & brn ('22) .90 .55
Never hinged 1.20
On cover 10.00
On cover, single franking 12.50
76 A17 30c brn org & brn 2.25 1.10
Never hinged 3.25
On cover 50.00
On cover, single franking 110.00
77 A17 30c dl red & brn ('22) .75 .65
Never hinged .95
On cover 25.00
On cover, single franking 95.00
78 A17 30c rose & ver ('24) .55 .55
Never hinged .80
On cover 7.50
On cover, single franking 10.00
79 A17 30c ol brn & brn ('25) .55 .55
Never hinged .95
On cover 6.00
On cover, single franking 8.75
80 A17 30c sl bl & bl grn ('27) 1.60 1.60
Never hinged 2.40
On cover 10.00
On cover, single franking 12.50
81 A17 35c vio & brn .90 .65
Never hinged 1.20
On cover 30.00
On cover, single franking 125.00
a. White chalky paper 4.50 2.75
Never hinged 7.00
82 A17 40c gray grn & brn .90 .65
Never hinged 1.20
On cover 30.00
On cover, single franking 62.50
83 A17 45c dk brn & brn .90 .65
Never hinged 1.20
On cover 30.00
On cover, single franking 75.00
a. White chalky paper 2.00 1.60
Never hinged 3.25
84 A17 50c rose & brn 2.25 1.10
Never hinged 3.25
On cover 45.00
On cover, single franking 95.00
a. 50c red and brown 2.40 1.20
Never hinged 4.00
On cover 45.00
On cover, single franking 95.00
85 A17 50c bl & brn ('22) 1.40 1.30
Never hinged 2.00
On cover 25.00
On cover, single franking 87.50
86 A17 50c org & grn ('25) .90 .40
Never hinged 1.20
On cover 12.50
87 A17 60c dk bl & lil rose ('25) .75 .75
Never hinged 2.00
On cover 30.00
On cover, single franking 105.00
88 A17 65c vio & ol brn ('27) 2.00 2.00
Never hinged 2.75
On cover 10.00
On cover, single franking 15.00
89 A17 75c slate & brn 1.40 1.10
Never hinged 2.15
On cover 50.00
On cover, single franking 105.00
90 A17 75c ind & dk bl ('25) .90 .90
Never hinged 1.20
On cover 25.00
On cover, single franking 95.00
91 A17 75c org brn & lt bl ('27) 2.75 2.75
Never hinged 4.25
On cover 16.00
92 A17 90c brn red & brt red ('30) 5.50 5.50
Never hinged 9.00
On cover 62.50
On cover, single franking 110.00
93 A18 1fr dl bl & brn 1.20 1.00
Never hinged 1.90
On cover 55.00
On cover, single franking 105.00
94 A18 1fr dk bl ('25) 1.00 .90
Never hinged 1.35
On cover 25.00
On cover, single franking 75.00
95 A18 1fr ver & ol grn ('27) 2.75 2.75
Never hinged 4.25
On cover 45.00
On cover, single franking 62.50
96 A18 1.10fr vio & dk brn ('28) 3.75 *4.50*
Never hinged 5.50
On cover 80.00
On cover, single franking 225.00
97 A18 1.50fr ind & ultra ('30) 5.50 5.50
Never hinged 9.00
On cover 55.00
On cover, single franking 95.00
98 A18 2fr gray & brn 4.50 2.00
Never hinged 7.00
On cover 55.00
On cover, single franking 95.00
99 A18 3fr red vio ('30) 9.50 9.50
Never hinged 14.50
On cover 95.00
On cover, single franking 160.00
100 A18 5fr org red & brn 10.50 8.00
Never hinged 18.00
On cover 125.00
On cover, single franking 200.00
Nos. 62-100 (39) 76.90 64.40

For surcharges see Nos. 105-128, B1.

Nos. 41, 43, 47 and 53 Surcharged in Carmine or Black

Spacing between figures of surcharge 1.5mm (5c), 2mm (10c)

1912, Aug.

101 A15 5c on 15c gray (C) 1.00 1.00
Never hinged 1.60
On cover 40.00
On cover, single franking 62.50
102 A15 5c on 25c blk, *rose* (C) 1.50 1.50
Never hinged 2.40
On cover 50.00
On cover, single franking 80.00
103 A15 10c on 40c red, *straw* 2.40 2.40
Never hinged 4.00
On cover 110.00
On cover, single franking 175.00
104 A15 10c on 5fr lil, *lav* 3.00 3.00
Never hinged 4.75
On cover 120.00
On cover, single franking 190.00
Nos. 101-104 (4) 7.90 7.90

Spacing between figures of surcharge 2.25mm (5c), 2.75mm (10c)

101a A15 5c on 15c gray (C) 37.50 37.50
Never hinged 92.50
102a A15 5c on 25c blk, *rose* (C) 77.50 77.50
Never hinged 190.00
103a A15 10c on 40c red, *straw* 125.00 125.00
Never hinged 280.00
104a A15 10c on 5fr lil, *lav* 77.50 77.50
Never hinged 280.00
Nos. 101a-104a (4) 317.50 317.50

Nos. 62, 63, 70 Surcharged

1920, June 15

105 A16 5c on 1c 2.10 2.10
Never hinged 3.15
On cover 35.00
On cover, single franking 50.00
a. Double surcharge 45.00 45.00
Never hinged 70.00
b. Inverted surcharge 32.50 32.50
Never hinged 57.50
On cover 75.00

106 A16 10c on 2c 2.10 2.10
Never hinged 3.15
On cover 40.00
On cover, single franking 62.50
a. Double surcharge 130.00
Never hinged 200.00
b. Inverted surcharge 45.00 45.00
Never hinged 70.00
c. Double surcharge, one inverted 95.00
Never hinged 150.00
107 A16 25c on 15c 2.25 2.25
Never hinged 3.25
On cover 62.50
a. Double surcharge 55.00 55.00
Never hinged 100.00
b. Inverted surcharge 55.00 55.00
Never hinged 100.00
c. Double surcharge, one inverted 100.00
Never hinged 150.00
d. Pair, one stamp without surcharge 160.00 160.00
Never hinged 275.00
Nos. 105-107 (3) 6.45 6.45

No. 70 Surcharged in Various Colors

1922, Dec.

108 A16 1c on 15c (Bk) .50 .50
Never hinged .65
On cover 75.00
On cover, single franking 110.00
a. Double surcharge 190.00 190.00
109 A16 2c on 15c (Bl) .50 .50
Never hinged .65
On cover 75.00
On cover, single franking 110.00
110 A16 5c on 15c (R) .65 .65
Never hinged .95
On cover 25.00
On cover, single franking 37.50
a. Imperf., pair 260.00
Never hinged 400.00
Nos. 108-110 (3) 1.65 1.65

Types of 1908-30 Surcharged

1923-25

111 A17 60c on 75c bl & rose .65 .65
Never hinged .95
On cover 30.00
On cover, single franking 60.00
112 A17 65c on 45c ol brn & brn ('25) 1.45 1.45
Never hinged 2.40
On cover 30.00
On cover, single franking 60.00
113 A17 85c on 75c blk & brn (R) ('25) 1.75 1.75
Never hinged 2.75
On cover 37.50
On cover, single franking 90.00
Nos. 111-113 (3) 3.85 3.85

Nos. 63, 73, 76-77, 84-85 Surcharged in Brown

Surcharge is horiz. on Nos. 114-115, vert. reading up on Nos. 116, 119 and down on Nos. 117-118.

1924, Feb. 14

114 A16 1c on 2c 3.25 3.25
Never hinged 5.75
On cover 75.00
On cover, single franking 125.00
a. Double surcharge 550.00 550.00
b. Inverted surcharge 100.00 100.00
Never hinged 160.00
On cover 275.00
On cover, single franking 295.00
115 A16 5c on 20c 4.00 4.00
Never hinged 6.50
On cover 150.00
On cover, single franking 450.00
a. Inverted surcharge 100.00 100.00
Never hinged 160.00
116 A17 15c on 30c (#76) 16.00 16.00
Never hinged 27.50
On cover 100.00
On cover, single franking 160.00
a. Surcharge reading down 57.50 57.50
Never hinged 90.00
117 A17 15c on 30c (#77) 22.50 22.50
Never hinged 37.50
On cover 125.00
On cover, single franking 210.00
a. Surcharge reading up 67.50 67.50
Never hinged 120.00
118 A17 25c on 50c (#84) 325.00 350.00
Never hinged 650.00
119 A17 25c on 50c (#85) 10.50 10.50
Never hinged 18.00
On cover 65.00
On cover, single franking 110.00
a. Double surcharge 400.00 400.00
b. Surcharge reading down 47.50
Never hinged 80.00
Nos. 114-119 (6) 381.25 406.25

Stamps and Types of 1908-30 Surcharged

1924-27

120 A16 25c on 15c brn vio & rose ('25) .55 .55
Never hinged .80
On cover 6.00
On cover, single franking 9.00
121 A18 25c on 2fr gray & brn .50 .50
Never hinged .65
On cover 6.00
On cover, single franking 9.00
122 A18 25c on 5fr org red & brn (Bl) 2.10 1.75
Never hinged 3.00
On cover 9.00
On cover, single franking 14.00
123 A17 90c on 75c brn red & red ('27) 3.75 2.75
Never hinged 5.75
On cover 27.50
On cover, single franking 45.00
124 A18 1.25fr on 1fr dk bl ('26) 1.10 1.00
Never hinged 1.75
On cover 24.00
On cover, single franking 37.50
125 A18 1.50fr on 1fr dk bl & ultra ('27) 2.00 1.10
Never hinged 2.75
On cover 50.00
On cover, single franking 125.00
126 A18 3fr on 5fr dl red & grn ('27) 3.00 3.00
Never hinged 4.25
On cover 55.00
On cover, single franking 140.00
a. Period after "F" omitted 13.50 13.50
Never hinged 24.00
127 A18 10fr on 5fr dl grn & dp red ('27) 12.00 12.00
Never hinged 19.00
On cover 75.00
On cover, single franking 175.00
a. Period after "F" omitted 35.00 35.00
Never hinged 57.50
128 A18 20fr on 5fr org brn & red vio ('27) 18.50 17.50
Never hinged 27.50
On cover 95.00
On cover, single franking 200.00
a. Period after "F" omitted 47.50 47.50
Never hinged 75.00
Nos. 120-128 (9) 43.50 40.15

Common Design Types pictured following the introduction.

Colonial Exposition Issue
Common Design Types

1931, Apr. 13 Engr. *Perf. 12½*
Name of Country in Black

129 CD70 40c deep green 5.25 5.25
Never hinged 7.25
On cover 37.50
On cover, single franking 62.50
130 CD71 50c violet 5.25 5.25
Never hinged 7.25
On cover 30.00
On cover, single franking 50.00
131 CD72 90c red orange 5.25 5.25
Never hinged 7.25
On cover 95.00
On cover, single franking 140.00
132 CD73 1.50fr dull blue 5.25 5.25
Never hinged 7.25
On cover 80.00
On cover, single franking 125.00
Nos. 129-132 (4) 21.00 21.00

Village of Basse-Pointe — A19

Government Palace, Fort-de-France — A20

Martinique Women A21

1933-40 Photo. *Perf. 13½*

133 A19 1c red, *pink* .25 .25
Never hinged .30
On cover 27.50
On cover, single franking 42.50
134 A20 2c dull blue .25 .25
Never hinged .30
On cover 27.50
On cover, single franking 42.50
135 A20 3c sepia ('40) .35 .35
Never hinged .40
On cover 30.00
On cover, single franking 50.00
136 A19 4c olive grn .25 .25
Never hinged .30
On cover 25.00
On cover, single franking 37.50
137 A20 5c dp rose .35 .35
Never hinged .45
On cover 20.00
On cover, single franking 30.00
138 A19 10c blk, *pink* .35 .35
Never hinged .45
On cover 15.00
On cover, single franking 25.00
139 A20 15c blk, *org* .35 .35
Never hinged .45
On cover 15.00
On cover, single franking 22.50
140 A21 20c org brn .35 .35
Never hinged .45
On cover 10.00
On cover, single franking 15.00
141 A19 25c brn vio .35 .35
Never hinged .45
On cover 8.00
On cover, single franking 10.00
142 A20 30c green .50 .50
Never hinged .65
On cover 8.00
On cover, single franking 12.50
143 A20 30c lt ultra ('40) .40 .40
Never hinged .60
On cover 20.00
On cover, single franking 30.00
144 A21 35c dl grn ('38) 1.00 .90
Never hinged 1.25
On cover 10.00
On cover, single franking 15.00
145 A21 40c olive brn .65 .50
Never hinged .80
On cover 5.00
On cover, single franking 6.25
146 A20 45c dk brn 2.00 1.90
Never hinged 2.40
On cover 12.50
On cover, single franking 19.00
147 A20 45c grn ('40) .65 .65
Never hinged .80
On cover 25.00
On cover, single franking 37.50
148 A20 50c red .50 .30
Never hinged .65
On cover 5.00
On cover, single franking 6.25
149 A19 55c brn red ('38) 1.30 1.00
Never hinged 1.75
On cover 10.00
On cover, single franking 12.50
150 A19 60c lt bl ('40) .95 .95
Never hinged 1.20
On cover 20.00
On cover, single franking 30.00
151 A21 65c red, *grn* .50 .50
Never hinged .65
On cover 7.50
On cover, single franking 10.00
152 A21 70c brt red vio ('40) .75 .75
Never hinged .95
On cover 7.50
On cover, single franking 12.50
153 A19 75c dk brn 1.10 .90
Never hinged 2.10
On cover 7.50
On cover, single franking 25.00
154 A20 80c vio ('38) .75 .65
Never hinged .90
On cover 7.50
On cover, single franking 12.50
155 A19 90c carmine 1.90 1.75
Never hinged 2.25
On cover 15.00
On cover, single franking 25.00
156 A19 90c brt red vio ('39) .95 .95
Never hinged 1.25
On cover 7.50
On cover, single franking 12.50
157 A20 1fr blk, *grn* 1.90 1.40
Never hinged 2.25
On cover 12.50
On cover, single franking 19.00
158 A20 1fr rose red ('38) .75 .65
Never hinged .90
On cover 12.50
On cover, single franking 21.00

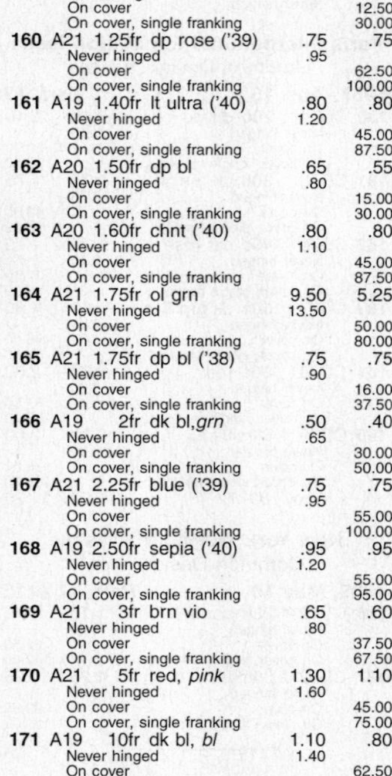

159 A21 1.25fr dk vio .80 .80
Never hinged 1.20
On cover 12.50
On cover, single franking 30.00
160 A21 1.25fr dp rose ('39) .75 .75
Never hinged .95
On cover 62.50
On cover, single franking 100.00
161 A19 1.40fr lt ultra ('40) .80 .80
Never hinged 1.20
On cover 45.00
On cover, single franking 87.50
162 A20 1.50fr dp bl .65 .55
Never hinged .80
On cover 15.00
On cover, single franking 30.00
163 A20 1.60fr chnt ('40) .80 .80
Never hinged 1.10
On cover 45.00
On cover, single franking 87.50
164 A21 1.75fr ol grn 9.50 5.25
Never hinged 13.50
On cover 50.00
On cover, single franking 80.00
165 A21 1.75fr dp bl ('38) .75 .75
Never hinged .90
On cover 16.00
On cover, single franking 37.50
166 A19 2fr dk bl,*grn* .50 .40
Never hinged .65
On cover 30.00
On cover, single franking 50.00
167 A21 2.25fr blue ('39) .75 .75
Never hinged .95
On cover 55.00
On cover, single franking 100.00
168 A19 2.50fr sepia ('40) .95 .95
Never hinged 1.20
On cover 55.00
On cover, single franking 95.00
169 A21 3fr brn vio .65 .60
Never hinged .80
On cover 37.50
On cover, single franking 67.50
170 A21 5fr red, *pink* 1.30 1.10
Never hinged 1.60
On cover 45.00
On cover, single franking 75.00
171 A19 10fr dk bl, *bl* 1.10 .80
Never hinged 1.40
On cover 62.50
On cover, single franking 100.00
172 A20 20fr red, *yel* 1.35 .95
Never hinged 1.90
On cover 80.00
On cover, single franking 125.00
Nos. 133-172 (40) 40.05 32.75

For surcharges see Nos. 190-195 in Scott Standard catalogue, Vol. 4.

Landing of Bélain d'Esnambuc — A22

Freed Slaves Paying Homage to Victor Schoelcher A23

1935, Oct. 22 Engr. *Perf. 13*

173 A22 40c blk brn 3.25 3.25
Never hinged 4.50
On cover 42.50
On cover, single franking 67.50
174 A22 50c dl red 3.25 3.25
Never hinged 4.50
On cover 35.00
On cover, single franking 57.50
175 A22 1.50fr ultra 12.00 12.00
Never hinged 16.50
On cover 95.00
On cover, single franking 140.00
176 A23 1.75fr lil rose 12.00 12.00
Never hinged 16.50
On cover 80.00
On cover, single franking 125.00
177 A23 5fr brown 12.00 12.00
Never hinged 16.50
On cover 80.00
On cover, single franking 125.00
a. 5fr ultramarine (error) 950.00
178 A23 10fr blue grn 9.50 9.50
Never hinged 12.50
On cover 105.00
On cover, single franking 150.00
Nos. 173-178 (6) 52.00 52.00

Tercentenary of French possessions in the West Indies.

Colonial Arts Exhibition Issue
Common Design Type
Souvenir Sheet

1937 *Imperf.*

179 CD74 3fr brt grn 8.75 *10.50*
Never hinged 11.00
On cover 140.00
On cover, single franking 200.00

a. "MARTINIQUE" omitted 3,100.
b. Inscriptions inverted 2,200.
Never hinged 3,250.

Paris International Exposition Issue
Common Design Types

1937, Apr. 15 ***Perf. 13***

180 CD74 20c dp vio 2.10 2.10
Never hinged 3.15
On cover 50.00
On cover, single franking 85.00
181 CD75 30c dk grn 1.75 1.75
Never hinged 2.75
On cover 42.50
On cover, single franking 70.00
182 CD76 40c car rose 1.75 1.75
Never hinged 2.75
On cover 37.50
On cover, single franking 62.50
183 CD77 50c dk brn & blk 1.60 1.60
Never hinged 2.50
On cover 40.00
On cover, single franking 50.00
184 CD78 90c red 2.00 2.00
Never hinged 3.00
On cover 87.50
On cover, single franking 160.00
185 CD79 1.50fr ultra 2.00 2.00
Never hinged 3.00
On cover 75.00
On cover, single franking 140.00
Nos. 180-185 (6) 11.20 11.20

New York World's Fair Issue
Common Design Type

1939, May 10 ***Perf. 12½x12***

186 CD82 1.25fr car lake 1.10 1.10
Never hinged 1.40
On cover 62.50
On cover, single franking 140.00
187 CD82 2.25fr ultra 1.25 1.25
Never hinged 1.60
On cover 62.50
On cover, single franking 125.00

SEMI-POSTAL STAMPS

Regular Issue of 1908 Surcharged in Red

Perf. 13½x14

1915, May 15 **Unwmk.**

B1 A16 10c + 5c car & brn 2.75 2.00
Never hinged 4.00
On cover 110.00

Curie Issue
Common Design Type

1938, Oct. 24 ***Perf. 13***

B2 CD80 1.75fr + 50c brt ultra 13.00 13.00
Never hinged 17.50
On cover 95.00
On cover, single franking 160.00

French Revolution Issue
Common Design Type
Photo.; Name & Value Typo. in Black

1939, July 5

B3 CD83 45c + 25c grn 10.50 10.50
Never hinged 15.00
On cover 125.00
B4 CD83 70c + 30c brn 10.50 10.50
Never hinged 15.00
On cover 95.00
B5 CD83 90c + 35c red org 10.50 10.50
Never hinged 15.00
On cover 87.50
B6 CD83 1.25fr + 1fr rose pink 10.50 10.50
Never hinged 15.00
On cover 125.00
On cover, single franking 200.00
B7 CD83 2.25fr + 2fr blue 10.50 10.50
Never hinged 15.00
On cover 110.00
On cover, single franking 190.00
Nos. B3-B7 (5) 52.50 52.50

POSTAGE DUE STAMPS

The set of 14 French Colonies postage due stamps (Nos. J1-J14) overprinted "MARTINIQUE" diagonally in red in 1887 was not an official issue.

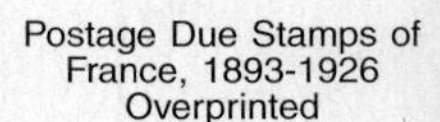

Postage Due Stamps of France, 1893-1926 Overprinted

1927, Oct. 10 ***Perf. 14x13½***

J15 D2 5c light blue 1.75 1.75
Never hinged 2.75
On cover 125.00
J16 D2 10c brown 2.10 2.00
Never hinged 3.75
On cover 125.00
J17 D2 20c olive green 2.10 2.00
Never hinged 3.75
On cover 125.00
J18 D2 25c rose 2.75 2.60
Never hinged 4.75
On cover 140.00
J19 D2 30c red 3.75 3.50
Never hinged 6.00
On cover 145.00
J20 D2 45c green 5.25 5.00
Never hinged 8.00
On cover 160.00
J21 D2 50c brn violet 6.50 6.00
Never hinged 11.00
On cover 165.00
J22 D2 60c blue green 6.50 6.00
Never hinged 11.00
On cover 175.00
J23 D2 1fr red brown 8.75 8.25
Never hinged 14.50
On cover 190.00
J24 D2 2fr bright vio 12.00 11.00
Never hinged 19.00
On cover 225.00
J25 D2 3fr magenta 13.00 12.00
Never hinged 21.00
On cover 250.00
Nos. J15-J25 (11) 64.45 60.10

Tropical Fruit — D3

1933, Feb. 15 **Photo.** ***Perf. 13½***

J26 D3 5c dk bl, *green* .50 .50
Never hinged .65
On cover 95.00
J27 D3 10c orange brown .50 .50
Never hinged .65
On cover 80.00
J28 D3 20c dk blue .95 .95
Never hinged 1.25
On cover 80.00
J29 D3 25c red, *pink* 1.40 1.40
Never hinged 1.75
On cover 75.00
J30 D3 30c dk vio 1.40 1.40
Never hinged 1.75
On cover 75.00
J31 D3 45c red, *yel* 1.10 1.10
Never hinged 1.40
On cover 75.00
J32 D3 50c dk brn 1.75 1.75
Never hinged 2.25
On cover 75.00
J33 D3 60c dl grn 1.75 1.75
Never hinged 2.25
On cover 80.00
J34 D3 1fr blk, *org* 1.75 1.75
Never hinged 2.25
On cover 95.00
J35 D3 2fr dp rose 1.75 1.75
Never hinged 2.25
On cover 110.00
J36 D3 3fr dk blue, *bl* 1.75 1.75
Never hinged 2.25
On cover 125.00
Nos. J26-J36 (11) 14.60 14.60

PARCEL POST STAMP

Postage Due Stamp of French Colonies Surcharged in Black

1903, Oct. **Unwmk.** ***Imperf.***

Q1 D1 5fr on 60c brn, *buff* 550.00 *675.00*
a. Inverted surcharge *875.00* *950.00*

MAURITANIA

mor-ə-ta-nē-ə

LOCATION — Northwestern Africa, bordering on the Atlantic Ocean
GOVT. — French Colony
AREA — 398,000 sq. mi.
POP. — 1,834,500 (est. 1984)
CAPITAL — Nouakchott

100 Centimes = 1 Franc

General Louis Faidherbe A1

Oil Palms — A2

Dr. Noel Eugène Ballay A3

Perf. 14x13½

1906-07 **Typo.** **Unwmk.**
"Mauritanie" in Red or Blue

1 A1 1c slate .70 .70
Never hinged 1.40
On cover 87.50
2 A1 2c chocolate 2.10 2.10
Never hinged 2.75
On cover 87.50
3 A1 4c choc, *gray bl* 2.75 2.75
Never hinged 4.25
On cover 87.50
4 A1 5c green 1.40 1.40
Never hinged 2.75
On cover 40.00
5 A1 10c carmine (B) 14.00 7.00
Never hinged 27.50
On cover 60.00
7 A2 20c black, *azure* 27.50 17.50
Never hinged 50.00
On cover 100.00
8 A2 25c blue, *pnksh* 10.00 7.00
Never hinged 14.00
On cover 50.00
9 A2 30c choc, *pnksh* 105.00 62.50
Never hinged 210.00
On cover 225.00
On cover, single franking 350.00
10 A2 35c black, *yellow* 10.00 7.00
Never hinged 17.50
On cover 130.00
11 A2 40c car, *az* (B) 10.00 10.00
Never hinged 17.50
On cover 130.00
12 A2 45c choc, *grnsh* ('07) 10.00 10.00
Never hinged 21.00
On cover 130.00
13 A2 50c deep violet 10.00 7.00
Never hinged 17.50
On cover 130.00
14 A2 75c blue, *org* 10.00 10.00
Never hinged 21.00
On cover 95.00
On cover, single franking 225.00
15 A3 1fr black, *azure* 27.50 27.50
Never hinged 50.00
On cover 150.00
On cover, single franking 300.00
16 A3 2fr blue, *pink* 55.00 55.00
Never hinged 140.00
On cover 225.00
On cover, single franking 400.00
17 A3 5fr car, *straw* (B) 140.00 150.00
Never hinged 275.00
On cover 475.00
On cover, single franking 625.00
Nos. 1-17 (16) 435.95 377.45

Crossing Desert A4

1913-38

18 A4 1c brn vio & brn .30 *.55*
Never hinged .70
On cover 70.00
19 A4 2c black & blue .30 *.55*
Never hinged .70
On cover 70.00
20 A4 4c violet & blk .30 *.55*
Never hinged .70
On cover 70.00
21 A4 5c yel grn & bl grn 1.00 .70
Never hinged 1.75
On cover 27.50
a. Chalky paper 2.10 1.40
Never hinged 3.50
On cover 37.50
22 A4 5c brn vio & rose ('22) .35 .35
Never hinged .70
On cover 25.00
23 A4 10c rose & red org 2.50 1.75
Never hinged 3.50
On cover 25.00
a. Chalky paper 3.50 2.50
Never hinged 5.50
On cover 25.00
24 A4 10c yel grn & bl grn ('22) .35 .70
Never hinged .70
On cover 45.00
25 A4 10c lil rose, *bluish* ('25) .70 1.00
Never hinged 1.00
On cover 47.50
26 A4 15c dk brn & blk ('17) .70 .70
Never hinged 1.00
On cover 15.00
a. Chalky paper 1.00 1.00
Never hinged 1.75
On cover 17.50
27 A4 20c bis brn & org .70 .70
Never hinged 1.00
On cover 27.50
28 A4 25c blue & vio 1.40 1.00
Never hinged 2.50
On cover 27.50
On cover, single franking 75.00
29 A4 25c grn & rose ('22) .35 .35
Never hinged .70
On cover 10.00
30 A4 30c bl grn & rose 1.40 1.50
Never hinged 2.50
On cover 35.00
On cover, single franking 87.50
31 A4 30c rose & red org ('22) 1.75 *2.10*
Never hinged 2.10
On cover 37.50
On cover, single franking 75.00
32 A4 30c black & yel ('26) .35 .35
Never hinged .70
On cover 16.00
33 A4 30c bl grn & yel grn ('28) 1.40 1.40
Never hinged 2.10
On cover 37.50
34 A4 35c brown & vio .70 .75
Never hinged 1.40
On cover 40.00
On cover, single franking 95.00
35 A4 35c dp grn & lt grn ('38) 1.40 1.40
Never hinged 2.10
On cover 45.00
36 A4 40c gray & bl grn 2.75 2.50
Never hinged 5.00
On cover 45.00
On cover, single franking 100.00
37 A4 45c org & bis brn 1.40 *1.75*
Never hinged 2.50
On cover 55.00
On cover, single franking 125.00
38 A4 50c brn vio & rose 1.00 *1.40*
Never hinged 1.75
On cover 62.50
On cover, single franking 140.00
39 A4 50c dk bl & ultra ('22) .70 *.70*
Never hinged .85
On cover 30.00
On cover, single franking 45.00
40 A4 50c gray grn & dp bl ('26) .35 .70
Never hinged .70
On cover 10.00
41 A4 60c vio, *pnksh* ('25) .70 *1.00*
Never hinged 1.00
On cover 27.50
On cover, single franking 80.00
42 A4 65c yel brn & lt bl ('26) 1.00 *1.75*
Never hinged 1.75
On cover 17.50
On cover, single franking 30.00
43 A4 75c ultra & brown 1.00 1.40
Never hinged 1.75
On cover 50.00
On cover, single franking 125.00
44 A4 85c myr grn & lt brn ('26) 1.40 *1.75*
Never hinged 1.75
On cover 35.00
On cover, single franking 100.00
45 A4 90c brn red & rose ('30) 2.10 2.10
Never hinged 3.50
On cover 50.00
On cover, single franking 95.00
46 A4 1fr rose & black 1.00 *1.40*
Never hinged 1.75
On cover 70.00
On cover, single franking 160.00
47 A4 1.10fr vio & ver ('28) 10.00 *14.00*
Never hinged 17.50
On cover 160.00
On cover, single franking 340.00
48 A4 1.25fr dk bl & blk brn ('33) 2.10 2.50
Never hinged 3.50
On cover 27.50
On cover, single franking 87.50
49 A4 1.50fr lt bl & dp bl ('30) 1.40 *1.40*
Never hinged 2.10
On cover 45.00
On cover, single franking 80.00
50 A4 1.75fr bl grn & brn red ('33) 2.10 2.50
Never hinged 2.75
On cover 22.50
On cover, single franking 35.00

51 A4 1.75fr dk bl & ultra ('38) 2.10 2.10
Never hinged 2.75
On cover 45.00
On cover, single franking 75.00
52 A4 2fr red org & vio 1.75 *2.10*
Never hinged 2.95
On cover 80.00
On cover, single franking 175.00
53 A4 3fr red violet ('30) 2.10 2.10
Never hinged 3.50
On cover 62.50
On cover, single franking 140.00
54 A4 5fr violet & blue 3.00 *3.75*
Never hinged 5.00
On cover 105.00
On cover, single franking 225.00
Nos. 18-54 (37) 53.90 63.30

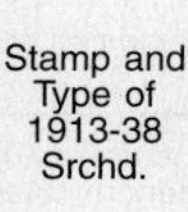

Stamp and Type of 1913-38 Srchd.

1922-25

55 A4 60c on 75c violet, *pnksh* 1.00 *1.40*
Never hinged 1.75
On cover 25.00
On cover, single franking 45.00
56 A4 65c on 15c dk brn & blk ('25) 1.75 *2.10*
Never hinged 2.50
On cover 62.50
On cover, single franking 140.00
57 A4 85c on 75c ultra & brn ('25) 1.75 *2.10*
Never hinged 2.75
On cover 45.00
On cover, single franking 87.50
Nos. 55-57 (3) 4.50 *5.60*

Type of 1913-38 Srchd.

1924-27

58 A4 25c on 2fr red org & vio 1.00 1.40
Never hinged 1.75
On cover 10.00
a. Left bars and "2" omitted 400.00
Never hinged 600.00
59 A4 90c on 75c brn red & cer ('27) 2.10 *2.75*
Never hinged 3.75
On cover 50.00
On cover, single franking 87.50
60 A4 1.25fr on 1fr dk bl & ultra ('26) .70 *.70*
Never hinged 1.00
On cover 55.00
On cover, single franking 105.00
61 A4 1.50fr on 1fr bl & dp bl ('27) 1.40 *1.75*
Never hinged 2.10
On cover 45.00
On cover, single franking 75.00
62 A4 3fr on 5fr ol brn & red vio ('27) 7.00 7.00
Never hinged 10.00
On cover 95.00
On cover, single franking 190.00
63 A4 10fr on 5fr mag & bl grn ('27) 7.00 7.75
Never hinged 10.00
On cover 105.00
On cover, single franking 225.00
64 A4 20fr on 5fr bl vio & dp org ('27) 7.00 *8.00*
Never hinged 12.50
On cover 120.00
On cover, single franking 250.00
a. Period after "F" omitted 27.50 32.50
Never hinged 50.00
Nos. 58-64 (7) 26.20 *29.35*

Common Design Types pictured following the introduction.

Colonial Exposition Issue

Common Design Types

Engr.; Name of Country Typo. in Black

1931, Apr. 13 *Perf. 12½*

65 CD70 40c deep green 7.00 7.00
Never hinged 10.00
On cover 110.00
66 CD71 50c violet 5.00 5.00
Never hinged 7.00
On cover 95.00
67 CD72 90c red orange 5.00 5.00
Never hinged 7.00
On cover 165.00
On cover, single franking 240.00
68 CD73 1.50fr dull blue 5.00 5.00
Never hinged 7.00
On cover 150.00
On cover, single franking 225.00
Nos. 65-68 (4) 22.00 22.00

Paris International Exposition Issue

Common Design Types

1937, Apr. 15 *Perf. 13*

69 CD74 20c deep violet 1.75 1.75
Never hinged 2.75
On cover 105.00
70 CD75 30c dark green 1.75 1.75
Never hinged 2.75
On cover 95.00
71 CD76 40c carmine rose 2.10 2.10
Never hinged 2.75
On cover 75.00
72 CD77 50c dk brn & blk 1.40 1.40
Never hinged 2.75
On cover 70.00
73 CD78 90c red 1.40 1.40
Never hinged 2.75
On cover 105.00
On cover, single franking 175.00
74 CD79 1.50fr ultra 2.10 2.10
Never hinged 2.75
On cover 95.00
On cover, single franking 160.00
Nos. 69-74 (6) 10.50 10.50

Colonial Arts Exhibition Issue

Common Design Type

Souvenir Sheet

1937 *Imperf.*

75 CD76 3fr dark blue 10.00 *14.00*
Never hinged 14.00
On cover 125.00
On cover, single franking 190.00
a. Marginal inscription inverted 1,100.
Never hinged 1,500.

Camel Rider — A5

Mauri Couple — A8

Mauris on Camels A6

Family Before Tent — A7

1938-40 *Perf. 13*

76 A5 2c violet blk .25 .25
Never hinged .35
On cover 35.00
77 A5 3c dp ultra .25 .25
Never hinged .35
On cover 35.00
78 A5 4c rose violet .30 .30
Never hinged .45
On cover 35.00
79 A5 5c orange red .30 .30
Never hinged .45
On cover 27.50
80 A5 10c brown car .35 .35
Never hinged .70
On cover 27.50
81 A5 15c dk violet .35 .35
Never hinged .70
On cover 22.50
82 A6 20c red .35 .35
Never hinged .70
On cover 16.00
83 A6 25c deep ultra .35 .35
Never hinged .70
On cover 21.00
84 A6 30c deep brown .25 .25
Never hinged .35
On cover 13.50
85 A6 35c Prus green .35 .70
Never hinged .70
On cover 35.00
86 A6 40c rose car ('40) .35 .35
Never hinged .70
On cover 14.50
87 A6 45c Prus grn ('40) .35 .35
Never hinged .70
On cover 30.00
88 A6 50c purple .35 .50
Never hinged .70
On cover 16.00
89 A7 55c rose violet .70 1.00
Never hinged 1.40
On cover 40.00
90 A7 60c violet ('40) .35 .35
Never hinged .70
On cover 25.00
91 A7 65c deep green .70 1.00
Never hinged 1.40
On cover 40.00
92 A7 70c red ('40) .70 .70
Never hinged 1.00
On cover 27.50
93 A7 80c deep blue 1.40 1.40
Never hinged 1.75
On cover 45.00
94 A7 90c rose violet ('39) .70 .70
Never hinged 1.00
On cover 45.00
On cover, single franking 100.00
95 A7 1fr red 2.75 2.10
Never hinged 3.50
On cover 40.00
On cover, single franking 75.00
96 A7 1fr dp green ('40) .70 1.00
Never hinged 1.00
On cover 7.50
97 A7 1.25fr rose car ('39) 1.40 1.40
Never hinged 1.75
On cover 62.50
On cover, single franking 125.00
98 A7 1.40fr dp blue ('40) .70 .70
Never hinged 1.00
On cover 45.00
On cover, single franking 100.00
99 A7 1.50fr violet .70 1.00
Never hinged 1.40
On cover 40.00
On cover, single franking 105.00
99A A7 1.50fr red brn ('40) 125.00
Never hinged 160.00
100 A7 1.60fr black brn ('40) 1.75 1.75
Never hinged 2.75
On cover 45.00
On cover, single franking 105.00
101 A8 1.75fr deep ultra 1.40 *1.40*
Never hinged 1.75
On cover 40.00
On cover, single franking 105.00
102 A8 2fr rose violet .35 *1.00*
Never hinged .70
On cover 27.50
On cover, single franking 50.00
103 A8 2.25fr dull ultra ('39) .70 .70
Never hinged 1.00
On cover 55.00
On cover, single franking 110.00
104 A8 2.50fr black brn ('40) 1.40 1.40
Never hinged 1.75
On cover 35.00
On cover, single franking 70.00
105 A8 3fr deep green .35 *.90*
Never hinged .70
On cover 45.00
On cover, single franking 80.00
106 A8 5fr scarlet .70 *1.00*
Never hinged 1.40
On cover 45.00
On cover, single franking 87.50
107 A8 10fr deep brown 1.75 *1.90*
Never hinged 2.10
On cover 55.00
On cover, single franking 105.00
108 A8 20fr brown car 2.10 *2.25*
Never hinged 2.50
On cover 70.00
On cover, single franking 120.00
Nos. 76-108 (34) 150.45 28.30

Nos. 91 and 109 surcharged with new values are listed under French West Africa.

For surcharges see Nos. B9-B12 in Scott Standard catalogue, Vol. 4.

Caillie Issue

Common Design Type

1939, Apr. 5 Engr. *Perf. 12½x12*

109 CD81 90c org brn & org .35 *1.00*
Never hinged 1.40
On cover 11.00
110 CD81 2fr brt violet .35 *1.40*
Never hinged .70
On cover 27.50
On cover, single franking 50.00
111 CD81 2.25fr ultra & dk bl .35 *1.40*
Never hinged .70
On cover 35.00
On cover, single franking 55.00
Nos. 109-111 (3) 1.05 3.80

New York World's Fair Issue

Common Design Type

1939, May 10

112 CD82 1.25fr carmine lake .70 1.40
Never hinged 1.00
On cover 75.00
On cover, single franking 160.00
113 CD82 2.25fr ultra .70 1.40
Never hinged 1.00
On cover 75.00
On cover, single franking 145.00

SEMI-POSTAL STAMPS

Nos. 23 and 26 Surcharged in Red

1915-18 Unwmk. *Perf. 14x13½*

B1 A4 10c + 5c rose & red org 1.75 *2.10*
Never hinged 2.75
On cover 60.00
a. Double surcharge 225.00
Never hinged 350.00
B2 A4 15c + 5c dk brn & blk ('18) 1.75 *2.10*
Never hinged 2.75
On cover 60.00
a. Double surcharge 190.00
Never hinged 290.00
b. Inverted surcharge 150.00
Never hinged 240.00
c. Pair, one normal, one inverted surcharge 350.00

Curie Issue

Common Design Type

1938, Oct. 24 *Perf. 13*

B3 CD80 1.75fr + 50c brt ultra 7.75 7.75
Never hinged 12.50
On cover 100.00
On cover, single franking 170.00

French Revolution Issue

Common Design Type

Photo.; Name and Value Typographed in Black

1939, July 5 **Unwmk.**

B4 CD83 45c + 25c grn 8.50 8.50
Never hinged 14.00
On cover 160.00
B5 CD83 70c + 30c brn 8.50 8.50
Never hinged 14.00
On cover 120.00
B6 CD83 90c + 35c red org 8.50 8.50
Never hinged 14.00
On cover 100.00
B7 CD83 1.25fr + 1fr rose pink 8.50 8.50
Never hinged 14.00
On cover 170.00
On cover, single franking 250.00
B8 CD83 2.25fr + 2fr bl 8.50 8.50
Never hinged 14.00
On cover 160.00
On cover, single franking 225.00
Nos. B4-B8 (5) 42.50 42.50

AIR POST STAMPS

Common Design Type

Perf. 12½x12

1940, Feb. 8 Engr. Unwmk.

C1 CD85 1.90fr ultra .35 .35
Never hinged .70
On cover 37.50
C2 CD85 2.90fr dk red .35 .35
Never hinged .70
On cover 37.50
a. "MAURITANIE" double 150.00
Never hinged 225.00
C3 CD85 4.50fr dk gray grn .70 .70
Never hinged 1.00
On cover 45.00
C4 CD85 4.90fr yel bister .70 .70
Never hinged 1.00
On cover 50.00
a. "MAURITANIE" inverted 225.00
Never hinged 300.00
C5 CD85 6.90fr deep org 1.40 1.40
Never hinged 1.75
On cover 62.50
Nos. C1-C5 (5) 3.50 3.50

POSTAGE DUE STAMPS

D1

Perf. 14x13½

1906-07 Unwmk. Typo.

J1 D1 5c grn, *grnsh* 3.50 3.50
Never hinged 7.00
On cover 200.00
J2 D1 10c red brn 5.00 5.00
Never hinged 10.00
On cover 200.00
J3 D1 15c dk bl 10.00 7.00
Never hinged 17.50
On cover 200.00
J4 D1 20c blk, *yellow* 12.00 10.00
Never hinged 23.00
On cover 200.00
J5 D1 30c red, *straw* 14.00 11.00
Never hinged 24.00
On cover 200.00
J6 D1 50c violet 20.00 19.00
Never hinged 40.00
On cover 200.00
J7 D1 60c blk, *buff* 16.00 14.00
Never hinged 32.50
On cover 200.00
J8 D1 1fr blk, *pinkish* 26.00 20.00
Never hinged 47.50
On cover 200.00
Nos. J1-J8 (8) 106.50 89.50

Issue dates: 20c, 1906; others 1907.

Regular postage stamps canceled "T" in a triangle were used for postage due.

D2

1914

J9 D2 5c green .25 *.35*
Never hinged .35
On cover 150.00
J10 D2 10c rose .30 *.50*
Never hinged .35
On cover 150.00
J11 D2 15c gray .35 *.70*
Never hinged .70
On cover 150.00
J12 D2 20c brown .35 *.70*
Never hinged .70
On cover 150.00
J13 D2 30c blue .70 *1.00*
Never hinged 1.40
On cover 150.00
J14 D2 50c black 1.75 *1.75*
Never hinged 2.10
On cover 150.00
J15 D2 60c orange 1.40 *1.40*
Never hinged 1.75
On cover 150.00
J16 D2 1fr violet 1.40 *1.40*
Never hinged 1.75
On cover 150.00
Nos. J9-J16 (8) 6.50 *7.80*

Type of 1914 Issue Surcharged

1927, Oct. 10

J17 D2 2fr on 1fr lil rose 3.50 3.50
Never hinged 5.00
a. Period after "F" omitted 14.00 *15.00*
Never hinged 24.00
J18 D2 3fr on 1fr org brn 3.50 *4.25*
Never hinged 5.50

MAURITIUS

mo-'ri-sh,ē-,əs

LOCATION — Island in the Indian Ocean about 550 miles east of Madagascar
GOVT. — British Colony
AREA — 720 sq. mi.
POP. — 969,191 (est. 1983)
CAPITAL — Port Louis

12 Pence = 1 Shilling
100 Cents = 1 Rupee (1878)

Nos. 1-6, 14-17 unused are valued without gum.

Nos. 3a-8, 14-15 are printed on fragile paper with natural irregularities which might be mistaken for faults.

Very fine examples of Nos. 22-58 will have perforations touching the design on one or more sides. Examples with perfs clear on four sides are scarce and will sell for more. Inferior examples will sell for much reduced prices.

Catalogue values for unused stamps in this country are for Never Hinged items, beginning with Scott 223 in the regular postage section, Scott J1 in the postage due section.

Queen Victoria — A1

1847 Unwmk. Engr. *Imperf.*

1 A1 1p orange *1,250,000. 1,250,000.*
2 A1 2p dark blue *1,700,000.*

Nos. 1 and 2 were engraved and printed in Port Louis. There is but one type of each value. The initials "J. B." on the bust are those of the engraver, J. Barnard.

All unused examples of the 2p are in museums. There is one unused example of the 1p in private hands. There are two used examples of the 1p in private hands, both of which have small faults and are valued thus.

Queen Victoria — A2

Earliest Impressions

1848 Thick Yellowish Paper

3 A2 1p orange *65,000. 18,000.*
4 A2 2p dark blue *62,500. 24,500.*
d. "PENOE" *125,000. 42,500.*

Early Impressions

Yellowish White Paper

3a A2 1p orange *32,500. 7,250.*
4a A2 2p blue *35,000. 8,500.*
e. "PENOE" *65,000. 16,000.*

Bluish Paper

5 A2 1p orange *32,500. 7,250.*
6 A2 2p blue *35,000. 8,500.*
c. "PENOE" *65,000. 16,000.*

Intermediate Impressions

Yellowish White Paper

3b A2 1p red orange *21,500.* 2,850.
4b A2 2p blue *22,500.* 3,600.
f. "PENOE" *40,000.* 7,500.
j. 2p pale blue *22,500.* 3,750.

Bluish Paper

5a A2 1p red orange *21,500.* 2,900.
6a A2 2p blue *22,500.* 3,750.
d. "PENOE" *40,000.* 7,500.
f. Double impression —

Worn Impressions

Yellowish White Paper

3c A2 1p orange red 7,500. 900.
d. 1p brownish red 7,500. 900.
4c A2 2p blue 9,250. 1,600.
g. "PENOE" *12,500.* 3,000.

Bluish Paper

5b A2 1p orange red 7,000. 850.
c. 1p brownish red 7,000. 850.
d. Double impression
6b A2 2p blue 9,500. 1,500.
e. "PENOE" *12,500.* 3,000.

Latest Impressions

Yellowish or Grayish Paper

3e A2 1p orange red 6,000. 750.
f. 1p brownish red 6,000. 750.
On cover, from *3,750.*
4h A2 2p blue 7,500. 1,100.
On cover, from *5,500.*
i. "PENOE" *14,000.* 2,100.

Bluish Paper

5e A2 1p orange red 6,000. 750.
f. 1p brownish red 6,000. 750.
6g A2 2p blue 7,500. 1,100.
On cover, from *5,500.*
h. "PENOE" 14,000. 2,000.

These stamps were printed in sheets of twelve, four rows of three, and each position differs in details. The "PENOE" error is the most pronounced variety on the plates and is from position 7.

The stamps were in use until 1859. Earliest impressions, Nos. 3-4, show the full background of diagonal and vertical lines with the diagonal lines predominant. Early impressions, Nos. 3a-4a, 5-6, show the full background with the vertical lines predominating. As the plate became worn the vertical lines disappeared, giving the intermediate impressions, Nos. 3b-4b, 5a-6a.

Worn impressions, Nos. 3c-4c, 5b-6b, have little background remaining, and latest impressions, Nos. 3e-4h, 5e-6g, have also lost details of the frame and head. The paper of the early impressions is usually rather thick, that of the worn impressions rather thin. Expect natural fibrous inclusions in the paper of all impressions.

"Britannia" — A3

1849-58

7 A3 red brown, *blue* 26.00
8 A3 blue ('58) 10.00

Nos. 7-8 were never placed in use.

1858-59

9 A3 (4p) green, *bluish* 550.00 225.00
On cover, from *625.00*
10 A3 (6p) red 60.00 *125.00*
On cover, from *450.00*
11 A3 (9p) magenta ('59) 850.00 225.00
On cover, from *750.00*
a. Used as 1p ('62) 180.00
On cover, from *750.00*

No. 11 was re-issued in Nov. 1862, as a 1p stamp (No. 11a). When used as such it is always canceled "B53." Price so used, $200.

"Britannia" — A4

1858 Black Surcharge

12 A4 4p green, *bluish* 1,650. 525.00
On cover, from *1,500.*

Queen Victoria — A5

1859, Mar. Early Impressions

14 A5 2p blue, *grayish* 16,500. 3,000.
On cover, from *15,000.*
a. 2p deep blue, *grayish* 18,500. 3,500.
14B A5 2p blue, *bluish* 16,500. 3,000.
On cover, from *15,000.*
c. Intermediate impression 9,000. 1,300.
On cover, from *6,500.*
d. Worn impression 4,500. 850.00
On cover, from *4,250.*

Type A5 was engraved by Lapirot, in Port Louis, and was printed locally. There were twelve varieties in the sheet.

Early impressions have clear and distinct background lines. In the intermediate impressions, the lines are somewhat blurred, and white patches appear. In the worn impressions, the background lines are discontinuous, with many white patches. Analogous wear is also obvious in the background of the inscriptions on all four sides. Values depend on the state of wear. One should expect natural fibrous inclusions in the paper on all printings.

A6

1859, Oct.

15 A6 2p blue, *bluish* *210,000.* 11,000.
On cover, from *35,000.*

No. 15 was printed from the plate of the 1848 issue after it had been entirely re-engraved by Sherwin. It is commonly known as the "fillet head." The plate of the 1p, 1848, was also re-engraved but was never put in use.

A7

1859, Dec. Litho. Laid Paper

16 A7 1p vermilion *9,000.* 1,350.
On cover, from *6,500.*
a. 1p deep red *15,000.* 2,350.
On cover, from *11,500.*
b. 1p red *11,250.* 1,675.
17 A7 2p pale blue *5,000.* 850.
On cover, from *8,000.*
a. 2p slate blue *9,250.* 1,250.
On cover, from *4,000.*
b. 2p blue 5,000. 950.
On cover, from *1,250.*
c. Retouched on neck 2,100.
d. Retouched below "TWO" 1,250.

Lithographed locally by Dardenne.

"Britannia" — A8

1859 Wove Paper Engr. *Imperf.*

18 A8 6p blue 800.00 57.50
On cover, from *300.00*
19 A8 1sh vermilion 3,150. 65.00
On cover, from *350.00*

1861

20 A8 6p gray violet 37.50 *110.00*
On cover, from *350.00*
21 A8 1sh green 675.00 160.00
On cover, from *650.00*

1862 *Perf. 14 to 16*

22 A8 6p slate 37.50 *110.00*
On cover, from *500.00*
a. Horiz. pair, imperf between *8,500.*
23 A8 1sh deep green 2,750. 350.00
On cover, from *1,750.*

Values for Nos. 22-23 are for examples with perfs. touching the design.

Following the change in currency in 1878, a number of issues denominated in sterling were overprinted "CANCELLED" in serifed type and sold as remainders.

A9

1860-63 Typo. *Perf. 14*

24 A9 1p brown lilac 400.00 42.50
On cover, from 125.00
25 A9 2p blue 425.00 60.00
On cover, from 175.00
26 A9 4p rose 425.00 42.50
On cover, from 125.00
27 A9 6p green ('62) 1,050. 175.00
On cover, from 500.00
28 A9 6p lilac ('63) 425.00 125.00
On cover, from 325.00
29 A9 9p dull lilac 190.00 42.50
On cover, from 125.00
Overprinted "CANCELLED" 120.00
30 A9 1sh buff ('62) 400.00 100.00
On cover, from 325.00
31 A9 1sh green ('63) 900.00 200.00
On cover, from 600.00

For surcharges see Nos. 43-45.

1863-72 Wmk. 1

32 A9 1p lilac brown 85.00 17.00
On cover, from 50.00
Overprinted "CANCELLED" 60.00
a. 1p bister brown 150.00 17.00
On cover, from 50.00
b. 1p brown 110.00 13.00
On cover, from 45.00
33 A9 2p blue 100.00 13.00
On cover, from 45.00
Overprinted "CANCELLED" 70.00
a. Imperf., pair 1,850. 2,350.
34 A9 3p vermilion 90.00 21.00
On cover, from 65.00
Overprinted "CANCELLED" 42.50
a. 3p deep red 180.00 42.50
On cover, from 135.00
35 A9 4p rose 100.00 4.00
On cover, from 20.00
Overprinted "CANCELLED" 75.00
36 A9 6p lilac ('64) 425.00 45.00
On cover, from 140.00
37 A9 6p blue grn ('65) 235.00 7.00
On cover, from 30.00
Overprinted "CANCELLED" 110.00
a. 6p yellow green ('65) 300.00 17.00
On cover, from 45.00
38 A9 9p green ('72) 190.00 *375.00*
On cover, from *1,250.*
39 A9 1sh org yel ('64) 365.00 29.00
On cover, from 100.00
Overprinted "CANCELLED" 150.00
a. 1sh yellow 285.00 13.50
On cover, from 100.00
40 A9 1sh blue ('70) 140.00 29.00
On cover, from 100.00
41 A9 5sh red violet 260.00 60.00
On cover, from *350.00*
Overprinted "CANCELLED" 130.00
a. 5sh bright violet 325.00 60.00
On cover, from 350.00
Overprinted "CANCELLED" 180.00
Nos. 32-41 (10) 1,990. 600.00

For surcharges see Nos. 48-49, 51-58, 87.

A10

1872

42 A10 10p claret 375.00 57.50
On cover, *from* 300.00
Overprinted "CANCELLED" 100.00

For surcharges see Nos. 46-47.

No. 29 Surcharged in Black or Red

a b

1876 **Unwmk.**

43 A9(a) ½p on 9p 24.00 24.00
On cover, *from* 125.00
Overprinted "CANCELLED" 20.00
a. Inverted surcharge 800.00
b. Double surcharge 2,350.
44 A9(b) ½p on 9p *5,000.*
Overprinted "CANCELLED" 300.00
45 A9(b) ½p on 9p (R) *3,400.*
Overprinted "CANCELLED" 150.00
a. "PRNNY" instead of "PENNY" —

Nos. 44 and 45 were never placed in use. No. 45 is valued with perfs cutting into the design.

Stamps of 1863-72 Surcharged in Black

c

d

1876-77 **Wmk. 1**

46 A10(a) ½p on 10p claret 4.75 *29.00*
On cover, *from* 150.00
47 A10(c) ½p on 10p cl ('77) 12.00 *50.00*
On cover, *from* 250.00
Overprinted "CANCELLED" 4.75
48 A9(d) 1p on 4p rose ('77) 25.00 27.50
On cover, *from* 150.00
49 A9(d) 1sh on 5sh red vio ('77) 350.00 125.00
On cover, *from* 750.00
Overprinted "CANCELLED" 60.00
a. 1sh on 5sh violet ('77) 340.00 160.00
On cover, *from* 750.00
Overprinted "CANCELLED" 50.00
Nos. 46-49 (4) 391.75 *231.50*

A16

1878 **Black Surcharge**

50 A16 2c claret 17.50 12.50
On cover, *from* 37.50

Stamps and Type of 1863-72 Surcharged in Black — e

51 A9 4c on 1p bister brn 27.50 10.00
On cover, *from* 45.00
52 A9 8c on 2p blue 90.00 4.25
On cover, *from* 20.00
53 A9 13c on 3p org red 26.00 52.50
On cover, *from* 325.00
54 A9 17c on 4p rose 200.00 4.50
On cover, *from* 35.00
55 A9 25c on 6p sl blue 275.00 8.00
On cover, *from* 45.00
56 A9 38c on 9p violet 50.00 *100.00*
On cover, *from* 625.00
57 A9 50c on 1sh green 100.00 5.75
On cover, *from* 150.00
58 A9 2r50c on 5sh violet 22.50 *26.00*
On cover, *from* 450.00
Nos. 50-58 (9) 808.50 *223.50*

For surcharge see No. 87.

A18

A19

A20

A21

A22

A23

A24

A25

A26

1879-80 **Wmk. 1**

59 A18 2c red brn ('80) 55.00 27.50
On cover, *from* 150.00
60 A19 4c orange 72.50 4.25
On cover, *from* 20.00
61 A20 8c blue ('80) 40.00 4.50
On cover, *from* 25.00
62 A21 13c slate ('80) 180.00 325.00
On cover, *from* —
63 A22 17c rose ('80) 95.00 10.00
On cover, *from* 75.00
64 A23 25c bister 475.00 18.00
On cover, *from* 150.00
65 A24 38c violet ('80) 200.00 375.00
On cover, *from* —
66 A25 50c green ('80) 6.50 5.50
On cover, *from* 200.00
67 A26 2r50c brn vio ('80) 57.50 *85.00*
On cover, *from* —
Nos. 59-67 (9) 1,182. 854.75

Nos. 59-67 are known imperforate.
For surcharges & overprints see Nos. 76-78, 83-86, 122-123.

1882-93 **Wmk. 2**

68 A18 1c violet ('93) 2.50 .55
On cover, *from* 10.00
Overprinted "SPECIMEN" 95.00
69 A18 2c red brown 40.00 7.00
On cover, *from* 35.00
70 A18 2c green ('85) 4.75 .75
On cover, *from* 10.00
Overprinted "SPECIMEN" 95.00
71 A19 4c orange 95.00 7.00
On cover, *from* 35.00
72 A19 4c rose ('85) 5.50 1.25
On cover, *from* 10.00
Overprinted "SPECIMEN" 95.00
73 A20 8c blue ('91) 5.00 1.80
On cover, *from* 15.00
74 A23 25c bister ('83) 14.00 4.00
75 A25 50c dp orange ('87) 45.00 20.00
On cover, *from* 100.00
Overprinted "SPECIMEN" 100.00
Nos. 68-75 (8) 211.75 42.35

For surcharges and overprint see Nos. 88-89, 121.

Nos. 63 and Type of 1882 Surcharged in Black

f

g

1883 **Wmk. 1**

Surcharge Measures 14x3½mm

76 A22(f) 16c on 17c rose 180.00 60.00
On cover, *from* —
a. Double surcharge 2,900.

Surcharge Measures 15½x3½mm

77 A22(f) 16c on 17c rose 190.00 60.00
On cover, *from* —
a. Double surcharge 3,150.
b. Horiz. pair (#76, #77) 850.00 750.00

Surcharge Measures 15½x2¾mm

78 A22(f) 16c on 17c rose *375.00* *140.00*

Wmk. 2

79 A22(g) 16c on 17c rose 115.00 2.40
Nos. 76-79 (4) *860.00* *262.40*

Queen Victoria — A29

1885-94

80 A29 15c orange brown ('92) 9.00 1.50
On cover, *from* 15.00
81 A29 15c blue ('94) 10.00 1.50
On cover, *from* 15.00
82 A29 16c orange brown 9.50 2.75
On cover, *from* 30.00
Nos. 80-82 (3) 28.50 5.75
Set of 3, ovptd "SPECIMEN" 345.00

For surcharges see Nos. 90, 116.

Various Stamps Surcharged in Black or Red

h

j

1885-87 **Wmk. 1**

83 A24(h) 2c on 38c violet 170.00 47.50
On cover, *from* *250.00*
a. Inverted surcharge 1,250. 1,000.
b. Double surcharge 1,350.
c. Without bar 275.00
84 A21(j) 2c on 13c sl (R) ('87) 80.00 *130.00*
On cover, *from* 625.00
a. Inverted surcharge 260.00 *300.00*
b. Double surcharge *975.00* 850.00
c. As "b," one on back *1,000.*
d. Double surcharge, both inverted *1,750.*

k

l

1891

85 A22(k) 2c on 17c rose 145.00 *155.00*
a. Inverted surcharge 575.00 575.00
b. Double surcharge 950.00 950.00
86 A24(k) 2c on 38c vio 11.50 16.00
On cover, *from* 135.00
a. Double surcharge 240.00 *260.00*
b. Dbl. surch., one invtd. 260.00 *300.00*
c. Inverted surcharge 1,250. —
87 A9(e+l) 2c on 38c on 9p vio 15.00 6.75
On cover, *from* *75.00*
a. Double surcharge 850.00 850.00
b. Inverted surcharge 625.00 —
c. Dbl. surch., one invtd. 200.00 *225.00*

Wmk. 2

88 A19(k) 2c on 4c rose 2.50 1.00
On cover, *from* 10.00
a. Double surcharge 95.00 90.00
b. Inverted surcharge 90.00 —
c. Dbl. surch., one invtd. 95.00 90.00
Nos. 85-88 (4) 174.00 178.75

m

n

1893, Jan.

89 A18(m) 1c on 2c violet 2.75 1.75
On cover, *from* 12.50
Overprinted "SPECIMEN" 37.50
90 A29(n) 1c on 16c org brown 3.25 *4.50*
On cover, *from* *50.00*

Coat of Arms — A38

1895-1904 **Wmk. 2**

91 A38 1c lilac & ultra .90 1.80
On cover, *from* 10.00
92 A38 1c gray blk & blk .60 .25
On cover, *from* 6.00
93 A38 2c lilac & orange 7.50 .60
On cover, *from* 6.00
94 A38 2c dull lil & vio 1.00 .25
On cover, *from* 6.00
95 A38 3c lilac .85 .60
On cover, *from* 5.00
96 A38 3c grn & scar, *yel* 4.50 1.50
On cover, *from* 7.50
97 A38 4c lilac & green 6.00 .60
On cover, *from* 6.00
98 A38 4c dull lil & car, *yel* 3.00 .50
On cover, *from* 6.00
99 A38 4c gray grn & pur 3.00 *2.40*
On cover, *from* 15.00

100 A38 4c blk & car, *blue* 18.00 .75
On cover, *from* 6.00
101 A38 5c lilac & vio, *buff* 12.00 *100.00*
On cover, *from* *450.00*
102 A38 5c lilac & blk, *buff* 3.00 3.00
On cover, *from* 15.00
103 A38 6c grn & rose 5.75 5.00
On cover, *from* 25.00
104 A38 6c vio & scar, *red* 4.75 1.00
On cover, *from* 10.00
105 A38 8c gray grn & blk, *buff* 4.50 *15.00*
On cover, *from* 90.00
106 A38 12c black & car rose 3.00 *3.00*
On cover, *from* 15.00
107 A38 15c grn & org 30.00 *10.00*
On cover, *from* 55.00
108 A38 15c blk & ultra, *blue* 65.00 1.50
On cover, *from* 15.00
109 A38 18c gray grn & ultra 22.50 4.25
On cover, *from* 20.00
110 A38 25c grn & car, *grn*, chalky paper 6.00 *27.50*
On cover, *from* *150.00*
a. Ordinary paper ('02) 22.50 *47.50*
On cover, *from* *275.00*
111 A38 50c green, *yel* 20.00 *80.00*
On cover, *from* *400.00*
Nos. 91-111 (21) 221.85 *259.50*
Set of 21, ovptd "SPECIMEN" 600.00

The 25c is on both ordinary and chalky paper. Ornaments in lower panel omitted on Nos. 106-111.

Year of issue: Nos. 103, 107, 1899; Nos. 92, 94, 98, 1900; Nos. 96, 99, 101-102, 104-106, 110-111, 1902; Nos. 100, 108, 1904; others, 1895.

See Nos. 128-135. For surcharges and overprints see Nos. 113, 114, 117-120.

Diamond Jubilee Issue

Arms A39

1898, May 23 **Wmk. 46**
112 A39 36c brown org & ultra 13.50 *27.50*
On cover, *from* *100.00*
Overprinted "SPECIMEN" 55.00

60th year of Queen Victoria's reign.
For surcharges see Nos. 114 and 127.

No. 109 Surcharged in Red

1899 **Wmk. 2**
113 A38 6c on 18c 1.40 1.25
On cover, *from* 15.00
a. Inverted surcharge 725.00 340.00

No. 112 Surcharged in Blue

Wmk. 46
114 A39 15c on 36c 3.50 2.10
On cover, *from* 17.50
a. Without bar 500.00

Admiral Mahe de La Bourdonnais A40

1899, Dec. **Engr.** **Wmk. 1**
115 A40 15c ultra 30.00 5.00
On cover, *from* 35.00
Overprinted "SPECIMEN" 85.00

Birth bicent. of Admiral Mahe de La Bourdonnais, governor of Mauritius, 1734-46.

No. 82 Surcharged in Black

1900 **Wmk. 2**
116 A29 4c on 16c orange brown 17.50 27.50
On cover, *from* *175.00*

No. 109 Surcharged in Black — r

1902
117 A38 12c on 18c grn & ultra 3.50 *11.00*
On cover, *from* 65.00

Preceding Issues Overprinted in Black

1902
118 A38 4c lilac & car, *yel* 1.50 .30
On cover, *from* 5.00
119 A38 6c green & rose 1.50 *3.25*
On cover, *from* 7.50
120 A38 15c green & org 6.25 1.35
On cover, *from* 10.00
121 A23 25c bister 8.00 3.25

Wmk. 1

On cover, *from* *90.00*
122 A25 50c green 20.00 6.25
On cover, *from* *50.00*
123 A26 2r50c brown violet 135.00 *225.00*
On cover, *from* *750.00*
Nos. 118-123 (6) 172.25 239.40

Coat of Arms — A41

1902 **Wmk. 1**
124 A41 1r blk & car rose 62.50 60.00
On cover, *from* *400.00*

Wmk. 2 Sideways

125 A41 2r50c grn & blk, *bl* 40.00 *160.00*
On cover, *from* *1,000.*
126 A41 5r blk & car, *red* 110.00 *180.00*
On cover, *from* —
Nos. 124-126 (3) 212.50 *400.00*
Set of 3, ovptd "SPECIMEN" 190.00

No. 112 Surcharged type "r" but with longer bar

1902 **Wmk. 46**
127 A39 12c on 36c 2.40 1.50
On cover, *from* 12.50
a. Inverted surcharge 775.00 525.00

Arms Type of 1895-1904

1904-07 **Wmk. 3** **Chalky Paper**
128 A38 1c gray blk & black ('07) 8.75 5.00
129 A38 2c dl lil & vio ('05) 35.00 3.00
130 A38 3c grn & scar, *yel* 22.50 13.00
131 A38 4c blk & car, *blue* 16.00 .25
132 A38 6c vio & scar, *red* ('06) 14.00 .35
133 A38 15c blk & ultra, *bl* 4.50 .40
135 A38 50c green, *yel* 3.00 *7.00*
136 A41 1r black & car rose ('07) 50.00 *65.00*
Nos. 128-136 (8) 153.75 *94.00*

The 2c, 4c, 6c also exist on ordinary paper.
Ornaments in lower panel omitted on 15c and 50c.

Arms — A42

Edward VII — A43

1910 **Wmk. 3** **Ordinary Paper**
137 A42 1c black 3.25 .30
138 A42 2c brown 3.00 .25
139 A42 3c green 3.25 .25
140 A42 4c ol grn & rose 4.00 .25
141 A43 5c gray & rose 3.00 *3.25*
142 A42 6c carmine 5.25 .25
a. A42 6c pale red 9.00 2.40
143 A42 8c brn org 3.25 *1.60*
144 A43 12c gray 3.75 *3.00*
145 A42 15c ultramarine 21.00 .25

Chalky Paper

146 A43 25c blk & scar, *yel* 2.25 *13.00*
147 A43 50c dull vio & blk 2.60 *20.00*
148 A43 1r blk, *green* 17.75 *13.00*
149 A43 2r50c blk & car, *bl* 27.50 *75.00*
150 A43 5r grn & car, *yel* 42.50 *100.00*
151 A43 10r grn & car, *grn* 165.00 *250.00*
Nos. 137-151 (15) 307.35 *480.40*

Numerals of 12c, 25c and 10r of type A43 are in color on plain tablet.
See Nos. 161-178.

King George V — A44

For description of dies I and II see "Dies of British Colonial Stamps" in table of contents.
Numeral tablet of 5c, 50c, 1r, 2.50r and 5r of type A44 has lined background with colorless denomination.

Die I

1912-22 **Wmk. 3** **Ordinary Paper**
152 A44 5c gray & rose 3.00 *4.50*
a. A44 5c slate gray & carmine 11.00 *11.50*
153 A44 12c gray 8.00 1.10

Chalky Paper

154 A44 25c blk & red, *yel* .45 1.50
a. 25c gray black & red, *yellow*, Die II 1.10 *25.00*
Overprinted "SPECIMEN" 47.50
155 A44 50c dull vio & blk 52.50 *125.00*
156 A44 1r black, *emerald*, die II 2.50 *8.00*
Overprinted "SPECIMEN" 50.00
a. 1r black, *emer*, olive back, die I ('21) 11.50 *60.00*
b. 1r blk, *bl grn*, olive back, die I 6.75 *21.00*
157 A44 2r50c blk & red, *bl* 42.50 *75.00*
158 A44 5r grn & red, *yel* 115.00 *175.00*
a. Die II ('22) 115.00 *200.00*
159 A44 10r grn & red, *emer*, die II ('21) 47.50 *180.00*
Overprinted "SPECIMEN" 67.50
a. 10r grn & red, *bl grn*, olive back, die I 1,150.
b. 10r green & red, *emer*, die I 85.00 *200.00*
c. 10r grn & red, *emer*, olive back, die I 145.00 *210.00*
d. 10r grn & red, *grn*, die I 105.00 *210.00*

Surface-colored Paper

160 A44 25c blk & red, *yel* ('16) 2.75 *21.00*
Nos. 152-160 (9) 274.20 *591.10*

1921-26 **Wmk. 4** **Ordinary Paper**
161 A42 1c black 1.10 1.10
162 A42 2c brown 1.10 .25
163 A42 2c violet, *yel* ('25) 3.50 2.00
164 A42 3c green ('25) 3.50 3.50
165 A42 4c ol grn & rose 1.60 *2.00*
166 A42 4c green 1.10 .25
167 A42 4c brown ('25) 4.50 2.50
168 A42 6c rose red 13.50 7.25
169 A42 6c violet 1.35 .25
170 A42 8c brown org ('25) 2.50 *24.00*
171 A42 10c gray ('22) 2.25 *3.75*
172 A42 10c rose red ('25) 12.00 6.75
173 A42 12c rose red 1.70 1.60
174 A42 12c gray ('25) 1.90 *5.00*
175 A42 15c ultramarine 6.00 5.50
176 A42 15c dull blue ('25) 1.60 .25
177 A42 20c ultra ('22) 2.25 .90
178 A42 20c dull vio ('25) 9.50 *16.00*
Nos. 161-178 (18) 70.95 *82.85*

Ornaments in lower panel omitted on Nos. 171-178.

For surcharges see Nos. 201-203.

Die II

1922-34 **Ordinary Paper**
179 A44 1c black 2.40 *3.00*
180 A44 2c brown 1.10 .25
181 A44 3c green 2.10 .45
182 A44 4c olive grn & red ('27) 3.25 .30
a. Die I ('32) 18.00 *62.50*
183 A44 4c green, die I ('33) 13.50 *.50*
184 A44 5c gray & car 1.10 .25
a. Die I ('32) 10.00 6.50
185 A44 6c olive brn ('28) 5.50 .65
186 A44 8c orange 2.10 *15.50*
187 A44 10c rose red ('26) 4.25 .25
a. Die I ('32) 15.50 *16.75*
188 A44 12c gray, small "c" ('22) 5.00 *23.00*
Overprinted "SPECIMEN" 47.50
189 A44 12c gray, "c" larger & thinner ('34) 17.50 .25
190 A44 12c rose red .70 *3.75*
191 A44 15c dk blue ('28) 4.75 .25
192 A44 20c dull vio 4.75 .45
193 A44 20c dk blue ('34) 28.00 .45
a. Die I ('27) 11.00 2.60
194 A44 25c black & red, *yel* 1.10 .25
a. Die I ('32) 7.25 *67.50*

Chalky Paper

195 A44 50c dull vio & blk 8.00 3.75
196 A44 1r blk, *emerald* 6.75 .55
a. Die I ('32) 25.00 *62.50*
197 A44 2r50c blk & red, *bl* 22.00 19.00
198 A44 5r green & red, *yel* 47.50 *95.00*
199 A44 10r green & red, *emer* ('28) 145.00 *340.00*
Nos. 179-199 (21) 326.35 *507.85*

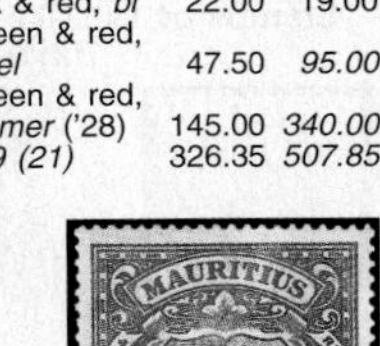

A45

1924
200 A45 50r lilac & green 1,000. *2,750.*
Overprinted "SPECIMEN" 400.00

Nos. 166, 173, 177 Surcharged

1925
201 A42 3c on 4c green 8.00 *6.25*
202 A42 10c on 12c rose red .50 *1.60*
203 A42 15c on 20c ultra .65 1.75
Nos. 201-203 (3) 9.15 9.60
Set, ovpted. "SPECIMEN" 92.50

Common Design Types pictured following the introduction.

Silver Jubilee Issue
Common Design Type

1935, May 6 **Engr.** ***Perf. 13½x14***
204 CD301 5c gray black & ultra .60 .25
205 CD301 12c indigo & green 5.50 .25
206 CD301 20c blue & brown 6.50 .25
207 CD301 1r brt vio & indigo 35.00 *57.50*
Nos. 204-207 (4) 47.60 58.25
Set, never hinged 60.00
Set, ovpted. "SPECIMEN" 145.00

Coronation Issue
Common Design Type

1937, May 12 **Wmk. 4** ***Perf. 13½x14***
208 CD302 5c dark purple .30 .25
Never hinged .45
209 CD302 12c carmine .50 2.40
Never hinged .90
210 CD302 20c bright ultra 1.25 1.10
Never hinged 1.90
Nos. 208-210 (3) 2.05 3.75
Set, never hinged 3.25
Set, perforated "SPECIMEN" 85.00
Set, never hinged, perforated "SPECIMEN" 110.00

King George VI — A46

1938-43 Typo. *Perf. 14*

211 A46 2c gray ('43) .25 .25
Never hinged .30
a. Perf. 15x14 ('43) .70 .25
Never hinged 1.10
212 A46 3c rose vio & car ('43) 1.50 2.15
Never hinged 2.10
213 A46 4c green ('43) 3.25 *2.15*
Never hinged 5.75
214 A46 5c violet ('43) 2.10 .25
Never hinged 3.50
a. Perf. 15x14 ('43) 40.00 .25
Never hinged 62.50
215 A46 10c carmine ('43) 1.90 .25
Never hinged 2.75
a. Perf. 15x14 ('43) 25.00 2.50
Never hinged 42.50
216 A46 12c sal pink ('43) .70 .25
Never hinged 1.10
a. Perf. 15x14 ('43) 40.00 1.35
Never hinged 60.00
217 A46 20c blue ('43) .70 .25
Never hinged 1.10
218 A46 25c maroon ('43) 6.00 .25
Never hinged 9.00
a. A46 25c brown purple, chalky paper ('38) 14.00 .25
Never hinged 20.00
219 A46 1r brn blk ('43) 14.00 2.00
Never hinged 20.00
a. A46 1r gray brown, chalky paper ('38) 30.00 3.25
Never hinged 45.00
220 A46 2.50r pale vio ('43) 25.00 26.00
Never hinged 37.50
a. A46 2.50r pale violet, chalky paper ('38) 40.00 28.00
Never hinged 62.50
221 A46 5r ol grn ('43) 21.00 42.50
Never hinged 30.00
a. A46 5r olive green, chalky paper ('38) 35.00 42.50
Never hinged 57.50
222 A46 10r rose vio ('43) 9.75 *42.50*
Never hinged 14.00
a. A46 10r reddish purple, chalky paper ('38) 52.50 57.50
Never hinged 80.00
Nos. 211-222 (12) 86.15 118.80
Set, never hinged 127.00
Set, perforated "SPECIMEN" 300.00
Set, never hinged, perforated "SPECIMEN" 400.00

Catalogue values for unused stamps in this section, from this point to the end of the section, are for Never Hinged items.

Peace Issue
Common Design Type
Perf. 13½x14

1946, Nov. 20 Engr. Wmk. 4

223 CD303 5c lilac .25 .80
224 CD303 20c deep blue .25 .25

"Post Office" Stamp of 1847 — A47

1948, Mar. 22 *Perf. 11½*

225 A47 5c red vio & orange .25 .55
226 A47 12c green & orange .25 .25
227 A47 20c blue & dp blue .25 .25
228 A47 1r lt red brn & dp blue .35 .35
Nos. 225-228 (4) 1.10 1.40

Cent. of the 1st Mauritius postage stamps.

Silver Wedding Issue
Common Design Types

1948, Oct. 25 Photo. *Perf. 14x14½*

229 CD304 5c violet .25 .25

Perf. 11½x11
Engraved; Name Typographed

230 CD305 10r lilac rose 17.50 45.00

UPU Issue
Common Design Types
Engr.; Name Typo. on 20c, 35c
Perf. 13½, 11x11½

1949, Oct. 10 Wmk. 4

231 CD306 12c rose carmine .65 2.10
232 CD307 20c indigo 2.40 2.75
233 CD308 35c rose violet .65 1.60
234 CD309 1r sepia .65 .25
Nos. 231-234 (4) 4.35 6.70

Sugar Factory — A48

Aloe Plant — A49

Designs: 2c, Grand Port. 4c, Tamarind Falls. 5c, Rempart Mountain. 10c, Transporting cane. 12c, Map and dodo. 20c, "Paul et Virginie." 25c, Statue of Mahe La Bourdonnais. 35c, Government House. 50c, Pieter Both Mountain. 1r, Sambar. 2.50r, Port Louis. 5r, Beach scene. 10r, Arms.

Perf. 13½x14½, 14½x13½

1950, July 1 Photo.

235 A48 1c red violet .25 .55
236 A48 2c cerise .25 .25
237 A49 3c yel green .70 *4.50*
238 A49 4c green .25 *3.25*
239 A48 5c greenish blue .25 .25
240 A48 10c red .30 *.80*
241 A48 12c olive green 1.60 *3.25*
242 A49 20c brt ultra 1.10 .25
243 A49 25c vio brown 2.15 .45
244 A48 35c rose violet .45 .25
245 A49 50c emerald 3.00 .55
246 A48 1r sepia 10.00 .25
247 A48 2.50r orange 22.00 17.50
248 A48 5r red brown 23.00 17.50
249 A48 10r gray blue 18.00 *37.50*
Nos. 235-249 (15) 83.30 87.10

SPECIAL DELIVERY STAMPS

SD1

1903 Wmk. 1 *Perf. 14*
Red Surcharge

E1 SD1 15c on 15c ultra 14.50 37.50

SD2

SD3

EXPRESS
DELIVERY
(INLAND)
15 c

New Setting with Smaller "15c" without period — SD3a

1904

E2 SD2 15c on 15c ultra 62.50 95.00
a. "INLAND" inverted 3,400.
b. Inverted "A" in "INLAND" 1,700. 1,250.
E3 SD3 15c on 15c ultra 9.00 3.75
a. Double surcharge, both inverted 1,875. 1,900.
b. Inverted surcharge 1,250. 800.00
c. Vert. pair, imperf between *6,250.*
E3F SD3a 15c on 15c ultra 840.00 800.00
g. Inverted surcharge 1,775.
h. Double surcharge 3,750.
i. Double surcharge, both inverted — 5,500.
j. "c" omitted 2,750.

To make No. E2 the word "INLAND" was printed on No. E1. For Nos. E3 and E3F, new settings of the surcharge were made with different spacing between the words.

SD4

SD5

E4 SD4 15c green & red 18.00 6.25
a. Double surcharge 800.00 800.00
b. Inverted surcharge 1,000. 900.00
c. "LNIAND." —
d. As "c," double surcharge *900.00* 800.00
E5 SD5 18c green & black 3.00 32.50
a. Exclamation point (!) instead of "I" in "FOREIGN" 800.00

POSTAGE DUE STAMPS

Catalogue values for unused stamps in this section are for Never Hinged items.

Numeral — D1

Perf. 14½x14

1933-54 Typo. Wmk. 4

J1 D1 2c black 1.50 .60
On cover *625.00*
J2 D1 4c violet .60 .80
On cover *625.00*
J3 D1 6c red .70 *.95*
On cover *625.00*
J4 D1 10c green .85 *2.40*
On cover *625.00*
J5 D1 20c ultramarine .75 *2.60*
On cover *750.00*
J6 D1 50c dp red lilac ('54) .65 *19.00*
On cover *900.00*
J7 D1 1r orange ('54) .85 *19.00*
On cover *1,000.*
Nos. J1-J7 (7) 5.90 *45.35*

Covers: Values are for properly franked commercial covers. Philatelic covers sell for less.

MAYOTTE

mä-ˈyät

LOCATION — One of the Comoro Islands situated in the Mozambique Channel midway between Madagascar and Mozambique (Africa)
GOVT. — French Colony
AREA — 140 sq. mi.
POP. — 13,783 (1914)
CAPITAL — Dzaoudzi
See Comoro Islands

100 Centimes = 1 Franc

Stamps of Mayotte were replaced successively by those of Madagascar, Comoro Islands and France.

Navigation and Commerce — A1

Perf. 14x13½

1892-1907 Typo. Unwmk.
Name of Colony in Blue or Carmine

1 A1 1c blk, *lil bl* 1.40 .90
Never hinged 2.40
On cover 190.00
2 A1 2c brn, *buff* 1.90 1.40
Never hinged 3.00
On cover 190.00
a. Name double 575.00 500.00
3 A1 4c claret, *lav* 2.40 1.75
Never hinged 4.00
On cover 190.00
4 A1 5c grn, *grnsh* 4.75 3.25
Never hinged 9.00
On cover 125.00
5 A1 10c blk, *lavender* 9.00 4.75
Never hinged 16.00
On cover 160.00
6 A1 10c red ('00) 75.00 52.50
Never hinged 155.00
On cover 190.00
7 A1 15c blue, quadrille paper 17.50 10.50
Never hinged 35.00
On cover 250.00
8 A1 15c gray ('00) 140.00 110.00
Never hinged 300.00
On cover 340.00
9 A1 20c red, *grn* 13.50 10.50
Never hinged 27.50
On cover 225.00
10 A1 25c blk, *rose* 14.50 9.75
Never hinged 30.00
On cover 225.00
On cover, single franking 310.00
11 A1 25c blue ('00) 16.00 13.50
Never hinged 35.00
On cover 95.00
On cover, single franking 160.00
12 A1 30c brn, *bis* 22.00 16.00
Never hinged 42.50
On cover 190.00
On cover, single franking 225.00
13 A1 35c blk, *yel* ('00) 11.00 8.00
Never hinged 24.00
On cover 62.50
On cover, single franking 110.00
14 A1 40c red, *straw* 22.50 16.00
Never hinged 42.50
On cover 225.00
On cover, single franking 310.00
15 A1 45c blk, *gray grn* ('07) 21.00 20.00
Never hinged 42.50
On cover 110.00
On cover, single franking 190.00
16 A1 50c carmine, *rose* 32.00 22.50
Never hinged 62.50
On cover 250.00
On cover, single franking 375.00
17 A1 50c brn, *az* ('00) 30.00 30.00
Never hinged 57.50
On cover 160.00
On cover, single franking 275.00
18 A1 75c dp vio, *org* 30.00 21.00
Never hinged 67.50
On cover 300.00
On cover, single franking 450.00
19 A1 1fr brnz grn, *straw* 32.00 22.50
Never hinged 67.50
On cover 310.00
On cover, single franking 440.00
20 A1 5fr red lil, *lav* ('99) 135.00 130.00
Never hinged 275.00
On cover 440.00
On cover, single franking 625.00
Nos. 1-20 (20) 631.45 504.80

Perf. 13½x14 stamps are counterfeits.

Issues of 1892-1907 Surcharged in Black or Carmine

1912
Spacing between figures of surcharge 1.5mm (5c), 2mm (10c)

22 A1 5c on 2c brn, *buff* 3.25 *4.00*
Never hinged 5.75
On cover 125.00
23 A1 5c on 4c cl, *lav* (C) 2.00 2.00
Never hinged 3.50
On cover 95.00
24 A1 5c on 15c bl (C) 2.00 2.00
Never hinged 3.50
On cover 95.00
25 A1 5c on 20c red, *grn* 2.00 *2.40*
Never hinged 3.50
On cover 105.00
26 A1 5c on 25c blk, *rose* (C) 1.60 1.60
Never hinged 2.50
On cover 95.00
a. Double surcharge 360.00
b. Pair, one stamp without surcharge 1,000.

27	A1	5c on 30c brn, *bis* (C)	2.00	2.00
		Never hinged	3.50	
		On cover		100.00
28	A1	10c on 40c red, *straw*	2.00	*2.40*
		Never hinged	3.50	
		On cover		110.00
a.		Double surcharge	360.00	
29	A1	10c on 45c blk, *gray grn* (C)	2.00	2.00
		Never hinged	3.50	
		On cover		105.00
a.		Double surcharge	360.00	*325.00*
30	A1	10c on 50c car, *rose*	4.50	*5.00*
		Never hinged	7.50	
		On cover		170.00
31	A1	10c on 75c dp vio, *org*	3.50	*4.25*
		Never hinged	6.50	
		On cover		160.00
32	A1	10c on 1fr brnz grn, *straw*	3.50	*4.25*
		Never hinged	6.50	
		On cover		160.00
		Nos. 22-32 (11)	28.35	*31.90*

Spacing between figures of surcharge 2.25mm (5c), 2.75mm (10c)

22a	A1	5c on 2c brn, *buff*	19.00	19.00
		Never hinged	30.00	
23a	A1	5c on 4c cl, *lav* (C)	13.50	13.50
		Never hinged	24.00	
24a	A1	5c on 15c bl (C)	13.50	13.50
		Never hinged	24.00	
25a	A1	5c on 20c red, *grn*	13.50	13.50
		Never hinged	24.00	
26c	A1	5c on 25c blk, *rose* (C)	13.00	13.00
		Never hinged	22.50	
d.		Double surcharge	2,800.	2,750.
27a	A1	5c on 30c brn, *bis* (C)	13.50	13.50
		Never hinged	24.00	
28b	A1	10c on 40c red, *straw*	65.00	65.00
		Never hinged	125.00	
c.		Double surcharge	3,500.	3,000.
29b	A1	10c on 45c blk, *gray grn* (C)	60.00	60.00
		Never hinged	115.00	
c.		Double surcharge	3,500.	*3,000.*
30a	A1	10c on 50c car, *rose*	87.50	87.50
		Never hinged	160.00	
31a	A1	10c on 75c dp vio, *org*	87.50	87.50
		Never hinged	160.00	
32a	A1	10c on 1fr brnz grn, *straw*	150.00	150.00
		Nos. 22a-32a (11)	536.00	536.00

Se-tenant Pairs, Both Ovpt. Settings

22b	A1	5c on 2c, #22 + #22a	22.50	22.50
		Never hinged	37.50	
23b	A1	5c on 4c, #23 + #23a	17.50	17.50
		Never hinged	27.50	
24b	A1	5c on 15c, #24 + #24a	17.50	17.50
		Never hinged	27.50	
25b	A1	5c on 20c, #25 + #25a	17.50	17.50
		Never hinged	27.50	
26b	A1	5c on 25c, #26 + #26a	16.50	16.50
		Never hinged	26.00	
27b	A1	5c on 30c, #27 + #27a	17.50	17.50
		Never hinged	27.50	
28b	A1	10c on 40c, #28 + #28a	75.00	75.00
		Never hinged	140.00	
29b	A1	10c on 45c, #29 + #29a	65.00	65.00
		Never hinged	125.00	
30b	A1	10c on 50c, #30 + #30a	95.00	95.00
		Never hinged	175.00	
31b	A1	10c on 75c, #31 + #31a	95.00	95.00
		Never hinged	175.00	
32b	A1	10c on 1fr, #32 + #32a	175.00	175.00
		Never hinged	280.00	
		Nos. 22b-32b (11)	614.00	614.00

Nos. 22-32 were available for use in Madagascar and the entire Comoro archipelago.

MEMEL

'mā-məl

LOCATION — In northern Europe, bordering on the Baltic Sea
GOVT. — Special commission (see below)
AREA — 1099 sq. mi.
POP. — 151,960

Following World War I this territory was detached from Germany and by Treaty of Versailles assigned to the government of a commission of the Allied and Associated Powers (not the League of Nations), which administered it until January, 1923, when it was forcibly occupied by Lithuania. In 1924 Memel became incorporated as a semi-autonomous district of Lithuania with the approval of the Allied Powers and the League of Nations.

100 Pfennig = 1 Mark
100 Centu = 1 Litas (1923)

Excellent counterfeits of all Memel stamps exist.

Stamps of Germany, 1905-20, Overprinted

Wmk. Lozenges (125)

1920, Aug. 1 ***Perf. 14, 14½***

No.	Type	Description	Unused	Used
1	A16	5pf green	1.50	*15.00*
		Never hinged	9.00	
		On cover		22.50
2	A16	10pf car rose	1.90	*9.00*
		Never hinged	9.00	
		On cover		18.00
3	A16	10pf orange	.30	*3.25*
		Never hinged	1.40	
		On cover		6.00
4	A22	15pf violet brown	2.60	*12.00*
		Never hinged	13.00	
		On cover		22.50
5	A16	20pf blue violet	1.10	*5.25*
		Never hinged	5.25	
		On cover		6.00
6	A16	30pf org & blk, *buff*	1.25	*8.25*
		Never hinged	7.50	
		On cover		8.00
7	A16	30pf dull blue	.40	*3.25*
		Never hinged	1.50	
		On cover		10.50
8	A16	40pf lake & blk	.25	*3.25*
		Never hinged	1.10	
		On cover		6.00
9	A16	50pf pur & blk, *buff*	.30	*3.25*
		Never hinged	1.40	
		On cover		8.00
10	A16	60pf olive green	1.50	*6.00*
		Never hinged	5.25	
		On cover		10.50
11	A16	75pf grn & blk	2.60	*22.50*
		Never hinged	13.50	
		On cover		30.00
12	A16	80pf blue violet	1.35	*9.75*
		Never hinged	7.50	
		On cover		19.00

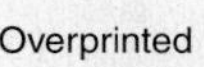
Overprinted

No.	Type	Description	Unused	Used
13	A17	1m car rose	.30	*3.25*
		Never hinged	1.40	
		On cover		20.00
14	A17	1.25m green	13.00	*50.00*
		Never hinged	45.00	
		On cover		100.00
15	A17	1.50m yel brn	4.50	*30.00*
		Never hinged	22.50	
		On cover		40.00
16	A21	2m blue	7.50	*13.50*
		Never hinged	52.50	
		On cover		32.50
17	A21	2.50m red lilac	11.50	*60.00*
		Never hinged	52.50	
		On cover		150.00
		Nos. 1-17 (17)	51.85	*257.50*

Stamps of France, Surcharged in Black

On A22

On A18

1920 **Unwmk.** ***Perf. 14x13½***

No.	Type	Description	Unused	Used
18	A22	5pf on 5c green	.75	*3.25*
		Never hinged	4.50	
		On cover		4.50
19	A22	10pf on 10c red	.60	*2.60*
		Never hinged	3.00	
		On cover		4.50
20	A22	20pf on 25c blue	1.10	*3.75*
		Never hinged	4.50	
		On cover		7.50
21	A22	30pf on 30c org	.75	*3.25*
		Never hinged	3.75	
		On cover		4.50
22	A22	40pf on 20c red brn	1.10	*3.25*
		Never hinged	5.00	
		On cover		7.50
23	A22	50pf on 35c vio	.30	*3.25*
		Never hinged	2.00	
		On cover		4.50
24	A18	60pf on 40c red & pale bl	.40	*3.75*
		Never hinged	2.25	
		On cover		6.00
25	A18	80pf on 45c grn & bl	1.10	*4.50*
		Never hinged	5.00	
		On cover		9.00
26	A18	1m on 50c brn & lav	.50	*3.75*
		Never hinged	3.00	
		On cover		9.00
27	A18	1m 25pf on 60c vio & ultra	1.20	*9.00*
		Never hinged	5.25	
		On cover		19.00
28	A18	2m on 1fr cl & ol grn	.60	*3.50*
		Never hinged	3.00	
		On cover		4.50
29	A18	3m on 5fr bl & buff	22.50	*67.50*
		Never hinged	97.50	
		On cover		140.00
		Nos. 18-29 (12)	30.90	*111.35*

For stamps with additional surcharges and overprints see Nos. 43-49, C1-C4.

French Stamps of 1900-20 Surcharged like Nos. 24 to 29 in Red or Black

On A18

Type I

Type II

1920-21 **Unwmk.** ***Perf. 14x13½***

No.	Type	Description	Unused	Used
30	A18	3m on 2fr org & pale bl	22.50	*67.50*
		Never hinged	90.00	
		On cover		125.00
31	A18	4m on 2fr org & pale bl (I) (Bk)	.45	*3.75*
		Never hinged	1.50	
		On cover		8.00
a.		Type II	.45	*3.75*
		Never hinged	1.50	
32	A18	10m on 5fr bl & buff	3.00	*15.00*
		Never hinged	12.00	
		On cover		72.50
33	A18	20m on 5fr bl & buff	37.50	*150.00*
		Never hinged	165.00	
		On cover		210.00
		Nos. 30-33 (4)	63.45	*236.25*

For stamps with additional overprints see Nos. C5, C19.

New Value with Initial Capital

1921

No.	Type	Description	Unused	Used
39	A18	60Pf on 40c red & pale bl	4.50	*19.00*
		Never hinged	19.00	
		On cover		32.50
40	A18	3M on 60c vio & ultra	2.25	*7.50*
		Never hinged	15.00	
		On cover		11.00
41	A18	10M on 5fr bl & buff	2.25	*8.25*
		Never hinged	15.00	
		On cover		20.00
42	A18	20M on 45c grn & bl	4.50	*26.00*
		Never hinged	26.50	
		On cover		72.50
		Nos. 39-42 (4)	13.50	*60.75*

The surcharged value on No. 40 is in italics. For stamps with additional overprints see Nos. C6-C7, C18.

Stamps of 1920 Surcharged with Large Numerals in Dark Blue or Red

No. 43

No. 49

1921-22

No.	Type	Description	Unused	Used
43	A22	15pf on 10pf on 10c	.40	*1.90*
		Never hinged	3.00	
		On cover		4.75
a.		Inverted surcharge	55.00	*225.00*
		Never hinged	160.00	
44	A22	15pf on 20pf on 25c	.40	*3.00*
		Never hinged	2.25	
		On cover		5.25
a.		Inverted surcharge	55.00	
		Never hinged	160.00	
45	A22	15pf on 50pf on 35c (R)	.40	*3.00*
		Never hinged	2.25	
		On cover		5.25
a.		Inverted surcharge	55.00	
		Never hinged	160.00	
46	A22	60pf on 40pf on 20c	.40	*1.90*
		Never hinged	3.00	
		On cover		4.00
a.		Inverted surcharge	55.00	*225.00*
		Never hinged	150.00	
47	A18	75pf on 60pf on 40c	.75	*3.75*
		Never hinged	5.25	
		On cover		16.00
48	A18	1.25m on 1m on 50c	.60	*3.00*
		Never hinged	3.75	
		On cover		7.50
49	A18	5.00m on 2m on 1fr	.90	*4.50*
		Never hinged	6.00	
		On cover		19.00
a.		Inverted surcharge	150.00	*525.00*
		Never hinged	375.00	
		Nos. 43-49 (7)	3.85	*21.05*

Stamps of France Surcharged in Black or Red

On A20, A22

1922

No.	Type	Description	Unused	Used
50	A22	5pf on 5c org	.25	*1.35*
		Never hinged	1.10	
		On cover		8.00
51	A22	10pf on 10c red	.75	*5.25*
		Never hinged	4.50	
		On cover		16.00
52	A22	10pf on 10c grn	.25	*1.35*
		Never hinged	1.10	
		On cover		8.00
53	A22	15pf on 10c grn	.25	*1.35*
		Never hinged	1.10	
		On cover		8.00
54	A22	20pf on 20c red brn	7.50	*37.50*
		Never hinged	35.00	
		On cover		67.50
55	A22	20pf on 25c bl	7.50	*37.50*
		Never hinged	35.00	
		On cover		67.50
56	A22	25pf on 5c org	.25	*1.35*
		Never hinged	1.10	
		On cover		8.00
57	A22	30pf on 30c red	1.10	*5.25*
		Never hinged	4.50	
		On cover		16.00
58	A22	35pf on 35c vio	.25	*.75*
		Never hinged	1.00	
		On cover		9.50
59	A20	50pf on 50c dl bl	.25	*1.35*
		Never hinged	1.10	
		On cover		6.00
60	A20	75pf on 15c grn	.30	*.75*
		Never hinged	1.00	
		On cover		8.00
61	A22	75pf on 35c vio	.30	*1.35*
		Never hinged	1.10	
		On cover		8.00
62	A22	1m on 25c blue	.30	*.75*
		Never hinged	1.00	
		On cover		6.00
63	A22	1¼m on 30c red	.25	*.75*
		Never hinged	1.00	
		On cover		8.00
64	A22	3m on 5c org	.40	*5.00*
		Never hinged	4.50	
		On cover		8.00
65	A20	6m on 15c grn (R)	.75	*5.00*
		Never hinged	5.25	
		On cover		8.00
66	A22	8m on 30c red	.75	*13.00*
		Never hinged	6.00	
		On cover		26.00

On A18

No.	Type	Description	Unused	Used
67	A18	40pf on 40c red & pale bl	.25	*1.35*
		Never hinged	1.10	
		On cover		8.00
68	A18	80pf on 45c grn & bl	.30	*1.35*
		Never hinged	1.10	
		On cover		4.50
69	A18	1m on 40c red & pale bl	.30	*2.25*
		Never hinged	1.10	
		On cover		4.50
70	A18	1.25m on 60c vio & ultra (R)	.30	*2.25*
		Never hinged	1.10	
		On cover		6.00
71	A18	1.50m on 45c grn & bl (R)	.30	*2.25*
		Never hinged	1.10	
		On cover		6.00
72	A18	2m on 45c grn & bl	.75	*2.60*
		Never hinged	3.00	
		On cover		6.00
73	A18	2m on 1fr cl & ol grn	.30	*2.25*
		Never hinged	1.10	
		On cover		4.50
74	A18	2¼m on 40c red & pale bl	.25	*.75*
		Never hinged	1.00	
		On cover		8.00
75	A18	2½m on 60c vio & ultra	.75	*2.50*
		Never hinged	3.00	
		On cover		16.00
76	A18	3m on 60c vio & ultra (R)	1.10	*5.25*
		Never hinged	4.50	
		On cover		9.00
77	A18	4m on 45c grn & bl	.25	*.75*
		Never hinged	1.00	
		On cover		8.00
78	A18	5m on 1fr cl & ol grn	.30	*3.00*
		Never hinged	1.25	
		On cover		6.00
79	A18	6m on 60c vio & ultra	.25	*.75*
		Never hinged	1.00	
		On cover		8.00
80	A18	6m on 2fr org & pale bl	.30	*3.00*
		Never hinged	1.25	
		On cover		8.00
81	A18	9m on 1fr cl & ol grn	.25	*.75*
		Never hinged	1.00	
		On cover		8.00
82	A18	9m on 5fr bl & buff (R)	.40	*3.00*
		Never hinged	2.25	
		On cover		9.50
83	A18	10m on 45c grn & bl (R)	.75	*5.00*
		Never hinged	6.00	
		On cover		8.00
84	A18	12m on 40c red & pale bl	.40	*2.25*
		Never hinged	2.00	
		On cover		8.00
85	A18	20m on 40c red & pale bl	.75	*5.00*
		Never hinged	6.00	
		On cover		8.00
86	A18	20m on 2fr org & pale bl	.25	*2.00*
		Never hinged	2.00	
		On cover		8.00
87	A18	30m on 60c vio & ultra	.75	*5.00*
		Never hinged	6.00	
		On cover		8.00
88	A18	30m on 5fr dk bl & buff	2.60	*19.00*
		Never hinged	15.00	
		On cover		60.00
89	A18	40m on 1fr cl & ol grn	.75	*6.50*
		Never hinged	6.00	
		On cover		11.00
90	A18	50m on 2fr org & pale bl	7.50	*45.00*
		Never hinged	45.00	
		On cover		90.00
91	A18	80m on 2fr org & pale bl (R)	.75	*6.50*
		Never hinged	6.00	
		On cover		11.00

92 A18 100m on 5fr bl & buff 1.10 *12.00*
Never hinged 7.50
On cover 47.50
Nos. 50-92 (43) 43.35 *261.90*

A 500m on 5fr dark blue and buff was prepared, but not officially issued. Value: unused $800; never hinged $2,000.

For stamps with additional surcharges and overprints see Nos. 93-99, C8-C17, C20-C29.

Nos. 52, 54, 67, 59 Surcharged "Mark"

1922-23

93 A22 10m on 10pf on 10c .75 *7.00*
Never hinged 3.75
On cover 24.00
a. Double surcharge 100.00 *500.00*
Never hinged 260.00
94 A22 20m on 20pf on 20c .40 *4.50*
Never hinged 2.25
On cover 11.00
95 A18 40m on 40pf on 40c ('23) .75 *5.00*
Never hinged 4.50
On cover 20.00
96 A20 50m on 50pf on 50c 2.25 *14.50*
Never hinged 15.00
On cover 26.00
Nos. 93-96 (4) 4.15 *31.00*

Nos. 72, 61, 70 Srchd. in Red or Black

1922-23

97 A18 10m on 2m on 45c 1.90 *13.00*
Never hinged 11.50
On cover 22.50
98 A22 25m on 1m on 25c 1.90 *13.00*
Never hinged 11.50
On cover 22.50
99 A18 80m on 1.25m on 60c (Bk) ('23) 1.10 *7.00*
Never hinged 6.00
On cover 72.50
Nos. 97-99 (3) 4.90 *33.00*

For No. 99 with additional surcharges see Nos. N28-N30.

AIR POST STAMPS

Nos. 24-26, 28, 31, 39-40 Ovptd. in Dark Blue

1921, July 6 Unwmk. *Perf. 14x13½*

C1 A18 60pf on 40c 30.00 *150.00*
Never hinged 120.00
On cover 225.00
C2 A18 80pf on 45c 3.75 *13.00*
Never hinged 15.00
On cover 75.00
C3 A18 1m on 50c 4.00 *13.00*
Never hinged 19.00
On cover 52.50
C4 A18 2m on 1fr 4.50 *13.50*
Never hinged 15.00
On cover 60.00
a. "Flugpost" inverted 150.00 *375.00*
Never hinged 375.00
C5 A18 4m on 2fr (I) 3.75 *19.00*
Never hinged 15.00
On cover 75.00
a. Type II 75.00 *260.00*
Never hinged 200.00
On cover 1,200.
b. Pair, type I and type II 100.00

New Value with Initial Capital

C6 A18 60Pf on 40c 3.75 *17.00*
Never hinged 15.00
On cover 75.00
a. "Flugpost" inverted 150.00 *375.00*
Never hinged 400.00
C7 A18 3M on 60c 2.60 *17.00*
Never hinged 13.00
On cover 60.00
a. "Flugpost" inverted 260.00 *600.00*
Never hinged 600.00
Nos. C1-C7 (7) 52.35 *242.50*

The surcharged value on No. C7 is in italics.

Nos. 67-71, 73, 76, 78, 80, 82 Ovptd. in Dark Blue

1922, May 12

C8 A18 40pf on 40c .40 *3.75*
Never hinged 5.75
On cover 40.00
C9 A18 80pf on 45c .40 *3.75*
Never hinged 5.75
On cover 40.00
C10 A18 1m on 40c .40 *3.75*
Never hinged 5.75
On cover 40.00
C11 A18 1.25m on 60c .75 *6.00*
Never hinged 9.00
On cover 40.00
C12 A18 1.50m on 45c .75 *6.00*
Never hinged 9.00
On cover 40.00
C13 A18 2m on 1fr .75 *6.00*
Never hinged 9.00
On cover 40.00
C14 A18 3m on 60c .75 *6.00*
Never hinged 9.00
On cover 40.00
C15 A18 5m on 1fr 1.10 *6.00*
Never hinged 9.00
On cover 60.00
C16 A18 6m on 2fr 1.10 *6.00*
Never hinged 9.00
On cover 60.00
C17 A18 9m on 5fr 1.10 *6.00*
Never hinged 9.00
On cover 60.00

Same Overprint On Nos. 40, 31

C18 A18 3m on 60c 120.00 *1,050.*
Never hinged 375.00
On cover 2,400.
C19 A18 4m on 2fr .75 *6.00*
Never hinged 9.00
On cover 47.50
Nos. C8-C17,C19 (11) 8.25 *59.25*

Nos. 67, 69-71, 73, 76, 78, 80, 82 Ovptd. in Black or Red

1922, Oct. 17

C20 A18 40pf on 40c 1.25 *15.00*
Never hinged 7.50
On cover 100.00
C21 A18 1m on 40c 1.25 *15.00*
Never hinged 7.50
On cover 100.00
C22 A18 1.25m on 60c (R) 1.25 *15.00*
Never hinged 7.50
On cover 100.00
C23 A18 1.50m on 45c (R) 1.25 *15.00*
Never hinged 7.50
On cover 100.00
C24 A18 2m on 1fr 1.25 *15.00*
Never hinged 7.50
On cover 100.00
C25 A18 3m on 60c (R) 1.25 *15.00*
Never hinged 7.50
On cover 100.00
C26 A18 4m on 2fr 1.25 *15.00*
Never hinged 7.50
On cover 100.00
C27 A18 5m on 1fr 1.25 *15.00*
Never hinged 7.50
On cover 100.00
C28 A18 6m on 2fr 1.25 *15.00*
Never hinged 7.50
On cover 100.00
C29 A18 9m on 5fr (R) 1.25 *15.00*
Never hinged 7.50
On cover 100.00
Nos. C20-C29 (10) 12.50 *150.00*

No. C26 is not known without the "FLUGPOST" overprint.

OCCUPATION STAMPS

Issued under Lithuanian Occupation

Surcharged in Various Colors on Unissued Official Stamps of Lithuania Similar to Type O4

On Nos. N1-N6

On Nos. N7-N11

Memel Printing

1923 Unwmk. Litho. *Perf. 11*

N1 O4 10m on 5c bl (Bk) 1.00 *10.00*
Never hinged 12.00
On cover 37.50
a. Double overprint 35.00 *230.00*
Never hinged 130.00
b. "Memel" and bars omitted 7.00 *52.50*
Never hinged 32.50
On cover 160.00
N2 O4 25m on 5c bl (R) 1.00 *10.00*
Never hinged 12.00
On cover 30.00
a. Double overprint 35.00 *230.00*
Never hinged 130.00
N3 O4 50m on 25c red (Bk) 1.00 *10.00*
Never hinged 12.00
On cover 32.50
a. Double overprint 35.00 *230.00*
Never hinged 130.00
N4 O4 100m on 25c red (G) 1.00 *10.00*
Never hinged 12.00
On cover 130.00
a. Double overprint 35.00 *230.00*
Never hinged 150.00
N5 O4 400m on 1 l brn (R) 1.30 *13.00*
Never hinged 17.00
On cover 60.00
a. Double overprint 35.00 *230.00*
Never hinged 130.00
N6 O4 500m on 1 l brn (Bl) 1.30 *13.00*
Never hinged 17.00
On cover 80.00
a. Double overprint 35.00 *230.00*
Never hinged 130.00
Nos. N1-N6 (6) 6.60 *66.00*

Kaunas Printing

Black Surcharge

N7 O4 10m on 5c blue .70 *6.00*
Never hinged 13.00
On cover 15.00
N8 O4 25m on 5c blue .70 *6.00*
Never hinged 13.00
On cover 15.00
N9 O4 50m on 25c red .70 *6.00*
Never hinged 13.00
On cover 15.00
N10 O4 100m on 25c red .80 *6.00*
Never hinged 17.00
On cover 16.00
N11 O4 400m on 1 l brn 1.30 *9.25*
Never hinged 22.50
On cover 40.00
Nos. N7-N11 (5) 4.20 *33.25*

No. N8 has the value in "Markes," others of the group have it in "Markiu."

For additional surcharge see No. N87.

Surcharged in Various Colors on Unissued Official Stamps of Lithuania Similar to Type O4

1923

N12 O4 10m on 5c bl (R) 1.30 *8.00*
Never hinged 18.00
On cover 60.00
a. "Markes" instead of "Markiu" 13.00 *92.50*
Never hinged 80.00
N13 O4 20m on 5c bl (R) 1.30 *8.00*
Never hinged 18.00
On cover 60.00
N14 O4 25m on 25c red (Bl) 1.30 *10.50*
Never hinged 18.00
On cover 60.00
N15 O4 50m on 25c red (Bl) 2.60 *10.50*
Never hinged 32.50
On cover 60.00
a. Inverted surcharge 32.50 *130.00*
Never hinged 130.00
N16 O4 100m on 1 l brn (Bk) 2.60 *15.00*
Never hinged 36.00
On cover 80.00
a. Inverted surcharge 32.50 130.00
Never hinged 130.00
N17 O4 200m on 1 l brn (Bk) 4.00 *17.00*
Never hinged 50.00
On cover 80.00
Nos. N12-N17 (6) 13.10 *69.00*

No. N14 has the value in "Markes," others of the group have it in "Markiu."

"Vytis"
O4 O5

1923, Mar.

N18 O4 10m lt brown .35 *5.50*
Never hinged 3.25
On cover 19.00
N19 O4 20m yellow .35 *5.50*
Never hinged 3.25
On cover 19.00
N20 O4 25m orange .35 *7.00*
Never hinged 3.25
On cover 19.00
N21 O4 40m violet .35 *5.50*
Never hinged 3.25
On cover 19.00
N22 O4 50m yellow grn 1.00 *12.00*
Never hinged 8.00
On cover 30.00
N23 O5 100m carmine .45 *6.00*
Never hinged 3.25
On cover 19.00
N24 O5 300m olive grn 5.00 *120.00*
Never hinged 60.00
On cover 275.00
N25 O5 400m olive brn .45 *6.00*
Never hinged 4.00
On cover 40.00
N26 O5 500m lilac 5.00 *120.00*
Never hinged 60.00
On cover 275.00
N27 O5 1000m blue .85 *10.00*
Never hinged 7.00
On cover 95.00
Nos. N18-N27 (10) 14.15 *297.50*

No. N20 has the value in "Markes."

For surcharges see Nos. N44-N69, N88-N114.

No. 99 Surcharged in Green

1923, Apr. 13

N28 A18 100m on No. 99 3.00 *60.00*
Never hinged 10.50
On cover 725.00
a. Inverted overprint 70.00
Never hinged 230.00
N29 A18 400m on No. 99 4.00 *60.00*
Never hinged 13.00
On cover 725.00
a. Inverted overprint 70.00
Never hinged 230.00
N30 A18 500m on No. 99 3.00 *60.00*
Never hinged 10.50
On cover 725.00
a. Inverted overprint 70.00
Never hinged 230.00
Nos. N28-N30 (3) 10.00 180.00

The normal position of the green surcharge is sideways, up-reading, with the top at the left. Inverted varieties are reversed, with the over-print down-reading.

Ship — O7

Seal — O8

Lighthouse — O9

1923, Apr. 12 Litho.

N31 O7 40m olive grn 3.75 *32.50*
Never hinged 26.00
On cover 275.00
N32 O7 50m brown 3.75 *32.50*
Never hinged 26.00
On cover 275.00
N33 O7 80m green 3.75 *32.50*
Never hinged 26.00
On cover 275.00
N34 O7 100m red 3.75 *32.50*
Never hinged 26.00
On cover 275.00
N35 O8 200m deep blue 3.75 *32.50*
Never hinged 26.00
On cover 275.00
N36 O8 300m brown 3.75 *32.50*
Never hinged 26.00
On cover 275.00
N37 O8 400m lilac 3.75 *32.50*
Never hinged 26.00
On cover 275.00
N38 O8 500m orange 3.75 *32.50*
Never hinged 26.00
On cover 275.00
N39 O8 600m olive grn 3.75 *32.50*
Never hinged 26.00
On cover 275.00
N40 O9 800m deep blue 3.75 *32.50*
Never hinged 26.00
On cover 275.00
N41 O9 1000m lilac 3.75 *32.50*
Never hinged 26.00
On cover 275.00
N42 O9 2000m red 3.75 *32.50*
Never hinged 26.00
On cover 275.00
N43 O9 3000m green 3.75 *32.50*
Never hinged 26.00
On cover 275.00
Nos. N31-N43 (13) 48.75 *422.50*

Union of Memel with Lithuania. Forgeries exist.

For surcharges see Nos. N70-N86.

Nos. N20, N24, N26 Surcharged in Various Colors

1923 Thin Figures

N44 O5 2c on 300m (R) 5.25 *13.00*
Never hinged 30.00
On cover 52.50
a. Double surcharge 70.00 *325.00*
Never hinged 200.00
N45 O5 3c on 300m (R) 6.00 *17.00*
Never hinged 32.50
On cover 52.50
a. Double surcharge 145.00 *400.00*
Never hinged 400.00
N46 O4 10c on 25m (Bk) 6.00 *13.00*
Never hinged 32.50
On cover 52.50
a. Double surcharge 70.00 *325.00*
Never hinged 200.00
b. Inverted surcharge 92.50 *260.00*
Never hinged 200.00
N47 O4 15c on 25m (Bk) 6.00 *13.00*
Never hinged 32.50
On cover 52.50
N48 O5 20c on 500m (Bl) 9.25 *26.00*
Never hinged 42.50
On cover 75.00
N49 O5 30c on 500m (Bk) 7.25 *13.00*
Never hinged 32.50
On cover 52.50
a. Double surcharge
On cover —
N50 O5 50c on 500m (G) 11.00 *26.00*
Never hinged 70.00
On cover 120.00
a. Inverted surcharge 52.50 *200.00*
Never hinged 165.00
b. Double surcharge 130.00 *600.00*
Never hinged 400.00
Nos. N44-N50 (7) 50.75 *121.00*

Nos. N19, N21-N27 Surcharged

N51 O4 2c on 20m yellow 3.25 *13.00*
Never hinged 17.00
On cover 32.50
N52 O4 2c on 50c yel grn 3.25 *13.00*
Never hinged 17.00
On cover 32.50
a. Double surcharge 50.00 *260.00*
Never hinged 145.00
b. Vert. pair, imperf between 70.00 *300.00*
Never hinged 200.00
N53 O4 3c on 40m violet 5.50 *12.00*
Never hinged 22.50
On cover 45.00
a. Double surcharge 57.50 *260.00*
Never hinged 160.00
N54 O5 3c on 300m ol grn 3.25 *10.00*
Never hinged 17.00
On cover 32.50
a. Double surcharge 130.00 *450.00*
Never hinged 400.00
N55 O5 5c on 100m carmine 8.00 *10.00*
Never hinged 42.50
On cover 32.50
N56 O5 5c on 300m ol grn (R) 3.25 *17.00*
Never hinged 22.50
On cover 50.00
a. Double surcharge 92.50 *325.00*
Never hinged 260.00
N57 O5 10c on 400m ol brn 17.00 *20.00*
Never hinged 82.50
On cover 52.50
N58 O5 30c on 500m lilac 5.25 *22.50*
Never hinged 37.50
On cover 67.50
a. Double surcharge 92.50 *325.00*
Never hinged 260.00
b. Inverted surcharge 100.00 *360.00*
Never hinged 300.00
N59 O5 1 l on 1000m blue 22.50 *65.00*
Never hinged 130.00
On cover 110.00
a. Double surcharge 130.00 *460.00*
Never hinged 400.00
Nos. N51-N59 (9) 71.25 *182.50*

There are several types of the numerals in these surcharges. Nos. N56 and N58 have "CENT" in short, thick letters, as on Nos. N44 to N50.

Nos. N18-N23, N25, N27 Surcharged

Thick Figures

N60 O4 2c on 10m lt brn 5.25 *65.00*
Never hinged 20.00
On cover 150.00
N61 O4 2c on 20m yellow 17.00 *120.00*
Never hinged 65.00
On cover 275.00
N62 O4 2c on 50m yel grn 6.50 *80.00*
Never hinged 32.50
On cover 150.00
N63 O4 3c on 10m lt brn 17.00 *110.00*
Never hinged 65.00
On cover 190.00
a. Double surcharge 130.00 *525.00*
Never hinged 400.00
N64 O4 3c on 40m violet 20.00 *190.00*
Never hinged 80.00
On cover 375.00
N65 O5 5c on 100m car 10.00 *32.50*
Never hinged 40.00
On cover 75.00
a. Double surcharge 92.50 *300.00*
Never hinged 260.00
N66 O5 10c on 400m ol brn 130.00 *550.00*
Never hinged 625.00
On cover 1,600.
N67 O4 15c on 25m orange 130.00 *550.00*
Never hinged 625.00
On cover 1,600.
N68 O5 50c on 1000m blue 5.25 *10.00*
Never hinged 20.00
On cover 32.50
a. Double surcharge 92.50 *300.00*
Never hinged 260.00
On cover 400.00
N69 O5 1 l on 1000m blue 6.50 *20.00*
Never hinged 32.50
On cover 60.00
a. Double surcharge 92.50 *300.00*
Never hinged 260.00
Nos. N60-N69 (10) 347.50 *1,728.*

No. N69 is surcharged like type "b" in the following group.

Nos. N31-N43 Surcharged

a

b

N70 O7(a) 15c on 40m ol grn 4.25 *26.00*
Never hinged 20.00
On cover 55.00
N71 O7(a) 30c on 50m brown 4.25 *20.00*
Never hinged 20.00
On cover 45.00
a. Double surcharge 52.50 *230.00*
Never hinged 165.00
N72 O7(a) 30c on 80m green 4.25 *32.50*
Never hinged 20.00
On cover 67.50
N73 O7(a) 30c on 100m red 4.25 *13.00*
Never hinged 20.00
On cover 37.50
N74 O8(a) 50c on 200m dp blue 4.25 *26.00*
Never hinged 20.00
On cover 55.00
N75 O8(a) 50c on 300m brn 4.25 *13.00*
Never hinged 20.00
On cover 37.50
a. Double surcharge 52.50 *230.00*
Never hinged 165.00
b. Inverted surcharge 52.50 *230.00*
Never hinged 165.00
N76 O8(a) 50c on 400m lilac 4.25 *22.50*
Never hinged 20.00
On cover 52.50
a. Inverted surcharge 60.00 *260.00*
Never hinged 200.00
N77 O8(a) 50c on 500m org 4.25 *13.00*
Never hinged 20.00
On cover 37.50
a. Double surcharge 52.50 *230.00*
Never hinged 165.00
N78 O8(b) 1 l on 600m ol grn 4.25 *30.00*
Never hinged 22.50
On cover 67.50
N79 O9(b) 1 l on 800m dp blue 5.00 *30.00*
Never hinged 22.50
On cover 67.50
N80 O9(b) 1 l on 1000m lil 4.50 *30.00*
Never hinged 22.50
On cover 67.50
N81 O9(b) 1 l on 2000m red 5.00 *30.00*
Never hinged 22.50
On cover 75.00
N82 O9(b) 1 l on 3000m grn 5.00 *30.00*
Never hinged 22.50
On cover 67.50
Nos. N70-N82 (13) 57.75 *316.00*

These stamps are said to have been issued to commemorate the institution of autonomous government.

Nos. N32, N34, N36, N38 Surcharged in Green

1923

N83 O7 15c on 50m brn 165. *1,650.*
Never hinged 1,200.
On cover 3,350.
a. Thick numerals in surcharge 1,000. *4,000.*
Never hinged 3,000.
N84 O7 25c on 100m red 70. *1,000.*
Never hinged 400.
On cover 2,500.
a. Thick numerals in surcharge 1,000. *2,600.*
Never hinged 4,000.
N85 O8 30c on 300m brn 130. *1,050.*
Never hinged 650.
On cover 2,800.
a. Thick numerals in surcharge 800. *3,000.*
Never hinged 2,000.
N86 O8 60c on 500m org 80. *1,000.*
Never hinged 400.
On cover 2,800.
a. Thick numerals in surcharge 525. *2,000.*
Never hinged 1,300.

Surcharges on Nos. N83-N86 are of two types, differing in width of numerals. Values are for stamps with narrow numerals, as illustrated.

Nos. N8, N10-N11, N3 Surcharged in Red or Green

N87 O4 10c on 25m on 5c bl (R) 26.00 *100.00*
Never hinged 325.00
On cover 225.00
N88 O4 15c on 100m on 25c red (G) 32.50 *300.00*
Never hinged 400.00
On cover 600.00
a. Inverted surcharge 325.00 *1,850.*
Never hinged 1,700.
N89 O4 30c on 400m on 1 l brn (R) 6.50 *40.00*
Never hinged 52.50
On cover 90.00
N90 O4 60c on 50m on 25c red (G) 32.50 *260.00*
Never hinged 375.00
On cover 600.00
Nos. N87-N90 (4) 97.50 *700.00*

Nos. N18-N22 Surcharged in Green or Red

N91 O4 15c on 10m 26.00 *200.00*
Never hinged 165.00
On cover 260.00
N92 O4 15c on 20m 2.60 *26.00*
Never hinged 17.00
On cover 110.00
N93 O4 15c on 25m 5.50 *52.50*
Never hinged 22.50
On cover 110.00
N94 O4 15c on 40m 1.65 *26.00*
Never hinged 10.00
On cover 110.00
N95 O4 15c on 50m (R) 2.40 *30.00*
Never hinged 10.00
On cover 90.00
a. Inverted surcharge 50.00
Never hinged 165.00
N96 O4 25c on 10m 9.25 *100.00*
Never hinged 45.00
On cover 260.00
N97 O4 25c on 20m 2.40 *26.00*
Never hinged 10.00
On cover 90.00
a. Double surcharge 160.00
Never hinged 600.00
N98 O4 25c on 25m 4.50 *40.00*
Never hinged 22.50
On cover 110.00
N99 O4 25c on 40m 4.00 *40.00*
Never hinged 22.50
On cover 90.00
a. Inverted surcharge 50.00
Never hinged 165.00
N100 O4 25c on 50m (R) 2.40 *20.00*
Never hinged 13.50
On cover 90.00
a. Inverted surcharge 50.00
Never hinged 165.00
N101 O4 30c on 10m 26.00 *200.00*
Never hinged 165.00
On cover 300.00
N102 O4 30c on 20m 4.00 *32.50*
Never hinged 20.00
On cover 140.00
N103 O4 30c on 25m 4.50 *52.50*
Never hinged 20.00
On cover 140.00
N104 O4 30c on 40m 3.25 *20.00*
Never hinged 13.00
On cover 140.00
N105 O4 30c on 50m (R) 2.60 *20.00*
Never hinged 17.00
On cover 140.00
a. Inverted surcharge 50.00
Never hinged 165.00
Nos. N91-N105 (15) 101.05 *885.50*

Nos. N23, N25, N27 Surcharged in Green or Red

N106 O5 15c on 100m 2.40 *20.00*
Never hinged 10.00
On cover 90.00
a. Inverted surcharge 50.00
Never hinged 165.00
N107 O5 15c on 400m 2.00 *17.00*
Never hinged 10.00
On cover 90.00
N108 O5 15c on 1000m (R) 52.50 *400.00*
Never hinged 325.00
On cover 875.00
a. Inverted surcharge 165.00 *700.00*
Never hinged 525.00
N109 O5 25c on 100m 2.00 *20.00*
Never hinged 10.00
On cover 90.00
N110 O5 25c on 400m 2.00 *20.00*
Never hinged 10.00
On cover 90.00
a. Double surcharge 100.00
Never hinged 300.00
N111 O5 25c on 1000m (R) 52.50 *400.00*
Never hinged 325.00
On cover 875.00
a. Inverted surcharge 165.00 *700.00*
Never hinged 525.00
N112 O5 30c on 100m 2.60 *20.00*
Never hinged 17.00
On cover 140.00
a. Inverted surcharge 50.00
Never hinged 165.00
N113 O5 30c on 400m 2.60 *20.00*
Never hinged 17.00
On cover 140.00
N114 O5 30c on 1000m (R) 52.50 *400.00*
Never hinged 325.00
On cover 875.00
a. Inverted surcharge 165.00 *700.00*
Never hinged 525.00
Nos. N106-N114 (9) 171.10 *1,317.*

Nos. N96 to N100 and N109 to N111 are surcharged "Centai," the others "Centu."

MESOPOTAMIA

ˌme-s̜ə-ˌpə-ˈtā-mē-ə

LOCATION — In Western Asia, bounded on the north by Syria and Turkey, on the east by Persia, on the south by Saudi Arabia and on the west by Trans-Jordan.
GOVT. — A former Turkish Province
AREA — 143,250 (1918) sq. mi.
POP. — 2,849,282 (1920)
CAPITAL — Baghdad

During World War I this territory was occupied by Great Britain. It was recognized as an independent state and placed under British Mandate but in 1932 the Mandate was terminated and the country admitted to membership in the League of Nations as the Kingdom of Iraq. Postage stamps of Iraq are now in use.

16 Annas = 1 Rupee

Watermark

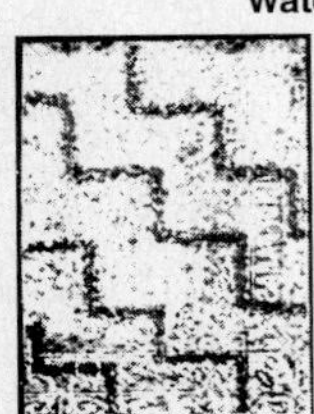

Wmk. 48 — Diagonal Zigzag Lines

Issued under British Occupation

Baghdad Issue

Stamps of Turkey 1901-16 Surcharged

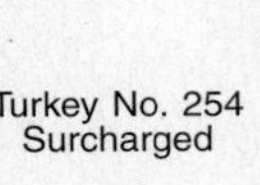

Turkey No. 254 Surcharged

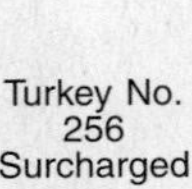

Turkey No. 256 Surcharged

Turkey No. 258 Surcharged

Turkey No. 259 Surcharged

Turkey No. 260 Surcharged

The surcharges were printed from slugs which were arranged to fit the various shapes of the stamps.

1917 Unwmk. *Perf. 12, 13½*

N1 ¼a on 2pa red lil 400.00 425.00
a. "IN BRITISH" omitted *17,500.*
N2 ¼a on 5pa vio brown 300.00 325.00
a. "¼ An" omitted *20,000.*
N3 ½a on 10pa green 1,450. *1,750.*
N4 1a on 20pa red 1,000. *1,100.*
a. "BAGHDAD" double 2,600.
N5 2a on 1pi blue 450.00 *500.00*
Nos. N1-N5 (5) 3,600. 4,100.

On Turkey No. 249

N6 A22 2a on 1pi ultra 1,150. *1,375.*
a. "IN BRITISH" omitted *17,500.*

Turkey No. 251 Surcharged

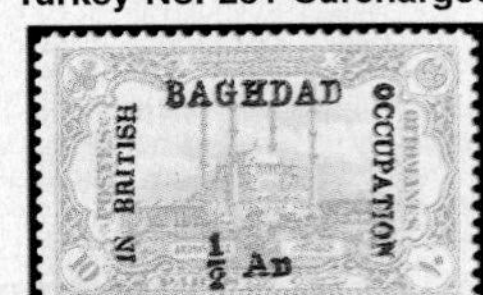

N7 A23 ½a on 10pa green 3,250. 3,500.

On Turkey Nos. 272-273

N8 A29 1a on 20pa red 675. *750.*
a. "OCCUPATION" omitted *20,000.*
b. "BAGHDAD" double 2,600.
N9 A30 2a on 1pi blue 5,250. *8,500.*

On Turkey Nos. 346-348

N10 A41 ½a on 10pa car, perf 12½ 1,000. *1,200.*
a. Perf 13½ 2,100. *2,400.*
N11 A41 1a on 20pa ultra, perf 13½ 2,650. 3,250.
a. "1 An" omitted *18,500.*
b. Perf 12½ *14,000.* 350.00
N12 A41 2a on 1pi vio & black, perf 13½ 325.00 *200.00*
a. "BAGHDAD" omitted *20,000.*
b. Perf 12½ *650.00* *700.00*

On Turkey Nos. 297, 300

N13 A17 ¼a on 5pa purple *20,000.*
N14 A17 2a on 1pi blue 450. 500.
a. "OCCUPATION" omitted 17,500.

On Turkey No. 306

N15 A18 1a on 20pa car 1,000. *1,150.*
a. Value omitted *17,500.*

On Turkey Nos. 329-331

N16 A22 ½a on 10pa bl grn 300.00 350.00
N17 A22 1a on 20pa car rose 1,000. *1,000.*
a. "1 An" omitted *10,000.* *7,500.*
b. With additional "Behie" *11,000.* *10,500.*
N18 A22 2a on 1pi ultra 325.00 350.00
a. "BAGHDAD" omitted —

On Turkey No. 337

N19 A22 1a on 20pa car rose *9,000.* *11,750.*

On Turkey No. P125

N20 A17 1a on 20pa car —

On Turkey Nos. B1, B8

Inscription in crescent is obliterated by another crescent handstamped in violet black on Nos. N21-N27.

N21 A18 ½a on 10pa dull grn 325.00 *375.00*
a. "OCCUPATION" omitted *16,000.*
N22 A21 1a on 20pa car rose 1,000. *1,100.*

On Turkey No. B29

N23 A21 2a on 1pi ultra 3,750. *4,000.*

On Turkey Nos. B33-B34

N24 A22 1a on 20pa car rose 325.00 *375.00*
N25 A22 2a on 1pi ultra 450.00 *500.00*
a. "OCCUPATION" omitted *17,500.*
b. "BAGHDAD" omitted *16,500.*

On Turkey No. B42

N26 A41 ½a on 10pa car, perf 12½ 450.00 *500.00*
a. "BAGHDAD" double
b. Perf 13½ 900.00 *1,000.*

On Turkey No. B38

N27 A11 1a on 10pa on 20pa vio brn 500.00 550.00
a. "OCCUPATION" omitted — *17,500.*

Iraq Issue

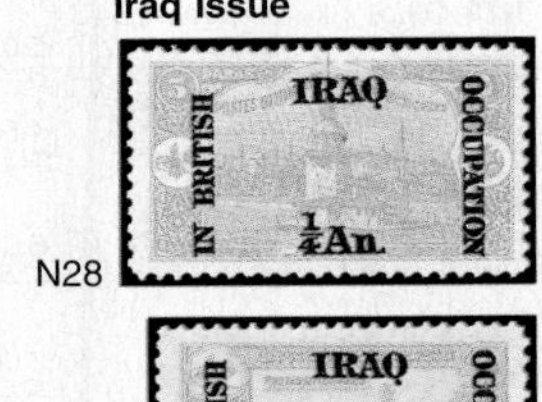

N28

N29

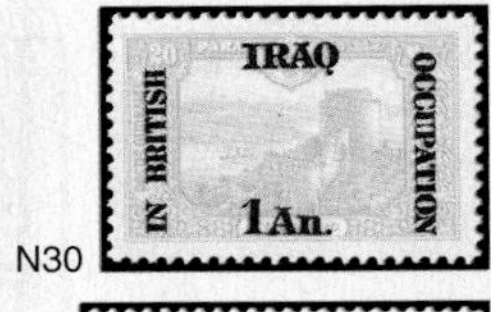

N30

N31

N32

N33

N34

N35

N36

N37

N38

N39

N40

N41

Turkey Nos. 256, 258-269 Surcharged

1918-20 *Perf. 12*

N28 ¼a on 5pa vio brn .55 *1.10*
N29 ½a on 10pa grn 1.00 .25
N30 1a on 20pa red .55 .25
N31 1½a on 5pa vio brn 16.50 .75
N32 2½a on 1pi blue 1.50 1.50
a. Inverted surcharge *11,500.*
N33 3a on 1½pi car & black 1.60 .25
a. Double surcharge, red & blk *4,500.* *5,500.*
N34 4a on 1¾pi slate & red brn 1.60 .30
a. Center inverted *37,500.*

N35		6a on 2pi grn & black	2.50	2.00
N36		8a on 2½pi org & ol grn	3.75	2.25
N37		12a on 5pi dl vio	2.00	6.50
N38		1r on 10pi red brown	2.75	1.50
N39		2r on 25pi ol grn	12.50	3.25
N40		5r on 50pi car	30.00	32.50
N41		10r on 100pi dp blue	100.00	18.50
		Nos. N28-N41 (14)	176.80	70.90

See #N50-N53. For overprints see #NO1-NO21.

Mosul Issue

A13 A14

A15

A16

A17

A18

A19

1919		Unwmk.		*Perf. 11½, 12*
N42	A13	½a on 1pi grn & brn red	2.40	2.10
N43	A14	1a on 20pa *rose*	1.50	1.90
a.		"POSTAGE" omitted		
N44	A15	1a on 20pa *rose*	4.50	4.50
a.		Double surcharge	725.00	

Turkish word at right of tughra ("reshad") is large on No. N43, small on No. N44.

Wmk. Turkish Characters

Perf. 12½

N45	A16	2½a on 1pi vio & yel	1.60	1.60
N46	A17	3a on 20pa grn & yel	90.00	*125.00*

Wmk. 48

N47	A17	3a on 20pa green	1.75	*4.25*
N48	A18	4a on 1pi dull vio	3.50	3.75
a.		Double surcharge	1,250.	
b.		"4" omitted	2,000.	
c.		As "b," double surcharge		
N49	A19	8a on 10pa claret	4.25	*5.50*
a.		Double surcharge	*750.00*	*875.00*
b.		Inverted surcharge	*900.00*	*1,000.*
c.		8a on 1pi dull violet	*3,500.*	
		Nos. N42-N49 (8)	109.50	148.60

Value for No. 49c is for a stamp with the perfs cutting into the design.

Iraq Issue

Types of 1918-20 Issue

1921		Wmk. 4		*Perf. 12*
N50	A28	½a on 10pa green	7.50	2.50
N51	A26	1½a on 5pa dp brn	5.00	1.35
N52	A37	2r on 25pi ol grn	37.50	14.00
		Nos. N50-N52 (3)	50.00	17.85
		Set of 3, ovptd "SPECIMEN"	175.00	

Type of 1918-20 without "Reshad"

1922				Unwmk.
N53	A36	1r on 10pi red brn	350.00	27.50

"Reshad" is the small Turkish word at right of the tughra in circle at top center.

For overprint see No. NO22.

OFFICIAL STAMPS

Nos. N29-N41 Overprinted

1920		Unwmk.		*Perf. 12*
NO1	A28	½a on 10pa grn	25.00	2.00
NO2	A29	1a on 20pa red	8.00	1.00
NO3	A26	1½a on 5pa vio brown	60.00	3.00
NO4	A30	2½a on 1pi blue	8.00	8.00
NO5	A31	3a on 1½pi car & black	27.50	1.00
NO6	A32	4a on 1¾pi sl & red brn	55.00	4.75
NO7	A33	6a on 2pi grn & black	42.50	10.00
NO8	A34	8a on 2½pi org & ol grn	55.00	6.00
NO9	A35	12a on 5pi dull vio	32.50	24.00
NO10	A36	1r on 10pi red brown	47.50	12.00
NO11	A37	2r on 25pi ol green	45.00	22.50
NO12	A38	5r on 50pi car	85.00	65.00
NO13	A39	10r on 100pi dp blue	125.00	*160.00*
		Nos. NO1-NO13 (13)	616.00	319.25

Same Overprint on Types of Regular Issue of 1918-20

1921-22				Wmk. 4
NO14	A28	½a on 10pa grn	1.10	1.10
NO15	A29	1a on 20pa red	11.50	1.10
NO16	A26	1½a on 5pa dp brn	3.00	1.25
NO17	A32	4a on 1¾pi gray & red brn	2.25	*3.25*
NO18	A33	6a on 2pi grn & black	42.50	*175.00*
NO19	A34	8a on 2½pi org & yel grn	3.50	2.25
NO20	A35	12a on 5pi dl vio	42.50	*95.00*
NO21	A37	2r on 25pi ol grn	125.00	*165.00*
		Nos. NO14-NO21 (8)	231.35	*443.95*
		Set of 8, ovptd "SPECIMEN"	325.00	

Same Overprint on No. N53

1922				Unwmk.
NO22	A36	1r on 10pi red brn	50.00	7.50

MEXICO

'mek-si-ˌkō

LOCATION — Extreme southern part of the North American continent, south of the United States
GOVT. — Republic
AREA — 756,198 sq. mi.
POP. — 76,791,819 (est. 1984)
CAPITAL — Mexico, D.F

8 Reales = 1 Peso
100 Centavos = 1 Peso

GREAT BRITAIN POST OFFICES IN MEXICO

British postal agencies were opened in Veracruz in 1825 and in Tampico in 1842. British stamps were used at Tampico from 1867 but were not provided for the agency at Veracruz. The British Veracruz office was closed in 1874 and the Tampico office in 1876.

Values are for clear cancellations on sound, fault-free stamps, with average to fine centering. In many cases, very fine copies are rare or non-existent.

TAMPICO

Pre-Stamp Postmark

1841

Crowned Circle Handstamp Type II

A1	Inscribed "PAID AT TAMPICO" in red, on cover	*2,250.*

Earliest known use 11/13/41.

Stamps of Great Britain Cancelled with barred oval "C63" obliterator

1859-85		
A4	1p rose red, plates 81, 89, 103, 117, 139, 147 (#33), *value from*	150.00
A5	2p blue, plate 9 (#29)	200.00
A6	2p blue, plate 14 (#30), *value from*	200.00
A7	4p vermilion, plates 7-14 (#43), *value from*	150.00
A8	1sh green, plates 4, 5, 7, 8 (#54), *value from*	200.00
A9	2sh blue (#55)	600.00

VERACRUZ

Pre-Stamp Postal Markings

1841-45

Crowned Circle Handstamp Type II

A10	Inscribed "PAID AT VERACRUZ" in red, on cover	*2,000.*
A11	Inscribed "PAID AT VERACRUZ" in black, on cover	*1,100.*

Earliest known use: A10, 11/13/41; A11, 1845.

Watermarks

Wmk. 150 — PAPEL SELLADO in Sheet

Wmk. 151 — R. P. S. in the Sheet (R.P.S. stands for "Renta Papel Sellado")

Wmk. 152 — "CORREOS E U M" on Every Horizontal Line of Ten Stamps

Wmk. 153 — "R M" Interlaced

Wmk. 154 — Eagle and R M

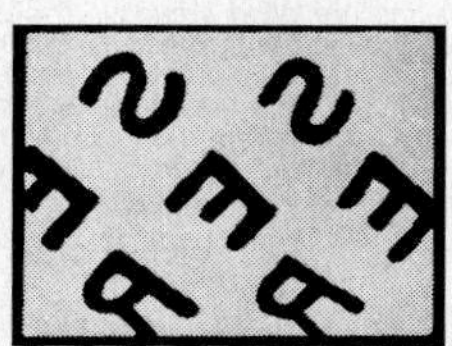

Wmk. 155 — SERVICIO POSTAL DE LOS ESTADOS UNIDOS MEXICANOS

Wmk. 156 — CORREOS MEXICO

Wmk. 248 — SECRETARIA DE HACIENDA MEXICO

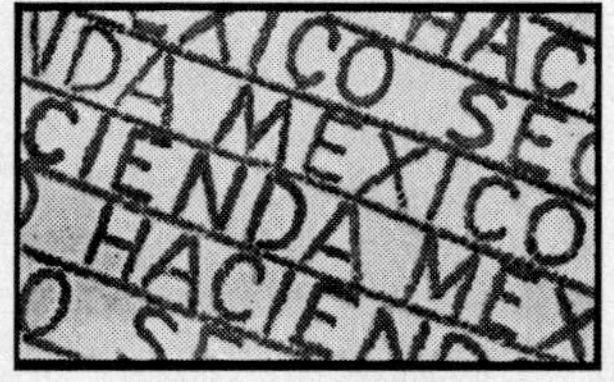

Wmk. 260 — Lines and SECRETARIA DE HACIENDA MEXICO

Miguel Hidalgo y Costilla — A1

Handstamped with District Name

1856		Unwmk.	Engr.	*Imperf.*
1	A1	½r blue	50.00	45.00
		2-4 stamps on cover		150.00
b.		Without overprint	45.00	50.00
c.		Double impression		150.00
2	A1	1r yellow	30.00	5.50
		On cover		15.00
b.		Half used as ½r on cover		*10,000.*
c.		Without overprint	25.00	30.00
d.		1r green (error)		
3	A1	2r yellow grn	27.50	5.50
		On cover		15.00
a.		2r deep blue green	275.00	45.00
b.		2r emerald	250.00	55.00
		On cover		75.00
c.		Half used as 1r on cover		600.00
d.		Without overprint	40.00	22.50
e.		As "a," without overprint	250.00	45.00
f.		As "b," without overprint		75.00
g.		Printed on both sides (yel green)	300.00	

4 A1 4r red 175.00 110.00
On cover 175.00
a. Half used as 2r on cover 250.00
b. Quarter used as 1r on cover 700.00
c. Without overprint 140.00 *160.00*
d. Three quarters used as 3r on cover *12,000.*
5 A1 8r red lilac 350.00 200.00
On cover 900.00
a. 8r violet 300.00 200.00
b. Without overprint 225.00 225.00
c. Eighth used as 1r on cover *17,500.*
d. Quarter used as 2r on cover 225.00
e. Half used as 4r on cover 900.00
Nos. 1-5 (5) 632.50 366.00

The 1r and 2r were printed in sheets of 60 with wide spacing between stamps, and in sheets of 190 or 200 with narrow spacing.

No. 3a can be distinguished from the other 2r stamps by the horizontal grain of the paper. The plate for No. 3b has framelines.

All values, except the 1r, have been reprinted, some of them several times. The reprints usually show signs of wear and the impressions are often smudgy. The paper is usually thicker than that of the originals. Reprints are usually on very white paper. Reprints are found with and without overprints and with cancellations made both from the original handstamps and from forged ones.

Counterfeits exist.

See Nos. 6-12. For overprints see Nos. 35-45.

1861

6 A1 ½r black, *buff* 50.00 45.00
On cover, 2 or 4 stamps 200.00
a. Without overprint 34.00 62.50
7 A1 1r black, *green* 20.00 5.50
On cover 15.00
a. Impression of 2r on back 750.00
b. Without overprint 5.00 22.50
d. As "b," blk, *pink* (error) 8,000 *9,000.*
f. Double impression 150.00
8 A1 2r black, *pink* 15.00 6.50
On cover 15.00
a. Impression of 1r on back 2,000.
b. Half used as 1r on cover 750.00
c. Without overprint 3.50 22.50
d. Printed on both sides 2,250.
e. Double impression 100.00
f. As "e," without overprint —
9 A1 4r black, *yellow* 200.00 100.00
On cover 150.00
a. Half used as 2r on cover 190.00
b. Without overprint 50.00 100.00
c. Quarter used as 1r on cover 700.00
d. Three-quarters used as 3r on cover *35,000.*
10 A1 4r dull rose, *yel* 200.00 80.00
On cover 175.00
a. Half used as 2r on cover *950.00*
b. Without overprint 110.00 140.00
c. Printed on both sides *9,000.*
d. Quarter used as 1r on cover *10,000.*
11 A1 8r black, *red brn* 375.00 250.00
On cover 1,100.
a. ⅛ used as 1R on cover front *11,000.*
b. Quarter used as 2r on cover 250.00
c. Half used as 4r on cover 750.00
d. Without overprint 110.00 225.00
e. Three quarters used as 6r on cover *45,000.*
12 A1 8r grn, *red brn* 500.00 240.00
On cover 1,000.
a. Half used as 4r on cover 30,000.
b. Without overprint 150.00 200.00
c. Quarter used as 2r on cover 40,000.
d. Printed on both sides *12,500.* *12,500.*
Nos. 6-12 (7) 1,360. 727.00

Nos. 6, 9, 10, 11 and 12 have been reprinted. Most reprints of the ½r, 4r and 8r are on vertically grained paper. Originals are on horizontally grained paper. The original ½r stamps are much worn but the reprints are unworn. The paper of the 4r is too deep and rich in color and No. 10 is printed in too bright red.

Reprints of the 8r can only be told by experts. All these reprints are found in fancy colors and with overprints and cancellations as in the 1856 issue.

Counterfeits exist.

Hidalgo — A3

With District Name

1864 ***Perf. 12***

14 A3 1r red *750.* *3,000.*
a. Without District Name .75
15 A3 2r blue *1,100.* *1,750.*
a. Without District Name .75
16 A3 4r brown *1,250.* *2,400.*
a. Without District Name 1.25
b. Vert. pair, imperf. between
17 A3 1p black *3,250.* —
a. Without District Name 2.00

Nos. 14 to 17 were issued with district overprints of Saltillo or Monterrey on the toned paper of 1864. Overprints on the 1867 white paper are fraudulent. Counterfeit cancellations are plentiful. The 1r red with "½" surcharge is bogus.

Coat of Arms — A4

Overprint of District Name, etc.

Five types of overprints:

I — District name only.

II — District name, consignment number and "1864" in large figures.

III — District name, number and "1864" in small figures.

IV — District name, number and "1865."

V — District name, number and "1866."

1864-66 ***Imperf.***

18 A4 3c brn (IV, V) 1,300. *3,250.*
a. Without overprint 700.00
b. Laid paper *4,500.* *6,000.*
19 A4 ½r brown (I) 400.00 250.00
On cover 800.00
a. Type II 2,200. 2,250.
b. Without overprint 200.00 *650.00*
20 A4 ½r lilac (IV) 60.00 55.00
On cover 700.00
a. Type III 140.00 75.00
b. Type II 200.00 200.00
c. Type V *3,000.*
d. ½r gray (V) 70.00 80.00
e. Without overprint 5.75
f. ½r gray lilac 250.00 100.00
21 A4 1r blue (IV, V) 15.00 9.00
On cover 75.00
a. Type III 80.00 40.00
b. Without overprint 2.50
c. Half used as ½r on cover *10,000.*
22 A4 1r ultra (I, II) 120.00 30.00
On cover 90.00
a. Type III 90.00 40.00
b. Without overprint 160.00 150.00
c. Half used as ½r on cover *7,250.*
23 A4 2r org (III, IV, V) 10.00 6.00
On cover 12.00
a. Type II 20.00 10.00
On cover 16.00
b. Type I 50.00 10.00
On cover 25.00
c. 2r dp org, without ovpt., early plate 175.00 65.00
d. Without ovpt., late plate 2.00
e. Half used as 1r on cover *6,000.*
24 A4 4r grn (III, IV, V) 100.00 50.00
On cover 150.00
a. Types I, II 160.00 77.50
b. 4r dk grn, without ovpt. 4.75 *1,700.*
d. Half used as 2r on cover *700.00*
25 A4 8r red (IV, V) 150.00 90.00
On cover 750.00
a. Types II, III 175.00 125.00
b. Type I 400.00 175.00
c. 8r dk red, without ovpt. 7.00 *575.00*
f. Quarter used as 2r on cover *15,000.*
g. Three-quarters used as 6r on cover

The 2r printings from the early plates are 25½mm high; those from the late plate, 24½mm.

Varieties listed as "Without overprint" in unused condition are remainders.

Besides the overprints of district name, number and date, Nos. 18-34 often received, in the district offices, additional overprints of numbers and sometimes year dates. Stamps with these "sub-consignment numbers" sell for more than stamps without them.

Genuine examples of No. 20c should bear Mexico district name overprint, together with consignment numbers 1-1866 or 17-1866. Gray lilac stamps of other consignments are examples of No. 20f.

Value unused for No. 18 is for an example without gum. Examples with original gum sell for more. Examples of No. 18a on laid paper are forgeries.

No. 25g does not exist on full cover.

Faked quarterlings and bisects of 1856-64 are plentiful.

The 3c has been reprinted from a die on which the words "TRES CENTAVOS," the outlines of the serpent and some of the background lines have been retouched.

Emperor Maximilian — A5

Overprinted with District Name, Number and Date 1866 or 866; also with Number and Date only, or with Name only

1866 **Litho.**

26 A5 7c lilac gray 65.00 125.00
a. 7c deep gray 85.00 140.00
27 A5 13c blue 35.00 35.00
a. Half used as 7c on cover —
b. 13c cobalt blue 25.00 25.00
c. Without overprint 2,500.
28 A5 25c buff 12.50 9.00
a. Half used as 13c on cover —
b. Without overprint 2,500.
29 A5 25c orange 12.00 12.00
a. 25c red orange 20.00 27.50
b. 25c red brown 85.00 47.50
c. 25c brown *110.00* 85.00
30 A5 50c green 25.00 30.00
Nos. 26-30 (5) 149.50 211.00

Litho. printings have round period after value numerals.

Overprinted with District Name, Number and Date 866 or 867; also with Number and Date only

Engr.

31 A5 7c lilac 450.00 *5,500.*
a. Without overprint 3.50
32 A5 13c blue 12.00 12.00
a. Without overprint 1.25
33 A5 25c orange brown 12.00 11.00
a. Without overprint 1.25
34 A5 50c green 700.00 70.00
a. Without overprint 2.50

See "sub-consignment" note after No. 25.

Engraved printings have square period after value numerals.

Varieties listed as "Without overprint" in unused condition are remainders.

1867

35 A1 ½r blk, *buff* 2,500. *5,000.*
36 A1 1r blk, *green* 60.00 10.00
37 A1 2r blk, *pink* 22.50 5.00
a. Printed on both sides 140.00
38 A1 4r red, *yel* 625.00 50.00
a. Printed on both sides 175.00
39 A1 4r red *6,000.* *3,250.*
40 A1 8r blk, *red brn* 3,500. 275.00
41 A1 8r grn, *red brn* *4,000.*

Dangerous counterfeits exist of the "Mexico" overprint.

Examples of No. 38 with yellow removed are offered as No. 39.

Same Overprint
Thin Gray Blue Paper
Wmk. 151

42 A1 ½r gray 275.00 190.00
a. Without overprint 175.00 175.00
43 A1 1r blue 400.00 65.00
b. Without overprint 300.00 125.00
44 A1 2r green 200.00 30.00
a. Printed on both sides 6,000. 3,500.
b. Without overprint 300.00 50.00
45 A1 4r rose 3,000. 75.00
a. Without overprint *5,000.* 225.00

Most examples of Nos. 42-45 do not show the watermark. Values are for such stamps. Examples showing the watermark sell for more.

Reprints of the ½r and 4r exist on watermarked paper. Reprints of ½r and 8r also exist in gray on thick grayish wove paper, unwatermarked.

Hidalgo — A6

Thin Figures of Value, without Period after Numerals

100 CENT.

Overprinted with District Name, Number and Abbreviated Date

1868 **Unwmk.** **Litho.** ***Imperf.***

46 A6 6c blk, *buff* 40.00 20.00
47 A6 12c blk, *green* 45.00 20.00
a. Period after "12" 65.00 55.00
48 A6 25c bl, *pink* 75.00 20.00
a. Without overprint 125.00
49 A6 50c blk, *yellow* 600.00 60.00
50 A6 100c blk, *brown* 775.00 140.00
a. Half used as 50c on cover 3,000.
51 A6 100c brn, *brn* 1,750. 500.00

Perf.

52 A6 6c blk, *buff* 35.00 35.00
a. Without overprint 150.00
b. Period after "6" 100.00 75.00
53 A6 12c blk, *green* 35.00 12.00
a. Period after "12" 85.00 30.00
b. Very thick paper 50.00 25.00
c. Without overprint 110.00
54 A6 25c blue, *pink* 55.00 10.00
b. Without overprint 150.00
55 A6 50c blk, *yellow* 325.00 45.00
a. Half used as 50c on cover 3,000.
56 A6 100c blk, *brown* 375.00 110.00
c. Without overprint 350.00
57 A6 100c brn, *brn* 1,000. 375.00
a. Printed on both sides 1,250. 1,000.

Four kinds of perforation are found in the 1868 issue: serrate, square, pin and regular. The narrow spacing between stamps was inadequate for some of these perforation types.

Thick Figures of Value, with Period after Numerals

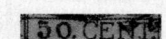

Overprinted with District Name, Number and Abbreviated Date

58 A6 6c blk, *buff* 9.50 4.50
59 A6 12c blk, *green* 4.25 1.25
a. Very thick paper 10.00
c. 12c black, *buff* (error) 575.00 575.00
d. Printed on both sides *3,000.*
e. No period after "12" —
61 A6 25c blue, *pink* 8.00 1.25
a. No period after "25" 90.00
c. Very thick paper 25.00 6.00
d. "85" for "25" 75.00 50.00
e. "35" for "25" 75.00
f. Printed on both sides —
62 A6 50c blk, *yellow* 125.00 15.00
a. No period after "50" 225.00 35.00
b. 50c blue, *lt pink* (error) *3,000.* *2,000.*
c. Half used as 25c on cover 1,000.
d. Very thick paper 50.00
e. "30" for "50" 750.00 750.00
64 A6 100c blk, *brown* 150.00 90.00
a. No period after "100" 175.00 100.00
b. Very thick paper 75.00
c. Quarter used as 25c on cover *2,000.*
d. Bisect used as 50c on cover 4,000.
Nos. 58-64 (5) 296.75 112.00

Perf.

65 A6 6c blk, *buff* 40.00 20.00
a. Very thick paper 60.00 35.00
66 A6 12c blk, *green* 5.50 5.50
a. Very thick paper 20.00 15.00
b. 12c black, *buff* (error) 575.00 575.00
c. No period after "12" —
68 A6 25c blue, *pink* 20.00 2.50
a. No period after "25" 80.00 80.00
c. Thick paper 30.00 15.00
d. "85" for "25" 80.00 40.00
69 A6 50c blk, *yellow* 200.00 25.00
a. No period after "50" 200.00 30.00
b. 50c blue, *lt pink* (error) *2,500.* *1,500.*
c. Thick paper 60.00
70 A6 100c blk, *brown* 200.00 60.00
a. No period after "100" 200.00 65.00
b. Very thick paper 80.00
Nos. 65-70 (5) 465.50 113.00

Postal forgeries of Nos. 58-70 were printed from original plates with district name overprints forged. These include the pelure paper varieties and some thick paper varieties. The "Anotado" handstamp was applied to some of the confiscated forgeries and they were issued, including Nos. 73a and 78a.

Stamps of 1868 Handstamped

Overprinted with District Name, Number and Abbreviated Date Thick Figures with Period

1872 *Imperf.*

71 A6 6c blk, *buff* 650.00 675.00
72 A6 12c blk, *green* 85.00 75.00
73 A6 25c bl, *pink* 40.00 45.00
a. Pelure paper 55.00 65.00
b. "85" for "25" 125.00
74 A6 50c blk, *yellow* 850.00 475.00
a. No period after "50" 900.00 475.00
75 A6 100c blk, *brown* 1,250. 1,000.
a. No period after "100" 1,100.

Perf.

76 A6 6c blk, *buff* 750.00
77 A6 12c blk, *green* 90.00 80.00
78 A6 25c blue, *pink* 35.00 42.50
a. Pelure paper 65.00 90.00
79 A6 50c blk, *yellow* 850.00 600.00
a. No period after "50" 550.00
80 A6 100c blk, *brown* 1,200.

Counterfeit "Anotado" overprints abound. Genuine cancellations other than Mexico City or of the Diligencias de Puebla are unknown. It is recommended that these be purchased accompanied by certificates of authenticity from competent experts.

The stamps of the 1872 issue are found perforated with square holes, pin-perf. 13, 14 or 15, and with serrate perforation.

Counterfeits of the 1868 6c, 12c buff, 50c and 100c (both colors) from new plates have clear, sharp impressions and more facial shading lines than the originals. These counterfeits are found perf. and imperf., with thick and thin numerals, and with the "Anotado" overprint.

Hidalgo — A8

Moiré on White Back Overprinted with District Name, Number and Abbreviated Date White Wove Paper

1872 **Litho.** **Wmk. 150** *Imperf.*

81 A8 6c green 325.00 275.00
82 A8 12c blue 250.00 125.00
a. Laid paper 2,000. 350.00
83 A8 25c red 400.00 125.00
a. Laid paper 2,000. 350.00
84 A8 50c yellow 2,000. 850.00
a. 50c blue (error) 3,000.
b. Laid paper 4,000.
c. As "a," without ovpt. 130.00
86 A8 100c gray lilac 1,000. 650.00
Nos. 81-86 (5) 3,975. 2,025.

Wmk. "LA + F"

81a A8 6c green 2,000. 1,000.
82b A8 12c blue 450.00 325.00
83b A8 25c red 575.00 575.00
c. Without overprint 500.00
84d A8 50c yellow 3,500. 2,000.
86a A8 100c gray lilac 4,000. 1,500.

1872 **Wmk. 150** *Pin-perf.*

87 A8 6c green 2,500. 2,000.
88 A8 12c blue 475.00 175.00
89 A8 25c red 550.00 275.00
b. Laid paper 1,000.
90 A8 50c yellow 1,500. 950.00
a. 50c blue (error) *1,000.* *1,250.*
b. As "a," without overprint 200.00
92 A8 100c gray lilac 1,200. 1,200.
Nos. 87-92 (5) 6,225. 4,600.

Wmk. "LA + F"

87a A8 6c green 2,500. 2,000.
88a A8 12c blue 450.00 *400.00*
89a A8 25c red 950.00 350.00
90c A8 50c yellow 4,000. 2,500.
92a A8 100c gray lilac 3,600. 2,750.

The watermark "LA+F" stands for La Croix Frères, the paper manufacturers, and is in double-lined block capitals 13mm high. A single stamp will show only part of this watermark.

Values for Nos. 87-92a are for examples with visible perfs on all sides.

1872 **Unwmk.** *Imperf.*

93 A8 6c green 12.50 12.50
a. Without moiré on back, without overprint 60.00 65.00
b. Vertically laid paper 3,000. 1,300.
c. Bottom label retouched 100.00 90.00
d. Very thick paper 37.50 37.50
94 A8 12c blue 2.00 1.75
a. Without moiré on back, without overprint 30.00 35.00
b. Vertically laid paper 350.00 210.00
c. Thin gray bl paper of 1867 (Wmk 151) 2,000.
95 A8 25c red 8.50 2.00
a. Without moiré on back, without overprint 30.00 35.00
b. Vertically laid paper 450.00 500.00
c. Thin gray bl paper of 1867 (Wmk 151) 1,500.
96 A8 50c yellow 140.00 35.00
a. 50c orange 140.00 35.00
b. Without moiré on back, without overprint 50.00 70.00
c. Vertically laid paper 2,000.
d. 50c blue (error) 650.00
e. As "d," without overprint 45.00
f. As "e," without moiré on back 65.00
g. Half used as 25c on cover *5,000.*
98 A8 100c gray lilac 90.00 50.00
a. 100c lilac 100.00 42.50
b. Without moiré on back, without overprint 50.00 110.00
c. Vertically laid paper 1,250.
Nos. 93-98 (5) 253.00 101.25

Counterfeits of these stamps are 24½mm high instead of 24mm. The printing is sharper and more uniform than the genuine. Forged district names and consignment numbers exist.

Pin-perf. and Serrate Perf.

99 A8 6c green 90.00 75.00
100 A8 12c blue 3.50 3.00
a. Vertically laid paper 350.00
b. Horiz. pair, imperf. vert. 100.00 100.00
c. Vert. pair, imperf. between 150.00
101 A8 25c red 3.25 1.50
a. Vertically laid paper 500.00
b. Horiz. pair, imperf. vert. 100.00 100.00
102 A8 50c yellow 175.00 50.00
a. 50c orange 160.00 50.00
b. 50c blue (error) 475.00 500.00
c. As "b," without overprint 45.00
104 A8 100c lilac 150.00 80.00
a. 100c gray lilac 125.00 80.00
Nos. 99-104 (5) 421.75 209.50

Values for Nos. 99-104a are for examples with visible perfs on all sides.

Hidalgo
A9 A10

A11 A12

A13 A14

Overprinted with District Name and Number and Date; also with Number and Date only Thick Wove Paper, Some Showing Vertical Ribbing

1874-80 **Unwmk.** **Engr.** *Perf. 12*

105 A9 4c org ('80) 12.50 12.00
a. Vert. pair, imperf. btwn. 60.00
b. Without overprint 6.50 12.50
c. Half used as 2c on cover 1,000.
106 A10 5c brown 4.50 3.00
a. Horizontally laid paper 100.00 55.00
b. Imperf., pair 60.00
c. Horiz. pair, imperf. btwn. 50.00 300.00
d. Vert. pair, imperf. btwn. 110.00 110.00
e. Without overprint 37.50 37.50
f. As "a," wmkd. "LACROIX" 1,750. 1,000.
107 A11 10c black 2.00 1.25
a. Horizontally laid paper 2.50 2.50
b. Horiz. pair, imperf. btwn. 75.00 75.00
c. Without overprint 35.00 27.50
d. Half used as 5c on cover 2,000.
e. Imperf., pair
f. As "a," wmkd. "LACROIX" 350.00 250.00
108 A11 10c org ('78) 2.00 1.25
a. 10c yellow bister 7.50 4.25
b. Imperf., pair
c. Without overprint 55.00 55.00
d. Half used as 5c on cover 100.00
109 A12 25c blue .85 .70
b. Horizontally laid paper 2.25 1.75
c. Imperf., pair 50.00 25.00
d. Without overprint 35.00 20.00
e. Horiz. pair, imperf. btwn. 125.00
f. As "b," horiz. pair, imperf. vert. 200.00
g. As "b," wmkd. "LACROIX" 300.00 250.00
h. Printed on both sides 1,500.
i. Half used as 10c on cover 2,000.
110 A13 50c green 13.00 13.00
a. Without overprint 50.00
b. Half used as 25c on cover 2,500.
111 A14 100c carmine 18.00 15.00
a. Imperf., pair 200.00 200.00
b. Without overprint 50.00
c. Quarter used as 25c on cover 3,000.
Nos. 105-111 (7) 52.85 46.20

The "LACROIX" watermark is spelled out "LACROIX FRERES" in 2 lines of block capitals without serifs once to a sheet of horiz. laid paper. 6-12 stamps may have a portion of the wmk.

1875-77 **Wmk. 150**

112 A10 5c brown 110.00 70.00
113 A11 10c black 110.00 70.00
114 A12 25c blue 110.00 70.00
115 A13 50c green 650.00 450.00
116 A14 100c carmine 600.00 400.00
Nos. 112-116 (5) 1,580. 1,060.

1881 **Unwmk.** **Thin Wove Paper**

117 A9 4c orange 70.00 70.00
a. Without overprint 20.00 20.00
118 A10 5c brown 10.00 6.50
a. Without overprint .50 20.00
b. As "a," vert. pair, imperf. horiz. 1,000.
119 A11 10c orange 6.00 3.50
a. Imperf., pair
b. Vert. pair, imperf. horiz.
c. Without overprint .75 4.50
d. Vert. pair, imperf. btwn.
e. Half used as 5c on cover 1,500.
120 A12 25c blue 4.00 2.25
a. Imperf., pair 100.00
b. Without overprint .50 8.00
c. Double impression 65.00
d. Printed on both sides *1,500.*
121 A13 50c green 45.00 40.00
a. Without overprint 4.00 30.00
122 A14 100c carmine 50.00 50.00
a. Without overprint 6.00 300.00

The stamps of 1874-81 are found with number and date wide apart, close together or omitted, and in various colors.

The thin paper is fragile and easily damaged. Values for Nos. 117-122 are for undamaged, fine examples.

Benito Juárez — A15

Overprinted with District Name and Number and Date; also with Number and Date only Thick Wove Paper, Some Showing Vertical Ribbing

1879 *Perf. 12*

123 A15 1c brown 4.00 4.00
a. Without overprint 75.00 140.00
b. 1c gray 20.00 15.00
124 A15 2c dk violet 4.00 4.50
a. Without overprint 75.00 150.00
b. Printed on both sides
c. 2c dark gray 20.00 14.00
125 A15 5c orange 2.25 1.50
a. Without overprint 75.00 90.00
b. Double impression *500.00*
126 A15 10c blue 3.00 2.50
a. Without overprint 75.00 150.00
b. 10c ultra 160.00 160.00
127 A15 25c rose 8.00 30.00
a. Without overprint 1.75 150.00
128 A15 50c green 15.00 50.00
a. Without overprint 1.25 150.00
b. Printed on both sides 165.00
129 A15 85c violet 20.00 250.00
a. Without overprint 2.50
130 A15 100c black 25.00 75.00
a. Without overprint 3.00 150.00
Nos. 123-130 (8) 81.25 417.50

Used values for Nos. 127-130 are for stamps with postal cancellations. Pen cancelled examples are worth the same as unused stamps.

Forged cancellations on Nos. 127-130 are plentiful.

1882 **Thin Wove Paper**

131 A15 1c brown 40.00 37.50
a. Without overprint 125.00
132 A15 2c dk violet 27.50 24.00
a. 2c slate 47.50 50.00
b. Without overprint 110.00
c. Half used as 1c on cover
133 A15 5c orange 9.00 6.00
a. Without overprint 1.25
b. Half used as 2c on cover
c. As "a," vert. pair, imperf. btwn.
134 A15 10c blue 9.00 6.00
a. Without overprint 1.25
b. Half used as 5c on cover
135 A15 10c brown 9.00
a. Imperf., pair 3.00
136 A15 12c brown 7.50 8.00
a. Without overprint 2.50 22.50
b. Imperf., pair 75.00
c. Half used as 6c on cover
137 A15 18c orange brn 9.00 15.00
a. Horiz. pair, imperf. btwn. 100.00
b. Without overprint 2.25 18.00
138 A15 24c violet 9.00 11.00
a. Without overprint 2.25 17.50
139 A15 25c rose 45.00 250.00
a. Without overprint 4.50
140 A15 25c orange brn 5.50
141 A15 50c green 45.00 75.00
a. Without overprint 6.25
142 A15 50c yellow 80.00 350.00
a. Without overprint 150.00
143 A15 85c red violet 55.00
144 A15 100c black 75.00 *250.00*
a. Without overprint 5.00
b. Vert. pair, imperf. btwn. 165.00 165.00
145 A15 100c orange 95.00 400.00
a. Without overprint 175.00
Nos. 131-145 (15) 520.50 1,433.

No. 135, 140 and 143 exist only without overprint. They were never placed in use.

Used values for Nos. 139, 141, 142, 144 and 145 are for postally used stamps. Forged cancellations are plentiful. Pen cancelled examples are worth the same as unused stamps.

See note on thin paper after No. 122.

A16

Overprinted with District Name, Number and Abbreviated Date

1882-83

146 A16 2c green 11.00 8.00
a. Without overprint 27.50 20.00
147 A16 3c car lake 11.00 8.00
a. Without overprint 5.25 8.50
148 A16 6c blue ('83) 30.00 40.00
a. Without overprint 30.00 50.00
149 A16 6c ultra 6.00 8.50
a. Without overprint 3.50 6.00
b. As "a," imperf pair 50.00
Nos. 146-149 (4) 58.00 64.50

See note on thin paper after No. 122.

Hidalgo — A17

1884 **Wove or Laid Paper** *Perf. 12*

150 A17 1c green 4.00 .75
a. Imperf., pair 125.00
b. 1c blue (error) 600.00 475.00
c. 1c black green 75.00 40.00
151 A17 2c green 6.75 2.00
a. Imperf., pair 200.00 225.00
b. Half used as 1c on cover
c. 2c black green 75.00 40.00
152 A17 3c green 12.50 2.00
a. Imperf., pair 200.00 250.00
b. Horiz. pair, imperf. vert. 225.00 250.00
c. 3c black green 75.00 40.00
153 A17 4c green 16.00 2.00
a. Imperf., pair 200.00 250.00
b. Half used as 2c on cover 400.00
c. Horiz. pair, imperf. btwn. 200.00 250.00
154 A17 5c green 17.50 1.50
a. Imperf., pair 200.00 250.00
b. 5c black green 75.00 40.00
c. Horiz. pair, imperf. btwn. 250.00
d. Vert. pair, imperf. btwn. 275.00
155 A17 6c green 15.00 1.50
a. Imperf., pair 200.00 250.00
b. 6c black green 80.00 50.00
156 A17 10c green 16.00 .75
a. Imperf., pair 125.00 150.00
b. 10c black green 50.00 25.00
157 A17 12c green 30.00 3.50
a. Vert. pair, imperf. between 250.00 350.00
b. Half used as 6c on cover 300.00
c. 12c black green 90.00 60.00
158 A17 20c green 90.00 2.50
a. Diagonal half used as 10c on cover 300.00
b. Imperf., pair 350.00 350.00
159 A17 25c green 100.00 5.00
a. Imperf., pair 300.00 300.00
160 A17 50c green .60 *5.00*
a. Imperf., pair 150.00 150.00
b. Horiz. pair, imperf. btwn. 300.00
c. Double impression 200.00 200.00
161 A17 1p blue .60 *11.00*
a. Imperf., pair 250.00 250.00
b. Vert. pair, imperf. between 100.00
c. 1p with 1c printed on back 300.00
d. Horiz. pair, imperf. btwn. 250.00
162 A17 2p blue .60 *22.50*
a. Imperf., pair 175.00 200.00

163 A17 5p blue 350.00 300.00
164 A17 10p blue 500.00 225.00
Nos. 150-162 (13) 359.55 *60.00*

Imperforate varieties should be purchased in pairs or larger. Single imperforates are usually trimmed perforated stamps.

Beware of examples of No. 150 that have been chemically changed to resemble No. 150b.

Bisects were not officially authorized. Nos. 155 and 160 exist as bisects on piece.

Forged cancels on Nos. 161-162 are plentiful.

Some values exist perf. 11.

See Nos. 165-173, 230-231.

1885

165 A17 1c pale green 35.00 7.00
166 A17 2c carmine 25.00 3.50
a. Diagonal half used as 1c on cover 350.00
167 A17 3c orange brn 25.00 6.00
a. Imperf., pair 250.00 250.00
b. Horiz. pair, imperf. btwn. 300.00
168 A17 4c red orange 42.50 19.00
a. Half used as 2c on cover 350.00
169 A17 5c ultra 27.50 3.50
170 A17 6c dk brown 32.50 6.00
a. Half used as 3c on cover 350.00
171 A17 10c orange 27.50 1.50
a. 10c yellow 30.00 1.50
b. Horiz. pair, imperf. btwn. 250.00 250.00
c. Imperf., pair 300.00
172 A17 12c olive brn 57.50 9.00
a. Printed on both sides 300.00
173 A17 25c grnsh blue 225.00 22.50
Nos. 165-173 (9) 497.50 78.00

Numeral of Value — A18

1886 ***Perf. 12***

174 A18 1c yellow green 2.25 .75
a. 1c blue grn 5.50 4.50
b. Horiz. pair, imperf. btwn. 200.00 200.00
c. Perf. 11 45.00 45.00
175 A18 2c carmine 2.60 .90
a. Horiz. pair, imperf. btwn. 80.00 75.00
b. Vert. pair, imperf. between 200.00 200.00
c. Perf. 11 45.00 45.00
d. Half used as 1c on cover 100.00
176 A18 3c lilac 12.00 7.50
177 A18 4c lilac 18.00 5.25
a. Perf. 11 50.00 *55.00*
b. Horiz. pair, imperf. btwn. 450.00
178 A18 5c ultra 2.25 1.00
a. 5c blue 2.25 .75
179 A18 6c lilac 30.00 7.50
180 A18 10c lilac 22.50 1.10
a. Perf. 11 125.00
181 A18 12c lilac 25.00 14.00
182 A18 20c lilac 190.00 110.00
183 A18 25c lilac 75.00 19.00
Nos. 174-183 (10) 379.60 167.00

Nos. 175, 191, 194B, 196, 202 exist with blue or black surcharge "Vale 1 Cvo." These were made by the Colima postmaster.

1887

184 A18 3c scarlet 1.90 .60
a. Imperf., pair 75.00
185 A18 4c scarlet 7.50 2.25
a. Imperf., pair 500.00
b. Horiz. pair, imperf. btwn. 400.00
186 A18 6c scarlet 12.50 2.25
a. Horiz. pair, imperf. btwn. 200.00
187 A18 10c scarlet 2.75 .60
a. Imperf., pair 75.00
b. Horiz. pair, imperf. btwn. 200.00
188 A18 20c scarlet 18.00 1.50
a. Horiz. pair, imperf. btwn. 275.00
b. Vert. pair, imperf. btwn. 350.00
189 A18 25c scarlet 15.00 4.00
Nos. 184-189 (6) 57.65 11.20

Perf. 6

190 A18 1c blue grn 45.00 45.00
191 A18 2c brown car 22.50 42.00
192 A18 5c ultra 15.00 4.50
a. 5c blue 15.00 4.50
193 A18 10c lilac 15.00 4.25
193A A18 10c brown lilac 15.00 3.00
194 A18 10c scarlet 35.00 15.00

Perf. 6x12

194A A18 1c blue grn 62.50 42.50
194B A18 2c brown car 85.00 75.00
194C A18 3c scarlet 300.00 350.00
194D A18 5c ultra 60.00 45.00
194E A18 10c lilac 90.00 75.00
194F A18 10c scarlet 80.00 60.00
194G A18 10c brown lilac 90.00 75.00

Many shades exist.

Paper with colored ruled lines on face or reverse of stamp

1887 ***Perf. 12***

195 A18 1c green 75.00 45.00
196 A18 2c brown car 190.00 47.50
198 A18 5c ultra 110.00 30.00
199 A18 10c scarlet 110.00 25.00

Perf. 6

201 A18 1c green 60.00 20.00
202 A18 2c brown car 60.00 24.00
204 A18 5c ultra 50.00 12.00
205 A18 10c brown lil 42.50 10.00
206 A18 10c scarlet 250.00 40.00
Nos. 201-206 (5) 462.50 106.00

Perf. 6x12

207 A18 1c green 225.00 140.00
208 A18 2c brown car 325.00 140.00
209 A18 5c ultra 225.00 140.00
210 A18 10c brown lil 290.00 135.00
211 A18 10c scarlet 350.00 225.00
Nos. 207-211 (5) 1,415. 780.00

1890-95 Wmk. 152 ***Perf. 11 & 12***

Wove or Laid Paper

212 A18 1c yellow grn .75 .35
a. 1c blue green .75 .35
b. Horiz. pair, imperf. btwn. 125.00 125.00
c. Laid paper 2.50 2.50
d. Horiz. pair, imperf. vert. 125.00 125.00
213 A18 2c carmine 1.50 .75
a. 2c brown car 1.25 1.00
b. Vert. pair, imperf. btwn. 150.00
c. Imperf., pair 200.00
214 A18 3c vermilion 1.00 .60
b. Horiz. pair, imperf. btwn. 200.00
215 A18 4c vermilion 3.25 2.10
a. Horiz. pair, imperf. btwn. 200.00
216 A18 5c ultra .60 .50
a. 5c dull blue 1.00 .50
217 A18 6c vermilion 3.75 2.75
a. Horiz. pair, imperf. btwn. 300.00
218 A18 10c vermilion .50 .35
b. Horiz. or vert. pair, imperf. btwn. 175.00 175.00
c. Vert. pair, imperf. horiz. 175.00
d. Imperf., pair 200.00
219 A18 12c ver ('95) 14.00 18.00
a. Horiz. pair, imperf. btwn. 450.00
220 A18 20c vermilion 3.50 1.50
220A A18 20c dk violet 160.00 *190.00*
221 A18 25c vermilion 5.00 2.50
Nos. 212-220,221 (10) 33.85 29.40

No. 219 has been reprinted in slightly darker shade than the original.

1892

222 A18 3c orange 4.00 2.00
223 A18 4c orange 4.25 3.00
224 A18 6c orange 5.75 2.00
225 A18 10c orange 27.50 2.00
226 A18 20c orange 50.00 6.00
227 A18 25c orange 16.00 4.50
Nos. 222-227 (6) 107.50 19.50

1892

228 A18 5p carmine 1,250. 900.
229 A18 10p carmine 1,900. 1,250.
230 A17 5p blue green 3,500. 1,200.
231 A17 10p blue green *7,000. 2,700.*

1894 ***Perf. 5½, 6***

232 A18 1c yellow grn 3.00 3.00
233 A18 3c vermilion 9.00 9.00
234 A18 4c vermilion 40.00 37.50
235 A18 5c ultra 12.50 5.00
236 A18 10c vermilion 7.50 3.00
236A A18 20c vermilion 110.00 110.00
237 A18 25c vermilion 62.50 62.50
Nos. 232-237 (7) 244.50 230.00

Perf. 5½x11, 11x5½, Compound and Irregular

238 A18 1c yellow grn 7.00 7.00
238A A18 2c brown car 16.00 16.00
238B A18 3c vermilion 47.50 32.50
238C A18 4c vermilion 55.00 55.00
239 A18 5c ultra 17.50 12.50
a. 5c blue 12.50 12.50
239C A18 6c vermilion 75.00 75.00
240 A18 10c vermilion 20.00 7.00
240A A18 20c vermilion 200.00 200.00
241 A18 25c vermilion 62.50 62.50
Nos. 238-241 (9) 500.50 467.50

The stamps of the 1890 to 1895 issues are also to be found unwatermarked, as part of the sheet frequently escaped the watermark.

Letter Carrier — A20

Mounted Courier with Pack Mule — A21

Statue of Cuauhtémoc A22

Mail Coach A23

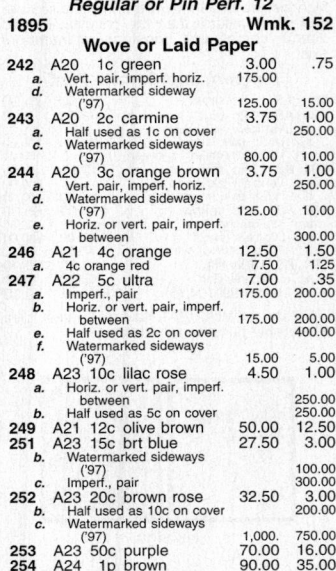

Mail Train — A24

Regular or Pin Perf. 12

1895 Wmk. 152

Wove or Laid Paper

242 A20 1c green 3.00 .75
a. Vert. pair, imperf. horiz. 175.00
d. Watermarked sideway ('97) 125.00 15.00
243 A20 2c carmine 3.75 1.00
a. Half used as 1c on cover 250.00
c. Watermarked sideways ('97) 80.00 10.00
244 A20 3c orange brown 3.75 1.00
a. Vert. pair, imperf. horiz. 250.00
d. Watermarked sideways ('97) 125.00 10.00
e. Horiz. or vert. pair, imperf. between 300.00
246 A21 4c orange 12.50 1.50
a. 4c orange red 7.50 1.25
247 A22 5c ultra 7.00 .35
a. Imperf., pair 175.00 200.00
b. Horiz. or vert. pair, imperf. between 175.00 200.00
e. Half used as 2c on cover 400.00
f. Watermarked sideways ('97) 15.00 5.00
248 A23 10c lilac rose 4.50 1.00
a. Horiz. or vert. pair, imperf. between 250.00
b. Half used as 5c on cover 250.00
249 A21 12c olive brown 50.00 12.50
251 A23 15c brt blue 27.50 3.00
b. Watermarked sideways ('97) 100.00
c. Imperf., pair 300.00
252 A23 20c brown rose 32.50 3.00
b. Half used as 10c on cover 200.00
c. Watermarked sideways ('97) 1,000. 750.00
253 A23 50c purple 70.00 16.00
254 A24 1p brown 90.00 35.00
a. Watermarked sideways ('97) 750.00 *900.00*
255 A24 5p scarlet 300.00 190.00
256 A24 10p deep blue 650.00 350.00
Nos. 242-256 (13) 1,255. 615.10

No. 248 exists in perf. 11.

Nos. 242d, 243c, 244d, 247f, 251b, 252c and 254a was a special printing, made in Jan. 1897. The watermark is sideways, the grain of the paper is horizontal (rather than vertical, as appears on Nos. 242-256), and the design is somewhat shorter than the other stamps in this series. The sideways orientation of the watermark is the most easily identifable feature of this printing.

Important: For unwatermarked examples of Nos. 242-256, see the footnote after No. 291.

Perf. 6

242b A20 1c green 60.00 35.00
243b A20 2c carmine 125.00 60.00
244b A20 3c orange brown 90.00 50.00
247c A22 5c ultra 90.00 50.00
248c A23 10c lilac rose 125.00 55.00
249a A21 12c olive brown 100.00 50.00

Perf. 6x12, 12x6 & Compound or Irregular

242c A20 1c green 30.00 20.00
244c A20 3c orange brown 35.00 20.00
246b A21 4c orange 75.00 50.00
247d A22 5c ultra 75.00 50.00
248d A23 10c lilac rose 35.00 20.00
249b A21 12c olive brown 50.00 25.00
251a A23 15c brt blue 60.00 40.00
252a A23 20c brown rose 100.00 70.00
253b A23 50c purple 150.00 100.00

See Nos. 257-291. For overprints see Nos. O10-O48A.

"Irregular" Perfs.

Some stamps perf. 6x12, 12x6, 5½x11 and 11x5½ have both perf. 6 and 12 or perf. 5½ and 11 on one or more sides of the stamp. These are known as irregular perfs.

1896-97 Wmk. 153 ***Perf. 12***

257 A20 1c green 14.00 1.25
c. Imperf., pair 250.00
258 A20 2c carmine 17.50 1.50
a. Horiz. pair, imperf. vert.
259 A20 3c orange brn 20.00 1.50
c. Horiz. pair, imperf. between 300.00
260 A21 4c orange 32.50 1.75
c. 4c deep orange 30.00 6.00
261 A22 5c ultra 9.00 1.25
a. Imperf., pair 200.00 200.00
b. Vert. pair, imperf. btwn. 200.00
262 A21 12c olive brn 160.00 80.00
263 A23 15c brt blue 200.00 13.00
264 A23 20c brown rose 750.00 275.00
265 A23 50c purple 175.00 110.00
266 A24 1p brown 300.00 250.00
267 A24 5p scarlet 800.00 600.00
268 A24 10p dp blue 900.00 525.00
Nos. 257-268 (12) 3,378. 1,860.

Perf. 6

257a A20 1c green 35.00 25.00
259a A20 3c orange brown 35.00 20.00
260a A21 4c orange 40.00 25.00
261c A22 5c ultra 110.00 70.00
263a A23 15c bright blue 75.00 35.00

Perf. 6x12, 12x6 and Compound or Irregular

257b A20 1c green 25.00 20.00
258b A20 2c carmine 50.00 25.00
259b A20 3c orange brown 40.00 20.00
260b A21 4c orange 45.00 20.00
261d A22 5c ultra 40.00 20.00
262a A21 12c olive brown 125.00 80.00
263b A23 15c bright blue 250.00 125.00
264a A23 20c brown rose
265a A23 50c purple

1897-98 Wmk. 154 ***Perf. 12***

269 A20 1c green 20.00 3.00
270 A20 2c scarlet 35.00 4.50
c. Horiz. pair, imperf. btwn. 250.00
271 A21 4c orange 52.50 3.75
a. Horizontal pair, imperf. vertical —
272 A22 5c ultra 50.00 3.75
a. Imperf., pair 85.00
273 A21 12c olive brown 200.00 45.00
275 A23 15c brt blue 275.00 85.00
276 A23 20c brown rose 175.00 15.00
c. Horiz. pair, imperf. btwn. 300.00
277 A23 50c purple 375.00 75.00
278 A24 1p brown 425.00 200.00
278A A24 5p scarlet — *4,000.*
Nos. 269-278 (9) 1,608. 435.00

Perf. 6

269a A20 1c green 45.00 25.00
270a A20 2c scarlet 45.00 25.00
272b A22 5c ultra 60.00 25.00
273a A21 12c olive brown 110.00 60.00
276a A23 20c brown rose *650.00*

Perf. 6x12, 12x6 and Compound or Irregular

269b A20 1c green 25.00 15.00
270b A20 2c scarlet 30.00 22.50
271b A21 4c orange 65.00 12.50
272c A22 5c ultra 50.00 15.00
273b A21 12c olive brown 125.00 65.00
275a A23 15c bright blue 125.00 65.00
276b A23 20c brown rose 240.00 30.00
277a A23 50c purple 125.00 50.00

1898 Unwmk. ***Perf. 12***

279 A20 1c green 3.00 .50
a. Horiz. pair, imperf. vert 300.00
b. Imperf., pair 250.00
280 A20 2c scarlet 6.25 .75
a. 2c green (error) *475.00*
281 A20 3c orange brn 6.00 .75
a. Imperf., pair 250.00 250.00
b. Pair, imperf. between 80.00 80.00
282 A21 4c orange 30.00 3.00
b. 4c deep orange 37.50 7.00
c. Imperf., pair 300.00
283 A22 5c ultra 2.00 .50
a. Imperf., pair 200.00 200.00
b. Pair, imperf. between 200.00
284 A23 10c lilac rose 550.00 175.00
285 A21 12c olive brn 80.00 27.50
a. Imperf., pair 200.00
286 A23 15c brt blue 175.00 8.00
287 A23 20c brown rose 35.00 3.00
a. Imperf., pair 250.00
288 A23 50c purple 150.00 42.50
289 A24 1p brown 175.00 80.00
290 A24 5p carmine rose 550.00 425.00
291 A24 10p deep blue 800.00 575.00
Nos. 279-291 (13) 2,562. 1,342.

Warning: Sheets of Nos. 242-256 (watermarked "CORREOS E U M") have a column of stamps without watermarks, because the watermark did not fit the sheet size. As a result, be careful not to confuse unwatermarked examples of Nos. 242-256 with Nos. 279-291. This is especially important for No. 284. Nos. 242-256 and the watermarked 1895-97 overprinted Officials, Nos. O10-O39, have a vertical grain or mesh to the paper. Nos. 279-291 and the unwatermarked 1898 overprinted Officials, Nos. O40-O48B, have a horizontal grain or mesh to the paper. Be careful not to confuse unwatermarked examples of Nos. O10-O39 with Nos. O40-O48B.

Perf. 6

No.	Type	Description	Unused	Used
279c	A20	1c green	85.00	35.00
280b	A20	2c scarlet	75.00	30.00
281c	A20	3c orange brown	50.00	35.00
283c	A22	5c ultra	65.00	30.00
287b	A23	20c brown rose	125.00	75.00
291a	A24	10p deep blue		

Perf. 6x12, 12x6 and Compound or Irregular

No.	Type	Description	Unused	Used
279d	A20	1c green	25.00	20.00
280c	A20	2c scarlet	25.00	20.00
281d	A20	3c orange brown	30.00	20.00
282a	A21	4c orange	40.00	25.00
283d	A22	5c ultra	20.00	10.00
284a	A23	10c lilac rose	125.00	85.00
285b	A21	12c olive brown	90.00	60.00
286a	A23	15c bright blue	75.00	50.00
287c	A23	20c brown rose	100.00	50.00
288a	A23	50c purple	575.00	575.00

Forgeries of the 6 and 6x12 perforations of 1895-98 are plentiful.

Coat of Arms
A25 A26

A27

A28

A29 A30

A31

Juanacatlán Falls — A32

View of Mt. Popocatépetl A33

Cathedral, Mexico, D. F. — A34

1899, Nov. 1 Wmk. 155 *Perf. 14, 15*

No.	Type	Description	Unused	Used
294	A25	1c green	1.90	.35
295	A26	2c vermilion	4.50	.35
296	A27	3c orange brn	3.00	.35
297	A28	5c dark blue	4.75	.35
298	A29	10c violet & org	6.00	.35
299	A30	15c lav & claret	8.00	.35
300	A31	20c rose & dk bl	9.00	.40
301	A32	50c red lil & blk	35.00	2.25
a.		50c lilac & black	42.50	2.25
302	A33	1p blue & blk	80.00	3.50
303	A34	5p carmine & blk	275.00	12.00
		Nos. 294-303 (10)	427.15	20.25
		Set, never hinged	1,500.	

See Nos. 304-305, 307-309. For overprints see Nos. 420-422, 439-450, 452-454, 482-483, 515-516, 539, 550, O49-O60, O62-O66, O68-O74, O101.

A35

1903

No.	Type	Description	Unused	Used
304	A25	1c violet	1.50	.35
a.		Booklet pane of 6	55.00	
305	A26	2c green	2.00	.35
a.		Booklet pane of 6	82.50	
306	A35	4c carmine	5.00	.45
307	A28	5c orange	1.25	.35
a.		Booklet pane of 6	82.50	
308	A29	10c blue & org	5.00	.35
309	A32	50c carmine & blk	75.00	6.50
		Nos. 304-309 (6)	89.75	8.35
		Set, never hinged	350.00	

For overprints see Nos. 451, O61, O67.

Independence Issue

Josefa Ortiz — A36

Leona Vicario — A37

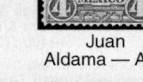

López Rayón — A38

Juan Aldama — A39

Miguel Hidalgo — A40

Ignacio Allende — A41

Epigmenio González A42

Mariano Abasolo A43

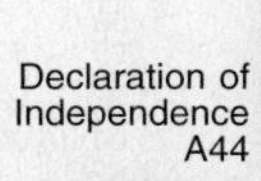

Declaration of Independence A44

Mass on the Mount of Crosses A45

Capture of Granaditas A46

1910 *Perf. 14*

No.	Type	Description	Unused	Used
310	A36	1c dull violet	.35	.35
a.		Booklet pane of 4	40.00	
311	A37	2c green	.35	.35
a.		Booklet pane of 8	40.00	
312	A38	3c orange brn	.60	.35
313	A39	4c carmine	2.50	.45
314	A40	5c orange	.35	.35
a.		Booklet pane of 8	27.50	
315	A41	10c blue & org	1.50	.35
316	A42	15c gray bl & cl	8.00	.50
317	A43	20c red & bl	5.00	.40
318	A44	50c red brn & blk	12.00	1.60
319	A45	1p blue & blk	15.00	2.00
320	A46	5p car & blk	57.50	16.50
		Nos. 310-320 (11)	103.15	23.20
		Set, never hinged	325.00	

Independence of Mexico from Spain, cent.

For overprints and surcharges see Nos. 370-380, 423-433, 455-465, 484-494, 517-538, 540-549, 551-558, 577-590, O75-O85, O102-O112, O191-O192, O195, RA13, Merida 1.

CIVIL WAR ISSUES

During the 1913-16 Civil War, provisional issues with various handstamped overprints were circulated in limited areas.

Sonora

A47

Seal

Typeset in a row of five varieties. Two impressions placed tête bêche (foot to foot) constitute a sheet. The settings show various wrong font and defective letters, "!" for "1" in "1913," etc. The paper occasionally has a manufacturer's watermark.

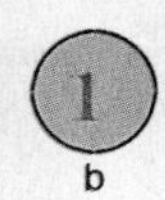

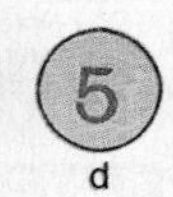

a b c d

Four Types of the Numerals.
a — Wide, heavy-faced numerals.
b — Narrow Roman numerals.
c — Wide Roman numerals.
d — Gothic or sans-serif numerals.

Nos. 321-346 Issued Without Gum Embossed "CONSTITUCIONAL"

1913 Typeset Unwmk. *Perf. 12*

No.	Type	Description	Unused	Used
321	A47 (a)	5c blk & red	*4,250.*	800.00
a.		"CENTAVOB"	*4,750.*	*850.00*

Colorless Roulette

No.	Type	Description	Unused	Used
322	A47(b)	1c blk & red	22.00	25.00
a.		With green seal	*1,500.*	*1,250.*
b.		Peerless Mills watermark	75.00	75.00
323	A47(a)	2c blk & red	18.00	15.00
a.		With green seal	*2,000.*	*2,000.*
b.		Peerless Mills watermark	75.00	75.00
324	A47(c)	2c blk & red	87.50	72.50
a.		With green seal	*5,000.*	*5,000.*
b.		Peerless Mills watermark	150.00	150.00
325	A47(a)	3c blk & red	97.50	77.50
a.		With green seal	*750.00*	*750.00*
b.		Peerless Mills watermark	250.00	250.00
326	A47(a)	5c blk & red	190.00	77.50
a.		"CENTAVOB"	200.00	50.00
b.		Peerless Mills watermark	800.00	800.00
327	A47(d)	5c blk & red	1,200.	350.00
a.		With green seal		*1,000.*
b.		Peerless Mills watermark	4,500.	1,500.
328	A47(b)	10c blk & red	35.00	*37.50*
a.		Peerless Mills watermark	75.00	75.00

Black Roulette

No.	Type	Description	Unused	Used
329	A47(d)	5c blk & red	300.00	140.00
a.		"MARO"	87.50	52.50
b.		Yukon Aurora watermark	2,500.	2,500.

Stamps are known with the embossing double or omitted.

The varieties with green seal are from a few sheets embossed "Constitucional" which were in stock at the time the green seal control was adopted.

Nos. 322-329 are known with papermakers' watermark ("Peerless Mills" or "Yukon Aurora").

No. 339

Without Embossing With Green Seal

Colorless Roulette

No.	Type	Description	Unused	Used
336	A47(b)	1c blk & red	15.00	10.00
a.		Peerless Mills watermark	60.00	40.00
337	A47(a)	3c blk & red	14.50	9.00
a.		Imperf.	*350.00*	
b.		Peerless Mills watermark	60.00	40.00
338	A47(a)	5c blk & red	750.00	250.00
a.		"CENTAVOB"	*800.00*	275.00
b.		Peerless Mills watermark	3,000.	1,000.
339	A47(b)	10c blk & red	8.00	7.50
a.		Peerless Mills watermark	35.00	35.00

Colored Roulette

No.	Type	Description	Unused	Used
340	A47(d)	5c brnsh blk & red	25.00	6.00
a.		5c lilac brown & red	75.00	22.50
b.		Double seal		*1,250.*
c.		Red printing omitted		*1,000.*
d.		Yukon Aurora watermark	3,500.	2,500.

Nos. 336-340 are known with papermaker's watermark ("Peerless Mills" or "Yukon Aurora").

1913-14 *Black Roulette* With Green Seal

No.	Type	Description	Unused	Used
341	A47(a)	1c black & red	4.00	4.00
b.		"erano" ('14)	100.00	60.00
342	A47(d)	2c black & red	4.50	4.00
a.		"erano" ('14)	30.00	35.00
343	A47(a)	3c black & red	4.75	4.00
a.		"CENTAVO"	25.00	25.00
b.		"erano" ('14)	35.00	35.00
344	A47(d)	5c black & red	4.75	4.00
b.		Heavy black penetrating roulette	2.75	1.75
c.		As "b," "MARO"	10.50	5.00
d.		Without green seal	*2,250.*	
		Nos. 341-344 (4)	18.00	16.00

Stamps without seal are unfinished remainders.

On Nos. 341-344 the rouletting cuts the paper slightly or not at all. On Nos. 344b-344c the rouletting is heavy, cutting deeply into the paper.

1914

No.	Type	Description	Unused	Used
345	A47(a)	5c black & red	5.00	5.00
346	A47(b)	10c black & red	4.25	5.00

Coat of Arms — A49

Revenue Stamps Used for Postage

1913 Litho. *Rouletted 14, 14x7*

No.	Type	Description	Unused	Used
347	A49	1c yellow grn	2.00	*2.50*
		Never hinged	7.00	
a.		With coupon	7.00	6.00
		Never hinged	40.00	
348	A49	2c violet	3.50	*4.00*
		Never hinged	14.00	
a.		With coupon	17.50	14.50
		Never hinged	95.00	

349 A49 5c brown .60 *.75*
Never hinged 2.50
a. With coupon 2.00 1.50
Never hinged 15.00
350 A49 10c claret 2.50 *3.50*
Never hinged 12.00
a. With coupon 15.00 12.00
Never hinged 100.00
351 A49 20c gray grn 3.00 *3.50*
Never hinged 12.00
a. With coupon 20.00 18.00
Never hinged 125.00
352 A49 50c ultra 11.00 *16.00*
Never hinged 47.50
a. With coupon 60.00 47.50
Never hinged 325.00
353 A49 1p orange 45.00 *55.00*
Never hinged 180.00
a. With coupon 175.00 120.00
Never hinged 750.00
Nos. 347-353 (7) 67.60 85.25

For a short time these stamps (called "Ejercitos") were used for postage with coupon attached. Later this was required to be removed unless they were to be used for revenue. Stamps overprinted with district names are revenues. Values above 1p were used for revenue. Imperfs exist of all values, but were not issued.

Many examples do not have gum because of a flood.

Use of typeset Sonora revenue stamps for postage was not authorized or allowed.

Coat of Arms
A50 A51

5c (A50): "CINCO CENTAVOS" 14x2mm

1914 ***Rouletted 9½x14***
354 A50 1c deep blue .45 .45
355 A50 2c yellow grn .60 .35
a. 2c green 3.00 1.75
356 A50 4c blue vio 11.00 2.50
a. Horiz. pair, imperf. btwn. 250.00
357 A50 5c gray grn 11.00 3.00
a. Horiz. pair imperf. btwn. 250.00
358 A50 10c red .45 .45
359 A50 20c yellow brn .60 .60
a. 20c deep brown 2.25 2.25
b. Horiz. pair, imperf. btwn. 250.00
360 A50 50c claret 2.50 3.50
a. Horiz. pair, imperf. btwn. 250.00
361 A50 1p brt violet 14.00 16.00
a. Horiz. pair, imperf. btwn. 250.00
Nos. 354-361 (8) 40.60 26.85
Set, never hinged 175.00

Nos. 354-361 (called "Transitorios") exist imperf. but were not regularly issued.

Many examples do not have gum because of a flood.

See Note after No. 465.

See No. 369. For overprints see Nos. 362-368, 559-565.

Overprinted in Black

1914
362 A50 1c deep blue 200.00 175.00
Never hinged 750.00
a. "1912" for "1914" *2,000.*
363 A50 2c yellow green 225.00 200.00
Never hinged 825.00
364 A50 4c blue violet 250.00 300.00
Never hinged 900.00
365 A50 5c gray green 35.00 50.00
Never hinged 115.00
a. Horiz. pair, imperf. btwn. 550.00
366 A50 10c red 150.00 150.00
Never hinged 560.00
a. "1912" for "1914" *2,000.*
367 A50 20c yellow brn *2,500.* *2,500.*
a. "1912" for "1914" *7,000.*
368 A50 50c claret *3,500.* *3,500.*

Values are for stamps with design close to, or just touching, the perfs.

Excellent counterfeits of this overprint exist.

Redrawn
"CINCO CENTAVOS" 16x2½mm

1914 ***Perf. 12***
369 A51 5c gray green 1.00 .35
Never hinged 1.50

Imperfs are printers' waste.

Regular Issue of 1910 Overprinted in Violet, Magenta, Black or Green

1914 **Wmk. 155** ***Perf. 14***
370 A36 1c dull violet 1.50 .60
a. Booklet pane of 4 75.00
371 A37 2c green 3.00 1.25
a. Booklet pane of 8 75.00
372 A38 3c orange brn 3.00 1.25
373 A39 4c carmine 5.00 2.00
374 A40 5c orange 1.00 .35
a. Booklet pane of 8 60.00
375 A41 10c blue & org 6.00 2.00
376 A42 15c gray bl & cl 10.00 3.00
377 A43 20c red & blue 20.00 6.00
378 A44 50c red brn & blk 25.00 8.00
379 A45 1p blue & blk 55.00 11.00
380 A46 5p carmine & blk 190.00 160.00
Nos. 370-380 (11) 319.50 195.45
Set, never hinged 1,000.

Overprinted On Postage Due Stamps of 1908
381 D1 1c blue 27.50 *30.00*
382 D1 2c blue 27.50 *30.00*
383 D1 4c blue 27.50 *30.00*
384 D1 5c blue 27.50 *30.00*
385 D1 10c blue 27.50 *30.00*
Nos. 381-385 (5) 137.50 150.00
Set, never hinged 375.00

This overprint is found double, inverted, sideways and in pairs with and without the overprint.

There are two or more types of this overprint.

The Postage Due Stamps and similar groups of them which follow were issued and used as regular postage stamps.

Values are for stamps where the overprint is clear enough to be expertised.

Counterfeits abound.

A52

1914 **Unwmk.** **Litho.** ***Perf. 12***
386 A52 1c pale blue .35 .50
387 A52 2c light green .35 .45
388 A52 3c orange .50 .50
389 A52 5c deep rose .50 .35
390 A52 10c rose .70 .85
391 A52 15c rose lilac 1.20 1.75
392 A52 50c yellow 2.00 2.50
a. 50c ocher 1.75
393 A52 1p violet 8.50 12.00
Nos. 386-393 (8) 14.10 18.90
Set, never hinged 50.00

Nos. 386-393, are known imperforate.

This set is usually called the Denver Issue because it was printed there.

See Note after No. 465.

For overprints and surcharges see Nos. 566-573, 591-592.

A53

Revenue Stamps Used for Postage

1914, July ***Perf. 12***
393A A53 1c rose 40.00
393B A53 2c lt green 35.00
393C A53 3c lt orange 75.00
393D A53 5c red 15.00
393E A53 10c gray green 70.00
393F A53 25c blue 150.00
Nos. 393A-393F (6) 385.00

Nos. 393A-393F were used in the northeast. Values are for examples with postal cancellations.

Unused examples are to be considered as revenues.

Pres. Madero

Stamps in this design, featuring Pres. Madero, within a frame very similar to that of the Denver Issue (Nos. 386-393), were ordered in 1915 by Francisco Villa, to be used by the Constitutionalist government. Five values (1c green, 2c brown, 3c carmine, 5c blue, and 10c yellow) were printed by Ellis Brothers & Co., El Paso, Texas. By the time of the stamps' arrival in Mexico City, the Constitutionalist regime had fallen, and the new Conventionist government returned them to the printer, who later sold the unissued stamps within the philatelic market. Value, set $10.

Background as A55 — A54

Nos. 394-413 Issued Without Gum

1914 ***Imperf.***

Values and Inscriptions in Black

Inscribed "SONORA"
394 A54 1c blue & red .35 .35
a. Double seal
b. Without seal 20.00
395 A54 2c green & org .35 .35
a. Without seal 100.00
396 A54 5c yellow & grn .35 .35
a. 5c orange & green 1.50 1.25
b. Without seal *300.00*
397 A54 10c lt bl & red 3.50 1.75
a. 10c blue & red 40.00 15.00
398 A54 20c yellow & grn 1.75 2.00
399 A54 20c orange & bl 15.00 17.50
400 A54 50c green & org 1.25 1.25
Nos. 394-400 (7) 22.55 23.55

Shades. Stamps of type A54 are usually termed the "Coach Seal Issue."

Inscribed "DISTRITO SUR DE LA BAJA CAL"
401 A54 1c yellow & blue 2.00 *30.00*
a. Without seal 50.00
402 A54 2c gray & ol grn 2.50 *25.00*
403 A54 5c olive & rose 2.00 *20.00*
a. Without seal 50.00
404 A54 10c pale red & dl vio 2.00 *20.00*
a. Without seal 50.00
Nos. 401-404 (4) 8.50 95.00

Counterfeit cancellations exist.

A55

Inscribed "SONORA"
405 A55 1c blue & red 6.00
a. Without seal 50.00
406 A55 2c green & org .50
407 A55 5c yellow & grn .50 *2.50*
a. Without seal 75.00
408 A55 10c blue & red .50 *2.50*
409 A55 20c yellow & grn 75.00 *15.00*
a. Without seal 95.00
b. Double seal *80.00*
Nos. 405-409 (5) *82.50* *20.00*

With "PLATA" added to the inscription
410 A55 1c blue & red 1.00
a. "PLATA" inverted 60.00
b. Pair, one without "PLATA" 15.00
411 A55 10c blue & red 1.00
412 A55 20c yellow & grn 2.50
a. "PLATA" double 50.00
413 A55 50c gray grn & org 1.75
a. Without seal 1.00
b. As "a," "P" of "PLATA" missing 150.00
Nos. 410-413 (4) 6.25

Stamps of type A55 are termed the "Anvil Seal Issue".

Nos. 410-413 were not placed in use.

Oaxaca

Coat of Arms — A56

5c:
Type I — Thick numerals, 2mm wide.
Type II — Thin numerals, 1½mm wide.

Perf. 8½ to 14
1915 **Typo.** **Unwmk.**
414 A56 1c dull violet 2.00 1.25
415 A56 2c emerald 3.00 2.25
a. Inverted numeral 30.00
e. Numeral omitted 35.00
416 A56 3c red brown 4.00 3.50
b. Inverted numeral 30.00
417 A56 5c org (type I) 77.50 77.50
a. Tête bêche pair 175.00 175.00
418 A56 5c org (type II) .50 .75
a. Types I and II in pair 70.00
419 A56 10c blue & car 4.00 4.00
Nos. 414-419 (6) 91.00 89.25
Set, never hinged 275.00

Many printing errors, imperfs and part perfs exist. Mostly these are printers' waste, private reprints or counterfeits.

Nos. 414-419 printed on backs of post office receipt forms.

Regular Issues of 1899-1910 Overprinted in Black

1914 **Wmk. 155** ***Perf. 14***

On Issues of 1899-1903
420 A28 5c orange
421 A30 15c lav & claret 250.00 250.00
Never hinged 700.00
422 A31 20c rose & dk bl *1,000.* 500.00

Counterfeits exist.

The listing of No. 420 is being re-evaluated. The Catalogue Editors would appreciate any information on the stamp.

On Issue of 1910
423 A36 1c dull violet .35 .35
424 A37 2c green .35 .35
425 A38 3c orange brown .40 .40
426 A39 4c carmine .50 .50
427 A40 5c orange .35 .35
428 A41 10c blue & orange .35 .35
429 A42 15c gray bl & claret .70 .60
430 A43 20c red & blue .75 .70

Overprinted

431 A44 50c red brn & blk 1.75 1.50
432 A45 1p blue & blk 8.00 5.50
433 A46 5p carmine & blk 42.50 32.50
Nos. 423-433 (11) 56.00 43.10
Set, never hinged 170.00

In the first setting of the overprint on 1c to 20c, the variety "GONSTITUCIONALISTA" occurs 4 times in each sheet of 100. In the second setting it occurs on the last stamp in each row of 10.

The overprint exists reading downward on Nos. 423-430; inverted on Nos. 431-433; double on Nos. 423-425, 427.

See Note after No. 465.

For overprints see Nos. 528-538.

Postage Due Stamps of 1908 Overprinted

434 D1 1c blue 4.75 5.00
435 D1 2c blue 6.00 5.00
436 D1 4c blue 25.00 25.00
437 D1 5c blue 25.00 25.00

438 D1 10c blue 5.50 5.00
a. Double overprint
Nos. 434-438 (5) 66.25 65.00
Set, never hinged 200.00

Preceding Issues Overprinted

This is usually called the "Villa" monogram. Counterfeits abound.

1915 **On Issue of 1899**
439 A25 1c green *210.00*
440 A26 2c vermilion *210.00*
441 A27 3c orange brn *175.00*
442 A28 5c dark blue *210.00*
443 A29 10c violet & org *210.00*
444 A30 15c lav & claret *750.00* 750.00
445 A31 20c rose & bl *1,000.* —
446 A32 50c red lil & blk *500.00* —
447 A33 1p blue & blk *500.00*
448 A34 5p car & blk *750.00* —
Nos. 439-448 (10) *4,515.*

On Issue of 1903
449 A25 1c violet *200.00*
450 A26 2c green *200.00*
451 A35 4c carmine *200.00*
452 A28 5c orange 45.00
a. Inverted overprint *75.00*
453 A29 10c blue & org *750.00* —
454 A32 50c car & blk — —
Nos. 449-453 (5) *1,395.*

In Sept. 1915 Postmaster Hinojosa ordered a special printing of Nos. 439-454 (as valued) for sale to collectors. Earlier a small quantity of Nos. 444-445, 448 and 452-454 was regularly issued. They are hard to distinguish and sell for much more. Counterfeits abound.

On Issue of 1910
455 A36 1c dull violet .85 1.00
456 A37 2c green .40 .60
457 A38 3c orange brown .60 .75
458 A39 4c carmine 4.00 4.50
459 A40 5c orange .35 .35
460 A41 10c blue & orange 7.00 7.50
461 A42 15c gray bl & cl 3.00 4.00
462 A43 20c red & blue 5.50 7.00
463 A44 50c red brn & blk 13.00 14.00
464 A45 1p blue & blk 17.00 20.00
465 A46 5p carmine & blk *150.00*
Never hinged 300.00
Nos. 455-464 (10) 51.70 59.70
Nos. 455-464, never hinged 175.00

Nos. 455-465 are known with overprint inverted, double and other variations. Most were ordered by Postmaster General Hinojosa for philtelic purposes. They were sold at a premium. This applies to Nos. 354-361, 386-393, 431-433 with this monogram as well.

Overprinted On Postage Due Stamps of 1908
466 D1 1c blue 15.00 20.00
467 D1 2c blue 15.00 20.00
468 D1 4c blue 15.00 20.00
469 D1 5c blue 15.00 20.00
470 D1 10c blue 15.00 20.00
Nos. 466-470 (5) 75.00 100.00
Set, never hinged 225.00

Nos. 466 to 470 are known with inverted overprint. All other values of the 1899 and 1903 issues exist with this overprint. See note after No. 465.

Issues of 1899-1910 Overprinted

This is called the "Carranza" or small monogram. Counterfeits abound.

On Issues of 1899-1903
482 A28 5c orange 40.00 20.00
Never hinged 125.00
483 A30 15c lav & claret 200.00 80.00
Never hinged 650.00

On Issue of 1910
484 A36 1c dull violet .70 .70
485 A37 2c green .70 .60
486 A38 3c orange brn .75 .75
487 A39 4c carmine 2.00 2.00
488 A40 5c orange .35 .35
489 A41 10c blue & org 1.50 1.50
a. Double ovpt., one invtd. 25.00
490 A42 15c gray bl & cl 1.50 1.50
491 A43 20c red & blue 1.50 1.50
492 A44 50c red brn & blk 10.00 10.00
493 A45 1p blue & blk 15.00 15.00
494 A46 5p car & blk 150.00 *150.00*
Nos. 484-494 (11) 184.00 *183.90*
Set, never hinged 550.00

All values exist with inverted overprint; all but 5p with double overprint.

Overprinted On Postage Due Stamps of 1908
495 D1 1c blue 22.00 *25.00*
496 D1 2c blue 22.00 *25.00*
497 D1 4c blue 22.00 *25.00*
498 D1 5c blue 22.00 *25.00*
499 D1 10c blue 22.00 *25.00*
Nos. 495-499 (5) 110.00 125.00
Set, never hinged 325.00

Nos. 495-499 exist with inverted overprint.

It is stated that, in parts of Mexico occupied by the revolutionary forces, instructions were given to apply a distinguishing overprint to all stamps found in the post offices. This overprint was usually some arrangement or abbreviation of "Gobierno Constitucionalista". Such overprints as were specially authorized or were in general use in large sections of the country are listed. Numerous other handstamped overprints were used in one town or locality. They were essentially military faction control marks necessitated in most instances by the chaotic situation following the split between Villa and Carranza. The fact that some were often struck in a variety of colors and positions suggests the influence of philatelists.

Coat of Arms A57

Statue of Cuauhtémoc A58

Ignacio Zaragoza A59

José María Morelos A60

Francisco Madero — A61

Benito Juárez — A62

1915 **Unwmk.** **Litho.** ***Rouletted 14***
500 A57 1c violet .25 .25
501 A58 2c green .25 .25
502 A59 3c brown .50 .25
503 A60 4c carmine .50 .25
504 A61 5c orange .75 .25
505 A62 10c ultra .35 .30
Nos. 500-505 (6) 2.60 1.55
Set, never hinged 4.00

Nos. 500-505 exists imperf.; some exist imperf. vertically or horizontally; some with rouletting and perforation combined. These probably were not regularly issued in these forms.

See Nos. 506-511. For overprints see Nos. O86-O97.

Map of Mexico — A63

Veracruz Lighthouse A64

Post Office, Mexico, D.F. — A65

TEN CENTAVOS:

Type I — Size 19½x24mm. Crossed lines on coat.

Type II — Size 19x23½mm. Diagonal lines only on coat.

1915-16 ***Perf. 12***
506 A57 1c violet .40 .25
507 A58 2c green .40 .30
508 A59 3c brown .50 .30
509 A60 4c carmine .50 .35
a. "CEATRO" 7.50 7.50
510 A61 5c orange .75 .35
511 A62 10c ultra, type I 1.00 .35
a. 10c ultra, type II .50 .25

Engr.
512 A63 40c slate .75 .35
513 A64 1p brown & blk 1.00 .75
a. Inverted center 200.00 275.00
514 A65 5p cl & ultra ('16) 12.00 4.00
a. Inverted center 450.00
Nos. 506-514 (9) 17.30 7.00
Set, never hinged 60.00

Nos. 507-508, 510-514, exist imperf; Nos. 513-514 imperf with inverted center. These varieties were not regularly issued.

See Nos. 626-628, 647. For overprints see Nos. O92-O100, O121-O123, O132-O133, O142-O144, O153-O154, O162-O164, O174, O188, O193, O207, O222.

Issues of 1899-1910 Overprinted in Blue, Red or Black

On Issues of 1899-1903
1916 **Wmk. 155** ***Perf. 14***
515 A28 5c orange (Bl) 125.00 175.00
Never hinged 400.00
516 A30 15c lav & cl (Bl) 775.00 775.00
Never hinged 2,250.

On Issue of 1910
517 A36 1c dull vio (R) 10.00 *10.00*
518 A37 2c green (R) .50 .35
519 A38 3c orange brn (Bl) .55 .40
a. Double overprint 500.00
520 A39 4c carmine (Bl) 6.00 *8.00*
521 A40 5c orange (Bl) .25 .25
a. Double overprint 75.00
522 A41 10c blue & org (R) 1.25 1.50
523 A42 15c gray bl & cl (Bk) 1.75 3.00
524 A43 20c red & bl (Bk) 1.75 3.00
525 A44 50c red brn & blk (R) 8.50 5.00
526 A45 1p blue & blk (R) 15.00 6.50
527 A46 5p car & blk (R) 175.00 175.00
Nos. 517-527 (11) 220.55 213.00
Nos. 517-527, never hinged 650.00

Nos. 519-524 exist with this overprint (called the "Corbata") reading downward and Nos. 525-527 with it inverted. Of these varieties only Nos. 519-521 were regularly issued.

On Nos. 423-430
528 A36 1c dull vio (R) 2.50 4.00
529 A37 2c green (R) .75 .60
530 A38 3c orange brn (Bl) .60 .60
531 A39 4c carmine (Bl) .60 .60
532 A40 5c orange (Bl) 1.00 .30
533 A41 10c blue & org (R) .75 .60
534 A42 15c gray bl & cl (Bk) .80 .80
535 A43 20c red & bl (Bk) .80 .80

On Nos. 431-433 in Red
536 A44 50c red brn & blk 7.50 6.00
537 A45 1p blue & blk 16.00 16.00
538 A46 5p carmine & blk 150.00 140.00
a. Tablet inverted 300.00
Nos. 528-538 (11) 181.30 170.30
Set, never hinged 550.00

Nos. 529 to 535 are known with the overprint reading downward and Nos. 536 to 538 with it inverted.

On No. 482
539 A28 5c orange (Bl) 400.00 *400.00*

On Nos. 484-494

540 A36 1c dull vio (R) 6.00 *6.00*
541 A37 2c green (R) .75 .75
a. Monogram inverted 100.00
542 A38 3c orange brn (Bl) .75 .75
543 A39 4c carmine (Bl) 8.50 *10.00*
544 A40 5c orange (Bl) 1.25 .35
545 A41 10c blue & org (R) 2.00 *2.50*
546 A42 15c gray bl & cl (Bk) 1.75 .75
a. Tablet double *750.00* *750.00*
b. Monogram double *750.00*
547 A43 20c red & bl (Bk) 1.75 1.50
548 A44 50c red brn & blk (R) 9.00 *10.00*
a. Monogram inverted 75.00
b. Tablet inverted 85.00
549 A45 1p blue & blk (R) 13.00 14.00
a. Tablet double 200.00
b. Monogram inverted 70.00
Nos. 539-549 (11) 444.75 *446.60*
Set, never hinged 1,300.

Nos. 541-547 exist with overprint reading downward. A few 5p were overprinted for the Post Office collection.

On No. 452
550 A28 5c orange (Bl) 125.00 *125.00*
Never hinged 275.00

On Nos. 455-462
551 A36 1c dull vio (R) 11.00 *15.00*
552 A37 2c green (R) 1.50 .90
553 A38 3c org brn (Bl) 3.25 *4.50*
554 A39 4c carmine (Bl) 13.00 *15.00*
555 A40 5c orange (Bl) 4.50 *6.00*
556 A41 10c bl & org (R) 12.00 *14.00*
a. Monogram inverted *250.00*
557 A42 15c gray bl & cl (Bk) 12.00 *14.00*
a. Monogram inverted *250.00*
558 A43 20c red & bl (Bk) 12.00 *14.00*
a. Monogram inverted *250.00*
Nos. 550-558 (9) 194.25 *208.40*
Set, never hinged 650.00

Stamps of 50c, 1p and 5p were overprinted for the Post Office collection but were not regularly issued.

Issues of 1914 Overprinted

On "Transitorio" Issue
Rouletted 9½x14
Unwmk.
559 A50 1c dp blue (R) 24.00 24.00
Never hinged 75.00
560 A50 2c yellow grn (R) 12.00 18.00
Never hinged 27.50
561 A50 4c blue vio (R) 425.00 375.00
Never hinged 1,200.
562 A50 10c red (Bl) 2.00 6.00
Never hinged 4.00
a. Vertical overprint 125.00
563 A50 20c yellow brn (Bl) 3.00 6.00
Never hinged 7.50
564 A50 50c claret (Bl) 15.00 20.00
Never hinged 45.00
565 A50 1p violet (Bl) 24.00 24.00
Never hinged 100.00
a. Horiz. pair, imperf. btwn.
Nos. 559-565 (7) 505.00 473.00

Overprinted in Blue On "Denver" Issue
Perf. 12
566 A52 1c pale blue 3.75
567 A52 2c lt green 3.75
568 A52 3c orange .45 *5.00*
569 A52 5c deep rose .45 *5.00*
570 A52 10c rose .45 *5.00*
571 A52 15c rose lilac .45 *5.00*
572 A52 50c yellow 1.10 *15.00*
573 A52 1p violet 9.50 *25.00*
Nos. 566-573 (8) 19.90
Set, never hinged 65.00

Many of the foregoing stamps exist with the "G. P. DE M." overprint printed in other colors than those listed. These "trial color" stamps were not regularly on sale at post offices but were available for postage and used stamps are known.

There appears to have been speculation in Nos. 516, 517, 520, 528, 539, 540, 543, 566, and 567. A small quantity of each of these stamps was sold at post offices but subsequently they could be obtained only from officials or their agents at advanced prices.

Venustiano Carranza — A66

1916, June 1 Engr. *Perf. 12*

574 A66 10c blue 1.75 1.00
a. Imperf., pair 25.00
575 A66 10c lilac brown 15.00 15.00
a. Imperf., pair 50.00
Nos. 574-575, never hinged 32.50

Entry of Carranza into Mexico, D.F.

Stamps of type A66 with only horizontal lines in the background of the oval are essays.

Coat of Arms — A67

1916

576 A67 1c lilac .35 .25
Never hinged .80

Issue of 1910 Surcharged in Various Colors

This overprint is called the "Barril."

1916 Wmk. 155 *Perf. 14*

577 A36 5c on 1c dl vio (Br) .50 .50
a. Vertical surcharge 1.25 1.25
b. Double surcharge 150.00
578 A36 10c on 1c dl vio (Bl) .50 .50
a. Double surcharge 100.00
579 A40 20c on 5c org (Br) .50 .50
a. Double surcharge 90.00
580 A40 25c on 5c org (G) .40 .50
581 A37 60c on 2c grn (R) 27.50 20.00
Nos. 577-581 (5) 29.40 22.00
Set, never hinged 100.00

On Nos. 423-424, 427

582 A36 5c on 1c (Br) .50 .50
a. Double tablet, one vertical 100.00
b. Inverted tablet 250.00 250.00
583 A36 10c on 1c (Bl) 1.00 1.00
584 A40 25c on 5c (G) .50 .50
a. Inverted tablet 225.00 225.00
585 A37 60c on 2c (R) 650.00 *425.00*
Never hinged 1,750.
Nos. 582-584, never hinged 4.50

No. 585 was not regularly issued.

The variety "GONSTITUCIONALISTA" is found on Nos. 582 to 585.

On No. 459

586 A40 25c on 5c org (G) .25 .25
Never hinged .70

On Nos. 484-485, 488

587 A36 5c on 1c (Br) 15.00 20.00
a. Vertical tablet 100.00 125.00
588 A36 10c on 1c (Bl) 5.00 7.50
589 A40 25c on 5c (G) 1.00 1.50
a. Inverted tablet 225.00
590 A37 60c on 2c (R) 650.00
Never hinged 1,750.
Nos. 587-589, never hinged 60.00

No. 590 was not regularly issued.

Surcharged on "Denver" Issue of 1914

1916 Unwmk. *Perf. 12*

591 A52 60c on 1c pale bl (Br) 3.00 6.00
592 A52 60c on 2c lt grn (Br) 3.00 6.00
a. Inverted surcharge *1,250.*
Set, never hinged 18.00

Postage Due Stamps Surcharged Like Nos. 577-581

1916 Wmk. 155 *Perf. 14*

593 D1 5c on 1c blue (Br) 2.50
594 D1 10c on 2c blue (V) 2.50
595 D1 20c on 4c blue (Br) 2.50
596 D1 25c on 5c blue (G) 2.50
597 D1 60c on 10c blue (R) 1.50
598 D1 1p on 1c blue (C) 1.50
599 D1 1p on 2c blue (C) 1.50
600 D1 1p on 4c blue (C) .80 .80
601 D1 1p on 5c blue (C) 2.50
602 D1 1p on 10c blue (C) 2.50
Nos. 593-602 (10) 20.30
Set, never hinged 60.00

There are numerous "trial colors" and "essays" of the overprints and surcharges on Nos. 577 to 602. They were available for postage though not regularly issued.

Postage Due Stamps Surcharged

1916

603 D1 2.50p on 1c blue 1.25 1.25
604 D1 2.50p on 2c blue 10.00
605 D1 2.50p on 4c blue 10.00 250.00
606 D1 2.50p on 5c blue 10.00
607 D1 2.50p on 10c blue 10.00
a. Inverted surcharge *1,500.*
Nos. 603-607 (5) 41.25
Set, never hinged 125.00

Regular Issue

Ignacio Zaragoza A68

Ildefonso Vázquez A69

J. M. Pino Suárez A70

Jesús Carranza A71

Maclovio Herrera — A72

F. I. Madero — A73

Belisario Domínguez A74

Aquiles Serdán A75

Rouletted 14½

1917-20 Engr. Unwmk.

Thick Paper

608 A68 1c dull violet 2.00 1.00
Never hinged 4.00
609 A68 1c lilac gray ('20) 5.00 .75
Never hinged 9.50
a. 1c gray ('20) 5.00 5.00
610 A69 2c gray green 1.50 .50
Never hinged 3.00
611 A70 3c bister brn 1.50 1.00
Never hinged 3.00
612 A71 4c carmine 2.50 1.00
Never hinged 7.50
613 A72 5c ultra 2.50 .50
Never hinged 5.00
a. Horiz. pair, imperf. btwn. 75.00
b. Imperf., pair 35.00 75.00
614 A73 10c blue 4.00 .50
Never hinged 10.00
a. Without imprint 7.50 1.00
Never hinged 16.00
615 A74 20c brown rose 40.00 2.00
Never hinged 90.00
a. 20c rose 40.00 2.00
Never hinged 80.00
616 A75 30c gray brown 90.00 3.00
Never hinged 250.00
617 A75 30c gray blk ('20) 100.00 4.00
Never hinged 250.00
Nos. 608-617 (10) 249.00 14.25

Perf. 12

Thick or Medium Paper

618 A68 1c dull violet 35.00 25.00
Never hinged 100.00
619 A69 2c gray green 10.00 6.00
Never hinged 20.00
620 A70 3c bis brn ('17) 200.00 200.00
Never hinged 400.00
622 A72 5c ultra 5.00 .25
Never hinged 10.00
623 A73 10c blue ('17) 5.00 .25
Never hinged 10.00
a. Without imprint ('17) 20.00 15.00
Never hinged 40.00
624 A74 20c rose ('20) 140.00 3.00
Never hinged 350.00
625 A75 30c gray blk ('20) 140.00 2.00
Never hinged 350.00

Thin or Medium Paper

626 A63 40c violet 65.00 1.00
Never hinged 200.00
627 A64 1p blue & blk 50.00 1.50
Never hinged 150.00
a. With center of 5p 800.00
b. 1p bl & dark blue (error) 500.00 20.00
c. Vert. pair, imperf. btwn. 250.00
628 A65 5p green & blk 1.50 *10.00*
Never hinged 3.00
a. With violet or red control number 25.00 10.00
b. With center of 1p 800.00

The 1, 2, 3, 5 and 10c are known on thin paper perforated. It is stated they were printed for Postal Union and "specimen" purposes.

All values exist imperf; these are not known to have been regularly issued. Nos. 627a and 628b were not regularly issued.

All values except 3c have an imprint.

For overprints and surcharges see Nos. B1-B2, O113-O165.

Meeting of Iturbide and Guerrero A77

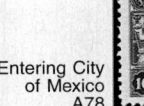

Entering City of Mexico A78

1921

632 A77 10c blue & brn 25.00 3.00
Never hinged 82.50
a. Center inverted *40,000.*
633 A78 10p black brn & blk 22.50 *37.50*
Never hinged 75.00

Commemorating the meeting of Agustín de Iturbide and Vicente Guerrero and the entry into City of Mexico in 1821.

For overprint see No. O194.

"El Salto de Agua," Public Fountain A79

Pyramid of the Sun at Teotihuacán A80

Chapultepec Castle A81

Columbus Monument A82

Juárez Colonnade, Mexico, D. F. A83

Monument to Josefa Ortiz de Dominguez A84

Cuauhtémoc Monument — A85

1923 Unwmk. *Rouletted 14½*

634 A79 2c scarlet 2.00 .25
635 A80 3c bister brn 2.00 .25
636 A81 4c green 2.50 .75
637 A82 5c orange 5.00 .25
638 A83 10c brown 3.75 .25
639 A85 10c claret 3.50 .25
640 A84 20c dk blue 52.50 1.75
641 A85 30c dk green 52.50 2.00
Nos. 634-641 (8) 123.75 5.75
Set, never hinged 300.00

See Nos. 642-646, 650-657, 688-692, 727A, 735A-736. For overprints see Nos. O166-O173, O178-O181, O183-O187, O196-O197, O199-O206, O210, O212-O214, O217-O222.

Communications Building — A87

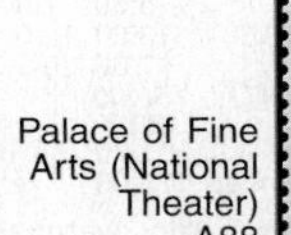

Palace of Fine Arts (National Theater) A88

Type I

Type II

Two types of 1p:
I — Eagle on palace dome.
II — Without eagle.

1923 Wmk. 156 *Perf. 12*

642 A79 2c scarlet 10.00 10.00
643 A81 4c green 1.40 .30
644 A82 5c orange 10.00 7.00
645 A85 10c brown lake 12.50 6.00
646 A83 30c dark green .95 .25
647 A63 40c violet 1.25 .25
648 A87 50c olive brn 1.00 .25
649 A88 1p red brn & bl (I) 1.00 1.00
a. Type II 3.00 *10.00*
Nos. 642-649 (8) 38.10 25.05
Set, never hinged 90.00

Most of Nos. 642-649 are known imperforate or part perforate but probably were not regularly issued.

For overprints see Nos. O175-O176, O189-O190, O208-O209, O223.

1923-34 *Rouletted 14½*

650 A79 2c scarlet .25 .25
651 A80 3c bis brn ('27) .25 .25
652 A81 4c green 47.50 35.00
653 A82 4c green ('27) .25 .25
654 A82 5c orange .25 .25
655 A85 10c lake .25 .25

656 A84 20c deep blue	.75	.30
657 A83 30c dk green ('34)	.75	.30
Nos. 650-657 (8)	50.25	36.85
Set, never hinged	125.00	

Nos. 650 to 657 inclusive exist imperforate.

Medallion A90

Map of Americas A91

Francisco García y Santos — A92

Post Office, Mexico, D. F. — A93

1926 ***Perf. 12***

658 A90 2c red	2.50	1.00
659 A91 4c green	2.50	1.00
660 A90 5c orange	2.50	.75
661 A91 10c brown red	4.00	1.00
662 A92 20c dk blue	4.00	1.25
663 A92 30c dk green	7.50	4.00
664 A92 40c violet	13.50	3.00
665 A93 1p brown & blue	27.50	10.00
a. 1p red & blue	37.50	15.00
Nos. 658-665 (8)	64.00	22.00
Set, never hinged	150.00	

Pan-American Postal Congress.

Nos. 658-665 were also printed in black, on unwatermarked paper, for presentation to delegates to the Universal Postal Congress at London in 1929. Remainders were overprinted in 1929 for use as airmail official stamps, and are listed as Nos. CO3-CO10.

For overprints see Nos. 667-674, 675A-682, CO3-CO10.

Benito Juárez — A94

1926 ***Rouletted 14½***

666 A94 8c orange	.30	.25
Never hinged	.70	

For overprint see No. O182.

Nos. 658-665 Overprinted

1930 ***Perf. 12***

667 A90 2c red	4.00	2.25
a. Reading down	15.00	15.00
668 A91 4c green	4.00	2.50
a. Reading down	15.00	15.00
669 A90 5c orange	4.00	2.00
a. Reading down	15.00	35.00
b. Double overprint	75.00	*75.00*
670 A91 10c brown red	7.50	2.50
671 A92 20c dk blue	9.50	3.50
672 A92 30c dk green	8.50	4.00
a. Reading down	10.00	12.00
673 A92 40c violet	12.50	8.50
a. Reading down	47.50	50.00
674 A93 1p red brn & bl	11.00	7.00
a. Double overprint	250.00	
b. Triple overprint	200.00	
Nos. 667-674 (8)	61.00	32.25
Set, never hinged	150.00	

Overprint horizontal on 1p.

Arms of Puebla — A95

1931, May 1 **Engr.**

675 A95 10c dk bl & dk brn	3.00	.50
Never hinged	7.50	

400th anniversary of Puebla.

Nos. 658-665a Overprinted

1931

676 A91 4c green	70.00	*75.00*
a. Inverted overprint	*750.00*	
677 A90 5c orange	13.00	*17.00*
678 A91 10c brown red	13.00	*14.00*
679 A92 20c dk blue	13.00	*18.00*
680 A92 30c dk green	22.50	*25.00*
681 A92 40c violet	32.50	*35.00*
682 A93 1p brown & bl	30.00	*35.00*
a. 1p red & blue	42.50	*45.00*
Nos. 676-682 (7)	194.00	219.00
Set, never hinged	475.00	

Overprint horizontal on 1p.

Nos. 676 and 682 are not known to have been sold to the public through post offices.

Forgeries of overprint exist.

Bartolomé de las Casas — A96

1933, Mar. 3 **Engr.** ***Rouletted 14½***

683 A96 15c dark blue	.30	.25
Never hinged	.70	

For overprint see No. O215.

Emblem of Mexican Society of Geography and Statistics — A97

1933, Oct. ***Rouletted 14½***

684 A97 2c deep green	1.50	.60
685 A97 5c dark brown	1.75	.50
686 A97 10c dark blue	.75	.25
687 A97 1p dark violet	100.00	65.00
Nos. 684-687 (4)	104.00	66.35
Set, never hinged	250.00	

XXI Intl. Congress of Statistics and the 1st centenary of the Mexican Society of Geography and Statistics.

Types of 1923 and PT1

1934 ***Perf. 10½, 11 (4c)***

687A PT1 1c brown	1.00	.30
688 A79 2c scarlet	.35	.25
689 A82 4c green	.35	.25
690 A85 10c brown lake	.35	.25
691 A84 20c dark blue	.75	.75
692 A83 30c dk blue grn	1.00	1.25
Nos. 687A-692 (6)	3.80	3.05
Set, never hinged	9.00	

See 2nd note after Postal Tax stamp No. RA3.

Indian Archer — A99

Indian — A100

Woman Decorating Pottery A101

Peon A102

Potter A103

Sculptor A104

Craftsman A105

Offering to the Gods A106

Worshiper — A107

1934, Sept. 1 **Wmk. 156** ***Perf. 10½***

698 A99 5c dk green	10.00	3.00
699 A100 10c brown lake	17.00	4.00
700 A101 20c ultra	30.00	20.00
701 A102 30c black	60.00	42.50
702 A103 40c black brn	37.50	25.00
703 A104 50c dull blue	175.00	160.00
704 A105 1p brn lake & blk	350.00	175.00
705 A106 5p brn blk & red brn	750.00	725.00
706 A107 10p brown & vio	2,000.	2,500.
a. Unwatermarked	*3,250.*	
Never hinged	5,000.	
Nos. 698-706 (9)	3,430.	3,655.
Set, never hinged	7,500.	

National University.

The design of the 1p is wider than the rest of the set. Values are for examples with perfs just touching the design.

See Nos. C54-C61, RA13B.

Yalalteca Indian — A108

Tehuana Indian — A109

Arch of the Revolution A110

Tower of Los Remedios A111

Cross of Palenque A112

Independence Monument A113

Independence Monument, Puebla A114

Monument to the Heroic Cadets A115

Stone of Tizoc — A116

Ruins of Mitla — A117

Coat of Arms A118

Charro A119

Imprint: "Oficina Impresora de Hacienda-Mexico"

1934-40 **Wmk. 156** ***Perf. 10½***

Size: 20x26mm

707 A108 1c orange	.65	.25
a. Unwmkd.		—
708 A109 2c green	.65	.25
a. Unwmkd.	3.75	3.75
709 A110 4c carmine	.90	.25
710 A111 5c olive brn	.65	.25
a. Unwmkd.	400.00	350.00
711 A112 10c dk blue	.80	.25
712 A112 10c violet ('35)	1.25	.25
a. Unwmkd.	200.00	40.00
713 A113 15c lt blue	4.00	.30
714 A114 20c gray green	1.90	.25
a. 20c olive green	2.00	.25
715 A114 20c ultra ('35)	1.40	.25
a. Unwmkd.		150.00
716 A115 30c lake	.90	.25
a. Unwmkd.	350.00	
716B A115 30c lt ultra ('40)	1.00	.25
717 A116 40c red brown	1.00	.25
718 A117 50c grnsh black	.90	.25
a. Imperf., pair	110.00	
b. Unwmkd.		375.00
719 A118 1p dk brn & org	2.50	.25
a. Imperf., pair	350.00	
720 A119 5p org & vio	7.75	.75
Nos. 707-720 (15)	26.25	4.30
Set, never hinged	70.00	

No. 718a was not regularly issued.

The existence of No. 707a has been questioned.

See Nos. 729-733, 733B, 735, 784-788, 795A-800A, 837-838, 840-841, 844, 846-851 (post 1940 listings are in Scott Standard catalogue, Vol. 4). For overprints see Nos. 728, O224-O232.

Tractor — A120

1935, Apr. 1 **Wmk. 156** ***Perf. 10½***

721 A120 10c violet	4.00	.50
Never hinged	9.00	

Industrial census of Apr. 10, 1935.

Arms of Chiapas — A121

1935, Sept. 14
722 A121 10c dark blue .50 .25
Never hinged 1.40
a. Unwmkd. 125.00 100.00

The 111th anniversary of the joining of the state of Chiapas with the federal republic of Mexico. See No. 734.

Emiliano Zapata — A122

1935, Nov. 20 **Wmk. 156**
723 A122 10c violet .75 .25
Never hinged 2.00

25th anniversary of the Plan of Ayala.

US and Mexico Joined by Highways A123

Matalote Bridge A124

View of Nuevo Laredo Highway — A125

1936 **Wmk. 248** ***Perf. 14***
725 A123 5c blue grn & rose .35 .25
726 A124 10c slate bl & blk .50 .25
727 A125 20c brn & dk grn 1.50 1.00
Nos. 725-727,C77-C79 (6) 3.60 2.50
Set, never hinged 8.50

Opening of the Mexico City - Nuevo Laredo Highway.

Monument Type of 1923
1936 **Wmk. 248** **Engr.** ***Perf. 10½***
727A A85 10c brown lake *2,500.* 650.00

No. 712 Overprinted in Green

1936, Dec. 15 **Wmk. 156**
728 A112 10c violet .60 .50
Never hinged 1.50

1st National Congress of Industrial Hygiene and Medicine.

Type of 1934
Redrawn size: 17½x21mm
Imprint: "Talleres de Imp. de Est. y Valores-Mexico"
1937 **Photo.** **Wmk. 156** ***Perf. 14***
729 A108 1c orange .60 .25
a. Imperf., pair 12.50 12.50
Never hinged 25.00
730 A109 2c dull green .60 .25
a. Imperf., pair 12.50 12.50
Never hinged 30.00
731 A110 4c carmine .90 .25
a. Imperf., pair 12.50 12.50
Never hinged 30.00
732 A111 5c olive brn .80 .25
a. Unwmkd. *300.00*

733 A112 10c violet .70 .25
a. Imperf., pair 10.00 12.50
Never hinged 12.00
Nos. 729-733 (5) 3.60 1.25
Set, never hinged 9.00

The imperfs were not regularly issued.

Types of 1934-35
1937 **Wmk. 260** **Size: 17½x21mm**
733B A111 5c olive brown *4,000.* 250.00
Never hinged *6,000.*

1937 **Engr.** ***Perf. 10½***
734 A121 10c dark blue 35.00 35.00
Never hinged 75.00

1937 **Size: 20x26mm**
735 A112 10c violet 350.00 55.00

Types of 1923
1934-37 **Wmk. 260** ***Perf. 10½***
735A A79 2c scarlet *6,000.*
735B A85 10c brown lake —

Forged perforations exist.

The listing of No. 735B is being re-evaluated. The Catalogue Editors would appreciate any information on the stamp.

Rouletted 14½
736 A85 10c claret *5,500. 175.00*

Blacksmith A126

Revolutionary Soldier A127

Revolutionary Envoy — A128

Wmk. 156
1938, Mar. 26 **Photo.** ***Perf. 14***
737 A126 5c black & brn .80 .25
738 A127 10c red brown .35 .25
739 A128 20c maroon & org 6.00 1.00
Nos. 737-739,C82-C84 (6) 13.15 5.00
Set, never hinged 32.00

Plan of Guadalupe, 25th anniv.

Arch of the Revolution A129

Independence Monument A131

Design: 10c, National Theater.

1938, July 1
740 A129 5c bister brn 4.25 .60
741 A129 5c red brown 25.00 2.25
742 A129 10c orange 15.00 11.00
743 A129 10c chocolate 1.00 .25
744 A131 20c brown lake 6.00 4.00
745 A131 20c black 18.00 15.00
Nos. 740-745 (6) 69.25 33.10
Nos. 740-745,C85-C90 (12) 129.60 63.35
Set, never hinged 275.00

16th Intl. Congress of Planning & Housing.

Arch of the Revolution A132

1939, May 1
746 A132 10c Prus blue .65 .25
Nos. 746,C91-C93 (4) 4.75 3.00
Set, never hinged 11.00

New York World's Fair.

Indian — A133

1939, May 17
747 A133 10c red orange .45 .25
Nos. 747,C94-C96 (4) 5.55 2.80
Set, never hinged 13.00

Tulsa World Philatelic Convention.

Juan Zumárraga A134

First Printing Shop in Mexico, 1539 A135

Design: 10c, Antonio de Mendoza.

1939, Sept. 1 **Engr.** ***Perf. 10½***
748 A134 2c brown blk .75 .25
749 A135 5c green .75 .25
750 A134 10c red brown .25 .25
Nos. 748-750,C97-C99 (6) 3.75 1.95
Set, never hinged 11.50

400th anniversary of printing in Mexico.

View of Taxco A137

Allegory of Agriculture A138

10c, Two hands holding symbols of commerce.

1939, Oct. 1 **Photo.** ***Perf. 12x13***
751 A137 2c dark carmine 1.25 .25
752 A138 5c sl grn & gray grn .25 .25
753 A138 10c org brn & buff .25 .25
Nos. 751-753,C100-C102 (6) 6.25 2.00
Set, never hinged 14.00

Census Taking.

"Penny Black" of 1840 — A140

1940, May ***Perf. 14***
754 A140 5c black & lemon .90 .50
755 A140 10c dark violet .25 .25
756 A140 20c lt blue & car .25 .25
757 A140 1p gray & red org 7.00 4.00
758 A140 5p black & Prus bl 50.00 50.00
Nos. 754-758,C103-C107 (10) 141.00 116.05
Set, never hinged 340.00

Postage stamp centenary.

Roadside Monument — A141

1940 **Wmk. 156**
759 A141 6c deep green .50 .25
Never hinged 1.25

Opening of the highway between Mexico, D. F., and Guadalajara. See Nos. 789, 842 in Scott Standard catalogue, Vol. 4.

Vasco de Quiroga — A142

Melchor Ocampo — A143

College Seal — A144

1940, July 15 **Engr.** ***Perf. 10½***
760 A142 2c violet 1.30 .50
761 A143 5c copper red .80 .25
762 A144 10c olive bister .80 .30
a. Imperf., pair 150.00
Nos. 760-762,C108-C110 (6) 5.10 2.60
Set, never hinged 11.00

Founding of the National College of San Nicolas de Hidalgo, 400th anniv.

Coat of Arms of Campeche A145

1940, Aug. 7 **Photo.** ***Perf. 12x13***
763 A145 10c bis brn & dk car 5.00 1.25
Never hinged 8.50
Nos. 763,C111-C113 (4) 12.60 6.70
Set, never hinged 30.00

400th anniversary of the founding of Campeche.

Man at Helm A146

1940, Dec. 1
764 A146 2c red org & blk 1.60 .60
765 A146 5c peacock bl & red brn 8.00 3.50
766 A146 10c slate grn & dk brn 4.00 .85
Nos. 764-766,C114-C116 (6) 21.00 9.45
Set, never hinged 45.00

Inauguration of Pres. Manuel Avila Camacho.

SEMI-POSTAL STAMPS

Nos. 622, 614 Surcharged in Red

1918, Dec. 25 Unwmk. *Perf. 12*
B1 A72 5c + 3c ultra 20.00 25.00

Rouletted 14½
B2 A73 10c + 5c blue 25.00 25.00
Set, never hinged 57.50

AIR POST STAMPS

Eagle AP1

Unwmk.

1922, Apr. 2 Engr. *Perf. 12*
C1 AP1 50c blue & red brn 67.50 50.00
Never hinged 160.00
a. 50c dark blue & claret ('29) 90.00 90.00
Never hinged 200.00

See Nos. C2-C3. For overprints and surcharges see Nos. C47-C48, CO1-CO2B, CO18-CO19, CO29.

1927, Oct. 13 Wmk. 156
C2 AP1 50c dk bl & red brn .75 .25
Never hinged 2.50
a. 50c dark blue & claret ('29) .75 .25
Never hinged 3.00
b. Vert. strip of 3, imperf. btwn. *7,500.*

The vignettes of Nos. C1a and C2a fluoresce a bright rose red under UV light.

1928
C3 AP1 25c brn car & gray brn .45 .25
C4 AP1 25c dk grn & gray brn .45 .25
Set, never hinged 2.50

On May 3, 1929, certain proofs or essays were sold at the post office in Mexico, D. F. They were printed in different colors from those of the regularly issued stamps. There were 7 varieties perf. and 2 imperf. and a total of 225 copies. They were sold with the understanding that they were for collections but the majority of them were used on air mail sent out that day.

Capt. Emilio Carranza and his Airplane "México Excelsior" AP2

1929, June 19
C5 AP2 5c ol grn & sepia 1.10 .65
C6 AP2 10c sep & brn red 1.25 .70
C7 AP2 15c vio & dk grn 3.00 1.25
C8 AP2 20c brown & blk 1.25 .75
C9 AP2 50c brn red & blk 7.50 5.00
C10 AP2 1p black & brn 15.00 10.00
Nos. C5-C10 (6) 29.10 18.35
Set, never hinged 75.00

1st anniv. of death of Carranza (1905-28). For overprints see Nos. C29-C36, C40-C44.

Coat of Arms and Airplane AP3

1929-34 *Perf. 11½, 12*
C11 AP3 10c violet .35 .25
C12 AP3 15c carmine 1.35 .25
C13 AP3 20c brown olive 37.50 1.25
C14 AP3 30c gray black .25 .25
C15 AP3 35c blue green .35 .25
a. Imperf., pair 1,200.
C16 AP3 50c red brn ('34) 1.25 .65
C17 AP3 1p blk & dk bl 1.25 .65
C18 AP3 5p claret & dp bl 4.00 3.50
C19 AP3 10p vio & ol brn 6.00 7.00
Nos. C11-C19 (9) 52.30 14.05
Set, never hinged 130.00

1930-32 *Rouletted 13, 13½*
C20 AP3 5c lt blue ('32) .35 .25
C21 AP3 10c violet .35 .25
C22 AP3 15c carmine .35 .25
a. 15c rose carmine .40 .25
C23 AP3 20c brown olive 1.50 .25
a. 20c brown .50 .25
b. 20c yellow brown .50 .25
c. Horiz. pair, imperf. btwn.
C24 AP3 25c violet .95 .80
C25 AP3 50c red brown .90 .75
Nos. C20-C25 (6) 4.40 2.55
Set, never hinged 13.00

Trial impressions of No. C20 were printed in orange but were never sold at post offices.
See Nos. C62-C64, C75. For overprints and surcharges see Nos. C28, C38-C39, C46, C49-C50, CO17, CO20-CO28, CO30.

Plane over Plaza, Mexico City — AP4

1929, Dec. 10 Wmk. 156 *Perf. 12*
C26 AP4 20c black violet 1.25 1.00
C27 AP4 40c slate green 85.00 75.00
Set, never hinged 210.00

Aviation Week, Dec. 10-16.
For overprint see No. CO11.

No. C21 Overprinted in Red

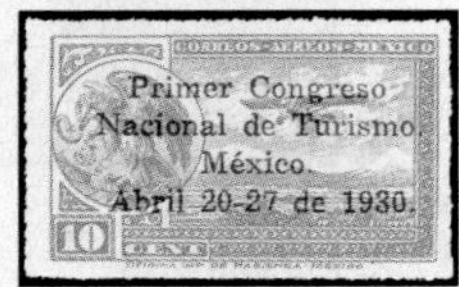

1930, Apr. 20 *Rouletted 13, 13½*
C28 AP3 10c violet 2.00 1.25
Never hinged 5.50

National Tourism Congress at Mexico, D. F., Apr. 20-27, 1930.

Nos. C5 and C7 Overprinted

1930, Sept. 1 *Perf. 12*
C29 AP2 5c ol grn & sepia 5.50 4.50
a. Double overprint 225.00 *250.00*
C30 AP2 15c violet & dk grn 9.00 7.75
Set, never hinged 45.00

Nos. C5-C10 Overprinted

1930, Dec. 18
C31 AP2 5c ol grn & sepia 7.00 6.50
C32 AP2 10c sep & brn red 3.50 4.00
a. Double overprint 60.00 60.00
C33 AP2 15c vio & dk grn 7.50 7.00
C34 AP2 20c brown & blk 7.00 5.50
C35 AP2 50c brn red & blk 14.00 10.00
C36 AP2 1p black & brn 4.00 2.75
Nos. C31-C36 (6) 43.00 35.75
Set, never hinged 130.00

Plane over Flying Field AP5

1931, May 15 Engr. *Perf. 12*
C37 AP5 25c lake 4.00 4.50
Never hinged 11.00
a. Imperf., pair 80.00 72.50
Never hinged 175.00

Aeronautic Exhibition of the Aero Club of Mexico. Of the 25c, 15c paid air mail postage and 10c went to a fund to improve the Mexico City airport.
For surcharge see No. C45.

Nos. C13 and C23 Srchd. in Red

1931
C38 AP3 15c on 20c brn ol 32.50 35.00
Never hinged 80.00

Rouletted 13, 13½
C39 AP3 15c on 20c brn ol .30 .25
Never hinged 1.00
a. Inverted surcharge 150.00 *200.00*
b. Double surcharge 150.00 *200.00*
c. Pair, one without surcharge 350.00

Nos. C5 to C9 Overprinted

1932, July 13 *Perf. 12*
C40 AP2 5c ol grn & sep 6.00 5.00
a. Imperf., pair 60.00 60.00
C41 AP2 10c sep & brn red 5.00 3.00
a. Imperf., pair 60.00 60.00
C42 AP2 15c vio & bk grn 6.00 4.00
a. Imperf., pair 60.00 60.00
C43 AP2 20c brn & blk 5.00 2.75
a. Imperf., pair 60.00 60.00
C44 AP2 50c brn red & blk 35.00 35.00
a. Imperf., pair 60.00 60.00
Nos. C40-C44 (5) 57.00 49.75
Set, never hinged 170.00
Set, C40a-C44a never hinged 650.00

Death of Capt. Emilio Carranza, 4th anniv.

No. C37 Surcharged

1932
C45 AP5 20c on 25c lake .70 .30
Never hinged 2.50
a. Imperf., pair 72.50 72.50
Never hinged 150.00

No. C13 Surcharged

C46 AP3 30c on 20c brn ol 30.00 30.00
Never hinged 75.00

Similar Surcharge on Nos. C3 and C4

C47 AP1 40c on 25c (#C3) .90 .90
Never hinged 3.00
a. Inverted surcharge *11,000.*
C48 AP1 40c on 25c (#C4) 50.00 50.00
Never hinged 125.00

Surcharged on Nos. C23 and C24 *Rouletted 13, 13½*

C49 AP3 30c on 20c brn ol .35 .25
Never hinged 1.00
a. Inverted surcharge *2,750.*
C50 AP3 80c on 25c dl vio 1.75 1.25
Never hinged 5.00
Nos. C45-C50 (6) 83.70 82.70

Palace of Fine Arts AP6

1933, Oct. 1 Engr. *Perf. 12*
C51 AP6 20c dk red & dl vio 3.50 1.40
C52 AP6 30c dk brn & dl vio 7.00 6.00
C53 AP6 1p grnsh blk & dl vio 72.50 70.00
Nos. C51-C53 (3) 83.00 77.40
Set, never hinged 190.00

21st Intl. Cong. of Statistics and the cent. of the Mexican Soc. of Geography and Statistics.

National University Issue

Nevado de Toluca AP7

Pyramids of the Sun and Moon AP8

View of Ajusco AP9

Volcanoes Popocatepetl and Iztaccíhuatl — AP10

Bridge over Tepecayo AP11

Chapultepec Fortress — AP12

Orizaba Volcano (Citlaltépetl) AP13

Mexican Girl and Aztec Calendar Stone AP14

1934, Sept. 1 Wmk. 156 *Perf. 10½*

No.	Description	Unused	Used
C54	AP7 20c orange	15.00	10.00
C55	AP8 30c red lilac & vio	20.00	20.00
C56	AP9 50c ol grn & bis brn	20.00	*25.00*
C57	AP10 75c blk & yel grn	25.00	*25.00*
C58	AP11 1p blk & pck bl	30.00	30.00
C59	AP12 5p bis brn & dk bl	225.00	*250.00*
C60	AP13 10p indigo & mar	550.00	525.00
C61	AP14 20p brn & brn lake	1,800.	*1,800.*
	Nos. C54-C61 (8)	2,685.	2,685.
	Set, never hinged	4,750.	

Type of 1929-34

1934-35 *Perf. 10½, 10½x10*

No.	Description	Unused	Used
C62	AP3 20c olive green	.35	.25
a.	20c slate	500.00	500.00
	Never hinged	600.00	
C63	AP3 30c slate	.40	.40
C64	AP3 50c red brn ('35)	2.00	2.00
	Nos. C62-C64 (3)	2.75	2.65
	Set, never hinged	7.00	

Symbols of Air Service AP15

Tláloc, God of Water (Quetzalcóatl Temple) — AP16

Orizaba Volcano (Citlaltépetl) AP17

"Eagle Man" AP18

Symbolical of Flight AP19

Aztec Bird-Man — AP20

Allegory of Flight and Pyramid of the Sun AP21

"Eagle Man" and Airplanes AP22

Natives Looking at Airplane and Orizaba Volcano — AP23

Imprint: "Oficina Impresora de Hacienda-Mexico"

Perf. 10½x10, 10x10½

1934-35 Wmk. 156

No.	Description	Unused	Used
C65	AP15 5c black	.45	.25
a.	Imperf., pair		
C66	AP16 10c red brown	.90	.25
C67	AP17 15c gray green	1.25	.25
a.	Imperf., pair	*400.00*	
C68	AP18 20c brown car	3.00	.25
a.	20c lake	4.00	.25
b.	Imperf., pair		
C69	AP19 30c brown olive	.70	.25
C70	AP20 40c blue ('35)	1.25	.25
C71	AP21 50c green	2.50	.25
a.	Imperf., pair	275.00	
C72	AP22 1p gray grn & red brn	3.50	.25
C73	AP23 5p dk car & blk	7.25	.70
	Nos. C65-C73 (9)	20.80	2.70
	Set, never hinged	45.00	

See Nos. C76A, C80, C81; C132-C140, C170-C177A in Scott Standard catalogue, Vol. 4. For overprint see No. C74.

No. C68 Overprinted in Violet

1935, Apr. 16

No.	Description	Unused	Used
C74	AP18 20c lake	*3,250.*	*4,000.*
	Never hinged	*6,000.*	

Amelia Earhart's goodwill flight to Mexico.

No. C74 with "Muestra" to left of "Mexico" was not issued for postage.

Arms-Plane Type of 1929-34

1935 Wmk. 248 *Perf. 10½x10*

No.	Description	Unused	Used
C75	AP3 30c slate	3.00	*5.00*
	Never hinged	5.00	

Francisco I. Madero AP24

1935, Nov. 20 Wmk. 156

No.	Description	Unused	Used
C76	AP24 20c scarlet	.30	.25
	Never hinged	.75	

Plan of San Luis, 25th anniv. See No. C76B.

Eagle Man Type of 1934-35

1936 Wmk. 260

No.	Description	Unused	Used
C76A	AP18 20c lake	*4,500.*	60.00
	Never hinged	7,500.	

Madero Type of 1935

1936

No.	Description	Unused	Used
C76B	AP24 20c scarlet	*12,500.*	

Tasquillo Bridge AP25

Corona River Bridge AP26

Bridge on Nuevo Laredo Highway AP27

Wmk. 248

1936, July 1 Photo. *Perf. 14*

No.	Description	Unused	Used
C77	AP25 10c slate bl & lt bl	.35	.25
C78	AP26 20c dl vio & org	.35	.25
C79	AP27 40c dk bl & dk grn	.55	.50
	Nos. C77-C79 (3)	1.25	.90
	Set, never hinged	2.75	

Opening of Nuevo Laredo Highway.

Eagle Man Type of 1934-35

Perf. 10½x10

1936, June 18 Engr. Unwmk.

No.	Description	Unused	Used
C80	AP18 20c brown carmine	10.00	7.00
	Never hinged	25.00	

Imprint: "Talleres de Imp. de Est. y Valores-Mexico"

1937 Wmk. 156 Photo. *Perf. 14*

No.	Description	Unused	Used
C81	AP18 20c rose red	1.25	.25
	Never hinged	2.50	
a.	20c brown carmine	1.50	.25
	Never hinged	3.00	
b.	20c dark carmine	2.00	.25
	Never hinged	4.50	
c.	Imperf., pair	37.50	50.00
	Never hinged	75.00	

There are two sizes of watermark 156. No. C81c was not regularly issued.

Cavalryman AP28

Early Biplane over Mountains AP29

Venustiano Carranza on Horseback AP30

1938, Mar. 26

No.	Description	Unused	Used
C82	AP28 20c org red & bl	.50	.25
C83	AP29 40c bl & org red	.75	*1.00*
C84	AP30 1p bl & bis brn	4.75	2.25
	Nos. C82-C84 (3)	6.00	3.45
	Set, never hinged	18.00	

Plan of Guadalupe, 25th anniversary.

Reconstructed edifices of Chichén Itzá — AP31

Designs: Nos. C85, C86, The Zócalo and Cathedral, Mexico City. Nos. C89, C90, View of Acapulco.

1938, July 1

No.	Description	Unused	Used
C85	AP31 20c carmine rose	.35	.25
C86	AP31 20c purple	20.00	10.00
C87	AP31 40c brt green	10.00	5.00
C88	AP31 40c dark green	10.00	5.00
C89	AP31 1p light blue	10.00	5.00
C90	AP31 1p slate blue	10.00	5.00
	Nos. C85-C90 (6)	60.35	30.25
	Set, never hinged	130.00	

16th Intl. Cong. of Planning & Housing.

Statue of José María Morelos — AP34

1939 Engr. *Perf. 10½*

No.	Description	Unused	Used
C91	AP34 20c green	.70	.50
	Never hinged	1.00	
C92	AP34 40c red violet	2.00	1.25
	Never hinged	5.00	
C93	AP34 1p vio brn & car	1.40	1.00
	Never hinged	1.75	
	Nos. C91-C93 (3)	4.10	2.75
	Set, never hinged	9.50	

New York World's Fair. Released in New York May 2, in Mexico May 24.

Type of 1939 Overprinted in Cerise

1939, May 23

No.	Description	Unused	Used
C93A	AP34 20c blue & red	425.00	425.00
	Never hinged	800.00	

Issued for the flight of Francisco Sarabia from Mexico City to New York on May 25.

Statue of Pioneer Woman, Ponca City, OK — AP35

1939, May 17

No.	Description	Unused	Used
C94	AP35 20c gray brown	1.00	.40
	Never hinged	2.00	
C95	AP35 40c slate green	2.50	1.25
	Never hinged	7.00	
C96	AP35 1p violet	1.60	.90
	Never hinged	3.00	
	Nos. C94-C96 (3)	5.10	2.55
	Set, never hinged	12.00	

Tulsa World Philatelic Convention.

First Engraving Made in Mexico, 1544 — AP36

First Work of Legislation Printed in America, 1563 — AP37

Designs: 1p, Reproduction of oldest preserved Mexican printing.

1939, Sept. 7 **Wmk. 156**
C97 AP36 20c slate blue .25 .25
a. Unwmkd. 50.00 *25.00*
C98 AP37 40c slate green .65 .25
a. Imperf., pair *700.00*
C99 AP37 1p dk brn & car 1.10 .70
Nos. C97-C99 (3) 2.00 1.10
Set, never hinged 8.00

400th anniversary of printing in Mexico.

Alternated Perforations

Nos. 763-766, 774-779, 792-795, 801-804, 806-811, 813-818, C100-C102, C111-C116, C123-C128, C143-C162, C430-C431 have alternating small and large perforations. See Scott Standard catalogue, Vol. 4, for post 1940 listings.

Transportation — AP39

Designs: 40c, Finger counting and factory. 1p, "Seven Censuses."

Perf. 12x13, 13x12

1939, Oct. 2 **Photo.**
C100 AP39 20c dk bl & bl 1.00 .25
C101 AP39 40c red org & org .75 .25
C102 AP39 1p ind & vio bl 2.75 .75
Nos. C100-C102 (3) 4.50 1.20
Set, never hinged 10.00

National Census of 1939-40.

Penny Black Type of Regular Issue, 1940

1940, May ***Perf. 14***
C103 A140 5c blk & dk grn .65 .55
C104 A140 10c bis brn & dp bl .55 .25
C105 A140 20c car & bl vio .40 .25
C106 A140 1p car & choc 6.00 5.00
C107 A140 5p gray grn & red brn 75.00 55.00
Nos. C103-C107 (5) 82.60 61.00
Set, never hinged 200.00

Issue dates: 5c-1p, May 2; 5p, May 15.

Part of Original College at Pátzcuaro AP43

College at Morelia (18th Century) — AP44

College at Morelia (1940) AP45

1940, July 15 **Engr.** ***Perf. 10½***
C108 AP43 20c brt green .45 .25
C109 AP44 40c orange .50 .30
C110 AP45 1p dp pur, red brn & org 1.25 1.00
Nos. C108-C110 (3) 2.20 1.50
Set, never hinged 5.00

400th anniv. of the founding of the National College of San Nicolas de Hidalgo.

Pirate Ship AP46

Designs: 40c, Castle of San Miguel. 1p, Temple of San Francisco.

Perf. 12x13, 13x12

1940, Aug. 7 **Photo.**
C111 AP46 20c red brn & bis brn 1.10 .70
C112 AP46 40c blk & sl grn 1.50 .75
C113 AP46 1p vio bl & blk 5.00 4.00
Nos. C111-C113 (3) 7.60 5.45
Set, never hinged 20.00

400th anniversary of Campeche.

Inauguration Type of Regular Issue, 1940

1940, Dec. 1 ***Perf. 12x13***
C114 A146 20c gray blk & red org 1.90 1.00
C115 A146 40c chnt brn & dk sl 2.00 1.50
C116 A146 1p brt vio bl & rose 3.50 2.00
Nos. C114-C116 (3) 7.40 4.50
Set, never hinged 20.00

AIR POST OFFICIAL STAMPS

Nos. C4 and C3 Overprinted in Black or Red

1929 **Wmk. 156** ***Perf. 12***
CO1 AP1 25c dk grn & gray brn 4.50 3.25
a. Without period 20.00 20.00
CO2 AP1 25c dk grn & gray brn (R) 4.00 *5.00*
a. Without period 21.00 21.00
CO2B AP1 25c brn car & gray brn 10.00 *12.50*
c. Without period 25.00 25.00
Nos. CO1-CO2B (3) 18.50 20.75
Set, never hinged 35.00

Types of Regular Issue of 1926 Overprinted in Red

1929, Oct. 15 **Unwmk.**
CO3 A90 2c black 75.00 *90.00*
CO4 A91 4c black 75.00 *90.00*
CO5 A90 5c black 75.00 *90.00*
CO6 A91 10c black 75.00 *90.00*
CO7 A92 20c black 75.00 *90.00*
CO8 A92 30c black 75.00 *90.00*
CO9 A92 40c black 75.00 *90.00*
Nos. CO3-CO9 (7) 525.00 630.00
Set, never hinged 1,100.

Horizontal Overprint

CO10 A93 1p black *2,250.* *2,250.*
Never hinged *4,000.*

Nos. CO3-CO9 also exist with overprint reading up.

No. C26 Overprinted in Black

1930 **Wmk. 156**
CO11 AP4 20c black violet 1.10 *1.75*
Never hinged 2.25
a. Without period 20.00 *20.00*
b. Inverted overprint 18.00 *18.00*
c. As "a," inverted overprint 210.00 210.00

No. CO11 with red overprint is believed not to have been issued for postal purposes.

Plane over Mexico City OA1

1930 **Engr.**
CO12 OA1 20c gray black 6.50 6.50
CO13 OA1 35c lt violet 1.10 *1.90*
CO14 OA1 40c ol brn & dp bl 1.25 *1.75*
CO15 OA1 70c vio & ol gray 1.50 *1.75*
Nos. CO12-CO15 (4) 10.35 *11.90*
Set, never hinged 23.50

No. CO12 Surcharged in Red

1931
CO16 OA1 15c on 20c .85 *1.40*
Never hinged 1.60
a. Inverted surcharge 140.00
b. Double surcharge 140.00

No. C20 Overprinted

1932 ***Rouletted 13, 13½***
CO17 AP3 5c light blue .80 *.90*
Never hinged 1.75

Air Post Stamps of 1927-32 Overprinted

On No. C1a

1932 **Unwmk.** ***Perf. 12***
CO18 AP1 50c dk bl & cl 1,000. 1,000.
Never hinged 2,000.

On Nos. C2, C2a
Wmk. 156

CO19 AP1 50c dk bl & red brn 1.25 *1.50*
Never hinged 2.25
a. 50c dark blue & claret 1.40 *1.60*

See note after No. C2.

On Nos. C11 and C12

1932 ***Perf. 12***
CO20 AP3 10c violet 22.50 *25.00*
Never hinged 45.00
CO21 AP3 15c carmine 350.00 *375.00*
Never hinged 700.00

On Nos. C21 to C23
Rouletted 13, 13½

CO22 AP3 10c violet .35 *.55*
CO23 AP3 15c carmine 1.40 *2.00*
CO24 AP3 20c brn olive 1.40 *2.00*

Nos. C20, C21 C23 and C25 Overprinted

1933-34 ***Rouletted 13½***
CO25 AP3 5c light blue .30 *.55*
CO26 AP3 10c violet ('34) .30 *.90*
CO27 AP3 20c brown olive .75 *1.25*
CO28 AP3 50c red brn ('34) 1.25 *1.90*

On No. C2
Perf. 12

CO29 AP1 50c dk bl & red brn 1.10 *2.00*
a. 50c dark blue & claret 1.60 *2.50*

On No. C11
Perf. 12

CO30 AP3 10c violet ('34) 140.00 *175.00*
a. Double overprint *325.00*

Forgeries exist.

SPECIAL DELIVERY STAMPS

Motorcycle Postman SD1

1919 **Unwmk.** **Engr.** ***Perf. 12***
E1 SD1 20c red & black 70.00 2.75

1923 **Wmk. 156**
E2 SD1 20c blk car & blk .30 .25

For overprint see No. E7

Messenger with Quipu — SD2

1934
E3 SD2 10c brn red & blue .30 .50

Indian Archer — SD3

Imprint: "Oficina Impresora de Hacienda Mexico."

1934 ***Perf. 10x10½***
E4 SD3 10c black violet 1.50 .50

See Nos. E5-E6, E8-E9 (in Scott Standard catalogue, Vol. 4).

Redrawn

Imprint: "Talleres de Imp. de Est. y Valores-Mexico."

1938-41 **Photo.** ***Perf. 14***
E5 SD3 10c slate violet .75 .25
a. Unwatermarked 50.00
E6 SD3 20c orange red ('41) .50 .25

Imperforate examples of No. E6 were not regularly issued.

No. E2 Overprinted "1940" in Violet

1940 **Engr.** ***Perf. 12***
E7 SD1 20c red & black .40 .25

INSURED LETTER STAMPS

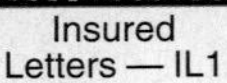

Insured Letters — IL1

Registered Mailbag — IL2

Safe — IL3

1935 Engr. Wmk. 156 *Perf. 10½*

No.	Type	Description	Unused	Used
G1	IL1	10c vermilion	1.75	.75
a.		Perf. 10x10½		
G2	IL2	50c dk bl	10.00	.60
G3	IL3	1p turq grn	1.25	.85
		Nos. G1-G3 (3)	13.00	2.20

Nos. G1 and G4 were issued both with and without imprint.

POSTAGE DUE STAMPS

D1

1908 Engr. Wmk. 155 *Perf. 14*

No.	Type	Description	Unused	Used
J1	D1	1c blue	1.00	*3.00*
J2	D1	2c blue	1.00	*3.00*
J3	D1	4c blue	1.00	*3.00*
J4	D1	5c blue	1.00	*3.00*
J5	D1	10c blue	1.00	*3.00*
		Nos. J1-J5 (5)	5.00	*15.00*

For overprints and surcharges see Nos. 381-385, 434-438, 466-470, 495-499, 593-607.

PORTE DE MAR STAMPS

These stamps were used to indicate the amount of cash to be paid to the captains of the mail steamers taking outgoing foreign mail.

PM2

1875 Unwmk. Litho. *Imperf.*

No.	Type	Description	Unused	Used
JX9	PM2	2c black	.60	*50.00*
a.		"5" added to make 25c	12.00	*100.00*
JX10	PM2	10c black	.80	*30.00*
JX11	PM2	12c black	.80	*50.00*
JX12	PM2	20c black	1.00	*50.00*
JX13	PM2	25c black	3.25	*50.00*
JX14	PM2	35c black	3.25	*60.00*
JX15	PM2	50c black	3.00	*60.00*
JX16	PM2	60c black	3.00	*75.00*
JX17	PM2	75c black	3.50	*75.00*
JX18	PM2	85c black	3.25	*100.00*
JX19	PM2	100c black	4.00	*100.00*
		Nos. JX9-JX19 (11)	26.45	700.00

Same, Numerals Larger

No.	Type	Description	Unused	Used
JX20	PM2	5c black	1.00	*50.00*
JX21	PM2	25c black	1.65	*50.00*
JX22	PM2	35c black	250.00	
JX23	PM2	50c black	1.00	*50.00*
JX24	PM2	60c black	125.00	
JX25	PM2	100c black	.60	*100.00*
		Nos. JX20-JX25 (6)	379.25	

In Nos. JX9-JX19 the figures of value are 7mm high and "CENTAVOS" is 7½mm long. On Nos. JX20-JX25 the figures of value are 8mm high and "CENTAVOS" is 9½mm long.

Nos. JX9-JX25 exist with overprints of district names.

Counterfeits exist of Nos. JX9-JX31.

PM3

1879

No.	Type	Description	Unused	Used
JX26	PM3	2c brown	.50	
JX27	PM3	5c yellow	.50	
JX28	PM3	10c red	.50	
JX29	PM3	25c blue	.50	
JX30	PM3	50c green	.50	
JX31	PM3	100c violet	.50	
		Nos. JX26-JX31 (6)	3.00	

Nos. JX26-JX31 were never put in use.

Nos. JX26-JX31 were printed on paper watermarked "ADMINISTRACION GENERAL DE CORREOS MEXICO." Aprroximately ¾ of the stamps do not show any of the watermark.

Stamps of this design were never issued. Examples appeared on the market in 1884. Value, set, $75. Value, full sheet $400.

All were printed in same sheet of 49 (7x7). Sheet consists of 14 of 10c; 7 each of 25c, 35c, 50c; 4 each of 60c, 85c; 3 each of 75c, 100c. There are four varieties of 10c, two of 25c, 35c and 50c.

OFFICIAL STAMPS

Hidalgo — O1

Wove or Laid Paper

1884-93 Unwmk. Engr. *Perf. 12*

No.	Type	Description	Unused	Used
O1	O1	red	1.40	1.00
a.		Vert. pair, imperf. betwn.	120.00	
O1B	O1	scarlet ('85)	1.40	1.00
O2	O1	olive brn ('87)	.90	.70
a.		Horiz. pair, imperf. betwn.		—
b.		Blue ruled lines on paper		
O3	O1	orange ('88)	2.50	.90
a.		Vert. pair, imperf. betwn.	110.00	
b.		Perf. 11	15.00	12.00
O4	O1	blue grn ('93)	1.40	.80
a.		Imperf., pair	15.00	12.00
b.		Perf. 11	15.00	12.00
		Nos. O1-O4 (5)	7.60	4.40

Pin-perf. 6

No.	Type	Description	Unused	Used
O5	O1	olive brown ('87)	100.00	50.00

Wmk. "Correos E U M" on every Vertical Line of Ten Stamps (152)

1894 *Perf. 5½*

No.	Type	Description	Unused	Used
O6	O1	ultra	3.00	2.75
a.		Vert. pair, imperf. horiz.	35.00	
b.		Imperf., pair	45.00	

Perf. 11, 12

No.	Type	Description	Unused	Used
O7	O1	ultra	1.75	1.60

Perf. 5½x11, 11x5½

No.	Type	Description	Unused	Used
O9	O1	ultra	12.00	8.00
		Nos. O6-O9 (3)	16.75	12.35

Regular Issues with Handstamped Overprint in Black

1895 Wmk. 152 *Perf. 12*

No.	Type	Description	Unused	Used
O10	A20	1c green	17.50	6.00
O11	A20	2c carmine	20.00	6.00
O12	A20	3c orange brn	17.50	6.00
O13	A21	4c red orange	26.00	12.00
a.		4c orange	42.50	14.00
O14	A22	5c ultra	35.00	12.00
O15	A23	10c lilac rose	32.50	3.00
O16	A21	12c olive brn	70.00	30.00
O17	A23	15c brt blue	42.50	18.00
O18	A23	20c brown rose	42.50	18.00
O19	A23	50c purple	90.00	42.50
O20	A24	1p brown	200.00	90.00
O21	A24	5p scarlet	475.00	250.00
O22	A24	10p deep blue	750.00	500.00
		Nos. O10-O22 (13)	1,819.	993.50

Similar stamps with red overprint were not officially placed in use. Nos. O10-O22 have a vertical grain or mesh to the paper.

1896-97 Wmk. 153

Black Overprint

No.	Type	Description	Unused	Used
O23	A20	1c green	60.00	10.00
O24	A20	2c carmine	60.00	12.00
O25	A20	3c orange brn	60.00	12.00
O26	A21	4c red orange	60.00	12.00
a.		4c orange	75.00	22.50
O27	A22	5c ultra	60.00	12.00
O28	A21	12c olive brn	80.00	30.00
O29	A23	15c brt blue	100.00	30.00
O29A	A23	50c purple	650.00	650.00
		Nos. O23-O29A (8)	1,130.	768.00

Nos. O23-O29A have a vertical grain or mesh to the paper.

1897 Wmk. 154 Black Overprint

No.	Type	Description	Unused	Used
O30	A20	1c green	100.00	30.00
O31	A20	2c scarlet	90.00	35.00
O33	A21	4c orange	125.00	60.00
O34	A22	5c ultra	100.00	35.00
O35	A21	12c olive brn	125.00	42.50
O36	A23	15c brt blue	160.00	42.50
O37	A23	20c brown rose	110.00	18.00
O38	A23	50c purple	150.00	30.00
O39	A24	1p brown	375.00	125.00
		Nos. O30-O39 (9)	1,335.	418.00

Nos. O30-O39 have a vertical grain or mesh to the paper.

1898 Unwmk. Black Overprint

No.	Type	Description	Unused	Used
O40	A20	1c green	35.00	9.50
O41	A20	2c scarlet	35.00	9.50
O42	A20	3c orange brn	35.00	9.50
O43	A21	4c orange	60.00	12.00
O44	A22	5c ultra	60.00	20.00
O45	A23	10c lilac rose	—	—
O46	A21	12c olive brn	125.00	30.00
O47	A23	15c brt blue	125.00	30.00
O48	A23	20c brown rose	225.00	75.00
O48A	A23	50c purple	375.00	150.00
O48B	A24	10p deep blue	*5,500.*	*5,500.*
		Nos. O40-O48A (10)	1,075.	345.50

The existence of No. O45 has been questioned by specialists. The editors would like to see authenticated evidence of this stamp.

See note following No. 291.

Black Overprint

1900 Wmk. 155 *Perf. 14, 15*

No.	Type	Description	Unused	Used
O49	A25	1c green	37.50	2.50
O50	A26	2c vermilion	50.00	4.00
O51	A27	3c yellow brn	50.00	2.50
O52	A28	5c dark blue	50.00	4.50
O53	A29	10c violet & org	65.00	5.50
O54	A30	15c lavender & cl	65.00	5.50
O55	A31	20c rose & dk bl	75.00	2.50
O56	A32	50c red lil & blk	150.00	25.00
O57	A33	1p blue & blk	300.00	25.00
O58	A34	5p carmine & blk	575.00	75.00
		Nos. O49-O58 (10)	1,418.	152.00

1903 Black Overprint

No.	Type	Description	Unused	Used
O59	A25	1c violet	35.00	4.00
O60	A26	2c green	35.00	4.00
O61	A35	4c carmine	65.00	2.50
O62	A28	5c orange	65.00	13.00
O63	A29	10c blue & org	70.00	4.00
O64	A32	50c carmine & blk	200.00	25.00
		Nos. O59-O64 (6)	470.00	52.50

Regular Issues Overprinted

1910 On Issues of 1899-1903

No.	Type	Description	Unused	Used
O65	A26	2c green	175.00	6.50
O66	A27	3c orange brn	175.00	4.00
O67	A35	4c carmine	200.00	10.00
O68	A28	5c orange	225.00	50.00
O69	A29	10c blue & org	200.00	4.00
O70	A30	15c lav & claret	225.00	6.50
O71	A31	20c rose & dk bl	275.00	3.00
O72	A32	50c carmine & blk	375.00	35.00
O73	A33	1p blue & blk	575.00	125.00
O74	A34	5p carmine & blk	200.00	125.00
		Nos. O65-O74 (10)	2,625.	369.00

1911 On Issue of 1910

No.	Type	Description	Unused	Used
O75	A36	1c violet	5.00	5.00
O76	A37	2c green	3.75	2.25
O77	A38	3c orange brn	5.00	2.50
O78	A39	4c carmine	5.50	2.25
O79	A40	5c orange	12.50	7.00
O80	A41	10c blue & org	5.50	2.50
O81	A42	15c gray bl & cl	13.00	8.50
O82	A43	20c red & blue	10.00	2.50
O83	A44	50c red brn & blk	35.00	15.00
O84	A45	1p blue & blk	60.00	25.00
O85	A46	5p carmine & blk	300.00	125.00
		Nos. O75-O85 (11)	455.25	197.50

Nos. 500 to 505 Overprinted

1915 Unwmk. *Rouletted 14½*

No.	Type	Description	Unused	Used
O86	A57	1c violet	1.00	*2.00*
O87	A58	2c green	1.00	*2.00*
O88	A59	3c brown	1.25	*2.00*
O89	A60	4c carmine	1.00	*2.00*
O90	A61	5c orange	1.00	*2.00*
O91	A62	10c ultra	1.25	*2.00*
		Nos. O86-O91 (6)	6.50	12.00

All values are known with inverted overprint. All values exist imperforate and part perforate but were not regularly issued in these forms.

On Nos. 506 to 514

1915-16 *Perf. 12*

No.	Type	Description	Unused	Used
O92	A57	1c violet	1.50	*2.00*
O93	A58	2c green	1.50	*2.00*
O94	A59	3c brown	1.50	*2.00*
O95	A60	4c carmine	1.50	*2.00*
a.		"CEATRO"	21.00	*30.00*
O96	A61	5c orange	1.50	*2.00*
O97	A62	10c ultra, type II	1.50	*2.00*
a.		Double overprint	*475.00*	
O98	A63	40c slate	8.00	*14.50*
a.		Inverted overprint	24.00	*25.00*
b.		Double overprint	40.00	
O99	A64	1p brown & blk	10.00	*14.50*
a.		Inverted overprint	27.50	27.50
O100	A65	5p claret & ultra	60.00	*60.00*
a.		Inverted overprint	80.00	
		Nos. O92-O100 (9)	87.00	101.00

Nos. O98 and O99 exist imperforate but probably were not issued in that form.

Preceding Issues Overprinted in Red, Blue or Black

On No. O74

1916 Wmk. 155

No.	Type	Description	Unused	Used
O101	A34	5p carmine & blk	900.00	

On Nos. O75 to O85

No.	Type	Description	Unused	Used
O102	A36	1c violet	6.50	
O103	A37	2c green	1.25	
O104	A38	3c orange brn (Bl)	1.75	
O105	A39	4c carmine (Bl)	7.00	
O106	A40	5c orange (Bl)	1.75	
O107	A41	10c blue & org	1.75	
O108	A42	15c gray bl & cl (Bk)	1.75	
O109	A43	20c red & bl (Bk)	1.90	
O110	A44	50c red brn & blk	200.00	
O111	A45	1p blue & blk	11.00	
O112	A46	5p carmine & blk	*3,250.*	
		Nos. O102-O111 (10)	234.65	

No. O102 with blue overprint is a trial color. Counterfeits exist of Nos. O110, O112.

Nos. 608, 610 to 612, 615 and 616 Overprinted Vertically in Red or Black

Thick Paper

1918 Unwmk. *Rouletted 14½*

O113 A68 1c violet (R) 60.00 35.00
O114 A69 2c gray grn (R) 65.00 35.00
O115 A70 3c bis brn (R) 60.00 35.00
O116 A71 4c carmine (Bk) 60.00 35.00
O117 A74 20c rose (Bk) 125.00 90.00
O118 A75 30c gray brn (R) 190.00 175.00

On Nos. 622-623
Medium Paper
Perf. 12

O119 A72 5c ultra (R) 40.00 40.00
O120 A73 10c blue (R) 35.00 25.00
a. Double overprint 400.00 *400.00*
Nos. O113-O120 (8) 635.00 470.00

Overprinted Horizontally in Red

On Nos. 626-628
Thin Paper

O121 A63 40c violet (R) 35.00 27.50
O122 A64 1p bl & blk (R) 85.00 70.00
O123 A65 5p grn & blk (R) *575.00 600.00*
Nos. O121-O123 (3) *695.00 697.50*

Nos. 608 and 610 to 615 Ovptd. Vertically Up in Red or Black

Thick Paper

1919 *Rouletted 14½*

O124 A68 1c dull vio (R) 6.00 6.00
a. "OFICIAN" 70.00 *80.00*
O125 A69 2c gray grn (R) 9.50 3.50
a. "OFICIAN" 70.00 *80.00*
O126 A70 3c bis brn (R) 14.00 6.00
a. "OFICIAN" 95.00 *100.00*
O127 A71 4c car (Bk) 29.00 13.00
c. "OFICIAN" —
O127A A72 5c ultra 200.00 125.00
b. "OFICIAN" *500.00*
O128 A73 10c blue (R) 9.50 2.50
a. "OFICIAN" 85.00 60.00
O129 A74 20c rose (Bk) 60.00 47.50
a. "OFICIAN" 140.00

On Nos. 618, 622
Perf. 12

O130 A68 1c dull violet (R) 47.50 47.50
a. "OFICIAN" 140.00 100.00
O131 A72 5c ultra (R) 47.50 22.50
a. "OFICIAN" 140.00 100.00

Overprinted Horizontally
On Nos. 626-627
Thin Paper

O132 A63 40c violet (R) 47.50 35.00
O133 A64 1p bl & blk (R) 60.00 50.00
Nos. O124-O133 (11) 530.50 358.50

Nos. 608 to 615 and 617 Ovptd. Vertically down in Black, Red or Blue

Size: 17½x3mm

1921 *Rouletted 14½*

O134 A68 1c gray (Bk) 30.00 12.00
a. 1c dull violet (Bk) 17.00 7.00
O135 A69 2c gray grn (R) 5.00 3.00
O136 A70 3c bis brn (R) 8.50 4.50
O137 A71 4c carmine (Bk) 27.50 21.00
O138 A72 5c ultra (R) 25.00 12.00
O139 A73 10c bl, reading down (R) 32.50 12.00
a. Overprint reading up 60.00 60.00
O140 A74 20c rose (R) 47.50 27.50
O141 A75 30c gray blk (R) 25.00 25.00

Overprinted Horizontally
On Nos. 626-628
Perf. 12

O142 A63 40c violet (R) 32.50 32.50
O143 A64 1p bl & blk (R) 25.00 25.00
O144 A65 5p grn & blk (Bk) *600.00 600.00*
Nos. O134-O144 (11) *858.50 774.50*

Nos. 609 to 615 Overprinted Vertically Down in Black

1921-30 *Rouletted 14½*

O145 A68 1c gray 5.00 2.50
a. 1c lilac gray 1.00 .70
O146 A69 2c gray green 1.75 .70
O147 A70 3c bister brn .80 .70
a. "OFICAL" 47.50 25.00
b. "OIFCIAL" 47.50 25.00
c. Double overprint 140.00
O148 A71 4c carmine 22.50 2.50
O149 A72 5c ultra 1.00 .70
O150 A73 10c blue 1.00 .70
a. "OIFCIAL" 50.00
O151 A74 20c brown rose 9.00 *9.50*
a. 20c rose 5.00 2.50

On No. 625
Perf. 12

O152 A75 30c gray black 7.25 2.50

Overprinted Horizontally
On Nos. 626, 628

O153 A63 40c violet 7.00 5.00
a. "OFICAL" 60.00 60.00
b. "OICIFAL" 60.00 60.00
c. Inverted overprint 90.00 *125.00*
O154 A65 5p grn & blk ('30) 375.00 *375.00*
Nos. O145-O154 (10) 430.30 *399.80*

Ovptd. Vertically Down in Red On Nos. 609, 610, 611, 613 and 614

1921-24 *Rouletted 14½*

O155 A68 1c lilac 1.60 1.00
O156 A69 2c gray green 1.50 .90
O157 A70 3c bister brown 4.00 1.00
O158 A72 5c ultra 1.60 .80
O159 A73 10c blue 35.00 3.50
a. Double overprint

On Nos. 624-625
Perf. 12

O160 A74 20c rose 7.25 1.60
O161 A75 30c gray black 19.00 5.00

Overprinted Horizontally
On Nos. 626-628

O162 A63 40c violet 14.00 7.50
a. Vert. pair, imperf. btwn.
O163 A64 1p blue & blk 35.00 25.00
O164 A65 5p green & blk 300.00 *300.00*

Overprinted Vertically Down in Blue on No. 612
Rouletted 14½

O165 A71 4c carmine 7.00 3.50
Nos. O155-O165 (11) 425.95 *349.80*

Same Overprint Vertically Down in Red on Nos. 635 and 637

1926-27 *Rouletted 14½*

O166 A80 3c bis brn, ovpt. horiz. 12.00 12.00
a. Period omitted 30.00 30.00
O167 A82 5c orange 27.50 *30.00*

Same Overprint Vertically Down in Blue or Red 0n Nos. 650, 651, 655 and 656
Wmk. 156

O168 A79 2c scarlet (Bl) 20.00 20.00
a. Overprint reading up 30.00 30.00
O169 A80 3c bis brn, ovpt. horiz. (R) 5.00 5.00
a. Inverted overprint 60.00
O170 A85 10c claret (Bl) 35.00 16.00
O171 A84 20c deep blue (R) 14.00 12.00
a. Overprint reading up 14.00 12.00

Overprinted Horizontally in Red On Nos. 643, 646-649
Perf. 12

O172 A81 4c green 6.00 6.00
O173 A83 30c dk grn 6.00 6.00
O174 A63 40c violet 16.00 16.00
a. Inverted overprint 80.00
O175 A87 50c olive brn 1.50 1.50
a. 50c yellow brown 18.00 18.00
O176 A88 1p red brn & bl 15.00 15.00
Nos. O168-O176 (9) 118.50 97.50

Same Overprint Horizontally on No. 651, Vertically Up on Nos. 650, 653-656, 666, RA1

1927-31 *Rouletted 14½*

O177 PT1 1c brown ('31) .70 *1.00*
O178 A79 2c scarlet .70 *1.00*
a. "OFICAIL" 30.00 30.00
b. Overprint reading down 1.50 *2.00*
O179 A80 3c bis brn 2.00 1.50
a. "OFICAIL" 40.00 30.00
O180 A82 4c green 1.50 1.00
a. "OFICAIL" 40.00 40.00
b. Overprint reading down 10.00 2.00
O181 A82 5c orange 4.00 3.00
a. Overprint reading down 4.00 2.50
O182 A94 8c orange 12.00 8.00
a. Overprint reading down 7.00 6.00
O183 A85 10c lake 2.00 2.00
a. Overprint reading down 2.00 2.00
O184 A84 20c dark blue 10.00 4.00
a. "OFICAIL" 40.00 40.00
b. Overprint reading down 20.00 20.00
Nos. O177-O184 (8) 32.90 21.50

Overprinted Vertically Up on #O186, Horizontally On Nos. 643 and 645 to 649

1927-33 *Perf. 12*

O185 A81 4c green 6.00 5.00
a. Inverted overprint 30.00 30.00
O186 A85 10c brown lake 55.00 45.00
O187 A83 30c dark green 1.40 1.00
a. Inverted overprint 30.00 30.00
b. Pair, tête bêche overprints 35.00 35.00
c. "OFICAIL" 35.00 35.00
O188 A63 40c violet 12.00 8.00
O189 A87 50c olive brn ('33) 3.25 *4.00*
O190 A88 1p red brn & bl 24.00 20.00
Nos. O185-O190 (6) 101.65 83.00

The overprint on No. O186 is vertical.

Nos. 320, 628, 633 Overprinted Horizontally

On Stamp No. 320

1927-28 Wmk. 155 *Perf. 14, 15*

O191 A46 5p car & blk (R) 175.00 *250.00*
O192 A46 5p car & blk (Bl) 175.00 *250.00*

Unwmk. *Perf. 12*

O193 A65 5p grn & blk (Bk) 375.00 *500.00*
a. Inverted overprint — —
O194 A78 10p blk brn & blk (Bl) 200.00 *300.00*

No. 320 Overprinted Horizontally

Wmk. 155 *Perf. 14*

O195 A46 5p carmine & blk 300.00

Nos. 650 and 655 Overprinted Horizontally

1928-29 Wmk. 156 *Rouletted 14½*
Size: 16x2½mm

O196 A79 2c dull red 18.00 12.00
O197 A85 10c rose lake 27.50 12.00

Nos. RA1, 650-651, 653-656 Overprinted

1932-33

O198 PT1 1c brown .70 *1.00*
O199 A79 2c dull red .80 *1.00*
O200 A80 3c bister brn 3.00 3.00
O201 A82 4c green 10.00 8.00
O202 A82 5c orange 12.00 8.00
O203 A85 10c rose lake 3.25 3.00
O204 A84 20c dark blue 15.00 10.00
a. Double overprint *200.00 90.00*
Nos. O198-O204 (7) 44.75 34.00

Nos. 651, 646-649 Overprinted Horizontally

1933 *Rouletted 14½*

O205 A80 3c bister brn 3.00 3.00

Perf. 12

O206 A83 30c dk green 8.00 3.00
O207 A63 40c violet 15.00 6.00
O208 A87 50c olive brn 2.50 3.00
a. "OFICIAL OFICIAL" 50.00 50.00
O209 A88 1p red brn & bl, type I 3.00 3.00
a. Type II 2.75 *3.50*

Overprinted Vertically On No. 656
Rouletted 14½

O210 A84 20c dark blue 18.00 10.00
Nos. O205-O210 (6) 49.50 28.00

Nos. RA1, 651, 653, 654, 683 Overprinted Horizontally

1934-37 *Rouletted 14½*
Size: 13x2mm

O211 PT1 1c brown 5.00 *6.00*
O212 A80 3c bister brn .70 .70
O213 A82 4c green 12.00 10.00
O214 A82 5c orange .70 .70
O215 A96 15c dk blue ('37) 1.00 1.00
Nos. O211-O215 (5) 19.40 18.40

See No. O217a.

Same Overprint on Nos. 687A-692

1934-37 *Perf. 10½*

O216 PT1 1c brown ('37) 1.00 *1.25*
O217 A79 2c scarlet 1.00 *1.50*
a. On No. 650 (error) 350.00
b. Double overprint 275.00
O218 A82 4c green ('35) 1.40 1.60
O219 A85 10c brown lake 1.00 1.00
O220 A84 20c dk blue ('37) 1.25 1.25
O221 A83 30c dk bl grn ('37) 2.00 2.00

On Nos. 647 and 649
Perf. 12, 11½x12

O222 A63 40c violet 3.00 3.50
O223 A88 1p red brn & bl (I) 5.00 *6.00*
a. Type II 4.00 4.00
Nos. O216-O223 (8) 15.65 18.10

On Nos. 707 to 709, 712, 715, 716, 717, 718 and 719

O224 A108 1c orange 2.00 *4.00*
O225 A109 2c green 1.25 *2.00*
O226 A110 4c carmine 1.25 *1.40*
O227 A112 10c violet 1.25 *2.50*
O228 A114 20c ultra 1.60 *2.50*
O229 A115 30c lake 2.00 *4.00*
O230 A116 40c red brown 2.50 *4.00*
O231 A117 50c black 2.75 *2.75*
O232 A118 1p dk brn & org 8.00 *12.00*
Nos. O224-O232 (9) 22.60 *35.15*

POSTAL TAX STAMPS

Morelos Monument — PT1

Rouletted 14½

1925 Engr. Wmk. 156

RA1 PT1 1c brown .35 .25
a. Imperf. 30.00

1926 ***Perf. 12***

RA2 PT1 1c brown	.75	*5.00*
a. Booklet pane of 2	12.00	

1925 Unwmk. *Rouletted 14½*

RA3 PT1 1c brown	75.00	19.00

It was obligatory to add a stamp of type PT1 to the regular postage on every article of domestic mail matter. The money obtained from this source formed a fund to combat a plague of locusts.

In 1931, 1c stamps of type PT1 were discontinued as Postal Tax stamps. It was subsequently used for the payment of postage on drop letters (announcement cards and unsealed circulars) to be delivered in the city of cancellation. See No. 687A.

For overprints see Nos. O177, O198, O211, O216, RA4.

No. RA1 Overprinted in Red

1929 **Wmk. 156**

RA4 PT1 1c brown	.35	.25
a. Overprint reading down	75.00	75.00

There were two settings of this overprint. They may be distinguished by the two lines being spaced 4mm or 6mm apart.

The money from sales of this stamp was devoted to child welfare work.

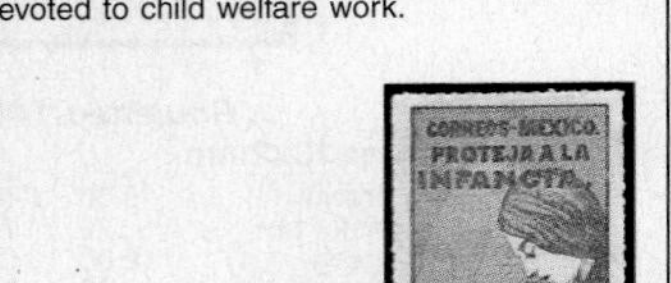

Mother and Child — PT3

1929 Litho. *Rouletted 13, 13½*

RA5 PT3 1c violet	.35	.25

PT4

1929 Size: 18x24½mm Unwmk.

RA6 PT4 2c deep green	.40	.25
RA7 PT4 5c brown	.40	.25
a. Imperf., pair	60.00	60.00

For surcharges see Nos. RA10-RA11.

PT5

Two types of 1c:

Type I — Background lines continue through lettering of top inscription. Denomination circle hangs below second background line. Paper and gum white.

Type II — Background lines cut away behind some letters. Circle rests on second background line. Paper and gum yellowish.

1929 Size: 19x25¼mm

RA8 PT5 1c violet, type I	.35	.25
a. Booklet pane of 4	10.00	
b. Booklet pane of 2	18.00	
c. Type II	.40	.25
d. Imperf., pair	50.00	50.00
RA9 PT5 2c deep green	.65	.25
a. Imperf., pair	12.00	

The use of these stamps, in addition to the regular postage, was compulsory. The money obtained from their sale was used for child welfare work.

For surcharge see No. RA12.

Nos. RA6, RA7, RA9 Surcharged

1930

RA10 PT4 1c on 2c dp grn	.75	.40
RA11 PT4 1c on 5c brown	1.00	.60
RA12 PT5 1c on 2c dp grn	2.00	1.00
Nos. RA10-RA12 (3)	3.75	2.00

Used stamps exist with surcharge double or reading down.

No. 423 Overprinted

1931, Jan. 30 Wmk. 155 *Perf. 14*

RA13 A36 1c dull violet	.40	.40
a. "PRO INFANCIA" double	50.00	

Indian Mother and Child — PT6

Wmk. 156

1934, Sept. 1 Engr. *Perf. 10½*

RA13B PT6 1c dull orange	.30	.25

Mosquito Attacking Man — PT7

1939 Photo. Wmk. 156 *Perf. 14*

RA14 PT7 1c Prus blue	1.50	.25
a. Imperf.	3.00	3.00

This stamp was obligatory on all mail, the money being used to aid in a drive against malaria.

See Nos. RA16, RA19 in Scott Standard catalogue, Vol. 4.

PROVISIONAL ISSUES

During the struggle led by Juarez to expel the Emperor Maximilian, installed June, 1864 by Napoleon III and French troops, a number of towns when free of Imperial forces issued provisional postage stamps. Maximilian was captured and executed June 19, 1867, but provisional issues continued current for a time pending re-establishment of Republican Government.

Campeche

A southern state in Mexico, comprising the western part of the Yucatan peninsula.

A1

White Paper
Numerals in Black

1876 Handstamped *Imperf.*

1	A1 5c gray blue & blue	*2,000.*
2	A1 25c gray blue & blue	*1,100.*
3	A1 50c gray blue & blue	*4,500.*

The stamps printed in blue-black and blue on yellowish paper, formerly listed as issued in 1867, are now known to be an unofficial production of later years. They are reprints, but produced without official sanction.

Chiapas

A southern state in Mexico, bordering on Guatemala and the Pacific Ocean.

A1

1866 Typeset

1	A1 ½r blk, *gray bl*	*2,000.*	*1,300.*
2	A1 1r blk, *lt grn*		*850.*
3	A1 2r blk, *rose*		*900.*
4	A1 4r blk, *lt buff*		*2,000.*
a.	Vertical half used as 2r on cover		*3,000.*
5	A1 8r blk, *rose*		*15,000.*
a.	Quarter used as 2r on cover		*4,000.*
b.	Half used as 4r on cover		*5,000.*

Chihuahua

A city of northern Mexico and capital of the State of Chihuahua.

A1

A2

1872 Handstamped

1	A1 12(c) black	*3,000.*
	On cover	—
2	A2 25(c) black	*3,000.*

Cuautla

A town in the state of Morelos.

A1

1867 Handstamped

1	A1 (2r) black	*7,000.*

All known examples on cover are uncanceled. Examples are known without the "73" inside the oval.

Cuernavaca

A city of Mexico, just south of the capital, and the capital of the State of Morelos.

A1

1867 Handstamped

1	A1 (1r) black	*1,750.*
2	A1 (2r) black	*40,000.*

No. 1 was canceled at Cuernavaca with the district name overprint. Supplies of overprinted stamps were sent to the Tetecala and Yguala sub-offices, where they were canceled with the usual local postmarks.

No. 2 was created by doubling the impression of the basic stamp and applying the district name overprint twice.

Unused examples of Nos. 1 and 2 do not exist.

Counterfeits exist.

Guadalajara

A city of Mexico and capital of the State of Jalisco.

A1

Dated "1867"
1st Printing
Medium Wove Paper

1867 Handstamped *Imperf.*

1	A1	Medio r blk, *white*	350.00	250.00
2	A1	un r blk, *gray bl*	750.00	350.00
a.		Overprinted "Cd. Guzman"		*1,000.*
3	A1	un r blk, *dk bl*		450.00
4	A1	un r blk, *white*		250.00
a.		Overprinted "Cd. Guzman"		*750.00*
5	A1	2r blk, *dk grn*	250.00	21.00
a.		Overprinted "Cd. Guzman"		*500.00*
6	A1	2r blk, *white*		125.00
a.		Overprinted "Cd. Guzman"		*400.00*
b.		Double print		250.00
7	A1	4r blk, *rose*	250.00	*300.00*
a.		Half used as 2r on cover		500.00
b.		Overprinted "Cd. Guzman"		*900.00*
8	A1	4r blk, *white*		500.00
a.		Half used as 2r on cover		2,500.
9	A1	un p blk, *lilac*	250.00	*300.00*

Serrate Perf.

10	A1	un r blk, *gray bl*	*900.00*
11	A1	2r blk, *dk grn*	700.00
12	A1	4r blk, *rose*	350.00
12A	A1	un p blk, *lilac*	*1,750.*

2nd Printing
No Period after "2" or "4"
Thin Quadrille Paper
Imperf

13	A1	2r blk, *green*	30.00	20.00
a.		Half used as 1r on cover		400.00

Serrate Perf.

14	A1	2r blk, *green*	225.00

Thin Laid Batonné Paper
Imperf

15	A1	2r blk, *green*	45.00	24.00

Serrate Perf.

16	A1	2r blk, *green*	225.00

3rd Printing
Capital "U" in "Un" on 1r, 1p
Period after "2" and "4"
Thin Wove Paper
Imperf

16A	A1	Un r blk, *white*		125.00
17	A1	Un r blk, *blue*		90.00
17A	A1	Un r blk, *lilac*	100.00	
18	A1	2r blk, *rose*		50.00
18A	A1	4r blk, *blue*	500.00	*1,000.*
18B	A1	Un p blue	1,750.	

Serrate Perf.

19	A1	Un r blk, *blue*	300.00
19A	A1	2r blk, *rose*	*750.00*
19B	A1	4r blue	*500.00*

Thin Quadrille Paper
Imperf

20	A1	2r blk, *rose*	42.50	42.50
21	A1	4r blk, *blue*	15.00	30.00
22	A1	4r blk, *white*	200.00	
23	A1	Un p blk, *lilac*	15.00	60.00
24	A1	Un p blk, *rose*	65.00	
24A	A1	Un p blk, *white*	1,500.	

Serrate Perf

24B A1 2r blk, *rose* *500.00*
25 A1 Un p blk, *lilac* 750.00 750.00
25A A1 Un p blk, *rose* 700.00 300.00

Thin Laid Batonné Paper

Imperf

26 A1 Un r blk, *green* 22.50 17.50
27 A1 2r blk, *rose* 27.50 22.50
27A A1 2r blk, *green* 47.50
28 A1 4r blk, *blue* 17.50 42.50
29 A1 4r blk, *white* 100.00
30 A1 Un p blk, *lilac* 30.00 52.50
31 A1 Un p blk, *rose* 65.00

Serrate Perf.

32 A1 Un r blk, *green* 300.00
33 A1 2r blk, *rose* 400.00 *200.00*
34 A1 4r blk, *blue* 425.00
34A A1 4r blk, *white* *1,750.*
34B A1 Un p blk, *lilac* 700.00

Thin Oblong Quadrille Paper

Imperf

35 A1 Un r blk, *blue* 250.00 22.50
35A A1 Un r blk, *white* 1,500.
36 A1 4r blk, *blue* 600.00

Serrate Perf.

37 A1 Un r blk, *blue* 300.00

4th Printing Dated "1868" Wove Paper

1868 ***Imperf.***

38 A1 2r blk, *lilac* 30.00 14.00
a. Half used as 1r on cover 500.00
39 A1 2r blk, *rose* 52.50 65.00

Serrate Perf.

40 A1 2r blk, *lilac* *300.00*
41 A1 2r blk, *rose* 750.00 300.00

Laid Batonné Paper

Imperf

42 A1 un r blk, *green* 12.50 12.50
43 A1 2r blk, *lilac* 12.50 12.50
a. Half used as 1r on cover 1,500.
43A A1 2r blk, *rose* 750.00

Serrate Perf.

44 A1 un r blk, *green* 250.00 200.00
44A A1 2r blk, *rose* 500.00

Quadrille Paper.

Imperf

45 A1 2r blk, *lilac* 25.00 14.00

Serrate Perf.

46 A1 2r blk, *lilac* 300.00 300.00

Laid Paper

Imperf

47 A1 un r blk, *green* 13.00 17.00
a. Watermarked "LA + F" *750.00* *1,000.*
b. "nu" instead of "un" 750.00
c. Dated "1863" 300.00
48 A1 2r blk, *lilac* 32.50 32.50
49 A1 2r blk, *rose* 37.50 37.50

Serrate Perf.

50 A1 un r blk, *green* 750.00 300.00
51 A1 2r blk, *rose* 475.00

Counterfeits of Nos. 1-51 abound.

Merida

A city of southeastern Mexico, capital of the State of Yucatan.

Mexico No. 521 Surcharged **25**

1916 **Wmk. 155** ***Perf. 14***

1 A40 25(c) on 5c org, on cover *500.00*

The G.P.DE.M. overprint reads down.

Authorities consider the Monterrey, Morelia and Patzcuaro stamps to be bogus.

Tlacotalpan

A village in the state of Veracruz.

A1

Handstamped Monogram, Value in Manuscript

1856, Oct.

1 A1 ½(r) black *30,000.*

Research suggests that this stamp was not an officially sanctioned issue, but was instead part of a postal fraud orchestrated by Tlacotalpan postmaster Angel Fernando and his assistant Ignacio Crespo to cover theft of funds in that post office. The initials IMC in the stamp are most likely those of Crespo.

REVOLUTIONARY ISSUES

SINALOA

A northern state in Mexico, bordering on the Pacific Ocean. Stamps were issued by a provisional government.

Coat of Arms — A1

1929 **Unwmk.** **Litho.** ***Perf. 12***

1 A1 10c blk, red & bl 5.00
a. Tête bêche pair 35.00
2 A1 20c blk, red & gray 5.00

Just as Nos. 1 and 2 were ready to be placed on sale the state was occupied by the Federal forces and the stamps could not be used. At a later date a few stamps were canceled by favor.

A recent find included a number of errors or printer's waste.

YUCATAN

A southeastern state of Mexico.

Chalchihuitlicue, Nahuatl Water Goddess — A1

"Casa de Monjas" — A2

Temple of the Tigers — A3

Without Gum

1924 **Unwmk.** **Litho.** ***Imperf.***

1 A1 5c violet 10.00 15.00
2 A2 10c carmine 40.00 50.00
3 A3 50c olive green 175.00

Perf. 12

4 A1 5c violet 50.00 60.00
5 A2 10c carmine 50.00 75.00
6 A3 50c olive green 200.00

Nos. 3 and 6 were not regularly issued.

MIDDLE CONGO

ˈmi-dᵊl ˈkäŋ-(ˌ)gō

LOCATION — Western Africa at the Equator, bordering on the Atlantic Ocean
GOVT. — French Colony
AREA — 166,069
POP. — 746,805 (1936)
CAPITAL — Brazzaville

In 1910 Middle Congo, formerly a part of French Congo, was declared a separate colony. It was grouped with Gabon and the Ubangi-Shari and Chad Territories and officially designated French Equatorial Africa. This group became a single administrative unit in 1934. See Gabon.

100 Centimes = 1 Franc

Leopard — A1

Bakalois Woman — A2

Coconut Grove — A3

Perf. 14x13½

1907-22 **Typo.** **Unwmk.**

1 A1 1c ol gray & brn .35 .45
Never hinged .70
On cover 87.50
a. Perf 11 40.00
Never hinged 55.00
b. Chalky paper .35 .45
Never hinged .70
On cover 87.50
2 A1 2c vio & brn .35 .45
Never hinged .70
On cover 87.50
a. Chalky paper .35 .45
Never hinged .70
On cover 87.50
3 A1 4c blue & brn .70 *.85*
Never hinged 1.40
On cover 87.50
a. Perf 11 40.00
Never hinged 55.00
b. Chalky paper .70 .85
Never hinged 1.40
On cover 87.50
4 A1 5c dk grn & bl .70 .70
Never hinged 1.40
On cover 35.00
a. Perf 11 40.00
Never hinged 55.00
b. Chalky paper .70 .70
Never hinged 1.40
On cover 35.00
5 A1 5c yel & bl ('22) .70 .75
Never hinged 1.20
On cover 25.00
6 A1 10c car & bl 1.00 .70
Never hinged 1.40
On cover 20.00
a. Perf 11 40.00
Never hinged 55.00
b. Chalky paper 1.00 .70
Never hinged 1.40
On cover 20.00
7 A1 10c dp grn & bl grn ('22) 4.00 4.00
Never hinged 6.25
On cover 50.00
a. Imperf pair 300.00
8 A1 15c brn vio & rose ('17) 2.10 1.00
Never hinged 3.50
On cover 20.00
9 A1 20c brown & bl 3.50 2.75
Never hinged 4.50
On cover 35.00
a. Chalky paper 3.50 2.75
Never hinged 4.50
On cover 35.00
10 A2 25c blue & grn 1.40 1.10
Never hinged 2.50
On cover 40.00
On cover, single franking 105.00
a. Chalky paper 1.40 1.10
Never hinged 2.75
On cover 40.00
11 A2 25c bl grn & gray ('22) 1.00 1.00
Never hinged 1.60
On cover 14.00
12 A2 30c scar & grn 2.10 1.75
Never hinged 3.50
On cover 45.00
On cover, single franking 87.50
a. Chalky paper 2.10 1.75
Never hinged 3.50
On cover 45.00
13 A2 30c dp rose & rose ('22) 1.75 *2.10*
Never hinged 2.75
On cover 45.00
On cover, single franking 80.00
14 A2 35c vio brn & bl 1.75 1.40
Never hinged 2.10
On cover 50.00
On cover, single franking 75.00
15 A2 40c dl grn & brn 1.75 1.75
Never hinged 2.75
On cover 55.00
On cover, single franking 105.00
a. Chalky paper 1.75 1.75
Never hinged 2.75
On cover 55.00
16 A2 45c violet & red 6.00 3.50
Never hinged 11.50
On cover 62.50
On cover, single franking 87.50
a. Chalky paper 6.00 3.50
Never hinged 11.50
On cover 62.50
17 A2 50c bl grn & red 2.10 2.10
Never hinged 3.50
On cover 70.00
On cover, single franking 140.00
a. Perf 11 37.50
Never hinged 55.00
b. Chalky paper 2.75 2.40
Never hinged 5.50
On cover 75.00
18 A2 50c bl & grn ('22) 1.75 2.10
Never hinged 3.50
On cover 37.50
On cover, single franking 75.00
19 A2 75c brown & bl 8.50 5.50
Never hinged 13.00
On cover 62.50
On cover, single franking 140.00
a. Chalky paper 8.50 5.00
Never hinged 13.00
On cover 62.50
20 A3 1fr dp grn & vio 13.00 9.00
Never hinged 19.00
On cover 75.00
On cover, single franking 175.00
a. Chalky paper 14.00 9.00
Never hinged 21.00
On cover 75.00
21 A3 2fr vio & gray grn 14.00 10.00
Never hinged 21.00
On cover 87.50
On cover, single franking 190.00
a. Chalky paper 14.00 10.00
Never hinged 21.00
On cover 87.50
22 A3 5fr blue & rose 42.50 37.50
Never hinged 70.00
On cover 140.00
On cover, single franking 250.00
a. Perf 11 70.00
Never hinged 110.00
b. Chalky paper 42.50 37.50
Never hinged 70.00
On cover 140.00
Nos. 1-22 (22) 111.00 90.45

For stamps of types A1-A3 in changed colors, see Chad and Ubangi-Shari. French Congo A4-A6 are similar but inscribed "Congo Francais."

For overprints and surcharges see Nos. 23-60, B1-B2.

Stamps and Types of 1907-22 Overprinted in Black, Blue or Red

1924-30

23 A1 1c ol gray & brn .35 .50
Never hinged .70
On cover 62.50
a. Double surcharge 150.00
Never hinged 175.00
24 A1 2c violet & brn .35 .50
Never hinged .70
On cover 62.50
a. Chalky paper .30 .50
Never hinged .45
On cover 62.50
25 A1 4c blue & brn .35 .50
Never hinged .70
On cover 62.50
a. Chalky paper .35 .50
Never hinged .70
On cover 62.50
b. Imperf pair 350.00
26 A1 5c yellow & bl .50 .50
Never hinged .70
On cover 27.50
27 A1 10c grn & bl grn (R) 1.10 .35
Never hinged 1.40
On cover 20.00
28 A1 10c car & gray ('25) .35 *.50*
Never hinged .70
On cover 25.00
29 A1 15c brn vio & rose (Bl) .70 .50
Never hinged 1.00
On cover 16.00
a. Double surcharge 175.00
Never hinged 175.00
30 A1 20c brown & blue .70 .65
Never hinged 1.40
On cover 27.50
a. Chalky paper .70 .65
Never hinged 1.40
On cover 27.50
31 A1 20c bl grn & yel grn ('26) .35 .35
Never hinged .70
On cover 19.00
32 A1 20c dp brn & rose lil ('27) 1.40 1.00
Never hinged 2.10
On cover 37.50

Nos. 10-22 Overprinted in Black, Red (R), and Blue (Bl)

33 A2 25c bl grn & gray 1.00 .40
Never hinged 1.40
On cover 14.00
34 A2 30c rose & pale rose (Bl) 1.40 .70
Never hinged 2.75
On cover 45.00
On cover, single franking 75.00
35 A2 30c gray & bl vio (R) ('25) .70 .65
Never hinged 1.00
On cover 12.50
36 A2 30c dk grn & grn ('27) 1.75 1.40
Never hinged 2.75
On cover 37.50
37 A2 35c choc & bl .70 .70
Never hinged 1.40
On cover 45.00
On cover, single franking 75.00
38 A2 40c ol grn & brn 1.40 1.40
Never hinged 2.75
On cover 50.00
On cover, single franking 80.00
a. Double overprint 300.00
Never hinged 425.00
39 A2 45c vio & pale red (Bl) 1.40 1.00
Never hinged 2.75
On cover 16.00
On cover, single franking 27.50
a. Inverted overprint 200.00
Never hinged 325.00
40 A2 50c blue & grn (R) 1.40 1.00
Never hinged 2.75
On cover 15.00
On cover, single franking 22.50
41 A2 50c org & blk ('25) .70 .65
Never hinged 1.00
On cover 12.50
a. Without overprint 220.00 *225.00*
Never hinged 300.00
42 A2 65c org brn & bl ('27) 2.75 2.10
Never hinged 4.25
On cover 30.00
On cover, single franking 62.50
43 A2 75c brown & blue 1.40 1.40
Never hinged 2.10
On cover 35.00
On cover, single franking 75.00
44 A2 90c brn red & pink ('30) 4.25 3.50
Never hinged 7.00
On cover 55.00
On cover, single franking 100.00
45 A3 1fr green & vio 1.40 1.40
Never hinged 2.75
On cover 35.00
On cover, single franking 70.00
a. Double overprint 275.00
Never hinged 425.00
46 A3 1.10fr vio & brn ('28) 3.50 4.25
Never hinged 5.50
On cover 160.00
On cover, single franking 340.00
47 A3 1.50fr ultra & bl ('30) 7.00 5.00
Never hinged 10.00
On cover 50.00
On cover, single franking 87.50
48 A3 2fr vio & gray grn 2.10 1.40
Never hinged 2.75
On cover 62.50
On cover, single franking 125.00
a. Chalky paper 2.10 1.40
Never hinged 2.75
On cover 62.50
b. Imperf pair 300.00
49 A3 3fr red violet ('30) 7.00 5.00
Never hinged 10.00
On cover 87.50
On cover, single franking 170.00
50 A3 5fr blue & rose 5.00 5.00
Never hinged 7.50
On cover 75.00
On cover, single franking 140.00
a. Chalky paper 5.00 4.50
Never hinged 7.50
On cover 75.00
Nos. 23-50 (28) 51.00 42.30

Nos. 48 and 50 Surcharged with New Values

1924

51 A3 25c on 2fr vio & gray grn 1.00 1.00
Never hinged 1.75
On cover 16.00
52 A3 25c on 5fr bl & rose (Bl) 1.25 1.25
Never hinged 2.00
On cover 16.00
a. Chalky paper 1.25 1.25
Never hinged 2.00
On cover 16.00

Types of 1924-27 Surcharged with New Values in Black or Red

1925-27

53 A3 65c on 1fr red org & ol brn 1.00 1.00
Never hinged 1.75
On cover 75.00
On cover, single franking 170.00
a. Without surcharge 275.00
Never hinged 425.00
54 A3 85c on 1fr red org & ol brn 1.00 1.00
Never hinged 1.75
On cover 62.50
On cover, single franking 125.00
a. Double surcharge 175.00
Never hinged 260.00
55 A2 90c on 75c brn red & rose red ('27) 2.00 *2.40*
Never hinged 3.50
On cover 62.50
On cover, single franking 110.00
56 A3 1.25fr on 1fr dl bl & ultra (R) 1.40 1.40
Never hinged 2.10
On cover 70.00
On cover, single franking 140.00
a. Without surcharge 200.00 200.00
Never hinged 300.00
57 A3 1.50fr on 1fr ultra & bl ('27) 2.00 2.00
Never hinged 3.50
On cover 55.00
On cover, single franking 100.00
a. Without surcharge 200.00 *200.00*
Never hinged 315.00
58 A3 3fr on 5fr org brn & dl red ('27) 4.00 *4.00*
Never hinged 7.00
On cover 105.00
On cover, single franking 225.00
a. Without surcharge 275.00
Never hinged 425.00
b. Period after "F" omitted 24.00 24.00
Never hinged 40.00
59 A3 10fr on 5fr ver & bl grn ('27) 13.00 13.00
Never hinged 19.00
On cover 125.00
On cover, single franking 225.00
60 A3 20fr on 5fr org brn & vio ('27) 13.50 13.50
Never hinged 21.00
On cover 140.00
On cover, single franking 275.00
a. Period after "F" omitted 40.00 40.00
Never hinged 65.00
Nos. 53-60 (8) 37.90 38.30

Bars cover old values on Nos. 56-60.

Common Design Types pictured following the introduction.

Colonial Exposition Issue
Common Design Types

1931 **Engr.** ***Perf. 12½***
Name of Country in Black

61 CD70 40c deep green 4.00 4.00
Never hinged 7.00
On cover 105.00
62 CD71 50c violet 5.50 5.50
Never hinged 7.25
On cover 87.50
63 CD72 90c red orange 5.50 5.50
Never hinged 7.25
On cover 150.00
On cover, single franking 225.00
64 CD73 1.50fr dull blue 5.50 5.50
Never hinged 7.25
On cover 140.00
On cover, single franking 210.00
Nos. 61-64 (4) 20.50 20.50

Viaduct at Mindouli A4

Pasteur Institute at Brazzaville A5

Government Building, Brazzaville — A6

1933 **Photo.** ***Perf. 13½***

65 A4 1c lt brown .25 .25
Never hinged .35
On cover 27.50
66 A4 2c dull blue .25 .25
Never hinged .35
On cover 27.50
67 A4 4c olive grn .30 .30
Never hinged .70
On cover 25.00
68 A4 5c red violet .50 .35
Never hinged .70
On cover 14.00
69 A4 10c slate .70 .40
Never hinged 1.40
On cover 16.00
70 A4 15c dk violet 1.40 1.00
Never hinged 3.50
On cover 22.50
71 A4 20c red, *pink* 8.50 6.00
Never hinged 14.00
On cover 45.00
72 A4 25c orange 1.00 1.00
Never hinged 2.10
On cover 27.50
73 A4 30c yellow grn 2.50 1.75
Never hinged 3.50
On cover 37.50
74 A5 40c orange brn 2.50 1.40
Never hinged 3.50
On cover 11.00
75 A5 45c blk, *green* 2.50 1.75
Never hinged 3.50
On cover 55.00
76 A5 50c black violet .90 .70
Never hinged 2.10
On cover 7.50
77 A5 65c brn red, *grn* 2.50 1.75
Never hinged 3.50
On cover 87.50
78 A5 75c black, *pink* 13.00 9.50
Never hinged 25.00
On cover 50.00
79 A5 90c carmine 2.50 1.75
Never hinged 3.50
On cover 45.00
On cover, single franking 125.00
80 A5 1fr dark red 1.00 .70
Never hinged 2.10
On cover 35.00
On cover, single franking 50.00
81 A5 1.25fr Prus blue 2.10 1.40
Never hinged 3.50
On cover 35.00
On cover, single franking 95.00
82 A5 1.50fr dk blue 14.00 7.00
Never hinged 21.00
On cover 75.00
On cover, single franking 190.00
83 A6 1.75fr dk violet 2.75 1.40
Never hinged 5.00
On cover 35.00
On cover, single franking 50.00
84 A6 2fr grnsh blk 2.10 1.40
Never hinged 4.00
On cover 35.00
On cover, single franking 62.50
85 A6 3fr orange 7.00 4.00
Never hinged 10.00
On cover 55.00
On cover, single franking 110.00
86 A6 5fr slate blue 35.00 25.00
Never hinged 52.50
On cover 140.00
On cover, single franking 240.00
87 A6 10fr black 50.00 35.00
Never hinged 95.00
On cover 170.00
On cover, single franking 275.00
88 A6 20fr dark brown 35.00 27.50
Never hinged 62.50
On cover 170.00
On cover, single franking 300.00
Nos. 65-88 (24) 188.25 131.55

SEMI-POSTAL STAMPS

No. 6 Surcharged in Black

1916 **Unwmk.** ***Perf. 14x13½***

B1 A1 10c + 5c car & blue 1.40 1.40
Never hinged 2.50
On cover 70.00
a. Double surcharge 140.00 140.00
Never hinged 210.00
b. Inverted surcharge 120.00 120.00
Never hinged 185.00
c. "c" omitted 50.00 50.00
Never hinged 75.00
d. Period below "c" omitted 45.00 45.00
Never hinged 70.00
e. As "a," One inverted 175.00 175.00
Never hinged 260.00
f. In pair with unsurcharged stamp 360.00
Never hinged 550.00

A printing with the surcharge placed lower and more to the left was made and used in Ubangi.

No. 6 Surcharged in Red

B2 A1 10c + 5c car & blue 1.40 1.40
Never hinged 2.50
On cover 70.00

POSTAGE DUE STAMPS

Postage Due Stamps of France Overprinted

1928 **Unwmk.** ***Perf. 14x13½***

J1 D2 5c light blue .50 *.70*
Never hinged .70
On cover 95.00
J2 D2 10c gray brn .60 *.70*
Never hinged 1.00
On cover 95.00
J3 D2 20c olive grn 1.00 *1.40*
Never hinged 1.75
On cover 95.00
J4 D2 25c brt rose 1.40 *1.75*
Never hinged 2.50
On cover 100.00
J5 D2 30c lt red 1.40 *1.75*
Never hinged 2.50
On cover 100.00
J6 D2 45c blue grn 1.40 *1.75*
Never hinged 2.75
On cover 105.00
J7 D2 50c brown vio 1.40 *1.75*
Never hinged 2.75
On cover 110.00
a. Period after "F" omitted 14.00 *17.50*
Never hinged 25.00
J8 D2 60c yellow brn 2.50 2.75
Never hinged 4.00
On cover 120.00
J9 D2 1fr red brn 2.50 *2.75*
Never hinged 4.00
On cover 125.00
J10 D2 2fr orange red 3.50 *4.00*
Never hinged 5.50
On cover 140.00
J11 D2 3fr brt violet 5.00 *7.00*
Never hinged 10.00
On cover 160.00
Nos. J1-J11 (11) 21.20 26.30

Village on Ubangi, Dance Mask — D3

Steamer on Ubangi River — D4

1930 ***Typo.***

J12 D3 5c dp bl & ol .70 *1.40*
Never hinged 1.40
On cover 37.50
J13 D3 10c dp red & brn 1.40 *1.40*
Never hinged 2.10
On cover 37.50
J14 D3 20c green & brn 2.75 *2.75*
Never hinged 4.00
On cover 37.50
J15 D3 25c lt bl & brn 3.50 *3.50*
Never hinged 5.50
On cover 45.00
J16 D3 30c bis brn & Prus bl 5.00 *5.00*
Never hinged 7.00
On cover 45.00
J17 D3 45c Prus bl & ol 6.00 *5.50*
Never hinged 10.00
On cover 50.00
J18 D3 50c red vio & brn 5.50 *6.00*
Never hinged 9.00
On cover 50.00
J19 D3 60c gray lil & bl blk 8.50 *9.00*
Never hinged 12.50
On cover 55.00
J20 D4 1fr bis brn & bl blk 10.00 *14.00*
Never hinged 17.50
On cover 70.00
J21 D4 2fr violet & brn 14.00 *14.00*
Never hinged 21.00
On cover 80.00
J22 D4 3fr dk red & brn 12.00 *10.00*
Never hinged 21.00
On cover 95.00
Nos. J12-J22 (11) 69.35 *72.55*

Rubber Trees and Djoué River — D5

1933 **Photo.** ***Perf. 13½***

J23 D5 5c apple green .70 .70
Never hinged 1.00
On cover 37.50
J24 D5 10c dk bl, *bl* .70 .70
Never hinged 1.00
On cover 37.50

J25 D5 20c red, *yel* 1.40 1.40
Never hinged 2.10
On cover 37.50
J26 D5 25c chocolate 1.40 1.40
Never hinged 2.10
On cover 37.50
J27 D5 30c orange red 1.75 *2.10*
Never hinged 2.50
On cover 45.00
J28 D5 45c dk violet 1.75 *2.10*
Never hinged 2.50
On cover 45.00
J29 D5 50c gray black 2.50 *2.75*
Never hinged 3.50
On cover 50.00
J30 D5 60c blk, *orange* 3.75 *4.00*
Never hinged 6.25
On cover 50.00
J31 D5 1fr brown rose 5.50 *6.25*
Never hinged 8.50
On cover 62.50
J32 D5 2fr orange yel 7.00 *8.50*
Never hinged 9.75
On cover 70.00
J33 D5 3fr Prus blue 12.00 *15.00*
Never hinged 17.00
On cover 87.50
Nos. J23-J33 (11) 38.45 44.90

MOHELI

mo-'ā-lē

LOCATION — One of the Comoro Islands, situated in the Mozambique Channel midway between Madagascar and Mozambique (Africa)
GOVT. — French Colony
AREA — 89 sq. mi.
POP. — 4,000
CAPITAL — Fomboni
See Comoro Islands

100 Centimes = 1 Franc

Navigation and Commerce — A1

Perf. 14x13½

1906-07 Typo. Unwmk.
Name of Colony in Blue or Carmine

1 A1 1c blk, *lil bl* 3.75 2.40
Never hinged 5.50
On cover 250.00
2 A1 2c brn, *buff* 2.50 1.75
Never hinged 3.00
On cover 250.00
3 A1 4c claret, *lav* 3.75 2.40
Never hinged 6.50
On cover 250.00
4 A1 5c yellow grn 4.25 2.40
Never hinged 7.50
On cover 225.00
5 A1 10c carmine 6.00 2.40
Never hinged 12.00
On cover 250.00
6 A1 20c red, *green* 13.00 7.25
Never hinged 24.00
On cover 250.00
On cover, single franking 440.00
7 A1 25c blue 13.00 5.50
Never hinged 24.00
On cover 125.00
On cover, single franking 225.00
8 A1 30c brn, *bister* 17.50 14.50
Never hinged 32.50
On cover 160.00
On cover, single franking 225.00
9 A1 35c blk, *yellow* 10.50 4.00
Never hinged 21.00
On cover 225.00
On cover, single franking 300.00
10 A1 40c red, *straw* 17.50 13.50
Never hinged 32.50
On cover 250.00
On cover, single franking 400.00
11 A1 45c blk, *gray grn* ('07) 75.00 60.00
Never hinged 150.00
On cover 500.00
On cover, single franking 690.00
a. Perf 11 300.00
12 A1 50c brn, *az* 24.00 14.50
Never hinged 47.50
On cover 300.00
On cover, single franking 440.00
13 A1 75c dp vio, *org* 27.50 24.00
Never hinged 55.00
On cover 375.00
On cover, single franking 525.00
14 A1 1fr brnz grn, *straw* 24.00 17.50
Never hinged 47.50
On cover 340.00
On cover, single franking 525.00
15 A1 2fr vio, *rose* 35.00 35.00
Never hinged 67.50
On cover 440.00
On cover, single franking 625.00
16 A1 5fr lil, *lavender* 140.00 140.00
Never hinged 280.00
On cover 800.00
On cover, single franking 1,100.
a. Imperf pair 700.00
Nos. 1-16 (16) 417.25 347.10

Perf. 13½x14 stamps are counterfeits.
No. 12, affixed to pressboard with animals printed on the back, was used as emergency currency in the Comoro Islands in 1920.

Issue of 1906-07 Surcharged in Carmine or Black

1912
Spacing between figures of surcharge 1.5mm (5c), 2mm (10c)

17 A1 5c on 4c cl, *lav* (C) 2.40 *3.25*
Never hinged 4.00
On cover 190.00
18 A1 5c on 20c red, *grn* 3.50 *3.50*
Never hinged 6.50
On cover 200.00
19 A1 5c on 30c brn, *bis* (C) 2.25 *3.50*
Never hinged 3.50
On cover 200.00
20 A1 10c on 40c red, *straw* 2.25 *3.50*
Never hinged 3.50
On cover 200.00
21 A1 10c on 45c blk, *gray grn* (C) 2.00 2.00
Never hinged 3.25
On cover 80.00
a. "Moheli" double 475.00
b. "Moheli" triple 475.00
d. As "a," in pair with normal stamp 850.00
e. As "b," in pair with normal stamp 850.00
22 A1 10c on 50c brn, *az* (C) 3.50 *4.50*
Never hinged 5.50
On cover 200.00
Nos. 17-22 (6) 15.90 20.25

Spacing between figures of surcharge 2.25mm (5c), 2.75mm (10c)

17a A1 5c on 4c cl, *lav* (C) 20.00 20.00
Never hinged 32.50
18a A1 5c on 20c red, *grn* 55.00 55.00
Never hinged 100.00
19a A1 5c on 30c brn, *bis* (C) 55.00 55.00
Never hinged 100.00
20a A1 10c on 40c red, *straw* 175.00 175.00
Never hinged 260.00
21c A1 10c on 45c blk, *gray grn* (C) 75.00 75.00
Never hinged 140.00
22a A1 10c on 50c brn, *az* (C) 150.00 150.00
Never hinged 240.00
Nos. 17a-22a (6) 530.00 530.00

Se-tenant Pairs, Both Ovpt. Settings

17b A1 5c on 4c, #17 + #17a 24.00 24.00
Never hinged 40.00
18b A1 5c on 20c, #18 + #18a 65.00 65.00
Never hinged 120.00
19b A1 5c on 30c, #19 + #19a 65.00 65.00
Never hinged 120.00
20b A1 10c on 40c, #20 + #20a 190.00 190.00
Never hinged 300.00
21f A1 10c on 45c, #21 + #21a 87.50 57.50
Never hinged 120.00
22b A1 10c on 50c, #22 + #22a 180.00 180.00
Never hinged 275.00

The stamps of Mohéli were supposed to have been superseded by those of Madagascar, January, 1908. However, Nos. 17-22 were surcharged in 1912 to use up remainders. These were available for use in Madagascar and the entire Comoro archipelago. In 1950 stamps of Comoro Islands came into use.

MONACO

'mä-nə-ˌkō

LOCATION — Southern coast of France, bordering on the Mediterranean Sea
GOVT. — Principality
AREA — 481 acres
POP. — 27,063 (1982)
CAPITAL — Monaco

100 Centimes = 1 Franc

STAMPS OF SARDINIA

CANCELED WITH SARDINIAN "MENTONE" C.D.S.

1851
A1 20c blue (#2) on cover, stamp pen cancelled *7,500.*

No. A1 is unique.

1853
A2 20c blue (#5) —

1854
A3 20c blue (#8) —

1855-60
A4 5c yellow green (#10a) 925.00
On cover —
A5 10c bister (#11) 450.00
On cover —
A6 20c light blue (#12b) 450.00
On cover *8,100.*
A7 40c red (#13) 600.00
On cover —
A8 80c orange yellow (#14) 2,750.
On cover —

With French Small Figures "4220" for Menton

A9 10c bister (#11) *1,500.*
A10 80c orange yellow (#14) *5,100.*

STAMPS OF SARDINIA CANCELED WITH SARDINIAN "MONACO" C.D.S.

1853
A12 20c blue (#5) on cover *9,000.*

One cover and four singles of No. A12 are known.

1854
A13 20c blue (#8) on cover —

One example of No. A13 is known.

1855-60
A14 5c yellow green (#10a) 1,900.
On cover *21,500.*
A15 10c bister (#11) 900.00
On cover, from *16,250.*
A16 20c light blue (#12b) 750.00
On cover, from *10,800.*
A17 40c red (#13) 1,200.
On cover, from *16,250.*
A18 80c orange yellow (#14) 5,400.
On cover *21,500.*

With French Small Figures "4222" for Monaco

A19 10c bister (#11) *2,200.*
A20 20c blue (#12a) *1,800.*
A21 40c red (#13) *2,900.*
A22 80c orange yellow (#14) *4,000.*

STAMPS OF FRANCE CANCELED WITH SARDINIAN "MENTONE" C.D.S.

A23 10c bister (#14) 875.00
On cover, from *4,800.*
A24 20c blue(#15) 425.00
On cover, from *3,000.*
A25 40c orange(#18) 1,450.
On cover, from *10,000.*
A26 80c carmine(#19) 1,450.
On cover, from *10,000.*

STAMPS OF FRANCE CANCELED WITH SARDINIAN "MONACO" C.D.S.

A27 10c bister (#14) 1,325.
On cover, from *11,000.*
A28 20c blue(#15) 725.00
On cover, from *11,000.*
A29 40c orange(#18) 1,600.
A30 80c carmine(#19) 2,900.

STAMPS OF FRANCE CANCELED WITH VARIOUS FRENCH POSTMARKS OF MONACO "4222" SMALL FIGURES

1853-60 ***Empire, Imperf***
A31 1c olive green (#12) 1,600.
A32 5c green (#13) 1,325.
A33 10c bister (#14) 550.
On cover, from *5,750.*
A34 20c blue (#15) 375.
On cover, from *3,300.*
A35 40c orange (#18) 1,100.
On cover, from *13,800.*
A36 80c carmine(#19) 1,750.
A37 20c blue (#26) *16,500.*

"2387" LARGE FIGURES

1853-60 ***Empire, Imperf***
A38 1c olive green (#12) —
A39 5c yellow green (#13) 1,000.
A40 10c bister (#14) 550.00
A41 20c blue (#15) 450.00
A42 40c orange (#18) 1,000.
A43 80c carmine(#19) —

1862-71 ***Empire, Perforated***
A44 1c olive green (#22) 725.00
A45 5c yellow green (#23) 300.00
On cover, from *2,600.*
A46 10c bister (#25) 60.00
On cover, from *725.00*
A47 20c blue (#26) 110.00
On cover, from *300.00*
A48 40c orange (#27) 210.00
On cover, from *3,600.*
A49 80c rose (#28) 850.00
On cover, from *10,800.*

1863-70 ***Empire, "Laureated"***
A50 1c bronze green, *pale blue* (#29) 210.00
On cover, from *3,000.*
A51 2c red brn, *yelsh* (#30) 290.00
A52 4c gray (#31) 325.00
On cover, from *3,300.*
A53 10c bister, *yellowish* (#32) 110.00
On cover, from *725.00*
A54 20c blue, *bluish* (#33) 70.00
On cover, from *290.00*
A55 30c brown, *yelsh* (#34) 160.00
On cover, from *1,450.*
A56 40c orange, *yelsh* (#35) 140.00
On cover, from *1,200.*
A57 80c rose, *pinkish* (#36) 210.00
On cover, from *1,900.*
A58 5fr gray lilac, *lav* (#37) 1,900.

1870-71 ***Bordeaux Issue***
A59 1c olive grn, *pale blue* (#38) 450.00
A60 2c red brn, *yelsh* (B) (#39) 1,000.
A61 4c gray (#40) 1,000.
A62 5c green, *grnsh* (#41) 400.00
On cover, from 400.00
A63 10c bister, *yelsh* (A) (#42) 290.00
On cover, from 2,150.
A64 20c blue, *bluish* (#43) 8,400.
A65 20c blue, *bluish* (#44) 290.00
On cover, from *2,200.*
A66 20c blue, *bluish* (#45) 290.00
On cover, from *2,150.*
A67 30c brown, *yelsh* (#46) 550.00
A68 40c orange, *yelsh* (#47) 450.00
A69 80c rose, *pinkish* (#48) 600.00

1870-73 ***Ceres***
A70 1c ol grn, *pale blue* (#50) 210.00
A71 2c red brn, *yelsh* (#51) 300.00
A72 4c gray (#52) 240.00
A73 5c yel grn, *pale blue* (#53) 140.00
On cover, from 1,600.
A74 10c bister, *yellowish* (#54) 700.00
A75 10c bister, *rose* ('73) (#55) 150.00
On cover, from 1,400.
A76 15c bister, *yelsh* ('71) (#56) 110.00
On cover, from 1,100.
A77 20c dull blue, *bluish* (#57) 200.00
On cover, from 1,950.
A78 40c org, *yelsh* (I) (#59) 110.00
On cover, from 1,100.

Ceres, Larger Figures of Value
1872-75
A79 10c bister, *rose* ('75) (#60) 150.00
On cover, from 1,500.
A80 15c bister ('73) (#61) 140.00
On cover, from 1,600.
A81 30c brn, *yelsh* (#62) 150.00
On cover, from 1,900.
A82 80c rose, *pinkish* (#63) 210.00
On cover, from 1,900.

"2387" SMALL FIGURES

1862-71 ***Empire, Imperf***
A83 10c bister (#25) 725.00
On cover, from 16,500.
A84 20c blue (#26) 450.00
On cover, from *7,200.*
A85 40c orange (#27) 450.00
On cover, from *7,200.*

1863-70 ***Empire, "Laureated"***
A86 20c blue, *bluish* (#33) 600.00
On cover, from *8,400.*
A87 30c brown, *yelsh* (#34) 450.00
On cover, from *6,600.*
A88 40c orange, *yelsh* (#35) 240.00
On cover, from *4,900.*
A89 80c rose, *pinkish* (#36) 290.00
A90 5fr gray lilac, *lav* (#37) 2,100.

1870-71 Bordeaux Issue
A91 5c grn, grnsh (#41) 925.00
A92 10c bister, yelsh (A) (#42) 325.00
On cover 7,200.
A93 20c blue, bluish (#43) 1,100.
A94 20c blue, bluish ('71) (#45) 1,100.
A95 30c brown, yelsh (#46) 1,100.
On cover 7,200.
A96 40c orange, yelsh (#47) 500.00
On cover 6,300.
A97 80c rose, pinkish (#48) 600.00
On cover 1,600.

Ceres, Larger Figures of Value
1872-75
A98 30c brn, yelsh (#62) 400.00
A99 80c rose, pinkish (#63) —

"MONACO / (87)" DOUBLE CIRCLE DATESTAMP, DATE IN 3 LINES, WITHOUT TIME INDICIA

1853-60 Empire, Imperf
A100 1c olive green (#12) 210.00
A101 5c yellow green (#13) 325.00
A102 10c bister (#14) 275.00
A103 20c blue (#15) 275.00
A104 40c orange (#18) —

1862-71 Empire, Perforated
A105 1c olive green (#22) 200.00
A106 5c yellow green (#23) 200.00
On cover, from 425.00
A107 5c green, pale blue ('71) (I) (#24) —
A108 10c bister (#25) 160.00
A109 20c blue (#26) 290.00
On cover, from 2,900.
A110 40c orange (#27) 200.00
On cover, from 2,900.
A111 80c rose (#28) 650.00

1863-70 Empire, "Laureated"
A112 1c bronze grn, pale blue (#29) —
A113 2c red brn, yelsh (#30) 87.50
On cover, from 1,600.
A114 4c gray (#31) 87.50
On cover, from 1,400.
A115 10c bister, yelsh (#32) 140.00
A116 20c blue, bluish (#33) 290.00
On cover, from 2,200.
A117 30c brown, yelsh (#34) —
A118 40c orange, yelsh (#35) —
A119 80c rose, pinkish (#36) —
A120 5fr gray lilac, lav (#37) 1,900.

"MONACO / (87)" SINGLE CIRCLE DATESTAMP, DATE IN 3 LINES, WITH TIME INDICIA

1862-71 Empire, Perforated
A121 10c bister (#25) 400.00

1863-70 Empire, "Laureated"
A122 1c brnz grn, pale blue (#29) 160.00
A123 2c red brn, yelsh (#30) 130.00
A124 4c gray (#31) 130.00
A125 10c bister, yelsh (#32) 400.00
A126 20c blue, bluish (#33) 325.00

1870-71 Bordeaux Issue
A127 5c grn, grnsh (#41) 500.00

1870-73 Ceres
A128 1c ol grn, pale blue (#50) 290.00
A129 2c red brn, yelsh (#51) 290.00
A130 4c gray (#52) 290.00
A131 5c yel grn, pale blue (#53) 290.00

"MONACO / (87)" DOUBLE CIRCLE DATESTAMP, DATE IN 3 LINES, WITH TIME INDICIA

1862-71 Empire, Perforated
A132 1c olive green (#22) 200.00
A133 5c yellow green (#23) 200.00
On cover, from 450.00
A134 5c green, pale blue ('71) (I) (#24) 210.00
A135 10c bister (#25) 200.00
A136 20c blue (#26) 300.00
A137 40c orange (#27) —
A138 80c rose (#28) —

1863-70 Empire, "Laureated"
A139 1c brnz grn, pale blue (#29) 125.00
A140 2c red brn, yelsh (#30) 85.00
On cover, from 1,000.
A141 4c gray (#31) 110.00
On cover, from 1,100.
A142 10c bister, yelsh (#32) 125.00
A143 20c blue, bluish (#33) 240.00
On cover, from 3,000.
A144 30c brown, yelsh (#34) 325.00
A145 40c orange, yelsh (#35) 240.00
A146 80c rose, pinkish (#36) 325.00
A147 5fr gray lilac, lav (#37) 1,900.

1870-71 Bordeaux Issue
A148 1c ol grn, pale blue (#38) 325.00
On cover, from 3,250.
A149 2c red brn, yelsh (B) (#39) 450.00
A150 4c gray (#40) 725.00
On cover, from 4,900.
A151 5c grn, grnsh (#41) 400.00
On cover —
A152 10c bister, yelsh (A) (#42) 210.00
On cover —
A153 20c blue, bluish (#44) 210.00
On cover, from 4,400.
A154 20c blue, bluish (#45) 210.00
On cover, from 3,800.
A155 30c brown, yelsh (#46) 725.00
A156 40c orange, yelsh (#47) 325.00
A157 80c rose, pinkish (#48) 500.00

1870-73 Ceres
A158 1c ol grn, pale blue (#50) 110.00
A159 2c red brn, yelsh (#51) 110.00
On cover, from 1,600.
A160 4c gray (#52) 110.00
A161 5c yel grn, pale blue (#53) 72.50
On cover, from 1,200.
A162 10c bister, rose ('73) (#55) 140.00
On cover 1,200.
A163 15c bister, yelsh ('71) (#56) 92.50
On cover, from 1,400.
A164 20c dull blue, bluish (#57) 160.00
A165 25c blue, bluish ('71) (#58) 92.50
On cover, from 725.00
A166 40c orange, yelsh (I) (#59) 190.00
On cover, from 2,100.

Ceres, Larger Figures of Value
1872-75
A167 10c bister, rose ('75) (#60) 140.00
On cover, from 1,200.
A168 15c bister ('73) (#61) 92.50
On cover, from 1,400.
A169 30c brn, yelsh (#62) 140.00
On cover, from 1,800.
A170 80c rose, pinkish (#63) 290.00
On cover —

"MONACO / PRINCIPAUTE" DOUBLE CIRCLE DATESTAMP, DATE IN 3 LINES, WITH TIME INDICIA

1863-70 Empire, "Laureated"
A171 5fr gray lilac, lav (#37) 1,600.

1870-73 Ceres
A172 1c ol grn, pale blue (#50) 110.00
A173 2c red brn, yelsh (#51) 110.00
On cover, from 1,600.
A174 4c gray (#52) 110.00
A175 5c yel grn, pale blue (#53) 85.00
On cover, from 1,200.
A176 15c bister, yelsh ('71) (#56) 140.00
On cover, from —
A177 20c dull blue, bluish (#57) —
A178 25c blue, bluish ('71) (#58) 85.00
On cover, from 725.00
A179 40c orange, yelsh (I) (#59) 290.00
On cover —

Ceres, Larger Figures of Value
1872-75
A180 10c bister, rose ('75) (#60) 140.00
On cover, from 1,200.
A181 15c bister ('73) (#61) 85.00
On cover, from 1,400.
A182 30c brn, yelsh (#62) 140.00
On cover, from 1,800.
A183 80c rose, pinkish (#63) 290.00
On cover —

"MONACO / PRINCIPAUTE" DOUBLE CIRCLE DATESTAMP, DATE IN 3 LINES, WITH TIME INDICIA IN SANS SERIF CHARACTERS

Peace & Commerce Issue, Type I ("N" under "B")
1876-78
A184 1c grn, grnsh (#64) 290.00
On cover —
A185 2c grn, grnsh (#65) 1,200.
On cover —
A186 4c grn, grnsh (#66) 210.00
On cover —
A187 5c grn, grnsh (#67) 210.00
On cover 6,600.
A188 10c grn, grnsh (#68) 2,100.
On cover —
A189 15c gray lil, grayish (#69) 160.00
On cover 875.00
A190 20c red brn, straw (#70) 210.00
On cover —
A191 25c ultra, bluish (#72) 210.00
On cover 1,200.
A192 30c brn, yelsh (#73) 140.00
On cover 875.00
A193 40c red, straw (#74) 150.00
On cover 1,200.
A194 75c carmine, rose (#75) 210.00
On cover 550.00
A195 1fr brnz grn, straw (#76) 110.00
On cover 2,100.

Peace & Commerce Issue, Type II ("N" under "U")
1876-90
A196 2c grn, grnsh (#77) 210.00
On cover —
A197 5c grn, grnsh (#78) 40.00
On cover 500.00
A198 10c grn, grnsh (#79) 725.00
On cover —
A199 15c gray lil, grayish (#80) 42.50
On cover 325.00
A200 25c ultra, bluish (#81) 42.50
On cover 210.00
A201 25c blue, bluish (#81a) 55.00
On cover 290.00
A202 30c yel brn, yelsh (#82) 110.00
On cover —
A203 75c car, rose ('77) (#83) —
On cover —
A204 1fr brnz grn, straw ('77) (#84) 110.00
On cover 1,400.
A205 1c blk, lil blue (#86) 210.00
On cover 2,800.
A206 2c brown, straw (#88) 160.00
On cover —
A207 3c yel, straw ('78) (#89) 210.00
On cover —
A208 4c claret, lav (#90) 72.50
On cover 1,600.
A209 10c black, lav (#91) 72.50
On cover 1,100.
A210 15c blue ('78) (#92) 40.00
On cover 210.00
A211 25c blk, red ('78) (#93) 85.00
On cover 1,300.
A212 35c blk, yel ('78) (#94) 725.00
On cover —
A213 40c red, straw ('80) (#95) 65.00
On cover 850.00
A214 5fr vio, lav (#96) 290.00
On cover 7,200.
A215 3c gray, grayish ('80) (#97) 160.00
On cover —
A216 20c red, yel grn (#98) 110.00
On cover —
A217 25c yellow, straw (#99) 42.50
On cover 425.00

"MONACO / ALPES-MARITIMES" DOUBLE CIRCLE DATESTAMP, DATE IN 3 LINES, WITH TIME INDICIA

1870-73 Ceres
A218 4c gray (#52) 1,900.
A219 5c yel grn, pale blue (#53) 1,900.
A220 25c blue, bluish ('71) (#58) 1,100.
On cover 10,000.

"MONTE-CARLO / PTE. DE MONACO" DOUBLE CIRCLE DATESTAMP, DATE IN 3 LINES, WITH TIME INDICIA

Peace & Commerce Issue, Type II ("N" under "U")
1876-90
A221 2c grn, grnsh (#77) —
A222 5c grn, grnsh (#78) 72.50
A223 10c grn, grnsh (#79) —
A224 15c gray lil, grayish (#80) —
A225 25c ultra, bluish (#81) —
A226 25c blue, bluish (#81a) —
A227 30c yel brn, yelsh (#82) 190.00
A228 75c carm, rose ('77) (#83) —
A229 1fr brnz grn, straw ('77) (#84) 110.00
A230 1c black, lil blue (#86) 110.00
A231 2c brown, straw (#88) 72.50
A232 3c yel, straw ('78) (#89) —
A233 4c claret, lav (#90) 72.50
A234 10c black, lav (#91) 72.50
A235 15c blue ('78) (#92) 65.00
On cover 875.00
A236 25c blk, red ('78) (#93) 85.00
On cover 1,100.
A237 35c blk, yel ('78) (#94) —
A238 40c red, straw ('80) (#95) 110.00
A239 5fr violet, lav (#96) 475.00
A240 3c gray, grayish ('80) (#97) 110.00
A241 20c red, yel grn (#98) 110.00
A242 25c yellow, straw (#99) 72.50

Other "Monte-Carlo" cancelations exist, used at mail transit offices.

POSTAGE DUE STAMPS OF FRANCE "MONACO / PRINCIPAUTE" DOUBLE CIRCLE DATESTAMP, DATE IN 3 LINES, WITH TIME INDICIA

1859-95 Empire, "Laureated"
AJ1 10c black (#J3) —
AJ2 15c black ('63) (#J4) 900.00
AJ3 25c black ('71) (#J6) 1,300.
AJ4 30c black ('78) (#J7) 1,300.
AJ5 1c black (#J11) 42.50
On cover 300.00
AJ6 2c black (#J12) 72.50
On cover 875.00
AJ7 3c black (#J13) 72.50
On cover 950.00
AJ8 4c black (#J14) 110.00
On cover —
AJ9 5c black (#J15) 35.00
On cover 290.00
AJ10 10c black (#J16) 35.00
On cover 290.00
AJ11 15c black (#J17) 55.00
On cover 325.00
AJ12 20c black (#J18) 160.00
On cover —
AJ13 30c black (#J19) 55.00
On cover 290.00
AJ14 40c black (#J20) 140.00
On cover —
AJ15 50c black ('92) (#J21) 160.00
On cover 1,100.
AJ16 60c black ('84) (#J22) 130.00
On cover 725.00
AJ17 2fr black ('84) (#J24) 850.00
AJ18 5fr black ('84) (#J25) 1,400.
AJ19 1fr brown (#J26) 475.00
AJ20 2fr brown (#J27) 475.00
AJ21 5fr brown (#J28) 725.00
AJ22 5c blue ('94) (#J29) 29.00
On cover 72.50
AJ23 10c brown (#J30) 29.00
On cover 90.00
AJ24 15c lt grn ('94) (#J31) 29.00
On cover 110.00
AJ25 30c red ('94) (#J34) 29.00
On cover 90.00
AJ26 50c brn vio ('95) (#J38) 35.00
On cover 140.00

"MONTE-CARLO / PTE. DE MONACO" DOUBLE CIRCLE DATESTAMP, DATE IN 3 LINES, WITH TIME INDICIA

1882-95
AJ27 1c black (#J11) 42.50
On cover 290.00
AJ28 2c black (#J12) 72.50
On cover 950.00
AJ29 3c black (#J13) 85.00
AJ30 4c black (#J14) —
AJ31 5c black (#J15) 55.00
On cover 325.00
AJ32 10c black (#J16) 55.00
On cover 290.00
AJ33 15c black (#J17) 32.50
On cover 290.00
AJ34 20c black (#J18) 240.00
On cover —
AJ35 30c black (#J19) 55.00
On cover 325.00
AJ36 40c black (#J20) 160.00
On cover —
AJ37 50c black ('92) (#J21) 160.00
On cover 875.00
AJ38 60c black ('84) (#J22) —
AJ39 1fr brown (#J26) 360.00
AJ40 2fr brown (#J27) —
AJ41 5fr brown (#J28) 475.00
AJ42 5c blue ('94) (#J29) 21.00
On cover 55.00
AJ43 10c brown (#J30) 29.00
On cover 85.00
AJ44 15c lt grn ('94) (#J31) 29.00
On cover 85.00
AJ45 30c red ('94) (#J34) 21.00
On cover 55.00
AJ46 50c brn vio ('95) (#J38) 35.00
On cover 110.00

Other "Monte-Carlo" cancelations exist, used at mail transit offices.

Issues of the Principality

Values for unused stamps are for examples with original gum as defined in the catalogue introduction. Very fine examples of Nos. 1-181, B1-B50, C1 and J1-J27 will have perforations clear of the design and/or frameline. Very well centered are worth more than the values quoted.

Prince Charles III — A1

1885 Unwmk. Typo. *Perf. 14x13½*

1 A1 1c olive green 25.00 17.50
Never hinged 37.50
On cover with other values 290.00
On postal stationery to up-grade rate 525.00
a. 1c bronze green 30.00 21.00
Never hinged 45.00
2 A1 2c dull lilac 57.50 27.50
Never hinged 72.50
On cover with other values 290.00
On postal stationery to up-grade rate 525.00
a. 2c slate violet 62.50 32.50
Never hinged 92.50
3 A1 5c blue 70.00 35.00
Never hinged 95.00
On cover with other values 175.00
On postal stationery to up-grade rate 290.00
4 A1 10c brown, *straw* 85.00 40.00
Never hinged 125.00
On cover with other values 225.00
On postal stationery to up-grade rate 225.00
5 A1 15c rose 350.00 18.00
Never hinged 490.00
On cover 175.00
6 A1 25c green 700.00 75.00
Never hinged 925.00
On cover 350.00
7 A1 40c slate, *rose* 85.00 45.00
Never hinged 110.00
On cover 225.00
On cover, single franking 400.00
8 A1 75c black, *rose* 275.00 125.00
Never hinged 400.00
On cover 800.00
On cover, single franking *1,150.*
9 A1 1fr black, *yellow* 1,750. 500.00
Never hinged 2,300.
On cover *4,000.*
Philatelic cover, single franking *2,900.*
10 A1 5fr rose, *green* 3,000. 2,000.
Never hinged 4,400.
On registered cover *11,500.*
On money letter *10,500.*
Philatelic cover, single franking *7,750.*

Values for blocks of 4

1 A1 1c olive green 125.00 110.00
Never hinged 190.00
On cover 190.00
2 A1 2c dull lilac 275.00 300.00
Never hinged 375.00
On cover 450.00
3 A1 5c blue 400.00 240.00
Never hinged 600.00
On cover 600.00
4 A1 10c brown, *straw* 400.00 250.00
Never hinged 600.00
On cover 625.00
5 A1 15c rose 2,200. 165.00
Never hinged 2,750.
6 A1 25c green 5,500. 800.00
Never hinged 7,000.
7 A1 40c slate, *rose* 425.00 375.00
Never hinged 550.00
On cover 1,450.
8 A1 75c black, *rose* 1,700. 750.00
Never hinged 2,400.
9 A1 1fr black, *yellow* *12,000.* *10,000.*
Never hinged —

No blocks of No. 10 are known. A few pairs do exist. Values: unused $17,500; used $6,750.

Prince Albert I — A2

1891-1921

11 A2 1c olive green .70 .70
Never hinged 1.20
On cover 8.50
On printed matter 175.00
12 A2 2c dull violet .80 .80
Never hinged 1.25
On cover 8.50
On printed matter 115.00
13 A2 5c blue 50.00 6.00
Never hinged 85.00
On cover 24.00
On cover, single franking 90.00
14 A2 5c yel grn ('01) .50 .35
Never hinged 1.00
On cover 7.00
On cover, single franking 57.50
15 A2 10c brown, *straw* 100.00 16.00
Never hinged 160.00
On cover 85.00
On cover, with #13 (15c rate) 175.00
On cover, single franking —
a. 10c dark brown, *yellow* 110.00 17.50
Never hinged 175.00
16 A2 10c carmine ('01) 4.00 .70
Never hinged 9.00
On cover 29.00
On postcard 29.00
a. 10c rose 3.50 .60
Never hinged 7.00
On cover 29.00

17 A2 15c rose 175.00 8.00
Never hinged 275.00
On cover 30.00
On cover, single franking 85.00
a. Double impression *1,400.*
18 A2 15c vio brn, *straw* ('01) 3.00 1.00
Never hinged 6.50
On cover 30.00
19 A2 15c gray grn ('21) 2.00 *2.50*
Never hinged 4.00
On cover 18.00
On cover, single franking 30.00
20 A2 25c green 275.00 32.50
Never hinged 425.00
On cover 90.00
On cover, single franking 175.00
21 A2 25c dp blue ('01) 15.00 5.00
Never hinged 27.50
On cover 57.50
22 A2 40c slate, *rose* ('94) 4.00 2.40
Never hinged 7.00
On cover 57.50
On cover, single franking 85.00
23 A2 50c vio brn (shades), *org* 7.00 4.75
Never hinged 12.00
On cover 29.00
On cover, single franking 57.50
a. 50c brown, *orange* 12.50 12.50
Never hinged 21.00
On cover 35.00
24 A2 75c vio brn, *buff* ('94) 27.50 18.00
Never hinged 50.00
On cover 140.00
On cover, single franking 290.00
a. 75c lilac brown, *buff* 36.00 27.50
Never hinged 65.00
On cover 50.00
25 A2 75c ol brn, *buff* ('21) 20.00 *24.00*
Never hinged 40.00
On cover 115.00
On cover, single franking —
26 A2 1fr black, *yellow* 19.00 11.00
Never hinged 32.50
On cover 115.00
On cover, single franking —
a. 1fr black, *pale yel straw* 17.00 11.50
Never hinged 32.50
On cover 125.00
27 A2 5fr rose, *grn* 100.00 87.50
Never hinged 175.00
On cover 975.00
Philatelic cover, over-franked 350.00
a. 5fr carmine rose, *green* 160.00 120.00
Never hinged 350.00
Philatelic cover, over-franked 350.00
b. Perf 11 *2,000.*
c. Double impression 1,500.
28 A2 5fr dull vio ('21) 200.00 *250.00*
Never hinged 350.00
On cover *1,600.*
Philatelic cover, over-franked 850.00
29 A2 5fr dk grn ('21) 22.50 *27.50*
Never hinged 47.50
On cover 290.00
Philatelic cover, over-franked 115.00
a. 5fr pale green ('21) 400.00 275.00
Never hinged 575.00
Nos. 11-29 (19) 1,026. 498.70

The handstamp "OL" in a circle of dots is a cancellation, not an overprint.

On cover values for Nos. 27-29 are for over-franked philatelic covers.

See No. 1782 in Scott Standard catalogue, Vol. 4. For overprints and surcharges see Nos. 30-35, 57-59, B1.

Stamps of 1901-21 Overprinted or Surcharged

1921, Mar. 5

30 A2 5c lt green .70 *.70*
Never hinged 1.20
On cover 40.00
31 A2 75c brown, *buff* 5.25 *6.25*
Never hinged 8.00
On cover 70.00
32 A2 2fr on 5fr dull vio 32.50 *52.50*
Never hinged 60.00
On cover 85.00
On cover, single franking© 225.00
Nos. 30-32 (3) 38.45 *59.45*

Issued to commemorate the birth of Princess Antoinette, daughter of Princess Charlotte and Prince Pierre, Comte de Polignac.

Stamps and Type of 1891-1921 Surcharged

1922

33 A2 20c on 15c gray green 1.10 *1.40*
Never hinged 2.00
On cover 17.50
34 A2 25c on 10c rose .70 *.90*
Never hinged 1.20
On cover 17.50
35 A2 50c on 1fr black, *yel* 6.00 *6.50*
Never hinged 9.50
On cover 35.00
Nos. 33-35 (3) 7.80 *8.80*

Prince Albert I — A5

Oceanographic Museum — A6

"The Rock" of Monaco — A7

Royal Palace — A8

1922-24 Engr. *Perf. 11*

40 A5 25c deep brown 4.00 *4.75*
Never hinged 6.75
On cover 7.25
a. 25c olive brown 12.00 12.00
Never hinged 21.00
On cover 24.00
41 A6 30c dark green .90 .90
Never hinged 1.75
On cover 12.00
a. 30c gray green 2.75 2.75
Never hinged 4.00
On cover 16.00
42 A6 30c scarlet ('23) .50 .45
Never hinged .75
On cover 2.00
a. 30c salmon .75 1.75
Never hinged 1.25
On cover 2.40
43 A6 50c ultra 4.25 4.25
Never hinged 8.00
On cover 8.00
a. 50c pale ultra 7.25 *7.50*
Never hinged 12.00
On cover 13.50
b. 50c greenish blue 5.50 6.00
Never hinged 9.50
On cover —
44 A7 60c black brown .35 .35
Never hinged .55
On cover 1.60
a. 60c pale gray .70 .70
Never hinged 1.20
On cover 2.40
45 A7 1fr black, *yellow* .25 .25
Never hinged .40
On cover 1.20
a. 1fr gray black, *yellow* .40 .25
Never hinged .70
On cover 1.60
46 A7 2fr scarlet ver .50 .45
Never hinged .85
On cover 4.00
a. 2fr carmine 2.50 *3.00*
Never hinged 4.50
On cover 6.50
47 A8 5fr red brown 32.50 *37.50*
Never hinged 55.00
On cover 92.50
a. 5fr deep brown 55.00 *65.00*
Never hinged 95.00
On cover 175.00
48 A8 5fr green, *bluish* 10.50 10.50
Never hinged 21.00
On cover 40.00
a. 5fr dk green, *lil* ('24) 12.00 *12.00*
Never hinged 24.00
On cover 35.00
49 A8 10fr carmine 14.00 18.00
Never hinged 30.00
On cover 40.00
a. 10fr rose 65.00 *72.50*
Never hinged 105.00
On cover 125.00
Nos. 40-49 (10) 67.75 *77.40*

Nos. 40-49 exist imperf.

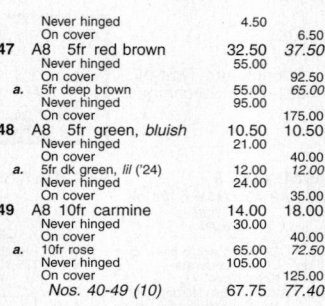

Prince Louis II
A9 A10

St. Dévote Viaduct ("Bridge of Suicides") A11

1923-24 Engr.

50 A9 10c deep green .35 *.55*
Never hinged .55
On cover 1.15
51 A9 15c car rose ('24) .45 *.70*
Never hinged .70
On cover 1.15
52 A9 20c red brown .35 *.55*
Never hinged .65
On cover 1.15
53 A9 25c violet .25 *.45*
Never hinged .45
On cover 1.15
a. Without engraver's name 27.50 27.50
Never hinged 40.00
On cover —
54 A11 40c orange brn ('24) .65 .55
Never hinged .85
On cover 1.15
55 A10 50c ultra .35 *.45*
Never hinged .55
On cover 1.60
Nos. 50-55 (6) 2.40 *3.25*

The 25c comes in 2 types, one with larger "5" and "c" touching frame of numeral tablet.

Stamps of the 1922-24 issues sometimes show parts of the letters of a papermaker's watermark.

The engraved stamps of type A11 measure 31x21½mm. The typographed stamps of that design measure 36x21½mm.

See #86-88. For surcharges see #95-96.

Stamps and Type of 1891-1921 Surcharged

1924, Aug. 5 ***Perf. 14x13½***

No.	Type	Description	Unused	Used
57	A2	45c on 50c brn ol, *buff*	.60	*.70*
		Never hinged	1.00	
		On cover		1.60
		On cover, single franking		3.25
a.		Double surcharge	775.00	775.00
		Never hinged	1,050.	
58	A2	75c on 1fr blk, *yel*	.60	*.70*
		Never hinged	1.50	
		On cover		2.00
		On cover, single franking		3.50
a.		Double surcharge	550.00	*550.00*
		Never hinged	1,050.	
59	A2	85c on 5fr dk green	.60	*.70*
		Never hinged	1.50	
		On cover		2.00
		On cover, single franking		3.25
a.		Double surcharge	*650.00*	*650.00*
		Never hinged	700.00	
		Nos. 57-59 (3)	1.80	2.10
		Set, never hinged	2.25	

Grimaldi Family Coat of Arms — A12

Prince Louis II — A13

Louis II — A14

View of Monaco A15

1924-33 **Typo.**

No.	Type	Description	Unused	Used
60	A12	1c gray black	.25	.25
61	A12	2c red brown	.25	.25
62	A12	3c brt violet ('33)	2.75	1.90
63	A12	5c orange ('26)	.35	.30
64	A12	10c blue	.25	.25
65	A13	15c apple green	.25	.25
66	A13	15c dull vio ('29)	2.75	1.90
67	A13	20c violet	.25	.25
68	A13	20c rose	.35	.25
69	A13	25c rose	.25	.25
70	A13	25c red, *yel*	.25	*.25*
71	A13	30c orange	.25	.25
72	A13	40c black brown	.25	.25
73	A13	40c lt bl, *bluish*	.35	.35
74	A13	45c gray blk ('26)	.90	.70
75	A14	50c myrtle grn ('25)	.25	*.25*
76	A13	50c brown, *org*	.25	.25
77	A14	60c yel brn ('25)	.25	*.25*
78	A13	60c ol grn, *grnsh*	.25	*.25*
79	A13	75c ol grn, *grnsh* ('26)	.70	.35
80	A13	75c car, *straw* ('26)	.35	.25
81	A13	75c slate	.90	.55
82	A13	80c red, *yel* ('26)	.40	.30
83	A13	90c rose, *straw* ('27)	2.00	1.60
84	A13	1.25fr bl, *bluish* ('26)	.25	.25
85	A13	1.50fr bl, *bluish* ('27)	3.75	1.90

Size: 36x21½mm

No.	Type	Description	Unused	Used
86	A11	1fr blk, *orange*	.25	*.25*
87	A11	1.05fr red violet ('26)	.25	*.25*
88	A11	1.10fr blue grn ('27)	8.00	6.00
89	A15	2fr vio & ol brn ('25)	2.75	1.00
90	A15	3fr rose & ultra, *yel* ('27)	22.50	11.00
91	A15	5fr grn & rose ('25)	8.50	6.00
92	A15	10fr yel brn & bl ('25)	25.00	17.50
		Nos. 60-92 (33)	86.30	55.85
		Set, never hinged	175.00	

Nos. 60 to 74 and 76 exist imperforate.
For surcharges see Nos. 93-94, 97-99, C1.

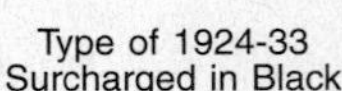

Type of 1924-33 Surcharged in Black

1926-31

No.	Type	Description	Unused	Used
93	A13	30c on 25c rose	.30	.25
94	A13	50c on 60c ol grn, *grnsh* ('28)	1.50	.35
95	A11	50c on 1.05fr red vio ('28)	1.10	.70
a.		Double surcharge	65.00	
96	A11	50c on 1.10fr bl grn ('31)	14.00	8.75
97	A13	50c on 1.25fr bl, *bluish* (R) ('28)	1.60	.65
98	A13	1.25fr on 1fr bl, *bluish*	.80	.50
99	A15	1.50fr on 2fr vio & ol brn ('28)	7.00	5.25
		Nos. 93-99 (7)	26.30	16.45
		Set, never hinged	40.00	

Princes Charles III, Louis II and Albert I A17

1928, Feb. 18 **Engr.** ***Perf. 11***

No.	Type	Description	Unused	Used
100	A17	50c dull carmine	2.50	*4.75*
101	A17	1.50fr dark blue	2.50	*4.75*
102	A17	3fr dark violet	2.50	*4.75*
		Nos. 100-102 (3)	7.50	14.25
		Set, never hinged	18.00	

Nos. 100-102 were sold exclusively at the Intl. Phil. Exhib. at Monte Carlo, Feb., 1928. One set was sold to each purchaser of a ticket of admission to the exhibition which cost 5fr.
Exist imperf. Value, set $27.50.

Old Watchtower A20

Royal Palace A21

Church of St. Dévote — A22

Prince Louis II — A23

"The Rock" of Monaco A24

Gardens of Monaco A25

Fortifications and Harbor — A26

1932-37 ***Perf. 13, 14x13½***

No.	Type	Description	Unused	Used
110	A20	15c lilac rose	.80	.25
111	A20	20c orange brn	.80	.25
112	A21	25c olive blk	1.10	.35
113	A22	30c yellow grn	1.40	.35
114	A23	40c dark brown	3.25	1.40
115	A24	45c brown red	3.50	1.10
a.		45c red	425.00	425.00
116	A23	50c purple	3.25	.85
117	A25	65c blue green	3.50	1.10
118	A26	75c deep blue	4.00	1.75
119	A23	90c red	9.50	3.25
120	A22	1fr red brn ('33)	27.50	7.75
121	A26	1.25fr rose lilac	6.75	4.50
122	A23	1.50fr ultra	40.00	10.50
123	A21	1.75fr rose lilac	35.00	9.50
124	A21	1.75fr car rose ('37)	24.00	13.00
125	A24	2fr dark blue	13.50	4.75
126	A20	3fr purple	20.00	9.00
127	A21	3.50fr orange ('35)	47.50	32.50
128	A22	5fr violet	27.50	20.00
129	A21	10fr deep blue	125.00	70.00
130	A25	20fr black	175.00	140.00
		Nos. 110-130 (21)	572.85	332.15
		Set, never hinged	1,150.	

Postage Due Stamps of 1925-32 Surcharged or Overprinted in Black

1937-38 ***Perf. 14x13***

No.	Type	Description	Unused	Used
131	D3	5c on 10c violet	1.00	1.00
132	D3	10c violet	1.00	1.00
133	D3	15c on 30c bister	1.00	1.00
134	D3	20c on 30c bister	1.00	1.00
135	D3	25c on 60c red	1.50	1.50
136	D3	30c bister	2.40	2.40
137	D3	40c on 60c red	2.40	2.40
138	D3	50c on 60c red	2.40	2.40
139	D3	65c on 1fr lt bl	2.25	2.00
140	D3	85c on 1fr lt bl	5.00	4.50
141	D3	1fr light blue	7.75	7.75
142	D3	2.15fr on 2fr dl red	7.75	7.75
143	D3	2.25fr on 2fr dl red ('38)	19.00	19.00
144	D3	2.50fr on 2fr dl red ('38)	29.00	29.00
		Nos. 131-144 (14)	83.45	82.70
		Set, never hinged	175.00	

Grimaldi Arms — A27

Prince Louis II — A28

1937-43 **Engr.**

No.	Type	Description	Unused	Used
145	A27	1c dk vio brn ('38)	.25	.25
146	A27	2c emerald	.25	.25
147	A27	3c brt red violet	.25	.25
148	A27	5c red	.25	.25
149	A27	10c ultra	.25	.25
149A	A27	10c black ('43)	.25	.25
150	A27	15c violet ('39)	1.75	1.50
150A	A27	30c dull grn ('43)	.25	.25
150B	A27	40c rose car ('43)	.25	.25
150C	A27	50c brt vio ('43)	.25	.25
151	A28	55c red brn ('38)	5.75	2.25
151A	A27	60c Prus blue ('43)	.25	.25
152	A28	65c violet ('38)	30.00	13.00
153	A28	70c red brn ('39)	.35	.35
153A	A27	70c red brn ('43)	.25	.25
154	A28	90c violet ('39)	.35	.30
155	A28	1fr rose red ('38)	18.50	10.50
156	A28	1.25fr rose red ('39)	.35	.35
157	A28	1.75fr ultra ('38)	18.50	10.50
158	A28	2.25fr ultra ('39)	.35	.25
		Nos. 145-158 (20)	78.65	41.75
		Set, never hinged	150.00	

Nos. 151, 152, 155, 157 exist imperf.

Souvenir Sheet

Prince Louis II — A29

1938, Jan. 17 **Unwmk.** ***Imperf.***

No.	Type	Description	Unused	Used
159	A29	10fr magenta	65.00	65.00
		Never hinged	175.00	

"Fête Nationale" 1/17/38. Size: 99x120mm.

Cathedral of Monaco — A30

St. Nicholas Square — A31

Palace Gate — A32

Palace of Monaco — A34

Panorama of Monaco A33

Harbor of Monte Carlo A35

1939-46 ***Perf. 13***

No.	Type	Description	Unused	Used
160	A30	20c rose lilac	.25	.25
161	A31	25c gldn brown	.45	.30
162	A32	30c dk blue grn	.35	.30
162A	A32	30c brown red ('40)	.35	.25
163	A31	40c henna brn	.70	.50
164	A33	45c brt red vio	.50	.50
165	A34	50c dk blue grn	.35	.25
166	A32	60c rose carmine	.40	.35
166A	A32	60c dk green ('40)	.90	.70
166B	A35	70c brt red vio ('41)	.40	.25
167	A35	75c dark green	.40	.25
167A	A30	80c dull green ('43)	.25	*.25*
168	A34	1fr brown black	.40	.25
168A	A33	1fr claret ('43)	.25	.25
168B	A35	1.20fr ultra ('46)	.25	*.35*
168C	A34	1.30fr brown blk ('41)	.40	.35
168D	A31	1.50fr ultra ('46)	.40	.40
169	A31	2fr rose violet	.40	.30
169A	A35	2fr lt ultra ('43)	.25	.25
169B	A34	2fr green ('46)	.35	.25
170	A33	2.50fr red	27.50	17.50
171	A33	2.50fr dp blue ('40)	1.75	1.75
172	A35	3fr brown red	.45	.35

172A A31 3fr black ('43) .25 .25
172B A30 4fr rose lilac ('46) 1.25 .55
172C A34 4.50fr brt violet ('43) .25 .25
173 A30 5fr Prus blue 5.25 4.00
173A A32 5fr deep green ('43) .25 .25
173B A34 6fr lt violet ('46) .70 .55
174 A33 10fr green 1.40 *1.60*
174A A30 10fr deep blue ('43) .25 *.25*
174B A35 15fr rose pink ('43) .40 *.25*
175 A32 20fr brt ultra 1.60 1.25
175A A33 20fr sepia ('43) .40 .25
175B A35 25fr blue green ('46) 1.40 1.25
Nos. 160-175B (35) 51.10 36.85
Set, never hinged 100.00

See Nos. 214-221, 228-232, 274-275, 319-320, 407-408, 423, 426, 428-429 in Scott Standard catalogue, Vol. 4; B36-B50.

Louis II Stadium A36

1939, Apr. 23 **Engr.**
176 A36 10fr dark green 100.00 *110.00*
Never hinged 175.00

Inauguration of Louis II Stadium.

Louis II Stadium A37

1939, Aug. 15
177 A37 40c dull green 1.25 1.25
178 A37 70c brown black 1.60 1.60
179 A37 90c dark violet 2.25 2.25
180 A37 1.25fr copper red 3.00 3.00
181 A37 2.25fr dark blue 4.25 4.25
Nos. 177-181 (5) 12.35 12.35
Set, never hinged 22.50

8th International University Games.

Imperforates

Many Monaco stamps from 1940 to 1999 exist imperforate. Officially 20 sheets, ranging from 25 to 100 subjects, were left imperforate.

SEMI-POSTAL STAMPS

No. 16 Surcharged in Red

1914, Oct. **Unwmk.** ***Perf. 14x13½***
B1 A2 10c + 5c carmine 5.00 5.00
Never hinged 13.50
On cover, 10c rate 57.50

View of Monaco — SP2

1919, Sept. 20 **Typo.**
B2 SP2 2c + 3c lilac 32.50 *32.50*
Never hinged 60.00
On Cover 55.00
B3 SP2 5c + 5c green 17.50 *17.50*
Never hinged 35.00
On Cover 40.00
B4 SP2 15c + 10c rose 17.50 *17.50*
Never hinged 35.00
On Cover 40.00
B5 SP2 25c + 15c blue 37.50 *37.50*
Never hinged 65.00
On Cover 65.00
B6 SP2 50c + 50c brn, *buff* 175.00 *150.00*
Never hinged 350.00
On Cover 240.00
B7 SP2 1fr + 1fr blk, *yel* 275.00 *150.00*
Never hinged 550.00
On Cover 550.00
B8 SP2 5fr + 5fr dull red 925.00 *1,050.*
Never hinged 1,850.
On Cover 2,000.
Nos. B2-B8 (7) 1,480. *1,455.*

Nos. B4-B8 Surcharged

20 mars
1920
2c + 3c

1920, Mar. 20
B9 SP2 2c + 3c on #B4 37.50 *37.50*
Never hinged 70.00
On Cover 80.00
a. "c" of "3c" inverted *1,500.* *1,500.*
Never hinged 2,400.
b. Pair, Nos. 9, 9a 2,250. *2,250.*
Never hinged 3,000.
B10 SP2 2c + 3c on #B5 37.50 *37.50*
Never hinged 70.00
On Cover 80.00
a. "c" of "3c" inverted *1,500.* *1,500.*
Never hinged 2,400.
b. Pair, Nos. 10, 10a 2,250. *2,250.*
Never hinged *3,000.*
B11 SP2 2c + 3c on #B6 37.50 *37.50*
Never hinged 70.00
On Cover 80.00
a. "c" of "3c" inverted *1,500.* *1,500.*
Never hinged *2,400.*
b. Pair, Nos. 11, 11a 2,250. *2,250.*
Never hinged *3,000.*
B12 SP2 5c + 5c on #B7 37.50 *37.50*
Never hinged 70.00
On Cover 80.00
B13 SP2 5c + 5c on #B8 37.50 *37.50*
Never hinged 70.00
On Cover 80.00

Overprinted

20 mars
1920

B14 SP2 15c + 10c rose 25.00 25.00
Never hinged 50.00
On Cover 40.00
B15 SP2 25c + 15c blue 10.50 10.50
Never hinged 18.00
On Cover 24.00
B16 SP2 50c + 50c brn, *buff* 50.00 50.00
Never hinged 90.00
On Cover 120.00
B17 SP2 1fr + 1fr blk, *yel* 67.50 67.50
Never hinged 140.00
On Cover 325.00
B18 SP2 5fr + 5fr red 5,800. 5,800.
Never hinged 8,900.
On Cover —
Nos. B9-B17 (9) 340.50 340.50

Marriage of Princess Charlotte to Prince Pierre, Comte de Polignac.

Palace Gardens SP3

"The Rock" of Monaco SP4

Bay of Monaco SP5

Prince Louis II — SP6

1937, Apr. **Engr.** ***Perf. 13***
B19 SP3 50c + 50c green 2.10 2.10
B20 SP4 90c + 90c car 2.10 2.10
B21 SP5 1.50fr + 1.50fr blue 5.00 5.00
B22 SP6 2fr + 2fr violet 8.50 8.50
B23 SP6 5fr + 5fr brn red 60.00 60.00
Nos. B19-B23 (5) 77.70 77.70
Set, never hinged 225.00

The surtax was used for welfare work.

Pierre and Marie Curie — SP7

Monaco Hospital, Date Palms SP8

1938, Nov. 15 ***Perf. 13***
B24 SP7 65c + 25c dp bl grn 9.00 9.00
B25 SP8 1.75fr + 50c dp ultra 9.00 9.00
Set, never hinged 35.00

B24 and B25 exist imperforate.

The surtax was for the International Union for the Control of Cancer.

Lucien — SP9

Honoré II — SP10

Louis I — SP11

Charlotte de Gramont — SP12

Antoine I — SP13

Marie de Lorraine — SP14

Jacques I SP15

Louise-Hippolyte SP16

Honoré III — SP17

"The Rock," 18th Century SP18

1939, June 26
B26 SP9 5c + 5c brn blk 1.25 .75
B27 SP10 10c + 10c rose vio 1.25 .75
B28 SP11 45c + 15c brt grn 4.50 3.50
B29 SP12 70c + 30c brt red vio 6.75 6.00
B30 SP13 90c + 35c vio 6.75 6.00
B31 SP14 1fr + 1fr ultra 17.00 16.00
B32 SP15 2fr + 2fr brn org 17.00 16.00
B33 SP16 2.25fr + 1.25fr Prus bl 20.00 20.00
B34 SP17 3fr + 3fr dp rose 27.50 *27.50*
B35 SP18 5fr + 5fr red 50.00 *50.00*
Nos. B26-B35 (10) 152.00 146.50
Set, never hinged 400.00

Types of Regular Issue, 1939 Surcharged in Red

1940, Feb. 10 **Engr.** ***Perf. 13***
B36 A30 20c + 1fr violet 1.75 1.75
B37 A31 25c + 1fr dk grn 1.75 1.75
B38 A32 30c + 1fr brn red 1.75 1.75
B39 A31 40c + 1fr dk blue 1.75 1.75
B40 A33 45c + 1fr rose car 1.75 1.75
B41 A34 50c + 1fr brown 1.75 1.75
B42 A32 60c + 1fr dk grn 2.25 2.25
B43 A35 75c + 1fr brn blk 2.25 2.25
B44 A34 1fr + 1fr scarlet 3.00 3.00
B45 A31 2fr + 1fr indigo 3.00 3.00
B46 A33 2.50fr + 1fr dk grn 7.00 7.00
B47 A35 3fr + 1fr dk blue 7.00 7.00
B48 A30 5fr + 1fr brn blk 9.50 9.50
B49 A33 10fr + 5fr lt blue 18.00 18.00
B50 A32 20fr + 5fr brn vio 18.00 18.00
Nos. B36-B50 (15) 80.50 80.50
Set, never hinged 240.00

The surtax was used to purchase ambulances for the French government.

AIR POST STAMPS

No. 91 Srchd. in Black

Perf. 14x13½

1933, Aug. 22 **Unwmk.**

C1	A15 1.50fr on 5fr		16.00	16.00
	a. Imperf., pair		350.00	

POSTAGE DUE STAMPS

D1

Perf. 14x13½

1905-43 **Unwmk.** **Typo.**

J1	D1	1c olive green	.45	.55
J2	D1	5c green	.45	.55
		On cover		57.50
J3	D1	10c rose	.45	.55
		On cover		57.50
J4	D1	10c brn ('09)	350.00	125.00
		On cover		175.00
J5	D1	15c vio brn, *straw*	3.50	1.75
J6	D1	20c bis brn, *buff* ('26)	.35	.35
J7	D1	30c blue	.45	.55
		On cover		57.50
J8	D1	40c red vio ('26)	.35	.35
J9	D1	50c brn, *org*	4.50	4.00
		On cover		57.50
J10	D1	50c blue grn ('27)	.35	.35
J11	D1	60c gray blk ('26)	.35	.65
J12	D1	60c brt vio ('34)	21.00	27.50
J13	D1	1fr red brn, *straw* ('26)	.35	.25
J14	D1	2fr red org ('27)	1.00	1.50
J15	D1	3fr mag ('27)	1.00	1.50
J15A	D1	5fr ultra ('43)	.80	1.00
		Nos. J1-J15A (16)	385.35	166.40

For surcharge see No. J27.

Prince Albert I — D2

1910

J16	D2	1c olive green	.25	.45
J17	D2	10c light violet	.45	.60
J18	D2	30c bister	190.00	160.00

In January, 1917, regular postage stamps overprinted "T" in a triangle were used as postage due stamps.

Nos. J17 and J18 Surcharged

1918

J19	D2 20c on 10c lt vio	3.75	7.50
	a. Double surcharge	*1,000.*	
J20	D2 40c on 30c bister	4.50	8.50

D3

1925-32

J21	D3	1c gray green	.40	.50
J22	D3	10c violet	.40	.55
J23	D3	30c bister	.50	.75
J24	D3	60c red	.70	.75
J25	D3	1fr lt bl ('32)	75.00	75.00
J26	D3	2fr dull red ('32)	75.00	75.00
		Nos. J21-J26 (6)	152.00	152.55

Nos. J25 and J26 have the numerals of value double-lined.

"Recouvrements" stamps were used to recover charges due on undelivered or refused mail which was returned to the sender.

No. J9 Surcharged

1925

J27	D1 1fr on 50c brn, *org*	.75	.50
	a. Double surcharge	*750.00*	

MONGOLIA

män-ˈgōl-yə

(Outer Mongolia)

LOCATION — Central Asia, bounded on the north by Siberia, on the west by Sinkiang, on the south and east by China proper and Manchuria
GOVT. — Republic
AREA — 604,250 sq. mi.
POP. — 1,820,000 (est. 1984)
CAPITAL — Ulan Bator

Outer Mongolia, which had long been under Russian influence although nominally a dependency of China, voted at a plebescite on October 20, 1945, to sever all ties with China and become an independent nation. See Tannu Tuva.

100 Cents = 1 Dollar
100 Mung = 1 Tugrik (1926)

Watermark

Wmk. 170 — Greek Border and Rosettes

Scepter of Indra — A1

1924 Litho. Unwmk. *Perf. 10, 13½*
Surface Tinted Paper

1	A1	1c multi, *bister*	12.00	12.00
2	A1	2c multi, *brnsh*	10.50	5.50
	a.	Perf. 13½	47.50	40.00
3	A1	5c multi	40.00	24.00
	a.	Perf. 10	47.50	35.00
4	A1	10c multi, *gray bl*	20.00	16.00
	a.	Perf. 10	20.00	16.00
5	A1	20c multi, *gray*	27.50	17.50
6	A1	50c multi, *salmon*	40.00	24.00
7	A1	$1 multi, *yellow*	55.00	40.00
	b.	Perf. 10	650.00	190.00
		Nos. 1-7 (7)	205.00	139.00

These stamps vary in size from 19x25mm (1c) to 30x39mm ($1). They also differ in details of the design.

Errors of perforating and printing exist.

Some quantities of Nos. 1-2, 4-7 were defaced with horizontal perforation across the center.

The 5c exists perf 11½. Value, $325 unused, hinged, $190 used.

Revenue Stamps Handstamp

A2

Sizes: 1c to 20c: 22x36mm
50c, $1: 26x43½mm
$5: 30x45½mm

Overprinted in Violet

1926 ***Perf. 11***

16	A2	1c blue	12.00	12.00
17	A2	2c orange	16.00	11.00
18	A2	5c plum	16.00	13.00
19	A2	10c green	20.00	17.00
20	A2	20c yel brn	24.00	20.00
21	A2	50c brn & ol grn	*190.00*	*175.00*
22	A2	$1 brn & salmon	*550.00*	*475.00*
23	A2	$5 red, yel & gray	*650.00*	—
		Nos. 16-23 (8)	*1,478.*	*723.00*

Black Overprint

16a	A2	1c blue	20.00	13.50
17a	A2	2c orange	32.50	20.00
18a	A2	5c plum	36.00	20.00
19a	A2	10c green	47.50	24.00
20a	A2	20c yellow brown	65.00	45.00
21a	A2	50c brown & olive grn	*1,200.*	*325.00*
22a	A2	$1 brown & salmon	*600.00*	*400.00*
23a	A2	$5 red, yellow & gray		
		Nos. 16a-22a (7)	*2,001.*	*847.50*

Red Overprint

16b	A2	1c blue
17b	A2	2c orange
18b	A2	5c plum
19b	A2	10c green
20b	A2	20c yellow brown

The preceding handstamped overprints may be found inverted, double, etc. Counterfeits abound.

For overprints and surcharges see #48-61.

A3

A4

Soyombo

TYPE I — The pearl above the crescent is solid. The devices in the middle of the stamp are not outlined.

TYPE II — The pearl is open. The devices and panels are all outlined in black.

1926-29 ***Perf. 11***

Type I
Size: 22x28mm

32	A3	5m lilac & blk	12.00	12.00
33	A3	20m blue & blk	20.00	24.00

Type II
Size: 22x29mm

34	A3	1m yellow & blk	3.25	3.25
35	A3	2m brn org & blk	4.00	3.25
36	A3	5m lilac & blk	4.75	4.00
37	A3	10m lt blue & blk	4.00	2.00
	a.	Imperf, pair		
39	A3	25m yel grn & blk	8.00	4.00
	a.	Imperf, pair	125.00	110.00

Size: 26x34mm

40	A3	40m lemon & blk	11.00	4.75
41	A3	50m buff & blk	16.00	6.50

Size: 28x37mm

42	A4	1t brown, grn & blk	32.50	12.00
43	A4	3t red, yel & blk	72.50	47.50
44	A4	5t brn vio, rose & blk	95.00	60.00
		Nos. 32-44 (12)	283.00	183.25

In 1929 a change was made in the perforating machine. Every fourth pin was removed, which left the perforation holes in groups of three with blank spaces between the groups. Nos. 44A-44D have only this interrupted perforation. Nos. 37 and 39 are found with both perforations.

For overprints and surcharges see #45-47.

Soyombo — A5

1929, July ***Interrupted Perf 11***

44A	A5 5m lilac & black	25.00	20.00
44B	A5 10m lt grnish blue & black	100.00	65.00
	a. imperf, pair	—	
44C	A5 20m blue & black	35.00	27.50
	a. imperf, pair	—	
	b. Horiz. pair, imperf btwn.		—
44D	A5 25m yel grn & black	32.50	27.50
	a. imperf, pair	—	

See note after No. 44.

Nos. 34, 35, 40 Handstamped With New Values in Black

1930

45	A3	10m on 1m	32.50	30.00
46	A3	20m on 2m	45.00	40.00
47	A3	25m on 40m	52.50	47.50
		Nos. 45-47 (3)	130.00	117.50

Soyombo — A6

Violet Overprint, Handstamped

1931

48	A6	1c blue	24.00	12.00
	a.	Blue overprint	87.50	47.50
49	A6	2c orange	27.50	9.50
50	A6	5c brown vio	35.00	9.50
	a.	Blue overprint	65.00	22.50
51	A6	10c green	32.50	9.50
	a.	Blue overprint	65.00	37.50
52	A6	20c bister brn	47.50	12.00
53	A6	50c brown & ol yel	130.00	120.00
54	A6	$1 brown & salmon	200.00	160.00
		Nos. 48-54 (7)	496.50	332.50

Soyombo — A7

Revenue Stamps Surcharged in Black, Red or Blue

1931

59	A7	5m on 5c brn vio (Bk)	40.00	16.00
	a.	Inverted surcharge		35.00
	b.	Imperf., pair	225.00	225.00
60	A7	10m on 10c grn (R)	55.00	27.50
	a.	Inverted surcharge	90.00	50.00
	b.	Imperf., pair	225.00	225.00
61	A7	20m on 20c bis brn (Bl)	65.00	35.00
	a.	Inverted surcharge		55.00
	b.	Imperf., pair	225.00	225.00
		Nos. 59-61 (3)	160.00	78.50

On Nos. 59-61, "Postage" is always diagonal, and may read up or down.

Weaver at Loom — A8

Telegrapher A9

Sukhe Bator A10

Lake and Mountains — A11

Designs: 5m, Mongol at lathe. 10m, Government building, Ulan Bator. 15m, Young Mongolian revolutionary. 20m, Studying Latin alphabet. 25m, Mongolian soldier. 50m, Monument to Sukhe Bator. 3t, Sheep shearing. 5t, Camel caravan. 10t, Chasing wild horses.

Perf. 12½x12

1932		Photo.		Wmk. 170
62	A8	1m brown	3.25	1.50
63	A9	2m red violet	3.25	1.50
64	A8	5m indigo	2.00	.80
65	A8	10m dull green	2.00	.80
66	A9	15m dp brown	2.00	.80
67	A9	20m rose red	2.40	.80
68	A9	25m dull violet	2.40	.80
69	A10	40m gray black	2.00	1.20
70	A10	50m dull blue	2.40	.80

Perf. 11x12

71	A11	1t dull green	2.75	1.20
72	A11	3t dull violet	5.50	2.00
73	A11	5t brown	19.50	12.00
74	A11	10t ultra	40.00	20.00
		Nos. 62-74 (13)	89.45	44.20

Used values are for canceled-to-order stamps.

MONTENEGRO

ˌmän-tə-ˈnē-ˌgrō

LOCATION — Southern Europe, bordering on the Adriatic Sea
GOVT. — Kingdom
AREA — 5,603 sq. mi.
POP. — 516,000 (estimated)
CAPITAL — Cetinje

This kingdom, formerly a Turkish Protectorate, later became independent. On December 1, 1918, Montenegro united with Serbia, Bosnia and Herzegovina, Croatia, Dalmatia and Slovenia to form the Kingdom of the Serbs, Croats and Slovenes which became Yugoslavia in 1929.

All stamps of the Kingdom of Montenegro were printed at the State Printing Works, Vienna, Later, overprints were applied at Cetinje.

100 Novcic = 1 Florin
100 Helera = 1 Kruna (1902)
100 Para = 1 Kruna (1907)
100 Para = 1 Perper (1910)

Canceled to Order

Used values for Nos. 1-110, H1-H5, and J1-J26 are for canceled-to-order stamps. Postally used examples sell for considerably more.

Watermarks

Wmk. 91 — "BRIEF-MARKEN" (#1-14) or "ZEITUNGS-MARKEN" (#15-21) in Double-lined Capitals once across sheet

Prince Nicholas I — A1

Early Printings
Narrow Spacing (2-2½mm)
Perf. 10½ Large Holes, pointed teeth

1874		Typo.		Wmk. 91
1	A1	2n yellow	40.00	45.00
2	A1	3n green	55.00	45.00
3	A1	5n rose red	50.00	45.00
4	A1	7n lt lilac	50.00	37.50
5	A1	10n blue	140.00	92.50
6	A1	15n yel bister	160.00	140.00
7	A1	25n lilac gray	325.00	225.00
		Nos. 1-7 (7)	820.00	630.00

Middle Printings (1879)
Narrow spacing
Perf. 12, 12½, 13 and Compound

8	A1	2n yellow	11.50	7.50
a.		Perf. 12-13x10½	190.00	140.00
9	A1	3n green	9.25	6.00
10	A1	5n red	9.25	6.00
11	A1	7n rose lilac	9.25	6.00
a.		7n lilac	19.00	14.00
12	A1	10n blue	19.00	8.00
a.		Perf. 12-13x10½	65.00	52.50
13	A1	15n bister brn	19.00	11.00
14	A1	25n gray lilac	25.00	16.00
		Nos. 8-14 (7)	102.25	60.50

Late Printings (1893?)
Narrow and wide spacing (2¾-3½mm)
Perf. 10½, 11½ Small holes, broad teeth
(Perf. 11½ also with pointed teeth)

15	A1	2n yellow	4.50	3.00
a.		Perf. 11 ('94)	32.50	23.00
16	A1	3n green	4.50	3.00
17	A1	5n red	3.50	2.75
18	A1	7n rose	3.50	2.75
a.		Perf. 11 ('94)	14.50	13.50
19	A1	10n blue	4.50	3.25
20	A1	15n brown	4.50	3.50
21	A1	25n brown violet	5.75	4.50
		Nos. 15-21 (7)	30.75	22.75

Dates of issue of the late printings are still being researched.

Types of 1874-93 Overprinted in Black or Red

1893			*Perf. 10½, 11½*	
22	A1	2n yellow	32.50	8.00
a.		Perf. 11	*75.00*	*30.00*
23	A1	3n green	6.50	3.25
24	A1	5n red	4.50	2.75
25	A1	7n rose	5.75	4.50
a.		Perf. 12	110.00	72.50
b.		7n rose lilac	5.00	3.00
c.		7n lilac, perf. 12	*125.00*	
d.		Perf. 11	*40.00*	*30.00*
26	A1	10n blue	5.75	4.50
27	A1	10n blue (R)	8.50	6.25
28	A1	15n brown	4.50	3.50
a.		Perf. 12	140.00	92.50
29	A1	15n brown (R)	*2,750.*	*1,900.*
30	A1	25n brown violet	4.50	3.50
31	A1	25n brn vio (R)	8.50	5.50
a.		Perf. 12½		*275.00*
		Nos. 22-28,30-31 (9)	81.00	41.75

Introduction of printing to Montenegro, 400th anniversary.

This overprint had many settings. Several values exist with "1494" or "1495" instead of "1493", or with missing letters or numerals due to wearing of the clichés. Double and inverted overprints exist. Some printings were made after 1893 to supply a philatelic demand, but were available for postage.

The 7n with red overprint was not issued.

1894-98		Wmk. 91		*Perf. 10½*
32	A1	1n gray blue	.65	.65
33	A1	2n emerald ('98)	.45	.45
34	A1	3n car rose ('98)	.45	.45
c.		3n analine red ('98)	.45	.75
35	A1	5n orange ('98)	2.75	.65
36	A1	7n gray lilac ('98)	.55	.55
37	A1	10n magenta ('98)	.65	.95
38	A1	15n red brn ('98)	.45	.65
39	A1	20n brown orange	.65	.65
40	A1	25n dull blue ('98)	.45	.65
41	A1	30n maroon	.65	.65
42	A1	50n ultra	.65	.45
43	A1	1fl deep green	.95	4.50
44	A1	2fl red brown	1.50	13.50
		Nos. 32-44 (13)	10.80	24.75

Perf. 11½, Small Holes

32a	A1	1n gray blue	.55	.60
33a	A1	2n emerald ('98)	.70	.65
34a	A1	3n carmine rose ('98)	.70	.65
c.		3n aniline red ('98)	8.00	1.40
35a	A1	5n orange ('98)	1.10	1.10
36a	A1	7n gray lilac ('98)	1.50	1.10
37a	A1	10n magenta ('98)	1.50	1.40
38a	A1	15n red brown ('98)	1.10	1.40
39a	A1	20n brown orange ('98)	.65	.65
40a	A1	25n dull blue ('98)	1.10	1.40
41a	A1	30n maroon	.65	.95
42a	A1	50n ultramarine	.75	1.40
43a	A1	1fl deep green	1.90	3.25
44a	A1	2fl red brown	1.90	4.00

Perf. 11½, Large Holes

32b	A1	1n gray blue	.45	.45
33b	A1	2n emerald ('98)	2.25	2.10
34b	A1	3n carmine rose ('98)	.70	.65
c.		3n aniline red ('98)	2.00	2.75
35b	A1	5n orange ('98)	8.00	1.40
36b	A1	7n gray lilac ('98)	1.10	1.10
37b	A1	10n magenta ('98)	1.40	1.10
38b	A1	15n red brown ('98)	1.10	1.40
39b	A1	20n brown orange ('98)	.45	.45
40b	A1	25n dull blue ('98)	1.10	1.40
41b	A1	30n maroon	.45	.55
42b	A1	50n ultramarine	2.75	.65
43b	A1	1fl deep green	4.25	6.25
44b	A1	2fl red brown	4.25	19.00

Monastery at Cetinje (Royal Mausoleum) A3

Perf. 10½

1896, Sept. 1		Litho.		Unwmk.
45	A3	1n dk blue & bis	.40	1.40
46	A3	2n magenta & yel	.40	1.40
47	A3	3n org brn & yel grn	.40	1.40
48	A3	5n bl grn & bis	.40	1.40
49	A3	10n yellow & ultra	.40	1.40
50	A3	15n dk blue & grn	.40	1.40
51	A3	20n bl grn & ultra	.40	1.50
52	A3	25n dk blue & yel	.50	1.50
53	A3	30n magenta & bis	.65	1.50
54	A3	50n red brn & gray bl	.65	1.50
55	A3	1fl rose & gray bl	1.10	1.90
56	A3	2fl brown & black	1.60	2.25
		Nos. 45-56 (12)	7.30	18.55

Perf. 11½

45a	A3	1n dark blue & bister	.95	2.25
46a	A3	2n magenta & yellow	.95	2.25
47a	A3	3n org brn & yel grn	.95	2.25
48a	A3	5n blue green & bister	.95	2.25
49a	A3	10n yellow & ultramarine	.45	1.40
50a	A3	15n dark blue & green	72.50	110.00
51a	A3	20n blue green & ultra	45.00	67.50
52a	A3	25n dk blue & yellow	1.40	2.75
53a	A3	30n magenta & bister	1.40	2.75
54a	A3	50n red brn & gray blue	1.40	2.75
55a	A3	1fl rose & gray blue	2.10	3.50
56a	A3	2fl brown & black	2.75	5.50

Bicentenary of the ruling dynasty, founded by the Vladika, Danilo Petrovich of Nyegosh.

Inverted centers and other errors exist, but experts believe these to be printer's waste.

Perf. 11½ counterfeits are common.

Prince Nicholas I — A4

Perf. 13x13½, 13x12½ (2h, 5h, 50h, 2k, 5k), 12½ (1h, 25h)

1902, July 12				
57	A4	1h ultra	.45	.45
58	A4	2h rose lilac	.45	.45
59	A4	5h green	.45	.45
a.		Pair, imperf.	5.75	
60	A4	10h rose	.45	.45
61	A4	25h dull blue	.95	1.10
a.		Perf. 12½	4.50	
62	A4	50h gray green	.95	1.10
63	A4	1k chocolate	.95	.95
64	A4	2k pale brown	.95	1.10
65	A4	5k buff	1.10	2.75
		Nos. 57-65 (9)	6.70	8.80

The 2h black brown and 25h indigo were not issued. Values: 2h, $95; 25h, $65. The 25h, perf. 12½, probably was never issued. Value, $4.50.

Constitution Issue

Same Overprinted in Red or Black "Constitution" 15mm

УСТАВ Type I

УСТАВ Type II

УСТАВ Type III

УСТАВ Type IV

1905, Dec. 5				
66	A4	1h ultra (R)	.45	.45
e.		Double overprint	14.00	14.00
67	A4	2h rose lilac	.45	.45
e.		Double overprint	14.00	14.00
68	A4	5h green (R)	.95	.95
e.		Double overprint	14.00	14.00
f.		Inverted overprint	37.50	
69	A4	10h rose	1.40	1.10
e.		Double overprint	14.00	
70	A4	25h dull blue (R)	.70	.65
e.		Double overprint	14.00	
71	A4	50h gray green (R)	.70	.65
e.		Double overprint	14.00	14.00
72	A4	1k chocolate (R)	.70	.65
e.		Double overprint	14.00	14.00
f.		Inverted overprint	37.50	
73	A4	2k pale brown (R)	.95	.95
e.		Double overprint	17.00	17.00
74	A4	5k buff	1.50	1.40
e.		Double overprint	17.00	
		Nos. 66-74 (9)	7.80	7.25

Overprints in other colors are proofs.

1906		"Constitution" 16½mm		

Type I

67a	A4	2h rose lilac	45.00	45.00
e.		Double overprint	—	
f.		Inverted overprint	—	
69a	A4	10h rose	325.00	
70a	A4	25h dull blue (R)	29.00	27.00
e.		Double overprint	—	
f.		Inverted overprint	—	
71a	A4	50h gray green (R)	29.00	27.00
e.		Double overprint	—	
f.		Inverted overprint	—	
72a	A4	1k chocolate (R)	29.00	27.00
73a	A4	2k pale brown (R)	29.00	27.00
f.		Inverted overprint	—	
74a	A4	5k buff	1.50	1.40
f.		Inverted overprint	—	
		Nos. 67a-74a (9)	488.90	155.80

Type II

66b	A4	1h ultra (R)	.45	.45
67b	A4	2h rose lilac	.45	.45
e.		Double overprint	19.00	
f.		Inverted overprint	47.50	
68b	A4	5h green (R)	.95	.95
e.		Double overprint	19.00	
69b	A4	10h rose	1.10	1.10
f.		Inverted overprint	47.50	
70b	A4	25h dull blue (R)	.70	.65
e.		Double overprint	19.00	
f.		Inverted overprint	47.50	
71b	A4	50h gray green (R)	.70	.65
e.		Double overprint	19.00	
72b	A4	1k chocolate (R)	.70	.65
73b	A4	2k pale brown (R)	.95	.95
f.		Inverted overprint	47.50	
74b	A4	5k buff	1.50	1.40
f.		Inverted overprint	55.00	
		Nos. 66b-74b (9)	7.50	7.25

Type III

66c	A4	1h ultra (R)	2.75	2.75
67c	A4	2h rose lilac	2.75	2.75
e.		Double overprint	—	
f.		Inverted overprint	—	
68c	A4	5h green (R)	5.75	5.50
e.		Double overprint	—	
69c	A4	10h rose	7.25	6.75
f.		Double overprint	—	
70c	A4	25h dull blue (R)	3.75	3.50
e.		Double overprint	—	
f.		Inverted overprint	—	
71c	A4	50h gray green (R)	3.75	3.50
e.		Double overprint	—	

72c A4 1k chocolate (R) 3.75 3.75
73c A4 2k pale brown (R) 4.75 4.75
f. Inverted overprint —
74c A4 5k buff 5.75 5.50
f. Inverted overprint —

Type IV

66d A4 1h ultra (R) .95 .95
g. "Constitutton" 22.50
h. "Coustitution" 22.50
67d A4 2h rose lilac .95 .95
g. "Constitutton" 22.50
h. "Coustitution" 22.50
68d A4 5h green (R) 2.40 2.40
e. Double overprint —
f. Inverted overprint —
g. "Constitutton" 22.50
h. "Coustitution" 22.50
69d A4 10h rose 2.25 6.75
f. Inverted overprint —
g. "Constitutton" 22.50
h. "Coustitution" 22.50
70d A4 25h dull blue (R) 1.90 1.90
e. Double overprint —
f. Inverted overprint —
g. "Constitutton" 37.50
h. "Coustitution" 37.50
71d A4 50h gray green (R) 2.40 2.40
f. Inverted overprint —
g. "Constitutton" 37.50
h. "Coustitution" 37.50
72d A4 1k chocolate (R) 2.40 2,40
g. "Constitutton" 47.50
h. "Coustitution" 47.50
73d A4 2k pale brown (R) 3.50 3.25
f. Inverted overprint —
g. "Constitutton" 47.50
h. "Coustitution" 47.50
74d A4 5k buff 3.75 3.50
f. Inverted overprint —
g. "Constitutton" 47.50
h. "Coustitution" 47.50

Many other overprint varieties exist, including reversed color overprints.

Prince Nicholas I — A5

1907, June 1 Engr. *Perf. 12½*

75 A5 1pa ocher .40 .25
76 A5 2pa black .40 .25
77 A5 5pa yellow green 1.60 .25
78 A5 10pa rose red 2.75 .25
79 A5 15pa ultra .45 .45
80 A5 20pa red orange .45 .45
81 A5 25pa indigo .45 .45
82 A5 35pa bister brown .70 .45
83 A5 50pa dull violet .70 .65
84 A5 1kr carmine rose .70 .65
85 A5 2kr green .70 .65
86 A5 5kr red brown 1.50 1.10
Nos. 75-86 (12) 10.80 5.85

Many Montenegro stamps exist imperforate or part perforate. Experts believe these to be printer's waste.

King Nicholas I as a Youth — A6

King Nicholas I and Queen Milena — A7

King Nicholas I — A11

Prince Nicholas — A12

5pa, 10pa, 25pa, 35pa, Nicholas in 1910. 15pa, Nicholas in 1878. 20pa, King and Queen, diff.

1910, Aug. 28 Engr.

87 A6 1pa black .75 .45
88 A7 2pa purple brown .75 .45
89 A6 5pa dark green .75 .45
90 A6 10pa carmine .75 .45
91 A6 15pa slate blue .75 .45
92 A7 20pa olive green .95 .65
93 A6 25pa deep blue .95 .65
94 A6 35pa chestnut 1.40 .95
95 A11 50pa violet 1.40 .95
96 A11 1per lake 1.40 .95
97 A11 2per yellow green 1.75 1.10

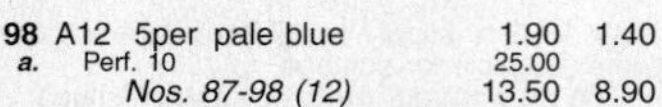
98 A12 5per pale blue 1.90 1.40
a. Perf. 10 25.00
Nos. 87-98 (12) 13.50 8.90

Proclamation of Montenegro as a kingdom, the 50th anniv. of the reign of King Nicholas and the golden wedding celebration of the King and Queen.

King Nicholas I — A13

1913, Apr. 1 Typo.

99 A13 1pa orange .45 .65
100 A13 2pa plum .45 .65
101 A13 5pa deep green .50 .65
102 A13 10pa deep rose .50 .65
103 A13 15pa blue gray .60 .65
104 A13 20pa dark brown .60 .65
105 A13 25pa deep blue .95 .95
106 A13 35pa vermilion .70 .65
107 A13 50pa pale blue .45 .95
108 A13 1per yellow brown .95 1.40
109 A13 2per gray violet .95 1.40
110 A13 5per yellow green .95 1.40
Nos. 99-110 (12) 8.05 10.65

ACKNOWLEDGMENT OF RECEIPT STAMPS

Prince Nicholas I — AR1

Perf. 10½, 11½

1895 Litho. Wmk. 91

H1 AR1 10n ultra & rose 1.10 1.10
a. Perf. 11½ 1.10 1.10

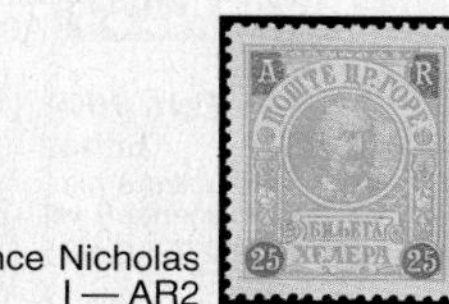
Prince Nicholas I — AR2

1902 Unwmk. *Perf. 12½*

H2 AR2 25h orange & carmine 1.10 1.10
a. Double print 29.00
b. Pair, imperf. 45.00

Constitution Issue

No. H2 Overprinted in Black

1905

"Constitution" 15mm

H3 AR2 25h orange & carmine 1.10 1.10
g. Inverted overprint 85.00
h. Double overprint 24.00

"Constitution" 16½mm ('06)

H3a Overprint Type I 32.50 35.00
H3b Overprint Type II 1.40 1.90
H3c Overprint Type III 5.75 6.50
H3d Overprint Type IV 3.25 3.50
e. "Constitutton" 22.00
f. "Coustitution" 22.00

See note after 74a.

AR3

1907 Engr.

H4 AR3 25pa olive .95 1.40

Nicholas I — AR4

1913 Typo.

H5 AR4 25pa olive green .95 3.50

POSTAGE DUE STAMPS

D1

Perf. 10½

1894, Nov. Litho. Wmk. 91

J1 D1 1n red 3.75 3.50
c. Pair, imperf. 42.50
J2 D1 2n yellow green 1.50 1.40
J3 D1 3n orange .95 .95
c. Double impression 8.50
J4 D1 5n olive green .70 .65
J5 D1 10n violet .70 .65
J6 D1 20n ultra .70 .65
c. Double impression 55.00
J7 D1 30n emerald .70 .65
c. Double impression 55.00
J8 D1 50n pale gray grn .70 .65
Nos. J1-J8 (8) 9.70 9.10

Perf. 11

J1a D1 1n red 7.25 6.75
J2a D1 2n yellow green 4.75 4.75
J3a D1 3n orange 5.75 5.50
J5a D1 10n violet 3.75 3.50
J6a D1 20n ultramarine 3.75 3.50
J7a D1 30n emerald 5.75 5.50
J8a D1 50n pale gray green 5.75 5.50
Nos. J1a-J8a (7) 36.75 35.00

Perf. 11½

J1b D1 1n red 3.75 3.50
J2b D1 2n yellow green 1.50 1.40
J3b D1 3n orange .95 .95
J4b D1 5n olive green .70 .65
J5b D1 10n violet .70 .65
J6b D1 20n ultramarine .70 .65
J7b D1 30n emerald .70 .65
J8b D1 50n pale gray green .70 .65
Nos. J1b-J8b (8) 9.70 9.10

D2

1902 Unwmk. *Perf. 12½*

J9 D2 5h orange .45 .65
J10 D2 10h olive green .45 .65
J11 D2 25h dull lilac .45 .65
J12 D2 50h emerald .45 .65
J13 D2 1k pale gray green .95 1.50
Nos. J9-J13 (5) 2.75 4.10

Constitution Issue

Postage Due Stamps of 1902 Overprinted in Black or Red "Constitution" 15mm

1905

J14 D2 5h orange .65 1.40
a. Inverted overprint 37.50
b. Double overprint 17.00
J15 D2 10h olive green (R) .95 2.75
a. Double overprint 17.00
b. Ovpt. 16¾mm, Type II 1.90 4.00
c. As "b," Type III 1.90 4.00
d. As "b," Type IV 1.90 4.00
e. As "d," "Constitutton" 37.50
f. As "d," "Coustitution" 37.50
J16 D2 25h dull lilac .65 1.40
a. Inverted overprint 37.50
b. Double overprint 17.00
J17 D2 50h emerald .65 1.40
a. Inverted overprint 37.50
b. Double overprint 14.00
J18 D2 1k pale gray green .95 1.90
a. Double overprint 14.00
Nos. J14-J18 (5) 3.85 8.85

D3

1907 Typo. *Perf. 13x13½*

J19 D3 5pa red brown .45 1.40
J20 D3 10pa violet .45 1.40
J21 D3 25pa rose .45 1.40
J22 D3 50pa green .45 1.40
Nos. J19-J22 (4) 1.80 5.60

D4

1913 *Perf. 12½*

J23 D4 5pa gray 1.40 1.90
J24 D4 10pa violet .95 1.40
J25 D4 25pa blue gray .95 1.40
J26 D4 50pa lilac rose 1.40 1.90
Nos. J23-J26 (4) 4.70 6.60

ISSUED UNDER AUSTRIAN OCCUPATION

Austrian Military Stamps of 1917 Overprinted

1917 Unwmk. *Perf. 12½*

1N1 M1 10h blue 14.50 12.00
1N2 M1 15h car rose 14.50 12.00

Austrian Military Stamps of 1917 Overprinted in Black

1918

1N3 M1 10h blue 40.00
1N4 M1 15h car rose 1.90

Nos. 1N3-1N4 were never placed in use.

This overprint exists on other stamps of Austria and Bosnia and Herzegovina, and in blue or red.

MONTSERRAT

ˌmänˌtˌ-sə-ˈrat

LOCATION — West Indies southeast of Puerto Rico
GOVT. — British Crown Colony
AREA — 39 sq. mi.
POP. — 12,074 (1980)
CAPITAL — Plymouth

Montserrat was one of the four presidencies of the former Leeward Islands colony until it became a colony itself in 1956.

Montserrat stamps were discontinued in 1890 and resumed in 1903. In the interim, stamps of Leeward Islands were used. In 1903-56, stamps of Montserrat and Leeward Islands were used concurrently.

12 Pence = 1 Shilling
20 Shillings = 1 Pound
100 Cents = 1 Dollar (1951)

Catalogue values for unused stamps in this country are for Never Hinged items, beginning with Scott 104 in the regular postage section.

PRE-STAMP POSTAL MARKINGS

Crowned Circle handstamp type VI is pictured in the Crowned Circle Handstamps and Great Britain Used Abroad section.

Plymouth

1852-58
A1 VI "Montserrat" crowned circle handstamp in red, on cover 4,500.

The handstamp was used, in black, as a provisional in 1886.

STAMPS OF GREAT BRITAIN USED IN MONTSERRAT

Numeral cancellation type A is pictured in the Crowned Circle Handstamps and Great Britain Used Abroad section.

1858-60

A08 (Plymouth)

A2 A 1p rose red (#20) 1,300.
A3 A 4p rose (#26) —
A4 A 6p lilac (#27) 550.00
A5 A 1sh green (#28) 2,750.

Issued under British Administration

Values for unused stamps are for examples with original gum as defined in the catalogue introduction. Very fine examples of Nos. 1-2, 6 and 11 will have perforations touching the design on at least one side due to the narrow spacing of the stamps on the plates. Stamps with perfs clear of the framelines on all four sides are scarce and will command higher prices.

Stamps of Antigua Overprinted in Black — a

1876 Engr. Wmk. 1 *Perf. 14*
1 A1 1p red 30.00 19.00
a. Vert. or diag. half used as ½p on cover 1,650.
c. "S" inverted 1,250. 875.00
2 A1 6p green 75.00 50.00
a. Vertical half used as 3p on cover —
b. Vertical third used as 2p on cover 6,500.
c. "S" inverted 1,900. 1,350.
d. 6p blue green 1,350.
e. As "d," "S" inverted *13,000.*

Some experts consider Nos. 2d, 2e to be from a trial printing.

Queen Victoria — A2

1880 Typo.
3 A2 2½p red brown 300.00 225.00
4 A2 4p blue 160.00 47.50

See Nos. 5, 7-10.

1884 Wmk. 2
5 A2 ½p green 1.25 *11.00*

Antigua No. 18 Overprinted type "a"

1884 Engr.
6 A1 1p rose red 28.00 20.00
a. Vert. half used as ½p on cover 1,550.
b. "S" inverted 1,100. 1,100.

Type of 1880

1884-85 Typo.
7 A2 2½p red brown 275.00 77.50
8 A2 2½p ultra ('85) 29.00 22.50
9 A2 4p blue 2,100. 300.00
10 A2 4p red lilac ('85) 6.00 3.50

Antigua No. 20 Overprinted type "a"

1884 Engr. *Perf. 12*
11 A1 1p red 82.50 65.00
a. "S" inverted 2,350. 1,550.
b. Vert. half used as ½p on cover 1,900.

Symbol of the Colony — A3

King Edward VII — A4

1903 Wmk. 2 Typo. *Perf. 14*
12 A3 ½p gray green .90 19.00
13 A3 1p car & black .90 .50
14 A3 2p brown & black 6.50 *50.00*
15 A3 2½p ultra & black 1.75 2.10
16 A3 3p dk vio & brn orange 8.50 *50.00*
17 A3 6p ol grn & vio 15.00 *65.00*
18 A3 1sh vio & gray grn 12.00 *26.00*
19 A3 2sh brn org & gray green 42.50 *27.50*
20 A3 2sh6p blk & gray grn 27.50 *60.00*

Wmk. 1
21 A4 5sh car & black 160.00 *225.00*
Nos. 12-21 (10) 275.55 *525.10*
Set of 10, ovptd "SPECIMEN" 190.00

1904-08 Wmk. 3 Chalky Paper
22 A3 ½p grn & gray grn ('06) 1.00 1.25
a. Ordinary paper 13.00 4.00
23 A3 1p car & blk ('07) 17.00 *30.00*
24 A3 2p brown & black ('06) 2.50 1.40
a. Ordinary paper 3.00 *13.00*
25 A3 2½p ultra & blk ('05) 3.00 *7.75*
26 A3 3p dk vio & brn orange ('08) 13.00 2.75
a. Ordinary paper 13.00 *8.00*
27 A3 6p ol grn & vio ('08) 16.00 *6.50*
a. Ordinary paper 13.00 *42.50*
28 A3 1sh violet & gray grn ('08) 12.00 8.50
29 A3 2sh brn org & gray grn ('08) 60.00 *55.00*
30 A3 2sh6p blk & gray grn ('08) 65.00 *60.00*
31 A4 5sh car & blk ('07) 160.00 *190.00*
Nos. 22-31 (10) 349.50 *363.15*
Set of 10, ovptd "SPECIMEN" 300.00

1908-13 Ordinary Paper
31A A3 ½p deep green 12.00 1.10
32 A3 1p carmine 1.75 .35
33 A3 2p gray 2.00 *22.50*
34 A3 2½p ultramarine 2.50 4.25

Chalky Paper
35 A3 3p vio, *yellow* 1.10 *22.50*
36 A3 6p red vio & gray vio 12.00 *60.00*
37 A3 1sh blk, *green* 10.00 *55.00*
38 A3 2sh bl & vio, *bl* 50.00 *67.50*
39 A3 2sh6p car & blk, *blue* 42.50 *87.50*
40 A4 5sh grn & scar, *yel* 65.00 92.50

Surface-colored Paper
41 A3 3p vio, *yel* ('13) 4.50 *40.00*
Overprinted "SPECIMEN" 26.00
Nos. 31A-41 (11) 203.35 *453.20*
#31A-40, ovptd "SPECIMEN" 250.00

King George V — A5

1913 Chalky Paper
42 A5 5sh green & scar, *yel* 90.00 *160.00*
Overprinted "SPECIMEN" 85.00

King George V — A6

1916-22 Wmk. 3 *Perf. 14*

Ordinary Paper
43 A6 ½p green .45 2.75
44 A6 1p scarlet 2.50 .90
a. 1p carmine red 28.00 9.00
45 A6 2p gray 2.75 *5.00*
46 A6 2½p ultramarine 2.50 *26.00*

Chalky Paper
47 A6 3p violet, *yel* 1.40 *23.00*
48 A6 4p blk & red, *yel* ('22) 8.50 *42.50*
49 A6 6p dl vio & red violet 3.50 *37.50*
50 A6 1sh blk, *bl grn*, ol back 3.50 *42.50*
51 A6 2sh vio & ultra, *bl* 22.00 *60.00*
52 A6 2sh6p blk & red, *bl* 40.00 *90.00*
53 A6 5sh grn & red, *yel* 55.00 *95.00*
Nos. 43-53 (11) 142.10 *425.15*
Set of 11, ovptd "SPECIMEN" 200.00

For overprints see Nos. MR1-MR3.

1922-29 Wmk. 4 Ordinary Paper
54 A6 ¼p brown .35 6.25
55 A6 ½p green ('23) .30 .30
56 A6 1p dp violet ('23) .80 .70
57 A6 1p carmine ('29) 1.10 1.75
58 A6 1½p orange 2.50 *11.00*
59 A6 1½p rose red ('23) .60 *5.00*
60 A6 1½p fawn ('29) 3.25 .55
61 A6 2p gray .80 *2.25*
62 A6 2½p ultramarine 9.25 18.00
63 A6 2½p orange ('23) 2.75 *21.00*
64 A6 3p ultra ('23) .80 *18.00*

Chalky Paper
65 A6 3p vio, *yel* ('26) 2.00 *6.50*
66 A6 4p black & red, *yel* ('23) 1.75 *14.00*
67 A6 5p dull vio & ol grn 5.50 *11.00*
68 A6 6p dull vio & red vio ('23) 3.50 *8.50*
69 A6 1sh blk, *emer* ('23) 3.50 *8.00*
70 A6 2sh vio & ultra, *bl* 8.00 *22.50*
71 A6 2sh6p blk & red, *bl* ('23) 14.00 *65.00*
72 A6 3sh green & vio 14.00 *22.50*
73 A6 4sh black & scar 17.50 *50.00*
74 A6 5sh grn & red, *yel* ('23) 37.50 *65.00*
Nos. 54-74 (21) 129.75 *357.80*
Set of 21, ovptd or perforated "SPECIMEN" 350.00

Tercentenary Issue

New Plymouth and Harbor — A7

1932, Apr. 18 Engr.
75 A7 ½p green 1.25 *16.00*
76 A7 1p red 1.25 *6.50*
77 A7 1½p orange brown 1.40 *3.00*
78 A7 2p gray 1.90 *23.00*
79 A7 2½p ultra 1.40 *21.00*
80 A7 3p orange 1.90 *21.00*
81 A7 6p violet 2.50 *37.50*
82 A7 1sh olive green 14.50 *50.00*
83 A7 2sh6p lilac rose 52.50 *87.50*
84 A7 5sh dark brown 115.00 *200.00*
Nos. 75-84 (10) 193.60 465.50
Set, never hinged 400.00
Set of 10, perforated "SPECIMEN" 250.00

300th anniv. of the colonization of Montserrat.

Common Design Types pictured following the introduction.

Silver Jubilee Issue
Common Design Type

1935, May 6 *Perf. 11x12*
85 CD301 1p car & dk blue 1.25 4.25
86 CD301 1½p gray blk & ultra 2.00 *3.75*
87 CD301 2½p ultra & brn 2.75 *4.25*
88 CD301 1sh brn vio & ind 4.25 *18.00*
Nos. 85-88 (4) 10.25 *30.25*
Set, never hinged 19.00
Set, perforated "SPECIMEN" 100.00

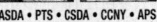

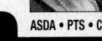

Coronation Issue
Common Design Type

1937, May 12 *Perf. 13½x14*

No.	Type	Description	Unused	Used
89	CD302	1p carmine	.25	1.50
90	CD302	1½p brown	.40	.35
91	CD302	2½p bright ultra	.35	1.50
		Nos. 89-91 (3)	1.00	3.35
		Set, never hinged	1.75	

Carr's Bay — A8

Sea Island Cotton — A9

Botanic Station A10

1941-48 *Perf. 14*

No.	Type	Description	Unused	Used
92	A8	½p dk grn ('42)	.25	.25
93	A9	1p car ('42)	.40	.35
94	A9	1½p rose vio ('42)	.40	*.55*
95	A10	2p red orange	1.20	.80
96	A9	2½p brt ultra ('43)	.40	.35
97	A8	3p brown ('42)	1.50	.45
98	A10	6p dull vio ('42)	2.00	.70
99	A8	1sh brn lake ('42)	1.75	.35
100	A10	2sh6p slate bl ('43)	13.50	3.00
101	A8	5sh car rose ('42)	16.00	3.50

Perf. 12

No.	Type	Description	Unused	Used
102	A10	10sh blue ('48)	10.00	*30.00*
103	A8	£1 black ('48)	10.00	*35.00*
		Nos. 92-103 (12)	57.40	*75.30*
		Set, never hinged	85.00	

1938, Aug. 2 *Perf. 13*

No.	Type	Description	Unused	Used
92a	A8	½p	2.50	*2.00*
93a	A8	1p	2.50	*.40*
94a	A9	1½p	11.00	*1.00*
95a	A10	2p	11.00	*1.00*
96a	A9	2½p	1.25	*1.50*
97a	A8	3p	3.00	*3.25*
98a	A10	6p	11.50	*1.25*
99a	A8	1sh	11.50	*1.25*
100a	A10	2sh6p	20.00	*1.00*
101a	A8	5sh	24.00	*10.00*
		Nos. 92a-101a (10)	98.25	*22.65*
		Set, never hinged	200.00	

Catalogue values for unused stamps in this section, from this point to the end of the section, are for Never Hinged items.

Peace Issue
Common Design Type

1946, Nov. 1 Engr. *Perf. 13½x14*

No.	Type	Description	Unused	Used
104	CD303	1½p deep magenta	.25	.25
105	CD303	3p brown	.25	.25

Silver Wedding Issue
Common Design Types

1949, Jan. 3 Photo. *Perf. 14x14½*

No.	Type	Description	Unused	Used
106	CD304	2½p brt ultra	.25	.25

Engraved; Name Typographed
Perf. 11½x11

No.	Type	Description	Unused	Used
107	CD305	5sh rose carmine	9.00	*18.00*

UPU Issue
Common Design Types
Engr.; Name Typo. on 3p and 6p
Perf. 13½, 11x11½

1949, Oct. 10 **Wmk. 4**

No.	Type	Description	Unused	Used
108	CD306	2½p ultramarine	.45	*1.00*
109	CD307	3p chocolate	1.10	.75
110	CD308	6p lilac	.75	.85
111	CD309	1sh rose violet	1.10	1.25
		Nos. 108-111 (4)	3.40	3.85

University Issue
Common Design Types

1951, Feb. 16 Engr. *Perf. 14x14½*

No.	Type	Description	Unused	Used
112	CD310	3c rose lil & gray blk	.25	*.60*
113	CD311	12c violet & black	.60	*.90*

Government House A11

Designs (portrait at right on 12c, 24c and $2.40): 2c, $1.20, Cotton field. 3c, Map of Presidency. 4c, 24c, Picking tomatoes. 5c, 12c, St. Anthony's Church. 6c, $4.80, Badge of Presidency. 8c, 60c, Cotton ginning.

Perf. 11½x11

1951, Sept. 17 Engr. Wmk. 4

No.	Type	Description	Unused	Used
114	A11	1c gray	.30	.30
115	A11	2c green	.30	.30
116	A11	3c orange brown	.30	.30
117	A11	4c rose carmine	.30	.30
118	A11	5c red violet	.30	.30
119	A11	6c dark brown	.40	.40
120	A11	8c dark blue	.60	.60
121	A11	12c red brn & blue	1.25	1.25
122	A11	24c emer & rose car	1.75	1.75
123	A11	60c rose car & gray black	3.50	3.50
124	A11	$1.20 dp bl & emer	11.00	11.00
125	A11	$2.40 dp grn & gray black	14.00	14.00
126	A11	$4.80 pur & gray blk	28.00	28.00
		Nos. 114-126 (13)	62.00	62.00

WAR TAX STAMPS

No. 43 Overprinted in Red or Black

1917-18 Wmk. 3 *Perf. 14*

No.	Type	Description	Unused	Used
MR1	A6	½p green (R)	.25	*1.75*
MR2	A6	½p green ('18)	.25	*2.00*

Type of Regular Issue of 1919 Overprinted

1918

No.	Type	Description	Unused	Used
MR3	A6	1½p orange & black	.30	*.35*
		Set of 3, ovptd "SPECIMEN"	100.00	

Denomination on No. MR3 in black on white ground. Two dots under "d."

MOROCCO

mə-'rä-ˌkō

LOCATION — Northwest coast of Africa
GOVT. — Kingdom
AREA — Approx. 170,000 sq. mi.
POP. — 4,442,000 (1912 est.)
CAPITAL — Rabat

In 1892 the Sultan of Morocco established a postal service for most of the country's chief towns and cities. This service, utilizing handstruck franks, carried official correspondence, as well as some private correspondence. With French guidance, it was reorganized as the *Administration Cherifienne des Postes, Telegraphes et Telephones* in Sept. 1911. In 1912 Morocco became a French protectorate, and on Oct. 1, 1913, the Cherifian PTT was merged with the French *Administration des Postes et Telegraphes.*

Stamps were issued by the Moroccan post office in 1912, and these remained in use throughout the country until 1915 and in Tangier until 1919.

400 Moussonats = 1 Rial

Aissaouas Mosque, Tangier — A1a

On White Paper
Narrow Margins

1912, May 25 Litho. *Perf. 11*

No.	Type	Description	Unused	Used
A1	A1a	1m light gray	8.00	8.00
		Never hinged	16.00	
		On cover		500.00
A2	A1a	2m lilac	9.00	8.00
		Never hinged	19.00	
		On cover		500.00
A3	A1a	5m blue green	12.00	8.00
		Never hinged	24.00	
		On cover		450.00
A4	A1a	10m vermilion	20.00	8.50
		Never hinged	40.00	
		On cover		450.00
A5	A1a	25m blue	29.00	24.00
		Never hinged	55.00	
		On cover		625.00
A6	A1a	50m violet	42.50	35.00
		Never hinged	85.00	
		On cover		750.00
		Nos. A1-A6 (6)	120.50	91.50

On Nos. A1-A12, the 5m and 10m values always have the name of the engraver beneath the design, while the 1m, 25m and 50m always lack name, and the 2m value exists both with and without name.

Aissaouas Mosque, Tangier — A1b

On Lightly Tinted Paper

1913, Feb. Wide Margins

No.	Type	Description	Unused	Used
A7	A1b	1m gray	1.75	1.75
		Never hinged	3.50	
		On cover		450.00
A8	A1b	2m brown lilac	1.75	1.75
		Never hinged	3.50	
		On cover		450.00
A9	A1b	5m blue green	2.00	2.00
		Never hinged	4.25	
		On cover		375.00
A10	A1b	10m vermilion	2.00	2.00
		Never hinged	4.25	
		On cover		375.00
A11	A1b	25m blue	4.25	4.25
		Never hinged	7.50	
		On cover		400.00
A12	A1b	50m gray violet	4.25	4.25
		Never hinged	8.50	
		On cover		500.00
		Nos. A7-A12 (6)	16.00	16.00

No. A6 Surcharged

1913, Nov.

No.	Type	Description	Unused	Used
A13	A1a	.05 on 50c violet	1,750.	*2,000.*
		On cover		4,250.
A14	A1a	.10 on 50c violet	1,750.	*2,000.*
		On cover		4,250.

MOZAMBIQUE

mō-zəm-'bēk

LOCATION — Southeastern Africa, bordering on the Mozambique Channel
GOVT. — Portuguese Colony
AREA — 308,642 sq. mi.
POP. — 14,140,000 (est. 1983)
CAPITAL — Maputo

Mozambique, or Portuguese East Africa, was divided into eight districts: Lourenco Marques, Inhambane, Quelimane, Tete, Mozambique, Zambezia, Nyassa and the Manica and Sofala region formerly administered by the Mozambique Company. At various times the districts issued their own stamps which were eventually replaced by those inscribed "Mocambique."

1000 Reis = 1 Milreis
100 Centavos = 1 Escudo (1913)

Portuguese Crown — A1

Perf. 12½, 13½

1877-85 Typo. Unwmk.

No.	Type	Description	Unused	Used
1	A1	5r black	2.00	1.00
a.		Perf. 13½	3.00	1.60
2	A1	10r yellow	18.00	4.50
3	A1	10r green ('81)	1.50	.60
4	A1	20r bister	1.50	.75
a.		Perf. 13½	3.00	2.00
5	A1	20r rose ('85)	400.00	*125.00*
6	A1	25r rose	1.00	.35
a.		Perf. 13½	6.75	1.60
7	A1	25r violet ('85)	3.00	2.00
8	A1	40r blue	25.00	15.00
9	A1	40r yel buff ('81)	2.00	1.60
a.		Perf. 12½	3.50	3.00
10	A1	50r green	60.00	20.00
a.		Perf. 13½	125.00	60.00
11	A1	50r blue ('81)	1.00	.40
12	A1	100r lilac	1.00	.50
13	A1	200r orange	2.00	1.40
a.		Perf. 12½	5.25	4.50
14	A1	300r chocolate	2.25	2.00
		Nos. 1-4,6-14 (13)	120.25	50.10

The reprints of the 1877-85 issues are printed on a smooth white chalky paper, ungummed, with rough perforation 13½, also on thin white paper, with shiny white gum and clean-cut perforation 13½.

King Luiz — A2

Typographed and Embossed

1886 *Perf. 12½*

No.	Type	Description	Unused	Used
15	A2	5r black	1.50	.60
16	A2	10r green	1.50	.70
17	A2	20r rose	2.00	1.50
18	A2	25r dull lilac	9.00	1.40
19	A2	40r chocolate	1.75	.85
20	A2	50r blue	2.25	.50
21	A2	100r yellow brn	2.50	.50
22	A2	200r gray violet	4.25	1.75
23	A2	300r orange	4.50	2.00
		Nos. 15-23 (9)	29.25	9.80

Perf. 13½

No.	Type	Description	Unused	Used
15a	A2	5r	4.00	2.75
16a	A2	10r	4.25	2.75
17a	A2	20r	13.00	6.00
18a	A2	25r	13.00	6.00
19a	A2	40r	15.00	9.50
20a	A2	50r	16.00	4.50
22a	A2	200r	15.00	12.50
		Nos. 15a-22a (7)	80.25	44.00

Nos. 15, 18, 19, 20, 21 and 23 have been reprinted. The reprints have shiny white gum and clean-cut perforation 13½. Many of the colors are paler than those of the originals.

For surcharges and overprints see Nos. 23A, 36-44, 46-48, 72-80, 192, P1-P5.

No. 19 Surcharged in Black

Type I

Type II

Type III

There are three varieties of No. 23A:
I — "PROVISORIO" 19mm long, numerals 4½mm high.
II — "PROVISORIO" 19½mm long, numerals 5mm high.
III — "PROVISORIO" 19½mm long, numerals of both sizes.

1893, Jan. *Perf. 12½*

Without Gum

No.	Type	Description	Unused	Used
23A	A2	5r on 40r choc	150.00	50.00

King Carlos I — A3

1894 Typo. *Perf. 11½, 12½*

No.	Type	Description	Unused	Used
24	A3	5r yellow	.50	.45
25	A3	10r red lilac	.50	.35
26	A3	15r red brown	1.25	.75
27	A3	20r gray lilac	1.25	.50
28	A3	25r blue green	1.25	.25
29	A3	50r lt blue	5.00	1.50
a.		Perf. 12½	7.50	2.00
30	A3	75r rose	1.75	1.25
31	A3	80r yellow grn	2.00	1.00
32	A3	100r brown, *buff*	1.75	1.25
33	A3	150r car, *rose*	8.00	4.00
a.		Perf. 11½		
34	A3	200r dk blue, *blue*	6.00	3.00
35	A3	300r dk blue, *salmon*	9.00	3.00
		Nos. 24-35 (12)	38.25	17.30

Nos. 28 and 31-33 have been reprinted with shiny white gum and clean-cut perf. 13½.

For surcharges and overprints see Nos. 45, 81-92, 193-198, 201-205, 226-228, 238-239.

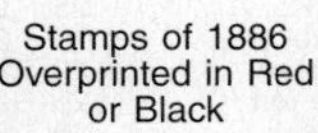

Stamps of 1886 Overprinted in Red or Black

1895, July 1 *Perf. 12½*

Without Gum

No.	Type	Description	Unused	Used
36	A2	5r black (R)	12.00	5.50
37	A2	10r green	14.00	6.50
38	A2	20r rose	15.00	6.00
39	A2	25r violet	16.00	6.50
a.		Double overprint	200.00	
40	A2	40r chocolate	20.00	7.50
41	A2	50r blue	22.00	7.50
a.		Perf. 13½	80.00	55.00
42	A2	100r yellow brown	22.00	8.25
43	A2	200r gray violet	30.00	13.00
a.		Perf. 13½	100.00	65.00
44	A2	300r orange	45.00	17.50
		Nos. 36-44 (9)	196.00	78.25

Birth of Saint Anthony of Padua, 7th cent.

No. 35 Surcharged in Black

1897, Jan. 2 *Perf. 12½*

Without Gum

No.	Type	Description	Unused	Used
45	A3	50r on 300r dk bl, *sal*	150.00	40.00

Nos. 17, 19 Surcharged

a

b

c

1898 Without Gum

No.	Type	Description	Unused	Used
46	A2 (a)	2½r on 20r rose	42.50	11.00
47	A2 (b)	2½r on 20r rose	30.00	10.00
a.		Inverted surcharge	55.00	45.00
48	A2 (c)	5r on 40r choc	60.00	10.00
a.		Inverted surcharge	90.00	45.00
		Nos. 46-48 (3)	132.50	31.00

King Carlos I — A4

Name and Value in Black except 500r

1898-1903 Typo. *Perf. 11½*

No.	Type	Description	Unused	Used
49	A4	2½r gray	.25	.25
50	A4	5r orange	.25	.25
51	A4	10r lt green	.25	.25
52	A4	15r brown	2.00	1.50
53	A4	15r gray grn ('03)	.70	.55
54	A4	20r gray violet	.85	.40
55	A4	25r sea green	.85	.40
56	A4	25r carmine ('03)	.70	.30
57	A4	50r dark blue	1.50	.50
58	A4	50r brown ('03)	2.00	1.50
59	A4	65r dull blue ('03)	20.00	12.00
60	A4	75r rose	7.00	2.75
61	A4	75r red lilac ('03)	3.00	1.75
62	A4	80r violet	6.00	3.25
63	A4	100r dk blue, *bl*	2.00	1.00
64	A4	115r org brn, *pink* ('03)	10.00	5.00
65	A4	130r brown, *straw* ('03)	10.00	5.00
66	A4	150r brown, *straw*	10.00	2.75
67	A4	200r red lilac, *pnksh*	2.00	1.40
68	A4	300r dk blue, *rose*	8.00	3.25
69	A4	400r dl bl, *straw* ('03)	13.00	7.50
70	A4	500r blk & red, *bl* ('01)	20.00	8.00
71	A4	700r vio, *yelsh* ('01)	25.00	9.00
		Nos. 49-71 (23)	145.35	68.55

For overprints and surcharges see Nos. 94-113, 200, 207-220.

Stamps of 1886-94 Surcharged

On Stamps of 1886

Red Surcharge

1902 *Perf. 12½, 13½*

No.	Type	Description	Unused	Used
72	A2	115r on 5r blk	5.00	2.00

Black Surcharge

No.	Type	Description	Unused	Used
73	A2	65r on 20r rose	5.00	2.50
a.		Double surcharge	50.00	50.00
74	A2	65r on 40r choc	6.00	4.00
75	A2	65r on 200r violet	5.00	1.75
76	A2	115r on 50r blue	2.00	1.00
77	A2	130r on 25r red vio	3.00	.90
78	A2	130r on 300r orange	3.00	.90
79	A2	400r on 10r green	7.50	3.25
80	A2	400r on 100r yel brn	40.00	25.00
		Nos. 72-80 (9)	76.50	41.30

The reprints of Nos. 74, 75, 76, 77, 79 and 80 have shiny white gum and clean-cut perforation 13½.

On Stamps of 1894

Perf. 11½

No.	Type	Description	Unused	Used
81	A3	65r on 10r red lil	3.50	2.00
82	A3	65r on 15r red brn	3.50	2.00
a.		Pair, one without surcharge		
83	A3	65r on 20r gray lil	3.75	2.00
84	A3	115r on 5r yel	4.00	2.00
a.		Inverted surcharge		
85	A3	115r on 25r bl grn	3.50	2.00
86	A3	130r on 75r rose	4.00	2.25
87	A3	130r on 100r brn, *buff*	6.00	5.00
88	A3	130r on 150r car, *rose*	4.00	2.00
89	A3	130r on 200r bl, *bl*	5.00	3.50
90	A3	400r on 50r lt bl	1.50	1.40
91	A3	400r on 80r yel grn	1.50	1.40
92	A3	400r on 300r bl, *sal*	1.50	1.40

On Newspaper Stamp of 1893

Perf. 13½

No.	Type	Description	Unused	Used
93	N3	115r on 2½r brn	2.00	2.25
		Nos. 81-93 (13)	43.75	29.20

Reprints of No. 87 have shiny white gum and clean-cut perforation 13½.

Overprinted in Black

On Stamps of 1898

Perf. 11½

No.	Type	Description	Unused	Used
94	A4	15r brown	2.00	.85
95	A4	25r sea green	2.50	.85
96	A4	50r blue	3.00	1.75
97	A4	75r rose	5.00	2.00
		Nos. 94-97 (4)	12.50	5.45

No. 59 Surcharged in Black

1905

No.	Type	Description	Unused	Used
98	A4	50r on 65r dull blue	4.00	2.00

Stamps of 1898-1903 Overprinted in Carmine or Green

1911

No.	Type	Description	Unused	Used
99	A4	2½r gray	.30	.25
a.		Inverted overprint	15.00	15.00
100	A4	5r orange	.30	.25
101	A4	10r lt green	2.00	.50
102	A4	15r gray grn	.30	.25
103	A4	20r gray vio	2.00	.40
104	A4	25r carmine (G)	.30	.25
a.		25r gray violet (error)		
105	A4	50r brown	.50	.25
106	A4	75r red lilac	1.00	.50
107	A4	100r dk blue, *bl*	1.00	.50
108	A4	115r org brn, *pink*	1.50	.85
109	A4	130r brown, *straw*	1.50	.85
a.		Double overprint		
110	A4	200r red lil, *pnksh*	3.00	.70
111	A4	400r dull bl, *straw*	3.50	.85
112	A4	500r blk & red, *bl*	4.00	.85
113	A4	700r vio, *straw*	4.50	.85
		Nos. 99-113 (15)	25.70	8.10

King Manuel II — A5

Overprinted in Carmine or Green

1912 *Perf. 11½x12*

No.	Type	Description	Unused	Used
114	A5	2½r violet	.25	.25
115	A5	5r black	.25	.25
116	A5	10r gray grn	.25	.25
117	A5	20r carmine (G)	.55	.40
118	A5	25r vio brn	.25	.25
119	A5	50r dp blue	.50	.35
120	A5	75r bis brn	.50	.35
121	A5	100r brn, *lt grn*	.50	.35
122	A5	200r dk grn, *salmon*	1.00	.70
123	A5	300r black, *azure*	1.00	.70

Perf. 14x15

No.	Type	Description	Unused	Used
124	A5	500r ol grn & vio brn	2.00	1.25
		Nos. 114-124 (11)	7.05	5.10

Vasco da Gama Issue of Various Portuguese Colonies Common Design Types Surcharged

1913 On Stamps of Macao

No.	Type	Description	Unused	Used
125	CD20	¼c on ½a bl grn	1.50	1.50
126	CD21	½c on 1a red	1.50	1.50
127	CD22	1c on 2a red vio	1.50	1.50
128	CD23	2½c on 4a yel grn	1.50	1.50
a.		Double surcharge	50.00	50.00
129	CD24	5c on 8a dk bl	2.50	2.50
130	CD25	7½c on 12a vio brn	2.00	2.00
131	CD26	10c on 16a bis brn	1.75	1.50
132	CD27	15c on 24a bis	1.50	1.50
		Nos. 125-132 (8)	13.75	13.50

On Stamps of Portuguese Africa

No.	Type	Description	Unused	Used
133	CD20	¼c on 2½r bl grn	1.25	1.25
134	CD21	½c on 5r red	1.25	1.25
135	CD22	1c on 10r red vio	1.25	1.25
a.		Inverted surcharge	45.00	45.00
136	CD23	2½c on 25r yel grn	1.25	1.25
137	CD24	5c on 50r dk bl	1.25	1.25
138	CD25	7½c on 75r vio brn	1.75	1.75
139	CD26	10c on 100r bis brn	1.50	1.50
140	CD27	15c on 150r bis	1.50	1.50
		Nos. 133-140 (8)	11.00	11.00

On Stamps of Timor

No.	Type	Description	Unused	Used
141	CD20	¼c on ½a bl grn	1.50	1.50
142	CD21	½c on 1a red	1.50	1.50
143	CD22	1c on 2a red vio	1.50	1.50
144	CD23	2½c on 4a yel grn	1.50	1.50
145	CD24	5c on 8a dk bl	1.50	1.50
146	CD25	7½c on 12a vio brn	3.00	3.00
147	CD26	10c on 16a bis brn	1.50	1.50
148	CD27	15c on 24a bis	2.00	2.00
		Nos. 141-148 (8)	14.00	14.00
		Nos. 125-148 (24)	38.75	38.50

Ceres — A6

1914 Typo. *Perf. 15x14*

Name and Value in Black

Chalky Paper

No.	Type	Description	Unused	Used
149	A6	¼c olive brown	.35	.25
		Never hinged	.55	
150	A6	½c black	.35	.25
		Never hinged	.55	
151	A6	1c blue green	.35	.25
		Never hinged	.55	
152	A6	1½c lilac brown	.35	.25
		Never hinged	.55	
153	A6	2c carmine	.40	.25
		Never hinged	.65	
154	A6	2½c lt vio	.40	.25
		Never hinged	.65	
155	A6	5c deep blue	.40	.25
		Never hinged	.65	
156	A6	7½c yel brn	1.45	.75
		Never hinged	2.25	
157	A6	8c slate	1.45	.75
		Never hinged	2.25	
158	A6	10c org brn	1.45	.75
		Never hinged	2.25	
159	A6	15c plum	3.00	1.40
		Never hinged	4.75	
160	A6	20c yellow green	1.45	.95
		Never hinged	2.25	
161	A6	30c brown, *grn*	2.00	1.10
		Never hinged	2.40	
163	A6	40c brn, *pink*	2.00	.85
		Never hinged	2.00	
164	A6	50c org, *salmon*	2.75	3.00
		Never hinged	4.50	
165	A6	1e grn, *bl,*	18.00	7.00
		Never hinged	29.00	
		Nos. 149-165 (16)	36.15	18.30

1919-26 Ordinary Paper

No.	Type	Description	Unused	Used
166	A6	¼c olive brown	.25	.25
		Never hinged	.40	
a.		Name and value printed twice	12.00	
		Never hinged	19.00	
b.		Name and value printed triple	—	
c.		Thick carton paper	8.00	
		Never hinged	13.00	
167	A6	½c black	.25	.25
		Never hinged	.40	
168	A6	1c blue green	.25	.25
		Never hinged	.40	
169	A6	1½c lilac brown	.25	.25
		Never hinged	.40	
170	A6	2c carmine	.25	.25
		Never hinged	.40	
171	A6	2½c lt vio	.25	.25
		Never hinged	.40	
172	A6	3c org ('21)	.25	.25
		Never hinged	.40	
a.		Name and value printed twice	—	
173	A6	4c pale rose ('21)	.25	.25
		Never hinged	.40	
174	A6	4½c gray ('21)	.25	.25
		Never hinged	.40	
175	A6	5c deep blue	.25	.25
		Never hinged	.40	
176	A6	7c ultra ('21)	.25	.25
		Never hinged	.40	
177	A6	7½c yel brn	.25	.25
		Never hinged	.40	
178	A6	8c slate	.25	.25
		Never hinged	.40	
179	A6	10c org brn	.25	.25
		Never hinged	.40	
180	A6	30c deep green ('21)	.75	.50
		Never hinged	1.20	
181	A6	1e rose	1.40	.85
		Never hinged	2.25	
		Nos. 166-181 (16)	5.65	4.85

Perf. 12x11½

No.	Type	Description	Unused	Used
182	A6	¼c olive brown	.30	.25
		Never hinged	.50	
183	A6	½c black	.25	.25
		Never hinged	.40	
184	A6	1c blue green	.50	.25
		Never hinged	.80	
a.		Name and value printed twice	16.00	
		Never hinged	26.00	
185	A6	1½c lilac brown	.25	.25
		Never hinged	.40	
186	A6	2c carmine	.25	.25
		Never hinged	.40	
187	A6	2c gray ('26)	.25	.25
		Never hinged	.40	
188	A6	2½c lt vio	.25	.25
		Never hinged	.40	
189	A6	3c org ('21)	.25	.25
		Never hinged	.40	

190 A6 4c pale rose ('21) .25 .25
Never hinged .40
a. Name and value printed twice 16.00
Never hinged 26.00
b. Value omitted 15.00
Never hinged 24.00
c. 4c carmine rose .25 .25
Never hinged .40
191 A6 4½c gray ('21) .25 .25
Never hinged .40
191A A6 6c lilac ('21) .25 .25
Never hinged .40
a. Name and value printed twice
191B A6 7c ultra ('21) .25 .25
Never hinged .40
191C A6 7½c yel brn .25 .25
Never hinged .40
191D A6 8c slate .25 .25
Never hinged .40
191E A6 10c org brn .25 .25
Never hinged .40
191F A6 12c gray brn ('21) .25 .25
Never hinged .40
191G A6 12c blue grn ('22) .25 .25
Never hinged .40
191H A6 15c plum .65 .35
Never hinged 1.05
191I A6 15c brn rose ('22) .25 .25
Never hinged .40
191J A6 20c yel grn .25 .25
Never hinged .40
191K A6 24c ultra ('26) 4.50 2.00
Never hinged 7.25
191L A6 25c choc ('26) 1.50 1.25
Never hinged 2.40
191M A6 30c deep green ('21) 1.00 .25
Never hinged 1.60
191N A6 40c turq blue ('22) 1.00 .30
Never hinged 1.60
191O A6 50c lt violet ('26) .50 .25
Never hinged .80
191P A6 60c dk blue ('22) 1.00 .30
Never hinged 1.60
191Q A6 60c rose ('26) 1.10 .25
Never hinged 1.75
191R A6 80c brt rose ('22) 1.60 1.25
Never hinged 2.50
191S A6 80c rose ('22) 1.00 .25
Never hinged 1.60
191T A6 1e rose ('22) 1.60 .50
Never hinged 2.50
Nos. 182-191T (30) 20.50 11.70

For surcharges see Nos. 232-234, 236-237, 249-250, J46-50.

1921 **Chalky Paper**

191U A6 40c brown, *pink* ('21) 1.25 .85
Never hinged 2.00
191V A6 60c red brn, *pink* 1.00 .60
Never hinged 1.60
191W A6 80c dk brn, *bl* ('21) 1.40 .60
Never hinged 2.25
191X A6 1e grn, *bl,* 1.40 .60
Never hinged 2.25
191Y A6 2e brt vio, *pink* 1.40 .60
Never hinged 2.25

Perf. 15x14

191Z A6 30c gray bl, *pink* ('21) 1.50 1.25
Never hinged 2.40
Nos. 191U-191Z (6) 7.95 4.50

Stamps of 1902 Overprinted Locally in Carmine

1915

On Provisional Stamps of 1902

192 A2 115r on 5r black 200.00 100.00
193 A3 115r on 5r yellow 1.25 .75
194 A3 115r on 25r bl grn 1.25 .75
195 A3 130r on 75r rose 1.25 .75
196 A3 130r on 100r brn, *buff* 1.25 .75
197 A3 130r on 150r car, *rose* 1.25 .75
198 A3 130r on 200r bl, *bl* 1.25 .75
199 N3 115r on 2½r brn .80 .40

On No. 97

200 A4 75r rose 1.50 1.10
Nos. 192-200 (9) 209.80 106.00

Stamps of 1902-05 Overprinted in Carmine

1915

On Provisional Stamps of 1902

201 A3 115r on 5r yellow .80 .50
202 A3 115r on 25r bl grn .80 .55
203 A3 130r on 75r rose .80 .55
204 A3 130r on 150r car, *rose* 1.00 .50
205 A3 130r on 200r bl, *bl* 1.00 .50
206 N3 115r on 2½r brn 1.00 .50

On No. 96

207 A4 50r blue 1.00 .50

On No. 98

208 A4 50r on 65r dull blue 1.00 .50
Nos. 201-208 (8) 7.40 4.10

Stamps of 1898-1903 Overprinted Locally in Carmine Like Nos. 192-200

1917

209 A4 2½r gray 20.00 17.50
210 A4 15r gray grn 15.00 12.50
211 A4 20r gray vio 15.00 12.50
212 A4 50r brown 14.00 11.00
213 A4 75r red lilac 32.50 25.00
214 A4 100r blue, *bl* 6.00 2.50
215 A4 115r org brn, *pink* 8.00 3.00
216 A4 130r brown, *straw* 7.50 3.00
217 A4 200r red lil, *pnksh* 7.50 2.50
218 A4 400r dull bl, *straw* 7.50 3.00
219 A4 500r blk & red, *bl* 7.00 2.50
220 A4 700r vio, *yelsh* 15.00 6.00
Nos. 209-220 (12) 155.00 101.00

War Tax Stamps of 1916-18 Surcharged

1918 ***Rouletted 7***

221 WT2 2½c on 5c rose 2.50 1.50

Perf. 11, 12

222 WT2 2½c on 5c red 1.10 .70
a. "PETRIA" 4.00 2.00
b. "PEPUBLICA" 4.00 2.00
c. "1910" for "1916" 9.00 4.00

War Tax Stamps of 1916-18 Surcharged

1919 ***Perf. 11***

224 WT1 1c on 1c gray grn .75 .40
a. "PEPUBLICA" 6.00 4.00
b. Rouletted 7 *300.00* *100.00*

Perf. 12

225 WT2 1½c on 5c red .40 .35
a. "PETRIA" 4.00 2.00
b. "PEPUBLICA" 4.00 2.50
c. "1910" for "1916" 7.50 3.75

Stamps of 1902 Overprinted Locally in Carmine Like Nos. 192-200

1920

226 A3 400r on 50r lt blue 1.25 1.25
227 A3 400r on 80r yel grn 1.25 1.25
228 A3 400r on 300r bl, *sal* 1.25 1.25
Nos. 226-228 (3) 3.75 3.75

War Tax Stamp of 1918 Surcharged in Green

1920 ***Perf. 12***

229 WT2 6c on 5c red .60 .50
a. "1910" for "1916" 9.00 5.00
b. "PETRIA" 3.00 2.00
c. "PEPUBLICA" 3.00 2.00

Lourenco Marques Nos. 117, 119 Surcharged in Red or Bue

1921 ***Perf. 15x14***

230 A4 10c on ½c blk (R) .75 .40
Never hinged 1.20
231 A4 30c on 1½c brn (Bl) 1.25 .70
Never hinged 2.00

Same Surcharge on Mozambique Nos. 150, 152, 155 in Red, Blue or Green

232 A6 10c on ½c blk (R) 1.00 .85
Never hinged 1.60
233 A6 30c on 1½c brn (Bl) 1.10 .70
Never hinged 1.75
a. Double surcharge 30.00 30.00
Never hinged 47.50
234 A6 60c on 2½c vio (G) 1.50 .80
Never hinged 2.40
Nos. 230-234 (5) 5.60 3.45

War Tax Stamp of 1918 Surcharged in Green

1921 ***Perf. 12***

235 WT2 2e on 5c red 1.00 .50
a. "PETRIA" 2.50 2.25
b. "PEPUBLICA" 4.25 2.50
c. "1910" for "1916" 9.00 6.50

No. 190 Surcharged

1923 ***Perf. 12x11½***

236 A6 50c on 4c pale rose 1.00 .55
Never hinged 1.60

No. 191R Overprinted in Green

1924

237 A6 80c bright rose 1.00 .60
Never hinged 1.60

4th centenary of the death of Vasco da Gama.

Nos. 90 and 91 Surcharged

1925 ***Perf. 11½***

238 A3 40c on 400r on 50r .70 .70
239 A3 40c on 400r on 80r .60 .50
a. "a" omitted 42.50 42.50

Glazed Paper

1922-26 ***Perf. 12x11½***

240 A6 1e blue ('26) 1.60 .65
Never hinged 2.50
241 A6 2e dk violet ('22) 1.00 .35
Never hinged 1.60
242 A6 5e buff ('26) 9.00 2.50
Never hinged 16.00
243 A6 10e pink ('26) 18.00 5.00
Never hinged 24.00
244 A6 20e pale turq ('26) 45.00 17.50
Never hinged 65.00

Postage Due Stamp of 1917 Overprinted in Black and Bars in Red

1929, Jan. ***Perf. 12***

247 D1 50c gray .85 .55

No. 191Y Surcharged

1931 ***Perf. 11½***

249 A6 70c on 2e dk vio 1.50 .50
Never hinged 1.60
250 A6 1.40e on 2e dk vio 2.00 .50
Never hinged 2.40

"Portugal" Holding Volume of the "Lusiads" — A7

Wmk. Maltese Cross (232)

1933, July 13 **Typo.** ***Perf. 14***

Value in Red or Black

251 A7 1c bister brn (R) .25 .25
252 A7 5c black brn .25 .25
253 A7 10c dp violet .25 .25
254 A7 15c black (R) .25 .25
255 A7 20c light gray .25 .25
256 A7 30c blue green .25 .25
257 A7 40c orange red .25 .25
258 A7 45c brt blue .40 .25
259 A7 50c dk brown .30 .25
260 A7 60c olive grn .25 .25
261 A7 70c orange brn .25 .25
262 A7 80c emerald .25 .25
263 A7 85c deep rose 1.00 .50
264 A7 1e red brown .75 .25
265 A7 1.40e dk blue (R) 7.00 1.10
266 A7 2e dk violet 2.00 .35
267 A7 5e apple green 4.00 .50
268 A7 10e olive bister 8.00 1.00
269 A7 20e orange 22.50 2.00
Nos. 251-269 (19) 48.45 8.70

See Nos. 298-299 in Scott Standard catalogue, Vol. 4.

Common Design Types pictured following the introduction.

Common Design Types

Perf. 13½x13

1938, Aug. **Engr.** **Unwmk.**

Name and Value in Black

270 CD34 1c gray green .25 .25
271 CD34 5c orange brn .25 .25
272 CD34 10c dk carmine .25 .25
273 CD34 15c dk vio brn .25 .25
274 CD34 20c slate .25 .25
275 CD35 30c rose vio .25 .25
276 CD35 35c brt green .30 .25
277 CD35 40c brown .40 .25
278 CD35 50c brt red vio .40 .25
279 CD36 60c gray black .50 .25
280 CD36 70c brown vio .50 .25
281 CD36 80c orange .75 .25
282 CD36 1e red .70 .25
283 CD37 1.75e blue 1.75 .30
284 CD37 2e brown car 1.50 .30
285 CD37 5e olive green 5.00 .50
286 CD38 10e blue vio 10.00 1.00
287 CD38 20e red brown 22.50 1.40
Nos. 270-287 (18) 45.80 6.75

For surcharges see Nos. 297, 301 in Scott Standard catalogue, Vol. 4.

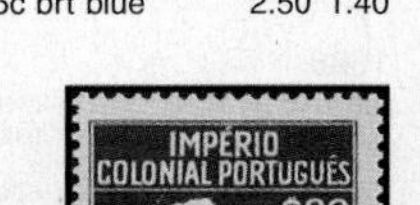

No. 258 Surcharged in Black

1938, Jan. 16 **Wmk. 232** ***Perf. 14***

288 A7 40c on 45c brt blue 2.50 1.40

Map of Africa — A7a

Perf. 11½x12

1939, July 17 Litho. Unwmk.

No.	Type	Description	Unused	Used
289	A7a	80c vio, *pale rose*	1.50	1.25
290	A7a	1.75e bl, *pale bl*	4.00	2.75
291	A7a	3e grn, *yel grn*	7.00	4.00
292	A7a	20e brn, *buff*	*35.00*	*50.00*
		Nos. 289-292 (4)	*47.50*	*58.00*

Presidential visit.

SEMI-POSTAL STAMPS

"History" Pointing out to "the Republic" Need for Charity SP1

Nurse Leading Wounded Soldiers SP2

Veteran Relating Experiences — SP3

Perf. 11½

1920, Dec. 1 Litho. Unwmk.

No.	Type	Description	Unused	Used
B1	SP1	¼c olive	5.00	3.50
B2	SP1	½c olive blk	5.00	3.50
B3	SP1	1c dp bister	5.00	3.50
B4	SP1	2c lilac brn	5.00	3.50
B5	SP1	3c lilac	5.00	3.50
B6	SP1	4c green	5.00	3.50
B7	SP2	5c grnsh blue	5.00	3.50
B8	SP2	6c light blue	5.00	3.50
B9	SP2	7½c red brown	5.00	3.50
B10	SP2	8c lemon	5.00	3.50
B11	SP2	10c gray lilac	5.00	3.50
B12	SP2	12c pink	5.00	3.50
B13	SP3	18c rose	5.00	3.50
B14	SP3	24c vio brn	5.00	3.50
B15	SP3	30c pale ol grn	5.00	3.50
B16	SP3	40c dull red	5.00	3.50
B17	SP3	50c yellow	5.00	3.50
B18	SP3	1e ultra	5.00	3.50
		Nos. B1-B18 (18)	90.00	63.00

Nos. B1-B18 were used Dec. 1, 1920, in place of ordinary stamps. The proceeds were for war victims.

AIR POST STAMPS

Common Design Type

Perf. 13½x13

1938, Aug. Engr. Unwmk.

Name and Value in Black

No.	Type	Description	Unused	Used
C1	CD39	10c scarlet	.30	.25
C2	CD39	20c purple	.30	.25
C3	CD39	50c orange	.30	.25
C4	CD39	1e ultra	.40	.30
C5	CD39	2e lilac brn	1.00	.30
C6	CD39	3e dk green	1.75	.40
C7	CD39	5e red brown	2.10	.70
C8	CD39	9e rose car	4.25	.75
C9	CD39	10e magenta	7.25	1.25
		Nos. C1-C9 (9)	17.65	4.45

No. C7 exists with overprint "Exposicao Internacional de Nova York, 1939-1940" and Trylon and Perisphere. Value $50.

POSTAGE DUE STAMPS

D1

1904 Unwmk. Typo. *Perf. 11½x12*

Name and Value in Black

No.	Type	Description	Unused	Used
J1	D1	5r yellow grn	.40	.25
J2	D1	10r slate	.40	.25
J3	D1	20r yellow brn	.40	.25
J4	D1	30r orange	.80	.70
J5	D1	50r gray brn	.70	.55
J6	D1	60r red brown	3.50	1.75
J7	D1	100r red lilac	3.00	1.75
J8	D1	130r dull blue	1.50	1.20
J9	D1	200r carmine	2.00	1.20
J10	D1	500r violet	2.50	1.20
		Nos. J1-J10 (10)	15.20	9.10

See J34-J43. For overprints see Nos. 247, J11-J30.

Same Overprinted in Carmine or Green

1911

No.	Type	Description	Unused	Used
J11	D1	5r yellow green	.25	.25
J12	D1	10r slate	.40	.25
J13	D1	20r yellow brn	.30	.25
J14	D1	30r orange	.30	.25
J15	D1	50r gray brown	.40	.30
J16	D1	60r red brown	.60	.35
J17	D1	100r red lilac	.80	.55
J18	D1	130r dull blue	1.10	.80
J19	D1	200r carmine (G)	1.20	.95
J20	D1	500r violet	1.60	.95
		Nos. J11-J20 (10)	6.95	4.90

Nos. J1-J10 Overprinted Locally in Carmine

1916

No.	Type	Description	Unused	Used
J21	D1	5r yellow grn	4.00	3.25
J22	D1	10r slate	5.50	3.25
J23	D1	20r yellow brn	80.00	60.00
J24	D1	30r orange	22.50	12.50
J25	D1	50r gray brown	80.00	55.00
J26	D1	60r red brown	65.00	45.00
J27	D1	100r red lilac	80.00	60.00
J28	D1	130r dull blue	2.40	2.25
J29	D1	200r carmine	2.75	3.00
J30	D1	500r violet	5.50	4.75
		Nos. J21-J30 (10)	347.65	249.00

War Tax Stamps of 1916 Ovptd. Diagonally

1918 *Rouletted 7*

No.	Type	Description	Unused	Used
J31	WT1	1c gray green	.95	.80
J32	WT2	5c rose	.95	.80
a.		Inverted overprint	8.25	7.50

Perf. 11

No.	Type	Description	Unused	Used
J33	WT1	1c gray green	.95	.80
a.		"PEPUBLICA"	50.00	40.00
		Nos. J31-J33 (3)	2.85	2.40

Type of 1904 Issue With Value in Centavos

1917 *Perf. 12*

No.	Type	Description	Unused	Used
J34	D1	½c yellow green	.30	.30
J35	D1	1c slate	.30	.30
J36	D1	2c orange brown	.30	.30
J37	D1	3c orange	.30	.30
J38	D1	5c gray brown	.30	.30
J39	D1	6c pale brn	.30	.30
J40	D1	10c red violet	.30	.30
J41	D1	13c deep blue	.55	.55
J42	D1	20c rose	.55	.55
J43	D1	50c gray	.55	.55
		Nos. J34-J43 (10)	3.75	3.75

Lourenco Marques Nos. 117, 119 Surcharged in Red

1921

No.	Type	Description	Unused	Used
J44	A4	5c on ½c blk	2.00	.95
J45	A4	10c on 1½c brn	2.00	.95

Same Surcharge on Mozambique Nos. 151, 154, 190 in Red or Green

Perf. 15x14

No.	Type	Description	Unused	Used
J46	A6	6c on 1c bl grn (R)	2.00	.95
		Never hinged	2.50	
J47	A6	20c on 2½c vio (R)	1.50	.85
		Never hinged	1.60	
a.		Inverted surcharge	7.50	7.50
		Never hinged	12.00	

Perf. 12x11½

No.	Type	Description	Unused	Used
J48	A6	50c on 4c rose (G)	1.50	.85
		Never hinged	1.60	
a.		Inverted surcharge	8.50	8.50
		Never hinged	13.50	
		Nos. J44-J48 (5)	9.00	4.55

Regular Issues of 1921-22 Surcharged in Black or Red

1924 *Perf. 12x11½*

No.	Type	Description	Unused	Used
J49	A6	20c on 30c ol grn (Bk)	1.50	.45
		Never hinged	1.75	
a.		Perf. 15x14	19.00	4.50
		Never hinged	30.00	
J50	A6	50c on 60c dk bl (R)	1.50	1.00
		Never hinged	1.60	

WAR TAX STAMPS

Coats of Arms of Portugal and Mozambique on Columns, Allegorical Figures of History of Portugal and the Republic Holding Scroll with Date of Declaration of War — WT1

Prow of Galley of Discoveries. Left, "Republic" Teaching History of Portugal; Right "History" with Laurels (Victory) and Sword (Symbolical of Declaration of War) — WT2

1916 Unwmk. Litho. *Rouletted 7*

No.	Type	Description	Unused	Used
MR1	WT1	1c gray green	2.25	.55
a.		Imperf., pair	15.00	
MR2	WT2	5c rose	2.25	.55
a.		Imperf., pair	15.00	

1918 *Perf. 11, 12*

No.	Type	Description	Unused	Used
MR3	WT1	1c gray green	.85	.55
a.		"PEPUBLICA"	8.50	4.75
MR4	WT2	5c red	1.00	.70
a.		"PETRIA"	4.00	4.00
b.		"PEPUBLICA"	4.00	4.00
c.		"1910" for "1916"	11.00	5.50
d.		Imperf., pair		
		Nos. MR1-MR4 (4)	6.35	2.35

For surcharges and overprints see Nos. 221-225, 229, 235, J31-J33.

NEWSPAPER STAMPS

No. 19 Surcharged in Black, Red or Blue

a

b

1893 Unwmk. *Perf. 11½, 12½, 13½*

No.	Type	Description	Unused	Used
P1	A2 (a)	2½r on 40r	200.00	90.00
P2	A2 (a)	5r on 40r	175.00	90.00
P3	A2 (a)	5r on 40r (R)	150.00	75.00
P4	A2 (a)	5r on 40r (Bl)	180.00	75.00
P5	A2 (b)	2½r on 40r	22.50	16.00
		Nos. P1-P5 (5)	727.50	346.00

Nos. P1-P5 exist with double surcharge, Nos. P2-P4 with inverted surcharge.

N3

1893 Typo. *Perf. 11½, 13½*

No.	Type	Description	Unused	Used
P6	N3	2½r brown	.35	.30

For surcharge and overprint see Nos. 93, 199, 206.

No. P6 has been reprinted on chalk-surfaced paper with clean-cut perforation 13½. Value, 50 cents.

POSTAL TAX STAMPS

Pombal Commemorative Issue

Common Design Types

1925 Engr. *Perf. 12½*

No.	Type	Description	Unused	Used
RA1	CD28	15c brown & black	.30	.25
RA2	CD29	15c brown & black	.30	.25
RA3	CD30	15c brown & black	.30	.25
		Nos. RA1-RA3 (3)	.90	.75

Seal of Local Red Cross Society — PT7

Surcharged in Various Colors

1925 Typo. *Perf. 11½*

No.	Type	Description	Unused	Used
RA4	PT7	50c slate & yel (Bk)	1.60	1.60

Seal of Local Red Cross Society — PT8

1926

No.	Type	Description	Unused	Used
RA5	PT8	40c slate & yel (Bk)	3.50	3.50
RA6	PT8	50c slate & yel (R)	3.50	3.50
RA7	PT8	60c slate & yel (V)	3.50	3.50
RA8	PT8	80c slate & yel (Br)	3.50	3.50
RA9	PT8	1e slate & yel (Bl)	3.50	3.50
RA10	PT8	2e slate & yel (G)	3.50	3.50
		Nos. RA5-RA10 (6)	21.00	21.00

Obligatory on mail certain days of the year. The tax benefited the Cross of the Orient Society.

Type of 1926 Issue

1927 Black Surcharge

No.	Type	Description	Unused	Used
RA11	PT8	5c red & yel	3.50	3.50
RA12	PT8	10c green & yel	3.50	3.50
RA13	PT8	20c gray & yel	3.50	3.50
RA14	PT8	30c lt bl & yel	3.50	3.50
RA15	PT8	40c vio & yel	3.50	3.50
RA16	PT8	50c car & yel	3.50	3.50
RA17	PT8	60c brown & yel	3.50	3.50
RA18	PT8	80c blue & yel	3.50	3.50
RA19	PT8	1e olive & yel	3.50	3.50
RA20	PT8	2e yel brn & yel	3.50	3.50
		Nos. RA11-RA20 (10)	35.00	35.00

See note after No. RA10.

PT9

1928 **Litho.**

No.	Type	Description	Unused	Used
RA21	PT9	5c grn, yel & blk	4.50	4.50
RA22	PT9	10c sl bl, yel & blk	4.50	4.50
RA23	PT9	20c gray blk, yel & blk	4.50	4.50
RA24	PT9	30c brn rose, yel & blk	4.50	4.50
RA25	PT9	40c cl brn, yel & blk	4.50	4.50
RA26	PT9	50c red org, yel & blk	4.50	4.50
RA27	PT9	60c brn, yel & blk	4.50	4.50
RA28	PT9	80c dk brn, yel & blk	4.50	4.50
RA29	PT9	1e gray, yel & blk	4.50	4.50
RA30	PT9	2e red, yel & blk	4.50	4.50
		Nos. RA21-RA30 (10)	45.00	45.00

See note after RA10.

Mother and Children — PT10

1929 **Photo.** ***Perf. 14***

No.	Type	Description	Unused	Used
RA31	PT10	40c ultra, cl & blk	3.00	3.00

The use of this stamp was compulsory on all correspondence to Portugal and Portuguese Colonies for eight days beginning July 24, 1929.

See Nos.RA39-RA47.

Mousinho de Albuquerque PT11

1930-31 ***Perf. 14½x14***

Inscribed: "MACONTENE"

No.	Type	Description	Unused	Used
RA32	PT11	50c lake, red & gray	3.50	4.00

Inscribed: "COOLELA"

No.	Type	Description	Unused	Used
RA33	PT11	50c red vio, red brn & gray	3.50	4.00

Inscribed: "MUJENGA"

No.	Type	Description	Unused	Used
RA34	PT11	50c org red, red & gray	3.50	4.00

Inscribed: "CHAIMITE"

No.	Type	Description	Unused	Used
RA35	PT11	50c dp grn, bl grn & gray	3.50	4.00

Inscribed: "IBRAHIMO"

No.	Type	Description	Unused	Used
RA36	PT11	50c dk bl, blk & gray	3.50	4.00

Inscribed: "MUCUTO-MUNO"

No.	Type	Description	Unused	Used
RA37	PT11	50c ultra, blk & gray	3.50	4.00

Inscribed: "NAGUEMA"

No.	Type	Description	Unused	Used
RA38	PT11	50c dk vio, lt vio & gray	3.50	4.00
		Nos. RA32-RA38 (7)	24.50	28.00

The portrait is that of Mousinho de Albuquerque, the celebrated Portuguese warrior, and the names of seven battles in which he took part appear at the foot of the stamps. The stamps were issued for the memorial fund bearing his name and their use was obligatory on all correspondence posted on eight specific days in the year.

Type of 1929 Issue

Denominations in Black

No. RA42 Without Denomination

1931 ***Perf. 14***

No.	Type	Description	Unused	Used
RA39	PT10	40c rose & vio	4.00	3.25
RA40	PT10	40c ol grn & vio ('32)	5.50	4.50
RA41	PT10	40c bis brn & rose ('33)	5.50	4.50
RA42	PT10	bl grn & rose ('34)	3.75	3.50
RA43	PT10	40c org & ultra ('36)	5.50	4.50
RA44	PT10	40c choc & ultra ('37)	5.50	4.50
RA45	PT10	40c grn & brn car ('38)	7.50	5.50
RA46	PT10	40c yel & blk ('39)	7.50	5.50
RA47	PT10	40c gray brn ('40)	7.50	5.50
		Nos. RA39-RA47 (9)	52.25	41.25

POSTAL TAX DUE STAMPS

Pombal Commemorative Issue

Common Design Types

1925 **Unwmk.** ***Perf. 12½***

No.	Type	Description	Unused	Used
RAJ1	CD28	30c brown & black	.55	.65
RAJ2	CD29	30c brown & black	.55	.65
RAJ3	CD30	30c brown & black	.55	.65
		Nos. RAJ1-RAJ3 (3)	1.65	1.95

MOZAMBIQUE COMPANY

mō-zəm-'bēk 'kəmp-nē

LOCATION — Comprises the territory of Manica and Sofala of the Mozambique Colony in southeastern Africa

GOVT. — A part of the Portuguese Colony of Mozambique

AREA — 51,881 sq. mi.

POP. — 368,447 (1939)

CAPITAL — Beira

The Mozambique Company was chartered by Portugal in 1891 for 50 years. The territory was under direct administration of the Company until July 18, 1941

1000 Reis = 1 Milreis

100 Centavos = 1 Escudo (1916)

Mozambique Nos. 15-23 Overprinted in Carmine or Black

1892 **Unwmk.** ***Perf. 12½, 13½***

No.	Type	Description	Unused	Used
1	A2	5r black (C)	4.00	.50
a.		Pair, one without overprint	50.00	22.50
2	A2	10r green	4.00	.50
3	A2	20r rose	4.00	.50
a.		Perf. 13½	45.00	30.00
4	A2	25r violet	4.00	.45
a.		Double overprint	27.50	
5	A2	40r chocolate	4.00	.45
a.		Double overprint	20.00	
6	A2	50r blue	4.00	.50
7	A2	100r yellow brown	4.00	.75
8	A2	200r gray violet	4.50	.90
9	A2	300r orange	5.00	.90
		Nos. 1-9 (9)	37.50	5.45

Nos. 1 to 6, 8-9 were reprinted in 1905. These reprints have white gum and clean-cut perf. 13½ and the colors are usually paler than those of the originals.

Company Coat of Arms — A2

Perf. 11½, 12½, 13½

1895-1907 **Typo.**

Black or Red Numerals

No.	Type	Description	Unused	Used
10	A2	2½r olive yellow	.25	.25
11	A2	2½r gray ('07)	1.50	1.50
12	A2	5r orange	.25	.25
a.		Value omitted	15.00	
b.		Perf. 13½	2.00	1.10
13	A2	10r red lilac	.40	.30
14	A2	10r yel grn ('07)	2.50	.40
a.		Value inverted at top of stamp	20.00	20.00
15	A2	15r red brown	1.00	.30
16	A2	15r dk green ('07)	2.50	.40
17	A2	20r gray lilac	1.50	.30
18	A2	25r green	.75	.30
a.		Perf. 13½	1.90	1.25
19	A2	25r carmine ('07)	2.50	.60
a.		Value omitted	15.00	10.00
20	A2	50r blue	.90	.30
21	A2	50r brown ('07)	2.50	.60
a.		Value omitted	15.00	
22	A2	65r slate blue ('02)	.75	.35
23	A2	75r rose	.70	.30
24	A2	75r red lilac ('07)	5.00	1.00
25	A2	80r yellow green	.50	.30
26	A2	100r brown, *buff*	1.00	.30
27	A2	100r dk bl, *bl* ('07)	4.00	1.00
28	A2	115r car, *pink* ('04)	1.25	.70
29	A2	115r org brn, *pink* ('07)	6.00	1.40
30	A2	130r grn, *pink* ('04)	1.50	.70
31	A2	130r brn, *yel* ('07)	6.00	1.40
32	A2	150r org brn, *pink*	1.00	.60
33	A2	200r dk blue, *bl*	1.00	.90
a.		Perf. 13½	2.00	1.60
34	A2	200r red lil, *pink* ('07)	7.00	1.40
35	A2	300r dk bl, *salmon*	1.10	.90
a.		Perf. 13½	2.50	1.40
36	A2	400r brn, *bl* ('04)	2.50	1.10
37	A2	400r dl bl, *yel* ('07)	9.00	3.25
38	A2	500r blk & red	1.10	.75
39	A2	500r blk & red, *bl* ('07)	9.00	1.90
a.		500r pur & red, *yel* (error)		
40	A2	700r slate, *buff* ('04)	9.00	2.00
41	A2	700r pur, *yel* ('07)	5.00	2.00
42	A2	1000r violet & red	1.50	1.00
		Nos. 10-42 (33)	90.45	28.75

#12b, 18a, 33a, 35a were issued without gum.

For overprints & surcharges see #43-107, B1-B7.

Nos. 25 and 6 Surcharged or Overprinted in Red

b

c

1895 ***Perf. 12½, 13½***

No.	Type	Description	Unused	Used
43	A2(b)	25r on 80r yel grn	22.50	16.00
44	A2(c)	50r blue	9.00	4.00

Overprint "c" on No. 44 also exists reading from upper left to lower right.

Stamps of 1895 Overprinted in Bister, Orange, Violet, Green, Black or Brown

1898 ***Perf. 12½, 13½***

Without Gum

No.	Type	Description	Unused	Used
45	A2	2½r olive yel (Bi)	6.00	1.50
a.		Double overprint	*40.00*	*25.00*
b.		Red overprint	*60.00*	*50.00*
46	A2	5r orange (O)	8.00	1.50
47	A2	10r red lilac (V)	8.00	1.50
48	A2	15r red brown (V)	10.00	3.00
a.		Red overprint		
49	A2	20r gray lilac (V)	10.00	3.00
50	A2	25r green (G)	12.00	3.00
a.		Inverted overprint	65.00	40.00
51	A2	50r blue (Bk)	12.00	4.00
a.		Inverted overprint	60.00	40.00
52	A2	75r rose (V)	14.00	5.00
a.		Inverted overprint	75.00	40.00
b.		Red overprint		
53	A2	80r yellow grn (G)	19.00	5.00
a.		Inverted overprint		
54	A2	100r brn, *buff* (Br)	19.00	5.00
55	A2	150r org brn, *pink* (O)	19.00	5.00
a.		Inverted overprint	75.00	30.00
b.		Double overprint		
56	A2	200r dk blue, *bl* (Bk)	17.00	7.50
57	A2	300r dk blue, *sal* (Bk)	22.50	10.00
a.		Inverted overprint	60.00	50.00
b.		Green overprint		
		Nos. 45-57 (13)	176.50	55.00

Vasco da Gama's discovery of route to India, 400th anniversary.

No. 57b was prepared but not issued.

Nos. 45 and 49 were also issued with gum.

The "Centenario" overprint on stamps perf. 11½ is forged.

Nos. 23, 12, 17 Surcharged in Black, Carmine or Violet

e

1899 ***Perf. 12½***

No.	Type	Description	Unused	Used
59	A2(e)	25r on 75r rose (Bk)	4.00	2.50

f g

1900 ***Perf. 12½, 12½x11½***

No.	Type	Description	Unused	Used
60	A2(f)	25r on 5r org (C)	2.10	1.40
61	A2(g)	50r on half of 20r gray lil (V)	2.00	1.00
b.		Entire stamp	15.00	9.00

No. 61b is perf. 11½ vertically through center.

Stamps of 1895-1907 Overprinted Locally in Carmine or Green

1911 ***Perf. 11½, 13½***

No.	Type	Description	Unused	Used
61A	A2	2½r gray (C)	7.00	3.00
62	A2	5r orange (G)	6.00	3.00
63	A2	10r yellow grn (C)	1.00	.50
64	A2	15r dk green (C)	1.00	.50
a.		Double overprint	40.00	20.00
65	A2	20r gray lilac (G)	2.00	.50
a.		Perf. 13½	3.00	.80
66	A2	25r carmine (G)	1.25	.60
67	A2	50r brown (G)	.70	.45
68	A2	75r red lilac (G)	2.00	.45
69	A2	100r dk bl, *bl* (C)	2.00	.50
70	A2	115r org brn, *pink* (G)	2.50	1.25
71	A2	130r brn, *yel* (G)	3.00	1.25
72	A2	200r red lil, *pink* (G)	3.00	1.25
73	A2	400r dull bl, *yel* (C)	3.00	.70
74	A2	500r blk & red, *bl* (C)	4.00	1.40
75	A2	700r pur, *yel* (G)	4.00	1.40
		Nos. 61A-75 (15)	42.45	16.75

Nos. 63, 67 and 71 exist with inverted overprint; Nos. 63, 72 and 75 with double overprint.

Overprinted in Lisbon in Carmine or Green

1911 ***Perf. 11½, 12½***

No.	Type	Description	Unused	Used
75B	A2	2½r gray	.30	.25
76	A2	5r orange	.30	.25
77	A2	10r yellow grn	.25	.25
78	A2	15r dark green	.35	.25
79	A2	20r gray lilac	.40	.25
80	A2	25r carmine (G)	.35	.25
a.		Value inverted at top of stamp	18.00	
81	A2	50r brown	.70	.25
82	A2	75r red lilac	.70	.25
a.		Value omitted	15.00	
83	A2	100r dk blue, *bl*	1.00	.25
84	A2	115r org brn, *pink*	2.50	.40
85	A2	130r brown, *yel*	3.00	.40
a.		Double overprint	30.00	
86	A2	200r red lil, *pink*	3.00	.40
87	A2	400r dull bl, *yel*	5.00	.40
88	A2	500r blk & red, *bl*	7.50	.40
89	A2	700r pur, *yel*	5.00	.55
		Nos. 75B-89 (15)	30.35	4.80

Nos. 75B-89 Surcharged

1916 *Perf. 11½*

No.	Type	Description	Unused	Used
90	A2	¼c on 2½r gray	.25	.25
91	A2	½c on 5r org	.25	.25
a.		"½c" double	20.00	
92	A2	1c on 10r yel grn	.40	.25
93	A2	1½c on 15r dk grn	.40	.25
a.		Imperf., pair	35.00	
94	A2	2c on 20r gray lil	.50	.25
95	A2	2½c on 25r car	1.00	.25
96	A2	5c on 50r brn	.40	.25
a.		Imperf., pair	40.00	
97	A2	7½c on 75r red lil	.65	.25
98	A2	10c on 100r dk bl, *bl*	1.25	.95
a.		Inverted surcharge	40.00	40.00
99	A2	11½c on 115r org brn, *pink*	3.50	.95
a.		Inverted surcharge	50.00	50.00
100	A2	13c on 130r brn, *yel*	6.50	.95
101	A2	20c on 200r red lil, *pink*	5.50	1.10
102	A2	40c on 400r dl bl, *yel*	6.50	.50
103	A2	50c on 500r blk & red, *bl* (R)	8.00	.70
104	A2	70c on 700r pur, *yel*	8.00	1.25
		Nos. 90-104 (15)	43.10	8.40

Nos. 87 to 89 Surcharged

1918 *Perf. 11½*

No.	Type	Description	Unused	Used
105	A2	½c on 700r pur, *yel*	2.50	1.30
106	A2	2½c on 500r blk & red, *bl* (Bl)	3.50	1.30
107	A2	5c on 400r dl bl, *yel*	4.50	1.30
		Nos. 105-107 (3)	10.50	3.90

Native and Village — A9

Man and Ivory Tusks — A10

Corn — A11

Tapping Rubber Tree — A12

Sugar Refinery — A13

Buzi River Scene — A14

Tobacco Field — A15

View of Beira — A16

Coffee Plantation A17

Orange Tree A18

Cotton Field A19

Sisal Plantation A20

Scene on Beira R. R. — A21

Court House at Beira — A22

Coconut Palm A23

Mangroves A24

Cattle — A25

Company Arms — A26

1918-31 **Engr.** *Perf. 14, 15, 12½*

No.	Type	Description	Unused	Used
108	A9	¼c brn & yel grn	.55	.50
109	A9	¼c ol grn & blk ('25)	.30	.25
110	A10	½c black	.55	.50
111	A11	1c green & blk	.55	.50
112	A12	1½c black & grn	.55	.50
113	A13	2c carmine & blk	.55	.50
114	A13	2c ol blk & blk ('25)	.30	.25
115	A14	2½c lilac & blk	.55	.50
116	A11	3c ocher & blk ('23)	.30	.25
a.		3p orange & black ('25)	.30	.25
117	A15	4c grn & brn ('21)	.30	.25
118	A15	4c red & blk ('25)	.30	.25
119	A9	4½c gray & blk ('23)	.30	.25
120	A16	5c blue & blk	.55	.50
121	A17	6c claret & bl ('21)	.80	.30
122	A17	6c lilac & blk ('25)	.30	.25
123	A21	7c ultra & blk ('23)	1.00	.50
124	A18	7½c orange & grn	.75	.70
125	A19	8c violet & blk	1.50	1.10
126	A20	10c red org & blk	1.50	1.10
128	A19	12c brn & blk ('23)	1.00	.70
129	A19	12c bl grn & blk ('25)	2.00	.35
130	A21	15c carmine & blk	1.00	.95
131	A22	20c dp green & blk	1.60	.65
132	A23	30c red brn & blk	3.50	.95
133	A23	30c gray grn & blk ('25)	2.00	.55
134	A23	30c bl grn & blk ('31)	3.50	.55
135	A24	40c yel grn & blk	1.90	1.10
136	A24	40c grnsh bl & blk ('25)	.70	.85
137	A25	50c orange & blk	3.00	1.10
138	A25	50c lt vio & blk ('25)	2.25	.80
139	A25	60c rose & brn ('23)	1.50	.80
140	A20	80c ultra & brn ('23)	4.00	.80
141	A20	80c car & blk ('25)	1.10	.80
142	A26	1e dk green & blk	2.25	2.00
143	A26	1e blue & blk ('25)	2.25	.80
144	A16	2e rose & vio ('23)	6.00	1.30
145	A16	2e lilac & blk ('25)	4.00	.80
		Nos. 108-145 (37)	55.05	24.80

Shades exist of several denominations.

For surcharges see Nos. 146-154, RA1.

Nos. 132, 142, 115, 120, 131, 135, 125, 137 Surcharged with New Values in Red, Blue, Violet or Black

h

i

j

1920 *Perf. 14, 15*

No.	Type	Description	Unused	Used
146	A23(h)	½c on 30c (Bk)	7.00	5.00
147	A26(h)	½c on 1e (R)	7.00	5.00
148	A14(h)	1½c on 2½c (Bl)	6.00	2.25
149	A16(h)	1½c on 5c (V)	6.00	2.25
150	A14(h)	2c on 2½c (R)	6.00	2.25
151	A22(i)	4c on 20c (V)	7.00	4.50
152	A24(i)	4c on 40c (V)	7.00	4.50
153	A19(j)	6c on 8c (R)	7.50	4.50
154	A25(j)	6c on 50c (Bk)	8.00	4.50
		Nos. 146-154 (9)	61.50	34.75

The surcharge on No. 148 is placed vertically between two bars. On No. 154 the two words of the surcharge are 13mm apart.

Native — A27

View of Beira — A28

Tapping Rubber Tree — A29

Picking Tea — A30

Zambezi River — A31

1925-31 **Engr.** *Perf. 12*

No.	Type	Description	Unused	Used
155	A27	24c ultra & blk	1.25	1.00
156	A28	25c choc & ultra	1.25	1.00
157	A27	85c brn red & blk ('31)	.95	.80
158	A28	1.40e dl bl & blk ('31)	.90	.80
159	A29	5e yel brn & ultra	1.75	.65
160	A30	10e rose & blk	2.75	.95
161	A31	20e green & blk	3.25	1.20
		Nos. 155-161 (7)	12.10	6.40

Ivory Tusks — A32

Panning Gold — A33

1931 **Litho.** *Perf. 14*

No.	Type	Description	Unused	Used
162	A32	45c lt blue	3.00	1.30
163	A33	70c yellow brn	2.00	.70

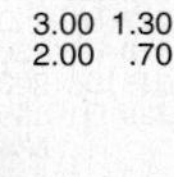

Zambezi Railroad Bridge A34

1935 **Engr.** *Perf. 12½*

No.	Type	Description	Unused	Used
164	A34	1e dk blue & blk	8.75	1.60

Opening of a new bridge over the Zambezi River.

Airplane over Beira — A35

1935

No.	Type	Description	Unused	Used
165	A35	5c blue & blk	.55	.55
166	A35	10c red org & blk	.55	.40
a.		Square pair, imperf. between	50.00	
167	A35	15c red & blk	.55	.40
a.		Square pair, imperf. between	50.00	
168	A35	20c yel grn & blk	.55	.40
169	A35	30c green & blk	.55	.40
170	A35	40c gray bl & blk	.70	.55
171	A35	45c blue & blk	.70	.55
172	A35	50c violet & blk	.70	.70
a.		Square pair, imperf. btwn.	60.00	
173	A35	60c carmine & brn	1.10	.65
174	A35	80c carmine & blk	1.10	.65
		Nos. 165-174 (10)	7.05	5.25

Issued to commemorate the opening of the Blantyre-Beira Salisbury air service.

Giraffe — A36

Thatched Huts — A37

Rock Python — A41

Coconut Palms A50

Zambezi Railroad Bridge A52

Sena Gate — A53

Company Arms — A54

Designs: 10c, Dhow. 15c, St. Caetano Fortress, Sofala. 20c, Zebra. 40c, Black rhinoceros. 45c, Lion. 50c, Crocodile. 60c, Leopard. 70c, Mozambique woman. 80c, Hippopotami. 85c, Vasco da Gama's flagship. 1e, Man in canoe. 2e, Greater kudu.

1937, May 16 *Perf. 12½*

No.	Type	Description	Unused	Used
175	A36	1c yel grn & vio	.30	.25
176	A37	5c blue & yel grn	.30	.25
177	A36	10c ver & ultra	.30	.25
178	A37	15c carmine & blk	.30	.25
179	A36	20c green & ultra	.30	.25
180	A41	30c dk grn & ind	.30	.30
181	A41	40c gray bl & blk	.30	.30
182	A41	45c blue & brn	.30	.30
183	A41	50c dk vio & emer	.30	.30
184	A37	60c carmine & bl	.30	.30
185	A36	70c yel brn & pale grn	.30	.30
186	A37	80c car & pale grn	.40	.35
187	A41	85c org red & blk	.50	.40
188	A41	1e dp bl & blk	.50	.40
189	A50	1.40e dk bl & pale grn	.90	.40
190	A41	2e pale lilac & brn	1.50	.50

191	A52	5e yel brn & bl	1.25	.75
192	A53	10e carmine & blk	2.25	1.50
193	A54	20e grn & brn vio	3.00	2.75
		Nos. 175-193 (19)	13.60	10.10

Stamps of 1937 Overprinted in Red or Black

1939, Aug. 28

194	A41	30c dk grn & ind (R)	3.00	.85
195	A41	40c gray bl & blk (R)	3.00	.85
196	A41	45c blue & brn (Bk)	3.00	.85
197	A41	50c dk vio & emer (R)	4.00	1.00
198	A41	85c org red & blk (Bk)	4.00	1.00
199	A41	1e dp bl & blk (R)	4.00	1.25
200	A41	2e pale lil & brn (Bk)	4.50	1.75
		Nos. 194-200 (7)	25.50	7.55

Visit of the President of Portugal to Beira in 1939.

King Alfonso Henriques — A55

1940, Feb. 16 Typo. *Perf. 11½x12*

201	A55	1.75e blue & lt blue	1.50	.75

800th anniv. of Portuguese independence.

King John IV — A56

1940, Oct. 10 Engr. *Perf. 12½*

202	A56	40c gray grn & blk	.65	.50
203	A56	50c dk vio & brt grn	.65	.50
204	A56	60c brt car & dp bl	.65	.50
205	A56	70c brn org & dk grn	.65	.50
206	A56	80c car & dp grn	.65	.50
207	A56	1e dk bl & blk	.65	.50
		Nos. 202-207 (6)	3.90	3.00

300th anniv. of the restoration of the Portuguese Monarchy.

Mozambique Company's charter terminated July 18th, 1941 after which date its stamps were superseded by those of the territory of Mozambique.

SEMI-POSTAL STAMPS

Lisbon Issue of 1911 Overprinted in Red

1917 Unwmk. *Perf. 11½*

B1	A2	2½r gray	9.00	*10.50*
a.		Double overprint	75.00	*75.00*
B2	A2	10r yellow grn	10.00	*15.00*
B3	A2	20r gray lilac	14.00	*20.00*
B4	A2	50r brown	20.00	*25.00*
B5	A2	75r red lilac	65.00	*70.00*
B6	A2	100r dk blue, *bl*	75.00	*80.00*
B7	A2	700r purple, *yel*	175.00	*225.00*
		Nos. B1-B7 (7)	368.00	*445.50*

Nos. B1-B7 were used on July 31, 1917, in place of ordinary stamps. The proceeds were given to the Red Cross.

AIR POST STAMPS

Airplane over Beira — AP1

1935 Unwmk. Engr. *Perf. 12½*

C1	AP1	5c blue & blk	.25	.25
C2	AP1	10c org red & blk	.25	.25
C3	AP1	15c red & blk	.25	.25
C4	AP1	20c yel grn & blk	.25	.25
C5	AP1	30c green & blk	.25	.25
C6	AP1	40c gray bl & blk	.25	.25
C7	AP1	45c blue & blk	.25	.25
C8	AP1	50c dk vio & blk	.40	.25
C9	AP1	60c car & brn	.40	.25
C10	AP1	80c car & blk	.50	.25
C11	AP1	1e blue & blk	.50	.25
C12	AP1	2e mauve & blk	1.50	.40
C13	AP1	5e bis brn & bl	1.50	.50
C14	AP1	10e car & blk	2.00	.75
C15	AP1	20e bl grn & blk	3.00	1.00
		Nos. C1-C15 (15)	11.55	5.40

POSTAGE DUE STAMPS

D1

1906 Unwmk. Typo. *Perf. 11½x12*
Denominations in Black

J1	D1	5r yellow grn	.70	.40
J2	D1	10r slate	.70	.55
J3	D1	20r yellow brn	1.25	.55
J4	D1	30r orange	1.50	1.00
J5	D1	50r gray brown	1.50	1.00
J6	D1	60r red brown	22.50	9.00
J7	D1	100r red lilac	4.00	2.50
J8	D1	130r dull blue	32.50	12.00
J9	D1	200r carmine	13.00	4.00
J10	D1	500r violet	18.00	5.00
		Nos. J1-J10 (10)	95.65	36.00

Nos. J1-J10 Overprinted in Carmine or Green

1911

J11	D1	5r yellow grn	.30	.30
J12	D1	10r slate	.30	.30
J13	D1	20r yellow brn	.30	.30
J14	D1	30r orange	.30	.30
J15	D1	50r gray brown	.30	.30
J16	D1	60r red brown	.50	.50
J17	D1	100r red lilac	.50	.50
J18	D1	130r dull blue	2.00	1.40
J19	D1	200r carmine (G)	1.30	1.35
J20	D1	500r violet	2.50	1.40
		Nos. J11-J20 (10)	8.30	6.65

D2

1916 Typo.
With Value in Centavos in Black

J21	D2	½c yellow grn	.30	.30
J22	D2	1c slate	.30	.30
J23	D2	2c orange brn	.30	.30
J24	D2	3c orange	.70	.30
J25	D2	5c gray brown	.70	.30
J26	D2	6c pale brown	.70	.35
J27	D2	10c red lilac	.70	.55
J28	D2	13c gray blue	1.40	1.30
J29	D2	20c rose	1.40	1.30
J30	D2	50c gray	3.25	1.50
		Nos. J21-J30 (10)	9.75	6.50

Company Arms — D3

1919 Engr. *Perf. 14, 15*

J31	D3	½c green	.25	.25
a.		Perf. 12½	.25	.25
J32	D3	1c slate	.25	.25
a.		Perf. 12½	.25	.25
J33	D3	2c red brown	.25	.25
a.		Perf. 12½	.25	.25
J34	D3	3c orange	.25	.25
a.		Perf. 12½	.25	.25
J35	D3	5c gray brown	.25	.25
a.		Perf. 12½	.25	.25
J36	D3	6c lt brown	.50	.50
a.		Perf. 12½	.50	.50
b.		Perf. 13½	.50	.50
J37	D3	10c lilac rose	.50	.50
a.		Perf. 12½	.50	.50
J38	D3	13c dull blue	.50	.50
a.		Perf. 12½	.50	.50
b.		Perf. 13½	.50	.50
J39	D3	20c rose	.50	.50
a.		Perf. 12½	.50	.50
J40	D3	50c gray	.50	.50
a.		Perf. 12½	.50	.50
		Nos. J31-J40 (10)	3.75	3.75

NEWSPAPER STAMP

Newspaper Stamp of Mozambique Overprinted

1894 Unwmk. *Perf. 11½*

P1	N3	2½r brown	.65	.55
a.		Inverted overprint	30.00	30.00
b.		Perf. 12½	1.50	1.10

Reprints are on stout white paper with clean-cut perf. 13½. Value $1.

POSTAL TAX STAMPS

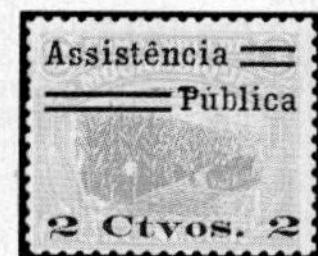

No. 116 Surcharged in Black

1932 *Perf. 12½*

RA1	A11	2c on 3c org & blk	1.40	*2.00*

Charity — PT2

1933 Litho. *Perf. 11*

RA2	PT2	2c magenta & blk	1.40	*2.00*

PT3

1940 Unwmk. *Perf. 10½*

RA3	PT3	2c black & ultra	15.00	*16.00*

NATAL

nə-'tal

LOCATION — Southern coast of Africa, bordering on the Indian Ocean
GOVT. — British Crown Colony
AREA — 35,284 sq. mi.
POP. — 1,206,386 (1908)
CAPITAL — Pietermaritzburg

Natal united with Cape of Good Hope, Orange Free State and the Transvaal in 1910 to form the Union of South Africa.

12 Pence = 1 Shilling
20 Shillings = 1 Pound

Values for Nos. 1-7 are for examples with complete margins and free from damage. Unused values for No. 8 on are for stamps with original gum as defined in the catalogue introduction. Very fine examples of Nos. 8-49, 61-63 and 79 will have perforations touching the design on one or more sides due to the narrow spacing of the stamps on the plates. Stamps with perfs clear of the design on all four sides are scarce and will command higher prices.

Watermark

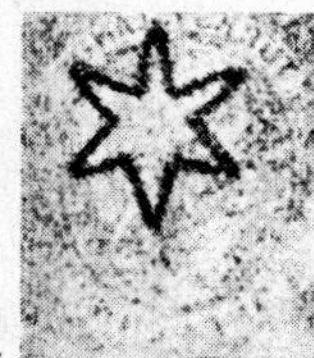

Wmk. 5 — Small Star

Crown and V R (Victoria Regina) — A1

Crown and V R (Victoria Regina) — A2

Crown and Laurel — A3

A4

A5

Colorless Embossing

1857 Unwmk. *Imperf.*

1 A1 3p *rose* 725.
 a. Tete beche pair *55,000.*
2 A2 6p *green* 2,000.
 a. Diagonal half used as 3p on cover *16,500.*
3 A3 9p *blue* 65,000. *13,000.*
4 A4 1sh *buff* *10,500.*

1858

5 A5 1p *blue* 1,400.
6 A5 1p *rose* 2,200.
 a. No. 1 embossed over No. 6 —
7 A5 1p *buff* 1,450.

Reprints: The paper is slightly glazed, the embossing sharper and the colors as follows: 1p pale blue, deep blue, carmine rose or yellow; 3p pale rose or carmine rose; 6p bright green or yellow green; 1sh pale buff or pale yellow. Bogus cancellations are found on the reprints.

The stamps printed on surface-colored paper are revenue stamps with trimmed perforations.

Queen Victoria — A6

1860 Engr. *Perf. 14*

8 A6 1p rose 190.00 95.00
9 A6 3p blue 225.00 60.00
 a. Vert. pair, imperf betwn. *13,000.*

1863 *Perf. 13*

10 A6 1p red 130.00 35.00
 a. 1p carmine lake 130.00 35.00

1861 *Clean-cut Perf. 14 to 16*

11 A6 3p blue 350.00 82.50

1862 *Rough Perf. 14 to 16*

12 A6 3p blue 175.00 45.00
 a. Imperf., pair *4,500.*
 b. Imperf. horiz. or vert., pair *6,500.*
13 A6 6p gray 275.00 75.00

1862 Wmk. 5

14 A6 1p rose 180.00 82.50

Imperforate stamps of the 1p and 3p on paper watermarked small star are proofs.

1864 Wmk. 1 *Perf. 12½*

15 A6 1p carmine red 140.00 50.00
 a. 1p brown red 200.00 50.00
 b. 1p rose 135.00 45.00
16 A6 6p violet 90.00 37.50
 a. 6p dull reddish violet 110.00 22.50

No. 15 imperf is a proof.

Queen Victoria — A7

1867 Typo. *Perf. 14*

17 A7 1sh green 275.00 52.50

For types A6 and A7 overprinted or surcharged see Nos. 18-50, 61-63, 76, 79.

Stamps of 1860-67 Overprinted

1869 Overprint 12¾mm

18 A6 1p carmine red (#15) 525.00 100.00
 a. 1p rose (#15b) 550.00 105.00
 b. Double overprint — —
19 A6 3p blue (#12) 700.00 110.00
19A A6 3p blue (#9) — 550.00
19B A6 3p blue (#11) 1,050. 325.00
20 A6 6p violet (#16) 650.00 110.00
 a. 6p dull reddish violet (#16a) 775.00 95.00
21 A7 1sh green (#17) *30,000.* 2,100.

Same Overprint 13¾mm

22 A6 1p rose (#15b) 1,200. 325.00
 a. 1p carmine red (#15) 1,200. 300.00
23 A6 3p blue (#12) 2,800. 550.00
 a. Inverted overprint
23B A6 3p blue (#9) — —
23C A6 3p blue (#11) — 1,100.
24 A6 6p violet (#16) 2,750. 225.00
 a. 6p dull reddish violet (#16a) 3,000. 225.00
25 A7 1sh green (#17) *35,000.* *3,250.*

Same Overprint 14½ to 15½mm

26 A6 1p rose (#15b) 1,050. 250.00
 a. 1p carmine red (#15) 1,050. 210.00
27 A6 3p blue (#12) — 450.00
27A A6 3p blue (#11) — 775.00
27B A6 3p blue (#9) — —
28 A6 6p violet (#16) 2,100. 140.00
 a. 6p dull reddish violet (#16a) — 150.00
29 A7 1sh green (#17) *32,000.* *2,750.*

Overprinted

30 A6 1p rose (#15b) 150.00 55.00
 a. 1p carmine red (#15) 210.00 55.00
 b. Inverted overprint
31 A6 3p blue (#12) 250.00 55.00
 a. Double overprint *1,800.*
31B A6 3p blue (#11) 225.00 62.50
31C A6 3p blue (#9) 400.00 95.00
32 A6 6p violet (#16) 210.00 77.50
 a. 6p dull reddish violet (#16a) 275.00 87.50
33 A7 1sh green (#17) 350.00 87.50

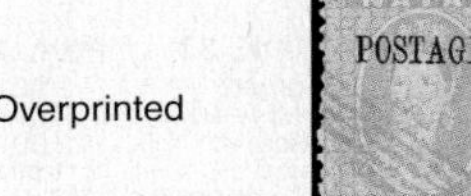

Overprinted

34 A6 1p rose (#15b) 650.00 120.00
 a. 1p carmine red (#15) 550.00 110.00
35 A6 3p blue (#12) 825.00 120.00
35A A6 3p blue (#11) 1,200. 375.00
35B A6 3p blue (#9) *4,250.* *925.00*
36 A6 6p violet (#16) 825.00 120.00
 a. 6p dull reddish violet (#16a) 875.00 100.00
 b. Inverted overprint
37 A7 1sh green (#17) *37,500.* *2,000.*

Overprinted in Black or Red

1870-73 Wmk. 1 *Perf. 12½*

38 A6 1p red 120.00 16.50
39 A6 3p ultra (R) ('72) 130.00 16.50
40 A6 6p lilac ('73) 250.00 45.00
 Nos. 38-40 (3) 500.00 78.00

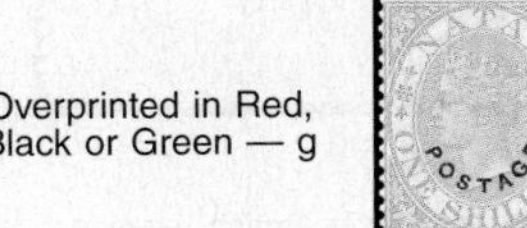

Overprinted in Red, Black or Green — g

1870 *Perf. 14*

41 A7 1sh green (R) — *9,500.*
42 A7 1sh green (Bk) — *1,750.*
 a. Double overprint *3,900.*
43 A7 1sh green (G) 150.00 13.00

See No. 76.

Type of 1867 Overprinted

1873

44 A7 1sh brown lilac 425.00 32.50

No. 44 without overprint is a revenue.

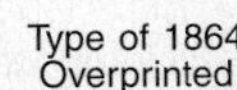

Type of 1864 Overprinted

1874 *Perf. 12½*

45 A6 1p rose red 400.00 95.00
 a. Double overprint

Overprinted

1875

46 A6 1p rose red 185.00 70.00
 a. 1p carmine 175.00 82.50
 b. Double overprint 1,900. 650.00

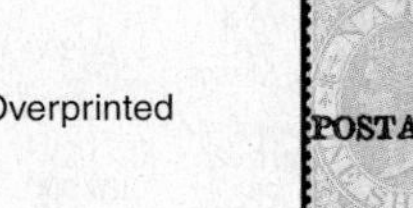

Overprinted

1875 Overprint 14½mm *Perf. 12½*

47 A6 1p yellow 100.00 100.00
 a. Double overprint, one albino 275.00 —
48 A6 1p rose red 140.00 87.50
 a. Inverted overprint 2,250. 575.00
49 A6 6p violet 95.00 10.00
 a. Inverted overprint 900.00 190.00
 b. Double overprint 1,050.

Perf. 14

50 A7 1sh green 140.00 9.00
 a. Double overprint 425.00
 Nos. 47-50 (4) 475.00 206.50

The 1p yellow without overprint is a revenue.

A8 A9

A10 A11

Queen Victoria — A12

1874-78 Typo. Wmk. 1 *Perf. 14*

51 A8 1p dull rose 60.00 8.50
 a. 1p bright rose 55.00 7.50
52 A9 3p ultramarine 190.00 40.00
 a. Perf. 14x12½ 2,500. 1,100.
53 A10 4p brown ('78) 210.00 18.00
54 A11 6p violet 110.00 9.00

Perf. 15½x15

55 A12 5sh claret 525.00 120.00

Perf. 14

56 A12 5sh claret ('78) 450.00 120.00
57 A12 5sh carmine 120.00 42.50
 Handstamped "SPECIMEN" 250.00
 a. 5sh rose ('78) 150.00 45.00

Perf. 12½

58 A10 4p brown ('78) 400.00 82.50

See Nos. 65-71. For types A8-A10 surcharged see Nos. 59-60, 72-73, 77, 80.

Surcharged in Black

n

No. 60

o

1877 *Perf. 14*

59 A8(n) ½p on 1p rose 45.00 *82.50*
 a. Double surcharge "1/2"
60 A8(n) ½p on 1p rose 110.00 —

Surcharge "n" exists in 3 or more types each of the large "1/2" (No. 59) and the small "1/2" (No. 60).

"HALF" and "½" were overprinted separately; "½" may be above, below or overlapping.

Perf. 12½

61 A6(o) ½p on 1p yel 13.00 *25.00*
 a. Double surcharge 400.00 230.00
 b. Inverted surcharge 400.00 240.00
 c. Pair, one without surcharge 4,750. 3,000.
 d. "POTAGE" 350.00 250.00
 e. "POSAGE" 350.00 325.00
 f. "POSTAGE" omitted 2,500. —
62 A6(o) 1p on 6p vio 82.50 13.00
 a. "POSTAGE" omitted
 b. "POTAGE" 650.00 190.00
63 A6(o) 1p on 6p rose 150.00 60.00
 a. Inverted surcharge 1,750. 600.00
 b. Double surcharge — 350.00
 c. Dbl. srch., one inverted 400.00 250.00
 d. Triple srch., one invtd.
 e. Quadruple surcharge 550.00 300.00
 f. "POTAGE" 1,000. 390.00
 Nos. 61-63 (3) 245.50 98.00

No. 63 without overprint is a revenue.

A14

1880 Typo. *Perf. 14*

64 A14 ½p blue green 27.50 35.00
 a. Vertical pair, imperf. between

1882-89 Wmk. Crown and CA (2)

65 A14 ½p blue green ('84) 120.00 20.00
66 A14 ½p gray green ('84) 6.00 1.40
67 A8 1p rose ('84) 7.50 .30
 a. 1p carmine 7.00 .40
68 A9 3p ultra ('84) 170.00 22.00
69 A9 3p gray ('89) 11.50 5.25
70 A10 4p brown 16.50 1.90
71 A11 6p violet 13.00 2.75
 Nos. 65-71 (7) 344.50 53.60

Surcharged in Black

p q

1885-86

72 A8(p) ½p on 1p rose 24.00 14.00
 a. Hyphen after "HALF" omitted 120.00 55.00
 b. Inverted surcharge —
73 A9(q) 2p on 3p gray ('86) 40.00 7.00

A17

1887

74 A17 2p olive green, die B ('89) 6.00 1.75
 Handstamped "SPECIMEN" 87.50
 a. Die A 60.00 3.00
 Overprinted "SPECIMEN" 110.00

For explanation of dies A and B see "Dies of British Colonial Stamps" in the catalogue introduction.

Type of 1867 Overprinted Type "g" in Red

1888

76 A7 1sh orange 12.00 1.90
Handstamped "SPECI-MEN" 130.00
a. Double overprint 3,250.

Surcharged in Black

1891

77 A10 2½p on 4p brown 17.50 17.50
Handstamped "SPECIMEN" 130.00
a. "PENGE" 77.50
b. "PENN" 325.00 275.00
c. Double surcharge 400.00 350.00
d. As "c," in vert. pair with normal stamp 650.00 750.00
e. Inverted surcharge 550.00 475.00
f. Vert. pair, surcharge tete-beche 2,250. 3,000.

A20

1891, June

78 A20 2½p ultramarine 12.00 1.60
Handstamped "SPECIMEN" 82.50

Surcharged in Red or Black

No. 79

No. 80

1895, Mar. Wmk. 1 *Perf. 12½*

79 A6 ½p on 6p vio (R) 3.00 10.00
Handstamped "SPECIMEN" 65.00
a. "Ealf" 27.50 75.00
b. "Penny" 27.50 75.00
c. Double surcharge, one vertical 350.00
d. Double surcharge 350.00

Stamps with fancy "P," "T" or "A" in surcharge sell for twice as much.

Wmk. 2 *Perf. 14*

80 A8 ½p on 1p rose (Bk) 3.50 2.50
Handstamped "SPECIMEN" 70.00
a. Double surcharge 525.00 550.00
b. Pair, one without surcharge and the other with double surcharge —

A23

King Edward VII — A24

1902-03 Typo. Wmk. 2 *Perf. 14*

81 A23 ½p blue green 7.50 .55
82 A23 1p rose 13.00 .25
83 A23 1½p blk & blue grn 4.50 6.00
84 A23 2p ol grn & scar 6.00 .45
85 A23 2½p ultramarine 1.90 6.00
86 A23 3p gray & red vio 1.60 2.75
87 A23 4p brown & scar 12.00 27.50
88 A23 5p org & black 4.50 4.00
89 A23 6p mar & bl grn 4.50 5.00
90 A23 1sh pale bl & dp rose 5.50 5.25
91 A23 2sh vio & bl grn 62.50 11.50
92 A23 2sh6p red violet 50.00 15.00
93 A23 4sh yel & dp rose 95.00 95.00
Nos. 81-93, ovptd. "SPECI-MEN" 225.00

Wmk. 1

94 A24 5sh car lake & dk blue 65.00 14.00
Overprinted "SPECI-MEN" 65.00
95 A24 10sh brn & dp rose 130.00 45.00
Overprinted "SPECI-MEN" 65.00
96 A24 £1 ultra & blk 350.00 85.50
Overprinted "SPECI-MEN" 65.00
97 A24 £1 10sh vio & bl grn 600.00 140.00
Overprinted "SPECI-MEN" 120.00
Revenue cancel 15.00
98 A24 £5 blk & vio *5,500.* *1,400.*
Overprinted "SPECI-MEN" 250.00
Revenue cancel 110.00
99 A24 £10 org & grn *14,000.* *6,500.*
Overprinted "SPECI-MEN" 450.00
Revenue cancel 180.00
100 A24 £20 grn & car *28,000.* *19,000.*
Overprinted "SPECI-MEN" 550.00
Revenue cancel 325.00
Nos. 81-96 (16) 813.50 323.75

1904-08 Wmk. 3

101 A23 ½p blue green 12.00 .25
102 A23 1p rose 12.00 .25
a. Booklet pane of 6 600.00
Complete booklet of 5 #102a 3,500.
b. Booklet pane of 5 + 1 label 500.00
Complete booklet of 5 #102b 3,500.
103 A23 2p ol grn & scar 18.50 4.00
104 A23 4p brn & scar 3.50 1.60
105 A23 5p org & blk ('08) 5.50 5.00
106 A23 1sh pale bl & dp rose 100.00 9.00
107 A23 2sh vio & bl grn 75.00 55.00
108 A23 2sh6p red violet 70.00 55.00
109 A24 £1 10sh vio & org brn, chalky paper 1,900. *5,000.*
Overprinted "SPECI-MEN" 350.00
Revenue cancel 55.00
Nos. 101-108 (8) 296.50 130.10

A25

A26

1908-09

110 A25 6p red violet 5.75 3.50
111 A25 1sh blk, *grn* 7.75 3.25
112 A25 2sh bl & vio, *bl* 19.00 3.75
113 A25 2sh6p red & blk, *bl* 32.00 3.75
114 A26 5sh red & grn, *yell* 30.00 45.00
115 A26 10sh red & grn, *grn* 135.00 135.00
116 A26 £1 blk & vio, *red* 440.00 400.00
Nos. 110-116 (7) 669.50 594.25

OFFICIAL STAMPS

Nos. 101-103, 106 and Type A23 Overprinted

1904 Wmk. 3 *Perf. 14*

O1 A23 ½p blue green 3.75 .45
O2 A23 1p rose 14.50 1.25
O3 A23 2p ol grn & scar 45.00 22.50
O4 A23 3p gray & red vio 27.50 *5.50*
O5 A23 6p mar & bl grn 87.50 82.50
O6 A23 1sh pale bl & dp rose 250.00 *275.00*
Nos. O1-O6 (6) 428.25 *387.20*

Stamps of Natal were replaced by those of the Union of South Africa.

NAURU

nä-'ü-(,)rü

LOCATION — An island on the Equator in the west central Pacific Ocean, midway between the Marshall and Solomon Islands.
GOVT. —
AREA — 8½ sq. mi.
POP. — 8,421 (est. 1983)
CAPITAL — None. Parliament House is in Yaren District.

The island, a German possession, was captured by Australian forces in 1914 and, following World War I, was mandated to the British Empire. It was administered jointly by Great Britain, Australia and New Zealand.

See North West Pacific Islands.

12 Pence = 1 Shilling

Great Britain Stamps of 1912-13 Overprinted at Bottom of Stamp

1916-23 Wmk. 33 *Perf. 14½x14*

1 A82 ½p green 3.50 *12.50*
a. Double ovpt, one albino 70.00
2 A83 1p scarlet 2.50 *14.50*
a. 1p carmine red 16.00
b. Double ovpt, one albino 260.00
3 A84 1½p red brn ('23) 57.50 *85.00*
4 A85 2p org (die I) 3.00 *15.00*
a. Double ovpt, one albino 135.00
b. Triple ovpt, two albino 350.00
c. 2p deep orange (die II) ('23) 75.00 *110.00*
6 A86 2½p ultra 3.00 *7.50*
a. Double ovpt, one albino 300.00
7 A87 3p violet 2.50 *6.50*
a. Double ovpt, one albino 375.00
8 A88 4p slate green 2.50 *9.00*
a. Double ovpt, one albino 260.00
9 A89 5p yel brown 2.75 *14.00*
a. Double ovpt, one albino 175.00
10 A89 6p dull violet 8.50 *11.00*
a. Double ovpt, one albino 400.00
11 A90 9p blk brn 10.00 *24.00*
a. Double ovpt, one albino 375.00
12 A90 1sh bister 8.50 *20.00*
a. Double ovpt, one albino 425.00
Nos. 1-12 (11) 104.25 *219.00*

Great Britain Stamps of 1915 Overprinted

Nos. of basic British stamps are in parentheses.

Wmk. 34 *Perf. 11x12*

13 A91 2sh6p lt brn (#173d) 80.00 *125.00*
a. 2sh6p black brown (#173e) 625.00 *1,600.*
b. As "a," double ovpt, one albino 1,950.
c. As "a," triple ovpt, two albino 1,950.
d. 2sh6p pale brown (worn plate) (#173a) 80.00 *115.00*
14 A91 5sh carmine (#174b) 125.00 *175.00*
a. As "a," triple ovpt, two albino 1,500.
b. 5sh rose carmine (#174) 3,000. 2,750.
15 A91 10sh lt blue (R) (#175a) 275.00 *375.00*
a. Double ovpt, one albino 1,500.
b. Triple ovpt, one black, one red, one albino 3,750.
c. 10sh indigo blue (#175) *12,500.* *6,000.*
d. Double ovpt, one albino 14,000. 8,000.
e. 10sh deep bright blue (#175c) 575.00 *625.00*

Same Ovpt. on Great Britain No. 179a and 179b

1920

16 A91 2sh6p gray brown (#179a) 85.00 *200.00*
a. Double ovpt, one albino 550.00
b. 2sh6p chocolate brown (#179b) 105.00 *175.00*
c. As "b", double ovpt, one albino 550.00
Nos. 13-16 (4) 565.00 *875.00*
Nos. 1-16 (15) 669.25 *1,094.*

1923 Overprint Centered

1b A82 ½p 5.00 *55.00*
2c A83 1p 20.00 *45.00*
3a A84 1½p 30.00 *57.50*
b. Double ovpt, one albino 200.00
4d A85 2p As No. 4a 32.50 *80.00*
Nos. 1b-4d (4) 87.50 *237.50*

On Nos. 1-12 "NAURU" is usually 12¾mm wide and at the foot of the stamp. In 1923 four values were overprinted with the word 13½mm wide and across the middle of the stamp.

Forged overprints exist.

Freighter — A1

1924-48 Unwmk. Engr. *Perf. 11*

Unsurfaced grayish paper '24-'34

17 A1 ½p orange brown 2.75 *3.00*
18 A1 1p green 4.00 3.00
19 A1 1½p red 4.50 4.50
20 A1 2p orange 4.50 *12.00*
21 A1 2½p blue 6.50 *27.50*
b. 2½ greenish blue ('34) 13.00 *25.00*
22 A1 3p pale blue 4.50 *14.50*
23 A1 4p olive green 8.50 *22.50*
24 A1 5p dk brown 4.50 *7.50*
25 A1 6p dark violet 5.25 *21.00*
26 A1 9p brown olive 11.00 *21.00*
27 A1 1sh brown red 7.00 *14.00*
28 A1 2sh6p slate green 32.50 *55.00*
29 A1 5sh claret 55.00 *110.00*
30 A1 10sh yellow 140.00 *200.00*
Nos. 17-30 (14) 290.50 *515.50*

Glazed surfaced white paper '37-'48

17a A1 ½p orange brown 4.75 *15.00*
b. Perf. 14 ('47) 1.75 *10.00*
18a A1 1p green 2.50 *4.00*
19a A1 1½p red 1.10 *2.00*
20a A1 2p orange 4.50 *8.00*
21a A1 2½p blue ('48) 4.00 *4.00*
c. Horiz. pair, imperf between *17,000.* *20,000.*
d. Vert. pair, imperf between *17,000.* *20,000.*
22a A1 3p grnsh gray ('47) 7.00 *23.00*
23a A1 4p olive green 7.00 *15.00*
24a A1 5p dk brown 5.25 *5.00*
25a A1 6p dark violet 5.75 *6.00*
26a A1 9p brown olive 9.50 *21.00*
27a A1 1sh brown red 14.00 3.25
28a A1 2sh6p slate green 34.00 *37.50*
29a A1 5sh claret 40.00 *55.00*
30a A1 10sh yellow 85.00 *110.00*
Nos. 17a-30a (14) 224.35 *308.75*
Set #17a-30a, never hinged 205.00

Stamps of Type A1 Overprinted in Black

1935, July 12 *Perf. 11*

Glazed Paper

31 A1 1½p red .90 .90
32 A1 2p orange 1.50 *3.75*
33 A1 2½p blue 1.50 *1.75*
34 A1 1sh brown red 6.00 *3.50*
Nos. 31-34 (4) 9.90 *9.90*
Set, never hinged 16.00

25th anniv. of the reign of George V.

George VI — A2

1937, May 10 Engr.

35 A2 1½p salmon rose .25 *1.00*
36 A2 2p dull orange .25 *2.00*
37 A2 2½p blue .25 *1.25*
38 A2 1sh brown violet .35 *1.25*
Nos. 35-38 (4) 1.10 *5.50*
Set, never hinged 1.75

Coronation of George VI & Elizabeth.

NEPAL

nə-'pol

LOCATION — In the Himalaya Mountains between India and Tibet
GOVT. — Kingdom
AREA — 56,136 sq. mi.
POP. — 16,100,000 (est. 1982)
CAPITAL — Kathmandu

Nepal stamps were valid only in Nepal and India until April 1959, when they became valid to all parts of the world.

4 Pice = 1 Anna
64 Pice = 16 Annas = 1 Rupee

Nos. 1-24, 29A were issued without gum.

Sripech and Crossed Khukris — A1

1881 Typo. Unwmk. *Pin-perf.*

European Wove Paper

1	A1	1a ultramarine	300.00	*475.00*
2	A1	2a purple	375.00	500.00
a.		Tete beche pair		—
3	A1	4a green	500.00	*650.00*

Imperf

4	A1	1a blue	175.00	140.00
5	A1	2a purple	200.00	*200.00*
a.		Tete beche pair	*800.00*	*800.00*
6	A1	4a green	275.00	*500.00*

No. 3 postally used is probably unique. Only 2 No. 5a are known unused. No. 5a is only known to exist used in a strip of three.

1886 Native Wove Paper *Imperf.*

7	A1	1a ultramarine	22.50	*32.50*
a.		Tete beche pair	*150.00*	*175.00*
8	A1	2a violet	37.50	37.50
a.		Tete beche pair	*200.00*	*200.00*
9	A1	4a green	55.00	55.00
a.		Tete beche pair	*300.00*	*250.00*
		Nos. 7-9 (3)	115.00	125.00

Nos. 7-10 are clear to mostly clear designs on good quality native paper. European wove paper is of substantially higher quality, white, and lacks the wood fibers of the native paper.

Used values for Nos. 10-49 are for telegraph cancels.

Siva's Bow and Two Khukris — A2

1899-1917 *Imperf.*

Native Wove Paper

10	A2	½a black, clear impression	20.00	13.50
a.		Tete beche pair	*100.00*	55.00
11	A2	½a red orange ('17)	*1,750.*	400.00
a.		Tete beche pair		—

Pin-perf.

12	A2	½a black	30.00	17.50
a.		Tete beche pair	*225.00*	55.00

No. 11 is known postally used on six covers.

11a unused is only known in larger blocks, no unused pairs currently exist.

Type of 1881

1898-1917 *Imperf.*

13	A1	1a pale blue	60.00	60.00
a.		1a bluish green	75.00	75.00
b.		Tete beche pair	*150.00*	*150.00*
c.		As "a," tete beche pair	*300.00*	*300.00*
14	A1	2a gray violet	60.00	60.00
a.		Tete beche pair	*140.00*	*140.00*
15	A1	2a claret ('17)	*100.00*	32.50
a.		Tete beche pair	*225.00*	*100.00*
16	A1	2a brown ('17)	25.00	12.00
a.		Tete beche pair	55.00	42.50
17	A1	4a dull green	70.00	70.00
a.		Tete beche pair	350.00	*350.00*
b.		Cliche of 1a in plate of 4a ('04)	*500.00*	*400.00*
c.		As "b," pair	—	—
		Nos. 13-17 (5)	315.00	234.50

No. 13-17 are blurry impressions on poor quality native paper.

#17b has the recut frame of the 1904 issue. #17b probably was used only on telegraph/telephone forms.

Pin-perf.

18	A1	1a pale blue	17.50	10.00
a.		Tete beche pair	*75.00*	*50.00*
19	A1	2a gray violet	90.00	90.00
a.		Tete beche pair	*300.00*	*300.00*
20	A1	2a claret ('17)	90.00	45.00
a.		Tete beche pair	250.00	—
21	A1	2a brown ('17)	90.00	45.00
a.		Tete beche pair	250.00	—
22	A1	4a dull green	150.00	150.00
a.		Tete beche pair	*900.00*	*900.00*

Frame Recut on All Cliches, Fewer Lines

1903-04 Native Wove Paper *Imperf.*

23	A1	1a bright blue	20.00	13.00
a.		Tete beche pair	60.00	42.50

Pin-perf.

24	A1	1a bright blue	30.00	
a.		Tete beche pair	*120.00*	

European Wove Paper

23b	A1	1a blue	*950.00*	1,000.
23c		Tete beche pair	*1,750.*	

Pin-perf.

24b	A1	1a blue	650.00	—
24c		Tete beche pair	*2,750.*	

Siva Mahadeva — A3

1907 Engr. *Perf. 13½*

European Wove Paper

26	A3	2p brown	9.00	2.50
27	A3	4p green	10.00	2.50
28	A3	8p carmine	14.00	2.50
29	A3	16p violet	27.50	6.00
		Nos. 26-29 (4)	60.50	13.50

Type A3 has five characters in bottom panel, reading "Gurkha Sirkar." Date divided in lower corners is "1964." Outer side panels carry denomination (also on A5).

A4

1917-18 *Imperf.*

29A	A4	1a bright blue	12.00	5.00
b.		1a indigo	12.00	6.00
c.		Pin-perf.	17.50	15.00

No. 29A may not have been used postally.

In 1917 a telephone and telegraph system was started and remainder stocks and further printings of designs A1 and A2 were used to pay telegrams fees. Design A4 was designed for telegraph use but was valid for postal use. After 1929 design A3 was used for telegrams. The usual telegraph cancellation is crescent-shaped.

Type of 1907 Redrawn

A5

Nine characters in bottom panel reading "Nepal Sirkar"

1930 *Perf. 14, 14½*

Size: 24¾x18¾mm

30	A5	2p dark brown	12.00	1.00
31	A5	4p green	12.00	1.25
32	A5	8p deep red	45.00	3.00
33	A5	16p dark red vio	32.50	3.00
34	A5	24p orange yellow	27.50	4.00
35	A5	32p dark ultra	32.50	4.00

Size: 26x19½mm

36	A5	1r orange red	40.00	9.00

Size: 28x21mm

37	A5	5r brown & black	47.50	*30.00*
		Nos. 30-37 (8)	249.00	*55.25*

On Nos. 30-37 the date divided in lower corners is "1986."

Type of 1929 Redrawn

Date characters in Lower Corners read "1992"

1935 Unwmk. Engr. *Perf. 14*

38	A5	2p dark brown	6.00	1.50
39	A5	4p green	6.00	2.00
40	A5	8p bright red	150.00	10.00
41	A5	16p dk red violet	15.00	3.00
42	A5	24p orange yellow	15.00	4.50
43	A5	32p dark ultra	16.00	5.00
		Nos. 38-43 (6)	208.00	26.00

NETHERLANDS

'ne-t͟hər-lən‚d‚z

(Holland)

LOCATION — Northwestern Europe, bordering on the North Sea
GOVT. — Kingdom
AREA — 13,203 sq. mi.
POP. — 14,394,589 (1984)
CAPITAL — Amsterdam

100 Cents = 1 Gulden
(Guilder or Florin)

Catalogue values for unused stamps in this country are for Never Hinged items, beginning with Scott 216 in the regular postage section, and Scott B123 in the semi-postal section.

Values for unused stamps are for examples with original gum as defined in the catalogue introduction. Very fine examples of Nos. 4-12 will have perforations touching the frameline on one or more sides due to the narrow spacing of the stamps on the plates. Stamps with perfs clear on all four sides are very scarce and command higher prices.

Watermarks

Wmk. 158

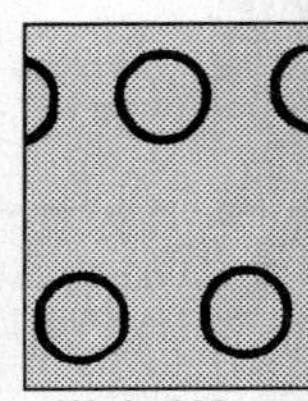

Wmk. 202 — Circles

King William III — A1

Wmk. 158

1852, Jan. 1 Engr. *Imperf.*

1	A1	5c blue	400.00	35.00
		No gum	200.00	
		On cover, single franking		95.00
		Handstamped "SPECIMEN"	1,900.	
a.		5c light blue	450.00	40.00
b.		5c steel blue (Plates 1-2, '53)	750.00	100.00
c.		5c dark blue	450.00	35.00
d.		5c greenish blue (Plate 5, '62)	—	125.00
e.		Thin paper (Plate 6, '63)	425.00	32.50
f.		Ribbed paper (Plate 2, '54)	—	200.00
2	A1	10c lake	450.00	27.50
		No gum	220.00	
		On cover, single franking		82.50
		Handstamped "SPECIMEN"	1,900.	
a.		10c deep rose red	575.00	47.50
b.		10c brownish red	700.00	77.50
c.		10c car lake (see "f.")	1,550.	40.00
d.		10c dp rose red, thin paper	525.00	35.00
e.		Ribbed paper (Plate 3, '54)	—	—
f.		As "c," horn on forehead	450.00	27.50
3	A1	15c orange yellow	775.00	130.00
		No gum	380.00	
		On cover, single franking		400.00
		Handstamped "SPECIMEN"	1,900.	
a.		15c dark orange yellow	950.00	175.00
b.		15c dark yel org, thin paper	950.00	300.00

Full margins = 1¼mm.

In 1895 the 10c was privately reprinted in several colors on unwatermarked paper by

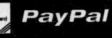

Joh. A. Moesman, whose name appears on the back.

Values for pairs

1 A1 5c blue 975.00 155.00
On cover 235.00
2 A1 10c lake 1,000. 140.00
On cover 225.00
3 A1 15c orange yellow 1,650. 350.00
On cover, single franking 550.00

Values for strips of 3

1 A1 5c blue 2,100. 425.00
On cover 750.00
2 A1 10c lake 2,100. 350.00
On cover 750.00
3 A1 15c orange yellow 2,750. 775.00
On cover 1,250.

Values for strips of 4

1 A1 5c blue *4,000.* 1,325.
2 A1 10c lake *3,000.* 775.00
3 A1 15c orange yellow *5,500.* 1,425.

Values for strips of 5

1 A1 5c blue *5,250.* 3,600.
2 A1 10c lake *4,500.* 2,750.
3 A1 15c orange yellow *7,000.* 2,500.

Values for blocks of 4

1 A1 5c blue *5,250.* 3,100.
2 A1 10c lake *5,250.* 3,000.
3 A1 15c orange yellow *6,500.* *5,750.*

Values for Vert. or Horiz. Gutter Pairs

1 A1 5c blue *12,500.*
2 A1 10c lake *24,000.*
3 A1 15c orange yellow *19,500.*

Gutter = 10mm.

King William III — A2

1864 Unwmk. *Perf. 12½x12*

4 A2 5c blue 300.00 16.00
No gum 100.00
On cover, single franking 40.00
Handstamped "SPECIMEN" 1,050.
5 A2 10c lake 425.00 8.00
No gum 150.00
On cover, single franking 30.00
Handstamped "SPECIMEN" 1,050.
6 A2 15c orange 1,050. 100.00
No gum 350.00
On cover, single franking 135.00
Handstamped "SPECIMEN" 1,050.
a. 15c yellow ('66) 1,350. 115.00
No gum 450.00
On cover, single franking 200.00

The paper varies considerably in thickness. It is sometimes slightly bluish, also vertically ribbed.

Values for used pairs

4 A2 5c blue 52.50
5 A2 10c lake 25.00
6 A2 15c orange 225.00

Values for used strips of 3

4 A2 5c blue 100.00
5 A2 10c lake 80.00
6 A2 15c orange 375.00

Values for used strips of 4

4 A2 5c blue 200.00
5 A2 10c lake 175.00
6 A2 15c orange 700.00

Values for blocks of 4

4 A2 5c blue *2,400.* 900.00
5 A2 10c lake *2,900.* 1,150.
6 A2 15c orange *5,500.* *2,750.*

William III — A3

1867 *Perf. 12¾x11¾*

7a A3 5c ultra 115.00 2.75
No gum 29.00
On cover, single franking 8.00
8a A3 10c lake 225.00 4.75
No gum 55.00
On cover, single franking 8.00
9 A3 15c orange brn 640.00 35.00
No gum 200.00
On cover, single franking 47.50
10 A3 20c dk green 625.00 24.00
No gum 175.00
On cover, single franking 37.50
Overprinted "SPECIMEN" 3,850.
11 A3 25c dk violet 2,100. 110.00
No gum 525.00
On cover, single franking 325.00
12 A3 50c gold 2,500. 160.00
No gum 625.00
On cover, single franking 1,125.

The paper of Nos. 7-22 sometimes has an accidental bluish tinge of varying strength.

During its manufacture a chemical whitener (bluing agent) was added in varying quantities. No particular printing was made on bluish paper.

Two varieties of numerals in each value, differing chiefly in the thickness.

Oxidized examples of the 50c are worth much less.

Imperforate varieties of Nos. 7-12 are proofs.

Values for blocks of 4

7a A3 5c ultra 600.00 110.00
8a A3 10c lake 1,000. 175.00
9 A3 15c orange brn *23,000.*
10 A3 20c dk green *7,000.* 7,000.
11 A3 25c dk violet *11,500.* 1,100.
12 A3 50c gold *12,500.* 1,100.

1867-68

Perf. 14

7 A3 5c ultra 115.00 2.75
8 A3 10c lake 225.00 4.75
9a A3 15c org brn 650.00 37.50
10a A3 20c dk grn 1,150. 24.00
11a A3 25c dk vio *4,000.*
12a A3 50c gold *11,500.*

Perf. 13½

7b A3 5c ultra 1,050. 700.00
d. 5c blue 115.00 2.40
8b A3 10c car lake 175.00 3.25
9b A3 15c org brn 675.00 32.50
10b A3 20c dk grn 1,150. 24.00
11b A3 25c dk vio *9,000.*

Perf. 10½x10

7c A3 5c ultra 225.00 11.50
8c A3 10c lake 230.00 7.75
9c A3 15c orange brown 2,700. 1,150.
10c A3 20c dark green 1,550. 155.00

Perf. 13¼x14

7e A3 5c ultra 97.50 2.40
8d A3 10c lake 160.00 3.25
9d A3 15c orange brown 650.00 32.50
10d A3 20c dark green 625.00 24.00

Coat of Arms — A4

1869-71 Typo. *Perf. 13¼, 14*

17 A4 ½c red brown ('71) 24.00 3.75
Never hinged 210.00
No gum 7.75
On cover, single franking 275.00
On cover, two singles 160.00
Overprinted "SPECIMEN" 250.00
c. Perf. 14 *2,300.* 875.00
18 A4 1c black 210.00 70.00
Never hinged 1,150.
No gum 85.00
On cover, single franking 220.00
On cover, two singles 500.00
Overprinted "SPECIMEN" 250.00
19 A4 1c green 15.50 2.25
Never hinged 190.00
No gum 5.00
On cover, single franking 85.00
On cover, two singles 37.50
Overprinted "SPECIMEN" 250.00
c. Perf. 14 27.50 5.50
20 A4 1½c rose 150.00 77.50
Never hinged 850.00
No gum 72.50
On cover, single franking 1,150.
On cover, two singles 750.00
Overprinted "SPECIMEN" 250.00
b. Perf. 14 175.00 97.50
21 A4 2c buff 60.00 15.00
Never hinged 275.00
No gum 19.00
On cover, single franking 140.00
On cover, two singles 275.00
Overprinted "SPECIMEN" 250.00
c. Perf. 14 55.00 14.00
22 A4 2½c violet ('70) 475.00 70.00
Never hinged 1,950.
No gum 115.00
On cover, single franking 175.00
On cover, two singles 200.00
Overprinted "SPECIMEN" 250.00
c. Perf. 14 775.00 425.00

Imperforate varieties are proofs.

Values for blocks of 4

17 A4 ½c red brown ('71) 115.00 77.50
18 A4 1c black 1,125. 775.00
19 A4 1c green 57.50 57.50
20 A4 1½c rose 875.00 575.00
21 A4 2c buff 250.00 155.00
22 A4 2½c violet ('70) 2,400. 775.00

A5 A6

Perf. 12½, 13, 13½, 13x14, 14, 12½x12 and 11½x12

1872-88

23 A5 5c blue 11.50 .30
Never hinged 130.00
No gum 3.00
On cover, single franking 4.00
On cover, two singles 7.00
Overprinted "SPECIMEN" 62.50
a. 5c ultra 14.00 1.25
Never hinged 77.50
No gum 3.50
On cover, single franking 20.00
On cover, two singles 27.50
24 A5 7½c red brn ('88) 35.00 18.00
Never hinged 200.00
No gum 15.00
On cover, single franking —
On cover, two singles 105.00
Overprinted "SPECIMEN" 40.00
25 A5 10c rose 57.50 1.60
Never hinged 275.00
No gum 14.50
On cover, single franking 7.75
On cover, two singles 32.00
Overprinted "SPECIMEN" 100.00
26 A5 12½c gray ('75) 62.50 2.40
Never hinged 275.00
No gum 16.00
On cover, single franking 22.50
On cover, two singles 37.50
Overprinted "SPECIMEN" 92.50
27 A5 15c brn org 350.00 5.25
Never hinged 2,750.
No gum 87.50
On cover, single franking 70.00
On cover, two singles 105.00
Overprinted "SPECIMEN" 92.50
28 A5 20c green 425.00 5.00
Never hinged 2,750.
No gum 105.00
On cover, single franking 70.00
On cover, two singles 105.00
Overprinted "SPECIMEN" 125.00
29 A5 22½c dk grn ('88) 77.50 42.50
Never hinged 750.00
No gum 40.00
On cover, single franking 575.00
On cover, two singles —
Overprinted "SPECIMEN" 80.00
30 A5 25c dull vio 525.00 4.00
Never hinged 2,950.
No gum 130.00
On cover, single franking 110.00
On cover, two singles 195.00
On parcel post receipt card 105.00
Overprinted "SPECIMEN" 125.00
31 A5 50c bister 650.00 11.00
Never hinged 3,750.
No gum 165.00
On cover, single franking 275.00
On cover, two singles —
On parcel post receipt card 125.00
Overprinted "SPECIMEN" 150.00
32 A5 1g gray vio ('88) 480.00 40.00
Never hinged 1,750.
No gum 120.00
On cover, single franking —
On cover, two singles —
On parcel post receipt card 175.00
Overprinted "SPECIMEN" 110.00
33 A6 2g50c rose & ultra 900.00 105.00
Never hinged 4,000.
No gum 425.00
On cover, single franking —
On cover, two singles —
On parcel post receipt card —
Overprinted "SPECIMEN" 550.00

Imperforate varieties are proofs.

Values for blocks of 4

23 A5 5c blue 57.50 20.00
a. 5c ultra 75.00 20.00
24 A5 7½c red brown 175.00 350.00
25 A5 10c rose 275.00 65.00
26 A5 12½c gray 325.00 70.00
27 A5 15c brown orange 2,300. 115.00
28 A5 20c green 2,450. 125.00
29 A5 22½c dark green 350.00 325.00
30 A5 25c dull violet 3,000. 75.00
31 A5 50c bister 3,250. 75.00
32 A5 1g gray violet 2,800. 750.00
33 A6 2g50c rose & ultra 4,400. 550.00

Numeral of Value — A7

HALF CENT:
Type I — Fraction bar 8 to 8½mm long.
Type II — Fraction bar 9mm long and thinner.

Perf. 12½, 13½, 14, 12½x12, 11½x12

1876-94

34 A7 ½c rose (II) 11.50 .30
Never hinged 40.00
On cover 47.50
On cover, single franking 70.00
a. ½c rose (I) 15.00 .50
Never hinged 45.00
On cover 57.50
On cover, single franking 77.50
c. Laid paper 60.00
d. Perf. 14 (I) 1,950. 575.00
35 A7 1c emer grn ('94) 2.75 .25
Never hinged 15.00
On cover, single franking 5.00
b. As "c," laid paper 70.00 7.25
c. 1c green 8.00 .25
Never hinged 75.00
On cover, single franking 5.50
36 A7 2c olive yel ('94) 32.50 2.75
Never hinged 145.00
On cover, single franking 55.00
a. 2c yellow 65.00 3.50
Never hinged 300.00
On cover, single franking 55.00
37 A7 2½c violet ('94) 14.00 .30
Never hinged 110.00
On cover, single franking 2.75
b. 2½c dark violet ('94) 17.50 .45
Never hinged 150.00
On cover, single franking 3.50
c. 2½c lilac 100.00 .80
Never hinged 700.00
On cover, single franking 4.00
d. Laid paper — —
Nos. 34-37 (4) 60.75 3.60

Imperforate varieties are proofs.

Values for blocks of 4

34 A7 ½c rose (II) 57.50 62.50
b. ½c red brn 525.00 175.00
35 A7 1c emerald grn 11.00 *25.00*
c. 1c grn 47.50 27.50
36 A7 2c ol yel 160.00 60.00
a. 2c yel 325.00 62.50
37 A7 2½c vio 70.00 *85.00*
b. 2½c dk vio 90.00 100.00
c. 2½c lilac 475.00 50.00

Princess Wilhelmina — A8

1891-94 *Perf. 12½*

40 A8 3c orange ('94) 8.00 2.30
Never hinged 35.00
On cover, single franking 52.50
Overprinted "SPECIMEN" 52.50
a. 3c orange yellow ('92) 11.50 2.75
Never hinged 52.50
On cover, single franking 57.50
41 A8 5c lt ultra ('94) 4.00 .25
Never hinged 26.00
On cover, single franking 2.75
Overprinted "SPECIMEN" 52.50
a. 5c dull blue 5.00 .25
Never hinged 29.00
On cover, single franking 3.00
42 A8 7½c brown ('94) 15.00 6.25
Never hinged 75.00
On postcard 42.50
On cover 50.00
On cover, single franking 190.00
Overprinted "SPECIMEN" 52.50
a. 7½c red brown 27.50 6.25
Never hinged 135.00
On postcard 42.50
On cover 50.00
On cover, single franking 190.00
43 A8 10c brt rose ('94) 23.50 1.60
Never hinged 125.00
On cover, single franking 9.25
Overprinted "SPECIMEN" 52.50
a. 10c brick red 45.00 2.40
Never hinged 175.00
On cover, single franking 14.00
44 A8 12½c bluish gray ('94) 23.50 1.60
Never hinged 130.00
On cover, single franking 12.50
Overprinted "SPECIMEN" 52.50
a. 12½c gray 40.00 1.75
Never hinged 175.00
On cover, single franking 30.00
45 A8 15c yel brn ('94) 60.00 5.00
Never hinged 300.00
On cover, single franking 100.00
Overprinted "SPECIMEN" 52.50
a. 15c orange brown 80.00 5.50
Never hinged 400.00
On cover, single franking 150.00
46 A8 20c green ('94) 70.00 3.00
Never hinged 325.00
On cover, single franking 125.00
Overprinted "SPECIMEN" 52.50
a. 20c yellow green 80.00 3.00
Never hinged 400.00
On cover, single franking 160.00
47 A8 22½c dk grn ('94) 32.50 13.50
Never hinged 165.00
On cover, single franking 175.00
Overprinted "SPECIMEN" 55.00
a. 22½c deep blue green 55.00 13.50
Never hinged 275.00
On cover, single franking 290.00
48 A8 25c dl vio ('94) 110.00 6.00
Never hinged 575.00
On cover, single franking 77.50
Overprinted "SPECIMEN" 77.50
a. 25c dark violet 110.00 6.00
Never hinged 575.00
On cover, single franking 77.50
49 A8 50c yel brn ('94) 550.00 20.00
Never hinged 2,600.
On parcel post receipt card 275.00
On cover, single franking 450.00
Overprinted "SPECIMEN" 150.00
a. 50c bister 575.00 27.50
Never hinged 2,750.
On parcel post receipt card 325.00
On cover, single franking 500.00
50 A8 1g gray vio 625.00 77.50
Never hinged 2,750.
On cover *875.00*
On cover, single franking *2,750.*
Overprinted "SPECIMEN" *1,250.*

The paper used in 1891-93 was white, rough and somewhat opaque. In 1894, a thinner, smooth and sometimes transparent paper was introduced.

The 5c orange was privately produced.

Values for blocks of 4

40 A8 3c org 50.00 14.00
a. 3c org yel 70.00 50.00
41 A8 5c lt ultra 21.00 11.50
a. 5c dull bl 32.50 11.50
42 A8 7½c brn 100.00 72.50
a. 7½c red brn 160.00 77.50

43 A8 10c br rose 145.00 40.00
a. 10c brick red 240.00 50.00
44 A8 12½c bluish gray 145.00 57.50
a. 12½c gray 200.00 70.00
45 A8 15c yel brn 325.00 85.00
a. 15c org brn 500.00 100.00
46 A8 20c green 400.00 57.50
a. 20c yel grn 475.00 77.50
47 A8 22½c dk grn 200.00 160.00
a. 22½c dp bl grn 225.00 155.00
48 A8 25c dull vio 625.00 57.50
a. 25c dk vio 625.00 57.50
49 A8 50c yel brn 2,750. 160.00
a. 50c bister *3,500.* 275.00
50 A8 1g gray vio *3,250.* 500.00

Princess Wilhelmina — A9

1893-96 ***Perf. 11½x11***

51 A9 50c emer & yel brn ('96) 80.00 15.00
On cover *550.00*
a. Perf. 11 *2,500.* 200.00
52 A9 1g brn & ol grn ('96) 200.00 22.50
On cover *2,200.*
a. Perf. 11 225.00 60.00
53 A9 2g 50c brt rose & ultra 400.00 130.00
On cover *6,000.*
a. 2g 50c lil rose & ultra, perf. 11 475.00 130.00
b. Perf. 11½ 500.00 140.00

Perf. 11

54 A9 5g brnz grn & red brn ('96) 700.00 425.00

Values for blocks of 4

51	A9	50c emer & yel brn	375.00	72.50
52	A9	1g brn & ol grn	850.00	200.00
a.		Perf. 11	1,100.	250.00
53	A9	2g 50c brt rose & ultra	1,900.	650.00
a.		2g 50c lil rose & ultra	2,250.	675.00
b.		Perf. 11½	2,250.	750.00
54	A9	5g brnz grn & red brn	3,500.	*2,600.*

A10

Queen Wilhelmina — A11

Perf. 12½ (#70, 73, 75-77, 81-82), 11½, 11½x11, 11x11½

1898-1924

55 A10 ½c violet .45 .25
Never hinged .80
On cover 2.50
On cover, single franking 50.00
56 A10 1c red .90 .25
Never hinged 3.00
On cover, pair 1.00
On cover, single franking .50
b. Imperf., pair 2,000. —
57 A10 1½c ultra ('08) 6.00 .85
Never hinged 15.00
On cover 3.25
On cover, single franking 2.50
58 A10 1½c dp blue ('13) 3.00 .35
Never hinged 8.00
On cover 2.00
On cover, single franking 1.00
59 A10 2c yellow brn 3.75 .25
Never hinged 16.00
On cover 3.25
On cover, single franking 1.75
60 A10 2½c deep green 3.25 .25
Never hinged 9.50
On cover, pair .75
On cover, single franking .50
b. Imperf., pair *6,250.*
61 A11 3c orange 16.50 3.25
Never hinged 70.00
On cover 30.00
On cover, single franking 25.00
62 A11 3c pale ol grn ('01) 1.10 .25
Never hinged 2.50
On cover 1.75
On cover, single franking .50
63 A11 4c claret ('21) 1.60 1.10
Never hinged 2.50
On cover 8.00
On cover, single franking 32.50
a. 4c lilac 2.50 1.50
64 A11 4½c violet ('19) 3.75 3.75
Never hinged 5.25
On cover 10.00
On cover, single franking 65.00
65 A11 5c car rose 1.60 .25
Never hinged 3.75
On cover 1.00
On cover, single franking .50
a. 5c pale rose 2.50 .25
66 A11 7½c brown .75 .25
Never hinged 1.60
On cover 1.00
On cover, single franking .50
a. Tête bêche pair ('24) 80.00 72.50
Never hinged 115.00
On cover, overfranked 325.00
b. 7½c dark brown 1.50 .30
67 A11 10c gray lilac 6.25 .25
Never hinged 15.00
On cover 6.50
On cover, single franking 1.00
a. 10c dark gray 7.25 .30
68 A11 12½c blue 3.25 .30
Never hinged 11.00
On cover 5.00
On cover, single franking 3.25
69 A11 15c yellow brn 100.00 3.25
Never hinged 500.00
On cover 32.50
On cover, single franking 65.00
70 A11 15c bl & car ('08) 6.25 .25
Never hinged 22.00
On cover 15.00
On cover, single franking 25.00
a. Perf 11½ 7.25 .80
b. Perf 11½x11 75.00 16.50
c. Perf 11x11½ 1,100. 525.00
71 A11 17½c vio ('06) 50.00 12.00
Never hinged 100.00
On cover 40.00
On cover, single franking 150.00
73 A11 17½c ultra & brn ('10) 15.00 .90
Never hinged 60.00
On cover 25.00
On cover, single franking 30.00
a. 17½c ultra & blk brn 18.00 .90
b. Perf 11½ 18.00 3.00
c. Perf 11½x11 18.00 3.00
74 A11 20c yellow green 150.00 .75
Never hinged 1,200.
On cover 35.00
On cover, single franking 65.00
75 A11 20c ol grn & gray ('08) 10.00 .50
Never hinged 45.00
On cover 30.00
On cover, single franking 25.00
a. Perf 11½ 12.00 1.40
76 A11 22½c brn & ol grn 9.25 .60
Never hinged 45.00
On cover 25.00
On cover, single franking 30.00
a. Perf 11½ 9.25 1.90
b. Perf 11½x11 9.25 .75
77 A11 25c car & blue 9.25 .45
Never hinged 45.00
On cover 16.50
On cover, single franking 22.50
a. 25c rose & blue 18.00 .50
b. Perf 11½ 10.00 .75
c. Perf 11½x11 10.00 .75
78 A11 30c lil & vio brn ('17) 24.00 .50
Never hinged 65.00
On cover 16.50
On cover, single franking 26.00
79 A11 40c grn & org ('20) 34.00 1.10
Never hinged 92.50
On cover 30.00
On cover, single franking 65.00
80 A11 50c brnz grn & red brn 110.00 1.10
Never hinged 400.00
On cover 32.50
On cover, single franking 100.00
81 A11 50c gray & vio ('14) 70.00 1.10
Never hinged 175.00
On cover 32.50
On cover, single franking 80.00
On parcel post receipt card, multiple 165.00
a. Perf 11½x11 70.00 16.50
On cover, single franking 125.00
b. 50c gray blk & vio 72.50 1.90
82 A11 60c ol grn & grn ('20) 34.00 1.10
Never hinged 92.50
On cover 50.00
On cover, single franking 115.00
a. Perf 11½ 200.00 20.00
b. Perf 11½x11 40.00 1.40
Nos. 55-82 (27) 673.90 35.20
Set, never hinged 3,000.

See Nos. 107-112. For overprints and surcharges see Nos. 102-103, 106, 117-123, 135-136, O1-O8.

Values for blocks of 4

55	A10	½c vio	2.25	*5.25*
56	A10	1c red	4.75	5.25
57	A10	1½c ultra	30.00	10.00
58	A10	1½c dp bl	14.00	5.25
59	A10	2c yel brn	19.00	5.25
60	A10	2½c dp grn	17.00	5.25
61	A11	3c org	85.00	60.00
62	A11	3c pale ol grn	5.50	3.00
63	A11	4c claret	7.50	5.00
64	A11	4½c vio	18.00	18.00
65	A11	5c car rose	7.00	1.50
66	A11	7½c brn	3.00	1.75
67	A11	10c gray lil	32.50	2.00
68	A11	12½c bl	17.00	5.25
69	A11	15c yel brn	450.00	45.00
70	A11	15c bl & car	30.00	4.50
71	A11	17½c vio	250.00	62.50
73	A11	17½c ultra & brn	75.00	11.00
74	A11	20c yel grn	725.00	32.50
75	A11	20c ol grn & gray	52.50	6.00
76	A11	22½c brn & ol grn	47.50	7.25
77	A11	25c car & bl	47.50	6.00
78	A11	30c lil & vio brn	120.00	9.00
79	A11	40c grn & org	175.00	15.00
80	A11	50c brnz grn & red brn	500.00	18.50
81	A11	50c gray & vio	350.00	11.00
82	A11	60c ol grn & grn	175.00	11.00

A12

I II

Type I — The figure "1" is 3¾mm high and 2¾mm wide.

Type II — The figure "1" is 3½mm high and 2½mm wide, it is also thinner than in type I.

Perf. 11, 11x11½, 11½, 11½x11

1898-1905 **Engr.**

83 A12 1g dk grn, II ('99) 52.50 .75
Never hinged 375.00
On parcel post receipt card 65.00
On parcel post receipt card, single franking 225.00
a. Type I ('98) 190.00 110.00
Never hinged 1,000.
On cover, overfranked 225.00
84 A12 2½g brn lil ('99) 100.00 3.25
Never hinged 275.00
On parcel post receipt card 100.00
On flight cover 55.00
85 A12 5g claret ('99) 225.00 6.00
Never hinged 675.00
On parcel post receipt card 150.00
On flight cover 100.00
86 A12 10g orange ('05) 775.00 675.00
Never hinged 1,650.
On parcel post receipt card —
On flight cover 675.00
Set, never hinged 2,975.

For surcharge see No. 104.

Values for blocks of 4

83	A12	1g dk grn (II)	240.00	5.00
a.		Type I	925.00	750.00
84	A12	2½g brnn lil	475.00	14.50
85	A12	5g claret	1,000.	30.00
86	A12	10g org	4,250.	3,400.

Admiral M. A. de Ruyter and Fleet — A13

1907, Mar. 23 **Typo.** ***Perf. 12x12½***

87 A13 ½c blue 2.00 1.25
Never hinged 5.25
On cover 22.50
On cover, single franking 65.00
88 A13 1c claret 3.50 2.25
Never hinged 15.00
On cover 19.00
On cover, single franking 27.50
89 A13 2½c vermilion 6.00 2.25
Never hinged 17.00
On cover 24.00
On cover, single franking 37.50
Nos. 87-89 (3) 11.50 5.75
Set, never hinged 37.00

De Ruyter (1607-1676), naval hero.
For surcharges see Nos. J29-J41.

King William I — A14

Designs: 2½c, 12½c, 1g, King William I. 3c, 20c, 2½g, King William II. 5c, 25c, 5g, King William III. 10c, 50c, 10g, Queen Wilhelmina.

Perf. 11½x11, 11½ (#97, 100-101)

1913, Nov. 29 **Engr.**

90 A14 2½c green, *grn* .80 .80
Never hinged 2.25
On cover 10.00
On cover, single franking 8.00
91 A14 3c buff, *straw* 1.80 1.50
Never hinged 1.60
On cover 20.00
On cover, single franking 20.00
92 A14 5c rose red, *sal* 1.25 .90
Never hinged 1.90
On cover 11.00
On cover, single franking 6.50
93 A14 10c gray blk 4.25 2.40
Never hinged 6.50
On cover 22.50
On cover, single franking 32.50
94 A14 12½c dp blue, *bl* 3.00 1.90
Never hinged 5.50
On cover 22.50
On cover, single franking 26.00
95 A14 20c orange brn 13.00 11.00
Never hinged 32.50
On cover 25.00
On cover, single franking 72.50
96 A14 25c pale blue 15.00 8.75
Never hinged 32.50
On cover 60.00
On cover, single franking 90.00
97 A14 50c yel grn 32.50 27.50
Never hinged 82.50
On cover 120.00
On cover, single franking 145.00
On parcel post receipt card 190.00
98 A14 1g claret 47.50 20.00
Never hinged 175.00
On cover 120.00
On cover, single franking 180.00
On parcel post receipt card 180.00
Never hinged *190.00*
99 A14 2½g dull violet 120.00 50.00
Never hinged 325.00
On parcel post receipt card 180.00
100 A14 5g yel, *straw* 225.00 40.00
Never hinged 525.00
On parcel post receipt card 160.00
101 A14 10g red, *straw* 800.00 725.00
Never hinged 1,500.
Nos. 90-101 (12) 1,264. 889.75
Set, never hinged 2,285.

Perf. 11½

90a	A14	2½c grn, *grn*	1.10	.90
91a	A14	5c buff, *straw*	1.40	1.35
92a	A14	5c rose red, *salmon*	1.50	.90
93a	A14	10c gray blk	4.25	2.50
94a	A14	12½c dp bl, *bl*	3.25	2.25
95a	A14	20c org brn	13.00	11.00
98a	A14	1g claret	60.00	20.00
		Never hinged	140.00	

Centenary of Dutch independence.
For surcharge see No. 105.

No. 78 Surcharged in Red or Black

a

b

1919, Dec. 1 ***Perf. 12½***

102 A11 (a) 40c on 30c (R) 22.50 3.25
Never hinged 80.00
On cover 75.00
On cover, single franking 110.00
103 A11 (b) 60c on 30c (Bk) 25.00 3.75
Never hinged 80.00
On cover 80.00
On cover, single franking 130.00
Set, never hinged 140.00
Set on overfranked philatelic cover 55.00

Nos. 86 and 101 Surcharged in Black

1920, Aug. 17 ***Perf. 11, 11½***

104 A12 2.50g on 10g 145.00 110.00
Never hinged 300.00
On parcel post receipt card, single franking 300.00
On parcel post receipt card, multiple franking 500.00
On overfranked philatelic cover 375.00
105 A14 2.50g on 10g 160.00 100.00
Never hinged 325.00
On parcel post receipt card, single franking 300.00
On parcel post receipt card, multiple franking 350.00
On overfranked philatelic cover 375.00
Set, never hinged 625.00
Set on overfranked philatelic cover 375.00

No. 64 Surcharged in Red

1921, Mar. 1 **Typo.** ***Perf. 12½***

106 A11 4c on 4½c vio 4.00 1.60
Never hinged 8.00
On cover 19.00
On cover, single franking 16.00

A17

1921-22 Typo. *Perf. 12½*
107 A17 5c green ('22) 11.00 .25
Never hinged 35.00
On cover 1.75
On cover, single franking 1.75
108 A17 12½c vermilion ('22) 18.00 1.75
Never hinged 55.00
On cover 10.00
On cover, single franking 8.00
109 A17 20c blue 27.50 .25
Never hinged 125.00
On cover 15.00
On cover, single franking 5.00
Nos. 107-109 (3) 56.50 2.25
Set, never hinged 215.00

Queen Type of 1898-99, 10c Redrawn

1922 *Perf. 12½*
110 A11 10c gray 29.00 .25
Never hinged 75.00

Imperf
111 A11 5c car rose 7.25 7.25
Never hinged 13.50
On cover 30.00
On cover, single franking 65.00
112 A11 10c gray 7.25 7.25
Never hinged 14.00
On cover 30.00
On cover, single franking 55.00
Nos. 110-112 (3) 43.50 14.75
Set (Nos. 111-112) on overfranked philatelic cover 35.00

In redrawn 10c the horizontal lines behind the Queen's head are wider apart.

Orange Tree and Lion of Brabant A18

Post Horn and Lion A19

Numeral of Value — A20

1923, Mar. 9 *Perf. 12½*
113 A18 1c dark violet .55 .60
Never hinged 1.75
On cover 7.25
On cover, single franking
114 A18 2c orange 6.00 .25
Never hinged 9.00
On cover 2.75
On cover, single franking .55
115 A19 2½c bluish green 1.75 .65
Never hinged 3.50
On cover 9.00
On cover, single franking —
116 A20 4c deep blue 1.25 .60
Never hinged 2.75
On cover —
On cover, single franking 13.00
Nos. 113-116 (4) 9.55 2.10
Set, never hinged 17.00
Set on overfranked philatelic cover 6.00

Nos. 56, 58, 62, 65, 68, 73, 76 Surcharged in Various Colors

c

d

1923, July *Perf. 12½*
117 A10(c) 2c on 1c (Bl) .45 .25
Never hinged .90
On cover 2.75
On cover, single franking 3.75
118 A10(c) 2c on 1½c (Bk) .45 .25
Never hinged .90
On cover 2.75
On cover, single franking 3.75
119 A11(d) 10c on 3c (Br) 4.25 .25
Never hinged 10.00
On cover 16.00
On cover, single franking 6.40
120 A11(d) 10c on 5c (Bk) 8.00 .50
Never hinged 17.50
On cover 22.50
On cover, single franking 9.00
121 A11(d) 10c on 12½c (R) 7.25 .90
Never hinged 19.00
On cover 22.50
On cover, single franking 15.00

Perf. 11½x11
122 A11(d) 10c on 17½c (R) 4.00 4.00
Never hinged 8.00
On cover 30.00
On cover, single franking 45.00
a. Perf. 11½ *1,600. 800.00*
b. Perf. 12½ 4.00 4.00
Never hinged 8.00
On cover 35.00
On cover, single franking 60.00
123 A11(d) 10c on 22½c (R) 4.00 4.00
Never hinged 6.50
On cover 30.00
On cover, single franking 45.00
a. Perf. 11½ 3.00 3.50
Never hinged 6.50
On cover 30.00
On cover, single franking 45.00
b. Perf. 12½ 4.00 4.00
Never hinged 8.00
On cover 35.00
On cover, single franking 55.00
Nos. 117-123 (7) 28.40 10.15
Set, never hinged 62.50
Set on overfranked philatelic cover 13.00

Queen Wilhelmina
A21 A22

Perf. 11½x12½, 11½x12 (5c)
1923, Oct. Engr.
124 A22 2c myrtle green .25 .25
Never hinged 1.10
On cover 5.50
On cover, single franking 1.15
a. Vert. pair, imperf. between *2,400.*
125 A21 5c green .35 .25
Never hinged 1.10
On cover 11.00
On cover, single franking 1.10
a. Vert. pair, imperf. between *1,800.*
126 A22 7½c carmine .50 .25
Never hinged 2.00
On cover 5.50
On cover, single franking 1.10
127 A22 10c vermilion .40 .25
Never hinged 1.50
On cover 3.75
On cover, single franking .90
a. Vert. pair, imperf. between *550.00 575.00*
128 A22 20c ultra 3.50 1.00
Never hinged 1.50
On cover 3.75
On cover, single franking .90
129 A22 25c yellow 5.50 1.10
Never hinged 15.00
On cover 32.50
On cover, single franking 65.00

Perf. 11½
130 A22 35c orange 5.00 3.00
Never hinged 15.00
On cover 35.00
On cover, single franking 30.00
131 A22 50c black 17.00 .50
Never hinged 45.00
On cover 100.00
On cover, single franking 150.00
132 A21 1g red 30.00 7.25
Never hinged 60.00
On cover 350.00
On cover, single franking 200.00
133 A21 2½g black 210.00 200.00
Never hinged 450.00
on parcel post receipt card, single franking 310.00
on parcel post receipt card, single franking 550.00
134 A21 5g dark blue 200.00 175.00
Never hinged 375.00
on parcel post receipt card, single franking 300.00
Nos. 124-134 (11) 472.50 388.85
Set, never hinged 975.00

25th anniv. of the assumption as monarch of the Netherlands by Queen Wilhelmina at the age of 18.

No. 119 Overprinted in Red

No. 73 With Additional Surcharge in Blue

1923 Typo. *Perf. 12½*
135 A11 10c on 3c 1.10 1.00
Never hinged 8.00
On cover 27.50
On cover, single franking 27.50
136 A11 1g on 17½c 62.50 15.00
Never hinged 160.00
On cover 240.00
On cover, single franking 320.00
a. Perf. 11½ 95.00 40.00
b. Perf. 11½x11 80.00 30.00

Stamps with red surcharge were prepared for use as Officials but were not issued.

Queen Wilhelmina — A23

1924, Sept. 6 Photo. *Perf. 12½*
137 A23 10c slate green 32.50 35.00
Never hinged 55.00
On cover 170.00
On cover, single franking 180.00
138 A23 15c gray black 42.50 45.00
Never hinged 80.00
On cover 200.00
On cover, single franking —
139 A23 35c brown orange 32.50 35.00
Never hinged 60.00
On cover 250.00
On cover, single franking —
Nos. 137-139 (3) 107.50 115.00

These stamps were available solely to visitors to the International Philatelic Exhibition at The Hague and were not obtainable at regular post offices. Set of three on international philatelic exhibition cover dataed Sept. 6-12, 15-17, 1924, value, $110. Set of three on Netherland Philatelic Exhibition cover dated Sept. 13-14, value, $150.

See Nos. 147-160, 172-193. For overprints and surcharge see Nos. 194, O11, O13-O15.

Ship in Distress — A23a

Lifeboat — A23b

1924, Sept. 15 Litho. *Perf. 11½*
140 A23a 2c black brn 3.75 2.50
Never hinged 7.25
On cover 7.25
On cover, single franking 13.00
141 A23b 10c orange brn 6.50 2.00
Never hinged 13.00
On cover 7.25
On cover, single franking 13.00

Centenary of Royal Dutch Lifeboat Society.

Type A23 and

Gull — A24

1924-26 Unwmk. *Perf. 12½*
142 A24 1c deep red .75 .90
Never hinged .90
On cover 1.90
On cover, single franking —
143 A24 2c red orange 2.50 .25
Never hinged 3.75
On cover .75
On cover, single franking .80
144 A24 2½c deep green 3.00 .80
Never hinged 5.00
On cover 1.75
On cover, single franking 4.50
145 A24 3c yel grn ('25) 15.00 1.00
Never hinged 50.00
On cover 2.75
On cover, single franking 5.50
146 A24 4c dp ultra 3.00 .70
Never hinged 15.00
On cover 2.00
On cover, single franking 7.25

Photo.
147 A23 5c dull green 3.50 .75
Never hinged 8.00
On cover 2.00
148 A23 6c org brn ('25) .75 .50
Never hinged 1.40
On cover 7.00
On cover, single franking 12.50
149 A23 7½c orange ('25) .35 .25
Never hinged 1.10
On cover .50
On cover, single franking 1.25
150 A23 9c org red & blk ('26) 1.50 1.25
Never hinged 3.00
On cover 27.50
On cover, single franking 110.00
151 A23 10c red, *shades* 1.50 .25
Never hinged 5.50
On cover .40
152 A23 12½c deep rose 1.60 .35
Never hinged 4.50
On cover 11.00
On cover, single franking 12.50
153 A23 15c ultra 6.00 .45
Never hinged 15.00
On cover, single franking .75
154 A23 20c dp blue ('25) 10.00 .60
Never hinged 22.00
On cover 7.00
On cover, single franking 12.50
155 A23 25c olive bis ('25) 22.50 .85
Never hinged 40.00
On cover 8.00
On cover, single franking 25.00
156 A23 30c violet 13.00 .65
Never hinged 40.00
On cover 20.00
On cover, single franking 25.00
157 A23 35c olive brn ('25) 30.00 6.00
Never hinged 80.00
On cover 20.00
On cover, single franking 85.00
158 A23 40c dp brown 35.00 .75
Never hinged 200.00
On cover 25.00
On cover, single franking 60.00
159 A23 50c blue grn ('25) 60.00 .60
Never hinged 275.00
On cover 25.00
On parcel post receipt card, single franking 70.00
160 A23 60c dk violet ('25) 27.50 .80
Never hinged 100.00
On cover 65.00
On cover, single franking 250.00
Nos. 142-160 (19) 237.45 17.70
Set, never hinged 725.00

See Nos. 164-171, 243A-243Q. For overprints and surcharges see Nos. 226-243, O9-O10.

Syncopated Perforations

Type A

Type B

Type C

These special "syncopated" or "interrupted" perforations, devised for coil stamps, are found on Nos. 142-156, 158-160, 164-166, 168-185, 187-193 and certain semipostals of 1925-33, between Nos. B9 and B69. There are four types:

A (1st stamp is #142a). On two shorter sides, groups of four holes separated by blank spaces equal in width to two or three holes.

B (1st stamp is #164a). As "A," but on all four sides.

C (1st stamp is #164b). On two shorter sides, end holes are omitted.

D (1st stamp is #174c). Four-hole sequence on horiz. sides, three-hole on vert. sides.

Syncopated, Type A (2 Sides)

1925-26
142a A24 1c deep red .75 .80
Never hinged 1.45
143a A24 2c red orange 2.75 2.50
Never hinged 4.50
144a A24 2½c deep green 2.75 1.25
Never hinged 4.50
145a A24 3c yellow green 18.00 20.00
Never hinged 40.00
146a A24 4c deep ultra 2.75 1.90
Never hinged 7.00
147a A23 5c dull green 5.50 2.50
Never hinged 10.00
148a A23 6c orange brown 110.00 100.00
Never hinged 190.00
149a A23 7½c orange 1.10 1.00
Never hinged 1.50
150a A23 9c org red & blk 1.75 1.25
Never hinged 2.50

151a A23 10c red 11.00 2.75
Never hinged 17.00
152a A23 12½c deep rose 1.75 1.50
Never hinged 3.50
153a A23 15c ultra 67.50 6.00
Never hinged 145.00
154a A23 20c deep blue 10.00 4.00
Never hinged 20.00
155a A23 25c olive bister 42.50 45.00
Never hinged 90.00
156a A23 30c violet 14.50 10.50
Never hinged 27.50
158a A23 40c deep brown 45.00 36.00
Never hinged 160.00
159a A23 50c blue green 55.00 20.00
Never hinged 240.00
160a A23 60c dark violet 27.50 11.00
Never hinged 70.00
Nos. 142a-160a (18) 420.10 267.95
Set, never hinged 1,035.

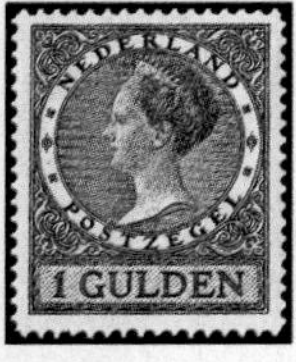

A25

1925-30 Engr. *Perf. 11½*

161 A25 1g ultra 8.00 .65
Never hinged 25.00
On cover 18.00
On parcel post receipt card, single franking 55.00
a. Perf 12½ ('30) 8.75 .75
Never hinged 27.50
As "a," on cover 20.00
As "a," pn parcel post receipt card, single franking 55.00
162 A25 2½g car ('27) 90.00 3.00
Never hinged 175.00
On cover 72.50
On parcel post receipt card, single franking 110.00
a. Perf 12½ ('30) 100.00 3.00
Never hinged 175.00
As "a," on cover 72.50
On parcel post receipt card, single franking 110.00
163 A25 5g gray blk 160.00 2.50
Never hinged 300.00
On cover 55.00
On parcel post receipt card, single franking 90.00
a. Perf 12½ ('30) 175.00 1.90
Never hinged 300.00
As "a," on cover 55.00
As "a," on parcel post receipt card, single franking 90.00
Nos. 161-163 (3) 258.00 6.15

Types of 1924-26 Issue

Perf. 12½, 13½x12½, 12½x13½

1926-39 Wmk. 202 Litho.

164 A24 ½c gray ('28) .90 1.00
Never hinged 1.60
On cover 4.00
165 A24 1c dp red ('27) .25 .25
Never hinged .35
On cover .80
166 A24 1½c red vio ('28) 1.10 .25
Never hinged 2.50
On cover .50
c. "CEN" for "CENT" 165.00 275.00
Never hinged *375.00*
On cover *500.00*
d. "GENT" for "CENT" 120.00 115.00
Never hinged *250.00*
167 A24 1½c gray ('35) .25 .25
Never hinged .35
On cover .50
a. 1½c dark gray .25 .25
Never hinged .35
On cover .50
168 A24 2c dp org .25 .25
Never hinged .35
On cover .50
a. 2c red orange .25 .25
Never hinged .35
On cover .50
169 A24 2½c green ('27) 2.75 .25
Never hinged 6.50
On cover .50
170 A24 3c yel grn ('27) .25 .25
Never hinged .35
On cover .65
171 A24 4c dp ultra ('27) .25 .25
Never hinged .35
On cover 1.00

Photo.

172 A23 5c dp green .25 .25
Never hinged .35
On cover .50
173 A23 6c org brn ('27) .25 .25
Never hinged .35
On cover .50
174 A23 7½c dk vio ('27) 3.25 .25
Never hinged 5.75
On cover .65
175 A23 7½c red ('28) .35 .25
Never hinged .65
On cover .65
176 A23 9c org red & blk ('28) 11.00 12.00
Never hinged 15.00
On cover 13.50
On cover, single franking 82.50
b. Value omitted *14,500.*
177 A23 10c red 1.30 .25
Never hinged 2.60
On cover .50
178 A23 10c dl vio ('29) 2.50 .25
Never hinged 5.00
On cover .50
179 A23 12½c dp rose ('27) 42.50 4.50
Never hinged 82.50
On cover 15.00
180 A23 12½c ultra ('28) .25 .25
Never hinged .50
On cover 3.25
181 A23 15c ultra 7.25 .25
Never hinged 11.50
On cover 3.25
182 A23 15c orange ('29) 1.30 .25
Never hinged 2.50
On cover 3.25
183 A23 20c dp blue ('28) 7.25 .25
Never hinged 12.00
On cover 3.25
184 A23 21c ol brn ('31) 25.00 .90
Never hinged 52.50
On cover 25.00
On cover, single franking 30.00
185 A23 22½c ol brn ('27) 7.25 3.00
Never hinged 17.00
On cover 25.00
On cover, single franking 62.50
186 A23 22½c dp org ('39) 15.50 16.00
Never hinged 20.00
On cover 40.00
On cover, single franking 75.00
187 A23 25c ol bis ('27) 4.50 .25
Never hinged 13.00
On cover 13.00
On cover, single franking 21.00
188 A23 27½c gray ('28) 4.50 .90
Never hinged 13.00
On cover 10.00
189 A23 30c violet 5.00 .25
Never hinged 13.00
On cover 16.50
190 A23 35c olive brn 62.50 12.50
Never hinged 145.00
On cover 22.50
191 A23 40c dp brown 9.00 .25
Never hinged 24.00
On cover 26.00
On cover, single franking 50.00
192 A23 50c blue grn 5.00 .25
Never hinged 13.00
On cover 32.50
On parcel post receipt card 50.00
193 A23 60c black ('29) 57.50 .90
Never hinged 180.00
On cover 50.00
On parcel post receipt card 75.00
On parcel post receipt card, single franking 120.00
Nos. 164-193 (30) 279.20 56.95
Set, never hinged 640.00

Syncopated, Type A (2 Sides), 12½

1926-27

168b A24 2c deep orange .40 .40
170a A24 3c yellow green .60 .60
171a A24 4c deep ultra .60 .60
172a A23 5c deep green .70 .60
173a A23 6c orange brown .40 .45
174a A23 7½c dark violet 4.50 2.00
177a A23 10c red 1.00 .85
181a A23 15c ultra 7.00 3.00
185a A23 22½c olive brown 7.00 2.50
187a A23 25c olive bister 20.00 18.00
189a A23 30c violet 19.00 12.00
190a A23 35c olive brown 77.50 22.50
191a A23 40c deep brown 50.00 40.00
Nos. 168b-191a (13) 188.70 103.50
Set, never hinged 360.00

1928 *Syncopated, Type B (4 Sides)*

164a A24 ½c gray .80 .65
165a A24 1c deep red .30 .30
166a A24 1½c red violet .80 .25
168c A24 2c deep orange 1.00 .60
169a A24 2½c green 2.75 .25
170b A24 3c yellow green .75 .75
171b A24 4c deep ultra .75 .65
172b A23 5c deep green 1.00 .75
173b A23 6c orange brown .75 .50
174b A23 7½c dark violet 4.25 2.00
175a A23 7½c red .25 .25
176a A23 9c org red & blk 10.00 12.50
178a A23 10c dull violet 5.25 5.00
179a A23 12½c deep rose 80.00 80.00
180a A23 12½c ultra 1.40 .40
181b A23 15c ultra 9.00 2.00
182a A23 15c orange .75 .30
183a A23 20c deep blue 7.00 3.00
187b A23 25c olive bister 17.00 10.00
188a A23 27½c gray 4.50 2.00
189b A23 30c violet 15.00 8.00
191b A23 40c deep brown 35.00 22.50
192a A23 50c blue green 55.00 45.00
193a A23 60c black 45.00 22.50
Nos. 164a-193a (24) 298.30 220.15
Set, never hinged 600.00

Syncopated, Type C (2 Sides, Corners Only)

1930

164b A24 ½c gray 1.00 .70
165b A24 1c deep red 1.00 .40
166b A24 1½c red violet .90 .25
168d A24 2c deep orange .80 .70
169b A24 2½c green 2.75 .25
170c A24 3c yellow green 1.10 .50
171c A24 4c deep ultra .50 .25
172c A23 5c deep green .70 .50
173c A23 6c orange brown .70 .70
178b A23 10c dull violet 8.00 7.00
183b A23 20c deep blue 7.75 3.75
184a A23 21c olive brown 25.00 9.00
189c A23 30c violet 12.00 7.00
192b A23 50c blue green 45.00 45.00
Nos. 164b-192b (14) 107.20 76.20
Set, never hinged 225.00

Syncopated, Type D (3 Holes Vert., 4 Holes Horiz.)

1927

174c A23 7½c dark violet *2,750.* *2,100.*
Never hinged *3,750.*

No. 185 Surcharged in Red

1929, Nov. 11 *Perf. 12½*

194 A23 21c on 22½c ol brn 21.00 1.50
Never hinged 47.50

Queen Wilhelmina — A26

1931, Oct. Photo. *Perf. 12½*

195 A26 70c dk bl & red 30.00 .80
Never hinged 120.00
a. Perf. 14½x13½ ('39) 36.00 8.00
Never hinged 140.00

See No. 201.

Arms of the House of Orange — A27

William I — A28

Designs: 5c, William I, Portrait by Goltzius. 6c, Portrait of William I by Van Key. 12½c, Portrait attributed to Moro.

1933, Apr. 1 Unwmk. Engr.

196 A27 1½c black .55 .40
197 A28 5c dark green 1.75 .40
198 A28 6c dull violet 2.75 .30
199 A28 12½c deep blue 17.00 3.50
Nos. 196-199 (4) 22.05 4.60
Set, never hinged 55.00

400th anniv. of the birth of William I, Count of Nassau and Prince of Orange, frequently referred to as William the Silent.

Star, Dove and Sword — A31

1933, May 18 Photo. Wmk. 202

200 A31 12½c dp ultra 9.00 .75
Never hinged 27.50

For overprint see No. O12.

Queen Wilhelmina Design of 1931

Queen Wilhelmina and ships.

Perf. 14½x13½

1933, July 26 Wmk. 202

201 A26 80c Prus bl & red 110.00 3.25
Never hinged 350.00

Willemstad Harbor — A33

Van Walbeeck's Ship — A34

Perf. 14x12½

1934, July 2 Engr. Unwmk.

202 A33 6c violet blk 3.50 .25
203 A34 12½c dull blue 22.00 3.00
Set, never hinged 77.50

Tercentenary of Curacao.

Minerva — A35

Design: 12½c, Gisbertus Voetius.

Wmk. 202

1936, May 15 Photo. *Perf. 12½*

204 A35 6c brown lake 2.50 .25
205 A35 12½c indigo 4.50 4.50
Set, never hinged 16.00

300th anniversary of the founding of the University at Utrecht.

Boy Scout Emblem A37

"Assembly" A38

Mercury — A39

1937, Apr. 1 *Perf. 14½x13½*

206 A37 1½c multicolored .40 .25
207 A38 6c multicolored 1.25 .25
208 A39 12½c multicolored 4.00 1.40
Nos. 206-208 (3) 5.65 1.90
Set, never hinged 12.00

Fifth Boy Scout World Jamboree, Vogelenzang, Netherlands, 7/31-8/13/37.

Wilhelmina — A40

1938, Aug. 27 *Perf. 12½x12*

209 A40 1½c black .25 .25
210 A40 5c red orange .30 .25
211 A40 12½c royal blue 4.00 1.60
Nos. 209-211 (3) 4.55 2.10
Set, never hinged 13.50

Reign of Queen Wilhelmina, 40th anniv.

St. Willibrord — A41

Design: 12½c, St. Willibrord as older man.

Perf. 12½x14

1939, June 15 Engr. Unwmk.

212 A41 5c dk slate grn .75 .25
213 A41 12½c slate blue 5.00 2.75
Set, never hinged 14.00

12th centenary of the death of St. Willibrord.

Woodburning Engine — A43

Design: 12½c, Streamlined electric car.

Perf. 14½x13½

1939, Sept. 1 Photo. Wmk. 202

214 A43 5c dk slate grn .80 .25
215 A43 12½c dark blue 8.00 4.00
Set, never hinged 22.50

Centenary of Dutch Railroads.

Catalogue values for unused stamps in this section, from this point to the end of the section, are for Never Hinged items.

Queen Wilhelmina — A45

1940-47 ***Perf. 13½x12½***

216 A45 5c dk green .25 .25
216B A45 6c hn brn ('47) .55 .25
217 A45 7½c brt red .25 .25
218 A45 10c brt red vio .25 .25
219 A45 12½c sapphire .25 .25
220 A45 15c light blue .25 .25
220B A45 17½c slate bl ('46) 1.25 .70
221 A45 20c purple .35 .25
222 A45 22½c olive grn 1.25 .85
223 A45 25c rose brn .35 .25
224 A45 30c bister .80 .35
225 A45 40c brt green 1.25 .60
225A A45 50c orange ('46) 9.50 .60
225B A45 60c pur brn ('46) 8.50 2.00
Nos. 216-225B (14) 25.05 7.10

Imperf. examples of Nos. 216, 218-220 were released through philatelic channels during the German occupation, but were never issued at any post office. Value, set, $1.

For overprints see Nos. O16-O24 (O20-O24 in Scott Standard catalogue, Vol. 5).

Type of 1924-26 Surcharged in Black or Blue

Perf. 12½x13½

1940, Oct. Photo. Wmk. 202

226 A24 2½c on 3c ver 2.00 .25
227 A24 5c on 3c lt grn .25 .25
228 A24 7½c on 3c ver .25 .25
a. Pair, #226, 228 4.00 1.50
229 A24 10c on 3c lt grn .25 .25
230 A24 12½c on 3c lt bl (Bl) .30 .25
231 A24 17½c on 3c lt grn .60 .65
232 A24 20c on 3c lt grn .40 .25
233 A24 22½c on 3c lt grn .80 .85
234 A24 25c on 3c lt grn .50 .25
235 A24 30c on 3c lt grn .65 .30
236 A24 40c on 3c lt grn .80 .60
237 A24 50c on 3c lt grn .70 .40
238 A24 60c on 3c lt grn 1.60 .85
239 A24 70c on 3c lt grn 3.75 1.75
240 A24 80c on 3c lt grn 5.50 4.00
241 A24 1g on 3c lt grn 35.00 32.50
242 A24 2.50g on 3c lt grn 40.00 37.50
243 A24 5g on 3c lt grn 37.50 35.00
Nos. 226-243 (18) 130.85 116.15
Set, hinged 70.00

No. 228a is from coils.

Gull Type of 1924-26

1941

243A A24 2½c dk green 1.25 .35
b. Booklet pane of 6 10.00
243C A24 5c brt green .25 .25
243E A24 7½c henna .25 .25
r. Pair, #243A, 243E 1.00 1.00
243G A24 10c brt violet .25 .25
243H A24 12½c ultra .25 .25
243J A24 15c lt blue .25 .25
243K A24 17½c red org .25 .25
243L A24 20c lt violet .25 .25
243M A24 22½c dk ol grn .25 .25
243N A24 25c lake .25 .25
243O A24 30c olive 3.50 .25
243P A24 40c emerald .25 .25
243Q A24 50c orange brn .25 .25
Nos. 243A-243Q (13) 7.50 3.35

No. 243Er is from coils.

SEMI-POSTAL STAMPS

Design Symbolical of the Four Chief Means for Combating Tuberculosis: Light, Water, Air and Food — SP1

Perf. 12½

1906, Dec. 21 Typo. Unwmk.

B1 SP1 1c (+1c) rose red 20.00 11.00
B2 SP1 3c (+3c) pale ol grn 30.00 26.00
B3 SP1 5c (+5c) gray 30.00 15.00
Nos. B1-B3 (3) 80.00 *52.00*
Set, never hinged 475.00

Surtax aided the Society for the Prevention of Tuberculosis.

Nos. B1-B3 canceled-to-order "AMSTERDAM 31.07 10-12 N," sell at $3 a set.

Symbolical of Charity SP2

SP3

1923, Dec. 15 ***Perf. 11½***

B4 SP2 2c (+5c) vio bl 17.00 17.00
B5 SP3 10c (+5c) org red 17.00 17.00
Set, never hinged 75.00

The surtax was for the benefit of charity.

Allegory, Charity Protecting Child — SP6

1924, Dec. 15 Photo. ***Perf. 12½***

B6 SP6 2c (+2c) emer 1.80 1.80
B7 SP6 7½c (+3½c) dk brn 6.75 8.00
B8 SP6 10c (+2½c) vermilion 4.00 1.80
Nos. B6-B8 (3) 12.55 11.60
Set, never hinged 26.00

These stamps were sold at a premium over face value for the benefit of Child Welfare Societies.

Arms of North Brabant SP7

Arms of Gelderland SP8

Arms of South Holland — SP9

1925, Dec. 17 ***Perf. 12½***

B9 SP7 2c (+2c) grn & org .85 .75
B10 SP8 7½c (+3½c) vio & bl 4.25 4.50
B11 SP9 10c (+2½c) red & org 3.50 .45
Nos. B9-B11 (3) 8.60 5.70
Set, never hinged 18.50

Surtax went to Child Welfare Societies.

Syncopated Perfs., Type A

B9a SP7 2c (+2c) 18.50 22.00
B10a SP8 7½c (+3½c) 37.50 37.50
B11a SP9 10c (+2½c) 65.00 52.00
Nos. B9a-B11a (3) 121.00 111.50
Set, never hinged 250.00

Arms of Utrecht SP10

Arms of Zeeland SP11

Arms of North Holland SP12

Arms of Friesland SP13

1926, Dec. 1 Wmk. 202 ***Perf. 12½***

B12 SP10 2c (+2c) sil & red .50 .40
B13 SP11 5c (+3c) grn & gray bl 1.40 1.10
B14 SP12 10c (+3c) red & gold 2.10 .25
B15 SP13 15c (+3c) ultra & yel 5.50 4.25
Nos. B12-B15 (4) 9.50 6.00
Set, never hinged 25.00

The surtax on these stamps was devoted to Child Welfare Societies.

Syncopated Perfs., Type A

B12a SP10 2c (+2c) 4.75 4.75
B13a SP11 5c (+3c) 7.25 7.25
B14a SP12 10c (+3c) 13.50 13.50
B15a SP13 15c (+3c) 14.50 14.50
Nos. B12a-B15a (4) 40.00 40.00
Set, never hinged 95.00

King William III — SP14

Red Cross and Doves — SP18

Designs: 3c, Queen Emma. 5c, Prince Consort Henry. 7½c, Queen Wilhelmina.

Perf. 11½, 11½x12 B

1927, June Photo. Unwmk.

B16 SP14 2c (+2c) scar 2.50 2.25

Engr.

B17 SP14 3c (+2c) dp grn 5.75 *8.00*
B18 SP14 5c (+3c) slate bl 1.00 1.00

Photo.

B19 SP14 7½c (+3½c) ultra 4.50 1.50
B20 SP18 15c (+5c) ultra & red 8.75 8.00
Nos. B16-B20 (5) 22.50 20.75
Set, never hinged 52.50

60th anniversary of the Netherlands Red Cross Society. The surtaxes in parentheses were for the benefit of the Society.

Arms of Drenthe SP19

Arms of Groningen SP20

Arms of Limburg SP21

Arms of Overijssel SP22

1927, Dec. 15 Wmk. 202 ***Perf. 12½***

B21 SP19 2c (+2c) dp rose & vio .35 .30
B22 SP20 5c (+3c) ol grn & yel 1.50 1.25
B23 SP21 7½c (+3½c) red & blk 3.25 .35
B24 SP22 15c (+3c) ultra & org brn 4.75 4.25
Nos. B21-B24 (4) 9.85 6.15
Set, never hinged 26.00

The surtax on these stamps was for the benefit of Child Welfare Societies.

Syncopated Perfs., Type A

B21a SP19 2c (+2c) 1.90 1.40
B22a SP20 5c (+3c) 3.50 1.75
B23a SP21 7½c (+3½c) 4.25 1.75
B24a SP22 15c (+3c) 12.50 9.00
Nos. B21a-B24a (4) 22.15 13.90
Set, never hinged 57.50

Rowing — SP23

Fencing — SP24

Soccer SP25

Yachting SP26

Putting the Shot SP27

Running SP28

Riding SP29

Boxing SP30

Perf. 11½, 12, 11½x12, 12x11½

1928, Mar. 27 Litho.

B25 SP23 1½c (+1c) dk grn 1.90 1.40
B26 SP24 2c (+1c) red vio 2.40 1.75
B27 SP25 3c (+1c) green 2.40 2.00
B28 SP26 5c (+1c) lt bl 3.00 1.40
B29 SP27 7½c (+2½c) org 3.00 1.75
B30 SP28 10c (+2c) scarlet 6.75 5.25
B31 SP29 15c (+2c) dk bl 6.75 3.75
B32 SP30 30c (+3c) dk brn 20.00 17.50
Nos. B25-B32 (8) 46.20 34.80
Set, never hinged 150.00

The surtax on these stamps was used to help defray the expenses of the Olympic Games of 1928.

Jean Pierre Minckelers — SP31

5c, Hermann Boerhaave. 7½c, Hendrik Antoon Lorentz. 12½c, Christian Huygens.

1928, Dec. 10 Photo. ***Perf. 12x12½***

B33 SP31 1½c (+1½c) vio .55 .40
B34 SP31 5c (+3c) grn 1.75 .60

Perf. 12

B35 SP31 7½c (+2½c) ver 3.50 .25
a. Perf. 12x12½ 4.75 .70
Never hinged 11.00
B36 SP31 12½c (+3½c) ultra 9.75 7.50
a. Perf. 12x12½ 77.50 7.75
Never hinged 175.00
Nos. B33-B36 (4) 15.55 8.75
Set, never hinged 37.50

The surtax on these stamps was for the benefit of Child Welfare Societies.

Child on Dolphin — SP35

1929, Dec. 10 Litho. ***Perf. 12½***

B37 SP35 1½c (+1½c) gray 2.10 .45
B38 SP35 5c (+3c) blue grn 3.50 .75
B39 SP35 6c (+4c) scarlet 2.10 .35
B40 SP35 12½c (+3½c) dk bl 13.50 11.00
Nos. B37-B40 (4) 21.20 12.55
Set, never hinged 62.50

Surtax for child welfare.

Syncopated Perfs., Type B

B37a SP35 1½c (+1½c) 3.00 1.25
B38a SP35 5c (+3c) 4.50 1.25
B39a SP35 6c (+4c) 3.25 1.25
B40a SP35 12½c (+3½c) 25.00 14.00
Nos. B37a-B40a (4) 35.75 17.75
Set, never hinged 72.50

Rembrandt and His "Cloth Merchants of Amsterdam" SP36

Perf. 11½

1930, Feb. 15 Engr. Unwmk.

B41 SP36 5c (+5c) bl grn 6.75 6.00
B42 SP36 6c (+5c) gray blk 5.25 3.50
B43 SP36 12½c (+5c) dp bl 9.00 8.00
Nos. B41-B43 (3) 21.00 17.50
Set, never hinged 52.50

Surtax for the benefit of the Rembrandt Soc.

"Spring" — SP37

5c, Summer. 6c, Autumn. 12½c, Winter.

1930, Dec. 10 ***Perf. 12½***

B44 SP37 1½c (+1½c) lt red 1.50 .45
B45 SP37 5c (+3c) gray grn 2.25 .60
B46 SP37 6c (+4c) claret 2.00 .45
B47 SP37 12½c (+3½c) lt ultra 16.00 8.50
Nos. B44-B47 (4) 21.75 10.00
Set, never hinged 52.50

Surtax was for Child Welfare work.

Syncopated Perfs., Type C

B44a SP37 1½c (+1½c) 2.40 1.25
B45a SP37 5c (+3c) 3.50 1.25
B46a SP37 6c (+4c) 2.40 1.25
B47a SP37 12½c (+3½c) 19.00 12.50
Nos. B44a-B47a (4) 27.30 16.25
Set, never hinged 55.00

Stained Glass Window and Detail of Repair Method — SP41

6c, Gouda Church and repair of window frame.

Wmk. 202

1931, Oct. 1 Photo. ***Perf. 12½***

B48 SP41 1½c (+1½c) bl grn 17.00 15.00
B49 SP41 6c (+4c) car rose 20.00 17.00
Set, never hinged 75.00

Deaf Mute Learning Lip Reading — SP43

Designs: 5c, Mentally retarded child. 6c, Blind girl learning to read Braille. 12½c, Child victim of malnutrition.

1931, Dec. 10 ***Perf. 12½***

B50 SP43 1½c (+1½c) ver & ultra 1.90 1.25
B51 SP43 5c (+3c) Prus bl & vio 5.25 1.25
B52 SP43 6c (+4c) vio & grn 5.25 1.25
B53 SP43 12½c (+3½c) ultra & dp org 29.00 21.00
Nos. B50-B53 (4) 41.40 24.75
Set, never hinged 95.00

The surtax was for Child Welfare work.

Syncopated Perfs., Type C

B50a SP43 1½c (+1½c) 1.90 1.25
B51a SP43 5c (+3c) 5.25 1.25
B52a SP43 6c (+4c) 5.50 1.25
B53a SP43 12½c (+3½c) 30.00 22.50
Nos. B50a-B53a (4) 42.65 26.25
Set, never hinged 105.00

Drawbridge — SP47

Designs: 2½c, Windmill and Dikes. 6c, Council House, Zierikzee. 12½c, Flower fields.

1932, May 23 ***Perf. 12½***

B54 SP47 2½c (+1½c) turq grn & blk 7.00 5.00
B55 SP47 6c (+4c) gray blk & blk 10.50 5.00
B56 SP47 7½c (+3½c) brt red & blk 30.00 12.50
B57 SP47 12½c (+2½c) ultra & blk 32.50 19.00
Nos. B54-B57 (4) 80.00 41.50
Set, never hinged 190.00

The surtax was for the benefit of the National Tourist Association.

Furze and Boy — SP51

Designs (Heads of children and flowers typifying the seasons): 5c, Cornflower. 6c, Sunflower. 12½c, Christmas rose.

1932, Dec. 10 ***Perf. 12½***

B58 SP51 1½c (+1½c) brn & yel 2.10 .45
B59 SP51 5c (+3c) red org & ultra 2.75 .75
B60 SP51 6c (+4c) dk grn & ocher 2.10 .35
B61 SP51 12½c (+3½c) ocher & ultra 27.50 18.00
Nos. B58-B61 (4) 34.45 19.55
Set, never hinged 90.00

The surtax aided Child Welfare Societies.

Syncopated Perfs., Type C

B58a SP51 1½c (+1½c) 2.75 1.60
B59a SP51 5c (+3c) 3.50 1.60
B60a SP51 6c (+4c) 3.50 1.60
B61a SP51 12½c (+3½c) 35.00 22.50
Nos. B58a-B61a (4) 44.75 27.30
Set, never hinged 100.00

Monument at Den Helder SP55

The "Hope," A Church and Hospital Ship SP56

Lifeboat in a Storm SP57

Dutch Sailor and Sailors' Home SP58

1933, June 10 ***Perf. 14½x13½***

B62 SP55 1½c (+1½c) dp red 3.50 1.60
B63 SP56 5c (+3c) bl grn & red org 10.50 3.00
B64 SP57 6c (+4c) dp grn 16.00 2.50
B65 SP58 12½c (+3½c) ultra 24.00 17.50
Nos. B62-B65 (4) 54.00 24.60
Set, never hinged 125.00

The surtax was for the aid of Sailors' Homes.

Child Carrying the Star of Hope, Symbolical of Christmas Cheer — SP59

1933, Dec. 11 ***Perf. 12½***

B66 SP59 1½c (+1½c) sl & org brn 1.50 .55
B67 SP59 5c (+3c) dk brn & ocher 2.00 .65
B68 SP59 6c (+4c) bl grn & gold 2.50 .55
B69 SP59 12½c (+3½c) dk bl & sil 25.00 18.00
Nos. B66-B69 (4) 31.00 19.75
Set, never hinged 75.00

The surtax aided Child Welfare Societies.

Syncopated Perfs., Type C

B66a SP59 1½c (+1½c) 1.90 .70
B67a SP59 5c (+3c) 2.60 .90
B68a SP59 6c (+4c) 3.25 .90
B69a SP59 12½c (+3½c) 26.00 20.00
Nos. B66a-B69a (4) 33.75 22.50
Set, never hinged 87.50

Queen Wilhelmina SP60

Princess Juliana SP61

Perf. 12½

1934, Apr. 28 Engr. Unwmk.

B70 SP60 5c (+4c) dk vio 11.50 3.25
B71 SP61 6c (+5c) blue 10.50 4.25
Set, never hinged 52.50

The surtax was for the benefit of the Anti-Depression Committee.

Dowager Queen Emma — SP62

1934, Oct. 1 ***Perf. 13x14***

B72 SP62 6c (+2c) blue 11.50 1.40
Never hinged 27.50

Surtax for the Fight Tuberculosis Society.

Poor Child — SP63

Perf. 13½x13

1934, Dec. 10 Photo. Wmk. 202

B73 SP63 1½c (+1½c) olive 1.40 .45
B74 SP63 5c (+3c) rose red 2.40 1.00
B75 SP63 6c (+4c) bl grn 2.40 .25
B76 SP63 12½c (+3½c) ultra 22.50 16.00
Nos. B73-B76 (4) 28.70 17.70
Set, never hinged 75.00

The surtax aided child welfare.

Henri D. Guyot SP64

A. J. M. Diepenbrock SP65

F. C. Donders SP66

J. P. Sweelinck SP67

Perf. 12½ x 12, 12

1935, June 17 Engr. Unwmk.

B77 SP64 1½c (+1½c) dk car 1.50 1.25
B78 SP65 5c (+3c) blk brn 4.00 3.50
B79 SP66 6c (+4c) myr grn 4.50 .70
B80 SP67 12½c (+3½c) dp bl 24.00 4.00
Nos. B77-B80 (4) 34.00 9.45
Set, never hinged 87.50

Surtax for social and cultural projects.

Netherlands Map, DC-3 Planes' Shadows SP68

Perf. 14x13

1935, Oct. 16 Photo. Wmk. 202

B81 SP68 6c (+4c) brn 24.00 7.50
Never hinged 60.00

Surtax for Natl. Aviation.

Girl Picking Apple — SP69

1935, Dec. 4 *Perf. 14½x13½*

No.	Type	Description	Unused	Used
B82	SP69	1½c (+1½c) crim	.50	.30
B83	SP69	5c (+3c) dk yel grn	1.40	1.10
B84	SP69	6c (+4c) blk brn	1.25	.30
B85	SP69	12½c (+3½c) ultra	20.00	7.00
		Nos. B82-B85 (4)	23.15	8.70
		Set, never hinged	80.00	

The surtax aided child welfare.

H. Kamerlingh Onnes — SP70

Dr. A. S. Talma — SP71

Msgr. H. J. A. M. Schaepman SP72

Desiderius Erasmus SP73

Perf. 12½x12

1936, May 1 **Engr.** **Unwmk.**

No.	Type	Description	Unused	Used
B86	SP70	1½c (+1½c) brn blk	.80	.75
B87	SP71	5c (+3c) dl grn	.80	*3.25*
B88	SP72	6c (+4c) dk red	3.50	.50
B89	SP73	12½c (+3½c) dl bl	13.00	2.50
		Nos. B86-B89 (4)	18.10	7.00
		Set, never hinged	60.00	

Surtax for social and cultural projects.

Cherub — SP74

Perf. 14½x13½

1936, Dec. 1 **Photo.** **Wmk. 202**

No.	Type	Description	Unused	Used
B90	SP74	1½c (+1½c) lil gray	.50	.30
B91	SP74	5c (+3c) turq grn	2.00	.75
B92	SP74	6c (+4c) dp red brn	1.90	.25
B93	SP74	12½c (+3½c) ind	14.00	4.75
		Nos. B90-B93 (4)	18.40	6.05
		Set, never hinged	45.00	

The surtax aided child welfare.

Jacob Maris — SP75

Franciscus de la Boe Sylvius — SP76

Joost van den Vondel SP77

Anthony van Leeuwenhoek SP78

Perf. 12½x12

1937, June 1 **Engr.** **Unwmk.**

No.	Type	Description	Unused	Used
B94	SP75	1½c (+1½c) blk brn	.50	.40
B95	SP76	5c (+3c) dl grn	4.00	2.75
B96	SP77	6c (+4c) brn vio	1.00	.25
B97	SP78	12½c (+3½c) dl bl	7.00	.85
		Nos. B94-B97 (4)	12.50	4.25
		Set, never hinged	35.00	

Surtax for social and cultural projects.

"The Laughing Child" after Frans Hals — SP79

Perf. 14½x13½

1937, Dec. 1 **Photo.** **Wmk. 202**

No.	Type	Description	Unused	Used
B98	SP79	1½c (+1½c) blk	.25	.25
B99	SP79	3c (+2c) grn	1.50	1.00
B100	SP79	4c (+2c) hn brn	.60	.45
B101	SP79	5c (+3c) bl grn	.50	.25
B102	SP79	12½c (+3½c) dk bl	7.25	1.40
		Nos. B98-B102 (5)	10.10	3.35
		Set, never hinged	32.50	

The surtax aided child welfare.

Marnix van Sint Aldegonde SP80

Otto Gerhard Heldring SP81

Maria Tesselschade SP82

Hermann Boerhaave SP84

Harmenszoon Rembrandt van Rijn — SP83

Perf. 12½x12

1938, May 16 **Engr.** **Unwmk.**

No.	Type	Description	Unused	Used
B103	SP80	1½c (+1½c) sep	.30	.50
B104	SP81	3c (+2c) dk grn	.55	.30
B105	SP82	4c (+2c) rose lake	1.75	1.50
B106	SP83	5c (+3c) dk sl grn	2.25	.30
B107	SP84	12½c (+3½c) dl bl	7.75	1.10
		Nos. B103-B107 (5)	12.60	3.70
		Set, never hinged	32.50	

The surtax was for the benefit of cultural and social relief.

Child with Flowers, Bird and Fish — SP85

Perf. 14½x13½

1938, Dec. 1 **Photo.** **Wmk. 202**

No.	Type	Description	Unused	Used
B108	SP85	1½c (+1½c) blk	.25	.25
B109	SP85	3c (+2c) mar	.30	.25
B110	SP85	4c (+2c) dk bl grn	.60	.80
B111	SP85	5c (+3c) hn brn	.25	.25
B112	SP85	12½c (+3½c) dp bl	9.00	1.75
		Nos. B108-B112 (5)	10.40	3.30
		Set, never hinged	35.00	

The surtax aided child welfare.

Matthijs Maris — SP86

Anton Mauve — SP87

Gerard van Swieten SP88

Nikolaas Beets SP89

Peter Stuyvesant — SP90

Perf. 12½x12

1939, May 1 **Engr.** **Unwmk.**

No.	Type	Description	Unused	Used
B113	SP86	1½c (+1½c) sepia	.60	.60
B114	SP87	2½c (+2½c) gray grn	3.00	2.75
B115	SP88	3c (+3c) ver	.80	1.00
B116	SP89	5c (+3c) dk sl grn	2.00	.30
B117	SP90	12½c (+3½c) indigo	5.00	.85
		Nos. B113-B117 (5)	11.40	5.50
		Set, never hinged	40.00	

The surtax was for the benefit of cultural and social relief.

Child Carrying Cornucopia — SP91

Perf. 14½x13½

1939, Dec. 1 **Photo.** **Wmk. 202**

No.	Type	Description	Unused	Used
B118	SP91	1½c (+1½c) blk	.25	.25
B119	SP91	2½c (+2½c) dk ol grn	3.75	2.00
B120	SP91	3c (+3c) hn brn	.40	.25
B121	SP91	5c (+3c) dk grn	.85	.25
B122	SP91	12½c (+3½c) dk bl	4.00	1.00
		Nos. B118-B122 (5)	9.25	3.75
		Set, never hinged	40.00	

The surtax was used for destitute children.

Catalogue values for unused stamps in this section, from this point to the end of the section, are for Never Hinged items.

Vincent van Gogh SP92

E. J. Potgieter SP93

Petrus Camper SP94

Jan Steen SP95

Joseph Scaliger — SP96

Perf. 12½x12

1940, May 11 **Engr.** **Wmk. 202**

No.	Type	Description	Unused	Used
B123	SP92	1½c +1½c brn blk	1.90	.25
B124	SP93	2½c +2½c dk grn	6.00	1.40
B125	SP94	3c +3c car	3.75	1.10
B126	SP95	5c +3c dp grn	7.75	.25
a.		Booklet pane of 4	250.00	
B127	SP96	12½c +3½c dp bl	6.75	.80

Surtax for social and cultural projects.

Type of 1940 Surcharged in Black

1940, Sept. 7

No.	Type	Description	Unused	Used
B128	SP95	7½c +2½c on 5c +3c dk red	.50	.25
		Nos. B123-B128 (6)	26.65	4.05

Child with Flowers and Doll — SP97

Perf. 14½x13½

1940, Dec. 2 **Photo.** **Wmk. 202**

No.	Type	Description	Unused	Used
B129	SP97	1½c +1½c dl bl gray	.65	.25
B130	SP97	2½c +2½c dp ol	2.50	.50
B131	SP97	4c +3c royal bl	2.50	.65
B132	SP97	5c +3c dk bl grn	2.50	.25
B133	SP97	7½c +3½c hn	.65	.25
		Nos. B129-B133 (5)	8.80	1.90

The surtax was used for destitute children.

AIR POST STAMPS

Stylized Seagull — AP1

Perf. 12½

1921, May 1 **Unwmk.** **Typo.**

No.	Type	Description	Unused	Used
C1	AP1	10c red	1.50	1.25
C2	AP1	15c yellow grn	6.25	2.50
C3	AP1	60c dp blue	19.00	.50
		Nos. C1-C3 (3)	26.75	4.25
		Set, never hinged	190.00	

Nos. C1-C3 were used to pay airmail fee charged by the carrier, KLM.

Lt. G. A. Koppen — AP2

Capt. Jan van der Hoop — AP3

Wmk. Circles (202)

1928, Aug. 20 Litho. *Perf. 12*

No.	Type	Description	Unused	Used
C4	AP2	40c orange red	.25	.25
C5	AP3	75c blue green	.25	.25
		Set, never hinged	1.25	

Mercury — AP4

Perf. 11½

1929, July 16 Unwmk. Engr.

No.	Type	Description	Unused	Used
C6	AP4	1½g gray	2.50	1.65
C7	AP4	4½g carmine	1.75	3.00
C8	AP4	7½g blue green	24.00	4.50
		Nos. C6-C8 (3)	28.25	9.15
		Set, never hinged	70.00	

Queen Wilhelmina — AP5

Perf. 12½, 14x13

1931, Sept. 24 Photo. Wmk. 202

No.	Type	Description	Unused	Used
C9	AP5	36c org red & dk bl	10.00	.60
		Never hinged	70.00	

Fokker Pander AP6

1933, Oct. 9 *Perf. 12½*

No.	Type	Description	Unused	Used
C10	AP6	30c dark green	.40	.60
		Never hinged	.80	

Nos. C10-C12 were issued for use on special flights.

Crow in Flight AP7

1938-53 *Perf. 13x14*

No.	Type	Description	Unused	Used
C11	AP7	12½c dk blue & gray	.35	.25
C12	AP7	25c dk bl & gray ('53)	1.50	1.50
		Set, never hinged	4.25	

MARINE INSURANCE STAMPS

Floating Safe Attracting Gulls — MI1

Floating Safe with Night Flare — MI2

Fantasy of Floating Safe — MI3

Perf. 11½

1921, Feb. 2 Unwmk. Engr.

No.	Type	Description	Unused	Used
GY1	MI1	15c slate grn	11.00	*75.00*
GY2	MI1	60c car rose	15.00	*75.00*
GY3	MI1	75c gray brn	18.50	*75.00*
GY4	MI2	1.50g dk blue	65.00	*425.00*
GY5	MI2	2.25g org brn	110.00	*550.00*
GY6	MI3	4½g black	165.00	*675.00*
GY7	MI3	7½g red	250.00	*925.00*
		Nos. GY1-GY7 (7)	634.50	*2,800.*
		Set, never hinged	1,500.	

POSTAGE DUE STAMPS

Postage due types of Netherlands were also used for Netherlands Antilles, Netherlands Indies and Surinam in different colors.

D1

Unwmk.

1870, May 15 Typo. *Perf. 13*

No.	Type	Description	Unused	Used
J1	D1	5c brown, *org*	72.50	15.00
		No gum	22.00	
		On cover		140.00
		On postcard		80.00
J2	D1	10c violet, *bl*	150.00	20.00
		No gum	47.50	
		On cover		225.00
a.		Perf 12½x12	300.00	32.50

D2

Type I — 34 loops. "T" of "BETALEN" over center of loop; top branch of "E" of "TE" shorter than lower branch.

Type II — 33 loops. "T" of "BETALEN" between two loops.

Type III — 32 loops. "T" of "BETALEN" slightly to the left of loop; top branch of first "E" of "BETALEN" shorter than lower branch.

Type IV — 37 loops. Letters of "PORT" larger than in the other three types.

Imperforate varieties are proofs.

Perf. 11½x12, 12½x12, 12½, 13½

1881-87 Value in Black

No.	Type	Description	Unused	Used
J3	D2	1c lt blue (III)	11.00	11.00
		No gum	4.00	
a.		Type I	15.00	18.00
b.		Type II	20.00	20.00
c.		Type IV	47.50	52.50
J4	D2	1½c lt blue (III)	15.00	15.00
		No gum	4.00	
a.		Type I	18.00	18.00
b.		Type II	24.00	24.00
c.		Type IV	75.00	75.00
J5	D2	2½c lt blue (III)	37.50	5.00
		No gum	8.00	
a.		Type I	45.00	5.50
b.		Type II	50.00	6.00
c.		Type IV	210.00	125.00
J6	D2	5c lt blue (III) ('87)	140.00	3.50
		No gum	20.00	
a.		Type I	50.00	5.00
b.		Type II	130.00	5.25
c.		Type IV	1,250.	350.00
J7	D2	10c lt blue (III) ('87)	92.50	4.00
		No gum	22.50	
a.		Type I	115.00	4.50
b.		Type II	125.00	5.00
c.		Type IV	2,500.	375.00
J8	D2	12½c lt blue (III)	95.00	25.00
		No gum	22.50	
a.		Type I	165.00	40.00
b.		Type II	130.00	45.00
c.		Type IV	350.00	100.00
J9	D2	15c lt blue (III)	90.00	4.00
		No gum	17.00	
a.		Type I	105.00	4.50
b.		Type II	120.00	5.00
c.		Type IV	130.00	25.00
J10	D2	20c lt blue (III)	35.00	4.00
		No gum	7.75	
a.		Type I	47.50	4.25
b.		Type II	50.00	5.50
c.		Type IV	137.50	27.50
J11	D2	25c lt blue (III)	210.00	3.50
		No gum	47.50	
a.		Type I	230.00	3.00
b.		Type II	275.00	4.50
c.		Type IV	425.00	170.00

Value in Red

No.	Type	Description	Unused	Used
J12	D2	1g lt blue (III)	85.00	30.00
		No gum	20.00	
a.		Type I	85.00	37.50
b.		Type II	100.00	40.00
c.		Type IV	175.00	75.00
		Nos. J3-J12 (10)	811.00	105.00

See Nos. J13-J26, J44-J60. For surcharges see Nos. J27-J28, J42-J43, J72-J75.

1896-1910 *Perf. 12½*

Value in Black

No.	Type	Description	Unused	Used
J13	D2	½c dk bl (I) ('01)	.40	.35
J14	D2	1c dk blue (I)	1.65	.35
a.		Type III	2.50	3.25
J15	D2	1½c dk blue (I)	.75	.35
a.		Type III	2.50	2.50
J16	D2	2½c dk blue (I)	1.50	.75
a.		Type III	3.25	.55
J17	D2	3c dk bl (I) ('10)	1.65	1.10
J18	D2	4c dk bl (I) ('09)	1.65	2.25
J19	D2	5c dk blue (I)	13.00	.35
a.		Type III	16.00	.55
J20	D2	6½c dk bl (I) ('07)	45.00	45.00
J21	D2	7½c dk bl (I) ('04)	1.75	.55
J22	D2	10c dk blue (I)	35.00	.55
a.		Type III	52.50	1.50
J23	D2	12½c dk blue (I)	30.00	1.10
a.		Type III	45.00	3.50
J24	D2	15c dk blue (I)	35.00	.90
a.		Type III	55.00	1.00
J25	D2	20c dk blue (I)	20.00	8.00
a.		Type III	20.00	8.75
J26	D2	25c dk blue (I)	45.00	.75
a.		Type III	50.00	1.00
		Nos. J13-J26 (14)	232.35	62.35

Surcharged in Black

1906, Jan. 10 *Perf. 12½*

No.	Type	Description	Unused	Used
J27	D2	50c on 1g lt bl (III)	125.00	110.00
a.		50c on 1g light blue (I)	165.00	140.00
b.		50c on 1g light blue (II)	175.00	150.00

Surcharged in Red

1906, Oct. 6

No.	Type	Description	Unused	Used
J28	D2	6½c on 20c dk bl (I)	5.50	5.00

Nos. 87-89 Surcharged

1907, Nov. 1

No.	Type	Description	Unused	Used
J29	A13	½c on 1c claret	1.25	1.25
J30	A13	1c on 1c claret	.50	.50
J31	A13	1½c on 1c claret	.50	.50
J32	A13	2½c on 1c claret	1.25	1.25
J33	A13	5c on 2½c ver	1.40	.40
J34	A13	6½c on 2½c ver	3.50	3.50
J35	A13	7½c on ½c blue	2.00	1.25
J36	A13	10c on ½c blue	1.75	.75
J37	A13	12½c on ½c blue	5.00	4.75
J38	A13	15c on 2½c ver	6.00	4.00
J39	A13	25c on ½c blue	9.00	8.50
J40	A13	50c on ½c blue	42.50	40.00
J41	A13	1g on ½c blue	60.00	55.00
		Nos. J29-J41 (13)	134.65	121.65

Two printings of the above surcharges were made. Some values show differences in the setting of the fractions; others are practically impossible to distinguish.

No. J20 Surcharged in Red

1909, June

No.	Type	Description	Unused	Used
J42	D2	4c on 6½c dark blue	5.50	5.00
		Never hinged	20.00	

No. J12 Surcharged in Black

1910, July 11

No.	Type	Description	Unused	Used
J43	D2	3c on 1g lt bl, type III	30.00	27.50
		Never hinged	100.00	
a.		Type I	37.50	40.00
		Never hinged	110.00	
b.		Type II	40.00	40.00
		Never hinged	125.00	

Type I

1912-21 *Perf. 12½, 13½x13*

Value in Color of Stamp

No.	Type	Description	Unused	Used
J44	D2	½c pale ultra	.25	.25
J45	D2	1c pale ultra ('13)	.25	.25
J46	D2	1½c pale ultra ('15)	1.90	1.50
J47	D2	2½c pale ultra	.25	.25
J48	D2	3c pale ultra	.40	.40
J49	D2	4c pale ultra ('13)	.25	.25
J50	D2	4½c pale ultra ('16)	5.25	5.00
J51	D2	5c pale ultra	.25	.25
J52	D2	5½c pale ultra ('16)	5.00	5.00
J53	D2	7c pale ultra ('21)	2.25	2.25
J54	D2	7½c pale ultra ('13)	2.50	1.00
J55	D2	10c pale ultra ('13)	.40	.40
J56	D2	12½c pale ultra ('13)	.40	.40
J57	D2	15c pale ultra ('13)	.40	.40
J58	D2	20c pale ultra ('20)	.40	.25
J59	D2	25c pale ultra ('17)	80.00	.60
J60	D2	50c pale ultra ('20)	.40	.25
		Nos. J44-J60 (17)	100.55	18.70
		Set, never hinged	450.00	

D3

1921-38 Typo. *Perf. 12½, 13½x12½*

No.	Type	Description	Unused	Used
J61	D3	3c pale ultra ('28)	.25	.25
J62	D3	6c pale ultra ('27)	.25	.25
J63	D3	7c pale ultra ('28)	.40	.40
J64	D3	7½c pale ultra ('26)	.40	.40
J65	D3	8c pale ultra ('38)	.40	.40
J66	D3	9c pale ultra ('30)	.40	.40
J67	D3	11c ultra ('21)	13.00	3.50
J68	D3	12c pale ultra ('28)	.40	.25
J69	D3	25c pale ultra ('25)	.40	.25
J70	D3	30c pale ultra ('35)	.40	.25
J71	D3	1g ver ('21)	.50	.25
		Nos. J61-J71 (11)	16.80	6.60
		Set, never hinged	50.00	

Stamps of 1912-21 Surcharged

1923, Dec. *Perf. 12½*

No.	Type	Description	Unused	Used
J72	D2	1c on 3c ultra	.75	.50
J73	D2	2½c on 7c ultra	1.20	.50
J74	D2	25c on 1½c ultra	8.00	.50
J75	D2	25c on 7½c ultra	10.00	.50
		Nos. J72-J75 (4)	19.95	2.00
		Set, never hinged	45.00	

Nos. 56, 58, 62, 65 Surcharged

1924, Aug.

No.	Type	Description	Unused	Used
J76	A11	4c on 3c olive grn	1.50	1.10
J77	A10	5c on 1c red	.75	.40
a.		Surcharge reading down	500.00	450.00
J78	A10	10c on 1½c blue	.95	.40
a.		Tête bêche pair	8.50	8.50
J79	A11	12½c on 5c carmine	.95	.50
a.		Tête bêche pair	10.00	10.00
		Nos. J76-J79 (4)	4.15	2.40

The 11c on 22½c and 15c on 17½c exist. These were used by the postal service for accounting of parcel post fees.

OFFICIAL STAMPS

Regular Issues of 1898-1908 Overprinted

1913 Typo. Unwmk. *Perf. 12½*

No.	Type	Description	Unused	Used
O1	A10	1c red	4.00	2.75
O2	A10	1½c ultra	1.00	2.25
O3	A10	2c yellow brn	7.00	7.00
O4	A10	2½c dp green	16.00	12.00
O5	A11	3c olive grn	4.00	1.00
O6	A11	5c carmine rose	4.00	4.50
O7	A11	10c gray lilac	35.00	37.50
		Nos. O1-O7 (7)	71.00	67.00

Same Overprint in Red on No. 58

1919

No.	Type	Description	Unused	Used
O8	A10	1½c deep blue (R)	100.00	110.00

Nos. O1 to O8 were used to defray the postage on matter relating to the Poor Laws.

Counterfeit overprints exist.

For the International Court of Justice

Regular Issue of 1926-33 Overprinted in Gold

1934 Wmk. 202 *Perf. 12½*

No.	Type	Description	Unused	Used
O9	A24	1½c red violet		1.50
O10	A24	2½c deep green		1.50
O11	A23	7½c red		2.25
O12	A31	12½c deep ultra		22.50
O13	A23	15c orange		2.00
O14	A23	30c violet		2.25
a.		Perf. 13½x12½		2.25
		Nos. O9-O14 (6)		32.00

Same Overprint on No. 180 in Gold

1937 *Perf. 13½x12½*

No.	Type	Description	Unused	Used
O15	A23	12½c ultra		16.00

"Mint" Officials

Nos. O9-O15, were sold to the public only canceled. Uncanceled, they were obtainable only by favor of an official or from UPU specimen stamps.

Same on Regular Issue of 1940 Overprinted in Gold

1940 *Perf. 13½x12½*

No.	Type	Description	Unused	Used
O16	A45	7½c bright red	22.50	8.75
O17	A45	12½c sapphire	22.50	8.75
O18	A45	15c lt blue	22.50	8.75
O19	A45	30c bister	22.50	8.75
		Nos. O16-O19 (4)	90.00	35.00

NETHERLANDS ANTILLES

ˈne-th̲ər-lənˌdz an-ˈti-lēz

(Curaçao)

LOCATION — Two groups of islands about 500 miles apart in the West Indies, north of Venezuela

GOVT. — Dutch Colony

AREA — 383 sq. mi.

POP. — 260,000 (est. 1983)

CAPITAL — Willemstad

100 Cents = 1 Gulden

Values for unused examples of Nos. 1-44 are for stamps without gum.

Watermark

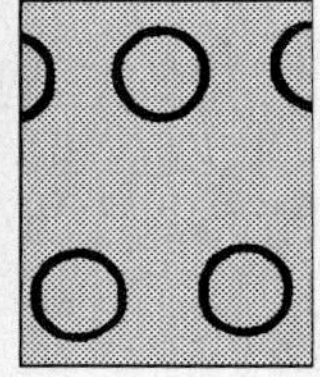

Wmk. 202 — Circles

King William III — A1

Regular Perf. 11½, 12½, 11½x12, 12½x12, 13½x13, 14

1873-79 Typo. Unwmk.

No.	Type	Description	Unused	Used
1	A1	2½c green	5.00	8.00
2	A1	3c bister	55.00	*110.00*
3	A1	5c rose	10.00	12.00
4	A1	10c ultra	60.00	17.00
5	A1	25c brown orange	45.00	10.00
6	A1	50c violet	1.75	2.50
7	A1	2.50g bis & pur ('79)	37.50	37.50
		Nos. 1-7 (7)	214.25	*197.00*

See bluish paper note with Netherlands #7-22.

The gulden denominations, Nos. 7 and 12, are of larger size.

See 8-12. For surcharges see #18, 25-26.

Perf. 14, Small Holes

No.	Type	Description	Unused	Used
1b	A1	2½c	12.00	15.00
2b	A1	3c	60.00	*140.00*
3b	A1	5c	14.50	21.00
4b	A1	10c	72.50	80.00
5b	A1	25c	65.00	45.00
6b	A1	50c	26.00	30.00
		Nos. 1b-6b (6)	250.00	*331.00*

"Small hole" varieties have the spaces between the holes wider than the diameter of the holes.

1886-89 *Perf. 11½, 12½, 12½x12*

No.	Type	Description	Unused	Used
8	A1	12½c yellow	95.00	52.50
9	A1	15c olive ('89)	27.50	19.00
10	A1	30c pearl gray ('89)	35.00	50.00
11	A1	60c olive bis ('89)	42.50	17.00
12	A1	1.50g lt & dk bl ('89)	100.00	80.00
		Nos. 8-12 (5)	300.00	218.50

Nos. 1-12 were issued without gum until 1890. Imperfs. are proofs.

Numeral — A2

1889 *Perf. 12½*

No.	Type	Description	Unused	Used
13	A2	1c gray	.85	1.00
14	A2	2c violet	.65	1.25
15	A2	2½c green	4.50	3.00
16	A2	3c bister	5.00	4.50
17	A2	5c rose	21.00	1.75
		Nos. 13-17 (5)	32.00	11.50

Black Handstamped Surcharge

1891 *Perf. 12½x12*

Without Gum

No.	Type	Description	Unused	Used
18	A1	25c on 30c pearl gray	15.00	14.00

No. 18 exists with double surcharge, value $225, and with inverted surcharge, value $275.

Queen Wilhelmina — A4

1892-96 *Perf. 12½*

No.	Type	Description	Unused	Used
19	A4	10c ultra ('95)	1.25	1.25
20	A4	12½c green	26.00	6.25
21	A4	15c rose ('93)	2.50	2.50
22	A4	25c brown orange	100.00	5.50
23	A4	30c gray ('96)	2.50	*5.50*
		Nos. 19-23 (5)	132.25	21.00

No. 4 Handstamped Surcharge in Magenta

No. 10 Handstamped Surcharge in Black

1895 *Perf. 12½, 13½x13*

No.	Type	Description	Unused	Used
25	A1	2½c on 10c ultra	13.00	8.00

Perf. 12½x12

No.	Type	Description	Unused	Used
26	A1	2½c on 30c gray	125.00	6.00

Nos. 25-26 exist with surcharge double or inverted.

No. 26 and No. 25, perf. 13½x13, were issued without gum.

Netherlands Nos. 77, 68 Surcharged in Black

1902, Jan. 1 *Perf. 12½*

No.	Type	Description	Unused	Used
27	A11	25c on 25c car & bl	2.00	2.00

Netherlands No. 84 Surcharged in Black

1901, May 1 Engr. *Perf. 11½x11*

No.	Type	Description	Unused	Used
28	A12	1.50g on 2.50g brn lil	20.00	21.00

1902, Mar. 1 Typo. *Perf. 12½*

No.	Type	Description	Unused	Used
29	A11	12½c on 12½c blue	25.00	7.00

A9

A10

1904-08

No.	Type	Description	Unused	Used
30	A9	1c olive green	1.40	.90
31	A9	2c yellow brown	12.00	3.00
32	A9	2½c blue green	4.00	.35
33	A9	3c orange	7.50	4.00
34	A9	5c rose red	7.00	.35
35	A9	7½c gray ('08)	27.50	6.00
36	A10	10c slate	11.00	3.00
37	A10	12½c deep blue	1.25	.50
38	A10	15c brown	14.00	10.00
39	A10	22½c brn & ol ('08)	14.00	8.50
40	A10	25c violet	14.00	1.90
41	A10	30c brown orange	32.50	13.00
42	A10	50c red brown	27.50	8.25
		Nos. 30-42 (13)	173.65	59.75

Queen Wilhelmina — A11

1906, Nov. 1 Engr. *Perf. 11½*

Without Gum

No.	Type	Description	Unused	Used
43	A11	1½g red brown	35.00	25.00
44	A11	2½g slate blue	35.00	24.00

A12

Queen Wilhelmina

A13 A14

Perf. 12½, 11, 11½, 11x11½

1915-33 Typo.

No.	Type	Description	Unused	Used
45	A12	½c lilac ('20)	1.60	1.10
46	A12	1c olive green	.25	.25
47	A12	1½c blue ('20)	.25	.25
48	A12	2c yellow brn	1.25	1.40
49	A12	2½c green	.90	.25
50	A12	3c yellow	2.25	1.50
51	A12	3c green ('26)	2.60	2.50
52	A12	5c rose	2.00	.25
53	A12	5c green ('22)	3.75	2.75
54	A12	5c lilac ('26)	2.00	.25
55	A12	7½c drab	1.10	.30
56	A12	7½c bister ('20)	1.10	.25
57	A12	10c lilac ('22)	5.00	4.50
58	A12	10c rose ('26)	4.25	1.25
59	A13	10c car rose	13.00	3.00
60	A13	12½c blue	2.25	.50
61	A13	12½c red ('22)	2.00	1.60
62	A13	15c olive grn	.65	.65
63	A13	15c lt blue ('26)	4.00	2.50
64	A13	20c blue ('22)	6.50	3.00
65	A13	20c olive grn ('26)	2.50	2.25
66	A13	22½c orange	2.50	2.25
67	A13	25c red violet	3.25	.90
68	A13	30c slate	3.25	.65
69	A13	35c sl & red ('22)	3.25	4.25

Perf. 11½x11, 11½, 12½, 11

Engr.

No.	Type	Description	Unused	Used
70	A14	50c green	4.00	.25
71	A14	1½g violet	13.00	11.00
72	A14	2½g carmine	21.00	20.00
a.		Perf. 12½ ('33)	140.00	*300.00*
		Nos. 45-72 (28)	109.45	69.60

Some stamps of 1915 were also issued without gum.

For surcharges see #74, 107-108, C1-C3.

A15

Laid Paper

Without Gum

1918, July 16 Typo. *Perf. 12*

No.	Type	Description	Unused	Used
73	A15	1c black, *buff*	6.75	3.75

"HAW" are the initials of Postmaster H. A. Willemsen.

No. 60 Surcharged in Black

1918, Sept. 1 *Perf. 12½*

No.	Type	Description	Unused	Used
74	A13	5c on 12½c blue	3.75	2.00
a.		"5" 2½mm wide	60.00	32.50
b.		Double surcharge		700.00

The "5" of No. 74 is 3mm wide. Illustration shows No. 74a surcharge.

Queen Wilhelmina — A16

1923 Engr. *Perf. 11½, 11x11½*

75 A16 5c green 1.00 2.00
76 A16 7½c olive grn 1.25 1.60
77 A16 10c car rose 1.75 2.00
78 A16 20c indigo 2.50 3.50
 a. Perf. 11x11½ 3.25 4.25
79 A16 1g brown vio 30.00 19.00
80 A16 2½g gray black 70.00 *170.00*
81 A16 5g brown 90.00 *200.00*
 a. Perf. 11x11½ 625.00
 Nos. 75-81 (7) 196.50 *398.10*

25th anniv. of the assumption of the government of the Netherlands by Queen Wilhelmina, at the age of 18.

Nos. 80-81 with clear cancel between Aug. 1, 1923 and Apr. 30, 1924, sell for considerably more.

Types of Netherlands Marine Insurance Stamps, Inscribed "CURACAO" Surcharged in Black

1927, Oct. 3

87 MI1 3c on 15c dk green .25 .30
88 MI1 10c on 60c car rose .25 .45
89 MI1 12½c on 75c gray brn .25 .45
90 MI2 15c on 1.50g dk bl 3.00 2.50
 a. Double surcharge *500.00*
91 MI2 25c on 2.25g org brn 6.50 6.25
92 MI3 30c on 4½g black 13.00 11.00
93 MI3 50c on 7½g red 7.50 7.25
 Nos. 87-93 (7) 30.75 28.20

Nos. 90, 91 and 92 have "FRANKEER-ZEGEL" in one line of small capitals. Nos. 90 and 91 have a heavy bar across the top of the stamp.

Queen Wilhelmina — A17

1928-30 Engr. *Perf. 11½, 12½*

95 A17 6c orange red ('30) 1.50 .40
 a. Booklet pane of 6
96 A17 7½c orange red .60 .45
97 A17 10c carmine 1.50 .35
98 A17 12½c red brown 1.50 1.00
 a. Booklet pane of 6
99 A17 15c dark blue 1.50 .35
 a. Booklet pane of 6
100 A17 20c blue black 5.75 .55
101 A17 21c yellow grn ('30) 9.25 14.00
102 A17 25c brown vio 3.50 1.40
103 A17 27½c black ('30) 12.00 14.00
104 A17 30c deep green 5.75 .55
105 A17 35c brnsh black 2.00 1.75
 Nos. 95-105 (11) 44.85 34.80

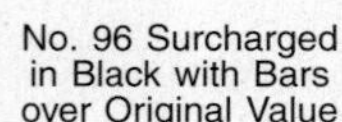

No. 96 Surcharged in Black with Bars over Original Value

1929, Nov. 1

106 A17 6c on 7½c org red 1.40 1.00
 a. Inverted surcharge 275.00 260.00

No. 51 Surcharged in Red

1931, Mar. 1 Typo. *Perf. 12½*

107 A12 2½c on 3c green 1.10 1.10

No. 49 Surcharged in Red

1932, Oct. 29

108 A12 1½c on 2½c grn 3.50 3.50

Prince William I, Portrait by Van Key — A18

1933 Photo. *Perf. 12½*

109 A18 6c deep orange 1.75 1.40

400th birth anniv. of Prince William I, Count of Nassau and Prince of Orange, frequently referred to as William the Silent.

Willem Usselinx — A19

Van Walbeeck's Ship — A22

Designs: 2½c, 5c, 6c, Frederik Hendrik. 10c, 12½c, 15c, Jacob Binckes. 27½c, 30c, 50c, Cornelis Evertsen the Younger. 1.50g, 2.50g, Louis Brion.

1934, Jan. 1 Engr. *Perf. 12½*

110 A19 1c black 1.00 1.25
111 A19 1½c dull violet .75 .30
112 A19 2c orange 1.00 1.25
113 A19 2½c dull green .85 1.25
114 A19 5c black brn .85 .85
115 A19 6c violet bl .75 .25
116 A19 10c lake 2.00 1.00
117 A19 12½c bister brn 6.50 7.00
118 A19 15c blue 1.60 1.00
119 A22 20c black 3.00 2.00
120 A22 21c brown 11.00 13.00
121 A22 25c dull green 11.00 11.00
122 A19 27½c brown vio 14.00 16.00

123 A19 30c scarlet 11.00 5.25
124 A19 50c orange 11.00 8.25
125 A19 1.50g indigo 47.50 50.00
126 A19 2.50g yellow grn 52.50 47.50
 Nos. 110-126 (17) 176.30 167.15

3rd centenary of the founding of the colony.

Numeral A25

Queen Wilhelmina A26

1936, Aug. 1 Litho. *Perf. 13½x13*

Size: 18x22mm

127 A25 1c brown black .25 .25
128 A25 1½c deep ultra .25 .25
129 A25 2c orange .25 .25
130 A25 2½c green .25 .25
131 A25 5c scarlet .35 .25

Engr.

Perf. 12½

Size: 20¼x30½mm

132 A26 6c brown vio .45 .25
133 A26 10c orange red .85 .25
134 A26 12½c dk bl grn 1.50 .95
135 A26 15c dark blue 1.25 .60
136 A26 20c orange yel 1.25 .60
137 A26 21c dk gray 2.25 2.25
138 A26 25c brown lake 1.50 .75
139 A26 27½c violet brn 2.50 2.75
140 A26 30c olive brn .60 .25

Perf. 13x14

Size: 22x33mm

141 A26 50c dull yel grn 3.00 .25
 a. Perf. 14 50.00 .25
142 A26 1.50g black brn 18.00 13.00
 a. Perf. 14 40.00 20.00
143 A26 2.50g rose lake 16.00 11.00
 a. Perf. 14 16.00 11.00
 Nos. 127-143 (17) 50.50 34.15

See Nos. 147-151 in Scott Standard catalogue, Vol. 5. For surcharges see Nos. B1-B3 in Scott Vol. 5.

Queen Wilhelmina — A27

Perf. 12½x12

1938, Aug. 27 Photo. Wmk. 202

144 A27 1½c dull purple .25 .25
145 A27 6c red orange .80 .75
146 A27 15c royal blue 1.50 1.25
 Nos. 144-146 (3) 2.55 2.25

Reign of Queen Wilhelmina, 40th anniv.

AIR POST STAMPS

Regular Issues of 1915-22 Surcharged in Black

Perf. 12½

1929, July 6 Typo. Unwmk.

C1 A13 50c on 12½c red 13.00 13.00
C2 A13 1g on 20c blue 13.00 13.00
C3 A13 2g on 15c ol grn 42.50 47.50
 Nos. C1-C3 (3) 68.50 73.50

Excellent forgeries exist.

Allegory, "Flight" — AP1

1931-39 Engr.

C4 AP1 10c Prus grn ('34) .25 .25
C5 AP1 15c dull blue ('38) .25 .25
C6 AP1 20c red .75 .25
C7 AP1 25c gray ('38) .75 .60
C8 AP1 30c yellow ('39) .30 .30
C9 AP1 35c dull blue .80 .90
C10 AP1 40c green .60 .40
C11 AP1 45c orange 2.25 2.25
C12 AP1 50c lake ('38) .75 .50
C13 AP1 60c brown vio .60 .35
C14 AP1 70c black 6.50 2.50
C15 AP1 1.40g brown 4.25 5.25
C16 AP1 2.80g bister 5.00 5.50
 Nos. C4-C16 (13) 23.05 19.30

No. C6 Surcharged in Black

1934, Aug. 25

C17 AP1 10c on 20c red 19.00 17.00

POSTAGE DUE STAMPS

D1

Type I — 34 loops. "T" of *"BETALEN"* over center of loop, top branch of "E" of *"TE"* shorter than lower branch.

Type II — 33 loops. "T" of *"BETALEN"* over center of two loops.

Type III — 32 loops. "T" of *"BETALEN"* slightly to the left of loop, top of first "E" of *"BETALEN"* shorter than lower branch.

Value in Black

1889 Unwmk. Typo. *Perf. 12½*

Type III

J1 D1 2½c green 3.00 3.25
J2 D1 5c green 2.00 1.75
J3 D1 10c green 32.50 27.50
J4 D1 12½c green 375.00 200.00
J5 D1 15c green 20.00 17.00
J6 D1 20c green 9.00 9.00
J7 D1 25c green 190.00 150.00
J8 D1 30c green 10.00 9.00
J9 D1 40c green 10.00 9.00
J10 D1 50c green 40.00 37.50

Nos. J1-J10 were issued without gum.

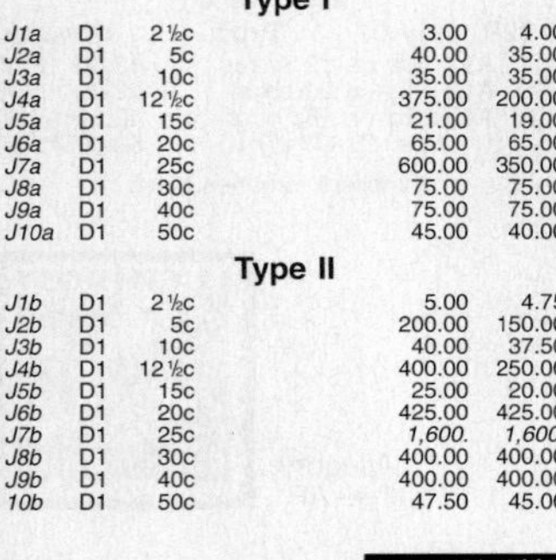

Type I

J1a	D1	2½c	3.00	4.00
J2a	D1	5c	40.00	35.00
J3a	D1	10c	35.00	35.00
J4a	D1	12½c	375.00	200.00
J5a	D1	15c	21.00	19.00
J6a	D1	20c	65.00	65.00
J7a	D1	25c	600.00	350.00
J8a	D1	30c	75.00	75.00
J9a	D1	40c	75.00	75.00
J10a	D1	50c	45.00	40.00

Type II

J1b	D1	2½c	5.00	4.75
J2b	D1	5c	200.00	150.00
J3b	D1	10c	40.00	37.50
J4b	D1	12½c	400.00	250.00
J5b	D1	15c	25.00	20.00
J6b	D1	20c	425.00	425.00
J7b	D1	25c	*1,600.*	*1,600.*
J8b	D1	30c	400.00	400.00
J9b	D1	40c	400.00	400.00
10b	D1	50c	47.50	45.00

D2

1892-98 Value in Black *Perf. 12½*

J11	D2	2½c green (III)	.25	.25
J12	D2	5c green (III)	.60	.45
J13	D2	10c green (III)	1.50	.40
J14	D2	12½c green (III)	1.60	.60
J15	D2	15c green (III) ('95)	2.50	1.10
J17	D2	25c green (III)	1.25	.95
		Nos. J11-J17 (6)	7.70	3.75

Type I

J11a	D2	2½c	.50	.50
J12a	D2	5c	2.50	2.50
J13a	D2	10c	2.75	2.00
J14a	D2	12½c	2.00	1.40
J16	D2	20c green ('95)	3.50	1.40
J17a	D2	25c	1.50	1.50
J18	D2	30c green ('95)	25.00	13.00
J19	D2	40c green ('95)	25.00	15.00
J20	D2	50c green ('95)	30.00	15.00

Type II

J11b	D2	2½c	20.00	20.00
J12b	D2	5c	1.00	1.00
J13b	D2	10c	1.75	1.10
J14b	D2	12½c	9.00	8.00
J17b	D2	25c	*12.50*	*12.50*
		Nos. J11b-J17b (5)	44.25	42.60

Type I
On Yellowish or White Paper
Value in Color of Stamp

1915 *Perf. 12½, 13½x12½*

J21	D2	2½c green	1.00	.95
J22	D2	5c green	1.00	.95
J23	D2	10c green	.90	.80
J24	D2	12½c green	1.25	1.10
J25	D2	15c green	1.90	2.00
J26	D2	20c green	1.00	1.75
J27	D2	25c green	.35	.25
J28	D2	30c green	3.00	3.25
J29	D2	40c green	3.00	3.25
J30	D2	50c green	2.50	3.00
		Nos. J21-J30 (10)	15.90	17.30

1944 *Perf. 11½*

J23a	D2	10c yellow green	20.00	18.00
J24a	D2	12½c yellow green	20.00	10.00
J27a	D2	25c yellow green	40.00	1.00
		Nos. J23a-J27a (3)	80.00	29.00

NETHERLANDS INDIES

'ne-th̲ər-lən‚d‚z 'in-dēs

(Dutch Indies)

LOCATION — East Indies
GOVT. — Dutch colony
AREA — 735,268 sq. mi.
POP. — 76,000,000 (estimated 1949)
CAPITAL — Jakarta (formerly Batavia)

Netherlands Indies consisted of the islands of Sumatra, Java, the Lesser Sundas, Madura, two thirds of Borneo, Celebes, the Moluccas, western New Guinea and many small islands.

100 Cents = 1 Gulden

Values for unused stamps are for examples with original gum as defined in the catalogue introduction. Very fine examples of No. 2 will have perforations touching the frameline on one or more sides due to the narrow spacing of the stamps on the plates. Stamps with perfs clear of the framelines on all four sides are scarce and will command higher prices.

Watermarks

Wmk. 202 — Circles

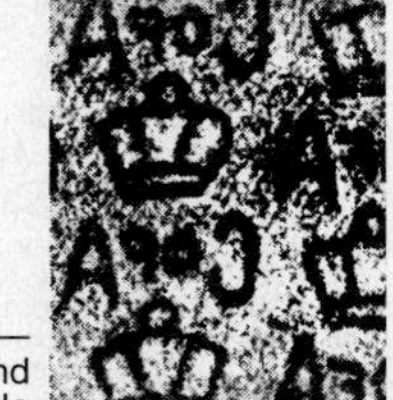

Wmk. 228 — Small Crown and C of A Multiple

King William III — A1

Unwmk.

1864, Apr. 1 Engr. *Imperf.*

1	A1	10c lake	450.00	100.00

1868 *Perf. 12½x12*

2	A1	10c lake	1,250.	150.00

Privately perforated examples of No. 1 sometimes are mistaken for No. 2.

King William III — A2

ONE CENT:
Type I — "CENT" 6mm long.
Type II — "CENT" 7½mm long.

Perf. 11½x12, 12½, 12½x12, 13x14, 13½, 14, 13½x14

1870-88 Typo.

3	A2	1c sl grn, type I	6.00	4.50
a.		Perf. 13x14, small holes	10.00	8.00
4	A2	1c sl grn, type II	2.75	1.75
5	A2	2c red brown	6.00	4.00
a.		2c fawn	6.00	4.00
6	A2	2c violet brn	110.00	95.00
7	A2	2½c orange	35.00	20.00
8	A2	5c pale green	50.00	3.50
a.		Perf. 14, small holes	60.00	4.00
b.		Perf. 13x14, small holes	50.00	5.00
9	A2	10c orange brn	13.00	.25
a.		Perf. 14, small holes	24.00	.80
b.		Perf. 13x14, small holes	35.00	.80
10	A2	12½c gray	3.50	1.50
a.		Perf. 12½x12		1,000.
11	A2	15c bister	17.00	1.50
a.		Perf. 13x14, small holes	27.50	1.75
12	A2	20c ultra	100.00	5.00
a.		Perf. 14, small holes	100.00	5.00
b.		Perf. 13x14, small holes	100.00	5.25
13	A2	25c dk violet	14.00	.55
b.		Perf. 13x14, small holes	25.00	2.50
c.		Perf. 14, large holes	450.00	100.00
14	A2	30c green	27.50	3.25
15	A2	50c carmine	17.00	1.50
a.		Perf. 14, small holes	22.50	1.50
b.		Perf. 13x14, small holes	17.00	1.50
c.		Perf. 14, large holes	25.00	2.50
16	A2	2.50g green & vio	100.00	17.50
b.		Perf. 14, small holes	100.00	17.50
c.		Perf. 14, large holes	110.00	17.50
		Nos. 3-16 (14)	501.75	159.80

Imperforate examples of Nos. 3-16 are proofs. The 1c red brown and 2c yellow are believed to be bogus.

"Small hole" varieties have the spaces between the holes wider than the diameter of the holes.

Numeral of Value — A3

1883-90 *Perf. 12½*

17	A3	1c slate grn ('88)	.75	.25
a.		Perf. 12½x12	1.10	.65
18	A3	2c brown ('84)	.75	.25
a.		Perf. 12½x12	.75	.30
b.		Perf. 11½x12	65.00	22.50
19	A3	2½c yellow	.75	.65
a.		Perf. 12½x12	1.25	.75
b.		Perf. 11½x12	20.00	7.50
20	A3	3c lilac ('90)	.85	.25
21	A3	5c green ('87)	45.00	27.50
22	A3	5c ultra ('90)	9.00	.25
		Nos. 17-22 (6)	57.10	29.15

For surcharges and overprint see Nos. 46-47, O4.

Queen Wilhelmina — A4

1892-97 *Perf. 12½*

23	A4	10c orange brn ('95)	5.00	.30
24	A4	12½c gray ('97)	9.00	*12.50*
25	A4	15c bister ('95)	15.00	1.75
26	A4	20c ultra ('93)	35.00	1.60
27	A4	25c violet	35.00	1.60
28	A4	30c green ('94)	42.50	2.00
29	A4	50c carmine ('93)	30.00	1.40
30	A4	2.50g org brn & ultra	165.00	40.00
		Nos. 23-30 (8)	336.50	61.15

For overprints see Nos. O21-O27.

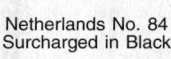

Netherlands Nos. 67-69, 74, 77, 80 Surcharged in Black

1900, July 1

31	A11	10c on 10c gray lil	1.40	.25
32	A11	12½c on 12½c blue	2.25	.55
33	A11	15c on 15c yel brn	2.50	.30
34	A11	20c on 20c yel grn	13.00	.60
35	A11	25c on 25c car & bl	13.00	.70
36	A11	50c on 50c brnz grn & red brn	22.50	.90

Netherlands No. 84 Surcharged in Black

1902 *Perf. 11½x11*

37	A12	2.50g on 2½g brn lil	45.00	11.00
a.		Perf. 11	50.00	12.50
		Nos. 31-37 (7)	99.65	14.30

A6

1902-09 *Perf. 12½*

38	A6	½c violet	.35	.25
39	A6	1c olive grn	.35	.25
a.		Booklet pane of 6		
40	A6	2c yellow brn	2.75	.25
41	A6	2½c green	1.75	.25
a.		Booklet pane of 6		
42	A6	3c orange	1.75	1.10
43	A6	4c ultra ('09)	11.00	9.00
44	A6	5c rose red	4.25	.25
a.		Booklet pane of 6		
45	A6	7½c gray ('08)	2.25	.30
		Nos. 38-45 (8)	24.45	11.65

For overprints see Nos. 63-69, 81-87, O1-O9.

Nos. 18, 20 Surcharged

1902

46	A3	½c on 2c yel brn	.25	.25
a.		Double surcharge	175.00	150.00
47	A3	2½c on 3c violet	.25	.25

Queen Wilhelmina — A9

1903-08

48	A9	10c slate	1.00	.25
a.		Booklet pane of 6		
49	A9	12½c deep blue ('06)	1.50	.25
a.		Booklet pane of 6		
50	A9	15c chocolate ('06)	7.25	2.00
a.		Ovptd. with 2 horiz. bars	2.50	1.00
51	A9	17½c bister ('08)	3.00	.25
52	A9	20c grnsh slate	1.50	1.50
53	A9	20c olive grn ('05)	30.00	.25
54	A9	22½c brn & ol grn ('08)	3.75	.25
55	A9	25c violet ('04)	12.50	.25
56	A9	30c orange brn	32.50	.30
57	A9	50c red brown ('04)	25.00	.30
		Nos. 48-57 (10)	118.00	5.60

For overprints and surcharges see Nos. 58, 70-78, 88-96, 139, O10-O18.

No. 52 Surcharged in Black

1905, July 6

58	A9	10c on 20c grnsh slate	3.75	1.90

Queen Wilhelmina — A10

1905-12 Engr. *Perf. 11x11½*

59	A10	1g dull lilac ('06)	60.00	.40
a.		Perf. 11½x11	60.00	.50
b.		Perf. 11	70.00	11.00
60	A10	1g dl lil, *bl* ('12)	60.00	6.50
a.		Perf. 11	70.00	*75.00*
61	A10	2½g slate bl ('05)	82.50	3.00
a.		Perf. 11½	82.50	3.50
b.		Perf. 11½x11	90.00	3.50
c.		Perf. 11	675.00	
62	A10	2½g sl bl, *bl* ('12)	90.00	40.00
a.		Perf. 11	100.00	100.00
		Nos. 59-62 (4)	292.50	49.90

Sheets of Nos. 60 & 62 were soaked in an indigo solution.

For overprints and surcharge see Nos. 79-80, 97-98, 140, O19-O20.

Previous Issues Overprinted

1908, July 1

63	A6	½c violet	.25	.25
64	A6	1c olive grn	.35	.25
65	A6	2c yellow brn	1.50	2.00
66	A6	2½c green	.75	.25
67	A6	3c orange	.65	1.10
68	A6	5c rose red	2.25	.40

No.	Type	Description	Unused	Used
69	A6	7½c gray	2.50	2.25
70	A9	10c slate	.55	.25
71	A9	12½c dp blue	12.00	3.50
72	A9	15c choc (#50a)	3.75	2.00
73	A9	17½c bister	1.40	.95
74	A9	20c olive grn	7.50	1.40
75	A9	22½c brn & ol grn	5.75	3.50
76	A9	25c violet	5.75	.30
77	A9	30c orange brn	20.00	3.25
78	A9	50c red brown	10.00	1.00
79	A10	1g dull lilac	90.00	4.50
80	A10	2½g slate blue	100.00	65.00
		Nos. 63-80 (18)	264.95	92.15

The above stamps were overprinted for use in the territory outside of Java and Madura, stamps overprinted "Java" being used in these latter places.

The 15c is overprinted, in addition, with two horizontal lines, 2½mm apart.

The overprint also exists on Nos. 59a-59b. Same values.

Overprint Reading Down

No.	Type	Description	Unused	Used
63a	A6	½c	.55	*3.25*
64a	A6	1c	.55	*2.50*
65a	A6	2c	2.25	*4.50*
66a	A6	2½c	.95	*3.00*
67a	A6	3c	15.00	*40.00*
68a	A6	5c	2.25	*2.50*
70a	A9	10c	.65	*1.90*
71a	A9	12½c	4.50	*8.00*
72a	A9	15c	32.50	*75.00*
74a	A9	20c	7.25	8.00
75a	A9	22½c	*1,400.*	*1,400.*
76a	A9	25c	5.50	7.25
77a	A9	30c	11.00	15.00
78a	A9	50c	7.50	9.00
79a	A10	1g	175.00	225.00
80a	A10	2½g	*2,250.*	*2,500.*

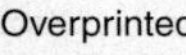
Overprinted

1908, July 1

No.	Type	Description	Unused	Used
81	A6	½c violet	.25	.25
b.		Double overprint	550.00	
82	A6	1c olive grn	.30	.30
83	A6	2c yellow brn	2.10	2.10
84	A6	2½c green	1.10	.25
85	A6	3c orange	.90	.90
86	A6	5c rose red	2.75	.25
87	A6	7½c gray	2.25	2.10
88	A9	10c slate	.75	.25
89	A9	12½c deep blue	2.50	.70
b.		Dbl. ovpt., one inverted	150.00	150.00
90	A9	15c choc (on No. 50a)	3.50	3.00
91	A9	17½c bister	1.90	.80
92	A9	20c olive grn	11.00	.90
93	A9	22½c brn & ol grn	4.75	2.50
94	A9	25c violet	4.75	.40
95	A9	30c orange brn	29.00	2.50
96	A9	50c red brown	18.00	.70
97	A10	1g dull lilac	45.00	3.00
b.		Perf. 11	57.50	5.00
98	A10	2½g slate blue	70.00	47.50
		Nos. 81-98 (18)	200.80	68.40

Inverted Overprint

No.	Type	Description	Unused	Used
81a	A6	½c	1.00	*2.75*
82a	A6	1c	1.00	*3.25*
83a	A6	2c	3.50	*7.25*
84a	A6	2½c	3.00	*4.00*
85a	A6	3c	20.00	27.50
86a	A6	5c	3.00	3.75
88a	A9	10c	2.00	*2.50*
89a	A9	12½c	3.25	5.75
90a	A9	15c	3.50	*11.00*
92a	A9	20c	11.00	12.00
94a	A9	25c	6.00	*11.00*
95a	A9	30c	29.00	29.00
96a	A9	50c	18.00	22.50
97a	A10	1g	180.00	180.00
98a	A10	2½g	*2,750.*	*3,000.*

A11

Queen Wilhelmina
A12 A13

Typo., Litho. (#114A)

1912-40 ***Perf. 12½***

No.	Type	Description	Unused	Used
101	A11	½c lt vio	.25	.25
102	A11	1c olive grn	.25	.25
103	A11	2c yellow brn	.50	.25
104	A11	2c gray blk ('30)	.50	.25
105	A11	2½c green	1.40	.25
106	A11	2½c lt red ('22)	.30	.25
107	A11	3c yellow	.50	.25
108	A11	3c green ('29)	.80	.25
109	A11	4c ultra	.75	.30
110	A11	4c dp grn ('28)	1.40	.25
111	A11	4c yellow ('30)	10.00	4.50
112	A11	5c rose	1.25	.25
113	A11	5c green ('22)	1.05	.25
114	A11	5c chlky bl ('28)	.65	.25
114A	A11	5c ultra ('40)	1.00	.25
115	A11	7½c bister	.45	.25
116	A11	10c lilac ('22)	1.10	.25
117	A12	10c car rose ('14)	.85	.25
118	A12	12½c dull bl ('14)	1.10	.25
119	A12	12½c red ('22)	1.10	.25
120	A12	15c blue ('29)	10.00	.30
121	A12	17½c red brn ('15)	1.10	.30
122	A12	20c green ('15)	2.00	.30
123	A12	20c blue ('22)	2.00	.30
124	A12	20c orange ('32)	17.00	.30
125	A12	22½c orange ('15)	2.00	.50
126	A12	25c red vio ('15)	2.00	.25
127	A12	30c slate ('15)	2.25	.25
128	A12	32½c vio & red ('22)	2.25	.25
129	A12	35c org brn ('29)	10.00	.70
130	A12	40c green ('22)	2.25	.25

Perf. 11½

Engr.

No.	Type	Description	Unused	Used
131	A13	50c green ('13)	4.75	.25
a.		Perf. 11x11½	5.00	.35
b.		Perf. 12½	5.00	.35
132	A13	60c dp blue ('22)	5.50	.25
133	A13	80c orange ('22)	4.75	.25
134	A13	1g brown ('13)	3.50	.25
a.		Perf. 11x11½	4.00	.25
135	A13	1.75g dk vio, p. 12½ ('31)	17.50	2.40
136	A13	2½g car ('13)	14.50	.50
a.		Perf. 11x11½	15.00	.75
b.		Perf. 12½	16.00	.70
		Nos. 101-136 (37)	128.55	16.90

For surcharges and overprints see Nos. 137-138, 144-150, 102a-123a, 158, 194-195, B1-B3, C1-C5.

Water Soluble Ink

Some values of types A11 and A12 and late printings of types A6 and A9 are in soluble ink. The design disappears when immersed in water.

Nos. 105, 109, 54, 59 Surcharged

1917-18 **Typo.** ***Perf. 12½***

No.	Type	Description	Unused	Used
137	A11	½c on 2½c	.30	.30
138	A11	1c on 4c ('18)	.55	.55
139	A9	17½c on 22½c ('18)	1.25	.55
a.		Inverted surcharge	350.00	425.00

Perf. 11x11½

No.	Type	Description	Unused	Used
140	A10	30c on 1g ('18)	10.00	2.25
a.		Perf. 11½x11	140.00	55.00
		Nos. 137-140 (4)	12.10	3.65

Nos. 121, 125, 131, 134 Surcharged in Red or Blue

On A12

On A13

Two types of 32½c on 50c:
I — Surcharge bars spaced as in illustration.
II — Bars more closely spaced.

1922, Jan. ***Perf. 12½***

No.	Type	Description	Unused	Used
144	A12	12½c on 17½c (R)	.30	.25
145	A12	12½c on 22½c (R)	.40	.25
146	A12	20c on 22½c (Bl)	.40	.25

Perf. 11½, 11x11½

No.	Type	Description	Unused	Used
147	A13	32½c on 50c (Bl) (I, perf. 11½)	1.25	.25
a.		Type II, perf. 11½	10.00	.25
b.		Type I, perf. 11x11½	1,000.	6.00
c.		Type II, perf. 11x11½	19.00	1.00
148	A13	40c on 50c (R)	3.75	.45
149	A13	60c on 1g (Bl)	6.00	.40
150	A13	80c on 1g (R)	6.75	.90
		Nos. 144-150 (7)	18.85	2.75

Stamps of 1912-22 Overprinted in Red, Blue, Green or Black

a

b

No. 145a

1922, Sept. 18 **Typo.** ***Perf. 12½***

No.	Type	Description	Unused	Used
102a	A11(a)	1c ol grn (R)	7.00	5.75
103a	A11(a)	2c yel brn (Bl)	7.00	5.75
106a	A11(a)	2½c lt red (G)	65.00	*72.50*
107a	A11(a)	3c yellow (R)	7.00	7.00
109a	A11(a)	4c ultra (R)	38.50	36.00
113a	A11(a)	5c green (R)	13.00	10.00
115a	A11(a)	7½c drab (Bl)	9.00	5.75
116a	A11(a)	10c lilac (Bk)	70.00	80.00
145a	A12(b)	12½c on 22½c org (Bl)	7.00	7.00
121a	A12(b)	17½c red brn (Bk)	7.00	5.75
123a	A12(b)	20c blue (Bk)	7.00	5.75
		Nos. 102a-123a (11)	237.50	241.25

Issued to publicize the 3rd Netherlands Indies Industrial Fair at Bandoeng, Java.

Nos. 102a-123a were sold at a premium for 3, 4, 5, 6, 8, 9, 10, 12½, 15, 20 and 22½ cents respectively.

Queen Wilhelmina — A15

1923, Aug. 31 **Engr.** ***Perf. 11½***

No.	Type	Description	Unused	Used
151	A15	5c myrtle green	.25	.25
a.		Perf. 11½x11	400.00	140.00
b.		Perf. 11x11½	4.50	.55
152	A15	12½c rose	.25	.25
a.		Perf. 11x11½	1.25	.25
b.		Perf. 11½x11	1.75	.25
153	A15	20c dark blue	.35	.25
a.		Perf. 11½x11	3.25	.40
154	A15	50c red orange	1.40	.60
a.		Perf. 11x11½	6.50	1.25
b.		Perf. 11½x11	2.00	.90
c.		Perf. 11	4.50	.85
155	A15	1g brown vio	2.75	.40
a.		Perf. 11½x11	7.50	.80
156	A15	2½g gray black	35.00	12.00
157	A15	5g orange brown	135.00	125.00
		Nos. 151-157 (7)	175.00	138.75

25th anniversary of the assumption of the government of the Netherlands by Queen Wilhelmina, at the age of 18.

No. 123 Surcharged

1930, Dec. 13 **Typo.** ***Perf. 12½***

No.	Type	Description	Unused	Used
158	A12	12½c on 20c bl (R)	.30	.25
a.		Inverted surcharge	375.00	475.00

Prince William I, Portrait by Van Key — A16

1933, Apr. 18 **Photo.**

No.	Type	Description	Unused	Used
163	A16	12½c deep orange	1.25	.25

400th anniv. of the birth of Prince William I, Count of Nassau and Prince of Orange, frequently referred to as William the Silent.

Rice Field Scene
A17

Queen Wilhelmina
A18

Queen Wilhelmina
A19

1933-37 **Unwmk.** ***Perf. 11½x12½***

No.	Type	Description	Unused	Used
164	A17	1c lilac gray ('34)	.25	.25
165	A17	2c plum ('34)	.25	.25
166	A17	2½c bister ('34)	.25	.25
167	A17	3c yellow grn ('34)	.25	.25
168	A17	3½c dark gray ('37)	.25	.25
169	A17	4c dk olive ('34)	1.00	.25
170	A17	5c ultra ('34)	.25	.25
171	A17	7½c violet ('34)	1.50	.25
172	A17	10c ver ('34)	2.10	.25
173	A18	10c ver ('37)	.30	.25
174	A18	12½c dp org ('34)	.30	.25
a.		12½c light orange, perf. 12½ ('33)	7.50	.40
175	A18	15c ultra ('34)	.30	.25
176	A18	20c plum ('34)	.50	.25
177	A18	25c blue grn ('34)	2.10	.25
178	A18	30c lilac gray ('34)	3.25	.25
179	A18	32½c bister ('34)	9.00	*10.00*
180	A18	35c violet ('34)	5.00	1.25
181	A18	40c yel grn ('34)	3.00	.25
182	A18	42½c yellow ('34)	3.00	.25

1934, Jan 16 ***Perf. 12½***

No.	Type	Description	Unused	Used
183	A19	50c lilac gray	5.00	.25
184	A19	60c ultra	6.00	.50
185	A19	80c vermilion	6.00	.60
186	A19	1g violet	6.25	.40
187	A19	1.75g yellow grn	20.00	15.00
188	A19	2.50g plum	22.50	2.00
		Nos. 164-188 (25)	98.60	34.25

See Nos. 200-225. For overprints and surcharges see Nos. 271-275 (in Scott Standard catalogue, Vol. 5), B48, B57 (in Scott Vol. 5).

Water Soluble Ink

Nos. 164-188 and the first printing of No. 163 have soluble ink and the design disappears when immersed in water.

Nos. C6-C7, C14, C9-C10 Surcharged in Black

a

b

1934 Typo. *Perf. 12½x11½, 12½*

189 AP1(a) 2c on 10c .30 .45
190 AP1(a) 2c on 20c .25 .25
191 AP3(b) 2c on 30c .40 .60
192 AP1(a) 42½c on 75c 4.25 .25
193 AP1(a) 42½c on 1.50g 4.25 .40
Nos. 189-193 (5) 9.45 1.95

Nos. 127-128 Surcharged with New Value in Red or Black

1937, Sept. *Perf. 12½*

194 A12 10c on 30c (R) 2.50 .25
a. Double surcharge 675.00
195 A12 10c on 32½c (Bk) 2.75 .30

Wilhelmina — A20

Perf. 12½x12

1938, Aug. 30 Photo. Wmk. 202

196 A20 2c dull purple .25 .25
197 A20 10c car lake .25 .25
198 A20 15c royal blue 1.25 .75
199 A20 20c red orange .50 .30
Nos. 196-199 (4) 2.25 1.55

40th anniv. of the reign of Queen Wilhelmina.

Types of 1933-37

1938-40 Photo. *Perf. 12½x12*

200 A17 1c lilac gray ('39) .30 *.80*
201 A17 2c plum ('39) .25 .25
202 A17 2½c bister ('39) .50 .50
203 A17 3c yellow grn ('39) 1.50 1.25
205 A17 4c gray ol ('39) 1.50 1.25
206 A17 5c ultra ('39) .25 .25
a. Perf. 12x12½ 1.25 .25
207 A17 7½c violet ('39) 2.50 1.00
208 A18 10c ver ('39) .25 .25
210 A18 15c ultra ('39) .25 .25
211 A18 20c plum ('39) .25 .25
a. Perf. 12x12½ 1.25 .25
212 A18 25c blue grn ('39) 25.00 24.00
213 A18 30c lilac gray ('39) 6.50 .80
215 A18 35c violet ('39) 2.75 .65
216 A18 40c dp yel grn ('40) 5.00 .25

Perf. 12½

218 A19 50c lilac gray ('40) 275.00
219 A19 60c ultra ('39) 10.50 1.25
220 A19 80c ver ('39) 62.50 26.00
221 A19 1g violet ('39) 27.50 .85
223 A19 2g Prus green 27.50 14.00
225 A19 5g yellow brn 25.00 6.00
Nos. 200-216,219-225 (19) 199.80 79.85

The note following No. 188 applies also to this issue.

The 50c was sold only at the philatelic window in Amsterdam.

SEMI-POSTAL STAMPS

Regular Issue of 1912-14 Surcharged in Carmine

1915, June 10 Unwmk. *Perf. 12½*

B1 A11 1c + 5c ol grn 4.50 4.50
B2 A11 5c + 5c rose 4.50 4.50
B3 A12 10c + 5c rose 7.25 7.25
Nos. B1-B3 (3) 16.25 16.25

Surtax for the Red Cross.

Bali Temple SP1

Watchtower SP2

Menangkabau Compound — SP3

Borobudur Temple, Java SP4

Perf. 11½x11, 11x11½

1930, Dec. 1 Photo.

B4 SP1 2c (+ 1c) vio & brn 1.00 .80
B5 SP2 5c (+ 2½c) dk grn & brn 4.75 2.50
B6 SP3 12½c (+ 2½c) dp red & brn 3.25 .50
B7 SP4 15c (+ 5c) ultra & brn 5.75 5.75
Nos. B4-B7 (4) 14.75 9.55

Surtax for youth care.

Farmer and Carabao SP5

5c, Fishermen. 12½c, Dancers. 15c, Musicians.

1931, Dec. 1 Engr. *Perf. 12½*

B8 SP5 2c (+ 1c) olive bis 3.00 2.00
B9 SP5 5c (+ 2½c) bl grn 4.25 3.75
B10 SP5 12½c (+ 2½c) dp red 3.25 .55
B11 SP5 15c (+ 5c) dl bl 8.25 7.00
Nos. B8-B11 (4) 18.75 13.30

The surtax was for the aid of the Leper Colony at Salatiga.

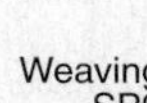
Weaving SP9

5c, Plaiting rattan. 12½c, Woman batik dyer. 15c, Coppersmith.

1932, Dec. 1 Photo. *Perf. 12½*

B12 SP9 2c (+ 1c) dp vio & bis .40 .40
B13 SP9 5c (+ 2½c) dp grn & bis 2.50 2.00
B14 SP9 12½c (+ 2½c) brt rose & bis .85 .30
B15 SP9 15c (+ 5c) bl & bis 3.25 3.00
Nos. B12-B15 (4) 7.00 5.70

The surtax was donated to the Salvation Army.

Woman and Lotus — SP13

Designs: 5c, "The Light that Shows the Way." 12½c, YMCA emblem. 15c, Jobless man.

1933, Dec. 1 *Perf. 12½*

B16 SP13 2c (+ 1c) red vio & ol bis .65 .30
B17 SP13 5c (+ 2½c) grn & ol bis 2.25 1.90
B18 SP13 12½c (+ 2½c) ver & ol bis 2.50 .30
B19 SP13 15c (+ 5c) bl & ol bis 2.75 2.00
Nos. B16-B19 (4) 8.15 4.50

The surtax was for the Amsterdam Young Men's Society for Relief of the Poor in Netherlands Indies.

Dowager Queen Emma — SP17

1934, Sept. 15 *Perf. 13x14*

B20 SP17 12½c (+ 2½c) blk brn 1.25 .45

Issued in memory of the late Dowager Queen Emma of Netherlands. The surtax was for the Anti-Tuberculosis Society.

A Pioneer at Work — SP18

Designs: 5c, Cavalryman rescuing wounded native. 12½c, Artilleryman under fire. 15c, Bugler.

1935 *Perf. 12½*

B21 SP18 2c (+ 1c) plum & ol bis 1.25 1.00
B22 SP18 5c (+ 2½c) grn & ol bis 3.25 2.25
B23 SP18 12½c (+ 2½c) red org & ol bis 3.25 .25
B24 SP18 15c (+ 5c) brt bl & ol bis 4.50 4.50
Nos. B21-B24 (4) 12.25 8.00

The surtax was for the Indies Committee of the Christian Military Association for the East and West Indies.

Child Welfare Work — SP22

1936, Dec. 1 Size: 23x20mm

B25 SP22 2c (+ 1c) plum 1.00 .60

Size: 30x26½mm

B26 SP22 5c (+ 2½c) gray vio 1.25 1.10
B27 SP22 7½c (+ 2½c) dk vio 1.25 1.25
B28 SP22 12½c (+ 2½c) red org 1.25 .30
B29 SP22 15c (+5c) brt bl 2.00 1.75
Nos. B25-B29 (5) 6.75 5.00

Surtax for Salvation Army.

Boy Scouts — SP23

1937, May 1

B30 SP23 7½c + 2½c dk ol brn 1.25 1.00
B31 SP23 12½c + 2½c rose car 1.25 .50

Fifth Boy Scout World Jamboree, Vogelenzang, Netherlands, July 31-Aug. 13, 1937. Surtax for Netherlands Indies Scout Association.

Sifting Rice — SP24

Designs: 3½c, Mother and children. 7½c, Plowing with carabao team. 10c, Carabao team and cart. 20c, Native couple.

1937, Dec. 1

B32 SP24 2c (+ 1c) dk brn & org 1.10 .80
B33 SP24 3½c (+ 1½c) gray 1.10 .80
B34 SP24 7½c (+ 2½c) Prus grn & org 1.25 .95
B35 SP24 10c (+ 2½c) car & org 1.25 .25
B36 SP24 20c (+ 5c) brt bl 1.25 1.10
Nos. B32-B36 (5) 5.95 3.90

Surtax for the Public Relief Fund for indigenous poor.

Modern Plane — SP28

Design: 20c, Plane nose facing left.

Wmk. 202

1938, Oct. 15 Photo. *Perf. 12½*

B36A SP28 17½c (+5c) olive brn .85 .85
B36B SP28 20c (+5c) slate .85 .55

10th anniversary of the Dutch East Indies Royal Air Lines (K. N. I. L. M.).

Surtax for the Aviation Fund in the Netherlands Indies.

Nun and Child
SP29 SP30

Designs: 7½c, Nurse examining child's arm. 10c, Nurse bathing baby. 20c, Nun bandaging child's head.

1938, Dec. 1 Wmk. 202 *Perf. 12½*

B37 SP29 2c (+ 1c) vio .60 .45

Perf. 11½x12

B38 SP30 3½c (+ 1½c) brt grn 1.00 .90

Perf. 12x11½

B39 SP30 7½c (+ 2½c) cop red .80 .85
B40 SP30 10c (+ 2½c) ver .90 .25
B41 SP30 20c (+ 5c) brt ultra 1.00 .95
Nos. B37-B41 (5) 4.30 3.40

The surtax was for the Central Mission Bureau in Batavia.

Social Workers SP34

Indonesian Nurse Tending Patient SP35

European Nurse Tending Patient — SP36

Perf. 13x11½, 11½x13

1939, Dec. 1 Photo.

B42 SP34 2c (+ 1c) purple .25 .25
B43 SP35 3½c (+ 1½c) bl grn & pale bl grn .30 .25
B44 SP34 7½c (+ 2½c) cop brn .25 .25
B45 SP35 10c (+ 2½c) scar & pink 1.40 .80

B46 SP36 10c (+ 2½c) scar 1.40 .80
B47 SP36 20c (+ 5c) dk bl .40 .35
Nos. B42-B47 (6) 4.00 2.70

No. B44 shows native social workers.

Nos. B45 and B46 were issued se-tenant vertically and horizontally. The surtax was used for the Bureau of Social Service.

No. 174 Surcharged in Brown

1940, Dec. 2 Unwmk. ***Perf. 12x12½***
B48 A18 10c + 5c on 12½c dp org 1.10 .40

AIR POST STAMPS

Regular Issues of 1913-1923 Surcharged in Black or Blue

Nos. 119 & 126 Surcharged

No. 133 Surcharged

No. 134 Surcharged

No. 136 Surcharged

Perf. 12½, 11½

1928, Sept. 20 Unwmk.
C1 A12 10c on 12½c red 1.00 1.00
C2 A12 20c on 25c red vio 2.25 2.25
C3 A13 40c on 80c org 1.90 1.50
C4 A13 75c on 1g brn (Bl) .90 .55
C5 A13 1½g on 2½g car 6.25 5.50
Nos. C1-C5 (5) 12.30 10.80

On Nos. C4 and C5 there are stars over the original values and the airplane is of different shape. On No. C3 there are no bars under "OST."

Planes over Temple AP1

1928, Dec. 1 Litho. ***Perf. 12½x11½***
C6 AP1 10c red violet .30 .25
C7 AP1 20c brown .85 .55
C8 AP1 40c rose 1.00 .55
C9 AP1 75c green 2.25 .25
C10 AP1 1.50g orange 4.00 .50
Nos. C6-C10 (5) 8.40 2.10

For surcharges see Nos. 189-190, 192-193, C11-C12, C17.

No. C8 Surcharged in Black or Green

1930-32
C11 AP1 30c on 40c rose .90 .25
C12 AP1 30c on 40c rose (G) ('32) 1.25 .25

Pilot at Controls of Plane AP2

1931, Apr. 1 Photo. ***Perf. 12½***
C13 AP2 1g blue & brown 11.00 11.00

Issued for the first air mail flight from Java to Australia.

Landscape and Garudas AP3

1931, May
C14 AP3 30c red violet 2.25 .25
C15 AP3 4½g bright blue 8.00 3.00
C16 AP3 7½g yellow green 10.00 3.25
Nos. C14-C16 (3) 20.25 6.50

For surcharge see No. 191.

No. C10 Surcharged in Blue

1932, July 21 ***Perf. 12½x11½***
C17 AP1 50c on 1.50g org 2.50 .40
a. Inverted surcharge *1,800. 2,000.*

Airplane AP4

1933, Oct. 18 Photo. ***Perf. 12½***
C18 AP4 30c deep blue 2.10 1.75

MARINE INSURANCE STAMPS

Floating Safe Attracting Gulls — MI1

Floating Safe with Night Flare — MI2

Artistic Fantasy of Floating Safe — MI3

Perf. 11½

1921, Nov. 1 Unwmk. Engr.
GY1 MI1 15c slate green 2.25 *40.00*
GY2 MI1 60c rose 4.00 *50.00*
GY3 MI1 75c gray brn 4.00 *55.00*
GY4 MI2 1.50g dark blue 25.00 *250.00*
GY5 MI2 2.25g org brn 32.50 *350.00*
GY6 MI3 4½g black 65.00 *600.00*
GY7 MI3 7½g red 80.00 *700.00*
Nos. GY1-GY7 (7) 212.75 *2,045.*

POSTAGE DUE STAMPS

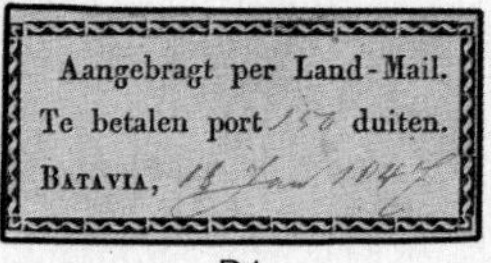

D1

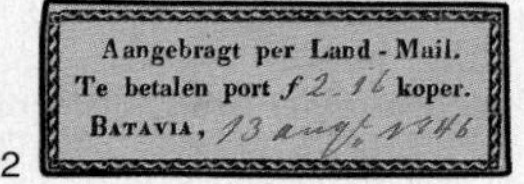

D2

1845-46 Unwmk. Typeset ***Imperf.***
Bluish Paper
J1 D1 black ('46) *1,650.*
J2 D2 black *2,000.*
a. "Maill" instead of "Mail" *3,200.*

D3

Perf. 12½x12, 13x14, 10½x12

1874 Typo.
J3 D3 5c ocher 300.00 275.00
J4 D3 10c green, *yel* 120.00 100.00
J5 D3 15c ocher, *org* 25.00 20.00
a. Perf. 11½x12 40.00 40.00
J6 D3 20c green, *blue* 40.00 17.50
a. Perf. 11½x12 80.00 25.00
Nos. J3-J6 (4) 485.00 412.50

D4

Type I — 34 loops. "T" of "Betalen" over center of loop, top branch of "E" of "Te" shorter than lower branch.

Type II — 33 loops. "T" of "Betalen" over center of two loops.

Type III — 32 loops. "T" of "Betalen" slightly to the left of loop, top branch of first "E" of "Betalen" shorter than lower branch.

Type IV — 37 loops and letters of "PORT" larger than in the other three types.

Value in Black

Perf. 11½x12, 12½, 12½x12, 13½

1882-88 Type III
J7 D4 2½c carmine .40 1.10
J8 D4 5c carmine .25 .40
J9 D4 10c carmine 2.50 3.00
J10 D4 15c carmine 3.00 3.00
J11 D4 20c carmine 135.00 1.00
J12 D4 30c carmine 1.75 2.50
J13 D4 40c carmine 1.25 2.00
J14 D4 50c deep salmon .75 .60
J15 D4 75c carmine .45 .50
Nos. J7-J15 (9) 145.35 14.10

Type I

J7a D4 2½c carmine .40 1.10
J8a D4 5c carmine .25 .45
J9a D4 10c carmine 3.25 4.00
J10a D4 15c carmine 3.25 3.50
J11a D4 20c carmine 95.00 .50
J12a D4 30c carmine 3.25 4.00
J13a D4 40c carmine 1.40 2.00
J14a D4 50c deep salmon .80 .60
J15a D4 75c carmine .50 .60
Nos. J7a-J15a (9) 108.10 16.75

Type II

J7b D4 2½c carmine .50 1.40
J8b D4 5c carmine .25 .50
J9b D4 10c carmine 3.50 4.50
J10b D4 15c carmine 3.75 4.00
J11b D4 20c carmine 165.00 1.00
J12b D4 30c carmine 7.00 7.50
J13b D4 40c carmine 1.50 2.50
J14b D4 50c deep salmon .85 .75
J15b D4 75c carmine .65 .85
Nos. J7b-J15b (9) 183.00 23.00

Type IV

J7c D4 2½c carmine 2.25 3.00
J8c D4 5c carmine 1.00 1.75
J9c D4 10c carmine 20.00 24.00
J10c D4 15c carmine 13.00 14.00
J11c D4 20c carmine 250.00 9.00
J13c D4 40c carmine 2.50 3.50
J14c D4 50c deep salmon 15.00 *20.00*
J15c D4 75c carmine 1.25 2.50
Nos. J7c-J15c (8) 305.00 77.75

D5

1892-95 Type I ***Perf. 12½***
J16 D5 10c carmine 2.25 .30
J17 D5 15c carmine ('95) 12.00 1.75
J18 D5 20c carmine 2.00 .25
Nos. J16-J18 (3) 16.25 2.30

Type III

J16a D5 10c dull red 2.75 2.00
J18a D5 20c dull red 3.75 1.40

Type II

J16b D5 10c dull red 13.00 13.00
J18b D5 20c dull red 18.00 6.50

1906-09 Type I
J19 D5 2½c carmine ('08) .50 .30
J20 D5 5c carmine ('09) 2.25 .25
J21 D5 30c carmine 17.50 5.75
J22 D5 40c carmine ('09) 12.50 1.50
J23 D5 50c carmine ('09) 8.50 .90
J24 D5 75c carmine ('09) 17.00 4.00
Nos. J19-J24 (6) 58.25 12.70

Value in Color of Stamp

1913-39 ***Perf. 12½***
J25 D5 1c salmon ('39) .25 *1.25*
J26 D5 2½c salmon .25 .25
J27 D5 3½c salmon ('39) .25 *1.25*
J28 D5 5c salmon .25 .25
J29 D5 7½c salmon ('22) .25 .25
J30 D5 10c salmon .25 .25
J31 D5 12½c salmon ('22) 2.75 .25
J32 D5 15c salmon 2.75 .25
J33 D5 20c salmon .25 .25
J34 D5 25c salmon ('22) .25 .25
J35 D5 30c salmon .25 .25
J36 D5 37½c salmon ('30) 22.50 22.50
J37 D5 40c salmon .25 .25
J38 D5 50c salmon 1.40 .25
J39 D5 75c salmon 2.50 .25
Nos. J25-J39 (15) 34.40 28.00

Thick White Paper
Invisible Gum
Numerals Slightly Larger

1941 Litho. ***Perf. 12½***
J25a D5 1c light red .60 *2.00*
J28a D5 5c light red .65 1.00
J30a D5 10c light red 10.50 10.00
J32a D5 15c light red 1.00 1.00
J33a D5 20c light red .80 .80
J35a D5 30c light red 1.25 1.00
J37a D5 40c light red 1.00 .80
Nos. J25a-J37a (7) 15.80 16.60

No. J36 Surcharged with New Value

1937, Oct. 1 Unwmk. ***Perf. 12½***
J40 D5 20c on 37½c salmon .25 .30

D6

1939-40
J41 D6 1g salmon 5.00 7.50
J42 D6 1g blue ('40) .30 *4.50*
a. 1g lt bl, thick paper, invisible gum .90 *1.00*

OFFICIAL STAMPS

Regular Issues of 1883-1909 Overprinted

Perf. 12½

1911, Oct. 1 Typo. Unwmk.
O1 A6 ½c violet .25 .30
O2 A6 1c olive grn .25 .25
O3 A6 2c yellow brn .25 .25
O4 A3 2½c yellow .75 .75
O5 A6 2½c blue grn 1.40 1.25
O6 A6 3c orange .40 .40
O7 A6 4c ultra .25 .25
O8 A6 5c rose red .80 .80
b. Double overprint *325.00*
O9 A6 7½c gray 2.75 2.75
O10 A9 10c slate .25 .25
O11 A9 12½c deep blue 2.00 2.25

O12	A9	15c chocolate	.65	.65
a.		Overprinted with two bars	32.50	
b.		As "a," "Dienst" inverted	52.50	
O13	A9	17½c bister	2.75	2.50
O14	A9	20c olive grn	.60	.50
O15	A9	22½c brn & ol grn	3.50	3.00
O16	A9	25c violet	2.00	2.00
O17	A9	30c orange brn	.90	.60
O18	A9	50c red brown	12.00	7.00
O19	A10	1g dull lilac	3.00	1.25
O20	A10	2½g slate blue	27.50	30.00
		Nos. O1-O20 (20)	62.25	57.00

The overprint reads diagonally downward on Nos. O1-O3 and O5-O9.

Overprint Inverted

O1a	A6	½c	45.00	*125.00*
O2a	A6	1c	3.00	*19.00*
O3a	A6	2c	3.00	*20.00*
O5a	A6	2½c	9.00	*30.00*
O6a	A6	3c	110.00	*40.00*
O8a	A6	5c	3.00	*20.00*
O10a	A9	10c	3.00	*7.00*
O11a	A9	12½c	32.50	*55.00*
O14a	A9	20c	175.00	70.00
O16a	A9	25c	*1,250.*	*1,000.*
O17a	A9	30c	225.00	140.00
O18a	A9	50c	32.50	32.50
O19a	A10	1g	*525.00*	*850.00*
O20a	A10	2½g	225.00	*625.00*

Regular Issue of 1892-1894 Overprinted

1911, Oct. 1

O21	A4	10c orange brn	1.25	.60
O22	A4	12½c gray	3.00	*5.50*
O23	A4	15c bister	3.00	3.00
O24	A4	20c blue	3.00	1.00
O25	A4	25c lilac	12.00	10.00
O26	A4	50c carmine	2.50	1.25
O27	A4	2.50g org brn & bl	55.00	55.00
		Nos. O21-O27 (7)	79.75	76.35

Inverted Overprints

O21a	A4	10c	15.00	*50.00*
O22a	A4	12½c	425.00	*400.00*
O23a	A4	15c	425.00	*325.00*
O24a	A4	20c	165.00	*175.00*
O25a	A4	25c	800.00	*900.00*
O26a	A4	50c	15.00	*75.00*
O27a	A4	2.50g	1,150.	*1,450.*

NEVIS

ˈnē-vəs

LOCATION — West Indies, southeast of Puerto Rico
GOVT. — Presidency of the Leeward Islands Colony (British)
AREA — 50 sq. mi.
POP. — 9,800 (1990)
CAPITAL — Charlestown

Nevis stamps were discontinued in 1890 and replaced by those of the Leeward Islands. From 1903 to 1956 stamps of St. Kitts-Nevis and Leeward Islands were used concurrently.

See Leeward Islands and St. Kitts-Nevis.

12 Pence = 1 Shilling

PRE-STAMP POSTAL MARKINGS

Crowned Circle handstamp type VI is pictured in the Crowned Circle Handstamps and Great Britain Used Abroad section.

Charlestown

1852

A1 VI "Nevis" crowned circle handstamp in red, on cover — *6,500.*

The handstamp was used, in black, as a provisional to 1886.

STAMPS OF GREAT BRITAIN USED IN NEVIS

Numeral cancellation type A is pictured in the Crowned Circle Handstamps and Great Britain Used Abroad section.

1858-60

A09 (Charlestown)

A2	A	1p rose red (#20)	700.00
A3	A	2p blue (#29, P7, 8)	2,250.
A4	A	4p rose (#26)	500.00
A5	A	6p lilac (#27)	350.00
A6	A	1sh green (#28)	2,750.

Issued under British Administration

Unused examples of Nos. 1-8 almost always have no original gum, and they are valued without gum. These stamps with original gum are worth more. Other issues are valued with original gum as defined in the catalogue introduction. Very fine examples of Nos. 1-8, will have perforations touching the design on at least one side due to the narrow spacing of the stamps on the plates. Stamps with perfs clear of the design on all four sides are scarce and will command higher prices.

Medicinal Spring
A1 A2

A3 A4

1861 Unwmk. Engr. *Perf. 13*

Bluish Wove Paper

1	A1	1p lake rose	325.00	140.00
2	A2	4p dull rose	950.00	200.00
3	A3	6p gray	775.00	260.00
4	A4	1sh green	1,100.	250.00

Grayish Wove Paper

5	A1	1p lake rose	110.00	60.00
6	A2	4p dull rose	175.00	80.00
7	A3	6p lilac gray	175.00	65.00
8	A4	1sh green	400.00	95.00

1867 White Wove Paper *Perf. 15*

9	A1	1p red	65.00	55.00
10	A2	4p orange	155.00	25.00
11	A4	1sh yellow green	925.00	125.00
a.		Imperf.		*7,500.*
12	A4	1sh blue green	325.00	45.00

Laid Paper

13	A4	1sh yel green	*25,000.*	6,750.
		Manuscript cancel		3,000.

No. 13 values are for stamps with design cut into on one or two sides.

1876 Wove Paper Litho.

14	A1	1p rose	32.50	25.00
14A	A1	1p red	45.00	30.00
b.		1p vermilion	45.00	45.00
c.		Imperf., pair	*1,900.*	
d.		Half used as ½p on cover		*4,500.*
15	A2	4p orange	190.00	45.00
a.		Imperf.		
b.		Vert. pair, imperf. between	*12,750.*	
16	A3	6p olive gray	250.00	250.00
17	A4	1sh gray green	100.00	*125.00*
a.		1sh dark green	135.00	*175.00*
b.		Horiz. strip of 3, perf. all around & imperf. btwn.	*20,000.*	

Perf. 11½

18	A1	1p vermilion	65.00	60.00
a.		Horiz. pair, imperf. btwn.		
b.		Half used as ½p on cover		*4,500.*
c.		Imperf., pair	1,000.	
		Nos. 14-18 (6)	682.50	535.00

Queen Victoria — A5

1879-80 Typo. Wmk. 1 *Perf. 14*

19	A5	1p violet ('80)	90.00	55.00
a.		Diagonal half used as ½p on cover		*1,500.*
20	A5	2½p red brown	175.00	100.00

1882-90 Wmk. Crown and CA (2)

21	A5	½p green ('83)	14.00	*27.50*
22	A5	1p violet	125.00	50.00
a.		Half used as ½p on cover		900.00
23	A5	1p rose ('83)	42.50	*35.00*
a.		1p carmine ('84)	20.00	20.00
24	A5	2½p red brown	140.00	55.00
25	A5	2½p ultra ('84)	24.00	27.50
26	A5	4p blue	400.00	55.00
27	A5	4p gray ('84)	25.00	10.00
28	A5	6p green ('83)	500.00	400.00
29	A5	6p brown org ('86)	27.50	*77.50*
30	A5	1sh violet ('90)	125.00	*225.00*
		Nos. 21-30 (10)	1,423.	*962.50*

Half of No. 22 Surcharged in Black or Violet

1883

31	A5	½p on half of 1p	1,100.	60.00
a.		Double surcharge		450.00
b.		Unsevered pair	*7,500.*	
c.		Surcharged on half of 1p revenue stamp		600.00
32	A5	½p on half of 1p (V)	1,250.	55.00
a.		Double surcharge		450.00
b.		Unsevered pair	*7,500.*	850.00
c.		Surcharged on half of 1p revenue stamp		600.00

Surcharge reads up or down.

NEW BRITAIN

ˈnü ˈbri-tᵊn

LOCATION — South Pacific Ocean, northeast of New Guinea
GOVT. — Australian military government
AREA — 13,000 sq. mi. (approx.)
POP. — 50,600 (approx.)
CAPITAL — Rabaul

The island Neu-Pommern, a part of former German New Guinea, was captured during World War I by Australian troops and named New Britain. Following the war it was mandated to Australia and designated a part of the Mandated Territory of New Guinea. See German New Guinea, North West Pacific Islands and New Guinea.

12 Pence = 1 Shilling

Stamps of German New Guinea, 1900, Surcharged

Kaiser's Yacht "The Hohenzollern"
A3 A4

First Setting

Surcharge lines spaced 6mm on 1p-8p, 4mm on 1sh-5sh

Perf. 14, 14½

1914, Oct. 17 Unwmk.

1	A3	1p on 3pf brown	750.00	*875.00*
a.		"1" for "I"	2,200.	2,500.
b.		Short "1"	2,200.	
c.		"1" with straight top serif	2,200.	
d.		"I" for "1" (setting 12)	3,800.	
2	A3	1p on 5pf green	95.00	*200.00*
a.		"1" for "I"	385.00	475.00
b.		Short "1"	385.00	465.00
c.		"1" with straight top serif (settings 6 & 9)	525.00	600.00
3	A3	2p on 10pf car	100.00	*260.00*
a.		"1" for "I"	440.00	550.00
4	A3	2p on 20pf ultra	100.00	*200.00*
a.		"2d." dbl., "G.R.I." omitted	*6,000.*	
b.		Inverted surcharge	16,500.	
c.		"1" for "I"	425.00	475.00
5	A3	2½p on 10pf car	105.00	*220.00*
a.		Fraction bar omitted (setting 9)	3,800.	3,850.
6	A3	2½p on 20pf ultra	120.00	*250.00*
a.		Inverted surcharge		
b.		Fraction bar omitted (setting 9)		10,500.
7	A3	3p on 25pf org & blk, *yel*	375.00	*475.00*
a.		"1" for "I"	1,200.	1,400.
8	A3	3p on 30pf org & blk, *sal*	475.00	*525.00*
a.		Double surcharge	*15,000.*	*15,000.*
b.		Triple surcharge		
c.		"1" for "I"	1,400.	1,650.
9	A3	4p on 40pf lake & black	475.00	*625.00*
a.		Double surcharge	4,100.	*5,000.*
b.		Inverted surcharge	*16,250.*	
c.		"4d." omitted		
d.		"1" for "I"	1,625.	
10	A3	5p on 50pf pur & blk, *sal*	850.00	*1,100.*
a.		Double surcharge	*16,250.*	
b.		"1" for "I"	2,500.	3,250.
11	A3	8p on 80pf lake & blk, *rose*	1,050.	*1,650.*
a.		No period after "8d"	*4,600.*	
b.		Surcharged "G.R.I. 4d" (error)	*15,250.*	
c.		"1" for "I"	3,500.	4,600.
12	A4	1sh on 1m car	5,500.	*4,750.*
a.		Large "s"	13,000.	*13,000.*
13	A4	2sh on 2m blue	3,750.	*4,500.*
a.		Surcharged "G.R.I. 5s" (error)	*45,000.*	
b.		Surcharged "G.R.I. 2d" corrected by handstamped "s"	*55,000.*	
c.		Large "s"	12,500.	15,000.
14	A4	3sh on 3m blk vio	6,000.	*7,750.*
a.		No period after "I"	14,000.	*14,000.*
b.		Large "s"	16,500.	
15	A4	5sh on 5m slate & car	14,000.	*16,500.*
a.		No period after "I"	18,500.	21,000.
b.		Surcharged "G.R.I. 1s" (error)	*87,500.*	
c.		Large "s"	*30,000.*	

"G.R.I." stands for Georgius Rex Imperator.

Second Setting

Surcharge lines spaced 5mm on 1p-8p, 5½mm on 1sh-5sh

1914, Dec. 16

16	A3	1p on 3pf brown	95.00	*100.00*
a.		Double surcharge	1,500.	*1,850.*
b.		"I" for "1"	825.00	
c.		"1" with straight top serif	140.00	170.00
d.		Inverted surcharge	6,000.	—
e.		"4" for "1"	*17,500.*	
f.		Small "1"	350.00	
g.		Double surcharge, one inverted	*8,000.*	
17	A3	1p on 5pf green	35.00	*55.00*
a.		Double surcharge	5,250.	
b.		"G. I. R."	*13,000.*	*14,000.*
c.		"d" inverted		3,750.
d.		No periods after "G R I"		*11,000.*
e.		Small "1"	140.00	210.00
f.		"1d" double		—
g.		No period after "1d"		
h.		Triple surcharge		
i.		No periods or spaces in "GRI"	*11,000.*	
j.		"1" with straight top serif	55.00	90.00
k.		"1d" inverted		*11,000.*
18	A3	2p on 10pf car	50.00	*65.00*
a.		Double surcharge	*16,250.*	*16,250.*
b.		Dbl. surch., one inverted		*13,000.*
c.		Surcharged "G. I. R., 3d" (error)	*13,000.*	
d.		Surcharged "1d" (error)	*12,000.*	*11,000.*
e.		Period before "G"	*11,000.*	
f.		No period after "2d"	200.00	*275.00*
g.		Inverted surcharge		
h.		"2d" double, one inverted		
j.		Pair, #18, 20	*30,000.*	
k.		Vertical pair, #18, 20	*22,000.*	
19	A3	2p on 20pf ultra	50.00	*75.00*
a.		Double surcharge	3,500.	*4,750.*
b.		Double surch., one inverted	5,000.	*6,500.*
c.		"R" inverted		*9,250.*
d.		Surcharged "1d" (error)	*13,000.*	*14,000.*
f.		Inverted surcharge	10,500.	
h.		Pair, one without surcharge	25,000.	
i.		Vertical pair, #19, 21	20,000.	23,000.
j.		No period after "d"	140.00	210.00
k.		No period after "I"	1,650.	
20	A3	2½p on 10pf car	250.00	375.00
21	A3	2½p on 20pf ultra	2,100.	*2,500.*
a.		Double surcharge, one invtd.		
b.		"2½" triple		
c.		Surcharged "3d" in pair with normal	*42,500.*	
22	A3	3p on 25pf org & blk, *yel*	190.00	*275.00*
a.		Double surcharge	*11,000.*	*13,000.*
b.		Inverted surcharge	*11,000.*	*13,000.*
c.		"G. R. I." only		
d.		"G. I. R."		
e.		Pair, one without surcharge	*15,000.*	
f.		Surcharged "G. I. R., 5d" (error)		
g.		Surcharged "1d" (error)	*22,000.*	
h.		Thick "3"	650.00	825.00

23 A3 3p on 30pf org & blk, *sal* 175.00 *220.00*
a. Double surcharge 4,000. *4,600.*
b. Double surcharge, one invtd. 4,500. *5,500.*
c. "d" inverted
d. Surcharged "1d" (error) *12,000.* *14,000.*
e. Triple surcharge
g. Double inverted surcharge *13,000.* *14,000.*
h. Pair, one without surcharge *14,000.*
i. No period after "3d" 875.00
j. Thick "3" 600.00
k. Inverted surcharge 10,000.

24 A3 4p on 40pf lake & blk 185.00 *300.00*
a. Double surcharge 3,500. —
b. Double surcharge, both invtd. *13,000.*
c. Double surcharge, one invtd. 5,250.
d. Inverted surcharge 9,250.
e. Surcharged "1d" (error) 9,000.
f. "1" on "4"
g. As "e," inverted *20,000.*
h. Surcharge "G.R.I. 3d," double (error) *27,500.*
i. No period after "I" 3,500.

25 A3 5p on 50pf pur & blk, *sal* 350.00 *400.00*
a. Double surcharge 4,500. *5,500.*
b. Double surcharge, one invtd. *10,500.* *10,500.*
c. "5" omitted
d. Inverted surcharge 10,000. *10,000.*
e. Double inverted surcharge 13,000. *14,000.*
f. "G. I. R."
g. Surcharge "G.R.I. 3d" (error) *23,000.*
h. Thin "5" 1,200. 2,750.

26 A3 8p on 80pf lake & blk, *rose* 475.00 *650.00*
a. Double surcharge 7,000. *8,250.*
b. Double surcharge, one invtd. 7,000. *8,250.*
c. Triple surcharge 9,500. *10,000.*
d. No period after "8d"
e. Inverted surcharge *14,000.* 14,000.
f. Surcharged "3d" (error) *18,500.* *18,500.*

27 A4 1sh on 1m car 5,250. *7,750.*
a. No period after "I" *12,000.*

28 A4 2sh on 2m bl 5,500. *8,750.*
a. Surcharged "5s" (error)
b. Double surcharge
c. No period after "I" *13,000.*

29 A4 3sh on 3m blk vio 10,000. *16,250.*
a. No periods after "R I"
b. "G.R.I." double *45,000.*

29C A4 5sh on 5m sl & car *42,500.* *45,000.*
d. No periods after "R I"
e. Surcharged "1s"

Nos. 18-19 Surcharged with Large "1"

1915, Jan.

29F A3 1(p) on 2p on 10pf carmine *32,500.* *30,000.*
29G A3 1(p) on 2p on 20pf ultramarine *30,000.* *17,500.*

Same Surcharge on Stamps of Marshall Islands

1914

30 A3 1p on 3pf brn 110.00 *170.00*
a. Inverted surcharge 9,250.
b. "1" with straight top serif 185.00 325.00
c. ".G.R.I." and "1" with straight top serif *14,000.*

31 A3 1p on 5pf green 90.00 *130.00*
a. Double surcharge 3,800. *5,000.*
b. No period after "d"
c. Inverted surcharge 5,250.
d. "1" with straight top serif 155.00 175.00
e. "I" for "1" 1,300.
f. Space between "1" and "d" 325.00 350.00

32 A3 2p on 10pf car 27.50 *50.00*
a. Double surcharge 3,800.
b. Double surcharge, one invtd. 5,500.
c. Surcharge sideways 10,500.
d. No period after "2d"
e. No period after "G" 875.00
f. Inverted surcharge 7,000.

33 A3 2p on 20 pf ultra 30.00 *50.00*
a. No period after "d" 80.00 *150.00*
b. Double surcharge 4,000. 5,250.
c. Double surcharge, one invtd. *9,750.* *10,500.*
d. Inverted surcharge *11,000.* *11,000.*
e. "I" omitted

34 A3 3p on 25pf org & blk, *yel* 475.00 *600.00*
a. Double surcharge 4,250. *5,000.*
b. Double surcharge, one invtd. 4,700.
c. No period after "d" 925.00 1,250.
d. Inverted surcharge 13,000.
e. Thick "3" 1,250. 1,500.

35 A3 3p on 30pf org & blk, *sal* 475.00 *600.00*
a. No period after "d" 925.00 1,200.
b. Inverted surcharge 9,000. 9,500.
c. Double surcharge 7,000.
d. Double surcharge, one invtd.
e. Thick "3" 1,250.

36 A3 4p on 40pf lake & blk 175.00 *250.00*
a. No period after "d" 475.00 *700.00*
b. Double surcharge 7,000. *8,000.*
c. "4d" omitted
d. "1d" on "4d"
e. No period after "R"
f. Inverted surcharge 9,750.
g. Surcharged "1d" (error) *17,500.*
h. Surcharged "G.R.I. 3d" double (error)
i. "d" omitted *7,750.*
j. Triple surcharge *14,000.*
k. Surcharged "3d" *17,500.*

37 A3 5p on 50pf pur & blk, *sal* 300.00 *375.00*
a. "d" omitted 2,250.
b. Double surcharge *10,500.*
c. "5d" double
d. Inverted surcharge *16,500.*
e. Thin "5" 4,000.

38 A3 8p on 80pf lake & blk, *rose* 525.00 775.00
a. Inverted surcharge *10,500.*
b. Double surcharge *10,000.*
c. Double surcharge, one invtd.
d. Triple surcharge *16,500.*
e. Double surcharge, both inverted *13,250.* *14,000.*

39 A4 1sh on 1m car 4,100. *5,500.*
a. Double surcharge *45,000.*
b. Dbl. surch., one with "s1" for "1s"
c. No period after "I" 6,500. 9,250.
d. Additional surcharge "1d" *50,000.*

40 A4 2sh on 2m blue 2,000. 4,500.
a. Double surcharge, one invtd. *45,000.* *45,000.*
b. Double surcharge *45,000.*
c. Large "S"
d. No period after "I" 3,750. *6,500.*

41 A4 3sh on 3m blk vio 6,500. *9,750.*
a. Double surcharge *42,500.* *45,000.*
b. No period after "I" 8,750.
c. No period after "R I"
d. Inverted surcharge

42 A4 5sh on 5m sl & car *14,000.* *15,000.*
a. Double surcharge, one invtd. *75,000.*

See Nos. 44-45.

A5

Surcharged in Black on Registration Label

Town Name in Sans-Serif Letters

1914 *Perf. 12*

43 A5 3p black & red (Rabaul) 300.00 *350.00*
a. Double surcharge (Rabaul) 5,500. *7,000.*
b. "(Deutsch-Neuguinea)" 475.00 600.00
c. No bracket before "Deutsch" 1,000. 1,400.
d. No bracket after "Neuguinea" 1,500. 2,250.
e. No bracket and double surcharge *16,500.*
f. "G.R.I. 3d" double *16,500.* *16,500.*
g. "G.R.I. 3d" inverted *16,500.*
h. No period after "I" 1,000.

44 A5 3p black & red (Friedrich Wilhelms-haven) 275.00 *875.00*
a. No period after "d" 475.00
b. "G" omitted 8,000.
c. Inverted surcharge *16,500.*
d. "(Deutsch-Neuguinea)" 300.00 875.00
e. As "d", no period after "d" 525.00

45 A5 3p black & red (Herbert-shohe) 325.00 *825.00*
a. No period after "d" 525.00
b. No period after "I" 1,000. 2,000.
c. "G" omitted 8,750.
d. Surcharge omitted (in horiz. pair with normal) 18,500.
e. "(Deutsch Neu-Guinea)" 550.00 1,100.
f. "(Deutsch-Neuguinea)"

46 A5 3p black & red (Kawieng) 350.00 *700.00*
a. Double surcharge
b. No period after "d" 600.00
c. "G.R.I." double 8,000.
d. "3d" double 8,250.
e. "G" omitted 8,750.
f. "(Deutsch-Neuguinea)" 1,100.
g. As "f", no bracket after "Neuguinea" 4,100.

47 A5 3p black & red (Kieta) 500.00 *875.00*
a. Pair, one without surcharge *16,500.*
b. No bracket before "Deutsch" 1,750. 3,000.
c. No period after "d" 925.00
d. No period after "I" 1,400.
e. "G" omitted 8,250.

48 A5 3p black & red (Manus) 325.00 *925.00*
a. Double surcharge *9,250.*
b. No bracket before "Deutsch" 1,300. 2,500.

49 A5 3p black & red (Deulon) 27,500. *30,000.*

50 A5 3p black & red (Stephan-sort) *4,500.*
a. No period after "d" 8,750.

Town Name in Letters with Serifs

44f Friedrich Wilhelm-shafen "(Deutsch-Newguinea)" 300.00 825.00
g. As (f), no period after "d" 500.00 1,200.
h. As (f), no period after "I" 925.00 1,750.
i. As (f), no bracket before "Deutsch" 1,500. 2,500.
j. As (f), no bracket after "Neuguinea" 1,500. 2,500.
46h Kawieng "(Deutsch Newguinea)" 300.00 725.00
i. As (h), no period after "d" 500.00
j. As (h), no period after "I"
48c Manus "(Deutsch-Newguinea)" 4,500. 5,500.
d. As (c), no period after "I" 8,750. 8,250.

Nos. 32-33 Surcharged with Large "1"

1915

51 A3 1p on 2p on 10pf 275. 300.
a. "1" double *16,500.*
b. "1" inverted *20,000.* *20,000.*
c. Small "1" 650.00

52 A3 1p on 2p on 20pf 4,000. 2,750.
a. "1" inverted *20,000.* *20,000.*
b. On #33a 10,000. 4,500.

The stamps of Marshall Islands surcharged "G. R. I." and new values in British currency were all used in New Britain and are therefore listed here.

Stamps of Marshall Islands Surcharged

Surcharge lines spaced 6mm apart

53 A3 1p on 3pf brown *3,750.*
a. Inverted surcharge *16,000.*
54 A3 1p on 5pf green *3,750.*
a. Inverted surcharge *16,500.*
55 A3 2p on 10pf car *4,750.*
56 A3 2p on 20pf ultra *4,250.*
a. Inverted surcharge *17,000.*
57 A3 2½p on 10pf car *30,000.*
58 A3 2½p on 20pf ultra *45,000.*
59 A3 3p on 25pf org & blk, *yel* *7,000.*
60 A3 3p on 30pf org & blk, *sal* *7,000.*
61 A3 4p on 40pf lake & blk *7,000.*
a. Inverted surcharge *18,000.*
62 A3 5p on 50pf pur & blk, *sal* *6,500.*
63 A3 8p on 80pf lake & blk, *rose* *7,500.*
a. Inverted surcharge *20,000.*

Surcharge lines spaced 5 ½mm apart

64 A4 1sh on 1m car *17,500.*
a. Large "S" *22,500.*
65 A4 2sh on 2m bl *14,500.*
a. Large "S" *20,000.*
66 A4 3sh on 3m blk vi-ol *30,000.*
a. Large "S" *40,000.*
67 A4 5sh on 5m sl & car *45,000.*
a. Large "S" *52,500.*

OFFICIAL STAMPS

O1

German New Guinea Nos. 7-8 Surcharged

1915 **Unwmk.** ***Perf. 14***

O1 O1 1p on 3pf brown 35.00 *80.00*
a. Double surcharge 5,500.
b. "1" and "d" spaced 100.00 190.00
O2 O1 1p on 5pf green 110.00 *150.00*
a. "1" and "d" spaced 210.00 325.00

NEW CALEDONIA

'nü ˌka-lə-'dō-nyə

LOCATION — Island in the South Pacific Ocean, east of Queensland, Australia
GOVT. — French Overseas Territory
AREA — 7,375 sq. mi.
POP. — 147,200 (est. 1984)
CAPITAL — Noumea

Dependencies of New Caledonia are the Loyalty Islands, Isle of Pines, Huon Islands and Chesterfield Islands.

100 Centimes = 1 Franc

STAMPS OF FRENCH COLONIES USED IN NEW CALEDONIA

1859-65 Typo. Unwmk. ***Imperf.***

Eagle and Crown Type A1

A4 1c olive green, *pale blue* ('62) (#1) 60.00
Noumea c.d.s. 110.00
On cover, from —
A5 5c yel grn, *grnsh* ('62) (#2) 55.00
Noumea c.d.s. 90.00
On cover, from 2,850.
A6 10c bister, *yel* (#3) 45.00
Noumea c.d.s. 90.00
On cover, from 1,750.
A7 20c bl, *bluish* ('65) (#4) 42.50
Noumea c.d.s. 85.00
On cover, from 1,150.
A8 40c org, *yelsh* (#5) 50.00
Noumea c.d.s. 90.00
On cover, from 1,650.
A9 80c car rose, *pnksh* ('65) (#6) 90.00
Noumea c.d.s. 150.00
On cover, from —

Values are for stamps cancelled with the losange of dots.

Rare stamps and covers of the French Colonies General Issues should be accompanied by certificates of authenticity issued by competent authorities and committees.

1871-72 ***Imperf.***

Ceres Type A4, Napoleon III Types A2, A3, A5

A10 1c ol grn, *pale bl* ('72) (#7) 225.00
On cover —
A11 5c yel grn, *grnsh* ('72) (#8) 800.00
On cover —
A12 10c bis, *yelsh* (#9) 325.00
On cover *2,750.*
A13 15c bis, *yelsh* ('72) (#10) 225.00
On cover —
A14 20c blue, *bluish* (#11) 275.00
On cover —
A15 25c blue, *bluish* ('72) (#12) 35.00
On cover —
A16 30c brn, *yelsh* (#13) 165.00
On cover —
A17 40c org, *yelsh* (I) (#14) 300.00
On cover —
A18 80c rose, *pinksh* (#15) 300.00
On cover —

1872-77 ***Imperf.***

Ceres Types A6, A7

A19 1c ol grn, *pale bl* ('72) (#16) 165.00
On cover —
A20 5c grn, *pale bl* (#19) 25.00
On cover —
A21 10c bis, *rosel* ('76) (#20) 80.00
On cover, from *1,950.*
A22 15c bister ('77) (#21) 340.00
On cover —
A23 30c brn, *yelsh* (#22) 275.00
On cover, from *650.00*
A24 80c rose, *pnksh* ('73) (#23) 350.00
On cover, from —

1877-78 ***Imperf.***

Peace & Commerce Type A8 - Type I

A25 1c grn, *grnsh* (#24) 250.00
On cover —
A26 4c grn, *grnsh* (#25) 225.00
On cover —
A27 30c brn, *yelsh* ('78) (#26) 45.00
On cover, from 200.00
A28 40c ver, *straw* (#27) 30.00
On cover, from 125.00
A29 75c rose, *rose* ('78) (#28) 80.00
On cover, from 500.00
a. 75c carmine, *rose* (#28a) 210.00
On cover, from 1,900.
A30 1fr brnz grn, *straw* (#29) 135.00
On cover —

Peace & Commerce - Type II

A31 2c grn, *grnsh* (#30) 250.00
On cover —
A32 5c grn, *grnsh* (#31) 20.00
On cover —
A33 10c grn, *grnsh* (#32) 40.00
On cover —
A34 15c gray, *grnsh* (#33) 100.00
On cover —
A35 20c red brn, *straw* (#34) 27.50
On cover —
A36 25c ultra, *bluish* (#35) 90.00
On cover —
a. 25c bl, *bluish* ('78) (#35a) 200.00
On cover, from *1,000.*
A37 35c vio blk, *org* (') (#36) 90.00
On cover —

1878-80 ***Imperf.***

Peace & Commerce Type A8 - Type II

A38 1c blk, *lil bl* (#38) 225.00
On cover —
A39 2c brn, *buff* (#39) 175.00
On cover, from 1,200.
A40 4c claret, *lav* (#40) 160.00
On cover, from 1,600.
A41 10c blk, *lav* ('79) (#41) 21.00
On cover, from 150.00
A42 15c blue ('79) (#42) 25.00
On cover, from 1,350.
A43 20c red, *grn* ('79) (#43) 80.00
On cover, from 1,450.
A44 25c blk, *red* ('79) (#44) 250.00
On cover 1,350.
A45 25c yel, *straw* ('80) (#45) 45.00
On cover, from 200.00

No. 44 was used at Mayotte, Nossi-Be and New Caledonia only. Beware of forgeries.

1881-86 ***Perf. 14x13½***

Commerce Type A9

A46 1c blk, *lil bl* (#46) 150.00
On cover *1,750.*
A47 2c brn, *buff* (#47) 150.00
On cover —
A48 4c claret, *lav* (#48) 125.00
On cover —
A49 5c grn, *grnsh* (#49) 65.00
On cover, from 200.00
A50 10c blk, *lav* (#50) 40.00
On cover —
A51 15c blue (#41) 45.00
On cover, from 600.00
A52 20c red, *yel grn* (#52) 60.00
On cover —
A53 25c yel, *straw* (#53) 60.00
On cover, from 1,100.
A54 25c blk, *rose* ('86) (#54) 75.00
On cover, from 1,250.
A55 30c brn, *bister* (#55) 60.00
On cover —
A56 35c vio blk, *yel org* (#56) 60.00
On cover —
a. 35c vio blk, *yel* (#56a) 100.00
On cover —
A57 40c ver, *straw* (#57) 90.00
On cover —
A58 75c car, *rose* (#58) 90.00
On cover, from 1,500.
A59 1fr brnz grn, *straw* (#59) 110.00
On cover —

Napoleon III — A1

1859 **Unwmk.** **Litho.** ***Imperf.***

Without Gum

1 A1 10c black 250.00 250.00
On cover, with New South Wales postage *30,000.*
On philatelic cover *2,500.*

Fifty varieties. Counterfeits abound.

See No. 315 in Scott Standard catalogue, Vol. 5.

Covers exist addressed to Australia, franked with No. 1, which might have paid local postage, and New South Wales stamps paying the maritime rate. Philatelic covers franked with No. 1 were made in the 1890s.

Covers addressed to Australia bearing stamps of Australian States canceled in Port-de-France or Noumea, from $30,000.

Covers addressed to Australia bearing stamps of Australian States in combination with stamps of French Colonies General issues, New Caledonia, canceled at Noumea, from $5,000.

Covers addressed to Australia bearing stamps of Australian States in combination with stamps of New Caledonia, canceled at Noumea, from $4,250.

Type of French Colonies, 1877 Surcharged in Black

Nos. 2-5

Nos. 6-7

1881-83

2 A8 5c on 40c red, *straw* ('82) 425.00 425.00
a. Inverted surcharge 1,600. 1,600.
b. Double surcharge 1,350.
c. Double surcharge, both inverted 1,900. 1,900.
3 A8 05c on 40c red, *straw* ('83) 40.00 40.00
On cover 700.00
4 A8 25c on 35c dp vio, *yel* 300.00 300.00
On cover 925.00
On cover 2,500.
a. Inverted surcharge 950.00 950.00
5 A8 25c on 75c rose car, *rose* ('82) 400.00 400.00
On cover 1,100.
a. Inverted surcharge 1,250. 1,250.

1883-84

6 A8 5c on 40c red, *straw* ('84) 26.50 26.50
Never hinged 52.50
On cover 600.00
a. Inverted surcharge 26.50 26.50
Never hinged 55.00
7 A8 5c on 75c rose car, *rose* ('83) 52.50 52.50
On cover 600.00
a. Inverted surcharge 75.00 75.00
Never hinged 110.00

In type "a" surcharge, the narrower-spaced letters measure 14½mm, and an early printing of No. 4 measures 13½mm. Type "b" letters measure 18mm.

French Colonies No. 59 Surcharged in Black

No. 8

Nos. 9-10

1886 ***Perf. 14x13½***

8 A9 5c on 1fr 32.50 26.50
Never hinged 52.50
On cover 475.00
a. Inverted surcharge 45.00 45.00
Never hinged 100.00
b. Double surcharge 200.00 200.00
c. Double surcharge, one inverted 225.00 225.00
9 A9 5c on 1fr 32.50 30.00
Never hinged 60.00
On cover 475.00
a. Inverted surcharge 60.00 60.00
Never hinged 125.00
b. Double surcharge 200.00 200.00
c. Double surcharge, one inverted 225.00 225.00

French Colonies No. 29 Surcharged

Imperf

10 A8 5c on 1fr *10,000.* *11,500.*
On cover —

Types of French Colonies, 1877-86, Surcharged in Black

Nos. 11, 13

No. 12

1891-92 ***Imperf.***

11 A8 10c on 40c red, *straw* ('92) 45.00 40.00
Never hinged 82.50
On cover 165.00
a. Inverted surcharge 42.50 37.50
Never hinged 82.50
b. Double surcharge 100.00 100.00
c. Double surcharge, one inverted 190.00 190.00
d. No period after "10c" 125.00 125.00

Perf. 14x13½

12 A9 10c on 30c brn, *bis* 25.00 22.50
Never hinged 45.00
On cover 300.00
a. Inverted surcharge 25.00 22.50
Never hinged 45.00
b. Double surcharge 67.50 67.50
c. Double surcharge, inverted 60.00 60.00
d. Double surcharge, one inverted 100.00 100.00
13 A9 10c on 40c red, *straw* ('92) 26.00 26.00
Never hinged 52.50
On cover 300.00
a. Inverted surcharge 26.00 26.00
b. No period after "10c" 60.00 60.00
c. Double surcharge 67.50 67.50
d. Double surcharge, one inverted 110.00 100.00
Nos. 11-13 (3) 96.00 88.50

Variety "double surcharge, one inverted" exists on Nos. 11-13. Value slightly higher than for "double surcharge."

Types of French Colonies, 1877-86, Handstamped in Black — g

1892 ***Imperf.***

16 A8 20c red, *grn* 350.00 *400.00*
On cover 675.00
a. Inverted surcharge 850.00 900.00
17 A8 35c violet, *org* 75.00 75.00
a. Pair, one stamp without surcharge 950.00
On cover 500.00
18 A8 40c red, *straw* *1,500.* —
On cover
19 A8 1fr bronz grn, *straw* 300.00 300.00
On cover 525.00

The 1c, 2c, 4c and 75c of type A8 are believed not to have been officially made or actually used.

1892 ***Perf. 14x13½***

23 A9 5c green, *grnsh* 19.00 15.00
Never hinged 30.00
On cover 300.00
a. Pair, one stamp without overprint 600.00
Never hinged 1,000.
24 A9 10c blk, *lavender* 140.00 82.50
Never hinged 210.00
On cover 300.00
25 A9 15c blue 110.00 60.00
Never hinged 190.00
On cover 375.00
a. Pair, one stamp without overprint 825.00
26 A9 20c red, *grn* 110.00 60.00
Never hinged 190.00
On cover 300.00
27 A9 25c yellow, *straw* 30.00 22.50
Never hinged 50.00
On cover 250.00
28 A9 25c black, *rose* 110.00 37.50
Never hinged 190.00
On cover 325.00
29 A9 30c brown, *bis* 90.00 75.00
Never hinged 175.00
On cover 400.00
30 A9 35c violet, *org* 240.00 190.00
On cover 725.00
a. Inverted overprint 650.00
b. Pair, one stamp without overprint 1,350.
32 A9 75c carmine, *rose* 225.00 190.00
On cover 700.00
a. Pair, one stamp without overprint 1,350.
33 A9 1fr bronz grn, *straw* 190.00 175.00
On cover 700.00
Nos. 23-33 (10) 1,264. 907.50

The note following No. 19 also applies to the 1c, 2c, 4c and 40c of type A9.

Surcharged in Blue or Black — h

1892-93 ***Imperf.***

34 A8 10c on 1fr brnz grn, *straw* (Bl) *5,250.* *4,500.*
On cover 6,000.

Perf. 14x13½

35 A9 5c on 20c red, *grn* (Bk) 27.50 22.50
Never hinged 55.00
On cover *375.00*
a. Inverted surcharge 125.00 125.00
Never hinged 225.00
b. Double surcharge 82.50 100.00
Never hinged 160.00
36 A9 5c on 75c car, *rose* (Bk) 22.50 16.50
Never hinged 45.00
On cover 300.00
a. Inverted surcharge 125.00 125.00
Never hinged 225.00
b. Double surcharge 82.50 82.50
Never hinged 150.00
37 A9 5c on 75c car, *rose* (Bl) 18.50 15.00
Never hinged 37.50
On cover 300.00
a. Inverted surcharge 125.00 125.00
Never hinged 225.00
b. Double surcharge 82.50 82.50
Never hinged 150.00
38 A9 10c on 1fr brnz grn, *straw* (Bk) 21.00 15.00
Never hinged 42.50
On cover 300.00
a. Inverted surcharge 600.00 600.00
39 A9 10c on 1fr brnz grn, *straw* (Bl) 22.50 21.00
Never hinged 45.00
On cover 300.00
a. Inverted surcharge 125.00 125.00
Never hinged 225.00
b. Double surcharge 85.00 85.00
Never hinged 150.00
Nos. 35-39 (5) 112.00 90.00

Navigation and Commerce — A12

1892-1904 **Typo.** ***Perf. 14x13½***

Name of Colony in Blue or Carmine

40 A12 1c black, *blue* 1.10 1.10
Never hinged 1.90
On cover or postcard 200.00
41 A12 2c brown, *buff* 1.90 1.90
Never hinged 3.00
On cover or postcard 200.00
42 A12 4c claret, *lav* 2.50 2.25
Never hinged 4.25
On cover or postcard 175.00
On cover, single franking 275.00
43 A12 5c green, *grnsh* 4.00 1.90
Never hinged 7.25
On cover 62.50
44 A12 5c yellow green ('00) 2.25 1.50
Never hinged 3.75
On cover 50.00
45 A12 10c blk, *lavender* 9.00 5.25
Never hinged 15.00
On cover 55.00
46 A12 10c rose red ('00) 11.00 1.50
Never hinged 17.50
On cover 50.00
47 A12 15c bl, quadrille paper 30.00 3.50
Never hinged 57.50
On cover 62.50
48 A12 15c gray ('00) 20.00 1.50
Never hinged 27.50
On cover 45.00
49 A12 20c red, *grn* 20.00 10.50
Never hinged 35.00
On cover 140.00
50 A12 25c black, *rose* 25.00 6.75
Never hinged 45.00
On cover 125.00
On cover, single franking 225.00
51 A12 25c blue ('00) 22.00 10.50
Never hinged 45.00
On cover 175.00
On cover, single franking 275.00
52 A12 30c brown, *bis* 25.00 13.50
Never hinged 45.00
On cover 125.00
On cover, single franking 175.00
53 A12 40c red, *straw* 26.00 13.50
Never hinged 45.00
On cover 160.00
On cover, single franking 190.00
54 A12 50c carmine, *rose* 67.50 37.50
Never hinged 135.00
On cover 275.00
On cover, single franking 450.00
55 A12 50c brn, *az* (name in car) ('00) 125.00 85.00
Never hinged 225.00
On cover 875.00
On cover, single franking 1,550.
56 A12 50c brn, *az* (name in bl) ('04) 65.00 42.50
Never hinged 125.00
On cover 550.00
On cover, single franking 875.00
57 A12 75c violet, *org* 37.50 26.50
Never hinged 75.00
On cover 375.00
On cover, single franking 625.00
58 A12 1fr bronz grn, *straw* 45.00 26.50
Never hinged 110.00
On cover 450.00
On cover, single franking 700.00
Nos. 40-58 (19) 539.75 293.15

Perf. 13½x14 stamps are counterfeits.

For overprints and surcharges see Nos. 59-87, 117-121.

Covers: Values for Nos. 40-42 are for covers or postcards with more than one stamp used to make the rate. This also applies to Nos. 66-68, 81-84, 88-90.

Nos. 41-42, 52, 57-58 Surcharged in Black

j

1900-01

59 A12 (h) 5c on 2c ('01) 22.50 19.00
Never hinged 37.50
On cover 225.00
a. Double surcharge 140.00 140.00
Never hinged 240.00
b. Inverted surcharge 125.00 125.00
Never hinged 210.00
60 A12 (h) 5c on 4c 4.50 4.50
Never hinged 9.00
On cover 125.00
a. Inverted surcharge 82.50 82.50
Never hinged 150.00
b. Double surcharge 87.50 87.50
Never hinged 160.00
61 A12 (j) 15c on 30c 5.25 4.50
Never hinged 10.50
On cover 125.00
a. Inverted surcharge 75.00 75.00
Never hinged 140.00
b. Double surcharge 67.50 67.50
Never hinged 125.00
c. "N.C.E." omitted from overprint 500.00 340.00
62 A12 (j) 15c on 75c ('01) 20.00 17.50
Never hinged 37.50
On cover 225.00
a. Pair, one without surcharge —
b. Inverted surcharge 130.00 130.00
Never hinged 225.00
c. Double surcharge 140.00 140.00
Never hinged 240.00

63 A12 (j) 15c on 1fr ('01) 26.50 26.50
Never hinged 45.00
On cover 300.00
a. Double surcharge 175.00 175.00
Never hinged 300.00
b. Inverted surcharge 175.00 175.00
Never hinged 300.00
Nos. 59-63 (5) 78.75 72.00

Nos. 52-53 Surcharged in Black

k

1902

64 A12 (k) 5c on 30c 10.50 9.00
Never hinged 17.50
On cover 125.00
a. Inverted surcharge 52.50 52.50
Never hinged 100.00
65 A12 (k) 15c on 40c 10.50 8.25
Never hinged 17.50
On cover 125.00
a. Inverted surcharge 52.50 52.50
Never hinged 100.00

Jubilee Issue

Stamps of 1892-1900 Overprinted in Blue, Red, Black or Gold

1903

66 A12 1c blk, *lil bl* (Bl) 3.00 3.00
Never hinged 5.25
On cover or postcard *300.00*
a. Inverted overprint *290.00 290.00*
b. "I" in "TENAIRE" omitted 30.00 30.00
Never hinged 57.50
67 A12 2c brown, *buff* (Bl) 5.25 4.50
Never hinged 9.00
On cover or postcard *300.00*
a. "I" in "TENAIRE" omitted 32.50 32.50
Never hinged 67.50
68 A12 4c claret, *lav* (Bl) 7.50 6.00
Never hinged 13.50
On cover or postcard *300.00*
a. Double overprint *375.00 375.00*
b. "I" in "TENAIRE" omitted 37.50 37.50
Never hinged 75.00
69 A12 5c dk grn, *grnsh* (R) 7.50 4.50
Never hinged 13.50
On cover 225.00
a. "I" in "TENAIRE" omitted 52.50 52.50
Never hinged 110.00
70 A12 5c yellow green (R) 10.00 9.00
Never hinged 19.00
On cover 225.00
a. "I" in "TENAIRE" omitted 60.00 60.00
Never hinged 130.00
71 A12 10c blk, *lav* (R) 19.00 16.00
Never hinged 35.00
On cover 275.00
a. "I" in "TENAIRE" omitted 110.00 110.00
Never hinged 225.00
72 A12 10c blk, *lav* (double G & Bk) 11.50 9.00
Never hinged 19.00
On cover 225.00
a. "I" in "TENAIRE" omitted 120.00 120.00
Never hinged 240.00
73 A12 15c gray (R) 15.00 11.50
Never hinged 26.00
On cover 210.00
a. "I" in "TENAIRE" omitted 125.00 125.00
Never hinged 245.00
74 A12 20c red, *grn* (Bl) 22.00 19.00
Never hinged 37.50
On cover 300.00
a. "I" in "TENAIRE" omitted 140.00 140.00
Never hinged 280.00
75 A12 25c blk, *rose* (Bl) 19.50 19.00
Never hinged 35.00
On cover 350.00
a. Double overprint 325.00
b. "I" in "TENAIRE" omitted 170.00 170.00
Never hinged 360.00
76 A12 30c brown, *bis* (R) 26.50 22.50
Never hinged 45.00
On cover 375.00
a. "I" in "TENAIRE" omitted 215.00 215.00
77 A12 40c red, *straw* (Bl) 34.00 30.00
Never hinged 55.00
On cover 450.00
a. "I" in "TENAIRE" omitted 260.00 260.00
78 A12 50c car, *rose* (Bl) 60.00 52.50
Never hinged 110.00
On cover 725.00
a. Pair, one without overprint *300.00*
a. "I" in "TENAIRE" omitted 280.00 280.00
79 A12 75c vio, *org* (Bk) 77.50 72.50
Never hinged 160.00
On cover 950.00
a. Dbl. ovpt. in blk and red *500.00*
a. "I" in "TENAIRE" omitted 280.00 280.00
80 A12 1fr brnz grn, *straw* (Bl) 120.00 115.00
Never hinged 240.00
On cover 1,100.
a. Dbl. ovpt., one in red *525.00 525.00*
b. "I" in "TENAIRE" omitted 450.00 450.00
Nos. 66-80 (15) 438.25 394.00

With Additional Surcharge of New Value in Blue

(a) (b)

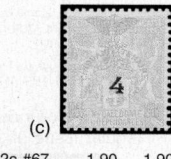

(c)

81 A12 (a) 1c on 2c #67 1.90 1.90
Never hinged 3.00
On cover or postcard *300.00*
a. Numeral double *115.00 115.00*
Never hinged 210.00
b. Numeral only 400.00
c. "I" in "TENAIRE" omitted 35.00 35.00
Never hinged 67.50
82 A12 (b) 2c on 4c #68 3.50 3.50
Never hinged 5.25
On cover or postcard *300.00*
a. "I" in "TENAIRE" omitted 35.00 35.00
Never hinged 67.50
83 A12 (a) 4c on 5c #69 2.25 2.25
Never hinged 3.75
On cover or postcard *275.00*
a. Small "4" *650.00 650.00*
b. "I" in "TENAIRE" omitted 35.00 35.00
Never hinged 67.50
84 A12 (c) 4c on 5c #70 3.00 3.00
Never hinged 5.25
On cover or postcard *950.00*
a. Pair, one without numeral
b. "I" in "TENAIRE" omitted 35.00 35.00
Never hinged 67.50
85 A12 (b) 10c on 15c #73 3.00 3.00
Never hinged 5.25
On cover 250.00
a. "I" in "TENAIRE" omitted 35.00 35.00
Never hinged 67.50
86 A12 (b) 15c on 20c #74 3.75 3.75
Never hinged 6.00
On cover 250.00
a. "I" in "TENAIRE" omitted 35.00 35.00
Never hinged 67.50
87 A12 (b) 20c on 25c #75 9.00 9.00
Never hinged 16.50
On cover 375.00
a. "I" in "TENAIRE" omitted 110.00 110.00
Never hinged 205.00
Nos. 81-87 (7) 26.40 26.40

50 years of French occupation.

Surcharge on Nos. 81-83, 85-86 is horizontal, reading down.

There are three types of numeral on No. 83. The numeral on No. 84 is identical with that of No. 83a except that its position is upright.

Nos. 66-87 are known with "I" of "TENAIRE" missing.

Kagu
A16

Landscape
A17

Ship — A18

1905-28 Typo. *Perf. 14x13½*

88 A16 1c blk, *green* .30 .30
Never hinged .45
On cover or postcard *95.00*
89 A16 2c red brown .30 .30
Never hinged .45
On cover or postcard *95.00*
90 A16 4c bl, *org* .45 .45
Never hinged .60
On cover or postcard *95.00*
91 A16 5c pale green .55 .55
Never hinged .75
On cover 45.00
92 A16 5c dl bl ('21) .40 .40
Never hinged .75
On cover 95.00
93 A16 10c carmine 1.90 1.25
Never hinged 2.60
On cover 32.50
94 A16 10c green ('21) .75 .75
Never hinged 1.10
On cover 37.50
95 A16 10c red, *pink* ('25) .85 .85
Never hinged 1.20
On cover 32.50
96 A16 15c violet .90 .85
Never hinged 1.40
On cover *45.00*
97 A17 20c brown .55 .55
Never hinged .75
On cover *45.00*
98 A17 25c blue, *grn* 1.05 .60
Never hinged 1.60
On cover 55.00
On cover, single franking 160.00
99 A17 25c red, *yel* ('21) .75 .75
Never hinged 1.10
On cover 32.50
100 A17 30c brn, *org* 1.40 .85
Never hinged 1.90
On cover *62.50*
On cover, single franking 190.00
101 A17 30c dp rose ('21) 2.50 2.50
Never hinged 4.25
On cover *50.00*
102 A17 30c org ('25) .60 .60
Never hinged 1.00
On cover *45.00*
103 A17 35c blk, *yellow* .75 .75
Never hinged 1.10
On cover *80.00*
On cover, single franking 250.00
104 A17 40c car, *grn* 1.25 1.05
Never hinged 1.75
On cover *62.50*
On cover, single franking 125.00
105 A17 45c vio brn, *lav* .75 .75
Never hinged 1.10
On cover *62.50*
On cover, single franking 125.00
106 A17 50c car, *org* 3.25 3.00
Never hinged 5.25
On cover *75.00*
On cover, single franking 190.00
107 A17 50c dk bl ('21) 1.75 1.75
Never hinged 2.40
On cover *50.00*
On cover, single franking 145.00
108 A17 50c gray ('25) 1.05 1.05
Never hinged 1.50
On cover *70.00*
On cover, single franking 170.00
109 A17 65c dp bl ('28) .90 .90
Never hinged 1.50
On cover *75.00*
On cover, single franking 190.00
110 A17 75c ol grn, *straw* .85 .70
Never hinged 1.20
On cover *95.00*
On cover, single franking 250.00
111 A17 75c bl, *bluish* ('25) .90 .90
Never hinged 1.20
On cover *62.50*
On cover, single franking 160.00
112 A17 75c violet ('27) 1.15 1.15
Never hinged 1.90
On cover *75.00*
On cover, single franking 225.00
113 A18 1fr bl, *yel grn* 1.30 1.05
Never hinged 1.75
On cover *95.00*
On cover, single franking 250.00
114 A18 1fr dp bl ('25) 1.90 1.90
Never hinged 3.25
On cover *95.00*
On cover, single franking 145.00
115 A18 2fr car, *bl* 3.50 2.25
Never hinged 5.00
On cover *105.00*
On cover, single franking 275.00
116 A18 5fr blk, *straw* 6.75 6.75
Never hinged 12.00
On cover *130.00*
On cover, single franking 350.00
Nos. 88-116 (29) 39.30 35.50

See Nos. 311, 317a in Scott Standard catalogue, Vol. 5. For surcharges see Nos. 122-135, B1-B3, Q1-Q3.

Nos. 96, 98, 103, 106, 113 and 115, pasted on cardboard and handstamped "TRESORIER PAYEUR DE LA NOUVELLE CALEDONIE" were used as emergency currency in 1914.

Stamps of 1892-1904 Surcharged in Carmine or Black

Spacing between figures of surcharge 1.5mm (5c), 2mm (10c)

1912

117 A12 5c on 15c gray (C) 1.50 *1.90*
Never hinged 2.25
On cover 105.00
a. Inverted surcharge 210.00 210.00
Never hinged 325.00
118 A12 5c on 20c red, *grn* 1.50 *1.90*
Never hinged 2.25
On cover 80.00
119 A12 5c on 30c brn, *bis* (C) 2.25 *3.00*
Never hinged 3.75
On cover 105.00
120 A12 10c on 40c red, *straw* 3.25 *3.25*
Never hinged 4.00
On cover 125.00
121 A12 10c on 50c brn, *az* (C) 3.25 *4.25*
Never hinged 4.00
On cover 145.00
Nos. 117-121 (5) 11.75 14.30

Spacing between figures of surcharge 2.25mm (5c), 2.75mm (10c)

117b A12 5c on 15c gray (C) 200.00 200.00
Never hinged 325.00
c. Inverted surcharge 4,000. 4,000.
Never hinged 5,750.
d. In pair with No. 117 210.00 210.00
Never hinged 340.00
118a A12 5c on 20c red, *grn* 130.00 130.00
Never hinged 200.00
d. In pair with No. 118 150.00 150.00
Never hinged 225.00
119a A12 5c on 30c brn, *bis* (C) 290.00 290.00
Never hinged 450.00
d. In pair with No. 119 300.00 300.00
Never hinged 500.00
120a A12 10c on 40c red, *straw* 200.00 200.00
Never hinged 325.00
d. In pair with No. 120 210.00 210.00
Never hinged 350.00
121a A12 10c on 50c brn, *az* (C) 240.00 240.00
Never hinged 400.00
d. In pair with No. 121 250.00 250.00
Never hinged 425.00
Nos. 117b-121a (5) 1,060. 1,060.

No. 96 Surcharged in Brown

1918

122 A16 5c on 15c violet 1.90 1.90
Never hinged 3.00
On cover 160.00
a. Double surcharge 75.00 75.00
Never hinged 140.00
b. Inverted surcharge 45.00 45.00
Never hinged 75.00

The color of the surcharge on No. 122 varies from red to dark brown.

No. 96 Surcharged

1922

123 A16 5c on 15c vio (R) .60 .60
Never hinged 1.00
On cover 80.00
a. Double surcharge 75.00 75.00
Never hinged 120.00

Stamps and Types of 1905-28 Surcharged in Red or Black

No. 124

No. 127

1924-27

124 A16 25c on 15c vio .75 .75
Never hinged 1.20
On cover 45.00
a. Double surcharge 75.00
Never hinged 120.00
b. Double surcharge, one inverted 110.00
Never hinged 190.00
125 A18 25c on 2fr car, *bl* .85 .85
Never hinged 1.20
On cover 45.00
126 A18 25c on 5fr blk, *straw* .90 .90
Never hinged 1.40
On cover 45.00
a. Double surcharge 125.00 125.00
Never hinged 300.00
b. Triple surcharge 225.00 210.00
Never hinged 425.00
127 A17 60c on 75c bl grn (R) .75 .75
Never hinged 1.20
On cover 55.00
On cover, single franking 190.00
128 A17 65c on 45c red brn 2.00 2.00
Never hinged 3.25
On cover 62.50
On cover, single franking 190.00
129 A17 85c on 45c red brn 2.00 2.00
Never hinged 3.50
On cover 70.00
On cover, single franking 200.00
130 A17 90c on 75c dp rose 1.05 1.05
Never hinged 1.60
On cover 55.00
On cover, single franking 190.00

131 A18 1.25fr on 1fr dp bl (R) .90 .90
Never hinged 1.40
On cover 80.00
On cover, single franking 170.00

132 A18 1.50fr on 1fr dp bl, *bl* 1.60 1.60
Never hinged 3.25
On cover 80.00
On cover, single franking 170.00

133 A18 3fr on 5fr red vio 2.10 2.10
Never hinged 3.50
On cover 95.00
On cover, single franking 190.00

134 A18 10fr on 5fr ol, *lav* (R) 7.50 7.50
Never hinged 12.00
On cover 105.00
On cover, single franking 250.00

135 A18 20fr on 5fr vio rose, *org* 14.50 14.50
Never hinged 25.00
On cover 120.00
On cover, single franking 275.00
a. Period after "F" omitted 52.50 52.50
Never hinged 82.50
Nos. 124-135 (12) 34.90 34.90

Issue years: Nos. 125-127, 1924. Nos. 124, 128-129, 1925. Nos. 131, 134, 1926. Nos. 130, 132-133, 135, 1927.

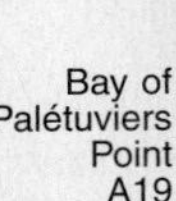

Bay of Palétuviers Point A19

Landscape with Chief's House A20

Admiral de Bougainville and Count de La Pérouse — A21

1928-40 **Typo.**

136 A19 1c brn vio & ind .25 .25
Never hinged .40
On cover 87.50

137 A19 2c dk brn & yel grn .25 .25
Never hinged .40
On cover 75.00

137B A19 3c brn vio & ind .30 .30
Never hinged .45
On cover 80.00

138 A19 4c org & Prus grn .25 .25
Never hinged .40
On cover 75.00

139 A19 5c Prus bl & dp ol .45 .45
Never hinged .75
On cover 70.00

140 A19 10c gray lil & dk brn .30 .30
Never hinged .45
On cover 62.50

141 A19 15c yel brn & dp bl .55 .55
Never hinged .85
On cover 62.50

142 A19 20c brn red & dk brn .55 .55
Never hinged .85
On cover 50.00

143 A19 25c dk grn & dk brn .70 .55
Never hinged 1.00
On cover 30.00

144 A20 30c gray grn & bl grn .60 .60
Never hinged .90
On cover 50.00

145 A20 35c blk & brt vio .90 .90
Never hinged 1.40
On cover 50.00

146 A20 40c brt red & olvn .55 .55
Never hinged .85
On cover 30.00

147 A20 45c dp bl & red org 1.60 1.30
Never hinged .85
On cover 30.00

147A A20 45c bl grn & dl grn 1.05 1.05
Never hinged 1.40
On cover 62.50

148 A20 50c vio & brn .85 .85
Never hinged 1.20
On cover 25.00

149 A20 55c vio bl & car 3.50 2.25
Never hinged 5.00
On cover 62.50

150 A20 60c vio bl & car .75 .75
Never hinged 1.00
On cover 50.00

151 A20 65c org brn & bl 1.30 1.15
Never hinged 1.90
On cover 55.00

152 A20 70c dp rose & brn .60 .60
Never hinged .90
On cover 55.00

153 A20 75c Prus bl & ol gray 1.40 1.15
Never hinged 2.10
On cover 37.50

154 A20 80c red brn & grn 1.15 1.00
Never hinged 1.60
On cover 55.00

155 A20 85c grn & brn 2.00 1.30
Never hinged 2.90
On cover 55.00

156 A20 90c dp red & brt red 1.30 .90
Never hinged 1.90
On cover 62.50
On cover, single franking 140.00

157 A20 90c ol grn & rose red 1.05 1.05
Never hinged 1.40
On cover 25.00

158 A21 1fr dp ol & sal red 7.25 4.25
Never hinged 11.00
On cover 95.00
On cover, single franking 170.00

159 A21 1fr rose red & dk car 2.25 1.75
Never hinged 3.25
On cover 70.00
On cover, single franking 125.00

160 A21 1fr brn red & grn 1.05 1.05
Never hinged 1.50
On cover 30.00

161 A21 1.10fr dp grn & brn 12.00 12.00
Never hinged 16.50
On cover 105.00
On cover, single franking 175.00

162 A21 1.25fr brn red & grn 1.20 1.20
Never hinged 1.90
On cover 50.00
On cover, single franking 110.00

163 A21 1.25fr rose red & dk car 1.15 1.15
Never hinged 1.50
On cover 45.00
On cover, single franking 160.00

164 A21 1.40fr dk bl & red org 1.20 1.20
Never hinged 1.60
On cover 50.00
On cover, single franking 110.00

165 A21 1.50fr dp bl & bl .90 .90
Never hinged 1.25
On cover 62.50
On cover, single franking 125.00

166 A21 1.60fr dp grn & brn 1.35 1.35
Never hinged 1.90
On cover 55.00
On cover, single franking 125.00

167 A21 1.75fr dk bl & red org 1.05 1.05
Never hinged 1.50
On cover 62.50
On cover, single franking 110.00

168 A21 1.75fr violet bl 1.50 1.05
Never hinged 1.50
On cover 62.50
On cover, single franking 110.00

169 A21 2fr red org & brn .90 .75
Never hinged 1.25
On cover 75.00
On cover, single franking 160.00

170 A21 2.25fr vio bl 1.20 1.20
Never hinged 1.60
On cover 62.50
On cover, single franking 140.00

171 A21 2.50fr brn & lt brn 1.75 1.75
Never hinged 2.60
On cover 70.00
On cover, single franking 190.00

172 A21 3fr mag & brn .75 .75
Never hinged 1.10
On cover 80.00
On cover, single franking 200.00

173 A21 5fr dk bl & brn 1.15 1.15
Never hinged 1.75
On cover 80.00
On cover, single franking 160.00

174 A21 10fr vio & brn, *pnksh* 1.30 1.30
Never hinged 1.90
On cover 95.00
On cover, single franking 190.00

175 A21 20fr red & brn, *yel* 2.75 2.75
Never hinged 4.25
On cover 105.00
On cover, single franking 250.00
Nos. 136-175 (42) 62.90 55.45

The 35c in Prussian green and dark green without overprint is listed as Wallis and Futuna No. 53a.

Issue years: 35c, 70c, 85c, #162, 167, 1933; 55c, 80c, #159, 168, 1938; #157, 163, 2.25fr, 1939; 3c, 60c, 1.40fr, 1.60fr, 2.50fr, 147A, 160, 1940; others, 1928.

Compare with Nos. 265A-265B.

For overprints see #180-207, 217-251 (in Scott Standard catalogue, Vol. 5), Q4-Q6.

Common Design Types pictured following the introduction.

Colonial Exposition Issue

Common Design Types

1931 **Engr.** ***Perf. 12½***

Country Name Typo. in Black

176 CD70 40c dp green 6.00 6.00
Never hinged 10.50
On cover 105.00

177 CD71 50c violet 6.00 6.00
Never hinged 10.50
On cover 87.50

178 CD72 90c red orange 6.00 6.00
Never hinged 10.50
On cover 160.00
On cover, single franking 225.00

179 CD73 1.50fr dull blue 6.00 6.00
Never hinged 10.50
On cover 140.00
On cover, single franking 190.00
Nos. 176-179 (4) 24.00 24.00

Paris-Nouméa Flight Issue

Regular Issue of 1928 Overprinted

1932 ***Perf. 14x13½***

180 A20 40c brt red & olvn 475.00 *500.00*
Never hinged 700.00
On cover 1,250.

181 A20 50c vio & brn 475.00 *500.00*
Never hinged 700.00
On cover 1,250.

Arrival on Apr. 5, 1932 at Nouméa, of the French aviators, Verneilh, Dévé and Munch.
Excellent forgeries exist of #180-181.

Types of 1928-33 Overprinted in Black or Red

1933

182 A19 1c red vio & dl bl 6.50 *7.00*
Never hinged 9.75
On cover 125.00

183 A19 2c dk brn & yel grn 6.50 *7.00*
Never hinged 9.75
On cover 125.00

184 A19 4c dl org & Prus bl 6.50 *7.00*
Never hinged 9.75
On cover 125.00

185 A19 5c Prus grn & ol (R) 6.50 *7.00*
Never hinged 9.75
On cover 125.00

186 A19 10c gray lil & dk brn (R) 6.50 *7.00*
Never hinged 9.75
On cover 125.00

187 A19 15c yel brn & dp bl (R) 6.50 *7.00*
Never hinged 9.75
On cover 125.00

188 A19 20c brn red & dk brn 6.50 *7.00*
Never hinged 9.75
On cover 125.00

189 A19 25c dk grn & dk brn (R) 6.50 *7.00*
Never hinged 9.75
On cover 125.00

190 A20 30c gray grn & bl grn (R) 6.75 *7.50*
Never hinged 10.50
On cover 125.00

191 A20 35c blk & lt vio 6.75 *7.50*
Never hinged 10.50
On cover 125.00

192 A20 40c brt red & olvn 6.75 *7.00*
Never hinged 10.50
On cover 125.00

193 A20 45c dp bl & red org 6.75 *7.50*
Never hinged 10.50
On cover 125.00

194 A20 50c vio & brn 6.75 *7.00*
Never hinged 10.50
On cover 125.00

195 A20 70c dp rose & brn 7.50 *8.00*
Never hinged 11.00
On cover 140.00

196 A20 75c Prus bl & ol gray (R) 7.50 *8.00*
Never hinged 11.00
On cover 125.00

197 A20 85c grn & brn 7.50 *8.00*
Never hinged 11.00
On cover 125.00

198 A20 90c dp red & brt red 9.50 *10.00*
Never hinged 13.00
On cover 160.00

199 A21 1fr dp ol & sal red 9.50 *10.00*
Never hinged 13.00
On cover 160.00

200 A21 1.25fr brn red & grn 9.50 *10.00*
Never hinged 13.50
On cover 165.00

201 A21 1.50fr dp bl & bl (R) 9.50 *10.00*
Never hinged 13.50
On cover 165.00

202 A21 1.75fr dk bl & red org 9.50 *10.00*
Never hinged 13.50
On cover 170.00

203 A21 2fr red org & brn 9.50 *10.00*
Never hinged 13.50
On cover 190.00

204 A21 3fr mag & brn 9.50 *10.00*
Never hinged 13.50
On cover 190.00

205 A21 5fr dk bl & brn (R) 9.50 *10.00*
Never hinged 13.50
On cover 200.00

206 A21 10fr vio & brn, *pnksh* 10.00 *11.00*
Never hinged 14.00
On cover 225.00

207 A21 20fr red & brn, *yel* 10.00 *11.00*
Never hinged 14.00
On cover 230.00
Nos. 182-207 (26) 204.25 218.50

1st anniv., Paris-Noumea flight. Plane centered on Nos. 190-207.

Paris International Exposition Issue

Common Design Types

1937 **Engr.** ***Perf. 13***

208 CD74 20c dp vio 2.75 2.75
Never hinged 4.00
On cover 105.00

209 CD75 30c dk grn 2.75 2.75
Never hinged 4.00
On cover 87.50

210 CD76 40c car rose 2.75 2.75
Never hinged 4.00
On cover 80.00

211 CD77 50c dk brn & bl 2.75 2.75
Never hinged 4.00
On cover 75.00

212 CD78 90c red 2.75 2.75
Never hinged 4.00
On cover 105.00
On cover, single franking 190.00

213 CD79 1.50fr ultra 2.75 2.75
Never hinged 4.00
On cover 95.00
On cover, single franking 160.00
Nos. 208-213 (6) 16.50 16.50

Colonial Arts Exhibition Issue Souvenir Sheet

Common Design Type

1937 ***Imperf.***

214 CD78 3fr sepia 22.50 *34.00*
Never hinged 35.00
On cover 190.00
On cover, single franking 250.00

New York World's Fair Issue

Common Design Type

1939 ***Perf. 12½x12***

215 CD82 1.25fr car lake 1.60 1.60
Never hinged 2.50
On cover 80.00
On cover, single franking 160.00

216 CD82 2.25fr ultra 1.75 1.75
Never hinged 2.50
On cover 80.00
On cover, single franking 145.00

SEMI-POSTAL STAMPS

No. 93 Surcharged

1915 **Unwmk.** ***Perf. 14x13½***

B1 A16 10c + 5c carmine 1.50 1.50
Never hinged 2.25
On cover 75.00
a. Inverted surcharge 75.00 75.00
Never hinged 140.00
b. Cross omitted 100.00 —
Never hinged 300.00
c. Double surcharge 160.00 160.00
Never hinged 275.00

Regular Issue of 1905 Surcharged

1917

B2 A16 10c + 5c rose 1.50 1.30
Never hinged 2.25
On cover 100.00
a. Double surcharge 130.00 —
Never hinged 225.00
B3 A16 15c + 5c violet 1.50 1.40
Never hinged 2.25
On cover 95.00

Curie Issue
Common Design Type

1938, Oct. 24 ***Perf. 13***

B4 CD80 1.75fr + 50c brt ultra 16.50 17.50
Never hinged 25.00
On cover 105.00
On cover, single franking 190.00

French Revolution Issue
Common Design Type

1939, July 5 Photo.
Name and Value Typo. in Black

B5 CD83 45c + 25c green 13.50 13.50
Never hinged 22.50
On cover 140.00
B6 CD83 70c + 30c brown 13.50 13.50
Never hinged 22.50
On cover 105.00
B7 CD83 90c + 35c red org 13.50 13.50
Never hinged 22.50
On cover 95.00
B8 CD83 1.25fr + 1fr rose pink 13.50 13.50
Never hinged 22.50
On cover 160.00
On cover, single franking 225.00
B9 CD83 2.25fr + 2fr blue 13.50 13.50
Never hinged 22.50
On cover 140.00
On cover, single franking 200.00
Nos. B5-B9 (5) 67.50 67.50

AIR POST STAMPS

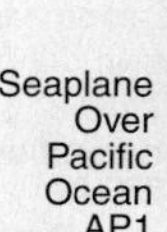

Seaplane Over Pacific Ocean AP1

1938-40 Unwmk. Engr. ***Perf. 13***

C1 AP1 65c deep violet 1.00 1.00
Never hinged 1.50
On cover 80.00
a. "65c" omitted 225.00
C2 AP1 4.50fr red 1.60 1.60
Never hinged 2.60
On cover 70.00
C3 AP1 7fr dk bl grn ('40) 1.15 .85
Never hinged 1.50
On cover 75.00
C4 AP1 9fr ultra 3.00 2.60
Never hinged 4.50
On cover 95.00
C5 AP1 20fr dk org ('40) 2.25 2.25
Never hinged 3.50
On cover 105.00
C6 AP1 50fr black ('40) 3.75 3.25
Never hinged 5.00
On cover 125.00
Nos. C1-C6 (6) 12.75 11.55

AIR POST SEMI-POSTAL STAMP

French Revolution Issue
Common Design Type
Unwmk.

1939, July 5 Photo. ***Perf. 13***
Name and Value Typo. in Orange

CB1 CD83 4.50fr + 4fr brn blk 34.00 34.00
Never hinged 52.50
On cover 190.00
On cover, single franking 300.00

POSTAGE DUE STAMPS

For a short time in 1894, 5, 10, 15, 20, 25 and 30c postage stamps (Nos. 43, 45, 47, 49, 50 and 52) were overprinted with a "T" in an inverted triangle and used as Postage Due stamps.

French Colonies Postage Due Stamps Overprinted in Carmine, Blue or Silver

1903 Unwmk. ***Imperf.***

J1 D1 5c blue (C) 3.75 3.75
Never hinged 6.75
On cover 300.00
a. "I" in "TENAIRE" omitted 37.50 37.50
Never hinged 67.50
J2 D1 10c brown (C) 11.50 11.50
Never hinged 20.00
On cover 375.00
a. "I" in "TENAIRE" omitted 50.00 50.00
Never hinged 95.00
J3 D1 15c yel grn (C) 22.50 11.50
Never hinged 45.00
On cover 375.00
a. "I" in "TENAIRE" omitted 100.00 100.00
Never hinged 200.00
J4 D1 30c carmine (Bl) 19.00 15.00
Never hinged 37.50
On cover 375.00
a. "I" in "TENAIRE" omitted 97.50 97.50
Never hinged 200.00
J5 D1 50c violet (Bl) 65.00 22.50
Never hinged 125.00
On cover 440.00
a. "I" in "TENAIRE" omitted 260.00 260.00
J6 D1 60c brn, *buff* (Bl) 260.00 95.00
On cover 800.00
a. "I" in "TENAIRE" omitted 1,200. 1,200.
J7 D1 1fr rose, *buff* (S) 42.50 26.00
Never hinged 75.00
On cover 500.00
a. "I" in "TENAIRE" omitted 225.00 225.00
b. Double overprint 225.00 225.00
J8 D1 2fr red brn (Bl) 1,300. 1,300.
a. "I" in "TENAIRE" omitted 6,500.
Nos. J1-J8 (8) 1,724. 1,485.

Fifty years of French occupation.

Men Poling Boat — D2

1906 Typo. ***Perf. 13½x14***

J9 D2 5c ultra, *azure* .70 .75
Never hinged 1.20
On cover 105.00
J10 D2 10c vio brn, *buff* .70 .75
Never hinged 1.20
On cover 100.00
J11 D2 15c grn, *greenish* 1.00 1.10
Never hinged 1.60
On cover 105.00
J12 D2 20c blk, *yellow* 1.00 1.10
Never hinged 1.60
On cover 125.00
J13 D2 30c carmine 1.35 1.50
Never hinged 2.25
On cover 140.00
J14 D2 50c ultra, *buff* 2.25 2.25
Never hinged 3.75
On cover 145.00
J15 D2 60c brn, *azure* 1.50 1.90
Never hinged 2.40
On cover 160.00
J16 D2 1fr dk grn, *straw* 2.25 2.75
Never hinged 4.00
On cover 190.00
Nos. J9-J16 (8) 10.75 12.10

Type of 1906 Issue Surcharged

1926-27

J17 D2 2fr on 1fr vio 5.75 6.25
Never hinged 8.25
On cover 250.00
J18 D2 3fr on 1fr org brn 5.75 6.25
Never hinged 8.25
On cover 275.00

Malayan Sambar — D3

1928 ***Typo.***

J19 D3 2c sl bl & dp brn .25 .40
Never hinged .40
On cover 125.00
J20 D3 4c brn red & bl grn .45 .60
Never hinged .75
On cover 125.00
J21 D3 5c red org & bl blk .60 .75
Never hinged 1.00
On cover 95.00
J22 D3 10c mag & Prus bl .60 .75
Never hinged 1.00
On cover 80.00
J23 D3 15c dl grn & scar .60 .75
Never hinged 1.00
On cover 80.00
J24 D3 20c mar & ol grn 1.05 1.10
Never hinged 1.50
On cover 95.00
J25 D3 25c bis brn & sl bl .75 .90
Never hinged 1.20
On cover 95.00
J26 D3 30c bl grn & ol grn 1.05 1.10
Never hinged 1.50
On cover 95.00
J27 D3 50c lt brn & dk red 1.35 1.50
Never hinged 1.90
On cover 105.00
J28 D3 60c mag & brt rose 1.35 1.50
Never hinged 1.90
On cover 125.00
J29 D3 1fr dl bl & Prus grn 1.75 1.90
Never hinged 2.60
On cover 140.00
J30 D3 2fr dk red & ol grn 1.90 2.25
Never hinged 2.90
On cover 170.00
J31 D3 3fr violet & brn 2.75 3.00
Never hinged 4.25
On cover 190.00
Nos. J19-J31 (13) 14.45 16.50

PARCEL POST STAMPS

Type of Regular Issue of 1905-28 Srchd. or Ovptd.

1926 Unwmk. ***Perf. 14x13½***

Q1 A18 50c on 5fr olive, *lav* 1.30 1.90
Never hinged 2.25
Q2 A18 1fr deep blue 1.75 2.75
Never hinged 3.25
Q3 A18 2fr car, *bluish* 2.10 3.00
Never hinged 3.75
Nos. Q1-Q3 (3) 5.15 7.65

Regular Issue of 1928 Overprinted

1930

Q4 A20 50c violet & brown 1.30 1.90
Never hinged 2.25
Q5 A21 1fr dp ol & sal red 1.75 2.75
Never hinged 3.25
Q6 A21 2fr red org & brn 2.10 3.00
Never hinged 3.75
Nos. Q4-Q6 (3) 5.15 7.65

NEW GUINEA

'nü 'gi-nē

LOCATION — On an island of the same name in the South Pacific Ocean, north of Australia.
GOVT. — Mandate administered by Australia
AREA — 93,000 sq. mi.
POP. — 675,369 (1940)
CAPITAL — Rabaul

The territory occupies the northeastern part of the island and includes New Britain and other nearby islands. It was formerly a German possession and should not be confused with British New Guinea (Papua) which is in the south-eastern part of the same island, nor Netherlands New Guinea. For previous issues see German New Guinea, New Britain, North West Pacific Islands.

12 Pence = 1 Shilling
20 Shillings = 1 Pound

Native Huts — A1

1925-28 Engr. ***Perf. 11***

1 A1 ½p orange 2.75 8.00
2 A1 1p yellow green 2.75 6.25
3 A1 1½p vermilion ('26) 3.75 3.00
4 A1 2p claret 7.25 5.00
5 A1 3p deep blue 8.00 4.50
6 A1 4p olive green 15.00 24.00
7 A1 6p yel bister ('28) 6.50 55.00
a. 6p light brown 22.50 55.00
b. 6p olive bister ('27) 13.00 52.50
8 A1 9p deep violet 15.00 50.00
9 A1 1sh gray green 17.50 30.00
10 A1 2sh red brown 35.00 55.00
11 A1 5sh olive bister 55.00 75.00
12 A1 10sh dull rose 120.00 200.00
13 A1 £1 grnsh gray 210.00 325.00
Nos. 1-13 (13) 498.50 840.75

For overprints see Nos. C1-C13, O1-O9.

Bird of Paradise — A2

1931, Aug. 2

18 A2 1p light green 4.50 6.50
19 A2 1½p red 5.75 11.50
20 A2 2p violet brown 5.75 2.50
21 A2 3p deep blue 5.75 5.50
22 A2 4p olive green 7.50 27.50
23 A2 5p slate green 8.00 22.50
24 A2 6p bister 8.00 25.00
25 A2 9p dull violet 9.50 21.00
26 A2 1sh bluish gray 7.00 17.00
27 A2 2sh red brown 11.50 47.50
28 A2 5sh olive brown 47.50 62.50
29 A2 10sh rose red 120.00 150.00
30 A2 £1 gray 250.00 300.00
Nos. 18-30 (13) 490.75 699.00

10th anniversary of Australian Mandate.
For overprints see #C14-C27, O12-O22.

Type of 1931 without date scrolls

1932-34 ***Perf. 11***

31 A2 1p light green 7.25 .25
32 A2 1½p violet brown 7.25 20.00
33 A2 2p red 5.50 .25
34 A2 2½p dp grn ('34) 7.50 27.50
35 A2 3p gray blue 8.00 1.25
36 A2 3½p magenta ('34) 15.00 22.50
37 A2 4p olive green 6.00 7.00
38 A2 5p slate green 7.00 .80
39 A2 6p bister 7.50 4.00
40 A2 9p dull violet 11.00 27.50
41 A2 1sh bluish gray 7.00 11.50
42 A2 2sh red brown 5.00 19.00
43 A2 5sh olive brown 32.50 50.00
44 A2 10sh rose red 60.00 80.00
45 A2 £1 gray 120.00 110.00
Nos. 31-45 (15) 306.50 381.55

For overprints see #46-47, C28-C43, O23-O35. See footnote following C43.

Silver Jubilee Issue

Stamps of 1932-34 Overprinted

1935, June 27 **Glazed Paper**

46 A2 1p light green 1.10 .85
47 A2 2p red 3.25 .85
Set, never hinged 6.50

King George VI — A3

1937, May 18 **Engr.**

48 A3 2p salmon rose .30 *1.60*
49 A3 3p blue .30 *1.90*
50 A3 5p green .35 *1.90*
51 A3 1sh brown violet .45 *2.50*
Nos. 48-51 (4) 1.40 *7.90*
Set, never hinged 2.50

Coronation of George VI and Queen Elizabeth.

AIR POST STAMPS

Regular Issues of 1925-28 Overprinted

1931, June ***Perf. 11***

C1 A1 ½p orange 1.75 *8.50*
C2 A1 1p yellow green 1.75 *5.75*
C3 A1 1½p vermilion 1.40 *7.00*
C4 A1 2p claret 1.40 *8.00*
C5 A1 3p deep blue 2.00 *15.00*
C6 A1 4p olive green 1.40 *10.00*
C7 A1 6p light brown 2.00 *16.00*
C8 A1 9p deep violet 3.50 *19.00*
C9 A1 1sh gray green 3.50 *19.00*
C10 A1 2sh red brown 8.00 *47.50*
C11 A1 5sh ol bister 22.50 *75.00*
C12 A1 10sh light red 92.50 *120.00*
C13 A1 £1 grnsh gray 170.00 *290.00*
Nos. C1-C13 (13) 311.70 *640.75*

Type of Regular Issue of 1931 and Nos. 18-30 Overprinted

1931, Aug.

C14 A2 ½p orange 3.75 3.75
C15 A2 1p light green 4.50 *7.50*
C16 A2 1½p red 4.25 *11.50*
C17 A2 2p violet brown 4.25 3.50
C18 A2 3p deep blue 7.00 *7.00*
C19 A2 4p olive green 7.00 7.00
C20 A2 5p slate green 7.00 12.50
C21 A2 6p bister 8.00 *30.00*
C22 A2 9p dull violet 9.00 *17.00*
C23 A2 1sh bluish gray 8.50 *17.00*
C24 A2 2sh red brown 18.00 *55.00*
C25 A2 5sh olive brown 47.50 *80.00*
C26 A2 10sh rose red 87.50 *140.00*
C27 A2 £1 gray 150.00 *290.00*
Nos. C14-C27 (14) 366.25 *681.75*

10th anniversary of Australian Mandate.

Same Overprint on Type of Regular Issue of 1932-34 and Nos. 31-45

1932-34 ***Perf. 11***

C28 A2 ½p orange .65 *1.75*
C29 A2 1p light green 1.40 *2.50*
C30 A2 1½p violet brown 2.00 *11.50*
C31 A2 2p red 2.00 *.35*
C32 A2 2½p dp grn ('34) 8.75 2.75
C33 A2 3p gray blue 3.75 3.50
C34 A2 3½p mag ('34) 5.25 *3.75*
C35 A2 4p olive green 5.00 *11.50*
C36 A2 5p slate green 8.00 *8.50*
C37 A2 6p bister 5.00 *17.00*
C38 A2 9p dull violet 7.00 *10.00*
C39 A2 1sh bluish gray 7.00 *12.50*
C40 A2 2sh red brown 14.00 *55.00*
C41 A2 5sh olive brown 55.00 *65.00*
C42 A2 10sh rose red 100.00 92.50
C43 A2 £1 gray 87.50 62.50
Nos. C28-C43 (16) 312.30 *360.60*

No. C28 exists without overprint, but is believed not to have been issued in this condition. Value $200.

Plane over Bulolo Goldfield AP1

1935, May 1 **Engr.** **Unwmk.**

C44 AP1 £2 violet 350.00 160.00
C45 AP1 £5 green 750.00 550.00

AP2

1939, Mar. 1

C46 AP2 ½p orange 2.50 *9.25*
C47 AP2 1p green 2.00 *5.00*
C48 AP2 1½p vio brown 2.25 *19.00*
C49 AP2 2p red orange 5.00 4.00
C50 AP2 3p dark blue 8.50 *21.00*
C51 AP2 4p ol bister 9.00 9.75
C52 AP2 5p slate grn 8.00 4.50
C53 AP2 6p bister brn 25.00 *30.00*
C54 AP2 9p dl violet 25.00 *45.00*
C55 AP2 1sh sage grn 25.00 32.50
C56 AP2 2sh car lake 30.00 *75.00*
C57 AP2 5sh ol brown 85.00 *160.00*
C58 AP2 10sh rose red 325.00 *425.00*
C59 AP2 £1 grnsh gray 95.00 *150.00*
Nos. C46-C59 (14) 647.25 *990.00*
Set, never hinged 1,100.

OFFICIAL STAMPS

Regular Issue of 1925 Overprinted

1925-29 **Unwmk.** ***Perf. 11***

O1 A1 1p yellow green 5.00 *5.00*
O2 A1 1½p vermilion ('29) 6.25 *19.00*
O3 A1 2p claret 3.25 *4.25*
O4 A1 3p deep blue 6.00 *10.00*
O5 A1 4p olive green 5.00 *9.75*
O6 A1 6p yel bister ('29) 8.00 *40.00*
a. 6p olive bister 29.00 *40.00*
O7 A1 9p deep violet 4.50 *40.00*
O8 A1 1sh gray green 6.25 *40.00*
O9 A1 2sh red brown 42.50 *70.00*
Nos. O1-O9 (9) 86.75 *238.00*

Nos. 18-28 Overprinted

1931, Aug. 2

O12 A2 1p light green 12.00 *14.00*
O13 A2 1½p red 12.00 *13.50*
O14 A2 2p violet brown 12.00 *8.00*
O15 A2 3p deep blue 7.50 *7.00*
O16 A2 4p olive green 7.00 *9.75*
O17 A2 5p slate green 11.50 *13.50*
O18 A2 6p bister 16.00 *19.00*
O19 A2 9p dull violet 18.00 *32.50*
O20 A2 1sh bluish gray 18.00 *32.50*
O21 A2 2sh red brown 45.00 *80.00*
O22 A2 5sh olive brown 110.00 *200.00*
Nos. O12-O22 (11) 269.00 *429.75*

10th anniversary of Australian Mandate.

Same Overprint on Nos. 31-43

1932-34

O23 A2 1p light green 19.00 *20.00*
O24 A2 1½p violet brown 19.00 *20.00*
O25 A2 2p red 19.50 *3.75*
O26 A2 2½p dp green ('34) 10.00 *12.50*
O27 A2 3p gray blue 11.50 *42.50*
O28 A2 3½p magenta ('34) 8.00 *10.00*
O29 A2 4p olive green 21.00 *32.50*
O30 A2 5p slate green 10.00 *30.00*
O31 A2 6p bister 25.00 *55.00*
O32 A2 9p dull violet 16.00 *47.50*
O33 A2 1sh bluish gray 17.50 *32.50*
O34 A2 2sh red brown 40.00 *85.00*
O35 A2 5sh olive brown 140.00 *190.00*
Nos. O23-O35 (13) 356.50 *581.25*

NEW HEBRIDES, BRITISH

'nü 'he-brə-ˌdēz

LOCATION — A group of islands in the South Pacific Ocean northeast of New Caledonia
GOVT. — Condominium under the joint administration of Great Britain and France
AREA — 5,790 sq. mi.
POP. — 100,000 (est. 1976)
CAPITAL — Vila (Port-Vila)

See French New Hebrides.

12 Pence = 1 Shilling
100 Centimes = 1 Franc

Catalogue values for unused stamps in this country are for Never Hinged items, beginning with Scott 62 in the regular postage section, Scott J11 in the postage due section.

British Issues

Stamps of Fiji, 1903-06, Overprinted

1908-09 **Wmk. 2** ***Perf. 14***

Colored Bar Covers "FIJI" on #2-6, 9

1 A22 ½p grn & pale grn ('09) 60.00 *87.50*
2 A22 2p vio & orange 1.50 *1.75*
3 A22 2½p vio & ultra, *bl* 1.50 *1.75*
4 A22 5p vio & green 1.60 *3.25*
5 A22 6p vio & car rose 3.75 *3.50*
6 A22 1sh grn & car rose 145.00 *300.00*
Nos. 1-6 (6) 213.35 *397.75*

Wmk. Multiple Crown and CA (3)

7 A22 ½p gray green 1.00 *5.00*
a. grn & pale grn 17.50 *26.00*
8 A22 1p carmine .80 *1.00*
a. Pair, one without overprint 10,000.
9 A22 1sh grn & car rose ('09) 25.00 *4.25*
Nos. 7-9 (3) 26.80 *10.25*

Nos. 2-6, 9 are on chalk-surfaced paper.

Stamps of Fiji, 1904-11, Overprinted in Black or Red

1910, Dec. 15

10 A22 ½p green 3.50 *25.00*
11 A22 1p carmine 11.00 *8.50*
12 A22 2p gray 1.00 *3.00*
13 A22 2½p ultra 1.10 *6.00*
14 A22 5p violet & ol grn 2.25 *5.50*
15 A22 6p violet 2.50 *7.50*
16 A22 1sh black, *grn* (R) 3.00 *7.50*
Nos. 10-16 (7) 24.35 *63.00*

Nos. 14-16 are on chalk-surfaced paper.

Native Idols — A1

1911, July 25 **Engr.** **Wmk. 3**

17 A1 ½p pale green 1.00 *1.75*
18 A1 1p red 3.00 2.00
19 A1 2p gray 6.00 3.00
20 A1 2½p ultramarine 4.00 *5.50*
21 A1 5p olive green 4.50 *5.25*
22 A1 6p claret 3.00 *5.00*
23 A1 1sh black, *green* 2.75 *12.00*
24 A1 2sh violet, *blue* 20.00 *20.00*
25 A1 5sh green, *yel* 30.00 *50.00*
Nos. 17-25 (9) 74.25 *104.50*

See Nos. 33-37. For surcharges see Nos. 26-29, 38-39, French Issues No. 36.

Surcharged

1920-21

26 A1 1p on 5p ol grn ('21) 10.00 *60.00*
a. Inverted surcharge 4,500.
27 A1 1p on 1sh blk, *grn* 4.00 *13.00*
28 A1 1p on 2sh vio, *blue* 1.50 *10.00*
29 A1 1p on 5sh grn, *yel* 1.25 *10.00*

On French Issue No. 16

30 A2 2p on 40c red, *yel* ('21) 2.00 *22.00*
Nos. 26-30 (5) 18.75 *115.00*

French Issue No. 27

Wmk. R F in Sheet

31 A2 2p on 40c red, *yel* ('21) 125.00 *700.00*

The letters "R.F." are the initials of "Republique Francaise." They are large double-lined Roman capitals, about 120mm high. About one-fourth of the stamps in each sheet show portions of the watermark, the other stamps are without watermark.

No. 26a is considered by some to be printers' waste.

Type of 1911 Issue

1921, Oct. **Wmk. 4**

33 A1 1p rose red 2.50 *14.50*
34 A1 2p gray 4.00 *45.00*
37 A1 6p claret 14.00 *80.00*
Nos. 33-37 (3) 20.50 *139.50*

For surcharge see No. 40.

Stamps of 1911-21 Surcharged with New Values as in 1920-21

1924, May 1 **Wmk. 3**

38 A1 1p on ½p pale green 4.00 *22.50*
39 A1 5p on 2½p ultra 7.50 *27.50*
a. Inverted surcharge 3,500.

Wmk. 4

40 A1 3p on 1p rose red 4.50 *10.00*
Nos. 38-40 (3) 16.00 *60.00*

No. 39a is considered by some to be printers' waste.

A3

The values at the lower right denote the currency and amount for which the stamps were to be sold. The English stamps could be bought at the French post office in French money.

1925 **Engr.**

41 A3 ½p (5c) black 1.25 *20.00*
42 A3 1p (10c) green 1.00 *17.50*
43 A3 2p (20c) grnsh gray 1.75 *2.75*
44 A3 2½p (25c) brown 1.00 *14.00*
45 A3 5p (50c) ultra 3.25 *2.75*
46 A3 6p (60c) claret 4.00 *15.00*
47 A3 1sh (1.25fr) blk, *grn* 3.50 *18.00*
48 A3 2sh (2.50fr) vio, *bl* 6.25 *20.00*
49 A3 5sh (6.25fr) grn, *yel* 6.25 *27.50*
Nos. 41-49 (9) 28.25 *137.50*

Beach Scene A5

1938, June 1 Wmk. 4 *Perf. 12*

50 A5 5c green 1.75 *4.00*
51 A5 10c dark orange 2.00 *2.00*
52 A5 15c violet 2.50 *3.00*
53 A5 20c rose red 2.75 *3.25*
54 A5 25c brown 1.50 *2.75*
55 A5 30c dark blue 3.00 2.50
56 A5 40c olive green 3.25 *5.50*
57 A5 50c brown vio 1.25 *1.50*
58 A5 1fr car, *emerald* 6.50 *9.00*
59 A5 2fr dk blue, *emer* 22.50 22.50
60 A5 5fr red, *yellow* 40.00 50.00
61 A5 10fr violet, *blue* 125.00 80.00
Nos. 50-61 (12) 212.00 186.00
Set, never hinged 300.00

Catalogue values for unused stamps in this section, from this point to the end of the section, are for Never Hinged items.

Common Design Types pictured following the introduction.

UPU Issue
Common Design Type

1949, Oct. 10 Engr. *Perf. 13½*

62 CD309 10c red orange .35 *.90*
63 CD309 15c violet .35 *1.00*
64 CD309 30c violet blue .40 *1.10*
65 CD309 50c rose violet .50 *1.25*
Nos. 62-65 (4) 1.60 *4.25*

Outrigger Canoes with Sails — A6

Designs: 25c, 30c, 40c and 50c, Native Carving. 1fr, 2fr and 5fr, Island couple.

1953, Apr. 30 *Perf. 12½*

66 A6 5c green 1.00 *1.25*
67 A6 10c red 1.10 .35
68 A6 15c yellow 1.10 .25
69 A6 20c ultramarine 1.10 .25
70 A6 25c olive .90 .25
71 A6 30c light brown .90 .25
72 A6 40c black brown 1.10 .40
73 A6 50c violet 1.40 .50
74 A6 1fr deep orange 5.75 1.75
75 A6 2fr red violet 6.00 *9.00*
76 A6 5fr scarlet 9.00 *22.50*
Nos. 66-76 (11) 29.35 *36.75*

POSTAGE DUE STAMPS

British Issues
Type of 1925 Overprinted

1925, June Engr. Wmk. 4 *Perf. 14*

J1 A3 1p (10c) green 37.50 1.25
J2 A3 2p (20c) gray 40.00 1.25
J3 A3 3p (30c) carmine 40.00 3.25
J4 A3 5p (50c) ultra 45.00 5.50
J5 A3 10p (1fr) car, *blue* 52.50 6.50
Nos. J1-J5 (5) 215.00 17.75

Values for Nos. J1-J5 are for toned stamps.

Regular Stamps of 1938 Overprinted in Black

1938, June 1 *Perf. 12*

J6 A5 5c green 20.00 *32.50*
J7 A5 10c dark orange 20.00 *32.50*
J8 A5 20c rose red 22.50 *50.00*
J9 A5 40c olive green 27.50 *57.50*
J10 A5 1fr car, *emerald* 35.00 *67.50*
Nos. J6-J10 (5) 125.00 *240.00*

Catalogue values for unused stamps in this section, from this point to the end of the section, are for Never Hinged items.

Regular Stamps of 1953 Overprinted in Black

1953, Apr. 30 *Perf. 12½*

J11 A6 5c green 4.75 *13.50*
J12 A6 10c red 2.25 *11.00*
J13 A6 20c ultramarine 6.00 *20.00*
J14 A6 40c black brown 8.50 *37.50*
J15 A6 1fr deep orange 5.50 *45.00*
Nos. J11-J15 (5) 27.00 *127.00*

NEW HEBRIDES, FRENCH

'nü 'he-brə-ˌdēz

LOCATION — A group of islands in the South Pacific Ocean lying north of New Caledonia
GOVT. — Condominium under the joint administration of Great Britain and France
AREA — 5,790 sq. mi.
POP. — 100,000 (est. 1976)
CAPITAL — Port-Vila (Vila)

Postage stamps are issued by both Great Britain and France. In 1911 a joint issue was made bearing the coats of arms of both countries. The British stamps bore the coat of arms of Great Britain and the value in British currency on the right and the French coat of arms and values at the left. On the French stamps the positions were reversed. This resulted in some confusion when the value of the French franc decreased following World War II but the situation was corrected by arranging that both series of stamps be sold for their value as expressed in French currency.

See British New Hebrides.

12 Pence = 1 Shilling
100 Centimes = 1 Franc

Covers
Values are for commercial covers paying correct rates. Philatelic covers sell for less.

French Issues
Stamps of New Caledonia, 1905, Overprinted in Black or Red

Nos. 1-4

No. 5

1908 Unwmk. *Perf. 14x13½*

1 A16 5c green 12.50 *5.00*
On cover —
2 A16 10c rose 12.50 *4.75*
On cover —
3 A17 25c blue, *grnsh* (R) 9.50 *6.00*
4 A17 50c carmine, *org* 8.50 *6.50*
On cover —
5 A18 1fr bl, *yel grn* (R) 26.00 *22.50*
On cover —
Nos. 1-5 (5) 69.00 *44.75*

For overprints and surcharges see #6-10, 33-35.

Stamps of 1908 with Additional Overprint

1910

6 A16 5c green 8.00 *3.00*
On cover —
7 A16 10c rose 8.00 *1.75*
On cover —
8 A17 25c blue, *grnsh* (R) 3.50 *6.00*
On cover 200.00
9 A17 50c car, *orange* 11.00 *25.00*
On cover —
10 A18 1fr bl, *yel grn* (R) 28.00 *22.50*
On cover —
Nos. 6-10 (5) 58.50 *58.25*

A2

Perf. 14

1911, July 12 Engr. Wmk. 3

11 A2 5c pale green 1.00 *3.00*
On cover 200.00
12 A2 10c red .55 *1.10*
On cover —
13 A2 20c gray 2.00 *4.00*
On cover 150.00
14 A2 25c ultramarine 2.75 *7.00*
On cover —
15 A2 30c vio, *yellow* 6.50 *8.00*
On cover —
16 A2 40c red, *yellow* 4.00 *8.00*
On cover —
17 A2 50c olive green 4.00 *8.00*
On cover —
18 A2 75c brn orange 7.00 *30.00*
On cover 150.00
19 A2 1fr brn red, *bl* 6.00 *7.00*
On cover —
20 A2 2fr violet 12.00 *22.50*
On cover 150.00
21 A2 5fr brn red, *grn* 14.00 *47.50*
Nos. 11-21 (11) 59.80 *146.10*

For surcharges see Nos. 36-37, 43 and British issue No. 30.

1912 Wmk. R F in Sheet

22 A2 5c pale green 1.75 *5.50*
On cover —
23 A2 10c red 1.75 *6.00*
On cover —
24 A2 20c gray 2.10 *2.40*
On cover —
25 A2 25c ultramarine 2.50 *7.00*
On cover —
26 A2 30c vio, *yellow* 2.50 *17.00*
On cover 125.00
27 A2 40c red, *yellow* 24.00 *80.00*
On cover 150.00
28 A2 50c olive green 18.00 *30.00*
On cover 150.00
29 A2 75c brn orange 9.00 *42.50*
On cover 150.00
30 A2 1fr brn red, *bl* 9.00 *10.00*
On cover —
31 A2 2fr violet 9.25 *47.50*
On cover —
32 A2 5fr brn red, *grn* 32.50 *55.00*
On cover —
Nos. 22-32 (11) 112.35 302.90

In the watermark, "R F" (République Française initials) are large double-lined Roman capitals, about 120mm high. About one-fourth of the stamps in each sheet show parts of the watermark. The other stamps are without watermark.

For surcharges see Nos. 38-42 and British issue No. 31.

Nos. 9 and 8 Surcharged

1920 Unwmk. *Perf. 14x13½*

33 A17 5c on 50c red, *org* 2.50 *22.00*
On cover 110.00
34 A17 10c on 25c bl, *grnsh* 1.00 *1.50*
On cover —

Same Surcharge on No. 4

35 A17 5c on 50c red, *org* 900.00 *1,100.*
On cover —

British Issue No. 21 and French Issue No. 15 Surcharged

1921 Wmk. 3 *Perf. 14*

36 A1 10c on 5p ol grn 16.00 *50.00*
On cover —
37 A2 20c on 30c vio, *yel* 15.00 *65.00*
On cover —

Nos. 27 and 26 Surcharged

1921 Wmk. R F in Sheet

38 A2 5c on 40c red, *yel* 27.50 *100.00*
On cover 120.00
39 A2 20c on 30c vio, *yel* 11.50 *80.00*
On cover —

Stamps of 1910-12 Surcharged with New Values as in 1920-21

1924

40 A2 10c on 5c pale grn 2.75 11.00
On cover —
41 A2 30c on 10c red 2.75 3.00
On cover —
42 A2 50c on 25c ultra 4.50 20.00
On cover 100.00

Wmk. 3

43 A2 50c on 25c ultra 40.00 *110.00*
On cover —
Nos. 40-43 (4) 50.00 144.00

A4

The values at the lower right denote the currency and amount for which the stamps were to be sold. The stamps could be purchased at the French post office and used to pay postage at the English rates.

1925 Engr. Wmk. R F in Sheet

44 A4 5c (½p) black .90 *13.00*
On cover 100.00
45 A4 10c (1p) green 1.00 *9.00*
On cover 100.00
46 A4 20c (2p) grnsh gray 3.75 *3.75*
On cover 100.00
47 A4 25c (2½p) brown 1.50 *9.00*
On cover 100.00
48 A4 30c (3p) carmine 1.75 *18.00*
On cover 100.00
49 A4 40c (4p) car, *org* 2.50 *16.00*
50 A4 50c (5p) ultra 2.00 *11.00*
51 A4 75c (7½p) bis brn 1.75 *22.00*
52 A4 1fr (10p) car, *blue* 3.00 *14.50*
53 A4 2fr (1sh 8p) gray vio 3.50 37.50
54 A4 5fr (4sh) car, *grnsh* 7.00 *37.50*
Nos. 44-54 (11) 28.65 *191.25*

For overprints see Nos. J1-J5.

Beach Scene A6

1938 *Perf. 12*

55 A6 5c green 2.50 *9.00*
56 A6 10c dark orange 2.50 *3.25*
57 A6 15c violet 2.50 *8.00*
58 A6 20c rose red 2.50 *5.50*
59 A6 25c brown 5.50 *7.50*
60 A6 30c dark blue 5.50 *8.00*
61 A6 40c olive grn 2.75 *15.00*
62 A6 50c brown violet 2.75 *5.00*
63 A6 1fr dk car, *grn* 3.75 *8.00*
64 A6 2fr blue, *grn* 25.00 *40.00*

65 A6 5fr red, *yellow* 37.50 *65.00*
66 A6 10fr vio, *blue* 80.00 *150.00*
Nos. 55-66 (12) 172.75 *324.25*
Set, never hinged 360.00

For overprints see Nos. 67-78 (in Scott Standard catalogue, Vol. 5), J6-J15 (J11-J15 in Scott Vol. 5).

POSTAGE DUE STAMPS

French Issues

Nos. 45-46, 48, 50, 52 Overprinted

1925 Wmk. R F in Sheet *Perf. 14*
J1 A4 10c green 50.00 4.75
J2 A4 20c greenish gray 50.00 4.75
J3 A4 30c carmine 50.00 4.75
J4 A4 50c ultramarine 50.00 4.75
J5 A4 1fr carmine, *blue* 50.00 4.75
Nos. J1-J5 (5) 250.00 23.75

Nos. 55-56, 58, 61, 63 Overprinted

1938 *Perf. 12*
J6 A6 5c green 11.00 *65.00*
J7 A6 10c dark orange 12.50 *65.00*
J8 A6 20c rose red 14.50 *70.00*
J9 A6 40c olive green 30.00 *140.00*
J10 A6 1fr dark car, *green* 35.00 *160.00*
Nos. J6-J10 (5) 103.00 *500.00*

NEW REPUBLIC

'nü ri-'pə-blik

LOCATION — In South Africa, located in the northern part of the present province of Natal
GOVT. — Republic
CAPITAL — Vryheid

New Republic was created in 1884 by Boer adventurers from Transvaal who proclaimed Dinizulu king of Zululand and claimed as their reward a large tract of country as their own, which they called New Republic. This area was excepted when Great Britain annexed Zululand in 1887, but New Republic became a part of Transvaal in 1888 and was included in the Union of South Africa.

12 Pence = 1 Shilling
20 Shillings = 1 Pound

New Republic stamps were individually handstamped on gummed and perforated sheets of paper. Naturally many of the impressions are misaligned and touch or intersect the perforations. Values are for stamps with good color and, for Nos. 37-64, sharp embossing. The alignment does not materially alter the value of the stamp.

A1

Handstamped

1886 Unwmk. *Perf. 11½*
1 A1 1p violet, *yel* 20.00 22.50
a. "d" omitted, in pair with normal 2,750.
1A A1 1p black, *yel* *3,250.*
2 A1 2p violet, *yel* 22.50 *27.50*
a. "d" omitterd 4,750.
b. As "a", without date
c. tete-beche pair —
3 A1 3p violet, *yel* 50.00 *60.00*
a. Double impression
b. "d" omitted (Oct. 13 '86) *4,750.*
c. Tete-beche pair
4 A1 4p violet, *yel* 85.00
a. Without date
b. "4d" omitted, in pair with normal *3,000.*
5 A1 6p violet, *yel* 65.00 *70.00*
a. Double impression
b. "6d" omitted in pair with normal —
6 A1 9p violet, *yel* 125.00
7 A1 1sh violet, *yel* 125.00
a. "1/S" 800.00
b. "1s" omitted in pair with normal —
8 A1 1/6 violet, *yel* 120.00
a. Without date
b. "1s6d" 600.00
c. as "b", tete-beche pair —
d. as "b", "d" omitted 150.00
9 A1 2sh violet, *yel* 75.00
a. tete-beche pair 875.00
10 A1 2sh6p violet, *yel* 190.00
a. Without date
b. "2/6" 190.00
11 A1 4sh violet, *yel*
a. "4/s" 825.00
12 A1 5sh violet, *yel* 55.00 *65.00*
a. Without date
b. "s" omitted, in pair with normal 3,500.
13 A1 5/6 violet, *yel* 300.00
a. "5s6d" 550.00
14 A1 7sh6p violet, *yel* 175.00
a. "7/6" 250.00
15 A1 10sh violet, *yel* 225.00 *275.00*
a. Tete-beche pair —
16 A1 10sh6p violet, *yel* 250.00
b. "d" omitted 225.00
16A A1 13sh violet, *yel* 600.00
17 A1 £1 violet, *yel* 150.00
a. Tete-beche pair 650.00
18 A1 30sh violet, *yel* 150.00
a. tete-beche pair 750.00

Granite Paper

19 A1 1p violet, *gray* 30.00 *35.00*
a. "d" omitted 750.00
b. "1" omitted in pair with normal —
20 A1 2p violet, *gray* 22.50 *25.00*
a. "ZUID AFRIKA" omitted
b. "d" omitted *1,350.*
c. "2d." omitted in pair with normal —
21 A1 3p violet, *gray* 40.00 37.50
a. tete-beche pair 375.00
22 A1 4p violet, *gray* 55.00 *60.00*
23 A1 6p violet, *gray* 95.00 *95.00*
a. "6" omitted in pair with normal *2,750.*
24 A1 9p violet, *gray* 150.00
25 A1 1sh violet, *gray* 45.00 50.00
a. tete-beche pair 425.00
b. "1s." omitted in pair with normal 2,750.
26 A1 1sh6p violet, *gray* 125.00
a. tete-beche pair 750.00
b. "1/6" 190.00
c. "d" omitted —
27 A1 2sh violet, *gray* 150.00
a. "2s." omitted in pair with normal *3,250.*
28 A1 2sh6p violet, *gray* 3,500.
a. "2/6" 250.00
29 A1 4sh violet, *gray* 525.00
30 A1 5sh6p violet, *gray* 425.00
a. "5/6" 325.00
b. As "a," "/" omitted
c. As "a," "6" omitted *4,500.*
31 A1 7/6 violet, *gray* 325.00
a. 7s. 6d violet gray 450.00
32 A1 10sh violet, *gray* 225.00 225.00
a. tete-beche pair 525.00
f. "s" omitted —
32B A1 10sh 6p vio, *gray* 275.00
c. Without date —
d. tete-beche pair —
e. "d" omitted 600.00
33 A1 12sh violet, *gray* 450.00
34 A1 13sh violet, *gray* 550.00
35 A1 £1 violet, *gray* 375.00
36 A1 30sh violet, *gray* 325.00

Same with Embossed Arms

37 A1 1p violet, *yel* 22.50 *25.00*
a. Arms inverted 30.00 35.00
b. Arms tete-beche, pair 125.00 *135.00*
c. tete-beche pair *950.00*
38 A1 2p violet, *yel* 27.50 *30.00*
a. Arms inverted 30.00 35.00
39 A1 4p violet, *yel* 80.00 85.00
a. Arms inverted 125.00 87.50
b. Arms tete-beche, pair 350.00
40 A1 6p violet, *yel* 375.00

Granite Paper

41 A1 1p violet, *gray* 30.00 30.00
a. Imperf. vert., pair
b. Arms inverted 40.00 45.00
c. Arms tete-beche, pair 550.00
42 A1 2p violet, *gray* 30.00 30.00
a. Imperf. horiz., pair
b. Arms inverted 55.00 *65.00*
c. Arms tete-beche, pair 550.00

There were several printings of the above stamps and the date upon them varies from "JAN 86" and "7 JAN 86" to "20 JAN 87."

Nos. 7, 8, 10, 13, 14, 26, 28 and 30 have the denomination expressed in two ways. Example: "1s 6d" or "1/6."

A2

1887 Arms Embossed
43 A2 3p violet, *yel* 27.50 *27.50*
a. Arms inverted 30.00 32.50
b. tete-beche pair 375.00 450.00
c. Imperf. vert., pair
d. Arms omitted
e. Arms tete-beche, pair 225.00
f. Arms sideways 375.00
44 A2 4p violet, *yel* 20.00 20.00
a. Arms inverted 25.00 25.00
45 A2 6p violet, *yel* 17.50 *17.50*
a. Arms inverted 50.00 50.00
b. Arms omitted 95.00
c. Arms tete-beche, pair 375.00
46 A2 9p violet, *yel* 17.50 *20.00*
a. Arms inverted 250.00
b. Arms tete-beche, pair 425.00
47 A2 1sh violet, *yel* 20.00 *20.00*
a. Arms inverted 75.00
b. Arms omitted
48 A2 1sh6p violet, *yel* 55.00 45.00
49 A2 2sh violet, *yel* 42.50 *45.00*
a. Arms inverted 65.00 60.00
b. Arms omitted 150.00
50 A2 2sh6p violet, *yel* 40.00 *40.00*
a. Arms inverted 45.00 *45.00*
50B A2 3sh violet, *yel* 65.00 65.00
c. Arms inverted 80.00 *80.00*
d. Arms tete-beche, pair 600.00
51 A2 4sh violet, *yel* 650.00
a. Arms omitted —
b. "4/s" 65.00 65.00
c. As "b," arms omitted 275.00
51B A2 4/s violet, *yel*
a. Arms omitted
52 A2 5sh violet, *yel* 60.00 60.00
a. Imperf. vert., pair
b. Arms inverted — 175.00
53 A2 5sh6p violet, *yel* 30.00 *35.00*
54 A2 7sh6p violet, *yel* 35.00 *37.50*
a. Arms inverted 125.00
b. Arms tete-beche, pair —
55 A2 10sh violet, *yel* 32.50 *35.00*
a. Arms inverted 40.00
b. Arms omitted 135.00 90.00
c. Imperf. vert., pair
d. Arms tete-beche, pair 150.00
56 A2 10sh6p violet, *yel* 30.00 *32.50*
a. Imperf. vert., pair
b. Arms inverted 55.00
c. Arms omitted
57 A2 £1 violet, *yel* 75.00 85.00
a. Arms inverted 80.00
b. tete-beche pair 650.00 750.00
58 A2 30sh violet, *yel* 225.00

Granite Paper

59 A2 1p violet, *gray* 32.50 20.00
a. Arms omitted 150.00 150.00
b. Arms inverted 30.00 30.00
c. Imperf. vert., pair
d. tete-beche pair 650.00
e. Arms tete-beche, pair —
f. Arms sideways —
60 A2 2p violet, *gray* 20.00 20.00
a. Arms omitted 135.00 125.00
b. Arms inverted 55.00 55.00
c. tete-beche pair 425.00
d. Arms tete-beche, pair —
61 A2 3p violet, *gray* 35.00 35.00
a. Arms inverted 65.00 65.00
b. tete-beche pair 450.00
c. Arms tete-beche, pair —
62 A2 4p violet, *gray* 30.00 27.50
a. Arms inverted 110.00
b. Tete-beche, pair 375.00
c. Arms tete-beche, pair 300.00
63 A2 6p violet, *gray* 35.00 35.00
a. Arms inverted 110.00
64 A2 1sh6p violet, *gray* 50.00 42.50
a. Arms inverted 175.00
b. Arms tete-beche, pair 475.00
65 A2 2/6 violet, *gray* — *1,150.*
Nos. 59-64 (6) 202.50 180.00

These stamps were valid only in New Republic.

All these stamps may have been valid for postage but bona-fide canceled examples of any but the 1p and 2p stamps are quite rare.

NEW ZEALAND

'nü 'zē-lənd

LOCATION — Group of islands in the south Pacific Ocean, southeast of Australia
GOVT. — Self-governing dominion of the British Commonwealth
AREA — 107,241 sq. mi.
POP. — 3,230,000 (est. 1983)
CAPITAL — Wellington

12 Pence = 1 Shilling
20 Shillings = 1 Pound

Catalogue values for unused stamps in this country are for Never Hinged items, beginning with Scott 246 in the regular postage section, Scott B9 in the semi-postal section, Scott J21 in the postage due section, Scott O92 in the officials section, Scott OY29 in the Life Insurance Department section.

Watermarks

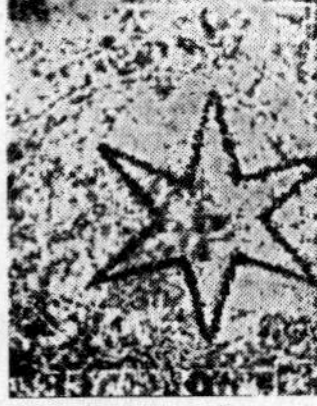
Wmk. 6 — Large Star

Wmk. 59 — N Z

Wmk. 60 — Lozenges

Wmk. 61 — N Z and Star Close Together

Wmk. 62 — N Z and Small Star Wide Apart

Wmk. 63 — Double-lined N Z and Star

Wmk. 64 — Small Star

Wmk. 253 — Multiple N Z and Star

PRE-STAMP POSTAL MARKINGS

Crowned Circle handstamp types I and III are pictured in the Crowned Circle Handstamps and Great Britain Used Abroad section.

Auckland

1846

A1 I "Auckland New Zealand" crowned circle handstamp in red, on cover 325.

Nelson

1846

A2 I "Nelson New Zealand" crowned circle handstamp in red, on cover 1,200.

New Plymouth

1846-54

A3 I "New Plymouth New Zealand" crowned circle handstamp in red, on cover 3,000.
A4 I "New Plymouth New Zealand" crowned circle handstamp in black, on cover 3,000.

Similar to type I, "PAID/AT" straight

A5 "New Plymouth New Zealand" crowned circle handstamp in red, on cover ('54) 3,500.
A6 "New Plymouth New Zealand" crowned circle handstamp in black, on cover ('54) 3,500.

The device used for Nos. A5-A6 was made locally.

Otago

1851

A7 III "Otago New Zealand" crowned circle handstamp in red, on cover 2,100.

Petre

1846

A8 I "Petre New Zealand" crowned circle handstamp in red, on cover 1,500.

Port Victoria

1851

A9 III "Port Victoria New Zealand" crowned circle handstamp in red, on cover 1,300.

Russell

1846

A10 I "Russell New Zealand" crowned circle handstamp in red, on cover 7,500.

Wellington

1846

A11 I "Wellington New Zealand" crowned circle handstamp in red, on cover 375.

Issued under British Administration

Values for unused stamps are for examples with original gum as defined in the catalogue introduction.

Very fine examples of the perforated issues between Nos. 7a-69, AR1-AR30, J1-J11, OY1-OY9 and P1-P4 will have perforations touching the framelines or design on one or more sides due to the narrow spacing of the stamps on the plates and imperfect perforating methods.

The rouletted and serrate rouletted stamps of the same period rarely have complete roulettes and are valued as sound and showing partial roulettes. Stamps with complete roulettes range from very scarce to very rare, are seldom traded, and command great premiums.

Victoria — A1

London Print
Wmk. 6

1855, July 20 Engr. *Imperf.*
White Paper

1 A1 1p dull carmine *85,000.* *20,000.*
 On cover —
 a. 1p orange ('57) 35,000.

Blued Paper

2 A1 2p deep blue *40,000.* 750.
 On cover, single franking 1,750.
3 A1 1sh yellow green *55,000.* *6,000.*
 On cover *45,000.*
 a. Half used as 6p on cover *42,500.*

The blueing of Nos. 2 and 3 was caused by chemical action in the printing process.

Auckland Print

1855-58 Blue Paper Unwmk.

4 A1 1p orange red 13,000. 2,150.
 On cover *7,250.*
 a. A1 1p orange *35,000.*
5 Al 2p blue ('56) 4,000. 325.
 On cover 1,300.
6 Al 1sh green ('58) *50,000.* 4,250.
 On cover *10,000.*
 a. Half used as 6p on cover *27,500.*

Nos. 4-6 may be found with parts of the papermaker's name in double-lined letters.

1857-61 Unwmk.
Thin Hard or Thick Soft White Paper

7 A1 1p orange ('58) 3,500. 825.
 e. 1p org vermilion, Wmk. 6 ('56) *35,000.*
 On cover, pair *65,000.*
8 A1 2p blue ('58) 1,300. 200.
 e. 2p pale blue ('57) 1,300. 195.
 f. 2p deep dull blue 1,725. 300.
 g. 2p deep ultra ('58) 3,000. 1,000.
9 A1 6p brown ('59) 3,000. 325.
 e. 6p bister brown ('59) 4,100. 550.
 f. 6p chestnut ('59) 5,000. 650.
 h. 6p pale brown 2,850. 325.
10 A1 1sh blue grn ('61) 18,500. 2,000.
 e. 1sh emerald ('58) 22,000. 2,000.

No. 7e is identical to a shade of No. 7. The only currently known example is a pair on a cover front. To qualify as No. 7e, a stamp must be on piece or on cover with a cancellation dated prior to 1862.

1859 *Pin Rouletted 9-10*

7a A1 1p dull orange 6,000.
8a A1 2p blue 3,800.
9a A1 6p brown 4,600.
10a A1 1sh greenish blue 8,250.

1859 *Serrate Rouletted 16, 18*

7b A1 1p dull orange 5,500.
8b A1 2p blue 4,100.
9b A1 6p brown 3,800.
 g. 6p chestnut 7,750.
10b A1 1sh greenish blue 7,000.

Value for No. 10b is for a damaged stamp.

1859 *Rouletted 7*

7c A1 1p dull orange *9,750.* 5,500.
 f. Pair, imperf between —
8c A1 2p blue *8,250.* 3,500.
9c A1 6p brown *7,750.* 3,000.
 l. Pair, imperf. between 27,500. 13,000.
10c A1 1sh greenish blue — 5,250.
10d A1 1sh emerald green — 5,250.

Roulettes are seldom complete or intact. Values for Nos. 7c to 10d are for stamps with partial roulettes.

1862 *Perf. 13*

7d A1 1p orange vermilion 8,000.
8d A1 2p blue 8,250. 3,800.
9d A1 6p brown *7,000.*

See No. 26.

"H" Rouletted 16

8i A1 2p blue 5,000.
9i A1 6p brown 5,250.

"Y" Rouletted 18

7j A1 1p orange *6,000.*
8j A1 2p blue *4,000.*
9j A1 6p brown *5,000.*
 k. 6d chestnut *5,250.*
10j A1 1sh blue green *8,250.*

Oblique Rouletted 13

7k A1 1p dull orange *6,500.*

1862-63 Wmk. 6 *Imperf.*

11 A1 1p orange ver 1,050. 275.00
 d. 1p carmine vermilion ('63) 475.00 300.00
 e. 1p vermilion 750.00 275.00
 f. 1p carmine 825.00 375.00
12 A1 2p deep blue 950.00 100.00
 d. 2p slate blue 2,000. 200.00
 e. Double impression 4,250.
 f. 2p milky blue, worn plate — 250.00
 g. 2p blue, worn plate 750.00 95.00
13 A1 3p brown lilac ('63) 750.00 95.00
14 A1 6p red brn ('63) 1,700. 115.00
 d. 6p black brown 2,000. 130.00
 e. 6p brown ('63) 2,100. 125.00
 f. 6p pale red brown 2,200. 170.00
 g. 6p gray brown 2,200. 180.00
15 A1 1sh yellow green 2,500. 375.00
 d. 1sh deep green 2,750. 400.00
 f. 1sh bronze green 2,000. 350.00
 g. 1sh olive green 2,850. 450.00

See No. 7e.

1862 *Pin Rouletted 9-10*

12a A1 2p deep blue — 3,100.
14a A1 6p black brown — 4,250.

1862 *Serrate Rouletted 16, 18*

11b A1 1p orange vermilion 11,000. 2,400.
12b A1 2p blue — 1,250.
13b A1 3p brown lilac 6,000. 1,850.
14b A1 6p black brown — 1,900.
 f. 6d brown 2,400.
15b A1 1sh yellow green 4,500.

1862 *Rouletted 7*

11c A1 1p vermilion 4,750. 850.
 g. 1p vermilion *3,500.* *850.*
 h. 1p carmine vermilion *5,000.* 1,050.
12c A1 2p blue 3,750. 500.
 h. 2p slate blue *4,500.* *1,050.*
 i. 2p pale blue *3,000.* *625.*
13c A1 3p brown lilac 3,800. 850.
14c A1 6p red brown 3,500. 525.
 h. 6p brown *3,800.* *600.*
 i. 6p black brown *3,800.* *525.*
 j. 6p gray brown *3,000.* *825.*
15c A1 1sh green 4,000. 950.
 h. 1sh green *4,000.* *950.*
 i. 1sh deep green *5,250.* *1,100.*
 j. 1sh bluish green *5,250.* *1,200.*

The 1p, 2p, 6p and 1sh come in two or more shades.

"H" Rouletted 16

12n A1 2p deep blue *2,200.*
14n A1 6p black brown *2,200.*
15n A1 1sh deep green *4,250.*
 o. 1sh bluish green *4,250.*

"Y" Rouletted 18

11p A1 1p orange vermilion *2,500.*
12p A1 2p deep blue *2,000.*
 t. 2p slate blue *2,100.*
13p A1 3p brown-lilac *2,600.*
14p A1 6p black brown *2,000.*
 t. 6p brown *2,250.*
15p A1 1sh yellowish green *4,400.*

Oblique Rouletted 13

12q A1 2p deep blue *2,400.*
 u. 2p slate blue —
13q A1 3p brown-lilac *3,250.*
14q A1 6p black brown *2,750.*

Square Rouletted 14

11r A1 1p orange vermilion *2,600.*
12r A1 2p deep blue *2,150.*
13r A1 3p brown lilac *3,250.*
14r A1 6p black brown *2,600.*

Serrate Rouletted 13

11s A1 1p orange vermilion *3,250.*
12s A1 2p deep blue *2,400.*
13s A1 3p brown lilac *4,500.* *2,200.*
14s A1 6p black brown *2,400.*
15s A1 1sh black brown *4,400.*

1863 *Perf. 13*

16 A1 1p carmine ver 2,850. 425.00
 a. 1p orange vermilion 2,850. 425.00
 b. 1p vermilion 2,850. 425.00
 c. As "a.," pair, imperf between 10,000.
17 A1 2p blue, no plate wear 2,850. 450.00
 a. 2p deep blue, no plate wear 1,050. 110.00
 b. 2p slate blue, slight plate wear — 750.00
 c. 2p milky blue, slight plate wear 350.00 525.00
18 A1 3p brown lilac 2,750. 525.00
19 A1 6p red brown 1,450. 120.00
 a. 6p brown 1,650. 165.00
 b. 6p black brown 1,900. 225.00
 c. As "b," horiz. pair, imperf. btwn. —
20 A1 1sh green 2,850. 375.00
 a. 1sh deep green 2,850. 425.00
 b. 1sh yellow green 3,100. 425.00
 c. 1sh bluish green 3,100. 425.00
 d. 1sh bronze green 3,250. 425.00

This issue was made at Dunedin by perforating stamps of the previous issue. Most of the shades known imperf also are known perf. 13.

1862 Unwmk. *Imperf.*
Pelure Paper

21 A1 1p vermilion 15,000. 2,500.
 b. Rouletted 7 6,500.
 c. Serrate rouletted 13 10,000.
22 A1 2p pale dull ultra 5,250. 1,000.
 c. 2p gray blue 6,000. 1,000.
23 A1 3p brown lilac *50,000.*
24 A1 6p black brown 3,300. 400.
 b. Rouletted 7 4,000. 500.
 c. Serrate rouletted 15 — *6,000.*
 d. Serrate rouletted 13 *6,250.*
25 A1 1sh deep yel green 14,500. 1,150.
 b. 1sh deep green 14,500. *1,150.*
 c. Rouletted 7 15,000. *1,900.*
 d. Serrate rouletted 15 *5,000.*
 e. "Y" rouletted 18 *5,000.*

No. 23 was never placed in use.

1863 *Perf. 13*

21a A1 1p vermilion 15,000. 3,500.
22a A1 2p gray blue 9,000. 1,100.
 b. 2p pale dull ultramarine 8,000. 1,100.
24a A1 6p black brown 8,000. 400.
25a A1 1sh deep green 14,000. 2,100.

1863 Unwmk. *Perf. 13*
Thick White Paper

26 A1 2p dull dark blue 3,750. 1,000.
 a. Imperf. 2,000. 1,000.
 b. Pin Roulette 9-10 *2,500.*

Nos. 26 and 26a differ from 8 and 8d by a white patch of wear at right of head.

1864 Wmk. 59 *Imperf.*
27 A1 1p carmine ver 950. 375.
28 A1 2p blue 1,650. 275.
d. 2p pale blue (advanced plate wear) 1,650. 275.
e. 2p deep blue (advanced plate wear) 1,650. 275.
29 A1 6p red brown 5,250. 750.
30 A1 1sh green 1,900. 315.

1864 *Rouletted 7*
27a A1 1p carmine vermilion 6,250. 3,100.
28a A1 2p blue 2,500. 775.
29a A1 6p deep red brown 7,250. 3,100.
30a A1 1sh green 4,250. 1,150.

1864 *Perf. 12½*
27B A1 1p carmine ver 12,000. 5,000.
28B A1 2p blue 450. 80.
29B A1 6p red brown 625. 70.
30B A1 1sh dp yel green 7,750. 3,100.

1864 *Perf. 13*
27C A1 1p carmine ver 11,500. 5,000.
d. "Y" roulette 18 *7,000.*
28C A1 2p blue 1,100. 210.
30C A1 1sh yellow green 2,400. 800.
d. Horiz. pair, imperf. btwn. *45,000.*
e. Perf. 6½x13 4,750.

1864-71 Wmk. 6 *Perf. 12½*
31 A1 1p vermilion 225.00 42.50
a. 1p orange ('71) 600.00 95.00
b. 1p pale org & ver 275.00 42.50
c. 1p Imperf. pair 4,500. 2,750.
d. 1p Vert. pair, imperf. btwn.
e. 1p carmine 250.00 125.00
32 A1 2p blue 225.00 22.00
a. 2p blue, worn plate 325.00 30.00
b. Horiz. pair, imperf. btwn. (#32) *5,250.*
c. Perf. 10x12½ 19,000.
d. Imperf., pair (#32) *2,750.* *2,000.*
e. indigo ('65), plate II 325.00 *75.00*
f. As "e", horiz. pair, imperf. btwn.
g. 2p greenish blue 325.00 75.00
33 A1 3p lilac 165.00 35.00
a. 3p mauve 850.00 90.00
b. Imperf. pair (#33) *4,500.* *2,000.*
c. As "a", imperf. pair *5,000.* *2,000.*
d. 3p brown lilac 2,600. 800.00
34 A1 4p deep rose ('65) 3,250. 275.00
35 A1 4p yellow ('65) 250.00 130.00
a. 4p orange yellow *2,350.* 1,000.
36 A1 6p red brown 325.00 27.50
a. 6p brown 375.00 42.50
b. Horiz. pair, imperf. btwn. 3,000. 3,000.
c. Imperf. pair 2,250. 3,250.
37 A1 1sh yellow green 325.00 125.00
a. 1sh green 700.00 135.00
b. 1sh deep green 1,300. 375.00
c. Imperf. pair 5,500. 4,250.

The 1p, 2p and 6p come in two or more shades.

The 2p plate used for No. 32 was damaged and retouched in the bottom quarter of the plate. This is found also on all subsequent 2p issues.

Imperforate examples of the 1p pale orange, worn plate; 2p dull blue and 6p dull chocolate brown are official reprints. Value, each $100.

1871 Wmk. 6 *Perf. 10*
38 A1 1p deep brown 950.00 130.00
38A A1 2p blue *29,000.*
38B A1 2p vermilion *24,000.*

There is only one known of both 38A and 38B.

1871 *Perf. 12½*
39 A1 1p brown 250.00 55.00
a. Imperf. pair 3,500. 2,250.
b. Vert. pair, imperf. horiz. 3,500. 5,750.
40 A1 2p orange 190.00 31.00
a. 2p vermilion 225.00 35.00
b. Imperf. pair 2,750. —
41 A1 6p blue 375.00 75.00
a. 6p pale blue 225.00 60.00
Nos. 39-41 (3) 815.00 161.00

1871 *Perf. 10x12½*
42 A1 1p brown 425.00 55.00
b. Perf. 12½ on 3 sides, 10 on 1 side 700.00 200.00
c. Perf. 12½x10 5,000.
42A A1 2p blue *14,000.*
43 A1 2p orange 300.00 42.50
a. Perf. 12½ on 3 sides, 10 on 1 side 1,900. 500.00
44 A1 6p blue 2,400. 575.00
a. 6p deep blue 3,250. 950.00
b. Perf. 12½ on 3 sides 10 on 1 side 1,700. 475.00
c. Vert. pair, imperf. btwn. *6,000.* —
d. Horiz. pair, imperf. vert. —
Nos. 42-44 (3) 3,125. 672.50

1873 Wmk. 59 *Perf. 12½*
45 A1 1p brown 8,500.
46 A1 2p vermilion 1,550. 400.00
a. Imperf. pair *4,750.*

1873 Unwmk. *Perf. 12½*
47 A1 1p brown 1,150. 260.00
48 A1 2p vermilion 160.00 60.00
49 A1 4p yellow orange 225.00 *925.00*

The watermark "T.H. SAUNDERS" in double-line capitals falls on 32 of the 240 stamps in a sheet. The 1p and 2p also are known with script "WT & CO" watermark.

1873 Wmk. 60
50 A1 2p vermilion *3,500.* 750.

A2

A3

A4

A5

A6

A7

1874 Typo. Wmk. 62 *Perf. 12½*
51 A2 1p violet 120.00 15.50
a. Bluish paper 240.00 45.00
b. Imperf. pair 750.00 1,650.
c. Perf. 12x12½ 1,650. 400.00
52 A3 2p rose 120.00 9.00
a. Bluish paper 240.00 42.50
b. Perf. 12 1,300. 210.00
c. Perf. 12x12½ 1,300. 350.00
53 A4 3p brown 210.00 85.00
a. Bluish paper 400.00 110.00
54 A5 4p claret 315.00 75.00
a. Bluish paper 625.00 125.00
55 A6 6p blue 275.00 13.50
a. Bluish paper 475.00 60.00
56 A7 1sh green 625.00 40.00
a. Bluish paper 1,150. 200.00
Nos. 51-56 (6) 1,665. 238.00

1874 *Perf. 12½, 10*
51f A2 1p violet 175.00 45.00
g. Bluish paper 275.00 65.00
52f A3 2p rose 250.00 95.00
g. Bluish paper 600.00 110.00
53f A4 3p brown 225.00 90.00
g. Bluish paper 425.00 125.00
54f A5 4p claret 850.00 165.00
g. Bluish paper 425.00 125.00
55f A6 6p blue 325.00 55.00
g. Bluish paper 475.00 110.00
56f A7 1sh green 700.00 150.00
g. Bluish paper 1,200. 275.00
h. Vert. pair, imperf. between *6,750.*

1878 *Perf. 12x11½*
51i A2 1p violet 65.00 9.00
52i A3 2p rose 70.00 8.00
54i A5 4p claret 210.00 60.00
55i A6 6p blue 140.00 12.50
56i A7 1sh green 225.00 50.00

1875 Wmk. 6 *Perf. 12½*
57 A2 1p violet 2,000. 310.00
58 A3 2p rose 775.00 45.00

A8

1878 Wmk. 62 *Perf. 12x11½*
59 A8 2sh deep rose 750.00 450.00
60 A8 5sh gray 800.00 500.00

No. 60 has numeral "5" in each of the four spandrels.

Beware of cleaned fiscally used examples of Nos. 59-60.

A9

A10

A11

A12

A13

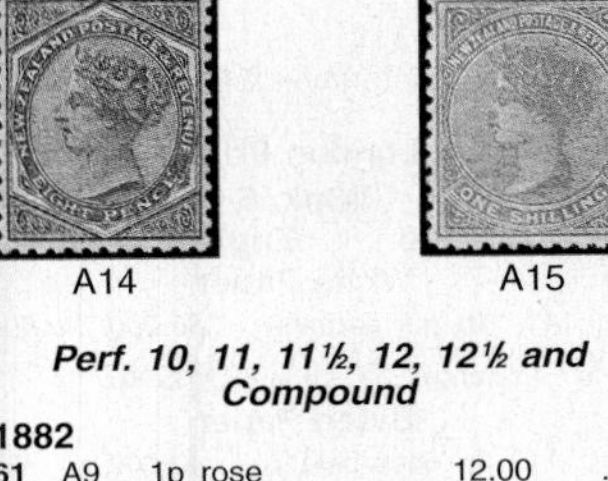
A14

A15

Perf. 10, 11, 11½, 12, 12½ and Compound

1882
61 A9 1p rose 12.00 .70
a. Vert. pair, imperf. horiz. *950.00*
b. Perf. 12x11½ 50.00 7.00
c. Perf. 12½ 300.00 175.00
d. Imperf., pair 900.00
e. 1p deep carmine, perf. 11 6.50 1.80
f. 1p deep carmine, thin course paper ('98) 16.50 3.50
62 A10 2p violet 13.50 .35
a. Vert. pair, imperf. btwn. *950.00*
b. Perf. 12½ 200.00 110.00
c. Imperf., pair 1,000.
d. 2p deep purple, thin course paper ('99) 22.50 6.50
63 A11 3p orange 60.00 9.50
a. 3p yellow ('99) 62.50 14.00
b. 3p pale yellow, thin course paper ('99) 110.00 25.00
64 A12 4p blue green 62.50 4.50
a. Perf. 10x11 95.00 13.00
b. 4p yellow green ('95) 65.00 6.50
65 A13 6p brown 80.00 8.00
a. 6p black brown ('97) 90.00 5.50
b. 6p brown, thin course paper ('98) 140.00 14.50
66 A14 8p blue 80.00 60.00
67 A15 1sh red brown 125.00 15.00
d. Vert. pair, imperf. btwn. *1,800.*
Nos. 61-67 (7) 433.00 98.05

See #87. For overprints see #O1-O2, O5, O7-O8.

A15a

A16

A17

1891-95
67A A15a ½p black ('95) 4.25 .25
b. Perf. 12x11½ 37.50 *90.00*
c. ½p black, thin course paper ('98) 42.50 6.50
68 A16 2½p ultramarine 57.50 5.00
a. Perf. 12½ 375.00 200.00
b. 2½p ultramarine, thin course paper ('98) 110.00 27.50
69 A17 5p olive gray 70.00 25.00
a. 5p olive gray, thin course paper ('99) 75.00 42.50
Nos. 67A-69 (3) 131.75 30.25

In 1893 advertisements were printed on the backs of Nos. 61-67, 68-69.

See #86C. For overprints see #O3-O4, O9.

Mt. Cook — A18

Lake Taupo — A19

Pembroke Peak — A20

Mt. Earnslaw, Lake Wakitipu — A21

Mt. Earnslaw, Lake Wakitipu — A22

Huia, Sacred Birds — A23

White Terrace, Rotomahana A24

Otira Gorge and Mt. Ruapehu A25

Kiwi A26

Maori Canoe A27

Pink Terrace, Rotomahana A28

Kea & Kaka (Hawk-billed Parrots) A29

Milford Sound — A30

Mt. Cook — A31

Perf. 12 to 16

1898, Apr. 5 Engr. Unwmk.
70 A18 ½p lilac gray 9.00 1.65
a. Horiz. or vert. pair, imperf. btwn. 1,750. 1,450.
b. ½p purple brown 9.00 1.65
c. ½p purple black 9.00 2.50
71 A19 1p yel brn & bl 6.00 .75
a. Horiz. or vert. pair, imperf. btwn. 1,350. 1,350.
b. Imperf. pair 950.00 850.00
c. 1p brown & blue 6.00 1.00
d. As "c," horiz. or vert. pair, imperf. btwn. 1,350. 1,350.
72 A20 2p rose brown 57.50 .30
a. Horiz. pair, imperf. vert. 650.00
b. Vert. pair, imperf. btwn. 1,300.
c. 2p lake 45.00 .30

d. As "c," horiz. pair, imperf. vert. 650.00
e. As "c," horiz. pair, imperf. btwn.
f. As "c," vert. pair, imperf. btwn.
73 A21 2½p bl (*Wakitipu*) 16.00 *47.50*
a. 2½p sky bl (*Wakitipu*) 14.00 50.00
74 A22 2½p bl (*Wakatipu*) 50.00 9.00
a. 2½p deep bl (*Wakitipu*) 50.00 9.00
75 A23 3p orange brn 35.00 9.00
76 A24 4p rose 17.00 *21.00*
a. 4p bright rose 17.00 21.00
b. 4p lake rose 22.50 25.00
77 A25 5p red brown 95.00 200.00
a. 5p violet brown 65.00 *25.00*
78 A26 6p green 85.00 50.00
a. 6p grass green 210.00 *240.00*
79 A27 8p dull blue 75.00 50.00
a. 8p indigo 75.00 50.00
b. 8p Prussian blue 75.00 50.00
80 A28 9p lilac 70.00 42.50
81 A29 1sh dull red 100.00 30.00
a. Pair, imperf. between 5,250.
b. 1sh vermilion 100.00 30.00
82 A30 2sh blue green 275.00 160.00
a. Vert. pair, imperf. btwn. 5,500. 5,250.
83 A31 5sh vermilion 375.00 *525.00*
Nos. 70-83 (14) 1,266. *1,147.*

The 5sh stamps are often found with revenue cancellations that are embossed or show a crown on the top of a circle. These are worth much less.

See Nos. 84, 88-89, 91-98, 99B, 102, 104, 106-107, 111-112, 114-121, 126-128, 1508-1521 (in Scott Standard catalogue, Vol. 5). For overprint see No. O10.

A32 A33

1900 Wmk. 63 *Perf. 11*
Thick Soft Wove Paper
84 A18 ½p green 9.00 2.00
a. ½p yellow-green 9.50 2.00
b. ½p pale yellow-green ('00) 20.00 6.25
c. ½p deep green 10.00 2.00
d. As "c," pair, imperf. btwn. 575.00
85 A32 1p carmine rose 14.00 .25
a. 1p lake 45.00 5.00
b. 1p crimson 14.00 .25
c. As "b," pair, imperf. btwn. 1,650. 1,750.
d. As "c," horiz. pair, imperf. vert. 650.00
86 A33 2p red violet 15.00 .75
a. Pair, imperf. btwn. 1,450.
b. 2p dull violet ('00) 19.00 .65
d. Pair, imperf. btwn. 1,550.
e. 2p mauve 22.00 1.50
Nos. 84-86 (3) 38.00 3.00

Nos. 84 and 86 are re-engravings of Nos. 70 and 72 and are slightly smaller.

See No. 110. For Handstamp see No. O18.

A34

1899-1900 Wmk. 63
86C A15a ½p black ('00) 9.00 *18.00*
87 A10 2p violet ('00) 30.00 19.00

Unwmk.
88 A22 2½p blue 21.00 4.00
a. Horiz. pair, imperf. vert. 1,500.
b. Vert. pair, imperf. btwn. 650.00 —
c. 2½p deep blue 21.50 4.00
89 A23 3p org brown 27.50 2.50
a. Horiz. pair, imperf. vert. 650.00
b. Horiz. pair, imperf. btwn. 1,525.
c. 3p deep brown 27.50 2.50
d. As "c," pair, imperf. btwn. 1,550. 2.50
90 A34 4p yel brn & bl ('00) 6.00 3.75
c. 4p chestnut & bright blue 6.00 3.75
d. 4p bister-brown & deep blue 6.00 3.75
91 A25 5p red brown 50.00 9.00
a. 5p violet brown 60.00 9.00
b. Pair, imperf. between *3,250.*
92 A26 6p green 70.00 *75.00*
a. 6p yellow-green 110.00 *125.00*
93 A26 6p rose ('00) 50.00 8.00
a. 6p carmine 50.00 8.00
b. 6p scarlet 80.00 27.00
c. As "b," double impression 875.00 *925.00*
d. As #93, horiz. pair, imperf. vert. 600.00
e. As "a", horiz. pair, imperf. vert. 500.00
f. As "b," horiz. pair, imperf. vert. 825.00
g. As #93, horiz. pair, imperf. btwn. 1,400.
h. As "a", vert. pair, imperf. btwn. 1,600.
94 A27 8p dark blue 50.00 20.00
a. 8p Prussian blue 50.00 20.00
95 A28 9p red lilac 60.00 37.50
a. 9p rosy purple 50.00 17.00
96 A29 1sh red 70.00 11.00
a. 1sh dull orange-red 70.00 6.50
b. 1sh dull brown-red 70.00 16.50
c. 1sh bright red 75.00 40.00
97 A30 2sh blue green 215.00 60.00
a. 2sh, "laid paper" 225.00 250.00
b. 2sh gray-green 150.00 65.00
98 A31 5sh vermilion 300.00 400.00
Revenue cancel 27.50
a. 5sh carmine red 325.00 450.00
Nos. 86C-98 (13) 958.50 667.75

See #113. For overprints see #O11-O15.

The 5sh stamps are often found with revenue cancellations that are embossed or show a crown on the top of a circle. These are worth much less.

"Commerce" — A35

1901, Jan. 1 Unwmk. *Perf. 12 to 16*
99 A35 1p carmine 7.00 4.50

Universal Penny Postage.

See Nos. 100, 103, 105, 108, 129. For overprint see Nos. 121a, O16, O18, O24, O32. Compare design A35 with A42.

Boer War Contingent A36

1901 Wmk. 63 *Perf. 11*
Thick Soft Paper
99B A18 ½p green 14.00 7.50
c. Pair, imperf. btwn. 650.00
100 A35 1p carmine 10.00 .25
a. Horiz. pair, imperf. vert. 425.00 325.00
b. 1p carmine-lake 26.00 12.00
101 A36 1½p brown org 10.00 4.00
a. Vert. pair, imperf. horiz. 1,200.
b. As "d," imperf. pair 1,250.
c. Horiz. pair, imperf. vert. 1,300.
d. 1½p pale chestnut 10.00 4.00
e. 1½p brown 50.00 55.00
f. 1½p khaki 1,200. 750.00
g. As "d," horiz. pair, imperf. vert. 1,300.
h. As "e," imperf. pair 1,300.
Nos. 99B-101 (3) 34.00 11.75

Perf. 14
99Bd A18 ½p green 24.00 7.00
100c A35 1p carmine 70.00 23.00
d. Horiz. pair, imperf. vert. 350.00

Perf. 14x11
99Be A18 ½p green 12.00 16.50
100e A35 1p carmine 300.00 125.00

Perf. 11x14
99Bf A18 ½p green 14.00 27.50
100f A35 1p carmine 2,400. 925.00

Perf. 11, 14 mixed
99Bg A18 ½p green 60.00 90.00
100g A35 1p carmine 300.00 125.00

No. 101 was issued to honor the New Zealand forces in the South African War.

See No. 109.

Thin Hard Paper
Perf. 14
102 A18 ½p green 42.50 42.50
a. Horiz. pair, imperf. vert. 400.00
103 A35 1p carmine 18.00 8.00
a. Horiz. pair, imperf. vert. 300.00
b. Vert. pair, imperf. horiz. 300.00

Perf. 11
102c A18 ½p green 95.00 125.00
103c A35 1p carmine 165.00 145.00

Perf. 14x11
102d A18 ½p green 50.00 70.00
103d A35 1p carmine 35.00 20.00

Perf. 11x14
102e A18 ½p green 26.00 55.00
103e A35 1p carmine 10.00 4.00

Perf. 11, 14 mixed
102f A18 ½p green 70.00 105.00
103f A35 1p carmine 82.50 87.50

1902 Unwmk. *Perf. 14*
104 A18 ½p green 35.00 8.50
105 A35 1p carmine 12.50 4.25

Perf. 11
104a A18 ½p green 200.00 210.00

Perf. 14x11
104b A18 ½p green 145.00 210.00
105b A35 1p carmine 125.00 145.00

Perf. 11x14
104c A18 ½p green 200.00 350.00
105c A35 1p carmine 145.00 200.00

Perf. 11, 14 mixed
104d A18 ½p green 175.00 250.00
105d A35 1p carmine 130.00 175.00

1902 *Perf. 11*
Thin White Wove Paper
106 A26 6p rose red 45.00 8.50
a. Watermarked letters 100.00 110.00

The sheets of No. 106 are watermarked with the words "LISBON SUPERFINE" in two lines, covering ten stamps.

1902-07 Wmk. 61 *Perf. 14*
107 A18 ½p green 9.00 2.75
a. Horiz. pair, imperf. vert. 300.00
108 A35 1p carmine 4.25 .25
a. 1p rose carmine 4.25 .25
d. Horiz. pair, imperf. vert. 200.00
e. Vert. pair, imperf. horiz. 200.00
f. Booklet pane of 6 275.00
g. As "a," horiz. pair, imperf. vert. 200.00
h. As "a," vert. pair, imperf. horiz. 200.00
i. As "a," booklet pane of 6 300.00
j. 1p deep carmine 35.00 4.50
109 A36 1½p brown org ('07) 25.00 *55.00*
110 A33 2p dull vio ('03) 12.00 2.75
a. 2p purple 12.00 2.75
b. As "a," horiz. pair, imperf. vert. 550.00 *800.00*
c. As "a," vert. pair, imperf. horiz. 775.00
111 A22 2½p blue 30.00 5.00
a. 2½p deep blue 30.00 5.00
112 A23 3p org brown 32.50 8.00
a. Horiz. pair, imperf. vert. 1,000.
113 A34 4p yel brn & bl 10.00 4.50
a. Horiz. pair, imperf. vert. 650.00
b. Vert. pair, imperf. horiz. 650.00
114 A25 5p red brown 40.00 16.00
a. 5p violet brown 60.00 37.50
115 A26 6p rose red 60.00 9.00
b. 6p pink 60.00 9.00
d. As, "b," horiz. pair, imperf. vert. 850.00
116 A27 8p steel blue 45.00 11.50
117 A28 9p red violet 45.00 8.00
118 A29 1sh pale red 175.00 60.00
a. 1sh orange red 80.00 8.00
b. 1sh orange brown 80.00 8.00
119 A30 2sh green 150.00 32.50
a. 2sh blue green 190.00 42.50
120 A31 5sh deep red 240.00 *300.00*
a. 5sh dull red 240.00 *300.00*
Nos. 107-120 (14) 877.75 515.25

The unique example of No. 113 with inverted center is used and is in the New Zealand National Philatelic Collection.

1902-03 *Perf. 11*
107e A18 ½p green 70.00 *120.00*
108k A35 1p carmine *800.00* *800.00*
111e A22 2½p blue 35.00 11.00
f. 2½p deep blue 35.00 11.00
112e A23 3p yellow brown 37.50 3.50
f. 3p bistre brown 45.00 3.50
g. 3p pale bistre 50.00 6.00
113e A34 4p yel brn & bl 6.00 *75.00*
f. Horiz. pair, imperf. vert. *650.00*
114e A25 5p deep brown 55.00 7.50
f. 5p red brown 55.00 9.00
g. 5p sepia 60.00 20.00
115e A26 6p rose 40.00 8.00
f. 6p bright carmine pink 65.00 9.00
g. 6p scarlet 75.00 17.50
h Horiz. pair, imperf. vert. 850.00
116e A27 8p deep blue 55.00 11.50
f. 8p steel blue 55.00 11.50
g. Horiz. pair, imperf. vert. 2,000.
h. Vert. pair, imperf. horiz. 2,000.
117e A28 9p red violet 70.00 11.00
118e A29 1sh orange red 75.00 7.50
f. 1sh brown red 75.00 14.00
g. 1sh bright red 75.00 14.00
h. Wmk. 62 — 2,000.
119e A30 2sh blue green 190.00 42.50
f. 2sh green 180.00 62.50
120e A31 5sh vermilion 275.00 *3.75*
f. 5sh deep red 300.00 *400.00*
Nos. (12) 1,709. 1,101.

1902-07 *Perf. compound 11 and 14*
107i A18 ½p green, perf. 14x11 ('02) 30.00 *125.00*
j. Perf 11x14 30.00 *90.00*
108l A35 1p carmine, perf 14x11 ('02) 100.00 *125.00*
m. Perf. 11x14 150.00 *150.00*
n. As "m," deep carmine 500.00 500.00
109i A36 1½p chestnut ('07) *1,600.*
110i A33 2p dull violet ('03) *500.00* *400.00*
112i A23 3p orange brown *1,000.* *750.00*
113i A34 4p yel brn & blue ('03) *450.00* *450.00*
114i A25 5p red brown ('06) *1,800.* *1,500.*
115i A26 6p rose carmine ('07) *450.00* *450.00*
116i A27 8p steel blue ('07) *1,500.* *1,500.*
117i A28 9p red violet ('06) *1,750.* *1,600.*
120i A31 5sh deep red ('06) *3,500.* *3,250.*

1903-07 *Perf. mixed 11 and 14*
107k A18 ½p green 40.00 *77.50*
108o A35 1p carmine 35.00 *55.00*
p. 1p rose carmine 35.00 *55.00*
q. 1p deep carmine 300.00 *325.00*
109k A36 1½p chestnut ('07) *1,600.*
110k A33 2p dull violet ('03) *450.00* *325.00*
112k A23 3p orange brown ('06) *1,000.* *750.00*
113k A34 4p yel brn & blue ('03) *425.00* *450.00*
114k A25 5p red brown ('06) *1,400.* *200.00*
115k A26 6p rose carmine ('07) *450.00* *450.00*
116k A27 8p steel blue ('07) *1,500.* *1,500.*
117k A28 9p red violet ('06) *1,650.* *1,600.*
119k A30 2sh blue green ('06) *1,750.* *1,800.*
120k A31 5sh deep red ('06) *3,500.* *3,250.*

Wmk. 61 is normally sideways on 3p, 5p, 6p, 8p and 1sh. The 6p exists with wmk. upright. The 1sh exists with wmk. upright and inverted.

See No. 129. For overprints see Nos. O17-O22.

The 5sh stamps are often found with revenue cancellations that are embossed or show a crown on the top of a circle. These are worth much less.

1903 Unwmk. *Perf. 11*
Laid Paper
121 A30 2sh blue green 225.00 *250.00*

No. 108a Overprinted in Green: "King Edward VII Land" in Two Lines Reading Up

1908, Jan. 15 *Perf. 14*
121a A35 1p rose carmine 475.00 42.50
b. Double overprint *1,600.*

In 1908 a quantity of the 1p carmine (A35) was overprinted "King Edward VII Land" and taken on a Shackleton expedition to the Antarctic. Because of the weather Shackleton landed at Victoria Land instead. The stamp was never sold to the public at face value. See No. 121a.

Similar conditions prevailed for the 1909-12½p green and 1p carmine overprinted "VICTORIA LAND." See Nos. 130d-131d.

Christchurch Exhibition Issue

Arrival of the Maoris A37

Maori Art — A38

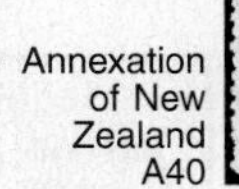

Landing of Capt. Cook A39

Annexation of New Zealand A40

Wmk. 61
1906, Nov. Typo. *Perf. 14*
122 A37 ½p emerald 37.50 *37.50*
123 A38 1p vermilion 18.00 27.50
a. 1p claret *15,000.* *25,000.*
124 A39 3p blue & brown 60.00 *115.00*
125 A40 6p gray grn & rose 220.00 *425.00*
Nos. 122-125 (4) 335.50 *605.00*

Value for No. 123a is for a fine example.

Designs of 1902-07 Issue, but smaller

1907-08 Engr. *Perf. 14x15*
126 A23 3p orange brown *55.00* 17.50
127 A26 6p carmine rose *55.00* 11.50
128 A29 1sh orange red *125.00* 26.00
Nos. 126-128 (3) *235.00* 55.00

Perf. 14x13, 13½ Compound
126a A23 3p orange brown 60.00 55.00
127a A26 6p carmine red 475.00 190.00
128a A29 1sh orange red 155.00 70.00

Perf. 14
126b A23 3p orange brown 100.00 30.00
127b A26 6p carmine red 50.00 11.00

The small stamps are about 21mm high, those of 1898-1902 about 23mm.

Type of 1902 Redrawn

1908 **Typo.** ***Perf. 14x14½***
129 A35 1p carmine 40.00 3.00

REDRAWN, 1p: The lines of shading in the globe are diagonal and the other lines of the design are generally thicker than on No. 108.

Edward VII
A41

"Commerce"
A42

1909-12 ***Perf. 14x14½***
130 A41 ½p yellow green 7.25 .55
a. Booklet pane of 6 *225.00*
b. Booklet pane 5 + label *775.00*
c. Imperf., pair 250.00
131 A42 1p carmine 2.00 .25
a. Imperf., pair 410.00
b. Booklet pane of 6 225.00

Perf. 14x14½
Engr.
Various Frames

132 A41 2p mauve 25.00 7.25
133 A41 3p orange brown 27.50 1.40
134 A41 4p red orange 32.50 *27.50*
135 A41 4p yellow ('12) 22.50 *13.50*
136 A41 5p red brown 22.00 5.00
137 A41 6p carmine rose 50.00 1.75
138 A41 8p deep blue 20.00 3.25
139 A41 1sh vermilion 75.00 6.75
Nos. 130-139 (10) 283.75 67.20

Perf. 14
133a A41 3p orange brown 55.00 22.00
134a A41 4p red orange 22.00 16.50
136a A41 5p red brown 29.00 5.00
137a A41 6p carmine rose 45.00 11.00
138a A41 8p deep blue 50.00 100.00
d. No wmk. 110.00 200.00
139a A41 1sh vermilion 65.00 15.00

Perf. 14x13½
133b A41 3p orange brown 82.50 145.00
c. Vert. pair, perf. 14x13½ and 14x14½ 275.00 475.00
136b A41 5p red brown 21.00 3.25
c. Vert. pair, perf. 14x13½ and 14x14½ 275.00 475.00
137b A41 6p carmine rose 82.50 145.00
c. Vert. pair, perf. 14x13½ and 14x14½ 275.00 475.00
138b A41 8p deep blue 50.00 3.25
c. Vert. pair, perf. 14x13½ and 14x14½ 275.00 475.00

See No. 177. For overprints see Nos. 130d-131d, 130e-137e, O33-O37, O49, O54; Cook Islands No. 49.

Nos. 130-131 Overprinted in Black: "VICTORIA LAND" in Two Lines

1911-13
130d A41 ½p yellow green *1,100.* *950.00*
131d A42 1p carmine 70.00 *150.00*

See note after No. 120.
Issue dates: 1p, Feb. 9; ½p, Jan. 18, 1913.

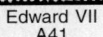

Stamps of 1909 Overprinted in Black

1913
130e A41 ½p yellow green 25.00 *55.00*
131e A42 1p carmine 35.00 *45.00*
133e A41 3p orange brown 250.00 *400.00*
137e A41 6p carmine rose 300.00 *500.00*
Nos. 130e-137e (4) 610.00 *1,000.*

This issue was valid only within New Zealand and to Australia from Dec. 1, 1913, to Feb. 28, 1914. The Auckland Stamp Collectors Club inspired this issue.

King George V — A43

1915 **Typo.** ***Perf. 14x15***
144 A43 ½p yellow green 2.00 .25
b. Booklet pane of 6 *150.00*

See Nos. 163-164, 176, 178. For overprints see Nos. O41, O45-O46, MR1; Cook Islands No. 48.

A44

A45

1915-22 **Engr.** ***Perf. 14x13½***
145 A44 1½p gray 4.25 2.00
a. Perf. 14x14½ 5.50 2.00
b. Vert. pair, both perfs 39.00 *110.00*
146 A45 2p purple 14.50 *45.00*
a. Perf. 14x14½ 7.75 *55.00*
b. Vert. pair, both perfs 30.00 *175.00*
147 A45 2p org yel ('16) 9.50 *35.00*
a. Perf. 14x14½ 9.50 *35.00*
b. Vert. pair, both perfs 23.00 *275.00*
148 A44 2½p dull blue 3.50 *7.50*
a. Perf. 14x14½ 10.00 *35.00*
b. Vert. pair, both perfs 45.00 *200.00*
149 A45 3p violet brown 16.50 1.40
a. Vert. pair, both perfs 55.00 *150.00*
b. Perf. 14x14½ 13.00 2.25
150 A45 4p orange yellow 4.75 *60.00*
a. Vert. pair, both perfs 30.00 *275.00*
b. Perf. 14x14½ 4.75 *60.00*
151 A45 4p purple ('16) 22.50 .55
a. Perf. 14x14½ 7.50 .55
b. Vert. pair, both perfs 65.00 *165.00*
c. 4p blackish violet 10.00 .55
d. Vert. pair, top stamp imperf., bottom stamp perf 3 sides *1,200.*
152 A44 4½p dark green 25.00 *26.00*
a. Perf. 14x14½ 15.00 *60.00*
b. Vert. pair, both perfs 60.00 *190.00*
153 A45 5p light blue ('21) 19.00 1.10
a. Imperf., pair 250.00 200.00
b. Perf. 14x14½ 13.00 *42.50*
c. Vert. pair, both perfs 90.00 *275.00*
154 A45 6p carmine rose 13.00 .55
a. Horiz. pair, imperf. vert.
b. Perf. 14x14½ 11.00 .65
c. Vert. pair, both perfs 70.00 *155.00*
155 A44 7½p red brown 22.50 *26.00*
a. Perf. 14x14½ 12.00 *90.00*
b. Vert. pair, both perfs 55.00 *250.00*
156 A45 8p blue ('21) 25.00 *50.00*
a. Perf. 14x14½ 9.50 *60.00*
b. Vert. pair, both perfs 42.50 *200.00*
157 A45 8p red brown ('22) 35.00 4.00
158 A45 9p olive green 30.00 5.00
a. Imperf., pair *1,500.*
b. Perf. 14x14½ 16.50 *32.50*
c. Vert. pair, both perfs 82.50 *250.00*
159 A45 1sh vermilion 30.00 .60
a. Imperf., pair 450.00
b. Perf. 14x14½ 15.00 .55
c. Vert. pair, both perfs 82.50 *300.00*
Nos. 145-159 (15) 275.00 264.70

Nos. 145-156, 158-159 exist in vert. pairs with perf 14x13½ on top and perf 14x14½ on the bottom. These sell for a premium. The 5p and No. 151c exist with the perf varieties reversed. These are rare. No. 157 only comes perf 14x13½.

The former Nos. 151a and 151b probably were listed from sheets with No. 151d. They probably do not exist.

For overprints see Nos. O47-O48, O50-O53; Cook Islands Nos. 53-60.

A46

A47

No. 160

No. 161

The engr. stamps have a background of geometric lathe-work; the typo. stamps have a background of crossed dotted lines.

Type A43 has three diamonds at each side of the crown, type A46 has two, and type A47 has one.

1916-19 **Typo.** ***Perf. 14x15***
160 A46 1½p gray black 9.00 1.40
161 A47 1½p gray black 11.00 .60
162 A47 1½p brown org ('18) 42.50 *100.00*
a. Perf. 14 9.50 *45.00*
163 A43 2p yellow 2.60 .25
a. Perf. 14 3.00 .25
164 A43 3p chocolate ('19) 12.00 1.50
a. Perf. 14 9.50 4.00
Nos. 160-164 (5) 77.10 103.75

In 1916 the 1½, 2, 3 and 6p of the 1915-16 issue and the 8p of the 1909 issue were printed on paper intended for the long rectangular stamps of the 1902-07 issue. In this paper the watermarks are set wide apart, so that the smaller stamps often show only a small part of the watermark or miss it altogether.

For overprints see Nos. O42-O44; Cook Islands Nos. 50-52.

Victory Issue

"Peace" and British Lion — A48

Peace and Lion — A49

Maori Chief — A50

British Lion — A51

"Victory" — A52

King George V, Lion and Maori Fern at Sides — A53

1920, Jan. 27 ***Perf. 14***
165 A48 ½p yellow green 3.25 2.75
166 A49 1p carmine 4.50 .65
167 A50 1½p brown orange 3.50 .55
168 A51 3p black brown 15.00 *16.00*
169 A52 6p purple 17.00 *19.00*
170 A53 1sh vermilion 25.00 *55.00*
Nos. 165-170 (6) 68.25 *93.95*

No. 165 Surcharged in Red

1922, Mar.
174 A48 2p on ½p yellow green 6.00 1.50

Map of New Zealand — A54

1923 **Typo.** ***Perf. 14x15***
175 A54 1p carmine rose 4.75 .70

Restoration of Penny Postage. The paper varies from thin to thick.

Types of 1909-15
N Z and Star 'watermark' printed on back, usually in blue

1925 **Unwmk.** ***Perf. 14x14½***
176 A43 ½p yellow green 3.50 *3.50*
177 A42 1p carmine 3.50 .90
178 A43 2p yellow 20.00 *62.50*
Nos. 176-178 (3) 27.00 *66.90*

Exhibition Buildings
A55

1925, Nov. 17 **Wmk. 61**
Surface Tinted Paper
179 A55 ½p yel green, *grnsh* 3.50 *16.50*
180 A55 1p car rose, *pink* 4.25 *7.50*
181 A55 4p red violet, *lilac* 37.50 *80.00*
Nos. 179-181 (3) 45.25 *104.00*

Dunedin Exhibition.

George V in Admiral's Uniform
A56

In Field Marshal's Uniform
A57

1926 ***Perf. 14***
182 A56 2sh blue 70.00 35.00
a. 2sh dark blue 65.00 *67.50*
183 A56 3sh violet 130.00 *175.00*
a. 3sh deep violet 110.00 *190.00*
184 A57 1p rose red 1.25 .25
a. Booklet pane of 6 150.00
b. Imperf., pair 250.00
c. Perf. 14x14½ .70 .55
Nos. 182-184 (3) 201.25 210.25

For overprints see Nos. O55-O56 and Cook Islands Nos. 74-75.

Pied Fantail and Clematis
A58

Kiwi and Cabbage Palm
A59

Maori Woman Cooking in Boiling Spring
A60

Maori Council House (Whare)
A61

Mt. Cook and Mountain Lilies
A62

Maori Girl Wearing Tiki — A63

Mitre Peak — A64

Striped Marlin
A65

Harvesting — A66

Tuatara Lizard — A67

Maori Panel from Door — A68

Tui or Parson Bird — A69

Capt. Cook Landing at Poverty Bay — A70

Mt. Egmont, North Island A71

Perf. 13½-14x13½, 13-14x13½ (189, 192, 197, 198), 13½x14 (193), 14x14½ (195), 14 (191)

1935, May 1 Engr. Wmk. 61

No.	Type	Description	Unused	Used
185	A58	½p bright green	3.00	1.50
186	A59	1p copper red	2.50	1.00
c.		Perf. 13½x14	82.50	65.00
186A	A59	1p copper red, re-engraved	9.00	4.00
b.		Booklet pane of 6 + ad labels	80.00	
187	A60	1½p red brown	16.00	*22.00*
a.		Perf. 13½x14	6.50	13.00
188	A61	2p red orange	4.00	2.50
189	A62	2½p dull blue & dk brown	15.00	*45.00*
a.		Perf. 13½x14	10.00	30.00
190	A63	3p chocolate	13.50	4.00
191	A64	4p blk brn & blk	5.00	3.25
192	A65	5p violet blue	26.00	*35.00*
a.		Perf. 13½x14	28.00	55.00
193	A66	6p red	9.00	*12.00*
194	A67	8p dark brown	14.00	*21.00*

Litho.

Size: 18x21½mm

No.	Type	Description	Unused	Used
195	A68	9p blk & scar	16.00	7.00

Engr.

No.	Type	Description	Unused	Used
196	A69	1sh dk sl green	25.00	20.00
197	A70	2sh olive green	50.00	50.00
a.		Perf. 13½x14	70.00	65.00
198	A71	3sh yel brn & brn black	25.00	*55.00*
a.		Perf. 13½x14	25.00	65.00
		Nos. 185-198 (15)	233.00	283.25
		Set, never hinged	500.00	

On No. 186A, the horizontal lines in the sky are much darker.

The 2½p, 5p, 2sh and 3sh are perf. 13½ vertically; perf. 13-14 horizontally on each stamp.

See Nos. 203-216, 244-245. For overprints see Nos. O58-O71, O90.

Silver Jubilee Issue

Queen Mary and King George V A72

1935, May 7 *Perf. 11x11½*

No.	Type	Description	Unused	Used
199	A72	½p blue green	.75	1.00
200	A72	1p dark car rose	1.00	.75
201	A72	6p vermilion	20.00	*30.00*
		Nos. 199-201 (3)	21.75	*31.75*
		Set, never hinged	29.00	

25th anniv. of the reign of King George V.

Types of 1935

Perf. 13½-14x13½

1936-42 Wmk. 253

No.	Type	Description	Unused	Used
203	A58	½p bright green	2.00	.25
204	A59	1p copper red	2.00	.25
205	A60	1½p red brown	9.50	6.00
206	A61	2p red orange	.25	.25
a.		Perf. 14	16.50	.90
b.		Perf. 14x14½-15	21.00	*25.00*
c.		Perf. 12½	4.00	.25
207	A62	2½p dull blue & dk brn	1.50	*6.00*
a.		Perf. 14	10.00	1.65
b.		Perf. 13-14x13½	12.00	28.00
208	A63	3p chocolate	20.00	1.50
209	A64	4p blk brn & blk	10.00	1.25
a.		Perf. 12½	50.00	20.00
b.		Perf. 14	70.00	145.00
c.		Perf. 14x14¼	1.25	.25
210	A65	5p violet blue	2.50	1.25
a.		Perf. 12½	16.00	14.00
b.		Perf. 13-14x13½	30.00	3.75
211	A66	6p red, perf. 13½x14	27.50	2.00
a.		Perf. 12½	1.75	5.00
b.		Perf. 14½x14	1.50	.25
212	A67	8p dark brown	17.50	7.75
a.		Perf. 12½	2.25	1.60
b.		Perf. 14½x14	4.50	1.75

Litho.

Size: 18x21½mm

No.	Type	Description	Unused	Used
213	A68	9p gray & scarlet, perf.14x15	30.00	4.00
a.		9p black & scarlet, perf. 14x14½	32.50	4.25

Engr.

No.	Type	Description	Unused	Used
214	A69	1sh dk sl grn	3.50	1.25
a.		Perf. 12½	35.00	25.00
215	A70	2sh olive green	6.50	1.50
a.		Perf. 13½x14	175.00	4.00
b.		Perf. 12½	12.50	9.50
c.		Perf. 13-14x13½	55.00	12.00
216	A71	3sh yel brn & blk brn	5.50	3.25
a.		Perf. 12½ ('41)	45.00	50.00
b.		Perf. 13-14x13½	55.00	14.00
		Nos. 203-216 (14)	138.25	36.50
		Set, never hinged	180.00	

Perf. 13-14x13½ is perforated 13 on half of each horizontal side and 14 on the other half.

Wool Industry A73

Butter Industry A74

Sheep Farming A75

Apple Industry A76

Shipping A77

1936, Oct. 1 Wmk. 61 *Perf. 11*

No.	Type	Description	Unused	Used
218	A73	½p deep green	.25	.30
219	A74	1p red	.25	.25
220	A75	2½p deep blue	1.25	*4.00*
221	A76	4p dark purple	1.00	*3.00*
222	A77	6p red brown	2.00	*3.50*
		Nos. 218-222 (5)	4.75	*11.05*
		Set, never hinged	6.50	

Congress of the Chambers of Commerce of the British Empire held in New Zealand.

Queen Elizabeth and King George VI A78

Perf. 13½x13

1937, May 13 Wmk. 253

No.	Type	Description	Unused	Used
223	A78	1p rose carmine	.25	.25
224	A78	2½p dark blue	.50	*1.25*
225	A78	6p vermilion	.65	*1.25*
		Nos. 223-225 (3)	1.40	*2.75*
		Set, never hinged	2.25	

Coronation of George VI and Elizabeth.

A79

A80

1938-44 Engr. *Perf. 13½*

No.	Type	Description	Unused	Used
226	A79	½p emerald	4.75	.25
226B	A79	½p brown org ('41)	.25	.30
227	A79	1p rose red	3.75	.25
227A	A79	1p lt blue grn ('41)	.25	.25
228	A80	1½p violet brown	19.00	3.25
228B	A80	1½p red ('44)	.25	.35
228C	A80	3p blue ('41)	.25	.25
		Nos. 226-228C (7)	28.50	4.90
		Set, never hinged	40.00	

See Nos. 258-264. For surcharges and overprints see Nos. 242-243, 279, 285, O72-O74 (in Scott Standard catalogue, Vol. 5).

Landing of the Maoris in 1350 A81

Captain Cook, His Map of New Zealand, 1769, H.M.S. Endeavour A82

Victoria, Edward VII, George V, Edward VIII and George VI — A83

Abel Tasman, Ship, and Chart of West Coast of New Zealand A84

Treaty of Waitangi, 1840 — A85

Pioneer Settlers Landing on Petone Beach, 1840 A86

The Progress of Transport A87

H.M.S. "Britomart" at Akaroa — A88

Route of Ship Carrying First Shipment of Frozen Mutton to England — A89

Maori Council A90

Gold Mining in 1861 and Modern Gold Dredge A91

Giant Kauri — A92

Perf. 13½x14 (236), 13x13½, 14x13½ (233)

1940, Jan. 2 Engr. Wmk. 253

No.	Type	Description	Unused	Used
229	A81	½p dk blue green	.30	.25
230	A82	1p scarlet & sepia	2.25	.25
231	A83	1½p brt vio & ultra	.25	.60
232	A84	2p blk brn & Prus grn	1.10	.25
233	A85	2½p dk bl & myr grn	1.50	1.00
234	A86	3p dp plum & dk vio	2.75	1.00
235	A87	4p dk red vio & vio brn	10.00	1.60
236	A88	5p brown & lt bl	6.00	4.00
237	A89	6p vio & brt grn	8.00	1.50
238	A90	7p org red & black	1.25	*4.50*
239	A90	8p org red & black	8.00	5.00
240	A91	9p dp org & olive	5.50	2.25
241	A92	1sh dk sl grn & ol	10.00	4.00
		Nos. 229-241 (13)	56.90	26.20
		Set, never hinged	95.00	

Centenary of British sovereignty established by the treaty of Waitangi.

Imperfs of #229-241 exist. These probably are plate proofs.

For surcharge and overprints see Nos. 246, O76-O86.

Stamps of 1938 Surcharged with New Values in Black

1941 Wmk. 253 *Perf. 13½*

No.	Type	Description	Unused	Used
242	A79	1p on ½p emerald	1.00	.25
243	A80	2p on 1½p violet brn	1.00	.25
		Set, never hinged	3.50	

Type of 1935 Redrawn

1941 Typo. Wmk. 61 *Perf. 14x15*

Size: 17½x20½mm

No.	Type	Description	Unused	Used
244	A68	9p int black & scarlet	70.00	30.00

Wmk. 253

No.	Type	Description	Unused	Used
245	A68	9p int black & scarlet	4.00	3.50
		Set, never hinged	160.00	

Catalogue values for unused stamps in this section, from this point to the end of the section, are for Never Hinged items.

No 231 Srchd. in Black

1944 *Perf. 13½x13*

246 A83 10p on 1½p brt vio & ultra .45 .45

Peace Issue

Lake Matheson A93

Parliament House, Wellington — A94

St. Paul's Cathedral, London — A95

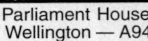

The Royal Family — A96

Badge of Royal New Zealand Air Force A97

New Zealand Army Overseas Badge A98

Badge of Royal Navy A99

New Zealand Coat of Arms A100

Knight, Window of Wellington Boys' College A101

Natl. Memorial Campanile, Wellington A103

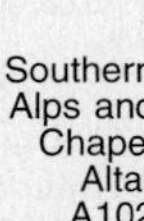

Southern Alps and Chapel Altar A102

Engr.; Photo. (1½p, 1sh)
Perf. 13x13½, 13½x13

1946, Apr. 1 **Wmk. 253**

No.	Type	Description	Unused	Used
247	A93	½p choc & dk bl grn	.25	.60
248	A94	1p emerald	.25	.25
249	A95	1½p scarlet	.25	.25
250	A96	2p rose violet	.25	.25
251	A97	3p dk grn & ultra	.25	.25
252	A98	4p brn org & ol grn	.25	.25
253	A99	5p ultra & blue grn	.80	.80
254	A100	6p org red & red brn	.25	.25
255	A101	8p brown lake & blk	.30	.30
256	A102	9p black & brt bl	.30	.30
257	A103	1sh gray black	.80	.40
		Nos. 247-257 (11)	3.95	3.90

Return to peace at the close of WWII.
Imperfs exist from the printer's archives.

George VI Type of 1938 and

King George VI — A104

1947 **Engr.** *Perf. 13½*

No.	Type	Description	Unused	Used
258	A80	2p orange	.30	.25
260	A80	4p rose lilac	.75	.50
261	A80	5p gray	1.00	.50
262	A80	6p rose carmine	1.00	.25
263	A80	8p deep violet	1.00	1.00
264	A80	9p chocolate	2.00	.40
		Perf. 14		
265	A104	1sh dk car rose & chnt	.75	.50
266	A104	1sh3p ultra & chnt	2.50	1.00
267	A104	2sh dk grn & brn org	6.25	2.00
268	A104	3sh gray blk & chnt	5.00	3.00
		Nos. 258-268 (10)	20.55	9.40

Nos. 265-267 have watermark either upright or sideways. On No. 268 watermark is always sideways.

For overprints see Nos. O98-O99.

"John Wickliffe" and "Philip Laing" A105

Cromwell, Otago A106

First Church, Dunedin — A107

University of Otago A108

1948, Feb. 23 *Perf. 13½*

No.	Type	Description	Unused	Used
269	A105	1p green & blue	.25	.25
270	A106	2p brown & green	.25	.25
271	A107	3p violet	.35	.35
272	A108	6p lilac rose & gray blk	.35	.35
		Nos. 269-272 (4)	1.20	1.20

Otago Province settlement, cent.

A Royal Visit set of four was prepared but not issued. Examples of the 3p have appeared in the stamp market.

A109

Black Surcharge

Wmk. 253

1950, July 28 **Typo.** *Perf. 14*

273 A109 1½p rose red .40 .40

See Nos. 367, 404A-404D, AR46-69 in Scott Standard catalogue, Vol. 5.

Cathedral at Christchurch — A110

"They Passed this Way" A111

3p, John Robert Godley. 6p, Canterbury University College. 1sh, View of Timaru.

1950, Nov. 20 **Engr.** *Perf. 13x13½*

No.	Type	Description	Unused	Used
274	A110	1p blue grn & blue	.50	.50
275	A111	2p car & red org	.50	.50
276	A110	3p indigo & blue	.50	.50
277	A111	6p brown & blue	.70	.70
278	A111	1sh claret & blue	.70	.70
		Nos. 274-278 (5)	2.90	2.90

Centenary of the founding of Canterbury Provincial District.

Imperfs of #274-278 exist.

No. 227A Surcharged in Black

1952, Dec. *Perf. 13½*

279 A79 3p on 1p lt blue green .30 .25

POSTAL-FISCAL STAMPS

In 1881 fiscal stamps of New Zealand of denominations over one shilling were made acceptable for postal duty. Values for canceled stamps are for postal cancellations. Denominations above £5 appear to have been used primarily for fiscal purposes.

Queen Victoria
PF1 PF2

Perf. 11, 12, 12½

1882 **Typo.** **Wmk. 62**

No.	Type	Description	Unused	Used
AR1	PF1	2sh blue	125.00	20.00
AR2	PF1	2sh6p dk brown	125.00	20.00
AR3	PF1	3sh violet	225.00	25.00
AR4	PF1	4sh brown vio	325.00	40.00
AR5	PF1	4sh red brn	275.00	40.00
AR6	PF1	5sh green	325.00	40.00
AR7	PF1	6sh rose	500.00	65.00
AR8	PF1	7sh ultra	550.00	150.00
AR9	PF1	7sh6p ol gray	1,500.	500.00
AR10	PF1	8sh dull blue	525.00	125.00
AR11	PF1	9sh org red	900.00	300.00
AR12	PF1	10sh red brn	350.00	75.00

1882-90

No.	Type	Description	Unused	Used
AR13	PF2	15sh dk grn	1,500.	400.00
AR15	PF2	£1 rose	700.00	150.00
AR16	PF2	25sh blue		—
AR17	PF2	30sh brown		—
AR18	PF2	£1 15sh yellow		—
AR19	PF2	£2 purple		—

PF3

PF4

No.	Type	Description	Unused	Used
AR20	PF3	£2 10sh red brn		—
AR21	PF3	£3 yel green		—
AR22	PF3	£3 10sh rose		—
AR23	PF3	£4 ultra		—
AR24	PF3	£4 10sh ol brn		—
AR25	PF3	£5 dark blue		—
AR26	PF4	£6 org red		—
AR27	PF4	£7 brn red		—
AR28	PF4	£8 green		—
AR29	PF4	£9 rose		—
AR30	PF4	£10 blue		—
AR30A	PF4	£20 yellow	—	—

No. AR31

With "COUNTERPART" at Bottom

1901

AR31 PF1 2sh6p brown 300.00 *400.00*

Perf. 11, 14, 14½x14

1903-15 **Wmk. 61**

No.	Type	Description	Unused	Used
AR32	PF1	2sh blue ('07)	80.00	12.00
AR33	PF1	2sh6p brown	80.00	12.00
AR34	PF1	3sh violet	175.00	14.00
AR35	PF1	4sh brn red	200.00	30.00
AR36	PF1	5sh grn ('06)	225.00	30.00
AR37	PF1	6sh rose	375.00	50.00
AR38	PF1	7sh dull blue	400.00	80.00
AR39	PF1	7sh6p ol gray ('06)	1,500.	400.00
AR40	PF1	8sh dk blue	450.00	75.00
AR41	PF1	9sh dl org ('06)	600.00	200.00
AR42	PF1	10sh dp clar	250.00	50.00
AR43	PF2	15sh blue grn	1,350.	350.00
AR44	PF2	£1 rose	500.00	150.00
		Perf. 14½		
AR45	PF2	£2 dp vio ('25)	600.00	150.00
a.		Perf. 14	700.00	150.00
		Nos. AR32-AR45 (14)	6,785.	1,603.

For overprints see Cook Islands Nos. 67-71.

Coat of Arms — PF5

1931-39 **Wmk. 61** *Perf. 14*

Type PF5 (Various Frames)

No.	Description	Unused	Used
AR46	1sh3p lemon	30.00	40.00
AR47	1sh3p org ('32)	8.00	9.00
AR48	2sh6p brown	16.00	5.25
AR49	4sh dull red ('32)	17.00	7.50
AR50	5sh green	21.00	12.50
AR51	6sh brt rose ('32)	37.50	15.00
AR52	7sh gray blue	32.50	25.00
AR53	7sh6p olive gray ('32)	75.00	92.50
AR54	8sh dark blue	50.00	37.50
AR55	9sh brn org	52.50	32.50
AR56	10sh dark car	27.50	10.50
AR57	12sh6p brn vio ('35)	250.00	250.00
AR58	15sh ol grn ('32)	70.00	42.50
AR59	£1 pink ('32)	75.00	22.50
AR60	25sh turq bl ('38)	550.00	600.00
AR61	30sh dk brn ('36)	300.00	200.00

AR62 35sh yel ('37) 6,000. *7,500.*
AR63 £2 vio ('33) 400.00 70.00
AR64 £2 10sh dk red ('36) 400.00 *550.00*
AR65 £3 lt grn ('32) 400.00 210.00
AR66 £3 10sh rose ('39) 2,250. 2,250.
AR67 £4 light blue 400.00 175.00
AR68 £4 10sh dk ol gray ('39) 2,500. 2,500.
AR69 £5 dk blue ('32) 400.00 100.00

For overprints see Cook Islands Nos. 80-83.

No. AR62 Surcharged in Black

1939 ***Perf. 14***
AR70 PF5 35sh on 35sh yel 500.00 350.00

Type PF5 Surcharged in Black

1940
AR71 3sh6p on 3sh6p dl green 28.50 21.00
AR72 5sh6p on 5sh6p rose lilac 60.00 57.50
AR73 11sh on 11sh pale yellow 125.00 150.00
AR74 22sh on 22sh scar 275.00 350.00
Nos. AR71-AR74 (4) 488.50 578.50

Type of 1931

1940-58 Wmk. 253 ***Perf. 14***

Type PF5 (Various Frames)

AR75 1sh3p orange 5.75 .60
AR76 2sh6p brown 5.75 .60
AR77 4sh dull red 6.75 .60
AR78 5sh green 11.50 .90
AR79 6sh brt rose 20.00 4.00
AR80 7sh gray bl 20.00 6.75
AR81 7sh6p ol gray ('50) 70.00 *70.00*
AR82 8sh dk blue 45.00 25.00
AR83 9sh orange ('46) 50.00 30.00
AR84 10sh dk carmine 25.00 3.25
AR85 15sh olive ('45) 55.00 20.00
AR86 £1 pink('45) 29.00 8.50
a. Perf. 14x13½ ('58) 32.50 15.00
AR87 25sh blue ('46) 500.00 *550.00*
AR88 30sh choc ('46) 250.00 200.00
AR89 £2 violet ('46) 100.00 60.00
AR90 £2 10sh dk red ('51) 400.00 *525.00*
AR91 £3 lt grn ('46) 150.00 125.00
AR92 £3 10sh rose ('48) 2,300. *2,500.*
AR93 £4 lt blue ('52) 150.00 160.00
AR94 £5 dk blue ('40) 175.00 150.00

Type PF5 Surcharged in Black

1942-45 Wmk. 253
AR95 3sh6p on 3sh6p grn 12.50 8.00
AR96 5sh6p on 5sh6p rose lil ('44) 26.00 8.50
AR97 11sh on 11sh yel 67.50 52.50
AR98 22sh on 22sh car ('45) 325.00 *275.00*
Nos. AR95-AR98 (4) 431.00 344.00

SEMI-POSTAL STAMPS

Nurse — SP1

Inscribed: "Help Stamp out Tuberculosis, 1929"

Wmk. 61

1929, Dec. 11 Typo. ***Perf. 14***
B1 SP1 1p + 1p scarlet 12.50 *20.00*

Nurse — SP2

Inscribed: "Help Promote Health, 1930"

1930, Oct. 29
B2 SP2 1p + 1p scarlet 30.00 *45.00*

Boy — SP3

1931, Oct. 31 ***Perf. 14½x14***
B3 SP3 1p + 1p scarlet 100.00 90.00
B4 SP3 2p + 1p dark blue 100.00 75.00

Hygeia, Goddess of Health — SP4

1932, Nov. 18 Engr. ***Perf. 14***
B5 SP4 1p + 1p carmine 22.50 *30.00*
Never hinged 55.00

Road to Health — SP5

1933, Nov. 8
B6 SP5 1p + 1p carmine 15.00 *20.00*
Never hinged 35.00

Crusader — SP6

1934, Oct. 25 ***Perf. 14x13½***
B7 SP6 1p + 1p dark carmine 12.50 *20.00*
Never hinged 25.00

Child at Bathing Beach — SP7

1935, Sept. 30 ***Perf. 11***
B8 SP7 1p + 1p scarlet 3.00 3.25
Never hinged 5.00

Catalogue values for unused stamps in this section, from this point to the end of the section, are for Never Hinged items.

Anzac — SP8

1936, Apr. 27
B9 SP8 ½p + ½p green .70 *2.00*
B10 SP8 1p + 1p red .70 *1.60*

21st anniv. of Anzac landing at Gallipoli.

"Health" SP9

1936, Nov. 2
B11 SP9 1p + 1p red 2.00 *4.25*

Boy Hiker — SP10

1937, Oct. 1
B12 SP10 1p + 1p red 3.00 *4.00*

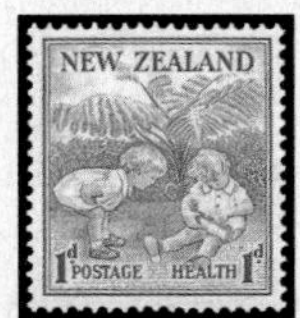

Children at Play — SP11

Perf. 14x13½

1938, Oct. 1 Wmk. 253
B13 SP11 1p + 1p red 6.25 3.25

Children at Play — SP12

Black Surcharge

1939, Oct. 16 Wmk. 61 ***Perf. 11½***
B14 SP12 1p on ½p + ½p grn 5.00 5.00
B15 SP12 2p on 1p + 1p scar 5.00 5.00

Children at Play — SP12a

1940, Oct. 1
B16 SP12a 1p + ½p green 16.00 17.50
B17 SP12a 2p + 1p org brown 16.00 17.50

The surtax was used to help maintain children's health camps.

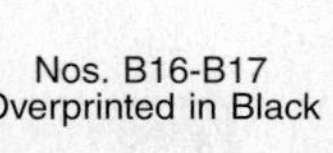

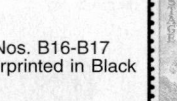

Nos. B16-B17 Overprinted in Black

1941, Oct. 4 ***Perf. 11½***
B18 SP12a 1p + ½p green 3.00 *3.50*
B19 SP12a 2p + 1p org brown 3.00 *3.50*

Children in Swing — SP13

1942, Oct. 1 Engr.
B20 SP13 1p + ½p green .35 *1.10*
B21 SP13 2p + 1p dp org brown .35 *1.10*

Imperf plate proofs on card exist for #B22-B27, B32-B33, B38-B39, B46-B48, B59-B60. Imperfs exist for B44-B45, B49-B51. These are from the printer's archives. See Scott Standard catalogue, Vol. 5, for listings after 1940.

Princess Elizabeth — SP14

Design: 1p+1/2p, Princess Margaret Rose.

1943, Oct. 1 Wmk. 253 ***Perf. 12***
B22 SP14 1p + ½p dark green .25 .40
a. Vert. pair, imperf. between 12,500.
B23 SP14 2p + 1p red brown .25 .40
a. Vert. pair, imperf. between 12,500.

Princesses Margaret Rose and Elizabeth SP16

1944, Oct. 9 ***Perf. 13½***
B24 SP16 1p + ½p blue green .35 .45
B25 SP16 2p + 1p chalky blue .35 .35

Peter Pan Statue, London — SP17

1945, Oct. 1
B26 SP17 1p + ½p gray grn & bis brn .25 .35
B27 SP17 2p + 1p car & ol bis .25 .35

Soldier Helping Child over Stile SP18

1946, Oct. 24 *Perf. 13½x13*
B28 SP18 1p + ½p dk grn & org brn .25 .35
B29 SP18 2p + 1p dk brn & org brn .25 .35

Statue of Eros, London — SP19

1947, Oct. 1 Engr. *Perf. 13x13½*
B30 SP19 1p + ½p deep green .25 .35
B31 SP19 2p + 1p deep carmine .25 .35

Children's Health Camp SP20

1948, Oct. 1 *Perf. 13½x13*
B32 SP20 1p + ½p blue grn & ultra .25 .35
B33 SP20 2p + 1p red & dk brn .25 .35

Nurse and Child — SP21

1949, Oct. 3 Photo. *Perf. 14x14½*
B34 SP21 1p + ½p deep green .30 .35
B35 SP21 2p + 1p ultramarine .30 .35

Princess Elizabeth and Prince Charles — SP22

1950, Oct. 2
B36 SP22 1p + ½p green .25 .35
B37 SP22 2p + 1p violet brown .25 .35

Racing Yachts SP23

Perf. 13½x13
1951, Nov. 1 Engr. Wmk. 253
B38 SP23 1½p + ½p red & yel .25 *.35*
B39 SP23 2p + 1p dp grn & yel .25 .35

Princess Anne SP24

Prince Charles SP25

Perf. 14x14½
1952, Oct. 1 Wmk. 253 Photo.
B40 SP24 1½p + ½p crimson .25 .35
B41 SP25 2p + 1p brown .25 .35

AIR POST STAMPS

Plane over Lake Manapouri AP1

Perf. 14x14½
1931, Nov. 10 Typo. Wmk. 61
C1 AP1 3p chocolate 27.50 22.50
a. Perf. 14x15 150.00 *500.00*
C2 AP1 4p dark violet 27.50 27.50
C3 AP1 7p orange 30.00 27.50
Nos. C1-C3 (3) 85.00 77.50

Most examples of No. C1a are poorly centered.

Type of 1931 Surcharged in Red

1931, Dec. 18 *Perf. 14x14½*
C4 AP1 5p on 3p yel green 20.00 25.00

Type of 1931 Overprinted in Dark Blue

1934, Jan. 17
C5 AP1 7p bright blue 50.00 55.00

1st official air mail flight between NZ and Australia.

Airplane over Landing Field AP2

1935, May 4 Engr. *Perf. 14*
C6 AP2 1p rose carmine 1.10 .80
C7 AP2 3p dark violet 5.75 3.75
C8 AP2 6p gray blue 11.50 5.75
Nos. C6-C8 (3) 18.35 10.30
Set, never hinged 40.00

SPECIAL DELIVERY STAMPS

SD1

Perf. 14x14½, 14x15
1903-26 Typo. Wmk. 61
E1 SD1 6p purple & red ('26) 60.00 40.00
a. 6p violet & red, perf. 11 70.00 50.00

Mail Car — SD2

1939, Aug. 16 Engr. *Perf. 14*
E2 SD2 6p violet 1.75 6.00
Never hinged 5.00

POSTAGE DUE STAMPS

D1

Wmk. 62
1899, Dec. 1 Typo. *Perf. 11*
J1 D1 ½p green & red 8.00 *19.00*
a. No period after "D" 75.00 60.00
J2 D1 1p green & red 12.50 2.10
J3 D1 2p green & red 40.00 6.25
J4 D1 3p green & red 20.00 6.00
J5 D1 4p green & red 42.50 25.00
J6 D1 5p green & red 45.00 *60.00*
J7 D1 6p green & red 45.00 *60.00*
J8 D1 8p green & red 110.00 *150.00*
J9 D1 10p green & red 175.00 *225.00*
J10 D1 1sh green & red 140.00 100.00
J11 D1 2sh green & red 225.00 *300.00*
Nos. J1-J11 (11) 863.00 953.35

Nos. J1-J11 may be found with N. Z. and D. varying in size.

D2

1902, Feb. 28 Unwmk.
J12 D2 ½p gray grn & red 3.00 7.50

Wmk. 61
J13 D2 ½p gray grn & red 3.00 2.10
J14 D2 1p gray grn & red 12.00 4.00
J15 D2 2p gray grn & red 150.00 150.00

1904-28 *Perf. 14, 14x14½*
J16 D2 ½p green & car 3.75 4.25
J17 D2 1p green & car 7.00 1.00
J18 D2 2p green & car 9.00 3.50
J19 D2 3p grn & rose ('28) 50.00 25.00
Nos. J16-J19 (4) 69.75 33.75

N Z and Star printed on the back in Blue
1925 Unwmk. *Perf. 14x14½, 14x15*
J20 D2 ½p green & rose 4.00 *26.00*
J21 D2 2p green & rose 9.00 *35.00*

Catalogue values for unused stamps in this section, from this point to the end of the section, are for Never Hinged items.

D3

1939 Wmk. 61 Typo. *Perf. 15x14*
J22 D3 ½p turquoise green 13.00 *9.00*
J23 D3 1p rose pink 5.00 .60
J24 D3 2p ultramarine 9.00 1.75
J25 D3 3p brown orange 26.00 29.00
Nos. J22-J25 (4) 53.00 40.35

1945-49 Wmk. 253
J27 D3 1p rose pink ('49) 5.00 25.00
J28 D3 2p ultramarine ('47) 7.00 9.00
J29 D3 3p brown orange 15.00 5.75
Nos. J27-J29 (3) 27.00 39.75

The use of postage due stamps was discontinued in Sept., 1951.

WAR TAX STAMP

No. 144 Overprinted in Black

Perf. 14x14½
1915, Sept. 24 Wmk. 61
MR1 A43 ½p green 2.10 .60

OFFICIAL STAMPS

Regular Issues of 1882-92 Overprinted & Handstamped

1892 Wmk. 62 *Perf as Before*
Rose or Magenta Handstamp
O1 A9 1p rose *600.*
O2 A10 2p violet *800.*
O3 A16 2½p ultramarine *700.*
O4 A17 5p olive gray *1,000.*
O5 A13 6p brown *1,200.*

Violet Handstamp
O6 N1 ½p rose *1,000.*
O7 A9 1p rose *600.*
O8 A10 2p violet

Handstamped on No. 67A in Rose
1899 *Perf. 10, 10x11*
O9 A15a ½p black *600.*

Handstamped on No. 79 in Violet
Unwmk. *Perf. 14, 15*
O10 A27 8p dull blue *1,200.*

Hstmpd. on Stamps of 1899-1900 in Violet

1902 *Perf. 11*
O11 A22 2½p blue *650.*
O12 A23 3p org brown *1,000.*
O13 A25 5p red brown *900.*
O14 A27 8p dark blue *1,000.*

Green Handstamp
O15 A25 5p red brown *900.*

Handstamped on Stamp of 1901 in Violet
Wmk. 63 *Perf. 11*
O16 A35 1p carmine *600.*

Handstamped on Stamps of 1902-07 in Violet or Magenta
1905-07 Wmk. 61 *Perf. 11, 14*
O17 A18 ½p green *600.*
O18 A35 1p carmine *600.*
O19 A22 2½p blue *700.*
O20 A25 5p red brown
O21 A27 8p deep blue
O22 A30 2sh blue green *5,000.*

The "O. P. S. O." handstamp is usually struck diagonally, reading up, but on No. O19 it also occurs horizontally. The letters stand for "On Public Service Only."

Overprinted in Black

On Stamps of 1902-07
1907 *Perf. 14, 14x13, 14x14½*
O23 A18 ½p green 12.00 2.00
O24 A35 1p carmine 12.00 1.00
a. Booklet pane of 6 110.00
O25 A33 2p violet 20.00 2.00
O26 A23 3p orange brn 60.00 6.00
O27 A26 6p carmine rose 250.00 40.00
a. Horiz. pair, imperf. vert. *925.00*
O28 A29 1sh brown red 125.00 25.00
O29 A30 2sh blue green 175.00 150.00
a. Horiz. pair, imperf. vert. *1,400.*
O30 A31 5sh vermilion 350.00 350.00
Nos. O23-O30 (8) 1,004. 576.00

On No. 127
Perf. 14x13, 14x14½
O31 A26 6p carmine rose 325.00 65.00

On No. 129

1909 ***Perf. 14x14½***
O32 A35 1p car (redrawn) 90.00 3.00

On Nos. 130-131, 133, 137, 139

1910 ***Perf. 14, 14x13½, 14x14½***
O33 A41 ½p yel grn 10.00 1.00
a. Inverted overprint 1,600.
O34 A42 1p carmine 3.75 .25
O35 A41 3p org brn 20.00 2.00
O36 A41 6p car rose 30.00 10.00
O37 A41 1sh vermilion 70.00 40.00
Nos. O33-O37 (5) 133.75 53.25

For 3p see note on perf varieties following No. 139.

On Postal-Fiscal Stamps Nos. AR32, AR36, AR44

1911-14
O38 PF1 2sh blue ('14) 75.00 52.50
O39 PF1 5sh green ('13) 125.00 *200.00*
O40 PF2 £1 rose 1,000. 625.00
Nos. O38-O40 (3) 1,200. 877.50

On Stamps of 1909-19
Perf. 14x13½, 14x14½

1915-19 **Typo.**
O41 A43 ½p green 1.60 .25
O42 A46 1½p gray black ('16) 8.00 3.00
O43 A47 1½p gray black ('16) 5.75 1.00
O44 A47 1½p brown org ('19) 5.75 .60
O45 A43 2p yellow ('17) 5.75 .50
O46 A43 3p chocolate ('19) 16.00 1.50

Engr.
O47 A45 3p vio brn ('16) 8.00 1.50
O48 A45 6p car rose ('16) 12.00 1.00
O49 A41 8p dp bl (R) ('16) 20.00 *30.00*
O50 A45 1sh vermilion ('16) 7.50 2.25
a. 1sh orange 15.00 *20.00*
Nos. O41-O50 (10) 90.35 *41.60*

For 8p see note on perf varieties following No. 139.

1922 **On No. 157**
O51 A45 8p red brown 125.00 *200.00*

1925 **On Nos. 151, 158**
O52 A45 4p purple 20.00 4.25
O53 A45 9p olive green 45.00 42.50

On No. 177

1925 ***Perf. 14x14½***
O54 A42 1p carmine 5.00 5.00

On Nos. 184, 182

1927-28 **Wmk. 61** ***Perf. 14, 14½x14***
O55 A57 1p rose red 2.50 .25
O56 A56 2sh blue 125.00 140.00

On No. AR50

1933 ***Perf. 14***
O57 PF5 5sh green 450.00 450.00

Nos. 186, 187, 196 Overprinted in Black

1936 ***Perf. 14x13½, 13½x14, 14***
O58 A59 1p copper red 2.00 1.40
O59 A60 1½p red brown 14.00 *30.00*
O60 A69 1sh dark slate grn 30.00 *52.50*
Nos. O58-O60 (3) 46.00 83.90
Set, never hinged 120.00

Same Overprint Horizontally in Black or Green on Stamps of 1936
Perf. 12½, 13½, 13x13½, 14x13½, 13½x14, 14

1936-42 **Wmk. 253**
O61 A58 ½p brt grn ('37) 1.50 5.25
O62 A59 1p copper red 3.00 .60
O63 A60 1½p red brown 4.00 5.25
O64 A61 2p red org ('38) 1.00 .25
a. Perf. 12½ ('42) 110.00 62.50
O65 A62 2½p dk gray & dk brown 8.00 24.00
O66 A63 3p choc ('38) 27.50 4.00
O67 A64 4p blk brn & blk 5.00 1.10
O68 A66 6p red ('37) 5.75 .35
O68B A67 8p dp brn ('42) 8.50 20.00
O69 A68 9p blk & scar (G) ('38) 80.00 45.00
O70 A69 1sh dk slate grn 14.00 1.60
a. Perf. 12½ ('42) 27.50 1.75

Overprint Vertical

O71 A70 2sh ol grn ('37) 24.00 8.50
a. Perf. 12½ ('42) 90.00 25.00
Nos. O61-O71 (12) 182.25 115.90
Set, never hinged 550.00

Same Overprint Horizontally in Black on Nos. 226, 227, 228

1938
O72 A79 ½p emerald 5.75 1.75
O73 A79 1p rose red 7.25 .30
O74 A80 1½p violet brn 37.50 10.50
Nos. O72-O74 (3) 50.50 12.55
Set, never hinged 95.00

Same Overprint on No. AR50

1938 **Wmk. 61** ***Perf. 14***
O75 PF5 5sh green 75.00 47.50
Never hinged 150.00

Nos. 229-235, 237, 239-241 Overprinted in Red or Black

Perf. 13½x13, 13x13½, 14x13½

1940 **Wmk. 253**
O76 A81 ½p dk bl grn (R) .60 .75
a. "ff" joined 29.00 70.00
O77 A82 1p scar & sepia 2.25 .30
a. "ff" joined 29.00 70.00
O78 A83 1½p brt vio & ultra 1.10 *4.25*
O79 A84 2p blk brn & Prus grn 2.25 .30
a. "ff" joined 35.00 70.00
O80 A85 2½p dk bl & myr grn 1.40 4.50
a. "ff" joined 29.00 77.50
O81 A86 3p dp plum & dk vio (R) 5.75 .95
a. "ff" joined 24.00 55.00
O82 A87 4p dk red vio & vio brn 14.50 1.60
a. "ff" joined 70.00 92.50
O83 A89 6p vio & brt grn 14.50 1.60
a. "ff" joined 40.00 80.00
O84 A90 8p org red & blk 14.50 13.00
a. "ff" joined 40.00 110.00
O85 A91 9p dp org & olive 5.75 5.75
O86 A92 1sh dk sl grn & ol 35.00 5.25
Nos. O76-O86 (11) 97.60 38.25
Set, never hinged 190.00

Nos. 227A, 228C Overprinted in Black

1941 **Wmk. 253** ***Perf. 13½***
O88 A79 1p light blue green .30 .30
O89 A80 3p blue .75 .30
Set, never hinged 2.25

Same Overprint on No. 245

1944 ***Perf. 14x15***
Size: 17¼x20¼mm
O90 A68 9p int black & scar 20.00 17.00
Never Hinged 60.00

Same Overprint on No. AR78
Perf. 14
O91 PF5 5sh green 12.00 7.00
Never Hinged 20.00

Catalogue values for unused stamps in this section, from this point to the end of the section, are for Never Hinged items.

Same Ovpt. on Stamps of 1941-47

1946-51 ***Perf. 13½, 14***
O92 A79 ½p brn org ('46) 1.75 1.25
O92B A80 1½p red 5.75 1.25
O93 A80 2p orange .90 .30
O94 A80 4p rose lilac 4.00 1.25
O95 A80 6p rose carmine 5.75 1.25
O96 A80 8p deep violet 10.00 4.50
O97 A80 9p chocolate 11.50 5.75
O98 A104 1sh dk car rose & chestnut 11.50 1.75
O99 A104 2sh dk grn & brn org 26.00 8.50
Nos. O92-O99 (9) 77.15 25.80

LIFE INSURANCE

Lighthouses — LI1

Perf. 10, 11, 10x11, 12x11½

1891, Jan. 2 **Typo.** **Wmk. 62**
OY1 LI1 ½p purple 110.00 7.00
OY2 LI1 1p blue 80.00 2.00
OY3 LI1 2p red brown 150.00 4.25
OY4 LI1 3p chocolate 425.00 22.50
OY5 LI1 6p green 550.00 70.00
OY6 LI1 1sh rose pink 800.00 140.00
Nos. OY1-OY6 (6) 2,115. 245.75

Stamps from outside rows of the sheets sometimes lack watermark.

1903-04 **Wmk. 61** ***Perf. 11, 14x11***
OY7 LI1 ½p purple 120.00 7.00
OY8 LI1 1p blue 75.00 1.10
OY9 LI1 2p red brown 200.00 10.00
Nos. OY7-OY9 (3) 395.00 18.10

Lighthouses — LI2

1905-32 ***Perf. 11, 14, 14x14½***
OY10 LI2 ½p yel grn ('13) 1.40 .90
OY11 LI2 ½p green ('32) 5.75 2.75
OY12 LI2 1p blue ('06) 375.00 29.00
OY13 LI2 1p dp rose ('13) 9.75 1.10
OY14 LI2 1p scarlet ('31) 4.25 2.00
OY15 LI2 1½p gray ('17) 14.00 4.25
OY16 LI2 1½p brn org ('19) 1.75 1.40
OY17 LI2 2p red brown 2,750. 200.00
OY18 LI2 2p violet ('13) 20.00 17.00
OY19 LI2 2p yellow ('21) 6.00 6.00
OY20 LI2 3p ocher ('13) 29.00 20.00
OY21 LI2 3p choc ('31) 11.00 26.00
OY22 LI2 6p car rose ('13) 20.00 26.00
OY23 LI2 6p pink ('31) 20.00 45.00
Nos. OY10-OY23 (14) 3,268. 381.40

#OY15, OY16 have "POSTAGE" at each side.
Stamps from outside rows of the sheets sometimes lack watermark.

1946-47 **Wmk. 253** ***Perf. 14x15***
OY24 LI2 ½p yel grn ('47) 1.90 1.90
OY25 LI2 1p scarlet 1.40 1.25
OY26 LI2 2p yellow 2.25 *15.00*
OY27 LI2 3p chocolate 10.50 *30.00*
OY28 LI2 6p pink ('47) 8.50 *25.00*
Nos. OY24-OY28 (5) 24.55 73.15
Set, never hinged 42.50

Catalogue values for unused stamps in this section, from this point to the end of the section, are for Never Hinged items.

New Zealand Lighthouses

Castlepoint LI3

Taiaroa — LI4

Cape Palliser LI5

Cape Campbell LI6

Eddystone (England) LI7

Stephens Island LI8

The Brothers LI9

Cape Brett — LI10

Perf. 13½x13, 13x13½

1947-65 **Engr.** **Wmk. 253**
OY29 LI3 ½p dk grn & red orange 1.75 1.70
OY30 LI4 1p dk ol grn & blue 1.75 1.10
OY31 LI5 2p int bl & gray .90 .90
OY32 LI6 2½p ultra & blk ('63) 11.00 15.00
OY33 LI7 3p red vio & bl 3.50 .75
OY34 LI8 4p dk brn & org 4.50 1.75
a. Wmkd. sideways ('65) 4.50 16.00
OY35 LI9 6p dk brn & bl 4.25 2.50
OY36 LI10 1sh red brn & bl 4.25 3.50
Nos. OY29-OY36 (8) 31.90 27.20

Set first issued Aug. 1, 1947.
Exist imperf.

NEWSPAPER STAMPS

Queen Victoria — N1

Wmk. 59

1873, Jan. 1 **Typo.** ***Perf. 10***
P1 N1 ½p rose 140.00 47.50
a. Perf. 12½x10 160.00 75.00
b. Perf. 12½ 210.00 75.00

The "N Z" watermark is widely spaced and intended for larger stamps. About a third of the stamps in each sheet are unwatermarked. They are worth a slight premium.
For overprint, see No. O6.

1875, Jan. **Wmk. 64** ***Perf. 12½***
P3 N1 ½p rose 25.00 5.00
a. Pair, imperf. between 800.00 500.00
b. Perf. 12 70.00 12.50

1892 **Wmk. 62** ***Perf. 12½***
P4 N1 ½p bright rose 11.00 1.50
a. Unwatermarked 20.00 10.00

NICARAGUA

ˌni-kə-ˈrä-gwə

LOCATION — Central America, between Honduras and Costa Rica
GOVT. — Republic
AREA — 57,143 sq. mi.
POP. — 2,908,000 (est. 1984)
CAPITAL — Managua

100 Centavos = 1 Peso
100 Centavos = 1 Córdoba (1913)

GREAT BRITAIN POST OFFICE IN GREYTOWN

British influence on the Mosquito coast of Nicaragua dated from the mid-17th century, and the local Mosquito Indians were under British protection until 1860. A British postal agency existed in the port of Greytown as early as 1842, and British stamps were used from 1865 to May 1, 1882.

Values are for clear cancellations on sound, fault-free stamps, with average to fine centering. In many cases, very fine examples are rare or non-existent.

Stamps of Great Britain Canceled with barred oval "C57" obliterator or with "GREYTOWN" circular date stamp

No. A22

1865-81

A1	½p rose red, plates 5, 10, 115 (#58), *value from*	85.00
A2	1p rose red, plates 180, 197, 210 (#33), *value from*	55.00
A3	1½p lake red, plate 3 (#32)	80.00
A4	2p blue, plate 9 (#29)	60.00
A5	2p blue, plates 14, 15 (#30), *value from*	60.00
A6	3p rose, plates 17-20 (#61), *value from*	60.00
A7	3p rose, plate 20 (#83)	—
A8	4p vermilion, plates 8, 10, 11, 13, 14 (#43), *value from*	60.00
A9	4p vermilion, plate 15 (#69)	325.00
A10	4p pale olive green, plate 15 (#70)	225.00
	Plate 16 (#70)	210.00
A11	4p gray brown, plate 17 (#71)	350.00
A12	4p gray brown, plate 17 (#84)	100.00
A13	6p gray, plates 14-17 (#62), *value from*	100.00
A14	8p orange (#73)	350.00
A15	1sh green, plate 4 (#48)	—
A16	1sh green, plates 6, 7 (#54), *value from*	—
A17	1sh green, plates 8, 10, 12, 13 (#64), *value from*	75.00
A18	1sh salmon, plate 13 (#65)	425.00
A19	1sh salmon, plate 13 (#87)	120.00
A20	2sh blue (#55)	175.00
A21	2sh brown (#56)	*2,500.*
A22	5sh rose, plate 1 (#57)	*500.00*
	Plate 2 (#57)	*675.00*
A23	5sh rose, plate 4 (#90a)	*2,500.*
A24	10shslate (#74)	*4,000.*

1880

A25	1p red brown (#79)	80.00
A26	1½p red brown (#80)	85.00

ISSUES OF THE REPUBLIC

Watermarks

Wmk. 117 — Liberty Cap

Wmk. 209 — Multiple Ovals

Liberty Cap on Mountain Peak; From Seal of Country — A1

Unwmk.

1862, Dec. 2 Engr. *Perf. 12*

Yellowish Paper

1	A1	2c dark blue	75.00	20.00
		On cover		*25,000.*
2	A1	5c black	150.00	60.00
		On cover		*10,000.*

Designs of Nos. 1-2 measure 22½x18½mm. Perforations are invariably rough.

Values are for stamps without gum. Examples with gum sell for more. Nos. 1-2 were canceled only by pen.

There is one reported cover of No. 1, two of No. 2.

See No. C509 in Scott Standard catalogue, Vol. 5.

A2

A3

1869-71 White Paper

3	A1	1c bister ('71)	3.00	1.25
		On cover		*7,500.*
4	A1	2c blue	3.00	1.25
		On cover		*7,500.*
5	A1	5c black	100.00	1.00
		On cover		*6,000.*
6	A2	10c vermilion	4.00	1.75
		On cover		*5,000.*
7	A3	25c green	7.50	4.00
		On cover		*7,500.*
		Nos. 3-7 (5)	117.50	9.25

Designs of Nos. 3-7 measure 22½x19mm. Perforations are clean cut.

There are two reported covers of No. 5, five of No. 7.

1878-80 *Rouletted 8½*

8	A1	1c brown	2.00	1.25
		On cover		*7,500.*
9	A1	2c blue	2.00	1.25
		On cover		*7,500.*
10	A1	5c black	50.00	1.00
		On cover		*6,000.*
11	A2	10c ver ('80)	2.50	1.50
		On cover		*5,000.*
12	A3	25c green ('79)	2.50	4.00
		On cover		*7,500.*
		Nos. 8-12 (5)	59.00	9.00

Most values exist on thicker soft paper.

Stamps with letter/numeral cancellations other than "3 G," "6 M," "9 C" sell for more.

Nos. 3-12 were reprinted in 1892. The corresponding values of the two series are printed in the same shades which is not usually true of the originals. They are, however, similar to some of the original shades and the only certain test is comparison. Originals have thin white gum; reprints have rather thick yellowish gum. Value 50c each. Unused examples of Nos. 3-12 without gum should be presumed to be reprints. Nos. 5 and 10 unused are extremely scarce and should be purchased with original gum and should be expertized.

Seal of Nicaragua — A4

1882 Engr. *Perf. 12*

13	A4	1c green	.25	.25
14	A4	2c carmine	.25	.25
15	A4	5c blue	.30	.25
16	A4	10c dull violet	.40	*.75*
17	A4	15c yellow	.80	*25.00*
18	A4	20c slate gray	1.60	*5.00*
19	A4	50c dull violet	2.25	*25.00*
		Nos. 13-19 (7)	5.85	*56.50*

Used Values

of Nos. 13-120 are for stamps with genuine cancellations applied while the stamps were valid. Various counterfeit cancellations exist.

Locomotive and Telegraph Key — A5

1890 Engr.

20	A5	1c yellow brown	.25	.30
21	A5	2c vermilion	.25	.30
22	A5	5c deep blue	.25	.30
23	A5	10c lilac gray	.25	.30
24	A5	20c red	.25	*.30*
25	A5	50c purple	.25	*.30*
26	A5	1p brown	.25	*.40*
27	A5	2p dark green	.25	*.40*
28	A5	5p lake	.25	*.50*
29	A5	10p orange	.25	*.50*
		Nos. 20-29 (10)	2.50	

The issues of 1890-1899 were printed by the Hamilton Bank Note Co., New York, to the order of N. F. Seebeck who held a contract for stamps with the government of Nicaragua. Reprints were made, for sale to collectors, of the 1896, 1897 and 1898, postage, postage due and official stamps. See notes following those issues.

For overprints see Nos. O1-O10.

Perforation Varieties

Imperfs and part perfs of all the Seebeck issues, Nos. 20-120, exist for all except originals of the 1898 issue, Nos. 99-109M.

Goddess of Plenty — A6

1891 Engr.

30	A6	1c yellow brn	.25	.35
31	A6	2c red	.25	.35
32	A6	5c dk blue	.25	.25
33	A6	10c slate	.25	.50
34	A6	20c plum	.25	*2.00*
35	A6	50c purple	.25	*5.00*
36	A6	1p black brn	.25	*5.00*
37	A6	2p green	.25	*8.50*
38	A6	5p brown red	.25	
39	A6	10p orange	.25	
		Nos. 30-39 (10)	2.50	

For overprints see Nos. O11-O20.

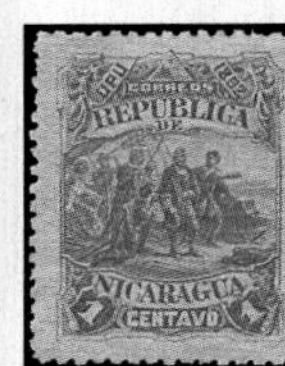

Columbus Sighting Land — A7

1892 Engr.

40	A7	1c yellow brn	.25	.25
41	A7	2c vermilion	.25	.25
42	A7	5c dk blue	.25	.25
43	A7	10c slate	.25	.25
44	A7	20c plum	.25	*2.00*
45	A7	50c purple	.25	*7.00*
46	A7	1p brown	.25	*7.00*
47	A7	2p blue grn	.25	*8.50*
48	A7	5p rose lake	.25	
49	A7	10p orange	.25	
		Nos. 40-49 (10)	2.50	

Commemorative of the 400th anniversary of the discovery of America by Columbus.

Stamps of the 1892 design were printed in other colors than those listed and overprinted "Telegrafos". The 1c blue, 10c orange, 20c slate, 50c plum and 2p vermilion are telegraph stamps which did not receive the overprint.

For overprints see Nos. O21-O30.

Arms — A8

1893 Engr.

51	A8	1c yellow brn	.25	.25
52	A8	2c vermilion	.25	.25
53	A8	5c dk blue	.25	.25
54	A8	10c slate	.25	.25
55	A8	20c dull red	.25	*1.50*
56	A8	50c violet	.25	*4.00*
57	A8	1p dk brown	.25	*7.00*
58	A8	2p blue green	.25	*8.50*
59	A8	5p rose lake	.25	
60	A8	10p orange	.25	
		Nos. 51-60 (10)	2.50	

The 1c blue and 2c dark brown are telegraph stamps which did not receive the "Telegrafos" overprint.

For overprints see Nos. O31-O41.

"Victory" — A9

1894 Engr.

61	A9	1c yellow brn	.25	*.30*
62	A9	2c vermilion	.25	*.30*
63	A9	5c dp blue	.25	*.30*
64	A9	10c slate	.25	*.30*
65	A9	20c lake	.25	*.30*
66	A9	50c purple	.25	*.30*
67	A9	1p brown	.25	*.40*
68	A9	2p green	.25	*.40*
69	A9	5p brown red	.25	*.50*
70	A9	10p orange	.25	*.50*
		Nos. 61-70 (10)	2.50	3.60

There were three printings of this issue. Only the first is known postally used. Unused values are for the third printing.

Used values are for stamps with "DIRECCION" cancels in black that were removed from post office new year cards.

Specialists believe the 25c yellow green, type A9, is a telegraph denomination never issued for postal purposes. Stamps in other colors are telegraph stamps without the usual "Telegrafos" overprint.

For overprints see Nos. O42-O51.

Coat of Arms — A10

1895 Engr.

71	A10	1c yellow brn	.25	.30
72	A10	2c vermilion	.25	.30
73	A10	5c deep blue	.25	.25
74	A10	10c slate	.25	.25
75	A10	20c claret	.25	*.75*
76	A10	50c light violet	50.00	*5.00*
77	A10	1p dark brown	.25	*5.00*
78	A10	2p deep green	.25	*8.00*
79	A10	5p brown red	.25	*11.00*
80	A10	10p orange	.25	
		Nos. 71-80 (10)	52.25	

Frames of Nos. 71-80 differ for each denomination.

A 50c violet blue exists. Its status is questioned. Value 25c.

There was little proper use of No. 80. Canceled examples are almost always c-t-o or have faked cancels.

For overprints see Nos. O52-O71.

Map of Nicaragua — A11

1896 **Engr.**

81 A11 1c violet .30 *1.00*
82 A11 2c blue grn .30 *.50*
83 A11 5c brt rose .30 *.30*
84 A11 10c blue .50 *.50*
85 A11 20c bister brn 3.00 *4.00*
86 A11 50c blue gray .60 *8.00*
87 A11 1p black .75 *11.00*
88 A11 2p claret .75 *15.00*
89 A11 5p deep blue .75 *15.00*
Nos. 81-89 (9) 7.25 *55.30*

There were two printings of this issue. Only the first is known postally used. Unused values are for the second printing.

See italic note after No. 109M.

For overprints see Nos. O82-O117.

Wmk. 117

89A A11 1c violet 3.75 .90
89B A11 2c bl grn 3.75 1.25
89C A11 5c brt rose 15.00 .30
89D A11 10c blue 25.00 .90
89E A11 20c bis brn 22.50 4.25
89F A11 50c bl gray 42.50 *9.00*
89G A11 1p black 37.50 *12.50*
89H A11 2p claret *18.00*
89I A11 5p dp bl *40.00*

Same, dated 1897

1897 **Engr.** **Unwmk.**

90 A11 1c violet .50 .50
91 A11 2c bl grn .50 .60
92 A11 5c brt rose .50 .30
93 A11 10c blue 6.25 .75
94 A11 20c bis brn 2.50 *3.75*
95 A11 50c bl gray 9.00 *9.50*
96 A11 1p black 9.00 *15.00*
97 A11 2p claret 20.00 *19.00*
98 A11 5p dp bl 20.00 *42.50*
Nos. 90-98 (9) 68.25 *91.90*

See italic note after No. 109M.

Wmk. 117

98A A11 1c violet 14.00 .50
98B A11 2c bl grn 14.00 .50
98C A11 5c brt rose 20.00 .40
98D A11 10c blue 22.50 .90
98E A11 20c bis brn 22.50 4.25
98F A11 50c bl gray 22.50 *8.00*
98G A11 1p black 25.00 *16.00*
98H A11 2p claret 25.00 *25.00*
98I A11 5p dp bl 125.00 *50.00*
Nos. 98A-98I (9) 290.50 *105.55*

Coat of Arms of "Republic of Central America" — A12

1898 **Engr.** **Wmk. 117**

99 A12 1c brown .25 .40
100 A12 2c slate .25 .40
101 A12 4c red brown .25 .50
102 A12 5c olive green 40.00 22.50
103 A12 10c violet 15.00 .60
104 A12 15c ultra .40 1.50
105 A12 20c blue 10.00 2.00
106 A12 50c yellow 10.00 *9.50*
107 A12 1p violet blue .40 *16.00*
108 A12 2p brown 19.00 *22.50*
109 A12 5p orange 25.00 *32.50*
Nos. 99-109 (11) 120.55 *108.40*

Unwmk.

109A A12 1c brown 1.25 .30
109B A12 2c slate 1.25
109D A12 4c red brown 2.25 .60
109E A12 5c olive green 25.00 .25
109G A12 10c violet 25.00 .60
109H A12 15c ultra 25.00
109I A12 20c blue 25.00
109J A12 50c yellow 25.00
109K A12 1p deep ultra 25.00
109L A12 2p olive brown 25.00
109M A12 5p orange 25.00
Nos. 109A-109M (11) 204.75

The paper of Nos. 109A to 109M is slightly thicker and more opaque than that of Nos. 81 to 89 and 90 to 98. The 5c and 10c also exist on very thin, semi-transparent paper.

Many reprints of Nos. 81-98, 98F-98H, 99-109M are on thick, porous paper, with and without watermark. The watermark is sideways. Paper of the originals is thinner for Nos. 81-109 but thicker for Nos. 109A-109M. Value 25c each.

In addition, reprints of Nos. 81-89 and 90-98 exist on thin paper, but with shades differing slightly from those of originals.

For overprints see Nos. O118-O128.

"Justice" — A13

1899 **Litho.**

110 A13 1c gray grn .25 *.35*
111 A13 2c brown .25 *.25*
112 A13 4c dp rose .35 *.40*
113 A13 5c dp bl .25 *.25*
114 A13 10c buff .25 *.30*
115 A13 15c chocolate .25 *.65*
116 A13 20c dk grn .35 *.75*
117 A13 50c brt rose .25 *3.00*
118 A13 1p red .25 *8.50*
119 A13 2p violet .25 *20.00*
120 A13 5p lt bl .25 *25.00*
Nos. 110-120 (11) 2.95 *59.45*

Nos. 110-120 exist imperf. and in horizontal pairs imperf. between.

Nos. 110-111, 113 exist perf 6x12 due to defective perforating equipment.

For overprints see Nos. O129-O139.

Mt. Momotombo A14

Imprint: "American Bank Note Co. NY"

1900, Jan. 1 **Engr.**

121 A14 1c plum .65 .25
122 A14 2c vermilion .65 .25
123 A14 3c green .90 .25
124 A14 4c ol grn 1.25 .25
125 A14 5c dk bl 4.00 .25
126 A14 6c car rose 14.00 5.00
127 A14 10c violet 7.00 .25
128 A14 15c ultra 8.00 .65
129 A14 20c brown 8.00 .65
130 A14 50c lake 7.00 1.10
131 A14 1p yellow 12.00 4.00
132 A14 2p salmon 10.00 2.25
133 A14 5p black 10.00 3.00
Nos. 121-133 (13) 83.45 18.15

Used values for #123, 126, 130-133 are for canceled to order examples.

See Nos. 159-161. For overprints and surcharges see Nos. 134-136, 144-151, 162-163, 175-178, O150-O154, 1L1-1L13, 1L16-1L19, 1L20, 2L1-2L10, 2L16-2L24, 2L36-2L39.

Mt. Momotombo — A14a

1902 **White Wove Paper** ***Imperf.***

Size: 55x52mm

133A A14a 5c blue
133B A14a 10c red violet
133C A14a 20c brown
133D A14a 30c black green
133E A14a 50c red

51x51mm

133F A14a 2c dk red, *buff*
133G A14a 4c red brown, *buff*

Nos. 133A-133G are documented on covers postmarked from 1902-04. Specimen pairs and blocks are from sheets of 35 (Nos. 133A-133E) or 28 (Nos. 133F-133G) sold in the 1990 American Bank Note Company archives sale. Nos. 133A-133G are not cutouts from similar postal envelopes issued in 1900.

Nos. 131-133 Surcharged in Black or Red

1901, Mar. 5

134 A14 2c on 1p yel 5.00 4.50
a. Bar below date 16.00 *9.00*
b. Inverted surcharge *35.00*
c. Double surcharge *50.00*
135 A14 10c on 5p blk (R) 12.00 4.50
a. Bar below date 17.50 8.00
136 A14 20c on 2p salmon 7.50 7.50
a. Bar below date 14.00 10.00
Nos. 134-136 (3) 24.50 16.50

A 2c surcharge on No. 121, the 1c plum, was not put on sale, though some are known used from a few sheets distributed by the post office to "government friends." Value, *$250.00.*

The 2c on 1p yellow without ornaments is a reprint.

Postage Due Stamps of 1900 Overprinted in Black or Gold

1901, Mar.

137 D3 1c plum 4.50 3.50
138 D3 2c vermilion 4.50 3.50
139 D3 5c dk bl 6.00 3.50
140 D3 10c pur (G) 8.50 8.50
a. Double overprint 14.00 14.00
141 D3 20c org brn 10.00 10.00
142 D3 30c dk grn 10.00 6.50
143 D3 50c lake 8.50 4.00
a. "1091" for "1901" 35.00 35.00
b. "Correo" 37.50
Nos. 137-143 (7) 52.00 39.50

In 1904 an imitation of this overprint was made to fill a dealer's order. The date is at top and "Correos" at bottom. The overprint is printed in black, sideways on the 1c and 2c and upright on the 5c and 10c. Some examples of the 2c were further surcharged "1 Centavo." None of these stamps was ever regularly used.

Nos. 126, 131-133 Surcharged

1901, Oct. 20 **Black Surcharge**

144 A14 3c on 6c rose 12.00 5.00
a. Bar below value 13.00 5.50
b. Inverted surcharge 14.00 8.00
c. Double surcharge 14.00 8.00
d. Double surch., one inverted 25.00 25.00
145 A14 4c on 6c rose 8.00 4.00
a. Bar below value 9.00 4.50
b. "1 cent" instead of "4 cent" 11.00 8.00
c. Double surcharge 20.00 20.00
146 A14 5c on 1p yellow 6.00 4.00
a. Three bars below value 7.00 4.50
b. Ornaments at each side of "1901" 30.00 4.50
c. Double surcharge, one in red 17.50 15.00
147 A14 10c on 2p salmon 6.50 4.00
a. Inverted surcharge 30.00 27.50
b. Double surcharge

Blue Surcharge

148 A14 3c on 6c rose 9.00 4.50
a. Bar below value 10.00 5.50
b. Double surcharge 11.00 8.00
149 A14 4c on 6c rose 12.00 5.00
a. Bar below value 13.00 7.50
b. "1 cent" instead of "4 cent" 20.00 10.00
c. Inverted surcharge 25.00 20.00

Red Surcharge

150 A14 5c on 1p yellow 8.00 6.50
a. Three bars below value 10.00 7.00
b. Ornaments at each side of "1901" 10.00 7.00
c. Inverted surcharge 20.00 12.00
d. Double surcharge, inverted 22.50 17.50
151 A14 20c on 5p black 5.50 3.50
a. Inverted surcharge 20.00 16.00
b. Double surcharge 22.50 22.50
c. Triple surcharge
Nos. 144-151 (8) 67.00 36.50

In 1904 a series was surcharged as above, but with "Centavos" spelled out. About the same time No. 122 was surcharged "1 cent." and "1901," "1902" or "1904." All of these surcharges were made to fill a dealer's order and none of the stamps was regularly issued or used.

Postage Due Stamps of 1900 Overprinted in Black

1901, Oct.

152 D3 1c red violet 1.00 .40
a. Ornaments at each side of the stamp 10.00 .65
b. Ornaments at each side of "1901" 1.10 .65
c. "Correos" in italics 1.50 1.50
d. Double overprint 14.00 14.00
153 D3 2c vermilion .75 .40
a. Double overprint 8.50 5.50
154 D3 5c dark blue 1.00 .60
a. Double overprint, one inverted
b. Double overprint 7.00 7.00
155 D3 10c purple 1.00 .60
b. Double overprint 10.00 10.00
c. Double overprint, one inverted 12.00 12.00
156 D3 20c org brn 1.50 1.25
b. Double overprint 7.00 7.00
157 D3 30c dk grn 1.00 1.10
a. Double overprint 9.00 9.00
b. Inverted overprint 19.00 19.00
158 D3 50c lake 1.00 1.10
a. Triple overprint 25.00 25.00
b. Double overprint 16.00 16.00
Nos. 152-158 (7) 7.25 5.45

One stamp in each group of 25 has the 2nd "o" of "Correos" italic. Value twice normal.

Momotombo Type of 1900

Without Imprint

1902 **Litho.** ***Perf. 14***

159 A14 5c blue .50 .25
a. Imperf., pair 3.75
160 A14 5c carmine .50 .25
a. Imperf., pair 3.75
161 A14 10c violet 1.50 .25
a. Imperf., pair 3.75
Nos. 159-161 (3) 2.50 .75

No. 161 was privately surcharged 6c, 1p and 5p in black in 1903. Not fully authorized but known postally used. Value of c-t-o peso denominations, $5 each.

Nos. 121 and 122 Surcharged in Black

1902, Oct. ***Perf. 12***

162 A14 15c on 2c ver 4.00 .75
a. Double surcharge 32.50
b. Blue surcharge 90.00
163 A14 30c on 1c plum 3.00 2.25
a. Double surcharge 12.00
b. Inverted surcharge 27.50

Counterfeits of No. 163 exist in slightly smaller type.

President José Santos Zelaya — A15

1903, Jan. **Engr.**

167 A15 1c emer & blk .45 .50
168 A15 2c rose & blk 1.00 .50
169 A15 5c ultra & blk .50 .50
170 A15 10c yel & blk .50 *.85*
171 A15 15c lake & blk 1.75 *2.00*
172 A15 20c vio & blk 1.75 *2.00*
173 A15 50c ol & blk 1.75 *5.00*
174 A15 1p red brn & blk 2.00 *6.00*
Nos. 167-174 (8) 9.70 *17.35*

10th anniv. of 1st election of Pres. Zelaya.

The so-called color errors-1c orange yellow and black, 2c ultramarine and black, 5c lake and black and 10c emerald and black-were also delivered to postal authorities. They were intended for official use though not issued as such. Value, $4 each.

No. 161 Surcharged in Blue

Nos. 175-176

No. 177

1904-05

175 A14 5c on 10c vio ('05) 1.75 .25
a. Inverted surcharge 5.50 3.00
b. Without ornaments 2.00 .70
c. Character for "cents" inverted 1.75 .40
d. As "b," inverted
e. As "c," inverted 2.75 2.75
f. Double surcharge 25.00 8.00
g. "5" omitted 2.75 2.75
176 A14 15c on 10c vio ('05) .90 .30
a. Inverted surcharge 4.00 1.40
b. Without ornaments 2.00 1.40
c. Character for "cents" inverted 2.50 1.10
d. As "b," inverted
e. As "c," inverted 5.00 1.75
f. Imperf. 7.00
h. As "a," imperf. 10.00 9.00
i. Double surcharge 16.00 14.00
177 A14 15c on 10c vio 4.50 2.75
a. Inverted surcharge 7.00 6.00
b. "Centcvos" 7.00 4.50
c. "5" of "15" omitted 12.50
d. As "b," inverted 8.50 8.50
e. Double surcharge 11.00 11.00
f. Double surcharge, inverted 13.00 13.00
g. Imperf., pair 9.00 9.00
Nos. 175-177 (3) 7.15 3.30

There are two settings of the surcharge on No. 175. In the 1st the character for "cents" and the figure "5" are 2mm apart and in the 2nd 4mm.

The 2c vermilion, No. 122, with surcharge "1 cent. / 1904" was not issued.

No. 161 Surcharged in Black

1905, June

178 A14 5c on 10c violet .60 .35
a. Inverted surcharge 13.50 10.00
b. Double surcharge 4.50 4.50
c. Surcharge in blue 75.00

Coat of Arms — A18

Imprint: "American Bank Note Co. NY"

1905, July 25 Engr. *Perf. 12*

179 A18 1c green .30 .25
180 A18 2c car rose .30 .25
181 A18 3c violet .45 .25
182 A18 4c org red .45 .25
183 A18 5c blue .45 .25
184 A18 6c slate .60 .40
185 A18 10c yel brn .85 .25
186 A18 15c brn olive .75 .35
187 A18 20c lake .60 .40
188 A18 50c orange 3.00 1.50
189 A18 1p black 1.50 1.50
190 A18 2p dk grn 1.50 2.00
191 A18 5p violet 1.75 2.50
Nos. 179-191 (13) 12.50 10.15

See Nos. 202-208, 237-248. For overprints and surcharges see Nos. 193-201, 212-216, 235-236, 249-265, O187-O198, O210-O222, 1L21-1L62, 1L73-1L95, 1LO1-1LO3, 2L26-2L35, 2L42-2L46, 2L48-2L72, 2LO1-2LO4.

Nos. 179-184 and 191 Surcharged in Black or Red Reading Up or Down

1906-08

193 A18 10c on 2c car rose (up) 7.00 4.50
a. Surcharge reading down 13.00 13.00
194 A18 10c on 3c vio (up) .80 .25
a. "¢" normal 2.75 1.35
b. Double surcharge 4.50 4.50
c. Double surch., up and down 7.00 5.00
d. Pair, one without surcharge 9.50
e. Surcharge reading down .30 .25
195 A18 10c on 4c org red (up) ('08) *35.00 20.00*
a. Surcharge reading down *32.50 26.00*
196 A18 15c on 1c grn (up) .60 .30
a. Double surcharge 7.50 7.50
b. Dbl. surch., one reading down 11.00 11.00
c. Surcharge reading down .70 .35
197 A18 20c on 2c car rose (down) ('07) .50 .30
a. Double surcharge 13.00 13.00
b. Surcharge reading up 37.50 32.50
c. "V" omitted 10.00 10.00
198 A18 20c on 5c bl (down) .90 .50
a. Surcharge reading up 35.00
199 A18 50c on 6c sl (R) (down) .80 .50
a. Double surcharge
b. Surcharge reading up 30.00 30.00
c. Yellow brown surcharge .80 .40
200 A18 1p on 5p vio (down) ('07) 42.50 25.00
Nos. 193-200 (8) 88.10 51.35

There are several settings of these surcharges and many varieties in the shapes of the figures, the spacing, etc.

Surcharged in Red Vertically Reading Up

1908, May

201 A18 35c on 6c slate 3.50 2.25
a. Double surcharge (R) 25.00
b. Double surcharge (R + Bk) 65.00
c. Carmine surcharge 3.50 2.25

Arms Type of 1905

Imprint: "Waterlow & Sons, Ltd."

1907, Feb. *Perf. 14 to 15*

202 A18 1c green .70 .40
203 A18 2c rose .80 .25
204 A18 4c brn org 2.00 .30
205 A18 10c yel brn 3.00 .25
206 A18 15c brn olive 4.50 .90
207 A18 20c lake 8.00 1.25
208 A18 50c orange 20.00 4.25
Nos. 202-208 (7) 39.00 7.60

Nos. 202-204, 207-208 Surcharged in Black or Blue (Bl) Reading Down

1907-08

212 A18 10c on 2c rose 1.50 .50
a. Double surcharge 10.00
b. "Vale" only 22.50
c. Surcharge reading up 14.00 6.50
213 A18 10c on 4c brn org (up) ('08) 2.25 .85
a. Double surcharge 10.00
b. Surcharge reading down 10.00
214 A18 10c on 20c lake ('08) 3.25 1.40
a. Surcharge reading up 80.00
215 A18 10c on 50c org (Bl) ('08) 2.00 .60
216 A18 15c on 1c grn ('08) 32.50 4.00
Nos. 212-216 (5) 41.50 7.35

Several settings of this surcharge provide varieties of numeral font, spacing, etc.

Revenue Stamps Overprinted "CORREO-1908" — A19

1908, June

217 A19 5c yel & blk .60 .40
a. "CORROE" 2.75 2.75
b. Overprint reading down 7.00
c. Double overprint 13.00
218 A19 10c lt bl & blk .50 .25
a. Double overprint 4.50 4.50
b. Overprint reading down .50 .25
c. Double overprint, up and down 13.00 13.00
219 A19 1p yel brn & blk .50 *2.00*
a. "CORROE" 10.00 *12.00*
220 A19 2p pearl gray & blk .50 *2.50*
a. "CORROE" 10.00 10.00
Nos. 217-220 (4) 2.10 *5.15*

The overprint exists on a 5p in green (value $200) and on a 50p in black (value $300).

Revenue Stamps Surcharged Vertically Reading Up in Red (1c, 15c), Blue(2c), Green (4c) or Orange (35c)

221 A19 1c on 5c yel & blk .40 .25
a. "1008" 2.00 *3.00*
b. "8908" 2.00 *3.00*
c. Surcharge reading down 4.00 4.00
d. Double surcharge 4.00 4.00
222 A19 2c on 5c yel & blk .50 .30
b. "ORREO" 1.75 1.75
c. "1008" 1.75 1.75
d. "8908" 2.50 *5.50*
f. Double surcharge 7.00 7.00
g. Double surcharge, one inverted 7.00 7.00
h. Surcharge reading down 9.00 9.00
223 A19 4c on 5c yel & blk .65 .35
a. "ORREO" 3.50 *7.50*
b. "1008" 2.00 2.00
c. "8908" 2.00 2.00
224 A19 15c on 50c ol & blk .60 .40
a. "1008" 7.50 *11.50*
b. "8908" 4.00 4.00
c. Surcharge reading down 10.00 10.00
225 A19 35c on 50c ol & blk 4.00 1.00
a. Double surcharge, one inverted 12.00 12.00
b. Surcharge reading down 12.00 12.00
c. Double surcharge, one in black
Nos. 221-225 (5) 6.15 2.30

For surcharges and overprints see Nos. 225D-225H, 230-234, 266-278, 1L63-1L72A, 1L96-1L106, 2L47.

Revenue Stamps Surcharged Vertically Reading Up in Blue, Black or Orange

1908, Nov.

225D A19 2c on 5c yel org & blk (Bl) 20.00 12.50
e. "9c" instead of "2c" 75.00 75.00
225F A19 10c on 50c ol & blk (Bk) *850.00 325.00*
g. Double surcharge *425.00*
225H A19 35c on 50c ol & blk (O) 17.50 10.00

In this setting there are three types of the character for "cents."

Revenue Stamps Overprinted or Surcharged in Various Colors

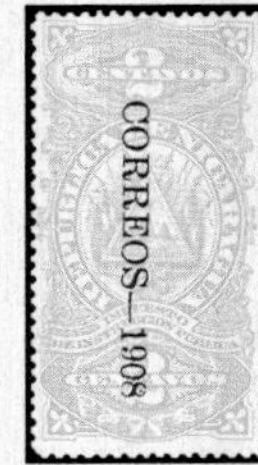

No. 226 No. 227

1908, Dec.

226 2c org (Bk) 3.50 2.00
a. Double overprint 6.00 6.00
b. Overprint reading up 5.00 5.00
227 4c on 2c org (Bk) 1.75 .90
a. Surcharge reading up 5.00 5.00
b. Blue surcharge 80.00 80.00
228 5c on 2c org (Bl) 1.50 .60
a. Surcharge reading up 6.00 6.00
229 10c on 2c org (G) 1.50 .30
a. "1988" for "1908" 4.00 3.00
b. Surcharge reading up 5.00 5.00
c. "¢" inverted 4.00 4.00
d. Double surcharge 7.50
Nos. 226-229 (4) 8.25 3.80

Two printings of No. 229 exist. In the first, the initial of "VALE" is a small capital, and in the second a large capital.

The overprint "Correos-1908." 35mm long, handstamped on 1c blue revenue stamp of type A20, is private and fraudulent.

Revenue Stamps Surcharged in Various Colors

1909, Feb. Color: Olive & Black

230 A19 1c on 50c (V) 4.00 1.60
231 A19 2c on 50c (Br) 7.00 3.00
232 A19 4c on 50c (G) 7.00 3.00
233 A19 5c on 50c (C) 4.00 1.75
a. Double surcharge 12.50 12.50
234 A19 10c on 50c (Bk) 1.10 .75
Nos. 230-234 (5) 23.10 10.10

Nos. 230 to 234 are found with three types of the character for "cents."

Nos. 190 and 191 Surcharged in Black

1909, Mar. *Perf. 12*

235 A18 10c on 2p dk grn 20.00 12.00
236 A18 10c on 5p vio *100.00 70.00*

There are three types of the character for "cents."

Arms Type of 1905

Imprint: "American Bank Note Co. NY"

1909, Mar.

237 A18 1c yel grn .35 .25
238 A18 2c vermilion .35 .25
239 A18 3c red org .35 .25
240 A18 4c violet .35 .25
241 A18 5c dp bl .35 .25
242 A18 6c gray brn 3.00 1.50
243 A18 10c lake .85 .25
244 A18 15c black .85 .25
245 A18 20c brn olive .85 .25
246 A18 50c dp grn 1.25 .40
247 A18 1p yellow 1.25 .40
248 A18 2p car rose 1.00 .40
Nos. 237-248 (12) 10.80 4.70

Nos. 239 and 244, Surcharged in Black or Red

1910, July

249 A18 2c on 3c red org 2.75 1.10
250 A18 10c on 15c blk (R) 1.25 .30
a. "VLEA" 3.50 2.00
b. Double surcharge 17.50 17.50

There are two types of the character for "cents."

Nos. 239, 244, 245 Surcharged in Black or Red

1910

252 A18 2c on 3c (Bk) 1.50 1.25
a. Double surcharge 6.00 6.00
b. Pair, one without surcharge
c. "Vale" omitted 10.00 10.00
254 A18 5c on 20c (R) .40 .30
a. Double surcharge (R) 6.00 5.00
b. Inverted surcharge (R) 10.00 *32.50*
c. Black surcharge 100.00
d. Double surcharge (Bk) 140.00
e. Inverted surcharge (Bk) 110.00

No.	Description	Unused	Used
255	A18 10c on 15c (Bk)	.90	.30
a.	"c" omitted	2.00	1.10
b.	"10c" omitted	2.50	1.50
c.	Inverted surcharge	4.00	4.00
d.	Double surcharge	6.00	6.00
e.	Double surch., one inverted	14.00	18.50
	Nos. 252-255 (3)	2.80	1.85

There are several minor varieties in this setting, such as italic "L" and "E" and fancy "V" in "VALE," small italic "C," and italic "I" for "1" in "10."

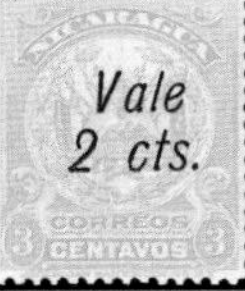

Nos. 239, 244, 246 and 247, Surcharged in Black

1910, Dec. 10

No.	Description	Unused	Used
256	A18 2c on 3c red org	.85	.45
a.	Without period	1.00	.75
b.	Inverted surcharge	6.00	6.00
c.	Double surcharge	6.00	6.00
257	A18 10c on 15c blk	2.00	.75
a.	Without period	3.50	1.25
b.	Double surcharge	6.00	3.00
c.	Inverted surcharge	10.00	18.00
258	A18 10c on 50c dp grn	1.25	.40
a.	Without period	1.50	.75
b.	Double surcharge	10.00	26.00
c.	Inverted surcharge	3.00	3.00
259	A18 10c on 1p yel	.90	.40
a.	Without period	1.25	.75
b.	Double surcharge	3.00	3.00
	Nos. 256-259 (4)	5.00	2.00

The 15c on 50c deep green is a telegraph stamp from which the "Telegrafos" overprint was omitted. It appears to have been pressed into postal service, as all examples are used with postal cancels. Value $450.

Nos. 240, 244-248 Surcharged in Black

Surcharge as on Nos. 256-259 but lines wider apart.

1911, Mar.

No.	Description	Unused	Used
260	A18 2c on 4c vio	.30	.25
a.	Without period	.35	.30
b.	Double surcharge	3.50	3.00
c.	Double surcharge, inverted	4.00	4.00
d.	Double surcharge, one invtd.	9.00	17.50
e.	Inverted surcharge	10.00	18.50
261	A18 5c on 20c brn ol	.30	.25
a.	Without period	.60	.50
b.	Double surcharge	2.50	2.50
c.	Inverted surcharge	2.50	2.00
d.	Double surcharge, one invtd.	6.00	6.00
262	A18 10c on 15c blk	.40	.25
a.	Without period	1.00	.50
b.	"Yale"	12.00	12.00
c.	Double surcharge	3.00	3.00
d.	Inverted surcharge	3.00	3.00
e.	Double surch., one inverted	5.00	4.00
f.	Double surch., both inverted	12.00	12.00
263	A18 10c on 50c dp grn	.25	.25
a.	Without period	1.00	.50
b.	Double surcharge	3.00	2.50
c.	Double surcharge, one invtd.	5.00	4.00
d.	Inverted surcharge	5.00	5.00
264	A18 10c on 1p yel	1.50	.40
a.	Without period	2.00	1.50
b.	Double surcharge	4.00	4.00
c.	Double surcharge, one invtd.	7.50	
265	A18 10c on 2p car rose	.60	.50
a.	Without period	2.00	1.50
b.	Double surcharge	2.50	2.50
c.	Double surcharge, one invtd.	6.00	6.00
d.	Inverted surcharge	6.00	6.00
	Nos. 260-265 (6)	3.35	1.90

Revenue Stamps Surcharged in Black

1911, Apr. 10 ***Perf. 14 to 15***

No.	Description	Unused	Used
266	A19 2c on 5p dl bl	1.00	1.25
a.	Without period	1.25	1.50
b.	Double surcharge	2.50	2.00
267	A19 2c on 5p ultra	.35	.40
a.	Without period	.75	1.25
b.	Double surcharge	3.50	
268	A19 5c on 10p pink	.75	.40
a.	Without period	1.50	1.00
b.	"cte" for "cts"	1.50	1.00
c.	Double surcharge	4.00	4.00
d.	Inverted surcharge	2.50	2.50
269	A19 10c on 25c lilac	.40	.25
a.	Without period	1.00	.75
b.	"cte" for "cts"	1.25	1.00
c.	Inverted surcharge	4.00	4.00
d.	Double surcharge	2.50	2.50
e.	Double surcharge, one inverted	4.00	4.00
270	A19 10c on 2p gray	.40	.25
a.	Without period	1.00	.75
b.	"cte" for "cts"	1.25	1.00
c.	Double surcharge	5.00	5.00
d.	Double surcharge, one inverted	4.00	3.00
271	A19 35c on 1p brown	.40	.30
a.	Without period	1.00	.75
b.	"cte" for "cts"	1.25	1.00
c.	"Corre"	1.50	1.50
d.	Double surcharge	2.50	2.50
e.	Double surcharge, one inverted	2.50	2.50
f.	Double surcharge inverted	3.00	3.00
g.	Inverted surcharge	5.00	
	Nos. 266-271 (6)	3.30	2.85

These surcharges are in settings of twenty-five. One stamp in each setting has a large square period after "cts" and two have no period. One of the 2c has no space between "02" and "cts" and one 5c has a small thin "s" in "Correos."

Surcharged in Black

1911, June

No.	Description	Unused	Used
272	A19 5c on 2p gray	1.50	1.00
a.	Inverted surcharge	6.00	5.00

In this setting one stamp has a large square period and another has a thick up-right "c" in "cts."

Surcharged in Black

1911, June 12

No.	Description	Unused	Used
273	A19 5c on 25c lilac	1.50	1.25
274	A19 5c on 50c ol grn	5.00	5.00
275	A19 5c on 5p blue	7.00	7.00
276	A19 5c on 5p ultra	7.50	6.00
a.	Inverted surcharge	45.00	
277	A19 5c on 50p ver	6.25	5.00
278	A19 10c on 50c ol grn	1.50	.50
	Nos. 273-278 (6)	28.75	24.75

This setting has the large square period and the thick "c" in "cts." Many of the stamps have no period after "cts." Owing to broken type and defective impressions letters sometimes appear to be omitted.

A21

Revenue Stamps Surcharged on the Back in Black

a

b

Railroad coupon tax stamps (1st class red and 2nd class blue) are the basic stamps of Nos. 279-294. They were first surcharged for revenue use in 1903 in two types: I — "Timbre Fiscal" and "cents" (originally intended for use in Bluefields).

1911, July

No.	Description	Unused	Used
279	A21 (a) 2c on 5c on 2 bl	.25	.30
a.	New value in yellow on face	6.00	6.00
b.	New value in black on face	10.00	5.00
c.	New value in red on face	100.00	
d.	Inverted surcharge	.75	
e.	Double surch., one inverted	7.50	7.50
f.	"TIMBRE FISCAL" in black	.75	.75
280	A21 (b) 2c on 5c on 2 bl	.25	.30
a.	New value in yellow on face	3.00	3.00
b.	New value in black on face	9.00	4.00
c.	New value in red on face	100.00	
d.	Inverted surcharge	.90	1.00
e.	Double surch., one inverted	7.50	7.50
f.	"TIMBRE FISCAL" in black	1.00	1.00
281	A21 (a) 5c on 5c on 2 bl	.25	.25
a.	Inverted surcharge	.50	.35
b.	"TIMBRE FISCAL" in black	1.00	1.00
c.	New value in yellow on face		
282	A21 (b) 5c on 5c on 2 bl	.25	.25
a.	Inverted surcharge	.40	.35
b.	"TIMBRE FISCAL" in black	1.00	1.00
c.	New value in yellow on face		
283	A21 (a) 10c on 5c on 2 bl	.25	.25
a.	Inverted surcharge	.75	.50
b.	"TIMBRE FISCAL" in black	1.00	1.00
c.	New value in yellow on face	100.00	
d.	Double surcharge	6.00	6.00
284	A21 (b) 10c on 5c on 2 bl	.25	.25
a.	Inverted surcharge	.75	.50
b.	"TIMBRE FISCAL" in black	1.00	1.00
c.	Double surcharge	6.00	6.00
d.	New value in yellow on face	110.00	
285	A21 (a) 15c on 10c on 1 red	.25	.25
a.	Inverted surcharge	1.00	1.25
b.	"Timbre Fiscal" double	5.00	
286	A21 (b) 15c on 10c on 1 red	.40	.35
a.	Inverted surcharge	1.00	1.00
b.	"Timbre Fiscal" double	5.00	
	Nos. 279-286 (8)	2.15	2.20

These surcharges are in settings of 20. For listing, they are separated into small and large figures, but there are many other varieties due to type and arrangement.

The colored surcharges on the face of the stamps were trial printings. These were then surcharged in black on the reverse. The olive yellow surcharge on the face of the 2c was later applied to prevent use as a 5c revenue stamps. Other colors known on the face are orange and green. Forgeries exist.

For overprints and surcharges see Nos. 287-294, O223-O244, 1L107-1L108.

Surcharged on the Face in Black

1911, Oct.

No.	Description	Unused	Used
287	A21 2c on 10c on 1 red	6.50	6.50
a.	Inverted surcharge	1.40	1.40
b.	Double surcharge	10.00	10.00
288	A21 20c on 10c on 1 red	4.50	4.50
a.	Inverted surcharge	5.25	5.00
289	A21 50c on 10c on 1 red	5.25	4.50
a.	Inverted surcharge	10.00	10.00
	Nos. 287-289 (3)	16.25	15.50

There are two varieties of the figures "2" and "5" in this setting.

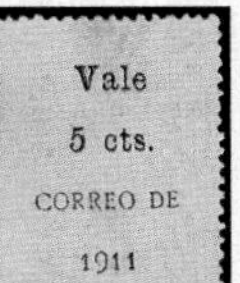

Surcharged on the Back in Black

1911, Nov.

No.	Description	Unused	Used
289B	A21 5c on 10c on 1 red	37.50	
c.	Inverted surcharge	20.00	
289D	A21 10c on 10c on 1 red	12.50	
e.	Inverted surcharge	24.00	

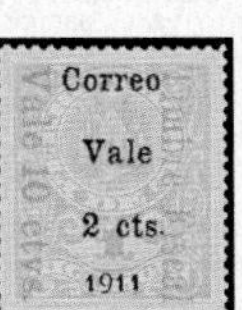

Surcharged on the Face

1911, Dec.

Dark Blue Postal Surcharge

No.	Description	Unused	Used
290	A21 2c on 10c on 1 red	.25	.25
a.	Inverted surcharge	2.50	2.50
b.	Double surcharge	5.00	5.00
291	A21 5c on 10c on 1 red	.30	.25
a.	Double surcharge	2.50	2.50
b.	Inverted surcharge	2.50	2.50
292	A21 10c on 10c on 1 red	.35	.25
a.	Inverted surcharge	2.50	2.50
b.	Double surcharge	2.50	2.50
c.	"TIMBRE FISCAL" on back	3.50	3.50

Black Postal Surcharge

No.	Description	Unused	Used
293	A21 10c on 10c on 1 red	1.50	1.00
a.	Inverted surcharge	7.00	7.00
b.	New value surch. on back	12.00	12.00

Red Postal Surcharge

No.	Description	Unused	Used
293C	A21 5c on 5c on 2 blue	1.40	1.25
d.	"TIMBRE FISCAL" in black	2.50	1.75
e.	"5" omitted	3.75	3.75
f.	Inverted surcharge	4.75	4.75
	Nos. 290-293C (5)	3.80	3.00

Bar Overprinted on No. O234 in Dark Blue

No.	Description	Unused	Used
294	A21 10c on 10c on 1 red	1.25	1.00
a.	Inverted surcharge	2.50	2.50
b.	Bar at foot of stamp	5.00	5.00

Nos. 290-294 each have three varieties of the numerals in the surcharge.

"Liberty" — A22

Coat of Arms — A23

1912, Jan. **Engr.** ***Perf. 14, 15***

No.	Description	Unused	Used
295	A22 1c yel grn	.30	.25
296	A22 2c carmine	.40	.25
297	A22 3c yel brn	.30	.25
298	A22 4c brn vio	.30	.25
299	A22 5c blue & blk	.25	.25
300	A22 6c olive bister	.30	.80
301	A22 10c red brn	.25	.25
302	A22 15c vio	.25	.25
303	A22 20c red	.25	.25
304	A22 25c blue grn & blk	.30	.25
305	A23 35c grn & chnt	2.00	1.50
306	A22 50c lt blue	1.00	.40
307	A22 1p org	1.40	2.00
308	A22 2p dark blue grn	1.50	2.25
309	A22 5p blk	3.50	3.50
	Nos. 295-309 (15)	12.30	12.70

For overprints and surcharges see Nos. 310-324, 337A-348, 395-396, O245-O259.

No. 305 Surcharged in Violet

1913, Mar.

No.	Description	Unused	Used
310	A23 15c on 35c	.40	.25
a.	"ats" for "cts"	7.50	6.00

Stamps of 1912 Surcharged in Red or Black

1913-14

No.	Description	Unused	Used
311	A22 ½c on 3c yel brn (R)	.40	.35
a.	"Corooba"	2.50	2.50
b.	"do" for "de"	2.50	2.50
c.	Inverted surcharge	22.50	
312	A22 ½c on 15c vio (R)	.25	.25
a.	"Corooba"	1.00	1.00
b.	"do" for "de"	1.25	1.25
313	A22 ½c on 1p org	.75	.25
a.	"VALB"	3.00	5.00
b.	"ALE"	4.00	3.50
c.	"LE"	6.00	5.00
d.	"VALE" omitted	3.50	3.50
314	A22 1c on 3c yel brn	.95	.60
315	A22 1c on 4c brn vio	.75	.25
316	A22 1c on 50c lt blue	.25	.25
317	A22 1c on 5p blk	.25	.25
318	A22 2c on 4c brn vio	.35	.25
a.	"do" for "de"	3.00	12.00
319	A22 2c on 20c red	3.50	4.50
a.	"do" for "de"	17.50	12.50
320	A22 2c on 25c blue grn & blk	.35	.25
a.	"do" for "de"	3.50	2.50

321 A23 2c on 35c grn & chnt .25 .40
a. "9131" 4.00 *7.50*
b. "do" for "de" 2.50 2.00
322 A22 2c on 50c lt blue .25 .25
a. "do" for "de" 2.00 *4.00*
323 A22 2c on 2p dark blue grn .25 .25
a. "VALB" 1.25 1.25
b. "ALE" 2.50 1.25
c. "VALE" omitted 6.00
d. "VALE" and "dos" omitted 6.00
324 A22 3c on 6c olive bis .25 .25
a. "VALB" *35.00*
Nos. 311-324 (14) 8.80 8.35

Nos. 311, 312 surcharged in black were not regularly issued.

Surcharged on Zelaya Issue of 1912

325 Z2 ½c on 2c ver .60 *1.25*
a. "Corooba" 1.25 1.25
b. "do" for "de" 1.25 1.25
326 Z2 1c on 3c org brn .50 .25
327 Z2 1c on 4c car .50 .25
328 Z2 1c on 6c red brn .40 .25
329 Z2 1c on 20c dark vio .50 .25
330 Z2 1c on 25c grn & blk .50 .25
331 Z2 2c on 1c yel grn ('14) 6.75 1.25
a. "Centavos" 7.50 1.50
332 Z2 2c on 25c grn & blk 2.25 *3.00*
333 Z2 5c on 35c brn & blk .40 .25
334 Z2 5c on 50c ol grn .40 .25
a. Double surcharge 22.50
335 Z2 6c on 1p org .50 .25
336 Z2 10c on 2p org brn .90 .25
337 Z2 1p on 5p dk bl grn 1.00 .40
Nos. 325-337 (13) 15.20 8.15

On No. 331 the surcharge has a space of 2½mm between "Vale" and "dos."

Space between "Vale" and "dos" 2½mm instead of 1mm, "de Cordoba" in different type.

1914, Feb.

337A A22 2c on 4c brn vio 27.50 4.00
b. "Ccntavos" 12.00
337C A22 2c on 20c red 13.00 3.75
d. "Ccntavos" 4.00
337E A22 2c on 25c bl grn & blk 6.00
f. "Ccntavos" 12.00
337G A23 2c on 35c grn & chnt 8.50
h. "Ccntavos" 15.00
337I A22 2c on 50c lt bl 22.50 4.00
j. "Ccntavos" 10.00

No. 310 with Additional Surcharge

1913, Dec.

337K A23 ½c on 15c on 35c *300.00*

The word "Medio" is usually in heavy-faced, shaded letters. It is also in thinner, unshaded letters and in letters from both fonts mixed.

No. 310 Surcharged in Black and Violet

338 A23 ½c on 15c on 35c .50 .25
a. Double surcharge 3.50
b. Inverted surcharge 3.50
c. Surcharged on No. 305 12.00
339 A23 1c on 15c on 35c .25 .25
a. Double surcharge 4.00

Official Stamps of 1912 Surcharged

1914, Feb.

340 A22 1c on 25c lt bl .40 .25
a. Double surcharge 9.00
341 A23 1c on 35c lt bl .40 .25
a. "0.10" for "0.01" 10.00 10.00
341B A22 1c on 50c lt bl *200.00*
342 A22 1c on 1p lt bl .25 .25
342A A22 2c on 20c lt bl *200.00* *150.00*
b. "0.12" for "0.02"
343 A22 2c on 50c lt bl .40 .25
a. "0.12" for "0.02" 150.00
344 A22 2c on 2p lt bl .40 .25
345 A22 2c on 5p lt bl *250.00*
346 A22 5c on 5p lt bl .25 .25

Red Surcharge

347 A22 5c on 1p lt bl *140.00*
348 A22 5c on 5p lt bl *500.00*

National Palace, Managua — A24

León Cathedral — A25

Various Frames

1914, May 13 Engr. *Perf. 12*

349 A24 ½c lt blue .85 .25
350 A24 1c dk green .85 .25
351 A25 2c red orange .85 .25
352 A24 3c red brown 1.25 .30
353 A25 4c scarlet 1.25 .40
354 A24 5c gray black .45 .25
355 A25 6c black brn 9.00 5.50
356 A25 10c orange yel .85 .25
357 A24 15c dp violet 5.75 2.00
358 A25 20c slate 11.00 5.50
359 A24 25c orange 1.50 .45
360 A25 50c pale blue 1.40 .40
Nos. 349-360 (12) 35.00 15.80

In 1924 the 5c, 10c, 25c, 50c were issued in slightly larger size, 27x22¾mm. The original set was 26x22½mm.

No. 356 with overprint "Union Panamericana 1890-1940" in green is of private origin.

See Nos. 408-415, 483-495, 513-523, 652-664. For overprints and surcharges see Nos. 361-394, 397-400, 416-419, 427-479, 500, 540-548, 580-586, 600-648, 671-673, 684-685, C1-C3, C9-C13, C49-C66, C92-C105, C121-C134, C147-C149, C155-C163, C174-C185, CO1-CO24, O260-O294, O296-O319, O332-O376, RA1-RA5, RA10-RA11, RA26-RA35, RA39-RA40, RA44, RA47, RA52.

No. 355 Surcharged in Black

1915, Sept.

361 A25 5c on 6c blk brn 1.50 .40
a. Double surcharge 7.00 7.00

Stamps of 1914 Surcharged in Black or Red

1918-19 New Value in Figures

362 A24 1c on 3c red brn 6.50 2.25
a. Double surch., one invtd. 12.50
363 A25 2c on 4c scarlet 32.50 22.50
364 A24 5c on 15c dp vio (R) 7.50 1.50
a. Double surcharge 12.00
364C A24 5c on 15c dp vio 350.00

Surcharged in Black

365 A25 2c on 20c slate 110.00 60.00
a. "ppr" for "por" *500.00* *300.00*
b. Double surcharge *300.00*
c. "Cordobo" *500.00* *300.00*
365D A25 5c on 20c slate — *200.00*
e. Double surcharge (Bk + R) *300.00*
f. "Cordobo" *300.00*

The surcharge on No. 365 is in blue black, and that on No. 365D usually has an admixture of red.

Used only at Bluefields and Rama.

Surcharged in Black, Red or Violet

New Value in Words

366 A25 ½c on 6c blk brn 4.00 1.50
a. "Meio" 15.00
b. Double surcharge 12.00
367 A25 ½c on 10c yellow 2.50 .30
a. "Val" for "Vale" 3.00
b. "Codoba" 3.00
c. Inverted surcharge 5.00
d. Double surch., one inverted 10.00
368 A24 ½c on 15c dp vio 2.50 .60
a. Double surcharge 7.50
b. "Codoba" 4.00
c. "Meio" 6.00
369 A24 ½c on 25c orange 5.00 2.00
a. Double surcharge 8.00
b. Double surch., one inverted 6.00
370 A25 ½c on 50c pale bl 2.50 .30
a. "Meio" 6.00
b. Double surcharge 5.00
c. Double surch., one inverted 7.00
371 A25 ½c on 50c pale bl (R) 4.50 1.50
a. Double surcharge 10.00
372 A24 1c on 3c red brn 3.00 .30
a. Double surcharge 3.50
373 A25 1c on 6c blk brn 12.50 3.50
a. Double surcharge 9.00
374 A25 1c on 10c yellow 24.00 8.00
a. "nu" for "un" 22.50
375 A24 1c on 15c dp vio 4.50 .75
a. Double surcharge 10.00
b. "Codoba" 6.00
376 A25 1c on 20c slate *200.00* *100.00*
a. Black surch. normal and red surch. invtd. *150.00*
b. Double surch., red & black *150.00*
c. Blue surcharge *200.00*
377 A25 1c on 20c sl (V) 110.00 70.00
a. Double surcharge (V + Bk) *150.00*
378 A25 1c on 20c sl (R) 2.50 .30
a. Double surch., one inverted
b. "Val" for "Vale" 3.50 3.00
379 A24 1c on 25c orange 4.50 1.00
a. Double surcharge 11.00
380 A25 1c on 50c pale bl 14.00 4.50
a. Double surcharge 17.50
381 A25 2c on 4c scarlet 3.50 .30
a. Double surcharge 10.00
b. "centavo" 5.00
c. "Val" for "Vale"
382 A24 2c on 6c blk brn 24.00 8.00
a. "Centavoss"
b. "Cordobas"
383 A25 2c on 10c yellow 24.00 4.50
a. "centavo"
384 A25 2c on 20c sl (R) 13.00 3.25
a. "pe" for "de" 15.00
b. Double surch., red & blk 27.50
c. "centavo" 12.00
d. Double surcharge (R) 17.50
385 A24 2c on 25c orange 5.50 .40
a. "Vle" for "Vale" 7.50
b. "Codoba" 7.50
c. Inverted surcharge 10.00
386 A25 5c on 6c blk brn 10.00 4.25
a. Double surcharge 13.50
387 A24 5c on 15c dp vio 3.50 .60
a. "cincoun" for "cinco" 15.00
b. "Vle" for "Vale" 12.50
c. "Codoba" 12.50
Nos. 366-387 (22) 479.50 215.85

No. 378 is surcharged in light red and brown red: the latter color is frequently offered as the violet surcharge (No. 377).

Official Stamps of 1915 Surcharged in Black or Blue

1919-21

388 A24 1c on 25c lt blue 1.50 .25
a. Double surcharge 10.00
b. Inverted surcharge 12.00
389 A25 2c on 50c lt blue 1.50 .25
a. "centavo" 4.00 4.00
b. Double surcharge 12.00
390 A25 10c on 20c lt blue 1.40 .40
a. "centavos" 5.00 5.00
b. Double surcharge 8.00
390F A25 10c on 20c lt bl (Bl) 65.00
Nos. 388-390 (3) 4.40 .90

There are numerous varieties of omitted, inverted and italic letters in the foregoing surcharges.

No. 358 Surcharged in Black

Types of the numerals

1919, May

391 A25 2c on 20c (I) *200.00* *150.00*
a. Type II
b. Type III
c. Type IV
d. Type VI
e. Type VIII
392 A25 5c on 20c (I) 110.00 50.00
a. Type II 110.00 45.00
b. Type III 125.00 55.00
c. Type IV 125.00 50.00
d. Type V 140.00 60.00
e. Type VI 140.00 60.00
f. Type VII 400.00 250.00
h. Double surch., one inverted

No. 358 Surcharged in Black

393 A25 2 Cents on 20c (I) *200.00* *150.00*
a. Type II
b. Type III
c. Type IV
d. Type V
e. Type VI
f. Type VII
393G A25 5 Cents on 20c sl, (VIII) 140.00 55.00

Nos. 391-393G used only at Bluefields and Rama.

No. 351 Surcharged in Black

1920, Jan.

394 A25 1c on 2c red org 1.50 .25
a. Inverted surcharge
b. Double surcharge

No. 394 stamps with uppercase "VALE" in surcharge are believed to be unauthorized surcharges.

Official Stamps of 1912 Overprinted in Carmine

1921, Mar.

395 A22 1c lt blue 1.50 .60
a. "Parricular" 5.00 5.00
b. Inverted overprint 10.00
396 A22 5c lt blue 1.50 .40
a. "Parricular" 5.00 5.00

Official Stamps of 1915 Surcharged in Carmine

1921, May

397 A25 ½c on 2c light blue .50 .25
a. "Mddio" 2.50 2.50
398 A25 ½c on 4c light blue 1.25 .25
a. "Mddio" 2.50 2.50
399 A24 1c on 3c light blue 1.25 .30
Nos. 397-399 (3) 3.00 .80

No. 354 Surcharged in Red

1921, Aug.

400 A24 ½c on 5c gray blk .75 .75

Trial printings of this stamp were surcharged in yellow, black and red, and yellow and red. Some of these were used for postage.

Gen. Manuel José Arce — A26

José Cecilio del Valle — A27

Miguel Larreinaga A28

Gen. Fernando Chamorro A29

Gen. Máximo Jérez — A30

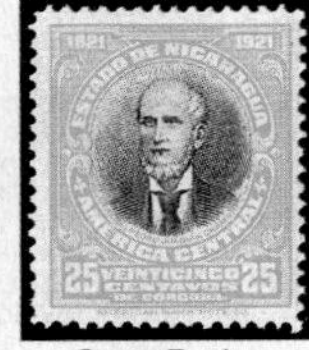

Gen. Pedro Joaquín Chamorro — A31

Rubén Darío — A32

1921, Sept. **Engr.**

401 A26 ½c lt bl & blk 1.60 1.60
402 A27 1c grn & blk 1.60 1.60
403 A28 2c rose red & blk 1.60 1.60
404 A29 5c ultra & blk 1.60 1.60
405 A30 10c org & blk 1.60 1.60
406 A31 25c yel & blk 1.60 1.60
407 A32 50c vio & blk 1.60 1.60
Nos. 401-407 (7) 11.20 11.20

Centenary of independence.

For overprints and surcharges see Nos. 420-421, RA12-RA16, RA19-RA23.

Types of 1914 Issue

1922 **Various Frames**

408 A24 ½c green .25 .25
409 A24 1c violet .25 .25
410 A25 2c car rose .25 .25
411 A24 3c ol gray .30 .25
411A A25 4c vermilion .35 .25
412 A25 6c red brn .25 .25
413 A24 15c brown .35 .25
414 A25 20c bis brn .50 .25
415 A25 1cor blk brn .90 .50
Nos. 408-415 (9) 3.40 2.50

In 1924 Nos. 408-415 were issued in slightly larger size, 27x22¾mm. The original set was 26x22½mm.

Nos. 408, 410 exist with signature controls. See note before No. 600. Same values.

No. 356 Surcharged in Black

1922, Nov.

416 A25 1c on 10c org yel 1.00 .35
417 A25 2c on 10c org yel 1.00 .25

Nos. 354 and 356 Surcharged in Red

1923, Jan.

418 A24 1c on 5c gray blk 1.25 .25
419 A25 2c on 10c org yel 1.25 .25
a. Inverted surcharge

Nos. 401 and 402 Overprinted in Red

1923

420 A26 ½c lt blue & blk 7.50 7.50
421 A27 1c green & blk 2.50 .85
a. Double overprint 7.50

Francisco Hernández de Córdoba — A33

1924 **Engr.**

422 A33 1c deep green 2.50 .30
423 A33 2c carmine rose 2.50 .30
424 A33 5c deep blue 2.00 .30
425 A33 10c bister brn 2.00 .60
Nos. 422-425 (4) 9.00 1.50

Founding of León & Granada, 400th anniv.

For overprint & surcharges see #499, 536, O295.

Stamps of 1914-22 Overprinted

Black, Red or Blue Overprint

1927, May 3

427 A24 ½c green (Bk) .25 .25
428 A24 1c violet (R) .25 .25
a. Double overprint 3.00
428B A24 1c violet (Bk) 85.00 55.00
429 A25 2c car rose (Bk) .25 .25
a. Inverted overprint 5.00
b. Double overprint 5.00
430 A24 3c ol gray (Bk) 1.25 1.25
a. Inverted overprint 5.00
b. Double overprint 6.00
c. Double ovpt., one inverted 9.00 7.00
430D A24 3c ol gray (Bl) 8.00 3.25
431 A25 4c ver (Bk) 16.00 13.00
a. Inverted overprint 30.00
432 A24 5c gray blk (R) 1.25 .25
a. Inverted overprint 7.50
432B A24 5c gray blk (Bk) .75 .25
c. Double ovpt., one inverted 8.00
d. Double overprint 8.00
433 A25 6c red brn (Bk) 13.00 11.00
a. Inverted overprint 17.50
b. Double overprint
c. "1297" for "1927" 250.00
434 A25 10c yellow (Bl) .65 .40
a. Double overprint 12.50
b. Double ovpt., one inverted 10.00
435 A24 15c brown (Bk) 6.00 2.50
436 A25 20c bis brn (Bk) 6.00 2.50
a. Double overprint 17.50
437 A24 25c orange (Bk) 27.50 5.00
438 A25 50c pale bl (Bk) 7.50 3.00
439 A25 1cor blk brn (Bk) 15.00 9.00
Nos. 427-439 (16) 188.65 107.15

Most stamps of this group exist with tall "1" in "1927." Counterfeits exist of normal stamps and errors of Nos. 427-478.

1927, May 19 **Violet Overprint**

440 A24 ½c green .25 .25
a. Inverted overprint 2.00 2.00
b. Double overprint 2.00 2.00
441 A24 1c violet .25 .25
a. Double overprint 2.00 2.00
442 A25 2c car rose .25 .25
a. Double overprint 2.00 2.00
b. "1927" double 5.00
d. Double ovpt., one inverted 2.00 2.00
443 A24 3c ol gray .25 .25
a. Inverted overprint 6.00
b. Overprinted "1927" only 12.00
c. Double ovpt., one inverted 9.00
444 A25 4c vermilion 37.50 27.50
a. Inverted overprint 75.00
445 A24 5c gray blk 1.00 .25
a. Double overprint, one inverted 6.00
446 A25 6c red brn 37.50 27.50
a. Inverted overprint 75.00
447 A25 10c yellow .35 .25
a. Double overprint 2.00 2.00
448 A24 15c brown .75 .30
a. Double overprint 5.00
b. Double overprint, one inverted 8.00
449 A25 20c bis brn .35 .25
a. Double overprint
450 A24 25c orange .40 .25
451 A25 50c pale bl .40 .25
a. Double ovpt., one inverted 4.00 4.00
452 A25 1cor blk brn .75 .25
a. Double overprint 3.00
b. "1927" double 5.00
c. Double ovpt., one inverted 6.00
Nos. 440-452 (13) 80.00 57.80

Stamps of 1914-22 Overprinted in Violet

1928, Jan. 3

453 A24 ½c green .25 .25
a. Double overprint 3.00
b. Double overprint, one inverted 4.00
454 A24 1c violet .25 .25
a. Inverted overprint 2.00
b. Double overprint 2.00
c. Double overprint, one inverted 2.00
d. "928" for "1928" 2.50
455 A25 2c car rose .25 .25
a. Inverted overprint 2.00
b. Double overprint 2.00
c. "1928" omitted 5.00
d. "928" for "1928" 2.50
e. As "d," inverted
f. "19" for "1928"
456 A24 3c ol gray .40 .25
457 A25 4c vermilion .25 .25
458 A24 5c gray blk .25 .25
a. Double overprint 5.00
b. Double overprint, one inverted 5.00
459 A25 6c red brn .25 .25
460 A25 10c yellow .25 .25
a. Double overprint 2.50
c. Inverted overprint
461 A24 15c brown .35 .25
462 A25 20c bis brn .50 .25
a. Double overprint
463 A24 25c orange .75 .25
a. Double overprint, one inverted 4.00
464 A25 50c pale bl 1.25 .25
465 A25 1cor blk brn 1.25 .35
Nos. 453-465 (13) 6.25 3.35

Stamps of 1914-22 Overprinted in Violet

1928, June 11

466 A24 ½c green .25 .25
467 A24 1c violet .25 .25
a. "928" omitted
469 A24 3c ol gray .75 .25
a. Double overprint 6.00
470 A25 4c vermilion .35 .25
471 A24 5c gray blk .25 .25
a. Double overprint 4.00
472 A25 6c red brn .40 .25
a. Double overprint 5.00
473 A25 10c yellow .50 .25
474 A24 15c brown 1.75 .25
a. Double overprint
475 A25 20c bis brn 2.00 .25
476 A24 25c orange 2.00 .25
a. Double overprint, one inverted 6.00
477 A25 50c pale bl 2.00 .25
478 A25 1cor blk brn 5.00 2.50
a. Double overprint 10.00
Nos. 466-478 (12) 15.50 5.25

No. 410 with above overprint in black was not regularly issued.

No. 470 with Additional Surcharge in Violet

1928

479 A25 2c on 4c ver 1.25 .35
a. Double surcharge 9.00

A34

Inscribed: "Timbre Telegrafico"

1928 **Red Surcharge**

480 A34 1c on 5c bl & blk .30 .25
a. Double surcharge 5.00
b. Double surcharge, one inverted
481 A34 2c on 5c bl & blk .30 .25
a. Double surcharge 5.00
482 A34 3c on 5c bl & blk .30 .25
Nos. 480-482 (3) .90 .75

Stamps similar to Nos. 481-482, but with surcharge in black and with basic stamp inscribed "Timbre Fiscal," are of private origin.

See designs A36, A37, A44, PT1, PT4, PT6, PT7.

Types of 1914 Issue

1928 **Various Frames**

483 A24 ½c org red .40 .25
484 A24 1c orange .40 .25
485 A25 2c green .40 .25
486 A24 3c dp vio .40 .25
487 A25 4c brown .40 .25
488 A24 5c yellow .40 .25
489 A25 6c lt bl .40 .25
490 A25 10c dk bl .90 .25
491 A24 15c car rose 1.40 .50
492 A25 20c dk grn 1.40 .50
493 A24 25c blk brn 27.50 6.00
494 A25 50c bis brn 3.25 1.00
495 A25 1cor dl vio 6.25 3.00
Nos. 483-495 (13) 43.50 13.00

No. 425 Overprinted in Violet

1929

499 A33 10c bis brn .75 .60

No. 408 Overprinted in Red

1929

500 A24 ½c green (R) .25 .25
a. Inverted overprint 5.50
b. Double overprint 5.00
c. Double overprint, one inverted 5.00

A36

Ovptd. Horiz. in Black "R. de T." Surcharged Vert. in Red

1929

504 A36 1c on 5c bl & blk (R) .25 .25
a. Inverted surcharge 3.00
b. Surcharged "0.10" for "0.01" 3.00
c. "0.0" instead of "0.01" 5.00

509 A36 2c on 5c bl & blk (R) .25 .25
a. Double surcharge 2.50
b. Double surcharge, one inverted 3.50
c. Inverted surcharge 5.00

Overprinted Horizontally in Black "R. de C." Surcharged Vertically in Red

510 A36 2c on 5c bl & blk (R) 22.50 1.25
a. Dbl. surcharge, one inverted 25.00

A37

Surcharged in Red

511 A37 1c on 10c dk grn & blk (R) .25 .25
a. Double surcharge
512 A37 2c on 5c bl & blk (R) .25 .25
Nos. 504-512 (5) 23.50 2.25

The varieties tall "1" in "0.01" and "O$" for "C$" are found in this surcharge.

Nos. 500, 504, 509-512 and RA38 were surcharged in red and sold in large quantities to the public. Surcharges in various other colors were distributed only to a favored few and not regularly sold at the post offices.

Types of 1914 Issue

1929-31 **Various Frames**

513 A24 1c ol grn .25 .25
514 A24 3c lt bl .30 .25
515 A25 4c dk bl ('31) .30 .25
516 A24 5c ol brn .40 .25
517 A25 6c bis brn ('31) .50 .30
518 A25 10c lt brn ('31) .60 .25
519 A24 15c org red ('31) .90 .25
520 A25 20c org ('31) 1.25 .35
521 A24 25c dk vio .25 .25
522 A25 50c grn ('31) .50 .25
523 A25 1cor yel ('31) 4.50 1.25
Nos. 513-523 (11) 9.75 3.90

Nos. 513-523 exist with signature controls. See note before No. 600. Same values.

New Post Office at Managua — A38

1930, Sept. 15 **Engr.**

525 A38 ½c olive gray 1.25 1.25
526 A38 1c carmine 1.25 1.25
527 A38 2c red org .90 .90
528 A38 3c orange 1.75 1.75
529 A38 4c yellow 1.75 1.75
530 A38 5c ol grn 2.25 2.25
531 A38 6c bl grn 2.25 2.25
532 A38 10c black 2.75 2.75
533 A38 25c dp bl 5.50 5.50
534 A38 50c ultra 9.00 9.00
535 A38 1cor dp vio 25.00 25.00
Nos. 525-535 (11) 53.65 53.65

Opening of the new general post office at Managua. The stamps were on sale on day of issuance and for an emergency in April, 1931.

No. 499 Surcharged in Black and Red

1931, May 29

536 A33 2c on 10c bis brn .50 1.60
a. Red surcharge omitted 2.50
b. Red surcharge double 5.00
c. Red surcharge inverted 6.00
d. Red surcharge double, one invtd.

Surcharge exists in brown.

Types of 1914-31 Issue Overprinted

1931, June 11

540 A24 ½c green .35 .25
a. Double overprint .80
b. Double ovpt., one inverted 1.40
c. Inverted overprint .80
541 A24 1c ol grn .35 .25
a. Double overprint .80
b. Double ovpt., one inverted 1.40
c. Inverted overprint
542 A25 2c car rose .35 .25
a. Double overprint .80
b. Double ovpt., both inverted 2.50
c. Inverted overprint 1.40
543 A24 3c lt bl .35 .25
a. Double overprint .80
b. Double ovpt., one inverted 1.40
c. Inverted overprint 1.40
544 A24 5c yellow 4.00 2.25
545 A24 5c ol brn 1.25 .25
a. Double overprint 4.50
b. Inverted overprint 4.50
546 A24 15c org red 1.50 .40
a. Double overprint 3.50
547 A24 25c blk brn 12.00 6.50
a. Double overprint 13.00 7.00
b. Inverted overprint 13.00 7.00
548 A24 25c dk vio 4.50 2.50
a. Double overprint 10.00
Nos. 540-548 (9) 24.65 12.90

Counterfeits exist of the scarcer values. The 4c brown and 6c light blue with this overprint are bogus.

Managua P.O. Before and After Earthquake A40

1932, Jan. 1 **Litho.** ***Perf. 11½***
Soft porous paper, Without gum

556 A40 ½c emerald 1.50
557 A40 1c yel brn 1.90
558 A40 2c dp car 1.50
559 A40 3c ultra 1.50
560 A40 4c dp ultra 1.50
561 A40 5c yel brn 1.60
562 A40 6c gray brn 1.60
563 A40 10c yel brn 2.50
564 A40 15c dl rose 3.75
565 A40 20c orange 3.50
566 A40 25c dk vio 2.50
567 A40 50c emerald 2.50
568 A40 1cor yellow 6.25
Nos. 556-568 (13) 32.10

Issued in commemoration of the earthquake at Managua, Mar. 31, 1931. The stamps were on sale on Jan. 1, 1932, only. The money received from this sale was for the reconstruction of the Post Office building and for the improvement of the postal service. Many shades exist.

Sheets of 10.

Reprints are on thin hard paper and do not have the faint horiz. ribbing that is on the front or back of the originals. Fake cancels abound. Value 75 cents each.

See Nos. C20-C24. For overprints and surcharges see Nos. C32-C43, C47-C48.

Rivas Railroad Issue

"Fill" at El Nacascolo — A41

1c, Wharf at San Jorge. 5c, Rivas Station. 10c, San Juan del Sur. 15c, Train at Rivas Station.

1932, Dec. 17 **Litho.** ***Perf. 12***
Soft porous paper

570 A41 1c yellow 16.00
a. 1c ocher 18.00
571 A41 2c carmine 16.00
572 A41 5c blk brn 16.00
573 A41 10c chocolate 16.00
574 A41 15c yellow 16.00
a. 15c deep orange 18.00
Nos. 570-574 (5) 80.00

Inauguration of the railroad from San Jorge to San Juan del Sur. On sale only on Dec. 17, 1932.

Sheets of 4, without gum. See #C67-C71.

Reprints exist on five different papers ranging from thick soft light cream to thin very hard paper and do not have the faint horiz. ribbing that is normally on the front or back of the originals. Originals are on very white paper. Value of reprints, $5 each.

Leon-Sauce Railroad Issue

Bridge No. 2 at Santa Lucia — A42

Designs: 1c, Environs of El Sauce. 5c, Santa Lucia. 10c, Works at Km. 64. 15c, Rock cut at Santa Lucia.

1932, Dec. 30 ***Perf. 12***
Soft porous paper

575 A42 1c orange 16.00
576 A42 2c carmine 16.00
577 A42 5c blk brn 16.00
578 A42 10c brown 16.00
579 A42 15c orange 16.00
Nos. 575-579 (5) 80.00

Inauguration of the railroad from Leon to El Sauce. On sale only on Dec. 30, 1932.

Sheets of 4, without gum. See #C72-C76.

Reprints exist on thin hard paper and do not have the faint horiz. ribbing that is on the front or back of the originals. Value $5 each.

Nos. 514-515, 543 Surcharged in Red

1932, Dec. 10

580 A24 1c on 3c lt bl (514) .35 .25
a. Double surcharge 3.50
581 A24 1c on 3c lt bl (543) 4.00 3.50
582 A25 2c on 4c dk bl (515) .25 .25
a. Double surcharge 2.50
Nos. 580-582 (3) 4.60 4.00

Nos. 514, 516, 545 and 518 Surcharged in Black or Red

1933

583 A24 1c on 3c lt bl (Bk) (514) .25 .25
a. "Censavo" 4.00 2.25
b. Double surcharge, one inverted 4.00
584 A24 1c on 5c ol brn (R) (516) .25 .25
a. Inverted surcharge
b. Double surcharge
585 A24 1c on 5c ol brn (R) (545) 6.50 5.00
a. Red surcharge double 12.00
586 A25 2c on 10c lt brn (Bk) (518) .25 .25
a. Double surcharge 7.00 2.50
b. Inverted surcharge 6.00 3.50
c. Double surcharge, one inverted 7.00 2.50
Nos. 583-586 (4) 7.25 5.75

On No. 586 "Vale Dos" measures 13mm and 14mm.

No. 583 with green surcharge and No. 586 with red surcharge are bogus.

Flag of the Race Issue

Flag with Three Crosses for Three Ships of Columbus A43

1933, Aug. 3 **Litho.** ***Rouletted 9***
Without gum

587 A43 ½c emerald 1.75 1.75
588 A43 1c green 1.50 1.50
589 A43 2c red 1.50 1.50
590 A43 3c dp rose 1.50 1.50
591 A43 4c orange 1.50 1.50
592 A43 5c yellow 1.75 1.75
593 A43 10c dp brn 1.75 1.75
594 A43 15c dk brn 1.75 1.75
595 A43 20c vio bl 1.75 1.75
596 A43 25c dl bl 1.75 1.75
597 A43 30c violet 4.50 4.50
598 A43 50c red vio 4.50 4.50
599 A43 1cor ol brn 4.50 4.50
Nos. 587-599 (13) 30.00 30.00

Commemorating the raising of the symbolical "Flag of the Race"; also the 441st anniversary of the sailing of Columbus for the New World, Aug. 3, 1492. Printed in sheets of 10.

See Nos. C77-C87, O320-O331.

In October, 1933, various postage, airmail and official stamps of current issues were overprinted with facsimile signatures of the Minister of Public Works and the Postmaster-General. These overprints are control marks.

Nos. 410 and 513 Overprinted in Black

1935 ***Perf. 12***

600 A24 1c ol grn .25 .25
a. Inverted overprint 1.40 1.60
b. Double overprint 1.40 1.60
c. Double overprint, one inverted 1.60 1.60
601 A25 2c car rose .25 .25
a. Inverted overprint 1.60
b. Double overprint 1.60
c. Double overprint, one inverted 1.60
d. Double overprint, both inverted 2.50 2.25

No. 517 Surcharged in Red as in 1932

1936, June

602 A25 ½c on 6c bis brn .35 .25
a. "Ccentavo" .80 .80
b. Double surcharge 3.50 3.50

Regular Issues of 1929-35 Overprinted in Blue

1935, Dec.

603 A25 ½c on 6c bis brn .65 .25
604 A24 1c ol grn (#600) .80 .25
605 A25 2c car rose (#601) .80 .25
a. Black overprint inverted 6.00
606 A24 3c lt bl .80 .25
607 A24 5c ol brn 1.00 .25
608 A25 10c lt brn 1.60 .80
Nos. 603-608 (6) 5.65 2.05

Nos. 606-608 have signature control overprint. See note before No. 600.

Same Overprint in Red

1936, Jan.

609 A24 ½c dk grn .25 .25
610 A25 ½c on 6c bis brn (602) .25 .25
a. Double surch., one inverted 6.00 6.00
611 A24 1c ol grn (513) .25 .25
612 A24 1c ol grn (600) .25 .25
613 A25 2c car rose (410) .50 .25
614 A25 2c car rose (601) .25 .25
a. Black overprint inverted 12.00 2.50
b. Black ovpt. double, one invtd. 12.00 3.50
615 A24 3c lt bl .25 .25
616 A25 4c dk bl .25 .25
617 A24 5c ol brn .25 .25
618 A25 6c bis brn .25 .25
619 A25 10c lt brn .50 .25
620 A24 15c org red .25 .25
621 A25 20c orange .80 .25
622 A24 25c dk vio .25 .25
623 A25 50c green .35 .25
624 A25 1cor yellow .40 .25
Nos. 609-624 (16) 5.30 4.00

Red or blue "Resello 1935" overprint may be found inverted or double. Red and blue overprints on same stamp are bogus.

Nos. 615-624 have signature control overprint. See note before No. 600.

Regular Issues of 1922-29 Overprinted in Carmine

1936, May

625 A24 ½c green .25 .25
626 A24 1c olive green .25 .25
627 A25 2c carmine rose .50 .25
628 A24 3c light blue .25 .25
Nos. 625-628 (4) 1.25 1.00

No. 628 has signature control overprint. See note before No. 600.

Nos. 514, 516 Surcharged in Black

1936, June

629 A24 1c on 3c lt bl .25 .25
a. "1396" for "1936" 1.00 1.00
b. "Un" omitted 4.50 1.40
c. Inverted surcharge 1.60 1.60
d. Double surcharge 1.60 1.60
630 A24 2c on 5c ol brn .25 .25
a. "1396" for "1936" 1.40 1.40
b. Double surcharge 3.50 3.50

Regular Issues of 1929-31 Surcharged in Black or Red

1936

631 A24 ½c on 15c org red (R) .25 .25
a. Double surcharge 5.00
632 A25 1c on 4c dk bl (Bk) .25 .25
633 A24 1c on 5c ol brn (Bk) .25 .25
634 A25 1c on 6c bis brn (Bk) .40 .25
a. "1939" instead of "1936" 2.50 1.60
635 A24 1c on 15c org red (Bk) .25 .25
a. "1939" instead of "1936" 2.50 1.60
636 A25 1c on 20c org (Bk) .25 .25
a. "1939" intead of "1936" 2.50 1.60
b. Double surcharge 4.00
637 A25 1c on 20c org (R) .25 .25
638 A25 2c on 10c lt brn (Bk) .25 .25
639 A24 2c on 15c org red (Bk) 1.00 .80
640 A25 2c on 20c org (Bk) .50 .25
641 A24 2c on 25c dk vio (R) .35 .25
642 A24 2c on 25c dk vio (Bk) .35 .25
a. "1939" instead of "1936" 2.50 1.60
643 A25 2c on 50c grn (Bk) .35 .25
a. "1939" instead of "1936" 2.50 1.60
644 A25 2c on 1 cor yel (Bk) .35 .25
a. "1939" instead of "1936" 2.50 1.60
645 A25 3c on 4c dk bl (Bk) .65 .50
a. "1939" instead of "1936" 2.50 1.60
b. "s" of "Centavos" omitted and "r" of "Tres" inverted 2.50
Nos. 631-645 (15) 5.70 4.55

Nos. 634, 639, 643-644 exist with and without signature controls. Same values, except for No. 639, which is rare without the signature control. Nos. 635-636, 642, 645 do not have signature controls. Others have signature controls only. See note before No. 600.

Regular Issues of 1929-31 Overprinted in Black

1936, Aug.

646 A24 3c lt bl .35 .25
647 A24 5c ol brn .25 .25
648 A25 10c lt brn .50 .35
Nos. 646-648 (3) 1.10 .85

No. 648 bears script control mark.

A44

1936, Oct. 19 Red Surcharge

649 A44 1c on 5c grn & blk .25 .25
650 A44 2c on 5c grn & blk .25 .25

Types of 1914

1937, Jan. 1 Engr.

652 A24 ½c black .25 .25
653 A24 1c car rose .25 .25
654 A25 2c dp bl .25 .25
655 A24 3c chocolate .25 .25
656 A25 4c yellow .25 .25
657 A24 5c org red .25 .25
658 A25 6c dl vio .25 .25
659 A25 10c ol grn .25 .25
660 A24 15c green .25 .25
661 A25 20c red brn .25 .25
663 A25 50c brown .35 .25
664 A25 1cor ultra .60 .25
Nos. 652-664 (12) 3.45 3.00

See note after No. 360.

Mail Carrier — A45

Designs: 1c, Mule carrying mail. 2c, Mail coach. 3c, Sailboat. 5c, Steamship. 7½c, Train.

1937, Dec. Litho. *Perf. 11*

665 A45 ½c green .25 .25
666 A45 1c magenta .25 .25
667 A45 2c brown .25 .25
668 A45 3c purple .25 .25
669 A45 5c blue .25 .25
670 A45 7½c red org .55 .35
Nos. 665-670 (6) 1.80 1.60

75th anniv. of the postal service in Nicaragua.

Nos. 665-670 exists printed on several different kinds of paper: medium thick porous white paper, a thinner whitish toned paper, and a thin hard brownish tone paper.

Nos. 665-670 were also issued in sheets of 4. Value, set of sheets $20.

The miniature sheets are ungummed, and also exist imperf. and part-perf.

Nos. 359, 663 and 664 Surcharged in Red

1938 *Perf. 12*

671 A24 3c on 25c org .25 .25
672 A25 5c on 50c brn .25 .25
a. "e" of "Vale" omitted 1.60 1.00
673 A25 6c on 1cor ultra .25 .25
Nos. 671-673 (3) .75 .75

No. 672 has a script signature control and the surcharge is in three lines.

Dario Park A46

1939, Jan. Engr. *Perf. 12½*

674 A46 1½c yel grn .25 .25
675 A46 2c dp rose .25 .25
676 A46 3c brt bl .25 .25
677 A46 6c brn org .25 .25
678 A46 7½c dp grn .25 .25
679 A46 10c blk brn .25 .25
680 A46 15c orange .25 .25
681 A46 25c lt vio .25 .25
682 A46 50c brt yel grn .25 .25
683 A46 1cor yellow .65 .40
Nos. 674-683 (10) 2.90 2.65

Nos. 660 and 661 Surcharged in Red

1939 *Perf. 12*

684 A24 1c on 15c grn .25 .25
a. Inverted surcharge 2.00 2.00
685 A25 1c on 20c red brn .25 .25

AIR POST STAMPS

Counterfeits exist of almost all scarce surcharges among Nos. C1-C66.

Regular Issues of 1914-28 Overprinted in Red

1929, May 15 Unwmk. *Perf. 12*

C1 A24 25c orange 1.75 1.75
a. Double overprint, one inverted 50.00
b. Inverted overprint 50.00
c. Double overprint 50.00
C2 A24 25c blk brn 2.25 2.25
a. Double overprint, one inverted 50.00
b. Double overprint 50.00
c. Inverted overprint 30.00

There are numerous varieties in the setting of the overprint. The most important are: Large "1" in "1929" and large "A" in "Aereo" and "P. A. A."

Similar Overprint on Regular Issue of 1929 in Red

1929, June

C3 A24 25c dk vio 1.25 .75
a. Double overprint 50.00
b. Inverted overprint 50.00
c. Double overprint, one inverted 50.00
Nos. C1-C3 (3) 5.25 4.75

The stamps in the bottom row of the sheet have the letters "P. A. A." larger than usual.

Similar overprints, some including an airplane, have been applied to postage issues of 1914-20, officials of 1926 and Nos. 401-407. These are, at best, essays.

Airplanes over Mt. Momotombo — AP1

1929, Dec. 15 Engr.

C4 AP1 25c olive blk .50 .40
C5 AP1 50c blk brn .75 .75
C6 AP1 1cor org red 1.00 1.00
Nos. C4-C6 (3) 2.25 2.15

See Nos. C18-C19, C164-C168. For surcharges and overprints see Nos. C7-C8, C14-C17, C25-C31, C106-C120, C135-C146, C150-C154, C169-C173, CO25-CO29.

No. C4 Surcharged in Red or Black

1930, May 15

C7 AP1 15c on 25c ol blk (R) .50 .40
a. "$" inverted 3.50
b. Double surcharge (R + Bk) 7.00
c. As "b," red normal, blk invtd. 7.00
d. Double red surch., one inverted 7.00
C8 AP1 20c on 25c ol blk (Bk) .75 .60
a. "$" inverted 7.00
b. Inverted surcharge 15.00

Nos. C1, C2 and C3 Surcharged in Green

1931, June 7

C9 A24 15c on 25c org 70.00 50.00
C10 A24 15c on 25c blk brn 100.00 100.00
C11 A24 15c on 25c dk vio 15.00 15.00
c. Inverted surcharge 47.50
C12 A24 20c on 25c dk vio 10.00 10.00
c. Inverted surcharge 100.00
d. Double surcharge 100.00
C13 A24 20c on 25c blk brn 375.00

No. C13 was not regularly issued.

"1391"

C9a A24 15c on 25c
C10a A24 15c on 25c
C11a A24 15c on 25c 60.00
d. As "a," inverted 400.00
C12a A24 20c on 25c *75.00*
e. As "a," inverted 400.00
g. As "a," double 400.00
C13a A24 20c on 25c

"1921"

C9b A24 15c on 25c
C10b A24 15c on 25c 400.00
C11b A24 15c on 25c 60.00
e. As "b," inverted 400.00
C12b A24 20c on 25c *100.00*
f. As "b," inverted 400.00
h. As "b," double 400.00
C13b A24 20c on 25c

Nos. C8, C4-C6 Surcharged in Blue

1931, June

C14 AP1 15c on 20c on 25c 26.00 9.00
b. Blue surcharge inverted 37.50
c. "$" in blk, surch. invtd. 50.00
d. Blue surch. dbl., one invtd. 30.00
C15 AP1 15c on 25c 5.50 5.50
b. Blue surcharge inverted 100.00
c. Double surch., one invtd. 25.00
C16 AP1 15c on 50c 40.00 40.00
C17 AP1 15c on 1cor 100.00 100.00
Nos. C14-C17 (4) 171.50 154.50

"1391"

C14a AP1 15c on 20c on 25c 50.00
C15a AP1 15c on 25c 30.00
C16a AP1 15c on 50c 80.00
C17a AP1 15c on 1cor 225.00
Nos. C14a-C17a (4) 385.00

Momotombo Type of 1929

1931, July 8

C18 AP1 15c deep violet .25 .25
C19 AP1 20c deep green .40 .40

Managua Post Office Before and After Earthquake AP2

Without gum, Soft porous paper

1932, Jan. 1 Litho. *Perf. 11*

C20 AP2 15c lilac 1.50 *1.25*
a. 15c violet 22.50
b. Vert. pair, imperf. btwn. 35.00
C21 AP2 20c emerald 2.00
b. Horizontal pair, imperf. between 35.00
C22 AP2 25c yel brn 6.50
b. Vertical pair, imperf. between 60.00
C23 AP2 50c yel brn 8.00
C24 AP2 1cor dp car 12.00
a. Vert. or horiz. pair, imperf. btwn. 80.00
Nos. C20-C24 (5) 30.00

Sheets of 10. See note after No. 568.

For overprint and surcharges see #C44-C46.

Reprints: see note following No. 568. Value $1 each.

Nos. C5 and C6 Surcharged in Red or Black

1932, July 12 *Perf. 12*

C25 AP1 30c on 50c (Bk) 1.50 1.50
a. "Valc" 25.00
b. Double surcharge 15.00
c. Double surch., one inverted 15.00
d. Period omitted after "O" 25.00
e. As "a," double 300.00
C26 AP1 35c on 50c (R) 1.50 1.50
a. "Valc" 30.00
b. Double surcharge 12.00
c. Double surch., one inverted 12.00
d. As "a," double 300.00

C27 AP1 35c on 50c (Bk) 35.00 35.00
a. "Valc" 250.00
C28 AP1 40c on 1cor (Bk) 1.75 1.75
a. "Valc" 25.00
b. Double surcharge 15.00
c. Double surch., one inverted 15.00
d. Inverted surcharge 15.00
e. As "a," inverted 300.00
f. As "a," double 300.00
C29 AP1 55c on 1cor (R) 1.75 1.75
a. "Valc" 25.00
b. Double surcharge 12.00
c. Double surch., one inverted 12.00
d. Inverted surcharge 12.00
e. As "a," inverted 300.00
f. As "a," double 300.00
Nos. C25-C29 (5) 41.50 41.50

No. C18 Overprinted in Red

1932, Sept. 11

C30 AP1 15c dp vio 70.00 70.00
a. "Aerreo" 150.00 150.00
b. Invtd. "m" in "Septiembre" 150.00

International Air Mail Week.

No. C6 Surcharged

1932, Oct. 12

C31 AP1 8c on 1 cor org red 20.00 20.00
a. "1232" 30.00 30.00
b. 2nd "u" of "Inauguracion" is an "n" 30.00 30.00

Inauguration of airmail service to the interior.

Regular Issue of 1932 Overprinted in Red

1932, Oct. 24 *Perf. 11½*

Without Gum

C32 A40 1c yel brn 20.00 20.00
a. Inverted overprint 125.00 125.00
C33 A40 2c carmine 20.00 20.00
a. Inverted overprint 125.00 125.00
b. Double overprint 100.00 100.00
C34 A40 3c ultra 9.50 9.50
a. Inverted overprint 150.00 150.00
b. As "a," vert. pair, imperf. btwn. 500.00
C35 A40 4c dp ultra 9.50 9.50
a. Inverted overprint 125.00 125.00
b. Double overprint 100.00 100.00
c. Vert. or horiz. pair, imperf. btwn. 300.00
C36 A40 5c yel brn 9.50 9.50
a. Inverted overprint 125.00 125.00
b. Vert. pair, imperf. btwn. 75.00
C37 A40 6c gray brn 9.50 9.50
a. Inverted overprint 100.00 100.00
C38 A40 50c green 9.00 9.00
a. Inverted overprint 125.00 125.00
C39 A40 1cor yellow 9.50 9.50
a. Inverted overprint 125.00 125.00
b. Horiz. pair, imperf. btwn. 200.00
Nos. C32-C39 (8) 96.50 96.50

Nos. 564, C20-C21 exist overprinted as C32-C39. The editors believe they were not regularly issued.

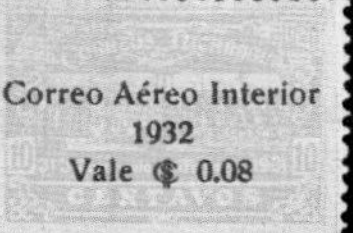

Surcharged in Red

1932, Oct. 24

C40 A40 8c on 10c yel brn 9.00 9.00
a. Inverted surcharge 125.00 125.00
C41 A40 16c on 20c org 9.00 9.00
a. Inverted surcharge 125.00 125.00
C42 A40 24c on 25c dp vio 9.00 9.00
a. Inverted surcharge 125.00 125.00
b. Horiz. pair, imperf. vert. 300.00

Surcharged in Red as No. C40 but without the word "Vale"

C43 A40 8c on 10c yel brn 45.00 45.00
a. Inverted surcharge 125.00 125.00
b. Horiz. pair, imperf. vert. 300.00

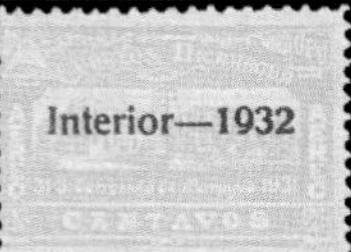

No. C22 Overprinted in Red

1932, Oct. 24

C44 AP2 25c yel brn 8.00 8.00
a. Inverted overprint 125.00 125.00

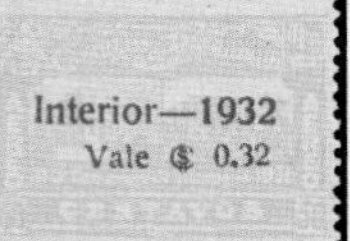

Nos. C23 and C24 Surcharged in Red

1932, Oct. 24

C45 AP2 32c on 50c yel brn 9.50 9.50
a. Inverted surcharge 125.00 125.00
b. "Interior-1932" inverted 150.00 150.00
c. "Vale $0.32" inverted 150.00 150.00
d. Horiz. pair, imperf. btwn. 200.00
C46 AP2 40c on 1cor car 7.00 7.00
a. Inverted surcharge 125.00 125.00
b. "Vale $0.40" inverted 200.00 200.00

Nos. 557-558 Overprinted in Black like Nos. C32 to C39

1932, Nov. 16

C47 A40 1c yel brn 25.00 22.50
a. "1232" 45.00 45.00
b. Inverted overprint 125.00 125.00
c. Double ovpt., one invtd. 125.00 125.00
d. As "a," inverted 500.00
C48 A40 2c dp car 20.00 17.50
a. "1232" 45.00 45.00
b. Inverted overprint 125.00 125.00
c. As "a," inverted 500.00

Excellent counterfeits exist of Nos. C27, C30-C48. Forged overprints and surcharges as on Nos. C32-C48 exist on reprints of Nos. C20-C24.

Regular Issue of 1914-32 Surcharged in Black

1932 *Perf. 12*

C49 A25 1c on 2c brt rose .65 .30
C50 A24 2c on 3c lt bl .65 .30
C51 A25 3c on 4c dk bl .65 .30
C52 A24 4c on 5c gray brn .65 .30
C53 A25 5c on 6c ol brn .65 .30
C54 A25 6c on 10c lt brn .65 .30
a. Double surcharge 25.00
C55 A24 8c on 15c org red .65 .30
C56 A25 16c on 20c org .65 .35
C57 A24 24c on 25c dk vio 2.50 1.00
C58 A24 25c on 25c dk vio 2.50 1.00
a. Double surcharge 25.00
C59 A25 32c on 50c grn 2.50 1.25
C60 A25 40c on 50c grn 3.00 1.40
C61 A25 50c on 1cor yel 4.25 2.25
C62 A25 1cor on 1cor yel 6.50 3.00
Nos. C49-C62 (14) 26.45 12.35

Nos. C49-C62 exist with inverted surcharge.

In addition to C49 to C62, four other stamps, Type A25, exist with this surcharge:

40c on 50c bister brown, black surcharge.
1cor on 2c bright rose, black surcharge.
1cor on 1cor yellow, red surcharge.
1cor on 1cor dull violet, black surcharge.

The editors believe they were not regularly issued.

Surcharged on Nos. 548, 547

1932

C65 A24 24c on 25c dk vio 45.00 45.00
C66 A24 25c on 25c blk brn 50.00 50.00

Counterfeits of Nos. C65 and C66 are plentiful.

Rivas Railroad Issue

La Chocolata Cut — AP3

El Nacascola — AP4

Designs: 25c, Cuesta cut. 50c, Mole of San Juan del Sur. 1cor, View of El Estero.

1932, Dec. **Litho.**

Soft porous paper

C67 AP3 15c dk vio 20.00
C68 AP4 20c bl grn 20.00
C69 AP4 25c dk brn 20.00
C70 AP4 50c blk brn 20.00
C71 AP4 1cor rose red 20.00
Nos. C67-C71 (5) 100.00

Inauguration of the railroad from San Jorge to San Juan del Sur, Dec. 18, 1932. Printed in sheets of 4, without gum.

Reprints: see note following No. 574. Value, $6 each.

Leon-Sauce Railroad Issue

"Fill" at Santa Lucia River — AP5

Designs: 15c, Bridge at Santa Lucia. 25c, Malpaicillo Station. 50c, Panoramic view. 1cor, San Andres.

1932, Dec. 30 **Soft porous paper**

C72 AP5 15c purple 20.00
C73 AP5 20c bl grn 20.00
C74 AP5 25c dk brn 20.00
C75 AP5 50c blk brn 20.00
C76 AP5 1cor rose red 20.00
Nos. C72-C76 (5) 100.00

Inauguration of the railroad from Leon to El Sauce, 12/30/32. Sheets of 4, without gum.

Reprints: see note following No. 579. Value, $6 each.

Flag of the Race Issue

1933, Aug. 3 **Litho.** *Rouletted 9*

Without gum

C77 A43 1c dk brn 1.50 1.50
C78 A43 2c red vio 1.50 1.50
C79 A43 4c violet 2.50 2.25
C80 A43 5c dl bl 2.25 2.25
C81 A43 6c vio bl 2.25 2.25
C82 A43 8c dp brn .70 .70
C83 A43 15c ol brn .70 .70
C84 A43 20c yellow 2.25 2.25
a. Horiz. pair, imperf. btwn. 15.00
b. Horiz. pair, imperf. vert. 15.00
C85 A43 25c orange 2.25 2.25
C86 A43 50c rose 2.25 2.25
C87 A43 1cor green 11.00 11.00
Nos. C77-C87 (11) 29.15 28.90

See note after No. 599. Printed in sheets of 10.

Reprints exist, shades differ from postage and official stamps.

Imperf., Pairs

C78a A43 2c 14.00
C79a A43 4c 10.00
C81a A43 6c 10.00
C82a A43 8c 10.00
C83a A43 15c 10.00
C87a A43 1cor 30.00

AP7

1933, Nov. *Perf. 12*

C88 AP7 10c bis brn 1.60 1.60
a. Vert. pair, imperf. between 35.00
C89 AP7 15c violet 1.25 1.25
a. Vert. pair, imperf. between 37.50
C90 AP7 25c red 1.50 1.50
a. Horiz. pair, imperf. between 22.50
C91 AP7 50c dp bl 1.60 1.60
Nos. C88-C91 (4) 5.95 5.95

Intl. Air Post Week, Nov. 6-11, 1933. Printed in sheets of 4. Counterfeits exist.

Stamps and Types of 1928-31 Surcharged in Black

1933, Nov. 3

C92 A25 1c on 2c grn .25 .25
C93 A24 2c on 3c ol gray .25 .25
C94 A25 3c on 4c car rose .25 .25
C95 A24 4c on 5c lt bl .25 .25
C96 A25 5c on 6c dk bl .25 .25
C97 A25 6c on 10c ol brn .25 .25
C98 A24 8c on 15c bis brn .25 .25
C99 A25 16c on 20c brn .25 .25
C100 A24 24c on 25c ver .25 .25
C101 A24 25c on 25c org .25 .25
C102 A25 32c on 50c vio .25 .25
C103 A25 40c on 50c grn .25 .25
C104 A25 50c on 1cor yel .25 .25
C105 A25 1cor on 1cor org red .35 .25
Nos. C92-C105 (14) 3.60 3.50

Nos. C100, C102-C105 exist without script control overprint. Value, each $1.50.

Type of Air Post Stamps of 1929 Surcharged in Black

1933, Oct. 28

C106 AP1 30c on 50c org red *2.00* .25
C107 AP1 35c on 50c lt bl *2.00* .25
C108 AP1 40c on 1cor yel *5.00* .25
C109 AP1 55c on 1cor grn *4.00* .25
Nos. C106-C109 (4) *13.00* 1.00

No. C19 Surcharged in Red

1934, Mar. 31

C110 AP1 10c on 20c grn .30 .25
a. Inverted surcharge 15.00
b. Double surcharge, one inverted 15.00
c. "Ceutroamericano" 10.00

No. C110 with black surcharge is believed to be of private origin.

No. C4 Surcharged in Red

1935, Aug.

C111 AP1 10c on 25c ol blk .25 .25
a. Small "v" in "vale" (R) 5.00
b. "centrvos" (R) 5.00
c. Double surcharge (R) 25.00
d. Inverted surcharge (R) 25.00
g. As "a," inverted 400.00
h. As "a," double 400.00

No. C111 with blue surcharge is believed to be private origin.

The editors do not recognize the Nicaraguan air post stamps overprinted in red "VALIDO 1935" in two lines and with or without script control marks as having been issued primarily for postal purposes.

Nos C4-C6, C18-C19 Overprinted Vertically in Blue, Reading Up:

1935-36

C112 AP1 15c dp vio 1.00 1.00
C113 AP1 20c dp grn 1.75 1.75
C114 AP1 25c ol blk 2.25 2.25
C115 AP1 50c blk brn 5.00 5.00
C116 AP1 1cor org red 40.00 40.00
Nos. C112-C116 (5) 50.00 50.00

Same Overprint on Nos. C106-C109 Reading Up or Down

C117 AP1 30c on 50c org red 1.50 1.40
C118 AP1 35c on 50c lt bl 6.50 6.50
C119 AP1 40c on 1cor yel 6.50 6.50
C120 AP1 55c on 1cor grn 6.50 6.50
Nos. C117-C120 (4) 21.00 20.90
Nos. C112-C120 (9) 71.00 70.90

Same Overprint in Red on Nos. C92-C105

1936

C121 A25 1c on 2c grn .25 .25
C122 A24 2c on 3c ol gray .25 .25
C123 A25 3c on 4c car rose .25 .25
C124 A24 4c on 5c lt bl .25 .25
C125 A25 5c on 6c dk bl .25 .25
C126 A25 6c on 10c ol brn .25 .25
C127 A24 8c on 15c bis brn .25 .25
C128 A25 16c on 20c brn .30 .25
C129 A24 24c on 25c ver .50 .30
C130 A24 25c on 25c org .35 .25
C131 A25 32c on 50c vio .35 .25
C132 A25 40c on 50c grn 1.00 .50
C133 A25 50c on 1cor yel .85 .25
C134 A25 1cor on 1cor org red 3.50 .65
Nos. C121-C134 (14) 8.60 4.20

Nos. C121 to C134 are handstamped with script control mark.

Overprint Reading Down on No. C110

C135 AP1 10c on 20c grn *350.00*

This stamp has been extensively counterfeited.

Overprinted in Red on Nos. C4 to C6, C18 and C19

C136 AP1 15c dp vio 1.00 .25
C137 AP1 20c dp grn 1.25 .60
C138 AP1 25c ol blk 1.25 .55
C139 AP1 50c blk brn 1.00 .55
C140 AP1 1cor org red 3.25 .55

On Nos. C106 to C109

C141 AP1 30c on 50c org red 2.25 .60
C142 AP1 35c on 50c lt bl 2.25 .40
C143 AP1 40c on 1cor yel 2.25 .55
C144 AP1 55c on 1cor grn 2.25 .50

Same Overprint in Red or Blue on No. C111 Reading Up or Down

C145 AP1 10c on 25c, down 3.00 .45
a. "Centrvos" 25.00
C146 AP1 10c on 25c (Bl), up 6.00 1.00
a. "Centrvos" 25.00
Nos. C136-C146 (11) 25.75 6.00

Overprint on No. C145 is at right, on No. C146 in center.

Nos. C92, C93 and C98 Overprinted in Black

1936

C147 A25 1c on 2c grn 2.00 .25
C148 A24 2c on 3c ol gray 2.00 .25
a. "Resello 1936" dbl., one invtd. 7.50
C149 A24 8c on 15c bis brn 2.00 .25
Nos. C147-C149 (3) 6.00 .75

With script control handstamp.

Nos. C5 and C6 Surcharged in Red

1936, Nov. 26

C150 AP1 15c on 50c blk brn .40 .25
C151 AP1 15c on 1cor org red .40 .25

Nos. C18 and C19 Overprinted in Carmine

1936, July 2

C152 AP1 15c dp vio .60 .25
C153 AP1 20c dp grn .60 .25

Overprint reading up or down.

No. C4 Surcharged and Overprinted in Red

C154 AP1 10c on 25c olive blk .50 .30
a. Surch. and ovpt. inverted 3.50

Same Overprint in Carmine on Nos. C92 to C99

C155 A25 1c on 2c green .75 .25
C156 A24 2c on 3c olive gray 4.00 2.00
C157 A25 3c on 4c car rose .75 .25
C158 A24 4c on 5c light blue .75 .25
C159 A25 5c on 6c dark blue .75 .25
C160 A25 6c on 10c olive brn .75 .25
C161 A24 8c on 15c bister brn .75 .25
C162 A25 16c on 20c brown .75 .25
Nos. C154-C162 (9) 9.75 4.05

No. 518 Overprinted in Black

C163 A25 10c lt brn .75 .25
a. Overprint inverted 3.50
b. Double overprint 3.50

Two fonts are found in the sheet of #C163.

Momotombo Type of 1929

1937

C164 AP1 15c yel org 1.00 .25
C165 AP1 20c org red 1.00 .25
C166 AP1 25c black 1.00 .25
C167 AP1 50c violet 1.00 .25
C168 AP1 1cor orange 4.50 .25
Nos. C164-C168 (5) 8.50 1.25

Surcharged in Black

1937

C169 AP1 30c on 50c car rose 1.25 .25
C170 AP1 35c on 50c olive grn 1.25 .25
C171 AP1 40c on 1cor green 1.25 .25
C172 AP1 55c on 1cor blue 1.25 .25
Nos. C169-C172 (4) 5.00 1.00

No. C168 Surcharged in Violet

1937 Unwmk. *Perf. 12*

C173 AP1 10c on 1cor org .45 .25
a. "Centauos" 10.00

No. C98 with Additional Overprint "1937"

C174 A24 8c on 15c bis brn .65 .25
a. "1937" double 6.50

Nos. C92-C102 with Additional Overprint in Blue reading "HABILITADO 1937"

C175 A25 1c on 2c grn .90 .25
a. Blue overprint double *3.50*
C176 A24 2c on 3c ol gray .90 .25
a. Double surch., one inverted *3.50*
C177 A25 3c on 4c car rose .90 .25
C178 A24 4c on 5c lt bl .90 .25
C179 A25 5c on 6c dk bl .90 .25
C180 A25 6c on 10c ol brn .90 .25
C181 A24 8c on 15c bis brn .90 .25
a. "Habilitado 1937" double 4.50
C182 A25 16c on 20c brn .90 .25
a. Double surcharge 3.50
C183 A24 24c on 25c ver .90 .25
C184 A24 25c on 25c org .90 .25
C185 A25 32c on 50c vio .90 .25
Nos. C175-C185 (11) 9.90 2.75

Map of Nicaragua AP8

For Foreign Postage

1937, July 30 Engr.

C186 AP8 10c green .40 .25
C187 AP8 15c dp bl .40 .25
C188 AP8 20c yellow .40 .25
C189 AP8 25c bl vio .40 .25
C190 AP8 30c rose car .40 .25
C191 AP8 50c org yel .50 .25
C192 AP8 1cor ol grn 1.00 .55
Nos. C186-C192 (7) 3.50 2.05

Presidential Palace AP9

For Domestic Postage

C193 AP9 1c rose car .40 .25
C194 AP9 2c dp bl .40 .25
C195 AP9 3c ol grn .40 .25
C196 AP9 4c black .40 .25
C197 AP9 5c dk vio .40 .25
C198 AP9 6c chocolate .40 .25
C199 AP9 8c bl vio .40 .25
C200 AP9 16c org yel .40 .25
C201 AP9 24c yellow .40 .25
C202 AP9 25c yel grn .40 .25
Nos. C193-C202 (10) 4.00 2.50

No. C201 with green overprint "Union Panamericana 1890-1940" is of private origin.

Managua AP10

Designs: 15c, Presidential Palace. 20c, Map of South America. 25c, Map of Central America. 30c, Map of North America. 35c, Lagoon of Tiscapa, Managua. 40c, Road Scene. 45c, Park. 50c, Another park. 55c, Scene in San Juan del Sur. 75c, Tipitapa River. 1cor, Landscape.

Wmk. 209

1937, Sept. 17 Typo. *Perf. 11*

Center in Dark Blue

C203 AP10 10c yel grn 2.25 1.20
C204 AP10 15c orange 2.25 1.40
C205 AP10 20c red 1.75 1.00
C206 AP10 25c vio brn 1.75 1.00
a. Center, double impression —
C207 AP10 30c bl grn 1.75 1.00
a. Great Lakes omitted 40.00 40.00
C208 AP10 35c lemon .75 .45
C209 AP10 40c green .75 .40
C210 AP10 45c brt vio .75 .35
C211 AP10 50c rose lil .75 .35
a. Vert. pair, imperf. btwn. 140.00
C212 AP10 55c lt bl .75 .35
C213 AP10 75c gray grn .75 .35

Center in Brown Red

C214 AP10 1cor dk bl 1.75 .50
Nos. C203-C214 (12) 16.00 8.35

150th anniv. of the Constitution of the US.

Diriangen — AP11

Designs: 4c, 10c, Nicarao. 5c, 15c, Bartolomé de Las Casas. 8c, 20c, Columbus.

For Domestic Postage

Without gum

1937, Oct. 12 Unwmk. *Perf. 11*

C215 AP11 1c green .25 .25
C216 AP11 4c brn car .25 .25
C217 AP11 5c dk vio .25 .25
a. Without imprint .40
C218 AP11 8c dp bl .25 .25
a. Without imprint .50

For Foreign Postage

Wmk. 209

With Gum

C219 AP11 10c lt brn .25 .25
C220 AP11 15c pale bl .25 .25
a. Without imprint 1.00
C221 AP11 20c pale rose .25 .25
Nos. C215-C221 (7) 1.75 1.75

Nos. C215-C221 printed in sheets of 4.

Imperf., Pairs

C215a AP11 1c .25 .25
C216a AP11 4c .25 .25
C217b AP11 5c .25 .25
C217c AP11 5c Without imprint
C218b AP11 8c .25
C218c AP11 8c Without imprint
C219a AP11 10c .25 .25
C220b AP11 15c .25 .25
C220c AP11 15c Without imprint
C221a AP11 20c .35 .35

Gen. Tomas Martinez — AP11a

Design: 10c-50c, Gen. Anastasio Somoza.

For Domestic Postage

Without Gum

Perf. 11½, Imperf.

1938, Jan. 18 Typo. Unwmk.

Center in Black

C221B AP11a 1c orange .25 .25
C221C AP11a 5c red vio .25 .25
C221D AP11a 8c dk bl .25 .25
C221E AP11a 16c brown .25 .25
f. Sheet of 4, 1c, 5c, 8c, 16c 2.25 2.25

For Foreign Postage

C221G AP11a 10c green .25 .25
C221H AP11a 15c dk bl .25 .25
C221J AP11a 25c violet .40 .40
C221K AP11a 50c carmine .50 .45
m. Sheet of 4, 10c, 15c, 25c, 50c 3.25 3.25
Nos. C221B-C221K (8) 2.40 2.35

75th anniv. of postal service in Nicaragua. Printed in sheets of four.

Stamps of type AP11a exist in changed colors and with inverted centers, double centers and frames printed on the back. These varieties were private fabrications.

Lake Managua AP12

President Anastasio Somoza — AP13

For Domestic Postage

1939	Unwmk.	Engr.	*Perf. 12½*	
C222	AP12	2c dp bl	.25	.25
C223	AP12	3c green	.25	.25
C224	AP12	8c pale lil	.25	.25
C225	AP12	16c orange	.25	.25
C226	AP12	24c yellow	.25	.25
C227	AP12	32c dk grn	.25	.25
C228	AP12	50c dp rose	.25	.25

For Foreign Postage

C229	AP13	10c dk brn	.25	.25
C230	AP13	15c dk bl	.25	.25
C231	AP13	20c org yel	.25	.25
C232	AP13	25c dk pur	.25	.25
C233	AP13	30c lake	.25	.25
C234	AP13	50c dp org	.25	.25
C235	AP13	1cor dk ol grn	.35	.40
		Nos. C222-C235 (14)	3.60	3.65

For Domestic Postage

Will Rogers and View of Managua AP14

Designs: 2c, Rogers standing beside plane. 3c, Leaving airport office. 4c, Rogers and US Marines. 5c, Managua after earthquake.

1939, Mar. 31		Engr.	*Perf. 12*	
C236	AP14	1c brt grn	.25	.25
C237	AP14	2c org red	.25	.25
C238	AP14	3c lt ultra	.25	.25
C239	AP14	4c dk bl	.25	.25
C240	AP14	5c rose car	.25	.25
		Nos. C236-C240 (5)	1.25	1.25

Will Rogers' flight to Managua after the earthquake, Mar. 31, 1931.

For surcharges see Nos. 686, 688 in Scott Standard catalogue, Vol. 5.

Pres. Anastasio Somoza in US House of Representatives — AP19

President Somoza and US Capitol AP20

President Somoza, Tower of the Sun and Trylon and Perisphere AP21

For Domestic Postage

1940, Feb. 1				
C241	AP19	4c red brn	.25	.25
C242	AP20	8c blk brn	.25	.25
C243	AP19	16c grnsh bl	.25	.25
C244	AP20	20c brt plum	.50	.30
C245	AP21	32c scarlet	.25	.25

For Foreign Postage

C246	AP19	25c dp bl	.25	.25
C247	AP19	30c black	.25	.25
C248	AP20	50c rose pink	.45	.40
C249	AP21	60c green	.50	.30
C250	AP19	65c dk vio brn	.50	.25
C251	AP19	90c ol grn	.65	.30
C252	AP21	1cor violet	1.00	.55
		Nos. C241-C252 (12)	5.10	3.60

Visit of Pres. Somoza to US in 1939.

For surcharge see No. C636 in Scott Standard catalogue, Vol. 5.

L. S. Rowe, Statue of Liberty, Nicaraguan Coastline, Flags of 21 American Republics, US Shield and Arms of Nicaragua — AP22

1940, Aug. 2		Engr.	*Perf. 12½*	
C253	AP22	1.25cor multi	2.00	1.00

50th anniversary of Pan American Union.

For overprint see No. C493 in Scott Standard catalogue, Vol. 5.

AIR POST OFFICIAL STAMPS

OA1

"Typewritten" Overprint on #O293

1929, Aug.		Unwmk.	*Perf. 12*	
CO1	OA1	25c orange	50.00	45.00

Excellent counterfeits of No. CO1 are plentiful.

Official Stamps of 1926 Ovptd. in Dark Blue

1929, Sept. 15				
CO2	A24	25c orange	.50	.50
a.		Inverted overprint	25.00	
b.		Double overprint	25.00	
CO3	A25	50c pale bl	.75	.75
a.		Inverted overprint	25.00	
b.		Double overprint	25.00	
c.		Double overprint, one inverted	25.00	

Nos. 519-523 Overprinted in Black

1932, Feb.				
CO4	A24	15c org red	.40	.40
a.		Inverted overprint	25.00	
b.		Double overprint	25.00	
c.		Double overprint, one invtd.	25.00	
CO5	A25	20c orange	.45	.45
a.		Double overprint	25.00	
CO6	A24	25c dk vio	.45	.45
CO7	A25	50c green	.55	.55
CO8	A25	1cor yellow	1.00	1.00
		Nos. CO4-CO8 (5)	2.85	2.85

Nos. CO4-CO5, CO7-CO8 exist with signature control overprint. Value, each, $2.50.

Overprinted on Stamp No. 547

CO9	A24	25c blk brn	42.50	42.50

The varieties "OFICAL", "OFIAIAL" and "CORROE" occur in the setting and are found on each stamp of the series.

Counterfeits of No. CO9 are plentiful.

Stamp No. CO4 with overprint "1931" in addition is believed to be of private origin.

Type of Regular Issue of 1914 Overprinted Like Nos. CO4-CO8

1933				
CO10	A24	25c olive	.25	.25
CO11	A25	50c ol grn	.25	.25
CO12	A25	1cor org red	.40	.40

On Stamps of 1914-28

CO13	A24	15c dp vio	.25	.25
CO14	A25	20c dp grn	.25	.25
		Nos. CO10-CO14 (5)	1.40	1.40

Nos. CO10-CO14 exist without signature control mark. Value, each $2.50.

Air Post Official Stamps of 1932-33 Ovptd. in Blue

1935				
CO15	A24	15c dp vio	1.00	.80
CO16	A25	20c dp grn	2.00	1.60
CO17	A24	25c olive	3.00	2.50
CO18	A25	50c ol grn	35.00	30.00
CO19	A25	1cor org red	40.00	37.50
		Nos. CO15-CO19 (5)	81.00	72.40

Overprinted in Red

CO20	A24	15c dp vio	.25	.25
CO21	A25	20c dp grn	.25	.25
CO22	A24	25c olive	.25	.25
CO23	A25	50c ol grn	.80	.80
CO24	A25	1cor org red	.80	.80
		Nos. CO20-CO24 (5)	2.35	2.35

Nos. CO15 to CO24 are handstamped with script control mark. Counterfeits of blue overprint are plentiful.

The editors do not recognize the Nicaraguan air post Official stamps overprinted in red "VALIDO 1935" in two lines and with or without script control marks as having been issued primarily for postal purposes.

Nos. C164-C168 Overprinted in Black

1937				
CO25	AP1	15c yel org	.80	.55
CO26	AP1	20c org red	.80	.60
CO27	AP1	25c black	.80	.70
CO28	AP1	50c violet	.80	.70
CO29	AP1	1cor orange	.80	.70
		Nos. CO25-CO29 (5)	4.00	3.25

Pres. Anastasio Somoza — OA2

1939, Feb. 7		Engr.	*Perf. 12½*	
CO30	OA2	10c brown	.25	.25
CO31	OA2	15c dk bl	.25	.25
CO32	OA2	20c yellow	.25	.25
CO33	OA2	25c dk pur	.25	.25
CO34	OA2	30c lake	.25	.25
CO35	OA2	50c dp org	.65	.65
CO36	OA2	1cor dk ol grn	1.25	1.25
		Nos. CO30-CO36 (7)	3.15	3.15

POSTAGE DUE STAMPS

D1

1896	Unwmk.	Engr.	*Perf. 12*	
J1	D1	1c orange	.50	*1.25*
J2	D1	2c orange	.50	*1.25*
J3	D1	5c orange	.50	*1.25*
J4	D1	10c orange	.50	*1.25*
J5	D1	20c orange	.50	*1.25*
J6	D1	30c orange	.50	*1.25*
J7	D1	50c orange	.50	*1.50*
		Nos. J1-J7 (7)	3.50	*9.00*

Wmk. 117

J8	D1	1c orange	1.00	*1.50*
J9	D1	2c orange	1.00	*1.50*
J10	D1	5c orange	1.00	*1.50*
J11	D1	10c orange	1.00	*1.50*
J12	D1	20c orange	1.25	*1.50*
J13	D1	30c orange	1.00	*1.50*
J14	D1	50c orange	1.00	*1.50*
		Nos. J8-J14 (7)	7.25	*10.50*

1897			Unwmk.	
J15	D1	1c violet	.50	*1.50*
J16	D1	2c violet	.50	*1.50*
J17	D1	5c violet	.50	*1.50*
J18	D1	10c violet	.50	*1.50*
J19	D1	20c violet	1.25	*2.00*
J20	D1	30c violet	.50	*1.50*
J21	D1	50c violet	.50	*1.50*
		Nos. J15-J21 (7)	4.25	*11.00*

Wmk. 117

J22	D1	1c violet	.50	*1.50*
J23	D1	2c violet	.50	*1.50*
J24	D1	5c violet	.50	*1.50*
J25	D1	10c violet	.50	*1.50*
J26	D1	20c violet	1.00	*2.00*
J27	D1	30c violet	.50	*1.50*
J28	D1	50c violet	.50	*1.50*
		Nos. J22-J28 (7)	4.00	*11.00*

Reprints of Nos. J8-J28 are on thick, porous paper. Color of 1896 reprints, reddish orange; or 1897 reprints, reddish violet. On watermarked reprints, liberty cap is sideways. Value 25c each.

D2

1898		Litho.	Unwmk.	
J29	D2	1c blue green	.25	*2.00*
J30	D2	2c blue green	.25	*2.00*
J31	D2	5c blue green	.25	*2.00*
J32	D2	10c blue green	.25	*2.00*
J33	D2	20c blue green	.25	*2.00*
J34	D2	30c blue green	.25	*2.00*
J35	D2	50c blue green	.25	*2.00*
		Nos. J29-J35 (7)	1.75	*14.00*

1899				
J36	D2	1c carmine	.25	*2.00*
J37	D2	2c carmine	.25	*2.00*
J38	D2	5c carmine	.25	*2.00*
J39	D2	10c carmine	.25	*2.00*
J40	D2	20c carmine	.25	*2.00*
J41	D2	50c carmine	.25	*2.00*
		Nos. J36-J41 (6)	1.50	*12.00*

Some denominations are found in se-tenant pairs.

Various counterfeit cancellations exist on #J1-J41.

D3

1900 **Engr.**

J42	D3	1c plum	.75	
J43	D3	2c vermilion	.75	
J44	D3	5c dk bl	.75	
J45	D3	10c purple	.75	
J46	D3	20c org brn	.75	
J47	D3	30c dk grn	1.50	
J48	D3	50c lake	1.50	
		Nos. J42-J48 (7)	6.75	

Nos. J42-J48 were not placed in use as postage due stamps. They were only issued with "Postage" overprints. See Nos. 137-143, 152-158, O72-O81, 2L11-2L15, 2L25, 2L40-2L41.

OFFICIAL STAMPS

Types of Postage Stamps Overprinted in Red Diagonally Reading up

1890 **Unwmk.** **Engr.** ***Perf. 12***

O1	A5	1c ultra	.25	*.30*
O2	A5	2c ultra	.25	*.30*
O3	A5	5c ultra	.25	*.30*
O4	A5	10c ultra	.25	*.40*
O5	A5	20c ultra	.25	*.45*
O6	A5	50c ultra	.25	*.75*
O7	A5	1p ultra	.25	*1.25*
O8	A5	2p ultra	.25	*1.60*
O9	A5	5p ultra	.25	*2.40*
O10	A5	10p ultra	.25	*4.00*
		Nos. O1-O10 (10)	2.50	*11.75*

All values of the 1890 issue are known without overprint and most of them with inverted or double overprint, or without overprint and imperforate. There is no evidence that they were issued in these forms.

Official stamps of 1890-1899 are scarce with genuine cancellations. Forged cancellations are plentiful.

Overprinted Vertically Reading Up

1891 **Litho.**

O11	A6	1c green	.25	*.30*
O12	A6	2c green	.25	*.30*
O13	A6	5c green	.25	*.30*
O14	A6	10c green	.25	*.30*
O15	A6	20c green	.25	*.50*
O16	A6	50c green	.25	*1.10*
O17	A6	1p green	.25	*1.25*
O18	A6	2p green	.25	*1.30*
O19	A6	5p green	.35	*2.40*
O20	A6	10p green	.50	*4.00*
		Nos. O11-O20 (10)	2.85	*11.75*

All values of this issue except the 2c and 5p exist without overprint and several with double overprint. They are not known to have been issued in this form.

Many of the denominations may be found in se-tenant pairs.

Overprinted in Dark Blue

1892 **Engr.**

O21	A7	1c yellow brown	.25	*.30*
O22	A7	2c yellow brown	.25	*.30*
O23	A7	5c yellow brown	.25	*.30*
O24	A7	10c yellow brown	.25	*.30*
O25	A7	20c yellow brown	.25	*.50*
O26	A7	50c yellow brown	.25	*1.00*
O27	A7	1p yellow brown	.25	*1.25*
O28	A7	2p yellow brown	.25	*1.60*
O29	A7	5p yellow brown	.25	*2.40*
O30	A7	10p yellow brown	.25	*4.00*
		Nos. O21-O30 (10)	2.50	*11.95*

The 2c and 1p are known without overprint and several values exist with double or inverted overprint. These probably were not regularly issued.

Commemorative of the 400th anniversary of the discovery of America by Christopher Columbus.

Overprinted in Red

1893 **Engr.**

O31	A8	1c slate	.25	*.30*
O32	A8	2c slate	.25	*.30*
O33	A8	5c slate	.25	*.30*
O34	A8	10c slate	.25	*.30*
O35	A8	20c slate	.25	*.50*
O36	A8	25c slate	.25	*.75*
O37	A8	50c slate	.25	*.85*
O38	A8	1p slate	.25	*1.00*
O39	A8	2p slate	.25	*2.00*
O40	A8	5p slate	.25	*5.50*
O41	A8	10p slate	.25	*5.50*
		Nos. O31-O41 (11)	2.75	*14.30*

The 2, 5, 10, 20, 25, 50c and 5p are known without overprint but probably were not regularly issued. Some values exist with double or inverted overprints.

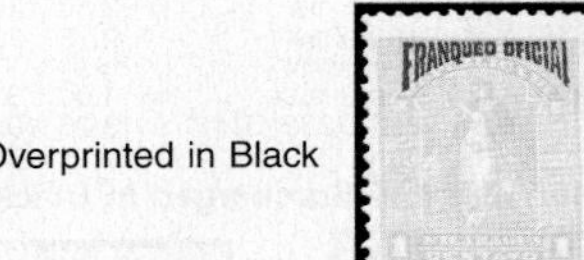

Overprinted in Black

1894

O42	A9	1c orange	.30	.35
O43	A9	2c orange	.30	.35
O44	A9	5c orange	.30	.35
O45	A9	10c orange	.30	.35
O46	A9	20c orange	.30	*.50*
O47	A9	50c orange	.30	*.75*
O48	A9	1p orange	.30	*1.50*
O49	A9	2p orange	.30	*2.00*
O50	A9	5p orange	2.00	*3.00*
O51	A9	10p orange	2.00	*4.00*
		Nos. O42-O51 (10)	6.40	*13.15*

Reprints are yellow.

Overprinted in Dark Blue

1895

O52	A10	1c green	.25	*.35*
O53	A10	2c green	.25	*.35*
O54	A10	5c green	.25	*.35*
O55	A10	10c green	.25	*.35*
O56	A10	20c green	.25	*.50*
O57	A10	50c green	.25	*1.00*
O58	A10	1p green	.25	*1.50*
O59	A10	2p green	.25	*2.00*
O60	A10	5p green	.25	*3.00*
O61	A10	10p green	.25	*4.00*
		Nos. O52-O61 (10)	2.50	*13.40*

Wmk. 117

O62	A10	1c green		
O63	A10	2c green		
O64	A10	5c green		
O65	A10	10c green		
O66	A10	20c green		
O67	A10	50c green		
O68	A10	1p green		
O69	A10	2p green		
O70	A10	5p green		
O71	A10	10p green		

Nos. O62-O71 probably exist only as reprints. Value, each 15 cents.

Postage Due Stamps of Same Date Handstamped in Violet

1896 **Unwmk.**

O72	D1	1c orange	7.00	
O73	D1	2c orange	7.00	
O74	D1	5c orange	5.00	
O75	D1	10c orange	5.00	
O76	D1	20c orange	10.00	
		Nos. O72-O76 (5)	34.00	

Wmk. 117

O77	D1	1c orange	7.00	
O78	D1	2c orange	7.00	
O79	D1	5c orange	4.00	
O80	D1	10c orange	4.00	
O81	D1	20c orange	4.00	
		Nos. O77-O81 (5)	26.00	

Nos. O72-O81 were handstamped in rows of five. Several handstamps were used, one of which had the variety "Oftcial." Most varieties are known inverted and double.

Forgeries exist.

Types of Postage Stamps Overprinted in Red

1896 **Unwmk.**

O82	A11	1c red	2.50	3.00
O83	A11	2c red	2.50	3.00
O84	A11	5c red	2.50	3.00
O85	A11	10c red	2.50	3.00
O86	A11	20c red	3.00	3.00
O87	A11	50c red	5.00	*5.00*
O88	A11	1p red	12.00	*12.00*
O89	A11	2p red	12.00	*12.00*
O90	A11	5p red	16.00	*16.00*
		Nos. O82-O90 (9)	58.00	*60.00*

Wmk. 117

O91	A11	1c red	3.00	3.50
O92	A11	2c red	3.00	3.50
O93	A11	5c red	3.00	3.50
O94	A11	10c red	3.00	3.50
O95	A11	20c red	5.00	5.00
O96	A11	50c red	3.00	*5.00*
O97	A11	1p red	14.00	*14.00*
O98	A11	2p red	16.00	*16.00*
O99	A11	5p red	25.00	*25.00*
		Nos. O91-O99 (9)	75.00	*79.00*

Used values for Nos. O88-O90, O97-O99 are for CTO examples. Postally used examples are not known.

Same, Dated 1897

1897 **Unwmk.**

O100	A11	1c red	3.00	3.00
O101	A11	2c red	3.00	3.00
O102	A11	5c red	3.00	2.50
O103	A11	10c red	3.00	3.00
O104	A11	20c red	3.00	4.00
O105	A11	50c red	5.00	*5.00*
O106	A11	1p red	12.00	*12.00*
O107	A11	2p red	12.00	*12.00*
O108	A11	5p red	16.00	*16.00*
		Nos. O100-O108 (9)	60.00	*60.50*

Wmk. 117

O109	A11	1c red	5.00	5.00
O110	A11	2c red	5.00	5.00
O111	A11	5c red	5.00	5.00
O112	A11	10c red	10.00	10.00
O113	A11	20c red	10.00	10.00
O114	A11	50c red	12.00	*12.00*
O115	A11	1p red	20.00	*20.00*
O116	A11	2p red	20.00	*20.00*
O117	A11	5p red	20.00	*20.00*
		Nos. O109-O117 (9)	107.00	*107.00*

Reprints of Nos. O82-O117 are described in notes after No. 109M. Value 15c each.

Used values for Nos. O106-O108, O115-O117 are for CTO examples. Postally used examples are not known.

Overprinted in Blue

1898 **Unwmk.**

O118	A12	1c carmine	3.25	3.25
O119	A12	2c carmine	3.25	3.25
O120	A12	4c carmine	3.25	3.25
O121	A12	5c carmine	2.50	2.50
O122	A12	10c carmine	4.00	4.00
O123	A12	15c carmine	6.00	6.00
O124	A12	20c carmine	6.00	6.00
O125	A12	50c carmine	8.50	*8.50*
O126	A12	1p carmine	11.00	*11.00*
O127	A12	2p carmine	11.00	*11.00*
O128	A12	5p carmine	11.00	*11.00*
		Nos. O118-O128 (11)	69.75	*69.75*

Stamps of this set with sideways watermark 117 or with black overprint are reprints. Value 25c each.

Used values for Nos. O126-O128 are for CTO examples. Postally used examples are not known.

Overprinted in Dark Blue

1899

O129	A13	1c gray grn	.35	*1.00*
O130	A13	2c bis brn	.35	*1.00*
O131	A13	4c lake	.35	*1.00*
O132	A13	5c dk bl	.35	*.50*
O133	A13	10c buff	.35	*1.00*
O134	A13	15c chocolate	.35	*2.00*
O135	A13	20c dk grn	.35	*3.00*
O136	A13	50c car rose	.35	*3.00*
O137	A13	1p red	.35	*10.00*
O138	A13	2p violet	.35	*10.00*
O139	A13	5p lt bl	.35	*15.00*
		Nos. O129-O139 (11)	3.85	*47.50*

Counterfeit cancellations on Nos. O129-O139 are plentiful.

"Justice" — O5

1900 **Engr.**

O140	O5	1c plum	.60	.60
O141	O5	2c vermilion	.50	.50
O142	O5	4c ol grn	.60	.60
O143	O5	5c dk bl	1.25	.45
O144	O5	10c purple	1.25	.35
O145	O5	20c brown	.90	.35
O146	O5	50c lake	1.25	.50
O147	O5	1p ultra	3.50	2.50
O148	O5	2p brn org	4.00	4.00
O149	O5	5p grnsh blk	5.00	5.00
		Nos. O140-O149 (10)	18.85	14.85

For surcharges see Nos. O155-O157.

Nos. 123, 161 Surcharged in Black

1903 ***Perf. 12, 14***

O150	A14	1c on 10c violet	.25	.30
a.		"Centovo"	1.00	
b.		"Contavo"	1.00	
c.		With ornaments	.30	
d.		Inverted surcharge	1.00	
e.		"1" omitted at upper left	2.00	
O151	A14	2c on 3c green	.30	.40
a.		"Centovos"	1.00	
b.		"Contavos"	1.00	
c.		With ornaments	.35	
d.		Inverted surcharge	1.00	
O152	A14	4c on 3c green	1.25	1.25
a.		"Centovos"	2.50	
b.		"Contavos"	2.50	
c.		With ornaments	2.50	
d.		Inverted surcharge		
O153	A14	4c on 10c violet	1.25	1.25
a.		"Centovos"	2.50	
b.		"Contavos"	2.50	
c.		With ornaments	2.00	
d.		Inverted surcharge		
O154	A14	5c on 3c green	.25	.25
a.		"Centovos"	1.00	
b.		"Contavos"	1.00	
c.		With ornaments	.30	
d.		Double surcharge	2.00	
e.		Inverted surcharge		
		Nos. O150-O154 (5)	3.30	3.45

These surcharges are set up to cover 25 stamps. Some of the settings have bars or pieces of fancy border type below "OFICIAL." There are 5 varieties on #O150, 3 on #O151, 1 each on #O152, O153, O154.

In 1904 #O151 was reprinted to fill a dealer's order. This printing lacks the small figure at the upper right. It includes the variety "OFICILA." At the same time the same setting was printed in carmine on official stamps of 1900, 1c on 10c violet and 2c on 1p ultramarine. Also the 1, 2 and 5p official stamps of 1900 were surcharged with new values and the dates 1901 or 1902 in various colors, inverted, etc. It is doubtful if any of these varieties were ever in Nicaragua and certain that none of them ever did legitimate postal duty.

No. O145 Surcharged in Black

1904 *Perf. 12*

O155 O5 10c on 20c brn .25 .25
a. No period after "Ctvs" 1.00 .75
O156 O5 30c on 20c brn .25 .25
O157 O5 50c on 20c brn .50 .35
b. Lower "50" omitted 2.50 2.50
b. Upper figures omitted 2.50 2.50
c. Top left and lower figures omitted 3.50 3.50
Nos. O155-O157 (3) 1.00 .85

Coat of Arms — O6

1905, July 25 **Engr.**

O158 O6 1c green .25 .25
O159 O6 2c rose .25 .25
O160 O6 5c blue .25 .25
O161 O6 10c yel brn .25 .25
O162 O6 20c orange .25 .25
O163 O6 50c brn ol .25 .25
O164 O6 1p lake .25 .25
O165 O6 2p violet .25 .25
O166 O6 5p gray blk .25 .25
Nos. O158-O166 (9) 2.25 2.25

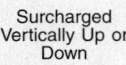

Surcharged Vertically Up or Down

1907

O167 O6 10c on 1c grn .75 .75
O168 O6 10c on 2c rose 25.00 22.50
O169 O6 20c on 2c rose 22.50 *26.00*
O170 O6 50c on 1c grn 1.50 1.50
O171 O6 50c on 2c rose 22.50 *23.00*

Surcharged

O172 O6 1p on 2c rose 1.50 1.50
O173 O6 2p on 2c rose 1.50 1.50
O174 O6 3p on 2c rose 1.50 1.50
O175 O6 4p on 2c rose
O176 O6 4p on 5c blue 2.25 2.25

The setting for this surcharge includes various letters from wrong fonts, the figure "1" for "l" in "Vale" and an "l" for "1" in "$1.00."

Surcharged

O177 O6 20c on 1c green 1.00 1.00
a. Double surcharge 5.00 5.00
Nos. O167-O174,O176-O177 (10) 80.00 81.50

The preceding surcharges are vertical, reading both up and down.

Revenue Stamps Surcharged

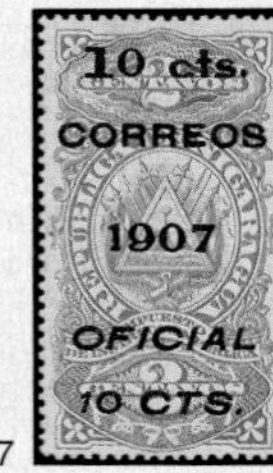

O7

1907 *Perf. 14 to 15*

O178 O7 10c on 2c org (Bk) .25 .25
O179 O7 35c on 1c bl (R) .25 .25
a. Inverted surcharge 3.00 3.00
O180 O7 70c on 1c bl (V) .25 .25
a. Inverted surcharge 3.00 3.00
O181 O7 70c on 1c bl (O) .25 .25
a. Inverted surcharge 3.00 3.00
O182 O7 1p on 2c org (G) .25 .25
a. Inverted surcharge 14.00 14.00
O183 O7 2p on 2c org (Br) .25 .25
O184 O7 3p on 5c brn (Bl) .25 .25
O185 O7 4p on 5c brn (G) .25 .25
a. Double surcharge 3.00 3.00
O186 O7 5p on 5c brn (G) .25 .25
a. Inverted surcharge 3.50 3.50
Nos. O178-O186 (9) 2.25 2.25

Letters and figures from several fonts were mixed in these surcharges.

See Nos. O199-O209.

No. 202 Surcharged

1907, Nov.

Black or Blue Black Surcharge

O187 A18 10c on 1c grn 15.00 15.00
O188 A18 15c on 1c grn 15.00 20.00
O189 A18 20c on 1c grn 15.00 15.00
O190 A18 50c on 1c grn 15.00 20.00

Red Surcharge

O191 A18 1(un)p on 1c grn 14.00 15.00
O192 A18 2(dos)p on 1c grn 14.00 15.00
Nos. O187-O192 (6) 88.00 100.00

No. 181 Surcharged

1908 **Yellow Surcharge** *Perf. 12*

O193 A18 10c on 3c vio 15.00 15.00
O194 A18 15c on 3c vio 15.00 15.00
O195 A18 20c on 3c vio 15.00 15.00
O196 A18 35c on 3c vio 15.00 15.00
O197 A18 50c on 3c vio 15.00 15.00
Nos. O193-O197 (5) 75.00 75.00

Black Surcharge

O198 A18 35c on 3c vio *100.00 100.00*

Revenue Stamps Surcharged like 1907 Issue Dated "1908"

1908 *Perf. 14 to 15*

O199 O7 10c on 1c bl (V) .75 .50
a. Inverted surcharge 3.50 3.50
O200 O7 35c on 1c bl (Bk) .75 .50
a. Inverted surcharge 3.50 3.50
b. Double surcharge 4.00 4.00
O201 O7 50c on 1c bl (R) .75 .50
O202 O7 1p on 1c bl (Br) 37.50 37.50
a. Inverted surcharge 65.00 65.00
O203 O7 2p on 1c bl (G) .90 .75
O204 O7 10c on 2c org (Bk) 1.10 .65
O205 O7 35c on 2c org (R) 1.10 .65
a. Double surcharge 3.50
O206 O7 50c on 2c org (Bk) 1.10 .65
O207 O7 70c on 2c org (Bl) 1.10 .65
O208 O7 1p on 2c org (G) 1.10 .65
O209 O7 2p on 2c org (Br) 1.10 .65
Nos. O199-O209 (11) 47.25 43.65

There are several minor varieties in the figures, etc., in these surcharges.

Nos. 243-248 Overprinted in Black

1909 *Perf. 12*

O210 A18 10c lake .25 .25
a. Double overprint 2.50 2.50
O211 A18 15c black .60 .50
O212 A18 20c brn ol 1.00 .75
O213 A18 50c dp grn 1.50 1.00
O214 A18 1p yellow 1.75 1.25
O215 A18 2p car rose 6.50 2.00
Nos. O210-O215 (6) 11.60 5.75

Overprinted in Black

1910

O216 A18 15c black 1.50 1.25
a. Double overprint 4.00 4.00
O217 A18 20c brn ol 2.50 2.00
O218 A18 50c dp grn 2.50 2.00
O219 A18 1p yellow 2.75 2.50
a. Inverted overprint 16.00 7.50
O220 A18 2p car rose 4.00 3.00
Nos. O216-O220 (5) 13.25 10.75

Nos. 239-240 Surcharged in Black

No. O221

No. O222

1911

O221 A18 5c on 3c red org 10.00 6.00
O222 A18 10c on 4c vio 12.00 5.00
a. Double surcharge 24.00 24.00
b. Pair, one without new value 35.00

Revenue Stamps Surcharged in Black

1911, Nov. *Perf. 14 to 15*

O223 A21 10c on 10c on 1 red 3.00 3.00
a. Inverted surcharge 4.50
b. Double surcharge 4.50
O224 A21 15c on 10c on 1 red 3.00 3.00
a. Inverted surcharge 5.00
b. Double surcharge 4.50
O225 A21 20c on 10c on 1 red 3.00 3.00
a. Inverted surcharge 5.00
O226 A21 50c on 10c on 1 red 3.75 3.75
a. Inverted surcharge 4.50
O227 A21 1p on 10c on 1 red 5.00 *7.00*
a. Inverted surcharge 6.00
O228 A21 2p on 10c on 1 red 5.50 *10.00*
a. Inverted surcharge 7.50
b. Double surcharge 7.50
Nos. O223-O228 (6) 23.25 29.75

Surcharged in Black

1911, Nov.

O229 A21 10c on 10c on 1 red 22.50
O230 A21 15c on 10c on 1 red 22.50
O231 A21 20c on 10c on 1 red 22.50
O232 A21 50c on 10c on 1 red 16.00
Nos. O229-O232 (4) 83.50

Surcharged in Black

1911, Dec.

O233 A21 5c on 10c on 1 red 4.50 *6.00*
a. Double surcharge 7.50
b. Inverted surcharge 7.50
c. "5" omitted 6.00
O234 A21 10c on 10c on 1 red 5.50 *7.00*
O235 A21 15c on 10c on 1 red 6.00 *7.50*
O236 A21 20c on 10c on 1 red 6.50 *8.50*
O237 A21 50c on 10c on 1 red 7.50 *10.00*
Nos. O233-O237 (5) 30.00 39.00

Nos. O233 to O237 have a surcharge on the back like Nos. 285 and 286 with "15 cts" obliterated by a heavy horizontal bar.

Surcharged Vertically in Black

1912

O238 A21 5c on 10c on 1 red 8.00 8.00
O239 A21 10c on 10c on 1 red 8.00 8.00
O240 A21 15c on 10c on 1 red 8.00 8.00
O241 A21 20c on 10c on 1 red 8.00 8.00
O242 A21 35c on 10c on 1 red 8.00 8.00
O243 A21 50c on 10c on 1 red 8.00 8.00
O244 A21 1p on 10c on 1 red 8.00 8.00
Nos. O238-O244 (7) 56.00 56.00

Nos. O238 to O244 are printed on Nos. 285 and 286 but the surcharge on the back is obliterated by a vertical bar.

Types of Regular Issue of 1912 Overprinted in Black

1912 *Perf. 12*

O245 A22 1c light blue .25 .25
O246 A22 2c light blue .25 .25
O247 A22 3c light blue .25 .25
O248 A22 4c light blue .25 .25
O249 A22 5c light blue .25 .25
O250 A22 6c light blue .35 .25
O251 A22 10c light blue .35 .25
O252 A22 15c light blue .35 .25
O253 A22 20c light blue .35 .25
O254 A22 25c light blue .35 .25
O255 A23 35c light blue .40 .25
O256 A22 50c light blue 3.75 2.00
O257 A22 1p light blue .65 .45
O258 A22 2p light blue .75 .55
O259 A22 5p light blue 1.00 .75
Nos. O245-O259 (15) 9.55 6.50

On the 35c the overprint is 15½mm wide, on the other values it is 13mm.

Types of Regular Issue of 1914 Overprinted in Black

1915, May

O260 A24 1c light blue .25 .25
O261 A25 2c light blue .25 .25
O262 A24 3c light blue .25 .25
O263 A25 4c light blue .25 .25
O264 A24 5c light blue .25 .25
O265 A25 6c light blue .25 .25
O266 A25 10c light blue .25 .25
O267 A24 15c light blue .25 .25
O268 A25 20c light blue .25 .25
O269 A24 25c light blue .30 .30
O270 A25 50c light blue .60 .60
Nos. O260-O270 (11) 3.15 3.15

Regular Issues of 1914-22 Overprinted in Red

1925

O271 A24 ½c dp grn .25 .25
a. Double overprint 2.50 2.50
O272 A24 1c violet .25 .25
O273 A25 2c car rose .25 .25
O274 A24 3c ol grn .25 .25
O275 A25 4c vermilion .25 .25
a. Double overprint *4.00 4.00*
O276 A24 5c black .25 .25
a. Double overprint *4.00 4.00*
O277 A25 6c red brn .25 .25
O278 A25 10c yellow .30 .30
a. Double overprint *4.25 4.25*
O279 A24 15c red brn .40 .40
O280 A25 20c bis brn .50 .50
O281 A24 25c orange .60 .60
a. Inverted overprint *60.00 40.00*
O282 A25 50c pale bl .75 .75
a. Double overprint *20.00 20.00*
Nos. O271-O282 (12) 4.30 4.30

Type II overprint has "f" and "i" separated. Comes on Nos. O272-O274 and O276.

Regular Issues of 1914-22 Overprinted in Black

1926

O283 A24 ½c dk grn .25 .25
O284 A24 1c dp vio .25 .25
O285 A25 2c car rose .25 .25
O286 A24 3c ol gray .25 .25
O287 A25 4c vermilion .25 .25
O288 A24 5c gray blk .25 .25
O289 A25 6c red brn .25 .25
O290 A25 10c yellow .25 .25
O291 A24 15c dp brn .25 .25
O292 A25 20c bis brn .25 .25
O293 A24 25c orange .25 .25
O294 A25 50c pale bl .25 .25
Nos. O283-O294 (12) 3.00 3.00

No. 499 Surcharged in Black

1931

O295 A33 5c on 10c bis brn .25 .25

Nos. 517-518 Overprinted in Red

1931

O296 A25 6c bis brn .25 .25
O297 A25 10c lt brn .25 .25

Nos. 541, 543, 545 With Additional Overprint in Red

O298 A24 1c ol grn .25 .25
O299 A24 3c lt bl .25 .25
a. "OFICIAL" inverted .80 .80
O300 A24 5c gray brn .25 .25
a. "1931" double .80 .80
Nos. O298-O300 (3) .75 .75

Regular Issues of 1914-31 Overprinted in Black

1932, Feb. 6

O301 A24 1c ol grn .25 .25
a. Double overprint 1.40 1.40
O302 A25 2c brt rose .25 .25
a. Double overprint 1.40 1.40
O303 A24 3c lt bl .25 .25
a. Double overprint .50 .50
O304 A25 4c dk bl .25 .25
O305 A24 5c ol brn .25 .25
O306 A25 6c bis brn .25 .25
a. Double overprint 2.00 2.00
O307 A25 10c lt brn .30 .25
O308 A24 15c org red .40 .25
a. Double overprint 2.25 2.25
O309 A25 20c orange .70 .35
O310 A24 25c dk vio 2.00 .50
O311 A25 50c green .25 .25
O312 A25 1cor yellow .25 .25
Nos. O301-O312 (12) 5.40 3.35

With Additional Overprint in Black

1932, Feb. 6

O313 A24 1c ol grn 5.50 5.50
O314 A25 2c brt rose 6.50 6.50
a. Double overprint 8.25 8.25
O315 A24 3c lt bl 5.00 5.00
O316 A24 5c ol brn 5.00 5.00
O317 A24 15c org red .65 .65
O318 A24 25c blk brn .65 .65
O319 A24 25c dk vio 1.50 1.50
Nos. O313-O319 (7) 24.80 24.80

The variety "OFIAIAL" occurs once in each sheet of Nos. O301 to O319 inclusive.

Despite the 1932 relase date, the "1931" overprint on Nos. O313-O319 is correct.

Flag of the Race Issue

1933, Aug. 9 Litho. ***Rouletted 9***
Without gum

O320 A43 1c orange 1.25 1.25
O321 A43 2c yellow 1.25 1.25
O322 A43 3c dk brn 1.25 1.25
O323 A43 4c dp brn 1.25 1.25
O324 A43 5c gray brn 1.25 1.25
O325 A43 6c dp ultra 1.50 1.50
O326 A43 10c dp vio 1.50 1.50
O327 A43 15c red vio 1.50 1.50
O328 A43 20c dp grn 1.50 1.50
O329 A43 25c green 2.50 2.50
O330 A43 50c carmine 3.00 3.00
O331 A43 1cor red 5.00 5.00
Nos. O320-O331 (12) 22.75 22.75

See note after No. 599.

Reprints of Nos. O320-O331 exist.

A 25c dull blue exists. Its status is questioned.

Regular Issue of 1914-31 Overprinted in Red

1933, Nov. ***Perf. 12***

O332 A24 1c ol grn .25 .25
O333 A25 2c brt rose .25 .25
O334 A24 3c lt bl .25 .25
O335 A25 4c dk bl .25 .25
O336 A24 5c ol brn .25 .25
O337 A25 6c bis brn .25 .25
O338 A25 10c lt brn .25 .25
O339 A24 15c red org .25 .25
O340 A25 20c orange .25 .25
O341 A24 25c dk vio .25 .25
O342 A25 50c green .25 .25
O343 A25 1cor yellow .35 .25
Nos. O332-O343 (12) 3.10 3.00

Nos. O332-O343 exist with or without signature control overprint. Values are the same.

Official Stamps of 1933 Overprinted as Nos. CO15-CO19 in Blue

1935, Dec.

O344 A24 1c ol grn .65 .40
O345 A25 2c brt rose .65 .50
O346 A24 3c lt bl 1.60 .50
O347 A25 4c dk bl 1.60 1.60
O348 A24 5c ol brn 1.60 1.60
O349 A25 6c bis brn 2.00 2.00
O350 A25 10c lt brn 2.00 2.00
O351 A24 15c org red 27.50 27.50
O352 A25 20c orange 27.50 27.50
O353 A24 25c dk vio 27.50 27.50
O354 A25 50c green 27.50 27.50
O355 A25 1cor yellow 27.50 27.50
Nos. O344-O355 (12) 147.60 146.10

Nos. O344-O355 have signature control overprints. Counterfeits of overprint abound.

Same Overprinted in Red

1936, Jan.

O356 A24 1c ol grn .25 .25
O357 A25 2c brt rose .25 .25
O358 A24 3c lt bl .25 .25
a. Double overprint
O359 A25 4c dk bl .25 .25
O360 A24 5c ol brn .25 .25
O361 A25 6c bis brn .25 .25
O362 A25 10c lt brn .25 .25
O363 A24 15c org red .25 .25
O364 A25 20c orange .25 .25
O365 A24 25c dk vio .25 .25
O366 A25 50c green .25 .25
O367 A25 1cor yellow .35 .35
Nos. O356-O367 (12) 3.10 3.10

Nos. O356-O367 have signature control overprints.

Nos. 653 to 655, 657, 659 660, 662 to 664 Overprinted in Black

1937

O368 A24 1c car rose .25 .25
O369 A25 2c dp bl .25 .25
O370 A24 3c chocolate .25 .25
O371 A24 5c org red .35 .25
O372 A25 10c ol grn .65 .40
O373 A24 15c green .80 .50
O374 A24 25c orange 1.00 .65
O375 A25 50c brown 1.40 .80
O376 A25 1cor ultra 2.50 1.25
Nos. O368-O376 (9) 7.45 4.60

Islands of the Great Lake O9

1939, Jan. Engr. ***Perf. 12½***

O377 O9 2c rose red 1.00 .25
O378 O9 3c lt bl 1.00 .25
O379 O9 6c brn org 1.00 .25
O380 O9 7½c dp grn 1.00 .25
O381 O9 10c blk brn 1.00 .25
O382 O9 15c orange 1.00 .25
O383 O9 25c dk vio 1.50 .25
O384 O9 50c brt yel grn 4.00 .75
Nos. O377-O384 (8) 11.50 2.50

POSTAL TAX STAMPS

Official Stamps of 1915 Surcharged in Black

1921, July Unwmk. ***Perf. 12***

RA1 A24 1c on 5c lt bl 1.50 .60
RA2 A25 1c on 6c lt bl .65 .25
a. Double surcharge, one inverted
RA3 A25 1c on 10c lt bl 1.00 .25
a. Double surcharge 3.50 3.50
RA4 A24 1c on 15c lt bl 1.50 .25
a. Double surcharge, one inverted 5.00 5.00
Nos. RA1-RA4 (4) 4.65 1.35

"R de C" signifies "Reconstruccion de Comunicaciones." The stamps were intended to provide a fund for rebuilding the General Post Office which was burned in April, 1921. One stamp was required on each letter or parcel, in addition to the regular postage. In the setting of one hundred there are five stamps with antique "C" and twenty-one with "R" and "C" smaller than in the illustration. One or more stamps in the setting have a dotted bar, as illustrated over No. 388, instead of the double bar.

The use of the "R de C" stamps for the payment of regular postage was not permitted.

Official Stamp of 1915 Overprinted in Black

1921, July

RA5 A24 1c light blue 6.00 1.75

This stamp is known with the dotted bar as illustrated over No. 388, instead of the double bar.

Coat of Arms — PT1

1921, Sept. **Red Surcharge**

RA6 PT1 1c on 1c ver & blk .25 .25
RA7 PT1 1c on 2c grn & blk .25 .25
a. Double surcharge 3.00 3.00
b. Double surcharge, one inverted 4.00 4.00
RA8 PT1 1c on 4c org & blk .25 .25
a. Double surcharge 4.00 4.00
RA9 PT1 1c on 15c dk bl & blk .25 .25
a. Double surcharge 3.00 3.00
Nos. RA6-RA9 (4) 1.00 1.00

PT2

1922, Feb. **Black Surcharge**

RA10 PT2 1c on 10c yellow .25 .25
a. Period after "de" .50 .40
b. Double surcharge 2.00 2.00
c. Double inverted surcharge 3.75 3.75
d. Inverted surcharge 3.00 3.00
e. Without period after "C" 1.00 1.00

No. 409 Overprinted in Black

1922

RA11 A24 1c violet .25 .25
a. Double overprint 2.00 2.00

This stamp with the overprint in red is a trial printing.

Nos. 402, 404-407 Surcharged in Black

1922, June

RA12 A27 1c on 1c grn & blk .75 .75
RA13 A29 1c on 5c ultra & blk .75 .75
RA14 A30 1c on 10c org & blk .75 .40
RA15 A31 1c on 25c yel & blk .75 .30
a. Inverted surcharge 5.00 5.00
RA16 A32 1c on 50c vio & blk .30 .25
a. Double surcharge 4.00 4.00
Nos. RA12-RA16 (5) 3.30 2.45

PT3

Surcharge in Red or Dark Blue

1922, Oct. ***Perf. 11½***

RA17 PT3 1c yellow (R) .25 .25
a. No period after "C" 1.00 1.00
RA18 PT3 1c violet (DBl) .25 .25
a. No period after "C" 1.00 1.00

Surcharge is inverted on 22 out of 50 of No. RA17, 23 out of 50 of No. RA18.

See No. RA24.

Nos. 403-407 Surcharged in Black

1923 *Perf. 12*

RA19 A28 1c on 2c rose red & black .50 .45
RA20 A29 1c on 5c ultra & blk .55 .25
RA21 A30 1c on 10c org & blk .25 .25
RA22 A31 1c on 25c yel & blk .35 .30
RA23 A32 1c on 50c vio & blk .25 .25
Nos. RA19-RA23 (5) 1.90 1.50

The variety no period after "R" occurs twice on each sheet.

Red Surcharge
Wmk. Coat of Arms in Sheet
Perf. 11½

RA24 PT3 1c pale blue .25 .25

Type of 1921 Issue

Without Surcharge of New Value

Unwmk.

RA25 PT1 1c ver & blk .25 .25
a. Double overprint, one inverted 3.00 3.00

No. 409 Overprinted in Blue

1924

RA26 A24 1c violet .25 .25
a. Double overprint 8.00 8.00

There are two settings of the overprint on No. RA26, with "1924" 5½mm or 6½mm wide.

No. 409 Overprinted in Blue

1925

RA27 A24 1c violet .25 .25

No. 409 Overprinted in Blue

1926

RA28 A24 1c violet .25 .25

No. RA28 Overprinted in Various Colors

1927

RA29 A24 1c vio (R) .25 .25
a. Double overprint (R) 2.00 2.00
b. Inverted overprint (R) 3.00 3.00
RA30 A24 1c vio (V) .25 .25
a. Double overprint 2.50 2.50
b. Inverted overprint 2.50 2.50
RA31 A24 1c vio (Bl) .25 .25
a. Double overprint 5.00 5.00
RA32 A24 1c vio (Bk) .25 .25
a. Double ovpt., one invtd. 4.25 4.25
b. Double overprint 4.25 4.25

Same Overprint on No. RA27

RA33 A24 1c vio (Bk) 15.00 10.00
Nos. RA29-RA33 (5) 16.00 11.00

No. RA28 Overprinted in Violet

1928

RA34 A24 1c violet .25 .25
a. Double overprint 2.00 2.00
b. "928" 1.00 1.00

Similar to No. RA34 but 8mm space between "Resello" and "1928"
Black Overprint

RA35 A24 1c violet .40 .25
a. "1828" 2.00 2.00

PT4

Inscribed "Timbre Telegrafico"
Horiz. Srch. in Black, Vert. Srch. in Red

RA36 PT4 1c on 5c bl & blk .60 .25
a. Comma after "R" 1.25 1.25
b. No period after "R" 1.25 1.25
c. No periods after "R" and "C" 1.25 1.25

("CORREOS" at right) — PT5

1928 **Engr.** *Perf. 12*

RA37 PT5 1c plum .25 .25

See Nos. RA41-RA43. For overprints see Nos. RA45-RA46, RA48-RA51.

PT6

1929 **Red Surcharge**

RA38 PT6 1c on 5c bl & blk .25 .25
a. Inverted surcharge 3.00 3.00
b. Double surcharge 2.00 2.00
c. Double surcharge, one inverted 2.00 2.00
d. Period after "de" 1.25 1.25
e. Comma after "R" 1.25 1.25

See note after No. 512.

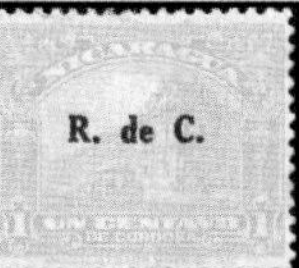

Regular Issue of 1928 Overprinted in Blue

RA39 A24 1c red orange .25 .25

No. RA39 exists both with and without signature control overprint.

An additional overprint, "1929" in black or blue on No. RA39, is fraudulent.

No. 513 Overprinted in Red

1929

RA40 A24 1c ol grn .25 .25
a. Double overprint .75 .75

No. RA40 is known with overprint in black, and with overprint inverted. These varieties were not regularly issued, but copies have been canceled by favor.

Type of 1928 Issue Inscribed at right "COMUNICACIONES"

1930-37

RA41 PT5 1c carmine .25 .25
RA42 PT5 1c orange ('33) .25 .25
RA43 PT5 1c green ('37) .25 .25
Nos. RA41-RA43 (3) .75 .75

No. RA42 has signature control. See note before No. 600.

No. RA39 Overprinted in Black

1931

RA44 A24 1c red orange .25 .25
a. "1931" double overprint .35 .35
b. "1931" double ovpt., one invtd. .40 .40

No. RA44 exists with signature control overprint. See note before No. 600. Value is the same.

No. RA42 Overprinted Vertically, up or down, in Black

1935

RA45 PT5 1c orange .25 .25
a. Double overprint 1.00 1.00
b. Double ovpt., one inverted

No. RA45 and RA45a Overprinted Vertically, Reading Down, in Blue

RA46 PT5 1c orange .50 .25
a. Black overprint double 2.00 2.00

Same Overprint in Red on Nos. RA39, RA42 and RA45

RA47 A24 1c red org (#RA39) *50.00 50.00*
RA48 PT5 1c org (#RA42) .25 .25
RA49 PT5 1c org (#RA45) .25 .25
a. Black overprint double .80 .80

Overprint is horizontal on No. RA47 and vertical, reading down, on Nos. RA48-RA49.

No. RA48 exists with signature control overprint. See note before No. 600. Same values.

No. RA42 Overprinted Vertically, Reading Down, in Carmine

1935 **Unwmk.** *Perf. 12*

RA50 PT5 1c orange .25 .25

No. RA45 with Additional Overprint "1936", Vertically, Reading Down, in Red

1936

RA51 PT5 1c orange .50 .25

No. RA39 with Additional Overprint "1936" in Red

RA52 A24 1c red orange .50 .25

No. RA52 exists only with script control mark.

PT7

1936 **Vertical Surcharge in Red**

RA53 PT7 1c on 5c grn & blk .25 .25
a. "Cenavo" 1.40 1.40
b. "Centavos" 1.40 1.40

Horizontal Surcharge in Red

RA54 PT7 1c on 5c grn & blk .25 .25
a. Double surcharge 1.40 1.40

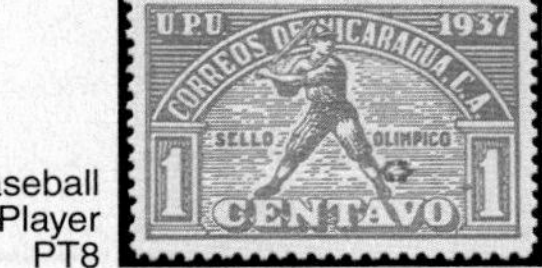

Baseball Player PT8

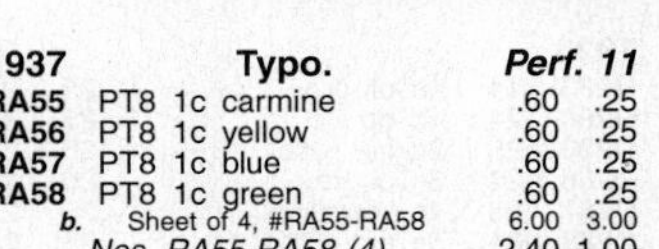

1937 **Typo.** *Perf. 11*

RA55 PT8 1c carmine .60 .25
RA56 PT8 1c yellow .60 .25
RA57 PT8 1c blue .60 .25
RA58 PT8 1c green .60 .25
b. Sheet of 4, #RA55-RA58 6.00 3.00
Nos. RA55-RA58 (4) 2.40 1.00

Issued for the benefit of the Central American Caribbean Games of 1937.

Control mark in red is variously placed. See dark oval below "OLIMPICO" in illustration.

Tête bêche Pairs

RA55a PT8 1c .75 .75
RA56a PT8 1c .75 .75
RA57a PT8 1c .75 .75
RA58a PT8 1c .75 .75
Nos. RA55a-RA58a (4) 3.00 3.00

PROVINCE OF ZELAYA

(Bluefields)

A province of Nicaragua lying along the eastern coast. Special postage stamps for this section were made necessary because for a period two currencies, which differed materially in value, were in use in Nicaragua. Silver money was used in Zelaya and Cabo Gracias a Dios while the rest of Nicaragua used paper money. Later the money of the entire country was placed on a gold basis.

Dangerous counterfeits exist of most of the Bluefields overprints.

Regular Issues of 1900-05 Handstamped in Black (4 or more types)

1904-05 **Unwmk.** *Perf. 12, 14*

On Engraved Stamps of 1900

1L1 A14 1c plum 1.50 .75
1L2 A14 2c vermilion 1.50 .75
1L3 A14 3c green 1.90 1.50
1L4 A14 4c ol grn 11.00 9.00
1L5 A14 15c ultra 3.00 1.90
1L6 A14 20c brown 3.00 1.90
1L7 A14 50c lake 10.50 9.00
1L8 A14 1p yellow 21.00
1L9 A14 2p salmon 30.00
1L10 A14 5p black 37.50
Nos. 1L1-1L10 (10) 120.90
Nos. 1L1-1L7 (7) 24.80

On Lithographed Stamps of 1902

1L11 A14 5c blue 3.00 .75
1L12 A14 5c carmine 1.90 .90
1L13 A14 10c violet 1.50 .75
Nos. 1L11-1L13 (3) 6.40 2.40

On Postage Due Stamps Overprinted "1901 Correos"

1L14 D3 20c brn (No. 156) 4.50 1.90
1L15 D3 50c lake (No. 158) — —

On Surcharged Stamps of 1904-05

1L16 A14 5c on 10c (#175) 1.50 1.10
1L17 A14 5c on 10c (#178) 3.00 1.50
1L18 A14 15c on 10c vio (#176) 1.50 1.50
1L19 A14 15c on 10c vio (#177) 14.00 4.50
Nos. 1L16-1L19 (4) 20.00 8.60

On Surcharged Stamp of 1901

1L20 A14 20c on 5p blk 18.00 3.00

On Regular Issue of 1905

1906-07 *Perf. 12*

1L21 A18 1c green .30 .30
1L22 A18 2c car rose .30 .30
1L23 A18 3c violet .30 .30
1L24 A18 4c org red .45 .45
1L25 A18 5c blue .25 .25
1L26 A18 10c yel brn 3.00 1.50
1L27 A18 15c brn ol 4.50 1.75
1L28 A18 20c lake 9.00 7.50
1L29 A18 50c orange 35.00 30.00
1L30 A18 1p black 30.00 27.50
1L31 A18 2p dk grn 37.50
1L32 A18 5p violet 45.00
Nos. 1L21-1L32 (12) 165.60
Nos. 1L21-1L30 (10) 69.85

On Surcharged Stamps of 1906-08

1L33 A18 10c on 3c vio .40 .40
1L34 A18 15c on 1c grn .50 .50
1L35 A18 20c on 2c rose 3.50 3.50
1L36 A18 20c on 5c bl 1.50 1.50
1L37 A18 50c on 6c sl (R) 1.50 3.00
Nos. 1L33-1L37 (5) 7.40 8.90

Handstamped

Stamps with the above overprints were made to fill dealers' orders but were never regularly issued or used. Stamps with similar overprints handstamped are bogus.

Surcharged Stamps of 1906 Overprinted in Red, Black or Blue

1L38 A18 15c on 1c grn (R) 2.75 2.75
a. Red overprint inverted
1L39 A18 20c on 2c rose (Bk) 1.90 1.90
1L40 A18 20c on 5c bl (R) 3.00 3.00
1L41 A18 50c on 6c sl (Bl) 14.00 14.00
Nos. 1L38-1L41 (4) 21.65 21.65

Stamps of the 1905 issue overprinted as above No. 1L38 or similarly overprinted but with only 2¼mm space between "B" and "Dpto. Zelaya" were made to fill dealers' orders but not placed in use.

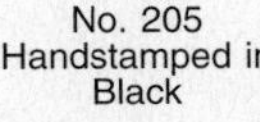

No. 205 Handstamped in Black

Perf. 14 to 15

1L42 A18 10c yel brn 24.00 24.00

Stamps of 1907 Overprinted in Red or Black

1L43 A18 15c brn ol (R) 3.00 3.00
1L44 A18 20c lake .90 .90
a. Inverted overprint 11.00 11.00

With Additional Surcharge

1L45 A18 5c brn org .50 .45
a. Inverted surcharge 7.50 7.50

With Additional Surcharge

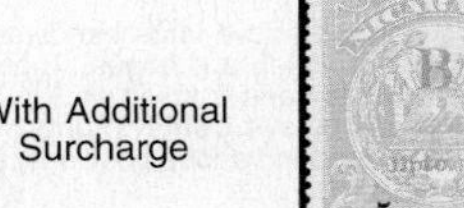

1L46 A18 5c on 4c brn org 12.00 12.00

On Provisional Postage Stamps of 1907-08 in Black or Blue

1L47 A18 10c on 2c rose (Bl) 4.50 4.50
1L48 A18 10c on 2c rose *300.00*
1L48A A18 10c on 4c brn org *300.00*
1L49 A18 10c on 20c lake 3.00 3.00
1L50 A18 10c on 50c org (Bl) 3.00 2.25

Arms Type of 1907 Overprinted in Black or Violet

1907

1L51 A18 1c green .30 .25
1L52 A18 2c rose .30 .25
1L53 A18 3c violet .40 .40
1L54 A18 4c brn org .45 .45
1L55 A18 5c blue 4.50 2.25
1L56 A18 10c yel brn .40 .30
1L57 A18 15c brn ol .75 .40
1L58 A18 20c lake .75 .45
1L59 A18 50c orange 2.25 1.50
1L60 A18 1p blk (V) 2.25 1.50
1L61 A18 2p dk grn 2.25 1.90
1L62 A18 5p violet 3.75 2.25
Nos. 1L51-1L62 (12) 18.35 11.90

Nos. 217-225 Overprinted in Green

1908

1L63 A19 1c on 5c yel & blk (R) .45 .40
1L64 A19 2c on 5c yel & blk (Bl) .45 .40
1L65 A19 4c on 5c yel & blk (G) .45 .40
a. Overprint reading down 11.00 11.00
b. Double overprint, reading up and down 18.00 18.00
1L66 A19 5c yel & blk .45 .45
a. "CORROE" 4.50
b. Double overprint 11.00 11.00
c. Double overprint, reading up and down 19.00 19.00
d. "CORREO 1908" double 15.00 15.00
1L67 A19 10c lt bl & blk .45 .45
a. Ovpt. reading down .50 .50
b. "CORREO 1908" triple 37.50

1L68 A19 15c on 50c ol & blk (R) .90 .90
a. "1008" 4.50
b. "8908" 4.50
1L69 A19 35c on 50c ol & blk 1.40 1.40
1L70 A19 1p yel brn & blk 1.90 1.90
a. "CORROE" 12.00 12.00
1L71 A19 2p pearl gray & blk 2.25 2.25
a. "CORROE" 15.00 15.00
Nos. 1L63-1L71 (9) 8.70 8.55

Overprinted Horizontally in Black or Green

1L72 A19 5c yel & blk 9.00 7.50
1L72A A19 2p pearl gray & blk (G) *300.00*

On Nos. 1L72-1L72A, space between "B" and "Dpto. Zelaya" is 13mm.

Nos. 237-248 Overprinted in Black

Imprint: "American Bank Note Co. NY"

1909 *Perf. 12*

1L73 A18 1c yel grn .25 .25
1L74 A18 2c vermilion .25 .25
a. Inverted overprint
1L75 A18 3c red org .25 .25
1L76 A18 4c violet .25 .25
1L77 A18 5c dp bl .30 .25
a. Inverted overprint 9.00 9.00
b. "B" inverted 7.50 7.50
c. Double overprint 12.00 12.00
1L78 A18 6c gray brn 4.50 3.00
1L79 A18 10c lake .30 .30
a. "B" inverted 9.00 9.00
1L80 A18 15c black .45 .40
a. "B" inverted 11.00 11.00
b. Inverted overprint 12.00 12.00
c. Double overprint 14.00 14.00
1L81 A18 20c brn ol .50 .50
a. "B" inverted 19.00 19.00
1L82 A18 50c dp grn 1.50 1.50
1L83 A18 1p yellow 5.00 2.25
1L84 A18 2p car rose 6.00 3.00
a. Double overprint 27.50 27.50
Nos. 1L73-1L84 (12) 19.55 12.20

One stamp in each sheet has the "o" of "Dpto." sideways.

Overprinted in Black

1910

1L85 A18 3c red org .40 .40
1L86 A18 4c violet .40 .40
a. Inverted overprint 14.00 14.00
1L87 A18 15c black 4.50 2.25
1L88 A18 20c brn ol .25 .30
1L89 A18 50c dp grn .30 .40
1L90 A18 1p yellow .30 .45
a. Inverted overprint 7.50
1L91 A18 2p car rose .40 .75
Nos. 1L85-1L91 (7) 6.55 4.95

Black Ovpt., Green Srch., Carmine Block-outs

Z1

1910

1L92 Z1 5c on 10c lake 3.75 3.00

There are three types of the letter "B." It is stated that this stamp was used exclusively for postal purposes and not for telegrams.

No. 247 Surcharged in Black

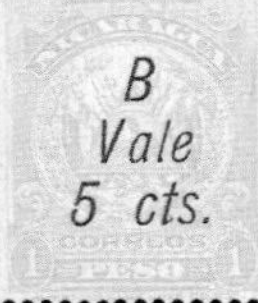

1911

1L93 A18 5c on 1p yellow .75 .75
a. Double surcharge 14.00
1L94 A18 10c on 1p yellow 1.50 1.50
1L95 A18 15c on 1p yellow .75 .75
a. Inverted surcharge 9.00
b. Double surcharge 9.00
c. Double surcharge, one invtd. 9.00
Nos. 1L93-1L95 (3) 3.00 3.00

Revenue Stamps Surcharged in Black

Perf. 14 to 15

1L96 A19 5c on 25c lilac .75 1.10
a. Without period 1.50 1.50
b. Inverted surcharge 9.00 9.00
1L97 A19 10c on 1p yel brn 1.10 .75
a. Without period 1.90 1.90
b. "01" for "10" 9.00 7.50
c. Inverted surcharge 13.00 13.00

Surcharged in Black

1L98 A19 5c on 1p yel brn 1.50 1.50
a. Without period 2.25
b. "50" for "05" 14.00 14.00
c. Inverted surcharge 15.00 15.00
1L99 A19 5c on 10p pink 1.50 1.50
a. Without period 2.25 2.25
b. "50" for "05" 11.00 11.00
1L100 A19 10c on 1p yel brn 82.50 82.50
a. Without period 95.00 95.00
1L101 A19 10c on 25p grn .75 .75
a. Without period 2.25 2.25
b. "1" for "10" 7.50
1L102 A19 10c on 50p ver 11.00 11.00
a. Without period 16.00
b. "1" for "10" 22.50
Nos. 1L98-1L102 (5) 97.25 97.25

With Additional Overprint "1904"

1L103 A19 5c on 10p pink 14.00 14.00
a. Without period 24.00 24.00
b. "50" for "05" 110.00 110.00
1L104 A19 10c on 2p gray .75 .75
a. Without period 1.90
b. "1" for "10" 7.50
1L105 A19 10c on 25p grn 92.50
a. Without period 100.00
1L106 A19 10c on 50p ver 7.50 7.50
a. Without period 14.00
b. "1" for "10" 18.00
c. Inverted surcharge

The surcharges on Nos. 1L96 to 1L106 are in settings of twenty-five. One stamp in each setting has a large square period after "cts" and another has a thick upright "c" in that word. There are two types of "1904".

No. 293C Overprinted

1911

1L107 A21 5c on 5c on 2 bl (R) 32.50
a. "5" omitted 37.50
b. Red overprint inverted 40.00
c. As "a" and "b" 47.50

Same Overprint On Nos. 290, 291, 292 and 289D with Lines of

Surcharge spaced 2½mm apart Reading Down

1L107D A21 2c on 10c on 1 red *250.00*
e. Overprint reading up *250.00*
1L107F A21 5c on 10c on 1 red *150.00*
1L107G A21 10c on 10c on 1 red (#292) *200.00*
1L108 A21 10c on 10c on 1 red (#289D) *200.00*

Locomotive — Z2

1912 **Engr.** ***Perf. 14***

1L109 Z2 1c yel grn 1.50 .50
1L110 Z2 2c vermilion 1.25 .25
1L111 Z2 3c org brn 1.50 .45
1L112 Z2 4c carmine 1.50 .30
1L113 Z2 5c dp bl 1.50 .45
1L114 Z2 6c red brn 9.00 3.50
1L115 Z2 10c slate 1.50 .30
1L116 Z2 15c dl lil 1.50 .60
1L117 Z2 20c bl vio 1.50 .60
1L118 Z2 25c grn & blk 2.25 .80
1L119 Z2 35c brn & blk 3.00 1.25
1L120 Z2 50c ol grn 3.00 1.25
1L121 Z2 1p orange 4.00 1.75
1L122 Z2 2p org brn 7.50 3.25
1L123 Z2 5p dk bl grn 18.00 7.50
Nos. 1L109-1L123 (15) 58.50 22.75

The stamps of this issue were for use in all places on the Atlantic Coast of Nicaragua where the currency was on a silver basis.

For surcharges see Nos. 325-337.

OFFICIAL STAMPS

Regular Issue of 1909 Overprinted in Black

1909 **Unwmk.** ***Perf. 12***

1LO1 A18 20c brn ol 15.00 12.00
a. Double overprint 30.00

No. O216 Overprinted in Black

1LO2 A18 15c black 15.00 10.00

Same Overprint on Official Stamp of 1911

1911

1LO3 A18 5c on 3c red org 22.50 17.50

CABO GRACIAS A DIOS

A cape and seaport town in the extreme northeast of Nicaragua. The name was coined by Spanish explorers who had great difficulty finding a landing place along the Nicaraguan coast and when eventually locating this harbor expressed their relief by designating the point "Cape Thanks to God." Special postage stamps came into use for the same reasons as the Zelaya issues. See Zelaya.

Dangerous counterfeits exist of most of the Cabo Gracias a Dios overprints. Special caution should be taken with double and inverted handstamps of Nos. 2L1-2L25, as most are counterfeits. Expert opinion is required.

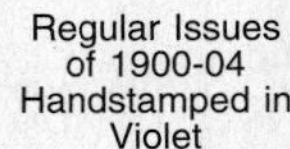

Regular Issues of 1900-04 Handstamped in Violet

On Engraved Stamps of 1900

1904-05 **Unwmk.** ***Perf. 12, 14***

2L1 A14 1c plum 2.25 1.10
2L2 A14 2c vermilion 4.50 1.25
2L3 A14 3c green 6.00 4.50
2L4 A14 4c ol grn 9.75 9.75
2L5 A14 15c ultra 35.00 22.50
2L6 A14 20c brown 3.00 2.25
Nos. 2L1-2L6 (6) 60.50 41.35

On Lithographed Stamps of 1902

2L7 A14 5c blue 24.00 24.00
2L8 A14 10c violet 24.00 24.00

On Surcharged Stamps of 1904

2L9 A16 5c on 10c vio 22.50 22.50
2L10 A16 15c on 10c vio

On Postage Due Stamps Violet Handstamp

2L11 D3 20c org brn (#141) 5.00 1.25
2L12 D3 20c org brn (#156) 3.50 1.25
2L13 D3 30c dk grn (#157) 14.00 14.00
2L14 D3 50c lake (#158) 3.75 .75
Nos. 2L11-2L14 (4) 26.25 17.25

Black Handstamp

2L15 D3 30c dk grn (#157) 24.00 24.00

Stamps of 1900-05 Handstamped in Violet

On Engraved Stamps of 1900

2L16 A14 1c plum 2.75 2.25
2L17 A14 2c vermilion 27.50 24.00
2L18 A14 3c green 37.50 27.50
2L19 A14 4c ol grn 40.00 37.50
2L20 A14 15c ultra 45.00 45.00
Nos. 2L16-2L20 (5) 152.75 136.25

On Lithographed Stamps of 1902

2L22 A14 5c dk bl 95.00 50.00
2L23 A14 10c violet 27.50 24.00

On Surcharged Stamp of 1904

2L24 A14 5c on 10c vio

On Postage Due Stamp

2L25 D3 20c org brn (#141)

The editors have no evidence that stamps with this handstamp were issued. Examples were sent to the UPU and covers are known.

Stamps of 1900-08 Handstamped in Violet

1905 **On Stamps of 1905**

2L26 A18 1c green 1.10 1.10
2L27 A18 2c car rose 1.50 1.50
2L28 A18 3c violet 1.50 1.50
2L29 A18 4c org red 3.75 3.75
2L30 A18 5c blue 1.50 1.10
2L31 A18 6c slate 3.75 3.75
2L32 A18 10c yel brn 3.00 1.90
2L33 A18 15c brn ol 4.50 4.50
2L34 A18 1p black 20.00 20.00
2L35 A18 2p dk grn 35.00 35.00
Nos. 2L26-2L35 (10) 75.60 74.10

Magenta Handstamp

2L26a A18 1c 3.75 3.00
2L27a A18 2c 3.00 2.75
2L28a A18 3c 3.75 3.00
2L30a A18 5c 7.50 6.00
2L33a A18 15c 13.50 11.00
Nos. 2L26a-2L33a (5) 31.50 25.75

On Stamps of 1900-04

2L36 A14 5c on 10c vio 14.00 14.00
2L37 A14 10c violet
2L38 A14 20c brown 12.00 12.00
2L39 A14 20c on 5p blk 95.00

On Postage Due Stamps Overprinted "Correos"

2L40 D3 20c org brn (#141) 9.00 9.00
2L41 D3 20c org brn (#156) 5.00 4.50

On Surcharged Stamps of 1906-08

2L42 A18 10c on 3c vio *250.00*
2L43 A18 20c on 5c blue 9.00 9.00
2L44 A18 50c on 6c slate 24.00 24.00

On Stamps of 1907

Perf. 14 to 15

2L44A A18 2c rose *250.00*
2L45 A18 10c yel brn *100.00 75.00*
2L46 A18 15c brn ol *90.00 75.00*

On Provisional Stamp of 1908 in Magenta

2L47 A19 5c yel & blk 7.50 7.50

Stamps with the above large handstamp in black instead of violet, are bogus. There are also excellent counterfeits in violet.

The foregoing overprints being handstamped are found in various positions, especially the last type.

Stamps of 1907 Type A18, Overprinted in Black or Violet

1907

2L48 A18 1c green .35 .30
a. Vert. pair, imperf. btwn. —
2L49 A18 2c rose .35 .30
2L50 A18 3c violet .35 .30
a. Vert. pair, imperf. btwn. *350.00*
2L51 A18 4c brn org .50 .40
2L52 A18 5c blue .60 .50
2L53 A18 10c yel brn .50 .40
2L54 A18 15c brn ol .85 .75
2L55 A18 20c lake .85 .75
2L56 A18 50c orange 2.25 1.50
2L57 A18 1p blk (V) 2.50 1.90
2L58 A18 2p dk grn 3.50 2.25
2L59 A18 5p violet 5.00 3.75
Nos. 2L48-2L59 (12) 17.60 13.10

Nos. 237-248 Overprinted in Black

Imprint: American Bank Note Co.

1909 ***Perf. 12***

2L60 A18 1c yel grn .35 .40
2L61 A18 2c vermilion .35 .40
2L62 A18 3c red org .35 .40
2L63 A18 4c violet .35 .40
2L64 A18 5c dp bl .35 .60
2L65 A18 6c gray brn 6.00 6.00
2L66 A18 10c lake .60 .75
2L67 A18 15c black .90 .90
2L68 A18 20c brn ol 1.00 *4.00*
2L69 A18 50c dp grn 2.50 2.50
2L70 A18 1p yellow 4.00 4.00
2L71 A18 2p car rose 5.75 5.75
Nos. 2L60-2L71 (12) 22.50 26.10

No. 199 Overprinted Vertically

2L72 A18 50c on 6c slate (R) 7.50 7.50

CABO GRACIAS A DIOS OFFICIAL STAMPS

Official Stamps of 1907 Overprinted in Red or Violet

1907

2LO1 A18 10c on 1c green *60.00*
2LO2 A18 15c on 1c green *75.00*
2LO3 A18 20c on 1c green *100.00*
2LO4 A18 50c on 1c green *125.00*

NIGER

'nī-jər

LOCATION — Northern Africa, directly north of Nigeria
GOVT. — Republic
AREA — 458,075 sq. mi.
POP. — 6,265,000 (est. 1984)
CAPITAL — Niamey

The colony, formed in 1922, was originally a military territory.

100 Centimes = 1 Franc

Stamps of Upper Senegal and Niger Type of 1914, Overprinted

Camel and Rider — A1

In the overprint, normal spacing between the words "DU" and "NIGER" is 2½mm. In one position (72) of all sheets in the first printing, the space between the two words is 3mm.

1921-26 Unwmk. *Perf. 13½x14*

1 A1 1c brn vio & vio .25 *.40*
Never hinged .40
On cover 87.50
a. Wide spacing in ovpt. 14.00 17.50
Never hinged 24.00
2 A1 2c dk gray & dl vio .25 *.40*
Never hinged .40
On cover 87.50
a. Wide spacing in ovpt. 14.00 17.50
Never hinged 24.00
3 A1 4c black & blue .35 *.50*
Never hinged .45
On cover 87.50
a. Wide spacing in ovpt. 14.00 17.50
Never hinged 24.00
4 A1 5c ol brn & dk brn .30 *.50*
Never hinged .45
On cover 42.50
a. Wide spacing in ovpt. 14.00 17.50
Never hinged 24.00
5 A1 10c yel grn & bl grn 1.60 *2.00*
Never hinged 2.75
On cover 95.00
a. Wide spacing in ovpt. 21.00 24.00
Never hinged 35.00
6 A1 10c mag, *bluish* ('26) .95 *1.20*
Never hinged 1.40
On cover 27.50
7 A1 15c red brn & org .40 *.55*
Never hinged .55
On cover 50.00
a. Wide spacing in ovpt. 14.00 17.50
Never hinged 24.00
8 A1 20c brn vio & blk .35 *.50*
Never hinged .45
On cover 42.50
a. Wide spacing in ovpt. 14.00 17.50
Never hinged 24.00
9 A1 25c blk & bl grn .80 *.80*
Never hinged 1.25
On cover 35.00
a. Wide spacing in ovpt. 14.00 17.50
Never hinged 24.00
10 A1 30c red org & rose 2.75 *3.50*
Never hinged 4.75
On cover 62.50
On cover, single franking 125.00
a. Wide spacing in ovpt. 27.50 30.00
Never hinged 50.00
11 A1 30c bl grn & red org ('26) .80 *.80*
Never hinged 1.25
On cover 16.00
a. Wide spacing in ovpt. 21.00 24.00
Never hinged 35.00
12 A1 35c rose & violet .95 *1.20*
Never hinged 1.50
On cover 55.00
On cover, single franking 80.00
a. Wide spacing in ovpt. 18.00 21.00
Never hinged 30.00
13 A1 40c gray & rose .95 *1.20*
Never hinged 1.60
On cover 45.00
On cover, single franking 55.00
a. Wide spacing in ovpt. 17.50 21.00
Never hinged 27.50
14 A1 45c blue & ol brn 1.40 *1.40*
Never hinged 2.10
On cover 70.00
On cover, single franking 110.00
a. Wide spacing in ovpt. 17.50 21.00
Never hinged 27.50
15 A1 50c ultra & bl .80 *1.20*
Never hinged 1.40
On cover 50.00
On cover, single franking 125.00
a. Wide spacing in ovpt. 17.50 21.00
Never hinged 27.50
16 A1 50c dk gray & bl vio ('25) 1.60 *1.60*
Never hinged 2.75
On cover 16.00
a. Wide spacing in ovpt. 27.50 32.50
Never hinged 47.50
17 A1 60c org red ('26) 1.40 *2.00*
Never hinged 2.00
On cover 42.50
On cover, single franking 80.00
18 A1 75c yel & ol brn 1.40 *1.60*
Never hinged 2.40
On cover 55.00
On cover, single franking 140.00
a. Wide spacing in ovpt. 17.50 21.00
Never hinged 27.50
19 A1 1fr dk brn & dl vio 1.60 *2.00*
Never hinged 2.75
On cover 75.00
On cover, single franking 170.00
a. Wide spacing in ovpt. 21.00 23.00
Never hinged 35.00
20 A1 2fr green & blue 1.60 *2.00*
Never hinged 2.75
On cover 87.50
On cover, single franking 190.00
a. Wide spacing in ovpt. 21.00 24.00
Never hinged 35.00
21 A1 5fr violet & blk 2.75 *4.00*
Never hinged 4.75
On cover 110.00
On cover, single franking 210.00
a. Wide spacing in ovpt. 27.50 30.00
Never hinged 50.00
Nos. 1-21 (21) 23.25 29.35

Types of 1921 Surcharged in Black or Red

1922-26

22 A1 25c on 15c red brn & org ('25) .95 .80
Never hinged 1.20
On cover 20.00
a. Multiple surcharge 260.00
Never hinged 375.00
b. "25c" inverted 140.00
Never hinged 190.00
c. Wide spacing in ovpt. 21.00 24.00
Never hinged 37.50
23 A1 25c on 2fr grn & bl (R) ('24) .90 .80
Never hinged 1.20
On cover 20.00
a. Wide spacing in ovpt. 21.00 24.00
Never hinged 37.50
24 A1 25c on 5fr vio & blk (R) ('24) .95 .80
Never hinged 1.25
On cover 20.00
a. Double surcharge 225.00
Never hinged 340.00
b. Wide spacing in ovpt. 27.50 32.50
Never hinged 50.00
25 A1 60c on 75c vio,*pnksh* .90 *1.20*
Never hinged 1.20
On cover 45.00
On cover, single franking 70.00
a. Wide spacing in ovpt. 24.00 30.00
Never hinged 42.50
26 A1 65c on 45c bl & ol brn ('25) 2.75 *3.50*
Never hinged 4.75
On cover 87.50
On cover, single franking 170.00
a. Wide spacing in ovpt. 40.00 42.50
Never hinged 62.50
27 A1 85c on 75c yel & ol brn ('25) 2.75 *3.50*
Never hinged 4.75
On cover 75.00
On cover, single franking 140.00
a. Wide spacing in ovpt. 40.00 42.50
Never hinged 62.50
28 A1 1.25fr on 1fr dp bl & lt bl (R) ('26) 1.10 *1.20*
Never hinged 1.60
On cover 80.00
On cover, single franking 140.00
a. Surcharge omitted 260.00
Never hinged 400.00
b. As "a," in pair with unsurcharged stamp 1,700.
Nos. 22-28 (7) 10.30 11.80

Nos. 22-24 are surcharged "25c," No. 28, "1f25." Nos. 25-27 are surcharged like illustration.

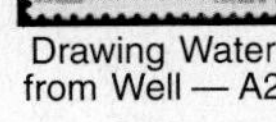

Drawing Water from Well — A2

Zinder Fortress — A4

Boat on Niger River — A3

Perf. 13x14, 13½x14, 14x13, 14x13½

1926-40 Typo.

29 A2 1c lil rose & ol .25 *.40*
Never hinged .40
On cover 70.00
30 A2 2c dk gray & dl red .25 *.40*
Never hinged .40
On cover 70.00
31 A2 3c red vio & ol gray ('40) .25 *.40*
Never hinged .40
On cover 50.00
32 A2 4c amber & gray .25 *.40*
Never hinged .40
On cover 70.00
33 A2 5c ver & yel grn .25 *.40*
Never hinged .40
On cover 42.50
34 A2 10c dp bl & Prus bl .25 *.40*
Never hinged .40
On cover 37.50
35 A2 15c gray grn & yel grn .55 *.80*
Never hinged .80
On cover 25.00
36 A2 15c gray lil & lt red ('28) .40 .40
Never hinged .80
On cover 22.50
37 A3 20c Prus grn & ol brn .40 *.55*
Never hinged .55
On cover 27.50
38 A3 25c black & dl red .40 .50
Never hinged .55
On cover 20.00
39 A3 30c bl grn & yel grn .80 *1.20*
Never hinged 1.20
On cover 37.50
40 A3 30c yel & red vio ('40) .30 *.50*
Never hinged .40
On cover 22.50
41 A3 35c brn org & turq bl, *bluish* .80 *1.20*
Never hinged 1.20
On cover 37.50
42 A3 35c bl grn & dl grn ('38) 1.20 *1.60*
Never hinged 1.60
On cover 42.50
43 A3 40c red brn & slate .40 *.50*
Never hinged .55
On cover 14.00
44 A3 45c yel & red vio 1.60 *1.90*
Never hinged 2.40
On cover 35.00
45 A3 45c bl grn & dl grn ('40) .30 *.50*
Never hinged .50
On cover 27.50
46 A3 50c scar & grn, *grnsh* .40 .40
Never hinged .55
On cover 14.00
47 A3 55c dk car & brn ('38) 2.00 2.00
Never hinged 2.75
On cover 14.00
48 A3 60c dk car & brn ('40) .55 *.70*
Never hinged .70
On cover 27.50
49 A3 65c ol grn & rose .40 *.55*
Never hinged .55
On cover 50.00
50 A3 70c ol grn & rose ('40) 2.00 *2.50*
Never hinged 2.40
On cover 37.50
51 A3 75c grn & vio, *pink* 2.00 *2.25*
Never hinged 3.25
On cover 25.00
On cover, single franking 35.00
a. Center and value double 225.00
Never hinged 340.00
52 A3 80c cl & ol grn ('38) 1.60 *2.00*
Never hinged 2.40
On cover 70.00
On cover, single franking 125.00
53 A3 90c brn red & ver 1.60 *1.90*
Never hinged 2.40
On cover 37.50
On cover, single franking 87.50
54 A3 90c brt rose & yel grn ('39) 2.00 *2.40*
Never hinged 2.50
On cover 42.50
On cover, single franking 95.00
55 A4 1fr rose & yel grn 8.00 8.75
Never hinged 18.00
On cover 30.00
On cover, single franking 50.00
56 A4 1fr dk red & red org ('38) 2.00 *2.40*
Never hinged 2.75
On cover 87.50
57 A4 1fr grn & red ('40) .80 .80
Never hinged 1.10
On cover 11.00
58 A4 1.10fr ol brn & grn 4.00 *6.50*
Never hinged 6.50
On cover 225.00
On cover, single franking 450.00
59 A4 1.25fr grn & red ('33) 2.40 2.40
Never hinged 3.25
On cover 25.00
On cover, single franking 70.00
60 A4 1.25fr dk red & red org ('39) .80 *1.20*
Never hinged 1.10
On cover 62.50
On cover, single franking 125.00
61 A4 1.40fr red vio & dk brn ('40) .80 *1.50*
Never hinged 1.10
On cover 50.00
On cover, single franking 105.00
62 A4 1.50fr dp bl & pale bl .55 *.70*
Never hinged .70
On cover 37.50
On cover, single franking 80.00
63 A4 1.60fr ol brn & grn ('40) 1.75 *2.00*
Never hinged 2.00
On cover 45.00
On cover, single franking 105.00
64 A4 1.75fr red vio & dk brn ('33) 1.60 2.40
Never hinged 2.40
On cover 19.00
On cover, single franking 25.00
65 A4 1.75fr dk bl & vio bl ('38) 1.25 *1.60*
Never hinged 1.75
On cover 42.50
On cover, single franking 80.00
66 A4 2fr red org & ol brn .30 *.50*
Never hinged .50
On cover 35.00
On cover, single franking 62.50
67 A4 2.25fr dk bl & vio bl ('39) 1.20 *1.60*
Never hinged 1.60
On cover 55.00
On cover, single franking 110.00
68 A4 2.50fr blk brn ('40) 1.20 *1.60*
Never hinged 1.60
On cover 35.00
On cover, single franking 70.00
69 A4 3fr dl vio & blk ('27) .55 *.80*
Never hinged .80
On cover 42.50
On cover, single franking 105.00
70 A4 5fr vio brn & blk, *pink* .80 *1.20*
Never hinged 1.20
On cover 50.00
On cover, single franking 100.00
71 A4 10fr chlky bl & mag 1.60 *2.00*
Never hinged 2.75
On cover 55.00
On cover, single franking 105.00
72 A4 20fr yel grn & red org 1.60 *2.00*
Never hinged 2.75
On cover 70.00
On cover, single franking 125.00
Nos. 29-72 (44) 52.40 *66.70*

For surcharges see Nos. B7-B10 in the *Scott Standard Postage Stamp Catalogue*, Vol. 5.

Common Design Types pictured following the introduction.

Colonial Exposition Issue
Common Design Types

1931 Typo. *Perf. 12½*
Name of Country in Black

73 CD70 40c deep green 5.00 5.00
Never hinged 8.00
On cover 105.00
74 CD71 50c violet 5.00 5.00
Never hinged 8.00
On cover 87.50
75 CD72 90c red orange 5.75 5.75
Never hinged 8.00
On cover 160.00
On cover, single franking 225.00
76 CD73 1.50fr dull blue 5.75 5.75
Never hinged 10.00
On cover 140.00
On cover, single franking 190.00
Nos. 73-76 (4) 21.50 21.50

Paris International Exposition Issue
Common Design Types

1937 *Perf. 13*

77 CD74 20c deep violet 2.00 2.00
Never hinged 3.25
On cover 120.00
78 CD75 30c dark green 2.00 2.00
Never hinged 3.25
On cover 100.00
79 CD76 40c carmine rose 2.00 2.00
Never hinged 3.25
On cover 87.50
80 CD77 50c dark brown 1.60 1.60
Never hinged 2.75
On cover 80.00
81 CD78 90c red 1.60 1.60
Never hinged 2.75
On cover 110.00
On cover, single franking 210.00
82 CD79 1.50fr ultra 2.00 2.00
Never hinged 3.25
On cover 105.00
On cover, single franking 190.00
Nos. 77-82 (6) 11.20 11.20

Colonial Arts Exhibition Issue
Souvenir Sheet
Common Design Type

1937 ***Imperf.***
83 CD74 3fr magenta 10.00 *14.00*
Never hinged 14.00
On cover 140.00
On cover, single franking 210.00

Caillie Issue
Common Design Type

1939 ***Perf. 12½x12***
84 CD81 90c org brn & org .35 .35
Never hinged .70
On cover 14.00
85 CD81 2fr brt violet .35 1.00
Never hinged .70
On cover 35.00
On cover, single franking 55.00
86 CD81 2.25fr ultra & dk bl .35 1.00
Never hinged .70
On cover 40.00
On cover, single franking 70.00
Nos. 84-86 (3) 1.05 2.35

New York World's Fair Issue
Common Design Type

1939, May 10
87 CD82 1.25fr car lake .70 1.40
Never hinged 1.00
On cover 87.50
On cover, single franking 170.00
88 CD82 2.25fr ultra .70 1.40
Never hinged 1.00
On cover 87.50
On cover, single franking 160.00

SEMI-POSTAL STAMPS

Curie Issue
Common Design Type

1938 Unwmk. Engr. *Perf. 13*
B1 CD80 1.75fr + 50c brt ultra 15.00 15.00
Never hinged 25.00
On cover 125.00
On cover, single franking 210.00

French Revolution Issue
Common Design Type

1939 Photo. *Perf. 13*
Name and Value Typo. in Black
B2 CD83 45c + 25c grn 12.00 12.00
Never hinged 20.00
On cover 160.00
B3 CD83 70c + 30c brn 12.00 12.00
Never hinged 20.00
On cover 110.00
B4 CD83 90c + 35c red org 12.00 12.00
Never hinged 20.00
On cover 100.00
B5 CD83 1.25fr + 1fr rose pink 12.00 12.00
Never hinged 20.00
On cover 170.00
On cover, single franking 250.00
B6 CD83 2.25fr + 2fr blue 12.00 12.00
Never hinged 20.00
On cover 160.00
On cover, single franking 225.00
Nos. B2-B6 (5) 60.00 60.00

AIR POST STAMPS

Common Design Type

1940 Unwmk. Engr. *Perf. 12½x12*
C1 CD85 1.90fr ultra .35 .35
Never hinged .70
On cover 50.00
C2 CD85 2.90fr dk red .35 .35
Never hinged .70
On cover 50.00
C3 CD85 4.50fr dk gray grn .70 .70
Never hinged 1.00
On cover 55.00
C4 CD85 4.90fr yel bis .70 .70
Never hinged 1.00
On cover 67.50
C5 CD85 6.90fr dp org 1.40 1.40
Never hinged 2.00
On cover 80.00
Nos. C1-C5 (5) 3.50 3.50

POSTAGE DUE STAMPS

1914 Upper Senegal and Niger Postage Due Stamps Ovptd.

1921 Unwmk. *Perf. 14x13½*
J1 D1 5c green .70 *.95*
Never hinged 1.10
On cover 50.00
J2 D1 10c rose .70 *.95*
Never hinged 1.10
On cover 50.00
J3 D1 15c gray .70 *1.05*
Never hinged 1.10
On cover 50.00
J4 D1 20c brown .70 *1.05*
Never hinged 1.10
On cover 55.00
J5 D1 30c blue .70 *1.20*
Never hinged 1.10
On cover 55.00
J6 D1 50c black .70 *1.20*
Never hinged 1.10
On cover 62.50
J7 D1 60c orange 1.40 *2.00*
Never hinged 2.10
On cover 75.00
J8 D1 1fr violet 1.40 *2.00*
Never hinged 2.10
On cover 95.00
Nos. J1-J8 (8) 7.00 *10.40*

Caravansary Near Timbuktu
D2

1927 **Typo.**
J9 D2 2c dk bl & red .35 *.35*
Never hinged .45
On cover 50.00
J10 D2 4c ver & blk .35 *.35*
Never hinged .45
On cover 50.00
J11 D2 5c org & vio .35 *.35*
Never hinged .70
On cover 42.50
J12 D2 10c red brn & blk vio .35 *.35*
Never hinged .70
On cover 42.50
J13 D2 15c grn & org .35 .35
Never hinged .70
On cover 42.50
J14 D2 20c cer & ol brn .35 .70
Never hinged .70
On cover 50.00
J15 D2 25c blk & ol brn .35 *.70*
Never hinged .70
On cover 50.00
J16 D2 30c dl vio & blk 1.40 *1.40*
Never hinged 1.75
On cover 55.00
J17 D2 50c dp red, *grnsh* .70 *1.10*
Never hinged 1.40
On cover 62.50
J18 D2 60c gray vio & org, *bluish* .70 .70
Never hinged 1.10
On cover 67.50
J19 D2 1fr ind & ultra, *bluish* 1.00 *1.20*
Never hinged 1.40
On cover 75.00
J20 D2 2fr rose red & vio 1.10 *1.40*
Never hinged 2.10
On cover 95.00
J21 D2 3fr org brn & ultra 1.75 2.00
Never hinged 2.10
On cover 100.00
Nos. J9-J21 (13) 9.10 *10.95*

NIGER COAST PROTECTORATE

ˈnī-jər ˈkōst prə-ˈtek-t(ə-)rət

(Oil Rivers Protectorate)

LOCATION — West coast of Africa on Gulf of Guinea
GOVT. — British Protectorate

This territory was originally known as the Oil Rivers Protectorate, and its affairs were conducted by the British Royal Niger Company. The Company surrendered its charter to the Crown in 1899. In 1900 all of the territories formerly controlled by the Royal Niger Company were incorporated into the two protectorates of Northern and Southern Nigeria, the latter absorbing the area formerly known as Niger Coast Protectorate. In 1914 Northern and Southern Nigeria joined to form the Crown Colony of Nigeria. (See Nigeria, Northern Nigeria, Southern Nigeria and Lagos.)

12 Pence = 1 Shilling

Stamps of Great Britain, 1881-87, Overprinted in Black

1892 Wmk. 30 *Perf. 14*
1 A54 ½p vermilion 22.50 13.00
2 A40 1p lilac 13.00 11.00
a. "OIL RIVERS" at top *10,000.*
b. Half used as ½p on cover *2,750.*
3 A56 2p green & car 40.00 9.50
a. Half used as 1p on cover *2,500.*
4 A57 2½p violet, *bl* 10.00 2.75
5 A61 5p lilac & blue 20.00 7.25
6 A65 1sh green 77.50 *100.00*
Nos. 1-6 (6) 183.00 143.50

For surcharges see Nos. 7-36, 50.

Dangerous forgeries exist of all surcharges.

No. 2 Surcharged in Red or Violet

1893
7 A40 ½p on half of 1p (R) 175. 160.
c. Unsevered pair 550. 500.
d. As "c," surcharge inverted and dividing line reversed *27,500.*
e. "½" omitted
f. Straight top to "1" in "½" 390. *400.*
g. Double surcharge in pair with normal *2,100.*
7A A40 ½p on half of 1p (V) *7,750.* *5,500.*
b. Surcharge double *27,500.*
c. Unsevered pair *20,000.* *17,500.*

Nos. 3-6 Handstamp Srchd. in Violet, Red, Carmine, Bluish Black, Deep Blue, Green or Black

1893 Wmk. 30 *Perf. 14*
8 A56 ½p on 2p (V) *525.* 325.
a. Surcharge inverted *19,000.*
b. Surcharge diagonal, inverted *18,500.*
9 A57 ½p on 2½p (V) 14,000.
10 A57 ½p on 2½p (R) 425. 275.
a. Surcharge inverted *12,500.*
b. Surcharge diagonal, inverted *14,500.*
11 A57 ½p on 2½p (C) *25,000.* *24,500.*
12 A57 ½p on 2½p (B) *40,000.* —
13 A57 ½p on 2½p (G) 550.

14 A56 ½p on 2p (V) 500. 375.
15 A56 ½p on 2p (Bl) 2,200. 825.
16 A57 ½p on 2½p (V) *7,750.*
17 A57 ½p on 2½p (R) 650. *775.*
18 A57 ½p on 2½p (Bl) 475. 450.
19 A57 ½p on 2½p (G) 500. *550.*

20 A56 ½p on 2p (V) 550. 775.
a. Surcharge inverted *17,500.*
21 A57 ½p on 2½p (R) 600. 475.
a. Surcharge inverted *20,000.*
b. Surcharge diagonal, inverted *8,250.*
22 A57 ½p on 2½p (C) 475. 500.
23 A57 ½p on 2½p (Bl Bk) *5,500.*
24 A57 ½p on 2½p (Bl) 475. *525.*
25 A57 ½p on 2½p (G) 325. 275.
a. Surcharge diagonal, inverted
26 A57 ½p on 2½p (Bk) *4,750.*
a. Surcharge inverted *15,500.*
b. Surcharge diagonal, inverted *13,500.*

27 A57 ½p on 2½p (R) *10,000.*
28 A57 ½p on 2½p (G) 550. 500.

29 A56 1sh on 2p (V) 500. 425.
a. Surcharge inverted *13,500.*
b. Surcharge diagonal, inverted *12,500.*
30 A56 1sh on 2p (R) 825. *4,500.*
a. Surcharge inverted *18,000.*
31 A56 1sh on 2p (Bk) *6,500.*
a. Surcharge inverted *21,000.*

32 A56 5sh on 2d (V) *10,000.* *11,500.*
a. Surcharge inverted *55,000.*
33 A61 10sh on 5p (R) *7,250.* *11,000.*
a. Surcharge inverted *55,000.*
34 A65 20sh on 1sh (V) *165,000.*
a. Surcharge inverted *190,000.*
35 A65 20sh on 1sh (R) *145,000.*
36 A65 20sh on 1sh (Bk) *145,000.*

The handstamped 1893 surcharges are known inverted, vertical, etc.

Queen Victoria
A8 A9

A10 A11

A12 A13

1893 Unwmk. *Perf. 12 to 15*
37 A8 ½p vermilion 10.00 *11.00*
38 A9 1p light blue 6.75 5.25
a. Half used as ½p on cover 825.00
39 A10 2p green 47.50 47.50
a. Half used as 1p on cover *1,000.*
b. Horiz. pair, imperf. between *17,500.*
40 A11 2½p car lake 20.00 4.50
41 A12 5p gray lilac 24.00 17.50
a. 5p lilac 16.50 24.00
42 A13 1sh black 15.50 16.00
Nos. 37-42 (6) 123.75 101.75

For surcharge see No. 49.

A15

A16

A17

A18

A19

A20

1894 **Engr.**
43 A15 ½p yel green 5.25 5.50
44 A16 1p vermilion 15.00 9.50
a. 1p orange vermilion 25.00 17.50
b. Diagonal half, used as ½p on cover 875.00
45 A17 2p car lake 35.00 7.25
a. Half used as 1p on cover —
46 A18 2½p blue 12.00 4.50
47 A19 5p dp violet 14.00 6.00
48 A20 1sh black 70.00 26.00
Nos. 43-48 (6) 151.25 58.75

See #55-59, 61. For surcharges see #51-54.

Halves of Nos. 38, 3 & 44 Srchd. in Red, Blue, Violet or Black

No. 49

No. 50

Nos. 51-53

1894
49 A9 ½p on half of 1p (R) 1,300. 425.
a. Inverted surcharge *15,500.*

Perf. 14
Wmk. 30
50 A56 1p on half of 2p (R) 1,950. 425.
a. Double surcharge 7,250. 1,350.
b. Inverted surcharge 2,250.

Perf. 12 to 15
Unwmk.
51 A16 ½p on half of 1p (Bl) 3,850. 550.
a. Double surcharge
52 A16 ½p on half of 1p (V) 4,400. 775.
53 A16 ½p on half of 1p (Bk) *6,000. 1,100.*

This surcharge is found on both vertical and diagonal halves of the 1p.

No. 46 Surcharged in Black

1894
54 A18 ½p on 2½p blue 475. 275.
a. Double surcharge 8,750. 2,500.

The surcharge is found in eight types. The "OIE" variety is broken type.

A27

A28

A29

1897-98 **Wmk. 2**
55 A15 ½p yel green 3.50 3.00
a. ½p green ('97) 9.00 1.50
56 A16 1p vermilion 9.00 1.60
57 A17 2p car lake 4.75 2.50
58 A18 2½p blue 17.50 3.25
a. 2½p slate blue 7.50 3.00
59 A19 5p dp violet 22.50 *90.00*
60 A27 6p yel brn ('98) 8.00 *10.00*
61 A20 1sh black 17.50 *32.50*
62 A28 2sh6p olive bister 24.00 *90.00*
63 A29 10sh dp pur ('98) 140.00 *250.00*
a. 10sh bright purple 135.00 *225.00*
Nos. 55-63 (9) 246.75 *482.85*

The stamps of Niger Coast Protectorate were superseded in Jan. 1900, by those of Northern and Southern Nigeria.

NIGERIA

nī-ˈjir-ē-ə

LOCATION — West coast of Africa, bordering on the Gulf of Guinea
GOVT. — Republic
AREA — 356,669 sq. mi.
POP. — 82,390,000 (est. 1983)
CAPITAL — Lagos

The colony and protectorate were formed in 1914 by the union of Northern and Southern Nigeria. The mandated territory of Cameroons (British) was also attached for administrative purposes. See Niger Coast Protectorate, Lagos, Northern Nigeria and Southern Nigeria.

12 Pence = 1 Shilling
20 Shillings = 1 Pound

Catalogue values for unused stamps in this country are for Never Hinged items, beginning with Scott 71 in the regular postage section.

King George V — A1

Numerals of 3p, 4p, 6p, 5sh and £1 of type A1 are in color on plain tablet.

Dies I and II are described at front of this volume.

Die I
Ordinary Paper
Wmk. Multiple Crown and CA (3)
1914-27 **Typo.** ***Perf. 14***
1 A1 ½p green 5.50 .70
a. Booklet pane of 6
2 A1 1p carmine 5.25 .25
a. Booklet pane of 6
b. 1p scarlet ('16) 13.00 .25
3 A1 2p gray 9.00 2.00
a. 2p slate gray ('18) 10.00 .85
4 A1 2½p ultramarine 10.00 5.50
a. 2½p dull blue ('15) 27.50 11.00

Chalky Paper
5 A1 3p violet, *yel* 1.60 3.00
6 A1 4p blk & red, *yel* 1.10 *4.75*
7 A1 6p dull vio & red vio 10.00 11.00
8 A1 1sh black, *green* 1.10 *10.00*
a. 1sh black, *emerald* 1.40 *15.00*
b. 1sh black, *bl grn*, ol back 60.00 *60.00*
c. As "a," olive back ('20) 9.00 *47.50*
9 A1 2sh6p blk & red, *bl* 17.50 7.25
10 A1 5sh grn & red, *yel*, white back 25.00 *65.00*
11 A1 10sh grn & red, *grn* 72.50 *100.00*
a. 10sh grn & red, *emer* 40.00 *110.00*
b. 10sh green & red, *blue grn*, olive back 1,000. *1,700.*
c. As "a," olive back 160.00 250.00
12 A1 £1 vio & blk, *red* 190.00 *275.00*
a. Die II ('27) 275.00 *350.00*
Nos. 1-12 (12) 348.55 *484.45*

Surface-colored Paper
13 A1 3p violet, *yel* 3.50 *12.00*
14 A1 4p black & red, *yel* 1.60 *11.50*
15 A1 1sh black, *green* 1.60 *25.00*
a. 1sh black, *emerald* *225.00*
16 A1 5sh grn & red, *yel* 21.00 *55.00*
17 A1 10sh grn & red, *grn* 50.00 *180.00*
Nos. 13-17 (5) 77.70 *283.50*

Die II
1921-33 **Ordinary Paper** **Wmk. 4**
18 A1 ½p green 6.50 .90
a. Die I 1.25 .40
19 A1 1p carmine 1.75 .55
a. Booklet pane of 6 27.50
b. Die I 3.25 .35
c. Booklet pane of 6, Die I 37.50
20 A1 1½p orange ('31) 8.75 .35
21 A1 2p gray 10.00 .50
a. Die I 1.60 *8.00*
b. Booklet pane of 6, Die I 55.00
22 A1 2p red brown ('27) 5.00 1.00
a. Booklet pane of 6 60.00
23 A1 2p dk brown ('28) 4.50 .25
a. Booklet pane of 6 50.00
b. Die I ('32) 6.00 .75
24 A1 2½p ultra (die I) 1.25 *13.50*
25 A1 3p dp violet 11.00 1.10
a. Die I ('24) 6.00 3.50
26 A1 3p ultra ('31) 10.00 1.10

Chalky Paper
27 A1 4p blk & red, *yel* .70 .60
a. Die I ('32) 6.25 7.75
28 A1 6p dull vio & red vio 8.00 *9.00*
a. Die I 14.00 *40.00*
29 A1 1sh black, *emerald* 6.50 2.25
30 A1 2sh6p blk & red, *bl* 7.25 *47.50*
a. Die I ('32) 50.00 *85.00*
31 A1 5sh green & red, *yel* ('26) 16.00 *80.00*
a. Die I ('32) 75.00 *250.00*
32 A1 10sh green & red, *emer* 67.50 *225.00*
a. Die I ('32) 130.00 *500.00*
Nos. 18-32 (15) 164.70 383.60

Silver Jubilee Issue
Common Design Type
1935, May 6 **Engr.** ***Perf. 11x12***
34 CD301 1½p black & ultra 1.00 *1.50*
35 CD301 2p indigo & green 2.00 *1.75*
36 CD301 3p ultra & brown 3.50 *19.00*
37 CD301 1sh brown vio & ind 6.75 *37.50*
Nos. 34-37 (4) 13.25 *59.75*
Set, never hinged 24.00

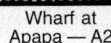

Wharf at Apapa — A2

Picking Cacao Pods — A3

Dredging for Tin — A4

Timber — A5

Fishing Village — A6

Ginning Cotton — A7

Minaret at Habe — A8

Fulani Cattle — A9

Victoria-Buea Road — A10

Oil Palms A11

View of Niger at Jebba A12

Nigerian Canoe A13

1936, Feb. 1 ***Perf. 11½x13***
38 A2 ½p green 1.50 1.40
39 A3 1p rose car .50 .40
40 A4 1½p brown 2.00 .40
a. Perf. 12½x13½ 85.00 4.50
41 A5 2p black .50 *.80*
42 A6 3p dark blue 2.00 1.50
a. Perf. 12½x13½ 150.00 25.00
43 A7 4p red brown 2.50 2.00
44 A8 6p dull violet .70 .60
45 A9 1sh olive green 2.25 *5.00*

Perf. 14
46 A10 2sh6p ultra & blk 8.00 *40.00*
47 A11 5sh ol grn & blk 22.00 *60.00*
48 A12 10sh slate & blk 90.00 *140.00*
49 A13 £1 orange & blk 130.00 *200.00*
Nos. 38-49 (12) 261.95 *452.10*
Set, never hinged 400.00

Common Design Types pictured following the introduction.

Coronation Issue
Common Design Type

1937, May 12 ***Perf. 11x11½***

50	CD302	1p dark carmine	.50	*2.00*
51	CD302	1½p dark brown	1.25	*2.50*
52	CD302	3p deep ultra	1.50	*4.00*
		Nos. 50-52 (3)	3.25	8.50
		Set, never hinged	6.50	

George VI — A14

Victoria-Buea Road — A15

Niger at Jebba A16

1938-51 **Wmk. 4** ***Perf. 12***

53	A14	½p deep green	.25	.25
a.		Perf. 11½ ('50)	1.40	*1.75*
54	A14	1p dk carmine	.40	.30
55	A14	1½p red brown	.25	.25
a.		Perf. 11½ ('50)	.25	.25
56	A14	2p black	.25	*3.00*
57	A14	2½p orange ('41)	.25	*3.00*
58	A14	3p deep blue	.25	.25
59	A14	4p orange	32.50	4.00
60	A14	6p brown violet	.30	.25
a.		Perf. 11½ ('51)	1.40	.60
61	A14	1sh olive green	.40	.25
a.		Perf. 11½ ('50)	.90	.25
62	A14	1sh3p turq blue ('40)	.60	.70
a.		Perf. 11½ ('50)	2.10	.70
63	A15	2sh6p ultra & blk ('51)	1.50	4.50
a.		Perf. 13½ ('42)	2.25	*7.00*
b.		Perf. 14 ('42)	2.00	*3.50*
c.		Perf. 13x11½	37.50	24.00
64	A16	5sh org & blk, perf. 13½ ('42)	4.50	*4.50*
a.		Perf. 12 ('49)	5.50	4.00
b.		Perf. 14 ('48)	6.75	3.00
c.		Perf. 13x11½	67.50	21.00

1944, Dec. 1 ***Perf. 12***

65	A14	1p red violet	.25	.30
a.		Perf. 11½ ('50)	.60	.60
66	A14	2p deep red	.25	*3.00*
a.		Perf. 11½ ('50)	.35	*.70*
67	A14	3p black	.25	*3.50*
68	A14	4p dark blue	.25	*4.00*
		Nos. 53-68 (16)	42.45	*32.05*
		Set, never hinged	75.00	

Issue date: Nos. 65a, 66a, Feb. 15.

Catalogue values for unused stamps in this section, from this point to the end of the section, are for Never Hinged items.

Peace Issue
Common Design Type

1946, Oct. 21 **Engr.** ***Perf. 13½x14***

71	CD303	1½p brown	.35	.25
72	CD303	4p deep blue	.35	*2.50*

Silver Wedding Issue
Common Design Types

1948, Dec. 20 **Photo.** ***Perf. 14x14½***

73	CD304	1p brt red violet	.35	.30

Perf. 11½x11

Engraved; Name Typographed

74	CD305	5sh brown orange	17.50	*22.50*

UPU Issue
Common Design Types
Engr.; Name Typo. on 3p, 6p
Perf. 13½, 11x11½

1949, Oct. 10 **Wmk. 4**

75	CD306	1p red violet	.25	.25
76	CD307	3p indigo	.35	*3.50*
77	CD308	6p rose violet	.80	*3.50*
78	CD309	1sh olive	1.40	*2.00*
		Nos. 75-78 (4)	2.80	*9.25*

NIUE

nē-'ü-ˌā

LOCATION — Island in the south Pacific Ocean, northeast of New Zealand
AREA — 100 sq. mi.
POP. — 3,019 (est. 1984)
CAPITAL — Alofi

Niue, also known as Savage Island, was annexed to New Zealand in 1901 with the Cook Islands.

12 Pence = 1 Shilling
20 Shillings = 1 Pound

Catalogue values for unused stamps in this country are for Never Hinged items, beginning with Scott 90 in the regular postage section.

Watermarks

Wmk. 61 — Single-lined NZ and Star Close Together

Wmk. 253 — NZ and Star

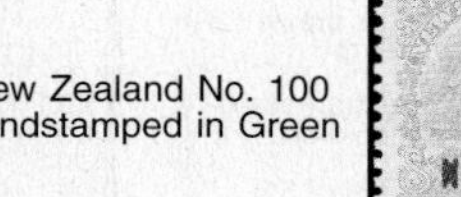
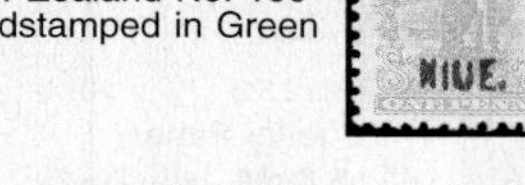
New Zealand No. 100 Handstamped in Green

1902 **Wmk. 63** ***Perf. 11***
Thick Soft Paper

1	A35	1p carmine	375.00	375.00

Stamps of New Zealand Surcharged in Carmine, Vermilion or Blue

1/2p

1p

2 1/2p

Perf. 14
Thin Hard Paper

3	A18	½p green (C)	5.50	*7.00*
a.		Inverted surcharge	325.00	*600.00*
b.		Double surcharge	1,200.	
4	A35	1p carmine (Bl), perf. 11x14	2.00	*3.75*
a.		No period after "PENI"	50.00	*70.00*
b.		Perf. 14	50.00	*55.00*
c.		As "a," perf. 14	500.00	600.00

Perf. 14
Wmk. 61

6	A18	½p green (V)	1.25	1.25
7	A35	1p carmine (Bl)	.85	1.10
a.		No period after "PENI"	9.00	*17.00*
b.		Double surcharge	*1,800.*	*2,000.*

Perf. 11
Unwmk.

8	A22	2½p blue (C)	2.50	*4.50*
a.		No period after "PENI"	35.00	*55.00*
9	A22	2½p blue (V)	1.75	4.25
a.		No period after "PENI"	30.00	55.00
b.		Double surcharge	2,500.	

The surcharge on the ½ & 1p stamps is printed in blocks of 60. Two stamps in each block have a space between the "U" and "E" of "NIUE" and one of the 1p stamps has a broken "E" like an "F."

Blue Surcharge on Stamps of New Zealand, Types of 1898

e

f

g

h

1903 **Wmk. 61** ***Perf. 11***

10	A23(e)	3p yellow brown	11.00	5.50
11	A26(f)	6p rose	15.00	12.50
13	A29(g)	1sh brown red	40.00	*47.50*
a.		1sh scarlet	40.00	*47.50*
b.		1sh orange red	50.00	*52.50*
c.		As "b," surcharge "h" (error)	750.00	
		Nos. 10-13 (3)	66.00	*65.50*

Surcharged in Carmine or Blue on Stamps of New Zealand — j

1911-12 ***Perf. 14, 14x14½***

14	A41(j)	½p yellow grn (C)	.60	.70
15	A41(f)	6p car rose (Bl)	2.50	*7.50*
16	A41(g)	1sh vermilion (Bl)	8.00	*50.00*
		Nos. 14-16 (3)	11.10	*58.20*

1915 ***Perf. 14***

18	A22(d)	2½p dark blue (C)	26.00	*55.00*

Surcharged in Brown or Dark Blue on Stamps of New Zealand

1917 ***Perf. 14x13½, 14x14½***

19	A42	1p carmine (Br)	24.00	6.25
a.		No period after "PENI"	850.00	
20	A45(e)	3p violet brn (Bl)	50.00	100.00
a.		No period after "Pene"	850.00	
b.		Perf. 14x13½	67.50	125.00
c.		Vert. pair, #20 & 20b	190.00	

New Zealand Stamps of 1909-19 Overprinted in Dark Blue or Red — k

1917-20 **Typo.**

21	A43	½p yellow grn (R)	.80	*2.75*
22	A42	1p carmine (Bl)	11.00	*14.00*
23	A47	1½p gray black (R)	1.10	*2.50*
24	A47	1½p brown org (R)	1.00	*8.50*
25	A43	3p chocolate (Bl)	1.60	*37.50*

Engr.

26	A44	2½p dull blue (R)	1.50	*16.00*
a.		Perf. 14x13½	4.75	*19.00*
b.		Vert. pair, #26-26a	19.00	*72.50*
27	A45	3p violet brown (Bl)	1.75	*2.25*
a.		Perf. 14x13½	3.50	2.25
b.		Vert. pair, #27-27a	22.50	*50.00*
28	A45	6p car rose (Bl)	6.00	*26.00*
a.		Perf. 14x13½	11.00	*25.00*
b.		Vert. pair, #28-28a	32.50	*125.00*
29	A45	1sh vermilion (Bl)	7.50	*30.00*
a.		Perf. 14x13½	17.00	*40.00*
b.		Vert. pair, #29-29a	47.50	*132.50*
		Nos. 21-29 (9)	32.25	*139.50*

Same Overprint On Postal-Fiscal Stamps of New Zealand, 1906-15

Perf. 14, 14½ and Compound

1918-23

30	PF1	2sh blue (R)	18.00	*35.00*
31	PF1	2sh6p bn (Bl) ('23)	24.00	*55.00*
32	PF1	5sh green (R)	29.00	*57.50*
a.		Perf. 14	115.00	*125.00*
b.		Perf. 14½x14 ('29)	27.50	*64.50*
33	PF1	10sh red brn (Bl) ('23)	145.00	*185.00*
a.		Perf. 14½x14 ('27)	100.00	*165.00*
34	PF2	£1 rose (Bl) ('23)	185.00	*275.00*
a.		Perf. 14½x14 ('28)	170.00	*300.00*
		Nos. 30-34 (5)	401.00	*607.50*

Nos. 32b, 33a and 34a come on thick paper and in different color varieties.

Landing of Captain Cook A16

Avarua Waterfront A17

Capt. James Cook — A18

Coconut Palm — A19

Arorangi Village — A20

Avarua Harbor — A21

Unwmk.

1920, Aug. 23 **Engr.** ***Perf. 14***

35	A16	½p yel grn & blk	4.25	4.25
36	A17	1p car & black	2.25	1.40
37	A18	1½p red & black	2.75	*18.00*
38	A19	3p pale blue & blk	1.90	*16.00*
39	A20	6p dp grn & red brn	5.25	*21.00*
a.		Center inverted	*1,000.*	
40	A21	1sh blk brn & blk	5.25	*21.00*
		Nos. 35-40 (6)	21.65	*81.65*

See Nos. 41-42. For surcharge see No. 48.

Types of 1920 Issue and

Rarotongan Chief (Te Po) — A22

Avarua Harbor — A23

1925-27 **Wmk. 61**

41	A16	½p yel grn & blk ('26)	2.75	*11.00*
42	A17	1p car & black	2.00	1.00
43	A22	2½p dk blue & blk ('27)	4.50	*13.00*
44	A23	4p dull vio & blk ('27)	8.00	*22.50*
		Nos. 41-44 (4)	17.25	*47.50*

New Zealand No. 182 Overprinted Type "k" in Red

1927

47	A56	2sh blue	18.00	*35.00*
a.		2sh dark blue	17.00	*47.50*

No. 37 Surcharged

1931 Unwmk. *Perf. 14*

48 A18 2p on 1½p red & blk 5.25 1.10

New Zealand Postal-Fiscal Stamps of 1931-32 Overprinted Type "k" in Blue or Red

1931, Nov. 12 Wmk. 61

49 PF5 2sh6p deep brown 5.00 13.00
50 PF5 5sh green (R) 40.00 *75.00*
51 PF5 10sh dark car 40.00 *110.00*
52 PF5 £1 pink ('32) 75.00 *160.00*
Nos. 49-52 (4) 160.00 *358.00*

See Nos. 86-89D, 116-119 (in Scott Standard catalogue, Vol. 5).

Landing of Captain Cook — A24

Capt. James Cook — A25

Polynesian Migratory Canoe — A26

Islanders Unloading Ship — A27

View of Avarua Harbor — A28

R.M.S. Monowai — A29

King George V — A30

Perf. 13, 14 (4p, 1sh)

1932, Mar. 16 Engr. Unwmk.

53 A24 ½p yel grn & blk 14.00 *25.00*
a. Perf. 14x13 275.00
54 A25 1p dp red & blk 1.10 .55
55 A26 2p org brn & blk 7.50 *4.50*
a. Perf. 14x13x13x13 150.00 *190.00*
56 A27 2½p indigo & blk 8.50 *80.00*
a. Center inverted 350.00
57 A28 4p Prus blue & blk 16.00 *60.00*
a. Perf. 13 15.00 *65.00*
58 A29 6p dp org & blk 2.75 2.25
59 A30 1sh dull vio & blk 3.75 *5.50*
Nos. 53-59 (7) 53.60 *177.80*

For types overprinted see Nos. 67-69.

1933-36 Wmk. 61 *Perf. 14*

60 A24 ½p yel grn & blk .50 *3.50*
61 A25 1p deep red & blk .50 *2.25*
62 A26 2p brown & blk ('36) .50 *1.75*
63 A27 2½p indigo & blk .50 *4.75*
64 A28 4p Prus blue & blk 2.00 *4.25*
65 A29 6p org & blk ('36) .80 *.90*
66 A30 1sh dk vio & blk ('36) 9.00 *25.00*
Nos. 60-66 (7) 13.80 *42.40*

See Nos. 77-82.

Silver Jubilee Issue

Types of 1932 Overprinted in Black or Red

1935, May 7 *Perf. 14*

67 A25 1p car & brown red .80 *3.50*
68 A27 2½p indigo & bl (R) 4.25 *13.00*
a. Vert. pair, imperf. horiz. 275.00
69 A29 6p dull org & grn 6.25 *10.00*
Nos. 67-69 (3) 11.30 *26.50*
Set, never hinged 16.00

The vertical spacing of the overprint is wider on No. 69.

No. 68a is from proof sheets.

Coronation Issue

New Zealand Stamps of 1937 Overprinted in Black

Perf. 13½x13

1937, May 13 Wmk. 253

70 A78 1p rose carmine .25 .25
71 A78 2½p dark blue .25 *1.50*
72 A78 6p vermilion .30 .30
Nos. 70-72 (3) .80 *2.05*
Set, never hinged 1.25

George VI — A31

Village Scene — A32

Coastal Scene with Canoe — A33

1938, May 2 Wmk. 61 *Perf. 14*

73 A31 1sh dp violet & blk 5.00 8.00
74 A32 2sh dk red brown & blk 6.50 *17.00*
75 A33 3sh yel green & blue 18.50 17.00
Nos. 73-75 (3) 30.00 42.00
Set, never hinged 55.00

See Nos. 83-85.

Mt. Ikurangi behind Avarua — A34

Perf. 13½x14

1940, Sept. 2 Engr. Wmk. 253

76 A34 3p on 1½p rose vio & blk .45 .25
Never hinged .75

Examples without surcharge are from printer's archives. Value, $250 unused.

Types of 1932-38

1944-46 Wmk. 253 *Perf. 14*

77 A24 ½p yel grn & blk .40 *2.25*
78 A25 1p dp red & blk ('45) .40 *1.25*
79 A26 2p org brn & blk ('46) 3.75 *6.00*
80 A27 2½p dk bl & blk ('45) .50 *1.00*
81 A28 4p Prus blue & blk 2.75 .90
82 A29 6p dp orange & blk 1.40 1.40
83 A31 1sh dp vio & blk .85 1.00
84 A32 2sh brn car & blk ('45) 8.50 3.75
85 A33 3sh yel grn & bl ('45) 11.00 8.50
Nos. 77-85 (9) 29.55 26.05
Set, never hinged 35.00

New Zealand Postal-Fiscal Stamps Overprinted Type "k" (narrow "E") in Blue or Red

1941-45 Wmk. 61 *Perf. 14*

86 PF5 2sh6p brown 65.00 *100.00*
87 PF5 5sh green (R) 140.00 300.00
88 PF5 10sh rose 85.00 *250.00*
89 PF5 £1 pink 125.00 *400.00*
Nos. 86-89 (4) 415.00 *1,050.*
Set, never hinged 750.00

Wmk. 253

89A PF5 2sh6p brown 2.75 *11.00*
89B PF5 5sh green (R) 5.50 *15.00*
e. 5sh light yellow green, wmkd. sideways ('67) 10.00 *80.00*
89C PF5 10sh rose 37.50 *135.00*
89D PF5 £1 pink 400.00 *80.00*
Nos. 89A-89D (4) 445.75 *241.00*
Set, never hinged 125.00

No. 89Be exists in both line and comb perf.

Catalogue values for unused stamps in this section, from this point to the end of the section, are for Never Hinged items.

Peace Issue

New Zealand Nos. 248, 250, 254 and 255 Overprinted in Black or Blue

p

q

1946, June 4 *Perf. 13x13½, 13½x13*

90 A94 (p) 1p emerald .40 .35
91 A96 (q) 2p rose violet (Bl) .40 .35
92 A100 (p) 6p org red & red brn .40 *.75*
93 A101 (p) 8p brn lake & blk (Bl) .50 *.75*
Nos. 90-93 (4) 1.70 *2.20*

Map of Niue — A35

H.M.S. Resolution — A36

Designs: 2p, Alofi landing. 3p, Thatched Dwelling. 4p, Arch at Hikutavake. 6p, Alofi bay. 9p, Fisherman. 1sh, Cave at Makefu. 2sh, Gathering bananas. 3sh, Matapa Chasm.

Perf. 14x13½, 13½x14

1950, July 3 Engr. Wmk. 253

94 A35 ½p red orange & bl .25 *1.25*
95 A36 1p green & brown 2.25 *2.50*
96 A36 2p rose car & blk 1.25 *2.00*
97 A36 3p blue vio & blue .25 .25
98 A36 4p brn vio & ol grn .30 .40
99 A36 6p brn org & bl grn .90 *1.40*
100 A35 9p dk brn & brn org .40 *1.40*
101 A36 1sh black & purple .45 .60
102 A35 2sh dp grn & brn org 4.00 *5.00*
103 A35 3sh black & dp blue 4.75 *5.00*
Nos. 94-103 (10) 14.80 *19.80*

For surcharges see Nos. 106-115 in Scott Standard catalogue, Vol. 5.

NORTH BORNEO

'north 'bor-nē-ˌō

LOCATION — Northeast part of island of Borneo, Malay archipelago
AREA — 29,388 sq. mi.
POP. — 470,000 (est. 1962)
CAPITAL — Jesselton

The British North Borneo Company administered North Borneo, under a royal charter granted in 1881.

100 Cents = 1 Dollar

Quantities of most North Borneo stamps through 1912 have been canceled to order with an oval of bars. Values given for used stamps beginning with No. 6 are for those with this form of cancellation. Stamps from No. 6 through Nos. 159 and J31 that do not exist cto have used values in italics. Stamps with dated town cancellations sell for much higher prices.

Catalogue values for unused stamps in this country are for Never Hinged items, beginning with Scott 238.

North Borneo

Coat of Arms — A1

1883-84 Unwmk. Litho. *Perf. 12*

1 A1 2c brown 47.50 *75.00*
a. Horiz. pair, imperf. btwn. 20,000.
2 A1 4c rose ('84) 65.00 *70.00*
3 A1 8c green ('84) 90.00 *60.00*
Nos. 1-3 (3) 202.50 *205.00*

For surcharges see Nos. 4, 19-21.

No. 1 Surcharged in Black

4 A1 8c on 2c brown 500.00 *210.00*
a. Double surcharge *6,000.*
4 A1 8c on 2c brown 500.00 *210.00*

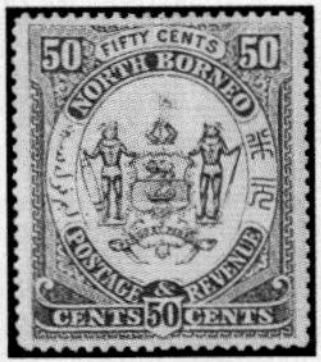

Coat of Arms with Supporters
A4 A5

Perf. 14

6 A4 50c violet 225.00 40.00
7 A5 $1 red 185.00 19.00

1886 *Perf. 14*

8 A1 ½c magenta 120.00 *200.00*
9 A1 1c orange *210.00* *350.00*
a. Imperf., pair 300.00
b. Vert. pair, imperf horiz. 1,500.
10 A1 2c brown 47.50 42.50
a. Horiz. pair, imperf. between 700.00
11 A1 4c rose 20.00 *55.00*
a. Horiz. pair, imperf. between — *1,700.*
12 A1 8c green 22.50 *50.00*
a. Horiz. pair, imperf. between *900.00*
13 A1 10c blue 55.00 *65.00*
a. Imperf., pair 375.00
Nos. 8-13 (6) 475.00 *762.50*

Nos. 8, 11, 12 and 13 Surcharged or Overprinted in Black

b

c

d

1886

14 A1 (b) ½c magenta 225.00 *325.00*
15 A1 (c) 3c on 4c rose 130.00 *150.00*
16 A1 (d) 3c on 4c rose 1,800.
17 A1 (c) 5c on 8c green 140.00 *150.00*
a. Inverted surcharge 2,750.
18 A1 (b) 10c blue 300.00 *375.00*

On Nos. 2 and 3

Perf. 12

19 A1 (c) 3c on 4c rose 325.00 *375.00*
20 A1 (d) 3c on 4c rose — *16,000.*
a. Double surcharge, both types of "3" —
21 A1 (c) 5c on 8c green 325.00 *375.00*

British North Borneo

A9

1886 Unwmk. Litho. *Perf. 12*

22 A9 ½c lilac rose 400.00 *700.00*
23 A9 1c orange 250.00 *400.00*

Perf. 14

25 A9 ½c rose 4.75 *21.00*
a. ½c lilac rose 21.00 *50.00*
b. Imperf., pair 70.00
26 A9 1c orange 2.25 *16.00*
a. Imperf., pair 80.00
b. Vert. pair, imperf. btwn. 425.00
27 A9 2c brown 2.25 *16.00*
a. Imperf., pair 50.00
28 A9 4c rose 6.50 *19.00*
a. Cliché of 1c in plate of 4c 350.00 *1,300.*
b. Imperf., pair 65.00
c. As "a," imperf. in pair with #28 7,500.
d. Horiz. pair, imperf vert. 425.00
29 A9 8c green 30.00 *28.00*
a. Imperf., pair 55.00 *55.00*
30 A9 10c blue 15.00 *45.00*
a. Imperf., pair 55.00
b. Vert. pair, imperf btwn. 425.00
Nos. 25-30 (6) 60.75 *145.00*

For surcharges see Nos. 54-55.

A10

A11

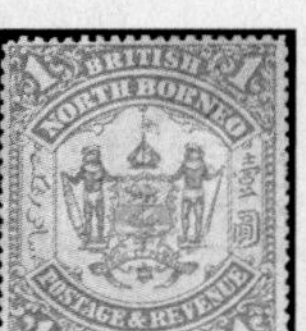
A12

A13

31 A10 25c slate blue 475.00 25.00
a. Imperf., pair 475.00 50.00
32 A11 50c violet 475.00 25.00
a. Imperf., pair 550.00 50.00
33 A12 $1 red 400.00 24.00
a. Imperf., pair 600.00 50.00
34 A13 $2 sage green 700.00 30.00
a. Imperf., pair 600.00 55.00
Nos. 31-34 (4) 2,050. 104.00
Nos. 22-34 (12) 2,761. *1,349.*

See Nos. 44-47.

A14

1887-92 *Perf. 14*

35 A14 ½c rose 1.50 .60
a. ½c magenta 4.00 *3.00*
36 A14 1c orange 6.50 .50
37 A14 2c red brown 7.50 .50
a. 2c brown 14.00 *1.00*
b. As "a," horiz. pair imperf. between 425.00
38 A14 3c violet 2.75 .50
39 A14 4c rose 14.50 .50
a. Horiz. pair, imperf. vert. *250.00*
40 A14 5c slate 3.00 .50
41 A14 6c lake ('92) 20.00 .50
42 A14 8c green 32.50 1.00
a. Horiz. pair, imperf. between
43 A14 10c blue 7.25 .50
Nos. 35-43 (9) 95.50 5.10

Exist imperf. Value $20 each, unused, $4.50 used. Forgeries exist, perf. 11½.

For surcharges see Nos. 52-53, 56-57.

Redrawn

25c. The letters of "BRITISH NORTH BORNEO" are 2mm high instead of 1½mm.

50c. The club of the native at left does not touch the frame. The 0's of "50" are flat at top and bottom instead of being oval.

$1.00. The spear of the native at right does not touch the frame. There are 14 pearls at each side of the frame instead of 13.

$2.00. "BRITISH" is 11mm long instead of 12mm. There are only six oars at the side of the dhow.

1888

44 A10 25c slate blue 115.00 .75
b. Horiz. pair, imperf. between *300.00*
c. Imperf., pair 500.00 22.50
45 A11 50c violet 135.00 .75
a. Imperf., pair 600.00 22.50
46 A12 $1 red 67.50 .75
a. Imperf., pair 450.00 22.50
47 A13 $2 sage green 250.00 1.50
a. Imperf., pair 750.00 25.00
Nos. 44-47 (4) 567.50 3.75

For surcharges see Nos. 50-51, 58.

A15

A16

1889

48 A15 $5 red violet 400.00 9.00
a. Imperf., pair 1,100. 80.00
49 A16 $10 brown 400.00 12.50
b. Imperf., pair 1,300. 90.00

No. 44 Surcharged in Red — e

1890

50 A10 2c on 25c slate blue 87.50 *100.00*
a. Inverted surcharge 450.00 *450.00*
b. With additional surcharge "2 cents" in black
51 A10 8c on 25c slate blue 135.00 *145.00*

Surcharged in Black On #42-43 — f

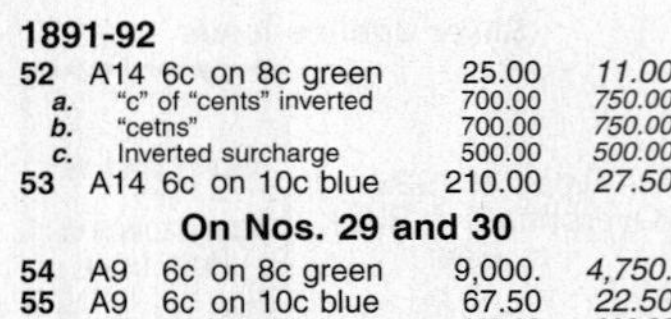

1891-92

52 A14 6c on 8c green 25.00 *11.00*
a. "c" of "cents" inverted 700.00 *750.00*
b. "cetns" 700.00 *750.00*
c. Inverted surcharge 500.00 *500.00*
53 A14 6c on 10c blue 210.00 *27.50*

On Nos. 29 and 30

54 A9 6c on 8c green 9,000. *4,750.*
55 A9 6c on 10c blue 67.50 *22.50*
a. Inverted surcharge 300.00 *300.00*
b. Double surcharge 1,500.
c. Triple surcharge 550.00

Nos. 39, 40 and 44 Surcharged in Red

1892

56 A14 1c on 4c rose 27.50 15.00
a. Double surcharge 1,650.
b. Surcharged on face & back *675.00*
57 A14 1c on 5c slate 8.00 6.50
58 A10 8c on 25c blue 185.00 *200.00*
Nos. 56-58 (3) 220.50 *221.50*

North Borneo

Dyak Chief — A21

Malayan Sambar — A22

Malay Dhow — A26

Sago Palm — A23

Saltwater Crocodile — A27

Argus Pheasant A24

Mt. Kinabalu A28

Coat of Arms — A25

Coat of Arms with Supporters — A29

A30

A31

A32

A33

A34

A35

Perf. 12 to 15 and Compound

1894 Engr. Unwmk.

59 A21 1c bis brn & blk 1.40 .50
a. Vert. pair, imperf. btwn. *950.00*
60 A22 2c rose & black 5.50 .75
a. Horiz. pair, imperf. btwn. *950.00 950.00*
b. Vert. pair, imperf. btwn. *950.00 950.00*
61 A23 3c vio & ol green 4.00 .55
a. Horiz. pair, imperf. btwn. — *850.00*
b. Vert. pair, imperf. btwn. 1,350.
62 A24 5c org red & blk 14.00 .75
a. Horiz. pair, imperf. btwn. 850.00
63 A25 6c brn ol & blk 4.50 .60
64 A26 8c lilac & black 6.50 .75
a. Vert. pair, imperf. btwn. 550.00 *350.00*
b. Horiz. pair, imperf. btwn. *750.00*
65 A27 12c ultra & black 47.50 3.00
a. 12c blue & black 30.00 2.75
66 A28 18c green & black 30.00 2.00
67 A29 24c claret & blue 25.00 2.00

Litho. *Perf. 14*

68 A30 25c slate blue 10.00 1.00
a. Imperf., pair 60.00 12.00
69 A31 50c violet 50.00 2.00
a. Imperf., pair 12.00
b. 50c dark ultra 50.00 2.00
70 A32 $1 red 14.50 1.25
a. Perf. 14x11 300.00
b. Imperf., pair 47.50 12.00
71 A33 $2 gray green 27.50 2.75
a. Imperf., pair 18.00
72 A34 $5 red violet 275.00 17.50
a. Imperf., pair 925.00 65.00
73 A35 $10 brown 325.00 16.00
a. Imperf., pair 950.00 60.00
Nos. 59-73 (15) 840.40 51.40

For #68-70 in other colors see Labuan #63b-65b.

For surcharges & overprints see #74-78, 91-94, 97-102, 115-119, 130-135, 115-119, 150-151, 158-159, J1-J8. In other colors see Labuan #63-65, 93-95, 116-118, and 120.

No. 70 Surcharged in Black

1895, June

74 A32 4c on $1 red 7.00 1.25
a. Double surcharge 1,000.
75 A32 10c on $1 red 27.50 .60
76 A32 20c on $1 red 57.50 .60
77 A32 30c on $1 red 52.50 2.00
78 A32 40c on $1 red 65.00 2.00
Nos. 74-78 (5) 209.50 6.45

See No. 99.

A37

A38

A39

A40

A41

A42

A43

"Postal Revenue" — A44

No "Postal Revenue" — A45

Perf. 13 to 16 and Compound

1897-1900 **Engr.**

79 A37 1c bis brn & blk 12.00 .55
a. Horiz. pair, imperf. btwn. 600.00
80 A38 2c dp rose & blk 25.00 .55
81 A38 2c grn & blk ('00) 72.50 .60
82 A39 3c lilac & ol green 36.00 .55
83 A40 5c orange & black 125.00 .85
84 A41 6c ol brown & blk 57.50 .50
85 A42 8c brn lilac & blk 16.50 .75
86 A43 12c blue & black 160.00 1.50
87 A44 18c green & black 40.00 4.50
a. Vert. pair, imperf. btwn. *350.00*
b. Horiz. pair, imperf. vert. *95.00*
c. Imperf, pair *200.00*
88 A45 24c claret & blue 40.00 4.25
Nos. 79-88 (10) 584.50 14.60

For overprints and surcharges see Nos. 105-107, 109-112, 124-127, J9-J17, J20-J22, J24-J26, J28.

"Postage & Revenue"
A46 A47

1897

89 A46 18c green & black 135.00 1.75
90 A47 24c claret & blue 62.50 2.10

For surcharges & overprints see #95-96, 128-129, 113-114, J18-J19, J30-J31.

Stamps of 1894-97 Surcharged in Black

1899

91 A40 4c on 5c org & blk 40.00 *12.50*
92 A41 4c on 6c ol brn & blk 20.00 *25.00*
93 A42 4c on 8c brn lil & blk 16.00 *13.00*
94 A43 4c on 12c bl & blk 29.00 *15.00*
a. Horiz. pair, imperf. btwn. 850.00
b. Vert. pair, imperf. btwn. 950.00
95 A46 4c on 18c grn & blk 16.00 *18.00*
96 A47 4c on 24c cl & blue 25.00 *20.00*
a. Perf. 16 55.00 *55.00*
97 A30 4c on 25c sl blue 6.00 *10.00*
98 A31 4c on 50c violet 18.00 *18.00*
a. 4c on 50c dark ultra 20.00 *36.00*
99 A32 4c on $1 red 6.25 *14.00*
100 A33 4c on $2 gray grn 6.25 *19.00*

"CENTS" 8½mm below "4"

101 A34 4c on $5 red vio 7.25 *18.00*
a. Normal spacing 170.00 *250.00*
102 A35 4c on $10 brown 7.25 *18.00*
a. Normal spacing 130.00 *250.00*
Nos. 91-102 (12) 197.00 *200.50*

No. 99 differs from No. 74 in the distance between "4" and "cents" which is 4¾mm on No. 99 and 3¾mm on No. 74.

Orangutan — A48

1899-1900 **Engr.**

103 A48 4c green & black 10.00 1.75
104 A48 4c dp rose & blk ('00) 40.00 .75

For overprints see Nos. 108, J13, J23.

Stamps of 1894-1900 Overprinted in Red, Black, Green or Blue — m

1901-05

105 A37 1c bis brn & blk (R) 4.00 .35
106 A38 2c grn & blk (R) 3.50 .35
107 A39 3c lil & ol grn (Bk) 2.00 .35
108 A48 4c dp rose & blk (G) 10.00 .35
109 A40 5c org & blk (G) 16.00 .35
110 A41 6c ol brn & blk (R) 4.50 .75
111 A42 8c brn & blk (Bl) 4.25 .55
a. Vert. pair, imperf. btwn. 425.00
112 A43 12c blue & blk (R) 60.00 1.50
113 A46 18c grn & blk (R) 15.00 1.40
114 A47 24c red & blue (Bk) 18.00 1.75
115 A30 25c slate blue (R) 3.00 .60
a. Inverted overprint 700.00
116 A31 50c violet (R) 3.00 .70
117 A32 $1 red (R) 20.00 3.75
118 A32 $1 red (Bk) 10.00 2.75
a. Double overprint 425.00
119 A33 $2 gray grn (R) 37.50 4.00
a. Double overprint 1,600.
Nos. 105-119 (15) 210.75 19.50

Nos. 110, 111 and 122 are known without period after "PROTECTORATE."
See Nos. 122-123, 150-151.

Bruang (Sun Bear) — A49

Railroad Train — A50

1902 **Engr.**

120 A49 10c slate & dk brn 130.00 3.25
a. Vertical pair, imperf. between 575.00
121 A50 16c yel brn & grn 150.00 3.75

Overprinted type "m" in Red or Black

122 A49 10c sl & dk brn (R) 75.00 1.10
a. Double overprint 900.00 350.00
123 A50 16c yel brn & grn (Bk) 150.00 2.50
Nos. 120-123 (4) 505.00 10.60

For overprints see Nos. J27, J29.

Stamps of 1894-97 Surcharged in Black

1904

124 A40 4c on 5c org & blk 50.00 14.00
125 A41 4c on 6c ol brn & blk 8.00 14.00
a. Inverted surcharge 350.00
126 A42 4c on 8c brn lil & blk 15.00 14.00
a. Inverted surcharge 350.00
127 A43 4c on 12c blue & blk 40.00 14.00
128 A46 4c on 18c grn & blk 16.00 14.00
129 A47 4c on 24c cl & bl 20.00 14.00
130 A30 4c on 25c sl blue 5.00 14.00
131 A31 4c on 50c violet 5.50 14.00
132 A32 4c on $1 red 7.00 14.00
133 A33 4c on $2 gray grn 10.50 14.00
134 A34 4c on $5 red vio 14.00 14.00
135 A35 4c on $10 brown 14.00 14.00
a. Inverted surcharge 2,750.
Nos. 124-135 (12) 205.00 168.00

Malayan Tapir — A51

Traveler's Palm — A52

Railroad Station — A53

Meeting of the Assembly — A54

Elephant and Mahout A55

Sumatran Rhinoceros A56

Natives Plowing — A57

Wild Boar — A58

Palm Cockatoo A59

Rhinoceros Hornbill A60

Banteng (Wild Ox)
A61 A62

Cassowary A63

1909-22 **Unwmk.** **Engr.** ***Perf. 14***
Center in Black

136 A51 1c chocolate 7.00 .30
b. Perf. 13½
c. Perf. 15 47.50 .40
137 A52 2c green 1.00 .30
b. Perf. 15 3.25 .30
138 A53 3c deep rose 3.25 .30
b. Perf. 15 42.50 .55
139 A53 3c green ('22) 42.50 *.40*
140 A54 4c dull red 2.75 .30
b. Perf. 13½ *11.00* *10.50*
c. Perf. 15 21.00 .40
141 A55 5c yellow brn 16.00 .40
b. Perf. 15
142 A56 6c olive green 13.00 .30
b. Perf. 15 80.00 1.00
143 A57 8c rose 4.00 .60
b. Perf 15 *12.00*
144 A58 10c blue 45.00 2.00
b. Perf. 13½ —
c. Perf. 15 70.00 *6.50*
145 A59 12c deep blue 42.50 1.00
c. Perf. 15 *12.00*
146 A60 16c red brown 26.00 1.25
b. Perf. 13½ 30.00 6.50
147 A61 18c blue green 120.00 1.25
148 A62 20c on 18c bl grn (R) 7.00 .55
b. Perf. 15 250.00 *75.00*
149 A63 24c violet 28.00 1.75
Nos. 136-149 (14) 358.00 10.70

Issued: #139, 1922; others, July 1, 1909.
See #167-178. #136a-149a follow #162.
For surcharges and overprints see #160-162, 166, B1-B12, B14-B24, B31-B41, J32-J49.

Nos. 72-73 Overprinted type "m" in Red

1910

150 A34 $5 red violet 325.00 9.00
151 A35 $10 brown 550.00 11.00
a. Double overprint
b. Inverted overprint 2,700. 450.00

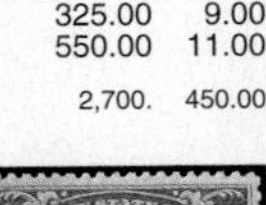

A64

A65

1911 Engr. *Perf. 14*

Center in Black

No.	Type	Description	Unused	Used
152	A64	25c yellow green	18.00	2.00
a.		Perf. 15	19.00	
b.		Imperf., pair	55.00	
153	A64	50c slate blue	18.00	2.25
a.		Perf. 15	24.00	*22.50*
b.		Imperf., pair	90.00	
154	A64	$1 brown	18.00	4.00
a.		Perf. 15	60.00	*8.00*
c.		Imperf., pair	180.00	
155	A64	$2 dk violet	75.00	5.00
156	A65	$5 claret	150.00	32.50
a.		Perf. 13½	*150.00*	
b.		Imperf., pair	200.00	
157	A65	$10 vermilion	500.00	90.00
a.		Imperf., pair	475.00	
		Nos. 152-157 (6)	779.00	*135.75*

See #179-184. #152c-153c follow #162.

For overprint and surcharges see Nos. B13, B25-B30, B42-B47.

Nos. 72-73 Overprinted in Red

1912

No.	Type	Description	Unused	Used
158	A34	$5 red violet	1,500.	9.25
159	A35	$10 brown	1,800.	9.25

Nos. 158 and 159 were prepared for use but not regularly issued.

Nos. 138, 142 and 145 Surcharged in Black or Red

1916 Center in Black *Perf. 14*

No.	Type	Description	Unused	Used
160	A53	2c on 3c dp rose	30.00	15.00
a.		Inverted "S"	110.00	95.00
161	A56	4c on 6c ol grn (R)	30.00	20.00
a.		Inverted "S"	110.00	100.00
162	A59	10c on 12c bl (R)	60.00	*70.00*
a.		Inverted "S"	180.00	*190.00*
		Nos. 160-162 (3)	120.00	105.00

Stamps and Types of 1909-11 Overprinted in Red or Blue

1922 Center in Black

No.	Type	Description	Unused	Used
136a	A51	1c brown	20.00	*70.00*
137a	A52	2c green	2.50	*25.00*
138a	A53	3c deep rose (B)	16.00	*65.00*
140a	A54	4c dull red (B)	3.75	*45.00*
141a	A55	5c yel brown (B)	9.50	*65.00*
142a	A56	6c olive green	9.50	*70.00*
143a	A57	8c rose (B)	8.50	*42.50*
144a	A58	10c gray blue	20.00	*65.00*
145a	A59	12c deep blue	12.00	*45.00*
146a	A60	16c red brown (B)	26.00	*75.00*
148a	A62	20c on 18c bl grn	27.50	*90.00*
149a	A63	24c violet	50.00	*75.00*
152c	A64	25c yel green	12.00	*65.00*
153c	A64	50c slate blue	17.50	*70.00*
		Nos. 136a-153c (14)	234.75	*867.50*

Industrial fair, Singapore, 3/31-4/15/22.

No. 140 Surcharged in Black

1923

No.	Type	Description	Unused	Used
166	A54	3c on 4c dull red & blk	2.75	*6.00*
a.		Double surcharge	*1,300.*	

Types of 1909-22 Issues

1926-28 Engr. *Perf. 12½*

Center in Black

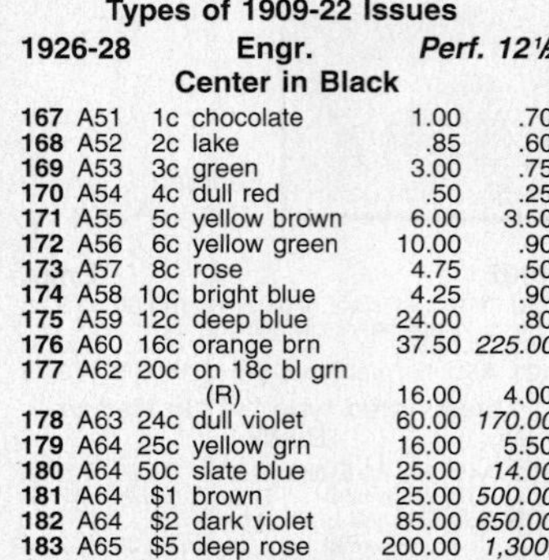

No.	Type	Description	Unused	Used
167	A51	1c chocolate	1.00	.70
168	A52	2c lake	.85	.60
169	A53	3c green	3.00	.75
170	A54	4c dull red	.50	.25
171	A55	5c yellow brown	6.00	3.50
172	A56	6c yellow green	10.00	.90
173	A57	8c rose	4.75	.50
174	A58	10c bright blue	4.25	.90
175	A59	12c deep blue	24.00	.80
176	A60	16c orange brn	37.50	*225.00*
177	A62	20c on 18c bl grn (R)	16.00	4.00
178	A63	24c dull violet	60.00	*170.00*
179	A64	25c yellow grn	16.00	5.50
180	A64	50c slate blue	25.00	*14.00*
181	A64	$1 brown	25.00	*500.00*
182	A64	$2 dark violet	85.00	*650.00*
183	A65	$5 deep rose	200.00	*1,300.*
184	A65	$10 dull vermilion	550.00	*1,500.*
		Nos. 167-184 (18)	1,069.	*4,377.*

Murut — A66

Orangutan — A67

Dyak — A68

Mt. Kinabalu A69

Clouded Leopard A70

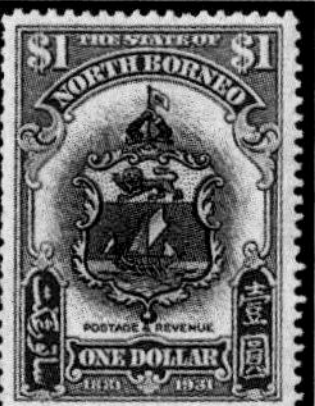

Coat of Arms — A71

Arms with Supporters and Motto A72

Arms with Supporters — A73

1931, Jan. 1 Engr. *Perf. 12½*

Center in Black

No.	Type	Description	Unused	Used
185	A66	3c blue green	1.50	*1.50*
186	A67	6c orange red	17.50	4.75
187	A68	10c carmine	4.50	*13.00*
188	A69	12c ultra	4.75	*8.00*
189	A70	25c deep violet	40.00	35.00
190	A71	$1 yellow green	27.50	*110.00*
191	A72	$2 red brown	47.50	*110.00*
192	A73	$5 red violet	160.00	*500.00*
		Nos. 185-192 (8)	303.25	*782.25*

50th anniv. of the North Borneo Co.

Buffalo Transport A74

Palm Cockatoo — A75

Murut — A76

Proboscis Monkey — A77

Bajaus — A78

Map of North Borneo and Surrounding Lands — A79

Orangutan — A80

Murut with Blowgun — A81

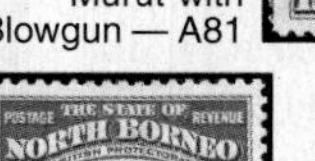

Dyak — A82

River Scene — A83

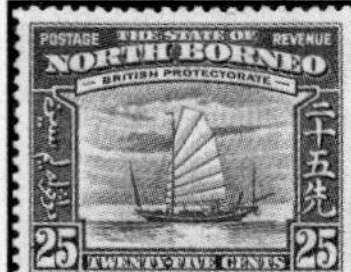

Proa — A84

Mt. Kinabalu — A85

Coat of Arms — A86

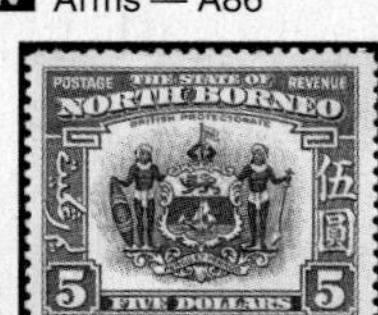

Arms with Supporters A87

1939, Jan. 1 *Perf. 12½*

No.	Type	Description	Unused	Used
193	A74	1c red brn & dk grn	2.75	2.25
194	A75	2c Prus bl & red vio	3.25	2.25
195	A76	3c dk grn & sl blue	3.50	2.50
196	A77	4c rose vio & ol grn	8.50	.50
197	A78	6c dp cl & dk blue	7.75	14.00
198	A79	8c red	11.00	2.00
199	A80	10c olive grn & vio	26.00	7.00
200	A81	12c ultra & grn	27.50	8.00
201	A82	15c bis brn & brt bl grn	21.00	13.00
202	A83	20c ind & rose vio	14.50	7.00
203	A84	25c dk brn & bl grn	21.00	15.00
204	A85	50c purple & brn	22.50	14.00
205	A86	$1 car & brown	72.50	22.50
206	A86	$2 ol grn & pur	120.00	*150.00*
207	A87	$5 blue & indigo	350.00	*375.00*
		Nos. 193-207 (15)	711.75	635.00
		Set, never hinged	1,200.	

For overprints see #208-237, MR1-MR2, N1-N15, N16-N31.

Nos. 193 to 207 Overprinted in Black

1945, Dec. 17 Unwmk. *Perf. 12½*

No.	Type	Description	Unused	Used
208	A74	1c red brn & dk grn	9.50	2.25
209	A75	2c Prus bl & red vio	10.00	2.00
210	A76	3c dk grn & sl bl	.90	1.25
211	A77	4c rose vio & ol grn	12.00	*16.00*
212	A78	6c dp cl & dk bl	.90	1.25
213	A79	8c red	2.10	.75
214	A80	10c ol green & vio	2.10	.40
215	A81	12c ultra & green	4.25	3.50
216	A82	15c bis brn & brt bl grn	1.20	1.10
217	A83	20c ind & rose vio	4.25	2.50
218	A84	25c dk brn & bl grn	4.75	1.50
219	A85	50c purple & brn	3.00	2.50
220	A86	$1 carmine & brn	35.00	*40.00*
221	A86	$2 ol green & pur	35.00	*42.50*
a.		Double overprint	4,000.	
222	A87	$5 blue & indigo	18.00	18.00
		Nos. 208-222 (15)	142.95	135.50
		Set, never hinged	235.00	

"BMA" stands for British Military Administration.

Nos. 193 to 207 Ovptd. in Black or Carmine

1947

223 A74 1c red brn & dk grn .25 1.00
224 A75 2c Prus bl & red vio 1.25 .80
225 A76 3c dk grn & sl bl (C) .25 .80
226 A77 4c rose vio & ol grn .50 .80
227 A78 6c dp cl & dk bl (C) .25 .25
228 A79 8c red .25 .25
229 A80 10c olive grn & vio 1.10 .35
230 A81 12c ultra & grn 2.40 2.75
231 A82 15c bis brn & brt bl grn 1.75 .30
232 A83 20c ind & rose vio 2.40 .85
233 A84 25c dk brn & bl grn 2.40 .50
234 A85 50c purple & brn 2.00 .85
235 A86 $1 carmine & brn 8.50 1.75
236 A86 $2 ol green & pur 11.50 *18.00*
237 A87 $5 blue & ind (C) 19.00 *25.00*
Nos. 223-237 (15) 53.80 54.25
Set, never hinged 80.00

The bars obliterate "The State of" and "British Protectorate."

Catalogue values for unused stamps in this section, from this point to the end of the section, are for Never Hinged items.

Silver Wedding Issue
Common Design Types
Perf. 14x14½

1948, Nov. 1 Wmk. 4 Photo.
238 CD304 8c scarlet .30 *.75*

Perf. 11½x11
Engraved; Name Typographed
239 CD305 $10 purple 35.00 *45.00*

Common Design Types pictured following the introduction.

UPU Issue
Common Design Types
Engr.; Name Typo. on 10c and 30c

1949, Oct. 10 *Perf. 13½, 11x11½*
240 CD306 8c rose carmine .65 .25
241 CD307 10c chocolate 3.25 1.75
242 CD308 30c deep orange 1.50 1.75
243 CD309 55c blue 1.75 *2.75*
Nos. 240-243 (4) 7.15 6.50

Mount Kinabalu — A88

Coconut Grove — A89

Designs: 2c, Musician. 4c, Hemp drying. 5c, Cattle at Kota Belud. 8c, Map. 10c, Logging. 15c, Proa at Sandakan. 20c, Bajau Chief. 30c, Suluk Craft. 50c, Clock tower. $1, Bajau horsemen. $2, Murut with blowgun. $5, Net fishing. $10, Arms.

Perf. 13½x14½, 14½x13½

1950, July 1 Photo.
244 A88 1c red brown .25 *1.25*
245 A88 2c blue .25 *.50*
246 A89 3c green .25 .25
247 A89 4c red violet .25 .25
248 A89 5c purple .25 .25
249 A88 8c red 1.25 .85
250 A88 10c violet brn 1.75 .25
251 A88 15c brt ultra 2.00 .65
252 A88 20c dk brown 2.25 .25
253 A89 30c brown 5.50 .25
254 A89 50c cer *(Jessleton)* 1.75 4.75
255 A89 $1 red orange 6.00 1.75
256 A88 $2 dark green 15.00 *20.00*
257 A88 $5 emerald 25.00 *30.00*
258 A88 $10 gray blue 65.00 *90.00*
Nos. 244-258 (15) 126.75 151.25

Redrawn

1952, May 1 *Perf. 14½x13½*
259 A89 50c cerise *(Jesselton)* 16.00 3.25

SEMI-POSTAL STAMPS

Nos. 136-138, 140-146, 148-149, 152 Ovptd. in Carmine or Vermilion

1916 Unwmk. *Perf. 14*
Center in Black
B1 A51 1c chocolate 7.50 *35.00*
B2 A52 2c green 30.00 *80.00*
a. Perf. 15 35.00 *80.00*
B3 A53 3c deep rose 27.50 *50.00*
B4 A54 4c dull red 7.25 *32.50*
a. Perf. 15 275.00 *180.00*
B5 A55 5c yellow brown 50.00 *55.00*
B6 A56 6c olive green 70.00 *75.00*
a. Perf. 15 225.00 *225.00*
B7 A57 8c rose 24.00 *60.00*
B8 A58 10c brt blue 55.00 *70.00*
B9 A59 12c deep blue 100.00 *100.00*
B10 A60 16c red brown 110.00 *110.00*
B11 A62 20c on 18c bl grn 55.00 *100.00*
B12 A63 24c violet 130.00 *130.00*

Perf. 15
B13 A64 25c yellow green 375.00 *425.00*
Nos. B1-B13 (13) 1,041. *1,323.*

All values exist with the vermilion overprint and all but the 4c with the carmine.

Of the total overprinting, a third was given to the National Philatelic War Fund Committee in London to be auctioned for the benefit of the wounded and veterans' survivors. The balance was lost en route from London to Sandakan when a submarine sank the ship. Very few were postally used.

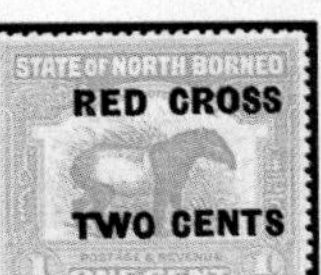

Nos. 136-138, 140-146, 149, 152-157 Surcharged

1918 Center in Black *Perf. 14*
B14 A51 1c + 2c choc 3.50 *14.00*
B15 A52 2c + 2c green 1.00 *8.50*
B16 A53 3c + 2c dp rose 14.00 *19.00*
a. Perf. 15 30.00 *65.00*
B17 A54 4c + 2c dull red .70 *5.00*
a. Inverted surcharge 450.00
B18 A55 5c + 2c yel brn 8.00 *29.00*
B19 A56 6c + 2c olive grn 5.00 *29.00*
a. Perf. 15 225.00 *250.00*
B20 A57 8c + 2c rose 5.50 *11.00*
B21 A58 10c + 2c brt blue 8.00 *27.50*
B22 A59 12c + 2c deep bl 21.00 *55.00*
a. Inverted surcharge 700.00
B23 A60 16c + 2c red brn 22.50 *45.00*
B24 A63 24c + 2c violet 22.50 *45.00*
B25 A64 25c + 2c yel grn 12.00 *42.50*
B26 A64 50c + 2c sl blue 14.00 *42.50*
B27 A64 $1 + 2c brown 50.00 *55.00*
B28 A64 $2 + 2c dk vio 75.00 *95.00*
B29 A65 $5 + 2c claret 425.00 *650.00*
B30 A65 $10 + 2c ver 475.00 *700.00*
Nos. B14-B30 (17) 1,163. *1,873.*

On Nos. B14-B24 the surcharge is 15mm high, on Nos. B25-B30 it is 19mm high.

Nos. 136-138, 140-146, 149, 152-157 Surcharged in Red

1918 Center in Black
B31 A51 1c + 4c choc .60 *5.00*
B32 A52 2c + 4c green .65 *8.00*
B33 A53 3c + 4c dp rose 1.00 *3.75*
B34 A54 4c + 4c dull red .40 *4.75*
B35 A55 5c + 4c yel brn 2.00 *22.50*
B36 A56 6c + 4c olive grn 2.00 *12.00*
a. Vert. pair, imperf. btwn. 2,500.
B37 A57 8c + 4c rose 1.25 *9.50*
B38 A58 10c + 4c brt blue 3.75 *12.00*
B39 A59 12c + 4c dp blue 14.00 *14.00*
B40 A60 16c + 4c red brn 8.00 *16.00*
B41 A63 24c + 4c violet 11.00 *20.00*
B42 A64 25c + 4c yel grn 9.00 *50.00*
B43 A64 50c + 4c sl blue 15.00 *45.00*
a. Perf. 15 60.00
B44 A64 $1 + 4c brown 22.50 *60.00*
a. Perf. 15 180.00
B45 A64 $2 + 4c dk vio 55.00 *80.00*
B46 A65 $5 + 4c claret 300.00 *400.00*
B47 A65 $10 + 4c ver 375.00 *450.00*
Nos. B31-B47 (17) 821.15 *1,213.*

POSTAGE DUE STAMPS

Regular Issues Overprinted

On Nos. 60 to 67
Reading Up Vert. (V), or Horiz. (H)

1895, Aug. 1 Unwmk. *Perf. 14, 15*
J1 A22 2c rose & blk (V) 30.00 2.50
J2 A23 3c vio & ol grn (V) 6.00 1.25
J3 A24 5c org red & blk (V) 60.00 3.25
a. Period after "DUE" (V) 275.00
J4 A25 6c ol brn & blk (V) 20.00 2.75
J5 A26 8c lilac & blk (H) 50.00 3.00
a. Double ovpt. (H) *400.00*
J6 A27 12c blue & blk (H) 70.00 3.00
a. Double overprint (H) *325.00*
J7 A28 18c green & blk (V) 70.00 4.25
a. Ovpt. reading down 600.00 *350.00*
b. Overprinted horizontally 70.00 4.25
c. Same as "b" inverted 375.00 *400.00*
J8 A29 24c claret & bl (H) 40.00 4.00
Nos. J1-J8 (8) 346.00 24.00

1897 On Nos. 80 and 85
J9 A38 2c dp rose & blk (V) 8.50 1.50
a. Overprinted horizontally 23.00 *15.00*
J10 A42 8c brn lil & blk (H) 65.00 *80.00*
a. Period after "DUE" 30.00 *75.00*

On Nos. 81-88 and 104 Vertically reading up

1901
J11 A38 2c green & blk 75.00 .70
a. Overprinted horizontally 225.00
J12 A39 3c lilac & ol grn 32.00 .50
a. Period after "DUE" 70.00 *70.00*
J13 A48 4c dp rose & blk 70.00 .50
J14 A40 5c orange & blk 28.00 .90
a. Period after "DUE" 90.00
J15 A41 6c olive brn & blk 7.00 .50
J16 A42 8c brown & blk 9.00 .50
a. Overprinted horizontally 30.00
b. Period after "DUE" (H) 23.00 75.00
J17 A43 12c blue & blk 150.00 4.00
J18 A46 18c green & blk 80.00 4.00
J19 A47 24c red & blue 50.00 2.50
Nos. J11-J19 (9) 501.00 14.10

On Nos. 105-114, 122-123 Horizontally

1903-11 *Perf. 14*
J20 A37 1c bis brn & blk, period after "DUE" 4.50 55.00
a. Period omitted
J21 A38 2c green & blk 27.50 .30
a. Ovpt. vert., perf. 16 550.00 *275.00*
b. Perf 15 (ovpt. horiz.) 55.00 *55.00*
J22 A39 3c lilac & ol grn 7.00 .35
a. Ovpt. vert. 140.00 *140.00*
b. Perf. 15 (ovpt. horiz.) 50.00 *45.00*
J23 A48 4c dp rose & blk, perf. 15 11.00 2.00
a. "Postage Due" double 550.00 170.00
b. Perf. 14 21.00 1.00
J24 A40 5c orange & blk 45.00 .45
a. Ovpt. vert., perf. 15 250.00 *160.00*
b. Perf. 13½ (ovpt. horiz.)
c. Perf. 15 (ovpt. horiz.) 85.00 *35.00*
J25 A41 6c olive brn & blk 24.00 .40
a. "Postage Due" double *750.00*
b. "Postage Due" inverted 500.00 *125.00*
c. Perf. 16 90.00 *37.50*
J26 A42 8c brown & blk 27.50 .50
a. Overprint vertical 200.00 *125.00*
J27 A49 10c slate & brn 130.00 1.60
J28 A43 12c blue & blk 42.50 3.75
J29 A50 16c yel brn & grn 85.00 3.75
J30 A46 18c green & blk 17.50 1.50
a. "Postage Due" double *500.00* *100.00*
J31 A47 24c claret & blue 17.50 3.75
a. "Postage Due" double *350.00* *125.00*
b. Overprint vertical 325.00 *140.00*
Nos. J20-J31 (12) 439.00 73.35

On Nos. 137 and 139-146

1921-31 *Perf. 14, 15*
J32 A52 2c green & blk 27.50 *80.00*
a. Perf. 13½ 11.00 *75.00*
J33 A53 3c green & blk 5.25 *50.00*
J34 A54 4c dull red & blk 1.25 1.25
J35 A55 5c yel brn & blk 9.50 *30.00*
J36 A56 6c olive grn & blk 17.00 17.00
J37 A57 8c rose & blk 2.00 2.00
J38 A58 10c blue & blk 16.00 *19.00*
a. Perf. 15 120.00 *200.00*
J39 A59 12c dp vio & blk 70.00 55.00
J40 A60 16c red brn & blk 26.00 65.00
Nos. J32-J40 (9) 174.50 319.25

On Nos. 168 to 176

1926-28 *Perf. 12½*
J41 A52 2c lake & blk .75 *2.00*
J42 A53 3c green & blk 10.00 *32.50*
J43 A54 4c dull red & blk 3.25 *2.00*
J44 A55 5c yel brown & blk 8.50 *90.00*
J45 A56 6c yel green & blk 14.00 3.00
J46 A57 8c rose & black 11.00 *22.50*
J47 A58 10c brt blue & blk 12.00 *90.00*
J48 A59 12c dp blue & blk 32.50 *160.00*
J49 A60 16c org brn & blk 75.00 *225.00*
Nos. J41-J49 (9) 167.00 *627.00*

Crest of British North Borneo Company — D1

1939, Jan. 1 Engr. *Perf. 12½*
J50 D1 2c brown 4.25 *80.00*
J51 D1 4c carmine 4.75 *110.00*
J52 D1 6c dp rose violet 17.50 *150.00*
J53 D1 8c dk blue green 22.50 *300.00*
J54 D1 10c deep ultra 50.00 *450.00*
Nos. J50-J54 (5) 99.00 *1,090.*
Set, never hinged 160.00

WAR TAX STAMPS

Nos. 193-194 Overprinted

No. MR1

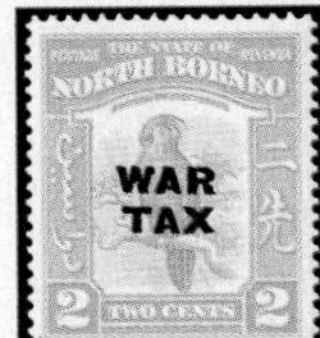

No. MR2

1941, Feb. 24 Unwmk. *Perf. 12½*
MR1 A74 1c red brn & dk grn 2.75 4.50
MR2 A75 2c Prus blue & red violet 11.00 4.75

For overprints see Nos. N15A-N15B.

OCCUPATION STAMPS

Issued under Japanese Occupation

Nos. 193-207 Handstamped in Violet or Black

On Nos. N1-N15B, the violet overprint is attributed to Jesselton, the black to Sandakan. Nos. N1-N15 are generally found with violet overprint, Nos. N15A-N15B with black.

1942 Unwmk. *Perf. 12½*
N1 A74 1c 200.00 250.00
N2 A75 2c 220.00 275.00
N3 A76 3c 175.00 300.00
N4 A77 4c 325.00 390.00
N5 A78 6c 200.00 355.00
N6 A79 8c 275.00 210.00
N7 A80 10c 250.00 360.00
N8 A81 12c 275.00 525.00
N9 A82 15c 220.00 525.00
N10 A83 20c 300.00 *650.00*
N11 A84 25c 300.00 *700.00*
N12 A85 50c 400.00 *775.00*

N13 A86 $1 440.00 *925.00*
N14 A86 $2 650.00 *1,250.*
N15 A87 $5 775.00 *1,350.*
Nos. N1-N15 (15) 5,005. *8,840.*

For overprints see Nos. N22a, N31a.

Same Overprint on Nos. MR1-MR2 in Black or Violet

1942
N15A A74 1c *775.00 325.00*
N15B A75 2c *2,100. 650.00*

Nos. 193 to 207 Overprinted in Black

1944, Sept. 30 Unwmk. *Perf. 12½*
N16 A74 1c 8.25 13.00
N17 A75 2c 8.25 10.00
N18 A76 3c 8.25 11.00
N19 A77 4c 16.50 25.00
N20 A78 6c 12.00 7.00
N21 A79 8c 11.00 *18.50*
N22 A80 10c 9.25 *14.50*
a. On No. N7 500.00
N23 A81 12c 17.50 *14.50*
N24 A82 15c 17.50 *17.50*
N25 A83 20c 35.00 *55.00*
N26 A84 25c 35.00 *55.00*
N27 A85 50c 87.50 *130.00*
N28 A86 $1 105.00 *165.00*
Nos. N16-N28 (13) 371.00 *536.00*

Nos. N1 and 205 Surcharged in Black

No. N30

No. N31

1944, May
N30 A74 $2 on 1c *5,500. 4,750.*
N31 A86 $5 on $1 5,000. 3,750.
a. On No. N13 10,000. 6,000.

Mt. Kinabalu
OS1

Boat and Traveler's Palm
OS2

1943, Apr. 29 Litho.
N32 OS1 4c dull rose red 30.00 60.00
N33 OS2 8c dark blue 25.00 55.00

Stamps of Japan, 1938-43, Overprinted in Black

1s, War factory girl. 2s, Gen. Maresuke Nogi. 3s, Power plant. 4s, Hyuga Monument and Mt. Fuji. 5s, Adm. Heihachiro Togo. 6s, Garambi Lighthouse, Formosa. 8s, Meiji Shrine, Tokyo. 10s, Palms and map of "Greater East Asia." 15s, Aviator saluting and Japanese flag. 20s, Mt. Fuji and cherry blossoms. 25s, Horyu Temple, Nara. 30s, Miyajima Torii, Itsukushima shrine. 50s, Golden Pavilion, Kyoto. 1y, Great Buddha, Kamakura. See Burma, Vol. 1, for illustrations of 2s, 3s, 5s, 8s, 20s and watermark. For others, see Japan.

Wmk. Curved Wavy Lines (257)
1944, Sept. 30 *Perf. 13*
N34 A144 1s orange brown 10.00 *35.00*
N35 A84 2s vermilion 8.25 *30.00*
N36 A85 3s green 10.00 *35.00*
N37 A146 4s emerald 18.50 *27.50*
N38 A86 5s brown lake 15.50 *30.00*
N39 A88 6s orange 24.00 *32.50*
N40 A90 8s dk purple & pale vio 7.00 *32.50*
N41 A148 10s crim & dull rose 15.00 *35.00*
N42 A150 15s dull blue 14.00 *32.50*
N43 A94 20s ultra 95.00 *100.00*
N44 A95 25s brown 65.00 *95.00*
N45 A96 30s peacock blue 195.00 *105.00*
N46 A97 50s olive 87.50 *87.50*
N47 A98 1y lt brown 95.00 *120.00*
Nos. N34-N47 (14) 659.75 *797.50*

The overprint translates "North Borneo."

OCCUPATION POSTAGE DUE STAMPS

Nos. J50-J51, J53 Handstamped in Black

1942, Sept. 30
NJ1 D1 2c brown — *5,000.*
NJ2 D1 4c carmine — *5,000.*
NJ3 D1 8c dk blue green — *5,000.*

NORTHERN NIGERIA

'nor-thər͵n nī-'jir-ē-ə

LOCATION — Western Africa
GOVT. — A former British Protectorate
AREA — 281,703 sq. mi.
POP. — 11,866,250
CAPITAL — Zungeru

In 1914 Northern Nigeria united with Southern Nigeria to form the Colony and Protectorate of Nigeria.

12 Pence = 1 Shilling
20 Shillings = 1 Pound

Victoria — A1

Numerals of 5p and 6p, types A1 and A2, are in color on plain tablet.

Wmk. Crown and C A (2)
1900, Mar. Typo. *Perf. 14*
1 A1 ½p lilac & grn 8.00 *22.00*
2 A1 1p lilac & rose 5.00 5.50
3 A1 2p lilac & yel 16.00 *60.00*
4 A1 2½p lilac & blue 13.00 *45.00*
5 A1 5p lilac & brn 30.00 *70.00*
6 A1 6p lilac & vio 30.00 *50.00*
7 A1 1sh green & blk 32.50 *85.00*
8 A1 2sh6p green & blue 180.00 *550.00*
9 A1 10sh green & brn 325.00 *900.00*
Nos. 1-9 (9) 639.50 *1,788.*
Set, ovptd. "SPECIMEN" 225.00

Edward VII — A2

1902, July 1
10 A2 ½p violet & green 2.00 1.25
11 A2 1p vio & car rose 5.00 1.00
12 A2 2p violet & org 2.50 *3.00*
13 A2 2½p violet & ultra 2.00 *11.00*
14 A2 5p vio & org brn 7.00 *7.50*
15 A2 6p violet & pur 20.00 *8.00*
16 A2 1sh green & black 8.50 *8.50*
17 A2 2sh6p green & ultra 19.00 *75.00*
18 A2 10sh green & brown 55.00 *60.00*
Nos. 10-18 (9) 121.00 *175.25*
Set, ovptd. "SPECIMEN" 175.00

1904, Apr. Wmk. 3
18A A2 £25 green & car *60,000.*

No. 18A was available for postage but probably was used only for fiscal purposes.

1905 Ordinary Paper
19 A2 ½p violet & grn 27.50 8.50
20 A2 1p violet & car rose 22.50 1.25
21 A2 2p violet & org 19.00 *32.50*
22 A2 2½p violet & ultra 7.25 *10.00*
23 A2 5p violet & org brn 32.50 *85.00*
24 A2 6p violet & pur 29.00 *65.00*
25 A2 1sh green & black 65.00 *100.00*
26 A2 2sh6p green & ultra 50.00 *60.00*
Nos. 19-26 (8) 252.75 *362.25*

1906-07 Chalky Paper
19a A2 ½p violet & grn 6.00 5.50
20a A2 1p violet & car rose 6.00 1.25
21a A2 2p violet & org 20.00 *30.00*
23a A2 5p violet & org brn 35.00 *75.00*
24a A2 6p violet & pur 45.00 45.00
25a A2 1sh green & black 24.00 *55.00*
26a A2 2sh6p green & ultra 45.00 60.00
Nos. 19a-26a (7) 181.00 *271.75*

1910-11 Ordinary Paper
28 A2 ½p green 2.25 1.25
29 A2 1p carmine 5.25 1.25
30 A2 2p gray 9.50 *4.50*
31 A2 2½p ultra 3.50 *9.50*

Chalky Paper
32 A2 3p violet, *yel* 4.50 1.00
33 A2 5p vio & ol grn 6.00 *16.00*
34 A2 6p vio & red vio ('11) 6.00 *6.00*
a. 6p violet & deep violet 7.50 *26.00*
35 A2 1sh black, *green* 4.75 .75
36 A2 2sh6p blk & red, *bl* 19.00 *50.00*
37 A2 5sh grn & red, *yel* 27.50 *75.00*
38 A2 10sh grn & red, *grn* 55.00 *50.00*
Nos. 28-38 (11) 143.25 215.25
Set, ovptd. "SPECIMEN" 325.00

George V — A3

For description of dies I and II, see A pages in front section of catalogue.

Die I

1912 Ordinary Paper
40 A3 ½p green 4.50 1.00
41 A3 1p carmine 4.50 .60
42 A3 2p gray 6.75 *17.00*

Chalky Paper
43 A3 3p violet, *yel* 2.25 1.25
44 A3 4p blk & red, *yel* 1.25 *2.25*
45 A3 5p vio & ol grn 4.50 *18.00*
46 A3 6p vio & red vio 4.25 *4.50*
47 A3 9p violet & scar 2.25 *12.00*
48 A3 1sh blk, *green* 5.00 2.25
49 A3 2sh6p blk & red, *bl* 10.00 *55.00*
50 A3 5sh grn & red, *yel* 25.00 *90.00*
51 A3 10sh grn & red, *grn* 45.00 *50.00*
52 A3 £1 vio & blk, *red* 200.00 120.00
Nos. 40-52 (13) 315.25 *373.85*
Set, ovptd. "SPECIMEN" 225.00

Numerals of 3p, 4p, 5p and 6p, type A3, are in color on plain tablet.

Stamps of Northern Nigeria were replaced in 1914 by those of Nigeria.

NORTHERN RHODESIA

'nor-thər͵n rō-'dē-zhē͵ə

LOCATION — In southern Africa, east of Angola and separated from Southern Rhodesia by the Zambezi River.
GOVT. — British Protectorate
AREA — 287,640 sq. mi.
POP. — 2,550,000 (est. 1962)
CAPITAL — Lusaka

Prior to April 1, 1924, Northern Rhodesia was administered by the British South Africa Company. See Rhodesia and Southern Rhodesia.

12 Pence = 1 Shilling
20 Shillings = 1 Pound

Catalogue values for unused stamps in this country are for Never Hinged items, beginning with Scott 46 in the regular postage section.

King George V
A1 A2

1925-29 Engr. Wmk. 4 *Perf. 12½*
1 A1 ½p dk green 1.75 .80
2 A1 1p dk brown 1.75 .25
3 A1 1½p carmine 4.25 .30
4 A1 2p brown org 4.50 .25
5 A1 3p ultra 4.50 1.30
6 A1 4p dk violet 7.50 .50
7 A1 6p gray 9.00 .40
8 A1 8p rose lilac 9.00 *60.00*
9 A1 10p olive grn 9.00 *50.00*
10 A2 1sh black & org 4.25 2.25
11 A2 2sh ultra & brn 27.50 *40.00*
12 A2 2sh6p green & blk 24.00 *15.00*
13 A2 3sh indigo & vio 40.00 25.00
14 A2 5sh dk vio & gray 50.00 22.50
15 A2 7sh6p blk & lil rose 160.00 *275.00*
16 A2 10sh black & green 100.00 *100.00*
17 A2 20sh rose lil & red 275.00 *325.00*
Nos. 1-17 (17) 732.00 *918.55*

High values with revenue cancellations are inexpensive.

Issue dates: 3sh, 1929; others, Apr. 1.

Common Design Types pictured following the introduction.

Silver Jubilee Issue
Common Design Type

1935, May 6 *Perf. 13½x14*
18 CD301 1p olive grn & ultra 1.50 1.50
19 CD301 2p indigo & grn 2.50 2.25
20 CD301 3p blue & brown 4.00 *10.00*
21 CD301 6p brt vio & indigo 8.75 2.50
Nos. 18-21 (4) 16.75 16.25
Set, never hinged 25.00

Coronation Issue
Common Design Type

1937, May 12 *Perf. 11x11½*
22 CD302 1½p dark carmine .25 .25
23 CD302 2p yellow brown .30 *.75*
24 CD302 3p deep ultra .40 *1.25*
Nos. 22-24 (3) .95 2.25
Set, never hinged 1.50

King George VI — A3

1938-52 Wmk. 4 *Perf. 12½*
Size: 19x24mm
25 A3 ½p green .25 .25
26 A3 ½p dk brn ('51) 1.40 *1.50*
a. Perf. 12½x14 1.00 *6.00*
27 A3 1p dk brown .25 .25
28 A3 1p green ('51) .90 *2.25*
29 A3 1½p carmine 30.00 .75
a. Horiz. pair, imperf. between *27,000.*
30 A3 1½p brn org ('41) .30 .25
31 A3 2p brown org 30.00 1.75
32 A3 2p carmine ('41) 1.00 .50
33 A3 2p rose lilac ('51) .40 *1.50*
34 A3 3p ultra .45 .30
35 A3 3p red ('51) .30 *3.00*
36 A3 4p dk violet .30 .40
37 A3 4½p dp blue ('52) 1.75 *12.00*
38 A3 6p dark gray .30 .25
39 A3 9p violet ('52) 1.75 *12.00*

Size: 21½x26¾mm
40 A3 1sh blk & brn org 2.50 .60
41 A3 2sh6p green & blk 7.50 7.00
42 A3 3sh ind & dk vio 14.00 *17.50*
43 A3 5sh violet & gray 15.00 *17.50*

44 A3 10sh black & green 18.00 *35.00*
45 A3 20sh rose lil & red 42.50 *80.00*
Nos. 25-45 (21) 168.85 *194.55*
Set, never hinged 275.00

Catalogue values for unused stamps in this section, from this point to the end of the section, are for Never Hinged items.

Peace Issue
Common Design Type

1946, Nov. 26 Engr. *Perf. 13½x14*
46 CD303 1½p deep orange 1.00 *1.50*
a. Perf. 13½ 14.00 *13.00*
47 CD303 2p carmine .25 *.50*

Silver Wedding Issue
Common Design Types

1948, Dec. 1 Photo. *Perf. 14x14½*
48 CD304 1½p orange .30 .25
Perf. 11½x11
Engr.
49 CD305 20sh rose brown 92.50 90.00

UPU Issue
Common Design Types
Engr.; Name Typo. on 3p, 6p
Perf. 13½, 11x11½

1949, Oct. 10 Wmk. 4
50 CD306 2p rose carmine .50 .50
51 CD307 3p indigo 2.00 *3.00*
52 CD308 6p gray 1.50 1.50
53 CD309 1sh red orange 1.00 *1.50*
Nos. 50-53 (4) 5.00 *6.50*

POSTAGE DUE STAMPS

D1

1929 Typo. Wmk. 4 *Perf. 14*
J1 D1 1p black 3.00 *2.75*
On cover *150.00*
a. Wmk. 4a (error) 6,000.
J2 D1 2p black 6.00 *3.50*
On cover *180.00*
a. Bisected, used as 1d, on cover *850.00*
J3 D1 3p black 3.50 *27.50*
On cover *350.00*
a. Crown in watermark missing 600.00
b. Wmk. 4a (error) 375.00
J4 D1 4p black 12.00 *42.50*
On cover *400.00*
Nos. J1-J4 (4) 24.50 *76.25*

NORTH INGERMANLAND

'north 'iŋ-gər-mən-,land

LOCATION — In Northern Russia lying between the River Neva and Finland
CAPITAL — Kirjasalo

In 1920 the residents of this territory revolted from Russian rule and set up a provisional government. The new State existed only a short period as the revolution was quickly quelled by Soviet troops.

100 Pennia = 1 Markka

Arms — A1

Perf. 11½
1920, Mar. 21 Unwmk. Litho.
1 A1 5p green 2.75 *3.50*
2 A1 10p rose red 2.75 *3.50*
b. Horiz. pair, imperf. btwn. 50.00
3 A1 25p bister 2.75 *3.50*
b. Horiz. pair, imperf. btwn. 50.00
c. Vert. pair, imperf. btwn. 50.00
4 A1 50p dark blue 2.50 *3.50*
5 A1 1m car & black 30.00 *42.50*
6 A1 5m lilac & black 175.00 160.00
7 A1 10m brown & blk 200.00 200.00
Nos. 1-7 (7) 415.75 *416.50*
Set, never hinged 1,100.

Well centered examples sell for twice the values shown.

Imperf., Pairs
1a A1 5p 45.00
2a A1 10p 100.00
3a A1 25p 50.00
4a A1 50p 50.00
5a A1 1m 65.00
6a A1 5m 200.00
7a A1 10m 350.00

Arms — A2

Peasant — A3

Plowing — A4

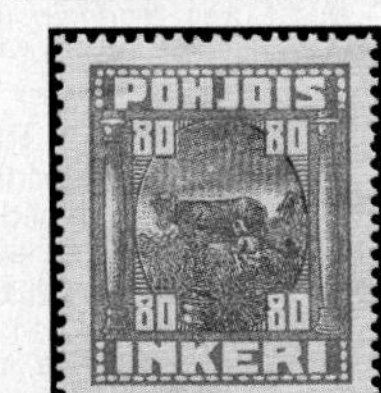

Milking — A5

Planting A6

Ruins of Church A7

Peasants Playing Zithers A8

1920, Aug. 2
8 A2 10p gray grn & ultra 3.50 *7.00*
9 A3 30p buff & gray grn 3.50 *7.00*
a. Horiz. pair, imperf. btwn. 100.00
10 A4 50p ultra & red brn 3.50 *7.00*
11 A5 80p claret & slate 3.50 *7.00*
12 A6 1m red & slate 20.00 *45.00*
13 A7 5m dk vio & dl rose 8.25 *18.00*
14 A8 10m brn & violet 8.25 *18.00*
a. Center inverted 1,000.
Nos. 8-14 (7) 50.50 *109.00*
Set, never hinged 120.00

Counterfeits abound.

Nos. 8-14 exist imperf. Value for set in pairs, $200.

NORTH WEST PACIFIC ISLANDS

'north 'west pə-'si-fik 'ī-ləndz

LOCATION — Group of islands in the West Pacific Ocean including a part of New Guinea and adjacent islands of the Bismarck Archipelago
GOVT. — Australian military government
AREA — 96,160 sq. mi.
POP. — 636,563

Stamps of Australia were overprinted for use in the former German possessions of Nauru and German New Guinea which Australian troops had captured. Following the League of Nations' decision which placed these territories under mandate to Australia, these provisional issues were discontinued. See German New Guinea, New Britain, Nauru and New Guinea.

12 Pence = 1 Shilling
20 Shillings = 1 Pound

Stamps of Australia Overprinted — a

Type a: "P" of "PACIFIC" above "S" of "ISLANDS."

There are two varieties of the letter "S" in the Type "a" overprint. These occur in three combinations: a, both normal "S"; b, 1st "S" with small head and long bottom stroke, 2nd "S" normal; c, both "S" with small head and long bottom stroke.

DESIGN A1
Die I — The inside frameline has a break at left, even with the top of the letters of the denomination.
Die II — The frameline does not show a break.
Die IV — As Die III, with a break in the top outside frameline above the "ST" of "AUSTRALIA." The upper right inside frameline has an incomplete corner.
Dies are only indicated when there are more than one for any denomination.

1915-16 Wmk. 8 *Perf. 12*

1 A1 2p gray 25.00 *75.00*
2 A1 2½p dark blue 5.00 *22.50*
3 A1 3p ol bis, die I 25.00 *65.00*
a. Die II 385.00 *600.00*
b. Pair, #3, 3a 825.00 *1,200.*
c. Pair, die I and die II 2,500.
d. 3p grnish olive (I) 210.00 300.00
e. As "c.," die II 120.00 150.00
4 A1 6p ultra 120.00 *130.00*
5 A1 9p violet 60.00 *72.50*
6 A1 1sh blue green 75.00 *77.50*
8 A1 5sh yel & gray ('16) 2,750. *3,850.*
9 A1 10sh pink & gray 170.00 *200.00*
Revenue cancel
10 A1 £1 ultra & brown *600.00* *775.00*
Nos. 1-6,8-10 (9) *3,830.* *5,268.*

For surcharge see No. 27.

Wmk. Wide Crown and Narrow A (9)
Perf. 12, 14

ONE PENNY
Die I — Normal die, having outside the oval band with "AUSTRALIA" a white line and a heavy colored line.
Die Ia — As die I with a small white spur below the right serif at foot of the "1" in left tablet.
Dies are only indicated when there are more than one for any denomination.

11 A4 ½p emerald 3.25 *10.00*
a. Double overprint
b. ½p bright green 3.25 11.00
12 A4 1p car (Die I) 7.75 7.25
a. 1p carmine rose (Die I) 120.00 *150.00*
b. 1p carmine (Die Ia) 110.00 *120.00*
13 A1 2p gray 20.00 *50.00*
14 A1 2½p dk bl ('16) *30,000.* *30,000.*
16 A4 4p orange 4.50 *17.50*
17 A4 5p org brown 2.75 *19.00*
18 A1 6p ultra 11.00 *13.00*
19 A1 9p violet 17.50 *24.00*
20 A1 1sh blue green 12.50 *27.50*
21 A1 2sh brown 110.00 *130.00*
22 A1 5sh yel & gray 82.50 *120.00*
Nos. 11-13,16-22 (10) *271.75* *418.25*

For surcharge see No. 28.

1915-16 Wmk. 10 *Perf. 12*

23 A1 2p gray, die I 9.00 *32.50*
24 A1 3p ol bis, die I 7.00 *15.00*
a. Die II 125.00 *190.00*
b. Pair, #24, 24a 250.00
25 A1 2sh brown ('16) 45.00 *65.00*
26 A1 £1 ultra & brn ('16) 400.00 *525.00*
Nos. 23-26 (4) *461.00* *637.50*

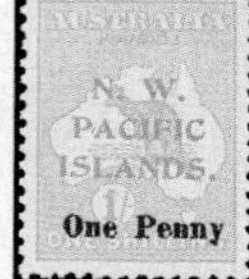

Nos. 6 and 17 Surcharged

1918, May 23 Wmk. 8 *Perf. 12*

27 A1 1p on 1sh bl grn 125.00 100.00

Wmk. 9 *Perf. 14*

28 A4 1p on 5p org brn 110.00 100.00

Stamps of Australia Overprinted — b

Type "b": "P" of "PACIFIC" above space between "I" and "S" of "ISLANDS."

1918-23 Wmk. 10 *Perf. 12*

29 A1 2p gray 8.50 *30.00*
a. Die II 13.50 *57.50*
30 A1 2½p dk bl ('19) 6.50 *19.00*
a. "1" of fraction omitted *13,000.* *16,500.*
31 A1 3p ol bis, die I 27.50 *30.00*
a. Die II 80.00 *100.00*
b. Pair, #31, 31a 500.00 *650.00*
32 A1 6p ultra ('19) 7.50 *16.50*
a. 6p chalky blue 50.00 *75.00*
33 A1 9p violet ('19) 11.50 *60.00*
34 A1 1sh bl grn ('18) 16.50 *37.50*
a. 1sh emerald green 7.00 *32.50*
35 A1 2sh brown 25.00 *42.50*
36 A1 5sh yel & gray ('19) 75.00 *80.00*
37 A1 10sh pink & gray ('19) 200.00 *275.00*
38 A1 £1 ultra & brn 4,500. *5,500.*
Nos. 29-37 (9) 378.00 *590.50*

1919 Wmk. 11 *Perf. 14*

39 A4 ½p emerald 5.00 *6.00*

1918-23 Wmk. 9

40 A4 ½p emerald 2.00 *4.00*
41 A4 1p car red, die 1 4.25 1.75
a. 1p carmine red, die Ia 125.00 90.00
42 A4 1p scar, die I, rough paper 1,000. 675.00
a. 1p rose red, die Ia, rough paper 1,000. 675.00
43 A4 1p violet ('22) 2.75 *7.25*
44 A4 2p orange 8.75 2.75
45 A4 2p red ('22) 10.50 2.25
46 A4 4p yel org 4.00 *17.50*
47 A4 4p violet ('22) 22.50 *45.00*
a. "Four Penc" in thinner letters 900.00 *1,550.*
48 A4 4p light ultra ('22) 12.50 *65.00*
a. "Four Penc" in thinner letters 1,000. *2,000.*
49 A4 5p brown 4.25 *13.50*
Nos. 40-41,43-49 (9) 71.50 *159.00*

North West Pacific Islands stamps were largely used in New Britain. Some were used in Nauru. They were intended to serve the Bismarck Archipelago and other places.

NORWAY

'nor-ˌwā

LOCATION — Western half of the Scandinavian Peninsula in northern Europe
GOVT. — Kingdom
AREA — 125,051 sq. mi.
POP. — 4,134,353 (1984)
CAPITAL — Oslo

120 Skilling = 1 Specie Daler
100 Ore = 1 Krone (1877)

Watermarks

Wmk. 159 — Lion

Wmk. 160 — Post Horn

Coat of Arms — A1

Wmk. 159

1855, Jan. 1 Typo. *Imperf.*

1 A1 4s blue *4,250.* 175.
On cover 375.
a. Double foot on right hind leg of lion 3,000.

Full margins = 1¾mm.

Values for multiples

Pair — 600.
Strip of 3 2,000.
Strip of 4 7,500.
Strip of 5 12,000.
Strip of 6 17,500.
Block of 4 22,500.

Only a few genuine unused examples of No. 1 exist. Stamps often offered have had pen-markings removed. The unused catalogue value is for a stamp without gum. Stamps with original gum sell for much more.

No. 1 was reprinted in 1914 and 1924 unwatermarked. Lowest value reprint, $75.

ROULETTED REPRINTS

The various reprints of the early issues were never valid for postage and are not known canceled.

1963: No. 1, value $25; Nos. 2-5, 15, value each $15.
1966: Nos. 57, 70a, 100, 152, J1, O1. Value each $12.
1969: Nos. 69, 92, 107, 114, 128, J12. Value each $12.

King Oscar I — A2

1856-57 Unwmk. *Perf. 13*

2 A2 2s yellow ('57) 800.00 160.00
On cover 375.00
a. 2s orange 800.00 200.00
On cover 600.00
3 A2 3s lilac ('57) 550.00 120.00
On cover 925.00
4 A2 4s blue 450.00 20.00
On cover 32.50
a. Imperf. *10,000.*
b. Half used as 2s on cover —
c. 4s blackish blue 600.00 35.00
On cover 100.00
d. 4s greenish blue 450.00 17.50
On cover 40.00
e. 4s pale greenish blue 1,500. 60.00
On cover 125.00
5 A2 8s dull lake 1,450. 65.00
On cover 300.00
a. 8s lilac red 1,900. 90.00
On cover 500.00

Nos. 2-5 were reprinted in 1914 and 1924, perf. 13½. Lowest valued reprint, $50 each.

A3

1863 Litho. *Perf. 14½x13½*

6 A3 2s yellow 1,250. 300.00
On cover 500.00
7 A3 3s gray lilac 850.00 600.00
On cover 925.00
8 A3 4s blue 275.00 18.00
On cover 25.00
a. 4s greenish blue 400.00 26.00
On cover 40.00
b. 4s dark blue 700.00 75.00
On cover —
c. Half used as 2s on cover —
9 A3 8s rose 1,200. 80.00
On cover 250.00
10 A3 24s brown 55.00 65.00
On cover 1,450.
On cover, single franking 1,900.
a. 24s dark brown 60.00 150.00
b. 24s reddish brown 72.50 180.00
Nos. 6-10 (5) 3,630. 1,063.

There are four types of the 2, 3, 8 and 24 skilling and eight types of the 4 skilling. See note on used value of No. 10 following No. 21.

No. 8 exists imperf. Value, unused $900.

A4

1867-68 Typo.

11 A4 1s black, coarse impression ('68) 100.00 70.00
On cover 140.00
a. 1s dark gray, fine impression ('68) 175.00 120.00
On cover —
12 A4 2s orange 35.00 30.00
On cover 175.00
a. 2s brt yellow orange 90.00 110.00
On cover —
b. Vert. pair, imperf between *1,750.*
13 A4 3s dl lil, coarse impression ('68) 600.00 160.00
On cover 250.00
a. 3s reddish violet, fine impression 1,200. 275.00
On cover 500.00
14 A4 4s blue, thin paper 175.00 15.00
On cover 25.00
a. 4s greenish blue, thick paper 250.00 12.00
On cover 25.00
15 A4 8s car rose 750.00 70.00
On cover 250.00
a. 8s rose, clear impression 1,900. 550.00
On cover 1,750.
Nos. 11-15 (5) 1,660. 345.00

See note on used value of #12 following #21.
For surcharges see Nos. 59-61, 149.

No. 15 was reprinted in 1914 and 1924, perf. 13½. Lowest valued reprint, $50.

Post Horn and Crown — A5

1872-75 Wmk. 160

16 A5 1s yel grn ('75) 13.50 *25.00*
On cover 35.00
a. 1s deep green ('73) 375.00 100.00
On cover 150.00
b. "E.EN" 25.00 *75.00*
c. 1s blue green, fine impression ('73) 350.00 105.00
On cover 175.00
d. Vert. pair, imperf between —
17 A5 2s ultra ('74) 20.00 *40.00*
On cover 50.00
a. 2s Prussian blue ('74) *17,000.* *5,000.*
b. 2s gray blue 15.00 *30.00*
On cover 350.00
18 A5 3s rose 85.00 35.00
On cover 17.50
a. 3s carmine 95.00 16.00
On cover 17.50
b. 3s carmine, *bluish* thin paper 450.00 50.00
On cover 42.50
19 A5 4s lilac, thin paper ('75) 19.00 *30.00*
On cover 50.00
a. 4s dark violet, *bluish*, thin paper 700.00 200.00
On cover 350.00
b. 4s brown violet, *bluish*, thin paper ('73) 700.00 250.00
On cover 350.00
c. 4s violet, *white*, thick paper ('73) 120.00 80.00
On cover 200.00
20 A5 6s org brn ('75) 675.00 90.00
On cover 425.00
21 A5 7s red brn ('73) 75.00 65.00
On cover 100.00
Nos. 16-21 (6) 887.50 285.00

In this issue there are 12 types each of Nos. 16, 17, 18 and 19; 12 types of No. 20 and 20 types of No. 21. The differences are in the words of value.

Nos. 10, 12, 16, 17, 19 and 21 were re-released in 1888 and used until March 31, 1908. Used values of these stamps are for examples canceled in this later period, usually with a two-ring cancellation. Examples bearing clear dated cancellations before 1888 are worth considerably more, as follows: No. 10 $165, No. 12 $70, No. 16 $60, No. 17 $100, No. 17b $450, No. 19 $90, No. 21 $100.

No. 21 exists imperf. Value, unused without gum $800.

No. 19 comes on thin and thick paper.

For surcharges see Nos. 62-63.

Post Horn — A6

King Oscar II — A7

"NORGE" in Sans-serif Capitals, Ring of Post Horn Shaded

1877-78

22 A6 1o drab 12.00 *14.00*
On cover 60.00
23 A6 3o orange 125.00 45.00
On cover 50.00
24 A6 5o ultra 40.00 18.00
On cover 42.50
a. 5o dull blue 800.00 125.00
On cover 175.00
b. 5o bright blue 300.00 70.00
On cover 120.00
c. No period after "Postfrim" 57.50 20.00
d. Retouched plate 200.00 25.00
On cover 60.00
e. As "c," retouched plate 225.00 27.50
f. 5o Prussian blue 120.00 24.00
On cover 72.50
g. As "f," retouched plate 150.00 18.00
On cover 75.00
25 A6 10o rose 120.00 4.50
On cover 9.00
b. Retouched plate 120.00 5.50
On cover 9.50
26 A6 12o lt green 150.00 30.00
On cover 90.00
27 A6 20o orange brn 450.00 20.00
On cover 90.00
28 A6 25o lilac 600.00 150.00
On cover 300.00
29 A6 35o bl grn ('78) 30.00 20.00
On cover 60.00
On cover, single franking 300.00
a. Retouched plate 250.00 110.00
b. 35o dark blue green, coarse impression 30.00 18.00
c. 35o pale blue green 2,400. 210.00
30 A6 50o maroon 65.00 12.50
On cover 110.00
On cover, single franking 200.00
31 A6 60o dk bl ('78) 70.00 12.50
On cover 110.00
On cover, single franking 425.00
a. 60o pale steel blue 175.00 60.00
32 A7 1k gray grn & grn ('78) 45.00 12.50
On cover 350.00
33 A7 1.50k ultra & bl ('78) 100.00 50.00
On cover 540.00
34 A7 2k rose & mar ('78) 55.00 25.00
On cover 540.00
Nos. 22-34 (13) 1,862. 414.00

In this issue there are 12 types each of Nos. 16, 17, 18 and 19; 12 types of No. 20 and 20 types of No. 21. The differences are in the words of value. There are 6 types each of Nos. 22, 26 and 28 to 34; 12 types each of Nos. 23, 24, 25 and 27. The differences are in the numerals.

A 2nd plate of the 5o ultramarine has 100 types, the 10o, 200 types.

The retouch on 5o, 10o and 35o shows as a thin white line between crown and post horn.

Philatelic covers exist, especially for Nos. 29-34. They sell for much less.

Post Horn — A8

"NORGE" in Sans-serif Capitals, Ring of Horn Unshaded

1882-93 Wmk. 160 *Perf. 14½x13½*

35 A8 1o blk brn ('86) 25.00 *30.00*
On cover 90.00
a. No period after "Post-frim" 60.00 60.00
b. Small "N" in "NORGE" 60.00 60.00
36 A8 1o gray ('93) 15.00 15.00
On cover 90.00
37 A8 2o brown ('90) 8.00 *10.00*
On cover 30.00
On cover, single franking 100.00
38 A8 3o yellow ('89) 100.00 12.50
On cover 35.00
a. 3o orange ('83) 300.00 25.00
On cover 55.00
b. Perf. 13½x12½ ('93) 12,000. 4,000.
39 A8 5o bl grn ('89) 95.00 4.00
On cover 15.00
a. 5o gray green ('86) 120.00 6.00
On cover 27.50
b. 5o emerald ('88) 300.00 12.50
On cover 35.00
c. 5o yellow green ('91) 100.00 4.50
On cover 15.00
d. Perf. 13½x12½ ('93) *5,000.* *1,200.*
On cover —
40 A8 10o rose 80.00 2.00
On cover 7.00
a. 10o rose red ('86) 80.00 2.00
On cover 7.50
b. 10o carmine ('91) 80.00 2.00
On cover 7.50
c. As "b," imperf. ('91) *3,000.* *2,750.*
41 A8 12o green ('84) 1,800. 500.00
On cover 3,000.
42 A8 12o org brn ('84) 50.00 35.00
On cover 1,450.
a. 12o bister brown ('83) 100.00 70.00
43 A8 20o brown 200.00 25.00
On cover 210.00
44 A8 20o blue ('86) 125.00 3.50
On cover 35.00
a. 20o ultramarine ('83) 500.00 25.00
On cover 175.00
b. No period after "Post-frim" ('85) 700.00 30.00
On cover 175.00
c. As "a," imperf. ('90) *2,500.* *3,000.*
d. 20o Prussian blue 350.00 30.00
45 A8 25o dull vio ('84) 25.00 30.00
On cover 350.00
On cover, single franking 600.00

Dies vary from 20 to 21mm high. Numerous types exist due to different production methods, including separate handmade dies for value figures. Many shades exist.

Philatelic covers bearing No. 45 sell for less.

No. 42 and 42a Surcharged in Black

1888 *Perf. 14½x13½*

46 A8 2o on 12o org brn 3.50 *4.50*
On cover 65.00
On cover, single franking 175.00
a. 2o on 12o bister brown 7.00 5.50

Post Horn — A10

"NORGE" in Roman instead of Sans-serif capitals

Perf. 14½x13½

1893-1908 Wmk. 160

Size: 16x20mm

47 A10 1o gray ('99) 4.50 *5.00*
On cover 7.00
48 A10 2o pale brn ('99) 3.25 *3.00*
On cover, single franking 27.50
49 A10 3o orange yel 2.75 .40
On cover 2.50
50 A10 5o dp green ('98) 7.00 .30
On cover 1.75
b. Booklet pane of 6 *800.00*
51 A10 10o carmine ('98) 16.00 .30
On cover 1.75
b. Booklet pane of 6 *1,100.*
d. 10o rose ('94) 350.00 4.00
e. Imperf *4,000.*
52 A10 15o brown ('08) 65.00 16.00
On cover 35.00
53 A10 20o dp ultra 30.00 .40
On cover 3.00
b. Booklet pane of 6
54 A10 25o red vio ('01) 85.00 5.00
On cover 24.00
55 A10 30o sl gray ('07) 65.00 5.50
On cover 30.00
56 A10 35o dk bl grn ('98) 18.00 12.50
On cover 47.50
57 A10 50o maroon ('94) 75.00 3.00
On cover 35.00
58 A10 60o dk blue ('00) 85.00 16.00
On cover 120.00
Nos. 47-58 (12) 456.50 67.40

Two dies exist of 3, 10 and 20o.

See Nos. 74-95, 162-166, 187-191, 193, 307-309, 325-326, 416-419, 606, 709-714, 960-968, 1141-1145. For overprints and surcharge see Nos. 99, 207-211, 220-224, 226, 329, 1282A-91. Post 1940 listings are in Scott Standard catalogue, Vol. 5.

Philatelic covers exist, especially for Nos. 54-58. They sell for less than values shown.

1893-98 Wmk. 160 *Perf. 13½x12½*

47a A10 1o gray ('95) 25.00 *45.00*
On cover 42.50
49a A10 3o orange ('95) 50.00 12.00
On cover 17.50
50a A10 5o green 35.00 1.75
On cover 9.00
51a A10 10o carmine ('96) 35.00 1.50
On cover 7.00
c. 10o rose ('95) 100.00 3.25
On cover 7.00
53a A10 20o dull ultra ('95) 110.00 7.50
On cover 30.00
54a A10 25o red violet ('98) 140.00 55.00
On cover 125.00
56a A10 35o dark blue green ('95) 100.00 30.00
On cover 140.00
57a A10 50o maroon ('97) 350.00 25.00
On cover 120.00
Nos. 47a-57a (8) 845.00 177.75

Two dies exist of each except 25 and 35o.

No. 12 Surcharged in Green, Blue or Carmine

1905 Unwmk. *Perf. 14½x13½*

59 A4 1k on 2s org (G) 57.50 50.00
On cover 150.00
60 A4 1.50k on 2s org (Bl) 100.00 85.00
On cover 225.00
61 A4 2k on 2s org (C) 110.00 100.00
On cover 175.00
Nos. 59-61 (3) 267.50 235.00

Used values are for stamps canceled after 1910. Stamps used before that sell for twice as much.

Philatelic covers sell for less.

Nos. 19 and 21 Surcharged in Black

1906-08 Wmk. 160 *Perf. 14½x13½*

62 A5 15o on 4s lilac ('08) 8.50 8.50
On cover 55.00
a. 15o on 4s violet ('08) 20.00 17.50
On cover 60.00
63 A5 30o on 7s red brn 16.00 12.00
On cover 95.00
a. Inverted overprint *10,000.*

Used values are for stamps canceled after 1914. Stamps used before that sell for twice as much.

Philatelic covers sell for less.

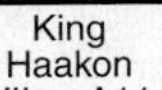

King Haakon VII — A11

Die A

Die B

Die C

Die A — Background of ruled lines. The coils at the sides are ornamented with fine cross-lines and small dots. Stamps 20¼mm high.

Die B — Background of ruled lines. The coils are ornamented with large white dots and dashes. Stamps 21¼mm high.

Die C — Solid background. The coils are without ornamental marks. Stamps 20¾mm high.

Die A

1907 Typo. *Perf. 14½x13½*

64 A11 1k yellow grn 70.00 40.00
On cover 425.00
65 A11 1.50k ultra 120.00 90.00
On cover 500.00
66 A11 2k rose 185.00 125.00
On cover 600.00
Nos. 64-66 (3) 375.00 255.00

Used values are for stamps postmarked after 1910. Stamps postmarked before that sell for twice as much. Stamps postmarked after 1914 sell for one-half the values listed. See note after No. 180.

1909-10 Die B

67 A11 1k green 225.00 130.00
On cover 600.00
68 A11 1.50k ultra 260.00 *375.00*
On cover 1,500.
69 A11 2k rose 200.00 8.00
On cover 300.00
Nos. 67-69 (3) 685.00 *513.00*

Used values are for stamps canceled after 1914. Stamps used before that sell for twice as much.

1911-18 Die C

70 A11 1k light green .90 .25
On cover 12.00
a. 1k dark green 90.00 3.50
On cover 50.00
71 A11 1.50k ultra 3.50 1.00
On cover 30.00
72 A11 2k rose ('15) 4.50 1.50
On cover 47.50
73 A11 5k dk violet ('18) 6.00 6.00
On cover 120.00
Nos. 70-73 (4) 14.90 8.75
Set, never hinged 40.00

See note following No. 180.

Philatelic covers sell for less.

Post Horn Type Redrawn

Original

Redrawn

In the redrawn stamps the white ring of the post horn is continuous instead of being broken by a spot of color below the crown. On the 3 and 30 ore the top of the figure "3" in the oval band is rounded instead of flattened.

1910-29 *Perf. 14½x13½*

74 A10 1o pale olive .40 *.75*
75 A10 2o pale brown .40 *.50*
76 A10 3o orange .40 *.50*
77 A10 5o green 4.50 .25
a. Booklet pane of 6 175.00
Complete booklet, 4 #77a 3,200.
78 A10 5o magenta ('22) .80 .25
79 A10 7o green ('29) .80 .25
80 A10 10o car rose 6.50 .25
a. Booklet pane of 6 100.00
Complete booklet, 2 #80a 500.00
81 A10 10o green ('22) 8.00 .50
82 A10 12o purple ('17) 1.00 1.50
83 A10 15o brown 8.00 .50
a. Booklet pane of 6 25.00
Complete booklet, 2 #83a 90.00
84 A10 15o indigo ('20) 9.00 .25
85 A10 20o deep ultra 9.00 .25
a. Booklet pane of 6 400.00
Complete booklet, 2 #85a *4,000.*
86 A10 20o ol grn ('21) 11.00 .30
87 A10 25o red lilac 55.00 .50
88 A10 25o car rose ('22) 9.00 .80
89 A10 30o slate gray 12.00 .50
90 A10 30o lt blue ('27) 10.00 8.00
91 A10 35o dk olive ('20) 15.00 .50
92 A10 40o ol grn ('17) 6.00 .50
93 A10 40o dp ultra ('22) 30.00 .30
94 A10 50o claret 25.00 .50
95 A10 60o deep blue 30.00 .50
Nos. 74-95 (22) 251.80 18.15
Set, never hinged 1,500.

Constitutional Assembly of 1814 — A12

1914, May 10 Engr. *Perf. 13½*

96 A12 5o green 1.25 .75
97 A12 10o car rose 3.00 .75
98 A12 20o deep blue 10.00 12.00
Nos. 96-98 (3) 14.25 13.50
Set, never hinged 80.00

Norway's Constitution of May 17, 1814.

No. 87 Surcharged

1922, Mar. 1 *Perf. 14½x13½*

99 A10 5o on 25o red lilac 1.00 *1.50*
Never hinged 2.00

Lion Rampant — A13

"NORGE" in Roman capitals, Line below "Ore"

1922-24 Typo. *Perf. 14½x13½*

100	A13	10o dp grn ('24)	10.00	.60
101	A13	20o dp vio	16.00	.25
102	A13	25o scarlet ('24)	27.50	.75
103	A13	45o blue ('24)	2.00	1.50
		Nos. 100-103 (4)	55.50	3.10
		Set, never hinged	250.00	

For surcharge see No. 129.

Polar Bear and Airplane — A14

1925, Apr. 1

104	A14	2o yellow brn	2.25	*3.50*
105	A14	3o orange	4.50	*6.00*
106	A14	5o magenta	12.00	*22.50*
107	A14	10o yellow grn	16.00	*35.00*
108	A14	15o dark blue	15.00	*32.50*
109	A14	20o plum	25.00	*40.00*
110	A14	25o scarlet	6.00	*8.00*
		Nos. 104-110 (7)	80.75	147.50
		Set, never hinged	180.00	

Issued to help finance Roald Amundsen's attempted flight to the North Pole.

A15

1925, Aug. 19

111	A15	10o yellow green	7.00	*15.00*
112	A15	15o indigo	5.00	*9.00*
113	A15	20o plum	7.00	*2.50*
114	A15	45o dark blue	6.00	*9.00*
		Nos. 111-114 (4)	25.00	35.50
		Set, never hinged	100.00	

Annexation of Spitsbergen (Svalbard).
For surcharge see No. 130.

A16

"NORGE" in Sans-serif Capitals, No Line below "Ore"

1926-34 Wmk. 160

Size: 16x19½mm

115	A16	10o yel grn	.70	.25
116	A16	14o dp org ('29)	2.25	3.00
117	A16	15o olive brown	.85	.25
118	A16	20o plum	30.00	.40
119	A16	20o scar ('27)	1.00	.25
a.		Booklet pane of 6	80.00	
		Complete booklet, 2 #119a	375.00	
120	A16	25o red	12.00	3.00
121	A16	25o org brn ('27)	1.25	.25
122	A16	30o dull bl ('28)	1.25	.25
123	A16	35o ol brn ('27)	75.00	.25
124	A16	35o red vio ('34)	2.00	.25
125	A16	40o dull blue	5.00	1.50
126	A16	40o slate ('27)	2.00	.25
127	A16	50o claret ('27)	2.00	.25
128	A16	60o Prus bl ('27)	2.00	.25
		Nos. 115-128 (14)	137.30	10.40
		Set, never hinged	675.00	

See Nos. 167-176, 192, 194-202A. For overprints and surcharges see Nos. 131, 212-219, 225, 227-234, 302-303. Post 1940 listings are in Scott Standard catalogue, Vol. 5.

Nos. 103 and 114 Surcharged

1927, June 13

129	A13	30o on 45o blue	13.00	3.00
130	A15	30o on 45o dk blue	7.00	10.00
		Set, never hinged	60.00	

No. 120 Surcharged

1928

131	A16	20o on 25o red	2.50	2.50
		Never hinged	15.00	

See Nos. 302-303 in Scott Standard catalogue, Vol. 5.

Henrik Ibsen — A17

1928, Mar. 20 Litho.

132	A17	10o yellow grn	10.00	5.00
133	A17	15o chnt brown	4.00	4.50
134	A17	20o carmine	3.50	.90
135	A17	30o dp ultra	7.00	5.00
		Nos. 132-135 (4)	24.50	15.40
		Set, never hinged	85.00	

Ibsen (1828-1906), dramatist.

Postage Due Stamps of 1889-1923 Overprinted

a

b

1929, Jan.

136	D1	(a)	1o gray	.90	*1.75*
137	D1	(a)	4o lilac rose	.60	.60
138	D1	(a)	10o green	2.50	*5.00*
139	D1	(b)	15o brown	3.50	*8.00*
140	D1	(b)	20o dull vio	1.25	1.00
141	D1	(b)	40o deep ultra	2.00	1.00
142	D1	(b)	50o maroon	10.00	10.00
143	D1	(a)	100o orange yel	4.25	*4.25*
144	D1	(b)	200o dk violet	5.50	5.00
			Nos. 136-144 (9)	30.50	36.60
			Set, never hinged	75.00	

Niels Henrik Abel — A18

1929, Apr. 6 Litho. *Perf. 14½x13½*

145	A18	10o green	3.50	1.00
146	A18	15o red brown	3.50	2.50
147	A18	20o rose red	1.25	.50
148	A18	30o deep ultra	3.25	3.00
		Nos. 145-148 (4)	11.50	7.00
		Set, never hinged	50.00	

Abel (1802-1829), mathematician.

No. 12 Surcharged

Perf. 14½x13½

1929, July 1 Unwmk.

149	A4	14o on 2s orange	3.50	*8.00*
		Never hinged	7.00	

Saint Olaf A19

Trondheim Cathedral A20

Death of Olaf in Battle of Stiklestad A21

Typo.; Litho. (15o)
Perf. 14½x13½

1930, Apr. 1 Wmk. 160

150	A19	10o yellow grn	14.00	.70
151	A20	15o brn & blk	1.75	1.00
152	A19	20o scarlet	1.25	.50

Engr.
Perf. 13½

153	A21	30o deep blue	4.50	5.00
		Nos. 150-153 (4)	21.50	7.20
		Set, never hinged	90.00	

King Olaf Haraldsson (995-1030), patron saint of Norway.

Björnson — A22

1932, Dec. 8 *Perf. 14½x13½*

154	A22	10o yellow grn	10.00	.75
155	A22	15o black brn	1.50	1.50
156	A22	20o rose red	1.00	.50
157	A22	30o ultra	3.50	*4.50*
		Nos. 154-157 (4)	16.00	7.25
		Set, never hinged	60.00	

Björnstjerne Björnson (1832-1910), novelist, poet and dramatist.

Holberg — A23

1934, Nov. 23

158	A23	10o yellow grn	4.50	.90
159	A23	15o brown	1.00	1.25
160	A23	20o rose red	18.00	.50
161	A23	30o ultra	4.00	4.50
		Nos. 158-161 (4)	27.50	7.15
		Set, never hinged	90.00	

Ludvig Holberg (1684-1754), Danish man of letters.

Types of 1893-1900, 1926-34 Second Redrawing

Perf. 13x13½

1937 Wmk. 160 Photo.

Size: 17x21mm

162	A10	1o olive	.70	2.00
163	A10	2o yellow brn	.70	1.75
164	A10	3o deep orange	1.75	*4.00*
165	A10	5o rose lilac	.55	.40
166	A10	7o brt green	.70	.40
167	A16	10o brt green	.45	.30
		Complete booklet, 2 panes of 6 #167	675.00	
168	A16	14o dp orange	3.00	6.00
169	A16	15o olive bis	1.75	.25
170	A16	20o scarlet	1.25	.25
		Complete booklet, 2 panes of 6 #170	1,250.	
		Complete booklet, panes of 6 ea of #165, 167, 170	500.00	
171	A16	25o dk org brn	6.00	.50
172	A16	30o ultra	3.50	.50
173	A16	35o brt vio	2.50	.25
174	A16	40o dk slate grn	3.50	.25
175	A16	50o deep claret	3.50	.75
176	A16	60o Prussian bl	2.50	.25
		Nos. 162-176 (15)	32.35	17.85
		Set, never hinged	125.00	

Nos. 162 to 166 have a solid background inside oval. Nos. 74, 75, 76, 78, 79 have background of vertical lines.

King Haakon VII — A24

1937-38

177	A24	1k dark green	.25	.25
178	A24	1.50k sapphire ('38)	1.00	2.00
179	A24	2k rose red ('38)	1.00	1.25
180	A24	5k dl vio ('38)	9.00	*10.00*
		Nos. 177-180 (4)	11.25	13.50
		Set, never hinged	25.00	

Nos. 64-66, 67-69, 70-73, 177-180 and B11-B14 were demonetized and banned on Sept. 30, 1940. Nos. 267, B19, B32-B34 and B38-B41 were demonetized on May 15, 1945. All of these stamps became valid again Sept. 1, 1981. Nos. 64-66, 67-69 and 70-73 rarely were used after 1981, and values represent stamps used in the earlier period. Values for Nos. B11-B14 used are for stamps used in the earlier period, and used examples in the later period are worth the same as mint stamps. Values for the other stamps used are for examples used in the later period, and stamps with dated cancellations prior to May 15, 1945 sell for more. False cancellations exist.

Reindeer — A25

Borgund Church — A26

Jolster in Sunnfiord A27

Perf. 13x13½, 13½x13

1938, Apr. 20 Wmk. 160

181	A25	15o olive brn	1.25	1.25
182	A26	20o copper red	4.00	.55
183	A27	30o brt ultra	4.00	2.50
		Nos. 181-183 (3)	9.25	4.30
		Set, never hinged	40.00	

1939, Jan. 16 Unwmk.

184	A25	15o olive brn	.50	.75
185	A26	20o copper red	.50	.25
186	A27	30o brt ultra	.50	.50
		Nos. 184-186 (3)	1.50	1.50
		Set, never hinged	3.00	

Types of 1937
Perf. 13x13½

1940-49 Unwmk. Photo.

Size: 17x21mm

187	A10	1o olive grn ('41)	.25	.25
188	A10	2o yel brn ('41)	.25	.25
189	A10	3o dp org ('41)	.25	.25
190	A10	5o rose lilac ('41)	.35	.25
191	A10	7o brt green ('41)	.40	.25
192	A16	10o brt green	.35	.25
		Complete booklet, 2 panes of 6 #192	50.00	
193	A10	12o brt vio	.80	2.00
194	A16	14o dp org ('41)	1.50	4.00
195	A16	15o olive bister	.50	.25
196	A16	20o red	.45	.25
		Complete booklet, 2 panes of 6 #196	60.00	
		Complete booklet, pane of 6 ea of #190, 192, 196	200.00	
		Complete booklet, pane of 10 ea of #190, 192, 196	125.00	
197	A16	25o dk org brn	1.25	.25
197A	A16	25o scarlet ('46)	.50	.25
		Complete booklet, pane of 10 ea of #190, 192, 197A	110.00	
		Complete booklet, pane of 10 ea of #192, 195, 197A	100.00	
198	A16	30o brt ultra ('41)	1.75	.40
198A	A16	30o gray ('49)	6.00	.25
199	A16	35o brt vio ('41)	1.75	.25
200	A16	40o dk sl grn ('41)	1.00	.25
200A	A16	40o dp ultra ('46)	3.75	.40
201	A16	50o dp claret ('41)	1.00	.25
201A	A16	55o dp org ('46)	15.00	.40

202 A16 60o Prus bl ('41) 1.25 .25
202A A16 80o dk org brn ('46) 14.00 .40
Nos. 187-202A (21) 52.35 11.35
Set, never hinged 150.00

Lion Rampant — A28

1940 Unwmk. Photo. *Perf. 13x13½*
203 A28 1k brt green 1.00 .25
204 A28 1½k deep blue 1.75 .30
205 A28 2k bright red 2.50 1.25
206 A28 5k dull purple 7.00 *7.00*
Nos. 203-206 (4) 12.25 8.80
Set, never hinged 40.00

For overprints see Nos. 235-238 in Scott Standard catalogue, Vol. 5.

SEMI-POSTAL STAMPS

North Cape Issue

North Cape — SP1

Perf. 13½x14
1930, June 28 Wmk. 160 Photo.
Size: 33¼x21½mm
B1 SP1 15o + 25o blk brn 2.00 *6.00*
B2 SP1 20o + 25o car 35.00 *80.00*
B3 SP1 30o + 25o ultra 90.00 *110.00*
Nos. B1-B3 (3) 127.00 *196.00*
Set, never hinged 275.00

The surtax was given to the Tourist Association. See No. B9-B10; Nos. B28-B30, B54-B56, B59-B61 in Scott Standard catalogue, Vol. 5.

Radium Hospital SP2

1931, Apr. 1 *Perf. 14½x13½*
B4 SP2 20o + 10o carmine 16.00 10.00
Never hinged 65.00

The surtax aided the Norwegian Radium Hospital.

Fridtjof Nansen — SP3

1935, Dec. 13 *Perf. 13½*
B5 SP3 10o + 10o green 3.50 *7.00*
B6 SP3 15o + 10o red brn 10.00 *15.00*
B7 SP3 20o + 10o crimson 5.00 4.50
B8 SP3 30o + 10o brt ultra 12.00 *16.00*
Nos. B5-B8 (4) 30.50 42.50
Set, never hinged 55.00

The surtax aided the International Nansen Office for Refugees.

North Cape Type of 1930

1938, June 20 *Perf. 13x13½*
Size: 27x21mm
B9 SP1 20o + 25o brn car 3.50 *9.00*
B10 SP1 30o + 25o dp ultra 13.50 32.50
Set, never hinged 27.50

Surtax given to the Tourist Assoc.

Queen Maud — SP4

Perf. 13x13½
1939, July 24 Photo. Unwmk.
B11 SP4 10o + 5o brt grn .40 10.00
B12 SP4 15o + 5o red brn .40 10.00
B13 SP4 20o + 5o scarlet .50 7.50
B14 SP4 30o + 5o brt ultra .40 12.00
Nos. B11-B14 (4) 1.70 39.50
Set, never hinged 4.00

The surtax was used for charities.

Fridtjof Nansen — SP5

1940, Oct. 21
B15 SP5 10o + 10o dk grn 3.50 4.50
B16 SP5 15o + 10o henna brn 4.00 6.00
B17 SP5 20o + 10o dark red .75 1.50
B18 SP5 30o + 10o ultra 2.50 4.50
Nos. B15-B18 (4) 10.75 16.50
Set, never hinged 16.00

The surtax was used for war relief work.

AIR POST STAMPS

Airplane over Akershus Castle — AP1

Perf. 13½x14½
1927-34 Typo. Wmk. 160
C1 AP1 45o lt bl, strong frame line ('34) 4.50 *5.00*
Never hinged 20.00
a. Faint or broken frame line 25.00 9.00
Never hinged 150.00

Airplane over Akershus Castle — AP2

1937, Aug. 18 Photo. *Perf. 13*
C2 AP2 45o Prussian blue .90 .70
Never hinged 4.50

POSTAGE DUE STAMPS

Numeral of Value — D1

Inscribed "at betale"

Perf. 14½x13½
1889-1914 Typo. Wmk. 160
J1 D1 1o olive green ('15) 1.25 *2.50*
Never hinged 2.40
a. 1o brown olive ('20) 7.00 18.00
Never hinged 24.00
b. 1o brownish gray ('89) 3.50 3.50
Never hinged 16.00
c. 1o gray ('93) 3.50 3.50
Never hinged 16.00
J2 D1 4o magenta ('11) 2.00 2.00
Never hinged 12.00
a. 4o brown lilac ('08) 15.00 6.00
Never hinged 75.00
b. 4o bluish violet ('93) 47.50 11.00
Never hinged 210.00
J3 D1 10o carmine rose ('99) 5.00 .90
Never hinged 15.00
a. 10o rose red ('89) 90.00 25.00
Never hinged 425.00
J4 D1 15o brown ('14) 4.50 1.75
Never hinged 13.00
J5 D1 20o ultra ('99) 3.50 .65
Never hinged 15.00
a. Perf. 13½x12½ ('95) 250.00 115.00
Never hinged 1,300.
J6 D1 50o maroon ('89) 6.50 4.00
Never hinged 30.00
Nos. J1-J6 (6) 22.75 11.80

See #J7-J12. For overprint see #136-144.

1922-23 Inscribed "a betale"
J7 D1 4o lilac rose 11.00 18.00
Never hinged 35.00
J8 D1 10o green 5.00 3.50
Never hinged 22.50
J9 D1 20o dull violet 8.00 8.00
Never hinged 30.00
J10 D1 40o deep ultra 12.00 1.50
Never hinged 40.00
J11 D1 100o orange yel 35.00 17.00
Never hinged 150.00
J12 D1 200o dark violet 75.00 30.00
Never hinged 160.00
Nos. J7-J12 (6) 146.00 78.00

OFFICIAL STAMPS

Coat of Arms — O1

Perf. 14½x13½
1926 Typo. Wmk. 160
O1 O1 5o rose lilac .75 *1.50*
O2 O1 10o yellow green .50 .50
O3 O1 15o indigo 2.00 *4.50*
O4 O1 20o plum .50 .25
O5 O1 30o slate 4.50 *10.00*
O6 O1 40o deep blue 2.50 *2.00*
O7 O1 60o Prussian blue 5.00 *10.00*
Nos. O1-O7 (7) 15.75 *28.75*
Set, never hinged 40.00

Official Stamp of 1926 Surcharged

1929, July 1
O8 O1 2o on 5o magenta .60 *1.75*
Never hinged 2.00

Coat of Arms — O2

Perf. 14½x13½
1933-34 Litho. Wmk. 160
Size: 35x19¼mm
O9 O2 2o ocher .60 *1.75*
O10 O2 5o rose lilac 4.50 *7.00*
O11 O2 7o orange 4.50 *10.00*
O12 O2 10o green 30.00 1.25
O13 O2 15o olive .60 *1.25*
O14 O2 20o vermilion 30.00 .60
O15 O2 25o yellow brn .60 *1.00*
O16 O2 30o ultra .90 *1.25*
O18 O2 40o slate 30.00 1.25
O19 O2 60o blue 18.00 2.00
O20 O2 70o olive brn 1.50 *4.00*
O21 O2 100o violet 2.00 3.50
Nos. O9-O16,O18-O21 (12) 123.20 34.85
Same, never hinged 600.00

On the lithographed stamps, the lion's left leg is shaded.

Typo.
Size: 34x18¾mm
O10a O2 5o rose lilac 1.50 4.00
O11a O2 7o orange 8.00 *22.50*
O12a O2 10o green .70 .60
O13a O2 15o olive 6.00 *20.00*
O14a O2 20o vermilion .70 .50
O17 O2 35o red violet ('34) .90 .90
O18a O2 40o slate 1.00 .90
O19a O2 60o blue 1.25 1.25
Nos. O10a-O14a,O17,O18a-O19a (8) 20.05 *50.65*
Same, never hinged 60.00

Coat of Arms — O3

1937-38 Photo. *Perf. 13½x13*
O22 O3 5o rose lilac ('38) .75 1.50
O23 O3 7o dp orange .75 4.00
O24 O3 10o brt green .40 .50
O25 O3 15o olive bister .55 1.00
O26 O3 20o carmine ('38) 2.50 5.00
O27 O3 25o red brown ('38) 1.00 1.00
O28 O3 30o ultra 1.00 1.00
O29 O3 35o red vio ('38) 1.75 .60
O30 O3 40o Prus grn ('38) 1.00 .60
O31 O3 60o Prus bl ('38) 1.25 .60
O32 O3 100o dk vio ('38) 2.00 1.50
Nos. O22-O32 (11) 12.95 *17.30*
Set, never hinged 35.00

See Nos. O33-O43, O55-O56. For surcharge see No. O57. Post 1940 listings are in Scott Standard catalogue, Vol. 5.

1939-47 Unwmk.
O33 O3 5o dp red lil ('41) .25 .25
O34 O3 7o dp orange ('41) .30 *1.50*
O35 O3 10o brt green ('41) .25 .25
O36 O3 15o olive ('45) .25 .25
O37 O3 20o carmine .25 .25
O38 O3 25o red brown 3.00 *20.00*
O38A O3 25o scarlet ('46) .25 .25
O39 O3 30o ultra 2.75 2.75
O39A O3 30o dk gray ('47) .65 .55
O40 O3 35o brt lilac ('41) .60 .50
O41 O3 40o grnsh blk ('41) .55 .25
O41A O3 40o dp ultra ('46) 3.00 .25
O42 O3 60o Prus blue ('41) .65 .50
O43 O3 100o dk violet ('41) 1.00 .25
Nos. O33-O43 (14) 13.75 *27.80*
Set, never hinged 40.00

NOSSI-BE

ˌno-sē-ˈbā

LOCATION — Island in the Indian Ocean, off the northwest coast of Madagascar
GOVT. — French Protectorate
AREA — 130 sq. mi.
POP. — 9,000 (approx. 1900)
CAPITAL — Hellville

In 1896 the island was placed under the authority of the Governor-General of Madagascar and postage stamps of Madagascar were placed in use.

100 Centimes = 1 Franc

Covers
Values are for commercial covers paying correct rates. Philatelic covers sell for less.

Stamps of French Colonies Surcharged in Blue

a

b

c

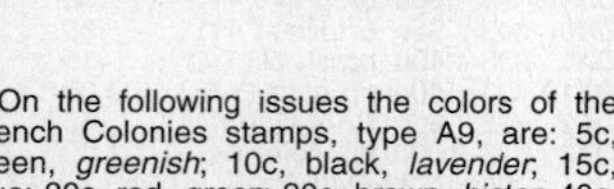

On the following issues the colors of the French Colonies stamps, type A9, are: 5c, green, *greenish*; 10c, black, *lavender*; 15c, blue; 20c, red, *green*; 30c, brown, *bister*; 40c, vermilion, *straw*; 75c, carmine, *rose*; 1fr, bronze green, *straw*.

1889 Unwmk. *Imperf.*

1 A8(a) 25 on 40c red, *straw* 2,600. 1,100.
On cover 2,400.
a. Double surcharge 3,400.
b. Inverted surcharge 3,750. 1,600.
2 A8(b) 25c on 40c red, *straw* 3,100. 2,000.
On cover 4,100.
a. Double surcharge 5,500. 2,800.
b. Inverted surcharge 5,500. 2,800.
c. Pair, "a" and "c"

Perf. 14x13½

3 A9(b) 5c on 10c 3,750. 1,450.
On cover 3,250.
a. Double surcharge 3,500.
b. Inverted surcharge 5,000. 3,100.
4 A9(b) 5c on 20c 4,000. 1,600.
On cover 3,250.
a. Inverted surcharge 5,000. 3,100.
5 A9(c) 5c on 10c 3,100. 1,100.
On cover 2,400.
a. Inverted surcharge 5,600.
6 A9(c) 5c on 20c 3,600. 2,400.
On cover
7 A9(a) 15 on 20c 2,800. 1,100.
On cover 2,400.
a. Double surcharge 2,400.
b. Inverted surcharge 4,250. 1,750.
c. 15 on 30c (error) *32,000.* *28,000.*
8 A9(a) 25 on 30c 2,800. 950.
On cover *2,500.*
a. Double surcharge 2,200.
b. Inverted surcharge 3,600. 1,600.
9 A9(a) 25 on 40c 2,400. 1,100.
On cover *2,500.*
a. Double surcharge 2,000.
b. Inverted surcharge 3,600. 1,600.

d

e

f

1890 Black Surcharge

10 A9(d) 25c on 20c 425.00 300.00
On cover 1,200.
11 A9(e) 0.25 on 20c 425.00 300.00
On cover 1,200.
a. In vert. pair with #10 925.00 675.00
12 A9(f) 25 on 20c 1,000. 675.00
On cover 2,100.
a. In vert. pair with #10 1,800. 1,350.
b. In vert. pair with #11 1,800. 1,350.
c. Vert. strip of 3, #10-12 4,200. 4,200.
13 A9(d) 25c on 75c 425.00 300.00
On cover 1,200.
14 A9(e) 0.25 on 75c 425.00 300.00
On cover 1,200.
a. In vert. pair with #13 925.00 675.00
15 A9(f) 25 on 75c 1,000. 675.00
On cover —
a. In vert. pair with #13 1,800. 1,350.
b. In vert. pair with #14 1,800. 1,350.
c. Vert. strip of 3, #13-15 4,200. 4,200.
16 A9(d) 25c on 1fr 425.00 300.00
On cover 1,200.
17 A9(e) 0.25 on 1fr 425.00 300.00
On cover 1,200.
a. In vert. pair with #16 925.00 675.00
18 A9(f) 25 on 1fr 1,000. 675.00
On cover —
a. In vert. pair with #16 1,800. 1,350.
b. In vert. pair with #17 1,800. 1,350.
c. Vert. strip of 3, #16-18 4,200. 4,200.

Nos. 10-18 were overprinted in forms of 25 (5x5), with five rows of types d, e, f, d, e, making possible the various setenant multiples listed above.

The 25c on 20c with surcharge composed of "25 c." as in "d," "N S B" as in "e," and frame as in "f" is an essay.

Surcharged or Overprinted in Black, Carmine, Vermilion or Blue

j

k

m

1893

23 A9(j) 25 on 20c (Bk) 52.50 45.00
No gum 40.00
On cover *450.00*
24 A9(j) 50 on 10c (Bk) 67.50 47.50
No gum 52.50
On cover *550.00*
a. Inverted surcharge 400.00 260.00
No gum 325.00
25 A9(j) 75 on 15c (Bk) 300.00 240.00
No gum 240.00
On cover *550.00*
26 A9(j) 1fr on 5c (Bk) 150.00 110.00
No gum 110.00
On cover *625.00*
a. Inverted surcharge 400.00 275.00
No gum 325.00
27 A9(k) 10c (C) 28.00 24.00
Never hinged 45.00
On cover *450.00*
a. Inverted overprint 130.00 120.00
28 A9(k) 10c (V) 27.50 24.00
Never hinged 45.00
On cover *450.00*
29 A9(k) 15c (Bk) 32.50 32.50
Never hinged 55.00
On cover *450.00*
a. Inverted overprint 140.00 130.00
b. As "a," in pair with normal stamp 225.00 225.00
30 A9(k) 20c (Bk) 500.00 75.00
On cover *600.00*
31 A9(m) 20c (Bl) 130.00 67.50
Never hinged 240.00
On cover *400.00*
a. Inverted overprint 190.00 180.00
b. As "a," in pair with normal stamp 450.00 450.00

Counterfeits exist of surcharges and overprints of Nos. 1-31.

Navigation and Commerce — A14

1894 Typo. *Perf. 14x13½*
Name of Colony in Blue or Carmine

32 A14 1c blk, *lil bl* 1.60 1.60
Never hinged 2.75
On cover 150.00
a. No accent on "E" of "NOSSI BE" 3.25 3.25
Never hinged 5.50
33 A14 2c brn, *buff* 2.00 2.00
Never hinged 3.25
On cover 150.00
a. No accent on "E" of "NOSSI BE" 4.00 4.00
Never hinged 7.25
34 A14 4c claret, *lav* 2.75 2.00
Never hinged 4.50
On cover 150.00
a. No accent on "E" of "NOSSI BE" 4.75 4.75
Never hinged 8.75
35 A14 5c grn, *greenish* 4.00 3.25
Never hinged 7.25
On cover 100.00
a. No accent on "E" of "NOSSI BE" 7.25 6.50
Never hinged 13.50
36 A14 10c blk, *lav* 9.50 6.50
Never hinged 17.50
On cover 100.00
a. No accent on "E" of "NOSSI BE" 20.00 16.00
Never hinged 32.50
37 A14 15c blue, quadrille paper 13.50 6.50
Never hinged 24.00
On cover 125.00
a. No accent on "E" of "NOSSI BE" 27.50 20.00
Never hinged 55.00
38 A14 20c red, *grn* 9.50 6.50
Never hinged 17.50
On cover 125.00
a. No accent on "E" of "NOSSI BE" 20.00 16.00
Never hinged 32.50
39 A14 25c blk, *rose* 16.00 9.50
Never hinged 32.50
On cover 125.00
a. No accent on "E" of "NOSSI BE" 30.00 24.00
Never hinged 60.00
40 A14 30c brn, *bister* 16.00 14.50
Never hinged 32.50
On cover 125.00
a. No accent on "E" of "NOSSI BE" 30.00 27.50
Never hinged 60.00
41 A14 40c red, *straw* 22.50 16.00
Never hinged 45.00
On cover *300.00*
a. No accent on "E" of "NOSSI BE" 40.00 32.50
Never hinged 80.00
42 A14 50c carmine, *rose* 22.50 16.00
Never hinged 45.00
On cover *300.00*
a. No accent on "E" of "NOSSI BE" 40.00 32.50
Never hinged 80.00
43 A14 75c dp vio, *orange* 37.50 37.50
Never hinged 75.00
On cover *450.00*
a. No accent on "E" of "NOSSI BE" 67.50 67.50
Never hinged 140.00
44 A14 1fr brnz grn, *straw* 27.50 27.50
Never hinged 55.00
On cover *450.00*
a. No accent on "E" of "NOSSI BE" 55.00 55.00
Never hinged 125.00
Nos. 32-44 (13) 184.85 149.35

Perf. 13½x14 stamps are counterfeits.

POSTAGE DUE STAMPS

Stamps of French Colonies Surcharged in Black

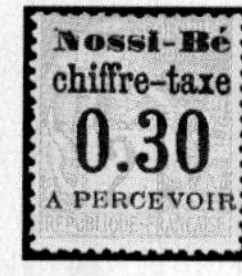
n

o

1891 Unwmk. *Perf. 14x13½*

J1 A9(n) 20 on 1c blk, *lil bl* 425.00 300.00
On cover *1,500.*
a. Inverted surcharge 925.00 675.00
b. Surcharged vertically 1,200. *1,400.*
c. Surcharge on back 1,050. 1,050.
J2 A9(n) 30 on 2c brn, *buff* 400.00 300.00
On cover *1,500.*
a. Inverted surcharge 875.00 675.00
b. Surcharge on back 1,000. *1,200.*
J3 A9(n) 50 on 30c brn, *bister* 120.00 105.00
On cover *900.00*
a. Inverted surcharge 925.00 675.00
b. Surcharge on back 1,050. *1,300.*
J4 A9(o) 35 on 4c cl, *lav* 450.00 325.00
On cover *1,500.*
a. Inverted surcharge 925.00 675.00
b. Surcharge on back 1,100. *1,300.*
c. Pair, one without surcharge
J5 A9(o) 35 on 20c red, *green* 450.00 325.00
On cover *1,500.*
a. Inverted surcharge 925.00 675.00
b. Surcharge on back 1,050. *1,200.*
J6 A9(o) 1fr on 35c vio, *orange* 325.00 240.00
On cover *1,500.*
a. Inverted surcharge 925.00 625.00
b. Surcharge on back 1,000. 1,100.

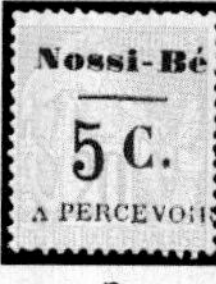
p

q

r

1891

J7 A9(p) 5c on 20c 225.00 225.00
On cover *1,250.*
J8 A9(q) 5c on 20c 275.00 275.00
On cover *1,250.*
b. In se-tenant pair with #J7 725.00
J9 A9(r) 0.10c on 5c 27.50 24.00
Never hinged 52.50
On cover *850.00*
J10 A9(p) 10c on 15c 225.00 225.00
On cover *1,250.*
J11 A9(q) 10c on 15c 275.00 275.00
On cover *1,500.*
b. In se-tenant pair with #J10 725.00
J12 A9(p) 15c on 10c 200.00 200.00
On cover *1,500.*
J13 A9(q) 15c on 10c 210.00 210.00
On cover *1,500.*
b. In se-tenant pair with #J12 725.00
J14 A9(r) 0.15c on 20c 32.50 32.50
Never hinged 65.00
On cover *1,250.*
a. 25c on 20c (error) *40,000.* *35,000.*
J15 A9(p) 25c on 5c 180.00 180.00
On cover *1,500.*
J16 A9(q) 25c on 5c 200.00 200.00
On cover *1,500.*
b. In se-tenant pair with #J15 700.00
J17 A9(r) 0.25c on 75c 650.00 575.00
On cover *3,000.*

Inverted Surcharge

J7a	A9(p)	5c on 20c	425.00	425.00
J8a	A9(q)	5c on 20c	425.00	425.00
J10a	A9(p)	10c on 15c	425.00	425.00
J11a	A9(q)	10c on 15c	425.00	425.00
J12a	A9(p)	15c on 10c	425.00	425.00
J13a	A9(q)	15c on 10c	425.00	425.00
J15a	A9(p)	25c on 5c	425.00	425.00
J16a	A9(q)	25c on 5c	425.00	425.00
J17a	A9(r)	0.25c on 75c	1,800.	1,500.

Stamps of Nossi-Be were superseded by those of Madagascar.

Counterfeits exist of surcharges on #J1-J17.

NYASALAND PROTECTORATE

nī-ˈa-sə-ˌland prə-ˈtek-t̯ə-ˌrət

LOCATION — In southern Africa, bordering on Lake Nyasa
GOVT. — British Protectorate
AREA — 49,000 sq. mi.
POP. — 2,950,000 (est. 1962)
CAPITAL — Zomba

For previous issues, see British Central Africa.

12 Pence = 1 Shilling
20 Shillings = 1 Pound

Catalogue values for unused stamps in this country are for Never Hinged items, beginning with Scott 68 in the regular postage section and Scott J1 in the postage due section.

A1

King Edward VII — A2

Wmk. Crown and C A (2)
1908, July 22 Typo. *Perf. 14*
Chalky Paper

1 A1 1sh black, *green* 6.00 *19.00*

Wmk. Multiple Crown and C A (3)
Ordinary Paper

2 A1 ½p green 2.00 2.25
3 A1 1p carmine 9.25 1.10

Chalky Paper

4 A1 3p violet, *yel* 1.75 *4.75*
5 A1 4p scar & blk, *yel* 2.25 *1.75*
6 A1 6p red vio & vio 6.25 *12.50*
7 A2 2sh6p car & blk, *bl* 75.00 *110.00*
8 A2 4sh black & car 110.00 *180.00*
9 A2 10sh red & grn, *grn* 200.00 *325.00*
10 A2 £1 blk & vio, *red* 650.00 *750.00*
11 A2 £10 ultra & lilac 12,000. *8,000.*
Nos. 1-10 (10) 1,063. *1,406.*

A3

King George V — A4

1913-19 Ordinary Paper

12 A3 ½p green 1.75 *2.25*
13 A3 1p scarlet 7.75 1.00
a. 1p carmine 4.00 2.00
14 A3 2p gray 10.00 1.00
15 A3 2½p ultra 2.50 *7.50*

Chalky Paper

16 A3 3p violet, *yel* 6.00 4.50
17 A3 4p scar & blk, *yel* 2.00 *2.50*
18 A3 6p red vio & dull vio 5.00 *10.00*
19 A3 1sh black, *green* 2.00 *9.00*
a. 1sh black, *emerald* 4.50 *7.00*
b. 1sh blk, *bl grn*, olive back 6.00 1.60
20 A4 2sh6p red & blk, *bl* ('18) 12.50 *29.00*
21 A4 4sh blk & red ('18) 50.00 *90.00*
22 A4 10sh red & grn, *grn* 130.00 *160.00*
23 A4 £1 blk & vio, *red* ('18) 200.00 170.00
24 A4 £10 brt ultra & slate vio ('19) *4,000.* *2,000.*
Revenue cancel 275.00
a. £10 pale ultra & dull vio ('14) 8,000.
Revenue cancel 300.00
Nos. 12-23 (12) 429.50 *486.75*

Stamps of Nyasaland Protectorate overprinted "N. F." are listed under German East Africa.

1921-30 Wmk. 4 Ordinary Paper

25 A3 ½p green 3.25 .50
26 A3 1p rose red 3.75 .50
27 A3 1½p orange 4.00 *17.50*
28 A3 2p gray 3.50 .50

Chalky Paper

29 A3 3p violet, *yel* 20.00 3.25
30 A3 4p scar & blk, *yel* 6.25 *11.00*
31 A3 6p red vio & dl vio 6.25 3.25
32 A3 1sh blk, *grn* ('30) 14.50 4.50
33 A4 2sh ultra & dl vio, *bl* 20.00 15.00
34 A4 2sh6p red & blk, *bl* ('24) 27.50 19.00
35 A4 4sh black & car 26.00 *45.00*
36 A4 5sh red & grn, *yel* ('29) 55.00 85.00
37 A4 10sh red & grn, *emer* 120.00 *120.00*
Nos. 25-37 (13) 310.00 *325.00*

George V and Leopard A5

1934-35 Engr. *Perf. 12½*

38 A5 ½p green .75 *1.25*
39 A5 1p dark brown .75 .75
40 A5 1½p rose .75 *3.50*
41 A5 2p gray 1.00 *1.25*
42 A5 3p dark blue 3.00 2.00
43 A5 4p rose lilac ('35) 7.25 4.00
44 A5 6p dk violet 3.50 1.00
45 A5 9p olive bis ('35) 8.50 *16.00*
46 A5 1sh orange & blk 24.00 *15.00*
Nos. 38-46 (9) 49.50 *44.75*

Common Design Types pictured following the introduction.

Silver Jubilee Issue
Common Design Type
1935, May 6 *Perf. 11x12*

47 CD301 1p gray blk & ultra 1.00 *2.50*
48 CD301 2p indigo & grn 2.75 2.75
49 CD301 3p ultra & brn 8.50 *20.00*
50 CD301 1sh brown vio & ind 27.50 *55.00*
Nos. 47-50 (4) 39.75 *80.25*
Set, never hinged 60.00

Coronation Issue
Common Design Type
1937, May 12 *Perf. 11x11½*

51 CD302 ½p deep green .25 .30
52 CD302 1p dark brown .40 .40
53 CD302 2p gray black .40 .60
Nos. 51-53 (3) 1.05 1.30
Set, never hinged 1.75

A6

King George VI — A7

1938-44 Engr. *Perf. 12½*

54 A6 ½p green .25 *2.00*
54A A6 ½p dk brown ('42) .25 *2.25*
55 A6 1p dark brown 2.50 .35
55A A6 1p green ('42) .25 *1.75*
56 A6 1½p dark carmine 5.00 *6.00*
56A A6 1½p gray ('42) .25 *5.75*
b. "A" of CA in watermark missing 1,600.
57 A6 2p gray 5.00 1.25
b. "A" of CA in watermark missing *1,300.*
57A A6 2p dark car ('42) .25 *2.00*
c. "A" of CA in watermark missing 1,600.
58 A6 3p blue .60 1.00
59 A6 4p rose lilac 1.75 2.00
60 A6 6p dark violet 2.00 2.00
61 A6 9p olive bister 2.00 *5.25*
62 A6 1sh orange & blk 2.10 *3.25*

Typo.
Perf. 14
Chalky Paper

63 A7 2sh ultra & dl vio, *bl* 7.00 *17.50*
64 A7 2sh6p red & blk, *bl* 9.00 *24.00*
65 A7 5sh red & grn, *yel* 35.00 30.00
a. 5sh dk red & dp grn, *yel* ('44) 55.00 *140.00*
66 A7 10sh red & grn, *grn* 35.00 *70.00*

Wmk. 3

67 A7 £1 blk & vio, *red* 30.00 *52.50*
Nos. 54-67 (18) 138.20 *228.85*
Set, never hinged 220.00

Catalogue values for unused stamps in this section, from this point to the end of the section, are for Never Hinged items.

Canoe on Lake Nyasa — A8

Soldier of King's African Rifles — A9

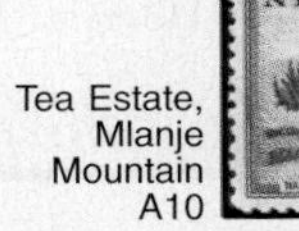
Tea Estate, Mlanje Mountain A10

Map and Coat of Arms — A11

Fishing Village, Lake Nyasa — A12

Tobacco Estate — A13

Arms of Nyasaland and George VI A14

1945, Sept. 1 Engr. *Perf. 12*

68 A8 ½p brn vio & blk .50 .25
69 A9 1p dp green & blk .25 .75
70 A10 1½p gray grn & blk .35 .45
71 A11 2p scarlet & blk 1.50 .90
72 A12 3p blue & blk .45 .30
73 A13 4p rose vio & blk 2.50 .80
74 A10 6p violet & blk 3.00 .90
75 A8 9p ol grn & blk 4.50 *3.00*
76 A11 1sh myr grn & ind 3.75 .55
77 A12 2sh dl red brn & grn 9.50 5.50
78 A13 2sh6p ultra & green 9.50 7.00
79 A14 5sh ultra & lt vio 7.00 *6.50*
80 A11 10sh green & lake 25.00 18.00
81 A14 20sh black & scar 29.00 *35.00*
Nos. 68-81 (14) 96.80 79.90

Peace Issue
Common Design Type
Perf. 13½x14
1946, Dec. 16 Wmk. 4

82 CD303 1p bright green .25 .25
83 CD303 2p red orange .25 .25

A15

1947, Oct. 20 *Perf. 12*

84 A15 1p emerald & org brn .65 .50

Silver Wedding Issue
Common Design Types
1948, Dec. 15 Photo. *Perf. 14x14½*

85 CD304 1p dark green .25 .25

Engr.; Name Typo.
Perf. 11½x11

86 CD305 10sh purple 18.00 *30.00*

UPU Issue
Common Design Types
Engr.; Name Typo. on 3p, 6p
Perf. 13½, 11x11½
1949, Nov. 21 Wmk. 4

87 CD306 1p blue green .35 .35
88 CD307 3p Prus blue 2.50 2.50
89 CD308 6p rose violet .85 .85
90 CD309 1sh violet blue .35 .35
Nos. 87-90 (4) 4.05 4.05

Arms of British Central Africa and Nyasaland Protectorate — A16

1951, May 15 Engr. *Perf. 11x12*
Arms in Black

91 A16 2p rose 1.25 1.25
92 A16 3p blue 1.25 1.25
93 A16 6p purple 1.50 *2.25*
94 A16 5sh deep blue 5.50 *8.00*
Nos. 91-94 (4) 9.50 *12.75*

60th anniv. of the Protectorate, originally British Central Africa.

POSTAGE DUE STAMPS

Catalogue values for unused stamps in this section are for Never Hinged items.

D1

Perf. 14
1950, July 1 Wmk. 4 Typo.

J1 D1 1p rose red 4.00 *32.50*
On cover *300.00*
J2 D1 2p ultramarine 18.00 *32.50*
On cover *300.00*
J3 D1 3p green 15.00 *8.00*
On cover *300.00*
J4 D1 4p claret 29.50 *60.00*
On cover *500.00*
J5 D1 6p ocher 40.00 *160.00*
On cover *750.00*
Nos. J1-J5 (5) 106.50 *293.00*

Covers: Cover values are for properly franked commercial items. Philatelic usages sell for less.

NYASSA

nī-ˈa-sə

LOCATION — In the northern part of Mozambique in southeast Africa
GOVT. — Part of Portuguese East Africa Colony
AREA — 73,292 sq. mi.
POP. — 3,000,000 (estimated)
CAPITAL — Porto Amelia

The district formerly administered by the Nyassa Company is now a part of Mozambique. Postage stamps of Mozambique are used.

1000 Reis = 1 Milreis
100 Centavos = 1 Escudo (1919)

Mozambique Nos. 24-35 Overprinted in Black

1898 Unwmk. *Perf. 11½, 12½*

No.	Type	Description	Unused	Used
1	A3	5r yellow	3.00	1.50
2	A3	10r redsh violet	3.00	1.50
3	A3	15r chocolate	3.00	1.50
4	A3	20r gray violet	3.00	1.50
5	A3	25r blue green	3.00	1.50
6	A3	50r light blue	3.00	1.50
a.		Inverted overprint		
b.		Perf. 12½	6.00	3.50
7	A3	75r rose	4.00	2.00
8	A3	80r yellow grn	4.00	2.00
9	A3	100r brown, *buff*	4.00	2.00
10	A3	150r car, *rose*	6.50	4.00
11	A3	200r dk blue, *blue*	5.00	3.00
12	A3	300r dk blue, *salmon*	5.00	3.00
		Nos. 1-12 (12)	46.50	25.00

Reprints of Nos. 1, 5, 8, 9, 10 and 12 have white gum and clean-cut perforation 13½. Value of No. 9, $15; others $3 each.

Same Overprint on Mozambique Issue of 1898

1898 *Perf. 11½*

No.	Type	Description	Unused	Used
13	A4	2½r gray	2.50	.80
14	A4	5r orange	2.50	.80
15	A4	10r light green	2.50	.80
16	A4	15r brown	3.00	1.00
17	A4	20r gray violet	3.00	1.00
18	A4	25r sea green	3.00	1.00
19	A4	50r blue	3.00	1.00
20	A4	75r rose	2.75	1.00
21	A4	80r violet	3.50	.80
22	A4	100r dk bl, *bl*	3.50	.80
23	A4	150r brown, *straw*	3.50	.80
24	A4	200r red lilac, *pnksh*	3.75	1.00
25	A4	300r dk blue, *rose*	4.00	1.00
		Nos. 13-25 (13)	40.50	11.80

Giraffe — A5

Camels — A6

1901 Engr. *Perf. 14*

No.	Type	Description	Unused	Used
26	A5	2½r blk & red brn	1.75	.55
27	A5	5r blk & violet	1.75	.55
28	A5	10r blk & dp grn	1.75	.55
29	A5	15r blk & org brn	1.75	.55
30	A5	20r blk & org red	1.75	.70
31	A5	25r blk & orange	1.75	.70
32	A5	50r blk & dl bl	1.75	.70
33	A6	75r blk & car lake	2.00	.70
34	A6	80r blk & lilac	2.00	.90
35	A6	100r blk & brn bis	2.00	.90
36	A6	150r blk & dp org	2.25	1.00
37	A6	200r blk & grnsh bl	2.50	1.00
38	A6	300r blk & yel grn	2.50	1.00
		Nos. 26-38 (13)	25.50	9.80

Nos. 26 to 38 are known with inverted centers but are believed to be purely speculative and never regularly issued. Value $80 each.

Perf 13½, 14½, 15½ & compound also exist.

For overprints and surcharges see Nos. 39-50, 63-80.

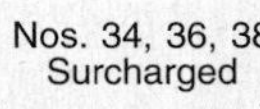

Nos. 34, 36, 38 Surcharged

1903

No.	Type	Description	Unused	Used
39	A6	65r on 80r	1.00	.75
40	A6	115r on 150r	1.00	.75
41	A6	130r on 300r	1.00	.75
		Nos. 39-41 (3)	3.00	2.25

Nos. 29, 31 Overprinted

1903

No.	Type	Description	Unused	Used
42	A5	15r black & org brn	1.00	.75
43	A5	25r black & orange	1.00	.75

Nos. 34, 36, 38 Surcharged

1903

No.	Type	Description	Unused	Used
44	A6	65r on 80r	32.50	15.00
45	A6	115r on 150r	32.50	15.00
46	A6	130r on 300r	32.50	15.00
		Nos. 44-46 (3)	97.50	45.00

Nos. 29, 31 Overprinted

1903

No.	Type	Description	Unused	Used
47	A5	15r black & org brn	500.00	100.00
48	A5	25r black & orange	150.00	100.00

Forgeries exist of Nos. 44-48.

Nos. 26, 35 Surcharged

1910

No.	Type	Description	Unused	Used
49	A5	5r on 2½r	1.00	.75
50	A6	50r on 100r	1.00	.75
a.		"50 REIS" omitted	300.00	

Reprints of Nos. 49-50, made in 1921, have 2mm space between surcharge lines, instead of 1½mm. Value, each 25 cents.

Zebra — A7

Vasco da Gama's Flagship "San Gabriel" — A8

Designs: Nos. 51-53, Camels. Nos. 57-59, Giraffe and palms.

1911 Red Overprint

No.	Type	Description	Unused	Used
51	A7	2½r blk & dl vio	1.25	.55
52	A7	5r black	1.25	.55
53	A7	10r blk & gray grn	1.25	.55
54	A7	20r blk & car lake	1.25	.55
55	A7	25r blk & vio brn	1.25	.55
56	A7	50r blk & dp bl	1.25	.55
57	A8	75r blk & brn	1.25	.55
58	A8	100r blk & brn, *grn*	1.25	.55
59	A8	200r blk & dp grn, *sal*	1.40	1.00
60	A8	300r blk, *blue*	2.40	1.60
61	A8	400r blk & dk brn	3.00	2.00
a.		Pair, one without overprint		
62	A8	500r ol & vio brn	4.00	3.00
		Nos. 51-62 (12)	20.80	12.00

Nos. 51-62 exist without overprint but were not issued in that condition. Value $7.50 each.

For surcharges see Nos. 81-105.

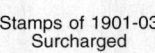

Stamps of 1901-03 Surcharged

1918 On Nos. 26-38

No.	Type	Description	Unused	Used
63	A5	¼c on 2½r	140.00	110.00
64	A5	½c on 5r	140.00	110.00
65	A5	1c on 10r	140.00	110.00
66	A5	1½c on 15r	2.10	1.10
67	A5	2c on 20r	1.25	1.00
68	A5	3½c on 25r	1.50	1.00
69	A5	5c on 50r	1.25	1.00
70	A6	7½c on 75r	1.25	1.00
71	A6	8c on 80r	1.25	1.00
72	A6	10c on 100r	1.25	1.00
73	A6	15c on 150r	2.10	2.00
74	A6	20c on 200r	2.00	2.00
75	A6	30c on 300r	3.25	2.40
		On Nos. 39-41		
76	A6	40c on 65r on 80r	18.00	16.50
77	A6	50c on 115r on 150r	3.00	2.00
78	A6	1e on 130r on 300r	5.00	2.00
		On Nos. 42-43		
79	A5	1½c on 15r	7.00	3.00
80	A5	3½c on 25r	2.00	1.00
		Nos. 63-80 (18)	472.20	368.00

On Nos. 70-78 there is less space between "REPUBLICA" and the new value than on the other stamps of this issue.

On Nos. 76-78 the 1903 surcharge is canceled by a bar.

The surcharge exists inverted on #64, 66-70, 72, 76, 78-80, and double on #64, 67, 69.

Nos. 51-62 Surcharged in Black or Red

Numerals: The "1" (large or small) is thin, sharp-pointed, and has thin serifs. The "2" is italic, with the tail thin and only slightly wavy. The "3" has a flat top. The "4" is open at the top. The "7" has thin strokes.

Centavos: The letters are shaded, i.e., they are thicker in some parts than in others. The "t" has a thin cross bar ending in a downward stroke at the right. The "s" is flat at the bottom and wider than in the next group.

1921 Lisbon Surcharges

No.	Type	Description	Unused	Used
81	A7	¼c on 2½r	5.00	2.75
83	A7	½c on 5r (R)	5.00	2.75
a.		½c on 2½r (R) (error)	275.00	250.00
84	A7	1c on 10r	5.00	2.75
a.		Pair, one without surcharge		
85	A8	1½c on 300r (R)	5.00	2.75
86	A7	2c on 20r	5.00	2.75
87	A7	2½c on 25r	5.00	2.75
88	A8	3c on 400r	5.00	2.75
a.		"Republica" omitted		
89	A7	5c on 50r	5.00	2.75
90	A8	7½c on 75r	5.00	2.75
91	A8	10c on 100r	5.00	2.75
92	A8	12c on 500r	5.00	2.75
93	A8	20c on 200r	5.00	2.75
		Nos. 81-93 (12)	60.00	33.00

The surcharge exists inverted on Nos. 83-85, 87-88 and 92, and double on Nos. 81, 83 and 86.

Forgeries exist of Nos. 81-93.

London Surcharges

Numerals — The "1" has the vertical stroke and serifs thicker than in the Lisbon printing. The "2" is upright and has a strong wave in the tail. The small "2" is heavily shaded. The "3" has a rounded top. The "4" is closed at the top. The "7" has thick strokes.

Centavos — The letters are heavier than in the Lisbon printing and are of even thickness throughout. The "t" has a thick cross bar with scarcely any down stroke at the end. The "s" is rounded at the bottom and narrower than in the Lisbon printing.

No.	Type	Description	Unused	Used
94	A7	¼c on 2½r	1.50	1.25
95	A7	½c on 5r (R)	1.50	1.25
96	A7	1c on 10r	1.50	1.25
97	A8	1½c on 300r (R)	1.50	1.25
98	A7	2c on 20r	1.50	1.25
99	A7	2½c on 25r	1.50	1.25
100	A8	3c on 400r	1.50	1.25
101	A7	5c on 50r	1.50	1.25
102	A8	7½c on 75r	1.50	1.25
a.		Inverted surcharge		
103	A8	10c on 100r	1.50	1.25
104	A8	12c on 500r	1.50	1.25
105	A8	20c on 200r	1.50	1.25
		Nos. 94-105 (12)	18.00	15.00

A9

Zebra and Warrior — A10

Designs: 2c-6c, Vasco da Gama. 7½c-20c, "San Gabriel." 2e-5e, Dhow and warrior.

Perf. 12½, 13½-15 & Compound

1921-23 Engr.

No.	Type	Description	Unused	Used
106	A9	¼c claret	1.25	.70
107	A9	½c steel blue	1.25	.70
108	A9	1c grn & blk	1.25	.70
109	A9	1½c blk & ocher	1.25	.70
110	A9	2c red & blk	1.25	.70
111	A9	2½c blk & ol grn	1.25	.70
112	A9	4c blk & org	1.25	.70
113	A9	5c ultra & blk	1.25	.70
114	A9	6c blk & vio	1.25	.70
115	A9	7½c blk & blk brn	1.25	.70
116	A9	8c blk & ol grn	1.25	.70
117	A9	10c blk & red brn	1.25	.70
118	A9	15c blk & carmine	1.25	.70
119	A9	20c blk & pale bl	1.25	.70
120	A10	30c blk & bister	1.25	.70
121	A10	40c blk & gray bl	1.25	.70
122	A10	50c blk & green	1.25	.70
123	A10	1e blk & red brn	1.25	.70
124	A10	2e red brn & blk ('23)	3.25	2.50
125	A10	5e ultra & red brn ('23)	3.00	2.25
		Nos. 106-125 (20)	28.75	17.35

POSTAGE DUE STAMPS

Giraffe — D1

½c, 1c, Giraffe. 2c, 3c, Zebra. 5c, 6c, 10c, "San Gabriel." 20c, 50c, Vasco da Gama.

1924 Unwmk. Engr. *Perf. 14*
J1 D1 ½c deep green 1.00 *1.75*
J2 D1 1c gray 1.00 *1.75*
J3 D1 2c red 1.00 *1.75*
J4 D1 3c red orange 1.00 *1.75*
J5 D1 5c dark brown 1.00 *1.75*
J6 D1 6c orange brown 1.00 *1.75*
J7 D1 10c brown violet 1.00 *1.75*
J8 D1 20c carmine 1.00 *1.75*
J9 D1 50c lilac gray 1.00 *1.75*
Nos. J1-J9 (9) 9.00 *15.75*

Used values are for c-t-o copies.

NEWSPAPER STAMP

Mozambique No. P6 Ovptd. Like Nos. 1-25 in Black

1898 Unwmk. *Perf. 13½*
P1 N3 2½r brown 2.00 1.00

Reprints have white gum and clean-cut perf. 13½. Value $1.

POSTAL TAX STAMPS

Pombal Issue

Mozambique Nos. RA1-RA3 Overprinted "NYASSA" in Red

1925 Unwmk. *Perf. 12½*
RA1 CD28 15c brown & blk 5.00 5.00
RA2 CD29 15c brown & blk 5.00 5.00
RA3 CD30 15c brown & blk 5.00 5.00
Nos. RA1-RA3 (3) 15.00 15.00

POSTAL TAX DUE STAMPS

Pombal Issue

Mozambique Nos. RAJ1-RAJ3 Overprinted "NYASSA" in Red

1925 Unwmk. *Perf. 12½*
RAJ1 CD28 30c brown & blk 12.50 7.75
RAJ2 CD29 30c brown & blk 12.50 7.75
RAJ3 CD30 30c brown & blk 12.50 7.75
Nos. RAJ1-RAJ3 (3) 37.50 23.25

OBOCK

'ō-,bäk

LOCATION — A seaport in eastern Africa on the Gulf of Aden, directly opposite Aden.

Obock was the point of entrance from which French Somaliland was formed. The port was acquired by the French in 1862 but was not actively occupied until 1884 when Sagallo and Tadjoura were ceded to France. In 1888 Djibouti was made into a port and the seat of government moved from Obock to the latter city. In 1902 the name Somali Coast was adopted on the postage stamps of Djibouti, these stamps superseding the individual issues of Obock.

100 Centimes = 1 Franc

Covers

Values are for commercial covers paying correct rates. Philatelic covers sell for less.

Counterfeits exist of Nos. 1-31.

Stamps of French Colonies Handstamped in Black

#1-11, J1-J4

#12-20, J5-J18

1892 Unwmk. *Perf. 14x13½*
1 A9 1c blk, *lil bl* 45.00 45.00
Never hinged 90.00
On cover —
2 A9 2c brn, *buff* 45.00 45.00
Never hinged 90.00
On cover —
3 A9 4c claret, *lav* 450.00 *475.00*
On cover —
4 A9 5c grn, *grnsh* 40.00 32.50
Never hinged 75.00
On cover —
5 A9 10c blk, *lavender* 80.00 47.50
On cover *700.00*
6 A9 15c blue 72.50 50.00
On cover *700.00*
7 A9 25c blk, *rose* 110.00 80.00
On cover *700.00*
8 A9 35c vio, *org* 450.00 450.00
On cover —
9 A9 40c red, *straw* 400.00 *425.00*
On cover —
10 A9 75c car, *rose* 450.00 *475.00*
On cover —
11 A9 1fr brnz grn, *straw* 500.00 550.00
On cover —
Nos. 1-11 (11) 2,643. 2,675.

No. 3 has been reprinted. On the reprints the second "O" of "OBOCK" is 4mm high instead of 3½mm. Value $32.50.

1892
12 A9 4c claret, *lav* 27.50 27.50
Never hinged 50.00
On cover —
13 A9 5c grn, *grnsh* 27.50 27.50
Never hinged 50.00
On cover —
14 A9 10c blk, *lavender* 27.50 27.50
Never hinged 50.00
On cover *700.00*
15 A9 15c blue 27.50 27.50
Never hinged 50.00
On cover *700.00*
16 A9 20c red, *grn* 47.50 45.00
Never hinged 175.00
On cover —
17 A9 25c blk, *rose* 35.00 27.50
Never hinged 110.00
On cover *700.00*
18 A9 40c red, *straw* 60.00 52.50
Never hinged 210.00
On cover —
19 A9 75c car, *rose* 325.00 275.00
On cover —
20 A9 1fr brnz grn, *straw* 87.50 80.00
On cover —
Nos. 12-20 (9) 665.00 590.00

Exists inverted or double on all denominations.

Nos. 14, 15, 17, 20 with Additional Surcharge Handstamped in Red, Blue or Black

Nos, 21-30

No. 31

1892
21 A9 1c on 25c blk, *rose* 20.00 20.00
Never hinged 40.00
On cover —
22 A9 2c on 10c blk, *lav* 72.50 60.00
Never hinged 80.00
On cover —
23 A9 2c on 15c blue 22.50 20.00
Never hinged 40.00
On cover —
24 A9 4c on 15c bl (Bk) 20.00 20.00
Never hinged 35.00
On cover —
25 A9 4c on 25c blk, *rose* (Bk) 20.00 20.00
Never hinged 35.00
On cover —
26 A9 5c on 25c blk, *rose* 27.50 27.50
Never hinged 50.00
On cover —
27 A9 20c on 10c blk, *lav* 95.00 95.00
On cover —
28 A9 30c on 10c blk, *lav* 120.00 110.00
On cover —
29 A9 35c on 25c blk, *rose* 100.00 92.50
On cover —
a. "3" instead of "35" 950.00 950.00
30 A9 75c on 1fr brnz grn, *straw* 110.00 110.00
On cover —
b. "57" instead of "75" *8,750.* *9,250.*
c. "55" instead of "75" *8,750.* *9,250.*
31 A9 5fr on 1fr brnz grn, *straw* (Bl) 775.00 700.00
On cover —
Nos. 21-31 (11) 1,383. 1,275.

Exists inverted on most denominations.

Navigation and Commerce — A4

Obock in Red (1c, 5c, 15c, 25c, 75c, 1fr) or Blue

1892 Typo. *Perf. 14x13½*
32 A4 1c blk, *lil bl* 2.75 2.75
Never hinged 4.00
On cover 190.00
33 A4 2c brn, *buff* 2.00 2.00
Never hinged 2.75
On cover 190.00
34 A4 4c claret, *lav* 2.75 2.75
Never hinged 4.00
On cover 170.00
35 A4 5c grn, *grnsh* 6.25 4.00
Never hinged 7.00
On cover 95.00
36 A4 10c blk, *lavender* 8.00 5.25
Never hinged 12.50
On cover 90.00
37 A4 15c bl, quadrille paper 19.50 11.50
Never hinged 30.00
On cover 125.00
38 A4 20c red, *grn* 27.50 27.50
Never hinged 45.00
On cover —
39 A4 25c blk, *rose* 27.50 24.00
Never hinged 45.00
On cover 100.00
40 A4 30c brn, *bis* 24.00 20.00
Never hinged 37.50
On cover —
41 A4 40c red, *straw* 24.00 20.00
Never hinged 37.50
On cover 225.00
42 A4 50c car, *rose* 28.00 24.00
Never hinged 45.00
On cover 190.00
43 A4 75c vio, *org* 32.50 24.00
Never hinged 52.50
On cover 500.00
a. Name double 350.00 350.00
b. Name inverted *5,500.* *5,500.*
44 A4 1fr brnz grn, *straw* 47.50 40.00
Never hinged 80.00
On cover —
Nos. 32-44 (13) 252.25 207.75

Perf. 13½x14 stamps are counterfeits.

Camel and Rider — A5

Quadrille Lines Printed on Paper

1893 Size: 32mm at base *Imperf.*
44A A5 2fr slate 65.00 55.00
Never hinged 130.00

Size: 45mm at base
45 A5 5fr red 140.00 125.00
Never hinged 160.00

Somali Warriors A7

A8

1894 *Imperf.*

Quadrille Lines Printed on Paper

46 A7 1c blk & rose 2.75 2.75
Never hinged 4.25
On cover 425.00
47 A7 2c vio brn & grn 2.75 2.75
Never hinged 4.25
On cover 425.00
48 A7 4c brn vio & org 2.75 2.75
Never hinged 4.25
On cover 425.00
49 A7 5c bl grn & brn 3.50 3.50
Never hinged 5.50
On cover 300.00
50 A7 10c blk & grn 9.50 8.00
Never hinged 14.00
On cover 300.00
a. Half used as 5c on cover ('01) 350.00
51 A7 15c bl & rose 9.50 7.25
Never hinged 14.00
On cover 110.00
52 A7 20c brn org & mar 9.50 8.00
Never hinged 14.00
On cover *250.00*
a. Half used as 10c on cover ('01) 325.00
53 A7 25c blk & bl 10.50 6.50
Never hinged 15.00
On cover 175.00
a. Right half used as 5c on cover ('01) 300.00
b. Left half used as 2c on cover ('03) 300.00
54 A7 30c bis & yel grn 20.00 14.50
Never hinged 30.00
On cover *225.00*
a. Half used as 15c on cover ('01) 2,200.
55 A7 40c red & bl grn 17.00 13.00
Never hinged 27.50
On cover 210.00
56 A7 50c rose & bl 15.00 12.00
Never hinged 25.00
On cover 250.00
a. Half used as 25c on cover 3,400.
57 A7 75c gray lil & org 20.00 13.00
Never hinged 30.00
On cover 500.00
58 A7 1fr ol grn & mar 17.00 10.50
Never hinged 27.50
On cover *650.00*

Size: 37mm at base
60 A8 2fr vio & org 120.00 120.00
Never hinged 180.00
On cover —

Size: 42mm at base
61 A8 5fr rose & bl 95.00 95.00
Never hinged 160.00
On cover —

Size: 46mm at base
62 A8 10fr org & red vio 160.00 160.00
Never hinged 270.00
On cover —
63 A8 25fr brn & bl 875.00 875.00
Never hinged 1,400.
On cover —
64 A8 50fr red vio & grn 1,000. 1,000.
Never hinged 1,275.
On cover —

Counterfeits exist of Nos. 63-64.

Stamps of Obock were replaced in 1901 by those of Somali Coast. The 5c on 75c, 5c on 25fr and 10c on 50fr of 1902 are listed under Somali Coast.

POSTAGE DUE STAMPS

Postage Due Stamps of French Colonies Handstamped Like #1-20

1892 Unwmk. *Imperf.*
J1 D1 5c black *11,000.*
J2 D1 10c black 240.00 *275.00*
J3 D1 30c black 375.00 *450.00*
J4 D1 60c black 475.00 *550.00*
J5 D1 1c black 55.00 55.00
Never hinged 120.00
On cover *350.00*
J6 D1 2c black 45.00 45.00
Never hinged 95.00
On cover *300.00*
J7 D1 3c black 52.50 52.50
Never hinged 110.00
On cover *350.00*
J8 D1 4c black 45.00 45.00
Never hinged 95.00
On cover *300.00*
J9 D1 5c black 16.00 16.00
Never hinged 35.00
On cover *200.00*
J10 D1 10c black 35.00 35.00
Never hinged 70.00
On cover *200.00*
J11 D1 15c black 24.00 24.00
Never hinged 45.00
On cover *225.00*
J12 D1 20c black 32.50 32.50
Never hinged 60.00
On cover *250.00*

J13 D1 30c black 32.50 32.50
Never hinged 60.00
On cover 250.00
J14 D1 40c black 60.00 60.00
Never hinged 75.00
On cover 400.00
J15 D1 60c black 80.00 80.00
On cover 500.00
J16 D1 1fr brown 225.00 225.00
J17 D1 2fr brown 240.00 240.00
J18 D1 5fr brown 525.00 525.00
Nos. J2-J18 (17) 2,558. 2,743.

Overprint Inverted

J5a D1 1c black *200.00 200.00*
J6a D1 2c black *200.00 200.00*
J7a D1 3c black *200.00 200.00*
J8a D1 4c black *200.00 200.00*
J9a D1 5c black *200.00 200.00*
J10a D1 10c black *250.00 250.00*
J11a D1 15c black *200.00 200.00*
J15a D1 60c black *275.00 275.00*
J16a D1 1fr brown *550.00 550.00*
J17a D1 2fr brown *550.00 550.00*

Double Overprint

J5b D1 1c black *200.00 200.00*
J6b D1 2c black *200.00 200.00*
J9b D1 5c black *250.00 250.00*
J10b D1 10c black *300.00 300.00*
J11b D1 15c black *250.00 250.00*
J12b D1 20c black *250.00 250.00*
J13b D1 30c black *300.00 300.00*

These handstamped overprints may be found double on some values. Counterfeits exist of Nos. J1-J18.

No. J1 has been reprinted. The overprint on the original measures 12½x3¾mm and on the reprint 12x3¼mm. Value, $325.

OLTRE GIUBA

ˌōl-trā-ˈjü-bə

(Italian Jubaland)

LOCATION — A strip of land, 50 to 100 miles in width, west of and parallel to the Juba River in East Africa
GOVT. — Italian Protectorate
AREA — 33,000 sq. mi.
POP. — 12,000
CAPITAL — Kismayu

Oltre Giuba was ceded to Italy by Great Britain in 1924 and in 1926 was incorporated with Italian Somaliland. In 1936 it became part of Italian East Africa.

100 Centesimi = 1 Lira

Watermark

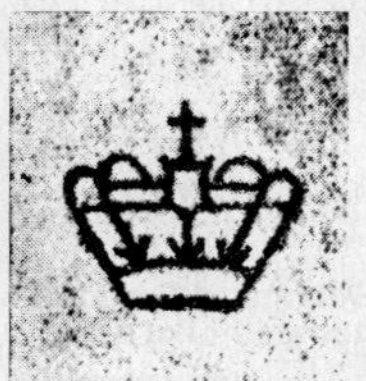

Wmk. 140 — Crown

Italian Stamps of 1901-26 Overprinted

On #1-15

On #16-20

1925, July 29 Wmk. 140 *Perf. 14*

1 A42 1c brown 5.50 *30.00*
Never hinged 14.00
On cover 350.00
a. Inverted overprint 475.00
2 A43 2c yel brown 4.25 *30.00*
Never hinged 11.00
On cover 350.00
3 A48 5c green 4.25 *12.50*
Never hinged 11.00
On cover 300.00
4 A48 10c claret 4.25 *12.50*
Never hinged 11.00
On cover 300.00
5 A48 15c slate 4.25 *17.50*
Never hinged 11.00
On cover 340.00
6 A50 20c brn orange 4.25 *17.50*
Never hinged 11.00
On cover 350.00
7 A49 25c blue 4.25 *17.50*
Never hinged 11.00
On cover 340.00
8 A49 30c org brown 5.50 *22.50*
Never hinged 14.00
On cover 350.00
9 A49 40c brown 11.00 *17.50*
Never hinged 28.00
On cover 475.00
10 A49 50c violet 11.00 *17.50*
Never hinged 28.00
On cover 350.00
11 A49 60c carmine 11.00 *22.50*
Never hinged 28.00
On cover 725.00
12 A46 1 l brn & green 16.00 30.00
Never hinged 40.00
On cover 650.00
13 A46 2 l dk grn & org 85.00 60.00
Never hinged 210.00
On cover —
14 A46 5 l blue & rose 110.00 87.50
Never hinged 275.00
On cover —
15 A51 10 l gray grn & red 21.00 *95.00*
Never hinged 52.50
On cover —
Nos. 1-15 (15) 301.50 *490.00*

1925-26

16 A49 20c green 7.00 *17.50*
Never hinged 16.00
On cover 400.00
17 A49 30c gray 10.00 *22.50*
Never hinged 22.50
On cover 525.00
18 A46 75c dk red & rose 42.50 *95.00*
Never hinged 100.00
On cover 600.00
19 A46 1.25 l bl & ultra 87.50 *160.00*
Never hinged 210.00
On cover 1,050.
20 A46 2.50 l dk grn & org 120.00 *275.00*
Never hinged 300.00
On cover 1,750.
Nos. 16-20 (5) 267.00 *570.00*

Issue years: #18-20, 1926; others 1925.

Victor Emmanuel Issue

Italian Stamps of 1925 Overprinted

1925-26 Unwmk. *Perf. 11*

21 A78 60c brown car 1.60 *16.00*
Never hinged 4.00
On cover 650.00
a. Perf. 13½ *12,000.*
Never hinged 18,000.
On cover —
22 A78 1 l dark blue 1.60 *25.00*
Never hinged 4.00
On cover 875.00
a. Perf. 13½ 650.00 *2,400.*
Never hinged 1,600.
On cover —
23 A78 1.25 l dk bl ('26) 6.50 *40.00*
Never hinged 16.00
On cover 1,300.
a. Perf. 13½ 6.50 *40.00*
Never hinged 16.00
On cover 1,300.
Nos. 21-23 (3) 9.70 *81.00*

Saint Francis of Assisi Issue

Italian Stamps and Type of 1926 Overprinted

1926, Apr. 12 Wmk. 140 *Perf. 14*

24 A79 20c gray green 2.50 *45.00*
Never hinged 6.25
On cover 725.00
25 A80 40c dark violet 2.50 *45.00*
Never hinged 6.25
On cover 725.00
26 A81 60c red brown 2.50 *65.00*
Never hinged 6.25
On cover 725.00

Overprinted in Red

Unwmk.

27 A82 1.25 l dk bl, perf. 11 2.50 *87.50*
Never hinged 6.25
On cover 1,200.
28 A83 5 l + 2.50 l ol grn, perf. 13½ 8.00 *135.00*
Never hinged 20.00
On cover —
Nos. 24-28 (5) 18.00 *377.50*
Set on overfranked philatelic cover *725.00*

Map of Oltre Giuba — A1

1926, Apr. 21 Typo. Wmk. 140

29 A1 5c yellow brown 1.60 *35.00*
Never hinged 4.00
On cover 475.00
30 A1 20c blue green 1.60 *35.00*
Never hinged 4.00
On cover 450.00
31 A1 25c olive brown 1.60 *35.00*
Never hinged 4.00
On cover 450.00
32 A1 40c dull red 1.60 *35.00*
Never hinged 4.00
On cover 450.00
33 A1 60c brown violet 1.60 *35.00*
Never hinged 4.00
On cover 550.00
34 A1 1 l blue 1.60 *35.00*
Never hinged 4.00
On cover 600.00
35 A1 2 l dark green 1.60 *35.00*
Never hinged 4.00
On cover —
Nos. 29-35 (7) 11.20 *245.00*
Set on overfranked philatelic cover *260.00*

Oltre Giuba was incorporated with Italian Somaliland on July 1, 1926, and stamps inscribed "Oltre Giuba" were discontinued.

SEMI-POSTAL STAMPS

Note preceding Italy semi-postals applies to No. 28.

Colonial Institute Issue

"Peace" Substituting Spade for Sword — SP1

Wmk. 140

1926, June 1 Typo. *Perf. 14*

B1 SP1 5c + 5c brown 1.20 *9.50*
Never hinged 3.00
On cover 475.00
B2 SP1 10c + 5c ol grn 1.20 *9.50*
Never hinged 3.00
On cover 400.00
B3 SP1 20c + 5c blue grn 1.20 *9.50*
Never hinged 3.00
On cover 450.00
B4 SP1 40c + 5c brn red 1.20 *9.50*
Never hinged 3.00
On cover 475.00
B5 SP1 60c + 5c orange 1.20 *9.50*
Never hinged 3.00
On cover 600.00
B6 SP1 1 l + 5c blue 1.20 *20.00*
Never hinged 3.00
On cover 650.00
Nos. B1-B6 (6) 7.20 *67.50*
Set on overfranked philatelic cover *260.00*

Surtax for Italian Colonial Institute.

SPECIAL DELIVERY STAMPS

Special Delivery Stamps of Italy Ovptd.

1926 Wmk. 140 *Perf. 14*

E1 SD1 70c dull red 32.50 *65.00*
Never hinged 80.00
E2 SD2 2.50 l blue & red 67.50 *180.00*
Never hinged 160.00

POSTAGE DUE STAMPS

Italian Postage Due Stamps of 1870-1903 Ovptd. Like Nos. E1-E2

1925, July 29 Wmk. 140 *Perf. 14*

J1 D3 5c buff & magenta 24.00 24.00
Never hinged 47.50
J2 D3 10c buff & magenta 24.00 24.00
Never hinged 47.50
J3 D3 20c buff & magenta 24.00 *40.00*
Never hinged 47.50
J4 D3 30c buff & magenta 24.00 *40.00*
Never hinged 47.50
J5 D3 40c buff & magenta 24.00 *45.00*
Never hinged 47.50
J6 D3 50c buff & magenta 32.50 *55.00*
Never hinged 65.00
J7 D3 60c buff & brown 32.50 *65.00*
Never hinged 65.00
J8 D3 1 l blue & magenta 35.00 *80.00*
Never hinged 65.00
J9 D3 2 l blue & magenta 175.00 *275.00*
Never hinged 350.00
J10 D3 5 l blue & magenta 225.00 275.00
Never hinged 450.00
Nos. J1-J10 (10) 620.00 *923.00*

PARCEL POST STAMPS

These stamps were used by affixing them to the waybill so that one half remained on it following the parcel, the other half staying on the receipt given the sender. Most used halves are right halves. Complete stamps were obtainable canceled, probably to order. Both unused and used values are for complete stamps.

Italian Parcel Post Stamps of 1914-22 Overprinted

1925, July 29 Wmk. 140 *Perf. 13½*

Q1 PP2 5c brown 21.00 *45.00*
Never hinged 37.50
Q2 PP2 10c blue 17.50 *45.00*
Never hinged 29.00
Q3 PP2 20c black 17.50 *45.00*
Never hinged 29.00
Q4 PP2 25c red 17.50 *45.00*
Never hinged 29.00
Q5 PP2 50c orange 21.00 *45.00*
Never hinged 37.50
Q6 PP2 1 l violet 17.50 *100.00*
Never hinged 29.00
a. Double overprint 550.00
Q7 PP2 2 l green 28.00 *100.00*
Never hinged 56.00
Q8 PP2 3 l bister 65.00 *130.00*
Never hinged 130.00
Q9 PP2 4 l slate 29.00 *130.00*
Never hinged 57.50
Q10 PP2 10 l rose lilac 95.00 *225.00*
Never hinged 190.00
Q11 PP2 12 l red brown 175.00 *350.00*
Never hinged 350.00
Q12 PP2 15 l olive green 160.00 *350.00*
Never hinged 325.00
Q13 PP2 20 l brown violet 160.00 *350.00*
Never hinged 325.00
Nos. Q1-Q13 (13) 824.00 1,960.

Halves Used

Q1-Q4	1.75
Q5-Q7	3.00
Q8-Q9	4.75
Q10	9.25
Q11	15.00
Q12-Q13	10.00

OMAN

'ō-ˌmän

Muscat and Oman

LOCATION — Southeastern corner of the Arabian Peninsula
GOVT. — Sultanate
AREA — 105,000 sq. mi.
POP. — 1,500,000 (est. 1982)
CAPITAL — Muscat

Nos. 16-93, the stamps with "value only" surcharges, were used not only in Muscat, but also in Dubai (Apr. 1, 1948 - Jan. 6, 1961), Qatar (Aug. 1950 - Mar. 31, 1957), and Abu Dhabi (Mar. 30, 1963 - Mar. 29, 1964). Occasionally they were also used in Bahrain and Kuwait.

12 Pies = 1 Anna
16 Annas = 1 Rupee

Catalogue values for all unused stamps in this country are for Never Hinged items, beginning with No. 25.

Muscat

Stamps of India 1937-43 Overprinted in Black

On #1-13 the overprint is smaller — 13x6mm.

Wmk. Multiple Stars (196)
1944, Nov. 20 *Perf. 13½x14*

1 A83 3p slate .40 *8.00*
Never hinged .75
2 A83 ½a rose violet .40 *8.00*
Never hinged .75
3 A83 9p lt green .40 *8.00*
Never hinged .75
4 A83 1a carmine rose .40 *8.00*
Never hinged .75
5 A84 1½a dark purple .40 *8.00*
Never hinged .75
a. Double overprint 300.00
Never hinged 425.00
6 A84 2a scarlet .50 *8.00*
Never hinged .85
7 A84 3a violet 1.00 *8.00*
Never hinged 1.75
8 A84 3½a ultra 1.00 *8.00*
Never hinged 1.75
9 A85 4a chocolate 1.10 *8.00*
Never hinged 2.00
10 A85 6a pck blue 1.25 *8.00*
Never hinged 2.25
11 A85 8a blue violet 1.40 *8.50*
Never hinged 2.50
12 A85 12a car lake 1.50 *8.50*
Never hinged 2.75
13 A81 14a rose violet 2.75 *13.50*
Never hinged 4.50
14 A82 1r brown & slate 1.75 *12.50*
Never hinged 5.50
15 A82 2r dk brn & dk vio 5.00 *20.00*
Never hinged 13.00
Nos. 1-15 (15) 19.25 *143.00*
Set, never hinged 40.00

200th anniv. of Al Busaid Dynasty.
Used values for Nos. 1-15 are for stamps canceled with contemporaneous postmarks of the Indian postal administration. Examples with later British post office cancellations are worth much less.

Great Britain, Nos. 258 to 263, 243, 248, 249A Surcharged
Perf. 14½x14
1948, Apr. 1 **Wmk. 251**

16 A101 ½a on ½p green 3.00 *8.00*
Never hinged 5.50
17 A101 1a on 1p vermilion 3.25 *.30*
Never hinged 6.00
18 A101 1½a on 1½p lt red brn 15.00 *4.25*
Never hinged 26.00
19 A101 2a on 2p lt org 2.25 *3.50*
Never hinged 4.00
20 A101 2½a on 2½p ultra 4.25 *8.50*
Never hinged 7.50
21 A101 3a on 3p violet 4.00 *.25*
Never hinged 7.00
22 A102 6a on 6p rose lilac 4.50 *.25*
Never hinged 8.00
23 A103 1r on 1sh brown 5.00 *.75*
Never hinged 9.00

Wmk. 259 ***Perf. 14***

24 A104 2r on 2sh6p yel grn 14.00 *52.50*
Never hinged 25.00
Nos. 16-24 (9) 55.25 *78.30*

Catalogue values for unused stamps in this section from this point to the end of the section are for Never Hinged items.

Silver Wedding Issue
Great Britain, Nos. 267 and 268, Surcharged with New Value in Black
Perf. 14½x14, 14x14½
1948, Apr. 26 **Wmk. 251**

25 A109 2½a on 2½p brt ultra 3.50 *5.00*
26 A110 15r on £1 dp chlky bl 42.50 *42.50*

Three bars obliterate the original denomination on No. 26.

Olympic Games Issue
Great Britain, Nos. 271 to 274, Surcharged with New Value in Black
1948, July 29 ***Perf. 14½x14***

27 A113 2½a on 2½p brt ultra .75 *2.75*
28 A114 3a on 3p dp violet .85 *2.75*
29 A115 6a on 6p red violet .95 *3.00*
30 A116 1r on 1sh dk brn 2.25 *4.25*
a. Double surcharge 1,500.
Nos. 27-30 (4) 4.80 12.75

A square of dots obliterates the original denomination on Nos. 28-30.

UPU Issue
Great Britain Nos. 276 to 279 Surcharged with New Value and Square of Dots in Black
1949, Oct. 10 **Photo.**

31 A117 2½a on 2½p brt ultra .75 *2.75*
32 A118 3a on 3p brt violet .95 *3.75*
33 A119 6a on 6p red violet 1.10 *2.50*
34 A120 1r on 1sh brown 2.75 *6.75*
Nos. 31-34 (4) 5.55 15.75

Great Britain Nos. 280-286 Surcharged with New Value in Black
1951

35 A101 ½a on ½p lt org 1.00 *9.00*
36 A101 1a on 1p ultra .60 *7.50*
37 A101 1½a on 1½p green 17.00 *35.00*
38 A101 2a on 2p lt red brn .85 *8.00*
39 A101 2½a on 2½p vermilion 1.50 *16.00*
40 A102 4a on 4p ultra 1.25 *3.25*

Perf. 11x12
Wmk. 259

41 A121 2r on 2sh6p green 45.00 7.00
Nos. 35-41 (7) 67.20 *85.75*

Two types of surcharge on No. 41.

Stamps of Great Britain, 1952-54, Srchd. with New Value in Black and Dark Blue
1952-54 **Wmk. 298** ***Perf. 14½x14***

42 A126 ½a on ½p red org ('53) .35 *2.00*
43 A126 1a on 1p ultra ('53) .35 *2.00*
44 A126 1½a on 1½p grn ('52) .40 *2.00*
45 A126 2a on 2p red brn ('53) .50 .25
46 A127 2½a on 2½p scar ('52) .35 .25
47 A127 3a on 3p dk pur (dk bl) .50 *1.00*
48 A128 4a on 4p ultra ('53) 2.25 *3.75*
49 A129 6a on 6p lilac rose .60 .45
50 A132 12a on 1sh3p dk grn ('53) 8.00 .90
51 A131 1r on 1sh6p dk bl ('53) 3.00 .75
Nos. 42-51 (10) 16.30 13.35

OFFICIAL STAMPS

Official Stamps of India 1938-43 Overprinted in Black

Perf. 13½x14
1944, Nov. 20 **Wmk. 196**

O1 O8 3p slate .80 *15.00*
O2 O8 ½a dk rose violet .80 *15.00*
O3 O8 9p green .80 *15.00*
O4 O8 1a carmine rose .80 *15.00*
O5 O8 1½a dull purple .80 *15.00*
O6 O8 2a scarlet .80 *15.00*
O7 O8 2½a purple 5.50 *15.00*
O8 O8 4a dark brown 2.00 *15.00*
O9 O8 8a blue violet 3.50 *17.50*
O10 A82 1r brown & slate 6.00 *27.50*
Nos. O1-O10 (10) 21.80 *165.00*
Set, never hinged 37.50

Al Busaid Dynasty, 200th anniv. On Nos. O1-O9 the overprint is smaller — 13x6mm.
Used values for Nos. O1-O10 are for stamps canceled with contemporaneous postmarks of the Indian postal administration. Examples with the later British post office cancellations are worth much less.

ORANGE RIVER COLONY

'är-inj 'ri-vər 'kä-lə-nē

(Orange Free State)

LOCATION — South Africa, north of the Cape of Good Hope between the Orange and Vaal Rivers
GOVT. — British Crown Colony
AREA — 49,647 sq. mi.
POP. — 528,174 (1911)
CAPITAL — Bloemfontein

Orange Free State was an independent republic, 1854-1900. Orange River Colony existed from May, 1900, to June, 1910, when it united with Cape of Good Hope, Natal and the Transvaal to form the Union of South Africa.

12 Pence = 1 Shilling

Values for unused stamps are for examples with original gum as defined in the catalogue introduction. Very fine examples of Nos. 1-60c will have perforations touching the design on one or more sides due to the narrow spacing of the stamps on the plates. Stamps with perfs clear of the design on all four sides are scarce and will command higher prices.

Een = 1
Twee = 2
Drie = 3
Vier = 4

Issues of the Republic

Orange Tree — A1

1868-1900 Unwmk. Typo. Perf. 14

1 A1 ½p red brown ('83) 7.50 .75
2 A1 ½p orange ('97) 3.00 .60
a. ½p yellow ('97) 3.00 .40
3 A1 1p red brown 22.50 .50
a. 1p pale brown 32.50 2.50
b. 1p deep brown 32.50 .60
4 A1 1p violet ('94) 5.00 .35
5 A1 2p violet ('83) 20.00 1.50
a. 2p pale mauve ('83-'84) 23.00 .50
6 A1 3p ultra ('83) 8.25 2.25
7 A1 4p ultra ('78) 5.75 4.50
a. 4p pale blue ('78) 26.00 5.25
8 A1 6p car rose ('90) 30.00 13.00
a. 6p rose ('71) 37.50 8.00
b. 6p pale rose ('68) 72.50 8.75
c. 6p bright carmine ('94) 18.50 2.25
9 A1 6p ultramarine ('00) 80.00
10 A1 1sh orange 65.00 1.75
a. 1sh orange buff *110.00* *7.25*
11 A1 1sh brown ('97) 32.50 1.75
12 A1 5sh green ('78) 14.00 *20.00*
Nos. 1-8,10-12 (11) 213.50 46.95

No. 8b was not placed in use without surcharge.
For surcharges see #13-53, 44j-53c, 57-60.

No. 13

No. 8a Surcharged in Four Different Types

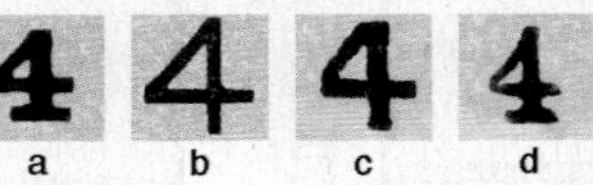

1877

13 (a) 4p on 6p rose 450.00 65.00
a. Inverted surcharge — 600.00
b. Double surcharge, one inverted ("a" + "c" inverted) *4,250.*
c. Double surcharge, one inverted ("a" inverted + "c") *6,000.*
14 (b) 4p on 6p rose 1,450. 225.00
a. Inverted surcharge — 1,250.
b. Double surcharge, one inverted ("b" and "d") —
15 (c) 4p on 6p rose 220.00 42.50
a. Inverted surcharge — 400.00
16 (d) 4p on 6p rose 325.00 50.00
a. Inverted surcharge *1,500.* 500.00
b. Double surcharge, one inverted ("d" and "c" inverted) — *4,250.*
c. Double surcharge, one inverted ("d" inverted and "c") — *6,500.*

No. 17

No. 12 Surcharged with Bar and

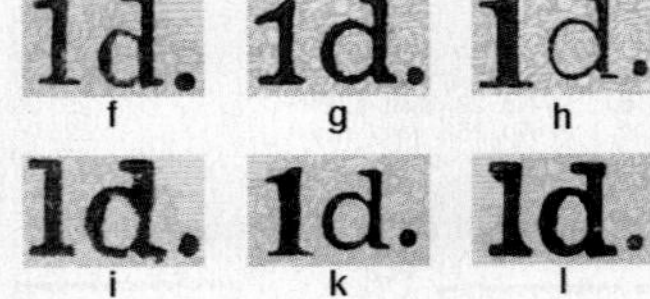

1881

First Printing

17 (f) 1p on 5sh green 120.00 32.50

Second Printing

18 (g) 1p on 5sh green 65.00 32.50
a. Inverted surcharge — *1,250.*
b. Double surcharge *1,450.*
19 (h) 1p on 5sh green 300.00 95.00
a. Inverted surcharge — *1,450.*
b. Double surcharge — *1,650.*
20 (i) 1p on 5sh green 100.00 32.50
a. Double surcharge — *1,325.*
b. Inverted surcharge *2,000.* *1,000.*
21 (k) 1p on 5sh green 600.00 275.00
a. Inverted surcharge — *2,500.*
b. Double surcharge *2,500.*

Third Printing

21C (l) 1p on 5sh green 95.00 32.50
d. Inverted surcharge — *875.00*
e. Double surcharge *900.00*
Nos. 17-21C (6) 1,280. 500.00

No. 12 Surcharged

1882

22 A1 ½p on 5sh green 25.00 5.50
a. Double surcharge 550.00 400.00
b. Inverted surcharge *1,500.* *1,000.*

No. 7 Surcharged with Thin Line and

m

n

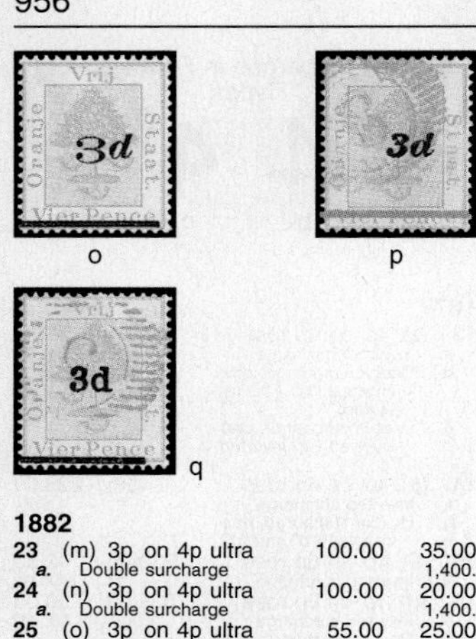

o p q

1882

23 (m) 3p on 4p ultra 100.00 35.00
  a. Double surcharge 1,400.
24 (n) 3p on 4p ultra 100.00 20.00
  a. Double surcharge 1,400.
25 (o) 3p on 4p ultra 55.00 25.00
  a. Double surcharge 1,400.
26 (p) 3p on 4p ultra 275.00 80.00
  a. Double surcharge 3,500.
27 (q) 3p on 4p ultra 100.00 24.00
  a. Double surcharge 1,400.
  Nos. 23-27 (5) 630.00 184.00

No. 6 Surcharged

1888

28 A1 2p on 3p ultra 60.00 2.25
  a. Wide "2" at top 77.50 10.00
  b. As No. 28, invtd. surch. 350.00
  c. As No. 28a, invtd. surch. 825.00
  d. Curved base on "2" *1,450.* *650.00*

Nos. 6 and 7 Surcharged

r s

t

1890-91

29 (r) 1p on 3p ultra ('91) 9.50 1.00
  a. Double surcharge 100.00 77.50
  b. "1" and "d" wide apart 170.00 135.00
30 (r) 1p on 4p ultra 45.00 12.50
  a. Double surcharge 170.00 135.00
  b. Triple surcharge *3,250.*
31 (s) 1p on 3p ultra ('91) 25.00 3.00
  a. Double surcharge 325.00 300.00
32 (s) 1p on 4p ultra 95.00 60.00
  a. Double surcharge 475.00 375.00
33 (t) 1p on 4p ultra *2,500.* *675.00*

No. 6 Surcharged

1892

34 A1 2½p on 3p ultra 21.00 .80
  a. Without period 92.50 55.00

No. 6 Surcharged

v

w

x y

z

1896

35 (v) ½p on 3p ultra 8.50 12.00
  a. Double surcharge "v" and "y" 15.50 15.50
36 (w) ½p on 3p ultra 14.50 3.00
  a. Double surcharge "w" and "y" 15.00 11.00
37 (x) ½p on 3p ultra 14.50 2.50
38 (y) ½p on 3p ultra 9.00 5.50
  a. Double surcharge 14.50 11.00
  b. Triple surcharge 77.50 77.50
39 (z) ½p on 3p ultra 14.50 2.50

Surcharged as "v" but "1" with Straight Serif

40 A1 ½p on 3p ultra 15.50 *16.50*
  a. Double surcharge, one type "y" 75.00 75.00

Surcharged as "z" but "1" with Straight Serif

41 A1 ½p on 3p ultra 15.50 15.50
  a. Double surcharge, one type "y" 75.00 75.00
  Nos. 35-41 (7) 92.00 57.50

No. 6 Surcharged

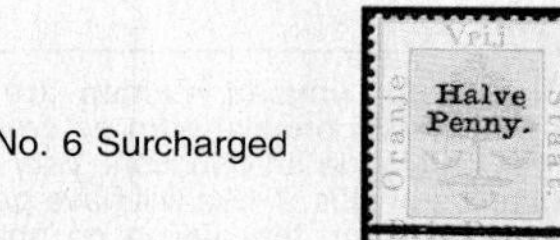

1896

42 A1 ½p on 3p ultra 1.10 .65
  a. No period after "Penny" 22.50 *35.00*
  b. "Peuny" 22.50 *35.00*
  c. Inverted surcharge 65.00 *72.50*
  d. Double surch., one inverted 200.00 *225.00*
  e. Without bar 10.00
  f. With additional surcharge as on Nos. 35-41 37.50
  g. As "a", inverted surcharge 2,250.
  h. As "b", inverted surcharge 1,750.

No. 6 Surcharged

1897

43 A1 2½p on 3p ultra 10.50 .90
  a. Roman "I" instead of "1" in "½" 185.00 100.00

Issued under British Occupation

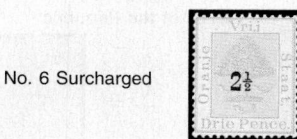

Nos. 2-8, 8a, 10-12 Surcharged or Overprinted

Periods in "V.R.I." Level with Bottoms of Letters

1900, Mar.-Apr. Unwmk. *Perf. 14*

44 A1 ½p on ½p org 5.00 *7.25*
  a. No period after "V" 25.00 *35.00*
  b. No period after "I" 175.00 175.00
  c. "I" and period after "R" omitted 300.00 275.00
  f. "½" omitted *210.00* *210.00*
  g. Small "½" 65.00 65.00
  h. Double surcharge 200.00
  i. As "g," double surcharge 575.00
45 A1 1p on 1p violet 3.00 2.00
  a. No period after "V" 20.00 18.50
  b. "I" and period after "R" omitted 300.00 300.00
  d. "1" of "1d" omitted 225.00 225.00
  e. "d" omitted 425.00 425.00
  f. "1d" omitted, "V.R.I." at top 475.00
45O A1 1p on 1p brown *675.00* *450.00*
  y. No period after "V" *4,000.*
46 A1 2p on 2p violet 4.75 3.00
  a. No period after "V" 20.00 24.00
  b. No period after "R" 360.00 360.00
  c. No period after "I" 360.00 360.00
47 A1 '2½' on 3p ultra 21.00 22.50
  a. No period after "V" 105.00 105.00
  b. Roman "I" in "½" 275.00 275.00
48 A1 3p on 3p ultra 3.25 4.75
  a. No period after "V" 25.00 30.00
  b. Dbl. surch. one diagonal 600.00
  c. Pair, one with surcharge omitted 725.00
  j. "3d" omitted 275.00 275.00
  k. "V.R.I." omitted 275.00 275.00
49 A1 4p on 4p ultra 11.00 *18.50*
  a. No period after "V" 72.50 *82.50*
50 A1 6p on 6p car rose 50.00 45.00
  a. No period after "V" 275.00 300.00
  b. "6" omitted 340.00 325.00
51 A1 6p on 6p ultra 14.50 6.50
  a. No period after "V" 55.00 55.00
  c. "6" omitted 95.00 *100.00*
  h. "V.R.I." omitted 550.00 425.00
52 A1 1sh on 1sh brown 8.00 3.00
  a. No period after "V" 55.00 35.00
  c. "1" of "1s" omitted 165.00 155.00
  j. "1s" omitted 225.00 220.00
  k. "V.R.I." omitted 225.00 220.00
52G A1 1sh on 1sh org *4,100.* *2,750.*
53 A1 5sh on 5sh green 32.50 60.00
  a. No period after "V" 300.00 *360.00*
  b. "5" omitted 1,100. 1,100.

#47, 47c overprinted "V.R.I." on #43.

No. 45f ("1d" omitted) with "V.R.I." at bottom is a shift which sells for a fifth of the value of the listed item. Varieties such as "V.R.I." omitted, denomination omitted and pair, one without surcharge are also the result of shifts.

For surcharges see Nos. 57, 60.

Nos. 2, 4-12 Surcharged or Overprinted

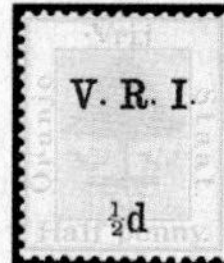

Periods in "V.R.I." Raised Above Bottoms of Letters

1900-01

44j A1 ½p on ½p orange .35 .25
  k. Mixed periods 3.25 2.25
  l. Pair, one with level periods 15.50 *20.00*
  m. No period after "V" 4.00 *4.25*
  n. No period after "I" 42.50 42.50
  o. "V" omitted 675.00
  p. Small "½" 20.00 *22.50*
  q. "1" for "I" in "V.R.I." 10.00
  r. Thick "V" 6.00 4.00
45i A1 1p on 1p violet .35 .25
  j. Mixed periods 2.00 *2.50*
  k. Pair, one with level periods 25.00 *25.00*
  l. No period after "V" 6.00 *7.00*
  m. No period after "R" 19.00 19.00
  n. No period after "I" 19.00 19.00
  p. Double surcharge 120.00 120.00
  q. Inverted surcharge 425.00
  s. Small "1" in "1d" 120.00 120.00
  t. "1" for "I" in "V.R.I." 13.00
  u. Thick "V" 7.50 .40
  v. As "u," invtd. "1" for "I" in "V.R.I." 24.00 24.00
  w. As "u," double surcharge 375.00 360.00
  z. As "u," no period after "R" 50.00 *55.00*
  za. Pair, one without surchage 275.00
  zb. Stamp double impression, one inverted 2,750.
  zc. Stamp double impression, one inverted, thick "V" 7,500.
46e A1 2p on 2p violet 3.50 .35
  f. Mixed periods 8.50 5.25
  g. Pair, one with level periods 15.00 *15.00*
  h. Inverted surcharge 360.00 360.00
  i. Thick "V" 16.50 15.50
  j. As "i," invtd. "1" for "I" in "V.R.I." 32.50 *35.00*
47c A1 '2½' on 3p ultra 250.00 250.00
  d. Thick "V" 4,250.
  f. As "d," Roman "I" on "½" —
48d A1 3p on 3p ultra 1.60 .35
  e. Mixed periods 9.50 9.50
  f. Pair, one with level periods 25.00 *25.00*
  g. Double surcharge 440.00
  h. Thick "V" 7.50 *17.50*
  i. As "h," invtd. "1" for "I" in "V.R.I." 72.50 *85.00*
  l. Double surcharge, one diagonal 450.00
  m. As "l", thick "V" *600.00*
  n. As "l", mixed periods *7,500.*
  o. As "n", thick "V" —
49b A1 4p on 4p ultra 3.25 *3.75*
  c. Mixed periods 11.00 *16.00*
  d. Pair, one with level periods 24.00 *35.00*
50c A1 6p on 6p car rose 45.00 *55.00*
  d. Mixed periods 160.00 *175.00*
  e. Pair, one with level periods 300.00 *350.00*
  f. Thick "V" *500.00* *525.00*
51d A1 6p on 6p ultra 1.10 .45
  e. Mixed periods 10.50 *11.00*
  f. Pair, one with level periods 25.00 *30.00*
  g. Thick "V" 25.00 35.00
  i. "6d" omitted 500.00
52e A1 1sh on 1sh brown 10.00 .50
  f. Mixed periods 27.50 25.00
  h. Pair, one with level periods 50.00 *55.00*
  i. Thick "V" 32.50 11.00
52j A1 1sh on 1sh orange *1,500.* *1,500.*
53c A1 5sh on 5sh green 10.50 *15.00*
  d. Mixed periods 400.00 400.00
  e. Pair, one with level periods *1,600.*
  f. "5" with short flag 65.00 *77.50*
  g. Thick "V" 72.50 *60.00*
  Handstamped "SPECIMEN" 60.00
  Handstamped "SPECIMEN", thick "V" 170.00

Stamps with mixed periods have one or two periods level with the bottoms of letters. One stamp in each pane had all periods level. Later settings had several stamps with thick "V." Forgeries of the scarcer varieties exist.

"V.R.I." stands for Victoria Regina Imperatrix. On No. 59, "E.R.I." stands for Edward Rex Imperator.

Cape of Good Hope Stamps of 1893-98 Overprinted

1900 Wmk. 16

54 A15 ½p green .65 .25
  a. No period after "COLONY" 12.00 *25.00*
  b. Double overprint 900.00 775.00
55 A13 2½p ultramarine 3.50 1.00
  a. No period after "COLONY" 82.50 82.50

Overprinted as in 1900

1902, May

56 A15 1p carmine rose 2.25 .25
  a. No period after "COLONY" 25.00 *30.00*

Nos. 51d, 53c, Surcharged and No. 8b Surcharged like No. 51 but Reading "E.R.I."

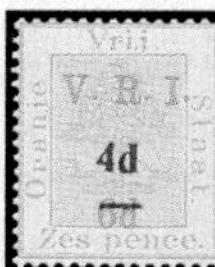

Carmine or Vermilion and Black Surcharges

1902 Unwmk.

57 A1 4p on 6p on 6p ultra 1.60 2.25
  a. Thick "V" 2.75 *8.25*
  b. As "a," invtd. "1" instead of "I" 7.25 *18.50*
  c. No period after "R" 42.50 *55.00*

Black Surcharge

59 A1 6p on 6p ultra 6.00 *19.00*
  a. Double surcharge, one invtd. — —

Orange Surcharge

60 A1 1sh on 5sh on 5sh grn 10.50 *25.00*
  a. Thick "V" 17.50 *55.00*
  b. "5" with short flag 80.00 *95.00*
  c. Double surcharge 1,100.
  Nos. 57-60 (3) 18.10 *46.25*

"E.R.I." stands for Edward Rex Imperator.

King Edward VII — A8

1903-04 Wmk. 2 Typo.

61 A8 ½p yellow green 10.00 2.50
  Never hinged 16.00
62 A8 1p carmine 8.50 .25
  Never hinged 10.50
63 A8 2p chocolate 10.00 1.00
  Never hinged 14.00
64 A8 2½p ultra 6.00 1.25
  Never hinged 5.75
65 A8 3p violet 10.50 1.25
  Never hinged 16.00
66 A8 4p olive grn & car 42.50 5.50
  Never hinged 15.00
  a. "IOSTAGE" for "POSTAGE" 1,000. 500.00
  Never hinged 1,600.
67 A8 6p violet & car 9.25 1.25
  Never hinged 15.00
68 A8 1sh bister & car 50.00 3.00
  Never hinged 67.50
69 A8 5sh red brn & bl ('04) 160.00 30.00
  Never hinged 170.00
  Nos. 61-69 (9) 306.75 46.00

Some of the above stamps are found with the overprint "C. S. A. R." for use by the Central South African Railway.

The "IOSTAGE" variety on the 4p is the result of filled in type.

Issue dates: 1p, Feb. 3. ½p, 2p, 2½p, 3p, 4p, 6p, 1sh, July 6. 5sh, Oct. 31.

1907-08 Wmk. 3

70 A8 ½p yellow green 16.50 1.10
  Never hinged 21.00
71 A8 1p carmine 10.50 .35
  Never hinged 17.00
72 A8 4p olive grn & car 5.00 5.25
  Never hinged 8.00
  a. "IOSTAGE" for "POSTAGE" 200.00 160.00
  Never hinged 350.00

73 A8 1sh bister & car 85.00 25.00
Never hinged 125.00
Nos. 70-73 (4) 117.00 31.70

The "IOSTAGE" variety on the 4p is the result of filled-in type.

Stamps of Orange River Colony were replaced by those of Union of South Africa.

MILITARY STAMP

M1

1899, Oct. 15 Unwmk. *Perf. 12*

M1 M1 black, *bister yellow* 50.00 60.00
Never hinged 90.00
On cover, *from* 1,200.

No. M1 was provided to members of the Orange Free State army on active service during the Second Boer War. Soldiers' mail carried free was required to bear either No. M1 or be signed by the sender's unit commander. The stamps were used extensively from Oct. 1899 until the fall of Kroonstad in May 1900.

No. M1 was typeset and printed by Curling & Co., Bloemfontein, in sheets of 20 (5x4), with each row of five containing slightly different types.

Forgeries exist. The most common counterfeits either have 17 pearls, rather than 16, in the top and bottom frames, or omit the periods after "BRIEF" and "FRANKO."

PAKISTAN

'pa-ki-ˌstan

LOCATION — In southern, central Asia
GOVT. — Republic
AREA — 307,293 sq. mi.
POP. — 88,000,000 (est. 1983)
CAPITAL — Islamabad

Pakistan was formed August 15, 1947, when India was divided into the Dominions of the Union of India and Pakistan, with some princely states remaining independent.

Pakistan had two areas made up of all or part of several predominantly Moslem provinces in the northwest and northeast corners of pre-1947 India. Western Pakistan consists of the entire provinces of Baluchistan, Sind (Scinde) and "Northwest Frontier," and 15 districts of the Punjab. Eastern Pakistan, consisting of the Sylhet district in Assam and 14 districts in Bengal Province, became independent as Bangladesh in December 1971.

The state of Las Bela was incorporated into Pakistan.

12 Pies = 1 Anna
16 Annas = 1 Rupee

Catalogue values for all unused stamps in this country are for Never Hinged items.

Stamps of India, 1937-43, Overprinted in Black

Nos. 1-12

Nos. 13-19

Perf. 13½x14

1947, Oct. 1 Wmk. 196

1 A83 3p slate .25 .25
On cover 5.00
2 A83 ½a rose violet .25 .25
On cover 5.00
3 A83 9p lt green .25 .25
On cover 5.00
4 A83 1a car rose .25 .25
On cover 5.00
4A A84 1a3p bister ('49) 4.75 *5.75*
Postally used 10.00
On cover 24.00
5 A84 1½a dk purple .25 .25
On cover 5.00
6 A84 2a scarlet .25 .40
On cover 5.00
7 A84 3a violet .25 .40
On cover 5.00
8 A84 3½a ultra 2.00 *3.00*
On cover 10.00
9 A85 4a chocolate .55 .30
On cover 5.00
10 A85 6a peacock blue 2.10 1.25
On cover 5.00
11 A85 8a blue violet .65 *.85*
On cover 5.00
12 A85 12a carmine lake 2.10 .40
On cover 5.00
13 A81 14a rose violet 5.75 3.50
On cover 12.00
14 A82 1r brn & slate 3.50 1.50
On cover 5.00
a. Inverted overprint 310.00
b. Pair, one without ovpt. 900.00
15 A82 2r dk brn & dk vio 6.50 3.25
On cover 9.00
16 A82 5r dp ultra & dk grn 8.00 5.00
On cover 17.00
17 A82 10r rose car & dk vio 10.00 6.50
On cover 32.50
18 A82 15r dk grn & dk brn 90.00 *110.00*
On cover 750.00
19 A82 25r dk vio & bl vio 70.00 70.00
On cover 650.00
Nos. 1-19 (20) 207.65 213.35
Set, hinged 135.00

Provisional use of stamps of India with handstamped or printed "PAKISTAN" was authorized in 1947-49. Nos. 4A, 14a 14b exist only as provisional issues.

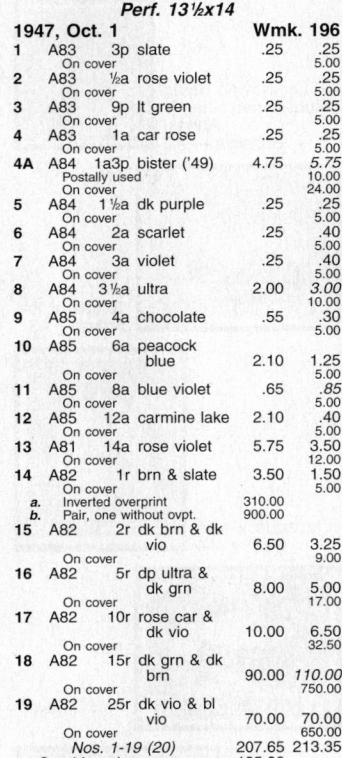

Constituent Assembly Building, Karachi A1

Crescent and Urdu Inscription — A2

Designs: 2½a, Karachi Airport entrance. 3a, Lahore Fort gateway.

Unwmk.

1948, July 9 Engr. *Perf. 14*

20 A1 1½a bright ultra 1.25 *2.00*
21 A1 2½a green 1.25 .25
22 A1 3a chocolate 1.25 .30

Perf. 12

23 A2 1r red 1.25 .85
a. Perf. 14 6.00 *10.00*
Nos. 20-23 (4) 5.00 3.40

Pakistan's independence, Aug. 15, 1947.

Examples of No. 23a used on cover are unknown. Used examples of No. 23a are cto.

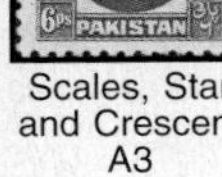

Scales, Star and Crescent A3

Star and Crescent A4

Karachi Airport Building A5

Karachi Port Authority Building — A6

Khyber Pass — A7

2½a, 3½a, 4a, Ghulan Muhammed Dam, Indus River, Sind. 1r, 2r, 5r, Salimullah Hostel.

Perf. 12½, 14 (3a, 10a), 14x13½ (2½a, 3½a, 6a, 12a)

1948-57 Unwmk.

24 A3 3p org red, perf. 12½ .25 .25
a. Perf. 13½ ('54) 2.00 1.00
25 A3 6p pur, perf. 12½ 1.25 .25
a. Perf. 13½ ('54) 4.00 3.50
26 A3 9p dk grn, perf. 12½ .55 .25
a. Perf. 13½ ('54) 3.50 1.75
27 A4 1a dark blue .25 .50
28 A4 1½a gray green .25 .25
29 A4 2a orange red 4.50 .70
30 A6 2½a green 6.50 *5.00*
31 A5 3a olive green 8.00 1.00
32 A6 3½a violet blue 6.50 *4.00*
33 A6 4a chocolate 1.25 .25
34 A6 6a deep blue 2.00 .55
35 A6 8a black 2.00 *1.25*
36 A5 10a red 8.00 *8.00*
37 A6 12a red 8.00 1.25

Perf. 14

38 A5 1r ultra 19.00 .25
a. Perf. 13½ ('54) 25.00 7.00
39 A5 2r dark brown 20.00 .80
a. Perf. 13½ ('54) 30.00 3.00

Perf. 13½

40 A5 5r car ('54) 13.00 .40
a. Perf. 13½x14 17.00 2.25

Perf. 13

41 A7 10r rose lilac ('51) 19.00 2.50
a. Perf. 14 14.00 *26.00*
b. Perf. 12 110.00 8.50
42 A7 15r blue green ('57) 20.00 16.00
a. Perf. 14 20.00 *65.00*
b. Perf. 12 32.50 20.00

Perf. 14

43 A7 25r purple 55.00 *67.50*
a. Perf. 13 ('54) 40.00 27.50
b. Perf. 12 32.50 *37.50*
Nos. 24-43 (20) 195.30 110.95
Set, hinged 100.00

Many compound perforations exist.

See No. 259, types A9-A11. For surcharges and overprints see Nos. 124, O14-O26, O35-O37, O41-O43A, O52, O63, O68.

Imperfs of Nos. 24-43 are from proof sheets improperly removed from the printer's archives.

"Quaid-i-Azam" (Great Leader), "Mohammed Ali Jinnah" — A8

1949, Sept. 11 Engr. *Perf. 13½x14*

44 A8 1½a brown 1.75 1.00
45 A8 3a dark green 2.25 1.25
46 A8 10a blk *(English inscriptions)* 6.00 *6.00*
Nos. 44-46 (3) 10.00 8.25

1st anniv. of the death of Mohammed Ali Jinnah (1876-1948), Moslem lawyer, president of All-India Moslem League and first Governor General of Pakistan.

Re-engraved (Crescents Reversed)

A9

A10

A11

Perf. 12½, 13½x14 (3a, 10a), 14x13½ (6a, 12a)

1949-53

47 A10 1a dk blue ('50) 2.50 .55
a. Perf. 13 ('52) 3.00 .25
48 A10 1½a gray green 7.00 2.00
a. Perf. 13 ('53) 2.50 .25
49 A10 2a orange red 2.50 .55
a. Perf. 13 ('53) 2.00 .25
b. As "a," printed on gum side 55.00
50 A9 3a olive green 7.50 1.00
51 A11 6a deep blue ('50) 14.00 .50
52 A11 8a black ('50) 6.00 1.10
53 A9 10a red 7.50 1.25
54 A11 12a red ('50) 27.50 .90
Nos. 47-54 (8) 74.50 7.85

For overprints see #O27-O31, O38-O40.

Vase and Plate — A12

Star and Crescent, Plane and Hour Glass — A13

Moslem Leaf Pattern — A14

Arch and Lamp of Learning A15

1951, Aug. 14 Engr. *Perf. 13*

55 A12 2½a dark red 1.90 1.25
56 A13 3a dk rose lake 1.00 .25
57 A12 3½a dp ultra (Urdu "½3") 1.25 *8.00*
57A A12 3½a dp ultra (Urdu "3½") ('56) 4.50 6.00
58 A14 4a deep green 1.50 .25
59 A14 6a red orange 1.50 .25
60 A15 8a brown 4.50 .35
61 A15 10a purple 2.25 1.00
62 A13 12a dk slate blue 2.00 .25
Nos. 55-62 (9) 20.40 17.60

Fourth anniversary of independence.

On No. 57, the characters of the Urdu denomination at right appears as "½3." On the reengraved No. 57A, they read "3½."

Issue date: Dec. 1956.

See Nos. 88, O32-O34.

For surcharges see Nos. 255, 257.

OFFICIAL STAMPS

Official Stamps of India, 1939-43, Overprinted in Black

1947-49 Wmk. 196 *Perf. 13½x14*

O1	O8	3p slate	1.50	.50
		On cover		5.00
O2	O8	½a dk rose vio	.60	.25
		On cover		5.00
O3	O8	9p green	4.00	1.50
		On cover		8.00
O4	O8	1a carmine rose	.60	.25
		On cover		5.00
O4A	O8	1a3p bister ('49)	*9.00*	*25.00*
		Postally used		30.00
		On cover		40.00
O5	O8	1½a dull purple	.60	.25
		On cover		5.00
O6	O8	2a scarlet	.60	.40
		On cover		5.00
O7	O8	2½a purple	7.00	*11.00*
		On cover		24.00
O8	O8	4a dk brown	1.40	*.50*
		On cover		5.00
O9	O8	8a blue violet	2.00	*.75*
		On cover		16.00
		Nos. O1-O9 (10)	27.30	40.40

India Nos. O100-O103 Overprinted in Black

O10	A82	1r brown & slate	1.00	*1.25*
		On cover		8.00
O11	A82	2r dk brn & dk vio	7.50	1.50
		On cover		25.00
O12	A82	5r dp ultra & dk grn	30.00	*55.00*
		On cover		550.00
		Telegraph cancel		7.50
O13	A82	10r rose car & dk vio	60.00	*30.00*
		On cover		600.00
		Telegraph cancel		*5.00*
		Nos. O1-O13 (14)	125.80	128.15
		Set, hinged	90.00	

Regular Issue of 1948 Overprinted in Black or Carmine — a

"C" in "SERVICE" is nearly round.

Perf. 12½, 13, 13½x14, 14x13½

1948, Aug. 14 Unwmk.

O14	A3	3p orange red	.25	.25
O15	A3	6p purple (C)	.25	.25
O16	A3	9p dk green (C)	.25	.25
O17	A4	1a dk blue (C)	4.25	.25
O18	A4	1½a gray grn (C)	4.00	.25
O19	A4	2a orange red	1.75	.25
O20	A5	3a olive green	29.00	14.00
O21	A6	4a chocolate	1.25	.25
O22	A6	8a black (C)	2.50	*10.00*
O23	A5	1r ultra	1.25	.30
O24	A5	2r dark brown	17.50	10.00
O25	A5	5r carmine	50.00	20.00
O26	A7	10r rose lil, perf. 14x13½	22.50	*60.00*
a.		Perf. 12	25.00	*65.00*
b.		Perf. 13	22.50	*70.00*
		Nos. O14-O26 (13)	134.75	116.05
		Set, hinged	72.50	

Issued: No. O26a, 10/10/51; No. O26b, 1954(?).

Nos. 47-50 and 52 Overprinted Type "a" in Black or Carmine

1949-50 *Perf. 12½, 13½x14*

O27	A10	1a dark blue (C)	2.10	.25
O28	A10	1½a gray green (C)	.65	.25
a.		Inverted ovpt.	275.00	45.00
O29	A10	2a orange red	2.10	.25
O30	A9	3a olive grn ('49)	37.50	7.50
O31	A11	8a black (C)	57.50	25.00
		Nos. O27-O31 (5)	99.85	33.25

Unwmk.

1951, Aug. 14 Engr. *Perf. 13*

O32	A13	3a dark rose lake	9.25	*10.00*
O33	A14	4a deep green	2.40	.40
O34	A15	8a brown	*10.00*	5.00
		Nos. O32-O34 (3)	21.65	*15.40*

See Nos. 56, 58, 60.

BAHAWALPUR

LOCATION — A State of Pakistan.
AREA — 17,494 sq. mi.
POP. — 1,341,209 (1941)
CAPITAL — Bahawalpur

Bahawalpur was an Indian princely state that was autonomous from Aug. 15-Oct. 3, 1947, when it united with Pakistan. These stamps had franking power solely within Bahawalpur.

Used values are for c-t-o or favor cancels.

India George VI stamps of 1937-40 and 1941-43 were overprinted for use in Bahawalpur during the brief period of that state's independence, following the creation of the separate dominions of India and Pakistan on Aug. 15, 1947. Stamps of Bahawalpur were replaced by stamps of Pakistan for external mail when the state united with Pakistan on Oct. 3, 1947. They continued to be used on internal mail until 1953.

Stamps of India Used in Bahawalpur

Overprinted in Red or Black

1947, Aug. 15

A1	A83	3p slate (R)	30.00	
		Never hinged	42.50	
A2	A83	½a rose vio	30.00	
		Never hinged	42.50	
A3	A83	9p light grn (R)	30.00	
		Never hinged	42.50	
A4	A83	1a car rose	30.00	
		Never hinged	42.50	
A5	A84	1½a dark pur (R)	30.00	
		Never hinged	42.50	
A6	A84	2a scarlet	30.00	
		Never hinged	42.50	
a.		Double overprint	3,500.	
		Never hinged	5,000.	
A7	A84	3a violet (R)	30.00	
		Never hinged	42.50	
A8	A84	3½a ultramarine (R)	30.00	
		Never hinged	42.50	
A9	A85	4a chocolate	30.00	
		Never hinged	42.50	
A10	A85	6a peacock bl (R)	30.00	
		Never hinged	42.50	
a.		Double overprint	3,500.	
		Never hinged	5,000.	
A11	A85	8a blue vio (R)	30.00	
		Never hinged	42.50	
A12	A85	12a carm lake	30.00	
		Never hinged	42.50	
A13	A81	14a rose vio	75.00	
		Never hinged	85.00	
A14	A82	1r brn & slate	35.00	
		Never hinged	55.00	
a.		Double overprint, one albino	400.00	
		Never hinged	550.00	
A15	A82	2r dk brn & dk vio (R)	2,250.	
		Never hinged	4,250.	
A16	A82	5r dp ultra & dk grn (R)	2,250.	
		Never hinged	4,250.	
A17	A82	10r rose car & dk vio	2,250.	
		Never hinged	4,250.	

Covers: Commercial covers of Nos. A1-A17 are very rare, with perhaps one to three covers known for each.

Numerous overprint forgeries exist. Most postmarks encountered are canceled to order.

Catalogue values for unused stamps in this section, from this point to the end of the section are for Never Hinged items.

Amir Muhammad Bahawal Khan I Abbasi — A1

Perf. 12½x12

1947, Dec. 1 Wmk. 274 Engr.

1	A1	½a brt car rose & blk	4.00	*8.00*

Bicentenary of the ruling family.

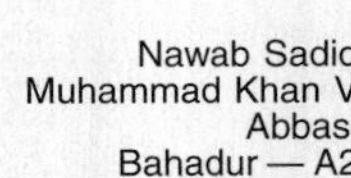

Nawab Sadiq Muhammad Khan V Abbasi Bahadur — A2

Tombs of the Amirs — A3

Mosque, Sadiq Garh — A4

Fort Dirawar A5

Nur-Mahal Palace — A6

Palace, Sadiq Garh — A7

Nawab Sadiq Muhammad Khan V Abbasi Bahadur — A8

A9

Perf. 12½ (A2), 12x12½ (A3, A5, A6, A7), 12½x12 (A4, A8), 13x13½ (A9)

1948, Apr. 1 Engr. Wmk. 274

2	A2	3p dp blue & blk	2.00	*11.00*
3	A2	½a lake & blk	2.00	*11.00*
4	A2	9p dk green & blk	2.00	*11.00*
5	A2	1a dp car & blk	2.00	*11.00*
6	A2	1½a violet & blk	3.00	*11.00*
7	A3	2a car & dp grn	3.00	*11.00*
8	A4	4a brn & org red	3.00	*11.00*
9	A5	6a dp bl & vio brn	3.50	*11.00*
10	A6	8a brt pur & car	3.75	*11.00*
11	A7	12a dp car & dk bl grn	4.50	*11.00*
12	A8	1r chocolate & vio	25.00	*35.00*
13	A8	2r dp mag & dk grn	50.00	*45.00*
14	A8	5r purple & black	50.00	*55.00*
15	A9	10r black & car	45.00	*65.00*
		Nos. 2-15 (14)	198.75	*310.00*

See #18-21. For overprints see #O17-O24.

Soldiers of 1848 and 1948 — A10

1948, Oct. 15 Engr. *Perf. 11½*

16	A10	1½a dp car & blk	1.75	*8.00*

Centenary of the Multan Campaign.

Amir Khan V and Mohammed Ali Jinnah — A11

1948, Oct. 3 *Perf. 13x12½*

17	A11	1½a grn & car rose	1.50	*5.25*

1st anniv. of the union of Bahawalpur with Pakistan.

Types of 1948

1948 *Perf. 12x11½*

18	A8	1r orange & dp grn	1.75	*17.00*
19	A8	2r carmine & blk	1.90	*21.00*
20	A8	5r ultra & red brn	2.25	*37.50*

Perf. 13½

21	A9	10r green & red brn	2.75	*50.00*
		Nos. 18-21 (4)	8.65	*125.50*

Panjnad Weir — A12

1949, Mar. 3 *Perf. 14*

22	A12	3p shown	.25	*8.00*
23	A12	½a Wheat	.25	*8.00*
24	A12	9p Cotton	.25	*8.00*
25	A12	1a Sahiwal Bull	.25	*8.00*
		Nos. 22-25 (4)	1.00	*32.00*

25th anniv. of the acquisition of full ruling powers by Amir Khan V.

UPU Monument, Bern — A13

1949, Oct. 10 *Perf. 13*

Center in Black

26	A13	9p green	.25	*3.00*
27	A13	1a red violet	.25	*3.00*
28	A13	1½a brown orange	.25	*3.00*
29	A13	2½a blue	.25	*3.00*
		Nos. 26-29 (4)	1.00	*12.00*

UPU, 75th anniv. Exist perf 17½x17; value, each $2. Exist imperf.

For overprints see Nos. O25-O28.

OFFICIAL STAMPS

Two printings of Nos. O1-O10 exist. The first printing has brownish, streaky gum, and the second printing has clear, even gum.

Panjnad Weir — O1

Camel and Colt — O2

Antelopes O3

Pelicans O4

Juma Masjid Palace, Fort Derawar O5

Temple at Pattan Munara O6

Red Overprint

Wmk. 274

1945, Jan. 1 Engr. *Perf. 14*

O1	O1	½a brt grn & blk	4.50	*12.50*
O2	O2	1a carmine & blk	5.75	*12.50*
O3	O3	2a violet & blk	5.00	*12.50*
O4	O4	4a olive & blk	12.50	*16.00*
O5	O5	8a brown & blk	22.00	20.00
O6	O6	1r orange & blk	22.00	20.00
		Nos. O1-O6 (6)	71.75	*93.50*

For types overprinted see Nos. O7-O9, O11-O13.

Types of 1945, Without Red Overprint, Srchd. in Black

1945 Unwmk.

O7	O5	½a on 8a lake & blk	*10.00*	*10.00*
O8	O6	1½a on 1r org & blk	35.00	*10.00*
O9	O1	1½a on 2r ultra & blk	200.00	20.00
		Nos. O7-O9 (3)	245.00	40.00

Camels — O7

1945, Mar. 10 Red Overprint

O10	O7	1a brown & black	80.00	*75.00*

Types of 1945, Without Red Overprint, Ovptd. in Black

1945

O11	O1	½a carmine & black	1.75	*7.00*
O12	O2	1a carmine & black	3.00	*7.00*
O13	O3	2a orange & black	5.25	*7.00*
		Nos. O11-O13 (3)	10.00	*21.00*

Nawab Sadiq Muhammad Khan V Abbasi Bahadur — O8

1945

O14	O8	3p dp blue & blk	4.50	*8.00*
O15	O8	1½a dp violet & blk	27.50	17.00

Flags of Allied Nations O9

1946, May 1

O16	O9	1½a emerald & gray	5.50	*7.00*

Victory of Allied Nations in World War II.

Stamps of 1948 Overprinted in Carmine or Black

Perf. 12½, 12½x12, 12x11½, 13½

1948 Wmk. 274

O17	A2	3p dp bl & blk (C)	1.00	*15.00*
O18	A2	1a dp carmine & blk	1.00	*15.00*
O19	A3	2a car & dp grn	1.00	*15.00*
O20	A4	4a brown & org red	1.00	*15.00*
O21	A8	1r org & dp grn (C)	1.00	*15.00*
O22	A8	2r car & blk (C)	1.00	*15.00*
O23	A8	5r ultra & red brn (C)	1.00	*15.00*
O24	A9	10r grn & red brn (C)	1.00	*15.00*
		Nos. O17-O24 (8)	8.00	*120.00*

Same Ovpt. in Carmine on #26-29

1949 Center in Black *Perf. 13, 18*

O25	A13	9p green	.25	*7.50*
O26	A13	1a red violet	.25	*7.50*
O27	A13	1½a brown orange	.25	*7.50*
O28	A13	2½a blue	.25	*7.50*
		Nos. O25-O28 (4)	1.00	*30.00*

75th anniv. of the UPU. Exist perf 17½x17; value, each *$10.* Exist imperf.

PALESTINE

ˈpa-lə-ˌstīn

LOCATION — Western Asia bordering on the Mediterranean Sea
GOVT. — British Mandate
AREA — 10,429 sq. mi.
POP. — 1,605,816 (estimated)
CAPITAL — Jerusalem

Formerly a part of Turkey, Palestine was occupied by the Egyptian Expeditionary Forces of the British Army in World War I and was mandated to Great Britain in 1923.

10 Milliemes = 1 Piaster
1000 Milliemes = 1 Egyptian Pound
1000 Mils = 1 Palestine Pound (1928)

Watermark

Wmk. 33

Issued under British Military Occupation

For use in Palestine, Transjordan, Lebanon, Syria and in parts of Cilicia and northeastern Egypt

A1

Wmk. Crown and "GvR" (33)

1918, Feb. 10 Litho. *Rouletted 20*

1	A1	1pi deep blue	190.00	105.00
2	A1	1pi ultra	2.50	2.50

Nos. 2 & 1 Surcharged in Black

1918, Feb. 16

3	A1	5m on 1pi ultra	8.50	4.25
a.		5m on 1pi gray blue	110.00	*600.00*

Nos. 1 and 3a were issued without gum. No. 3a is on paper with a surface sheen.

1918 Typo. *Perf. 15x14*

4	A1	1m dark brown	.35	*.45*
		Never hinged	.55	
5	A1	2m blue green	.35	*.50*
		Never hinged	.55	
6	A1	3m light brown	.40	.40
		Never hinged	.60	
7	A1	4m scarlet	.40	*.45*
		Never hinged	.60	
8	A1	5m orange	.75	.35
		Never hinged	1.15	
9	A1	1pi indigo	.50	.30
		Never hinged	.75	
10	A1	2pi olive green	3.50	1.00
		Never hinged	4.50	
11	A1	5pi plum	3.75	2.50
		Never hinged	4.75	
12	A1	9pi bister	11.50	7.50
		Never hinged	16.50	
13	A1	10pi ultramarine	12.00	4.50
		Never hinged	18.00	
14	A1	20pi gray	16.00	*20.00*
		Never hinged	24.00	
		Nos. 4-14 (11)	49.50	37.95

Many shades exist.

Nos. 4-11 exist with rough perforation.

Issued: 1m, 2m, 4m, 2pi, 5pi, 7/16; 5m, 9/25; 1pi, 11/9; 3m, 9pi, 10pi, 12/17; 20pi, 12/27.

Nos. 4-11 with overprint "O. P. D. A." (Ottoman Public Debt Administration) or "H.J.Z." (Hejaz-Jemen Railway) are revenue stamps; they exist postally used.

For overprints on stamps and types see #15-62 & Jordan #1-63, 73-90, 92-102, 130-144, J12-J23.

Issued under British Administration

Overprinted at Jerusalem

Stamps and Type of 1918 Overprinted in Black or Silver

1920, Sept. 1 Wmk. 33 *Perf. 15x14*

Arabic Overprint 8mm long

15	A1	1m dark brown	9.00	2.25
16	A1	2m bl grn, perf 14	4.50	1.75
d.		Perf 15x14	14.00	6.00
17	A1	3m lt brown	17.50	8.50
d.		Perf 14	110.00	62.50
e.		Inverted overprint	550.00	*700.00*
18	A1	4m scarlet	5.25	1.75
19	A1	5m org, perf 14	8.00	.75
e.		Perf 15x14	27.50	10.00
20	A1	1pi indigo (S)	5.75	1.25
21	A1	2pi olive green	7.00	2.50
22	A1	5pi plum	27.50	*30.00*
23	A1	9pi bister	15.00	*23.00*
24	A1	10pi ultra	13.00	*19.50*
25	A1	20pi gray	35.00	*50.00*
		Nos. 15-25 (11)	147.50	141.25

Forgeries exist of No. 17e.

Similar Ovpt., with Arabic Line 10mm Long, Arabic "S" and "T" Joined, ".." at Left Extends Above Other Letters

1920-21 *Perf. 15x14*

15a	A1	1m dark brown	2.25	1.20
e.		Perf. 14	700.00	850.00
g.		As "a," invtd. ovpt.	450.00	
16a	A1	2m blue green	10.00	4.50
e.		"PALESTINE" omitted	*2,500.*	*1,500.*
f.		Perf. 14	4.75	4.50
17a	A1	3m light brown	3.75	1.20
18a	A1	4m scarlet	5.50	1.40
b.		Perf. 14	70.00	87.50
19a	A1	5m orange	2.60	.90
f.		Perf. 14	9.50	1.25
20a	A1	1pi indigo, perf. 14 (S) ('21)	57.50	1.40
d.		Perf. 15x14	525.00	32.50
21a	A1	2pi olive green ('21)	75.00	30.00
22a	A1	5pi plum ('21)	52.50	11.00
d.		Perf. 14	225.00	*525.00*
		Nos. 15a-22a (8)	209.10	51.60

This overprint often looks grayish to grayish black. In the English line the letters are frequently uneven and damaged.

Similar Ovpt., with Arabic Line 10mm Long, Arabic "S" and "T" Separated and 6mm Between English and Hebrew Lines

1920, Dec. 6

15b	A1	1m dk brn, perf 14	57.50	37.50
17b	A1	3m lt brn, perf 15x14	60.00	37.50
19b	A1	5m orange, perf 14	400.00	37.50
d.		Perf. 15x14	*16,000.*	*13,750.*
		Nos. 15b-19b (3)	517.50	112.50

Overprinted as Before, 7½mm Between English and Hebrew Lines, ".." at Left Even With Other Letters

1921 *Perf. 15x14*

15c	A1	1m dark brown	15.00	4.00
f.		1m dull brown, perf 14		*2,300.*
16c	A1	2m blue green	25.00	6.25
17c	A1	3m light brown	35.00	3.50
18c	A1	4m scarlet	35.00	4.00
19c	A1	5m orange	70.00	1.10
20c	A1	1pi indigo (S)	21.00	.90
21c	A1	2pi olive green	26.50	7.00
22c	A1	5pi plum	29.00	9.25
23c	A1	9pi bister	57.50	*100.00*
24c	A1	10pi ultra	70.00	16.00
25c	A1	20pi pale gray	100.00	57.50
d.		Perf. 14	*13,750.*	*2,900.*
		Nos. 15c-25c (11)	484.00	*209.50*

Overprinted at London

Stamps of 1918 Overprinted

1921 *Perf. 15x14*

37	A1	1m dark brown	1.50	.35
38	A1	2m blue green	2.50	.35
39	A1	3m light brown	2.75	.35
40	A1	4m scarlet	3.25	.70
41	A1	5m orange	3.00	.35
42	A1	1pi bright blue	2.25	.40
43	A1	2pi olive green	3.75	.45
44	A1	5pi plum	10.00	5.75
45	A1	9pi bister	20.00	16.00
46	A1	10pi ultra	26.00	*600.00*
47	A1	20pi gray	65.00	*1,600.*
		Nos. 37-47 (11)	140.00	
		Nos. 37-45 (9)		24.70

The 2nd character from left on bottom line that looks like quotation marks consists of long thin lines.

Deformed or damaged letters exist in all three lines of the overprint.

Similar Overprint on Type of 1921

1922 Wmk. 4 *Perf. 14*

No.	Type	Description	Unused	Used
48	A1	1m dark brown	1.75	.35
a.		Inverted overprint	—	*13,750.*
b.		Double overprint	260.00	500.00
49	A1	2m yellow	2.50	.35
50	A1	3m Prus blue	2.75	.25
51	A1	4m rose	2.75	.25
52	A1	5m orange	3.25	.35
53	A1	6m blue green	2.50	.35
54	A1	7m yellow brown	2.50	.35
55	A1	8m red	2.50	.35
56	A1	1pi gray	3.00	.35
57	A1	13m ultra	3.50	.25
58	A1	2pi olive green	3.50	.40
a.		Inverted overprint	350.00	*575.00*
b.		2pi yellow bister	*140.00*	*7.50*
59	A1	5pi plum	5.50	1.40
a.		Perf. 15x14	62.50	4.50

Perf. 15x14

No.	Type	Description	Unused	Used
60	A1	9pi bister	10.00	10.00
a.		Perf. 14	1,050.	225.00
61	A1	10pi light blue	8.50	3.00
a.		Perf. 14	75.00	15.00
62	A1	20pi violet	10.50	6.25
a.		Perf. 14	180.00	120.00
		Nos. 48-62 (15)	65.00	24.25

The 2nd character from left on bottom line that looks like quotation marks consists of short thick lines.

The "E. F. F." for "E. E. F." on No. 61 is caused by damaged type.

Rachel's Tomb — A3

Mosque of Omar (Dome of the Rock) — A4

Citadel at Jerusalem A5

Tiberias and Sea of Galilee A6

1927-42 Typo. *Perf. 13½x14½*

No.	Type	Description	Unused	Used
63	A3	2m Prus blue	2.75	.25
		Never hinged	4.25	
64	A3	3m yellow green	1.75	.25
		Never hinged	2.75	
65	A4	4m rose red	9.00	1.40
		Never hinged	13.50	
66	A4	4m violet brn ('32)	2.50	.25
		Never hinged	3.75	
67	A5	5m brown org	4.25	.25
		Never hinged	6.50	
c.		Perf. 14½x14 (coil stamp) ('36)	16.00	*21.00*
		Never hinged	24.00	
68	A4	6m deep green	1.50	.25
		Never hinged	2.25	
69	A5	7m deep red	12.00	.70
		Never hinged	18.00	
70	A5	7m dk violet ('32)	1.00	.25
		Never hinged	1.50	
71	A4	8m yellow brown	18.50	7.00
		Never hinged	28.50	
72	A4	8m scarlet ('32)	1.50	.25
		Never hinged	2.25	
73	A3	10m deep gray	1.75	.25
		Never hinged	2.75	
a.		Perf. 14½x14 (coil stamp) ('38)	23.50	*27.50*
74	A4	13m ultra	17.50	.40
		Never hinged	27.00	
75	A4	13m olive bister ('32)	2.75	.25
		Never hinged	4.25	
76	A4	15m ultra ('32)	4.75	.50
		Never hinged	7.25	
77	A5	20m olive green	1.75	.25
		Never hinged	2.75	

Perf. 14

No.	Type	Description	Unused	Used
78	A6	50m brown purple	3.50	.40
		Never hinged	5.50	
79	A6	90m bister	87.50	*60.00*
		Never hinged	130.00	
80	A6	100m bright blue	2.60	.80
		Never hinged	4.00	
81	A6	200m dk violet	9.25	5.75
		Never hinged	14.00	
82	A6	250m dp brown ('42)	7.50	3.50
		Never hinged	11.00	
83	A6	500m red ('42)	9.00	3.50
		Never hinged	11.00	
84	A6	£1 gray black ('42)	13.00	4.00
		Never hinged	17.50	
		Nos. 63-84 (22)	215.60	90.45

Issued: 3m, #74, 6/1; 2m, 5m, 6m, 10m, #65, 69, 71, 77-81, 8/14; #70, 72, 6/1/32; #75, 15m, 8/1/32; #66, 11/1/32; #82-84, 1/15/42.

POSTAGE DUE STAMPS

D1

1923 Unwmk. Typo. *Perf. 11*

No.	Type	Description	Unused	Used
J1	D1	1m bister brown	27.50	*40.00*
		Never hinged	30.00	
b.		Horiz. pair, imperf. btwn.	1,300.	*750.00*
J2	D1	2m green	16.00	11.50
		Never hinged	24.00	
J3	D1	4m red	12.00	*13.50*
		Never hinged	18.00	
J4	D1	8m violet	8.50	*8.50*
		Never hinged	13.00	
b.		Horiz. pair, imperf. btwn.		*2,300.*
J5	D1	13m dark blue	7.50	*8.50*
		Never hinged	11.50	
a.		Horiz. pair, imperf. btwn.	1,050.	
		Nos. J1-J5 (5)	71.50	*82.00*

Imperfs. of 1m, 2m, 8m, are from proof sheets.

Values for Nos. J1-J5 are for fine centered copies.

D2

1924, Dec. 1 Wmk. 4

No.	Type	Description	Unused	Used
J6	D2	1m brown	1.10	2.00
		Never hinged	1.60	
J7	D2	2m yellow	4.00	1.75
		Never hinged	6.00	
J8	D2	4m green	2.00	1.50
		Never hinged	3.00	
J9	D2	8m red	3.00	1.00
		Never hinged	4.50	
J10	D2	13m ultramarine	3.50	2.50
		Never hinged	4.25	
J11	D2	5pi violet	15.00	1.75
		Never hinged	19.50	
		Nos. J6-J11 (6)	28.60	10.50

D3

1928-45 *Perf. 14*

No.	Type	Description	Unused	Used
J12	D3	1m lt brown	2.75	1.00
		Never hinged	3.50	
a.		Perf. 15x14 ('45)	42.50	80.00
J13	D3	2m yellow	3.00	.70
		Never hinged	4.75	
J14	D3	4m green	3.50	1.60
		Never hinged	5.50	
a.		4m bluish grn, perf. 15x14 ('45)	75.00	*97.50*
J15	D3	6m brown org ('33)	19.00	5.00
		Never hinged	27.00	
J16	D3	8m red	2.75	1.25
		Never hinged	4.25	
J17	D3	10m light gray	2.00	.70
		Never hinged	3.00	
J18	D3	13m ultra	4.50	2.25
		Never hinged	7.00	
J19	D3	20m olive green	4.50	1.25
		Never hinged	7.00	
J20	D3	50m violet	5.00	2.50
		Never hinged	7.00	
		Nos. J12-J20 (9)	47.00	16.25

The Hebrew word for "mil" appears below the numeral on all values but the 1m.

Issued: 6m, Oct. 1933; others, Feb. 1, 1928.

PANAMA

'pa-nə-ˌmä

LOCATION — Central America between Costa Rica and Colombia
GOVT. — Republic
AREA — 30,134 sq. mi.
POP. — 1,970,000 (est. 1983)
CAPITAL — Panama

Formerly a department of the Republic of Colombia, Panama gained its independence in 1903. Dividing the country at its center is the Panama Canal.

100 Centavos = 1 Peso
100 Centesimos = 1 Balboa (1904)

Watermark

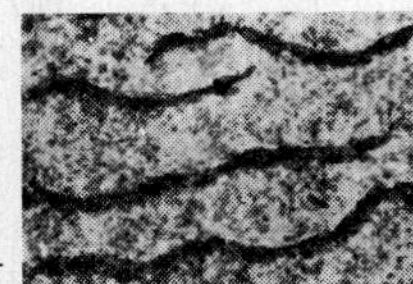

Wmk. 229 — Wavy Lines

Wmk. 233 — "Harrison & Sons, London." in Script

GREAT BRITAIN USED in PANAMA

Stamps of Great Britain cancelled "C35" were used in Panama. Listings appear in the "Stamps of Great Britain Used in Colombia" section, at the beginning of Colombian listings.

Issues of the Sovereign State of Panama Under Colombian Dominion

Valid only for domestic mail.

Coat of Arms
A1 A2

1878 Unwmk. Litho. *Imperf.*

Thin Wove Paper

No.	Type	Description	Unused	Used
1	A1	5c gray green	25.00	30.00
a.		5c yellow green	25.00	30.00
2	A1	10c blue	60.00	60.00
3	A1	20c rose red	40.00	32.50
		Nos. 1-3 (3)	125.00	122.50

Very Thin Wove Paper

No.	Type	Description	Unused	Used
4	A2	50c buff	*1,500.*	

All values of this issue are known rouletted unofficially.

Medium Thick Paper

No.	Type	Description	Unused	Used
5	A1	5c blue green	25.00	30.00
6	A1	10c blue	65.00	70.00
7	A2	50c orange	13.00	
		Nos. 5-7 (3)	103.00	100.00

Nos. 5-7 were printed before Nos. 1-4, according to Panamanian archives.

Values for used Nos. 1-5 are for handstamped postal cancellations.

These stamps have been reprinted in a number of shades, on thin to moderately thick, white or yellowish paper. They are without gum or with white, crackly gum. All values have been reprinted from new stones made from retouched dies. The marks of retouching are plainly to be seen in the sea and clouds. On the original 10c the shield in the upper left corner has two blank sections; on the reprints the design of this shield is completed. The impression of these reprints is frequently blurred.

Reprints of the 50c are rare. Beware of remainders of the 50c offered as reprints.

Issues of Colombia for use in the Department of Panama

Issued because of the use of different currency.

Map of Panama — A3

1887-88 *Perf. 13½*

No.	Type	Description	Unused	Used
8	A3	1c black, *green*	.90	.80
9	A3	2c black, *pink* ('88)	1.60	1.25
a.		2c black, *salmon*	1.60	
10	A3	5c black, *blue*	.90	.35
11	A3	10c black, *yellow*	.90	.40
a.		Imperf., pair		
12	A3	20c black, *lilac*	1.00	.50
13	A3	50c brown ('88)	2.00	1.00
a.		Imperf.		
		Nos. 8-13 (6)	7.30	4.30

See No. 14. For surcharges and overprints see Nos. 24-30, 107-108, 115-116, 137-138.

1892 Pelure Paper

No.	Type	Description	Unused	Used
14	A3	50c brown	2.50	1.10

The stamps of this issue have been reprinted on papers of slightly different colors from those of the originals.

These are: 1c yellow green, 2c deep rose, 5c bright blue, 10c straw, 20c violet.

The 50c is printed from a very worn stone, in a lighter brown than the originals. The series includes a 10c on lilac paper.

All these stamps are to be found perforated, imperforate, imperforate horizontally or imperforate vertically. At the same time that they were made, impressions were struck upon a variety of glazed and surface-colored papers.

Map of Panama — A4

Wove Paper

1892-96 Engr. *Perf. 12*

No.	Type	Description	Unused	Used
15	A4	1c green	.25	.25
16	A4	2c rose	.40	.25
17	A4	5c blue	1.50	.50
18	A4	10c orange	.35	.25
19	A4	20c violet ('95)	.50	.35
20	A4	50c bister brn ('96)	.50	.40
21	A4	1p lake ('96)	6.50	4.00
		Nos. 15-21 (7)	10.00	6.00

In 1903 Nos. 15-21 were used in Cauca and three other southern Colombia towns. Stamps canceled in these towns are worth much more.

For surcharges and overprints see Nos. 22-23, 51-106, 109-114, 129-136, 139, 151-161, 181-184, F12-F15, H4-H5.

Nos. 16, 12-14 Surcharged

a

b

c

d

e

f

g

1894 Black Surcharge

22 (a) 1c on 2c rose .50 .40
a. Inverted surcharge 2.50 2.50
b. Double surcharge
23 (b) 1c on 2c rose .40 .50
a. "CCNTAVO" 2.50 2.50
b. Inverted surcharge 2.50 2.50
c. Double surcharge

Red Surcharge

24 (c) 5c on 20c black, *lil* 2.50 1.50
a. Inverted surcharge 12.50 12.50
b. Double surcharge
c. Without "HABILITADO"
25 (d) 5c on 20c black, *lil* 3.50 3.00
a. "CCNTAVOS" 7.50 7.50
b. Inverted surcharge 12.50 12.50
c. Double surcharge
d. Without "HABILITADO"
26 (e) 5c on 20c black, *lil* 6.00 5.00
a. Inverted surcharge 12.50 12.50
b. Double surcharge
27 (f) 10c on 50c brown 3.00 3.00
a. "1894" omitted
b. Inverted surcharge
c. "CCNTAVOS" 15.00
28 (g) 10c on 50c brown 12.50 12.50
a. "CCNTAVOS" 32.50
b. Inverted surcharge

Pelure Paper

29 (f) 10c on 50c brown 4.00 3.00
a. "1894" omitted 7.50
b. Inverted surcharge 12.50 12.50
c. Double surcharge
30 (g) 10c on 50c brown 10.00 10.00
a. "CCNTAVOS"
b. Without "HABILITADO"
c. Inverted surcharge 25.00 25.00
d. Double surcharge
Nos. 22-30 (9) 42.40 38.90

There are several settings of these surcharges. Usually the surcharge is about 15½mm high, but in one setting, it is only 13mm. All the types are to be found with a comma after "CENTAVOS." Nos. 24, 25, 26, 29 and 30 exist with the surcharge printed sideways. Nos. 23, 24 and 29 may be found with an inverted "A" instead of "V" in "CENTAVOS." There are also varieties caused by dropped or broken letters.

Issues of the Republic Issued in the City of Panama

Stamps of 1892-96 Overprinted

1903, Nov. 16 Rose Handstamp

51 A4 1c green 2.00 1.50
52 A4 2c rose 5.00 3.00
53 A4 5c blue 2.00 1.25
54 A4 10c yellow 2.00 2.00
55 A4 20c violet 4.00 3.50
56 A4 50c bister brn 10.00 7.00
57 A4 1p lake 50.00 40.00
Nos. 51-57 (7) 75.00 58.25

Blue Black Handstamp

58 A4 1c green 2.00 1.25
59 A4 2c rose 1.00 1.00
60 A4 5c blue 7.00 6.00
61 A4 10c yellow 5.00 3.50
62 A4 20c violet 10.00 7.50
63 A4 50c bister brn 10.00 7.50
64 A4 1p lake 50.00 42.50
Nos. 58-64 (7) 85.00 69.25

The stamps of this issue are to be found with the handstamp placed horizontally, vertically or diagonally; inverted; double; double, one inverted; double, both inverted; in pairs, one without handstamp; etc.

This handstamp is known in brown rose on the 1, 5, 20 and 50c, in purple on the 1, 2, 50c and 1p, and in magenta on the 5, 10, 20 and 50c.

Reprints were made in rose, black and other colors when the handstamp was nearly worn out, so that the "R" of "REPUBLICA" appears to be shorter than usual, and the bottom part of "LI" has been broken off. The "P" of "PANAMA" leans to the left and the tops of "NA" are broken. Many of these varieties are found inverted, double, etc.

Overprinted

Bar in Similar Color to Stamp

1903, Dec. 3 Black Overprint

65 A4 2c rose 2.50 2.50
a. "PANAMA" 15mm long 3.50
b. Violet bar 5.00
66 A4 5c blue 100.00
a. "PANAMA" 15mm long 100.00
67 A4 10c yellow 2.50 2.50
a. "PANAMA" 15mm long 6.00
b. Horizontal overprint 17.50

Gray Black Overprint

68 A4 2c rose 2.00 2.00
a. "PANAMA" 15mm long 2.50

Carmine Overprint

69 A4 5c blue 2.50 2.50
a. "PANAMA" 15mm long 3.50
b. Bar only 75.00 75.00
c. Double overprint
70 A4 20c violet 7.50 6.50
a. "PANAMA" 15mm long 10.00
b. Double overprint, one in black 150.00
Nos. 65,67-70 (5) 17.00 16.00

This overprint was set up to cover fifty stamps. "PANAMA" is normally 13mm long and 1¾mm high but, in two rows in each sheet, it measures 15 to 16mm.

This word may be found with one or more of the letters taller than usual; with one, two or three inverted "V's" instead of "A's"; with an inverted "Y" instead of "A"; an inverted "N"; an "A" with accent; and a fancy "P."

Owing to misplaced impressions, stamps exist with "PANAMA" once only, twice on one side, or three times.

Overprinted in Red

1903, Dec.

71 A4 1c green .75 .60
a. "PANAMA" 15mm long 1.25
b. "PANAMA" reading down 3.00 .75
c. "PANAMA" reading up and down 3.00
d. Double overprint 8.00
72 A4 2c rose .50 .40
a. "PANAMA" 15mm long 1.00
b. "PANAMA" reading down .75 .50
c. "PANAMA" reading up and down 4.00
d. Double overprint 8.00
73 A4 20c violet 1.50 1.00
a. "PANAMA" 15mm long 2.25
b. "PANAMA" reading down
c. "PANAMA" reading up and down 8.00 8.00
d. Double overprint 18.00 18.00
74 A4 50c bister brn 3.00 2.50
a. "PANAMA" 15mm long 5.00
b. "PANAMA" reading up and down 12.00 12.00
c. Double overprint 6.00 6.00
75 A4 1p lake 6.00 4.50
a. "PANAMA" 15mm long 6.25
b. "PANAMA" reading up and down 15.00 15.00
c. Double overprint 15.00
d. Inverted overprint 25.00
Nos. 71-75 (5) 11.75 9.00

This setting appears to be a re-arrangement (or two very similar re-arrangements) of the previous overprint. The overprint covers fifty stamps. "PANAMA" usually reads upward but sheets of the 1, 2 and 20c exist with the word reading upward on one half the sheet and downward on the other half.

In one re-arrangement one stamp in fifty has the word reading in both directions. Nearly all the varieties of the previous overprint are repeated in this setting excepting the inverted "Y" and fancy "P." There are also additional varieties of large letters and "PANAMA" occasionally has an "A" missing or inverted. There are misplaced impressions, as the previous setting.

Overprinted in Red

1904-05

76 A4 1c green .25 .25
a. Both words reading up 1.50
b. Both words reading down 2.75
c. Double overprint
d. Pair, one without overprint 15.00
e. "PANAAM" 20.00
f. Inverted "M" in "PANAMA" 5.00
77 A4 2c rose .25 .25
a. Both words reading up 2.50
b. Both words reading down 2.50
c. Double overprint 10.00
d. Double overprint, one inverted 14.00
e. Inverted "M" in "PANAMA" 5.00
78 A4 5c blue .30 .25
a. Both words reading up 3.00
b. Both words reading down 4.25
c. Inverted overprint 12.50
d. "PANAAM" 25.00
e. "PANANA" 8.00
f. "PAMANA" 5.00
g. Inverted "M" in "PANAMA" 5.00
h. Double overprint 20.00
79 A4 10c yellow .30 .25
a. Both words reading up 5.00
b. Both words reading down 5.00
c. Double overprint 15.00
d. Inverted overprint 6.75
e. "PAMANA" 8.00
f. Inverted "M" in "PANAMA" 15.00
g. Red brown overprint 7.50 3.50
80 A4 20c violet 2.00 1.00
a. Both words reading up 5.00
b. Both words reading down 10.00
81 A4 50c bister brn 2.00 1.60
a. Both words reading up 10.50
b. Both words reading down 10.00
c. Double overprint
82 A4 1p lake 5.00 5.00
a. Both words reading up 12.50
b. Both words reading down 12.50
c. Double overprint
d. Double overprint, one inverted 20.00
e. Inverted "M" in "PANAMA" 45.00
Nos. 76-82 (7) 10.10 8.60

This overprint is also set up to cover fifty stamps. One stamp in each fifty has "PANAMA" reading upward at both sides. Another has the word reading downward at both sides, a third has an inverted "V" in place of the last "A" and a fourth has a small thick "N." In a resetting all these varieties are corrected except the inverted "V." There are misplaced overprints as before.

Later printings show other varieties and have the bar 2½mm instead of 2mm wide. The colors of the various printings of Nos. 76-82 range from carmine to almost pink.

Experts consider the black overprint on the 50c to be speculative.

The 20c violet and 50c bister brown exist with bar 2½mm wide, including the error "PAMANA," but are not known to have been issued. Some examples have been canceled "to oblige."

Issued in Colon

Handstamped in Magenta or Violet

1903-04 On Stamps of 1892-96

101 A4 1c green .75 .75
102 A4 2c rose .75 .75
103 A4 5c blue 1.00 1.00
104 A4 10c yellow 3.50 3.00
105 A4 20c violet 8.00 6.50
106 A4 1p lake 80.00 70.00

On Stamps of 1887-92

Ordinary Wove Paper

107 A3 50c brown 25.00 20.00
Nos. 101-107 (7) 119.00 102.00

Pelure Paper

108 A3 50c brown 70.00

Handstamped in Magenta, Violet or Red

On Stamps of 1892-96

109 A4 1c green 5.50 5.00
110 A4 2c rose 5.50 5.00
111 A4 5c blue 5.50 5.00
112 A4 10c yellow 8.25 7.00
113 A4 20c violet 12.00 9.00
114 A4 1p lake 70.00 60.00

On Stamps of 1887-92

Ordinary Wove Paper

115 A3 50c brown 35.00 25.00
Nos. 109-115 (7) 141.75 116.00

Pelure Paper

116 A3 50c brown 50.00 37.50

The first note after No. 64 applies also to Nos. 101-116.

The handstamps on Nos. 109-116 have been counterfeited.

Stamps with this overprint were a private speculation. They exist on cover. The overprint was to be used on postal cards.

Overprinted On Stamps Of 1892-96

On Stamps of 1892-96

Carmine Overprint

129 A4 1c green .40 .40
a. Inverted overprint 6.00
b. Double overprint 2.25
c. Double overprint, one inverted 6.00
130 A4 5c blue .50 .50

Brown Overprint

131 A4 1c green 12.00
a. Double overprint, one inverted

Black Overprint

132 A4 1c green 60.00 30.00
a. Vertical overprint 42.50
b. Inverted overprint 42.50
c. Double overprint, one inverted 42.50
133 A4 2c rose .50 .50
a. Inverted overprint
134 A4 10c yellow .50 .50
a. Inverted overprint 4.00
b. Double overprint 16.00
c. Double overprint, one inverted 6.00
135 A4 20c violet .50 .50
a. Inverted overprint 4.00
b. Double overprint 5.50
136 A4 1p lake 16.00 14.00

On Stamps of 1887-88

Blue Overprint

Ordinary Wove Paper

137 A3 50c brown 3.00 3.00

Pelure Paper

138 A3 50c brown 3.00 3.00
a. Double overprint 14.00

This overprint is set up to cover fifty stamps. In each fifty there are four stamps without accent on the last "a" of "Panama," one with accent on the "a" of "Republica" and one with a thick, upright "i."

Overprinted in Carmine

On Stamp of 1892-96

139 A4 20c violet *200.00*
a. Double overprint

Unknown with genuine cancels.

Issued in Bocas del Toro

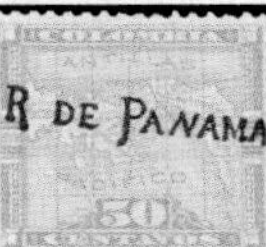

Stamps of 1892-96 Overprinted Handstamped in Violet

1903-04

151 A4 1c green 20.00 14.00
152 A4 2c rose 20.00 14.00
153 A4 5c blue 25.00 16.00
154 A4 10c yellow 15.00 8.25
155 A4 20c violet 50.00 30.00
156 A4 50c bister brn 100.00 55.00
157 A4 1p lake 140.00 110.00
Nos. 151-157 (7) 370.00 247.25

The handstamp is known double and inverted. Counterfeits exist.

Handstamped in Violet

158 A4 1c green *100.00*
159 A4 2c rose *70.00*
160 A4 5c blue *80.00*
161 A4 10c yellow *100.00*
Nos. 158-161 (4) *350.00*

This handstamp was applied to these 4 stamps only by favor, experts state. Counterfeits are numerous. The 1p exists only as a counterfeit.

General Issues

A5

1905, Feb. 4 **Engr.** ***Perf. 12***

179 A5 1c green .60 .40
180 A5 2c rose .80 .50

Panama's Declaration of Independence from the Colombian Republic, Nov. 3, 1903.

Surcharged in Vermilion on Stamps of 1892-96 Issue

1906

181 A4 1c on 20c violet .25 .25
a. "Panrma" 2.25 2.25
b. "Pnnama" 2.25 2.25
c. "Pauama" 2.25 2.25
d. Inverted surcharge 4.00 4.00
e. Double surcharge 3.50 3.50
f. Double surcharge, one inverted

Stamps of 1892-96 Surcharged in Vermilion

182 A4 2c on 50c bister brn .25 .25
a. 3rd "A" of "PANAMA" inverted 2.25 2.25
b. Both "PANAMA" reading down 4.00 4.00
c. Double surcharge
d. Inverted surcharge 2.50

The 2c on 20c violet was never issued to the public. All examples are inverted. Value, 75c.

Carmine Surcharge

183 A4 5c on 1p lake .60 .40
a. Both "PANAMA" reading down 6.00 6.00
b. "5" omitted
c. Double surcharge
d. Inverted surcharge
e. 3rd "A" of "PANAMA" inverted 5.50 5.50

On Stamp of 1903-04, No. 75

184 A4 5c on 1p lake .60 .40
a. "PANAMA" 15mm long
b. "PANAMA" reading up and down
c. Both "PANAMA" reading down
d. Inverted surcharge
e. Double surcharge
f. 3rd "A" of "PANAMA" inverted
Nos. 181-184 (4) 1.70 1.30

National Flag — A6

Vasco Núñez de Balboa — A7

Fernández de Córdoba — A8

Coat of Arms — A9

Justo Arosemena A10

Manuel J. Hurtado A11

José de Obaldía — A12

Tomás Herrera — A13

José de Fábrega — A14

1906-07 **Engr.** ***Perf. 11½***

185 A6 ½c orange & multi .70 .35
186 A7 1c dk green & blk ('07) .70 .35
187 A8 2c scarlet & blk 1.00 .35
188 A9 2½c red orange 1.00 .35
189 A10 5c blue & black 1.75 .35
a. 5c ultramarine & black 2.00 .50
190 A11 8c purple & blk 1.50 .65
191 A12 10c violet & blk 1.50 .50
192 A13 25c brown & blk 3.50 1.10
193 A14 50c black 9.00 3.50
Nos. 185-193 (9) 20.65 7.50

Inverted centers exist of Nos. 185-187, 189, 189a, 190-193, Value, each $25. Nos. 185-193 exist imperf.

For surcharge see No. F29.

Issued: Nos. 185, 188-193, 11/20; No. 187, 9/1.

Map — A17

Balboa — A18

Córdoba — A19

Arms — A20

Arosemena A21

Obaldía A23

1909-16 ***Perf. 12***

195 A17 ½c org ('11) 1.00 .30
196 A17 ½c rose ('15) .70 .60
197 A18 1c dk grn & blk 1.00 .50
a. Inverted center 7,500. 7,500.
b. Booklet pane of 6 ('16) *160.00*
Complete booklet, 4 #197b —
198 A19 2c ver & blk 1.00 .30
a. Booklet pane of 6 *160.00*
199 A20 2½c red orange 1.50 .30
200 A21 5c blue & blk 2.00 .30
a. Booklet pane of 6 ('16) *350.00*
201 A23 10c violet & blk 3.75 1.10
Complete booklet, panes of 6 (3x2) of #195 (3), 197 (3), 199 (2), 200, 201 ('11) —
Nos. 195-201 (7) 10.95 3.40

Value for No. 197a used is for an off-center example with faults.

The panes contained in the booklet listed following No. 201 are marginal blocks of 6 (3x2), without gum, stapled within the booklet cover, with advertising paper interleaving. The complete booklet was sold for B1.50.

Nos. 197b and 198a are gummed panes of 6 (2x3), imperf on outside edges.

For overprints and surcharges see #H23, I4-I7.

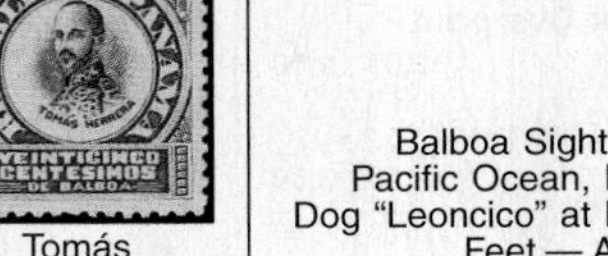

Balboa Sighting Pacific Ocean, His Dog "Leoncico" at His Feet — A24

1913, Sept. 1

202 A24 2½c dk grn & yel grn 1.75 .65

400th anniv. of Balboa's discovery of the Pacific Ocean.

Panama-Pacific Exposition Issue

Chorrera Falls — A25

Map of Panama Canal — A26

Balboa Taking Possession of the Pacific A27

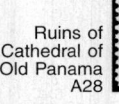

Ruins of Cathedral of Old Panama A28

Palace of Arts — A29

Gatun Locks — A30

Culebra Cut — A31

Santo Domingo Monastery's Flat Arch — A32

1915, Mar. 1 ***Perf. 12***

204 A25 ½c ol grn & blk .40 .30
205 A26 1c dk grn & blk .95 .30
206 A27 2c car & blk .75 .30
a. 2c ver & blk ('16) .75 .30
208 A28 2½c scarlet & blk .95 .35
209 A29 3c violet & blk 1.60 .55
210 A30 5c blue & blk 2.10 .35
a. Center inverted 1,500. 650.00
211 A31 10c orange & blk 2.10 .70
212 A32 20c brown & blk 10.50 3.25
a. Center inverted 300.00
Nos. 204-212 (8) 19.35 6.10

For surcharges and overprints see Nos. 217, 233, E1-E2.

Manuel J. Hurtado — A33

1916

213 A33 8c violet & blk 9.00 4.25

For surcharge see No. F30.

S. S. Panama in Culebra Cut Aug. 11, 1914 A34

S. S. Panama in Culebra Cut Aug. 11, 1914 A35

S. S. Cristobal in Gatun Lock — A36

1918, Aug. 23

214 A34 12c purple & blk 15.00 5.75
215 A35 15c brt blue & blk 10.00 3.50
216 A36 24c yellow brn & blk 15.00 3.50
Nos. 214-216 (3) 40.00 12.75

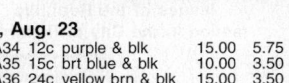

No. 208 Surcharged in Dark Blue

1919, Aug. 15

217 A28 2c on 2½c scar & blk .35 .35
a. Inverted surcharge 11.00 5.00
b. Double surcharge 15.00 6.00

City of Panama, 400th anniversary.

Dry Dock at Balboa A38

Ship in Pedro Miguel Lock — A39

1920, Sept. 1 **Engr.**

218 A38 50c orange & blk 30.00 22.50
219 A39 1b dk violet & blk 40.00 27.50

For overprint and surcharge see Nos. C6, C37.

Arms of Panama City — A40

José Vallarino — A41

"Land Gate" — A42

Simón Bolivar — A43

Statue of Cervantes — A44

Bolívar's Tribute — A45

Carlos de Ycaza — A46

Municipal Building in 1821 and 1921 — A47

Statue of Balboa — A48

Villa de Los Santos Church — A49

Herrera — A50

Fábrega — A51

1921, Nov.

220 A40 ½c orange .80 .25
221 A41 1c green 1.00 .25
222 A42 2c carmine 1.25 .25
223 A43 2½c red 2.75 1.10
224 A44 3c dull violet 2.75 1.10
225 A45 5c blue 2.75 .35
226 A46 8c olive green 10.00 3.50
227 A47 10c violet 6.75 1.50
228 A48 15c lt blue 8.00 2.00
229 A49 20c olive brown 14.50 3.50
230 A50 24c black brown 14.50 4.25
231 A51 50c black 25.00 8.00
Nos. 220-231 (12) 90.05 26.05

Centenary of independence.
For overprints and surcharges see Nos. 264, 275-276, 299, 304, 308-310, C35.

Hurtado — A52

1921, Nov. 28

232 A52 2c dark green .65 .65

Manuel José Hurtado (1821-1887), president and folklore writer.
For overprints see Nos. 258, 301.

No. 208 Surcharged in Black

1923

233 A28 2c on 2½c scar & blk .45 .45
a. "1923" omitted 4.00
b. Bar over "CENTESIMOS" 4.00
c. Inverted surcharge 4.00
d. Double surcharge 4.00
e. Pair, one without surcharge 4.00

Two stamps in each sheet have a bar above "CENTESIMOS" (No. 233b).

Arms — A53

1924, May **Engr.**

234 A53 ½c orange .25 .25
235 A53 1c dark green .25 .25
236 A53 2c carmine .25 .25
237 A53 5c dark blue .45 .25
238 A53 10c dark violet .60 .25
239 A53 12c olive green .75 .40
240 A53 15c ultra .95 .40
241 A53 24c yellow brown 1.90 .60
242 A53 50c orange 4.50 1.10
243 A53 1b black 6.75 2.50
Nos. 234-243 (10) 16.65 6.25

For overprints & surcharges see Nos. 277, 321A, 331-338, 352, C19-C20, C68, RA5, RA10-RA22. Post 1940 listings in Scott Standard catalogue, Vol. 5.

Bolívar — A54

Statue of Bolívar — A55

Bolívar Hall — A56

1926, June 10 ***Perf. 12½***

244 A54 ½c orange .55 .25
245 A54 1c dark green .55 .25
246 A54 2c scarlet .70 .30
247 A54 4c gray .90 .35
248 A54 5c dark blue 1.40 .50
249 A55 8c lilac 2.25 .80
250 A55 10c dull violet 1.60 .80
251 A55 12c olive green 2.50 1.00
252 A55 15c ultra 3.25 1.25
253 A55 20c brown 6.75 1.60
254 A56 24c black violet 8.00 2.00
255 A56 50c black 13.50 5.00
Nos. 244-255 (12) 41.95 14.10

Bolivar Congress centennial.
For surcharges and overprints see Nos. 259-263, 266-267, 274, 298, 300, 302-303, 305-307, C33-C34, C36, C38-C39.

Lindbergh's Airplane, "The Spirit of St. Louis" — A57

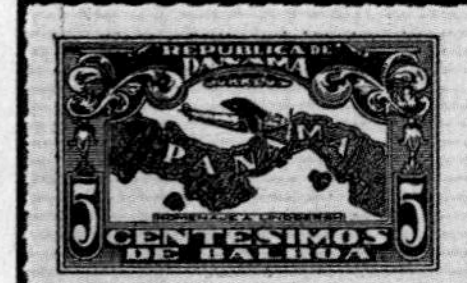

Lindbergh's Airplane and Map of Panama — A58

1928, Jan. 9 **Typo.** ***Rouletted 7***

256 A57 2c dk red & blk, *salmon* .40 .25
257 A58 5c dk blue, *grn* .60 .40

Visit of Colonel Charles A. Lindbergh to Central America by airplane.
No. 256 has black overprint.

No. 232 Overprinted in Red

1928, Nov. 1 ***Perf. 12***

258 A52 2c dark green .25 .25

25th anniversary of the Republic.

No. 247 Surcharged in Black

1930, Dec. 17 ***Perf. 12½, 13***

259 A54 1c on 4c gray .25 .25

Centenary of the death of Simón Bolívar, the Liberator.

Nos. 244-246 Overprinted in Red or Blue

1932 ***Perf. 12½***

260 A54 ½c orange (R) .25 .25
261 A54 1c dark green (R) .35 .25
a. Double overprint 18.00
262 A54 2c scarlet (Bl) .35 .25

No. 252 Surcharged in Red

263 A55 10c on 15c ultra 1.00 .50
a. Double surcharge 55.00
Nos. 260-263 (4) 1.95 1.25

No. 220 Overprinted as in 1932 in Black

1933, May 25 ***Perf. 12***

Overprint 19mm Long

264 A40 ½c orange .35 .25
a. Overprint 17mm long —

Dr. Manuel Amador Guerrero — A60

1933, June 30 **Engr.** ***Perf. 12½***

265 A60 2c dark red .50 .25

Centenary of the birth of Dr. Manuel Amador Guerrero, founder of the Republic of Panama and its first President.

No. 251 Surcharged in Red

1933

266 A55 10c on 12c olive grn 1.25 .65

No. 253 Overprinted in Red

267 A55 20c brown 2.25 1.75

José Domingo de Obaldía — A61

Quotation from Emerson — A63

National Institute — A64

Designs: 2c, Eusebio A. Morales. 12c, Justo A. Facio. 15c, Pablo Arosemena.

1934, July 24 **Engr.** ***Perf. 14***

268 A61 1c dark green 1.00 .50
269 A61 2c scarlet 1.00 .45
270 A63 5c dark blue 1.25 .80
271 A64 10c brown 3.25 1.50
272 A61 12c yellow green 6.50 2.00
273 A61 15c Prus blue 8.50 2.50
Nos. 268-273 (6) 21.50 7.75

25th anniv. of the Natl. Institute.

Nos. 248, 227 Overprinted in Black or Red

1935-36 ***Perf. 12½, 12***

274 A54 5c dark blue .90 .30
275 A47 10c violet (R) ('36) 1.25 .60

No. 225 Surcharged in Red

1936. Sept. 19 ***Perf. 11½***

276 A45 1c on 5c blue .40 .40
a. Lines of surcharge 1½mm btwn. 6.50

No. 241 Surcharged in Blue

1936, Sept. 24 *Perf. 12*

277	A53	2c on 24c yellow brn	.60	.50
a.		Double surcharge	20.00	

Centenary of the birth of Pablo Arosemena, president of Panama in 1910-12. See Nos. C19-C20.

Panama Cathedral A67

Designs: ½c, Ruins of Custom House, Portobelo. 1c, Panama Tree. 2c, "La Pollera." 5c, Simon Bolivar. 10c, Cathedral Tower Ruins. Old Panama. 15c, Francisco Garcia y Santos, 20c, Madden Dam, Panama Canal. 25c, Columbus. 50c, Gaillard Cut. 1b, Panama Cathedral.

1936, Dec. 1 **Engr.** *Perf. 11½*

278	A67	½c yellow org	.55	.25
279	A67	1c blue green	.55	.25
280	A67	2c carmine rose	.55	.25
281	A67	5c blue	.80	.50
282	A67	10c dk violet	1.75	.75
283	A67	15c turq blue	1.75	.75
284	A67	20c red	2.00	1.50
285	A67	25c black brn	3.50	2.00
286	A67	50c orange	7.75	5.00
287	A67	1b black	18.00	12.00
		Nos. 278-287,C21-C26 (16)	62.70	40.00

4th Postal Congress of the Americas and Spain.

Stamps of 1936 Overprinted in Red or Blue

1937, Mar. 9

288	A67	½c yellow org (R)	.35	.30
a.		Inverted overprint	25.00	
289	A67	1c blue green (R)	.45	.25
290	A67	2c car rose (Bl)	.45	.25
291	A67	5c blue (R)	.70	.25
292	A67	10c dk vio (R)	1.10	.35
293	A67	15c turq bl (R)	5.25	3.25
294	A67	20c red (Bl)	2.00	1.25
295	A67	25c black brn (R)	2.75	1.25
296	A67	50c orange (Bl)	9.00	6.00
297	A67	1b black (R)	14.50	10.00
		Nos. 288-297,C27-C32 (16)	84.60	54.15

Stamps of 1921-26 Overprinted in Red or Blue

1937, July *Perf. 12, 12½*

298	A54	½c orange (R)	1.10	.80
a.		Inverted overprint	30.00	
299	A41	1c green (R)	.35	.25
a.		Inverted overprint	30.00	
300	A54	1c dk green (R)	.35	.25
301	A52	2c dk green (R)	.45	.35
302	A54	2c scarlet (Bl)	.55	.35

Stamps of 1921-26 Surcharged in Red

303	A54	2c on 4c gray	.70	.45
304	A46	2c on 8c ol grn	.70	.60
305	A55	2c on 8c lilac	.70	.45
306	A55	2c on 10c dl vio	.70	.50
307	A55	2c on 12c ol grn	.70	.45
308	A48	2c on 15c lt blue	.70	.60
309	A50	2c on 24c blk brn	.70	.75
310	A51	2c on 50c black	.70	.35
		Nos. 298-310 (13)	8.40	6.15

Ricardo Arango A77

Juan A. Guizado A78

La Concordia Fire — A79

Modern Fire Fighting Equipment A80

Firemen's Monument A81

David H. Brandon A82

Perf. 14x14½, 14½x14

1937, Nov. 25 **Photo.** **Wmk. 233**

311	A77	½c orange red	2.10	.35
312	A78	1c green	2.10	.35
313	A79	2c red	2.10	.25
314	A80	5c brt blue	4.00	.50
315	A81	10c purple	7.25	1.25
316	A82	12c yellow grn	11.50	2.00
		Nos. 311-316,C40-C42 (9)	49.30	7.05

50th anniversary of the Fire Department.

Old Panama Cathedral Tower and Statue of Liberty Enlightening the World, Flags of Panama and US — A83

Engr. & Litho.

1938, Dec. 7 **Unwmk.** *Perf. 12½*

Center in Black; Flags in Red and Ultramarine

317	A83	1c deep green	.35	.25
318	A83	2c carmine	.55	.25
319	A83	5c blue	.80	.30
320	A83	12c olive	1.40	.75
321	A83	15c brt ultra	1.75	1.25
		Nos. 317-321,C49-C53 (10)	22.45	15.35

150th anniv. of the US Constitution.

No. 236 Overprinted in Black

1938, June 5 *Perf. 12*

321A	A53	2c carmine	.45	.25
b.		Inverted overprint	22.50	
		Nos. 321A,C53A-C53B (3)	1.25	1.05

Opening of the Normal School at Santiago, Veraguas Province, June 5, 1938.

Gatun Lake — A84

Designs: 1c, Pedro Miguel Locks. 2c, Allegory. 5c, Culebra Cut. 10c, Ferryboat. 12c, Aerial View of Canal. 15c, Gen. William C. Gorgas. 50c, Dr. Manuel A. Guerrero. 1b, Woodrow Wilson.

1939, Aug. 15 **Engr.** *Perf. 12½*

322	A84	½c yellow	.35	.25
323	A84	1c dp blue grn	.55	.25
324	A84	2c dull rose	.65	.25
325	A84	5c dull blue	1.00	.25
326	A84	10c dk violet	1.10	.35
327	A84	12c olive green	1.10	.50
328	A84	15c ultra	1.10	.80
329	A84	50c orange	2.75	1.60
330	A84	1b dk brown	5.75	3.00
		Nos. 322-330,C54-C61 (17)	34.35	14.45

25th anniversary of the opening of the Panama Canal. For surcharges see Nos. C64, G2 (in Scott Standard catalogue, Vol. 5).

AIR POST STAMPS

Special Delivery Stamp No. E3 Srchd. in Dark Blue

1929, Feb. 8 **Unwmk.** *Perf. 12½*

C1	SD1	25c on 10c org	1.00	.80
a.		Inverted surcharge	22.50	22.50

Nos. E3-E4 Overprinted in Blue

1929, May 22

C2	SD1	10c orange	.50	.50
a.		Inverted overprint	20.00	17.50
b.		Double overprint	20.00	17.50

Some specialists claim the red overprint is a proof impression.

With Additional Surcharge of New Value

C3	SD1	15c on 10c org	.50	.50
C4	SD1	25c on 20c dk brn	1.10	1.00
a.		Double surcharge	20.00	20.00
		Nos. C2-C4 (3)	2.10	2.00

No. E3 Surcharged in Blue

1930, Jan. 25

C5	SD1	5c on 10c org	.50	.50

No. 219 Overprinted in Red

1930, Feb. 28 *Perf. 12*

C6	A39	1b dk vio & blk	16.00	12.50

AP5

1930-41 **Engr.** *Perf. 12*

C6A	AP5	5c blue ('41)	.25	.25
C6B	AP5	7c rose car ('41)	.25	.25
C6C	AP5	8c gray blk ('41)	.25	.25
C7	AP5	15c dp grn	.30	.25
C8	AP5	20c rose	.35	.25
C9	AP5	25c deep blue	.65	.65
		Nos. C6A-C9 (6)	2.05	1.90

Issued: Nos. C7-C9, 1/20; Nos. C6A-C6C, 7/1/41. See No. C112. For surcharges and overprints see Nos. 353, C16-C16A, C53B, C69, C82-C83, C109, C122, C124. Post 1940 listings are in Scott Standard catalogue, Vol. 5.

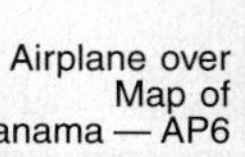

Airplane over Map of Panama — AP6

1930, Aug. 4 *Perf. 12½*

C10	AP6	5c ultra	.25	.25
C11	AP6	10c orange	.30	.25
C12	AP6	30c dp vio	5.50	4.00
C13	AP6	50c dp red	1.50	.50
C14	AP6	1b black	5.50	4.00
		Nos. C10-C14 (5)	13.05	9.00

For surcharge and overprints see Nos. C53A, C70-C71, C115. Post 1940 listings are in Scott Standard catalogue, Vol. 5.

Amphibian AP7

1931, Nov. 28 **Typo.**

Without Gum

C15	AP7	5c deep blue	.80	1.00
a.		5c gray blue	.80	1.00
b.		Horiz. pair, imperf. btwn.	50.00	

For the start of regular airmail service between Panama City and the western provinces, but valid only on Nov. 28-29 on mail carried by hydroplane "3 Noviembre."

Many sheets have a papermaker's watermark "DOLPHIN BOND" in double-lined capitals.

No. C9 Surcharged in Red 19mm long

1932, Dec. 14 *Perf. 12*

C16	AP5	20c on 25c dp bl	6.25	.70

Surcharge 17mm long

C16A	AP5	20c on 25c dp bl	200.00	2.50

Special Delivery Stamp No. E4 Overprinted in Red or Black

1934 *Perf. 12½*

C17	SD1	20c dk brn	1.00	.50
C17A	SD1	20c dk brn (Bk)	100.00	55.00

Issued: No. C17, 7/31.

Surcharged In Black

1935, June

C18	SD1	10c on 20c dk brn	.80	.50

Same Surcharge with Small "10"

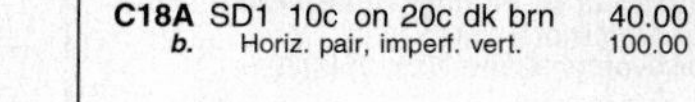

C18A	SD1	10c on 20c dk brn	40.00	5.00
b.		Horiz. pair, imperf. vert.	100.00	

Nos. 234 and 242 Surcharged in Blue

1936, Sept. 24

C19 A53 5c on ½c org	400.00	250.00
C20 A53 5c on 50c org	1.00	.80
a. Double surcharge	60.00	60.00

Centenary of the birth of President Pablo Arosemena.

It is claimed that No. C19 was not regularly issued. Counterfeits of No. C19 exist.

Urracá Monument AP8

Palace of Justice AP9

10c, Human Genius Uniting the Oceans. 20c, Panama City. 30c, Balboa Monument. 50c, Pedro Miguel Locks.

1936, Dec. 1 Engr. *Perf. 12*

C21 AP8 5c blue	.65	.40
C22 AP9 10c yel org	.85	.60
C23 AP9 20c red	3.00	1.50
C24 AP8 30c dk vio	3.50	2.50
C25 AP9 50c car rose	8.00	5.75
C26 AP9 1b black	9.50	6.00
Nos. C21-C26 (6)	25.50	16.75

4th Postal Congress of the Americas and Spain.

Nos. C21-C26 Overprinted in Red or Blue

1937, Mar. 9

C27 AP8 5c blue (R)	.55	.30
a. Inverted overprint	50.00	
C28 AP9 10c yel org (Bl)	.75	.45
C29 AP9 20c red (Bl)	1.75	1.00
a. Double overprint	50.00	
C30 AP8 30c dk vio (R)	4.50	3.25
C31 AP8 50c car rose (Bl)	18.00	13.00
a. Double overprint	175.00	
C32 AP9 1b black (R)	22.50	13.00
Nos. C27-C32 (6)	48.05	31.00

Regular Stamps of 1921-26 Surcharged in Red

1937, June 30 *Perf. 12, 12½*

C33 A55 5c on 15c ultra	.75	.75
C34 A55 5c on 20c brn	.75	.75
C35 A47 10c on 10c vio	1.75	1.50

Regular Stamps of 1920-26 Surcharged in Red

C36 A56 5c on 24c blk vio	.75	.75
C37 A39 5c on 1b dk vio & blk	.75	.50
C38 A56 10c on 50c blk	2.25	2.00
a. Inverted surcharge	30.00	

No. 248 Overprinted in Red

C39 A54 5c dark blue	.75	.75
a. Double overprint	18.00	
Nos. C33-C39 (7)	7.75	7.00

Fire Dept. Badge AP14

Florencio Arosemena AP15

José Gabriel Duque — AP16

Perf. 14x14½

1937, Nov. 25 Photo. Wmk. 233

C40 AP14 5c blue	4.50	.60
C41 AP15 10c orange	6.75	1.00
C42 AP16 20c crimson	9.00	.75
Nos. C40-C42 (3)	20.25	2.35

50th anniversary of the Fire Department.

Basketball — AP17

Baseball AP18

1938, Feb. 12 *Perf. 14x14½, 14½x14*

C43 AP17 1c shown	2.25	.25
C44 AP18 2c shown	2.25	.25
C45 AP18 7c Swimming	3.00	.25
C46 AP18 8c Boxing	3.00	.25
C47 AP17 15c Soccer	5.00	1.25
a. Souv. sheet of 5, #C43-C47	18.00	18.00
b. As "a," No. C43 omitted	*3,500.*	
Nos. C43-C47 (5)	15.50	2.25

4th Central American Caribbean Games.

US Constitution Type

Engr. & Litho.

1938, Dec. 7 Unwmk. *Perf. 12½*

Center in Black, Flags in Red and Ultramarine

C49 A83 7c gray	.35	.25
C50 A83 8c brt ultra	.55	.35
C51 A83 15c red brn	.70	.45
C52 A83 50c orange	8.00	5.75
C53 A83 1b black	8.00	5.75
Nos. C49-C53 (5)	17.60	12.55

Nos. C12 and C7 Surcharged in Red

1938, June 5 *Perf. 12½, 12*

C53A AP6 7c on 30c dp vio	.40	.40
c. Double surcharge	27.50	
d. Inverted surcharge	27.50	
C53B AP5 8c on 15c dp grn	.40	.40
e. Inverted surcharge	22.50	

Opening of the Normal School at Santiago, Veraguas Province, June 5, 1938. The 8c surcharge has no bars.

Belisario Porras AP23

Designs: 2c, William Howard Taft. 5c, Pedro J. Sosa. 10c, Lucien Bonaparte Wise. 15c, Armando Reclus. 20c, Gen. George W. Goethals. 50c, Ferdinand de Lesseps. 1b, Theodore Roosevelt.

1939, Aug. 15 Engr.

C54 AP23 1c dl rose	.40	.25
C55 AP23 2c dp bl grn	.40	.25
C56 AP23 5c indigo	.65	.25
C57 AP23 10c dk vio	.70	.25
C58 AP23 15c ultra	1.60	.35
C59 AP23 20c rose pink	4.00	1.40
C60 AP23 50c dk brn	5.00	.70
C61 AP23 1b black	7.25	3.75
Nos. C54-C61 (8)	20.00	7.00

Opening of Panama Canal, 25th anniv.

For surcharges see Nos. C63, C65; Nos. G1, G3 in Scott Standard catalogue, Vol. 5.

Flags of the 21 American Republics AP31

1940, Apr. 15 Unwmk.

C62 AP31 15c blue	.40	.35

Pan American Union, 50th anniversary.

For surcharge see No. C66.

Stamps of 1939-40 Surcharged in Black

a

b

c

d

1940, Aug. 12

C63 AP23 (a) 5c on 15c lt ultra	.25	.25
a. "7 AEREO 7" on 15c	60.00	60.00
C64 A84 (b) 7c on 15c ultra	.40	.25
C65 AP23 (c) 7c on 20c rose pink	.40	.25
C66 AP31 (d) 8c on 15c blue	.40	.25
Nos. C63-C66 (4)	1.45	1.00

SPECIAL DELIVERY STAMPS

Nos. 211-212 Overprinted in Red

1926 Unwmk. *Perf. 12*

E1 A31 10c org & blk	7.50	3.25
a. "EXRPESO"	40.00	
E2 A32 20c brn & blk	10.00	3.25
a. "EXRPESO"	40.00	
b. Double overprint	35.00	35.00

Bicycle Messenger SD1

1929, Feb. 8 Engr. *Perf. 12½*

E3 SD1 10c orange	1.25	1.00
E4 SD1 20c dk brn	4.75	2.50

For surcharges and overprints see Nos. C1-C5, C17-C18A, C67 (in Scott Standard catalogue, Vol. 5).

REGISTRATION STAMPS

Issued under Colombian Dominion

R1

1888 Unwmk. Engr. *Perf. 13½*

F1 R1 10c black, *gray*	8.00	5.25

Imperforate and part-perforate copies without gum and those on surface-colored paper are reprints.

Magenta, Violet or Blue Black Handstamped Overprint

1898 *Perf. 12*

F2 A4 10c orange	7.00	6.50

The handstamp on No. F2 was also used as a postmark.

R3

1900 **Litho.** ***Perf. 11***

F3 R3 10c blk, *lt bl* 4.00 3.50

1901

F4 R3 10c brown red 30.00 20.00

R4

1902 **Blue Black Surcharge**

F5 R4 20c on 10c brn red 20.00 16.00

Issues of the Republic Issued in the City of Panama

Registration Stamps of Colombia Handstamped in Blue Black or Rose

1903-04 ***Imperf.***

F6 R9 20c red brn, *bl* 45.00 42.50
F7 R9 20c blue, *blue* (R) 45.00 42.50

For surcharges and overprints see Nos. F8-F11, F16-F26.

Reprints exist of Nos. F6 and F7; see note after No. 64.

With Additional Surcharge in Rose

F8 R9 10c on 20c red brn, *bl* 60.00 55.00
b. "10" in blue black 60.00 55.00
F9 R9 10c on 20c bl, *bl* 60.00 45.00

Handstamped in Rose

F10 R9 10c on 20c red brn, *bl* 60.00 55.00
F11 R9 10c on 20c blue, *blue* 45.00 42.50

Issued in Colon

Regular Issues Handstamped "R/COLON" in Circle (as on F2) Together with Other Overprints and Surcharges

Handstamped

1903-04 ***Perf. 12***

F12 A4 10c orange 3.00 2.50

Handstamped

F13 A4 10c orange 22.50

Overprinted in Red

F14 A4 10c orange 3.00 2.50

Overprinted in Black

F15 A4 10c orange 7.50 5.00

The handstamps on Nos. F12 to F15 are in magenta, violet or red; various combinations of these colors are to be found. They are struck in various positions, including double, inverted, one handstamp omitted, etc.

Colombia No. F13 Handstamped Like No. F12 in Violet

Imperf

F16 R9 20c red brn, *bl* 60.00 55.00

Overprinted Like No. F15 in Black

F17 R9 20c red brn, *bl* 6.00 5.75

No. F17 Surcharged in Manuscript

F18 R9 10c on 20c red brn, *bl* 60.00 55.00

No. F17 Surcharged in Purple **10**

F19 R9 10c on 20c 82.50 80.00

No. F17 Surcharged in Violet

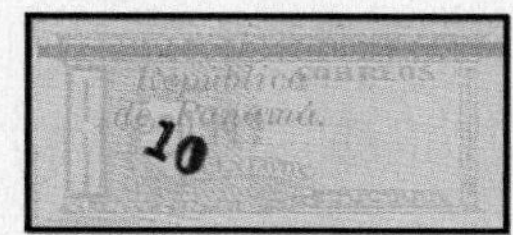

F20 R9 10c on 20c 82.50 80.00

The varieties of the overprint which are described after No. 138 are also to be found on the Registration and Acknowledgment of Receipt stamps. It is probable that Nos. F17 to F20 inclusive owe their existence more to speculation than to postal necessity.

Issued in Bocas del Toro

Colombia Nos. F17 and F13 Handstamped in Violet

R DE PANAMA

1903-04

F21 R9 20c blue, *blue* 125.00 125.00
F22 R9 20c red brn, *bl* 125.00 125.00

No. F21 Surcharged in Manuscript in Violet or Red

F23 R9 10c on 20c bl, *bl* 150.00 140.00

Colombia Nos. F13, F17 Handstamped in Violet

Surcharged in Manuscript (a) "10" (b) "10cs" in Red

F25 R9 10 on 20c red brn, *bl* 70.00 65.00
F26 R9 10cs on 20c bl, *bl* 55.00 50.00
Nos. F21-F26 (5) 525.00 505.00

No. F25 without surcharge is bogus, according to leading experts.

General Issue

R5

1904, Aug. 1 **Engr.** ***Perf. 12***

F27 R5 10c green 1.00 .50

Nos. 190 and 213 Surcharged in Red

#F29-F30

#F29b

1916-17

F29 A11 5c on 8c pur & blk 3.00 2.25
a. "5" inverted 75.00
b. Large, round "5" 50.00
c. Inverted surcharge 12.50 11.00
d. Tête bêche surcharge
e. Pair, one without surcharge 10.00
F30 A33 5c on 8c vio & blk 3.50 .80
a. Inverted surcharge 13.00 8.25
b. Tête bêche surcharge
c. Double surcharge 60.00

Issued: No. F29, 1/1/16; No. F30, 1/28/17.

Stamps similar to No. F30, overprinted in green were unauthorized.

ACKNOWLEDGMENT OF RECEIPT STAMPS

Issued under Colombian Dominion

Experts consider this handstamp- "A.R. / COLON / COLOMBIA"-to be a cancellation or a marking intended for a letter to receive special handling. It was applied at Colon to various stamps in 1897-1904 in different colored inks for philatelic sale. It exists on cover, usually with the bottom line removed by masking the handstamp.

Nos. 17-18 Handstamped in Rose

1902

H4 A4 5c blue 5.00 5.00
H5 A4 10c yellow 10.00 10.00

This handstamp was also used as a postmark.

Issues of the Republic Issued in the City of Panama

Colombia No. H3 Handstamped in Rose

1903-04 **Unwmk.** ***Imperf.***

H9 AR2 10c blue, *blue* 10.00 8.00

Reprints exist of No. H9, see note after No. 64.

No. H9 Surcharged

H10 AR2 5c on 10c bl, *bl* 5.00 5.00

Colombia No. H3 Handstamped in Rose

H11 AR2 10c blue, *blue* 17.50 14.00

Issued in Colon

Handstamped in Magenta or Violet

Imperf

H17 AR2 10c blue, *blue* 15.00 15.00

Handstamped

H18 AR2 10c blue, *blue* 82.50 70.00

Overprinted in Black

H19 AR2 10c blue, *blue* 11.00 8.00

No. H19 Surcharged in Manuscript

H20 AR2 10c on 5c on 10c 100.00 82.50

Issued in Bocas del Toro

Colombia No. H3 Handstamped in Violet and Surcharged in Manuscript in Red Like Nos. F25-F26

1904

H21 AR2 5c on 10c blue, *blue*

No. H21, unused, without surcharge is bogus.

General Issue

AR3

1904, Aug. 1 **Engr.** ***Perf. 12***

H22 AR3 5c blue 1.00 .80

No. 199 Overprinted in Violet

1916, Jan. 1
H23 A20 2½c red orange 1.00 .80
a. "R.A." for "A.R." 50.00
b. Double overprint 8.00
c. Inverted overprint 8.00

LATE FEE STAMPS

Issues of the Republic Issued in the City of Panama

Colombia No. I4 Handstamped in Rose or Blue Black

REPUBLICA DE PANAMA

LF3

1903-04 Unwmk. *Imperf.*
I1 LF3 5c pur, *rose* 12.50 9.00
I2 LF3 5c pur, *rose* (Bl Blk) 17.50 12.50

Reprints exist of #I1-I2; see note after #64.

General Issue

LF4

1904 Engr. *Perf. 12*
I3 LF4 2½c lake 1.00 .65

No. 199 Overprinted with Typewriter

1910, Aug. 12
I4 A20 2½c red orange 125.00 100.00

Used only on Aug. 12-13. Counterfeits abound.

Handstamped

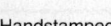

1910
I5 A20 2½c red orange 60.00 50.00

Counterfeits abound.

No. 195 Surcharged in Green

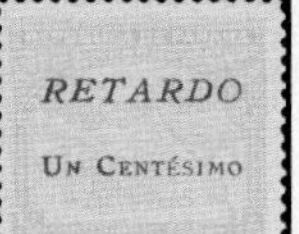

1917, Jan. 1
I6 A17 1c on ½c orange .80 .80
a. "UN CENTESIMO" inverted 50.00
b. Double surcharge 10.00
c. Inverted surcharge 6.50 6.50

No. 196 Surcharged in Green

1921
I7 A17 1c on ½c rose 25.00 20.00

POSTAGE DUE STAMPS

San Lorenzo Castle Gate, Mouth of Chagres River D1

Statue of Columbus D2

Pedro J. Sosa — D4

Design: 4c, Capitol, Panama City.

Unwmk.
1915, Mar. 25 Engr. *Perf. 12*
J1 D1 1c olive brown 3.50 .75
J2 D2 2c olive brown 5.25 .65
J3 D1 4c olive brown 7.25 1.25
J4 D4 10c olive brown 5.25 1.75
Nos. J1-J4 (4) 21.25 4.40

Type D1 was intended to show a gate of San Lorenzo Castle, Chagres, and is so inscribed.

D5

1930, Dec. 30 *Perf. 12½*
J5 D5 1c emerald 1.00 .60
J6 D5 2c dark red 1.00 .60
J7 D5 4c dark blue 1.60 .80
J8 D5 10c violet 1.60 .80
Nos. J5-J8 (4) 5.20 2.80

POSTAL TAX STAMPS

Pierre and Marie Curie — PT1

Unwmk.
1939, June 15 Engr. *Perf. 12*
RA1 PT1 1c rose carmine .65 .25
RA2 PT1 1c green .65 .25
RA3 PT1 1c orange .65 .25
RA4 PT1 1c blue .65 .25
Nos. RA1-RA4 (4) 2.60 1.00

See Nos. RA6-RA18, RA24-RA27, RA30. Post 1940 listings are in Scott Standard catalogue, Vol. 5.

Stamp of 1924 Overprinted in Black

1940, Dec. 20
RA5 A53 1c dark green 1.40 .75

PAPUA

'pa-pyə-wə

LOCATION — The southeastern portion of the island of New Guinea, north of Australia
AREA — 90,540 sq. mi.
POP. — 276,488 (1940)
CAPITAL — Port Moresby

In 1884 a British Protectorate was proclaimed over this part of the island, called "British New Guinea." In 1905 the administration was transferred to Australia and in 1906 the name was changed to Territory of Papua.

12 Pence = 1 Shilling
20 Shillings = 1 Pound

Watermarks

Wmk. 13 — Crown and Double-Lined A

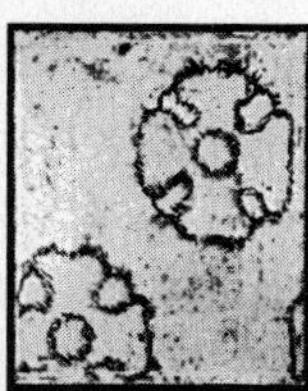

Wmk. 47 — Multiple Rosette

Wmk. 74 — Crown and Single-Lined A Sideways

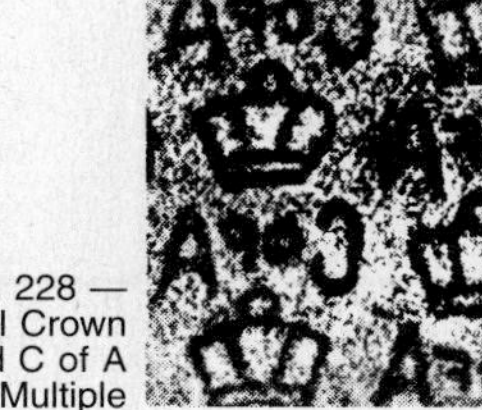

Wmk. 228 — Small Crown and C of A Multiple

British New Guinea

Lakatoi — A1

Wmk. 47
1901, July 1 Engr. *Perf. 14*
Center in Black
1 A1 ½p yellow green 24.00 6.00
2 A1 1p carmine 12.50 5.50
3 A1 2p violet 13.50 7.50
4 A1 2½p ultra 37.50 12.00
5 A1 4p black brown 45.00 40.00
a. Deformed "d" at left (pl.3, pos.4 right pane) 310.00 260.00
6 A1 6p dark green 65.00 40.00
7 A1 1sh orange 65.00 *75.00*
8 A1 2sh6p brown ('05) 700.00 *700.00*
Nos. 1-8 (8) 962.50 *886.00*

The paper varies in thickness and the watermark is found in two positions, with the greater width of the rosette either horizontal or vertical.

For stamps inscribed "Papua New Guinea" see Nos. 1024-1029.

For overprints see Nos. 11-26.

Papua

Stamps of British New Guinea, Overprinted

Large Overprint

1906, Nov. 8 Wmk. 47 *Perf. 14*
Center in Black
11 A1 ½p yellow green 12.00 *25.00*
12 A1 1p carmine 20.00 *22.50*
13 A1 2p violet 19.00 5.00
14 A1 2½p ultra 12.00 *18.00*
15 A1 4p black brown 250.00 160.00
e. Deformed "d" at left 260.00 *350.00*
16 A1 6p dark green 47.50 *50.00*
17 A1 1sh orange 30.00 *50.00*
18 A1 2sh6p brown 225.00 *240.00*
Nos. 11-18 (8) 615.50 *570.50*

Small Overprint

1907 Center in Black
19 A1 ½p yel grn 24.00 *29.00*
a. Double overprint 3,500.
20 A1 1p carmine 12.00 *7.50*
a. Vertical overprint, up 7,500. 4,500.
21 A1 2p violet 8.00 4.00
a. Double overprint 4,250.
22 A1 2½p ultra 21.00 *24.00*
a. Double overprint
b. 2½p dull blue & blk 175.00 *190.00*
23 A1 4p blk brn 50.00 *70.00*
a. Deformed "d" at left 600.00
24 A1 6p dk grn 50.00 *55.00*
a. Double overprint 7,000. *13,000.*
25 A1 1sh orange 55.00 *60.00*
a. Double overprint *21,000.* *14,000.*
26 A1 2sh6p brown 60.00 *75.00*
b. Vert. ovpt., down *8,500.*
d. Double horiz. ovpt. 4,500.
e. Triple horiz. ovpt. 3,100.
Nos. 19-26 (8) 280.00 *324.50*

A2

Small "PAPUA"

Perf. 11, 12½
1907-08 Litho. Wmk. 13
Center in Black
28 A2 1p carmine ('08) 7.50 *5.75*
29 A2 2p violet ('08) 27.50 8.00
30 A2 2½p ultra ('08) 17.50 *9.00*
31 A2 4p black brown 9.00 *15.00*
b. Deformed "d" at left 35.00 *62.50*
32 A2 6p dk green ('08) 17.50 *18.50*
33 A2 1sh orange ('08) 57.50 *25.00*
Nos. 28-33 (6) 136.50 *81.25*

Perf. 12½
30a A2 2½p 180.00 *190.00*
31a A2 4p 13.00 *13.00*
c. Deformed "d" at left 62.50 62.50
33a A2 1sh 77.50 *100.00*
Nos. 30a-33a (3) 270.50 *303.00*

1909-10 Wmk. Sideways
Center in Black
34 A2 ½p yellow green 5.50 *6.50*
a. Perf. 11x12½ *5,000.* *5,000.*
b. Perf. 11 6.00 *7.50*
35 A2 1p carmine 10.00 *14.00*
a. Perf. 11 11.00 9.25
36 A2 2p violet ('10) 10.00 *15.00*
a. Perf. 11x12½ 1,700.
b. Perf. 11 27.50 *10.50*
37 A2 2½p ultra ('10) 7.00 *26.00*
a. Perf. 12½ 13.00 *45.00*
38 A2 4p black brn ('10) 6.50 *12.00*
a. Perf. 11x12½ *16,000.*
b. As "#38," deformed "d" at left 32.50 *52.50*
39 A2 6p dark green 12.50 22.50
a. Perf. 12½ 5,500. *14,000.*
40 A2 1sh orange ('10) 25.00 *65.00*
a. Perf. 11 65.00 *85.00*
Nos. 34-40 (7) 76.50 *161.00*

One stamp in each sheet has a white line across the upper part of the picture which is termed the "rift in the clouds."

Large "PAPUA"

2sh6p:
Type I — The numerals are thin and irregular. The body of the "6" encloses a large spot of color. The dividing stroke is thick and uneven.

Type II — The numerals are thick and well formed. The "6" encloses a narrow oval of color. The dividing stroke is thin and sharp.

1910 **Wmk. 13**

Center in Black

41 A2 ½p yellow green 6.00 *14.00*
42 A2 1p carmine 15.00 16.00
43 A2 2p violet 7.50 *8.00*
44 A2 2½p blue violet 13.00 *22.50*
45 A2 4p black brown 13.50 *14.00*
46 A2 6p dark green 11.00 *13.00*
47 A2 1sh orange 14.00 *22.50*
48 A2 2sh6p brown, type II 77.50 *75.00*
a. Type I 60.00 *60.00*
Nos. 41-48 (8) 157.50 *185.00*

Wmk. Sideways

49 A2 2sh6p choc, type I 85.00 *100.00*

1911 **Typo.** **Wmk. 74** ***Perf. 12½***
50 A2 ½p yellow green 1.25 *4.00*
51 A2 1p lt red 1.50 2.00
52 A2 2p lt violet 4.00 2.00
53 A2 2½p ultra 6.50 *11.00*
a. 2½p dull ultra 6.25 9.50
54 A2 4p olive green 4.75 *18.00*
55 A2 6p orange brown 5.00 *6.50*
56 A2 1sh yellow 14.00 *20.00*
57 A2 2sh6p rose 46.00 *50.00*
Nos. 50-57 (8) 83.00 *113.50*

For surcharges see Nos. 74-79.

1915, June ***Perf. 14***
59 A2 1p light red 22.50 3.00

A3

1916-31
60 A3 ½p pale yel grn & myr grn ('19) 1.00 1.50
61 A3 1p rose red & blk 2.50 1.50
62 A3 1½p yel brn & gray bl ('25) 2.50 1.00
63 A3 2p red vio & vio brn ('19) 2.75 1.25
64 A3 2p red brn & vio brn ('31) 4.00 1.50
a. 2p cop red & vio brn ('31) 29.00 2.25
65 A3 2½p ultra & dk grn ('19) 5.75 *15.00*
66 A3 3p emerald & blk 4.75 3.00
a. 3p dp bl grn & blk 5.75 9.25
67 A3 4p org & lt brn ('19) 5.75 7.00
68 A3 5p ol brn & sl ('31) 5.50 *18.00*
69 A3 6p vio & dl vio ('23) 5.50 *11.00*
70 A3 1sh ol grn & dk brn ('19) 7.00 *9.00*
71 A3 2sh6p rose & red brn ('19) 27.50 *47.50*
72 A3 5sh dp grn & blk 55.00 *60.00*
73 A3 10sh gray bl & grn ('25) 175.00 *200.00*
Nos. 60-73 (14) 304.50 *377.25*

Type A3 is a redrawing of type A2. The lines of the picture have been strengthened, making it much darker, especially the sky and water.

See Nos. 92-93. For surcharges & overprints see Nos. 88-91, O1-O10.

Stamps of 1911 Surcharged

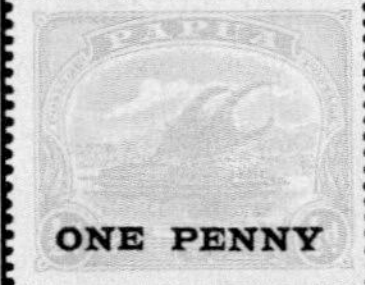

1917 ***Perf. 12½***
74 A2 1p on ½p yellow grn 1.75 *1.90*
75 A2 1p on 2p lt violet 14.50 *17.50*
76 A2 1p on 2½p ultra 1.50 *4.50*
77 A2 1p on 4p olive green 2.10 *5.25*
78 A2 1p on 6p org brn 10.00 *24.50*
79 A2 1p on 2sh6p rose 4.00 *7.00*
Nos. 74-79 (6) 33.85 *60.65*

No. 62 Surcharged

1931, Jan. 1 ***Perf. 14***
88 A3 2p on 1½p yellow brn & gray blue 1.50 *2.25*

Nos. 70, 71 and 72 Surcharged in Black

1931
89 A3 5p on 1sh #70 1.75 *3.00*
90 A3 9p on 2sh6p #71 10.00 *18.00*
91 A3 1sh3p on 5sh #72 7.50 *14.00*
Nos. 89-91 (3) 19.25 *35.00*

Type of 1916 Issue

1932 **Wmk. 228** ***Perf. 11***
92 A3 9p dp violet & gray 9.50 *37.50*
93 A3 1sh3p pale bluish grn & grayish vio 14.50 *37.50*

For overprints see Nos. O11-O12.

Motuan Girl — A5

Bird of Paradise and Boar's Tusk — A6

Mother and Child — A7

Papuan Motherhood — A8

Dubu (Ceremonial Platform) — A9

Fire Maker — A10

Designs: 1p, Steve, son of Oala. 1½p, Tree houses. 3p, Papuan dandy. 5p, Masked dancer. 9p, Shooting fish. 1sh3p, Lakatoi. 2sh, Delta art. 2sh6p, Pottery making. 5sh, Sgt.-Major Simoi. £1, Delta house.

Unwmk.

1932, Nov. 14 **Engr.** ***Perf. 11***
94 A5 ½p orange & blk 4.50 4.00
a. ½p orange brown & black 4.00 *26.00*
95 A5 1p yel grn & blk 4.00 .70
96 A5 1½p red brn & blk 4.50 *9.25*
97 A6 2p light red 12.50 .35
98 A5 3p blue & blk 4.25 *7.50*
99 A7 4p olive green 12.00 *12.00*
100 A5 5p grnsh sl & blk 7.00 3.50
101 A8 6p bister brown 8.50 6.25
102 A5 9p lilac & blk 11.50 *24.00*
103 A9 1sh bluish gray 10.00 *10.00*
104 A5 1sh3p brown & blk 19.00 *29.00*
105 A5 2sh bluish slate & blk 19.00 *26.00*
106 A5 2sh6p rose lilac & blk 29.00 *42.50*
107 A5 5sh olive & blk 70.00 62.50
108 A10 10sh gray lilac 150.00 120.00
109 A5 £1 lt gray & black 275.00 180.00
Nos. 94-109 (16) 640.75 *537.55*

For overprints see Nos. 114-117.

Hoisting Union Jack at Port Moresby A21

H. M. S. "Nelson" at Port Moresby A22

1934, Nov. 6
110 A21 1p dull green 3.00 *3.50*
111 A22 2p red brown 2.75 *3.00*
112 A21 3p blue 3.00 *3.00*
113 A22 5p violet brown 12.00 *22.50*
Nos. 110-113 (4) 20.75 *32.00*
Set, never hinged 27.50

Declaration of British Protection, 50th anniv.

Silver Jubilee Issue

Stamps of 1932 Issue Overprinted in Black

a

b

1935, July 9 **Glazed Paper**
114 A5(a) 1p yellow grn & blk 1.20 *4.00*
115 A6(b) 2p light red 3.50 *5.00*
116 A5(a) 3p lt blue & blk 2.25 *4.00*
117 A5(a) 5p grnsh slate & blk 2.25 *4.00*
Nos. 114-117 (4) 9.20 *17.00*
Set, never hinged 16.50

25th anniv. of the reign of George V.

Coronation Issue

King George VI — A22a

Unwmk.

1937, May 14 **Engr.** ***Perf. 11***
118 A22a 1p green .40 .25
119 A22a 2p salmon rose .40 *1.50*
120 A22a 3p blue .40 *1.50*
121 A22a 5p brown violet .40 *2.00*
Nos. 118-121 (4) 1.60 *5.25*
Set, never hinged 2.50

AIR POST STAMPS

Regular Issue of 1916 Overprinted

1929 **Wmk. 74** ***Perf. 14***
C1 A3 3p blue grn & dk gray 2.00 *12.50*
b. Vert. pair, one without ovpt. *6,000.*
c. Horiz. pair, one without ovpt. *6,500.*
d. 3p blue grn & sepia blk 57.50 *75.00*
e. Overprint on back, vert. *5,000.*

No. C1 exists on white and on yellowish paper, No. C1d on yellowish paper only.

Regular Issues of 1916-23 Overprinted in Red

1930, Sept. 15 **Wmk. 74**
C2 A3 3p blue grn & blk 2.00 *7.00*
a. Yellowish paper 2,200. *3,750.*
b. Double overprint 1,500.
C3 A3 6p violet & dull vio 8.00 *12.00*
a. Yellowish paper 5.00 *19.00*
C4 A3 1sh ol grn & ol brn 6.00 *17.50*
a. Inverted overprint *14,500.*
b. Yellowish paper 10.00 26.00
Nos. C2-C4 (3) 16.00 *36.50*

Port Moresby AP1

Unwmk.

1938, Sept. 6 **Engr.** ***Perf. 11***
C5 AP1 2p carmine 2.75 3.25
C6 AP1 3p ultra 2.75 2.50
C7 AP1 5p dark green 2.75 *3.50*
C8 AP1 8p red brown 6.50 *21.00*
C9 AP1 1sh violet 17.50 22.50
Nos. C5-C9 (5) 32.25 *52.75*
Set, never hinged 65.00

Papua as a British possession, 50th anniv.

Papuans Poling Rafts — AP2

1939-41
C10 AP2 2p carmine 3.00 6.00
C11 AP2 3p ultra 3.00 *11.00*
C12 AP2 5p dark green 3.00 2.25
C13 AP2 8p red brown 7.50 3.25
C14 AP2 1sh violet 9.00 9.00
C15 AP2 1sh6p lt olive ('41) 27.50 *40.00*
Nos. C10-C15 (6) 53.00 *71.50*
Set, never hinged 90.00

OFFICIAL STAMPS

Nos. 60-63, 66-71, 92-93 Overprinted

1931 **Wmk. 74** ***Perf. 14½***
O1 A3 ½p #60 2.50 *5.50*
O2 A3 1p #61 5.00 *13.00*
O3 A3 1½p #62 2.00 *14.00*

O4 A3 2p #63 4.50 *14.00*
O5 A3 3p #66 3.00 *25.00*
O6 A3 4p #67 3.00 *21.00*
O7 A3 5p #68 7.00 *42.50*
O8 A3 6p #69 5.00 *9.75*
O9 A3 1sh #70 11.00 *35.00*
O10 A3 2sh6p #71 47.50 *97.50*

1932 Wmk. 228 *Perf. 11½*

O11 A3 9p #92 37.50 *55.00*
O12 A3 1sh3p #93 37.50 *55.00*
Nos. O1-O12 (12) 165.50 *387.25*

PARAGUAY

'par-ə-ˌgwī

LOCATION — South America, bounded by Bolivia, Brazil and Argentina
GOVT. — Republic
AREA — 157,042 sq. mi.
POP. — 3,477,000 (1983)
CAPITAL — Asuncion

10 Reales = 100 Centavos = 1 Peso

Vigilant Lion Supporting Liberty Cap
A1 A2

A3

1870, Aug. Unwmk. Litho. *Imperf.*

1 A1 1r rose 6.50 *10.00*
On cover *2,000.*
On cover, pen canceled *1,000.*
a. 1r bright rose 4.50 *9.*
On cover *2,100.*
On cover, pen canceled *1,100.*
2 A2 2r blue 120.00 *120.00*
On cover *4,000.*
a. 2r dark blue *125.*
On cover *5,000.*
3 A3 3r black 225.00 *250.00*
On cover *8,000.*
On cover, pen canceled *1,000.*
Nos. 1-3 (3) 351.50 *380.00*

Counterfeits of 2r in blue and other colors are on thicker paper than originals. They show a colored dot in upper part of "S" of "DOS" in upper right corner.
For surcharges see Nos. 4-9, 19.

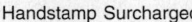

Handstamp Surcharged

1878 Black Surcharge

4 A1 5c on 1r rose 100. *120.*
On cover (see footnote) *10,000.*
5 A2 5c on 2r blue 450. 400.
On cover *13,000.*
5E A3 5c on 3r black 550. 550.
On cover *15,000.*
Nos. 4-5E (3) 1,100. 1,070.

Blue Surcharge

5F A1 5c on 1r rose 100. *120.*
On cover (see footnote) *10,000.*
5H A2 5c on 2r blue *1,200.* *1,200.*
On cover *13,000.*
6 A3 5c on 3r black 675. 650.
On cover *15,000.*
Nos. 5F-6 (3) *1,975.* *1,970.*

The surcharge may be found inverted, double, sideways and omitted.
Remainders of Nos. 4 and 5F were placed on sale at Post Offices during 1892. Covers dated 1892 are worth about $7,500.
The originals are surcharged in dull black or dull blue. The reprints are in intense black and bright blue. The reprint surcharges are over-inked and show numerous breaks in the handstamp.

Handstamp Surcharged

Black Surcharge

7 A2 5c on 2r blue 450.00 350.00
On cover *13,000.*
8 A3 5c on 3r black 575.00 550.00
On cover *15,000.*

Blue Surcharge

9 A3 5c on 3r black 550.00 550.00
On cover *15,000.*
a. Dbl. surch., large & small "5" —
Nos. 7-9 (3) 1,575. 1,450.

The surcharge on Nos. 7, 8 and 9 is usually placed sideways. It may be found double or inverted on Nos. 8 and 9.
Nos. 4 to 9 have been extensively counterfeited.
Two examples recorded of No. 9a, one without gum, the other with full but disturbed original gum.

A4

1879 Litho. *Perf. 12½*
Thin Paper

10 A4 5r orange .80
11 A4 10r red brown .90
a. Imperf.
b. Horiz. pair, imperf. vert. 60.00

Nos. 10 and 11 were never placed in use.
For surcharges see Nos. 17-18.

A4a

1879-81 Thin Paper

12 A4a 5c orange brown 2.50 2.00
On cover 500.00
a. 5c reddish brown 2.00 2.00
On cover 525.00
13 A4a 10c blue grn ('81) 3.50 3.00
On cover 700.00
a. Imperf., pair 50.00 *60.00*

Reprints of Nos. 10-13 are imperf., perf. 11½, 12, 12½ or 14. They have yellowish gum and the 10c is deep green.

A5 A6

A7

1881, Aug. Litho. *Perf. 11½-13½*

14 A5 1c blue .80 .70
On cover —
a. Imperf., pair —
b. Horiz. pair, imperf. btwn. —
15 A6 2c rose red .80 .70
On cover *300.00*
a. 2c dull orange red 1.00 .90
On cover *300.00*
b. Imperf., pair —
c. Horiz. pair, imperf. vert. 25.00 25.00
d. Vert. pair, imperf. horiz. 25.00 25.00
16 A7 4c brown .80 .70
On cover *650.00*
a. Imperf., pair —
b. Horiz. pair, imperf. vert. 25.00 25.00
c. Vert. pair, imperf. horiz. 25.00 25.00

No. 11 Handstamped Surcharge in Black or Gray

1881, July *Perf. 12½*

17 A4 1c on 10c blue grn 16.00 14.00
On cover 400.00
18 A4 2c on 10c blue grn 16.00 14.00
On cover 450.00

Gray handstamps sell for 10 times more than black as many specialists consider the black to be reprints.

No. 1 Handstamped Surcharge in Black

1884, May 8 *Imperf.*

19 A1 1c on 1r rose 10.00 8.00
On cover *1,750.*

The surcharges on Nos. 17-19 exist double, inverted and in pairs with one omitted. Counterfeits exist.

Seal of the Treasury — A11

1884, Aug. 3 Litho. *Perf. 12½*

20 A11 1c green 1.00 .80
On cover 35.00
21 A11 2c rose pink, thin paper 1.00 .80
b. 2c rose red, thin paper .85 .85
c. 2c red, thick paper, perf. 11½ .70 .85

Perf. 11½

22 A11 5c pale blue, yellowish paper 1.00 .80
b. 5c blue, thin paper, perf. 12½ .65 .65
On cover 45.00
c. 5c pale blue, thin paper, perf. 12½ .65 .65
d. 5c blue, thin paper 3.75 3.75
e. 5c pale blue, thin paper 2.50 2.50
f. 5c blue, thick paper 11.50 9.00
Nos. 20-22 (3) 3.00 2.40

There are two types of each value differing mostly in the shape of the numerals. In addition, there are numerous small flaws in the lithographic transfers.
For overprints see Nos. O1, O8, O15.

Imperf., Pairs

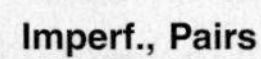

20a A11 1c green 12.50
21a A11 2c rose red 16.00
d. 2c red, thick paper 10.00
22a A11 5c blue 16.00
Nos. 20a-22a (3) 44.50

Seal of the Treasury — A12

Perf. 11½, 11½x12, 12½x11½

1887 Typo.

23 A12 1c green .30 .25
24 A12 2c rose .30 .25
25 A12 5c blue .50 .35
26 A12 7c brown .90 .50
27 A12 10c lilac .60 .35
28 A12 15c orange .60 .35
29 A12 20c pink .60 .35
Nos. 23-29 (7) 3.80 2.40

See #42-45. For surcharges & overprints see #46, 49-50, 71-72, 167-170A, O20-O41, O49.

Symbols of Liberty from Coat of Arms — A13

1889, Feb. Litho. *Perf. 11½*

30 A13 15c red violet 2.50 2.00
a. Imperf., pair 10.00 8.00

For overprints see Nos. O16-O19.

Overprint Handstamped in Violet

1892, Oct. 12 *Perf. 12x12½*

31 A15 10c violet blue 10.00 5.00

Discovery of America by Columbus, 400th anniversary. Overprint reads: "1492 / 12 DE OCTUBRE / 1892." Sold only on day of issue.

Cirilo A. Rivarola — A15

Designs: 2c, Salvador Jovellanos. 4c, Juan B. Gil. 5c, Higinio Uriarte. 10c, Cándido Bareiro. 14c, Gen. Bernardino Caballero. 20c, Gen. Patricio Escobar. 30c, Juan G. González.

1892-96 Litho. *Perf. 12x12½*

32 A15 1c gray (centavos) .25 .25
33 A15 1c gray (centavo) ('96) .25 .25
34 A15 2c green .25 .25
a. Chalky paper ('96) .25 .25
35 A15 4c carmine .25 .25
a. Chalky paper ('96) .25 .25
36 A15 5c violet ('93) .25 .25
a. Chalky paper ('96) .25 .25
37 A15 10c vio bl (punched) ('93) .25 .25
Unpunched ('96) 5.00
38 A15 10c dull blue ('96) .25 .25
39 A15 14c yellow brown .75 .50
40 A15 20c red ('93) 1.25 .50
41 A15 30c light green 2.00 .80
Nos. 32-41 (10) 5.75 3.55

The 10c violet blue (No. 37) was, until 1896, issued punched with a circular hole in order to prevent it being fraudulently overprinted as No. 31.
Nos. 33 and 38 are on chalky paper.
For surcharge see No. 70.

Seal Type of 1887

1892 Typo.

42 A12 40c slate blue 3.00 1.25
43 A12 60c yellow 1.50 .50
44 A12 80c light blue 1.40 .50
45 A12 1p olive green 1.40 .50
Nos. 42-45 (4) 7.30 2.75

For surcharges see Nos. 71-72.

No. 26 Surcharged in Black

1895, Aug. 1 *Perf. 11½x12*

46 A12 5c on 7c brown .75 .75

Telegraph Stamps Surcharged

1896, Apr. Engr. *Perf. 11½*
Denomination in Black

47 5c on 2c brown & gray .90 .60
a. Inverted surcharge 10.00 10.00
48 5c on 4c yellow & gray .90 .60
a. Inverted surcharge 7.50 7.50

Nos. 28, 42 Surcharged

1898-99 **Typo.**

49 A12 10c on 15c org ('99) .75 .45
a. Inverted surcharge 17.50 17.50
b. Double surcharge 11.00 11.00
50 A12 10c on 40c slate bl .35 .25

Surcharge on No. 49 has small "c."

Telegraph Stamps Surcharged

1900, May 14 **Engr.** ***Perf. 11½***

50A 5c on 30c grn, gray & blk 2.75 1.50
50B 10c on 50c dl vio, gray & blk 6.00 3.75

The basic telegraph stamps are like those used for Nos. 47-48, but the surcharges on Nos. 50A-50B consist of "5 5" and "10 10" above a blackout rectangle covering the engraved denominations.

A 40c red, bluish gray and black telegraph stamp (basic type of A24) was used provisionally in August, 1900, for postage. Value, postally used, $5.

Seal of the Treasury — A25

1900, Sept. **Engr.** ***Perf. 11½, 12***

51 A25 2c gray .40 .30
52 A25 3c orange brown .40 .30
53 A25 5c dark green .40 .30
54 A25 8c dark brown .40 .30
55 A25 10c carmine rose 1.00 .30
56 A25 24c deep blue 1.20 .30
Nos. 51-56 (6) 3.80 1.80

See Nos. 57-67. For surcharges see Nos. 69, 74, 76, 156-157.

Small Figures

1901, Apr. **Litho.** ***Perf. 11½***

57 A25 2c rose .25 .25
58 A25 5c violet brown .25 .25
59 A25 40c blue .85 .30
Nos. 57-59 (3) 1.35 .80

1901-02 **Larger Figures**

60 A25 1c gray green ('02) .30 .30
61 A25 2c gray .30 .30
a. Half used as 1c on cover 10.00
62 A25 4c pale blue .30 .30
63 A25 5c violet .30 .30
64 A25 8c gray brown ('02) .30 .30
65 A25 10c rose red ('02) .75 .30
66 A25 28c orange ('02) 1.50 .30
67 A25 40c blue .75 .30
Nos. 60-67 (8) 4.50 2.40

For surcharges see Nos. 74, 76.

J. B. Egusquiza — A26

Chalky Paper

1901, Sept. 24 **Typo.** ***Perf. 12x12½***

68 A26 1p slate .30 .25

For surcharge see No. 73.

No. 56 Surcharged in Red

1902, Aug.

69 A25 20c on 24c dp blue .50 .40
a. Inverted surcharge 6.25

Counterfeit surcharges exist.

Nos. 39, 43-44 Surcharged

1902, Dec. 22 ***Perf. 12x12½***

70 A15 1c on 14c yellow brn .25 .25
a. No period after "cent" .90 .75
b. Comma after "cent" .65 .50
c. Accent over "Un" .65 .50

1903 ***Perf. 11½***

71 A12 5c on 60c yellow .35 .30
72 A12 5c on 80c lt blue .30 .30

Nos. 68, 64, 66 Surcharged

No. 73

No. 74

No. 76

1902-03 ***Perf. 12***

73 A26 1c on 1p slate ('03) .40 .40
a. No period after "cent" 3.25 3.00

Perf. 11½

74 A25 5c on 8c gray brown .50 .40
a. No period after "cent" 1.75 1.50
b. Double surcharge 7.00 6.00
76 A25 5c on 28c orange .50 .40
a. No period after "cent" 1.75 1.50
b. Comma after "cent" .80 .60
Nos. 73-76 (3) 1.40 1.20

The surcharge on Nos. 73 and 74 is found reading both upward and downward.

Sentinel Lion with Right Paw Ready to Strike for "Peace and Justice" — A32

Perf. 11½

1903, Feb. 28 **Litho.** **Unwmk.**

77 A32 1c gray .30 .30
78 A32 2c blue green .45 .30
79 A32 5c blue .60 .30
80 A32 10c orange brown .75 .30
81 A32 20c carmine .75 .30
82 A32 30c deep blue .90 .30
83 A32 60c purple 2.10 1.00
Nos. 77-83 (7) 5.85 2.80

For surcharges and overprints see Nos. 139-140, 166, O50-O56.

Sentinel Lion with Right Paw Ready to Strike for "Peace and Justice" — A33

1903, Sept.

84 A33 1c yellow green .30 .30
85 A33 2c red orange .30 .30
86 A33 5c dark blue .45 .30
87 A33 10c purple .45 .30
88 A33 20c dark green 5.00 .45
89 A33 30c ultramarine 1.50 .30
90 A33 60c ocher 1.75 .75
Nos. 84-90 (7) 9.75 2.70

Nos. 84-90 exist imperf. Value for pairs, $3 each for 1c-20c, $4 for 30c, $5 for 60c.

The three-line overprint "Gobierno provisorio Ago. 1904" is fraudulent.

Sentinel Lion at Rest — A35

Perf. 11½, 12, 11½x12

1905-10 **Engr.**

Dated "1904"

91 A35 1c orange .30 .25
92 A35 1c vermilion ('07) .30 .25
93 A35 1c grnsh bl ('07) .30 .25
94 A35 2c vermilion ('06) .30 .25
95 A35 2c olive grn ('07) 60.00
96 A35 2c car rose ('08) .45 .25
97 A35 5c dark blue .30 .25
98 A35 5c slate blue ('06) .30 .25
99 A35 5c yellow ('06) .30 .25
100 A35 10c bister ('06) .30 .25
101 A35 10c emerald ('07) .30 .25
102 A35 10c dp ultra ('08) .30 .25
103 A35 20c violet ('06) .45 .25
104 A35 20c bister ('07) .45 .25
105 A35 20c apple grn ('07) .45 .25
106 A35 30c turq bl ('06) .65 .25
107 A35 30c blue gray ('07) .65 .25
108 A35 30c dull lilac ('08) .90 .25
109 A35 60c chocolate ('07) .60 .25
110 A35 60c org brn ('07) 5.25 1.60
111 A35 60c salmon pink ('10) 5.25 1.60
Nos. 91-111 (21) 78.10
Nos. 91-94,96-111 (20) 18.10 7.70

All but Nos. 92 and 104 exist imperf. Value for pair, $10 each, except No. 95 at $35.00 and Nos. 109-111 at $15.00 each pair.

For surcharges and overprints see Nos. 129-130, 146-155, 174-190, 266.

Sentinel Lion at Rest — A36

1904, Aug. **Litho.** ***Perf. 11½***

112 A36 10c light blue .50 .40
a. Imperf., pair 6.00

No. 112 Surcharged in Black

1904, Dec.

113 A36 30c on 10c light blue .80 .50

Peace between a successful revolutionary party and the government previously in power.

Governmental Palace, Asunción — A37

Dated "1904"

Center in Black

1906-10 **Engr.** ***Perf. 11½, 12***

114 A37 1p bright rose 2.50 1.50
115 A37 1p brown org ('07) 1.00 .50
116 A37 1p ol gray ('07) 1.00 .50
117 A37 2p turquoise ('07) .50 .40
118 A37 2p lake ('09) .50 .40
119 A37 2p brn org ('10) .60 .40
120 A37 5p red ('07) 1.50 1.00
121 A37 5p ol grn ('10) 1.50 1.00
122 A37 5p dull bl ('10) 1.50 1.00
123 A37 10p brown org ('07) 1.40 1.00
124 A37 10p dp blue ('10) 1.40 1.00
125 A37 10p choc ('10) 1.50 1.00
126 A37 20p olive grn ('07) 3.50 3.25
127 A37 20p violet ('10) 3.50 3.25
128 A37 20p yellow ('10) 3.50 3.25
Nos. 114-128 (15) 25.40 19.45

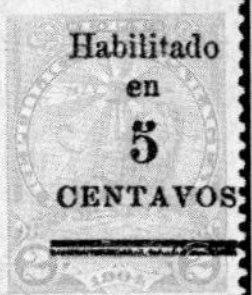

Nos. 94 and 95 Surcharged

1907

129 A35 5c on 2c vermilion .45 .30
a. "5" omitted 1.50 1.50
b. Inverted surcharge 5.25 5.25
c. Double surcharge
d. Double surcharge, one inverted 1.50 1.50
e. Double surcharge, both invtd. 9.00 9.00
130 A35 5c on 2c olive grn .60 .30
a. "5" omitted 1.50 1.50
b. Inverted surcharge 1.50 1.50
c. Double surcharge 3.00 3.00
d. Bar omitted 3.00 3.00

Official Stamps of 1906-08 Surcharged

1908

131 O17 5c on 10c bister .45 .30
a. Double surcharge 4.50 4.50
132 O17 5c on 10c violet .45 .30
a. Inverted surcharge 3.50 3.50
133 O17 5c on 20c emerald .45 .30
134 O17 5c on 20c violet .45 .30
a. Inverted surcharge 3.50 3.50
135 O17 5c on 30c slate bl 1.50 1.00
136 O17 5c on 30c turq bl 1.50 1.00
a. Inverted surcharge
b. Double surcharge 9.00 9.00
137 O17 5c on 60c choc .45 .30
a. Double surcharge 9.00 9.00
138 O17 5c on 60c red brown .90 .30
a. Inverted surcharge 1.60 1.60
Nos. 131-138 (8) 6.15 3.80

Same Surcharge on Official Stamps of 1903

139 A32 5c on 30c dp blue 3.75 3.25
140 A32 5c on 60c purple 1.50 .90
a. Double surcharge 7.50 7.50

Official Stamps of 1906-08 Overprinted

141 O17 5c deep blue .40 .40
a. Inverted overprint 3.00 3.00
b. Bar omitted 9.00 9.00
c. Double overprint 4.00 4.00
142 O17 5c slate blue .50 .40
a. Inverted overprint 4.00 4.00
b. Double overprint 3.50 3.50
c. Bar omitted 9.00 9.00
143 O17 5c greenish blue .40 .40
a. Inverted overprint 2.50 2.50
b. Bar omitted 7.50 7.50
144 O18 1p brown org & blk .50 .50
a. Double overprint 2.00 2.00
b. Double overprint, one inverted 2.50 2.50
c. Triple overprint, two inverted 4.50 4.50
145 O18 1p brt rose & blk .90 .70
a. Bar omitted
Nos. 141-145 (5) 2.70 2.40

Regular Issues of 1906-08 Surcharged

1908

146 A35 5c on 1c grnsh bl .30 .30
a. Inverted surcharge 1.50 1.50
b. Double surcharge 2.25 2.25
c. "5" omitted 2.25 2.25
147 A35 5c on 2c car rose .30 .30
a. Inverted surcharge 2.50 2.50
b. "5" omitted 3.00 3.00
c. Double surcharge 5.25 5.25
d. Double surcharge, one invtd,
148 A35 5c on 60c org brn .30 .30
a. Inverted surcharge 3.75 3.75
b. "5" omitted 1.50 1.50
149 A35 5c on 60c sal pink .30 .30
a. Double surcharge .75 .75
b. Double surcharge, one invtd. 5.25 5.25
150 A35 5c on 60c choc .30 .30
a. Inverted surcharge 7.50 7.50

151 A35 20c on 1c grnsh bl .30 .30
a. Inverted surcharge 2.25 2.25
152 A35 20c on 2c ver 9.00 7.50
153 A35 20c on 2c car rose 5.25 4.50
a. Inverted surcharge 19.00
154 A35 20c on 30c dl lil .30 .30
a. Inverted surcharge 2.25 2.25
b. Double surcharge
155 A35 20c on 30c turq bl 2.25 2.25
Nos. 146-155 (10) 18.60 16.35

Same Surcharge on Regular Issue of 1901-02

156 A25 5c on 28c org 1.90 1.60
157 A25 5c on 40c dk bl .60 .45
a. Inverted surcharge 6.00 6.00

Same Surcharge on Official Stamps of 1908

158 O17 5c on 10c emer .40 .40
a. Double surcharge 14.00
159 O17 5c on 10c red lil .40 .40
a. Double surcharge 4.00 4.00
b. "5" omitted 3.00 3.00
160 O17 5c on 20c bis .80 .60
a. Double surcharge 2.50 2.50
161 O17 5c on 20c sal pink .80 .60
a. "5" omitted 3.50 3.50
162 O17 5c on 30c bl gray .40 .40
163 O17 5c on 30c yel .40 .40
a. "5" omitted 3.00 3.00
b. Inverted surcharge 2.50 2.50
164 O17 5c on 60c org brn .40 .40
a. Double surcharge 12.00 12.00
165 O17 5c on 60c dp ultra .40 .40
a. Inverted surcharge 5.00 5.00
b. "5" omitted 3.00
Nos. 158-165 (8) 4.00 3.60

Same Surcharge on No. O52

166 A32 20c on 5c blue 2.50 2.00
a. Inverted surcharge 6.00 7.50

Stamp of 1887 Surcharged

1908 **On Stamp of 1887**
167 A12 20c on 2c car 6.50 3.00
a. Inverted surcharge 22.50

On Official Stamps of 1892

168 A12 5c on 15c org 7.50 5.25
169 A12 5c on 20c pink 120.00 95.00
170 A12 5c on 50c gray 52.50 37.50
170A A12 20c on 5c blue 4.50 3.75
b. Inverted surcharge 25.00 25.00
Nos. 167-170A (5) 191.00 144.50

Nos. 151, 152, 153, 155, 167, 170A, while duly authorized, all appear to have been sold to a single individual, and although they paid postage, it is doubtful whether they can be considered as ever having been placed on sale to the public.

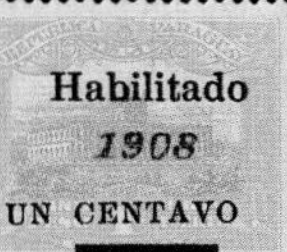

Nos. O82-O84 Surcharged (Date in Red)

1908-09
171 O18 1c on 1p brt rose & blk .50 .50
172 O18 1c on 1p lake & blk .50 .50
173 O18 1c on 1p brn org & blk ('09) 5.00 5.00
Nos. 171-173 (3) 6.00 6.00

Varieties of surcharge on Nos. 171-173 include: "CETTAVO"; date omitted, double or inverted; third line double or omitted.

Types of 1905-1910 Overprinted

1908, Mar. 5 ***Perf. 11½***
174 A35 1c emerald .30 .30
175 A35 5c yellow .30 .30
176 A35 10c lilac brown .30 .30
177 A35 20c yellow orange .30 .30
178 A35 30c red .40 .30
179 A35 60c magenta .30 .30
180 A37 1p light blue .30 .30
Nos. 174-180 (7) 2.20 2.10

Overprinted

1909, Sept.
181 A35 1c blue gray .40 .40
182 A35 1c scarlet .40 .40
183 A35 5c dark green .40 .40
184 A35 5c deep orange .40 .40
185 A35 10c rose .40 .40
186 A35 10c bister brown .40 .40
187 A35 20c yellow .40 .40
188 A35 20c violet .40 .40
189 A35 30c orange brown .60 .40
190 A35 30c dull blue .60 .40
Nos. 181-190 (10) 4.40 4.00

Counterfeits exist.

Coat of Arms above Numeral of Value — A38

1910-21 **Litho.** ***Perf. 11½***
191 A38 1c brown .40 .25
192 A38 5c bright violet .40 .25
a. Pair, imperf. between 2.00 2.00
193 A38 5c blue grn ('19) .40 .25
194 A38 5c lt blue ('21) .40 .25
195 A38 10c yellow green .40 .25
196 A38 10c dp vio ('19) .40 .25
197 A38 10c red ('21) .40 .25
198 A38 20c red .40 .25
199 A38 50c car rose .60 .25
200 A38 75c deep blue .40 .25
a. Diag. half perforated ('11) .40 .25
Nos. 191-200 (10) 4.20 2.50

Nos. 191-200 exist imperforate.
No. 200a was authorized for use as 20c.
For surcharges see Nos. 208, 241, 261, 265.

"The Republic" — A39

1911 **Engr.**
201 A39 1c olive grn & blk .30 .30
202 A39 2c dk blue & blk .45 .30
203 A39 5c carmine & indigo .45 .30
204 A39 10c dp blue & brn .45 .30
205 A39 20c olive grn & ind .60 .30
206 A39 50c lilac & indigo .75 .30
207 A39 75c ol grn & red lil .75 .30
Nos. 201-207 (7) 3.75 2.10

Centenary of National Independence.
The 1c, 2c, 10c and 50c exist imperf. Value for pairs, $2.25 each.

No. 199 Surcharged

1912
208 A38 20c on 50c car rose .30 .30
a. Inverted surcharge 1.90 1.90
b. Double surcharge 1.90 1.90
c. Bar omitted 2.50 2.50

National Coat of Arms — A40

1913 **Engr.** ***Perf. 11½***
209 A40 1c gray .30 .25
210 A40 2c orange .30 .25
211 A40 5c lilac .30 .25
212 A40 10c green .30 .25
213 A40 20c dull red .30 .25
214 A40 40c rose .30 .25
215 A40 75c deep blue .30 .25
216 A40 80c yellow .30 .25
217 A40 1p light blue .45 .25
218 A40 1.25p pale blue .45 .25
219 A40 3p greenish blue .45 .25
Nos. 209-219 (11) 3.75 2.75

For surcharges see Nos. 225, 230-231, 237, 242, 253, 262-263, L3-L4.

Nos. J7-J10 Overprinted

1918
220 D2 5c yellow brown .25 .25
221 D2 10c yellow brown .25 .25
222 D2 20c yellow brown .25 .25
223 D2 40c yellow brown .25 .25

Nos. J10 and 214 Surcharged

224 D2 5c on 40c yellow brn .25 .25
225 A40 30c on 40c rose .25 .25
Nos. 220-225 (6) 1.50 1.50

Nos. 220-225 exist with surcharge inverted, double and double with one inverted.
The surcharge "Habilitado-1918-5 cents 5" on the 1c gray official stamps of 1914, is bogus.

No. J11 Overprinted

1920
229 D2 1p yellow brown .25 .25
a. Inverted overprint .65 .65
e. As "g," "AABILITADO" .75 .75
f. As "g," "1929" for "1920" .75 .75
g. Overprint lines 8mm apart .25 .25

Nos. 216 and 219 Surcharged

230 A40 50c on 80c yellow .25 .25
231 A40 1.75p on 3p grnsh bl .75 .65

Same Surcharge on No. J12

232 D2 1p on 1.50p yel brn .25 .25
Nos. 229-232 (4) 1.50 1.40

Nos. 229-232 exist with various surcharge errors, including inverted, double, double inverted and double with one inverted. Those that were issued are listed.

Parliament Building A41

1920 **Litho.** ***Perf. 11½***
233 A41 50c red & black .35 .30
a. "CORRLOS" 5.00 5.00
234 A41 1p lt blue & blk 1.00 .45
235 A41 1.75p dk blue & blk .30 .30
236 A41 3p orange & blk 1.50 .30
Nos. 233-236 (4) 3.15 1.35

50th anniv. of the Constitution.
All values exist imperforate and Nos. 233, 235 and 236 with center inverted. It is doubtful that any of these varieties were regularly issued.

No. 215 Surcharged

1920
237 A40 50c on 75c deep blue .60 .40

Nos. 200, 215 Surcharged

1921
241 A38 50c on 75c deep blue .40 .40
242 A40 50c on 75c deep blue .40 .40

A42

1922, Feb. 8 **Litho.** ***Perf. 11½***
243 A42 50c car & dk blue .40 .40
a. Imperf. pair 2.00
b. Center inverted 25.00 25.00
244 A42 1p dk blue & brn .40 .40
a. Imperf. pair 2.00
b. Center inverted 30.00 30.00
c. As "b," imperf. pair 110.00

For overprints see Nos. L1-L2.

Rendezvous of Conspirators A43

1922-23
245 A43 1p deep blue .40 .40
246 A43 1p scar & dk bl ('23) .40 .40
247 A43 1p red vio & gray ('23) .40 .40
248 A43 1p org & gray ('23) .40 .40
249 A43 5p dark violet 1.20 .40
250 A43 5p dk bl & org brn ('23) 1.20 .40
251 A43 5p dl red & lt bl ('23) 1.20 .40
252 A43 5p emer & blk ('23) 1.20 .40
Nos. 245-252 (8) 6.40 3.20

National Independence.

No. 218 Surcharged "Habilitado en $1:-1924" in Red

1924
253 A40 1p on 1.25p pale blue .40 .40

This stamp was for use in Asunción. Nos. L3 to L5 were for use in the interior, as is indicated by the "C" in the surcharge.

Map of Paraguay — A44

1924 **Litho.** ***Perf. 11½***
254 A44 1p dark blue .40 .40
255 A44 2p carmine rose .40 .40
256 A44 4p light blue .40 .40
a. Perf. 12 .80 .40
Nos. 254-256 (3) 1.20 1.20

#254-256 exist imperf. Value $3 each pair.
For surcharges and overprint see Nos. 267, C5, C15-C16, C54-C55, L7.

Gen. José E. Díaz — A45

1925-26 *Perf. 11½, 12*

257	A45	50c	red	.25	.25
258	A45	1p	dark blue	.25	.25
259	A45	1p	emerald ('26)	.25	.25
			Nos. 257-259 (3)	.75	.75

#257-258 exist imperf. Value $1 each pair.
For overprints see Nos. L6, L8, L10.

Columbus — A46

1925 *Perf. 11½*

260	A46	1p	blue	.50	.40
a.			Imperf., pair	3.00	

For overprint see No. L9.

Nos. 194, 214-215, J12 Surcharged in Black or Red

1926

261	A38	1c	on 5c lt blue	.25	.25
262	A40	7c	on 40c rose	.25	.25
263	A40	15c	on 75c dp bl (R)	.25	.25
264	D2	1.50p	on 1.50p yel brn	.25	.25
			Nos. 261-264 (4)	1.00	1.00

Nos. 194, 179 and 256 Surcharged "Habilitado" and New Values

1927

265	A38	2c	on 5c lt blue	.25	.25
266	A35	50c	on 60c magenta	.25	.25
a.			Inverted surcharge	2.00	
267	A44	1.50p	on 4p lt blue	.25	.25

Official Stamp of 1914 Surcharged "Habilitado" and New Value

268	O19	50c	on 75c dp bl	.25	.25
			Nos. 265-268 (4)	1.00	1.00

National Emblem — A47

Pedro Juan Caballero — A48

Map of Paraguay — A49

Fulgencio Yegros — A50

Ignacio Iturbe — A51

Oratory of the Virgin, Asunción — A52

Perf. 12, 11, 11½, 11x12

1927-38 **Typo.**

269	A47	1c	lt red ('31)	.25	.25
270	A47	2c	org red ('30)	.25	.25
271	A47	7c	lilac	.25	.25
272	A47	7c	emerald ('29)	.25	.25
273	A47	10c	gray grn ('28)	.25	.25
a.			10c light green ('31)	.25	.25
274	A47	10c	lil rose ('30)	.25	.25
275	A47	10c	light bl ('35)	.25	.25
276	A47	20c	dull bl ('28)	.25	.25
277	A47	20c	lil brn ('30)	.25	.25
278	A47	20c	lt vio ('31)	.25	.25
279	A47	20c	rose ('35)	.25	.25
280	A47	50c	ultramarine	.25	.25
281	A47	50c	dl red ('28)	.25	.25
282	A47	50c	orange ('30)	.25	.25
283	A47	50c	gray ('31)	.25	.25
284	A47	50c	brn vio ('34)	.25	.25
285	A47	50c	rose ('36)	.25	.25
286	A47	70c	ultra ('28)	.25	.25
287	A48	1p	emerald	.25	.25
288	A48	1p	org red ('30)	.25	.25
289	A48	1p	brn org ('34)	.25	.25
290	A49	1.50p	brown	.25	.25
291	A49	1.50p	lilac ('28)	.25	.25
292	A49	1.50p	rose red ('32)	.25	.25
293	A50	2.50p	bister	.25	.25
294	A51	3p	gray	.25	.25
295	A51	3p	rose red ('36)	.25	.25
296	A51	3p	brt vio ('36)	.25	.25
297	A52	5p	chocolate	.25	.25
298	A52	5p	violet ('36)	.25	.25
299	A52	5p	pale org ('38)	.25	.25
300	A49	20p	red ('29)	7.00	5.50
301	A49	20p	emerald ('29)	7.00	5.50
302	A49	20p	vio brn ('29)	7.00	5.50
			Nos. 269-302 (34)	28.75	24.25

No. 281 is also known perf. 10½x11½.
Papermaker's watermarks are sometimes found on No. 271 ("GLORIA BOND" in double-lined circle) and No. 280 ("Extra Vencedor Bond" or "ADBANCE/M M C").
For surcharges and overprints see Nos. 312, C4, C6, C13-C14, C17-C18, C25-C32, C34-C35, L11-L30, O94-O96, O98.

Arms of Juan de Salazar de Espinosa — A53

1928, Aug. 15 *Perf. 12*

303	A53	10p	violet brown	3.00	2.00

Juan de Salazar de Espinosa, founder of Asunción.
A papermaker's watermark ("INDIAN BOND EXTRA STRONG S.&C") is sometimes found on Nos 303, 305-307.

Columbus — A54

1928 **Litho.**

304	A54	10p	ultra	2.40	1.50
305	A54	10p	vermilion	2.40	1.50
306	A54	10p	deep red	2.40	1.50
			Nos. 304-306 (3)	7.20	4.50

For surcharge and overprint see Nos. C33, L37.

President Rutherford B. Hayes of US and Villa Occidental — A55

1928, Nov. 20 *Perf. 12*

307	A55	10p	gray brown	10.00	3.50
308	A55	10p	red brown	10.00	3.50

50th anniv. of the Hayes' Chaco decision.

Portraits of Archbishop Bogarin — A56

1930, Aug. 15

309	A56	1.50p	lake	2.00	1.50
310	A56	1.50p	turq blue	2.00	1.50
311	A56	1.50p	dull vio	2.00	1.50
			Nos. 309-311 (3)	6.00	4.50

Archbishop Juan Sinforiano Bogarin, first archbishop of Paraguay.
For overprints see Nos. 321-322.

No. 272 Surcharged

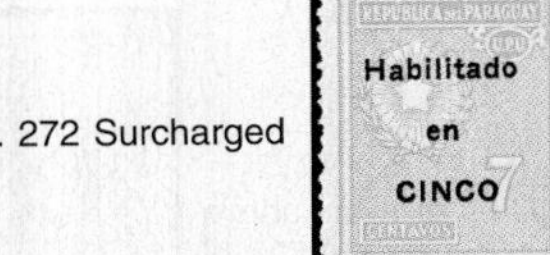

1930

312	A47	5c	on 7c emer	.25	.25

A57

1930-39 **Typo.** *Perf. 11½, 12*

313	A57	10p	brown	1.00	.40
314	A57	10p	brn red, *bl* ('31)	1.00	.40
315	A57	10p	dk bl, *pink* ('32)	1.00	.40
316	A57	10p	gray brn ('36)	.80	.40
317	A57	10p	gray ('37)	.80	.40
318	A57	10p	blue ('39)	.40	.40
			Nos. 313-318 (6)	5.00	2.40

1st Paraguayan postage stamp, 60th anniv.
For overprint see No. L31.

Gunboat "Humaitá" — A58

1931 *Perf. 12*

319	A58	1.50p	purple	.80	.50
			Nos. 319,C39-C53 (16)	25.75	18.05

Constitution, 60th anniv.
For overprint see No. L33.

View of San Bernardino — A59

1931, Aug.

320	A59	1p	light green	.50	.40

Founding of San Bernardino, 50th anniv.
For overprint see No. L32.

Nos. 309-310 Overprinted in Blue or Red

1931, Dec. 31

321	A56	1.50p	lake (Bl)	3.00	3.00
322	A56	1.50p	turq blue (R)	3.00	3.00

Map of the Gran Chaco — A60

1932-35 **Typo.** *Perf. 12*

323	A60	1.50p	deep violet	.40	.40
324	A60	1.50p	rose ('35)	.40	.40

For overprints see Nos. L34-L36, O97.

Nos. C74-C78 Surcharged

1933 **Litho.**

325	AP18	50c	on 4p ultra	.50	.40
326	AP18	1p	on 8p red	1.00	.80
327	AP18	1.50p	on 12p bl grn	1.00	.80
328	AP18	2p	on 16p dk vio	1.00	.80
329	AP18	5p	on 20p org brn	2.25	1.75
			Nos. 325-329 (5)	5.75	4.55

Flag of the Race Issue

Flag with Three Crosses: Caravels of Columbus — A61

1933, Oct. 10 **Litho.** *Perf. 11*

330	A61	10c	multicolored	.50	.40
331	A61	20c	multicolored	.75	.40
332	A61	50c	multicolored	.75	.40
333	A61	1p	multicolored	.75	.40
334	A61	1.50p	multicolored	.75	.40
335	A61	2p	multicolored	.90	.50
336	A61	5p	multicolored	1.40	1.00
337	A61	10p	multicolored	1.75	1.00
			Nos. 330-337 (8)	7.55	4.50

441st anniv. of the sailing of Christopher Columbus from the port of Palos, Aug. 3, 1492, on his first voyage to the New World.
Nos. 332, 334 and 335 exist with Maltese crosses omitted.

Monstrance — A62

1937, Aug. Unwmk. *Perf. 11½*

338 A62 1p dk blue, yel & red .40 .40
339 A62 3p dk blue, yel & red .40 .40
340 A62 10p dk blue, yel & red .40 .40
Nos. 338-340 (3) 1.20 1.20

1st Natl. Eucharistic Congress, Asuncion.

Arms of Asunción — A63

1937, Aug.

341 A63 50c violet & buff .60 .40
342 A63 1p bis & lt grn .60 .40
343 A63 3p red & lt bl .60 .40
344 A63 10p car rose & buff .60 .40
345 A63 20p blue & drab .60 .40
Nos. 341-345 (5) 3.00 2.00

Founding of Asuncion, 400th anniv.

Oratory of the Virgin, Asunción — A64

1938-39 Typo. *Perf. 11, 12*

346 A64 5p olive green .60 .40
347 A64 5p pale rose ('39) .60 .40
348 A64 11p violet brown .80 .50
Nos. 346-348 (3) 2.00 1.30

Founding of Asuncion, 400th anniv.

Carlos Antonio Lopez — A65

José Eduvigis Diaz — A66

1939 *Perf. 12*

349 A65 2p lt ultra & pale brn .90 .60
350 A66 2p lt ultra & brn .90 .60

Reburial of ashes of Pres. Carlos Antonio Lopez (1790-1862) and Gen. José Eduvigis Diaz in the National Pantheon, Asuncion.

Pres. Patricio Escobar and Ramon Zubizarreta A67

Design: 5p, Pres. Bernardino Caballero and Senator José S. Decoud.

1939-40 Litho. *Perf. 11½*
Heads in Black

351 A67 50c dull org ('40) .60 .60
352 A67 1p lt violet ('40) .60 .60
353 A67 2p red brown ('40) .60 .60
354 A67 5p lt ultra .75 .60
Nos. 351-354,C122-C123,O99-O104 (12) 27.55 26.20

Founding of the University of Asuncion, 50th anniv.

Varieties of this issue include inverted heads (50c, 1p, 2p); doubled heads; Caballero and Decoud heads in 50c frame: imperforates and part-perforates. Examples with inverted heads were not officially issued.

Coats of Arms — A69

Flags of Paraguay, United States — A70

Designs: 1p, Pres. Baldomir, flags of Paraguay, Uruguay. 2p, Pres. Benavides, flags of Paraguay, Peru. 5p, Pres. Alessandri, flags of Paraguay, Chile. 6p, Pres. Vargas, flags of Paraguay, Brazil. 10p, Pres. Ortiz, flags of Paraguay, Argentina.

1939 Engr.; Flags Litho. *Perf. 12*
Flags in National Colors

355 A69 50c violet blue .30 .30
356 A70 1p olive .30 .30
357 A70 2p blue green .30 .30
358 A70 3p sepia .35 .35
359 A70 5p orange .30 .30
360 A70 6p dull violet .75 .60
361 A70 10p bister brn .60 .35
Nos. 355-361,C113-C121 (16) 42.30 28.25

First Buenos Aires Peace Conference.
For overprint and surcharge, see Nos. 387, B10.

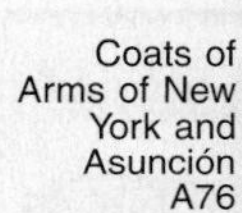

Coats of Arms of New York and Asunción A76

1939, Nov. 30

362 A76 5p scarlet .80 .80
363 A76 10p deep blue 1.20 .80
364 A76 11p dk blue grn 1.20 1.20
365 A76 22p olive blk 2.00 1.60
Nos. 362-365,C124-C126 (7) 33.95 31.40

New York World's Fair.

Paraguayan Soldier — A77

Paraguayan Woman — A78

Cowboys — A79

Plowing — A80

View of Paraguay River — A81

Oxcart A82

Pasture A83

Pireretá Falls — A84

1940, Jan. 1 Photo. *Perf. 12½*

366 A77 50c deep orange .40 .25
367 A78 1p brt red violet .40 .25
368 A79 3p bright green .40 .25
369 A80 5p chestnut .40 .25
370 A81 10p magenta .40 .25
371 A82 20p violet 1.00 .30
372 A83 50p cobalt blue 2.00 .45
373 A84 100p black 4.00 1.40
Nos. 366-373 (8) 9.00 3.40

Second Buenos Aires Peace Conference.
For surcharge see No. 386.

Map of the Americas — A85

1940, May Engr. *Perf. 12*

374 A85 50c red orange .30 .25
375 A85 1p green .30 .25
376 A85 5p dark blue .50 .25
377 A85 10p brown 1.00 .50
Nos. 374-377,C127-C130 (8) 12.20 9.20

Pan American Union, 50th anniversary.

Reproduction of Type A1 — A86

Sir Rowland Hill — A87

Designs: 6p, Type A2. 10p, Type A3.

1940, Aug. 15 Photo. *Perf. 13½*

378 A86 1p aqua & brt red vio .50 .25
379 A87 5p dp yel grn & red brn .65 .30
380 A86 6p org brn & ultra 1.50 .65
381 A86 10p ver & black 1.50 1.00
Nos. 378-381 (4) 4.15 2.20

Postage stamp centenary.

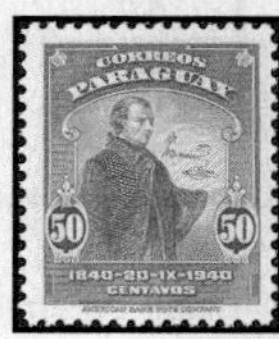

Dr. José Francia
A90 A91

1940, Sept. 20 Engr. *Perf. 12*

382 A90 50c carmine rose .30 .25
383 A91 50c plum .30 .25
384 A90 1p bright green .30 .25
385 A91 5p deep blue .30 .25
Nos. 382-385 (4) 1.20 1.00

Centenary of the death of Dr. Jose Francia (1766-1840), dictator of Paraguay, 1814-1840.

No. 366 Surcharged in Black

1940, Sept. 7 *Perf. 12½*

386 A77 5p on 50c dp org .40 .25

In honor of Pres. Jose F. Estigarribia who died in a plane crash Sept. 7, 1940.

SEMI-POSTAL STAMPS

Red Cross Nurse SP1

Unwmk.
1930, July 22 Typo. *Perf. 12*

B1 SP1 1.50p + 50c gray violet 2.00 1.20
B2 SP1 1.50p + 50c deep rose 2.00 1.20
B3 SP1 1.50p + 50c dark blue 2.00 1.20
Nos. B1-B3 (3) 6.00 3.60

The surtax was for the benefit of the Red Cross Society of Paraguay.

College of Agriculture — SP2

1930

B4 SP2 1.50p + 50c blue, *pale pink* .60 .50

Surtax for the Agricultural Institute.

The sheet of No. B4 has a papermaker's watermark: "Vencedor Bond."

A 1.50p+50c red on pale yellow was prepared but not regularly issued. Value, 40 cents.

Red Cross Headquarters SP3

1932

B5 SP3 50c + 50c rose .60 .60

AIR POST STAMPS

Official Stamps of 1913 Surcharged

Correo Aéreo Habilitado en $ 2:85

1929, Jan. 1 Unwmk. *Perf. 11½*

C1 O19 2.85p on 5c lilac 2.25 1.50
C2 O19 5.65p on 10c grn 1.25 1.50
C3 O19 11.30p on 50c rose 2.00 1.25
Nos. C1-C3 (3) 5.50 4.25

Counterfeits of surcharge exist.

Regular Issues of 1924-27 Surcharged

1929, Feb. 26 *Perf. 12*

C4 A51 3.40p on 3p gray 4.50 4.00
a. Surch. "Correo / en $3.40 / Habilitado / Aereo" 8.75
b. Double surcharge 8.75
c. "Aéro" instead of "Aéreo"
C5 A44 6.80p on 4p lt bl 4.50 3.25
a. Surch. "Correo / Aereo / en $6.80 / Habilitado" 8.75
C6 A52 17p on 5p choc 4.50 3.25
a. Surch. "Correo / Habilitado / Habilitado / en 17p" 4.50
b. Double surcharge 25.00 25.00
Nos. C4-C6 (3) 13.50 10.50

Wings — AP1

Pigeon with Letter AP2

Airplanes — AP3

1929-31 **Typo.** *Perf. 12*

C7 AP1 2.85p gray green 1.75 1.25
a. Imperf., pair 37.50
C8 AP1 2.85p turq grn ('31) .50 .50
C9 AP2 5.65p brown 2.00 1.25
C10 AP2 5.65p scar ('31) 1.00 .50
C11 AP3 11.30p chocolate 1.75 1.25
a. Imperf., pair 37.50
C12 AP3 11.30p dp blue ('31) .50 .50
Nos. C7-C12 (6) 7.50 5.25

Sheets of these stamps sometimes show portions of a papermaker's watermark "Indian Bond C. Extra Strong."

Excellent counterfeits are plentiful.

Regular Issues of 1924-28 Surcharged in Black or Red

1929 *Perf. 11½, 12*

C13 A47 95c on 7c lilac .35 .30
C14 A47 1.90p on 20c dull bl .35 .30
C15 A44 3.40p on 4p lt bl (R) .45 .30
a. Double surcharge 3.00
C16 A44 4.75p on 4p lt bl (R) .90 .75
a. Double surcharge 3.00
C17 A51 6.80p on 3p gray 1.00 .90
a. Double surcharge 4.50
C18 A52 17p on 5p choc 3.00 3.00
a. Horiz. pair, imperf. between 37.50
Nos. C13-C18 (6) 6.05 5.55

Six stamps in the sheet of No. C17 have the "$" and numerals thinner and narrower than the normal type.

Airplane and Arms — AP4

Cathedral of Asunción AP5

Airplane and Globe — AP6

1930 *Perf. 12*

C19 AP4 95c dp red, *pink* 1.50 .90
C20 AP4 95c dk bl, *blue* 1.50 .90
C21 AP5 1.90p lt red, *pink* 1.50 .90
C22 AP5 1.90p violet, *blue* 1.50 .90
C23 AP6 6.80p blk, *lt bl* 1.50 .90
C24 AP6 6.80p green, *pink* 1.50 .90
Nos. C19-C24 (6) 9.00 5.40

Sheets of Nos. C19-C24 have a papermaker's watermark: "Extra Vencedor Bond."

Counterfeits exist.

Stamps and Types of 1927-28 Overprinted in Red

1930

C25 A47 10c olive green .60 .40
a. Double overprint 6.00
C26 A47 20c dull blue .60 .40
a. "CORREO CORREO" instead of "CORREO AEREO" 5.00
b. "AEREO AEREO" instead of "CORREO AEREO" 5.00
C27 A48 1p emerald 1.40 1.40
C28 A51 3p gray 1.40 1.40
Nos. C25-C28 (4) 4.00 3.60

Counterfeits of Nos. C26a and C26b exist.

Nos. 273, 282, 286, 288, 300, 302, 305 Surcharged in Red or Black

#C29-C30, C32

#C31

#C33

#C34-C35

1930 **Red or Black Surcharge**

C29 A47 5c on 10c gray grn (R) .50 .50
a. "AEREO" omitted 30.00
C30 A47 5c on 70c ultra (R) .50 .50
a. Vert. pair, imperf. between 40.00
C31 A48 20c on 1p org red .60 .50
a. "CORREO" double 6.00 6.00
b. "AEREO" double 6.00 6.00
C32 A47 40c on 50c org (R) .60 .50
a. "AEREO" omitted 9.00 9.00
b. "CORREO" double 6.00 6.00
c. "AEREO" double 6.00 6.00
C33 A54 6p on 10p red 2.50 2.00
C34 A49 10p on 20p red 10.00 10.00
C35 A49 10p on 20p vio brn 10.00 10.00
Nos. C29-C35 (7) 24.70 24.00

Declaration of Independence AP11

1930, May 14 **Typo.**

C36 AP11 2.85p dark blue .70 .50
C37 AP11 3.40p dark green .70 .40
C38 AP11 4.75p deep lake .70 .40
Nos. C36-C38 (3) 2.10 1.30

Natl. Independence Day, May 14, 1811.

Gunboat Type

Gunboat "Paraguay."

1931-39 *Perf. 11½, 12*

C39 A58 1p claret .60 .60
C40 A58 1p dk blue ('36) .60 .60
C41 A58 2p orange .60 .60
C42 A58 2p dk brn ('36) .60 .60
C43 A58 3p turq green .75 .75
C44 A58 3p lt ultra ('36) .90 .75
C45 A58 3p brt rose ('39) .60 .60
C46 A58 6p dk green 1.20 .90
C47 A58 6p violet ('36) 1.40 .90
C48 A58 6p dull bl ('39) 1.20 .75
C49 A58 10p vermilion 3.00 1.75
C50 A58 10p bluish grn ('35) 4.50 3.00
C51 A58 10p yel brn ('36) 3.25 2.25
C52 A58 10p dk blue ('36) 2.75 1.50
C53 A58 10p lt pink ('39) 3.00 2.00
Nos. C39-C53 (15) 24.95 17.55

1st constitution of Paraguay as a Republic and the arrival of the "Paraguay" and "Humaita."

Counterfeits of #C39-C53 are plentiful.

Regular Issue of 1924 Surcharged

1931, Aug. 22

C54 A44 3p on 4p lt bl 17.50 17.50

Overprinted

C55 A44 4p lt blue 15.00 15.00

On Nos. C54-C55 the Zeppelin is handstamped. The rest of the surcharge or overprint is typographed.

War Memorial AP13

Orange Tree and Yerba Mate — AP14

Yerba Mate — AP15

Palms — AP16

Eagle — AP17

1931-36 **Litho.**

C56 AP13 5c lt blue .25 .40
a. Horiz. pair, imperf. btwn. 6.25
C57 AP13 5c dp grn ('33) .25 .40
C58 AP13 5c lt red ('33) .30 .40
C59 AP13 5c violet ('35) .25 .40
C60 AP14 10c dp violet .25 .40
C61 AP14 10c brn lake ('33) .25 .40
C62 AP14 10c yel brn ('33) .25 .40
C63 AP14 10c ultra ('35) .25 .40
a. Imperf., pair 5.50
C64 AP15 20c red .25 .40
C65 AP15 20c dl blue ('33) .30 .40
C66 AP15 20c emer ('33) .25 .40
C67 AP15 20c yel brn ('35) .25 .40
a. Imperf., pair 3.75
C68 AP16 40c dp green .25 .40
C69 AP16 40c slate bl ('35) .25 .40
C70 AP16 40c red ('36) .30 .40
C71 AP17 80c dull blue .25 .40
C72 AP17 80c dl grn ('33) .50 .40
C73 AP17 80c scar ('33) .30 .40
Nos. C56-C73 (18) 4.95 7.20

Airship "Graf Zeppelin" — AP18

1932, Apr. **Litho.**

C74 AP18 4p ultra 3.75 3.75
a. Imperf., pair 35.00
C75 AP18 8p red 6.25 5.00
C76 AP18 12p blue grn 5.00 5.00
C77 AP18 16p dk violet 8.75 6.25
C78 AP18 20p orange brn 8.75 6.25
Nos. C74-C78 (5) 32.50 26.25

For surcharges see Nos. 325-329.

"Graf Zeppelin" over Brazilian Terrain AP19

"Graf Zeppelin" over Atlantic — AP20

1933, May 5

C79 AP19 4.50p dp blue 4.00 3.00
C80 AP19 9p dp rose 7.00 5.00
a. Horiz. pair, imperf. between 150.00
C81 AP19 13.50p blue grn 8.00 6.00
C82 AP20 22.50p bis brn 18.00 14.00
C83 AP20 45p dull vio 24.00 24.00
Nos. C79-C83 (5) 61.00 52.00

Excellent counterfeits are plentiful.

For overprints see Nos. C88-C97.

Posts and Telegraph Building, Asunción — AP21

1934-37 *Perf. 11½*

C84	AP21	33.75p ultra	6.00	5.25
C85	AP21	33.75p car ('35)	6.00	5.25
a.		33.75p rose ('37)	5.25	4.50
C86	AP21	33.75p emerald ('36)	7.50	6.00
C87	AP21	33.75p bis brn ('36)	2.25	2.25
		Nos. C84-C87 (4)	21.75	18.75

Excellent counterfeits exist.
For surcharge see No. C107.

Nos. C79-C83 Overprinted in Black

1934, May 26

C88	AP19	4.50p deep bl	3.00	2.25
C89	AP19	9p dp rose	3.75	3.00
C90	AP19	13.50p blue grn	10.50	7.50
C91	AP20	22.50p bis brn	9.00	6.00
C92	AP20	45p dull vio	13.50	10.50
		Nos. C88-C92 (5)	39.75	29.25

Types of 1933 Issue Overprinted in Black

1935

C93	AP19	4.50p rose red	3.50	2.50
C94	AP19	9p lt green	4.50	3.00
C95	AP19	13.50p brown	9.50	7.00
C96	AP20	22.50p violet	7.50	5.50
C97	AP20	45p blue	22.50	13.00
		Nos. C93-C97 (5)	47.50	31.00

Tobacco Plant — AP22

1935-39 **Typo.**

C98	AP22	17p lt brown	12.50	12.50
C99	AP22	17p carmine	21.00	21.00
C100	AP22	17p dark blue	15.00	15.00
C101	AP22	17p pale yel grn ('39)	8.00	8.00
		Nos. C98-C101 (4)	56.50	56.50

Excellent counterfeits are plentiful.

Church of Incarnation AP23

1935-38

C102	AP23	102p carmine	7.50	5.00
C103	AP23	102p blue	7.50	5.00
C103A	AP23	102p indigo ('36)	4.50	4.50
C104	AP23	102p yellow brn	5.50	4.75
a.		Imperf., pair	30.00	
C105	AP23	102p violet ('37)	2.50	2.50
C106	AP23	102p brn org ('38)	2.25	2.25
		Nos. C102-C106 (6)	29.75	24.00

Excellent counterfeits are plentiful.
For surcharges see Nos. C108-C109.

Types of 1934-35 Surcharged in Red

1937, Aug. 1

C107	AP21	24p on 33.75p sl bl	1.00	.70
C108	AP23	65p on 102p ol bis	2.50	1.75
C109	AP23	84p on 102p bl grn	2.50	1.50
		Nos. C107-C109 (3)	6.00	3.95

Plane over Asunción AP24

1939, Aug. 3 **Typo.** *Perf. 10½, 11½*

C110	AP24	3.40p yel green	1.00	1.00
C111	AP24	3.40p orange brn	.60	.50
C112	AP24	3.40p indigo	.60	.50
		Nos. C110-C112 (3)	2.20	2.00

Buenos Aires Peace Conference Type and

Map of Paraguay with New Chaco Boundary AP28

Designs: 1p, Flags of Paraguay and Bolivia. 3p, Coats of Arms. 5p, Pres. Ortiz of Argentina, flags of Paraguay, Argentina. 10p, Pres. Vargas, Brazil. 30p, Pres. Alessandri, Chile. 50p, US Eagle and Shield. 100p, Pres. Benavides, Peru. 200p, Pres. Baldomir, Uruguay.

Engr.; Flags Litho.

1939, Nov. *Perf. 12½*

Flags in National Colors

C113	A69	1p red brown	.60	.60
C114	A69	3p dark blue	.60	.60
C115	A70	5p olive blk	.60	.60
C116	A70	10p violet	.60	.60
C117	A70	30p orange	.60	.60
C118	A70	50p black brn	.90	.60
C119	A70	100p brt green	1.25	.90
C120	A70	200p green	6.75	3.75
C121	AP28	500p black	27.50	17.50
		Nos. C113-C121 (9)	39.40	25.75

For overprints see Nos. 388-390 in Scott Standard catalogue, Vol. 5.

University of Asuncion Type

Pres. Bernardino Caballero and Senator José S. Decoud.

1939, Sept. **Litho.** *Perf. 12*

C122	A67	28p rose & blk	10.00	10.00
C123	A67	90p yel grn & blk	12.00	12.00

Map with Asunción to New York Air Route — AP35

1939, Nov. 30 **Engr.**

C124	AP35	30p brown	7.75	6.00
C125	AP35	80p orange	9.00	9.00
C126	AP35	90p purple	12.00	12.00
		Nos. C124-C126 (3)	28.75	27.00

New York World's Fair.

Pan American Union Type

1940, May *Perf. 12*

C127	A85	20p rose car	.60	.60
C128	A85	70p violet bl	1.25	.60
C129	A85	100p Prus grn	1.50	1.50
C130	A85	500p dk violet	6.75	5.25
		Nos. C127-C130 (4)	10.10	7.95

POSTAGE DUE STAMPS

D1

1904 **Unwmk.** **Litho.** *Perf. 11½*

J1	D1	2c green	1.00	*2.00*
J2	D1	4c green	1.00	*2.00*
J3	D1	10c green	1.00	*2.00*
J4	D1	20c green	1.00	*2.00*
		Nos. J1-J4 (4)	4.00	8.00

D2

1913 **Engr.**

J5	D2	1c yellow brown	1.00	1.00
J6	D2	2c yellow brown	1.00	1.00
J7	D2	5c yellow brown	1.00	1.00
J8	D2	10c yellow brown	1.00	1.00
J9	D2	20c yellow brown	1.00	1.00
J10	D2	40c yellow brown	1.00	1.00
J11	D2	1p yellow brown	1.00	1.00
J12	D2	1.50p yellow brown	1.00	1.00
		Nos. J5-J12 (8)	8.00	8.00

For overprints and surcharges see Nos. 220-224, 229, 232, 264, L5.

INTERIOR OFFICE ISSUES

The "C" signifies "Campana" (rural). These stamps were sold by Postal Agents in country districts, who received a commission on their sales. These stamps were available for postage in the interior but not in Asunción or abroad.

Nos. 243-244 Overprinted in Red

1922

L1	A42	50c car & dk bl	.50	.50
L2	A42	1p dk bl & brn	.50	.50

The overprint on Nos. L2 exists double or inverted. Counterfeits exist. Double or inverted overprints on No. L1 and all overprints in black are counterfeit.

Nos. 215, 218, J12 Surcharged

1924

L3	A40	50c on 75c deep bl	.50	.50
L4	A40	1p on 1.25p pale bl	.50	.50
L5	D2	1p on 1.50p yel brn	.50	.50
		Nos. L3-L5 (3)	1.50	1.50

Nos. L3-L4 exist imperf.

Nos. 254, 257-260 Overprinted in Black or Red

1924-26

L6	A45	50c red ('25)	1.00	1.00
L7	A44	1p dk blue (R)	1.00	1.00
L8	A45	1p dk bl (R) ('25)	1.00	1.00
L9	A46	1p blue (R) ('25)	1.00	1.00
L10	A45	1p emerald ('26)	2.00	.75
		Nos. L6-L10 (5)	6.00	4.75

Nos. L6, L8-L9 exist imperf. Value $2.50 each pair.

Same Overprint on Stamps and Type of 1927-36 in Red or Black

1927-39

L11	A47	50c ultra (R)	.50	.50
L12	A47	50c dl red ('28)	.50	.50
L13	A47	50c orange ('29)	.50	.50
L14	A47	50c lt bl ('30)	.50	.50
L15	A47	50c gray (R) ('31)	.50	.50
L16	A47	50c bluish grn (R) ('33)	.50	.50
L17	A47	50c vio (R) ('34)	.50	.50
L18	A48	1p emerald	.50	.50
L19	A48	1p org red ('29)	.50	.50
L20	A48	1p lil brn ('31)	.50	.50
L21	A48	1p dk bl (R) ('33)	.50	.50
L22	A48	1p brt vio (R) ('35)	.50	.50
L23	A49	1.50p brown	.50	.50
a.		Double overprint	3.00	
L24	A49	1.50p lilac ('28)	.50	.50
L25	A49	1.50p dull bl (R)	.50	.50
L26	A50	2.50p bister ('28)	.50	.50
L27	A50	2.50p vio (R) ('36)	.50	.50
L28	A51	3p gray (R)	.50	.50
L29	A51	3p rose red ('39)	.50	.50
L30	A52	5p vio (R) ('36)	.50	.50
L31	A57	10p gray brn (R) ('36)	5.00	3.00
		Nos. L11-L31 (21)	15.00	13.00

Types of 1931-35 and No. 305 Overprinted in Black or Red

1931-36

L32	A59	1p light red	2.00	1.00
L33	A58	1.50p dp bl (R)	1.00	.75
L34	A60	1.50p bis brn ('32)	2.00	1.00
L35	A60	1.50p grn (R) ('34)	2.00	1.00
L36	A60	1.50p bl (R) ('36)	2.00	1.00
L37	A54	10p vermilion	8.00	2.50
		Nos. L32-L37 (6)	17.00	7.25

OFFICIAL STAMPS

O1

O3

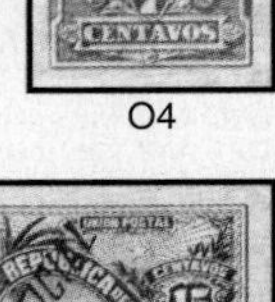

O4

O5

O6

O2

O7

Unwmk.

1886, Aug. 20 Litho. *Imperf.*
O1 O1 1c orange 7.00 7.00
O2 O2 2c violet 7.00 7.00
O3 O3 5c red 7.00 7.00
O4 O4 7c green 7.00 7.00
O5 O5 10c brown 7.00 7.00
O6 O6 15c slate blue 7.00 7.00
a. Wavy lines on face of stamp
b. "OFICIAL" omitted 1.25
O7 O7 20c claret 7.00 7.00
Nos. O1-O7 (7) 49.00 49.00

Nos. O1 to O7 have the date and various control marks and letters printed on the back of each stamp in blue and black.

The overprints exist inverted on all values.

Nos. O1 to O7 have been reprinted from new stones made from slightly retouched dies.

Types of 1886 With Overprint

1886 *Perf. 11½*
O8 O1 1c dark green 1.50 1.50
O9 O2 2c scarlet 1.50 1.50
O10 O3 5c dull blue 1.50 1.50
O11 O4 7c orange 1.50 1.50
O12 O5 10c lake 1.50 1.50
O13 O6 15c brown 1.50 1.50
O14 O7 20c blue 1.50 1.50
Nos. O8-O14 (7) 10.50 10.50

The overprint exists inverted on all values. Value, each $1.50.

No. 20 Overprinted

1886, Sept. 1
O15 A11 1c dark green 4.00 4.00

Types of 1889 Regular Issue Surcharged

Handstamped Surcharge in Black

1889 *Imperf.*
O16 A13 3c on 15c violet 3.75 2.75
O17 A13 5c on 15c red brn 3.75 2.25

Perf. 11½
O18 A13 1c on 15c maroon 4.00 2.25
O19 A13 2c on 15c maroon 4.00 2.25
Nos. O16-O19 (4) 15.50 9.50

Counterfeits of Nos. O16-O19 abound.

Regular Issue of 1887 Handstamp Overprinted in Violet

Perf. 11½-12½ & Compounds

1890 Typo.
O20 A12 1c green .35 .30
O21 A12 2c rose red .35 .30
O22 A12 5c blue .35 .30
O23 A12 7c brown 10.00 8.00
O24 A12 10c lilac .35 .35
O25 A12 15c orange .75 .45
O26 A12 20c pink .65 .45
Nos. O20-O26 (7) 12.80 10.15

Nos. O20-O26 exist with double overprint and all but the 20c with inverted overprint.

Nos. O20-O22, O24-O26 exist with blue overprint. The status is questioned. Value, set $15.

Stamps and Type of 1887 Regular Issue Overprinted in Black

1892
O33 A12 1c green .30 .30
O34 A12 2c rose red .30 .30
O35 A12 5c blue .30 .30
O36 A12 7c brown 4.00 1.75
O37 A12 10c lilac 1.25 .55
O38 A12 15c orange .35 .30
O39 A12 20c pink .65 .35
O40 A12 50c gray .75 .35
Nos. O33-O40 (8) 7.90 4.20

No. 26 Overprinted

1893
O41 A12 7c brown 17.50 8.00

Counterfeits of No. O41 exist.

O16

1901, Feb. Engr. *Perf. 11½, 12½*
O42 O16 1c dull blue .75 .50
O43 O16 2c rose red .75 .50
O44 O16 4c dark brown .75 .50
O45 O16 5c dark green .75 .50
O46 O16 8c orange brn .75 .50
O47 O16 10c car rose 2.50 1.00
O48 O16 20c deep blue 2.50 1.00
Nos. O42-O48 (7) 8.75 4.50

A 12c deep green, type O16, was prepared but not issued.

No. 45 Overprinted

1902 *Perf. 12x12½*
O49 A12 1p olive grn 2.00 2.00
a. Inverted overprint 10.00

Counterfeits of No. O49a exist.

Regular Issue of 1903 Overprinted

1903 *Perf. 11½*
O50 A32 1c gray .90 .35
O51 A32 2c blue green .90 .35
O52 A32 5c blue .90 .35
O53 A32 10c orange brn .90 .35
O54 A32 20c carmine .90 .35
O55 A32 30c deep blue .90 .35
O56 A32 60c purple .90 .35
Nos. O50-O56 (7) 6.30 2.45

O17

1905-08 Engr. *Perf. 11½, 12*
O57 O17 1c gray grn .50 .30
O58 O17 1c ol grn ('05) .90 .30
O59 O17 1c brn org ('06) .80 .30
O60 O17 1c ver ('08) .50 .30
O61 O17 2c brown org .35 .30
O62 O17 2c gray grn ('05) .35 .30
O63 O17 2c red ('06) 2.00 .75
O64 O17 2c gray ('08) 1.00 .50
O65 O17 5c deep bl ('06) .50 .35
O66 O17 5c gray bl ('08) 4.00 2.00
O67 O17 5c grnsh bl ('08) 2.00 1.50
O68 O17 10c violet ('06) .35 .50
O69 O17 20c violet ('08) 2.00 1.25
Nos. O57-O69 (13) 15.25 8.65

O18

1908
O70 O17 10c bister 10.50
O71 O17 10c emerald 10.50
O72 O17 10c red lilac 13.50
O73 O17 20c bister 9.00
O74 O17 20c salmon pink 10.50
O75 O17 20c green 10.50
O76 O17 30c turquoise bl 10.50
O77 O17 30c blue gray 10.50
O78 O17 30c yellow 4.50
O79 O17 60c chocolate 12.00
O80 O17 60c orange brn 15.00
O81 O17 60c deep ultra 12.00
O82 O18 1p brt rose & blk 72.50
O83 O18 1p lake & blk 72.50
O84 O18 1p brn org & blk 75.00
Nos. O70-O84 (15) 349.00

Nos. O70-O84 were not issued, but were surcharged or overprinted for use as regular postage stamps. See Nos. 131-138, 141-145, 158-165, 171-173.

O19

1913 *Perf. 11½*
O85 O19 1c gray .30 .35
O86 O19 2c orange .30 .35
O87 O19 5c lilac .30 .35
O88 O19 10c green .30 .35
O89 O19 20c dull red .30 .35
O90 O19 50c rose .30 .35
O91 O19 75c deep blue .30 .35
O92 O19 1p dull blue 1.00 .50
O93 O19 2p yellow 1.00 .50
Nos. O85-O93 (9) 4.10 3.45

For surcharges see Nos. 268, C1-C3.

Type of Regular Issue of 1927-38 Overprinted in Red

1935
O94 A47 10c light ultra .35 .30
O95 A47 50c violet .35 .30
O96 A48 1p orange .35 .30
O97 A60 1.50p green .35 .30
O98 A50 2.50p violet .35 .30
Nos. O94-O98 (5) 1.75 1.50

Overprint is diagonal on 1.50p.

University of Asunción Type

1940 Litho. *Perf. 12*
O99 A67 50c red brn & blk .50 .30
O100 A67 1p rose pink & blk .50 .30
O101 A67 2p lt bl grn & blk .50 .30
O102 A67 5p ultra & blk .50 .30
O103 A67 10p lt vio & blk .50 .30
O104 A67 50p dp org & blk .50 .30
Nos. O99-O104 (6) 3.00 1.80

PENRHYN ISLAND

pen-ˈrin ˈī-lənd

(Tongareva)

AREA — 3 sq. mi.
POP. — 395 (1926)

Stamps of Cook Islands were used in Penrhyn from 1932 until 1973.

12 Pence = 1 Shilling

Watermarks

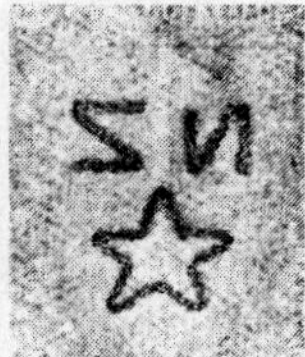

Wmk. 61 — N Z and Star Close Together

Wmk. 63 — Double-lined N Z and Star

On watermark 61 the margins of the sheets are watermarked "NEW ZEALAND POSTAGE" and parts of the double-lined letters of these words are frequently found on the stamps. It occasionally happens that a stamp shows no watermark whatever.

Stamps of New Zealand Surcharged in Carmine, Vermilion, Brown or Blue

½ pence

1 pence

2½ pence

1902 Wmk. 63 *Perf. 14*
1 A18 ½p green (C) 1.00 *14.00*
a. No period after "ISLAND" 175.00 *325.00*
2 A35 1p carmine (Br) 3.75 *27.50*
a. Perf. 11 *1,000.* *1,200.*
b. Perf. 11x14 *1,200.* *1,400.*

Wmk. 61 *Perf. 14*
5 A18 ½p green (V) 4.75 *16.00*
a. No period after "ISLAND" 180.00 *375.00*
6 A35 1p carmine (Bl) 1.50 *9.50*
a. No period after "ISLAND" 60.00 *170.00*
b. Perf. 11x14 *15,000.* *8,500.*

Unwmk. *Perf. 11*
8 A22 2½p blue (C) 14.50 13.00
a. "½" and "PENI" 2mm apart 30.00 *35.00*
9 A22 2½p blue (V) 14.50 13.00
a. "½" and "PENI" 2mm apart 30.00 *35.00*
Nos. 1-9 (6) 40.00 *93.00*

Stamps with compound perfs. also exist perf. 11 or 14 on one or more sides.

d

e

f

1903 Wmk. 61
10 A23(d) 3p yel brn (Bl) 11.50 *42.50*
11 A26(e) 6p rose (Bl) 17.50 *50.00*
12 A29(f) 1sh org red (Bl) 65.00 *65.00*
a. 1sh bright red (Bl) 47.50 *47.50*
b. 1sh brown red (Bl) 65.00 *65.00*
Nos. 10-12 (3) 94.00 *157.50*

1914-15 *Perf. 14, 14x14½*
13 A41(a) ½p yel grn (C) .90 *12.00*
a. No period after "ISLAND" 29.00 *110.00*
b. No period after "PENI" 110.00 *350.00*
14 A41(a) ½p yel grn (V) ('15) .90 *9.25*
a. No period after "ISLAND" 11.50 *65.00*
b. No period after "PENI" 55.00 *190.00*
15 A41(e) 6p car rose (Bl) 27.50 *82.50*
16 A41(f) 1sh ver (Bl) 50.00 *110.00*
Nos. 13-16 (4) 79.30 *213.75*

New Zealand Stamps of 1915-19 Overprinted in Red or Dark Blue

Perf. 14x13½, 14x14½

1917-20 Typo.
17 A43 ½p yel grn (R) ('20) 1.10 *2.25*
18 A47 1½p gray black (R) 7.50 *27.50*
19 A47 1½p brn org (R) ('19) .70 *27.50*
20 A43 3p choc (Bl) ('19) 4.00 *45.00*

Engr.
21 A44 2½p dull bl (R) ('20) 2.25 *10.00*
22 A45 3p vio brn (Bl) ('18) 12.00 *80.00*
23 A45 6p car rose (Bl) ('18) 5.75 *21.00*
24 A45 1sh vermilion (Bl) 14.00 *37.50*
Nos. 17-24 (8) 47.30 *250.75*

Landing of Capt. Cook
A10

Avarua Waterfront
A11

Capt. James Cook — A12

Coconut Palm — A13

Arorangi Village, Rarotonga — A14

Avarua Harbor — A15

1920 Unwmk. *Perf. 14*
25 A10 ½p emerald & blk 1.25 *23.00*
a. Center inverted 1,000.
26 A11 1p red & black 2.00 *19.00*
a. Center inverted 1,000.
27 A12 1½p violet & blk 7.75 *24.00*
28 A13 3p red org & blk 3.25 *15.00*
29 A14 6p dk brn & red brn 4.00 *24.00*
30 A15 1sh dull bl & blk 12.00 *32.50*
Nos. 25-30 (6) 30.25 *137.50*

Rarotongan Chief (Te Po) — A16

1927 Engr. Wmk. 61
31 A16 2½p blue & red brn 17.50 *47.50*

Types of 1920 Issue

1928-29
33 A10 ½p yellow grn & blk 6.50 *25.00*
34 A11 1p carmine rose & blk 6.50 *22.50*

PERU

pə-ˈrü

LOCATION — West coast of South America
GOVT. — Republic
AREA — 496,093 sq. mi.
POP. — 18,300,000 (est. 1982)
CAPITAL — Lima

8 Reales = 1 Peso (1857)
100 Centimos = 8 Dineros =
4 Pesetas = 1 Peso (1858)
100 Centavos = 1 Sol (1874)

GREAT BRITAIN POST OFFICES IN PERU

British postal agencies operated in a number of Peruvian cities from 1846: Arica (1846-79), Callao (1846-79), Paita (1848-79), Pisco (1868-70), Iquique (1869-79), Islay (1869-77), and Mollendo (1877-79). British stamps were in use at these offices from 1865.

Values are for clear cancellations on sound, fault-free stamps, with average to fine centering. In many cases, very fine examples are rare or non-existent.

ARICA
Pre-Stamp Postmark

1850

Crowned Circle Handstamp Type I
A1 Inscribed "PAID AT ARICA" in red, on cover *5,000.*

Earliest known use 11/5/50.

Stamps of Great Britain Cancelled with "C36"

1865-79
A2 ½p rose red, plates 5, 6, 10, 11, 13 (#58), *value from* 85.00
A3 1p rose red, plates 102, 139, 140, 163, 167 (#33), *value from* 62.50
A4 1½p lake red, plate 3 (#32) —
A5 2p blue, plate 14 (#30) 85.00
A6 3p rose, plates 5, 9 (#49) —
A7 3p rose, plates 11, 12, 17-19 (#61), *value from* 62.50
A8 4p vermilion, plates 10-14 (#43), *value from* 62.50
A9 4p vermilion, plate 15 (#69) —
A10 4p pale olive green, plates 15, 16 (#70) 250.00
A11 6p lilac, plate 3 (#39) —
a. 6p lilac, plate 4 (#39b) —
A12 6p lilac, plate 5 (#45) —
A13 6p dull violet, plate 6 (#50) —
A14 6p violet, plates 8, 9 (#51) 90.00
A15 6p brown plate 11 (#59) 115.00
a. 6p pale buff, plate 11 (#59b) 110.00
A16 6p gray, plate 12 (#60) 240.00
A17 6p gray, plates 13-16 (#62), *value from* 62.50
A18 8p orange (#73) —
A19 9p straw (#40) —
A20 9p straw (#46) —
A21 9p bister, plate 4 (#52) 250.00
A22 10p red brown (#53) —
A23 1sh green (#42) —
A24 1sh green, plate 4 (#48) —
A25 1sh green, plates 4-7 (#54) 62.50
A26 1sh green, plates 8-13 (#64), *value from* 80.00
A27 2sh blue (#55) 200.00
A28 5sh rose, plate 1 (#57) *600.00*
Plate 2 (#57) *800.00*

CALLAO
Pre-Stamp Postmark

1846

Crowned Circle Handstamp Type I
A32 Inscribed "PAID AT CALLAO" in red, straight-line "CALLAO", on cover 1,250.
a. Used in 1865 or after on cover with stamps of Peru, *value from* 350.00
A33 Inscribed "PAID AT CALLAO" in red, curved "CALLAO", on cover 725.00
a. Used in 1865 or after on cover with stamps of Peru, *value from* 350.00

Earliest known use 7/16/46.

Stamps of Great Britain Cancelled with barred oval "C38" obliterator, either single or in duplex

No. A63

1865-79
A34 ½p rose red, plates 5, 6, 10-14 (#58), *value from* 50.00
A35 1p rose red, plates 74, 88, 89, 93, 94, 97, 108, 123, 127, 128, 130, 134, 137, 139-141, 143-146, 148, 149, 157, 160, 163, 167, 171-173, 175, 176, 180-183, 185, 187, 190, 193, 195, 198-201, 204, 206, 209, 210, 212, 213, 215 (#33), *value from* 37.50
A36 1½p lake red, plate 3 (#32) —
A37 2p blue, plates 9, 12 (#29) 37.50
A38 2p blue, plates 13-15 (#30) 37.50
A39 3p rose (#37) —
A40 3p rose, plate 4 (#44) 110.00
A41 3p rose, plates 5-10 (#49), *value from* 50.00
A42 3p rose, plates 11, 12, 14-19 (#61), *value from* 50.00
A43 4p vermilion, plate 3 (#34) —
a. 4p vermilion, plate 4 (#34a) —
A44 4p vermilion, plates 8, 10-14 (#43), *value from* 42.50
A45 4p vermilion, plate 15 (#69) 350.00
A46 4p pale olive green, plates 15, 16 (#70) 225.00
A47 6p lilac, plate 3 (#39) —
a. 6p lilac, plate 4 (#39b) —
A48 6p lilac, plates 5, 6 (#45) —
A49 6p dull violet, plate 6 (#50) —
A50 6p violet, plates 8, 9 (#51), *value from* 80.00
A51 6p brown plate 11 (#59) 55.00
a. 6p pale buff, plates 11, 12 (#59b), *value from* 80.00
A52 6p gray, plate 12 (#60) 240.00
A53 6p gray, plates 13-16 (#62), *value from* 55.00
A54 8p orange (#73) 300.00
A55 9p straw (#40) —
A56 9p straw, plate 4 (#46) 450.00
A57 9p bister, plate 4 (#52) 350.00
A58 10p red brown (#53) 300.00
A59 1sh green, plate 4 (#48) —
A60 1sh green, plates 4-7 (#54), *value from* 42.50
A61 1sh green, plates 8-13 (#64), *value from* 62.50
A62 2sh blue (#55) 140.00
A63 5sh rose, plate 1 (#57) 525.00
Plate 2 (#57) 675.00

IQUIQUE
Stamps of Great Britain Cancelled with "D87" Type B obliterator

1865-79
A69 ½p rose red, plates 5, 6, 13, 14 (#58), *value from* 85.00
A70 1p rose red, plates 76, 179, 185, 205 (#33), *value from* 55.00
A71 2p blue, plates 9, 12 (#29) —
A72 2p blue, plates 13-15 (#30) 55.00
A73 3p rose, plates 5-9 (#49), *value from* 67.50
A74 3p rose, plates 12, 18, 19 (#61), *value from* 85.00

A75 4p vermilion, plates 12-14 (#43), *value from* 75.00
A76 4p vermilion, plate 15 (#69) 350.00
A77 4p pale olive green, plates 15, 16 (#70) 225.00
A78 6p violet, plates 8, 9 (#51) —
A79 6p brown plate 11 (#59) —
a. 6p pale buff, plates 11, 12 (#59b), *value from* 125.00
A80 6p gray, plate 12 (#60) 250.00
A81 6p gray, plates 13-16 (#62) 90.00
A82 8p orange (#73) 375.00
A83 9p bister, plate 4 (#52) 225.00
A84 10p red brown (#53) —
A85 1sh green, plates 4, 6, 7 (#54) 67.50
A86 1sh green, plates 8-13 (#64), *value from* 90.00
A87 2sh blue (#55) 250.00

ISLAY / MOLLENDO
Pre-Stamp Postmark

1850
Crowned Circle Handstamp Type I

A90 Inscribed "PAID AT ISLAY" in red, curved "ISLAY", on cover 6,000.

Earliest known use 10/23/50.

Stamps of Great Britain Cancelled with Type A barred oval "C42" obliterator or with circular date stamp

1865-79
A91 1p rose red, plates 78, 84, 87, 88, 96, 103, 125, 134 (#33), *value from* 62.50
A92 1½p lake red, plate 3 (#32) —
A93 2p blue, plate 9 (#29) 62.50
A94 2p blue, plates 13, 15 (#30), *value from* 62.50
A95 3p rose (#37) —
A96 3p rose, plate 4 (#44) 125.00
A97 3p rose, plates 4-6, 10 (#49), *value from* 67.50
A98 4p vermilion, plate 3 (#34) 150.00
a. 4p vermilion, plate 4 (#34a) 175.00
A99 4p vermilion, plates 9-13 (#43), *value from* 70.00
A100 4p vermilion, plate 15 (#69) —
A101 4p pale olive green, plates 15, 16 (#70), *value from* 225.00
A102 6p lilac, plate 3 (#39) 100.00
a. 6p lilac, plate 4 (#39b) 150.00
A103 6p lilac, plate 5 (#45) 90.00
A104 6p bright violet, plate 6 (#50a) 100.00
A105 6p violet, plates 8, 9 (#51), *value from* 90.00
A106 6p brown plate 11 (#59) —
a. 6p pale buff, plate 12 (#59b) —
A107 6p gray, plate 12 (#60) —
A108 6p gray, plates 13-16 (#62), *value from* 75.00
A109 9p straw (#46) 425.00
A110 9p bister, plate 4 (#52) 225.00
A111 10p red brown (#53) 325.00
A112 1sh green, plate 4 (#48) —
A113 1sh green, plates 4-7 (#54), *value from* 67.50
A114 1sh green, plates 8, 10, 12, 13 (#64), *value from* 90.00
A115 2sh blue (#55) —
A116 5sh rose, plate 1 (#57) —
Plate 2 (#57) —

PAITA
Pre-Stamp Postmarks

1850
Crowned Circle Handstamp Type I

A122 Inscribed "PAID AT PAITA" in black, curved "ISLAY", on cover *7,500.*
A123 Inscribed "PAID AT PAITA" in red, curved "ISLAY", on cover *7,500.*

Earliest known use 11/5/50.

Stamps of Great Britain Cancelled with Type A barred oval "C43" obliterator or with circular date stamp

1865-79
A121 1p rose red, plates 127, 147 (#33) 75.00
A122 2p blue, plate 9 (#29) 75.00
A123 2p blue, plate 14 (#30) 75.00
A124 3p rose, plates 5, 6 (#49) 85.00
A125 3p rose, plates 17-19 (#61) 85.00
A126 4p vermilion, plates 10-14 (#43), *value from* 85.00
A127 4p pale olive green, plate 15 (#70) —
A128 6p lilac, plate 3 (#39) 130.00

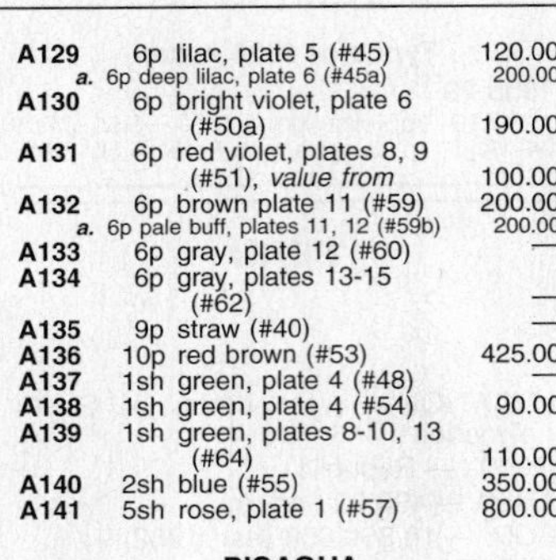

A129 6p lilac, plate 5 (#45) 120.00
a. 6p deep lilac, plate 6 (#45a) 200.00
A130 6p bright violet, plate 6 (#50a) 190.00
A131 6p red violet, plates 8, 9 (#51), *value from* 100.00
A132 6p brown plate 11 (#59) 200.00
a. 6p pale buff, plates 11, 12 (#59b) 200.00
A133 6p gray, plate 12 (#60) —
A134 6p gray, plates 13-15 (#62) —
A135 9p straw (#40) —
A136 10p red brown (#53) 425.00
A137 1sh green, plate 4 (#48) —
A138 1sh green, plate 4 (#54) 90.00
A139 1sh green, plates 8-10, 13 (#64) 110.00
A140 2sh blue (#55) 350.00
A141 5sh rose, plate 1 (#57) 800.00

PISAGUA
Stamps of Great Britain Cancelled with Type B barred oval "D65" obliterator

1867
A150 1p rose red (#33) —
A151 2p blue (#30) —
A152 2sh blue (#55) —

PISCO AND CHINCHA ISLANDS
Stamps of Great Britain Cancelled with Type B barred oval "D74" obliterator

1865-70
A160 2p blue, plate 9 (#29) —
A161 4p vermilion, plates 10, 12 (#43) *1,000.*
A162 6p bright violet, plate 6 (#50a) *1,750.*
A163 1sh green, plate 4 (#54) —
A164 2sh blue (#55) *2,500.*

ISSUES OF THE REPUBLIC

Sail and Steamship — A1

Design: 2r, Ship sails eastward.

Unwmk.

1857, Dec. 1 **Engr.** ***Imperf.***
1 A1 1r blue, *blue* 1,700. 2,250.
2 A1 2r brn red, *blue* 1,900. 3,000.

The Pacific Steam Navigation Co. gave a quantity of these stamps to the Peruvian government so that a trial of prepayment of postage by stamps might be made.

Stamps of 1 and 2 reales, printed in various colors on white paper, laid and wove, were prepared for the Pacific Steam Navigation Co. but never put in use. Value $50 each on wove paper, $400 each on laid paper.

Coat of Arms
A2 A3

A4

Wavy Lines in Spandrels

1858, Mar. 1 **Litho.**
3 A2 1d deep blue 275.00 47.50
4 A3 1p rose red 1,100. 160.00
5 A4 ½ peso rose red *6,500.* *4,750.*
6 A4 ½ peso buff *2,750.* 375.00
a. ½ peso orange yellow *2,750.* 375.00

A5 A6

Large Letters

1858, Dec. **Double-lined Frame**
7 A5 1d slate blue 450.00 45.00
8 A6 1p red 450.00 65.00

A7 A8

1860-61
Zigzag Lines in Spandrels
9 A7 1d blue 175.00 10.50
a. 1d Prussian blue 175.00 20.00
b. Cornucopia on white ground 375.00 80.00
c. Zigzag lines broken at angles 225.00 22.50
10 A8 1p rose 450.00 42.50
a. 1p brick red 450.00 42.50
b. Cornucopia on white ground 450.00 42.50

Retouched, 10 lines instead of 9 in left label
11 A8 1p rose 250.00 27.50
a. Pelure paper 425.00 32.50
Nos. 9-11 (3) 875.00 80.50

A9 A10

1862-63 **Embossed**
12 A9 1d red 14.50 4.50
a. Arms embossed sideways 550.00 150.00
b. Thick paper 120.00 37.50
c. Diag. half used on cover 350.00
13 A10 1p brown ('63) 120.00 37.50
a. Diag. half used on cover 1,000.

Counterfeits of Nos. 13 and 15 exist.

A11

1868-72
14 A11 1d green 19.00 3.75
a. Arms embossed inverted *2,250.* *1,200.*
b. Diag. half used on cover *2,000.*
15 A10 1p orange ('72) 150.00 55.00
a. Diag. half used on cover *1,100.*

Nos. 12-15, 19 and 20 were printed in horizontal strips. Stamps may be found printed on two strips of paper where the strips were joined by overlapping.

Llamas — A12 A13

A14

1866-67 **Engr.** ***Perf. 12***
16 A12 5c green 10.50 .95
17 A13 10c vermilion 10.50 2.25
18 A14 20c brown 35.00 7.00
a. Diagonal half used on cover 675.00
Nos. 16-18 (3) 56.00 10.20

See Nos. 109, 111, 113.

Locomotive and Arms — A15

1871, Apr. **Embossed** ***Imperf.***
19 A15 5c scarlet 125.00 42.50
a. 5c pale red 125.00 42.50

20th anniv. of the first railway in South America, linking Lima and Callao.

The so-called varieties "ALLAO" and "CALLA" are due to over-inking.

Llama — A16

1873, Mar. ***Rouletted Horiz.***
20 A16 2c dk ultra 50.00 *325.00*

Counterfeits are plentiful.

Sun God of the Incas — A17

Coat of Arms
A18 A19

A20 A21

A22 A23

Embossed with Grill

1874-84 **Engr.** ***Perf. 12***
21 A17 1c orange ('79) .90 .65
22 A18 2c dk violet 1.25 .95
23 A19 5c blue ('77) 1.40 .45
24 A19 5c ultra ('79) 13.00 3.25
25 A20 10c green ('76) .45 .30
a. Imperf., pair 35.00
26 A20 10c slate ('84) 2.00 .45
a. Diag. half used as 5c on cover —
27 A21 20c brown red 3.50 1.10
28 A22 50c green 15.00 4.25
29 A23 1s rose 2.40 2.40
Nos. 21-29 (9) 39.90 13.80

No. 25a lacks the grill.

No. 26 with overprint "DE OFICIO" is said to have been used to frank mail of Gen. A. A. Caceres during the civil war against Gen. Miguel Iglesias, provisional president. Experts question its status.

1880
30 A17 1c green 2.50
31 A18 2c rose 2.50

Nos. 30 and 31 were prepared for use but not issued without overprint.

See Nos. 104-108, 110, 112, 114-115.

For overprints see Nos. 32-103, 116-128, J32-J33, O2-O22, N11-N23, 1N1-1N9, 3N11-3N20, 5N1, 6N1-6N2, 7N1-7N2, 8N7, 8N10-8N11, 9N1-9N3, 10N3-10N8, 10N10-10N11, 11N1-11N5, 12N1-12N3, 13N1, 14N1-14N16, 15N5-15N8, 15N13-15N18, 16N1-16N22.

Stamps of 1874-80 Overprinted in Red, Blue or Black

1880, Jan. 5

32 A17 1c green (R) .90 .65
a. Inverted overprint 10.00 10.00
b. Double overprint 13.50 13.50
33 A18 2c rose (Bl) 1.75 1.10
a. Inverted overprint 10.00 10.00
b. Double overprint 14.00 12.00
34 A18 2c rose (Bk) 75.00 60.00
a. Inverted overprint
b. Double overprint
35 A19 5c ultra (R) 3.50 1.75
a. Inverted overprint 10.00 10.00
b. Double overprint 14.00 14.00
36 A22 50c green (R) 45.00 27.50
a. Inverted overprint 45.00 45.00
b. Double overprint 55.00 55.00
37 A23 1s rose (Bl) 70.00 50.00
a. Inverted overprint 110.00 110.00
b. Double overprint 110.00 110.00
Nos. 32-37 (6) 196.15 141.00

Stamps of 1874-80 Overprinted in Red or Blue

1881, Jan. 28

38 A17 1c green (R) 1.25 .95
a. Inverted overprint 8.25 8.25
b. Double overprint 14.00 14.00
39 A18 2c rose (Bl) 24.00 15.00
a. Inverted overprint 17.50 15.00
b. Double overprint 25.00 20.00
40 A19 5c ultra (R) 2.75 1.25
a. Inverted overprint 14.00 14.00
b. Double overprint 20.00 20.00
41 A22 50c green (R) 750.00 425.00
a. Inverted overprint 850.00
42 A23 1s rose (Bl) 140.00 90.00
a. Inverted overprint 175.00

Reprints of Nos. 38 to 42 were made in 1884. In the overprint the word "PLATA" is 3mm high instead of 2½mm. The cross bars of the letters "A" of that word are set higher than on the original stamps. The 5c is printed in blue instead of ultramarine.

For stamps of 1874-80 overprinted with Chilean arms or small UPU "horseshoe," see Nos. N11-N23.

Stamps of 1874-79 Handstamped in Black or Blue

1883

65 A17 1c orange (Bk) 1.25 1.10
66 A17 1c orange (Bl) 50.00 50.00
68 A19 5c ultra (Bk) 13.00 7.00
69 A20 10c green (Bk) 1.25 1.10
70 A20 10c green (Bl) 5.00 4.00
71 A22 50c green (Bk) 7.00 4.25
73 A23 1s rose (Bk) 10.00 8.00
Nos. 65-73 (7) 87.50 75.45
Nos. 65,68-73 (6) 37.50 25.45

This overprint is found in 11 types.

The 1c green, 2c dark violet and 20c brown red, overprinted with triangle, are fancy varieties made for sale to collectors and never placed in regular use.

Overprinted Triangle and "Union Postal Universal Peru" in Oval

1883

77 A22 50c grn (R & Bk) 210.00 110.00
78 A23 1s rose (Bl & Bk) 250.00 160.00

The 1c green, 2c rose and 5c ultramarine, over printed with triangle and "U. P. U. Peru" oval, were never placed in regular use.

Overprinted Triangle and "Union Postal Universal Lima" in Oval

1883

79 A17 1c grn (R & Bl) 70.00 70.00
80 A17 1c grn (R & Bk) 7.00 7.00
a. Oval overprint inverted
b. Double overprint of oval
81 A18 2c rose (Bl & Bk) 7.00 7.00
82 A19 5c ultra (R & Bk) 11.00 10.00
83 A19 5c ultra (R & Bl) 17.00 10.00

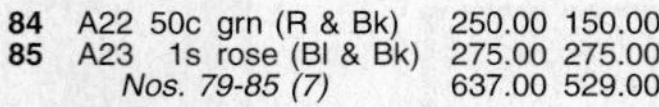

84 A22 50c grn (R & Bk) 250.00 150.00
85 A23 1s rose (Bl & Bk) 275.00 275.00
Nos. 79-85 (7) 637.00 529.00

Some authorities question the status of No. 79.

Nos. 80, 81, 84, and 85 were reprinted in 1884. They have the second type of oval overprint with "PLATA" 3mm high.

Overprinted Triangle and

86 A17 1c grn (Bk & Bk) 1.75 1.25
a. Horseshoe inverted 10.00
87 A17 1c grn (Bl & Bk) 5.00 3.50
88 A18 2c ver (Bk & Bk) 1.75 1.25
89 A19 5c bl (Bk & Bk) 2.25 1.60
90 A19 5c bl (Bl & Bk) 12.00 10.50
91 A19 5c bl (R & Bk) *1,500. 1,100.*

Overprinted Horseshoe Alone

1883, Oct. 23

95 A17 1c green 2.25 2.25
96 A18 2c vermilion 2.25 *6.50*
a. Double overprint
97 A19 5c blue 3.50 3.50
98 A19 5c ultra 20.00 15.00
99 A22 50c rose 57.50 57.50
100 A23 1s ultra 55.00 22.50
Nos. 95-100 (6) 140.50 107.25

The 2c dark violet overprinted with the above design in red and triangle in black also the 1c green overprinted with the same combination plus the horseshoe in black, are fancy varieties made for sale to collectors.

No. 23 Overprinted in Black

1884, Apr. 28

103 A19 5c blue .65 .40
a. Double overprint 5.00 5.00

Stamps of 1c and 2c with the above overprint, also with the above and "U. P. U. LIMA" oval in blue or "CORREOS LIMA" in a double-lined circle in red, were made to sell to collectors and were never placed in use.

Without Overprint or Grill

1886-95

104 A17 1c dull violet .90 .30
105 A17 1c vermilion ('95) .65 .30
106 A18 2c green 1.25 .30
107 A18 2c dp ultra ('95) .55 .30
108 A19 5c orange 1.00 .45
109 A12 5c claret ('95) 2.25 .85
110 A20 10c slate .65 .30
111 A13 10c orange ('95) 1.00 .55
112 A21 20c blue 8.75 1.10
113 A14 20c dp ultra ('95) 10.50 2.25
114 A22 50c red 2.75 1.10
115 A23 1s brown 2.25 .85
Nos. 104-115 (12) 32.50 8.65

Overprinted Horseshoe in Black and Triangle in Rose Red

1889

116 A17 1c green .75 .75
a. Horseshoe inverted 7.50

Nos. 30 and 25 Overprinted "Union Postal Universal Lima" in Oval in Red

1889, Sept. 1

117 A17 1c green 2.00 1.60
117A A20 10c green 2.00 2.00

The overprint on Nos. 117 and 117A is of the second type with "PLATA" 3mm high.

Stamps of 1874-80 Overprinted in Black

Pres. Remigio Morales Bermúdez

1894, Oct. 23

118 A17 1c orange 1.00 .65
a. Inverted overprint 7.00 7.00
b. Double overprint 7.00 7.00
119 A17 1c green .65 .55
a. Inverted overprint 3.50 3.50
b. Dbl. inverted ovpt. 5.00 5.00
120 A18 2c violet .65 .55
a. Diagonal half used as 1c
b. Inverted overprint 7.00 7.00
c. Double overprint 7.00 7.00
121 A18 2c rose .65 .55
a. Double overprint 7.00 7.00
b. Inverted overprint 9.75 7.00
122 A19 5c blue 4.50 2.75
122A A19 5c ultra 7.25 3.50
b. Inverted overprint 10.00 10.00
123 A20 10c green .65 .55
a. Inverted overprint 7.00 7.00
124 A22 50c green 2.40 2.00
a. Inverted overprint 10.00 10.00
Nos. 118-124 (8) 17.75 11.10

Same, with Additional Ovpt. of Horseshoe

125 A18 2c vermilion .55 .45
a. Head inverted 2.50 2.50
b. Head double 5.00 5.00
126 A19 5c blue 1.75 .85
a. Head inverted 7.00 7.00
127 A22 50c rose 70.00 42.50
a. Head double 55.00 45.00
b. Head inverted 75.00 60.00
128 A23 1s ultra 175.00 150.00
a. Both overprints inverted 200.00 110.00
b. Head double 200.00 110.00
Nos. 125-128 (4) 247.30 193.80

A23a

Vermilion Surcharge

1895 ***Perf. 11½***

129 A23a 5c on 5c grn 18.00 13.00
130 A23a 10c on 10c ver 13.00 10.00
131 A23a 20c on 20c brn 14.00 10.00
132 A23a 50c on 50c ultra 18.00 13.00
133 A23a 1s on 1s red brn 18.00 13.00
Nos. 129-133 (5) 81.00 59.00

Nos 129-133 were used only in Tumbes. The basic stamps were prepared by revolutionaries in northern Peru.

A23b

"Liberty" — A23c

1895, Sept. 8 **Engr.**

134 A23b 1c gray violet 1.90 1.10
135 A23b 2c green 1.90 1.10
136 A23b 5c yellow 1.90 1.10
137 A23b 10c ultra 1.90 1.10
138 A23c 20c orange 1.90 1.25
139 A23c 50c dark blue 10.00 7.00
140 A23c 1s car lake 55.00 35.00
Nos. 134-140 (7) 74.50 47.65

Success of the revolution against the government of General Caceres and of the election of President Pierola.

Manco Capac, Founder of Inca Dynasty — A24

Francisco Pizarro Conqueror of the Inca Empire — A25

General José de La Mar — A26

1896-1900

141 A24 1c ultra .90 .30
a. 1c blue (error) 70.00 60.00
142 A24 1c yel grn ('98) .90 .30
143 A24 2c blue .90 .30
144 A24 2c scar ('99) .90 .30
145 A25 5c indigo 1.25 .30
146 A25 5c green ('97) 1.25 .30
147 A25 5c grnsh bl ('99) .90 .55
148 A25 10c yellow 1.75 .45
149 A25 10c gray blk ('00) 1.75 .30
150 A25 20c orange 3.50 .45
151 A26 50c car rose 8.75 1.60
152 A26 1s orange red 13.00 1.60
153 A26 2s claret 3.50 1.25
Nos. 141-153 (13) 39.25 8.00

The 5c in black is a chemical changeling.

For surcharges and overprints see Nos. 187-188, E1, O23-O26.

Paucartambo Bridge A27

Post and Telegraph Building, Lima — A28

Pres. Nicolás de Piérola — A29

1897, Dec. 31

154 A27 1c dp ultra 1.25 .60
155 A28 2c brown 1.25 .40
156 A29 5c bright rose 1.75 .60
Nos. 154-156 (3) 4.25 1.60

Opening of new P.O. in Lima.

No. J1 Overprinted in Black

1897, Nov. 8

157 D1 1c bister .90 .75
a. Inverted overprint 4.50 4.50
b. Double overprint 17.50 17.50

A31

1899

158	A31	5s orange red	2.75	2.75
159	A31	10s blue green	850.00	600.00

For surcharge see No. J36.

Pres. Eduardo de Romaña — A32

1900 Frame Litho., Center Engr.

160	A32	22c yel grn & blk	13.00	1.40

Admiral Miguel L. Grau — A33

2c, Col. Francisco Bolognesi. 5c, Pres. Romaña.

1901, Jan.

161	A33	1c green & blk	1.75	.75
162	A33	2c red & black	1.75	.75
163	A33	5c dull vio & blk	1.75	.75
		Nos. 161-163 (3)	5.25	2.25

Advent of 20th century.

A34

1902 Engr.

164	A34	22c green	.55	.30

Municipal Hygiene Institute Lima — A35

1905

165	A35	12c dp blue & blk	1.75	.50

For surcharges see Nos. 166-167, 186, 189.

Same Surcharged in Red or Violet

1907

166	A35	1c on 12c (R)	.35	.30
a.		Inverted surcharge	8.00	8.00
b.		Double surcharge	8.00	8.00
167	A35	2c on 12c (V)	.65	.45
a.		Double surcharge	8.00	8.00
b.		Inverted surcharge	8.00	8.00

Monument of Bolognesi — A36

Admiral Grau — A37

Llama — A38

Statue of Bolivar — A39

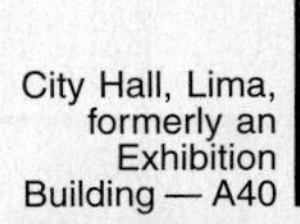

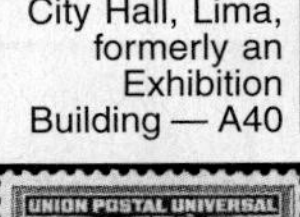

City Hall, Lima, formerly an Exhibition Building — A40

School of Medicine, Lima — A41

Post and Telegraph Building, Lima — A42

Grandstand at Santa Beatrix Race Track — A43

Columbus Monument — A44

1907

168	A36	1c yel grn & blk	.55	.30
169	A37	2c red & violet	.55	.30
170	A38	4c olive green	9.25	1.25
171	A39	5c blue & blk	1.00	.30
172	A40	10c red brn & blk	1.75	.45
173	A41	20c dk grn & blk	40.00	.75
174	A42	50c black	40.00	1.60
175	A43	1s purple & grn	200.00	3.75
176	A44	2s dp bl & blk	200.00	160.00
		Nos. 168-176 (9)	493.10	168.70

For surcharges and overprint see #190-195, E2.

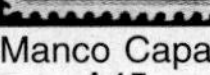

Manco Capac A45

Columbus A46

Pizarro A47

San Martin A48

Bolívar A49

La Mar A50

Ramón Castilla A51

Grau A52

Bolognesi — A53

1909

177	A45	1c gray	.35	.25
178	A46	2c green	.35	.25
179	A47	4c vermilion	.45	.30
180	A48	5c violet	.35	.25
181	A49	10c deep blue	.75	.30
182	A50	12c pale blue	1.75	.30
183	A51	20c brown red	1.90	.45
184	A52	50c yellow	8.25	.55
185	A53	1s brn red & blk	17.00	.65
		Nos. 177-185 (9)	31.15	3.30

See types A54, A78-A80, A81-A89.

For surcharges and overprint see Nos. 196-200, 208, E3.

No. 165 Surcharged in Red

1913, Jan.

186	A35	8c on 12c dp bl & blk	.90	.35

Stamps of 1899-1908 Surcharged in Red

a

b

c

1915 On Nos. 142, 149

187	A24(a)	1c on 1c	27.50	22.50
a.		Inverted surcharge	32.50	37.50
188	A25(a)	1c on 10c	1.75	1.25
a.		Inverted surcharge	4.50	4.50

On No. 165

189	A35(c)	2c on 12c	.45	.30
a.		Inverted surcharge	7.75	7.75

On Nos. 168-170, 172-174

190	A36(a)	1c on 1c	1.10	1.10
a.		Inverted surcharge	3.50	3.50
191	A37(a)	1c on 2c	1.75	1.60
a.		Inverted surcharge	4.50	4.50
192	A38(b)	1c on 4c	3.25	2.75
a.		Inverted surcharge	10.50	10.50
193	A40(b)	1c on 10c	1.75	1.25
a.		Inverted surcharge	3.75	3.75
193C	A40(c)	2c on 10c	175.00	125.00
b.		Inverted surcharge	*175.00*	
194	A41(c)	2c on 20c	22.50	21.00
a.		Inverted surcharge	45.00	45.00
195	A42(c)	2c on 50c	3.25	3.25
a.		Inverted surcharge	13.00	13.00
		Nos. 187-195 (10)	238.30	180.00

Nos. 182-184, 179, 185 Surcharged in Red, Green or Violet

d

e

f

1916

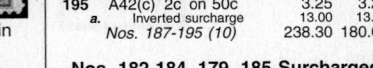

196	A50(d)	1c on 12c (R)	.35	.25
a.		Double surcharge	5.00	5.00
b.		Green surcharge	7.50	7.50
197	A51(d)	1c on 20c (G)	.35	.25
198	A52(d)	1c on 50c (G)	.35	.25
a.		Inverted surcharge	5.00	5.00
199	A47(e)	2c on 4c (V)	.35	.25
a.		Green surcharge	1.60	1.25
200	A53(f)	10c on 1s (G)	1.10	.25
a.		"VALF"	10.50	10.50
		Nos. 196-200 (5)	2.50	1.25

Official Stamps of 1909-14 Ovptd. or Srchd. in Green or Red

g

h

1916

201	O1(g)	1c red (G)	.25	.25
202	O1(h)	2c on 50c ol grn (R)	.35	.25
203	O1(g)	10c bis brn (G)	.35	.25

Postage Due Stamps of 1909 Surcharged in Violet-Black

204	D7	2c on 1c brown	.65	.65
205	D7	2c on 5c brown	.25	.25
206	D7	2c on 10c brown	.25	.25
207	D7	2c on 50c brown	.25	.25
		Nos. 201-207 (7)	2.35	2.15

Many examples of Nos. 187 to 207 have a number of pin holes. It is stated that these holes were made at the time the surcharges were printed.

The varieties listed of the 1915 and 1916 issues were sold to the public at post offices. Many other varieties which were previously listed are now known to have been delivered to one speculator or to have been privately printed by him from the surcharging plates which he had acquired.

No. 179 Surcharged in Black

1917

208	A47	1c on 4c ver	.55	.55
a.		Double surcharge	8.25	8.25
b.		Inverted surcharge	8.25	8.25

San Martin — A54

Columbus at Salamanca — A62

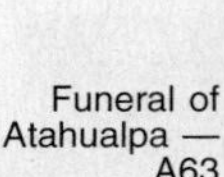

Funeral of Atahualpa — A63

Battle of Arica, "Arica, the Last Cartridge" A64

Designs: 2c, Bolívar. 4c, José Gálvez. 5c, Manuel Pardo. 8c, Grau. 10c, Bolognesi. 12c, Castilla. 20c, General Cáceres.

1918 Centers in Black Engr.

No.	Type	Description	Unused	Used
209	A54	1c orange	.35	.25
210	A54	2c green	.35	.25
211	A54	4c lake	.45	.30
212	A54	5c dp ultra	.45	.30
213	A54	8c red brn	1.25	.45
214	A54	10c grnsh bl	.55	.30
215	A54	12c dl vio	1.75	.30
216	A54	20c ol grn	2.10	.30
217	A62	50c vio brn	8.25	.55
218	A63	1s greenish bl	21.00	.75
219	A64	2s deep ultra	35.00	1.10
		Nos. 209-219 (11)	71.50	4.85

For surcharges see Nos. 232-233, 255-256.

Augusto B. Leguía — A65

1919, Dec. Litho.

No.	Type	Description	Unused	Used
220	A65	5c bl & blk	.35	.30
a.		Imperf.	.35	.35
b.		Center inverted	15.00	15.00
221	A65	5c brn & blk	.35	.30
a.		Imperf.	.35	.35
b.		Center inverted	15.00	15.00

Constitution of 1919.

San Martín — A66

Thomas Cochrane — A70

Oath of Independence — A69

Designs: 2c, Field Marshal Arenales. 4c, Field Marshal Las Heras. 10c, Martin Jorge Guisse. 12c, Vidal. 20c, Leguia. 50c, San Martin monument. 1s, San Martin and Leguia.

1921, July 28 Engr.; 7c Litho.

No.	Type	Description	Unused	Used
222	A66	1c ol brn & red brn	.45	.25
a.		Center inverted	600.00	600.00
223	A66	2c green	.55	.30
224	A66	4c car rose	1.90	.90
225	A69	5c ol brn	.60	.25
226	A70	7c violet	1.90	.65
227	A66	10c ultra	1.90	.65
228	A66	12c blk & slate	4.50	.90
229	A66	20c car & gray blk	4.50	1.10
230	A66	50c vio brn & dl vio	13.00	3.75
231	A69	1s car rose & yel grn	19.00	8.00
		Nos. 222-231 (10)	48.30	16.75

Centenary of Independence.

Nos. 213, 212 Surcharged in Black or Red Brown

1923-24

No.	Type	Description	Unused	Used
232	A54	5c on 8c No. 213	.75	.55
233	A54	4c on 5c (RB) ('24)	.55	.25
a.		Inverted surcharge	5.00	5.00
b.		Double surcharge, one inverted	6.00	6.00

A78

A79

Simón Bolívar — A80

Perf. 14, 14x14½, 14½, 13½

1924 Engr.; Photo. (4c, 5c)

No.	Type	Description	Unused	Used
234	A78	2c olive grn	.40	.25
235	A79	4c yellow grn	.65	.25
236	A79	5c black	2.25	.25
237	A80	10c carmine	.80	.25
238	A78	20c ultra	2.25	.30
239	A78	50c dull violet	5.50	1.10
240	A78	1s yellow brn	13.00	4.25
241	A78	2s dull blue	35.00	18.00
		Nos. 234-241 (8)	59.85	24.65

Centenary of the Battle of Ayacucho which ended Spanish power in South America.

No. 237 exists imperf.

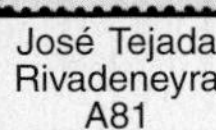

José Tejada Rivadeneyra A81

Mariano Melgar A82

Iturregui A83

Leguía A84

José de La Mar — A85

Monument of José Olaya — A86

Statue of María Bellido — A87

De Saco — A88

José Leguía — A89

1924-29 Engr. *Perf. 12*

Size: 18½x23mm

No.	Type	Description	Unused	Used
242	A81	2c olive gray	.35	.25
243	A82	4c dk grn	.35	.25
244	A83	8c black	3.25	3.25
245	A84	10c org red	.35	.25
245A	A85	15c dp bl ('28)	1.00	.30
246	A86	20c blue	1.75	.30
247	A86	20c yel ('29)	2.75	.30
248	A87	50c violet	8.25	.45
249	A88	1s bis brn	15.00	1.60
250	A89	2s ultra	40.00	8.00
		Nos. 242-250 (10)	73.05	14.95

See Nos. 258, 260, 276-282.

For surcharges and overprint see Nos. 251-253, 257-260, 262, 268-271, C1.

No. 246 Surcharged in Red

a

b

1925

No.	Type	Description	Unused	Used
251	A86(a)	2c on 20c blue	550.00	550.00
252	A86(b)	2c on 20c blue	1.75	1.10
a.		Inverted surcharge	50.00	50.00
b.		Double surch., one inverted	50.00	50.00

No. 245 Overprinted

1925

No.	Type	Description	Unused	Used
253	A84	10c org red	1.75	1.75
a.		Inverted overprint	21.00	21.00

This stamp was for exclusive use on letters from the plebiscite provinces of Tacna and Arica, and posted on the Peruvian transport "Ucayali" anchored in the port of Arica.

No. 213 Surcharged

a

Habilitada 2 centavos 1929

b

1929

No.	Type	Description	Unused	Used
255	A54(a)	2c on 8c	1.25	1.25
256	A54(b)	2c on 8c	1.25	1.25

No. 247 Surcharged

Habilitada 15 cts. 1929

No.	Type	Description	Unused	Used
257	A86	15c on 20c yellow	1.25	1.25
a.		Inverted surcharge	13.00	13.00
		Nos. 255-257 (3)	3.75	3.75

Types of 1924 Coil Stamps

1929 *Perf. 14 Horizontally*

No.	Type	Description	Unused	Used
258	A81	2c olive gray	65.00	40.00
260	A84	10c orange red	70.00	37.50

Postal Tax Stamp of 1928 Overprinted

1930 *Perf. 12*

No.	Type	Description	Unused	Used
261	PT6	2c dark violet	.55	.55
a.		Inverted overprint	3.25	3.25

No. 247 Surcharged

Habilitada 2 Cts. 1930

No.	Type	Description	Unused	Used
262	A86	2c on 20c yellow	.55	.55

Air Post Stamp of 1928 Surcharged

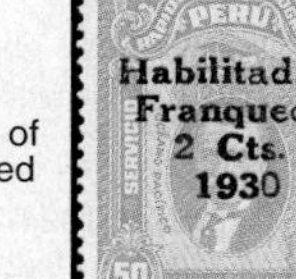

No.	Type	Description	Unused	Used
263	AP1	2c on 50c dk grn	.55	.55
a.		"Habitada"	2.10	2.10

Coat of Arms — A91

Lima Cathedral A92

10c, Children's Hospital. 50c, Madonna & Child.

Perf. 12x11½, 11½x12

1930, July 5 Litho.

No.	Type	Description	Unused	Used
264	A91	2c green	1.75	.95
265	A92	5c scarlet	3.75	2.10
266	A92	10c dark blue	2.25	1.60
267	A91	50c bister brown	30.00	19.00
		Nos. 264-267 (4)	37.75	23.65

6th Pan American Congress for Child Welfare. By error the stamps are inscribed "Seventh Congress."

Type of 1924 Overprinted in Black, Green or Blue

1930, Dec. 22 Photo. *Perf. 15x14*

Size: 18¼x22mm

No.	Type	Description	Unused	Used
268	A84	10c orange red (Bk)	1.00	.80
a.		Inverted overprint	14.00	14.00
b.		Without overprint	8.50	8.50
c.		Double surcharge	7.00	7.00

Same with Additional Surcharge of Numerals in Each Corner

No.	Type	Description	Unused	Used
269	A84	2c on 10c org red (G)	.35	.25
a.		Inverted surcharge	17.00	
270	A84	4c on 10c org red (G)	.35	.25
a.		Double surcharge	12.50	12.50

Engr.

Perf. 12

Size: 19x23½mm

No.	Type	Description	Unused	Used
271	A84	15c on 10c org red (Bl)	.35	.25
a.		Inverted surcharge	14.00	14.00
b.		Double surcharge	14.00	14.00
		Nos. 268-271 (4)	2.05	1.55

Bolívar — A95

1930, Dec. 16 **Litho.**

272	A95	2c buff	.55	.55
273	A95	4c red	.90	.75
274	A95	10c blue green	.45	.30
275	A95	15c slate gray	.90	.90
		Nos. 272-275 (4)	2.80	2.50

Death cent. of General Simón Bolivar.
For surcharges see Nos. RA14-RA16.

Types of 1924-29 Issues

Size: 18x22mm

1931 **Photo.** ***Perf. 15x14***

276	A81	2c olive green	.45	.30
277	A82	4c dark green	.45	.30
279	A85	15c deep blue	1.25	.30
280	A86	20c yellow	2.10	.30
281	A87	50c violet	2.10	.45
282	A88	1s olive brown	3.25	.55
		Nos. 276-282 (6)	9.60	2.20

Pizarro — A96

Old Stone Bridge, Lima — A97

1931, July 28 **Litho.** ***Perf. 11***

283	A96	2c slate blue	2.10	1.75
284	A96	4c deep brown	2.10	1.75
285	A96	15c dark green	2.10	1.75
286	A97	10c rose red	2.10	1.75
287	A97	10c mag & lt grn	2.10	1.75
288	A97	15c yel & bl gray	2.10	1.75
289	A97	15c dk slate & red	2.10	1.75
		Nos. 283-289 (7)	14.70	12.25

1st Peruvian Phil. Exhib., Lima, July, 1931.

Manco Capac A99

Oil Refinery A100

Sugar Cane Field A102

Picking Cotton A103

Guano Deposits A104

Mining A105

Llamas — A106

1931-32 ***Perf. 11, 11x11½***

292	A99	2c olive black	.35	.25
293	A100	4c dark green	.65	.30
295	A102	10c red orange	1.75	.25
a.		Vertical pair, imperf. between	30.00	
296	A103	15c turq blue	2.00	.30
297	A104	20c yellow	8.25	.30
298	A105	50c gray lilac	8.25	.30
299	A106	1s brown olive	20.00	1.40
		Nos. 292-299 (7)	41.25	3.10

Arms of Piura — A107

1932, July 28 ***Perf. 11½x12***

300	A107	10c dark blue	8.25	8.00
301	A107	15c deep violet	8.25	8.00
		Nos. 300-301,C3 (3)	42.50	38.50

400th anniv. of the founding of the city of Piura. On sale one day. Counterfeits exist.
See No. C7.

Parakas A108

Chimu A109

Inca — A110

1932, Oct. 15 ***Perf. 11½, 12, 11½x12***

302	A108	10c dk vio	.35	.25
303	A109	15c brn red	.65	.30
304	A110	50c dk brn	1.50	.30
		Nos. 302-304 (3)	2.50	.85

4th cent. of the Spanish conquest of Peru.

Arequipa and El Misti — A111

President Luis M. Sánchez Cerro — A112

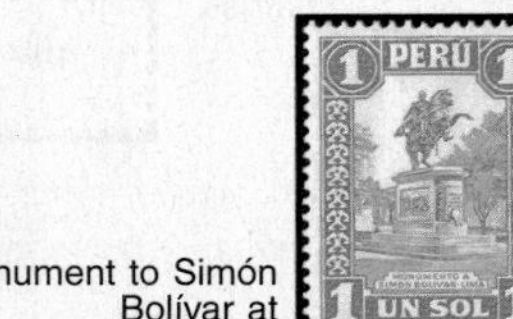

Monument to Simón Bolívar at Lima — A115

1932-34 **Photo.** ***Perf. 13½***

305	A111	2c black	.25	.25
306	A111	2c blue blk	.25	.25
307	A111	2c grn ('34)	.25	.25
308	A111	4c dk brn	.25	.25
309	A111	4c org ('34)	.25	.25
310	A112	10c vermilion	27.50	16.00
311	A115	15c ultra	.60	.25
312	A115	15c mag ('34)	.60	.25
313	A115	20c red brn	1.25	.25
314	A115	20c vio ('34)	1.25	.25
315	A115	50c dk grn ('33)	1.25	.25
316	A115	1s dp org	11.00	1.60
317	A115	1s org brn	12.00	1.10
		Nos. 305-317 (13)	56.70	21.20

For overprint see No. RA24.

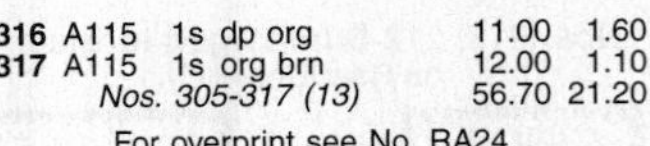

Statue of Liberty — A116

1934

318	A116	10c rose	.75	.25

Pizarro — A117

The Inca — A119

Coronation of Huascar — A118

1934-35 ***Perf. 13***

319	A117	10c crimson	.40	.25
320	A117	15c ultra	1.10	.25
321	A118	20c deep bl ('35)	2.00	.25
322	A118	50c dp red brn	1.60	.25
323	A119	1s dark vio	11.00	1.10
		Nos. 319-323 (5)	16.10	2.10

For surcharges and overprint see Nos. 354-355, J54, O32.

Pizarro and the Thirteen A120

Belle of Lima — A122

Francisco Pizarro — A123

4c, Lima Cathedral. 1s, Veiled woman of Lima.

1935, Jan. 18 ***Perf. 13½***

324	A120	2c brown	.55	.30
325	A120	4c violet	.60	.45
326	A122	10c rose red	.60	.30
327	A123	15c ultra	1.10	.75
328	A120	20c slate gray	2.25	.95
329	A122	50c olive grn	3.25	1.90
330	A122	1s Prus bl	6.00	3.75
331	A123	2s org brn	14.50	10.00
		Nos. 324-331,C6-C12 (15)	91.05	60.50

Founding of Lima, 4th cent.

View of Ica — A125

Lake Huacachina, Health Resort — A126

Grapes — A127

Cotton Boll — A128

Zuniga y Velazco and Philip IV — A129

Supreme God of the Nazcas — A130

Engr.; Photo. (10c)

1935, Jan. 17 ***Perf. 12½***

332	A125	4c gray blue	.45	1.25
333	A126	5c dark car	.45	1.25
334	A127	10c magenta	6.50	3.25
335	A126	20c green	2.25	2.25
336	A128	35c dark car	11.00	8.00
337	A129	50c org & brn	7.75	7.00
338	A130	1s pur & red	22.50	17.00
		Nos. 332-338 (7)	50.90	40.00

Founding of the City of Ica, 300th anniv.

Pizarro and the Thirteen — A131

1935-36 **Photo.** ***Perf. 13½***

339	A131	2c dp claret	.25	.25
340	A131	4c bl grn ('36)	.25	.25

For surcharge and overprints see Nos. 353, J53, RA25-RA26.

"San Cristóbal," First Peruvian Warship — A132

Naval College at Punta A133

Independence Square, Callao — A134

Aerial View of Callao A135

Plan of Walls of Callao in 1746 A137

Grand Marshal José de La Mar — A138

Packetboat "Sacramento" — A139

Viceroy José Antonio Manso de Velasco — A140

Fort Maipú — A141

Plan of Fort Real Felipe A142

Design: 15c, Docks and Custom House.

1936, Aug. 27 Photo. *Perf. 12½*

341 A132 2c black .75 .30
342 A133 4c bl grn .75 .30
343 A134 5c yel brn .75 .30
344 A135 10c bl gray .75 .30
345 A135 15c green .75 .30
346 A137 20c dk brn 1.00 .30
347 A138 50c purple 1.90 .55
348 A139 1s olive grn 12.00 1.75

Engr.

349 A140 2s violet 20.00 9.00
350 A141 5s carmine 27.50 19.00
351 A142 10s red org & brn 65.00 55.00
Nos. 341-351,C13 (12) 134.40 88.85

Province of Callao founding, cent.

Nos. 340, 321 and 323 Surcharged in Black

1936 *Perf. 13½, 13*

353 A131 2c on 4c bl grn .35 .25
a. "0.20" for "0.02" 4.25 4.25
354 A118 10c on 20c dp bl .35 .25
a. Double surcharge 4.25 4.25
b. Inverted surcharge 4.25 4.25
355 A119 10c on 1s dk vio .55 .55
Nos. 353-355 (3) 1.25 1.05

Many varieties of the surcharge are found on these stamps: no period after "S," no period after "Cts," period after "2," "S" omitted, various broken letters, etc.

The surcharge on No. 355 is horizontal.

Peruvian Cormorants (Guano Deposits) — A143

Oil Well at Talara — A144

Avenue of the Republic, Lima A146

San Marcos University at Lima A148

Post Office, Lima — A149

Viceroy Manuel de Amat y Junyent — A150

Designs: 10c, "El Chasqui" (Inca Courier). 20c, Municipal Palace and Museum of Natural History. 5s, Joseph A. de Pando y Riva. 10s, Dr. José Dávila Condemarin.

1936-37 Photo. *Perf. 12½*

356 A143 2c lt brn .75 .30
357 A143 2c grn ('37) 1.00 .30
358 A144 4c blk brn .75 .30
359 A144 4c int blk ('37) .45 .30
360 A143 10c crimson .45 .30
361 A143 10c ver ('37) .35 .30
362 A146 15c ultra .90 .30
363 A146 15c brt bl ('37) .45 .30
364 A146 20c black .90 .30
365 A146 20c blk brn ('37) .35 .30
366 A148 50c org yel 3.25 .85
367 A148 50c dk gray vio ('37) 1.00 .30
368 A149 1s brn vio 6.50 1.10
369 A149 1s ultra ('37) 1.90 .30

Engr.

370 A150 2s ultra 13.00 2.75
371 A150 2s dk vio ('37) 4.50 .85
372 A150 5s slate bl 13.00 2.75
373 A150 10s dk vio & brn 75.00 37.50
Nos. 356-373 (18) 124.50 49.40

No. 370 Surcharged in Black

1937

374 A150 1s on 2s ultra 3.25 3.25

Children's Holiday Center, Ancón — A153

Chavin Pottery — A154

Highway Map of Peru — A155

Archaeological Museum, Lima — A156

Industrial Bank of Peru — A157

Worker's Houses, Lima — A158

Toribio de Luzuriaga A159

Historic Fig Tree A160

Idol from Temple of Chavin — A161

Mt. Huascarán — A162

Imprint: "Waterlow & Sons Limited, Londres"

1938, July 1 Photo. *Perf. 12½, 13*

375 A153 2c emerald .25 .25
376 A154 4c org brn .25 .25
377 A155 10c scarlet .35 .25
378 A156 15c ultra .40 .25
379 A157 20c magenta .25 .25
380 A158 50c greenish blue .50 .25
381 A159 1s dp claret 1.60 .25
382 A160 2s green 6.50 .25

Engr.

383 A161 5s dl vio & brn 13.00 .75
384 A162 10s blk & ultra 27.50 1.25
Nos. 375-384 (10) 50.60 4.00

See Nos. 410-418, 426-433, 438-441. For surcharges see Nos. 388, 406, 419, 445-446A, 456, 758. Post 1940 listings are in Scott Standard catalogue, Vol. 5.

Palace Square A163

Lima Coat of Arms A164

Government Palace — A165

1938, Dec. 9 Photo. *Perf. 12½*

385 A163 10c slate green .65 .45

Engraved and Lithographed

386 A164 15c blk, gold, red & bl 1.10 .55

Photo.

387	A165	1s olive	2.75	1.60
		Nos. 385-387,C62-C64 (6)	9.30	5.90

8th Pan-American Conf., Lima, Dec. 1938.

No. 377 Surcharged in Black

1940 ***Perf. 13***

388	A155	5c on 10c scarlet	.25	.25
a.		Inverted surcharge		

AIR POST STAMPS

No. 248 Overprinted in Black

1927, Dec. 10 **Unwmk.** ***Perf. 12***

C1	A87	50c violet	50.00	26.00
a.		Inverted overprint	500.00	—

Two types of overprint: first printing, dull black ink; second printing, shiny black ink. Values are the same. No. C1a occurs in the first printing.

Counterfeits exist.

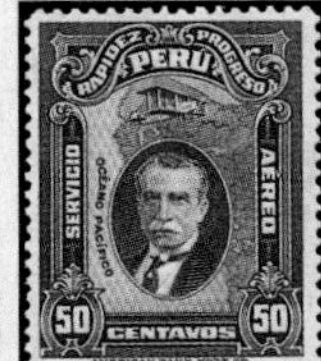

President Augusto Bernardino Leguía — AP1

1928, Jan. 12 **Engr.**

C2	AP1	50c dark green	1.10	.55

For surcharge see No. 263.

Coat of Arms of Piura Type

1932, July 28 **Litho.**

C3	A107	50c scarlet	26.00	22.50

Counterfeits exist.

Airplane in Flight — AP3

1934, Feb. **Engr.** ***Perf. 12½***

C4	AP3	2s blue	6.50	.60
C5	AP3	5s brown	15.00	1.25

For surcharges see Nos. C14-C15.

Funeral of Atahualpa AP4

Palace of Torre-Tagle AP7

Designs: 35c, Mt. San Cristobal. 50c, Avenue of Barefoot Friars. 10s, Pizarro and the Thirteen.

1935, Jan. 18 **Photo.** ***Perf. 13½***

C6	AP4	5c emerald	.35	.25
C7	AP4	35c brown	.45	.45
C8	AP4	50c orange yel	.90	.75
C9	AP4	1s plum	1.75	1.25
C10	AP7	2s red orange	2.75	2.40
C11	AP4	5s dp claret	11.00	7.00
C12	AP4	10s dk blue	45.00	30.00
		Nos. C6-C12 (7)	62.20	42.10

4th centenary of founding of Lima.

Nos. C6-C12 overprinted "Radio Nacional" are revenue stamps.

"La Callao," First Locomotive in South America AP9

1936, Aug. 27 ***Perf. 12½***

C13	AP9	35c gray black	3.25	1.75

Founding of the Province of Callao, cent.

Nos. C4-C5 Surcharged "Habilitado" and New Value, like Nos. 353-355

1936, Nov. 4

C14	AP3	5c on 2s blue	.55	.30
C15	AP3	25c on 5s brown	1.10	.55
a.		Double surcharge	14.00	14.00
b.		No period btwn. "O" & "25 Cts"	1.60	1.60
c.		Inverted surcharge	21.00	

There are many broken letters in this setting.

Mines of Peru AP10

Jorge Chávez AP14

Aerial View of Peruvian Coast AP16

View of the "Sierra" — AP17

St. Rosa of Lima — AP22

Designs: 5c, La Mar Park, Lima. 15c, Mail Steamer "Inca" on Lake Titicaca. 20c, Native Queña (flute) Player and Llama. 30c, Ram at Model Farm, Puno. 1s, Train in Mountains. 1.50s, Jorge Chavez Aviation School. 2s, Transport Plane. 5s, Aerial View of Virgin Forests.

1936-37 **Photo.** ***Perf. 12½***

C16	AP10	5c brt green	.35	.25
C17	AP10	5c emer ('37)	.35	.25
C18	AP10	15c lt ultra	.55	.25
C19	AP10	15c blue ('37)	.35	.25
C20	AP10	20c gray blk	1.50	.25
C21	AP10	20c pale ol grn ('37)	1.00	.30
C22	AP14	25c mag ('37)	.45	.25
C23	AP10	30c henna brn	4.75	1.10
C24	AP10	30c dk ol brn ('37)	1.50	.25
C25	AP14	35c brown	2.75	2.25
C26	AP10	50c yellow	.45	.30
C27	AP10	50c brn vio ('37)	.65	.25
C28	AP16	70c Prus grn	5.50	5.00
C29	AP16	70c pck grn ('37)	1.00	.85
C30	AP17	80c brn blk	6.50	5.00
C31	AP17	80c ol blk ('37)	1.25	.55
C32	AP10	1s ultra	4.75	.45
C33	AP10	1s red brn ('37)	2.40	.30
C34	AP14	1.50s red brn	7.75	6.00
C35	AP14	1.50s org yel ('37)	4.75	.45
		Engr.		
C36	AP10	2s deep blue	13.00	7.75
C37	AP10	2s yel grn ('37)	9.25	.80
C38	AP16	5s green	17.00	3.75
C39	AP22	10s car & brn	125.00	110.00
		Nos. C16-C39 (24)	212.80	146.85

Nos. C23, C25, C28, C30, C36 Surcharged in Black or Red

1936, June 26

C40	AP10	15c on 30c hn brn	.65	.45
C41	AP14	15c on 35c brown	.65	.45
C42	AP16	15c on 70c Prus grn	4.50	3.50
C43	AP17	25c on 80c brn blk (R)	4.50	3.50
C44	AP10	1s on 2s dp bl	7.75	6.50
		Nos. C40-C44 (5)	18.05	14.40

Surcharge on No. C43 is vertical, reading down.

First Flight in Peru, 1911 — AP23

Jorge Chávez — AP24

Airport of Limatambo at Lima — AP25

Map of Aviation Lines from Peru — AP26

Designs: 10c, Juan Bielovucic (1889-?) flying over Lima race course, Jan. 14, 1911. 15c, Jorge Chavez-Dartnell (1887-1910), French-born Peruvian aviator who flew from Brixen to Domodossola in the Alps and died of plane-crash injuries.

1937, Sept. 15 **Engr.** ***Perf. 12***

C45	AP23	10c violet	.65	.25
C46	AP24	15c dk green	.90	.25
C47	AP25	25c gray brn	.65	.25
C48	AP26	1s black	3.00	2.10
		Nos. C45-C48 (4)	5.20	2.85

Inter-American Technical Conference of Aviation, Sept. 1937.

Government Restaurant at Callao — AP27

Monument on the Plains of Junin — AP28

Rear Admiral Manuel Villar — AP29

View of Tarma — AP30

Dam, Ica River — AP31

View of Iquitos AP32

Highway and Railroad Passing AP33

Mountain Road — AP34

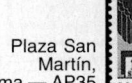

Plaza San Martín, Lima — AP35

National Radio of Peru AP36

Stele from Chavin Temple AP37

Ministry of Public Works, Lima — AP38

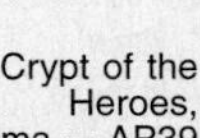

Crypt of the Heroes, Lima — AP39

Imprint: "Waterlow & Sons Limited, Londres."

1938, July 1 Photo. *Perf. 12½, 13*

C49 AP27 5c violet brn .25 .25
C50 AP28 15c dk brown .25 .25
C51 AP29 20c dp magenta .55 .30
C52 AP30 25c dp green .25 .25
C53 AP31 30c orange .25 .25
C54 AP32 50c green .45 .30
C55 AP33 70c slate bl .65 .30
C56 AP34 80c olive 1.25 .30
C57 AP35 1s slate grn 10.00 4.25
C58 AP36 1.50s purple 2.25 .30

Engr.

C59 AP37 2s ind & org brn 3.75 .95
C60 AP38 5s brown 18.00 1.75
C61 AP39 10s ol grn & ind 70.00 37.50
Nos. C49-C61 (13) 107.90 46.95

See Nos. C73-C75, C89-C93, C103 in Scott Standard catalogue, Vol. 5.
For surcharges see Nos. C65, C76-C77, C82-C88, C108 in Scott Vol. 5.

Torre-Tagle Palace — AP40

National Congress Building — AP41

Manuel Ferreyros, José Gregorio Paz Soldán and Antonio Arenas — AP42

1938, Dec. 9 Photo. *Perf. 12½*

C62 AP40 25c brt ultra .90 .65
C63 AP41 1.50s brown vio 2.40 1.90
C64 AP42 2s black 1.50 .75
Nos. C62-C64 (3) 4.80 3.30

8th Pan-American Conference at Lima.

SPECIAL DELIVERY STAMPS

No. 149 Overprinted in Black

1908 Unwmk. *Perf. 12*

E1 A25 10c gray black 25.00 19.00

No. 172 Overprinted in Violet

1909

E2 A40 10c red brn & blk 40.00 22.50

No. 181 Handstamped in Violet

1910

E3 A49 10c deep blue 24.00 20.00

Two handstamps were used to make No. E2. Impressions from them measure 22½x6½mm and 24x6½mm.
Counterfeits exist of Nos. E1-3.

POSTAGE DUE STAMPS

Coat of Arms — D1

Steamship and Llama
D2 D3

D4 D5

With Grill

1874-79 Unwmk. Engr. *Perf. 12*

J1 D1 1c bister ('79) .45 .30
On cover, postage due usage 1,000.
On cover, postage usage 500.
J2 D2 5c vermilion .55 .30
On cover, postage due usage 350.
On cover, postage usage 500.
J3 D3 10c orange .65 .30
On cover, postage due usage 350.
On cover, postage usage 500.
J4 D4 20c blue 1.10 .55
On cover, postage due usage 750.
On cover, postage usage —
J5 D5 50c brown 17.00 6.50
On cover, postage due usage 1,000.
On cover, postage usage —
Nos. J1-J5 (5) 19.75 7.95

A 2c green exists, but was not regularly issued.
For overprints and surcharges see Nos. 157, J6-J31, J37-J38, 8N14-8N15, 14N18.

1902-07 Without Grill

J1a D1 1c bister .35
On cover, postage due usage 250.00
On cover, postage usage 250.00
J2a D2 5c vermilion .55
On cover, postage due usage 250.00
On cover, postage usage 250.00
J3a D3 10c orange .55
On cover, postage due usage 500.00
On cover, postage usage 250.00
J4a D4 20c blue .65
On cover, postage due usage 500.00
On cover, postage usage —
Nos. J1a-J4a (4) 2.10

Nos. J1-J5 Overprinted in Blue or Red

1881 "PLATA" 2½mm High

J6 D1 1c bis (Bl) 6.00 5.00
J7 D2 5c ver (Bl) 12.00 11.00
a. Double overprint
b. Inverted overprint 24.00 24.00
J8 D3 10c org (Bl) 12.00 11.00
a. Inverted overprint 24.00 24.00
J9 D4 20c bl (R) 45.00 32.50
J10 D5 50c brn (Bl) 100.00 90.00
Nos. J6-J10 (5) 175.00 149.50

In the reprints of this overprint "PLATA" is 3mm high instead of 2½mm. Besides being struck in the regular colors it was also applied to the 1, 5, 10 and 50c in red and the 20c in blue.

Overprinted in Red

1881

J11 D1 1c bister 9.00 9.00
J12 D2 5c vermilion 11.00 10.00
J13 D3 10c orange 13.00 13.00
J14 D4 20c blue 55.00 37.50
J15 D5 50c brown 125.00 125.00
Nos. J11-J15 (5) 213.00 194.50

Originals of Nos. J11 to J15 are overprinted in brick-red, oily ink; reprints in thicker, bright red ink. The 5c exists with reprinted overprint in blue.

Overprinted "Union Postal Universal Lima Plata" in Oval in first named color and Triangle in second named color

1883

J16 D1 1c bis (Bl & Bk) 9.00 6.50
J17 D1 1c bis (Bk & Bl) 13.00 13.00
J18 D2 5c ver (Bl & Bk) 13.00 13.00
On cover, postage due usage —
On cover, postage usage 500.00
J19 D3 10c org (Bl & Bk) 13.00 13.00
On cover, postage due usage —
On cover, postage usage 500.00
J20 D4 20c bl (R & Bk) *850.00 850.00*
On cover, postage due usage —
On cover, postage usage 500.00
J21 D5 50c brn (Bl & Bk) 60.00 60.00

Reprints of Nos. J16 to J21 have the oval overprint with "PLATA" 3mm. high. The 1c also exists with the oval overprint in red.

Overprinted in Black

1884

J22 D1 1c bister .90 .90
On cover, postage due usage 500.00
On cover, postage usage 500.00
J23 D2 5c vermilion .90 .90
On cover, postage due usage 250.00
On cover, postage usage 250.00
J24 D3 10c orange .90 .90
On cover, postage due usage 250.00
On cover, postage usage 350.00
J25 D4 20c blue 1.90 .90
On cover, postage due usage 500.00
On cover, postage usage 500.00
J26 D5 50c brown 5.50 1.75
On cover, postage due usage 500.00
On cover, postage usage —
Nos. J22-J26 (5) 10.10 5.35

The triangular overprint is found in 11 types.

Overprinted "Lima Correos" in Circle in Red and Triangle in Black

1884

J27 D1 1c bister 42.50 42.50

Reprints of No. J27 have the overprint in bright red. At the time they were made the overprint was also printed on the 5, 10, 20 and 50c Postage Due stamps.
Postage Due stamps overprinted with Sun and "CORREOS LIMA" (as shown above No. 103), alone or in combination with the "U. P. U. LIMA" oval or "LIMA CORREOS" in double-lined circle, are fancy varieties made to sell to collectors and never placed in use.

Overprinted

1896-97

J28 D1 1c bister .65 .55
On cover, postage due usage 500.00
On cover, postage usage —
a. Double overprint
J29 D2 5c vermilion .75 .45
On cover, postage due usage 500.00
On cover, postage usage 150.00
a. Double overprint
b. Inverted overprint
J30 D3 10c orange 1.00 .65
On cover, postage due usage 500.00
On cover, postage usage 300.00
a. Inverted overprint
J31 D4 20c blue 1.25 .85
On cover, postage due usage 500.00
On cover, postage usage 300.00
a. Double overprint
J32 A22 50c red ('97) 1.25 .85
On cover, postage due usage 750.00
On cover, postage usage —
J33 A23 1s brown ('97) 1.90 1.25
On cover, postage due usage 750.00
On cover, postage usage —
a. Double overprint
b. Inverted overprint
Nos. J28-J33 (6) 6.80 4.60

Liberty — D6

1899 Engr.

J34 D6 5s yel grn 1.90 *10.50*
J35 D6 10s dl vio 1,700. 1,700.

For surcharge see No. J39.

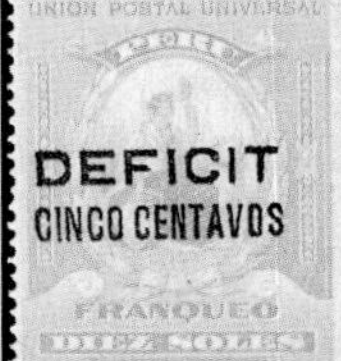

No. J36

No. J37

1902 On No. 159

J36 A31 5c on 10s bl grn 1.90 1.50
a. Double surcharge 20.00 20.00

On No. J4

J37 D4 1c on 20c blue 1.10 .75
On cover, postage due usage 750.00
On cover, postage usage —
a. "DEFICIT" omitted 15.00 3.50
b. "DEFICIT" double 15.00 3.50
c. "UN CENTAVO" double 15.00 3.50

d. "UN CENTAVO" omitted 18.00 10.00

Surcharged Vertically

J38 D4 5c on 20c blue 2.75 1.75

No. J35 Surcharged Diagonally

J39 D6 1c on 10s dull vio .75 .75
Nos. J36-J39 (4) 6.50 4.75

D7

1909 Engr. *Perf. 12*

J40 D7 1c red brown .90 .30
On cover, postage due usage 100.00
On cover, postage usage 20.00
J41 D7 5c red brown .90 .30
On cover, postage due usage 50.00
On cover, postage usage 10.00
J42 D7 10c red brown 1.10 .45
On cover, postage due usage 50.00
On cover, postage usage 10.00
J43 D7 50c red brown 1.75 .45
On cover, postage due usage 200.00
On cover, postage usage 30.00
Nos. J40-J43 (4) 4.65 1.50

1921 Size: 18¼x22mm

J44 D7 1c violet brown .45 .30
On cover, postage due usage 100.00
On cover, postage usage 20.00
J45 D7 2c violet brown .45 .30
On cover, postage due usage 50.00
On cover, postage usage 10.00
J46 D7 5c violet brown .65 .30
On cover, postage due usage 50.00
On cover, postage usage 10.00
J47 D7 10c violet brown .90 .45
On cover, postage due usage 50.00
On cover, postage usage 10.00
J48 D7 50c violet brown 2.75 1.25
On cover, postage due usage 200.00
On cover, postage usage 30.00
J49 D7 1s violet brown 13.00 5.25
On cover, postage due usage —
On cover, postage usage 30.00
J50 D7 2s violet brown 22.50 6.50
On cover, postage due usage —
On cover, postage usage 30.00
Nos. J44-J50 (7) 40.70 14.35

Nos. J49 and J50 have the circle at the center replaced by a shield containing "S/.", in addition to the numeral.

In 1929 during a shortage of regular postage stamps, some of the Postage Due stamps of 1921 were used instead.

See Nos. J50A-J52, J55-J56. For surcharges see Nos. 204-207, 757 (in Scott Standard catalogue, Vol. 5).

Type of 1909-22
Size: 18¾x23mm

J50A D7 2c violet brown 1.25 .30
On cover, postage due usage 50.00
On cover, postage usage 10.00
J50B D7 10c violet brown 1.75 .45
On cover, postage due usage 50.00
On cover, postage usage 10.00

Type of 1909-22 Issues

1932 Photo. *Perf. 14½x14*

J51 D7 2c violet brown 1.25 .45
On cover, postage due usage 50.00
On cover, postage usage 10.00
J52 D7 10c violet brown 1.25 .45
On cover, postage due usage 50.00
On cover, postage usage 10.00

Regular Stamps of 1934-35 Overprinted in Black

1935 *Perf. 13*

J53 A131 2c deep claret 1.25 .50
On cover, postage due usage 100.00
On cover, postage usage —
J54 A117 10c crimson 1.25 .50
On cover, postage due usage 100.00
On cover, postage usage —

Type of 1909-32
Size: 19x23mm
Imprint: "Waterlow & Sons, Limited, Londres."

1936 Engr. *Perf. 12½*

J55 D7 2c light brown .45 .45
On cover, postage due usage 50.00
On cover, postage usage 100.00
J56 D7 10c gray green .90 .90
On cover, postage due usage 50.00
On cover, postage usage 100.00

OFFICIAL STAMPS

Regular Issue of 1886 Overprinted in Red

1890, Feb. 2

O2 A17 1c dl vio 2.40 2.40
On cover 150.00
a. Double overprint 14.00 14.00
O3 A18 2c green 2.40 2.40
On cover 150.00
a. Double overprint
b. Inverted overprint 14.00 14.00
O4 A19 5c orange 3.50 2.75
On cover 150.00
a. Inverted overprint 14.00 14.00
b. Double overprint 14.00 14.00
O5 A20 10c slate 2.00 1.25
On cover 150.00
a. Double overprint 14.00 14.00
b. Inverted overprint 14.00 14.00
O6 A21 20c blue 5.50 3.50
On cover 200.00
a. Double overprint 14.00 14.00
b. Inverted overprint 14.00 14.00
O7 A22 50c red 7.25 3.25
a. Inverted overprint 20.00
b. Double overprint
O8 A23 1s brown 9.00 8.00
a. Double overprint 27.50 27.50
b. Inverted overprint 27.50 27.50
Nos. O2-O8 (7) 32.05 23.55

Nos. 118-124 (Bermudez Ovpt.) Overprinted Type "a" in Red

1894, Oct.

O9 A17 1c green 2.40 2.40
On cover 300.00
a. "Gobierno" and head invtd. 11.00 9.25
b. Dbl. ovpt. of "Gobierno"
O10 A17 1c orange 40.00 32.50
On cover 300.00
O11 A18 2c rose 2.40 2.40
On cover 300.00
a. Overprinted head inverted 17.00 17.00
b. Both overprints inverted
O12 A18 2c violet 2.40 2.40
On cover 300.00
a. "Gobierno" double
O13 A19 5c ultra 40.00 32.50
On cover 300.00
a. Both overprints inverted
O14 A19 5c blue 19.00 16.00
On cover 300.00
O15 A20 10c green 6.00 6.00
On cover 300.00
O16 A22 50c green 9.00 9.00
Nos. O9-O16 (8) 121.20 103.20

Nos. 125-126 ("Horseshoe" Ovpt.) Overprinted Type "a" in Red

O17 A18 2c vermilion 3.50 3.50
O18 A19 5c blue 3.50 3.50

Nos. 105, 107, 109, 113 Overprinted Type "a" in Red

1895, May

O19 A17 1c vermilion 13.00 13.00
On cover 300.00
O20 A18 2c dp ultra 13.00 13.00
On cover 300.00
O21 A12 5c claret 11.00 11.00
On cover 300.00
O22 A14 20c dp ultra 11.00 11.00
On cover 300.00
Nos. O19-O22 (4) 48.00 48.00

Nos. O2-O22 have been extensively counterfeited.

Nos. 141, 148, 149, 151 Overprinted in Black

1896-1901

O23 A24 1c ultra .35 .30
On cover 30.00
O24 A25 10c yellow 1.00 .50
On cover 30.00
a. Double overprint 22.50
O25 A25 10c gray blk ('01) .35 .30
On cover 30.00
O26 A26 50c brt rose 5.00 5.00
On cover 60.00
Nos. O23-O26 (4) 6.70 6.10

O1

1909-14 Engr. *Perf. 12*
Size: 18½x22mm

O27 O1 1c red .55 .30
On cover 30.00
a. 1c brown red .55 .30
On cover 30.00
O28 O1 1c orange ('14) .90 .65
On cover 30.00
O29 O1 10c bis brn ('14) .35 .30
On cover 30.00
a. 10c violet brown .90 .45
On cover 30.00
O30 O1 50c ol grn ('14) 1.25 .65
On cover 60.00
a. 50c blue green 2.00 .65
On cover 60.00

Size: 18¾x23½mm

O30B O1 10c vio brn .90 .30
On cover 30.00
Nos. O27-O30B (5) 3.95 2.20

See Nos. O31, O33-O34. For overprints and surcharge see Nos. 201-203, 760 (in Scott Standard catalogue, Vol. 5).

1933 Photo. *Perf. 15x14*

O31 O1 10c violet brown 1.25 .45
On cover 40.00

No. 319 Overprinted in Black

1935 Unwmk. *Perf. 13*

O32 A117 10c crimson .35 .25
On cover 40.00

Type of 1909-33
Imprint: "Waterlow & Sons, Limited, Londres."

1936 Engr. *Perf. 12½*
Size: 19x23mm

O33 O1 10c light brown .25 .25
On cover 60.00
O34 O1 50c gray green .65 .65
On cover 60.00

PARCEL POST STAMPS

PP1

PP2

PP3

1897 Typeset Unwmk. *Perf. 12*

Q1 PP1 1c dull lilac 4.00 3.50
Q2 PP2 2c bister 5.50 3.75
a. 2c olive 5.50 3.75
b. 2c yellow 5.50 3.75
c. Laid paper 65.00 65.00
Q3 PP3 5c dk bl 19.00 10.50
a. Tête bêche pair *375.00*
Q4 PP3 10c vio brn 24.00 18.00
Q5 PP3 20c rose red 29.00 22.50
Q6 PP3 50c bl grn 85.00 75.00
Nos. Q1-Q6 (6) 166.50 133.25

Surcharged in Black

1903-04

Q7 PP3 1c on 20c rose red 12.00 10.00
Q8 PP3 1c on 50c bl grn 12.00 10.00
Q9 PP3 5c on 10c vio brn 80.00 65.00
a. Inverted surcharge 125.00 110.00
b. Double surcharge
Nos. Q7-Q9 (3) 104.00 85.00

POSTAL TAX STAMPS

Plebiscite Issues

These stamps were not used in Tacna and Arica (which were under Chilean occupation) but were used in Peru to pay a supplementary tax on letters, etc.

It was intended that the money derived from the sale of these stamps should be used to help defray the expenses of the plebiscite.

Morro Arica — PT1

Adm. Grau and Col. Bolognesi Reviewing Troops — PT2

Bolognesi Monument PT3

1925-26 Unwmk. Litho. *Perf. 12*

RA1 PT1 5c dp bl 2.75 .75
RA2 PT1 5c rose red 1.40 .55
RA3 PT1 5c yel grn 1.25 .55
RA4 PT2 10c brown 5.50 *22.50*
RA5 PT3 50c bl grn 35.00 17.00
Nos. RA1-RA5 (5) 45.90 41.35

PT4

1926

RA6	PT4 2c orange	1.10	.30

PT5

1927-28

RA7	PT5 2c dp org	1.10	.30
RA8	PT5 2c red brn	1.10	.30
RA9	PT5 2c dk bl	1.10	.30
RA10	PT5 2c gray vio	1.10	.30
RA11	PT5 2c bl grn ('28)	1.10	.30
RA12	PT5 20c red	5.50	1.75
	Nos. RA7-RA12 (6)	11.00	3.25

PT6

1928 **Engr.**

RA13	PT6 2c dk vio	.55	.25

The use of the Plebiscite stamps was discontinued July 26, 1929, after the settlement of the Tacna-Arica controversy with Chile.

For overprint see No. 261.

Unemployment Fund Issues

These stamps were required in addition to the ordinary postage, on every letter or piece of postal matter. The money obtained by their sale was to assist the unemployed.

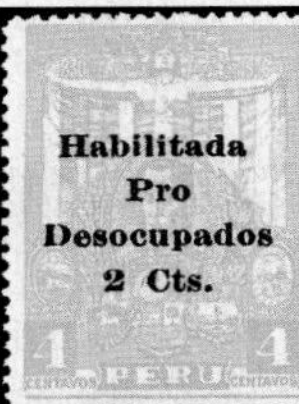

Nos. 273-275 Surcharged

1931

RA14	A95 2c on 4c red	1.75	.75
a.	Inverted surcharge	4.25	4.25
RA15	A95 2c on 10c bl grn	.75	.75
a.	Inverted surcharge	4.25	4.25
RA16	A95 2c on 15c sl gray	.75	.75
a.	Inverted surcharge	4.25	4.25
	Nos. RA14-RA16 (3)	3.25	2.25

"Labor" — PT7

Two types of Nos. RA17-RA18:
I — Imprint 15mm.
II — Imprint 13¾mm.

Perf. 12x11½, 11½x12

1931-32 **Litho.**

RA17	PT7 2c emer (I)	.25	.25
a.	Type II	.25	
RA18	PT7 2c rose car (I) ('32)	.25	.25
a.	Type II	.25	

Blacksmith — PT8

1932-34

RA19	PT8 2c dp gray	.25	.25
RA20	PT8 2c pur ('34)	.35	.25

Monument of 2nd of May — PT9

Perf. 13, 13½, 13x13½

1933-35 **Photo.**

RA21	PT9 2c bl vio	.25	.25
RA22	PT9 2c org ('34)	.25	.25
RA23	PT9 2c brn vio ('35)	.25	.25
	Nos. RA21-RA23 (3)	.75	.75

For overprint see No. RA27.

No. 307 Overprinted in Black

1934 ***Perf. 13½***

RA24	A111 2c green	.25	.25
a.	Inverted overprint	2.25	2.00

No. 339 Overprinted in Black

1935

RA25	A131 2c deep claret	.25	.25

No. 339 Overprinted Type "a" in Black

1936 **Unwmk.** ***Perf. 13½***

RA26	A131 2c deep claret	.25	.25

No. RA23 Overprinted in Black

1936 ***Perf. 13x13½***

RA27	PT9 2c brn vio	.25	.25
a.	Double overprint	3.50	
b.	Overprint reading down	3.50	
c.	Overprint double, reading down	3.50	

St. Rosa of Lima — PT10

1937 **Engr.** ***Perf. 12***

RA28	PT10 2c car rose	.25	.25

Nos. RA27 and RA28 represented a tax to help erect a church.

"Protection" by John Q. A. Ward — PT11

Imprint: "American Bank Note Company"

1938 **Litho.**

RA29	PT11 2c brown	.35	.25

The tax was to help the unemployed.

See Nos. RA30, RA34, RA40 in Scott Standard catalogue, Vol. 5.

OCCUPATION STAMPS

Issued under Chilean Occupation

Stamps formerly listed as Nos. N1-N10 are regular issues of Chile canceled in Peru.

Stamps of Peru, 1874-80, Overprinted in Red, Blue or Black

1881-82 ***Perf. 12***

N11	A17 1c org (Bl)	.50	1.00
a.	Inverted overprint		
N12	A18 2c dk vio (Bk)	.50	4.00
a.	Inverted overprint	16.50	
b.	Double overprint	22.50	
N13	A18 2c rose (Bk)	1.60	*18.00*
a.	Inverted overprint		
N14	A19 5c bl (R)	55.00	62.50
a.	Inverted overprint		
N15	A19 5c ultra (R)	90.00	100.00
N16	A20 10c grn (R)	.50	*1.60*
a.	Inverted overprint	6.50	6.50
b.	Double overprint	12.00	12.00
N17	A21 20c brn red (Bl)	80.00	125.00
	Nos. N11-N17 (7)	228.10	312.10

Reprints of No. N17 have the overprint in bright blue; on the originals it is in dull ultramarine. Nos. N11 and N12 exist with reprinted overprint in red or yellow. There are numerous counterfeits with the overprint in both correct and fancy colors.

Same, with Additional Overprint in Black

1882

N19	A17 1c grn (R)	.50	.80
a.	Arms inverted	8.25	10.00
b.	Arms double	5.50	6.50
c.	Horseshoe inverted	12.00	13.50
N20	A19 5c bl (R)	.80	.80
a.	Arms inverted	13.50	15.00
b.	Arms double	13.50	15.00
N21	A22 50c rose (Bk)	1.60	2.00
a.	Arms inverted	10.00	
N22	A22 50c rose (Bl)	1.60	2.75
N23	A23 1s ultra (R)	3.25	4.50
a.	Arms inverted	13.50	
b.	Horseshoe inverted	16.50	
c.	Arms and horseshoe inverted	20.00	
d.	Arms double	13.50	
	Nos. N19-N23 (5)	7.75	10.85

PROVISIONAL ISSUES

Stamps Issued in Various Cities of Peru during the Chilean Occupation of Lima and Callao

During the Chilean-Peruvian War which took place in 1879 to 1882, the Chilean forces occupied the two largest cities in Peru, Lima & Callao. As these cities were the source of supply of postage stamps, Peruvians in other sections of the country were left without stamps and were forced to the expedient of making provisional issues from whatever material was at hand. Many of these were former canceling devices made over for this purpose. Counterfeits exist of many of the overprinted stamps.

ANCACHS

(See Note under "Provisional Issues")

Regular Issue of Peru, Overprinted in Manuscript in Black

1884 **Unwmk.** ***Perf. 12***

1N1	A19 5c blue	57.50	55.00

Regular Issues of Peru, Overprinted in Black

1N2	A19 5c blue	18.00	16.50

Regular Issues of Peru, Overprinted in Black

1N3	A19 5c blue	90.00	82.50
1N4	A20 10c green	55.00	40.00
1N5	A20 10c slate	55.00	35.00

Same, with Additional Overprint "FRANCA"

1N6	A20 10c green	82.50	42.50

Overprinted

1N7	A19 5c blue	30.00	25.00
1N8	A20 10c green	30.00	25.00

Same, with Additional Overprint "FRANCA"

1N9	A20 10c green		

Revenue Stamp of Peru, 1878-79, Ovptd. in Black "CORREO Y FISCAL" or "FRANCA" — A1

1N10	A1 10c yellow	37.50	37.50

APURIMAC

(See Note under "Provisional Issues")

Provisional Issue of Arequipa Overprinted in Black

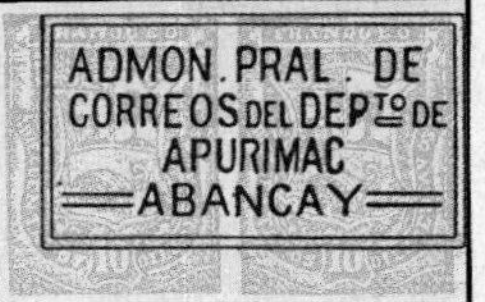

Overprint Covers Two Stamps

1885 **Unwmk.** ***Imperf.***

2N1	A6 10c gray	100.00	90.00

Some experts question the status of No. 2N1.

AREQUIPA

(See Note under "Provisional Issues")

Coat of Arms
A1 A2

Overprint ("PROVISIONAL 1881-1882") in Black

1881, Jan. Unwmk. *Imperf.*

3N1 A1 10c blue 2.50 3.50
a. 10c ultramarine 2.50 4.00
b. Double overprint 12.00 13.50
c. Overprinted on back of stamp 8.25 10.00
3N2 A2 25c rose 2.50 6.00
a. "2" in upper left corner invtd. 8.25
b. "Cevtavos" 8.25 10.00
c. Double overprint 12.00 13.50

The overprint also exists on 5s yellow.
The overprints "1883" in large figures or "Habilitado 1883" are fraudulent.
For overprints see Nos. 3N3, 4N1, 8N1, 10N1, 15N1-15N3.

With Additional Overprint Handstamped in Red

1881, Feb.

3N3 A1 10c blue 3.50 3.50
a. 10c ultramarine 13.50 11.50

A4

1883 Litho.

3N7 A4 10c dull rose 3.50 5.00
a. 10c vermilion 3.50 5.00

Overprinted in Blue like No. 3N3

3N9 A4 10c vermilion 5.00 4.00
a. 10c dull rose 5.00 4.00

See No. 3N10. For overprints see Nos. 8N2, 8N9, 10N2, 15N4.
Reprints of No. 3N9 are in different colors from the originals, orange, bright red, etc. They are printed in sheets of 20 instead of 25.

Redrawn

3N10 A4 10c brick red (Bl) 160.00

The redrawn stamp has small triangles without arabesques in the lower spandrels. The palm branch at left of the shield and other parts of the design have been redrawn.

Same Overprint in Black, Violet or Magenta On Regular Issues of Peru

1884 Embossed with Grill *Perf. 12*

3N11 A17 1c org (Bk, V or M) 6.50 6.50
3N12 A18 2c dk vio (Bk) 6.50 6.50
3N13 A19 5c bl (Bk, V or M) 2.00 1.40
a. 5c ultramarine (Bk or M) 8.25 6.50
3N15 A20 10c sl (Bk) 3.50 2.50
3N16 A21 20c brn red (Bk, V or M) 25.00 25.00
3N18 A22 50c grn (Bk or V) 25.00 25.00
3N20 A23 1s rose (Bk or V) 35.00 35.00
Nos. 3N11-3N20 (7) 103.50 101.90

A5 A6

Rear Admiral M. L. Grau
A7

Col. Francisco Bolognesi
A8

Same Overprint as on Previous Issues

1885 *Imperf.*

3N22 A5 5c olive (Bk) 5.25 5.25
3N23 A6 10c gray (Bk) 5.25 4.75
3N25 A7 5c blue (Bk) 5.25 4.75
3N26 A8 10c olive (Bk) 5.25 3.25
Nos. 3N22-3N26 (4) 21.00 18.00

For overprints see Nos. 2N1, 8N5-8N6, 8N12-8N13, 10N9, 10N12, 15N10-15N12.
These stamps have been reprinted without overprint; they exist however with forged overprint. Originals are on thicker paper with distinct mesh, reprints on paper without mesh.

Without Overprint

3N22a A5 5c olive 5.25 5.25
3N23a A6 10c gray 4.00 3.25
3N25a A7 5c blue 4.00 3.25
3N26a A8 10c olive 4.00 3.25
Nos. 3N22a-3N26a (4) 17.25 15.00

AYACUCHO

(See Note under "Provisional Issues")

Provisional Issue of Arequipa Overprinted in Black

1881 Unwmk. *Imperf.*

4N1 A1 10c blue 150.00 125.00
a. 10c ultramarine 150.00 125.00

CHACHAPOYAS

(See Note under "Provisional Issues")

Regular Issue of Peru Overprinted in Black

1884 Unwmk. *Perf. 12*

5N1 A19 5c ultra 190.00 160.00

CHALA

(See Note under "Provisional Issues")

Regular Issues of Peru Overprinted in Black

1884 Unwmk. *Perf. 12*

6N1 A19 5c blue 17.00 13.00
6N2 A20 10c slate 22.50 16.00

CHICLAYO

(See Note under "Provisional Issues")

Regular Issue of Peru Overprinted in Black

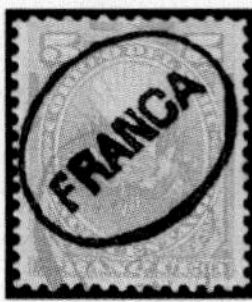

1884 Unwmk. *Perf. 12*

7N1 A19 5c blue 29.00 18.00

Same, Overprinted **FRANCA**

7N2 A19 5c blue 65.00 37.50

CUZCO

(See Note under "Provisional Issues")

Provisional Issues of Arequipa Overprinted in Black

1881-85 Unwmk. *Imperf.*

8N1 A1 10c blue 125.00 110.00
8N2 A4 10c red 125.00 110.00

Overprinted "CUZCO" in an oval of dots

8N5 A5 5c olive 200.00 175.00
8N6 A6 10c gray 200.00 175.00

Regular Issue of Peru Overprinted in Black "CUZCO" in a Circle

Perf. 12

8N7 A19 5c blue 50.00 50.00

Provisional Issues of Arequipa Overprinted in Black

1883 *Imperf.*

8N9 A4 10c red 18.00 18.00

Same Overprint in Black on Regular Issues of Peru

1884 *Perf. 12*

8N10 A19 5c blue 29.00 18.00
8N11 A20 10c slate 29.00 18.00

Same Overprint in Black on Provisional Issues of Arequipa

Imperf

8N12 A5 5c olive 27.50 27.50
8N13 A6 10c gray 8.00 8.00

Postage Due Stamps of Peru Surcharged in Black

Perf. 12

8N14 D1 10c on 1c bis 200.00 175.00
8N15 D3 10c on 10c org 200.00 175.00

HUACHO

(See Note under "Provisional Issues")

Regular Issues of Peru Overprinted in Black

1884 Unwmk. *Perf. 12*

9N1 A19 5c blue 16.00 16.00
9N2 A20 10c green 13.00 13.00
9N3 A20 10c slate 27.50 27.50
Nos. 9N1-9N3 (3) 56.50 56.50

MOQUEGUA

(See Note under "Provisional Issues")

Provisional Issues of Arequipa Overprinted in Violet

Overprint 27mm wide.

1881-83 Unwmk. *Imperf.*

10N1 A1 10c blue 75.00 70.00
10N2 A4 10c red ('83) 75.00 70.00

Same Overprint on Regular Issues of Peru in Violet

1884 *Perf. 12*

10N3 A17 1c orange 75.00 70.00
10N4 A19 5c blue 55.00 35.00

Red Overprint

10N5 A19 5c blue 65.00 55.00

Same Overprint in Violet on Provisional Issues of Peru of 1880

Perf. 12

10N6 A17 1c grn (R) 12.00 9.75
10N7 A18 2c rose (Bl) 15.00 15.00
10N8 A19 5c bl (R) 30.00 30.00

Same Overprint in Violet on Provisional Issue of Arequipa

1885 *Imperf.*

10N9 A6 10c gray 85.00 42.50

Regular Issues of Peru Overprinted in Violet

10N10 A19 5c blue 200.00 125.00
10N11 A20 10c slate 85.00 42.50

Same Overprint in Violet on Provisional Issue of Arequipa

Imperf

10N12 A6 10c gray 125.00 110.00

PAITA

(See Note under "Provisional Issues")

Regular Issues of Peru Overprinted

Black Overprint

1884 Unwmk. *Perf. 12*

11N1 A19 5c blue 40.00 40.00
a. 5c ultramarine 40.00 40.00
11N2 A20 10c green 27.50 27.50
11N3 A20 10c slate 40.00 40.00

Red Overprint

11N4 A19 5c blue 40.00 40.00

Overprint lacks ornaments on #11N4-11N5.

Violet Overprint Letters 5½mm High

11N5	A19	5c ultra	40.00	40.00
a.		5c blue		

PASCO

(See Note under "Provisional Issues")

Regular Issues of Peru Overprinted in Magenta or Black

1884		Unwmk.		*Perf. 12*
12N1	A19	5c blue (M)	27.50	12.50
a.		5c ultramarine (M)	42.50	22.50
12N2	A20	10c green (Bk)	65.00	55.00
12N3	A20	10c slate (Bk)	125.00	90.00
		Nos. 12N1-12N3 (3)	217.50	157.50

PISCO

(See Note under "Provisional Issues")

Regular Issue of Peru Overprinted in Black

1884		Unwmk.		*Perf. 12*
13N1	A19	5c blue	350.00	275.00

PIURA

(See Note under "Provisional Issues")

Regular Issues of Peru Overprinted in Black

1884		Unwmk.		*Perf. 12*
14N1	A19	5c blue	35.00	21.00
a.		5c ultramarine	45.00	27.50
14N2	A21	20c brn red	150.00	150.00
14N3	A22	50c green	350.00	350.00

Same Overprint in Black on Provisional Issues of Peru of 1881

14N4	A17	1c grn (R)	35.00	35.00
14N5	A18	2c rose (Bl)	55.00	55.00
14N6	A19	5c ultra (R)	70.00	70.00

Regular Issues of Peru Overprinted in Violet, Black or Blue **PIURA**

14N7	A19	5c bl (V)	27.50	18.00
a.		5c ultramarine (V)	27.50	18.00
b.		5c ultramarine (Bk)	27.50	18.00
14N8	A21	20c brn red (Bk)	150.00	150.00
14N9	A21	20c brn red (Bl)	150.00	150.00

Same Overprint in Black on Provisional Issues of Peru of 1881

14N10	A17	1c grn (R)	35.00	35.00
14N11	A19	5c bl (R)	42.50	42.50
a.		5c ultramarine (R)	70.00	70.00

Regular Issues of Peru Overprinted in Black

14N13	A19	5c blue	7.25	6.50
14N14	A21	20c brn red	150.00	150.00

Regular Issues of Peru Overprinted in Black

14N15	A19	5c ultra	110.00	100.00
14N16	A21	20c brn red	250.00	225.00

Same Overprint on Postage Due Stamp of Peru

14N18	D3	10c orange	125.00	125.00

PUNO

(See Note under "Provisional Issues")

Provisional Issue of Arequipa Overprinted in Violet or Blue

Diameter of outer circle 20½mm, PUNO 11½mm wide, M 3½mm wide.

Other types of this overprint are fraudulent.

1882-83		Unwmk.		*Imperf.*
15N1	A1	10c blue (V)	29.00	29.00
a.		10c ultramarine (V)	35.00	35.00
15N3	A2	25c red (V)	45.00	35.00
15N4	A4	10c dl rose (Bl)	29.00	29.00
a.		10c vermilion (Bl)	29.00	29.00

The overprint also exists on 5s yellow of Arequipa.

Same Overprint in Magenta on Regular Issues of Peru

1884				*Perf. 12*
15N5	A17	1c orange	19.00	15.00
15N6	A18	2c violet	65.00	65.00
15N7	A19	5c blue	10.00	10.00

Violet Overprint

15N8	A19	5c blue	10.00	10.00
a.		5c ultramarine	20.00	20.00

Same Overprint in Black on Provisional Issues of Arequipa

1885				*Imperf.*
15N10	A5	5c olive	16.00	13.50
15N11	A6	10c gray	10.00	10.00
15N12	A8	10c olive	19.00	19.00

Regular Issues of Peru Overprinted in Magenta

1884				*Perf. 12*
15N13	A17	1c orange	21.00	21.00
15N14	A18	2c violet	24.00	21.00
15N15	A19	5c blue	10.00	10.00
a.		5c ultramarine	20.00	20.00
15N16	A20	10c green	29.00	22.50
15N17	A21	20c brn red	150.00	150.00
15N18	A22	50c green		

YCA

(See Note under "Provisional Issues")

Regular Issues of Peru Overprinted in Violet

1884		Unwmk.		*Perf. 12*
16N1	A17	1c orange	70.00	70.00
16N3	A19	5c blue	22.50	18.00

Black Overprint

16N5	A19	5c blue	19.00	9.00

Magenta Overprint

16N6	A19	5c blue	19.00	9.00
16N7	A20	10c slate	55.00	55.00

Regular Issues of Peru Overprinted in Black

16N12	A19	5c blue	275.00	225.00
16N13	A21	20c brown	350.00	275.00

Regular Issues of Peru Overprinted in Carmine

16N14	A19	5c blue	275.00	225.00
16N15	A20	10c slate	350.00	275.00

Same, with Additional Overprint

16N21	A19	5c blue	275.00	275.00
16N22	A21	20c brn red	475.00	450.00

Various other stamps exist with the overprints "YCA" and "YCA VAPOR" but they are not known to have been issued. Some of them were made to fill a dealer's order and others are reprints or merely cancellations.

PHILIPPINES

ˌfi-lə-ˈpēnz

LOCATION — Group of about 7,100 islands and islets in the Malay Archipelago, north of Borneo, in the North Pacific Ocean

AREA — 115,830 sq. mi.

POP. — 53,350,000 (est. 1984)

CAPITAL — Quezon City

The islands were ceded to the United States by Spain in 1898. On November 15, 1935, they were given their independence, subject to a transition period which ended July 4, 1946.

20 Cuartos = 1 Real

100 Centavos de Peso = 1 Peso (1864)

100 Centimos de Escudo = 1 Escudo (1871)

100 Centimos de Peseta = 1 Peseta (1872)

1000 Milesimas de Peso = 100 Centimos or Centavos = 1 Peso (1878)

100 Cents = 1 Dollar (1899)

100 Centavos = 1 Peso (1906)

Watermarks

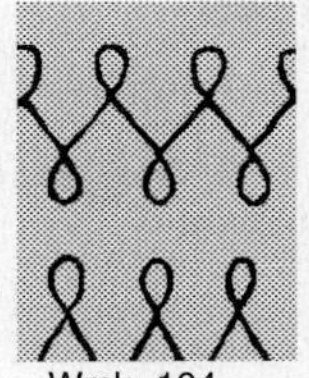

Wmk. 104 — Loops

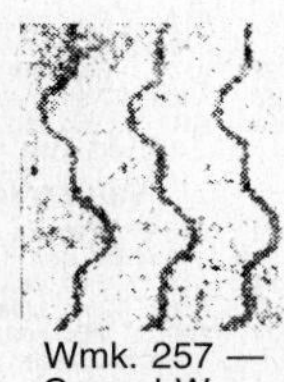

Wmk. 257 — Curved Wavy Lines

Watermark 104: loops from different watermark rows may or may not be directly opposite each other.

Wmk. 190PI — Single-lined PIPS

Wmk. 191PI — Double-lined PIPS

Watermark 191 has double-lined USPS.

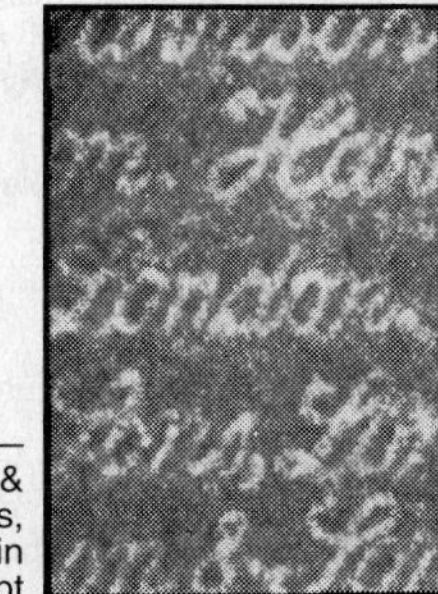

Wmk. 233 — "Harrison & Sons, London." in Script

Issued under Spanish Dominion

The stamps of Philippine Islands punched with a round hole were used on telegraph receipts or had been withdrawn from use and punched to indicate that they were no longer available for postage. In this condition they sell for less, as compared to postally used copies.

Many color varieties exist of Nos. 1-88. Only major varieties are listed.

Queen Isabella II
A1 A2

1854		Unwmk.	Engr.	*Imperf.*
1	A1	5c orange	4,000.	350.
		On cover		*3,000.*
2	A1	10c carmine	700.	250.
		On cover		*25,000.*
a.		10c pale rose	950.	400.
		As "a," on cover		*30,000.*
d.		10c carmine, half used as 5c on cover		50,000.
4	A2	1r blue	1,000.	300.
a.		1r slate blue	800.	300.
		On cover		—
c.		"CORROS" (#4, pos. 26)	4,500.	4,900.
d.		"CORROS" (#4a, pos. 26)	4,500.	4,000.
5	A2	2r slate green	1,000.	250.
		On cover		*50,000.*
a.		2r green	1,000.	750.

Forty plate varieties of each value. Many color varieties exist.

A 10c black exists. This is a proof or an unissued trial color. Value about $8,000.

For overprints see Nos. 24A-25A.

Covers: There are two covers recorded with No. 2; two with No. 2a; seven with No. 4 and shades; two with No. 5 and shades. Forged covers for Nos. 1-5 exist.

Values for pairs

1	A1	5c orange	5,000.	650.
2	A1	10c carmine	1,550.	525.
a.		10c pale rose	2,100.	875.
4	A2	1r blue	1,500.	600.
a.		1r slate blue	1,900.	825.
c.		"CORROS" (#4, pos. 26)	*7,250.*	*4,900.*
5	A2	2r slate green	2,300.	440.

Values for blocks of 4

1	A1	5c orange	16,500.	2,200.
2	A1	10c carmine	6,900.	1,550.
a.		10c pale rose	5,000.	2,200.
4	A2	1r blue	4,200.	1,650.
a.		1r slate blue	5,100.	3,500.
c.		"CORROS"(#4, pos. 26)	—	—
5	A2	2r slate green	6,500.	4,500.

A3

1855				Litho.
6	A3	5c pale red	1,600.	500.
		On cover		*8,000.*

Four varieties.

A3a

Redrawn

7 A3a 5c vermilion *7,000.* *1,100.*
On cover *45,000.*

In the redrawn stamp the inner circle is smaller and is not broken by the labels at top and bottom. Only one variety.

Covers: There are 10 covers recorded with singles of No. 6, two with pairs; four covers with No. 7, including one with a pair.

Values for pairs

6	A3	5c red	4,200.	1,600.
7	A3	5c vermilion	22,000.	—

Values for blocks of 4

6	A3	5c pale red	21,000.	7,000.
7	A3	5c vermilion	—	—

Queen Isabella II — A4

Blue Paper

1856 Typo. Wmk. 104

8 A4 1r green 100.00 *75.00*
On cover *200.00*
9 A4 2r carmine 400.00 200.00
On cover *700.00*

Nos. 8 and 9 used can be distinguished from Cuba Nos. 2 and 3 only by the cancellations.

For overprints, see Nos. 26-27.

Queen Isabella II — A5

Dot After "CORREOS"

1859, Jan. 1 Litho. Unwmk.

10 A5 5c vermilion 15.00 8.00
On cover 600.00
a. 5c scarlet 24.00 12.00
On cover 750.00
b. 5c orange 32.50 17.50
On cover 1,000.
11 A5 10c lilac rose 17.00 *35.00*
On cover 2,000.

Four varieties of each value, repeated in the sheet.

For overprint see No. 28.

Covers: Only two covers recorded bearing No. 11a.

Values for pairs

10	A5	5c vermilion	42.50	22.00
a.		5c scarlet	57.50	22.00
b.		5c orange	77.50	42.50
11	A5	10c lilac rose	40.00	*62.50*

Values for blocks of 4

10	A5	5c vermilion	87.50	47.50
a.		5c scarlet	120.00	65.00
b.		5c orange	160.00	95.00
11	A5	10c lilac rose	85.00	*1,900.*

Covers

Values are for commercial covers paying correct rates. Philatelic covers sell for less.

Dot after CORREOS
A6 A7

1861-62

12 A6 5c vermilion 40.00 40.00
On cover *4,000.*
13 A7 5c dull red ('62) 190.00 95.00
On cover *3,000.*

No. 12, one variety only, repeated in the sheet.

For overprint see No. 29.

Covers: There are about seven covers recorded with No. 12; 15 with No. 13.

Values for pairs

12	A6	5c vermilion	85.00	*92.50*
13	A7	5c dull red	475.00	240.00

Values for blocks of 4

12	A6	5c vermilion	190.00	*210.00*
13	A7	5c dull red	1,150.	600.00

Colon after CORREOS — A8

A8a

A9

1863

14 A8 5c vermilion 13.50 8.25
On cover *3,000.*
15 A8 10c carmine 37.50 *250.00*
16 A8 1r violet 850.00 *3,000.*
17 A8 2r blue 650.00 *2,000.*
18 A8a 1r gray grn 500.00 140.00
On cover *3,000.*
a. 1r deep gray green 350.00 175.00
On cover 3,500.
20 A9 1r green 200.00 60.00
On cover 2,000.
Nos. 14-20 (6) 2,251. 5,458.

No. 18 has "CORREOS" 10½mm long, the point of the bust is rounded and is about 1mm from the circle which contains 94 pearls.

No. 20 has "CORREOS" 11mm long, and the bust ends in a sharp point which nearly touches the circle of 76 pearls.

For overprints see Nos. 30-34.

Values for pairs

14	A8	5c vermilion	55.00	15.00
15	A8	10ccarmine	105.00	—
16	A8	1r violet	1,700.	—
17	A8	2r blue	1,450.	—
18	A8a	1r gray grn	700.00	300.00
a.		1r deep gray green	750.00	375.00
20	A9	1r green	375.00	110.00

Values for blocks of 4

14	A8	5c vermilion	100.00	60.00
15	A8	10ccarmine	225.00	*400.00*
16	A8	1r violet	3,750.	*3,900.*
17	A8	2r blue	3,250.	3,000.
18	A8a	1r gray grn	1,600.	775.00
a.		1r deep gray green	1,750.	1,000.
20	A9	1r green	875.00	300.00

A10

1864 Typo.

21 A10 3 1/8c blk, *yellow* 4.75 2.00
On cover 400.00
a. 3 1/8c blk, *buff* 7.00 3.75
On cover 400.00
22 A10 6 2/8c grn, *rose* 6.75 2.00
On cover 500.00
23 A10 12 4/8c blue, *sal* 9.00 1.75
On cover 200.00
24 A10 25c red, *buff* 12.00 3.75
On cover 700.00
a. 25c red, *rose* 17.50 7.25
On cover *800.00*
Nos. 21-24 (4) 32.50 9.50

For overprints see Nos. 35-38.

Values for pairs

21	A10	3 1/8c blk, *yellow*	9.50	6.50
a.		3 1/8c blk, *buff*	18.50	11.00
22	A10	6 2/8c grn, *rose*	16.00	7.00
23	A10	12 4/8c blue, *sal*	18.50	6.00
24	A10	25c red, *buff*	25.00	11.00
a.		25c red, *rose*	45.00	21.00

Values for blocks of 4

21	A10	3 1/8c blk, *yellow*	22.50	16.00
a.		3 1/8c blk, *buff*	42.50	27.50
22	A10	6 2/8c grn, *rose*	35.00	15.00
23	A10	12 4/8c blue, *sal*	42.50	13.50
24	A10	25c red, *buff*	55.00	26.00
a.		25c red, *rose*	100.00	50.00

Preceding Issues Handstamped

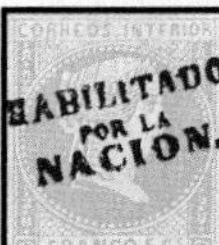

1868-74

24A A1 5c orange ('74) *8,000.* *6,750.*
25 A2 1r sl bl ('74) *2,800.* *1,050.*
b. "CORROS" (pos. 26) 4,500. *3,100.*
25A A2 2r grn ('74) *9,000.* *8,000.*
26 A4 1r grn, *bl* ('73) 180.00 80.00
27 A4 2r car, *bl* ('73) 325.00 225.00
27A A5 5c vermilion ('74) *8,000.* *10,000.*
28 A5 10c rose ('74) 80.00 45.00
29 A7 5c dull red ('73) 250.00 175.00
30 A8 5c ver ('72) 115.00 35.00
On cover *3,500.*
30A A8 10c car ('72) *6,000.* —
31 A8 1r vio ('72) 700.00 600.00
On cover *20,000.*
32 A8 2r bl ('72) 500.00 425.00
33 A8a 1r gray grn ('71) 175.00 85.00
34 A9 1r grn ('71) 50.00 30.00
On cover 800.00
35 A10 3 1/8c blk, *yellow* 9.50 4.75
On cover 400.00
36 A10 6 2/8c grn, *rose* 9.50 4.75
On cover 400.00
37 A10 12 4/8c bl, *salmon* 27.50 12.00
On cover 500.00
38 A10 25c red, *buff* 29.00 15.00
On cover 1,500.

Covers: There is one cover recorded with No. 31.

Reprints exist of #24A-38. These have crisp, sharp letters and usually have a broken first "A" of "HABILITADO."

Imperforates

Imperforates of designs A11-A16 probably are from proof or trial sheets.

"Spain" — A11

1871 Typo. *Perf. 14*

39 A11 5c blue 95.00 9.25
On cover 1,000.
40 A11 10c deep green 15.00 6.00
On cover 1,000.
41 A11 20c brown 110.00 50.00
On cover —
42 A11 40c rose 170.00 60.00
On cover —
Nos. 39-42 (4) 390.00 125.25

King Amadeo — A12

1872

43 A12 12c rose 20.00 5.50
On cover 400.00
44 A12 16c blue 190.00 37.50
On cover *5,000.*
45 A12 25c gray lilac 13.50 5.50
On cover 400.00
46 A12 62c violet 40.00 9.75
On cover 500.00
47 A12 1p25c yellow brn 85.00 42.50
On cover *3,000.*
Nos. 43-47 (5) 348.50 100.75

A 12c in deep blue and a 62c in rose exist but were not issued. Value $30 each.

Covers: There are two covers recorded with No. 47.

"Peace" — A13

1874

48 A13 12c gray lilac 22.50 5.50
On cover 600.00
49 A13 25c ultra 8.25 2.75
On cover 600.00
50 A13 62c rose 65.00 5.50
On cover 600.00
51 A13 1p25c brown 300.00 82.50
On cover *4,000.*
Nos. 48-51 (4) 395.75 96.25

King Alfonso XII — A14

1875-77

52 A14 2c rose 3.50 .95
On cover 400.00
53 A14 2c dk blue ('77) 260.00 100.00
On cover *2,500.*
54 A14 6c orange ('77) 14.00 *16.00*
On cover 1,000.
55 A14 10c blue ('77) 4.50 .85
On cover 400.00
56 A14 12c lilac ('76 4.50 .85
On cover 300.00
57 A14 20c vio brn ('76 20.00 5.00
On cover *3,000.*
58 A14 25c dp green ('76 25.00 5.00
On cover *3,000.*
Nos. 52-58 (7) 331.50 128.65

Imperforates of type A14 are from proof or trial sheets.

Nos. 52, 63 Handstamp Surcharged in Black or Blue

1877-79

59 A14 12c on 2c rose (Bk) 85.00 22.50
On cover *3,000.*
a. Surcharge inverted *600.00* *375.00*
b. Surcharge double *475.00* *350.00*
60 A16 12c on 25m blk (Bk) ('79) 105.00 47.50
On cover *4,000.*
a. Surcharge inverted *875.00* *650.00*
61 A16 12c on 25m blk (Bl) ('79) 350.00 225.00
On cover —
Nos. 59-61 (3) 540.00 295.00

Forgeries of Nos. 59-61 exist.

A16

1878-79 Typo.

62 A16 25m black 3.50 .45
On cover 300.00
63 A16 25m green ('79) 67.50 *62.50*
64 A16 50m dull lilac 34.00 10.00
On cover 400.00
65 A16 0.0625 (62½m) gray 65.00 15.00
66 A16 100m car ('79) 110.00 37.50
67 A16 100m yel grn ('79) 10.00 2.75
On cover 350.00
68 A16 125m blue 6.00 .50
On cover 250.00
69 A16 200m rose ('79) 37.50 5.75
On cover 400.00
70 A16 200m vio rose ('79) 350.00 *900.00*
On cover 5,000.
71 A16 250m bister ('79) 13.00 2.75
On cover 400.00
Nos. 62-71 (10) 696.50 *1,037.*

Imperforates of type A16 are from proof or trial sheets.

For surcharges see Nos. 60-61, 72-75.

Covers: There is one cover recorded with No. 70.

Stamps of 1878-79 Surcharged

a

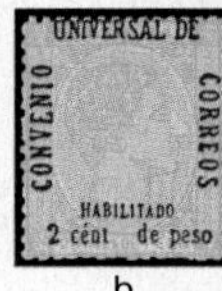

b

1879

72 A16 (a) 2c on 25m grn 55.00 11.00
b. Inverted surcharge 425.00 325.00
73 A16 (a) 8c on 100m car 52.50 6.50
On cover *2,000.*
a. "COREROS" 150.00 80.00
b. Surcharge double *400.00* —

74 A16 (b) 2c on 25m grn 300.00 57.50
75 A16 (b) 8c on 100m car 400.00 57.50
Nos. 72-75 (4) 807.50 132.50

Covers: There are four covers recorded with No. 73.

A19

Original state: The medallion is surrounded by a heavy line of color of nearly even thickness, touching the line below "Filipinas"; the opening in the hair above the temple is narrow and pointed.

1st retouch: The line around the medallion is thin, except at the upper right, and does not touch the horizontal line above it; the opening in the hair is slightly wider and rounded; the lock of hair above the forehead is shaped like a broad "V" and ends in a point; there is a faint white line below it, which is not found on the original. The shape of the hair and the width of the white line vary.

2nd retouch: The lock of hair is less pointed; the white line is much broader.

1880-86 Typo.

76 A19 2c carmine .90 *.80*
On cover 150.00
77 A19 2 1/2c brown 8.00 1.90
On cover 275.00
78 A19 2 4/8c ultra ('82) 1.25 2.25
On cover 200.00
79 A19 2 4/8c ultra, 1st retouch ('83) .90 1.90
On cover 300.00
80 A19 2 4/8c ultra, 2nd retouch ('86) 10.50 4.25
On cover 300.00
81 A19 5c gray blue ('82) .90 *1.90*
On cover 300.00
82 A19 6 2/8c dp grn ('82) 7.00 11.00
On cover *1,000.*
83 A19 8c yellow brn 36.00 6.25
On cover 200.00
84 A19 10c green 400.00 500.00
85 A19 10c brn lil ('82) 3.75 *4.25*
On cover 300.00
86 A19 12 4/8c brt rose ('82) 1.90 1.90
On cover 250.00
87 A19 20c bis brn ('82) 3.50 1.75
On cover 600.00
88 A19 25c dk brn ('82) 4.75 1.90
On cover 800.00
Nos. 76-88 (13) 479.35 540.05

See #137-139. For surcharges see #89-108, 110-111.

Surcharges exist double or inverted on many of Nos. 89-136. Several different surcharge types exist. There are many forgeries of the surcharges.

Stamps and Type of 1880-86 Handstamp Surcharged in Black, Green or Red

c

d

e

f

Design A19

1881-88 Black Surcharge

89 (c) 2c on 2 1/2c 4.25 2.25
On cover 300.00
91 (f) 10c on 2 4/8c (#80) ('87) 6.25 2.10
92 (d) 20c on 8c brn ('83) 10.00 3.25
93 (d) 1r on 2c ('83) 190.00 *325.00*
94 (d) 2r on 2 4/8c (#78; '83) 6.25 2.10
On cover *175.00*
a. On No. 79 57.50 *100.00*
b. On No. 80 110.00 *200.00*

Most used examples of No. 93 are hole punched. Postally used examples are rare.

Green Surcharge

95 (e) 8c on 2c ('83) 11.00 2.25
95A (d+e) 8c on 1r on 2c ('83) 200.00 *275.00*
96 (d) 10c on 2c ('83) 5.50 2.25
97 (d) 1r on 2c ('83) 190.00 *225.00*
98 (d) 1r on 5c gray bl ('83) 8.00 3.25
99 (d) 1r on 8c brn ('83) 10.00 3.25

Red Surcharge

100 (f) 1c on 2 4/8c (#79; '87) 1.25 *2.00*
101 (f) 1c on 2 4/8c (#80; '87) 3.50 3.00
102 (d) 16c on 2 4/8c (#78; '83) 10.00 3.25
103 (d) 1r on 2c ('83) 6.25 3.25
On cover 550.00
104 (d) 1r on 5c bl gray ('83) 12.00 5.25

Handstamp Surcharged in Magenta

g

h

1887

105 A19 (g) 8c on 2 4/8c (#79) 1.25 .90
On cover *200.00*
106 A19 (g) 8c on 2 4/8c (#80) 3.50 2.00
On cover *300.00*

1888

107 A19 (h) 2 4/8c on 1c gray grn 1.75 1.00
108 A19 (h) 2 4/8c on 5c bl gray 1.90 .90
109 N1 (h) 2 4/8c on 1/8c grn 1.90 1.40
110 A19 (h) 2 4/8c on 50m bis 1.90 .80
111 A19 (h) 2 4/8c on 10c grn 1.75 .65
Nos. 107-111 (5) 9.20 4.75

No. 109 is surcharged on a newspaper stamp of 1886-89 and has the inscriptions shown on cut N1.

On Revenue Stamps

R1

R2

R3(d)

Handstamp Surcharged in Black, Yellow, Green, Red, Blue or Magenta

j

k

m

1881-88 Black Surcharge

112 R1(c) 2c on 10c bis 50.00 12.50
113 R1(j) 2 4/8c on 10c bis 12.00 1.75
On cover *300.00*
114 R1(j) 2 4/8c on 2r bl 200.00 140.00
On cover *1,000.*
115 R1(j) 8c on 10c bis *450.00* *6,000.*
On cover *30,000.*
116 R1(j) 8c on 2r bl 8.50 2.10
On cover *500.00*
118 R1(d) 1r on 12 4/8c gray bl ('83) 7.75 3.75
On cover *600.00*
119 R1(d) 1r on 10c bis ('82) 11.50 4.00

One example of No. 115 on cover is reported.

Yellow Surcharge

120 R2(e) 2c on 200m grn ('82) 6.25 *8.00*
121 R1(d) 16c on 2r bl ('83) 6.00 *7.00*

Green Surcharge

122 R1(d) 1r on 10c bis ('83) 11.50 4.00

Red Surcharge

123 R1(d+e) 2r on 8c on 2r blue 55.00 35.00
a. On 8c on 2r blue (d+d) 80.00 75.00
124 R1(d) 1r on 12 4/8c gray bl ('83) 16.50 13.00
125 R1(k) 6 2/8c on 12 4/8c gray bl ('85) 5.00 *24.00*
126 R3(d) 1r on 10p bis ('83) 95.00 23.00
127 R1(m) 1r green 350.00 *700.00*
127A R1(m) 2r blue 900.00 *1,150.*
127B R1(d) 1r on 1r grn ('83) 700.00 *800.00*
128 R2(d) 1r on 1p grn ('83) 150.00 65.00
129 R2(d) 1r on 200m grn ('83) 600.00 *800.00*
129A R1(d) 2r on 2r blue *900.00* *900.00*

The surcharge on No. 129A is pale red.

Blue Surcharge

129B R1(m) 10c bister ('81) *700.00* —

Magenta Surcharge

130 R2(h) 2 4/8c on 200m grn ('88) 4.25 2.10
131 R2(h) 2 4/8c on 20c brn ('88) 12.50 5.75

On Telegraph Stamps

T1

T2

Surcharged in Red, or Black

1883-88

132 T1(d) 2r on 250m ultra (R) 7.75 3.00
133 T1(d) 20c on 250m ultra *750.00* 375.00
134 T1(d) 2r on 250m ultra 10.00 4.75
135 T1(d) 1r on 20c on 250m ultra (R & Bk) 9.25 3.75

Magenta Surcharge

136 T2(h) 2 4/8c on 1c bis ('88) .95 .90

Most, if not all, used stamps of No. 133 are hole-punched. Used value is for examples with hole punches.

Type of 1880-86 Redrawn

1887-89

137 A19 50m bister .65 *6.00*
On cover *500.00*
138 A19 1c gray grn ('88) .65 *5.00*
On cover *400.00*
a. 1c yellow green ('89) .70 *6.00*
On cover *500.00*
139 A19 6c yel brn ('88) 10.00 *47.50*
On cover —
Nos. 137-139 (3) 11.30 *58.50*

King Alfonso XIII — A36

1890-97 Typo.

140 A36 1c violet ('92) 1.00 .75
On cover *500.00*
141 A36 1c rose ('94) 17.50 *40.00*
142 A36 1c bl grn ('96) 2.25 1.00
On cover *500.00*
143 A36 1c claret ('97) 16.00 10.00
144 A36 2c claret ('94) .25 .25
On cover *100.00*
145 A36 2c violet ('92) .25 .25
On cover *100.00*
146 A36 2c dk brn ('94) .25 *3.50*
On cover *300.00*
147 A36 2c ultra ('96) .35 .35
On cover *100.00*
148 A36 2c gray brn ('96) .85 *2.25*
On cover *400.00*
149 A36 2 4/8c dull blue .55 .30
On cover *100.00*
150 A36 2 4/8c ol gray ('92) .30 *1.40*
On cover *400.00*
151 A36 5c dark blue .50 *1.40*
On cover *300.00*
152 A36 5c slate green .85 *1.40*
On cover *500.00*
153 A36 5c green ('92) .80 .55
On cover *300.00*
155 A36 5c vio brn ('96) 9.50 4.00
On cover *500.00*
a. 5c dk vio *750.00* *300.00*
156 A36 5c blue grn ('96) 6.00 3.00
157 A36 6c brown vio ('92) .30 *1.40*
158 A36 6c red orange ('94) .95 2.25
159 A36 6c car rose ('96) 6.00 4.00
160 A36 8c yellow grn .30 .30
On cover *600.00*
161 A36 8c ultra ('92) .75 .30
On cover *150.00*
162 A36 8c red brn ('94) .85 .30
On cover *150.00*
163 A36 10c blue grn 1.75 1.25
On cover *400.00*
164 A36 10c pale cl ('91) 1.60 .40
On cover *250.00*
165 A36 10c claret ('94) .75 .40
On cover *250.00*
166 A36 10c yel brn ('96) .85 .30
On cover *200.00*
167 A36 12 4/8c yellow grn .30 .25
On cover *400.00*
168 A36 12 4/8c org ('92) .85 .25
On cover *500.00*
169 A36 15c red brn ('92) .85 .30
On cover *150.00*
170 A36 15c rose ('94) 2.10 .75
On cover *400.00*
171 A36 15c bl grn ('96) 2.60 2.10
On cover *800.00*
172 A36 20c pale vermilion 30.00 *45.00*
174 A36 20c gray brn ('92) 2.75 .45
On cover *700.00*
175 A36 20c dk vio ('94) 15.00 8.00
On cover *600.00*
176 A36 20c org ('96) 4.50 2.25
On cover *500.00*

177 A36 25c brown 9.50 2.00
On cover *700.00*
178 A36 25c dull bl ('91) 2.50 .50
On cover *700.00*
179 A36 40c dk vio ('97) 13.50 *35.00*
180 A36 80c claret ('97) 30.00 40.00
Nos. 140-180 (39) 185.75 218.15

Many of Nos. 140-180 exist imperf and in different colors. These are considered to be proofs. Only major varieties are listed. Color varieties of most issues exist.

Stamps of Previous Issues Handstamp Surcharged in Blue, Red, Black or Violet

1897 **Blue Surcharge**

181 A36 5c on 5c green 2.00 *5.00*
On cover *2,500.*
182 A36 15c on 15c red brn 5.50 3.00
On cover *2,000.*
183 A36 20c on 20c gray brn 12.00 *12.00*

Red Surcharge

185 A36 5c on 5c green 4.50 4.75
On cover *2,500.*

Black Surcharge

187 A36 5c on 5c green 100.00 *300.00*
188 A36 15c on 15c rose 5.50 3.00
On cover *3,000.*
189 A36 20c on 20c dk vio 35.00 18.00
190 A36 20c on 25c brown 25.00 *40.00*

Violet Surcharge

191 A36 15c on 15c rose *15.00* *30.00*
On cover *3,000.*
Nos. 181-191 (9) 204.50 415.75

Inverted, double and other variations of this surcharge exist.

The 5c on 5c blue gray (#81a) was released during US Administration. The surcharge is a mixture of red and black inks.

Impressions in violet black are believed to be reprints. The following varieties are known: 5c on 2⅘c olive gray, 5c on 5c blue green, 5c on 25c brown, 15c on 15c rose, 15c on 15c red brown, 15c on 25c brown, 20c on 20c gray brown, 20c on 20c dark violet, 20c on 25c brown. Value: each $40. These surcharges are to be found double, inverted, etc.

King Alfonso XIII — A39

1898 **Typo.**

192 A39 1m orange brown .25 *1.25*
On cover *500.00*
193 A39 2m orange brown .25 *1.75*
On cover *600.00*
194 A39 3m orange brown .25 *1.75*
On cover *600.00*
195 A39 4m orange brown 13.00 *40.00*
On cover *2,000.*
196 A39 5m orange brown .25 *2.75*
On cover *300.00*
197 A39 1c black violet .25 *.60*
On cover *500.00*
198 A39 2c dk bl grn .25 *.60*
On cover *200.00*
199 A39 3c dk brown .25 *.60*
On cover *150.00*
200 A39 4c orange 20.00 *40.00*
201 A39 5c car rose .25 *.60*
On cover *500.00*
202 A39 6c dk blue 1.15 *1.75*
203 A39 8c gray brown .60 .35
On cover *100.00*
204 A39 10c vermilion 2.75 1.25
On cover *300.00*
205 A39 15c dull ol grn 2.25 1.10
On cover *400.00*
206 A39 20c maroon 2.50 1.60
On cover *600.00*
207 A39 40c violet 1.25 *1.75*
208 A39 60c black 6.00 4.00
209 A39 80c red brown 8.00 7.00
210 A39 1p yellow green 20.00 *10.00*
211 A39 2p slate blue 40.00 *12.00*
Nos. 192-211 (20) 119.50 *130.70*

One cliche of No. 197 was included in error within the sheet of Puerto Rico No. 140. Pairs showing this error se-tenant are known. See Puerto Rico No. 140b.

Nos. 192-211 exist imperf. Value, set $2,000.

Issued under U.S. Administration

Regular Issues of the United States Overprinted in Black

1899-1901 **Unwmk.** ***Perf. 12***

On U.S. Stamp No. 260

212 A96 50c orange 300. 225.
Never hinged 775.
On cover —

On U.S. Stamps Nos. 279, 279B, 279Bd, 279Bj, 279Bf, 279Bc, 268, 281, 282C, 283, 284, 275, 275a

Wmk. Double-lined USPS (191)

213 A87 1c yellow green 3.50 .60
Never hinged 10.00
On cover 10.00
214 A88 2c red, type IV 1.75 .60
Never hinged 4.25
On cover 10.00
a. 2c orange red, type IV, ('01) 1.75 .60
Never hinged 4.25
b. Bklt. pane of 6, red, type IV ('00) 200.00 *300.00*
Never hinged 450.00
c. 2c reddish carmine, type IV 2.50 1.00
Never hinged 6.00
On cover 12.50
d. 2c rose carmine, type IV 3.00 1.10
Never hinged 7.25
On cover 15.00
215 A89 3c purple 9.00 1.25
Never hinged 21.50
On cover 50.00
216 A91 5c blue 9.00 1.00
Never hinged 21.50
On cover 20.00
a. Inverted overprint *6,500.*

No. 216a is valued in the grade of fine.

217 A94 10c brown, type I 35.00 4.00
Never hinged 80.00
On cover 100.00
217A A94 10c orange brown, type II 125.00 27.50
Never hinged 325.00
On cover 250.00

No. 217A was overprinted on U.S. No. 283a, vertical watermark.

218 A95 15c olive green 40.00 8.00
Never hinged 95.00
On cover 110.00
219 A96 50c orange 125.00 37.50
Never hinged 300.00
On cover *400.00*
a. 50c red orange 250.00 55.00
Never hinged 600.00
Nos. 213-219 (8) 348.25 80.45

Regular Issue

Same Overprint in Black On U.S. Stamps Nos. 280b, 282 and 272

1901, Aug. 30

220 A90 4c orange brown 35.00 5.00
Never hinged 80.00
On cover 50.00
221 A92 6c lake 40.00 7.00
Never hinged 95.00
On cover 65.00
222 A93 8c violet brown 40.00 7.50
Never hinged 95.00
On cover 50.00
Nos. 220-222 (3) 115.00 19.50

Same Overprint in Red On U.S. Stamps Nos. 276, 276A, 277a and 278

223 A97 $1 black, type I 300.00 200.00
Never hinged 1,000.
On cover *800.00*
223A A97 $1 black, type II 2,000. 750.00
Never hinged 5,000.
On cover —
224 A98 $2 dark blue 350.00 325.00
Never hinged 1,150.
On cover 3,250.
225 A99 $5 dark green 600.00 *900.00*
Never hinged 1,600.
On cover *12,500.*

Regular Issue

Same Overprint in Black On U.S. Stamps Nos. 300 to 310 and Shades

1903-04

226 A115 1c blue green 7.00 .40
Never hinged 15.50
On cover 8.25
227 A116 2c carmine 9.00 1.10
Never hinged 20.00
On cover 10.00
228 A117 3c bright violet 67.50 12.50
Never hinged 150.00
On cover 55.00
229 A118 4c brown 80.00 22.50
Never hinged 175.00
a. 4c orange brown 80.00 20.00
Never hinged 175.00
On cover 40.00
230 A119 5c blue 17.50 1.00
Never hinged 40.00
On cover 22.50
231 A120 6c brownish lake 85.00 22.50
Never hinged 190.00
On cover 65.00
232 A121 8c violet black 50.00 15.00
Never hinged 125.00
On cover 300.00
233 A122 10c pale red brown 35.00 2.25
Never hinged 80.00
On cover 27.50
a. 10c red brown 35.00 3.00
Never hinged 80.00
On cover 35.00
b. Pair, one without overprint *1,500.*
234 A123 13c purple black 35.00 17.50
Never hinged 80.00
a. 13c brown violet 35.00 17.50
Never hinged 80.00
On cover 55.00
235 A124 15c olive green 60.00 15.00
Never hinged 135.00
On cover 100.00
236 A125 50c orange 125.00 35.00
Never hinged 275.00
On cover 300.00
Nos. 226-236 (11) 571.00 144.75
Set, never hinged 1,285.

Same Overprint in Red On U.S. Stamps Nos. 311, 312 and 313

237 A126 $1 black 300.00 200.00
Never hinged 800.00
On cover *1,000.*
238 A127 $2 dark blue 550.00 *800.00*
Never hinged 1,500.
239 A128 $5 dark green 800.00 *2,750.*
Never hinged 2,000.
240 A129 2c carmine 8.00 2.25
Never hinged 17.50
On cover 3.50
a. Booklet pane of 6 *2,000.*
b. 2c scarlet 8.00 2.75
Never hinged 19.00
On cover 4.00
c. As "b," booklet pane of 6 —

José Rizal — A40

Designs: 4c, McKinley. 6c, Ferdinand Magellan. 8c, Miguel Lopez de Legaspi. 10c, Gen. Henry W. Lawton. 12c, Lincoln. 16c, Adm. William T. Sampson. 20c, Washington. 26c, Francisco Carriedo. 30c, Franklin. 1p-10p, Arms of City of Manila.

Wmk. Double-lined PIPS (191PI)

1906, Sept. 8 ***Perf. 12***

241 A40 2c deep green .40 .25
Never hinged 1.00
a. 2c yellow green ('10) .60 .25
Never hinged 1.50
b. Booklet pane of 6 750.00 *800.00*
Never hinged *1,500.*
242 A40 4c carmine .50 .25
Never hinged 1.25
a. 4c carmine lake ('10) 1.00 .25
Never hinged 2.50
b. Booklet pane of 6 *650.00* *700.00*
Never hinged *1,250.*
243 A40 6c violet 2.50 .25
Never hinged 6.25
244 A40 8c brown 4.50 .90
Never hinged 11.00
245 A40 10c blue 3.50 .30
Never hinged 8.75
a. 10c dark blue 3.50 .30
Never hinged 8.75
246 A40 12c brown lake 9.00 2.50
Never hinged 22.50
247 A40 16c violet black 6.00 .35
Never hinged 15.00
248 A40 20c orange brown 7.00 .35
Never hinged 17.50
249 A40 26c vio brn 11.00 3.00
Never hinged 27.50
250 A40 30c olive green 6.50 1.75
Never hinged 16.00
251 A40 1p orange 55.00 17.50
Never hinged 130.00
252 A40 2p black 50.00 1.75
Never hinged 130.00
253 A40 4p dark blue 160.00 20.00
Never hinged 375.00
254 A40 10p dark green 225.00 80.00
Never hinged 575.00
Nos. 241-254 (14) 540.90 129.15
Set, never hinged 1,316.

1909-13 **Change of Colors**

255 A40 12c red orange 11.00 3.00
Never hinged 27.50
256 A40 16c olive green 6.00 .75
Never hinged 15.00
257 A40 20c yellow 9.00 1.25
Never hinged 22.50
258 A40 26c blue green 3.50 1.25
Never hinged 8.75
259 A40 30c ultramarine 13.00 3.50
Never hinged 32.50
260 A40 1p pale violet 45.00 5.00
Never hinged 110.00
260A A40 2p violet brown ('13) 100.00 12.00
Never hinged 250.00
Nos. 255-260A (7) 187.50 26.75
Set, never hinged 466.25

Wmk. Single-lined PIPS (190PI)

1911

261 A40 2c green .75 .25
Never hinged 1.80
On cover 4.00
a. Booklet pane of 6 *800.00* *900.00*
Never hinged *1,400.*
262 A40 4c carmine lake 3.00 .25
Never hinged 6.75
On cover 6.00
a. 4c carmine — —
b. Booklet pane of 6 *600.00* *700.00*
Never hinged *1,100.*
263 A40 6c deep violet 3.00 .25
Never hinged 6.75
264 A40 8c brown 9.50 .50
Never hinged 21.50
265 A40 10c blue 4.00 .25
Never hinged 9.00
266 A40 12c orange 4.00 .45
Never hinged 9.00
267 A40 16c olive green 4.50 .40
Never hinged 10.00
a. 16c pale olive green 4.50 .50
Never hinged 10.00
268 A40 20c yellow 3.50 .25
Never hinged 7.75
a. 20c orange 4.00 .30
Never hinged 9.00
269 A40 26c blue green 6.00 .30
Never hinged 13.50
270 A40 30c ultramarine 6.00 .50
Never hinged 13.50
271 A40 1p pale violet 27.50 .60
Never hinged 62.50
272 A40 2p violet brown 45.00 1.00
Never hinged 100.00
273 A40 4p deep blue 550.00 110.00
Never hinged 1,100.
274 A40 10p deep green 200.00 30.00
Never hinged 400.00
Nos. 261-274 (14) 866.75 145.00
Set, never hinged 1,862.

1914

275 A40 30c gray 12.00 .50
Never hinged 27.50

1914 ***Perf. 10***

276 A40 2c green 3.00 .25
Never hinged 7.00
a. Booklet pane of 6 *750.00* *800.00*
Never hinged *1,250.*
277 A40 4c carmine 4.00 .30
Never hinged 9.00
a. Booklet pane of 6 *750.00*
Never hinged *1,300.*
278 A40 6c light violet 45.00 9.50
Never hinged 100.00
a. 6c deep violet 50.00 6.25
Never hinged 110.00
279 A40 8c brown 55.00 10.50
Never hinged 125.00
280 A40 10c dark blue 30.00 .25
Never hinged 67.50
281 A40 16c olive green 100.00 5.00
Never hinged 225.00
282 A40 20c orange 40.00 1.00
Never hinged 85.00
283 A40 30c gray 60.00 4.50
Never hinged 130.00
284 A40 1p pale violet 150.00 3.75
Never hinged 350.00
Nos. 276-284 (9) 487.00 35.05
Set, never hinged 1,020.

Wmk. Single-lined PIPS (190PI)

1918 ***Perf. 11***

285 A40 2c green 21.00 4.25
Never hinged 40.00
a. Booklet pane of 6 *750.00* *800.00*
Never hinged *1,300.*
286 A40 4c carmine 26.00 6.00
Never hinged 55.00
a. Booklet pane of 6 *1,350.* *2,000.*
287 A40 6c deep violet 40.00 6.00
Never hinged 90.00
287A A40 8c light brown 220.00 25.00
Never hinged 400.00
288 A40 10c dark blue 60.00 3.00
Never hinged 140.00
289 A40 16c olive green 110.00 10.00
Never hinged 250.00
289A A40 20c orange 175.00 12.00
Never hinged 400.00
289C A40 30c gray 95.00 18.00
Never hinged 215.00
289D A40 1p pale violet 100.00 25.00
Never hinged 225.00
Nos. 285-289D (9) 847.00 109.25
Set, never hinged 1,815.

1917 **Unwmk.** ***Perf. 11***

290 A40 2c yellow green .25 .25
Never hinged .55
On cover 4.00
Never hinged 25.00
a. 2c dark green .30 .25
Never hinged .65
b. Vert. pair, imperf. horiz. *2,000.*
c. Horiz. pair, imperf. between *1,500.* —
d. Vertical pair, imperf. btwn. *1,750.* *1,000.*
e. Booklet pane of 6 27.50 *30.00*
Never hinged 60.00
291 A40 4c carmine .30 .25
Never hinged .65
On cover 6.00
a. 4c light rose .30 .25
Never hinged .65

b. Booklet pane of 6 20.00 *22.50*
Never hinged 35.00
292 A40 6c deep violet .35 .25
Never hinged .70
a. 6c lilac .40 .25
Never hinged .80
b. 6c red violet .40 .25
Never hinged .70
c. Booklet pane of 6 *550.00* *800.00*
Never hinged *900.00*
293 A40 8c yellow brown .30 .25
Never hinged .50
a. 8c orange brown .30 .25
Never hinged .50
294 A40 10c deep blue .30 .25
Never hinged .65
295 A40 12c red orange .35 .25
Never hinged .75
296 A40 16c light olive green 65.00 .25
Never hinged 130.00
a. 16c olive bister 65.00 .50
Never hinged 130.00
297 A40 20c orange yellow .35 .25
Never hinged .75
298 A40 26c green .50 .45
Never hinged 1.10
a. 26c blue green .60 .25
Never hinged 1.35
299 A40 30c gray .55 .25
Never hinged 1.35
300 A40 1p pale violet 40.00 1.00
Never hinged 90.00
a. 1p red lilac 40.00 1.00
Never hinged 90.00
b. 1p pale rose lilac 40.00 1.10
Never hinged 90.00
301 A40 2p violet brown 35.00 1.00
Never hinged 77.50
302 A40 4p blue 32.50 .50
Never hinged 72.50
a. 4p dark blue 35.00 .55
Never hinged 77.50
Nos. 290-302 (13) 175.75 5.20
Set, never hinged 377.00

1923-26

Design: 16c, Adm. George Dewey.

303 A40 16c olive bister 1.00 .25
Never hinged 2.25
a. 16c olive green 1.25 .25
Never hinged 2.75
304 A40 10p dp grn ('26) 50.00 20.00
Never hinged 110.00

Legislative Palace
A42

1926, Dec. 20 ***Perf. 12***

319 A42 2c green & black .50 .25
Never hinged 1.25
a. Horiz. pair, imperf. between *300.00*
b. Vert. pair, imperf. between *575.00*
320 A42 4c car & blk .55 .40
Never hinged 1.20
a. Horiz. pair, imperf. between *325.00*
b. Vert. pair, imperf. between *600.00*
321 A42 16c ol grn & blk 1.00 .65
Never hinged 2.25
a. Horiz. pair, imperf. between *350.00*
b. Vert. pair, imperf. between *625.00*
c. Double impression of center *675.00*
322 A42 18c lt brn & blk 1.10 .50
Never hinged 2.50
a. Double impression of center *1,250.*
b. Vertical pair, imperf. between *675.00*
323 A42 20c orange & black 2.00 1.00
Never hinged 4.50
a. 20c orange & brown *600.00* —
b. As No. 323, imperf., pair *575.00* *575.00*
c. As "a," imperf., pair *1,750.*
d. Vert. pair, imperf. between *700.00*
324 A42 24c gray & black 1.00 .55
Never hinged 2.25
a. Vert. pair, imperf. between *700.00*
325 A42 1p rose lil & blk 47.50 50.00
Never hinged 70.00
a. Vert. pair, imperf. between *700.00*
Nos. 319-325 (7) 53.65 53.35
Set, never hinged 83.95

Opening of the Legislative Palace.
No. 322a is valued in the grade of fine.
For overprints, see Nos. O1-O4.

Rizal Type of 1906
Coil Stamp

1928 ***Perf. 11 Vertically***

326 A40 2c green 7.50 *12.50*
Never hinged 19.00
On cover 100.00

Types of 1906-1923

1925-31 ***Imperf.***

340 A40 2c yel green ('31) .50 .50
Never hinged .90
a. 2c green ('25) .80 .75
Never hinged 1.80
341 A40 4c car rose ('31) .50 *1.00*
Never hinged 1.00
a. 4c carmine ('25) 1.20 1.00
Never hinged 2.75
342 A40 6c violet ('31) 3.00 3.75
Never hinged 5.00
a. 6c deep violet ('25) 12.00 8.00
Never hinged 26.00
343 A40 8c brown ('31) 2.00 *5.00*
Never hinged 4.00
a. 8c yellow brown ('25) 13.00 8.00
Never hinged 26.00
344 A40 10c blue ('31) 5.00 *7.50*
Never hinged 12.00
a. 10c deep blue ('25) 45.00 20.00
Never hinged 100.00
345 A40 12c dp orange ('31) 8.00 10.00
Never hinged 15.00
a. 12c red orange ('25) 60.00 35.00
Never hinged 135.00
346 A40 16c olive green 6.00 7.50
Never hinged 11.00
a. 16c bister green ('25) 42.50 18.00
Never hinged 100.00
347 A40 20c dp yel org ('31) 5.00 *7.50*
Never hinged 11.00
a. 20c yellow orange ('25) 45.00 20.00
Never hinged 100.00
348 A40 26c green ('31) 6.00 *9.00*
Never hinged 11.00
a. 26c blue green ('25) 45.00 25.00
Never hinged 110.00
349 A40 30c light gray ('31) 8.00 10.00
Never hinged 16.00
a. 30c gray ('25) 45.00 25.00
Never hinged 110.00
350 A40 1p light violet ('31) 10.00 *15.00*
Never hinged 20.00
a. 1p violet ('25) 200.00 100.00
Never hinged 425.00
351 A40 2p brn vio ('31) 30.00 *45.00*
Never hinged 80.00
a. 2p violet brown ('25) 400.00 400.00
Never hinged 675.00
352 A40 4p blue ('31) 80.00 90.00
Never hinged 150.00
a. 4p deep blue ('25) 2,200. 1,100.
Never hinged 3,500.
353 A40 10p green ('31) 175.00 *225.00*
Never hinged 300.00
a. 10p deep green ('25) 2,750. *2,950.*
Never hinged 4,250.
Nos. 340-353 (14) 339.00 436.75
Set, never hinged 636.90
Nos. 340a-353a (14) 5,860. 4,711.

Nos. 340a-353a were the original post office issue. These were reprinted twice in 1931 for sale to collectors (Nos. 340-353).

Mount Mayon, Luzon
A43

Post Office, Manila
A44

Pier No. 7, Manila Bay — A45

(See footnote) — A46

Rice Planting
A47

Rice Terraces
A48

Baguio Zigzag
A49

1932, May 3 ***Perf. 11***

354 A43 2c yellow green .75 .30
Never hinged 1.25
355 A44 4c rose carmine .75 .30
Never hinged 1.25
356 A45 12c orange .90 .75
Never hinged 1.30
357 A46 18c red orange 45.00 15.00
Never hinged 72.50
358 A47 20c yellow 1.00 .75
Never hinged 1.60
359 A48 24c deep violet 1.60 1.00
Never hinged 2.75
360 A49 32c olive brown 1.60 1.00
Never hinged 2.75
Nos. 354-360 (7) 51.60 19.10
Set, never hinged 83.40

The 18c vignette was intended to show Pagsanjan Falls in Laguna, central Luzon, and is so labeled. Through error the stamp pictures Vernal Falls in Yosemite National Park, California.

For overprints see #C29-C35, C47-C51, C63 (in Scott Standard catalogue, Vol. 5).

Nos. 302, 302a Surcharged in Orange or Red

1932

368 A40 1p on 4p blue (O) 6.00 1.00
Never hinged 9.75
On cover 1.00
a. 1p on 4p dark blue (O) 6.00 1.00
Never hinged 9.25
369 A40 2p on 4p dark blue (R) 9.00 1.50
Never hinged 15.00
a. 2p on 4p blue (R) 9.00 1.00
Never hinged 15.00
On cover 2.00

Far Eastern Championship

Issued in commemoration of the Tenth Far Eastern Championship Games.

Baseball Players
A50

Tennis Player — A51

Basketball Players — A52

1934, Apr. 14 ***Perf. 11½***

380 A50 2c yellow brown 1.50 .80
Never hinged 2.25
381 A51 6c ultramarine .25 .25
Never hinged .30
a. Vertical pair, imperf. between *700.00*
382 A52 16c violet brown .50 .50
Never hinged .75
a. Vert. pair, imperf. horiz. *950.00*
Nos. 380-382 (3) 2.25 1.55
Set, never hinged 3.30

José Rizal — A53

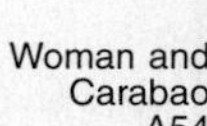

Woman and Carabao
A54

La Filipina — A55

Pearl Fishing
A56

Fort Santiago
A57

Salt Spring — A58

Magellan's Landing, 1521 — A59

"Juan de la Cruz" — A60

Rice Terraces
A61

"Blood Compact," 1565 — A62

Barasoain Church, Malolos
A63

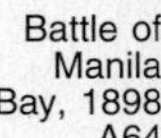
Battle of Manila Bay, 1898
A64

Montalban Gorge A65

George Washington A66

1935, Feb. 15 *Perf. 11*

383 A53 2c rose .25 .25
Never hinged .25
384 A54 4c yellow green .25 .25
Never hinged .25
385 A55 6c dark brown .25 .25
Never hinged .35
386 A56 8c violet .25 .25
Never hinged .35
387 A57 10c rose carmine .30 .25
Never hinged .45
388 A58 12c black .35 .25
Never hinged .50
389 A59 16c dark blue .35 .25
Never hinged .55
390 A60 20c light olive green .35 .25
Never hinged .45
391 A61 26c indigo .40 .40
Never hinged .60
392 A62 30c orange red .40 .40
Never hinged .60
393 A63 1p red org & blk 2.00 1.25
Never hinged 3.00
394 A64 2p bis brn & blk 12.00 2.00
Never hinged 16.00
395 A65 4p blue & black 12.00 4.00
Never hinged 16.00
396 A66 5p green & black 25.00 5.00
Never hinged 50.00
Nos. 383-396 (14) 54.15 15.05
Set, never hinged 74.45

For overprints & surcharges see Nos. 411-424, 433-446, 449, 463-466, 468, 472-474, 478-484, 485-494, C52-C53, O15-O36, O38, O40-O43, N2-N9, N28, NO2-NO6. Post 1940 listings are in Scott Standard catalogue, Vol. 5.

Issues of the Commonwealth

Issued to commemorate the inauguration of the Philippine Commonwealth, Nov. 15, 1935.

The Temples of Human Progress — A67

1935, Nov. 15

397 A67 2c carmine rose .25 .25
Never hinged .35
398 A67 6c deep violet .25 .25
Never hinged .35
399 A67 16c blue .25 .25
Never hinged .40
400 A67 36c yellow green .40 .30
Never hinged .65
401 A67 50c brown .70 .55
Never hinged 1.00
Nos. 397-401 (5) 1.85 1.60
Set, never hinged 2.75

Jose Rizal Issue

75th anniversary of the birth of Jose Rizal (1861-1896), national hero of the Filipinos.

Jose Rizal — A68

1936, June 19 *Perf. 12*

402 A68 2c yellow brown .25 .25
Never hinged .25

403 A68 6c slate blue .25 .25
Never hinged .25
a. Imperf. vertically, pair 1,000.
Never hinged 1,500.
404 A68 36c red brown .50 *.70*
Never hinged .75
Nos. 402-404 (3) 1.00 1.20
Set, never hinged 1.25

Commonwealth Anniversary Issue

Issued in commemoration of the first anniversary of the Commonwealth.

President Manuel L. Quezon — A69

1936, Nov. 15 *Perf. 11*

408 A69 2c orange brown .25 .25
Never hinged .30
409 A69 6c yellow green .25 .25
Never hinged .30
410 A69 12c ultramarine .25 .25
Never hinged .30
Nos. 408-410 (3) .75 .75
Set, never hinged .90

Stamps of 1935 Overprinted in Black

a

b

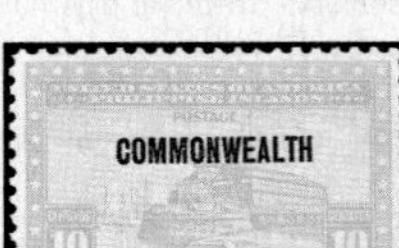

1936-37

411 A53(a) 2c rose .25 .25
Never hinged .25
a. Bklt. pane of 6 ('37) 2.50 2.00
Never hinged 4.00
b. Hyphen omitted 125.00 100.00
412 A54(b) 4c yel grn ('37) .45 *4.00*
Never hinged .70
413 A55(a) 6c dark brown .25 .25
Never hinged .25
414 A56(b) 8c violet ('37) .25 .25
Never hinged .35
On cover .75
415 A57(b) 10c rose carmine .25 .25
Never hinged .25
a. "COMMONWEALT" 20.00 —
Never hinged 30.00
416 A58(b) 12c black ('37) .25 .25
Never hinged .30
On cover .75
417 A59(b) 16c dark blue .25 .25
Never hinged .40
On cover .75
418 A60(a) 20c lt ol grn ('37) .90 .40
Never hinged 1.50
On cover .85
419 A61(b) 26c indigo ('37) .80 .35
Never hinged 1.40
On cover .85
420 A62(b) 30c orange red .45 .25
Never hinged .75
421 A63(b) 1p red org & blk .90 .25
Never hinged 1.50
On cover .75
422 A64(b) 2p bis brn & blk ('37) 12.50 4.00
Never hinged 21.00
On cover 6.00
423 A65(b) 4p bl & blk ('37) 45.00 8.00
Never hinged 72.50
On cover *50.00*
424 A66(b) 5p grn & blk ('37) 12.50 *25.00*
Never hinged 21.00
On cover *40.00*
Nos. 411-424 (14) 75.00 43.75
Set, never hinged 122.15

Eucharistic Congress Issue

Issued to commemorate the 33rd International Eucharistic Congress held at Manila, Feb. 3-7, 1937.

Map of Philippines — A70

1937, Feb. 3

425 A70 2c yellow green .25 .25
Never hinged .25
426 A70 6c light brown .25 .25
Never hinged .25
427 A70 12c sapphire .25 .25
Never hinged .25
428 A70 20c deep orange .30 .25
Never hinged .50
429 A70 36c deep violet .55 .40
Never hinged .80
430 A70 50c carmine .70 .35
Never hinged 1.10
Nos. 425-430 (6) 2.30 1.75
Set, never hinged 3.15

Arms of Manila — A71

1937, Aug. 27

431 A71 10p gray 5.00 2.00
Never hinged 7.25
432 A71 20p henna brown 4.00 1.40
Never hinged 6.50

Stamps of 1935 Overprinted in Black

a

b

1938-40

433 A53(a) 2c rose ('39) .25 .25
Never hinged .25
a. Booklet pane of 6 3.50 3.50
Never hinged 5.50
b. As "a," lower left-hand stamp overprinted "WEALTH COMMON-" 2,500.
c. Hyphen omitted 100.00 50.00
434 A54(b) 4c yel grn ('40) 3.00 *30.00*
Never hinged 4.75
435 A55(a) 6c dk brn ('39) .25 .25
Never hinged .40
a. 6c golden brown .25 .25
Never hinged .40
436 A56(b) 8c violet ('39) .25 *1.75*
Never hinged .25
a. "COMMONWEALT" (LR 31) 90.00
Never hinged 140.00
437 A57(b) 10c rose car ('39) .25 .25
Never hinged .25
a. "COMMONWEALT" (LR 31) 65.00 —
Never hinged 100.00
438 A58(b) 12c black ('40) .25 *1.00*
Never hinged .25
439 A59(b) 16c dark blue .25 .25
Never hinged .25
440 A60(a) 20c lt ol grn ('39) .25 .25
Never hinged .25
441 A61(b) 26c indigo ('40) 1.00 *2.50*
Never hinged 1.50
442 A62(b) 30c org red ('39) 3.00 .70
Never hinged 5.00
443 A63(b) 1p red org & blk .60 .25
Never hinged 1.00
444 A64(b) 2p bis brn & blk ('39) 10.00 1.00
Never hinged 15.00
445 A65(b) 4p bl & blk ('40) 175.00 250.00
Never hinged 350.00
On cover 500.00
446 A66(b) 5p grn & blk ('40) 20.00 8.00
Never hinged 35.00
Nos. 433-446 (14) 214.35 *296.45*
Set, never hinged 414.15

Overprint "b" measures 18½x1¾mm.

No. 433b occurs in booklet pane, No. 433a, position 5; all examples are straight-edged, left and bottom.

First Foreign Trade Week Issue

Nos. 384, 298a and 432 Surcharged in Red, Violet or Black

a

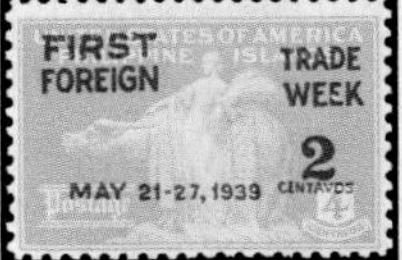

b

c

1939, July 5

449 A54(a) 2c on 4c yel grn (R) .25 .25
Never hinged .35
450 A40(b) 6c on 26c blue grn (V) .25 .50
Never hinged .35
a. 6c on 26c green 3.00 1.00
Never hinged 5.00
451 A71(c) 50c on 20p henna brn (Bk) 1.25 1.00
Never hinged 2.00 5.00
Nos. 449-451 (3) 1.75 1.75
Set, never hinged 2.70

Commonwealth 4th Anniversary Issue (#452-460)

Triumphal Arch — A72

1939, Nov. 15

452 A72 2c yellow green .25 .25
Never hinged .25
453 A72 6c carmine .25 .25
Never hinged .25
454 A72 12c bright blue .25 .25
Never hinged .25
Nos. 452-454 (3) .75 .75
Set, never hinged .75

For overprints see Nos. 469, 476 in Scott Standard catalogue, Vol. 5.

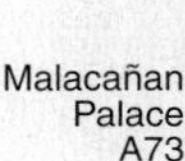

Malacañan Palace A73

1939, Nov. 15

455 A73 2c green .25 .25
Never hinged .25
456 A73 6c orange .25 .25
Never hinged .25
457 A73 12c carmine .25 .25
Never hinged .25
Nos. 455-457 (3) .75 .75
Set, never hinged .75

For overprint, see No. 470 in Scott Standard catalogue, Vol. 5.

Pres. Quezon Taking Oath of Office — A74

1940, Feb. 8

458 A74 2c dark orange .25 .25
Never hinged .25
459 A74 6c dark green .25 .25
Never hinged .25
460 A74 12c purple .25 .25
Never hinged .30
Nos. 458-460 (3) .75 .75
Set, never hinged .80

For overprints, see Nos. 471, 477 in Scott Standard catalogue, Vol. 5.

AIR POST STAMPS

Madrid-Manila Flight Issue

Issued to commemorate the flight of Spanish aviators Gallarza and Loriga from Madrid to Manila.

Regular Issue of 1917-26 Overprinted in Red or Violet

Designs: Nos. C7-C8, Adm. William T. Sampson. No. C9, Adm. George Dewey.

1926, May 13 Unwmk. *Perf. 11*

C1 A40 2c green (R) 20.00 17.50
Never hinged 45.00
C2 A40 4c carmine (V) 30.00 20.00
Never hinged 55.00
a. Inverted overprint *3,000.* —
C3 A40 6c lilac (R) 75.00 75.00
Never hinged 125.00
C4 A40 8c org brn (V) 75.00 60.00
Never hinged 125.00
C5 A40 10c deep blue (R) 75.00 60.00
Never hinged 140.00
C6 A40 12c red org (V) 80.00 65.00
Never hinged 150.00
C7 A40 16c lt ol grn (V) *3,250.* *3,250.*
C8 A40 16c ol bister (R) *5,000.* *5,000.*
C9 A40 16c ol grn (V) 100.00 70.00
Never hinged 160.00
C10 A40 20c org yel (V) 100.00 80.00
Never hinged 160.00
C11 A40 26c blue grn (V) 100.00 80.00
Never hinged 160.00
C12 A40 30c gray (V) 100.00 80.00
Never hinged 160.00
C13 A40 2p vio brn (R) 600.00 600.00
Never hinged 1,100.
On cover 800.00
C14 A40 4p dk blue (R) 750.00 750.00
Never hinged 1,300.
On cover —
C15 A40 10p dp grn (V) 1,350. 1,350.
On cover —

Same Overprint on No. 269

Wmk. Single-lined PIPS (190)

Perf. 12

C16 A40 26c blue grn (V) *6,250.*

Same Overprint on No. 284

Perf. 10

C17 A40 1p pale violet (V) 300.00 225.00
Never hinged 450.00
On cover —

London-Orient Flight Issue

Issued Nov. 9, 1928, to celebrate the arrival of a British squadron of hydroplanes.

Regular Issue of 1917-25 Overprinted in Red

1928, Nov. 9 *Perf. 11*

C18 A40 2c green 1.00 1.00
Never hinged 2.00
C19 A40 4c carmine 1.25 1.50
Never hinged 2.00
C20 A40 6c violet 5.00 3.00
Never hinged 10.00
On cover 4.00
C21 A40 8c orange brown 5.00 3.00
Never hinged 10.00
On cover 5.00
C22 A40 10c deep blue 5.00 3.00
Never hinged 10.00
On cover 5.00
C23 A40 12c red orange 8.00 4.00
Never hinged 12.00
On cover 6.00
C24 A40 16c ol grn (Dewey) 8.00 4.00
Never hinged 12.00
On cover 6.00
C25 A40 20c orange yellow 8.00 4.00
Never hinged 12.00
On cover 6.00
C26 A40 26c blue green 20.00 8.00
Never hinged 35.00
On cover 12.00
C27 A40 30c gray 20.00 8.00
Never hinged 35.00
On cover 12.00

Same Overprint on No. 271

Wmk. Single-lined PIPS (190)

Perf. 12

C28 A40 1p pale violet 55.00 30.00
Never hinged 90.00
On cover 34.00
Nos. C18-C28 (11) 136.25 69.50
Set, never hinged 230.00

Von Gronau Issue

Commemorating the visit of Capt. Wolfgang von Gronau's airplane on its round-the-world flight.

Nos. 354-360 Overprinted

1932, Sept. 27 Unwmk. *Perf. 11*

C29 A43 2c yellow green .90 .60
Never hinged 1.40
C30 A44 4c rose carmine .90 .40
Never hinged 1.40
C31 A45 12c orange 1.25 .65
Never hinged 2.00
On cover 1.00
C32 A46 18c red orange 5.00 5.00
Never hinged 8.00
On cover 7.00
C33 A47 20c yellow 3.50 3.50
Never hinged 5.75
On cover 6.00
C34 A48 24c deep violet 3.50 4.00
Never hinged 5.75
On cover 6.00
C35 A49 32c olive brown 3.50 3.00
Never hinged 5.75
On cover 7.00
Nos. C29-C35 (7) 18.55 17.15
Set, never hinged 31.55

Rein Issue

Commemorating the flight from Madrid to Manila of the Spanish aviator Fernando Rein y Loring.

Regular Issue of 1917-25 Overprinted

1933, Apr. 11

C36 A40 2c green .75 .45
Never hinged 1.10
C37 A40 4c carmine .90 .45
Never hinged 1.40
C38 A40 6c deep violet 1.10 .80
Never hinged 1.75
C39 A40 8c orange brown 3.75 2.00
Never hinged 5.75
C40 A40 10c dark blue 3.75 2.25
Never hinged 5.75
C41 A40 12c orange 3.75 2.00
C42 A40 16c ol grn (Dewey) 3.50 2.00
Never hinged 5.25
C43 A40 20c yellow 3.75 2.00
Never hinged 5.75
C44 A40 26c green 3.75 2.75
Never hinged 5.75
a. 26c blue green 4.00 2.00
Never hinged 6.00
C45 A40 30c gray 4.00 3.00
Never hinged 6.00
Nos. C36-C45 (10) 29.00 17.70
Set, never hinged 44.25

No. 290a Overprinted

1933, May 26

C46 A40 2c green .65 .40
Never hinged 1.00

Regular Issue of 1932 Overprinted

C47 A44 4c rose carmine .30 .25
Never hinged .45
C48 A45 12c orange .60 .25
Never hinged .90
C49 A47 20c yellow .60 .25
Never hinged .90
C50 A48 24c deep violet .65 .25
Never hinged 1.00
C51 A49 32c olive brown .85 .35
Never hinged 1.40
Nos. C46-C51 (6) 3.65 1.75
Set, never hinged 5.65

Transpacific Issue

Issued to commemorate the China Clipper flight from Manila to San Francisco, Dec. 2-5, 1935.

Nos. 387, 392 Overprinted in Gold

1935, Dec. 2

C52 A57 10c rose carmine .40 .25
Never hinged .60
C53 A62 30c orange red .60 .35
Never hinged .90

Manila-Madrid Flight Issue

Issued to commemorate the Manila-Madrid flight by aviators Antonio Arnaiz and Juan Calvo.

Regular Issue of 1917-25 Surcharged in Various Colors

1936, Sept. 6

C54 A40 2c on 4c carmine (Bl) .25 .25
Never hinged .25
C55 A40 6c on 12c red org (V) .25 .25
Never hinged .30
C56 A40 16c on 26c blue grn (Bk) .25 .25
Never hinged .40
a. 16c on 26c green 2.00 .70
Never hinged 3.00
Nos. C54-C56 (3) .75 .75
Set, never hinged .95

Air Mail Exhibition Issue

Issued to commemorate the first Air Mail Exhibition, held Feb. 17-19, 1939.

Regular Issue of 1917-37 Surcharged in Black or Red

1939, Feb. 17

C57 A40 8c on 26c blue grn (Bk) 2.00 2.00
Never hinged 4.00
a. 8c on 26c green (Bk) 10.00 4.00
Never hinged 16.00
C58 A71 1p on 10p gray (R) 8.00 4.00
Never hinged 12.00

SPECIAL DELIVERY STAMPS

United States No. E5 Overprinted in Red

Wmk. Double-lined USPS (191)

1901, Oct. 15 *Perf. 12*

E1 SD3 10c dark blue 100. 80.
Never hinged 185.
On cover 350.
a. Dots in curved frame above messenger (Pl. 882) *175.* *160.*

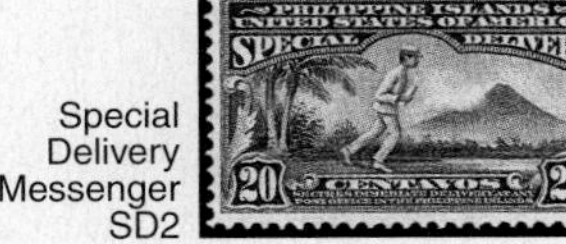

Special Delivery Messenger SD2

Wmk. Double-lined PIPS (191PI)

1906, Sept. 8

E2 SD2 20c deep ultra 45.00 8.00
Never hinged 90.00
On cover 17.50
b. 20c pale ultramarine 35.00 8.00
Never hinged 70.00
On cover 17.50

See Nos. E3-E6. For overprints see Nos. E7-E10, EO1. Post 1940 listings are in Scott Standard catalogue, Vol. 5.

SPECIAL PRINTING

U.S. No. E6 Overprinted in Red

Wmk. Double-lined USPS (191)

1907

E2A SD4 10c ultramarine *3,250.*

Wmk. Single-lined PIPS (190PI)

1911, Apr.

E3 SD2 20c deep ultra 22.00 1.75
Never hinged 42.00
On cover 12.50

1916 *Perf. 10*

E4 SD2 20c deep ultra 175.00 150.00
Never hinged 275.00
On cover 200.00

1919 Unwmk. *Perf. 11*

E5 SD2 20c ultramarine .60 .25
Never hinged .90
On cover 5.00
a. 20c pale blue .75 .25
Never hinged 1.00
On cover 5.25
b. 20c dull violet .60 .25
Never hinged .90
On cover 5.00

Type of 1906 Issue

1925-31 *Imperf.*

E6 SD2 20c dull violet ('31) 27.50 *75.00*
Never hinged 40.00
On cover 250.00
a. 20c violet blue ('25) 50.00 —
Never hinged 80.00
On cover —

Type of 1919 Overprinted in Black

1939, Apr. 27 *Perf. 11*

E7 SD2 20c blue violet .25 .25
Never hinged .40
On cover 5.00

SPECIAL DELIVERY OFFICIAL STAMP

Type of 1906 Issue Overprinted

1931 Unwmk. *Perf. 11*

EO1 SD2 20c dull violet 3.00 *75.00*
Never hinged 4.50
a. No period after "B" 50.00 *250.00*
Never hinged 75.00
b. Double overprint —

It is strongly recommended that expert opinion be acquired for Nos. EO1 and EO1a used.

POSTAGE DUE STAMPS

U.S. Nos. J38-J44 Overprinted in Black

Wmk. Double-lined USPS (191)

1899, Aug. 16 *Perf. 12*

J1 D2 1c deep claret 7.50 2.50
Never hinged 15.00
On cover 30.00
J2 D2 2c deep claret 7.50 2.50
Never hinged 15.00
On cover 37.50
J3 D2 5c deep claret 15.00 2.50
Never hinged 30.00
On cover *70.00*
J4 D2 10c deep claret 19.00 5.50
Never hinged 37.50
On cover 100.00

J5 D2 50c deep claret 250.00 100.00
Never hinged 425.00
On cover —

No. J1 was used to pay regular postage Sept. 5-19, 1902.

1901, Aug. 31

J6 D2 3c deep claret 17.50 7.00
Never hinged 35.00
On cover 60.00
J7 D2 30c deep claret 250.00 110.00
Never hinged 415.00
On cover —
Nos. J1-J7 (7) 566.50 230.00
Set, never hinged 882.50

Post Office Clerk — D3

1928, Aug. 21 Unwmk. *Perf. 11*

J8 D3 4c brown red .25 .25
Never hinged .25
J9 D3 6c brown red .30 .75
Never hinged .45
J10 D3 8c brown red .25 .75
Never hinged .35
J11 D3 10c brown red .30 .75
Never hinged .45
J12 D3 12c brown red .25 .75
Never hinged .35
J13 D3 16c brown red .30 .75
Never hinged .45
J14 D3 20c brown red .30 .75
Never hinged .45
Nos. J8-J14 (7) 1.95 4.75
Set, never hinged 2.75

No. J8 Surcharged in Blue

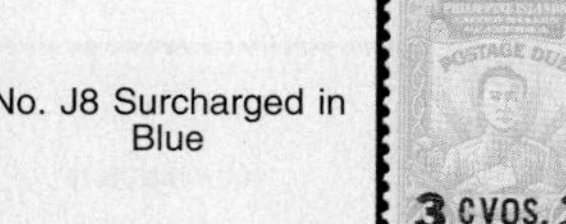

1937, July 29 Unwmk. *Perf. 11*

J15 D3 3c on 4c brown red .25 .25
Never hinged .35

See note after No. NJ1 in Scott Standard catalogue, Vol. 5.

OFFICIAL STAMPS

Official Handstamped Overprints

"Officers purchasing stamps for government business may, if they so desire, surcharge them with the letters O.B. either in writing with black ink or by rubber stamps but in such a manner as not to obliterate the stamp that postmasters will be unable to determine whether the stamps have been previously used." C.M. Cotterman, Director of Posts, December 26, 1905.

Beginning January 1, 1906, all branches of the Insular Government used postage stamps to prepay postage instead of franking them as before. Some officials used manuscript, some utilized the typewriting machines but by far the larger number provided themselves with rubber stamps. The majority of these read "O.B." but other forms were: "OFFICIAL BUSINESS" or "OFFICIAL MAIL" in two lines, with variations on many of these.

These "O.B." overprints are known on U.S. 1899-1901 stamps; on 1903-06 stamps in red and blue; on 1906 stamps in red, blue, black, yellow and green.

"O.B." overprints were also made on the centavo and peso stamps of the Philippines, per order of May 25, 1907.

Beginning in 1926 the Bureau of Posts issued press-printed official stamps, but many government offices continued to handstamp ordinary postage stamps "O.B." The press-printed "O.B." overprints are listed below.

During the Japanese occupation period 1942-45, the same system of handstamped official overprints prevailed, but the handstamp usually consisted of "K.P.", initials of the Tagalog words, "Kagamitang Pampamahalaan" (Official Business), and the two Japanese characters used in the printed overprint on Nos. NO1 to NO4.

Regular Issue of 1926 Ovptd. in Red

1926, Dec. 20 Unwmk. *Perf. 12*

O1 A42 2c green & black 3.00 1.00
Never hinged 4.50
On cover 2.00
O2 A42 4c car & blk 3.00 1.25
Never hinged 4.50
On cover 2.00
a. Vertical pair, imperf. between 750.00
O3 A42 18c lt brn & blk 8.00 4.00
Never hinged 12.00
On cover 6.50
O4 A42 20c org & blk 7.75 1.75
Never hinged 11.50
On cover 3.00
Nos. O1-O4 (4) 21.75 8.00
Set, never hinged 32.50

Opening of the Legislative Palace.

Regular Issue of 1917-26 Overprinted by the U.S. Bureau of Engraving and Printing

1931 *Perf. 11*

O5 A40 2c green .40 .25
Never hinged .65
a. No period after "B" 17.50 17.50
Never hinged 27.50
b. No period after "O" 40.00 30.00
O6 A40 4c carmine .45 .25
Never hinged .70
a. No period after "B" 40.00 20.00
Never hinged 60.00
O7 A40 6c deep violet .75 .25
Never hinged 1.25
O8 A40 8c yellow brown .75 .25
Never hinged 1.25
O9 A40 10c deep blue 1.20 .25
Never hinged 1.90
O10 A40 12c red orange 2.00 .25
Never hinged 3.00
a. No period after "B" 80.00 80.00
Never hinged 120.00
O11 A40 16c lt ol grn (Dewey) 1.00 .25
Never hinged 1.50
a. 16c olive bister 2.00 .25
Never hinged 3.00
O12 A40 20c orange yellow 1.25 .25
Never hinged 1.90
a. No period after "B" 80.00 80.00
Never hinged 120.00
O13 A40 26c green 2.00 1.00
Never hinged 3.25
a. 26c blue green 2.50 1.50
Never hinged 4.00
O14 A40 30c gray 2.00 .25
Never hinged 3.25
Nos. O5-O14 (10) 11.80 3.25
Set, never hinged 18.65

Overprinted on Nos. 383-392

1935

O15 A53 2c rose .25 .25
Never hinged .30
a. No period after "B" 15.00 10.00
Never hinged 22.50
b. No period after "O" — —
O16 A54 4c yellow green .25 .25
Never hinged .30
a. No period after "B" 15.00 *40.00*
Never hinged 22.50
O17 A55 6c dark brown .25 .25
Never hinged .40
a. No period after "B" 35.00 35.00
Never hinged 52.50
O18 A56 8c violet .30 .25
Never hinged .45
O19 A57 10c rose carmine .30 .25
Never hinged .45
O20 A58 12c black .75 .25
Never hinged 1.10
O21 A59 16c dark blue .55 .25
Never hinged .85
O22 A60 20c light olive green .60 .25
Never hinged .90
O23 A61 26c indigo .90 .25
Never hinged 1.50
O24 A62 30c orange red .80 .25
Never hinged 1.20
Nos. O15-O24 (10) 4.95 2.50
Set, never hinged 7.40

Nos. 411 and 418 with Additional Overprint in Black

1937-38

O25 A53 2c rose .25 .25
Never hinged .30
a. No period after "B" 25.00 25.00
Never hinged 45.00
b. Period after "B" raised (UL 4) 150.00
O26 A60 20c lt ol grn ('38) .70 .50
Never hinged 1.10

Regular Issue of 1935 Overprinted In Black

a

b

1938-40

O27 A53(a) 2c rose .25 .25
Never hinged .30
a. Hyphen omitted 10.00 10.00
Never hinged 15.00
b. No period after "B" 20.00 *30.00*
Never hinged 30.00
O28 A54(b) 4c yellow green .75 1.00
Never hinged 1.10
O29 A55(a) 6c dark brown .30 .25
Never hinged .45
O30 A56(b) 8c violet .75 .85
Never hinged 1.10
O31 A57(b) 10c rose carmine .25 .25
Never hinged .30
a. No period after "O" 50.00 40.00
Never hinged 75.00
O32 A58(b) 12c black .30 .25
Never hinged .45
O33 A59(b) 16c dark blue .30 .25
Never hinged .45
O34 A60(a) 20c lt ol grn ('40) .55 .85
Never hinged .85
O35 A61(b) 26c indigo 1.50 *2.00*
Never hinged 2.25
O36 A62(b) 30c orange red .75 .85
Never hinged 1.10
Nos. O27-O36 (10) 5.70 6.80
Set, never hinged 8.25

NEWSPAPER STAMPS

N1

1886-89 Unwmk. Typo. *Perf. 14*

P1 N1 ⅛c yellow green .30 *7.50*
On cover or wrapper *500.00*
P2 N1 1m rose ('89) .30 *15.00*
On cover or wrapper *500.00*
P3 N1 2m blue ('89) .30 *15.00*
On cover or wrapper *800.00*
P4 N1 5m dk brown ('89) .30 *15.00*
On cover or wrapper *1,000.*
Nos. P1-P4 (4) 1.20 *52.50*

N2

1890-96

P5 N2 ⅛c dark violet .25 .25
On cover or wrapper *400.00*
P6 N2 ⅛c green ('92) 6.75 *10.00*
On cover or wrapper *600.00*
P7 N2 ⅛c org brn ('94) .25 .25
On cover or wrapper *200.00*
P8 N2 ⅛c dull blue ('96) .85 .60
On cover or wrapper *200.00*
P9 N2 1m dark violet .25 .25
On cover or wrapper *200.00*
P10 N2 1m green ('92) 2.25 *5.50*
On cover or wrapper *400.00*
P11 N2 1m olive gray ('94) .25 .45
On cover or wrapper *200.00*
P12 N2 1m ultra ('96) .35 .25
On cover or wrapper *200.00*
P13 N2 2m dark violet .25 .45
On cover or wrapper *200.00*
P14 N2 2m green ('92) 2.50 *13.00*
On cover or wrapper *500.00*
P15 N2 2m olive gray ('94) .25 *.45*
On cover or wrapper *200.00*
P16 N2 2m brown ('96) .30 .25
On cover or wrapper *200.00*
P17 N2 5m dark violet .25 *1.10*
On cover or wrapper *500.00*
P18 N2 5m green ('92) 150.00 55.00
P19 N2 5m olive gray ('94) .25 *.45*
On cover or wrapper *500.00*
P20 N2 5m dp blue grn ('96) 2.50 1.40
On cover or wrapper *600.00*
Nos. P5-P20 (16) 167.50 *89.65*

Imperfs. exist of Nos. P8, P9, P11, P12, P16, P17 and P20.

FILIPINO REVOLUTIONARY GOVERNMENT

The Filipino Republic was instituted by Gen. Emilio Aguinaldo on June 23, 1899. At the same time he assumed the office of President. Aguinaldo dominated the greater part of the island of Luzon and some of the smaller islands until late in 1899. He was taken prisoner by United States troops on March 23, 1901.

The devices composing the National Arms, adopted by the Filipino Revolutionary Government, are emblems of the Katipunan political secret society or of Katipunan origin. The letters "K K K" on these stamps are the initials of this society whose complete name is "Kataas-taasang, Kagalang-galang Katipunan nang Mañga Anak nang Bayan," meaning "Sovereign Worshipful Association of the Sons of the Country."

The regular postage and telegraph stamps were in use on Luzon as early as Nov. 10, 1898. Owing to the fact that stamps for the different purposes were not always available together with a lack of proper instructions, any of the adhesives were permitted to be used in the place of the other. Hence telegraph and revenue stamps were accepted for postage and postage stamps for revenue or telegraph charges. In addition to the regular postal emission, there are a number of provisional stamps, issues of local governments of islands and towns.

POSTAGE ISSUES

A1

A2

Coat of Arms — A3

1898-99 Unwmk. *Perf. 11½*

Y1 A1 2c red 175.00 125.00
On cover *1,500.*
a. Double impression *325.00*
Y2 A2 2c red .30 4.00
On cover 350.00
b. Double impression —
d. Horiz. pair, imperf. between —
e. Vert. pair, imperf. between *225.00*
Y3 A3 2c red 150.00 *200.00*
On cover *2,000.*

Imperf pairs and pairs, imperf horizontally, have been created from No. Y2e.

REGISTRATION STAMP

RS1

YF1	RS1	8c green	5.00	*30.00*
		On cover with #Y2		*3,500.*
a.		Imperf., pair	400.00	
b.		Imperf. vertically, pair		—

NEWSPAPER STAMP

N1

YP1	N1	1m black	2.00	*20.00*
a.		Imperf., pair	5.00	*20.00*

PITCAIRN ISLANDS

'pit-ˌkarn 'ī-lənds

LOCATION — South Pacific Ocean, nearly equidistant from Australia and South America

GOVT. — British colony under the British High Commissioner in New Zealand

AREA — 1.75 sq. mi.

POP. — 57 (1984)

The district of Pitcairn also includes the uninhabited islands of Ducie, Henderson and Oeno.

Postal affairs are administered by Fiji.

12 Pence = 1 Shilling

Catalogue values for all unused stamps in this country are for Never Hinged items.

Cluster of Oranges A1

Fletcher Christian with Crew and View of Pitcairn Island — A2

John Adams and His House A3

William Bligh and H. M. Armed Vessel "Bounty" A4

Map of Pitcairn and Pacific Ocean — A5

Bounty Bible — A6

H.M. Armed Vessel "Bounty" A7

Pitcairn School, 1949 — A8

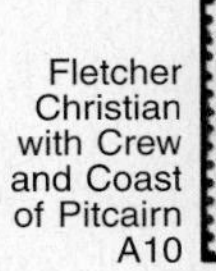
Fletcher Christian and View of Pitcairn Island — A9

Fletcher Christian with Crew and Coast of Pitcairn A10

Perf. 12½, 11½x11

1940-51		**Engr.**		**Wmk. 4**
1	A1	½p blue grn & org	.75	*.95*
2	A2	1p red lil & rose vio	.95	*.80*
3	A3	1½p rose car & blk	.95	.50
4	A4	2p dk brn & brt grn	2.25	1.40
5	A5	3p dk blue & yel grn	1.25	1.25
5A	A6	4p dk blue grn & blk	21.00	12.00
6	A7	6p sl grn & dp brn	6.00	1.50
6A	A8	8p lil rose & grn	22.50	8.00
7	A9	1sh slate & vio	5.25	1.50
8	A10	2sh6p dk brn & brt grn	15.00	4.00
		Nos. 1-8 (10)	75.90	31.90

Nos. 1-5, 6 and 7-8 exist in a booklet of eight panes of one. Value $2,750.

Issued: 4p, 8p, 9/1/51; others, 10/15/40.

Common Design Types pictured following the introduction.

Peace Issue
Common Design Type

1946, Dec. 2			*Perf. 13½x14*	
9	CD303	2p brown	.65	.65
10	CD303	3p deep blue	.75	.75

Silver Wedding Issue
Common Design Types

1949, Aug. 1		**Photo.**	*Perf. 14x14½*	
11	CD304	1½p scarlet	1.75	1.00

Perf. 11½x11

Engraved; Name Typographed

12	CD305	10sh purple	43.00	47.50

UPU Issue
Common Design Types

Engr.; Name Typo. on 3p & 6p

1949, Oct. 10			*Perf. 13½, 11x11½*	
13	CD306	2½p red brown	2.25	4.00
14	CD307	3p indigo	8.00	4.00
15	CD308	6p green	4.00	4.00
16	CD309	1sh rose violet	4.25	4.50
		Nos. 13-16 (4)	18.50	16.50

POLAND

'pō-lənd

LOCATION — Europe between Russia and Germany

GOVT. — Republic

AREA — 120,628 sq. mi.

POP. — 36,399,000 (est. 1983)

CAPITAL — Warsaw

100 Kopecks = 1 Ruble
100 Fenigi = 1 Marka (1918)
100 Halerzy = 1 Korona (1918)
100 Groszy = 1 Zloty (1924)

Watermarks

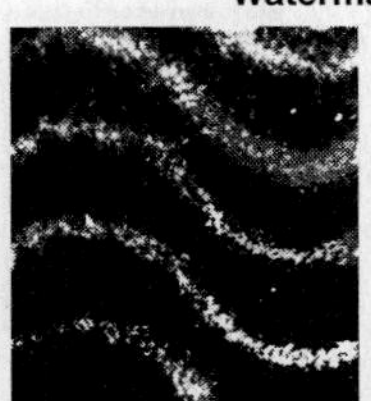
Wmk. 145 — Wavy Lines

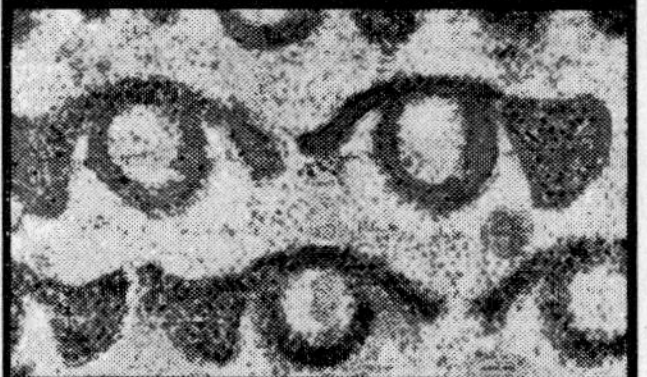
Wmk. 234 — Multiple Post Horns

Issued under Russian Dominion

Coat of Arms — A1

Perf. 11½ to 12½

1860		**Typo.**		**Unwmk.**
1	A1	10k blue & rose	2,400.	250.
		On cover		1,000.
a.		10k blue & carmine	2,500.	325.
b.		10k dark blue & rose	3,000.	350.
c.		Added blue frame for inner oval	6,000.	850.
d.		Imperf.	—	7,500.

Used for letters within the Polish territory and to Russia. Postage on all foreign letters was paid in cash.

These stamps were superseded by those of Russia in 1865.

Counterfeits exist.

Issues of the Republic

Local issues were made in various Polish cities during the German occupation.

In the early months of the Republic many issues were made by overprinting the German occupation stamps with the words "Poczta Polska" and an eagle or bars often with the name of the city.

These issues were not authorized by the Government but were made by the local authorities and restricted to local use. In 1914 two stamps were issued for the Polish Legion and in 1918 the Polish Expeditionary Force used surcharged Russian stamps. The regularity of these issues is questioned.

Numerous counterfeits of these issues abound.

Warsaw Issues
Stamps of the Warsaw Local Post Surcharged

Statue of Sigismund III — A2

Coat of Arms of Warsaw — A3

Polish Eagle A4

Sobieski Monument A5

1918, Nov. 17		**Wmk. 145**	*Perf. 11½*	
11	A2	5f on 2gr brn & buff	1.40	1.00
a.		Inverted surcharge	200.00	200.00
12	A3	10f on 6gr grn & buff	.70	.70
a.		Inverted surcharge	15.00	15.00
13	A4	25f on 10gr rose & buff	7.00	3.50
a.		Inverted surcharge	27.50	27.50
14	A5	50f on 20gr bl & buff	8.50	7.00
a.		Inverted surcharge	350.00	350.00
		Nos. 11-14 (4)	17.60	12.20

Counterfeits exist.

Occupation Stamps Nos. N6-N16 Overprinted or Surcharged

a

b

1918-19		**Wmk. 125**	*Perf. 14, 14½*	
15	A16	3pf brown ('19)	35.00	27.50
16	A22	5pf on 2½pf gray	1.40	.70
17	A16	5pf on 3pf brown	5.00	3.50
18	A16	5pf green	1.75	.70
19	A16	10pf carmine	1.40	.50
20	A22	15pf dark violet	1.00	.50
21	A16	20pf blue	1.40	.50
a.		20pf ultramarine	*775.00*	*2,250.*
23	A22	25pf on 7½pf org	1.00	.50
24	A16	30pf org & blk, *buff*	1.00	.50
25	A16	40pf lake & black	1.75	1.25
26	A16	60pf magenta	1.40	.50
		Nos. 15-26 (11)	52.10	36.65

There are two settings of this overprint. The first printing, issued Dec. 5, 1918, has space of 3½mm between the middle two bars. The second printing, issued Jan. 15, 1919, has space of 4mm. No. 15 comes only in the second setting; all others in both. The German overprint on No. 21a is very glossy.

Varieties of this overprint and surcharge are numerous: double; inverted; misspellings (Pocata, Poczto, Pelska); letters omitted, inverted or wrong font; 3 bars instead of 4, etc.

No. 21a requires competent expertization. A number of shades of the blue No. 21 exist. Counterfeits exist.

Lublin Issue

Austrian Military Semi-Postal Stamps of 1918 Overprinted

1918, Dec. 5		**Unwmk.**	*Perf. 12½x13*	
27	MSP7	10h gray green	8.50	7.50
a.		Inverted overprint	80.00	80.00
b.		Double overprint	1,750.	700.00
c.		Double ovpt., one inverted	2,100.	850.00
28	MSP8	20h magenta	6.50	7.50
a.		Inverted overprint	50.00	50.00
b.		Double ovpt., one inverted	1,750.	500.00

29 MSP7 45h blue 6.50 7.50
a. Inverted overprint 50.00 50.00
b. Double ovpt., one inverted 1,750. 500.00
Nos. 27-29 (3) 21.50 22.50

Austrian Military Stamps of 1917 Surcharged

1918-19 ***Perf. 12½***

30 M3 3hal on 3h ol gray 27.50 20.00
a. Inverted surcharge 3,500. 3,500.
b. Perf. 11½ 50.00 27.50
c. Perf. 11½x12½ 30.00 27.50
31 M3 3hal on 15h brt rose 7.00 7.00
a. Inverted surcharge 22.50 30.00

Surcharged in Black

32 M3 10hal on 30h sl grn 7.00 7.00
a. Inverted surcharge 22.50 30.00
b. Brown surcharge (error) 75.00 65.00
34 M3 25hal on 40h ol bis 15.00 12.00
a. Inverted surcharge 37.50 42.50
b. Perf. 11½ 50.00 27.50
c. As "b," inverted surcharge 175.00 175.00
35 M3 45hal on 60h rose 7.00 7.00
a. Inverted surcharge 25.00 27.50
36 M3 45hal on 80h dl blue 8.50 8.50
a. Inverted surcharge 35.00 35.00
37 M3 50hal on 60h rose 14.00 14.00
a. Inverted surcharge 50.00 35.00

Similar surcharge with bars instead of stars over original value

38 M3 45hal on 80h dl blue 12.00 10.00
a. Inverted surcharge 40.00 35.00
b. Double srch., one inverted 1,350. —

Overprinted

39 M3 50h deep green 27.50 27.50
a. Inverted overprint 100.00 100.00
40 M3 90h dark violet 7.00 7.00
a. Inverted overprint 100.00 100.00
Nos. 30-40 (10) 132.50 120.00

Counterfeits

All Cracow issues, Nos. 41-60, J1-J12 and P1-P5, have been extensively counterfeited. Competent expertization is necessary. Prices apply only for authenticated stamps with identified plating position. Cost of certificate is not included in the catalogue value.

Cracow Issues

Austrian Stamps of 1916-18 Overprinted

1919, Jan. 17 **Typo.**

41 A37 3h brt violet 500.00 450.00
42 A37 5h lt green 625.00 475.00
43 A37 6h deep orange 70.00 65.00
a. Inverted overprint 50,000.
44 A37 10h magenta 500.00 450.00
45 A37 12h lt blue 70.00 70.00
46 A39 40h olive green 35.00 30.00
a. Inverted overprint 350.00 —
b. Double overprint 2,000.
47 A39 50h blue green 20.00 14.00
a. Inverted overprint 35,000.
48 A39 60h deep blue 17.50 14.00
a. Inverted overprint 350.00 —
49 A39 80h orange brown 14.00 14.00
a. Inverted overprint. 300.00 250.00
b. Double overprint 1,750. —
50 A39 90h red violet 1,200. 1,000.
51 A39 1k carmine, *yel* 30.00 27.50

Engr.

52 A40 2k blue 12.00 14.00
a. On gray paper 60.00 60.00
53 A40 3k carmine rose 190.00 175.00
54 A40 4k yellow green 200.00 175.00
55 A40 10k deep violet *12,000.* *13,000.*

The 3k is on granite paper.

The overprint on Nos. 52-55 is litho. and slightly larger than illustration with different ornament between lines of type.

Same Overprint on Nos. 168-171

1919 **Typo.**

56 A42 15h dull red 67.50 35.00
57 A42 20h dark green 300.00 140.00
58 A42 25h blue *1,900.* 1,900.
59 A42 30h dull violet 550.00 350.00

Austria No. 157 Surcharged

1919, Jan. 24

60 A39 25h on 80h org brn 10.00 10.00
a. Inverted surcharge 240.00 150.00

Excellent counterfeits of Nos. 27 to 60 exist.

Polish Eagle — A9

1919, Feb. 25 **Litho.** ***Imperf.***

Without gum

Yellowish Paper

61 A9 2h gray 1.75 1.40
62 A9 3h dull violet 1.00 1.00
63 A9 5h green 1.00 .70
64 A9 6h orange 17.50 20.00
65 A9 10h lake 1.00 .70
66 A9 15h brown 1.00 .70
67 A9 20h olive green 1.00 1.00

Bluish Paper

68 A9 25h carmine .70 .70
69 A9 50h indigo 1.00 1.00
70 A9 70h deep blue 1.75 1.40
71 A9 1k ol gray & car 1.75 1.75
Nos. 61-71 (11) 29.45 30.35

Nos. 61-71 exist with privately applied perforations.

Counterfeits exist.

For surcharges see Nos. J35-J39.

Posen (Poznan) Issue

Germany Nos. 84-85, 87, 96, 98 Overprinted in Black

Perf. 14, 14½

1919, Aug. 5 **Wmk. 125**

72 A22 5pf on 2pf gray 30.00 24.00
73 A22 5pf on 7½pf org 2.00 1.40
a. Double surcharge 1,000.
74 A16 5pf on 20pf bl vio 2.00 1.25
75 A16 10pf on 25pf org & blk, *yel* 6.00 3.50
76 A16 10pf on 40pf lake & blk 3.50 1.40
Nos. 72-76 (5) 43.50 31.55

Counterfeits exist.

Germany Nos. 96 and 98 Surcharged in Red or Green

a

b

1919, Sept. 15

77 A22 5pf on 2pf (R) 275.00 175.00
a. Inverted surcharge *27,500.*
78 A22 10pf on 7½pf (G) 400.00 125.00

Nos. 77-78 are a provisional issue for use in Gniezno. Counterfeit surcharges abound.

Eagle and Fasces, Symbolical of United Poland
A10 A11

"Agriculture" A12

"Peace" — A13

Polish Cavalryman A14

For Northern Poland

Denominations as "F" or "M"

1919, Jan. 27 ***Imperf.***

Wove or Ribbed Paper

81 A10 3f bister brn .25 .35
82 A10 5f green .25 .35
83 A10 10f red violet .25 .35
84 A10 15f deep rose .25 .25
85 A11 20f deep blue .25 .50
86 A11 25f olive green .25 .50
87 A11 50f blue green .25 .50
88 A12 1m violet 2.50 3.75
89 A12 1.50m deep green 4.25 7.00
90 A12 2m dark brown 4.25 8.50
91 A13 2.50m orange brn 8.50 22.50
92 A14 5m red violet 17.50 40.00
Nos. 81-92 (12) 38.75 84.55

Perf. 10, 11, 11½, 10x11½, 11½x10

1919-20

93 A10 3f bister brn .25 .25
94 A10 5f green .25 .25
95 A10 10f red violet .25 .25
96 A10 10f brown ('20) .25 .25
97 A10 15f deep rose .25 .25
98 A10 15f vermilion ('20) .25 .25
99 A11 20f deep blue .25 .25
100 A11 25f olive green .25 .25
101 A11 40f brt violet ('20) .25 .25
102 A11 50f blue green .25 .25
103 A12 1m violet .70 .25
105 A12 1.50m deep green .70 .35
106 A12 2m dark brown 1.75 .50
107 A13 2.50m orange brn 1.00 .70
108 A14 5m red violet 2.00 1.50
Nos. 93-108 (15) 8.65 5.80

No. 108 exists in various shades of brown and violet.

Several denominations among Nos. 81-132 are found with double impression or in pairs imperf. between. See Nos. 109-132, 140-152C, 170-175. For surcharges & overprints, see Nos. 153, 199-200, B1-B14, 2K1-2K12, Eastern Silesia 41-50.

For Southern Poland

Denominations as "H" or "K"

1919, Jan. 27 ***Imperf.***

109 A10 3h red brown .35 .35
110 A10 5h emerald .35 .25
111 A10 10h orange .35 .25
112 A10 15h vermilion .35 .25
113 A11 20h gray brown .35 .25
114 A11 25h light blue .35 .25
115 A11 50h orange brn .35 .70
116 A12 1k dark green .35 1.40
117 A12 1.50k red brown 1.50 4.00
118 A12 2k dark blue 1.50 3.50
119 A13 2.50k dark violet 6.50 10.00
120 A14 5k slate blue 15.00 20.00
Nos. 109-120 (12) 27.30 41.20

Perf. 10, 11½, 10x11½, 11½x10

121 A10 3h red brown .25 .25
122 A10 5h emerald .25 .25
123 A10 10h orange .25 .25
124 A10 15h vermilion .25 .25
125 A11 20h gray brown .25 .25
126 A11 25h light blue .25 .25
127 A11 50h orange brn .25 .25
128 A12 1k dark green .25 .25
129 A12 1.50k red brown .35 .25
130 A12 2k dark blue .70 .25
131 A13 2.50k dark violet 1.40 .70
132 A14 5k slate blue 1.40 1.10
Nos. 121-132 (12) 5.85 4.30

National Assembly Issue

A20

Ignacy Jan Paderewski — A21

Adalbert Trampczynski — A22

Eagle Watching Ship — A24

25f, Gen. Josef Pilsudski. 1m, Griffin.

1919-20 ***Perf. 11½***

Wove or Ribbed Paper

133 A20 10f red violet .35 .25
134 A21 15f brown red .35 .25
a. Imperf., pair 25.00
135 A22 20f dp brown (21x25mm) .35 .25
136 A22 20f dp brown (17x20mm) ('20) .75 1.60
137 A21 25f olive green .35 .25
138 A24 50f Prus blue .35 .25
139 A24 1m purple 1.00 .35
Nos. 133-139 (7) 3.50 3.20

First National Assembly of Poland.

General Issue

1919 ***Perf. 9 to 14½ and Compound***

Thin Laid Paper

140 A11 25f olive green .25 .25
141 A11 50f blue green .25 .25
142 A12 1m dark gray .25 .25
143 A12 2m bister brn .25 .25
144 A13 3m red brown 2.00 .35
a. Pair, imperf. vert. 8.00 8.00
145 A14 5m red violet 1.25 .25
146 A14 6m deep rose 1.40 .25
a. Pair, imperf. vert. 8.00 8.00
147 A14 10m brown red .50 .30
a. Horizontal pair, imperf. 8.00 8.00
148 A14 20m gray green 1.40 .50
Nos. 140-148 (9) 7.55 2.65

Type of 1919 Redrawn

Perf. 9 to 14½ and Compound

1920-22 **Thin Laid or Wove Paper**

149 A10 1m red .25 .25
150 A10 2m gray green .25 .25
151 A10 3m light blue .50 .35
152 A10 4m rose red .25 .25

152A A10 5m dark violet .25 .25
b. Horiz. pair, imperf. vert. 8.00 8.00
152C A10 8m gray brown ('22) .50 .50
Nos. 149-152C (6) 2.00 1.85

The word "POCZTA" is in smaller letters and the numerals have been enlarged.

The color of No. 152A varies from dark violet to red brown.

No. 101 Surcharged

Perf. 10, 11½, 10x11½, 11½x10

1921, Jan. 25 Thick Wove Paper

153 A11 3m on 40f brt vio .30 .25
a. Double surcharge 25.00 25.00
b. Inverted surcharge — —

Sower and Rainbow of Hope — A27

Thin Laid or Wove Paper

Perf. 9 to 14½ and Compound

1921 Size: 28x22mm Litho.

154 A27 10m grnsh blue .50 .25
155 A27 15m light brown .25 .25
155A A27 20m red .80 .25
Nos. 154-155A (3) 1.55 .75

Signing of peace treaty with Russia.

Nos. 154-155A exist imperf. Value, unused, each $6.

See No. 191. For surcharges see Nos. 196-198.

Sun (Peace) Breaking into Darkness (Despair) — A28

"Peace" and "Agriculture" A29

"Peace" A30

Perf. 11, 11½, 12, 12½, 13 and Compound

1921, May 2

156 A28 2m green .40 9.50
157 A28 3m blue 1.50 10.00
158 A28 4m red .35 .70
a. 4m carmine rose (error) *600.00*
159 A29 6m carmine rose .35 1.50
160 A29 10m slate blue 1.25 .80
161 A30 25m dk violet 2.00 .70
162 A30 50m slate bl & buff 1.25 .70
Nos. 156-162 (7) 7.10 23.90

Issued to commemorate the Constitution.

Polish Eagle — A31

Perf. 9 to 14½ and Compound

1921-23

163 A31 25m violet & buff .80 .25
164 A31 50m carmine & buff .80 .25
a. Vert. pair, imperf. horiz.
165 A31 100m blk brn & org .80 .25
166 A31 200m black & rose ('23) .80 .25
167 A31 300m olive grn ('23) .40 .25
168 A31 400m brown ('23) .55 .25
169 A31 500m brn vio ('23) .70 .25
169A A31 1000m orange ('23) 1.25 .25
169B A31 2000m dull blue ('23) .35 .25
Nos. 163-169B (9) 6.45 2.25

For surcharge see No. 195.

Type of 1919 and

Miner — A32

Perf. 9 to 14½ and Compound

1922-23

170 A10 5f blue .25 1.00
171 A10 10f lt violet .25 1.00
172 A11 20f pale red .25 2.00
173 A11 40f violet brn .25 2.00
174 A11 50f orange .25 2.00
175 A11 75f blue green .25 3.00
176 A32 1m black .25 2.00
177 A32 1.25m dark green .25 4.50
178 A32 2m deep rose .25 2.00
179 A32 3m emerald .25 2.00
180 A32 4m deep ultra .25 4.00
181 A32 5m yellow brn .25 2.00
182 A32 6m red orange .25 8.50
183 A32 10m lilac brn .25 3.50
184 A32 20m deep violet .25 4.00
185 A32 50m olive green .25 3.50
187 A32 80m vermilion ('23) 1.00 27.50
188 A32 100m violet ('23) .60 40.00
189 A32 200m orange ('23) 2.50 40.00
190 A32 300m pale blue ('23) 6.00 60.00
Nos. 170-190 (20) 14.10 214.50

Union of Upper Silesia with Poland.

There were 2 printings of Nos. 176 to 190, the 1st being from flat plates, the 2nd from rotary press on thin paper, perf. 12½.

Nos. 173 and 175 are printed from new plates showing larger value numerals and a single "f."

Sower Type Redrawn

Size: 25x21mm

1922 Thick or Thin Wove Paper

191 A27 20m carmine .75 .25

In this stamp the design has been strengthened and made more distinct, especially the ground and the numerals in the upper corners.

Nicolaus Copernicus A33

Father Stanislaus Konarski — A34

1923 ***Perf. 10 to 12½***

192 A33 1000m indigo .35 .35
193 A34 3000m brown .35 .70
a. "Konapski" 17.00 19.00
194 A33 5000m rose .35 .35
Nos. 192-194 (3) 1.05 1.40

Nicolaus Copernicus (1473-1543), astronomer (Nos. 192, 194); Stanislaus Konarski (1700-1773), educator, and the creation by the Polish Parliament of the Commission of Public Instruction (No. 193).

No. 163 Surcharged

1923 ***Perf. 9 to 14½ and Compound***

195 A31 10000m on 25m .50 .25
a. Double surcharge 60.00
b. Inverted surcharge 35.00

Stamps of 1921 Surcharged

196 A27 25000m on 20m red 2.00 1.00
a. Double surcharge 60.00 —
b. Inverted surcharge 35.00 —
197 A27 50000m on 10m grnsh bl .80 .25
a. Double surcharge 60.00 —
b. Inverted surcharge 35.00 —

No. 191 Surcharged

198 A27 25000m on 20m car .60 .25
a. Double surcharge 60.00 —
b. Inverted surcharge 35.00 —

No. 150 Surcharged with New Value

1924

199 A10 20000m on 2m gray grn .80 .25
a. Inverted surcharge 35.00 —
b. Double surcharge 60.00 —

Type of 1919 Issue Surcharged with New Value

200 A10 100000m on 5m red brn .80 .25
a. Double surcharge 60.00 —
b. Inverted surcharge 35.00 —
Nos. 195-200 (6) 5.50 2.25

Arms of Poland — A35

Perf. 10 to 14½ and Compound

1924 Thin Paper Litho.

205 A35 10,000m lilac brn 1.10 .50
206 A35 20,000m ol grn .70 .35
207 A35 30,000m scarlet 1.25 .25
208 A35 50,000m apple grn 2.75 .25
209 A35 100,000m brn org 1.00 .25
210 A35 200,000m lt blue 1.10 .25
211 A35 300,000m red vio 2.75 1.00
212 A35 500,000m brn 2.50 1.00
213 A35 1,000,000m ple rose .35 *35.00*
214 A35 2,000,000m dk grn .35 *225.00*
Nos. 205-214 (10) 13.85 263.85
Set, never hinged 50.00

Arms of Poland A36

President Stanislaus Wojciechowski A37

Perf. 10 to 13½ and Compound

1924

215 A36 1g orange brown .35 .50
216 A36 2g dark brown .35 .25
217 A36 3g orange .35 .25
218 A36 5g olive green .35 .25
219 A36 10g blue green .75 .25
220 A36 15g red .75 .25
221 A36 20g blue 2.50 .25
222 A36 25g red brown 6.50 .25
a. 25g indigo *12,000.* *6,000.*
223 A36 30g deep violet 10.00 .25
a. 30g gray blue *250.00* *125.00*
224 A36 40g indigo 2.50 .70
225 A36 50g magenta .50 .25

Perf. 11½, 12

226 A37 1z scarlet 17.50 1.40
Nos. 215-226 (12) 42.40 4.85
Set, never hinged 265.00

For overprints see Nos. 1K1-1K11.

Holy Gate of Wilno (Vilnius) — A38

Poznan Town Hall — A39

Sigismund Monument, Warsaw — A40

Wawel Castle at Cracow — A41

Sobieski Statue at Lwow — A42

Ship of State — A43

1925-27 ***Perf. 10 to 13***

227 A38 1g bister brown .55 .25
228 A42 2g brown olive .65 .50
229 A40 3g blue 2.00 .25
230 A39 5g yellow green 2.75 .25
231 A40 10g violet 2.00 .25
232 A41 15g rose red 3.00 .25
233 A43 20g dull red 13.00 .25
234 A38 24g gray blue 5.50 .75
235 A42 30g dark blue 1.60 .25
236 A41 40g lt blue ('27) 1.60 .25
237 A43 45g dark violet 11.00 .25
Nos. 227-237 (11) 43.65 3.50
Set, never hinged 110.00

For overprints see Nos. 1K11A-1K17.

1926-27 Redrawn

238 A40 3g blue .65 .25
239 A39 5g yellow green 1.00 .25
240 A40 10g violet .85 .25
241 A41 15g rose red .85 .25
Nos. 238-241 (4) 3.35 1.00
Set, never hinged 7.50

On Nos. 229-232 the lines representing clouds touch the numerals. On the redrawn stamps the numerals have white outlines, separating them from the cloud lines.

Marshal Pilsudski — A44

Frederic Chopin — A45

1927 Typo. ***Perf. 12½, 11½***

242 A44 20g red brown 2.00 .25
243 A45 40g deep ultra 8.50 .75
Set, never hinged 35.00

See No. 250. For overprint see No. 1K18.

President Ignacy Moscicki — A46

1927, May 4 *Perf. 11½*

245 A46 20g red 3.00 1.00
Never hinged 10.00

Dr. Karol Kaczkowski — A47

1927, May 27 *Perf. 11½, 12½*

246 A47 10g gray green 3.00 3.50
247 A47 25g carmine 4.50 3.50
248 A47 40g dark blue 6.00 1.75
Nos. 246-248 (3) 13.50 8.75
Set, never hinged 50.00

4th Intl. Congress of Millitary Medicine and Pharmacy, Warsaw, May 30-June 4.

Juliusz Slowacki — A48

1927, June 28 *Perf. 12½*

249 A48 20g rose 2.75 .70
Never hinged 12.00

Transfer from Paris to Cracow of the remains of Julius Slowacki, poet.

Pilsudski Type of 1927
Design Redrawn

1928 *Perf. 11½, 12x11½, 12½x13*

250 A44 25g yellow brown 2.00 .25
Never hinged 8.50

Souvenir Sheet

A49

1928, May 3 Engr. *Perf. 12½*

251 A49 Sheet of 2 250.00 325.00
Never hinged 475.00
a. 50g black brown 25.00 85.00
b. 1z black brown 25.00 85.00

1st Natl. Phil. Exhib., Warsaw, May 3-13.
Sold to each purchaser of a 1.50z ticket to the Warsaw Philatelic Exhibition.
Counterfeits exist.

Marshal Pilsudski — A49a

Perf. 10½ to 14 and Compound

1928-31 **Wove Paper**

253 A49a 50g bluish slate 3.00 .25
254 A49a 50g blue grn ('31) 20.00 .35
Set, never hinged 70.00

See No. 315.

Pres. Moscicki — A50

Perf. 12x12½, 11½ to 13½ and Compound

1928 **Laid Paper**

255 A50 1z black, *cream* 15.00 .70
Never hinged 50.00
a. Horizontally laid paper ('30) 40.00 1.75
Never hinged 120.00

See Nos. 305, 316. For surcharges and overprints see Nos. J92-J94, 1K19, 1K24.

General Josef Bem — A51

Wove Paper

1928, May Typo. *Perf. 12½*

256 A51 25g rose red 2.00 .35
Never hinged 8.50

Return from Syria to Poland of the ashes of General Josef Bem.

Henryk Sienkiewicz — A52

1928, Oct.

257 A52 15g ultra .75 .25
Never hinged 3.25

For overprint see No. 1K23.

Eagle Arms — A53

1928-29 *Perf. 12x12½*

258 A53 5g dark violet .25 .25
259 A53 10g green .25 .25
260 A53 25g red brown .25 .25
Nos. 258-260 (3) .75 .75
Set, never hinged 4.00

See design A58. For overprints see Nos. 1K20-1K22.

"Swiatowid," Ancient Slav God — A54

1928, Dec. 15 *Perf. 12½x12*

261 A54 25g brown .50 .25
Never hinged 3.50

Poznan Agricultural Exhibition.

King John III Sobieski — A55

1930, July *Perf. 12x12½*

262 A55 75g claret 1.50 .25
Never hinged 6.00

Stylized Soldiers — A56

1930, Nov. 1 *Perf. 12½*

263 A56 5g violet brown .35 .25
264 A56 15g dark blue 2.75 .25
265 A56 25g red brown .25 .25
266 A56 30g dull red 5.00 2.25
Nos. 263-266 (4) 8.35 3.00
Set, never hinged 25.00

Centenary of insurrection of 1830.

Kosciuszko, Washington, Pulaski — A57

Laid Paper

1932, May 3 *Perf. 11½*

267 A57 30g brown 1.00 .35
Never hinged 3.50

200th birth anniv. of George Washington.

A58

Perf. 12x12½

1932-33 Typo. Wmk. 234

268 A58 5g dull vio ('33) .35 .25
269 A58 10g green .35 .25
270 A58 15g red brown ('33) .35 .25
271 A58 20g gray .75 .25
272 A58 25g buff .75 .25
273 A58 30g deep rose .85 .25
274 A58 60g blue 3.75 .50
Nos. 268-274 (7) 7.15 2.00
Set, never hinged 27.50

For overprints and surcharge see Nos. 280-281, 284, 292, 1K25-1K27.

Torun City Hall — A59

1933, Jan. 2 Engr. *Perf. 11½*

275 A59 60g blue 27.50 1.00
Never hinged 90.00

700th anniversary of the founding of the City of Torun by the Grand Master of the Knights of the Teutonic Order.
See No. B28.

Altar Panel of St. Mary's Church, Cracow — A60

Perf. 11½-12½ & Compound

1933, July 10 Laid Paper Unwmk.

277 A60 80g red brown 8.50 .70
Never hinged 30.00

400th death anniv. of Veit Stoss, sculptor and woodcarver.
For surcharge see No. 285.

John III Sobieski and Allies before Vienna, painted by Jan Matejko — A61

1933, Sept. 12 **Laid Paper**

278 A61 1.20z indigo 20.00 2.00
Never hinged 70.00

250th anniv. of the deliverance of Vienna by the Polish and allied forces under command of John III Sobieski, King of Poland, when besieged by the Turks in 1683.
For surcharge see No. 286.

Cross of Independence A62

Wmk. 234

1933, Nov. 11 Typo. *Perf. 12½*

279 A62 30g scarlet 1.75 .30
Never hinged 6.25

15th anniversary of independence.

Type of 1932 Overprinted in Red or Black

1934, May 5 *Perf. 12*

280 A58 20g gray (R) 20.00 40.00
281 A58 30g deep rose 30.00 45.00
Set, never hinged 175.00

Katowice Philatelic Exhibition. Counterfeits exist.

Josef Pilsudski — A63

Perf. 11½ to 12½ and Compound

1934, Aug. 6 Engr. Unwmk.

282 A63 25g gray blue 1.25 .70
283 A63 30g black brown 1.75 .70
Set, never hinged 17.50

Polish Legion, 20th anniversary.
For overprint see No. 293.

Nos. 274, 277-278 Surcharged in Black or Red

1934 Wmk. 234 *Perf. 12x12½*

284 A58 55g on 60g blue 1.75 .25

Perf. 11½-12½ & Compound

Unwmk.

285 A60 25g on 80g red brn 2.50 .25
286 A61 1z on 1.20z ind (R) 9.50 4.25
a. Figure "1" in surcharge 5mm high instead of 4½mm 9.50 4.25
Never hinged 50.00
Nos. 284-286 (3) 13.75 4.75
Set, never hinged 75.00

Surcharge of No. 286 includes bars.

Marshal Pilsudski — A64

1935 *Perf. 11 to 13 and Compound*

No.	Type	Description	Unused	Used
287	A64	5g black	.35	.25
288	A64	15g black	.35	.25
289	A64	25g black	.45	.25
290	A64	45g black	2.75	.50
291	A64	1z black	5.00	3.50
		Nos. 287-291 (5)	8.90	4.75
		Set, never hinged	30.00	

Pilsudski mourning issue.

Nos. 287-288 are typo., Nos. 290-291 litho. No. 289 exists both typo. and litho.

See No. B35b.

Nos. 270, 282 Overprinted in Blue or Red

1935 Wmk. 234 *Perf. 12x12½*

No.	Type	Description	Unused	Used
292	A58	15g red brown	.75	.25

Perf. 11½, 11½x12½

Unwmk.

No.	Type	Description	Unused	Used
293	A63	25g gray blue (R)	2.00	.85
		Set, never hinged	12.00	

Issued in connection with the proposed memorial to Marshal Pilsudski, the stamps were sold at Cracow exclusively.

"The Dog Cliff" — A65 President Ignacy Moscicki — A75

Designs: 10g, "Eye of the Sea." 15g, M. S. "Pilsudski." 20g, View of Pieniny. 25g, Belvedere Palace. 30g, Castle in Mira. 45g, Castle at Podhorce. 50g, Cloth Hall, Cracow. 55g, Raczynski Library, Poznan. 1z, Cathedral, Wilno.

1935-36 Typo. *Perf. 12½x13*

No.	Type	Description	Unused	Used
294	A65	5g violet blue	.25	.25
295	A65	10g yellow green	.40	.25
296	A65	15g Prus green	1.90	.25
297	A65	20g violet black	.95	.25
		Engr.		
298	A65	25g myrtle green	.30	.30
299	A65	30g rose red	.75	.25
300	A65	45g plum ('36)	.25	.25
301	A65	50g black ('36)	.25	.25
302	A65	55g blue ('36)	1.25	.25
303	A65	1z brown ('36)	3.50	3.50
304	A75	3z black brown	1.00	5.25
		Nos. 294-304 (11)	10.80	11.05
		Set, never hinged	40.00	

See Nos. 308-311. For overprints see Nos. 306-307, 1K28-1K32.

Type of 1928 inscribed "1926. 3. VI. 1936" on Bottom Margin

1936, June 3

No.	Type	Description	Unused	Used
305	A50	1z ultra	2.00	4.00
		Never hinged	6.50	

Presidency of Ignacy Moscicki, 10th anniv.

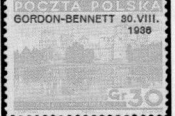

Nos. 299, 302 Overprinted in Blue or Red

1936, Aug. 15

No.	Type	Description	Unused	Used
306	A65	30g rose red	3.50	3.50
307	A65	55g blue (R)	5.50	2.25
		Set, never hinged	30.00	

Gordon-Bennett Intl. Balloon Race. Counterfeits exist.

Scenic Type of 1935-36

Designs: 5g, Church at Czestochowa. 10g, Maritime Terminal, Gdynia. 15g, University, Lwow. 20g, Municipal Building, Katowice.

1937 Engr. *Perf. 12½*

No.	Type	Description	Unused	Used
308	A65	5g violet blue	.25	.25
309	A65	10g green	.40	.25
310	A65	15g red brown	.35	.25
311	A65	20g orange brown	.35	.25
		Nos. 308-311 (4)	1.35	1.00
		Set, never hinged	5.00	

For overprints see Nos. 1K31-1K32.

Marshal Smigly-Rydz — A80

1937 *Perf. 12½x13*

No.	Type	Description	Unused	Used
312	A80	25g slate green	.25	.25
313	A80	55g blue	.25	.25
		Set, never hinged	2.00	

For surcharges see Nos. N30, N32.

Types of 1928-37

1937 Souvenir Sheets

No.	Description	Unused	Used
314	Sheet of 4	14.00	20.00
a.	A80 25g, dark brown	1.75	2.75
315	Sheet of 4	14.00	20.00
a.	A49a 50g, deep blue	1.75	2.75
316	Sheet of 4	12.50	20.00
a.	A50 1z, gray black	1.75	2.75
	Set, never hinged	120.00	

Visit of King Carol of Romania to Poland, June 26-July 1.

See No. B35c.

President Moscicki — A81

1938, Feb. 1 *Perf. 12½*

No.	Type	Description	Unused	Used
317	A81	15g slate green	.70	.25
318	A81	30g rose violet	.35	.25
		Set, never hinged	3.00	

71st birthday of President Moscicki.

For surcharge see No. N31.

Kosciuszko, Paine and Washington and View of New York City — A82

1938, Mar. 17 *Perf. 12x12½*

No.	Type	Description	Unused	Used
319	A82	1z gray blue	1.40	.70
		Never hinged	5.00	

150th anniv. of the US Constitution.

Boleslaus I and Emperor Otto III at Gnesen — A83 Marshal Pilsudski — A95

Designs: 10g, King Casimir III. 15g, King Ladislas II Jagello and Queen Hedwig. 20g, King Casimir IV. 25g, Treaty of Lublin. 30g, King Stephen Bathory commending Wielock, the peasant. 45g, Stanislas Zolkiewski and Jan Chodkiewicz. 50g, John III Sobieski entering Vienna. 55g, Union of nobles, commoners and peasants. 75g, Dabrowski, Kosciuszko and Poniatowski. 1z, Polish soldiers. 2z, Romuald Traugutt.

1938, Nov. 11 Engr. *Perf. 12½*

No.	Type	Description	Unused	Used
320	A83	5g red orange	.25	.25
321	A83	10g green	.25	.25
322	A83	15g fawn	.25	.25
323	A83	20g peacock blue	.25	.25
324	A83	25g dull violet	.35	.25
325	A83	30g rose red	.35	.25
326	A83	45g black	.45	.25
327	A83	50g brt red vio	.35	.25
328	A83	55g ultra	.35	.25
329	A83	75g dull green	1.40	1.00
330	A83	1z orange	1.60	1.75
331	A83	2z carmine rose	6.50	15.00
332	A95	3z gray black	3.00	10.00
		Nos. 320-332 (13)	15.35	30.00
		Set, never hinged	57.50	

20th anniv. of Poland's independence. See No. 339. For surcharges see Nos. N33-N47.

Souvenir Sheet

Marshal Pilsudski, Gabriel Narutowicz, President Moscicki, Marshal Smigly-Rydz — A96

1938, Nov. 11 *Perf. 12½*

No.	Type	Description	Unused	Used
333	A96	Sheet of 4	10.00	18.00
		Never hinged	35.00	
a.		25g dull violet (Pilsudski)	1.10	1.75
b.		25g dull violet (Narutowicz)	1.10	1.75
c.		25g dull violet (Moscicki)	1.10	1.75
d.		25g dull violet (Smigly-Rydz)	1.10	1.75

20th anniv. of Poland's independence.

Poland Welcoming Teschen People — A97

1938, Nov. 11

No.	Type	Description	Unused	Used
334	A97	25g dull violet	1.75	.50
		Never hinged	5.00	

Restoration of the Teschen territory ceded by Czechoslovakia.

Skier — A98

1939, Feb. 6

No.	Type	Description	Unused	Used
335	A98	15g orange brown	.50	.70
336	A98	25g dull violet	.50	.70
337	A98	30g rose red	1.40	.70
338	A98	55g brt ultra	3.25	1.25
		Nos. 335-338 (4)	5.65	3.35
		Set, never hinged	20.00	

Intl. Ski Meet, Zakopane, Feb. 11-19.

Type of 1938

15g, King Ladislas II Jagello, Queen Hedwig.

Re-engraved

1939, Mar. 2 *Perf. 12½*

No.	Type	Description	Unused	Used
339	A83	15g redsh brown	.25	.25
		Never hinged	.70	

No. 322 with crossed swords and helmet at lower left. No. 339, swords and helmet have been removed.

Marshal Pilsudski Reviewing Troops — A99

1939, Aug. 1 Engr.

No.	Type	Description	Unused	Used
340	A99	25g dull rose violet	.25	.90
		Never hinged	1.00	

Polish Legion, 25th anniv. See No. B35a.

SEMI-POSTAL STAMPS

Regular Issue of 1919 Surcharged in Violet

a

b

1919, May 3 Unwmk. *Imperf.*

No.	Type	Description	Unused	Used
B1	A10(a)	5f + 5f grn	.35	.35
B2	A10(a)	10f + 5f red vio	.35	.50
B3	A10(a)	15f + 5f dp red	.35	.50
B4	A11(b)	25f + 5f ol grn	.35	.35
B5	A11(b)	50f + 5f bl grn	.35	.70
		Perf. 11½		
B6	A10(a)	5f + 5f grn	.25	.25
B7	A10(a)	10f + 5f red vio	.50	.50
B8	A10(a)	15f + 5f dp red	.25	.25
B9	A11(b)	25f + 5f ol grn	.25	.25
B10	A11(b)	50f + 5f bl grn	.35	.35
		Nos. B1-B10 (10)	3.35	4.00
		Set, never hinged	15.00	

First Polish Philatelic Exhibition. The surtax benefited the Polish White Cross Society.

Regular Issue of 1920 Surcharged in Red and Carmine

1921, Mar. 5 *Perf. 9*

Thin Laid Paper

No.	Type	Description	Unused	Used
B11	A14	5m + 30m red vio	1.50	8.50
B12	A14	6m + 30m dp rose	1.50	8.50
B13	A14	10m + 30m lt red	3.00	*8.50*
B14	A14	20m + 30m gray grn	65.00	*120.00*
		Nos. B11-B14 (4)	71.00	145.50
		Set, never hinged	125.00	

Counterfeits, differently perforated, exist of Nos. B11-B14.

SP1

1925, Jan. 1 Typo. *Perf. 12½*

No.	Type	Description	Unused	Used
B15	SP1	1g orange brn	4.50	35.00
B16	SP1	2g dk brown	4.50	35.00
B17	SP1	3g orange	4.50	35.00
B18	SP1	5g olive grn	4.50	35.00
B19	SP1	10g blue grn	4.50	35.00
B20	SP1	15g red	4.50	35.00
B21	SP1	20g blue	4.50	35.00
B22	SP1	25g red brown	4.50	35.00
B23	SP1	30g dp violet	4.50	35.00

B24 SP1 40g indigo 110.00 35.00
B25 SP1 50g magenta 4.50 35.00
Nos. B15-B25 (11) 155.00 385.00
Set, never hinged 350.00

"Na Skarb" means "National Funds." These stamps were sold at a premium of 50 groszy each, for charity.

Light of Knowledge — SP2

1927, May 3 ***Perf. 11½***
B26 SP2 10g + 5g choc & grn 6.25 7.00
B27 SP2 20g + 5g dk bl & buff 7.50 12.00
Set, never hinged 37.50

"NA OSWIATE" means "For Public Instruction." The surtax aided an Association of Educational Societies.

Torun Type of 1933

1933, May 21 **Engr.**
B28 A59 60g (+40g) red brn, *buff* 8.50 10.00
Never hinged 30.00

Philatelic Exhibition at Torun, May 21-28, 1933, and sold at a premium of 40g to aid the exhibition funds.

Souvenir Sheet

Stagecoach and Wayside Inn — SP3

1938, May 3 **Engr.** ***Imperf.***
B29 SP3 Sheet of 4 52.50 100.00
Never hinged 125.00
a. 45g green 5.25 7.00
b. 55g blue 5.25 7.00

Perf. 12
B29C SP3 Sheet of 4 67.50 120.00
Never hinged 150.00
d. 45g green 6.50 8.50
e. 55g blue 6.50 8.50

5th Phil. Exhib., Warsaw, May 3-8. The sheets each contain two 45g and two 55g stamps. Sold for 3z.

Souvenir Sheet

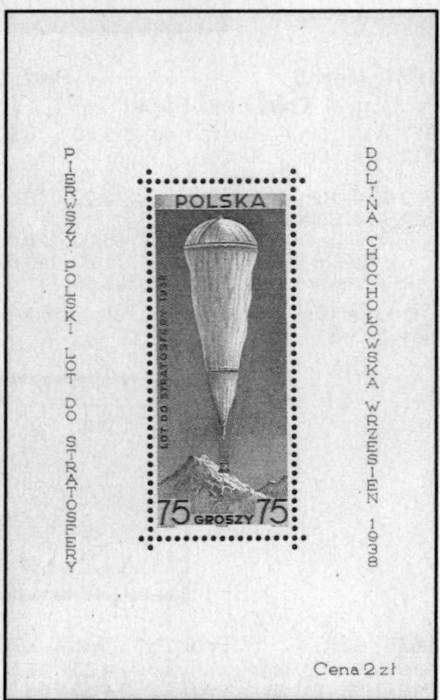
Stratosphere Balloon over Mountains — SP4

1938, Sept. 15 ***Perf. 12½***
B31 SP4 75g dp vio, sheet 40.00 65.00
Never hinged 120.00

Issued in advance of a proposed Polish stratosphere flight. Sold for 2z.

Winterhelp Issue

SP5

1938-39
B32 SP5 5g + 5g red org .45 *.25*
B33 SP5 25g + 10g dk vio ('39) .90 *.25*
B34 SP5 55g + 15g brt ultra ('39) 1.10 *3.00*
Nos. B32-B34 (3) 2.45 *3.50*
Set, never hinged 9.50

For surcharges see Nos. N48-N50.

Souvenir Sheet

SP6

1939, Aug. 1
B35 SP6 Sheet of 3, dark blue gray 15.00 24.00
Never hinged 40.00
a. 25g Marshal Pilsudski Reviewing Troops 3.50 2.75
b. 25g Marshal Pilsudski 3.50 2.75
c. 25g Marshal Smigly-Rydz 3.50 2.75

25th anniv. of the founding of the Polish Legion. The sheets sold for 1.75z, the surtax going to the National Defense fund.
See types A64, A80, A99.

AIR POST STAMPS

Biplane — AP1

Perf. 12½
1925, Sept. 10 **Typo.** **Unwmk.**
C1 AP1 1g lt blue .65 10.00
C2 AP1 2g orange .65 10.00
C3 AP1 3g yellow brn .65 10.00
C4 AP1 5g dk brown .65 .85
C5 AP1 10g dk green .65 .85
C6 AP1 15g red violet 3.25 .85
C7 AP1 20g olive grn 7.50 4.50
C8 AP1 30g dull rose 7.50 2.50
C9 AP1 45g dk violet 8.50 4.25
Nos. C1-C9 (9) 30.00 43.80
Set, never hinged 95.00

Counterfeits exist.
Nos. C1-C9 exist imperf. Value, set $125.
For overprint see No. C11.

Capt. Franciszek Zwirko and Stanislaus Wigura — AP2

Perf. 11½ to 12½ and Compound
1933, Apr. 15 **Engr.** **Wmk. 234**
C10 AP2 30g gray green 14.00 1.00
Never hinged 42.50

Winning of the circuit of Europe flight by two Polish aviators in 1932. The stamp was available for both air mail and ordinary postage.
For overprint see No. C12.

Nos. C7 and C10 Ovptd. in Red

Nos. C7 and C10 Ovptd. in Red

1934, Aug. 28 **Unwmk.** ***Perf. 12½***
C11 AP1 20g olive green 5.00 7.00

Wmk. 234
Perf. 11½
C12 AP2 30g gray green 6.00 2.00
Set, never hinged 50.00

POSTAGE DUE STAMPS

Cracow Issues

Postage Due Stamps of Austria, 1916, Overprinted in Black or Red

1919, Jan. 10 **Unwmk.** ***Perf. 12½***
J1 D4 5h rose red 17.50 20.00
J2 D4 10h rose red *5,250.* *8,500.*
J3 D4 15h rose red 12.00 *10.00*
a. Inverted overprint 3,500. *3,000.*
J4 D4 20h rose red 825.00 *650.00*
J5 D4 25h rose red 40.00 *40.00*
J6 D4 30h rose red *1,900.* *1,500.*
J7 D4 40h rose red *400.00* *400.00*
J8 D5 1k ultra (R) *5,500.* *6,250.*
J9 D5 5k ultra (R) *5,500.* *6,250.*
J10 D5 10k ultra (R) *22,500.* *25,000.*
a. Black overprint *85,000.* *100,000.*

Overprint on Nos. J1-J7, J10a is type. Overprint on Nos. J8-J10 is slightly larger than illustration, has a different ornament between lines of type and is litho.

Type of Austria, 1916-18, Surcharged in Black

D6

1919, Jan. 10
J11 D6 15h on 36h vio *525.00* 425.00
J12 D6 50h on 42h choc 70.00 *50.00*
a. Double surcharge 3,500. *5,500.*

See note above No. 41.
Counterfeits exist of Nos. J1-J12.

Regular Issues

Numerals of Value — D7

1919 **Typo.** ***Perf. 11½***
For Northern Poland
J13 D7 2f red orange .25 .25
J14 D7 4f red orange .25 .25
J15 D7 5f red orange .25 .25
J16 D7 10f red orange .25 .25
J17 D7 20f red orange .25 .25
J18 D7 30f red orange .25 .25
J19 D7 50f red orange .25 .25
J20 D7 100f red orange .50 .35
J21 D7 500f red orange 2.50 2.40

For Southern Poland
J22 D7 2h dark blue .25 .25
J23 D7 4h dark blue .25 .25
J24 D7 5h dark blue .25 .25
J25 D7 10h dark blue .25 .25
J26 D7 20h dark blue .25 .25
J27 D7 30h dark blue .25 .25
J28 D7 50h dark blue .35 .25
J29 D7 100h dark blue .45 .80
J30 D7 500h dark blue 1.40 1.60
Nos. J13-J30 (18) 8.45 8.65
Set, never hinged 33.00

Counterfeits exist.

1920 ***Perf. 9, 10, 11½***
Thin Laid Paper
J31 D7 20f dark blue .25 .25
J32 D7 100f dark blue .25 .25
J33 D7 200f dark blue .35 .25
J34 D7 500f dark blue .35 .25
Nos. J31-J34 (4) 1.20 1.00
Set, never hinged 4.25

Regular Issue of 1919 Surcharged

1921, Jan. 25 ***Imperf.***
Wove Paper
J35 A9 6m on 15h brown .75 .75
J36 A9 6m on 25h car .75 .75
J37 A9 20m on 10h lake 5.00 7.00
J38 A9 20m on 50h indigo 4.00 3.75
J39 A9 35m on 70h dp bl 7.00 9.00
Nos. J35-J39 (5) 17.50 21.25
Set, never hinged 60.00

Counterfeits exist.

Numerals of Value — D8

Thin Laid or Wove Paper
Size: 17x22mm

Perf. 9 to 14½ and Compound
1921-22 **Typo.**
J40 D8 1m indigo .25 .25
J41 D8 2m indigo .25 .25
J42 D8 4m indigo .25 .25
J43 D8 6m indigo .45 .25
J44 D8 8m indigo .45 .25
J45 D8 20m indigo .45 .25
J46 D8 50m indigo .45 .25
J47 D8 100m indigo .70 .35
Nos. J40-J47 (8) 3.25 2.10
Set, never hinged 13.00

Nos. J44-J45, J41 Surcharged
Perf. 9 to 14½ and Compound
1923, Nov.
J48 D8 10,000(m) on 8m indigo .35 .25
J49 D8 20,000(m) on 20m indigo .35 .25
J50 D8 50,000(m) on 2m indigo .45 .45
Nos. J48-J50 (3) 1.15 .95
Set, never hinged 5.75

Type of 1921-22 Issue
Size: 19x24mm

1923 **Typo.** ***Perf. 12½***
J51 D8 50m indigo .25 .25
J52 D8 100m indigo .25 .25
J53 D8 200m indigo .25 .25
J54 D8 500m indigo .60 .25
J55 D8 1000m indigo .35 .25
J56 D8 2000m indigo .40 .30
J57 D8 10,000m indigo .25 .25
J58 D8 20,000m indigo .35 .25
J59 D8 30,000m indigo .35 .25
J60 D8 50,000m indigo .35 .25
J61 D8 100,000m indigo .40 .25
J62 D8 200,000m indigo .40 .25
J63 D8 300,000m indigo 5.00 .35
J64 D8 500,000m indigo 1.75 .25
J65 D8 1,000,000m indigo 1.00 .30
J66 D8 2,000,000m indigo 1.75 .35
J67 D8 3,000,000m indigo 3.00 1.40
Nos. J51-J67 (17) 16.70 5.70
Set, never hinged 60.00

D9

Perf. 10 to 13½ and Compound

1924 **Size: 20x25½mm**

J68 D9 1g brown .25 .25
J69 D9 2g brown .25 .25
J70 D9 4g brown .30 .25
J71 D9 6g brown .30 .25
J72 D9 10g brown 1.25 .25
J73 D9 15g brown 4.50 .25
J74 D9 20g brown 3.25 .25
J75 D9 25g brown 6.25 .25
J76 D9 30g brown .75 .25
J77 D9 40g brown 1.00 .25
J78 D9 50g brown 1.00 .25
J79 D9 1z brown .45 .25
J80 D9 2z brown .45 .25
J81 D9 3z brown .75 1.50
J82 D9 5z brown .40 .60
Nos. J68-J82 (15) 21.15 5.35
Set, never hinged 92.50

Nos. J68-J69 and J72-J75 exist measuring 19½x24½mm.

For surcharges see Nos. J84-J91.

D10

1930, July ***Perf. 12½***

J83 D10 5g olive brown .70 .25
Never hinged 1.00

Postage Due Stamps of 1924 Surcharged

Perf. 10 to 13½ and Compound

1934-38

J84 D9 10g on 2z brown ('38) .25 .25
J85 D9 15g on 2z brown .25 .25
J86 D9 20g on 1z brown .40 .25
J87 D9 20g on 5z brown 6.00 .25
J88 D9 25g on 40g brown .85 .25
J89 D9 30g on 40g brown 1.40 .25
J90 D9 50g on 40g brown 1.40 .50
J91 D9 50g on 3z brown ('35) .85 .35
Nos. J84-J91 (8) 11.40 2.35
Set, never hinged 12.00

No. 255a Surcharged in Red or Indigo

1934-36 **Laid Paper**

J92 A50 10g on 1z (R) ('36) .80 .25
a. Vertically laid paper (No. 255) 25.00 18.00
J93 A50 20g on 1z (R) ('36) 2.50 .80
J94 A50 25g on 1z (I) .80 .30
a. Vertically laid paper (No. 255) 30.00 18.00
Nos. J92-J94 (3) 4.10 1.35
Set, never hinged 10.00

D11

1938-39 **Typo.** ***Perf. 12½x12***

J95 D11 5g dark blue green .25 .25
J96 D11 10g dark blue green .25 .25
J97 D11 15g dark blue green .25 .25
J98 D11 20g dark blue green .35 .25
J99 D11 25g dark blue green .35 .25
J100 D11 30g dark blue green .60 .25
J101 D11 50g dark blue green .95 .25
J102 D11 1z dark blue green 5.00 1.65
Nos. J95-J102 (8) 8.00 3.40
Set, never hinged 14.00

For surcharges see Nos. N51-N55.

OFFICIAL STAMPS

O1

Perf. 10, 11½, 10x11½, 11½x10

1920, Feb. 1 **Litho.** **Unwmk.**

O1 O1 3f vermilion .25 *.25*
O2 O1 5f vermilion .25 *.25*
O3 O1 10f vermilion .25 *.25*
O4 O1 15f vermilion .25 *.25*
O5 O1 25f vermilion .25 *.25*
O6 O1 50f vermilion .25 *.25*
O7 O1 100f vermilion .25 *.25*
O8 O1 150f vermilion .25 .25
O9 O1 200f vermilion .65 .45
O10 O1 300f vermilion .75 .50
O11 O1 600f vermilion 1.40 1.75
Nos. O1-O11 (11) 4.80 4.70
Set, never hinged 14.00

The stars on either side of the denomination do not appear on Nos. O7-O11.

Numerals Larger
Stars inclined outward

1920, Nov. 20 ***Perf. 11½***

Thin Laid Paper

O12 O1 5f red .25 .25
O13 O1 10f red .25 .25
O14 O1 15f red .25 .25
O15 O1 25f red .60 .25
O16 O1 50f red .35 .25
Nos. O12-O16 (5) 1.70 1.25
Set, never hinged 5.25

Polish Eagle — O3

Perf. 12x12½

1933, Aug. 1 **Typo.** **Wmk. 234**

O17 O3 (30g) vio (Zwyczajna) .35 .25
O18 O3 (80g) red (Polecona) .35 .25
Set, never hinged 3.00

Polish Eagle — O4

1935, Apr. 1

O19 O4 (25g) bl vio (Zwyczajna) .25 .25
O20 O4 (55g) car (Polecona) .25 .25
Set, never hinged 1.40

Stamps inscribed "Zwyczajna" or "Zwykla" were for ordinary official mail. Those with "Polecona" were for registered official mail.

NEWSPAPER STAMPS

Austrian Newspaper Stamps of 1916 Overprinted

1919, Jan. 10 **Unwmk.** ***Imperf.***

P1 N9 2h brown 19.00 *19.00*
P2 N9 4h green 18.00 *15.00*
P3 N9 6h dark blue 15.00 *14.00*
P4 N9 10h orange 275.00 200.00
P5 N9 30h claret 19.00 17.00
Nos. P1-P5 (5) 346.00 265.00

See note above No. 41.
Counterfeits exist of Nos. P1-P5.

OCCUPATION STAMPS

Issued under German Occupation

German Stamps of 1905 Overprinted

Perf. 14, 14½

1915, May 12 **Wmk. 125**

N1 A16 3pf brown .60 .50
N2 A16 5pf green 1.25 .50
N3 A16 10pf carmine 1.25 .50
N4 A16 20pf ultra 2.50 .75
N5 A16 40pf lake & blk 7.50 3.75
Nos. N1-N5 (5) 13.10 6.00
Set, never hinged 40.00

German Stamps of 1905-17 Overprinted

1916-17

N6 A22 2½pf gray 1.25 *2.50*
N7 A16 3pf brown 1.25 *2.50*
N8 A16 5pf green 1.25 *2.50*
N9 A22 7½pf orange 1.25 *2.50*
N10 A16 10pf carmine 1.25 *2.50*
N11 A22 15pf yel brn 3.50 3.50
N12 A22 15pf dk vio ('17) 1.25 *2.50*
N13 A16 20pf ultra 1.75 *2.50*
N14 A16 30pf org & blk, *buff* 7.00 *15.00*
N15 A16 40pf lake & blk 2.50 2.50
N16 A16 60pf magenta 3.00 *3.50*
Nos. N6-N16 (11) 25.25 42.00
Set, never hinged 70.00

For overprints and surcharges see #15-26.

German Stamps of 1934 Surcharged in Black

1939, Dec. 1 **Wmk. 237** ***Perf. 14***

N17 A64 6g on 3pf bister .25 *.40*
N18 A64 8g on 4pf dl bl .25 *.40*
N19 A64 12g on 6pf dk grn .25 *.40*
N20 A64 16g on 8pf vermilion .50 1.00
N21 A64 20g on 10pf choc .25 .40
N22 A64 24g on 12pf dp car .25 .25
N23 A64 30g on 15pf maroon .50 .90
N24 A64 40g on 20pf brt bl .50 .40
N25 A64 50g on 25pf ultra .50 .75
N26 A64 60g on 30pf ol grn .50 .40
N27 A64 80g on 40pf red vio .55 .80
N28 A64 1z on 50pf dk grn & blk 1.10 1.00
N29 A64 2z on 100(pf) org & blk 2.25 *3.00*
Nos. N17-N29 (13) 7.65 10.10
Set, never hinged 25.00

Stamps of Poland 1937, Surcharged in Black or Brown

1940 **Unwmk.** ***Perf. 12½, 12½x13***

N30 A80 24g on 25g sl grn 1.25 *3.25*
N31 A81 40g on 30g rose vio .40 1.25
N32 A80 50g on 55g blue .30 *.70*

Similar Surcharge on Stamps of 1938-39

N33 A83 2g on 5g red org .25 *.40*
N34 A83 4(g) on 5g red org .25 *.40*
N35 A83 6(g) on 10g grn .25 *.40*
N36 A83 8(g) on 10g grn (Br) .25 *.40*
N37 A83 10(g) on 10g grn .25 *.40*
N38 A83 12(g) on 15g redsh brn (#339) .25 *.40*
N39 A83 16(g) on 15g redsh brn (#339) .25 *.40*
N40 A83 24g on 25g dl vio .25 *.40*
N41 A83 30(g) on 30g rose red .25 *.40*
N42 A83 50(g) on 50g brt red vio .25 *.65*
N43 A83 60(g) on 55g ultra 6.00 *17.00*
N44 A83 80(g) on 75g dl grn 6.00 *17.00*
N45 A83 1z on 1z org 6.25 *17.00*
N46 A83 2z on 2z car rose 3.00 *7.50*
N47 A95 3z on 3z gray blk 4.00 *10.00*

Similar Surcharge on Nos. B32-B34

N48 SP5 30g on 5g+5g .25 .65
N49 SP5 40g on 25g+10g .25 .65
N50 SP5 1z on 55g+15g 4.00 *10.00*

Similar Surcharge on Nos. J98-J102

Perf. 12½x12

N51 D11 50(g) on 20g 1.25 *3.25*
N52 D11 50(g) on 25g 6.00 *17.50*
N53 D11 50(g) on 30g 14.00 *37.50*
N54 D11 50(g) on 50g .75 *2.40*
N55 D11 50(g) on 1z 1.75 *4.75*
Nos. N30-N55 (26) 57.95 *154.65*
Set, never hinged 160.00

The surcharge on Nos. N30 to N55 is arranged to fit the shape of the stamp and obliterate the original denomination. On some values, "General Gouvernement" appears at the bottom. Counterfeits exist.

St. Florian's Gate, Cracow — OS1

Palace, Warsaw — OS13

Designs: 8g, Watch Tower, Cracow. 10g, Cracow Gate, Lublin. 12g, Courtyard and statue of Copernicus. 20g, Dominican Church, Cracow. 24g, Wawel Castle, Cracow. 30g, Church, Lublin. 40g, Arcade, Cloth Hall, Cracow. 48g, City Hall, Sandomierz. 50g, Court House, Cracow. 60g, Courtyard, Cracow. 80g, St. Mary's Church, Cracow.

1940-41 **Unwmk.** **Photo.** ***Perf. 14***

N56 OS1 6g brown .25 *.75*
N57 OS1 8g brn org .25 *.75*
N58 OS1 8g bl blk ('41) .45 *.50*
N59 OS1 10g emerald .25 *.25*
N60 OS1 12g dk grn 2.00 .70
N61 OS1 12g dp vio ('41) .30 *.25*
N62 OS1 20g dk ol brn .25 .25
N63 OS1 24g henna brn .25 .25
N64 OS1 30g purple .25 .25
N65 OS1 30g vio brn ('41) .30 *.25*
N66 OS1 40g slate blk .25 .25
N67 OS1 48g chnt brn ('41) .60 *1.50*
N68 OS1 50g brt bl .25 .25
N69 OS1 60g slate grn .25 *.25*
N70 OS1 80g dull pur .25 *.50*
N71 OS13 1z rose lake 2.00 1.25
N72 OS13 1z Prus grn ('41) .55 *1.00*
Nos. N56-N72 (17) 8.70 9.20
Set, never hinged 16.00

For surcharges see Nos. NB1-NB4.

OCCUPATION SEMI-POSTAL STAMPS

Issued under German Occupation

Types of 1940 Occupation Postage Stamps Surcharged in Red

Unwmk.

1940, Aug. 17 Photo. *Perf. 14*

NB1	OS1	12g + 8g olive gray	1.60	*3.50*
NB2	OS1	24g + 16g olive gray	1.60	*3.50*
NB3	OS1	50g + 50g olive gray	2.00	*4.00*
NB4	OS1	80g + 80g olive gray	2.00	*5.25*
		Nos. NB1-NB4 (4)	7.20	*16.25*
		Set, never hinged	15.00	

German Peasant Girl in Poland OSP1

Designs: 24g+26g, Woman wearing scarf. 30g+20g, Similar to type OSP4.

1940, Oct. 26 Engr. *Perf. 14½*

Thick Paper

NB5	OSP1	12g + 38g dk sl grn	1.10	2.75
NB6	OSP1	24g + 26g cop red	1.10	2.75
NB7	OSP1	30g + 20g dk pur	2.00	*5.00*
		Nos. NB5-NB7 (3)	4.20	10.50
		Set, never hinged	8.50	

1st anniversary of the General Government.

German Peasant OSP4

1940, Dec. 1 *Perf. 12*

NB8	OSP4	12g + 8g dk grn	.50	*1.40*
NB9	OSP4	24g + 16g rose red	.50	*1.75*
NB10	OSP4	30g + 30g vio brn	1.10	*2.50*
NB11	OSP4	50g + 50g ultra	1.25	*3.00*
		Nos. NB8-NB11 (4)	3.35	*8.65*
		Set, never hinged	7.00	

The surtax was for war relief.

OCCUPATION RURAL DELIVERY STAMPS

Issued under German Occupation

OSD1

Perf. 13½

1940, Dec. 1 Photo. Unwmk.

NL1	OSD1	10g red orange	.45	*1.00*
NL2	OSD1	20g red orange	.45	*1.25*
NL3	OSD1	30g red orange	.45	*1.25*
NL4	OSD1	50g red orange	1.10	*3.00*
		Nos. NL1-NL4 (4)	2.45	*6.50*
		Set, never hinged	6.00	

OCCUPATION OFFICIAL STAMPS

Issued under German Occupation

Eagle and Swastika OOS1

Perf. 12, 13½x14

1940, Apr. Photo. Unwmk.

Size: 31x23mm

NO1	OOS1	6g lt brown	.60	*1.00*
NO2	OOS1	8g gray	.60	*1.00*
NO3	OOS1	10g green	.60	*1.00*
NO4	OOS1	12g dk green	.60	*1.75*
NO5	OOS1	20g dk brown	.60	*3.00*
NO6	OOS1	24g henna brn	10.00	1.75
NO7	OOS1	30g rose lake	.80	*2.75*
NO8	OOS1	40g dl violet	.80	*5.00*
NO9	OOS1	48g dl olive	3.25	*5.00*
NO10	OOS1	50g royal bl	.80	2.75
NO11	OOS1	60g dk ol grn	.60	*2.00*
NO12	OOS1	80g rose vio	.60	*2.00*

Size: 35x26mm

NO13	OOS1	1z gray blk & brn vio	1.50	*4.75*
NO14	OOS1	3z gray blk & chnt	1.50	*4.75*
NO15	OOS1	5z gray blk & org brn	2.40	*5.50*
		Nos. NO1-NO15 (15)	25.25	44.00
		Set, never hinged	70.00	

1940 Size: 21¼x16¼mm *Perf. 12*

NO16	OOS1	6g brown	.40	*1.10*
NO17	OOS1	8g slate	.50	*1.25*
NO18	OOS1	10g dp grn	1.00	*2.50*
NO19	OOS1	12g slate grn	.50	*1.25*
NO20	OOS1	20g blk brn	.50	*1.10*
NO21	OOS1	24g cop brn	1.00	*1.10*
NO22	OOS1	30g rose lake	.60	*1.25*
NO23	OOS1	40g dl pur	.60	*2.00*
NO24	OOS1	50g royal blue	.60	*2.00*
		Nos. NO16-NO24 (9)	5.70	*13.55*
		Set, never hinged	20.00	

POLISH OFFICES ABROAD

OFFICES IN DANZIG

Poland Nos. 215-225 Overprinted

1925, Jan. 5 Unwmk. *Perf. 11½x12*

1K1	A36	1g orange brn	.35	3.75
1K2	A36	2g dk brown	.35	2.00
1K3	A36	3g orange	.35	1.40
1K4	A36	5g olive grn	12.00	2.25
1K5	A36	10g blue grn	3.50	1.25
1K6	A36	15g red	20.00	2.25
1K7	A36	20g blue	1.10	.70
1K8	A36	25g red brown	1.40	.70
1K9	A36	30g dp violet	1.40	.70
1K10	A36	40g indigo	1.40	.70
1K11	A36	50g magenta	1.75	1.00
		Nos. 1K1-1K11 (11)	43.60	16.70
		Set, never hinged	300.00	

Same Ovpt. on Poland Nos. 230-231

1926 *Perf. 11½, 12*

1K11A	A39	5g yellow grn	32.50	37.50
1K12	A40	10g violet	12.50	15.00
		Set, never hinged	125.00	

Counterfeit overprints are known on Nos. 1K1-1K32.

No. 232 Overprinted

1926-27

1K13	A41	15g rose red	42.50	50.00
		Never hinged	165.00	

Same Overprint on Redrawn Stamps of 1926-27

Perf. 13

1K14	A39	5g yellow grn	1.10	1.60
1K15	A40	10g violet	2.00	2.25
1K16	A41	15g rose red	3.50	1.60
1K17	A43	20g dull red	2.25	2.25
		Nos. 1K14-1K17 (4)	8.85	7.70
		Set, never hinged	28.00	

Same Ovpt. on Poland Nos. 250, 255a

1928-30 *Perf. 12½*

1K18	A44	25g yellow brn	3.50	2.75
		Never hinged	17.50	

Laid Paper

Perf. 11½x12, 12½x11½

1K19	A50	1z blk, *cr* ('30)	20.00	32.50
		Never hinged	55.00	

Poland Nos. 258-260 Overprinted

1929-30 *Perf. 12x12½*

1K20	A53	5g dk violet	1.00	*1.75*
1K21	A53	10g green ('30)	1.00	*1.75*
1K22	A53	25g red brown	2.00	1.75
		Nos. 1K20-1K22 (3)	4.00	*5.25*
		Set, never hinged	27.50	

Same Overprint on Poland No. 257

1931, Jan. 5 *Perf. 12½*

1K23	A52	15g ultra	2.75	*5.25*
		Never hinged	17.50	

Poland No. 255 Overprinted in Dark Blue

1933, July 1 Laid Paper *Perf. 11½*

1K24	A50	1z black, *cream*	52.50	*110.00*
		Never hinged	120.00	

Poland Nos. 268-270 Overprinted in Black

1934-36 Wmk. 234 *Perf. 12x12½*

1K25	A58	5g dl violet	2.50	5.00
1K26	A58	10g green ('36)	24.50	*90.00*
1K27	A58	15g red brown	2.50	5.00
		Nos. 1K25-1K27 (3)	29.50	*100.00*
		Set, never hinged	100.00	

Poland Nos. 294, 296, 298 Overprinted in Black in one or two lines

1935-36 Unwmk. *Perf. 12½x13*

1K28	A65	5g violet blue	2.00	4.00
1K29	A65	15g Prus green	2.00	6.00
1K30	A65	25g myrtle green	3.00	3.00
		Nos. 1K28-1K30 (3)	7.00	13.00
		Set, never hinged	30.00	

Same Overprint in Black on Poland Nos. 308, 310

1937, June 5

1K31	A65	5g violet blue	1.10	*2.50*
1K32	A65	15g red brown	1.10	*2.50*
		Set, never hinged	7.00	

Polish Merchants Selling Wheat in Danzig, 16th Century — A2

1938, Nov. 11 Engr. *Perf. 12½*

1K33	A2	5g red orange	.30	3.00
1K34	A2	15g red brown	.30	3.00
1K35	A2	25g dull violet	.70	3.00
1K36	A2	55g brt ultra	1.10	3.00
		Nos. 1K33-1K36 (4)	2.40	12.00
		Set, never hinged	10.00	

OFFICES IN THE TURKISH EMPIRE

Stamps of Poland 1919, Overprinted in Carmine

1919, May Unwmk. *Perf. 11½*

Wove Paper

2K1	A10	3f bister brn	55.00	100.00
2K2	A10	5f green	55.00	100.00
2K3	A10	10f red vio	55.00	100.00
2K4	A10	15f red	55.00	100.00
2K5	A11	20f dp blue	55.00	100.00
2K6	A11	25f olive grn	55.00	100.00
2K7	A11	50f blue grn	55.00	100.00

Overprinted

2K8	A12	1m violet	140.00	120.00
2K9	A12	1.50m dp green	140.00	120.00
2K10	A12	2m dk brown	140.00	140.00
2K11	A13	2.50m orange brn	140.00	120.00
2K12	A14	5m red violet	140.00	140.00
		Nos. 2K1-2K12 (12)	1,085.	1,340.

Counterfeit cancellations are plentiful. Counterfeits exist of Nos. 2K1-2K12.

Reissues are lighter, shiny red. Value, set $25.

Polish stamps with "P.P.C." overprint (Poste Polonaise Constantinople) were used on consular mail for a time.

Seven stamps with these overprints were not issued. Value, set: unused $10, never hinged $35.

PONTA DELGADA

ˌpän-tə del-ˈgä-də

LOCATION — Administrative district of the Azores comprising the islands of Sao Miguel and Santa Maria
GOVT. — A district of Portugal
AREA — 342 sq. mi.
POP. — 124,000 (approx.)
CAPITAL — Ponta Delgada

1000 Reis = 1 Milreis

STAMPS OF PORTUGAL USED IN PONTA DELGADA

Barred Numeral "50"

1853 **Queen Maria II**

A1 5r org brn (#1) 1,300.
A2 25r blue (#2) 75.
A3 50r dp yel grn (#3) 1,350.
a. 50r blue grn (#3a) 2,000.
A4 100r lilac (#4) 2,750.

1855 **King Pedro V (Straight Hair)**

A5 5r red brn (#5) 1,400.
A6 25r blue, type II (#6) 70.00
a. Type I (#6a) 70.00
A7 50r green (#7) 110.00
A8 100r lilac (#8) 140.00

1856-58
King Pedro V (Curled Hair)

A9 5r red brn (#9) 150.00
A10 25r blue, type II (#10) 110.00
a. Type I (#10a) 80.00
A11 25r rose, type II (#11; '58) 24.00

1862-64 **King Luiz**

A12 5r brown (#12) 77.50
A13 10r orange (#13) 85.00
A14 25r rose (#14) 15.00
A15 50r yel green (#15) 110.00
A16 100r lilac (#16; '64) 125.00

1866-67 **King Luiz**
Imperf.

A17 5r black (#17) 75.00
A18 10r yellow (#18) 160.00
A19 20r bister (#19) 150.00
A20 25r rose (#20) 50.00
A21 50r green (#21) 150.00
A22 80r orange (#22) 150.00
A23 100r dk lilac (#23; '67) 190.00
A24 120r blue (#24) 140.00

Perf. 12½

A28 25r rose (#28) 130.00

Issued under Portuguese Administration

King Carlos — A1

1892-93 **Typo.** **Unwmk.**
Enamel Surfaced Paper
Perf. 12½

1 A1 5r yellow 2.75 1.60
Never hinged 3.75
c. Diagonal half used as 2½r on piece 17.50
2 A1 10r reddish vio 2.75 1.60
Never hinged 3.75
3 A1 15r chocolate 3.50 2.25
Never hinged 4.75
4 A1 20r lavender 5.00 2.25
Never hinged 6.75
5a A1 25r deep green 7.50 1.60
Never hinged 11.00
6 A1 50r ultra 10.00 3.25
Never hinged 14.50
7a A1 75r carmine 7.75 5.25
Never hinged 11.00
8 A1 80r yellow grn 10.00 9.00
Never hinged 14.50
9 A1 100r brn, *yel* 11.00 5.50
Never hinged 15.00
11 A1 200r dk bl, *bl* 50.00 30.00
Never hinged 80.00
12 A1 300r dk bl, *salmon* 50.00 30.00
Never hinged 80.00
Nos. 1-12 (11) 160.25 92.30

Perf. 13½

1a A1 5r yellow 3.00 1.60
Never hinged 4.00
2a A1 10r reddish vio 4.00 2.25
Never hinged 5.25
3a A1 15r chocolate 3.75 2.25
Never hinged 5.25
4a A1 20r lavender 9.00 2.00
Never hinged 11.50
6a A1 50r blue 11.00 5.50
Never hinged 16.50
7 A1 75r carmine 10.00 5.50
Never hinged 14.50
8a A1 80r yellow grn 15.50 8.75
Never hinged 22.50
9a A1 100r brn, *yel* 15.50 7.50
Never hinged 22.50
10 A1 150r car, *rose* 30.00 30.00
Never hinged 87.50

Perf. 11½

1b A1 5r yellow 8.50 5.50
Never hinged 14.50
5 A1 25r green 7.50 1.60
Never hinged 12.00
6b A1 50r blue 10.50 3.00
Never hinged 17.50

Chalky Paper
Perf. 11½

1d A1 5r yellow 5.00 1.50
Never hinged 6.75
5b A1 25r green 12.50 3.25
Never hinged 17.50

Perf. 12½

5c A1 25r green 10.00 4.75
Never hinged 13.00

Perf. 13½

1e A1 5r yellow 3.00 .80
Never hinged 4.00
5d A1 25r green 7.50 1.10
Never hinged 11.00

The 5r and 25r values were issued on two types of paper: enamel surfaced, which is white, with a uniform low gloss; and chalky, which bears a low-gloss application in a pattern of tiny lozenges, producing a somewhat duller appearance.

Nos. 1, 4 and 9-12 were reprinted in 1900 (perf. 11½). Value, each $50. All values were reprinted in 1905 (perf. 13½). Value, each $25. The reprints are on paper slightly thinner than that of the originals, and unsurfaced. They have white gum and clean-cut perfs.

King Carlos — A2

Name and Value in Black except Nos. 25 and 34

1897-1905 ***Perf. 11½***

13 A2 2½r gray .60 .35
Never hinged .95
14 A2 5r orange .60 .35
Never hinged .95
15 A2 10r lt green .60 .35
Never hinged .95
16 A2 15r brown 4.00 2.00
Never hinged 10.50
17 A2 15r gray grn ('99) 2.25 1.10
Never hinged 2.75
18 A2 20r dull violet 2.25 1.25
Never hinged 2.75
19 A2 25r sea green 3.00 1.25
Never hinged 3.75
20 A2 25r rose red ('99) 2.25 .40
Never hinged 2.75
21 A2 50r blue 3.00 1.25
Never hinged 3.75
22 A2 50r ultra ('05) 24.00 11.00
Never hinged 28.00
23 A2 65r slate blue ('98) 2.00 .45
Never hinged 2.50
24 A2 75r rose 7.00 1.25
Never hinged 8.75
25 A2 75r brn & car, *yel* ('05) 16.00 8.75
Never hinged 19.00
26 A2 80r violet 2.00 1.25
Never hinged 2.40
27 A2 100r dk bl, *bl* 4.25 1.25
Never hinged 5.25
28 A2 115r org brn, *rose* ('98) 5.00 1.60
Never hinged 5.75
29 A2 130r gray brn, *buff* ('98) 5.00 1.60
Never hinged 6.00
30 A2 150r lt brn, *buff* 5.00 2.25
Never hinged 6.00
31 A2 180r sl, *pnksh* ('98) 5.00 2.25
Never hinged 6.00
32 A2 200r red vio, *pnksh* 7.75 5.50
Never hinged 9.25
33 A2 300r blue, *rose* 10.00 5.50
Never hinged 11.00
a. Perf. 12½ 50.00 30.00
Never hinged 62.50
34 A2 500r blk & red, *bl* 25.00 10.00
Never hinged 30.00
a. Perf. 12½ 45.00 13.00
Never hinged 55.00
Nos. 13-34 (22) 136.55 60.95

Yellowish Paper

14a A2 5r orange .55 .30
Never hinged .75
15a A2 10r lt green .55 .30
Never hinged .75
23a A2 65r slate blue ('98) 1.25 .45
Never hinged 1.60

Imperfs are proofs.

The stamps of Ponta Delgada were superseded by those of the Azores, which in 1931 were replaced by those of Portugal.

PORTUGAL

ˈpōr-chi-gəl

LOCATION — Southern Europe, on the western coast of the Iberian Peninsula
GOVT. — Republic
AREA — 35,516 sq. mi.
POP. — 9,930,000 (est. 1983)
CAPITAL — Lisbon

Figures for area and population include the Azores and Madeira, which are integral parts of the republic. The republic was established in 1910. See Azores, Funchal, Madeira.

1000 Reis = 1 Milreis
10 Reis = 1 Centimo
100 Centavos = 1 Escudo (1912)

Queen Maria II
A1 A2

A3 A4

Typo. & Embossed
1853 **Unwmk.** ***Imperf.***

1 A1 5r reddish brown 2,850. 850.00
On newspaper or wrapper 3,500.
a. 5r orange brown 3,250. 1,000.
On newspaper or wrapper 3,900.
b. Double impression *4,250.*
On cover *24,000.*
2 A2 25r blue 925. 19.00
On cover 75.00
a. 25r greenish blue 1,600. 32.50
On cover 125.00
b. Double impression *4,750.* *1,500.*
On cover *6,200.*
3 A3 50r dp yellow grn 3,400. 875.00
On cover 3,500.
a. 50r blue green 6,750. 1,650.
On cover 6,500.
b. 50r green 3,400. 875.00
On cover 3,500.
c. Double impression *14,000.* *6,000.*
On cover *24,000.*
4 A4 100r lilac 31,000. 1,900.
On cover *9,000.*

Full margins = 2mm.

Values for pairs

1	A1	5r reddish brown	2,600.
1a	A1	5r orange brown	2,900.
2	A2	25r blue	57.50
2a	A2	25r greenish blue	100.00
3	A3	50r deep yellow green	2,650.
3a	A3	50r blue green	4,800.
3b	A3	50r green	2,650.
4	A4	100r lilac	*5,750.*

Values for blocks of 4

1	A1	5r reddish brown	*6,900.*
1a	A1	5r orange brown	*7,750.*
2	A2	25r blue	150.00
2a	A2	25r greenish blue	275.00
3	A3	50r deep yellow green	*7,000.*
3a	A3	50r blue green	*13,000.*
3b	A3	50r green	*7,000.*
4	A4	100r lilac	*15,000.*

The stamps of the 1853 issue were reprinted in 1864, 1885, 1905 and 1953. Many stamps of subsequent issues were reprinted in 1885 and 1905. The reprints of 1864 are on thin white paper with white gum. The originals have brownish gum which often stains the paper. The reprints of 1885 are on a stout, very white paper. They are usually ungummed, but occasionally have a white gum with yellowish spots. The reprints of 1905 are on creamy white paper of ordinary quality with shiny white gum.

When perforated the reprints of 1885 have a rather rough perforation 13½ with small holes; those of 1905 have a clean-cut perforation 13½ with large holes making sharp pointed teeth.

The colors of the reprints usually differ from those of the originals, but actual comparison is necessary.

The reprints are often from new dies which differ slightly from those used for the originals.

5 reis: There is a defect in the neck which makes the Adam's apple appear very large in the first reprint. The later ones can be distinguished by the paper and the shades and by the absence of the pendant curl.

25 reis: The burelage of the ground work in the original is sharp and clear, while in the 1864 reprints it is blurred in several places; the upper and lower right hand corners are very thick and blurred. The central oval is less than ½mm from the frame at the sides in the originals and fully ¾mm in the 1885 and 1905 reprints.

50 reis: In the reprints of 1864 and 1885 there is a small break in the upper right hand diagonal line of the frame, and the initials of the engraver (F. B. F.), which in the originals are plainly discernible in the lower part of the bust, do not show. The reprints of 1905 have not the break in the frame and the initials are distinct.

100 reis: The small vertical lines at top and bottom at each side of the frame are heavier in the reprints of 1864 than in the originals. The reprints of 1885 and 1905 can be distinguished only by the paper, gum and shades.

Reprints of 1953 have thick paper, no gum and dates "1853/1953" on back. Value $55 each.

Values of lowest-cost earlier reprints (1905) of Nos. 1, $100; No. 2, $120; Nos. 3, 4, $150.

King Pedro V
A5 A6

A7 A8

1855 **With Straight Hair**

TWENTY-FIVE REIS:

Type I — Pearls mostly touch each other and oval outer line.

Type II — Pearls are separate from each other and oval outer line.

5 A5 5r red brown 8,250. 900.00
On newspaper or wrapper 3,500.
6 A6 25r blue, type II 950.00 25.00
On cover 100.00
a. 25r blue, type I 1,150. 30.00
On cover 125.00
7 A7 50r green 600.00 70.00
On cover 275.00
a. 50r blue green 825.00 100.00
On cover 400.00
b. Double impression 1,900. 725.00
On cover —
8 A8 100r lilac 800.00 90.00
On cover 375.00
On cover, single franking 600.00

Full margins = 2mm.

Values for pairs

5	A5	5r red brown	*2,650.*
6	A6	25r blue, type II	72.50
6a	A6	25r blue, type I	87.50
7	A7	50r green	210.00
7a	A7	50r blue green	300.00
8	A8	100r lilac	275.00

Values for blocks of 4

5	A5	5r red brown	*7,000.*
6	A6	25r blue, type II	200.00
6a	A6	25r blue, type I	250.00
7	A7	50r green	550.00
7a	A7	50r ble green	800.00
8	A8	100r lilac	725.00

Several types of No. 5 exist, differing in number of pearls encircling head (74 to 89) and other details.

All values were reprinted in 1885 and 1905. Value for lowest-cost, $60 each.

See note after No. 4.

1856 **With Curled Hair**

TWENTY-FIVE REIS:

Type I — The network is fine (single lines).

Type II — The network is coarse (double lines).

9 A5 5r brown 500.00 70.00
On cover 275.00
On newspaper or wrapper 550.00
a. 5r yellow brown 525.00 140.00
On cover 575.00
b. 5r red brown 475.00 92.50
On cover 375.00
c. 5r rose brown 475.00 92.50
On cover 375.00
d. 5r bister brown 475.00 92.50
On cover 375.00
e. 5r gray brown 475.00 92.50
On cover 375.00
f. 5r dark brown 475.00 92.50
On cover 375.00
g. Double impression 1,400. 375.00
On cover *1,500.*
10 A6 25r blue, type II 400.00 13.50
On cover 52.50
a. 25r blue, type I *9,500.* 55.00
On cover 225.00

Full margins = 2mm.

Values for pairs

9	A5	5r brown	400.00
9a	A5	5r yellow brown	275.00
9b	A5	5r red brown	275.00
9c	A5	5r rose brown	275.00
9d	A5	5r bister brown	275.00
9e	A5	5r gray brown	275.00
9f	A5	5r dark brown	275.00
10	A6	25r blue, type II	40.00
10a	A6	25r blue, type I	175.00

Values for blocks of 4

9	A5	5r brown	1,100.
9a	A5	5r yellow brown	750.00
9b	A5	5r red brown	750.00
9c	A5	5r rose brown	750.00
9d	A5	5r bister brown	750.00
9e	A5	5r gray brown	750.00
9f	A5	5r dark brown	750.00
10	A6	25r blue, type II	100.00
10a	A6	25r blue, type I	450.00

1858

11 A6 25r rose, type II 275.00 6.50
On cover 19.00
Pair 13.50
Block of 4 42.50
a. Double impression 525.00 *275.00*
On cover *1,100.*

Full margins = 2mm.

The 5r dark brown, formerly listed and sold at about $1, is now believed by the best authorities to be a reprint made before 1866. It is printed on thin yellowish white paper with yellowish white gum and is known only unused. The same remarks will apply to a 25r blue which is common unused but not known used. It is printed from a die which was not used for the issued stamps but the differences are slight and can only be told by expert comparison.

Nos. 9 and 10, also 10a in rose, were reprinted in 1885 and Nos. 9, 10, 10a and 11 in 1905. Value of lowest-cost reprints, $40 each.

See note after No. 4.

King Luiz
A9 A10

A11 A12

A13

FIVE REIS:

Type I — The distance between "5" and "reis" is 3mm.

Type II — The distance between "5" and "reis" is 2mm.

1862-64

12 A9 5r brown, type I 125.00 10.00
On cover 40.00
On newspaper or wrapper 325.00
a. 5r brown, type II 160.00 25.00
On cover 110.00
On newspaper or wrapper 410.00
b. Double impression, type II 650.00 350.00
On cover 1,300.
c. 5r reddish brown — 125.00
On cover 500.00
d. Double embossing, type I — 275.00
On cover 1,100.
13 A10 10r orange 125.00 40.00
On cover 275.00
14 A11 25r rose 100.00 4.75
On cover 17.50
a. Double impression 1,350. 375.00
On cover 1,400.
b. Double embossing, type I 1,350. 375.00
On cover 1,400.
15 A12 50r yellow green 725.00 77.50
On cover 360.00
a. 50r blue green 850.00 100.00
On cover 450.00
16 A13 100r lilac ('64) 900.00 90.00
On cover 400.00
Nos. 12-16 (5) 1,975. 222.25

Full margins = 2mm.

Values for pairs

12	A9	5r brown, type I	30.00
12a	A9	5r brown, type II	75.00
12c	A9	5r reddish brown	375.00
13	A10	10r orange	140.00
14	A11	25r rose	14.00
15	A12	50r yellow green	225.00
15a	A12	50r blue green	300.00
16	A13	100r lilac ('64)	275.00

Values for blocks of 4

12	A9	5r brown, type I	80.00
12a	A9	5r brown, type II	210.00
12c	A9	5r reddish brown	1,000.
13	A10	10r orange	375.00
14	A11	25r rose	37.50
15	A12	50r yellow green	600.00
15a	A12	50r blue green	800.00
16	A13	100r lilac ('64)	700.00

All values were reprinted in 1885 and all except the 25r in 1905. Value of lowest-cost reprints, $10 each.

See note after No. 4.

King Luiz — A14

1866-67 ***Imperf.***

17 A14 5r black 100.00 10.00
On cover 40.00
a. Double impression 275.00 190.00
On cover 750.00
18 A14 10r yellow 225.00 140.00
On cover 575.00
19 A14 20r bister 175.00 67.50
On cover 260.00
On cover, single franking 550.00
20 A14 25r rose ('67) 200.00 6.00
On cover 32.50
a. Double impression 225.00
On cover 800.00
21 A14 50r green 250.00 50.00
On cover 260.00
On cover, single franking 550.00
22 A14 80r orange 250.00 50.00
On cover 260.00
23 A14 100r dk lilac ('67) 300.00 75.00
On cover 500.00
24 A14 120r blue 325.00 70.00
On cover 275.00
a. Double impression 725.00 450.00
On cover 1,800.
Nos. 17-24 (8) 1,825. 468.50

Full margins = 1¾mm.

Some values with unofficial percé en croix (diamond) perforation were used in Madeira.

All values were reprinted in 1885 and 1905. Value: Nos. 17-23, each $30-$40; No. 24, $100.

See note after No. 4.

Typographed & Embossed

1867-70 ***Perf. 12½***

25 A14 5r black 125.00 42.50
On cover 225.00
a. Double impression 225.00 110.00
On cover 425.00
26 A14 10r yellow 250.00 110.00
On cover 425.00
27 A14 20r bister ('69) 300.00 110.00
On cover 425.00
28 A14 25r rose 65.00 5.00
On cover 25.00
a. Double impression 550.00 200.00
On cover 800.00
29 A14 50r green ('68) 250.00 100.00
On cover 425.00
30 A14 80r orange ('69) 350.00 100.00
On cover 425.00
31 A14 100r lilac ('69) 250.00 100.00
On cover 425.00
32 A14 120r blue 300.00 67.50
On cover 260.00
a. Double impression 625.00 160.00
On cover 650.00
33 A14 240r pale violet ('70) 1,000. 475.00
On cover 1,900.
Nos. 25-33 (9) 2,890. 1,110.

Nos. 25-33 frequently were separated with scissors. Slightly blunted perfs on one or two sides are to be expected for stamps of this issue.

Two types each of 5r and 100r differ in the position of the "5" at upper right and the "100" at lower right in relation to the end of the label.

Nos. 25-33 were reprinted in 1885 and 1905. Some of the 1885 reprints were perforated 12½ as well as 13½. Value of the lowest-cost reprints, $40 each.

See note after No. 4.

King Luiz — A15

Typographed & Embossed

1870-84 ***Perf. 12½***

Plain Paper

34 A15 5r black 55.00 5.00
On newspaper or wrapper 55.00
f. Double impression 275.00 67.50
On cover 260.00
35 A15 10r yellow ('71) 77.50 27.50
On cover 150.00
f. Double impression 300.00 125.00
On cover 500.00
36 A15 10r blue grn ('79) 375.00 175.00
On cover 1,000.
37 A15 10r yellow grn ('80) 110.00 24.00
On newspaper or wrapper 125.00
On post card 160.00
d. Double impression 250.00 130.00
On cover 575.00
38 A15 15r lilac brn ('75) 100.00 29.00
On cover 110.00
39 A15 20r bister 72.50 25.00
On cover 150.00
g. Double impression — 175.00
On cover
40 A15 20r rose ('84) 325.00 55.00
On cover 400.00
41 A15 25r rose 30.00 3.75
On cover 15.00
f. Double impression 240.00 30.00
On cover 120.00
42 A15 50r pale green 140.00 40.00
On cover 150.00
43 A15 50r blue ('79) 350.00 50.00
On cover 210.00
44 A15 80r orange 140.00 30.00
On cover 120.00
45 A15 100r pale lilac ('71) 110.00 21.00
On cover 85.00
46 A15 120r blue ('71) 300.00 62.50
On cover 275.00
47 A15 150r pale bl ('76) 375.00 110.00
On cover 460.00
d. Double impression 1,050. 390.00
On cover 1,550.
48 A15 150r yellow ('80) 140.00 15.00
On cover 500.00
49 A15 240r pale violet ('73) 1,700. 1,050.
On cover *4,100.*
50 A15 300r dull violet ('76) 110.00 27.50
On cover 550.00
51 A15 1000r black ('84) 275.00 77.50
On cover 410.00
On cover, single franking 1,100.

Perf. 13½

34d A15 5r black 65.00 8.25
On newspaper or wrapper 32.50
35d A15 10r yellow 95.00 35.00
On cover 150.00
36a A15 10r blue green 675.00 300.00
On cover 1,250.
37a A15 10r yellow grn ('80) 125.00 27.50
On newspaper or wrapper 110.00
On post card 165.00
38a A15 15r lilac brown 140.00 57.50
On cover 225.00
39c A15 20r bister 110.00 27.50
On cover 160.00
40a A15 20r rose ('84) 350.00 85.00
On cover 425.00
b. Double impression — *1,050.*
On cover —
41d A15 25r rose 30.00 4.00
On cover 16.00
g. Double impression — *32.50*
On cover —
42a A15 50r pale green 160.00 40.00
On cover 160.00
43a A15 50r blue ('79) 325.00 52.50
On cover 210.00
44c A15 80r orange 165.00 40.00
On cover 160.00
45b A15 100r pale lilac 165.00 50.00
On cover 200.00
46a A15 120r blue 3,500.
On cover —
47b A15 150r blue 750.00 300.00
On cover 1,200.
48a A15 150r yellow ('80) 175.00 77.50
On cover 300.00
50a A15 300r dull violet ('76) 110.00 27.50
On cover 360.00
51a A15 1000r black ('84) 400.00 77.50
On cover 325.00
On cover, single franking *1,350.*

Perf. 11

34b A15 5r black *550.00*
On newspaper or wrapper —
35b A15 10r yellow *550.00*
On cover —
39b A15 20r bister *550.00*
On cover —
41b A15 25r rose *3,500.*
On cover —
42b A15 50r pale green *550.00*
On cover —
44b A15 80r orange *550.00*
On cover —
49b A15 240r pale violet — —
On cover —

Perf. 14¼

34c A15 5r black 225.00 *125.00*
On newspaper or wrapper 600.00
35c A15 10r yellow 425.00 *275.00*
On cover 1,600.
41c A15 25r rose 425.00 25.00
On cover 110.00

44c A15 80r orange 1,050. 800.00
On cover 3,200.
45a A15 100r pale lilac 1,300. 800.00
On cover 3,200.

Imperforate

34a A15 5r black 550.00
35a A15 10r yellow 550.00
39a A15 20r bister 550.00
41a A15 25r rose 550.00

Ribbed Paper

Perf. 12½

34e A15 5r black 150.00 22.50
On cover 92.50
35e A15 10r yellow 210.00 110.00
On cover 450.00
39d A15 20r bister 300.00 100.00
On cover 400.00
41e A15 25r rose 125.00 21.00
On cover 85.00
42c A15 50r pale green 400.00 90.00
On cover 350.00
44d A15 80r orange 400.00 100.00
On cover 425.00
45c A15 100r pale lilac 400.00 100.00
On cover 400.00
46b A15 120r blue 950.00 225.00
On cover 950.00
49c A15 240r pale violet 3,250. 2,100.
On cover 8,750.

Enamel Surfaced Paper

Perf. 12½

37b A15 10r yellow grn ('80) 110.00 24.00
On newspaper or wrapper 125.00
On post card 175.00
38b A15 15r lilac brown 110.00 30.00
On cover 125.00
d. Double impression 500.00 260.00
On cover 1,050.
39e A15 20r bister 100.00 25.00
On cover 110.00
44e A15 80r orange 125.00 19.00
On cover 75.00
45e A15 100r pale lilac ('71) 65.00 12.00
On cover 75.00
48b A15 150r yellow ('80) 125.00 13.50
On cover 55.00
50b A15 300r dull violet ('76) 110.00 30.00
On cover 225.00

Perf. 13½

37c A15 10r yellow grn ('80) 140.00 45.00
On newspaper or wrapper 175.00
On post card 190.00
38c A15 15r lilac brown 110.00 30.00
On cover 125.00
39f A15 20r bister 140.00 30.00
On cover 125.00
44f A15 80r orange 140.00 30.00
On cover 120.00
45f A15 100r pale lilac 160.00 42.50
On cover 175.00
48c A15 150r yellow ('80) 150.00 35.00
On cover 250.00
50c A15 300r dull violet ('76) 150.00 40.00
On cover 250.00

Two types each of 15r, 20r and 80r differ in the distance between the figures of value.

Imperfs probably are proofs.

For overprints and surcharges see Nos. 86-87, 94-96.

All values of the issues of 1870-84 were reprinted in 1885 and 1905. Value of the lowest-cost reprints, $30 each.

See note after No. 4.

King Luiz

A16 A17

A18 A19

1880-81 Typo. *Perf. 12½, 13½*

52 A16 5r black 40.00 4.00
On newspaper or wrapper 32.50
a. Enamel surfaced paper, perf 12½ *150.00* *50.00*
On cover *200.00*
b. Enamel surfaced paper, perf 13½ *140.00* *50.00*
On cover *200.00*
53 A17 25r bluish gray 300.00 29.00
On cover 110.00
54 A18 25r gray 45.00 3.50
On cover 15.00
55 A18 25r brown vio ('81) 45.00 3.50
On cover 15.00
56 A19 50r blue ('81) 300.00 15.00
On cover 75.00
Nos. 52-56 (5) 730.00 55.00

All values were reprinted in 1885 and 1905. Value of the lowest-cost reprints, $15 each.

See note after No. 4.

A20 A21

King Luiz

A22 A23

A24 A24a

1882-87 *Perf. 12½*

Plain Paper

57 A20 2r black ('84) 20.00 15.00
On cover 110.00
60a A23 25r brown 42.50 3.00
On cover 13.50
61a A23 50r blue 52.50 3.00
On cover 25.00
62 A24a 500r black ('84) 600.00 300.00
On cover 500.00
63 A24a 500r violet ('87) 300.00 52.50
On cover 1,200.
Nos. 57-63 (5) 1,015. 373.50

Perf. 13½

57a A20 2r black ('84) 25.00 16.00
On cover 110.00
60b A23 25r brown 37.50 3.60
On cover 15.00
61b A23 50r blue 52.50 4.00
On cover 27.50
62a A24a 500r black ('84) 900.00 725.00
On cover 2,900.
63a A24a 500r violet ('87) 825.00 275.00
On cover 1,800.

Perf. 11½

57b A20 2r black ('84) — —
On cover —
58c A21 5r black ('84) 32.50 3.25
On newspaper or wrapper 27.50
60 A23 25r brown 27.50 2.25
On cover 10.00

Enamel Surfaced Paper

Perf. 12½

58a A21 5r black ('84) 30.00 3.00
On newspaper or wrapper 22.50
58d A21 5r gray ('83) 32.50 3.50
On newspaper or wrapper 27.50
59a A22 10r green ('84) 50.00 4.00
On newspaper or wrapper 55.00
60c A23 25r brown 32.50 2.60
On cover 10.00
61c A23 50r blue 52.50 3.25
On cover 25.00

Perf. 13½

58b A21 5r black ('84) 35.00 7.25
On newspaper or wrapper 45.00
58e A21 5r gray ('83) 37.50 7.25
On newspaper or wrapper 45.00
59b A22 10r green ('84) 62.50 7.25
On newspaper or wrapper 100.00
60d A23 25r brown 37.50 3.50
On cover 13.50
61d A23 50r blue 50.00 10.00
On cover 42.50

Perf. 11½

58 A21 5r black ('84) 32.50 3.50
On newspaper or wrapper 11.00
58f A21 5r gray ('83) 50.00 11.00
On newspaper or wrapper 55.00
59 A22 10r green ('84) 35.00 4.00
On newspaper or wrapper 55.00
60e A23 25r brown 32.50 2.25
On cover 10.00
61 A24 50r blue 45.00 3.00
On cover 22.50

For overprints see Nos. 79-82, 85, 88-89, 93.

The stamps of the 1882-87 issues were reprinted in 1885, 1893 and 1905. Value of the lowest-cost reprints, $20 each.

See note after No. 4.

Covers: The values for Nos. 57, 57a and 57b are for philatelic covers or post cards.

A25 A26

1887 *Perf. 11½*

64 A25 20r rose 50.00 17.00
On cover 65.00
65 A26 25r violet 40.00 3.00
On cover 12.00
66 A26 25r lilac rose 30.00 3.00
On cover 11.00
Nos. 64-66 (3) 120.00 23.00

For overprints see Nos. 83-84, 90-92.

Nos. 64-66 were reprinted in 1905. Value $22.50 each. See note after No. 4.

King Carlos — A27

1892-93 *Perf. 12½*

Enamel Surfaced Paper

68 A27 10r redsh violet 30.00 4.00
On cover 55.00
69 A27 15r chocolate 27.50 6.00
On cover 55.00
70 A27 20r lavender 35.00 9.25
On cover 55.00
72 A27 50r blue 35.00 9.25
On cover 65.00
73 A27 75r carmine ('93) 67.50 8.00
On cover 82.50
74 A27 80r yellow grn 100.00 52.50
On cover 325.00
75 A27 100r brn, *buff* ('93) 65.00 6.25
On cover 110.00
76a A27 150r car, *rose* ('93) 250.00 100.00
On cover *400.00*
77 A27 200r dk bl, *bl* ('93) 160.00 35.00
On cover 550.00
78 A27 300r dk bl, *sal* ('93) 175.00 57.50
On cover 550.00
Nos. 67-78 (10) 945.00 287.75

Perf. 13½

68b A27 10r reddish violet 30.00 6.50
On cover 65.00
69a A27 15r chocolate 32.50 8.50
On cover 70.00
70a A27 20r lavender 50.00 11.50
On cover 65.00
72b A27 50r blue 100.00 12.00
On cover 72.50
73a A27 75r carmine ('93) 175.00 30.00
On cover *225.00*
74a A27 80r yellow green 85.00 42.50
On cover 325.00
75b A27 100r brown, *buff* ('93) 100.00 12.50
On cover *175.00*
76 A27 150r car, *rose* ('93) 160.00 42.50
On cover 225.00
77a A27 200r dk blue, *blue* ('93) 175.00 65.00
On cover *650.00*
78a A27 300r dk bl, *sal* ('93) 175.00 65.00
On cover *650.00*

Perf. 11½

67 A27 5r orange 11.00 2.00
On newspaper or wrapper *11.00*
68a A27 10r reddish violet 1,700. 45.00
On cover 275.00
71 A27 25r dark green 37.50 2.50
On cover 10.00
72a A27 50r blue 52.50 6.00
On cover 55.00
73b A27 75r carmine ('93) 350.00 13.00
On cover 110.00
75a A27 100r brown, *buff* ('93) 400.00 16.00
On cover *200.00*

Chalky Paper

Perf. 12½

68d A27 10r reddish violet 275.00 42.50
On cover *325.00*
70b A27 20r lavender 1,100. 550.00
On cover *2,250.*
73c A27 75r carmine ('93) 225.00 37.50
On cover *275.00*

Perf. 13½

68e A27 10r reddish violet 37.50 8.00
On cover 65.00
69b A27 15r chocolate 27.50 5.00
On cover 55.00
73d A27 75r carmine ('93) 225.00 18.00
On cover 140.00

Perf. 11½

67a A27 5r orange 13.00 2.00
On newspaper or wrapper 11.00
68c A27 10r reddish violet 35.00 2.00
On cover 55.00
71a A27 25r dark green 27.50 2.00
On cover 8.25

Nos. 67-78 were issued on two types of paper: enamel surfaced, which is white, with a uniform low gloss; and chalky, which bears a low-gloss application in a pattern of tiny lozenges, producing a somewhat duller appearance.

Nos. 76-78 were reprinted in 1900 (perf. 11½). Value, each $100. All values were reprinted in 1905 (perf. 13½). Value, each $50.

See note after No. 4.

Stamps and Types of Previous Issues Overprinted in Black or Red

a

b

c

1892

79 A21 (a) 5r gray blk 16.00 8.75
On newspaper or wrapper 45.00
a. Double overprint 650.00 450.00
80 A22 (b) 10r green 16.00 8.75
On newspaper or wrapper 110.00
a. Inverted overprint — —
b. Double overprint 650.00 450.00

1892-93

81 A21 (c) 5r gray blk (R) 13.50 6.75
On newspaper or wrapper 55.00
82 A22 (c) 10r green (R) 16.00 9.25
On newspaper or wrapper 110.00
a. Inverted overprint 160.00 160.00
83 A25 (c) 20r rose 42.50 22.50
On cover 160.00
a. Inverted overprint 225.00 225.00
84 A26 (c) 25r rose lilac, perf. 11½ 14.50 5.25
On cover 160.00
a. Perf. 12½ 475.00 70.00
On cover 275.00
85 A24 (c) 50r blue (R) ('93) 77.50 62.50
On cover 375.00
Nos. 81-85 (5) 164.00 106.25

1893

86 A15 (c) 15r bister brn, plain paper, perf 12½ (R) 20.00 12.00
On cover *120.00*
a. Perf 13½ 550.00 310.00
On cover *1,250.*
b. Surfaced paper, perf 12½ 20.00 11.50
On cover 110.00
c. Surfaced paper, perf 13½ 27.50 22.50
On cover *175.00*
87 A15 (c) 80r yellow 110.00 87.50
On cover *275.00*

Nos. 86-87 are found in two types each. See note below No. 51.

Some of Nos. 79-87 were reprinted in 1900 and all values in 1905. Value of lowest-cost reprint, $10.

See note after No. 4.

Stamps and Types of Previous Issues Overprinted or Surcharged in Black or Red

d

e

1893 *Perf. 11½, 12½*

88 A21 (d) 5r gray blk (R) 30.00 22.50
On cover 160.00
89 A22 (d) 10r grn, perf. 11½ (R) 24.00 20.00
On cover 160.00
a. "1938" 300.00 300.00
On cover *3,250.*
b. "1863" 300.00 300.00
On cover *3,250.*
c. "1838" 300.00 300.00
On cover *3,250.*
d. Perf. 12½ 1,650. 1,100.
On cover —
90 A25 (d) 20r rose 45.00 32.50
On cover 160.00
a. Inverted overprint 125.00 100.00
b. "1938" 300.00 300.00
On cover *3,250.*
91 A26 (e) 20r on 25r lil rose 60.00 47.50
On cover 190.00
92 A26 (d) 25r lilac rose 110.00 100.00
On cover 350.00
a. Inverted overprint 275.00 275.00

93 A24 (d) 50r blue (R) 125.00 110.00
On cover 450.00

Perf. 12½

94 A15 (e) 50r on 80r yel 150.00 100.00
On cover 275.00
95 A15 (e) 75r on 80r yel 100.00 72.50
On cover 375.00
a. "1893" and "50rs" double 350.00 200.00
On cover —
96 A15 (d) 80r yellow 150.00 95.00
On cover 375.00
a. "1893" double 450.00 450.00
On cover —
Nos. 88-96 (9) 794.00 600.00

Nos. 94-96 are found in two types each. See note below No. 51.

Some of Nos. 88-96 were reprinted in 1900 and all values in 1905. Value of lowest-cost reprint, $45 each.

See note after No. 4.

Covers: Values for Nos. 89a and 89b are for philatelic covers.

Prince Henry on his Ship — A46

Prince Henry Directing Fleet Maneuvers A47

Symbolic of Prince Henry's Studies — A48

1894 Litho. *Perf. 14*

97 A46 5r orange 4.00 .65
Never hinged 15.00
On cover or post card 82.50
98 A46 10r magenta 4.00 .65
Never hinged 15.00
On cover or post card 82.50
99 A46 15r red brown 11.00 3.25
Never hinged 45.00
On cover 225.00
100 A46 20r dull violet 11.00 4.00
Never hinged 45.00
On cover 225.00
101 A47 25r gray green 10.00 1.40
Never hinged —
On cover 110.00
102 A47 50r blue 27.50 6.00
Never hinged —
On cover 110.00
103 A47 75r car rose 52.50 11.50
Never hinged —
On cover 225.00
104 A47 80r yellow grn 52.50 14.00
Never hinged —
On cover 225.00
105 A47 100r lt brn, *pale buff* 50.00 10.00
Never hinged —
On cover 110.00

Engr.

106 A48 150r lt car, *pale rose* 175.00 32.50
Never hinged —
On cover 225.00
107 A48 300r dk bl, *sal buff* 200.00 37.50
Never hinged —
On cover 225.00
108 A48 500r dp vio, *pale lil* 400.00 77.50
Never hinged —
On cover 300.00
109 A48 1000r gray blk, *grysh* 600.00 110.00
Never hinged —
On cover 300.00
Nos. 97-109 (13) 1,598. 308.95

5th centenary of the birth of Prince Henry the Navigator.

Covers: Values for Nos. 99-100, 103-104, 106-109 are for overfranked covers, usually philatelic.

King Carlos — A49

1895-1905 Typo. *Perf. 11½*

Value in Black or Red (#122, 500r)

110 A49 2½r gray .25 .25
Never hinged .50
On newspaper or wrapper 5.50
111 A49 5r orange .25 .25
Never hinged .80
On newspaper or wrapper 5.50
112 A49 10r lt green .50 .25
Never hinged 1.10
On postcard 5.50
113 A49 15r brown 90.00 3.50
Never hinged 160.00
On cover 110.00
114 A49 15r gray grn ('99) 47.50 2.40
Never hinged 85.00
On cover 11.00
115 A49 20r gray violet .85 .35
Never hinged 1.40
On cover or postcard 5.50
116 A49 25r sea green 65.00 .25
Never hinged 120.00
On cover 5.50
117 A49 25r car rose ('99) .40 .25
Never hinged .70
On cover 4.50
118 A49 50r blue 82.50 .40
Never hinged 150.00
On cover 22.50
119 A49 50r ultra ('05) .55 .25
Never hinged 1.10
On cover 11.00
120 A49 65r slate bl ('98) .55 .25
Never hinged 1.10
On cover 11.00
121 A49 75r rose 110.00 4.50
Never hinged 225.00
On cover 110.00
122 A49 75r brn, *yel* ('05) 1.75 .65
Never hinged 3.00
On cover 55.00
123 A49 80r violet 2.10 1.25
Never hinged 4.50
On cover 110.00
124 A49 100r dk bl, *bl* 1.00 .40
Never hinged 2.00
On cover 55.00
125 A49 115r org brn, *pink* ('98) 4.75 2.75
Never hinged 9.50
On cover 110.00
126 A49 130r gray brn, *straw* ('98) 3.75 1.40
Never hinged 7.25
On cover 160.00
127 A49 150r lt brn, *straw* 140.00 22.50
Never hinged 275.00
On cover 325.00
128 A49 180r sl, *pnksh* ('98) 15.00 9.00
Never hinged 30.00
On cover 225.00
129 A49 200r red lil, *pnksh* 5.00 1.25
Never hinged 10.00
On cover 110.00
a. 200r brown violet, *rose* 16.00 2.25
Never hinged 32.50
On cover *190.00*
130 A49 300r blue, *rose* 3.75 2.00
Never hinged 7.50
On cover 275.00
131 A49 500r blk, *bl* ('96) 9.75 4.50
Never hinged 19.00
On cover 275.00
a. Perf. 12½ 110.00 26.00
Never hinged 225.00
On cover —
Nos. 110-131 (22) 585.20 58.60

Several values of the above type exist without figures of value, also with figures inverted or otherwise misplaced but they were not regularly issued.

St. Anthony and his Vision — A50

St. Anthony Preaching to Fishes — A51

St. Anthony Ascends to Heaven — A52

St. Anthony, from Portrait — A53

Perf. 11½, 12½ and Compound

1895 Typo.

132 A50 2½r black 4.00 1.10
Never hinged 16.00
On newspaper or wrapper 225.00

Litho.

133 A51 5r brown org 4.00 1.10
Never hinged 16.00
On newspaper or wrapper 160.00
134 A51 10r red lilac 13.50 8.25
Never hinged 55.00
On newspaper or wrapper 160.00
135 A51 15r chocolate 14.50 8.25
Never hinged 60.00
On cover 225.00
136 A51 20r gray violet 14.50 8.25
Never hinged 60.00
On cover 225.00
137 A51 25r grn & vio 13.00 1.00
Never hinged 52.50
On cover 225.00
138 A52 50r blue & brn 32.50 22.50
Never hinged 125.00
On cover 225.00
139 A52 75r rose & brn 50.00 40.00
Never hinged 200.00
On cover 225.00
140 A52 80r lt grn & brn 80.00 60.00
Never hinged —
On cover 225.00
141 A52 100r choc & blk 90.00 30.00
Never hinged —
On cover 225.00
142 A53 150r car & bis 200.00 100.00
Never hinged —
On cover 225.00
143 A53 200r blue & bis 200.00 125.00
Never hinged —
On cover 450.00
144 A53 300r slate & bis 400.00 140.00
Never hinged —
On cover 550.00
145 A53 500r vio brn & grn 600.00 300.00
Never hinged —
On cover 1,100.
146 A53 1000r vio & grn 700.00 375.00
Never hinged —
On cover *1,300.*
Nos. 132-146 (15) 2,416. 1,220.

7th centenary of the birth of Saint Anthony of Padua. Stamps have eulogy in Latin printed on the back.

Covers: Values for Nos. 135-136, 139-140, 142 are for overfranked covers, usually philatelic.

Vasco da Gama Issue

Common Design Types

1898 Engr. *Perf. 12½ to 16*

147 CD20 2½r blue green 1.40 .35
On newspaper or wrapper 55.00
148 CD21 5r red 1.40 .35
On cover 55.00
149 CD22 10r red violet 8.50 1.25
On cover or postcard 55.00
150 CD23 25r yel grn 5.00 .50
On cover 55.00
151 CD24 50r dark blue 10.50 3.00
On cover 110.00
152 CD25 75r violet brown 45.00 9.00
On cover 82.50
153 CD26 100r bister brown 30.00 9.00
On cover 110.00
154 CD27 150r bister 67.50 20.00
On cover 160.00
Nos. 147-154 (8) 169.30 43.45

For overprints and surcharges see Nos. 185-192, 199-206.

King Manuel II
A62 A63

1910 Typo. *Perf. 14½x15*

156 A62 2½r violet .25 .25
157 A62 5r black .25 .25
158 A62 10r gray green .25 .25
159 A62 15r lilac brown 2.75 1.40
160 A62 20r carmine .80 .65
161 A62 25r violet brn .60 .25
162 A62 50r dark blue 1.50 .65
163 A62 75r bister brn 9.25 5.00
164 A62 80r slate 2.50 2.25
165 A62 100r brn, *lt grn* 10.00 3.00
166 A62 200r dk grn, *sal* 6.00 4.25
167 A62 300r blk, *azure* 6.75 5.00
168 A63 500r ol grn & vio brn 13.50 11.50
169 A63 1000r dk bl & blk 30.00 24.00
Nos. 156-169 (14) 84.40 58.70

For overprint see No. RA1.

Preceding Issue Overprinted in Carmine or Green

1910

170 A62 2½r violet .25 .25
171 A62 5r black .25 .25
172 A62 10r gray green 3.50 1.25
173 A62 15r lilac brn 1.25 .85
174 A62 20r carmine (G) 4.25 1.50
175 A62 25r violet brn .80 .25
176 A62 50r dk blue 6.00 2.00
177 A62 75r bister brn 9.00 3.75
178 A62 80r slate 3.25 2.40
179 A62 100r brn, *lt grn* 2.00 .75
180 A62 200r dk grn, *sal* 2.50 1.60
181 A62 300r blk, *azure* 3.75 2.75
182 A63 500r ol grn & vio brn 9.50 8.25
183 A63 1000r dk bl & blk 24.00 24.00
Nos. 170-183 (14) 70.30 49.85

The numerous inverted and double overprints on this issue were unofficially and fraudulently made.

The 50r with blue overprint is a fraud.

Vasco da Gama Issue Overprinted or Surcharged

a

b

c

1911 *Perf. 12½ to 16*

185 CD20(a) 2½r blue grn .45 .25
a. Inverted overprint 14.00 12.00
186 CD21(b) 15r on 5r red .80 .35
a. Inverted surcharge 10.50 9.00
187 CD23(a) 25r yel grn .45 .25
188 CD24(a) 50r dk blue 3.25 1.60
a. Inverted overprint
189 CD25(a) 75r vio brn 42.50 32.50
190 CD27(b) 80r on 150r bis 9.00 4.75
191 CD26(a) 100r bis brn 9.00 3.00
a. Inverted overprint 40.00 24.00
192 CD22(c) 1000r on 10r red vio 62.50 37.50
Nos. 185-192 (8) 127.95 80.20

Postage Due Stamps of 1898 Overprinted or Surcharged for Regular Postage

d

e

1911 *Perf. 12*

193 D1(d) 5r black .85 .35
a. Double ovpt., one inverted 60.00 25.00
194 D1(d) 10r magenta 2.00 .65
195 D1(d) 20r orange 6.00 3.00
196 D1(d) 200r brn, *buff* 125.00 67.50
197 D1(e) 300r on 50r slate 90.00 42.50
198 D1(e) 500r on 100r car, *pink* 60.00 24.00
a. Inverted surcharge 125.00 87.50
Nos. 193-198 (6) 283.85 138.00

Vasco da Gama Issue of Madeira Ovptd. or Srchd. Types "a," "b" and "c"

1911 *Perf. 12½ to 16*

199 CD20(a) 2½r blue grn 11.50 8.25
a. Double overprint
200 CD21(b) 15r on 5r red 4.00 2.00
a. Inverted surcharge 12.50 11.00

No.	Type	Description	Unused	Used
201	CD23(a)	25r yellow grn	6.00	4.75
202	CD24(a)	50r dk blue	11.00	8.25
a.		Inverted overprint		
203	CD25(a)	75r violet brn	11.00	5.50
a.		Inverted overprint	35.00	30.00
204	CD27(b)	80r on 150r bis	12.50	11.00
a.		Inverted surcharge	47.50	40.00
205	CD26(a)	100r bister brn	40.00	8.25
a.		Inverted overprint	125.00	100.00
206	CD22(c)	1000r on 10r red vio	40.00	50.00
		Nos. 199-206 (8)	136.00	98.00

Ceres — A64

Chalky Paper
With Imprint

1912-20 Typo. *Perf. 15x14*

No.	Type	Description	Unused	Used
207	A64	¼c dark olive	8.00	5.00
		Never hinged	16.00	
208	A64	½c black	8.00	5.00
		Never hinged	16.00	
209	A64	1c deep green	6.50	2.50
		Never hinged	13.00	
210	A64	1½c chocolate	20.00	9.00
		Never hinged	40.00	
211	A64	2c carmine	20.00	9.00
		Never hinged	40.00	
212	A64	2½c violet	9.50	9.50
		Never hinged	20.00	
213	A64	5c dp blue	5.50	.55
		Never hinged	11.00	
214	A64	7½c yellow brn	65.00	13.50
		Never hinged	130.00	
215	A64	8c slate	3.00	3.00
		Never hinged	6.00	
216	A64	10c org brn	45.00	25.00
		Never hinged	90.00	
217	A64	15c plum	300.00	75.00
		Never hinged	600.00	
218	A64	20c vio brn, *grn*	13.00	1.50
		Never hinged	26.00	
219	A64	20c brn, *buff* ('20)	15.00	3.50
		Never hinged	30.00	
220	A64	30c brn, *pink*	100.00	9.50
		Never hinged	200.00	
221	A64	30c lt brn, *yel* ('17)	8.75	1.60
		Never hinged	17.50	
222	A64	50c org, *sal* ('18)	12.00	1.10
		Never hinged	24.00	
a.		50c orange, *yellow*	15.00	1.10
		Never hinged	30.00	
223	A64	1e dp grn, *bl*	19.00	1.40
		Never hinged	40.00	
		Nos. 207-223 (17)	658.25	175.65

1920 Typo. *Perf. 12x11½*

No.	Type	Description	Unused	Used
224	A64	14c dk bl, *yel*	3.25	1.25
		Never hinged	5.00	
225	A64	20c choc, *buff*	800.00	200.00
		Never hinged	1,300.	
226	A64	50c org, *salmon*	225.00	30.00
		Never hinged	450.00	
		Nos. 224-226 (3)	1,028.	231.25

1917-26 Typo. *Perf. 15x14*
Ordinary Paper

No.	Type	Description	Unused	Used
227	A64	¼c dk ol ('18)	.65	.25
		Never hinged	1.00	
a.		Thick carton paper	35.00	7.25
		Never hinged	52.50	
228	A64	½c black ('18)	.40	.25
a.		Thick carton paper	35.00	7.25
		Never hinged	52.50	
b.		Bluish paper	.95	.55
		Never hinged	1.40	
229	A64	1c deep green	.65	.25
		Never hinged	1.00	
a.		"CORREIC" for "CORREIO"	700.00	700.00
230	A64	1c chocolate	.25	.25
		Never hinged	.40	
a.		Thick carton paper	30.00	7.50
		Never hinged	45.00	
231	A64	1½c chocolate	5.50	2.50
		Never hinged	8.75	
232	A64	1½c dp grn ('18)	.30	.25
		Never hinged	.50	
233	A64	2c carmine	5.50	2.50
		Never hinged	8.75	
234	A64	2c orange ('18)	.25	.25
		Never hinged	.40	
235	A64	2½c violet	.25	.25
		Never hinged	.40	
236	A64	3c car rose	.25	.25
		Never hinged	.40	
237	A64	3c ultra ('21)	200.00	80.00
		Never hinged	400.00	
238	A64	3½c lt grn ('18)	.25	.25
		Never hinged	.40	
239	A64	4c lt grn ('19)	.40	.30
		Never hinged	.65	
a.		Thick carton paper	30.00	7.50
		Never hinged	50.00	
240	A64	5c yel brn	.50	.30
		Never hinged	.80	
240A	A64	5c deep blue	2.40	.25
		Never hinged	4.00	
241	A64	6c pale rose ('20)	.25	.25
		Never hinged	.40	
a.		Thick carton paper	1.75	.95
		Never hinged	2.75	
242	A64	7½c dp blue	.50	.45
		Never hinged	.80	
243	A64	7½c yellow brn	12.00	2.50
		Never hinged	20.00	
244	A64	8c slate	5.50	.75
		Never hinged	8.75	
245	A64	10c org brn	25.00	1.50
		Never hinged	40.00	
246	A64	12c bl gray ('20)	1.25	.65
		Never hinged	2.00	
247	A64	15c plum	3.25	.85
		Never hinged	5.25	
248	A64	20c choc ('20)	60.00	5.00
		Never hinged	95.00	
249	A64	30c gray brown	120.00	21.00
		Never hinged	240.00	
250	A64	36c red ('21)	4.50	1.25
		Never hinged	7.00	
251	A64	60c blue ('21)	4.00	1.90
		Never hinged	6.50	
252	A64	80c brn rose ('21)	1.40	1.10
		Never hinged	2.25	
253	A64	90c blue ('21)	5.50	4.75
		Never hinged	8.75	
254	A64	1e violet ('21)	185.00	65.00
		Never hinged	300.00	
		Nos. 227-254 (29)	645.70	195.05

1920-26 *Perf. 12x11½*
Ordinary Paper

No.	Type	Description	Unused	Used
255	A64	¼c dark olive	.40	.25
		Never hinged	.65	
256	A64	½c black	.40	.25
		Never hinged	.65	
a.		Thick carton paper	13.50	2.00
		Never hinged	22.00	
257	A64	1c chocolate	.25	.25
		Never hinged	.40	
a.		Thick carton paper	70.00	21.00
		Never hinged	140.00	
258	A64	1½c dp grn	.25	.25
		Never hinged	.40	
259	A64	2c orange	.70	.40
		Never hinged	1.10	
a.		Thick carton paper	110.00	14.50
		Never hinged	225.00	
b.		2c orange yellow	1.50	.30
		Never hinged	1.50	
c.		As "b," thick carton paper	110.00	14.50
		Never hinged	225.00	
260	A64	2c yellow	.55	.25
		Never hinged	.90	
261	A64	2c choc ('26)	1.40	*8.00*
		Never hinged	2.25	
262	A64	2½c violet	4.00	2.25
		Never hinged	6.25	
263	A64	3c car rose	.30	.30
		Never hinged	.50	
264	A64	3c ultra ('21)	.50	.25
		Never hinged	.80	
265	A64	4c lt grn ('19)	.25	.25
		Never hinged	.40	
a.		Thick carton paper	150.00	90.00
		Never hinged	240.00	
266	A64	4c org ('26)	1.40	1.60
		Never hinged	2.25	
267	A64	5c yel brn	1.00	.40
		Never hinged	2.25	
268	A64	5c ol brn ('23)	.25	.25
		Never hinged	.40	
269	A64	6c pale rose	.40	.40
		Never hinged	.65	
a.		Thick carton paper	1.60	.90
		Never hinged	2.50	
270	A64	6c brown ('24)	.55	.25
		Never hinged	.90	
271	A64	7½c dp blue	.25	.25
		Never hinged	.40	
272	A64	8c slate	.25	.25
		Never hinged	.40	
273	A64	8c bl grn ('22)	.45	.25
		Never hinged	.70	
274	A64	8c org ('24)	.45	.45
		Never hinged	.70	
275	A64	10c org brn	.45	.25
		Never hinged	.70	
a.		Thick carton paper	42.50	3.50
		Never hinged	65.00	
276	A64	12c dp grn ('21)	.45	.40
		Never hinged	.70	
277	A64	13½c chlky bl	1.40	.45
		Never hinged	2.25	
278	A64	14c brt vio ('21)	1.10	.55
		Never hinged	1.75	
a.		Thick carton paper	250.00	175.00
		Never hinged	400.00	
279	A64	15c black ('23)	.40	.25
		Never hinged	.65	
280	A64	16c brt ultra ('24)	.90	.65
		Never hinged	1.45	
a.		16c pale blue ('26)	.90	.65
		Never hinged	1.45	
281	A64	20c dk brn	.50	.25
		Never hinged	.80	
a.		Thick carton paper	60.00	10.00
		Never hinged	100.00	
282	A64	20c dp grn ('23)	.45	.25
		Never hinged	.70	
283	A64	20c gray ('24)	.25	.25
		Never hinged	.40	
284	A64	24c grnsh bl ('21)	.45	.25
		Never hinged	.70	
285	A64	25c sal pink ('23)	.45	.25
		Never hinged	.70	
286	A64	25c lt gray ('26)	.45	.25
		Never hinged	.70	
287	A64	30c gray brn ('21)	.50	.25
		Never hinged	.80	
288	A64	30c dk brn ('24)	20.00	4.00
		Never hinged	30.00	
289	A64	32c dp grn ('24)	1.10	.40
		Never hinged	1.75	
290	A64	36c red ('21)	1.75	.45
		Never hinged	2.75	
291	A64	40c dk bl ('23)	.90	.55
		Never hinged	1.45	
a.		"CORREIC" for "CORREIO"	225.00	140.00
292	A64	40c choc ('24)	.45	.45
		Never hinged	.70	
a.		"CORREIC" for "CORREIO"	32.50	57.50
293	A64	40c green ('26)	.25	.25
		Never hinged	.40	
294	A64	48c rose ('24)	7.50	4.00
		Never hinged	12.00	
295	A64	50c yellow ('21)	1.90	.70
		Never hinged	3.00	
296	A64	60c blue ('21)	1.40	.60
		Never hinged	2.25	
297	A64	64c pale ultra ('24)	9.50	5.50
		Never hinged	14.50	
298	A64	75c dull rose ('23)	15.00	7.50
		Never hinged	27.00	
298A	A64	80c brn rose ('21)	32.50	9.50
		Never hinged	45.00	
298B	A64	80c violet ('24)	1.00	.55
		Never hinged	1.60	
298C	A64	90c chalky bl ('21)	1.60	.85
		Never hinged	2.50	
298D	A64	96c dp rose ('26)	42.50	35.00
		Never hinged	70.00	
298E	A64	1e violet ('21)	4.50	1.90
		Never hinged	7.00	
298F	A64	1.10e yel brn ('21)	4.50	1.60
		Never hinged	7.00	
298G	A64	1.20e yel grn ('21)	2.50	1.40
		Never hinged	4.00	
298H	A64	2e sl grn ('21)	45.00	5.50
		Never hinged	100.00	
		Nos. 255-298H (52)	215.60	101.80

1923-26 *Perf. 12x11½*
Glazed Paper

No.	Type	Description	Unused	Used
298I	A64	1e dk blue	5.00	2.25
		Never hinged	9.00	
298J	A64	1e gray vio ('24)	1.50	1.10
		Never hinged	2.75	
298K	A64	1.20e buff ('24)	50.00	32.50
		Never hinged	90.00	
298L	A64	1.50e blk vio	17.50	3.25
		Never hinged	30.00	
298M	A64	1.50e lilac ('24)	30.00	5.00
		Never hinged	55.00	
298N	A64	1.60e dp bl ('24)	19.00	5.00
		Never hinged	35.00	
298O	A64	2e sl grn ('24)	37.50	5.50
		Never hinged	145.00	
298P	A64	2.40e ap grn ('26)	160.00	110.00
		Never hinged	190.00	
298Q	A64	3e pink ('26)	160.00	100.00
		Never hinged	190.00	
298R	A64	3.20e gray grn ('24)	32.50	12.00
		Never hinged	57.50	
298S	A64	5e emer ('24)	35.00	9.00
		Never hinged	65.00	
298T	A64	10e pink ('24)	175.00	50.00
		Never hinged	250.00	
298U	A64	20e pale turq ('24)	300.00	160.00
		Never hinged	500.00	
		Nos. 298I-298U (13)	1,023.	495.60

See design A85. For surcharges & overprints see Nos. 453-495, RA2.
See 496A-496R.

Presidents of Portugal and Brazil and Aviators Cabral and Coutinho A65

1923 Litho. *Perf. 14*

No.	Type	Description	Unused	Used
299	A65	1c brown	.25	*.65*
300	A65	2c orange	.25	*.65*
301	A65	3c ultra	.25	*.65*
302	A65	4c yellow grn	.25	*.65*
303	A65	5c bister brn	.25	*.65*
304	A65	10c brown org	.25	*.65*
305	A65	15c black	.25	*.65*
306	A65	20c blue grn	.25	*.65*
307	A65	25c rose	.25	*.65*
308	A65	30c olive brn	.60	*1.90*
309	A65	40c chocolate	.25	*.65*
310	A65	50c yellow	.50	*.85*
311	A65	75c violet	.50	*1.00*
312	A65	1e dp blue	.50	*2.00*
313	A65	1.50e olive grn	.75	*2.50*
314	A65	2e myrtle grn	1.00	*6.00*
		Nos. 299-314 (16)	6.35	*20.75*

Flight of Sacadura Cabral and Gago Coutinho from Portugal to Brazil.

Camoens at Ceuta A66

Camoens Saving the Lusiads — A67

Luis de Camoens — A68

First Edition of the Lusiads — A69

Camoens Dying — A70

Tomb of Camoens A71

Monument to Camoens — A72

Engr.; Values Typo. in Black
1924, Nov. 11 *Perf. 14, 14½*

No.	Type	Description	Unused	Used
315	A66	2c lt blue	.25	.25
316	A66	3c orange	.25	.25
317	A66	4c dk gray	.25	.25
318	A66	5c yellow grn	.25	.25
319	A66	6c lake	.25	.25
320	A67	8c orange brn	.25	.25
321	A67	10c gray vio	.25	.25
322	A67	15c olive grn	.25	.25
323	A67	16c violet brn	.25	.25
324	A67	20c dp orange	.30	.25
325	A68	25c lilac	.30	.25
326	A68	30c dk brown	.30	.25
327	A68	32c dk green	.90	1.00
328	A68	40c ultra	.30	.25
329	A68	48c red brown	1.25	1.25
330	A69	50c red orange	1.40	.90
331	A69	64c green	1.40	.90
332	A69	75c dk violet	1.40	.90
333	A69	80c bister	1.10	.90
334	A69	96c lake	1.10	.90
335	A70	1e slate	1.10	.80
336	A70	1.20e lt brown	5.25	4.75
337	A70	1.50e red	1.25	.90
338	A70	1.60e dk blue	1.25	.90
339	A70	2e apple grn	5.25	4.75
340	A71	2.40e green, *grn*	3.75	2.75
341	A71	3e dk bl, *bl*	1.60	1.00
a.		Value double	125.00	125.00
b.		Value omitted		
342	A71	3.20e blk, *green*	1.60	1.00
343	A71	4.50e blk, *orange*	5.00	2.75
344	A71	10e dk brn, *pnksh*	10.00	8.00
345	A72	20e dk vio, *lil*	10.00	7.00
		Nos. 315-345 (31)	58.05	44.60

Birth of Luis de Camoens, poet, 400th anniv.
For overprints see Nos. 1S6-1S71.

Castello-Branco's House at Sao Miguel de Seide — A73

Castello-Branco's Study — A74

Camillo Castello-Branco A75

Teresa de Albuquerque A76

Mariana and Joao de Cruz — A77

Simao de Botelho — A78

1925, Mar. 26 *Perf. 12½*

346	A73	2c orange	.25	.25
347	A73	3c green	.25	.25
348	A73	4c ultra	.25	.25
349	A73	5c scarlet	.25	.25
350	A73	6c brown vio	.25	.25
a.		"6" and "C" omitted		
351	A73	8c black brn	.25	.25
352	A74	10c pale blue	.25	.25
353	A75	15c olive grn	.25	.25
354	A74	16c red orange	.30	.30
355	A74	20c dk violet	.30	.30
356	A75	25c car rose	.30	.30
357	A74	30c bister brn	.30	.30
358	A74	32c green	1.10	1.00
359	A75	40c green & blk	.65	.65
360	A74	48c red brn	3.00	3.00
361	A76	50c blue green	.65	.65
362	A76	64c orange brn	3.00	3.00
363	A76	75c gray blk	.60	.60
364	A75	80c brown	.60	.60
365	A76	96c car rose	1.50	1.50
366	A76	1e gray vio	1.50	1.50
367	A76	1.20e yellow grn	1.50	1.50
368	A77	1.50e dk bl, *bl*	25.00	13.50
369	A75	1.60e indigo	4.75	3.75
370	A77	2e dk grn, *grn*	6.25	4.25
371	A77	2.40e red, *org*	52.50	32.50
372	A77	3e lake, *bl*	67.50	40.00
373	A77	3.20e *green*	32.50	32.50
374	A75	4.50e red & blk	12.50	3.00
375	A77	10e brn, *yel*	13.00	3.00
376	A78	20e *orange*	13.50	3.00
		Nos. 346-376 (31)	244.80	152.70
		Set, never hinged	400.00	

Centenary of the birth of Camillo Castello-Branco, novelist.

First Independence Issue

Alfonso the Conqueror, First King of Portugal — A79

Batalha Monastery and King John I — A80

Battle of Aljubarrota A81

Filipa de Vilhena Arming her Sons A82

King John IV (The Duke of Braganza) A83

Independence Monument, Lisbon — A84

Center in Black

1926, Aug. 13 *Perf. 14, 14½*

377	A79	2c orange	.25	.25
378	A80	3c ultra	.25	.25
379	A79	4c yellow grn	.25	.25
380	A80	5c black brn	.25	.25
381	A79	6c ocher	.25	.25
382	A80	15c dk green	.25	.25
383	A79	16c dp blue	.70	.65
384	A81	20c dull violet	.70	.65
385	A82	25c scarlet	.70	.65
386	A81	32c dp green	.90	.90
387	A82	40c yellow brn	.55	.55
388	A80	46c carmine	3.25	3.25
389	A82	50c olive bis	3.25	3.25
390	A83	64c blue green	4.50	4.50
391	A82	75c brown red	4.50	4.50
392	A84	96c dull red	6.75	6.75
393	A83	1e black vio	7.00	7.00
394	A81	1.60e myrtle grn	9.25	9.25
395	A84	3e plum	27.50	27.50
396	A84	4.50e olive grn	35.00	35.00
397	A81	10e carmine	55.00	55.00
		Nos. 377-397 (21)	161.05	160.90
		Set, never hinged	275.00	

The use of these stamps instead of the regular issue was obligatory on Aug. 13th and 14th, Nov. 30th and Dec. 1st, 1926.

Stamps of 1926 Surcharged in Black

No. 397A

No. 397D

No. 397K

1926 Center in Black *Perf. 13½x14*

397A	A80	2c on 5c blk brn	1.50	1.10
		Never hinged	1.90	
397B	A80	2c on 46c car	1.50	1.10
		Never hinged	1.90	
397C	A83	2c on 64c bl grn	2.00	1.50
		Never hinged	2.50	
397D	A82	3c on 75c brn red	2.00	1.50
		Never hinged	2.50	
397E	A84	3c on 96c dull red	2.00	2.00
		Never hinged	2.50	
397F	A83	3c on 1e blk vio	2.00	1.60
		Never hinged	2.50	
397G	A81	4c on 1.60e myr grn	11.50	11.50
		Never hinged	14.00	
397H	A84	4c on 3e plum	6.00	4.00
		Never hinged	7.50	
397J	A84	6c on 4.50e ol grn	6.00	4.00
		Never hinged	7.50	
397K	A81	6c on 10e carmine	6.00	4.00
		Never hinged	7.50	
		Nos. 397A-397K (10)	40.50	32.30
		Set, never hinged	60.00	

There are two styles of the ornaments in these surcharges.

Ceres — A85

Without Imprint

1926, Dec. 2 **Typo.** *Perf. 13½x14*

398	A85	2c chocolate	.25	.25
		Never hinged	.50	
399	A85	3c brt blue	.25	.25
		Never hinged	.50	
400	A85	4c dp orange	.25	.25
		Never hinged	.50	
401	A85	5c dp brown	.25	.25
		Never hinged	.50	
402	A85	6c orange brn	.25	.25
		Never hinged	.50	
403	A85	10c orange red	.25	.25
		Never hinged	.50	
404	A85	15c black	.25	.25
		Never hinged	.50	
405	A85	16c ultra	.25	.25
		Never hinged	.50	
406	A85	25c gray	.25	.25
		Never hinged	.50	
407	A85	32c dp green	.55	.35
		Never hinged	1.10	
408	A85	40c blue green	.35	.25
		Never hinged	.70	
409	A85	48c rose	1.10	.90
		Never hinged	2.25	
410	A85	50c ocher	2.00	1.60
		Never hinged	4.00	
411	A85	64c deep blue	2.00	1.60
		Never hinged	4.00	
412	A85	80c violet	3.75	.55
		Never hinged	7.50	
413	A85	96c car rose	2.10	1.10
		Never hinged	4.25	
414	A85	1e red brown	10.00	1.00
		Never hinged	20.00	
415	A85	1.20e yellow brn	10.00	1.00
		Never hinged	20.00	
416	A85	1.60e dark blue	2.40	.55
		Never hinged	4.75	
417	A85	2e green	14.50	1.00
		Never hinged	32.50	
418	A85	3.20e olive grn	5.50	1.00
		Never hinged	11.00	
419	A85	4.50e yellow	5.50	1.00
		Never hinged	11.00	
420	A85	5e brown olive	60.00	3.75
		Never hinged	130.00	
421	A85	10e red	8.75	2.00
		Never hinged	17.50	
		Nos. 398-421 (24)	130.75	19.90
		Set, never hinged	275.00	

See design A64.

Second Independence Issue

Gonçalo Mendes da Maia — A86

Dr. Joao das Regras — A88

Guimaraes Castle — A87

Battle of Montijo — A89

Brites de Almeida — A90

Joao Pinto Ribeiro — A91

Center in Black

1927, Nov. 29 **Engr.** *Perf. 14*

422	A86	2c brown	.25	.25
423	A87	3c ultra	.25	.25
424	A86	4c orange	.25	.25
425	A88	5c olive brn	.25	.25
426	A89	6c orange brn	.25	.25
427	A87	15c black brn	.45	.35
428	A88	16c deep blue	1.00	.35
429	A86	25c gray	1.25	1.10
430	A89	32c blue grn	2.50	1.60
431	A90	40c yellow grn	.65	.50
432	A86	48c brown red	11.50	10.00
433	A87	80c dk violet	8.25	7.00
434	A90	96c dull red	14.50	13.50
435	A88	1.60e myrtle grn	15.00	14.50
436	A91	4.50e bister	22.50	22.50
		Nos. 422-436 (15)	78.85	72.65
		Set, never hinged	140.00	

The use of these stamps instead of the regular issue was compulsory on Nov. 29-30, Dec. 1-2, 1927. The money derived from their sale was used for the purchase of a palace for a war museum, the organization of an international exposition in Lisbon, in 1940, and for fêtes to be held in that year in commemoration of the 8th cent. of the founding of Portugal and the 3rd cent. of its restoration.

Third Independence Issue

Gualdim Paes — A93

The Siege of Santarem — A94

Battle of Rolica — A95

Battle of Atoleiros A96

Joana de Gouveia A97

Matias de Albuquerque A98

1928, Nov. 28 **Center in Black**

437	A93	2c lt blue	.25	.25
438	A94	3c lt green	.25	.25
439	A95	4c lake	.25	.25
440	A96	5c olive grn	.25	.25
441	A97	6c orange brn	.25	.25
442	A94	15c slate	.75	.75

443 A95 16c dk violet .75 .75
444 A93 25c ultra .75 .75
445 A97 32c dk green 3.75 3.75
446 A96 40c olive brn .75 .75
447 A95 50c red orange 9.25 5.75
448 A94 80c lt gray 9.75 7.00
449 A97 96c carmine 17.50 15.00
450 A96 1e claret 27.50 27.50
451 A93 1.60e dk blue 13.00 11.50
452 A98 4.50e yellow 14.00 13.50
Nos. 437-452 (16) 99.00 88.25
Set, never hinged 150.00

Obligatory Nov. 27-30. See note after No. 436.

Type and Stamps of 1912-28 Surcharged in Black

1928-29 ***Perf. 12x11½, 15x14***

453 A64 4c on 8c orange .40 .35
Never hinged .50
454 A64 4c on 30c dk brn .40 .35
Never hinged .50
455 A64 10c on ¼c dk ol .40 .35
Never hinged .50
a. Inverted surcharge 110.00 100.00
Never hinged 230.00
456 A64 10c on ½c blk (R) .60 .45
Never hinged 1.10
a. Perf. 15x14 17.50 12.50
Never hinged 37.50
457 A64 10c on 1c choc .60 .45
Never hinged 1.10
a. Perf. 15x14 *75.00* *55.00*
Never hinged 150.00
458 A64 10c on 4c grn .45 .35
Never hinged .90
a. Perf. 15x14 *87.50* *67.50*
Never hinged 180.00
459 A64 10c on 4c orange .45 .35
Never hinged .90
460 A64 10c on 5c ol brn .45 .35
Never hinged .90
461 A64 15c on 16c blue 1.10 .80
Never hinged 2.00
462 A64 15c on 16c ultra 1.10 .80
Never hinged 2.00
463 A64 15c on 20c brown 32.50 32.50
Never hinged 65.00
464 A64 15c on 20c gray .45 .35
Never hinged .90
465 A64 15c on 24c grnsh bl 2.10 1.60
Never hinged 4.00
466 A64 15c on 25c gray .45 .35
Never hinged .90
467 A64 15c on 25c sal pink .45 .35
Never hinged .90
468 A64 16c on 32c dp grn .90 .80
Never hinged 1.90
469 A64 40c on 2c orange .45 .35
Never hinged .90
a. Thick carton paper 165.00 32.50
Never hinged 265.00
470 A64 40c on 2c yellow 4.50 3.25
Never hinged 9.50
471 A64 40c on 2c choc .40 .35
Never hinged .80
472 A64 40c on 3c ultra .45 .35
Never hinged .90
473 A64 40c on 50c yellow .40 .25
Never hinged .80
474 A64 40c on 60c dull bl .90 .65
Never hinged 1.90
a. Perf. 15x14 10.00 8.00
Never hinged 20.00
475 A64 40c on 64c pale ultra .90 .80
Never hinged 1.90
476 A64 40c on 75c dl rose .90 .90
Never hinged 1.90
477 A64 40c on 80c violet .65 .55
Never hinged 1.40
478 A64 40c on 90c chlky bl 4.50 3.25
Never hinged 9.50
a. Perf. 15x14 11.50 8.75
Never hinged 24.00
479 A64 40c on 1e gray vio .85 .85
Never hinged 1.75
480 A64 40c on 1.10e yel brn .90 .80
Never hinged 1.90
481 A64 80c on 6c pale rose .85 .70
Never hinged 1.60
a. Thick carton paper 5.75 5.00
Never hinged 12.00
482 A64 80c on 6c choc .85 .70
Never hinged 1.75
483 A64 80c on 48c rose 2.00 1.10
Never hinged 2.00
484 A64 80c on 1.50e lilac 4.00 1.25
Never hinged 6.00
485 A64 96c on 1.20e yel grn 4.00 2.40
Never hinged 7.00
486 A64 96c on 1.20e buff 4.00 2.75
Never hinged 7.00
487 A64 1.60e on 2e slate grn 35.00 27.50
Never hinged 70.00
487A A64 1.60e on 2e sl grn, *glazed paper* 37.50 25.00
Never hinged 80.00
488 A64 1.60e on 3.20e gray grn 15.00 7.25
Never hinged 30.00
489 A64 1.60e on 20e pale turq 20.00 10.00
Never hinged 37.50
Nos. 453-489 (37) 144.30 106.55
Set, never hinged 360.00 .45

Stamps of 1912-26 Overprinted in Black or Red

1929 ***Perf. 12x11½***

490 A64 10c orange brn .45
Never hinged .65
a. Perf. 15x14 275.00 275.00
Never hinged 425.00
491 A64 15c black (R) .40 .35
Never hinged .60
492 A64 40c lt green .65 .55
Never hinged .95
493 A64 40c chocolate .55 .45
Never hinged .80
494 A64 96c dp rose 5.50 4.50
Never hinged 8.00
495 A64 1.60e brt blue 22.50 15.00
Never hinged 32.50
a. Double overprint 110.00 100.00
Never hinged 160.00
Nos. 490-495 (6) 30.05 20.85
Set, never hinged 45.00

Liberty — A100

1929, May ***Perf. 12x11½***

496 A100 1.60e on 5c red brn 11.50 7.00

Types of 1912-20 Issues With Imprint
Perf. 12x11½

1930-31 **Typo.** **Wove Paper**

496A A64 4c orange .25 .25
Never hinged .45
496B A64 5c blk brn ('31) .25 .25
Never hinged .45
496C A64 6c red brn .25 .25
Never hinged .45
496D A64 10c red ('31) .45 .25
Never hinged .75
496E A64 15c black 2.50 .50
Never hinged 4.25
496F A64 25c lt gray .90 .45
Never hinged 1.50
496G A64 25c blue grn .90 .45
Never hinged 1.50
496H A85 32c dp green .90 .45
Never hinged 1.50
496I A64 40c green 3.50 1.25
Never hinged 6.00
496J A64 50c bister 2.25 1.40
Never hinged 3.75
496K A64 50c red brn ('30) 2.25 1.40
Never hinged 3.75
496L A64 75c car rose 2.25 1.40
Never hinged 3.75
496M A64 80c dk grn 2.25 1.40
Never hinged 3.75
496N A64 1e brn lake 6.50 1.10
Never hinged 11.00
496O A64 1.20e pur brn ('31) 4.50 1.10
Never hinged 7.50
496P A64 1.25e dk bl ('31) 4.50 1.10
Never hinged 7.50
496Q A64 2e red vio ('31) 19.00 6.50
Never hinged 32.50
496R A64 4.50e org ('31) 65.00 45.00
Never hinged 110.00
Nos. 496A-496R (18) 118.40 64.50
Set, never hinged 200.00

Nos. 496A-496R were printed at the Lisbon Mint from new plates produced from the original dies. The paper is whiter than the paper used for earlier Ceres stamps. The gum is white.

"Portugal" Holding Volume of "Lusiads" — A101

1931-38 **Typo.** ***Perf. 14***

497 A101 4c bister brn .25 .25
498 A101 5c olive gray .25 .25
499 A101 6c lt gray .25 .25
500 A101 10c dk violet .25 .25
501 A101 15c gray blk .25 .25
502 A101 16c brt blue 1.25 .65
503 A101 25c deep green 3.00 .35
504 A101 25c brt bl ('33) 3.50 .40
505 A101 30c dk grn ('33) 1.90 .40
506 A101 40c orange red 6.25 .25
507 A101 48c fawn 1.25 .95
508 A101 50c lt brown .30 .25
509 A101 75c car rose 5.00 1.10
510 A101 80c emerald .40 .25
511 A101 95c car rose ('33) 16.00 6.75
512 A101 1e claret 30.00 .25
513 A101 1.20e olive grn 2.10 .95
514 A101 1.25e dk blue 1.90 .25
515 A101 1.60e dk blue ('33) 32.50 4.25
516 A101 1.75e dk blue ('38) .65 .25
517 A101 2e dull violet .75 .25
518 A101 4.50e orange 1.50 .25
519 A101 5e yellow grn 1.50 .25
Nos. 497-519 (23) 111.00 19.30
Set, never hinged 175.00

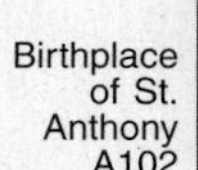

Birthplace of St. Anthony A102

Font where St. Anthony was Baptized A103

Lisbon Cathedral A104

St. Anthony with Infant Jesus A105

Santa Cruz Cathedral A106

St. Anthony's Tomb at Padua A107

1931, June **Typo.** ***Perf. 12***

528 A102 15c plum 1.00 .25

Litho.

529 A103 25c gray & pale grn 1.50 .25
530 A104 40c gray brn & buff 1.00 .25
531 A105 75c dl rose & pale rose 22.50 14.00
532 A106 1.25e gray & pale bl 52.50 30.00
533 A107 4.50e gray vio & lil 25.00 3.50
Nos. 528-533 (6) 103.50 48.25
Set, never hinged 190.00

7th centenary of the death of St. Anthony of Padua and Lisbon.
For surcharges see Nos. 543-548.

Nuno Alvares Pereira (1360-1431), Portuguese Warrior and Statesman — A108

1931, Nov. 1 **Typo.** ***Perf. 12x11½***

534 A108 15c black 2.00 1.10
535 A108 25c gray grn & blk 10.50 1.10
536 A108 40c orange 4.00 .50
a. Value omitted 150.00 150.00
537 A108 75c car rose 25.00 21.00
538 A108 1.25e dk bl & pale bl 30.00 20.00
539 A108 4.50e choc & lt grn 125.00 52.50
a. Value omitted 350.00 350.00
Nos. 534-539 (6) 196.50 96.20
Set, never hinged 325.00

For surcharges see Nos. 549-554.

Nos. 528-533 Surcharged

1933 ***Perf. 12***

543 A104 15c on 40c 2.00 .35
544 A102 40c on 15c 4.00 1.25
545 A103 40c on 25c 3.00 .35
546 A105 40c on 75c 20.00 5.25
547 A106 40c on 1.25e 20.00 5.25
548 A107 40c on 4.50e 20.00 5.25
Nos. 543-548 (6) 69.00 17.70
Set, never hinged 80.00

Nos. 534-539 Surcharged

1933 ***Perf. 12x11½***

549 A108 15c on 40c 1.00 .35
550 A108 40c on 15c 3.75 2.40
551 A108 40c on 25c 2.00 .80
552 A108 40c on 75c 17.00 4.00
553 A108 40c on 1.25e 17.00 4.00
554 A108 40c on 4.50e 17.00 4.00
Nos. 549-554 (6) 57.75 15.55
Set, never hinged 80.00

President Carmona — A109

1934, May 28 **Typo.** ***Perf. 11½***

556 A109 40c brt violet 18.00 .35
Never hinged 32.50

Head of a Colonial — A110

1934, July ***Perf. 11½x12***

558 A110 25c dk brown 3.00 1.60
559 A110 40c scarlet 19.00 .40
560 A110 1.60e dk blue 29.00 2.00
Nos. 558-560 (3) 51.00 4.00
Set, never hinged 125.00

Colonial Exposition.

Roman Temple, Evora A111

Prince Henry the Navigator A112

"All for the Nation"
A113

Coimbra Cathedral
A114

1935-41 ***Perf. 11½x12***

561 A111 4c black .45 .25
562 A111 5c blue .50 .25
563 A111 6c choc ('36) .75 .35

Perf. 11½, 12x11½ (1.75e)

564 A112 10c turq grn .65 .25
565 A112 15c red brown .35 .25
a. Booklet pane of 4
566 A113 25c dp blue 6.00 .45
a. Booklet pane of 4
567 A113 40c brown 2.00 .25
a. Booklet pane of 4
568 A113 1e rose red 9.25 .50
568A A114 1.75e blue 85.00 1.25
568B A113 10e gray blk ('41) 50.00 2.50
569 A113 20e turq grn ('41) 70.00 2.10
Nos. 561-569 (11) 224.95 8.40
Set, never hinged 400.00

For overprint see No. O1.

Queen Maria — A115

Typographed, Head Embossed

1935, June 1 ***Perf. 11½***

570 A115 40c scarlet 1.40 .25
Never hinged 2.10

First Portuguese Philatelic Exhibition.

Rod and Bowl of Aesculapius — A116

1937, July 24 **Typo.** ***Perf. 11½x12***

571 A116 25c blue 8.00 .85
Never hinged 15.00

Centenary of the establishment of the School of Medicine in Lisbon and Oporto.

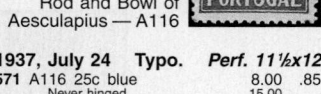

Gil Vicente — A117

1937

572 A117 40c dark brown 10.00 .25
573 A117 1e rose red 2.00 .25
Set, never hinged 32.50

400th anniversary of the death of Gil Vicente (1465-1536), Portuguese playwright. Design shows him in cowherd role in his play, "Auto do Vaqueiro."

Grapes — A118

1938 ***Perf. 11½***

575 A118 15c brt purple 1.40 .55
576 A118 25c brown 3.00 1.60
577 A118 40c dp red lilac 10.00 .35
578 A118 1.75e dp blue 30.00 5.00
Nos. 575-578 (4) 44.40 7.50
Set, never hinged 70.00

International Vineyard and Wine Congress.

Emblem of Portuguese Legion — A119

1940, Jan. 27 **Unwmk.** ***Perf. 11½***

579 A119 5c dull yellow .50 .25
580 A119 10c violet .50 .25
581 A119 15c brt blue .50 .25
582 A119 25c brown 22.50 1.10
583 A119 40c dk green 37.50 .40
584 A119 80c yellow grn 2.40 .55
585 A119 1e brt red 57.50 3.50
586 A119 1.75e dark blue 8.00 2.75
a. Souv. sheet of 8, #579-586 250.00 250.00
Never hinged 600.00
Nos. 579-586 (8) 129.40 9.05
Set, never hinged 190.00

Issued in honor of the Portuguese Legion.
No. 586a sold for 5.50e, the proceeds going to various charities.

Portuguese World Exhibition A120

King John IV — A121

Discoveries Monument, Belém — A122

King Alfonso I — A123

1940 **Engr.** ***Perf. 12x11½, 11½x12***

587 A120 10c brown violet .40 .25
588 A121 15c dk grnsh bl .40 .25
589 A122 25c dk slate grn 1.40 .25
590 A121 35c yellow green 1.10 .35
591 A123 40c olive bister 2.75 .25
592 A120 80c dk violet 5.25 .35
593 A122 1e dark red 12.00 1.60
594 A123 1.75e ultra 7.00 2.75
a. Souv. sheet of 8, #587-594 ('41) 140.00 110.00
Never hinged 275.00
Nos. 587-594 (8) 30.30 6.05
Set, never hinged 50.00

Portuguese Intl. Exhibition, Lisbon (10c, 80c); restoration of the monarchy, 300th anniv (15c, 35c); Portuguese independence, 800th anniv (40c, 1.75e).
No. 594a sold for 10e.

Sir Rowland Hill — A124

1940, Aug. 12 **Typo.** ***Perf. 11½x12***

595 A124 15c dk violet brn .40 .25
596 A124 25c dp org brn .40 .25
597 A124 35c green .40 .25
598 A124 40c brown violet .50 .25
599 A124 50c turq green 18.00 4.25
600 A124 80c lt blue 3.00 1.10
601 A124 1e crimson 21.00 3.50
602 A124 1.75e dk blue 6.75 3.50
a. Souv. sheet of 8, #595-602 ('41) 75.00 75.00
Never hinged 125.00
Nos. 595-602 (8) 50.45 13.35
Set, never hinged 75.00

Postage stamp centenary.
No. 602a sold for 10e.

AIR POST STAMPS

Symbol of Aviation AP1

Perf. 12x11½

1936-41 **Unwmk.** **Typo.**

C1 AP1 1.50e dark blue .75 .30
C2 AP1 1.75e red orange 1.00 .35
C3 AP1 2.50e rose red 1.00 .35
C4 AP1 3e brt blue ('41) 14.00 12.00
C5 AP1 4e dp yel grn ('41) 18.00 18.00
C6 AP1 5e car lake 1.75 1.25
C7 AP1 10e brown lake 3.00 1.25
C8 AP1 15e orange ('41) 11.50 7.00
C9 AP1 20e black brn 9.00 2.75
C10 AP1 50e brn vio ('41) 160.00 75.00
Nos. C1-C10 (10) 220.00 118.25
Set, never hinged 390.00

Stamps issued in 1941 have decimals '00' in the denomination.
Nos. C1-C10 exist imperf.

POSTAGE DUE STAMPS

Vasco da Gama Issue

The Zamorin of Calicut Receiving Vasco da Gama — D1

Unwmk.

1898, May 1 **Typo.** ***Perf. 12***

Denomination in Black

J1 D1 5r black 2.40 1.25
On cover —
a. Value and "Continente" omitted 50.00 5.00
J2 D1 10r lilac & blk 4.00 1.75
On cover 1,100.
J3 D1 20r orange & blk 6.50 2.50
On cover 550.00
J4 D1 50r slate & blk 50.00 11.00
On cover 1,100.
J5 D1 100r car & blk, *pink* 87.50 40.00
On cover 1,100.
J6 D1 200r brn & blk, *buff* 92.50 60.00
On cover —

For overprints and surcharges see Nos. 193-198.

D2

1904 ***Perf. 11½x12***

J7 D2 5r brown .45 .40
J8 D2 10r orange 2.75 .90
a. Imperf. —
J9 D2 20r lilac 8.00 3.75
J10 D2 30r gray green 5.75 2.75
J11 D2 40r gray violet 7.00 2.75
J12 D2 50r carmine 52.50 4.50
a. Imperf. —
J13 D2 100r dull blue 8.75 6.50
a. Imperf. —
Nos. J7-J13 (7) 85.20 21.55

Preceding Issue Overprinted in Carmine or Green

1910

J14 D2 5r brown .40 .25
J15 D2 10r orange .40 .25
J16 D2 20r lilac 1.40 1.00
J17 D2 30r gray green 1.25 .25
J18 D2 40r gray violet 1.40 .25
J19 D2 50r carmine (G) 6.00 4.50
J20 D2 100r dull blue 6.50 5.25
Nos. J14-J20 (7) 17.35 11.75

See note after No. 183.

D3

1915, Mar. 18 **Typo.**

J21 D3 ½c brown .60 .60
J22 D3 1c orange .60 .60
J23 D3 2c claret .60 .60
J24 D3 3c green .60 .60
J25 D3 4c gray violet .60 .60
J26 D3 5c carmine .60 .60
J27 D3 10c dark blue .60 .60
Nos. J21-J27 (7) 4.20 4.20

1921-27

J28 D3 ½c gray green ('22) .35 .35
J29 D3 4c gray green ('27) .35 .35
J30 D3 8c gray green ('23) .35 .35
J31 D3 10c gray green ('22) .35 .35
J32 D3 12c gray green .50 .50
J33 D3 16c gray green ('23) .50 .50
J34 D3 20c gray green .50 .50
J35 D3 24c gray green .50 .50
J36 D3 32c gray green ('23) .50 .50
J37 D3 36c gray green 1.50 .75
J38 D3 40c gray green ('23) 1.50 .75
J39 D3 48c gray green ('23) .65 .65
J40 D3 50c gray green .65 .65
J41 D3 60c gray green .65 .65
J42 D3 72c gray green .65 .65
J43 D3 80c gray green ('23) 7.50 7.50
J44 D3 1.20e gray green 3.00 3.00
Nos. J28-J44 (17) 20.00 18.50

D4

1932-33

J45 D4 5c buff .50 .45
J46 D4 10c lt blue .50 .45
J47 D4 20c pink 1.25 1.00
J48 D4 30c blue green 1.50 1.00
J49 D4 40c lt green 1.50 1.00
a. Figure of value inverted —
J50 D4 50c gray 1.60 1.00
J51 D4 60c rose 4.25 2.00

J52	D4	80c violet brn	10.00	4.00
J53	D4	1.20e gray ol ('33)	13.00	12.00
		Nos. J45-J53 (9)	34.10	22.90

D5

1940, Feb. 1 Unwmk. *Perf. 12½*

J54	D5	5c bister, perf. 14	.50	.35
J55	D5	10c rose lilac	.30	.25
J56	D5	20c dk car rose	.30	.25
J57	D5	30c purple	.30	.25
J58	D5	40c cerise	.30	.25
J59	D5	50c brt blue	.30	.25
J60	D5	60c yellow grn	.30	.25
J61	D5	80c scarlet	.30	.25
J62	D5	1e brown	.30	.25
J63	D5	2e dk rose vio	.55	.45
J64	D5	5e org yel, perf. 14	11.00	9.00
a.		Perf. 12½	175.00	125.00
		Nos. J54-J64 (11)	14.45	11.80

Nos. J54-J64 were first issued perf. 14. In 1955 all but the 5c were reissued in perf. 12½.

OFFICIAL STAMPS

No. 567 Overprinted in Black

1938 Unwmk. *Perf. 11½*

O1 A113 40c brown .45 .25

NEWSPAPER STAMPS

N1

Perf. 11½, 12½, 13½

1876 Typo. Unwmk.

P1	N1	2½r bister	9.50	1.40
		On newspaper or wrapper		5.00
a.		2½r olive green	9.50	1.40
		On newspaper or wrapper		5.00

Various shades.

PARCEL POST STAMPS

Mercury and Commerce PP1

1920-22 Unwmk. Typo. *Perf. 12*

Q1	PP1	1c lilac brown	.25	.25
Q2	PP1	2c orange	.25	.25
Q3	PP1	5c lt brown	.25	.25
Q4	PP1	10c red brown	.25	.25
Q5	PP1	20c gray blue	.30	.25
Q6	PP1	40c carmine rose	.35	.25
Q7	PP1	50c black	.50	.45
Q8	PP1	60c dk blue ('21)	.50	.45
Q9	PP1	70c gray brn ('21)	3.00	2.00
Q10	PP1	80c ultra ('21)	3.50	3.25
Q11	PP1	90c lt vio ('21)	3.50	2.25
Q12	PP1	1e lt green	4.00	2.25
Q13	PP1	2e pale lilac ('22)	11.00	3.50
Q14	PP1	3e olive ('22)	21.00	4.00
Q15	PP1	4e ultra ('22)	42.50	7.00
Q16	PP1	5e gray ('22)	55.00	4.75
Q17	PP1	10e chocolate ('22)	82.50	9.25
		Nos. Q1-Q17 (17)	228.65	40.65

Parcel Post Package PP2

1936 *Perf. 11½*

Q18	PP2	50c olive brown	.65	.50
Q19	PP2	1e bister brown	.65	.50
Q20	PP2	1.50e purple	.65	.50
Q21	PP2	2e carmine lake	2.75	.60
Q22	PP2	2.50e olive green	2.75	.60
Q23	PP2	4.50e brown lake	5.75	.65
Q24	PP2	5e violet	9.00	.75
Q25	PP2	10e orange	12.00	1.75
		Nos. Q18-Q25 (8)	34.20	5.85

POSTAL TAX STAMPS

These stamps represent a special fee for the delivery of postal matter on certain days in each year. The money derived from their sale is applied to works of public charity.

Regular Issues Overprinted in Carmine

1911, Oct. 4 Unwmk. *Perf. 14½x15*

RA1 A62 10r gray green 8.50 2.25

The 20r carmine of this type was for use on telegrams. Value, $10.

1912, Oct. 4 *Perf. 15x14½*

RA2 A64 1c deep green 6.00 1.75

The 2c carmine of this type was for use on telegrams. Value, $10.

"Lisbon" — PT1

1913, June 8 Litho. *Perf. 12x11½*

RA3 PT1 1c dark green .95 .70

The 2c dark brown of this type was for use on telegrams. Value, $5.

"Charity" — PT2

1915, Oct. 4 Typo.

RA4 PT2 1c carmine .35 .30

The 2c plum of this type was for use on telegrams. Value, $5.

See No. RA6.

No. RA4 Surcharged

1924, Oct. 4

RA5 PT2 15c on 1c dull red 1.25 .70

The 30c on 2c claret of this type was for use on telegrams. Value, $3.

Charity Type of 1915 Issue

1925, Oct. 4 *Perf. 12½*

RA6 PT2 15c carmine .35 .35

The 30c brown violet of this type was for use on telegrams. Value, $2.

Comrades of the Great War Issue

Muse of History with Tablet — PT3

1925, Apr. 8 Litho. *Perf. 11*

RA7	PT3	10c brown	1.10	1.10
RA8	PT3	10c green	1.10	1.10
RA9	PT3	10c rose	1.10	1.10
RA10	PT3	10c ultra	1.10	1.10
		Nos. RA7-RA10 (4)	4.40	4.40

The use of these stamps, in addition to the regular postage, was obligatory on certain days of the year. If the tax represented by these stamps was not prepaid, it was collected by means of Postal Tax Due Stamp No. RAJ1.

Pombal Issue
Common Design Types

Engraved; Value and "Continente" Typographed in Black

1925, May 8 *Perf. 12½*

RA11	CD28	15c ultra	.50	.40
RA12	CD29	15c ultra	1.00	.75
RA13	CD30	15c ultra	1.00	.75
		Nos. RA11-RA13 (3)	2.50	1.90

Olympic Games Issue

Hurdler — PT7

1928 Litho. *Perf. 12*

RA14 PT7 15c dull red & blk 10.00 *2.75*

The use of this stamp, in addition to the regular postage, was obligatory on May 22-24, 1928. 10% of the money thus obtained was retained by the Postal Administration; the balance was given to a Committee in charge of Portuguese participation in the Olympic games at Amsterdam.

POSTAL TAX DUE STAMPS

Comrades of the Great War Issue

PTD1

1925 Unwmk. Typo. *Perf. 11x11½*

RAJ1 PTD1 20c brown orange .55 .45

See Note after No. RA10.

Pombal Issue
Common Design Types

1925 *Perf. 12½*

RAJ2	CD28	30c ultra	1.10	1.10
RAJ3	CD29	30c ultra	1.10	1.10
RAJ4	CD30	30c ultra	1.10	1.10
		Nos. RAJ2-RAJ4 (3)	3.30	3.30

When the compulsory tax was not paid by the use of stamps #RA11-RA13, double the amount was collected by means of #RAJ2-RAJ4.

Olympic Games Issue

PTD2

1928 Litho. *Perf. 11½*

RAJ5 PTD2 30c lt red & blk 8.00 1.75

FRANCHISE STAMPS

These stamps are supplied by the Government to various charitable, scientific and military organizations for franking their correspondence. This franking privilege was withdrawn in 1938.

FOR THE RED CROSS SOCIETY

F1

Perf. 11½

1889-1915 Unwmk. Typo.

1S1	F1	rose & blk ('15)	.45	.40
		On cover or postcard		82.50
a.		Vermilion & black ('08)	5.75	1.25
		On cover or postcard		82.50
b.		Red & black, perf. 12½	65.00	6.25
		On cover or postcard		*190.00*

No. 1S1 Overprinted in Green

1917

1S3	F1	rose & black	90.00	77.50
a.		Inverted overprint	150.00	150.00

"Charity" Extending Hope to Invalid — F1a

1926 Litho. *Perf. 14*

Inscribed "LISBOA"

1S4 F1a black & red 9.00 9.00

Inscribed "DELEGACOES"

1S5 F1a black & red 9.00 9.00

No. 1S4 was for use in Lisbon. No. 1S5 was for the Red Cross chapters outside Lisbon.

For overprints see Nos. 1S72-1S73.

Camoens Issue of 1924 Overprinted in Black or Red

1927

1S6	A68	40c ultra	1.10	1.00
1S7	A68	48c red brown	1.10	1.00
1S8	A69	64c green	1.10	1.00
1S9	A69	75c dk violet	1.10	1.00
1S10	A71	4.50e blk, *org* (R)	1.10	1.00
1S11	A71	10e dk brn, *pnksh*	1.10	1.00
		Nos. 1S6-1S11 (6)	6.60	6.00

Camoens Issue of 1924 Overprinted in Red

1928

1S12	A67	15c olive grn	1.10	1.00
1S13	A67	16c violet brn	1.10	1.00
1S14	A68	25c lilac	1.10	1.00
1S15	A68	40c ultra	1.10	1.00
1S16	A70	1.20e lt brown	1.10	1.00
1S17	A70	2e apple green	1.10	1.00
		Nos. 1S12-1S17 (6)	6.60	6.00

Camoens Issue of 1924 Overprinted in Red

1929

1S18	A68	30c dk brown	1.10	1.00
1S19	A68	40c ultra	1.10	1.00
1S20	A69	80c bister	1.10	1.00
1S21	A70	1.50e red	1.10	1.00
1S22	A70	1.60e dark blue	1.10	1.00
1S23	A71	2.40e green, *grn*	1.10	1.00
		Nos. 1S18-1S23 (6)	6.60	6.00

Same Overprint Dated "1930"

1930

1S24	A68	40c ultra	1.10	1.00
1S25	A69	50c red orange	1.10	1.00
1S26	A69	96c lake	1.10	1.00
1S27	A70	1.60e dk blue	1.10	1.00
1S28	A71	3e dk blue, *bl*	1.10	1.00
1S29	A72	20e dk violet, *lil*	1.10	1.00
		Nos. 1S24-1S29 (6)	6.60	6.00

Camoens Issue of 1924 Overprinted in Red

1931

1S30	A68	25c lilac	1.25	1.10
1S31	A68	32c dk green	1.25	1.10
1S32	A68	40c ultra	1.25	1.10
1S33	A69	96c lake	1.25	1.10
1S34	A70	1.60e dark blue	1.25	1.10
1S35	A71	3.20e black, *green*	1.25	1.10
		Nos. 1S30-1S35 (6)	7.50	6.60

Same Overprint Dated "1932"

1931

1S36	A67	20c dp orange	1.75	1.75
1S37	A68	40c ultra	1.75	1.75
1S38	A68	48c red brown	1.75	1.75
1S39	A69	64c green	1.75	1.75
1S40	A70	1.60e dark blue	1.75	1.75
1S41	A71	10e dk brown, *pnksh*	1.75	1.75
		Nos. 1S36-1S41 (6)	10.50	10.50

Nos. 1S6-1S11 Overprinted in Red

1932

1S42	A68	40c ultra	1.75	1.75
1S43	A68	48c red brown	1.75	1.75
1S44	A69	64c green	1.75	1.75
1S45	A69	75c dk violet	1.75	1.75
1S46	A71	4.50e blk, *orange*	1.75	1.75
1S47	A71	10e dk brn, *pnksh*	1.75	1.75
		Nos. 1S42-1S47 (6)	10.50	10.50

1933 **Dated "1934"**

1S48	A68	40c ultra	2.25	2.25
1S49	A68	48c red brown	2.25	2.25
1S50	A69	64c green	2.25	2.25
1S51	A69	75c dark violet	2.25	2.25
1S52	A71	4.50e blk, *orange*	2.25	2.25
1S53	A71	10e dk brown, *pnksh*	2.25	2.25
		Nos. 1S48-1S53 (6)	13.50	13.50

1935 **Dated "1935"**

1S54	A68	40c ultra	2.60	2.60
1S55	A68	48c red brown	2.60	2.60
1S56	A69	64c green	2.60	2.60
1S57	A69	75c dk violet	2.60	2.60
1S58	A71	4.50e black, *orange*	2.60	2.60
1S59	A71	10e dk brn, *pnksh*	2.60	2.60
		Nos. 1S54-1S59 (6)	15.60	15.60

Camoens Issue of 1924 Overprinted in Black or Red

1935

1S60	A68	25c lilac	1.10	1.00
1S61	A68	40c ultra (R)	1.10	1.00
1S62	A69	50c red orange	1.10	1.00
1S63	A70	1e slate	1.10	1.00
1S64	A70	2e apple green	1.10	1.00
1S65	A72	20e dk violet, *lilac*	1.10	1.00
		Nos. 1S60-1S65 (6)	6.60	6.00

Camoens Issue of 1924 Overprinted in Red

1936

1S66	A68	30c dk brown	1.10	1.10
1S67	A68	32c dk green	1.10	1.10
1S68	A69	80c bister	1.10	1.10
1S69	A70	1.20e lt brown	1.10	1.10
1S70	A71	3e dk blue, *bl*	1.10	1.10
1S71	A71	4.50e black, *yel*	1.10	1.10
		Nos. 1S66-1S71 (6)	6.60	6.60

No. 1S4 Overprinted "1935"

1936 **Unwmk.** ***Perf. 14***

1S72	F1a	black & red	10.00	10.00

Same Stamp with Additional Overprint "Delegacoes"

1S73	F1a	black & red	10.00	10.00

After the government withdrew the franking privilege in 1938, the Portuguese Red Cross Society distributed charity labels which lacked postal validity.

FOR CIVILIAN RIFLE CLUBS

Rifle Club Emblem — F2

Perf. 11½x12

1899-1910 **Typo.** **Unwmk.**

2S1	F2	bl grn & car ('99)	10.00	10.00
2S2	F2	brn & yel grn ('00)	10.00	10.00
2S3	F2	car & buff ('01)	1.00	1.00
2S4	F2	bl & org ('02)	1.00	1.00
2S5	F2	grn & org ('03)	1.00	1.00
2S6	F2	lt brn & car ('04)	1.60	1.60
2S7	F2	mar & ultra ('05)	4.25	4.25
2S8	F2	ultra & buff ('06)	1.00	1.00
2S9	F2	choc & yel ('07)	1.00	1.00
2S10	F2	car & ultra ('08)	1.60	1.60
2S11	F2	bl & yel grn ('09)	1.00	1.00
2S12	F2	bl grn & brn, *pink* ('10)	4.00	4.00
		Nos. 2S1-2S12 (12)	37.45	37.45

FOR THE GEOGRAPHICAL SOCIETY OF LISBON

Coat of Arms

F3 F4

1903-34 **Unwmk.** **Litho.** ***Perf. 11½***

3S1	F3	blk, rose, bl & red	9.00	5.00
3S2	F3	bl, yel, red & grn ('09)	12.00	5.00
3S3	F4	blk, org, bl & red ('11)	5.50	4.00
3S4	F4	blk & brn org ('22)	6.75	4.75
3S5	F4	blk & bl ('24)	15.00	8.50
3S6	F4	blk & rose ('26)	6.75	4.75
3S7	F4	blk & grn ('27)	6.75	4.75
3S8	F4	bl, yel & red ('29)	4.75	3.50
3S9	F4	bl, red & vio ('30)	4.75	3.50
3S10	F4	dp bl, lil & red ('31)	4.75	3.50
3S11	F4	bis brn & red ('32)	4.75	3.50
3S12	F4	lt grn & red ('33)	4.75	3.50
3S13	F4	blue & red ('34)	4.75	3.50
		Nos. 3S1-3S13 (13)	90.25	57.75

No. 3S12 with three-line overprint, "C.I.C.I. Portugal 1933," was not valid for postage and was sold only to collectors.

No. 3S2 was reprinted in 1933. Green vertical lines behind "Porte Franco" omitted. Value $7.50.

F5

1934 **Litho.** ***Perf. 11½***

3S15	F5	blue & red	6.00	3.50

1935-38 ***Perf. 11***

3S16	F5	blue	18.00	5.25
3S17	F5	dk bl & red ('36)	4.75	4.25
3S18	F5	lil & red ('37)	3.50	2.75
3S19	F5	blk, grn & car ('38)	3.50	2.75
		Nos. 3S16-3S19 (4)	29.75	15.00

The inscription in the inner circle is omitted on No. 3S16.

FOR THE NATIONAL AID SOCIETY FOR CONSUMPTIVES

F10

Perf. 11½x12

1904, July **Typo.** **Unwmk.**

4S1	F10	brown & green	5.00	5.00
4S2	F10	carmine & yellow	5.00	5.00

PORTUGUESE AFRICA

'pōr-chə-,gēz 'a-fri-kə

For use in any of the Portuguese possessions in Africa.

1000 Reis = 1 Milreis
100 Centavos = 1 Escudo

Common Design Types pictured following the introduction.

Vasco da Gama Issue
Common Design Types
Inscribed "Africa - Correios"

Perf. 13½ to 15½

1898, Apr. 1 **Engr.** **Unwmk.**

1	CD20	2½r blue green	1.00	.90
		Never hinged	1.30	
2	CD21	5r red	1.00	.90
		Never hinged	1.30	
3	CD22	10r red violet	1.00	.90
		Never hinged	1.30	
4	CD23	25r yellow green	1.00	.90
		Never hinged	1.30	
5	CD24	50r dark blue	1.50	1.10
		Never hinged	1.80	
6	CD25	75r violet brown	6.25	6.25
		Never hinged	7.50	
7	CD26	100r bister brown	5.00	4.50
		Never hinged	7.00	
8	CD27	150r bister	8.00	6.25
		Never hinged	10.50	
		Nos. 1-8 (8)	24.75	21.70
		Set, never hinged	32.00	

Vasco da Gama's voyage to India.

WAR TAX STAMPS

Liberty WT1

Overprinted in Black, Orange or Carmine

Perf. 12x11½, 15x14

1919 **Typo.** **Unwmk.**

MR1	WT1	1c green (Bk)	.75	.75
a.		Figures of value omitted	40.00	
MR2	WT1	4c green (O)	2.00	
MR3	WT1	5c green (C)	.75	.75
		Nos. MR1-MR3 (3)	3.50	1.50

Values the same for either perf.

No. MR2 used is known only with fiscal cancelation. Some authorities consider No. MR2 a revenue stamp.

PORTUGUESE CONGO

'pōr-chi-gēz 'käŋ-gō

LOCATION — The northernmost district of the Portuguese Angola Colony on the southwest coast of Africa
CAPITAL — Cabinda

Stamps of Angola replaced those of Portuguese Congo.

1000 Reis = 1 Milreis
100 Centavos = 1 Escudo (1913)

King Carlos — A1

Perf. 12½

1894, Aug. 5 Typo. Unwmk.

1 A1 5r yellow 1.25 .75
a. 5r orange yellow .90 .75
b. As "a," Perf. 13½ 17.00 12.50
2 A1 10r redsh violet 2.00 .80
a. Perf. 13½ 17.50 12.50
3 A1 15r chocolate 3.00 2.00
a. Perf. 11½ 5.00 2.10
4 A1 20r lav, ordinary paper 2.50 2.00
a. Paper with enamel lozenges 2.50 1.75
b. Perf. 11½ 5.00 2.10
5 A1 25r green 2.00 .80
a. Paper with enamel lozenges 3.50 .85
b. Perf. 11½ 3.25 .85

Perf. 13½

6 A1 50r light blue 6.00 2.00
a. Perf. 11½ 13.00 4.50

Perf. 11½

7 A1 75r rose 8.00 3.75
a. Perf. 12½ 20.00 15.00
8 A1 80r yellow green 10.00 6.00
a. Perf. 12½ 60.00 37.50
9 A1 100r brown, *yel* 8.00 3.75
a. Perf. 13½ 32.50 19.00

Perf. 12½

10 A1 150r carmine, *rose* 15.00 9.00
11 A1 200r dk blue, *bl* 16.00 9.00
12 A1 300r dk blue, *salmon* 18.00 11.00
Nos. 1-12 (12) 91.75 50.85

For surcharges and overprints see Nos. 36-47, 127-131.

King Carlos — A2

Name & Value in Black except 500r

1898-1903 *Perf. 11½*

13 A2 2½r gray .35 .30
14 A2 5r orange .35 .30
15 A2 10r lt green .55 .30
16 A2 15r brown 1.50 1.25
17 A2 15r gray grn ('03) 1.00 .55
18 A2 20r gray violet 1.00 .70
19 A2 25r sea green 1.40 .90
20 A2 25r car rose ('03) .90 .45
21 A2 50r deep blue 1.60 1.25
22 A2 50r brown ('03) 2.75 1.75
23 A2 65r dull blue ('03) 30.00 6.50
24 A2 75r rose 4.00 2.25
25 A2 75r red lilac ('03) 2.75 2.25
26 A2 80r violet 3.00 2.50
27 A2 100r dk bl, *bl* 2.40 1.75
28 A2 115r org brn, *pink* ('03) 6.50 5.00
29 A2 130r brn, *straw* ('03) 30.00 11.00
30 A2 150r brown, *buff* 4.00 2.50
31 A2 200r red lilac, *pnksh* 5.00 3.00
32 A2 300r dk blue, *rose* 6.00 3.25
33 A2 400r dl bl, *straw* ('03) 15.00 9.50
34 A2 500r blk & red, *bl* ('01) 25.00 9.00
35 A2 700r vio, *yelsh* ('01) 30.00 17.50
Nos. 13-35 (23) 175.05 83.75

For overprints and surcharges see Nos. 49-53, 60-74, 117-126, 136-138.

Surcharged in Black

Perf. 12½, 11½ (#41, 43), 13½ (#44)

1902 On Issue of 1894

36 A1 65r on 15r choc 3.50 3.00
a. Perf. 11½ 17.00 9.00
37 A1 65r on 20r lav (#4) 4.00 3.00
a. Lozenge paper (#4a) 13.50 11.00
38 A1 65r on 25r green (#5) 4.00 3.00
a. Perf. 11½ 17.00 12.50
b. Lozenge paper (#5a) 4.75 4.50
39 A1 65r on 300r bl, *sal* 5.00 4.50
40 A1 115r on 10r red vio 4.00 3.00
41 A1 115r on 50r lt bl 4.00 2.50
a. Perf. 13½ 4.00 2.75
42 A1 130r on 5r yellow 5.00 2.75
a. Inverted surcharge 27.50 27.50
b. Perf. 13½ 4.00 2.75
43 A1 130r on 75r rose 5.00 3.00
a. Perf. 12½ 7.00 6.00
44 A1 130r on 100r brn, *yel* 5.00 3.75
a. Inverted surcharge 40.00 35.00
b. Perf. 11½ 20.00 12.50
45 A1 400r on 80r yel grn 1.75 1.25
a. Perf. 12½ 5.00 3.50
46 A1 400r on 150r car, *rose* 2.25 1.90
47 A1 400r on 200r bl, *bl* 2.25 1.90

On Newspaper Stamps of 1894

48 N1 115r on 2½r brn 3.75 2.50
a. Inverted surcharge 25.00 25.00
b. Perf. 13½ 3.75 3.25
Nos. 36-48 (13) 49.50 36.05

Nos. 16, 19, 21 and 24 Overprinted in Black

1902 *Perf. 11½*

49 A2 15r brown 3.00 1.25
50 A2 25r sea green 3.00 1.40
51 A2 50r blue 3.00 1.40
a. Double overprint 20.00 18.00
52 A2 75r rose 4.00 2.75
a. Double ovpt, one albino 10.00 6.00
Nos. 49-52 (4) 13.00 6.80

No. 23 Surcharged

1905

53 A2 50r on 65r dull blue 7.00 2.50

Angola Stamps of 1898-1903 (Port. Congo type A2) Overprinted or Surcharged

a

b

1911

54 (a) 2½r gray 1.50 .90
55 (a) 5r orange 2.00 1.25
56 (a) 10r lt green 2.00 1.25
a. "REPUBLICA" inverted 17.50 17.50
57 (a) 15r gray green 2.00 1.25
a. "REPUBLICA" inverted 17.50 17.50
58 (b) 25r on 200r red vio, *pnksh* 3.00 2.00
a. "REPUBLICA" inverted 17.50 17.50
b. "CONGO" double 17.50 17.50

Thin Bar and "CONGO" as Type "b"

59 (a) 2½r gray 1.25 .90
Nos. 54-59 (6) 11.75 7.55

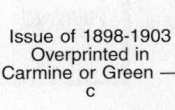

Issue of 1898-1903 Overprinted in Carmine or Green — c

1911

60 A2 2½r gray .25 .25
61 A2 5r orange .25 .25
62 A2 10r lt green .25 .25
63 A2 15r gray grn .25 .25
64 A2 20r gray vio .45 .25
65 A2 25r car rose (G) 2.00 .90
66 A2 50r brown .65 .35
67 A2 75r red lilac 1.10 .55
68 A2 100r dk bl, *bl* 1.00 .60
69 A2 115r org brn, *pink* 2.10 1.40
70 A2 130r brown, *straw* 2.10 1.40
71 A2 200r red vio, *pnksh* 3.00 1.90
72 A2 400r dull bl, *straw* 5.25 2.50
73 A2 500r blk & red, *bl* 5.75 2.25
74 A2 700r violet, *yelsh* 5.75 2.25
Nos. 60-74 (15) 30.15 15.35

Numerous inverts and doubles exist. These are printer's waste or made to order.

Common Design Types pictured following the introduction.

Vasco da Gama Issue of Various Portuguese Colonies Surcharged

1913 On Stamps of Macao

75 CD20 ¼c on ½a bl grn 2.00 1.25
76 CD21 ½c on 1a red 2.00 1.25
77 CD22 1c on 2a red vio 2.00 1.25
78 CD23 2½c on 4a yel grn 2.00 1.25
79 CD24 5c on 8a dk blue 2.00 1.25
80 CD25 7½c on 12a vio brn 3.00 2.50
81 CD26 10c on 16a bis brn 2.50 1.75
82 CD27 15c on 24a bister 2.50 1.75
Nos. 75-82 (8) 18.00 12.25

On Stamps of Portuguese Africa

83 CD20 ¼c on 2½r bl grn 2.00 .80
84 CD21 ½c on 5r red 2.00 .80
85 CD22 1c on 10r red vio 2.00 .80
86 CD23 2½c on 25r yel grn 2.00 .80
87 CD24 5c on 50r dk bl 2.00 1.10
88 CD25 7½c on 75r vio brn 2.00 1.90
89 CD26 10c on 100r bis brn 1.50 1.25
a. Inverted surcharge 25.00 25.00
90 CD27 15c on 150r bister 2.00 1.50
Nos. 83-90 (8) 15.50 8.95

On Stamps of Timor

91 CD20 ¼c on ½a bl grn 2.00 1.25
92 CD21 ½c on 1a red 2.00 1.25
93 CD22 1c on 2a red vio 2.00 1.25
94 CD23 2½c on 4a yel grn 2.00 1.25
95 CD24 5c on 8a dk blue 2.00 1.25
a. Double surcharge 25.00 25.00
96 CD25 7½c on 12a vio brn 2.50 2.50
97 CD26 10c on 16a bis brn 2.25 2.25
98 CD27 15c on 24a bister 2.25 2.25
Nos. 91-98 (8) 17.00 13.25
Nos. 75-98 (24) 50.50 34.45

Ceres — A3

Name and Value in Black
Chalky Paper

1914 Typo. *Perf. 15x14*

99 A3 ¼c olive brn .35 .50
Never hinged .55
a. Inscriptions inverted 20.00
100 A3 ½c black .75 1.00
Never hinged 1.20
101 A3 1c blue grn 3.00 4.25
Never hinged 4.75
102 A3 1½c lilac brn 2.00 1.40
Never hinged 3.25
103 A3 2c carmine 2.00 1.40
Never hinged 3.25
104 A3 2½c lt violet .75 .90
Never hinged 1.20
105 A3 5c dp blue 1.00 1.40
Never hinged 1.60
106 A3 7½c yellow brn 1.50 1.40
Never hinged 2.40
107 A3 8c slate 3.00 3.25
Never hinged 3.25
108 A3 10c orange brn 3.00 3.25
Never hinged 3.25
109 A3 15c plum 3.00 3.25
Never hinged 3.25
110 A3 20c yellow grn 3.00 3.25
Never hinged 3.50
111 A3 30c brown, *grn* 4.00 5.00
Never hinged 4.50
112 A3 40c brown, *pink* 5.00 9.00
Never hinged 8.00
113 A3 50c orange, *salmon* 9.00 9.00
Never hinged 9.50
114 A3 1e green, *blue* 10.00 10.00
Never hinged 13.00
Nos. 99-114 (16) 51.35 58.25

1920 Ordinary Paper

115 A3 ¼c olive brn .40 .55
Never hinged .65
116 A3 2c carmine .75 1.15
Never hinged 1.20

Issue of 1898-1903 Overprinted Locally in Green or Red

1914-18 *Perf. 11½*

117 A2 50r brown (G) 1.00 .65
118 A2 75r rose (G) 500.00
119 A2 75r red lilac (G) 3.00 1.50
120 A2 100r blue, *bl* (R) 1.00 .80
121 A2 200r red vio, *pink* (G) 2.00 1.25
122 A2 400r dl bl, *straw* (R) ('18) 80.00 55.00
123 A2 500r blk & red, *bl* (R) 65.00 42.50

Same on Nos. 51-52

124 A2 50r blue (R) 1.00 .70
125 A2 75r rose (G) 1.50 1.10

Same on No. 53

126 A2 50r on 65r dl bl (R) 1.25 1.10
Nos. 117,119-126 (9) 155.75 104.60

No. 118 was not regularly issued.

Provisional Issue of 1902 Overprinted Type "c" in Red

1915 *Perf. 11½, 12½, 13½*

127 A1 115r on 10r red vio .75 .25
a. Perf. 13½ 17.00 14.00
128 A1 115r on 50r lt bl 2.00 .25
a. Perf. 11½ 2.00 .65
129 A1 130r on 5r yellow 1.00 .25
130 A1 130r on 75r rose 2.00 .65
131 A1 130r on 100r brn, *buff* 1.00 .40
135 N1 115r on 2½r brn .80 .40

Nos. 49, 51 Overprinted Type "c"

136 A2 15r brown .85 .55
137 A2 50r blue .85 .40

No. 53 Overprinted Type "c"

138 A2 50r on 65r dull blue 1.25 .40
Nos. 127-138 (9) 10.50 3.55

NEWSPAPER STAMP

N1

Perf. 12½

1894, Aug. 5 Typo. Unwmk.

P1 N1 2½r brown 1.50 .60
a. Perf. 13½ 1.50 .60

For surcharge and overprint see Nos. 48, 135.

PORTUGUESE GUINEA

'pōr-chi-gēz 'gi-nē

LOCATION — On the west coast of Africa between Senegal and Guinea
GOVT. — Portuguese Overseas Territory
AREA — 13,944 sq. mi.
POP. — 560,000 (est. 1970)
CAPITAL — Bissau

1000 Reis = 1 Milreis
100 Centavos = 1 Escudo (1913)

STAMPS OF CAPE VERDE USED IN PORTUGUESE GUINEA

Before Mar. 19, 1879, Portuguese Guinea was an administrative dependency of Cape Verde. Cape Verde stamps Nos. 1-4, 4a, 5-7 and 14 were used in Portuguese Guinea in 1877-1881, overlapping slightly with the issues of Portuguese Guinea.

Use in Portuguese Guinea can be distinguished by the cancellations composed of several concentric rings, with or without a heavy dot at the center. There are several types of these canceling devices, and some similar ones were also at Cape Verde. Identification of the cancellations by experts is advised.

1877-81

A1 A1 5r black (#1)
A2 A1 10r yellow (#2)
A3 A1 20r bister (#3)
A4 A1 25r rose, perf 12½ (#4)
A1 25r rose, perf 13½ (#4a)
A5 A1 40r blue, perf 12½ (#5)
A6 A1 50r green (#6)
A7 A1 50r blue (#14)
A8 A1 100r lilac (#7)

Issued under Portuguese Administration

Nos. 1-7 are valued with small faults such as short perfs or small thins. Completely fault-free examples of any of these stamps are very scarce and are worth more than the values given.

Stamps of Cape Verde, 1877-85 Overprinted in Black

1881 Unwmk. *Perf. 12½*
Without Gum (Nos. 1-7)

1 A1 5r black *1,000.* *800.*
1A A1 10r yellow *2,000.* *800.*
2 A1 20r bister *500.* *250.*
3 A1 25r rose *1,400.* *775.*
4 A1 40r blue *1,250.* *800.*
a. Cliché of Mozambique in Cape Verde plate *16,500.* *15,250.*
4B A1 50r green *2,000.* *725.*
5 A1 100r lilac 300. 175.
6 A1 200r orange *600.* *475.*
7 A1 300r brown *600.* *475.*

Excellent forgeries exist of Nos. 1-7.

Overprinted in Red or Black

1881-85 *Perf. 12½*

8 A1 5r black (R) 6.00 2.75
10 A1 10r green ('85) 6.00 5.50
11 A1 20r bister 4.00 2.25
12 A1 20r rose ('85) 6.75 5.00
a. Double overprint
13 A1 25r carmine 3.00 1.75
14 A1 25r violet ('85) 4.00 1.90
a. Double overprint
15b A1 40r blue 180.00 115.00
c. Cliché of Mozambique in Cape Verde plate *1,350.* *900.00*
16 A1 40r yellow ('85) 1.90 1.60
a. Cliché of Mozambique in Cape Verde plate 50.00 45.00
b. Imperf.
c. As "a," imperf.
g. Double overprint
17a A1 50r green 180.00 115.00
18 A1 50r blue ('85) 5.75 2.75
a. Imperf.
b. Double overprint
19 A1 100r lilac 7.75 6.00
a. Inverted overprint
b. 100r lilac 7.75 6.00
20 A1 200r orange 11.50 8.00
21 A1 300r yellow brn 14.00 11.00
a. 300r lake brown 16.00 12.50

Perf. 13½

8a A1 5r black (R) 4.00 3.00
9 A1 10r yellow 160.00 160.00
10a A1 10r green ('85) 6.75 5.00
11a A1 20r bister 3.25 2.25
12b A1 20r rose ('85) 6.75 5.50
13a A1 25r rose 67.50 37.50
15 A1 40r blue 175.00 110.00
a. Cliché of Mozambique in Cape Verde plate *1,500.* *875.00*
16d A1 40r yellow ('85) 4.00 3.00
e. Cliché of Mozambique in Cape Verde plate 50.00 45.00
f. Imperf.
17 A1 50r green 175.00 110.00
18c A1 50r blue ('85) 10.50 4.00
19c A1 100r pale lilac 9.00 5.50
d. 100r gray lilac 9.00 5.50

Varieties of this overprint may be found without accent on "E" of "GUINE," or with grave instead of acute accent.

Stamps of the 1881-85 issues were reprinted on a smooth white chalky paper, ungummed, and on thin white paper with shiny white gum and clean-cut perforation 13½.

King Luiz — A3

1886 Typo. *Perf. 12½, 13½*

22 A3 5r gray black 6.00 5.50
a. Imperf.
23 A3 10r green 7.25 4.00
a. Perf. 13½ 8.25 6.75
b. Imperf.
24 A3 20r carmine 10.50 4.00
25 A3 25r red lilac 10.50 6.25
a. Imperf.
26 A3 40r chocolate 8.50 6.25
a. Perf. 12½ 82.50 60.00
27 A3 50r blue 17.00 6.25
a. Imperf.
28 A3 80r gray 18.00 10.00
a. Perf. 12½ 82.50 60.00
29 A3 100r brown 18.00 10.00
a. Perf. 12½ 37.50 22.50
30 A3 200r gray lilac 40.00 20.00
31 A3 300r orange 50.00 30.00
a. Perf. 13½ 210.00 210.00
Nos. 22-31 (10) 185.75 102.25

For surcharges and overprints see Nos. 67-76, 180-183.

Reprinted in 1905 on thin white paper with shiny white gum and clean-cut perforation 13½.

King Carlos — A4

1893-94 *Perf. 11½*

32 A4 5r yellow 1.90 1.10
a. Perf. 12½ 2.00 1.25
33 A4 10r red violet 1.90 1.10
34 A4 15r chocolate 2.40 1.60
35 A4 20r lavender 2.40 1.60
36 A4 25r blue green 2.40 1.60
37 A4 50r lt blue 5.00 3.75
a. Perf. 12½ 17.00 12.50
b. Perf. 11½, lozenge paper 175.00 125.00
38 A4 75r rose 12.00 7.50
39 A4 80r lt green 12.00 7.50
40 A4 100r brn, *buff* 12.00 7.50
41 A4 150r car, *rose* 12.00 8.00
42 A4 200r dk bl, *bl* 20.00 15.00
43 A4 300r dk bl, *sal* 20.00 15.00
Nos. 32-43 (12) 104.00 71.25

Almost all of Nos. 32-43 were issued without gum.

For surcharges and overprints see #77-88, 184-188, 203-205.

King Carlos — A5

1898-1903 *Perf. 11½*
Name & Value in Black except 500r

44 A5 2½r gray .50 .35
45 A5 5r orange .50 .35
46 A5 10r lt green .50 .35
47 A5 15r brown 3.25 2.25
48 A5 15r gray grn ('03) 1.75 1.25
49 A5 20r gray violet 1.40 1.10
50 A5 25r sea green 1.75 .90
51 A5 25r carmine ('03) 1.00 .55
52 A5 50r dark blue 2.75 1.40
53 A5 50r brown ('03) 3.25 2.25
54 A5 65r dl blue ('03) 25.00 8.75
55 A5 75r rose 20.00 8.00
56 A5 75r lilac ('03) 4.00 2.25
57 A5 80r brt violet 3.00 1.90
58 A5 100r dk bl, *bl* 2.75 1.90
a. Perf. 12½ 52.50 22.50
59 A5 115r org brn, *pink* ('03) 8.50 6.00
a. 115r orange brown, *yellowish* 8.25 5.00
60 A5 130r brn, *straw* ('03) 10.00 7.50
61 A5 150r lt brn, *buff* 11.00 3.25
62 A5 200r red lilac, *pnksh* 10.00 3.25
63 A5 300r blue, *rose* 11.00 4.25
64 A5 400r dl bl, *straw* ('03) 16.00 10.00
65 A5 500r blk & red, *bl* ('01) 18.00 7.75
66 A5 700r vio, *yelsh* ('01) 25.00 10.00
Nos. 44-66 (23) 180.90 85.55

Stamps issued in 1903 were without gum.

For overprints and surcharges see Nos. 90-115, 190-194, 197.

Issue of 1886 Surcharged in Black or Red

1902, Oct. 20 *Perf. 12½*

67 A3 65r on 10r green 6.50 5.50
a. Inverted surcharge 30.00 25.00
68 A3 65r on 20r car 6.50 5.00
69 A3 65r on 25r red lilac 6.50 5.00
70 A3 115r on 40r choc 5.75 4.50
a. Perf. 13½ 13.00 9.50
71 A3 115r on 50r blue 5.75 4.50
a. Inverted surcharge 30.00 25.00
72 A3 115r on 300r orange 7.25 5.75
73 A3 130r on 80r gray 7.25 5.00
a. Perf. 13½ 14.00 5.75
74 A3 130r on 100r brown 7.75 5.75
a. Perf. 13½ 20.00 14.00
75 A3 400r on 200r gray lil 13.00 8.75
76 A3 400r on 5r gray blk (R) 32.50 24.00
Nos. 67-76 (10) 98.75 73.75

Reprints of No. 76 are in black and have clean-cut perforation 13½.

Same Surcharge on Issue of 1893-94

Perf. 11½, 12½ (#80)

77 A4 65r on 10r red vio 5.75 3.50
78 A4 65r on 15r choc 5.75 3.50
79 A4 65r on 20r lav 5.75 3.50
80 A4 65r on 50r lt bl 3.00 2.25
a. Perf. 13½ 3.25 2.50
81 A4 115r on 5r yel 5.50 3.00
a. Inverted surcharge 45.00 45.00
b. Perf. 12½ 55.00 40.00
82 A4 115r on 25r bl grn 6.00 3.25
83 A4 130r on 150r car, *rose* 6.00 3.25
84 A4 130r on 200r dk bl, *bl* 6.50 4.50
85 A4 130r on 300r dk bl, *sal* 6.50 4.50
86 A4 400r on 75r rose 4.50 3.00
87 A4 400r on 80r lt grn 3.00 1.60
88 A4 400r on 100r brn, *buff* 4.00 1.60

Same Surcharge on No. P1

Perf. 13½

89 N1 115r on 2½r brn 4.50 3.25
a. Inverted surcharge 30.00 25.00
b. Perf. 12½ 4.75 3.50
c. As "b," inverted surcharge 30.00 25.00
Nos. 77-89 (13) 66.75 40.70

Issue of 1898 Overprinted in Black

1902, Oct. 20 *Perf. 11½*

90 A5 15r brown 2.50 1.25
91 A5 25r sea green 2.50 1.60
92 A5 50r dark blue 3.00 1.60
93 A5 75r rose 5.75 4.00
Nos. 90-93 (4) 13.75 8.45

No. 54 Surcharged in Black

1905

94 A5 50r on 65r dull blue 6.00 2.50

Issue of 1898-1903 Overprinted in Carmine or Green

1911 *Perf. 11½*

95 A5 2½r gray .40 .35
a. Inverted overprint 19.00 19.00
96 A5 5r orange .40 .35
97 A5 10r lt green .70 .50
98 A5 15r gray green .70 .50
99 A5 20r gray violet .70 .50
100 A5 25r carmine (G) .70 .50
a. Double overprint 15.00 15.00
101 A5 50r brown .45 .40
102 A5 75c lilac .45 .40
103 A5 100r dk bl, *bl* 1.50 .75
104 A5 115r org brn, *pink* 1.50 1.00
105 A5 130r brn, *straw* 1.50 1.00
106 A5 200r red lil, *pink* 6.50 3.25
107 A5 400r dl bl, *straw* 2.50 1.50
108 A5 500r blk & red, *bl* 2.75 1.50
109 A5 700r vio, *yelsh* 4.25 2.25
Nos. 95-109 (15) 25.00 14.75

Issued without gum: #101-102, 104-105, 107.

Issue of 1898-1903 Overprinted in Red

1913 *Perf. 11½*
Without Gum (Nos. 110-115)

110 A5 15r gray grn 14.00 6.50
111 A5 75r lilac 14.00 6.50
a. Inverted overprint 35.00 35.00
112 A5 100r bl, *bl* 10.00 4.50
a. Inverted overprint 35.00 35.00
113 A5 200r red lil, *pnksh* 40.00 25.00
a. Inverted overprint 82.50 82.50

Same Overprint on Nos. 90, 93 in Red

114 A5 15r brown 11.00 7.25
a. "REPUBLICA" double *35.00* *35.00*
b. "REPUBLICA" inverted *30.00* *30.00*
115 A5 75r rose 11.00 7.25
a. "REPUBLICA" inverted 35.00 35.00
Nos. 110-115 (6) 100.00 57.00

Vasco da Gama Issue of Various Portuguese Colonies Surcharged

1913 On Stamps of Macao

116 CD20 ¼c on ½a bl grn 2.00 1.60
117 CD21 ½c on 1a red 2.00 1.60
118 CD22 1c on 2a red vio 2.00 1.60
119 CD23 2½c on 4a yel grn 2.00 1.60
120 CD24 5c on 8a dk bl 2.00 1.60
121 CD25 7½c on 12a vio brn 3.25 3.25
122 CD26 10c on 16a bis brn 2.00 1.60
a. Inverted surcharge 30.00 30.00
123 CD27 15c on 24a bis 2.75 2.75
Nos. 116-123 (8) 18.00 15.60

On Stamps of Portuguese Africa

124 CD20 ¼c on 2½c bl grn 2.00 1.40
125 CD21 ½c on 5r red 2.00 1.40
126 CD22 1c on 10r red vio 2.00 1.40
127 CD23 2½c on 25r yel grn 2.00 1.40
128 CD24 5c on 50r dk bl 2.00 1.40
129 CD25 7½c on 75r vio brn 3.00 3.00
130 CD26 10c on 100r bis brn 2.00 1.40
131 CD27 15c on 150r bis 4.00 4.00
Nos. 124-131 (8) 19.00 15.40

On Stamps of Timor

132 CD20 ¼c on ½a bl grn 2.00 1.60
133 CD21 ½c on 1a red 2.00 1.60
134 CD22 1c on 2a red vio 2.00 1.60
135 CD23 2½c on 4a yel grn 2.00 1.60
136 CD24 5c on 8a dk blue 2.00 1.60
137 CD25 7½c on 12a vio brn 3.00 3.00
138 CD26 10c on 16a bis brn 2.00 1.60
139 CD27 15c on 24a bister 3.00 3.00
Nos. 132-139 (8) 18.00 15.60
Nos. 116-139 (24) 55.00 46.60

Ceres — A6

Name and Value in Black

1914 Chalky Paper *Perf. 15x14*
140 A6 ¼c olive brown .25 .25
Never hinged .40
141 A6 ½c black .40 .30
Never hinged .65
142 A6 1c blue green 1.40 1.40
Never hinged 2.25
143 A6 1½c lilac brn .60 .60
Never hinged .95
144 A6 2c carmine .65 .65
Never hinged 1.05
145 A6 2½c lt violet 1.00 1.00
Never hinged 1.60
146 A6 5c deep blue .65 .55
Never hinged 1.05
147 A6 7½c yellow brn .95 .40
Never hinged 1.50
148 A6 8c slate .65 .55
Never hinged 1.05
149 A6 10c orange brn .80 .65
Never hinged 1.30
150 A6 15c plum 8.25 7.25
Never hinged 13.00
151 A6 20c yellow grn 1.15 .85
Never hinged 1.75
152 A6 30c brown, *grn* 7.00 6.00
Never hinged 11.00
153 A6 40c brown, *pink* 3.50 3.25
Never hinged 5.50
154 A6 50c orange, *salmon* 3.50 3.25
Never hinged 5.50
155 A6 1e green, *blue* 5.00 3.50
Never hinged 6.50
Nos. 140-155 (16) 35.75 30.45

1919-20 Ordinary Paper
156 A6 ¼c olive brown .40 .35
Never hinged .65
157 A6 ½c black ('20) .25 .25
Never hinged .40
158 A6 1c blue green 2.75 2.50
Never hinged 4.50
159 A6 2c carmine .65 .65
Never hinged 1.05
Nos. 156-159 (4) 4.05 3.75

1921-26 *Perf. 12x11½*
160 A6 ¼c olive brown 3.00 2.25
Never hinged 4.75
161 A6 ½c black .25 .25
Never hinged .40
162 A6 1c yellow green ('22) .25 .25
Never hinged .40
163 A6 1½c lilac brn .25 .25
Never hinged .40
164 A6 2c carmine .25 .25
Never hinged .40
165 A6 2c gray ('25) .25 *1.60*
Never hinged .40
166 A6 2½c lt violet .25 .25
Never hinged .40
167 A6 3c orange ('22) .25 *1.60*
Never hinged .40
168 A6 4c deep red ('22) .25 *1.60*
Never hinged .40
169 A6 4½c gray ('22) .25 *1.60*
Never hinged .40
170 A6 5c brt blue ('22) .25 .25
Never hinged .40
171 A6 6c lilac ('22) .25 *1.60*
Never hinged .40
172 A6 7c ultra ('22) .30 *1.60*
Never hinged .50
173 A6 7½c yellow brn .25 .25
Never hinged .40
174 A6 8c slate .25 .25
Never hinged .40
175 A6 10c orange brn .25 .25
Never hinged .40
176 A6 12c blue grn ('22) .65 .50
Never hinged 1.05
177 A6 15c brn rose ('22) .50 .35
Never hinged .80
178 A6 20c yellow grn .25 .25
Never hinged .40
179 A6 24c ultra ('25) 1.90 1.60
Never hinged 3.00
179A A6 25c brown ('25) 2.50 2.25
Never hinged 4.00
179B A6 30c gray grn ('22) .90 .25
Never hinged 1.45
179C A6 40c turq bl ('22) .90 .40
Never hinged 1.45
179D A6 50c violet ('25) 1.90 .90
Never hinged 3.00
179E A6 60c dk blue ('22) 1.90 .95
Never hinged 3.00
179F A6 60c dp rose ('26) 2.50 1.75
Never hinged 4.00
179G A6 80c brt rose ('22) 1.60 1.00
Never hinged 2.50
179H A6 1e indigo ('26) 4.00 2.75
Never hinged 5.50
Nos. 160-179H (28) 26.30 27.05

1922-25 Glazed Paper
179I A6 1e pale rose 4.00 1.50
Never hinged 4.00
179J A6 2e dk violet 4.00 1.50
Never hinged 4.75
179K A6 5e buff ('25) 20.00 15.00
Never hinged 21.00
179L A6 10e pink ('25) 40.00 20.00
Never hinged 47.50
179M A6 20e pale turq ('25) 100.00 50.00
Never hinged 125.00
Nos. 179I-179M (5) 168.00 88.00

For surcharges see Nos. 195-196, 211-213.

Provisional Issue of 1902 Overprinted in Carmine

1915 *Perf. 11½, 12½, 13½*
180 A3 115r on 40r choc 1.10 .65
a. Perf. 13½ 13.00 8.50
181 A3 115r on 50r blue 1.40 .75
182 A3 130r on 80r gray 4.50 1.90
a. Perf. 12½ 27.50 22.50
183 A3 130r on 100r brn 3.50 1.90
a. Perf. 13½ 14.50 11.00
184 A4 115r on 5r yellow .80 .65
a. Perf. 11½ 5.00 4.50
185 A4 115r on 25r bl grn .75 .65
186 A4 130r on 150r car, *rose* 1.25 .80
187 A4 130r on 200r bl, *bl* .80 .70
188 A4 130r on 300r dk bl, *sal* 1.10 .80
189 N1 115r on 2½r brn 1.25 .90
a. Perf. 13½ 13.00 11.00
b. Inverted overprint 22.50 22.50

Nos. 90, 92, 94 Overprinted

Perf. 11½
190 A5 15r brown .80 .70
191 A5 50r dark blue .80 .70
192 A5 50r on 65r dl bl .80 .70
Nos. 180-192 (13) 18.85 11.80

Nos. 64, 66 Overprinted

1919 Without Gum *Perf. 11½*
193 A5 400r dl bl, *straw* 175.00 21.00
194 A5 700r vio, *yelsh* 15.00 10.00

Nos. 140, 141 and 59 Surcharged

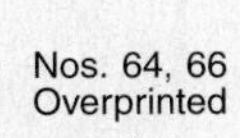

a

b

1920, Sept. *Perf. 15x14, 11½*
Without Gum
195 A6(a) 4c on ¼c 3.25 2.75
Never hinged 5.25
196 A6(a) 6c on ½c 4.00 2.75
Never hinged 6.50
197 A5(b) 12c on 115r 8.00 5.50
Never hinged 13.00
Nos. 195-197 (3) 15.25 11.00

Nos. 86-88 Surcharged

1925 *Perf. 11½*
203 A4 40c on 400r on 75r .95 .80
204 A4 40c on 400r on 80r .95 .80
205 A4 40c on 400r on 100r .95 .80
Nos. 203-205 (3) 2.85 2.40

Nos. 179F-179G, 179J Surcharged

1931 *Perf. 12x11½*
211 A6 50c on 60c dp rose 3.25 1.60
Never hinged 5.25
212 A6 70c on 80c pink 3.25 1.90
Never hinged 5.25
213 A6 1.40e on 2e dk vio 6.50 4.00
Never hinged 10.50
213A A6 1.40e on 2e dk vio (glazed paper) 6.50 4.00
Never hinged 10.50
Nos. 211-213A (4) 19.50 11.50

Ceres — A7

1933 Wmk. 232
214 A7 1c bister .25 .25
Never hinged .40
215 A7 5c olive brn .25 .25
Never hinged .40
216 A7 10c violet .25 .25
Never hinged .40
217 A7 15c black .25 .25
Never hinged .40
218 A7 20c gray .25 .25
219 A7 30c dk green .25 .25
Never hinged .40
220 A7 40c red orange .45 .25
Never hinged .70
221 A7 45c lt blue 1.10 .80
Never hinged 1.75
222 A7 50c lt brown 1.10 .55
Never hinged 1.75
223 A7 60c olive grn 1.40 .55
Never hinged 2.25
224 A7 70c orange brn 2.75 .65
Never hinged 4.50
225 A7 80c emerald 1.50 .80
Never hinged 2.40
226 A7 85c deep rose 3.00 1.40
Never hinged 4.75
227 A7 1e red brown 1.40 .90
Never hinged 2.25
228 A7 1.40e dk blue 6.50 2.25
Never hinged 10.50
229 A7 2e red violet 4.50 1.90
Never hinged 7.25
230 A7 5e apple green 10.00 5.75
Never hinged 16.00
231 A7 10e olive bister 17.50 9.50
Never hinged 28.00
232 A7 20e orange 55.00 25.00
Never hinged 87.50
Nos. 214-232 (19) 107.70 51.80

Common Design Types pictured following the introduction.

Common Design Types
Engr.; Name & Value Typo. in Black
1938 Unwmk. *Perf. 13½x13*
233 CD34 1c gray grn .25 .25
234 CD34 5c orange brn .25 .25
235 CD34 10c dk carmine .25 .25
236 CD34 15c dk vio brn .25 .25
237 CD34 20c slate .40 .25
238 CD35 30c rose violet .60 .25
239 CD35 35c brt green .65 .35
240 CD35 40c brown 1.10 .35
241 CD35 50c brt red vio 1.10 .35
242 CD36 60c gray black 1.60 .35
243 CD36 70c brown vio 1.60 .35
244 CD36 80c orange 1.90 .70
245 CD36 1e red 1.50 .50
246 CD37 1.75e blue 2.10 1.00
247 CD37 2e brown car 5.00 1.40
248 CD37 5e olive grn 5.50 2.25
249 CD38 10e blue vio 7.50 2.75
250 CD38 20e red brown 22.50 4.50
Nos. 233-250 (18) 54.05 16.35

AIR POST STAMPS

Common Design Type
Perf. 13½x13
1938, Sept. 19 Engr. Unwmk.
Name and Value in Black
C1 CD39 10c red orange .60 .45
C2 CD39 20c purple .60 .45
C3 CD39 50c orange .65 .45
C4 CD39 1e ultra .65 .50
C5 CD39 2e lilac brown 6.00 3.50
C6 CD39 3e dark green 2.00 1.25
C7 CD39 5e red brown 5.00 1.25
C8 CD39 9e rose carmine 7.00 3.00
C9 CD39 10e magenta 11.50 3.50
Nos. C1-C9 (9) 34.00 14.35

No. C7 exists with overprint "Exposicao Internacional de Nova York, 1939-1940" and Trylon and Perisphere. Value $300.

POSTAGE DUE STAMPS

D1

Without Gum
1904 Unwmk. Typo. *Perf. 12*
J1 D1 5r yellow green .60 .45
J2 D1 10r slate .60 .45
J3 D1 20r yellow brown .65 .55
J4 D1 30r red orange 1.90 1.60
J5 D1 50r gray brown 1.90 1.60
J6 D1 60r red brown 4.25 2.75
J7 D1 100r lilac 4.25 2.75
J8 D1 130r dull blue 3.25 2.10
J9 D1 200r carmine 6.50 5.25
J10 D1 500r violet 11.00 6.00
Nos. J1-J10 (10) 34.90 23.50

Same Overprinted in Carmine or Green

1911 Without Gum
J11 D1 5r yellow green .25 .25
J12 D1 10r slate .25 .25
J13 D1 20r yellow brown .35 .35
J14 D1 30r red orange .35 .35
J15 D1 50r gray brown .35 .35
J16 D1 60r red brown 1.00 .80
J17 D1 100r lilac 1.90 1.40
J18 D1 130r dull blue 1.90 1.00
J19 D1 200r carmine (G) 1.90 1.50
J20 D1 500r violet 1.10 1.00
Nos. J11-J20 (10) 9.35 7.25

Nos. J2-J10 Overprinted

1919 Without Gum
J21 D1 10r slate 8.25 8.25
J22 D1 20r yellow brown 9.00 9.00
J23 D1 30r red orange 6.50 5.75
J24 D1 50r gray brown 2.50 2.10
J25 D1 60r red brown 800.00 500.00
J26 D1 100r lilac 2.25 1.90
J27 D1 130r dull blue 22.50 19.00
J28 D1 200r carmine 2.75 2.50
J29 D1 500r violet 24.00 20.00
Nos. J21-J24,J26-J29 (8) 77.75 68.50

No. J25 was not regularly issued but exists on genuine covers.

D2

1921

J30	D2	½c yellow green	.25	.25
J31	D2	1c slate	.25	.25
J32	D2	2c orange brown	.25	.25
J33	D2	3c orange	.25	.25
J34	D2	5c gray brown	.25	.25
J35	D2	6c light brown	.25	.25
J36	D2	10c red violet	.60	.60
J37	D2	13c dull blue	.60	.60
J38	D2	20c carmine	.60	.60
J39	D2	50c gray	.60	.60
		Nos. J30-J39 (10)	3.90	3.90

WAR TAX STAMPS

WT1

Perf. 11½x12

1919, May 20 Typo. Unwmk.

MR1	WT1	10r brn, buff & blk	45.00	27.50
MR2	WT1	40r brn, buff & blk	40.00	22.50
MR3	WT1	50r brn, buff & blk	42.50	25.00
		Nos. MR1-MR3 (3)	127.50	75.00

The 40r is not overprinted "REPUBLICA."

Some authorities consider Nos. MR2-MR3 to be revenue stamps.

NEWSPAPER STAMP

N1

1893 Typo. Unwmk. *Perf. 12½*

P1	N1	2½r brown	1.25	.75
a.		Perf. 13½	1.25	.90

For surcharge and overprint see Nos. 89, 189.

POSTAL TAX STAMPS

Pombal Issue

Common Design Types

1925 Unwmk. Engr. *Perf. 12½*

RA1	CD28	15c red & black	.55	.45
RA2	CD29	15c red & black	.55	.45
RA3	CD30	15c red & black	.55	.45
		Nos. RA1-RA3 (3)	1.65	1.35

Coat of Arms — PT7

Without Gum

1934, Apr. 1 Typo. *Perf. 11½*

RA4	PT7	50c red brn & grn	7.50	5.00
a.		Tête beche pair		450.00

Coat of Arms — PT8

1938-40 Without Gum

RA5	PT8	50c ol bis & citron	6.50	3.25
RA6	PT8	50c lt grn & ol brn ('40)	6.50	3.25

POSTAL TAX DUE STAMPS

Pombal Issue

Common Design Types

1925 Unwmk. *Perf. 12½*

RAJ1	CD28	30c red & black	.55	.45
RAJ2	CD29	30c red & black	.55	.45
RAJ3	CD30	30c red & black	.55	.45
		Nos. RAJ1-RAJ3 (3)	1.65	1.35

PORTUGUESE INDIA

'pōr-chi-gēz 'in-dē-ə

LOCATION — West coast of the Indian peninsula

GOVT. — Portuguese colony

AREA — 1,537 sq. mi.

POP. — 649,000 (1958)

CAPITAL — Panjim (Nova-Goa)

1000 Reis = 1 Milreis

12 Reis = 1 Tanga (1881-82)

(Real = singular of Reis)

16 Tangas = 1 Rupia

Expect Nos. 1-55, 70-112 to have rough perforations. Stamps frequently were cut apart because of the irregular and missing perforations. Scissor separations that do not remove perfs do not negatively affect value.

Numeral of Value — A1

A1: Large figures of value.

"REIS" in Roman capitals. "S" and "R" of "SERVICO" smaller and "E" larger than the other letters. 33 lines in background. Side ornaments of four dashes.

A2: Large figures of value.

"REIS" in block capitals. "S," "E" and "R" same size as other letters of "SERVICO." 44 lines in background. Side ornaments of five dots.

Handstamped from a Single Die

Perf. 13 to 18 & Compound

1871, Oct. 1 Unwmk.

Thin Transparent Brittle Paper

1	A1	10r black	625.00	325.00
2	A1	20r dk carmine	1,350.	300.00
a.		20r orange vermilion	1,350.	300.00
3	A1	40r Prus blue	475.00	325.00
4	A1	100r yellow grn	550.00	375.00
5	A1	200r ocher yel	850.00	450.00

1872 Thick Soft Wove Paper

5A	A1	10r black	*1,500.*	350.00
6	A1	20r dk carmine	*1,650.*	400.00
7	A1	20r orange ver	*1,800.*	400.00
7A	A1	100r yellow grn		—
8	A1	200r ocher yel	*1,700.*	1,000.
9	A1	300r dp red violet		*3,000.*

The 600r and 900r of type A1 are bogus.

See Nos. 24-28. For surcharges see Nos. 70-71, 73, 83, 94, 99, 104, 108.

Numeral of Value — A2

Perf. 12½ to 14½ & Compound

1872

10	A2	10r black	260.00	100.00
11	A2	20r vermilion	225.00	85.00
a.		"20" omitted		*1,000.*
12	A2	40r blue	70.00	60.00
a.		Tête bêche pair	*5,750.*	*5,750.*
b.		40r dark blue	85.00	60.00
13	A2	100r deep green	70.00	60.00
14	A2	200r yellow	275.00	250.00
15	A2	300r red violet	275.00	225.00
a.		Imperf.		
16	A2	600r red violet	175.00	140.00
a.		"600" double	*700.00*	
17	A2	900r red violet	200.00	175.00
		Nos. 10-17 (8)	1,550.	1,095.

An unused 100r blue green exists with watermark of lozenges and gray burelage on back. Experts believe it to be a proof.

White Laid Paper

18	A2	10r black	37.50	32.50
a.		Tête bêche pair	*14,000.*	*8,500.*
b.		10r brownish black	37.50	30.00
19	A2	20r vermilion	35.00	27.50
20	A2	40r blue	70.00	57.50
a.		"40" double		—
b.		Tête bêche pair	—	—
21	A2	100r green	62.50	45.00
a.		"100" double	*450.00*	
22	A2	200r yellow	175.00	175.00
		Nos. 18-22 (5)	380.00	337.50

See No. 23. For surcharges see Nos. 72, 82, 95-96, 100-101, 105-106, 109-110.

Re-issues

1873 Thin Bluish Toned Paper

23	A2	20r vermilion	200.00	160.00
24	A1	10r black	14.00	8.50
a.		"1" inverted	125.00	100.00
b.		"10" double	400.00	
25	A1	20r vermilion	17.00	11.50
a.		"20" double	400.00	
b.		"20" inverted		
26	A1	300r dp violet	110.00	85.00
a.		"300" double	475.00	
27	A1	600r dp violet	140.00	100.00
a.		"600" double	575.00	
b.		"600" inverted	575.00	
28	A1	900r dp violet	140.00	100.00
a.		"900" double	675.00	
b.		"900" triple	1,000.	
		Nos. 23-28 (6)	621.00	465.00

Nos. 23 to 26 are re-issues of Nos. 11, 5A, 7, and 9. The paper is thinner and harder than that of the 1871-72 stamps and slightly transparent. It was originally bluish white but is frequently stained yellow by the gum.

Nos. 23 to 26 may be found with part of the papermaker's watermark "ORIGINAL TURKISH MILL KENT."

A3

A3: Same as A1 with small figures.

1874 Thin Bluish Toned Paper

29	A3	10r black	35.00	27.50
a.		"10" and "20" superimposed	475.00	*450.00*
30	A3	20r vermilion	550.00	350.00
a.		"20" double		*625.00*

For surcharge see No. 84.

Nos. 29 and 30 may be found with part of the papermaker's watermark "ORIGINAL TURKISH MILL KENT."

A4

A4: Same as A2 with small figures.

1875

31	A4	10r black	37.50	22.50
a.		Value sideways		550.00
32	A4	15r rose	12.50	9.00
a.		"15" inverted	475.00	
b.		"15" double		
c.		Value omitted		1,150.
33	A4	20r vermilion	70.00	42.50
a.		"0" missing	850.00	575.00
b.		"20" sideways	*850.00*	
c.		"20" double		
		Nos. 31-33 (3)	120.00	74.00

For surcharges see Nos. 74, 78, 85.

Nos. 31 to 33 may be found with part of the papermaker's watermark "HODGKINSON & CO."

A5

A6

A5: Re-cutting of A1.

Small figures. "REIS" in Roman capitals. Letters larger. "V" of "SERVICO" barred. 33 lines in background. Side ornaments of five dots.

A6: First re-cutting of A2.

Small figures. "REIS" in block capitals. Letters re-cut. "V" of "SERVICO" barred. 41 lines above and 43 below "REIS." Side ornaments of five dots.

Perf. 12½ to 13½ & Compound

1876

34	A5	10r black	20.00	14.00
35	A5	20r vermilion	16.00	11.50
a.		"20" double		—
36	A6	10r black	6.25	4.25
a.		Double impression	525.00	
b.		"10" double	525.00	
37	A6	15r rose	425.00	325.00
a.		"15" omitted	—	*1,000.*
38	A6	20r vermilion	22.50	17.00
39	A6	40r blue	110.00	85.00
40	A6	100r green	160.00	150.00
a.		Imperf.		
41	A6	200r yellow	1,000.	675.00
42	A6	300r violet	550.00	450.00
a.		"300" omitted		
43	A6	600r violet	*800.00*	*675.00*
44	A6	900r violet	*1,200.*	*750.00*
a.		"900" omitted		

For surcharges see Nos. 75-76, 78C-80, 86-87, 91-92, 98, 102, 107, 111.

Nos. 34 to 44 may be found with part of the papermaker's watermark "SPICER BROTHERS."

A7

A8

A9

A7: Same as A5 with addition of a star above and a bar below the value.

A8: Second re-cutting of A2. Same as A6 but 41 lines both above and below "REIS." Star above and bar below value.

A9: Third re-cutting of A2. 41 lines above and 38 below "REIS." Star above and bar below value. White line around central oval.

1877

45	A7	10r black	30.00	25.00
46	A8	10r black	42.50	37.50
47	A9	10r black	29.00	25.00
a.		"10" omitted		
48	A9	15r rose	32.50	27.50
49	A9	20r vermilion	8.50	8.00
50	A9	40r blue	17.00	16.00
a.		"40" omitted	42.50	35.00
51	A9	100r green	100.00	60.00
a.		"100" omitted		
52	A9	200r yellow	100.00	70.00
53	A9	300r violet	150.00	85.00
54	A9	600r violet	150.00	85.00
55	A9	900r violet	150.00	85.00
		Nos. 45-55 (11)	809.50	524.00

For surcharges see Nos. 77, 81, 88-90, 93, 112.

No. 47, 20r, 40r and 200r exist imperf.

Nos. 45 to 55 may be found with part of the papermaker's watermark "SPICER BROTHERS."

Portuguese Crown — A10

Perf. 12½, Thin paper

1877, July 15 **Typo.**
56 A10 5r black 5.00 3.50
57 A10 10r yellow 9.00 7.25
a. Imperf.
58 A10 20r bister 9.50 7.00
59 A10 25r rose 10.00 8.00
60a A10 40r blue 175.00 140.00
61 A10 50r yellow grn 32.50 20.00
62 A10 100r lilac 16.00 11.50
63 A10 200r orange 22.50 17.50

Perf 13½, Thin paper

56a A10 5r black 5.00 3.50
57b A10 10r yellow 10.00 8.50
58a A10 20r bister 9.50 6.00
59a A10 25r rose 10.00 8.00
60 A10 40r blue 14.00 11.00
61a A10 50r yellow grn 32.50 20.00
62a A10 100r lilac 15.00 11.50
64 A10 300r yel brn 29.00 25.00

Perf 13½, Medium paper

56b A10 5r black 5.00 3.50
57c A10 10r yellow 9.00 7.25
58b A10 20r bister 9.50 6.00
59b A10 25r rose 10.00 8.00
60b A10 40r blue 13.50 11.00
63a A10 200r orange 22.50 17.00
63b A10 200r pale orange 22.50 17.00
64a A10 300r yel brn 29.00 25.00

1880-81

Perf 12½, Thin Paper

65 A10 10r green 17.00 13.50
66a A10 25r slate 72.50 55.00
67 A10 25r violet 37.50 25.00
68 A10 40r yellow 37.50 25.00
69 A10 50r dk blue 37.50 25.00

Perf 13½, Thin Paper

65a A10 10r green 10.00 8.50
66 A10 25r slate 37.50 27.50
67a A10 25r violet 27.50 20.00
68a A10 40r yellow 35.00 27.50
69a A10 50r dk blue 17.50 16.00
Nos. 65a-69a (5) 127.50 99.50

Perf 13½, Medium Paper

65b A10 10r green 10.00 8.50
66b A10 25r slate 37.50 27.50
67b A10 25r violet 27.50 20.00
68b A10 40r yellow 32.50 25.00
69b A10 50r blue 17.50 15.00
c. 50c dark blue 19.00 16.00

For surcharges see Nos. 113-161.

The stamps of the 1877-81 issues were reprinted in 1885, on stout very white paper, ungummed and with rough perforation 13½. They were again reprinted in 1905 on thin white paper with shiny white gum and clean-cut perforation 13½ with large holes. Value of the lowest-cost reprint, $3 each.

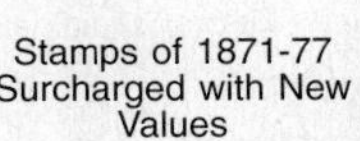
Stamps of 1871-77 Surcharged with New Values

1881 **Black Surcharge**
70 A1 1½r on 20r (#2) *1,500.*
71 A1 1½r on 20r (#7) *1,000.*
72 A2 1½r on 20r (#11) *800.00*
73 A1 1½r on 20r (#25) 225.00 200.00
74 A4 1½r on 20r (#33) 140.00 125.00
a. Inverted surcharge 250.00
75 A5 1½r on 20r (#35) 110.00 85.00
76 A6 1½r on 20r (#38) 125.00 110.00
77 A9 1½r on 20r (#49) 200.00 140.00
78 A4 5r on 15r (#32) 4.00 2.50
a. Double surcharge 10.00
b. Inverted surcharge 10.00
78C A6 5r on 15r (#37) 4.00 2.50
79 A5 5r on 20r (#35) 4.00
a. Double surcharge 14.00
b. Inverted surcharge —
80 A6 5r on 20r (#38) 4.00 2.50
a. Double surcharge —
b. Inverted surcharge —
81 A9 5r on 20r (#49) 10.00 4.00
a. Double surcharge —
b. Invtd. surcharge —

Red Surcharge

82 A2 5r on 10r (#18) *600.00 350.00*
83 A1 5r on 10r (#24) *600.00 300.00*
84 A3 5r on 10r (#29) *1,750.*
85 A4 5r on 10r (#31) *125.00 125.00*
86 A5 5r on 10r (#34) 6.00 6.00
a. Double surcharge 17.00
87 A6 5r on 10r (#36) 9.50 7.75
a. Inverted surcharge
88 A7 5r on 10r (#45) 90.00 50.00
a. Inverted surcharge 175.00
89 A8 5r on 10r (#46) 190.00 82.50
90 A9 5r on 10r (#47) 40.00 35.00
a. Inverted surcharge 82.50
b. Double surcharge 82.50

Similar Surcharge, Handstamped Black Surcharge

1883
91 A5 1½r on 10r (#34) 1,650. *825.00*
92 A6 1½r on 10r (#36) 1,100. *825.00*
93 A9 1½r on 10r (#47) *825.00 600.00*
94 A1 4½r on 40r (#3) 2,500. *775.00*
95 A2 4½r on 40r (#12) 35.00 35.00
96 A2 4½r on 40r (#20) 35.00 35.00
98 A6 4½r on 40r (#39) 35.00 35.00
99 A1 4½r on 100r (#4) 2,500. *775.00*
100 A2 4½r on 100r (#13) 45.00 42.50
101 A2 4½r on 100r (#21) 45.00 42.50
102 A6 4½r on 100r (#40) 45.00 42.50
104 A1 6r on 100r (#4) 2,200. *1,200.*
105 A2 6r on 100r (#13) 375.00 *275.00*
106 A2 6r on 100r (#21) *275.00 225.00*
107 A6 6r on 100r (#40) *350.00 275.00*
108 A1 6r on 200r (#5) *825.00 600.00*
109 A2 6r on 200r (#14) *275.00*
110 A2 6r on 200r (#22) *275.00 275.00*
111 A6 6r on 200r (#41) *450.00*
112 A9 6r on 200r (#52) *550.00 500.00*

Stamps of 1877-81 Surcharged in Black

1881-82
113 A10 1½r on 5r blk 1.40 1.10
a. With additional surcharge "4½" in blue 150.00 125.00
114 A10 1½r on 10r grn 1.40 1.10
a. With additional surch. "6" 160.00 110.00
115 A10 1½r on 20r bis 11.50 8.75
a. Inverted surcharge 27.50
b. Double surcharge 27.50
c. Pair, one without surcharge —
116 A10 1½r on 25r slate 40.00 35.00
117 A10 1½r on 100r lil 60.00 47.50
118 A10 4½r on 10r grn 190.00 160.00
119 A10 4½r on 20r bis 4.00 2.75
a. Inverted surcharge 82.50 65.00
120 A10 4½r on 25r vio 11.50 11.00
121 A10 4½r on 100r lil 225.00 160.00
122 A10 6r on 10r yel 47.50 45.00
123 A10 6r on 10r grn 10.00 8.00
124 A10 6r on 20r bis 17.00 15.00
125 A10 6r on 25r slate 35.00 27.50
126 A10 6r on 25r vio 2.25 1.75
127 A10 6r on 40r blue 82.50 70.00
128 A10 6r on 40r yel 42.50 35.00
129 A10 6r on 50r grn 47.50 38.50
130 A10 6r on 50r blue 110.00 90.00
Nos. 113-130 (18) 939.05 757.95

Surcharged in Black

131 A10 1t on 10r grn 450.00 325.00
a. With additional surch. "6" 900.00 775.00
132 A10 1t on 20r bis 47.50 42.50
133 A10 1t on 25r slate 35.00 30.00
134 A10 1t on 25r vio 13.00 9.00
135 A10 1t on 40r blue 19.00 17.50
136 A10 1t on 50r grn 55.00 47.50
137 A10 1t on 50r blue 25.00 19.00
138 A10 1t on 100r lil 24.00 13.00
139 A10 1t on 200r org 47.50 42.50
140 A10 2t on 25r slate 35.00 35.00
a. Small "T" 55.00 40.00
141 A10 2t on 25r vio 14.00 11.50
142 A10 2t on 40r blue 42.50 35.00
143 A10 2t on 40r yel 52.50 42.50
144 A10 2t on 50r grn 15.00 13.00
a. Inverted surcharge 110.00 100.00
145 A10 2t on 50r blue 90.00 75.00
146 A10 2t on 100r lil 11.50 9.25
147 A10 2t on 200r org 40.00 35.00
148 A10 2t on 300r brn 35.00 30.00
149 A10 4t on 10r grn 14.00 11.50
a. Inverted surcharge 45.00 45.00
150 A10 4t on 50r grn 13.00 10.00
a. With additional surch. "2" 200.00 110.00
151 A10 4t on 200r org 40.00 35.00
152 A10 8t on 20r bis 35.00 24.00
153 A10 8t on 25r rose 250.00 160.00
154 A10 8t on 40r blue 47.50 40.00
155 A10 8t on 100r lil 40.00 35.00
156 A10 8t on 200r org 35.00 30.00
157 A10 8t on 300r brn 47.50 40.00
Nos. 131-157 (27) 1,574. 1,218.

1882 **Blue Surcharge**
158 A10 4½r on 5r black 12.00 10.50

Similar Surcharge, Handstamped

1883
159 A10 1½r on 5r black 55.00 35.00
160 A10 1½r on 10r grn 82.50 45.00
161 A10 4½r on 100r lil *500.00 325.00*

The "2" in "½" is 3mm high, instead of 2mm as on Nos. 113, 114 and 121.

The handstamp is known double on #159-161.

A12

With or Without Accent on "E" of "REIS"

1882-83 **Typo.**
162 A12 1½r black .55 .45
a. "½" for "1½"
163 A12 4½r olive bister .95 .45
164 A12 6r green .80 .45
165 A12 1t rose .80 .45
166 A12 2t blue .80 .45
167 A12 4t lilac 3.25 2.75
168 A12 8t orange 3.25 2.75
Nos. 162-168 (7) 10.40 7.75

There were three printings of the 1882-83 issue. The first had "REIS" in thick letters with acute accent on the "E." The second had "REIS" in thin letters with accent on the "E." The third had the "E" without accent. In the first printing the "E" sometimes had a grave or circumflex accent.

The third printing may be divided into two sets, with or without a small circle in the cross of the crown.

Stamps doubly printed or with value omitted, double, inverted or misplaced are printer's waste.

Nos. 162-168 were reprinted on thin white paper, with shiny white gum and clean-cut perforation 13½. Value of lowest-cost reprint, $1 each.

"REIS" no serifs — A13

"REIS" with serifs — A14

1883 **Litho.** ***Imperf.***
169 A13 1½r black 1.40 1.10
a. Tête bêche pair
b. "1 ½" double 425.00 325.00
170 A13 4½r olive grn 14.00 11.00
a. "4 ½" omitted 350.00 275.00
171 A13 6r green 14.00 11.00
a. Tête bêche pair 1,200.
b. "6" omitted 400.00 300.00
172 A14 1½r black 125.00 55.00
a. "1 ½" omitted 350.00 325.00
173 A14 6r green 62.50 47.50
a. "6" omitted 425.00 350.00
Nos. 169-173 (5) 216.90 125.60

Nos. 169-171 exist with unofficial perf. 12.

King Luiz — A15

Perf. 12½, 13½

1886, Apr. 29 **Embossed**
174 A15 1½r black 3.00 1.40
a. Perf. 13½ 150.00 87.50
175 A15 4½r bister 4.00 1.50
a. Perf. 13½ 30.00 14.00
176 A15 6r dp green 5.00 1.75
a. Perf. 13½ 35.00 15.00
177 A15 1t brt rose 7.00 3.00
178 A15 2t deep blue 9.00 4.50
179 A15 4t gray vio 11.00 4.50
180 A15 8t orange 10.00 4.75
Nos. 174-180 (7) 49.00 21.40

For surcharges and overprints see Nos. 224-230, 277-278, 282, 317-323, 354, 397.

Nos. 178-179 were reprinted. Originals have yellow gum. Reprints have white gum and clean-cut perforation 13½. Value, $4 each.

King Carlos — A16

1895-96 **Typo.** ***Perf. 11½, 12½, 13½***
181 A16 1½r black 3.00 .65
182 A16 4½r pale orange 3.00 .65
a. Perf. 13½ 8.00 1.60
183 A16 6r green 3.00 .65
a. Perf. 12½ 3.50 1.10
184 A16 9r gray lilac 5.00 3.00
185 A16 1t lt blue 3.00 .55
a. Perf. 12½ 5.50 2.50
186 A16 2t rose 2.00 .65
a. Perf. 12½ 4.25 2.25
187 A16 4t dk blue 3.00 .80
a. Perf. 12½ 5.25 3.25
188 A16 8t brt violet 5.00 2.75
Nos. 181-188 (8) 27.00 9.70

For surcharges and overprints see Nos. 231-238,275-276, 279-281, 324-331, 352.

No. 184 was reprinted. Reprints have white gum, and clean-cut perforation 13½. Value $10.

Common Design Types pictured following the introduction.

Vasco da Gama Issue

Common Design Types

1898, May 1 **Engr.** ***Perf. 14 to 15***
189 CD20 1½r blue green 1.00 .90
190 CD21 4½r red 1.00 .90
191 CD22 6r red violet 1.25 .75
192 CD23 9r yellow green 1.50 1.00
193 CD24 1t dk blue 3.00 1.60
194 CD25 2t violet brn 3.75 1.90
195 CD26 4t bister brn 3.75 1.90
196 CD27 8t bister 5.00 4.00
Nos. 189-196 (8) 20.25 12.95

For overprints and surcharges see Nos. 290-297, 384-389.

King Carlos — A17

Name and Value in Black except No. 219

1898-1903 **Typo.** ***Perf. 11½***
197 A17 1r gray ('02) .35 .25
198 A17 1½r orange .35 .25
199 A17 1½r slate ('02) .45 .25
200 A17 2r orange ('02) .35 .25
201 A17 2½r yel brn ('02) .45 .25
202 A17 3r dp blue ('02) .45 .25
203 A17 4½r lt green .70 .55
204 A17 6r brown .70 .55
205 A17 6r gray grn ('02) .45 .25
206 A17 9r dull vio .80 .55
a. 9r gray lilac 1.75 1.75
208 A17 1t sea green .80 .50
209 A17 1t car rose ('02) .60 .25
210 A17 2t blue 1.40 .55
a. Perf. 13½ 30.00 7.75
211 A17 2t brown ('02) 3.25 2.10
212 A17 2½t dull bl ('02) 15.00 6.50
213 A17 4t blue, *blue* 3.25 2.25
214 A17 5t brn, *straw* ('02) 4.50 2.10
215 A17 8t red lil, *pnksh* 5.50 1.40
216 A17 8t red vio, *pink* ('02) 5.00 3.00
217 A17 12t blue, *pink* 12.00 2.25
218 A17 12t grn, *pink* ('02) 9.00 3.25
219 A17 1rp blk & red, *bl* 12.00 6.50
220 A17 1rp dl bl, *straw* ('02) 18.00 7.25
221 A17 2rp vio, *yelsh* 20.00 8.25
222 A17 2rp gray blk, *straw* ('03) 20.00 12.00
Nos. 197-222 (25) 135.35 61.55

Several stamps of this issue exist without value or with value inverted but they are not known to have been issued in this condition. The 1r and 6r in carmine rose are believed to be color trials.

For surcharges and overprints see Nos. 223, 239-259, 260C-274, 283-289, 300-316, 334-350, 376-383, 390-396, 398-399.

No. 210 Surcharged in Black

1900

223 A17 1½r on 2t blue 6.00 2.00
a. Inverted surcharge 100.00
b. Perf. 13½ 35.00 22.50

Stamps of 1885-96 Surcharged in Black or Red

On Stamps of 1886

1902 ***Perf. 12½, 13½***

224 A15 1r on 2t blue 1.10 .50
225 A15 2r on 4½r bis .65 .50
a. Inverted surcharge 22.50 22.50
b. Double surcharge
226 A15 2½r on 6r green .55 .25
227 A15 3r on 1t rose .55 .25
228 A15 2½t on 1½r blk (R) 3.00 1.40
229 A15 2½t on 4t gray vio 5.00 2.75
230 A15 5t on 8t orange 3.00 .65
a. Perf. 12½ 27.50 17.00

On Stamps of 1895-96

Perf. 11½, 12½, 13½

231 A16 1r on 6r green .50 .25
232 A16 2r on 8t brt vio .35 .25
233 A16 2½r on 9r gray vio .35 .35
234 A16 3r on 4½r yel 2.00 1.00
a. Inverted surcharge 24.00 24.00
235 A16 3r on 1t lt bl 2.00 .90
236 A16 2½t on 1½r blk (R) 3.00 .80
237 A16 5t on 2t rose 3.00 .80
a. Perf. 12½ 35.00 22.50
238 A16 5t on 4t dk bl 3.00 .80
a. Perf. 12½ 35.00 22.50
Nos. 224-238 (15) 28.05 11.45

Nos. 224, 229, 231, 233, 234, 235 and 238 were reprinted in 1905. They have whiter gum than the originals and very clean-cut perf. 13½. Value $2.50 each.

Nos. 204, 208, 210 Overprinted

1902 ***Perf. 11½***

239 A17 6r brown 3.00 1.40
a. Inverted overprint
240 A17 1t sea green 4.00 1.40
241 A17 2t blue 3.00 1.40
a. Perf. 13½ 150.00 100.00
Nos. 239-241 (3) 10.00 4.20

No. 212 Surcharged in Black

1905

243 A17 2t on 2½t dull blue 2.25 1.60

Stamps of 1898-1903 Overprinted in Lisbon in Carmine or Green

1911

244 A17 1r gray .25 .25
a. Inverted overprint 11.00 11.00
245 A17 1½r slate .25 .25
a. Double overprint 11.00 11.00
246 A17 2r orange .25 .25
a. Double overprint 15.00 15.00
b. Inverted overprint 11.00 11.00
247 A17 2½r yellow brn .25 .25
248 A17 3r deep blue .25 .25
249 A17 4½r light green .35 .25
250 A17 6r gray green .25 .25
251 A17 9r gray lilac .35 .25
252 A17 1t car rose (G) .50 .25
253 A17 2t brown .50 .25
254 A17 4t blue, *blue* 1.40 1.00
255 A17 5t brn, *straw* 1.40 1.00
256 A17 8t vio, *pink* 4.25 2.50
257 A17 12t grn, *pink* 4.50 2.50
258 A17 1rp dl bl, *straw* 7.00 4.75
259 A17 2rp gray blk, *straw* 8.75 7.50
Nos. 244-259 (16) 30.50 21.75

A18

Values are for pairs, both halves.

1911 **Perforated Diagonally**

260 A18 1r on 2r orange .80 .70
a. Without diagonal perf. 4.50 4.00
b. Cut diagonally instead of perf. 3.50 3.25

Stamps of Preceding Issues Perforated Vertically through the Middle and Each Half Surcharged

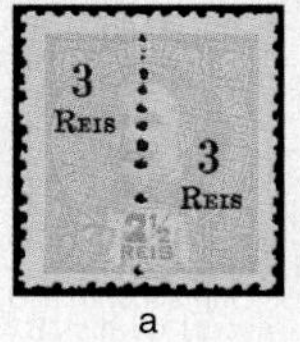

a

b

Values are for pairs, both halves of the stamp.

1912-13 **On Issue of 1898-1903**

260C A17(a) 1r on 2r org .25 .25
261 A17(a) 1r on 1t car .25 .25
262 A17(a) 1r on 5t brn, *straw* 300.00 225.00
263 A17(b) 1r on 5t brn, *straw* 7.75 6.00
264 A17(a) 1½r on 2½r yel brn .75 .65
264C A17(a) 1½r on 4½r lt grn 12.00 7.75
265 A17(a) 1½r on 9r gray lil .55 .45
266 A17(a) 1½r on 4t bl, *bl* .55 .45
267 A17(a) 2r on 2½r yel brn .70 .45
268 A17(a) 2r on 4t bl, *bl* 1.00 .70
269 A17(a) 3r on 2½r yel brn .70 .45
270 A17(a) 3r on 2t brown .70 .50
271 A17(a) 6r on 4½r lt grn .70 .60
272 A17(a) 6r on 9r gray lil .70 .55
273 A17(a) 6r on 9r dull vio 4.50 3.50
274 A17(b) 6r on 8t red vio, *pink* 1.60 1.00

On Nos. 237-238, 230, 226, 233

275 A16(b) 1r on 5t on 2t 20.00 17.00
276 A16(b) 1r on 5t on 4t 10.00 9.25
277 A15(b) 1r on 5t on 8t 5.00 3.25
278 A15(a) 2r on 2½r on 6r 4.25 3.25
279 A16(a) 2r on 2½r on 9r 25.00 24.00
280 A16(b) 3r on 5t on 2t 7.75 6.25
281 A16(b) 3r on 5t on 4t 7.75 6.25
282 A15(b) 3r on 5t on 8t 2.50 1.60

On Issue of 1911

283 A17(a) 1r on 1r gray .25 .25
283B A17(a) 1r on 2r org .25 .25
284 A17(a) 1r on 1t car .35 .25
285 A17(a) 1r on 5t brn, *straw* .35 .25
285A A17(b) 1r on 5t brn, *straw* 825.00 550.00
285B A17(a) 1½r on 4½r lt grn .65 .50
286 A17(a) 3r on 2t brn 11.50 8.50
289 A17(a) 6r on 9r gray lil .55 .45

There are several settings of these surcharges and many minor varieties of the letters and figures, notably a small "6." Nos. 260-289 were issued mostly without gum.

More than half of Nos. 260C-289 exist with inverted or double surcharge, or with bisecting perforation omitted. The legitimacy of these varieties is questioned. Price of inverted surcharges, $3-$15; double surcharges, $1-$4; perf. omitted, $1.50-$15.

Similar surcharges made without official authorization on stamps of type A17 are: 2r on 2½r, 3r on 2½r, 3r on 5t, and 6r on 4½r.

Vasco da Gama Issue Overprinted

1913

290 CD20 1½r blue green .35 .25
291 CD21 4½r red .35 .25
a. Double overprint 22.50
292 CD22 6r red violet .45 .40
a. Double overprint 22.50
293 CD23 9r yellow grn .45 .40
294 CD24 1t dark blue 1.00 .55
295 CD25 2t violet brown 2.25 1.25
296 CD26 4t orange brn 1.25 1.00
297 CD27 8t bister 2.25 1.40
Nos. 290-297 (8) 8.35 5.50

Issues of 1898-1913 Overprinted Locally in Red

1913-15 **On Issues of 1898-1903**

300 A17 2r orange 10.00 10.00
301 A17 2½r yellow brn .95 .80
302 A17 3r dp blue 19.00 17.00
303 A17 4½r lt green 1.90 1.60
304 A17 6r gray grn 25.00 20.00
305 A17 9r gray lilac 1.90 1.40
306 A17 1t sea green 45.00 35.00
307 A17 2t blue 50.00 35.00
309 A17 4t blue, *blue* 40.00 27.50
310 A17 5t brn, *straw* 55.00 35.00
311 A17 8t red vio, *pink* 65.00 45.00
312 A17 12t grn, *pink* 3.50 2.50
313 A17 1rp blk & red, *bl* 100.00 82.50
314 A17 1rp dl bl, *straw* 65.00 45.00
315 A17 2rp gray blk, *straw* 82.50 55.00
316 A17 2rp vio, *yelsh* 77.50 45.00
Nos. 300-316 (16) 642.25 458.30

Inverted or double overprints exist on 2½r, 4½r, 9r, 1rp and 2rp.

Nos. 300-316 were issued without gum except 4½r and 9r.

Nos. 302, 304, 306, 307, 310, 311 and 313 were not regularly issued. Nor were the 1½r, 2t brown and 12t blue on pink with preceding overprint.

Same Overprint in Red or Green on Provisional Issue of 1902

317 A15 1r on 2t blue 45.00 27.50
a. "REPUBLICA" inverted 140.00
318 A15 2r on 4½r bis 45.00 27.50
a. "REPUBLICA" inverted 140.00
319 A15 2½r on 6r grn .75 .65
a. "REPUBLICA" inverted 19.00 19.00
320 A15 3r on 1t rose (R) 11.00 8.75
321 A15 2½t on 4t gray vio 110.00 45.00
323 A15 5t on 8t org (G) 15.00 8.25
a. Red overprint 27.50 22.50
324 A16 1r on 6r grn 35.00 22.50
325 A16 2r on 8t vio 35.00 22.50
a. Inverted surcharge 110.00
327 A16 3r on 4½r yel 82.50 55.00
328 A16 3r on 1t lt bl 82.50 55.00
329 A16 5t on 2t rose (G) 10.00 3.00
330 A16 5t on 4t bl (G) 10.00 3.00
331 A16 5t on 4t bl (R) 10.00 4.25
a. "REPUBLICA" inverted 55.00
b. "REPUBLICA" double 55.00
Nos. 317-331 (13) 491.75 282.90

The 2½r on 1½r of types A15 and A16, the 3r on 1t (A15) and 2½r on 9r (A16) were clandestinely printed.

Some authorities question the status of No. 317-318, 320-321, 324, 327-328.

Same Overprint on Nos. 240-241

1913-15

334 A17 1t sea green 15.00 5.00
335 A17 2t blue 15.00 6.00

This overprint was applied to No. 239 without official authorization. Value $35.

On Issue of 1912-13 Perforated through the Middle

Values are for pairs, both halves of the stamp.

336 A17(a) 1r on 2r org 17.00 11.00
340 A17(a) 1½r on 4½r lt grn 17.00 11.00
341 A17(a) 1½r on 9r gray lil 20.00
342 A17(a) 1½r on 4t bl, *bl* 27.50
343 A17(a) 2r on 2½r yel brn 20.00
344 A17(a) 2r on 4t bl, *bl* 27.50 7.25
345 A17(a) 3r on 2½r yel brn 22.50
346 A17(a) 3r on 2t brn 17.00 5.25
347 A17(a) 6r on 4½r lt grn 1.10 .90
348 A17(a) 6r on 9r gray lil 1.60 1.60
350 A17(b) 6r on 8t red vio, *pink* 1.60 1.60
352 A16(b) 1r on 5t on 4t bl 110.00
354 A15(a) 2r on 2½r on 6r grn 13.00
Nos. 334-354 (15) 325.80

The 1r on 5t (A15), 1r on 1t (A17), 1½r on 2½r (A17), 3r on 5t on 8t (A15), and 6r on 9r (A17) were clandestinely printed.

Nos. 336, 347 exist with inverted surcharge.

Some authorities question the status of Nos. 341-345, 352 and 354.

Ceres — A21

Name and Value in Black
Chalky Paper

1914 **Typo.** ***Perf. 15x14***

357 A21 1r olive brn .35 *.55*
Never hinged .55
358 A21 1½r yellow grn .35 .55
Never hinged .55
359 A21 2r black .70 .40
Never hinged 1.10
360 A21 2½r olive grn .70 .40
Never hinged 1.10
361 A21 3r lilac .70 .40
Never hinged 1.10
362 A21 4½r orange brn .70 .40
Never hinged 1.10
363 A21 5r blue green .70 .50
Never hinged 1.10
364 A21 6r lilac brown .70 .40
Never hinged 1.10
365 A21 9r ultra .70 .40
Never hinged 1.10
366 A21 10r carmine .95 .55
Never hinged 1.50
367 A21 1t lt violet 1.25 .55
Never hinged 2.00
368 A21 2t deep blue 1.25 .55
Never hinged 2.00
369 A21 3t yellow brown 1.90 .95
Never hinged 3.00
370 A21 4t slate 2.25 1.25
Never hinged 3.50
371 A21 8t plum 4.50 4.00
Never hinged 7.25
372 A21 12t brown, *green* 4.00 3.25
Never hinged 6.50
373 A21 1rp brown, *pink* 40.00 *50.00*
Never hinged 65.00
374 A21 2rp org, *salmon* 30.00 *60.00*
Never hinged 47.50
375 A21 3rp green, *blue* 40.00 60.00
Never hinged 65.00
Nos. 357-375 (19) 131.70 185.10

The 1r, 2r, 2½r, 3r, 4½r, 5r, 6r and 10r, 1t and 3t exist on glazed paper.

1916-20 **Ordinary Paper**

375A A21 1r olive brn .80 *1.25*
Never hinged 1.30
375B A21 1½r yellow grn .80 *1.25*
Never hinged 1.30
b. Imperf.
375C A21 2r black ('19) .80 *1.25*
Never hinged 1.30
375D A21 2½r olive grn ('19) .80 *1.25*
Never hinged 1.30
375E A21 3r lilac ('16) .80 *1.25*
Never hinged 1.30
375F A21 4½r orange brn ('19) .80 *1.25*
Never hinged 1.30
375G A21 6r lilac brown ('16) .80 *1.25*
Never hinged 1.30
375H A21 1t lt violet ('16) .80 *1.25*
Never hinged 1.30
375I A21 2t deep blue ('16) .80 *1.25*
Never hinged 1.30
Nos. 375A-375I (9) 7.20 11.25

1921-23 ***Perf. 12x11½***

375J A21 1r olive brn .80 *1.25*
Never hinged 1.30
375K A21 1½r yellow grn .80 *1.25*
Never hinged 1.30
375L A21 2r black 1.50 *1.50*
Never hinged 2.40
375M A21 3r lilac ('22) .80 *1.25*
Never hinged 1.30
375N A21 4r blue ('22) 1.40 1.25
Never hinged 2.25
375O A21 4½r orange brn 2.75 1.60
Never hinged 4.50
375P A21 5r blue green 10.00 6.00
Never hinged 16.00
375Q A21 6r lilac brown .80 .70
Never hinged 1.30
375R A21 9r ultra 1.60 .95
Never hinged 2.50
375S A21 10r carmine 2.50 1.45
Never hinged 4.00
375T A21 1t lt violet 2.75 1.25
Never hinged 4.00
375U A21 1½t gray green ('22) 1.40 .95
Never hinged 2.25
375V A21 2t deep blue 2.75 1.25
Never hinged 4.50

375W A21 2½t turquoise blue ('22) 1.50 1.25
Never hinged 2.40
375X A21 3t4r yellow brown ('23) 5.50 4.50
Never hinged 8.75
375Y A21 4t slate 2.25 1.25
Never hinged 3.50
375Z A21 8t plum 7.75 5.50
Never hinged 12.50
Nos. 375J-375Z (17) 46.85 33.15

The 1, 2, 2½, 3, 4½r, 1, 2, and 4t exist with the black inscriptions inverted and the 2½r with them double, one inverted, but it is not known that any of these were regularly issued.

For surcharges see Nos. 400, 400A, 420, 421, 423.

Nos. 249, 251-253, 256-259 Surcharged in Black

1914

376 A17 1½r on 4½r grn .35 .25
377 A17 1½r on 9r gray lil .45 .35
378 A17 1½r on 12t grn, *pink* .55 .50
379 A17 3r on 1t car rose .45 .40
380 A17 3r on 2t brn 3.25 2.75
381 A17 3r on 8t red vio, *pink* 2.50 2.25
382 A17 3r on 1rp dl bl, *straw* 1.00 .60
383 A17 3r on 2rp gray blk, *straw* 1.10 .80

There are 3 varieties of the "2" in "1½."
Nos. 376-377 exist with inverted surcharge.

Vasco da Gama Issue Surcharged in Black

384 CD21 1½r on 4½r red .40 .35
385 CD23 1½r on 9r yel grn .50 .35
386 CD24 3r on 1t dk bl .40 .35
387 CD25 3r on 2t vio brn .60 .50
388 CD26 3r on 4t org brn .35 .25
389 CD27 3r on 8t bister 1.40 1.25
Nos. 376-389 (14) 13.30 10.95

Double, inverted and other surcharge varieties exist on Nos. 384-386, 389.

Nos. 303, 305, 312 and 315 Surcharged in Black

1915

390 A17 1½r on 4½r grn 45.00 22.50
a. "REPUBLICA" omitted 77.50 47.50
b. "REPUBLICA" inverted 82.50
391 A17 1½r on 9r gray lil 14.00 8.25
a. "REPUBLICA" omitted 35.00
392 A17 1½r on 12t grn, *pink* 1.40 1.10
396 A17 3r on 2rp gray blk, *straw* 55.00 22.50
Nos. 390-396 (4) 115.40 54.35

Nos. 390, 390a, 390b, 391, and 391a were not regularly issued. The 3r on 2½r (A17) was surcharged without official authorization.

Preceding Issues Overprinted in Carmine

1915 **On No. 230**

397 A15 5t on 8t org 2.75 1.50

On Nos. 241, 243

398 A17 2t blue 2.25 1.40
399 A17 2t on 2½t dl bl 2.75 1.40
Nos. 397-399 (3) 7.75 4.30

Nos. 375C, 359 Surcharged in Carmine

1922

400 A21 1½r on 2r black (ordinary paper) .75 .60
Never hinged 1.25
400A A21 1½r on 2r black (chalky paper) .50 .40
Never hinged .80

No. 400 also exists on glazed paper.

Ceres Type of 1913-23
Name and Value in Black

1922 **Typo.** ***Perf. 12x11½***
Glazed Paper

407 A21 1rp gray brn 17.50 17.00
Never hinged 28.00
408 A21 2rp yellow 30.00 *90.00*
Never hinged 47.50
409 A21 3rp bluish grn 40.00 *100.00*
Never hinged 65.00
410 A21 5rp carmine rose 50.00 *150.00*
Never hinged 80.00
Nos. 407-410 (4) 137.50 357.00

Vasco da Gama and Flagship A22

1925, Jan. 30 **Litho.**
Without Gum

411 A22 6r brown 5.00 3.25
412 A22 1t red violet 7.00 5.00

400th anniv. of the death of Vasco da Gama (1469?-1524), Portuguese navigator.

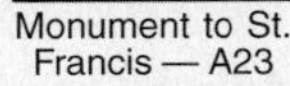

Monument to St. Francis — A23

Image of St. Francis — A25

Autograph of St. Francis A24

Image of St. Francis — A26

Tomb of St. Francis — A28

Church of Bom Jesus at Goa — A27

1931, Dec. 3 ***Perf. 14***

414 A23 1r gray green 1.00 .80
415 A24 2r brown 1.00 .80
416 A25 6r red violet 2.00 .80
417 A26 1½t yellow brn 7.00 3.50
418 A27 2t deep blue 10.00 4.75
419 A28 2½t light red 12.00 5.50
Nos. 414-419 (6) 33.00 16.15

Exposition of St. Francis Xavier at Goa, in December, 1931.

Nos. 371 and 375X Surcharged

1931-32 ***Perf. 15x14***
Chalky Paper

420 A21 1½r on 8t plum ('32) 2.25 1.60

Ordinary Paper
Perf. 12x11½

421 A21 1½r on 8t plum ('32) 1.50 1.10
423 A21 2½t on 3t4r yel brn 90.00 50.00

"Portugal" and Vasco da Gama's Flagship "San Gabriel" — A29

Perf. 11½x12

1933 **Typo.** **Wmk. 232**

424 A29 1r bister .25 .25
425 A29 2r olive brn .25 .25
426 A29 4r violet .25 .25
427 A29 6r dk green .25 .25
428 A29 8r black .40 .30
429 A29 1t gray .40 .30
430 A29 1½t dp rose .40 .30
431 A29 2t brown .40 .30
432 A29 2½t dk blue 2.25 .55
433 A29 3t brt blue 2.50 .55
434 A29 5t red orange 2.50 .55
435 A29 1rp olive grn 11.00 3.25
436 A29 2rp maroon 27.50 7.50
437 A29 3rp orange 40.00 8.75
438 A29 5rp apple grn 55.00 25.00
Nos. 424-438 (15) 143.35 48.35

For surcharges see Nos. 454-463, 472-474, J34-J36 in Scott Standard catalogue, Vol. 5.

Common Design Types
Perf. 13½x13

1938, Sept. 1 **Engr.** **Unwmk.**
Name and Value in Black

439 CD34 1r gray grn .30 .25
440 CD34 2r orange brn .30 .25
441 CD34 3r dk vio brn .30 .25
442 CD34 6r brt green .30 .25
443 CD35 10r dk carmine .40 .30
444 CD35 1t brt red vio .55 .30
445 CD35 1½t red .90 .30
446 CD37 2t orange .90 .30
447 CD37 2½t blue .90 .30
448 CD37 3t slate 1.75 .35
449 CD36 5t rose vio 2.75 .50
450 CD36 1rp brown car 4.50 .90
451 CD36 2rp olive grn 7.75 2.75
452 CD38 3rp blue vio 13.00 6.50
453 CD38 5rp red brown 22.50 6.50
Nos. 439-453 (15) 57.10 20.00

For surcharges see Nos. 492-495, 504-505.

AIR POST STAMPS

Common Design Type
Perf. 13½x13

1938, Sept. 1 **Engr.** **Unwmk.**
Name and Value in Black

C1 CD39 1t red orange .70 .40
C2 CD39 2½t purple .80 .40
C3 CD39 3½t orange .80 .40
C4 CD39 4½t ultra 1.60 .45
C5 CD39 7t lilac brown 1.75 .55
C6 CD39 7½t dark green 2.50 .80
C7 CD39 9t red brown 4.50 1.25
C8 CD39 11t magenta 5.00 1.25
Nos. C1-C8 (8) 17.65 5.50

No. C4 exists with overprint "Exposicao Internacional de Nova York, 1939-1940" and Trylon and Perisphere. Value, unused $90, never hinged $125.

POSTAGE DUE STAMPS

D1

1904 **Unwmk.** **Typo.** ***Perf. 11½***
Name and Value in Black

J1 D1 2r gray green .50 .35
J2 D1 3r yellow grn .50 .35
J3 D1 4r orange .50 .45
J4 D1 5r slate .50 .50
J5 D1 6r gray .50 .50
J6 D1 9r yellow brn .60 .60
J7 D1 1t red orange 2.25 .80
J8 D1 2t gray brown 3.25 1.60
J9 D1 5t dull blue 4.50 3.00
J10 D1 10t carmine 7.75 3.50
J11 D1 1rp dull vio 13.00 7.50
Nos. J1-J11 (11) 33.85 19.15

Nos. J1-J11 Overprinted in Carmine or Green

1911

J12 D1 2r gray grn .25 .25
J13 D1 3r yellow grn .25 .25
J14 D1 4r orange .25 .25
J15 D1 5r slate .25 .25
J16 D1 6r gray .45 .25
J17 D1 9r yellow brn .55 .35
J18 D1 1t red org .65 .35
J19 D1 2t gray brn .90 .55
J20 D1 5t dull blue 2.25 1.40
J21 D1 10t carmine (G) 3.25 1.90
J22 D1 1rp dull violet 7.75 3.25
Nos. J12-J22 (11) 16.80 9.05

Nos. J1-J11 Overprinted

1914

J23 D1 2r gray grn 1.50 1.10
J24 D1 3r yellow grn 1.50 1.10
J25 D1 4r orange 1.50 1.10
J26 D1 5r slate 1.50 1.10
J27 D1 6r gray 1.60 1.10
J28 D1 9r yellow brn 1.60 1.10
J29 D1 1t red org 3.25 1.10
J30 D1 2t gray brn 20.00 3.25
J31 D1 5t dull blue 21.00 4.50
J32 D1 10t carmine 25.00 6.50
J33 D1 1rp dull violet 45.00 8.75
Nos. J23-J33 (11) 123.45 30.70

WAR TAX STAMPS

Overprinted in Black or Carmine

WT1

Denomination in Black
Perf. 15x14

1919, Apr. 15 **Typo.** **Unwmk.**

MR1 WT1 0:00:05,48rp grn 2.25 1.50
MR2 WT1 0:01:09,94rp grn 4.75 3.00
MR3 WT1 0:02:03,43rp grn (C) 4.75 3.00
Nos. MR1-MR3 (3) 11.75 7.50

Some authorities consider No. MR2 a revenue stamp.

POSTAL TAX STAMPS

Pombal Issue
Common Design Types

1925	Unwmk.	Perf. 12½	
RA1	CD28 6r rose & black	.50	.50
RA2	CD29 6r rose & black	.50	.50
RA3	CD30 6r rose & black	.50	.50
	Nos. RA1-RA3 (3)	1.50	1.50

POSTAL TAX DUE STAMPS

Pombal Issue
Common Design Types

1925	Unwmk.	Perf. 12½	
RAJ1	CD28 1t rose & black	.65	.65
RAJ2	CD29 1t rose & black	.65	.65
RAJ3	CD30 1t rose & black	.65	.65
	Nos. RAJ1-RAJ3 (3)	1.95	1.95

See note after Portugal No. RAJ4.

PUERTO RICO

ˌpwer-tə-ˈrē-ˌ(ˌ)kō

(Porto Rico)

LOCATION — A large island in the West Indies, east of Hispaniola
GOVT. — Former Spanish Colony
AREA — 3,435 sq. mi.
POP. — 953,243 (1899)
CAPITAL — San Juan

The island was ceded to the United States by the Treaty of 1898.

100 Centimes = 1 Peseta
1000 Milesimas = 100 Centavos = 1 Peso (1881)
100 Cents = 1 Dollar (1898)

Puerto Rican stamps of 1855-73, a part of the Spanish colonial period, were also used in Cuba. They are listed as Cuba Nos. 1-4, 9-14, 18-21, 31-34, 39-41, 47-49, 51-53, 55-57.

STAMPS OF CUBA USED IN PUERTO RICO

Values for Stamps on Cover

1855-73

A1	½r p blue green (#1)	100.00
A2	1r p gray green (#2)	200.00
A3	2r p carmine (#3)	500.00
A4	½r p yel grn (#9)	50.00
a.	½r p greenish blue (#9a)	60.00
A5	1r p green (#10)	75.00
A6	2r p orange red (#11)	300.00
A7	½r p blue (#12)	25.00
a.	½r p milky blue (#12a)	30.00
A8	1r p gray green (#13)	25.00
c.	1r p pale green (#13c)	30.00
A9	2r p dull rose (#14)	150.00
A10	½r p green (#18)	10.00
A11	½r p green, *pale rose* (#19)	15.00
a.	½r p green, *rose lilac* (#19a)	15.00
A12	1r p blue, *salmon* (#20)	50.00
A13	2r p vermilion, *buff* (#21)	150.00
a.	2r p red, *buff* (#21a)	175.00
A14	5c dull violet (#31)	300.00
A15	10c blue (#32)	20.00
A16	20c green (#33)	30.00
A17	40c rose (#34)	200.00
A18	5c rose (#38)	—
A18A	10c red brown (#39)	15.00
A19	20c orange (#40)	25.00
A20	40c dull violet (#41)	150.00
A21	10c green (#47)	15.00
A22	20c red brown (#48)	25.00
A23	40c rose (#49)	150.00
A24	25c ultramarine (#51)	15.00
A25	50c gray green (#52)	40.00
A26	1p pale brown (#53)	150.00
A27	25c gray (#55)	20.00
a.	25c lilac (#55b)	30.00
A28	50c brown (#56)	50.00
A29	1p red brown (#57)	200.00

Most local inland covers of this period (1855-73) are official fronts of covers only. The values stated above for lower denominations are for such fronts. Complete covers with the same stamps are worth at least double these values.

OFFICIAL STAMPS OF SPAIN USED IN PUERTO RICO

1858

A30	½o black, *yellow*, (#O5)	30.00
	On cover or wrapper	200.00
	On cover in combination with Cuba #18 (A10) or #19 (A11)	300.00
a.	½o black, *straw*, (#O5a)	30.00
	On cover or wrapper	200.00
A31	1o black, *rose*, (#O6)	30.00
	On cover or wrapper	300.00
a.	1o black, *salmon rose*, (#O6a)	30.00
	On cover or wrapper	300.00
A32	1o black, *blue green*, (#O7)	175.00
	On cover or wrapper	500.00
a.	4o black, *green*, (#O7a)	150.00
	On cover or wrapper	500.00
A33	1 l black, *blue*, (#O8)	375.00
	On wrapper	1,000.

Values are for stamps with clear readable or identifiable cancellations of Puerto Rico.

Values for Pairs

A30	½o black, *yellow*,	75.00
A30a	½o black, *straw*, (#O5a)	75.00
A31	1o black, *rose*, (#O6)	75.00
A31a	1o black, *salmon rose*, (#O6a)	75.00
A32	4o black, *blue green* (#O7)	375.00
A32a	4o black, *blue*, (#O8)	775.00
A33	1 l black, *blue*, (O8)	775.00

Values for Blocks of 4

A30	½o black, *yellow* (#O5)	150.00
A30a	½o black, *straw*, (#O5a)	150.00
A31	1o black, *rose*, (#O6)	150.00
A31a	1o black, *salmon rose*, (#O6a)	225.00
A32	4o black, *blue green*, (#O7)	850.00
A32a	4o black, *green*, (#O7a)	900.00
A33	1l black, *blue*, (#O8)	1,650.

STAMPS OF GREAT BRITAIN USED IN PUERTO RICO

Aguadilla
Stamps of Great Britain Cancelled Type B "F84"

1873-77

A34	½p rose red (#58, plate 6)	115.00
A35	1p rose red (#33, plates 119, 122, 139, 149, 156, 160)	72.50
A36	2p blue (#30, plate 14)	—
A37	3p rose (#49, plates 7-9)	—
A38	3p rose (#61, plate 12)	—
A39	4p vermilion (#43, plates 12-14)	85.00
A40	4p vermilion (#69, plate 15)	400.00
A41	6p buff (#59b, plate 11)	—
A42	6p gray (#62, plates 13, 14)	—
A43	9p bister (#52, plate 4)	450.00
A44	10p red brown (#53)	450.00
A45	1sh green (#54, plates 4-7)	77.50
A46	1sh green (#64, plates 8-12)	90.00
A47	2sh blue (#55, plate 55)	350.00

Nos. A34-A47 on cover are valued from $1,500.

Arroyo
Stamps of Great Britain Cancelled Type B "F83" in black or red or with circular date stamp

1873-77

A48	½p rose red (#58, plate 5)	77.50
A49	1p rose red (#33, plates 149-151, 156, 164, 174, 175)	72.50
A50	1 ½p lake red (#32, plates 1, 3)	—
A51	2p blue (#30, plate 14)	—
A52	3p rose (#49, plates 5, 7, 10)	77.50
A53	3p rose (#61, plates 11, 12, 14, 16, 18)	72.50
A54	4p vermilion (#43, plates 12-14)	72.50
A55	4p vermilion (#69, plate 15)	400.00
A56	6p brown (#59, plate 11)	85.00
A57	6p buff (#59b, plate 11)	105.00
A58	6p gray (#60, plate 12)	—
A59	6p gray (#62, plates 13-15)	77.50
A60	9p bister (#52, plate 4)	400.00
A61	10p red brown (#53)	400.00
A62	1sh green (#48, plate 4)	—
A63	1sh green (#54, plates 4-7)	77.50
A64	1sh green (#64, plates 8-13)	92.50
A65	2sh blue (#55)	300.00
A66	5sh rose (#57, plate 2)	—

Nos. A48-A66 on cover are valued from $2,000.

Mayaguez
Stamps of Great Britain Cancelled Type B "F85" in black or blue

1873-77

A67	½p rose red (#58, plates 4-6, 8, 10, 11)	72.50
A68	1p rose red (#33, plates 76, 120-124, 134, 137, 140, 146, 149-151, 154-157, 160, 167, 170, 174-176, 178, 180, 182, 185, 186, 189)	50.00
A69	1 ½p lake red (#32, plates 1, 3)	65.00
A70	2p blue (#30, plates 13-15)	65.00
A71	3p rose (#49, plates 7-10)	72.50
A72	3p rose (#61, plates 11, 12, 14, 16-19)	65.00
A73	4p vermilion (#43, plates 11-14)	65.00
A74	4p vermilion (#69, plate 15)	400.00
A75	4p pale olive green (#70, plate 15)	—
A76	6p bright violet (#51, plate 9)	—
A77	6p buff (#59b, plate 11)	105.00
A78	6p brown (#59, plate 11)	92.50
A79	6p gray (#60, plate 12)	260.00
A80	6p gray (#62, plates 13-16)	65.00
A81	8p orange (#73)	400.00
A82	9p bister (#52, plate 4)	300.00
A83	10p red brown (#53)	400.00
A84	1sh green (#54, plates 4-7)	57.50
A85	1sh green (#64, plates 8-12)	77.50
A86	2sh blue (#55)	240.00
A87	5sh rose (#57, plate 1)	—
A88	5sh rose (#57, plate 2)	—

Nos. A67-A88 on cover are valued from $500.

Naguabo
Stamps of Great Britain Cancelled Type B "582"

1875-77

A89	½p rose red (#58, plates 2, 12, 14)	—
A90	1p rose red (#33, plates 159, 165)	*450.00*
A91	3p rose (#61, plates 17, 18)	*725.00*
A92	4p vermilion (#43, plates 13, 14)	*650.00*
A93	4p vermilion (#69, plate 15)	—
A94	6p gray (#62, plates 14, 15)	—
A95	9p bister (#52, plate 4)	—
A96	10p red brown (#53)	*1,250.*
A97	1sh green (#64, plates 11, 12)	—
A98	2sh blue (#55)	*1,000.*

Only two covers bearing British stamps canceled "582" are known. Values from $10,000.

Ponce
Stamps of Great Britain Cancelled Type B "F88"

1873-77

A99	½p rose red (#58, plates 5, 10, 12)	72.50
A100	1p rose red (#33, plates 120-124, 146, 148, 154, 156-158, 160, 167, 171, 174, 175, 179, 186, 187)	*57.50*
A101	1 ½p lake red (#32, plate 3)	145.00
A102	2p blue (#30, plates 13, 14)	72.50
A103	3p rose (#49, plates 7-9)	—
A104	3p rose (#61, plates 12, 16-19)	65.00
A105	4p vermilion (#43, plates 8, 9, 12-14)	72.50
A106	4p vermilion (#69, plate 15)	400.00
A107	4p pale olive green (#70, plates 15, 16)	275.00
A108	6p buff (#59b, plates 11, 12)	97.50
A109	6p brown (#59, plate 11)	85.00
A110	6p gray (#60, plate 12)	—
A111	6p gray (#62, plates 13-15)	72.50
A112	9p bister (#52, plate 4)	350.00
A113	10p red brown (#53)	400.00
A114	1sh green (#54, plates 4, 6, 7)	65.00
A115	1sh green (#64, plates 8-13)	77.50
A116	2sh blue (#55)	—
A117	5sh rose (#57, plate 1)	500.00
A118	5sh rose (#57, plate 2)	700.00

Nos. A99-A118 on cover are valued from $1,000.

San Juan
Crowned Circle Type I

1844

A119 I	Crowned circle handstamp "Paid at San Juan," double circle curved "PAID" in black, on cover	1,000.
	As #A119, with additional local postage, cover	1,200.
A120 I	Crowned circle handstamp "Paid at San Juan," double circle curved "PAID" in red, on cover	1,000.
	As #A120, with additional local postage, cover	1,500.

Stamps of Great Britain Cancelled Type A or B "C61"

1865-77

A121	½p rose red (#58, plates 5, 10, 15)	65.00
A122	1p rose red (#33, plates 73, 73, 81, 84, 90, 94, 100-102, 107, 117, 122, 124, 125, 127, 130, 137-140, 145, 146, 149, 153, 156, 159, 160, 162, 163, 169, 171-175, 179, 180, 182, 186)	50.00
A123	1 ½p lake red (#32, plates 1, 3)	85.00
A124	2p blue (#29, plate 9)	50.00
A125	2p blue (#30, plates 13, 14)	45.00
A126	3p rosee (#44, plate 4)	120.00
A127	3p rose (#49, plates 4-10)	65.00
A128	3p rose (#61, plates 11, 12, 14-18)	60.00
A129	4p vermilion (#43, plates 7-14)	65.00
A130	4p vermilion (#69, plate 15)	400.00
A131	6p lilac (#45, plates 5, 6)	97.50
A132	6p lilac (#50, plate 6)	92.50
A133	6p bright violet (#50a, plate 6)	100.00
A134	6p bright violet (#51, plates 8, 9)	92.50
A135	6p buff (#59b, plates 11, 12)	97.50
A136	6p brown (#59, plate 11)	65.00
A137	6p gray (#60, plate 12)	—
A138	6p gray (#62, plates 13-15)	65.00
A139	9p straw (#40)	400.00
A140	9p straw (#46, plate 4)	500.00
A141	9p bister (#52, plate 4)	275.00
A142	10p red brown (#53)	350.00
A143	1sh green (#48, plate 4)	185.00
A144	1sh green (#54, plates 4-7)	57.50
A145	1sh green (#64, plates 8-13)	77.50
A146	2sh blue (#55)	175.00
A147	5sh rose (#57, plate 1)	600.00
A148	5sh rose (#57, plate 2)	750.00

Nos. A121-A148 on cover are valued from $300.

Issued under Spanish Dominion

Values for unused stamps are for examples with original gum as defined in the catalogue introduction. Very fine examples of Nos. 1-170, MR1-MR13 will have perforations clear of the design but will be noticeably poorly centered. Extremely fine examples will be well centered; these are scarce and command substantial premiums.

Stamps of Cuba Overprinted in Black

a

b

c

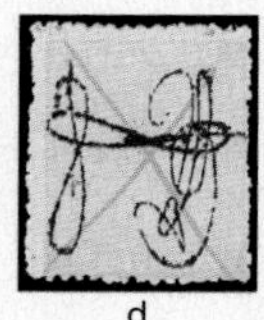
d

1873 **Unwmk.** ***Perf. 14***

1	A10 (a) 25c gray	62.50	2.10
	On cover		50.00
a.	25c lilac	67.50	3.25
	On cover		75.00
2	A10 (a) 50c brown	140.00	6.25
	On cover		200.00
3	A10 (a) 1p red brown	600.00	21.00
	On cover		500.00
	Nos. 1-3 (3)	802.50	29.35

1874

4	A11 (b) 25c ultra	47.50	10.00
	On cover		50.00
a.	Double overprint	275.00	
b.	Inverted overprint	275.00	

1875

5	A12 (b) 25c ultra	37.50	3.25
	On cover		50.00
a.	Inverted overprint	95.00	55.00
6	A12 (b) 50c green	45.00	3.50
	On cover		200.00
a.	Inverted overprint	*210.00*	*105.00*
7	A12 (b) 1p brown	160.00	17.50
	On cover		500.00
	Nos. 5-7 (3)	242.50	24.25

1876

8	A13 (c) 25c pale violet	4.25	1.90
	On cover		50.00
a.	25c bluish gray	5.50	2.75
	On cover		60.00
9	A13 (c) 50c ultra	10.50	3.25
	On cover		200.00
10	A13 (c) 1p black	75.00	12.00
	On cover		700.00

11 A13 (d) 25c pale violet 35.00 1.40
On cover 100.00
12 A13 (d) 1p black 75.00 11.00
On cover 500.00
Nos. 8-12 (5) 199.75 29.55

Varieties of overprint on Nos. 8-11 include: inverted, double, partly omitted and sideways. Counterfeit overprints exist.

King Alfonso XII — A5

1877 **Typo.**

13 A5 5c yellow brown 10.00 2.75
On cover 100.00
a. 5c carmine (error) 300.00 —
14 A5 10c carmine 40.00 7.50
On cover 100.00
a. 10c brown (error) 300.00 —
15 A5 15c deep green 60.00 15.50
On cover 200.00
16 A5 25c ultra 25.00 2.60
On cover 50.00
17 A5 50c bister 40.00 6.50
On cover 300.00
Nos. 13-17 (5) 175.00 34.85

Imperf. examples of Nos. 13-17 are from proof or trial sheets. Value, set $400.

1878 **Dated "1878"**

18 A5 5c ol bister 22.00 22.00
On cover 300.00
19 A5 10c red brown 350.00 120.00
On cover 500.00
20 A5 25c deep green 2.75 1.75
On cover 50.00
21 A5 50c ultra 9.00 3.50
On cover 200.00
22 A5 1p bister 18.00 8.50
On cover 500.00
Nos. 18-22 (5) 401.75 155.75

Imperf. examples of Nos. 18-22 are from proof or trial sheets. Value, set $600.

1879 **Dated "1879"**

23 A5 5c lake 20.00 6.50
On cover 200.00
24 A5 10c dark brown 20.00 6.50
On cover 300.00
25 A5 15c dk olive grn 20.00 6.50
On cover 300.00
26 A5 25c blue 5.00 2.25
On cover 50.00
27 A5 50c dark green 20.00 6.50
On cover 200.00
28 A5 1p gray 110.00 30.00
On cover 500.00
Nos. 23-28 (6) 195.00 58.25

Imperf. examples of Nos. 23-28 are from proof or trial sheets.

King Alfonso XII — A6

1880

29 A6 ¼c deep green 37.50 25.00
On cover 400.00
30 A6 ½c brt rose 9.00 3.25
On cover 300.00
31 A6 1c brown lilac 16.50 13.00
On cover 300.00
32 A6 2c gray lilac 8.50 5.50
On cover 300.00
33 A6 3c buff 9.50 6.00
On cover 300.00
34 A6 4c black 9.50 6.00
On cover 300.00
35 A6 5c gray green 4.75 2.50
On cover 200.00
36 A6 10c rose 5.25 3.00
On cover 200.00
37 A6 15c yellow brn 9.50 4.50
On cover 200.00
38 A6 25c gray blue 4.75 2.10
On cover 50.00
39 A6 40c gray 18.00 22.00
On cover 100.00
40 A6 50c dark brown 40.00 20.00
On cover 400.00
41 A6 1p olive bister 150.00 26.50
On cover 700.00
Nos. 29-41 (13) 322.75 139.35

1881 **Dated "1881"**

42 A6 ½m lake .55 .50
On cover 300.00
a. ½m carmine rose .55 .50
On cover 300.00
43 A6 1m violet .55 .30
On cover 200.00
a. 1m reddish violet .70 .45
On cover 200.00
44 A6 2m pale rose .75 .50
On cover 200.00
a. 2m deep rose .70 .50
On cover 200.00
45 A6 4m brt yellowish green 1.30 .30
On cover 200.00
a. 4m emerald green 3.50 1.40
On cover 200.00
46 A6 6m brown lilac 1.30 .70
On cover 200.00
a. 6m pale lilac 3.50 1.40
On cover 200.00
47 A6 8m ultra 3.25 1.75
On cover 200.00
a. 8m steel blue 5.50 2.10
On cover 200.00
48 A6 1c gray green 4.25 1.50
On cover 100.00
49 A6 2c lake 5.75 4.75
On cover 75.00
50 A6 3c dark brown 12.50 7.75
On cover 100.00
a. 3c chestnut brown 14.50 7.75
On cover 100.00
b. Double impression of top inscriptions 30.00 15.00
51 A6 5c grayish ultra 4.75 .55
On cover 50.00
a. 5c blue 6.50 2.25
On cover 60.00
52 A6 8c brown 4.75 2.25
On cover 100.00
53 A6 10c slate 75.00 11.50
On cover 400.00
54 A6 20c olive bister 90.00 21.00
On cover 700.00
Nos. 42-54 (13) 204.70 53.35

Alfonso XII — A7

1882-86

55 A7 ½m rose .30 .25
On cover 200.00
a. ½m salmon rose .55 .35
On cover 200.00
56 A7 ½m lake ('84) .90 .40
On cover 200.00
57 A7 1m pale lake .90 1.10
On cover 200.00
58 A7 1m brt rose ('84) .30 .25
On cover 200.00
59 A7 2m violet .30 .25
On cover 200.00
60 A7 4m brown lilac .30 .25
On cover 150.00
61 A7 6m brown .45 .25
On cover 150.00
62 A7 8m yellow green .45 .25
On cover 300.00
63 A7 1c gray green .30 .25
On cover 100.00
64 A7 2c rose 1.15 .25
On cover 100.00
65 A7 3c yellow 4.25 2.25
On cover 100.00
a. Cliché of 8c in plate of 3c 120.00
66 A7 3c yellow brn ('84) 4.25 .90
On cover 100.00
a. Cliché of 8c in plate of 3c 25.00
67 A7 5c gray blue 15.00 1.25
On cover 50.00
68 A7 5c gray bl, 1st retouch ('84) 15.00 3.00
On cover *75.00*
69 A7 5c gray bl, 2nd retouch ('86) 115.00 5.75
On cover *75.00*
70 A7 8c gray brown 3.75 .25
On cover 75.00
71 A7 10c dark green 3.75 .30
On cover 200.00
72 A7 20c gray lilac 5.50 .30
On cover 500.00
a. 20c olive brown (error) *120.00*
73 A7 40c blue 65.00 15.00
On cover —
74 A7 80c olive bister 70.00 21.00
On cover —
Nos. 55-74 (20) 306.85 53.50

For differences between the original and the retouched stamps see note on the 1883-86 issue of Cuba.

Alfonso XIII — A8

1890-97

75 A8 ½m black .30 .25
On cover 150.00
a. ½m jet black .25 .25
On cover 150.00
76 A8 ½m olive gray ('92) .25 .25
On cover 150.00
a. ½m bronze green .25 .25
On cover 150.00
77 A8 ½m red brn ('94) .25 .25
On cover 150.00
78 A8 ½m dull vio ('96) .25 .25
On cover 150.00
79 A8 1m emerald .25 .25
On cover 150.00
80 A8 1m dk violet ('92) .25 .25
On cover 150.00
81 A8 1m ultra ('94) .25 .25
On cover 100.00
82 A8 1m dp brown ('96) .25 .25
On cover 100.00
83 A8 2m lilac rose .25 .25
On cover 100.00
84 A8 2m violet brn ('92) .25 .25
On cover 100.00
85 A8 2m red orange ('94) .25 .25
On cover 100.00
86 A8 2m yellow grn ('96) .25 .25
On cover 100.00
87 A8 4m dk olive grn 11.50 5.75
On cover 200.00
88 A8 4m ultra ('92) .25 .25
On cover 150.00
89 A8 4m yellow brn ('94) .25 .25
On cover 100.00
90 A8 4m blue grn ('96) 1.00 .35
On cover 100.00
91 A8 6m dk brown 50.00 15.00
On cover 200.00
92 A8 6m pale rose ('92) .25 .25
On cover 150.00
93 A8 8m olive bister 35.00 22.00
On cover 200.00
94 A8 8m yellow grn ('92) .25 .25
On cover 150.00
95 A8 1c yellow brown .30 .25
On cover 100.00
96 A8 1c blue grn ('91) .55 .25
On cover 100.00
97 A8 1c violet brn ('94) 6.00 .45
On cover 100.00
98 A8 1c claret ('96) .65 .25
On cover 100.00
99 A8 2c brownish violet 1.00 .85
On cover 150.00
a. 2c blackish violet 1.40 1.10
On cover 150.00
100 A8 2c red brown ('92) .95 .25
On cover 100.00
101 A8 2c lilac ('94) 2.25 .45
On cover 75.00
102 A8 2c orange brn ('96) .65 .25
On cover 50.00
103 A8 3c slate blue 7.50 1.00
On cover 150.00
104 A8 3c orange ('92) .90 .25
On cover 100.00
105 A8 3c ol gray ('94) 6.00 .45
On cover 100.00
106 A8 3c blue ('96) 22.00 .35
On cover 100.00
107 A8 3c claret brn ('97) .30 .25
On cover 100.00
108 A8 4c slate bl ('94) 1.50 .45
On cover 75.00
109 A8 4c gray brn ('96) .70 .25
On cover 75.00
110 A8 5c brown violet 13.00 .45
On cover 50.00
111 A8 5c yellow grn ('94) 5.75 1.10
On cover 50.00
112 A8 5c blue green ('92) .90 .25
On cover 50.00
113 A8 5c blue ('96) .30 .25
On cover 50.00
114 A8 6c orange ('94) .45 .25
On cover 100.00
115 A8 6c violet ('96) .35 .25
On cover 100.00
116 A8 8c ultra 16.00 1.75
On cover 150.00
117 A8 8c gray brown ('92) .25 .25
On cover 100.00
118 A8 8c dull vio ('94) 13.00 5.00
On cover 75.00
119 A8 8c car rose ('96) 3.00 1.50
On cover 75.00
120 A8 10c rose 4.75 1.10
On cover 150.00
a. 10c salmon rose 11.50 2.75
On cover 150.00
b. 10c carmine rose 6.00 1.20
On cover 150.00
121 A8 10c lilac rose ('92) 1.50 .35
On cover 150.00
122 A8 20c red orange 5.25 4.75
On cover 400.00
123 A8 20c lilac ('92) 2.50 .55
On cover 400.00
a. 20c violet 2.50 .55
On cover 400.00
124 A8 20c car rose ('94) 1.50 .45
On cover 400.00
125 A8 20c olive gray ('96) 6.75 1.50
On cover 300.00
126 A8 40c orange 200.00 57.50
On cover —
127 A8 40c slate blue ('92) 5.75 4.00
On cover —
128 A8 40c claret ('94) 7.50 13.50
On cover 800.00
129 A8 40c salmon ('96) 7.00 1.60
On cover 500.00
130 A8 80c yellow green 700.00 240.00
On cover 5,000.
131 A8 80c orange ('92) 14.50 11.50
On cover —
132 A8 80c black ('97) 27.50 23.50
On cover —

Imperforates of type A8 were not issued and are variously considered to be proofs or printer's waste.

For overprints see Nos. 154A-170, MR1-MR13.

Landing of Columbus on Puerto Rico — A9

1893 **Litho.** ***Perf. 12***

133 A9 3c dark green 300.00 60.00
On cover, philatelic 200.00
On cover, commercial 500.00

400th anniversary, landing of Columbus on Puerto Rico. Counterfeits exist.

Alfonso XIII — A10

1898 **Typo.**

135 A10 1m orange brown .25 .25
On cover 100.00
136 A10 2m orange brown .25 .25
On cover 100.00
137 A10 3m orange brown .25 .25
On cover 150.00
138 A10 4m orange brown 2.40 .75
On cover 150.00
139 A10 5m orange brown .25 .25
On cover 150.00
140 A10 1c black violet .25 .25
On cover 100.00
a. Tête bêche pair *1,700.*
b. Pair, #140 & Philippines #197 (cliche error) *1,500.*
141 A10 2c dk blue green .25 .25
On cover 100.00
142 A10 3c dk brown .25 .25
On cover 75.00
143 A10 4c orange 2.40 1.60
On cover 100.00
144 A10 5c brt rose .30 .25
On cover 75.00
145 A10 6c dark blue .85 .25
On cover 100.00
146 A10 8c gray brown .30 .25
On cover 100.00
147 A10 10c vermilion .30 .25
On cover 150.00
148 A10 15c dull olive grn .30 .25
On cover 200.00
149 A10 20c maroon 3.00 .75
On cover 200.00
150 A10 40c violet 2.25 2.00
On cover 500.00
151 A10 60c black 2.25 2.00
On cover —
152 A10 80c red brown 8.50 7.25
On cover —
153 A10 1p yellow green 18.00 14.50
On cover —
154 A10 2p slate blue 50.00 22.00
On cover —
Nos. 135-154 (20) 92.60 53.85

Nos. 135-154 exist imperf. Value, set $1,300.

Stamps of 1890-97 Handstamped in Rose or Violet

1898

154A A8 ½m dull violet 27.50 11.00
On cover 300.00
155 A8 1m deep brown 2.00 1.75
On cover 300.00
156 A8 2m yellow green .50 .50
On cover 200.00
157 A8 4m blue green .50 .50
On cover 300.00
158 A8 1c claret 6.00 5.00
On cover 300.00
159 A8 2c orange brown .75 *1.00*
On cover 300.00
160 A8 3c blue 55.00 18.00
On cover 300.00
161 A8 3c claret brn 4.00 3.25
On cover 300.00
162 A8 4c gray brn .80 .80
On cover 300.00
163 A8 4c slate blue 29.00 16.50
On cover

164 A8 5c yellow grn 13.00 8.50
On cover —
165 A8 5c blue 1.00 .80
On cover 300.00
166 A8 6c violet 1.00 .55
On cover 300.00
a. Inverted Ovpt., on cover —
167 A8 8c car rose (V) 2.00 1.00
On cover 200.00
a. Rose overprint 26.00 21.00
On cover 1,000.
168 A8 20c olive gray 2.50 1.40
On cover —
169 A8 40c salmon 4.50 3.25
On cover —
170 A8 80c black 60.00 27.50
On cover 2,000.
Nos. 154A-170 (17) 210.05 101.30

As usual with handstamps there are many inverted, double and similar varieties. Counterfeits of Nos. 154A-170 abound.

Issued under U.S. Administration
PROVISIONAL ISSUES
Ponce Issue

A11

Handstamped

1898 Unwmk. *Imperf.*
200 A11 5c violet, *yellowish* *7,500.* —

The only way No. 200 is known used is handstamped on envelopes. Unused stamps always have a violet control mark. Used envelopes do not have the control mark. The same handstamp used to prepare No. 200 also is known handstamped on an unused envelope, also without the control mark. Research into whether the envelopes represent prepaid postmaster provisional usage is ongoing.

Uses on 2c U.S. stamps on cover were strictly as a cancellation, not as provisional postage.

Dangerous forgeries exist.

Coamo Issue

A12

Types of "5":
I — Curved flag. Pos. 2, 3, 4, 5.
II — Flag turns down at right. Pos. 1, 9, 10.
III — Fancy outlined "5." Pos. 6, 7.
IV — Flag curls into ball at right. Pos. 8.

Coamo Issue
Typeset, setting of 10

1898, Aug. Unwmk. *Imperf.*
201 A12 5c black 700. *1,250.*
On cover *27,500.*

See the Scott U.S. Specialized Catalogue for more detailed listings.

The stamps bear the control mark "F. Santiago" in violet. About 500 were issued.

Dangerous forgeries exist.

Regular Issue

United States Nos. 279, 279Bf, 281, 272 and 282C Overprinted in Black at 36 degree angle

1899 Wmk. 191 *Perf. 12*
210 A87 1c yellow green 6.00 1.40
Never hinged 13.00
a. Overprint at 25 degree angle 8.00 2.25
Never hinged 17.50
211 A88 2c redsh car, type IV 5.00 1.25
Never hinged 11.00
a. Overprint at 25 degree angle, *Mar. 15* 6.50 2.25
Never hinged 14.00
212 A91 5c blue 12.50 2.50
Never hinged 27.50
213 A93 8c violet brown 40.00 17.50
Never hinged 90.00
a. Overprint at 25 degree angle 45.00 19.00
Never hinged 100.00
c. "PORTO RIC" 150.00 110.00
214 A94 10c brown, type I 22.50 6.00
Never hinged 50.00
Nos. 210-214 (5) 86.00 28.65

Misspellings of the overprint on Nos. 210-214 (PORTO RICU, PORTU RICO, FORTO RICO) are actually broken letters.

United States Nos. 279 and 279B Overprinted Diagonally in Black

1900
215 A87 1c yellow green 7.50 1.40
Never hinged 17.50
On cover 50.00
216 A88 2c red, type IV 5.50 2.00
Never hinged 12.50
On cover 50.00
b. Inverted overprint *12,500.*

No. 216b is unique.

Stamps of Puerto Rico were replaced by those of the United States.

POSTAGE DUE STAMPS

United States Nos. J38, J39 and J42 Overprinted in Black at 36 degree angle

1899 Wmk. 191 *Perf. 12*
J1 D2 1c deep claret 22.50 5.50
Never hinged 50.00
On cover 125.00
a. Overprint at 25 degree angle 22.50 7.50
Never hinged 50.00
J2 D2 2c deep claret 20.00 6.00
Never hinged 45.00
On cover 250.00
a. Overprint at 25 degree angle 20.00 7.00
Never hinged 45.00
J3 D2 10c deep claret 180.00 55.00
Never hinged 375.00
On cover —
a. Overprint at 25 degree angle 160.00 75.00
Never hinged 330.00
Nos. J1-J3 (3) 222.50 66.50

WAR TAX STAMPS

Stamps of 1890-94 Overprinted or Surcharged by Handstamp

1898 Unwmk. *Perf. 14*
Purple Overprint or Surcharge
MR1 A8 1c yellow brn 8.00 5.75
On cover —
MR2 A8 2c on 2m orange 3.75 3.00
On cover —
MR3 A8 2c on 5c blue grn 5.00 3.50
On cover —
MR4 A8 2c dark violet .95 .95
On cover 300.00
MR5 A8 2c lilac .90 .90
On cover 300.00
MR6 A8 2c red brown .50 .30
On cover 200.00
MR7 A8 5c blue green 1.90 1.90
On cover 300.00
MR8 A8 5c on 5c bl grn 8.75 6.00
On cover 300.00

Rose Surcharge
MR9 A8 2c on 2m orange 1.90 1.90
On cover 300.00
MR10 A8 5c on 1m dk vio .30 .30
On cover 300.00
MR11 A8 5c on 1m dl bl .85 .85
On cover 300.00

Magenta Surcharge
MR12 A8 5c on 1m dk vio .50 .30
On cover 300.00
MR13 A8 5c on 1m dl bl 3.00 3.00
On cover 300.00
Nos. MR1-MR13 (13) 36.30 28.65

Nos. MR2-MR13 were issued as War Tax Stamps (2c on letters or sealed mail; 5c on telegrams) but, during the early days of the American occupation, they were accepted for ordinary postage.

Double, inverted and similar varieties of overprints are numerous in this issue.

Counterfeit overprints exist.

QUELIMANE

ˌkel-ə-ˈmän-ə

LOCATION — A district of the Mozambique Province in Portuguese East Africa
GOVT. — Part of the Portuguese East Africa Colony
AREA — 39,800 sq. mi.
POP. — 877,000 (approx.)
CAPITAL — Quelimane

This district was formerly a part of Zambezia. Quelimane stamps were replaced by those of Mozambique.

100 Centavos = 1 Escudo

Vasco da Gama Issue

Various Portuguese Colonies Surcharged

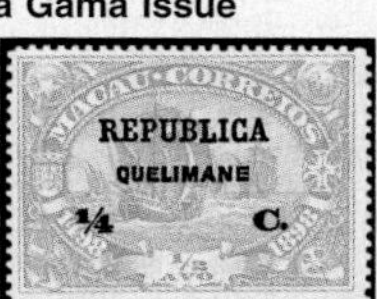

1913 Unwmk. *Perf. 12½ to 16*
On Stamps of Macao
1 CD20 ¼c on ½a bl grn 4.00 4.00
2 CD21 ½c on 1a red 3.00 3.00
3 CD22 1c on 2a red vio 3.00 3.00
4 CD23 2½c on 4a yel grn 3.00 3.00
5 CD24 5c on 8a dk bl 3.00 3.00
6 CD25 7½c on 12a vio brn 5.00 *5.00*
7 CD26 10c on 16a bis brn 3.00 3.00
a. Inverted surcharge 50.00
8 CD27 15c on 24a bister 3.00 3.00
Nos. 1-8 (8) 27.00 27.00
Set, never hinged 42.50

On Stamps of Portuguese Africa
9 CD20 ¼c on 2½r bl grn 3.00 *3.00*
10 CD21 ½c on 5r red 3.00 *3.00*
11 CD22 1c on 10r red vio 3.00 *3.00*
12 CD23 2½c on 25r yel grn 3.00 *3.00*
13 CD24 5c on 50r dk bl 3.00 *3.00*
14 CD25 7½c on 75r vio brn 5.00 *4.50*
15 CD26 10c on 100r bister 3.25 *3.00*
16 CD27 15c on 150r bister 3.25 *3.00*
Nos. 9-16 (8) 26.50 25.50
Set, never hinged 40.00

On Stamps of Timor
17 CD20 ¼c on ½a bl grn 3.00 *3.00*
18 CD21 ½c on 1a red 3.00 *3.00*
19 CD22 1c on 2a red vio 3.00 *3.00*
20 CD23 2½c on 4a yel grn 3.00 *3.00*
21 CD24 5c on 8a dk bl 3.00 *3.00*
22 CD25 7½c on 12a vio brn 5.00 *4.50*
23 CD26 10c on 16a bis brn 3.25 *3.00*
24 CD27 15c on 24a bister 3.25 *3.00*
Nos. 17-24 (8) 26.50 25.50
Set, never hinged 42.50
Nos. 1-24 (24) 80.00 78.00
Set, never hinged 125.00

Ceres — A1

1914 Typo. *Perf. 15x14*
Name and Value in Black
Chalky Paper
25 A1 ¼c olive brown 2.00 *2.75*
Never hinged 2.75
26 A1 ½c black 2.00 *2.75*
Never hinged 4.50
27 A1 1c blue green 3.00 *2.75*
Never hinged 6.75
a. Imperf.
28 A1 1½c lilac brown 3.00 *3.00*
Never hinged 6.75
29 A1 2c carmine 3.00 *3.00*
Never hinged 6.75
30 A1 2½c light violet 2.00 *1.50*
Never hinged 4.25
31 A1 5c deep blue 3.00 *3.00*
Never hinged 6.75
32 A1 7½c yellow brown 5.00 *3.00*
Never hinged 10.00
33 A1 8c slate 5.00 *3.00*
Never hinged 10.00
34 A1 10c orange brown 5.00 *3.00*
Never hinged 10.00
35 A1 15c plum 5.00 *4.50*
Never hinged 10.00
36 A1 20c yellow green 8.00 *2.50*
Never hinged 15.00
37 A1 30c brown, *green* 9.00 *8.00*
Never hinged 17.00
38 A1 40c brown, *pink* 9.00 *9.00*
Never hinged 17.00
39 A1 50c orange, *salmon* 10.00 *10.00*
Never hinged 18.00
40 A1 1e green, *blue* 12.50 *11.00*
Never hinged 20.00
Nos. 25-40 (16) 86.50 *72.75*

Ordinary Paper
25B A1 ¼c olive brown 1.75 *2.75*
Never hinged 2.50
27B A1 1c blue green 2.50 *2.75*
Never hinged 4.00
32B A1 7½c yellow brown 4.00 3.00
Never hinged 6.00
34B A1 10c orange brown 3.00 3.00
Never hinged 5.00
36B A1 20c yellow green 5.00 *2.50*
Never hinged 8.00
Nos. 25B-36B (5) 16.25 14.00

REUNION

LOCATION — An island in the Indian Ocean about 400 miles east of Madagascar
GOVT. — French Colony
AREA — 970 sq. mi.
POP. — 490,000 (est. 1974)
CAPITAL — St. Denis

100 Centimes = 1 Franc

A1

A2

1852 Unwmk. Typo. *Imperf.*

1 A1 15c black, *blue* *39,000.* *25,000.*
On cover *45,000.*
2 A2 30c black, *blue* *39,000.* *25,000.*
On cover *35,000.*

Four varieties of each value.

The reprints are printed on a more bluish paper than the originals. They have a frame of a thick and a thin line, instead of one thick and two thin lines. Value, $62.50 each.

Stamps of French Colonies Surcharged or Overprinted in Black

a

Overprint Type "a"

1885

3 A1(a) 5c on 40c org, *yelsh* 450.00 375.00
On cover 1,200.
a. Inverted surcharge 2,250. 2,100.
b. Double surcharge 2,250. 2,100.
4 A1(a) 25c on 40c org, *yelsh* 70.00 55.00
On cover 950.00
a. Inverted surcharge 1,000. 900.00
b. Double surcharge 1,000. 900.00
5 A5(a) 5c on 30c brn, *yelsh* 70.00 57.50
On cover 950.00
a. "5" inverted 3,500. 3,000.
b. Double surcharge 1,100. 900.00
c. Inverted surcharge 1,000. 900.00
6 A4(a) 5c on 40c org, *yelsh* (I) 62.50 45.00
On cover 950.00
a. 5c on 40c org, *yelsh* (II) 2,500. 2,500.
b. Inverted surcharge (I) 1,100. 900.00
c. Double surcharge (I) 1,100. 900.00
7 A8(a) 5c on 30c brn, *yelsh* 22.50 18.00
On cover 950.00
8 A8(a) 5c on 40c ver, *straw* 135.00 115.00
On cover 950.00
a. Inverted surcharge 950.00 850.00
b. Double surcharge 925.00 850.00
9 A8(a) 10c on 40c ver, *straw* 27.50 22.50
On cover 950.00
a. Inverted surcharge 950.00 850.00
b. Double surcharge 950.00 850.00
10 A8(a) 20c on 30c brn, *yelsh* 90.00 75.00
On cover 1,050.

b

Overprint Type "b" With or Without Accent on "E"

1891

11 A4 40c org, *yelsh* (I) 575.00 550.00
On cover *1,750.*
a. 40c orange, *yelsh* (II) *6,750.* *6,750.*
b. Double overprint 750.00 750.00
12 A7 80c car, *pnksh* 80.00 62.50
Never hinged 150.00
On cover *400.00*
13 A8 30c brn, *yelsh* 52.50 52.50
Never hinged 100.00
On cover *325.00*
14 A8 40c ver, *straw* 42.50 42.50
Never hinged 80.00
On cover 825.00
a. With accent on "E" 260.00 210.00
15 A8 75c car, *rose* 475.00 475.00
a. With accent on "E" 1,200. 1,200.
16 A8 1fr brnz grn, *straw* 62.50 52.50
Never hinged 110.00
On cover *325.00*
a. With accent on "E" 425.00 425.00

Perf. 14x13½

17 A9 1c blk, *lil bl* 4.75 4.00
Never hinged 10.50
On cover 475.00
a. Inverted overprint 60.00 60.00
Never hinged 125.00
b. Double overprint 52.50 52.50
Never hinged 110.00
18 A9 2c brn, *buff* 6.50 5.00
Never hinged 13.50
On cover 475.00
a. Inverted overprint 40.00 40.00
Never hinged 85.00
19 A9 4c claret, *lav* 10.00 8.00
Never hinged 21.00
On cover 475.00
a. Inverted overprint 72.50 72.50
Never hinged 150.00
20 A9 5c grn, *grnsh* 11.50 9.00
Never hinged 22.50
On cover 300.00
a. Inverted overprint 60.00 60.00
Never hinged 125.00
b. Double overprint 60.00 57.50
Never hinged 125.00
21 A9 10c blk, *lav* 40.00 8.00
Never hinged 80.00
On cover 300.00
a. Inverted overprint 90.00 80.00
Never hinged 180.00
b. Double overprint 100.00 80.00
Never hinged 200.00
22 A9 15c blue 57.50 9.00
On cover 300.00
a. Inverted overprint 120.00 110.00
23 A9 20c red, *grn* 45.00 30.00
Never hinged 85.00
On cover 190.00
a. Inverted overprint 175.00 150.00
b. Double overprint 175.00 150.00
24 A9 25c blk, *rose* 50.00 7.25
Never hinged 92.50
On cover 240.00
a. Inverted overprint 125.00 120.00
25 A9 35c dp vio, *yel* 45.00 35.00
Never hinged 85.00
On cover 300.00
b. Inverted overprint 180.00 175.00
26 A9 40c red, *straw* 72.50 62.50
Never hinged 150.00
On cover 475.00
a. Inverted overprint 240.00 225.00
27 A9 75c car, *rose* 675.00 575.00
On cover 1,100.
a. Inverted overprint 1,600. 1,400.
28 A9 1fr brnz grn, *straw* 575.00 500.00
On cover 1,500.
a. Inverted overprint 1,600. 1,500.
b. Double overprint 1,500. 1,400.

For surcharges see Nos. 29-33, 53-55.

Overprinted "RUNION"

17c A9 1c blk, *lil bl* 27.50 27.50
Never hinged 57.50
18c A9 2c brn, *buff* 32.50 32.50
Never hinged 70.00
19c A9 4c claret, *lav* 37.50 37.50
Never hinged 80.00
20c A9 5c grn, *grnsh* 37.50 32.50
Never hinged 80.00
21c A9 10c blk, *lav* 72.50 70.00
Never hinged 150.00
22c A9 15c blue 90.00 85.00
Never hinged 180.00
23c A9 20c red, *grn* 100.00 100.00
24c A9 25c blk, *rose* 80.00 70.00
Never hinged 160.00
25c A9 35c dp vio, *yel* 72.50 72.50
Never hinged 150.00
26c A9 40c red, *straw* 240.00 240.00
27c A9 75c car, *rose* *1,600.* *1,500.*
28c A9 1fr brnz grn, *straw* *1,600.* *1,500.*

Overprinted "REUNIONR"

13d A8 30c brn, *yelsh* 525.00 525.00
14d A8 40c ver, *straw* 500.00 500.00
15d A8 75c car, *rose* *1,600.* *1,600.*
16d A8 1fr brnz grn, *straw* *1,000.* *1,000.*
17d A9 1c blk, *lil bl* 32.50 32.50
Never hinged 70.00
18d A9 2c brn, *buff* 32.50 32.50
Never hinged 70.00
19d A9 4c claret, *lav* 37.50 37.50
Never hinged 80.00
20d A9 5c grn, *grnsh* 37.50 32.50
Never hinged 80.00
21d A9 10c blk, *lav* 72.50 70.00
Never hinged 150.00
22d A9 15c blue 90.00 85.00
Never hinged 190.00
23d A9 20c red, *grn* 100.00 100.00
24d A9 25c blk, *rose* 80.00 70.00
Never hinged 160.00
25d A9 35c dp vio, *yel* 72.50 72.50
Never hinged 150.00
26d A9 40c red, *straw* 200.00 200.00
27d A9 75c car, *rose* *1,600.* *1,500.*
28d A9 1fr brnz grn, *straw* *1,600.* *1,500.*

Overprinted "REUNIOU"

17e A9 1c blk, *lil bl* 35.00 35.00
Never hinged 72.50
20e A9 5c grn, *grnsh* 35.00 35.00
Never hinged 80.00
24e A9 25c blk, *rose* 97.50 90.00
Never hinged 190.00
27e A9 75c car, *rose* *1,700.* *1,500.*
28e A9 1fr brnz grn, *straw* *1,750.* *1,500.*

Overprinted "REUNOIN"

17f A9 1c blk, *lil bl* 32.50 15.00
Never hinged 70.00
18f A9 2c brn, *buff* 32.50 15.00
Never hinged 70.00
19f A9 4c claret, *lav* 35.00 20.00
Never hinged 80.00
20f A9 5c grn, *grnsh* 40.00 17.50
Never hinged 85.00
21f A9 10c blk, *lav* 72.50 45.00
Never hinged 150.00
22f A9 15c blue 90.00 50.00
Never hinged 180.00
23f A9 20c red, *grn* 100.00 60.00
24f A9 25c blk, *rose* 100.00 45.00
Never hinged 200.00
25f A9 35c dp vio, *yel* 90.00 45.00
Never hinged 190.00
26f A9 40c red, *straw* 225.00 225.00
27f A9 75c car, *rose* *1,750.* *1,500.*
28f A9 1fr brnz grn, *straw* *1,750.* *1,500.*

Overprinted "RUENION"

15g A8 75c car, *rose* *2,350.* *2,350.*
17g A9 1c blk, *lil bl* 27.50 27.50
Never hinged 55.00
18g A9 2c brn, *buff* 45.00 45.00
Never hinged 92.50
19g A9 4c claret, *lav* 45.00 45.00
Never hinged 92.50
20g A9 5c grn, *grnsh* 72.50 65.00
Never hinged 150.00
21g A9 10c blk, *lav* 80.00 72.50
Never hinged 160.00
22g A9 15c blue 110.00 100.00
26g A9 40c red, *straw* 200.00 200.00

Overprinted "EUNION"

11h A4 40c org, *yelsh* (I) *4,500.* *4,500.*
12h A7 80c car, *pnksh* *650.00* *450.00*
14h A8 40c ver, *straw* 190.00 125.00
15h A8 75c car, *rose* *2,400.* *1,750.*
17h A9 1c blk, *lil bl* 27.50 15.00
Never hinged 55.00
18h A9 2c brn, *buff* 37.50 15.00
Never hinged 80.00
19h A9 4c claret, *lav* 52.50 27.50
Never hinged 110.00
20h A9 5c grn, *grnsh* 60.00 27.50
Never hinged 125.00
21h A9 10c blk, *lav* 80.00 72.50
Never hinged 160.00
22h A9 15c blue 90.00 50.00
Never hinged 180.00
23h A9 20c red, *grn* 90.00 50.00
Never hinged 180.00
24h A9 25c blk, *rose* 110.00 55.00
25h A9 35c dp vio, *yel* 90.00 50.00
Never hinged 180.00
26h A9 40c red, *straw* 200.00 110.00
27h A9 75c car, *rose* 1,750. 1,500.
28h A9 1fr brnz grn, *straw* 1,750. 1,500.

Overprinted "ERUNION"

17i A9 1c blk, *lil bl* 27.50 27.50
Never hinged 55.00
18i A9 2c brn, *buff* 32.50 32.50
Never hinged 70.00
19i A9 4c claret, *lav* 52.50 52.50
Never hinged 110.00
20i A9 5c grn, *grnsh* 60.00 57.50
Never hinged 125.00
21i A9 10c blk, *lav* 72.50 72.50
Never hinged 150.00
22i A9 15c blue 90.00 72.50
Never hinged 180.00
23i A9 20c red, *grn* 110.00 100.00
24i A9 25c blk, *rose* 110.00 90.00
Never hinged 225.00
25i A9 35c dp vio, *yel* 90.00 90.00
Never hinged 180.00
26i A9 40c red, *straw* 200.00 200.00
27i A9 75c car, *rose* 1,750. 1,500.
28i A9 1fr brnz grn, *straw* 1,750. 1,500.

Overprinted "REUNIN"

18j A9 2c brn, *buff* 32.50 32.50
Never hinged 70.00
23j A9 20c red, *grn* 87.50 80.00
Never hinged 70.00

For surcharges see Nos. 29-33, 53-55.

No. 23 with Additional Surcharge in Black

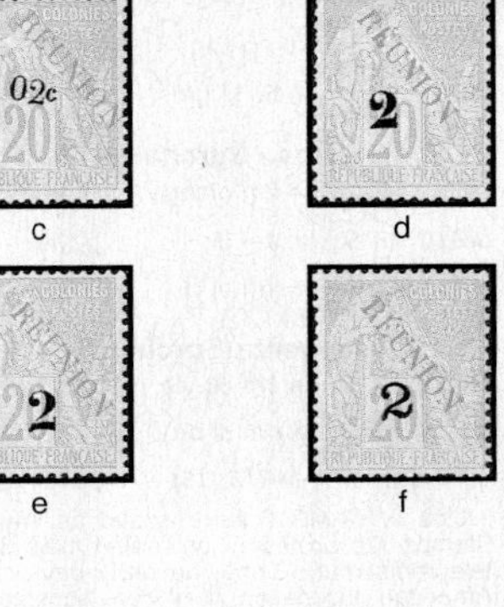

c d e f

1891

29 A9(c) 02c on 20c red, *grn* 14.50 14.50
Never hinged 27.50
On cover 300.00
a. Inverted surcharge 90.00 90.00
Never hinged 140.00
b. No "c" after "02" 57.50 57.50
Never hinged 100.00
c. Overprinted "RUNION" 90.00 90.00
Never hinged 180.00
30 A9(c) 15c on 20c red, *grn* 18.00 18.00
Never hinged 35.00
On cover 300.00
a. Inverted surcharge 70.00 70.00
Never hinged 125.00
b. No "c" after "15" 60.00 60.00
Never hinged 120.00
c. Overprinted "RUNION" 140.00 140.00
31 A9(d) 2c on 20c red, *grn* 5.00 5.00
Never hinged 10.00
On cover 300.00
32 A9(e) 2c on 20c red, *grn* 6.00 5.75
Never hinged 11.50
On cover 300.00
a. Overprinted "RUENION" 52.50 52.50
Never hinged 110.00
b. Overprinted "RUNOIN" 52.50 52.50
Never hinged 110.00
33 A9(f) 2c on 20c red, *grn* 10.00 10.00
On cover 300.00
Nos. 29-33 (5) 53.50 53.25

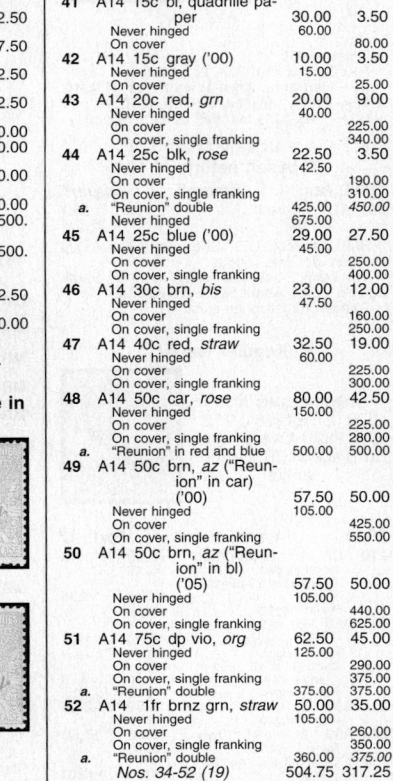

Navigation and Commerce — A14

1892-1905 Typo. *Perf. 14x13½*
Name of Colony in Blue or Carmine

34 A14 1c blk, *lil bl* 2.00 1.25
Never hinged 3.25
On cover 125.00
35 A14 2c brn, *buff* 2.00 1.25
Never hinged 3.25
On cover 125.00
36 A14 4c claret, *lav* 3.25 2.25
Never hinged 4.50
On cover 125.00
37 A14 5c grn, *grnsh* 7.25 2.25
Never hinged 12.50
On cover 105.00
38 A14 5c yel grn ('00) 1.75 1.75
Never hinged 2.40
On cover 12.50
39 A14 10c blk, *lav* 9.50 3.50
Never hinged 17.50
On cover 92.50
40 A14 10c red ('00) 4.50 4.50
Never hinged 5.50
On cover 25.00
41 A14 15c bl, quadrille paper 30.00 3.50
Never hinged 60.00
On cover 80.00
42 A14 15c gray ('00) 10.00 3.50
Never hinged 15.00
On cover 25.00
43 A14 20c red, *grn* 20.00 9.00
Never hinged 40.00
On cover 225.00
On cover, single franking 340.00
44 A14 25c blk, *rose* 22.50 3.50
Never hinged 42.50
On cover 190.00
On cover, single franking 310.00
a. "Reunion" double 425.00 *450.00*
Never hinged 675.00
45 A14 25c blue ('00) 29.00 27.50
Never hinged 45.00
On cover 250.00
On cover, single franking 400.00
46 A14 30c brn, *bis* 23.00 12.00
Never hinged 47.50
On cover 160.00
On cover, single franking 250.00
47 A14 40c red, *straw* 32.50 19.00
Never hinged 60.00
On cover 225.00
On cover, single franking 300.00
48 A14 50c car, *rose* 80.00 42.50
Never hinged 150.00
On cover 225.00
On cover, single franking 280.00
a. "Reunion" in red and blue 500.00 500.00
49 A14 50c brn, *az* ("Reunion" in car) ('00) 57.50 50.00
Never hinged 105.00
On cover 425.00
On cover, single franking 550.00
50 A14 50c brn, *az* ("Reunion" in bl) ('05) 57.50 50.00
Never hinged 105.00
On cover 440.00
On cover, single franking 625.00
51 A14 75c dp vio, *org* 62.50 45.00
Never hinged 125.00
On cover 290.00
On cover, single franking 375.00
a. "Reunion" double 375.00 375.00
52 A14 1fr brnz grn, *straw* 50.00 35.00
Never hinged 105.00
On cover 260.00
On cover, single franking 350.00
a. "Reunion" double 360.00 *375.00*
Nos. 34-52 (19) 504.75 317.25

Perf. 13½x14 stamps are counterfeits.

For surcharges and overprint see Nos. 56-59, 99-106, Q1.

French Colonies No. 52 Surcharged in Black

g

h

j

1893

53 A9(g) 2c on 20c red, *grn* 3.25 3.25
Never hinged 5.50
On cover 250.00
54 A9(h) 2c on 20c red, *grn* 6.00 6.00
Never hinged 9.50
On cover 250.00
55 A9(j) 2c on 20c red, *grn* 22.50 22.50
Never hinged 45.00
On cover 250.00
Nos. 53-55 (3) 31.75 31.75

Reunion Nos. 47-48, 51-52 Surcharged in Black

1901

56 A14 5c on 40c red, *straw* 7.00 7.00
Never hinged 11.00
On cover 60.00
a. Inverted surcharge 47.50 47.50
Never hinged 92.50
b. No bar 240.00 240.00
c. Thin "5" — —
d. "5" inverted 1,400. 1,200.
57 A14 5c on 50c car, *rose* 7.75 7.25
Never hinged 13.50
On cover 80.00
a. Inverted surcharge 47.50 47.50
Never hinged 92.50
b. No bar 240.00 240.00
c. Thin "5" —
58 A14 15c on 75c vio, *org* 22.50 22.50
Never hinged 37.50
On cover 150.00
a. Inverted surcharge 57.50 57.50
Never hinged 105.00
b. No bar 240.00 240.00
c. Thin "5" and small "1" 47.50 47.50
Never hinged 87.50
d. As "c," inverted 800.00 800.00
59 A14 15c on 1fr brnz grn, *straw* 19.00 19.00
Never hinged 35.00
On cover 150.00
a. Inverted surcharge 57.50 57.50
Never hinged 105.00
b. No bar 240.00 240.00
c. Thin "5" and small "1" 47.50 47.50
Never hinged 85.00
d. As "c," inverted —
Nos. 56-59 (4) 56.25 55.75

Map of Réunion
A19

Coat of Arms and View of St. Denis
A20

View of St. Pierre
A21

1907-30 **Typo.**

60 A19 1c vio & lt rose .30 .30
Never hinged .45
On cover 42.50
a. 1c violet & dark rose .45 .45
Never hinged .70
On cover 42.50
61 A19 2c brn & ultra .30 .30
Never hinged .45
On cover 42.50
On cover, single franking 400.00
62 A19 4c ol grn & red .40 .40
Never hinged .65
On cover 42.50
a. Center double 225.00
Never hinged 350.00
63 A19 5c grn & red 1.35 .40
Never hinged 2.00
On cover 50.00
64 A19 5c org & vio ('22) .30 .30
Never hinged .55
On cover 12.50
65 A19 10c car & grn 2.75 .40
Never hinged 4.00
On cover 19.00
66 A19 10c grn ('22) .30 .30
Never hinged .55
On cover 10.00
a. 10c green & blue green 14.00 14.00
Never hinged 21.00
67 A19 10c brn red & org red, *bluish* ('26) .70 .70
Never hinged 1.00
On cover 12.50
68 A19 15c blk & ultra ('17) .55 .40
Never hinged .80
On cover 12.50
a. Center double 250.00 250.00
Never hinged 400.00
69 A19 15c gray grn & bl grn ('26) .40 .40
Never hinged .70
On cover 8.75
70 A19 15c bl & lt red ('28) .55 .45
Never hinged .70
On cover 10.00
71 A20 20c gray grn & bl grn .45 .45
Never hinged .70
On cover 15.00
a. Center omitted 1,100. 1,100.
72 A20 25c dp bl & vio brn 7.00 4.00
Never hinged 11.00
On cover 29.00
On cover, single franking 80.00
73 A20 25c lt brn & bl ('22) .55 .55
Never hinged .85
On cover 8.75
74 A20 30c yel brn & grn 1.50 1.00
Never hinged 2.10
On cover 30.00
On cover, single franking 92.50
75 A20 30c rose & pale rose ('22) 1.50 1.50
Never hinged 2.25
On cover 22.50
On cover, single franking 80.00
76 A20 30c gray & car rose ('26) .55 .55
Never hinged .70
On cover 10.00
77 A20 30c dp grn & yel grn ('28) 1.20 1.20
Never hinged 1.75
On cover 10.00
78 A20 35c ol grn & bl 1.75 1.10
Never hinged 2.50
On cover 37.50
On cover, single franking 105.00
79 A20 40c gray grn & brn ('25) .70 .70
Never hinged 1.00
On cover 19.00
80 A20 45c vio & car rose 1.90 1.10
Never hinged 2.75
On cover 25.00
On cover, single franking 62.50
81 A20 45c red brn & ver ('25) .90 .90
Never hinged 1.25
On cover 22.50
82 A20 45c vio & red org ('28) 3.00 2.75
Never hinged 4.50
On cover 12.50
83 A20 50c red brn & ultra 5.00 1.75
Never hinged 6.50
On cover 37.50
On cover, single franking 80.00
84 A20 50c bl & ultra ('22) 1.40 1.40
Never hinged 2.10
On cover 32.50
On cover, single franking 80.00
85 A20 50c yel & vio ('26) 1.10 1.10
Never hinged 1.75
On cover 30.00
86 A20 60c dk bl & yel brn ('25) 1.10 1.10
Never hinged 1.75
On cover 32.50
On cover, single franking 92.50
87 A20 65c vio & lt bl ('28) 1.60 1.40
Never hinged 2.00
On cover 15.00
88 A20 75c red & car rose .80 .70
Never hinged 1.25
On cover 42.50
On cover, single franking 92.50
89 A20 75c ol brn & red vio ('28) 2.50 2.25
Never hinged 3.25
On cover 12.50
90 A20 90c brn red & brt red ('30) 9.00 8.25
Never hinged 12.00
On cover 50.00
On cover, single franking 92.50
91 A21 1fr ol grn & bl 1.50 1.40
Never hinged 2.00
On cover 50.00
On cover, single franking 105.00
92 A21 1fr blue ('25) .95 .95
Never hinged 1.60
On cover 25.00
On cover, single franking 62.50
93 A21 1fr yel brn & lav ('28) 1.50 .70
Never hinged 2.40
On cover 32.50
On cover, single franking 62.50
94 A21 1.10fr org brn & rose lil ('28) 1.50 1.40
Never hinged 2.00
On cover 62.50
On cover, single franking 190.00
95 A21 1.50fr dk bl & ultra ('30) 16.00 16.00
Never hinged 19.00
On cover 75.00
On cover, single franking 110.00
96 A21 2fr red & grn 6.75 4.25
Never hinged 7.25
On cover 55.00
On cover, single franking 92.50
97 A21 3fr red vio ('30) 14.50 9.50
Never hinged 17.50
On cover 67.50
On cover, single franking 110.00
98 A21 5fr car & vio brn 11.50 6.75
Never hinged 14.50
On cover 87.50
On cover, single franking 160.00
Nos. 60-98 (39) 105.60 79.05

For surcharges see Nos. 107-121, 178-180 (in Scott Standard catalogue, Vol. 5), B1-B3.

Stamps of 1892-1900 Surcharged in Black or Carmine

1912

Spacing between figures of surcharge 1.5mm (5c), 2mm (10c)

99 A14 5c on 2c brn, *buff* 1.60 1.60
Never hinged 2.25
On cover 42.50
100 A14 5c on 15c gray (C) 1.40 1.40
Never hinged 2.25
On cover 42.50
a. Inverted surcharge 210.00 210.00
101 A14 5c on 20c red, *grn* 2.40 2.40
Never hinged 4.00
On cover 105.00
102 A14 5c on 25c blk, *rose* (C) 1.60 1.60
Never hinged 2.50
On cover 92.50
103 A14 5c on 30c brn, *bis* (C) 1.40 1.40
Never hinged 2.40
On cover 80.00
104 A14 10c on 40c red, *straw* 1.40 1.40
Never hinged 2.40
On cover 80.00
105 A14 10c on 50c brn, *az* (C) 5.75 5.75
Never hinged 9.50
On cover 105.00
106 A14 10c on 75c dp vio, *org* 9.50 9.50
Never hinged 14.50
On cover 110.00
Nos. 99-106 (8) 25.05 25.05

Spacing between figures of surcharge 2.25mm (5c), 2.75mm (10c)

99a A14 5c on 2c brn, *buff* 30.00 30.00
Never hinged 55.00
100b A14 5c on 15c gray (C) 30.00 30.00
Never hinged 55.00
101a A14 5c on 20c red, *grn* 325.00 325.00
Never hinged 550.00
102a A14 5c on 25c blk, *rose* (C) 105.00 105.00
Never hinged 190.00
103a A14 5c on 30c brn, *bis* (C) 105.00 105.00
Never hinged 190.00
104a A14 10c on 40c red, *straw* 65.00 65.00
Never hinged 120.00
105a A14 10c on 50c brn, *az* (C) 105.00 105.00
Never hinged 190.00
106a A14 10c on 75c dp vio, *org* 275.00 275.00
Never hinged 450.00
Nos. 99a-106a (8) 1,040. 1,040.

Se-tenant Pairs, Both Ovpt. Settings

99b A4 5c on 2c, #59 + #59a 35.00 35.00
Never hinged 65.00
100c A14 5c on 15c, #100 + #100a 35.00 35.00
Never hinged 65.00
101b A14 5c on 20c, #101 + #101a 375.00 375.00
Never hinged 600.00
102b A14 5c on 25c, #102 + #102a 140.00 140.00
Never hinged 225.00
103b A14 5c on 30c, #103 + #103a 140.00 140.00
Never hinged 225.00
104b A14 10c on 40c, #104 + #104a 72.50 72.50
Never hinged 130.00
105b A14 10c on 50c, #105 + #105a 140.00 140.00
Never hinged 225.00
106b A14 10c on 75c, #106 + #106a 300.00 300.00
Never hinged 475.00
Nos. 99b-106b (8) 1,238. 1,238.

No. 62 Surcharged

1917

107 A19 1c on 4c ol grn & red 2.00 2.00
Never hinged 2.75
On cover 62.50
a. Inverted surcharge 80.00 80.00
Never hinged 140.00
On cover 275.00
b. Double surcharge 70.00 70.00
Never hinged 100.00
c. In pair with unsurcharged #62 625.00 625.00

Stamps and Types of 1907-30 Surcharged in Black or Red

1922-33

108 A20 40c on 20c grn & yel .80 .80
Never hinged 1.10
On cover 10.00
a. Double surcharge, one inverted 175.00 175.00
Never hinged 300.00
b. Center double 175.00 175.00
Never hinged 300.00
c. Surcharge omitted 1,200. 1,200.
109 A20 50c on 45c red brn & ver ('33) 1.20 1.20
Never hinged 2.005
On cover 8.75
109A A20 50c on 45c vio & red org ('33) 325.00 275.00
Never hinged 500.00
b. Double surcharge 1,750.
Never hinged 2,500.
110 A20 50c on 65c vio & lt bl ('33) 1.20 1.20
Never hinged 2.00
On cover 10.00
111 A20 60c on 75c red & rose .85 .85
Never hinged 1.25
On cover 25.00
On cover, single franking 62.50
a. Double surcharge 225.00 225.00
Never hinged 350.00

112 A19 65c on 15c blk & ultra (R) ('25) 2.00 2.00
Never hinged 2.90
On cover 42.50
On cover, single franking 80.00

113 A19 85c on 15c blk & ultra (R) ('25) 2.00 2.00
Never hinged 2.90
On cover 42.50
On cover, single franking 92.50

114 A20 85c on 75c red & cer ('25) 2.25 2.25
Never hinged 3.00
On cover 42.50
On cover, single franking 92.50

115 A20 90c on 75 brn red & rose red ('27) 2.25 2.25
Never hinged 2.90
On cover 37.50
On cover, single franking 92.50

Nos. 108-109,110-115 (8) 12.55 12.55

Stamps and Type of 1907-30 Srchd. in Black or Red

1924-27

116 A21 25c on 5fr car & brn 1.10 1.10
Never hinged 1.50
On cover 8.75
a. Double surcharge 110.00
Never hinged 160.00

117 A21 1.25fr on 1fr bl (R) ('26) 1.10 1.10
Never hinged 1.50
On cover 32.50
On cover, single franking 80.00
a. Double surcharge 125.00
Never hinged 180.00

118 A21 1.50fr on 1fr ind & ultra, *bluish* ('27) 1.50 1.50
Never hinged 2.10
On cover 30.00
On cover, single franking 50.00
a. Double surcharge 140.00
Never hinged 210.00
b. Surcharge omitted 200.00
Never hinged 300.00

119 A21 3fr on 5fr dl red & lt bl ('27) 4.25 3.00
Never hinged 5.25
On cover 40.00
On cover, single franking 105.00
a. No period after "F" 14.50 14.50
Never hinged 24.00

120 A21 10fr on 5fr bl grn & brn red ('27) 19.50 17.00
Never hinged 25.00
On cover 62.50
On cover, single franking 140.00

121 A21 20fr on 5fr blk brn & rose ('27) 24.00 19.00
Never hinged 30.00
On cover 75.00
On cover, single franking 170.00

Nos. 116-121 (6) 51.45 42.70

Colonial Exposition Issue

Common Design Types

1931 **Engr.** ***Perf. 12½***

Name of Country Typo. in Black

122 CD70 40c dp green 5.50 5.50
Never hinged 7.50
On cover 50.00

123 CD71 50c violet 5.50 5.50
Never hinged 7.50
On cover 42.50

124 CD72 90c red orange 5.50 5.50
Never hinged 7.50
On cover 80.00
On cover, single franking 125.00

125 CD73 1.50fr dull blue 5.50 5.50
Never hinged 7.50
On cover 75.00
On cover, single franking 110.00

Nos. 122-125 (4) 22.00 22.00

Cascade of Salazie — A22

Waterfowl Lake and Anchain Peak — A23

Léon Dierx Museum, St. Denis — A24

Perf. 12, 12½ and Compound

1933-40 **Engr.**

126 A22 1c violet .25 .25
Never hinged .40
On cover 30.00

127 A22 2c dark brown .25 .25
Never hinged .40
On cover 30.00

128 A22 3c rose vio ('40) .25 .25
Never hinged .40
On cover 37.50

129 A22 4c olive green .25 .25
Never hinged .40
On cover 30.00

130 A22 5c red orange .25 .25
Never hinged .40
On cover 25.00

131 A22 10c ultramarine .25 .25
Never hinged .40
On cover 22.50

132 A22 15c black .25 .25
Never hinged .40
On cover 21.00

133 A22 20c indigo .30 .25
Never hinged .45
On cover 10.00

134 A22 25c red brown .40 .30
Never hinged .55
On cover 19.00

135 A22 30c dark green .40 .40
Never hinged .55
On cover 19.00

136 A23 35c green ('38) .55 .55
Never hinged .80
On cover 25.00

137 A23 40c ultramarine .55 .55
Never hinged .80
On cover 5.00

138 A23 40c brn blk ('40) .40 .40
Never hinged .55
On cover 30.00

139 A23 45c red violet 1.00 1.00
Never hinged 1.20
On cover 12.50

140 A23 45c green ('40) .45 .45
Never hinged .65
On cover 30.00

141 A23 50c red .30 .25
Never hinged .45
On cover 5.00

142 A23 55c brn org ('38) 1.50 1.00
Never hinged 1.80
On cover 5.00

143 A23 60c dull bl ('40) .45 .45
Never hinged .65
On cover 25.00

144 A23 65c olive green 1.10 .80
Never hinged 1.25
On cover 7.50

145 A23 70c ol grn ('40) .65 .65
Never hinged .85
On cover 10.00

146 A23 75c dark brown 5.00 4.25
Never hinged 6.00
On cover 15.00

147 A23 80c black ('38) 1.00 .80
Never hinged 1.25
On cover 10.00

148 A23 90c carmine 2.50 2.10
Never hinged 3.50
On cover 22.50
On cover, single franking 62.50

149 A23 90c dl rose vio ('39) 1.00 1.00
Never hinged 1.20
On cover 8.75

150 A23 1fr green 2.00 .70
Never hinged 2.50
On cover 15.00
On cover, single franking 37.50

151 A23 1fr dk car ('38) 2.50 .70
Never hinged 3.50
On cover 16.00
On cover, single franking 37.50

152 A23 1fr black ('40) .70 .70
Never hinged 1.10
On cover 12.50

153 A24 1.25fr orange brown .70 .55
Never hinged 1.10
On cover 10.00
On cover, single franking 25.00

154 A24 1.25fr brt car rose ('39) 1.00 1.00
Never hinged 1.20
On cover 42.50
On cover, single franking 62.50

155 A22 1.40fr pck bl ('40) 1.00 1.00
Never hinged 1.20
On cover 37.50
On cover, single franking 62.50

156 A24 1.50fr ultramarine .40 .40
Never hinged .55
On cover 12.50
On cover, single franking 30.00

157 A22 1.60fr dk car rose ('40) 1.40 1.40
Never hinged 1.65
On cover 42.50
On cover, single franking 75.00

158 A24 1.75fr olive green 1.00 .65
Never hinged 1.25
On cover 19.00
On cover, single franking 42.50

159 A22 1.75fr dk bl ('38) 1.40 .85
Never hinged 2.10
On cover 19.00
On cover, single franking 42.50

160 A24 2fr vermilion .55 .55
Never hinged .80
On cover 25.00
On cover, single franking 62.50

161 A22 2.25fr brt ultra ('39) 2.00 2.00
Never hinged 2.40
On cover 42.50
On cover, single franking 80.00

162 A22 2.50fr chnt ('40) 1.40 1.40
Never hinged 1.65
On cover 50.00
On cover, single franking 75.00

163 A24 3fr purple .55 .55
Never hinged .80
On cover 30.00
On cover, single franking 62.50

164 A24 5fr magenta .55 .55
Never hinged .80
On cover 37.50
On cover, single franking 67.50

165 A24 10fr dark blue 1.10 1.10
Never hinged 1.40
On cover 50.00
On cover, single franking 92.50

166 A24 20fr red brown 1.50 1.50
Never hinged 2.25
On cover 60.00
On cover, single franking 105.00

Nos. 126-166 (41) 39.05 32.55

For overprints and surcharges see Nos. 177A, 181-220, 223 in Scott Standard catalogue, Vol. 5; C1.

Paris International Exposition Issue

Common Design Types

1937 ***Perf. 13***

167 CD74 20c dp vio 2.25 2.25
Never hinged 3.50
On cover 62.50

168 CD75 30c dk grn 2.25 2.25
Never hinged 3.50
On cover 50.00

169 CD76 40c car rose 2.25 2.25
Never hinged 3.50
On cover 42.50

170 CD77 50c dk brn & blk 2.10 2.10
Never hinged 3.25
On cover 42.50

171 CD78 90c red 2.10 2.10
Never hinged 3.25
On cover 67.50
On cover, single franking 125.00

172 CD79 1.50fr ultra 2.25 2.25
Never hinged 3.25
On cover 62.50
On cover, single franking 110.00

Nos. 167-172 (6) 13.20 13.20
Set, never hinged 20.00

Colonial Arts Exhibition Issue

Souvenir Sheet

Common Design Type

1937 ***Imperf.***

173 CD74 3fr ultra 8.50 *10.00*
Never hinged 16.00
On cover 105.00
On cover, single franking 165.00

New York World's Fair Issue

Common Design Type

1939 **Engr.** ***Perf. 12½x12***

174 CD82 1.25fr car lake 1.40 1.40
Never hinged 2.25
On cover 50.00
On cover, single franking 110.00

175 CD82 2.25fr ultra 1.40 1.40
Never hinged 2.25
On cover 50.00
On cover, single franking 110.00

Set, never hinged 4.50

For overprints, see Nos. 221-222 in Scott Standard catalogue, Vol. 5.

SEMI-POSTAL STAMPS

No. 65 Surcharged in Black or Red

1915 **Unwmk.** ***Perf. 14x13½***

B1 A19 10c + 5c (Bk) 160.00 120.00
Never hinged 250.00
On cover 200.00
a. Inverted surcharge 450.00 350.00

B2 A19 10c + 5c (R) 1.75 1.75
Never hinged 6.75
On cover 35.00
a. Inverted surcharge 77.50 77.50
Never hinged 175.00
b. Double surcharge, both inverted 675.00 675.00

No. 65 Surcharged in Red

1916

B3 A19 10c + 5c 1.90 1.90
Never hinged 2.40
On cover 27.50

Curie Issue

Common Design Type

1938 ***Perf. 13***

B4 CD80 1.75fr + 50c brt ultra 14.00 14.00
Never hinged 24.00
On cover 52.50
On cover, single franking 80.00

French Revolution Issue

Common Design Type

1939 **Photo.** **Unwmk.**

Name and Value Typo. in Black

B5 CD83 45c + 25c grn 12.50 12.50
Never hinged 21.00
On cover 67.50

B6 CD83 70c + 30c brn 12.50 12.50
Never hinged 21.00
On cover 52.50

B7 CD83 90c + 35c red org 12.50 12.50
Never hinged 21.00
On cover 40.00

B8 CD83 1.25fr + 1fr rose pink 12.50 12.50
Never hinged 21.00
On cover 67.50

B9 CD83 2.25fr + 2fr blue 12.50 12.50
Never hinged 21.00
On cover 60.00

Nos. B5-B9 (5) 62.50 62.50
Set, never hinged 110.00

See CB1.

AIR POST STAMPS

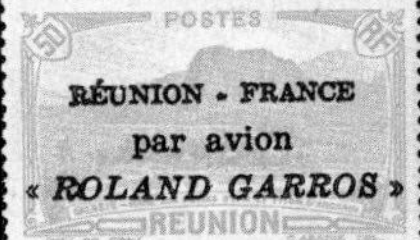

No. 141 Ovptd. in Blue

1937, Jan. 23 **Unwmk.** ***Perf. 12½***

C1 A23 50c red 290.00 250.00
Never hinged 500.00
On cover 600.00
a. Vert. pair, one without overprint 1,800. 1,800.
b. Inverted overprint 6,000.
c. As "b," in pair with unoverprinted stamp 26,000.

Flight of the "Roland Garros" from Reunion to France by aviators Laurent, Lenier and Touge in Jan.-Feb., 1937.

Airplane and Landscape — AP2

1938, Mar. 1 **Engr.** ***Perf. 12½***

C2 AP2 3.65fr slate blue & car 1.00 .90
Never hinged 1.40
On cover 55.00

C3 AP2 6.65fr brown & org red 1.00 .90
Never hinged 1.40
On cover 55.00

C4 AP2 9.65fr car & ultra 1.00 .90
Never hinged 1.40
On cover 62.50

C5 AP2 12.65fr brown & green 2.00 1.50
Never hinged 2.90
On cover 75.00

Nos. C2-C5 (4) 5.00 4.20
Set, never hinged 7.00

For overprints see Nos. C14-C17 in Scott Standard catalogue, Vol. 5.

AIR POST SEMI-POSTAL STAMP

French Revolution Issue
Common Design Type

1939 Unwmk. *Perf. 13*
Name and Value Typo. in Orange

CB1 CD83 3.65fr + 4fr brn blk	25.00	25.00
Never hinged	37.50	
On cover		92.50
On cover, single franking		165.00

POSTAGE DUE STAMPS

D1

1889-92 Unwmk. Type-set *Imperf.*
Without Gum

J1 D1 5c black	29.00	16.00
On cover		*800.00*
a. Missing "ti" of "Centimes" and "à"	190.00	190.00
b. Double impression	150.00	150.00
J2 D1 10c black	35.00	16.00
On cover		700.00
a. Double impression	150.00	150.00
b. Triple impression	300.00	300.00
J3 D1 15c black ('92)	67.50	42.50
a. Missing "ti" of "Centimes"	225.00	225.00
b. Missing "ti" of "Centimes" and "à"	225.00	225.00
c. Double impression	210.00	210.00
J4 D1 20c black	50.00	27.50
a. Double impression	210.00	210.00
J5 D1 30c black	45.00	27.50
a. Double impression	150.00	150.00
Nos. J1-J5 (5)	226.50	129.50

Ten varieties of each value.

Nos. J1-J2, J4-J5 issued on yellowish paper in 1889; Nos. J1-J3, J5 on bluish white paper in 1892.

Many small printing varieties exist, as well as intermediate stages of the plate deterioration that resulted in Nos. J1a and J3a, Which appear in one position in the second printing of the 5c and 15c values.

D2

1907 Typo. *Perf. 14x13½*

J6 D2 5c carmine, *yel*	.90	.90
Never hinged	1.60	
On cover		150.00
J7 D2 10c blue, *bl*	.90	.90
Never hinged	1.60	
On cover		150.00
J8 D2 15c black, *bluish*	1.50	1.50
Never hinged	2.40	
On cover		150.00
J9 D2 20c carmine	1.50	1.50
Never hinged	2.40	
On cover		150.00
J10 D2 30c green, *grnsh*	2.25	2.25
Never hinged	3.50	
On cover		*175.00*
J11 D2 50c red, *green*	2.60	2.60
Never hinged	4.00	
On cover		*210.00*
J12 D2 60c carmine, *bl*	2.60	2.60
Never hinged	4.00	
On cover		*210.00*
J13 D2 1fr violet	3.00	3.00
Never hinged	5.25	
On cover		*300.00*
Nos. J6-J13 (8)	15.25	15.25
Set, never hinged	27.50	

Type of 1907 Issue Surcharged

1927

J14 D2 2fr on 1fr org red	12.50	12.50
Never hinged	19.00	
On cover		190.00
J15 D2 3fr on 1fr org brn	12.50	12.50
Never hinged	19.00	
On cover		190.00
a. No period after "F"	52.50	52.50
Never hinged	87.50	
Set, never hinged	40.00	

Arms of Réunion — D3

1933 Engr. *Perf. 13x13½*

J16 D3 5c deep violet	.25	.25
Never hinged	.40	
J17 D3 10c dark green	.25	.25
Never hinged	.40	
J18 D3 15c orange brown	.25	.25
Never hinged	.40	
J19 D3 20c light red	.35	.35
Never hinged	.55	
J20 D3 30c olive green	.35	.35
Never hinged	.55	
J21 D3 50c ultramarine	.80	.80
Never hinged	1.20	
J22 D3 60c black brown	.80	.80
Never hinged	1.20	
J23 D3 1fr light violet	.80	.80
Never hinged	1.20	
J24 D3 2fr deep blue	.80	.80
Never hinged	1.25	
J25 D3 3fr carmine	1.00	1.00
Never hinged	1.60	
Nos. J16-J25 (10)	5.65	5.65
Set, never hinged	8.75	

PARCEL POST STAMP

No. 40 Overprinted

1906 Unwmk. *Perf. 14x13½*

Q1 A14 10c red	22.50	22.50
Never hinged	47.50	

RHODESIA

rō-ˈdē-zhˌē-ˌə

(British South Africa)

LOCATION — Southeastern Africa
GOVT. — Administered by the British South Africa Company
AREA — 440,653 sq. mi.
POP. — 1,738,000 (estimated 1921)
CAPITAL — Salisbury

In 1923 the area was divided and the portion south of the Zambezi River became the British Crown Colony of Southern Rhodesia. In the following year the remaining territory was formed into the Protectorate of Northern Rhodesia.

12 Pence = 1 Shilling
20 Shillings = 1 Pound

A1

A2

Coat of Arms — A3

Thin Paper
Engr. (A1, A3); Engr., Typo. (A2)
1890-94 Unwmk. *Perf. 14, 14½*

1 A2 ½p blue & ver ('91)	4.75	*5.25*
a. ½p dp blue & ver ('93)	5.00	*7.75*
2 A1 1p black	17.50	4.00
3 A2 2p gray grn & ver ('91)	28.00	8.00
4 A2 3p gray & grn ('91)	25.00	5.00
5 A2 4p red brn & blk ('91)	47.50	6.50
6 A1 6p ultra	80.00	28.00
7 A1 6p deep blue	50.00	4.25
8 A2 8p rose & bl ('91)	22.50	24.00
a. 8p red & ultramarine ('92)	16.50	*24.00*
9 A1 1sh gray brown	55.00	16.00
10 A1 2sh vermilion	77.50	42.50
11 A1 2sh6p dull lilac	47.50	55.00
Revenue cancellation		1.00
a. 2sh6p lilac ('93)	65.00	60.00
Revenue cancellation		1.50
12 A2 3sh brn & grn ('94)	195.00	100.00
Revenue cancellation		2.50
13 A2 4sh gray & ver ('93)	48.00	60.00
Revenue cancellation		1.00
14 A1 5sh yellow	92.50	65.00
Revenue cancellation		1.50
15 A1 10sh deep green	130.00	*110.00*
Revenue cancellation		1.25
16 A3 £1 dark blue	*325.00*	*175.00*
Revenue cancellation		6.75
17 A3 £2 rose	*550.00*	*200.00*
Revenue cancellation		22.50
18 A3 £5 yellow grn	*1,775.*	*500.00*
Revenue cancellation		50.00
19 A3 £10 orange brn	*3,000.*	*800.00*
Revenue cancellation		75.00
Nos. 1-16 (16)	1,246.	*708.50*

The paper of the 1891 issue has the trademark and initials of the makers in a monogram watermarked in each sheet. Some of the lower values were also printed on a slightly thicker paper without watermark.

Examples of Nos. 16-19 with cancellations removed are frequently offered as unused specimens.

See Nos. 24-25, 58.

For surcharges see Nos. 20-23, 40-42. For overprints see British Central Africa Nos. 1-20.

Nos. 6 and 9 Surcharged in Black

1891, Mar.

20 A1 ½p on 6p ultra	150.00	*525.00*
21 A1 2p on 6p ultra	195.00	*700.00*
22 A1 4p on 6p ultra	210.00	*825.00*
23 A1 8p on 1sh brown	225.00	*925.00*
Nos. 20-23 (4)	780.00	*2,975.*

Beware of forged surcharges.

1895 Thick Soft Paper *Perf. 12½*

24 A2 2p green & red	32.50	20.00
25 A2 4p ocher & black	32.50	21.00
a. Imperf., pair	2,250.	

A4

Die I — Small dot at the right of the tail of the supporter at the right of the shield, and the body of the lion is not fully shaded.

Die II — No dot and the lion is heavily shaded.

1896 Engraved, Typo. *Perf. 14*

26 A4 ½p slate & vio	5.00	*3.75*
27 A4 1p scar & emer	14.00	5.50
a. 1p scarlet & emerald (I)	27.50	5.00
b. 1p car red & emerald green (I)		—
28 A4 2p brn & rose lil (II)	30.00	4.00
a. 2p brown & rose lilac (I)	32.50	5.75
29 A4 3p red brn & ultra	11.00	2.50
30 A4 4p blue & red lil	24.00	.60
a. 4p ultra & red lilac (II)	85.00	14.00
b. 4p blue & red lilac (I)	42.50	24.00
c. 4p ultra & red lilac (I)	62.50	
d. Horiz. pair, imperf. btwn. (I)		
31 A4 6p vio & pale rose (II)	19.00	1.10
a. 6p violet & pink (I)	87.50	26.00
32 A4 8p dp grn & vio, *buff* (I)	20.00	.70
a. Imperf. pair	*4,500.*	
b. Horiz. pair, imperf. btwn.		
33 A4 1sh brt grn & ultra	27.50	4.00
34 A4 2sh dk bl & grn, *buff*	55.00	14.00
35 A4 2sh6p brn & vio, *yel*	92.50	65.00
36 A4 3sh grn & red vio, *bl*	90.00	47.50
a. Imperf. pair	*13,000.*	
37 A4 4sh red & bl, *grn*	75.00	4.00
38 A4 5sh org red & grn	65.00	14.00
39 A4 10sh sl & car, *rose*	150.00	75.00
Nos. 26-39 (14)	678.00	241.65

See type A7.

Nos. 4, 13-14 Surcharged in Black

1896, Apr. *Perf. 14*

40 A2 1p on 3p	650.00	850.00
a. "P" of "Penny" inverted	*50,000.*	
b. "y" of "Penny" inverted		—
c. Double surcharge		—
41 A2 1p on 4sh	325.00	350.00
a. "P" of "Penny" inverted	*37,500.*	
b. Single bar in surch.	*1,250.*	*1,400.*
c. "y" of "Penny" inverted	*37,500.*	
42 A1 3p on 5s yellow	225.00	*275.00*
a. "T" of "THREE" inverted	*50,000.*	
b. "R" of "THREE" inverted	*37,500.*	
Nos. 40-42 (3)	*1,200.*	*1,475.*

Cape of Good Hope Stamps Overprinted in Black

1896, May 22 Wmk. 16

43 A6 ½p slate	20.00	*25.00*
44 A15 1p carmine	22.50	*29.00*
45 A6 2p bister brown	27.50	15.00
46 A6 4p deep blue	34.00	27.50
a. "COMPANY" omitted	*11,000.*	
47 A3 6p violet	77.50	*90.00*
48 A6 1sh yellow buff	175.00	*165.00*

Wmk. 2

49 A6 3p claret	60.00	*85.00*
Nos. 43-49 (7)	416.50	*436.50*

Nos. 42-49 were used at Bulawayo during the Matabele Rebellion.

Forgeries are known.

Remainders

Rhodesian authorities made available remainders in large quantities of all stamps in 1897, 1898-1908, 1905, 1909 and 1910 issues, CTO. Some varieties exist only as remainders. See notes following Nos. 100 and 118.

A7

Type A7 differs from type A4 in having the ends of the scroll which is below the shield curved between the hind legs of the supporters instead of passing behind one leg of each. There are other minor differences.

Perf. 13½ to 16
1897 Unwmk. Engr.

50 A7 ½p slate & violet	7.00	*9.50*
51 A7 1p ver & gray grn	10.00	*10.00*
52 A7 2p brn & lil rose	22.50	4.25
53 A7 3p red brn & gray bl	8.50	.55
a. Vert. pair, imperf. btwn.	*5,000.*	
54 A7 4p ultra & red lil	28.00	4.50
a. Horiz. pair, imperf. btwn.	*18,000.*	*17,500.*
55 A7 6p vio & sal	18.00	4.00
56 A7 8p dk grn & vio, *buff*	28.00	.55
a. Vert. pair, imperf. btwn.	—	*4,000.*
57 A7 £1 blk & red, *grn*	450.00	250.00
Revenue cancellation		12.00
Nos. 50-56 (7)	122.00	*33.35*

Thick Paper

Perf. 15

58 A3 £2 bright red 1,900. 500.00
Revenue cancellation 65.00

See note on remainders following No. 49.

A8 A9

A10

1898-1908 *Perf. 13½ to 16*

59 A8 ½p yel grn ('04) 6.00 3.25
a. Imperf. pair 1,000.
b. Horiz. pair, imperf. vert. 975.00
c. Vert. pair, imperf between 1,675.
d. ½p dull blue green 15.00 3.25
e. ½p deep green (shades) ('08) 35.00 3.75
60 A8 1p rose (shades) 12.00 .60
a. Horiz. pair, imperf. btwn. 1,150.
b. Vert. pair, imperf between 825.00
c. Imperf. pair 1,000. 900.00
d. 1p red (shades) ('05) 10.50 .55
e. As "d," horiz. pair, imperf vert. 450.00 500.00
f. As "d," vert. pair, imperf horiz. 1,100.
g. As "d," imperf, pair 675.00 650.00
h. As "d," horiz. pair, imperf between 900.00 550.00
i. As "d," vert. strip of 4, imperf between 3,000.
61 A8 2p brown 11.00 2.00
62 A8 2½p dull blue (shades) 22.50 2.00
a. Horiz. pair, imperf vert. 1,100. 1,300.
b. 2½p gray blue (shades) ('03) 19.00 1.90
63 A8 3p clar ('08) 20.00 .90
a. Vert. pair, imperf between 800.00
64 A8 4p ol grn 18.00 .35
a. Vert. pair, imperf. between 800.00
65 A8 6p lilac 23.00 3.00
a. 6p reddish mauve ('02) 26.00 7.00
66 A9 1sh bister 32.50 4.50
a. Vert. pair, imperf. btwn. 3,500. 3,500.
b. Horiz. pair, imperf between 4,000. 4,000.
c. 1sh deep olive bister ('07) 400.00 375.00
d. As "c," imperf., pair 3,500.
e. As "c," horiz. pair, imperf between 4,750.
f. 1sh bister brown ('08) 75.00 17.50
g. 1sh brownish yellow ('08) 30.00 12.50
67 A9 2sh6p bluish gray ('06) 75.00 2.25
a. Vert. pair, imperf. between 1,300. 575.00
68 A9 3sh pur ('02) 32.50 4.00
a. 2sh6p deep blue violet ('08) 82.50 16.00
69 A9 5sh org ('01) 70.00 25.00
70 A9 7sh6p blk ('01) 110.00 32.50
71 A9 10sh bluish grn ('08) 65.00 2.50
72 A10 £1 gray vio, perf 15½ ('01) 425.00 170.00
Revenue cancellation 17.50
a. £1 blackish purple, perf 14 ('02) 725.00 150.00
Revenue cancellation 9.50
73 A10 £2 red brn ('08) 130.00 7.50
74 A10 £5 dk blue ('01) 3,750. 3,000.
Revenue cancellation 125.00
75 A10 £10 blue lil ('01) 3,750. 3,000.
Revenue cancellation 125.00
75A A10 £20 bister ('01?) 22,500.
Revenue cancellation 175.00
75B A10 £100 cherry red ('01) 185,000. —
Revenue cancellation 900.00
Nos. 59-73 (15) 1,053. 260.35

For overprints and surcharges see #82-100.
See note on remainders following #49.

Victoria Falls — A11

Perf. 14, 14½x15 (#78)

1905, July 13

76 A11 1p rose red 8.50 10.00
a. Perf 14½x15 19.00 20.00
77 A11 2½p ultra 18.00 12.00
a. Perf 14½x15 30.00 20.00
78 A11 5p magenta 35.00 60.00
a. Perf 14 70.00 90.00
79 A11 1sh blue green 42.50 57.50
a. Imperf., pair 35,000.
b. Horiz. pair, imperf. vert. 37,500.
c. Horiz. pair, imperf. btwn. 45,000.
d. Vert. pair, imperf. btn. 45,000.
e. Perf 14½x15 — 425.00
80 A11 2sh6p black 135.00 180.00
81 A11 5sh violet 125.00 50.00
a. Perf 14½x15 475.00
Nos. 76-81 (6) 364.00 369.50
Nos. 76-81 overprinted "SPECIMEN" 400.00

Opening of the Victoria Falls bridge across the Zambezi River.
See note on remainders following No. 49.

Stamps of 1898-1908 Overprinted or Surcharged

1909 *Perf. 14, 15*

82 A8 ½p green (shades) 5.00 3.00
a. No period after "RHODESIA" 90.00 45.00
b. ½p yellow green ('11) 45.00 30.00
83 A8 1p car rose 10.00 1.75
a. Horiz. pair, imperf between 525.00
b. No period after "RHODESIA" 95.00 35.00
c. 1p deep carmine rose 10.00 1.75
d. As "c," horiz. pair, imperf between 525.00
84 A8 2p brown 5.00 7.25
a. No period after "RHODESIA" 155.00 100.00
85 A8 2½p cobalt blue 3.50 .90
a. No period after "RHODESIA" 60.00 32.50
86 A8 3p claret 3.50 3.00
a. Double overprint 1,600. 1,600.
b. Inverted overprint 20.00 20.00
c. No period after "RHODESIA" 180.00 85.00
87 A8 4p ol grn 15.00 3.75
a. Inverted overprint 16.50
b. No period after "RHODESIA" 100.00 75.00
88 A8 5p on 6p lilac 12.50 20.00
a. Violet surcharge 100.00
b. 5p on 6p dull purple 24.00 20.00
89 A8 6p lilac 8.50 9.00
a. No period after "RHODESIA" 90.00
b. 6p dull purple 25.00 9.00
c. As "b," no period after "RHODESIA" 110.00 65.00
90 A9 7½p on 2sh6p 4.50 4.25
a. Violet surcharge 25.00 11.00
b. Double surcharge 10,000.
91 A9 10p on 3sh pur, vio srch. 7.75 4.50
a. Black surcharge 16.50 20.00
92 A9 1sh dp brnsh bister 14.00 9.00
a. No period after "RHODESIA" 110.00 60.00
b. 1sh bister 30.00
c. As "b," no period after "RHODESIA" 200.00
93 A9 2sh on 5sh org 14.00 8.50
94 A9 2sh6p bluish gray 30.00 12.00
a. No period after "RHODESIA" 135.00 75.00
b. Inverted overprint 25.00
95 A9 3sh purple 25.00 12.50
96 A9 5sh orange 50.00 80.00
a. No period after "RHODESIA" 225.00 225.00
97 A9 7sh6p black 110.00 30.00
98 A9 10sh bluish grn 70.00 22.50
a. No period after "RHODESIA" 400.00 250.00
99 A10 £1 gray vio 220.00 110.00
a. Vert. pair, lower stamp without overprint 47,500.
b. Violet overprint 425.00 220.00
100 A10 £2 red brn, *bluish*, perf 14½x15 ('12) 4,500. 330.00
a. £2 brown 4,750. 375.00
100B A10 £5 dp blue, *bluish* 9,000. 5,000.
Nos. 82-99 (18) 608.25 341.90

See note on remainders following No. 49. Nos. 86b, 87a and 94b are from the remainders.

Queen Mary and King George V — A12

1910 Engr. *Perf. 14, 15x14, 14x15*

101 A12 ½p green 15.00 2.50
a. ½p olive green 45.00 5.50
b. Perf. 15 350.00 14.50
c. Imperf., pair 16,000. 8,000.
d. Perf. 13½ 350.00 55.00
102 A12 1p rose car 37.50 4.50
a. Vertical pair, imperf. btwn. 22,500. 14,500.
b. Perf. 15 350.00 10.00
c. Perf. 13½ 2,250. 55.00
103 A12 2p gray & blk 60.00 12.50
b. Perf. 15 1,000. 47.50
104 A12 2½p ultra 27.50 12.00
a. 2½p light blue 29.00 24.00
b. Perf. 15 82.50 45.00
c. Perf. 13½ 45.00 77.50
105 A12 3p ol yel & vio 50.00 52.00
a. Perf. 15 3,650. 82.50
b. Perf. 14x15 7,750. 325.00
106 A12 4p org & blk 55.00 27.50
a. 4p orange & violet black 95.00 72.50
b. Perf. 15x14 550.00
c. Perf. 15 65.00 82.50
107 A12 5p ol grn & brn 60.00 60.00
a. 5p olive yel & brn (error) 725.00 165.00
b. Perf. 15 875.00 115.00
108 A12 6p claret & brn 72.50 25.00
a. Perf. 15 1,000. 67.50
109 A12 8p brn vio & gray blk 190.00 110.00
a. Perf. 13½ 67.50 275.00
110 A12 10p plum & rose red 55.00 55.00
111 A12 1sh turq grn & black 72.50 24.00
a. Perf. 14x15 32,500. 3,250.
b. Perf. 15 1,325. 62.50
112 A12 2sh gray bl & black 125.00 82.50
a. Perf. 15 2,500 400.00
113 A12 2sh6p car rose & blk 400.00 450.00
114 A12 3sh vio & bl grn 250.00 210.00
115 A12 5sh yel grn & brn red 325.00 225.00
116 A12 7sh6p brt bl & car 725.00 500.00
117 A12 10sh red org & bl grn 475.00 550.00
a. 10sh red org & myrtle grn 725.00 325.00
118 A12 £1 bluish sl & car 1,650. 775.00
a. £1 black & red 1,550. 425.00
c. Perf. 15 19,000. 4,750.
d. As "a," carmine and reddish mauve (error) 14,500.
Nos. 101-118 (18) 4,645. 3,178.

See note on remainders following No. 49. The £1 in plum and red is from the remainders.

King George V — A13

Three dies were used for Nos. 122, 124-138: I, Outline at top of cap absent or very faint and broken. Left ear not shaded or outlined and appears white; II, Outline at top of cap faint and broken. Ear shaded all over, with no outline; III, Outline at top of cap continuous. Ear shaded all over, with continuous outline. Die types are noted in parentheses.

1913-23 *Perf. 14*

119 A13 ½p dp grn 9.25 2.50
a. Vert. pair, imperf horiz. 925.00
b. Vert. strip of 5, imperf between 4,250.
c. ½p blue green 12.00 2.50
d. As "c," perf 15 9.50 30.00
e. ½p yellow green 24.00 2.50
f. Horiz. pair, imperf between 1,000.
g. ½p dull green 13.50 2.50
h. As "g," horiz. pair, imperf vert. 1,000. 1,000.
i. As "g," horiz. pair, imperf between 1,300.
j. ½p bright green 28.00 2.50
k. As "j," vert. pair, imperf between 1,750.
l. ½p green, perf 15 16.00 24.00
m. As "l," perf 14x15 7,750. 225.00
n. As "l," perf 15x14 7,750. 400.00
120 A13 1p brn rose 4.50 4.00
a. Perf. 15 7.50 10.00
b. 1p bright rose 7.25 2.50
c. As "b," horiz. pair, imperf btwn. 1,100. 950.00
d. 1p carmine red (shades) 12.50 4.00
e. As "d," pair, imperf between 1,650.
f. 1p red 8.00 2.50
g. As "f," horiz. pair, imperf btwn. 1,250.
h. As "f," perf. 13½ 600.00
i. 1p scarlet 24.00 3.00
j. As "i," horiz. pair, imperf btwn. 1,350.
k. 1p rose red 12.50 2.50
l. As "k," horiz. pair, imperf btwn. 1,000. 1,000.
m. As "k," vert. pair, imperf btwn. 3,000.
n. As "k," perf. 15 675.00 24.50
o. As "n," horiz. pair, imperf between 19,000.
p. 1p bright rose red (rosine) 550.00 22.50
q. 1p cherry red —
121 A13 1½p bis brn ('17) 6.00 2.50
a. Horiz. pair, imperf between 900.00 900.00
b. Perf. 15 ('19) 50.00 8.00
c. As "b," horiz. pair, imperf between 26,500.
d. 1½p brown ocher ('19) 5.50 2.50
e. As "d," horiz. pair, imperf between 875.00 900.00
f. As "d," perf 15 ('17) 55.00 16.00
g. 1½p drab brown ('17) 7.25 2.50
h. As "g," horiz. pair, imperf between 875.00
i. As "g," vert. pair, imperf between 2,500.
122 A13 2p vio blk & blk (III) '22 13.50 9.00
a. 2p gray & black (III) 11.50 4.00
b. Perf. 15 (II) 13.50 25.00
c. Horiz. pair, imperf. btwn. (III) 6,750.
d. 2p gray & brnish blk (III), perf 15 6,500.
123 A13 2½p ultra 8.25 40.00
a. Perf. 15 17.50 65.00
124 A13 3p org yel & blk (III) 20.00 4.75
a. 3p yellow & black (III) 17.50 4.25
b. Perf. 15 (I) 9.00 27.50
125 A13 4p org red & blk (I) 12.00 42.50
a. Perf. 15 (I) 175.00 32.50
126 A13 5p yel grn & blk (I) 7.25 22.50
127 A13 6p lilac & blk (III) 16.50 8.75
a. Perf. 15 (I) 10.50 12.00
128 A13 8p gray grn & vio (II) 19.00 82.50
a. Perf. 15 (III) 77.50
b. 8p green & violet (II) 225.00 190.00
129 A13 10p car rose & bl, perf. 15 (II) 16.50 50.00
a. Perf. 14 (III) '22 18.50 75.00
130 A13 1sh turq bl & blk (III) '22 15.00 22.50
a. 1sh lt grn & blk (III) ('19) 95.00 60.00
b. Perf. 15 (II) 77.50 22.50
132 A13 2sh brn & blk, perf. 14 (III)('19) 22.50 20.00
a. Perf. 15 (I) 17.50 55.00
133 A13 2sh6p ol gray & vio bl (III) '22 65.00 110.00
a. 2sh6p gray & blue (II) 82.50 60.00
b. Perf. 15 (II) 55.00 105.00
134 A13 3sh brt blue & red brn (II) 130.00 165.00
a. Perf. 15 (III) '23 195.00
b. 3sh blue & chocolate (II) 775.00 325.00
135 A13 5sh grn & bl (II) 95.00 100.00
a. Perf. 15 (II) 210.00 225.00
136 A13 7sh6p blk & vio, perf. 15 (II) 175.00 300.00
a. Perf. 14 (III) '22 250.00 425.00
137 A13 10sh yel grn & car (III) '23 275.00 360.00
a. Perf. 15 (II) 250.00 425.00
138 A13 £1 vio & blk (II) 450.00 675.00
a. £1 magenta & black (III) '23 950.00 1,250.
b. Perf. 15 (III) '23 1,100.
c. Perf. 15, black & purple (II) 1,750. 1,750.
Nos. 119-138 (19) 1,360. 2,022.

No. 120 Surcharged in Dark Violet

No. 139

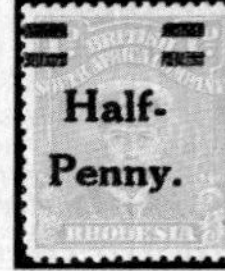
No. 140

1917

No.	Type	Description	Unused	Used
139	A13	½p on 1p	2.75	10.50
a.		Inverted surcharge	*1,600.*	*1,650.*
140	A13	½p on 1p	2.00	10.00

RIO DE ORO

ˌrē-ō dē ˈōr-ˌō

LOCATION — On the northwest coast of Africa, bordering on the Atlantic Ocean
GOVT. — Spanish Colony
AREA — 71,600 sq. mi.
POP. — 24,000
CAPITAL — Villa Cisneros

Prior to the issuance of Rio de Oro stamps, Spanish stamps were used 1901-1904, canceled "Rio de Oro."

Rio de Oro became part of Spanish Sahara in 1924.

100 Centimos = 1 Peseta

King Alfonso XIII — A1

Control Numbers on Back in Blue

1905 Unwmk. Typo. *Perf. 14*

No.	Type	Description	Unused	Used
1	A1	1c blue green	4.00	3.00
2	A1	2c claret	5.00	3.00
3	A1	3c bronze green	5.00	3.00
4	A1	4c dark brown	5.00	3.00
5	A1	5c orange red	5.00	3.00
6	A1	10c dk gray brown	5.00	3.00
7	A1	15c red brown	5.00	3.00
8	A1	25c dark blue	95.00	32.50
9	A1	50c dark green	45.00	13.50
10	A1	75c dark violet	45.00	19.00
11	A1	1p orange brown	32.50	8.00
12	A1	2p buff	100.00	57.50
13	A1	3p dull violet	70.00	20.00
14	A1	4p blue green	70.00	20.00
15	A1	5p dull blue	100.00	45.00
16	A1	10p pale red	250.00	150.00
		Nos. 1-16 (16)	841.50	386.50
		Set, never hinged	1,700.	

For surcharges see Nos. 17, 34-36, 60-66.

No. 8 Handstamp Surcharged in Rose — a

1907

No.	Type	Description	Unused	Used
17	A1	15c on 25c dk blue	250.00	60.00
		Never hinged	400.00	

The surcharge exists inverted, double and in violet, normally positioned. Value for each, $450.

King Alfonso XIII — A2

Control Numbers on Back in Blue

1907 Typo.

No.	Type	Description	Unused	Used
18	A2	1c claret	3.00	2.75
19	A2	2c black	3.50	2.75
20	A2	3c dark brown	3.50	2.75
21	A2	4c red	3.50	2.75
22	A2	5c black brown	3.50	2.75
23	A2	10c chocolate	3.50	2.75
24	A2	15c dark blue	3.50	2.75
25	A2	25c deep green	9.50	2.75
26	A2	50c black violet	9.50	2.75
27	A2	75c orange brown	9.50	2.75
28	A2	1p orange	16.00	2.75
29	A2	2p dull violet	5.50	2.75
30	A2	3p blue green	5.50	2.75
a.		Cliché of 4p in plate of 3p	400.00	260.00
31	A2	4p dark blue	9.00	5.00
32	A2	5p red	9.00	5.25
33	A2	10p deep green	9.00	12.00
		Nos. 18-33 (16)	106.50	58.00
		Set, never hinged	250.00	

For surcharges see Nos. 38-43, 67-70.

Nos. 9-10 Handstamp Surcharged in Red

1907

No.	Type	Description	Unused	Used
34	A1	10c on 50c dk green	100.00	30.00
		Never hinged	175.00	
a.		"10" omitted	175.00	100.00
		Never hinged	250.00	
35	A1	10c on 75c dk violet	100.00	32.00
		Never hinged	175.00	

No. 12 Handstamp Surcharged in Violet

1908

No.	Type	Description	Unused	Used
36	A1	2c on 2p buff	52.50	24.00
		Never hinged	100.00	

No. 36 is found with "1908" measuring 11mm and 12mm.

Same Surcharge in Red on No. 26

No.	Type	Description	Unused	Used
38	A2	10c on 50c blk vio	22.50	3.75
		Never hinged	37.50	

A 5c on 10c (No. 23) was not officially issued.

Nos. 25, 27-28 Handstamp Surcharged Type "a" in Red, Violet or Green

1908

No.	Type	Description	Unused	Used
39	A2	15c on 25c dp grn (R)	25.00	3.75
40	A2	15c on 75c org brn (V)	32.50	17.50
a.		Green surcharge	50.00	6.75
		Never hinged	72.50	
41	A2	15c on 1p org (V)	37.50	15.00
42	A2	15c on 1p org (R)	35.00	15.00
43	A2	15c on 1p org (G)	25.00	12.00
		Nos. 39-43 (5)	155.00	63.25
		Set, never hinged	325.00	

As this surcharge is handstamped, it exists in several varieties: double, inverted, in pairs with one surcharge omitted, etc.

A3

Revenue stamps overprinted and surcharged

1908 *Imperf.*

No.	Type	Description	Unused	Used
44	A3	5c on 50c green (C)	90.00	30.00
		Never hinged	160.00	
45	A3	5c on 50c green (V)	130.00	52.50
		Never hinged	225.00	

The surcharge, which is handstamped, exists in many variations.

Nos. 44-45 are found with and without control numbers on back. Stamps with control numbers sell at about double the above values. Counterfeits exist.

See Spanish Guinea Nos. 98-101C for additional revenue stamps surcharged for postal use.

King Alfonso XIII — A4

Control Numbers on Back in Blue

1909 Typo. *Perf. 14½*

No.	Type	Description	Unused	Used
46	A4	1c red	.85	.50
47	A4	2c orange	.85	.50
48	A4	5c dark green	.85	.50
49	A4	10c orange red	.85	.50
50	A4	15c blue green	.85	.50
51	A4	20c dark violet	2.10	.70
52	A4	25c deep blue	2.10	.70
53	A4	30c claret	2.10	.70
54	A4	40c chocolate	2.10	.70
55	A4	50c red violet	4.00	.70
56	A4	1p dark brown	5.25	3.25
57	A4	4p carmine rose	6.25	4.75
58	A4	10p claret	14.00	7.75
		Nos. 46-58 (13)	42.15	21.75
		Set, never hinged	80.00	

Stamps of 1905 Handstamped in Black

1910

No.	Type	Description	Unused	Used
60	A1	10c on 5p dull bl	21.00	8.50
a.		Red surcharge	90.00	55.00
		Never hinged	145.00	
62	A1	10c on 10p pale red	21.00	8.50
a.		Violet surcharge	145.00	62.50
		Never hinged	210.00	
b.		Green surcharge	145.00	62.50
		Never hinged	210.00	
65	A1	15c on 3p dull vio	21.00	8.50
a.		Imperf.	110.00	
		Never hinged	190.00	
66	A1	15c on 4p blue grn	21.00	8.50
a.		10c on 4p bl grn	925.00	275.00
		Never hinged	1,300.	
		Nos. 60-66 (4)	84.00	34.00
		Set, never hinged	160.00	

See note after No. 43.

Nos. 31 and 33 Surcharged in Red or Violet

1911-13

No.	Type	Description	Unused	Used
67	A2	2c on 4p dk blue (R)	12.50	9.00
68	A2	5c on 10p dp grn (V)	37.50	9.00

Nos. 29-30 Surcharged in Black

No.	Type	Description	Unused	Used
69	A2	10c on 2p dull vio	19.00	8.25
69A	A2	10c on 3p bl grn ('13)	225.00	50.00

Nos. 30, 32 Handstamped Type "a"

No.	Type	Description	Unused	Used
69B	A2	15c on 3p bl grn ('13)	200.00	24.00
70	A2	15c on 5p red	13.50	9.00
		Nos. 67-70 (6)	507.50	109.25
		Set, never hinged	650.00	

King Alfonso XIII — A5

Control Numbers on Back in Blue

1912 Typo. *Perf. 13½*

No.	Type	Description	Unused	Used
71	A5	1c carmine rose	.40	.35
72	A5	2c lilac	.40	.35
73	A5	5c deep green	.40	.35
74	A5	10c red	.40	.35
75	A5	15c brown orange	.40	.35
76	A5	20c brown	.40	.35
77	A5	25c dull blue	.40	.35
78	A5	30c dark violet	.40	.35
79	A5	40c blue green	.40	.35
80	A5	50c lake	.40	.35
81	A5	1p red	4.00	.80
82	A5	4p claret	7.50	4.00
83	A5	10p dark brown	11.00	6.00
		Nos. 71-83 (13)	26.50	14.30
		Set, never hinged	60.00	

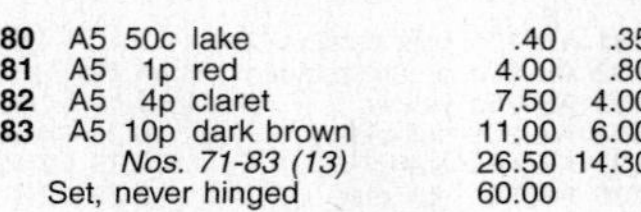

For overprints see Nos. 97-109.

King Alfonso XIII — A6

Control Numbers on Back in Blue

1914 *Perf. 13*

No.	Type	Description	Unused	Used
84	A6	1c olive black	.40	.35
85	A6	2c maroon	.40	.35
86	A6	5c deep green	.40	.35
87	A6	10c orange red	.40	.35
88	A6	15c orange red	.40	.35
89	A6	20c deep claret	.40	.35
90	A6	25c dark blue	.40	.35
91	A6	30c blue green	.40	.35
92	A6	40c brown orange	.40	.35
93	A6	50c dark brown	.40	.35
94	A6	1p dull lilac	3.00	2.40
95	A6	4p carmine rose	7.25	6.25
96	A6	10p dull violet	7.50	6.25
		Nos. 84-96 (13)	21.75	18.40
		Set, never hinged	50.00	

Nos. 71-83 Overprinted in Black

1917 *Perf. 13½*

No.	Type	Description	Unused	Used
97	A5	1c carmine rose	17.50	1.40
98	A5	2c lilac	17.50	1.40
99	A5	5c deep green	3.50	1.40
100	A5	10c red	3.50	1.40
101	A5	15c orange brn	3.50	1.40
102	A5	20c brown	3.50	1.40
103	A5	25c dull blue	3.50	1.40
104	A5	30c dark violet	3.50	1.40
105	A5	40c blue green	3.50	1.40
106	A5	50c lake	3.50	1.40
107	A5	1p red	19.00	4.75
108	A5	4p claret	22.50	6.25
109	A5	10p dark brown	42.50	9.25
		Nos. 97-109 (13)	147.00	34.25
		Set, never hinged	300.00	

Nos. 97-109 exist with overprint inverted or double (value 50 percent over normal) and in dark blue (value twice normal). Forgeries exist.

King Alfonso XIII — A7

Control Numbers on Back in Blue

1919 Typo. *Perf. 13*

No.	Type	Description	Unused	Used
114	A7	1c brown	1.25	.55
115	A7	2c claret	1.25	.55
116	A7	5c light green	1.25	.55
117	A7	10c carmine	1.25	.55
118	A7	15c orange	4.00	2.00
119	A7	20c orange	1.25	.55
120	A7	25c blue	1.25	.55
121	A7	30c green	1.25	.55
122	A7	40c vermilion	1.25	.55
123	A7	50c brown	1.25	.55
124	A7	1p lilac	8.00	4.50
125	A7	4p rose	14.50	7.50
126	A7	10p violet	25.00	10.00
		Nos. 114-126 (13)	62.75	28.95
		Set, never hinged	100.00	

A8

Control Numbers on Back in Blue

1920 *Perf. 13*

No.	Type	Description	Unused	Used
127	A8	1c gray lilac	1.10	.55
128	A8	2c rose	1.10	.55
129	A8	5c light red	1.10	.55
130	A8	10c lilac	1.10	.55

131 A8	15c light brown	1.10	.55
132 A8	20c greenish blue	1.10	.55
133 A8	25c yellow	1.10	.55
134 A8	30c dull blue	6.25	4.50
135 A8	40c orange	3.75	2.10
136 A8	50c dull rose	3.75	2.10
137 A8	1p gray green	5.25	2.10
138 A8	4p lilac rose	7.00	4.25
139 A8	10p brown	25.00	10.00
	Nos. 127-139 (13)	58.70	28.90
	Set, never hinged	100.00	

A9

Control Numbers on Back in Blue

1922

140 A9	1c yellow	1.00	.60
141 A9	2c red brown	1.00	.60
142 A9	5c blue green	1.00	.60
143 A9	10c pale red	1.00	.60
144 A9	15c myrtle green	1.00	.60
145 A9	20c turq blue	1.00	.65
146 A9	25c deep blue	1.00	.65
147 A9	30c deep rose	1.75	1.25
148 A9	40c violet	1.75	1.25
149 A9	50c orange	1.75	1.25
150 A9	1p lilac	5.50	1.75
151 A9	4p claret	12.00	4.00
152 A9	10p dark brown	20.00	8.25
	Nos. 140-152 (13)	49.75	22.05
	Set, never hinged	100.00	

For subsequent issues see Spanish Sahara.

ROMANIA

rō-ˈmā-nēə

(Rumania, Roumania)

LOCATION — Southeastern Europe, bordering on the Black Sea
GOVT. — Kingdom
AREA — 91,699 sq. mi.
POP. — 22,600,000 (est. 1984)
CAPITAL — Bucharest

Romania was formed in 1861 from the union of the principalities of Moldavia and Walachia in 1859. It became a kingdom in 1881. Following World War I, the original territory was considerably enlarged by the addition of Bessarabia, Bukovina, Transylvania, Crisana, Maramures and Banat.

40 Parale = 1 Piaster
100 Bani = 1 Leu (plural "Lei") (1868)

Catalogue values for unused stamps in this country are for Never Hinged items, beginning with Scott 475 in the regular postage section, Scott B82 in the semi-postal section, Scott CB1 in the airpost semi-postal section, Scott J82 in the postage due section, Scott O1 in the official section, Scott RA16 in the postal tax section, and Scott RAJ1 in the postal tax postage due section.

Watermarks

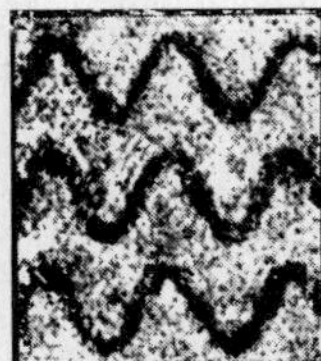
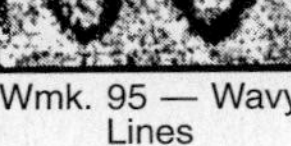

Wmk. 95 — Wavy Lines

Wmk. 163 — Coat of Arms

Wmk. 164 — PR

Wmk. 165 — PR Interlaced

Wmk. 167 — Coat of Arms Covering 25 Stamps

Wmk. 200 — PR

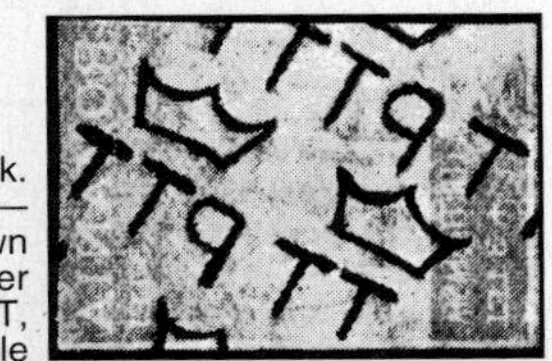

Wmk. 225 — Crown over PTT, Multiple

Wmk. 230 — Crowns and Monograms

Values for unused stamps are for examples with original gum as defined in the catalogue introduction except for Nos. 1-4 which are valued without gum.

Moldavia

Coat of Arms — A1

Laid Paper

Handstamped

1858, July Unwmk. *Imperf.*

1 A1	27pa blk, *rose*	*60,000.*	*25,000.*
a.	Tête bêche pair		
2 A1	54pa blue, *grn*	*15,500.*	*10,000.*
3 A1	108pa blue, *rose*	*35,000.*	*16,000.*

Wove Paper

4 A1	81pa blue, *bl*	*50,000.*	*55,000.*

Full margins = 3mm.

Cut to shape or octagonally, Nos. 1-4 sell for one-fourth to one-third of these values.

Coat of Arms — A2

1858 Bluish Wove Paper

5 A2	5pa black	*15,000.*	*15,000.*
a.	Tête bêche pair		
6 A2	40pa blue	275.	225.
a.	Tête bêche pair	*1,300.*	*2,650.*
7 A2	80pa red	*7,750.*	*875.*
a.	Tête bêche pair		

Full margins = 3mm.

1859 White Wove Paper

8 A2	5pa black	*15,000.*	*10,000.*
a.	Tête bêche pair		
b.	Frame broken at bottom	175.	
c.	As "b," tête bêche pair	600.	
9 A2	40pa blue	175.	190.
b.	Tête bêche pair	650.	*1,500.*
10 A2	80pa red	475.	300.
b.	Tête bêche pair	*1,750.*	*3,250.*

Full margins = 3mm.

No. 8b has a break in the frame at bottom below "A." It was never placed in use.

Moldavia-Walachia

Coat of Arms — A3

Printed by Hand from Single Dies

1862 White Laid Paper

11 A3	3pa orange	300.00	*2,250.*
a.	3pa yellow	300.00	*2,250.*
12 A3	6pa carmine	300.00	475.00
13 A3	6pa red	300.00	475.00
14 A3	30pa blue	87.50	115.00
	Nos. 11-14 (4)	987.50	3,315.

White Wove Paper

15 A3	3pa orange yel	85.00	*275.00*
a.	3pa lemon	85.00	*275.00*
16 A3	6pa carmine	95.00	*275.00*
17 A3	6pa vermilion	77.50	*225.00*
18 A3	30pa blue	60.00	65.00
	Nos. 15-18 (4)	317.50	840.00

Greenish-Blue Paper

15C A3	3pa orange yel	—	2,500.
	On cover		109,000.

Only one cover is known with No. 15C: 10 examples prepaying the single letter rate of 30pa. On cover value is based on 2011 Swiss auction price realized.

Tête bêche pairs

11b A3	3pa orange	1,550.	
12a A3	6pa carmine	1,000.	1,250.
14a A3	30pa blue	190.00	1,550.
15b A3	3pa orange yellow	210.00	*1,600.*
16a A3	6pa carmine	275.00	1,750.
17a A3	6pa vermilion	190.00	1,600.
18a A3	30pa blue	175.00	1,600.

Full margins = 2mm.

Nos. 11-18 were printed with a hand press, one at a time, from single dies. The impressions were very irregularly placed and occasionally overlapped. Sheets of 32 (4x8). The 3rd and 4th rows were printed inverted, making the second and third rows tête bêche. All values come in distinct shades, frequently even on the same sheet. The paper of this and the following issues through No. 52 often shows a bluish, grayish or yellowish tint.

White Wove Paper

1864 Typographed from Plates

19 A3	3pa yellow	60.00	*1,500.*
a.	Tête bêche pair	350.00	
b.	Pair, one sideways	150.00	
20 A3	6pa deep rose	22.50	
a.	Tête bêche pair	52.50	
b.	Pair, one sideways	52.50	
21 A3	30pa deep blue	17.50	*100.00*
a.	Tête bêche pair	57.50	
b.	Pair, one sideways	57.50	2,650.
c.	Bluish wove paper	*150.00*	
	Nos. 19-21 (3)	100.00	

Full margins = 1 ¼mm.

Stamps of 1862 issue range from very clear to blurred impressions but rarely have broken or deformed characteristics. The 1864 issue, though rarely blurred, usually have various imperfections in the letters and numbers. These include breaks, malformations, occasional dots at left of the crown or above the "R" of "PAR," a dot on the middle stroke of the "F," and many other bulges, breaks and spots of color.

The 1864 issue were printed in sheets of 40 (5x8). The first and second rows were inverted. Clichés in the third row were placed sideways, 4 with head to right and 4 with head to left, making one tête bêche pair. The fourth and fifth rows were normally placed.

No. 20 was never placed in use.

All values exist in shades, light to dark.

Counterfeit cancellations exist on #11-21.

Three stamps in this design- 2pa, 5pa, 20pa- were printed on white wove paper in 1864, but never placed in use. Value, set $12.

Romania

Prince Alexandru Ioan Cuza — A4

TWENTY PARALES:

Type I — The central oval does not touch the inner frame. The "I" of "DECI" extends above and below the other letters.

Type II — The central oval touches the frame at the bottom. The "I" of the "DECI" is the same height as the other letters.

1865, Jan. Unwmk. Litho. *Imperf.*

22 A4	2pa orange	70.00	*250.00*
a.	2pa yellow	77.50	*325.00*
b.	2pa ocher	325.00	*325.00*
23 A4	5pa blue	45.00	*275.00*
24 A4	20pa red, type I	35.00	47.50
a.	Bluish paper	350.00	
25 A4	20pa red, type II	35.00	40.00
a.	Bluish paper	350.00	
	Nos. 22-25 (4)	185.00	612.50

Full margins = 1 ¼mm.

The 20pa types are found se-tenant.

White Laid Paper

26 A4	2pa orange	60.00	*275.00*
a.	2pa ocher	125.00	
27 A4	5pa blue	95.00	*450.00*

Full margins = 1 ¼mm.

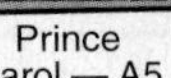

Prince Carol — A5

Type I — A6

Type II — A7

TWENTY PARALES:

Type I — A6. The Greek border at the upper right goes from right to left.

Type II — A7. The Greek border at the upper right goes from left to right.

1866-67 Thin Wove Paper

29 A5	2pa blk, *yellow*	35.00	*95.00*
a.	Thick paper	65.00	*400.00*
30 A5	5pa blk, *dk bl*	60.00	*575.00*
a.	5pa black, *indigo*	100.00	—
b.	Thick paper	70.00	*525.00*
31 A6	20pa blk, *rose,* (I)	30.00	26.50
a.	Dot in Greek border, thin paper	400.00	150.00
b.	Thick paper	175.00	87.50
c.	Dot in Greek border, thick paper	125.00	72.50
32 A7	20pa blk, *rose,* (II)	30.00	26.50
a.	Thick paper	175.00	87.50
	Nos. 29-32 (4)	155.00	723.00

Full margins = 1 ¼mm.

The 20pa types are found se-tenant.

Faked cancellations are known on Nos. 22-27, 29-32.

The white dot of Nos. 31a and 31c occurs in extreme upper right border.

Thick paper was used in 1866, thin in 1867.

Prince Carol — A8

1868-70

No.	Type	Description	Unused	Used
33	A8	2b orange	42.50	40.00
a.		2b yellow	45.00	40.00
34	A8	3b violet ('70)	42.50	40.00
35	A8	4b dk blue	55.00	47.50
36	A8	18b scarlet	225.00	30.00
a.		18b rose	225.00	30.00
		Nos. 33-36 (4)	365.00	157.50

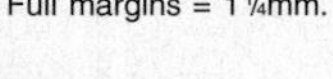

Full margins = 1¼mm.

Prince Carol — A9

1869

No.	Type	Description	Unused	Used
37	A9	5b orange yel	72.50	42.50
a.		5b deep orange	75.00	*42.50*
38	A9	10b blue	40.00	35.00
a.		10b ultramarine	77.50	52.50
b.		10b indigo	85.00	40.00
40	A9	15b vermilion	40.00	35.00
41	A9	25b orange & blue	40.00	26.50
42	A9	50b blue & red	150.00	52.50
a.		50b indigo & red	175.00	55.00
		Nos. 37-42 (5)	342.50	191.50

Full margins = 1mm.

No. 40 on vertically laid paper was not issued. Value $1,250.

Prince Carol — A10

1871-72 ***Imperf.***

No.	Type	Description	Unused	Used
43	A10	5b rose	42.50	35.00
a.		5b vermilion	45.00	45.00
44	A10	10b orange yel	55.00	35.00
a.		Vertically laid paper	*450.00*	*450.00*
45	A10	10b blue	125.00	70.00
46	A10	15b red	210.00	210.00
47	A10	25b olive brown	47.50	47.50
		Nos. 43-47 (5)	480.00	397.50

Full margins = 1mm.

1872

No.	Type	Description	Unused	Used
48	A10	10b ultra	42.50	52.50
a.		Vertically laid paper	175.00	300.00
b.		10b greenish blue	150.00	175.00
49	A10	50b blue & red	225.00	240.00

Full margins = 1mm.

No. 48 is a provisional issue printed from a new plate in which the head is placed further right.

Faked cancellations are found on No. 49.

1872 **Wove Paper** ***Perf. 12½***

No.	Type	Description	Unused	Used
50	A10	5b rose	65.00	52.50
a.		5b vermilion	*1,300.*	*700.00*
51	A10	10b blue	57.50	52.50
a.		10b ultramarine	60.00	25.00
52	A10	25b dark brown	47.50	47.50
		Nos. 50-52 (3)	170.00	152.50

No. 43a with faked perforation is frequently offered as No. 50a.

Prince Carol — A11

Paris Print, Fine Impression
Tinted Paper

1872 **Typo.** ***Perf. 14x13½***

No.	Type	Description	Unused	Used
53	A11	1½b brnz grn, *bluish*	25.00	5.00
54	A11	3b green, *bluish*	32.50	5.00
55	A11	5b bis, *pale buff*	21.00	4.50
56	A11	10b blue	21.00	5.00
57	A11	15b red brn, *pale buff*	140.00	15.00
58	A11	25b org, *pale buff*	145.00	18.50
59	A11	50b rose, *pale rose*	150.00	42.50
		Nos. 53-59 (7)	534.50	95.50

Nos. 53-59 exist imperf.

Bucharest Print, Rough Impression
Perf. 11, 11½, 13½, and Compound

1876-79

No.	Type	Description	Unused	Used
60	A11	1½b brnz grn, *bluish*	6.50	4.25
61	A11	5b bis, *yelsh*	17.00	3.25
b.		Printed on both sides		*75.00*
62	A11	10b bl, *yelsh* ('77)	27.50	5.00
a.		10b pale bl, *yelsh*	25.00	5.00
b.		10b dark blue, *yelsh*	42.50	5.00
d.		Cliché of 5b in plate of 10b ('79)	425.00	425.00
63	A11	10b ultra, *yelsh* ('77)	47.50	5.00
64	A11	15b red brn, *yelsh*	72.50	9.25
a.		Printed on both sides		*100.00*
65	A11	30b org red, *yelsh* ('78)	190.00	50.00
a.		Printed on both sides		*210.00*
		Nos. 60-65 (6)	361.00	76.75

#60-65 are valued in the grade of fine.

#62d has been reprinted in dark blue. The originals are in dull blue. Value of reprint, $175.

Perf. 11, 11½, 13½ and Compound

1879

No.	Type	Description	Unused	Used
66	A11	1½b blk, *yelsh*	6.25	4.25
b.		Imperf.		12.00
67	A11	3b ol grn, *bluish*	17.50	12.50
a.		Diagonal half used as 1½b on cover		
68	A11	5b green, *bluish*	6.75	4.25
69	A11	10b rose, *yelsh*	13.50	2.50
b.		Cliché of 5b in plate of 10b	3.75.00	*475.00*
70	A11	15b rose red, *yelsh*	50.00	12.50
71	A11	25b blue, *yelsh*	140.00	25.00
72	A11	50b bister, *yelsh*	120.00	35.00
		Nos. 66-72 (7)	354.00	96.00

#66-72 are valued in the grade of fine.

There are two varieties of the numerals on the 15b and 50b.

No. 69b has been reprinted in dark rose. Originals are in pale rose. Value of reprint, $40.

King Carol I — A12

1880 **White Paper**

No.	Type	Description	Unused	Used
73	A12	15b brown	12.50	2.50
74	A12	25b blue	23.50	3.25

#73-74 are valued in the grade of fine.

No. 74 exists imperf.

King Carol I — A13

Perf. 13½, 11½ & Compound

1885-89

No.	Type	Description	Unused	Used
75	A13	1½b black	3.50	1.75
a.		Printed on both sides		
76	A13	3b violet	5.00	1.75
a.		Half used as 1½b on cover		21.00
77	A13	5b green	75.00	1.75
78	A13	15b red brown	14.50	2.50
79	A13	25b blue	17.00	6.00
		Nos. 75-79 (5)	115.00	13.75

Tinted Paper

No.	Type	Description	Unused	Used
80	A13	1½b blk, *bluish*	5.00	1.75
81	A13	3b vio, *bluish*	5.00	1.75
82	A13	3b ol grn, *bluish*	5.00	1.75
83	A13	5b bl grn, *bluish*	5.00	1.75
84	A13	10b rose, *pale buff*	5.00	2.50
85	A13	15b red brn, *pale buff*	18.50	2.75
86	A13	25b bl, *pale buff*	18.50	6.00
87	A13	50b bis, *pale buff*	75.00	21.00
		Nos. 80-87 (8)	137.00	39.25

Thin Pale Yellowish Paper

1889 **Wmk. 163**

No.	Type	Description	Unused	Used
88	A13	1½b black	30.00	6.00
89	A13	3b violet	21.00	6.00
90	A13	5b green	21.00	6.00
91	A13	10b rose	21.00	6.00
92	A13	15b red brown	72.50	13.00
93	A13	25b dark blue	47.50	10.00
		Nos. 88-93 (6)	213.00	47.00

King Carol I — A14

1890 ***Perf. 13½, 11½ & Compound***

No.	Type	Description	Unused	Used
94	A14	1½b maroon	5.00	3.50
95	A14	3b violet	25.00	3.50
96	A14	5b emerald	12.00	3.50
97	A14	10b red	13.00	5.00
a.		10b rose	17.00	6.75
98	A14	15b dk brown	30.00	3.50
99	A14	25b gray blue	25.00	3.50
100	A14	50b orange	65.00	32.50
		Nos. 94-100 (7)	175.00	55.00

1891 **Unwmk.**

No.	Type	Description	Unused	Used
101	A14	1½b lilac rose	1.75	1.25
b.		Printed on both sides		*65.00*
102	A14	3b lilac	2.00	1.75
a.		3b violet	2.25	2.25
b.		Printed on both sides		
c.		Impressions of 5b on back	*100.00*	*75.00*
103	A14	5b emerald	3.50	1.75
104	A14	10b pale red	21.00	1.75
a.		Printed on both sides	*140.00*	*110.00*
105	A14	15b gray brown	13.00	1.25
106	A14	25b gray blue	13.00	1.75
107	A14	50b orange	85.00	13.00
		Nos. 101-107 (7)	139.25	22.50

Nos. 101-107 exist imperf.

King Carol I — A15

1891

No.	Type	Description	Unused	Used
108	A15	1½b claret	6.00	7.00
109	A15	3b lilac	6.00	7.00
110	A15	5b emerald	7.50	8.50
111	A15	10b red	7.50	8.50
112	A15	15b gray brown	7.50	8.50
		Nos. 108-112 (5)	34.50	39.50

25th year of the reign of King Carol I.

1894 **Wmk. 164**

No.	Type	Description	Unused	Used
113	A14	3b lilac	9.25	5.00
114	A14	5b pale green	9.25	5.00
115	A14	25b gray blue	13.50	6.25
116	A14	50b orange	27.50	12.50
		Nos. 113-116 (4)	59.50	28.75

King Carol I

A17 A18

A19

A20

A21

A23

1893-98 **Wmk. 164 & 200**

No.	Type	Description	Unused	Used
117	A17	1b pale brown	1.25	1.25
118	A17	1½b black	.85	1.25
119	A18	3b chocolate	1.25	.85
120	A19	5b blue	1.75	.85
a.		Cliché of the 25b in the plate of 5b	185.00	*200.00*
121	A19	5b yel grn ('98)	5.00	3.00
a.		5b emerald	5.00	3.00
122	A20	10b emerald	2.50	1.75
123	A20	10b rose ('98)	6.00	2.50
124	A21	15b rose	2.50	.85
125	A21	15b black ('98)	6.00	2.00
126	A19	25b violet	3.75	1.25
127	A19	25b indigo ('98)	9.25	3.25
128	A19	40b gray grn	21.00	3.50
129	A19	50b orange	12.50	2.00
130	A23	1 l bis & rose	30.00	2.00
131	A23	2 l orange & brn	35.00	3.25
		Nos. 117-131 (15)	138.60	29.55

This watermark may be found in four versions (Wmks. 164, 200 and variations). The paper also varies in thickness.

A 3b orange of type A18; 10b brown, type A20; 15b rose, type A21, and 25b bright green with similar but different border, all watermarked "P R," were prepared but never issued. Value, each $15.

See Nos. 132-157, 224-229. For overprints and surcharges see Romanian Post Offices in the Turkish Empire Nos. 1-6, 10-11.

King Carol I — A24

Thin Paper, Tinted Rose on Back
Perf. 11½, 13½ and Compound

1900-03 **Unwmk.**

No.	Type	Description	Unused	Used
132	A17	1b pale brown	1.75	1.75
133	A24	1b brown ('01)	1.75	1.25
134	A24	1b black ('03)	1.75	1.25
135	A18	3b red brown	1.75	.85
136	A19	5b emerald	2.50	.85
137	A20	10b rose	3.00	1.25
138	A21	15b black	2.50	.85
139	A21	15b lil gray ('01)	2.50	.85
140	A21	15b dk vio ('03)	2.50	1.25
141	A19	25b blue	4.25	1.75
142	A19	40b gray grn	8.50	1.75
143	A19	50b orange	17.00	1.75
144	A23	1 l bis & rose ('01)	34.00	3.00
145	A23	1 l grn & blk ('03)	30.00	3.50
146	A23	2 l org & brn ('01)	30.00	3.50
147	A23	2 l red brn & blk ('03)	25.00	4.25
		Nos. 132-147 (16)	168.75	29.65

#132 inscribed BANI; #133-134 BAN.

1900, July **Wmk. 167**

No.	Type	Description	Unused	Used
148	A17	1b pale brown	12.00	5.00
149	A18	3b red brown	12.00	5.50
150	A19	5b emerald	10.00	5.00
151	A20	10b rose	15.00	6.00
152	A21	15b black	17.00	7.25
153	A19	25b blue	19.00	12.50
154	A19	40b gray grn	30.00	12.50
155	A19	50b orange	30.00	12.50
156	A23	1 l bis & rose	34.00	17.00
157	A23	2 l orange & brn	42.50	21.00
		Nos. 148-157 (10)	221.50	104.25

Mail Coach Leaving PO — A25

Thin Paper, Tinted Rose on Face

1903 **Unwmk.** ***Perf. 14x13½***

No.	Type	Description	Unused	Used
158	A25	1b gray brown	*2.25*	1.60
159	A25	3b brown violet	*3.75*	1.60
160	A25	5b pale green	*7.50*	2.50
161	A25	10b rose	*4.50*	2.50
162	A25	15b black	*4.50*	3.25
163	A25	25b blue	*22.50*	9.50
164	A25	40b dull green	*32.50*	12.50
165	A25	50b orange	*37.50*	16.00
		Nos. 158-165 (8)	*115.00*	49.45

Counterfeits are plentiful. See note after No. 172. See No. 428.

King Carol I and Façade of New Post Office — A26

Thick Toned Paper

1903 **Engr.** ***Perf. 13½x14***

No.	Type	Description	Unused	Used
166	A26	15b black	5.00	3.75
167	A26	25b blue	11.00	6.50
168	A26	40b gray grn	19.00	9.00
169	A26	50b orange	21.00	11.00
170	A26	1 l dk brown	16.00	9.00
171	A26	2 l dull red	130.00	65.00
a.		2 l orange (error)	180.00	150.00
172	A26	5 l dull violet	160.00	110.00
a.		5 l red violet	80.00	32.50
		Nos. 166-172 (7)	362.00	214.25

Opening of the new PO in Bucharest (Nos. 158-172).
Counterfeits exist.

Prince Carol Taking Oath of Allegiance, 1866 — A27

Prince in Royal Carriage A28

Prince Carol at Calafat in 1877 — A29

Prince Carol Shaking Hands with His Captive, Osman Pasha — A30

Carol I as Prince in 1866 and King in 1906 — A31

Romanian Army Crossing Danube A32

Romanian Troops Return to Bucharest in 1878 — A33

Prince Carol at Head of His Command in 1877 — A34

King Carol I at the Cathedral in 1896 — A35

King Carol I at Shrine of St. Nicholas, 1904 — A36

1906 **Engr.** ***Perf. 12***

No.	Type	Description	Unused	Used
176	A27	1b bister & blk	.65	.45
177	A28	3b red brn & blk	1.40	.45
178	A29	5b dp grn & blk	1.75	.45
179	A30	10b carmine & blk	1.10	.45
180	A31	15b dull vio & blk	1.10	.45
181	A32	25b ultra & blk	7.00	5.25
a.		25b olive green & black	9.00	5.25
182	A33	40b dk brn & blk	1.90	1.60
183	A34	50b bis brn & blk	2.00	1.60
184	A35	1 l vermilion & blk	2.25	1.90
185	A36	2 l orange & blk	2.50	2.40
		Nos. 176-185 (10)	21.65	15.00

40 years' rule of Carol I as Prince & King.
No. 181a was never placed in use. Cancelations were by favor.

King Carol I — A37

1906

No.	Type	Description	Unused	Used
186	A37	1b bister & blk	.90	.45
187	A37	3b red brn & blk	2.25	.85
188	A37	5b dp grn & blk	1.50	.75
189	A37	10b carmine & blk	1.50	.75
190	A37	15b dl vio & blk	1.50	.75
191	A37	25b ultra & blk	13.50	7.00
192	A37	40b dk brn & blk	6.00	1.50
193	A37	50b bis brn & blk	6.00	1.50
194	A37	1 l red & blk	6.00	1.50
195	A37	2 l orange & blk	6.00	1.50
		Nos. 186-195 (10)	45.15	16.55

25th anniversary of the Kingdom.

Plowman and Angel — A38

Exposition Building — A39

Exposition Buildings
A40 A41

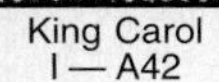
King Carol I — A42

Queen Elizabeth (Carmen Sylva) — A43

1906 **Typo.** ***Perf. 11½, 13½***

No.	Type	Description	Unused	Used
196	A38	5b yel grn & blk	4.50	1.40
197	A38	10b car & blk	4.50	1.40
198	A39	15b violet & blk	6.50	2.25
199	A39	25b blue & blk	6.50	2.25
200	A40	30b red & blk brn	8.75	2.25
201	A40	40b grn & blk brn	9.50	2.75
202	A41	50b orange & blk	8.75	3.25
203	A41	75b lt brn & dk brn	7.75	3.25
204	A42	1.50 l red lil & blk brn	97.50	45.00
a.		Center inverted		
205	A42	2.50 l yellow & brn	37.50	26.00
a.		Center inverted		
206	A43	3 l brn org & brn	28.00	26.00
		Nos. 196-206 (11)	219.75	115.80

General Exposition. They were sold at post offices July 29-31, 1906, and were valid only for those three days. Those sold at the exposition are overprinted "S E" in black. Remainders were sold privately, both unused and canceled to order, by the Exposition promoters. Value, set: unused or used, $450.

A44

A45

Perf. 11½, 13½ & Compound

1908-18 **Engr.**

No.	Type	Description	Unused	Used
207	A44	5b pale yel grn	2.50	.25
208	A44	10b carmine	.70	.25
209	A45	15b purple	11.50	2.25
210	A44	25b deep blue	1.75	.25
211	A44	40b brt green	.85	.25
212	A44	40b dk brn ('18)	5.25	2.25
213	A44	50b orange	.65	.25
214	A44	50b lt red ('18)	2.00	.70
215	A44	1 l brown	2.00	.40
216	A44	2 l red	10.00	2.50
		Nos. 207-216 (10)	37.20	9.35

King Carol I — A46

Perf. 13½x14, 11½, 13½ & Compound

1909-18 **Typo.**

No.	Type	Description	Unused	Used
217	A46	1b black	.60	.25
218	A46	3b red brown	1.25	.25
219	A46	5b yellow grn	.60	.25
220	A46	10b rose	1.25	.25
221	A46	15b dull violet	21.00	12.50
222	A46	15b olive green	1.25	.25
223	A46	15b red brn ('18)	1.10	.65
		Nos. 217-223 (7)	27.05	14.40

Nos. 217-219, 222 exist imperf.
No. 219 in black is a chemical changeling.
For surcharge and overprints see Nos. 240-242, 245-247, J50-J51, RA1-RA2, RA11-RA12, Romanian Post Offices in the Turkish Empire 7-9.

Types of 1893-99

1911-19 **White Paper** **Unwmk.**

No.	Type	Description	Unused	Used
224	A17	1½b straw	1.75	.45
225	A19	25b deep blue ('18)	1.00	.85
226	A19	40b gray brn ('19)	1.25	.85
227	A19	50b dull red ('19)	1.75	.85
228	A23	1 l gray grn ('18)	2.25	.50
229	A23	2 l orange ('18)	2.25	.85
		Nos. 224-229 (6)	10.25	4.35

For overprints see Romanian Post Offices in the Turkish Empire Nos. 10-11.

Romania Holding Flag — A47

Romanian Crown and Old Fort on Danube — A48

Troops Crossing Danube — A49

View of Turtucaia — A50

Mircea the Great and Carol I — A51

View of Silistra — A52

Perf. 11½x13½, 13½x11½

1913, Dec. 25

No.	Type	Description	Unused	Used
230	A47	1b black	.85	.40
231	A48	3b ol gray & choc	2.25	.85
232	A49	5b yel grn & blk brn	1.75	.40
233	A50	10b org & gray	.85	.40
234	A51	15b bister & vio	2.25	.85
235	A52	25b blue & choc	3.00	1.25
236	A49	40b bis & red vio	6.00	4.75
237	A48	50b yellow & bl	16.00	6.50
238	A48	1 l bl & ol bis	25.00	14.50
239	A48	2 l org red & rose	40.00	20.00
		Nos. 230-239 (10)	97.95	49.90

Romania's annexation of Silistra.

No. 217 Handstamped in Red

Perf. 13½x14, 11½, 13½ & Compound

1918, May 1

No.	Type	Description	Unused	Used
240	A46	25b on 1b black	2.25	2.25

This handstamp is found inverted.

No. 219 and 220 Overprinted in Black

1918

No.	Type	Description	Unused	Used
241	A46	5b yellow green	.60	.55
a.		Inverted overprint	3.25	3.25
b.		Double overprint	3.25	3.25
242	A46	10b rose	.60	.55
a.		Inverted overprint	3.25	3.25
b.		Double overprint	3.25	3.25

Nos. 217, 219 and 220 Overprinted in Red or Black

1919, Nov. 8

No.	Type	Description	Unused	Used
245	A46	1b black (R)	.40	.25
a.		Inverted overprint	6.75	
b.		Double overprint	10.00	2.25
246	A46	5b yel grn (Bk)	.40	.25
a.		Double overprint	10.00	3.25
b.		Inverted overprint	6.75	2.00

247 A46 10b rose (Bk) .40 .25
a. Inverted overprint 6.75 2.00
b. Double overprint 10.00 3.00
Nos. 245-247 (3) 1.20 .75

Recovery of Transylvania and the return of the King to Bucharest.

King Ferdinand — A53

1920-22 **Typo.**

248 A53 1b black .25 .25
249 A53 5b yellow grn .25 .25
250 A53 10b rose .25 .25
251 A53 15b red brown .75 .25
252 A53 25b deep blue 1.50 .40
253 A53 25b brown .75 .25
254 A53 40b gray brown 1.25 .35
255 A53 50b salmon .35 .25
256 A53 1 l gray grn 1.25 .25
257 A53 1 l rose .75 .25
258 A53 2 l orange 1.25 .25
259 A53 2 l dp blue 1.25 .25
260 A53 2 l rose ('22) 3.00 1.75
Nos. 248-260 (13) 12.85 5.00

Nos. 248-260 are printed on two papers: coarse, grayish paper with bits of colored fiber, and thinner white paper of better quality.
Nos. 248-251, 253 exist imperf.

King Ferdinand — A54

Type I Type II Type III

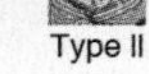
Type I Type II Type I Type II

TWO LEI:
Type I — The "2" is thin, with tail 2½mm wide. Top of "2" forms a hook.
Type II — The "2" is thick, with tail 3mm wide. Top of "2" forms a ball.
Type III — The "2" is similar to type II. The "E" of "LEI" is larger and about 2mm wide.

THREE LEI:
Type I — Top of "3" begins in a point. Top and middle bars of "E" of "LEI" are without serifs.
Type II — Top of "3" begins in a ball. Top and middle bars of "E" of "LEI" have serifs.

FIVE LEI:
Type I — The "5" is 2½mm wide. The end of the final stroke of the "L" of "LEI" almost touches the vertical stroke.
Type II — The "5" is 3mm wide and the lines are broader than in type I. The end of the final stroke of the "L" of "LEI" is separated from the vertical by a narrow space.

Perf. 13½x14, 11½, 13½ & Compound

1920-26

261 A54 3b black .25 .25
262 A54 5b black .25 .25
263 A54 10b yel grn ('25) .25 .25
a. 10b olive green ('25) .40
264 A54 25b bister brn .25 .25
265 A54 25b salmon .25 .25
266 A54 30b violet .25 .25
267 A54 50b orange .25 .25
268 A54 60b gray grn 1.00 .55
269 A54 1 l violet .25 .25
270 A54 2 l rose (I) 1.25 .25
a. 2 l claret (I) *47.50*
271 A54 2 l lt green (II) .70 .25
a. 2 l light green (I) .95 .40
b. 2 l light green (III) .80 .25
272 A54 3 l blue (I) 2.60 .80
273 A54 3 l buff (II) 2.60 .80
a. 3 l buff (I) *12.50* 2.25
274 A54 3 l salmon (II) .25 .25
a. 3 l salmon (I) 1.60 1.25
275 A54 3 l car rose (II) .65 .25
276 A54 5 l emer (I) 2.10 .50
277 A54 5 l lt brn (II) .45 .25
a. 5 l light brown (I) 1.60 .80

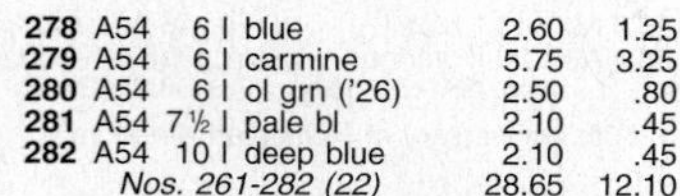
278 A54 6 l blue 2.60 1.25
279 A54 6 l carmine 5.75 3.25
280 A54 6 l ol grn ('26) 2.50 .80
281 A54 7½ l pale bl 2.10 .45
282 A54 10 l deep blue 2.10 .45
Nos. 261-282 (22) 28.65 12.10

#273 and 273a, 274 and 274a, exist se-tenant. The 50b exists in three types.
For surcharge see No. Q7.

Alba Iulia Cathedral A55

King Ferdinand A56

Coat of Arms — A57

Queen Marie as Nurse — A58

Michael the Brave and King Ferdinand A59

King Ferdinand A60

Queen Marie — A61

Perf. 13½x14, 13½, 11½ & Compound

1922, Oct. 15 **Photo.** **Wmk. 95**

283 A55 5b black .40 .30
a. Engraver's name omitted *.40* .30
284 A56 25b chocolate 1.25 .40
285 A57 50b dp green 1.25 .60
286 A58 1 l olive grn 1.50 .85
287 A59 2 l carmine 1.50 .85
288 A60 3 l blue 4.00 1.25
289 A61 6 l violet 11.50 8.00
Nos. 283-289 (7) 21.40 12.25

Coronation of King Ferdinand I and Queen Marie on Oct. 15, 1922, at Alba Iulia. All values exist imperforate. Value, set $150, unused or used.

King Ferdinand
A62 A63

1926, July 1 **Unwmk.** ***Perf. 11***

291 A62 10b yellow grn .35 .25
292 A62 25b orange .35 .25
293 A62 50b orange brn .35 .25
294 A63 1 l dk violet .50 .25
295 A63 2 l dk green .50 .25
296 A63 3 l brown car .50 .50
297 A63 5 l black brn .50 .50
298 A63 6 l dk olive .50 .50
a. 6 l bright blue (error) 150.00 175.00
300 A63 9 l slate .75 .50
301 A63 10 l brt blue .75 .50
b. 10 l brown carmine (error) 150.00 175.00
Nos. 291-301 (10) 5.05 3.75

60th birthday of King Ferdinand.

Exist imperf. Value, set unused $150; used $175. Imperf. examples with watermark 95 are proofs.

King Carol I and King Ferdinand A69

King Ferdinand A70

A71

1927, Aug. 1 ***Perf. 13½***

308 A69 25b brown vio .50 .35
309 A70 30b gray blk .50 .35
310 A71 50b dk green .50 .35
311 A69 1 l bluish slate .50 .35
312 A70 2 l dp green .50 .45
313 A70 3 l violet .50 .55
314 A71 4 l dk brown .50 .65
315 A71 4.50 l henna brn 3.00 2.25
316 A70 5 l red brown .50 .55
317 A71 6 l carmine 2.00 1.25
318 A69 7.50 l grnsh bl .50 .55
319 A69 10 l brt blue 3.00 1.10
Nos. 308-319 (12) 12.50 8.75

50th anniversary of Romania's independence from Turkish suzerainty.
Some values exist imperf. All exist imperf. and with value numerals omitted.

King Michael
A72 A73

Perf. 13½x14 (25b, 50b); 13½

1928-29 **Typo.** **Unwmk.**

Size: 19x25mm

320 A72 25b black .25 .25
321 A72 30b fawn ('29) .40 .25
322 A72 50b olive grn .25 .25

Photo.

Size: 18½x24½mm

323 A73 1 l violet .45 .25
324 A73 2 l dp green .45 .25
325 A73 3 l brt rose .90 .25
326 A73 5 l red brown 1.40 .25
327 A73 7.50 l ultra 6.25 .90
328 A73 10 l blue 5.25 .35
Nos. 320-328 (9) 15.60 3.00

See Nos. 343-345, 353-357. For overprints see Nos. 359-368A.

Parliament House, Bessarabia — A74

Designs: 1 l, 2 l, Parliament House, Bessarabia. 3 l, 5 l, 20 l, Hotin Fortress. 7.50 l, 10 l, Fortress Cetatea Alba.

1928, Apr. 29 **Wmk. 95** ***Perf. 13½***

329 A74 1 l deep green 1.75 .65
330 A74 2 l deep brown 1.75 .65
331 A74 3 l black brown 1.75 .65
332 A74 5 l carmine lake 2.25 .80
333 A74 7.50 l ultra 2.25 .80
334 A74 10 l Prus blue 5.00 2.00
335 A74 20 l black vio 8.00 2.75
Nos. 329-335 (7) 22.75 8.30

Reunion of Bessarabia with Romania, 10th anniv.

King Carol I and King Michael A77

View of Constanta Harbor A78

Trajan's Monument at Adam Clisi A79

Cernavoda Bridge — A80

1928, Oct. 25

336 A77 1 l blue green 1.10 .45
337 A78 2 l red brown 1.10 .45
338 A77 3 l gray black 1.40 .50
339 A79 5 l dull lilac 1.75 .60
340 A79 7.50 l ultra 2.10 .80
341 A80 10 l blue 3.25 1.90
342 A80 20 l carmine rose 5.50 3.25
Nos. 336-342 (7) 16.20 7.95

Union of Dobruja with Romania, 50th anniv.

Michael Types of 1928-29

Perf. 13½x14

1928, Sept. 1 **Typo.** **Wmk. 95**

343 A72 25b black .60 .25

Photo.

344 A73 7.50 l ultra 2.00 .75
345 A73 10 l blue 4.00 .60
Nos. 343-345 (3) 6.60 1.60

Ferdinand I; Stephen the Great; Michael the Brave; Corvin and Constantine Brancoveanu — A81

Union with Transylvania A82

Avram Jancu — A83

Prince Michael the Brave — A84

Castle Bran — A85

King Ferdinand I — A86

1929, May 10 Photo. Wmk. 95

347 A81 1 l dark violet 2.25 1.75
348 A82 2 l olive green 2.25 1.75
349 A83 3 l violet brown 2.50 1.75
350 A84 4 l cerise 2.75 2.25
351 A85 5 l orange 4.50 2.25
352 A86 10 l brt blue 7.50 4.25
Nos. 347-352 (6) 21.75 14.00

Union of Transylvania and Romania.

Michael Type of 1928

1930 Unwmk. *Perf. 14½x14*

Size: 18x23mm

353 A73 1 l deep violet .80 .25
354 A73 2 l deep green 1.25 .25
355 A73 3 l carmine rose 2.40 .25
356 A73 7.50 l ultra 5.00 1.10
357 A73 10 l deep blue 16.00 7.00
Nos. 353-357 (5) 25.45 8.85

Stamps of 1928-30 Overprinted

On Nos. 320-322, 326, 328

Perf. 13½x14, 13½

1930, June 8 Typo.

359 A72 25b black .40 .25
360 A72 30b fawn .80 .25
361 A72 50b olive green .80 .25

Photo.

Size: 18½x24½mm

362 A73 5 l red brown 1.60 .25
362A A73 10 l brt blue 8.25 1.50

On Nos. 353-357

Perf. 14½x14

Size: 18x23mm

363 A73 1 l deep violet .80 .25
364 A73 2 l deep green .80 .25
365 A73 3 l carmine rose 1.60 .25
366 A73 7.50 l ultra 4.00 .75
367 A73 10 l deep blue 3.25 .75

On Nos. 343-344

Perf. 13½x14, 13½

Typo. Wmk. 95

368 A72 25b black 1.25 .35

Photo.

Size: 18½x24½mm

368A A73 7.50 l ultra 5.00 1.50
Nos. 359-368A (12) 28.55 6.60

Accession to the throne by King Carol II. This overprint exists on Nos. 323, 345.

A87

A88

King Carol II — A89

Perf. 13½, 14, 14x13½

1930 Wmk. 225

369 A87 25b black 1.10 .25
370 A87 50b chocolate 3.25 .45
371 A87 1 l dk violet 2.25 .25
372 A87 2 l gray green 2.75 .25
373 A88 3 l carmine rose 2.25 .25
374 A88 4 l orange red 3.25 .25
375 A88 6 l carmine brn 4.25 .25
376 A88 7.50 l ultra 4.25 .30
377 A89 10 l deep blue 2.25 .25
378 A89 16 l peacock grn 4.75 .25
379 A89 20 l orange 1.40 .60
Nos. 369-379 (11) 31.75 3.35

Exist imperf. Value, unused or used, $250.
See Nos. 405-414.

A90

A91

1930, Dec. 24 Unwmk. *Perf. 13½*

380 A90 1 l dull violet 1.25 .45
381 A91 2 l green 2.25 .50
382 A91 4 l vermilion 2.50 .35
383 A91 6 l brown carmine 6.50 .45
Nos. 380-383 (4) 12.50 1.75

First census in Romania.

King Carol II — A92

King Carol I — A93

King Ferdinand — A96

King Carol II — A94

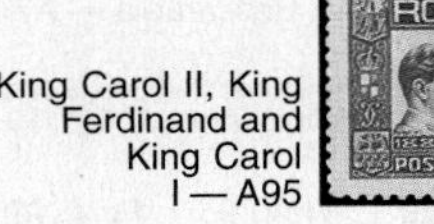
King Carol II, King Ferdinand and King Carol I — A95

1931, May 10 Photo. Wmk. 225

384 A92 1 l gray violet 2.50 1.75
385 A93 2 l green 4.25 2.00
386 A94 6 l red brown 11.00 3.25

387 A95 10 l blue 16.00 6.00
388 A96 20 l orange 22.50 8.50
Nos. 384-388 (5) 56.25 21.50

50th anniversary of Romanian Kingdom.

Using Bayonet — A97

Romanian Infantryman 1870 — A98

Romanian Infantry 1830 — A99

King Carol I A100

Infantry Advance A101

King Ferdinand A102

King Carol II A103

1931, May 10

389 A97 25b gray black 1.40 .75
390 A98 50b dk red brn 2.10 1.10
391 A99 1 l gray violet 2.75 1.10
392 A100 2 l deep green 4.25 1.50
393 A101 3 l carmine rose 10.00 3.50
394 A102 7.50 l ultra 13.00 9.00
395 A103 16 l blue green 16.00 4.00
Nos. 389-395 (7) 49.50 20.95

Centenary of the Romanian Army.

Naval Cadet Ship "Mircea" A104

10 l, Ironclad. 16 l, Light cruiser. 20 l, Destroyer.

1931, May 10

396 A104 6 l red brown 7.00 4.00
397 A104 10 l blue 9.50 4.50
398 A104 16 l blue green 40.00 6.00
399 A104 20 l orange 17.50 10.00
Nos. 396-399 (4) 74.00 24.50

50th anniversary of the Romanian Navy.

King Carol II — A108

1931 Unwmk. Engr. *Perf. 12*

400 A108 30 l ol bis & dk bl 1.75 1.00
401 A108 50 l red & dk bl 4.50 1.50
402 A108 100 l dk grn & dk bl 7.25 3.50
Nos. 400-402 (3) 13.50 6.00

Exist imperf. Value, unused or used, $150.

Carol II, Ferdinand, Carol I — A109

Wmk. 230

1931, Nov. 1 Photo. *Perf. 13½*

403 A109 16 l Prus green 12.00 .90

Exists imperf. Value, unused or used, $300.

Carol II Types of 1930

Perf. 13½, 14, 14½ and Compound

1932 Wmk. 230

405 A87 25b black .50 .25
406 A87 50b dark brown 1.00 .25
407 A87 1 l dark violet 1.40 .25
408 A87 2 l gray green 1.75 .25
409 A88 3 l carmine rose 2.25 .25
410 A88 4 l orange red 5.25 .25
411 A88 6 l carmine brn 12.50 .25
412 A88 7.50 l ultra 21.50 .75
413 A89 10 l deep blue 125.00 .90
414 A89 20 l orange 110.00 9.00
Nos. 405-414 (10) 281.15 12.40

Alexander the Good — A110

1932, May *Perf. 13½*

415 A110 6 l carmine brown 12.00 6.00

500th death anniv. of Alexander the Good, Prince of Moldavia, 1400-1432.

King Carol II — A111

1932, June

416 A111 10 l brt blue 12.00 .45

Exists imperf. Value, unused or used, $200.

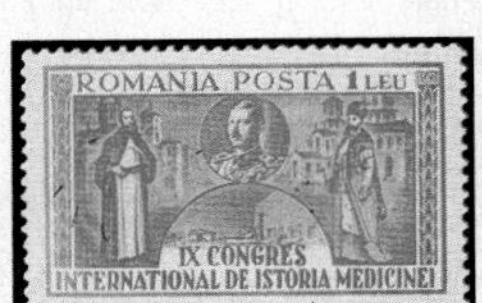
Cantacuzino and Gregory Ghika, Founders of Coltea and Pantelimon Hospitals — A112

Session of the Congress A113

Aesculapius and Hygeia — A114

1932, Sept. *Perf. 13½*

No.	Type	Value	Color	Unused	Used
417	A112	1 l	carmine rose	7.50	7.50
418	A113	6 l	deep orange	20.00	11.00
419	A114	10 l	brt blue	34.00	18.50
			Nos. 417-419 (3)	61.50	37.00

9th Intl. History of Medicine Congress, Bucharest.

Bull's Head and Post Horn A116

Lion Rampant and Bridge A117

Dolphins A118

Eagle and Castles A119

Coat of Arms — A120

Eagle and Post Horn — A121

Bull's Head and Post Horn — A122

1932, Nov. 20 **Typo.** *Imperf.*

No.	Type	Value	Color	Unused	Used
421	A116	25b	black	.85	.40
422	A117	1 l	violet	2.00	.70
423	A118	2 l	green	2.50	.90
424	A119	3 l	car rose	2.80	1.10
425	A120	6 l	red brown	3.50	1.25
426	A121	7.50 l	lt blue	4.25	1.75
427	A122	10 l	dk blue	8.00	3.00
			Nos. 421-427 (7)	23.90	9.10

75th anniv. of the first Moldavian stamps.

Mail Coach Type of 1903

1932, Nov. 20 *Perf. 13½*

No.	Type	Value	Color	Unused	Used
428	A25	16 l	blue green	11.00	5.50

30th anniv. of the opening of the new post office, Bucharest, in 1903.

Arms of City of Turnu-Severin, Ruins of Tower of Emperor Severus — A123

Inauguration of Trajan's Bridge — A124

Prince Carol Landing at Turnu-Severin — A125

Bridge over the Danube A126

1933, June 2 **Photo.** *Perf. 14½x14*

No.	Type	Value	Color	Unused	Used
429	A123	25b	gray green	.75	.30
430	A124	50b	dull blue	1.10	.45
431	A125	1 l	black brn	1.75	.75
432	A126	2 l	olive blk	3.25	1.10
			Nos. 429-432 (4)	6.85	2.60

Centenary of the incorporation in Walachia of the old Roman City of Turnu-Severin.
Exist imperf. Value, unused or used, $150.

Queen Elizabeth and King Carol I — A127

Profiles of Kings Carol I, Ferdinand and Carol II — A128

Castle Peles, Sinaia A129

1933, Aug.

No.	Type	Value	Color	Unused	Used
433	A127	1 l	dark violet	2.50	2.00
434	A128	3 l	olive brown	3.00	2.75
435	A129	6 l	vermilion	4.25	3.25
			Nos. 433-435 (3)	9.75	8.00

50th anniversary of the erection of Castle Peles, the royal summer residence at Sinaia.
Exist imperf. Value, unused or used, $125.

A130

A131

King Carol II — A132

1934, Aug. *Perf. 13½*

No.	Type	Value	Color	Unused	Used
436	A130	50b	brown	1.00	.40
437	A131	2 l	gray green	2.00	.40
438	A131	4 l	red	3.50	.55
439	A132	6 l	deep claret	8.00	.40
			Nos. 436-439 (4)	14.50	1.75

See Nos. 446-460 for stamps inscribed "Posta." Nos. 436, 439 exist imperf. Value for both, unused or used, $100.

Child and Grapes — A133

Woman and Fruit — A134

1934, Sept. 14

No.	Type	Value	Color	Unused	Used
440	A133	1 l	dull green	5.00	2.25
441	A134	2 l	violet brown	5.00	2.25

Natl. Fruit Week, Sept. 14-21. Exist imperf. Value, unused or used, $125.

Crisan, Horia and Closca A135

1935, Feb. 28

No.	Type	Value	Color	Unused	Used
442	A135	1 l	shown	.65	.50
443	A135	2 l	Crisan	.90	.60
444	A135	6 l	Closca	2.25	1.00
445	A135	10 l	Horia	5.00	2.25
			Nos. 442-445 (4)	8.80	4.35

150th anniversary of the death of three Romanian martyrs. Exist imperf. Value, unused or used, $110.

A139

A140

A141

A142

King Carol II — A143

Wmk. 230

1935-40 **Photo.** *Perf. 13½*

No.	Type	Value	Color	Unused	Used
446	A139	25b	black brn	.25	.25
447	A142	50b	brown	.25	.25
448	A140	1 l	purple	.25	.25
449	A141	2 l	green	.45	.25
449A	A141	2 l	dk bl grn ('40)	.65	.25
450	A142	3 l	deep rose	.70	.25
450A	A142	3 l	grnsh bl ('40)	.85	.30
451	A141	4 l	vermilion	1.25	.25
452	A140	5 l	rose car ('40)	1.25	.80
453	A143	6 l	maroon	1.60	.25
454	A140	7.50 l	ultra	1.90	.30
454A	A142	8 l	magenta ('40)	1.90	.70
455	A141	9 l	brt ultra ('40)	2.50	.80
456	A142	10 l	brt blue	1.00	.25
456A	A143	12 l	slate bl ('40)	1.60	1.25
457	A139	15 l	dk brn ('40)	1.60	.95
458	A143	16 l	Prus blue	2.10	.25
459	A143	20 l	orange	1.25	.35
460	A143	24 l	dk car ('40)	2.10	.95
			Nos. 446-460 (19)	23.45	8.90

Exist imperf. Value, unused or used, $240.

Nos. 454, 456 Overprinted in Red

1936, Dec. 5

No.	Type	Value	Color	Unused	Used
461	A140	7.50 l	ultra	9.25	6.50
462	A142	10 l	brt blue	9.25	6.50

16th anniversary of the Little Entente.
Overprints in silver or gold are fraudulent.

Birthplace of Ion Creanga A144

Ion Creanga A145

1937, May 15

No.	Type	Value	Color	Unused	Used
463	A144	2 l	green	1.25	.80
464	A145	3 l	carmine rose	1.75	.90
465	A144	4 l	dp violet	2.00	1.10
466	A145	6 l	red brown	5.00	2.50
			Nos. 463-466 (4)	10.00	5.30

Creanga (1837-89), writer. Exist imperf. Value, unused or used, $125.

Cathedral at Curtea de Arges — A146

1937, July 1

No.	Type	Value	Color	Unused	Used
467	A146	7.50 l	ultra	2.50	1.10
468	A146	10 l	blue	3.25	.80

The Little Entente (Romania, Czechoslovakia, Yugoslavia). Exist imperf. Value, unused or used, $125.

Souvenir Sheet

A146a

Surcharged in Black with New Values

1937, Oct. 25 **Unwmk.** *Perf. 13½*

No.	Type	Description	Unused	Used
469	A146a	Sheet of 4	9.00	9.00
a.		2 l on 20 l orange	.35	.35
b.		6 l on 10 l bright blue	.35	.35
c.		10 l on 6 l maroon	.45	.45
d.		20 l on 2 l green	1.00	1.00

Promotion of the Crown Prince Michael to the rank of Lieutenant on his 17th birthday.

Arms of Romania, Greece, Turkey and Yugoslavia A147

Perf. 13x13½

1938, Feb. 10 **Wmk. 230**

No.	Type	Value	Color	Unused	Used
470	A147	7.50 l	ultra	1.50	.90
471	A147	10 l	blue	2.00	.80

The Balkan Entente.
Exist imperf. Value, unused or used, $100.

A148

King Carol II

A149 A150

1938, May 10 ***Perf. 13½***

No.	Type	Value	Color	Unused	Used
472	A148	3 l	dk carmine	.75	.50
473	A149	6 l	violet brn	1.25	.50
474	A150	10 l	blue	2.00	.90
			Nos. 472-474 (3)	4.00	1.90

New Constitution of Feb. 27, 1938.
Exist imperf. Value, unused or used, $100.

Catalogue values for unused stamps in this section, from this point to the end of the section, are for Never Hinged items.

Prince Carol's Calatorie, 1866
A151

Examining Plans for a Monastery
A153

Prince Carol and Carmen Sylva (Queen Elizabeth)
A155

Sigmaringen and Peles Castles — A154

Prince Carol, Age 6 — A156

Equestrian Statue — A159

Battle of Plevna — A160

On Horseback
A161

Cathedral of Curtea de Arges
A164

King Carol I and Queen Elizabeth
A163

Designs: 50b, At Calafat. 4 l, In 1866. 5 l, In 1877. 12 l, in 1914.

Perf. 14, 13½

1939, Apr. 10 **Wmk. 230**

No.	Type	Value	Color	Unused	Used
475	A151	25b	olive blk	.25	.25
476	A151	50b	violet brn	.25	.25
477	A153	1 l	dk purple	.25	.25
478	A154	1.50 l	green	.25	.25
479	A155	2 l	myrtle grn	.25	.25
480	A156	3 l	red orange	.25	.25
481	A156	4 l	rose lake	.25	.25
482	A156	5 l	black	.25	.25
483	A159	7 l	olive blk	.25	.25
484	A160	8 l	dark blue	.25	.25
485	A161	10 l	deep mag	.80	.25
486	A161	12 l	dull blue	1.20	.25
487	A163	15 l	ultra	1.20	.25
488	A164	16 l	Prus green	1.20	.60
			Nos. 475-488 (14)	6.90	3.85

Centenary of the birth of King Carol I.
Nos 475-488 exist imperf. Value, unused or used, $150.

Souvenir Sheets

1939 ***Perf. 14x13½***

No.	Description	Unused	Used
488A	Sheet of 3, #475-476, 478	3.50	3.50
d.	Imperf. ('40)	7.00	7.00

Perf. 14x15½

No.	Description	Unused	Used
488B	Sheet of 4, #480-482, 486	3.50	3.50
e.	Imperf. ('40)	7.00	7.00
488C	Sheet of 4, #479, 483-485	3.50	3.50
f.	Imperf. ('40)	7.00	7.00

No. 488A sold for 20 l, Nos. 488B-488C for 50 l, the surtax for national defense.

Nos. 488A-488C and 488Ad-488Cf were overprinted "PRO-PATRIA 1940" to aid the armament fund. Value, set of 6, $100.

Nos. 488A-488C exist with overprint of "ROMA BERLIN 1940" and bars, but these are not recognized as having been officially issued.

Romanian Pavilion
A165

Romanian Pavilion
A166

1939, May 8 ***Perf. 14x13½, 13½***

No.	Type	Value	Color	Unused	Used
489	A165	6 l	brown carmine	1.25	.60
490	A166	12 l	brt blue	1.25	.60

New York World's Fair.

Nos 489-490 exist imperf. Value, unused or used, $250.

Mihail Eminescu

A167 A168

1939, May 22 ***Perf. 13½***

No.	Type	Value	Color	Unused	Used
491	A167	5 l	olive gray	3.00	1.75
492	A168	7 l	brown carmine	3.00	1.75

Mihail Eminescu, poet, 50th death anniv.
Nos 491-492 exist imperf. Value, unused or used, $300.

Three Types of Locomotives — A169

Modern Train
A170

Wood-burning Locomotive
A171

Streamlined Locomotive
A172

Railroad Terminal
A173

1939, June 10 **Typo.** ***Perf. 14***

No.	Type	Value	Color	Unused	Used
493	A169	1 l	red violet	1.75	.60
494	A170	4 l	deep rose	1.75	.60
495	A171	5 l	gray lilac	1.75	.60
496	A171	7 l	claret	1.75	.60
497	A172	12 l	blue	3.50	1.75
498	A173	15 l	green	3.50	2.40
			Nos. 493-498 (6)	14.00	6.55

Romanian Railways, 70th anniversary.
Nos 493-498 exist imperf. Value, unused or used, $200.

Arms of Romania, Greece, Turkey and Yugoslavia — A174

Wmk. 230

1940, May 27 **Photo.** ***Perf. 13½***

No.	Type	Value	Color	Unused	Used
504	A174	12 l	lt ultra	1.25	.75
505	A174	16 l	dull blue	1.25	.75

The Balkan Entente.
Nos 504-505 exist imperf. Value, unused or used, $125.

King Michael — A175

1940-42 **Wmk. 230** ***Perf. 14***

No.	Type	Value	Color	Unused	Used
506	A175	25b	Prus green	.25	.25
506A	A175	50b	dk grn ('42)	.25	.25
507	A175	1 l	purple	.25	.25
508	A175	2 l	red orange	.25	.25
508A	A175	4 l	slate ('42)	.25	.25
509	A175	5 l	rose pink	.25	.25
509A	A175	7 l	dp blue ('42)	.25	.25
510	A175	10 l	dp magenta	.40	.25
511	A175	12 l	dull blue	.25	.25
511A	A175	13 l	dk vio ('42)	.25	.25
512	A175	16 l	Prus blue	.55	.25
513	A175	20 l	brown	1.75	.25
514	A175	30 l	yellow grn	.25	.25
515	A175	50 l	olive brn	.25	.25
516	A175	100 l	rose brown	.75	.25
			Nos. 506-516 (15)	6.20	3.75

See Nos. 535A-553 in Scott Standard catalogue, Vol. 5.

SEMI-POSTAL STAMPS

Queen Elizabeth Spinning — SP1

Perf. 11½, 11½x13½

1906, Jan. 14 **Typo.** **Unwmk.**

No.	Type	Value	Color	Unused	Used
B1	SP1	3b (+ 7b)	brown	6.00	3.75
B2	SP1	5b (+ 10b)	lt grn	6.00	3.75
B3	SP1	10b (+ 10b)	rose red	29.00	11.00
B4	SP1	15b (+ 10b)	violet	20.00	7.50
			Nos. B1-B4 (4)	61.00	26.00

The Queen Weaving — SP2

1906, Mar. 18

No.	Type	Value	Color	Unused	Used
B5	SP2	3b (+ 7b)	org brn	6.00	3.75
B6	SP2	5b (+ 10b)	bl grn	6.00	3.75
B7	SP2	10b (+ 10b)	car	29.00	11.00
B8	SP2	15b (+ 10b)	red vio	20.00	7.50
			Nos. B5-B8 (4)	61.00	26.00

Queen as War Nurse
SP3

1906, Mar. 23 ***Perf. 11½, 13½x11½***

No.	Type	Value	Color	Unused	Used
B9	SP3	3b (+ 7b)	org brn	6.00	3.75
B10	SP3	5b (+ 10b)	bl grn	6.00	3.75
B11	SP3	10b (+ 10b)	car	29.00	11.00
B12	SP3	15b (+ 10b)	red vio	20.00	7.50
			Nos. B9-B12 (4)	61.00	26.00
			Nos. B1-B12 (12)	183.00	78.00

Booklet panes of 4 exist of Nos. B1-B3, B5-B7, B9-B12.

Counterfeits of Nos. B1-B12 are plentiful. Examples of Nos. B1-B12 with smooth, even gum are counterfeits.

SP4

1906, Aug. 4 *Perf. 12*

B13 SP4	3b (+ 7b) ol brn, buff & bl	3.25	1.50
B14 SP4	5b (+ 10b) grn, rose & buff	3.25	1.50
B15 SP4	10b (+ 10b) rose red, buff & bl	5.00	3.00
B16 SP4	15b (+ 10b) vio, buff & bl	13.00	3.75
	Nos. B13-B16 (4)	24.50	9.75

Guardian Angel Bringing Poor to Crown Princess Marie SP5

1907, Feb. **Engr.** *Perf. 11*

Center in Brown

B17 SP5	3b (+ 7b) org brn	4.00	1.50
B18 SP5	5b (+ 10b) dk grn	4.00	1.50
B19 SP5	10b (+ 10b) dk car	4.00	1.50
B20 SP5	15b (+ 10b) dl vio	4.00	1.50
	Nos. B17-B20 (4)	16.00	6.00

Nos. B1-B20 were sold for more than face value. The surtax, shown in parenthesis, was for charitable purposes.

Map of Romania SP9

Stephen the Great SP10

Michael the Brave SP11

Kings Carol I and Ferdinand SP12

Adam Clisi Monument — SP13

1927, Mar. 15 **Typo.** *Perf. 13½*

B21 SP9	1 l + 9 l lt vio	4.25	1.60
B22 SP10	2 l + 8 l Prus grn	4.25	1.60
B23 SP11	3 l + 7 l dp rose	4.25	1.60
B24 SP12	5 l + 5 l dp bl	4.25	1.60
B25 SP13	6 l + 4 l ol grn	6.25	2.50
	Nos. B21-B25 (5)	23.25	8.90

50th anniv. of the Royal Geographical Society. The surtax was for the benefit of that society. The stamps were valid for postage only from 3/15-4/14.

Boy Scouts in Camp — SP15

The Rescue — SP16

Designs: 3 l+3 l, Swearing in a Tenderfoot. 4 l+4 l, Prince Nicholas Chief Scout. 6 l+6 l, King Carol II in Scout's Uniform.

1931, July 15 **Photo.** **Wmk. 225**

B26 SP15	1 l + 1 l car rose	3.75	2.50
B27 SP16	2 l + 2 l dp grn	5.00	3.00
B28 SP15	3 l + 3 l ultra	6.00	3.00
B29 SP16	4 l + 4 l ol gray	7.50	8.00
B30 SP16	6 l + 6 l red brn	10.00	8.00
	Nos. B26-B30 (5)	32.25	24.50

The surtax was for the benefit of the Boy Scout organization.

Boy Scout Jamboree Issue

Scouts in Camp SP20

Semaphore Signaling SP21

Trailing — SP22

Camp Fire — SP23

King Carol II — SP24

King Carol II and Prince Michael — SP25

1932, June 8 **Wmk. 230**

B31 SP20	25b + 25b pck grn	3.00	1.10
B32 SP21	50b + 50b brt bl	4.00	2.25
B33 SP22	1 l + 1 l ol grn	4.50	3.25
B34 SP23	2 l + 2 l org red	7.50	4.50
B35 SP24	3 l + 3 l Prus bl	14.00	9.00
B36 SP25	6 l + 6 l blk brn	16.00	11.50
	Nos. B31-B36 (6)	49.00	31.60

For overprints see Nos. B44-B49.

Tuberculosis Sanatorium — SP26

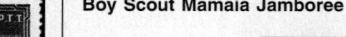

Memorial Tablet to Postal Employees Who Died in World War I — SP27

Carmen Sylva Convalescent Home — SP28

1932, Nov. 1

B37 SP26	4 l + 1 l dk grn	5.00	4.00
B38 SP27	6 l + 1 l chocolate	5.50	4.75
B39 SP28	10 l + 1 l dp bl	10.00	8.00
	Nos. B37-B39 (3)	20.50	16.75

The surtax was given to a fund for the employees of the postal and telegraph services.

Philatelic Exhibition Issue

Souvenir Sheet

King Carol II — SP29

1932, Nov. 20 **Unwmk.** *Imperf.*

B40 SP29	6 l + 5 l dk ol grn	50.00	50.00

Intl. Phil. Exhib. at Bucharest, Nov. 20-24, 1932. Each holder of a ticket of admission to the exhibition could buy an example of No. B40. The ticket cost 20 lei.

Roadside Shrine — SP31

Woman Spinning — SP33

Woman Weaving SP32

1934, Apr. 16 **Wmk. 230** *Perf. 13½*

B41 SP31	1 l + 1 l dk brn	1.00	.90
B42 SP32	2 l + 1 l blue	1.25	1.10
B43 SP33	3 l + 1 l slate grn	1.75	1.50
	Nos. B41-B43 (3)	4.00	3.50

Weaving Exposition.

Boy Scout Mamaia Jamboree Issue

Semi-Postal Stamps of 1932 Overprinted in Black or Gold

1934, July 8

B44 SP20	25b + 25b pck grn	3.75	2.50
B45 SP21	50b + 50b brt bl (G)	5.00	3.00
B46 SP22	1 l + 1 l ol grn	6.00	4.75
B47 SP23	2 l + 2 l org red	7.50	5.50
B48 SP24	3 l + 3 l Prus bl (G)	16.00	7.00
B49 SP25	6 l + 6 l blk brn (G)	18.00	9.50
	Nos. B44-B49 (6)	56.25	32.25

Sea Scout Saluting SP34

Scout Bugler SP35

Sea and Land Scouts SP36

King Carol II — SP37

Sea, Land and Girl Scouts — SP38

1935, June 8

B50 SP34	25b ol blk	1.25	1.00
B51 SP35	1 l violet	2.75	2.25
B52 SP36	2 l green	3.50	3.00
B53 SP37	6 l + 1 l red brn	5.00	4.50
B54 SP38	10 l + 2 l dk ultra	14.00	13.00
	Nos. B50-B54 (5)	26.50	23.75

Fifth anniversary of accession of King Carol II, and a national sports meeting held June 8. Surtax aided the Boy Scouts.

Nos. B50-B54 exist imperf. Value $250.

King Carol II — SP39

1936, May

B55 SP39	6 l + 1 l rose car	.75	.55

Bucharest Exhibition and 70th anniversary of the dynasty. Exists imperf. Value $125

Girl of Oltenia — SP40

Girl of Saliste — SP42

Youth from Gorj — SP44

Designs: 1 l+1 l, Girl of Banat. 3 l+1 l, Girl of Hateg. 6 l+3 l, Girl of Neamt. 10 l+5 l, Youth and girl of Bucovina.

1936, June 8

No.	Design	Denomination	Unused	Used
B56	SP40	50b + 50b brown	.60	.60
B57	SP40	1 l + 1 l violet	.60	.60
B58	SP42	2 l + 1 l Prus grn	.60	*.70*
B59	SP42	3 l + 1 l car rose	.60	*.90*
B60	SP44	4 l + 2 l red org	1.00	.90
B61	SP40	6 l + 3 l ol gray	1.00	*1.20*
B62	SP42	10 l + 5 l brt bl	2.25	*2.40*
		Nos. B56-B62 (7)	6.65	*7.30*

6th anniv. of accession of King Carol II. The surtax was for child welfare. Exist imperf. Value $300, unused or used.

Insignia of Boy Scouts
SP47 SP48

Jamboree Emblem — SP49

1936, Aug. 20

No.	Design	Denomination	Unused	Used
B63	SP47	1 l + 1 l brt bl	3.00	*5.25*
B64	SP48	3 l + 3 l ol gray	4.50	*5.25*
B65	SP49	6 l + 6 l car rose	6.00	*5.25*
		Nos. B63-B65 (3)	13.50	*15.75*

Boy Scout Jamboree at Brasov (Kronstadt). Exist imperf. Value $350, unused or used.

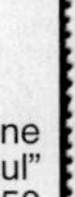

Submarine "Delfinul" SP50

Designs: 3 l+2 l, Training ship "Mircea." 6 l+3 l, Steamship "S.M.R."

1936, Oct.

No.	Design	Denomination	Unused	Used
B66	SP50	1 l + 1 l pur	2.75	2.50
B67	SP50	3 l + 2 l ultra	2.50	*3.00*
B68	SP50	6 l + 3 l car rose	3.50	*4.25*
		Nos. B66-B68 (3)	8.75	*9.75*

Marine Exhibition at Bucharest. Exist imperf. Value $325, unused or used.

Soccer SP53

Swimming SP54

Throwing the Javelin — SP55

Skiing — SP56

King Carol II Hunting — SP57

Rowing SP58

Horsemanship SP59

Founding of the U.F.S.R. SP60

1937, June 8 Wmk. 230 *Perf. 13½*

No.	Design	Denomination	Unused	Used
B69	SP53	25b + 25b ol blk	1.00	.35
B70	SP54	50b + 50b brown	1.00	.45
B71	SP55	1 l + 50b violet	1.20	.50
B72	SP56	2 l + 1 l slate grn	1.50	.55
B73	SP57	3 l + 1 l rose lake	2.20	.70
B74	SP58	4 l + 1 l red org	3.60	1.10
B75	SP59	6 l + 2 l dp claret	4.25	1.90
B76	SP60	10 l + 4 l brt blue	5.25	2.25
		Nos. B69-B76 (8)	20.00	7.80

25th anniversary of the Federation of Romanian Sports Clubs (U.F.S.R.); 7th anniversary of the accession of King Carol II. Exist imperf. Value $200, unused or used.

Start of Race — SP61

Javelin Thrower — SP62

Designs: 4 l+1 l, Hurdling. 6 l+1 l, Finish of race. 10 l+1 l, High jump.

1937, Sept. 1 Wmk. 230 *Perf. 13½*

No.	Design	Denomination	Unused	Used
B77	SP61	1 l + 1 l purple	.75	*.90*
B78	SP62	2 l + 1 l green	.95	*1.25*
B79	SP61	4 l + 1 l vermilion	1.25	*1.75*
B80	SP62	6 l + 1 l maroon	1.40	*1.90*
B81	SP61	10 l + 1 l brt bl	4.25	3.50
		Nos. B77-B81 (5)	8.60	*9.30*

8th Balkan Games, Bucharest. Exist imperf. Value $200, unused or used.

Catalogue values for unused stamps in this section, from this point to the end of the section, are for Never Hinged items.

King Carol II — SP66

1938, May 24

No.	Design	Denomination	Unused	Used
B82	SP66	6 l + 1 l deep magenta	1.50	.45

Bucharest Exhibition (for local products), May 19-June 19, celebrating 20th anniversary of the union of Rumanian provinces. Exists imperf. Value $200, unused or used.

Dimitrie Cantemir — SP67

Maria Doamna — SP68

Mircea the Great SP69

Constantine Brancoveanu SP70

Stephen the Great — SP71

Prince Cuza — SP72

Michael the Brave — SP73

Queen Elizabeth — SP74

King Carol II — SP75

King Ferdinand I — SP76

King Carol I — SP77

1938, June 8 *Perf. 13½*

No.	Design	Denomination	Unused	Used
B83	SP67	25b + 25b ol blk	.80	.35
B84	SP68	50b + 50b brn	1.25	.35
B85	SP69	1 l + 1 l blk vio	1.25	.35
B86	SP70	2 l + 2 l dk yel grn	1.40	.35
B87	SP71	3 l + 2 l dp mag	1.40	.35
B88	SP72	4 l + 2 l scarlet	1.40	.35
B89	SP73	6 l + 2 l vio brn	1.50	.45
B90	SP74	7.50 l gray bl	1.75	.60
B91	SP75	10 l brt bl	2.25	.60
B92	SP76	16 l dk slate grn	3.50	2.00
B93	SP77	20 l vermilion	4.75	2.00
		Nos. B83-B93 (11)	21.25	7.75

8th anniv. of accession of King Carol II. Surtax was for Straja Tarii, a natl. org. for boys. Exist imperf. Value $175, unused or used.

"The Spring" — SP78

"Escorting Prisoners" SP79

"Rodica, the Water Carrier" SP81

Nicolae Grigorescu SP82

Design: 4 l+1 l, "Returning from Market."

1938, June 23 *Perf. 13½*

No.	Design	Denomination	Unused	Used
B94	SP78	1 l + 1 l brt bl	2.25	.70
B95	SP79	2 l + 1 l yel grn	2.25	1.25
B96	SP79	4 l + 1 l vermilion	2.25	1.25
B97	SP81	6 l + 1 l lake	3.00	2.25
B98	SP82	10 l + 1 l brt bl	6.75	2.50
		Nos. B94-B98 (5)	16.50	7.95

Birth centenary of Nicolae Grigorescu, Romanian painter. Exist imperf. Value $200, unused or used.

St. George and the Dragon — SP83

1939, June 8 Photo.

No.	Design	Denomination	Unused	Used
B99	SP83	25b + 25b ol gray	.60	.45
B100	SP83	50b + 50b brn	.60	.45
B101	SP83	1 l + 1 l pale vio	.60	.45
B102	SP83	2 l + 2 l lt grn	.60	.45
B103	SP83	3 l + 2 l red vio	1.00	.45
B104	SP83	4 l + 2 l red org	1.40	.55
B105	SP83	6 l + 2 l car rose	1.50	.55
B106	SP83	8 l gray vio	1.75	.55
B107	SP83	10 l brt bl	1.90	.70
B108	SP83	12 l brt ultra	2.10	1.40
B109	SP83	16 l bl grn	2.25	1.75
		Nos. B99-B109 (11)	14.30	7.75

9th anniv. of accession of King Carol II. Exist imperf. Value $175, unused or used.

King Carol II
SP87 SP88

SP89

SP90

SP91

Wmk. 230

1940, June 8 Photo. *Perf. 13½*

No.	Type	Description	Unused	Used
B113	SP87	1 l + 50b dl pur	.75	.30
B114	SP88	4 l + 1 l fawn	.75	.45
B115	SP89	6 l + 1 l blue	.75	.45
B116	SP90	8 l rose brn	1.10	.65
B117	SP89	16 l ultra	1.25	.90
B118	SP91	32 l dk vio brn	2.00	1.25
		Nos. B113-B118 (6)	6.60	4.00

10th anniv. of accession of King Carol II.
Exist imperf. Value $200, unused or used.

King Carol II
SP92 SP93

1940, June 1

No.	Type	Description	Unused	Used
B119	SP92	1 l + 50b dk grn	.25	.25
B120	SP92	2.50 l + 50b Prus grn	.25	.25
B121	SP93	3 l + 1 l rose car	.35	.25
B122	SP92	3.50 l + 50b choc	.35	.35
B123	SP93	4 l + 1 l org brn	.50	.35
B124	SP93	6 l + 1 l sapphire	.75	.25
B125	SP93	9 l + 1 l brt bl	.85	.70
B126	SP93	14 l + 1 l dk bl grn	1.10	.90
		Nos. B119-B126 (8)	4.40	3.30

Surtax was for Romania's air force. Exist imperf. Value $200, unused or used.

View of Danube
SP94

Greco-Roman Ruins — SP95

Designs: 3 l+1 l, Hotin Castle. 4 l+1 l, Hurez Monastery. 5 l+1 l, Church in Bucovina. 8 l+1 l, Tower. 12 l+2 l, Village church, Transylvania. 16 l+2 l, Arch in Bucharest.

Inscribed: "Straja Tarii 8 Junie 1940"

1940, June 8 *Perf. 14½x14, 14x14½*

No.	Type	Description	Unused	Used
B127	SP94	1 l + 1 l dp vio	.40	.25
B128	SP95	2 l + 1 l red brn	.45	.30
B129	SP94	3 l + 1 l yel grn	.50	.35
B130	SP94	4 l + 1 l grnsh blk	.55	.40
B131	SP95	5 l + 1 l org ver	.60	.45
B132	SP95	8 l + 1 l brn car	.85	.60
B133	SP95	12 l + 2 l ultra	1.75	1.10
B134	SP95	16 l + 2 l dk bl gray	3.00	2.00
		Nos. B127-B134 (8)	8.10	5.45

Issued to honor Straja Tarii, a national organization for boys. Exist imperf. Value $140, unused or used.

King Michael — SP102

1940-42 Photo. Wmk. 230

No.	Type	Description	Unused	Used
B138	SP102	1 l + 50b yel grn	.25	.25
B138A	SP102	2 l + 50b yel grn	.25	.25
B139	SP102	2.50 l + 50b dk bl grn	.25	.25
B140	SP102	3 l + 1 l pur	.25	.25
B141	SP102	3.50 l + 50b rose pink	.25	.25
B141A	SP102	4 l + 50b org ver	.25	.25
B142	SP102	4 l + 1 l brn	.25	.25
B142A	SP102	5 l + 1 l dp plum	1.25	.25
B143	SP102	6 l + 1 l lt ultra	.25	.25
B143A	SP102	7 l + 1 l sl grn	.50	.25
B143B	SP102	8 l + 1 l dp vio	.25	.25
B143C	SP102	12 l + 1 l brn vio	.50	.25
B144	SP102	14 l + 1 l brt bl	.50	.25
B144A	SP102	19 l + 1 l lil rose	1.00	.25
		Nos. B138-B144A (14)	6.00	3.50

Issue years: Nos. B138A, B141A, B142A, B143A, B143B, B143C, B144A, 1942; others, 1940.

Corneliu Codreanu — SP103

1940, Nov. 8 Unwmk. *Perf. 13½*

No.	Type	Description	Unused	Used
B145	SP103	7 l + 30 l dk grn	6.00	*9.00*

13th anniv. of the founding of the Iron Guard by Corneliu Codreanu.

AIR POST STAMPS

Capt. C. G. Craiu's Airplane
AP1

Wmk. 95 Vertical

1928 Photo. *Perf. 13½*

No.	Type	Description	Unused	Used
C1	AP1	1 l red brown	3.00	2.50
C2	AP1	2 l brt blue	3.00	2.50
C3	AP1	5 l carmine rose	3.00	2.50

Wmk. 95 Horizontal

No.	Type	Description	Unused	Used
C4	AP1	1 l red brown	4.00	3.25
C5	AP1	2 l brt blue	4.00	3.25
C6	AP1	5 l carmine rose	4.00	3.25
		Nos. C1-C6 (6)	21.00	17.25

Nos. C4-C6 also come with white gum.

Nos. C4-C6 Overprinted

1930

No.	Type	Description	Unused	Used
C7	AP1	1 l red brown	8.00	6.75
C8	AP1	2 l brt blue	8.00	6.75
a.		Vert. pair, imperf. btwn.	*175.00*	
C9	AP1	5 l carmine rose	8.00	6.75
		Nos. C7-C9 (3)	24.00	20.25

Same Overprint on Nos. C1-C3

Wmk. 95 Vertical

No.	Type	Description	Unused	Used
C10	AP1	1 l red brown	50.00	50.00
C11	AP1	2 l brt blue	50.00	50.00
C12	AP1	5 l carmine rose	50.00	50.00
		Nos. C10-C12 (3)	150.00	150.00
		Nos. C7-C12 (6)	174.00	170.25

Nos. C7-C12 for the accession of King Carol II.

Excellent connterfeits are known of Nos. C10-C12.

King Carol II — AP2

Bluish Paper

1930, Oct. 4 Unwmk.

No.	Type	Description	Unused	Used
C13	AP2	1 l dk violet	2.00	3.50
C14	AP2	2 l gray green	2.50	3.50
C15	AP2	5 l red brown	5.00	3.50
C16	AP2	10 l brt blue	9.00	3.50
		Nos. C13-C16 (4)	18.50	14.00
		Set, never hinged	36.50	

Junkers Monoplane
AP3

Monoplanes
AP7

Designs: 3 l, Monoplane with biplane behind. 5 l, Biplane. 10 l, Monoplane flying leftward.

1931, Nov. 4 Wmk. 230

No.	Type	Description	Unused	Used
C17	AP3	2 l dull green	1.50	1.25
C18	AP3	3 l carmine	2.00	1.75
C19	AP3	5 l red brown	2.50	2.00
C20	AP3	10 l blue	6.00	4.50
C21	AP7	20 l dk violet	15.00	6.00
		Nos. C17-C21 (5)	27.00	15.50
		Set, never hinged	40.00	

Exist imperforate. Value $350, unused or used.

AIR POST SEMI-POSTAL STAMPS

Catalogue values for unused stamps in this section are for Never Hinged items.

Corneliu Codreanu
SPAP1

Unwmk.

1940, Dec. 1 Photo. *Perf. 14*

No.	Type	Description	Unused	Used
CB1	SPAP1	20 l + 5 l Prus grn	4.50	3.25

Propaganda for the Rome-Berlin Axis.
No. CB1 exists with overprint "1 Mai 1941 Jamboreea Nationala."

POSTAGE DUE STAMPS

D1

Perf. 11, 11½, 13½ and Compound

1881 Typo. Unwmk.

No.	Type	Description	Unused	Used
J1	D1	2b brown	4.00	1.50
J2	D1	5b brown	22.50	2.50
a.		Tête bêche pair	*190.00*	*75.00*
J3	D1	10b brown	30.00	1.50
J4	D1	30b brown	32.50	1.50
J5	D1	50b brown	26.00	2.75
J6	D1	60b brown	21.00	4.00
		Nos. J1-J6 (6)	136.00	13.75

1885

No.	Type	Description	Unused	Used
J7	D1	10b pale red brown	8.00	.50
J8	D1	30b pale red brown	8.00	.50

1887-90

No.	Type	Description	Unused	Used
J9	D1	2b gray green	4.00	1.00
J10	D1	5b gray green	8.00	3.50
J11	D1	10b gray green	8.00	3.50
J12	D1	30b gray green	8.00	1.00
		Nos. J9-J12 (4)	28.00	9.00

1888

No.	Type	Description	Unused	Used
J14	D1	2b green, *yellowish*	.90	.75
J15	D1	5b green, *yellowish*	2.25	2.25
J16	D1	10b green, *yellowish*	32.50	2.75
J17	D1	30b green, *yellowish*	17.50	1.25
		Nos. J14-J17 (4)	53.15	7.00

1890-96 Wmk. 163

No.	Type	Description	Unused	Used
J18	D1	2b emerald	1.60	.45
J19	D1	5b emerald	.80	.45
J20	D1	10b emerald	1.25	.45
J21	D1	30b emerald	2.00	.45
J22	D1	50b emerald	6.50	.95
J23	D1	60b emerald	8.75	3.25
		Nos. J18-J23 (6)	20.90	6.00

1898 Wmk. 200

No.	Type	Description	Unused	Used
J24	D1	2b blue green	.70	.45
J25	D1	5b blue green	.90	.30
J26	D1	10b blue green	1.40	.30
J27	D1	30b blue green	1.90	.30
J28	D1	50b blue green	4.75	.90
J29	D1	60b blue green	5.50	1.75
		Nos. J24-J29 (6)	15.15	4.00

1902-10 Unwmk.

Thin Paper, Tinted Rose on Back

No.	Type	Description	Unused	Used
J30	D1	2b green	.85	.25
J31	D1	5b green	.50	.25
J32	D1	10b green	.40	.25
J33	D1	30b green	.50	.25
J34	D1	50b green	2.50	.90
J35	D1	60b green	5.25	2.25
		Nos. J30-J35 (6)	10.00	4.15

1908-11 White Paper

No.	Type	Description	Unused	Used
J36	D1	2b green	.80	.50
J37	D1	5b green	.60	.50
a.		Tête bêche pair	12.00	12.00
J38	D1	10b green	.40	.30
a.		Tête bêche pair	12.00	12.00
J39	D1	30b green	.50	.30
a.		Tête bêche pair	12.00	12.00
J40	D1	50b green	2.00	1.25
		Nos. J36-J40 (5)	4.30	2.85

D2

1911 Wmk. 165

No.	Type	Description	Unused	Used
J41	D2	2b dark blue, *green*	.25	.25
J42	D2	5b dark blue, *green*	.25	.25
J43	D2	10b dark blue, *green*	.25	.25
J44	D2	15b dark blue, *green*	.25	.25
J45	D2	20b dark blue, *green*	.25	.25
J46	D2	30b dark blue, *green*	.25	.25
J47	D2	50b dark blue, *green*	.50	.30
J48	D2	60b dark blue, *green*	.60	.40
J49	D2	2 l dark blue, *green*	1.00	.80
		Nos. J41-J49 (9)	3.60	3.00

The letters "P.R." appear to be embossed instead of watermarked. They are often faint or entirely invisible.

The 20b, type D2, has two types, differing in the width of the head of the "2." This affects Nos. J45, J54, J58, and J63.

See Nos. J52-J77, J82, J87-J88 (in Scott Standard catalogue, Vol. 5). For overprints see Nos. J78-J81, RAJ1-RAJ2, RAJ20-RAJ21, 3NJ1-3NJ7.

Regular Issue of 1908 Overprinted

1918 **Unwmk.**
J50 A46 5b yellow green 1.40 .40
a. Inverted overprint 5.00 5.00
J51 A46 10b rose 1.40 .40
a. Inverted overprint 3.75 3.75

Postage Due Type of 1911

1920 **Wmk. 165**
J52 D2 5b black, *green* .25 .25
J53 D2 10b black, *green* .25 .25
J54 D2 20b black, *green* 4.00 .60
J55 D2 30b black, *green* 1.10 .40
J55A D2 50b black, *green* 3.00 .90
Nos. J52-J55A (5) 8.60 2.40

Perf. 11½, 13½ and Compound

1919 **Unwmk.**
J56 D2 5b black, *green* .30 .25
J57 D2 10b black, *green* .30 .25
J58 D2 20b black, *green* 1.00 .25
J59 D2 30b black, *green* .90 .25
J60 D2 50b black, *green* 2.25 .40
Nos. J56-J60 (5) 4.75 1.40

1920-26 **White Paper**
J61 D2 5b black .25 .25
J62 D2 10b black .25 .25
J63 D2 20b black .25 .25
J64 D2 30b black .25 .25
J65 D2 50b black .40 .40
J66 D2 60b black .25 .25
J67 D2 1 l black .30 .30
J68 D2 2 l black .25 .25
J69 D2 3 l black ('26) .25 .25
J70 D2 6 l black ('26) .30 .30
Nos. J61-J70 (10) 2.75 2.75

1923-24
J74 D2 1 l black, *pale green* .25 .25
J75 D2 2 l black, *pale green* .45 .25
J76 D2 3 l black, *pale green* ('24) 1.25 .60
J77 D2 6 l blk, *pale green* ('24) 1.75 .60
Nos. J74-J77 (4) 3.70 1.70

Postage Due Stamps of 1920-26 Overprinted

1930 ***Perf. 13½***
J78 D2 1 l black .25 .25
J79 D2 2 l black .25 .25
J80 D2 3 l black .35 .25
J81 D2 6 l black .60 .30
Nos. J78-J81 (4) 1.45 1.05

Accession of King Carol II.

Catalogue values for unused stamps in this section, from this point to the end of the section, are for Never Hinged items.

Type of 1911 Issue

1931 **Wmk. 225**
J82 D2 2 l black .90 .35

D3

1932-37 **Wmk. 230**
J83 D3 1 l black .25 .25
J84 D3 2 l black .25 .25
J85 D3 3 l black ('37) .25 .25
J86 D3 6 l black ('37) .25 .25
Nos. J83-J86 (4) 1.00 1.00

See Nos. J89-J98 in Scott Standard catalogue, Vol. 5.

OFFICIAL STAMPS

Catalogue values for unused stamps in this section are for Never Hinged items.

Eagle Carrying National Emblem — O1

1929 **Photo.** **Wmk. 95** ***Perf. 13½***
O1 O1 25b red orange .25 .25
O2 O1 50b dk brown .25 .25
O3 O1 1 l dk violet .30 .25
O4 O1 2 l olive grn .30 .25
O5 O1 3 l rose car .45 .25
O6 O1 4 l dk olive .45 .25
O7 O1 6 l Prus blue 2.50 .25
O8 O1 10 l deep blue .80 .25
O9 O1 25 l carmine brn 1.60 1.25
O10 O1 50 l purple 4.75 3.50
Nos. O1-O10 (10) 11.65 6.75

Type of Official Stamps of 1929 Overprinted

1930 **Unwmk.**
O11 O1 25b red orange .25 .25
O12 O1 50b dk brown .25 .25
O13 O1 1 l dk violet .35 .25
O14 O1 3 l rose carmine .50 .25
Nos. O11-O14 (4) 1.35 1.00

Nos. O11-O14 were not placed in use without overprint.

Same Overprint on Nos. O1-O10 Wmk. 95

O15 O1 25b red orange .25 .25
O16 O1 50b dk brown .25 .25
O17 O1 1 l dk violet .25 .25
O18 O1 2 l dp green .25 .25
O19 O1 3 l rose carmine .60 .25
O20 O1 4 l olive black .75 .25
O21 O1 6 l Prus blue 2.00 .25
O22 O1 10 l deep blue .80 .25
O23 O1 25 l carmine brown 3.00 2.50
O24 O1 50 l purple 4.00 3.50
Nos. O15-O24 (10) 12.15 8.00

Accession of King Carol II to the throne of Romania (Nos O11-O24).

Coat of Arms — O2

Perf. 13½, 13½x14½

1931-32 **Typo.** **Wmk. 225**
O25 O2 25b black .30 .25
O26 O2 1 l lilac .30 .25
O27 O2 2 l emerald .60 .40
O28 O2 3 l rose 1.00 .70
Nos. O25-O28 (4) 2.20 1.60

1932 **Wmk. 230** ***Perf. 13½***
O29 O2 25b black .30 .25
O30 O2 1 l violet .40 .35
O31 O2 2 l emerald .65 .55
O32 O2 3 l rose .80 .65
O33 O2 6 l red brown 1.25 1.00
Nos. O29-O33 (5) 3.40 2.80

PARCEL POST STAMPS

PP1

Perf. 11½, 13½ and Compound

1895 **Wmk. 163** **Typo.**
Q1 PP1 25b brown red 12.50 2.25

1896
Q2 PP1 25b vermilion 10.00 1.25

Perf. 13½ and 11½x13½

1898 **Wmk. 200**
Q3 PP1 25b brown red 7.00 1.25
a. Tête bêche pair
Q4 PP1 25b vermilion 7.00 .90

Thin Paper
Tinted Rose on Back

1905 **Unwmk.** ***Perf. 11½***
Q5 PP1 25b vermilion 7.50 1.25

1911 **White Paper**
Q6 PP1 25b pale red 7.50 1.25

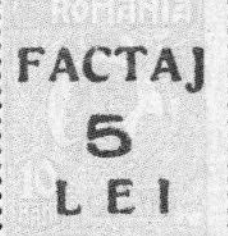

No. 263 Surcharged in Carmine

1928 ***Perf. 13½***
Q7 A54 5 l on 10b yellow green 1.50 .30

POSTAL TAX STAMPS

Regular Issue of 1908 Overprinted

Perf. 11½, 13½, 11½x13½

1915 **Unwmk.**
RA1 A46 5b green .25 .25
RA2 A46 10b rose .40 .25

The "Timbru de Ajutor" stamps represent a tax on postal matter. The money obtained from their sale was turned into a fund for the assistance of soldiers' families.

Until 1923 the only "Timbru de Ajutor" stamps used for postal purposes were the 5b and 10b. Stamps of higher values with this inscription were used to pay the taxes on railway and theater tickets and other fiscal taxes. In 1923 the postal rate was advanced to 25b.

The Queen Weaving — PT1

1916-18 **Typo.**
RA3 PT1 5b gray blk .25 .25
RA4 PT1 5b green ('18) .70 .40
RA5 PT1 10b brown .40 .25
RA6 PT1 10b gray blk ('18) 1.00 .45
Nos. RA3-RA6 (4) 2.35 1.35

For overprints see Nos. RA7-RA8, RAJ7-RAJ9, 3NRA1-3NRA8.

Stamps of 1916 Overprinted in Red or Black

1918 ***Perf. 13½***
RA7 PT1 5b gray blk (R) .70 .25
a. Double overprint 5.00
c. Black overprint 5.00
RA8 PT1 10b brn (Bk) .70 .25
a. Double overprint 5.00
b. Double overprint, one inverted 5.00
c. Inverted overprint 5.00

Same Overprint on RA1 and RA2

1919
RA11 A46 5b yel grn (R) *19.00 12.50*
RA12 A46 10b rose (Bk) *19.00 12.50*

Charity — PT3

Perf. 13½, 11½, 13½x11½

1921-24 **Typo.** **Unwmk.**
RA13 PT3 10b green .25 .25
RA14 PT3 25b blk ('24) .25 .25

Type of 1921-24 Issue

1928 **Wmk. 95**
RA15 PT3 25b black 1.00 .45

Nos. RA13, RA14 and RA15 are the only stamps of type PT3 issued for postal purposes. Other denominations were used fiscally.

Catalogue values for unused stamps in this section, from this point to the end of the section, are for Never Hinged items.

Airplane — PT4

1931 **Photo.** **Unwmk.**
RA16 PT4 50b Prus bl .45 .25
a. Double impression 15.00
RA17 PT4 1 l dk red brn .75 .25
RA18 PT4 2 l ultra 1.00 .25
Nos. RA16-RA18 (3) 2.20 .75

The use of these stamps, in addition to the regular postage, was obligatory on all postal matter for the interior of the country. The money thus obtained was to augment the National Fund for Aviation. When the stamps were not used to prepay the special tax, it was collected by means of Postal Tax Due stamps Nos. RAJ20 and RAJ21.

Nos. RA17 and RA18 were also used for other than postal tax.

Head of Aviator — PT5

1932 **Wmk. 230** ***Perf. 14 x 13½***
RA19 PT5 50b Prus bl .30 .25
RA20 PT5 1 l red brn .45 .25
RA21 PT5 2 l ultra .70 .25
Nos. RA19-RA21 (3) 1.45 .75

See notes after No. RA18.

After 1937 use of Nos. RA20-RA21 was limited to other than postal matter.

Nos. RA19-RA21 exist imperf.

Four stamps similar to type PT5, but inscribed "Fondul Aviatiei," were issued in 1936: 10b sepia, 20b violet, 3 l green and 5 l red. These were used for purposes other than postal tax.

Aviator — PT6

1937 ***Perf. 13½***
RA22 PT6 50b Prus grn .25 .25
RA23 PT6 1 l red brn .35 .25
RA24 PT6 2 l ultra .45 .25
Nos. RA22-RA24 (3) 1.05 .75

Stamps overprinted or inscribed "Fondul Aviatiei" other than Nos. RA22, RA23 or RA24 were used to pay taxes on other than postal matters.

POSTAL TAX DUE STAMPS

Catalogue values for unused stamps in this section are for Never Hinged items.

Postage Due Stamps of 1911 Overprinted

Perf. 11½, 13½, 11½x13½

1915 **Unwmk.**

RAJ1 D2 5b dk bl, *grn* .75 .25
RAJ2 D2 10b dk bl, *grn* .75 .25
a. Wmk. 165 10.00 1.00

PTD1

1916 **Typo.** **Unwmk.**

RAJ3 PTD1 5b brn, *grn* .40 .25
RAJ4 PTD1 10b red, *grn* .40 .25

See Nos. RAJ5-RAJ6, RAJ10-RAJ11. For overprint see No. 3NRAJ1.

1918

RAJ5 PTD1 5b red, *grn* .25 .25
a. Wmk. 165 1.00 .25
RAJ6 PTD1 10b brn, *grn* .25 .25
a. Wmk. 165 1.75 .25

Postal Tax Stamps of 1916, Overprinted in Red, Black or Blue

RAJ7 PT1 5b gray blk (R) .40 .25
a. Inverted overprint 7.50
RAJ8 PT1 10b brn (Bk) .80 .25
a. Inverted overprint 7.50
RAJ9 PT1 10b brn (Bl) *5.00* *5.00*
a. Vertical overprint *20.00* *15.00*
Nos. RAJ7-RAJ9 (3) 6.20 5.50

Type of 1916

1921

RAJ10 PTD1 5b red .50 .25
RAJ11 PTD1 10b brown .50 .25

PTD2

1922-25 **Greenish Paper** **Typo.**

RAJ12 PTD2 10b brown .25 .25
RAJ13 PTD2 20b brown .25 .25
RAJ14 PTD2 25b brown .25 .25
RAJ15 PTD2 50b brown .25 .25
Nos. RAJ12-RAJ15 (4) 1.00 1.00

1923-26

RAJ16 PTD2 10b lt brn .25 .25
RAJ17 PTD2 20b lt brn .25 .25
RAJ18 PTD2 25b brown ('26) .25 .25
RAJ19 PTD2 50b brown ('26) .25 .25
Nos. RAJ16-RAJ19 (4) 1.00 1.00

J82 and Type of 1911 Postage Due Stamps Overprinted in Red

1931 **Wmk. 225** ***Perf. 13½***

RAJ20 D2 1 l black .25 .25
RAJ21 D2 2 l black .25 .25

When the Postal Tax stamps for the Aviation Fund issue (Nos. RA16 to RA18) were not used to prepay the obligatory tax on letters, etc., it was collected by affixing Nos. RAJ20 and RAJ21.

OCCUPATION STAMPS

ISSUED UNDER AUSTRIAN OCCUPATION

Emperor Karl of Austria
OS1 OS2

1917 **Unwmk.** **Engr.** ***Perf. 12½***

1N1 OS1 3b ol gray 2.00 3.00
1N2 OS1 5b ol grn 2.00 3.00
1N3 OS1 6b violet 2.00 3.00
1N4 OS1 10b org brn .40 .70
1N5 OS1 12b dp bl 1.50 2.50
1N6 OS1 15b brt rose 1.50 2.50
1N7 OS1 20b red brn .40 .70
1N8 OS1 25b ultra .40 .70
1N9 OS1 30b slate .70 1.00
1N10 OS1 40b olive bis .70 1.00
a. Perf. 11½ 100.00 175.00
b. Perf. 11½x12½ 100.00 175.00
1N11 OS1 50b dp grn .40 .70
1N12 OS1 60b rose .40 .70
1N13 OS1 80b dl bl .35 .65
1N14 OS1 90b dk vio .70 1.00
1N15 OS2 2 l rose, *straw* 1.10 1.60
1N16 OS2 3 l grn, *bl* 1.10 2.00
1N17 OS2 4 l rose, *grn* 1.50 2.50
Nos. 1N1-1N17 (17) 17.15 27.25

Nos. 1N1-1N14 have "BANI" surcharged in red.

Nos. 1N1-1N17 also exist imperforate. Value, set $125.

OS3 OS4

1918

1N18 OS3 3b ol gray .35 .85
1N19 OS3 5b ol grn .35 .85
1N20 OS3 6b violet .35 .85
1N21 OS3 10b org brn .35 .85
1N22 OS3 12b dp bl .35 .85
1N23 OS3 15b brt rose .35 .85
1N24 OS3 20b red brn .35 .85
1N25 OS3 25b ultra .35 .85
1N26 OS3 30b slate .35 .85
1N27 OS3 40b ol bis .35 .85
1N28 OS3 50b dp grn .35 .85
1N29 OS3 60b rose .35 .85
1N30 OS3 80b dl bl .35 .85
1N31 OS3 90b dk vio .35 .85
1N32 OS4 2 l rose, *straw* .35 .85
1N33 OS4 3 l grn, *bl* .75 2.25
1N34 OS4 4 l rose, *grn* 1.00 2.25
Nos. 1N18-1N34 (17) 7.00 17.25

Exist. imperf. Value, set $80.

The complete series exists with "BANI" or "LEI" inverted, also with those words and the numerals of value inverted. Neither of these sets was regularly issued.

Austrian Nos. M69-M82 Overprinted In Black

1918 **Typo.** ***Perf. 12½***

1N35 M5 1h grnsh blue 40.00
Never hinged 87.50
1N36 M5 2h orange 25.00
Never hinged 50.00
1N37 M5 3h olive gray 47.50
Never hinged 87.50
1N38 M5 5h yellow green 25.00
Never hinged 50.00
1N39 M5 10h dark brown 70.00
Never hinged 140.00
1N40 M5 20h red 70.00
Never hinged 140.00
1N41 M5 25h blue 27.50
Never hinged 55.00
1N42 M5 30h bister 47.50
Never hinged 95.00
1N43 M5 45h dark slate 52.50
Never hinged 105.00
1N44 M5 50h deep green 60.00
Never hinged 120.00
1N45 M5 60h violet 80.00
Never hinged 160.00
1N46 M5 80h rose 1,000.
Never hinged 2,000.
1N47 M5 90h brown violet 80.00
Never hinged 160.00
Nos. 1N35-1N47 (13) 1,625.

Nos. 1N35-1N47 were on sale at the Vienna post office for a few days before the Armistice signing. They were never issued at the Army Post Offices.

ISSUED UNDER BULGARIAN OCCUPATION

Dobruja District

Bulgarian Stamps of 1915-16 Overprinted in Red or Blue

1916 **Unwmk.** ***Perf. 11½, 14***

2N1 A20 1s dk blue grn (R) .25 .25
2N2 A23 5s grn & vio brn (R) 3.00 1.75
2N3 A24 10s brn & brnsh blk (Bl) .30 .25
2N4 A26 25s indigo & blk (Bl) .30 .25
Nos. 2N1-2N4 (4) 3.85 2.50

Many varieties of overprint exist.

ISSUED UNDER GERMAN OCCUPATION

German Stamps of 1905-17 Surcharged

1917 **Wmk. 125** ***Perf. 14***

3N1 A22 15b on 15pf dk vio (R) 1.00 1.00
3N2 A16 25b on 20pf ultra (Bk) 1.00 1.00
3N3 A16 40b on 30pf org & blk, *buff* (R) 17.50 17.50
Nos. 3N1-3N3 (3) 19.50 19.50

"M.V.iR." are the initials of "Militär Verwaltung in Rumänien" (Military Administration of Romania).

German Stamps of 1905-17 Surcharged

1917-18

3N4 A16 10b on 10pf car 1.10 1.40
3N5 A22 15b on 15pf dk vio 5.50 4.50
3N6 A16 25b on 20pf ultra 3.00 4.00
3N7 A16 40b on 30pf org & blk, *buff* 1.00 1.40
a. "40" omitted 90.00 *350.00*
Nos. 3N4-3N7 (4) 10.60 11.30

German Stamps of 1905-17 Surcharged

1918

3N8 A16 5b on 5pf grn .60 1.75
3N9 A16 10b on 10pf car .60 1.50
3N10 A22 15b on 15pf dk vio .25 .40
3N11 A16 25b on 20pf bl vio .60 1.50
a. 25b on 20pf blue 2.50 8.00
3N12 A16 40b on 30pf org & blk, *buff* .30 .35
Nos. 3N8-3N12 (5) 2.35 5.50

German Stamps of 1905-17 Overprinted

1918

3N13 A16 10pf carmine 8.75 *40.00*
3N14 A22 15pf dk vio 13.00 *35.00*
3N15 A16 20pf blue 1.25 *1.75*
3N16 A16 30pf org & blk, *buff* 13.00 *22.50*
Nos. 3N13-3N16 (4) 36.00 *99.25*

POSTAGE DUE STAMPS ISSUED UNDER GERMAN OCCUPATION

Postage Due Stamps and Type of Romania Overprinted in Red

Perf. 11½, 13½ and Compound

1918 **Wmk. 165**

3NJ1 D2 5b dk bl, *grn* 20.00 60.00
3NJ2 D2 10b dk bl, *grn* 20.00 60.00

The 20b, 30b and 50b with this overprint are fraudulent.

Unwmk.

3NJ3 D2 5b dk bl, *grn* 8.00 10.50
3NJ4 D2 10b dk bl, *grn* 8.00 10.50
3NJ5 D2 20b dk bl, *grn* 3.00 2.75
3NJ6 D2 30b dk bl, *grn* 3.00 2.75
3NJ7 D2 50b dk bl, *grn* 3.00 2.75
Nos. 3NJ1-3NJ7 (7) 65.00 149.25

POSTAL TAX STAMPS ISSUED UNDER GERMAN OCCUPATION

Romanian Postal Tax Stamps and Type of 1916

Overprinted in Red or Black

Perf. 11½, 13½ and Compound

1917 **Unwmk.**

3NRA1 PT1 5b gray blk (R) .80 2.75
3NRA2 PT1 10b brown (Bk) .80 2.75

Same, Overprinted

1917-18

3NRA3 PT1 5b gray blk (R) 1.50 3.50
a. Black overprint 57.00 *750.00*
3NRA4 PT1 10b brown (Bk) 9.00 19.00
3NRA5 PT1 10b violet (Bk) 1.50 5.00
Nos. 3NRA3-3NRA5 (3) 12.00 27.50

Same, Overprinted in Red or Black

1918

3NRA6 PT1 5b gray blk (R) *45.00* 30.00
3NRA7 PT1 10b brown (Bk) *45.00* 30.00

Same, Overprinted

1918

3NRA8 PT1 10b violet (Bk) .80 2.75

POSTAL TAX DUE STAMP ISSUED UNDER GERMAN OCCUPATION

Type of Romanian Postal Tax Due Stamp of 1916 Overprinted

Perf. 11½, 13½, and Compound

1918 **Wmk. 165**

3NRAJ1 PTD1 10b red, *green* 2.50 3.00

ROMANIAN POST OFFICES IN THE TURKISH EMPIRE

40 Paras = 1 Piaster

King Carol I
A1 A2

Perf. 11½, 13½ and Compound

1896 **Wmk. 200** **Black Surcharge**

1	A1	10pa on 5b blue	32.50	30.00
2	A2	20pa on 10b emer	24.00	22.50
3	A1	1pa on 25b violet	24.00	22.50
		Nos. 1-3 (3)	80.50	75.00

Violet Surcharge

4	A1	10pa on 5b blue	17.00	15.00
5	A2	20pa on 10b emer	17.00	15.00
6	A1	1pa on 25b violet	17.00	15.00
		Nos. 4-6 (3)	51.00	45.00

Romanian Stamps of 1908-18 Overprinted in Black or Red

1919 **Typo.** **Unwmk.**

7	A46	5b yellow grn	.50	.50
8	A46	10b rose	.65	.65
9	A46	15b red brown	.75	.75
10	A19	25b dp blue (R)	1.00	1.00
11	A19	40b gray brn (R)	2.75	2.75
		Nos. 7-11 (5)	5.65	5.65

All values exist with inverted overprint.

ROMANIAN POST OFFICES IN THE TURKISH EMPIRE POSTAL TAX STAMP

Romanian Postal Tax Stamp of 1918 Overprinted

1919 **Unwmk.** ***Perf. 11½, 11½x13½***

RA1 PT1 5b green 2.50 2.50

ROUAD, ILE

ēl-ru-ad

(Arwad)

LOCATION — An island in the Mediterranean, off the coast of Latakia, Syria

GOVT. — French Mandate

In 1916, while a French post office was maintained on Ile Rouad, stamps were issued by France.

25 Centimes = 1 Piaster

French Offices in the Levant 1902-06 Stamps Ovptd.

Perf. 14x13½

1916, Jan. 12 **Unwmk.**

1	A2	5c green	550.00	275.00
		On cover		1,250.
2	A3	10c rose red	550.00	275.00
		On cover		1,250.
3	A5	1pi on 25c blue	550.00	275.00
		On cover		1,250.

Dangerous counterfeits exist.

A 40c and 2pi-on-50c exist but were not regularly issued. Most examples have favor cancels. Value so canceled, $700 each.

Stamps of French Offices in the Levant, 1902-06, Overprinted Horizontally

1916, Dec.

4	A2	1c gray	1.40	1.40
		Never hinged	2.25	
		On cover		55.00
a.		Grayish paper (GC) ('18)	3.00	2.75
		Never hinged	5.00	
b.		1c slate ('20)	3.00	2.75
		Never hinged	5.00	
5	A2	2c lilac brown	1.50	1.50
		Never hinged	2.25	
		On cover		55.00
a.		Grayish paper (GC) ('18)	3.00	3.00
		Never hinged	5.00	
b.		2c violet brown ('20)	3.00	3.00
		Never hinged	5.00	
6	A2	3c red orange	1.60	1.60
		Never hinged	2.25	
		On cover		55.00
a.		Double overprint	210.00	
b.		Grayish paper (GC) ('19)	1.75	1.75
		Never hinged	3.00	
7	A2	5c green	1.75	1.75
		Never hinged	3.00	
		On cover		45.00
8	A3	10c rose	2.00	2.00
		Never hinged	3.25	
		On cover		37.50
9	A3	15c pale red	2.00	2.00
		Never hinged	3.25	
		On cover		30.00
10	A3	20c brown violet	3.75	3.75
		Never hinged	6.25	
		On cover		50.00
		On cover, single franking		95.00
a.		Grayish paper (GC) ('19)	5.00	5.00
		Never hinged	8.25	
		On cover		62.50
		On cover, single franking		105.00
11	A5	1pi on 25c blue	2.75	2.75
		Never hinged	4.50	
		On cover		45.00
		On cover, single franking		62.50
12	A3	30c violet	2.50	2.50
		Never hinged	4.00	
		On cover		50.00
		On cover, single franking		67.50
13	A4	40c red & pale bl	6.00	6.00
		Never hinged	9.00	
		On cover		62.50
		On cover, single franking		80.00
14	A6	2pi on 50c bis brn & lavender	9.00	9.00
		Never hinged	14.50	
		On cover		105.00
		On cover, single franking		170.00
15	A6	4pi on 1fr cl & ol grn	16.00	16.00
		Never hinged	27.00	
		On cover		170.00
		On cover, single franking		275.00
16	A6	20pi on 5fr dk bl & buff	40.00	40.00
		Never hinged	67.50	
		On cover		440.00
		On cover, single franking		1,100.
		Nos. 4-16 (13)	90.25	90.25

There is a wide space between the two words of the overprint on Nos. 13 to 16 inclusive.

(Note on G. C. paper follows France No. 184.)

RUANDA-URUNDI

rü-ˌän-də ü'rün-dē

(Belgian East Africa)

LOCATION — In central Africa, bounded by Congo, Uganda and Tanganyika

AREA — 20,540 sq. mi.

POP. — 4,700,000 (est. 1958)

CAPITAL — Usumbura

See German East Africa for stamps issued under Belgian occupation.

100 Centimes = 1 Franc

Stamps of Belgian Congo, 1923-26, Overprinted

1924-26 ***Perf. 12***

6	A32	5c orange yel	.25	.25
		Never hinged	.40	
7	A32	10c green	.25	.25
		Never hinged	.55	
		On cover		2.75
a.		Double overprint	70.00	70.00
		Never hinged	125.00	
8	A32	15c olive brn	.25	.25
		Never hinged	.55	
		On cover		2.75
9	A32	20c olive grn	.25	.25
		Never hinged	.55	
		On cover		23.00
10	A44	20c green ('26)	.25	.25
		Never hinged	.35	
		On cover		27.50
11	A44	25c red brown	.40	.25
		Never hinged	.80	
		On cover		30.00
12	A44	30c rose red	.35	.35
		Never hinged	1.50	
		On cover		30.00
13	A44	30c olive grn ('25)	.25	.25
		Never hinged	.35	
		On cover		23.00
14	A32	40c violet ('25)	.35	.35
		Never hinged	.75	
		On cover		30.00
a.		Inverted overprint	95.00	95.00
		Never hinged	170.00	
15	A44	50c gray blue	.35	.35
		Never hinged	1.50	
		On cover		2.75
16	A44	50c buff ('25)	.40	.35
		Never hinged	.75	
		On cover		17.00
17	A44	75c red org	.65	.60
		Never hinged	1.90	
		On cover		2.75
18	A44	75c gray blue ('25)	.60	.45
		Never hinged	1.00	
		On cover		27.50
19	A44	1fr bister brown	.70	.60
		Never hinged	1.50	
		On cover		47.50
20	A44	1fr dull blue ('26)	.75	.50
		Never hinged	1.00	
		On cover		30.00
21	A44	3fr gray brown	6.00	2.50
		Never hinged	16.50	
		On cover		110.00
22	A44	5fr gray	12.00	9.00
		Never hinged	30.00	
23	A44	10fr gray black	22.50	20.00
		Never hinged	82.50	
		Nos. 6-23 (18)	46.55	36.80
		Set, never hinged	140.00	

Belgian Congo Nos. 112-113 Overprinted in Red or Black

1925-27 ***Perf. 12½***

24	A44	45c dk vio (R) ('27)	.35	.35
		Never hinged	.75	
		On cover		23.00
25	A44	60c car rose (Bk)	.60	.50
		Never hinged	1.00	
		On cover		15.00
		Set, never hinged	1.75	

Stamps of Belgian Congo, 1923-1927, Overprinted

1927-29

26	A32	10c green ('29)	.65	.65
		Never hinged	1.60	
		On cover		19.00
27	A32	15c ol brn ('29)	1.75	1.75
		Never hinged	3.25	
		On cover		19.00
28	A44	35c green	.35	.35
		Never hinged	.70	
		On cover		30.00
29	A44	75c salmon red	.50	.45
		Never hinged	.90	
		On cover		27.50
30	A44	1fr rose red	.60	.50
		Never hinged	1.50	
		On cover		30.00
31	A32	1.25fr dull blue	.95	.70
		Never hinged	3.00	
		On cover		40.00
32	A32	1.50fr dull blue	.95	.65
		Never hinged	3.00	
		On cover		47.50
33	A32	1.75fr dull blue	2.50	1.60
		Never hinged	6.25	
		On cover		47.50

No. 32 Surcharged

34	A32	1.75fr on 1.50fr dl bl	.95	.70
		Never hinged	3.00	
		On cover		47.50
		Nos. 26-34 (9)	9.20	7.35
		Set, never hinged	23.50	

Nos. 30 and 33 Surcharged

1931

35	A44	1.25fr on 1fr rose red	3.50	2.00
		Never hinged	7.50	
		On cover		47.50
36	A32	2fr on 1.75fr dl bl	5.50	3.00
		Never hinged	12.50	
		On cover		75.00
		Set, never hinged	20.00	

Porter — A1

Mountain Scene — A2

Designs: 5c, 60c, Porter. 15c, Warrior. 25c, Kraal. 40c, Cattle herders. 50c, Cape buffalo. 75c, Bahutu greeting. 1fr, Urundi women. 1.25fr, Bahutu mother. 1.50fr, 2fr, Making wooden vessel. 2.50fr, 3.25fr, Preparing hides. 4fr, Watuba potter. 5fr, Mututsi dancer. 10fr, Watusi warriors. 20fr, Urundi prince.

1931-38 **Engr.** ***Perf. 11½***

37	A1	5c dp lil rose ('38)	.25	.25
		Never hinged	.40	
		On cover		30.00
38	A2	10c gray	.25	.25
		Never hinged	.40	
		On cover		22.50
39	A2	15c pale red	.25	.25
		Never hinged	.40	
		On cover		25.00
40	A2	25c brown vio	.25	.25
		Never hinged	.40	
		On cover		22.50

41 A1 40c green .50 .50
Never hinged 1.00
On cover 19.00
42 A2 50c gray lilac .25 .25
Never hinged .40
On cover 19.00
43 A1 60c lilac rose .25 .25
Never hinged .40
On cover 12.50
44 A1 75c gray black .25 .25
Never hinged .65
On cover 12.50
45 A2 1fr rose red .40 .25
Never hinged .90
On cover 12.50
46 A1 1.25fr red brown .40 .25
Never hinged .90
On cover 15.00
47 A2 1.50fr brown vio ('37) .25 .25
Never hinged .40
On cover 30.00
48 A2 2fr deep blue .50 .25
Never hinged .90
On cover 19.00
49 A2 2.50fr dp blue ('37) .60 .60
Never hinged 1.75
On cover 37.50
50 A2 3.25fr brown vio .65 .30
Never hinged 1.75
On cover 27.50
51 A2 4fr rose .65 .45
Never hinged 1.75
On cover 27.50
52 A1 5fr gray .65 .50
Never hinged 1.75
On cover 55.00
53 A1 10fr brown violet .90 .90
Never hinged 2.75
On cover 62.50
54 A1 20fr brown 3.25 3.00
Never hinged 7.75
Nos. 37-54 (18) 10.50 9.00
Set, never hinged 25.00

King Albert Memorial Issue

King Albert — A16

1934 **Photo.**
55 A16 1.50fr black .65 .65
Never hinged 2.50
On cover 12.50

SEMI-POSTAL STAMPS

Belgian Congo Nos. B10-B11 Overprinted

1925 **Unwmk.** ***Perf. 12½***
B1 SP1 25c + 25c car & blk .75 .50
Never hinged 1.90
B2 SP1 25c + 25c car & blk .75 .50
Never hinged 1.90
Set, never hinged 3.75

No. B2 inscribed "BELGISCH CONGO."
Commemorative of the Colonial Campaigns in 1914-1918. Nos. B1 and B2 alternate in the sheet.

Belgian Congo Nos. B12-B20 Overprinted in Blue or Red

1930 ***Perf. 11½***
B3 SP3 10c + 5c ver 1.00 1.00
Never hinged 1.35
B4 SP3 20c + 10c dk brn 1.50 1.50
Never hinged 4.50
B5 SP5 35c + 15c dp grn 2.00 2.00
Never hinged 1.25
B6 SP5 60c + 30c dl vio 2.25 2.25
Never hinged 10.00
B7 SP3 1fr + 50c dk car 3.75 3.75
Never hinged 19.00
B8 SP5 1.75fr + 75c dp bl (R) 9.75 9.75
Never hinged 25.00
B9 SP5 3.50fr + 1.50fr rose lake 15.00 15.00
Never hinged 47.50
B10 SP5 5fr + 2.50fr red brn 15.00 15.00
Never hinged 30.00
B11 SP5 10fr + 5fr gray blk 16.00 16.00
Never hinged 32.50
Nos. B3-B11 (9) 66.25 66.25
Set, never hinged 170.00

On Nos. B3, B4 and B7 there is a space of 26mm between the two words of the overprint.
The surtax was for native welfare.

Queen Astrid with Native Children — SP1

1936 **Photo.**
B12 SP1 1.25fr + 5c dk brn .75 .75
Never hinged 2.25
On cover 30.00
B13 SP1 1.50fr + 10c dl rose .75 .75
Never hinged 2.25
On cover 30.00
B14 SP1 2.50fr + 25c dk bl 1.50 1.50
Never hinged 4.50
On cover 37.50
Nos. B12-B14 (3) 3.00 3.00
Set, never hinged 9.00

Issued in memory of Queen Astrid. The surtax was for the National League for Protection of Native Children.

POSTAGE DUE STAMPS

Belgian Congo Nos. J1-J7 Overprinted

1924-27 **Unwmk.** ***Perf. 14***
J1 D1 5c black brn .25 .25
Never hinged .30
a. Double overprint 60.00 60.00
J2 D1 10c deep rose .25 .25
Never hinged .30
J3 D1 15c violet .30 .25
Never hinged .55
a. Double overprint 60.00 60.00
J4 D1 30c green .50 .30
Never hinged .70
J5 D1 50c ultra .50 .40
Never hinged .70
J6 D1 50c brt blue ('27) .80 .45
Never hinged 1.05
J7 D1 1fr gray .70 .55
Never hinged .90
Nos. J1-J7 (7) 3.30 2.45
Set, never hinged 4.50

RUSSIA

'rəsh-ə

(Union of Soviet Socialist Republics)

LOCATION — Eastern Europe and Northern Asia
GOVT. — Republic
AREA — 8,650,000 sq. mi.
POP. — 276,300,000 (est. 1985)
CAPITAL — Moscow

An empire until 1917, the government was overthrown in that year and a socialist union of republics was formed under the name of the Union of Soviet Socialist Republics. The USSR includes the following autonomous republics which have issued their own stamps: Armenia, Azerbaijan, Georgia and Ukraine.

100 Kopecks = 1 Ruble

Watermarks

Wmk. 166 — Colorless Numerals ("1" for Nos. 1-2, "2" for No. 3, "3" for No. 4)

Wmk. 168 — Cyrillic EZGB & Wavy Lines

Initials are those of the State Printing Plant.

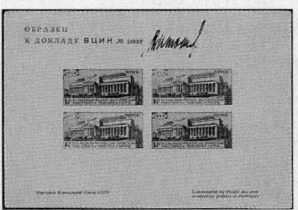

Wmk. 169 — Lozenges

Wmk. 171 — Diamonds

Wmk. 170 — Greek Border and Rosettes

Wmk. 226 — Diamonds Enclosing Four Dots

Empire

Coat of Arms — A1

Wmk. 166

1857, Dec. 10 Typo. *Imperf.*
1 A1 10k brown & blue *62,500.* 775.
No gum *21,000.*
Pen cancellation 475.
Penmark & postmark 475.
Straight line town cancellation, *from* 650.
Circular datestamp cancellation, *from* 900.
Pair, postal cancellation, *from* 3,250.
On cover, postal cancellation only, *from* *3,500.*
On cover, pen cancellation *1,750.*
On cover, pen & postal cancellations *3,000.*
a. Small "1" at upper-right corner *1,175.*
b. Broken "0" at bottom-left corner *1,450.*
c. Dot near "o" in "10 kop" *3,750.*

Full margins = ¾mm.

Genuine unused examples of No. 1 are exceedingly rare. Most of those offered are used with pen cancellation removed. The unused value is for an example without gum. The very few known stamps with original gum sell for much more.

See Poland for similar stamp inscribed "ZALOT KOP. 10."

1858, Jan. 10 *Perf. 14½, 15*
2 A1 10k brown & blue 14,000. 140.
No gum *4,400.*
On cover 650.
3 A1 20k blue & orange 13,000. 1,600.
No gum *4,250.*
On cover *13,500.*
4 A1 30k carmine & green 18,500. 2,750.
No gum *5,750.*
On cover *3,000.*

No. 3 exists in green & violet. It is an essay, value with or without watermark, about $1,000.

Coat of Arms — A2

Wove Paper

1858-64 Unwmk. *Perf. 12½*
5 A2 1k blk & yel ('64) 170.00 67.50
Never hinged *400.00*
On cover 425.00
a. 1k black & orange 340.00 55.00
Never hinged *675.00*
On cover 450.00
6 A2 3k blk & grn ('64) 1,100. 100.00
Never hinged *2,350.*
On cover 800.00
7 A2 5k blk & lil ('64) 1,000. 90.00
Never hinged *2,100.*
On cover 975.00
8 A1 10k brown & blue 275.00 13.50
Never hinged *925.00*
On cover 160.00
Half used as 5k on cover —
9 A1 20k blue & orange 1,000. 80.00
Never hinged *2,100.*
On cover 750.00
a. Half used as 10k on cover —
10 A1 30k car & grn 1,175. 125.00
Never hinged *2,600.*
On cover 1,250.
Nos. 5-10 (6) 4,720. 476.00

Coat of Arms — A3

1863
11 A3 5k black & blue 30.00 *160.00*
Never hinged 52.50
On cover, local use, dated 1863-July 1864 *4,500.*
On cover, dated after July 1864, *from* *2,100.*

No. 11 was issued to pay local postage in St. Petersburg and Moscow. It is known to have been used in other cities. In Aug. 1864 it was authorized for use on mail addressed to other destinations. No. 11 was withdrawn from use 12/21/84.

1865, June 2 *Perf. 14½, 15*
12 A2 1k black & yellow 375.00 37.50
Never hinged 1,000.
On cover 100.00
On cover, single franking 110.00
a. 1k black & orange 400.00 42.50
Never hinged 1,100.
On cover 110.00
On cover, single franking 120.00
13 A2 3k black & green 250.00 17.50
Never hinged 650.00
On cover 50.00
14 A2 5k black & lilac 375.00 40.00
Never hinged 1,000.
On cover 60.00
15 A1 10k brown & blue 925.00 3.00
Never hinged 3,100.
On cover 15.00
a. Thick paper 975.00 7.50
On cover 35.00
b. 10k redsh brn & bl 925.00 2.75
On cover 15.00
17 A1 20k blue & orange 2,750. 40.00
Never hinged 6,750.
On cover 210.00
a. Thick paper 3,000. 45.00
On cover 225.00
18 A1 30k car & grn 1,950. 40.00
Never hinged 2,600.
On cover 850.00
a. Thick paper 2,100. 45.00
On cover 950.00
Nos. 12-18 (6) 6,625. 178.00

Horizontally Laid Paper

1866-70 Wmk. 168
19 A2 1k blk & yel 6.50 1.10
Never hinged 18.50
On cover 8.00
On cover, single franking 37.50
a. 1k black & orange 12.00 1.25
Never hinged 30.00
On cover 10.00
On cover, single franking 42.50
b. Imperf. *3,000.*
c. Vertically laid 315.00 45.00
Never hinged 640.00
On cover 275.00
On cover, single franking 300.00
d. Groundwork inverted *5,500.* *5,500.*
e. Thick paper 75.00 55.00
f. As "c," imperf. 7,500. 7,250.
g. As "b," "c" & "d" *11,000.* *17,000.*
h. 1k blk & org, vert. laid paper 350.00 42.50
Never hinged 800.00
On cover 300.00
On cover, single franking 350.00
i. As "c," groundwork inverted 5,500. 5,500.
20 A2 3k blk & dp grn 11.00 1.50
Never hinged 27.50
On cover 12.50
a. 3k black & yellow green 12.50 1.50
Never hinged 40.00
On cover 12.50
b. Imperf. *3,400.*
c. Vertically laid 400.00 50.00
Never hinged 800.00
On cover 275.00
d. V's in groundwork (error) ('70) 1,000. 40.00
On cover 450.00
e. 3k black & blue green 12.50 1.50
On cover 12.50
22 A2 5k black & lilac 15.00 2.00
Never hinged 45.00
On cover 12.50
a. 5k black & gray 240.00 32.50
Never hinged 400.00
On cover 175.00
b. Imperf. 4,250.
c. Vertically laid 10,000. 160.00
Never hinged —
On cover 750.00
d. As "c," imperf. — —
23 A1 10k brn & blue 45.00 1.75
Never hinged 160.00
On cover 17.50
a. Vertically laid 525.00 16.50
Never hinged 1,000.
On cover 130.00
b. Center inverted *50,000.*
c. Imperf. *22,500.*
24 A1 20k blue & org 105.00 15.00
Never hinged 290.00
On cover 77.50
a. Vertically laid 5,250. 160.00
Never hinged —
On cover 850.00
25 A1 30k car & grn 100.00 30.00
Never hinged 275.00
On cover 250.00
On cover, single franking 475.00
a. Vertically laid 1,000. 120.00
Never hinged *2,150.*
On cover 1,250.
On cover, single franking 1,500.
Nos. 19-25 (6) 282.50 51.35

Arms — A4

1875-82 Horizontally Laid Paper
26 A2 2k black & red 25.00 1.60
Never hinged 67.50
On cover 125.00
On cover, single franking 175.00
a. Vertically laid 6,750. 160.00
Never hinged 8,500.
No gum 1,275.
On cover 850.00
On cover, single franking 1,000.
b. Groundwork inverted *57,500.*
27 A4 7k gray & rose ('79) 16.00 1.00
Never hinged 40.00
On cover 22.50
a. Imperf. *8,500.*
b. Vertically laid 2,000. 65.00
Never hinged 5,100.
No gum 600.00
On cover 300.00
c. Wmkd. hexagons ('79) *170,000.*
d. Center inverted —
e. Center omitted — —
f. 7k black & carmine ('80) 21.00 .85
Never hinged 35.00
On cover 22.50
g. 7k pale gray & carmine ('82) 21.00 .85
Never hinged 40.00
On cover 22.50
28 A4 8k gray & rose 25.00 1.60
Never hinged 80.00
On cover 17.50
a. Vertically laid 2,500. 82.50
Never hinged 3,500.
No gum 600.00
On cover 1,000.
b. Imperf. *22,500.*
c. "C" instead of "B" in "Bocem" 650.00 *250.*
Never hinged 1,275.
29 A4 10k brn & blue 50.00 5.75
Never hinged 160.00
On cover 85.00
a. Center inverted *60,000.*
30 A4 20k blue & org 67.50 10.00
Never hinged 210.00
On cover 67.50
a. Cross-shaped "T" in bottom word 170.00 27.50
Never hinged 400.00
b. Center inverted *75,000.*
c. Center double *90,000.*
d. As "a," center inverted —
Nos. 26-30 (5) 183.50 19.95

The hexagon watermark of No. 27c is that of revenue stamps. Four examples of No. 27c are recorded, all used at Perm. One example of No. 27d is recorded.

See Finland for stamps similar to designs A4-A15, which have "dot in circle" devices or are inscribed "Markka," "Markkaa," "Pen.," or "Pennia."

Imperial Eagle and Post Horns
A5 A6

Perf. 14 to 15 and Compound
1883-88 Wmk. 168
Horizontally Laid Paper
31 A5 1k orange 7.25 1.20
Never hinged 12.00
On cover 65.00
a. Imperf. 62,500.
b. Groundwork inverted *9,000.*
c. 1k yellow 6.75 1.20
Never hinged 13.50
On cover —
32 A5 2k dark green 4.00 1.20
Never hinged 12.00
On cover 65.00
a. 2k yellow green ('88) 26.50 4.00
Never hinged 50.00
On cover —
b. Imperf. 1,100. 700.00
c. Wove paper —
d. Groundwork inverted *31,500.*
33 A5 3k carmine 7.50 1.20
Never hinged 19.00
On cover 10.00
a. Imperf. —
b. Groundwork inverted *30,000.*
On cover 32,500.
c. Wove paper —
34 A5 5k red violet 4.00 .90
Never hinged 12.50
On cover —
a. Groundwork inverted *8,500.*
35 A5 7k blue 7.50 .90
Never hinged 19.00
On cover 10.00
a. Imperf. 800.00 475.00

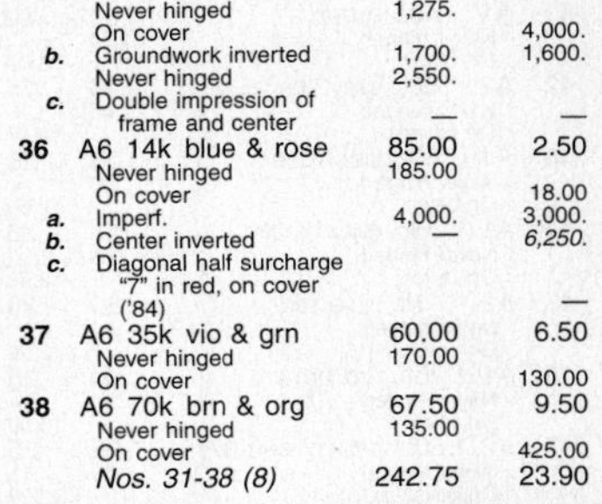

Never hinged 1,275.
On cover 4,000.
b. Groundwork inverted 1,700. 1,600.
Never hinged 2,550.
c. Double impression of frame and center — —
36 A6 14k blue & rose 85.00 2.50
Never hinged 185.00
On cover 18.00
a. Imperf. 4,000. 3,000.
b. Center inverted — *6,250.*
c. Diagonal half surcharge "7" in red, on cover ('84) —
37 A6 35k vio & grn 60.00 6.50
Never hinged 170.00
On cover 130.00
38 A6 70k brn & org 67.50 9.50
Never hinged 135.00
On cover 425.00
Nos. 31-38 (8) 242.75 23.90

Before 1882 the 1, 2, 3 and 5 kopecks had small numerals in the background; beginning with No. 31 these denominations have a background of network, like the higher values.

No. 36c is handstamped. It is known with cancellations of Tiflis and Kutais, both in Georgia. It is believed to be of philatelic origin.

A7

1884 *Perf. 13½, 13½x11½*
Vertically Laid Paper
39 A7 3.50r blk & gray 1,200. 625.
Never hinged 2,900.
a. Horiz. laid *175,000.* 15,000.
b. Inverted center — —
40 A7 7r blk & org 800. 675.
Never hinged 2,400.

Forgeries exist, both unused and used.

A8

Imperial Eagle and Post Horns with Thunderbolts — A9

With Thunderbolts Across Post Horns

Perf. 14 to 15 and Compound
1889, May 14
Horizontally Laid Paper
41 A8 4k rose 12.00 .45
Never hinged 34.00
On cover 8.50
a. Groundwork inverted — *16,000.*
b. Double impression of center — —
c. Double impression of frame — —
42 A8 10k dark blue 20.00 .45
Never hinged 50.00
On cover 8.50
43 A8 20k blue & carmine 21.00 1.20
Never hinged 60.00
On cover 12.50
a. Groundwork inverted — —
44 A8 50k violet & green 16.00 1.50
Never hinged 47.50
On cover 100.00

Perf. 13½
45 A9 1r lt brn, brn & org 47.50 2.50
Never hinged 140.00
On cover 260.00
a. Horiz. pair, imperf. btwn. 900.00 450.00
b. Vert. pair, imperf. btwn. 850.00 425.00
c. Center omitted — —
Nos. 41-45 (5) 116.50 6.10

See #57C, 60, 63, 66, 68, 82, 85, 87, 126, 129, 131. For surcharges see #216, 219, 223, 226.

A10

A11

A12

With Thunderbolts Across Post Horns

1889-92 *Perf. 14½x15*

Horizontally Laid Paper

46 A10 1k orange 3.25 .50
Never hinged 13.50
On cover 42.50
a. Imperf. 850.00 —
Never hinged 1,275.
47 A10 2k green 4.00 .50
Never hinged 13.50
On cover 42.50
a. Imperf. 800.00
Never hinged 1,200.
b. Groundwork inverted 800.00 *17,000.*
Never hinged 1,200.
48 A10 3k carmine 8.00 .50
Never hinged 50.00
On cover 5.00
a. Imperf. 425.00 350.00
Never hinged 525.00
49 A10 5k red vio 8.00 .60
Never hinged 13.50
On cover 5.00
b. Groundwork omitted or inverted 850.00 650.00
Never hinged 1,000.
50 A10 7k dk blue 5.25 .50
Never hinged 14.50
On cover 5.00
a. Imperf. 425.00 *9,000.*
Never hinged 500.00
b. Groundwork inverted *16,000.* *11,250.*
Never hinged —
c. Groundwork omitted 250.00 200.00
Never hinged 500.00
51 A11 14k blue & rose 16.00 .50
Never hinged 50.00
On cover 13.00
a. Center inverted *6,750.* *4,500.*
Never hinged —
b. Center omitted 850.00
Never hinged 1,000.
52 A11 35k vio & grn 67.50 6.00
Never hinged 135.00
On cover 42.50

Perf. 13½

53 A12 3.50r blk & gray 19.00 8.00
Never hinged 50.00
On cover 275.00
a. Center inverted — *12,750.*
54 A12 7r blk & yel 190.00 11.00
Never hinged 650.00
On cover 300.00
a. Dbl. impression of black *45,000.*
Nos. 46-54 (9) 321.00 28.10

Perf. 14 to 15 and Compound

1902-05 **Vertically Laid Paper**

55 A10 1k orange 4.50 .35
Never hinged 19.00
On cover 42.50
a. Imperf. 1,100. *1,100.*
Never hinged 1,550.
b. Groundwork inverted — —
c. Groundwork omitted — —
56 A10 2k yel grn 4.50 .35
Never hinged 19.00
On cover 42.50
a. 2k deep green 8.00 .70
b. Groundwork omitted — —
c. Groundwork inverted — —
d. Groundwork double *375.00* *375.00*
Never hinged *450.00*
57 A10 3k rose red 10.50 .35
Never hinged 27.00
On cover 5.00
a. Groundwork omitted — —
b. Double impression 275.00 250.00
d. Imperf. *1,350.* —
Never hinged *1,650.*
e. Groundwork inverted — —
f. Groundwork double 275.00
Never hinged *350.00*
57C A8 4k rose red ('04) 9.00 .85
Never hinged 27.50
On cover 5.00
f. Double impression 340.00 275.00
Never hinged 425.00
g. Groundwork inverted — —
58 A10 5k red vio 19.00 .60
Never hinged 80.00
On cover 10.00
a. 5k dull violet 12.50 2.25
b. Groundwork inverted — —
c. Imperf. — —
d. Groundwork omitted 675.00 150.00
Never hinged 850.00
e. Groundwork double *1,350.* 100.00
Never hinged *1,500.*

59 A10 7k dk blue 10.50 .35
Never hinged 27.50
On cover 10.00
a. Groundwork omitted 315.00 *275.00*
Never hinged 375.00
b. Imperf. 675.00 600.00
c. Groundwork inverted — —
60 A8 10k dk blue ('04) 4.00 .50
Never hinged 26.00
On cover 5.00
a. Groundwork inverted 42.50 17.50
Never hinged 70.00
b. Groundwork omitted 600.00 85.00
Never hinged 850.00
c. Groundwork double 175.00 85.00
Never hinged 225.00
61 A11 14k blue & rose 22.50 .80
Never hinged 67.50
On cover 17.50
a. Center inverted — *4,000.*
On cover *10,500.*
b. Center omitted 1,100. 700.00
Never hinged 1,350.
62 A11 15k brn vio & blue ('05) 20.00 2.00
Never hinged 50.00
On cover 42.50
a. Center omitted — —
b. Center inverted *4,500.* *4,000.*
Never hinged 5,000.
63 A8 20k blue & car ('04) 11.00 .85
Never hinged 50.00
On cover 13.00
64 A11 25k dull grn & lil ('05) 45.00 2.50
Never hinged 150.00
On cover 42.50
a. Center inverted *7,250.* 6,000.
b. Center omitted — —
65 A11 35k dk vio & grn 55.00 1.80
Never hinged 210.00
On cover 42.50
a. Center inverted 2,500. *2,000.*
Never hinged 3,000.
b. Center omitted — —
66 A8 50k vio & grn ('05) 35.00 1.00
Never hinged 400.00
On cover 27.50
67 A11 70k brn & org 45.00 3.25
Never hinged 160.00
On cover 125.00

Perf. 13½

68 A9 1r lt brn, brn & org 90.00 2.00
Never hinged 190.00
On cover 225.00
a. Perf. 11½ 700.00 50.00
Never hinged 1,350.
b. Perf. 13½x11½, 11½x13½ 340.00 525.00
Never hinged 500.00
c. Imperf. — —
d. Center inverted — —
e. Center omitted 675.00 250.00
Never hinged 850.00
f. Horiz. pair, imperf. btwn. 1,100. 350.00
Never hinged 1,250.
g. Vert. pair, imperf. btwn. 900.00 340.00
Never hinged 1,000.
69 A12 3.50r blk & gray 55.00 4.00
Never hinged 65.00
On cover 130.00
a. Center inverted *13,000.*
b. Imperf., pair 2,000. 2,000.
70 A12 7r blk & yel 14.00 4.75
Never hinged 40.00
On cover 175.00
a. Center inverted *7,000.* *13,500.*
Never hinged *7,500.*
b. Horiz. pair, imperf. btwn. 3,000. 1,450.
Never hinged *3,250.*
c. Vert. pair, imperf. btwn. 1,200. 800.00
Never hinged *1,500.*
d. Imperf., pair — —

A13

1906 *Perf. 13½*

71 A13 5r dk blue, grn & pale blue 50.00 4.50
Never hinged 160.00
On cover 42.50
a. Perf. 11½ 500.00 275.00
Never hinged 1,450.
72 A13 10r car rose, yel & gray 350.00 10.50
Never hinged 1,050.
On cover 100.00
Nos. 55-72 (19) 854.50 41.30

The design of No. 72 differs in many details from the illustration. Nos. 71-72 were printed in sheets of 25.

See Nos. 80-81, 83-84, 86, 108-109, 125, 127-128, 130, 132-135, 137-138. For surcharges see Nos. 217-218, 220-222, 224-225, 227-229.

A14

A15

Vertical Lozenges of Varnish on Face

1909-12 **Unwmk.** *Perf. 14x14½*

Wove Paper

73 A14 1k dull org yel .45 .45
Never hinged 1.60
On cover 85.00
a. 1k orange yellow ('09) 2.50 .45
Never hinged 6.50
On cover 85.00
c. Double impression 90.00 —
Never hinged 130.00
74 A14 2k dull green .25 .25
Never hinged .25
On cover 85.00
a. 2k green ('09) 1.60 .25
Never hinged 2.50
On cover 85.00
b. Double impression 100.00 —
Never hinged 170.00
75 A14 3k carmine .25 .25
Never hinged .50
On cover 8.50
a. 3k rose red ('09) 1.40 .25
Never hinged 5.75
On cover 8.50
76 A15 4k carmine .25 .25
Never hinged .35
On cover 8.50
a. 4k carmine rose ('09) 1.40 .25
Never hinged 2.50
On cover 8.50
77 A14 5k claret 2.50 .25
Never hinged 5.50
On cover 8.50
a. 5k lilac ('12) .25 .25
Never hinged .50
On cover 8.50
b. Double impression 95.00
Never hinged 115.00
78 A14 7k blue .25 .25
Never hinged .50
On cover 127.50
a. 7k light blue ('09) 2.50 .45
Never hinged 8.50
On cover 127.50
b. Imperf. 1,450.
79 A15 10k dark blue .25 .25
Never hinged .50
On cover 5.00
a. 10k light blue ('09) *80.00* *8.00*
Never hinged 140.00
On cover *100.00*
b. 10k pale blue 8.00 2.00
On cover 25.00
80 A11 14k dk blue & car .85 .25
Never hinged 4.00
On cover 10.00
a. 14k blue & rose ('09) 1.40 .25
Never hinged 3.25
On cover 10.00
81 A11 15k red brn & dp blue .25 .25
Never hinged .25
On cover 5.00
a. 15k dull violet & blue ('09) 1.40 .25
Never hinged 6.50
On cover 5.00
c. Center omitted 170.00
Never hinged 260.00
d. Center double 50.00 —
Never hinged 100.00
82 A8 20k dull bl & dk car .25 .25
Never hinged .25
On cover 1.00
a. 20k blue & carmine ('10) 1.40 .45
Never hinged 3.25
On cover 2.00
b. Groundwork omitted 42.50
Never hinged 85.00
c. Center double 175.00
Never hinged 250.00
d. Center and value omitted — —
83 A11 25k dl grn & dk vio .25 .25
Never hinged .25
On cover 1.00
a. 25k green & violet ('09) 1.40 .45
Never hinged 3.25
On cover 2.00
b. Center omitted 170.00
Never hinged 250.00
c. Center double 175.00 —
Never hinged 225.00
84 A11 35k red brn & grn .25 .25
Never hinged .25
On cover 1.00
a. 35k brown vio & yel green .55 .40
Never hinged .65
On cover 1.50
b. 35k violet & green ('09) 1.40 .45
Never hinged 3.25
On cover 2.00
c. Center double 25.00 —
Never hinged 42.50
85 A8 50k red brn & grn .25 .25
Never hinged .45
On cover 1.00
a. 50k violet & green ('09) 3.25 .45
Never hinged 8.00
On cover 2.00
b. Groundwork omitted 30.00
Never hinged 45.00
c. Center double 175.00 —
Never hinged 225.00
d. Center and value omitted — —
86 A11 70k brn & red org .25 .25
Never hinged .45
On cover 1.00
a. 70k lt brown & orange ('09) 2.50 .45
Never hinged 4.00
On cover 2.00
b. Center double 175.00 —
Never hinged 225.00
c. Center omitted 115.00 115.00
Never hinged 145.00

Perf. 13½

87 A9 1r pale brn, dk brn & org .50 .35
Never hinged 1.65
On cover 1.00
a. 1r pale brn, brn & org ('10) 1.65 .45
Never hinged 4.75
On cover 2.00
b. Perf. 12½ 80.00 —
Never hinged 135.00
c. Groundwork inverted 25.00 —
Never hinged 42.50
d. Horiz. pair, imperf. between 25.00 —
Never hinged 42.50
e. Vert. pair, imperf. between 25.00 —
Never hinged 42.50
f. Center inverted 40.00 —
Never hinged 145.00
g. Center double 25.00 —
Never hinged 95.00
Nos. 73-87 (15) 7.05 4.05

See Nos. 119-124. For surcharges see Nos. 117-118, B24-B29.

No. 87a was issued in sheets of 40 stamps, while Nos. 87 and 87b came in sheets of 50. Nos. 87g-87k are listed below No. 138a.

Nearly all values of this issue are known without the lines of varnish.

The 7k has two types:

I — The scroll bearing the top inscription ends at left with three short lines of shading beside the first letter. Four pearls extend at lower left between the leaves and denomination panel.

II — Inner lines of scroll at top left end in two curls; three pearls at lower left.

Three clichés of type II (an essay) were included by mistake in the plate used for the first printing. Value of pair, type I with type II, unused $4,500.

SURCHARGES

Russian stamps of types A6-A15 with various surcharges may be found listed under Armenia, Batum, Far Eastern Republic, Georgia, Latvia, Siberia, South Russia, Transcaucasian Federated Republics, Ukraine, Russian Offices in China, Russian Offices in the Turkish Empire and Army of the Northwest.

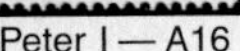
Peter I — A16

Alexander II — A17

Alexander III — A18

Peter I — A19

Nicholas II
A20 A21

Catherine II — A22

Nicholas I — A23

Alexander I — A24

Alexis Mikhailovich A25

Paul I A26

Elizabeth Petrovna A27

Michael Feodorovich A28

The Kremlin — A29

Winter Palace — A30

Romanov Castle — A31

Nicholas II — A32

Without Lozenges of Varnish

1913, Jan. 2 Typo. *Perf. 13½*
88 A16 1k brn org 1.60 .25
Never hinged 4.00
On cover 7.50
89 A17 2k yellow green 4.25 .25
Never hinged 9.25
On cover 7.50
90 A18 3k rose red 4.25 .25
Never hinged 13.50
On cover 7.50
b. Double impression 600.00
Never hinged 700.00
91 A19 4k dull red 1.60 .25
Never hinged 8.00
On cover 8.00
92 A20 7k brown 1.60 .25
Never hinged 4.00
On cover 8.00
b. Double impression 675.00 —
Never hinged 900.00
93 A21 10k deep blue 4.25 .25
Never hinged 9.50
On cover 8.00
94 A22 14k blue green 4.25 .40
Never hinged 8.50
On cover 35.00
95 A23 15k yellow brown 8.00 .60
Never hinged 21.00
On cover 37.50
96 A24 20k olive green 26.50 .70
Never hinged 80.00
On cover 40.00
97 A25 25k red violet 8.00 1.10
Never hinged 24.00
On cover 40.00
98 A26 35k gray vio & dk grn 2.50 .70
Never hinged 10.50
On cover 27.50
99 A27 50k brn & slate 10.75 1.90
Never hinged 30.00
On cover 45.00
100 A28 70k yel grn & brn 8.00 1.90
Never hinged 19.00
On cover 50.00

Engr.

101 A29 1r deep green 40.00 6.25
Never hinged 95.00
On cover 250.00
On postal money order receipt card 135.00
102 A30 2r red brown 65.00 11.00
Never hinged 135.00
On cover 425.00
On postal money order receipt card 175.00
103 A31 3r dark violet 50.00 11.00
Never hinged 110.00
On cover 425.00
On postal money order receipt card 175.00
104 A32 5r black brown 40.00 19.00
Never hinged 80.00
On cover 900.00
On postal money order receipt card 240.00
Nos. 88-104 (17) 280.55 56.05

Imperf

88a A16 1k brown orange 900.00 —
Never hinged 1,200.
89a A17 2k yellow green 900.00 —
Never hinged 1,200.
90a A18 3k rose red 900.00
Never hinged 1,200.
91a A19 4k dull red 2,150.
Never hinged 3,250.
92a A20 7k brown 500.00
Never hinged 750.00
93a A21 10k deep blue 900.00
Never hinged 1,200.
94a A22 14k blue green 2,150.
Never hinged 3,250.
101a A29 1r deep green 1,750.
Never hinged 2,500.
102a A30 2r red brown 900.00
Never hinged 1,000.
103b A31 3r dark violet 900.00
Never hinged 1,000.
104a A32 5r dark violet 2,150.
Never hinged 3,250.

Tercentenary of the founding of the Romanov dynasty.

See Nos. 105-107, 112-116, 139-141. For surcharges see Nos. 110-111, Russian Offices in the Turkish Empire 213-227.

Arms and 5-line Inscription on Back

Имѣетъ хожде-
ніе наравнѣ съ
размѣнной се-
ребряной моне-
той.

No. 107 Back

Thin Cardboard Without Gum

1915, Oct. Typo. *Perf. 13½*
105 A21 10k blue 2.50 32.50
On cover 50.00
106 A23 15k brown 2.50 32.50
On cover 50.00
107 A24 20k olive green 2.50 32.50
On cover 50.00
Nos. 105-107 (3) 7.50 97.50

Imperf

105a A21 10k 550.00
106a A23 15k 200.00 —
107a A24 20k 175.00

Nos. 105-107, 112-116 and 139-141 were issued for use as paper money, but contrary to regulations were often used for postal purposes. Back inscription means: "Having circulation on par with silver subsidiary coins."

Types of 1906 Issue Vertical Lozenges of Varnish on Face

1915 *Perf. 13½, 13½x13*
108 A13 5r ind, grn & lt blue 1.40 .50
Never hinged 3.25
On cover 42.50
a. 5r dk bl, grn & pale bl ('15) 13.50 1.60
Never hinged 27.50
On cover 75.00
b. Perf. 12½ 16.50 6.75
Never hinged 32.50
On cover 47.50
c. Center double 60.00
Never hinged 175.00
d. Pair, imperf. between 100.00 —
Never hinged 200.00
109 A13 10r car lake, yel & gray 2.00 .50
Never hinged 3.00
On cover 10.00
a. 10r carmine, yel & light gray 2.00 .50
Never hinged 3.00
On cover 10.00
b. 10r rose red, yel & gray ('15) 6.75 .85
Never hinged 14.00
On cover 12.50
c. 10r car, yel & gray blue (error) 2,700.
Never hinged 3,000.
d. Groundwork inverted 450.00
Never hinged 500.00
e. Center double 60.00 —
Never hinged 85.00

Nos. 108a and 109b were issued in sheets of 25. Nos. 108, 108b, 109 and 109a came in sheets of 50. Chemical forgeries of No. 109c exist. Genuine examples usually are centered to upper right.

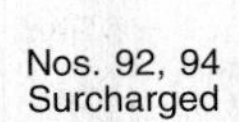

Nos. 92, 94 Surcharged

1916
110 A20 10k on 7k brown .85 .50
Never hinged 1.60
On cover 15.00
a. Inverted surcharge 210.00
Never hinged 250.00
111 A22 20k on 14k bl grn .85 .45
Never hinged 1.60
On cover 15.00

Imperf

110b A20 10k on 7k brown 425.00 —
Never hinged 850.00
111a A22 20k on 14k bl grn 425.00 —
Never hinged 850.00

Types of 1913 Issue Arms, Value & 4-line inscription on Back Surcharged Large Numerals on Nos. 112-113 Thin Cardboard

1916-17 Without Gum
112 A16 1 on 1k brn org ('17) 2.50 *40.00*
On cover 140.00
113 A17 2 on 2k yel green ('17) 2.50 *40.00*
On cover 150.00

Without Surcharge

114 A16 1k brown orange 50.00 —
On cover *200.00*
115 A17 2k yellow green 52.50 —
On cover *200.00*
116 A18 3k rose red 2.50 *32.50*
On cover *50.00*

See note after No. 107.

Nos. 78a, 80a Surcharged

a

b

1917 *Perf. 14x14½*
117 A14 10k on 7k lt blue .85 .45
Never hinged 1.65
On cover 15.00
a. Inverted surcharge 150.00 —
Never hinged *225.00*
b. Double surcharge 60.00 —
Never hinged 90.00
c. Imperforate *375.00* —
Never hinged *450.00*
118 A11 20k on 14k bl & rose 1.20 .45
Never hinged 2.40
On cover 13.00
a. Inverted surcharge 250.00 —
Never hinged *350.00*

Provisional Government Civil War Type of 1889-1912 Issues Vertical Lozenges of Varnish on Face

Two types of 7r:
Type I — Single outer frame line.
Type II — Double outer frame line.

Wove Paper

1917 Typo. *Imperf.*
119 A14 1k orange 1.10 .25
Never hinged 2.25
On cover 17.50
120 A14 2k gray green .25 .25
Never hinged .50
On cover 17.50
121 A14 3k red .25 .25
Never hinged .50
On cover 5.00
122 A15 4k carmine .85 2.50
Never hinged 2.25
On cover 7.50
123 A14 5k claret .25 .25
Never hinged .50
On cover 5.00
124 A15 10k dark blue 22.50 22.50
Never hinged 50.00
On cover *75.00*
125 A11 15k red brn & dp blue .40 .25
Never hinged .70
On cover 5.00
a. Center omitted 175.00
Never hinged 225.00
126 A8 20k blue & car .35 .35
Never hinged .70
On cover 5.00
a. Groundwork omitted 42.50 —
Never hinged 55.00
127 A11 25k grn & gray vio .50 1.00
Never hinged 1.10
On cover 5.00
128 A11 35k red brn & grn .50 .35
Never hinged 1.10
On cover 5.00
129 A8 50k brn vio & grn .45 .25
Never hinged .85
On cover 5.00
a. Groundwork omitted 42.50 —
Never hinged 127.50
130 A11 70k brn & org .45 .35
Never hinged .85
On cover 60.00
a. Center omitted 100.00 —
Never hinged *145.00*
131 A9 1r pale brn, brn & red org .35 .25
Never hinged .70
On cover 135.00
a. Center inverted 25.00 —
Never hinged *35.00*
b. Center omitted 25.00 —
Never hinged *35.00*
c. Center double 25.00 —
Never hinged *35.00*

d. Groundwork double 150.00 —
Never hinged *200.00*
e. Groundwork inverted 60.00 —
Never hinged *75.00*
f. Groundwork omitted 60.00 —
Never hinged *75.00*
g. Frame double 25.00 —
Never hinged *35.00*
132 A12 3.50r mar & lt grn 1.10 .25
Never hinged 2.25
On cover 60.00
133 A13 5r dk blue, grn & pale blue 1.25 .35
Never hinged 2.75
On cover 62.50
a. 5r dk bl, grn & yel (error) 900.00
b. Groundwork inverted *3,600.*
134 A12 7r dk grn & pink (I) 1.20 1.15
Never hinged 2.75
On cover 50.00
a. Center inverted *6,750.*
135 A13 10r scar, yel & gray 55.00 40.00
Never hinged 150.00
On cover 135.00
a. 10r scarlet, green & gray (error) 1,125.
Nos. 119-135 (17) 86.75 70.55

Beware of trimmed examples of No. 109 offered as No. 135.

Vertical Lozenges of Varnish on Face

1917 ***Perf. 13½, 13½x13***

137 A12 3.50r mar & lt grn .50 .25
Never hinged 1.10
138 A12 7r dk grn & pink (II) 2.50 .50
Never hinged 5.50
d. Type I 40.00 6.75
Never hinged 80.00

Perf. 12½

137a A12 3.50r maroon & lt grn 14.00 2.75
Never hinged 28.00
138a A12 7r dk grn & pink (II) 17.00 4.75
Never hinged 35.00

Horizontal Lozenges of Varnish on Face

Perf. 13½x13

87g A9 1r pale brown, brn & red orange 1.35 .30
Never hinged 2.50
On cover 10.00
h. Imperf. 17.50 —
Never hinged 27.50
i. As "h," center omitted 45.00 —
Never hinged 67.50
j. As "h," center inverted 22.50 —
Never hinged 27.50
k. As "h," center double 22.50 —
Never hinged 27.50
137b A12 3.50r mar & lt green 2.50 .50
Never hinged 5.50
On cover 24.00
d. Imperf. 2,250.
Never hinged 4,000.
138b A12 7r dk grn & pink (II) 1.35 .25
Never hinged 2.75
On cover 32.50
c. Imperf. 1,550.
Never hinged 2,100.

Nos. 87g, 137b and 138b often show the eagle with little or no embossing.

Types of 1913 Issue

No. 88 Surcharged Large Numeral

No. 139 Back

No. 140 Back

The backside of Nos. 139-140 have surcharge & 4-line inscription.

1917

Thin Cardboard, Without Gum

139 A16 1 on 1k brown org 2.50 *40.00*
On cover 135.00
140 A17 2 on 2k yel green 2.50 *40.00*
On cover 150.00
a. Imperf. 525.00 —
Pair *1,700.*

Without Surcharge

141 A18 3k rose red 2.50 *40.00*
On cover 90.00
Nos. 139-141 (3) 7.50 *120.00*

See note after No. 107.

Stamps overprinted with a Liberty Cap on Crossed Swords or with reduced facsimiles of pages of newspapers were a private speculation and without official sanction.

RUSSIAN TURKESTAN

Russian stamps of 1917-18 surcharged as above are frauds.

Russian Soviet Federated Socialist Republic

Severing Chain of Bondage — A33

1918 **Typo.** ***Perf. 13½***

149 A33 35k blue .45 *6.25*
Never hinged .85
a. Imperf., pair 1,600.
Never hinged 2,250.
150 A33 70k brown .50 *7.25*
Never hinged 1.10
a. Imperf., pair *16,500.*
Never hinged *52,500.*

For surcharges see Nos. B18-B23, J1-J9 and note following No. B17.

A 15k stamp exists but was not regularly issued. Value, $30,000.

During 1918-22, the chaotic conditions of revolution and civil war brought the printing of stamps by the central government to a halt. Stocks of old tsarist Arms type stamps and postal stationery remained in use, and postal savings and various revenue stamps were authorized for postage use. During this period, stamps were sold and used at different rates at different times: 1918-20, sold at face value; from March, 1920, sold at 100 times face value; from Aug. 15, 1921, sold at 250r each, regardless of face value; from April, 1922, sold at 10,000r per 1k or 1r. In Oct. 1922, these issues were superseded by gold currency stamps.

See Nos. AR1-AR25 for fiscal stamps used as postage stamps during this period.

Symbols of Agriculture — A40

Symbols of Industry — A41

Soviet Symbols of Agriculture and Industry — A42

Science and Arts — A43

1921 **Unwmk.** **Litho.** ***Imperf.***

177 A40 1r orange .85 *140.00*
Never hinged 2.75
178 A40 2r lt brown .85 *140.00*
Never hinged 2.75
a. Double impression 800.00
Never hinged 1,450.
179 A41 5r dull ultra 2.10 *140.00*
Never hinged 4.75
a. Double impression —
180 A42 20r blue 2.50 *140.00*
Never hinged 6.75
a. Double impression 240.00
Never hinged 325.00
b. Pelure paper 10.00 *175.00*
Never hinged 17.00
c. As "b," double impression 275.00 —
Never hinged 425.00
181 A40 100r orange .25 *.25*
Never hinged .25
a. Double impression 200.00
b. Pelure paper .25 .45
Never hinged .45
c. As "b," double impression 200.00
182 A40 200r lt brown .45 *.25*
Never hinged .70
a. Double impression 180.00
b. Triple impression 150.00
c. 200r gray brown 25.00
Never hinged 57.50
183 A43 250r dull violet .25 *.25*
Never hinged .45
a. Tête bêche pair 25.00
Never hinged 50.00
b. Double impression 90.00
Never hinged 110.00
c. Pelure paper .25 *.45*
Never hinged .50
d. As "c," tête bêche pair 32.50 —
Never hinged 45.00
e. As "c," double impression 100.00
f. Chalk surfaced paper 12.50 *5.00*
Never hinged 25.00
184 A40 300r green .50 *1.10*
Never hinged 1.35
a. Double impression 425.00
Never hinged 525.00
b. Pelure paper 8.00 22.50
Never hinged 16.50
185 A41 500r blue .85 .30
Never hinged 2.00
a. Double impression —
186 A41 1000r carmine .25 *.30*
Never hinged .50
a. Double impression 110.00
Never hinged 135.00
b. Triple impression 135.00
Never hinged 150.00
c. Pelure paper .85 *.30*
Never hinged 2.75
d. As "c," double impression 90.00
Never hinged 110.00
e. Thick paper 2.50 *2.75*
Never hinged 6.75
f. Chalk surfaced paper .25 *.50*
Never hinged 1.60
Nos. 177-186 (10) 8.85 562.45

Nos. 177-180 were on sale only in Petrograd, Moscow and Kharkov. Used values are for cancelled-to-order stamps. Postally used examples are worth substantially more.

Nos. 183a and 183d are from printings in which one of the two panes of 25 in the sheet were inverted. Thus, they are horizontal pairs, with a vertical gutter.

See Nos. 203, 205. For surcharges see Nos. 191-194, 196-199, 201, 210, B40, B43-B47, J10.

New Russia Triumphant A44

Type I — 37½mm by 23½mm.
Type II — 38½mm by 23¼mm.

1921, Aug. 10 **Wmk. 169** **Engr.**

187 A44 40r slate, type II 1.90 *160.00*
Never hinged 4.00
a. Type I 1.90 *160.00*
Never hinged 4.00

The types are caused by paper shrinkage. One type has the watermark sideways in relation to the other.

For surcharges see Nos. 195, 200.

Initials Stand for Russian Soviet Federated Socialist Republic — A45

1921 **Litho.** **Unwmk.**

188 A45 100r orange .85 .85
Never hinged 1.35
189 A45 250r violet .85 .85
Never hinged 1.35
190 A45 1000r carmine rose 1.75 1.40
Never hinged 2.75
Nos. 188-190 (3) 3.45 3.10

4th anniversary of Soviet Government.

A 200r was not regularly issued. Values: unused $60, never hinged $100.

Nos. 177-179 Surcharged in Black

1922

191 A40 5000r on 1r org 3.00 .80
Never hinged 3.75
a. Inverted surcharge 140.00 32.50
Never hinged 180.00
b. Double surch., red & blk 800.00 —
Never hinged 1,600.
c. Pair, one without surcharge 250.00 —
192 A40 5000r on 2r lt brn 3.00 1.10
Never hinged 3.75
a. Inverted surcharge 110.00 90.00
b. Double surcharge 145.00
193 A41 5000r on 5r ultra 3.00
Never hinged 4.00
a. Inverted surcharge — *450.00*
b. Double surcharge 145.00
Never hinged 200.00

Beware of digitally created forgeries of the errors of Nos. 191-193 and 196-199.

No. 180 Surcharged

194 A42 5000r on 20r blue 2.10 2.25
Never hinged 4.00
a. Pelure paper 16.50 3.25
Never hinged 27.50
b. Pair, one without surcharge *125.00*
Never hinged *150.00*

Nos. 177-180, 187-187a Surcharged in Black or Red

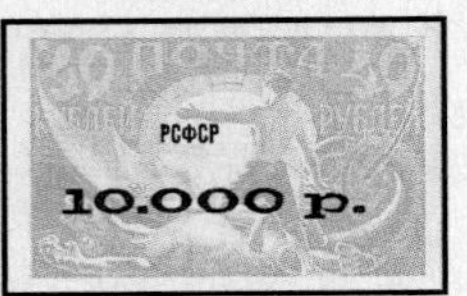

Wmk. Lozenges (169)

195 A44 10,000r on 40r, type I 95.00 50.00
Never hinged 160.00
a. Inverted surcharge 225.00
Never hinged 350.00
b. Type II 67.50 50.00
Never hinged 110.00
c. "1.0000" instead of "10.000" 2,750.
Never hinged 4,250.
d. Double surcharge *8,500.*
Never hinged —

Red Surcharge
Unwmk.

196 A40 5000r on 1r org 5.75 5.75
Never hinged 6.50
a. Inverted surcharge 50.00 25.00
Never hinged 75.00
197 A40 5000r on 2r lt brn 5.75 5.75
Never hinged 6.75
a. Inverted surcharge 125.00 30.00
Never hinged 160.00
198 A41 5000r on 5r ultra 5.75 5.75
Never hinged 6.75
199 A42 5000r on 20r blue 3.00 2.25
Never hinged 4.00
a. Inverted surcharge 200.00 50.00
Never hinged 275.00
b. Pelure paper 4.00 5.00
Never hinged 5.00

Wmk. Lozenges (169)

200 A44 10,000r on 40r, type I (R) 2.25 1.25
Never hinged 4.00
a. Inverted surcharge 160.00 40.00
Never hinged 250.00
b. Double surcharge 125.00 —
Never hinged 160.00
c. With periods after Russian letters 1,100. 450.00
Never hinged 1,650.
d. Type II 2.25 2.75
Never hinged 4.00
e. As "a," type II 125.00 40.00
Never hinged 150.00
f. As "c," type II 200.00 —
Never hinged 375.00

No. 183 Surcharged in Black or Blue Black

1922, Mar. Unwmk.

201 A43 7500r on 250r (Bk) .25 .25
Never hinged .50
a. Pelure paper .25 .25
Never hinged .50
b. Chalk surfaced paper .45 .45
Never hinged .50
c. Blue black surcharge .50 .25
Never hinged .85
d. Surch. typographed 250.00 —
Never hinged 450.00
e. As "c," surch. lithographed 850.00 —
Never hinged 1,000.
f. As "d," surch. inverted *3,250.* —
Never hinged *5,500.*
Nos. 191-201 (11) 128.85 75.15

Nos. 201, 201a and 201b exist with surcharge inverted (value about $20 each), and double (about $25 each).

The horizontal surcharge was prepared but not issued. Values: $11 unused, $20 never hinged. The horizontal surcharge also exists on pelure paper. Values: $70 unused, $175 never hinged.

Type of 1921 and

"Workers of the World Unite" A46

1922 Litho. Wmk. 171

202 A46 5000r dark violet 1.90 .60
Never hinged 4.00
203 A42 7500r blue .50 .50
Never hinged 1.10
204 A46 10,000r blue 17.50 3.00
Never hinged 32.50

Unwmk.

205 A42 7500r blue, *buff* .50 .50
Never hinged 1.25
a. Double impression 250.00
Never hinged 325.00
206 A46 22,500r dk violet, *buff* .50 .60
Never hinged 1.25
Nos. 202-206 (5) 20.90 5.20

For surcharges see Nos. B41-B42.

No. 183 Surcharged Diagonally

1922 Unwmk. *Imperf.*

210 A43 100,000r on 250r .50 .50
Never hinged .75
a. Inverted surcharge 200.00 .50
Never hinged 375.00
b. Pelure paper .50 .50
Never hinged 1.00
c. Chalk surfaced paper 2.25 1.65
Never hinged 4.00
d. As "b," inverted surcharge 225.00 —
Never hinged 375.00

Marking 5th Anniversary of October Revolution — A48

1922 Typo.

211 A48 5r ocher & black .60 *.25*
Never hinged 1.20
212 A48 10r brown & black .60 *.25*
Never hinged 1.20
213 A48 25r violet & black 1.60 *.60*
Never hinged 4.00
214 A48 27r rose & black 5.50 *2.00*
Never hinged 17.00
215 A48 45r blue & black 3.60 *2.00*
Never hinged 8.00
Nos. 211-215 (5) 11.90 *5.10*

Pelure Paper

211a A48 5r ocher & black 82.50
Never hinged 200.00
212a A48 10r brown & black 120.00
Never hinged 200.00
213a A48 25r violet & black 82.50
Never hinged 175.00
214a A48 27r rose & black 82.50
Never hinged 225.00
215a A48 45r blue & black 60.00
Never hinged 180.00

5th anniv. of the October Revolution. Sold in the currency of 1922 which was valued at 10,000 times that of the preceding years.

For surcharges see Nos. B38-B39.

Nos. 81, 82a, 85-86, 125-126, 129-130 Surcharged

1922-23 *Perf. 14½x15*

216 A8 5r on 20k .45 6.00
Never hinged .85
a. Inverted surcharge 50.00 *90.00*
Never hinged 95.00
b. Double surcharge 100.00 —
Never hinged 140.00
c. Pair, one without surch. 165.00
Never hinged 275.00
217 A11 20r on 15k 1.90 2.00
Never hinged 3.00
a. Inverted surcharge 120.00 *90.00*
Never hinged 175.00
b. Pair, one without surch. 165.00
Never hinged 275.00
218 A11 20r on 70k .25 .35
Never hinged .50
a. Inverted surcharge 60.00 *45.00*
Never hinged 75.00
b. Double surcharge 50.00 50.00
Never hinged 100.00
c. Pair, one without surch. 165.00
Never hinged 275.00
219 A8 30r on 50k 1.75 .50
Never hinged 2.75
a. Inverted surcharge *67.50* *67.50*
Never hinged 82.50
c. Groundwork omitted *50.00* *50.00*
Never hinged *100.00*
d. Double surcharge *100.00* *100.00*
Never hinged *150.00*
220 A11 40r on 15k 1.00 .35
Never hinged 6.50
a. Inverted surcharge 67.50 *67.50*
Never hinged 80.00
b. Double surcharge *90.00* *90.00*
Never hinged *100.00*
c. Pair, one without surch. 165.00
Never hinged 275.00
221 A11 100r on 15k 1.00 .35
Never hinged 1.10
a. Inverted surcharge *90.00* *67.50*
Never hinged *100.00*
b. Double surcharge *90.00* *67.50*
Never hinged *100.00*
c. Pair, one without surch. 225.00
Never hinged 340.00
222 A11 200r on 15k 2.75 .35
Never hinged 5.50
a. Inverted surcharge 57.50 *45.00*
Never hinged 85.00
b. Double surcharge 67.50 *45.00*
Never hinged 85.00
c. Pair, one without surch. 225.00
Never hinged 340.00

Nos. 221-222 exist with triple surcharge; No. 221 with double surcharge, one inverted. Value, each $100.

Imperf

223 A8 5r on 20k 32.50 25.00
Never hinged 52.50
224 A11 20r on 15k *9,500.*
Never hinged *20,000.*
225 A11 20r on 70k .90 1.75
Never hinged 1.00
a. Inverted surcharge 82.50
Never hinged 140.00
226 A8 30r on 50k brn vio & grn .50 1.00
Never hinged .90
227 A11 40r on 15k .30 .30
Never hinged .50
a. Inverted surcharge 140.00 —
Never hinged 225.00
b. Double surcharge 100.00 —
Never hinged 240.00
228 A11 100r on 15k 1.00 .50
Never hinged 1.75
a. Inverted surcharge 190.00 —
Never hinged 325.00
229 A11 200r on 15k .75 .50
Never hinged 1.25
a. Inverted surcharge — —
Never hinged —
b. Double surcharge 140.00 —
Never hinged 250.00
Nos. 216-223,225-229 (13) 45.05 38.95

Forgeries of No. 223-229 exist, including a dangerous digital forgery of No. 224.

Worker A49

Soldier A50

1922-23 Typo. *Imperf.*

230 A49 10r blue .25 .25
Never hinged .50
231 A50 50r brown .25 .25
Never hinged .50
232 A50 70r brown violet .25 .25
Never hinged .50
233 A50 100r red .25 .25
Never hinged .50
Nos. 230-233 (4) 1.00 1.00

1923 *Perf. 14x14½*

234 A49 10r dp bl, perf. 13½ .25 2.75
Never hinged .25
a. Perf. 14 32.50 4.00
Never hinged 70.00
b. Perf. 12½ 1.40 2.75
Never hinged 2.75
235 A50 50r brown .25 2.75
Never hinged .25
a. Perf. 12½ 7.50 3.25
Never hinged 16.50
b. Perf. 13½ 2.25 2.75
Never hinged 4.00
236 A50 70r brown violet .25 2.75
Never hinged .25
a. Perf. 12½ 4.00 2.75
Never hinged 8.00
237 A50 100r red .25 .25
Never hinged .25
a. Cliché of 70r in plate of 100r 50.00 30.00
Never hinged 85.00
b. Corrected cliché — —
Nos. 234-237 (4) 1.00 8.50

No. 237b has extra broken line at right.

Nos. 230-233 were surcharged for use in Far Eastern Republic. See Far Eastern Republic Nos. 66-70.

Soldier — Worker — Peasant
A51 A52 A53

1923 *Perf. 14½x15*

238 A51 3r rose .25 .25
Never hinged .45
b. 3r pale rose 52.50
Never hinged 100.00
239 A52 4r brown .25 .25
Never hinged .45
240 A53 5r light blue .25 .25
Never hinged .45
a. Double impression *82.50* —
Never hinged 140.00
241 A51 10r gray .25 .25
Never hinged .45
e. Double impression 95.00 —
Never hinged 175.00
g. 10r pale green 52.50
Never hinged 100.00
241A A51 20r brown violet .50 .35
Never hinged .85
b. Double impression *140.00* —
Never hinged 250.00
c. 20r pale lilac 52.50
Never hinged 100.00
Nos. 238-241A (5) 1.50 1.35

Imperf

238a A51 3r rose 12.50 —
Never hinged 15.00
239a A52 4r brown 30.00 —
Never hinged 47.50
b. As "a," double impression *150.00*
Never hinged 225.00
240b A53 5r light blue 8.00 —
Never hinged 10.50
241d A51 10r gray 8.00 —
Never hinged 10.50
f. As "d," double impression 115.00 —
Never hinged 200.00
241c A51 20r brown violet 275.00 —
Never hinged 500.00

Stamps of 1r buff, type A52, and 2r green, type A53, perf. 12 and imperf. were prepared but not put in use.

The imperfs of Nos. 238-241A were sold only by the philatelic bureau in Moscow.

Stamps of 20r, type A51, printed in gray black or dull violet are essays. Value, $200 each.

The stamps of this and the following issues were sold for the currency of 1923, one ruble of which was equal to 100 rubles of 1922 and 1,000,000 rubles of 1921.

Union of Soviet Socialist Republics

Reaping — A54

Sowing — A55

Fordson Tractor A56

Symbolical of the Exhibition — A57

1923, Aug. 19		Litho.		*Imperf.*
242	A54	1r brown & orange	4.50	2.50
		Never hinged	6.75	
243	A55	2r dp grn & pale grn	5.00	2.00
		Never hinged	9.50	
244	A56	5r dp bl & pale blue	5.00	3.75
		Never hinged	9.50	
245	A57	7r rose & pink	5.00	4.50
		Never hinged	9.50	

Perf. 12½, 13½

246	A54	1r brown & orange	5.00	*3.75*
		Never hinged	9.50	
a.		Perf. 12½	42.50	*37.50*
		Never hinged	85.00	
247	A55	2r dp grn & pale grn, perf. 12½	6.00	*3.75*
		Never hinged	12.00	
248	A56	5r dp bl & pale bl	14.00	*3.75*
		Never hinged	27.50	
a.		Perf. 13½	13.50	*8.00*
		Never hinged	22.50	
249	A57	7r rose & pink	5.00	*6.00*
		Never hinged	9.50	
a.		Perf. 12½	24.00	*12.50*
		Never hinged	24.00	
		Nos. 242-249 (8)	49.50	*30.00*

1st Agriculture and Craftsmanship Exhibition, Moscow.

Worker — Soldier — Peasant
A58 A59 A60

1923		Unwmk. Litho.		*Imperf.*
250	A58	1k orange	2.50	.45
		Never hinged	4.00	
251	A60	2k green	2.50	.45
		Never hinged	4.00	
252	A59	3k red brown	2.50	1.40
		Never hinged	4.00	
253	A58	4k deep rose	24.00	1.25
		Never hinged	40.00	
254	A58	5k lilac	2.50	.65
		Never hinged	4.00	
255	A60	6k light blue	2.75	.45
		Never hinged	4.50	
256	A59	10k dark blue	35.00	3.75
		Never hinged	50.00	
257	A58	20k yellow green	12.00	.75
		Never hinged	21.00	
258	A60	50k dark brown	19.00	2.50
		Never hinged	30.00	
259	A59	1r red & brown	50.00	5.00
		Never hinged	75.00	
		Nos. 250-259 (10)	152.75	16.65

1924				*Perf. 14½x15*
261	A58	4k deep rose	110.00	—
		Never hinged	225.00	
262	A59	10k dark blue	165.00	—
		Never hinged	325.00	
263	A60	30k violet	25.00	*4.00*
		Never hinged	50.00	
264	A59	40k slate gray	25.00	*4.00*
		Never hinged	50.00	
		Nos. 261-264 (4)	325.00	*8.00*

See Nos. 273-290, 304-321. For surcharges see Nos. 349-350.

Vladimir Ilyich Ulyanov (Lenin) — A61

1924				*Imperf.*
265	A61	3k red & black	8.25	2.40
		Never hinged	16.50	
266	A61	6k red & black	7.00	2.00
		Never hinged	17.50	
267	A61	12k red & black	5.50	2.00
		Never hinged	11.00	
268	A61	20k red & black	11.50	2.00
		Never hinged	22.50	
		Nos. 265-268 (4)	32.25	8.40

Three printings of Nos. 265-268 differ in size of red frame.

Perf. 13½

269	A61	3k red & black	6.75	4.00
		Never hinged	14.00	
270	A61	6k red & black	6.75	2.00
		Never hinged	14.00	
271	A61	12k red & black	12.00	2.00
		Never hinged	24.00	
272	A61	20k red & black	8.00	2.50
		Never hinged	16.50	
		Nos. 269-272 (4)	33.50	10.50
		Nos. 265-272 (8)	65.75	18.90

Death of Lenin (1870-1924).
Forgeries of Nos. 265-272 exist.

Types of 1923 and

Worker — A62

There are small differences between the lithographed stamps of 1923 and the typographed of 1924-25. On a few values this may be seen in the numerals.

Type A58: Lithographed. The two white lines forming the outline of the ear are continued across the cheek. Typographed. The outer lines of the ear are broken where they touch the cheek.

Type A59: Lithographed. At the top of the right shoulder a white line touches the frame at the left. Counting from the edge of the visor of the cap, lines 5, 6 and sometimes 7 touch at their upper ends. Typographed. The top line of the shoulder does not reach the frame. On the cap lines 5, 6 and 7 run together and form a white spot.

Type A60: In the angle above the first letter "C" there is a fan-shaped ornament enclosing four white dashes. On the lithographed stamps these dashes reach nearly to the point of the angle. On the typographed stamps the dashes are shorter and often only three are visible.

On unused examples of the typographed stamps the raised outlines of the designs can be seen on the backs of the stamps.

1924-25		Typo.		*Imperf.*
273	A59	3k red brown	6.75	1.40
		Never hinged	16.50	
274	A58	4k deep rose	3.00	1.50
		Never hinged	8.00	
275	A59	10k dark blue	4.00	1.25
		Never hinged	8.00	
275A	A60	50k brown	*6,750.*	25.00
		Never hinged	*10,500.*	

Other typographed and imperf. values include: 2k green, 5k lilac, 6k light blue, 20k green and 1r red and brown. Value, unused: $150, $100, $150, $200 and $1,000, respectively.

Nos. 273-275A were regularly issued. The 7k, 8k, 9k, 30k, 40k, 2r, 3r, and 5r also exist imperf. Value, set of 8, $75.

Perf. 14½x15

Typo.

276	A58	1k orange	160.00	8.00
		Never hinged	260.00	
277	A60	2k green	2.00	.45
		Never hinged	3.25	
278	A59	3k red brown	2.00	.45
		Never hinged	3.25	
279	A58	4k deep rose	2.00	.45
		Never hinged	3.25	
280	A58	5k lilac	160.00	5.00
		Never hinged	325.00	
281	A60	6k lt blue	2.00	.45
		Never hinged	4.00	
282	A59	7k chocolate	2.00	.45
		Never hinged	4.00	
283	A58	8k brn ol	1.80	.45
		Never hinged	3.25	
284	A60	9k orange red	4.50	.45
		Never hinged	8.00	
285	A59	10k dark blue	4.00	.45
		Never hinged	8.00	
286	A58	14k slate blue	225.00	2.50
		Never hinged	325.00	
287	A60	15k yellow	*25,000.*	*165.00*
		Never hinged	*40,000.*	
288	A58	20k gray green	5.25	.45
		Never hinged	11.00	
288A	A60	30k violet	400.00	*4.00*
		Never hinged	675.00	
288B	A59	40k slate gray	800.00	*4.00*
		Never hinged	1,375.	
289	A60	50k brown	225.00	*10.00*
		Never hinged	425.00	
290	A59	1r red & brn	19.00	*1.00*
		Never hinged	40.00	
291	A62	2r grn & rose	12.00	*2.00*
		Never hinged	25.00	
		Nos. 276-286,288-291 (17)	2,027.	40.55

See No. 323. Forgeries of No. 287 exist.

1925				*Perf. 12*
276a	A58	1k orange	2.50	1.00
		Never hinged	5.50	
277a	A60	2k green	21.50	1.00
		Never hinged	42.50	
278a	A59	3k red brown	3.50	9.00
		Never hinged	5.50	
279a	A58	4k deep rose	275.00	*25.00*
		Never hinged	500.00	
280a	A58	5k lilac	5.50	1.00
		Never hinged	11.00	
282a	A59	7k chocolate	10.00	1.00
		Never hinged	12.50	
283a	A58	8k brown olive	1,375.	5.00
		Never hinged	2,000.	
284a	A60	9k orange red	*20.00*	*2.50*
		Never hinged	*32.50*	
285a	A59	10k dark blue	*5.00*	2.00
		Never hinged	*8.00*	
286a	A58	14k slate blue	2.50	1.00
		Never hinged	4.50	
287a	A60	15k yellow	6.75	1.00
		Never hinged	14.00	
288c	A58	20k gray green	27.50	1.00
		Never hinged	52.50	
288d	A60	30k violet	22.50	*1.50*
		Never hinged	32.50	
288e	A59	40k slate gray	110.00	*2.50*
		Never hinged	225.00	
289a	A60	50k brown	16.50	*1.00*
		Never hinged	32.50	
290a	A59	1r red & brown	*2,000.*	*3,000.*
		Never hinged	*2,750.*	
		Nos. 276a-290a (16)	3,904.	3,056.

Soldier — A63

Worker — A64

1924-25				*Perf. 13½*
292	A63	3r blk brn & grn	19.00	2.50
		Never hinged	37.50	
a.		Perf. 10	5,500.	145.00
		Never hinged	10,000.	
b.		Perf. 13½x10	*2,750.*	—
		Never hinged	5,250.	
293	A64	5r dk bl & gray brn	200.00	12.50
		Never hinged	375.00	
a.		Perf. 10½	70.00	—
		Never hinged	82.50	

See Nos. 324-325.

Lenin Mausoleum, Moscow — A65

Wmk. 170

1925, Jan.		Photo.		*Imperf.*
294	A65	7k deep blue	9.00	2.50
		Never hinged	12.00	
295	A65	14k dark green	25.00	4.00
		Never hinged	40.00	
296	A65	20k carmine rose	14.00	5.00
		Never hinged	22.50	
297	A65	40k red brown	25.00	7.00
		Never hinged	40.00	
		Nos. 294-297 (4)	73.00	18.50

Perf. 13½x14

298	A65	7k deep blue	5.50	4.50
		Never hinged	10.00	
299	A65	14k dark green	25.00	6.75
		Never hinged	40.00	
300	A65	20k carmine rose	20.00	5.25
		Never hinged	27.50	
301	A65	40k red brown	26.00	6.25
		Never hinged	40.00	
		Nos. 298-301 (4)	76.50	22.75
		Nos. 294-301 (8)	149.50	41.25

First anniversary of Lenin's death.

Nos. 294-301 are found on both ordinary and thick paper. Those on thick paper sell for twice as much, except for No. 301, which is scarcer on ordinary paper.

Lenin — A66

Wmk. 170

1925, July		Engr.		*Perf. 13½*
302	A66	5r red brown	40.00	6.75
		Never hinged	85.00	
a.		Perf. 12½	165.00	25.00
		Never hinged	325.00	
b.		Perf. 10½ ('26)	82.50	11.00
		Never hinged	165.00	
303	A66	10r indigo	40.00	10.00
		Never hinged	82.50	
a.		Perf. 12½	1,250.	175.00
		Never hinged	1,750.	
b.		Perf. 10½ ('26)	200.00	11.00
		Never hinged	400.00	

Imperfs. exist. Value, set $75.
See Nos. 407-408, 621-622

Types of 1923 Issue

1925-27		Wmk. 170 Typo.		*Perf. 12*
304	A58	1k orange	1.60	.35
		Never hinged	2.60	
305	A60	2k green	1.60	.35
		Never hinged	2.60	
306	A59	3k red brown	1.60	.35
		Never hinged	2.60	
307	A58	4k deep rose	1.60	.35
		Never hinged	2.60	
308	A58	5k lilac	1.60	.35
		Never hinged	2.60	
309	A60	6k lt blue	1.60	.75
		Never hinged	2.60	
310	A59	7k chocolate	3.25	.75
		Never hinged	5.50	
311	A58	8k brown olive	17.00	1.40
		Never hinged	27.50	
a.		Perf. 14½x15	325.00	27.50
		Never hinged	575.00	
312	A60	9k red	6.50	.75
		Never hinged	10.00	
313	A59	10k dark blue	3.50	.75
		Never hinged	5.50	
a.		10k pale blue ('27)	9.00	4.50
		Never hinged	17.00	
314	A58	14k slate blue	4.00	1.25
		Never hinged	5.50	
315	A60	15k yellow	9.50	1.25
		Never hinged	16.50	
316	A59	18k violet	17.00	1.75
		Never hinged	27.50	
317	A58	20k gray green	9.50	1.25
		Never hinged	16.50	
318	A60	30k violet	17.00	1.25
		Never hinged	27.50	
319	A59	40k slate gray	17.00	1.75
		Never hinged	27.50	
320	A60	50k brown	17.00	1.75
		Never hinged	27.50	
321	A59	1r red & brown	19.00	4.00
		Never hinged	32.50	
a.		Perf. 14½x15	325.00	*50.00*
		Never hinged	575.00	
323	A62	2r grn & rose red	75.00	11.00
		Never hinged	125.00	
a.		Perf. 14½x15	18.00	5.00
		Never hinged	32.50	

Perf. 13½

324	A63	3r blk brn & grn	27.50	9.50
		Never hinged	50.00	
a.		Perf. 12½	*475.00*	82.50
		Never hinged	800.00	
325	A64	5r dk blue & gray brn	35.00	12.50
		Never hinged	70.00	
		Nos. 304-325 (21)	287.35	53.40

Nos. 304-315, 317-325 exist imperf. Value, set $125.

Mikhail V. Lomonosov and Academy of Sciences — A67

1925, Sept. Photo. *Perf. 12½, 13½*

326 A67 3k orange brown 7.50 2.00
Never hinged 11.00
a. Perf. 12½x12 40.00 6.75
Never hinged 82.50
c. Perf. 13½ 50.00 9.00
Never hinged 110.00
327 A67 15k dk olive green 14.00 2.25
Never hinged 27.50
a. Perf. 12½ 20.00 5.00
Never hinged 42.50

Russian Academy of Sciences, 200th anniv. Exist unwatermarked, on thick paper with yellow gum, perf. 13½. These are essays, later perforated and gummed. Value, each $50.

Prof. Aleksandr S. Popov (1859-1905), Radio Pioneer — A68

1925, Oct. *Perf. 13½*

328 A68 7k deep blue 6.25 1.00
Never hinged 14.00
329 A68 14k green 10.00 1.50
Never hinged 19.00

For surcharge see No. 353.

Decembrist Exiles — A69

Street Rioting in St. Petersburg — A70

Revolutionist Leaders — A71

1925, Dec. 28 *Imperf.*

330 A69 3k olive green 5.00 *1.00*
Never hinged 6.50
331 A70 7k brown 32.50 *3.50*
Never hinged 52.50
332 A71 14k carmine lake 19.00 *5.00*
Never hinged 27.50

Perf. 13½

333 A69 3k olive green 4.50 1.25
Never hinged 6.75
a. Perf. 12½ *100.00* *50.00*
Never hinged 190.00
334 A70 7k brown 16.50 *3.50*
Never hinged 32.50
335 A71 14k carmine lake 19.50 5.50
Never hinged 35.00
Nos. 330-335 (6) 97.00 19.75

Centenary of Decembrist revolution.
For surcharges see Nos. 354, 357.

Revolters Parading — A72

Speaker Haranguing Mob — A73

Street Barricade, Moscow — A74

1925, Dec. 20 *Imperf.*

336 A72 3k olive green 5.00 *7.50*
Never hinged 7.50
337 A73 7k brown 17.50 *8.75*
Never hinged 27.50
338 A74 14k carmine lake 12.50 *2.75*
Never hinged 22.50

Perf. 12½, 12x12½

339 A72 3k olive green 5.50 *3.00*
Never hinged 11.00
a. Perf. 13½ 37.50 *8.00*
Never hinged 82.50
340 A73 7k brown 35.00 *5.00*
Never hinged 72.50
a. Perf. 13½ 17.50 *5.25*
Never hinged 40.00
b. Horiz. pair, imperf. btwn. — —
Never hinged —
341 A74 14k carmine lake 6.75 3.75
Never hinged 11.00
a. Perf. 13½ 40.00 7.50
Never hinged 82.50
Nos. 336-341 (6) 82.25 30.75

20th anniversary of Revolution of 1905.
For surcharges see Nos. 355, 358.

Lenin — A75

1926 Wmk. 170 Engr. *Perf. 10½*

342 A75 1r dark brown 37.50 4.00
Never hinged 77.50
a. Perf. 12½ 2,250. —
Never hinged *3,250.*
343 A75 2r black violet 35.00 5.75
Never hinged 67.50
a. Perf. 12½ 2,250. —
Never hinged *3,250.*
344 A75 3r dark green 37.50 5.75
Never hinged 82.50
a. Perf. 12½ 4,250. —
Never hinged *5,250.*
b. Horiz. pair, imperf. btwn. — *5,000.*
Never hinged *6,000.*
Nos. 342-344 (3) 110.00 15.50

Nos. 342-343 exist imperf.
See Nos. 406, 620.

Liberty Monument, Moscow — A76

1926, July Litho. *Perf. 12x12½*

347 A76 7k blue green & red 10.00 2.75
Never hinged 19.00
348 A76 14k blue green & violet 12.50 2.75
Never hinged 25.00

6th International Esperanto Congress at Leningrad. Exist perf. 11½. Value, set $8,500.
For surcharge see No. 356.

Nos. 282, 282a and 310 Surcharged in Black

Two types of overprint: Type I, 2mm space between lines of surcharge; Type II, .7mm space between lines of surcharge.

1927, June Unwmk. *Perf. 14½x15*

349 A59 8k on 7k chocolate (I) 22.50 4.00
Never hinged 42.50
a. Perf. 12x12¼ 27.50 3.75
Never hinged 52.50
b. Inverted surcharge *300.00* —
Never hinged 400.00
c. Type II *2,750.* 140.00
Never hinged *10,000.*
d. As "b," surcharge inverted *275.00*

Perf. 12

Wmk. 170

350 A59 8k on 7k chocolate 8.00 2.50
Never hinged 14.50
a. Inverted surcharge *150.00*
Never hinged *200.00*
b. Type II *10,500.* 70.00
Never hinged *27,500.*
c. As "b," surcharge inverted *350.00*

The surcharge on Nos. 349-350 comes in two types: With space of 2mm between lines, and with space of ¾mm. The latter is much scarcer.

Same Surcharge on Stamps of 1925-26 in Black or Red

Perf. 13½, 12½, 12x12½

353 A68 8k on 7k dp bl (R) 6.75 2.25
Never hinged 15.00
a. Inverted "8" 110.00 *50.00*
Never hinged 190.00
354 A70 8k on 7k brown 12.50 *4.75*
Never hinged 22.50
355 A73 8k on 7k brown 20.00 *6.25*
Never hinged 32.50
356 A76 8k on 7k blue green & red 21.50 8.50
Never hinged 42.50

Imperf

357 A70 8k on 7k brown 11.00 4.00
Never hinged 19.00
358 A73 8k on 7k brown 19.00 7.00
Never hinged 32.50
Nos. 349-350,353-358 (8) 121.25 39.25

Postage Due Stamps of 1925 Surcharged

Two settings: A's aligned (shown), bottom A to left.

Lithographed or Typographed

1927, June Unwmk. *Perf. 12*

359 D1 8k on 1k red, typo. 4.50 *2.00*
Never hinged 9.50
a. Litho. *2,750.* *150.00*
Never hinged 5,500.
360 D1 8k on 2k violet 4.50 *2.00*
Never hinged 9.50
a. Inverted surcharge 275.00 —
Never hinged —

Perf. 12, 14½x14

361 D1 8k on 3k lt blue 4.50 *2.00*
Never hinged 10.50
a. Inverted surcharge 275.00 —
Never hinged —
362 D1 8k on 7k orange 4.25 *1.25*
Never hinged 6.75
363 D1 8k on 8k green 4.50 *2.00*
Never hinged 9.50
a. Inverted surcharge — *1,750.*
Never hinged —
364 D1 8k on 10k dk blue 4.00 *1.25*
Never hinged 6.75
a. Inverted surcharge 275.00 —
Never hinged —
365 D1 8k on 14k brown 3.75 4.00
Never hinged 10.00
a. Inverted surcharge 350.00 —
Never hinged —
Nos. 359-365 (7) 30.00 14.50

Wmk. 170

1927, June Typo. *Perf. 12*

366 D1 8k on 1k red 4.50 *1.00*
Never hinged 9.50
367 D1 8k on 2k violet 4.50 *1.00*
Never hinged 9.50
368 D1 8k on 3k lt blue 4.50 *1.00*
Never hinged 9.50
369 D1 8k on 7k orange 4.50 *1.00*
Never hinged 9.50
370 D1 8k on 8k green 4.50 *1.00*
Never hinged 9.50
371 D1 8k on 10k dk blue 4.50 *1.00*
Never hinged 9.50
a. Inverted surcharge *3,500.* —
Never hinged —
372 D1 8k on 14k brown 4.50 *1.00*
Never hinged 9.50
a. Inverted surcharge — *1,750.*
Never hinged —
Nos. 366-372 (7) 31.50 *7.00*

Nos. 366, 368-370 exist with inverted surcharge.

Dr. L. L. Zamenhof A77

1927 Photo. *Perf. 10½*

373 A77 14k yel grn & brn 11.00 2.25
Never hinged 22.50

Unwmk.

374 A77 14k yel grn & brn 11.00 2.25
Never hinged 22.50
a. Perf. 10 325.00 52.50
Never hinged 550.00
b. Perf. 10x10½ 175.00 75.00
Never hinged 325.00
c. Imperf. 950.00 —
Never hinged 1,375.
d. Vert. pair, imperf. btwn., never hinged *8,250.* —

40th anniversary of creation of Esperanto.

Worker, Soldier, Peasant — A78

Worker and Sailor — A81

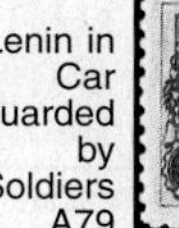

Lenin in Car Guarded by Soldiers A79

Smolny Institute, Leningrad A80

Map of the USSR A82

Men of Various Soviet Republics — A83

Workers of Different Races; Kremlin in Background — A84

Typo. (3k, 8k, 18k), Engr. (7k), Litho. (14k), Photo. (5k, 28k)

Perf. 13½, 12½x12, 11

1927, Oct. Unwmk.

375 A78 3k bright rose 5.50 1.10
Never hinged 9.50
a. Imperf., pair *5,000.*
376 A79 5k deep brown 14.00 2.25
Never hinged 27.50
a. Imperf. 1,650. *500.00*
Never hinged 2,500.
b. Perf. 12½ 125.00 12.50
Never hinged 250.00
c. Perf. 12½x10½ 55.00 5.00
Never hinged 110.00
377 A80 7k myrtle green 14.00 4.00
Never hinged 27.50
a. Perf. 11½ 32.50 7.50
Never hinged 55.00
b. Imperf., pair *1,500.*
Never hinged *2,900.*
378 A81 8k brown & black 8.00 1.50
Never hinged 16.50
a. Perf. 10½x12½ *42.50* *2.75*
Never hinged 82.50
379 A82 14k dull blue & red 6.75 2.75
Never hinged 14.00
380 A83 18k blue 4.75 1.25
Never hinged 6.50
a. Imperf. 275.00
Never hinged 425.00

381 A84 28k olive brown 18.00 5.00
Never hinged 25.00
a. Perf. 10 45.00 8.00
Never hinged 95.00
Nos. 375-381 (7) 71.00 17.85

10th anniversary of October Revolution.
The paper of No. 375 has an overprint of pale yellow wavy lines.
No. 377b exists with watermark 170. Value, $1,000.

Worker — A85

Peasant — A86

Lenin — A87

1927-28 Typo. *Perf. 13½*
Chalk Surfaced Paper

382 A85 1k orange 1.10 .35
Never hinged 1.90
a. Imperf. 1,750. —
Never hinged 2,750.
383 A86 2k apple green 4.25 .35
Never hinged 7.50
a. Imperf. 1,750. —
Never hinged 2,750.
385 A85 4k bright blue 1.10 .35
Never hinged 1.90
386 A86 5k brown 1.10 .35
Never hinged 1.90
a. Imperf. 1,750. —
Never hinged 2,750.
388 A86 7k dark red ('28) 1.10 .35
Never hinged 1.90
a. Double impression 475.00 —
Never hinged 675.00
389 A85 8k green 7.00 .60
Never hinged 14.00
391 A85 10k light brown 5.00 .35
Never hinged 9.75
a. Imperf. 1,325. —
Never hinged 2,250.
392 A87 14k dark green ('28) 10.75 4.00
Never hinged 19.00
393 A87 18k olive green 12.00 1.25
Never hinged 12.50
a. Imperf. *3,750.* —
Never hinged *5,400.*
394 A87 18k dark blue ('28) 11.00 1.70
Never hinged 27.50
395 A86 20k dark gray green 16.50 .35
Never hinged 27.50
396 A85 40k rose red 20.00 2.00
Never hinged 40.00
397 A86 50k bright blue 24.00 1.10
Never hinged 37.50
399 A85 70k gray green 11.00 2.00
Never hinged 22.50
400 A86 80k orange 15.00 2.75
Never hinged 27.50
Nos. 382-400 (15) 140.90 17.85

Soldier and Kremlin — A88

Sailor and Flag — A89

Cavalryman A90

Aviator A91

1928, Feb. 6
Chalk Surfaced Paper

402 A88 8k light brown 4.75 .85
Never hinged 8.25
a. Imperf. 1,200. —
Never hinged 1,650.
403 A89 14k deep blue 12.00 1.50
Never hinged 22.50
404 A90 18k carmine rose 6.50 1.60
Never hinged 11.00
a. Imperf. *7,000.*
405 A91 28k yellow green 15.00 2.25
Never hinged 27.50
Nos. 402-405 (4) 38.25 6.20

10th anniversary of the Soviet Army.

Lenin Types of 1925-26
Wmk. 169
1928-29 Engr. *Perf. 10½*

406 A75 3r dark green ('29) 52.50 3.50
Never hinged 105.00
a. Perf. 10 52.50 6.75
Never hinged 120.00
b. Imperf. 3,250. —
Never hinged *5,500.*
407 A66 5r red brown 19.00 3.75
Never hinged 35.00
a. Perf. 10 105.00 14.00
Never hinged 190.00
b. Imperf. *20,000.* —
Never hinged —
408 A66 10r indigo 19.00 *4.50*
Never hinged 35.00
a. Perf. 10 27.50 6.75
Never hinged 70.00
b. Imperf. *20,000.* —
Never hinged —
Nos. 406-408 (3) 90.50 11.75

Bugler Sounding Assembly
A92 A93

Perf. 12½x12
1929, Aug. 18 Photo. Wmk. 170

411 A92 10k olive brown 32.50 6.25
Never hinged 70.00
a. Perf. 10½ 140.00 27.50
Never hinged 240.00
b. Perf. 12½x12x10½x12 140.00 75.00
Never hinged 240.00
412 A93 14k slate 5.50 2.75
Never hinged 14.00
a. Perf. 12½x12x10½x12 425.00 95.00
Never hinged 800.00

First All-Soviet Assembly of Pioneers.

Factory Worker A95

Peasant A96

Farm Worker A97

Soldier A98

Worker, Soldier, Peasant A100

Worker A103

Lenin A104

Peasant A107

Factory Worker A109

Farm Worker A111

Perf. 12x12½
1929-31 Typo. Wmk. 170

413 A103 1k orange 1.25 .25
Never hinged 2.50
a. Perf. 10½ 19.00 4.00
Never hinged 32.50
b. Perf. 12x12¼ 8.00 1.60
Never hinged 12.50
414 A95 2k yellow green 1.25 .25
Never hinged 2.50
415 A96 3k blue 2.75 .25
Never hinged 5.00
a. Perf. 12x12¼ 82.50 *25.00*
Never hinged 140.00
416 A97 4k claret 2.75 .45
Never hinged 5.00
417 A98 5k orange brown 2.75 .45
Never hinged 5.00
a. Perf. 10½ 190.00 *25.00*
Never hinged 315.00
418 A100 7k scarlet 2.75 .90
Never hinged 5.00
419 A103 10k olive green 2.75 .50
Never hinged 5.00
a. Perf. 10½ 400.00 40.00
Never hinged 650.00

Unwmk.

420 A104 14k indigo 5.50 1.00
Never hinged 12.00
a. Perf. 10½ 17.50 3.25
Never hinged 37.50

Wmk. 170

421 A100 15k dk ol grn ('30) 2.75 .85
Never hinged 5.00
422 A107 20k green 2.75 .85
Never hinged 5.00
a. Perf. 10½ — —
Never hinged —
423 A109 30k dk violet 14.00 1.75
Never hinged 25.00
424 A111 50k dp brown 14.00 2.50
Never hinged 25.00
425 A98 70k dk red ('30) 8.00 2.50
Never hinged 15.00
426 A107 80k red brn ('31) 8.00 2.50
Never hinged 15.00
Nos. 413-426 (14) 71.25 15.00

Nos. 422, 423, 424 and 426 have a background of fine wavy lines in pale shades of the colors of the stamps.
See Nos. 456-466, 613A-619A. For surcharge see No. 743.

Symbolical of Industry A112

Tractors Issuing from Assembly Line — A113

Iron Furnace (Inscription reads, "More Metal More Machines") A114

Blast Furnace and Chart of Anticipated Iron Production A115

1929-30 *Perf. 12x12½*

427 A112 5k orange brown 3.25 *.90*
Never hinged 5.50
428 A113 10k olive green 9.50 *1.80*
Never hinged 17.00

Perf. 12½x12

429 A114 20k dull green 9.50 *3.00*
Never hinged 17.00
a. Perf. 10¾ *8,000.* 400.00
Never hinged *10,000.*
430 A115 28k violet black 4.25 2.00
Never hinged 6.75
Nos. 427-430 (4) 26.50 7.70

Publicity for greater industrial production.
No. 429 exists perf. 10½. Value *$4,000.*

Red Cavalry in Polish Town after Battle A116

Cavalry Charge A117

Staff Officers of 1st Cavalry Army A118

Plan of Action for 1st Cavalry Army — A119

1930, Feb. *Perf. 12x12½*

431 A116 2k yellow green 3.25 *1.80*
Never hinged 5.50
432 A117 5k light brown 7.00 *1.80*
Never hinged 13.00
433 A118 10k olive gray 14.00 *2.75*
Never hinged 27.50
434 A119 14k indigo & red 5.50 *2.50*
Never hinged 10.00
Nos. 431-434 (4) 29.75 *8.85*

1st Red Cavalry Army, 10th anniversary.

Students Preparing a Poster Newspaper A120

1930, Aug. 15

435 A120 10k olive green 8.00 *1.80*
Never hinged 16.50

Educational Exhibition, Leningrad, 7/1-8/15/30.

Telegraph Office, Moscow A121

Lenin Hydroelectric Power Station on Volkhov River A122

1930 Photo. Wmk. 169 *Perf. 12¼*

436 A121 1r deep blue 19.00 *5.00*
Never hinged 40.00

Wmk. 170

437 A122 3r yel grn & blk brn 10.50 *5.00*
Never hinged 20.00

See Nos. 467, 469.

Battleship Potemkin A123

Inside Presnya Barricade A124

Moscow Barricades in 1905 — A125

1930 Typo. *Perf. 12x12½, 12½x12*

438	A123 3k red	1.75	.50
	Never hinged	2.75	
439	A124 5k blue	3.25	.70
	Never hinged	5.50	
440	A125 10k dk green & red	9.50	1.75
	Never hinged	17.00	
	Nos. 438-440 (3)	14.50	2.95

1931 ***Imperf.***

452	A123 3k red	11.00	*5.00*
	Never hinged	19.00	
453	A124 5k deep blue	11.00	*9.00*
	Never hinged	19.00	
454	A125 10k dk green & red	22.00	*17.50*
	Never hinged	37.50	
	Nos. 452-454 (3)	44.00	*31.50*
	Nos. 438-454 (6)	58.50	34.45

Revolution of 1905, 25th anniversary.

Types of 1929-31 Regular Issue

1931-32 ***Imperf.***

456	A103 1k orange	4.00	1.00
	Never hinged	7.00	
457	A95 2k yellow green	4.00	1.00
	Never hinged	7.00	
458	A96 3k blue	5.50	1.00
	Never hinged	11.00	
459	A97 4k claret	47.50	14.00
	Never hinged	85.00	
460	A98 5k orange brown	5.50	2.50
	Never hinged	10.50	
462	A103 10k olive green	55.00	22.50
	Never hinged	100.00	
464	A100 15k dk olive green	35.00	*25.00*
	Never hinged	55.00	
466	A109 30k dull violet	40.00	*35.00*
	Never hinged	75.00	
467	A121 1r dark blue	200.00	*35.00*
	Never hinged	350.00	
	Nos. 456-467 (9)	396.50	137.00

Nos. 459, 462-467 were sold only by the philatelic bureau.

Type of 1930 Issue

1931 Wmk. 170 *Perf. 12x12½*

469	A121 1r dark blue	8.00	1.50
	Never hinged	12.00	

Maxim Gorki — A133

1932-33 Photo.

470	A133 15k dark brown	8.00	*1.75*
	Never hinged	16.50	
a.	Imperf.	140.00	*67.50*
	Never hinged	225.00	
471	A133 35k dp ultra ('33)	35.00	*14.50*
	Never hinged	75.00	

40th anniversary of Gorki's literary activity.

Lenin Addressing the People A134

Revolution in Petrograd (Leningrad) A135

Dnieper Hydroelectric Power Station A136

Asiatics Saluting the Soviet Flag — A139

Designs (dated 1917 1932): 15k, Collective farm. 20k, Magnitogorsk metallurgical plant in Urals. 30k, Radio tower and heads of 4 men.

1932-33 *Perf. 12½x12; 12½ (30k)*

472	A134 3k dark violet	4.25	1.25
	Never hinged	8.50	
473	A135 5k dark brown	4.25	1.25
	Never hinged	13.00	
474	A136 10k ultra	7.00	4.25
	Never hinged	12.00	
475	A136 15k dark green	4.25	1.50
	Never hinged	8.50	
476	A136 20k lake ('33)	4.25	1.50
	Never hinged	8.50	
477	A136 30k dk gray ('33)	55.00	*15.00*
	Never hinged	100.00	
478	A139 35k gray black	95.00	*55.00*
	Never hinged	180.00	
	Nos. 472-478 (7)	174.00	79.75

October Revolution, 15th anniversary.

Breaking Prison Bars — A140

1932, Nov. Litho. *Perf. 12½x12*

479	A140 50k dark red	32.50	9.50
	Never hinged	67.50	

Intl. Revolutionaries' Aid Assoc., 10th anniv.

Trier, Birthplace of Marx — A141

Grave, Highgate Cemetery, London — A142

35k, Portrait & signature of Karl Marx (1818-83).

Perf. 12x12½, 12½x12

1933, Mar. Photo.

480	A141 3k dull green	4.00	1.80
	Never hinged	7.50	
481	A142 10k black brown	10.00	2.25
	Never hinged	22.50	
482	A142 35k brown violet	67.50	14.50
	Never hinged	115.00	
	Nos. 480-482 (3)	81.50	18.55

Fine Arts Museum, Moscow — A145

1932, Dec. *Perf. 12½*

485	A145 15k black brown	5.00	6.00
	Never hinged	9.50	
486	A145 35k ultra	90.00	52.50
	Never hinged	140.00	
a.	Perf. 10½	67.50	32.50
	Never hinged	95.00	

Moscow Philatelic Exhibition, 1932.

Nos. 485 and 486 were also issued in imperf. sheets of 4 containing 2 of each value, on thick paper for presentation purposes. They were not valid for postage. Value, from $25,000. Replicas of the sheet were made for Moscow 97 by the Canadian Society of Russian Philately.

Nos. 485 and 486a Surcharged

1933, Mar. *Perf. 12½*

487	A145 30k on 15k blk brn	50.00	15.00
	Never hinged	82.50	
	Perf. 10½		
488	A145 70k on 35k ultra	275.00	200.00
	Never hinged	425.00	

Leningrad Philatelic Exhibition, 1933.

Peoples of the Soviet Union

Kazaks A146

Lezghians A147

Tungus A150

Crimean Tartars A148

Jews, Birobidzhan A149

Buryats — A151

Yakuts — A156

Chechens A152

Abkhas A153

Georgians A154

Nientzians A155

Great Russians — A157

Tadzhiks — A158

Transcaucasians — A159

Turkmen — A160

Ukrainians — A161

Uzbeks — A162

Byelorussians — A163

Koryaks A164

Bashkirs A165

Chuvashes A166

Perf. 12, 12x12½, 12½x12, 11x12, 12x11

1933, Apr. **Photo.**

No.	Type	Description	Unused	Used
489	A146	1k black brown	9.00	2.00
		Never hinged	15.50	
490	A147	2k ultra	5.00	2.00
		Never hinged	9.50	
491	A148	3k gray green	18.00	2.00
		Never hinged	32.50	
492	A149	4k gray black	5.00	2.00
		Never hinged	32.50	
493	A150	5k brown violet	5.00	2.00
		Never hinged	9.50	
494	A151	6k indigo	5.00	2.00
		Never hinged	9.50	
495	A152	7k black brown	5.00	2.00
		Never hinged	9.50	
496	A153	8k rose red	11.00	2.00
		Never hinged	18.00	
497	A154	9k ultra	35.00	2.00
		Never hinged	60.00	
498	A155	10k black brown	5.00	2.00
		Never hinged	9.50	
499	A156	14k olive green	5.00	2.00
		Never hinged	9.50	
500	A157	15k orange	16.00	2.00
		Never hinged	27.50	
501	A158	15k ultra	13.00	2.00
		Never hinged	25.00	
502	A159	15k dark brown	13.00	2.00
		Never hinged	32.50	
503	A160	15k rose red	13.00	2.00
		Never hinged	25.00	
504	A161	15k violet brown	16.00	2.00
		Never hinged	27.50	
505	A162	15k gray black	13.00	2.00
		Never hinged	25.00	
506	A163	15k dull green	16.00	2.00
		Never hinged	27.50	
507	A164	20k dull blue	18.00	*2.00*
		Never hinged	32.50	
508	A165	30k brown violet	15.00	*3.00*
		Never hinged	30.00	
509	A166	35k black	15.00	*3.00*
		Never hinged	30.00	
		Nos. 489-509 (21)	256.00	44.00

V. V. Vorovsky A169

3k, V. M. Volodarsky. 5k, M. S. Uritzky.

1933, Oct. ***Perf. 12x12½***

No.	Type	Description	Unused	Used
514	A169	1k dull green	4.00	1.00
		Never hinged	8.50	
515	A169	3k blue black	8.00	1.25
		Never hinged	17.00	
516	A169	5k olive brown	9.00	2.00
		Never hinged	17.50	
		Nos. 514-516 (3)	21.00	4.25

10th anniv. of the murder of Soviet Representative Vorovsky; 15th anniv. of the murder of the Revolutionists Volodarsky and Uritzky.

See Nos. 531-532, 580-582.

Order of the Red Banner, 15th Anniv. — A173

1933, Nov. 17 **Unwmk.** ***Perf. 14***

No.	Type	Description	Unused	Used
518	A173	20k black, red & yel	15.00	3.50
		Never hinged	40.00	

No. 518, perf. 9½, is a proof. Values: unused, $4,000; never hinged, $8,000.

Commissar Schaumyan A174

Commissar Prokofii A. Dzhaparidze A175

Commissars Awaiting Execution — A176

Designs: 35k, Monument to the 26 Commissars. 40k, Worker, peasant and soldier dipping flags in salute.

1933, Dec. 1

No.	Type	Description	Unused	Used
519	A174	4k brown	30.00	2.00
		Never hinged	85.00	
520	A175	5k dark gray	25.00	2.00
		Never hinged	77.50	
521	A176	20k purple	8.00	2.00
		Never hinged	27.50	
522	A176	35k ultra	80.00	*17.50*
		Never hinged	200.00	
523	A176	40k carmine	25.00	*7.00*
		Never hinged	50.00	
		Nos. 519-523 (5)	168.00	30.50

15th anniv. of the execution of 26 commissars at Baku. No. 521 exists imperf. Many part-perf varieties exist on all values of this issue, including imperf between pairs of several values.

Lenin's Mausoleum A179

1934, Feb. 7 **Engr.** ***Perf. 14***

No.	Type	Description	Unused	Used
524	A179	5k brown	20.00	2.50
		Never hinged	37.50	
a.		Imperf.	675.00	—
		Never hinged	1,050.	
525	A179	10k slate blue	90.00	10.00
		Never hinged	190.00	
a.		Imperf.	675.00	—
		Never hinged	1,050.	
526	A179	15k dk carmine	32.50	7.00
		Never hinged	67.50	
527	A179	20k green	6.00	5.25
		Never hinged	13.00	
528	A179	35k dark brown	32.50	8.00
		Never hinged	55.00	
		Nos. 524-528 (5)	181.00	32.75

10th anniversary of Lenin's death.

Ivan Fedorov A180

1934, Mar. 5

No.	Type	Description	Unused	Used
529	A180	20k carmine rose	55.00	10.00
		Never hinged	120.00	
a.		Imperf.	675.00	—
		Never hinged	1,000.	
530	A180	40k indigo	17.50	10.00
		Never hinged	32.50	
a.		Imperf.	675.00	—
		Never hinged	1,000.	

350th anniv. of the death of Ivan Fedorov, founder of printing in Russia.

Portrait Type of 1933

Designs: 10k, Yakov M. Sverdlov. 15k, Victor Pavlovich Nogin.

1934, Mar. **Photo.** **Wmk. 170**

No.	Type	Description	Unused	Used
531	A169	10k ultra	27.50	6.00
		Never hinged	55.00	
532	A169	15k red	200.00	37.50
		Never hinged	425.00	

Deaths of Yakov M. Sverdlov, chairman of the All-Russian Central Executive Committee of the Soviets, 15th anniv., Victor Pavlovich Nogin, chairman Russian State Textile Syndicate, 10th anniv.

A184

Dmitri Ivanovich Mendeleev A185

1934, Sept. 15 **Wmk. 170** ***Perf. 14***

No.	Type	Description	Unused	Used
536	A184	5k emerald	22.00	3.00
		Never hinged	42.50	
537	A185	10k black brown	100.00	13.00
		Never hinged	190.00	
538	A185	15k vermilion	140.00	18.00
		Never hinged	275.00	
539	A184	20k ultra	22.00	5.50
		Never hinged	22.50	
		Nos. 536-539 (4)	284.00	39.50

Prof. D. I. Mendeleev (1834-1907), chemist who discovered the Periodic Law of Classification of the Elements.

Imperfs. exist of 5k (value $400) and 15k (value $400).

Lenin as Child and Youth A186 A187

Demonstration before Lenin Mausoleum — A190

Designs: 5k, Lenin in middle age. 10k, Lenin the orator. 30k, Lenin and Stalin.

1934, Nov. 23 **Unwmk.** ***Perf. 14***

No.	Type	Description	Unused	Used
540	A186	1k indigo & black	22.00	4.00
		Never hinged	40.00	
541	A187	3k indigo & black	11.00	4.00
		Never hinged	21.00	
a.		Horiz. pair, imperf. btwn.	—	*5,000.*
		Never hinged	—	
542	A187	5k indigo & black	50.00	3.00
		Never hinged	100.00	
543	A187	10k indigo & black	16.50	2.50
		Never hinged	32.50	
544	A190	20k brn org & ultra	11.00	8.50
		Never hinged	21.00	
545	A190	30k brn org & car	240.00	35.00
		Never hinged	550.00	
		Nos. 540-545 (6)	350.50	57.00

First decade without Lenin.

See Nos. 931-935, 937 in Scott Standard catalogue, Vol. 5.

Bombs Falling on City A192

"Before War and Afterwards" A194

Designs: 10k, Refugees from burning town. 20k, "Plowing with the sword." 35k, "Comradeship."

1935, Jan. 1 **Wmk. 170** ***Perf. 14***

No.	Type	Description	Unused	Used
546	A192	5k violet black	28.00	3.00
		Never hinged	50.00	
547	A192	10k ultra	130.00	15.00
		Never hinged	200.00	
548	A194	15k green	150.00	20.00
		Never hinged	275.00	
549	A194	20k dark brown	19.00	3.75
		Never hinged	50.00	
550	A194	35k carmine	220.00	30.00
		Never hinged	500.00	
		Nos. 546-550 (5)	547.00	71.75

Anti-war propaganda, the designs symbolize the horrors of modern warfare.

Subway Tunnel A197

Subway Station Cross Section A198

Subway Station A199

Train in Station — A200

1935, Feb. 25 **Wmk. 170** ***Perf. 14***

No.	Type	Description	Unused	Used
551	A197	5k orange	42.50	7.50
		Never hinged	95.00	
552	A198	10k dark ultra	32.50	8.50
		Never hinged	65.00	
553	A199	15k rose carmine	300.00	32.50
		Never hinged	600.00	

554 A200 20k emerald 32.50 10.00
Never hinged 65.00
Nos. 551-554 (4) 407.50 58.50

Completion of Moscow subway.

Friedrich Engels (1820-1895), German Socialist and Collaborator of Marx — A201

1935, May Wmk. 170 *Perf. 14*

555 A201 5k carmine 14.00 4.00
Never hinged 24.00
556 A201 10k dark green 25.00 6.00
Never hinged 47.50
557 A201 15k dark blue 70.00 14.00
Never hinged 140.00
558 A201 20k brown black 13.50 6.00
Never hinged 24.00
Nos. 555-558 (4) 122.50 30.00

Running — A202

Designs: 2k, Diving. 3k, Rowing. 4k, Soccer. 5k, Skiing. 10k, Bicycling. 15k, Tennis. 20k, Skating. 35k, Hurdling. 40k, Parade of athletes.

1935, Apr. 22 Unwmk. *Perf. 14*

559 A202 1k orange & ultra 20.00 4.25
Never hinged 40.00
560 A202 2k black & ultra 16.00 2.50
Never hinged 30.00
561 A202 3k grn & blk brn 22.00 3.00
Never hinged 35.00
562 A202 4k rose red & ultra 17.00 5.25
Never hinged 32.50
563 A202 5k pur & blk brn 20.00 2.50
Never hinged 42.50
564 A202 10k rose red & vio 20.00 5.25
Never hinged 42.50
565 A202 15k blk & blk brn 190.00 42.50
Never hinged 400.00
566 A202 20k blk brn & ultra 22.00 5.00
Never hinged 37.50
567 A202 35k ultra & blk brn 125.00 35.00
Never hinged 250.00
568 A202 40k blk brn & car 20.00 8.50
Never hinged 30.00
Nos. 559-568 (10) 472.00 113.75

International Spartacist Games, Moscow. The games never took place.

Silver Plate of Sassanian Dynasty A212

1935, Sept. 10 Wmk. 170

569 A212 5k orange red 57.50 3.50
Never hinged 110.00
570 A212 10k dk yel grn 22.50 5.25
Never hinged 45.00
571 A212 15k dark violet 22.50 8.50
Never hinged 45.00
572 A212 35k black brown 57.50 10.00
Never hinged 110.00
Nos. 569-572 (4) 160.00 27.25

3rd International Congress of Persian Art, Leningrad, Sept. 12-18, 1935.

Kalinin, the Worker — A213

Mikhail Kalinin — A216

Kalinin as: 5k, farmer. 10k, orator.

1935, Nov. 20 Unwmk. *Perf. 14*

573 A213 3k rose lilac 3.75 1.25
Never hinged 7.00
a. Horiz. pair, imperf. btwn. — *4,500.*
Never hinged —
574 A213 5k green 3.75 1.25
Never hinged 7.00
575 A213 10k blue slate 7.50 1.75
Never hinged 13.00
576 A216 20k brown black 16.00 3.50
Never hinged 26.00
a. Imperf. *1,500.*
Never hinged *2,100.*
Nos. 573-576 (4) 31.00 7.75

60th birthday of Mikhail Kalinin, chairman of the Central Executive Committee of the USSR.

A217

Leo Tolstoy — A218

Design: 20k, Statue of Tolstoy.

1935, Dec. 4 *Perf. 14*

577 A217 3k ol black & vio 7.00 2.50
Never hinged 13.00
b. Horiz. pair, imperf. btwn. — *2,000.*
Never hinged —
578 A218 10k vio blk & blk brn 11.00 1.50
Never hinged 21.00
b. Vert. pair, imperf. btwn. — *2,250.*
Never hinged —
579 A217 20k dk grn & blk brn 12.50 3.00
Never hinged 25.00
Nos. 577-579 (3) 30.50 7.00

Perf. 11

577a A217 3k 7.00 4.00
Never hinged 11.00
c. Horiz. pair, imperf. btwn. *2,000.* *850.00*
Never hinged *3,000.*
578a A218 10k 26.00 3.00
Never hinged 52.50
579a A217 20k 9.00 4.50
Never hinged 17.50
b. Vert. pair, imperf. btwn. *1,600.* *1,100.*
Never hinged *2,500.*
Nos. 577a-579a (3) 42.00 11.50

25th anniv. of the death of Count Leo N. Tolstoy (1828-1910).

Portrait Type of 1933

Designs: 2k, Mikhail V. Frunze. 4k, N. E. Bauman. 40k, Sergei M. Kirov.

1935, Nov. Wmk. 170 *Perf. 11*

580 A169 2k purple 11.00 5.50
Never hinged 22.00
581 A169 4k brown violet 7.00 5.00
Never hinged 13.00
582 A169 40k black brown 19.00 5.00
Never hinged 32.50
Nos. 580-582 (3) 37.00 15.50

Perf. 14

580a A169 2k 10.00 1.50
Never hinged 25.00
b. Vert. pair, imperf. btwn. *2,250.* —
Never hinged *3,350.*
581a A169 4k 22.50 3.00
Never hinged 70.00
582a A169 40k 60.00 4.00
Never hinged 110.00
b. Vert. pair, imperf. btwn. — *2,750.*
Never hinged —
Nos. 580a-582a (3) 92.50 8.50

Death of three revolutionary heroes.

Nos. 580-582 exist imperf. but were not regularly issued. Values, set: unused, $1,800; never hinged, $3,250.

Pioneers Preventing Theft from Mailbox A223

Designs: 3k, 5k, Pioneers preventing destruction of property. 10k, Helping recover kite. 15k, Girl Pioneer saluting.

1936, Apr. Unwmk. *Perf. 14*

583 A223 1k yellow green 2.00 1.00
Never hinged 3.50
b. Vert. pair, imperf. btwn. — *1,650.*
Never hinged —
584 A223 2k copper red 2.50 .85
Never hinged 3.50
b. Vert. pair, imperf. btwn. *1,750.* *1,650.*
Never hinged *2,750.*
585 A223 3k slate blue 2.75 .85
Never hinged 3.50
586 A223 5k rose lake 4.50 1.40
Never hinged 6.75
587 A223 10k gray blue 6.75 2.50
Never hinged 10.00
b. Horiz. pair, imperf. btwn. *2,650.* —
Never hinged *3,900.*
588 A223 15k brown olive 40.00 10.00
Never hinged 110.00
Nos. 583-588 (6) 58.50 16.60

Perf. 11

583a A223 1k 2.00 1.00
Never hinged 3.50
c. Vert. pair, imperf. btwn. — *1,200.*
Never hinged —
584a A223 2k 2.50 1.00
Never hinged 3.50
c. Vert. pair, imperf. btwn. *1,750.* *1,900.*
Never hinged *2,750.*
585a A223 3k 2.25 1.00
Never hinged 3.50
b. Vert. pair, imperf. btwn. *1,750.* *1,650.*
Never hinged *2,750.*
586a A223 5k 22.50 2.25
Never hinged 37.50
587a A223 10k 11.50 3.00
Never hinged 27.50
c. Vert. pair, imperf. btwn. — *2,750.*
Never hinged —
d. Horiz. pair, imperf. btwn. *1,750.* *1,650.*
Never hinged *2,750.*
588a A223 15k 17.50 5.50
Never hinged 30.00
Nos. 583a-588a (6) 58.25 13.75

Nikolai A. Dobrolyubov, Writer and Critic, Birth Cent. — A227

1936, Aug. 13 Typo. *Perf. 11½*

589 A227 10k rose lake 10.50 5.50
Never hinged 20.00
a. Perf. 14 8.50 3.50
Never hinged 17.00

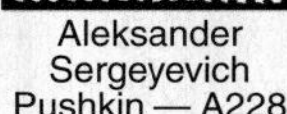

Aleksander Sergeyevich Pushkin — A228

Statue of Pushkin, Moscow — A229

Chalky Paper

1937, Feb. 1

Line Perf 12¼

590 A228 10k yellow brown 3.50 .75
Never hinged 6.75
591 A228 20k Prus green 3.50 .75
Never hinged 6.75
592 A228 40k rose lake 3.50 .75
Never hinged 6.75
593 A229 50k blue 8.25 2.00
Never hinged 14.50
594 A229 80k carmine rose 42.50 6.00
Never hinged 75.00
595 A229 1r green 82.50 8.50
Never hinged 145.00
Nos. 590-595 (6) 143.75 18.75

Chalky or Ordinary Paper

Comb Perf 12¼x11¾

590A A228 10k yellow brown 7.00 2.00
Never hinged 13.00
591A A228 20k Prus green 7.00 3.00
Never hinged 13.00
592A A228 40k rose lake 12.00 3.00
Never hinged 21.00
593A A229 50k blue 21.00 7.00
Never hinged 40.00
594A A229 80k carmine rose 7.00 2.00
Never hinged 13.00
Nos. 590A-594A (5) 54.00 17.00

Line Perf 13¾x12¼

590B A228 10k yellow brown 9.50 .75
Never hinged 17.00
591B A228 20k Prus green 6.00 .75
Never hinged 9.50
592B A228 40k rose lake 2.00 1.75
Never hinged 17.00
593B A229 50k blue 27.00 4.75
Never hinged 50.00
594B A229 80k carmine rose 22.50 6.00
Never hinged 35.00
595B A229 1r green 52.50 8.50
Never hinged 100.00
Nos. 590B-595B (6) 119.50 22.50

Line Perf 11x12¼

590C A228 10k yellow brown 37.50 2.25
Never hinged 72.50
591C A228 20k Prus green 165.00 14.50
Never hinged 300.00
592C A228 40k rose lake 145.00 14.50
Never hinged 255.00
593C A229 50k blue 37.50 11.00
Never hinged 72.50
594C A229 80k carmine rose 35.00 2.25
Never hinged 60.00
595C A229 1r green 42.50 5.50
Never hinged 72.50
Nos. 590C-595C (6) 462.50 50.00

Line Perf 13¾

590D A228 10k yellow brown 82.50 —
Never hinged 145.00
591D A228 20k Prus green 60.00 —
Never hinged 120.00
592D A228 40k rose lake 82.50 —
Never hinged 165.00
Nos. 590D-592D (3) 225.00

Line Perf 11

590E A228 10k yellow brown 187.50 *22.50*
Never hinged 330.00
592E A228 40k rose lake 140.00 *22.50*
Never hinged 240.00
Nos. 590E-592E (2) 327.50 45.00

Souvenir Sheet

Imperf

596 Sheet of 2 25.00 *75.00*
Never hinged 50.00
a. A228 10k brown 4.00 *20.00*
b. A229 50k brown 4.00 *27.50*

Pushkin (1799-1837), writer and poet.

Tchaikovsky Concert Hall — A230

Designs: 5k, 15k, Telegraph Agency House. 10k, Tchaikovsky Concert Hall. 20k, 50k, Red Army Theater. 30k, Hotel Moscow. 40k, Palace of the Soviets.

Unwmk.

1937, June Photo. *Perf. 12*

597 A230 3k brown violet 5.75 .75
Never hinged 11.50
b. Imperf. 285.00 145.00
Never hinged 475.00
598 A230 5k henna brown 2.90 1.75
Never hinged 4.75
b. Imperf. 285.00 105.00
Never hinged 500.00
599 A230 10k dark brown 6.00 .75
Never hinged 11.50
b. Imperf. 700.00 285.00
Never hinged 1,050.
600 A230 15k black 65.00 .75
Never hinged 120.00
b. Imperf. 1,050. 475.00
Never hinged 1,650.

601 A230 20k olive green 11.50 1.75
Never hinged 19.00
b. Imperf. 82.50 325.00
Never hinged 105.00
602 A230 30k gray black 8.25 2.25
Never hinged 14.50
a. Perf. 11 82.50 *12.50*
Never hinged 165.00
b. Imperf. — —
Never hinged —
603 A230 40k violet 11.50 1.75
Never hinged 22.50
a. Souv. sheet of 4, imperf. 29.00 *25.00*
Never hinged 55.00
b. Imperf. 1,425. —
Never hinged 2,350.
604 A230 50k dark brown 11.50 6.00
Never hinged 27.50
b. Imperf. 1,650. 425.00
Never hinged 3,000.
Nos. 597-604 (8) 122.40 15.75

First Congress of Soviet Architects. The 30k is watermarked Greek Border and Rosettes (170).

Feliks E. Dzerzhinski — A235

1937, July 27 Typo. *Perf. 12*
606 A235 10k yellow brown 3.00 1.20
Never hinged 6.00
a. Imperf. 1,500.
Never hinged 2,100.
607 A235 20k Prus green 6.75 1.20
Never hinged 12.00
a. Imperf. 1,500.
Never hinged 2,100.
608 A235 40k rose lake 14.00 2.25
Never hinged 32.50
a. Imperf. 1,500.
Never hinged 2,100.
609 A235 80k carmine 12.00 3.75
Never hinged 29.00
a. Imperf. 1,500.
Never hinged 2,100.
Nos. 606-609 (4) 35.75 8.40

Dzerzhinski, organizer of Soviet secret police, 10th death anniv.

Shota Rustaveli — A236

Line Perf 12¼
1938, Feb. Unwmk. Photo.
610 A236 20k deep green 7.25 1.00
Never hinged 13.00
a. Comb perf. 12½x12 *1,450.* 375.00
Never hinged *2,400.*
b. Imperf. *2,100.* —
Never hinged *4,250.*

750th anniversary of the publication of the poem "Knight in the Tiger Skin," by Shota Rustaveli, Georgian poet.

Statue Surmounting Pavilion A237

Soviet Pavilion at Paris Exposition A238

1938 Typo.
611 A237 5k red 1.25 .60
Never hinged 2.25
a. Imperf. *1,650.*
Never hinged *2,850.*
612 A238 20k rose 1.75 .50
Never hinged 3.00
613 A237 50k dark blue 19.50 3.75
Never hinged 37.50
Nos. 611-613 (3) 22.50 4.85

USSR participation in the 1937 International Exposition at Paris.

Types of 1929-32 and Lenin Types of 1925-26

1937-52 Unwmk. *Perf. 11½x12, 12*
613A A103 1k dull org ('40) 7.50 *2.50*
Never hinged 13.00
614 A95 2k yel grn ('39) 6.75 *1.00*
Never hinged 13.00
615 A97 4k claret ('40) 65.00 *3.50*
Never hinged 125.00
b. Imperf. 950.00
Never hinged 1,450.
615A A98 5k org brn ('46) 65.00 *10.00*
Never hinged 125.00
616 A109 10k blue ('38) 1.25 *.50*
Never hinged 2.75
b. Imperf. 725.00
Never hinged 1,450.
616A A103 10k olive ('40) 145.00 *12.50*
Never hinged 260.00
b. Imperf. 1,875.
Never hinged 2,850.
616B A109 10k black ('52) .25 .25
Never hinged .40
617 A97 20k dull green 1.25 .40
Never hinged 2.75
b. Imperf. 2,950.
Never hinged 4,750.
617A A107 20k green ('39) 100.00 *6.25*
Never hinged 150.00
b. Imperf. 600.00
Never hinged 950.00
618 A109 30k claret ('39) 45.00 1.75
Never hinged 95.00
b. Imperf. 600.00
Never hinged 950.00
619 A104 40k indigo ('38) 6.50 *.75*
Never hinged 11.00
b. Imperf. 375.00
Never hinged 600.00
619A A111 50k dp brn ('40) 6.50 *1.00*
Never hinged 12.00

Engr.
620 A75 3r dk grn ('39) 2.50 .50
Never hinged 4.75
a. Horiz. pair, imperf. btwn. *2,850.* —
Never hinged *4,750.*
621 A66 5r red brn ('39) 8.50 2.50
Never hinged 18.00
622 A66 10r indigo ('39) 3.75 1.50
Never hinged 7.50
Nos. 613A-622 (15) 464.75 44.90

No. 616B was re-issued in 1954-56 in slightly smaller format, 14½x21mm, and in gray black. See note after No. 738.

Airplane Route from Moscow to North Pole — A239

Soviet Flag and Airplanes at North Pole — A240

1938, Feb. 25 Litho. *Perf. 12*
625 A239 10k brn & black 3.75 .75
Never hinged 6.75
626 A239 20k blue gray & blk 7.25 2.25
Never hinged 15.00

Typo.
627 A240 40k dl grn & car 18.00 3.75
Never hinged 29.00
a. Imperf. 1,450.
Never hinged 2,850.
628 A240 80k rose car & car 4.00 .80
Never hinged 6.75
a. Imperf. 150.00
Never hinged 240.00
b. Double impression of flag *2,000.*
Never hinged *3,000.*
Nos. 625-628 (4) 33.00 7.55

Soviet flight to the North Pole.

Infantryman A241

Soldier A242

Stalin Reviewing Cavalry A246

Chapayev and Boy — A247

Designs: 30k, Sailor, 40k, Aviator. 50k, Antiaircraft soldier.

Unwmk.
1938, Mar. Photo. *Perf. 12*
629 A241 10k gray blk & dk red 5.50 .75
Never hinged 9.50
630 A242 20k gray blk & dk red 8.25 .80
Never hinged 14.50
631 A242 30k gray blk & dk red 10.50 1.20
Never hinged 21.00
632 A242 40k gray blk & dk red 14.50 1.90
Never hinged 25.00
633 A242 50k gray blk & dk red 14.50 1.90
Never hinged 25.00
634 A246 80k gray blk & dk red 19.00 3.75
Never hinged 37.50

Typo.
Perf. 12x12½
635 A247 1r black & carmine 6.00 2.00
Never hinged 9.50
a. Imperf. 1,150. —
Never hinged 1,900.
Nos. 629-635 (7) 78.25 12.30

Workers' & Peasants' Red Army, 20th anniv.

Aviators Chkalov, Baidukov, Beliakov and Flight Route — A248

1938, Apr. 10 Photo.
636 A248 10k black & red 8.25 .75
Never hinged 16.50
a. Imperf. 5,250. 3,600.
Never hinged 7,250.
637 A248 20k brn blk & red 12.00 .75
Never hinged 24.00
a. Imperf. 1,050. 375.00
Never hinged 1,875.
638 A248 40k brown & red 12.00 2.00
Never hinged 24.00
a. Imperf. 1,050. 375.00
Never hinged 1,875.
639 A248 50k brown vio & red 15.00 3.75
Never hinged 30.00
a. Imperf. 1,050. 375.00
Never hinged 1,875.
Nos. 636-639 (4) 47.25 7.25

First Trans-Polar flight, June 18-20, 1937, from Moscow to Vancouver, Wash.

Aviators Gromov, Danilin, Yumashev and Flight Route — A249

1938, Apr. 13
640 A249 10k claret 10.00 .75
Never hinged 16.50
a. Imperf. 825.00
Never hinged 1,175.
641 A249 20k brown black 12.00 1.75
Never hinged 21.00
a. Imperf. 725.00 —
Never hinged 950.00
642 A249 50k dull violet 13.00 5.00
Never hinged 24.00
a. Imperf. *23,000.*
Never hinged —
Nos. 640-642 (3) 35.00 7.50

First Trans-Polar flight, July 12-14, 1937, from Moscow to San Jacinto, Calif.

Arrival of the Rescuing Ice-breakers Taimyr and Murmansk A250

Ivan Papanin and His Men Aboard Ice-breaker Yermak — A251

1938, June 21 Typo. *Perf. 12, 12½*
643 A250 10k violet brown 6.00 1.25
Never hinged 12.00
a. Imperf. 2,250.
Never hinged 3,600.
644 A250 20k dark blue 8.25 1.50
Never hinged 18.00
a. Imperf. 2,250.
Never hinged 3,600.

Photo.
645 A251 30k olive brown 21.00 3.75
Never hinged 45.00
a. Imperf. 3,250.
Never hinged 4,750.
646 A251 50k ultra 16.50 6.00
Never hinged 35.00
a. Imperf. 2,350.
Never hinged 4,250.
Nos. 643-646 (4) 51.75 12.50

Rescue of Papanin's North Pole Expedition.

Arms of Armenia — A252

Arms of USSR A253

No. 650

No. 651

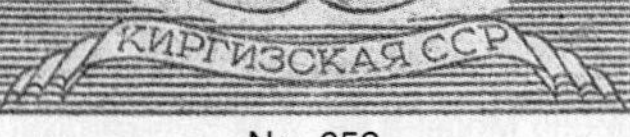

No. 652

No. 653

No. 654

No. 655

No. 656

Designs: Different arms on each stamp.

Perf. 12, 12½
1937-38 Unwmk. Typo.
647 A252 20k dp bl (Armenia) 10.50 2.00
Never hinged 19.50

No.	Type	Description	Unused	Used
648	A252	20k dl vio (Azerbaijan)	10.50	2.00
		Never hinged	19.50	
649	A252	20k brn org (Byelorussia)	10.50	2.00
		Never hinged	19.50	
650	A252	20k car rose (Georgia)	10.50	2.00
		Never hinged	19.50	
651	A252	20k bl grn (Kazakh)	10.50	2.00
		Never hinged	19.50	
652	A252	20k emer (Kirghiz)	10.50	2.00
		Never hinged	19.50	
653	A252	20k yel org (Uzbek)	10.50	2.00
		Never hinged	19.50	
654	A252	20k bl (R.S.F.S.R.)	10.50	2.00
		Never hinged	19.50	
655	A252	20k claret (Tadzhik)	10.50	2.00
		Never hinged	19.50	
656	A252	20k car (Turkmen)	10.50	2.00
		Never hinged	19.50	
657	A252	20k red (Ukraine)	10.50	2.00
		Never hinged	30.00	

Engr.

No.	Type	Description	Unused	Used
658	A253	40k brown red	9.25	2.00
		Never hinged	17.50	
		Nos. 647-658 (12)	124.75	24.00

Constitution of USSR. No. 649 has inscriptions in Yiddish, Polish, Byelorussian and Russian.

Issue dates: 40k, 1937. Others, 1938. See Nos. 841-842 in Scott Standard catalogue, Vol. 5.

Nurse Weighing Child — A264

Children at Lenin's Statue — A265

Biology Lesson A266

Health Camp A267

Young Model Builders A268

1938, Sept. 15 Unwmk. *Perf. 12*

No.	Type	Description	Unused	Used
659	A264	10k dk blue green	12.00	2.00
		Never hinged	21.00	
660	A265	15k dk blue green	3.50	3.50
		Never hinged	6.00	
661	A266	20k violet brown	13.00	2.50
		Never hinged	24.00	
662	A267	30k claret	13.00	2.50
		Never hinged	24.00	
663	A266	40k light brown	13.00	2.50
		Never hinged	24.00	
664	A268	50k deep blue	12.00	*5.00*
		Never hinged	21.00	
665	A268	80k light green	13.00	*4.50*
		Never hinged	25.00	
		Nos. 659-665 (7)	79.50	22.50

Child welfare.

View of Yalta A269

Crimean Shoreline — A272

Designs: No. 667, View along Crimean shore. No. 668, Georgian military highway. No, 670, View near Yalta. No. 671, "Swallows' Nest" Castle. 20k, Dzerzhinski Rest House for workers. 30k, Sunset in Crimea. 40k, Alupka. 50k, Gursuf. 80k, Crimean Gardens. 1r, "Swallows' Nest" Castle, horiz.

Unwmk.

1938, Sept. 21 Photo. *Perf. 12*

No.	Type	Description	Unused	Used
666	A269	5k brown	4.75	*1.00*
		Never hinged	9.50	
667	A269	5k black brown	4.75	*1.00*
		Never hinged	9.50	
668	A269	10k slate green	4.75	*1.00*
		Never hinged	9.50	
669	A272	10k brown	4.75	*1.00*
		Never hinged	9.50	
670	A269	15k black brown	6.00	*1.75*
		Never hinged	12.00	
671	A272	15k black brown	6.00	*1.75*
		Never hinged	12.00	
672	A269	20k dark brown	10.00	*1.75*
		Never hinged	19.00	
673	A272	30k black brown	12.00	*1.75*
		Never hinged	24.00	
674	A269	40k brown	12.00	*1.75*
		Never hinged	24.00	
675	A272	50k slate green	12.00	*1.75*
		Never hinged	24.00	
a.		Horiz. pair, imperf. btwn.	2,175.	
		Never hinged	3,500.	
b.		Vert. pair, imperf. btwn.	2,175.	
		Never hinged	3,500.	
676	A269	80k brown	12.00	*1.75*
		Never hinged	24.00	
677	A269	1r slate green	120.00	*20.00*
		Never hinged	225.00	
		Nos. 666-677 (12)	209.00	36.25

Children Flying Model Plane A281

Glider A282

Captive Balloon — A283

Dirigible over Kremlin — A284

Parachute Jumpers — A285

Hydroplane A286

Balloon in Flight — A287

Balloon Ascent — A288

Four-motor Plane A289

Unwmk.

1938, Oct. 7 Typo. *Perf. 12*

No.	Type	Description	Unused	Used
678	A281	5k violet brown	3.75	1.50
		Never hinged	7.00	
679	A282	10k olive gray	3.75	1.50
		Never hinged	7.00	
680	A283	15k pink	6.00	1.50
		Never hinged	11.00	
681	A284	20k deep blue	6.00	1.50
		Never hinged	11.00	
682	A285	30k claret	12.00	1.50
		Never hinged	21.00	
683	A286	40k deep blue	14.50	1.50
		Never hinged	26.00	
684	A287	50k blue green	12.00	2.50
		Never hinged	21.00	
685	A288	80k brown	14.50	2.50
		Never hinged	21.00	
686	A289	1r blue green	82.50	10.00
		Never hinged	145.00	
		Nos. 678-686 (9)	155.00	24.00

For overprints see Nos. C76-C76D.

Mayakovsky Station, Moscow Subway — A290

Sokol Terminal — A291

Kiev Station — A292

Dynamo Station A293

Train in Tunnel A294

Revolution Square Station A295

Unwmk.

1938, Nov. 7 Photo. *Perf. 12*

No.	Type	Description	Unused	Used
687	A290	10k deep red violet	3.00	2.00
		Never hinged	4.75	
a.		Vert. pair, imperf. btwn.	2,175.	—
		Never hinged	3,500.	
688	A291	15k dark brown	6.00	2.00
		Never hinged	9.50	
689	A292	20k black brown	14.50	2.50
		Never hinged	24.00	
690	A293	30k dark red violet	21.00	4.75
		Never hinged	37.50	
a.		Vert. pair, imperf. btwn.	—	*3,600.*
		Never hinged		
691	A294	40k black brown	21.00	4.75
		Never hinged	37.50	
692	A295	50k dark brown	24.00	7.25
		Never hinged	42.50	
		Nos. 687-692 (6)	89.50	23.25

Second line of the Moscow subway opening.

Girl with Parachute A296

Young Miner A297

Harvesting A298

Designs: 50k, Students returning from school. 80k, Aviator and sailor.

1938, Dec. 7 Typo. *Perf. 12*

No.	Type	Description	Unused	Used
693	A296	20k deep blue	13.00	2.50
		Never hinged	24.00	
694	A297	30k deep claret	13.00	2.50
		Never hinged	24.00	
695	A298	40k violet brown	10.50	2.50
		Never hinged	19.00	
696	A296	50k deep rose	35.00	8.25
		Never hinged	60.00	
697	A298	80k deep blue	8.25	6.00
		Never hinged	14.50	
		Nos. 693-697 (5)	79.75	21.75

20th anniv. of the Young Communist League (Komsomol).

Diving — A301

Discus Thrower — A302

Designs: 15k, Tennis. 20k, Acrobatic motorcyclists. 30k, Skier. 40k, Runners. 50k, Soccer. 80k, Physical culture.

Unwmk.

1938, Dec. 28 Photo. *Perf. 12*

No.	Type	Description	Unused	Used
698	A301	5k scarlet	3.50	1.25
		Never hinged	6.00	
699	A302	10k black	3.50	1.25
		Never hinged	6.00	
700	A302	15k brown	6.00	1.75
		Never hinged	11.50	
701	A302	20k green	6.00	1.75
		Never hinged	11.50	
702	A302	30k dull violet	30.00	2.00
		Never hinged	57.50	
703	A302	40k deep green	15.00	2.00
		Never hinged	30.00	
704	A302	50k blue	82.50	10.00
		Never hinged	150.00	
705	A302	80k deep blue	10.50	5.00
		Never hinged	20.00	
		Nos. 698-705 (8)	157.00	25.00

Gorki Street, Moscow — A309

Dynamo Subway Station A315

Moscow scenes: 20k, Council House & Hotel Moscow. 30k, Lenin Library. 40k, Crimea Bridge. 50k, Bridge over Moscow River. 80k, Khimki River Terminal.

Paper with network as in parenthesis

1939, Mar. Typo. *Perf. 12*

706 A309 10k brn *(red brown)* 3.75 1.25
Never hinged 7.00
707 A309 20k dk sl grn *(lt blue)* 3.75 1.50
Never hinged 7.00
708 A309 30k brn vio *(red brn)* 3.75 1.50
Never hinged 7.00
709 A309 40k blue *(lt blue)* 12.50 2.50
Never hinged 24.00
710 A309 50k rose lake *(red brn)* 12.50 3.00
Never hinged 24.00
711 A309 80k gray ol *(lt blue)* 12.50 5.75
Never hinged 24.00
712 A315 1r dk blue *(lt blue)* 70.00 7.50
Never hinged 130.00
Nos. 706-712 (7) 118.75 23.00

"New Moscow." On 30k, denomination is at upper right.

Foundry-man — A316

1939, Mar.

713 A316 15k dark blue 7.50 .75
Never hinged 14.50
a. Imperf. 2,000.
Never hinged 3,000.

Statue on USSR Pavilion — A317

USSR Pavilion A318

1939, May Photo.

714 A317 30k indigo & red 2.75 1.00
Never hinged 4.75
a. Imperf. ('40) 3.00 1.00
Never hinged 5.00
715 A318 50k blue & bister brn 5.50 1.00
Never hinged 10.00
a. Imperf. ('40) 6.00 1.25
Never hinged 11.00

Russia's participation in the NY World's Fair.

Paulina Osipenko A318a

Marina Raskova A318b

Design: 60k, Valentina Grizodubova.

1939, Mar.

718 A318a 15k green 8.25 2.00
Never hinged 16.50
719 A318b 30k brown violet 14.50 3.75
Never hinged 25.00
720 A318b 60k red 14.50 7.50
Never hinged 25.00
Nos. 718-720 (3) 37.25 13.25

Non-stop record flight from Moscow to the Far East.

Exist imperf. Value, each unused $2,100.

Shevchenko, Early Portrait — A319

Monument at Kharkov — A321

30k, Shevchenko portrait in later years.

1939, Mar. 9

721 A319 15k black brn & blk 7.50 1.50
Never hinged 16.50
722 A319 30k dark red & blk 13.00 2.25
Never hinged 32.50
723 A321 60k green & dk brn 14.50 3.00
Never hinged 32.50
Nos. 721-723 (3) 35.00 6.75

Taras G. Shevchenko (1814-1861), Ukrainian poet and painter.

Milkmaid with Prize Cow — A322

Tractor-plow at Work on Abundant Harvest A323

Designs: 20k, Shepherd tending sheep. No. 727, Fair pavilion. No. 728, Fair emblem. 45k, Turkmen picking cotton. 50k, Drove of horses. 60k, Symbolizing agricultural wealth. 80k, Kolkhoz girl with sugar beets. 1r, Hunter with Polar foxes.

1939, Aug.

724 A322 10k rose pink 3.50 .45
Never hinged 6.00
725 A323 15k red brown 3.50 .45
Never hinged 6.00
726 A323 20k slate black 9.50 2.00
Never hinged 19.00
727 A323 30k purple 5.75 1.00
Never hinged 9.50
728 A322 30k red orange 3.50 .45
Never hinged 6.00
729 A322 45k dark green 9.50 1.25
Never hinged 19.00
a. Horiz. pair, imperf. btwn. *1,750.*
Never hinged 2,850.
730 A322 50k copper red 2.00 .45
Never hinged 3.50
a. Horiz. pair, imperf. btwn. *1,500.*
731 A322 60k bright purple 7.00 1.00
Never hinged 12.00
732 A322 80k dark violet 7.00 1.00
Never hinged 12.00
733 A322 1r dark blue 19.00 2.00
Never hinged 35.00
a. Horiz. pair, imperf. btwn. *2,350.*
b. Vert. pair, imperf. btwn. *1,500.*
Nos. 724-733 (10) 70.25 10.05

Soviet Agricultural Fair.

Worker A331

Soldier A332

Aviator — A333

Perf. 11¾x12¼

Arms of USSR A334 A335

Perf. 11¾x12¼

1939-43 Unwmk. Typo.

734 A331 5k red .75 .25
Never hinged 1.50
a. Perf. 12¼ 37.50 30.00
Never hinged 95.00
735 A332 15k dark green 1.25 .25
Never hinged 2.25
a. Perf. 12¼ 60.00 35.00
Never hinged 150.00
736 A333 30k deep blue 2.00 .25
Never hinged 3.50
a. Perf. 12¼ 11.50 7.25
Never hinged 24.00
737 A334 60k fawn ('43) 9.50 .75
Never hinged 19.00

Photo.

738 A335 60k rose carmine 2.50 .45
Never hinged 5.00
a. Perf. 12¼ 12.00 .75
Never hinged 24.00
Nos. 734-738 (5) 16.00 1.95

No. 734 was re-issued in 1954-56 in slightly smaller format: 14x21½mm, instead of 14¾x22¼mm. Other values reissued in smaller format: 10k, 15k, 20k, 25k, 30k, 40k and 1r. (See notes following No. 622; Nos. 1260, 1347 and 1689 in Scott Standard catalogue, Vol. 5.)

No. 416 Surcharged with New Value in Black

1939 Wmk. 170 *Perf. 12x12½*

743 A97 30k on 4k claret 25.00 12.50
Never hinged 50.00
a. Unwmkd. 250.00 37.50
Never hinged 525.00

M.E. Saltykov (N. Shchedrin) A336 A337

Unwmk.

1939, Sept. Typo. *Perf. 12*

745 A336 15k claret 3.00 .75
Never hinged 5.00
746 A337 30k dark green 3.75 .75
Never hinged 7.25
747 A336 45k olive gray 8.75 1.50
Never hinged 16.50
748 A337 60k dark blue 8.75 2.25
Never hinged 16.50
Nos. 745-748 (4) 24.25 5.25

Mikhail E. Saltykov (1826-89), writer & satirist who used pen name of N. Shchedrin.

Sanatorium of the State Bank — A338

Designs: 10k, 15k, Soviet Army sanatorium. 20k, Rest home, New Afyon. 30k, Clinical Institute. 50k, 80k, Sanatorium for workers in heavy industry. 60k, Rest home, Sukhumi.

1939, Nov. Photo. *Perf. 12*

749 A338 5k dull brown 2.00 .25
Never hinged 3.50
750 A338 10k carmine 2.00 .25
Never hinged 3.50
751 A338 15k yellow green 3.50 .45
Never hinged 6.00
752 A338 20k dk slate green 7.00 .45
Never hinged 12.00
753 A338 30k bluish black 3.50 .45
Never hinged 6.00
a. Horiz. pair, imperf. between *2,500.*
Never hinged *3,500.*
754 A338 50k gray black 3.50 1.75
Never hinged 6.00
755 A338 60k brown violet 9.50 1.75
Never hinged 16.50
756 A338 80k orange red 7.00 1.75
Never hinged 12.50
Nos. 749-756 (8) 38.00 7.10

Mikhail Y. Lermontov (1814-1841), Poet and Novelist, in 1837 — A346

Portrait in 1838 — A347

Portrait in 1841 — A348

1939, Dec.

757 A346 15k indigo & sepia 8.25 1.25
Never hinged 14.50
a. Vert. pair, imperf. between — 1,650.
758 A347 30k dk grn & dull blk 12.00 3.00
Never hinged 24.00
a. Vert. pair, imperf. between — 1,650.
759 A348 45k brk red & indigo 8.25 1.25
Never hinged 14.50
Nos. 757-759 (3) 28.50 5.50

Nikolai Chernyshevski A349

1939, Dec. Photo.

760 A349 15k dark green 9.50 1.25
Never hinged 14.50
a. Perf. 12¼ 4.50 1.25
Never hinged 8.25
761 A349 30k dull violet 14.50 1.25
Never hinged 24.00
a. Perf. 12¼ 500.00 *145.00*
Never hinged 1,000.
762 A349 60k Prus green 14.50 3.00
Never hinged 24.00
a. Perf. 12¼ 90.00 12.00
Never hinged 165.00
Nos. 760-762 (3) 38.50 5.50

50th anniversary of the death of Nikolai Chernyshevski, scientist and critic.

Anton Chekhov — A350

Design: 20k, 30k, Portrait with hat.

1940, Feb. Unwmk. *Perf. 12*

763 A350 10k dark yellow green 2.00 1.50
Never hinged 3.50
764 A350 15k ultra 3.75 1.50
Never hinged 7.25
765 A350 20k violet 3.75 1.50
Never hinged 7.25
766 A350 30k copper brown 14.50 1.50
Never hinged 26.00
Nos. 763-766 (4) 24.00 6.00

Chekhov (1860-1904), playwright.

Welcome to Red Army by Western Ukraine and Western Byelorussia A352

Designs: 30k, Villagers welcoming tank crew. 50k, 60k, Soldier giving newspapers to crowd. 1r, Crowd waving to tank column.

1940, Apr.

767 A352 10k deep rose 1.90 .75
Never hinged 3.00
768 A352 30k myrtle green 3.25 1.00
Never hinged 6.50
a. Horiz. pair, imperf. between *950.00*
769 A352 50k gray black 3.75 1.25
Never hinged 6.50
770 A352 60k indigo 13.00 2.50
Never hinged 24.00
a. Horiz. pair, imperf. between *600.00*
771 A352 1r red 9.75 2.00
Never hinged 19.00
Nos. 767-771 (5) 31.65 7.50

Liberation of the people of Western Ukraine and Western Byelorussia.

Ice-breaker "Josef Stalin," Captain Beloussov and Chief Ivan Papanin A356

Badigin and Papanin A358

Map of the Drift of the Sedov and Crew Members — A359

Design: 30k, Icebreaker Georgi Sedov, Captain Vadygin and First Mate Trofimov.

1940, Apr.

772 A356 15k dull yel green 3.50 .75
Never hinged 4.75
773 A356 30k dull purple 10.50 1.25
Never hinged 19.00
a. Line perf. 12¼ 675.00 —
Never hinged 1,250.
b. Vert. pair, imperf. between — *7,250.*
774 A358 50k copper brown 6.50 1.50
Never hinged 12.00
775 A359 1r dark ultra 12.50 2.50
Never hinged 22.50
a. Vert. pair, imperf. between *3,300.* —
Never hinged *4,750.*
b. Horiz. pair, imperf. between — *6,000.*
Nos. 772-775 (4) 33.00 6.00

Heroism of the Sedov crew which drifted in the Polar Basin for 812 days.

A360

Vladimir V. Mayakovsky — A361

1940, June *Line Perf. 12¼*

776 A360 15k deep red 4.75 1.25
Never hinged 4.75
a. Comb perf. 11¾x12¼ 21.00 3.00
Never hinged 37.50
777 A360 30k copper brown 4.75 1.25
Never hinged 19.00
a. Comb perf. 11¾x12¼ 70.00 8.50
Never hinged 135.00
778 A361 60k dark gray blue 12.00 2.00
Never hinged 12.00
a. Comb perf. 12¼x11¾ 425.00 35.00
Never hinged 825.00
779 A361 80k bright ultra 9.50 1.25
Never hinged 22.50
Nos. 776-779 (4) 31.00 5.75

Mayakovsky, poet (1893-1930).

K.A. Timiryazev and Academy of Agricultural Sciences A362

In the Laboratory of Moscow University A363

Last Portrait A364

Monument in Moscow — A365

1940, June

780 A362 10k indigo 3.00 1.25
Never hinged 4.75
781 A363 15k purple 12.00 1.25
Never hinged 21.00
782 A364 30k dk violet brown 4.75 1.75
Never hinged 9.00
a. Horiz. pair, imperf. between — 2,500.
b. Horiz. pair, imperf. between and at right — 3,750.
783 A365 60k dark green 4.75 2.50
Never hinged 9.00
Nos. 780-783 (4) 24.50 6.75

20th anniversary of the death of K. A. Timiryasev, scientist and professor of agricultural and biological sciences.

Relay Race — A366

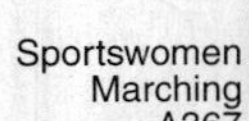

Sportswomen Marching A367

Children's Sport Badge — A368

Skier A369

Throwing the Grenade A370

1940, July 21 *Line Perf. 12½*

784 A366 15k carmine rose 4.25 .75
Never hinged 7.25
785 A367 30k sepia 8.25 3.00
Never hinged 15.00
786 A368 50k dk violet blue 4.75 .75
Never hinged 7.25
787 A369 60k dk violet blue 12.00 3.00
Never hinged 21.00
788 A370 1r grayish green 14.50 .75
Never hinged 32.50
Nos. 784-788 (5) 43.75 8.25

Perf. 11¾x12¼, 12¼x11¾ (#786)

784a A366 15k carmine rose 10.50 1.00
Never hinged 19.00
785a A367 30k sepia 8.25 1.00
Never hinged 14.50
786a A368 50k dk violet blue 4.75 1.50
Never hinged 8.25
787a A369 60k dk violet blue 8.25 1.00
Never hinged 14.50
788a A370 1r grayish green 350.00 22.50
Never hinged 700.00

2nd All-Union Physical Culture Day.

Tchaikovsky Museum at Klin A371

Tchaikovsky & Passage from his Fourth Symphony A372

Peter Ilich Tchaikovsky and Excerpt from Eugene Onegin — A373

Comb Perf. 12¼x11¾

1940, Aug. Unwmk. Typo.

789 A371 15k Prus green 5.50 1.50
Never hinged 10.00
790 A372 20k brown 6.00 1.50
Never hinged 12.00
791 A372 30k dark blue 5.50 2.00
Never hinged 12.00
792 A371 50k rose lake 14.50 3.50
Never hinged 10.00
793 A373 60k red 12.00 7.00
Never hinged 22.50
Nos. 789-793 (5) 43.50 15.50

Tchaikovsky (1840-1893), composer.

Volga Provinces Pavilion A374

Northeast Provinces Pavilion — A376

ПАВИЛЬОН МОСКОВСКОЙ, РЯЗАНСКОЙ И ТУЛЬСКОЙ ОБЛ.

No. 797

ПАВИЛЬОН УКРАИНСКОЙ ССР

No. 798

ПАВИЛЬОН БЕЛОРУССКОЙ ССР

No. 799

ПАВИЛЬОН АЗЕРБАЙДЖАНСКОЙ ССР

No. 800

ПАВИЛЬОН ГРУЗИНСКОЙ ССР

No. 801

ПАВИЛЬОН АРМЯНСКОЙ ССР

No. 802

ВХОДА В ПАВИЛЬОН УЗБЕКСКОЙ ССР

No. 803

ПАВИЛЬОН ТУРКМЕНСКОЙ ССР

No. 804

ПАВИЛЬОН ТАДЖИКСКОЙ ССР

No. 805

ПАВИЛЬОН КИРГИЗСКОЙ ССР

No. 806

ПАВИЛЬОН КАЗАХСКОЙ ССР

No. 807

ПАВИЛЬОН КАРЕЛО-ФИНСКОЙ ССР

No. 808

No. 795, Far East Provinces. No. 797, Central Regions. No. 798, Ukrainian. No. 799, Byelorussian. No. 800, Azerbaijan. No. 801, Georgian. No. 802, Armenian. No. 803, Uzbek. No. 804, Turkmen. No. 805, Tadzhik. No. 806, Kirghiz. No. 807, Kazakh. No. 808, Karelian Finnish. No. 809, Main building. No. 810, Mechanizaton Pavilion, Stalin statue.

1940, Oct. Typo. *Line Perf. 12¼*

794 A374 10k shown 9.50 .55
Never hinged 15.00
795 A374 15k multicolored 9.50 .55
Never hinged 15.00
796 A376 30k shown 12.00 .55
Never hinged 19.00
797 A376 30k multicolored 14.50 .55
Never hinged 22.50
798 A376 30k multicolored 3.50 .55
Never hinged 5.50
799 A376 30k multicolored 3.50 .55
Never hinged 5.50
800 A376 30k multicolored 3.50 .55
Never hinged 5.50
801 A374 30k multicolored 7.00 .55
Never hinged 12.00
802 A376 30k multicolored 7.00 .55
Never hinged 12.00
803 A376 30k multicolored 3.50 .55
Never hinged 5.50
804 A374 30k multicolored 9.50 .55
Never hinged 12.50
805 A376 30k multicolored 3.50 .55
Never hinged 5.50
806 A376 30k multicolored 3.50 .55
Never hinged 5.50
807 A376 30k multicolored 3.50 .55
Never hinged 5.50
808 A376 30k multicolored 9.50 .55
Never hinged 15.00
809 A376 50k multicolored 16.50 1.50
Never hinged 29.00

810 A376 60k multicolored 19.00 2.50
Never hinged 30.00
Nos. 794-810 (17) 138.50 12.25

All-Union Agricultural Fair.

Nos. 796-808 printed in three sheet formats with various vertical and horizontal se-tenant combinations.

Monument to Red Army Heroes — A391

Map of War Operations and M. V. Frunze — A393

Heroic Crossing of the Sivash A394

Designs: 15k, Grenade thrower. 60k, Frunze's headquarters, Stroganovka. 1r, Victorious soldier.

1940 ***Imperf.***

811 A391 10k dark green 2.25 .55
Never hinged 3.75
812 A391 15k orange ver 2.25 .55
Never hinged 3.50
813 A393 30k dull brown & car 6.25 1.50
Never hinged 11.00
814 A394 50k violet brn 3.50 1.00
Never hinged 5.50
815 A394 60k indigo 3.50 1.00
Never hinged 5.50
816 A391 1r gray black 4.25 1.50
Never hinged 7.00
Nos. 811-816 (6) 22.00 6.10

Perf. 12

811A A391 10k dark green 2.75 .55
Never hinged 4.50
812A A391 15k orange ver 2.75 .55
Never hinged 4.50
813A A393 30k dull brown & car 3.75 1.00
Never hinged 6.50
814A A394 50k violet brn 2.75 .65
Never hinged 4.50
815A A394 60k indigo 3.75 1.00
Never hinged 6.50
816A A391 1r gray black 3.75 1.00
Never hinged 6.50
Nos. 811A-816A (6) 19.50 4.75

20th anniversary of battle of Perekop.

POSTAL-FISCAL STAMPS

During 1918-22, Postal Savings stamps and Control stamps were authorized for postal use. Because of hyper-inflation during 1920-22, Russian Arms stamps and these postal-fiscal stamps were sold and used at different rates at different times: 1918-20, sold at face value; from March, 1920, sold at 100 times face value; from Aug. 15, 1921, sold at 250r each, regardless of face value; from April, 1922, sold at 10,000r per 1k or 1r. In Oct. 1922, these issues were superseded by gold currency stamps.

Postal Savings Stamps

PF1

Perf. 14½x14¾

1918, Jan. 12 Wmk. 171 Typo.

AR1 PF1 1k dp red, *buff* .60 *1.00*
Never hinged 1.10
AR2 PF1 5k green, *buff* .60 *1.00*
Never hinged 1.10
AR3 PF1 10k chocolate, *buff* 1.20 *1.00*
Never hinged 2.25
Nos. AR1-AR3 (3) 2.40 *3.00*

Nos. AR1-AR14 have a faint burelé background, which is noted as the paper color in these listings.

For surcharges of Nos. AR1-AR3, see Armenia Nos. 250-253, Far Eastern Republic Nos. 35 and 36, South Russia Nos. 47-49 and numerous Ukraine issues beginning with Nos. 45e-47e.

Postal Savings Stamps

PF2

PF3

1918, June 5 Litho. *Perf. 13*

AR4 PF2 25k black, *rose* 11.00 *37.50*
Never hinged 35.00
AR5 PF2 50k brn, *pale brn* 24.00 *50.00*
Never hinged 72.50
AR6 PF3 50k brn, *pale brn* 35.00 *62.50*
Never hinged 125.00
Nos. AR4-AR6 (3) 70.00 *150.00*

Inverted Background

AR4a PF2 25k black, *rose* 45.00 —
Never hinged 100.00
AR5a PF2 50k brn, *pale brn* — —
AR6a PF3 50k brn, *pale brn* 200.00 —
Never hinged 250.00

Control Stamps

PF4

PF5

PF6

PF7

PF8

1918, June 5 Litho. *Perf. 13*

AR7 PF4 25k blk, *pale brn* 24.00 *32.50*
Never hinged 45.00
AR8 PF4 50k brn, *buff* 17.50 *50.00*
Never hinged 37.50
AR9 PF5 1r org, *buff* 1.50 *3.50*
Never hinged 2.25
AR10 PF5 3r grn, *buff* 1.50 *3.50*
Never hinged 2.25
AR11 PF5 5r dp blue, *buff* 1.50 *3.75*
Never hinged 2.25
AR12 PF6 10r dp red, *buff* 1.50 *3.75*
Never hinged 2.25
AR13 PF7 25r dp brn, *buff* 5.00 *15.00*
Never hinged 10.00
AR14 PF8 100r blk, *blue & car* 3.75 *6.25*
Never hinged 7.50
Nos. AR7-AR14 (8) 56.25 *118.25*

Inverted Background

AR9a PF5 1r org, *buff* 60.00 —
AR10a PF5 3r grn, *buff* 300.00 —
AR12a PF6 10r red, *buff* —
AR13a PF7 25r dp brn, *buff* 175.00 —
AR14a PF8 100r blk, *blue & car* 200.00 —

General Revenue Stamps

PF9

1918 Litho. *Perf. 12x12½*

AR15 PF9 5k lil brn, *buff* 1.50 —
Never hinged 2.25
AR16 PF9 10k ol brn, *lt blue* 1.50 —
Never hinged 2.25
AR17 PF9 15k dp blue, *pink* 1.50 —
Never hinged 2.25
AR18 PF9 20k reddish brn, *buff* 1.50 —
Never hinged 2.25
AR19 PF9 50k org red, *gray* 1.50 —
Never hinged 2.25
AR20 PF9 75k ol grn, *buff* 3.25 —
Never hinged 6.25
AR21 PF9 1r red, *pale blue* 6.25 —
Never hinged 12.50
AR22 PF9 1.25r dk brn, *redsh brn* 30.00 —
Never hinged 45.00
AR23 PF9 2r vio, *dk grn* 30.00 —
Never hinged 50.00
AR24 PF9 3r dp vio blue, *rose lil* 3.50 —
Never hinged 7.25
AR25 PF9 5r dp blue grn, *lt grn* 6.50 —
Never hinged 13.50
Nos. AR15-AR25 (11) 87.00

Nos, AR15-AR25 exist in tête-bêche vertical pairs and in tête-bêche vertical gutter pairs.

SEMI-POSTAL STAMPS

Empire

Admiral Kornilov Monument, Sevastopol SP1

Pozharski and Minin Monument, Moscow SP2

Statue of Peter the Great, Leningrad SP3

Alexander II Memorial and Kremlin, Moscow SP4

1905 Typo. Unwmk. *Perf. 12x12½*

B1 SP1 3k red, brn & grn 24.00 5.25
Never hinged 72.50
B2 SP2 5k lil, vio & straw 5.00 3.50
Never hinged 10.00
B3 SP3 7k lt bl, dk bl & pink 5.00 3.50
Never hinged 10.00
B4 SP4 10k lt blue, dk bl & yel 7.50 .50
Never hinged 15.00
Nos. B1-B4 (4) 41.50 12.75

Line Perf. 13¼

B1a SP1 3k red, brn & grn 40.00 1.25
Never hinged 120.00
B3a SP3 7k lt bl, dk bl & pink 82.50 1.25
Never hinged 260.00
B4a SP4 10k lt bl, dk bl & yel 7.50 .50
Never hinged 15.00

Line Perf. 11½

B1b SP1 3k red, brn & grn 16.50 5.00
Never hinged 45.00

Perf. 13¼x11½

B1c SP1 3k red, brn & grn 200.00 *200.00*
Never hinged 250.00

Perf. 11½x13¼

B1d SP1 3k red, brn & grn 200.00 *200.00*
Never hinged 250.00

These stamps were sold for 3 kopecks over face value. The surtax was donated to a fund for the orphans of soldiers killed in the Russo-Japanese war.

Ilya Murometz Legendary Russian Hero — SP5

Designs: 3k, Don Cossack Bidding Farewell to His Sweetheart. 7k, Symbolical of Charity. 10k, St. George Slaying the Dragon.

1914 Colored Papers *Perf. 11½*

B5 SP5 1k red brn & dk grn, *straw* 2.00 2.00
Never hinged 3.75
B6 SP5 3k mar & gray grn, *pink* 3.00 3.00
Never hinged 6.00
B7 SP5 7k dk brn & dk grn, *buff* 3.50 2.00
Never hinged 7.00
B8 SP5 10k dk bl & brn, *blue* 12.00 4.50
Never hinged 24.00
Nos. B5-B8 (4) 20.50 11.50

Perf. 12½

B5a SP5 1k red brn & dk grn, *straw* 3.75 3.25
Never hinged 6.00
B6a SP5 3k mar & gray grn, *pink* 4.25 3.25
Never hinged 6.00
B7a SP5 7k dk brn & dk grn, *buff* 9.50 7.50
Never hinged 17.50
B8a SP5 10k dk bl & brn, *blue* 21.00 7.50
Never hinged 45.00
Nos. B5a-B8a (4) 38.50 21.50

Perf. 13¼

B5b SP5 1k red brn & dk grn, *straw* 8.50 2.00
Never hinged 15.00
B6b SP5 3k mar & gray grn, *pink* 225.00 45.00
Never hinged 600.00
B7b SP5 7k dk brn & dk grn, *buff* 3.75 3.75
Never hinged 6.00
B8b SP5 10k dk bl & brn, *blue* 24.00 5.50
Never hinged 60.00

Imperf

B5c SP5 1k red brn & dk grn, *straw* 600.00 200.00
B6c SP5 3k mar & gray grn, *pink* 600.00 200.00
B7c SP5 7k dk brn & dk grn, *buff* 600.00 200.00
B8c SP5 10k dk bl & brn, *blue* 600.00 200.00

For expanded listings, see the *Scott Classic Specialized Catalogue of Stamps and Covers 1840-1940.*

1915 White Paper *Perf. 11½*

B9 SP5 1k org brn & gray 2.25 2.00
Never hinged 5.00
B10 SP5 3k car & gray blk 2.25 2.00
Never hinged 5.00
B12 SP5 10k dk bl & dk brn 4.25 2.25
Never hinged 8.25
Nos. B9-B12 (3) 8.75

Perf. 12½

B9a SP5 1k org brn & gray 3.50 2.00
Never hinged 7.00
B10a SP5 3k car & gray blk 3.50 2.00
Never hinged 7.00
d. Horiz. pair, imperf. between 175.00
Never hinged 350.00

B11 SP5 7k dk brn & dk grn 12.00
Never hinged 30.00

B12a SP5 10k dk bl & dk brn 4.25 2.25
Never hinged 8.50
Nos. B9a-B12a+B11 (3) 11.25 6.25

Perf. 13¼

B9b SP5 1k org brn & gray 2.25 2.00
Never hinged 5.00
B10b SP5 3k car & gray blk 2.25 2.00
Never hinged 5.00
B12b SP5 10k dk bl & dk brn 5.00 2.25
Never hinged 10.00
Nos. B9b-B12b (3) 9.50 6.25

Imperf

B9c SP5 1k org brn & gray 425.00 225.00
B10c SP5 3k car & gray blk 425.00 225.00
B11c SP5 7k dk brn & dk grn 425.00 225.00
B12c SP5 10k dk bl & dk brn 425.00 225.00
Nos. B9c-B12c (3) 1,275. 675.00

These stamps were sold for 1 kopeck over face value. The surtax was donated to charities connected with the war of 1914-17.

No. B11 not regularly issued. It exists only perf 11½ (with Specimen overprint) and 12½.

For surcharges of Nos. B5-B13, see Armenia Nos. 255-265 and Siberia No. 64.

Russian Soviet Federated Socialist Republic
Volga Famine Relief Issue

Relief Work on Volga River — SP9

Administering Aid to Famine Victim — SP10

1921 Litho. *Imperf.*

B14 SP9 2250r green 3.75 6.00
Never hinged 7.25
a. Pelure paper 165.00 125.00
Never hinged 290.00
B15 SP9 2250r deep red 2.00 11.00
Never hinged 4.75
a. Pelure paper 19.00 15.00
Never hinged 35.00
B16 SP9 2250r brown 3.75 11.00
Never hinged 7.00
B17 SP10 2250r dark blue 9.50 30.00
Never hinged 21.00
a. 2250r dark blue 20.00 —
Never hinged 35.00
b. 2250r pale blue 35.00 —
Never hinged 60.00
Nos. B14-B17 (4) 19.00 58.00

Forged cancels and counterfeits of Nos. B14-B17 are plentiful.

Stamps of type A33 with this overprint were not charity stamps nor did they pay postage in any form.

They represent taxes paid on stamps exported from or imported into Russia. In 1925 the semi-postal stamps of 1914-15 were surcharged for the same purpose. Stamps of the regular issues 1918 and 1921 have also been surcharged with inscriptions and new values, to pay the importation and exportation taxes.

Nos. 149-150 Surcharged in Black, Red, Blue or Orange

1922, Feb. *Perf. 13½*

B18 A33 100r + 100r on 70k 1.60 1.25
Never hinged 3.50
c. "100 p. + p. 100" 225.00 290.00
Never hinged 600.00
B19 A33 100r + 100r on 70k (R) 1.60 1.25
Never hinged 3.50
B20 A33 100r + 100r on 70k (Bl) 1.00 1.25
Never hinged 2.25
B21 A33 250r + 250r on 35k .50 .75
Never hinged 1.20
B22 A33 250r + 250r on 35k (R) 1.00 2.00
Never hinged 2.25
B23 A33 250r + 250r on 35k (O) 1.60 5.00
Never hinged 3.50
Nos. B18-B23 (6) 7.30 11.50

Surcharge Inverted

B18a A33 100r + 100r on 70k 160.00 1.00
Never hinged 240.00
B19a A33 100r + 100r on 70k (R) 140.00 60.00
Never hinged 210.00
B20a A33 100r + 100r on 70k (Bl) 70.00 45.00
Never hinged 100.00
B21a A33 250r + 250r on 35k 70.00 —
Never hinged 100.00
B22a A33 250r + 250r on 35k (R) 200.00 45.00
Never hinged 290.00
B23a A33 250r + 250r on 35k (O) 225.00 100.00
Never hinged 340.00

Surcharge Double

B18b A33 100r + 100r on 70k *200.00* —
Never hinged 300.00
B19b A33 100r + 100r on 70k (R) *200.00* —
Never hinged 300.00
B21b A33 250r + 250r on 35k *200.00* —
Never hinged 300.00
B22b A33 250r + 250r on 35k (R) *200.00* —
Never hinged 300.00

Issued to raise funds for Volga famine relief.

Regular Issues of 1909-18 Overprinted

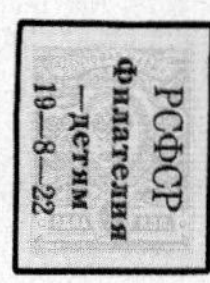

1922, Aug. 19 *Perf. 14*

B24 A14 1k orange 550.00 425.00
Never hinged 725.00
B25 A14 2k green 22.50 *22.50*
Never hinged 45.00
B26 A14 3k red 22.50 *22.50*
Never hinged 45.00
B27 A14 5k claret 22.50 *22.50*
Never hinged 45.00
B28 A15 10k dark blue 22.50 *22.50*
Never hinged 45.00

Imperf

B29 A14 1k orange 425.00 375.00
Never hinged 725.00
Nos. B24-B29 (6) 1,065. 890.00

Overprint Inverted (Reading Up)

B24a A14 1k orange 825.00
Never hinged 1,750.
B25a A14 2k green 325.00
Never hinged 500.00
B26a A14 3k red 825.00
Never hinged 1,750.
B27a A14 5k claret 825.00
Never hinged 1,750.
B28a A15 10k dark blue 825.00
Never hinged 1,900.
B29a A14 1k orange 825.00
Never hinged 1,750.

Double Overprint

B25b A14 2k green 600.00 900.00
Never hinged 500.00
B26b A14 3k red 1,450.
Never hinged 2,400.
B27b A14 5k claret 725.00
Never hinged 1,200.
B28b A15 10k dark blue 1,200.
Never hinged 1,750.
B29b A14 1k orange 2,400.
Never hinged 4,750.

The overprint means "Philately for the Children". The stamps were sold at five million times their face values and 80% of the amount was devoted to child welfare. The stamps were sold only at Moscow and for one day.

Nos. B24-B26 were reprinted ("second issue"). Values are for the second issue. The 1k from the first issue are worth about 3 times the values shown. Expertization is recommended to distinguish the two printings.

Worker and Peasant (Industry and Agriculture) — SP11

Allegory: Agriculture Will Help End Distress SP12

Star of Hope, Wheat and Worker-Peasant Handclasp — SP13

Sower — SP14

1922 Litho. *Imperf.*
Without Gum

B30 SP11 2t (2000r) green 15.00 *250.00*
B31 SP12 2t (2000r) rose 29.00 *125.00*
B32 SP13 4t (4000r) rose 42.50 *125.00*
B33 SP14 6t (6000r) green 22.50 *125.00*
Nos. B30-B33 (4) 109.00 625.00

Double Impression

B30a SP11 (2000r) green *475.00*
B31a SP12 (2000r) rose *650.00*
B32a SP13 (4000r) rose *725.00*
B33a SP14 (6000r) green *575.00*

Triple Impression

B30b SP11 (2000r) green *450.00*
B31b SP12 (2000r) rose *600.00*
B32b SP13 (4000r) rose *675.00*
B33b SP14 (6000r) green *500.00*

Nos. B30-B33 exist with double impression.

Counterfeits of Nos. B30-B33 exist; beware also of forged cancellations.

Miniature examples of Nos. B30-B33 exist, taken from the 1933 Soviet catalogue.

Automobile SP15

Steamship SP16

Railroad Train SP17

Airplane SP18

1922 *Imperf.*

B34 SP15 (20r+5r) light violet .40 .75
Never hinged .75
B35 SP16 (20r+5r) violet .50 .75
Never hinged 1.00
B36 SP17 (20r+5r) gray blue .40 .75
Never hinged .75
B37 SP18 (20r+5r) blue gray 2.25 *4.25*
Never hinged 4.75
Nos. B34-B37 (4) 3.55 *6.50*

Inscribed "For the Hungry." Each stamp was sold for 200,000r postage and 50,000r charity.

Counterfeits of Nos. B34-B37 exist.

Nos. 212, 183, 202 Surcharged in Bronze, Gold or Silver

1923 *Imperf.*

B38 A48 1r +1r on 10r 400.00 400.00
Never hinged 625.00
a. Inverted surcharge 1,250. 1,000.
Never hinged 2,000.
B39 A48 1r +1r on 10r (G) 40.00 25.00
Never hinged 75.00
a. Inverted surcharge 325.00 225.00
Never hinged 725.00
B40 A43 2r +2r on 250r 40.00 25.00
Never hinged 75.00
a. Pelure paper 40.00 25.00
Never hinged 75.00
b. Inverted surcharge 325.00 200.00
Never hinged 725.00
c. Double surcharge —

Wmk. 171

B41 A46 4r +4r on 5000r 40.00 25.00
Never hinged 75.00
a. Date spaced "1 923" 425.00 375.00
Never hinged 625.00
b. Inverted surcharge 1,150. 1,150.
Never hinged 1,600.
B42 A46 4r +4r on 5000r (S) 1,100. 850.00
Never hinged 1,800.
a. Inverted surcharge 4,750. 2,500.
Never hinged 11,500.
b. Date spaced "1 923" 2,500. 1,850.
Never hinged 3,750.
c. As "b," inverted surch. *22,500.* 8,000.
Never hinged 45,000.
Nos. B38-B42 (5) 1,620. 1,325.

The inscriptions mean "Philately's Contribution to Labor." The stamps were on sale only at Moscow and for one day. The surtax was for charitable purposes.

Counterfeits of No. B42 exist.

Leningrad Flood Issue

Nos. 181-182, 184-186 Surcharged

1924 Unwmk. *Imperf.*

B43 A40 3k + 10k on 100r 3.50 1.50
Never hinged 12.50
a. Pelure paper 2.50 4.00
Never hinged 3.75
b. Inverted surcharge 250.00 —
Never hinged 500.00
B44 A40 7k + 20k on 200r 3.75 1.50
Never hinged 6.00
a. Inverted surcharge 300.00 —
Never hinged 625.00
B45 A40 14k + 30k on 300r 3.75 2.25
Never hinged 6.25
a. Pelure paper 625.00 —

Never hinged 1,150.

Similar Surcharge in Red or Black

B46 A41 12k + 40k on 500r (R) 3.75 1.75
Never hinged 6.00
a. Double surcharge 1,600. —
Never hinged 3,000.
b. Inverted surcharge 1,550. —
Never hinged 2,750.
B47 A41 20k + 50k on 1000r 3.00 1.25
Never hinged 5.00
a. Thick paper 20.00 25.00
Never hinged 40.00
b. Pelure paper 10.00 10.00
Never hinged 25.00
c. Chalk surface paper 60.00 25.00
Never hinged 115.00
Nos. B43-B47 (5) 17.75 8.25

The surcharge on Nos. B43 to B45 reads: "S.S.S.R. For the sufferers by the inundation at Leningrad." That on Nos. B46 and B47 reads: "S.S.S.R. For the Leningrad Proletariat, 23, IX, 1924."

No. B46 is surcharged vertically, reading down, with the value as the top line.

Orphans
SP19

Lenin as a Child
SP20

1926 **Typo.** ***Perf. 13½***
B48 SP19 10k brown *14.50* *8.75*
Never hinged 30.00
B49 SP20 20k deep blue *60.00* *16.00*
Never hinged 115.00

Wmk. 170

B50 SP19 10k brown 3.00 1.50
Never hinged 5.00
B51 SP20 20k deep blue 7.50 3.50
Never hinged 18.50
Nos. B48-B51 (4) *85.00* *29.75*

Two kopecks of the price of each of these stamps was donated to organizations for the care of indigent children.

Types of 1926 Issue

1927
B52 SP19 8k + 2k yel green 1.75 .50
Never hinged 3.75
B53 SP20 18k + 2k deep rose 15.00 5.00
Never hinged 30.00

Surtax was for child welfare.

Industrial Training
SP21

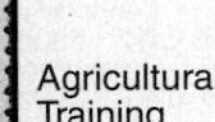

Agricultural Training
SP22

Perf. 10, 10½, 12½
1929-30 **Photo.** **Unwmk.**
B54 SP21 10k +2k ol brn & org brn 14.50 *3.00*
Never hinged 30.00
a. Perf. 10½ 200.00 *25.00*
Never hinged 350.00
B55 SP21 10k +2k ol grn ('30) 6.00 *1.50*
Never hinged 12.00
B56 SP22 20k +2k blk brn & bl, perf. 10½ 200.00 25.00
Never hinged 350.00
a. Perf. 12½ 125.00 37.50
Never hinged 225.00
b. Perf. 10 20.00 7.50
Never hinged 37.50
B57 SP22 20k +2k bl grn ('30) 8.50 *2.25*
Never hinged 17.50
Nos. B54-B57 (4) 229.00 31.75

Surtax was for child welfare.

AIR POST STAMPS

AP1

Plane Overprint in Red

1922 **Unwmk.** ***Imperf.***
C1 AP1 45r green & black 12.50 —
Never hinged 22.50
a. Translucent paper 85.00 —
Never hinged 200.00

5th anniversary of October Revolution.

No. C1 was on sale only at the Moscow General Post Office. Counterfeits exist.

Fokker F-111 — AP2

1923 **Photo.**
C2 AP2 1r red brown 14.50
Never hinged 29.00
C3 AP2 3r deep blue 14.50
Never hinged 29.00
C4 AP2 5r green 4.75
Never hinged 9.50
a. Wide "5" *40,000.*
C5 AP2 10r carmine 4.75
Never hinged 9.50
Nos. C2-C5 (4) 38.50

Nos. C2-C5 were not placed in use.

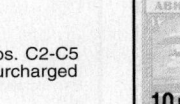

Nos. C2-C5 Surcharged

1924
C6 AP2 5k on 3r dp blue 8.25 3.75
Never hinged 14.50
C7 AP2 10k on 5r green 3.75 1.25
Never hinged 6.50
a. Wide "5" *1,250.* *700.00*
Never hinged 2,250.
b. Inverted surcharge *2,750.* —
C8 AP2 15k on 1r red brown 15.00 4.00
Never hinged 25.00
a. Inverted surcharge *1,400.* *500.00*
Never hinged *7,750.*
C9 AP2 20k on 10r car 3.75 1.00
Never hinged 6.50.
a. Inverted surcharge *4,000.* *2,500.*
Nos. C6-C9 (4) 30.75 10.00

Airplane over Map of World
AP3

1927, Sept. 1 **Litho.** ***Perf. 13x12***
C10 AP3 10k dk bl & yel brn 18.00 *7.50*
Never hinged 32.50
C11 AP3 15k dp red & ol grn 30.00 *10.00*
Never hinged 60.00

1st Intl. Air Post Cong. at The Hague, initiated by the USSR.

Graf Zeppelin and "Call to Complete 5-Year Plan in 4 Years" — AP4

1930 **Photo.** **Wmk. 226** ***Perf. 12½***
C12 AP4 40k dark blue 60.00 24.00
Never hinged 125.00
a. Perf. 10½ 72.50 24.00
Never hinged 145.00
b. Imperf. *1,650.* *1,325.*
Never hinged 2,850.
C13 AP4 80k carmine 60.00 24.00
Never hinged 125.00
a. Perf. 10½ 72.50 24.00
Never hinged 145.00
b. Imperf. *1,650.* *1,325.*
Never hinged 2,850.

Flight of the Graf Zeppelin from Friedrichshafen to Moscow and return.

Symbolical of Airship Communication from the Tundra to the Steppes — AP5

Airship over Dneprostroi Dam — AP6

Airship over Lenin Mausoleum — AP7

Airship Exploring Arctic Regions — AP8

Constructing an Airship
AP9

1931-32 **Wmk. 170** **Photo.** ***Imperf.***
C15 AP5 10k dark violet 40.00 30.00
Never hinged 75.00

Litho.

C16 AP6 15k gray blue 40.00 30.00
Never hinged 75.00

Typo.

C17 AP7 20k dk carmine 40.00 30.00
Never hinged 80.00

Photo.

C18 AP8 50k black brown 40.00 30.00
Never hinged 80.00
a. 50k gray blue (error) *85,000.*
Never hinged *125,000.*
C19 AP9 1r dark green 40.00 32.50
Never hinged 80.00
Nos. C15-C19 (5) 200.00 152.50

Perf. 12x12¼, 12¼x12½x12 (#C21, C23)

C20 AP5 10k dark violet 3.00 1.75
Never hinged 7.50

Litho.

C21 AP6 15k gray blue 120.00 19.00
Never hinged 225.00

Typo.

C22 AP7 20k dk carmine 3.00 1.75
Never hinged 7.50
a. 20k light red 3.00 —
Never hinged 7.50

Photo.

C23 AP8 50k black brown 14.50 4.00
Never hinged 27.50
a. 50k gray blue (error) 500.00 300.00
Never hinged *900.00*
C24 AP9 1r dark green 15.00 2.50
Never hinged 30.00

Perf. 12½
Unwmk. **Engr.**
C25 AP6 15k gray blk ('32) 6.00 1.25
Never hinged 12.00
a. Perf. 10½ *2,000.* *135.00*
Never hinged 8,000.
b. Perf. 14 17.50 22.50
Never hinged 85.00
c. Imperf. — *3,250.*
Nos. C20-C25 (6) 161.50 30.25

The 11½ perforation on Nos. C20-C25 is of private origin; beware also of bogus perforation "errors."

North Pole Issue

Graf Zeppelin and Icebreaker "Malygin" Transferring Mail — AP10

1931 **Wmk. 170** ***Imperf.***
C26 AP10 30k dark violet 35.00 *17.50*
Never hinged 65.00
C27 AP10 35k dark green 7.25 *4.25*
Never hinged 12.00
C28 AP10 1r gray black 48.00 *17.50*
Never hinged 95.00
C29 AP10 2r deep ultra 24.00 17.50
Never hinged 45.00
Nos. C26-C29 (4) 114.25 56.75

Perf. 12x12¼

C30 AP10 30k dark violet 45.00 *15.00*
Never hinged 80.00
C31 AP10 35k dark green 60.00 *12.50*
Never hinged 100.00
C32 AP10 1r gray black 105.00 *35.00*
Never hinged 210.00
C33 AP10 2r deep ultra 45.00 *15.00*
Never hinged 80.00
Nos. C30-C33 (4) 255.00 *77.50*

Perf. 12¼

C30a AP10 30k dark violet 40.00 17.50
Never hinged 70.00
C31a AP10 35k dark green 37.50 25.00
Never hinged 70.00
C32a AP10 1r gray black 60.00 60.00
Never hinged 120.00
C33a AP10 2r deep ultra 45.00 20.00
Never hinged 75.00

Map of Polar Region, Airplane and Icebreaker "Sibiryakov" — AP11

Perf. 12, 10½
1932, Aug. 26 **Wmk. 170**
C34 AP11 50k car rose 75.00 12.50
Never hinged 150.00
a. Perf. 10½ *30,000.* *14,000.*
Never hinged *46,500.*
b. Perf. 10½x12 *20,000.*
Never hinged *46,500.*
C35 AP11 1r green 37.50 22.50
Never hinged 75.00
a. Perf. 12 75.00 *37.50*
Never hinged 165.00

2nd International Polar Year in connection with proposed flight from Franz-Josef Land to Archangel which, being impossible, actually went from Archangel to Moscow to destinations.

Stratostat "U.S.S.R." — AP12

1933 **Photo.** ***Perf. 14***
C37 AP12 5k ultra 125.00 10.00
Never hinged 275.00
C38 AP12 10k carmine 27.50 10.00
Never hinged 75.00
C39 AP12 20k violet 11.50 9.50
Never hinged 22.50
Nos. C37-C39 (3) 164.00 29.50

Pairs, Imperf. Between

C37a Vert. pair, imperf. between *11,250.* —
Never hinged *17,500.*
C37b Horiz. pair, imperf. between *6,500.* *2,500.*
Never hinged *10,500.*
C38a Horiz. pair, imperf. between — *12,750.*

C38b	Vert, pair, imperf. between	*11,500.*	—
	Never hinged	*17,500.*	
C39a	Vert, pair, imperf. between	*11,500.*	—
	Never hinged	*17,500.*	

Ascent into the stratosphere by Soviet aeronauts, Sept. 30th, 1933.

Furnaces of Kuznetsk AP13

Designs: 10k, Oil wells. 20k, Collective farm. 50k, Map of Moscow-Volga Canal project. 80k, Arctic cargo ship.

1934, Feb. Wmk. 170 ***Perf. 14***

C40	AP13 5k ultra	27.50	6.00
	Never hinged	37.50	
C41	AP13 10k green	27.50	6.75
	Never hinged	37.50	
C42	AP13 20k carmine	60.00	7.50
	Never hinged	120.00	
C43	AP13 50k dull blue	175.00	35.00
	Never hinged	375.00	
C44	AP13 80k purple	60.00	9.00
	Never hinged	120.00	
	Nos. C40-C44 (5)	350.00	64.25

Unwmk.

C45	AP13 5k ultra	22.50	*4.00*
	Never hinged	37.50	
C46	AP13 10k green	22.50	*3.75*
	Never hinged	37.50	
a.	Horiz. pair, imperf. btwn.	2,000.	*1,250.*
	Never hinged	4,000.	
C47	AP13 20k carmine	30.00	*6.00*
	Never hinged	50.00	
C48	AP13 50k dull blue	160.00	*28.50*
	Never hinged	375.00	
C49	AP13 80k purple	18.00	*6.00*
	Never hinged	30.00	
	Nos. C45-C49 (5)	253.00	*48.25*

10th anniversary of Soviet civil aviation and airmail service. Counterfeits exist, perf 11½.

I. D. Usyskin AP18

10k, A. B. Vasenko. 20k, P. F. Fedosenko.

1934 Wmk. 170 ***Perf. 11***

C50	AP18 5k vio brown	17.50	6.00
	Never hinged	35.00	
C51	AP18 10k brown	115.00	6.00
	Never hinged	210.00	
C52	AP18 20k ultra	27.50	8.25
	Never hinged	50.00	
	Nos. C50-C52 (3)	160.00	20.25

Perf. 13¾

C50a	AP18 5k	135.	
	Never hinged	275.00	
C51a	AP18 10k	—	*4,500.*
C52a	AP18 20k	10,000.	
	Never hinged	*19,500.*	
	Nos. C50a-C52a (3)	10,135.	*4,500.*

Honoring victims of the stratosphere disaster. See Nos. C77-C79 in Scott Standard catalogue, Vol. 5.

Beware of examples of Nos. C50-C52 reperforated to resemble Nos. C50a-C52a.

Airship "Pravda" — AP19

Airship Landing — AP20

Airship "Voroshilov" — AP21

Sideview of Airship — AP22

Airship "Lenin" — AP23

1934 ***Perf. 14***

C53	AP19 5k red orange	25.00	*2.40*
	Never hinged	50.00	
C54	AP20 10k claret	27.50	*3.75*
	Never hinged	55.00	
C55	AP21 15k brown	75.00	*10.00*
	Never hinged	135.00	
C56	AP22 20k black	15.00	*7.50*
	Never hinged	30.00	
C57	AP23 30k ultra	375.00	*55.00*
	Never hinged	750.00	
	Nos. C53-C57 (5)	517.50	78.65

Capt. V. Voronin and "Chelyuskin" — AP24

Prof. Otto Y. Schmidt — AP25

A. V. Lapidevsky AP26

S. A. Levanevsky AP27

"Schmidt Camp" — AP28

Designs: 15k, M. G. Slepnev. 20k, I. V. Doronin. 25k, M. V. Vodopianov. 30k, V. S. Molokov. 40k, N. P. Kamanin.

1935 ***Perf. 14***

C58	AP24 1k red orange	12.50	2.25
	Never hinged	24.00	
C59	AP25 3k rose car	12.50	2.25
	Never hinged	24.00	
C60	AP26 5k emerald	7.50	2.25
	Never hinged	15.00	
C61	AP27 10k dark brown	17.50	2.25
	Never hinged	37.50	
C62	AP27 15k black	17.50	3.75
	Never hinged	37.50	
C63	AP27 20k deep claret	22.50	3.75
	Never hinged	47.50	
C64	AP27 25k indigo	120.00	17.50
	Never hinged	225.00	
C65	AP27 30k dull green	750.00	50.00
	Never hinged	1,500.	
C66	AP27 40k purple	22.00	12.00
	Never hinged	47.50	
C67	AP28 50k dark ultra	50.00	30.00
	Never hinged	100.00	
	Nos. C58-C67 (10)	1,032.	126.00

Aerial rescue of ice-breaker Chelyuskin crew and scientific expedition.

No. C61 Surcharged in Red

1935, Aug.

C68	AP27 1r on 10k dk brn	725.00	525.00
	Never hinged	1,275.	
a.	Inverted surcharge	*90,000.*	
	Never hinged	*150,000.*	
b.	Lower case Cyrillic "F"	1,500.	1,450.
	Never hinged	2,250.	
c.	As "b," inverted surcharge	*600,000.*	
	Never hinged	*800,000.*	

Moscow-San Francisco flight. Counterfeits exist.

Single-Engined Monoplane — AP34

Five-Engined Transport — AP35

20k, Twin-engined cabin plane. 30k, 4r-motored transport. 40k, Single-engined amphibian. 50k, Twin-motored transport. 80k, 8-motored transport.

1937 Unwmk. ***Perf. 12***

C69	AP34 10k yel brn & blk	3.00	1.00
	Never hinged	6.00	
a.	Imperf.		—
C70	AP34 20k gray grn & blk	3.00	1.00
	Never hinged	6.00	
C71	AP34 30k red brn & blk	3.00	1.00
	Never hinged	6.00	
C72	AP34 40k vio brn & blk	5.25	1.00
	Never hinged	9.00	
C73	AP34 50k dk vio & blk	16.50	2.00
	Never hinged	28.50	
C74	AP35 80k bl vio & brn	16.50	6.00
	Never hinged	28.50	
C75	AP35 1r blk, brn & buff	45.00	8.50
	Never hinged	90.00	
a.	Sheet of 4, imperf.	175.00	*215.00*
	Never hinged	450.00	

Vertical Pairs, Imperf. Between

C69b	AP34 10k yel brn & blk	—	*62.50*
C70a	AP34 20k gray grn & blk	*3,250.*	*3,250.*
	Never hinged	*5,000.*	
C71a	AP34 30k red brn & blk	—	*4,250.*
C72a	AP34 40k vio brn & blk	*3,250.*	*3,250.*
	Never hinged	*5,000.*	
C73a	AP34 50k dk vio & blk	—	*4,500.*
	Nos. C69-C75 (7)	92.25	20.50

Jubilee Aviation Exhib., Moscow, Nov. 15-20.

Vertical pairs, imperf. between, exist for No. C71, value $4,000; No. C72, value $5,750; No. C73, value $2,300.

Types of 1938 Regular Issue Overprinted in Various Colors

1939 ***Typo.***

C76	A282 10k red (C)	4.00	1.00
	Never hinged	6.50	
C76A	A285 30k blue (R)	6.75	1.00
	Never hinged	13.00	
C76B	A286 40k dl grn (Br)	8.25	1.20
	Never hinged	15.00	
C76C	A287 50k dl vio (R)	6.75	2.00
	Never hinged	13.00	
C76D	A289 1r brown (Bl)	12.50	2.50
	Never hinged	25.00	
a.	Double overprint		1,500.
	Nos. C76-C76D (5)	38.25	7.70

Soviet Aviation Day, Aug. 18, 1939.

AIR POST OFFICIAL STAMPS

Used on mail from Russian embassy in Berlin to Moscow. Surcharged on Consular Fee stamps. Currency: the German mark.

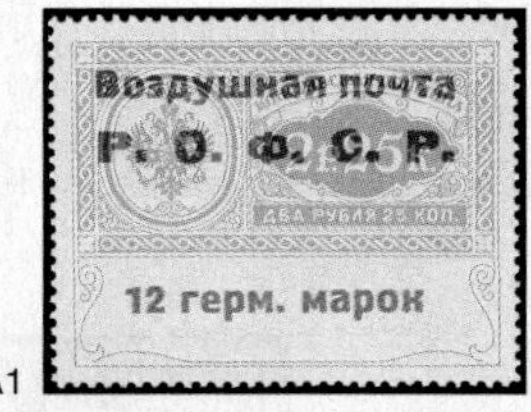

OA1

Surcharge in Carmine Bicolored Burelage

1922, July Litho. ***Perf. 13½***

CO1	OA1 12m on 2.25r	105.00	—
	Never hinged	180.00	
a.	Inverted surcharge	7,500.	—
CO2	OA1 24m on 3r	130.00	—
	Never hinged	260.00	
a.	Inverted surcharge	7,500.	—
CO3	OA1 120m on 2.25r	195.00	—
	Never hinged	310.00	
CO4	OA1 600m on 3r	260.00	—
	Never hinged	440.00	
CO5	OA1 1200m on 10k	725.00	—
	Never hinged	1,150.	
CO6	OA1 1200m on 50k	*37,500.*	—
	Never hinged	*60,000.*	
CO7	OA1 1200m on 2.25r	1,300.	—
	Never hinged	1,775.	
CO8	OA1 1200m on 3r	2,250.	—
	Never hinged	3,500.	

Three types of each denomination, distinguished by shape of "C" in surcharge and length of second line of surcharge. Used stamps have pen or crayon cancel. Forgeries exist.

SPECIAL DELIVERY STAMPS

Motorcycle Courier — SD1

Express Truck — SD2

Design: 80k, Locomotive.

Perf. 12½x12, 12x12½

1932 Photo. Wmk. 170

E1 SD1 5k dull brown 7.25 3.00
Never hinged 17.50
E2 SD2 10k violet brown 28.50 10.00
Never hinged 95.00
E3 SD2 80k dull green 60.00 8.50
Never hinged 225.00
Nos. E1-E3 (3) 95.75 21.50

Used values are for c-t-o.

POSTAGE DUE STAMPS

Regular Issue of 1918 Surcharged in Red or Carmine

1924-25 Unwmk. *Perf. 13½*

J1 A33 1k on 35k blue 2.00 *.50*
Never hinged 2.50
J2 A33 3k on 35k blue 2.00 *.50*
Never hinged 2.50
J3 A33 5k on 35k blue 2.00 *.50*
Never hinged 2.50
a. Imperf. *450.00*
J4 A33 8k on 35k blue ('25) 2.00 *.50*
Never hinged 3.50
a. Imperf. *450.00*
J5 A33 10k on 35k blue 2.00 *.50*
Never hinged 2.50
a. Pair, one without surcharge *550.00*
J6 A33 12k on 70k brown 2.00 *.50*
Never hinged 2.50
J7 A33 14k on 35k blue ('25) 2.00 *.50*
Never hinged 2.50
a. Imperf. *450.00*
J8 A33 32k on 35k blue 2.50 *.50*
Never hinged 3.50
J9 A33 40k on 35k blue 2.50 *.50*
Never hinged 3.50
a. Imperf. *450.00*
c. Pair, one without surcharge *675.00*
Nos. J1-J9 (9) 19.00 *4.50*

Inverted Surcharge

J1b A33 1k on 35k blue *150.00* —
Never hinged 200.00
J2b A33 3k on 35k blue *150.00* —
Never hinged 200.00
J3b A33 5k on 35k blue *150.00* —
Never hinged 200.00
J4b A33 8k on 35k blue *150.00* —
Never hinged 200.00
J6b A33 12k on 70k brown *200.00* —
Never hinged 250.00
J7b A33 14k on 35k brown *150.00* —
Never hinged 200.00
J8b A33 32k on 35k brown *150.00* —
Never hinged 200.00
J9b A33 40k on 35k brown *175.00* —
Never hinged 225.00

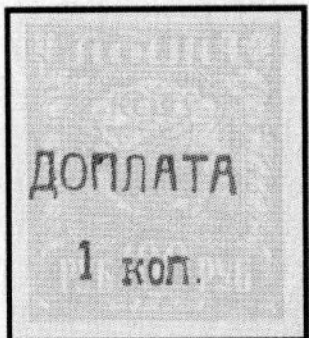

Regular Issue of 1921 Surcharged in Violet

1924 *Imperf.*

J10 A40 1k on 100r orange 6.75 *8.00*
Never hinged 9.00
a. 1k on 100r yellow 8.75 *8.00*
Never hinged 10.00
b. Pelure paper 6.75 *8.00*
Never hinged 10.00
c. Inverted surcharge *225.00*

D1

Lithographed or Typographed

1925 *Perf. 12*

J11 D1 1k red 2.00 .75
Never hinged 4.00
J12 D1 2k violet 2.00 .75
Never hinged 4.00
J13 D1 3k light blue 2.00 .75
Never hinged 4.00
J14 D1 7k orange 2.00 .75
Never hinged 4.00
J15 D1 8k green 2.00 .75
Never hinged 4.00
J16 D1 10k dark blue 2.00 .75
Never hinged 5.50
J17 D1 14k brown 2.00 .75
Never hinged 14.00
Nos. J11-J17 (7) 14.00 5.25

Perf. 14½x14

J13a D1 3k 12.50 1.00
Never hinged 19.00
J14a D1 7k 20.00 1.00
Never hinged 35.00
J16a D1 10k — —
Never hinged *10,000.*
J17a D1 14k 5.00 1.00
Never hinged 8.50
Nos. J13a-J17a (4) 37.50 3.00

Value of No. J16a unused is based on 2012 auction realization.

1925 Wmk. 170 Typo. *Perf. 12*

J18 D1 1k red 1.60 .40
Never hinged 3.50
J19 D1 2k violet 1.75 .40
Never hinged 3.50
J20 D1 3k light blue 1.75 .40
Never hinged 3.50
J21 D1 7k orange 1.75 .40
Never hinged 3.50
J22 D1 8k green 1.75 .40
Never hinged 3.50
J23 D1 10k dark blue 1.75 .40
Never hinged 3.50
J24 D1 14k brown 1.75 .40
Never hinged 3.50
Nos. J18-J24 (7) 12.10 2.80

For surcharges see Nos. 359-372.

WENDEN (LIVONIA)

A former district of Livonia, a province of the Russian Empire, which became part of Latvia, under the name of Vidzeme.

Used values for Nos. L2-L12 are for pen-canceled stamps. Postmarked examples sell for considerably more.

A1

1862 Unwmk. *Imperf.*

L1 A1 (2k) blue 30.00
a. Tête bêche pair *350.00*

No. L1 may have been used for a short period of time but withdrawn because of small size. Some consider it an essay.

A2

A3

1863

L2 A2 (2k) rose & black 240.00 240.00
a. Background inverted 600.00 600.00
L3 A3 (4k) blue grn & blk 175.00 250.00
a. (4k) yellow green & black 300.00 300.00
b. Half used as 2k on cover *2,500.*
c. Background inverted 950.00 500.00
d. As "a," background inverted 650.00 400.00

The official imitations of Nos. L2 and L3 have a single instead of a double hyphen after "WENDEN." Value, each $20.

Coat of Arms
A4 A5 A6

1863-71

L4 A4 (2k) rose & green 90.00 90.00
a. Yellowish paper
b. Green frame around central oval 95.00 60.00
c. Tête bêche pair *2,500.*
L5 A5 (2k) rose & grn ('64) 100.00 75.00
L6 A6 (2k) rose & green 75.00 75.00
Nos. L4-L6 (3) 265.00 240.00

Official imitations of Nos. L4b and L5 have a rose instead of a green line around the central oval. The first official imitation of No. L6 has the central oval 5½mm instead of 6¼mm wide; the second imitation is less clearly printed than the original and the top of the "f" of "Briefmarke" is too much hooked. Value, each $20.

Coat of Arms
A7 A8

1872-75 *Perf. 12½*

L7 A7 (2k) red & green 75.00 *75.00*
L8 A8 2k yel grn & red ('75) 8.50 *11.00*
a. Numeral in upper right corner resembles an inverted "3" 30.00 *30.00*

Reprints of No. L8 have no horizontal lines in the background. Those of No. L8a have the impression blurred and only traces of the horizontal lines.

A9

1878-80

L9 A9 2k green & red 8.50 *10.00*
a. Imperf.
L10 A9 2k blk, grn & red ('80) 10.00 10.00
a. Imperf., pair 35.00

No. L9 has been reprinted in blue green and yellow green with perforation 11½ and in gray green with perforation 12½ or imperforate.

1884 *Perf. 11½*

L11 A9 2k black, green & red 10.00 3.00
a. Green arm omitted 21.00
b. Arm inverted 21.00
c. Arm double 27.50
d. Imperf., pair 150.00

Wenden Castle — A10

1901 Litho.

L12 A10 2k dk green & brown 12.00 10.00
a. Tête bêche pair 45.00
b. Imperf., pair 120.00

OCCUPATION STAMPS

ISSUED UNDER GERMAN OCCUPATION

German Stamps Overprinted in Black

On Stamps of 1905-17

1916-17 Wmk. 125 *Perf. 14, 14½*

N1 A22 2½pf gray .65 *1.00*
N2 A16 3pf brown .25 .25
N3 A16 5pf green .65 *1.00*
N4 A22 7½pf orange .65 *1.00*
N5 A16 10pf carmine .65 *1.00*
N6 A22 15pf yel brn 3.00 2.00
N7 A22 15pf dk vio ('17) .65 *1.00*
N8 A16 20pf ultra 1.00 1.00
N9 A16 25pf org & blk, *yel* .50 *.50*
N10 A16 40pf lake & blk 1.00 *3.75*
N11 A16 50pf vio & blk, *buff* 1.00 *1.50*
N12 A17 1m car rose 12.00 3.50
Nos. 1N1-1N12 (12) 22.00 *17.50*
Set, never hinged 40.00

These stamps were used in the former Russian provinces of Suvalki, Vilnius, Kaunas, Kurland, Estland and Lifland.

ISSUED UNDER FINNISH OCCUPATION

Finnish Stamps of 1917-18 Overprinted

1919 Unwmk. *Perf. 14*

N13 A19 5p green 12.50 15.00
N14 A19 10p rose 12.50 15.00
N15 A19 20p buff 12.50 15.00
N16 A19 40p red violet 12.50 15.00
N17 A19 50p orange brn 150.00 150.00
N18 A19 1m dl rose & blk 140.00 140.00
N19 A19 5m violet & blk 425.00 425.00
N20 A19 10m brown & blk 725.00 725.00
Nos. N13-N20 (8) 1,490. 1,500.
Set, never hinged 3,000.

"Aunus" is the Finnish name for Olonets, a town of Russia.

Counterfeits overprints exist.

ARMY OF THE NORTHWEST

(Gen. Nicolai N. Yudenich)

Russian Stamps of 1909-18 Overprinted in Black or Red

On Stamps of 1909-12

Perf. 14 to 15 and Compound

1919, Aug. 1

1 A14 2k green 5.00 *10.00*
2 A14 5k claret 5.00 *10.00*
3 A15 10k dk blue (R) 10.00 *15.00*
4 A11 15k red brn & bl 5.00 *8.00*
5 A8 20k blue & car 8.00 *15.00*
6 A11 25k grn & gray vio 15.00 *20.00*
7 A8 50k brn vio & grn 10.00 *15.00*

Perf. 13½

8 A9 1r pale brn, dk brn & org 25.00 *50.00*
9 A13 10r scar, yel & gray 75.00 *125.00*

On Stamps of 1917

Imperf

10 A14 3k red 5.00 *10.00*
11 A12 3.50r mar & lt grn 17.50 *35.00*
12 A13 5r dk blue, grn & pale bl 17.50 *30.00*
13 A12 7r dk grn & pink 150.00 *200.00*

No. 2 Surcharged

Perf. 14, 14½x15

14 A14 10k on 5k claret 12.00 *24.00*
Nos. 1-14 (14) 360.00 *567.00*

Nos. 1-14 exist with inverted overprint or surcharge. The 1, 3½, 5, 7 and 10 rubles with red overprint are trial printings (value $150 each). The 20k on 14k, perforated, and the 1, 2, 5, 15, 70k and 1r imperforate were overprinted but never placed in use. Value: $300, $30, $45, $45, $45 and $65.

These stamps were in use from Aug. 1 to Oct. 15, 1919.

Counterfeits of Nos. 1-14 abound.

ARMY OF THE NORTH

A1

A2

A3

A4

A5

1919, Sept. Typo. *Imperf.*

1 A1 5k brown violet .60 *1.00*
2 A2 10k blue .60 *1.00*
3 A3 15k yellow .60 *1.00*
4 A4 20k rose .60 *1.00*
5 A5 50k green .60 *1.00*
Nos. 1-5 (5) 3.00 *5.00*

The letters OKCA are the initials of Russian words meaning "Special Corps, Army of the North." The stamps were in use from about the end of September to the end of December, 1919.

Used values are for c-t-o stamps.

(General Miller)

A set of seven stamps of this design was prepared in 1919, but not issued. Value, set $35. Counterfeits exist.

RUSSIA OFFICES ABROAD

For various reasons the Russian Empire maintained Post Offices to handle its correspondence in several foreign countries. These were similar to the Post Offices in foreign countries maintained by other world powers.

OFFICES IN CHINA

100 Kopecks = 1 Ruble
100 Cents = 1 Dollar (1917)

Russian Stamps Overprinted in Blue or Red

On Issues of 1889-92
Horizontally Laid Paper

1899-1904 Wmk. 168 *Perf. 14½x15*

1 A10 1k orange (Bl) .75 *1.00*
2 A10 2k yel green (R) .75 *1.00*
3 A10 3k carmine (Bl) .75 *1.00*
4 A10 5k red violet (Bl) .75 *1.00*
5 A10 7k dk blue (R) 1.50 *2.50*
a. Inverted overprint *500.00*
6 A8 10k dk blue (R) 1.50 *2.50*
7 A8 50k vio & grn (Bl) ('04) 12.00 *8.50*

Perf. 13½

8 A9 1r lt brn, brn & org (Bl) ('04) 150.00 150.00
Nos. 1-8 (8) 168.00 167.50

On Issues of 1902-05
Overprinted in Black, Red or Blue
Perf. 14½ to 15 and Compound

1904-08 Vertically Laid Paper

9 A8 4k rose red (Bl) 6.00 *3.50*
10 A10 7k dk blue (R) 15.00 15.00
11 A8 10k dk blue (R) 1,500. 1,300.
a. Groundwork inverted *14,500.*
12 A11 14k bl & rose (R) 10.00 10.00
13 A11 15k brn vio & blue (Bl) ('08) 35.00 *30.00*
14 A8 20k blue & car (Bl) 5.00 5.00
15 A11 25k dull grn & lil (R) ('08) 50.00 50.00
16 A11 35k dk vio & grn (R) 10.00 10.00
17 A8 50k vio & grn (Bl) 100.00 125.00
18 A11 70k brn & org (Bl) 15.00 13.00

Perf. 13½

19 A9 1r lt brn, brn & org (Bl) 25.00 25.00
20 A12 3.50r blk & gray (R) 5.00 *5.00*
21 A13 5r dk bl, grn & pale bl (R) ('07) 8.50 *12.00*
a. Inverted overprint *2,500.*
22 A12 7r blk & yel (Bl) 25.00 12.00
23 A13 10r scar, yel & gray (Bl) ('07) 100.00 *100.00*
Nos. 9-10,12-23 (14) 409.50 415.50

On Issues of 1909-12
Wove Paper
Lozenges of Varnish on Face

1910-16 Unwmk. *Perf. 14x14½*

24 A14 1k orange yel (Bl) .50 .50
25 A14 1k org yel (Bl Bk) 6.00 5.00
26 A14 2k green (Bk) 1.00 1.00
27 A14 2k green (Bl) 7.50 *15.00*
a. Double ovpt. (Bk and Bl)
28 A14 3k rose red (Bl) 2.00 *5.00*
29 A14 3k rose red (Bk) 12.00 12.00
30 A15 4k carmine (Bl) 1.00 2.00
31 A15 4k carmine (Bk) 10.00 10.00
32 A14 7k lt blue (Bk) 1.00 *1.00*
33 A15 10k blue (Bk) 1.00 1.00
34 A11 14k blue & rose (Bk) 10.00 5.00
35 A11 14k blue & rose (Bl)
36 A11 15k dl vio & bl (Bk) 1.00 *1.25*
37 A8 20k blue & car (Bk) *5.00* *7.00*
38 A11 25k green & vio (Bl) 3.50 *6.00*
39 A11 25k grn & vio (Bk) 1.00 *1.60*
40 A11 35k vio & grn (Bk) 1.00 1.00
42 A8 50k vio & grn (Bl) 2.00 *2.00*
43 A8 50k brn vio & grn (Bk) 18.00 *20.00*
44 A11 70k lt brn & org (Bl) 1.00 *2.00*

Perf. 13½

45 A9 1r pale brn, brn & org (Bl) 1.25 *2.40*
47 A13 5r dk bl, grn & pale bl (R) 25.00 15.00
Nos. 24-34,36-47 (21) 110.75 115.75

The existence of #35 is questioned.

Russian Stamps of 1902-12 Surcharged

a

b

c

On Stamps of 1909-12

1917 *Perf. 11½, 13½, 14, 14½x15*

50 A14(a) 1c on 1k dl org yel .60 *5.50*
51 A14(a) 2c on 2k dull grn .60 *5.50*
a. Inverted surcharge 100.00
52 A14(a) 3c on 3k car .60 *5.50*
a. Inverted surcharge 100.00
b. Double surcharge 150.00
53 A15(a) 4c on 4k car 1.25 *4.25*
54 A14(a) 5c on 5k claret 1.25 *15.00*
55 A15(b) 10c on 10k dk blue 1.25 *15.00*
a. Inverted surcharge 100.00 100.00
b. Double surcharge 115.00
56 A11(b) 14c on 14k dk blue & car 1.25 *10.00*
a. Imperf. 6.00
b. Inverted surcharge 100.00
57 A11(a) 15c on 15k brn lil & dp blue 1.25 *15.00*
a. Inverted surcharge 50.00
58 A8(b) 20c on 20k bl & car 1.25 *15.00*
59 A11(a) 25c on 25k grn & vio 1.25 *15.00*
60 A11(a) 35c on 35k brn vio & grn 1.50 *15.00*
a. Inverted surcharge 50.00
61 A8(a) 50c on 50k brn vio & grn 1.25 *15.00*
62 A11(a) 70c on 70k brn & red org 1.25 *15.00*
63 A9(c) $1 on 1r pale brn, brn & org 1.25 *15.00*
Nos. 50-63 (14) 15.80

On Stamps of 1902-05
Vertically Laid Paper
Perf. 11½, 13, 13½, 13½x11½
Wmk. Wavy Lines (168)

64 A12 $3.50 on 3.50r blk & gray 20.00 *40.00*
65 A13 $5 on 5r dk bl, grn & pale blue 20.00 *40.00*
66 A12 $7 on 7r blk & yel 10.00 *32.50*

On Stamps of 1915
Wove Paper

Unwmk. *Perf. 13½*

68 A13 $5 on 5r ind, grn & lt blue 25.00 *50.00*
a. Inverted surcharge 500.00
70 A13 $10 on 10r car lake, yel & gray 50.00 *100.00*
Nos. 64-70 (5) 125.00 262.50

The surcharge on Nos. 64-70 is in larger type than on the $1.

Russian Stamps of 1909-18 Surcharged in Black or Red

On Stamps of 1909-12

1920 *Perf. 14, 14½x15*

72 A14 1c on 1k dull org yel 175.00 *275.00*
73 A14 2c on 2k dull grn (R) 16.00 *27.50*
74 A14 3c on 3k car 16.00 *37.50*
75 A15 4c on 4k car 18.00 22.50
a. Inverted surcharge 130.00 150.00
76 A14 5c on 5k claret 60.00 90.00
77 A15 10c on 10k dk bl (R) 150.00 225.00
78 A14 10c on 10k on 7k blue (R) 125.00 190.00

On Stamps of 1917-18
Imperf

79 A14 1c on 1k orange 42.50 37.50
a. Inverted surcharge 125.00 *150.00*
80 A14 5c on 5k claret 35.00 55.00
a. Inverted surcharge 150.00
b. Double surcharge 250.00
c. Surcharged "Cent" only 95.00
Nos. 72-80 (9) 637.50 960.00

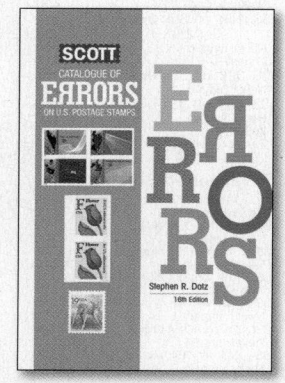

OFFICES IN THE TURKISH EMPIRE

Various powers maintained post offices in the Turkish Empire before World War I by authority of treaties which ended with the signing of the Treaty of Lausanne in 1923. The foreign post offices were closed Oct. 27, 1923.

100 Kopecks = 1 Ruble
40 Paras = 1 Piaster (1900)

The editors recommend that the stamps of Russian Offices in the Turkish Empire, 1863-1879, be purchased accompanied by certificates of authenticity.

Coat of Arms
A1

1863 Unwmk. Typo. *Imperf.*

1 A1 6k blue 325.00 *3,000.*
- *a.* 6k light blue, thin paper 350.00 *1,350.*
- *b.* 6k light blue, medium paper 325.00 *3,000.*
- *c.* 6k dark blue, chalky paper ('66) 165.00 —

Values are for stamps without faults. Most stamps from this set have faults. Forgeries exist.
No. 1c was unissued.

A2

A3

1865 Litho.

2 A2 (2k) brown & blue 800.00 750.00
3 A3 (20k) blue & red 900.00 850.00

Twenty-eight varieties of each.

A4

A5

1866 Horizontal Network

4 A4 (2k) rose & pale bl 25.00 *30.00*
- *a.* (2k) pale rose & blue 50.00 *75.00*

5 A5 (20k) deep blue & rose 40.00 *50.00*
- *a.* (20k) pale blue & rose 67.50 *70.00*

1867 Vertical Network

6 A4 (2k) rose & pale bl 75.00 *100.00*
- *a.* (2k) pale rose & deep blue 80.00 *95.00*

7 A5 (20k) dp blue & rose 200.00 *100.00*

The initials inscribed on Nos. 2 to 7 are those of the Russian Company of Navigation and Trade.

The official imitations of Nos. 2 to 7 are on yellowish white paper. The colors are usually paler than those of the originals and there are minor differences in the designs.

A6

Horizontally Laid Paper

1868 Typo. Wmk. 168 *Perf. 11½*

8 A6 1k brown 50.00 20.00
9 A6 3k green 60.00 25.00
10 A6 5k blue 60.00 25.00
11 A6 10k car & green 75.00 25.00
Nos. 8-11 (4) 245.00 95.00

Colors of Nos. 8-11 dissolve in water.

1872-90 *Perf. 14½x15*

12 A6 1k brown 10.00 2.00
13 A6 3k green 25.00 3.00
14 A6 5k blue 5.00 1.00
15 A6 10k pale red & grn ('90) 1.25 .60
- *b.* 10k carmine & green 24.00 3.75

Nos. 12-15 (4) 41.25 6.60

Vertically Laid Paper

12a A6 1k 75.00 18.00
13a A6 3k 75.00 18.00
14a A6 5k 75.00 18.00
15a A6 10k 190.00 47.50
Nos. 12a-15a (4) 415.00 101.50

Nos. 12-15 exist imperf.

No. 15 Surcharged in Black or Blue

a

b

c

1876

16 A6(a) 8k on 10k (Bk) 75.00 45.00
- *a.* Vertically laid *2,750.*
- *b.* Inverted surcharge 400.00

17 A6(a) 8k on 10k (Bl) 90.00 75.00
- *a.* Vertically laid
- *b.* Inverted surcharge

1879

18 A6(b) 7k on 10k (Bk) 80.00 65.00
- *a.* Vertically laid 750.00 750.00
- *b.* Inverted surcharge

19 A6(b) 7k on 10k (Bl) 125.00 85.00
- *a.* Vertically laid 1,750. 1,750.
- *b.* Inverted surcharge 500.00

19C A6(c) 7k on 10k (Bl) 1,250. 1,250.
19D A6(c) 7k on 10k (Bk) 1,250. 1,250.

Nos. 16-19D have been extensively counterfeited.

1879 *Perf. 14½x15*

20 A6 1k black & yellow 3.00 1.00
- *a.* Vertically laid 10.00 5.00

21 A6 2k black & rose 5.00 3.00
- *a.* Vertically laid 10.00 5.00

22 A6 7k carmine & gray 9.00 1.00
- *a.* Vertically laid 42.50 15.00

Nos. 20-22 (3) 17.00 5.00

1884

23 A6 1k orange .75 .50
24 A6 2k green 1.00 .75
25 A6 5k pale red violet 4.00 2.00
26 A6 7k blue 2.00 1.50
Nos. 23-26 (4) 7.75 4.75

Nos. 23-26 imperforate are believed to be proofs.

No. 23 surcharged "40 PARAS" is bogus, though some examples were postally used.

Russian Company of Navigation and Trade

This overprint, in two sizes, was privately applied in various colors to Russian Offices in the Turkish Empire stamps of 1900-1910.

A7

A8

Surcharged in Blue, Black or Red

1900 Horizontally Laid Paper

27 A7 4pa on 1k orange (Bl) 1.25 1.25
- *a.* Inverted surcharge 30.00 30.00

28 A7 4pa on 1k orange (Bk) 1.25 1.25
- *a.* Inverted surcharge 30.00 30.00

29 A7 10pa on 2k green .25 .25
- *a.* Inverted surcharge

30 A8 1pi on 10k dk blue .50 .60
- *a.* Inverted surcharge

Nos. 27-30 (4) 3.25 3.35

A9

A10

A11

1903-05 Vertically Laid Paper

31 A7 10pa on 2k yel green .60 *.40*
- *a.* Inverted surcharge 75.00

32 A8 20pa on 4k rose red (Bl) .60 *.40*
- *a.* Inverted surcharge 95.00

33 A8 1pi on 10k dk blue .60 *.40*
- *a.* Groundwork inverted 50.00 *15.00*

34 A8 2pi on 20k blue & car (Bk) 1.40 *.75*
35 A8 5pi on 50k brn vio & grn 3.50 *1.25*
36 A9 7pi on 70k brn & org (Bl) 4.00 *2.00*

Perf. 13½

37 A10 10pi on 1r lt brn, brn & org (Bl) 6.50 *4.00*
38 A11 35pi on 3.50r blk & gray 20.00 *10.00*
39 A11 70pi on 7r blk & yel 24.00 *12.50*
Nos. 31-39 (9) 61.20 31.70

A12

A13

A14

Wove Paper
Lozenges of Varnish on Face

1909 Unwmk. *Perf. 14½x15*

40 A12 5pa on 1k orange .30 *.40*
41 A12 10pa on 2k green .35 *.65*
- *a.* Inverted surcharge 30.00 *30.00*

42 A12 20pa on 4k carmine .70 *1.00*
43 A12 1pi on 10k blue .75 *1.20*
44 A12 5pi on 50k vio & grn 1.40 *1.60*
45 A12 7pi on 70k brn & org 2.00 *2.75*

Perf. 13½

46 A13 10pi on 1r brn & org 3.00 *5.00*
47 A14 35pi on 3.50r mar & lt grn 12.00 *14.00*
48 A14 70pi on 7r dk grn & pink 20.00 *25.00*
Nos. 40-48 (9) 40.50 *51.60*

50th anniv. of the establishing of the Russian Post Offices in the Levant.

Nos. 40-48 Overprinted with Names of Various Cities Overprinted "Constantinople" in Black

1909-10 *Perf. 14½x15*

61 A12 5pa on 1k .40 *.40*
- *c.* Inverted overprint 50.00

62 A12 10pa on 2k .40 *.40*
- *c.* Inverted overprint 30.00

63 A12 20pa on 4k .75 *.75*
- *c.* Inverted overprint 30.00

64 A12 1pi on 10k .75 *.75*
65 A12 5pi on 50k 1.50 *1.50*
66 A12 7pi on 70k 3.00 *3.00*

Perf. 13½

67 A13 10pi on 1r 15.00 *15.00*
- *a.* "Constanttnople" 100.00 100.00

68 A14 35pi on 3.50r 50.00 *30.00*
- *c.* "Constautinople" 100.00 100.00
- *d.* "Constantjnople" 100.00 100.00

69 A14 70pi on 7r 45.00 *42.50*
- *c.* "Constautinople" 100.00 100.00
- *d.* "Constantjnople" 100.00 100.00

Blue Overprint
Perf. 14½x15

70 A12 5pa on 1k 8.00 *8.00*
Nos. 61-70 (10) 124.80 *102.30*

"Consnantinople"

61a A12 5pa on 1k 10.00
62a A12 10pa on 2k 10.00
63a A12 20pa on 4k 10.00
64a A12 1pi on 10k 10.00
65a A12 5pi on 50k 10.00
66a A12 7pi on 70k 12.00
68a A14 35pi on 3.50r 50.00
69a A14 70pi on 7r 90.00
70a A12 5pa on 1k 10.00
Nos. 61a-70a (9) 212.00

"Constantinopie"

61b A12 5pa on 1k 25.00
- *d.* Inverted overprint 50.00

62b A12 10pa on 2k 25.00
- *d.* Inverted overprint 50.00

63b A12 20pa on 4k 30.00
- *d.* Inverted overprint 60.00

64b A12 1pi on 10k 30.00
65b A12 5pi on 50k 30.00
66b A12 7pi on 70k 30.00
68b A14 35pi on 3.50r 60.00
69b A14 70pi on 7r 90.00
Nos. 61b-69b (8) 320.00

Overprinted "Jaffa"
Black Overprint

71 A12 5pa on 1k 2.10 *3.75*
- *a.* Inverted overprint 75.00

72 A12 10pa on 2k 2.50 *4.00*
- *a.* Inverted overprint 50.00

73 A12 20pa on 4k 3.00 *5.25*
- *a.* Inverted overprint 60.00

74 A12 1pi on 10k 3.75 *5.25*
- *a.* Double overprint 95.00

75 A12 5pi on 50k 9.00 *10.50*
76 A12 7pi on 70k 11.00 *14.00*

Perf. 13½

77 A13 10pi on 1r 50.00 50.00
78 A14 35pi on 3.50r 100.00 100.00
79 A14 70pi on 7r 125.00 *150.00*

Blue Overprint
Perf. 14½x15

80 A12 5pa on 1k 12.00 12.00
Nos. 71-80 (10) 318.35 *354.75*

Overprinted "Ierusalem" in Black
Black Overprint

81 A12 5pa on 1k 2.10 *2.75*
- *a.* Inverted overprint 60.00
- *b.* "erusalem" 25.00
- *c.* As "b," overprint inverted 50.00

82 A12 10pa on 2k 2.75 *4.25*
- *a.* Inverted overprint 30.00
- *b.* "erusalem" 25.00
- *c.* As "b," overprint inverted 50.00

83 A12 20pa on 4k 4.25 *5.50*
- *a.* Inverted overprint 30.00
- *b.* "erusalem" 25.00
- *c.* As "b," overprint inverted 50.00

84 A12 1pi on 10k 4.25 *5.50*
- *a.* "erusalem" 30.00

85 A12 5pi on 50k 7.25 *11.00*
- *a.* "erusalem" 35.00

86 A12 7pi on 70k 14.00 *17.50*
- *a.* "erusalem" 35.00

Perf. 13½

87 A13 10pi on 1r 50.00 *50.00*
88 A14 35pi on 3.50r 125.00 125.00
89 A14 70pi on 7r 125.00 *150.00*

Blue Overprint
Perf. 14½x15

90 A12 5pa on 1k 15.00 25.00
Nos. 81-90 (10) 349.60 *396.50*

Overprinted "Kerassunde"
Black Overprint

91 A12 5pa on 1k .60 *.80*
- *a.* Inverted overprint 50.00

92 A12 10pa on 2k .60 *.80*
- *a.* Inverted overprint 50.00

93 A12 20pa on 4k 1.00 *1.10*
a. Inverted overprint 50.00
94 A12 1pi on 10k 1.25 *1.25*
95 A12 5pi on 50k 2.25 *2.50*
96 A12 7pi on 70k 3.50 *4.00*

Perf. 13½

97 A13 10pi on 1r 13.00 *15.00*
98 A14 35pi on 3.50r 42.50 *42.50*
99 A14 70pi on 7r 65.00 *52.50*

Blue Overprint

Perf. 14½x15

100 A12 5pa on 1k 15.00 *15.00*
Nos. 91-100 (10) 144.70 *135.45*

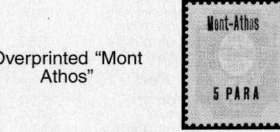

Overprinted "Mont Athos"

Black Overprint

101 A12 5pa on 1k 1.00 *1.50*
b. Inverted overprint 50.00
102 A12 10pa on 2k 1.00 *1.50*
b. Inverted overprint 50.00
103 A12 20pa on 4k 1.50 *3.00*
b. Inverted overprint 50.00
104 A12 1pi on 10k 2.00 *4.00*
b. Double overprint 60.00
105 A12 5pi on 50k 6.50 *7.00*
106 A12 7pi on 70k 8.00 *8.00*
b. Pair, one without "Mont Athos" 60.00

Perf. 13½

107 A13 10pi on 1r 30.00 *35.00*
108 A14 35pi on 3.50r 70.00 *80.00*
109 A14 70pi on 7r 130.00 *145.00*

Blue Overprint

Perf. 14½x15

110 A12 5pa on 1k 10.00 *15.00*
Nos. 101-110 (10) 260.00 *300.00*

"Mont Atho"

101a A12 5pa on 1k 25.00
102a A12 10pa on 2k 25.00
103a A12 20pa on 4k 25.00
c. Inverted overprint 100.00
104a A12 1pi on 10k 25.00
c. As "a," double overprint 125.00
105a A12 5pi on 50k 25.00
106a A12 7pi on 70k 25.00
110a A12 5pa on 1k 35.00

"M nt Athos"

101d A12 5pa on 1k 25.00
102d A12 10pa on 2k 25.00
103d A12 20pa on 4k 25.00
105d A12 5pi on 50k 50.00
106d A12 7pi on 70k 75.00

Overprinted

111 A12 5pa on 1k 1.50 *2.00*
a. Pair, one without overprint 50.00
112 A12 10pa on 2k 1.50 *2.00*
a. Pair, one without overprint 65.00
113 A12 20pa on 4k 2.50 *3.50*
a. Pair, one without overprint 65.00
114 A12 1pi on 10k 4.50 *6.00*
a. Pair, one without overprint 75.00
115 A12 5pi on 50k 7.00 *9.50*
a. Pair, one without overprint 100.00
116 A12 7pi on 70k 13.00 *17.50*
a. Pair, one without overprint 125.00

Perf. 13½

117 A13 10pi on 1r 80.00 *80.00*
Nos. 111-117 (7) 110.00 *120.50*

The overprint is larger on No. 117.

Overprinted "Salonique"

Black Overprint

Perf. 14½x15

131 A12 5pa on 1k 1.50 *2.00*
a. Inverted overprint 55.00
b. Pair, one without overprint 60.00
132 A12 10pa on 2k 2.00 *4.00*
a. Inverted overprint 55.00
b. Pair, one without overprint 60.00
133 A12 20pa on 4k 2.50 *5.00*
a. Inverted overprint 55.00
b. Pair, one without overprint 60.00
134 A12 1pi on 10k 3.00 *6.00*
a. Pair, one without overprint 75.00
135 A12 5pi on 50k 3.50 *8.00*
136 A12 7pi on 70k 5.00 *10.00*

Perf. 13½

137 A13 10pi on 1r 32.50 40.00
138 A14 35pi on 3.50r 80.00 *85.00*
139 A14 70pi on 7r 100.00 115.00

Blue Overprint

Perf. 14½x15

140 A12 5pa on 1k 15.00 *15.00*
Nos. 131-140 (10) 245.00 *290.00*

Overprinted "Smyrne"

Black Overprint

141 A12 5pa on 1k .65 *1.25*
a. Double overprint
b. Inverted overprint 10.00
142 A12 10pa on 2k .65 *1.25*
a. Inverted overprint 25.00
143 A12 20pa on 4k 1.40 *1.60*
a. Inverted overprint 17.50
144 A12 1pi on 10k 1.40 *1.75*
145 A12 5pi on 50k 3.00 *3.00*
146 A12 7pi on 70k 4.50 *6.00*

Perf. 13½

147 A13 10pi on 1r 18.00 *22.50*
148 A14 35pi on 3.50r 37.50 *40.00*
149 A14 70pi on 7r 55.00 *62.50*

Blue Overprint

Perf. 14½x15

150 A12 5pa on 1k 11.00 *11.00*
Nos. 141-150 (10) 133.10 150.85

"Smyrn"

141c A12 5pa on 1k 18.00 *20.00*
142b A12 10pa on 2k 18.00 *20.00*
143b A12 20pa on 4k 18.00 *20.00*
144a A12 1pi on 10k 20.00 *25.00*
145a A12 5pi on 50k 20.00 *25.00*
146a A12 7pi on 70k 20.00 25.00
Nos. 141c-146a (6) 114.00 135.00

Overprinted "Trebizonde"

Black Overprint

151 A12 5pa on 1k .80 *1.00*
a. Inverted overprint 25.00
b. Pair, one without overprint 60.00
152 A12 10pa on 2k .80 *1.00*
a. Inverted overprint 25.00
b. Pair, one without "Trebizonde" 60.00
153 A12 20pa on 4k .95 .95
a. Inverted overprint 25.00
b. Pair, one without overprint 100.00
154 A12 1pi on 10k .95 *1.50*
a. Pair, one without "Trebizonde" 35.00
155 A12 5pi on 50k 2.10 *2.50*
156 A12 7pi on 70k 4.25 *5.50*

Perf. 13½

157 A13 10pi on 1r 19.00 *20.00*
158 A14 35pi on 3.50r 37.50 *37.50*
159 A14 70pi on 7r 52.50 *55.00*

Blue Overprint

Perf. 14½x15

160 A12 5pa on 1k 6.25 *7.50*
Nos. 151-160 (10) 125.10 *132.45*

On Nos. 158 and 159 the overprint is spelled "Trebisonde".

Overprinted "Beyrouth"

Black Overprint

1910

161 A12 5pa on 1k .50 *.85*
162 A12 10pa on 2k .50 *.85*
a. Inverted overprint 25.00
163 A12 20pa on 4k .80 *1.10*
164 A12 1pi on 10k .80 *1.40*
165 A12 5pi on 50k 1.90 *2.75*
166 A12 7pi on 70k 4.00 *5.50*

Perf. 13½

167 A13 10pi on 1r 19.00 *21.00*
168 A14 35pi on 3.50r 40.00 *42.50*
169 A14 70pi on 7r 55.00 *60.00*
Nos. 161-169 (9) 122.50 135.95

Overprinted "Dardanelles"

Perf. 14½x15

171 A12 5pa on 1k 1.25 *2.50*
a. Pair, one without overprint 60.00
172 A12 10pa on 2k 1.25 *2.50*
a. Pair, one without overprint 60.00
173 A12 20pa on 4k 3.25 3.25
a. Inverted overprint 25.00
174 A12 1pi on 10k 3.50 *3.50*
175 A12 5pi on 50k 6.50 *7.50*
176 A12 7pi on 70k 14.00 14.00

Perf. 13½

177 A13 10pi on 1r 21.00 *21.00*
178 A14 35pi on 3.50r 37.50 *40.00*
a. Center and ovpt. inverted *5,000.* *2,750.*
179 A14 70pi on 7r 60.00 *65.00*
Nos. 171-179 (9) 148.25 159.25

Overprinted "Metelin"

Perf. 14½x15

181 A12 5pa on 1k 1.00 *2.00*
a. Inverted overprint 50.00
182 A12 10pa on 2k 1.00 *2.00*
a. Inverted overprint 50.00
183 A12 20pa on 4k 2.00 *5.00*
a. Inverted overprint 50.00
184 A12 1pi on 10k 3.00 *6.00*
185 A12 5pi on 50k 5.00 *8.00*
186 A12 7pi on 70k 8.00 *10.00*

Perf. 13½

187 A13 10pi on 1r 20.00 *30.00*
188 A14 35pi on 3.50r 70.00 70.00
189 A14 70pi on 7r 80.00 *85.00*

Blue Overprint

Perf. 14½x15

190 A12 5pa on 1k 10.00 *15.00*
Nos. 181-190 (10) 200.00 *233.00*

Overprinted "Rizeh"

Perf. 14½x15

191 A12 5pa on 1k .65 *1.00*
a. Inverted overprint 30.00
192 A12 10pa on 2k .65 *1.00*
a. Inverted overprint 30.00
193 A12 20pa on 4k 1.10 *1.40*
a. Inverted overprint 30.00
194 A12 1pi on 10k 1.10 *1.40*
195 A12 5pi on 50k 1.75 *3.75*
196 A12 7pi on 70k 3.25 *6.00*

Perf. 13½

197 A13 10pi on 1r 17.50 *21.00*
198 A14 35pi on 3.50r 27.50 *35.00*
199 A14 70pi on 7r 44.00 *52.50*
Nos. 191-199 (9) 97.50 123.05

Nos. 61-199 for the establishing of Russian Post Offices in the Levant, 50th anniv.

A15

Vertically Laid Paper

1910 **Wmk. 168** ***Perf. 14½x15***

200 A15 20pa on 5k red violet (Bl) .60 .60

A16

A17

Wove Paper

Vertical Lozenges of Varnish on Face

1910 **Unwmk.** ***Perf. 14x14½***

201 A16 5pa on 1k org yel (Bl) .40 *.50*
202 A16 10pa on 2k green (R) .40 *.50*
a. Inverted overprint 25.00
203 A17 20pa on 4k car rose (Bl) .40 *.50*
204 A17 1pi on 10k blue (R) .40 *.50*
a. Inverted overprint 25.00
205 A8 5pi on 50k vio & grn (Bl) .75 *1.20*
206 A9 7pi on 70k lt brn & org (Bl) 1.00 *1.25*

Perf. 13½

207 A10 10pi on 1r pale brn, brn & org (Bl) 1.40 *1.50*
Nos. 201-207 (7) 4.75 *5.95*

Russian Stamps of 1909-12 Surcharged in Black

No. 208

Nos. 209-212

1912 ***Perf. 14x14½***

208 A14 20pa on 5k claret .80 .60
209 A11 1½pi on 15k dl vio & blue .80 .75
210 A8 2pi on 20k bl & car .80 .90
211 A11 2½pi on 25k grn & vio 1.00 1.25
a. Double surcharge 150.00 150.00
212 A11 3½pi on 35k vio & grn 1.60 1.60
Nos. 208-212 (5) 5.00 5.10

Russia Nos. 88-91, 93, 95-104 Surcharged

c

d

e

f

g

1913 ***Perf. 13½***

213 A16(c) 5pa on 1k .25 .25
Never hinged .40
214 A17(d) 10pa on 2k .25 .25
Never hinged .40
215 A18(c) 15pa on 3k .25 .25
Never hinged .40
216 A19(c) 20pa on 4k .25 .25
Never hinged .40
217 A21(e) 1pi on 10k .25 .25
Never hinged .40
218 A23(f) 1½pi on 15k .50 *.50*
Never hinged .70
219 A24(f) 2pi on 20k .50 *.50*
Never hinged .70
220 A25(f) 2½pi on 25k .75 *.75*
Never hinged .90
221 A26(f) 3½pi on 35k 1.60 1.60
Never hinged 2.25
222 A27(e) 5pi on 50k 2.00 2.00
Never hinged 2.75
223 A28(f) 7pi on 70k 8.00 15.00
Never hinged 10.50
224 A29(e) 10pi on 1r 9.00 15.00
Never hinged 10.50
225 A30(e) 20pi on 2r 1.60 8.00
Never hinged 2.25
226 A31(g) 30pi on 3r 2.75 250.00
Never hinged 3.50
227 A32(e) 50pi on 5r 150.00 500.00
Never hinged 225.00
Nos. 213-227 (15) 177.95 794.60

Romanov dynasty tercentenary.
Forgeries exist of overprint on No. 227.

Russia Nos. 75, 71, 72 Surcharged

h

i

Perf. 14x14½

Wove Paper

228 A14(h) 15pa on 3k .25 .25
Never hinged .40

Perf. 13, 13½

230 A13(i) 50pi on 5r 3.00 *10.00*
Never hinged 7.50

Vertically Laid Paper

Wmk. Wavy Lines (168)

231 A13(i) 100pi on 10r 7.00 *20.00*
Never hinged 15.00
a. Double surcharge 750.00 —
Nos. 228-231 (3) 10.25 30.25

No. 228 has lozenges of varnish on face but No. 230 has not.

Wrangel Issues

For the Posts of Gen. Peter Wrangel's army and civilian refugees from South Russia, interned in Turkey, Serbia, etc.

Very few of the Wrangel overprints were actually sold to the public, and many of the covers were made up later with the original cancels. Reprints abound. Values probably are based on sales of reprints in most cases.

Russian Stamps of 1902-18 Surcharged in Blue, Red or Black

On Russia Nos. 69-70
Vertically Laid Paper

1921 **Wmk. 168** ***Perf. 13½***

232 A12 10,000r on 3.50r 250.00 250.00
233 A12 10,000r on 7r 250.00 250.00
234 A12 20,000r on 3.50r 250.00 250.00
235 A12 20,000r on 7r 250.00 250.00
Nos. 232-235 (4) 1,000. 1,000.

On Russia Nos. 71-86, 87a, 117-118, 137-138
Wove Paper
Perf. 14x14½, 13½
Unwmk.

236 A14 1000r on 1k 3.25 3.25
237 A14 1000r on 2k (R) 3.25 3.25
237A A14 1000r on 2k (Bk) 47.50 47.50
238 A14 1000r on 3k 1.10 1.10
a. Inverted surcharge 10.00 10.00
239 A15 1000r on 4k 1.10 1.10
a. Inverted surcharge 10.00 10.00
240 A14 1000r on 5k 1.10 1.10
a. Inverted surcharge 10.00 10.00
241 A14 1000r on 7k 1.10 1.10
a. Inverted surcharge 10.00 10.00
242 A15 1000r on 10k 1.10 1.10
a. Inverted surcharge 10.00 10.00
243 A14 1000r on 10k on 7k 1.10 1.10
244 A14 5000r on 3k 1.10 1.10
245 A11 5000r on 14k 10.00 10.00
246 A11 5000r on 15k 1.10 1.10
a. "PYCCKIN" 12.00 12.00
247 A8 5000r on 20k 3.50 3.50
a. "PYCCKIN" 12.00 12.00
248 A11 5000r on 20k on 14k 3.50 3.50
249 A11 5000r on 25k 1.10 1.10
250 A11 5000r on 35k 1.10 1.10
a. Inverted surcharge 10.00 10.00
b. New value omitted 10.00 10.00
251 A8 5000r on 50k 1.10 1.10
a. Inverted surcharge 10.00 10.00
252 A11 5000r on 70k 1.10 1.10
a. Inverted surcharge 10.00 10.00
253 A9 10,000r on 1r (Bl) 1.10 1.10
254 A9 10,000r on 1r (Bk) 8.25 8.25
255 A12 10,000r on 3.50r 3.50 3.50
256 A13 10,000r on 5r 45.00 45.00
257 A13 10,000r on 10r 4.25 4.25
258 A9 20,000r on 1r 2.50 2.50
259 A12 20,000r on 3.50r 2.50 2.50
a. Inverted surcharge 10.00 10.00
b. New value omitted 20.00 20.00
260 A12 20,000r on 7r 92.50 92.50
261 A13 20,000r on 10r 2.50 2.50
Nos. 236-261 (27) 246.30 246.30

On Russia No. 104

261A A32 20,000r on 5r 950.00

On Russia Nos. 119-123, 125-135
Imperf

262 A14 1000r on 1k 1.20 1.20
263 A14 1000r on 2k (R) 1.20 1.20
263A A14 1000r on 2k (Bk) 1.50 1.50
264 A14 1000r on 3k 1.20 1.20
265 A15 1000r on 4k 40.00 40.00
266 A14 1000r on 5k 1.50 1.50
267 A14 5000r on 3k 1.20 1.20
268 A11 5000r on 15k 1.50 1.50
268A A8 5000r on 20k 60.00
268B A11 5000r on 25k 60.00
269 A11 5000r on 35k 3.00 3.00
270 A8 5000r on 50k 3.00 3.00
271 A11 5000r on 70k 1.20 1.20
272 A9 10,000r on 1r (Bl) 1.20 1.20
a. Inverted surcharge 10.00 10.00
273 A9 10,000r on 1r (Bk) 1.20 1.20
274 A12 10,000r on 3.50r 1.20 1.20
275 A13 10,000r on 5r 10.00 10.00
276 A12 10,000r on 7r 60.00 60.00
276A A13 10,000r on 10r *200.00*
277 A9 20,000r on 1r (Bl) 1.20 1.20
a. Inverted surcharge 10.00 10.00
278 A9 20,000r on 1r (Bk) 1.20 1.20
279 A12 20,000r on 3.50r 10.00 10.00
280 A13 20,000r on 5r 1.20 1.20
281 A12 20,000r on 7r 47.50 47.50
281A A13 20,000r on 10r *275.00*
Nos. 262-268,269-276,277-281 (21) 191.20 191.20

A18

A19

On Russia AR1-AR3
Perf. 14½x15
Wmk. 171

282 A18 10,000r on 1k red, *buff* 6.50 6.50
283 A19 10,000r on 5k grn, *buff* 6.50 6.50
a. Inverted surcharge 10.00
284 A19 10,000r on 10k brn, *buff* 6.50 6.50
a. Inverted surcharge 10.00
Nos. 282-284 (3) 19.50 19.50

On Stamps of Russian Offices in Turkey On No. 38-39
Vertically Laid Paper
Wmk. Wavy Lines (168)

284B A11 20,000r on 35pi on 3.50r 300.00
284C A11 20,000r on 70pi on 7r 400.00

On Nos. 200-207
Vertically Laid Paper

284D A15 1000r on 20pa on 5k 5.00 5.00

Wove Paper
Unwmk.

285 A16 1000r on 5pa on 1k 2.50 2.50
286 A16 1000r on 10pa on 2k 2.50 2.50
287 A17 1000r on 20pa on 4k 2.50 2.50
288 A17 1000r on 1pi on 10k 2.50 2.50
289 A8 5000r on 5pi on 50k 2.50 2.50
290 A9 5000r on 7pi on 70k 2.50 2.50
291 A10 10,000r on 10pi on 1r 12.50 12.50
a. Inverted surcharge 25.00 25.00
b. Pair, one without surcharge 20.00 20.00
292 A10 20,000r on 10pi on 1r 2.50 2.50
a. Inverted surcharge 25.00 25.00
b. Pair, one without surcharge 25.00 25.00
Nos. 284D-292 (9) 35.00 35.00

On Nos. 208-212

293 A14 1000r on 20pa on 5k 2.50 2.50
294 A11 5000r on 1½pi on 15k 2.50 2.50
295 A8 5000r on 2pi on 20k 2.50 2.50
296 A11 5000r on 2½pi on 25k 2.50 2.50
297 A11 5000r on 3½pi on 35k 2.50 2.50
Nos. 293-297 (5) 12.50 12.50

On Nos. 228, 230-231

298 A14 1000r on 15pa on 3k 1.00 1.00
299 A13 10,000r on 50pi on 5r 65.00 65.00
300 A13 10,000r on 100pi on 10r 92.50 92.50
301 A13 20,000r on 50pi on 5r 1.00 1.00
302 A13 20,000r on 100pi on 10r 92.50 92.50
Nos. 298-302 (5) 252.00 252.00

On Stamps of South Russia Denikin Issue
Imperf

303 A5 5000r on 5k org 1.00 1.00
a. Inverted surcharge 10.00
304 A5 5000r on 10k green 1.00 1.00
305 A5 5000r on 15k red 1.00 1.00
306 A5 5000r on 35k lt bl 1.00 1.00
307 A5 5000r on 70k dk blue 1.00 1.00
307A A5 10,000r on 70k dk blue 50.00 50.00
308 A6 10,000r on 1r brn & red 1.00 1.00
309 A6 10,000r on 2r gray vio & yel 1.00 1.00
a. Inverted surcharge 30.00 30.00
310 A6 10,000r on 3r dull rose & grn 3.50 3.50
311 A6 10,000r on 5r slate & vio 2.50 2.50
312 A6 10,000r on 7r gray grn & rose 100.00 100.00
313 A6 10,000r on 10r red & gray 2.00 2.00
314 A6 20,000r on 1r brn & red 1.00 1.00
315 A6 20,000r on 2r gray vio & yel (Bl) 35.00 35.00
a. Inverted surcharge 30.00 30.00
315B A6 20,000r on 2r gray vio & yel (Bk) 1.00 1.00
316 A6 20,000r on 3r dull rose & grn (Bl) 50.00 50.00
316A A6 20,000r on 3r dull rose & grn (Bk) 30.00 30.00
317 A6 20,000r on 5r slate & vio 1.00 1.00
318 A6 20,000r on 7r gray grn & rose 60.00 60.00
319 A6 20,000r on 10r red & gray 1.00 1.00
Nos. 303-319 (20) 344.00 344.00

Trident Stamps of Ukraine Surcharged in Blue, Red, Black or Brown

1921 ***Perf. 14, 14½x15***

320 A14 10,000r on 1k org .45 .45
321 A14 10,000r on 2k grn 5.00 5.00
322 A14 10,000r on 3k red .45 .45
a. Inverted surcharge 10.00 10.00
323 A15 10,000r on 4k car .45 .45
324 A14 10,000r on 5k cl .45 .45
325 A14 10,000r on 7k lt bl .45 .45
a. Inverted surcharge 10.00 10.00
326 A15 10,000r on 10k dk bl .45 .45
a. Inverted surcharge 10.00 10.00
327 A14 10,000r on 10k on 7k lt bl .45 .45
a. Inverted surcharge 10.00 10.00
328 A8 20,000r on 20k bl & car (Br) .45 .45
a. Inverted surcharge 10.00 10.00
329 A8 20,000r on 20k bl & car (Bk) .45 .45
a. Inverted surcharge 35.00 35.00
330 A11 20,000r on 20k on 14k bl & rose .45 .45
331 A11 20,000r on 35k red brn & grn 75.00 75.00
332 A8 20,000r on 50k brn vio & grn .45 .45
a. Inverted surcharge 10.00 10.00
Nos. 320-332 (13) 84.95 84.95

Imperf

333 A14 10,000r on 1k org .75 .75
a. Inverted surcharge 10.00
334 A14 10,000r on 2k grn 2.00 2.00
335 A14 10,000r on 3k red .75 .75
336 A8 20,000r on 20k bl & car .75 .75
337 A11 20,000r on 35k red brn & grn 40.00 40.00
338 A8 20,000r on 50k brn vio & grn 2.00 2.00
Nos. 333-338 (6) 46.25 46.25

There are several varieties of the trident surcharge on Nos. 320 to 338.

Same Surcharge on Russian Stamps
On Stamps of 1909-18
Perf. 14x14½

338A A14 10,000r on 1k dl org yel 2.50 2.50
339 A14 10,000r on 2k dl grn 2.50 2.50
340 A14 10,000r on 3k car .50 .50
341 A15 10,000r on 4k car .50 .50
342 A14 10,000r on 5k dk cl .50 .50
343 A14 10,000r on 7k blue .50 .50
344 A15 10,000r on 10k dk bl 2.50 2.50
344A A14 10,000r on 10k on 7k bl 3.75 3.75
344B A11 20,000r on 14k dk bl & car 35.00 35.00
345 A11 20,000r on 15k red brn & dp bl .50 .50
346 A8 20,000r on 20k dl bl & dk car .50 .50
347 A11 20,000r on 20k on 14k dk bl & car 3.50 3.50
348 A11 20,000r on 35k red brn & grn 2.00 2.00
349 A8 20,000r on 50k brn vio & grn .50 .50
349A A11 20,000r on 70k brn & red org 2.50 2.50
Nos. 338A-349A (15) 57.75 57.75

On Stamps of 1917-18
Imperf

350 A14 10,000r on 1k org .75 .75
351 A14 10,000r on 2k gray grn .75 .75
352 A14 10,000r on 3k red .75 .75
353 A15 10,000r on 4k car 40.00 40.00
354 A14 10,000r on 5k claret .75 .75
355 A11 20,000r on 15k red brn & dp bl .75 .75
356 A8 20,000r on 50k brn vio & grn 2.00 2.00
357 A11 20,000r on 70k brn & org .75 .75
Nos. 350-357 (8) 46.50 46.50

Same Surcharge on Stamps of Russian Offices in Turkey
On Nos. 40-45
Perf. 14½x15

358 A12 10,000r on 5pa on 1k 5.00 5.00
359 A12 10,000r on 10pa on 2k 5.00 5.00
360 A12 10,000r on 20pa on 4k 5.00 5.00
361 A12 10,000r on 1pi on 10k 5.00 5.00
362 A12 20,000r on 5pi on 50k 5.00 5.00
363 A12 20,000r on 7pi on 70k 5.00 5.00
Nos. 358-363 (6) 30.00 30.00

On Nos. 201-206

364 A16 10,000r on 5pa on 1k 6.00 6.00
365 A16 10,000r on 10pa on 2k 6.00 6.00
366 A17 10,000r on 20pa on 4k 6.00 6.00
367 A17 10,000r on 1pi on 10k 6.00 6.00
368 A8 20,000r on 5pi on 50k 6.00 6.00
369 A9 20,000r on 7pi on 70k 6.00 6.00
Nos. 364-369 (6) 36.00 36.00

On Nos. 228, 208-212, Stamps of 1912-13

370 A14 10,000r on 15pa on 3k 5.00 5.00
371 A14 10,000r on 20pa on 5k 5.00 5.00
372 A11 20,000r on 1½pi on 15k 5.00 5.00
373 A8 20,000r on 2pi on 20k 5.00
374 A11 20,000r on 2½pi on 25k 5.00
375 A11 20,000r on 3½pi on 35k 5.00

Same Surcharge on Stamp of South Russia, Crimea Issue

376 A8 20,000r on 5r on 20k bl & car 750.00
Nos. 370-376 (7) 780.00 15.00

SAAR

'sär

LOCATION — On the Franco-German border southeast of Luxembourg
GOVT. — A German state
POP. — 1,400,000 (1959)
AREA — 991 sq. mi.
CAPITAL — Saarbrücken

A former German territory, the Saar was administered by the League of Nations 1920-35. After a January 12, 1935, plebiscite, it returned to Germany, and the use of German stamps was resumed.

100 Pfennig = 1 Mark
100 Centimes = 1 Franc (1921)

German Stamps of 1906-19 Overprinted

Nos. 1-16 exist in three types. Type I: larger letters, "Sarre" 10.7mm wide, no control mark below bar. Type II: as Type I, control mark (a short, thin line) below bar. Type III: smaller letters, "Sarre" 10.5mm wide, control mark below bar.

Type I

Perf. 14, 14½

1920, Jan. 30 **Wmk. 125**

1 A22 2pf gray 1.60 *4.50*
Never hinged 4.50
On cover 8.00
c. Inverted overprint 325.00 *550.00*
Never hinged 525.00
On cover 725.00
2 A22 2½pf gray 9.50 *27.50*
Never hinged 24.00
On cover 35.00
c. Inverted overprint 350.00 *650.00*
Never hinged 600.00
On cover 800.00
d. 2½pf deep greenish gray or bronze 97.50 *250.00*
Never hinged 200.00
On cover 325.00
3 A16 3pf brown 1.00 *2.75*
Never hinged 2.25
On cover 4.00
c. Inverted overprint 325.00 *550.00*
Never hinged 525.00
On cover 725.00
4 A16 5pf deep green .50 *1.00*
Never hinged .95
On cover 1.60
c. Inverted overprint 600.00 —
Never hinged 1,050.
d. 5pf dark bluish green 1.40 *3.60*
Never hinged 2.60
On cover 5.00
5 A22 7½pf orange .65 *1.75*
Never hinged 1.10
On cover 3.00
c. Inverted overprint — 800.00
Never hinged —
d. 7½pf red orange 3.40 *11.00*
Never hinged 6.50
On cover 20.00
e. 7½pf pale reddish orange 2.00 *6.25*
Never hinged 3.25
On cover 13.50
6 A16 10pf carmine .55 *1.25*
Never hinged 1.10
On cover 1.60
c. Inverted overprint 550.00 *1,050.*
Never hinged 975.00
d. Double overprint 725.00 *1,200.*
Never hinged 1,200.
On cover 1,450.
e. 10pf rose red 2.00 *4.50*
Never hinged 3.75
On cover 6.75
f. As "e," double overprint 750.00 *1,250.*
Never hinged 1,200.
On cover 1,450.
g. 10pf scarlet red 130.00 *240.00*
Never hinged 240.00
On cover 280.00
7 A22 15pf dk violet .50 *1.00*
Never hinged 1.10
On cover 1.60
c. Double overprint 800.00 *1,450.*
Never hinged 1,350.
On cover 1,500.
d. 15pf blackish violet 7.25 *17.00*
Never hinged 14.50
On cover 28.00
e. 15pf bluish violet 20.00 *110.00*
Never hinged 40.00
On cover 170.00
8 A16 20pf blue violet .50 *1.00*
Never hinged 1.10
On cover 1.60
c. Double overprint 600.00 *950.00*
Never hinged 950.00
On cover 1,200.
9 A16 25pf red org & blk, *yellow* 9.50 20.00
Never hinged 24.00
On cover 28.00
c. Inverted overprint 800.00 *2,400.*
Never hinged 1,350.
d. 25pf yel org & blk, *yellow* 30.00 *110.00*
Never hinged 57.50
On cover 135.00
10 A16 30pf org & blk, *yel buff* 17.50 *35.00*
Never hinged 35.00
On cover 57.50
d. 30pf org & blk, *org buff* 240.00 *500.00*
Never hinged 400.00
On cover 725.00
11 A22 35pf red brown .55 *1.25*
Never hinged 1.10
On cover 1.60
c. Inverted overprint 475.00 *1,050.*
Never hinged 900.00
On cover 1,200.
12 A16 40pf dp lake & blk .55 *1.25*
Never hinged 1.20
On cover 1.60
c. Inverted overprint 475.00 *1,050.*
Never hinged 900.00
On cover 1,200.
d. 40pf reddish lake & blk 5.50 *8.50*
Never hinged 11.00
On cover 13.50
13 A16 50pf pur & blk, *yel buff* .55 *1.60*
Never hinged 1.45
On cover 1.75
c. Inverted overprint 400.00 *725.00*
Never hinged 725.00
On cover 800.00
d. 50pf pur & blk, *org buff* 22.00 *75.00*
Never hinged 50.00
On cover 115.00
14 A16 60pf dp gray lilac .55 *1.25*
Never hinged 1.10
On cover 2.00
c. 60pf red lilac 300.00 *750.00*
Never hinged 600.00
On cover 1,350.
15 A16 75pf green & blk .55 *1.25*
Never hinged 1.00
On cover 2.50
c. Inverted overprint 240.00 *400.00*
Never hinged 400.00
On cover 500.00
16 A16 80pf lake & blk, *rose* 190.00 *275.00*
Never hinged 525.00
On cover 1,050.

Type II

1a A22 2pf gray 160.00 *450.00*
Never hinged 375.00
On cover 600.00
2a A22 2½pf olive gray 525.00 *975.00*
Never hinged 1,050.
On cover 2,500.
2e A22 2½pf dp grnsh gray or bronze 1,600. *3,400.*
Never hinged 3,400.
On cover —
3a A16 3pf brown 175.00 *360.00*
Never hinged 340.00
On cover 575.00
4a A16 5pf deep green 11.00 *65.00*
Never hinged 19.50
On cover 100.00
4e A16 5pf dark bluish green 55.00 *145.00*
Never hinged 115.00
On cover 200.00
5a A22 7½pf yellow orange 50.00 *180.00*
Never hinged 100.00
On cover 260.00
5f A22 7½pf red orange 1,600. *3,400.*
Never hinged 3,400.
On cover —
12a A16 40pf deep lake & blk 1.80 *6.00*
Never hinged 4.50
On cover 10.00
13a A16 50pf pur & blk, *yel buff* 1.60 *5.25*
Never hinged 3.75
On cover 11.00

Type III

1b A22 2pf gray 5.00 *20.00*
Never hinged 11.50
On cover 32.50
d. Double overprint 2,000. *2,600.*
Never hinged 3,500.
2b A22 2½pf olive gray 1.60 *5.75*
Never hinged 4.50
On cover 8.00
2f A22 2½pf dp grnsh gray or bronze 52.50 *115.00*
Never hinged 92.50
On cover 145.00
3b A16 3pf brown 1.30 *4.50*
Never hinged 2.60
On cover 6.50
4b A16 5pf deep green .50 *1.00*
Never hinged 1.00
On cover 1.60
f. Double overprint 800.00 *1,450.*
Never hinged 1,450.
4g A16 5pf dk bluish green 1.30 *3.75*
Never hinged 2.10
On cover 5.00
h. Double overprint 1,000. *1,450.*
Never hinged 1,800.
5b A22 7½pf yellow orange 4.75 *25.00*
Never hinged 10.00
On cover 40.00
5g A22 7½pf red orange 24.00 *65.00*
Never hinged 47.50
On cover 100.00
5h A22 7½pf pale reddish org 16.00 *2,400.*
Never hinged 32.50
On cover 3,600.
6b A16 10pf carmine .60 *1.10*
Never hinged 1.10
On cover 1.50
6h A16 10pf rose red 1.75 *6.00*
Never hinged 3.50
On cover 9.00
6i A16 10pf scarlet red 67.50 *120.00*
Never hinged 130.00
On cover 200.00
7b A22 15pf dk violet .50 *1.10*
Never hinged 1.10
On cover 1.50
7f A22 15pf blackish violet 1.50 *5.00*
Never hinged 3.00
On cover 8.00
8b A16 20pf blue violet .50 *1.25*
Never hinged 1.10
On cover 2.00
9b A16 25pf red org & blk, *yellow* 115.00 350.00
Never hinged 260.00
On cover 575.00
9e A16 25pf yel org & blk, *yel* 60.00 *120.00*
Never hinged 120.00
On cover 180.00
10b A16 30pf org & blk, *yel buff* 45.00 *100.00*
Never hinged 90.00
On cover 120.00
10c A16 30pf org & blk, *org buff* 210.00 *500.00*
Never hinged 400.00
On cover 725.00
11b A22 35pf red brown 16.00 *47.50*
Never hinged 32.00
On cover 110.00
12b A16 40pf deep lake & blk 2.50 *8.00*
Never hinged 4.50
On cover 12.00
e. Inverted overprint 575.00 *975.00*
Never hinged 975.00
On cover 1,200.
13b A16 50pf pur & blk, *yel buff* .60 *1.10*
Never hinged 1.45
On cover 2.00
14b A16 60pf dp gray lilac .50 *1.10*
Never hinged 1.00
On cover 1.60
15b A16 75pf green & blk .65 *1.20*
Never hinged 1.15
On cover 1.60
d. Double overprint 2,000. —
Never hinged 3,500.
16b A16 80pf lake & blk, *rose* 200.00 *300.00*
Never hinged 575.00
On cover 1,000.

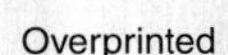

Overprinted

Type I

17 A17 1m carmine rose (25x17 holes) 27.50 *40.00*
Never hinged 57.50
On cover 115.00
a. Inverted overprint 725.00 *1,450.*
Never hinged 1,200.
On cover 1,800.
b. Double overprint 800.00 *1,450.*
Never hinged 1,350.
On cover 1,800.
c. 1m carmine rose (26x17 holes) 1,050. *1,550.*
Never hinged 2,800.
On cover 3,250.
d. As "c," double overprint *8,000.* *15,000.*
Never hinged *14,500.*

Type II

17f A17 1m carmine rose 40.00 *80.00*
Never hinged 100.00
On cover 160.00
17g A17 1m Inverted overprint 975.00 *1,800.*
Never hinged 1,600.
On cover
17h A17 1m Double overprint 1,050. *1,950.*
Never hinged 1,800.
On cover
Nos. 1-17 (17) 262.05 417.35

The 3m type A19 exists overprinted like No. 17, but was not issued. Value, $16,000 unused, $33,000 never hinged.
Overprint forgeries exist.

Bavarian Stamps of 1914-16 Overprinted

Perf. 14x14½

1920, Mar. 1 **Wmk. 95**

19 A10 2pf gray *900.00* *4,750.*
Never hinged 2,000.
On cover *6,500.*
20 A10 3pf brown 80.00 *650.00*
Never hinged 225.00
On cover 975.00
21 A10 5pf yellow grn .75 *1.60*
Never hinged 1.60
On cover 5.00
a. Double overprint 800.00
b. Pair, one stamp without ovpt. — —
22 A10 7½pf green 32.50 *275.00*
Never hinged 72.50
On cover 450.00
23 A10 10pf carmine rose .75 *1.60*
Never hinged 1.60
On cover 4.00
a. Double overprint 325.00 *650.00*
Never hinged 500.00
b. Pair, one stamp without ovpt. —
Never hinged —
24 A10 15pf vermilion .95 *1.90*
Never hinged 1.60
On cover 5.00
a. Double overprint 400.00 *800.00*
Never hinged 575.00
25 A10 15pf carmine 7.25 *16.00*
Never hinged 16.00
On cover 24.00
26 A10 20pf blue .65 *1.60*
Never hinged 1.60
On cover 4.00
a. Double overprint 325.00 *650.00*
Never hinged 500.00
27 A10 25pf gray 11.00 *16.00*
Never hinged 22.50
On cover 32.50
28 A10 30pf orange 6.50 *11.00*
Never hinged 14.50
On cover 24.00
30 A10 40pf olive green 10.50 *16.00*
Never hinged 21.00
On cover 32.50
31 A10 50pf red brown 2.00 *4.50*
Never hinged 4.50
On cover 5.75
a. Double overprint 350.00 *650.00*
Never hinged 575.00
32 A10 60pf dark green 3.25 *8.00*
Never hinged 6.50
On cover 24.00
a. 60pf blackish green on thick paper 3.40 *10.00*
Never hinged 7.25
On cover 28.00

Overprinted

Perf. 11½

35 A11 1m brown 24.00 *35.00*
Never hinged 52.50
On cover 130.00
a. 1m dark brown 16.00 *32.50*
Never hinged 40.00
On cover 120.00
36 A11 2m dk gray violet 60.00 *140.00*
Never hinged 130.00
On cover 350.00
a. 2m dk purple violet 1,850. 2,900.
Never hinged 3,250.
On cover 3,250.
37 A11 3m scarlet 120.00 *160.00*
Never hinged 275.00
On cover 1,450.
Nos. 35-37 (3) 204.00 *335.00*

Overprinted

38 A12 5m deep blue 800.00 *875.00*
Never hinged 2,000.
On cover 3,200.
39 A12 10m yellow green 140.00 *250.00*
Never hinged 360.00
On cover 1,000.
a. Double overprint *3,400.* *8,500.*
Never hinged *6,000.* —

Nos. 19, 20 and 22 were not officially issued, but were available for postage. Examples are known legitimately used on cover. The 20m type A12 was also overprinted in small quantity. Values: unused $125,000; never hinged $200,000.
No. 21a is valued without gum.
Overprint forgeries exist.

German Stamps of 1906-20 Overprinted

Perf. 14, 14½

1920, Mar. 26 **Wmk. 125**

41 A16 5pf green .25 *.50*
Never hinged .50
On cover 3.00
a. Inverted overprint 16.00 *160.00*
Never hinged 32.50
On cover 240.00

42 A16 5pf red brown .50 .80
Never hinged 1.10
On cover 2.40
b. 5pf brown 4.00 *13.00*
Never hinged 10.00
On cover 20.00
43 A16 10pf carmine .25 *.50*
Never hinged .50
On cover 3.00
a. Inverted overprint 47.50 *325.00*
Never hinged 97.50
On cover 500.00
44 A16 10pf orange .45 .50
Never hinged 1.10
On cover 2.40
a. Inverted overprint 16.00
Never hinged 28.00
b. Double ovpt., never hinged 80.00
45 A22 15pf dk violet .25 *.50*
Never hinged .65
On cover 3.00
a. Inverted overprint 27.50 *240.00*
Never hinged 55.00
On cover 325.00
46 A16 20pf blue violet .25 *.50*
Never hinged .65
On cover 3.00
a. Inverted overprint 35.00 —
Never hinged 72.50
47 A16 20pf green .95 .50
Never hinged 1.90
On cover 2.50
a. Double overprint, never hinged 80.00
48 A16 30pf org & blk, *buff* .40 *.50*
Never hinged 1.00
On cover 3.00
a. Double overprint 65.00
Never hinged 120.00
b. Inverted overprint —
Never hinged —
49 A16 30pf dull blue .55 *.75*
Never hinged 1.40
On cover 3.25
50 A16 40pf lake & blk .30 *.50*
Never hinged .65
On cover 3.00
51 A16 40pf car rose 1.00 .75
Never hinged 2.00
On cover 3.25
52 A16 50pf pur & blk, *buff* .55 .50
Never hinged 1.10
On cover 3.00
a. Double overprint 65.00 *400.00*
Never hinged 120.00
c. 50pf pur & blk, *orange buff* 3.25 *22.50*
Never hinged 6.50
On cover 40.00
53 A16 60pf red violet .65 .50
Never hinged 1.60
On cover 3.25
a. Inverted overprint 80.00 *325.00*
Never hinged 175.00
On cover 500.00
54 A16 75pf green & blk .75 .50
Never hinged 1.60
On cover 3.25
a. Double overprint 110.00 *400.00*
Never hinged 200.00
b. Inverted overprint 110.00
Never hinged 240.00
55 A17 1.25m green 2.75 1.25
Never hinged 5.75
On cover 7.25
a. Inverted overprint 95.00
Never hinged 200.00
56 A17 1.50m yellow brn 2.00 1.25
Never hinged 4.50
On cover 7.25
a. Inverted overprint 95.00 800.00
Never hinged 200.00
57 A21 2.50m lilac red 4.75 *13.50*
Never hinged 9.50
On cover 24.00
a. 2.50m lilac rose 12.50 *62.50*
Never hinged 27.50
On cover 80.00
b. 2.50m lilac 100.00 *925.00*
Never hinged 200.00
On cover *1,200.*
c. 2.50m brown lilac 10.00 *55.00*
Never hinged 20.00
On cover 85.00
58 A16 4m black & rose 8.75 *22.50*
Never hinged 20.00
On cover 72.50
a. Double overprint, never hinged 110.00
Nos. 41-58 (18) 25.35 *46.30*

On No. 57 the overprint is placed vertically at each side of the stamp.

Counterfeit overprints exist.

Germany No. 90 Surcharged in Black

1921, Feb.

65 A16 20pf on 75pf grn & blk .40 *1.25*
Never hinged 1.20
On cover 4.00
a. Inverted surcharge 24.00 *72.50*
Never hinged 50.00
On cover 110.00
b. Double surcharge 55.00 *125.00*
Never hinged 100.00
On cover 160.00

Germany No. 120 Surcharged

66 A22 5m on 15pf vio brn 5.50 *16.00*
Never hinged 20.00
On cover 80.00
67 A22 10m on 15pf vio brn 6.00 *19.00*
Never hinged 20.00
On cover 100.00
Nos. 65-67 (3) 11.90 *36.25*

Forgeries exist of Nos. 66-67.

Old Mill near Mettlach — A3

Miner at Work — A4

Entrance to Reden Mine — A5

Saar River Traffic — A6

Saar River near Mettlach — A7

Slag Pile at Völklingen — A8

Signal Bridge, Saarbrücken — A9

Church at Mettlach — A10

"Old Bridge," Saarbrücken A11

Cable Railway at Ferne — A12

Colliery Shafthead — A13

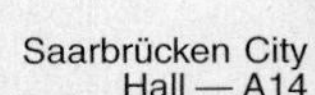

Saarbrücken City Hall — A14

Pottery at Mettlach — A15

St. Ludwig's Cathedral — A16

Presidential Residence, Saarbrücken A17

Burbach Steelworks, Dillingen A18

1921 Unwmk. Typo. *Perf. 12½*

68 A3 5pf ol grn & vio .35 *.50*
Never hinged .65
On cover 5.00
a. Tête bêche pair 3.50 *20.00*
Never hinged 7.25
On cover 65.00
c. Center inverted 100.00 *340.00*
Never hinged 210.00
d. Center printed in green 85.00 300.00
Never hinged 190.00
On cover 500.00
69 A4 10pf org & ultra .35 *.50*
Never hinged .80
On cover 5.00
70 A5 20pf grn & slate .35 *1.00*
Never hinged .65
On cover 11.50
a. Tête bêche pair 6.50 *40.00*
Never hinged 12.50
On cover 120.00
c. Perf. 10½ 22.50 *225.00*
Never hinged 40.00
On cover 280.00
d. As "c," tête bêche pair 140.00 *675.00*
Never hinged 200.00
On cover —
71 A6 25pf brn & dk bl .40 *.80*
Never hinged .85
On cover 12.00
a. Tête bêche pair 7.25 *40.00*
Never hinged 14.50
On cover 125.00
72 A7 30pf gray grn & brn .40 *.75*
Never hinged .85
On cover 7.50
a. Tête bêche pair 12.00 *60.00*
Never hinged 22.50
On cover 200.00
c. 30pf ol grn & blk 2.40 *22.50*
Never hinged 5.00
On cover 60.00
d. As "c," tête bêche pair 12.50 *72.50*
Never hinged 24.00
On cover 225.00
e. As "c," imperf., pair 120.00
Never hinged 250.00
73 A8 40pf vermilion .40 .50
Never hinged .85
On cover 5.00
a. Tête bêche pair 19.00 *80.00*
Never hinged 36.00
On cover 250.00
74 A9 50pf gray & blk .95 *4.00*
Never hinged 2.00
On cover 12.50
75 A10 60pf red & dk brn 1.60 *3.50*
Never hinged 3.75
On cover 20.00
76 A11 80pf deep blue .75 *1.00*
Never hinged 1.40
On cover 12.00
a. Tête bêche pair 21.00 *110.00*
Never hinged 42.50
On cover 200.00
77 A12 1m lt red & blk .80 *1.60*
Never hinged 1.60
On cover 12.00
a. 1m grn & blk *450.00*
Never hinged 1,000.
78 A13 1.25m lt brn & dk grn .95 *2.00*
Never hinged 2.40
On cover 20.00
79 A14 2m red & blk 2.40 *4.00*
Never hinged 6.00
On cover 20.00
80 A15 3m brn & dk ol 3.25 *9.50*
Never hinged 8.00
On cover 28.00
a. Center inverted 125.00
Never hinged 300.00
b. 3m orange brown & black 27.50 *85.00*
Never hinged 55.00
On cover 125.00
81 A16 5m yel & vio 12.00 *24.00*
Never hinged 20.00
On cover 90.00
82 A17 10m grn & red brn 12.00 *24.00*
Never hinged 25.00
On cover 115.00
83 A18 25m ultra, red & blk 32.50 *80.00*
Never hinged 90.00
On cover 325.00
a. 25m deep gray blue, deep cinnamon & black *2,400.* *3,750.*
Never hinged *3,750.*
On cover
Nos. 68-83 (16) 69.45 *157.65*

Values for tête bêche pairs are for vertical pairs. Horizontal pairs sell for about twice as much.

The ultramarine ink on No. 69 appears to be brown where it overlays the orange.

Exist imperf but were not regularly issued. Value $1,400. (hinged).

Nos. 70-83 Surcharged in Red, Blue or Black

a

b

c

1921, May 1

85 A5(a) 3c on 20pf (R) .40 *.50*
Never hinged .75
On cover 2.00
a. Tête bêche pair 4.75 *32.50*
Never hinged 10.00
On cover 100.00
b. Inverted surcharge 95.00
Never hinged 180.00
d. Perf. 10½ 4.75 *160.00*
Never hinged 12.50
On cover 225.00
e. As "d," tête bêche pair 21.00 —
Never hinged 40.00
86 A6(a) 5c on 25pf (R) .40 *.50*
Never hinged .85
On cover .85
a. Tête bêche pair 95.00 *400.00*
Never hinged 150.00
On cover 1,250.
87 A7(a) 10c on 30pf (Bl) .40 *.50*
Never hinged .85
On cover 1.60
a. Tête bêche pair 4.75 *25.00*
Never hinged 9.75
On cover 72.50
b. Inverted surcharge 95.00 *450.00*
Never hinged 180.00
c. Double surcharge 95.00 *475.00*
Never hinged 180.00
On cover —
88 A8(a) 15c on 40pf (Bk) .50 .50
Never hinged 1.20
On cover 1.60
a. Tête bêche pair 95.00 *400.00*
Never hinged 160.00
On cover 1,200.
b. Inverted surcharge 95.00 *450.00*
Never hinged 180.00
89 A9(a) 20c on 50pf (R) .40 *.50*
Never hinged .85
On cover 1.25

90 A10(a) 25c on 60pf (Bl) .50 .50
Never hinged 1.10
On cover 1.25

91 A11(a) 30c on 80pf (Bk) 1.60 1.00
Never hinged 4.00
On cover 2.00
a. Tête bêche pair 12.50 *60.00*
Never hinged 25.00
On cover 225.00
c. Inverted surcharge 140.00 *600.00*
Never hinged 240.00
d. Double surcharge *140.00* *600.00*
Never hinged 250.00

92 A12(a) 40c on 1m (Bl) 2.00 .50
Never hinged 5.75
On cover 2.00
a. Inverted surcharge 110.00 *450.00*
Never hinged 180.00
On cover —
b. Double surcharge 140.00 *600.00*
Never hinged 250.00

93 A13(a) 50c on 1.25m (Bk) 3.25 1.00
Never hinged 10.00
On cover 3.00
a. Double surcharge *275.00* *950.00*
Never hinged 500.00
b. Perf. 10½ 72.50 *140.00*
Never hinged 145.00
On cover 325.00

94 A14(a) 75c on 2m (Bl) 4.75 2.00
Never hinged 16.00
On cover 6.50
a. Inverted surcharge 110.00
Never hinged 200.00

95 A15(b) 1fr on 3m (Bl) 4.50 2.40
Never hinged 16.00
On cover 5.75
a. On No. 80b 22.50 *125.00*
Never hinged 60.00
On cover 260.00

96 A16(b) 2fr on 5m (Bl) 12.00 6.50
Never hinged 36.00
On cover 16.00

97 A17(b) 3fr on 10m (Bk) 17.50 *25.00*
Never hinged 52.50
On cover 72.50
b. Double surcharge 200.00 *800.00*
Never hinged 325.00

98 A18(c) 5fr on 25m (Bl) 17.50 *35.00*
Never hinged 52.50
On cover 250.00
Nos. 85-98 (14) 65.70 *76.40*

In these surcharges the period is occasionally missing and there are various wrong font and defective letters.

Values for tête bêche pairs are for vertical pairs. Horizontal pairs sell for about twice as much.

Nos. 85-89, 91, 93, 97-98 exist imperforate but were not regularly issued.

Cable Railway, Ferne — A19

Miner at Work — A20

"Old Bridge," Saarbrücken A21

Saarbrücken City Hall — A22

Slag Pile at Völklingen A23

Pottery at Mettlach — A24

Saar River Traffic — A25

St. Ludwig's Cathedral A26

Colliery Shafthead A27

Mettlach Church — A28

Burbach Steelworks, Dillingen A29

Perf. 12½x13½, 13½x12½

1922-23 **Typo.**

99 A19 3c ol grn & straw .40 *.65*
Never hinged .75
On cover 2.50

100 A20 5c orange & blk .40 .40
Never hinged .75
On cover 1.25

101 A21 10c blue green .40 .40
Never hinged .75
On cover 1.25

102 A19 15c deep brown 1.25 .40
Never hinged 3.00
On cover 1.60

103 A19 15c orange ('23) 2.40 .40
Never hinged 7.00
On cover 2.50

104 A22 20c dk bl & lem 13.50 .40
Never hinged 40.00
On cover 2.50

105 A22 20c brt bl & straw ('23) 4.00 .40
Never hinged 9.50
On cover 2.50

106 A22 25c red & yellow 6.50 2.25
Never hinged 16.00
On cover 7.50

107 A22 25c mag & straw ('23) 2.40 .40
Never hinged 7.00
On cover 1.25

108 A23 30c carmine & yel 2.00 2.10
Never hinged 5.25
On cover 3.25

109 A24 40c brown & yel 1.60 .40
Never hinged 4.00
On cover 1.60

110 A25 50c dk bl & straw .95 .40
Never hinged 2.00
On cover 1.60

111 A24 75c dp grn & straw 13.50 *24.00*
Never hinged 40.00
On cover 65.00

112 A24 75c blk & straw ('23) 32.50 3.25
Never hinged 77.50
On cover 7.25

113 A26 1fr brown red 2.40 .80
Never hinged 10.00
On cover 2.50

114 A27 2fr deep violet 6.50 3.25
Never hinged 16.00
On cover 5.00

115 A28 3fr org & dk grn 24.00 6.50
Never hinged 65.00
On cover 8.50

116 A29 5fr brn & red brn 24.00 *45.00*
Never hinged 65.00
On cover 100.00
Nos. 99-116 (18) 138.70 *91.40*

Nos. 99-116 exist imperforate but were not regularly issued.

For overprints see Nos. O1-O15.

Madonna of Blieskastel — A30

1925, Apr. 9 **Photo.** ***Perf. 13½x12½***

Size: 23x27mm

118 A30 45c lake brown 2.75 *5.25*
Never hinged 7.00
On cover 20.00

Size: 31½x36mm

Perf. 12

119 A30 10fr black brown 16.00 *24.00*
Never hinged 30.00
On cover 90.00

Nos. 118-119 exist imperforate but were not regularly issued.

For overprint see No. 154.

Market Fountain, St. Johann — A31

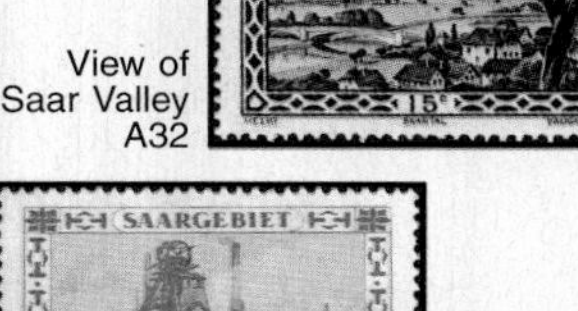

View of Saar Valley A32

Colliery Shafthead A35

Burbach Steelworks A36

Designs: 15c, 75c, View of Saar Valley. 20c, 40c, 90c, Scene from Saarlouis fortifications. 25c, 50c, Tholey Abbey.

1927-32 ***Perf. 13½***

120 A31 10c deep brown .75 .50
Never hinged 1.40
On cover 1.60

121 A32 15c olive black .40 *1.10*
Never hinged 1.10
On cover 3.25

122 A32 20c brown org .40 *.50*
Never hinged 1.10
On cover 1.60

123 A32 25c bluish slate .75 .50
Never hinged 1.25
On cover 3.25

124 A31 30c olive green .95 .50
Never hinged 1.60
On cover 1.60

125 A32 40c olive brown .75 .50
Never hinged 1.40
On cover 3.25

126 A32 50c magenta .95 .50
Never hinged 2.00
On cover 1.60

127 A35 60c red org ('30) 4.00 .55
Never hinged 10.00
On cover 3.25

128 A32 75c brown violet .75 .50
Never hinged 1.30
On cover 2.50

129 A35 80c red orange 2.40 *8.75*
Never hinged 6.50
On cover 20.00

130 A32 90c dp red ('32) 12.00 *17.50*
Never hinged 37.50
On cover 57.50

131 A35 1fr violet 2.40 .50
Never hinged 5.75
On cover 2.50

132 A36 1.50fr sapphire 6.50 .50
Never hinged 17.50
On cover 2.50

133 A36 2fr brown red 6.50 .50
Never hinged 17.50
On cover 3.25

134 A36 3fr dk olive grn 14.50 1.25
Never hinged 35.00
On cover 5.00

135 A36 5fr deep brown 14.50 7.25
Never hinged 35.00
On cover 20.00
Nos. 120-135 (16) 68.50 *41.40*

For surcharges and overprints see Nos. 136-153, O16-O26.

Nos. 126 and 129 Surcharged

1930-34

136 A32 40c on 50c mag ('34) 1.60 *1.60*
Never hinged 4.00
On cover 10.00

137 A35 60c on 80c red orange 2.00 *2.40*
Never hinged 5.00
On cover 8.00

Plebiscite Issue

Stamps of 1925-32 Ovptd. in Various Colors

Perf. 13½, 13½x13, 13x13½

1934, Nov. 1

139 A31 10c brown (Br) .40 *.55*
Never hinged 1.25
On cover 2.10

140 A32 15c black grn (G) .40 *.55*
Never hinged 1.25
On cover 2.10

141 A32 20c brn org (O) .65 *1.40*
Never hinged 1.60
On cover 3.00

142 A32 25c bluish sl (Bl) .65 *1.40*
Never hinged 1.60
On cover 3.00

143 A31 30c olive grn (G) .40 *.55*
Never hinged 1.25
On cover 1.25

144 A32 40c olive brn (Br) .40 *.75*
Never hinged 1.10
On cover 2.00

145 A32 50c magenta (R) .75 *1.40*
Never hinged 2.00
On cover 3.00

146 A35 60c red orge (O) .65 *.55*
Never hinged 1.10
On cover 1.60

147 A32 75c brown vio (V) .75 *1.25*
Never hinged 2.00
On cover 4.25

148 A32 90c deep red (R) .75 *1.40*
Never hinged 2.00
On cover 4.25

149 A35 1fr violet (V) .75 *1.60*
Never hinged 2.00
On cover 4.25

150 A36 1.50fr sapphire (Bl) 1.25 *3.25*
Never hinged 4.25
On cover 10.00

151 A36 2fr brn red (R) 2.00 *4.75*
Never hinged 5.75
On cover 14.50

152 A36 3fr dk ol grn (G) 4.75 *9.50*
Never hinged 12.00
On cover 25.00

153 A36 5fr dp brn (Br) 20.00 *32.50*
Never hinged 52.50
On cover 85.00

Size: 31½x36mm

Perf. 12

154 A30 10fr blk brn (Br) 24.00 *60.00*
Never hinged 57.50
On cover 200.00
Nos. 139-154 (16) 58.55 *121.40*

SEMI-POSTAL STAMPS

Red Cross Dog Leading Blind Man — SP1

Maternity Nurse with Child — SP4

Designs: No. B2, Nurse and invalid. No. B3, Children getting drink at spring.

Perf. 13½

1926, Oct. 25 Photo. Unwmk.

B1 SP1 20c + 20c dk ol grn 8.00 *20.00*
Never hinged 20.00
On cover 65.00
B2 SP1 40c + 40c dk brn 8.00 *20.00*
Never hinged 20.00
On cover 65.00
B3 SP1 50c + 50c red org 8.00 *20.00*
Never hinged 20.00
On cover 57.50
B4 SP4 1.50fr + 1.50fr brt bl 19.00 *47.50*
Never hinged 45.00
On cover 160.00
Nos. B1-B4 (4) 43.00 *107.50*

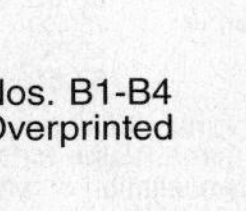

Nos. B1-B4 Overprinted

1927, Oct. 1

B5 SP1 20c + 20c dk ol grn 12.50 *35.00*
Never hinged 32.50
On cover 110.00
B6 SP1 40c + 40c dk brn 12.50 *35.00*
Never hinged 32.50
On cover 145.00
B7 SP1 50c + 50c red org 11.00 *32.50*
Never hinged 24.00
On cover 110.00
B8 SP4 1.50fr + 1.50fr brt bl 17.50 *72.50*
Never hinged 40.00
On cover 280.00
Nos. B5-B8 (4) 53.50 *175.00*

"The Blind Beggar" by Dyckmans SP5

"Almsgiving" by Schiestl SP6

"Charity" by Raphael — SP7

1928, Dec. 23 Photo.

B9 SP5 40c (+40c) blk brn 12.00 *72.50*
Never hinged 30.00
On cover 100.00
B10 SP5 50c (+50c) brn rose 12.00 *72.50*
Never hinged 30.00
On cover 100.00
B11 SP5 1fr (+1fr) dl vio 12.00 *72.50*
Never hinged 30.00
On cover 125.00
B12 SP6 1.50fr (+1.50fr) cob bl 12.00 *72.50*
Never hinged 30.00
On cover 135.00
B13 SP6 2fr (+2fr) red brn 14.00 *100.00*
Never hinged 32.50
On cover 200.00
B14 SP6 3fr (+3fr) dk ol grn 14.00 *135.00*
Never hinged 32.50
On cover 375.00
B15 SP7 10fr (+10fr) dk brn 360.00 *4,000.*
Never hinged 725.00
On cover *6,250.*
Nos. B9-B15 (7) 436.00 4,525.
Set of first day covers (7) *8,500.*
Set of one first day cover *6,500.*

"Orphaned" by Kaulbach SP8

"St. Ottilia" by Feuerstein SP9

"Madonna" by Ferruzzio — SP10

1929, Dec. 22

B16 SP8 40c (+15c) ol grn 2.00 *5.50*
Never hinged 5.25
On cover 30.00
B17 SP8 50c (+20c) cop red 4.00 *9.50*
Never hinged 10.00
On cover 45.00
B18 SP8 1fr (+50c) vio brn 4.00 *11.00*
Never hinged 10.00
On cover 70.00
B19 SP9 1.50fr (+75c) Prus bl 4.00 *11.00*
Never hinged 10.00
On cover 90.00
B20 SP9 2fr (+1fr) brn car 4.00 *11.00*
Never hinged 10.00
On cover 110.00
B21 SP9 3fr (+2fr) sl grn 8.00 *25.00*
Never hinged 16.00
On cover 145.00
B22 SP10 10fr (+8fr) blk brn 47.50 *135.00*
Never hinged 110.00
On cover 575.00
Nos. B16-B22 (7) 73.50 *208.00*

"The Safety-Man" SP11

"The Good Samaritan" SP12

"In the Window" — SP13

1931, Jan. 20

B23 SP11 40c (+15c) 8.00 *24.00*
Never hinged 20.00
On cover 65.00
B24 SP11 60c (+20c) 8.00 *24.00*
Never hinged 20.00
On cover 65.00
B25 SP12 1fr (+50c) 8.00 *47.50*
Never hinged 20.00
On cover 145.00
B26 SP11 1.50fr (+75c) 8.00 *47.50*
Never hinged 28.00
On cover 200.00
B27 SP12 2fr (+1fr) 8.00 *47.50*
Never hinged 28.00
On cover 225.00
B28 SP12 3fr (+2fr) 20.00 *47.50*
Never hinged 40.00
On cover 300.00
B29 SP13 10fr (+10fr) 95.00 *290.00*
Never hinged 210.00
On cover 800.00
Nos. B23-B29 (7) 155.00 *528.00*
Set on first day cover 1,250.

St. Martin of Tours — SP14

Nos. B33-B35, Charity. No. B36, The Widow's Mite.

1931, Dec. 23

B30 SP14 40c (+15c) 12.50 *35.00*
Never hinged 35.00
On cover 65.00
B31 SP14 60c (+20c) 12.50 *35.00*
Never hinged 35.00
On cover 65.00
B32 SP14 1fr (+50c) 16.00 *55.00*
Never hinged 40.00
On cover 130.00
B33 SP14 1.50fr (+75c) 19.00 *55.00*
Never hinged 45.00
On cover 210.00
B34 SP14 2fr (+1fr) 22.50 *55.00*
Never hinged 55.00
On cover 225.00
B35 SP14 3fr (+2fr) 27.50 *95.00*
Never hinged 72.50
On cover 350.00
B36 SP14 5fr (+5fr) 95.00 *325.00*
Never hinged 260.00
On cover 1,200.
Nos. B30-B36 (7) 205.00 *655.00*
Set on first day cover 2,000.

Ruins at Kirkel — SP17

Illingen Castle, Kerpen SP23

Designs: 60c, Church at Blie. 1fr, Castle Ottweiler. 1.50fr, Church of St. Michael, Saarbrucken. 2fr, Statue of St. Wendel. 3fr, Church of St. John, Saarbrucken.

1932, Dec. 20

B37 SP17 40c (+15c) 9.50 *22.50*
Never hinged 32.50
On cover 80.00
B38 SP17 60c (+20c) 9.50 *22.50*
Never hinged 32.50
On cover 100.00
B39 SP17 1fr (+50c) 14.00 *40.00*
Never hinged 32.50
On cover 130.00
B40 SP17 1.50fr (+75c) 20.00 *47.50*
Never hinged 60.00
On cover 160.00
B41 SP17 2fr (+1fr) 20.00 *55.00*
Never hinged 60.00
On cover 180.00
B42 SP17 3fr (+2fr) 55.00 *175.00*
Never hinged 130.00
On cover 575.00
B43 SP23 5fr (+5fr) 125.00 *290.00*
Never hinged 260.00
On cover 1,000.
Nos. B37-B43 (7) 253.00 *652.50*
Set on first day cover 1,700.

Scene of Neunkirchen Disaster — SP24

1933, June 1

B44 SP24 60c (+ 60c) org red 16.00 20.00
Never hinged 40.00
On cover 57.50
B45 SP24 3fr (+ 3fr) ol grn 35.00 *72.50*
Never hinged 90.00
On cover 140.00
B46 SP24 5fr (+ 5fr) org brn 35.00 *72.50*
Never hinged 90.00
On cover 250.00
Nos. B44-B46 (3) 86.00 *165.00*
Set on first day cover 525.00

The surtax was for the aid of victims of the explosion at Neunkirchen, Feb. 10.

"Love" — SP25

Designs: 60c, "Anxiety." 1fr, "Peace." 1.50fr, "Solace." 2fr, "Welfare." 3fr, "Truth." 5fr, Figure on Tomb of Duchess Elizabeth of Lorraine

1934, Mar. 15 Photo.

B47 SP25 40c (+15c) blk brn 5.50 *16.00*
Never hinged 14.50
On cover 40.00
B48 SP25 60c (+20c) red org 5.50 *16.00*
Never hinged 14.50
On cover 40.00
B49 SP25 1fr (+50c) dl vio 7.25 *20.00*
Never hinged 20.00
On cover 60.00
B50 SP25 1.50fr (+75c) blue 14.00 *35.00*
Never hinged 35.00
On cover 125.00
B51 SP25 2fr (+1fr) car rose 12.50 *35.00*
Never hinged 32.50
On cover 120.00
B52 SP25 3fr (+2fr) ol grn 14.00 *35.00*
Never hinged 35.00
On cover 135.00
B53 SP25 5fr (+5fr) red brn 32.50 *87.50*
Never hinged 80.00
On cover 350.00
Nos. B47-B53 (7) 91.25 *244.50*
Set on first day cover 850.00

Nos. B47-B53 Overprinted like Nos. 139-154 in Various Colors Reading up

1934, Dec. 1 ***Perf. 13x13½***

B54 SP25 40c (+15c) (Br) 3.50 *14.00*
Never hinged 8.00
On cover 40.00
B55 SP25 60c (+20c) (R) 3.50 *14.00*
Never hinged 8.00
On cover 40.00
B56 SP25 1fr (+50c) (V) 11.00 *25.00*
Never hinged 21.00
On cover 72.50
B57 SP25 1.50fr (+75c) (Bl) 7.25 *25.00*
Never hinged 18.00
On cover 80.00
B58 SP25 2fr (+1fr) (R) 11.00 *35.00*
Never hinged 26.00
On cover 90.00
B59 SP25 3fr (+2fr) (G) 10.00 *32.50*
Never hinged 25.00
On cover 100.00
B60 SP25 5fr (+5fr) (Br) 15.00 *40.00*
Never hinged 40.00
On cover 130.00
Nos. B54-B60 (7) 61.25 *185.50*

AIR POST STAMPS

Airplane over Saarbrücken — AP1

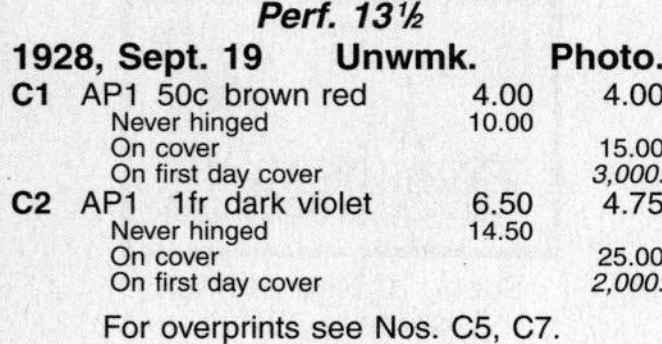

Perf. 13½

1928, Sept. 19 Unwmk. Photo.

C1 AP1 50c brown red 4.00 4.00
Never hinged 10.00
On cover 15.00
On first day cover *3,000.*
C2 AP1 1fr dark violet 6.50 4.75
Never hinged 14.50
On cover 25.00
On first day cover *2,000.*

For overprints see Nos. C5, C7.

Saarbrücken Airport and Church of St. Arnual — AP2

1932, Apr. 30

C3 AP2 60c orange red 6.50 4.75
Never hinged 16.00
On cover 20.00
On first day cover 62.50
C4 AP2 5fr dark brown 45.00 *95.00*
Never hinged 130.00
On cover 200.00
On first day cover 240.00

For overprints see Nos. C6, C8.

Nos. C1-C4 Overprinted like Nos. 139-154 in Various Colors

1934, Nov. 1 ***Perf. 13½, 13½x13***

C5 AP1 50c brn red (R) 4.00 *7.25*
Never hinged 10.00
On cover 20.00
On first day cover 40.00
C6 AP2 60c org red (O) 3.25 *2.75*
Never hinged 7.50
On cover 8.00
On first day cover 40.00
C7 AP1 1fr dk vio (V) 7.25 *9.50*
Never hinged 16.00
On cover 32.50
On first day cover 80.00
C8 AP2 5fr dk brn (Br) 9.50 *14.00*
Never hinged 20.00
On cover 65.00
On first day cover 100.00
Nos. C5-C8 (4) 24.00 *33.50*
Set on first day cover 250.00

OFFICIAL STAMPS

Regular Issue of 1922-1923 Ovptd. Diagonally in Red or Blue

Nos. O1-O15 have two types of overprint: Type I, center bar of "E" slightly above center, "S" has rounded bottom, "A" symetrical; Type 2, center bar of "E" centered, "S" has flat bottom, "A" slightly inclined to right. Overprints are Type I unless noted.

Perf. 12½x13½, 13½x12½

1922-23 Unwmk.

O1 A19 3c ol grn & straw (R) .95 *35.00*
Never hinged 2.75
On cover 120.00
O2 A20 5c org & blk (R) .40 *.40*
Never hinged 1.10
On cover 6.50
a. Pair, one without overprint 275.00
Never hinged 575.00
O3 A21 10c bl grn (R) .40 .35
Never hinged 1.10
On cover 6.50
a. Inverted overprint 32.50
Never hinged 80.00
O4 A19 15c dp brn (Bl) .40 .35
Never hinged 1.10
On cover 6.50
a. Pair, one without overprint 290.00
Never hinged 600.00
b. Double overprint 65.00
Never hinged 180.00
O5 A19 15c org (Bl) ('23) 2.40 .50
Never hinged 5.75
On cover 10.00
O6 A22 20c dk bl & lem (R) .40 .35
Never hinged 1.10
On cover 6.50
a. Inverted overprint 32.50
Never hinged 80.00
b. Double overprint 65.00
Never hinged 160.00
O7 A22 20c brt bl & straw (R) ('23) 2.40 .50
Never hinged 5.75
On cover 10.00
O8 A22 25c red & yel (Bl) 4.00 1.20
Never hinged 11.50
On cover 20.00
O9 A22 25c mag & straw (Bl) ('23) 2.40 .50
Never hinged 5.75
On cover 10.00
a. Overprint Type II ('24) 16.00 2.50
Never hinged 40.00
On cover 50.00
O10 A23 30c car & yel (Bl) .40 .35
Never hinged 1.20
On cover 8.00
a. Inverted overprint 52.50
Never hinged 140.00
O11 A24 40c brn & yel (Bl) .55 .35
Never hinged 1.60
On cover 8.50
O12 A25 50c dk bl & straw (R) .55 .35
Never hinged 1.70
On cover 6.50
a. Inverted overprint 32.50
Never hinged 80.00
O13 A24 75c dp grn & straw (R) 24.00 27.50
Never hinged 80.00
On cover 150.00
O14 A24 75c blk & straw (R) ('23) 4.75 2.40
Never hinged 12.00
On cover 20.00
O15 A26 1fr brn red (Bl) 47.50 16.00
Never hinged 145.00
On cover 100.00
a. Inverted overprint 150.00
Never hinged 400.00
b. Double overprint 150.00
Never hinged 400.00
c. Overprint Type II ('24) 12.00 2.40
Never hinged 32.50
On cover 32.50
Nos. O1-O15 (15) 91.50 *86.10*

The set (Type I) exists imperf. Value, hinged $1850. No. O15c (Type II) exists imperf. Value, hinged $325.

Regular Issue of 1927-30 Overprinted in Various Colors

Two types of overprint: Type I, overprint at 32 degree angle ('27-'32); Type II, overprint at 23 to 25 degree angle ('29-'34).

1927-34 ***Perf. 13½***

O16 A31 10c dp brn (Bl) (II) ('34) 2.00 2.40
Never hinged 8.00
On cover 17.00
O17 A32 15c ol blk (Bl) (II) ('34) 2.00 *6.50*
Never hinged 8.00
On cover 50.00
O18 A32 20c brn org (Bk) (II) ('31) 2.00 1.60
Never hinged 8.00
On cover 17.00
O19 A32 25c bluish sl (Bl) (II) 2.40 *6.50*
Never hinged 8.50
On cover 17.00
O20 A31 30c ol grn (C) (I) 5.75 .80
Never hinged 16.00
On cover 6.50
a. Orange red ovpt. (II) 2.00 .50
Never hinged 8.00
On cover 6.50
b. Carmine ovpt. (II) 4.00 2.10
Never hinged 11.50
On cover 12.50
O21 A32 40c ol brn (C) (I) 5.75 .80
Never hinged 16.00
On cover 6.50
a. Double overprint 80.00
b. 40c olive brown (C) (II) 2.00 .35
Never hinged 8.00
On cover 6.75
c. As "b," double overprint 100.00
Never hinged 240.00
O22 A32 50c mag (Bl) (I) 20.00 .65
Never hinged 65.00
On cover 6.50
a. Double overprint 80.00
b. 50c magenta (Bl) (II) 4.00 .40
Never hinged 13.00
On cover 6.50
c. As "b," double overprint 55.00
Never hinged 100.00
O23 A35 60c red org (Bk) (II) ('30) 1.20 .35
Never hinged 4.00
On cover 6.50
a. Double overprint 55.00
Never hinged 100.00
O24 A32 75c brn vio (C) (I) 5.75 .85
Never hinged 14.50
On cover 20.00
a. Double overprint 85.00
b. 75c brown violet (C) (II) 2.40 .80
Never hinged 8.00
On cover 16.00
O25 A35 1fr vio (RO) (I) 5.75 .85
Never hinged 16.00
On cover 4.25
a. Double overprint 85.00
b. 1fr violet (RO) (II) 2.40 .40
Never hinged 16.00
On cover 8.50
c. As "b," double overprint 85.00
Never hinged 160.00
O26 A36 2fr brn red (Bl) (I) 14.50 1.60
Never hinged 50.00
On cover 12.00
a. Double overprint 80.00
b. 2fr brown red (Bl) (II) 2.40 .40
Never hinged 16.00
On cover 8.00
c. As "b," double overprint 75.00
Never hinged 125.00
Nos. O16-O26 (11) 67.10 *22.90*

The overprint on Nos. O16 and O20 is known only inverted.

ST. CHRISTOPHER

sānt 'kris-tə-fər

LOCATION — Island in the West Indies, southeast of Puerto Rico
GOVT. — A Presidency of the Leeward Islands Colony
AREA — 68 sq. mi.
POP. — 18,578 (estimated)
CAPITAL — Basseterre

Stamps of St. Christopher were discontinued in 1890 and replaced by those of Leeward Islands. For later issues see St. Kitts-Nevis.

12 Pence = 1 Shilling

STAMPS OF GREAT BRITAIN USED IN ST. CHRISTOPHER

Numeral cancellation type A is pictured in the Crowned Circle Handstamps and Great Britain Used Abroad section.

1858-60

A12 (Basseterre)

A1 A 1p rose red (#20) 775.00
A2 A 2p blue (#29, P7) 2,000.
A3 A 4p rose (#26) 450.00
A4 A 6p lilac (#27) 300.00
A5 A 1sh green (#28) 2,500.

See footnote after No. 23.

Issued under British Administration

Queen Victoria — A1

Wmk. Crown and C C (1)

1870, Apr. 1 Typo. ***Perf. 12½***

1 A1 1p dull rose 95.00 52.50
2 A1 1p lilac rose 82.50 35.00
3 A1 6p green ('71) 140.00 8.75
a. 6p yellow green ('70) 140.00 21.00
Nos. 1-3 (3) 317.50 96.25

1875-79 ***Perf. 14***

4 A1 1p lilac rose 80.00 8.00
b. Half used as ½p on cover (2½p rate) *2,500.*
c. Half used as ½p on newsprint (½p rate) *2,500.*
5 A1 2½p red brown ('79) 200.00 *275.00*
6 A1 4p blue ('79) 225.00 16.00
7 A1 6p green 60.00 6.00
a. Horiz. pair, imperf. vert. —
Nos. 4-7 (4) 565.00 305.00

The value for No. 4b is for covers dated between March and June, 1882.
For surcharges see Nos. 18-20.

1882-90 Wmk. Crown and C A (2)

8 A1 ½p green 6.75 4.25
9 A1 1p rose 3.50 2.25
a. Half used as ½p on cover —
10 A1 1p lilac rose 600.00 77.50
a. Diagonal half used as ½p on cover —
11 A1 2½p red brown 200.00 67.50
a. 2½p deep red brown 210.00 72.50
12 A1 2½p ultra ('84) 5.25 2.00
13 A1 4p blue 550.00 27.50
14 A1 4p gray ('84) 1.75 1.10
15 A1 6p olive brn ('90) 95.00 *425.00*
16 A1 1sh violet ('87) 105.00 75.00
a. 1sh bright mauve ('90) 95.00 180.00
Nos. 8-16 (9) 1,567. 682.10

For surcharges see Nos. 17, 21-23.

No. 9 Bisected and Handstamp Surcharged in Black

1885, Mar.

17 A1 ½p on half of 1p 29.00 *45.00*
b. Inverted surcharge 250.00 125.00
c. Unsevered pair 140.00 *140.00*
d. As "c," one surcharge inverted *450.00* *325.00*
e. Double surcharge — —

No. 7 Surcharged in Black

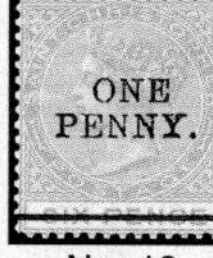

No. 18

No. 19

No. 20

1884-86 Wmk. 1

18 A1 1p on 6p grn ('86) 22.50 *50.00*
a. Inverted surcharge 10,000.
b. Double surcharge 1,650.
19 A1 4p on 6p green 75.00 57.50
a. Period after "PENCE" 75.00 57.50
b. Double surcharge — 3,000.
20 A1 4p on 6p grn ('86) 60.00 105.00
a. Without period after "d" 250.00 325.00
b. Double surcharge *2,750.* *3,000.*
Nos. 18-20 (3) 157.50 212.50

The line through original value on Nos. 18 and 20 was added by hand. Value for No. 18b is for stamp with pen cancellation or with violet handstamp (revenue cancels).

Nos. 8 and 12 Surcharged in Black Like No. 18 or

No. 21

No. 22

1887-88 Wmk. 2

21 A1 1p on ½p green 50.00 *60.00*
22 A1 1p on 2½p ('88) 72.50 72.50
a. Inverted surcharge *27,500.* *11,000.*
23 A1 1p on 2½p, no line over original value ('88) *22,000.* *15,000.*

Nos. 18 and 21 have the same type of One Penny surcharge. The line through the original value on Nos. 21 and 22 were added by hand. No. 23 probably is a sheet that was meant to be No. 22 but was missed when the bars were added.

Antigua No. 18 was used in St. Christopher in 1890. It is canceled "A12" instead of "A02." Values: used $140, on cover $850.

POSTAL FISCAL ISSUES

Nevis Nos. 22 and 28 Overprinted "REVENUE" Horizontally and "Saint Christopher" Diagonally

1883

AR1 A5 1p violet 425.00
AR2 A5 6p green 130.00 *170.00*

Stamps of St. Christopher Ovptd. "SAINT KITTS / NEVIS / REVENUE" in 3 Lines

1885

AR3 A1 1p rose 3.00 *19.00*
AR4 A1 3p violet 17.50 *72.50*
AR5 A1 6p orange brown 20.00 *55.00*
AR6 A1 1sh olive 3.75 *47.50*

Other values exist with the above overprints but were not available for postal purposes.

ST. HELENA

sānt 'he-lə-nə

LOCATION — Island in the Atlantic Ocean, 1,200 miles west of Angola
GOVT. — British Crown Colony
AREA — 47 sq. mi.
POP. — 5,499 (1982)
CAPITAL — Jamestown

12 Pence = 1 Shilling
20 Shillings = 1 Pound

Catalogue values for unused stamps in this country are for Never Hinged items, beginning with Scott 128 in the regular postage section.

Values for unused stamps are for examples with original gum as defined in the catalogue introduction. Very fine examples of Nos. 2-7, 11-39a and 47-47b will have perforations touching the design on one or more sides due to the narrow spacing of the stamps on the plates. Stamps with perfs clear of the design on all four sides are scarce and will command higher prices.

Watermark

Wmk. 6 — Star

Queen Victoria — A1

1856, Jan. Wmk. 6 Engr. *Imperf.*
1 A1 6p blue 600.00 225.00

For types surcharged see Nos. 8-39, 47.

1861 *Clean-Cut Perf. 14 to 15½*
2 A1 6p blue 2,100. 325.00

1863 *Rough Perf. 14 to 15½*
2B A1 6p blue 525.00 160.00

1871-74 Wmk. 1 *Perf. 12½*
3 A1 6p dull blue 900.00 125.00
4 A1 6p ultra ('73) 500.00 97.50

1879 *Perf. 14x12½*
5 A1 6p gray blue 475.00 60.00

1889 *Perf. 14*
6 A1 6p gray blue 550.00 60.00

1889 Wmk. Crown and C A (2)
7 A1 6p gray 42.50 6.00

Type of 1856 Surcharged

a

b

Long Bar, 16, 17, 18 or 19mm

1863 Wmk. 1 *Imperf.*
8 A1(a) 1p on 6p brn red (srch. 17mm) 150.00 *250.00*
a. Double surcharge 6,750. 4,250.
b. Surcharge omitted *23,000.*
9 A1(a) 1p on 6p brn red (srch. 19mm) 150.00 *275.00*
a. Vertical pair, #8, 9 *11,500.*
10 A1(b) 4p on 6p car 600.00 300.00
b. Double surcharge *16,000.* *10,000.*

1864-73 *Perf. 12½*
11 A1(a) 1p on 6p brn red 70.00 35.00
a. Double surcharge *12,000.*
12 A1(b) 1p on 6p brn red ('71) 140.00 21.00
a. Blue black surcharge *1,200.* *675.00*
13 A1(b) 2p on 6p yel ('73) 160.00 50.00
a. Blue black surcharge *4,800.* *2,700.*
14 A1(b) 3p on 6p dk vio ('73) 140.00 72.50
15 A1(b) 4p on 6p car 175.00 60.00
a. Double surcharge *6,750.*
16 A1(b) 1sh on 6p grn (bar 16 to 17mm) 450.00 35.00
a. Double surcharge *24,000.*
17 A1(b) 1sh on 6p dp grn (bar 18mm) ('73) 750.00 20.00
a. Blue black surcharge —

1868 Short Bar, 14 or 15mm
18 A1(a) 1p on 6p brn red 225.00 67.50
a. Imperf., pair *6,000.*
b. Double surcharge —
19 A1(b) 2p on 6p yel 200.00 72.50
a. Imperf 12,000.
20 A1(b) 3p on 6p dk vio 120.00 60.00
a. Double surcharge 7,250.
b. Imperf., pair *2,000.*
c. 3p on 6p pale purple 3,300. 900.00
21 A1(b) 4p on 6p car (words 18mm) 140.00 72.50
a. Double surcharge *6,000.*
b. Imperf, single 14,500.
22 A1(b) 4p on 6p car (words 19mm) 325.00 150.00
a. Words double, 18mm and 19mm *26,000.* *11,000.*
b. Imperf. —
c. Surcharge omitted *6,000.*
23 A1(a) 1sh on 6p yel grn 750.00 160.00
a. Double surcharge *19,500.*
b. Pair, one without surcharge *19,500.*
c. Imperf *17,000.*
24 A1(a) 5sh on 6p org 67.50 77.50
a. 5sh on 6p yellow 550.00 450.00

1882 *Perf. 14x12½*
25 A1(a) 1p on 6p brown red 90.00 18.00
26 A1(b) 2p on 6p yellow 140.00 60.00
27 A1(b) 3p on 6p violet 350.00 85.00
28 A1(b) 4p on 6p carmine (words 16½mm) 170.00 72.50

1883 *Perf. 14*
29 A1(a) 1p on 6p brown red 120.00 22.50
30 A1(b) 2p on 6p yellow 150.00 37.50
31 A1(a) 1sh on 6p yel grn 25.00 15.00

Long Bar, 18mm

1882 *Perf. 14x12½*
32 A1(b) 1sh on 6p dp grn 900.00 30.00

Short Bar, 14 or 14½mm

1884-94 Wmk. 2 *Perf. 14*
33 A1(b) ½p on 6p grn (words 17mm) 12.00 20.00
a. ½p on 6p emer, blurred print (words 17mm) ('84) 16.00 23.00
b. Double surcharge 1,450. 1,575.
c. "N" and "Y" spaced .8mm (#33) 550.00 *800.00*
d. "N" and "Y" spaced .8mm (#33a) 1,300.
e. As "d," double surcharge 13,500.
34 A1(b) ½p on 6p grn (words 15mm) ('94) 3.25 3.50
a. "N" and "Y" spaced .8mm 1,800.
35 A1(a) 1p on 6p red ('87) 5.75 4.50
a. 1p on 6p pale red 7.75 3.75
36 A1(b) 2p on 6p yel ('94) 3.25 9.50
37 A1(b) 3p on 6p dp vio ('87) 9.00 13.50
a. 3p on 6p red violet 6.00 6.00
b. Double surcharge,#37a *11,500.* *7,250.*
c. Double surcharge, #37 *11,000.*
38 A1(b) 4p on 6p pale brn (words 16½mm; '90) 37.50 *35.00*
a. 4p on 6p dk brn (words 17mm; '94) 30.00 21.00
b. With thin bar below thick one 850.00

The spacing between "N" and "Y" in surcharges on Nos. 33 and 34 is normally .5mm. Examples with .8mm spacing are from one position within the pane.

1894 Long Bar, 18mm
39 A1(b) 1sh on 6p yel grn 65.00 30.00
a. Double surcharge *5,750.*

See note after No. 47.

Queen Victoria — A3

1890-97 Typo. *Perf. 14*
40 A3 ½p green ('97) 3.25 7.75
41 A3 1p rose ('96) 20.00 2.40
42 A3 1½p red brn & grn 5.50 12.00
43 A3 2p yellow ('96) 6.00 14.50
44 A3 2½p ultra ('96) 18.00 14.50
45 A3 5p violet ('96) 13.50 37.50
46 A3 10p brown ('96) 29.00 *72.50*
Nos. 40-46 (7) 95.25 *161.15*
Set, ovptd. "SPECIMEN" 360.00

Type of 1856 Surcharged

1893 Engr. Wmk. 2
47 A1 2½p on 6p blue 3.75 6.75
a. Double surcharge *24,000.*
b. Double impression *11,500.*

In 1905 remainders of Nos. 34-47 were sold by the postal officials. They are canceled with bars, arranged in the shape of diamonds, in purple ink. No such cancellation was ever used on the island and the stamps so canceled are of slight value. With this cancellation removed, these remainders are sometimes offered as unused. Some have been recanceled with a false dated postmark.

King Edward VII — A5

1902 Typo. Wmk. 2
48 A5 ½p green 2.00 *3.00*
49 A5 1p carmine rose 13.00 .85
Nos. 48, 49, ovptd. "SPECIMEN" 90.00

Government House — A6

"The Wharf" — A7

1903, June Wmk. 1
50 A6 ½p gray grn & brn 2.40 4.00
51 A7 1p carmine & blk 1.90 .50
52 A6 2p ol grn & blk 12.00 1.50
53 A7 8p brown & blk 26.50 *37.50*
54 A6 1sh org buff & brn 27.50 *47.50*
55 A7 2sh violet & blk 65.00 *100.00*
Nos. 50-55 (6) 135.30 *191.00*
Set, ovptd. "SPECIMEN" 275.00

A8

1908, May Wmk. 3

Ordinary Paper

56 A8 2½p ultra 2.00 *1.90*
57 A8 4p black & red, *yel* ('11) 7.00 *21.00*
a. Chalky paper 10.00 *24.00*
58 A8 6p dull violet ('11) 7.75 *17.00*
a. Chalky paper 20.00 *37.50*
Nos. 56-58 (3) 16.75 *39.90*

Wmk. 2
Chalky Paper

60 A8 10sh grn & red, *grn* 275.00 *325.00*
Set, ovptd. "SPECIMEN" 300.00

Nos. 57 and 58 exist on both ordinary and chalky paper; No. 56 on ordinary and No. 60 on chalky paper.

Government House — A9

"The Wharf" — A10

1912-16 Ordinary Paper Wmk. 3
61 A9 ½p green & blk 3.25 12.00
62 A10 1p carmine & blk 5.75 2.00
a. 1p scarlet & black ('16) 14.50 *24.00*
63 A10 1½p orange & blk 4.25 9.00
64 A9 2p gray & black 6.75 2.00
65 A10 2½p ultra & blk 4.25 7.25
66 A9 3p vio & blk, *yel* 4.25 6.00
67 A10 8p dull vio & blk 12.00 60.00
68 A9 1sh black, *green* 11.00 42.50
69 A10 2sh ultra & blk, *bl* 50.00 *100.00*
70 A10 3sh violet & blk 75.00 *160.00*
Nos. 61-70 (10) 176.50 *400.75*
Set, ovptd. "SPECIMEN" 360.00

See Nos. 75-77.

King Edward VII — A11

Die I

For description of dies I and II see "Dies of British Colonial Stamps" in the front of the catalogue.

1912 Chalky Paper
71 A11 4p black & red, *yel* 15.00 *30.00*
72 A11 6p dull vio & red vio 4.75 *6.00*
Set, ovptd. "SPECIMEN" 110.00

A12

1913 Ordinary Paper
73 A12 4p black & red, *yel* 10.00 3.25
74 A12 6p dull vio & red vio 16.00 *35.00*
Set, ovptd. "SPECIMEN" 110.00

1922 **Wmk. 4**

No.	Type	Denom.	Color	Unused	Used
75	A10	1p	green	3.25	*55.00*
76	A10	1½p	rose red	12.00	*52.50*
77	A9	3p	ultra	25.00	*95.00*
			Nos. 75-77 (3)	40.25	*202.50*
			Set, ovptd. "SPECIMEN"	140.00	

Badge of the Colony — A13

1922-27 **Chalky Paper** **Wmk. 4**

No.	Type	Denom.	Color	Unused	Used
79	A13	½p	blk & gray	4.00	4.00
80	A13	1p	grn & blk	3.25	2.00
81	A13	1½p	rose red	3.75	*15.00*
82	A13	2p	pale gray & gray	4.50	2.40
83	A13	3p	ultra	2.40	*4.75*
84	A13	5p	red & grn, *emer*	5.00	*6.75*
85	A13	6p	red vio & blk	5.50	*9.75*
86	A13	8p	vio & blk	4.50	*8.50*
87	A13	1sh	dk brn & blk	7.75	*11.00*
88	A13	1sh6p	grn & blk, *emer*	18.00	*60.00*
89	A13	2sh	ultra & vio, *bl*	22.50	*55.00*
90	A13	2sh6p	car & blk, *yel*	17.00	*77.50*
91	A13	5sh	grn & blk, *yel*	45.00	*90.00*
92	A13	7sh6p	org & blk	140.00	*200.00*
93	A13	10sh	ol grn & blk	170.00	*250.00*
94	A13	15sh	vio & blk, *bl*	1,100.	*2,750.*
			Nos. 79-93 (15)	453.15	*796.65*
			Set, ovptd. "SPECIMEN"	1,450.	

Nos. 88, 90, and 91 are on ordinary paper.

Wmk. 3

Chalky Paper

No.	Type	Denom.	Color	Unused	Used
95	A13	4p	black, *yel*	15.00	*7.25*
96	A13	1sh6p	bl grn & blk, *grn*	26.50	*72.50*
97	A13	2sh6p	car & blk, *yel*	30.00	*77.50*
98	A13	5sh	grn & blk, *yel*	50.00	*120.00*
99	A13	£1	red vio & blk, *red*	475.00	*700.00*
			Nos. 95-99 (5)	596.50	*977.25*
			Set, ovptd. "SPECIMEN"	600.00	

Issue dates: ½p, 1½p, 2p, 3p, 4p, 8p, February, 1923; 5p, Nos. 88-91, 1927; others, June 1922.

Centenary Issue

Lot and Lot's Wife — A14

Plantation; Queen Victoria and Kings William IV, Edward VII, George V A15

Map of the Colony A16

Quay, Jamestown A17

View of James Valley — A18

View of Jamestown A19

View of Mundens A20

St. Helena — A21

View of High Knoll — A22

Badge of the Colony A23

Perf. 12

1934, Apr. 23 **Engr.** **Wmk. 4**

No.	Type	Denom.	Color	Unused	Used
101	A14	½p	dk vio & blk	1.25	*1.00*
102	A15	1p	green & blk	.80	*1.00*
103	A16	1½p	red & blk	3.00	*4.00*
104	A17	2p	orange & blk	3.75	*1.50*
105	A18	3p	blue & blk	1.75	*5.50*
106	A19	6p	lt blue & blk	4.00	*3.75*
107	A20	1sh	dk brn & blk	8.00	*22.50*
108	A21	2sh6p	car & blk	50.00	*60.00*
109	A22	5sh	choc & blk	100.00	*100.00*
110	A23	10sh	red vio & blk	300.00	*350.00*
			Nos. 101-110 (10)	472.55	*549.25*
			Set, never hinged	725.00	
			Set, perf. "SPECIMEN"	450.00	

Common Design Types

For description of dies I and II see "Dies of British Colonial Stamps" in Table of Contents.

Silver Jubilee Issue

Common Design Type

1935, May 6 ***Perf. 13½x14***

No.	Type	Denom.	Color	Unused	Used
111	CD301	1½p	car & dk blue	1.25	*6.75*
112	CD301	2p	gray blk & ultra	2.40	1.25
113	CD301	6p	indigo & grn	8.50	4.25
114	CD301	1sh	brt vio & ind	19.00	*21.00*
			Nos. 111-114 (4)	31.15	*33.25*
			Set, never hinged	52.50	
			Set, perf. "SPECIMEN"	170.00	

Coronation Issue

Common Design Type

1937, May 19

No.	Type	Denom.	Color	Unused	Used
115	CD302	1p	deep green	.45	*.90*
116	CD302	2p	deep orange	.40	*.55*
117	CD302	3p	bright ultra	.60	.60
			Nos. 115-117 (3)	1.45	2.05
			Set, never hinged	2.00	
			Set, perf. "SPECIMEN"	100.00	

Badge of the Colony — A24

1938-40 ***Perf. 12½***

No.	Type	Denom.	Color	Unused	Used
118	A24	½p	purple	.25	.75
119	A24	1p	dp green	7.00	2.40
119A	A24	1p	org yel ('40)	.25	.30
120	A24	1½p	carmine	.30	.40
121	A24	2p	orange	.25	.25
122	A24	3p	ultra	55.00	18.00
122A	A24	3p	gray ('40)	.35	.30
122B	A24	4p	ultra ('40)	1.10	.85
123	A24	6p	gray blue	1.10	1.40
123A	A24	8p	olive ('40)	1.75	1.00
124	A24	1sh	sepia	1.10	.35
125	A24	2sh6p	deep claret	11.00	6.75
126	A24	5sh	brown	11.00	12.50
127	A24	10sh	violet	11.00	*18.00*
			Nos. 118-127 (14)	101.45	63.25
			Set, never hinged	160.00	
			Set, perf. "SPECIMEN"	450.00	

Issue dates: May 12, 1938, July 8, 1940.

See Nos. 136-138.

Catalogue values for unused stamps in this section, from this point to the end of the section, are for Never Hinged items.

Peace Issue

Common Design Type

Perf. 13½x14

1946, Oct. 21 **Wmk. 4** **Engr.**

No.	Type	Denom.	Color	Unused	Used
128	CD303	2p	deep orange	.30	.40
129	CD303	4p	deep blue	.35	.30
			Set, perf. "SPECIMEN"	100.00	

Silver Wedding Issue

Common Design Types

1948, Oct. 20 **Photo.** ***Perf. 14x14½***

No.	Type	Denom.	Color	Unused	Used
130	CD304	3p	black	.30	.30

Perf. 11½x11

Engr.; Name Typo.

No.	Type	Denom.	Color	Unused	Used
131	CD305	10sh	blue violet	32.50	*42.50*

UPU Issue

Common Design Types

Engr.; Name Typo. on 4p, 6p

1949, Oct. 10 ***Perf. 13½, 11x11½***

No.	Type	Denom.	Color	Unused	Used
132	CD306	3p	rose carmine	.30	1.00
133	CD307	4p	indigo	3.50	1.60
134	CD308	6p	olive	.65	*3.25*
135	CD309	1sh	slate	.40	*1.25*
			Nos. 132-135 (4)	4.85	7.10

George VI Type of 1938

1949, Nov. 1 **Engr.** ***Perf. 12½***

Center in Black

No.	Type	Denom.	Color	Unused	Used
136	A24	1p	blue green	1.35	1.60
137	A24	1½p	carmine rose	1.35	1.60
138	A24	2p	carmine	1.35	1.60
			Nos. 136-138 (3)	4.05	4.80

WAR TAX STAMPS

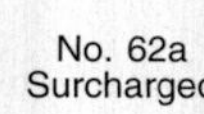

No. 62a Surcharged

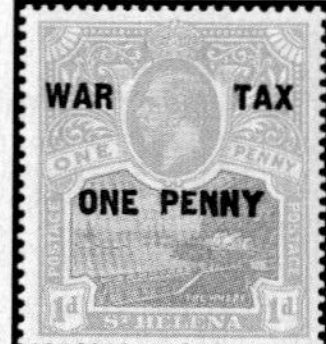

1916 **Wmk. 3** ***Perf. 14***

No.	Type	Denom.	Color	Unused	Used
MR1	A10	1p + 1p	scar & blk	3.00	4.00
			Ovptd. "SPECIMEN"	67.50	
a.			Double surcharge		*20,000.*

No. 62 Surcharged

1919

No.	Type	Denom.	Color	Unused	Used
MR2	A10	1p + 1p	car & blk	2.10	5.50
			Ovptd. "SPECIMEN"	67.50	

ST. KITTS-NEVIS

sānt 'kits-'nē-vəs

LOCATION — West Indies southeast of Puerto Rico
GOVT. — Associated State in British Commonwealth
AREA — 153 sq. mi.
POP. — 48,000, excluding Anguilla (est. 1976)
CAPITAL — Basseterre, St. Kitts

A presidency of the Leeward Islands colony.

See "St. Christopher" for stamps used in St. Kitts before 1890. From 1890 until 1903, stamps of the Leeward Islands were used. From 1903 until 1956, stamps of St. Kitts-Nevis and Leeward Islands were used concurrently.

12 Pence = 1 Shilling
20 Shillings = 1 Pound
100 Cents = 1 Dollar (1951)

Catalogue values for unused stamps in this country are for Never Hinged items, beginning with Scott 91 in the regular postage section.

Columbus Looking for Land — A1

Medicinal Spring — A2

Wmk. Crown and C A (2)

1903 Typo. *Perf. 14*

No.	Type	Description	Unused	Used
1	A1	½p grn & vio	2.00	.80
2	A2	1p car & black	5.25	.25
3	A1	2p brn & vio	3.50	12.00
4	A1	2½p ultra & black	20.00	6.00
5	A2	3p org & green	25.00	32.50
6	A1	6p red vio & blk	8.00	47.50
7	A1	1sh org & grn	7.75	12.00
8	A2	2sh blk & grn	13.50	22.50
9	A1	2sh6p violet & blk	20.00	50.00
10	A2	5sh ol grn & gray vio	70.00	62.50
		Nos. 1-10 (10)	175.00	246.05
		Set, ovptd. "SPECIMEN"	170.00	

1905-18 Wmk. 3

No.	Type	Description	Unused	Used
11	A1	½p green & violet	15.00	7.50
12	A1	½p green ('07)	1.10	.65
a.		½p dl blue grn ('16)	1.00	3.25
13	A2	1p carmine & blk	9.50	.30
14	A2	1p carmine ('07)	2.50	.25
a.		1p scarlet ('16)	1.00	.25
15	A1	2p brn & vio, ordinary paper	11.00	9.00
a.		Chalky paper	7.25	9.00
16	A1	2½p ultra & blk	40.00	6.00
17	A1	2½p ultra	4.00	.60
18	A2	3p org & grn, chalky paper	3.25	3.00
a.		Ordinary paper	30.00	18.00
19	A1	6p red violet & gray blk ('16)	12.00	35.00
a.		6p purple & gray, chalky paper ('08)	24.00	32.50
b.		6p dp vio & gray blk, ordinary paper	27.50	55.00
20	A1	1sh org & grn, chalky paper ('09)	4.00	35.00
a.		Ordinary paper ('09)	50.00	65.00
21	A2	5sh ol grn & gray vio ('18)	47.50	120.00
		Nos. 11-21 (11)	149.85	217.30

Nos. 13, 19a and 21 are on chalky paper only and Nos. 15, 18 and 20 are on both ordinary and chalky paper.

For stamp and type overprinted see #MR1-MR2.

King George V — A3

A4

1920-22 Ordinary Paper

No.	Type	Description	Unused	Used
24	A3	½p green	4.25	6.00
25	A4	1p carmine	3.50	6.75
26	A3	1½p orange	1.40	2.00
27	A4	2p gray	3.25	7.50
28	A3	2½p ultramarine	7.50	10.00
a.		"A" missing from watermark	600.00	

Chalky Paper

No.	Type	Description	Unused	Used
29	A4	3p vio & dull vio, *yel*	2.00	12.00
30	A3	6p red vio & dull vio	4.00	12.00
31	A4	1sh blk, *gray grn*	4.00	4.50
32	A3	2sh ultra & dull vio, *bl*	25.00	50.00
33	A4	2sh 6p red & blk, *bl*	5.50	40.00
34	A3	5sh red & grn, *yel*	5.50	45.00
35	A4	10sh red & grn, *grn*	14.50	52.50
36	A3	£1 blk & vio, *red* ('22)	300.00	375.00
		Nos. 24-36 (13)	380.40	623.25
		Set, ovptd. "SPECIMEN"	375.00	

1921-29 Ordinary Paper Wmk. 4

No.	Type	Description	Unused	Used
37	A3	½p yel green	2.50	1.50
a.		½p blue green	2.50	1.60
38	A4	1p rose red	1.25	.25
39	A4	1p dp violet ('22)	7.50	1.10
a.		1p pale violet ('29)	7.75	1.75
40	A3	1½p rose red ('25)	6.00	2.00
41	A3	1½p fawn ('28)	1.50	.35
42	A4	2p gray	1.00	.65
43	A3	2½p pale bright blue ('22)	1.75	2.50
44	A3	2½p brown ('22)	4.00	10.00

Chalky Paper

No.	Type	Description	Unused	Used
43a	A3	2½p ultra ('27)	1.75	2.00
45	A4	3p ultra ('22)	1.25	4.75
46	A4	3p vio & dl vio, *yel*	2.00	3.00
47	A3	6p red vio & dl vio ('24)	1.50	6.75
48	A4	1sh blk, *grn* ('29)	6.50	5.00
49	A3	2sh ultra & vio, *bl* ('22)	15.00	35.00
50	A4	2sh6p red & blk, *bl* ('27)	22.50	29.00
51	A3	5sh red & grn, *yel* ('29)	55.00	100.00
		Nos. 37-51 (16)	131.00	203.85
		Set, ovptd. "SPEICMEN"	450.00	

No. 43 exists on ordinary and chalky paper.

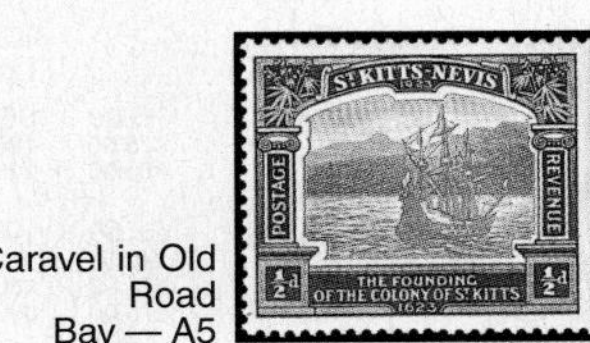

Caravel in Old Road Bay — A5

1923 Wmk. 4

No.	Type	Description	Unused	Used
52	A5	½p green & blk	2.50	8.25
53	A5	1p violet & blk	5.00	1.75
54	A5	1½p car & blk	5.00	11.00
55	A5	2p dk gray & blk	4.25	1.75
56	A5	2½p brown & blk	6.50	35.00
57	A5	3p ultra & blk	6.50	16.00
58	A5	6p red vio & blk	10.50	35.00
59	A5	1sh ol grn & blk	15.00	35.00
60	A5	2sh ultra & blk, *bl*	52.50	85.00
61	A5	2sh6p red & blk, *blue*	55.00	100.00
62	A5	10sh red & blk, *emer*	325.00	600.00

Wmk. 3

No.	Type	Description	Unused	Used
63	A5	5sh red & blk, *yel*	92.50	225.00
64	A5	£1 vio & blk, *red*	825.00	1,775.
		Nos. 52-63 (12)	580.25	1,154.
		Set, ovptd. "SPECIMEN"	850.00	

Tercentenary of the founding of the colony of St. Kitts (or St. Christopher).

Common Design Types pictured following the introduction.

Silver Jubilee Issue
Common Design Type
Inscribed "St. Christopher and Nevis"

Perf. 11x12

1935, May 6 Engr. Wmk. 4

No.	Type	Description	Unused	Used
72	CD301	1p car & dk blue	1.10	.75
73	CD301	1½p gray blk & ultra	.85	.85
74	CD301	2½p ultra & brown	1.10	.90
75	CD301	1sh brn vio & ind	8.50	16.00
		Nos. 72-75 (4)	11.55	18.50
		Set, never hinged	19.50	
		Set, ovptd. "SPECIMEN"	105.00	

Coronation Issue
Common Design Type
Inscribed "St. Christopher and Nevis"

1937, May 12 *Perf. 13½x14*

No.	Type	Description	Unused	Used
76	CD302	1p carmine	.25	.30
77	CD302	1½p brown	.30	.25
78	CD302	2½p bright ultra	.40	1.50
		Nos. 76-78 (3)	.95	2.05
		Set, never hinged	1.25	
		Set, ovptd. "SPECIMEN"	95.00	

George VI A6

Medicinal Spring A7

Columbus Looking for Land — A8

Map Showing Anguilla A9

Perf. 13½x14 (A6, A9), 14 (A7, A8)

1938-48 Typo.

No.	Type	Description	Unused	Used
79	A6	½p green	.25	.25
80	A6	1p carmine	1.00	.55
81	A6	1½p orange	.25	.30
82	A7	2p gray & car	.90	1.40
83	A6	2½p ultra	.50	.35
84	A7	3p car & pale lilac	2.75	5.50
85	A8	6p rose lil & dl grn	5.00	1.60
86	A7	1sh green & gray blk	3.00	1.00
87	A7	2sh6p car & gray blk	8.50	4.50
88	A8	5sh car & dull grn	17.50	13.00

Typo., Center Litho.
Chalky Paper

No.	Type	Description	Unused	Used
89	A9	10sh brt ultra & blk	9.50	21.00
90	A9	£1 brown & blk	9.50	25.00
		Nos. 79-90 (12)	58.65	74.45
		Set, never hinged	85.00	
		Set, ovptd. "SPECIMEN"	250.00	

Issued: ½, 1, 1½, 2½p, 8/15/38; 2p, 1941; 3, 6p, 2sh6p, 5sh, 1942; 1sh, 1943; 10sh, £1, 9/1/48.

For types overprinted see Nos. 99-104.

1938, Aug. 15 *Perf. 13x11½*

No.	Type	Description	Unused	Used
82a	A7	2p	18.00	3.00
84a	A7	3p	16.00	7.50
85a	A8	6p	6.50	3.00
86a	A7	1sh	8.50	1.50
87a	A7	2sh6p	22.50	10.00
88a	A8	5sh	47.50	23.00
		Nos. 82a-88a (6)	119.00	48.00

Catalogue values for unused stamps in this section, from this point to the end of the section, are for Never Hinged items.

Peace Issue
Common Design Type
Inscribed "St. Kitts-Nevis"

1946, Nov. 1 Engr. *Perf. 13½x14*

No.	Type	Description	Unused	Used
91	CD303	1½p deep orange	.25	.25
92	CD303	3p carmine	.25	.25
		Set, perf "SPECIMEN"	95.00	

Silver Wedding Issue
Common Design Types
Inscribed: "St. Kitts-Nevis"

1949, Jan. 3 Photo. *Perf. 14x14½*

No.	Type	Description	Unused	Used
93	CD304	2½p bright ultra	.25	.50

Perf. 11½x11

Engraved; Name Typographed

No.	Type	Description	Unused	Used
94	CD305	5sh rose carmine	11.00	6.75

UPU Issue
Common Design Types
Inscribed: "St. Kitt's-Nevis"

Engr.; Name Typo. on 3p, 6p

1949, Oct. 10 *Perf. 13½, 11x11½*

No.	Type	Description	Unused	Used
95	CD306	2½p ultra	.25	.35
96	CD307	3p deep carmine	2.50	2.50
97	CD308	6p red lilac	.25	1.40
98	CD309	1sh blue green	.35	.45
		Nos. 95-98 (4)	3.35	4.70

Types of 1938 Overprinted in Black or Carmine

On A6

On A7-A8

Perf. 13½x14, 13x12½

1950, Nov. 10 Wmk. 4

No.	Type	Description	Unused	Used
99	A6	1p carmine	.25	.25
100	A6	1½p orange	.25	.55
a.		Wmk. 4a (error)	3,000.	
101	A6	2½p ultra	.25	.25
102	A7	3p car & pale lilac	.80	.85
103	A8	6p rose lil & dl grn	.45	.25
104	A7	1sh grn & gray blk (C)	1.50	.40
		Nos. 99-104 (6)	3.50	2.55

300th anniv. of the settlement of Anguilla.

University Issue
Common Design Types
Inscribed: "St. Kitts-Nevis"

Perf. 14x14½

1951, Feb. 16 Engr. Wmk. 4

No.	Type	Description	Unused	Used
105	CD310	3c org yel & gray blk	.45	.25
106	CD311	12c red violet & aqua	.45	1.25

St. Christopher-Nevis-Anguilla

Bath House and Spa, Nevis — A10

Map — A11

Designs: 2c, Warner Park, St. Kitts. 4c, Brimstone Hill, St. Kitts. 5c, Nevis. 6c, Pinney's Beach, Nevis. 12c, Sir Thomas Warner's Tomb. 24c, Old Road Bay, St. Kitts. 48c, Picking Cotton. 60c, Treasury, St. Kitts. $1.20, Salt Pond, Anguilla. $4.80, Sugar Mill, St. Kitts.

1952, June 14 *Perf. 12½*

No.	Type	Description	Unused	Used
107	A10	1c ocher & dp grn	.25	1.75
108	A10	2c emerald	1.00	1.00
109	A11	3c purple & red	.40	1.25
110	A10	4c red	.25	.25
111	A10	5c gray & ultra	.40	.25
112	A10	6c deep ultra	.40	.25
113	A11	12c redsh brn & dp blue	1.25	.25
114	A10	24c car & gray blk	.40	.25
115	A10	48c vio brn & ol bis	3.00	4.75
116	A10	60c dp grn & och	2.25	4.50
117	A10	$1.20 dp ultra & dp green	8.00	4.75
118	A10	$4.80 car & emer	15.00	20.00
		Nos. 107-118 (12)	32.60	39.25

WAR TAX STAMPS

No. 12 Overprinted

1916 Wmk. 3 *Perf. 14*

MR1 A1 ½p deep green 1.10 .55
a. ½p dull blue green 2.40 .55
Overprinted "SPECIMEN" 50.00

Type of 1905-18 Issue Overprinted

1918

MR2 A1 1½p orange 1.75 1.00
Overprinted "SPECIMEN" 55.00

ST. LUCIA

sānt 'lü-shə

LOCATION — Island in the West Indies, one of the Windward group
GOVT. — British Colony
AREA — 240 sq. mi.
POP. — 126,800 (est. 1984)
CAPITAL — Castries

12 Pence = 1 Shilling
100 Cents = 1 Dollar (1949)

Catalogue values for unused stamps in this country are for Never Hinged items, beginning with Scott 127 in the regular postage section, Scott J3 in the postage due section.

Watermark

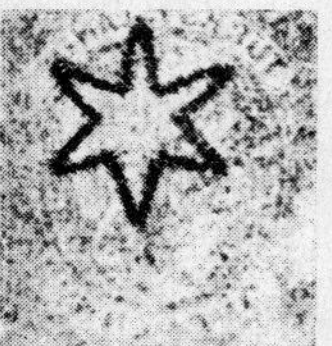

Wmk. 5 — Small Star

PRE-STAMP POSTAL MARKINGS

Crowned Circle handstamp type I is pictured in the Crowned Circle Handstamps and Great Britain Used Abroad section.

Castries

1844

A1 I "St. Lucia" crowned circle handstamp in red, on cover 1,400.

The handstamp was used, in black, as a provisional in April and May 1904, due to a stamp shortage. Value, on cover $375.

STAMPS OF GREAT BRITAIN USED IN ST. LUCIA

Numeral cancellation type A is pictured in the Crowned Circle Handstamps and Great Britain Used Abroad section.

1858-60

A11 (Castries)

A2 A 1p rose red (#20) 1,400.
A3 A 2p blue (#29, P7, 8) —
A4 A 4p rose (#26) 500.00
A5 A 6p lilac (#27) 300.00
A6 A 1sh green (#28) 2,400.

Issued under British Administration

Values for unused stamps are for examples with original gum as defined in the catalogue introduction. Very fine examples of Nos. 1-26 will have perforations touching the design on at least one side due to the narrow spacing of the stamps on the plates. Stamps with perfs clear of the framelines on all four sides are very scarce and will command higher prices.

Queen Victoria — A1

Perf. 14 to 16

1860, Dec. 18 Engr. Wmk. 5

1 A1 (1p) rose red 110.00 75.00
a. Double impression 2,500.
b. Horiz. pair, imperf vert. —
2 A1 (4p) blue 250.00 175.00
a. Horiz. pair, imperf vert. —
b. 4p deep blue — —
3 A1 (6p) green 325.00 225.00
a. Horiz. pair, imperf vert. —
b. 6p deep green 400.00 275.00
Nos. 1-3 (3) 685.00 475.00

For types overprinted see Nos. 15, 17, 19-26.

1863 Wmk. 1 *Perf. 12½*

4 A1 (1p) lake 95.00 *110.00*
a. (1p) brownish lake 120.00 120.00
5 A1 (4p) slate blue 140.00 150.00
6 A1 (6p) emerald 225.00 225.00
a. Watermark inverted —
Nos. 4-6 (3) 460.00 485.00

Nos. 4-6 exist imperforate on stamp paper, from proof sheets.

1864

7 A1 (1p) black 30.00 14.00
a. (1p) deep black 27.50 13.00
8 A1 (4p) yellow 190.00 50.00
a. (4p) olive yellow 425.00 100.00
b. (4p) lemon yellow 1,750.
c. (4p) chrome yellow 225.00 45.00
d. Watermark reversed
9 A1 (6p) violet 140.00 42.50
a. (6p) lilac 210.00 32.50
b. (6p) deep lilac 160.00 42.50
10 A1 (1sh) red orange 250.00 32.50
a. (1sh) orange 275.00 32.50
b. (1sh) brown orange 360.00 32.50
c. Horiz. pair, imperf between —
Nos. 7-10 (4) 610.00 139.00

Nos. 7-10 exist imperforate on stamp paper, from proof sheets.

Perf. 14

11 A1 (1p) deep black 50.00 22.00
a. Horiz. pair, imperf between —
12 A1 (4p) yellow 130.00 24.00
a. (4p) olive yellow 325.00 105.00
13 A1 (6p) pale lilac 125.00 24.00
a. (6p) deep lilac 125.00 45.00
b. (6p) violet 275.00 77.50
14 A1 (1sh) deep orange 175.00 19.00
a. (1sh) orange 250.00 25.00
Nos. 11-14 (4) 480.00 89.00

Type of 1860 Surcharged in Black or Red

a

b

1881

15 A1(a) ½p green 85.00 *120.00*
17 A1(b) 2½p scarlet 60.00 27.50

1883-84 Wmk. Crown and CA (2)

19 A1(a) ½p green 32.50 *47.50*
20 A1(a) 1p black (R) 52.50 16.00
a. Half used as ½p on cover —
21 A1(a) 4p yellow 325.00 24.00
22 A1(a) 6p violet 50.00 50.00
23 A1(a) 1sh orange 310.00 190.00
Nos. 19-23 (5) 770.00 327.50

1884 *Perf. 12*

24 A1(a) 4p yellow 300.00 32.50

Nos. 5 & 6 Surcharged

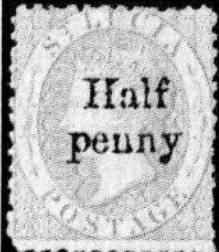

1885 Wmk. 1 *Perf. 12½*

25 A1 ½p emerald 77.50
26 A1 6p slate blue 1,500.

Nos. 25 and 26 were prepared for use but not issued.

A5

Die A

For explanation of dies A and B see "Dies of British Colonial Stamps..." in the catalogue Table of Contents.

1883-98 Typo. Wmk. 2 *Perf. 14*

27a A5 ½p green 17.50 10.00
28 A5 1p rose 55.00 19.00
29a A5 1p lilac ('86) 15.00 7.25
b. Imperf., pair 900.00
31a A5 2½p ultra 75.00 3.00
32a A5 3p lilac & grn ('86) 150.00 20.00
33a A5 4p brown ('85) 50.00 1.50
b. Imperf., pair 1,050.
34 A5 6p violet ('86) 300.00 240.00
a. Imperf., pair 2,000.
35 A5 6p lilac & blue ('87) 7.00 *18.00*
36 A5 1sh brn org ('85) 450.00 175.00
37a A5 1sh lil & red ('87) 150.00 37.50
Nos. 27a-37a (10) 1,224. 515.50
Nos. 27-39 (4) 812.00 452.00

Die B

27 A5 ½p green ('91) 4.00 1.25
29 A5 1p lilac ('91) 7.00 .35
30 A5 2p ultra & brn org ('98) 6.00 1.25
31 A5 2½p ultra ('91) 14.00 1.25
32 A5 3p lilac & grn ('91) 10.00 6.50
33 A5 4p brown ('93) 8.00 3.00
35a A5 6p lilac & blue ('91) 40.00 29.00
37 A5 1sh lil & red ('91) 14.00 6.00
38 A5 5sh lil & org ('91) 60.00 *175.00*
39 A5 10sh lil & blk ('91) 110.00 *175.00*
Nos. 27-39 (10) 273.00 398.60

Nos. 32, 32a, 35a and 33a Surcharged in Black

No. 40 No. 41 No. 42

Die A

1892

40a A5 ½p on 3p lil & grn 175.00 85.00
e. Small "A" in "HALF" 425.00 180.00
f. Small "O" in "ONE" 425.00 180.00
41 A5 ½p on half of 6p lilac & blue 32.50 4.00
a. Slanting serif 240.00 150.00
c. Without the bar of "½" 325.00 160.00
d. "2" of "½" omitted 575.00 600.00
e. Surcharged sideways 1,700.
f. Double surcharge 725.00 725.00
g. Triple surcharge 1,450.
h. Figure "1" used as fraction bar 575.00 325.00
42 A5 1p on 4p brown 9.00 *4.75*
b. Double surcharge 275.00
c. Inverted surcharge 1,100. 950.00
d. Thick diagonal stroke in first "N" 30.00 24.00
e. Thick diagonal stroke in second "N" 30.00 24.00

Die B

40 A5 ½p on 3p lil & grn 95.00 30.00
b. Double surcharge 1,000. 800.00
c. Inverted surcharge 2,450. 800.00
d. Triple surcharge, one on back 1,350. 1,500.
g. Small "O" in "ONE" 240.00 110.00
h. Small "A" in "HALF" 240.00 110.00
i. "O" over "H" shift 240.00 110.00
Nos. 40-42 (3) 216.50 93.75

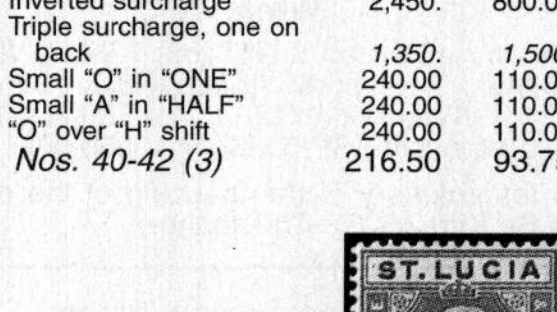

Edward VII — A9

Numerals of 3p, 6p, 1sh and 5sh of type A9 are in color on plain tablet.

1902-03 Typo.

43 A9 ½p violet & green 4.50 1.90
44 A9 1p violet & car rose 6.50 .90
46 A9 2½p violet & ultra 40.00 8.00
47 A9 3p violet & yellow 9.50 *10.00*
48 A9 1sh green & black 17.00 *50.00*
Nos. 43-48 (5) 77.50 *70.80*
Set, ovptd. "SPECIMEN" 130.00

The Pitons — A10

Wmk. 1 sideways

1902, Dec. 16 Engr.

49 A10 2p brown & green 16.00 2.50
Overprinted "SPECIMEN" 70.00

Fourth centenary of the discovery of the island by Columbus.

1904-05 Typo. Wmk. 3

50 A9 ½p violet & green 11.50 .65
a. Chalky paper 13.00 1.40
51 A9 1p violet & car rose 9.00 1.40
a. Chalky paper 12.00 1.40
52 A9 2½p violet & ultra 40.00 2.75
a. Chalky paper 18.00 5.00
53 A9 3p violet & yellow 13.00 3.25
54 A9 6p vio & dp vio ('05) 27.50 *35.00*
a. Chalky paper 21.00 47.50
55 A9 1sh green & blk ('05) 50.00 32.50
56 A9 5sh green & car ('05) 85.00 *200.00*
Nos. 50-56 (7) 236.00 *275.55*

No. 55 is on chalky paper only.

1907-10

57 A9 ½p green 2.00 1.10
58 A9 1p carmine 4.75 .35
59 A9 2½p ultra 4.25 2.00

Chalky Paper

60 A9 3p violet, *yel* ('09) 3.25 *19.00*
61 A9 6p violet & red vio 9.25 *40.00*
a. 6p violet & dull vio ('10) 75.00 *90.00*
62 A9 1sh black, *grn* ('09) 5.25 *8.75*
63 A9 5sh grn & red, *yel* 67.50 *77.50*
Nos. 57-63 (7) 96.25 *148.70*
Set, ovptd. "SPECIMEN" 300.00

King George V
A11 A12

Numerals of 3p, 6p, 1sh and 5sh of type A11 are in color on plain tablet.

For description of dies I and II see "Dies of British Colonial Stamps" in Table of Contents.

Die I

1912-19 Ordinary Paper

64 A11 ½p deep green .75 .50
a. ½p yellow green ('16) 2.50 .35
65 A11 1p scarlet 9.00 .25
a. 1p carmine 2.00 .25
b. 1p rose red 10.00 1.10
66 A12 2p gray ('13) 1.60 *4.50*
a. 2p slate gray ('16) 25.00 17.50
67 A11 2½p bright blue 4.50 3.00
a. 2½p ultra 4.00 3.00
b. 2½p deep blue ('16) 18.00 11.00

Chalky Paper

Numeral on White Tablet

68 A11 3p violet, *yel* 1.40 *2.50*
a. Die II 30.00 *60.00*
69 A11 6p vio & red vio 2.25 *21.00*
a. 6p gray purple & purple ('18) 17.50 27.50
70 A11 1sh black, *green* 7.00 *5.50*
a. 1sh black, *bl grn*, ol back 17.50 *19.00*
71 A11 1sh fawn 20.00 *50.00*
72 A11 5sh grn & red, *yel* 26.50 *85.00*
Nos. 64-72 (9) 73.00 *172.25*

A13

A14

1913-14 Chalky Paper

73 A13 4p scar & blk, *yel* 1.00 *2.25*
a. 4p white back .75 1.60
As "a," overprinted "SPECIMEN" 32.50
74 A14 2sh6p blk & red, *bl* 25.00 *50.00*
Nos. 64-74, ovptd. "SPECIMEN" 250.00

Surface-colored Paper

75 A13 4p scarlet & blk, *yel* .75 *1.60*
Overprinted "SPECIMEN" 32.50

Die II

1921-24 Wmk. 4 Ordinary Paper

76 A11 ½p green 1.25 .55
77 A11 1p carmine 14.50 *20.00*
78 A11 1p dk brn ('22) 1.60 .25
79 A13 1½p rose red ('22) .85 *2.75*
80 A12 2p gray .85 .25
81 A11 2½p ultra 7.50 *3.00*
82 A11 2½p orange ('24) 16.00 *60.00*
83 A11 3p dull blue ('24) 7.00 *12.00*
a. 3p bright blue ('22) 8.50 21.50

Chalky Paper

84 A11 3p violet, *yel* 3.75 *13.50*
85 A13 4p scar & blk, *yel* ('24) 1.40 *2.75*
86 A11 6p vio & red vio 2.50 *5.25*
87 A11 1sh fawn 7.50 *3.50*
88 A14 2sh6p blk & red, *bl* ('24) 20.00 *36.00*
89 A11 5sh grn & red, *yel* 60.00 *95.00*
Nos. 76-89 (14) 144.70 *254.80*
Set, ovptd. "SPECIMEN" 350.00

Common Design Types
For description of dies I and II see "Dies of British Colonial Stamps" in Table of Contents.

Silver Jubilee Issue
Common Design Type

1935, May 6 Engr. *Perf. 13½x14*

91 CD301 ½p green & blk .30 2.00
92 CD301 2p gray blk & ultra .95 1.40
93 CD301 2½p blue & brn 1.25 1.40
94 CD301 1sh brt vio & ind 13.50 *16.00*
Nos. 91-94 (4) 16.00 *20.80*
Set, never hinged 26.00
Set, perforated "SPECIMEN" 100.00

Port Castries A15

Columbus Square, Castries A16

Ventine Falls A17

Soldiers' Monument A19

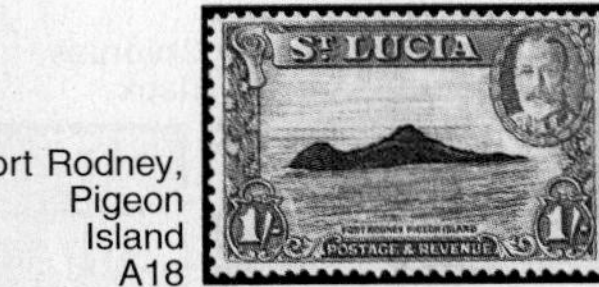
Fort Rodney, Pigeon Island A18

Government House A20

Seal of the Colony A21

Center in Black

1936, Mar. 1 *Perf. 14*

95 A15 ½p light green .35 .55
a. Perf. 13x12 5.50 *26.00*
96 A16 1p dark brown .45 .25
a. Perf. 13x12 10.00 4.25
97 A17 1½p carmine .70 .35
a. Perf. 12x13 17.50 2.50
98 A15 2p gray .60 .25
99 A16 2½p blue .60 .25
100 A17 3p dull green 1.50 .75
101 A15 4p brown 2.00 *1.25*
102 A16 6p orange 2.00 1.25
103 A18 1sh lt bl, perf. 13x12 3.50 2.50
104 A19 2sh6p ultra 15.00 14.00
105 A20 5sh violet 19.00 *25.00*
106 A21 10sh car rose, perf. 13x12 60.00 *100.00*
Nos. 95-106 (12) 105.70 *146.40*
Set, never hinged 225.00
Set, perforated "SPECIMEN" 325.00

Nos. 95a, 96a and 97a are coils.
Issue date: Nos. 95a, 96a, Apr. 8.

Coronation Issue
Common Design Type

1937, May 12 *Perf. 11x11½*

107 CD302 1p dark purple .25 .40
108 CD302 1½p dark carmine .40 .25
109 CD302 2½p deep ultra .40 1.40
Nos. 107-109 (3) 1.05 2.05
Set, never hinged 1.75
Set, perforated "SPECIMEN" 95.00

King George VI — A22

Columbus Square, Castries A23

Government House A24

The Pitons A25

Loading Bananas A26

Arms of the Colony — A27

Perf. 12½ (#110-111, 1½p-3½p, 8p, 3sh, 5sh, £1), 12 (6p, 1sh, 2sh, 10sh)

1938-48

110 A22 ½p green ('43) .25 .25
a. Perf. 14½x14 1.40 .25
111 A22 1p deep violet .25 .25
a. Perf. 14½x14 2.00 .85
112 A22 1p red, Perf. 14½x14 ('47) .25 .25
a. Perf. 12½ .65 .25
113 A22 1½p carmine ('43) 1.00 1.40
a. Perf. 14½x14 1.40 .50
114 A22 2p gray ('43) .25 .25
a. Perf. 14½x14 2.25 *1.75*
115 A22 2½p ultra ('43) .25 .25
a. Perf. 14½x14 3.00 .25
116 A22 2½p violet ('47) .85 .25
117 A22 3p red org ('43) .25 .25
a. Perf. 14½x14 1.00 .25
118 A22 3½p brt ultra ('47) .85 .25
119 A23 6p magenta ('48) 6.50 1.75
a. Perf. 13½ 2.00 .50
120 A22 8p choc ('46) 2.75 .40
121 A24 1sh lt brn ('48) .75 .40
a. Perf. 13½ 1.10 .40
122 A25 2sh red vio & sl bl 3.50 1.50
123 A22 3sh brt red vio ('46) 6.75 2.00
124 A26 5sh rose vio & blk 10.00 11.00
125 A27 10sh black, *yel* 7.50 *9.00*
126 A22 £1 sepia ('46) 9.00 8.00
Nos. 110-126 (17) 50.95 37.45
Set, never hinged 75.00
Set, perforated "SPECIMEN" 500.00

See Nos. 135-148.

Catalogue values for unused stamps in this section, from this point to the end of the section, are for Never Hinged items.

Peace Issue
Common Design Type
Perf. 13½x14

1946, Oct. 8 Wmk. 4 Engr.

127 CD303 1p lilac .25 .30
128 CD303 3½p deep blue .25 .30
Set, perforated "SPECIMEN" 85.00

Silver Wedding Issue
Common Design Types

1948, Nov. 26 Photo. *Perf. 14x14½*

129 CD304 1p scarlet .25 .25

Perf. 11½x11
Engraved; Name Typographed

130 CD305 £1 violet brown 22.00 *45.00*

UPU Issue
Common Design Types
Engr.; Name Typo. on 6c, 12c.
Perf. 13½, 11x11½

1949, Oct. 10 Wmk. 4

131 CD306 5c violet .25 *.85*
132 CD307 6c deep orange 1.60 *2.50*
133 CD308 12c red lilac .30 .25
134 CD309 24c blue green .40 .25
Nos. 131-134 (4) 2.55 *3.85*

Types of 1938
Values in Cents and Dollars

1949, Oct. 1 Engr. *Perf. 12½*

135 A22 1c green .35 .25
a. Perf. 14 3.25 .50
136 A22 2c rose lilac 1.25 .25
a. Perf. 14½x14 4.50 1.25
137 A22 3c red 1.60 *2.50*
138 A22 4c gray .95 .25
a. Perf. 14½x14 *18,800.*
139 A22 5c violet 1.75 .25
140 A22 6c red orange 1.25 *3.50*
141 A22 7c ultra 4.00 3.00
142 A22 12c rose lake 6.75 4.00
a. Perf. 14½x14 ('50) 750.00 550.00
143 A22 16c brown 5.75 .65

Perf. 11½

144 A27 24c Prus blue .75 .25
145 A27 48c olive green 1.75 1.60
146 A27 $1.20 purple 2.75 *10.00*
147 A27 $2.40 blue green 4.50 *20.00*
148 A27 $4.80 dk car rose 11.50 *21.00*
Nos. 135-148 (14) 44.90 *67.50*

Nos. 144 to 148 are of a type similar to A27, but with the denomination in the top corners and "St. Lucia" at the bottom.
For overprints see Nos. 152-155.

University Issue
Common Design Types
Perf. 14x14½

1951, Feb. 16 Wmk. 4

149 CD310 3c red & gray black .55 .75
150 CD311 12c brn car & blk .85 .75

Phoenix Rising from Burning Buildings — A28

Engr. & Typo.

1951, June 19 *Perf. 13½x13*

151 A28 12c dp blue & car .50 1.10

Reconstruction of Castries.

Nos. 136, 138, 139 and 142 Overprinted in Black

1951, Sept. 25 *Perf. 12½*

152 A22 2c rose lilac .25 .85
153 A22 4c gray .25 .60
154 A22 5c violet .25 .85
155 A22 12c rose lilac .45 .60
Nos. 152-155 (4) 1.20 2.90

Adoption of a new constitution for the Windward Islands, 1951.

POSTAGE DUE STAMPS

D1

Type I — "No." 3mm wide (shown).
Type II — "No." 4mm wide.

Rough Perf. 12

1931 Unwmk. Typeset

J1 D1 1p blk, *gray bl*, type I 10.00 *20.00*
a. Type II 24.00 *47.50*
b. Missing period after "ST" 325.00 475.00
c. Missing period after "LUCIA" 275.00 500.00
d. Serial number double 950.00
e. Serial number triple 2,100.
f. Two different numbers on the same stamp 2,100.
g. Serial number omitted 4,250.
J2 D1 2p blk, *yel*, type I 22.00 *47.50*
a. Type II 45.00 *105.00*
b. Vertical pair, imperf. btwn. *7,500.*
c. Missing period after "ST" 625.00 950.00
d. Missing period after "LUCIA" 900.00
e. Serial number double 2,000.
f. Two different numbers on the same stamp 2,400.

The serial numbers are handstamped. Type II has round "o" and period. Type I has tall "o" and square period.

Catalogue values for unused stamps in this section, from this point to the end of the section, are for Never Hinged items.

D2

1933-47 Typo. Wmk. 4 *Perf. 14*
Chalky Paper

J3 D2 1p black 15.00 *8.00*
J4 D2 2p black 40.00 *10.00*
J5 D2 4p black ('47) 11.00 *50.00*
J6 D2 8p black ('47) 11.00 *60.00*
Nos. J3-J6 (4) 77.00 *128.00*
Set, perforated "SPECIMEN" 160.00

Issue date: June 28, 1947.

Chalky Paper

1952, Nov. 27 Values in Cents

J7 D2 2c black .25 *9.50*
a. Ordinary paper ('49) 1.90 30.00
J8 D2 4c black .60 *14.00*
a. Ordinary paper ('49) 3.75 24.00
J9 D2 8c black 3.50 *50.00*
a. Ordinary paper ('49) 3.50 30.00
J10 D2 16c black 5.00 *65.00*
a. Ordinary paper ('49) 16.00 75.00
Nos. J7-J10 (4) 9.35 *138.50*

Nos. J7a-J10a issued 10/1/1949.

Wmk. 4a (error)

J7a D2 2c 40.00
J8a D2 4c 55.00
J9a D2 8c 350.00
J10a D2 16c 475.00
Nos. J7a-J10a (4) 920.00

WAR TAX STAMPS

No. 65 Overprinted

1916 Wmk. 3 *Perf. 14*

MR1 A11 1p scarlet 13.00 *19.00*
  a. Double overprint 550.00 *650.00*
  b. 1p carmine 67.50 55.00

Overprinted

MR2 A11 1p scarlet 1.40 .35
  a. Overprinted "SPECIMEN" 55.00

STE. MARIE DE MADAGASCAR

sănt-mə-rē-də-ˌmad-ə-ˈgas-kər

LOCATION — An island off the east coast of Madagascar
GOVT. — French Possession
AREA — 64 sq. mi.
POP. — 8,000 (approx.)

In 1896 Ste.-Marie de Madagascar was attached to the colony of Madagascar for administrative purposes.

100 Centimes = 1 Franc

Navigation and Commerce — A1

1894 Unwmk. Typo. *Perf. 14x13½*
Name of Colony in Blue or Carmine

1 A1 1c black, *lil bl* 1.75 1.75
  Never hinged 3.00
  On cover 190.00
2 A1 2c brown, *buff* 2.75 2.75
  Never hinged 5.25
  On cover 190.00
3 A1 4c claret, *lavender* 5.00 5.00
  Never hinged 9.25
  On cover 190.00
4 A1 5c green, *grnsh* 12.00 11.00
  Never hinged 24.00
  On cover 80.00
5 A1 10c black, *lavender* 13.50 10.50
  Never hinged 27.50
  On cover 70.00
6 A1 15c blue 40.00 36.00
  Never hinged 80.00
  On cover 110.00
7 A1 20c red, *green* 30.00 28.00
  Never hinged 62.50
  On cover 150.00
  On cover, single franking 275.00
8 A1 25c black, *rose* 25.00 22.00
  Never hinged 52.50
  On cover 80.00
  On cover, single franking 140.00
9 A1 30c brown, *bister* 17.50 16.00
  Never hinged 35.00
  On cover 140.00
  On cover, single franking 190.00
10 A1 40c red, *straw* 17.50 16.00
  Never hinged 35.00
  On cover 140.00
  On cover, single franking 250.00
11 A1 50c carmine, *rose* 52.50 52.50
  Never hinged 125.00
  On cover 250.00
  On cover, single franking 350.00
12 A1 75c violet, *org* 100.00 72.50
  Never hinged 195.00
  On cover 450.00
  On cover, single franking 550.00
13 A1 1fr brnz grn, *straw* 52.50 47.50
  Never hinged 110.00
  On cover 425.00
  On cover, single franking 690.00
  Nos. 1-13 (13) 370.00 321.50

Perf. 13½x14 stamps are counterfeits.

Covers: Values are for usages on Ste. Marie de Madagascar. These stamps were also used on Madagascar.

Values are for commercial covers paying correct rates. Philatelic covers sell for less.

These stamps were replaced by those of Madagascar.

ST. PIERRE & MIQUELON

sănt-ˈpi̯ə̦r and ˈmik-ə-ˌlän

LOCATION — Two small groups of islands off the southern coast of Newfoundland
GOVT. — French Colony
AREA — 93 sq. mi.
POP. — 6,051 (est. 1984)
CAPITAL — St. Pierre

100 Centimes = 1 Franc

STAMPS OF FRENCH COLONIES GENERAL ISSUES USED IN ST. PIERRE & MIQUELON

Canceled SPM in Lozenge of Dots

On Eagle & Crown Type, #1-6

1859-65

A1 A1 1c ol grn, *pale bl* ('62) 400.00
  On cover —
A2 A1 5c yel grn, *grnsh* ('62) 390.00
  On cover —
A3 A1 10c bister, *yel* 175.00
  On cover 3,500.
A4 A1 20c bl, *bluish* ('65) 190.00
  On cover 3,500.
A5 A1 40c org, *yelsh* 170.00
  On cover 3,500.
A6 A1 80c car rose, *pnksh* ('65) 140.00
  On cover 925.00

On Ceres and Napoleon III Types, #7//15

1871-72

A7 A2 1c ol grn, *pale bl* ('72) 325.00
  On cover —
A10 A4 15c bis, *yelsh* ('72) 900.00
  On cover —
A12 A4 25c bl, *bluish* ('72) 575.00
  On cover *9,250.*
  a. With circular date stamp *625.00*
  On cover —
A13 A5 30c brn, *yelsh* 325.00
  On cover *8,000.*
A14 A4 40c org, *yelsh* (I) 140.00
  On cover 2,000.
  a. With circular date stamp *190.00*
  On cover —
A15 A5 80c rose, *pnksh* 325.00
  On cover *9,250.*

On Ceres Type, #16//23

1872-77

A16 A6 1c ol grn, *pale bl* ('73) 325.00
  On cover —
A19 A6 5c grn, *pale bl* 150.00
  On cover 1,700.
  a. With circular date stamp 170.00
  On cover —
A20 A7 10c bis, *rose* ('76) 97.50
  On cover 1,100.
  a. With circular date stamp 125.00
  On cover 1,350.
A22 A7 30c brn, *yelsh* 240.00
  On cover —
  a. With circular date stamp 275.00
  On cover —
A23 A7 80c rose, *pnksh* ('73) 150.00
  On cover 2,200.
  a. With circular date stamp 175.00
  On cover —

Cancelled with Circular Date Stamps
On Peace & Commerce Types, #24//59

1877-78

Type I

A24 A8 1c grn, *grnsh* 425.00
  On cover —
A25 A8 4c grn, *grnsh* 425.00
  On cover —
A26 A8 30c brn, *yelsh* ('78) 225.00
  On cover —
A27 A8 40c ver, *straw* 125.00
  On cover —
A28 A8 75c rose, *rose* ('78) 325.00
  On cover —
A29 A8 1fr brnz grn, *straw* 325.00
  On cover —

Type II

A30 A8 2c grn, *grnsh* 375.00
  On cover —
A31 A8 5c grn, *grnsh* 125.00
  On cover —
A32 A8 10c grn, *grnsh* 160.00
  On cover —
A33 A8 15c gray, *grnsh* 200.00
  On cover —
A34 A8 20c red brn, *straw* 150.00
  On cover —
A35 A8 25c ultra *bluish* 275.00
  On cover —
A36 A8 35c vio blk, *org* ('78) 95.00
  On cover —

On Peace & Commerce Type, #38//45

1878-80

Type II

A38 A8 1c blk, *lil bl* 290.00
  On cover —
A40 A8 4c claret, *lav* 290.00
  On cover —
A41 A8 10c blk, *lav* ('79) 250.00
  On cover —
A42 A8 15c blue ('79) 90.00
  On cover —
A43 A8 20c red, *grn* ('79) 225.00
  On cover —
A45 A8 25c yel, *straw* ('80) 70.00
  On cover *500.00*

On Commerce Type, #46-59

1881-86

A46 A9 1c blk, *lil bl* 275.00
  On cover —
A47 A9 2c brn, *buff* 275.00
  On cover —
A48 A9 4c claret, *lav* 225.00
  On cover —
A49 A9 5c grn, *grnsh* 82.50
  On cover 1,000.
A50 A9 10c blk, *lavender* 100.00
  On cover 1,250.
A51 A9 15c blue 100.00
  On cover —
A52 A9 20c red, *yel grn* 150.00
  On cover 2,000.
A53 A9 25c yel, *straw* 40.00
  On cover —
A54 A9 25c blk, *rose* ('86) 32.50
  On cover 725.00
A55 A9 30c brn, *bis* 82.50
  On cover —
A56 A9 35c vio blk, *yel org* 140.00
  On cover —
  a. 35c violet black, *yellow* 200.00
  On cover —
A57 A9 40c ver, *straw* 200.00
  On cover —
A58 A9 75c car, *rose* 100.00
  On cover —
A59 A9 1fr brnz grn, *straw* 160.00
  On cover —

Covers
Values are for commercial covers bearing correct frankings. Philatelic covers generally sell for less.

REGULAR ISSUES

Stamps of French Colonies Handstamp Surcharged in Black

1885 Unwmk. *Imperf.*

1 A8 05c on 40c ver, *straw* 150.00 60.00
  On cover 1,000.
  a. Surcharge "05" missing 240.00
  b. Surcharge "05" double 375.00 325.00
2 A8 10c on 40c ver, *straw* 45.00 35.00
  On cover 850.00
  a. "M" inverted 375.00 350.00
  b. Surcharge "10" double 225.00 190.00
  c. As "b," one inverted 1,050.
3 A8 15c on 40c ver, *straw* 45.00 35.00
  On cover 850.00
  a. Double surcharge 525.00 500.00
  Nos. 1-3 (3) 240.00 130.00

Nos. 2 and 3 exist with "SPM" 17mm wide instead of 15½mm.

Nos. 1-3 exist with surcharge inverted and with it doubled.

Handstamp Surcharged in Black

b

c

d

1885

4 A8 (b) 05c on 35c blk, *yel* 160.00 110.00
  On cover 950.00
  a. Double surcharge 800.00
5 A8 (b) 05c on 75c car, *rose* 375.00 300.00
  On cover 1,100.
  a. Double surcharge 1,400.
6 A8 (b) 05c on 1fr brnz grn, *straw* 40.00 32.50
  On cover 850.00
  a. Double surcharge 360.00 325.00
  b. "SPM" omitted 260.00
7 A8 (c) 25c on 1fr brnz grn, *straw* *14,000.* *2,800.*
  On cover —
  a. "25" sideways *4,000.*
  b. "25" reversed *5,800.*
  c. Surcharge reversed *5,250.*
8 A8 (d) 25c on 1fr brnz grn, *straw* *2,700.* *1,925.*
  On cover —
  a. Surcharge sideways *5,500.* *2,900.*
  b. "SPM" reversed 5,500.

Nos. 7 and 8 exist with surcharge inverted, and with it vertical. No. 7 exists with "S P M" above "25" (the handstamping was done in two steps).

1885 *Perf. 14x13½*

9 A9 (c) 5c on 2c brn, *buff* *7,250.* *2,700.*
  On cover —
  a. Surcharge upright *16,500.*
10 A9 (d) 5c on 4c cl, *lav* 550.00 350.00
  On cover —
  a. Surcharge inverted 1,325. 1,100.
  b. "SPM" double 1,325. 1,100.
11 A9 (b) 05c on 20c red, *grn* 47.50 47.50
  On cover 850.00
  a. Double surcharge 360.00 325.00
  b. "SPM" in larger letters 240.00 200.00

A15

1886, Feb. Typo. *Imperf.*
Without Gum

12 A15 5c black 1,500.
  On cover *5,000.*
13 A15 10c black 1,600.
  On cover *5,000.*
14 A15 15c black 1,400.
  On cover *3,000.*
  Nos. 12-14 (3) 4,500.

Used values for Nos. 12-14 are for examples canceled with c.d.s. "St. Pierre et Miquelon." Stamps canceled at Langlade, Miquelon or Ile des Chiens sell for about double these values.

"P D" are the initials for "Payé a destination." Excellent forgeries exist.

Stamps of French Colonies Surcharged in Black

e

f

1891 *Perf. 14x13½*

15 A9 (e) 15c on 30c brn, *bis* 52.50 40.00
  On cover 700.00
  a. Inverted surcharge *310.00* *260.00*
  b. Double surcharge 260.00 210.00
16 A9 (e) 15c on 35c blk, *org* 725.00 575.00
  On cover *1,500.*
  a. Inverted surcharge *875.00* *700.00*
17 A9 (f) 15c on 35c blk, *org* 2,000. 1,650.
  On cover —
  a. Inverted surcharge *2,100.*
18 A9 (e) 15c on 40c red, *straw* 125.00 95.00
  On cover 700.00
  a. Inverted surcharge *300.00* *250.00*

Stamps of French Colonies Overprinted in Black or Red

1891, Oct. 15

19 A9 1c blk, *lil bl* 17.00 13.50
Never hinged 30.00
On cover 450.00
a. Inverted overprint 40.00 40.00
b. "S" omitted in "ST" 100.00 100.00
20 A9 1c blk, *lil bl* (R) 17.00 15.00
Never hinged 32.50
On cover 450.00
a. Inverted overprint 40.00 40.00
Never hinged 80.00
21 A9 2c brn, *buff* 17.00 13.50
Never hinged 32.50
On cover 450.00
a. Inverted overprint 40.00 40.00
b. "S" omitted in "ST" 110.00 110.00
22 A9 2c brn, *buff* (R) 32.50 30.00
Never hinged 65.00
On cover 450.00
a. Inverted overprint 82.50 82.50
Never hinged 130.00
23 A9 4c claret, *lav* 17.00 13.50
Never hinged 32.50
On cover 450.00
a. Inverted overprint 40.00 40.00
b. "S" omitted in "ST" 110.00 110.00
24 A9 4c claret, *lav* (R) 32.50 30.00
Never hinged 65.00
On cover 450.00
a. Inverted overprint 65.00 65.00
Never hinged 120.00
25 A9 5c grn, *grnsh* 27.50 19.00
Never hinged 45.00
On cover 400.00
a. Double surcharge 260.00
b. "S" omitted in "ST" 130.00 130.00
26 A9 10c blk, *lav* 47.50 40.00
Never hinged 80.00
On cover 400.00
a. Inverted overprint 95.00 *95.00*
b. "S" omitted in "ST" 160.00 160.00
27 A9 10c blk, *lav* (R) 32.50 30.00
Never hinged 65.00
On cover 400.00
a. Inverted overprint 65.00 *65.00*
Never hinged 120.00
28 A9 15c blue 45.00 32.50
Never hinged 72.50
On cover 300.00
a. "S" omitted in "ST" 160.00 160.00
29 A9 20c red, *grn* 110.00 100.00
Never hinged —
On cover *400.00*
a. "S" omitted in "ST" 300.00 300.00
30 A9 25c blk, *rose* 40.00 27.50
Never hinged 65.00
On cover 250.00
a. "S" omitted in "ST" 160.00 160.00
31 A9 30c brn, *bis* 150.00 125.00
Never hinged —
On cover *450.00*
a. "S" omitted in "ST" 400.00 400.00
32 A9 35c vio, *org* 525.00 400.00
Never hinged —
On cover —
a. "S" omitted in "ST" 925.00
33 A9 40c red, *straw* 100.00 80.00
Never hinged —
On cover 450.00
a. Double surcharge 500.00
b. "S" omitted in "ST" 340.00 340.00
34 A9 75c car, *rose* 140.00 130.00
Never hinged —
On cover 475.00
a. Inverted overprint 240.00 225.00
b. "S" omitted in "ST" 425.00 425.00
35 A9 1fr brnz grn, *straw* 120.00 105.00
Never hinged —
On cover *525.00*
a. Inverted overprint 220.00 220.00
b. "S" omitted in "ST" 350.00 350.00
Nos. 19-35 (17) 1,471. 1,205.

Numerous varieties of mislettering occur in the preceding overprint: "ST," "P," "M," "ON," or "-" missing; "-" instead of "ON"; "=" instead of "-" These varieties command values double or triple those of normal stamps.

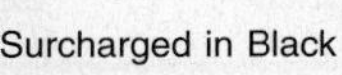

Surcharged in Black

1891-92

36 A9 1c on 5c grn, *grnsh* 16.00 16.00
Never hinged 22.50
On cover *450.00*
37 A9 1c on 10c blk, *lav* 18.00 16.50
Never hinged 26.00
On cover *450.00*
a. Double surcharge 175.00 175.00
38 A9 1c on 25c blk, *rose* ('92) 12.50 12.00
Never hinged 19.00
On cover *450.00*
39 A9 2c on 10c blk, *lav* 16.00 16.00
Never hinged 22.50
On cover *450.00*
a. Double surcharge 170.00 170.00
b. Triple surcharge 350.00 350.00
40 A9 2c on 15c bl 18.00 16.50
Never hinged 26.00
On cover *450.00*
41 A9 2c on 25c blk, *rose* ('92) 12.50 12.00
Never hinged 19.00
On cover *450.00*
42 A9 4c on 20c red, *grn* 16.00 16.00
Never hinged 22.50
On cover *450.00*
b. "S" omitted in "ST" 120.00 120.00
43 A9 4c on 25c blk, *rose* ('92) 12.50 12.00
Never hinged 19.00
On cover *450.00*
a. Double surcharge 160.00 160.00
b. As "a," in pair with normal stamp 325.00
44 A9 4c on 30c brn, *bis* 32.50 26.00
Never hinged 52.50
On cover *450.00*
a. "S" omitted in "ST" 150.00 150.00
b. "ST PIERRE M-on" double 275.00
45 A9 4c on 40c red, *straw* 32.50 26.00
Never hinged 52.50
On cover *450.00*
Nos. 36-45 (10) 186.50 169.00

See note after No. 35.

French Colonies 1881-86 Stamps Surcharged in Black

j

k

1892, Nov. 4

46 A9 (j) 1c on 5c grn, *grnsh* 16.00 14.00
Never hinged 22.50
On cover *450.00*
47 A9 (j) 2c on 5c grn, *grnsh* 16.00 14.00
Never hinged 22.50
On cover *450.00*
48 A9 (j) 4c on 5c grn, *grnsh* 16.00 14.00
Never hinged 22.50
On cover *450.00*
49 A9 (k) 1c on 25c blk, *rose* 12.50 12.00
Never hinged 19.00
On cover *450.00*
50 A9 (k) 2c on 25c blk, *rose* 12.50 12.00
Never hinged 19.00
On cover *450.00*
51 A9 (k) 4c on 25c blk, *rose* 12.50 12.00
Never hinged 19.00
On cover *450.00*
Nos. 46-51 (6) 85.50 78.00

See note after No. 35.

Postage Due Stamps of French Colonies Overprinted in Red

1892, Dec. 1 ***Imperf.***

52 D1 10c black 60.00 40.00
Never hinged 75.00
On cover *450.00*
53 D1 20c black 40.00 35.00
Never hinged 62.50
On cover *450.00*
54 D1 30c black 37.50 37.50
Never hinged 62.50
On cover *500.00*
55 D1 40c black 32.50 32.50
Never hinged 47.50
On cover *500.00*
56 D1 60c black 140.00 140.00
Never hinged —
On cover —

Black Overprint

57 D1 1fr brown 190.00 190.00
Never hinged —
On cover —
58 D1 2fr brown 325.00 325.00
Never hinged —
On cover —
59 D1 5fr brown 500.00 475.00
Never hinged —
On cover —
Nos. 52-59 (8) 1,325. 1,275.

See note after No. 35. "T P" stands for "Timbre Poste."

Navigation and Commerce — A16

1892-1908 Typo. *Perf. 14x13½*

60 A16 1c blk, *lil bl* 1.90 1.90
Never hinged 3.00
On cover 290.00
61 A16 2c brown, *buff* 1.90 1.90
Never hinged 3.00
On cover 290.00
62 A16 4c claret, *lav* 3.00 3.00
Never hinged 5.25
On cover 250.00
63 A16 5c green, *grnsh* 4.50 3.75
Never hinged 7.50
On cover 95.00
64 A16 5c yel grn ('08) 6.00 3.75
Never hinged 10.50
On cover 62.50
65 A16 10c black, *lav* 8.25 6.75
Never hinged 14.00
On cover 200.00
66 A16 10c red ('00) 6.00 3.75
Never hinged 10.50
On cover 62.50
67 A16 15c bl, quadrille paper 19.00 6.00
Never hinged 32.50
On cover 125.00
68 A16 15c gray, *lt gray* ('00) 100.00 65.00
Never hinged 200.00
On cover 600.00
69 A16 20c red, *grn* 30.00 24.00
Never hinged 55.00
On cover 425.00
On cover, single franking 550.00
70 A16 25c black, *rose* 13.50 3.75
Never hinged 25.00
On cover 95.00
On cover, single franking 160.00
71 A16 25c blue ('00) 25.00 15.00
Never hinged 35.00
On cover 125.00
On cover, single franking 200.00
72 A16 30c brown, *bis* 13.50 9.00
Never hinged 25.00
On cover 250.00
On cover, single franking 340.00
73 A16 35c blk, *yel* ('06) 8.00 7.25
Never hinged 13.50
On cover 150.00
On cover, single franking 250.00
74 A16 40c red, *straw* 9.75 9.00
Never hinged 15.00
On cover 250.00
On cover, single franking 340.00
75 A16 50c car, *rose* 52.50 42.50
Never hinged 95.00
On cover 440.00
On cover, single franking 550.00
76 A16 50c brown, *az* ('00) 40.00 37.50
Never hinged 75.00
On cover 500.00
On cover, single franking 625.00
77 A16 75c violet, *org* 35.00 30.00
Never hinged 60.00
On cover 500.00
On cover, single franking 625.00
78 A16 1fr brnz grn, *straw* 35.00 26.00
Never hinged 60.00
On cover 550.00
On cover, single franking 675.00
Nos. 60-78 (19) 412.80 299.80

Perf. 13½x14 stamps are counterfeits.

For surcharges and overprints see Nos. 110-120, Q1-Q2.

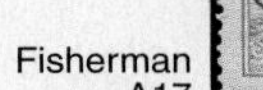

Fisherman A17

Fulmar Petrel A18

Fishing Schooner A19

1909-30

79 A17 1c org red & ol .40 *.50*
Never hinged .65
On cover 110.00
80 A17 2c olive & dp bl .40 *.50*
Never hinged .65
On cover 105.00
81 A17 4c violet & ol .55 *.75*
Never hinged .85
On cover 80.00
a. Perf 11 160.00
Never hinged 240.00
82 A17 5c bl grn & ol grn 1.20 .75
Never hinged 1.90
On cover 62.50
83 A17 5c blue & blk ('22) .55 *.75*
Never hinged 1.20
On cover 105.00
On cover, single franking 190.00
84 A17 10c car rose & red 1.20 1.10
Never hinged 2.00
On cover 62.50
85 A17 10c bl grn & ol grn ('22) .75 .75
Never hinged 1.40
On cover 95.00
86 A17 10c bis & mag ('25) .55 *.75*
Never hinged 1.20
On cover 62.50
86A A17 15c dl vio & rose ('17) .80 .75
Never hinged 1.25
On cover 75.00
87 A17 20c bis brn & vio brn 1.25 1.10
Never hinged 2.00
On cover 95.00
88 A18 25c dp blue & blue 4.50 3.00
Never hinged 7.50
On cover 110.00
On cover, single franking 225.00
a. 25c dp blue & dp blue 12.00 8.25
Never hinged 22.50
On cover 190.00
b. Perf 11 160.00
Never hinged 240.00
89 A18 25c ol brn & bl grn ('22) 1.25 *1.50*
Never hinged 2.00
On cover 62.50
90 A18 30c org & vio brn 2.60 2.60
Never hinged 4.00
On cover 105.00
On cover, single franking 225.00
91 A18 30c rose & dull red ('22) 1.75 *2.25*
Never hinged 2.60
On cover 110.00
92 A18 30c red brn & bl ('25) 1.00 1.00
Never hinged 1.60
On cover 105.00
93 A18 30c gray grn & bl grn ('26) 1.50 *2.25*
Never hinged 2.25
On cover 110.00
94 A18 35c ol grn & vio brn .80 .80
Never hinged 1.25
On cover 105.00
On cover, single franking 250.00
95 A18 40c vio brn & ol grn 4.00 3.00
Never hinged 6.00
On cover 80.00
On cover, single franking 150.00
96 A18 45c vio & ol grn 1.10 *1.50*
Never hinged 1.90
On cover 80.00
On cover, single franking 150.00
97 A18 50c ol & ol grn 2.25 2.25
Never hinged 3.75
On cover 125.00
On cover, single franking 275.00
98 A18 50c bl & pale bl ('22) 1.75 *2.25*
Never hinged 2.75
On cover 110.00
On cover, single franking 200.00
99 A18 50c yel brn & mag ('25) 1.60 *2.25*
Never hinged 2.40
On cover 62.50
On cover, single franking 150.00
100 A18 60c dk bl & ver ('25) 1.40 *1.90*
Never hinged 2.25
On cover 95.00
On cover, single franking 200.00
101 A18 65c vio & org brn ('28) 2.50 *3.00*
Never hinged 4.00
On cover 105.00
On cover, single franking 225.00
102 A18 75c brn & ol 1.90 *2.25*
Never hinged 3.00
On cover 125.00
On cover, single franking 275.00
103 A18 90c brn red & org red ('30) 35.00 *37.50*
Never hinged 47.50
On cover 340.00
On cover, single franking 475.00
104 A19 1fr ol grn & dp bl 5.00 3.75
Never hinged 8.25
On cover 105.00
On cover, single franking 200.00
a. Perf 11 160.00
Never hinged 225.00
105 A19 1.10fr bl grn & org red ('28) 5.50 *7.50*
Never hinged 9.25
On cover 190.00
On cover, single franking 375.00
106 A19 1.50fr bl & dp bl ('30) 15.00 15.00
Never hinged 20.00
On cover 275.00
On cover, single franking 375.00
107 A19 2fr violet & brn 6.00 4.50
Never hinged 9.75
On cover 125.00
On cover, single franking 225.00
108 A19 3fr red vio ('30) 18.00 *22.50*
Never hinged 30.00
On cover 300.00
On cover, single franking 400.00
109 A19 5fr vio brn & ol grn 13.50 12.50
Never hinged 20.00
On cover 190.00
On cover, single franking 300.00
a. Perf 11 160.00
Never hinged 240.00
Nos. 79-109 (32) 135.55 142.75

For overprints and surcharges see Nos. 121-131, 206C-206D, B1-B2, Q3-Q5. Post 1940 listings are in Scott Standard catalogue, Vol. 5.

Stamps of 1892-1906 Surcharged in Carmine or Black

1912

Spacing between figures of surcharge 1.5mm (5c), 2mm (10c)

110 A16 5c on 2c brn, *buff* 3.75 *4.00*
Never hinged 6.00
On cover 125.00
111 A16 5c on 4c claret, *lav* (C) 1.10 *1.50*
Never hinged 1.90
On cover 80.00
112 A16 5c on 15c blue (C) 1.10 *1.50*
Never hinged 1.90
On cover 95.00
113 A16 5c on 20c red, *grn* .90 *1.10*
Never hinged 1.50
On cover 67.50
114 A16 5c on 25c blk, *rose* (C) .90 *1.10*
Never hinged 1.40
On cover 55.00
115 A16 5c on 30c brn, *bis* (C) 1.10 *1.50*
Never hinged 1.50
On cover 110.00
116 A16 5c on 35c blk, *yel* (C) 1.90 *2.25*
Never hinged 3.00
On cover 110.00
117 A16 10c on 40c red, *straw* 1.50 *1.90*
Never hinged 1.90
On cover 95.00
b. Pair, one stamp without surcharge 625.00
118 A16 10c on 50c car, *rose* 1.50 *1.90*
Never hinged 2.75
On cover 105.00
119 A16 10c on 75c dp vio, *org* 3.75 *4.50*
Never hinged 6.00
On cover 125.00
120 A16 10c on 1fr brnz grn, *straw* 5.25 *6.25*
Never hinged 9.00
On cover 160.00
Nos. 110-120 (11) 22.75 *27.50*

Spacing between figures of surcharge 2.25mm (5c), 2.75mm (10c)

110a A16 5c on 2c brn, *buff* 400.00 400.00
Never hinged 775.00
111a A16 5c on 4c claret, *lav* (C) 37.50 37.50
Never hinged 75.00
112a A16 5c on 15c blue (C) 60.00 60.00
Never hinged 125.00
113a A16 5c on 20c red, *grn* 26.00 26.00
Never hinged 52.50
114a A16 5c on 25c blk, *rose* (C) 26.00 26.00
Never hinged 52.50
115a A16 5c on 30c brn, *bis* (C) 55.00 55.00
Never hinged 110.00
116a A16 5c on 35c blk, *yel* (C) 22.50 22.50
Never hinged 40.00
117a A16 10c on 40c red, *straw* 26.00 26.00
Never hinged 52.50
118a A16 10c on 50c car, *rose* 37.50 37.50
Never hinged 75.00
119a A16 10c on 75c dp vio, *org* 95.00 95.00
Never hinged 190.00
120a A16 10c on 1fr brnz grn, *straw* 95.00 95.00
Never hinged 190.00
Nos. 110a-120a (11) 880.50 880.50

Se-tenant Pairs, Both Ovpt. Settings

110b A16 5c on 2c, #110 + #110a 440.00 440.00
111b A16 5c on 4c, #111 + #111a 40.00 40.00
Never hinged 80.00
112b A16 5c on 15c, #112 + #112a 67.50 67.50
Never hinged 150.00
113b A16 5c on 20c, #113 + #113a 30.00 30.00
Never hinged 60.00
114b A16 5c on 25c, #114 + #114a 30.00 30.00
Never hinged 60.00
115b A16 5c on 30c, #115 + #115a 62.50 62.50
Never hinged 120.00
116b A16 5c on 35c, #116 + #116a 26.00 26.00
Never hinged 50.00
117c A16 10c on 40c, #117 + #117a 30.00 30.00
Never hinged 60.00
118b A16 10c on 50c, #118 + #118a 45.00 45.00
Never hinged 85.00
119b A16 10c on 75c, #119 + #119a 100.00 100.00
Never hinged 200.00
120b A16 10c on 1fr, #118 + #118a 100.00 100.00
Never hinged 200.00

Stamps and Types of 1909-17 Surcharged in Black, Blue (Bl) or Red

1924-27

121 A17 25c on 15c dl vio & rose ('25) .55 *.75*
Never hinged 1.20
On cover 62.50
a. Double surcharge 190.00
Never hinged 240.00
b. Triple surcharge 210.00
Never hinged 260.00
c. In pair with unovptd. stamp 700.00
Never hinged 1,000.
122 A19 25c on 2fr vio & lt brn (Bl) .80 *1.10*
Never hinged 1.25
On cover 62.50
123 A19 25c on 5fr brn & ol grn (Bl) .90 *1.10*
Never hinged 1.25
On cover 62.50
a. Triple surcharge 210.00
Never hinged 250.00
124 A18 65c on 45c vio & ol grn ('25) 2.25 *3.00*
Never hinged 3.75
On cover 110.00
On cover, single franking 210.00
125 A18 85c on 75c brn & ol ('25) 2.25 *3.00*
Never hinged 3.75
On cover 140.00
On cover, single franking 250.00
126 A18 90c on 75c brn red & dp org ('27) 3.00 *3.75*
Never hinged 4.75
On cover 125.00
On cover, single franking 225.00
127 A19 1.25fr on 1fr dk bl & ultra (R) ('26) 3.00 *3.75*
Never hinged 4.75
On cover 75.00
On cover, single franking 140.00
128 A19 1.50fr on 1fr ultra & dk bl ('27) 4.00 *4.50*
Never hinged 6.00
On cover 87.50
On cover, single franking 200.00
129 A19 3fr on 5fr ol brn & red vio ('27) 5.25 *6.00*
Never hinged 8.25
On cover 105.00
On cover, single franking 225.00
130 A19 10fr on 5fr ver & ol grn ('27) 25.00 *29.00*
Never hinged 40.00
On cover 210.00
On cover, single franking 375.00
131 A19 20fr on 5fr vio & ver ('27) 32.50 *40.00*
Never hinged 52.50
On cover 260.00
On cover, single franking 475.00
Nos. 121-131 (11) 79.50 95.95

Common Design Types pictured following the introduction.

Colonial Exposition Issue

Common Design Types

1931, Apr. 13 Engr. *Perf. 12½*

Name of Country in Black

132 CD70 40c deep green 6.00 6.00
Never hinged 9.75
On cover 105.00
133 CD71 50c violet 6.00 *6.00*
Never hinged 9.75
On cover 87.50
134 CD72 90c red orange 6.00 *6.00*
Never hinged 9.75
On cover 150.00
On cover, single franking 210.00
135 CD73 1.50fr dull blue 6.00 *6.00*
Never hinged 9.75
On cover 150.00
On cover, single franking 200.00
Nos. 132-135 (4) 24.00 24.00

Map and Fishermen — A20

Lighthouse and Fish — A21

Fishing Steamer and Sea Gulls A22

Perf. 13½x14, 14x13½

1932-33 Typo.

136 A20 1c red brn & ultra .25 *.35*
Never hinged .40
On cover 150.00
137 A21 2c blk & dk grn .40 *.50*
Never hinged .65
On cover 150.00
138 A22 4c mag & ol brn .40 *.60*
Never hinged .60
On cover 140.00
139 A22 5c vio & dk brn .80 *1.10*
Never hinged 1.20
On cover 125.00
140 A21 10c red brn & blk .80 *1.10*
Never hinged 1.20
On cover 105.00
141 A21 15c dk blue & vio 1.60 *2.25*
Never hinged 2.60
On cover 95.00
142 A20 20c blk & red org 1.90 *2.25*
Never hinged 3.00
On cover 75.00
143 A20 25c lt vio & lt grn 1.90 *2.25*
Never hinged 3.00
On cover 62.50
144 A22 30c ol grn & bl grn 1.90 *2.25*
Never hinged 3.00
On cover 62.50
145 A22 40c dp bl & dk brn 1.90 *2.25*
Never hinged 3.00
On cover 62.50
146 A21 45c ver & dp grn 1.90 2.25
Never hinged 3.00
On cover 62.50
147 A21 50c dk brn & dk grn 2.25 *2.60*
Never hinged 3.25
On cover 55.00
148 A22 65c ol brn & org 2.60 *3.00*
Never hinged 4.00
On cover 110.00
149 A20 75c grn & red org 2.25 *2.60*
Never hinged 3.25
On cover 75.00
150 A20 90c dull red & red 2.75 *3.75*
Never hinged 4.00
On cover 85.00
On cover, single franking 150.00
151 A22 1fr org brn & org red 2.60 *3.00*
Never hinged 3.75
On cover 75.00
On cover, single franking 140.00
152 A20 1.25fr dp bl & lake ('33) 2.60 *3.00*
Never hinged 4.00
On cover 95.00
On cover, single franking 190.00
153 A20 1.50fr dp blue & blue 2.60 *3.00*
Never hinged 4.00
On cover 105.00
On cover, single franking 200.00
154 A22 1.75fr blk & dk brn ('33) 3.25 *3.75*
Never hinged 4.75
On cover 110.00
On cover, single franking 210.00
155 A22 2fr bl blk & Prus bl 12.00 *13.50*
Never hinged 17.50
On cover 140.00
On cover, single franking 250.00
156 A21 3fr dp grn & dk brn 15.00 *19.00*
Never hinged 21.00
On cover 190.00
On cover, single franking 300.00
157 A21 5fr brn red & dk brn 32.50 *37.50*
Never hinged 42.50
On cover 340.00
On cover, single franking 500.00
158 A22 10fr dk grn & vio 75.00 *82.50*
Never hinged 120.00
On cover 500.00
On cover, single franking 675.00

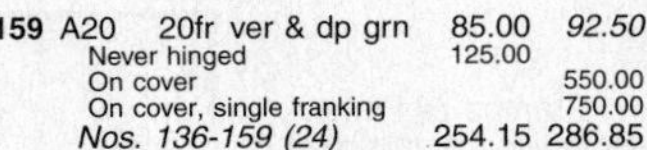

159 A20 20fr ver & dp grn 85.00 *92.50*
Never hinged 125.00
On cover 550.00
On cover, single franking 750.00
Nos. 136-159 (24) 254.15 286.85

For overprints and surcharges see Nos. 160-164, 207-221 (in Scott Standard catalogue, Vol. 5).

Nos. 147, 149, 153-154, 157 Overprinted in Black, Red or Blue

p

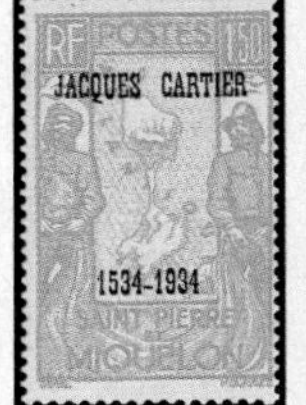

q

1934, Oct. 18

160 A21(p) 50c (Bk) 6.50 *7.50*
Never hinged 10.00
On cover 105.00
161 A20(q) 75c (Bk) 9.50 *10.50*
Never hinged 13.50
On cover 125.00
162 A20(q) 1.50fr (Bk) 9.50 *10.50*
Never hinged 16.00
On cover 170.00
On cover, single franking 250.00
163 A22(p) 1.75fr (R) 10.00 *12.50*
Never hinged 17.00
On cover 160.00
On cover, single franking 225.00
164 A21(p) 5fr (Bl) 45.00 *47.50*
Never hinged 75.00
On cover 300.00
On cover, single franking 500.00
Nos. 160-164 (5) 80.50 88.50

400th anniv. of the landing of Jacques Cartier.

Paris International Exposition Issue

Common Design Types

1937 *Perf. 13*

165 CD74 20c deep violet 2.40 *2.75*
Never hinged 3.25
On cover 105.00
166 CD75 30c dark green 2.40 *2.75*
Never hinged 3.25
On cover 87.50
167 CD76 40c carmine rose 2.40 *2.75*
Never hinged 3.25
On cover 80.00
168 CD77 50c dk brn & bl 2.40 *2.75*
Never hinged 3.25
On cover 75.00
169 CD78 90c red 2.50 *2.75*
Never hinged 3.50
On cover 140.00
On cover, single franking 225.00
170 CD79 1.50fr ultra 2.50 *2.75*
Never hinged 3.50
On cover 125.00
On cover, single franking 200.00
Nos. 165-170 (6) 14.60 16.50

Colonial Arts Exhibition Issue

Souvenir Sheet

Common Design Type

1937 *Imperf.*

171 CD78 3fr dark ultra 35.00 *47.50*
Never hinged 52.50
On cover 190.00
On cover, single franking 250.00

Dog Team A23

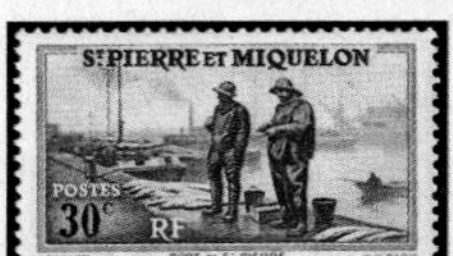

Port St. Pierre A24

Tortue Lighthouse A25

Soldiers' Bay at Langlade A26

1938-40 Photo. *Perf. 13½x13*

172 A23 2c dk bl grn .25 *.35*
Never hinged .40
On cover 105.00
a. Value omitted *425.00*
Never hinged 540.00
173 A23 3c brown violet .25 *.35*
Never hinged .40
On cover 105.00
174 A23 4c dk red violet .30 *.40*
Never hinged .45
On cover 105.00
175 A23 5c carmine lake .30 *.40*
Never hinged .45
On cover 95.00
176 A23 10c bister brown .30 *.40*
Never hinged .45
On cover 87.50
177 A23 15c red violet .65 *.80*
Never hinged .95
On cover 85.00
178 A23 20c blue violet .90 *1.10*
Never hinged 1.25
On cover 75.00
179 A23 25c Prus blue 2.50 *3.00*
Never hinged 3.40
On cover 62.50
180 A24 30c dk red violet .65 *.80*
Never hinged .95
On cover 62.50
181 A24 35c deep green .90 *1.10*
Never hinged 1.25
On cover 62.50
182 A24 40c slate blue ('40) .25 *.35*
Never hinged .40
On cover 62.50
183 A24 45c dp grn ('40) .50 *.60*
Never hinged .65
On cover 67.50
a. Value omitted *110.00*
Never hinged 175.00
184 A24 50c carmine rose .90 *1.10*
Never hinged 1.25
On cover 75.00
185 A24 55c Prus blue 4.25 *4.50*
Never hinged 6.00
On cover 80.00
186 A24 60c violet ('39) .65 *.90*
Never hinged 1.00
On cover 62.50
187 A24 65c brown 6.50 *6.75*
Never hinged 8.75
On cover 100.00
188 A24 70c org yel ('39) .75 *1.00*
Never hinged 1.10
On cover 55.00
189 A25 80c violet 1.60 *1.90*
Never hinged 2.50
On cover 62.50
190 A25 90c ultra ('39) 1.00 *1.25*
Never hinged 1.40
On cover 55.00
191 A25 1fr brt pink 13.00 *14.00*
Never hinged 16.50
On cover 150.00
On cover, single franking 250.00
192 A25 1fr pale ol grn ('40) 1.00 *1.25*
Never hinged 1.40
On cover 55.00
193 A25 1.25fr brt rose ('39) 2.40 *2.75*
Never hinged 3.00
On cover 105.00
On cover, single franking 150.00
194 A25 1.40fr dk brn ('40) 1.25 *1.50*
Never hinged 1.60
On cover 75.00
On cover, single franking 110.00
195 A25 1.50fr blue green 1.25 *1.50*
Never hinged 1.75
On cover 75.00
On cover, single franking 150.00
196 A25 1.60fr rose vio ('40) 1.25 *1.50*
Never hinged 1.60
On cover 75.00
On cover, single franking 150.00
197 A25 1.75fr deep blue 3.50 *4.50*
Never hinged 5.25
On cover 105.00
On cover, single franking 190.00
198 A26 2fr rose violet .90 *1.10*
Never hinged 1.25
On cover 75.00
On cover, single franking 125.00
199 A26 2.25fr brt blue ('39) 1.25 *1.60*
Never hinged 1.75
On cover 95.00
On cover, single franking 140.00
200 A26 2.50fr org yel ('40) 1.25 *1.50*
Never hinged 1.90
On cover 100.00
On cover, single franking 150.00
201 A26 3fr gray brown 1.10 *1.50*
Never hinged 1.60
On cover 75.00
On cover, single franking 125.00
202 A26 5fr henna brown 1.25 *1.50*
Never hinged 1.60
On cover 85.00
On cover, single franking 140.00
203 A26 10fr dk bl, *bluish* 1.90 *2.25*
Never hinged 2.60
On cover 95.00
On cover, single franking 150.00
204 A26 20fr slate green 2.50 *3.00*
Never hinged 3.25
On cover 110.00
On cover, single franking 190.00
Nos. 172-204 (33) 57.20 66.50

For overprints and surcharges see Nos. 222-255, 260-299, B9-B10 in Scott Standard catalogue, Vol. 5.

New York World's Fair Issue
Common Design Type

1939, May 10 Engr. *Perf. 12½x12*

205 CD82 1.25fr carmine lake 2.40 *3.00*
Never hinged 3.40
On cover 100.00
On cover, single franking 190.00
206 CD82 2.25fr ultra 2.40 *3.00*
Never hinged 3.40
On cover 95.00
On cover, single franking 140.00

For overprints and surcharges see Nos. 256-259 in Scott Standard catalogue, Vol. 5.

SEMI-POSTAL STAMPS

Regular Issue of 1909-17 Surcharged in Red

1915-17 Unwmk. *Perf. 14x13½*

B1 A17 10c + 5c car rose & red 3.00 *3.75*
Never hinged 4.50
On cover 95.00
B2 A17 15c + 5c dl vio & rose ('17) 3.00 *3.75*
Never hinged 4.50
On cover 95.00

Curie Issue
Common Design Type

1938, Oct. 24 Engr. *Perf. 13*

B3 CD80 1.75fr + 50c brt ultra 21.00 *22.50*
Never hinged 29.00
On cover 140.00
On cover, single franking 250.00

French Revolution Issue
Common Design Type

1939, July 5 Photo.
Name and Value Typo. in Black

B4 CD83 45c + 25c green 13.50 *14.50*
Never hinged 19.00
On cover 140.00
B5 CD83 70c + 30c brown 13.50 *14.50*
Never hinged 19.00
On cover 105.00
B6 CD83 90c + 35c red org 13.50 *14.50*
Never hinged 19.00
On cover 95.00
B7 CD83 1.25fr + 1fr rose pink 13.50 *14.50*
Never hinged 19.00
On cover 150.00
On cover, single franking 225.00
B8 CD83 2.25fr + 2fr blue 13.50 *14.50*
Never hinged 19.00
On cover 140.00
On cover, single franking 200.00
Nos. B4-B8 (5) 67.50 72.50

POSTAGE DUE STAMPS

Postage Due Stamps of French Colonies Overprinted in Red

1892 Unwmk. *Imperf.*

J1 D1 5c black 85.00 85.00
On cover —
J2 D1 10c black 26.00 26.00
Never hinged 55.00
On cover *1,000.*
J3 D1 15c black 26.00 26.00
Never hinged 55.00
On cover *1,000.*
J4 D1 20c black 26.00 26.00
Never hinged 55.00
On cover *1,000.*
J5 D1 30c black 26.00 26.00
Never hinged 55.00
On cover *1,000.*
J6 D1 40c black 26.00 26.00
Never hinged 55.00
On cover *1,000.*
J7 D1 60c black 82.50 90.00
On cover *1,200.*

Black Overprint

J8 D1 1fr brown 200.00 200.00
On cover —
J9 D1 2fr brown 200.00 200.00
On cover —
Nos. J1-J9 (9) 697.50 705.00

These stamps exist with and without hyphen. See note after No. 59.

Postage Due Stamps of France, 1893-1924, Overprinted

1925-27 *Perf. 14x13½*

J10 D2 5c blue .75 *1.10*
Never hinged 1.10
On cover 190.00
J11 D2 10c dark brown .75 *1.10*
Never hinged 1.10
On cover 200.00
J12 D2 20c olive green .80 *1.10*
Never hinged 1.10
On cover 210.00
J13 D2 25c rose 1.10 *1.50*
Never hinged 1.50
On cover 210.00
J14 D2 30c red 1.90 *2.25*
Never hinged 2.60
On cover 210.00
J15 D2 45c blue green 1.90 *2.25*
Never hinged 2.60
On cover 240.00
J16 D2 50c brown vio 2.60 *3.75*
Never hinged 4.50
On cover 275.00
J17 D2 1fr red brn, *straw* 3.50 *4.00*
Never hinged 4.75
On cover 300.00
J18 D2 3fr magenta ('27) 12.00 *15.00*
Never hinged 20.00
On cover 350.00

Surcharged

J19 D2 60c on 50c buff 2.75 *3.75*
Never hinged 4.75
On cover 275.00
J20 D2 2fr on 1fr red 4.50 *5.50*
Never hinged 8.25
On cover 300.00
Nos. J10-J20 (11) 32.55 41.30

Newfoundland Dog — D3

1932, Dec. 5 Typo.

J21 D3 5c dk blue & blk 1.50 *1.90*
Never hinged 2.25
On cover 125.00
J22 D3 10c green & blk 1.50 *1.90*
Never hinged 2.25
On cover 125.00
J23 D3 20c red & blk 1.75 *2.25*
Never hinged 2.75
On cover 140.00
J24 D3 25c red vio & blk 1.75 *2.25*
Never hinged 2.75
On cover 140.00
J25 D3 30c orange & blk 3.50 *4.50*
Never hinged 5.25
On cover 150.00
J26 D3 45c lt blue & blk 5.50 *6.75*
Never hinged 8.75
On cover 170.00
J27 D3 50c blue grn & blk 8.50 *10.50*
Never hinged 12.00
On cover 190.00
J28 D3 60c brt rose & blk 12.00 *15.00*
Never hinged 18.00
On cover 210.00
J29 D3 1fr yellow brn & blk 22.50 *30.00*
Never hinged 32.50
On cover 250.00
J30 D3 2fr dp violet & blk 32.50 *37.50*
Never hinged 55.00
On cover 300.00
J31 D3 3fr dk brown & blk 45.00 *55.00*
Never hinged 65.00
On cover 375.00
Nos. J21-J31 (11) 136.00 167.55

For overprints and surcharge see Nos. J42-J46 in Scott Standard catalogue, Vol. 5.

Codfish — D4

1938, Nov. 17 Photo. *Perf. 13*

J32 D4 5c gray black .40 *.50*
Never hinged .65
On cover 80.00
J33 D4 10c dk red violet .40 *.50*
Never hinged .65
On cover 80.00
J34 D4 15c slate green .50 *.75*
Never hinged .70
On cover 95.00
J35 D4 20c deep blue .55 *.75*
Never hinged .75
On cover 95.00
J36 D4 30c rose carmine .55 *.75*
Never hinged .70
On cover 95.00
J37 D4 50c dk blue green .70 *.80*
Never hinged .95
On cover 100.00
J38 D4 60c dk blue .95 *1.10*
Never hinged 1.25
On cover 110.00
J39 D4 1fr henna brown 1.90 *2.25*
Never hinged 2.50
On cover 140.00
J40 D4 2fr gray brown 4.50 *5.25*
Never hinged 6.00
On cover 175.00
J41 D4 3fr dull violet 4.75 *6.00*
Never hinged 7.00
On cover 210.00
Nos. J32-J41 (10) 15.20 18.65

For overprints see Nos. J48-J67 in Scott Standard catalogue, Vol. 5.

PARCEL POST STAMPS

No. 65 Overprinted

1901 Unwmk. *Perf. 14x13½*

Q1 A16 10c blk, *lav* 140.00 140.00
Never hinged 225.00
a. Inverted overprint 1,250. 1,250.
b. Double overprint 600.00 600.00

No. 66 Overprinted

Q2 A16 10c red 30.00 *32.50*
Never hinged 52.50

Nos. 84 and 87 Overprinted

1917-25

Q3 A17 10c car rose & red 4.50 *6.00*
Never hinged 6.75
a. Double overprint 300.00
Never hinged 360.00
Q4 A17 20c bis brn & vio brn ('25) 3.75 *5.25*
Never hinged 5.25
a. Double overprint 190.00
Never hinged 260.00

ST. THOMAS & PRINCE ISLANDS

sānt-'täm-əs and 'prin‸t‸s 'ī-lənd

LOCATION — Two islands in the Gulf of Guinea, 125 miles off the west coast of Africa
GOVT. — Portuguese Colony
AREA — 372 sq. mi.
POP. — 102,000 (est. 1984)
CAPITAL — Sao Tome

1000 Reis = 1 Milreis
100 Centavos = 1 Escudo (1913)

Portuguese Crown — A1

5, 25, 50 REIS:
Type I — "5" is upright.
Type II — "5" is slanting.

10 REIS:
Type I — "1" has short serif at top.
Type II — "1" has long serif at top.

40 REIS:
Type I — "4" is broad.
Type II — "4" is narrow.

Perf. 12½, 13½

1869-75 Unwmk. Typo.

1 A1 5r black, I 4.00 1.90
a. Type II 4.00 1.90
2 A1 10r yellow, I 14.00 8.50
a. Type II 17.50 10.50
3 A1 20r bister 3.50 2.75
4 A1 25r rose, I 2.00 1.10
a. 25r red 4.50 1.50
5 A1 40r blue ('75), I 5.00 3.50
a. Type II 5.50 4.50
6 A1 50r gray grn, II 9.00 7.00
a. Type I 15.00 14.00
7 A1 100r gray lilac 6.00 5.50
8 A1 200r red orange ('75) 9.00 6.25
9 A1 300r chocolate ('75) 9.00 7.00
Nos. 1-9 (9) 61.50 43.50

1881-85

10 A1 10r gray grn, I 8.00 6.75
a. Type II 9.50 6.00
b. Perf. 13½, I 11.00 8.00
11 A1 20r car rose ('85) 4.00 3.00
12 A1 25r vio ('85), II 2.25 1.75
13 A1 40r yel buff, II 5.00 4.00
a. Perf. 13½ 6.00 4.50
14 A1 50r dk blue, I 3.00 2.25
a. Type II 3.00 2.25
Nos. 10-14 (5) 22.25 17.75

For surcharges and overprints see Nos. 63-64, 129-129B, 154.

Nos. 1-14 have been reprinted on stout white paper, ungummed, with rough perforation 13½, also on ordinary paper with shiny white gum and clean-cut perforation 13½ with large holes.

King Luiz — A2

Typo., Head Embossed

1887 Perf. 12½, 13½

15 A2 5r black 6.00 2.50
16 A2 10r green 6.00 2.50
17 A2 20r brt rose 6.00 3.00
a. Perf. 12½ 55.00 55.00
18 A2 25r violet 6.00 1.60
19 A2 40r brown 6.00 2.25
20 A2 50r blue 6.00 2.50
21 A2 100r yellow brn 6.00 2.00
22 A2 200r gray lilac 15.00 10.50
23 A2 300r orange 15.00 10.50
Nos. 15-23 (9) 72.00 37.35

For surcharges and overprints see Nos. 24-26, 62, 65-72, 130-131, 155-158, 234-237.

Nos. 15, 16, 19, 21, 22, and 23 have been reprinted in paler colors than the originals, with white gum and cleancut perforation 13½. Value $1.50 each.

Nos. 16-17, 19 Surcharged

a

c

b: 5 cinco réis

1889-91 Without Gum

24 A2(a) 5r on 10r 35.00 20.00
25 A2(b) 5r on 20r 25.00 20.00
26 A2(c) 50r on 40r ('91) 240.00 50.00
Nos. 24-26 (3) 300.00 90.00

Varieties of Nos. 24-26, including inverted and double surcharges, "5" inverted, "Cinoc" and "Cinco," were deliberately made and unofficially issued.

King Carlos — A6

1895 Typo. Perf. 11½, 12½

27 A6 5r yellow 1.50 .60
28 A6 10r red lilac 2.00 1.00
29 A6 15r red brown 2.00 1.10
30 A6 20r lavender 2.50 1.10
31 A6 25r green 2.50 .75
32 A6 50r light blue 2.50 .70
a. Perf. 13½ 3.00 1.50
33 A6 75r rose 8.00 3.25
34 A6 80r yellow grn 8.00 6.25
35 A6 100r brn, *yel* 4.00 3.00
36 A6 150r car, *rose* 6.00 5.00
37 A6 200r dk bl, *bl* 7.75 6.50
38 A6 300r dk bl, *sal* 8.50 7.75
Nos. 27-38 (12) 55.25 37.00

For surcharges and overprints see Nos. 73-84, 132-137, 159-165, 238-243, 262-264, 268-274.

King Carlos — A7

1898-1903 Perf. 11½

Name and Value in Black except 500r

39 A7 2½r gray .30 .25
40 A7 5r orange .30 .25
41 A7 10r lt green .40 .30
42 A7 15r brown 2.00 1.75
43 A7 15r gray grn ('03) 1.10 1.10
44 A7 20r gray violet .90 .50
45 A7 25r sea green .70 .25
46 A7 25r carmine ('03) 1.10 .30
47 A7 50r blue 1.00 .50
48 A7 50r brown ('03) 4.50 4.50
49 A7 65r dull blue ('03) 22.50 9.00
50 A7 75r rose 10.00 6.50
51 A7 75r red lilac ('03) 2.50 1.40
52 A7 80r brt violet 5.00 5.00
53 A7 100r dk blue, *bl* 3.00 2.00
54 A7 115r org brn, *pink* ('03) 10.00 8.00
55 A7 130r brn, *straw* ('03) 10.00 6.00
56 A7 150r brn, *buff* 5.00 2.25
57 A7 200r red lil, *pnksh* 6.00 2.75
58 A7 300r dk blue, *rose* 8.00 5.00
59 A7 400r dull bl, *straw* ('03) 15.00 8.50
60 A7 500r blk & red, *bl* ('01) 12.00 5.00
61 A7 700r vio, *yelsh* ('01) 20.00 12.00
Nos. 39-61 (23) 141.30 83.10

For overprints and surcharges see Nos. 86-105, 116-128, 138-153, 167-169, 244-249, 255-261, 265-267.

Stamps of 1869-95 Surcharged in Red or Black

1902 On Stamp of 1887

62 A2 130r on 5r blk (R) 6.00 5.00
a. Perf. 13½ 32.50 32.50

On Stamps of 1869

63 A1 115r on 50r grn 10.00 7.50
64 A1 400r on 10r yel 25.00 12.00
a. Double surcharge 75.00 50.00

On Stamps of 1887

65 A2 65r on 20r rose 7.00 4.50
a. Perf. 13½ 8.50 7.00
66 A2 65r on 25r violet 6.00 4.00
a. Inverted surcharge 35.00 25.00
67 A2 65r on 100r yel brn 6.00 4.75
68 A2 115r on 10r blue grn 6.00 4.00
69 A2 115r on 300r orange 6.00 4.00
70 A2 130r on 200r gray lil 7.00 5.00
71 A2 400r on 40r brown 8.00 7.00
72 A2 400r on 50r blue 14.00 12.00
a. Perf. 13½ 110.00 90.00

On Stamps of 1895

73 A6 65r on 5r yellow 7.00 3.00
74 A6 65r on 10r red vio 7.00 3.00
75 A6 65r on 15r choc 7.00 3.00
76 A6 65r on 20r lav 7.00 3.00
77 A6 115r on 25r grn 7.00 3.00
78 A6 115r on 150r car, *rose* 7.00 3.00
79 A6 115r on 200r bl, *bl* 7.00 3.00
80 A6 130r on 75r rose 7.00 3.00
81 A6 130r on 100r brn, *yel* 7.00 3.50
a. Double surcharge 30.00 20.00
82 A6 130r on 300r bl, *sal* 7.00 3.00
83 A6 400r on 50r lt blue 1.10 .95
a. Perf. 13½ 2.00 1.60
84 A6 400r on 80r yel grn 2.00 1.50

On Newspaper Stamp No. P12

85 N3 400r on 2½r brown 1.10 .95
a. Double surcharge
Nos. 62-85 (24) 175.20 103.65

Reprints of Nos. 63, 64, 67, 71, and 72 have shiny white gum and clean-cut perf. 13½.

Stamps of 1898 Overprinted

1902

86 A7 15r brown 3.00 1.50
87 A7 25r sea green 3.00 1.25
88 A7 50r blue 3.00 1.25
89 A7 75r rose 5.00 3.50
Nos. 86-89 (4) 14.00 7.50

No. 49 Surcharged in Black

1905

90 A7 50r on 65r dull blue 5.00 2.75

Stamps of 1898-1903 Overprinted in Carmine or Green

1911

91 A7 2½r gray .25 .25
a. Inverted overprint 15.00 11.00
92 A7 5r orange .25 .25
93 A7 10r lt green .25 .25
a. Inverted overprint 15.00 12.00
94 A7 15r gray green .25 .25
95 A7 20r gray violet .25 .25
96 A7 25r carmine (G) .60 .25
97 A7 50r brown .30 .25
a. Inverted overprint 15.00 12.00
98 A7 75r red lilac .40 .25
99 A7 100r dk bl, *bl* .75 .50
a. Inverted overprint 17.50 14.00
100 A7 115r org brn, *pink* 1.50 .95
101 A7 130r brown, *straw* 1.50 .95
102 A7 200r red lil, *pnksh* 6.00 4.25
103 A7 400r dull blue, *straw* 2.00 1.00
104 A7 500r blk & red, *bl* 2.00 1.00
105 A7 700r violet, *yelsh* 2.00 1.00
Nos. 91-105 (15) 18.30 11.65

King Manuel II — A8

Overprinted in Carmine or Green

1912 Perf. 11½, 12

106 A8 2½r violet .25 .25
a. Double overprint 16.00 16.00
b. Double overprint, one inverted 25.00
107 A8 5r black .25 .25
108 A8 10r gray green .25 .25
a. Double overprint 14.00 14.00
109 A8 20r carmine (G) 1.00 .75
110 A8 25r violet brn .60 .45
111 A8 50r dk blue .60 .55
112 A8 75r bister brn .90 .55
113 A8 100r brn, *lt grn* 1.10 .50
114 A8 200r dk grn, *sal* 2.00 1.40
115 A8 300r black, *azure* 2.00 2.00
Nos. 106-115 (10) 8.95 6.95

Stamps of 1898-1905 Overprinted in Black

1913 On Stamps of 1898-1903

116 A7 2½r gray 4.00 1.00
a. Inverted overprint 20.00 20.00
b. Double overprint 20.00 20.00
117 A7 5r orange 2.00 1.00
118 A7 15r gray green 30.00 17.50
a. Inverted overprint 75.00
119 A7 20r gray violet 6.00 1.50
a. Inverted overprint 15.00
120 A7 25r carmine 10.00 4.50
a. Inverted overprint 30.00
b. Double overprint 30.00
121 A7 75r red lilac 7.00 5.00
122 A7 100r bl, *bluish* 10.00 7.50
123 A7 115r org brn, *pink* 37.50 35.00
a. Double overprint 75.00 60.00
124 A7 130r brn, *straw* 13.00 13.00
125 A7 200r red lil, *pnksh* 20.00 13.00
126 A7 400r dl bl, *straw* 14.00 12.50
127 A7 500r blk & red, *gray* 40.00 42.50
128 A7 700r vio, *yelsh* 50.00 40.00
Nos. 116-128 (13) 243.50 194.00

On Provisional Issue of 1902

129 A1 115r on 50r grn 125.00 85.00
a. Inverted overprint
129B A1 400r on 10r yel 700.00 500.00
130 A2 115r on 10r blue grn 3.00 2.50
a. Inverted overprint 25.00
131 A2 400r on 50r blue 80.00 75.00
132 A6 115r on 25r grn 2.00 1.75
a. Inverted overprint 20.00
133 A6 115r on 150r car, *rose* 60.00 40.00
a. Inverted overprint 100.00
134 A6 115r on 200r bl, *bl* 3.00 2.00
135 A6 130r on 75r rose 3.00 2.00
a. Inverted overprint 50.00
136 A6 400r on 50r lt bl 4.00 4.00
a. Perf. 13½ 20.00 10.00
137 A6 400r on 80r yel grn 5.00 4.25

Same Overprint on Nos. 86, 88, 90

138 A7 15r brown 5.00 1.75
139 A7 50r blue 5.00 2.00
140 A7 50r on 65r dl bl 16.00 12.00
Nos. 138-140 (3) 26.00 15.75

No. 123-125, 130-131 and 137 were issued without gum.

Stamps of 1898-1905 Overprinted in Black

On Stamps of 1898-1903

141 A7 2½r gray .60 .50
a. Inverted overprint 9.00
b. Double overprint 20.00 20.00
c. Double overprint inverted 30.00
142 A7 5r orange 30.00 22.50
143 A7 15r gray green 2.00 1.50
a. Inverted overprint 25.00
144 A7 20r gray violet 450.00 200.00
a. Inverted overprint 600.00

145 A7 25r carmine 50.00 27.50
a. Inverted overprint 75.00
146 A7 75r red lilac 5.00 2.25
a. Inverted overprint 5.00
147 A7 100r blue, *bl* 3.00 1.75
148 A7 115r org brn, *pink* 10.00 8.00
a. Inverted overprint 25.00
149 A7 130r brown, *straw* 8.00 7.00
a. Inverted overprint 25.00
150 A7 200r red lil, *pnksh* 4.00 1.75
a. Inverted overprint 10.00
151 A7 400r dull bl, *straw* 10.00 8.00
152 A7 500r blk & red, *gray* 9.00 8.50
153 A7 700r violet, *yelsh* 9.00 8.50

On Provisional Issue of 1902

154 A1 115r on 50r green 200.00 150.00
155 A2 115r on 10r bl grn 2.50 2.25
156 A2 115r on 300r org 250.00 125.00
157 A2 130r on 5r black 300.00 125.00
158 A2 400r on 50r blue 200.00 90.00
159 A6 115r on 25r green 3.00 1.75
160 A6 115r on 150r car, *rose* 3.00 2.25
a. "REPUBLICA" inverted 20.00
161 A6 115r on 200r bl, *bl* 3.00 2.25
162 A6 130r on 75r rose 3.00 2.00
a. Inverted surcharge 20.00
163 A6 130r on 100r brn, *yel* 900.00 500.00
164 A6 400r on 50r lt bl 3.50 3.00
a. Perf. 13½ 17.50 6.00
165 A6 400r on 80r yel grn 3.00 2.25
166 N3 400r on 2½r brn 2.00 1.75

Same Overprint on Nos. 86, 88, 90

167 A7 15r brown 1.50 1.25
a. Inverted overprint 20.00
168 A7 50r blue 1.50 1.25
a. Inverted overprint 20.00
169 A7 50r on 65r dull bl 2.25 1.50
Nos. 167-169 (3) 5.25 4.00

Most of Nos. 141-169 were issued without gum.

Common Design Types pictured following the introduction.

Vasco da Gama Issue of Various Portuguese Colonies Surcharged

On Stamps of Macao

170 CD20 ¼c on ½a bl grn 1.60 1.40
171 CD21 ½c on 1a red 1.60 1.40
172 CD22 1c on 2a red vio 1.60 1.40
173 CD23 2½c on 4a yel grn 1.60 1.40
174 CD24 5c on 8a dk bl 1.90 1.60
175 CD25 7½c on 12a vio brn 3.00 3.00
176 CD26 10c on 16a bis brn 1.90 1.60
177 CD27 15c on 24a bister 1.90 1.60
Nos. 170-177 (8) 15.10 13.40

On Stamps of Portuguese Africa

178 CD20 ¼c on 2½r bl grn 1.25 1.00
179 CD21 ½c on 5r red 1.25 1.00
180 CD22 1c on 10r red vio 1.25 1.00
181 CD23 2½c on 25r yel grn 1.25 1.00
182 CD24 5c on 50r dk bl 1.25 1.00
183 CD25 7½c on 75r vio brn 2.10 2.00
184 CD26 10c on 100r bis brn 1.25 1.00
185 CD27 15c on 150r bister 1.40 1.00
Nos. 178-185 (8) 11.00 9.00

On Stamps of Timor

186 CD20 ¼c on ½a bl grn 1.40 1.25
187 CD21 ½c on 1a red 1.40 1.25
188 CD22 1c on 2a red vio 1.40 1.25
a. Double surcharge 30.00
189 CD23 2½c on 4a yel grn 1.40 1.25
190 CD24 5c on 8a dk bl 1.75 1.60
191 CD25 7½c on 12a vio brn 2.50 2.50
192 CD26 10c on 16a bis brn 1.40 1.40
193 CD27 15c on 24a bister 1.40 1.40
Nos. 186-193 (8) 12.65 11.90
Nos. 170-193 (24) 38.75 34.30

Ceres — A9

Name and Value in Black
Chalky Paper

1914 **Typo.** ***Perf. 15x14***

194 A9 ¼c olive brown .40 .40
Never hinged .60
195 A9 ½c black .40 .40
Never hinged .60
196 A9 1c blue green .50 .40
Never hinged .75
197 A9 1½c lilac brn .30 .25
Never hinged .45
198 A9 2c carmine .40 .40
Never hinged .60
199 A9 2½c lt violet .40 .40
Never hinged .60
200 A9 5c deep blue .45 .35
Never hinged .70
201 A9 7½c yellow brn .65 .50
Never hinged 1.00
202 A9 8c slate .65 .50
Never hinged 1.00
203 A9 10c orange brn .65 .50
Never hinged 1.00
204 A9 15c plum 2.00 1.25
Never hinged 3.00
205 A9 20c yellow green 1.25 .75
Never hinged 1.90
206 A9 30c brown, *grn* 2.00 1.40
Never hinged 3.00
207 A9 40c brown, *pink* 1.75 1.40
Never hinged 2.75
208 A9 50c orange, *sal* 4.00 3.00
Never hinged 6.00
209 A9 1e green, *blue* 4.00 3.00
Never hinged 6.00
Nos. 194-209 (16) 19.80 14.90

For surcharges see Nos. 250-253, 281-282.

1920

Ordinary Paper

210 A9 ¼c olive brown .25 .25
Never hinged .40
211 A9 1½c lilac brn .75 .75
Never hinged 1.15
212 A9 7½c yellow brn 1.25 1.25
Never hinged 1.90
213 A9 10c orange brn 1.50 1.25
Never hinged 2.25
Nos. 210-213 (4) 3.75 3.50

1922-26 ***Perf. 12x11½***

214 A9 ¼c olive brown .25 .25
Never hinged .40
a. ¼c olive .25 .25
Never hinged .40
215 A9 ½c black .25 .25
Never hinged .40
216 A9 1c yellow grn ('22) .25 .25
Never hinged .40
217 A9 1½c lilac brn .30 .25
Never hinged .45
218 A9 2c carmine .25 .25
Never hinged .40
219 A9 2c gray ('26) .25 .25
Never hinged .40
220 A9 2½c lt violet .25 .25
Never hinged .40
221 A9 3c orange ('22) .25 .25
Never hinged .40
222 A9 4c rose ('22) .25 .25
Never hinged .40
223 A9 4½c gray ('22) .25 .25
Never hinged .40
224 A9 5c brt blue ('22) .25 .25
Never hinged .40
225 A9 6c lilac ('22) .25 .25
Never hinged .40
226 A9 7c ultra ('22) .25 .25
Never hinged .40
227 A9 7½c yellow brn .25 .25
Never hinged .40
228 A9 8c slate .25 .25
Never hinged .40
229 A9 10c orange brn .30 .25
Never hinged .45
230 A9 12c blue green ('22) .40 .40
Never hinged .60
231 A9 15c brn rose ('22) .25 .25
Never hinged .40
232 A9 20c yellow green .45 .45
Never hinged .70
233 A9 24c ultra ('26) 3.00 2.00
Never hinged 4.50
233A A9 25c choc ('26) 3.00 2.00
Never hinged 4.50
233B A9 30c gray grn ('22) .40 .30
Never hinged .60
233C A9 40c turq bl ('22) .40 .30
Never hinged .60
233D A9 50c lt violet ('26) .40 .30
Never hinged .60
233E A9 60c dk blue ('22) 2.00 .75
Never hinged 3.00
233F A9 60c rose ('26) 3.00 .75
Never hinged 3.00
233G A9 80c brt rose ('22) 3.00 .50
Never hinged 2.40

Glazed Paper

233H A9 1e pale rose ('22) 3.00 1.40
Never hinged 3.75
233I A9 1e blue ('26) 3.00 1.00
Never hinged 3.00
233J A9 2e dk violet ('22) 3.00 1.50
Never hinged 4.25
233K A9 5e buff ('26) 18.00 7.50
Never hinged 22.50
233L A9 10e pink ('26) 30.00 14.00
Never hinged 37.50
233M A9 20e pale turq ('26) 80.00 40.00
Never hinged 105.00
Nos. 214-233M (33) 157.40 77.40

Preceding Issues Overprinted in Bt. Red

1915

On Provisional Issue of 1902

234 A2 115r on 10r green 1.75 1.60
235 A2 115r on 300r org 1.75 1.75
236 A2 130r on 5r black 4.00 2.75
237 A2 130r on 200r gray lil 1.40 1.25
238 A6 115r on 25r green .60 .40
239 A6 115r on 150r car, *rose* .60 .40
240 A6 115r on 200r bl, *bl* .60 .40
241 A6 130r on 75r rose .60 .40
242 A6 130r on 100r brn, *yel* 1.10 1.25
243 A6 130r on 300r bl, *sal* 1.00 .75

Same Overprint on Nos. 88 and 90

244 A7 50r blue .70 .55
245 A7 50r on 65r dull bl .70 .55
Nos. 234-245 (12) 14.80 12.05

No. 86 Overprinted in Blue and Surcharged in Black

1919

246 A7 2½c on 15r brown .60 .55

No. 91 Surcharged in Black

247 A7 ½c on 2½r gray 3.00 2.75
248 A7 1c on 2½r gray 2.25 2.00
249 A7 2½c on 2½r gray 1.10 .65

No. 194 Surcharged in Black

250 A9 ½c on ¼c ol brn 2.00 1.75
Never hinged 3.00
251 A9 2c on ¼c ol brn 2.25 1.90
Never hinged 3.50
252 A9 2½c on ¼c ol brn 6.00 5.00
Never hinged 9.00

No. 199 Surcharged in Black

253 A9 4c on 2½c lt vio .90 .75
Nos. 246-253 (8) 18.10 15.35

Nos. 246-253 were issued without gum.

Stamps of 1898-1905 Overprinted in Green or Red

1920 **On Stamps of 1898-1903**

255 A7 75r red lilac (G) .55 .50
256 A7 100r blue, *blue* (R) .80 .75
257 A7 115r org brn, *pink* (G) 2.00 1.40
258 A7 130r brn, *straw* (G) 100.00 50.00
259 A7 200r red lil, *pnksh* (G) 2.00 1.00
260 A7 500r blk, & red, *gray* (G) 1.50 1.00
261 A7 700r vio, *yelsh* (G) 2.00 1.25

On Stamps of 1902

262 A6 115r on 25r grn (R) 1.00 .60
263 A6 115r on 200r bl, *bl* (R) 1.50 1.00
264 A6 130r on 75r rose (G) 2.00 1.50

On Nos. 88-89

265 A7 50r blue (R) 1.50 1.10
266 A7 75r rose (G) 25.00 7.00

On No. 90

267 A7 50r on 65r dl bl (R) 25.00 7.00
Nos. 255-257,259-267 (12) 64.85 24.10

Nos. 238-243 Surcharged in Blue or Red

1923 **Without Gum**

268 A6 10c on 115r on 25r (Bl) 1.00 .50
269 A6 10c on 115r on 150r (Bl) 1.00 .50
270 A6 10c on 115r on 200r (R) 1.00 .50
271 A6 10c on 130r on 75r (Bl) 1.00 .50
272 A6 10c on 130r on 100r (Bl) 1.00 .50
273 A6 10c on 130r on 300r (R) 1.00 .50
Nos. 268-273 (6) 6.00 3.00

Nos. 268-273 are usually stained and discolored.

Nos. 84-85 Surcharged

1925

274 A6 40c on 400r on 80r yel grn .90 .45
275 N3 40c on 400r on 2½r brn .90 .45

Nos. 233H and 233J Surcharged

1931

281 A9 70c on 1e pale rose 2.50 1.25
Never hinged 3.00
282 A9 1.40e on 2e dk vio 3.00 2.50
Never hinged 4.00

Ceres — A11

Perf. 12x11½

1934 **Typo.** **Wmk. 232**

283 A11 1c bister .25 .25
Never hinged .40
284 A11 5c olive brown .25 .25
Never hinged .40
285 A11 10c violet .25 .25
Never hinged .40
286 A11 15c black .25 .25
Never hinged .40
287 A11 20c gray .25 .25
Never hinged .40
288 A11 30c dk green .25 .25
Never hinged .40
289 A11 40c red orange .25 .25
Never hinged .40
290 A11 45c brt blue .50 .50
Never hinged .75
291 A11 50c brown .25 .25
Never hinged .40
292 A11 60c olive grn .50 .50
Never hinged .75
293 A11 70c brown org .50 .50
Never hinged .75
294 A11 80c emerald .50 .50
Never hinged .75
295 A11 85c deep rose 2.25 1.60
Never hinged 3.50
296 A11 1e maroon .95 .65
Never hinged 1.45
297 A11 1.40e dk blue 2.50 2.10
Never hinged 3.75
298 A11 2e dk violet 2.50 1.75
Never hinged 3.75
299 A11 5e apple green 10.00 3.75
Never hinged 15.00
300 A11 10e olive bister 20.00 6.00
Never hinged 27.00
301 A11 20e orange 50.00 18.00
Never hinged 75.00
Nos. 283-301 (19) 92.20 37.85

Common Design Types
Inscribed "S. Tomé"

1938 Unwmk. *Perf. 13½x13*
Name and Value in Black

302	CD34	1c gray green	.25	.25
303	CD34	5c orange brown	.25	.25
304	CD34	10c dk carmine	.25	.25
305	CD34	15c dk violet brn	.25	.25
306	CD34	20c slate	.25	.25
307	CD35	30c rose violet	.25	.25
308	CD35	35c brt green	.25	.25
309	CD35	40c brown	.25	.25
310	CD35	50c brt red vio	.25	.25
311	CD36	60c gray black	.25	.25
312	CD36	70c brown violet	.25	.25
313	CD36	80c orange	.45	.25
314	CD36	1e red	2.25	1.10
315	CD37	1.75e blue	2.00	1.50
316	CD37	2e brown car	15.00	5.00
317	CD37	5e olive green	15.00	5.50
318	CD38	10e blue violet	17.00	7.50
319	CD38	20e red brown	30.00	9.50
		Nos. 302-319 (18)	84.45	33.10

Marble Column and Portuguese Arms with Cross — A12

1938 *Perf. 12½*

320	A12	80c blue green	2.75	1.40
321	A12	1.75e deep blue	10.50	4.00
322	A12	20e brown	40.00	17.50
		Nos. 320-322 (3)	53.25	22.90

Visit of the President of Portugal in 1938.

Common Design Types
Inscribed "S. Tomé e Principe"

1939 *Perf. 13½x13*
Name and Value in Black

323	CD34	1c gray grn	.25	.25
324	CD34	5c orange brn	.25	.25
325	CD34	10c dk carmine	.25	.25
326	CD34	15c dk vio brn	.25	.25
327	CD34	20c slate	.45	.25
328	CD35	30c rose violet	.25	.25
329	CD35	35c brt green	.25	.25
330	CD35	40c brown	.45	.25
331	CD35	50c brt red vio	.45	.25
332	CD36	60c gray black	.45	.25
333	CD36	70c brown violet	.45	.25
334	CD36	80c orange	.45	.25
335	CD36	1e red	.90	.60
336	CD37	1.75e blue	1.50	.60
337	CD37	2e brown car	2.40	1.50
338	CD37	5e olive green	6.25	2.75
339	CD38	10e blue violet	9.00	4.00
340	CD38	20e red brown	15.00	5.50
		Nos. 323-340 (18)	39.25	17.95

AIR POST STAMPS

Common Design Type
Inscribed "S. Tomé"

1938 *Perf. 13½x13*
Name and Value in Black

C1	CD39	10c red orange	62.50	45.00
C2	CD39	20c purple	30.00	22.50
C3	CD39	50c orange	3.00	2.50
C4	CD39	1e ultra	5.25	4.00
C5	CD39	2e lilac brown	7.75	6.25
C6	CD39	3e dark green	12.00	8.00
C7	CD39	5e red brown	15.00	13.00
C8	CD39	9e rose carmine	17.50	13.00
C9	CD39	10e magenta	19.00	13.00
		Nos. C1-C9 (9)	172.00	127.25

Common Design Type
Inscribed "S. Tomé e Principe"

1939 Engr. Unwmk.
Name and Value Typo. in Black

C10	CD39	10c scarlet	.60	.30
C11	CD39	20c purple	.60	.30
C12	CD39	50c orange	.60	.30
C13	CD39	1e deep ultra	.60	.30
C14	CD39	2e lilac brown	1.75	1.25
C15	CD39	3e dark green	2.40	1.50
C16	CD39	5e red brown	3.50	2.10
C17	CD39	9e rose carmine	6.25	3.00
C18	CD39	10e magenta	7.25	3.00
		Nos. C10-C18 (9)	23.55	12.05

No. C16 exists with overprint "Exposicao International de Nova York, 1939-1940" and Trylon and Perisphere.

POSTAGE DUE STAMPS

"S. Thomé" — D1

1904 Unwmk. Typo. *Perf. 12*

J1	D1	5r yellow green	.55	.55
J2	D1	10r slate	.65	.65
J3	D1	20r yellow brown	.65	.65
J4	D1	30r orange	1.00	.65
J5	D1	50r gray brown	1.75	1.40
J6	D1	60r red brown	2.50	1.60
J7	D1	100r red lilac	3.00	1.75
J8	D1	130r dull blue	4.00	3.25
J9	D1	200r carmine	4.50	3.50
J10	D1	500r gray violet	8.00	5.00
		Nos. J1-J10 (10)	26.60	19.00

Overprinted in Carmine or Green

1911

J11	D1	5r yellow green	.30	.30
J12	D1	10r slate	.30	.30
J13	D1	20r yellow brown	.30	.30
J14	D1	30r orange	.30	.30
J15	D1	50r gray brown	.30	.30
J16	D1	60r red brown	.65	.65
J17	D1	100r red lilac	.80	.80
J18	D1	130r dull blue	.80	.80
J19	D1	200r carmine (G)	.80	.80
J20	D1	500r gray violet	1.25	1.25
		Nos. J11-J20 (10)	5.80	5.80

Nos. J1-J10 Overprinted in Black

1913 Without Gum

J21	D1	5r yellow green	6.00	3.75
J22	D1	10r slate	8.00	4.50
J23	D1	20r yellow brown	5.00	2.50
J24	D1	30r orange	5.00	2.50
J25	D1	50r gray brown	5.00	2.50
J26	D1	60r red brown	6.00	3.00
J27	D1	100r red lilac	6.00	4.00
J28	D1	130r dull blue	35.00	35.00
a.		Inverted overprint	70.00	70.00
J29	D1	200r carmine	50.00	50.00
J30	D1	500r gray violet	75.00	40.00
		Nos. J21-J30 (10)	201.00	147.75

Nos. J1-J10 Overprinted in Black

1913 Without Gum

J31	D1	5r yellow green	7.00	3.00
a.		Inverted overprint	50.00	40.00
J32	D1	10r slate	7.00	4.00
J33	D1	20r yellow brown	7.00	3.00
J34	D1	30r orange	7.00	3.00
a.		Inverted overprint	55.00	
J35	D1	50r gray brown	7.00	3.00
J36	D1	60r red brown	8.00	4.00
J37	D1	100r red lilac	8.00	4.00
J38	D1	130r dull blue	8.00	4.00
J39	D1	200r carmine	9.00	6.00
J40	D1	500r gray violet	17.00	15.00
		Nos. J31-J40 (10)	85.00	49.00

No. J5 Overprinted "Republica" in Italic Capitals like Regular Issue in Green

1920 Without Gum

J41	D1	50r gray brn	40.00	35.00

"S. Tomé" — D2

1921 Typo. *Perf. 11½*

J42	D2	½c yellow green	.25	.25
J43	D2	1c slate	.25	.25
J44	D2	2c orange brown	.25	.25
J45	D2	3c orange	.25	.25
J46	D2	5c gray brown	.25	.25
J47	D2	6c lt brown	.25	.25
J48	D2	10c red violet	.25	.25
J49	D2	13c dull blue	.25	.25
J50	D2	20c carmine	.25	.25
J51	D2	50c gray	.35	.40
		Nos. J42-J51 (10)	2.60	2.65

In each sheet one stamp is inscribed "S. Thomé" instead of "S. Tomé." Value, set of 10, $60.

NEWSPAPER STAMPS

N1

N2

Perf. 11½, 12½ and 13½
1892 Without Gum Unwmk.
Black Surcharge

P1	N1	2½r on 10r green	95.00	55.00
P2	N1	2½r on 20r rose	125.00	57.50
P3	N2	2½r on 10r green	125.00	57.50
P4	N2	2½r on 20r rose	125.00	57.50
		Nos. P1-P4 (4)	470.00	227.50

Green Surcharge

P5	N1	2½r on 5r black	67.50	30.00
P6	N1	2½r on 20r rose	125.00	57.50
P8	N2	2½r on 5r black	125.00	60.00
P9	N2	2½r on 10r green	125.00	62.50
P10	N2	2½r on 20r rose	125.00	77.50
		Nos. P5-P10 (5)	567.50	287.50

Both surcharges exist on No. 18 in green.

N3

1893 Typo. *Perf. 11½, 13½*

P12	N3	2½r brown	.45	.40

For surcharges and overprints see Nos. 85, 166, 275, P13.

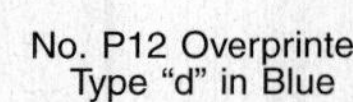

No. P12 Overprinted Type "d" in Blue

1899 Without Gum

P13	N3	2½r brown	40.00	16.00

POSTAL TAX STAMPS

Pombal Issue
Common Design Types

1925 Unwmk. *Perf. 12½*

RA1	CD28	15c orange & black	.45	.45
RA2	CD29	15c orange & black	.45	.45
RA3	CD30	15c orange & black	.45	.45
		Nos. RA1-RA3 (3)	1.35	1.35

Certain revenue stamps (5e, 6e, 7e, 8e and other denominations) were surcharged in 1946 "Assistencia," 2 bars and new values (1e or 1.50e) and used as postal tax stamps.

POSTAL TAX DUE STAMPS

Pombal Issue
Common Design Types

1925 Unwmk. *Perf. 12½*

RAJ1	CD28	30c orange & black	.75	.75
RAJ2	CD29	30c orange & black	.75	.75
RAJ3	CD30	30c orange & black	.75	.75
		Nos. RAJ1-RAJ3 (3)	2.25	2.25

ST. VINCENT

sānt 'vin(t)-sənt

LOCATION — Island in the West Indies
GOVT. — British Colony
AREA — 150 sq. mi.
POP. — 123,000 (est. 1984)
CAPITAL — Kingstown

12 Pence = 1 Shilling
20 Shillings = 1 Pound
100 Cents = 1 Dollar (1949)

Catalogue values for unused stamps in this country are for Never Hinged items, beginning with Scott 152 in the regular postage section.

PRE-STAMP POSTAL MARKINGS

Crowned Circle handstamp type I is pictured in the Crowned Circle Handstamps and Great Britain Used Abroad section.

1852
A1 I "St. Vincent" crowned circle handstamp in red, on cover 1,150.

STAMPS OF GREAT BRITAIN USED IN ST. VINCENT

Numeral cancellation type A is pictured in the Crowned Circle Handstamps and Great Britain Used Abroad section.

1858-60

A10

A2 A 1p rose red (#20) 725.
A3 A 2p blue (#29, p7, 8) —
A4 A 4p rose (#26) 440.
A5 A 6p lilac (#27) 325.
A6 A 1sh green (#28) 2,000.

Issued under British Administration

Values for unused stamps are for examples with original gum as defined in the catalogue introduction. Early stamps were spaced extremely narrowly on the plates, and the perforations were applied irregularly.

Therefore, very fine examples of Nos. 1-28, 30-39 will have perforations that cut into the design slightly on one or more sides. Also, very fine examples of Nos. 40-53, 55-60 will have perforations touching the design on at least one side. These stamps with perfs clear of the design on all four sides, especially Nos. 1-28, 30-39, are extremely scarce and command substantially higher prices.

Watermark

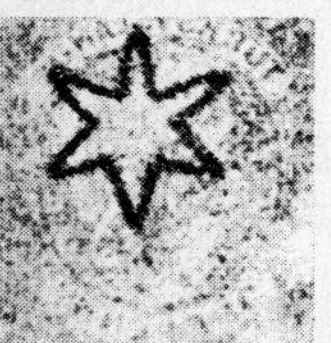

Wmk. 5 — Small Star

Queen Victoria — A1

1861 Engr. Unwmk. *Perf. 14 to 16*
1 A1 1p rose *62.50* 20.00
a. Imperf., pair 300.00
c. Horiz. pair, imperf. vert. *400.00*
1B A1 6p yellow green *8,250.* 250.00

Perfs on Nos. 1-1B are not clean cut. See Nos. 2-3 for rough perfs.

1862-66 *Rough Perf. 14 to 16*
2 A1 1p rose 60.00 20.00
a. Horiz. pair, imperf. vert. 400.00
3 A1 6p dark green 65.00 21.00
a. Imperf., pair 1,250.
b. Horiz. pair, imperf. between *14,500.* *15,500.*
4 A1 1sh slate ('66) 425.00 160.00
Nos. 2-4 (3) 550.00 201.00

1863-69 *Perf. 11 to 13*
5 A1 1p rose 45.00 22.50
6 A1 4p blue ('66) 300.00 125.00
a. Horiz. pair, imperf. vert.
7 A1 4p orange ('69) 400.00 175.00
8 A1 6p deep green 250.00 82.50
8A A1 1sh slate ('66) *2,750.* 1,000.
9 A1 1sh indigo ('69) 425.00 100.00
10 A1 1sh brown ('69) 550.00 175.00

Perf. 11 to 13x14 to 16
11 A1 1p rose *6,500.* 1,250.
12 A1 1sh slate 300.00 140.00

Rough Perf. 14 to 16
1871-78 Wmk. 5
13 A1 1p black 65.00 15.50
a. Vert. pair, imperf. btwn. *20,000.*
14 A1 6p dk blue green 350.00 77.50
a. Watermark sideways 100.00

Clean-Cut Perf. 14 to 16
14A A1 1p black 65.00 15.50
14B A1 6p dp bl grn 1,650. 55.00
c. 6p dull blue green 2,250. 55.00
15 A1 6p pale yel green ('78) 800.00 32.50
15A A1 1sh vermilion ('77) *50,000.*

For surcharge see No. 30.

Perf. 11 to 13
16 A1 4p dk bl ('77) 600.00 110.00
17 A1 1sh dp rose ('72) 825.00 160.00
18 A1 1sh claret ('75) 675.00 300.00

Perf. 11 to 13x14 to 16
20 A1 1p black 95.00 16.50
a. Horiz. pair, imperf. btwn. *25,000.*
21 A1 6p pale yel grn ('77) 725.00 55.00
22 A1 1sh lilac rose ('72) *6,250.* 400.00
23 A1 1sh vermilion ('77) 1,100. 100.00
a. Horiz. pair, imperf. vert. —

See Nos. 25-28A, 36-39, 42-53. For surcharges see Nos. 30, 32-33, 40, 55-60.

Victoria
A2

Seal of Colony
A3

1880-81 *Perf. 11 to 13*
24 A2 ½p org ('81) 8.00 8.75
25 A1 1p gray green 190.00 5.50
26 A1 1p drab ('81) 800.00 15.50
27 A1 4p ultra ('81) 1,350. 130.00
a. Horiz. pair, imperf. btwn.
28 A1 6p yel grn 550.00 77.50
a. Horiz. pair, imperf. btwn. *27,500.*
28A A1 1sh vermilion 900.00 65.00
29 A3 5sh rose 1,275. *1,650.*
a. Imperf *8,250.*

No. 29 is valued well centered with design well clear of the perfs.

See Nos. 35, 41, 54, 598 (in Scott Standard catalogue, Vol. 5). For surcharges see Nos. 31-33.

No. 14B Bisected and Surcharged in Red

1880, May *Perf. 14 to 16*
30 A1 1p on half of 6p 600.00 425.00
a. Unsevered pair *2,250.* *1,350.*

No. 28 Bisected and Surcharged in Red

1881, Sept. 1
31 A1 ½p on half of 6p yel grn ('81) 150. 190.
a. Unsevered pair 525. 550.
b. "1" with straight top 1,100.
c. Without fraction bar, pair, #31, 31c 4,750. *5,500.*

Nos. 28 and 28A Surcharged in Black

c

d

1881, Nov. *Perf. 11 to 13*
32 A1(c) 1p on 6p yel grn 500. 400.
33 A1(d) 4p on 1sh ver 1,850. 925.
a. 3 mm spacing between "4d" and bar *3,500.* *2,500.*

1883-84 Wmk. 2 *Perf. 12*
35 A2 ½p green ('84) 110.00 40.00
36 A1 4p ultra 825.00 55.00
37 A1 4p dull blue ('84) 2,500. 275.00
38 A1 6p yellow grn 175.00 350.00
39 A1 1sh orange ver 175.00 65.00
a. Imperf., pair

The ½p orange, 1p rose red, 1p milky blue and 5sh carmine lake were never placed in use. Some authorities believe them to be color trials.

Nos. 35-60 may be found watermarked with single straight line. This is from the frame which encloses each group of 60 watermark designs.

Type of A1 Surcharged in Black — e

1883 *Perf. 14*
40 A1(e) 2½p on 1p lake 27.50 1.75

1883-97
41 A2 ½p green ('85) 1.10 .65
a. ½p deep green 2.75 .65
42 A1 1p drab 80.00 3.50
43 A1 1p rose red ('85) 3.00 1.00
44 A1 1p pink ('86) 6.75 1.90
a. 1p carmine red ('89) 27.50 4.25
45 A1 2½p brt blue ('97) 10.00 2.25
46 A1 4p ultra 725.00 85.00
a. 4p dull ultramarine 1,100. 400.00
47 A1 4p red brn ('85) 1,100. 25.00
48 A1 4p lake brn ('86) 100.00 1.60
a. 4p purple brown ('86) 100.00 1.00
49 A1 4p yellow ('93) 2.00 *15.00*
Ovptd. "SPECIMEN" 40.00
a. 4p olive yellow *350.00* *350.00*
50 A1 5p gray brn ('97) 8.75 *32.50*
a. 5p black brown 10.00 *30.00*
51 A1 6p violet ('88) 225.00 *225.00*
52 A1 6p red violet ('91) 3.00 *25.00*
53 A1 1sh org ver ('91) 6.00 17.50
a. 1sh red orange 15.00 *22.50*
54 A3 5sh car lake ('88) 32.50 *60.00*
a. 5sh brown lake 35.00 *60.00*
b. Printed on both sides *8,250.*

Grading footnote after No. 29 applies equally to Nos. 54-54a.

No. 40 Resurcharged in Black

1885, Mar.
55 A1 1p on 2½p on 1p lake 37.50 27.50

Examples with 3-bar cancel are proofs.

Stamps of Type A1 Surcharged in Black or Violet

g

h

j

1890-91
56 A1(e) 2½p on 1p brt blue 2.00 .40
a. 2½p on 1p milky blue 27.50 9.50
b. 2½p on 1p gray blue 27.50 .75
57 A1(g) 2½p on 4p vio brn ('90) 90.00 *130.00*
a. Without fraction bar 475.00 *575.00*

1892-93
58 A1(h) 5p on 4p lake brn (V) 40.00 *55.00*
59 A1(j) 5p on 6p dp lake ('93) *2.00* *1.90*
a. 5p on 6p carmine lake 22.50 *32.50*
Ovptd. "SPECIMEN" 55.00
b. Double surcharge *7,750.* *4,500.*

1897
60 A1(j) 3p on 1p lilac 6.00 *26.50*
a. 3p on 1p reddish lilac 15.50 *52.50*
Ovptd. "SPECIMEN" 50.00

Victoria — A13

Numerals of 1sh and 5sh, type A13, and of 2p, 1sh, 5sh and £1, type A14, are in color on plain tablet.

1898 Typo. *Perf. 14*

No.	Type			Unused	Used
62	A13	½p	lilac & grn	3.00	3.00
63	A13	1p	lil & car rose	5.00	1.70
64	A13	2½p	lilac & ultra	6.50	2.25
65	A13	3p	lilac & ol grn	4.50	*21.00*
66	A13	4p	lilac & org	7.25	*25.00*
67	A13	5p	lilac & blk	8.25	*21.00*
68	A13	6p	lilac & brn	14.50	*55.00*
69	A13	1sh	grn & car rose	18.50	*60.00*
70	A13	5sh	green & ultra	100.00	*175.00*
			Nos. 62-70 (9)	167.50	*363.95*
			Set, ovptd. "SPECIMEN"	200.00	

Edward VII — A14

1902

No.	Type			Unused	Used
71	A14	½p	violet & green	4.75	.75
72	A14	1p	vio & car rose	4.75	.35
73	A14	2p	violet & black	6.50	*7.50*
74	A14	2½p	violet & ultra	5.50	4.00
75	A14	3p	violet & ol grn	5.50	*7.25*
76	A14	6p	violet & brn	12.00	*50.00*
77	A14	1sh	grn & car rose	30.00	*70.00*
78	A14	2sh	green & violet	27.50	*65.00*
79	A14	5sh	green & ultra	82.50	*140.00*
			Nos. 71-79 (9)	179.00	*344.85*
			Set, ovptd. "SPECIMEN"	175.00	

1904-11 Wmk. 3 Chalky Paper

No.	Type			Unused	Used
82	A14	½p	vio & grn	1.50	1.50
a.			Ordinary paper	9.00	5.50
83	A14	1p	vio & car rose	26.00	1.75
a.			Ordinary paper	29.00	1.90
84	A14	2½p	vio & ultra	19.00	*52.50*
85	A14	6p	vio & brn	19.00	*55.00*
86	A14	1sh	grn & car rose	15.50	*17.50*
a.			Ordinary paper	24.00	*57.50*
87	A14	2sh	vio & bl, *bl*	25.00	*52.50*
88	A14	5sh	grn & red, *yel*	19.00	*55.00*
89	A14	£1	vio & blk, *red*	300.00	*400.00*
			Nos. 82-88 (7)	125.00	*235.75*
			Nos. 87-89, ovptd. "SPECIMEN"	225.00	

Issued: 1p, 1904, ½p, 6p, 1905; 2½p, 1906; 1sh, 1908; 2sh, 5sh, 1909; £1, July 22, 1911.

"Peace and Justice" — A15

1907 Engr. Ordinary Paper

No.	Type			Unused	Used
90	A15	½p	yellow green	4.00	2.75
91	A15	1p	carmine	4.25	.25
92	A15	2p	orange	1.75	*7.75*
93	A15	2½p	ultra	45.00	10.00
94	A15	3p	dark violet	9.50	*18.00*
			Nos. 90-94 (5)	64.50	*38.75*
			Set, ovptd. "SPECIMEN"	145.00	

"Peace and Justice" — A16

1909 Without Dot under "d"

No.	Type			Unused	Used
95	A16	1p	carmine	1.50	.35
96	A16	6p	red violet	9.25	*50.00*
97	A16	1sh	black, *green*	5.50	*11.00*
			Nos. 95-97 (3)	16.25	*61.35*
			Set, ovptd. "SPECIMEN"	90.00	

1909-11 With Dot under "d"

No.	Type			Unused	Used
98	A16	½p	yel grn ('10)	2.50	.70
99	A16	1p	carmine	4.00	.25
100	A16	2p	gray ('11)	6.50	12.00
101	A16	2½p	ultra	9.50	4.50
102	A16	3p	violet, *yel*	3.00	*14.50*
103	A16	6p	red violet	20.00	11.00
			Nos. 98-103 (6)	45.50	*42.95*

King George V — A17

1913-17 *Perf. 14*

No.	Type			Unused	Used
104	A17	½p	gray green	.75	.25
105	A17	1p	carmine	1.00	.90
a.			1p rose red	1.10	.85
b.			1p scarlet	20.00	6.00
106	A17	2p	slate	3.50	*42.50*
a.			2p gray	8.75	*42.50*
107	A17	2½p	ultra	.60	.90
108	A17	3p	violet, *yellow*	1.00	*7.50*
a.			3p violet, *lemon*	3.25	*14.00*
b.			3p violet, *pale yellow*	2.75	*10.50*
109	A17	4p	red, *yellow*	1.00	*2.40*
110	A17	5p	olive green	2.50	*17.00*
111	A17	6p	claret	2.50	*5.00*
112	A17	1sh	black, *green*	1.75	*4.25*
113	A17	1sh	bister ('14)	4.75	*35.00*
114	A16	2sh	vio & ultra	5.75	*40.00*
115	A16	5sh	dk grn & car	15.00	*60.00*
116	A16	£1	black & vio	125.00	*200.00*
			Nos. 104-116 (13)	165.10	*415.70*
			Set, ovptd. "SPECIMEN"	300.00	

Issued: 5p, 11/7; #113, 5/1/14; others, 1/1/13.

For overprints see Nos. MR1-MR2.

No. 112 Surcharged in Carmine

1915

No.	Type			Unused	Used
117	A17	1p	on 1sh blk, *grn*	11.00	*45.00*
a.			"PENNY" & bar double	750.00	725.00
b.			Without period	15.00	
c.			"ONE" omitted	1,550.	1,350.
d.			"ONE" double	750.00	
e.			"PENNY" & bar omitted	1,450.	

Space between surcharge lines varies from 8 to 10mm.

1921-32 Wmk. 4

No.	Type			Unused	Used
118	A17	½p	green	2.10	.35
119	A17	1p	carmine ('21)	1.15	1.00
a.			1p red	2.75	.25
120	A17	1½p	yel brn ('32)	4.00	.25
121	A17	2p	gray	3.00	1.00
122	A17	2½p	ultra ('26)	1.50	1.75
123	A17	3p	ultra	1.15	*7.25*
124	A17	3p	vio, *yel* ('27)	1.15	*1.75*
125	A17	4p	red, *yel* ('30)	2.10	*7.25*
126	A17	5p	olive green	1.15	*7.75*
127	A17	6p	claret ('27)	1.75	*4.25*
128	A17	1sh	ocher ('27)	4.00	*20.00*
a.			1sh bistre	7.50	*30.00*
129	A16	2sh	brn vio & ultra	9.00	*15.00*
130	A16	5sh	dk grn & car	21.00	*37.50*
131	A16	£1	blk & vio ('28)	110.00	*150.00*
			Nos. 118-131 (14)	163.05	*255.10*
			Set, ovptd. or perf "SPECIMEN"	360.00	

Common Design Types pictured following the introduction.

Silver Jubilee Issue
Common Design Type

1935, May 6 *Perf. 11x12*

No.	Type			Unused	Used
134	CD301	1p	car & dk bl	.55	*4.75*
135	CD301	1½p	gray blk & ultra	1.40	*4.50*
136	CD301	2½p	ultra & brn	2.50	*5.00*
137	CD301	1sh	brn vio & ind	5.00	*7.00*
			Nos. 134-137 (4)	9.45	*21.25*
			Set, never hinged	16.00	
			Set, perforated "SPECIMEN"	110.00	

Coronation Issue
Common Design Type

1937, May 12 *Perf. 11x11½*

No.	Type			Unused	Used
138	CD302	1p	dark purple	.25	*1.25*
139	CD302	1½p	dark carmine	.25	*1.25*
140	CD302	2½p	deep ultra	.30	*2.25*
			Nos. 138-140 (3)	.80	*4.75*
			Set, never hinged	1.50	
			Set, perforated "SPECIMEN"	87.50	

Seal of the Colony — A18

Young's Island and Fort Duvernette — A19

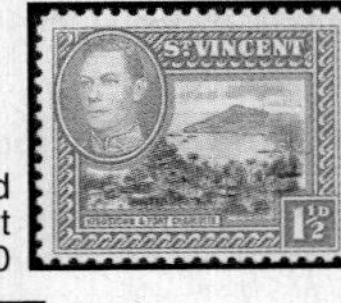
Kingstown and Fort Charlotte — A20

Villa Beach — A21

Victoria Park, Kingstown — A22

1938-47 Wmk. 4 *Perf. 12*

No.	Type			Unused	Used
141	A18	½p	grn & brt bl	.25	.25
142	A19	1p	claret & blue	.25	.25
143	A20	1½p	scar & lt grn	.25	.25
144	A18	2p	black & green	.30	.25
145	A21	2½p	pck bl & ind	.25	.25
145A	A22	2½p	choc & grn ('47)	.25	.25
146	A18	3p	dk vio & org	.25	.25
146A	A21	3½p	dp bl grn & ind ('47)	.40	*2.25*
147	A18	6p	claret & blk	.70	.40
148	A22	1sh	green & vio	.70	.75
149	A18	2sh	dk vio & brt blue	5.25	1.00
149A	A18	2sh6p	dp bl & org brn ('47)	.95	*4.25*
150	A18	5sh	dk grn & car	8.75	3.00
150A	A18	10sh	choc & dp vio ('47)	7.50	*10.00*
151	A18	£1	black & vio	22.50	*18.00*
			Nos. 141-151 (15)	48.55	*41.40*
			Set, never hinged	55.00	

Issue date: Mar. 11, 1938.

See Nos. 156-169, 180-184.

Catalogue values for unused stamps in this section, from this point to the end of the section, are for Never Hinged items.

Peace Issue
Common Design Type

1946, Oct. 15 Engr. *Perf. 13½x14*

No.	Type			Unused	Used
152	CD303	1½p	carmine	.25	.25
153	CD303	3½p	deep blue	.25	.25

Silver Wedding Issue
Common Design Types

1948, Nov. 30 Photo. *Perf. 14x14½*

No.	Type			Unused	Used
154	CD304	1½p	scarlet	.25	.25

Engraved; Name Typographed

Perf. 11½x11

No.	Type			Unused	Used
155	CD305	£1	red violet	27.50	*30.00*

Types of 1938

1949, Mar. 26 Engr. *Perf. 12*

No.	Type			Unused	Used
156	A18	1c	grn & brt bl	.25	*1.75*
157	A19	2c	claret & bl	.25	*.50*
158	A20	3c	scar & lt grn	.55	*1.00*
159	A18	4c	gray blk & grn	.40	.25
160	A22	5c	choc & grn	.25	.25
161	A18	6c	dk vio & org	.55	*1.25*
162	A21	7c	pck blue & ind	5.50	1.50
163	A18	12c	claret & blk	.50	.25
164	A22	24c	green & vio	.50	.55
165	A18	48c	dk vio & brt bl	4.50	*6.00*
166	A18	60c	dp bl & org brn	2.00	*5.50*
167	A18	$1.20	dk grn & car	4.75	4.75
168	A18	$2.40	choc & dp vio	6.75	*10.00*
169	A18	$4.80	gray blk & vio	13.00	*20.00*
			Nos. 156-169 (14)	39.75	*53.55*

For overprints see Nos. 176-179.

UPU Issue
Common Design Types

Engr.; Name Typo. on 6c, 12c

Perf. 13½, 11x11½

1949, Oct. 10 Wmk. 4

No.	Type			Unused	Used
170	CD306	5c	blue	.25	.25
171	CD307	6c	dp rose violet	.55	2.00
172	CD308	12c	red lilac	.30	2.00
173	CD309	24c	blue green	1.10	.80
			Nos. 170-173 (4)	2.20	*5.05*

University Issue
Common Design Types

1951, Feb. 16 Engr. *Perf. 14x14½*

No.	Type			Unused	Used
174	CD310	3c	red & blue green	.50	.65
175	CD311	12c	rose lilac & blk	.50	*1.50*

Nos. 158-160 and 163 Overprinted in Black

1951, Sept. 21 *Perf. 12*

No.	Type			Unused	Used
176	A20	3c	scarlet & lt grn	.30	*1.60*
177	A18	4c	gray blk & grn	.30	.60
178	A22	5c	chocolate & grn	.30	.60
179	A18	12c	claret & blk	.95	*1.25*
			Nos. 176-179 (4)	1.85	*4.05*

Adoption of a new constitution for the Windward Islands, 1951.

Type of 1938-47

1952

No.	Type			Unused	Used
180	A18	1c	gray black & green	.30	*2.25*
181	A18	3c	dk violet & orange	.30	*2.25*
182	A18	4c	green & brt blue	.30	.25
183	A20	6c	scarlet & dp green	.30	*2.00*
184	A21	10c	peacock blue & ind	.45	.35
			Nos. 180-184 (5)	1.65	*7.10*

WAR TAX STAMPS

No. 105 Overprinted

Type I — Words 2 to 2½mm apart.
Type II — Words 1½mm apart.
Type III — Words 3½mm apart.

1916 Wmk. 3 *Perf. 14*

No.	Type			Unused	Used
MR1	A17	1p	car, type III	3.25	*25.00*
a.			Double ovpt., type III	275.00	250.00
b.			1p carmine, type I	12.50	*18.50*
c.			Comma after "STAMP", type I	12.50	*30.00*
d.			Double ovpt., type I	200.00	200.00
e.			1p carmine, type II	135.00	87.50
f.			Double ovpt., type II	*1,450.*	

Overprinted

No.	Type			Unused	Used
MR2	A17	1p	carmine	1.40	*2.25*
			Ovptd. "SPECIMEN"	55,00	

SALVADOR, EL

ˈel ˈsal-və-ˌdor

LOCATION — On the Pacific coast of Central America, between Guatemala, Honduras and the Gulf of Fonseca
GOVT. — Republic
AREA — 8,236 sq. mi.
POP. — 5,300,000 (est. 1984)
CAPITAL — San Salvador

8 Reales = 100 Centavos = 1 Peso
100 Centavos = 1 Colón

Watermarks

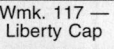

Wmk. 117 — Liberty Cap

Position of wmk. on reprints

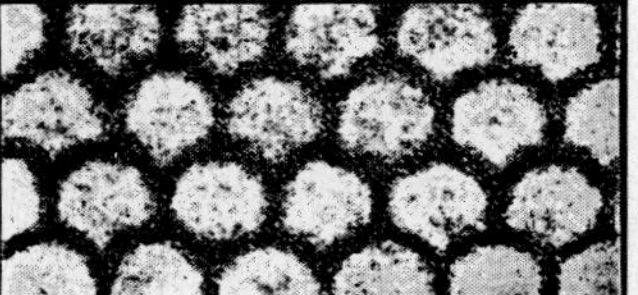

Wmk. 172 — Honeycomb

Wmk. 173 — S

Wmk. 240 — REPUBLICA DE EL SALVADOR in Sheet

Volcano San Miguel — A1

1867 Unwmk. Engr. *Perf. 12*

1	A1	½r dk gray blue	7.00	*4.00*
2	A1	1r dark red	7.00	4.00
3	A1	2r dark green	8.50	4.50
4	A1	4r dp ol brn	32.50	17.50
		Nos. 1-4 (4)	55.00	30.00

Nos. 1-4 when overprinted "Contra Sello" and shield with 14 stars, are telegraph stamps. For similar overprint see Nos. 5-12.

Counterfeits exist.

1873

1a	A1	½r blue (shades)	.45	.50
2a	A1	1r light red	.45	.50
3a	A1	2r green	1.75	2.25
4a	A1	4r yel brn (shades)	3.50	3.00

Nos. 1-4 Handstamped Either Type I or Type II in Black

Type I

Type II

Type II

1874

5	A1	½r blue	30.00	10.00
6	A1	1r red	20.00	10.00
7	A1	2r green	30.00	10.00
8	A1	4r bister	40.00	20.00
		Nos. 5-8 (4)	120.00	50.00

Nos. 1-4 Handstamped Type III in Black

Type III

9	A1	½r blue	8.00	6.00
10	A1	1r red	8.00	3.00
11	A1	2r green	10.00	3.00
12	A1	4r bister	12.00	10.00
		Nos. 9-12 (4)	38.00	22.00

The overprints on Nos. 5-12 exist double. Counterfeits are plentiful.

Coat of Arms
A2 A3

A4

A5

A6

1879 Litho. *Perf. 12½*

13	A2	1c green	3.00	1.75
a.		Invtd. "V" for 2nd "A" in "SALVADOR"	6.00	3.00
b.		Invtd. "V" for "A" in "REPUBLICA"	6.00	3.00
c.		Invtd. "V" for "A" in "UNIVERSAL"	6.00	3.00
d.		Thin paper	—	—
14	A3	2c rose	4.25	2.25
a.		Invtd. scroll in upper left corner	12.00	7.50
15	A4	5c blue	7.50	1.90
a.		5c ultra	12.00	6.00
16	A5	10c black	15.00	5.25
17	A6	20c violet	24.00	15.00
		Nos. 13-17 (5)	53.75	26.15

There are fifteen varieties of the 1c and 2c, twenty-five of the 5c and five each of the 10 and 20c.

In 1881 the 1c, 2c and 5c were redrawn, the 1c in fifteen varieties and the 2c and 5c in five varieties each.

No. 15 comes in a number of shades from light to dark blue.

These stamps, when overprinted "Contra sello" and arms, are telegraph stamps.

Counterfeits of No. 14 exist.

For overprints see Nos. 25D-25E, 28A-28C.

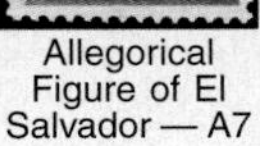

Allegorical Figure of El Salvador — A7

Volcano — A8

1887 Engr. *Perf. 12*

18	A7	3c brown	2.00	2.00
a.		Imperf., pair	10.00	10.00
19	A8	10c orange	30.00	3.00

For surcharges and overprints see Nos. 25, 26C-28, 30-32.

A9

1888 *Rouletted*

20	A9	5c deep blue	1.50	1.50

For overprints see Nos. 35-36.

A10

1889 *Perf. 12*

21	A10	1c green	.40	
22	A10	2c scarlet	.40	

Nos. 21-22 Overprinted in Black

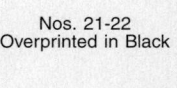

23	A10	1c green	.40	3.00
24	A10	2c scarlet	.40	

Nos. 21, 22 and 24 were never placed in use.

For overprints see Nos. 26, 29.

No. 18 Surcharged

Type I

Type II

Type I — thick numerals, heavy serifs.
Type II — thin numerals, straight serifs.

25	A7	1c on 3c brn, type II	4.00	*7.00*
a.		Double surcharge	1.50	
b.		Triple surcharge	3.50	
c.		Type I	.65	

The 1c on 2c scarlet is bogus.

Handstamped

1889 Violet Handstamp

25D	A2	1c green	19.00	19.00
25E	A6	20c violet	45.00	45.00
26	A10	1c green, #23	10.50	*15.00*
26C	A7	1c on 3c, #25	50.00	50.00
27	A7	3c brown	7.50	*15.00*
28	A8	10c orange	10.00	*12.50*

Black Handstamp

28A	A2	1c green	22.50	21.00
28B	A3	2c rose	26.00	26.00
28C	A6	20c violet	45.00	45.00
29	A10	1c green, #23	10.50	*15.00*
30	A7	3c brown	10.50	*15.00*
31	A7	1c on 3c, #25	40.00	40.00
32	A8	10c orange	15.00	12.50

Rouletted

Black Handstamp

35	A9	5c deep blue	9.00	*15.00*

Violet Handstamp

36	A9	5c deep blue	9.00	*15.00*

The 1889 handstamps as usual, are found double, inverted, etc. Counterfeits are plentiful.

A13

1890 Engr. *Perf. 12*

38	A13	1c green	.50	.50
39	A13	2c bister brown	.50	.50
40	A13	3c yellow	.50	.50
41	A13	5c blue	.50	.50
42	A13	10c violet	.50	.50
43	A13	20c orange	.75	*3.00*
44	A13	25c red	1.50	*5.00*
45	A13	50c claret	2.00	*7.50*
46	A13	1p carmine	5.00	*30.00*
		Nos. 38-46 (9)	11.75	*48.00*

The issues of 1890 to 1899 inclusive were printed by the Hamilton Bank Note Co., New York, to the order of N. F. Seebeck, who held a contract for stamps with the government of El Salvador. This contract gave the right to make reprints of the stamps and such were subsequently made in some instances, as will be found noted in italic type.

Used values of 1890-1899 issues are for stamps with genuine cancellations applied while the stamps were valid. Various counterfeit cancellations exist.

A14

1891

47	A14	1c vermilion	.50	.50
48	A14	2c yellow green	.50	.50
49	A14	3c violet	.50	.50
50	A14	5c carmine lake	2.00	.50
51	A14	10c blue	.50	.50
52	A14	11c violet	.50	.50
53	A14	20c green	.50	*.50*
54	A14	25c yellow brown	.50	*2.50*
55	A14	50c dark blue	2.00	*7.50*
56	A14	1p dark brown	.75	*25.00*
		Nos. 47-56 (10)	8.25	*38.50*

For surcharges see Nos. 57-59.

Nos. 47 and 56 have been reprinted in thick toned paper with dark gum.

A15

Nos. 48, 49 Surcharged in Black or Violet

b

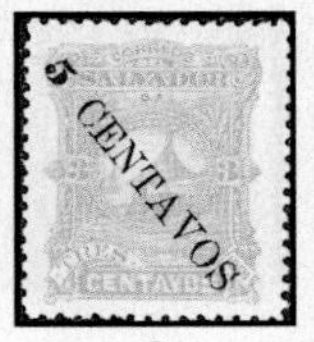

c

1891

57	A15	1c on 2c yellow grn	2.25	2.00
a.		Inverted surcharge	8.00	
b.		Surcharge reading up	12.00	

58 A14 (b) 1c on 2c yellow grn 1.60 1.40
59 A14 (c) 5c on 3c violet 4.00 3.25
Nos. 57-59 (3) 7.85 6.65

Landing of Columbus — A18

1892 **Engr.**

60 A18 1c blue green .50 .50
61 A18 2c orange brown .50 .50
62 A18 3c ultra .50 .50
63 A18 5c gray .50 .50
64 A18 10c vermilion .50 .50
65 A18 11c brown .50 .50
66 A18 20c orange .50 *.75*
67 A18 25c maroon .50 *2.00*
68 A18 50c yellow .50 *7.00*
69 A18 1p carmine lake .50 *25.00*
Nos. 60-69 (10) 5.00 *37.75*

400th anniversary of the discovery of America by Columbus.

Nos. 63, 66-67 Surcharged

Nos. 70, 72

Nos. 73-75

Surcharged in Black, Red or Yellow

1892

70 A18 1c on 5c gray (Bk) (down) 3.00 .75
a. Surcharge reading up 5.00 2.00
72 A18 1c on 5c gray (R) (up) 1.00 *3.00*
a. Surcharge reading down
73 A18 1c on 20c org (Bk) 1.50 .75
a. Inverted surcharge 3.50 2.50
b. "V" of "CENTAVO" inverted 3.50 2.50
Nos. 70-73 (3) 5.50 4.50

Similar Surcharge in Yellow or Blue, "centavo" in lower case letters

74 A18 1c on 25c mar (Y) 1.50 1.25
a. Inverted surcharge 2.50 2.50
75 A18 1c on 25c mar (Bl) *250.00 250.00*
a. Double surcharge (Bl + Bk) *275.00 275.00*

Counterfeits exist of Nos. 75 and 75a. Nos. 75, 75a have been questioned.

Pres. Carlos Ezeta — A21

1893 **Engr.**

76 A21 1c blue .50 .50
77 A21 2c brown red .50 .50
78 A21 3c purple .50 .50
79 A21 5c deep brown .50 .50
80 A21 10c orange brown .50 .50
81 A21 11c vermilion .50 .50
82 A21 20c green .50 *1.00*
83 A21 25c dk olive gray .50 *2.25*
84 A21 50c red orange .50 *5.00*
85 A21 1p black .50 *20.00*
Nos. 76-85 (10) 5.00 *31.25*

For surcharge see No. 89.

Founding City of Isabela — A22

Columbus Statue, Genoa — A23

Departure from Palos — A24

1893

86 A22 2p green .75 —
87 A23 5p violet .75
88 A24 10p orange .75
Nos. 86-88 (3) 2.25

Discoveries by Columbus. No. 86 is known on cover, but experts are not positive that Nos. 87 and 88 were postally used.

No. 77 Surcharged "UN CENTAVO"

1893

89 A21 1c on 2c brown red 1.00 *1.25*
a. "CENTNVO" 6.00 5.00

Liberty — A26

Columbus before Council of Salamanca — A27

Columbus Protecting Indian Hostages A28

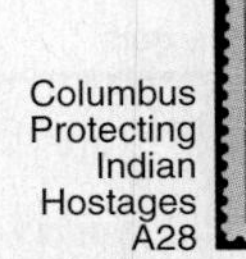
Columbus Received by Ferdinand and Isabella A29

1894, Jan.

91 A26 1c brown .75 .50
92 A26 2c blue .75 .50
93 A26 3c maroon .75 .50
94 A26 5c orange brn .75 .50
95 A26 10c violet .75 *.75*
96 A26 11c vermilion .75 *.75*
97 A26 20c dark blue .75 *1.00*
98 A26 25c orange .75 *5.00*
99 A26 50c black .75 *10.00*
100 A26 1p slate blue 1.10 *20.00*
101 A27 2p deep blue 1.10
102 A28 5p carmine lake 1.10
103 A29 10p deep brown 1.10
Nos. 91-103 (13) 11.15
Nos. 91-100 (10) *39.50*

Nos. 101-103 for the discoveries by Columbus. Experts are not positive that these were postally used.

No. 96 Surcharged

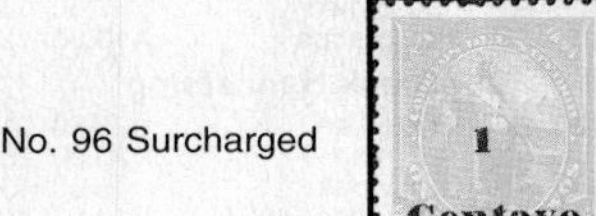

1894, Dec.

104 A26 1c on 11c vermilion 4.50 .65
a. "Ccntavo" *40.00 40.00*
b. Double surcharge

Coat of Arms — A31

Arms Overprint in Second Color Various Frames

1895, Jan. 1

105 A31 1c olive & green .50 *.25*
106 A31 2c dk green & bl .25 —
a. 2c dark green & green .50 .85
107 A31 3c brown & brown .50 —
108 A31 5c blue & brown .50 —
109 A31 10c orange & brn .50 —
110 A31 12c magenta & brn .50 —
111 A31 15c ver & ver .50 —
112 A31 20c yellow & brn .50 —
a. Inverted overprint 2.00
113 A31 24c violet & brn .50 —
114 A31 30c dp blue & blue .50 —
115 A31 50c carmine & brn .50 —
116 A31 1p black & brn .50 —
Nos. 105-116 (12) 5.75

As printed, Nos. 105-116 portrayed Gen. Antonio Ezeta, brother of Pres. Carlos Ezeta. Before issuance, Ezeta's overthrow caused the government to obliterate his features with the national arms overprint. The 3c, 10c, 30c exist without overprint. Value $1 each.

All values have been reprinted. Reprints of 2c are in dark yellow green on thick paper. Value, 25c each.

Coat of Arms — A32

Various Frames

1895 **Engr.** ***Perf. 12***

117 A32 1c olive 7.25 .50
118 A32 2c dk blue grn 7.25 .50
119 A32 3c brown 10.00 .75
120 A32 5c blue 2.00 .75
121 A32 10c orange 5.00 .75
122 A32 12c claret 17.50 1.00
123 A32 15c vermilion 22.00 1.00
124 A32 20c deep green 30.00 2.00
125 A32 24c violet 22.50 4.00
126 A32 30c deep blue 30.00 5.00
127 A32 50c carmine lake 3.00 35.00
128 A32 1p gray black 10.00 *35.00*
Nos. 117-128 (12) 166.50 *86.25*

The reprints are on thicker paper than the originals, and many of the shades differ. Value 25c each.

Nos. 122, 124-126 Surcharged in Black or Red

1895

129 A32 1c on 12c claret (Bk) 2.00 1.75
130 A32 1c on 24c violet 2.00 1.75
131 A32 1c on 30c dp blue 2.00 1.75
132 A32 2c on 20c dp grn 2.00 1.75
133 A32 3c on 30c dp blue 3.00 2.75
a. Double surcharge 9.00
Nos. 129-133 (5) 11.00 9.75

"Peace" — A45

1896, Jan. 1 **Engr.** **Unwmk.**

134 A45 1c blue 2.00 .50
135 A45 2c dark brown .50 .50
136 A45 3c blue green .50 .50
137 A45 5c brown olive 2.00 .50
138 A45 10c yellow .50 .50
139 A45 12c dark blue 4.00 *1.00*
140 A45 15c brt ultra .25 —
a. 15c light violet 1.10 *2.00*
141 A45 20c magenta 4.00 *3.00*
142 A45 24c vermilion 1.50 *5.00*
143 A45 30c orange 1.50 *5.00*
144 A45 50c black brn 3.00 *7.50*
145 A45 1p rose lake 6.00 *20.00*
Nos. 134-145 (12) 25.75 *44.00*

The frames of Nos. 134-145 differ slightly on each denomination.

For overprints see Nos. O1-O12, O37-O48.

Wmk. 117

145B A45 2c dark brown .25 .25

All values have been reprinted. The paper is thicker than that of the originals and the shades are different. The watermark is always upright on original stamps of Salvador, sideways on the reprints. Value 25c each.

Coat of Arms — A46

"White House" — A47

Locomotive A48

Mt. San Miguel A49

Ocean Steamship A50 A51

Post Office A52

Lake Ilopango A53

Atehausillas Waterfall A54

Coat of Arms A55

Coat of Arms A56

Columbus A57

1896

146 A46 1c emerald .50 *1.50*
147 A47 2c lake .50 *.90*
148 A48 3c yellow brn .75 .75
149 A49 5c deep blue .90 .50
150 A50 10c brown 2.00 .90
151 A51 12c slate 2.00 .90
152 A52 15c blue green 1.75 .75
153 A53 20c carmine rose 2.00 1.25
154 A54 24c violet *8.00* 1.25
155 A55 30c deep green 5.00 2.00
156 A56 50c orange 10.00 5.00
157 A57 100c dark blue 15.00 *12.50*
Nos. 146-157 (12) 48.40 *28.20*

Nos. 146-157 exist imperf.

Unwmk.

157B A46 1c emerald 3.75 .90
157C A47 2c lake 3.75 .50
157D A48 3c yellow brn 6.00 .50
157E A49 5c deep blue 4.00 .75

157F A50 10c brown 7.50 .75
157G A51 12c slate 10.00 1.00
157I A52 15c blue green 20.00 1.75
157J A53 20c carmine rose 7.50 1.00
157K A54 24c violet 10.00 1.25
157M A55 30c deep green 10.00 2.50
157N A56 50c orange 15.00 7.00
157O A57 100c dark blue 20.00 15.00
Nos. 157B-157O (12) 117.50 *32.90*

See Nos. 159-170L. For surcharges and overprints see Nos. 158, 158D, 171-174C, O13-O36, O49-O72, O79-O126.

All values have been reprinted, the 15c, 30c, 50c and 100c on watermarked and the 1c, 2c, 3c, 5c, 12c, 20c, 24c and 100c on unwatermarked paper. The papers of the reprints are thicker than those of the originals and the shades are different. Value, 25c each.

Black Surcharge on Nos. 154, 157K

1896 **Wmk. 117**
158 A54 15c on 24c violet 4.00 4.00
a. Double surcharge 20.00 *30.00*
b. Inverted surcharge 15.00

Unwmk.

158D A54 15c on 24c violet 4.00 3.00

Exist spelled "Qnince."

Types of 1896

1897 **Engr.** **Wmk. 117**
159 A46 1c scarlet 2.75 .90
160 A47 2c yellow grn 2.75 .50
161 A48 3c bister brn 2.50 .50
162 A49 5c orange 2.50 .75
163 A50 10c blue grn 3.00 .75
164 A51 12c blue 8.00 1.00
165 A52 15c black 20.00 10.00
166 A53 20c slate 8.00 2.00
167 A54 24c yellow 20.00 20.00
168 A55 30c rose 15.00 5.00
169 A56 50c violet 15.00 5.00
170 A57 100c brown lake 30.00 15.00
Nos. 159-170 (12) 129.50 61.40

Unwmk.

170A A46 1c scarlet 2.00 *1.50*
170B A47 2c yellow grn 1.00 *.90*
170C A48 3c bister brn .75 .75
170D A49 5c orange .90 .50
170E A50 10c blue grn 5.00 .90
170F A51 12c blue 1.00 2.00
170G A52 15c black 10.00 10.00
170H A53 20c slate 10.00 10.00
170I A54 24c yellow 20.00 20.00
170J A55 30c rose 10.00 10.00
170K A56 50c violet 9.50 10.00
170L A57 100c brown lake 50.00 *50.00*
Nos. 170A-170L (12) 120.15 116.55

All values have been have been reprinted. The papers of the reprints are thicker than those of the originals. Value, 25c each.

Surcharged in Red or Black

1897 **Wmk. 117**
171 A54 13c on 24c yel (R) 2.50 2.50
172 A55 13c on 30c rose (Bk) 2.50 2.50
173 A56 13c on 50c vio (Bk) 2.50 2.50
174 A57 13c on 100c brn lake (Bk) 2.50 2.50

Unwmk.

174A A54 13c on 24c yel (R) 2.50 2.50
174B A55 13c on 30c rose (Bk) 2.50 2.50
174C A56 13c on 50c vio (Bk) 2.50 2.50
Nos. 171-174C (7) 17.50 17.50

Coat of Arms of "Republic of Central America" — A59

ONE CENTAVO:
Originals: The mountains are outlined in red and blue. The sea is represented by short red and dark blue lines on a light blue background.

Reprints: The mountains are outlined in red only. The sea is printed in green and dark blue, much blurred.

FIVE CENTAVOS:
Originals: The sea is represented by horizontal and diagonal lines of dark blue on a light blue background.
Reprints: The sea is printed in green and dark blue, much blurred. The inscription in gold is in thicker letters.

1897 **Litho.**
175 A59 1c bl, gold, rose & grn 1.00 —
176 A59 5c rose, gold, bl & grn 2.00 —

Forming of the "Republic of Central America."
For overprints see Nos. O73-O76.
Stamps of type A59 formerly listed as "Type II" are now known to be reprints.

Allegory of Central American Union — A60

1898 **Engr.** **Wmk. 117**
177 A60 1c orange ver 2.25 .50
178 A60 2c rose 2.25 .50
179 A60 3c pale yel grn 2.00 .50
180 A60 5c blue green 2.00 .75
181 A60 10c gray blue 7.50 .75
182 A60 12c violet 8.50 1.00
183 A60 13c brown lake 8.50 1.00
184 A60 20c deep blue 9.50 2.00
185 A60 24c deep ultra 7.50 5.25
186 A60 26c bister brn 10.00 5.00
187 A60 50c orange 10.00 5.00
188 A60 1p yellow 25.00 15.00
Nos. 177-188 (12) 95.00 *37.25*

For overprints and surcharges see Nos. 189-198A, 224-241, 269A-269B, O129-O142.
The entire set has been reprinted. The shades of the reprints are not the same as those of the originals, and the paper is thicker. Value, 25c each.

No. 180 Overprinted Vertically, up or down in Black, Violet, Red, Magenta and Yellow

1899
189 A60 5c blue grn (Bk) 7.50 6.25
a. Italic 3rd "r" in "Territorial" 12.50 12.50
b. Double ovpt. (Bk + Y) 37.50 37.50
190 A60 5c blue grn (V) *82.50* *82.50*
191 A60 5c blue grn (R) *70.00* *70.00*
191A A60 5c blue grn (M) *70.00* *70.00*
191B A60 5c blue grn (Y) *75.00* *75.00*
Nos. 189-191B (5) *305.00* *303.75*

Counterfeits exist.

Nos. 177-184 Overprinted in Black

1899
192 A60 1c orange ver 2.00 .50
193 A60 2c rose 2.50 1.00
194 A60 3c pale yel grn 2.50 .50
195 A60 5c blue green 2.50 .50
196 A60 10c gray blue 4.00 1.25
197 A60 12c violet 6.50 2.50
198 A60 13c brown lake 6.50 2.00
198A A60 20c deep blue *75.00* *75.00*
Nos. 192-198 (7) 26.50 8.25

The overprint on No. 198A is only seen on the reprints.
Counterfeits exist of the "wheel" overprint used in 1899-1900.

Ceres ("Estado") — A61

Inscribed: "Estado de El Salvador"

1899 **Unwmk.** **Litho.** ***Perf. 12***
199 A61 1c brown .25
200 A61 2c gray green .25
201 A61 3c blue .25
202 A61 5c brown org .25
203 A61 10c chocolate .25
204 A61 12c dark green .25
205 A61 13c deep rose .25
206 A61 24c light blue .25
207 A61 26c carmine rose .25
208 A61 50c orange red .25
209 A61 100c violet .25
Nos. 199-209 (11) 2.75

Nos. 208-209 were probably not placed in use.
For overprints and surcharges see Nos. 210-223, 242-252D, O143-O185.

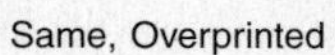
Same, Overprinted

Red Overprint

210 A61 1c brown 60.00 40.00

Blue Overprint

211 A61 1c brown 2.00 1.50
212 A61 5c brown org 2.00 1.50
212A A61 10c chocolate 15.00 10.00

Black Overprint

213 A61 1c brown 1.50 .75
214 A61 2c gray grn 2.00 .40
215 A61 3c blue 2.25 1.00
216 A61 5c brown org 1.50 .65
217 A61 10c chocolate 1.50 .80
218 A61 12c dark green 4.00 4.00
219 A61 13c deep rose 3.50 3.50
220 A61 24c light blue 30.00 27.50
221 A61 26c car rose 7.50 5.00
222 A61 50c orange red 9.00 7.50
223 A61 100c violet 10.00 9.00
Nos. 213-223 (11) 72.75 60.10

"Wheel" overprint exists double and triple.

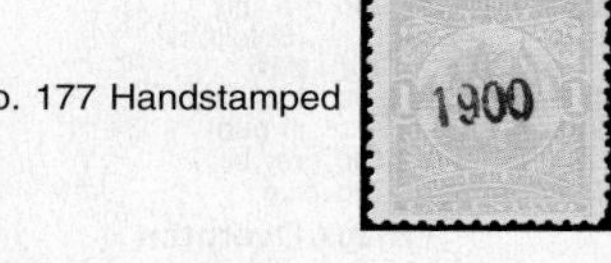

No. 177 Handstamped

1900 **Wmk. 117**
224 A60 1c orange ver 1.00 1.00

No. 177 Overprinted

225 A60 1c orange ver 15.00 15.00

Stamps of 1898 Surcharged in Black

1900
226 A60 1c on 10c gray blue 15.00 15.00
a. Inverted surcharge 15.00 15.00
227 A60 1c on 13c brn lake *100.00*
228 A60 2c on 12c vio 50.00 50.00
a. "eentavo"
b. Inverted surcharge
c. "centavos" 90.00
d. As "c," double surcharge
e. Vertical surcharge
229 A60 2c on 13c brn lake 5.00 5.00
a. "eentavo" 8.00 7.00
b. Inverted surcharge 12.50 10.00
c. "1900" omitted 7.50 7.50
230 A60 2c on 20c dp blue 5.00 5.00
a. Inverted surcharge 8.00 8.00
230B A60 2c on 26c bis brn — —
231 A60 3c on 12c vio *90.00* —
a. "eentavo"
b. Inverted surcharge — —
c. Double surcharge
232 A60 3c on 50c org 35.00 35.00
a. Inverted surcharge 35.00 35.00
233 A60 5c on 12c vio — —
234 A60 5c on 24c ultra 50.00 50.00
a. "eentavo"
b. "centavos" 70.00
235 A60 5c on 26c bis brn *150.00* *150.00*
a. Inverted surcharge *35.00* *35.00*
236 A60 5c on 1p yel 50.00 35.00
a. Inverted surcharge 60.00 60.00

With Additional Overprint in Black

237 A60 2c on 12c vio 2.50 2.50
a. Inverted surcharge 2.50 2.50
b. "eentavo" 8.00
c. "centavos" (plural) 75.00
d. "1900" omitted
237H A60 2c on 13c brn lake
238 A60 3c on 12c vio 125.00 125.00
a. "eentavo" 75.00 75.00
239 A60 5c on 26c bis brn 150.00 150.00
a. Inverted surcharge

Vertical Surcharge "Centavos" in the Plural

240 A60 2c on 12c vio 125.00 125.00
b. Without wheel
240A A60 5c on 24c dp ultra 125.00 125.00

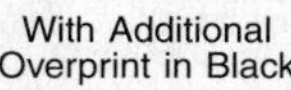
With Additional Overprint in Black

241 A60 5c on 12c vio 50.00 50.00
a. Surcharge reading downward

Counterfeits exist of the surcharges on Nos. 226-241 and the "wheel" overprint on Nos. 237-239, 241.

Same Surcharge on Stamps of 1899 Without Wheel

1900 **Unwmk.**
242 A61 1c on 13c dp rose 1.50 1.50
a. Inverted surcharge 4.00 3.00
b. "eentavo" 4.00 3.00
c. "ecntavo" 5.00 3.00
d. "1 centavo 1" 15.00 10.00
e. Double surcharge
243 A61 2c on 12c dk grn 8.00 8.00
a. Inverted surcharge 15.00 15.00
b. "eentavo"
244 A61 2c on 13c dp rose 3.00 2.50
a. "eentavo" 3.00 4.00
b. "ecntavo" 6.00 2.50
c. Inverted surcharge 9.00
245 A61 3c on 12c dk grn 3.00 2.50
a. Inverted surcharge 9.00 5.00
b. "eentavo" 12.00 12.00
c. Double surcharge 9.00
Nos. 242-245 (4) 15.50 14.50

With Additional Overprint in Black

246 A61 1c on 2c gray grn 1.00 1.00
a. "eentavo" 4.00 3.00
b. Inverted surcharge 10.00 9.00
247 A61 1c on 13c dp rose 4.00 4.00
a. "eentavo" 15.00
b. "1 centavo 1"
248 A61 2c on 12c dk grn 5.00 4.00
a. "eentavo" 15.00
b. Inverted surcharge 4.00 4.00
c. Double surcharge 8.00
249 A61 2c on 13c dp rose 100.00 100.00
a. "eentavo"
b. Double surcharge 150.00 150.00
250 A61 3c on 12c dk grn 5.00 3.00
a. Inverted surcharge 5.50 4.00
b. "eentavo" 8.00 7.00
c. Date double 15.00
251 A61 5c on 24c lt bl 12.00 5.00
a. "eentavo" 20.00 20.00
252 A61 5c on 26c car rose 4.00 4.00
a. Inverted surcharge 12.00 9.00
b. "eentavo" 6.00 5.00
252D A61 5c on 1c on 26c car rose
Nos. 246-248,250-252 (6) 31.00 21.00

Counterfeits exist of the surcharges on Nos. 242-252D and the "wheel" overprint on Nos. 246-252D.

Ceres ("Republica") — A63

There are two varieties of the 1c, type A63, one with the word "centavo" in the middle of the label (#253, 263, 270, 299, 305, 326), the other with "centavo" nearer the left end than the right (#270, 299, 305, 326).

The stamps of type A63 are found in a great variety of shades. Stamps of type A63 without handstamp were not regularly issued.

Handstamped in Violet or Black
Inscribed: "Republica de El Salvador"

1900

253	A63	1c blue green	.90	.90
a.		1c yellow green	.90	.90
254	A63	2c rose	1.50	1.00
255	A63	3c gray black	1.25	1.00
256	A63	5c pale blue	1.00	.60
a.		5c deep blue	5.00	.60
257	A63	10c deep blue	2.00	.60
258	A63	12c yel green	5.00	3.50
259	A63	13c yel brown	4.00	3.00
260	A63	24c gray	15.00	15.00
261	A63	26c yel brown	7.00	7.00
262	A63	50c rose red	2.00	2.00
		Nos. 253-262 (10)	39.65	34.60

For overprints and surcharges see Nos. 263-269, 270-282, 293A-311B, 317, 326-335, O223-O242, O258-O262, O305-O312.

Handstamped in Violet or Black

263	A63	1c lt green	10.00	4.00
264	A63	2c pale rose	10.00	3.00
265	A63	3c gray black	10.00	3.00
266	A63	5c slate blue	14.00	3.00
267	A63	10c deep blue	—	—
268	A63	13c yellow brn	35.00	35.00
269	A63	50c dull rose	15.00	15.00
		Nos. 263-266,268-269 (6)	94.00	63.00

Handstamped on 1898 Stamps
Wmk. 117

269A	A60	2c rose	30.00	30.00
269B	A60	10c gray blue	30.00	30.00

The overprints on Nos. 253 to 269B are handstamped and, as usual with that style of overprint, are to be found double, inverted, omitted, etc.

Specialists have questioned the existence of No. 267. The editors would like to see authenticated evidence of the existence of a genuine example.

Stamps of Type A63 Overprinted in Black

1900 **Unwmk.**

270	A63	1c light green	1.50	1.00
271	A63	2c rose	7.50	2.00
272	A63	3c gray black	1.50	1.00
273	A63	5c pale blue	7.50	2.00
a.		5c dark blue	6.00	1.00
274	A63	10c deep blue	7.50	2.00
a.		10c pale blue	7.50	2.00
275	A63	12c light green	2.25	1.50
276	A63	13c yellow brown	1.50	1.00
277	A63	24c gray	1.75	1.25
278	A63	26c yellow brown	3.00	2.00
		Nos. 270-278 (9)	34.00	13.75

This overprint is known double, inverted, etc.

Nos. 271-273 Surcharged in Black

1902

280	A63	1c on 2c rose	8.25	6.75
281	A63	1c on 3c black	6.00	4.25
282	A63	1c on 5c blue	3.75	3.00
		Nos. 280-282 (3)	18.00	14.00

Morazán Monument — A64

Perf. 14, 14½

1903 **Engr.** **Wmk. 173**

283	A64	1c green	1.00	.60
284	A64	2c carmine	1.00	.60
285	A64	3c orange	10.00	2.00
286	A64	5c dark blue	1.00	.60
287	A64	10c dull violet	1.00	.60
288	A64	12c slate	1.25	.60
289	A64	13c red brown	1.25	.60
290	A64	24c scarlet	7.50	3.75
291	A64	26c yellow brn	7.50	3.75
292	A64	50c bister	3.75	2.25
293	A64	100c grnsh blue	11.00	7.50
		Nos. 283-293 (11)	46.25	22.85

For surcharges and overprint see Nos. 312-316, 318-325, O253.

Stamps of 1900 with Shield in Black Overprinted

(5¾x13½mm) — a

1905

(5x14¾mm) — b

(4½x16mm) — c

1905

(4½x13½mm) — d

(5x14½mm) — e

1905

1905-06 **Unwmk.** ***Perf. 12***

Blue Overprint

293A	A63 (a)	2c rose	—	—
294	A63 (a)	3c gray blk	8.00	6.00
a.		Without shield		
295	A63 (a)	5c blue	10.00	7.50

Purple Overprint

296	A63 (b)	3c gray blk (Shield in pur)	—	—
296A	A63 (b)	5c bl (Shield in pue)	—	—
297	A63 (b)	3c gray blk	—	—
298	A63 (b)	5c blue	—	—

Black Overprint

298A	A63 (b)	5c blue	—	—

Blue Overprint

299	A63 (c)	1c green	10.00	5.00
299B	A63 (c)	2c rose	.50	.40
c.		"1905" vert.	1.00	
300	A63 (c)	5c blue	6.00	4.00
301	A63 (c)	10c deep blue	2.00	1.00

Black Overprint

302	A63 (c)	2c rose	10.00	5.00
303	A63 (c)	5c blue	25.00	25.00
304	A63 (c)	10c deep blue	12.00	7.00

Blue Overprint

305	A63 (d)	1c green	15.00	10.00
306	A63 (d)	2c rose, ovpt. vert.	9.00	5.00
a.		Overprint horiz.		
306B	A63 (d)	3c gray black	8.00	4.00
307	A63 (d)	5c blue	3.00	1.50

Blue Overprint

311	A63 (e)	2c rose	10.00	8.00
a.		Without shield	15.00	12.00

Black Overprint

311B	A63 (e)	5c blue	30.00	20.00
		Nos. 294-295,299-311B (15)	158.50	109.40

These overprints are found double, inverted, omitted, etc. Counterfeits exist.

Regular Issue of 1903 Surcharged

f

g

h

1905-06 **Wmk. 173** ***Perf. 14, 14½***

Black Surcharge

312	A64 (f)	1c on 2c car	4.00	2.00
a.		Double surcharge	20.00	20.00

Red Surcharge

312B	A64 (g)	5c on 12c slate	5.00	4.00
c.		Double surcharge		
d.		Black surcharge	15.00	15.00
e.		As "d," double surcharge		

Blue Handstamped Surcharge

313	A64 (h)	1c on 2c car	2.00	2.00
314	A64 (h)	1c on 10c vio	2.00	2.00
315	A64 (h)	1c on 12c sl ('06)	2.00	2.00
316	A64 (h)	1c on 13c red brn	22.50	15.00

No. 271 with Handstamped Surcharge in Blue
Unwmk.

317	A63 (h)	1c on 2c rose	—	—
		Nos. 312-316 (6)	37.50	27.00

The "h" is handstamped in strips of four stamps each differing from the others in the size of the upper figures of value and in the letters of the word "CENTAVO," particularly in the size of the "N" and the "O" of that word. The surcharge is known inverted, double, etc.

Regular Issue of 1903 with Handstamped Surcharge

i

j

k

Wmk. 173
Red Handstamped Surcharge

318	A64 (i)	5c on 12c slate	4.00	3.00
319	A64 (j)	5c on 12c slate	6.00	5.00
a.		Blue surcharge		

Blue Handstamped Surcharge

320	A64 (k)	5c on 12c slate	3.50	2.50
		Nos. 318-320 (3)	13.50	10.50

One or more of the numerals in the handstamped surcharges on Nos. 318, 319 and 320 are frequently omitted, inverted, etc.

Regular Issue of 1903 Surcharged

l

m

Blue Handstamped Surcharge

321	A64 (l)	6c on 12c slate	.75	.50
322	A64 (l)	6c on 13c red brn	1.50	.60

Red Handstamped Surcharge

323	A64 (l)	6c on 12c slate	27.50	15.00

Type "l" is handstamped in strips of four varieties, differing in the size of the numerals and letters. The surcharge is known double and inverted.

Black Surcharge

324	A64 (m)	1c on 13c red brn	2.25	1.50
a.		Double surcharge	6.00	4.50
b.		Right "1" & dot omitted		
c.		Both numerals omitted		
325	A64 (m)	3c on 13c red brn	.75	.60

Stamps of 1900, with Shield in Black, Overprinted — n

1905 **Unwmk.** ***Perf. 12***

Blue Overprint

326	A63 (n)	1c green	9.00	6.00
a.		Inverted overprint		
327	A63 (n)	2c rose	5.00	5.00
a.		Vertical overprint	12.50	12.50
b.		Imperforate	9.00	6.00
327B	A63 (n)	3c black	50.00	30.00
327C	A63 (n)	5c blue	25.00	20.00
328	A63 (n)	10c deep blue	15.00	9.00

Black Overprint

328A	A63 (n)	10c deep blue	20.00	15.00
		Nos. 326-328A (6)	124.00	85.00

Counterfeits of Nos. 326-335 abound.

Stamps of 1900, with Shield in Black Surcharged or Overprinted

o

1906

p

q

1906 **Blue and Black Surcharge**

329	A63 (o)	2c on 26c brn org	1.00	.80
a.		"2" & dot double	15.00	15.00
330	A63 (o)	3c on 26c brn org	8.00	6.50
a.		"3" & dot double		

Black Surcharge or Overprint

331	A63 (o)	3c on 26c brn org	9.00	7.00
a.		Disks & numerals omitted		
b.		"3" and disks double		
c.		"1906" omitted		
333	A63 (p)	10c deep blue	6.00	4.00
334	A63 (q)	10c deep blue	6.00	4.00
334A	A63 (q)	26c brown org	50.00	45.00
b.		"1906" in blue		

No. 257 Overprinted in Black

335	A63 (q)	10c dp bl (Shield in violet)	—	—
a.		Overprint type "p"		
		Nos. 329-334A (6)	80.00	67.30

There are numerous varieties of these surcharges and overprints.

Pres. Pedro José Escalón — A65

1906 **Engr.** ***Perf. 11½***

Glazed Paper

336	A65	1c green & blk	.25	.25
a.		Thin paper	.75	.25
337	A65	2c red & blk	.25	.25
338	A65	3c yellow & blk	.25	.25
339	A65	5c ultra & blk	.25	.25
a.		5c dark blue & black	.25	.25
340	A65	6c carmine & blk	.25	.25
341	A65	10c violet & blk	.25	.25
342	A65	12c violet & blk	.25	.25
343	A65	13c dk brn & blk	.25	.25
345	A65	24c carmine & blk	.35	.35
346	A65	26c choc & blk	.35	.35
347	A65	50c yellow & blk	.35	.45
348	A65	100c blue & blk	*3.00*	*3.00*
		Nos. 336-348 (12)	*6.05*	*6.15*

All values of this set are known imperforate but are not believed to have been issued in this condition.

See Nos. O263-O272. For overprints and surcharges see Nos. 349-354.

The entire set has been reprinted, perforated 11.8. Value, set of 12, $1.20.

Nos. 336-338 Overprinted in Black

1907

349 A65 1c green & blk .25 .25
a. Shield in red 3.50
350 A65 2c red & blk .25 .25
a. Shield in red 3.50
351 A65 3c yellow & blk .25 .25
Nos. 349-351 (3) .75 .75

Reprints of Nos. 349 to 351 have the same characteristics as the reprints of the preceding issue. Value, set of 3, 15c.

Stamps of 1906 Surcharged with Shield and

352 A65 1c on 5c ultra & blk .25 .25
a. 1c on 5c dark blue & black .25 .25
b. Inverted surcharge .35 .35
c. Double surcharge .45 .45
352D A65 1c on 6c rose & blk .25 .25
e. Double surcharge 1.25 1.25
353 A65 2c on 6c rose & blk 2.00 1.00
354 A65 10c on 6c rose & blk .50 .35
Nos. 352-354 (4) 3.00 1.85

The above surcharges are frequently found with the shield double, inverted, or otherwise misplaced.

National Palace — A66

Overprinted with Shield in Black

1907 Engr. Unwmk.

Paper with or without colored dots

355 A66 1c green & blk .25 .25
356 A66 2c red & blk .25 .25
357 A66 3c yellow & blk .25 .25
358 A66 5c blue & blk .25 .25
a. 5c ultramarine & black .25 .25
359 A66 6c ver & blk .25 .25
a. Shield in red 3.25
360 A66 10c violet & blk .25 .25
361 A66 12c violet & blk .25 .25
362 A66 13c sepia & blk .25 .25
363 A66 24c rose & blk .25 .25
364 A66 26c yel brn & blk .30 .25
365 A66 50c orange & blk .50 .35
a. 50c yellow & black 3.50
366 A66 100c turq bl & blk 1.00 .50
Nos. 355-366 (12) 4.05 3.35

Most values exist without shield, also with shield inverted, double, and otherwise misprinted. Many of these were never sold to the public.

See 2nd footnote following No. 421.

See Nos. 369-373, 397-401. For surcharges and overprints see Nos. 367-368A, 374-77, 414-421, 443-444, J71-J74, J76-J80, O329-O331.

No. 356 With Additional Surcharge in Black

1908

367 A66 1c on 2c red & blk .25 .25
a. Double surcharge 1.00 1.00
b. Inverted surcharge .50 .50
c. Double surcharge, one inverted .50 .50
d. Red surcharge

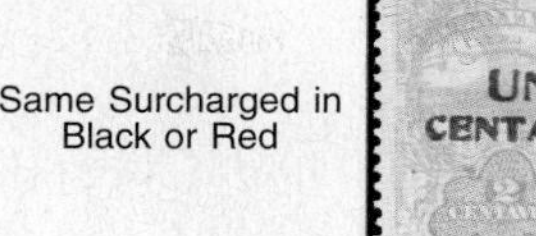

Same Surcharged in Black or Red

368 A66 1c on 2c *19.00 17.50*
368A A66 1c on 2c (R) *27.50 25.00*

Counterfeits exist of the surcharges on Nos. 368-368A.

Type of 1907

1909 Engr. Wmk. 172

369 A66 1c green & blk .25 .25
370 A66 2c rose & blk .25 .25
371 A66 3c yellow & blk .25 .25
372 A66 5c blue & blk .25 .25
373 A66 10c violet & blk .30 .25
Nos. 369-373 (5) 1.30 1.25

The note after No. 366 will apply here also.

Nos. 355, 369 Overprinted in Red

1909, Sept. Unwmk.

374 A66 1c green & blk 2.25 1.10
a. Inverted overprint 10.00

Wmk. 172

375 A66 1c green & blk 1.75 1.40
a. Inverted overprint

88th anniv. of El Salvador's independence.

Nos. 362, 364 Surcharged

1909 Unwmk.

376 A66 2c on 13c sep & blk 1.50 1.25
a. Inverted surcharge
377 A66 3c on 26c yel brn & blk 1.75 1.40
a. Inverted surcharge

A67

Design: Pres. Fernando Figueroa.

1910 Engr. Wmk. 172

378 A67 1c sepia & blk .25 .25
379 A67 2c dk grn & blk .25 .25
380 A67 3c orange & blk .25 .25
381 A67 4c carmine & blk .25 .25
a. 4c scarlet & black .25 .25
382 A67 5c purple & blk .25 .25
383 A67 6c scarlet & blk .25 .25
384 A67 10c purple & blk .25 .25
385 A67 12c dp bl & blk .25 .25
386 A67 17c ol grn & blk .25 .25
387 A67 19c brn red & blk .25 .25
388 A67 29c choc & blk .25 .25
389 A67 50c yellow & blk .25 .25
390 A67 100c turq bl & blk .25 .25
Nos. 378-390 (13) 3.25 3.25

A68

5c, José Matías Delgado. 6c, Manuel José Arce. 12c, Centenary Monument.

Paper with colored dots

1911 Unwmk.

391 A68 5c dp blue & brn .25 .25
392 A68 6c orange & brn .25 .25
393 A68 12c violet & brn .25 .25

Wmk. 172

394 A68 5c dp blue & brn .25 .25
395 A68 6c orange & brn .25 .25
396 A68 12c violet & brn .25 .25
Nos. 391-396 (6) 1.50 1.50

Centenary of the insurrection of 1811.

Palace Type of 1907 without Shield

1911 Paper without colored dots

397 A66 1c scarlet .25 .25
398 A66 2c chocolate .30 .30
a. Paper with brown dots
399 A66 13c deep green .25 .25
400 A66 24c yellow .25 .25
401 A66 50c dark brown .25 .25
Nos. 397-401 (5) 1.30 1.30

José Matías Delgado — A71

Manuel José Arce — A72

Francisco Morazán — A73

Rafael Campo — A74

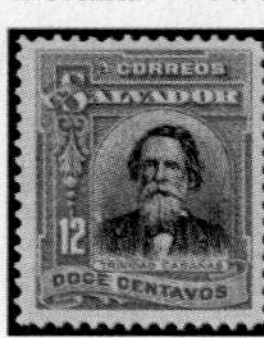

Trinidad Cabañas A75

Monument of Gerardo Barrios A76

Centenary Monument A77

National Palace A78

Rosales Hospital — A79

Coat of Arms — A80

1912 Unwmk. *Perf. 12*

402 A71 1c dp bl & blk 1.00 .25
403 A72 2c bis brn & blk 1.00 .25
404 A73 5c scarlet & blk 1.00 .25
405 A74 6c dk grn & blk 1.00 .25
406 A75 12c ol grn & blk 3.00 .25
407 A76 17c violet & slate 10.00 .25
408 A77 19c scar & slate 3.00 .30
409 A78 29c org & slate 5.00 .30
410 A79 50c blue & slate 5.00 .45
411 A80 1col black & slate 10.00 1.00
Nos. 402-411 (10) 40.00 3.55

Juan Manuel Rodríguez A81

Pres. Manuel E. Araujo A82

1914 *Perf. 11½*

412 A81 10c orange & brn 5.00 1.50
413 A82 25c purple & brn 5.00 1.50

Type of 1907 without Shield Overprinted in Black

1915

Paper overlaid with colored dots

414 A66 1c gray green .25 .25
415 A66 2c red .25 .25
416 A66 5c ultra .25 .25
417 A66 6c pale blue .25 .25
418 A66 10c yellow .60 .30
419 A66 12c brown .50 .25
420 A66 50c violet .25 .25
421 A66 100c black brn 1.40 1.40
Nos. 414-421 (8) 3.75 3.20

Varieties such as center omitted, center double, center inverted, imperforate exist with or without date, date inverted, date double, etc., but are believed to be entirely unofficial.

Preceding the stamps with the "1915" overprint a quantity of stamps of this type was overprinted with the letter "S." Evidence is lacking that they were ever placed in use. The issue was demonetized in 1916.

National Theater — A83

Various frames.

1916 Engr. *Perf. 12*

431 A83 1c deep green .25 .25
432 A83 2c vermilion .25 .25
433 A83 5c deep blue .25 .25
434 A83 6c gray violet .25 .25
435 A83 10c black brn .25 .25
436 A83 12c violet 2.50 .50
437 A83 17c orange .35 .25
438 A83 25c dk brown .80 .25
439 A83 29c black 5.00 .75
440 A83 50c slate 20.00 10.00
Nos. 431-440 (10) 29.90 13.00

Watermarked letters which occasionally appear are from the papermaker's name.

For surcharges and overprints see Nos. 450-455, 457-466, O332-O341.

Nos. O324-O325 with "OFICIAL" Barred out in Black

1917

441 O3 2c red .90 .90
a. Double bar
442 O3 5c ultramarine 1.00 .70
a. Double bar

Regular Issue of 1915 Overprinted "OFICIAL" and Re-overprinted In Red

443 A66 6c pale blue 1.25 1.00
a. Double bar

444 A66 12c brown 1.75 1.25
a. Double bar
b. "CORRIENTE" inverted

Same Overprint in Red On Nos. O323-O327

445 O3 1c gray green 3.50 2.50
a. "CORRIENTE" inverted
b. Double bar
c. "CORRIENTE" omitted
446 O3 2c red 3.50 2.50
a. Double bar
447 O3 5c ultra 18.00 12.00
a. Double bar, both in black
448 O3 10c yellow 2.00 1.00
a. Double bar
b. "OFICIAL" and bar omitted
449 O3 50c violet 1.00 1.00
a. Double bar
Nos. 443-449 (7) 31.00 21.25

Nos. O334-O335 Overprinted or Surcharged in Red

a

b

450 A83 (a) 5c deep blue 3.00 2.00
a. "CORRIENTE" double
451 A83 (b) 1c on 6c gray vio 2.00 1.50
a. "CORRIERTE"
b. "CORRIENRE" 5.00
c. "CORRIENTE" double

No. 434 Surcharged in Black

1918

452 A83 1c on 6c gray vio 1.75 1.00
a. Double surcharge
b. Inverted surcharge

No. 434 Surcharged in Black

1918

453 A83 1c on 6c gray vio 1.50 .75
a. "Centado" 2.25 1.50
b. Double surcharge 2.50 1.75
c. Inverted surcharge

No. 434 Surcharged in Black or Red

454 A83 1c on 6c gray vio 10.00 6.00
a. Double surcharge
b. Inverted surcharge 5.00 5.00
455 A83 1c on 6c gray vio (R) 10.00 6.00
a. Double surcharge
b. Inverted surcharge 5.00 5.00
Nos. 454-455 (2) 20.00 12.00

Counterfeits exist of Nos. 454-455.

Pres. Carlos Meléndez — A85

1919 **Engr.**

456 A85 1col dk blue & blk .50 .50

For surcharge see No. 467.

No. 437 Surcharged in Black

1919

457 A83 1c on 17c orange .25 .25
a. Inverted surcharge 1.00 1.00
b. Double surcharge 1.00 1.00

Nos. 435-436, 438, 440 Surcharged in Black or Blue

1920-21

458 A83 1c on 12c violet .25 .25
a. Double surcharge 1.00 1.00
459 A83 2c on 10c dk brn .25 .25
460 A83 5c on 50c slate ('21) .40 .25
461 A83 6c on 25c dk brn (Bl) ('21) 2.00 1.00

Same Srch. in Black on No. O337

462 A83 1c on 12c violet 1.00 1.00
a. Double surcharge
Nos. 458-462 (5) 3.90 2.75

No. 460 surcharged in yellow and 461 surcharged in red are essays.

No. 462 is due to some sheets of Official Stamps being mixed with the ordinary 12c stamps at the time of surcharging. The error stamps were sold to the public and used for ordinary postage.

Surcharged in Red, Blue or Black

15c Types:

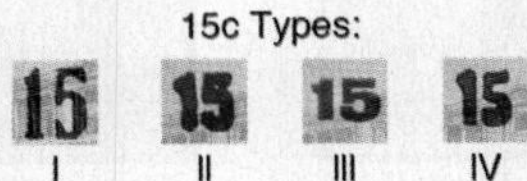

463 A83 15c on 29c blk (III) ('21) 1.00 .40
a. Double surcharge 2.00
b. Type I 1.50 1.00
c. Type II 1.00 .75
d. Type IV 2.50
464 A83 26c on 29c blk (Bl) 1.00 .60
a. Double surcharge
466 A83 35c on 50c slate (Bk) 1.00 .60
467 A85 60c on 1col dk bl & blk (R) .30 .25
Nos. 463-467 (4) 3.30 1.85

Surcharge on No. 464 differs from 15c illustration in that bar at bottom extends across stamp and denomination includes "cts." One stamp in each row of ten of No. 464 has the "t" of "cts" inverted and one stamp in each row of ten has the letters "c" in "cinco" larger than the normal.

No. 466 has the letters "c" in "cinco" larger than the normal.

Setting for No. 467 includes three types of numerals and "CENTAVOS" measuring from 16mm to 20mm wide.

No. 464 surcharged in green or yellow and the 35c on 29c black are essays.

A93

1921

468 A93 1c on 1c ol grn .25 .25
a. Double surcharge .75
469 A93 1c on 5c yellow .25 .25
a. Inverted surcharge
b. Double surcharge
470 A93 1c on 10c blue .25 .25
a. Double surcharge .50
471 A93 1c on 25c green .25 .25
a. Double surcharge
472 A93 1c on 50c olive .25 .25
a. Double surcharge
473 A93 1c on 1p gray blk .25 .25
a. Double surcharge
Nos. 468-473 (6) 1.50 1.50

The frame of No. 473 differs slightly from the illustration.

Setting includes many wrong font letters and numerals.

Francisco Menéndez A94

Manuel José Arce A95

Confederation Coin — A96

Delgado Addressing Crowd — A97

Coat of Arms of Confedera-tion A98

Francisco Morazán A99

Independence Monument A100

Columbus A101

1921 **Engr.** ***Perf. 12***

474 A94 1c green 2.50 .25
475 A95 2c black 5.00 .25
476 A96 5c orange 2.00 .25
477 A97 6c carmine rose 2.00 .25
478 A98 10c deep blue 2.00 .25
479 A99 25c olive grn 4.00 .25
480 A100 60c violet 9.00 .50
481 A101 1col black brn 15.00 .75
Nos. 474-481 (8) 41.50 2.75

For overprints and surcharges see Nos. 481A-485, 487-494, 506, O342-O349.

Nos. 474-477 Overprinted in Red, Black or Blue

a

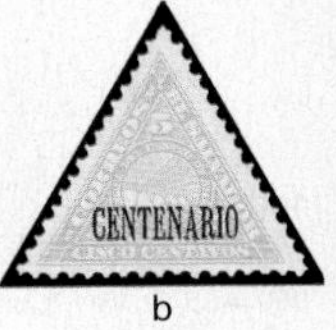

b

1921

481A A94 (a) 1c green (R) 5.00 4.00
481B A95 (a) 2c black (R) 5.00 4.00
481C A96 (b) 5c orange (Bk) 5.00 4.00
481D A97 (b) 6c car rose (Bl) 5.00 4.00
Nos. 481A-481D (4) 20.00 16.00

Centenary of independence.

No. 477 Surcharged

a

b

1923

482 A97 (a) 5c on 6c 4.00 .25
483 A97 (b) 5c on 6c 4.00 .25
484 A97 (b) 20c on 6c 4.00 .25
Nos. 482-484 (3) 12.00 .75

Nos. 482-484 exist with double surcharge.

No. 475 Surcharged in Red

1923

485 A95 10c on 2c black 4.00 .25

José Simeón Cañas y Villacorta — A102

1923 **Engr.** ***Perf. 11½***

486 A102 5c blue .60 .30

Centenary of abolition of slavery.
For surcharge see No. 571.

Nos. 479, 481 Surcharged in Red or Black

1924 ***Perf. 12***

487 A99 1c on 25c ol grn (R) .30 .25
a. Numeral at right inverted
b. Double surcharge
488 A99 6c on 25c ol grn (R) .25 .25
489 A99 20c on 25c ol grn (R) .60 .25
490 A101 20c on 1col blk brn (Bk) .75 .35
Nos. 487-490 (4) 1.90 1.10

Nos. 476, 478 Surcharged

1924

491 A96 1c on 5c orange (Bk) .40 .25
492 A98 6c on 10c dp bl (R) .40 .25

Nos. 491-492 exist with double surcharge.

A stamp similar to No. 492 but with surcharge "6 centavos 6" is an essay.

No. 476 Surcharged

493 A96 2c on 5c orange .40 .40
a. Top ornament omitted 2.00 2.00
Nos. 491-493 (3) 1.20 .90

No. 480 Surcharged

1924 **Red Surcharge**

494 A100 5c on 60c violet 6.00 5.00
a. "1781" for "1874" 13.00 12.00
b. "1934" for "1924" 13.00 12.00

Universal Postal Union, 50th anniversary.

This stamp with black surcharge is an essay. Examples have been passed through the post.

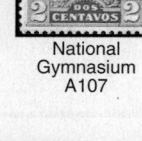

Daniel Hernández Monument A106

National Gymnasium A107

Atlacatl — A108

Conspiracy of 1811 — A109

Bridge over Lempa River — A110

Map of Central America — A111

Balsam Tree — A112

Tulla Serra — A114

Columbus at La Rábida — A115

Coat of Arms — A116

Photogravure; Engraved (35c, 1col)

1924-25 ***Perf. 12½; 14 (35c, 1col)***

495 A106 1c red violet .25 .25
496 A107 2c dark red .40 .25
497 A108 3c chocolate .30 .25
498 A109 5c olive blk .30 .25
499 A110 6c grnsh blue .40 .25
500 A111 10c orange .85 .25
a. "ATLANT CO" 8.00 8.00
501 A112 20c deep green 1.50 .40
502 A114 35c scar & grn 3.50 .50
503 A115 50c orange brown 2.75 .35
504 A116 1col grn & vio ('25) 4.00 .50
Nos. 495-504 (10) 14.25 3.25

For overprints and surcharges see Nos. 510-511, 520-534, 585, C1-C10, C19, O350-O361, RA1-RA4.

No. 480 Surcharged in Red

1925, Aug. ***Perf. 12***

506 A100 2c on 60c violet 1.50 1.25

City of San Salvador, 400th anniv.

The variety with dates in black is an essay.

View of San Salvador — A118

1925 **Photo.** ***Perf. 12½***

507 A118 1c blue 1.10 1.00
508 A118 2c deep green 1.10 1.00
509 A118 3c Mahogany red 1.10 1.00
Nos. 507-509 (3) 3.30 3.00

#506-509 for the 4th centenary of the founding of the City of San Salvador.

Black Surcharge

1928, July 17

510 A111 3c on 10c orange 1.25 .75
a. "ATLANT CO" 20.00 20.00

Industrial Exhibition, Santa Ana, July 1928.

Red Surcharge

1928

511 A109 1c on 5c olive black .45 .25
a. Bar instead of top left "1" .60 .25

Pres. Pío Romero Bosque, Salvador, and Pres. Lázaro Chacón, Guatemala A121

1929 **Litho.** ***Perf. 11½***

Portraits in Dark Brown

512 A121 1c dull violet .60 .45
a. Center inverted 11.50 11.50
513 A121 3c bister brn .60 .45
a. Center inverted 35.00 35.00
514 A121 5c gray grn .60 .45
515 A121 10c orange .60 .45
Nos. 512-515 (4) 2.40 1.80

Opening of the international railroad connecting El Salvador and Guatemala.

Nos. 512-515 exist imperforate. No. 512 in the colors of No. 515.

Tomb of Menéndez A122

1930, Dec. 3

516 A122 1c violet 4.50 3.50
517 A122 3c brown 4.50 3.50
518 A122 5c dark green 4.50 3.50
519 A122 10c yellow brn 4.50 3.50
Nos. 516-519 (4) 18.00 14.00

Centenary of the birth of General Francisco Menéndez.

Stamps of 1924-25 Issue Overprinted

1932 ***Perf. 12½, 14***

520 A106 1c deep violet .30 .25
521 A107 2c dark red .30 .25
522 A108 3c chocolate .45 .25
523 A109 5c olive blk .45 .25
524 A110 6c deep blue .60 .25
525 A111 10c orange 1.50 .25
a. "ATLANT CO" 12.00 9.00
526 A112 20c deep green 2.40 .75
527 A114 35c scar & grn 3.25 1.00
528 A115 50c orange brown 4.50 1.50
529 A116 1col green & vio 7.50 3.25
Nos. 520-529 (10) 21.25 8.00

Values are for the overprint measuring 7½x3mm. It is found in two other sizes: 7½x3¼mm and 8x3mm.

Types of 1924-25

Surcharged with New Values in Red or Black

1934 ***Perf. 12½***

530 A109 2(c) on 5c grnsh blk .25 .25
a. Double surcharge
531 A111 3(c) on 10c org (Bk) .45 .25
a. "ATLANT CO" 6.00 6.00

Nos. 503, 504, 502 Surcharged with New Values in Black

Perf. 12½, 14½

532 A115 2(c) on 50c .45 .25
a. Double surcharge 3.00
533 A116 8(c) on 1col .25 .25
534 A114 15(c) on 35c .45 .45
Nos. 530-534 (5) 1.85 1.45

Police Barracks, Type I — A123

Type II

Two types of the 2c:

Type I — The clouds have heavy lines of shading.

Type II — The lines of shading have been removed from the clouds.

Wmk. 240

1934-35 **Litho.** ***Perf. 12½***

535 A123 2c gray brn, type I .25 .25
a. 2c brown, type II .25 .25
536 A123 5c car, type II .25 .25
537 A123 8c lt ultra, type II .25 .25
Nos. 535-537,C33-C35 (6) 4.70 2.45

Discus Thrower A124

1935, Mar. 16 **Engr.** **Unwmk.**

538 A124 5c carmine 3.00 2.25
539 A124 8c blue 3.25 2.75
540 A124 10c orange yel 4.50 3.00
541 A124 15c bister 4.50 3.25
542 A124 37c green 6.00 4.50
Nos. 538-542,C36-C40 (10) 64.75 38.50

3rd Central American Games.

Same Overprinted in Black

1935, June 27

543 A124 5c carmine 5.00 3.00
544 A124 8c blue 7.00 3.00
545 A124 10c orange yel 7.00 3.50
546 A124 15c bister 7.00 3.50
547 A124 37c green 12.00 5.50
Nos. 543-547,C41-C45 (10) 71.50 42.70

Flag of El Salvador — A125

1935, Oct. 26 **Litho.** **Wmk. 240**

548 A125 1c gray blue .30 .25
549 A125 2c black brn .30 .25
550 A125 3c plum .30 .25
551 A125 5c rose carmine .45 .25
552 A125 8c ultra .45 .25
553 A125 15c fawn .60 .45
Nos. 548-553,C46 (7) 2.80 2.05

Tree of San Vicente — A126

Numerals in Black, Tree in Yellow Green

1935, Dec. 26

554 A126 2c black brn .85 .45
555 A126 3c dk blue grn .85 .45
556 A126 5c rose red .85 .45
557 A126 8c dark blue .85 .55
558 A126 15c brown .60 .45
Nos. 554-558,C47-C51 (10) 7.75 5.35

Tercentenary of San Vicente.

Volcano of Izalco — A127

Wharf at Cutuco — A128

Doroteo Vasconcelos A129

Parade Ground A130

Dr. Tomás G. Palomo — A131

Sugar Mill — A132

Coffee at Pier — A133

Gathering Balsam — A134

Pres. Manuel E. Araujo — A135

1935, Dec. Engr. Unwmk.

559	A127	1c deep violet	.25	.25
560	A128	2c chestnut	.25	.25
561	A129	3c green	.25	.25
562	A130	5c carmine	.60	.25
563	A131	8c dull blue	.25	.25
564	A132	10c orange	.60	.25
565	A133	15c dk olive bis	.60	.25
566	A134	50c indigo	3.00	1.75
567	A135	1col black	7.50	4.50
		Nos. 559-567 (9)	13.30	8.00

Paper has faint imprint "El Salvador" on face.
For surcharges and overprint see Nos. 568-570, 573, 583-584, C52.

Stamps of 1935 Surcharged with New Value in Black

1938 Perf. 12½

568	A130	1c on 5c carmine	.25	.25
569	A132	3c on 10c orange	.25	.25
570	A133	8c on 15c dk ol bis	.30	.25
		Nos. 568-570 (3)	.80	.75

No. 486 Surcharged with New Value in Red

1938 Perf. 11½

571	A102	3c on 5c blue	.30	.25

Centenary of the death of José Simeón Cañas, liberator of slaves in Latin America.

Map and Flags of US and El Salvador — A136

Engraved and Lithographed

1938, Apr. 21 Perf. 12

572	A136	8c multicolored	.95	.70

US Constitution, 150th anniv. See #C61.

No. 560 Surcharged with New Value in Black

1938 Perf. 12½

573	A128	1c on 2c chestnut	.25	.25

Indian Sugar Mill — A137

Designs: 2c, Indian women washing. 3c, Indian girl at spring. 5c, Indian plowing. 8c, Izote flower. 10c, Champion cow. 20c, Extracting balsam. 50c, Maquilishuat in bloom. 1col, Post Office, San Salvador.

1938-39 Engr. Perf. 12

574	A137	1c dark violet	.25	.25
575	A137	2c dark green	.25	.25
576	A137	3c dark brown	.30	.25
577	A137	5c scarlet	.30	.25
578	A137	8c dark blue	2.00	.25
579	A137	10c yel org ('39)	3.00	.25
580	A137	20c bis brn ('39)	2.75	.25
581	A137	50c dull blk ('39)	3.25	.70
582	A137	1col black ('39)	3.00	1.00
		Nos. 574-582 (9)	15.10	3.45

For surcharges & overprints see Nos. 591-592, C96 in Scott Standard catalogue, Vol. 5.

Nos. 566-567, 504 Surcharged in Red

1939, Sept. 25 Perf. 12½, 14

583	A134	8c on 50c indigo	.45	.25
584	A135	10c on 1col blk	.80	.25
585	A116	50c on 1col grn & vio	4.50	3.25
		Nos. 583-585 (3)	5.75	3.75

Battle of San Pedro Perulapán, 100th anniv.

Sir Rowland Hill — A146

1940, Mar. 1 Perf. 12½

586	A146	8c dk bl, lt bl & blk	6.00	2.00
		Nos. 586,C69-C70 (3)	36.50	22.00

Postage stamp centenary.

AIR POST STAMPS

Regular Issue of 1924-25 Overprinted in Black or Red

Back of No. C1

First Printing.
15c on 10c: "15 QUINCE 15" measures 22½mm.
20c: Shows on the back of the stamp an albino impression of the 50c surcharge.
25c on 35c: Original value canceled by a long and short bar.
40c on 50c: Only one printing.
50c on 1col: Surcharge in dull orange red.

Perf. 12½, 14

1929, Dec. 28 Unwmk.

C1	A112	20c dp green (Bk)	6.00	5.00
a.		Red overprint	850.00	850.00

Counterfeits exist of No. C1a.

Additional Surcharge of New Values and Bars in Black or Red

No. C3

No. C4

No. C5

C3	A111	15c on 10c org	1.10	1.10
a.		"ALTANT CO"	37.50	35.00
C4	A114	25c on 35c scar & grn	2.50	2.25
a.		Bars inverted	10.00	10.00
C5	A115	40c on 50c org brn	.85	.55
C6	A116	50c on 1col grn & bl vio (R)	15.00	10.00
		Nos. C1-C6 (5)	25.45	18.90

Back of No. C7

No. C7

No. C9

No. C10

Second Printing.
15c on 10c: "15 QUINCE 15" measures 20½mm.
20c: Has not the albino impression on the back of the stamp.
25c on 35c: Original value cancelled by two bars of equal length.
50c on 1col: Surcharge in carmine rose.

1930, Jan. 10

C7	A112	20c deep green	1.00	1.00
C8	A111	15c on 10c org	.75	.75
a.		"ATLANT CO"	37.50	35.00
b.		Double surcharge	20.00	
c.		As "a," double surcharge	75.00	
d.		Pair, one without surcharge	*175.00*	
C9	A114	25c on 35c scar & grn	.90	.90
C10	A116	50c on 1col grn & bl vio (C)	2.00	2.00
a.		Without bars over "UN COLON"	4.50	
b.		As "a," without block over "1"	4.50	
		Nos. C7-C10 (4)	4.65	4.65

Numerous wrong font and defective letters exist in both printings of the surcharges.
No. C10 with black surcharge is bogus.

Mail Plane over San Salvador AP1

1930, Sept. 15 Engr. Perf. 12½

C11	AP1	15c deep red	.40	.25
C12	AP1	20c emerald	.40	.25
C13	AP1	25c brown violet	.40	.25
C14	AP1	40c ultra	.60	.25
		Nos. C11-C14 (4)	1.80	1.00

Simón Bolivar — AP2

1930, Dec. 17 Litho. Perf. 11½

C15	AP2	15c deep red	6.00	5.00
a.		"15" double	82.50	
C16	AP2	20c emerald	6.00	5.00
C17	AP2	25c brown violet	6.00	5.00
a.		Vert. pair, imperf. btwn.	175.00	
b.		Imperf., pair		
C18	AP2	40c dp ultra	6.00	5.00
		Nos. C15-C18 (4)	24.00	20.00

Centenary of death of Simón Bolivar. Counterfeits of Nos. C15-C18 exist.

No. 504 Overprinted in Red

1931, June 29 Engr. Perf. 14

C19	A116	1col green & vio	4.50	3.00

Tower of La Merced Church — AP3

1931, Nov. 5 Litho. Perf. 11½

C20	AP3	15c dark red	4.50	3.25
a.		Imperf., pair	50.00	
C21	AP3	20c blue green	4.50	3.25
C22	AP3	25c dull violet	4.50	3.25
a.		Vert. pair, imperf. btwn.	110.00	
C23	AP3	40c ultra	4.50	3.25
a.		Imperf., pair	60.00	
		Nos. C20-C23 (4)	18.00	13.00

120th anniv. of the 1st movement toward the political independence of El Salvador. In the tower of La Merced Church (AP3) hangs the bell which José Matias Delgado-called the Father of his Country-rang to initiate the movement for liberty.

José Matias Delgado — AP4

1932, Nov. 12 Wmk. 271 Perf. 12½

C24	AP4	15c dull red & vio	1.25	1.10
C25	AP4	20c blue grn & bl	1.60	1.40
C26	AP4	25c dull vio & brn	1.60	1.40
C27	AP4	40c ultra & grn	1.90	1.75
		Nos. C24-C27 (4)	6.35	5.65

1st centenary of the death of Father José Matías Delgado, who is known as the Father of El Salvadoran Political Emancipation.

Nos. C24-C27 show cheek without shading in the 72nd stamp of each sheet.

Airplane and Caravels of Columbus — AP5

1933, Oct. 12 Wmk. 240 *Perf. 13*

C28 AP5 15c red orange 2.00 1.75
C29 AP5 20c blue green 3.00 2.50
C30 AP5 25c lilac 3.00 2.50
C31 AP5 40c ultra 3.00 2.50
C32 AP5 1col black 3.00 2.50
Nos. C28-C32 (5) 14.00 11.75

Saling of Chistopher Columbus from Palos, Spain, for the New World, 441st anniv.

Police Barracks Type

1934, Dec. 16 *Perf. 12½*

C33 A123 25c lilac .60 .25
C34 A123 30c brown .95 .45
a. Imperf., pair 80.00
C35 A123 1col black 2.40 1.00
Nos. C33-C35 (3) 3.95 1.70

Runner AP7

1935, Mar. 16 Engr. Unwmk.

C36 AP7 15c carmine 3.75 2.25
C37 AP7 25c violet 3.75 2.25
C38 AP7 30c brown 3.00 1.75
C39 AP7 55c blue 20.00 8.50
C40 AP7 1col black 13.00 8.00
Nos. C36-C40 (5) 43.50 22.75

Third Central American Games.
For overprints and surcharge see Nos. C41-C45, C53.

Nos. C36-C40 Overprinted in Black

1935, June 27

C41 AP7 15c carmine 3.00 1.40
C42 AP7 25c violet 3.00 1.40
C43 AP7 30c brown 3.00 1.40
C44 AP7 55c blue 17.00 14.00
C45 AP7 1col black 7.50 6.00
Nos. C41-C45 (5) 33.50 24.20

Flag of El Salvador Type

1935, Oct. 26 Litho. Wmk. 240

C46 A125 30c black brown .40 .35

Tree of San Vicente Type

1935, Dec. 26 *Perf. 12½*

Numerals in Black, Tree in Yellow Green

C47 A126 10c orange .75 .60
C48 A126 15c brown .75 .60
C49 A126 20c dk blue grn .75 .60
C50 A126 25c dark purple .75 .60
C51 A126 30c black brown .75 .60
Nos. C47-C51 (5) 3.75 3.00

Tercentenary of San Vicente.

No. 565 Overprinted in Red

1937 Engr. Unwmk.

C52 A133 15c dk olive bis .35 .25
a. Double overprint 25.00

No. C44 Surcharged in Red

C53 AP7 30c on 55c blue 1.50 .60

Panchimalco Church — AP10

1937, Dec. 3 Engr. *Perf. 12*

C54 AP10 15c orange yel .30 .25
C55 AP10 20c green .30 .25
C56 AP10 25c violet .30 .25
C57 AP10 30c brown .30 .25
C58 AP10 40c blue .30 .25
C59 AP10 1col black 1.40 .45
C60 AP10 5col rose carmine 4.50 3.25
Nos. C54-C60 (7) 7.40 4.95

US Constitution Type of Regular Issue

1938, Apr. 22 Engr. & Litho.

C61 A136 30c multicolored .95 .70

José Simeón Cañas y Villacorta — AP12

1938, Aug. 18 Engr.

C62 AP12 15c orange 1.40 1.25
C63 AP12 20c brt green 1.75 1.25
C64 AP12 30c redsh brown 1.90 1.25
C65 AP12 1col black 6.00 4.50
Nos. C62-C65 (4) 11.05 8.25

José Simeón Cañas y Villacorta (1767-1838), liberator of slaves in Central America.

Golden Gate Bridge, San Francisco Bay — AP13

1939, Apr. 14 *Perf. 12½*

C66 AP13 15c dull yel & blk .45 .25
C67 AP13 30c dk brown & blk .45 .25
C68 AP13 40c dk blue & blk .60 .45
Nos. C66-C68 (3) 1.50 .95

Golden Gate Intl. Exposition, San Francisco.
For surcharges see Nos. C86-C91 in Scott Standard catalogue, Vol. 5.

Sir Rowland Hill Type

1940, Mar. 1 Engr.

C69 A146 30c dk brn, buff & blk 8.00 2.50
C70 A146 80c org red & blk 22.50 17.50

Centenary of the postage stamp. Covers postmarked Feb. 29 were predated. Actual first day was Mar. 1.

Map of the Americas, Figure of Peace, Plane — AP15

1940, May 22 *Perf. 12*

C71 AP15 30c brown & blue .45 .25
C72 AP15 80c dk rose & blk .85 .55

Pan American Union, 50th anniversary.

Coffee Tree in Bloom — AP16

Coffee Tree with Ripe Berries — AP17

1940, Nov. 27

C73 AP16 15c yellow orange 1.60 .45
C74 AP16 20c deep green 2.25 .45
C75 AP16 25c dark violet 2.50 .55
C76 AP17 30c copper brown 3.00 .25
C77 AP17 1col black 9.00 .70
Nos. C73-C77 (5) 18.35 2.40

REGISTRATION STAMPS

Gen. Rafael Antonio Gutiérrez — R1

1897 Engr. Wmk. 117 *Perf. 12*

F1 R1 10c dark blue 125.00
F2 R1 10c brown lake .25

Unwmk.

F3 R1 10c dark blue .25
F4 R1 10c brown lake .25

Nos. F1 and F3 were probably not placed in use without the overprint "FRANQUEO OFICIAL" (Nos. O127-O128).

The reprints are on thick unwatermarked paper. Value, set of 2, 16c.

ACKNOWLEDGMENT OF RECEIPT STAMPS

AR1

1897 Engr. Wmk. 117 *Perf. 12*

H1 AR1 5c dark green .25

Unwmk.

H2 AR1 5c dark green .25

No. H2 has been reprinted on thick paper. Value 20c.

POSTAGE DUE STAMPS

D1

1895 Unwmk. Engr. *Perf. 12*

J1 D1 1c olive green .40 —
J2 D1 2c olive green .40 —
J3 D1 3c olive green .40 —
J4 D1 5c olive green .40 —
J5 D1 10c olive green .40 —
J6 D1 15c olive green .40 —
J7 D1 25c olive green .40 —
J8 D1 50c olive green .90 —
Nos. J1-J8 (8) 3.70

See Nos. J9-J56. For overprints see Nos. J57-J64, O186-O214.

1896 Wmk. 117

J9 D1 1c red .60 —
J10 D1 2c red .60 —
J11 D1 3c red .90 —
J12 D1 5c red 1.10 —
J13 D1 10c red 1.10 —
J14 D1 15c red 1.25 —
J15 D1 25c red 1.25 —
J16 D1 50c red 1.25 —
Nos. J9-J16 (8) 8.05

Unwmk.

J17 D1 1c red .40 —
J18 D1 2c red .40 —
J19 D1 3c red .40 —
J20 D1 5c red .40 —
J21 D1 10c red .40 —
J22 D1 15c red .50 —
J23 D1 25c red .50 —
J24 D1 50c red .50 —
Nos. J17-J24 (8) 3.50

Nos. J17-J24 exist imperforate.

1897

J25 D1 1c deep blue .40 —
J26 D1 2c deep blue .40 —
J27 D1 3c deep blue .40 —
J28 D1 5c deep blue .40 —
J29 D1 10c deep blue .50 —
J30 D1 15c deep blue .50 —
J31 D1 25c deep blue .40 —
J32 D1 50c deep blue .40 —
Nos. J25-J32 (8) 3.40

1898

J33 D1 1c violet 3.00
J34 D1 2c violet 1.00
J35 D1 3c violet 1.00
J36 D1 5c violet 5.00
J37 D1 10c violet 1.00
J38 D1 15c violet 1.00
J39 D1 25c violet 1.00
J40 D1 50c violet 1.00
Nos. J33-J40 (8) 14.00

Reprints of Nos. J1 to J40 are on thick paper, often in the wrong shades and usually with the impression somewhat blurred. Value, set of 40, $2, watermarked or unwatermarked.

1899 Wmk. 117 Sideways

J41 D1 1c orange .40
J42 D1 2c orange .40
J43 D1 3c orange .40
J44 D1 5c orange .40
J45 D1 10c orange .40
J46 D1 15c orange .40
J47 D1 25c orange .40
J48 D1 50c orange .40
Nos. J41-J48 (8) 3.20

Unwmk.

Thick Porous Paper

J49 D1 1c orange .40
J50 D1 2c orange .40
J51 D1 3c orange .40
J52 D1 5c orange .40
J53 D1 10c orange .40
J54 D1 15c orange .40

J55 D1 25c orange .40
J56 D1 50c orange .40
Nos. J49-J56 (8) 3.20

Nos. J41-J56 were probably not put in use without the wheel overprint.

Nos. J49-J56 Overprinted in Black

1900

J57 D1 1c orange 2.00
J58 D1 2c orange 2.00
J59 D1 3c orange 2.00
J60 D1 5c orange 3.00
J61 D1 10c orange 4.00
J62 D1 15c orange 4.00
J63 D1 25c orange 5.00
J64 D1 50c orange 6.00
Nos. J57-J64 (8) 28.00

See note after No. 198A.

Morazán Monument — D2

Perf. 14, 14½

1903 Engr. Wmk. 173

J65 D2 1c yellow green 1.75 1.25
J66 D2 2c carmine 2.75 1.75
J67 D2 3c orange 2.75 1.75
J68 D2 5c dark blue 2.75 1.75
J69 D2 10c dull violet 2.75 1.75
J70 D2 25c blue green 2.75 1.75
Nos. J65-J70 (6) 15.50 10.00

Nos. 355, 356, 358 and 360 Overprinted

1908 Unwmk. *Perf. 11½*

J71 A66 1c green & blk .80 .70
J72 A66 2c red & blk .60 .25
J73 A66 5c blue & blk 1.50 1.00
J74 A66 10c violet & blk 2.25 2.00

Same Overprint on No. O275

J75 O3 3c yellow & blk 1.50 1.25
Nos. J71-J75 (5) 6.65 5.20

Nos. 355-358, 360 Overprinted

J76 A66 1c green & blk .50 .50
J77 A66 2c red & blk .60 .60
J78 A66 3c yellow & blk .70 .70
J79 A66 5c blue & blk 1.00 1.00
J80 A66 10c violet & blk 2.00 2.00
Nos. J76-J80 (5) 4.80 4.80

It is now believed that stamps of type A66, on paper with Honeycomb watermark, do not exist with genuine overprints of the types used for Nos. J71-J80.

Pres. Fernando Figueroa — D3

1910 Engr. Wmk. 172

J81 D3 1c sepia & blk .30 .30
J82 D3 2c dk grn & blk .30 .30
J83 D3 3c orange & blk .30 .30
J84 D3 4c scarlet & blk .30 .30
J85 D3 5c purple & blk .30 .30
J86 D3 12c deep blue & blk .30 .30
J87 D3 24c brown red & blk .30 .30
Nos. J81-J87 (7) 2.10 2.10

OFFICIAL STAMPS

Nos. 134-157O Overprinted — a

Type a

1896 Unwmk. *Perf. 12*

O1 A45 1c blue .25
O2 A45 2c dk brown .25
a. Double overprint
O3 A45 3c blue grn 1.00
O4 A45 5c brown ol .25
O5 A45 10c yellow .25
O6 A45 12c dk blue .30
O7 A45 15c blue vio .25
O8 A45 20c magenta 1.00
O9 A45 24c vermilion .25
O10 A45 30c orange 1.00
O11 A45 50c black brn .45
O12 A45 1p rose lake .30
Nos. O1-O12 (12) 5.55

Nos. O1-O12 were not issued.
The 1c has been reprinted on thick unwatermarked paper. Value 25c.

Wmk. 117

O13 A46 1c emerald 4.75 3.00
O14 A47 2c lake 4.75 3.50
O15 A48 3c yellow brn 6.00 4.00
a. Inverted overprint — —
O16 A49 5c dp blue 5.00 5.00
O17 A50 10c brown 7.00 3.75
a. Inverted overprint —
O18 A51 12c slate 10.50 8.00
O19 A52 15c blue grn 12.50 8.75
O20 A53 20c car rose 12.50 8.00
a. Inverted overprint
O21 A54 24c violet 12.50 9.00
O22 A55 30c dp green 15.00 12.50
O23 A56 50c orange 25.00 17.00
O24 A57 100c dk blue 40.00 25.00
Nos. O13-O24 (12) 155.50 107.50

Unwmk.

O25 A46 1c emerald 2.50 *3.50*
a. Double overprint — —
O26 A47 2c lake 2.75 *175.00*
O27 A48 3c yellow brn 3.00 *2.50*
O28 A49 5c dp blue 3.00 .90
O29 A50 10c brown 2.50 2.50
a. Inverted overprint
O30 A51 12c slate 10.00 7.00
O31 A52 15c blue grn 12.00 7.75
O32 A53 20c car rose 20.00 11.00
a. Inverted overprint
O33 A54 24c violet 20.00 11.00
O34 A55 30c dp green — —
O35 A56 50c orange — —
O36 A57 100c dk blue — —
Nos. O25-O36 (12) 75.75 221.15

All values have been reprinted. Value 25c each.

Nos. 134-145 Handstamped in Black or Violet — b

1896 Type b

O37 A45 1c blue 11.00
O38 A45 2c dk brown 11.00
O39 A45 3c blue green 11.00
O40 A45 5c brown olive 11.00
O41 A45 10c yellow 13.00
O42 A45 12c dk blue 16.00
O43 A45 15c blue violet 16.00
O44 A45 20c magenta 16.00
O45 A45 24c vermilion 16.00
O46 A45 30c orange 16.00
O47 A45 50c black brown 22.50
O48 A45 1p rose lake 22.50
Nos. O37-O48 (12) 182.00

Reprints of the 1c and 2c on thick paper exist with this handstamp. Value, 25c each.
The legitimacy of the "De Officio" handstamp has been questioned. The editors would like to see evidence regarding the authorized use of this handstamp.

Forged overprints exist of Nos. O37-O76, O103-O126 and of the higher valued stamps of O141-O214.

Nos. 146-157F, 157I-157O, 158D Handstamped Type b in Black or Violet

1896 Wmk. 117

O49 A46 1c emerald 9.00
O50 A47 2c lake 9.00
O51 A48 3c yellow brn 9.00
O52 A49 5c deep blue 9.00
O53 A50 10c brown 9.00
O54 A51 12c slate 16.00
O55 A52 15c blue green 16.00
O56 A53 20c carmine rose 16.00
O57 A54 24c violet 16.00
O58 A55 30c deep green 16.00
O59 A56 50c orange 16.00
O60 A57 100c dark blue 16.00
Nos. O49-O60 (12) 157.00

Unwmk.

O61 A46 1c emerald 9.00
O62 A47 2c lake 9.00
O63 A48 3c yellow brn 9.00
O64 A49 5c deep blue 9.00
O65 A50 10c brown 13.50
O66 A52 15c blue green 16.00
O67 A58 15c on 24c vio 11.50
O68 A53 20c carmine rose 16.00
O69 A54 24c violet 16.00
O70 A55 30c deep green 16.00
O71 A56 50c orange 19.00
O72 A57 100c dark blue 19.00
Nos. O61-O72 (12) 163.00

Nos. 175-176 Overprinted Type a in Black

1897

O73 A59 1c bl, gold, rose & grn .30
O74 A59 5c rose, gold, bl & grn .30

These stamps were probably not officially issued.

Nos. 175-176 Handstamped Type b in Black or Violet

1900

O75 A59 1c bl, gold, rose & grn 22.50
O76 A59 5c rose, gold, bl & grn 22.50

Nos. 159-170L Overprinted Type a in Black

1897 Wmk. 117

O79 A46 1c scarlet 8.00 8.00
O80 A47 2c yellow green 8.00 8.00
O81 A48 3c bister brown 7.00 7.00
O82 A49 5c orange 7.00 7.00
O83 A50 10c blue green 9.00 9.00
O84 A51 12c blue 20.00 20.00
O85 A52 15c black 40.00 40.00
O86 A53 20c slate 20.00 20.00
O87 A54 24c yellow 40.00 40.00
a. Inverted overprint
O88 A55 30c rose 40.00 40.00
O89 A56 50c violet 40.00 40.00
O90 A57 100c brown lake 100.00 100.00
Nos. O79-O90 (12) 339.00

Unwmk.

O91 A46 1c scarlet 5.00 5.00
O92 A47 2c yellow green 3.00 3.00
O93 A48 3c bister brown 2.00 2.00
O94 A49 5c orange 3.00 3.00
O95 A50 10c blue green 10.00 10.00
O96 A51 12c blue 3.00 3.00
O97 A52 15c black 30.00 30.00
O98 A53 20c slate 20.00 20.00
O99 A54 24c yellow 30.00 30.00
O100 A55 30c rose 30.00 30.00
O101 A56 50c violet 20.00 20.00
O102 A57 100c brown lake 50.00 50.00
Nos. O91-O102 (12) 206.00

All values have been reprinted. Value 25c each.

Nos. 159-170L Handstamped Type b in Violet or Black

1897 Wmk. 117

O103 A46 1c scarlet 7.50
O104 A47 2c yellow green 7.50
O105 A48 3c bister brown 7.50
O106 A49 5c orange 7.50
O107 A50 10c blue green 8.75
O108 A51 12c blue
O109 A52 15c black
O110 A53 20c slate 15.00
O111 A54 24c yellow 17.50
O112 A55 30c rose
O113 A56 50c violet
O114 A57 100c brown lake

Unwmk.

O115 A46 1c scarlet 7.50
O116 A47 2c yellow grn 7.50
O117 A48 3c bister brn 7.50
O118 A49 5c orange 7.50
O119 A50 10c blue green 7.50
O120 A51 12c blue
O121 A52 15c black
O122 A53 20c slate
O123 A54 24c yellow
O124 A55 30c rose 15.00
O125 A56 50c violet
O126 A57 100c brown lake 17.50

Reprints of the 1 and 15c on thick watermarked paper and the 12, 30, 50 and 100c on thick unwatermarked paper are known with this overprint. Value, 25c each.

Nos. F1, F3 Overprinted Type a in Red

Wmk. 117

O127 R1 10c dark blue .30

Unwmk.

O128 R1 10c dark blue .30

The reprints are on thick paper. Value 15c.
Originals of the 10c brown lake Registration Stamp and the 5c Acknowledgment of Receipt stamp are believed not to have been issued with the "FRANQUEO OFICIAL" overprint. They are believed to exist only as reprints.

Nos. 177-188 Overprinted Type a

1898 Wmk. 117

O129 A60 1c orange ver 4.50 4.50
O130 A60 2c rose 4.50 4.50
O131 A60 3c pale yel grn 4.00 4.00
O132 A60 5c blue green 4.00 4.00
O133 A60 10c gray blue 15.00 15.00
O134 A60 12c violet 17.00 17.00
O135 A60 13c brown lake 17.00 17.00
O136 A60 20c deep blue 19.00 19.00
O137 A60 24c ultra 15.00 15.00
O138 A60 26c bister brn 20.00 20.00
O139 A60 50c orange 20.00 20.00
O140 A60 1p yellow 50.00 50.00
Nos. O129-O140 (12) 190.00 190.00

Reprints of the above set are on thick paper. Value, 25c each.

No. 177 Handstamped Type b in Violet

O141 A60 1c orange ver 35.00 —

No. O141 with Additional Overprint Type c in Black

c

Type "c" is called the "wheel" overprint.

O142 A60 1c orange ver — —

Counterfeits exist of the "wheel" overprint.

Nos. 204-205, 207 and 209 Overprinted

1899 Unwmk.

O143 A61 12c dark green — 50.00
O144 A61 13c deep rose 50.00 —
O145 A61 26c carmine rose 50.00 —
O146 A61 100c violet 100.00 —

Nos. O143-O144 Punched With Twelve Small Holes

O147 A61 12c dark green
O148 A61 13c deep rose

Official stamps punched with twelve small holes were issued and used for ordinary postage.

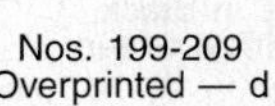

Nos. 199-209 Overprinted — d

1899 Blue Overprint

O149 A61 1c brown .30
O150 A61 2c gray green .30
O151 A61 3c blue .30
O152 A61 5c brown orange .30
O153 A61 10c chocolate .30
O154 A61 13c deep rose .30
O155 A61 26c carmine rose .30
O156 A61 50c orange red .30
O157 A61 100c violet .30

Black Overprint

O158 A61 3c blue .30
O159 A61 12c dark green .30
O160 A61 24c lt blue .30
Nos. O149-O160 (12) 3.60

Nos. O149-O160 were probably not placed in use.

With Additional Overprint Type c in Black

O161 A61 1c brown .60 .60
O162 A61 2c gray green 1.10 1.10
O163 A61 3c blue .60 .60
O164 A61 5c brown org .60 .60
O165 A61 10c chocolate .75 .75
O166 A61 12c dark green — —
O167 A61 13c deep rose 1.50 1.50
O168 A61 24c lt blue 30.00 30.00
O169 A61 26c carmine rose .75 .75
O170 A61 50c orange red 1.50 1.50
O171 A61 100c violet 1.50 1.50
Nos. O161-O165,O167-O171 (10) 38.90 38.90

Nos. O149-O155, O159-O160 Punched With Twelve Small Holes

Blue Overprint

O172 A61 1c brown 5.00 1.00
O173 A61 2c gray green 3.25 5.00
O174 A61 3c blue 8.00 3.75
O175 A61 5c brown org 10.00 3.00
O176 A61 10c chocolate 15.00 5.00
O177 A61 13c deep rose 7.50 7.00
O177A A61 24c lt blue
O178 A61 26c car rose 100.00 35.00

Black Overprint

O179 A61 12c dark green 6.00 4.50
Nos. O172-O177,O178-O179 (8) 154.75 64.25

It is stated that Nos. O172-O214 inclusive were issued for ordinary postage and not for use as Official stamps.

Nos. O161-O167, O169 Punched With Twelve Small Holes

O180 A61 1c brown 1.25 1.10
O180A A61 2c gray green
O181 A61 3c blue
O182 A61 5c brown orange 1.25
O182A A61 10c chocolate
O182B A61 12c dark green
O183 A61 13c deep rose 4.00 *5.00*
O184 A61 26c carmine rose

No. 209 Ovptd. Types a and e in Black

e

O185 A61 100c violet

Nos. J49-J56 Overprinted in Black

1900

O186 D1 1c orange 27.50
O187 D1 2c orange 27.50
O188 D1 3c orange 27.50
O189 D1 5c orange 27.50
O190 D1 10c orange 27.50
O191 D1 15c orange 62.50
O192 D1 25c orange 62.50
O193 D1 50c orange 62.50
Nos. O186-O193 (8) 325.00

Nos. O186-O189, O191-O193 Overprinted Type c in Black

O194 D1 1c orange *25.00*
O195 D1 2c orange *25.00*
O196 D1 3c orange *25.00*
O197 D1 5c orange *25.00*
O198 D1 15c orange 16.00 *25.00*
O199 D1 25c orange 19.00 *25.00*
O200 D1 50c orange 160.00 —

Nos. O186-O189 Punched With Twelve Small Holes

O201 D1 1c orange 45.00
O202 D1 2c orange 45.00
O203 D1 3c orange 45.00
O204 D1 5c orange 45.00
Nos. O201-O204 (4) 180.00

Nos. O201-O204 Overprinted Type c in Black

O205 D1 1c orange 9.00 6.50
O206 D1 2c orange 6.50
O207 D1 3c orange 6.50
O208 D1 5c orange 20.00 6.50

Overprinted Type a in Violet and Type c in Black

O209 D1 2c orange *25.00*
a. Inverted overprint *25.00*
O210 D1 3c orange *25.00*
O211 D1 10c orange 3.00

Nos. O186-O188 Handstamped Type e in Violet

O212 D1 1c orange 9.00 7.50
O213 D1 2c orange 9.00 7.50
O214 D1 3c orange 9.00 9.00
Nos. O212-O214 (3) 27.00 24.00

See note after No. O48.

Type of Regular Issue of 1900 Overprinted Type a in Black

O223 A63 1c lt green 22.50 —
a. Inverted overprint
O224 A63 2c rose 27.50 —
a. Inverted overprint
O225 A63 3c gray black 17.50 —
a. Overprint vertical
O226 A63 5c blue 17.50 —
O227 A63 10c blue 45.00 —
a. Inverted overprint
O228 A63 12c yellow grn 45.00 —
O229 A63 13c yellow brn 45.00 —
O230 A63 24c gray black 32.50 —
O231 A63 26c yellow brn 30.00 —
a. Inverted overprint
O232 A63 50c dull rose
a. Inverted overprint
Nos. O223-O231 (9) 282.50

Nos. O223-O224, O231-O232 Overprinted in Violet — f

O233 A63 1c lt green 4.75 4.00
O234 A63 2c rose 25.00
a. "FRANQUEO OFICIAL" invtd.
O235 A63 26c yellow brown .50 .50
O236 A63 50c dull rose .75 .55

Nos. O223, O225-O228, O232 Overprinted in Black — g

O237 A63 1c lt green 5.00 5.00
O238 A63 3c gray black
O239 A63 5c blue 40.00
O240 A63 10c blue
O241 A63 12c yellow green

Violet Overprint

O242 A63 50c dull rose 10.00

The shield overprinted on No. O242 is of the type on No. O212.

O1

1903 Wmk. 173 *Perf. 14, 14½*

O243 O1 1c yellow green .45 .25
O244 O1 2c carmine .45 .25
O245 O1 3c orange 5.00 .85
O246 O1 5c dark blue 5.00 .25
O247 O1 10c dull violet .70 .35
O248 O1 13c red brown .70 .35
O249 O1 15c yellow brown 5.00 1.75
O250 O1 24c scarlet .45 .35
O251 O1 50c bister .70 .35
O252 O1 100c grnsh blue .70 .75
Nos. O243-O252 (10) 19.15 5.50

For surcharges see Nos. O254-O257.

No. 285 Handstamped Type b in Black

1904

O253 A64 3c orange 35.00

Nos. O246-O248 Surcharged in Black

1905

O254 O1 2c on 5c dark blue 6.50 5.50
O255 O1 3c on 5c dark blue
a. Double surcharge
O256 O1 3c on 10c dl vio 18.00 12.00
O257 O1 3c on 13c red brn 1.75 1.40

A 2c surcharge of this type exists on No. O247.

No. O225 Overprinted in Blue

a

b

1905 Unwmk.

O258 A63(a) 3c gray black 4.00 3.50
O259 A63(b) 3c gray black 3.50 3.00

Nos. O224-O225 Overprinted in Blue

c

d

1906

O260 A63(c) 2c rose 22.50 20.00
O261 A63(c) 3c gray black 2.50 2.00
a. Overprint "1906" in blk
O262 A63(d) 3c gray black 2.75 2.50
Nos. O260-O262 (3) 27.75 24.50

Escalón — O2

1906 Engr. *Perf. 11½*

O263 O2 1c green & blk .40 .25
O264 O2 2c carmine & blk .40 .25
O265 O2 3c yellow & blk .40 .25
O266 O2 5c blue & blk .40 *.75*
O267 O2 10c violet & blk .40 .25
O268 O2 13c dk brown & blk .40 .25
O269 O2 15c red org & blk .50 .25
O270 O2 24c carmine & blk .60 *.35*
O271 O2 50c orange & blk .60 *1.50*
O272 O2 100c dk blue & blk .70 *4.50*
Nos. O263-O272 (10) 4.80 *8.60*

The centers of these stamps are also found in blue black.

Nos. O263 to O272 have been reprinted, perforated 11.8. Value, set of 10, $2.50.

National Palace — O3

1908

O273 O3 1c green & blk .25 .25
O274 O3 2c red & blk .25 .25
O275 O3 3c yellow & blk .25 .25
O276 O3 5c blue & blk .25 .25
O277 O3 10c violet & blk .25 .25
O278 O3 13c violet & blk .25 .25
O279 O3 15c pale brn & blk .25 .25
O280 O3 24c rose & blk .25 .25
O281 O3 50c yellow & blk .25 .25
O282 O3 100c turq blue & blk .35 .35
Nos. O273-O282 (10) 2.60 2.60

For overprints see Nos. 441-442, 445-449, J75, O283-O292, O323-O328.

Nos. O273-O282 Overprinted Type g in Black

O283 O3 1c green & blk 3.00
O284 O3 2c red & blk 4.00
O285 O3 3c yellow & blk 4.00
O286 O3 5c blue & blk 5.00
O287 O3 10c violet & blk 5.00
O288 O3 13c violet & blk 6.00
O289 O3 15c pale brn & blk 6.00
O290 O3 24c rose & blk 8.00
O291 O3 50c yellow & blk 9.00
O292 O3 100c turq & blk 10.00
Nos. O283-O292 (10) 60.00

Pres. Figueroa — O4

1910 Engr. Wmk. 172

O293 O4 2c dk green & blk .30 .25
O294 O4 3c orange & blk .30 .25
O295 O4 4c scarlet & blk .30 .25
a. 4c carmine & black
O296 O4 5c purple & blk .30 .25
O297 O4 6c scarlet & blk .30 .25
O298 O4 10c purple & blk .30 .25
O299 O4 12c dp blue & blk .30 .25
O300 O4 17c olive grn & blk .30 .25
O301 O4 19c brn red & blk .30 .25
O302 O4 29c choc & blk .30 .25
O303 O4 50c yellow & blk .30 .25
O304 O4 100c turq & blk .30 .25
Nos. O293-O304 (12) 3.60 3.00

Regular Issue, Type A63, Overprinted or Surcharged

a

b

c

1911 Unwmk.

O305 A63(a) 1c lt green .25 .25
O306 A63(b) 3c on 13c yel brn .25 .25
O307 A63(b) 5c on 10c dp bl .25 .25
O308 A63(a) 10c deep blue .25 .25
O309 A63(a) 12c lt green .25 .25
O310 A63(a) 13c yellow brn .25 .25
O311 A63(b) 50c on 10c dp bl .25 .25
O312 A63(c) 1col on 13c yel brn .25 .25
Nos. O305-O312 (8) 2.00 2.00

O5

1914 Typo. *Perf. 12*

Background in Green, Shield and "Provisional" in Black

O313	O5	2c yellow brn	.50	.25
O314	O5	3c yellow	.50	.25
O315	O5	5c dark blue	.50	.25
O316	O5	10c red	.50	.25
O317	O5	12c green	.50	.25
O318	O5	17c violet	.50	.25
O319	O5	50c brown	.50	.25
O320	O5	100c dull rose	.50	.25
		Nos. O313-O320 (8)	4.00	2.00

Stamps of this issue are known imperforate or with parts of the design omitted or misplaced. These varieties were not regularly issued.

O6

1914 Typo.

O321	O6	2c blue green	.50	.25
O322	O6	3c orange	.50	.25

Type of Official Stamps of 1908 With Two Overprints

1915

O323	O3	1c gray green	1.00	.60
a.		"1915" double		
b.		"OFICIAL" inverted		
O324	O3	2c red	1.00	.60
O325	O3	5c ultra	.35	*.70*
O326	O3	10c yellow	.35	*.60*
a.		Date omitted		
O327	O3	50c violet	.90	*1.50*
O328	O3	100c black brown	1.90	*3.25*
		Nos. O323-O328 (6)	5.50	7.25

Same Overprint on #414, 417, 429

O329	A66	1c gray green	10.00	1.60
O330	A66	6c pale blue	1.00	.45
a.		6c ultramarine		
O331	A66	12c brown	1.00	.75
		Nos. O329-O331 (3)	12.00	2.80

O323-O327, O329-O331 exist imperf.

Nos. O329-O331 exist with "OFICIAL" inverted and double. See note after No. 421.

Nos. 431-440 Overprinted in Blue or Red

1916

O332	A83	1c deep green	.45	.75
O333	A83	2c vermilion	1.60	1.60
O334	A83	5c dp blue (R)	1.25	1.60
O335	A83	6c gray vio (R)	.45	.75
O336	A83	10c black brown	.45	.75
O337	A83	12c violet	2.00	3.25
O338	A83	17c orange	.45	.75
O339	A83	25c dark brown	.45	.75
O340	A83	29c black (R)	.45	.75
O341	A83	50c slate (R)	2.00	.75
		Nos. O332-O341 (10)	9.55	11.70

Nos. 474-481 Overprinted

a

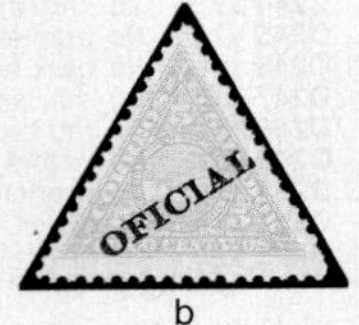

b

1921

O342	A94(a)	1c green	.25	.25
O343	A95(a)	2c black	.25	.25
a.		Inverted overprint		
O344	A96(b)	5c orange	.25	.25
O345	A97(a)	6c carmine rose	.25	.25
O346	A98(a)	10c deep blue	.30	.25
O347	A99(a)	25c olive green	.75	.35
O348	A100(a)	60c violet	1.00	.60
O349	A101(a)	1col black brown	1.10	.70
		Nos. O342-O349 (8)	4.15	2.90

Nos. 498 and 500 Overprinted in Black or Red

1925

O350	A109	5c olive black	.45	.25
O351	A111	10c orange (R)	.85	.25
a.		"ATLANT CO"	13.00	11.00

Inverted overprints exist.

Regular Issue of 1924-25 Overprinted in Black or Red

1927

O352	A106	1c red violet	.25	.25
O353	A107	2c dark red	.45	.25
O354	A109	5c olive blk (R)	.45	.25
O355	A110	6c dp blue (R)	5.25	4.50
O356	A111	10c orange	.50	.30
a.		"ATLANT CO"	22.50	19.00
O357	A116	1col grn & vio (R)	2.25	1.40
		Nos. O352-O357 (6)	9.15	6.95

Inverted overprints exist on 1c, 2c, 5c, 10c.

Regular Issue of 1924-25 Overprinted in Black

1932 *Perf. 12½*

O358	A106	1c deep violet	.25	.25
O359	A107	2c dark red	.45	.25
O360	A109	5c olive black	.25	.25
O361	A111	10c orange	.85	.35
a.		"ATLANT CO"	22.50	19.00
		Nos. O358-O361 (4)	1.80	1.10

PARCEL POST STAMPS

Mercury
PP1

1895 Unwmk. Engr. *Perf. 12*

Q1	PP1	5c brown orange	.45
Q2	PP1	10c dark blue	.45
Q3	PP1	15c red	.45
Q4	PP1	20c orange	.45
Q5	PP1	50c blue green	.45
		Nos. Q1-Q5 (5)	2.25

POSTAL TAX STAMPS

PT1

Overprinted "REVISADO" in Violet, Black or Red

1900-04 Typo. *Perf. 11½*

RA1	PT1	1c black
RA2	PT1	1c black, dated "1903"
RA3	PT1	1c black, dated "1904"

Use of these stamps was obligatory on all domestic letters. The funds raised were used to maintain the public schools.

Nos. 503, 501 Surcharged

1931 Unwmk. *Perf. 12½*

RA4	A115	1c on 50c org brn	.50	.40
a.		Double surcharge	5.00	5.00
RA5	A112	2c on 20c dp grn	.50	.40

Nos. 501, 503 Surcharged

RA6	A112	1c on 20c dp grn	.50	.40
RA7	A115	2c on 50c org brn	.50	.40
a.		Without period in "0.02"	3.00	

The use of these stamps was obligatory, in addition to the regular postage, on letters and other postal matter. The money obtained from their sale was to be used to erect a new post office in San Salvador.

SAMOA

sə-ˈmō-ə

(Western Samoa)

LOCATION — An archipelago in the South Pacific Ocean, east of Fiji

GOVT. — Monarchy and (partially) German possession

AREA — 1,130 sq. mi.

POP. — 39,000 (est. 1910)

CAPITAL — Apia

In 1861-99, Samoa was an independent kingdom under the influence of the US, to which the harbor of Pago Pago had been ceded, and that of Great Britain and Germany. In 1898 a disturbance arose, resulting in the withdrawal of Great Britain, and the partitioning of the islands between Germany and the US. Early in World War I the islands under German domination were occupied by New Zealand troops and in 1920 the League of Nations declared them a mandate to New Zealand.

12 Pence = 1 Shilling

20 Shillings = 1 Pound

100 Pfennig = 1 Mark (1900)

Catalogue values for unused stamps in this country are for Never Hinged items, beginning with Scott 191 in the regular postage section.

Watermarks

Wmk. 61 — N Z and Star Close Together

Wmk. 62 — N Z and Star Wide Apart

On watermark 61 the margins of the sheets are watermarked "NEW ZEALAND POSTAGE" and parts of the double-lined letters of these words are frequently found on the stamps. It occasionally happens that a stamp shows no watermark whatever.

Wmk. 253 — Multiple N Z and Star

Issues of the Kingdom

A1

Type I

Type II

Type III

Type IV

Type I

Line above "X" is usually unbroken. Dots over "SAMOA" are uniform and evenly spaced. Upper right serif of "M" is horizontal.

Printed in sheets of 20 (5x4), imperf on outer edges. Only six stamps may be perforated all around. Eight stamps in each pane of the 1p have a stop after "PENNY."

1877 Litho. Unwmk. *Perf. 12½*

1c	A1	1p sky blue	300.00	*400.00*
3c	A1	3p vermilion	450.00	*250.00*
4b	A1	6p bright violet	300.00	*350.00*
4c	A1	6p pale lilac	400.00	350.00

No. 6a shows the line above "X" unbroken, but has the dot between "M" and "O" characteristic of type I.

Stamps were pen cancelled from October 1877 to March 1878, when the circular date stamp arrived.

Type II

Line above "X" is usually broken. Small dot near upper right serif of letter "M." Printed in sheets of 10 (5x2), imperf on outer edges, so that all stamps have at least one straight edge.

1878-79 *Perf. 12½*

1b A1 1p sky blue 150.00 *250.00*
3b A1 3p vermilion 400.00 *750.00*
4a A1 6p violet 900.00 *1,000.*
6 A1 1sh orange yellow 325.00 135.00
6a A1 1sh dull yellow 400.00 100.00
6b A1 1sh lemon yellow 400.00 100.00
6c A1 1sh gldn yel, Perf 11¾ ('79) 110.00 *260.00*
7a A1 2sh red brown 450.00 *750.00*
7b A1 2sh chocolate 450.00 *750.00*
8b A1 5sh gray green 4,000. 1,500.

Type III

Line above "X" roughly retouched. Upper right serif of letter "M" bends down (joined to dot).

Printed in sheets of 10 (5x2), except the 1p, which was printed in sheets of 20 (5x4).

1879 *Perf. 12½*

1a A1 1p sky blue 260.00 125.00
3 A1 3p vermilion 550.00 300.00
4 A1 6p lilac 550.00 135.00
7 A1 2sh deep brown 370.00 *500.00*
7c A1 2sh chocolate 450.00 *500.00*
8 A1 5sh emerald green 1,875. 850.00
8c A1 5sh line above "X" not repaired (pos. 2/3) —

1879-82 *Perf. 11¾*

1 A1 1p blue 37.50 *1,000.*
1d A1 1p ultramarine 75.00
1e A1 1p deep blue 35.00
3a A1 3p scar ver, clean-cut perfs 120.00
3d A1 3p ver, rough perfs 65.00 —
4d A1 6p bright violet 40.00 *800.00*
4e A1 6p dull lilac 55.00 *100.00*
7d A1 2sh deep brown 275.00 —
8a A1 5sh yellow green 725.00
8d A1 5sh deep green 1,000.
8e A1 5sh line above "X" not repaired (pos. 2/3) —

Nos. 1-8e are found with either clean-cut or rough-cut perforations.

Only the 6p and 1sh denominations of the type III, perf 11¾ issue are known used.

Type IV

Speck of color on curved line below center of "M."

1880-82 *Perf. 11¾*

2 A1 2p lilac rose ('82) 25.00 —
5 A1 9p pale chestnut 80.00 *425.00*
5a A1 9p pale org brown 100.00 *800.00*

The 2p was never placed in use since the Samoa Express service was discontinued late in 1881.

Some examples of Nos. 1-8 appear with portions of the papermaker's watermark.

Imperforates of this issue are proofs.

Reprints are of type IV and nearly always perforated on all sides. They have a spot of color at the edge of the panel below the "M." This spot is not on any originals except the 2p, which may be distinguished by its color, and the 9p which may be distinguished by having a rough blind perf. 12.

Forgeries abound.

Covers: Covers with Nos. 1-8 are rare. Last known date is Sept. 24, 1881, although the service officially ended Aug. 31st.

Palms — A2

Three forms of watermark 62 are found on stamps of type A2:

1 — Wide "N Z" and wide star, 6mm apart (used 1886-87).

2 — Wide "N Z" and narrow star, 4mm apart (1890).

3 — Narrow "NZ" and narrow star, 7mm apart (1890-1900).

Wmk. 62, Type 1 (6mm spacing)

1886 **Typo.** *Perf. 12½*

9 A2 ½p purple brown 40.00 40.00
11 A2 1p yellow green 20.00 20.00
13 A2 2p brown orange 20.00 20.00
16 A2 4p blue 55.00 13.50
18 A2 1sh rose carmine 67.50 13.50
a. Diagonal half canceled in blue, on cover (Apr-June '95) 375.00
19 A2 2sh6p violet 50.00 *40.00*

No. 18e was authorized for use between April 24 and June, 1895, after stocks of other values were destroyed in a fire, and was canceled in blue. No. 18a was used to pay various rates, most commonly 2½p. Value is for examples paying this rate.

No. 18 was later bisected for sale to collectors. These stamps were canceled in black, and most were bisected vertically. Value on piece $7.50.

Wmk. 62, Type 1 (6mm spacing)

1887 *Perf. 12x11½*

9a A2 ½p purple brown 40.00 *100.00*
11a A2 1p yellow green 100.00 40.00
13a A2 2p yellow 40.00 *100.00*
16a A2 4p blue 100.00 100.00
17 A2 6p brown lake 20.00 20.00
18b A2 1sh rose carmine 100.00
19a A2 2sh6p violet 2,000.

Wmk. 62, Type 2 (4 mm spacing)

1890, May *Perf. 12x11½*

9b A2 ½p dp pur brown 100.00 40.00
11b A2 1p yellow green 20.00 20.00
13b A2 2p orange brown 40.00 10.00
16b A2 4p deep blue 100.00 10.00
17a A2 6p maroon 325.00 12.50
18c A2 1sh rose 200.00 20.00
19b A2 2sh6p bright violet 100.00 10.00

King Malietoa Laupepa — A3

Wmk. 62, Type 3 (7 mm spacing)

1890-92 *Perf. 12x11½*

9c A2 ½p purple brown 10.00 10.00
11c A2 1p green ('91) 20.00 10.00
d. 1p blue green 20.00 10.00
13c A2 2p orange 10.00 10.00
14 A3 2½p rose ('92) 80.00 6.00
16c A2 4p blue 100.00 20.00
17b A2 6p brown lake 40.00 10.00
18d A2 1sh rose 100.00 10.00
19c A2 2sh6p violet 100.00 10.00

Wmk. 62, Type 3 (7 mm spacing)

1891-92 *Perf. 12½*

13d A2 2p orange yellow 750.00
14a A3 2½p rose ('92) 10.00 *20.00*
16d A2 4p blue 750.00
17c A2 6p brown lake 3,000. 1,250.
18e A2 1sh rose 2,500. 1,500.
19d A2 2sh6p violet *2,500.*

1/2p and 1p values, perf 12½ with watermark 62 type 3, may exist. The editors would like to examine any documentation of certified examples.

Wmk. 62, Type 3 (7 mm spacing)

1895, May-1900 *Perf. 11*

9d A2 ½p purple brown 5.75 *2.10*
e. ½p deep purple brown ('00) 2.00 *100.00*
10 A2 ½p dl bl grn ('99) 4.00 *4.50*
11e A2 1p green 10.00 *20.00*
f. 1p bluish green ('97) 4.00 *2.00*
g. 1p deep green ('00) 2.00 *100.00*
12 A2 1p red brown 4.25 *20.00*
13e A2 2p yellow 40.00 40.00
f. 2p orange yellow ('96) 20.00 20.00
g. 2p bright yellow ('97) 16.00 *10.00*
h. 2p pale ocher ('97) 2.00 *20.00*
i. 2p brown ocher ('00) 2.00
14b A3 2½p rose 4.25 *10.50*
c. 2½p dp rose carmine ('00) 2.00 *100.00*
15 A3 2½p black, perf 10x11 ('96) 2.25 *3.25*
a. Perf 11 ('96) 150.00 100.00
b. Mixed perfs, 10 and 11 100.00 —
16e A2 4p blue 40.00 20.00
f. 4p deep blue ('00) 1.60 *52.50*
17d A2 6p brown lake 20.00 20.00
e. 6p maroon ('00) 2.00 *62.50*
18f A2 1sh rose 10.00 *20.00*
g. 1sh carmine ('00) 1.80 —
19e A2 2sh6p reddish lilac 10.00 20.00
f. 2sh6p purple ('97) 10.00 *20.00*
g. 2sh6p slate violet ('97) 40.00 —
h. 2sh6p deep purple ('98) 5.00 *10.00*
i. As "h," vert. pair, imperf. btw. 475.00

Watermark is inverted on No. 19d and reversed on No. 19g.

The 1900 printings are on a coarse paper.

For surcharges or overprints on stamps or types of design A2 see Nos. 20-22, 24-38.

Nos. 16b and 16c Handstamp Surcharged in Black or Red

a

b

c

1893 *Perf. 12x11½*

20 A2(a) 5p on 4p blue (#16c) 65.00 *100.00*
a. On 4p deep blue (#16b) 100.00 100.00
21 A2(b) 5p on 4p blue (#16c) 75.00 —
a. On 4p deep blue (#16b) 100.00 *110.00*
22 A2(c) 5p on 4p blue (#16c) (R) 42.50 *37.50*
a. On 4p deep blue (#16b) 47.50 *50.00*
Nos. 20-22 (3) 182.50 *137.50*

As the surcharges on Nos. 20-21 were handstamped in two steps, with bars of differing lengths, and on No. 22 in three steps. Various varieties exist.

Flag Design — A7

1894-95 **Typo.** *Perf. 11½x12*

23 A7 5p vermilion 35.00 7.50
a. Perf. 11 ('95) 70.00 15.00
b. As "a," deep red ('00) 5.00 *20.00*

Types of 1887-1895 Surcharged in Blue, Black, Red or Green

1½p, 2½p

R 3d.
3p

Handstamped Surcharges

1895 *Perf. 11*

24 A2 1½p on 2p org (Bl) 7.50 *10.00*
a. 1½p on 2p brn org, perf 12x11½ (Bl) 27.50 20.00
b. 1½p on 2p yellow, "2" ends with vertical stroke 5.00 *27.50*
c. As No. 24, pair, one without surcharge 650.00
25 A2 3p on 2p org (Bk) 10.00 *15.00*
a. 3p on 2p brn org, perf. 12x11½ (Bk) 60.00 25.00
b. 3p on 2p org yellow, narrow "R" (Bk) 6.00 *50.00*
c. Vert. pair, imperf. btwn. 650.00
d. As "b," pair, one without surcharge

Typographed Surcharges (#26 Handstamped)

1898-1900 *Perf. 11*

26 A2 2½p on 1sh rose (Bk), hstmpd. srch. 50.00 *50.00*
a. 2½p, typo surcharge 13.00 *15.00*
b. As "a," double surcharge 500.00 500.00
27 A2 2½p on 2sh6p vio (Bk) 13.00 *20.00*
28 A2 2½p on 1p bl grn (R) 1.75 *5.00*
a. Inverted surcharge 850.00 *425.00*
29 A2 2½p on 1sh rose car (R) 8.50 *20.00*
a. Double surcharge 400.00
30 A2 3p on 2p dp red org (G) 5.00 *130.00*
Nos. 26-30 (5) 78.25 *225.00*

No. 30 was a reissue, available for postage. The surcharge is not as tall as the 3p surcharge illustrated, which is the surcharge on No. 25. As Nos. 24-26 are handstamped, various varieties exist.

Stamps of 1886-99 Overprinted in Red or Blue

1899

31 A2 ½p dl bl grn (R) 3.50 *8.00*
32 A2 1p red brown (Bl) 4.25 *20.00*
33 A2 2p br orange (R) 2.50 *20.00*
a. 2p deep ocher 4.00 *20.00*
34 A2 4p blue (R) 1.00 *20.00*
35 A7 5p dp scarlet (Bl) 3.75 *20.00*
36 A2 6p maroon (Bl) 2.00 *20.00*
37 A2 1sh rose car (Bl) 2.00 *25.00*
38 A2 2sh6p mauve (R) 4.75 *40.00*
Nos. 31-38 (8) 23.75 *173.00*

In 1900 the Samoan islands were partitioned between the US and Germany. The part which became American has since used US stamps.

Issued under German Dominion

Stamps of Germany Overprinted

1900 **Unwmk.** *Perf. 13½x14½*

51 A9 3pf dark brown 11.00 *15.00*
Never hinged 32.50
On cover 82.50
52 A9 5pf green 14.00 *20.00*
Never hinged 45.00
On cover 82.50
53 A10 10pf carmine 11.00 *20.00*
Never hinged 25.00
On cover 65.00
54 A10 20pf ultra 21.00 *32.50*
Never hinged 57.50
On cover 125.00
55 A10 25pf orange 42.50 *85.00*
Never hinged 115.00
On cover 400.00
56 A10 50pf red brown 42.50 *80.00*
Never hinged 125.00
On cover 115.00
Nos. 51-56 (6) 142.00 *252.50*

Covers: Value for No. 56 on cover is for overfranked complete cover, usually philatelic.

Kaiser's Yacht "Hohenzollern"
A12 A13

1900 **Typo.** *Perf. 14*

57 A12 3pf brown 1.25 *1.40*
Never hinged 2.00
On cover 57.50
58 A12 5pf green 1.25 *1.40*
Never hinged 2.00
On cover 25.00
59 A12 10pf carmine 1.25 *1.40*
Never hinged 2.00
On cover 29.00
60 A12 20pf ultra 1.25 *2.75*
Never hinged 1.80
On cover 52.50
61 A12 25pf org & blk, *yel* 1.40 *14.00*
Never hinged 2.25
On cover 90.00
62 A12 30pf org & blk, *sal* 1.40 *13.00*
Never hinged 2.90
On cover 90.00
63 A12 40pf lake & blk 1.50 *14.00*
Never hinged 2.90
On cover 90.00
64 A12 50pf pur & blk, *sal* 1.50 *15.00*
Never hinged 2.90
On cover 37.50
65 A12 80pf lake & blk, *rose* 3.50 *37.50*
Never hinged 5.25
On cover 70.00

Perf. 14½x14

Engr.

66 A13 1m carmine 3.75 *70.00*
Never hinged 15.00
On cover 100.00
67 A13 2m blue 5.00 *120.00*
Never hinged 25.00
On cover 175.00
68 A13 3m black vio 9.00 *175.00*
Never hinged 32.50
On cover 180.00
69 A13 5m slate & car 140.00 *600.00*
Never hinged 500.00
On cover 800.00
Nos. 57-69 (13) 172.05

Covers: Values for Nos. 64-69 on cover are for overfranked complete covers, usually philatelic.

1915 Wmk. 125 Typo. *Perf. 14*

70 A12 3pf brown 1.25
Never hinged 2.50
71 A12 5pf green 1.50
Never hinged 2.90
72 A12 10pf carmine 1.50
Never hinged 3.00

Perf. 14½x14

Engr.

73 A13 5m slate & car, 25x17 holes ('19) 32.50
Never hinged 100.00
a. 26x17 holes ('15) 40.00
Never hinged 160.00

Nos. 70-73 were never put in use.

Issued under British Dominion
Nos. 57-69 Surcharged

On A12

On A13

1914 Unwmk. *Perf. 14*

101 A12 ½p on 3pf brn 60.00 16.00
a. Double surcharge 800.00 625.00
b. Fraction bar omitted 90.00 42.50
c. Comma after "I" 750.00 450.00
102 A12 ½p on 5pf grn 65.00 20.00
a. Double surcharge 800.00 625.00
b. Fraction bar omitted 140.00 62.50
d. Comma after "I" 450.00 190.00
103 A12 1p on 10pf car 110.00 42.50
a. Double surcharge 850.00 675.00
104 A12 2½p on 20pf ultra 62.50 14.00
a. Fraction bar omitted 95.00 45.00
b. Inverted surcharge 1,150. 1,050.
c. Double surcharge 800.00 675.00
d. Commas after "I" 575.00 375.00
105 A12 3p on 25pf org & blk, *yel* 80.00 42.50
a. Double surcharge 1,150. 850.00
b. Comma after "I" 5,250. 1,150.
106 A12 4p on 30pf org & blk, *sal* 135.00 62.50
107 A12 5p on 40pf lake & blk 135.00 75.00
108 A12 6p on 50pf pur & blk, *sal* 67.50 37.50
a. Inverted "9" for "6" 190.00 110.00
b. Double surcharge 1,250. 1,150.
109 A12 9p on 80pf lake & blk, *rose* 210.00 110.00

Perf. 14½x14

110 A13 1sh on 1m car ("1 Shillings") 3,500. *3,750.*
a. "1 Shilling." *11,500.* *7,500.*
111 A13 2sh on 2m blue 4,000. 3,500.
112 A13 3sh on 3m blk vio 1,600. 1,500.
a. Double surcharge *10,500.* *11,500.*
113 A13 5sh on 5m slate & car 1,200. 1,100.
a. Double surcharge 15,000. 15,000.

G.R.I. stands for Georgius Rex Imperator.

The 3d on 30pf and 4d on 40pf were produced at a later time.

Unauthorized overprints, created as favors, exist on Nos. 101-113.

Stamps of New Zealand Overprinted in Red or Blue

k

m

Perf. 14, 14x13½, 14x14½

1914, Sept. 29 Wmk. 61

114 A41(k) ½p yel grn (R) 1.50 .35
115 A42(k) 1p carmine 1.40 .25
116 A41(k) 2p mauve (R) 1.40 1.10
117 A22(m) 2½p blue (R) 2.00 2.00
118 A41(k) 6p car rose, perf. 14x14½ 2.25 2.00
a. Perf. 14x13½ 19.00 26.00
119 A41(k) 1sh vermilion 11.00 *22.00*
Nos. 114-119 (6) 19.55 *27.70*

Overprinted Type "m"

1914-25 *Perf. 14, 14½x14*

120 PF1 2sh blue (R) 7.00 6.25
121 PF1 2sh6p brown (Bl) 6.25 *15.00*
122 PF1 3sh vio (R) ('22) 18.00 *65.00*
123 PF1 5sh green (R) 22.50 *11.00*
124 PF1 10sh red brn (Bl) 45.00 *42.50*
125 PF2 £1 rose (Bl) 100.00 85.00
126 PF2 £2 vio (R) ('25) 400.00
Nos. 120-126 (7) 598.75
Nos. 120-125 (6) *224.75*

Postal use of the £2 is questioned.

Overprinted Type "k"

Perf. 14x13½, 14x14½

1916-19 Typo.

127 A43 ½p yellow grn (R) 1.00 *1.40*
128 A47 1½p gray blk (R) ('17) .55 .25
129 A47 1½p brn org (R) ('19) .35 .50
130 A43 2p yellow (R) ('18) 2.00 .25
131 A43 3p chocolate (Bl) 3.50 *22.50*

Engr.

132 A44 2½p dull blue (R) 1.25 .60
133 A45 3p violet brn (Bl) .65 *1.10*
134 A45 6p carmine rose (Bl) 2.25 *2.50*
135 A45 1sh vermilion (Bl) 4.75 1.75
Nos. 127-135 (9) 16.30 30.85

New Zealand Victory Issue of 1919 Overprinted Type "k"

1920, June *Perf. 14*

136 A48 ½p yellow grn (R) 6.50 *16.00*
137 A49 1p carmine (Bl) 3.00 *20.00*
138 A50 1½p brown org (R) 2.00 *11.00*
139 A51 3p black brn (Bl) 9.25 *10.50*
140 A52 6p purple (R) 5.25 *8.00*
141 A53 1sh vermilion (Bl) 15.00 12.50
Nos. 136-141 (6) 41.00 78.00

British Flag and Samoan House — A22

1921, Dec. 23 Engr. *Perf. 14x13½*

142 A22 ½p green 5.50 *2.00*
a. Perf. 14x14½ 5.50 *15.00*
143 A22 1p lake 6.50 .25
a. Perf. 14x14½ 9.00 1.75
144 A22 1½p org brn, perf. 14x14½ 1.50 *20.00*
a. Perf. 14x13½ 20.00 13.00
145 A22 2p yel, perf. 14x14½ 3.00 3.00
a. Perf. 14x13½ 15.00 .90
146 A22 2½p dull blue 2.00 *9.50*
147 A22 3p dark brown 2.00 *6.00*
148 A22 4p violet 2.00 *4.00*
149 A22 5p brt blue 2.00 *9.00*
150 A22 6p carmine rose 2.00 *8.00*
151 A22 8p red brown 2.25 *16.00*
152 A22 9p olive green 2.50 *40.00*
153 A22 1sh vermilion 2.25 *32.50*
Nos. 142-153 (12) 33.50 *150.25*

For overprints see Nos. 163-165.

New Zealand Nos. 182-183 Overprinted Type "m" in Red

1926-27 *Perf. 14½x14*

154 A56 2sh dark blue 5.75 *21.00*
a. 2sh blue ('27) 7.00 *50.00*
155 A56 3sh deep violet 25.00 *50.00*
a. 3sh violet ('27) 62.50 *110.00*

Issued: 2sh, Nov.; 3sh, Oct.; Nos. 154a, 155a, 11/10.

New Zealand Postal-Fiscal Stamps, Overprinted Type "m" in Blue or Red

1932, Aug. *Perf. 14*

156 PF5 2sh6p brown 18.00 *55.00*
157 PF5 5sh green (R) 30.00 *57.50*
158 PF5 10sh lake 55.00 *110.00*
159 PF5 £1 pink 80.00 *160.00*
160 PF5 £2 violet (R) *1,000.*
161 PF5 £5 dk bl (R) *2,600.*
Nos. 156-159 (4) 183.00 *382.50*

See Nos. 175-180, 195-202, 216-219 (in Scott Standard catalogue, Vol. 5).

Silver Jubilee Issue

Stamps of 1921 Overprinted in Black

1935, May 7 *Perf. 14x13½*

163 A22 1p lake .40 *.50*
a. Perf. 14x14½ *110.00* *200.00*
164 A22 2½p dull blue .75 *1.00*
165 A22 6p carmine rose 3.25 *4.00*
Nos. 163-165 (3) 4.40 5.50
Set, never hinged 9.00

25th anniv. of the reign of George V.

Western Samoa

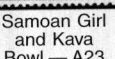

Samoan Girl and Kava Bowl — A23

View of Apia — A24

River Scene — A25

Samoan Chief and Wife — A26

Samoan Canoe and House — A27

"Vailima," Stevenson's Home — A28

Stevenson's Tomb — A29

Lake Lanuto'o — A30

Falefa Falls — A31

Perf. 14x13½, 13½x14

1935, Aug. 7 Engr. Wmk. 61

166 A23 ½p yellow grn .25 .40
167 A24 1p car lake & blk .25 .25
168 A25 2p red org & blk, perf. 14 4.00 4.00
a. Perf. 13½x14 5.00 *4.25*
169 A26 2½p dp blue & blk .25 .25
170 A27 4p blk brn & dk gray .50 .35
171 A28 6p plum .70 .35
172 A29 1sh brown & violet .50 .50
173 A30 2sh red brn & yel grn 1.10 .80
174 A31 3sh org brn & brt bl 2.50 *3.50*
Nos. 166-174 (9) 10.05 *10.40*
Set, never hinged 20.00

See Nos. 186-188.

Postal-Fiscal Stamps of New Zealand Overprinted in Blue or Carmine

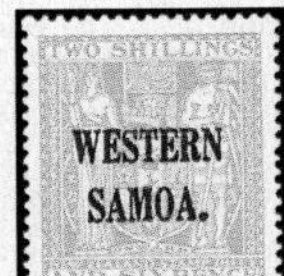

1935 *Perf. 14*

175 PF5 2sh6p brown 11.00 *18.00*
176 PF5 5sh green 24.00 *32.50*
177 PF5 10sh dp car 70.00 *85.00*
178 PF5 £1 pink 62.50 *110.00*
179 PF5 £2 violet (C) 180.00 *400.00*
180 PF5 £5 dk bl (C) 260.00 *525.00*
Nos. 175-180 (6) 607.50 *1,171.*

See Nos. 195-202, 216-219 (in Scott Standard catalogue, Vol. 5).

Samoan Coastal Village — A32

Map of Western Samoa — A33

Samoan Dancing Party A34

Robert Louis Stevenson A35

Perf. 13½x14

1939, Aug. 29 Engr. Wmk. 253

181 A32 1p scar & olive .60 .35
182 A33 1½p copper brn & bl 1.00 .90
183 A34 2½p dk blue & brn 1.10 1.00

Perf. 14x13½

184 A35 7p dp sl grn & vio 4.25 4.25
Nos. 181-184 (4) 6.95 6.50
Set, never hinged 12.00

25th anniv. of New Zealand's control of the mandated territory of Western Samoa.

Samoan Chief — A36

1940, Sept. 2 *Perf. 14x13½*

185 A36 3p on 1½p brown .50 .35
Never hinged .85

Issued only with surcharge. Examples without surcharge are from printer's archives.

Types of 1935 and

Apia Post Office — A37

1944-49 Wmk. 253 *Perf. 14*

186 A23 ½p yellow green .30 *21.00*
187 A25 2p red orange & blk 2.00 *7.00*
188 A26 2½p dp blue & blk ('48) 5.00 *40.00*

Perf. 13½x14

189 A37 5p dp ultra & ol brn ('49) 1.40 1.00
Nos. 186-189 (4) 8.70 *69.00*
Set, never hinged 14.50

Issue date: 5p, June 8.

Catalogue values for unused stamps in this section, from this point to the end of the section, are for Never Hinged items.

Peace Issue

New Zealand Nos. 248, 250, 254, and 255 Overprinted in Black or Blue

p

q

1946, June 1 *Perf. 13x13½, 13½x13*

191 A94(p) 1p emerald .40 .25
192 A96(q) 2p rose violet (Bl) .40 .25
193 A100(p) 6p org red & red brn .80 .25
194 A101(p) 8p brn lake & blk (Bl) .45 .25
Nos. 191-194 (4) 2.05 1.00

Stamps and Type of New Zealand, 1931-50 Overprinted Like Nos. 175-180 in Blue or Carmine

1945-50		**Wmk. 253**		***Perf. 14***
195	PF5	2sh6p brown	15.00	*27.50*
196	PF5	5sh green	21.00	18.00
197	PF5	10sh car ('48)	23.00	19.00
198	PF5	£1 pink ('48)	130.00	*200.00*
199	PF5	30sh choc ('48)	200.00	*350.00*
200	PF5	£2 violet (C)	210.00	*310.00*
201	PF5	£3 lt grn ('50)	300.00	*425.00*
202	PF5	£5 dk bl (C) ('50)	425.00	*500.00*

Making Siapo Cloth — A38

Western Samoa and New Zealand Flags, Village A39

Thatching Hut A40

Samoan Chieftainess A41

Designs: 2p, Western Samoa seal. 3p, Aleisa Falls (actually Malifa Falls). 5p, Manumea (tooth-billed pigeon). 6p, Fishing canoe. 8p, Harvesting cacao. 2sh, Preparing copra.

Perf. 13, 13½x13

1952, Mar. 10		**Engr.**	**Wmk. 253**	
203	A38	½p org brn & claret	.25	*2.00*
204	A39	1p green & olive	.25	.25
205	A38	2p deep carmine	.25	.25
206	A39	3p indigo & blue	.45	.25
207	A38	5p dk grn & org brn	9.00	.80
208	A39	6p dp rose pink & bl	1.00	.25
209	A39	8p rose carmine	.35	.30
210	A40	1sh blue & brown	.25	.25
211	A39	2sh yellow brown	1.10	.50
212	A41	3sh ol gray & vio brn	2.75	*2.75*
		Nos. 203-212 (10)	15.65	7.60

SAN MARINO

ˌsan mə-ˈrē-ˌnō

LOCATION — Eastern Italy, about 20 miles inland from the Adriatic Sea
GOVT. — Republic
AREA — 24.1 sq. mi.
POP. — 21,622 (1981)
CAPITAL — San Marino

100 Centesimi = 1 Lira

Watermarks

Wmk. 140 — Crown

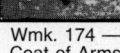

Wmk. 174 — Coat of Arms

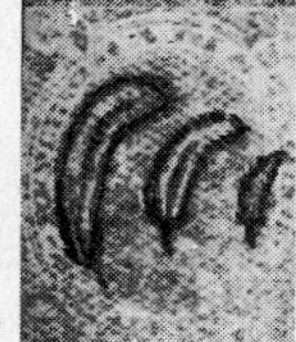

Wmk. 217 — Three Plumes

Nos. 1-28 were spaced very narrowly on the plates, so that perforations often cut into the design on one or two sides. Values are for very fine stamps, with perforations clear of the design. Examples with perfs cutting in the design sell for less, while examples with four clear, full margins sell for substantially more than the values shown. Never hinged premiums do not apply to stamps with perforations cutting the design.

Numeral — A1

Coat of Arms — A2

Coat of Arms — A3

1877-99	**Typo.**	**Wmk. 140**		***Perf. 14***
1	A1	2c green	37.50	19.00
		Never hinged	95.00	
		No gum	7.50	
		On cover		225.00
2	A1	2c blue ('94)	15.00	19.00
		Never hinged	42.50	
		No gum	3.40	
		On cover		225.00
3	A1	2c claret ('95)	13.50	19.00
		Never hinged	35.00	
		No gum	2.75	
		On cover		200.00
4	A2	5c orange ('90)	180.00	50.00
		Never hinged	475.00	
		No gum	37.50	
		On cover		350.00
5	A2	5c olive grn ('92)	9.00	9.25
		Never hinged	24.00	
		No gum	1.90	
		On cover		90.00
6	A2	5c green ('99)	9.25	14.00
		Never hinged	24.00	
		No gum	1.90	
		On cover		135.00
7	A2	10c ultra	350.00	115.00
		Never hinged	875.00	
		No gum	70.00	
		On cover		575.00
	a.	10c blue ('90)	3,600.	300.00
		Never hinged	9,000.	
		No gum	190.00	
		On cover		3,100.
8	A2	10c dk green ('92)	9.25	11.00
		Never hinged	24.00	
		No gum	1.90	
		On cover		110.00
9	A2	10c claret ('99)	9.25	13.50
		Never hinged	24.00	
		No gum	1.90	
		On cover		140.00
10	A2	15c claret ('94)	170.00	120.00
		Never hinged	425.00	
		No gum	42.50	
		On cover		1,250.
11	A2	20c vermilion	45.00	19.00
		Never hinged	115.00	
		No gum	9.50	
		On cover		225.00
12	A2	20c lilac ('95)	9.25	19.00
		Never hinged	24.00	
		No gum	1.90	
		On cover		165.00
13	A2	25c maroon ('90)	150.00	90.00
		Never hinged	390.00	
		No gum	30.00	
		On cover		450.00
14	A2	25c blue ('99)	9.25	17.00
		Never hinged	24.00	
		No gum	1.90	
		On cover		165.00
15	A2	30c brown	925.00	125.00
		Never hinged	2,800.	
		No gum	185.00	
		On cover		1,250.
16	A2	30c org yel ('92)	9.25	19.00
		Never hinged	24.00	
		No gum	1.90	
		On cover		190.00
	a.	30c yellow ochre	10.50	21.50
		On cover		210.00
17	A2	40c violet	925.00	125.00
		Never hinged	2,800.	
		No gum	185.00	
		On cover		1,250.
18	A2	40c dk brn ('92)	9.25	19.00
		Never hinged	24.00	
		No gum	1.90	
		On cover		190.00
19	A2	45c gray grn ('92)	9.25	19.00
		Never hinged	24.00	
		No gum	1.90	
		On cover		190.00
	a.	45c deep olive green	9.25	19.00
		On cover		190.00
20	A2	65c red brn ('92)	9.25	19.00
		Never hinged	22.50	
		No gum	1.90	
		On cover		190.00
21	A3	1 l car & yel ('92)	1,825.	950.00
		Never hinged	4,750.	
		No gum	650.00	
		On cover		3,750.
22	A3	1 l lt blue ('95)	1,675.	750.00
		Never hinged	4,250.	
		No gum	550.00	
		On cover		3,000.
23	A3	2 l brn & yel ('94)	90.00	120.00
		Never hinged	240.00	
		No gum	22.50	
		On cover		1,250.
24	A3	5 l vio & grn ('94)	225.00	450.00
		Never hinged	575.00	
		No gum	55.00	
		On cover		3,750.

Cover values are for properly franked covers, paying correct postage rates. Overfranked covers and other philatelic covers sell for about one-half of the values quoted.

Values for never-hinged stamps are for examples with very fine centering. Premiums do not apply to stamps with perforations cutting the design.

Values for Blocks of 4
(2 stamps never hinged)
(Average to Fine Centering)

1	A1	2c green	275.00	90.00
2	A1	2c blue ('94)	135.00	135.00
3	A1	2c claret ('95)	120.00	110.00
4	A2	5c orange ('90)	1,500.	*1,425.*
5	A2	5c olive grn ('92)	75.00	90.00
6	A2	5c green ('99)	75.00	97.50
7	A2	10c ultra	2,500.	*1,250.*
	a.	10c blue ('90)	12,000.	*3,000.*
8	A2	10c dk green ('92)	75.00	90.00
9	A2	10c claret ('99)	75.00	97.50
10	A2	15c claret ('94)	1,300.	*925.00*
11	A2	20c vermilion	350.00	110.00
12	A2	20c lilac ('95)	75.00	110.00
13	A2	25c maroon ('90)	1,250.	*1,350.*
14	A2	25c blue ('99)	75.00	110.00
15	A2	30c brown	8,250.	*3,200.*
16	A2	30c org yel ('92)	75.00	135.00
17	A2	40c violet	8,250.	*3,200.*
18	A2	40c dk brown ('92)	75.00	135.00
19	A2	45c gray grn ('92)	75.00	135.00
20	A2	65c red brown ('92)	75.00	135.00
21	A2	1 l car & yel ('92)	*17,500.*	*19,000.*
22	A2	1 l lt blue ('95)	*16,000.*	*14,500.*
23	A2	2 l brn & yel ('94)	725.00	*925.00*
24	A2	5 l vio & grn ('94)	1,800.	*5,000.*

See Nos. 911-915 in Scott Standard catalogue, Vol. 6.

Nos. 7a, 15, 11 Surcharged in Black

1892				
25	A2	5c on 10c blue	90.00	26.00
		Never hinged	225.00	
		No gum	22.50	
		On cover		265.00
	a.	Inverted surcharge	110.00	34.00
		Never hinged	275.00	
		On cover		340.00
	b.	5c on 10c ultramarine	*50,000.*	*12,000.*
		Never hinged	*62,500.*	
		No gum	*13,750.*	
	c.	As "b," inverted surch.	—	—
	d.	Double surcharge, one inverted	—	
		On cover		—
	e.	Pair, one without surcharge	2,250.	
		Never hinged	*4,500.*	
	f.	Pair, one without surcharge, surcharge inverted	2,250.	
		Never hinged	*4,500.*	
26	A2	5c on 30c brn	300.00	135.00
		Never hinged	750.00	
		No gum	75.00	
		On cover		*1,325.*
	a.	Inverted surcharge	375.00	170.00
		Never hinged	950.00	
		On cover		1,700.
	b.	Double surch., one inverted	375.00	210.00
		Never hinged	950.00	
	c.	Double invtd. surcharge	375.00	210.00
		Never hinged	950.00	
27	A2	10c on 20c ver	67.50	15.00
		Never hinged	175.00	
		No gum	17.00	
		On cover		150.00
	a.	Inverted surcharge	75.00	22.50
		Never hinged	190.00	
		On cover		225.00
	b.	Double surch., one inverted	82.50	30.00
		Never hinged	210.00	
		On cover		300.00
	c.	Double surcharge	82.50	30.00
		Never hinged	210.00	
		On cover		300.00

Ten to twelve varieties of each surcharge.

No. 11 Surcharged

28	A2	10c on 20c ver	300.00	19.00
		Never hinged	750.00	
		No gum	75.00	
		On cover		190.00
	a.	Only one "10" in surcharge	600.00	
		Never hinged	1,500.	

Values for never-hinged stamps are for examples with very fine centering. Premiums do not apply to stamps with perforations cutting the design.

Values for Blocks of 4
(2 stamps never hinged)

25	A2	5c on 10c blue	685.00	120.00
	b.	5c on 10c ultramarine		*45,000.*
26	A2	5c on 30c brown	2,250.	610.00
27	A2	10c on 20c ver	525.00	70.00
28	A2	10c on 20c ver	2,250.	85.00

Government Palace and Portraits of Regents, Tonnini and Marcucci
A6 A7

Portraits of Regents and View of Interior of Palace — A8

Wmk. 174

1894, Sept. 30		**Litho.**		***Perf. 15½***
29	A6	25c blue & dk brn	7.50	3.00
		Never hinged	52.50	
		On cover		60.00
30	A7	50c dull red & dk brn	45.00	9.50
		Never hinged	320.00	
		On cover		190.00
31	A8	1 l green & dk brown	35.00	11.50
		Never hinged	240.00	
		On cover		225.00
		Nos. 29-31 (3)	87.50	24.00

Opening of the new Government Palace and the installation of the new Regents.

Statue of Liberty — A9

Wmk. 140

1899-1922		**Typo.**		***Perf. 14***
32	A9	2c brown	3.75	1.90
		Never hinged	9.50	
		On cover		37.50
33	A9	2c claret ('22)	.75	.75
		Never hinged	1.90	
		On cover		20.00
34	A9	5c brown org	7.50	4.50
		Never hinged	19.00	
		On cover		45.00
35	A9	5c olive grn ('22)	.75	.75
		Never hinged	1.90	
		On cover		4.00
36	A9	10c brown org ('22)	.75	.75
		Never hinged	1.90	
		On cover		15.00
37	A9	20c dp brown ('22)	.75	.75
		Never hinged	1.90	
		On cover		15.00
38	A9	25c ultra ('22)	1.50	1.50
		Never hinged	3.75	
		On cover		22.50
39	A9	45c red brown ('22)	3.00	3.00
		Never hinged	7.50	
		On cover		22.50
		Nos. 32-39 (8)	18.75	13.90

Numeral of Value — A10

Mt. Titano — A11

1903-25 ***Perf. 14, 14½x14***

40 A10 2c violet 22.50 12.00
Never hinged 55.00
On cover 75.00
41 A10 2c org brn ('21) 1.50 1.10
Never hinged 3.75
On cover 37.50
42 A11 5c blue grn 11.00 7.50
Never hinged 28.00
On cover 37.50
43 A11 5c olive grn ('21) 1.50 1.10
Never hinged 3.75
On cover 19.00
a. Imperforate 85.00
Never hinged 175.00
44 A11 5c red brn ('25) .75 .75
Never hinged 1.90
On cover 7.50
45 A11 10c claret 11.50 7.50
Never hinged 29.00
On cover 37.50
46 A11 10c brown org ('21) 1.50 1.20
Never hinged 3.75
On cover 18.00
a. Imperforate 85.00
Never hinged 175.00
47 A11 10c olive grn ('25) .75 .75
Never hinged 1.90
On cover 7.50
48 A11 15c blue grn ('22) 1.50 1.10
Never hinged 3.75
On cover 18.00
49 A11 15c brown vio ('25) .75 .75
Never hinged 1.90
On cover 7.50
50 A11 20c brown orange 150.00 60.00
Never hinged 375.00
On cover 600.00
51 A11 20c brown ('21) 1.50 1.20
Never hinged 3.75
On cover 26.00
52 A11 20c blue grn ('25) .75 .75
Never hinged 1.90
On cover 11.00
53 A11 25c blue 27.50 12.00
Never hinged 70.00
On cover 37.50
54 A11 25c gray ('21) 1.50 1.10
Never hinged 3.75
On cover 26.00
55 A11 25c violet ('25) .75 .75
Never hinged 1.90
On cover 7.50
56 A11 30c brown red 12.00 *18.50*
Never hinged 30.00
On cover 82.50
57 A11 30c claret ('21) 1.50 1.20
Never hinged 3.75
On cover 75.00
58 A11 30c orange ('25) 22.50 3.75
Never hinged 57.50
On cover 45.00
59 A11 40c orange red 22.50 18.50
Never hinged 57.50
On cover 75.00
60 A11 40c dp rose ('21) 1.50 1.20
Never hinged 3.75
On cover 26.00
61 A11 40c brown ('25) .75 .75
Never hinged 1.90
On cover 10.50
62 A11 45c yellow 16.50 18.50
Never hinged 42.50
On cover 75.00
63 A11 50c brown vio ('23) 3.00 3.00
Never hinged 7.50
On cover 67.50
64 A11 50c gray blk ('25) .75 .75
Never hinged 1.90
On cover 7.50
65 A11 60c brown red ('25) 1.50 .75
Never hinged 3.75
On cover 45.00
66 A11 65c chocolate 17.00 18.50
Never hinged 42.50
On cover 75.00
67 A11 80c blue ('21) 6.00 6.00
Never hinged 15.00
On cover 67.50
68 A11 90c brown ('23) 6.00 6.00
Never hinged 15.00
On cover 67.50
69 A11 1 l olive green 60.00 30.00
Never hinged 150.00
On cover 600.00
70 A11 1 l ultra ('21) 6.00 6.00
Never hinged 15.00
On cover 67.50
71 A11 1 l lt blue ('25) 1.50 .75
Never hinged 3.75
On cover 45.00
72 A11 2 l violet 1,000. 425.00
Never hinged 2,000.
On cover 3,500.
73 A11 2 l orange ('21) 22.50 27.00
Never hinged 55.00
On cover 375.00
74 A11 2 l lt green ('25) 7.50 7.50
Never hinged 19.00
On cover 325.00
75 A11 5 l slate 275.00 300.00
Never hinged 700.00
On cover 1,850.

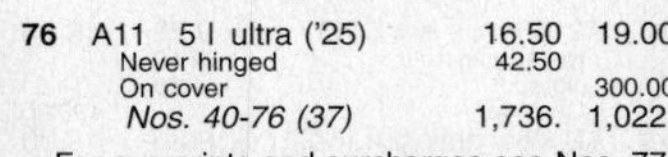

76 A11 5 l ultra ('25) 16.50 19.00
Never hinged 42.50
On cover 300.00
Nos. 40-76 (37) 1,736. 1,022.

For overprints and surcharges see Nos. 77, 93-96, 103, 107, 188-189 (in Scott Standard catalogue, Vol. 6), B1-B2, E2, E4.

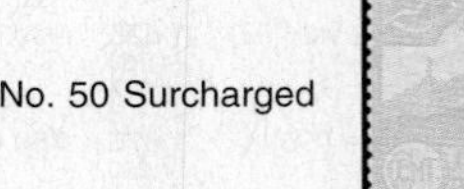

No. 50 Surcharged

1905, Sept. 1

77 A11 15c on 20c brown org 15.00 10.50
Never hinged 37.50
On cover 52.50
a. Large 5 in 1905 on level with 9 92.50 45.00

Coat of Arms
A12 A13

Two types:
I — Width 18½mm.
II — Width 19mm.

1907-10 Unwmk. Engr. ***Perf. 12***

78 A12 1c brown, II ('10) 8.00 2.00
Never hinged 20.00
On cover 45.00
a. Type I 16.00 3.00
Never hinged 40.00
On cover 45.00
79 A13 15c gray, I 37.50 6.00
Never hinged 95.00
On cover 60.00
a. Imperforate 140.00 140.00
Never hinged 275.00
b. Type II ('10) 300.00 32.50
Never hinged 725.00
On cover 225.00
c. As "b," imperforate 600.00 600.00
Never hinged 1,250.
Nos. 78a, 79 on overfranked philatelic cover 70.00
Nos. 78, 79a on overfranked philatelic cover 275.00

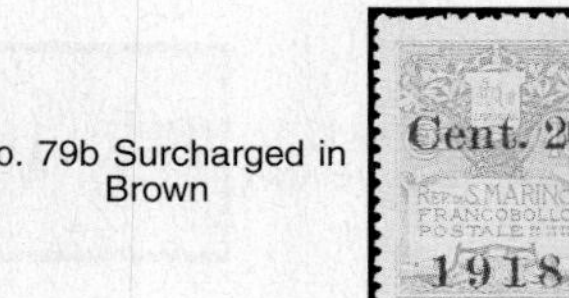

No. 79b Surcharged in Brown

1918, Mar. 15

80 A13 20c on 15c gray 6.00 3.75
Never hinged 16.00
On cover 32.50

St. Marinus — A14

Perf. 14½x14, 14x14½

1923, Aug. 11 Typo. Wmk. 140

81 A14 30c dark brown .75 .75
Never hinged 2.00
On cover 20.00

San Marino Intl. Exhib. of 1923. Proceeds from the sale of this stamp went to a mutual aid society.

Imperforate examples on chalky paper are proofs. Value, $175.

Italian Flag and Views of Arbe and Mt. Titano
A15

1923, Aug. 6

82 A15 50c olive green .75 .75
Never hinged 2.00
On cover 20.00
a. Reverse printing omitted 215.00
Never hinged 425.00
b. Gummed on both sides 15.00
Never hinged 30.00

Presentation to San Marino of the Italian flag which had flown over the island of Arbe, the birthplace of the founder of San Marino. Inscribed on back: "V. Moraldi dis. Blasi inc. Petiti impr.-Roma."

Imperfroate examples on chalky paper are proofs. Value, $175.

Mt. Titano and Sword — A16

1923, Sept. 29 ***Perf. 14x14½***

83 A16 1 l dark brown 22.50 22.50
Never hinged 60.00
On cover 100.00

In honor of the San Marino Volunteers who were killed or wounded in WWI.

Giuseppe Garibaldi
A17

Allegory-San Marino Sheltering Garibaldi
A18

1924, Sept. 25 ***Perf. 14***

84 A17 30c dark violet 3.75 4.00
Never hinged 9.50
On cover 10.00
85 A17 50c olive brown 3.75 4.00
Never hinged 9.00
On cover 10.00
86 A17 60c dull red 5.00 5.00
Never hinged 12.00
On cover 12.00
87 A18 1 l deep blue 9.00 9.00
Never hinged 22.50
On cover 22.50
88 A18 2 l gray green 11.00 11.00
Never hinged 27.50
On cover 120.00
Nos. 84-88 (5) 32.50 33.00
Set on overfranked philatelic cover 90.00

75th anniv. of Garibaldi's taking refuge in San Marino.

No. B8 Surcharged in Black

1924, Oct. 9

89 SP1 30c on 45c yel brn & blk 3.00 3.00
Never hinged 7.50
On cover 22.50
a. Pair, one stamp without surcharge 1,100. 1,100.
Never hinged 2,200.

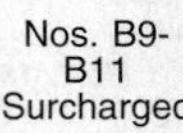

Nos. B9-B11 Surcharged

90 SP2 60c on 1 l bl grn & blk 10.50 10.50
Never hinged 26.50
On cover 55.00
91 SP2 1 l on 2 l vio & blk 29.00 29.00
Never hinged 72.50
On cover 95.00
92 SP2 2 l on 3 l claret & blk 22.00 22.00
Never hinged 52.50
On cover 215.00
Nos. 89-92 (4) 64.50 64.50
Set on overfranked philatelic cover 245.00

Nos. 67 and 68 Surcharged in Black or Red

1926, July 1

93 A11 75c on 80c blue 2.25 2.50
Never hinged 6.00
On cover 22.50
94 A11 1.20 l on 90c brown 2.25 2.50
Never hinged 6.00
On cover 22.50
95 A11 1.25 l on 90c brn (R) 3.75 3.75
Never hinged 9.50
On cover 40.00
96 A11 2.50 l on 80c blue (R) 8.00 8.00
Never hinged 20.00
On cover 45.00
Nos. 93-96 (4) 16.25 16.75
Set on overfranked philatelic cover 67.50

Antonio Onofri — A19

Unwmk.

1926, July 29 Engr. ***Perf. 11***

97 A19 10c dk blue & blk .75 .75
Never hinged 1.90
On cover 4.00
98 A19 20c olive grn & blk 1.50 1.50
Never hinged 3.75
On cover 6.00
99 A19 45c dk vio & blk .75 .75
Never hinged 1.90
On cover 22.50
100 A19 65c green & blk .75 .75
Never hinged 1.90
On cover 22.50
101 A19 1 l orange & blk 5.50 5.50
Never hinged 13.50
On cover 37.50
102 A19 2 l red vio & blk 5.50 5.50
Never hinged 13.50
On cover 45.00
Nos. 97-102 (6) 14.75 14.75
Set on overfranked philatelic cover 75.00

For surcharges see Nos. 104-106, 181-182.

Special Delivery Stamp No. E2 Surcharged

Perf. 14½x14

1926, Nov. 25 Wmk. 140

103 A11 1.85 l on 60c violet .80 .80
Never hinged 2.00
On cover 25.00

Nos. 101 and 102 Surcharged

13 Dots in Curved Row in Surcharge

1927, Mar. 10 Unwmk. *Perf. 11*

104 A19 1.25 l on 1 l 9.50 9.50
Never hinged 22.50
On cover 40.00
105 A19 2.50 l on 2 l 19.00 19.00
Never hinged 45.00
On cover 75.00
106 A19 5 l on 2 l 55.00 55.00
Never hinged 135.00
On cover 275.00
Nos. 104-106 (3) 83.50 83.50
Set on overfranked philatelic cover 250.00

14 Dots in Surcharge (Position 29)

104a A19 1.25 l on 1 l 30.00
Never hinged 60.00
105a A19 2.50 l on 2 l 60.00
Never hinged 120.00
106a A19 5 l on 2 l 185.00
Never hinged 375.00

12 Dots in Surcharge (Position 9, 22, 32)

104b A19 1.25 l on 1 l 20.00
Never hinged 40.00
105b A19 2.50 l on 2 l 37.50
Never hinged 75.00
106b A19 5 l on 2 l 125.00
Never hinged 250..00

11 Dots in Surcharge (Position 20)

104c A19 1.25 l on 1 l 30.00
Never hinged 60.00

9 Dots in Surcharge (Position 2)

106d A19 5 l on 2 l 225.00
Never hinged 450.00

Type of Special Delivery Stamp of 1923 Surcharged

1927, Sept. 15 Wmk. 140 *Perf. 14*

107 A11 1.75 l on 50c on 25c vio 1.25 1.25
Never hinged 3.25
On cover 27.50

The 50c on 25c violet was not issued without 1.75-lire surcharge.

War Memorial A21

Unwmk.

1927, Sept. 28 Engr. *Perf. 12*

108 A21 50c brown violet 2.25 2.25
Never hinged 8.50
109 A21 1.25 l blue 3.25 3.25
Never hinged 8.50
110 A21 10 l gray 27.50 27.50
Never hinged 67.50
Nos. 108-110 (3) 33.00 33.00
Set on overfranked philatelic cover 150.00

Erection of a cenotaph in memory of the San Marino volunteers in WWI.

Capuchin Church and Convent A22

Design: 2.50 l, 5 l, Death of St. Francis.

1928, Jan. 2

111 A22 50c red 25.00 10.00
Never hinged 62.50
112 A22 1.25 l dp blue 12.00 12.00
Never hinged 30.00
113 A22 2.50 l dk brown 12.00 12.00
Never hinged 30.00
114 A22 5 l dull violet 35.00 32.50
Never hinged 87.50
Nos. 111-114 (4) 84.00 66.50
Set on overfranked philatelic cover 225.00

7th centenary of the death of St. Francis of Assisi.

For surcharges see Nos. 183-184.

The Rocca (State Prison) A24

Government Palace A25

Statue of Liberty — A26

1929-35 Wmk. 217

115 A24 5c vio brn & ultra 1.50 .75
Never hinged 4.25
116 A24 10c grnsh blue & red vio 2.00 1.25
Never hinged 5.25
117 A24 15c dp org & emer 1.50 .75
Never hinged 4.25
118 A24 20c dk bl & org red 1.50 .75
Never hinged 4.25
119 A24 25c grn & gray blk 1.50 .75
Never hinged 4.25
120 A24 30c gray brn & red 1.50 .75
Never hinged 4.25
121 A24 50c red vio & ol gray 1.50 .75
Never hinged 4.25
122 A24 75c dp red & gray blk 1.50 .75
Never hinged 4.25
123 A25 1 l dk brn & emer 1.50 .75
Never hinged 4.25
124 A25 1.25 l dk blue & blk 1.50 .75
Never hinged 4.25
125 A25 1.75 l green & org 4.00 2.00
Never hinged 10.00
126 A25 2 l bl gray & red 2.00 1.25
Never hinged 5.25
127 A25 2.50 l car rose & ultra 2.00 1.25
Never hinged 5.25
128 A25 3 l dp org & bl 2.00 1.25
Never hinged 5.25
129 A25 3.70 l ol blk & red brn ('35) 2.00 1.25
Never hinged 5.25
130 A26 5 l dk vio & dk grn 4.00 3.75
Never hinged 10.00
131 A26 10 l bis brn & dk bl 16.00 15.00
Never hinged 40.00
132 A26 15 l grn & red vio 75.00 *90.00*
Never hinged 210.00
On cover 375.00
133 A26 20 l dk bl & red 325.00 325.00
Never hinged 825.00
On cover 1,150.
Nos. 115-133 (19) 447.50 448.75

General Post Office — A27

1932, Feb. 4

134 A27 20c blue green 27.50 21.00
Never hinged 70.00
135 A27 50c dark red 35.00 25.00
Never hinged 87.50
136 A27 1.25 l dark blue 225.00 175.00
Never hinged 575.00
137 A27 1.75 l dark brown 140.00 75.00
Never hinged 350.00
138 A27 2.75 l dark violet 70.00 42.50
Never hinged 175.00
Nos. 134-138 (5) 497.50 338.50
Set on overfranked philatelic cover 675.00

Opening of new General Post Office.

For surcharges see Nos. 151-160.

San Marino-Rimini Electric Railway — A28

1932, June 11

139 A28 20c deep green 4.25 4.25
Never hinged 10.00
140 A28 50c dark red 7.00 7.00
Never hinged 17.50
141 A28 1.25 l dark blue 17.50 17.50
Never hinged 45.00
142 A28 5 l deep brown 100.00 100.00
Never hinged 250.00
Nos. 139-142 (4) 128.75 128.75
Set on overfranked philatelic cover 350.00

Opening of the new electric railway between San Marino and Rimini.

Giuseppe Garibaldi — A29

Garibaldi's Arrival at San Marino — A30

1932, July 30

143 A29 10c violet brown 10.00 4.25
Never hinged 25.00
144 A29 20c violet 10.00 4.25
Never hinged 25.00
145 A29 25c green 10.00 4.25
Never hinged 25.00
146 A29 50c yellow brn 14.00 8.50
Never hinged 35.00
147 A30 75c dark red 35.00 17.50
Never hinged 87.50
148 A30 1.25 l dark blue 42.50 25.00
Never hinged 110.00
149 A30 2.75 l brown org 85.00 50.00
Never hinged 210.00
150 A30 5 l olive green 325.00 *400.00*
Never hinged 800.00
Nos. 143-150 (8) 531.50 513.75
Set on overfranked philatelic cover 650.00

Garibaldi (1807-1882), Italian patriot.

Nos. 138 and 137 Surcharged

1933, May 27

151 A27 25c on 2.75 l 14.00 14.00
Never hinged 35.00
152 A27 50c on 1.75 l 27.50 27.50
Never hinged 70.00
153 A27 75c on 2.75 l 55.00 55.00
Never hinged 140.00
154 A27 1.25 l on 1.75 l 400.00 400.00
Never hinged 1,000.
Nos. 151-154 (4) 496.50 496.50
Set on overfranked philatelic cover 575.00

Convention of philatelists, San Marino, May 28.

Nos. 134-137 Surcharged in Black

1934, Apr. 12

155 A27 25c on 1.25 l 2.75 2.75
Never hinged 7.00
156 A27 50c on 1.75 l 4.25 4.25
Never hinged 10.00
157 A27 75c on 50c 10.00 10.00
Never hinged 25.00
158 A27 1.25 l on 20c 35.00 35.00
Never hinged 87.50
Nos. 155-158 (4) 52.00 52.00
Set on overfranked philatelic cover 135.00

San Marino's participation (with a philatelic pavilion) in the 15th annual Trade Fair at Milan, Apr. 12-27.

Nos. 136 and 138 Surcharged Wheel and New Value

1934, Apr. 12

159 A27 3.70 l on 1.25 l 67.50 67.50
Never hinged 150.00
160 A27 3.70 l on 2.75 l 77.50 77.50
Never hinged 190.00
Set on overfranked philatelic cover 450.00

Ascent to Mt. Titano A31

Unwmk.

1935, Feb. 7 Engr. *Perf. 14*

161 A31 5c choc & blk .70 .70
Never hinged 1.75
162 A31 10c dk vio & blk .70 .70
Never hinged 1.75
163 A31 20c orange & blk .70 .70
Never hinged 1.75
164 A31 25c green & blk .70 .70
Never hinged 1.75
165 A31 50c olive bis & blk .70 .70
Never hinged 1.75
166 A31 75c brown red & blk 2.75 2.75
Never hinged 7.00
167 A31 1.25 l blue & blk 5.50 5.50
Never hinged 14.00
Nos. 161-167 (7) 11.75 11.75
Set on overfranked philatelic cover 42.50

12th anniv. of the founding of the Fascist Movement.

Melchiorre Delfico — A32

Statue of Delfico — A33

1935, Apr. 15 Wmk. 217 *Perf. 12*
Center in Black

169 A32 5c brown lake 2.10 2.10
Never hinged 5.25
170 A32 7½c lt brown 2.10 2.10
Never hinged 5.25
171 A32 10c dk blue grn 2.10 2.10
Never hinged 5.25
172 A32 15c rose carmine 42.50 25.00
Never hinged 110.00
173 A32 20c orange 3.00 2.50
Never hinged 7.50
174 A32 25c green 3.00 2.50
Never hinged 7.50
175 A33 30c dull violet 3.00 2.50
Never hinged 7.50
176 A33 50c olive green 4.25 4.25
Never hinged 11.00
177 A33 75c red 12.50 12.50
Never hinged 30.00
178 A33 1.25 l dark blue 3.50 3.50
Never hinged 8.75
179 A33 1.50 l dk brown 57.50 *62.50*
Never hinged 145.00

180 A33 1.75 l brown org 85.00 *97.50*
Never hinged 210.00
Nos. 169-180 (12) 220.55 219.05
Set on overfranked philatelic cover 475.00

Melchiorre Delfico (1744-1835), historian.
For surcharges see Nos. 202, 277 in Scott Standard catalogue, Vol. 6.

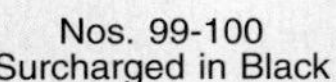
Nos. 99-100 Surcharged in Black

Nos. 112-113 Surcharged in Black

1936 **Unwmk.** ***Perf. 11***
181 A19 80c on 45c dk vio & blk 3.50 3.50
Never hinged 8.75
182 A19 80c on 65c grn & blk 3.50 3.50
Never hinged 8.75

Perf. 12

183 A22 2.05 l on 1.25 l 8.50 8.50
Never hinged 21.00
184 A22 2.75 l on 2.50 l 20.00 20.00
Never hinged 50.00
Nos. 181-184 (4) 35.50 35.50
Nos. 181-182 on overfranked philatelic cover 32.50
Nos. 183-184 on overfranked philatelic cover 110.00

Issued: Nos. 181-182, 4/14; Nos. 183-184, 8/23.

Souvenir Sheet

Design from Base of Roman Column — A34

1937, Aug. 23 **Engr.** **Wmk. 217**
185 A34 5 l steel blue 15.00 12.50
Never hinged 25.00
On first day cover 20.00

Unveiling of the Roman Column at San Marino. The date "1636 d. F. R." means the 1,636th year since the founding of the republic.
No. 185 was privately surcharged "+ 10 L 1941."

Souvenir Sheets

Abraham Lincoln — A35

1938, Apr. 7 **Wmk. 217** ***Perf. 13***
186 A35 3 l dark blue 2.75 2.75
Never hinged 3.75
187 A35 5 l rose red 18.00 18.00
Never hinged 37.50
Nos. 186-187 on first day cover 47.50

Dedication of a Lincoln bust, Sept. 3, 1937.

SEMI-POSTAL STAMPS

Regular Issue of 1903 Surcharged

a

b

1917, Dec. 15 **Wmk. 140** ***Perf. 14***
B1 A10(a) 25c on 2c violet 15.00 15.00
Never hinged 37.50
B2 A11(b) 50c on 2 l violet 60.00 60.00
Never hinged 150.00
Nos. B1-B2 on overfranked philatelic cover 350.00

Statue of Liberty — SP1

View of San Marino SP2

1918, June 1 **Typo.**
B3 SP1 2c dl vio & blk 3.75 3.75
Never hinged 9.50
B4 SP1 5c bl grn & blk 3.75 3.75
Never hinged 9.50
B5 SP1 10c lake & blk 3.75 3.75
Never hinged 9.50
B6 SP1 20c brn org & blk 3.75 3.75
Never hinged 9.50
B7 SP1 25c ultra & blk 3.75 3.75
Never hinged 9.50
B8 SP1 45c yel brn & blk 3.75 3.75
Never hinged 9.50
B9 SP2 1 l bl grn & blk 20.00 *24.00*
Never hinged 50.00
B10 SP2 2 l vio & blk 17.00 *21.00*
Never hinged 42.50
B11 SP2 3 l claret & blk 17.00 *21.00*
Never hinged 42.50
Nos. B3-B11 (9) 76.50 88.50
Set on overfranked philatelic cover 300.00

These stamps were sold at an advance of 5c each over face value, the receipts from that source being devoted to the support of a hospital for Italian soldiers.
For surcharges see Nos. 89-92.

Nos. B6-B8 Overprinted

1918, Dec. 12
B12 SP1 20c brn org & blk 6.00 6.00
Never hinged 15.00
B13 SP1 25c ultra & blk 6.00 6.00
Never hinged 15.00
B14 SP1 45c yel brn & blk 6.00 6.00
Never hinged 15.00

Nos. B9-B11 Ovptd.

B15 SP2 1 l blue grn & blk 10.50 10.50
Never hinged 25.00
B16 SP2 2 l violet & blk 19.00 20.00
Never hinged 47.50
B17 SP2 3 l claret & blk 19.00 20.00
Never hinged 47.50
Nos. B12-B17 (6) 66.50 68.50
Set on overfranked philatelic cover 240.00

Celebration of Italian Victory over Austria.
Inverted overprints were privately produced.

Coat of Arms SP3

Liberty SP4

1923, Sept. 20 **Engr.**
B18 SP3 5c + 5c olive grn .80 .80
Never hinged 2.00
B19 SP3 10c + 5c orange .80 .80
Never hinged 2.00
B20 SP3 15c + 5c dk green .80 .80
Never hinged 2.00
B21 SP3 25c + 5c brn lake .80 .80
Never hinged 2.00
B22 SP3 40c + 5c vio brn 4.00 4.00
Never hinged 10.00
B23 SP3 50c + 5c gray 2.40 .80
Never hinged 6.00
B24 SP4 1 l + 5c blk & bl 8.00 8.00
Never hinged 20.00
Nos. B18-B24 (7) 17.60 16.00
Set on overfranked philatelic cover 145.00

AIR POST STAMPS

View of San Marino AP1

Wmk. 217

1931, June 11 **Engr.** ***Perf. 12***
C1 AP1 50c blue grn 32.50 22.50
Never hinged 80.00
C2 AP1 80c red 32.50 22.50
Never hinged 80.00
C3 AP1 1 l bister brn 9.50 11.00
Never hinged 24.00
C4 AP1 2 l brt violet 9.50 11.00
Never hinged 24.00
C5 AP1 2.60 l Prus bl 65.00 *80.00*
Never hinged 160.00
C6 AP1 3 l dk gray 55.00 62.50
Never hinged 140.00
C7 AP1 5 l olive grn 9.50 11.00
Never hinged 24.00
C8 AP1 7.70 l dk brown 19.00 22.50
Never hinged 47.50
C9 AP1 9 l dp orange 19.00 22.50
Never hinged 47.50
C10 AP1 10 l dk blue 325.00 *500.00*
Never hinged 825.00
Nos. C1-C10 (10) 576.50 765.50
Set, never hinged 1,400.
Set on overfranked philatelic cover 2,150.

Exist imperf. Value, set $15,000.
For surhcarges see Nos. C11-C20.

Graf Zeppelin Issue

Stamps of Type AP1 Surcharged in Blue or Black

1933, Apr. 28
C11 AP1 3 l on 50c org 8.50 *155.00*
Never hinged 17.00
On flown cover 300.00
C12 AP1 5 l on 80c ol grn 42.50 *155.00*
Never hinged 85.00
On flown cover 350.00
C13 AP1 10 l on 1 l dk bl (Bk) 42.50 *200.00*
Never hinged 85.00
On flown cover *700.00*
C14 AP1 12 l on 2 l yel brn 42.50 *250.00*
Never hinged 85.00
On flown cover *1,150.*
C15 AP1 15 l on 2.60 l dl red (Bk) 42.50 *260.00*
Never hinged 85.00
On flown cover *1,400.*
C16 AP1 20 l on 3 l bl grn (Bk) 42.50 *425.00*
Never hinged 85.00
On flown cover *1,400.*
Nos. C11-C16 (6) 221.00 *1,445.*
Set, never hinged 440.00
Set, on single overfranked flight cover *4,500.*

Exist imperf.

Nos. C1 and C2 Surcharged

1936, Apr. 14
C17 AP1 75c on 50c blue grn 2.10 2.10
Never hinged 5.25
C18 AP1 75c on 80c red 12.50 12.50
Never hinged 32.50
Set, never hinged 37.50
Set, on single overfranked flight cover 65.00

SPECIAL DELIVERY STAMPS

SD1

Unwmk.

1907, Apr. 25 **Engr.** ***Perf. 12***
E1 SD1 25c carmine 35.00 17.50
Never hinged 110.00

For surcharges see Nos. E3, E5.

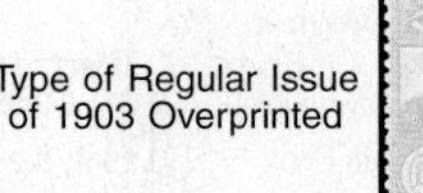
Type of Regular Issue of 1903 Overprinted

Perf. 14½x14

1923, May 30 **Wmk. 140**
E2 A11 60c violet 1.75 1.25
Never hinged 3.75

For surcharge see No. 103.

Type of 1907 Issue Surcharged

1923, July 26 ***Perf. 14***
E3 SD1 60c on 25c carmine 1.50 1.25
Never hinged 3.75
a. Vert. pair, imperf. between 275.00
Never hinged 550.00

No. E2 Surcharged

1926, Nov. 25 *Perf. 14½x14*

E4 A11 1.25 l on 60c violet 1.90 1.90
Never hinged 5.00

No. E3 Surcharged

1927, Sept. 15

E5 SD1 1.25 l on 60c on 25c 1.50 1.25
Never hinged 3.75
a. Inverted surcharge 175.00
Never hinged 350.00
b. Vert. pair, imperf. between 800.00
Never hinged 1,600.
c. Double surcharge 190.00
Never hinged 380.00

Statue of Liberty and View of San Marino — SD2

Wmk. 217

1929, Aug. 29 Engr. *Perf. 12*

E6 SD2 1.25 l green .65 .50
Never hinged 1.90

Overprinted in Red

E7 SD2 2.50 l deep blue 1.00 1.00
Never hinged 3.00

SEMI-POSTAL SPECIAL DELIVERY STAMP

SPSD1

Wmk. 140

1923, Sept. 20 Engr. *Perf. 14*

EB1 SPSD1 60c + 5c brown red 1.75 1.75
Never hinged 4.25

POSTAGE DUE STAMPS

D1

D2

D3

D4

Wmk. 140

1897-1920 Typo. *Perf. 14*

J1 D1 5c bl grn & dk brn 1.25 1.25
Never hinged 3.25
On cover 12.00
J2 D2 10c bl grn & dk brn 1.25 1.25
Never hinged 3.25
On cover 12.00
a. Numerals inverted 375.00 —
J3 D2 30c bl grn & dk brn 3.25 3.00
Never hinged 6.50
On cover 12.00
J4 D2 50c bl grn & dk brn 3.50 3.50
Never hinged 8.00
On cover 27.50
a. Numerals inverted 375.00 —
J5 D2 60c bl grn & dk brn 40.00 20.00
Never hinged 95.00
On cover 100.00
J6 D3 1 l claret & dk brn 7.50 7.50
Never hinged 19.00
On cover 47.50
J7 D4 3 l claret & brn ('20) 20.00 25.00
Never hinged 65.00
On cover 160.00
J8 D4 5 l claret & dk brn 80.00 55.00
Never hinged 190.00
On cover 275.00
J9 D2 10 l claret & dk brn 40.00 35.00
Never hinged 80.00
On cover 225.00
Nos. J1-J9 (9) 196.75 151.50

See Nos. J10-J36, J61. For surcharges see Nos. J37-J60, J64.

1924

J10 D1 5c rose & brown 1.75 1.75
Never hinged 4.75
On cover 24.00
J11 D2 10c rose & brown 1.75 1.75
Never hinged 4.75
On cover 16.00
J12 D2 30c rose & brown 3.00 3.00
Never hinged 8.00
On cover 24.00
J13 D2 50c rose & brown 3.25 3.25
Never hinged 9.50
On cover 27.50
J14 D2 60c rose & brown 12.00 12.00
Never hinged 32.50
On cover 80.00
J15 D3 1 l green & brown 20.00 20.00
Never hinged 47.50
On cover 120.00
J16 D4 3 l green & brown 55.00 55.00
Never hinged 130.00
On cover 360.00
J17 D4 5 l green & brown 70.00 70.00
Never hinged 160.00
On cover 440.00
J18 D2 10 l green & brown 325.00 325.00
Never hinged 750.00
On cover —
Nos. J10-J18 (9) 491.75 491.75

Postage Due Types of 1897 and

D5

1925-39 *Perf. 14*

J19 D1 5c blue & brn 1.50 .75
Never hinged 3.50
a. Numerals inverted 300.00 —
J20 D2 10c blue & brn 1.50 .75
Never hinged 3.50
a. Numerals inverted 300.00 —
J21 D2 15c blue & brn ('39) 1.00 .80
Never hinged 3.50
J22 D2 20c blue & brn ('39) 1.00 .80
Never hinged 1.60
J23 D2 25c blue & brn ('39) 1.50 1.25
Never hinged 2.40
J24 D2 30c blue & brn 1.50 .80
Never hinged 3.25
J25 D2 40c blue & brn ('39) 7.50 9.00
Never hinged 19.00
J26 D2 50c blue & brn 2.50 1.25
Never hinged 5.00
a. Numerals inverted 300.00 —
J27 D2 60c blue & brn 6.50 1.60
Never hinged 13.00
J28 D3 1 l buff & brn 9.50 1.60
Never hinged 19.00
J29 D4 2 l buff & brn ('39) 4.00 3.00
Never hinged 9.50
J30 D4 3 l buff & brn 125.00 50.00
Never hinged 250.00
J31 D4 5 l buff & brn 35.00 7.50
Never hinged 70.00
J32 D2 10 l buff & brn 47.50 20.00
Never hinged 95.00
J33 D5 15 l buff & brn ('28) 5.50 2.00
Never hinged 8.00
J34 D5 25 l buff & brn ('28) 67.50 40.00
Never hinged 135.00
J35 D5 30 l buff & brn ('28) 11.50 18.00
Never hinged 29.00
J36 D5 50 l buff & brn ('28) 13.50 18.00
Never hinged 32.50
Nos. J19-J36 (18) 343.50 177.10

Postage Due Stamps of 1925 Surcharged in Black and Silver

1931, May 18

J37 D1 15c on 5c bl & brn 1.50 1.50
Never hinged 3.25
J38 D2 15c on 10c bl & brn 1.50 1.50
Never hinged 3.25
J39 D2 15c on 30c bl & brn 1.50 1.50
Never hinged 3.25
J40 D1 20c on 5c bl & brn 1.50 1.50
Never hinged 3.25
J41 D2 20c on 10c bl & brn 1.50 1.50
Never hinged 3.25
J42 D2 20c on 30c bl & brn 1.50 1.50
Never hinged 3.25
J43 D1 25c on 5c bl & brn 4.50 3.00
Never hinged 8.00
J44 D2 25c on 10c bl & brn 4.50 3.00
Never hinged 8.00
J45 D2 25c on 30c bl & brn 25.00 20.00
Never hinged 65.00
J46 D1 40c on 5c bl & brn 4.50 1.50
Never hinged 8.00
J47 D2 40c on 10c bl & brn 5.50 1.50
Never hinged 9.50
J48 D2 40c on 30c bl & brn 5.50 1.50
Never hinged 9.50
J49 D1 2 l on 5c bl & brn 55.00 55.00
Never hinged 130.00
J50 D2 2 l on 10c bl & brn 140.00 100.00
Never hinged 300.00
J51 D2 2 l on 30c bl & brn 90.00 75.00
Never hinged 190.00
Nos. J37-J51 (15) 343.50 269.50

Nos. J19, J24-J25, J30, J34, J33, J22 Surcharged in Black

Perf. 14, 14½x14

1936-40 Wmk. 140

J52 D1 10c on 5c ('38) 5.50 3.00
Never hinged 9.50
J53 D2 25c on 30c ('38) 17.50 16.00
Never hinged 35.00
J54 D1 50c on 5c ('37) 17.50 16.00
Never hinged 35.00
J55 D2 1 l on 30c 67.50 11.00
Never hinged 160.00
J56 D2 1 l on 40c ('40) 11.50 12.00
Never hinged 27.50
J57 D4 1 l on 3 l ('37) 67.50 4.75
Never hinged 160.00
J58 D5 1 l on 25 l ('39) 110.00 30.00
Never hinged 250.00
J59 D5 2 l on 15 l ('38) 55.00 35.00
Never hinged 110.00
J60 D2 3 l on 20c ('40) 35.00 35.00
Never hinged 90.00
Nos. J52-J60 (9) 387.00 162.75

Postage Due Type of 1897

1939 Typo. *Perf. 14*

J61 D2 5c blue & brown 1.25 .50
Never hinged 1.60

Nos. J61 and J36 Surcharged

1940-43

J62 D2 10c on 5c .80 .40
Never hinged 1.60
J63 D2 50c on 5c 4.00 1.50
Never hinged 6.50
J64 D5 25 l on 50 l ('43) 3.50 3.50
Never hinged 9.50
Nos. J62-J64 (3) 8.30 5.40

PARCEL POST STAMPS

These stamps were used by affixing them to the way bill so that one half remained on it following the parcel, the other half staying on the receipt given the sender. Most used halves are right halves. Complete stamps were and are obtainable canceled, probably to order. Both unused and used values are for complete stamps. Most exist imperf and are scarce to rare thus.

PP1

Engraved, Typographed

1928, Nov. 22 Unwmk. *Perf. 12*

Pairs are imperforate between

Q1 PP1 5c blk brn & bl .60 .60
Never hinged 1.60
a. Imperf. 75.00
Q2 PP1 10c dk bl & bl .60 .60
Never hinged 1.60
Q3 PP1 20c gray blk & bl .60 .60
Never hinged 1.60
a. Imperf. 75.00
Q4 PP1 25c car & blue .60 .60
Never hinged 1.60
Q5 PP1 30c ultra & blue .60 .60
Never hinged 1.60
Q6 PP1 50c orange & bl .60 .60
Never hinged 1.60
Q7 PP1 60c rose & blue .60 .60
Never hinged 1.60
Q8 PP1 1 l violet & brn .60 .60
Never hinged 1.60
a. Imperf. 75.00
Q9 PP1 2 l green & brn 1.50 1.00
Never hinged 3.25
Q10 PP1 3 l bister & brn 1.75 1.25
Never hinged 4.00
Q11 PP1 4 l gray & brn 2.25 1.50
Never hinged 4.75
Q12 PP1 10 l rose lilac & brn 4.75 3.00
Never hinged 9.50
Q13 PP1 12 l red brn & brn 18.00 18.00
Never hinged 35.00
Q14 PP1 15 l olive grn & brn 27.50 27.50
Never hinged 55.00
a. Imperf. 75.00
Q15 PP1 20 l brn vio & brn 45.00 45.00
Never hinged 90.00
Nos. Q1-Q15 (15) 105.55 102.05

Halves Used

Q1-Q8	.25
Q9-Q10	.25
Q11	.25
Q12	.35
Q13	.65
Q14	2.75
Q15	3.00

SARAWAK

sə-ˈrä-ˌ(ˌ)wäˌk

LOCATION — Northwestern part of the island of Borneo, bordering on the South China Sea
GOVT. — British Crown Colony
AREA — 48,250 sq. mi. (approx.)
POP. — 975,918 (1970)
CAPITAL — Kuching

The last ruling Raja, who retired in 1946 when he ceded Sarawak to the British Crown, was Sir Charles Vyner Brooke, an Englishman. He inherited the title from his father, Sir Charles Johnson Brooke, who in turn received it from his uncle, Sir James Brooke. The title of Raja was conferred on Sir James by Raja Muda Hassim after Sir James had aided him in subduing a rebellion. The title and right of succession were duly recognized by the Sultan of Brunei and by Great Britain.

100 Cents = 1 Dollar

Catalogue values for unused stamps in this country are for Never Hinged items, beginning with Scott 155.

Watermarks

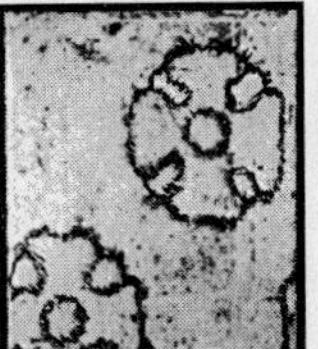

Wmk. 47 — Multiple Rosettes

Wmk. 71 — Rosette

Wmk. 231 — Oriental Crown

Unused examples of Nos. 1-7, 25 and 32-35 are valued without gum. Stamps with original gum are worth more.

Sir James Brooke — A1

Unwmk.

1869, Mar. 1 Litho. *Perf. 11*

1 A1 3c brown, *yellow* 60.00 *240.00*
On cover —

Covers: Only one authenticated cover is recorded with No. 1.

Sir Charles Johnson Brooke — A2

1871, Jan.

2 A2 3c brown, *yellow* 3.50 *4.00*
On cover —
a. Vertical pair, imperf between *600.00*
b. Horizontal pair, imperf between *1,000.*
c. Period after "THREE" 70.00 *85.00*

No. 2 surcharged "TWO CENTS" is believed to be bogus.

There are a number of lithographic flaws, including narrow A, "period" after THREE, etc.

Imperfs. of Nos. 1, 2 are proofs.

A papermaker's watermark, "LNL," usually appears once or twice in each pane.

For surcharges see Nos. 25, 32.

Covers: Only one authenticated cover is recorded with No. 2.

1875, Jan. 1 *Perf. 12*

3 A2 2c gray lilac, *lilac* 26.00 *22.00*
4 A2 4c brown, *yellow* 7.50 4.00
b. Vertical pair, imperf between *925.00* *975.00*
5 A2 6c green, *green* 6.00 5.00
6 A2 8c blue, *blue* 6.25 *7.50*
7 A2 12c red, *rose* 12.50 *9.00*
Nos. 3-7 (5) 58.25 *47.50*

Nos. 3-7 have each five varieties of the words of value.

Imperfs are proofs.

A papermaker's watermark usually appears once or twice in each pane of Nos. 3-7, "LNT" on No. 5, "LNL" on others.

Some examples of No. 7 have the appearance of being on laid paper, but the lines are accidental and not constant within the sheets.

For surcharges see Nos. 33-35.

Sir Charles Johnson Brooke — A4

1888-97 Typo. *Perf. 14*

8 A4 1c lilac & blk ('92) 6.50 1.60
9 A4 2c lilac & carmine 7.50 5.00
a. 2c pur & rose ('97) 17.50 6.00
10 A4 3c lilac & blue 11.00 *5.75*
11 A4 4c lilac & yellow 45.00 *70.00*
12 A4 5c lilac & grn ('91) 40.00 5.50
13 A4 6c lilac & brown 32.50 *70.00*
14 A4 8c green & car 21.00 6.00
a. 8c green & rose ('97) 40.00 19.00
15 A4 10c grn & vio ('91) 62.50 16.50
16 A4 12c green & blue 20.00 *16.00*
17 A4 16c gray grn & org ('97) 72.50 *95.00*
18 A4 25c green & brown 82.50 *52.50*
19 A4 32c gray grn & blk ('97) 62.50 *77.50*
20 A4 50c gray green ('97) 87.50 *130.00*
21 A4 $1 gray grn & blk ('97) 125.00 *135.00*
Nos. 8-21 (14) 676.00 *686.35*

No. 21 shows the numeral on white tablet.

Three higher values — $2, $5, $10 — were prepared but not issued. Value $950 each.

For surcharges see Nos. 22-24, 26-27.

Nos. 14 and 16 Surcharged in Black

No. 22

No. 23

No. 24

1889-91

22 A4 2c on 8c 4.50 *12.00*
a. Double surcharge 525.00
b. Pair, one without surcharge 8,500.
c. Inverted surcharge 4,500.
23 A4 5c on 12c ('91) 40.00 *62.50*
a. Double surcharge 1,400. *1,400.*
b. Pair, one without surcharge *13,000.*
c. No period after "C" 45.00 *70.00*
d. Without "C" 850.00 975.00
e. Double surch., one vert. 4,250.
24 A4 5c on 12c ('91) 350.00 *375.00*
a. No period after "C" 190.00 *200.00*
b. Double surcharge 1,500.
c. "C" omitted 1,400. *1,500.*

No. 2 Surcharged in Black

1892, May 23 *Perf. 11*

25 A2 1c on 3c brown, *yel* 2.50 *3.00*
b. Without bar 275.00 *275.00*
c. Period after "THREE" 57.50 *70.00*
d. Double surcharge 475.00 550.00
e. Vertical pair, imperf between *800.00*
f. Vertical pair, imperf horiz. *800.00*

Examples of No. 25b must be from the first printing, wherein the bar was applied after the surcharge. Examples of No. 25 with parts of the surcharge and/or bar omitted are stamps that had gum on the face prior to the surcharging operation. The ink was removed when the gum was washed off.

No. 10 Surcharged in Black

e

f

1892 *Perf. 14*

26 A4(e) 1c on 3c lil & bl 3.75 *3.75*
a. No period after "cent" 275.00 *300.00*
27 A4(f) 1c on 3c lil & bl 80.00 50.00
b. Double surcharge 800.00 850.00

Issued: #26, Feb.; #27, Jan. 12.

Sir Charles Johnson Brooke
A11 A12

A13

A14

1895, Jan. 1 Engr. *Perf. 11½, 12*

28 A11 2c red brn 17.50 *9.75*
a. Perf. 12½ 27.00 5.00
b. Vertical pair, imperf between *650.00*
c. Horizontal pair, imperf between *500.00*
d. As "a," horiz. pair, imperf between *750.00*
29 A12 4c black 17.50 3.75
a. Horizontal pair, imperf between *875.00*
30 A13 6c violet 20.00 *9.75*
31 A14 8c deep green 45.00 6.00
Nos. 28-31 (4) 100.00 29.25

The 2c and 8c imperf are proofs. Perforated stamps of these designs in other colors are color trials, which exist surcharged with new values in pence. These surcharged varieties were used in trial printings of a British South African issue.

Stamps of 1871-75 Surcharged in Black or Red

1899 *Perf. 11*

32 A2 2c on 3c brown, *yel* 4.25 *2.00*
a. Period after "THREE" 90.00 *90.00*
b. Vertical pair, imperf between *1,000.*

Perf. 12

33 A2 2c on 12c red, *rose* 4.00 *5.00*
a. Inverted surcharge 1,000. *1,400.*
34 A2 4c on 6c grn, *grn* (R) 62.50 *125.00*
35 A2 4c on 8c blue, *bl* (R) 10.00 *16.00*
Nos. 32-35 (4) 80.75 *148.00*

Sir Charles J. Brooke — A16

1899-1908 Typo. *Perf. 14*

36 A16 1c blue & car ('01) 1.75 *1.75*
a. 1c ultra & pink 12.00 3.75
37 A16 2c gray green 2.25 1.00
38 A16 3c dull violet ('08) 26.00 .75
39 A16 4c aniline car 2.75 .25
a. 4c rose ('99) 17.00 2.90
40 A16 8c yellow & black 2.75 .90
41 A16 10c ultra 7.00 1.10
42 A16 12c light violet ('99) 7.00 7.00
a. 12c bright purple ('05) 50.00 13.00
43 A16 16c org brn & grn 8.50 1.90
44 A16 20c brn ol & vio ('00) 8.00 7.50
45 A16 25c brown & ultra 11.00 *7.00*
46 A16 50c ol grn & rose 35.00 *40.00*
47 A16 $1 rose & green 100.00 *130.00*
a. $1 pink & pale green 100.00 *140.00*
Nos. 36-47 (12) 212.00 *199.15*

A 5c was prepared but not issued. Value $16.

1901 Wmk. 71

48 A16 2c gray green 62.50 23.00

Sir Charles Vyner Brooke — A17

1918-23 Unwmk.

50 A17 1c slate bl & rose 2.60 *3.25*
51 A17 2c deep green 3.00 1.75
52 A17 2c violet ('23) 2.25 *3.00*
53 A17 3c violet brown 3.75 3.00
54 A17 3c dp grn ('22) 5.00 1.40
55 A17 4c carmine rose 9.00 4.25
56 A17 4c purple brn ('23) 2.50 *2.75*
57 A17 5c orange ('23) 3.00 2.75
58 A17 6c lake brn ('22) 2.25 *1.60*
59 A17 8c yellow & blk 17.50 *75.00*
60 A17 8c car rose ('22) 5.25 *35.00*
61 A17 10c ultra 7.00 6.50
a. 10c blue 7.00 6.50
62 A17 10c black ('23) 4.50 *5.00*
63 A17 12c violet 22.50 *57.50*
64 A17 12c ultra ('22) 12.50 *21.00*
65 A17 16c brn & blue grn 7.00 *8.50*
66 A17 20c olive bis & vio 9.50 *7.50*
a. 20c olive green & violet 9.50 *7.50*
67 A17 25c brown & blue 4.75 *25.00*
68 A17 30c bis & gray ('22) 4.25 *4.75*
69 A17 50c ol grn & rose 11.50 *17.00*
70 A17 $1 car rose & grn 42.50 *32.50*
Nos. 50-70 (21) 182.10 *319.00*

In 1918 a supply of the 1c (No. 50) had the value tablet printed, by error, in slate blue instead of rose. It is officially stated that this stamp was never issued and had no franking power. Value $22.

The $1 denomination shows numeral of value in color on white tablet.

Nos. 61 and 63 Surcharged

1st Printing — Bars 1¼mm apart.
2nd Printing — Bars ¾mm apart.

1923, Jan.

77 A17 1c on 10c ultra 16.50 *62.50*
a. "cnet" 25,000.
b. Bars ¾mm apart 180.00 *500.00*
78 A17 2c on 12c violet 11.00 *55.00*
a. Bars ¾mm apart 92.50 *350.00*

No. 77b was created with "cnet" by the post office to sell additional error sheets to dealers after No. 77a had been corrected.Sale of these items was quickly discontinued.

Type of 1918 Issue

1928-29 Typo. Wmk. 47

79 A17 1c slate blue & rose 1.75 .80
80 A17 2c dull violet 2.75 1.80
81 A17 3c deep green 4.50 *5.75*
82 A17 4c purple brown 2.10 .25
83 A17 5c orange ('29) 14.00 5.75
84 A17 6c brown lake 1.50 .35
85 A17 8c carmine 4.00 *35.00*
86 A17 10c black 2.00 1.40
87 A17 12c ultra 4.00 *45.00*
88 A17 16c dp brn & bl grn 4.00 *4.50*
89 A17 20c dp olive & vio 4.00 *10.00*
90 A17 25c dk brown & ultra 7.00 *9.75*
91 A17 30c olive bis & gray 5.50 *11.50*
92 A17 50c olive grn & rose 15.00 *26.00*
93 A17 $1 car rose & grn 22.50 *27.50*
Nos. 79-93 (15) 94.60 *185.35*
Set, never hinged 170.00

Sir Charles Vyner Brooke — A18

Wmk. 231

1932, Jan. 1 Engr. *Perf. 12½*

94 A18 1c indigo 1.00 1.10
95 A18 2c dark green 1.25 *2.25*
96 A18 3c deep violet 5.00 1.10
97 A18 4c deep orange 12.00 .85
98 A18 5c brown lake 8.50 1.40
99 A18 6c deep red 9.75 *11.00*
100 A18 8c orange yel 11.00 *9.75*
101 A18 10c black 2.75 *3.75*
102 A18 12c violet blue 5.00 *11.00*
103 A18 15c orange brown 8.25 *11.00*
104 A18 20c violet & org 8.00 *9.00*
105 A18 25c org brn & yel 15.00 *25.00*
106 A18 30c org red & ol brn 12.50 *42.50*
107 A18 50c olive grn & red 17.50 *15.00*
108 A18 $1 car & green 25.00 *40.00*
Nos. 94-108 (15) 142.50 *184.70*

Sir Charles Vyner Brooke — A19

1934-41 Unwmk. *Perf. 12*

109 A19 1c brown violet 1.50 .25
110 A19 2c blue green 1.75 .25
111 A19 2c black ('41) 4.75 *1.75*
112 A19 3c black 1.40 .25
113 A19 3c blue grn ('41) 8.00 *5.00*
114 A19 4c magenta 2.25 .25
115 A19 5c violet 2.25 .25
116 A19 6c deep rose 3.00 .70
117 A19 6c red brn ('41) 8.75 *9.00*
118 A19 8c red brown 2.50 .25
119 A19 8c dp rose ('41) 9.25 .25
120 A19 10c red 5.00 .45
121 A19 12c deep ultra 3.50 .30
122 A19 12c orange ('41) 7.50 *6.25*
123 A19 15c orange 8.00 *12.00*
124 A19 15c deep blue ('41) 9.75 *20.00*
125 A19 20c dp rose & olive 8.50 1.50
126 A19 25c orange & vio 8.50 *2.00*
127 A19 30c vio & red brn 8.50 *3.25*
128 A19 50c red & violet 12.50 1.00
129 A19 $1 dk brn & red 7.00 1.00
130 A19 $2 violet & mag 30.00 34.00
131 A19 $3 bl grn & rose 50.00 *55.00*
132 A19 $4 red & ultra 50.00 *80.00*
133 A19 $5 red brn & red 80.00 *85.00*
134 A19 $10 orange & blk 35.00 *85.00*
Nos. 109-134 (26) 369.15 *404.95*

Issue dates: May 1, 1934, Mar. 1, 1941.
For overprints see #135-154, 159-173, N1-N22.

Stamps of 1934-41 Overprinted in Black or Red

1945, Dec. 17

135 A19 1c brown violet .85 .70
136 A19 2c black (R) 3.00 *1.50*
137 A19 3c blue green .85 *2.00*
138 A19 4c magenta 2.25 .35
139 A19 5c violet (R) 3.00 1.50
140 A19 6c red brown 3.50 .90
141 A19 8c deep rose 9.50 *23.00*
142 A19 10c red 1.50 .80
143 A19 12c orange 4.00 *4.25*
144 A19 15c deep blue 6.00 .45
145 A19 20c dp rose & ol 4.00 *5.50*
146 A19 25c org & vio (R) 4.50 *3.50*
147 A19 30c vio & red brn 4.75 *4.25*
148 A19 50c red & violet 1.50 .40
149 A19 $1 dk brn & red 2.00 *5.00*
150 A19 $2 violet & mag 6.75 *21.00*
151 A19 $3 bl grn & rose 19.00 *92.50*
152 A19 $4 red & ultra 24.00 *65.00*
153 A19 $5 red brn & red 125.00 *275.00*
154 A19 $10 org & blk (R) 110.00 *250.00*
Nos. 135-154 (20) 335.95 *757.60*
Set, never hinged 500.00

Catalogue values for unused stamps in this section, from this point to the end of the section, are for Never Hinged items.

Sir James Brooke, Sir Charles V. Brooke and Sir Charles J. Brooke A20

1946, May 18

155 A20 8c dark carmine 4.75 1.75
156 A20 15c dark blue 5.00 2.50
157 A20 50c red & black 5.00 3.00
158 A20 $1 sepia & black 5.00 *42.50*
Nos. 155-158 (4) 19.75 *49.75*

Type of 1934-41 Overprinted in Blue or Red

1947, Apr. 16 Wmk. 4 *Perf. 12*

159 A19 1c brown violet .25 *.30*
160 A19 2c black (R) .25 .25
161 A19 3c blue green (R) .25 .25
162 A19 4c magenta .30 .25
163 A19 6c red brown .50 *.90*
164 A19 8c deep rose 1.00 .25
165 A19 10c red .50 .25
166 A19 12c orange .70 *1.00*
167 A19 15c deep blue (R) .50 *.55*
168 A19 20c dp rose & ol (R) 2.00 .65
169 A19 25c orange & vio (R) .65 .55
170 A19 50c red & violet (R) 1.25 .80
171 A19 $1 dk brown & red 1.50 *1.00*
172 A19 $2 violet & magenta 3.75 *6.50*
173 A19 $5 red brown & red 9.00 3.25
Nos. 159-173 (15) 22.40 16.75

Common Design Types pictured following the introduction.

Silver Wedding Issue
Common Design Types

1948, Oct. 25 Photo. *Perf. 14x14½*

174 CD304 8c scarlet .40 .40

Perf. 11½x11

Engraved; Name Typographed

175 CD305 $5 light brown 50.00 *52.50*

UPU Issue
Common Design Types

Engr.; Name Typo. on 15c, 25c
Perf. 13½, 11x11½

1949, Oct. 10 Wmk. 4

176 CD306 8c rose carmine 1.40 .60
177 CD307 15c indigo 3.25 2.25
178 CD308 25c green 1.75 1.50
179 CD309 50c violet 1.75 *6.50*
Nos. 176-179 (4) 8.15 10.85

Troides Brookiana A21

Western Tarsier — A22

Designs: 3c, Kayan tomb. 4c, Kayan girl and boy. 6c, Bead work. 8c, Dyak dancer. 10c, Scaly anteater. 12c, Kenyah boys. 15c, Fire making. 20c, Kelemantan rice barn. 25c, Pepper vines. 50c, Iban woman. $1, Kelabit smithy. $2, Map of Sarawak. $5, Arms of Sarawak.

Perf. 11½x11, 11x11½

1950, Jan. 3 Engr.

180 A21 1c black .75 .30
181 A22 2c orange red .45 *.50*
182 A22 3c green .60 *1.00*
183 A22 4c brown 1.00 .25
184 A22 6c aquamarine .75 .25
185 A21 8c red 1.00 .30
186 A21 10c orange 3.00 *5.50*
187 A21 12c purple 3.25 1.40
188 A21 15c deep blue 4.25 .25
189 A21 20c red org & brn 2.50 .50
190 A21 25c carmine & grn 3.75 .60
191 A22 50c purple & brn 8.00 .45
192 A21 $1 dk brn & bl grn 25.00 4.25
193 A21 $2 rose car & blue 40.00 16.00

Engr. and Typo.

194 A21 $5 dp vio, blk, red & yel 30.00 18.00
Nos. 180-194 (15) 124.30 49.55

1952, Feb. 1

195 A21 10c orange *(Map)* 2.00 .65

OCCUPATION STAMPS

Issued under Japanese Occupation

Stamps of 1934-41 Handstamped in Violet

1942 Unwmk. *Perf. 12*

N1 A19 1c brown vio 45.00 *85.00*
N2 A19 2c blue green 125.00 *200.00*
N3 A19 2c black 170.00 *200.00*
N3A A19 3c black *500.00* *500.00*
N4 A19 3c blue green 100.00 *110.00*
N5 A19 4c magenta 130.00 *140.00*
N6 A19 5c violet 160.00 *170.00*
N7 A19 6c deep rose 225.00 180.00
N8 A19 6c red brown 120.00 *160.00*
N8A A19 8c red brown *500.00* *500.00*
N9 A19 8c deep rose 100.00 *120.00*
N10 A19 10c red 130.00 *150.00*
N11 A19 12c deep ultra 250.00 *250.00*
N12 A19 12c orange 200.00 *200.00*
N12A A19 15c orange *600.00* *600.00*
N13 A19 15c deep blue 180.00 *190.00*
N14 A19 20c dp rose & ol 95.00 *120.00*
N15 A19 25c org & vio 130.00 *150.00*
N16 A19 30c vio & red brn 100.00 *120.00*
N17 A19 50c red & vio 100.00 *120.00*
N18 A19 $1 dk brn & red 150.00 *170.00*
N19 A19 $2 vio & mag 375.00 *475.00*
N19A A19 $3 blue grn & rose *3,750.* *3,750.*
N20 A19 $4 red & ultra 325.00 *475.00*
N21 A19 $5 red brn & red 325.00 *475.00*
N22 A19 $10 org & blk 325.00 *475.00*
Nos. N1-N22 (26) *9,210.* *10,085.*

Stamps overprinted with Japanese characters in oval frame or between 2 vertical black lines were not for paying postage.

SASENO

ˈsə-ˈzā-ˌnō

LOCATION — An island in the Adriatic Sea, lying at the entrance of Valona Bay, Albania
GOVT. — Italian possession
AREA — 2 sq. mi.

Italy occupied this Albanian islet in 1914, and returned it to Albania in 1947.

100 Centesimi = 1 Lira

Used values in italics are for postally used stamps. CTO's sell for about the same as unused, hinged stamps.

Italian Stamps of 1901-22 Overprinted

1923 Wmk. 140 *Perf. 14*

1 A48 10c claret 32.50 *82.50*
Never hinged 75.00
a. Double overprint —
2 A48 15c slate 32.50 *82.50*
Never hinged 75.00
3 A50 20c brown orange 32.50 *82.50*
Never hinged 75.00
4 A49 25c blue 32.50 *82.50*
Never hinged 75.00
5 A49 30c yellow brown 32.50 *82.50*
Never hinged 75.00
6 A49 50c violet 32.50 *82.50*
Never hinged 75.00
7 A49 60c carmine 32.50 *82.50*
Never hinged 75.00
8 A46 1 l brown & green 32.50 *82.50*
Never hinged 75.00
a. Double overprint 475.00
b. Vertical overprint 190.00
Nos. 1-8 (8) 260.00 *660.00*
Set, never hinged 600.00

Superseded by postage stamps of Italy.

SAUDI ARABIA

ˈsau-dē ə-ˈrā-bē-ə

LOCATION — Southwestern Asia, on the Arabian Peninsula between the Red Sea and the Persian Gulf
GOVT. — Kingdom
AREA — 927,000 sq. mi.
POP. — 8,400,000 (est. 1984)
CAPITAL — Riyadh

In 1916 the Grand Sherif of Mecca declared the Sanjak of Hejaz independent of Turkish rule. In 1925, Ibn Saud, then Sultan of the Nejd, captured the Hejaz after a prolonged siege of Jedda, the last Hejaz stronghold.

The resulting Kingdom of the Hejaz and Nejd was renamed Saudi Arabia in 1932.

40 Paras = 1 Piaster = 1 Guerche (Garch, Qirsh)
11 Guerche = 1 Riyal (1928)
110 Guerche = 1 Sovereign (1931)

HEJAZ

Sherifate of Mecca

Adapted from Carved Door Panels of Mosque El Salih Talay, Cairo — A1

Taken from Page of Koran in Mosque of El Sultan Barquq, Cairo — A2

Taken from Details of an Ancient Prayer Niche in the Mosque of El Amri at Qus in Upper Egypt — A3

Perf. 10, 12

1916, Oct. Unwmk. Typo.

L1 A1 ¼pi green 60.00 50.00
Never hinged 90.00
L2 A2 ½pi red 60.00 45.00
Never hinged 90.00
a. Perf. 10 225.00 90.00
L3 A3 1pi blue 20.00 18.00
Never hinged 30.00
On cover 150.00
a. Perf. 12 250.00 200.00
b. Perf. 10x12 1,450. 1,450.
Nos. L1-L3 (3) 140.00 113.00

Exist imperf. Forged perf. exist.
See Nos. L5-L7, L10-L12. For overprints see Nos. L16-L18, L26-L28, L52-L54, L57-L59, L61-L66, L67, L70-L72, L77-L81, 37.

Central Design Adapted from a Koran Design for a Tomb. Background is from Stone Carving on Entrance Arch to the Ministry of Wakfs — A4

1916-17 *Roulette 20*

L4 A4 ⅛pi orange ('17) 5.50 2.00
Never hinged 8.25
On cover 150.00
L5 A1 ¼pi green 8.00 2.00
Never hinged 12.00
On cover 200.00
L6 A2 ½pi red 9.75 2.00
Never hinged 14.75
L7 A3 1pi blue 10.50 2.00
Never hinged 15.00
On cover, single franking 100.00
Nos. L4-L7 (4) 33.75 8.00

See No. L9. For overprints & surcharge see Nos. L15c, L16c, L17b, L18d, L25, L51, L56, L69, 33.

Adapted from Stucco Work above Entrance to Cairo R. R. Station A5

Adapted from First Page of the Koran of Sultan Farag — A6

1917 *Serrate Roulette 13*

L8 A5 1pa lilac brown 5.75 2.00
Never hinged 8.50
On cover 75.00
L9 A4 ⅛pi orange 6.25 3.00
Never hinged 9.50
On cover 75.00
L10 A1 ¼pi green 6.25 3.00
Never hinged 9.50
On cover 75.00
L11 A2 ½pi red 7.00 4.40
Never hinged 10.50
On cover 150.00
L12 A3 1pi blue 7.25 4.40
Never hinged 10.50
On cover, single franking 100.00
L13 A6 2pi magenta 32.50 14.50
Never hinged 50.00
On cover, single franking *425.00*
Nos. L8-L13 (6) 65.00 31.30

Designs A1-A6 are inscribed "Hejaz Postage."
For overprints and surcharge see Nos. L14-L31, L55-60, L62, L65--L75, L79a-81.

Kingdom of the Hejaz

Stamps of 1917-18 Overprinted in Black, Red or Brown

1921, Dec. 21 *Serrate Roulette 13*

L14 A5 1pa lilac brown 45.00 24.00
Never hinged 65.00
a. Date omitted at right 200.00
b. Date omitted at left 250.00
L15 A4 ⅛pi orange 87.50 27.50
Never hinged 130.00
a. Inverted overprint 175.00
b. Double overprint 265.00
c. Roulette 20 1,000. 1,000.
d. As "c," invtd. overprint 1,825. *1,825.*
e. Double overprint, one inverted 900.00
f. Double overprint, both inverted 900.00
g. Date omitted at right 185.00
h. Date omitted at left 500.00
L16 A1 ¼pi green 20.00 9.00
Never hinged 35.00
On cover 250.00
a. Inverted overprint 110.00
b. Double overprint 225.00
c. Roulette 20 1,100. 1,100.
d. As "c," invtd. overprint 2,050. 2,050.
e. Double overprint, one inverted 825.00
f. Double overprint, both inverted 225.00
g. Date omitted at right 60.00
h. Date omitted at left 200.00
L17 A2 ½pi red 21.00 6.75
Never hinged 35.00
On cover 325.00
a. Inverted overprint 200.00 77.50
b. Roulette 20 1,000. 1,000.
c. Double overprint 600.00
d. Double overprint, both inverted 600.00
e. Date omitted at right 100.00
L18 A3 1pi blue (R) 20.00 10.00
Never hinged 35.00
On cover 325.00
a. Brown overprint 85.00 37.50
b. Black overprint 155.00 82.50
c. As "b," invtd. overprint 500.00
d. Roulette 20 1,000. 1,000.
e. Date omitted at right 400.00
L19 A6 2pi magenta 25.00 15.00
Never hinged 40.00
a. Double overprint *3,500.*
b. Date omitted at right 150.00
c. As "a," date omitted at right 12,500.
Nos. L14-L19 (6) 218.50 92.25

Nos. L15-L17, L18b and L19 exist with date (1340) omitted at left or right side.
All values except No. L15 exist with gold overprint.
No. L19c is unique.
For errors and varieties in never hinged condition add 50%.

No. L14 With Additional Surcharge

a

b

L22 A5(a) ½pi on 1pa 500.00 225.00
Never hinged 750.00
No gum 75.00
L23 A5(b) 1pi on 1pa 500.00 225.00
Never hinged 750.00
No gum 75.00

Forgeries of Nos. L14-L23 abound.

Stamps of 1917-18 Overprinted in Black

1922, Jan. 7

L24 A5 1pa lilac brown 12.50 4.50
Never hinged 19.00
a. Inverted overprint 150.00
b. Double overprint 150.00
c. Double ovpt., one inverted 250.00
L25 A4 ⅛pi orange 20.00 12.50
Never hinged 30.00
a. Inverted overprint 175.00
b. Double ovpt., one inverted 250.00
L26 A1 ¼pi green 5.75 4.50
Never hinged 10.00
a. Inverted overprint 175.00
b. Double ovpt., one inverted 250.00
L27 A2 ½pi red 10.00 3.25
Never hinged 15.00
a. Inverted overprint 135.00
b. Double ovpt., one inverted 275.00
L28 A3 1pi blue 5.00 1.40
Never hinged 7.50
a. Double overprint 275.00
b. Inverted overprint 165.00
L29 A6 2pi magenta 10.00 10.00
Never hinged 15.00
a. Double overprint 275.00

With Additional Surcharge of New Value

L30 A5(a) ½pi on 1pa lil brn 40.00 21.00
Never hinged 30.00
L31 A5(b) 1pi on 1pa lil brn 4.00 1.50
Never hinged 6.00
On cover, single franking 325.00
a. Inverted surcharge 145.00
b. Double surcharge 165.00
c. Dbl. surch., one invtd., ovpt. invtd. 300.00
d. Inverted overprint 145.00
e. Inverted overprint and surcharge 300.00
f. Inverted overprint, double surcharge 300.00
g. Words of surcharge transposed 300.00
h. Overprint and surcharge inverted, words of surcharge transposed 500.00
i. Right hand character of surcharge inverted 110.00
Nos. L24-L31 (8) 107.25 58.65

The 1921 and 1922 overprints read: "The Arab Hashemite Government, 1340."
The overprint on No. L28 in red is bogus.
Forgeries abound.
For errors and varieties in never hinged condition add 50%.

Types A7 and A8
Very fine examples will be somewhat off center but perforations will be clear of the framelines.

Arms of Sherif of Mecca — A7

1922, Feb. Typo. *Perf. 11½*

L32 A7 ⅛pi red brown 3.00 .85
Never hinged 4.50
L34 A7 ½pi red 3.25 .60
Never hinged 4.75
On cover 125.00
a. Horiz. pair, imperf. btwn. 87.50 *35.00*
Never hinged 175.00
b. Vert. pair, imperf. btwn. — —
c. ½pi deep rose 15.50 2.00
Never hinged 23.50
L35 A7 1pi dark blue 3.50 .60
Never hinged 5.00
On cover 125.00
a. Vert. pair, imperf. btwn. 87.50
Never hinged 175.00
L36 A7 1½pi violet 4.00 .85
Never hinged 6.00
On cover, single franking 200.00
L37 A7 2pi orange 4.00 .90
Never hinged 6.00
On cover, single franking 75.00
L38 A7 3pi olive brown 4.00 .85
Never hinged 6.00
a. 3pi brown 30.00 15.00
Never hinged 45.00
L39 A7 5pi olive green 4.25 .85
Never hinged 6.25
Nos. L32-L39 (7) 26.00 5.50

Numerous shades exist. Some values were printed in other colors in 1925 for handstamping by the Nejdi authorities in Mecca. These exist without handstamps.
Exist imperf.
Forgeries exist, usually perf. 11.
Reprints of Nos. L32, L35 exist; paper and shades differ.
See Nos. L48A-L49. For surcharges and overprints see Nos. L40-L48, L76, L82-L159, 7-20, 38A-48, 55A-58A, LJ11-LJ16, LJ26-LJ39, J1-J8, J10-J11, P1-P3, Jordan 64-72, 91, 103-120, J1-J17, O1.

Stamps of 1922 Surcharged with New Values in Arabic

c

d

1923
L40 A7(c) ¼pi on ⅛pi org brn 55.00 50.00
Never hinged 82.50
On cover 300.00
a. Double surcharge 375.00
b. Double inverted surcharge 8.00
No gum 80.00
c. Double surch., one invtd. 475.00
No gum 50.00
d. Inverted surcharge — —
L41 A7(d) 10pi on 5pi ol grn 82.50 42.50
Never hinged 125.00
a. Double surch., one invtd. 375.00
b. Inverted surcharge 800.00

Forgeries exist.

Caliphate Issue

Stamps of 1922 Overprinted in Gold

1924
L42 A7 ⅛pi orange brown 7.00 *15.00*
Never hinged 14.00
On cover 700.00
L43 A7 ½pi red 4.50 *15.00*
Never hinged 9.00
L44 A7 1pi dark blue 7.00 *12.50*
Never hinged 14.00
On cover 700.00
a. Inverted overprint 375.00
L45 A7 1½pi violet 7.00 *12.50*
Never hinged 14.00
On cover 1,250.
L46 A7 2pi orange 7.00 *10.00*
Never hinged 14.00
On cover 1,250.
a. Inverted overprint 375.00
b. 2pi deep ochre 9.50 15.00
Never hinged 19.00
L47 A7 3pi olive brown 9.50 *15.00*
Never hinged 19.00
L48 A7 5pi olive green 8.25 *15.00*
Never hinged 16.50
a. Inverted overprint 400.00
Nos. L42-L48 (7) 50.25 95.00

Assumption of the Caliphate by King Hussein in Mar., 1924. The overprint reads "In commemoration of the Caliphate, Shaaban, 1342."

The overprint was typographed in black and dusted with "gold" powder while wet. Inverted overprints on other values are forgeries. So-called black overprints are either forgeries or gold overprints with the gold rubbed off. No genuine black overprints are known.

The overprint is 18-20mm wide. The 1st setting of the ½p is 16mm.

Forgeries exist.

Nos. L43-L44, L46 exist with postage due overprint as on Nos. LJ11-LJ13.

Type of 1922 and

Arms of Sherif of Mecca — A8

1924 *Perf. 11½*
L48A A7 ¼pi yellow green 9.00 *9.00*
Never hinged 17.50
b. Tête bêche pair *155.00* 125.00
Never hinged 275.00
c. Cracked plate (pos. 13) *50.00*
Never hinged *75.00*
d. Cracked plate in tête-bêche pair *350.00*
Never hinged *700.00*
L49 A7 3pi brown red 30.00 *14.50*
Never hinged 45.00
a. 3pi dull red 5.00 *7.50*
Never hinged 7.50
L50 A8 10pi vio & dk brn 7.00 *7.00*
Never hinged 12.50
a. Center inverted *100.00* 90.00
Never hinged 175.00
c. 10pi purple & sepia 7.00 *7.50*
Never hinged 12.50
Nos. L48A-L50 (3) 46.00 30.50

Nos. L48A, L50, L50a exist imperf.

Several printings of Nos. L48A-L50 exist; paper and shades differ.

A plate flaw in position 13 of No. L48A, which appears as a large white gash in the upper left portion of the stamp, exists. Values: unused single, $50; unused tête-bêche pair, $250.

Forgeries exist, usually perf. 11.

For overprint see Nos. L76A, Jordan 121.

Jedda Issues

Stamps of 1916-17 Overprinted

The Jedda overprints on Nos. L51-L159 read: "Al-hukuma al Hejaziyeh, 5 Rabi al'awwal 1343"

(The Hejaz Government, October 4, 1924). This is the date of the accession of King Ali.

Counterfeits exist of all Jedda overprints.

Jedda issues were also used in Medina and Yambo.

Used values for #L51-L186 and LJ17-LJ39 are for genuine cancels. Privately applied cancels exist for "Mekke" (Mecca, bilingual or all Arabic), Khartoum, Cairo, as well as for Jeddah. Many private cancels have wrong dates, some as early as 1916. These are worth half the used values.

Red Overprint

1925, Jan. *Roulette 20*
L51 A4 ⅛pi orange 27.50 *27.50*
Never hinged 40.00
a. Inverted overprint 135.00
b. Ovptd. on face and back 250.00
c. Normal ovpt. on face, double ovpt. on back — —
d. Inverted ovptd. on face and back 350.00
e. Dbl. ovpt., both invert. 500.00
L52 A1 ¼pi green 27.50 *22.00*
Never hinged 40.00
a. Inverted overprint 82.50
b. Double overprint 82.50
c. Double overprint, one invtd. 210.00
L53 A2 ½pi red 100.00 *100.00*
Never hinged 150.00
a. Inverted overprint 185.00
L54 A3 1pi blue 55.00 *55.00*
Never hinged 90.00
a. Inverted overprint *185.00*
b. Double ovpt., one invtd. 185.00
Nos. L51-L53 (3) 155.00 *149.50*

Serrate Roulette 13

L55 A5 1pa lilac brown 30.00 *20.00*
Never hinged 45.00
a. Inverted overprint 82.50
b. Double overprint 87.50
c. Ovptd. on face and back *200.00*
d. Normal ovpt. on face, double ovpt. on back 210.00
L56 A4 ⅛pi orange 72.50 *55.00*
Never hinged 110.00
a. Inverted overprint 120.00
L57 A1 ¼pi green 37.50 *30.00*
Never hinged 57.50
a. Pair, one without overprint *2,000.*
b. Inverted overprint 120.00
c. Double ovpt., one inverted 325.00
L58 A2 ½pi red 55.00 *45.00*
Never hinged 82.50
a. Inverted overprint *175.00*
L59 A3 1pi blue 60.00 *50.00*
Never hinged 90.00
a. Inverted overprint *150.00*
L60 A6 2pi magenta 55.00 *50.00*
Never hinged 85.00
a. Inverted overprint *155.00*
Nos. L55-L60 (6) 310.00 *250.00*

Gold Overprint

Roulette 20

L61 A1 ¼pi green, gold on red ovpt. *2,750.*
Never hinged 4,000.
No gum 1,000.
a. Gold on blue ovpt. 4,250. *7,000.*
On cover front 125,000.

Serrate Roulette 13

L62 A1 ¼pi green, gold on red ovpt. 45.00 *35.00*
Never hinged 67.50
a. Inverted overprint *300.00*

The overprint on No. L61 was typographed in red or blue (No. L62 only in red) and dusted with "gold" powder while wet.

For errors and varieties in never hinged condition add 50%.

Blue Overprint

Roulette 20

L63 A1 ¼pi green 150.00 *35.00*
Never hinged 225.00
a. Inverted overprint 185.00
b. Ovptd. on face and back 250.00 *550.00*
L64 A2 ½pi red, invtd. ovpt. 225.00 *80.00*
Never hinged 325.00
a. Upright overprint 200.00

Serrate Roulette 13

L65 A1 ¼pi green 35.00 *25.00*
Never hinged 52.50
a. Inverted overprint 77.50
b. Vert. ovpt. reading down 1,100.
c. Vert. ovpt. reading up 1,400.
L66 A2 ½pi red 55.00 *45.00*
Never hinged 82.50
a. Inverted overprint *135.00*
L66B A6 2pi mag, invtd. ovpt. *2,275.*

Blue overprint on Nos. L4, L8, L9 are bogus.

Same Overprint in Blue on Provisional Stamps of 1922

Overprinted on No. L17

L67 A2 ½pi red *4,250.*
No gum 600.00

Overprinted on Nos. L24-L29

L68 A5 1pa lilac brn 250.00 *250.00*
Never hinged *500.00*
L69 A4 ⅛pi orange *3,750.* *3,000.*
No gum 575.00
a. Inverted overprint 7,000.
L70 A1 ¼pi green 100.00 *100.00*
Never hinged 150.00
a. Inverted overprint 1,550.
No gum 275.00
L71 A2 ½pi red 145.00 *135.00*
Never hinged 225.00
a. Inverted overprint 1,675.
No gum 275.00
L72 A3 1pi blue 145.00 *145.00*
Never hinged 225.00
L73 A6 2pi magenta 250.00 *250.00*
Never hinged 375.00
a. Inverted overprint 1,825.
No gum 275.00

Same Overprint on Nos. L30 and L31

L74 A5(a) ½pi on 1pa 145.00 *145.00*
Never hinged 225.00
L75 A5(b) 1pi on 1pa 110.00 *110.00*
Never hinged 165.00
a. Inverted overprint 2,100.
No gum 325.00

Same Overprint in Blue Vertically, Reading Up or Down, on Stamps of 1922-24

Perf. 11½

L76 A7 ½pi red *1,600.* *1,600.*
Never hinged *2,750.*
L76A A8 10pi vio & dk brn *3,250.* *3,000.*
Never hinged *5,000.*

Nos. L5, L10 Overprinted Reading Up in Blue or Red

(Overprint reads up in illustration.)

Small three-line overprint. Top line 14mm long.

Roulette 20

L77a A1 ¼pi green (Bl) *775.00* *775.00*
L78 A1 ¼pi green (R) *725.00* *725.00*

Serrate Roulette 13

L79a A1 ¼pi green (Bl) 450.00 *450.00*
L80 A1 ¼pi green (R) 100.00 *100.00*

Overprint Reading Down

Roulette 20

L77 A1 ¼pi green (Bl) *1,550.* —

Serrate Roulette 13

L79 A1 ¼pi green (Bl) 725.00 —
L80a A1 ¼pi green (R) 385.00 —
L80b A1 ¼pi green (R), double ovpt. 725.00
L80c A1 ¼pi green (R), double ovpt., 1 reading up and 1 reading down 1,625.
L80d A1 ¼pi green (R), triple ovpt., all reading up — —

Nos. L10, L32-L39, L48A, L49a, L50 Overprinted

Large three-line overprint. Top line 16mm long.

Serrate Roulette 13

Red Overprint (vertical, reading down)

L81 A1 ¼pi green *1,850.*
a. Overprint reading up 1,500.
b. Overprint horizontal 1,750.
c. As "b," overprint inverted 1,750.

Perf. 11½

Blue Overprint

L82 A7 ⅛pi red brown 7.75 *7.00*
Never hinged 14.00
a. Inverted overprint 75.00
L83 A7 ½pi red 15.00 *7.25*
Never hinged 22.50
a. Double overprint 90.00
b. Inverted overprint 75.00 *45.00*
c. Double ovpt., one invtd. 135.00
d. Overprint reading up 190.00
L84 A7 1pi dark blue *900.00*
Never hinged *1,350.*
a. Inverted overprint *1,100.*
L85 A7 1½pi violet 22.50 *20.00*
Never hinged 35.00
a. Inverted overprint 140.00 *45.00*
b. Horiz. pair, imperf. vert. *175.00*
c. Pair, one with invert. ovpt., one without ovpt. *1,825.*
L86 A7 2pi orange 12.50 *12.50*
Never hinged 22.50
On cover, single franking 200.00
a. Double ovpt., one invtd. 145.00
b. Inverted overprint 125.00
c. Double overprint 135.00
d. Pair, one without overprint 1,375.
L87 A7 3pi olive brown 12.00 *10.00*
Never hinged 20.00
a. Inverted overprint 80.00
b. Double ovpt., one invtd. 135.00
c. Overprint reading up 275.00
d. Dbl. ovpt., both invtd. 175.00
L88 A7 3pi dull red 12.50 *12.50*
Never hinged 24.00
a. Inverted overprint 80.00
b. Double ovpt., one invtd. 135.00
c. Pair, one without ovpt. *550.00*
L89 A7 5pi olive green 16.00 *15.00*
Never hinged 24.00
a. Inverted overprint 145.00

For errors and varieties in never hinged condition add 50%.

Black Overprint

L90 A7 ⅛pi red brown *75.00*
Never hinged 125.00
a. Inverted overprint *275.00*
L91 A7 ½pi red 7.50 7.25
Never hinged 12.50
a. Inverted overprint 85.00
L92 A7 1pi dark blue *900.00*
Never hinged *1,350.*
a. Inverted overprint *1,100.*
L93 A7 1½pi violet 20.00 *20.00*
Never hinged 30.00
a. Inverted overprint 135.00
L94 A7 2pi orange 11.50 *11.50*
Never hinged 17.50
On cover 125.00
a. Inverted overprint 55.00
b. Horiz. pair, imperf. btwn. 155.00
L95 A7 3pi olive brown 12.00 *9.25*
Never hinged 18.00
a. Inverted overprint 87.50 *87.50*
b. 3pi brown 6.00 3.00
Never hinged 10.00
L96 A7 3pi dull red 15.00 *12.00*
Never hinged 22.50
a. Inverted overprint 90.00
L97 A7 5pi olive green 16.00 *15.00*
Never hinged 27.50
a. Inverted overprint 67.50
b. Double ovpt., one invert. 350.00

Red Overprint

L98 A7 ⅛pi red brn, invtd. *1,600.*
L99 A7 ¼pi yellow grn 26.00 *26.00*
Never hinged 40.00
a. Tête bêche pair 100.00
b. Inverted overprint 55.00
c. Tête bêche pair, one with inverted overprint 125.00
d. Double overprint 155.00
L100 A7 ½pi red *1,750.* *800.00*
Never hinged *2,750.*
a. Inverted overprint *2,250.* —
L101 A7 1pi dark blue 13.50 *13.50*
Never hinged 20.00
a. Inverted overprint 55.00
b. Double ovpt., one invtd. 80.00
c. Vert. pair, imperf. horiz. 155.00
L102 A7 1½pi violet 7.25 *7.25*
Never hinged 12.50
a. Inverted overprint 90.00
b. Horiz. pair, imperf. vert. 60.00
L103 A7 2pi orange 20.00 *20.00*
Never hinged 30.00
a. Inverted overprint 90.00
b. Overprint reading up 350.00
L104 A7 3pi olive brown 20.00 *20.00*
Never hinged 30.00
a. Inverted overprint 40.00
b. Vert. pair, imperf. btwn. 155.00
L105 A7 3pi dull red, invtd. *1,700.*
L106 A7 5pi olive green 20.00 *11.50*
Never hinged 30.00
a. Inverted overprint 90.00
b. Overprint reading up 365.00
c. Overprint reading down 365.00
d. Pair, one without overprint 400.00
L107 A8 10pi vio & dk brn 26.00 *27.50*
Never hinged 40.00
a. Inverted overprint 155.00
b. Center inverted 155.00

c. As "b," invtd. ovpt. 250.00
d. Ovpt. reading up 190.00
e. Ovpt. reading down 300.00

Nos. L98, L105 with normal overprint are fakes.

Gold Overprint

L108 A7 ⅛pi red brown 45.00 *42.50*
Never hinged 67.50
L109 A7 ½pi red 45.00 *42.50*
Never hinged 67.50
L110 A7 1pi dark blue 45.00 *42.50*
Never hinged 67.50
L111 A7 1½pi violet 185.00 *180.00*
Never hinged 290.00
L112 A7 2pi orange 145.00 *150.00*
Never hinged 225.00
L113 A7 3pi olive brown 55.00 *55.00*
Never hinged 85.00
L114 A7 3pi dull red 165.00 *160.00*
Never hinged 250.00
L115 A7 5pi olive green 155.00 *140.00*
Never hinged 240.00
Nos. L108-L115 (8) 840.00 *812.50*

Inverted overprints are forgeries.

Same Overprint on Nos. L42-L48

Blue Overprint

L116 A7 ⅛pi red brown 60.00 *60.00*
Never hinged *120.00*
a. Double ovpt., one invtd. *350.00*
L117 A7 ½pi red 135.00 *135.00*
Never hinged *270.00*
L118 A7 1pi dark blue 92.50 *85.00*
Never hinged *185.00*
L119 A7 1½pi violet 110.00 *100.00*
Never hinged *220.00*
L120 A7 2pi orange 460.00 *440.00*
Never hinged *900.00*
a. Inverted overprint *500.00*
L121 A7 3pi olive brown 165.00 *165.00*
Never hinged *330.00*
a. Inverted overprint *230.00*
L122 A7 5pi olive green 60.00 *60.00*
Never hinged *120.00*
a. Inverted overprint *250.00*
Never hinged *500.00*
Nos. L116-L122 (7) 1,083. *1,045.*

Black Overprint

L123 A7 ⅛pi red brown 75.00 *65.00*
Never hinged *150.00*
a. Inverted overprint *275.00*
L125 A7 1½pi violet 250.00 *210.00*
Never hinged *500.00*
a. Inverted overprint *300.00*
L127 A7 3pi olive brown 165.00 *175.00*
Never hinged *330.00*
a. Inverted overprint *300.00*
L128 A7 5pi olive green 250.00 *210.00*
Never hinged *500.00*
a. Inverted overprint *300.00*
Nos. L123-L128 (4) 740.00 *660.00*

Red Overprint

L129 A7 1pi dark blue 165.00 *145.00*
Never hinged *330.00*
L130 A7 1½pi violet 165.00 *165.00*
Never hinged 330.00
L131 A7 2pi orange 165.00 *150.00*
Never hinged 330.00
Nos. L129-L131 (3) 495.00 *460.00*

Overprints on stamps or in colors other than those listed are forgeries.

For errors and varieties in never hinged condition add 50%.

Stamps of 1922-24 Surcharged

a

and Handstamp Surcharged

b — 1/4pi

b — 1pi

b — 10pi

1925 **Litho.** ***Perf. 11½***

L135 A7 ¼pi on ¼pi on ⅛pi red brn 77.50 *77.50*
Never hinged 120.00
b. 1pi on ¼pi on ⅛pi red brown 225.00
Never hinged 450.00
c. Pair, one without handstamp *275.00*
d. Overprint inverted 155.00
e. Double overprint 185.00
f. Violet handstamp overprint 190.00
g. As "f," dbl. ovpt., both inverted 190.00
h. As "g," overprinted on both sides inverted on back 190.00
L136 A7 ¼pi on ¼pi on ½pi red 45.00 *45.00*
Never hinged 90.00
c. 1pi on ¼pi on ½pi 160.00 *65.00*
d. As "c," handstamped in violet *750.00*
e. Pair, one without handstamp 250.00
f. Overprint inverted 150.00
g. Double overprint 175.00
h. Dbl. ovpt., one inverted 325.00
i. Ovpt. on both sides 350.00
j. ¼pi on ¼pi on ½pi deep rose 95.00
k. As "j," handstamped in violet 190.00
l. As "j," ovpt. on both sides 190.00
L138 A7 1pi on 1pi on 2pi orange 45.00 *45.00*
Never hinged 90.00
a. ¼pi on ¼pi on 2pi org 125.00
b. 10pi on 1pi on 2pi org 125.00
c. ¼pi on 1pi on 2pi org 75.00
d. 1pi on ¼pi on 2pi org *125.00*
f. Pair, one without handstamp 350.00
g. Overprint inverted 145.00
h. Double overprint 175.00
i. Violet handstamp 190.00
j. As "i," inverted overprint 190.00
L139 A7 1pi on 1pi on 3pi ol brn 40.00 *40.00*
b. Pair, one without handstamp 210.00
c. Overprint inverted 125.00
d. Dbl. ovpt., one inverted 275.00
e. Violet handstamp 150.00
L140 A7 1pi on 1pi on 3pi dl red 55.00 *55.00*
Never hinged 90.00
b. ¼pi on 1pi on 3pi dl red 350.00
c. Pair, one without handstamp *275.00*
d. Overprint inverted 150.00
e. Double overprint 175.00
f. Violet handstamp 275.00
g. As"f," inverted overprint 275.00
L141 A7 10pi on 10pi on 5pi ol grn 27.50 *27.50*
Never hinged 55.00
b. 1pi on 10 pi on 5 pi 350.00
c. Pair, one without handstamp *275.00*
d. Overprint inverted 150.00
e. Dbl ovpt., one inverted 300.00
f. Violet handstamp 200.00
Nos. L135-L141 (6) 290.00 *290.00*

The printed surcharge (a) reads "The Hejaz Government. October 4, 1924." with new denomination in third line. This surcharge alone was used for the first issue (Nos. L135a-L141a). The new denomination was so small and indistinct that its equivalent in larger characters was soon added by handstamp (b) at bottom of each stamp for the second issue (Nos. L135-L141).

The handstamped surcharge (b) is found double, inverted, etc. It is also known in dark violet.

Without Handstamp "b"

L135a A7 ¼pi on ⅛pi red brn 155.00
Never hinged 225.00
i. Overprint inverted 425.00
j. Double overprint 600.00
k. Dbl. ovpt., both invert. 750.00
L136b A7 ¼pi on ½pi red 155.00
Never hinged 225.00
m. Overprint inverted 350.00
n. Double overprint 475.00
o. Dbl. ovpt., one invert. 750.00
L138e A7 1pi on 2pi orange 155.00
Never hinged 225.00
k. Double overprint 600.00
L139a A7 1pi on 3pi olive brn 155.00
Never hinged 225.00
L140a A7 1pi on 3pi dull red 155.00
Never hinged 225.00
h. Overprint inverted 475.00
i. Double overprint —
L141a A7 10pi on 5pi olive grn 155.00
Never hinged 225.00
Nos. L135a-L141a (6) 930.00

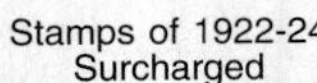

Stamps of 1922-24 Surcharged

Black Surcharge

L142 A7 ⅛pi on ½pi red 13.50 13.50
Never hinged 20.00
a. Inverted surcharge 60.00
L143 A7 ¼pi on ½pi red 13.50 13.50
Never hinged 20.00
a. Inverted surcharge 60.00
L144 A7 1pi on ½pi red 13.50 13.50
Never hinged 20.00
a. Inverted surcharge 60.00
L145 A7 1pi on 1½pi vio 13.50 13.50
Never hinged 20.00
a. Inverted surcharge 60.00
L146 A7 1pi on 2pi org 13.50 13.50
Never hinged 20.00
a. "10pi" 100.00
b. Inverted surcharge 70.00
c. As "a," inverted surcharge 185.00
L147 A7 1pi on 3pi olive brn 13.50 13.50
Never hinged 20.00
a. "10pi" 100.00
b. Inverted surcharge 70.00
c. As "a," inverted surcharge 185.00
d. Horiz. pair, imperf. vert. 150.00
L148 A7 10pi on 5pi olive grn 22.00 24.00
Never hinged 35.00
a. Inverted surcharge 90.00
Nos. L142-L148 (7) 103.00 *105.00*

Blue Surcharge

L149 A7 ⅛pi on ½pi red 22.50 *17.00*
Never hinged 35.00
a. Inverted surcharge 90.00
b. Double surcharge 350.00
L150 A7 ¼pi on ½pi red 22.50 *17.00*
a. Inverted surcharge 90.00
L151 A7 1pi on ½pi red 22.50 *17.00*
Never hinged 35.00
a. Inverted surcharge 90.00
b. Double surcharge 125.0275.000
L152 A7 1pi on 1½pi vio 22.50 *20.00*
Never hinged 35.00
a. Inverted surcharge 290.00
L153 A7 1pi on 2pi org 27.50 *27.50*
Never hinged 40.00
a. "10pi" 100.00
b. Inverted surcharge 90.00
c. As "a," inverted surcharge 290.00
L154 A7 1pi on 3pi olive brn 37.50 *37.50*
Never hinged 60.00
a. "10pi" 110.00
b. Inverted surcharge 140.00
L155 A7 10pi on 5pi olive grn 40.00 *40.00*
Never hinged 65.00
a. Inverted surcharge 110.00
Nos. L149-L155 (7) 195.00 *176.00*

Red Surcharge

L156 A7 1pi on 1½pi vio 30.00 *30.00*
Never hinged 50.00
a. Inverted surcharge 110.00
L157 A7 1pi on 2pi org 30.00 *30.00*
Never hinged 50.00
a. "10pi" 110.00
b. Inverted surcharge 120.00
L158 A7 1pi on 3pi olive brn 30.00 *30.00*
Never hinged 50.00
a. "10pi" 140.00
b. Inverted surcharge 110.00
L159 A7 10pi on 5pi olive grn 32.50 *22.50*
Never hinged 50.00
a. Inverted surcharge 110.00
Nos. L156-L159 (4) 122.50 *112.50*
Nos. L142-L159 (18) 420.50 *393.50*

The "10pi" surcharge is found inverted on Nos. L146a, L147a. The existence of genuine inverted "10pi" surcharges on Nos. L153a, L154a, L157a and L158a is in doubt.

The 10pi on 1½pi is bogus.

Forr errors and varieties in never hinged condition add 50%.

King Ali Issue

A9

A10

A11

A12

1925, May-June ***Perf. 11½***

Black Overprint

L160 A9 ⅛pi chocolate 2.25 *1.50*
L161 A9 ¼pi ultra 2.25 *1.50*
L162 A9 ½pi car rose 2.25 *1.50*
L163 A10 1pi yellow green 3.00 *1.75*
L164 A10 1½pi orange 3.00 *1.75*
L165 A10 2pi blue 3.50 *2.25*
L166 A11 3pi dark green 3.50 *2.25*
L167 A11 5pi orange brn 3.50 *2.25*
L168 A12 10pi red & green 6.00 *4.50*
a. Center inverted 90.00
Nos. L160-L168 (9) 29.25 *19.25*

Red Overprint

L169 A9 ⅛pi chocolate 4.00 *2.75*
L170 A9 ¼pi ultra 2.50 *1.60*
L171 A10 1pi yellow green 3.00 *2.00*
L172 A10 1½pi orange 3.00 *2.00*
L173 A10 2pi deep blue 3.50 *2.50*
On cover, single franking 650.00
L174 A11 3pi dark green 3.25 *2.75*
a. Horiz. pair, imperf. vert. 75.00
L175 A11 5pi org brn 4.00 *2.75*
L176 A12 10pi red & green 6.50 *5.50*
Nos. L169-L176 (8) 29.75 *21.85*

Blue Overprint

L177 A9 ⅛pi chocolate 2.75 *1.75*
L179 A9 ½pi car rose 2.75 *1.75*
L180 A10 1pi yellow green 2.75 *1.75*
L181 A10 1½pi orange 2.75 *1.75*
L182 A11 3pi dark green 2.75 *1.75*
L183 A11 5pi orange brn 6.75 *5.50*
L184 A12 10pi red & green 9.00 *7.25*
L185 A12 10pi red & org 275.00
Nos. L177-L184 (7) 29.50 *21.50*

Without Overprint

L186 A12 10pi red & green 8.00 *6.75*
a. Dbl. impression of center *90.00*

The overprint in the tablets on Nos. L160-L185 reads: "5 Rabi al'awwal, 1343" (Oct. 4, 1924), the date of the accession of King Ali.

The tablet overprints vary slightly in size. Each is found reading upward or downward and at either side of the stamp. These control overprints were first applied in Jedda by the government press.

They were later made from new plates by the stamp printer in Cairo. In the Jedda overprint, the bar over the "0" figure extends to the left.

Some values exist with 13m or 15mm instead of 18mm between tablets. They sell for more. The lines of the Cairo overprinting are generally wider, but more lightly printed, usually appearing slightly grayish and the bar is at center right. The Cairo overprints are believed not to have been placed in use.

Imperforates exist.

Nos. L160-L168 are known with the overprints spaced as on type D3 and aligned horizontally.

Examples of these stamps (perforated or imperforate) without the overprint, except No. L186 were not regularly issued and not available for postage.

No. L185 exists only with Cairo overprint. Imperfs of No. L185 sell for much less than No. L185. Fake perfs have been added to the imperfs.

The ¼pi with blue overprint is bogus.

No. L186 in other colors are color trials.

For overprints see #58B-58D, Jordan 122-129.

NEJDI ADMINISTRATION OF HEJAZ

Handstamped in Blue, Red, Black or Violet

The overprint reads: "1343. Barid al Sultanat an Nejdia" (1925. Post of the Sultanate of Nejd).

The overprints on this and succeeding issues are handstamped and, as usual, are found double, inverted, etc. These variations are scarce.

On Stamp of Turkey, 1915, With Crescent and Star in Red

1925, Mar.-Apr. Unwmk. ***Perf. 12***

1 A22 5pa ocher (Bl) 30.00 27.50
Never hinged 50.00
2 A22 5pa ocher (R) 30.00 20.00
Never hinged 50.00
3 A22 5pa ocher (Bk) 30.00 22.50
Never hinged 50.00
4 A22 5pa ocher (V) 30.00 18.00
Never hinged 50.00

On Stamp of Turkey, 1913

5 A28 10pa green (Bl) 40.00 16.00
Never hinged 60.00
a. Inverted overprint 500.00
Never hinged 1,000.
6 A28 10pa green (R) 40.00 12.50
Never hinged 60.00

On Stamps of Hejaz, 1922-24

Perf. 11½

7 A7 ⅛pi red brn (R) 70.00 24.00
Never hinged 110.00
8 A7 ⅛pi red brn (Bk) 70.00 35.00
Never hinged 110.00
9 A7 ⅛pi red brn (V) 50.00 24.00
Never hinged 75.00
10 A7 ⅛pi car (R) 70.00 30.00
Never hinged 110.00
11 A7 ⅛pi car (Bk) 70.00 35.00
Never hinged 110.00
12 A7 ⅛pi car (V) *50.00 27.50*
Never hinged 75.00
13 A7 ½pi red (Bl) 40.00 22.50
Never hinged 60.00
14 A7 ½pi red (V) 40.00 18.00
Never hinged 60.00
15 A7 1½pi vio (R) 60.00 24.00
Never hinged 90.00
16 A7 2pi yel buff (R) 85.00 57.50
Never hinged 140.00
a. 2pi orange (R) 110.00
Never hinged 160.00
17 A7 2pi yel buff (V) 85.00 57.50
Never hinged 140.00
a. 2pi orange (V) 100.00 32.50
Never hinged 150.00
18 A7 3pi brn red (Bl) 70.00 30.00
Never hinged 110.00
19 A7 3pi brn red (R) 70.00 22.50
Never hinged 110.00
20 A7 3pi brn red (V) 70.00 25.00
Never hinged 110.00

Many Hejaz stamps of the 1922 type were especially printed for this and following issues. The re-impressions are usually more clearly printed, in lighter shades than the 1922 stamps, and some are in new colors.

Counterfeits exist.

Arabic Inscriptions
R1 R2

On Hejaz Bill Stamp

22 R1 1pi violet (R) 40.00 15.00
Never hinged 60.00

On Hejaz Notarial Stamps

23 R2 1pi violet (R) 50.00 20.00
Never hinged 75.00
24 R2 2pi blue (R) 50.00 30.00
Never hinged 75.00
25 R2 2pi blue (V) 50.00 27.50
Never hinged 75.00

For overprint see No. 49.

On Hejaz Railway Tax Stamps

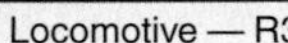

Locomotive — R3

Type I

Type II

Two design types appear on the basic revenue stamps. Type 1 depicts the cab's window and the band at the center of the boiler as a series of horizontal lines, the top of the cab does not touch the frame line above it, and the coupler at rear of car appears as a fine hook that does not touch the right frame. Type 2 depicts the cab's window and band on boiler as open vertical spaces, the top of the cab touches the frame line above it, and the coupler appears as a blob connected to the right frame line. Type 2 appears in position 12 in the sheet of 18 (6x3) of the 500pi value, and in position 30 in the 36-stamp (6x6) sheets in which the other values were printed.

Type 1

26 R3 1pi blue (R) 40.00 9.00
Never hinged 60.00
a. Type 2 60.00
Never hinged 90.00
27 R3 2pi ocher (R) 60.00 14.00
Never hinged 90.00
a. Type 2 90.00
Never hinged 140.00
28 R3 2pi ocher (V) 60.00 14.00
Never hinged 90.00
a. Type 2 90.00
Never hinged 140.00
29 R3 3pi lilac (R) 60.00 20.00
Never hinged 90.00
a. Type 2 90.00
Never hinged 140.00
Nos. 1-20,22-29 (28) 1,510. 698.50

For overprints and surcharges see Nos. 34, 50-54, 55, 59-68, J12-J15.

Pilgrimage Issue

Various Stamps Handstamp Surcharged in Blue and Red in Types "a" and "b" and with Tablets with New Values

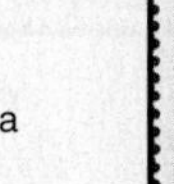
a

b

Surcharge "a" reads: "Tezkar al Hajj al Awwal Fi 'ahd al Sultanat al Nejdia, 1343" (Commemorating the first pilgrimage under the Nejdi Sultanate, 1925).

"b" reads: "Al Arba" (Wednesday.)

On Stamps of Turkey, 1913

1925, July 1 ***Perf. 12***

30 A28 1pi on 10pa grn (Bl & R) 100.00 55.00
Never hinged 150.00
31 A30 5pi on 1pi bl (Bl & R) 100.00 55.00
Never hinged 150.00

On Stamps of Hejaz, 1917-18

Serrate Roulette 13

32 A5 2pi on 1pa lil brn (R & Bl) 125.00 67.50
Never hinged 175.00
33 A4 4pi on ⅛pi org (R & Bl) 400.00 350.00
Never hinged 500.00

On Hejaz Railway Tax Stamp

Perf. 11½

34 R3 3pi lilac, type 1 (Bl & R) 200.00 40.00
Never hinged 300.00
On cover 425.00
a. Type 2 300.00
Never hinged 450.00
Nos. 30-34 (5) 925.00 567.50

No. 30 with handstamp "a" in black was a favor item. Nos. 30 and 33 with both handstamps in red are forgeries.

Handstamped in Blue, Red, Black or Violet

This overprint has practically the same meaning as that described over No. 1. The Mohammedan year (1343) is omitted.

This handstamp is said to be in private hands at this time. Extreme caution is advised before buying rare items.

On Stamp of Turkey, 1915, with Crescent and Star in Red

1925, July-Aug. ***Perf. 12***

35 A22 5pa ocher (Bl) 50.00 24.00
Never hinged 75.00

On Stamps of Turkey, 1913

36 A28 10pa green (Bl) 60.00 20.00
Never hinged 90.00
a. Black overprint 120.00
b. As "a," overprint inverted 650.00

On Stamps of Hejaz, 1922 (Nos. L28-L29)

Serrate Roulette 13

37 A3 1pi blue (R) 120.00 *67.50*
Never hinged 180.00
38 A6 2pi magenta (Bl) 120.00 *67.50*
Never hinged 180.00

On Stamps of Hejaz, 1922-24

Perf. 11½

38A A7 ⅛pi red brn (Bk) *4,500.*
No gum 1,500.
38B A7 ⅛pi red brn (Bl) *3,750.*
No gum 1,000.
39 A7 ½pi red (Bl) 12.50 10.00
On cover 75.00
a. Imperf., pair 25.00 22.50
39B A7 ½pi red (Bk) 20.00 18.00
c. Imperf., pair 50.00 37.50
40 A7 1pi gray vio (R) 50.00 29.00
Never hinged 75.00
a. 1pi black violet (R) *50.00*
Never hinged 75.00
41 A7 1½pi dk red (Bk) 50.00 30.00
Never hinged 75.00
a. 1½pi brick red (Bk) 50.00
Never hinged 75.00
42 A7 2pi yel buff (Bl) 80.00 47.50
Never hinged 120.00
a. 2pi orange (Bl) 110.00 55.00
Never hinged 160.00
43 A7 2pi deep vio (Bl) 85.00 52.50
Never hinged 125.00
44 A7 3pi brown red (Bl) 50.00 30.00
Never hinged 75.00
45 A7 5pi scarlet (Bl) 70.00 37.50
Never hinged 110.00
Nos. 35-38,39-45 (12) 767.50 *433.50*

Overprint on Nos. 38A, 39B, 39C is blue-black.

See note above No. 35.

With Additional Surcharge of New Value Typo. in Black

c

d

e

Color in parenthesis is that of overprint on basic stamp.

46 A7(c) 1pi on ½pi (Bl) 12.50 1.75
On cover, single franking 75.00
a. Imperf, pair 40.00
b. Ovpt. & surch. inverted 90.00
47 A7(d) 1½pi on ½pi (Bl) 17.50 7.25
On cover, pair 325.00
a. Imperf., pair 30.00
48 A7(e) 2pi on 3pi (Bl) 17.50 16.00
On cover 500.00
Nos. 46-48 (3) 47.50 25.00

Several variations in type settings of "c," "d" and "e" exist, including inverted letters and values.

On Hejaz Notarial Stamp

49 R2 2pi blue (Bk) 50.00 20.00
Never hinged 75.00
On cover 125.00
On cover, single franking 425.00

On Hejaz Railway Tax Stamps

50 R3 1pi blue, type 1 (R) 40.00 25.00
Never hinged 60.00
On cover 100.00
a. Type 2 60.00
Never hinged 90.00
51 R3 1pi blue, type 1 (Bk) 60.00 9.00
Never hinged 90.00
On cover 125.00
a. Type 2 90.00
Never hinged 140.00
52 R3 2pi ocher, type 1 (Bl) 60.00 9.00
Never hinged 90.00
On cover 125.00
a. Type 2 90.00
Never hinged 140.00
53 R3 3pi lilac, type 1 (Bl) 70.00 22.50
Never hinged 110.00
a. Type 2 100.00
Never hinged 150.00
54 R3 5pi green, type 1 (Bl) 60.00 20.00
Never hinged 90.00
a. Type 2 90.00
Never hinged 140.00
Nos. 49-54 (6) 340.00 105.50

Hejaz Railway Tax Stamp Handstamped in Black

This overprint reads: "Al Saudia. — Al Sultanat al Nejdia." (The Saudi Sultanate of Nejd.)

1925-26 **Small Handstamp**

55 R3 1pi blue, type 1 — *200.00*
b. Type 2 400.00

On Nos. L34, L36-L37, L41

55A A7 ½ pi red — *350.00*
56 A7 1½pi violet — *375.00*
57 A7 2pi orange — *375.00*
57A A7 10pi on 5pi ol green — *375.00*

On Nos. L95 and L97

58 A7 3pi olive brown — *400.00*
58A A7 5pi olive green — *400.00*

On Nos. L162-L163, L173

Perf. 11½

58B A9 ½pi car rose 350.00 —
58C A10 1pi yel grn — *225.00*
58D A10 2pi blue — *350.00*

Large Handstamp

58K R3 1pi blue *7,000.*
58L A7 3pi brn (#L95b) reading up *1,000.*
a. Overprint reading down 1,000.
58M A10 1pi yel grn (#L163) 1,500. *1,000.*

Nos. 55-58M were provisionally issued at Medina after its capitulation.

Only one example of No. 58K, a single stamp used on piece, is known.

This overprint exists on Nos. L160-L161, L164-L172, L174-L175, L180-L183. These 17 are known as bogus items, but may exist genuine.

Lithographed overprints are forgeries.

Medina Issue

Hejaz Railway Tax Stamps Handstamped

and Handstamp Surcharged in Various Colors

The large overprint reads: "The Nejdi Posts — 1344 — Commemorating Medina, the Illustrious." The tablet shows the new value.

1925

59 R3 1pi on 10pi vio, type 1 (Bk & V) 70.00 70.00
Never hinged 95.00
a. Type 2 100.00
Never hinged 150.00
60 R3 2pi on 50pi lt bl, type 1 (R & Bl) 70.00 70.00
Never hinged 95.00
a. Type 2 100.00
Never hinged 150.00
61 R3 3pi on 100pi red brn, type 1 (Bl & Bk) 70.00 70.00
Never hinged 95.00
a. Type 2 100.00
Never hinged 150.00
62 R3 4pi on 500pi dull red, type 1 (Bl & Bk) 70.00 70.00
Never hinged 95.00
a. Type 2 100.00
Never hinged 150.00
63 R3 5pi on 1000pi dp red, type 1 (Bl & Bk) 70.00 70.00
Never hinged 95.00
a. Type 2 100.00
Never hinged 150.00
Nos. 59-63 (5) 350.00 350.00

JEDDA ISSUE

Hejaz Railway Tax Stamps Handstamped and Tablet with New Value in Various Colors

This handstamp reads: "Commemorating Jedda — 1344 — The Nejdi Posts."

1925

64 R3 1pi on 10pi vio, type 1 (Bk & Bl) 70.00 70.00
Never hinged 95.00
a. Horiz. pair, imperf between 450.00
b. Type 2 100.00
Never hinged 150.00
65 R3 2pi on 50pi lt bl, type 1 (R & Bk) 70.00 70.00
Never hinged 95.00
a. Type 2 100.00
Never hinged 150.00
66 R3 3pi on 100pi red brn, type 1 (R & Bl) 70.00 70.00
Never hinged 95.00
a. Type 2 100.00
Never hinged 150.00
67 R3 4pi on 500pi dl red, type 1 (Bk & Bl) 70.00 70.00
Never hinged 95.00
a. Type 2 100.00
Never hinged 150.00
68 R3 5pi on 1000pi dp red, type 1 (Bk & Bl) 70.00 70.00
Never hinged 95.00
a. Type 2 100.00
Never hinged 150.00
Nos. 64-68 (5) 350.00 350.00

Nos. 59-63 and 64-68 were prepared in anticipation of the surrender of Medina and Jedda.

Kingdom of Hejaz-Nejd

Arabic Inscriptions and Value — A1

A2

Inscriptions in upper tablets: "Barid al Hejaz wa Nejd" (Posts of the Hejaz and Nejd)

1926, Feb. Typo. Unwmk. *Perf. 11*

69 A1 ¼pi violet 45.00 18.00
Never hinged 60.00
70 A1 ½pi gray 45.00 18.00
Never hinged 60.00
71 A1 1pi deep blue 45.00 22.00
Never hinged 60.00
72 A2 2pi blue green 45.00 18.00
Never hinged 60.00
73 A2 3pi carmine 45.00 19.00
Never hinged 60.00
74 A2 5pi maroon 45.00 20.00
Never hinged 60.00
Nos. 69-74 (6) 270.00 115.00

Nos. 69-72, 74 exist imperf. Value, each $40.
Used values are for favor cancels.

1926, Mar. *Perf. 11*

75 A1 ¼pi orange 12.00 10.00
On cover 75.00
a. Horiz. pair, imperf between 100.00
76 A1 ½pi blue green 5.25 *15.00*
a. Horiz. pair, imperf between 100.00
b. Vertz. pair, imperf between 100.00
77 A1 1pi carmine 4.25 *7.50*
On cover 125.00
a. Horiz. pair, imperf between 100.00
b. Vert. pair, imperf between 100.00
78 A2 2pi violet 5.25 *12.50*
a. Horiz. pair, imperf between 100.00
b. Vert. pair, imperf between 100.00
79 A2 3pi dark blue 5.25 *7.50*
a. Horiz. pair, imperf between 100.00
b. Vert. pair, imperf between 100.00
80 A2 5pi lt brown 10.00 *20.00*
On cover 550.00
a. 5pi olive brown
b. Horiz. pair, imperf between 100.00
c. Vert. pair, imperf between 100.00
Nos. 75-80 (6) 42.00 72.50

Nos. 75-80 also exist imperf. Value, twice the values shown above. Examples that are perforated 14, 14x11 and 11x14 were privately produced.

Counterfeits of types A1 and A2 are perf. 11½. They exist with and without overprints.

Types A1 and A2 in colors other than listed are proofs.

Pan-Islamic Congress Issue

Stamps of 1926 Hstmpd.

1926 *Perf. 11*

92 A1 ¼pi orange 12.00 5.00
Never hinged 24.00
93 A1 ½pi blue green 12.00 5.00
Never hinged 24.00
94 A1 1pi carmine 12.00 5.00
Never hinged 24.00
95 A2 2pi violet 12.00 5.00
Never hinged 24.00
On cover 150.00
96 A2 3pi dark blue 12.00 5.00
Never hinged 24.00
On cover, single franking 200.00
97 A2 5pi light brown 12.00 5.00
Never hinged 24.00
Nos. 92-97 (6) 72.00 30.00

The overprint reads: "al Mootamar al Islami 20 Zilkada, Sanat 1344." (The Islamic Congress, June 1, 1926.)

See counterfeit note after No. 80.

Tughra of King Abdul Aziz — A3

1926-27 Typo. *Perf. 11½*

98 A3 ⅛pi ocher 5.00 .60
Never hinged 7.50
99 A3 ¼pi gray green 6.00 1.50
Never hinged 9.00
100 A3 ½pi dull red 6.00 1.50
Never hinged 9.00
On paper wrapper 75.00
On cover 100.00
On cover, single franking 200.00
b. Horiz. pair, imperf between 400.00
101 A3 1pi deep violet 6.50 1.50
Never hinged 10.00
102 A3 1½pi gray blue 18.00 2.25
Never hinged 27.00
103 A3 3pi olive green 14.00 4.75
Never hinged 21.00
104 A3 5pi brown orange 27.50 5.00
Never hinged 40.00
105 A3 10pi dark brown 70.00 7.00
Never hinged 105.00
Nos. 98-105 (8) 153.00 24.10

Inscription at top reads: "Al Hukumat al Arabia" (The Arabian Government). Inscription below tughra reads: "Barid al Hejaz wa Nejd" (Post of the Hejaz and Nejd).

Stamps of 1926-27 Handstamped in Black or Red

1927

107 A3 ⅛pi ocher 13.00 4.75
108 A3 ¼pi gray grn 13.00 4.75
109 A3 ½pi dull red 13.00 4.75
110 A3 1pi deep violet 13.00 4.75
111 A3 1½pi gray bl (R) 13.00 4.75
112 A3 3pi olive green 13.00 4.75
113 A3 5pi brown orange 14.50 4.75
114 A3 10pi dark brown 16.00 4.75
On cover 100.00
Nos. 107-114 (8) 108.50 38.00
Set, never hinged 175.00

The overprint reads: "In commemoration of the Kingdom of Nejd and Dependencies, 25th Rajab 1345."

Inverted varieties have not been authenticated.

Turkey No. 258 Surcharged in Violet

1925 *Perf. 12*

115 A28 1g on 10pa green 175.00
Never hinged 225.00
No gum 50.00

Similar surcharges of 6g and 20g were made in red, but were not known to have been issued. Values: 6g, $350; 20g, $500.

A4

1929-30 Typo. *Perf. 11½*

117 A4 1¾g gray blue 40.00 4.50
Cover, single franking 50.00
119 A4 20g violet 50.00 12.50
120 A4 30g green 80.00 25.00

A5

1930 *Perf. 11, 11½*

125 A5 ½g rose 19.00 3.25
126 A5 1½g violet 19.00 2.10
127 A5 1¾g ultra 19.00 2.75
128 A5 3½g emerald 19.00 4.25

Perf. 11

129 A5 5g black brown 30.00 6.50
Nos. 125-129 (5) 106.00 18.85

Anniversary of King Ibn Saud's accession to the throne of the Hejaz, January 8, 1926.

A6

1931-32 *Perf. 11½*

130 A6 ⅛g ocher ('32) 22.50 3.25
131 A6 ¼g blue green 22.50 2.50
133 A6 1¾g ultra 37.50 3.25
On cover 50.00
Nos. 130-133 (3) 82.50 9.00

A7

1932 *Perf. 11½*

135 A7 ¼g blue green 16.00 32.50
a. Perf 11
136 A7 ½g scarlet 47.50 5.25
a. Perf 11
137 A7 2¼g ultra 90.00 8.50
a. Perf 11
Nos. 135-137 (3) 153.50 46.25

Kingdom of Saudi Arabia

A8

1934, Jan. *Perf. 11½, Imperf.*

138 A8 ¼g yellow green 11.00 10.00
Never hinged 15.00
139 A8 ½g red 11.00 10.00
Never hinged 15.00
140 A8 1½g light blue 21.00 19.00
Never hinged 27.50
141 A8 3g blue green 21.00 19.00
Never hinged 27.50
142 A8 3½g ultra 37.50 7.75
Never hinged 47.50
143 A8 5g yellow 50.00 37.50
Never hinged 65.00
144 A8 10g red orange 90.00
Never hinged 120.00
145 A8 20g bright violet 110.00
Never hinged 150.00
146 A8 ¼s claret 225.00
Never hinged 300.00
147 A8 30g dull violet 140.00
Never hinged 180.00
148 A8 ½s chocolate 475.00
Never hinged 700.00
149 A8 1s violet brown 1,075.
Never hinged 1,750.
Nos. 138-149 (12) 2,267.

Proclamation of Emir Saud as Heir Apparent of Arabia. Perf. and imperf. stamps were issued in equal quantities.

Favor cancels exist on Nos. 144-149.

Tughra of King Abdul Aziz — A9

1934-57 *Perf. 11, 11½*

159 A9 ⅛g yellow 5.25 .45
160 A9 ¼g yellow grn 5.25 .45
161 A9 ½g rose red ('43) 3.75 .25
a. ½g dark carmine 12.00 1.40
162 A9 ⅞g lt blue ('56) 6.50 .55
163 A9 1g blue green 5.25 .45
164 A9 2g olive grn ('57) 9.00 2.25
a. 2g olive bister ('57) 25.00 7.25
165 A9 2⅞g violet ('57) 6.50 .55
166 A9 3g ultra ('38) 6.50 .25
a. 3g light blue 20.00 1.75
167 A9 3½g lt ultra 35.00 2.25
168 A9 5g orange 6.50 .55
169 A9 10g violet 19.00 1.75

170 A9 20g purple brn 32.50 1.10
a. 20g purple black 25.00 2.25
171 A9 100g red vio ('42) 90.00 5.25
172 A9 200g vio brn ('42) 115.00 7.00
Nos. 159-172 (14) 346.00 23.10
Set, never hinged 450.00

The ½g has two types differing in position of the tughra.

No. 162 measures 31x22mm. No. 164 30½x21½mm. No. 165, 30½x22mm. No. 166 30x21mm. No. 171, 31x22mm. No. 172, 30½x21½mm. Rest of set, 29x20½mm. Grayish paper was used in 1946-49 printings.

No. 168 exists with pin-perf 6.

For overprint see No. J24.

HEJAZ POSTAGE DUE STAMPS

From Old Door at El Ashraf Barsbai in Shari el Ashrafiya, Cairo — D1

Serrate Roulette 13

1917, June 27 Typo. Unwmk.
LJ1 D1 20pa red 4.25 *4.00*
Never hinged 6.50
LJ2 D1 1pi blue 4.25 *4.00*
Never hinged 6.50
LJ3 D1 2pi magenta 4.25 *4.00*
Never hinged 6.50
Nos. LJ1-LJ3 (3) 12.75 *12.00*

For overprints see Nos. LJ4-LJ10, LJ17-LJ25, J9.

Nos. LJ1-LJ3 Overprinted in Black or Red — a

1921, Dec. Type a
LJ4 D1 20pa red 27.50 4.25
Never hinged 40.00
a. Double overprint, one at left 225.00
b. Overprint at left 55.00 32.50
Never hinged 86.00
LJ5 D1 1pi blue (R) 9.00 5.50
Never hinged 15.00
a. Date at top omitted 15.00
LJ6 D1 1pi bl, ovpt. at left 42.50 50.00
Never hinged 65.00
a. Overprint at right 30.00 32.50
Never hinged 47.50
LJ7 D1 2pi magenta 15.00 11.00
Never hinged 24.00
a. Double overprint, one at left 225.00
b. Overprint at left 72.50
Never hinged 100.00
c. Date at top omitted 72.50
Nos. LJ4-LJ7 (4) 94.00 70.75

Nos. LJ1-LJ3 Overprinted in Black — b

1922, Jan. Type b
LJ8 D1 20pa red 35.00 40.00
Never hinged 55.00
a. Overprint at left 60.00
LJ9 D1 1pi blue 5.00 5.00
Never hinged 8.00
a. Overprint at left 85.00
LJ10 D1 2pi magenta 5.00 5.00
Never hinged 8.00
a. Overprint at left 55.00
Nos. LJ8-LJ10 (3) 45.00 50.00

Regular issue of 1922 Overprinted

1923 Black Overprint *Perf. 11½*
LJ11 A7 ½pi red 5.50 2.00
Never hinged 9.00
a. Inverted overprint 67.50
Never hinged 100.00
LJ12 A7 1pi dark blue 10.00 2.25
Never hinged 16.00
a. Inverted overprint 100.00
Never hinged 155.00
b. Double overprint 165.00
LJ13 A7 2pi orange 5.50 3.00
Never hinged 9.00
a. Inverted overprint 60.00
Never hinged 100.00
Nos. LJ11-LJ13 (3) 21.00 7.25

1924 Blue Overprint
LJ14 A7 ½pi red 25.00 4.25
Never hinged 40.00
a. Inverted overprint 110.00
LJ15 A7 1pi dark blue 55.00 4.25
Never hinged 85.00
a. Inverted overprint 145.00
LJ16 A7 2pi orange 42.50 7.00
Never hinged 67.50
a. Inverted overprint 110.00
Nos. LJ14-LJ16 (3) 122.50 15.50

This overprint reads "Mustahaq" (Due).

1924 Gold Caliphate Overprint
LJ16A A7 ½pi As No. LJ11 1,000.
LJ16B A7 1pi As No. LJ12 1,000.
LJ16C A7 2pi As No. LJ13 1,000.

See note after No. L48.

Jedda Issues

Nos. LJ1-LJ3 Overprinted in Red or Blue (Overprint reads up in illustration)

Jedda issues were also used in Medina and Yambo. **Used values for #L51-L186 and LJ17-LJ39 are for genuine cancels. Privately applied cancels exist for "Mekke" (Mecca, bilingual or all Arabic), Khartoum, Cairo, as well as for Jeddah. Many private cancels have wrong dates, some as early as 1916. These are worth half the used values.**

1925, Jan. *Serrate Roulette 13*
LJ17 D1 20pa red (R) 550.00 *550.00*
LJ18 D1 20pa red (Bl) *725.00* 725.00
LJ19 D1 1pi blue (R) 27.50 *27.50*
LJ20 D1 1pi blue (Bl) 45.00 *45.00*
LJ21 D1 2pi mag (Bl) 21.00 *21.00*

Overprint Reading Down
LJ17a D1 20pa *550.00 550.00*
LJ18a D1 20pa 825.00
LJ19a D1 1pi 25.00 *25.00*
LJ20a D1 1pi 155.00 *80.00*
LJ21a D1 2pi 125.00 *60.00*

Nos. LJ1-LJ3 Overprinted in Blue or Red

1925
LJ22 D1 20pa red (Bl) 725.00 *725.00*
a. Inverted overprint 350.00 *325.00*
LJ24 D1 1pi blue (R) 35.00 *35.00*
a. Inverted overprint 40.00 *32.50*
LJ25 D1 2pi magenta (Bl) 40.00 *40.00*
a. Inverted overprint 27.50 *45.00*
b. Double overprint 375.00

No. LJ2 with this overprint in blue is bogus.

Regular Issues of 1922-24 Overprinted

and Handstamped — b

1925 *Perf. 11½*
LJ26 A7 ⅛pi red brown 30.00 *30.00*
Never hinged 45.00
b. Pair, one without handstamp *250.00* —
c. Overprint inverted 100.00 —
d. Violet handstamp 150.00 —
e. Double overprint 150.00 —
LJ27 A7 ½pi red 37.50 *37.50*
Never hinged 42.50
b. Pair, one without handstamp *250.00* —
c. Overprint inverted 100.00 —
d. Double overprint 125.00 —
LJ28 A7 1pi dark blue 27.50 *30.00*
Never hinged 42.50
b. Pair, one without handstamp *250.00* —
c. Overprint inverted 120.00 —
d. Double overprint 120.00 —
LJ29 A7 1½pi violet 30.00 *18.00*
Never hinged 45.00
b. Pair, one without handstamp *200.00* —
c. Overprint inverted 100.00 —
d. Violet handstamp 110.00 —
e. Horiz. pair, imperf. vert. *175.00*
f. Double ovpt., one invert. 225.00
g. Double ovpt., one vert. up 325.00
h. Double ovpt., one vert. down 325.00
i. Ovpt. on both sides, invert. on back 300.00
LJ30 A7 2pi orange 30.00 *30.00*
Never hinged 45.00
b. Pair, one without handstamp 200.00 —
c. Overprint inverted 110.00 —
d. Violet handstamp 125.00 —
LJ31 A7 3pi olive brown 30.00 *30.00*
Never hinged 45.00
b. Pair, one without handstamp *250.00* —
c. Overprint inverted 110.00 —
LJ32 A7 3pi dull red 72.50 *72.50*
Never hinged 115.00
b. Pair, one without handstamp *250.00* —
c. Overprint inverted 110.00 —
d. Violet handstamp 120.00 —
e. Double ovpt., one invert. 275.00
LJ33 A7 5pi olive green 30.00 *30.00*
Never hinged 45.00
b. Pair, one without handstamp *250.00* —
c. Overprint inverted 90.00 —
LJ34 A7 10pi vio & dk brn 45.00 *40.00*
Never hinged 67.50
b. Pair, one without handstamp *250.00* —
c. Overprint inverted 110.00 —
d. Violet handstamp 110.00 —
Nos. LJ26-LJ34 (9) 332.50 *318.00*

The printed overprint *(a)*, consisting of the three top lines of Arabic, was used alone for the first issue (Nos. LJ26a-LJ34a). The "postage due" box was so small and indistinct that its equivalent in larger characters was added by boxed handstamp *(b)* at bottom of each stamp for the second issue (Nos. LJ26-LJ34).

The handstamped overprint *(b)* is found double, inverted, etc. It is also known in dark violet.

Counterfeits exist of both overprint and handstamp.

Without Boxed Handstamp "b"
LJ26a A7 ⅛pi red brown 55.00
f. Triple ovpt., one vert. up, one vert. down 275.00
g. Double ovpt., one vert. up 400.00
LJ27a A7 ½pi red 60.00
e. Inverted overprint 90.00
f. Double ovpt., one vert. up 175.00
g. Triple ovpt., one vert. up, one vert. down 250.00
LJ28a A7 1pi dark blue 60.00
e. Inverted overprint 90.00
LJ29a A7 1½pi violet 60.00
j. Inverted overprint 100.00
LJ30a A7 2pi orange 60.00
e. Inverted overprint 100.00
f. Double ovpt., one invert. 250.00
g. Double ovpt., one vert. up 225.00
h. Triple ovpt., one vert. up, one vert. down 300.00
LJ31a A7 3pi olive brown 60.00
LJ32a A7 3pi dull red 60.00
f. Inverted overprint 135.00
g. Double ovpt., one vert. up 240.00
h. Double ovpt., one vert. down 240.00
i. Triple ovpt., one vert. up, one vert. down 300.00
LJ33a A7 5pi olive green 87.50
d. Inverted overprint 150.00
LJ34a A7 10pi vio & dk brn 87.50
e. Double overprint 300.00
Nos. LJ26a-LJ34a (9) 590.00

Regular Issue of 1922 Overprinted

and Handstamped

LJ35 A7 ½pi red *150.00 140.00*
LJ36 A7 1½pi violet *150.00 140.00*
a. Overprint in red, boxed handstamp violet *3,500. 1,400.*
LJ37 A7 2pi orange *200.00 175.00*
LJ38 A7 3pi olive brown *150.00 140.00*
a. Violet handstamp *300.00*
LJ39 A7 5pi olive green *125.00 140.00*
Nos. LJ35-LJ39 (5) *775.00 735.00*
Set, never hinged 1,000.

Counterfeits exist of Nos. LJ4-LJ39.

Arabic Numeral of Value — D2

1925, May-June *Perf. 11½*
LJ40 D2 ½pi light blue 3.00
LJ41 D2 1pi orange 3.00
LJ42 D2 2pi lt brown 3.00
LJ43 D2 3pi pink 3.00
Nos. LJ40-LJ43 (4) 12.00

Nos. LJ40-LJ43 have no overprint and were not officially issued. No. LJ40 exists only on cover.

Nos. LJ40-LJ43 exist imperforate. Impressions in colors other than issued are trial color proofs.

Arabic Numeral of Value — D3

1925 Black Overprint
LJ44 D3 ½pi light blue 4.50
Never hinged 6.75
LJ45 D3 1pi orange 4.50
Never hinged 6.75
LJ46 D3 2pi light brown 4.50
Never hinged 6.75
LJ47 D3 3pi pink 4.50
Never hinged 6.75
Nos. LJ44-LJ47 (4) 18.00

Nos. LJ44-LJ47 exist with either Jedda or Cairo overprints and the tablets normally read upward. Values are for Cairo overprints; Jedda overprints sell for more.

Red Overprint

LJ48 D3 ½pi light blue 3.75
Never hinged 6.00
LJ49 D3 1pi orange 3.75
Never hinged 6.00
LJ50 D3 2pi light brown 3.75
Never hinged 6.00
LJ51 D3 3pi pink 3.75
Never hinged 6.00

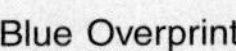

Blue Overprint

LJ52 D3 ½pi light blue 3.75
Never hinged 6.00
LJ53 D3 1pi orange 3.75
Never hinged 6.00
LJ54 D3 2pi light brown 3.75
Never hinged 6.00
LJ55 D3 3pi pink 3.75
Never hinged 6.00
Nos. LJ40-LJ55 (16) 60.00

Red and blue overprints are from Cairo. Nos. LJ44-LJ55 exist imperf.

NEJDI ADMINISTRATION OF HEJAZ POSTAGE DUE STAMPS

Nos. LJ11-LJ16 Handstamped in Blue, Red or Black

1925, Apr.-June Unwmk. *Perf. 11½*

J1 A7 ½pi red (Bl) 27.50 27.50
J2 A7 1pi lt blue (R) 55.00 55.00
a. 1pi dark blue (R) 35.00 35.00
J3 A7 2pi yel buff (Bl) 55.00 55.00
a. 2pi orange (Bl) 47.50 47.50
Nos. J1-J3 (3) 137.50 137.50

The original boxed overprint is printed on Nos. J1, J2a and J3a. Nos. J2-J3 are overprinted on a new printing of the basic stamps with handstamped boxed overprints.

Same, with Postage Due Overprint in Blue

J4 A7 ½pi red (Bl) *140.00*
J5 A7 1pi dk blue (R) *650.00*
J6 A7 2pi orange (Bl) *175.00*

On Hejaz Stamps of 1922-24 Handstamped in Blue

J7 A7 ½pi red (Bl & Bl) 16.00 16.00
J8 A7 3pi brn red (Bl & Bl) 19.00 19.00

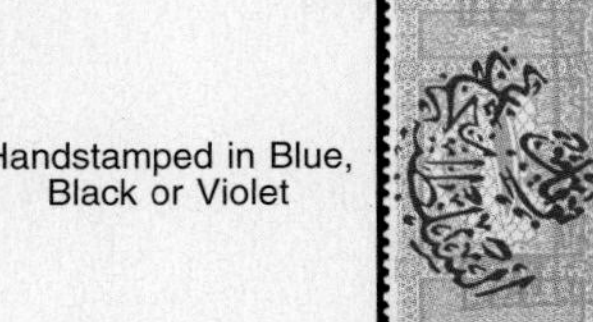

Handstamped in Blue, Black or Violet

On Hejaz No. LJ9
Serrate Roulette 13½

J9 D1 1pi blue (V) 60.00 27.50

See note before No. 35.

Same Overprint on Hejaz Stamps of 1924 with additional Handstamp in Black, Blue or Red

Perf. 11½

J10 A7 3pi brn red (Bl & Bk) 11.00 11.00
J11 A7 3pi brn red (Bk & Bl) 11.00 11.00

Same Handstamps on Hejaz Railway Tax Stamps

J12 R3 1pi blue, type 1 (Bk & R) 12.00 12.00
a. Type 2 40.00
Never hinged 60.00
J13 R3 2pi ocher, type 1 (Bl & Bk) 12.00 12.00
a. Type 2 40.00
Never hinged 60.00
J14 R3 5pi green, type 1 (Bk & R) 20.00 20.00
a. Type 2 60.00
Never hinged 90.00
J15 R3 5pi green, type 1 (V & BK) 20.00 9.00
a. Type 2 60.00
Never hinged 90.00
Nos. J10-J15 (6) 86.00 75.00

The second handstamp, which is struck on the lower part of the Postage Due Stamps, is the word Mustahaq (Due) in various forms.
#J13 exists with 2nd handstamp in blue.

Hejaz-Nejd

D1

1926 Typo. *Perf. 11*

J16 D1 ½pi carmine 4.00 *10.00*
On cover 200.00
J17 D1 2pi orange 4.00 *10.00*
On cover 175.00
On cover, single franking 425.00
J18 D1 6pi light brown 4.00 *10.00*
Nos. J16-J18 (3) 12.00 *30.00*
Set, never hinged 22.00

Nos. J16-J18 exist with perf. 14, 14x11 and 11x14, and imperf. These sell for six times the values quoted.

Nos. J16-J18 in colors other than listed (both perf. and imperf.) are proofs.

Counterfeit note after No. 80 also applies to Nos. J16-J21.

Pan-Islamic Congress Issue

Postage Due Stamps of 1926 Handstamped like Regular Issue

J19 D1 ½pi carmine 5.50 4.50
Never hinged 8.00
J20 D1 2pi orange 5.50 4.50
Never hinged 8.00
J21 D1 6pi light brown 5.50 4.50
Never hinged 8.00
Nos. J19-J21 (3) 16.50 13.50

D2

1927 *Perf. 11½*

J22 D2 1pi slate 18.00 .45
Never hinged 27.00
a. Inscription reads "2 piastres" in upper right circle 200.00 100.00
J23 D2 2pi dark violet 5.75 .45
Never hinged 9.00

Saudi Arabia

Saudi Arabia No. 161 Handstamped in Black

1935

J24 A9 ⅛g dark carmine 450.00

Two types of overprint.

D3

1937-39 Unwmk.

J25 D3 ⅛g org brn ('39) 20.00 20.00
Never hinged 20.00
J26 D3 1g light blue 20.00 20.00
Never hinged 20.00
J27 D3 2g rose vio ('39) 29.00 13.50
Never hinged 25.00
Nos. J25-J27 (3) 69.00 53.50

OFFICIAL STAMPS

Official stamps were normally used only on external correspondence.

O1

1939 Unwmk. Typo. *Perf. 11½*

O1 O1 3g deep ultra 5.25 2.40
On cover, single franking 15.00

Perf. 11, 11½

O2 O1 5g red violet 6.75 3.00
On cover, single franking 10.00

Perf. 11

O3 O1 20g brown 14.00 6.25
O4 O1 50g blue green 27.50 13.00
O5 O1 100g olive grn 110.00 60.00
O6 O1 200g purple 90.00 40.00
Nos. O1-O6 (6) 253.50 124.65

No. O1 on royal cover is valued at $50.

NEWSPAPER STAMPS

Nos. 8, 9 and 14 with Additional Overprint in Black

1925 Unwmk. *Perf. 11½*

P1 A7 ⅛pi red brown (Bk) *1,800. 1,800.*
P2 A7 ⅛pi red brown (V) *1,400. 900.*
P3 A7 ½pi red (V) *2,750. 1,800.*

Overprint reads: "Matbu'a" (Newspaper), but these stamps were normally used for regular postage. Counterfeits exist.

The status of this set in question. The government may have declared it to be unauthorized.

POSTAL TAX STAMPS

PT1

1934, May 15 Unwmk. *Perf. 11½*

RA1 PT1 ½g scarlet *100.00* 4.50
Never hinged 190.00
On cover 75.00

No. RA1 collected a "war tax" to aid wounded of the 1934 Saudi-Yemen war.

Nos. RA2-RA8 raised funds for the Medical Aid Society. Nos. RA4-RA8 in Scott Standard catalogue, Vol. 6.

General Hospital, Mecca
PT2

PT2a

1936, Oct. Size: 37x20mm

RA2 PT2 ⅛g scarlet *400.00* 9.00
Never hinged 625.00
On cover 100.00

Type of 1936, Redrawn

1937-42 Size: 30½x18mm

RA3 PT2a ⅛g scarlet 35.00 .90
Never hinged 75.00
On cover 10.00
a. ⅛g rose ('39) *60.00* 1.75
Never hinged 125.00
On cover 20.00
b. ⅛g rose car, perf. 11 ('42) *125.00* *6.75*
Never hinged 225.00

SCHLESWIG

ˈshles-ˌwig

LOCATION — In the northern part of the former Schleswig-Holstein Province, in northern Germany.

Schleswig was divided into North and South Schleswig after the Versailles Treaty, and plebiscites were held in 1920. North Schleswig (Zone 1) voted to join Denmark, South Schleswig to stay German.

100 Pfennig = 1 Mark
100 Ore = 1 Krone

Watermark

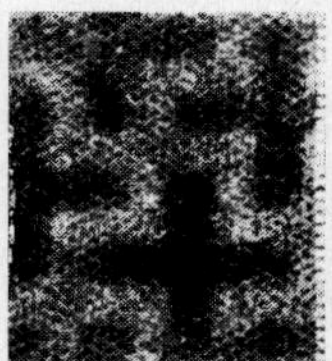

Wmk. 114 — Multiple Crosses

Plebiscite Issue

Arms — A11

View of Schleswig A12

Perf. 14x15

1920, Jan. 25 Typo. Wmk. 114

No.	Type	Description	Unused	Used
1	A11	2½pf gray	.25	*.85*
		Never hinged	.80	
		On cover		6.75
2	A11	5pf green	.25	*.85*
		Never hinged	.80	
		On cover		4.25
3	A11	7½pf yellow brown	.25	*.85*
		Never hinged	.80	
		On cover		6.75
4	A11	10pf deep rose	.25	*.85*
		Never hinged	.80	
		On cover		4.25
5	A11	15pf red violet	.25	*.85*
		Never hinged	.80	
		On cover		4.25
6	A11	20pf deep blue	.25	*.85*
		Never hinged	.80	
		On cover		4.25
7	A11	25pf orange	.35	.85
		Never hinged	1.60	
		On cover		8.50
8	A11	35pf brown	.45	*1.10*
		Never hinged	2.50	
		On cover		17.00
9	A11	40pf violet	.35	*.85*
		Never hinged	1.60	
		On cover		10.00
10	A11	75pf greenish blue	.45	*1.10*
		Never hinged	2.50	
		On cover		21.00
11	A12	1m dark brown	.45	*.85*
		Never hinged	2.50	
		On cover		21.00
12	A12	2m deep blue	.70	*1.50*
		Never hinged	4.25	
		On cover		60.00
13	A12	5m green	1.50	1.75
		Never hinged	6.75	
		On cover		135.00
14	A12	10m red	3.25	*3.50*
		Never hinged	16.00	
		On cover		—
		Nos. 1-14 (14)	9.00	*16.60*
		Set, never hinged	42.50	

The colored areas of type A11 are white, and the white areas are colored, on Nos. 7-10.

Types of 1920 Overprinted in Blue

1920, May 20

No.	Type	Description	Unused	Used
15	A11	1o dark gray	.25	*2.40*
		Never hinged	.75	
		On cover		21.00
16	A11	5o green	.25	*1.75*
		Never hinged	.75	
		On cover		21.00
17	A11	7o yellow brn	.25	*1.60*
		Never hinged	.75	
		On cover		21.00
18	A11	10o rose red	.25	*1.60*
		Never hinged	.75	
		On cover		21.00
19	A11	15o lilac rose	.25	*2.50*
		Never hinged	.75	
		On cover		21.00
20	A11	20o dark blue	.25	*2.75*
		Never hinged	.75	
		On cover		30.00
21	A11	25o orange	.25	*8.00*
		Never hinged	1.20	
		On cover		67.50
22	A11	35o brown	.85	*14.50*
		Never hinged	6.00	
		On cover		85.00
23	A11	40o violet	.25	*4.75*
		Never hinged	2.60	
		On cover		85.00
24	A11	75o greenish blue	.45	*8.00*
		Never hinged	3.25	
		On cover		120.00
25	A12	1k dark brown	.65	*13.00*
		Never hinged	4.00	
		On cover		150.00
a.		Double overprint		—
26	A12	2k deep blue	7.00	*47.50*
		Never hinged	40.00	
		On cover		—
27	A12	5k green	3.50	*47.50*
		Never hinged	30.00	
		On cover		—
28	A12	10k red	8.00	*87.50*
		Never hinged	40.00	
		On cover		—
		Nos. 15-28 (14)	22.45	*243.35*
		Set, never hinged	165.00	

OFFICIAL STAMPS

Nos. 1-14 Overprinted

1920 Wmk. 114 *Perf. 14x15*

No.	Type	Description	Unused	Used
O1	A11	2½pf gray	65.00	*92.50*
		Never hinged	125.00	
		On cover		*500.00*
O2	A11	5pf green	65.00	*110.00*
		Never hinged	125.00	
		On cover		*475.00*
O3	A11	7½pf yellow brn	65.00	*92.50*
		Never hinged	125.00	
		On cover		*600.00*
O4	A11	10pf deep rose	65.00	*120.00*
		Never hinged	125.00	
		On cover		*550.00*
O5	A11	15pf red violet	42.50	*60.00*
		Never hinged	85.00	
		On cover		*275.00*
O6	A11	20pf dp blue	65.00	*67.50*
		Never hinged	125.00	
		On cover		*275.00*
a.		Double overprint	1,500.	
O7	A11	25pf orange	125.00	*175.00*
		Never hinged	290.00	
		On cover		*625.00*
a.		Inverted overprint	*1,050.*	
O8	A11	35pf brown	125.00	*175.00*
		Never hinged	290.00	
		On cover		*725.00*
O9	A11	40pf violet	110.00	100.00
		Never hinged	210.00	
		On cover		*550.00*
O10	A11	75pf grnsh blue	125.00	*250.00*
		Never hinged	250.00	
		On cover		*850.00*
O11	A12	1m dark brown	125.00	*250.00*
		Never hinged	250.00	
		On cover		*850.00*
O12	A12	2m deep blue	185.00	*275.00*
		Never hinged	375.00	
		On cover		*1,100.*
O13	A12	5m green	275.00	*425.00*
		Never hinged	550.00	
		On cover		—
O14	A12	10m red	500.00	*625.00*
		Never hinged	1,000.	
		On cover		—
		Nos. O1-O14 (14)	1,938.	*2,818.*
		Set, never hinged	3,800.	

The letters "C.I.S." are the initials of "Commission Interalliée Slesvig," under whose auspices the plebiscites took place.

Counterfeit overprints exist.

SENEGAL

ˌse-ni-ˈgäl

LOCATION — West coast of Africa, bordering on the Atlantic Ocean
GOVT. — Republic
AREA — 76,000 sq. mi.
POP. — 6,300,000 (est. 1984)
CAPITAL — Dakar

The former French colony of Senegal became part of French West Africa in 1943. The Republic of Senegal was established Nov. 25, 1958. From Apr. 4, 1959, to June 20, 1960, the Republic of Senegal and the Sudanese Republic together formed the Mali Federation. After its breakup, Senegal resumed issuing its own stamps in 1960.

100 Centimes = 1 Franc

French Colonies Nos. 48, 49, 51, 52, 55, Type A9, Surcharged

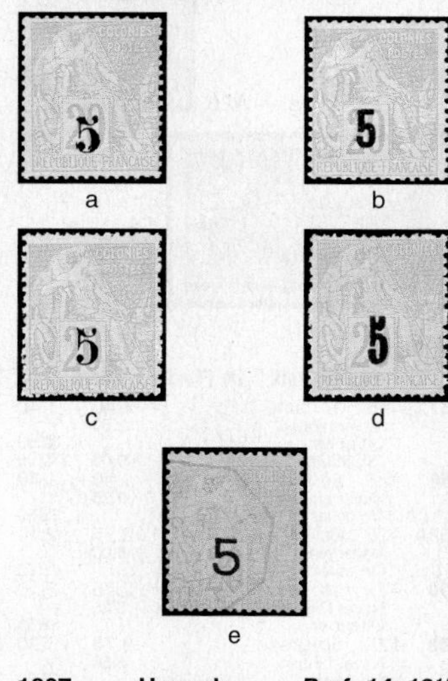

a b c d e

1887 Unwmk. *Perf. 14x13½*

Black Surcharge

No.	Type	Description	Unused	Used
1	(a)	5c on 20c red, *grn*	210.00	210.00
		On cover		*550.00*
a.		Double surcharge	550.00	
2	(b)	5c on 20c red, *grn*	375.00	375.00
		On cover		*600.00*
3	(c)	5c on 20c red, *grn*	1,250.	1,250.
		On cover		*2,000.*
4	(d)	5c on 20c red, *grn*	260.00	260.00
		On cover		*400.00*
5	(e)	5c on 20c red, *grn*	475.00	475.00
		On cover		*800.00*
6	(a)	5c on 30c brn, *bis*	325.00	325.00
		On cover		*750.00*
7	(b)	5c on 30c brn, *bis*	1,500.	1,500.
		On cover		*2,250.*
8	(d)	5c on 30c brn, *bis*	475.00	475.00
		On cover		*800.00*
		Nos. 1-8 (8)	4,870.	4,870.

See Madagascar #6-7 for stamps with surcharge like "d" on 10c and 25c stamps.

f g h i j k l m

No.	Type	Description	Unused	Used
9	(f)	10c on 4c cl, *lav*	160.00	160.00
		Never hinged	300.00	
		On cover		*500.00*
10	(g)	10c on 4c cl, *lav*	240.00	240.00
		On cover		*500.00*
11	(h)	10c on 4c cl, *lav*	120.00	120.00
		Never hinged	225.00	
		On cover		*500.00*
12	(i)	10c on 4c cl, *lav*	120.00	120.00
		On cover		*600.00*
a.		"1" without top stroke		
13	(f)	10c on 20c red, *grn*	725.00	725.00
		On cover		*1,500.*
14	(g)	10c on 20c red, *grn*	750.00	750.00
		On cover		*1,500.*
15	(h)	10c on 20c red, *grn*	650.00	650.00
		On cover		*1,350.*
16	(i)	10c on 20c red, *grn*	*4,250.*	*4,250.*
		On cover		*7,500.*
17	(j)	10c on 20c red, *grn*	750.00	750.00
		On cover		*1,500.*
18	(k)	10c on 20c red, *grn*	3,000.	3,000.
		On cover		*5,000.*
19	(l)	10c on 20c red, *grn*	750.00	750.00
		On cover		*1,500.*
20	(m)	10c on 20c red, *grn*	750.00	750.00
		On cover		*1,500.*

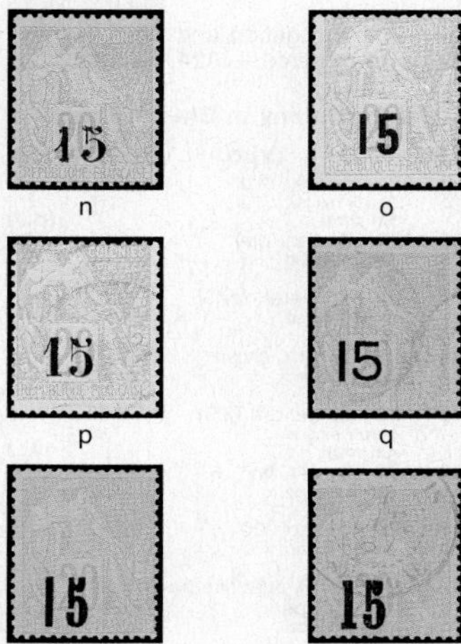

n o p q r s

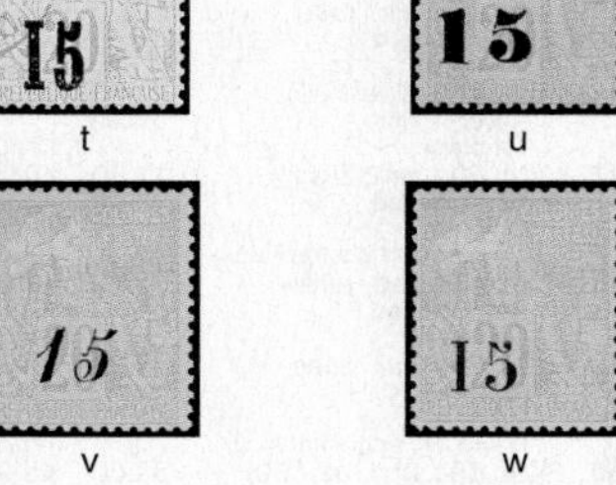

t u v w

No.	Type	Description	Unused	Used
21	(n)	15c on 20c red, *grn*	130.00	130.00
		Never hinged	250.00	
		On cover		*500.00*
22	(o)	15c on 20c red, *grn*	110.00	110.00
		Never hinged	225.00	
		On cover		*500.00*
23	(p)	15c on 20c red, *grn*	87.50	87.50
		Never hinged	175.00	
		On cover		*500.00*
24	(q)	15c on 20c red, *grn*	160.00	160.00
		On cover		*500.00*
25	(r)	15c on 20c red, *grn*	100.00	100.00
		Never hinged	190.00	
		On cover		*500.00*
26	(s)	15c on 20c red, *grn*	100.00	100.00
		Never hinged	190.00	
		On cover		*500.00*
27	(t)	15c on 20c red, *grn*	260.00	260.00
		On cover		*750.00*
28	(u)	15c on 20c red, *grn*	87.50	87.50
		Never hinged	175.00	
		On cover		*500.00*
29	(v)	15c on 20c red, *grn*	120.00	120.00
		Never hinged	225.00	
		On cover		*500.00*
30	(w)	15c on 20c red, *grn*	425.00	425.00
		On cover		—
		Nos. 21-30 (10)	1,580.	1,580.

Counterfeits exist of Nos. 1-34.

French Colonies Stamps of 1881-86 Surcharged

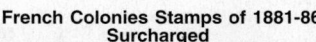

1892 **Black Surcharge**
31 A9 75c on 15c blue 450.00 200.00
On cover 650.00
a. "SENEGAL" double 950.00
32 A9 1fr on 5c grn, *grnsh* 450.00 200.00
On cover 650.00
a. "SENEGAL" double 14,750.
b. "SENEGAL" omitted 2,800.
c. "1F" double 325.00

"SENEGAL" in Red

33 A9 75c on 15c blue *16,500.* *5,750.*
On cover *13,000.*
34 A9 1fr on 5c grn, *grnsh* *7,500.* *1,600.*
On cover *3,900.*

Navigation and Commerce — A24

Name of Colony in Blue or Carmine

1892-1900 **Typo.** ***Perf. 14x13½***
35 A24 1c blk, *lil bl* 1.60 1.20
Never hinged 3.50
On cover 95.00
36 A24 2c brn, *buff* 2.25 2.25
Never hinged 7.00
On cover 95.00
37 A24 4c claret, *lav* 3.50 1.75
Never hinged 7.00
On cover 95.00
38 A24 5c grn, *grnsh* 3.50 2.25
Never hinged 7.00
On cover 50.00
39 A24 5c yel grn ('00) 3.50 1.40
Never hinged 7.00
On cover 19.00
40 A24 10c blk, *lav* 10.00 5.50
Never hinged 14.50
On cover 37.50
41 A24 10c red ('00) 7.00 1.40
Never hinged 10.00
On cover 19.00
42 A24 15c bl, quadrille paper 15.00 2.25
Never hinged 27.50
On cover 45.00
43 A24 15c gray ('00) 7.25 2.50
Never hinged 14.00
On cover 19.00
44 A24 20c red, *grn* 10.50 7.00
Never hinged 22.50
On cover 80.00
On cover, single franking 140.00
45 A24 25c blk, *rose* 17.50 7.25
Never hinged 32.50
On cover 37.50
46 A24 25c blue ('00) 40.00 35.00
Never hinged 80.00
On cover 250.00
47 A24 30c brn, *bis* 17.50 10.00
Never hinged 35.00
On cover 62.50
On cover, single franking 105.00
48 A24 40c red, *straw* 25.00 21.00
Never hinged 50.00
On cover 80.00
49 A24 50c car, *rose* 45.00 30.00
Never hinged 92.50
On cover 100.00
On cover, single franking 125.00
50 A24 50c brn, *az* ('00) 50.00 45.00
Never hinged 100.00
On cover 300.00
On cover, single franking 375.00
51 A24 75c vio, *org* 22.50 17.50
Never hinged 45.00
On cover 125.00
On cover, single franking 190.00
52 A24 1fr brnz grn, *straw* 25.00 21.00
Never hinged 55.00
On cover 140.00
On cover, single franking 225.00
Nos. 35-52 (18) 306.60 214.25

Perf. 13½x14 stamps are counterfeits.
For surcharges see Nos. 53-56, 73-78.

Stamps of 1892 Surcharged

1903
53 A24 5c on 40c red, *straw* 17.50 17.50
Never hinged 30.00
On cover 95.00
54 A24 10c on 50c car, *rose* 25.00 25.00
Never hinged 42.50
On cover 125.00
55 A24 10c on 75c vio, *org* 25.00 25.00
Never hinged 45.00
On cover 110.00
56 A24 10c on 1fr brnz grn, *straw* 80.00 80.00
Never hinged 160.00
On cover 300.00
Nos. 53-56 (4) 147.50 147.50

General Louis Faidherbe A25

Oil Palms — A26

Dr. Noel Eugène Ballay A27

1906 **Typo.**

"SÉNÉGAL" in Red or Blue

57 A25 1c slate 1.40 1.40
Never hinged 2.50
On cover 62.50
a. "SENEGAL" omitted 140.00 140.00
58 A25 2c choc (R) 1.40 1.40
Never hinged 3.25
On cover 62.50
58A A25 2c choc (Bl) 2.75 2.10
Never hinged 5.00
On cover 75.00
59 A25 4c choc, *gray bl* 2.75 2.10
Never hinged 5.25
On cover 62.50
60 A25 5c green 2.75 1.20
Never hinged 5.50
On cover 37.50
a. "SENEGAL" omitted 130.00
61 A25 10c car (Bl) 14.00 1.20
Never hinged 25.00
On cover 21.00
a. "SENEGAL" omitted 450.00 450.00
62 A25 15c violet 7.00 3.50
Never hinged 14.00
On cover 50.00
63 A26 20c blk, *az* 10.50 4.25
Never hinged 18.00
On cover 30.00
64 A26 25c bl, *pnksh* 3.50 2.75
Never hinged 7.00
On cover 45.00
65 A26 30c choc, *pnksh* 10.50 5.50
Never hinged 17.50
On cover 37.50
On cover, single franking 70.00
66 A26 35c blk, *yellow* 27.50 2.75
Never hinged 62.50
On cover 37.50
On cover, single franking 55.00
a. "SENEGAL" double 210.00 *225.00*
67 A26 40c car, *az* (Bl) 14.00 6.25
Never hinged 25.00
On cover 62.50
On cover, single franking 140.00
67A A26 45c choc, *grnsh* 25.00 15.00
Never hinged 52.50
On cover 80.00
On cover, single franking 110.00
68 A26 50c dp violet 14.00 6.25
Never hinged 27.50
On cover 62.50
On cover, single franking 105.00
69 A26 75c bl, *org* 10.50 7.75
Never hinged 21.00
On cover 95.00
On cover, single franking 225.00
70 A27 1fr blk, *azure* 27.50 27.50
Never hinged 60.00
On cover 140.00
On cover, single franking 275.00
71 A27 2fr blue, *pink* 35.00 35.00
Never hinged 80.00
On cover 175.00
On cover, single franking 300.00
72 A27 5fr car, *straw* (Bl) 72.50 62.50
Never hinged 140.00
On cover 250.00
On cover, single franking 475.00
Nos. 57-72 (18) 282.55 188.40

Stamps of 1892-1900 Surcharged in Carmine or Black

Spacing between figures of surcharge 1.5mm (5c), 2mm (10c)

1912
73 A24 5c on 15c gray (C) 1.10 1.10
Never hinged 1.75
On cover 50.00
74 A24 5c on 20c red, *grn* 2.10 *2.10*
Never hinged 3.50
On cover 100.00
75 A24 5c on 30c brn, *bis* (C) 1.40 1.40
Never hinged 2.50
On cover 62.50
76 A24 10c on 40c red, *straw* 1.75 1.75
Never hinged 2.75
On cover 75.00
77 A24 10c on 50c car, *rose* 4.25 *5.00*
Never hinged 7.00
On cover 100.00
78 A24 10c on 75c vio, *org* 7.00 *7.75*
Never hinged 10.50
On cover 110.00
Nos. 73-78 (6) 17.60 19.10

Spacing between figures of surcharge 2.25mm (5c), 2.75mm (10c)

73a A24 5c on 15c gray (C) 25.00 25.00
Never hinged 42.50
74a A24 5c on 20c red, *grn* 260.00 260.00
75a A24 5c on 30c brn, *bis* (C) 87.50 87.50
Never hinged 175.00
76a A24 10c on 40c red, *straw* 42.50 42.50
Never hinged 77.50
77a A24 10c on 50c car, *rose* 87.50 87.50
Never hinged 175.00
78a A24 10c on 75c vio, *org* 220.00 220.00
Nos. 73a-78a (6) 722.50 722.50

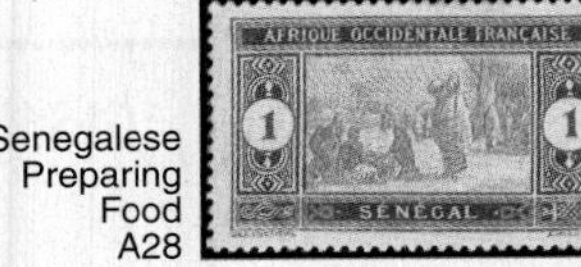
Senegalese Preparing Food A28

1914-33 **Typo.**
79 A28 1c ol brn & vio .25 .25
Never hinged .35
On cover 62.50
a. Chalky paper .25 .25
Never hinged .35
On cover 62.50
80 A28 2c black & blue .25 .25
Never hinged .35
On cover 62.50
81 A28 4c gray & brn .25 .25
Never hinged .35
On cover 62.50
82 A28 5c yel grn & bl grn .35 .25
Never hinged .70
On cover 21.00
a. Chalky paper 1.10 .50
Never hinged 1.75
On cover 25.00
83 A28 5c blk & rose ('22) .25 .25
Never hinged .35
On cover 25.00
a. Center double 300.00
Never hinged 450.00
84 A28 10c org red & rose 1.45 .25
Never hinged 2.25
On cover 12.50
a. Chalky paper 1.25 .25
Never hinged 2.00
On cover 12.50
85 A28 10c yel grn & bl grn ('22) .35 .30
Never hinged .70
On cover 37.50
86 A28 10c red brn & bl ('25) .35 .35
Never hinged .70
On cover 40.00
87 A28 15c red org & brn vio ('17) .35 .35
Never hinged .70
On cover 12.50
88 A28 20c choc & blk .35 .30
Never hinged .70
On cover 21.00
89 A28 20c grn & bl grn ('26) .35 .35
Never hinged .70
On cover 5.25
90 A28 20c db & lt bl ('27) .70 .70
Never hinged 1.10
On cover 16.50
91 A28 25c ultra & bl 1.10 .45
Never hinged 1.75
On cover 22.50
On cover, single franking 55.00
92 A28 25c red & blk ('22) .70 .30
Never hinged 1.10
On cover 6.25
93 A28 30c black & rose .75 .35
Never hinged 1.40
On cover 25.00
On cover, single franking 70.00
94 A28 30c red org & rose ('22) .70 .30
Never hinged 1.10
On cover 25.00
On cover, single franking 50.00
95 A28 30c gray & bl ('26) .35 .35
Never hinged .70
On cover 9.00
96 A28 30c dl grn & dp grn ('28) .70 .70
Never hinged 1.40
On cover 37.50
97 A28 35c orange & vio .70 .45
Never hinged 1.40
On cover 30.00
On cover, single franking 62.50
a. Chalky paper 2.75 2.10
Never hinged 5.00
On cover 45.00
98 A28 40c violet & grn 1.10 .45
Never hinged 1.40
On cover 37.50
On cover, single franking 80.00
99 A28 45c bl & ol brn 1.75 1.40
Never hinged 3.50
On cover 50.00
On cover, single franking 110.00
100 A28 45c rose & bl ('22) 1.10 .45
Never hinged 1.40
On cover 50.00
On cover, single franking 110.00
101 A28 45c rose & ver ('25) .70 .70
Never hinged 1.10
On cover 35.00
102 A28 45c ol brn & org ('28) 3.50 2.75
Never hinged 5.50
On cover 35.00
On cover, single franking 50.00
103 A28 50c vio brn & bl 1.75 1.10
Never hinged 3.50
On cover 55.00
On cover, single franking 125.00
104 A28 50c ultra & bl ('22) 2.75 1.75
Never hinged 3.50
On cover 22.50
On cover, single franking 50.00
105 A28 50c red org & grn ('26) .70 .35
Never hinged 1.10
On cover 6.25
106 A28 60c vio, *pnksh* ('26) .70 .35
Never hinged 1.10
On cover 25.00
On cover, single franking 55.00
107 A28 65c rose red & dp grn ('28) 2.10 1.40
Never hinged 3.50
On cover 40.00
On cover, single franking 75.00
108 A28 75c gray & rose 1.40 .70
Never hinged 2.10
On cover 37.50
On cover, single franking 70.00
109 A28 75c dk bl & lt bl ('25) 1.10 1.10
Never hinged 1.75
On cover 22.50
On cover, single franking 45.00
110 A28 75c rose & gray bl ('26) 2.10 1.05
Never hinged 2.75
On cover 11.00
111 A28 90c brn red & rose ('30) 5.00 5.00
Never hinged 9.00
On cover 55.00
On cover, single franking 140.00
112 A28 1fr violet & blk 1.40 .70
Never hinged 2.00
On cover 55.00
On cover, single franking 140.00
113 A28 1fr blue ('26) 1.05 1.05
Never hinged 1.40
On cover 35.00
On cover, single franking 87.50
114 A28 1fr blk & gray bl ('26) 1.75 1.05
Never hinged 3.00
On cover 14.00
On cover, single franking 20.00
115 A28 1.10fr bl grn & blk ('28) 4.25 *4.50*
Never hinged 7.25
On cover 105.00
On cover, single franking 275.00
116 A28 1.25fr dp grn & dp org ('33) 1.40 1.40
Never hinged 2.10
On cover 19.00
On cover, single franking 62.50
117 A28 1.50fr dk bl & bl ('30) 3.25 3.25
Never hinged 5.00
On cover 50.00
On cover, single franking 125.00
118 A28 1.75fr dk brn & Prus bl ('33) 7.25 1.40
Never hinged 10.50
On cover 15.00
On cover, single franking 21.00
119 A28 2fr carmine & bl 3.50 2.50
Never hinged 7.00
On cover 70.00
On cover, single franking 140.00
120 A28 2fr lt bl & brn ('22) 2.75 .90
Never hinged 4.25
On cover 42.50
On cover, single franking 125.00
121 A28 3fr red vio ('30) 3.50 2.10
Never hinged 7.25
On cover 67.50
On cover, single franking 170.00
122 A28 5fr green & vio 5.00 1.75
Never hinged 11.00
On cover 80.00
On cover, single franking 150.00
Nos. 79-122 (44) 71.10 45.90

For surcharges see Nos. 123-137, B1-B2.

No. 108 and Type of 1914 Srchd.

1922-25

123 A28 60c on 75c vio, *pnksh* 1.40 .90
Never hinged 2.10
On cover 15.00
On cover, single franking 25.00
a. Double surcharge 125.00
Never hinged 210.00
124 A28 65c on 15c red org & dl vio ('25) 1.40 1.40
Never hinged 2.10
On cover 55.00
On cover, single franking 125.00
125 A28 85c on 15c red org & dl vio ('25) 1.40 1.40
Never hinged 2.10
On cover 37.50
On cover, single franking 70.00
126 A28 85c on 75c ('25) 1.40 1.40
Never hinged 2.10
On cover 37.50
On cover, single franking 70.00

No. 87 Srchd. in Various Colors

1922

127 A28 1c on 15c (Bk) .70 .70
Never hinged 1.10
On cover 75.00
128 A28 2c on 15c (Bl) .70 .70
Never hinged 1.10
On cover 75.00
129 A28 4c on 15c (G) .70 .70
Never hinged 1.10
On cover 75.00
130 A28 5c on 15c (R) .70 .70
Never hinged 1.10
On cover 30.00
Nos. 123-130 (8) 8.40 7.90

Stamps and Type of 1914 Surcharged with New Value and Bars in Black or Red

1924-27

131 A28 25c on 5fr grn & vio .85 .85
Never hinged 1.40
On cover 6.25
132 A28 90c on 75c brn red & cer ('27) 1.40 1.10
Never hinged 2.10
On cover 42.50
On cover, single franking 75.00
a. Double surcharge 125.00
Never hinged 2.10
133 A28 1.25fr on 1fr bl & lt bl (R) ('26) 1.40 1.10
Never hinged 2.10
On cover 42.50
On cover, single franking 87.50
134 A28 1.50fr on 1fr dk bl & ultra ('27) 1.40 1.10
Never hinged 2.10
On cover 37.50
On cover, single franking 62.50
a. Surcharge omitted 160.00
Never hinged 275.00
135 A28 3fr on 5fr mag & ol brn ('27) 3.50 2.25
Never hinged 7.00
On cover 70.00
On cover, single franking 140.00
a. Period after "F" omitted 14.00 12.50
Never hinged 25.00
136 A28 10fr on 5fr dk bl & red org ('27) 7.75 3.50
Never hinged 14.00
On cover 87.50
On cover, single franking 160.00
137 A28 20fr on 5fr vio & ol bis ('27) 7.00 7.00
Never hinged 14.00
On cover 100.00
On cover, single franking 200.00
a. Period after "F" omitted 27.50 25.00
Never hinged 45.00
Nos. 131-137 (7) 23.30 16.90

Common Design Types pictured following the introduction

Colonial Exposition Issue

Common Design Types

Name of Country Typographed in Black

1931 Engr. *Perf. 12½*

138 CD70 40c deep green 5.00 5.00
Never hinged 7.00
On cover 80.00
139 CD71 50c violet 5.00 5.00
Never hinged 7.00
On cover 70.00
140 CD72 90c red orange 5.00 5.00
Never hinged 7.00
On cover 110.00
a. "SENEGAL" double 175.00
Never hinged 250.00
141 CD73 1.50fr dull blue 5.00 5.00
Never hinged 7.00
On cover 105.00
On cover, single franking 165.00
Nos. 138-141 (4) 20.00 20.00

Faidherbe Bridge, St. Louis A29

Diourbel Mosque A30

1935-40 *Perf. 12½x12*

142 A29 1c violet blue .25 .25
Never hinged .35
On cover 27.50
143 A29 2c brown .25 .25
Never hinged .35
On cover 27.50
144 A29 3c violet ('40) .25 .25
Never hinged .35
On cover 27.50
145 A29 4c gray blue .25 .25
Never hinged .35
On cover 27.50
146 A29 5c orange red .25 .25
Never hinged .35
On cover 22.50
147 A29 10c violet .25 .25
Never hinged .35
On cover 20.00
148 A29 15c black .25 .25
Never hinged .35
On cover 16.00
149 A29 20c dk carmine .30 .25
Never hinged .45
On cover 16.00
150 A29 25c black brn .30 .25
Never hinged .45
On cover 12.50
151 A29 30c green .30 .30
Never hinged .45
On cover 20.00
152 A29 40c rose lake .35 .30
Never hinged .50
On cover 8.75
153 A29 45c dk blue grn .35 .30
Never hinged .50
On cover 22.50
154 A30 50c red orange .35 .25
Never hinged .50
On cover 6.25
155 A30 60c violet ('40) .25 .30
Never hinged .35
On cover 20.00
156 A30 65c dk violet .35 .30
Never hinged .50
On cover 27.50
157 A30 70c red brn ('40) .70 .70
Never hinged 1.10
On cover 22.50
158 A30 75c brown .70 .55
Never hinged 1.10
On cover 10.00
159 A30 90c rose car 2.10 1.40
Never hinged 2.50
On cover 27.50
On cover, single franking 70.00
160 A30 1fr violet 10.50 2.50
Never hinged 12.50
On cover 12.50
On cover, single franking 19.00
161 A30 1.25fr redsh brn 1.40 1.10
Never hinged 2.50
On cover 21.00
On cover, single franking 42.50
162 A30 1.25fr rose car ('39) .85 .85
Never hinged 1.40
On cover 55.00
On cover, single franking 105.00
163 A30 1.40fr dk bl grn ('40) .70 .85
Never hinged 1.10
On cover 32.50
On cover, single franking 80.00
164 A30 1.50fr dk blue .35 .35
Never hinged .50
On cover 25.00
On cover, single franking 62.50
165 A30 1.60fr pck bl ('40) .70 .85
Never hinged 1.10
On cover 32.50
On cover, single franking 92.50
166 A30 1.75fr dk blue grn .35 .35
Never hinged .50
On cover 8.25
On cover, single franking 15.00
167 A30 2fr blue .70 .35
Never hinged 1.10
On cover 14.00
On cover, single franking 21.00
168 A30 3fr green .70 .45
Never hinged 1.10
On cover 32.50
On cover, single franking 62.50
169 A30 5fr black brn .70 .70
Never hinged 1.10
On cover 40.00
On cover, single franking 75.00
170 A30 10fr rose lake 1.75 1.10
Never hinged 2.25
On cover 45.00
On cover, single franking 87.50
171 A30 20fr grnsh slate 1.75 1.10
Never hinged 2.25
On cover 62.50
On cover, single franking 105.00
Nos. 142-171 (30) 28.25 17.20

Nos. 143, 148 and 156 surcharged with new values are listed under French West Africa in Scott Standard catalogue, Vol. 2.

For surcharges see Nos. B9, B11-B12 in Scott Standard catalogue, Vol. 6.

Paris International Exposition Issue

Common Design Types

1937 *Perf. 13*

172 CD74 20c deep violet 1.75 1.75
Never hinged 2.75
On cover 87.50
a. Sénégal omitted 90.00 *100.00*
Never hinged 130.00
On cover 300.00
173 CD75 30c dark green 1.75 1.75
Never hinged 2.75
On cover 70.00
174 CD76 40c car rose 1.75 1.75
Never hinged 2.75
On cover 55.00
175 CD77 50c dark brown 1.75 1.40
Never hinged 2.75
On cover 50.00
176 CD78 90c red 1.75 1.40
Never hinged 2.75
On cover 95.00
On cover, single franking 165.00
177 CD79 1.50fr ultra 1.75 1.75
Never hinged 2.75
On cover 80.00
On cover, single franking 140.00
Nos. 172-177 (6) 10.50 9.80

Colonial Arts Exhibition Issue

Souvenir Sheet

Common Design Type

1937 Unwmk. *Imperf.*

178 CD76 3fr rose violet 10.50 14.00
Never hinged 14.00
On cover 110.00
On cover, single franking 165.00
a. Inscriptions inverted 1,400.
Never hinged 1,900.

Senegalese Woman — A31

1938-40 *Perf. 12x12½, 12½x12*

179 A31 35c green .35 .55
Never hinged 1.10
On cover 27.50
180 A31 55c chocolate .70 .55
Never hinged 1.10
On cover 7.50
181 A31 80c violet 1.10 .65
Never hinged 1.60
On cover 50.00
On cover, single franking 70.00
182 A31 90c lt rose vio ('39) .70 .70
Never hinged 1.10
On cover 37.50
On cover, single franking 87.50
183 A31 1fr car lake 1.75 1.10
Never hinged 2.75
On cover 32.50
On cover, single franking 62.50
184 A31 1fr cop brn ('40) .35 .65
Never hinged .70
On cover 7.00
185 A31 1.75fr ultra 1.10 .70
Never hinged 1.40
On cover 30.00
On cover, single franking 55.00
186 A31 2.25fr ultra ('39) .90 .90
Never hinged 1.40
On cover 37.50
On cover, single franking 70.00
187 A31 2.50fr black ('40) 1.40 1.40
Never hinged 1.75
On cover 30.00
On cover, single franking 55.00
Nos. 179-187 (9) 8.35 7.20

For surcharge see No. B10 in Scott Standard catalogue, Vol. 6.

Caillié Issue

Common Design Type

1939 Engr. *Perf. 12½x12*

188 CD81 90c org brn & org .35 .70
Never hinged .70
On cover 6.00
189 CD81 2fr brt vio .35 1.10
Never hinged .70
On cover 22.50
On cover, single franking 42.50
190 CD81 2.25fr ultra & dk bl .35 1.10
Never hinged .70
On cover 27.50
On cover, single franking 50.00
Nos. 188-190 (3) 1.05 2.90
Set, never hinged 2.40

For No. 188 surcharged 20fr and 50fr, see French West Africa in Scott Standard catalogue, Vol. 2.

New York World's Fair Issue

Common Design Type

1939 *Perf. 12½x12*

191 CD82 1.25fr car lake .70 1.40
Never hinged 1.10
On cover 62.50
On cover, single franking 140.00
192 CD82 2.25fr ultra .70 1.40
Never hinged 1.10
On cover 62.50
On cover, single franking 125.00

SEMI-POSTAL STAMPS

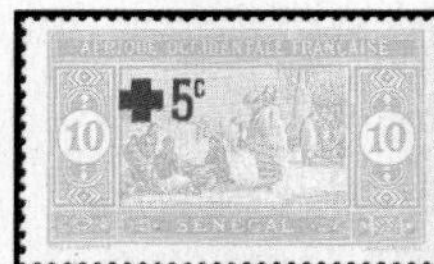

No. 84 Surcharged in Red

1915 Unwmk. *Perf. 14x13½*

B1 A28 10c + 5c org red & rose 1.75 1.75
Never hinged 2.75
On cover 37.50
a. Chalky paper 1.75 1.75
Never hinged 2.75
On cover 37.50
b. Double surcharge 190.00
Never hinged 300.00

No. B1 is on both ordinary and chalky paper.

Same Surcharge on No. 87

1918

B2 A28 15c + 5c red org & brn vio 1.75 1.75
Never hinged 2.75
On cover 37.50
a. Double surcharge 190.00
Never hinged 300.00
b. Inverted surcharge 190.00
Never hinged 300.00
c. Double surcharge, one inverted 225.00

Curie Issue

Common Design Type

1938 Engr. *Perf. 13*

B3 CD80 1.75fr + 50c brt ultra 10.50 10.50
Never hinged 17.50
On cover 80.00
On cover, single franking 150.00

French Revolution Issue

Common Design Type

Photo., Name & Value Typo. in Black

1939

B4 CD83 45c + 25c green 8.50 8.50
Never hinged 12.50
On cover 140.00
B5 CD83 70c + 30c brown 8.50 8.50
Never hinged 12.50
On cover 95.00
B6 CD83 90c + 35c red org 8.50 8.50
Never hinged 12.50
On cover 80.00
B7 CD83 1.25fr + 1fr rose pink 8.50 8.50
Never hinged 12.50
On cover 140.00
On cover, single franking 200.00
B8 CD83 2.25fr + 2fr blue 8.50 8.50
Never hinged 12.50
Nos. B4-B8 (5) 42.50 42.50

AIR POST STAMPS

Landscape AP1

Caravan AP2

Perf. 12½x12, 12x12½

1935 Engr. Unwmk.

C1	AP1 25c dk brown	.30	.30
	Never hinged	.35	
	On cover		19.00
C2	AP1 50c red orange	.35	.45
	Never hinged	.35	
	On cover		15.00
C3	AP1 1fr rose lilac	.30	.30
	Never hinged	.35	
	On cover		21.00
C4	AP1 1.25fr yellow grn	.30	.30
	Never hinged	.35	
	On cover		25.00
C5	AP1 2fr blue	.30	.30
	Never hinged	.35	
	On cover		30.00
C6	AP1 3fr olive grn	.30	.30
	Never hinged	.35	
	On cover		50.00
C7	AP2 3.50fr violet	.35	.30
	Never hinged	.70	
	On cover		45.00
C8	AP2 4.75fr orange	.35	.45
	Never hinged	.70	
	On cover		55.00
C9	AP2 6.50fr dk blue	1.10	1.10
	Never hinged	2.10	
	On cover		62.50
C10	AP2 8fr black	1.10	1.75
	Never hinged	2.10	
	On cover		75.00
C11	AP2 15fr rose lake	1.40	1.40
	Never hinged	2.75	
	On cover		75.00
	Nos. C1-C11 (11)	6.15	6.95

No. C8 surcharged "ENTR' AIDE FRANCAIS + 95f 25" in green, red violet or blue, was never issued in this colony.

Common Design Type

1940 Engr. Perf. 12½x12

C12	CD85 1.90fr ultra	.50	.50
	Never hinged	.70	
	On cover		35.00
C13	CD85 2.90fr dk red	.50	.50
	Never hinged	.70	
	On cover		35.00
C14	CD85 4.50fr dk gray grn	.55	.55
	Never hinged	.70	
	On cover		40.00
C15	CD85 4.90fr yellow bis	.85	.85
	Never hinged	1.10	
	On cover		45.00
a.	"SENEGAL" double	350.00	
	Never hinged	425.00	
C16	CD85 6.90fr dp orange	1.10	1.10
	Never hinged	1.60	
	On cover		62.50
	Nos. C12-C16 (5)	3.50	3.50

AIR POST SEMI-POSTAL STAMPS

French Revolution Issue

Common Design Type

1939 Unwmk. Photo. Perf. 13

Name and Value Typo. in Orange

CB1	CD83 4.75 + 4fr brn blk	14.00	14.00
	Never hinged	27.50	
	On cover		110.00
	On cover, single franking		200.00

Surtax used for the defense of the colonies.

POSTAGE DUE STAMPS

Postage Due Stamps of French Colonies Surcharged

1903 Unwmk. Imperf.

J1	D1 10c on 50c lilac	105.00	105.00
	Never hinged	250.00	
	On cover		450.00
J2	D1 10c on 60c brown, *buff*	105.00	105.00
	Never hinged	250.00	
	On cover		450.00
J3	D1 10c on 1fr rose, *buff*	425.00	425.00
	Nos. J1-J3 (3)	635.00	635.00

D2

1906 Typo. Perf. 14x13½

J4	D2 5c green, *grnsh*	7.00	4.25
	Never hinged	10.50	
	On cover		87.50
J5	D2 10c red brown	7.00	5.00
	Never hinged	14.00	
	On cover		87.50
J6	D2 15c dark blue	7.00	6.25
	Never hinged	14.00	
	On cover		100.00
J7	D2 20c black, *yellow*	10.50	6.25
	Never hinged	17.50	
	On cover		100.00
J8	D2 30c red, *straw*	10.50	10.00
	Never hinged	17.50	
	On cover		125.00
J9	D2 50c violet	10.50	7.50
	Never hinged	25.00	
	On cover		140.00
J10	D2 60c black, *buff*	17.00	15.00
	Never hinged	35.00	
	On cover		145.00
J11	D2 1fr black, *pinkish*	27.50	22.50
	Never hinged	50.00	
	On cover		175.00
	Nos. J4-J11 (8)	97.00	76.75

D3

1914

J12	D3 5c green	.70	.45
	Never hinged	1.10	
	On cover		42.50
J13	D3 10c rose	.70	.45
	Never hinged	1.10	
	On cover		42.50
J14	D3 15c gray	1.10	.70
	Never hinged	1.40	
	On cover		42.50
J15	D3 20c brown	1.10	1.10
	Never hinged	1.40	
	On cover		50.00
J16	D3 30c blue	1.40	1.10
	Never hinged	2.75	
	On cover		50.00
J17	D3 50c black	1.75	1.40
	Never hinged	2.75	
	On cover		55.00
J18	D3 60c orange	2.10	1.40
	Never hinged	3.50	
	On cover		62.50
J19	D3 1fr violet	2.10	1.75
	Never hinged	3.50	
	On cover		75.00
	Nos. J12-J19 (8)	10.95	8.35

Type of 1914 Issue Surcharged

1927

J20	D3 2fr on 1fr lilac rose	10.50	7.00
	Never hinged	14.00	
	On cover		95.00
a.	Period after "F" omitted	27.50	
	Never hinged	45.00	
J21	D3 3fr on 1fr org brn	10.50	7.00
	Never hinged	14.00	
	On cover		105.00

D4

1935 Engr. Perf. 12½x12

J22	D4 5c yellow green	.25	.25
	Never hinged	.50	
	On cover		32.50
J23	D4 10c red orange	.25	.25
	Never hinged	.50	
	On cover		32.50
J24	D4 15c violet	.25	.25
	Never hinged	.50	
	On cover		32.50
J25	D4 20c olive green	.25	.25
	Never hinged	.50	
	On cover		32.50
J26	D4 30c reddish brown	.25	.25
	Never hinged	.50	
	On cover		32.50
J27	D4 50c rose lilac	1.40	1.40
	Never hinged	1.40	
	On cover		24.00
J28	D4 60c orange	1.40	1.40
	Never hinged	1.75	
	On cover		45.00
J29	D4 1fr black	1.10	1.10
	Never hinged	1.40	
	On cover		45.00
J30	D4 2fr dark blue	1.10	1.10
	Never hinged	1.40	
	On cover		75.00
J31	D4 3fr dark carmine	1.40	1.40
	Never hinged	2.10	
	Nos. J22-J31 (10)	7.65	7.65

SENEGAMBIA & NIGER

ˌse-nə-ˈgam-bē-ə and ˈnī-jər

A French Administrative unit for the Senegal and Niger possessions in Africa during the period when the French possessions in Africa were being definitively divided into colonies and protectorates. The name was dropped in 1904 when this territory was consolidated with part of French Sudan, under the name Upper Senegal and Niger.

100 Centimes = 1 Franc

Covers

Values are for commercial covers bearing correct frankings. Philatelic covers sell for less.

Navigation and Commerce — A1

1903 Unwmk. Typo. Perf. 14x13½

Name of Colony in Blue or Carmine

1	A1 1c black, *lil bl*	2.10	*2.75*
	Never hinged	3.50	
	On cover		340.00
a.	Accent omitted from first "e" of "Sénégambie"	12.50	*17.50*
	Never hinged	21.00	
2	A1 2c brown, *buff*	2.10	*2.75*
	Never hinged	3.50	
	On cover		340.00
a.	Accent omitted from first "e" of "Sénégambie"	12.50	*17.50*
	Never hinged	21.00	
3	A1 4c claret, *lav*	5.75	*6.25*
	Never hinged	10.50	
	On cover		310.00
a.	Accent omitted from first "e" of "Sénégambie"	27.50	*40.00*
	Never hinged	55.00	
4	A1 5c yel grn	7.00	*7.00*
	Never hinged	10.50	
	On cover		225.00
5	A1 10c red	7.00	*7.75*
	Never hinged	10.50	
	On cover		175.00
6	A1 15c gray	14.50	14.50
	Never hinged	22.00	
	On cover		275.00
7	A1 20c red, *green*	12.50	*12.50*
	Never hinged	21.00	
	On cover		400.00
	On cover, single franking		550.00
8	A1 25c blue	21.00	17.50
	Never hinged	35.00	
	On cover		250.00
9	A1 30c brn, *bister*	17.50	*19.00*
	Never hinged	32.50	
	On cover		325.00
	On cover, single franking		400.00
10	A1 40c red, *straw*	21.00	*25.00*
	Never hinged	45.00	
	On cover		340.00
	On cover, single franking		425.00
11	A1 50c brn, *azure*	45.00	*50.00*
	Never hinged	90.00	
	On cover		310.00
	On cover, single franking		425.00
12	A1 75c deep vio, *org*	52.50	*52.50*
	Never hinged	110.00	
	On cover		425.00
	On cover, single franking		675.00
13	A1 1fr brnz grn, *straw*	70.00	*70.00*
	Never hinged	125.00	
	On cover		550.00
	On cover, single franking		925.00
	Nos. 1-13 (13)	277.95	287.50

Perf. 13½x14 stamps are counterfeits.

SERBIA

ˈsər-bē-ə

LOCATION — In southeastern Europe, bounded by Romania and Bulgaria on the east, the former Austro-Hungarian Empire on the north, Greece on the south, and Albania and Montenegro on the west.

GOVT. — Kingdom

AREA — 18,650 sq. mi.

POP. — 2,911,701 (1910)

CAPITAL — Belgrade

Following World War I, Serbia united with Montenegro, Bosnia and Herzegovina, Croatia, Dalmatia and Slovenia to form Yugoslavia.

100 Paras = 1 Dinar

Coat of Arms — A1

Prince Michael (Obrenovich III) — A2

1866 Unwmk. Typo. Imperf.

Paper colored Through

1	A1 1p dk green, *dk vio rose*	72.50	

Surface Colored Paper, Thin or Thick

2	A1 1p dk green, *lil rose*	72.50	
a.	1p olive green, *rose*	72.50	
b.	1p deep grn, *pale rose* (thick paper)	2,750.	
c.	1p lt olive grn, *pale rose*	72.50	
3	A1 2p red brown, *lilac*	72.50	
a.	2p red brn, *lil gray* (thick paper)	450.00	
b.	2p dl grn, *lil gray* (thick paper)	2,750.	
	Nos. 1-3 (3)	217.50	

Vienna Printing

Perf. 12

4	A2 10p orange	1,400.	850.00
5	A2 20p rose	925.00	375.00
6	A2 40p blue	1,000.	160.00
a.	Half used as 20p on cover		
	Nos. 4-6 (3)	3,325.	1,385.

Belgrade Printing

Perf. 9½

7	A2 1p green	24.00	725.00
8	A2 2p bister brn	37.50	725.00
9	A2 20p rose	19.00	29.00
a.	Vert. pair, imperf. between		
10	A2 40p ultra	300.00	325.00
a.	Half used as 20p on cover		17,000.
	Nos. 7-10 (4)	380.50	

Pelure Paper

11	A2 10p orange	110.00	140.00
12	A2 20p rose	95.00	19.00
a.	Pair, imperf. between		
13	A2 40p ultra	75.00	50.00
a.	Horiz. pair, imperf. between	5,500.	6,250.
b.	Half used as 20p on cover		12,000.
	Nos. 11-13 (3)	280.00	209.00

Nos. 1-3, 7-8, 14-16, 25-26 were used only as newspaper tax stamps.

1868-69 Ordinary Paper Imperf.

14	A2 1p green	67.50	
a.	1p olive green ('69)	*3,750.*	
15	A2 2p brown	95.00	
a.	2p bister brown ('69)	425.00	

Counterfeits of type A2 are common.

Prince Milan (Obrenovich IV) — A3

Perf. 9½, 12 and Compound

1869-78

16	A3 1p yellow	5.50	*110.00*
17	A3 10p red brown	9.00	4.75
a.	10p yellow brown	*475.00*	75.00
18	A3 10p orange ('78)	2.25	6.00
19	A3 15p orange	85.00	30.00
20	A3 20p gray blue	1.50	2.50
a.	20p ultramarine	4.50	2.25
b.	Half used as 10p on cover		
21	A3 25p rose	2.25	7.50
22	A3 35p lt green	4.50	4.50

23 A3 40p violet 2.25 3.00
a. Half used as 20p on cover
24 A3 50p blue green 11.00 7.50
Nos. 16-24 (9) 123.25 *175.75*

The first setting, which included all values except No. 18, had the stamps 2-2½mm apart.

A new setting, introduced in 1878, had the stamps 3-4mm apart, providing wider margins. Only Nos. 17, 18, 20 and 21 exist in this new setting, which differs also in shades from the earlier setting.

The narrow-spaced Nos. 17, 20 and 21 are rarer, especially unused, as are the early shades of Nos. 23 and 24.

All values except Nos. 19 and 24 are known in various partly perforated varieties.

Counterfeits exist.

See No. 25.

Prince Milan (Obrenovich IV) — A4

1872-79 ***Imperf.***

25 A3 1p yellow 8.50 24.00
a. Tête bêche pair
26 A4 2p blk, thin paper ('79) 1.90 .85
a. Thick paper ('73) 4.50 *24.00*

Used value of No. 26 is for canceled-to-order.

King Milan I — A5

1880 ***Perf. 13x13½***

27 A5 5p pale green 1.25 .45
a. 5p blue green 1.90 .45
b. 5p gray green 3.25 .95
c. 5p deep green 1.90 .45
d. 5p olive green 725.00 4.50
28 A5 10p carmine 2.75 .45
a. 10p rose 3.75 .95
29 A5 20p orange 1.40 .95
a. 20p yellow 4.50 1.90
30 A5 25p ultra 1.90 1.40
a. 25p blue 2.25 1.40
31 A5 50p brown 1.90 *6.00*
a. 50p brown violet 275.00 5.75
32 A5 1d violet 13.50 14.50
Nos. 27-32 (6) 22.70 23.75

King Alexander (Obrenovich V) — A6

1890

33 A6 5p green .45 .25
34 A6 10p rose red 1.60 .25
35 A6 15p red violet 1.40 .25
36 A6 20p orange .95 .25
37 A6 25p blue 1.90 .45
38 A6 50p brown 3.75 3.75
39 A6 1d dull lilac 14.50 11.50
Nos. 33-39 (7) 24.55 16.70

King Alexander — A7

1894-96 ***Perf. 13x13½***

Granite Paper

40 A7 5p green 5.25 .25
a. Perf. 11½ 9.50 .45
41 A7 10p car rose 7.25 .25
b. Perf. 11½ 110.00 1.90
42 A7 15p violet 11.00 .30
43 A7 20p orange 85.00 .95
a. Half used as 10p on cover *450.00*
44 A7 25p blue 24.00 .45
45 A7 50p brown 29.00 .95
46 A7 1d dk green 1.90 3.75
47 A7 1d red brn, *bl* ('96) 24.00 3.75
Nos. 40-47 (8) 187.40 10.65

1896-1900 ***Perf. 13x13½***

Ordinary Paper

48 A7 1p dull red .40 .25
49 A7 5p green ('98) 4.50 .25
a. Compound perf., with 11½ 19.00 1.50
50 A7 10p rose ('98) 110.00 .30
a. Compound perf., with 11½ 25.00 9.00
51 A7 15p violet ('00) 140,00 1.90
a. Compound perf., with 11½ 225.00 11.50
53 A7 25p deep blue ('00) 45.00 1.60
a. Compound perf., with 11½ 190,00 37.50
Nos. 48-53 (5) 160.04 4.30

1898-1906 ***Perf. 11½***

48b A7 1p dull red ('06) .40 .25
49b A7 5p green 4,50 .25
50b A7 10p rose 75.00 .25
51b A7 15p violet ('00) 9.25 .30
52 A7 20p orange ('00) 7.25 .30
53b A7 25p deep blue ('00) 2.25 .45
c. 25p ultramarine ('02) 7.25 .45
54 A7 50p brown ('00) 29,00 4.50
c. 50p red brown ('02) 19,00 2.25
Nos. 48b-54 (7) 94.89 6.30

Nos. 49-54 exist imperf.

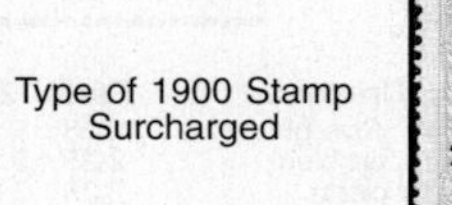

Type of 1900 Stamp Surcharged

1900

56 A7 10p on 20p rose 7.25 .95

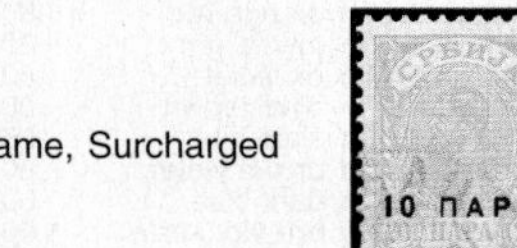

Same, Surcharged

1901

57 A7 10p on 20p rose 7.50 .95
58 A7 15p on 1d red brn, *bl* 6.50 1.90
a. Inverted surcharge *100.00 110.00*

King Alexander (Obrenovich V)
A8 A9

1901-03 **Typo.** ***Perf. 11½***

59 A8 5p green ('01) .80 .35
a. 5p pale yel grn ('01) .40 .35
60 A8 10p rose ('02) .35 .35
61 A8 15p red violet ('03) .35 .35
62 A8 20p orange ('03) .35 .35
63 A8 25p ultra ('(03) .35 .35
64 A8 50p bister ('03) .75 .75
65 A9 1d brown ('03) 1.10 1.90
66 A9 3d brt rose 22.50 10.00
a. 3d pink ('02) 11.00 15.00
67 A9 5d deep violet 20.00 10.00
a. 5d violet ('02) 12.00 15.00
Nos. 59-67 (9) 46.55 24.40

Counterfeits of Nos. 66-67 exist. Nos. 59-67 imperf. value of set of pairs, $100.

Arms of Serbia on Head of King Alexander — A10

Type I

Type II

Two Types of the Overprint

Type I — Overprint 12mm wide. Bottom of mantle defined by a single line. Wide crown above shield.

Type II — Overprint 10mm wide. Double line at bottom of mantle. Smaller crown above shield.

Arms Overprinted in Blue, Black, Red and Red Brown

1903-04 **Type I** ***Perf. 13½***

68 A10 1p red lil & blk (Bl) 1.10 1.40
a. Inverted overprint 24.00
69 A10 5p yel grn & blk (Bl) .95 .45
70 A10 10p car & blk (Bk) .70 .45
a. Double overprint 24.00
71 A10 15p ol gray & blk (Bk) .70 .45
a. Double overprint 24.00
72 A10 20p org & blk (Bk) .95 .45
73 A10 25p bl & blk (Bk) .95 .45
a. Double overprint 24.00
74 A10 50p gray & blk (R) 5.75 1.40

There were two printings of the type I overprint on Nos. 68-74, one typographed and one lithographed.

Type II

75 A10 1d bl grn & blk (Bk) 14.50 5.75

#68-75 with overprint omitted are from the remainders. Value, set $75.

Perf. 11½

Type I

75A A10 5p (Bl) .95 1.90
75B A10 50p (R) 1.90 9.25
75C A10 1d (Bk) 2.75 19.00

Type II

76 A10 3d vio & blk (R Br) 4.00 4.25
a. Perf. 13½ *140.00*
77 A10 5d lt brn & blk (Bl) 4.00 4.50

Type I With Additional Surcharge

78 A10 1p on 5d (R) 2.75 *14.50*
a. Perf. 13½ *925.00*
Nos. 68-78 (14) 41.95 64.20

Karageorge and Peter I — A11

Insurgents, 1804 A12

1904 **Typo.**

79 A11 5p yellow green .95 .45
80 A11 10p rose red .95 .45
81 A11 15p red violet .95 .45
82 A11 25p blue 1.75 .95
83 A11 50p gray brown 1.90 1.90
84 A12 1d bister 2.75 6.50
85 A12 3d blue green 3.75 9.25
86 A12 5d violet 4.50 11.50
Nos. 79-86 (8) 17.50 31.45

Centenary of the Karageorgevich dynasty and the coronation of King Peter. Counterfeits of Nos. 79-86 exist.

King Peter I Karageorgevich — A13

1905 **Thin Wove Paper** ***Perf. 11½***

87 A13 1p gray & blk .30 .25
88 A13 5p yel grn & blk 1.40 .25
89 A13 10p red & blk 3.25 .25
90 A13 15p red lil & blk 3.75 .25
91 A13 20p yellow & blk 6.50 .30
92 A13 25p ultra & blk 9.25 .30
93 A13 30p sl grn & blk 5.75 .30
94 A13 50p dk brown & blk 7.25 .65
95 A13 1d bister & blk 24.00 2.25
96 A13 3d blue grn & blk 2.25 2.25
97 A13 5d violet & blk 16.00 5.75
Nos. 87-97 (11) 79.70 12.80

Counterfeits of Nos. 87-97 abound.

Perf. 12x11½

Thick Wove Paper

87a A13 1p gray & black .30 .25
88a A13 5p yel grn & blk 1.10 .25
89a A13 10p red & blk 3.25 .25
90a A13 15p red lilac & blk 4.50 .30
91a A13 20p yellow & blk 8.50 .30
92a A13 25p ultra & blk 8.00 .30
93a A13 30p sl green & blk 8.00 .30
94a A13 50p dk brown & blk 8.00 .45
95a A13 1d bister & blk 1.00 .45
96a A13 3d blue grn & blk 1.00 1.10
97a A13 3d violet & blk 4.50 3.25

1907-11 **Horiz. Laid Paper**

87b A13 1p gray & black ('08) .45 .25
88b A13 5p yel grn & blk 2.75 .30
89b A13 10p red & blk 8,00 .25
90b A13 15p red lilac & blk ('08) 11.50 .30
91b A13 20p yellow & blk ('08) 8.00 .30
92b A13 25p ultra & blk ('08) 8.00 .30
93b A13 30p sl green & blk ('08) 10,50 .45
94b A13 50p dk brown & blk ('11) 15.00 .95

1911 **Vert. Laid Paper**

87c A13 1p gray & black 3.75 1.10
88c A13 5p yel grn & blk 5.75 .95
89c A13 10p red & blk 45.00 1.90
93c A13 30p sl green & blk 72,50 7.25

1908 **Laid Paper**

98 A13 1p gray & blk .35 .25
99 A13 5p yel grn & blk 2.25 .25
100 A13 10p red & blk 6.75 .25
101 A13 15p red lilac & blk 9.00 .25
102 A13 20p yellow & blk 9.00 .35
103 A13 25p ultra & blk 6.75 .35
104 A13 30p gray grn & blk 10.00 .35
105 A13 50p dk brn & blk 13.00 .75
Nos. 98-105 (8) 57.10 2.80

Nos. 90, 98-100, 102-104 are known imperforate but are not believed to have been issued in this condition.

Values of Nos. 98-105 are for horizontally laid paper. Four values also exist on vertically laid paper (1p, 5p, 10p, 30p).

King Peter I Karageorgevich A14

1911-14 **Thick Wove Paper**

108 A14 1p slate green .25 .25
109 A14 2p dark violet .25 .25
110 A14 5p green .25 .25
111 A14 5p pale yel grn ('14) .40 .25
112 A14 10p carmine .25 .25
113 A14 10p red ('14) .25 .25
114 A14 15p red violet .40 .25
115 A14 15p slate blk ('14) .25 .25
a. 15p red (error) *1,100.* —
116 A14 20p yellow .40 .25
117 A14 20p brown ('14) .65 .40
118 A14 25p deep blue .55 .25
119 A14 25p indigo ('14) .25 .40
120 A14 30p blue green .40 .30
121 A14 30p olive grn ('14) .25 .40
122 A14 50p dk brown .65 .45
123 A14 50p brn red ('14) .55 .45
124 A14 1d orange 29.00 *55.00*
125 A14 1d slate ('14) 4.50 *9.25*
126 A14 3d lake 37.50 *110.00*
127 A14 3d olive yel ('14) 190.00 *1,400.*
128 A14 5d violet 29.00 *80.00*
129 A14 5d dk violet ('14) 7.50 *24.00*
Nos. 108-129 (22) 303.50 *1,683.*

Counterfeits exist.

King Peter and Military Staff — A15

1915 ***Perf. 11½***

132 A15 5p yellow green .45 —
133 A15 10p scarlet .45 —
134 A15 15p slate 7.25
135 A15 20p brown 1.90
136 A15 25p blue 14.50
137 A15 30p olive green 9.25
138 A15 50p orange brown 37.50
Nos. 132-138 (7) 71.30

Nos. 134-138 were prepared but not issued for postal use. Instead they were permitted to be used as wartime emergency currency. Some are known imperf. The 15p also exists in blue from an erroneous cliche in the 25p plate; value $425.

Stamps of France, 1900-1907, with this handstamped control were used in 1916-1918 by the Serbian Postal Bureau on the Island of Corfu. On the 1c to 35c, the handstamp covers 2 or 3 stamps. It was applied after the stamps were on the cover.

King Peter and Prince Alexander — A16

Paris Printing

Clear Impression, Medium White Paper

1918, Jan. 10 Typo. *Perf. 11*

155 A16 1p black .25 .25
a. Horiz. pair, imperf. between 11.00
156 A16 2p olive brown .25 .25
a. Horiz. pair, imperf. between 11.00
157 A16 5p apple green .25 .25
158 A16 10p red .25 .25
a. Horiz. pair, imperf. between 14.00
159 A16 15p black brown .25 .25
160 A16 20p red brown .25 .25
162 A16 25p deep blue .25 .25
163 A16 30p olive green .25 .25
164 A16 50p violet .25 .25
a. Horiz. pair, imperf. between 14.00
165 A16 1d violet brown .95 .55
166 A16 3d slate green 1.40 1.10
167 A16 5d red brown 2.25 1.40
Nos. 155-167 (13) 11.35 6.40

Nos. 157-160, 164 exist imperf. Value each $9.

First Belgrade Printing

1919, Sept. *Rough Perf. 11½*

Coarse Impression, Thick White Paper

155b A16 1p black .95 .30
159b A16 15p pale red brown 4.50 2.25
161 A16 20p violet 4.50 1.10
165b A16 1d pale red brown 7.50 2.25

Second Belgrade Printing

1920 *Perf. 11½*

Poor Impression, Rough Perf, Small Holes

Pelure Paper

155c A16 1p black .25 .25
156c A16 2p olive brown .25 .25

Medium to Thick Paper

157c A16 5p yellow green .25 .25
d. Perf. 9 72.50 275.00
158c A16 10p red .25 .25
159c A16 15p black brown .25 .25
160c A16 20p red brown .25 .25
d. 20p chestnut .25 .25
162c A16 25p dull blue .25 .25
163c A16 30p pale olive gray .25 .25
164c A16 50p pale violet .25 .25
165c A16 1d deep brown .45 .30
166c A16 3d dp blue green 2.00 1.40
167c A16 5d red brown 3.50 2.25

Medium to Thin Oily Paper

159e A16 15d black brown .95 .95
160e A16 20d pale red brown — .95
162e A16 25d dull blue — 1.90

Clean-Cut Perfs, Large Hole

155f A16 1p black .25 .25
156f A16 2p olive brown .25 .25

Medium to Thick Paper

157f A16 5p yellow green .25 .25
158f A16 10p red .25 .25
159f A16 15p black brown .25 .25
160f A16 20p red brown .25 .25
g. 20p chestnut .25 .25
162f A16 25p dull blue .25 .25
163f A16 30p pale olive gray .25 .25
164f A16 50p pale violet .25 .25
165f A16 1d deep brown .45 .30
166f A16 3d dp blue green 2.25 1.25

Medium to Thin Oily Paper

159h A16 15p black brown 1.75 .90
160h A16 20p red brown .90 .90
i. 20p chestnut 1.75 1.40
162h A16 25p dull blue — 1.40

Paris Printing

Clear Impression, Clean-Cut Perfs

1920 *Perf. 11½*

Pelure Paper

169 A16 1p black .25 .25
170 A16 2p olive brown .25 .25

POSTAGE DUE STAMPS

Coat of Arms — D1

1895 Unwmk. Typo. *Perf. 13x13½*

Granite Paper

J1 D1 5p red lilac 6.50 1.00
J2 D1 10p blue 7.25 .45
J3 D1 20p orange brown 55.00 9.25
J4 D1 30p green .75 .95
J5 D1 50p rose .75 1.25
a. Cliché of 5p in plate of 50p 100.00 *190.00*
Nos. J1-J5 (5) 70.25 12.90

No. J1 exists imperf. Value $75.

1898-1904 Ordinary Paper

J6 D1 5p magenta ('04) .70 .45
J7 D1 20p brown 10.50 1.10
a. Tête bêche pair 150.00 *150.00*
J8 D1 20p dp brn ('04) 7.25 1.00
Nos. J6-J8 (3) 18.45 2.55

1906 Granite Paper *Perf. 11½*

J9 D1 5p magenta 14.50 3.75

1909 Laid Paper

J10 D1 5p magenta .95 .65
J11 D1 10p pale blue 5.75 9.25
J12 D1 20p pale brown .45 .95
Nos. J10-J12 (3) 7.15 10.85

1914 White Wove Paper

J13 D1 5p rose .45 2.25
J14 D1 10p deep blue 7.25 11.50

Coat of Arms — D2

1918-20 *Perf. 11*

Paris Printing

Clear Impression, Clean-Cut Perfs

J15 D2 5p red .45 .90
J16 D2 10p yellow green .45 .90
J17 D2 20p olive brown .45 .90
J18 D2 30p slate green .45 .90
J19 D2 50p chocolate .90 1.50
Nos. J15-J19 (5) 2.70 5.10

Belgrade Printing

Coarse Impression, Rough Perfs

J15a D2 5p red brown .45 .90
J18a D2 30p olive black .90 1.25
J19a D2 50p yellow brown 1.25 1.75

NEWSPAPER STAMPS

N1

Overprinted with Crown-topped Shield in Black

1911 Unwmk. Typo. *Perf. 11½*

P1 N1 1p gray .95 .95
P2 N1 5p green .95 .95
P3 N1 10p orange .95 .95
a. Cliché of 1p in plate of 10p *1,100.*
P4 N1 15p violet .95 .95
P5 N1 20p yellow .95 .95
a. Cliché of 50p in plate of 20p 110.00 *140.00*
P6 N1 25p blue .95 .95
P7 N1 30p slate 9.25 9.25
P8 N1 50p brown 7.50 7.50
P9 N1 1d bister 7.50 7.50
P10 N1 3d rose red 7.50 7.50
P11 N1 5d gray vio 7.50 7.50
Nos. P1-P11 (11) 44.95 44.95

ISSUED UNDER AUSTRIAN OCCUPATION

100 Heller = 1 Krone

Stamps of Bosnia, 1912-14, Overprinted

1916 Unwmk. *Perf. 12½*

1N1 A23 1h olive green 2.25 5.25
1N2 A23 2h brt blue 2.25 5.25
1N3 A23 3h claret 2.25 5.25
1N4 A23 5h green .40 .75
1N5 A23 6h dk gray 1.50 3.75
1N6 A23 10h rose carmine .40 .75
1N7 A23 12h dp olive grn .80 2.25
1N8 A23 20h orange brown .80 1.40
1N9 A23 25h ultra .80 2.25
1N10 A23 30h orange red .80 2.25
1N11 A24 35h myrtle grn .80 2.25
1N12 A24 40h dk violet .80 2.25
1N13 A24 45h olive brown .80 2.25
1N14 A24 50h slate blue .80 2.25
1N15 A24 60h brown violet .80 2.25
1N16 A24 72h dark blue .80 2.25
1N17 A25 1k brn vio, *straw* 1.50 2.25
1N18 A25 2k dk gray, *bl* 1.50 2.25
1N19 A26 3k carmine, *grn* 1.50 2.25
1N20 A26 5k dk vio, *gray* 1.50 2.25
1N21 A25 10k dk ultra, *gray* 15.00 30.00
Nos. 1N1-1N21 (21) 38.05 81.65

Stamps of Bosnia, 1912-14, Overprinted "SERBIEN" Horizontally at Bottom

1916

1N22 A23 1h olive green 8.00 19.00
1N23 A23 2h bright blue 8.00 19.00
1N24 A23 3h claret 8.00 19.00
1N25 A23 5h green .50 3.00
1N26 A23 6h dark gray 8.00 19.00
1N27 A23 10h rose carmine .50 3.00
1N28 A23 12h dp olive grn 8.00 19.00
1N29 A23 20h orange brn 8.00 19.00
1N30 A23 25h ultra 8.00 19.00
1N31 A23 30h orange red 8.00 19.00
1N32 A24 35h myrtle green 8.00 19.00
1N33 A24 40h dark violet 8.00 19.00
1N34 A24 45h olive brown 8.00 19.00
1N35 A24 50h slate blue 8.00 19.00
1N36 A24 60h brown violet 8.00 19.00
1N37 A24 72h dark blue 8.00 19.00
1N38 A25 1k brn vio, *straw* 19.00 40.00
1N39 A25 2k dk gray, *bl* 19.00 40.00
1N40 A26 3k carmine, *grn* 22.50 47.50
1N41 A26 5k dk vio, *gray* 27.50 60.00
1N42 A25 10k dk ultra, *gray* 52.50 100.00
Nos. 1N22-1N42 (21) 253.50 559.50

Nos. 1N22-1N42 were prepared in 1914, at the time of the 1st Austrian occupation of Serbia. They were not issued at that time because of the retreat. The stamps were put on sale in 1916, at the same time as Nos. 1N1-1N21.

SEYCHELLES

sā-ˈshel͜z

LOCATION — A group of islands in the Indian Ocean, off the coast of Africa north of Madagascar.
GOVT. — British Colony
AREA — 156 sq. mi.
POP. — 64,718 (est. 1984)
CAPITAL — Victoria

The islands were attached to the British colony of Mauritius from 1810 to 1903, when they became a separate colony.

100 Cents = 1 Rupee

Catalogue values for unused stamps in this country are for Never Hinged items, beginning with Scott 149 in the regular postage section and Scott J1 in the postage due section.

STAMPS OF MAURITIUS USED IN SEYCHELLES

Various Issues Canceled B64

1861 Post Paid

A1 2p blue (#4b) *11,000.*

1861 Britannia *Imperf.*

A2 6p blue (#18) 975.00
A3 6p gray violet (#20) *2,500.*
A4 1sh vermilion (#19) *1,600.*

1861-63 *Perf. 14*

A5 1p brown lilac (#24) 260.00
A6 2p blue (#25) 300.00
A7 4p rose (#26) 260.00
A8 6p green (#27) 1,100.
A9 6p lilac (#28) 750.00
A10 9p dull lilac (#29) 140.00
A11 1sh buff (#30) 375.00
A12 1sh green (#31) 850.00

1862 *Perf. 14 to 16*

A13 6p slate (#22) *925.00*

1863-72 Wmk. 1

A14 1p lilac brown (#32) 140.00
a. 1p bister brown (#32a) 125.00
b. 1p brown (#32b) 110.00
A15 2p pale blue (#33) 150.00
a. 2p bright blue (#33) 150.00
A16 3p vermilion (#34) 100.00
a. 3p deep red (#34a) 180.00
A17 4p rose (#35) 55.00
A18 6p lilac (#36) 275.00
A19 6p blue grn (#37) 85.00
a. 6p yellow green (#37a) 125.00
A20 9p green (#38) 1,800.
A21 10p claret (#42) 375.00
A22 1sh org yel (#39) 125.00
a. 1sh yellow (#39a) 120.00
A23 1sh blue (#40) 350.00
A24 5sh red violet (#41) 1,000.
a. 5sh bright violet (#41a) *1,000.*

1876-77 Surcharges

A25 ½p on 9p (#43) *375.00*
A26 ½p on 10p claret (#46) *350.00*
A27 ½p on 10p claret (#47) *750.00*
A28 1p on 4p rose (#48) —
A29 1sh on 5sh red vio (#49) —
a. 1sh on 5sh violet (#49a) —

1878 Decimal Surcharges

A30 2c claret (#50) 110.00
A31 4c on 1p bister brn (#51) 425.00
A32 8c on 2p blue (#52) 47.50
A33 13c on 3p org red (#53) 140.00
A34 17c on 4p rose (#54) 47.50
A35 25c on 6p sl blue (#55) 125.00
A36 38c on 9p violet (#56) *575.00*
A37 50c on 1sh green (#57) 125.00
A38 2r50c on 5sh violet (#58) 575.00

1879-80 Wmk. 1 New Designs

A39 2c red brown (#59) 150.00
A40 4c orange (#60) 150.00
A41 8c blue (#61) 47.50
A42 13c slate (#62) 1,500.
A43 17c rose (#63) 100.00
A44 25c bister (#64) 210.00
A45 38c violet (#65) 1,900.
A46 50c green (#66) 975.00
A47 2r50c brn vio (#67) *975.00*

1882-93 Wmk. 2

A48 2c red brown (#69) 110.00
A49 2c green (#70) 200.00
A50 4c orange (#71) 75.00
A51 4c rose (#72) 110.00
A52 25c bister (#74) 125.00
A53 50c deep orange (#75) 1,000.

1883 Surcharges

A54 16c on 17c rose, "16 CENTS" (#76) 150.00
A55 16c on 17c rose, "SIX-TEEN CENTS" (#79) 50.00

1885

A56 16c orange brown (#82) 62.50

1885-87 Wmk. 1

A57 2c on 38c violet (#64) —
A58 2c on 13c slate (R) (#84) —

Issued under British Administration

Queen Victoria — A1

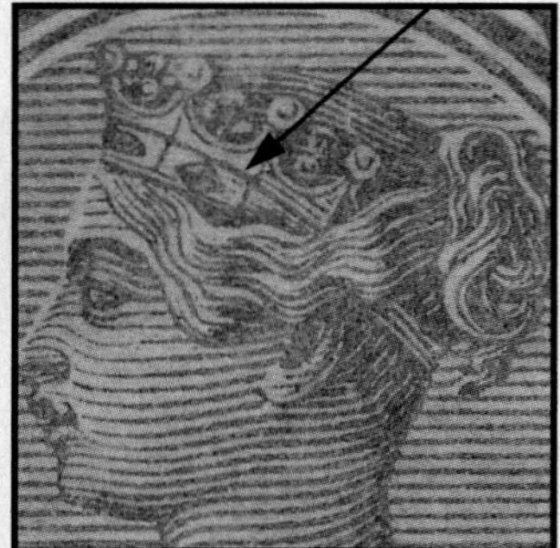

Die I

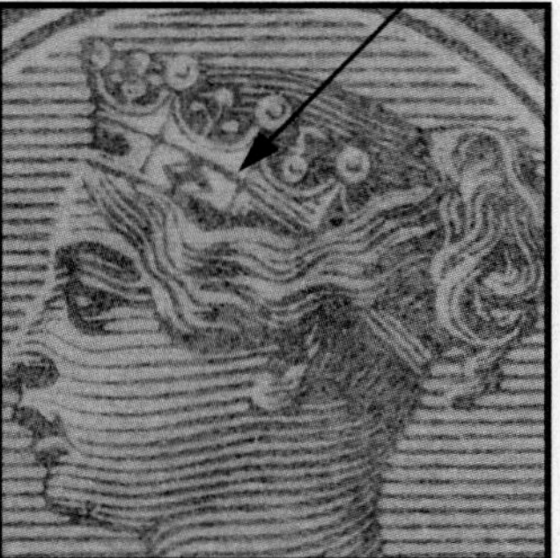

Die II

Two dies of 2c, 4c, 8c, 10c, 13c, 16c:

Die I — Shading lines at right of diamond in tiara band.

Die II — No shading lines in this rectangle.

1890-1900 Typo. Wmk. 2 *Perf. 14*

1 A1 2c grn & rose (II) 3.50 1.25
a. Die I 8.50 *21.00*
2 A1 2c org brn & grn ('00) 2.50 *3.25*
3 A1 3c dk vio & org ('93) 2.00 .75
4 A1 4c car rose & grn (II) 3.50 1.75
a. Die I 50.00 *21.00*
5 A1 6c car rose ('00) 4.50 .75
6 A1 8c brn vio & ultra (II) 17.50 2.50
a. 8c brn vio & bl (I) 18.50 *4.50*
7 A1 10c ultra & brn (II) 17.50 4.25
a. 10c bl & brn (I) 18.50 *42.50*
8 A1 12c ol gray & grn ('93) 3.50 1.25
9 A1 13c slate & blk (II) 8.50 2.50
a. Die I 8.00 *21.00*
10 A1 15c ol grn & vio ('93) 9.50 2.75
11 A1 15c ultra ('00) 11.00 8.50
12 A1 16c org brn & bl (I) 16.00 5.50
a. 16c org brn & ultra (II) 52.50 14.50
13 A1 18c ultra ('97) 14.00 1.75
14 A1 36c brn & rose ('97) 50.00 8.00
15 A1 45c brn & rose ('93) 30.00 *45.00*
16 A1 48c ocher & green 27.50 15.00
17 A1 75c yel & pur ('00) 60.00 *87.50*
18 A1 96c violet & car 72.50 60.00
19 A1 1r vio & red ('97) 16.00 8.50
20 A1 1.50r blk & rose ('00) 90.00 *100.00*
21 A1 2.25r vio & grn ('00) 115.00 *100.00*
Nos. 1-21 (21) 574.50 460.75

Numerals of 75c, 1r, 1.50r and 2.25r of type A1 are in color on plain tablet.

The 10c in ultramarine and orange brown, Die I, is known only with "SPECIMEN" overprint. Value $800.

For surcharges see Nos. 22-37.

Surcharged in Black

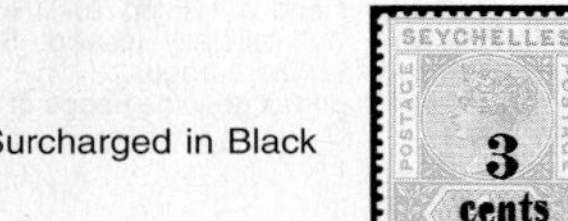

1893

22 A1 3c on 4c car rose & grn (II) 1.50 2.00
a. Inverted surcharge 375.00 *450.00*
b. Double surcharge 600.00
d. Pair, one without surcharge *14,000.*

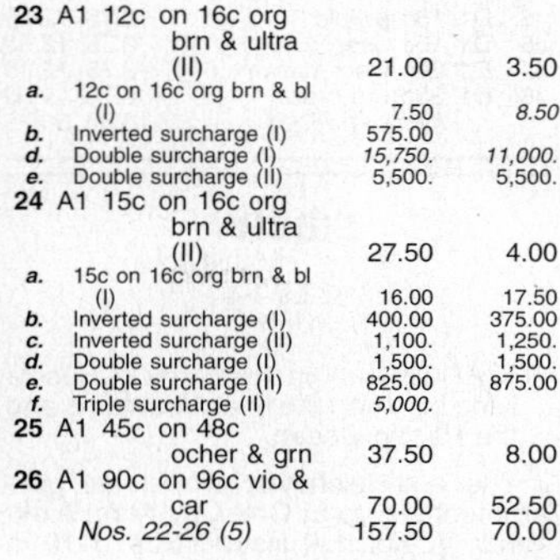

23 A1 12c on 16c org brn & ultra (II) 21.00 3.50
a. 12c on 16c org brn & bl (I) 7.50 *8.50*
b. Inverted surcharge (I) 575.00
d. Double surcharge (I) *15,750.* *11,000.*
e. Double surcharge (II) 5,500. 5,500.
24 A1 15c on 16c org brn & ultra (II) 27.50 4.00
a. 15c on 16c org brn & bl (I) 16.00 17.50
b. Inverted surcharge (I) 400.00 375.00
c. Inverted surcharge (II) 1,100. 1,250.
d. Double surcharge (I) 1,500. 1,500.
e. Double surcharge (II) 825.00 875.00
f. Triple surcharge (II) *5,000.*
25 A1 45c on 48c ocher & grn 37.50 8.00
26 A1 90c on 96c vio & car 70.00 52.50
Nos. 22-26 (5) 157.50 70.00

No. 15 Surcharged in Black

1896

27 A1 18c on 45c brn & rose 11.50 4.25
a. Double surcharge 1,850. 1,850.
b. Triple surcharge *2,750.*
28 A1 36c on 45c brn & rose 12.00 *70.00*
a. Double surcharge 1,850.
Nos. 27-28, ovptd. "SPECIMEN" 75.00

Surcharged in Black

1901

29 A1 3c on 10c bl & brn (II) 3.50 .90
a. Double surcharge 950.00
b. Triple surcharge 3,250.
30 A1 3c on 16c org brn & ultra (II) 7.00 *9.50*
a. "3 cents" omitted (II) 675.00 675.00
b. Inverted surcharge (II) 800.00 800.00
c. Double surcharge (II) 625.00 650.00
31 A1 3c on 36c brn & rose 2.10 1.10
a. Without bars — —
b. Double surcharge 950.00 *1,100.*
c. "3 cents" omitted 800.00 850.00
32 A1 6c on 8c brn vio & ultra (II) 7.00 4.00
a. Inverted surcharge 800.00 *925.00*
Nos. 29-32 (4) 19.60 *15.50*
Set, ovptd. "SPECIMEN" 110.00

Stamps of 1890-1900 Surcharged

1902, June

33 A1 2c on 4c car rose & grn (II) 5.00 3.50
34 A1 30c on 75c yel & pur 3.00 *7.50*
a. Narrow "0" in "30" 10.00 *50.00*
35 A1 30c on 1r vio & red 20.00 *52.50*
a. Narrow "0" in "30" 40.00 *120.00*
b. Double surcharge *1,750.*
36 A1 45c on 1r vio & red 9.50 *60.00*
37 A1 45c on 2.25r vio & grn 52.50 *160.00*
a. Narrow "5" in "45" 250.00 450.00
Nos. 33-37 (5) 90.00 *283.50*
Set, opt. "SPECIMEN" 140.00

King Edward VII — A6

Numerals of 75c, 1.50r and 2.25r of type A6 are in color on plain tablet.

1903, May 26 Typo. Wmk. 2

38 A6 2c red brn & grn 2.25 2.50
39 A6 3c green 1.25 *1.60*
40 A6 6c carmine rose 3.50 1.60
41 A6 12c ol gray & grn 5.25 3.25
42 A6 15c ultra 7.00 3.25
43 A6 18c pale yel grn & rose 5.25 *8.25*
44 A6 30c purple & grn 10.00 *19.00*
45 A6 45c brown & rose 8.75 *19.00*
46 A6 75c yel & pur 12.50 *35.00*
47 A6 1.50r black & rose 55.00 *87.50*
48 A6 2.25r red vio & grn 50.00 *110.00*
Nos. 38-48 (11) 160.75 *290.95*
Set, ovptd. "SPECIMEN" 225.00

Nos. 42-43, 45 Surcharged

1903

49 A6 3c on 15c 1.40 *4.25*
50 A6 3c on 18c 4.00 *52.50*
51 A6 3c on 45c 4.25 *4.25*
Nos. 49-51 (3) 9.65 *61.00*
Set, ovptd. "SPECIMEN" 90.00

Type of 1903

1906 Wmk. 3

52 A6 2c red brn & grn 1.90 *5.50*
53 A6 3c green 1.90 1.90
54 A6 6c car rose 2.50 1.00
55 A6 12c ol gray & grn 4.00 4.00
56 A6 15c ultra 4.00 *2.50*
57 A6 18c pale yel grn & rose 4.00 *8.00*
58 A6 30c purple & grn 7.75 *10.00*
59 A6 45c brown & rose 4.00 *14.00*
60 A6 75c yellow & pur 11.00 *67.50*
61 A6 1.50r black & rose 65.00 *72.50*
62 A6 2.25r red vio & grn 55.00 *72.50*
Nos. 52-62 (11) 161.05 *259.40*

King George V — A7

Numerals of 75c, 1.50r and 2.25r of type A7 are in color on plain tablet.

1912 *Perf. 14*

63 A7 2c org brn & grn 1.00 *7.50*
64 A7 3c green 6.25 .70
65 A7 6c car rose 4.75 3.00
66 A7 12c ol gray & grn 1.50 *6.75*
67 A7 15c ultra 5.00 1.75
68 A7 18c pl yel grn & rose 3.50 *12.50*
69 A7 30c pur & grn 14.00 3.00
70 A7 45c brn & rose 3.00 *50.00*
71 A7 75c yell & pur 3.25 *7.00*
72 A7 1.50r blk & rose 13.00 1.10
73 A7 2.25r vio & grn 75.00 3.25
Nos. 63-73 (11) 130.25 96.55
Set, ovptd. "SPECIMEN" 250.00

King George V — A8

For description of dies I and II see Dies of British Colonial Stamps in the Table of Contents.

The 5c of type A8 has a colorless numeral on solid-color tablet. Numerals of 9c, 20c, 25c, 50c, 75c, and 1r to 5r of type A8 are in color on plain tablet.

1917-20 Die I

74 A8 2c org brn & grn .55 *3.00*
75 A8 3c green 2.25 1.40
76 A8 5c brown ('20) 4.50 *14.00*
77 A8 6c carmine rose 4.75 1.60
78 A8 12c gray 2.60 1.75
79 A8 15c ultra 1.90 1.60
80 A8 18c violet, *yel* 4.75 *60.00*
a. Die II ('20) 4.25 *27.50*
81 A8 25c blk & red, *yel* ('20) 4.25 *52.50*
a. Die II ('20) 5.25 *19.00*
82 A8 30c dull vio & ol grn 1.60 *16.00*
83 A8 45c dull vio & org 3.75 *50.00*
84 A8 50c dull vio & blk ('20) 13.00 *62.50*
85 A8 75c blk, *bl grn*, ol back 2.25 *27.50*
a. 75c blk, *emer* (Die II) ('20) 1.50 *25.00*
86 A8 1r dl vio & red ('20) 23.00 *70.00*
87 A8 1.50r vio & bl, *bl* 10.00 *57.50*
a. Die II ('20) 22.00 *35.00*
88 A8 2.25r gray grn & dp vio 55.00 *160.00*

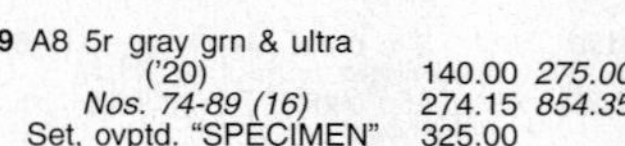

89 A8 5r gray grn & ultra ('20) 140.00 *275.00*
Nos. 74-89 (16) 274.15 *854.35*
Set, ovptd. "SPECIMEN" 325.00

Die II

1921-32 Ordinary Paper Wmk. 4

91 A8 2c org brn & grn .30 .25
92 A8 3c green 1.90 .25
93 A8 3c black ('22) 1.10 .35
94 A8 4c green ('22) 1.10 *2.75*
95 A8 4c ol grn & rose red ('28) 7.25 *21.00*
96 A8 5c dk brown 1.25 *6.00*
97 A8 6c car rose 4.75 *10.00*
98 A8 6c violet ('22) 1.60 .25
99 A8 9c rose red ('27) 4.00 *4.75*
100 A8 12c gray 3.00 .25
a. Die I ('32) 32.50 .70
101 A8 12c carmine ('22) 2.25 .35
102 A8 15c ultra 2.25 *65.00*
103 A8 15c yellow ('22) 1.10 *3.00*
104 A8 18c violet, *yel* 2.75 *17.00*
105 A8 20c ultra ('22) 1.60 .40

Chalky Paper

106 A8 25c blk & red, *yel* ('25) 3.00 *28.00*
107 A8 30c dull vio & ol grn 1.60 *17.00*
108 A8 45c dull vio & org 1.40 *5.75*
109 A8 50c dull vio & blk 2.75 2.50
110 A8 75c blk, *emer* ('24) 9.00 *24.00*
111 A8 1r dull vio & red 29.00 *20.00*
a. Die I ('32) 12.50 *37.50*
112 A8 1.50r vio & bl, *bl* ('24) 17.50 *25.00*
113 A8 2.25r green & vio 21.00 *16.00*
114 A8 5r green & ultra 120.00 *175.00*
Nos. 91-114 (24) 241.45 *444.85*
Set, ovptd. "SPECIMEN" 425.00

Common Design Types pictured following the introduction.

Silver Jubilee Issue

Common Design Type

1935, May 6 Engr. *Perf. 11x12*

118 CD301 6c black & ultra 1.25 *2.75*
Never hinged 2.75
119 CD301 12c indigo & grn 4.75 1.75
Never hinged 7.50
120 CD301 20c ultra & brown 3.50 4.00
Never hinged 5.50
121 CD301 1r brn vio & indigo 8.00 *24.00*
Never hinged 15.00
Nos. 118-121 (4) 17.50 *32.50*
Set, never hinged 30.00
Set, perf "SPECIMEN" 170.00

Coronation Issue

Common Design Type

1937, May 12 *Perf. 11x11½*

122 CD302 6c olive green .30 .25
Never hinged .45
123 CD302 12c deep orange .45 *.55*
Never hinged .70
124 CD302 20c deep ultra .45 *1.10*
Never hinged .75
Nos. 122-124 (3) 1.20 *1.90*
Set, never hinged 2.00
Set, perf "SPECIMEN" 110.00

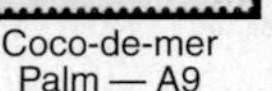

Coco-de-mer Palm — A9

Seychelles Giant Tortoise — A10

Fishing Canoe — A11

Perf. 13½x14½, 14½x13½

1938-41 Photo. Wmk. 4

Chalky Paper

125a A9 2c pur brn 1.00 .40
Never hinged 1.60
126 A10 3c green 7.25 3.00
Never hinged 9.00
128 A11 6c orange 10.00 3.75
Never hinged 14.00
130 A9 9c rose red 11.00 4.25
Never hinged 14.50
132 A10 12c violet 30.00 1.75
Never hinged 50.00
134a A9 18c rose lake 7.00 .65
Never hinged 10.50

135 A11 20c brt bl ('41) 27.50 6.50
Never hinged 45.00
137 A9 25c ocher 30.00 15.00
Never hinged 52.50
138 A10 30c rose lake 30.00 12.00
Never hinged 52.50
140a A11 45c chocolate 15.00 2.75
Never hinged 22.50
141a A9 50c dp reddish vio 9.00 .65
Never hinged 15.00
142 A10 75c gray blue 52.50 52.50
Never hinged 87.50
144 A11 1r yel grn 90.00 *90.00*
Never hinged 125.00
146a A9 1.50r ultra 19.00 4.75
Never hinged 27.50
147a A10 2.25r olive bister 35.00 11.50
Never hinged 52.50
148 A11 5r copper red 19.50 *16.00*
Never hinged 17.50

Issued: 3c, 6c, 12c, 20c, 25c, 1/1/38; 2c, 9c, 30c-5r, 2/10/38; 18c. 8/8/41.

New Values and Color Changes

1941-49

Chalky Paper

127a A10 3c orange .90 *1.10*
Never hinged 1.40
129 A11 6c grayish grn 2.75 1.40
Never hinged 4.25
129a A11 6c green ('49) 5.75 1.40
Never hinged 8.25
131a A9 9c gray blue 10.75 .40
Never hinged 20.00
133a A10 15c brn carmine 14.00 .45
Never hinged 20.00
134b A9 18c rose carmine ('49) 15.00 12.50
Never hinged 25.00
136a A11 20c brn ocher 10.00 .70
Never hinged 15.00
139a A9 30c blue 10.50 .55
Never hinged 21.00
140b A11 45c pur brn ('49) 17.00 13.50
Never hinged 26.00
141b A9 50c br lil ('49) 2.50 2.50
Never hinged 4.25
143a A10 75c dp sla lilac 11.00 4.25
Never hinged 16.50
145a A11 1r gray black 20.00 3.50
Never hinged 37.50

Issued: 3c, 6c (#129), 9c, 15c, 20c, 30c, 75c, 1r, 8/8/41; 6c (#129a), 45c, 4/5/49; 50c, 6/13/49.

1942-45

Ordinary Paper

125 A9 2c violet brown .25 *1.75*
Never hinged .75
127 A10 3c orange ('41) .75 *1.50*
Never hinged .65
129b A11 6c green ('41) 1.50 *2.40*
Never hinged .60
131 A9 9c peacock blue ('45) 4.75 3.25
Never hinged 6.75
131b A9 9c gray blue ('45) 11.00 1.60
Never hinged 16.00
133 A10 15c copper red 5.75 *4.75*
Never hinged 6.75
134 A9 18c rose lake 5.50 3.75
Never hinged 7.25
136 A11 20c ocher 2.00 *3.25*
Never hinged 2.75
139 A10 30c bright blue 1.90 *6.50*
140 A11 45c brown 3.00 3.00
Never hinged 3.00
141 A9 50c dl lil ('49) 3.50 4.00
Never hinged 3.00
143 A10 75c dull violet 2.50 *9.00*
Never hinged 2.75
145 A11 1r gray 3.50 *7.50*
Never hinged 2.50
146 A9 1.50r ultra 5.75 *18.00*
Never hinged 4.75
147 A10 2.25r olive bister 19.50 *29.00*
Never hinged 25.00
148a A11 5r copper red 17.50 *35.00*
Never hinged 25.00

Issued: all except No. 131, 11/18/42; No. 131, 11/19/45.

See Nos. 158-169, 174-188 (in Scott Standard catalogue, Vol. 6).

Catalogue values for unused stamps in this section, from this point to the end of the section, are for Never Hinged items.

Peace Issue

Common Design Type

Perf. 13½x14

1946, Sept. 23 Engr. Wmk. 4
149 CD303 9c light blue .25 .25
150 CD303 30c dark blue .30 .25

Silver Wedding Issue

Common Design Types

1948, Nov. 11 Photo. *Perf. 14x14½*
151 CD304 9c bright ultra .25 .75

Engraved; Name Typographed

Perf. 11½x11

152 CD305 5r rose carmine 16.00 *45.00*

UPU Issue

Common Design Types

Perf. 13½, 11x11½

1949, Oct. 10 Engr.
153 CD306 18c red violet .25 .25
154 CD307 50c dp rose violet 2.00 2.25
155 CD308 1r gray .55 .35
156 CD309 2.25r olive .45 *1.25*
Nos. 153-156 (4) 3.25 4.10

Types of 1938-41 Redrawn and

Sailfish — A12

Map — A13

Perf. 14½x13½, 13½x14½

1952, Mar. 3 Photo. Wmk. 4
157 A12 2c violet .75 .75
158 A10 3c orange .75 .30
159 A9 9c peacock blue .70 *1.75*
160 A11 15c yellow green .60 *1.00*
161 A13 18c rose lake 1.75 .25
162 A11 20c ocher 2.00 1.50
163 A10 25c bright red .80 2.25
164 A12 40c ultra 1.25 2.00
165 A11 45c violet brown 1.50 .35
166 A9 50c brt violet 1.40 1.75
167 A13 1r gray 4.75 4.25
168 A9 1.50r brt blue 11.00 *16.00*
169 A10 2.25r olive bister 17.50 *18.00*
170 A13 5r copper red 18.00 *19.00*
171 A12 10r green 25.00 *45.00*
Nos. 157-171 (15) 87.75 *114.15*

Wmk. 4a (Error)

157a A12 2c violet 140.00 *200.00*
b. Crown omitted in wmk. 825.00
158a A10 3c orange 190.00 190.00
b. Crown omitted in wmk. 600.00 600.00
159a A9 9c peacock blue 325.00 *400.00*
b. Crown omitted in wmk. 1,300.
160a A11 15c yellow green 275.00 *325.00*
b. Crown omitted in wmk. 825.00
161a A13 18c rose lake 375.00 325.00
b. Crown omitted in wmk. 1,200.
162a A11 20c ocher 450.00 450.00
b. Crown omitted in wmk. 1,300. 1,100.
163a A10 25c bright red 450.00
b. Crown omitted in wmk. 1,600.
164a A12 40c ultra 775.00
b. Crown omitted in wmk. 1,750.
165a A11 45c violet brown 525.00 525.00
b. Crown omitted in wmk. 1,750.
166a A9 50c brt violet 600.00 *725.00*
b. Crown omitted in wmk. 1,900. 1,750.
167a A13 1r gray 1,450.
168a A9 1.50r brt blue 3,000.
169a A10 2.25r olive bister 1,500.
170a A13 5r copper red 1,200.

The redrawn design shows a new portrait of King George VI surmounted by crown, as on type A12.

POSTAGE DUE STAMPS

Catalogue values for unused stamps in this section are for Never Hinged items.

D1

Engr.; Denomination Typo. in Carmine

1951, Mar. 1 Wmk. 4 *Perf. 11½*
J1 D1 2c carmine 1.50 *3.00*
J2 D1 3c blue green 2.25 *3.00*
J3 D1 6c ocher 2.25 *2.25*
J4 D1 9c brown orange 2.25 *4.00*
J5 D1 15c purple 2.10 *12.50*
J6 D1 18c deep blue 2.75 *12.50*
J7 D1 20c black brown 2.75 *12.50*
J8 D1 30c red brown 2.75 *9.00*
Nos. J1-J8 (8) 18.60 *58.75*

SIBERIA

sī-ˈbir-ē-ə

LOCATION — A vast territory of Russia lying between the Ural Mountains and the Pacific Ocean.

The anti-Bolshevist provisional government set up at Omsk by Adm. Aleksandr V. Kolchak issued Nos. 1-10 in 1919. The monarchist, anti-Soviet government in Priamur province issued Nos. 51-118 in 1921-22.

(Stamps of the Czechoslovak Legion are listed under Czechoslovakia.)

100 Kopecks = 1 Ruble

Russian Stamps of 1909-18 Surcharged

a

b

On Stamps of 1909-12

1919 Unwmk. *Perf. 14x14½*

Wove Paper

Lozenges of Varnish on Face

1 A14(a) 35k on 2k dull grn .60 *2.00*
a. Inverted surcharge 75.00
b. "5" omitted 150.00
c. Double surcharge —
2 A14(a) 50k on 3k car .60 *2.00*
a. Inverted surcharge 75.00
3 A14(a) 70k on 1k dl org yel 1.00 *4.25*
a. Inverted surcharge 75.00
4 A15(b) 1r on 4k car 1.25 *2.00*
a. Dbl. surch., one inverted 150.00 *110.00*
b. Inverted surcharge 75.00
c. Double surcharge 200.00
5 A14(b) 3r on 7k blue 7.00 *9.00*
a. Double surcharge 75.00 *30.00*
b. Inverted surcharge 75.00 *100.00*
c. Pair, one without surcharge 400.00
d. "3" omitted —
6 A11(b) 5r on 14k dk bl & car 9.50 *17.50*
a. Double surcharge 75.00 *40.00*
b. Inverted surcharge 100.00 *40.00*

On Stamps of 1917

Imperf

7 A14(a) 35k on 2k gray grn 1.25 *4.25*
a. Inverted surcharge *100.00*
8 A14(a) 50k on 3k red 1.00 *4.25*
a. Inverted surcharge 150.00
b. Double surcharge *100.00*
9 A14(a) 70k on 1k orange .75 *4.25*
a. Inverted surcharge 100.00
b. Dbl. surch., one inverted —
10 A15(b) 1r on 4k car 9.50 *14.00*
Nos. 1-10 (10) 32.45 *63.50*

Nos. 1-10 were first issued in Omsk during the regime of Admiral Kolchak. Later they were used along the line of the Trans-Siberian railway to Vladivostok.

Some experts question the postal use of most off-cover canceled examples of Nos. 1-10.

25Р 1-

Similar surcharges, handstamped as above are bogus.

Priamur Government Issues

Nikolaevsk Issue

A5

A6

A7

1909-17 Russian Stamps Handstamp Surcharged or Overprinted

1921 Unwmk. *Perf. 14x14½, 13½*
51 A5 10k on 4k carmine *250.00*
52 A5 10k on 10k dark blue *1,500.*
53 A6 15k on 14k dk blue & car *200.00*
a. Inverted surcharge *750.00*
54 A6 15k on 15k red brn & dp blue *75.00*
55 A6 15k on 35k red brn & grn *75.00*
56 A6 15k on 50k brn vio & grn *75.00*
57 A6 15k on 70k brn & red org *150.00 200.00*
58 A7 15k on 1r brn & org *200.00*
59 A5 on 20k dl bl & dk car *300.00 350.00*
60 A5 on 20k on 14k dk bl & car (#118) *200.00*
a. 15k on 20k on 14k dk bl & car (error) *1,100.*
61 A7 20k on 3½r mar & lt grn *250.00*
62 A7 20k on 5r indigo, grn & lt bl *850.00 950.00*
63 A7 20k on 7r dk grn & pink *900.00 950.00*

Nos. 59-60 are overprinted with initials but original denominations remain.

A 10k on 5k claret (Russia No. 77) and a 15k on 20k blue & carmine (Russia No. 82a) were not officially issued. Some authorities consider them bogus.

Reprints exist.

On Russian Semi-Postal Stamp No. B6

64 SP5 20k on 3k mar & gray grn, *pink 750.00*

On Stamps of 1917

Imperf

65 A5 10k on 1k orange *100.00*
66 A5 10k on 2k gray green *75.00*
67 A5 10k on 3k red *100.00*
68 A5 10k on 5k claret — *700.00*
69 A6 15k on 1r pale brn, brn & red org *150.00*
70 A7 20k on 1r pale brn, brn & red org *200.00*
71 A7 20k on 3½r mar & lt grn *325.00*
72 A7 20k on 7r dk grn & pink *950.00 950.00*

The letters of the overprint are the initials of the Russian words for "Nikolaevsk on Amur Priamur Provisional Government."

As the surcharges on Nos. 51-72 are handstamped, a number exist inverted or double.

A 20k blue & carmine (Russia No. 126) with Priamur overprint and a 15k on 20k (Russia No. 126) were not officially issued. Some authorities consider them bogus.

No evidence found of genuine usage of Nos. 51-72.

Stamps of Far Eastern Republic Overprinted

1922
78 A2 2k gray green 25.00 25.00
a. Inverted overprint 200.00
79 A2a 4k rose 25.00 25.00
a. Inverted overprint *250.00*

80	A2	5k claret	25.00	25.00
81	A2a	10k blue	25.00	25.00
		Nos. 78-81 (4)	100.00	100.00

Anniv. of the overthrow of the Bolshevik power in the Priamur district.

The letters of the overprint are the initials of "Vremeno Priamurski Pravitel'stvo" i.e. Provisional Priamur Government, 26th May.

Russian Stamps of 1909-21 Overprinted in Dark Blue or Vermilion

On Stamps of 1909-18

1922 — *Perf. 14x14½*

85	A14	1k dull org yel	75.00	100.00
86	A14	2k dull green	125.00	110.00
87	A14	3k carmine	30.00	50.00
88	A15	4k carmine	25.00	35.00
89	A14	5k dk claret	35.00	40.00
90	A14	7k blue (V)	100.00	45.00
91	A15	10k dark blue (V)	60.00	70.00
92	A11	14k dk bl & car	75.00	85.00
93	A11	15k red brn & dp bl	10.00	15.00
94	A8	20k dl bl & dk car	50.00	25.00
95	A11	20k on 14k dk bl & car	120.00	150.00
96	A11	25k dl grn & dk vio (V)	50.00	50.00
97	A11	35k red brn & grn	20.00	15.00
a.		Inverted overprint	200.00	
98	A8	50k brn vio & grn	20.00	50.00
99	A11	70k brn & red org	55.00	55.00
		Nos. 85-99 (15)	850.00	895.00

On Stamps of 1917

Imperf

100	A14	1k orange	15.00	*25.00*
a.		Inverted overprint	200.00	100.00
101	A14	2k gray green	15.00	25.00
102	A14	3k red	20.00	25.00
103	A15	4k carmine	100.00	100.00
104	A14	5k claret	35.00	25.00
105	A11	15k red brn & dp bl	*100.00*	125.00
106	A8	20k blue & car	125.00	75.00
107	A9	1r pale brn, brn & red org	40.00	*50.00*
		Nos. 100-107 (8)	450.00	450.00

On Stamps of Siberia, 1919

Perf. 14½x15

108	A14	35k on 2k green	100.00	100.00

Imperf

109	A14	70k on 1k orange	250.00	120.00

On Stamps of Far Eastern Republic, 1921

110	A2	2k gray green	20.00	*25.00*
111	A2a	4k rose	20.00	10.00
112	A2	5k claret	20.00	*25.00*
a.		Inverted overprint	100.00	
113	A2a	10k blue (R)	20.00	*30.00*
		Nos. 109-113 (5)	330.00	210.00

Same, Surcharged with New Values

114	A2	1k on 2k gray grn	20.00	*25.00*
115	A2a	3k on 4k rose	20.00	*25.00*

The overprint is in a rectangular frame on stamps of 1k to 10k and 1r; on the other values the frame is omitted. It is larger on the 1 ruble than on the smaller stamps.

The overprint reads "Priamurski Zemski Krai," Priamur Rural Province.

Far Eastern Republic Nos. 30-32 Overprinted in Blue

Perf. 14½x15

116	A14	35k on 2k green	20.00	*25.00*

Imperf

117	A14	35k on 2k green	60.00	*120.00*
118	A14	70k on 1k orange	30.00	15.00
		Nos. 116-118 (3)	110.00	160.00

Counterfeits of Nos. 51-118 abound.

SIERRA LEONE

sē-ˌer-ə lē-ˈōn

LOCATION — West coast of Africa, between Guinea and Liberia
GOVT. — British Colony
AREA — 27,925 sq. mi.
POP. — 3,354,000 (est. 1982)
CAPITAL — Freetown

Sierra Leone was a British colony and protectorate.

12 Pence = 1 Shilling
20 Shillings = 1 Pound

Catalogue values for unused stamps in this country are for Never Hinged items, beginning with Scott 186 in the regular postage section.

Queen Victoria — A1

1859-74 Unwmk. Typo. *Perf. 14*

1	A1	6p bright violet ('74)	77.50	30.00
a.		6p dull violet ('59)	275.00	55.00
b.		6p gray lilac ('65)	300.00	45.00

1872 — *Perf. 12½*

5	A1	6p violet	425.00	70.00

Queen Victoria — A2

1872 Wmk. 1 Sideways *Perf. 12½*

6	A2	1p rose	85.00	50.00
8	A2	3p yellow buff	160.00	42.50
9	A2	4p blue	200.00	45.00
10	A2	1sh yellow green	525.00	62.50

1873 Wmk. 1 Upright

6a	A2	1p	140.00	35.00
7	A2	2p magenta	150.00	55.00
8a	A2	3p	550.00	95.00
9a	A2	4p	375.00	57.50
10a	A2	1sh	675.00	110.00

1876-96 Wmk. 1 Upright *Perf. 14*

11	A2	½p bister	5.50	14.50
12	A2	1p rose	60.00	16.00
13	A2	1½p violet ('77)	55.00	10.00
14	A2	2p magenta	75.00	4.50
15	A2	3p yellow buff	65.00	8.00
16	A2	4p blue	225.00	7.25
17	A1	6p brt violet ('85)	72.50	27.50
a.		Half used as 3p on cover		2,750.
18	A1	6p violet brn ('90)	27.50	16.00
19	A1	6p brown vio ('96)	3.00	*11.00*
20	A2	1sh green	92.50	7.25
		Nos. 11-20 (10)	681.00	122.00

For surcharge see No. 32.

1883-93 Wmk. Crown and C A (2)

21	A2	½p bister	50.00	65.00
22	A2	½p dull green ('84)	3.50	3.00
23	A2	1p carmine ('84)	17.50	1.60
a.		1p rose carmine	32.50	9.50
b.		1p rose	225.00	40.00
24	A2	1½p violet ('93)	3.50	9.00
25	A2	2p magenta	77.50	9.50
26	A2	2p slate ('84)	62.50	4.50
27	A2	2½p ultra ('91)	18.50	2.00
28	A2	3p org yel ('92)	4.00	*16.00*
29	A2	4p blue	1,150.	32.50
30	A2	4p bister ('84)	2.75	3.00
31	A2	1sh org brn ('88)	27.50	22.00
		Nos. 21-28,30-31 (10)	267.25	135.60

For surcharge see No. 33.

Nos. 13 and 24 Surcharged in Black

1893 Wmk. 1

32	A2	½p on 1½p violet	575.00	*800.00*
a.		"PFNNY"	3,750.	*4,500.*

Wmk. 2

33	A2	½p on 1½p violet	9.25	4.00
a.		"PFNNY"	85.00	*82.50*
b.		Inverted surcharge	125.00	125.00
c.		Same as "a," inverted	4,000.	*5,500.*
d.		Double surcharge	*1,200.*	

A4

1896-97

34	A4	½p lilac & grn ('97)	2.75	3.50
35	A4	1p lilac & car	5.00	2.00
36	A4	1½p lilac & blk ('97)	4.50	24.00
37	A4	2p lilac & org	2.75	5.50
38	A4	2½p lilac & ultra	2.75	1.40
39	A4	3p lilac & sl ('97)	9.50	7.75
40	A4	4p lilac & car ('97)	10.50	14.50
41	A4	5p lilac & blk	14.50	16.00
42	A4	6p lilac ('97)	9.00	27.50
43	A4	1sh green & blk	6.75	22.50
44	A4	2sh green & ultra	34.00	*80.00*
45	A4	5sh green & car	90.00	*250.00*
46	A4	£1 violet, *red*	325.00	*600.00*
		Nos. 34-46 (13)	517.00	1,055.

Numerals of Nos. 39-46 of type A4 are in color on plain tablet.

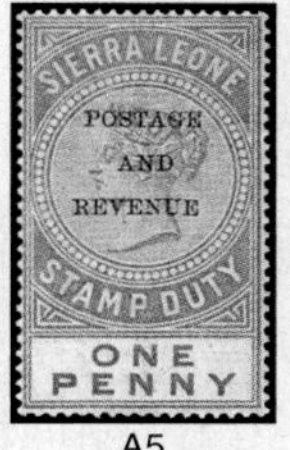

A5

A6

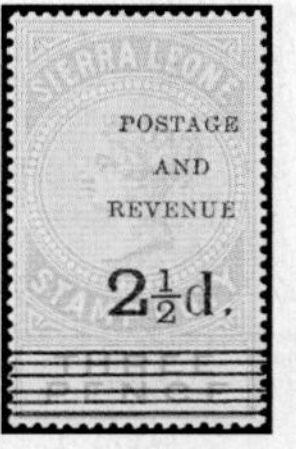

a

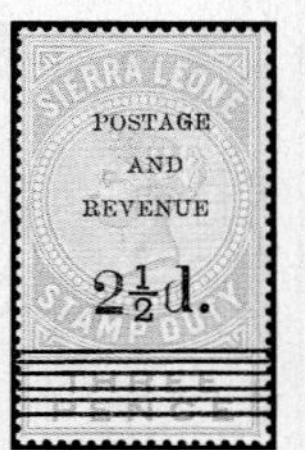

b

c

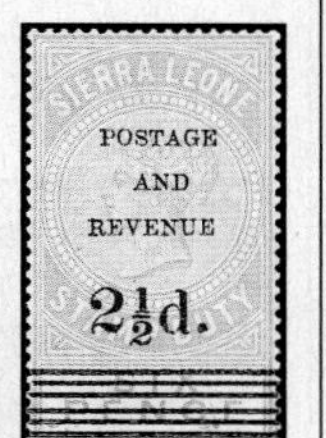

d

e

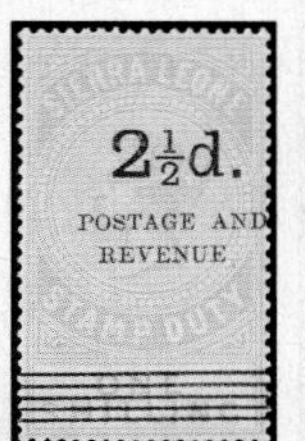

f

1897 Wmk. C A over Crown (46)

47	A5	1p lilac & grn	8.50	4.25
a.		Double overprint	*2,000.*	*2,000.*
48	A6(a)	2½p on 3p lil & grn	13.50	*22.50*
a.		Double surcharge	*40,000.*	
b.		Double surcharge, types "a" and "b"	*32,000.*	
c.		Double surcharge, types "a" and "c"	*55,000.*	
d.		Surcharge bars omitted	*2,000.*	
49	A6(b)	2½p on 3p	70.00	*95.00*
50	A6(c)	2½p on 3p	200.00	*250.00*
51	A6(d)	2½p on 3p	400.00	*525.00*
52	A6(a)	2½p on 6p lil & grn	10.50	*22.50*
53	A6(b)	2½p on 6p	55.00	*85.00*
54	A6(c)	2½p on 6p	150.00	190.00
55	A6(d)	2½p on 6p	325.00	*400.00*
56	A6(a)	2½p on 1sh lilac	110.00	80.00
57	A6(b)	2½p on 1sh lilac	1,100.	1,100.
58	A6(c)	2½p on 1sh lilac	550.00	500.00
a.		Italic "N" in "REVENUE"	1,750.	1,400.
59	A6(e)	2½p on 1sh lilac	1,750.	2,000.
59A	A6(f)	2½p on 1sh lilac	1,800.	1,500.
60	A6(a)	2½p on 2sh lilac	2,500.	*3,000.*
61	A6(b)	2½p on 2sh lilac	*20,000.*	
62	A6(c)	2½p on 2sh lilac	*12,000.*	*17,000.*
a.		Italic "N" in "REVENUE"	50,000.	50,000.
63	A6(e)	2½p on 2sh lilac	*47,500.*	
63A	A6(f)	2½p on 2sh lilac	*47,500.*	*50,000.*

The words "POSTAGE AND REVENUE" on Nos. 56-63A are set in two lines and overprinted below instead of above "2½d."

The "d" in type "f" is 3½mm wide; that in type "a" is 3mm.

Very fine examples of Nos. 47-63A will have perforations touching the frameline on one or more sides.

Nos. 56-59A are often found discolored. Such stamps sell for about half the values quoted.

King Edward VII — A7

Numerals of 3p to £1 of type A7 are in color on plain tablet.

1903 Wmk. Crown and C A (2)

64	A7	½p violet & grn	3.25	*6.50*
65	A7	1p violet & car	2.25	1.10
67	A7	2p violet & brn org	4.50	*17.50*
68	A7	2½p violet & ultra	5.00	*9.00*
69	A7	3p violet & gray	17.50	*22.50*
70	A7	4p violet & car	8.00	*19.00*
71	A7	5p violet & blk	16.00	*50.00*
72	A7	6p violet & dull vio	12.50	*40.00*
73	A7	1sh green & blk	26.00	*80.00*
74	A7	2sh green & ultra	55.00	*80.00*
75	A7	5sh green & car	80.00	*140.00*
76	A7	£1 violet, *red*	275.00	350.00
		Nos. 64-76 (12)	505.00	815.60

1904-05 Wmk. 3 Chalky Paper

77	A7	½p violet & grn	5.75	5.25
78	A7	1p violet & car	7.25	1.75
a.		On ordinary paper	1.75	1.00
79	A7	1½p violet & blk	3.50	*17.50*
80	A7	2p violet & brn org	4.75	4.50
81	A7	2½p violet & ultra	8.25	2.25
82	A7	3p violet & gray	55.00	4.00
83	A7	4p violet & car	14.00	8.00
84	A7	5p violet & blk	16.00	*40.00*
85	A7	6p violet & dl vio	9.00	*3.75*
86	A7	1sh green & blk	8.50	*10.00*
87	A7	2sh green & ultra	36.00	*40.00*
88	A7	5sh green & car	50.00	65.00
89	A7	£1 violet, *red*	300.00	350.00
		Nos. 77-89 (13)	518.00	552.00

1907-10 Ordinary Paper

90	A7	½p green	1.00	.60
91	A7	1p carmine	18.50	.80
92	A7	1½p orange ('10)	3.50	2.25
93	A7	2p gray	3.50	1.75
94	A7	2½p ultra	4.00	3.25

Chalky Paper

95	A7	3p violet, *yel*	14.00	*3.25*
a.		On ordinary paper	12.50	*15.00*
96	A7	4p blk & red, *yel*	2.60	1.75
97	A7	5p vio & ol grn	27.00	8.50
98	A7	6p vio & red vio	22.50	9.00
99	A7	1sh black, *green*	6.25	5.75
100	A7	2sh vio & bl, *bl*	26.00	22.50
101	A7	5sh grn & red, *yel*	50.00	70.00
102	A7	£1 vio & blk, *red*	300.00	250.00
		Nos. 90-102 (13)	478.85	379.40

King George V and Seal of the Colony

A8 A9

Die I

For description of dies I and II see "Dies of British Colonial Stamps" in Table of Contents.

Numerals of 3p, 4p, 5p, 6p and 10p of type A8 are in color on plain tablet. Numerals of 7p and 9p are on solid-color tablet.

1912-24 Ordinary Paper Wmk. 3

103	A8	½p green	5.00	3.50
104	A8	1p scarlet	10.00	1.00
a.		1p carmine	2.25	.45
105	A8	1½p orange	2.25	*2.75*
106	A8	2p gray	1.50	.25
107	A8	2½p ultra	1.25	1.00
a.		2½p deep blue	10.50	3.00

Chalky Paper

108	A9	3p violet, *yel*	6.25	3.75
109	A8	4p blk & red, *yel*	3.25	*17.50*
a.		Die II ('24)	6.50	*6.00*
110	A8	5p violet & ol grn	1.50	*7.00*
111	A8	6p vio & red vio	5.00	*6.75*
112	A8	7p violet & org	3.50	*12.00*
113	A8	9p violet & blk	5.75	*14.00*
114	A8	10p violet & red	3.50	*20.00*
115	A9	1sh black, *green*	10.00	*5.25*
a.		1sh black, *emerald*		*190.00*
116	A9	2sh vio & ultra, *bl*	29.00	7.00
117	A9	5sh grn & red, *yel*	27.50	*40.00*
118	A9	10sh grn & red, *grn*	110.00	*160.00*
119	A9	£1 vio & blk, *red*	250.00	*325.00*
120	A9	£2 violet & ultra	950.00	*1,400.*
121	A9	£5 gray grn & org	*3,500.*	*4,500.*
		Nos. 103-119 (17)	475.25	626.75

The status of #115a has been questioned.

Die II

1921-27 Ordinary Paper Wmk. 4

122	A8	½p green	2.50	1.10
123	A8	1p violet ('26)	8.25	.25
a.		Die I ('24)	5.25	*2.50*
124	A8	1½p scarlet	2.00	1.50
125	A8	2p gray ('22)	1.50	.25
126	A8	2½p ultra	3.50	*21.00*
127	A8	3p ultra ('22)	1.75	1.40
128	A8	4p blk & red, *yel*	5.75	3.75
129	A8	5p vio & ol grn	1.50	1.40

Chalky Paper

130	A8	6p dp vio & red vio	1.50	*3.25*
131	A8	7p vio & org ('27)	5.25	*30.00*
132	A8	9p dl vio & blk ('22)	6.25	*26.00*
133	A8	10p violet & red	6.25	*37.50*
134	A9	1sh blk, *emerald*	16.00	8.50
135	A9	2sh vio & ultra, *bl*	12.50	11.50
136	A9	5sh grn & red, *yel*	12.50	*62.50*
137	A9	10sh grn & red, *grn*	175.00	*350.00*
138	A9	£2 violet & ultra	900.00	*1,300.*
139	A9	£5 gray grn & org	*3,400.*	*4,500.*
		Nos. 122-137 (16)	262.00	559.90

Rice Field — A10

Palms and Kola Tree — A11

1932, Mar. 1 Engr. *Perf. 12½*

140	A10	½p green	.25	.50
141	A10	1p dk violet	.40	.30
142	A10	1½p rose car	.50	*3.00*
143	A10	2p yellow brn	.75	.30
144	A10	3p ultra	2.25	*3.25*
145	A10	4p orange	1.50	*16.00*
146	A10	5p olive green	3.00	*8.25*
147	A10	6p light blue	1.50	*5.25*
148	A10	1sh red brown	7.50	*16.00*

Perf. 12

149	A11	2sh dk brown	7.25	*8.75*
150	A11	5sh indigo	21.00	*28.00*
151	A11	10sh deep green	90.00	*130.00*
152	A11	£1 deep violet	180.00	*260.00*
		Nos. 140-152 (13)	315.90	479.60

Wilberforce Issue

Arms of Sierra Leone — A12

Slave Throwing Off Shackles — A13

Map of Sierra Leone — A14

Old Slave Market, Freetown A15

Fruit Seller — A16

Government Sanatorium — A17

Bullom Canoe — A18

Punting near Banana Islands — A19

Government Buildings, Freetown A20

Old Slavers' Resort, Bunce Island — A21

African Elephant — A22

George V A23

Freetown Harbor — A24

1933, Oct. 2

153	A12	½p dp grn	1.00	*1.25*
154	A13	1p brn & blk	.85	.25
155	A14	1½p org brn	8.50	4.75
156	A15	2p violet	3.50	.25
157	A16	3p ultra	6.50	1.75
158	A17	4p dk brn	7.00	*10.00*
159	A18	5p red brn & sl grn	7.50	*11.00*
160	A19	6p dp org & blk	14.00	7.00
161	A20	1sh dk vio	5.00	*18.00*
162	A21	2sh bl & dk brn	42.50	*50.00*
163	A22	5sh red vio & blk	160.00	*200.00*
164	A23	10sh grn & blk	300.00	*525.00*
165	A24	£1 yel & dk vio	650.00	*850.00*
		Nos. 153-165 (13)	1,206.	*1,679.*

Abolition of slavery in the British colonies and cent. of the death of William Wilberforce, English philanthropist and agitator against the slave trade.

Common Design Types

For description of dies I and II see "Dies of British Colonial Stamps" in Table of Contents.

Silver Jubilee Issue

Common Design Type

1935, May 6 *Perf. 11x12*

166	CD301	1p black & ultra	2.00	*2.50*
167	CD301	3p ultra & brown	3.00	*8.50*
168	CD301	5p indigo & green	4.25	*25.00*
169	CD301	1sh brn vio & ind	15.00	*20.00*
		Nos. 166-169 (4)	24.25	*56.00*
		Set, never hinged	42.50	

Coronation Issue

Common Design Type

1937, May 12 *Perf. 11x11½*

170	CD302	1p deep orange	.40	.90
171	CD302	2p dark violet	.65	1.00
172	CD302	3p deep ultra	.90	3.75
		Nos. 170-172 (3)	1.95	5.65
		Set, never hinged	3.75	

Freetown Harbor A25

Rice Harvesting A26

1938-44 *Perf. 12½*

173	A25	½p grn & blk	.25	.50
174	A25	1p dp cl & blk	.30	.70
175	A26	1½p rose red	12.50	1.25
175A	A26	1½p red vio ('41)	.25	*.70*
176	A26	2p red violet	30.00	3.00
176A	A26	2p dk red ('41)	.25	*2.10*
177	A25	3p ultra & blk	.35	*.60*
178	A25	4p red brn & blk	1.50	*4.50*
179	A26	5p olive green	2.25	4.00
180	A26	6p gray	.90	.60
181	A25	1sh ol grn & blk	2.25	.90
181A	A26	1sh3p org yel ('44)	.45	.60
182	A25	2sh sepia & blk	2.75	2.75
183	A26	5sh red brown	8.00	*17.50*
184	A26	10sh emerald	22.50	20.00
185	A25	£1 dk blue	13.00	*35.00*
		Nos. 173-185 (16)	97.50	94.70
		Set, never hinged	150.00	

Catalogue values for unused stamps in this section, from this point to the end of the section, are for Never Hinged items.

Peace Issue

Common Design Type

Perf. 13½x14

1946, Oct. 1 Engr. Wmk. 4

186	CD303	1½p lilac	.25	.25
187	CD303	3p bright ultra	.25	.25

Silver Wedding Issue

Common Design Types

1948, Dec. 1 Photo. *Perf. 14x14½*

188	CD304	1½p brt red violet	.25	.25

Engraved; Name Typographed

Perf. 11½x11

189	CD305	£1 dark blue	24.50	*26.00*

UPU Issue

Common Design Types

Engr.; Name Typo. on 3p, 6p

1949, Oct. 10 *Perf. 13½, 11x11½*

190	CD306	1½p rose violet	.25	.35
191	CD307	3p indigo	.50	1.75
192	CD308	6p gray	.85	2.00
193	CD309	1sh olive	1.40	1.00
		Nos. 190-193 (4)	3.00	5.10

SINGAPORE

'siŋ-ə-ˌpor

LOCATION — An island just off the southern tip of the Malay Peninsula, south of Johore
GOVT. — British Colony
AREA — 239 sq. mi.
POP. — 2,529,100 (est. 1984)
CAPITAL — Singapore

Singapore, Malacca and Penang were the British settlements which, together with the Federated Malay States, composed the former colony of Straits Settlements. On April 1, 1946, Singapore became a separate colony when the Straits Settlements colony was dissolved. Malacca and Penang joined the Malayan Union, which was renamed the Federation of Malaya in 1948.

See Straits Settlements for stamps of India canceled Singapore.

100 Cents = 1 Dollar

Catalogue values for all unused stamps in this country are for Never Hinged items.

King George VI — A1

1948 Wmk. 4 Typo. *Perf. 14*

No.	Type	Description	Unused	Used
1	A1	1c black	.25	*.50*
2	A1	2c orange	.25	*.50*
3	A1	3c green	.75	*.80*
4	A1	4c chocolate	.50	*.50*
6	A1	6c gray	.60	*.65*
7	A1	8c rose red	1.10	*.95*
9	A1	10c plum	.50	.25
11	A1	15c ultra	8.50	.40
12	A1	20c dk green & blk	5.00	.55
14	A1	25c org & rose lilac	6.00	.60
16	A1	40c dk vio & rose red	10.00	8.00
17	A1	50c ultra & black	5.50	.40
18	A1	$1 vio brn & ultra	14.00	4.50
19	A1	$2 rose red & emer	50.00	8.00
20	A1	$5 chocolate & emer	120.00	9.00
		Nos. 1-20 (15)	222.95	35.60
		Set, hinged	130.00	

1949-52 *Perf. 18*

No.	Type	Description	Unused	Used
1a	A1	1c black ('52)	.75	1.75
2a	A1	2c orange	1.50	1.50
4a	A1	4c chocolate	2.00	.25
5	A1	5c rose violet ('52)	4.75	1.00
6a	A1	6c gray ('52)	2.00	2.00
8	A1	8c green ('52)	9.00	3.00
9a	A1	10c plum ('50)	.70	.25
10	A1	12c rose red ('52)	14.00	12.50
11a	A1	15c ultra ('50)	22.50	.50
12a	A1	20c dark green & black	12.00	4.00
13	A1	20c ultra ('52)	10.00	.75
14a	A1	25c org & rose lil ('50)	4.00	.25
15	A1	35c dk vio & rose red ('52)	10.00	2.50
16a	A1	40c dk vio & rose red ('51)	42.50	18.00
17a	A1	50c ultra & black ('50)	7.50	.30
18a	A1	$1 violet brown & ultra	16.50	.90
b.		Wmk. 4a (error)	*16,500.*	*6,500.*
19a	A1	$2 rose red & emer ('51)	95.00	3.25
b.		Wmk. 4a (error)	*21,000.*	
20a	A1	$5 choc & emerald ('51)	200.00	4.00
		Nos. 1a-20a (18)	454.70	56.70
		Set, hinged	225.00	

Common Design Types pictured following the introduction.

Silver Wedding Issue

Common Design Types
Inscribed: "Singapore"

1948, Oct. 25 Photo. *Perf. 14x14½*

No.	Type	Description	Unused	Used
21	CD304	10c purple	1.00	.40

Perf. 11½x11

Engraved; Name Typographed

No.	Type	Description	Unused	Used
22	CD305	$5 light brown	115.00	45.00

UPU Issue

Common Design Types
Inscribed: "Malaya-Singapore"
Engr.; Name Typo. on 15c, 25c
Perf. 13½, 11x11½

1949, Oct. 10 Wmk. 4

No.	Type	Description	Unused	Used
23	CD306	10c rose violet	1.00	.70
24	CD307	15c indigo	4.75	3.00
25	CD308	25c orange	5.75	4.50
26	CD309	50c slate	6.50	5.00
		Nos. 23-26 (4)	18.00	13.20

SLOVAKIA

slō-'vä-kē-ə

LOCATION — Central Europe
GOVT. — Independent republic
AREA — 18,932 sq. mi.
POP. — 5,296,768 (est. 1992)
CAPITAL — Bratislava

Formerly a province of Czechoslovakia, Slovakia declared its independence in Mar., 1939. A treaty was immediately concluded with Germany guaranteeing Slovakian independence but providing for German "protection" for 25 years.

100 Halierov = 1 Koruna

Catalogue values for unused stamps in this country are for never hinged items, beginning with Scott 26 in the regular postage section, Scott B1 in the semi-postal section, Scott C1 in the airmail section, Scott EX1 in the personal delivery section, Scott J1 in the postage due section, and Scott P10 in the newspaper section.

Watermark

Wmk. 263 — Double-Barred Cross Multiple

Stamps of Czechoslovakia, 1928-39, Overprinted in Red or Blue

1939 *Perf. 10, 12½, 12x12½*

No.	Type	Description	Unused	Used
2	A29	5h dk ultra	1.50	1.40
3	A29	10h brown	.25	.25
4	A29	20h red (Bl)	.25	.25
5	A29	25h green	6.00	5.00
6	A29	30h red vio (Bl)	.25	.25
7	A61a	40h dark blue	.25	.25
8	A73	50h deep green	.25	.25
9	A63	50h deep green	.25	.25
10	A63	60h dull violet	.25	.25
11	A63	60h dull blue	9.50	*10.25*
12	A60	1k rose lake (Bl) (On No. 212)	.25	.25

Overprinted Diagonally

No.	Type	Description	Unused	Used
13	A64	1.20k rose lil (Bl)	1.25	1.25
14	A65	1.50k carmine (Bl)	1.25	1.25
15	A79	1.60k ol grn (Bl)	2.00	*2.75*
16	A66	2k dk bl grn	2.00	*2.75*
17	A67	2.50k dark blue	1.25	1.25
18	A68	3k brown	1.25	1.25
19	A69	3.50k dk violet	27.50	27.50
20	A69	3.50k dk vio (Bl)	40.00	40.00
21	A70	4k dk violet	17.50	17.50
22	A71	5k green	22.50	*22.50*
23	A72	10k blue	200.00	175.00
		Nos. 2-23 (22)	335.50	*311.65*

Excellent counterfeit overprints exist.

Stefánik Type of Czechoslovakia

Gen. Milan Stefánik

1939, Mar. 30 Engr. *Perf. 12½*

No.	Type	Description	Unused	Used
23A	A63	60h dark blue	45.00	37.50

Prepared by Czechoslovakia prior to the German occupation March 15, 1939. Subsequently issued for use in Slovakia.

Andrej Hlinka — A1

Overprinted in Red or Blue

Perf. 12½

1939, Apr. Unwmk. Photo.

No.	Type	Description	Unused	Used
24	A1	50h dark green (R)	.70	.70
a.		Perf. 10½	5.00	2.50
b.		Perf. 10½x12½	25.00	12.50
25	A1	1k dk car rose (Bl)	.75	.65
a.		Perf. 10½	1,200.	*1,000.*
		Never hinged	2,100.	
b.		Perf. 10½x12½	30.00	17.50

Catalogue values for unused stamps in this section, from this point to the end of the section, are for Never Hinged items.

Andrej Hlinka — A2

1939 Unwmk. *Perf. 12½*

No.	Type	Description	Unused	Used
26	A2	5h brt ultra	.55	.45
27	A2	10h olive green	.90	.70
a.		Perf. 10½x12½	200.00	120.00
b.		Perf. 10½	600.00	100.00
28	A2	20h orange red	.90	.70
a.		Imperf.	.85	.80
29	A2	30h dp violet	.90	.70
a.		Imperf.	1.00	*1.25*
b.		Perf. 10½x12½	45.00	20.00
c.		Perf. 10½	55.00	20.00
30	A2	50h dk green	.90	.70
31	A2	1k dk carmine rose	1.25	.70
32	A2	2.50k brt blue	1.25	.30
a.		Perf. 10½x12½	225.00	130.00
33	A2	3k black brown	3.00	.50
a.		Perf. 10½x12½	15.00	7.00
b.		Perf. 10½	15.00	7.00
		Nos. 26-33 (8)	9.65	*4.75*

On Nos. 32 and 33 a pearl frame surrounds the medallion. See Nos. 55-57, 69 (in Scott Standard catalogue, Vol. 6).

General Stefánik and Memorial Tomb — A3

1939, May *Perf. 12½*

Size: 25x20mm

No.	Type	Description	Unused	Used
34	A3	40h dark blue	1.10	
35	A3	60h slate green	1.10	
36	A3	1k gray violet	1.10	

Size: 30x23¾mm

No.	Type	Description	Unused	Used
37	A3	2k bl vio & sepia	1.25	
		Nos. 34-37 (4)	4.55	

20th anniv. of the death of Gen. Milan Stefánik, but not issued. Exists favor-canceled. Values, same as mint stamps.

Rev. Josef Murgas and Radio Towers — A4

1939 Unwmk.

No.	Type	Description	Unused	Used
38	A4	60h purple	.40	.30
39	A4	1.20k slate black	.75	.25

10th anniv. of the death of Rev. Josef Murgas. See No. 65 in Scott Standard catalogue, Vol. 6.

Girl Embroidering A5

Woodcutter A6

Girl at Spring — A7

1939-44 Wmk. 263 *Perf. 12½*

No.	Type	Description	Unused	Used
40	A5	2k dk blue green	6.25	.50
41	A6	4k copper brown	1.40	1.00
42	A7	5k orange red	1.00	.50
a.		Perf. 10 ('44)	1.25	1.00
		Nos. 40-42 (3)	8.65	2.00

Dr. Josef Tiso — A8

1939-44 Wmk. 263 *Perf. 12½*

No.	Type	Description	Unused	Used
43	A8	50h slate green	.45	.30
43A	A8	70h dk red brn ('42)	.35	.25
b.		Perf. 10½ ('44)	.35	.25

See No. 88 in Scott Standard catalogue, Vol. 6.

Presidential Residence — A9

1940, Mar. 14

No.	Type	Description	Unused	Used
44	A9	10k deep blue	1.00	.75

Tatra Mountains A10

Krivan Peak A11

Edelweiss in the Tatra Mountains
A12

Chamois
A13

Church at Javorina — A14

1940-43 Wmk. 263 *Perf. 12½*

Size: 17x21mm

No.	Type	Description	Unused	Used
45	A10	5h dk olive grn	.30	.25
46	A11	10h deep brown	.25	.25
47	A12	20h blue black	.25	.25
48	A13	25h olive brown	.55	.25
49	A14	30h chestnut brown	.35	.25
a.		Perf. 10½ ('43)	2.50	1.00
		Nos. 45-49 (5)	1.70	1.25

See Nos. 84-87, 103-107 in Scott Standard catalogue, Vol. 6.

Hlinka Type of 1939

1940-42 Wmk. 263 *Perf. 12½*

No.	Type	Description	Unused	Used
55	A2	1k dk car rose	.90	.60
56	A2	2.50k brt blue ('42)	1.25	.75
a.		Perf. 10½	.60	.60
57	A2	3k black brn ('41)	2.00	1.00
a.		Perf. 10½	2.00	.90

On Nos. 56 and 57 a pearl frame surrounds the medallion.

SEMI-POSTAL STAMPS

Catalogue values for unused stamps in this section are for Never Hinged items.

Josef Tiso — SP1

Wmk. 263

1939, Nov. 6 Photo. *Perf. 12½*

No.	Type	Description	Unused	Used
B1	SP1	2.50k + 2.50k royal blue	3.75	*4.00*

The surtax was used for Child Welfare.

AIR POST STAMPS

Catalogue values for unused stamps in this section are for Never Hinged items.

Planes over Tatra Mountains
AP1 AP2

Perf. 12½

1939, Nov. 20 Photo. Unwmk.

No.	Type	Description	Unused	Used
C1	AP1	30h violet	.40	.40
C2	AP1	50h dark green	.40	.40
C3	AP1	1k vermilion	.40	.40
C4	AP2	2k grnsh black	.65	.65
C5	AP2	3k dark brown	1.00	1.00
C6	AP2	4k slate blue	1.90	1.90
		Nos. C1-C6 (6)	4.75	4.75

See No. C10 in Scott Standard catalogue, Vol. 6.

Plane in Flight — AP3

1940, Nov. 30 Wmk. 263 *Perf. 12½*

No.	Type	Description	Unused	Used
C7	AP3	5k dk violet brn	1.50	1.50
C8	AP3	10k gray black	1.75	1.75
C9	AP3	20k myrtle green	2.25	2.25
		Nos. C7-C9 (3)	5.50	5.50

PERSONAL DELIVERY STAMPS

Catalogue values for unused stamps in this section are for Never Hinged items.

PD1

1940 Wmk. 263 Photo. *Imperf.*

No.	Type	Description	Unused	Used
EX1	PD1	50h indigo & blue	1.00	*1.75*
EX2	PD1	50h carmine & rose	1.00	*1.75*

POSTAGE DUE STAMPS

Catalogue values for unused stamps in this section are for Never Hinged items.

D1

1939 Unwmk. Photo. *Perf. 12½*

No.	Type	Description	Unused	Used
J1	D1	5h bright blue	1.00	.55
J2	D1	10h bright blue	.50	.55
J3	D1	20h bright blue	.50	.55
J4	D1	30h bright blue	3.00	1.00
J5	D1	40h bright blue	.70	.75
J6	D1	50h bright blue	2.50	.80
J7	D1	60h bright blue	2.00	.80
J8	D1	1k dark carmine	14.00	8.25
J9	D1	2k dark carmine	14.00	2.50
J10	D1	5k dark carmine	8.00	2.50
J11	D1	10k dark carmine	55.00	7.50
J12	D1	20k dark carmine	18.00	9.25
		Nos. J1-J12 (12)	119.20	35.00

1940-41 Wmk. 263

No.	Type	Description	Unused	Used
J13	D1	5h bright blue ('41)	.75	.55
J14	D1	10h bright blue ('41)	.30	.30
J15	D1	20h bright blue ('41)	.50	.30
J16	D1	30h bright blue ('41)	4.00	2.00
J17	D1	40h bright blue ('41)	.60	.55
J18	D1	50h bright blue ('41)	.75	.95
J19	D1	60h bright blue	.90	.95
J20	D1	1k dk car ('41)	.90	1.10
J21	D1	2k dk car ('41)	20.00	9.00
J22	D1	5k dk car ('41)	4.00	2.75
J23	D1	10k dk car ('41)	3.00	3.25
		Nos. J13-J23 (11)	35.70	21.70

NEWSPAPER STAMPS

Newspaper Stamps of Czechoslovakia, 1937, Overprinted in Red or Blue

1939, Apr. Unwmk. *Imperf.*

No.	Type	Description	Unused	Used
P1	N2	2h bister brn (Bl)	.50	.40
P2	N2	5h dull blue (R)	.50	.40
P3	N2	7h red org (Bl)	.50	.40
P4	N2	9h emerald (R)	.50	.40
P5	N2	10h henna brn (Bl)	.50	.40
P6	N2	12h ultra (R)	.50	.40
P7	N2	20h dk green (R)	1.10	.95
P8	N2	50h dk brown (Bl)	3.00	2.50
P9	N2	1k grnsh gray (R)	11.00	10.00
		Nos. P1-P9 (9)	18.10	15.85

Excellent counterfeits exist of Nos. P1-P9.

Catalogue values for unused stamps in this section, from this point to the end of the section, are for Never Hinged items.

Arms of Slovakia — N1

1939 Typo.

No.	Type	Description	Unused	Used
P10	N1	2h ocher	.30	.25
P11	N1	5h ultra	.45	.40
P12	N1	7h red orange	.35	.30
P13	N1	9h emerald	.35	.30
P14	N1	10h henna brown	1.60	1.10
P15	N1	12h dk ultra	.40	.35
P16	N1	20h dark green	1.60	1.10
P17	N1	50h red brown	1.90	1.25
P18	N1	1k grnsh gray	1.60	1.10
		Nos. P10-P18 (9)	8.55	6.15

1940-41 Wmk. 263

No.	Type	Description	Unused	Used
P20	N1	5h ultra	.25	.25
P23	N1	10h henna brown	.25	.25
P24	N1	15h brt purple ('41)	.30	.25
P25	N1	20h dark green	.60	.50
P26	N1	25h lt blue ('41)	.60	.50
P27	N1	40h red org ('41)	.60	.50
P28	N1	50h chocolate	1.10	.75
P29	N1	1k grnsh gray ('41)	1.10	.75
P30	N1	2k emerald ('41)	2.25	1.60
		Nos. P20-P30 (9)	7.05	5.35

SOLOMON ISLANDS

'sä-lə-mən 'ī-ləndz

British Solomon Islands

LOCATION — West Pacific Ocean, east of Papua
GOVT. — British Protectorate
AREA — 11,500 sq. mi.
POP. — 258,193 (1984)
CAPITAL — Honiara

The Solomons include 10 large islands and four groups of small islands extending over an area of 375,000 square miles.

12 Pence = 1 Shilling
20 Shillings = 1 Pound

Catalogue values for unused stamps in this country are for Never Hinged items, beginning with Scott 80 in the regular postage section.

War Canoe — A1

Unwmk.

1907, Feb. 14 Litho. *Perf. 11*

No.	Type	Description	Unused	Used
1	A1	½p ultra	11.00	*16.00*
2	A1	1p red	27.50	*30.00*
3	A1	2p dull blue	50.00	*35.00*
a.		Horiz. pair, imperf. btwn.	*15,000.*	
4	A1	2½p orange	38.50	*50.00*
a.		Vert. pair, imperf. btwn.	*7,500.*	
b.		Horiz. pair, imperf. btwn.	*12,000.*	*7,000.*
5	A1	5p yellow green	67.50	*80.00*
6	A1	6p chocolate	75.00	*77.50*
a.		Vertical pair, imperf. btwn.	*7,000.*	
7	A1	1sh violet	97.50	*110.00*
		Nos. 1-7 (7)	367.00	398.50

Imperf. between varieties should be accompanied by certificates of authenticity issued by competent authorities. Excellent counterfeits are plentiful.

War Canoe — A2

Wmk. Multiple Crown and CA (3)

1908-11 Engr. *Perf. 14*

No.	Type	Description	Unused	Used
8	A2	½p green	1.75	1.25
9	A2	1p carmine	1.50	1.25
10	A2	2p gray	1.50	1.25
11	A2	2½p ultra	4.25	2.50
12	A2	4p red, *yel* ('11)	3.75	13.50
13	A2	5p olive green	10.50	8.75
14	A2	6p claret	11.50	8.25
15	A2	1sh black, *green*	9.75	*9.25*
16	A2	2sh vio, *bl* ('10)	50.00	*70.00*
17	A2	2sh6p red, *bl* ('10)	62.50	*95.00*
18	A2	5sh bl, *yel* ('10)	115.00	*140.00*
		Nos. 8-18 (11)	272.00	*351.00*
		Set, ovptd. "SPECIMEN"	325.00	

George V — A3

Inscribed "POSTAGE - POSTAGE"

1913-24 Typo.

No.	Type	Description	Unused	Used
19	A3	½p green	1.10	*4.00*
20	A3	1p carmine	6.75	*17.50*
21	A3	3p violet, *yel*	2.00	*4.75*
a.		3p violet, *orange buff*	12.00	*27.50*
22	A3	11p dull violet & red	5.75	*14.00*

Wmk. 4

No.	Type	Description	Unused	Used
23	A3	1½p scarlet ('24)	2.50	.80
		Nos. 19-23 (5)	18.10	*41.05*
		Nos. 19-22, ovptd. "SPECIMEN"	80.00	

Inscribed "POSTAGE - REVENUE"

1914-23 Wmk. 3

No.	Type	Description	Unused	Used
28	A3	½p green	1.90	*13.50*
a.		½p yellow green ('17)	6.75	*21.00*
29	A3	1p carmine	1.75	1.50
a.		1p scarlet ('17)	7.25	*7.50*
30	A3	2p gray	4.75	*10.50*
31	A3	2½p ultra	5.00	*5.75*

Chalky Paper

No.	Type	Description	Unused	Used
32	A3	3p vio, *yel* ('23)	29.00	*140.00*
33	A3	4p blk & red, *yel*	2.25	*3.00*
34	A3	5p dull vio & ol grn	24.00	*35.00*
a.		5p brown purple & olive green	24.00	*35.00*
35	A3	6p dull vio & red vio	7.00	*16.00*
36	A3	1sh blk, *green*	5.50	*8.00*
a.		1sh blk, *bl grn, ol back*	8.50	*27.50*
37	A3	2sh dull vio & ultra, *bl*	8.50	*11.50*
38	A3	2sh6p blk & red, *bl*	11.00	*22.50*
39	A3	5sh grn & red, *yel*	50.00	*55.00*
a.		5sh green & red, *orange buff*	55.00	*80.00*
40	A3	10sh grn & red, *grn*	97.50	*100.00*
41	A3	£1 vio & blk, *red*	300.00	150.00
		Nos. 28-41 (14)	548.15	*572.25*
		Set, ovptd. "SPECIMEN"	450.00	

Inscribed "POSTAGE - REVENUE"

1922-31 Wmk. 4

No.	Type	Description	Unused	Used
43	A3	½p green	.50	*4.00*
44	A3	1p carmine ('23)	12.50	12.50
45	A3	1p violet ('27)	1.10	*8.50*
46	A3	2p gray ('23)	5.50	*17.00*
47	A3	3p ultra ('23)	.85	*5.25*

Chalky Paper

No.	Type	Description	Unused	Used
48	A3	4p blk & red, *yel* ('27)	4.25	*26.00*
49	A3	4½p red brn ('31)	3.75	*22.50*
50	A3	5p dull vio & ol grn	3.75	*32.50*
51	A3	6p dull vio & red vio	4.50	*32.50*
52	A3	1sh black, *emer*	3.75	*15.00*
53	A3	2sh dull vio & ultra, *bl* ('27)	25.00	*45.00*
54	A3	2sh6p blk & red, *bl*	8.75	*55.00*
55	A3	5sh grn & red, *yel*	40.00	*65.00*

56	A3	10sh grn & red, *emer* ('25)	150.00	*130.00*
		Nos. 43-56 (14)	264.20	*470.75*

No. 49 is on ordinary paper.

Common Design Types pictured following the introduction.

Silver Jubilee Issue

Common Design Type

1935, May 6 Engr. *Perf. 13½x14*

60	CD301	1½p car & dk bl	1.25	1.50
61	CD301	3p bl & brn	5.25	*7.50*
62	CD301	6p ol grn & lt bl	14.00	*12.00*
63	CD301	1sh brt vio & ind	6.75	*17.00*
		Nos. 60-63 (4)	27.25	38.00
		Set, never hinged	44.00	
		Set, perforated "SPECIMEN"	140.00	

Coronation Issue

Common Design Type

1937, May 13 *Perf. 11x11½*

64	CD302	1p dark purple	.25	*1.00*
65	CD302	1½p dk car	.25	*.55*
66	CD302	3p deep ultra	.40	*.45*
		Nos. 64-66 (3)	.90	2.00
		Set, never hinged	1.40	
		Set, perforated "SPECIMEN"	110.00	

Spears and Shield — A4

Policeman and Chief — A5

Artificial Island, Malaita — A6

Canoe House, New Georgia A7

Roviana War Canoe — A8

View of Munda Point — A9

Meeting House, Reef Islands A10

Coconut Plantation A11

Breadfruit A12

Tinakula Volcano, Santa Cruz Islands A13

Scrub Fowl — A14

Malaita Canoe — A15

Perf. 12½, 13½ (A7, A13, A14)

1939-51 Wmk. 4

67	A4	½p deep grn & ultra	.25	*1.25*
		Never hinged	.40	
68	A5	1p dk pur & choc	.25	*1.50*
		Never hinged	.40	
69	A6	1½p car & sl grn	1.00	*1.75*
		Never hinged	2.00	
70	A7	2p blk & org brn	1.50	*1.75*
		Never hinged	3.00	
a.		2p black & red brown ('43)	.35	*1.75*
		Never hinged	.75	
b.		Perf. 12 ('51)	.50	*1.50*
		Never hinged	1.00	
71	A8	2½p ol grn & rose vio	2.25	*2.25*
		Never hinged	3.75	
a.		Vert. pair, imperf. horiz.	*31,600.*	
72	A9	3p ultra & blk, perf. 13½	.60	*2.00*
		Never hinged	1.50	
a.		Perf. 12 ('51)	.85	*2.50*
		Never hinged	2.00	
73	A10	4½p dk brn & yel grn	3.25	*13.00*
		Never hinged	5.25	
74	A11	6p rose lil & dk pur	1.50	*1.00*
		Never hinged	2.75	
75	A12	1sh blk & grn	1.50	*1.00*
		Never hinged	2.50	
76	A13	2sh dp org & blk	6.50	*6.00*
		Never hinged	12.00	
a.		2sh dp org & vio blk ('43)	4.75	*6.50*
		Never hinged	13.00	
77	A14	2sh6p dull vio & blk	18.00	*4.50*
		Never hinged	30.00	
78	A15	5sh red & brt bl grn	18.00	13.00
		Never hinged	32.50	
79	A10	10sh red lil & ol ('42)	2.50	*8.50*
		Never hinged	5.00	
		Nos. 67-79 (13)	57.10	57.50
		Set, never hinged	100.00	

Catalogue values for unused stamps in this section, from this point to the end of the section, are for Never Hinged items.

Peace Issue

Common Design Type

Perf. 13½x14

1946, Oct. 15 Wmk. 4 Engr.

80	CD303	1½p carmine	.25	1.25
81	CD303	3p deep blue	.25	.25
		Set, perforated "SPECIMEN"	92.50	

Silver Wedding Issue

Common Design Types

1949, Mar. 14 Photo. *Perf. 14x14½*

82	CD304	2p black	.40	.40

Perf. 11½x11

Engr.; Name Typo.

83	CD305	10sh red violet	13.00	13.00

UPU Issue

Common Design Types

Engr.; Name Typo. on 3p and 5p

Perf. 13½, 11x11½

1949, Oct. 10 Wmk. 4

84	CD306	2p red brown	.60	.85
85	CD307	3p indigo	2.25	1.25
86	CD308	5p green	.60	*1.40*
87	CD309	1sh slate	.60	*1.40*
		Nos. 84-87 (4)	4.05	4.90

POSTAGE DUE STAMPS

D1

Perf. 12

1940, Sept. 1 Typo. Wmk. 4

J1	D1	1p emerald	4.50	*8.00*
J2	D1	2p dark red	4.75	*8.00*
J3	D1	3p chocolate	4.75	*13.00*
J4	D1	4p dark blue	7.25	*13.00*
J5	D1	5p deep green	8.00	*27.50*
J6	D1	6p brt red vio	8.00	*20.00*
J7	D1	1sh dull violet	10.00	*32.50*
J8	D1	1sh6p turq green	17.50	*60.00*
		Nos. J1-J8 (8)	64.75	*182.00*
		Set, never hinged	120.00	
		Set, perforated "SPECIMEN"	225.00	

SOMALIA

sō-'mä-lē-ə

(Italian Somaliland)

(Benadir)

LOCATION — Eastern Africa, bordering on the Indian Ocean and the Gulf of Aden
GOVT. — Italian Colony
AREA — 246,201 sq. mi.
POP. — 3,862,000 (est. 1982)
CAPITAL — Mogadiscio

The former Italian colony which included the territory west of the Juba River became known as Oltre Giuba (Trans-Juba), was absorbed into Italian East Africa in 1936.

4 Besas = 1 Anna
16 Annas = 1 Rupee
100 Besas = 1 Rupee (1922)
100 Centesimi = 1 Lira (1905, 1925)

Used values in italics are for postally used Italian Somalia stamps. CTO's sell for about the same as unused, hinged stamps.

Watermark

Wmk. 140 — Crown

Italian Somaliland

Elephant — A1

Lion — A2

Wmk. 140

1903, Oct. 12 Typo. *Perf. 14*

1	A1	1b brown	140.00	26.00
		Never hinged	350.00	
		On cover		375.00
2	A1	2b blue green	1.60	*15.00*
		Never hinged	3.75	
		On cover		265.00
3	A2	1a claret	1.60	*19.00*
		Never hinged	3.75	
		On cover		340.00
4	A2	2a orange brown	2.00	*37.50*
		Never hinged	4.50	
		On cover		525.00
5	A2	2½a blue	1.60	*37.50*
		Never hinged	3.75	
		On cover		1,000.
6	A2	5a orange	2.00	*75.00*
		Never hinged	4.50	
		On cover		2,000.
7	A2	10a lilac	2.00	*75.00*
		Never hinged	4.50	
		On cover		—
		Nos. 1-7 (7)	150.80	*285.00*
		Set on overfranked cover		*1,000.*

Covers: Cover values are for properly franked and traveled covers. Overpaid and other philatelic souvenirs sell for much less.

For surcharges see Nos. 8-27, 40-50, 70-77.

Surcharged

1905, Dec. 29

8	A2	15c on 5a org	*3,500.*	1,300.
		Never hinged	6,750.	
		On cover		5,000.
9	A2	40c on 10a lilac	1,100.	450.00
		Never hinged	2,250.	
		On cover		2,800.

Covers: Cover values are for properly franked and traveled covers, generally abroad. Internal covers, normally overpaid and not traveled, and other philatelic souvenirs sell for much less.

Surcharged

1906-07

10	A1	2c on 1b brown	6.00	*18.00*
		Never hinged	15.00	
		On cover		240.00
11	A1	5c on 2b blue grn	6.00	*13.50*
		Never hinged	15.00	
		On cover		115.00
a.		Double surcharge	350.00	
b.		Double surcharge, one invtd.		*5,250.*
c.		Pair, one without surcharge	*5,000.*	

Surcharges on No. 11c are virtually on top of each other. Certificates are necessary.

Surcharged

12	A2	10c on 1a claret	6.00	*13.50*
		Never hinged	15.00	
		On cover		110.00
13	A2	15c on 2a brn org ('06)	6.00	*13.50*
		Never hinged	15.00	
		On cover		150.00
14	A2	25c on 2½a blue	15.00	*14.00*
		Never hinged	37.50	
		On cover		165.00
15	A2	50c on 5a yellow	*30.00*	*35.00*
		Never hinged	75.00	
		On cover		300.00

Surcharged

16 A2 1 l on 10a lilac 30.00 45.00
Never hinged 75.00
On cover 825.00
Nos. 10-16 (7) 99.00 152.50

Covers: Cover values are for properly franked and traveled covers. Overpaid and other philatelic souvenirs sell for much less.

Nos. 15 and 16 With Bars Over Former Surcharge and

1916, Apr.

18 A2 5c on 50c on 5a yel 47.50 52.50
Never hinged 110.00
On cover 300.00
a. Double surcharge, one invtd. 5,000.
b. Lower left bar of surcharge omitted 120.00

19 A2 20c on 1 l on 10a dl lil 9.50 35.00
Never hinged 22.50
On cover 210.00
a. Bar of surcharge at top of stamp 125.00 125.00
b. Bar of surcharge omitted 675.00

No. 4 Surcharged

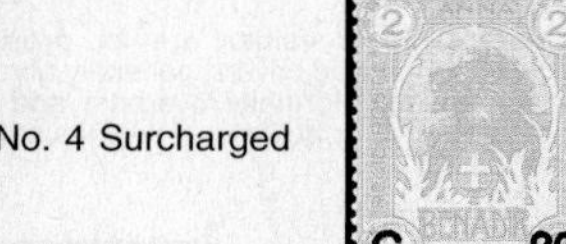

20 A2 20c on 2a org brn 22.50 15.00
Never hinged 55.00
On cover 150.00
Nos. 18-20 (3) 79.50 102.50

Nos. 11-16 Surcharged

a

b

1922, Feb. 1

22 A1(a) 3b on 5c on 2b 12.00 22.50
Never hinged 30.00
On cover 165.00

23 A2(b) 6c on 10c on 1a 22.50 18.00
Never hinged 55.00
On cover 180.00

24 A2(b) 9b on 15c on 2a 22.50 22.50
Never hinged 55.00
On cover 180.00

25 A2(b) 15b on 25c on 2½a 22.50 18.00
Never hinged 55.00
On cover 240.00
a. "15" at left omitted 300.00

26 A2(b) 30b on 50c on 5a 24.00 50.00
Never hinged 60.00
On cover 300.00

27 A2(b) 60b on 1 l on 10a 24.00 82.50
Never hinged 60.00
On cover 650.00
Nos. 22-27 (6) 127.50 213.50

Victory Issue

Italy Nos. 136-139 Surcharged

1922, Apr. *Perf. 14*

28 A64 3b on 5c olive grn 2.00 7.25
Never hinged 4.50
On cover 125.00
c. Surcharge denomination omitted 750.00

29 A64 6b on 10c red 2.00 7.25
Never hinged 4.50
On cover 225.00

30 A64 9b on 15c slate grn 2.00 11.00
Never hinged 4.50
On cover 240.00

31 A64 15b on 25c ultra 2.00 11.00
Never hinged 4.50
On cover 275.00
Nos. 28-31 (4) 8.00 36.50

Perf. 14x13½

28a A64 3b on 5c olive grn 4.75 16.00
Never hinged 9.00
29a A64 6b on 10c red 4.75 16.00
Never hinged 9.00
30a A64 9b on 15c slate grn 4.75 24.00
Never hinged 9.00
31a A64 15b on 25c ultra 4.75 24.00
Never hinged 9.00
Nos. 28a-31a (4) 19.00 80.00

Perf. 13½

29b A64 6b on 10c red 125.00 250.00
Never hinged 250.00
31b A64 15b on 25c ultra 125.00
Never hinged 250.00

Nos. 10-16 Surcharged with Bars and

c

d

1923, July 1

40 A1 1b brown 9.50 37.50
Never hinged 25.00
On cover 250.00

41 A1(c) 2b on 2c on 1b 9.50 37.50
Never hinged 25.00
On cover 175.00

42 A1(c) 3b on 2c on 1b 9.50 18.00
Never hinged 25.00
On cover 175.00

43 A2(d) 5b on 50c on 5a 9.50 19.00
Never hinged 25.00
On cover 125.00

44 A1(c) 6b on 5c on 2b 17.50 19.00
Never hinged 40.00
On cover 145.00

45 A2(d) 18b on 10c on 1a 17.50 19.00
Never hinged 40.00
On cover 190.00

46 A2(d) 20b on 15c on 2a 21.00 19.00
Never hinged 45.00
On cover 250.00

47 A2(d) 25b on 15c on 2a 21.00 19.00
Never hinged 45.00
On cover 250.00

48 A2(d) 30b on 25c on 2½a 24.00 24.00
Never hinged 55.00
On cover 225.00

49 A2(d) 60b on 1 l on 10a 24.00 52.50
Never hinged 55.00
On cover 475.00

50 A2(d) 1r on 1 l on 10a 65.00 65.00
Never hinged 135.00
On cover 675.00
Nos. 40-50 (11) 228.00 329.50

No. 40 is No. 10 with bars over the 1907 surcharge.

Propagation of the Faith Issue

Italy Nos. 143-146 Surcharged

1923, Oct. 24 **Wmk. 140**

51 A68 6b on 20c ol grn & brn org 11.50 50.00
Never hinged 25.00
On cover —

52 A68 13b on 30c cl & brn org 11.50 50.00
Never hinged 25.00
On cover —

53 A68 20b on 50c vio & brn org 7.50 57.50
Never hinged 14.50
On cover —

54 A68 30b on 1 l bl & brn org 7.50 87.50
Never hinged 14.50
On cover —
Nos. 51-54 (4) 38.00 245.00

Fascisti Issue

Italy Nos. 159-164 Surcharged in Red or Black

1923, Oct. 29 **Unwmk.** *Perf. 14*

55 A69 3b on 10c dk grn (R) 15.00 19.00
Never hinged 37.50
On cover 300.00

56 A69 13b on 30c dk vio (R) 15.00 19.00
Never hinged 37.50
On cover 300.00

57 A69 20b on 50c brn car 15.00 26.00
Never hinged 37.50
On cover 300.00

Wmk. 140

58 A70 30b on 1 l blue 15.00 50.00
Never hinged 37.50
On cover 575.00

59 A70 1r on 2 l brown 15.00 60.00
Never hinged 37.50
On cover 825.00

60 A71 3r on 5 l blk & bl (R) 15.00 90.00
Never hinged 37.50
On cover —
Nos. 55-60 (6) 90.00 264.00
Set on overfranked philatelic cover 750.00

Manzoni Issue

Italy Nos. 165-170 Surcharged in Red

1924, Apr. 1

61 A72 6b on 10c brn red & blk 11.00 75.00
Never hinged 30.00

62 A72 9b on 15c bl grn & blk 11.00 75.00
Never hinged 30.00

63 A72 13b on 30c blk & sl 11.00 75.00
Never hinged 30.00

64 A72 20b on 50c org brn & blk 11.00 75.00
Never hinged 30.00

Surcharged in Red

65 A72 30b on 1 l bl & blk 67.50 450.00
Never hinged 185.00

66 A72 3r on 5 l vio & blk 475.00 3,000.
Never hinged 1,200.
Nos. 61-66 (6) 586.50 3,750.

Covers bearing stamps of this issue are very scarce.

Victor Emmanuel Issue

Italy Nos. 175-177 Overprinted

1925-26 **Unwmk.** *Perf. 13½, 11*

67 A78 60c brown car 2.25 13.50
Never hinged 4.00
On cover 160.00
a. Perf. 11 180.00 375.00
Never hinged 350.00
On cover 475.00

68 A78 1 l dk bl, perf. 11 3.00 19.00
Never hinged 6.00
On cover 240.00
a. Perf. 13½ 10.50 57.50
Never hinged 24.00
On cover 475.00

69 A78 1.25 l dk blue ('26) 2.25 30.00
Never hinged 4.00
On cover 325.00
a. Perf. 11 1,050. 1,875.
Never hinged 1,900.
On cover 2,800.
Nos. 67-69 (3) 7.50 62.50

Stamps of 1907-16 with Bars over Original Values

1926, Mar. 1 **Wmk. 140** *Perf. 14*

70 A1 2c on 1b brown 26.00 52.50
Never hinged 75.00
On cover 275.00

71 A1 5c on 2b blue grn 18.00 26.00
Never hinged 50.00
On cover 175.00

72 A2 10c on 1a rose red 12.00 10.50
Never hinged 32.50
On cover 140.00

73 A2 15c on 2a org brn 12.00 13.50
Never hinged 32.50
On cover 160.00

74 A2 20c on 2a org brn 13.50 13.50
Never hinged 37.50
On cover 140.00

75 A2 25c on 2½a blue 13.50 18.00
Never hinged 37.50
On cover 200.00

76 A2 50c on 5a yellow 18.00 35.00
Never hinged 50.00
On cover 325.00

77 A2 1 l on 10a dull lil 26.00 45.00
Never hinged 75.00
On cover 600.00
Nos. 70-77 (8) 139.00 214.00

Saint Francis of Assisi Issue

Italy Nos. 178-180 Overprinted

1926, Apr. 12 *Perf. 14*

78 A79 20c gray green 2.25 13.50
Never hinged 6.00
On cover 125.00

79 A80 40c dark violet 2.25 13.50
Never hinged 6.00
On cover 140.00

80 A81 60c red brown 2.25 24.00
Never hinged 6.00
On cover 140.00

Italy Nos. 182 and Type of 1926 Overprinted in Red

Unwmk. *Perf. 11*

81 A82 1.25 l dark blue 2.25 35.00
Never hinged 6.00
On cover 260.00

Perf. 14

82 A83 5 l + 2.50 l ol grn 6.50 67.50
Never hinged 16.00
On cover —
Nos. 78-82 (5) 15.50 153.50
Set on overfranked philatelic cover 425.00

Italian Stamps of 1901-26 Overprinted

1926-30 **Wmk. 140**

83 A43 2c org brn 7.50 6.50
Never hinged 12.00
On cover 65.00

84 A48 5c green 7.50 6.50
Never hinged 12.00
On cover 55.00

85 A48 10c claret 7.50 .40
Never hinged 9.50
On cover 55.00

86 A49 20c violet brown 11.00 2.40
Never hinged 9.50
On cover 100.00

87 A46 25c grn & pale grn 7.50 1.60
Never hinged 9.50
On cover 72.50

88 A49 30c gray ('30) 20.00 50.00
Never hinged 47.50
On cover 275.00

89 A49 60c brn org 9.00 12.00
Never hinged 14.50
On cover 325.00
a. Double overprint 4,000.

90 A46 75c dk red & rose 160.00 50.00
Never hinged 325.00
On cover 300.00

91 A46 1 l brown & grn 9.00 .80
Never hinged 14.50
On cover 105.00

92 A46 1.25 l blue & ultra 19.00 2.40
Never hinged 32.50
On cover 250.00
93 A46 2 l dk grn & org 42.50 16.00
Never hinged 82.50
On cover 550.00
94 A46 2.50 l dk grn & org 42.50 24.00
Never hinged 82.50
On cover 675.00
95 A46 5 l blue & rose 90.00 57.50
Never hinged 215.00
On cover 2,800.
96 A51 10 l gray grn & red 90.00 *97.50*
Never hinged 215.00
On cover —
Nos. 83-96 (14) 523.00 327.60

Volta Issue

Type of Italy, 1927, Overprinted

1927, Oct. 10
97 A84 20c purple 6.00 *37.50*
Never hinged 12.00
On cover 240.00
98 A84 50c deep orange 9.00 *27.50*
Never hinged 20.00
On cover 240.00
a. Double overprint 175.00
Never hinged 375.00
b. As "#98" with "Tripolitania" inverted 525.00
99 A84 1.25 l brt blue 13.50 *60.00*
Never hinged 27.50
On cover 450.00
Nos. 97-99 (3) 28.50 *125.00*
Set on overfranked philatelic cover *350.00*

Italian Stamps of 1927-28 Overprinted in Black or Red

1928-30
100 A86 7½c lt brown 34.00 *75.00*
Never hinged 47.50
On cover 300.00
a. Double overprint 550.00
Never hinged 1,000.
101 A85 50c brn & sl (R) 34.00 6.00
Never hinged 47.50
On cover 60.00
102 A86 50c brt vio ('30) 60.00 *90.00*
Never hinged 100.00
On cover 160.00

Perf. 11
Unwmk.
103 A85 1.75 l deep brown 105.00 19.00
Never hinged 190.00
On cover 95.00
Nos. 100-103 (4) 233.00 *190.00*

Monte Cassino Issue

Monte Cassino Issue of Italy Overprinted in Red or Blue

1929, Oct. 14 Wmk. 140 *Perf. 14*
104 A96 20c dk green (R) 6.00 *21.00*
Never hinged 16.00
On cover 240.00
105 A96 25c red org (Bl) 6.00 *21.00*
Never hinged 16.00
On cover 175.00
106 A98 50c + 10c crim (Bl) 6.00 *22.50*
Never hinged 16.00
On cover 125.00
107 A98 75c + 15c ol brn (R) 6.00 *22.50*
Never hinged 16.00
On cover 240.00
108 A96 1.25 l + 25c dk vio (R) 13.50 *42.50*
Never hinged 37.50
On cover 300.00
109 A98 5 l + 1 l saph (R) 13.50 *45.00*
Never hinged 37.50
On cover —

Overprinted in Red

Unwmk.
110 A100 10 l + 2 l gray brn 13.50 *67.50*
Never hinged 37.50
On cover —
Nos. 104-110 (7) 64.50 *242.00*

Royal Wedding Issue

Type of Italian Royal Wedding Stamps of 1930 Overprinted

1930, Mar. 17 Wmk. 140
111 A101 20c yellow green 3.00 *9.00*
Never hinged 4.00
On cover 110.00
112 A101 50c + 10c dp org 2.25 *9.00*
Never hinged 3.00
On cover 145.00
113 A101 1.25 l + 25c rose red 2.25 *18.00*
Never hinged 3.00
On cover 240.00
Nos. 111-113 (3) 7.50 *36.00*
Set on overfranked philatelic cover *160.00*

Ferrucci Issue

Types of Italian Stamps of 1930 Overprinted in Red or Blue

1930, July 26
114 A102 20c violet (R) 6.00 *6.00*
Never hinged 13.00
On cover 120.00
115 A103 25c dk grn (R) 6.00 *6.00*
Never hinged 13.00
On cover 145.00
116 A103 50c black (R) 6.00 *11.00*
Never hinged 13.00
On cover 120.00
117 A103 1.25 l dp bl (R) 6.00 *21.00*
Never hinged 13.00
On cover 275.00
118 A104 5 l + 2 l dp car (bl) 13.50 *45.00*
Never hinged 26.00
On cover —
Nos. 114-118 (5) 37.50 *89.00*
Set on overfranked philatelic cover *275.00*

Virgil Issue

Types of Italian Stamps of 1930 Overprinted in Red or Blue

1930, Dec. 4 Photo. Wmk. 140
119 A106 15c violet blue 1.10 *11.00*
Never hinged 2.75
On cover 150.00
120 A106 20c org brn 1.10 *4.50*
Never hinged 2.75
On cover 90.00
121 A106 25c dark green 1.10 *4.50*
Never hinged 2.75
On cover 82.50
122 A106 30c lt brown 1.10 *4.50*
Never hinged 2.75
On cover 90.00
123 A106 50c dull violet 1.10 *4.50*
Never hinged 2.75
On cover 75.00
124 A106 75c rose red 1.10 *9.00*
Never hinged 2.75
On cover 175.00
125 A106 1.25 l gray blue 1.10 *11.00*
Never hinged 2.75
On cover 275.00

Engr.
Unwmk.
126 A106 5 l + 1.50 l dk vio 4.50 *45.00*
Never hinged 8.75
On cover —
127 A106 10 l + 2.50 l ol brn 4.50 *67.50*
Never hinged 8.75
On cover —
Nos. 119-127 (9) 16.70 *161.50*
Set on overfranked philatelic cover *450.00*

Saint Anthony of Padua Issue

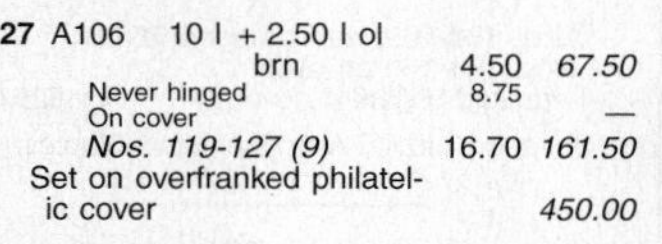

Types of Italian Stamps of 1931 Overprinted in Blue or Red

1931, May 7 Photo. Wmk. 140
129 A116 20c brown (Bl) 1.50 *21.00*
Never hinged 3.75
On cover 110.00
130 A116 25c green (R) 1.50 *7.50*
Never hinged 3.75
On cover 110.00
131 A118 30c gray brn (Bl) 1.50 *7.50*
Never hinged 3.75
On cover 175.00
132 A118 50c dull vio (Bl) 1.50 *7.50*
Never hinged 3.75
On cover 110.00
133 A120 1.25 l slate bl (R) 1.50 *37.50*
Never hinged 3.75
On cover 360.00

Overprinted in Red or Black

Engr. Unwmk.
134 A121 75c black (R) 1.50 *21.00*
Never hinged 3.75
On cover 300.00
135 A122 5 l + 2.50 l dk brn (Bk) 10.50 *75.00*
Never hinged 19.00
On cover —
Nos. 129-135 (7) 19.50 *177.00*
Set on overfranked philatelic cover *475.00*

Italy Nos. 218, 221 Overprinted in Red

1931 Wmk. 140
136 A94 25c dk green (R) 15.00 *25.00*
Never hinged 35.00
On cover 260.00
137 A95 50c purple (R) 15.00 4.50
Never hinged 35.00
On cover 125.00

Lighthouse at Cape Guardafui — A3

Tower at Mnara Ciromo — A4

Governor's Palace at Mogadishu — A5

Termite Nest — A6

Ostrich — A7

Hippopotamus — A8

Greater Kudu — A9

Lion — A10

1932 Wmk. 140 Photo. *Perf. 12*
138 A3 5c dp brn 12.00 *15.00*
Never hinged 32.50
On cover 65.00
139 A3 7½c violet 19.00 *37.50*
Never hinged 45.00
On cover 200.00
140 A3 10c gray black 26.00 .40
Never hinged 65.00
On cover 4.75
141 A3 15c olive green 9.50 1.20
Never hinged 25.00
On cover 26.00
142 A4 20c carmine 400.00 .40
Never hinged 935.00
On cover 2.40
143 A4 25c dp grn 9.50 .40
Never hinged 25.00
On cover 2.40
144 A4 30c dk brn 105.00 1.20
Never hinged 190.00
On cover 7.25
145 A5 35c dark blue 11.00 *22.50*
Never hinged 30.00
On cover 90.00
146 A5 50c violet 475.00 .40
Never hinged 1,150.
On cover 2.40
147 A5 75c carmine 11.00 .80
Never hinged 30.00
On cover 12.00
148 A6 1.25 l dark blue 37.50 .80
Never hinged 92.50
On cover 12.00
149 A6 1.75 l red orange 26.00 .80
Never hinged 60.00
On cover 12.00
150 A6 2 l carmine 11.00 .40
Never hinged 30.00
On cover 14.50
151 A7 2.55 l indigo 60.00 *135.00*
Never hinged 150.00
On cover 800.00
152 A7 5 l carmine 34.00 15.00
Never hinged 87.50
On cover 400.00
153 A8 10 l violet 52.50 37.50
Never hinged 125.00
On cover 1,750.
154 A9 20 l dark green 110.00 *150.00*
Never hinged 290.00
On cover —
155 A10 25 l dark blue 110.00 *290.00*
Never hinged 290.00
On cover —
Nos. 138-155 (18) 1,519. *709.30*
Set, never hinged 3,750.
Set on overfranked philatelic cover *2,600.*

1934-37 *Perf. 14*
138a A3 5c deep brown 3.75 .80
Never hinged 7.50
On cover 8.00
139a A3 7½c violet 3.75 *50.00*
Never hinged 7.50
On cover 110.00
140a A3 10c gray black 3.75 .40
Never hinged 7.50
On cover 2.40
141a A3 15c olive green 3.75 *2.40*
Never hinged 7.50
On cover 26.00
142a A4 20c carmine 3.75 .25
Never hinged 7.50
On cover 5.50
143a A4 25c deep green 3.75 .40
Never hinged 7.50
On cover 4.00
144a A4 30c dark brown 7.50 .40
Never hinged 15.00
On cover 6.50
145a A5 35c dark blue 19.00 *57.50*
Never hinged 27.50
On cover 80.00
146a A5 50c violet 50.00 .40
Never hinged 92.50
On cover 2.40
147a A5 75c carmine 67.50 .40
Never hinged 150.00
On cover 12.50
148a A6 1.25 l dark blue 135.00 1.20
Never hinged 260.00
On cover 12.50
149a A6 1.75 l red orange 340.00 42.50
Never hinged 650.00
On cover 40.00
150a A6 2 l carmine 82.50 .80
Never hinged 165.00
On cover 20.00
151a A7 2.55 l indigo 375.00 *975.00*
Never hinged 750.00
On cover 3,000.
152a A7 5 l carmine 37.50 3.25
Never hinged 75.00
On cover 120.00

153a A8 10 l violet 290.00 45.00
Never hinged 500.00
On cover 675.00
154a A9 20 l dark green *15,000.* *2,500.*
Never hinged *20,000.*
On cover —
155a A10 25 l dark blue 950.00 825.00
Never hinged 2,250.
On cover —
Nos. 138a-153a,155a (17) 2,377. 2,006.
Set, never hinged 5,650.

Perf. 12x14 or 14x12 (20c, 25c, 75c-2 l)

1932

139b A3 7½c violet 95.00 *160.00*
140b A3 10c gray black — 1,000.
142b A4 20c carmine 2,000. 1,000.
143b A4 25c deep green 160.00 65.00
145b A5 35c dark blue 110.00 *140.00*
146b A5 50c violet 80.00 40.00
c. Perf 14x12 —
147b A5 75c carmine 120.00 95.00
148b A6 1.25 l dark blue — 1,200.
149b A6 1.75 l red orange 525.00 525.00
150b A6 2 l carmine 525.00 525.00
151b A7 2.55 l indigo 2,700. —
153b A8 10 l violet 95.00 *120.00*

Perf 12 on 3 sides, Perf 14 on either top or bottom

140c A3 15c olive green — 675.00
142c A4 20c carmine 1,200. 1,100.
143c A4 25c deep green 160.00 160.00

Perf 12 on 3 sides, Perf 14 on left

147c A5 75c carmine 2,400. 1,100.

Types of 1932 Issue Overprinted in Black or Red

1934, May ***Perf. 14***

156 A3 10c brown (Bk) 21.00 *50.00*
Never hinged 30.00
On cover 400.00
157 A4 25c green 21.00 *50.00*
Never hinged 30.00
On cover 400.00
158 A5 50c dull vio (Bk) 21.00 *50.00*
Never hinged 30.00
On cover 275.00
159 A6 1.25 l blue 21.00 *50.00*
Never hinged 30.00
On cover 475.00
160 A7 5 l brown black 21.00 *50.00*
Never hinged 30.00
On cover —
161 A8 10 l car rose (Bk) 21.00 *97.50*
Never hinged 30.00
On cover —
162 A9 20 l dull blue 21.00 *97.50*
Never hinged 30.00
On cover —
163 A10 25 l dark green 21.00 *97.50*
Never hinged 30.00
On cover —
Nos. 156-163 (8) 168.00 *542.50*
Set, never hinged 375.00
Set on overfranked philatelic cover(s) *725.00*

Duke of the Abruzzi (Luigi Amadeo, 1873-1933).

Mother and Child A11

1934, Oct.

164 A11 5c ol grn & brn 5.25 *21.00*
Never hinged 10.00
On cover 325.00
165 A11 10c yel brn & blk 5.25 *21.00*
Never hinged 10.00
On cover 275.00
166 A11 20c scarlet & blk 5.25 *19.00*
Never hinged 10.00
On cover 275.00
167 A11 50c dk violet & brn 5.25 *19.00*
Never hinged 10.00
On cover 250.00
168 A11 60c org brn & blk 5.25 *26.00*
Never hinged 10.00
On cover 325.00
169 A11 1.25 l dk blue & grn 5.25 *45.00*
Never hinged 10.00
On cover 400.00
Nos. 164-169,C1-C6 (12) 63.00 *302.00*

Nos. 164-169, never hinged 75.00
Nos. 164-169 on overfranked philatelic cover(s) *325.00*

Second Colonial Arts Exhibition, Naples.

SEMI-POSTAL STAMPS

Italy Nos. B1-B3 Overprinted

Italy No. B4 Surcharged

1916 **Wmk. 140** ***Perf. 14***

B1 SP1 10c + 5c rose 16.00 *40.00*
Never hinged 50.00
On cover 175.00
B2 SP2 15c + 5c slate 67.50 *57.50*
Never hinged 125.00
On cover 250.00
B3 SP2 20c + 5c orange 16.00 *50.00*
Never hinged 50.00
On cover 275.00
B4 SP2 20c on 15c + 5c slate 67.50 *90.00*
Never hinged 125.00
On cover 325.00
Nos. B1-B4 (4) 167.00 *237.50*
Set on overfranked philatelic cover(s) 350.00

Holy Year Issue

Italy Nos. B20-B25 Surcharged in Black or Red

1925, June 1 ***Perf. 12***

B5 SP4 6b + 3b on 20c + 10c 3.75 *22.50*
Never hinged 8.00
On cover 200.00
B6 SP4 13b + 6b on 30c + 15c 3.75 *24.00*
Never hinged 8.00
On cover 200.00
B7 SP4 15b + 8b on 50c + 25c 3.75 *22.50*
Never hinged 8.00
On cover 200.00
B8 SP4 18b + 9b on 60c + 30c 3.75 *30.00*
Never hinged 8.00
On cover 275.00
B9 SP8 30b + 15b on 1 l +50c (R) 3.75 *37.50*
Never hinged 8.00
On cover —
B10 SP8 1r + 50b on 5 l +2.50 l (R) 3.75 *57.50*
Never hinged 8.00
On cover —
Nos. B5-B10 (6) 22.50 *194.00*
Set on overfranked philatelic cover(s) 450.00

Colonial Institute Issue

"Peace" Substituting Spade for Sword — SP10

1926, June 1 **Typo.** ***Perf. 14***

B11 SP10 5c + 5c brown 1.10 *9.00*
Never hinged 2.40
On cover 175.00
B12 SP10 10c + 5c olive grn 1.10 *9.00*
Never hinged 2.40
On cover 125.00
B13 SP10 20c + 5c blue grn 1.10 *9.00*
Never hinged 2.40
On cover 100.00
B14 SP10 40c + 5c brn red 1.10 *9.00*
Never hinged 2.40
On cover 100.00
B15 SP10 60c + 5c orange 1.10 *9.00*
Never hinged 2.40
On cover 175.00
B16 SP10 1 l + 5c blue 1.10 *20.00*
Never hinged 2.40
On cover 275.00
Nos. B11-B16 (6) 6.60 *65.00*
Set on overfranked philatelic cover(s) 250.00

The surtax was for the Italian Colonial Institute.

Italian Semi-Postal Stamps of 1926 Overprinted

1927, Apr. 21 **Unwmk.** ***Perf. 11½***

B17 SP10 40c + 20c dk brn & blk 3.75 *42.50*
Never hinged 6.00
On cover 175.00
B18 SP10 60c + 30c brn red & ol brn 3.75 *42.50*
Never hinged 6.00
On cover 190.00
B19 SP10 1.25 l + 60c dp bl & blk 3.75 *60.00*
Never hinged 6.00
On cover 350.00
B20 SP10 5 l + 2.50 l dk grn & blk 6.00 *92.50*
Never hinged 10.00
On cover —
Nos. B17-B20 (4) 17.25 *237.50*
Set on overfranked philatelic cover(s) 500.00

The surtax was for the charitable work of the Voluntary Militia for Italian National Defense. Nos. B19 and B20 in light blue and black and slate and black, respectively, were designed but not issued. Value, set of two, $2,500.

Allegory of Fascism and Victory — SP11

1928, Oct. 15 **Wmk. 140** ***Perf. 14***

B21 SP11 20c + 5c blue grn 3.00 *13.50*
Never hinged 7.00
On cover 160.00
B22 SP11 30c + 5c red 3.00 *13.50*
Never hinged 7.00
On cover 160.00
B23 SP11 50c + 10c purple 3.00 *22.50*
Never hinged 7.00
On cover 150.00
B24 SP11 1.25 l + 20c dk blue 3.75 *30.00*
Never hinged 8.50
On cover 400.00
Nos. B21-B24 (4) 12.75 *79.50*
Set on overfranked philatelic cover(s) 300.00

46th anniv. of the Societa Africana d'Italia. The surtax aided that society.

Italian Semi-Postal Stamps of 1928 Overprinted

1929, Mar. 4 **Unwmk.** ***Perf. 11***

B25 SP10 30c + 10c red & blk 4.50 *26.00*
Never hinged 10.00
On cover 175.00
B26 SP10 50c + 20c vio & blk 4.50 *28.00*
Never hinged 10.00
On cover 175.00
B27 SP10 1.25 l + 50c brn & bl 6.75 *50.00*
Never hinged 12.00
On cover 450.00
B28 SP10 5 l + 2 l ol grn & blk 6.75 *97.50*
Never hinged 12.00
On cover —
Nos. B25-B28 (4) 22.50 *201.50*
Set on overfranked philatelic cover(s) 475.00

The surtax was for the charitable work of the Voluntary Militia for Italian National Defense.

Italian Semi-Postal Stamps of 1926 Ovptd. in Black or Red

1930, Oct. 20 ***Perf. 14***

B29 SP10 30c + 10c dk grn & bl grn (Bk) 35.00 *60.00*
Never hinged 62.50
On cover 275.00
B30 SP10 50c + 10c dk grn & vio (R) 35.00 *97.50*
Never hinged 62.50
On cover 300.00
B31 SP10 1.25 l + 30c ol brn & red brn (R) 35.00 *97.50*
Never hinged 62.50
On cover 500.00
B32 SP10 5 l + 1.50 l ind & grn (R) 110.00 *260.00*
Never hinged 215.00
On cover —
Nos. B29-B32 (4) 215.00 *515.00*
Set on overfranked philatelic cover(s) 800.00

The surtax was for the charitable work of the Voluntary Militia for Italian National Defense.

Irrigation Canal SP14

1930, Nov. 27 **Photo.** **Wmk. 140**

B33 SP14 50c + 20c ol brn 3.75 *24.00*
Never hinged 9.50
On cover *200.00*
B34 S414 1.25 l + 20c dp blue 3.75 *24.00*
Never hinged 9.50
On cover *275.00*
B35 SP14 1.75 l + 20c green 3.75 *26.00*
Never hinged 9.50
On cover *350.00*
B36 SP14 2.55 l + 50c purple 9.00 *42.50*
Never hinged 16.00
On cover *550.00*
B37 SP14 5 l + 1 l dp car 9.00 *65.00*
Never hinged 16.00
On cover —
Nos. B33-B37 (5) 29.25 *181.50*
Set on overfranked philatelic cover(s) *325.00*

25th anniv. of the Italian Colonial Agricultural Institute. The surtax was for the aid of that institution.

SP15

King Victor Emmanuel III — SP16

1935, Jan. 1

B38 SP15 5c + 5c blk brn 6.00 *34.00*
Never hinged 12.50
On cover *300.00*
B39 SP15 7½c + 7½c vio 6.00 *34.00*
Never hinged 12.50
On cover *350.00*
B40 SP15 15c + 10c ol blk 6.00 *34.00*
Never hinged 12.50
On cover *260.00*
B41 SP15 20c + 10c rose red 6.00 *34.00*
Never hinged 12.50
On cover *260.00*
B42 SP15 25c + 10c dp grn 6.00 *34.00*
Never hinged 12.50
On cover *275.00*

B43 SP15 30c + 10c brn 6.00 *34.00*
Never hinged 12.50
On cover *300.00*
B44 SP15 50c + 10c pur 6.00 *34.00*
Never hinged 12.50
On cover *300.00*
B45 SP15 75c + 15c rose car 6.00 *34.00*
Never hinged 12.50
On cover *350.00*
B46 SP15 1.25 l + 15c dp bl 6.00 *34.00*
Never hinged 12.50
On cover *475.00*
B47 SP15 1.75 l + 25c red org 6.00 *34.00*
Never hinged 12.50
On cover *675.00*
B48 SP15 2.75 l + 25c gray 37.50 *135.00*
Never hinged 77.50
On cover —
B49 SP15 5 l + 1 l dp cl 37.50 *135.00*
Never hinged 77.50
On cover —
B50 SP15 10 l + 1.80 l red brn 37.50 *135.00*
Never hinged 77.50
On cover —
B51 SP16 25 l + 2.75 l brn & red 200.00 *500.00*
Never hinged 440.00
On cover —
Nos. B38-B51 (14) 372.50 *1,245.*
Set, never hinged 850.00
Set on overfranked philatelic cover(s) *2,800.*

Visit of King Victor Emmanuel III.

AIR POST STAMPS

View of Coast AP1

Cheetahs AP2

Wmk. 140

1934, Oct. Photo. *Perf. 14*

C1 AP1 25c sl bl & red org 5.25 *21.00*
Never hinged 10.00
On cover 250.00
C2 AP1 50c dk grn & blk 5.25 *19.00*
Never hinged 10.00
On cover 200.00
C3 AP1 75c brn & red org 5.25 *19.00*
Never hinged 10.00
On cover 275.00
a. Imperf. 3,000.
Never hinged 3,000.
C4 AP2 80c org brn & blk 5.25 *21.00*
Never hinged 10.00
On cover 325.00
C5 AP2 1 l scar & blk 5.25 *26.00*
Never hinged 10.00
On cover 350.00
C6 AP2 2 l dk bl & brn 5.25 *45.00*
Never hinged 10.00
On cover 525.00
Nos. C1-C6 (6) 31.50 *151.00*
Set, never hinged 80.00
Set, on flown cover 400.00

2nd Colonial Arts Exhibition, Naples.
For overprint see No. CO1.

Banana Tree and Airplane AP3

Designs: 25c, 1.50 l, Banana tree and plane. 50c, 2 l, Plane over cotton field. 60c, 5 l, Plane over orchard. 75c, 10 l, Plane over field workers. 1 l, 3 l, Small girl watching plane.

1936 Photo.

C7 AP3 25c slate green 3.50 *9.00*
Never hinged 5.50
On cover 100.00
C8 AP3 50c brown 2.00 .25
Never hinged 3.75
On cover 2.40
C9 AP3 60c red orange 4.00 *13.50*
Never hinged 7.50
On cover 200.00
C10 AP3 75c orange brn 3.50 2.40
Never hinged 5.50
On cover 20.00
C11 AP3 1 l deep blue 2.00 .25
Never hinged 3.75
On cover 2.40
C12 AP3 1.50 l purple 3.50 .80
Never hinged 5.50
On cover 20.00
C13 AP3 2 l slate blue 7.50 1.20
Never hinged 20.00
On cover 160.00
C14 AP3 3 l copper red 26.00 15.00
Never hinged 52.50
On cover 275.00
C15 AP3 5 l yellow green 30.00 18.00
Never hinged 60.00
On cover 475.00
C16 AP3 10 l dp rose red 37.50 34.00
Never hinged 75.00
On cover 950.00
Nos. C7-C16 (10) 119.50 *94.40*
Set, never hinged 260.00
Set, on flown cover 475.00

AIR POST SEMI-POSTAL STAMPS

King Victor Emmanuel III — SPAP1

Wmk. 140

1934, Nov. 5 Photo. *Perf. 14*

CB1 SPAP1 25c + 10c gray grn 9.00 *26.00*
Never hinged 16.00
On cover 300.00
CB2 SPAP1 50c + 10c brn 9.00 *26.00*
Never hinged 16.00
On cover 300.00
CB3 SPAP1 75c + 15c rose red 9.00 *26.00*
Never hinged 16.00
On cover 325.00
CB4 SPAP1 80c + 15c blk brn 9.00 *26.00*
Never hinged 16.00
On cover 400.00
CB5 SPAP1 1 l + 20c red brn 9.00 *26.00*
Never hinged 16.00
On cover 450.00
CB6 SPAP1 2 l + 20c brt bl 9.00 *26.00*
Never hinged 16.00
On cover —
CB7 SPAP1 3 l + 25c pur 26.00 *120.00*
Never hinged 55.00
On cover —
CB8 SPAP1 5 l + 25c org 26.00 *120.00*
Never hinged 55.00
On cover —
CB9 SPAP1 10 l + 30c rose vio 26.00 *120.00*
Never hinged 55.00
On cover —
CB10 SPAP1 25 l + 2 l dp grn 26.00 *120.00*
Never hinged 55.00
On cover —
Nos. CB1-CB10 (10) 158.00 *636.00*
Set, never hinged 375.00
Set, on flown cover 1,500.

65th birthday of King Victor Emmanuel III; non-stop flight from Rome to Mogadishu.
For overprint see No. CBO1.

AIR POST OFFICIAL STAMP

No. C1 Overprinted

Wmk. 140

1934, Nov. 11 Photo. *Perf. 14*

CO1 AP1 25c sl bl & red org *2,800. 5,250.*
Never hinged 4,900.
On flown cover *7,200.*
Pair on flown cover *14,500.*

Forgeries of this overprint exist.

AIR POST SEMI-POSTAL OFFICIAL STAMP

Air Post Semi-Postal Stamps of 1934 Overprinted in Black

1934, Nov. 5 Wmk. 140 *Perf. 14*

CBO1 SPAP1 25 l + 2 l cop red 2,950. *6,000.*
Never hinged 5,250.
On flown cover *8,000.*

SPECIAL DELIVERY STAMPS

Italy No. E3 Surcharged

1923, July 16 Wmk. 140 *Perf. 14*

E1 SD1 30b on 60c dl red 32.50 *30.00*
Never hinged 62.50
On cover 250.00

Italy, Type of 1908 Special Delivery Stamp Surcharged

E2 SD2 60b on 1.20 l bl & red 47.50 *57.50*
Never hinged 92.50
On cover 600.00

"Italia" SD3

1924, June Engr. Unwmk.

E3 SD3 30b dk red & brn 13.00 *24.00*
Never hinged 25.00
On cover 250.00
E4 SD3 60b dk blue & red 24.00 *35.00*
Never hinged 50.00
On cover 550.00

Nos. E3-E4 Surcharged in Black or Red

1926, Oct.

E5 SD3 70c on 30b (Bk) 15.00 *21.00*
Never hinged 30.00
On cover 325.00
E6 SD3 2.50 l on 60b (R) 17.00 *29.00*
Never hinged 45.00
On cover 550.00
a. Imperf., pair 1,200.

No. E3 Surcharged in Blue

1927 *Perf. 11*

E7 SD3 1.25 l on 30b 16.50 19.00
Never hinged 40.00
On cover 160.00
a. Perf. 14 300.00 *975.00*
Never hinged 600.00
On cover 4,000.
b. Imperf., pair 1,050.
Never hinged 1,500.

AUTHORIZED DELIVERY STAMP

Italy No. EY2 Overprinted in Black

1939 Wmk. 140 *Perf. 14*

EY1 AD2 10c brown 80.00 —
Never hinged 200.00
On cover *600.00*

No. EY1 has yellowish gum. A 1941 printing in grayish brown, with white gum, was not issued. The overprint on the 1939 printing is located between the "OS" and "AN" of POSTE ITALIANE, while the overprint on the 1941 printing is centered. Value: unused, 80 cents; never hinged, $2.00.

POSTAGE DUE STAMPS

Values for Nos. J1-J41 are for examples with perforations touching or cutting into the design on at least one side. Examples with perforations clear of the design on all four sides are scarce and command considerable premiums.

Postage Due Stamps of Italy Overprinted

1906-08 Wmk. 140 *Perf. 14*

J1 D3 5c buff & mag 26.00 *52.50*
Never hinged 32.50
On cover 750.00
J2 D3 10c buff & mag 75.00 75.00
Never hinged 105.00
On cover 550.00
J3 D3 20c org & mag 52.50 *90.00*
Never hinged 77.50
On cover 490.00
J4 D3 30c buff & mag 52.50 *105.00*
Never hinged 62.50
On cover 650.00
J5 D3 40c buff & mag 375.00 105.00
Never hinged 435.00
On cover 750.00
J6 D3 50c buff & mag 82.50 *120.00*
Never hinged 115.00
On cover 750.00
J7 D3 60c buff & mag ('08) 75.00 *120.00*
Never hinged 100.00
On cover —

J8 D3 1 l blue & mag 1,500. 550.00
Never hinged 1,900.
On cover —
J9 D3 2 l blue & mag 1,500. 550.00
Never hinged 1,900.
On cover —
J10 D3 5 l blue & mag 1,500. 550.00
Never hinged 1,900.
On cover —
J11 D3 10 l blue & mag 300.00 *500.00*
Never hinged 360.00
On cover —
Nos. J1-J11 (11) 5,539. *2,818.*

Postage Due Stamps of Italy Overprinted at Top of Stamps

1909-19
J12 D3 5c buff & mag 9.50 *30.00*
Never hinged 14.00
On cover 550.00
c. Overprint at center of stamp 27.50
Never hinged 42.50
J13 D3 10c buff & mag 9.50 *30.00*
Never hinged 14.00
On cover 400.00
J14 D3 20c buff & mag 20.00 *60.00*
Never hinged 30.00
On cover 450.00
J15 D3 30c buff & mag 60.00 *60.00*
Never hinged 82.50
On cover 550.00
J16 D3 40c buff & mag 60.00 *82.50*
Never hinged 82.50
On cover 650.00
J17 D3 50c buff & mag 60.00 *105.00*
Never hinged 82.50
On cover 450.00
J18 D3 60c buff & mag ('19) 82.50 *90.00*
Never hinged 100.00
On cover —
J19 D3 1 l blue & mag 170.00 105.00
Never hinged 250.00
On cover 650.00
J20 D3 2 l blue & mag 240.00 *240.00*
Never hinged 365.00
On cover —
J21 D3 5 l blue & mag 275.00 325.00
Never hinged 415.00
On cover —
J22 D3 10 l blue & mag 55.00 *110.00*
Never hinged 82.50
On cover —
Nos. J12-J22 (11) 1,042. *1,238.*

Same with Overprint at Bottom of Stamps

1920
J12a D3 5c buff & magenta 150.00 225.00
Never hinged 260.00
On cover 650.00
b. Double overprint 550.00
Never hinged 850.00
J13a D3 10c buff & magenta 150.00 225.00
Never hinged 260.00
On cover 550.00
J14a D3 20c buff & magenta 210.00 150.00
Never hinged 390.00
On cover 400.00
J15a D3 30c buff & magenta 210.00 150.00
Never hinged 425.00
On cover 475.00
J16a D3 40c buff & magenta 210.00 225.00
Never hinged 425.00
On cover 725.00
J17a D3 50c buff & magenta 210.00 210.00
Never hinged 425.00
On cover 525.00
J18a D3 60c buff & magenta 210.00 210.00
Never hinged 425.00
On cover —
J19a D3 1 l blue & magenta 210.00 300.00
Never hinged 425.00
On cover 950.00
b. Overprint at center of stamp 350.00
Never hinged 850.00
J20a D3 2 l blue & magenta 210.00 300.00
Never hinged 425.00
On cover —
J21a D3 5 l blue & magenta 210.00 375.00
Never hinged 425.00
On cover —
Nos. J12a-J21a (10) 1,980. 2,370.

D4

1923, July 1
J23 D4 1b buff & black 3.00 *11.50*
Never hinged 4.50
On cover 525.00
J24 D4 2b buff & black 3.00 *11.50*
Never hinged 4.50
On cover 400.00
a. Inverted numeral and ovpt. 550.00
Never hinged 850.00
J25 D4 3b buff & black 3.00 *11.50*
Never hinged 4.50
On cover 400.00
J26 D4 5b buff & black 4.50 *11.50*
Never hinged 5.00
On cover 400.00
J27 D4 10b buff & black 4.50 *11.50*
Never hinged 5.00
On cover 550.00
J28 D4 20b buff & black 4.50 *11.50*
Never hinged 5.00
On cover 550.00
J29 D4 40b buff & black 4.50 *11.50*
Never hinged 5.00
On cover 900.00
J30 D4 1r blue & black 4.50 *62.50*
Never hinged 10.00
On cover —
Nos. J23-J30 (8) 31.50 *143.00*

Nos. J23-J30 were overprinted on unde-nominated postage due stamps of Italy. They were surcharged in Somalian currencies of besas and rupees,

Type of Postage Due Stamps of Italy Overprinted

1926, Mar. 1
J31 D3 5c buff & black 30.00 *37.50*
Never hinged 57.50
On cover 550.00
J32 D3 10c buff & black 30.00 26.00
Never hinged 57.50
On cover 350.00
J33 D3 20c buff & black 30.00 *45.00*
Never hinged 57.50
On cover 325.00
J34 D3 30c buff & black 30.00 26.00
Never hinged 57.50
On cover 400.00
J35 D3 40c buff & black 30.00 26.00
Never hinged 57.50
On cover 475.00
J36 D3 50c buff & black 45.00 26.00
Never hinged 60.00
On cover 325.00
J37 D3 60c buff & black 45.00 26.00
Never hinged 60.00
On cover 650.00
J38 D3 1 l blue & black 67.50 45.00
Never hinged 125.00
On cover 725.00
J39 D3 2 l blue & black 105.00 45.00
Never hinged 190.00
On cover —
J40 D3 5 l blue & black 115.00 60.00
Never hinged 225.00
On cover —
J41 D3 10 l blue & black 150.00 82.50
Never hinged 260.00
On cover —
Nos. J31-J41 (11) 677.50 445.00

Numerals and Ovpt. Invtd.

J32a D3 10c 260.00
Never hinged 350.00
J33a D3 20c 825.00
Never hinged 1,100.
J34a D3 30c 260.00
Never hinged 350.00
J35a D3 40c 260.00
Never hinged 350.00
J36a D3 50c 260.00
Never hinged 350.00
J37a D3 60c 260.00
Never hinged 350.00

Postage Due Stamps of Italy, 1934, Overprinted in Black

1934, May 12
J42 D6 5c brown 1.50 *7.50*
Never hinged 2.40
On cover 550.00
J43 D6 10c blue 1.50 *7.50*
Never hinged 2.40
On cover 350.00
J44 D6 20c rose red 4.00 15.00
Never hinged 9.50
On cover 300.00
J45 D6 25c green 4.00 15.00
Never hinged 9.50
On cover 250.00
J46 D6 30c red orange 12.00 *19.00*
Never hinged 20.00
On cover 350.00
J47 D6 40c black brown 12.00 *26.00*
Never hinged 24.00
On cover 550.00
J48 D6 50c violet 20.00 9.00
Never hinged 42.50
On cover 250.00
J49 D6 60c black 20.00 *45.00*
Never hinged 50.00
On cover 600.00
J50 D7 1 l red orange 27.50 22.50
Never hinged 65.00
On cover 325.00
J51 D7 2 l green 50.00 45.00
Never hinged 125.00
On cover 550.00
J52 D7 5 l violet 52.50 *105.00*
Never hinged 125.00
On cover —
J53 D7 10 l blue 52.50 *110.00*
Never hinged 125.00
On cover —
J54 D7 20 l carmine 60.00 *170.00*
Never hinged 140.00
On cover —
Nos. J42-J54 (13) 317.50 *596.50*

PARCEL POST STAMPS

These stamps were used by affixing them to the way bill so that one half remained on it following the parcel, the other half staying on the receipt given the sender. Most used halves are right halves. Complete stamps were and are obtainable canceled, probably to order. Both unused and used values are for complete stamps.

Parcel Post Stamps of Italy, 1914-17, Overprinted

1917-19 Wmk. 140 *Perf. 13½*
Q1 PP2 5c brown 8.00 *67.50*
Never hinged 16.00
a. Double overprint 500.00 —
Never hinged 650.00
Q2 PP2 10c blue 9.50 *45.00*
Never hinged 19.00
Q3 PP2 20c black ('19) 375.00 225.00
Never hinged 700.00
Q4 PP2 25c red 16.00 *80.00*
Never hinged 32.50
a. Double overprint — —
Never hinged —
Q5 PP2 50c orange 165.00 97.50
Never hinged 325.00
Q6 PP2 1 l lilac 52.50 *97.50*
Never hinged 100.00
Q7 PP2 2 l green 72.50 *97.50*
Never hinged 150.00
Q8 PP2 3 l bister 80.00 *170.00*
Never hinged 160.00
Q9 PP2 4 l slate 87.50 *170.00*
Never hinged 175.00
Nos. Q1-Q9 (9) 866.00 *1,050.*

Halves Used

Q1	1.60
Q2	1.60
Q3	7.25
Q4	3.50
Q5	6.00
Q6	4.75
Q7	4.75
Q8	4.75
Q9	4.75

Nos. Q5-Q9 were overprinted in 1922 with a slightly different type in which the final "A" of SOMALIA is directly over the final "A" of ITALIANA. They were not regularly issued. Value for set: unused $1,600; never hinged $2,400.

Parcel Post Stamps of Italy, 1914-17, Overprinted

1923
Q10 PP2 25c red 75.00 *165.00*
Never hinged 145.00
Q11 PP2 50c orange 110.00 *165.00*
Never hinged 225.00
Q12 PP2 1 l violet 135.00 275.00
Never hinged 250.00
Q13 PP2 2 l green 135.00 275.00
Never hinged 250.00
Q14 PP2 3 l bister 210.00 275.00
Never hinged 400.00
Q15 PP2 4 l slate 210.00 275.00
Never hinged 400.00
Nos. Q10-Q15 (6) 875.00 *1,430.*

Halves Used

Q10	4.75
Q11	4.75
Q12	3.00
Q13	3.00
Q14	4.75
Q15	5.50

Parcel Post Stamps of Italy, 1914-17, Surcharged

1923
Q16 PP2 3b on 5c brown 27.50 *37.50*
Never hinged 55.00
Q17 PP2 5b on 5c brown 27.50 *37.50*
Never hinged 55.00
Q18 PP2 10b on 10c blue 27.50 34.00
Never hinged 55.00
Q19 PP2 25b on 25c red 27.50 52.50
Never hinged 55.00
Q20 PP2 50b on 50c org 35.00 *75.00*
Never hinged 70.00
Q21 PP2 1r on 1 l lilac 47.50 75.00
Never hinged 95.00
Q22 PP2 2r on 2 l green 80.00 120.00
Never hinged 160.00
Q23 PP2 3r on 3 l bister 80.00 120.00
Never hinged 160.00
Q24 PP2 4r on 4 l slate 95.00 120.00
Never hinged 190.00
Nos. Q16-Q24 (9) 447.50 671.50

Halves Used

Q16	1.60
Q17	1.60
Q18	1.60
Q19	3.25
Q20	3.25
Q21	3.25
Q22	3.25
Q23	3.25
Q24	3.25

No. Q16 has the numeral "3" at the left also.

Parcel Post Stamps of Italy, 1914-22 Overprinted

Nos. Q25-Q31 come with two types of overprint:

Type I — The first "I" and last "A" of ITALIANA extend slightly at both sides of SOMALIA.

Type II — Only the "I" extends.

1926-31 Red Overprint
Q25 PP2 5c brown 34.00 *82.50*
Never hinged 65.00
Q26 PP2 10c blue 32.50 *82.50*
Never hinged 65.00
Q27 PP2 20c black 72.50 82.50
Never hinged 145.00
Q28 PP2 25c red 72.50 82.50
Never hinged 145.00
Q29 PP2 50c orange 72.50 82.50
Never hinged 145.00
Q30 PP2 1 l violet 97.50 82.50
Never hinged 190.00
Q31 PP2 2 l green 160.00 82.50
Never hinged 325.00
Q32 PP2 3 l yellow 30.00 *82.50*
Never hinged 55.00
Q33 PP2 4 l slate 30.00 *82.50*
Never hinged 55.00
Q34 PP2 10 l vio brn ('30) 55.00 *105.00*
Never hinged 110.00
Q35 PP2 12 l red brn '31) 55.00 *105.00*
Never hinged 110.00
Q36 PP2 15 l olive ('31) 55.00 *190.00*
Never hinged 110.00
Q37 PP2 20 l dull vio ('31) 55.00 *190.00*
Never hinged 110.00
Nos. Q25-Q37 (13) 821.50 *1,333.*

Halves Used

Q25	2.00
Q26	2.00
Q27	3.25
Q28	3.25
Q29	3.25
Q30	3.25
Q31	3.25
Q32	3.25
Q33	3.25
Q34	4.00
Q35	4.00
Q36	4.00
Q37	4.00

These seven stamps with type I overprint were not regularly issued, and Nos. Q27-Q31 (type I) sell for less than with type II overprint.

Black Overprint

Q38 PP2 10 l violet brown 82.50 87.50
Never hinged 160.00
Q39 PP2 12 l red brown 55.00 87.50
Never hinged 110.00
Q40 PP2 15 l olive 55.00 87.50
Never hinged 110.00
Q41 PP2 20 l dull violet 55.00 87.50
Never hinged 110.00
Nos. Q38-Q41 (4) 247.50 350.00

Halves Used

Q38	4.00
Q39	4.00
Q40	4.00
Q41	4.00

Same Overprint on Parcel Post Stamps of Italy, 1927-38

1928-39 Black Overprint
Q42 PP3 25c red, type I ('31) 45.00 *52.50*
Never hinged 80.00
a. Type II 80.00 *160.00*
Never hinged 160.00
Q43 PP3 30c ultra 6.00 *7.50*
Never hinged 6.50
Q43A PP3 50c orange *12,750.*
Never hinged *18,000.*
Q44 PP3 60c red 6.00 *8.00*
Never hinged 6.50
Q45 PP3 1 l lilac brn, type II ('31) 40.00 *52.50*
Never hinged 80.00
a. Type I 875.00 *2,400.*
Never hinged 1,750.
b. 1 l lilac, type I 2,250.
Never hinged 3,400.
Q46 PP3 2 l green, type II ('31) 40.00 *52.50*
Never hinged 80.00
a. Type I 800.00 *3,250.*
Never hinged 1,600.
Q47 PP3 3 l bister 15.00 *20.00*
Never hinged 13.00
Q48 PP3 4 l gray black 15.00 *20.00*
Never hinged 13.00

Q49 PP3 10 l rose lil ('34) 475.00 *675.00*
Never hinged 900.00
Q50 PP3 20 l lil brn ('34) 475.00 *750.00*
Never hinged 900.00
Nos. Q42-Q43,Q44-Q50 (9) 1,117. *1,638.*

Halves Used

Q42	8.75
Q43	.45
Q43A	160.00
Q44	.45
Q45	2.75
Q46	2.75
Q47	.80
Q48	.80
Q49	20.00
Q50	20.00

The 25c, 1 l and 2 l come with both types of overprint (see note below No. Q37). Both types were regularly issued. Values are for type I on 25c, type II on 1 l and 2 l.

Red Overprint

Q51 PP3 5c brown ('39) 16.00
Never hinged 24.00
Q52 PP3 3 l bister ('30) 32.50 *80.00*
Never hinged 47.50
Half stamp 2.00
Q53 PP3 4 l gray black ('30) 32.50 *80.00*
Never hinged 47.50
Half stamp 2.00
Nos. Q51-Q53 (3) 81.00

Same Overprint in Black on Italy Nos. Q24-Q25

1940 *Perf. 13*
Q54 PP3 5c brown 6.00 *13.50*
Never hinged 4.75
Half stamp .50
Q55 PP3 10c deep blue 7.50 *13.50*
Never hinged 6.00
Half stamp .50

SOMALI COAST

sō-ˈmä-lē ˈkōst

(Djibouti)

LOCATION — Eastern Africa, bordering on the Gulf of Aden
GOVT. — French Overseas Territory
AREA — 8,500 sq. mi.
POP. — 86,000 (est. 1963)
CAPITAL — Djibouti (Jibuti)

The port of Obock, which issued postage stamps in 1892-1894, was included in the territory and began to use stamps of Somali Coast in 1902.

100 Centimes = 1 Franc

Obock Nos. 32-33, 35, 45 with Overprint or Surcharge Handstamped in Black, Blue or Red

Navigation and Commerce
A1 A2

A3

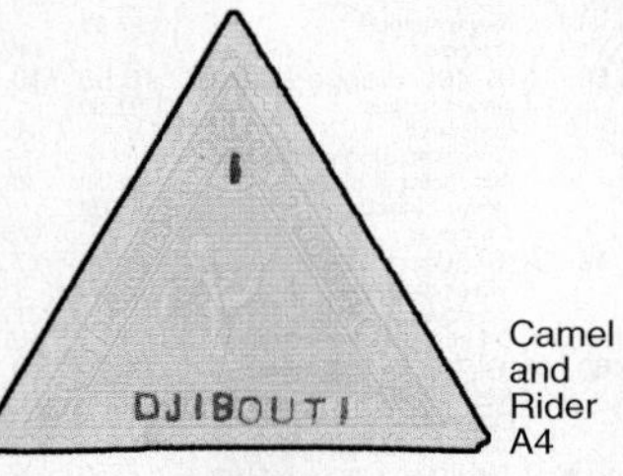

Camel and Rider
A4

1894 **Unwmk.** *Perf. 14x13½*
1 A1 5c grn & red, *grnsh* (with bar) 165.00 140.00
On cover 1,500.
a. Without bar 1,250. 800.00
b. Bar double 700.00 400.00
c. "D" omitted 1,100. 800.00
d. "D" double 1,100. 775.00
e. "D" inverted 1,100. 800.00
f. "J" omitted 975.00 625.00
g. Ovpt. "JD" 1,200. 850.00
2 A2 25c on 2c brn & bl, *buff* (Bl & Bk) 350.00 225.00
On cover 1,000.
a. "25" omitted 1,000. 950.00
b. "25" double 1,600.
c. "DJIBOUTI" omitted 1,000. 850.00
d. "DJIBOUTI" inverted 1,100. 975.00
e. "DJIBOUTI" double 1,600. 1,250.
3 A3 50c on 1c blk & red, *bl* (R & Bl) 350.00 250.00
On cover 1,250.
a. "5" instead of "50" 1,600. 1,150.
b. "0" instead of "50" 1,600. 1,150.
c. "DJIBOUTI" omitted 1,600. 1,250.

Imperf

4 A4 1fr on 5fr car 625.00 500.00
a. "DJIBOUTI" omitted 4,500.
b. "DJIBOUTI" double 1,900. 1,650.
c. "1" double 1,900. 1,650.
5 A4 5fr carmine 1,900. 1,350.

Counterfeits exist of Nos. 4-5.

View of Djibouti, Somali Warriors — A5

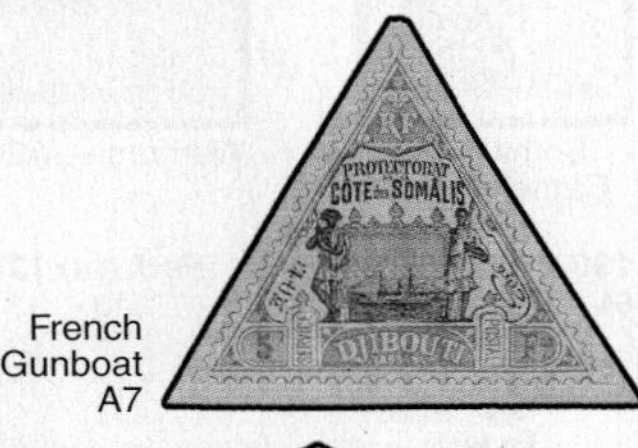

French Gunboat
A7

Crossing Desert (Size: 66mm wide, including simulated perfs.) — A8

Designs: 15c, 25c, 30c, 40c, 50c, 75c, Different views of Djibouti. 1fr, 2fr, Djibouti quay.

Imperf. (Simulated Perforations in Frame Color)

1894-1902 **Typo.**

Quadrille Lines Printed on Paper

6 A5 1c blk & claret 3.50 2.75
Never hinged 6.25
On cover 150.00
Ovpt. "Specimen" 160.00
a. Thick paper 17.50 17.50
Never hinged 35.00
7 A5 2c claret & blk 3.50 3.50
Never hinged 7.00
On cover 150.00
Ovpt. "Specimen" 160.00
a. Thick paper 17.50 17.50
Never hinged 35.00
8 A5 4c vio brn & bl 14.00 10.50
Never hinged 27.50
On cover 190.00
Ovpt. "Specimen" 190.00
a. Thick paper 40.00 27.50
Never hinged 85.00
9 A5 5c bl grn & red 14.00 7.00
Never hinged 27.50
On cover 110.00
Ovpt. "Specimen" 190.00
10 A5 5c grn & yel grn ('02) 10.50 7.75
Never hinged 21.00
On cover 110.00
Ovpt. "Specimen" 225.00
11 A5 10c brown & grn 17.50 10.50
Never hinged 35.00
On cover 105.00
Ovpt. "Specimen" 225.00
a. Half used as 5c on cover 200.00
12 A5 15c violet & grn 17.50 10.50
Never hinged 35.00
On cover 105.00
Ovpt. "Specimen" 225.00
13 A5 25c rose & blue 27.50 10.50
Never hinged 55.00
On cover 300.00
Ovpt. "Specimen" 225.00
14 A5 30c gray brn & rose 25.00 10.50
Never hinged 35.00
On cover 250.00
Ovpt. "Specimen" 225.00
a. Half used as 15c on cover 600.00
15 A5 40c org & bl ('00) 52.50 35.00
Never hinged 110.00
On cover 300.00
Ovpt. "Specimen" 225.00
a. Half used as 20c on cover 950.00
16 A5 50c blue & rose 27.50 17.50
Never hinged 55.00
On cover 375.00
Ovpt. "Specimen" 225.00
a. Half used as 25c on cover 2,000.
17 A5 75c violet & org 50.00 35.00
Never hinged 100.00
On cover 425.00
Ovpt. "Specimen" 300.00
18 A5 1fr ol grn & blk 25.00 21.00
Never hinged 50.00
On cover 500.00
Ovpt. "Specimen" 225.00
19 A5 2fr gray brn & rose 90.00 70.00
On cover 625.00
Ovpt. "Specimen" 475.00
a. Half used as 1fr on cover 2,400.
20 A7 5fr rose & blue 180.00 140.00
Ovpt. "Specimen" 575.00
21 A8 25fr rose & blue 1,000. *1,050.*
Ovpt. "S" (Specimen) 400.00
22 A8 50fr blue & rose 600.00 *675.00*
Ovpt. "S" (Specimen) 400.00
Nos. 6-20 (15) 558.00 392.00

High values are found with the overprint "S" (Specimen) erased and, usually, a cancellation added.

Values for bisects are for complete covers, newspapers or other printed matter.

For surcharges see Nos. 24-27B.

1899 **Black Surcharge**
23 A5 40c on 4c vio brn & bl *3,000.* 32.50
On cover 250.00
a. Double surcharge *5,500.* 1,400.
b. Pair, one without surcharge 4,250.
c. Inverted surcharge 1,600.
d. Double surcharge, both inverted 3,000.

Nos. 17-20 Surcharged

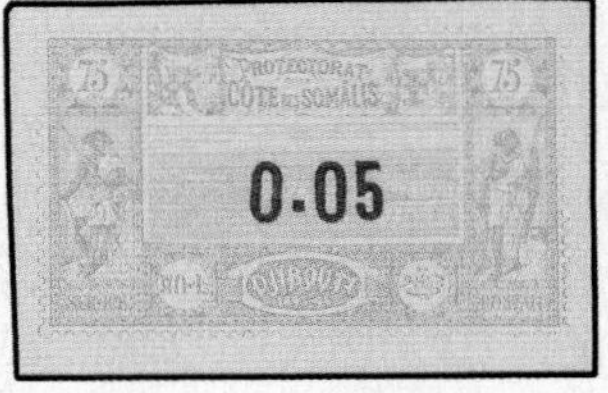

1902 **Blue Surcharge**
24 A5 0.05c on 75c 70.00 42.50
Never hinged 140.00
On cover 250.00
a. Inverted surcharge 550.00 500.00
b. Double surcharge 550.00 500.00
c. Pair, one without surcharge 2,500.
d. Comma instead of period in surcharge 105.00 42.50
On cover 275.00
e. As "d," double surcharge 875.00 875.00
25 A5 0.10c on 1fr 80.00 62.50
Never hinged 165.00
On cover 300.00
a. Inverted surcharge 510.00 400.00
b. Double surcharge 510.00 400.00
26 A5 0.40c on 2fr 550.00 400.00
On cover *1,500.*
a. Double surcharge 2,000. 1,850.

Black Surcharge

27 A7 0.75c on 5fr 525.00 400.00
On cover *1,900.*
a. Inverted surcharge 2,600. 2,100.
c. Double surcharge 2,600. 2,100.

Obock No. 57 Surcharged in Blue

27B A7 0.05c on 75c gray lil & org 1,500. 1,050.
On cover *2,250.*

A10

Nos. 15-16 Surcharged in Black

28 A10 5c on 40c 10.50 7.00
Never hinged 25.00
On cover 250.00
a. Double surcharge 130.00 130.00
29 A10 10c on 50c 27.50 27.50
Never hinged 55.00
On cover 375.00
a. Inverted surcharge 510.00 500.00
b. Double surcharge 600.00

Stamps of Obock Surcharged

Group of Warriors
A11

Black Surcharge

30 A11 5c on 30c bis & yel grn 17.50 10.50
Never hinged 35.00
On cover 350.00
a. Inverted surcharge 275.00 275.00
b. Double surcharge 325.00 275.00
c. Triple surcharge 1,500.

A12

Red Surcharge

31 A12 10c on 25c blk & bl 21.00 14.00
Never hinged 35.00
On cover 350.00
Ovpt. "Specimen" 275.00
a. Inverted surcharge 275.00 275.00
b. Double surcharge 325.00 325.00
c. Triple surcharge 1,600. 1,600.
d. "Djibouti" omitted 875.00 *1,250.*

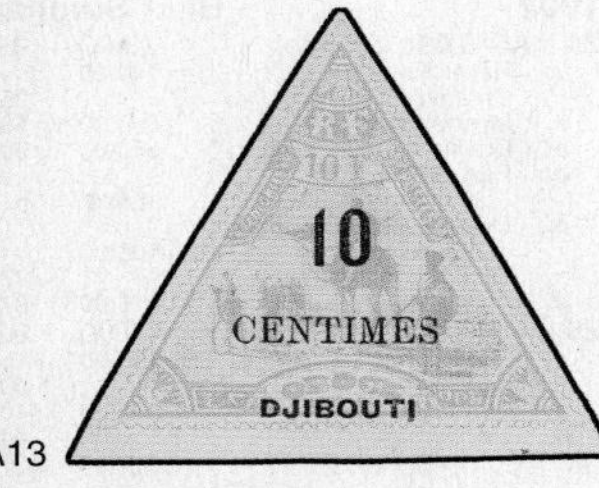
A13

Black Surcharge

32 A13 10c on 10fr org & red vio 40.00 32.50
Never hinged 85.00
On cover 375.00
a. Double surcharge 250.00 200.00
b. Double surch., one invtd. 2,200. 2,100.
c. Triple surcharge 1,500. 1,500.
d. "Djibouti" omitted 115.00 80.00

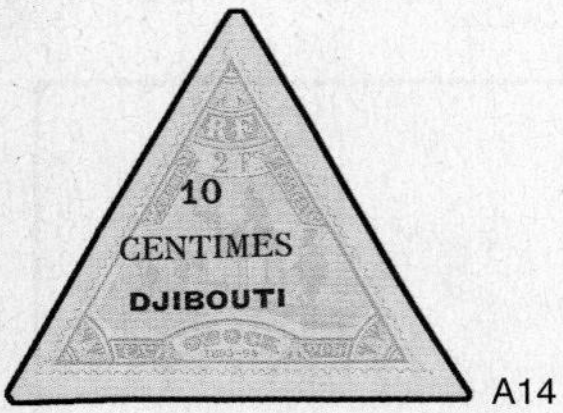
A14

Black Surcharge

33 A14 10c on 2fr dl vio & org 62.50 52.50
Never hinged 140.00
On cover 450.00
Ovpt. "Specimen" 375.00
a. Double surcharge 450.00 435.00
b. Double surcharge, one inverted 2,200. 2,200.
c. Triple surcharge, one inverted 2,700. 2,700.
d. "DJIBOUTI" inverted 250.00 225.00
e. Large "0" in "10" 160.00 125.00
f. As "e," double surcharge 1,500. 1,100.
g. As "e," inverted surcharge 1,700. 1,300.

Same Surcharge on Obock No. 53 in Red

33D A7 10c on 25c blk & bl *32,500.* *22,500.*

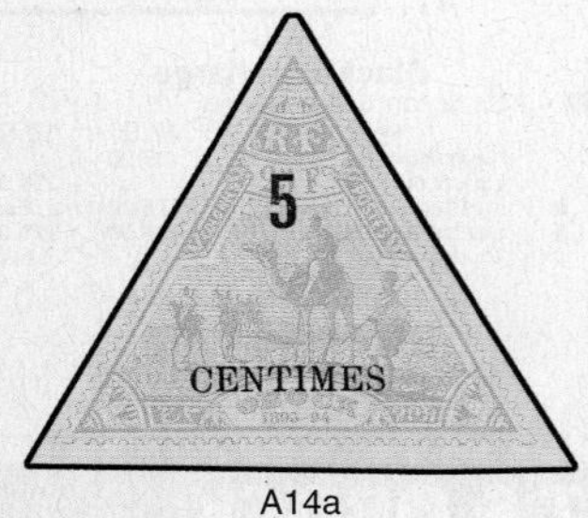
A14a

Black Surcharge on Obock Nos. 63-64

33E A14a 5c on 25fr brn & bl 62.50 55.00
Never hinged 130.00
On cover 450.00
n. "5" omitted 1,750. 1,500.
o. "5" inverted 4,250.
33F A14a 10c on 50fr red vio & grn 80.00 60.00
Never hinged 160.00
On cover 500.00
g. "01" instead of "10" 225.00 210.00
h. "CENTIMES" inverted 2,750. 2,750.
i. Double surcharge 2,750. 2,100.
k. Double surcharge, one inverted 2,750. 2,250.
l. "01" double, one inverted 6,650. 7,750.
m. "centimes" inverted 2,750. 2,750.

Tadjoura Mosque
A15

Somalis on Camel
A16

Warriors — A17

1902 Engr. *Perf. 11½*

34 A15 1c brn vio & org 1.40 1.10
Never hinged 2.10
On cover 110.00
a. 1c rose lilac & orange ('03) 1.75 1.75
Never hinged 3.25
On cover 140.00
35 A15 2c yel brn & yel grn 2.10 1.40
Never hinged 2.75
On cover 110.00
36 A15 4c bl & carmine 3.50 2.10
Never hinged 4.25
On cover 110.00
37 A15 5c bl grn & yel grn 3.50 1.75
Never hinged 5.00
On cover 95.00
38 A15 10c car & red org 7.00 4.25
Never hinged 14.00
On cover 62.50
39 A15 15c brn org & bl 7.00 4.25
Never hinged 14.00
On cover 60.00
40 A16 20c vio & green 17.50 7.75
Never hinged 32.50
On cover 95.00
41 A16 25c blue 25.00 12.50
Never hinged 45.00
On cover 62.50
a. 25c indigo & blue ('03) 25.00 15.00
42 A16 30c red & black 12.50 5.00
Never hinged 14.00
On cover 105.00
On cover, single franking 150.00
43 A16 40c orange & blue 17.50 10.00
Never hinged 35.00
On cover 105.00
On cover, single franking 150.00
44 A16 50c grn & red org 45.00 37.50
Never hinged 95.00
On cover 190.00
On cover, single franking 250.00
45 A16 75c orange & vio 10.50 7.00
Never hinged 21.00
On cover 250.00
On cover, single franking 375.00
46 A17 1fr red org & vio 35.00 17.50
Never hinged 55.00
On cover 300.00
On cover, single franking 475.00
47 A17 2fr yel grn & car 42.50 32.50
Never hinged 95.00
On cover 375.00
On cover, single franking 550.00
a. Without names of designer and engraver at bottom 140.00 140.00
48 A17 5fr orange & blue 35.00 27.50
Never hinged 55.00
On cover 425.00
On cover, single franking 700.00
Nos. 34-48 (15) 265.00 172.10

1903

49 A15 1c brn vio & blk 1.40 1.10
Never hinged 3.50
On cover 95.00
50 A15 2c yel brn & blk 1.40 1.10
Never hinged 3.50
On cover 95.00
51 A15 4c lake & blk 2.10 2.10
Never hinged 3.50
On cover 95.00
a. 4c red & black 2.75 2.50
Never hinged 5.25
On cover 100.00
52 A15 5c bl grn & blk 4.25 3.50
Never hinged 7.00
On cover 60.00
53 A15 10c carmine & blk 8.50 3.50
Never hinged 17.50
On cover 60.00
a. 10c red & black 8.50 3.50
Never hinged 15.00
On cover 60.00
54 A15 15c org brn & blk 25.00 10.50
Never hinged 40.00
On cover 60.00
a. 15c brown & black 21.00 10.50
Never hinged 37.50
On cover 60.00
55 A16 20c dl vio & blk 25.00 17.50
Never hinged 55.00
On cover 85.00
56 A16 25c ultra & blk 25.00 14.00
Never hinged 30.00
On cover 85.00
a. 25c dp blue & black 15.00 10.50
Never hinged 27.50
On cover 140.00
58 A16 40c orange & blk 10.50 10.50
Never hinged 21.00
On cover 85.00
On cover, single franking 110.00
a. 40c bister & black 22.50 22.50
Never hinged 45.00
On cover 125.00
59 A16 50c green & blk 25.00 17.50
Never hinged 50.00
On cover 85.00
On cover, single franking 125.00
60 A16 75c buff & blk 14.00 10.50
Never hinged 25.00
On cover 200.00
On cover, single franking 350.00
a. 75c brown orange & black 77.50 77.50
Never hinged 165.00
On cover 500.00
61 A17 1fr orange & blk 21.00 21.00
Never hinged 42.50
On cover 275.00
On cover, single franking 450.00
a. 1fr dp red & black 45.00 42.50
Never hinged 95.00
On cover 500.00
62 A17 2fr yel grn & blk 14.00 10.50
Never hinged 27.50
On cover 300.00
On cover, single franking 500.00
a. Without names of designer and engraver at bottom 50.00 50.00
Never hinged 105.00
63 A17 5fr red org & blk 25.00 21.00
Never hinged 55.00
On cover 375.00
On cover, single franking 625.00
a. 5fr ocher & black 35.00 32.50
Never hinged 70.00
On cover 450.00
Nos. 49-63 (14) 202.15 144.30

Imperforates, transposed colors and inverted centers exist in the 1902 and 1903 issues. Most of these were issued from Paris and some are said to have been fraudulently printed.

Tadjoura Mosque
A18

Somalis on Camel — A19

Warriors — A20

1909 Typo. *Perf. 14x13½*

64 A18 1c maroon & brn 1.10 1.10
Never hinged 1.75
On cover 62.50
65 A18 2c vio & ol gray 1.10 1.10
Never hinged 1.75
On cover 62.50
66 A18 4c ol gray & bl 1.40 1.10
Never hinged 2.50
On cover 62.50
67 A18 5c grn & gray grn 1.75 1.10
Never hinged 2.75
On cover 37.50
68 A18 10c car & ver 4.50 1.75
Never hinged 7.50
On cover 20.00
69 A18 20c blk & red brn 7.00 5.50
Never hinged 12.50
On cover 40.00
70 A19 25c bl & pale bl 5.00 4.00
Never hinged 10.00
On cover 45.00
On cover, single franking 95.00
71 A19 30c brn & scar 7.75 5.50
Never hinged 12.50
On cover 70.00
On cover, single franking 95.00
72 A19 35c vio & grn 10.50 7.00
Never hinged 17.50
On cover 40.00
On cover, single franking 60.00
73 A19 40c rose & vio 10.50 6.25
Never hinged 17.50
On cover 62.50
On cover, single franking 140.00
74 A19 45c brn & bl grn 10.50 6.25
Never hinged 17.50
On cover 62.50
On cover, single franking 110.00
75 A19 50c maroon & brn 10.50 7.00
Never hinged 17.50
On cover 80.00
On cover, single franking 160.00
76 A19 75c scarlet & grn 21.00 14.00
Never hinged 42.50
On cover 100.00
On cover, single franking 200.00
77 A20 1fr vio & brn 27.50 22.50
Never hinged 50.00
On cover 125.00
On cover, single franking 240.00
78 A20 2fr brn & rose 42.50 32.50
Never hinged 85.00
On cover 140.00
On cover, single franking 275.00
79 A20 5fr vio brn & bl grn 70.00 45.00
Never hinged 125.00
On cover 190.00
On cover, single franking 350.00
Nos. 64-79 (16) 232.60 161.65

Drummer
A21

Somali Girl
A22

Djibouti-Addis Ababa Railroad Bridge — A23

1915-33 *Perf. 13½x14*

Chalky Paper

80 A21 1c brt vio & red brn .25 .30
Never hinged .35
On cover 55.00
a. Ordinary paper .25 .30
Never hinged .35
On cover 55.00
81 A21 2c ocher & ind .25 .30
Never hinged .35
On cover 55.00
a. Ordinary paper .25 .30
Never hinged .35
On cover 55.00
82 A21 4c dk brn & red .35 .35
Never hinged .70
On cover 55.00
a. Ordinary paper .35 .35
Never hinged .70
On cover 55.00
83 A21 5c yel grn & grn 1.10 1.10
Never hinged 1.75
On cover 21.00
a. Ordinary paper 2.50 2.50
Never hinged 3.75
On cover 25.00
84 A21 5c org & dl red ('22) .70 .70
Never hinged 1.10
On cover 30.00
85 A22 10c car & dk red 2.10 1.10
Never hinged 2.75
On cover 12.50
a. Ordinary paper 2.10 1.10
Never hinged 2.75
On cover 12.50
86 A22 10c ap grn & grn ('22) 1.40 1.40
Never hinged 1.75
On cover 30.00
87 A22 10c ver & grn ('25) .35 .70
Never hinged .70
On cover 40.00
88 A22 15c brn vio & car ('18) 1.10 .70
Never hinged 1.40
On cover 12.50
a. Ordinary paper 1.10 .70
Never hinged 1.40
On cover 12.50
89 A22 20c org & blk brn .35 .35
Never hinged .70
On cover 21.00
a. Ordinary paper .35 .35
Never hinged .70
On cover 21.00
90 A22 20c dp grn & bl grn ('25) .35 .35
Never hinged .70
On cover 9.00
91 A22 20c dk grn & red ('27) .70 .70
Never hinged 1.10
On cover 25.00
92 A22 25c ultra & dl bl 1.10 .85
Never hinged 1.75
On cover 21.00
On cover, single franking 50.00
a. Ordinary paper 1.10 .85
Never hinged 1.75
On cover 21.00
93 A22 25c blk & bl grn ('22) 1.40 1.40
Never hinged 1.75
On cover 6.25
94 A22 30c blk & bl grn 2.75 2.10
Never hinged 3.50
On cover 25.00
On cover, single franking 65.00
95 A22 30c rose & red brn ('22) 1.40 1.40
Never hinged 2.75
On cover 30.00
On cover, single franking 60.00

96 A22 30c vio & ol grn ('25) .35 .70
Never hinged .70
On cover 9.00

97 A22 30c grn & dl grn ('27) .70 .70
Never hinged 1.10
On cover 30.00

98 A22 35c lt grn & dl rose .70 .70
Never hinged 1.10
On cover 20.00
On cover, single franking 30.00

99 A22 40c bl & brn vio 1.10 .70
Never hinged 1.75
On cover 30.00
On cover, single franking 50.00

100 A22 45c red brn & dk bl 1.10 .70
Never hinged 1.75
On cover 40.00
On cover, single franking 75.00

101 A22 50c car rose & blk 10.50 7.00
Never hinged 17.50
On cover 55.00
On cover, single franking 125.00

102 A22 50c ultra & ind ('24) 1.40 1.40
Never hinged 2.75
On cover 30.00
On cover, single franking 60.00

103 A22 50c dk brn & red vio ('25) 1.10 .70
Never hinged 1.40
On cover 6.00

104 A22 60c ol grn & red vio ('25) .70 .70
Never hinged 1.10
On cover 21.00
On cover, single franking 50.00

105 A22 65c car rose & ol grn ('25) .70 .70
Never hinged 1.10
On cover 20.00
On cover, single franking 30.00

106 A22 75c dl vio & choc .70 .70
Never hinged 1.10
On cover 40.00
On cover, single franking 100.00
a. Ordinary paper 1.10 .90
Never hinged 1.75
On cover 45.00

107 A22 75c ind & ultra ('25) .70 .70
Never hinged 1.10
On cover 21.00
On cover, single franking 50.00

108 A22 75c brt vio & ol brn ('27) 2.10 1.75
Never hinged 3.50
On cover 11.00

109 A22 85c vio brn & bl grn ('25) 1.10 1.10
Never hinged 1.75
On cover 40.00
On cover, single franking 70.00

110 A22 90c brn red & brt red ('30) 7.75 5.50
Never hinged 12.00
On cover 55.00
On cover, single franking 125.00

111 A23 1fr bis brn & red 2.10 1.40
Never hinged 3.50
On cover 55.00
On cover, single franking 140.00
a. Ordinary paper 2.10 1.40
Never hinged 3.50
On cover 55.00

112 A23 1.10fr red brn & blue ('28) 4.25 5.50
Never hinged 7.00
On cover 110.00
On cover, single franking 300.00

113 A23 1.25fr dk bl & blk brn ('33) 10.50 8.50
Never hinged 15.00
On cover 55.00
On cover, single franking 140.00

114 A23 1.50fr lt bl & dk bl ('30) 1.40 1.40
Never hinged 2.10
On cover 50.00
On cover, single franking 110.00

115 A23 1.75fr gray grn & lt red ('33) 9.00 5.50
Never hinged 14.00
On cover 35.00
On cover, single franking 45.00

116 A23 2fr bl vio & blk 3.50 2.75
Never hinged 7.00
On cover 70.00
On cover, single franking 140.00
a. Ordinary paper 3.50 2.75
Never hinged 7.00
On cover 70.00

117 A23 3fr red vio ('30) 10.50 8.50
Never hinged 17.50
On cover 80.00
On cover, single franking 160.00

118 A23 5fr rose red & blk 7.00 4.25
Never hinged 14.00
On cover 80.00
On cover, single franking 160.00
a. Ordinary paper 7.00 4.25
Never hinged 14.00
On cover 80.00
Nos. 80-118 (39) 94.60 75.35

No. 99 is on ordinary paper.

For surcharges and overprints see Nos. 119-134, 183-193 (in Scott Standard catalogue, Vol. 6).

Nos. 83, 92 Surcharged in Green or Blue

1922

119 A21 10c on 5c, ordinary paper (G) .70 .70
Never hinged 1.40
On cover 40.00
a. Double surcharge 110.00
Never hinged 190.00
b. Chalky paper 1.10 1.10
Never hinged 1.75
On cover 45.00

120 A22 50c on 25c (Bl) .70 .70
Never hinged 1.40
On cover 22.50
On cover, single franking 45.00

Type of 1915 Surcharged in Various Colors

1922

Ordinary Paper

121 A22 0,01c on 15c vio & rose (Bk) .35 *.45*
Never hinged .70
On cover 70.00
a. Chalky paper 5.00 5.00
Never hinged 7.75
On cover 100.00

122 A22 0,02c on 15c vio & rose (Bl) .35 *.65*
Never hinged .70
On cover 70.00
a. Chalky paper 5.00 5.00
Never hinged 7.75
On cover 100.00

123 A22 0,04c on 15c vio & rose (G) .70 .70
Never hinged 1.10
On cover 70.00
a. Chalky paper 3.50 3.50
Never hinged 5.50
On cover 90.00

124 A22 0,05c on 15c vio & rose (R) .70 .70
Never hinged 1.10
On cover 27.50
Nos. 121-124 (4) 2.10 2.50

Nos. 88, 99 and Type of 1915 Surcharged

1923-27

Ordinary Paper

125 A22 60c on 75c ol grn & vio .70 .70
Never hinged 1.10
On cover 16.00
On cover, single franking 27.50

126 A22 65c on 15c ('25) 2.75 2.75
Never hinged 3.50
On cover 55.00
On cover, single franking 125.00
a. Chalky paper 4.25 4.25
Never hinged 7.00
On cover 70.00

127 A22 85c on 40c ('25) 2.10 2.10
Never hinged 2.75
On cover 40.00
On cover, single franking 75.00

128 A22 90c on 75c brn red & red ('27) 5.50 5.50
Never hinged 7.75
On cover 55.00
On cover, single franking 105.00
a. Double surcharge 80.00
Never hinged 130.00
Nos. 125-128 (4) 11.05 11.05

No. 118 and Type of 1915-17 Surcharged with New Value and Bars in Black or Red

1924-27

129 A23 25c on 5fr 1.40 1.40
Never hinged 2.10
On cover 6.25
a. Chalky paper 7.75 7.75
Never hinged 13.50
On cover 65.00

130 A23 1.25fr on 1fr dk bl & ultra (R) ('26) 1.40 1.10
Never hinged 1.75
On cover 50.00
On cover, single franking 95.00

131 A23 1.50fr on 1fr lt bl & dk bl ('27) 1.40 1.40
Never hinged 1.75
On cover 40.00
On cover, single franking 55.00

132 A23 3fr on 5fr ver & red vio ('27) 7.00 7.00
Never hinged 7.75
On cover 70.00
On cover, single franking 140.00
a. Period after "F" omitted 27.50 27.50
Never hinged 45.00

133 A23 10fr on 5fr brn red & ol brn ('27) 10.50 10.50
Never hinged 14.00
On cover 90.00
On cover, single franking 175.00

134 A23 20fr on 5fr gray grn & lil rose ('27) 14.00 *17.50*
Never hinged 25.00
On cover 110.00
On cover, single franking 225.00
Nos. 129-134 (6) 35.70 38.90

Common Design Types pictured following the introduction.

Colonial Exposition Issue
Common Design Types

Engr., Name of Country Typo. in Black

1931 ***Perf. 12½***

135 CD70 40c deep green 5.50 5.50
Never hinged 9.00
On cover 95.00

136 CD71 50c violet 5.50 5.50
Never hinged 9.00
On cover 80.00

137 CD72 90c red orange 5.50 5.50
Never hinged 9.00
On cover 125.00
On cover, single franking 190.00
a. Country name omitted, in pair with normal stamp 1,250.

138 CD73 1.50fr dull blue 5.50 5.50
Never hinged 9.00
On cover 110.00
On cover, single franking 165.00
Nos. 135-138 (4) 22.00 22.00

Paris International Exposition Issue
Common Design Types

1937 **Engr.** ***Perf. 13***

139 CD74 20c deep violet 1.90 1.90
Never hinged 2.75
On cover 90.00

140 CD75 30c dark green 1.90 1.90
Never hinged 2.75
On cover 70.00

141 CD76 40c car rose 1.90 1.90
Never hinged 2.75
On cover 55.00
a. Country name double 190.00
Never hinged 290.00

142 CD77 50c dk brn & bl 1.90 1.90
Never hinged 3.25
On cover 50.00

143 CD78 90c red 1.90 1.90
Never hinged 3.25
On cover 95.00
On cover, single franking 160.00

144 CD79 1.50fr ultra 2.10 2.10
Never hinged 3.25
On cover 80.00
On cover, single franking 140.00
a. Country name inverted 125.00 130.00
Never hinged 190.00
On cover 225.00
Nos. 139-144 (6) 11.60 11.60

Colonial Arts Exhibition Issue
Souvenir Sheet
Common Design Type

1937 ***Imperf.***

145 CD75 3fr dull violet 14.00 *21.00*
Never hinged 21.00
On cover 140.00
On cover, single franking 210.00

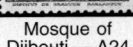

Mosque of Djibouti — A24

Somali Warriors — A25

Governor Léonce Lagarde — A26

View of Djibouti — A27

1938-40 ***Perf. 12x12½, 12½***

146 A24 2c dull red vio .25 .25
Never hinged .35
On cover 25.00

147 A24 3c slate grn ('40) .25 .25
Never hinged .35
On cover 30.00

148 A24 4c dull red brn .25 .25
Never hinged .35
On cover 25.00

149 A24 5c carmine .25 .25
Never hinged .35
On cover 21.00

150 A24 10c blue gray .25 .25
Never hinged .35
On cover 19.00

151 A24 15c slate black .35 .30
Never hinged .70
On cover 19.00

152 A24 20c dark orange .35 .30
Never hinged .70
On cover 19.00

153 A25 25c dark brown .70 .70
Never hinged 1.10
On cover 15.00

154 A25 30c dark blue .35 .35
Never hinged .70
On cover 15.00

155 A25 35c olive grn 1.10 .70
Never hinged 1.40
On cover 25.00

156 A24 40c org brn ('40) .35 .35
Never hinged .70
On cover 14.00

157 A24 45c dull grn ('40) .35 .35
Never hinged .70
On cover 22.50

158 A25 50c red .70 .70
Never hinged 1.10
On cover 12.50

159 A25 55c dull red vio 1.10 .70
Never hinged 1.40
On cover 7.50

160 A25 60c black ('40) .70 .70
Never hinged 1.10
On cover 20.00

161 A25 65c orange brown 1.10 1.10
Never hinged 1.40
On cover 12.50

162 A25 70c lt violet ('40) 1.40 1.40
Never hinged 1.75
On cover 22.50

163 A26 80c gray blk 2.75 2.10
Never hinged 3.50
On cover 45.00
On cover, single franking 75.00

164 A25 90c rose vio ('39) 1.40 1.40
Never hinged 2.10
On cover 55.00
On cover, single franking 105.00

165 A26 1fr carmine 3.50 2.10
Never hinged 5.00
On cover 30.00
On cover, single franking 55.00

166 A26 1fr black ('40) .55 .55
Never hinged .75
On cover 7.00

167 A26 1.25fr magenta ('39) 1.10 1.10
Never hinged 1.40
On cover 55.00
On cover, single franking 105.00

168 A26 1.40fr pck bl ('40) 1.10 1.10
Never hinged 1.40
On cover 35.00
On cover, single franking 80.00

169 A26 1.50fr dull green 1.10 1.10
Never hinged 1.40
On cover 15.00
On cover, single franking 25.00

170 A26 1.60fr brn car ('40) 1.10 1.10
Never hinged 1.40
On cover 35.00
On cover, single franking 95.00

171 A26 1.75fr ultra 1.40 1.10
Never hinged 2.10
On cover 27.50
On cover, single franking 50.00

172 A26 2fr dk orange 1.10 1.10
Never hinged 1.40
On cover 19.00
On cover, single franking 30.00

173 A26 2.25fr ultra ('39) 1.75 1.75
Never hinged 2.50
On cover 50.00
On cover, single franking 95.00

174 A26 2.50fr org brn ('40) 1.75 1.75
Never hinged 2.50
On cover 30.00
On cover, single franking 55.00

175 A26 3fr dull violet 1.10 1.10
Never hinged 1.40
On cover 30.00
On cover, single franking 55.00

176 A27 5fr brn & pale cl 2.10 2.10
Never hinged 3.50
On cover 40.00
On cover, single franking 70.00
177 A27 10fr ind & pale bl 2.50 2.75
Never hinged 3.50
On cover 45.00
On cover, single franking 90.00
178 A27 20fr car lake & gray 2.50 2.75
Never hinged 3.50
On cover 55.00
On cover, single franking 100.00
Nos. 146-178 (33) 36.60 33.85

For overprints and surcharge see Nos. 194-223 in the Scott Standard Catalogue, Vol. 6.

New York World's Fair Issue
Common Design Type

1939 Engr. *Perf. 12½x12*
179 CD82 1.25fr car lake .70 1.40
Never hinged 1.10
On cover 62.50
On cover, single franking 125.00
180 CD82 2.25fr ultra .70 1.40
Never hinged 1.10
On cover 62.50
On cover, single franking 110.00

SEMI-POSTAL STAMPS

Somali Girl — SP1

1915 Unwmk. *Perf. 13½x14*
Chalky Paper
B1 SP1 10c + 5c car & dk red 9.00 8.50
Never hinged 15.00
On cover 60.00

Curie Issue
Common Design Type

1938 Engr. *Perf. 13*
B2 CD80 1.75fr + 50c brt ultra 7.75 7.75
Never hinged 12.50
On cover 90.00
On cover, single franking 150.00

French Revolution Issue
Common Design Type

Photo., Name and Value Typo. in Black

1939
B3 CD83 45c + 25c green 9.00 9.00
Never hinged 15.00
On cover 140.00
B4 CD83 70c + 30c brown 9.00 9.00
Never hinged 15.00
On cover 100.00
B5 CD83 90c + 35c red org 9.00 9.00
Never hinged 15.00
On cover 90.00
B6 CD83 1.25fr + 1fr rose pink 9.00 9.00
Never hinged 17.50
On cover 90.00
On cover, single franking 225.00
B7 CD83 2.25fr + 2fr blue 9.00 9.00
Never hinged 15.00
On cover 140.00
On cover, single franking 200.00
Nos. B3-B7 (5) 45.00 45.00

POSTAGE DUE STAMPS

D1

1915 Unwmk. Typo. *Perf. 14x13½*
Chalky Paper
J1 D1 5c deep ultra .35 .55
Never hinged .55
On cover 45.00
a. Ordinary paper 1.10 1.10
Never hinged 1.75
On cover 50.00
J2 D1 10c brown red .55 .70
Never hinged .85
On cover 45.00
a. Ordinary paper 2.10 2.10
Never hinged 3.50
On cover 55.00
J3 D1 15c black .85 1.20
Never hinged 1.40
On cover 45.00
a. Ordinary paper 2.10 2.10
Never hinged 3.50
On cover 55.00
J4 D1 20c purple 1.75 2.10
Never hinged 2.50
On cover 50.00
J5 D1 30c orange 1.75 2.10
Never hinged 2.50
On cover 50.00
J6 D1 50c maroon 2.75 3.25
Never hinged 5.00
On cover 55.00
J7 D1 60c green 4.25 5.00
Never hinged 2.00
On cover 62.50
J8 D1 1fr dark blue 5.25 6.25
Never hinged 8.50
On cover 75.00
Nos. J1-J8 (8) 17.50 21.15

See Nos. J11-J20.

Type of 1915 Issue Surcharged

1927
J9 D1 2fr on 1fr light red 10.50 10.50
Never hinged 14.00
On cover 90.00
J10 D1 3fr on 1fr lilac rose 10.50 10.50
Never hinged 14.00
On cover 100.00

Type of 1915

1938 Engr. *Perf. 12½x13*
J11 D1 5c light ultra .25 .30
Never hinged .35
On cover 35.00
J12 D1 10c dark carmine .25 .30
Never hinged .35
On cover 35.00
J13 D1 15c brown black .30 .35
Never hinged .45
On cover 35.00
J14 D1 20c violet .30 .35
Never hinged .45
On cover 35.00
J15 D1 30c orange yellow 1.00 1.10
Never hinged 1.40
On cover 35.00
J16 D1 50c brown .65 .70
Never hinged .85
On cover 40.00
J17 D1 60c emerald 1.00 1.10
Never hinged 1.40
On cover 45.00
J18 D1 1fr indigo 2.00 2.00
Never hinged 2.90
On cover 45.00
J19 D1 2fr red .90 1.00
Never hinged 1.40
On cover 55.00
J20 D1 3fr dark brown 1.25 1.40
Never hinged 2.00
On cover 75.00
Nos. J11-J20 (10) 7.90 8.60
Set, never hinged 11.00

Inscribed "Inst de Grav" below design.

SOMALILAND PROTECTORATE

sō-ˈmä-lē-ˌland

prə-ˈtek-tˌə-ˌrət

LOCATION — Eastern Africa, bordering on the Gulf of Aden
GOVT. — British Protectorate
AREA — 68,000 sq. mi.
POP. — 640,000 (estimated)
CAPITAL — Hargeisa

Formerly administered by the Indian Government, the territory was taken over by the British Foreign Office in 1898 and transferred to the Colonial Office in 1905.

16 Annas = 1 Rupee
100 Cents = 1 Shilling (1951)

Catalogue values for unused stamps in this country are for Never Hinged items, beginning with Scott 108.

Stamps of India, 1882-1900, Overprinted at Top of Stamp

1903 Wmk. 39 *Perf. 14*
1 A17 ½a light green 3.00 5.00
Never hinged 5.25
2 A19 1a carmine rose 3.00 4.50
Never hinged 5.25
3 A21 2a violet 2.50 1.75
Never hinged 4.50
a. Double overprint 800.00
b. Double overprint, one albino
4 A28 2½a ultra 2.25 2.10
Never hinged 4.00
5 A22 3a brn org 3.50 3.50
Never hinged 6.25
6 A23 4a olive green 4.00 3.50
Never hinged 7.00
7 A25 8a red violet 4.25 6.00
8 A26 12a brown, *red* 6.75 9.00
Never hinged 12.00
a. Inverted overprint 1,200.
9 A29 1r car rose & grn 7.50 12.50
Never hinged 13.50
10 A30 2r yel brn & car rose 38.00 55.00
Never hinged 67.50
11 A30 3r grn & brn 36.00 67.50
Never hinged 62.50
12 A30 5r violet & blue 59.00 77.50
Never hinged 105.00

Wmk. Elephant's Head (38)
13 A14 6a bister 7.50 5.25
Never hinged 14.00
Nos. 1-13 (13) 177.25 253.10

Nos. 1-5 exist without the 2nd "I" of "BRITISH."

"BRIT SH" for "BRITISH"
1b A17 ½a light green 180.00 275.00
2b A19 1a carmine rose 225.00 300.00
3b A21 2a violet 400.00 500.00
4b A28 2½a ultra 650.00
5b A22 3a brown orange 800.00

"BR1TISH" for "BRITISH"
1c A17 ½a light green 200.00 275.00
2c A19 1a carmine rose 200.00
3c A21 2a violet 325.00
4c A28 2½a ultra 400.00
5c A22 3a brown orange 400.00 450.00
6c A23 4a olive green 425.00 475.00
7c A25 8a red violet 425.00 550.00
8c A26 12a brown, *red* 500.00 600.00
9c A29 1r car rose & grn 500.00
13c A14 6a bister 300.00 350.00

Curved Overprint
10d A30 2r yel brn & car rose 700.00
11d A30 3r green & brown 700.00
12d A30 5r violet & blue 700.00

"SOMAL.LAND"
13e A14 6a bister 175.00

Same, but Overprinted at Bottom of Stamp

1903 Wmk. 39
14 A28 2½a ultra 6.50 8.50
Never hinged 10.50
15 A26 12a violet, *red* 13.00 14.00
Never hinged 23.00
16 A29 1r car rose & grn 10.00 15.00
Never hinged 17.00
17 A30 2r yel brn & car rose 130.00 200.00
Never hinged 235.00
18 A30 3r green & brn 140.00 200.00
Never hinged 250.00
a. Double overprint, both inverted, one albino 1,000.
19 A30 5r violet & blue 130.00 180.00
Never hinged 225.00

Wmk. 38
20 A14 6a bister 8.50 7.50
Never hinged 15.00
Nos. 14-20 (7) 438.00 625.00

"BRIT SH" for "BRITISH"
14b A28 2½a ultra 1,500.

"BR1TISH" for "BRITISH"
14c A28 2½a ultra 200.00
15c A26 12a violet, *red* 425.00
16c A29 1r car rose & grn 475.00

Curved Overprint
17d A30 2r yel brn & car rose 850.00 1,300.
18d A30 3r green & brn 900.00
19d A30 5r violet & blue 900.00

"SOMAL.LAND"
14e A28 2½a ultra 275.00
15e A26 12a violet, *red* 375.00
16e A29 1r car rose & grn 500.00
17e A30 2r yel brn & car rose 850.00
18e A30 3r green & brn 900.00
19e A30 5r violet & blue 900.00

"SUMALILAND"
14f A28 2½a ultra 275.00
15f A26 12a violet, *red* 350.00 500.00
16f A29 1r car rose & grn 475.00
17f A30 2r yel brn & car rose 850.00
18f A30 3r green & brn 900.00
19f A30 5r violet & blue 900.00

Stamps of India, 1902-03, Ovptd.

1903 Wmk. 39
21 A33 ½a light green 3.25 .60
Never hinged 5.75
22 A34 1a car rose 1.40 .35
Never hinged 2.50
23 A35 2a violet 2.75 2.75
Never hinged 3.75
24 A37 3a brown orange 2.75 2.75
Never hinged 5.00
25 A38 4a olive green 1.60 3.50
Never hinged 3.00
26 A40 8a red violet 3.50 2.50
Never hinged 5.00
Nos. 21-26 (6) 15.25 12.45

"BRIT SH" for "BRITISH"
21b A33 ½a light green 550.00
22b A34 1a car rose 350.00
23b A35 2a violet 1,300.

"BR1TISH" for "BRITISH"
21c A33 ½a light green 130.00
22c A34 1a car rose 130.00 140.00
23c A35 2a violet 250.00
24c A37 3a brown orange 275.00 350.00
25c A38 4a olive green 200.00
26c A40 8a red violet 375.00

"SOMAL.LAND"
21e A33 ½a light green 80.00 95.00
22e A34 1a car rose 60.00 70.00
23e A35 2a violet 120.00
24e A37 3a brown orange 140.00 170.00
25e A38 4a olive green 140.00
26e A40 8a red violet 225.00

"SUMALILAND"
21f A33 ½a light green 250.00
22f A34 1a car rose 130.00 140.00
23f A35 2a violet 225.00
24f A37 3a brown orange 225.00
25f A38 4a olive green 200.00
26f A40 8a red violet 375.00

The above overprints vary in length, also in the relative positions of the letters.

A1

King Edward VII — A2

1904 Wmk. 2 Typo.
27 A1 ½a dl grn & grn 2.75 4.50
Never hinged 5.00
28 A1 1a carmine & blk 19.00 3.50
Never hinged 38.00
29 A1 2a red vio & dull vio 2.25 2.60
Never hinged 4.50
30 A1 2½a ultramarine 9.50 4.00
Never hinged 19.00
31 A1 3a gray grn & vio brn 2.50 6.25
Never hinged 5.00
32 A1 4a blk & gray grn 4.00 9.00
Never hinged 8.00
33 A1 6a vio & gray grn 11.50 18.00
Never hinged 22.00
34 A1 8a pale blue & blk 8.50 9.50
Never hinged 17.00
35 A1 12a ocher & blk 14.00 11.50
Never hinged 28.00

Wmk. Crown and C C (1)
36 A2 1r gray grn 20.00 47.50
Never hinged 36.00
37 A2 2r red vio & dull vio 60.00 90.00
Never hinged 120.00
38 A2 3r blk & gray grn 70.00 130.00
Never hinged 140.00
39 A2 5r carmine & blk 70.00 140.00
Never hinged 140.00
Nos. 27-39 (13) 294.00 476.35
Set, ovptd. "SPECIMEN" 225.00

1905 Wmk. 3
Ordinary Paper
40 A1 ½a dl grn & grn 2.00 8.00
41 A1 1a carmine & blk 22.50 1.75
42 A1 2a red vio & dull vio 9.00 19.00
43 A1 2½a ultramarine 4.50 11.00
44 A1 3a gray grn & vio brn 2.50 16.00
45 A1 4a blk & gray grn 5.00 26.00
46 A1 6a vio & gray grn 3.00 27.50
47 A1 8a pale blue & blk 8.00 11.00
48 A1 12a ocher & black 7.25 11.00
Nos. 40-48 (9) 63.75 131.25

Nos. 41, 42, 44-48 are on both ordinary and chalky paper, values are for lower value.

Chalky Paper

41a A1 1a carmine & black ('06) 21.00 1.75
42a A1 2a red vio & dull vio ('09) 20.00 *16.00*
44a A1 3a gray grn & vio brn ('11) 16.00 *50.00*
45a A1 4a blk & gray grn ('11) 22.50 *55.00*
46a A1 6a vio & gray grn ('11) 40.00 *80.00*
47a A1 8a blue & black ('11) 30.00 *80.00*
48a A1 12a org brn & blk ('11) 19.00 *75.00*

1909

49 A1 ½a bluish green 45.00 *40.00*
50 A1 1a carmine 3.00 2.25
Ovptd. "SPECIMEN" 40.00

For overprints see Nos. O11-O16.

A3

King George V — A4

The ½, 1 and 2½a of type A3 are on ordinary paper, the other values of types A3 and A4 are on chalky paper.

1912-19

51 A3 ½a green .90 *13.00*
52 A3 1a carmine 3.00 .60
a. 1p scarlet ('17) 3.50 1.40
53 A3 2a red vio & dull vio 4.25 *16.00*
a. 2a violet purple & dull purple ('19) 27.50 *50.00*
54 A3 2½a ultramarine 1.25 *9.75*
55 A3 3a gray grn & vio brn 2.75 *10.00*
56 A3 4a blk & grn ('13) 3.00 *11.50*
57 A3 6a violet & green 3.00 *11.50*
58 A3 8a lt blue & blk 4.25 *17.50*
59 A3 12a ocher & blk 4.00 *24.00*
60 A4 1r dull grn & grn 22.50 *27.50*
61 A4 2r red vio & dull vio ('19) 28.00 *80.00*
62 A4 3r blk & gray grn ('19) 85.00 *175.00*
63 A4 5r car & blk ('19) 90.00 *250.00*
Nos. 51-63 (13) 251.90 *646.35*
Set, ovptd. "SPECIMEN" 300.00

1921 **Wmk. 4**

64 A3 ½a blue green 3.75 *17.00*
65 A3 1a scarlet 4.25 .80
66 A3 2a vio & dull vio 5.00 1.10
67 A3 2½a ultramarine 1.25 *11.00*
68 A3 3a gray grn & vio brn 3.00 *8.50*
69 A3 4a black & grn 3.00 *15.00*
70 A3 6a violet & grn 2.00 *15.00*
71 A3 8a lt blue & blk 2.50 *12.50*
72 A3 12a ocher & blk 11.00 *17.50*
73 A4 1r dull grn & grn 10.00 *55.00*
74 A4 2r vio & dull vio 30.00 *62.50*
75 A4 3r blk & gray grn 42.50 *125.00*
76 A4 5r scarlet & blk 95.00 *200.00*
Nos. 64-76 (13) 213.25 *540.90*
Set, ovptd. "SPECIMEN" 300.00

Common Design Types

pictured following the introduction.

Silver Jubilee Issue

Common Design Type

1935, May 6 Engr. *Perf. 11x12*

77 CD301 1a car & dk blue 2.50 *4.00*
78 CD301 2a black & ultra 3.00 *4.25*
79 CD301 3a ultra & brown 2.50 *19.00*
80 CD301 1r brn vio & ind 9.00 *21.00*
Nos. 77-80 (4) 17.00 *48.25*
Set, never hinged 34.00
Set, perf "SPECIMEN" 110.00

Coronation Issue

Common Design Type

1937, May 13 *Perf. 13½x14*

81 CD302 1a carmine .25 *.40*
82 CD302 2a black .35 *2.00*
83 CD302 3a bright ultra .50 *1.00*
Nos. 81-83 (3) 1.10 *3.40*
Set, never hinged 2.00
Set, perf "SPECIMEN" 95.00

Blackhead Sheep — A5

Greater Kudu — A6

Map of Somaliland Protectorate A7

1938, May 10 Wmk. 4 *Perf. 12½*

84 A5 ½a green 1.25 *5.75*
Never hinged 2.50
85 A5 1a carmine .75 *1.75*
Never hinged 1.40
86 A5 2a deep claret 2.50 *4.50*
Never hinged 4.00
87 A5 3a ultra 10.00 *17.50*
Never hinged 17.50
88 A6 4a dark brown 3.50 *12.00*
Never hinged 6.00
89 A6 6a purple 9.00 *13.00*
Never hinged 15.00
90 A6 8a gray black 4.75 *13.50*
Never hinged 8.00
91 A6 12a orange 11.00 *35.00*
Never hinged 18.00
92 A7 1r green 8.50 *80.00*
Never hinged 14.00
93 A7 2r rose violet 15.00 *80.00*
Never hinged 25.00
94 A7 3r ultramarine 13.50 *45.00*
Never hinged 22.50
95 A7 5r black 18.00 *45.00*
Never hinged 30.00
a. Horiz. pair, imperf. btwn. *30,000.*
Nos. 84-95 (12) 97.75 *353.00*
Set, never hinged 163.90
Set, perf "SPECIMEN" 325.00

A8

A9

A10

1942, Apr. 22

96 A8 ½a green .25 *.50*
97 A8 1a carmine .25 .25
98 A8 2a deep claret .45 .25
99 A8 3a ultramarine 1.50 .25
100 A9 4a dark brown 1.75 .25
101 A9 6a purple 2.00 .25
102 A9 8a gray 2.40 *.25*
103 A9 12a orange 2.00 *1.50*
104 A10 1r green 2.25 *2.75*
105 A10 2r rose violet 3.75 *9.50*
106 A10 3r ultra 6.75 *16.00*
107 A10 5r black 10.00 *11.00*
Nos. 96-107 (12) 33.35 *42.75*
Set, never hinged 55.00
Set, perf "SPECIMEN" 300.00

For surcharges see Nos. 116-126.

Catalogue values for unused stamps in this section, from this point to the end of the section, are for Never Hinged items.

Peace Issue

Common Design Type

Perf. 13¾x14

1946, Oct. 15 Engr. Wmk. 4

108 CD303 1a carmine .35 .25
Hinged .25
a. Perf. 13½ 19.00 *65.00*
Hinged 11.50
109 CD303 3a deep blue .35 .25
Hinged .25
Set, perf "SPECIMEN" 85.00

Silver Wedding Issue

Common Design Types

1949, Jan. 28 Photo. *Perf. 14x14½*

110 CD304 1a scarlet .40 .25
Hinged .25

Perf. 11½x11

Engraved; Name Typographed

111 CD305 5r gray black 8.00 *8.50*
Hinged 6.00

UPU Issue

Common Design Types

Surcharged in Black or Carmine with New Values in Annas

Engr.; Name Typo. on 3a, 6a

1949, Oct. 10 *Perf. 13½, 11x11½*

112 CD306 1a on 10c rose car .40 *.35*
Hinged .25
113 CD307 3a on 30c ind (C) 2.00 *4.50*
Hinged 1.25
114 CD308 6a on 50c rose vio .55 *3.25*
Hinged .35
115 CD309 12a on 1sh red org 1.00 .60
Hinged .60
Nos. 112-115 (4) 3.95 8.70

Nos. 96 and 98 to 107 Surcharged with New Value in Black or Carmine

1951, Apr. 2 Wmk. 4 *Perf. 12½*

116 A8 5c on ½a green .40 *2.25*
117 A8 10c on 2a deep claret .40 *1.00*
118 A8 15c on 3a ultramarine 1.60 2.25
119 A9 20c on 4a dark brown 2.25 .25
120 A9 30c on 6a purple 1.80 1.50
121 A9 50c on 8a gray 2.50 .25
122 A9 70c on 12a red 4.00 *9.00*
123 A10 1sh on 1r green 2.25 2.00
124 A10 2sh on 2r rose violet 5.25 *22.50*
125 A10 2sh on 3r ultra 13.00 10.00
126 A10 5sh on 5r black (C) 22.50 15.00
Nos. 116-126 (11) 55.95 66.00

OFFICIAL STAMPS

Official Stamps of India, 1883-1900, Overprinted

1903, June 1 Wmk. 39 *Perf. 14*

O1 A17 ½a light green 9.50 *55.00*
Never hinged 17.00
O2 A19 1a carmine rose 22.50 *12.50*
Never hinged 40.00
O3 A21 2a violet 15.00 *55.00*
Never hinged 25.00
O4 A25 8a red violet 19.00 *450.00*
Never hinged 30.00
a. No period after "M" of "O.H.M.S." 4,250.
O5 A29 1r car rose & grn 20.00 *750.00*
Never hinged 30.00
Nos. O1-O5 (5) 86.00 *1,323.*

"BRITIS H" for "BRITISH"

O1b A17 ½a light green 350.00 *800.00*
O2b A19 1a carmine rose 350.00 *450.00*
O3b A21 2a violet 475.00
O4b A25 8a red violet 1,300.
O5b A29 1r car rose & grn 1,500.

"BR1TISH" for "BRITISH"

O1c A17 ½a light green 475.00
O2c A19 1a carmine rose 475.00 *550.00*
O3c A21 2a violet 600.00
O4c A25 8a red violet 1,600.
O5c A29 1r car rose & grn 1,800.

India Nos. 61-63, 68, 49 Overprinted

SERVICE BRITISH SOMALILAND

1903

O6 A33 ½a green .90
Never hinged 1.50
O7 A34 1a carmine rose .95
Never hinged 1.50
O8 A35 2a violet 1.60
Never hinged 2.50
O9 A40 8a red violet 8.00
Never hinged 13.00
O10 A29 1r car rose & grn 22.50
Never hinged 40.00
Nos. O6-O10 (5) 33.95

Nos. O6-O10 were not regularly issued, although used examples are known.

"BRIT SH" for "BRITISH"

O6b A33 ½a green 95.00
O7b A34 1a carmine rose 95.00
O8b A35 2a violet 130.00
O9b A40 8a red violet 2,750.
O10b A29 1r car rose & grn 2,750.

"BR1TISH" for "BRITISH"

O6c A33 ½a green 85.00
O7c A34 1a carmine rose 85.00
O8c A35 2a violet 120.00
O9c A40 8a red violet 2,250.
O10c A29 1r car rose & grn 2,250.

"SOMAL.LAND"

O6e A33 ½a green 85.00
O7e A34 1a carmine rose 85.00
O10e A29 1r car rose & grn 2,250.

"SUMALILAND"

O6f A33 ½a green 85.00
O7f A34 1a carmine rose 85.00
O8f A35 2a violet 120.00
O9f A40 8a red violet 2,250.
O10f A29 1r car rose & grn 2,250.

Regular Issue of 1904 Overprinted

1904 Wmk. Crown and C A (2)

O11 A1 ½a gray green 11.00 *55.00*
Never hinged 14.00
a. No period after "M" 300.00
O12 A1 1a carmine & blk 5.00 *8.00*
Never hinged 7.50
a. No period after "M" 250.00 *325.00*
O13 A1 2a red vio & dull vio 300.00 70.00
Never hinged 500.00
a. No period after "M" 3,250. 850.00
O14 A1 8a pale blue & blk 80.00 *150.00*
Never hinged 140.00
a. No period after "M" 650.00 *950.00*
Nos. O11-O14 (4) 396.00 *283.00*

Wmk. Crown and C C (1)

O15 A2 1r gray green 300.00 *1,100.*

Same Overprint on No. 42

1905 Wmk. 3

O16 A1 2a red vio & dull vio 140.00 *1,100.*
a. No period after "M" 2,500.

The period after "M" may be found missing on Nos. O11-O14 and O16.

SOUTH AFRICA

sauth 'a-fri-kə

LOCATION — Southern Africa
GOVT. — Republic
AREA — 433,678 sq. mi.
POP. — 26,749,000 (est. 1984)
CAPITAL — Pretoria (administrative); Cape Town (legislative)

The union was formed on May 31, 1910, comprising the former British colonies of Cape of Good Hope, Natal, Transvaal and the Orange Free State, which became provinces.

For previous listings, see individual headings.

12 Pence = 1 Shilling
20 Shillings = 1 Pound

Catalogue values for unused stamps in this country are for Never Hinged items, beginning with Scott 74 in the regular postage section, Scott B1 in the semi-postal section, Scott J22 in the postage due section, and Scott O21 in the officials section.

Watermarks

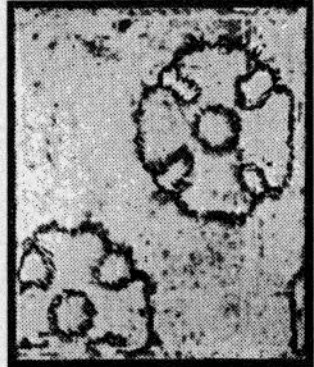

Wmk. 47 — Multiple Rosette

Wmk. 177 — Springbok's Head

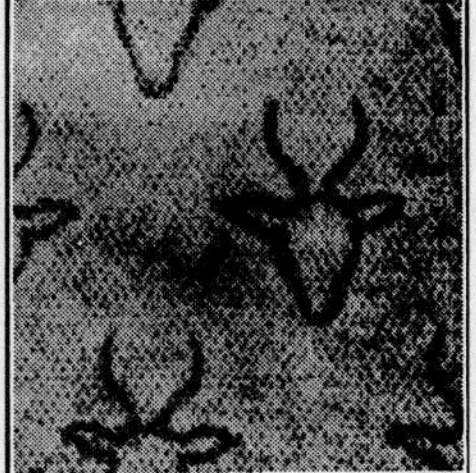

Wmk. 201 — Multiple Springbok's Head

STAMPS OF GREAT BRITAIN USED IN SOUTH AFRICA

Stamps of Great Britain used in South Africa during the Boer War, 1899-1902, with circular or octagonal postmarks "British Army South Africa" or "Natal Field Force" in several types.

1881

A1 1p lilac (16 dots) (#89) 6.25

1883-84

A2 2sh6p lilac (#96) 375.00
A3 5sh rose (#108) 475.00
A4 10sh ultramarine (#109) 950.00

1887-92

A5 ½p vermilion (#111) 7.50
A6 1½p violet & green (#112) 42.50
A7 2p green & carmine rose (#113) 21.00
A8 2½p violet, *blue* (#114) 7.50
A9 3p violet, *yellow* (#115) 17.00
A10 4p brown & green (#116) 30.00
A11 4½p carmine rose & green (#117) 120.00
A12 5p lilac blue, type II (#118) 21.00
A13 6p violet, *rose* (#119) 17.00
A14 9p blue & lilac (#120) 110.00
A15 10p carmine rose & lilac (#121) 100.00
A16 1sh green (#122) 160.00
A17 £1 green (#142) 1,700.

1900

A18 ½p blue green (#125) 7.50
A19 1sh carmine rose & green (#126) 240.00

1902

A20 ½p blue green (#127a) 17.50
A21 1p scarlet(#128) 12.00
A22 1½p violet & green (#129) 90.00
A23 2p yellow green & carmine (#130) 65.00
A24 2½p ultramarine (#131) 26.00
A25 3p dull purple *orange yellow* (#132) 80.00
A26 4p gray brown & green (#133) 90.00
A27 5p dull purple & ultramarine (#134) 90.00
A28 6p pale dull violet (#135) 42.50
A29 9p ultramarine & dull violet (#136) 160.00
A30 10p carmine & dull purple (#137) 170.00
A31 1sh carmine & dull green (#138) 110.00

ARMY OFFICIAL STAMPS

1896-1901

AO1 ½p vermilion (#O54) 125.00
AO2 ½p blue green (#O57) 125.00
AO3 1p lilac (#O55) 100.00
AO4 6p purple, *rose red* (#O58) —

From Aug. 19, 1910, through December 31, 1937, the stamps of the provinces (Cape of Good Hope, Natal, Orange River Colony and Transvaal) were valid for postage throughout South Africa. They were demonetized effective Jan. 1, 1938.

Union of South Africa

George V — A1

1910 Engr. Wmk. 47 *Perf. 14*

1 A1 2½p blue 3.25 1.75
Never hinged 7.00
a. 2½ deep blue 3.50 2.75
Never hinged 11.00
Handstamped "SPECIMEN" *525.00*

Union Parliament opening, Nov. 4, 1910.

Type A2 stamps have very small margins at top and bottom. Values are for examples with perfs close to, or touching the frame.

George V — A2

1913-24 Typo. Wmk. 177

2 A2 ½p green 1.75 .30
Never hinged 2.50
a. Double impression *12,000.*
b. ½p blue green 2.00 .25
c. ½p yellow green 2.75 1.00
d. ½p dark mossy green *500.00* *190.00*
e. Printed on gummed side *1,500.*
3 A2 1p rose red 1.75 .25
Never hinged 2.00
a. 1p scarlet 4.00 1.00
b. 1p carmine red 2.25 .25
c. 1p deep carmine lake 12.50 4.50
d. Printed on gummed side *925.00*
4 A2 1½p org brn ('20) .80 .25
a. Tête bêche pair 2.00 *18.00*
b. 1½p dark chestnut 4.50 15.00
c. Printed on gummed side *1,000.*
5 A2 2p dull violet 2.25 .25
Never hinged 4.50
a. 2p deep purple 2.50 .25
b. 2p reddish purple 3.00 .65
c. 2p deep plum *385.00* *190.00*
d. Printed on gummed side *1,000.*
6 A2 2½p ultra 5.50 1.60
Never hinged 10.50
a. 2½p deep blue 5.50 3.00
7 A2 3p brn org & blk 13.00 .55
Never hinged 25.00
a. 3p dull orange red & black 10.00 .70
8 A2 3p ultra ('22) 4.75 1.75
Never hinged 10.00
a. 3p dk ultramarine 6.50 2.50
9 A2 4p ol grn & org 11.00 .55
Never hinged 20.00
a. 4p sage green & orange 7.00 .55
10 A2 6p violet & black 9.50 .70
Never hinged 20.00
a. 6p bright violet & black 10.00 1.50
b. 6p reddish violet & black 10.00 1.00
c. "Z" of "ZUID" missing 80.00 37.50
11 A2 1sh orange 20.00 .90
Never hinged 32.50
a. 1sh orange yellow 22.50 1.00
12 A2 1sh3p violet ('20) 17.50 11.00
Never hinged 37.50
a. 1sh3p deep violet 17.00 11.00
13 A2 2sh6p green & cl 60.00 5.50
Never hinged 115.00
14 A2 5sh blue & claret 125.00 9.00
Never hinged 250.00
a. 5sh light blue & reddish purple 120.00 10.00
15 A2 10sh ol grn & blue 250.00 14.50
Never hinged 450.00
16 A2 £1 red & dp grn ('16) 850.00 1,600.
Never hinged 1,400.
a. £1 lt red & gray green ('24) 1,100. *1,600.*
Never hinged 1,650.
Nos. 2-16 (15) 1,373. 1,647.
Set, ovptd. or handstamped "SPECIMEN" 1,600.

The ½p, 1p and 1½p have the words "Revenue" and "Inkomst" on the stamps. On other stamps of this type these words are replaced by short vertical lines.

All values exist in many shades. No. 4a exists with and without gutter between.

Unwatermarked examples of the 1p are the result of misplaced watermarks.

Scott values watermarked stamps of South Africa in the normal upright position. Many issues exist with the watermark inverted, and some sideways. These varieties usually sell for a premium over the Scott values; however, in some instances the inverted watermarks sell for substantially less.

Nos. 3, 7 and 8 exist bisected. These are philatelic creations and have little value.

For overprint see No. O1.

Coil Stamps

Perf. 14 Horizontally

17 A2 ½p green 9.25 1.90
a. ½p blue green 11.00 2.50
b. ½p yellow green 11.00 2.50
18 A2 1p rose red ('14) 20.00 6.25
a. 1p scarlet 25.00 8.75
b. 1p carmine red 16.50 9.00
19 A2 1½p org brown ('20) 17.00 27.50
20 A2 2p dull violet ('21) 18.00 5.00
a. 2p deep purple 22.50 7.50
b. 2p reddish purple 22.50 7.50
Nos. 17-20 (4) 64.25 40.65

"Hope" — A3

Design: No. 22, inscribed SUIDAFRIKA.

1926 Engr. Wmk. 201 *Imperf.*

21 A3 4p blue gray 2.00 1.40
22 A3 4p blue gray 2.00 1.40

Nos. 21 and 22 were privately roulettted and perforated, but such varieties were not officially made.

No. 21 (English inscription) was printed in a separate sheet from No. 22 (Afrikaans inscription).

English-Afrikaans Se-Tenant

Stamps with English inscriptions and with Afrikaans inscriptions were printed alternately in the same sheets, starting with No. 23. Major-number listings and values are for horizontal pairs (vertical pairs sell for about one-third less) of such stamps consisting of one English and one Afrikaans-inscribed stamp, unless otherwise described.

Values are for pairs with no fold marks between stamps and no perf separations.

Beware of pairs that have been rejoined.

Springbok A5

Jan van Riebeek's Ship, Drommedaris — A6

Orange Tree — A7

1926 Typo. *Perf. 14½x14*

23 A5 ½p dk grn & blk, pair 3.00 *4.00*
a. Single, English .25 .25
b. Single, Afrikaans .25 .25
c. Tete beche pair ('27) 1,500.
d. Center omitted 2,000.
e. Booklet pane of 6 225.00
f. As "e," perf. 14 350.00
g. Missing "1" in "1/2" (Afrikaans only) 2,000.
h. Perf 13½x14 ('27) 85.00 85.00
i. As "h," single, English 4.00
j. As "h," single, Afrikaans 4.00
24 A6 1p car & blk, pair 3.00 *3.00*
a. Single, English .25 .25
b. Single, Afrikaans .25 .25
c. Imperf., pair 1,350.
d. Tete beche pair ('27) 1,750.
f. Booklet pane of 6 200.00
g. As "f," perf. 14 300.00
h. Imperf on three sides, vert. pair 700.00 800.00
i. Perf 13½x14 ('27) 110.00 85.00
j. As "h," single, English 4.00
k. As "h," single, Afrikaans 4.00
25 A7 6p org & grn, pair 42.50 *47.50*
a. Single, English 3.00 2.25
b. Single, Afrikaans 3.00 2.25
Nos. 23-25 (3) 48.50 54.50

Nos. 23c and 24d are from uncut sheets printed for the perf. 14 booklet panes of 1928, Nos. 23f and 24g.

See Nos. 33-35, 42, 45-50, 59-61, 98-99. For overprints see Nos. O2-O4, O6-O9, O12-O15, O18, O21-O25, O30-O32, O42-O45, O48.

Government Buildings, Pretoria — A8

"Groote Schuur," Rhodes's Home — A9

Native Kraal — A10

Gnu — A11

Trekking — A12

Ox Wagon — A13

Cape Town and Table Mountain — A14

Perf. 14, 14x13½

1927-28 Engr. Wmk. 201

26 A8 2p vio brn & gray, pair 14.00 *30.00*
a. Single, English 3.50 1.40
b. Single, Afrikaans 3.50 1.40
c. Perf. 14x13½, pair 45.00 *47.50*
d. As "c," single, English 6.00 .75
e. As "c," single, Afrikaans 6.00 .75
27 A9 3p red & blk, pair 24.00 *37.50*
a. Single, English 2.75 1.40
b. Single, Afrikaans 2.75 1.40
c. Perf. 14x13½, pair 80.00 *82.50*
d. As "c," single, English 6.50 2.75
e. As "c," single, Afrikaans 6.50 2.75
28 A10 4p brn, pair ('28) 32.50 *67.50*
a. Single, English 3.75 1.90
b. Single, Afrikaans 3.75 1.90
c. Perf. 14x13½, pair 67.50 *82.50*
d. As "c," single, English 5.00 2.75
e. As "c," single, Afrikaans 5.00 2.75
29 A11 1sh dp bl & bis brn, pair 47.50 *87.50*
a. Single, English 7.50 2.75
b. Single, Afrikaans 7.50 2.75
c. Perf. 14x13½, pair ('30) 75.00 *90.00*
d. As "c," single, English 7.50 2.00
e. As "c," single, Afrikaans 7.50 2.00
30 A12 2sh6p brn & bl grn, pair 150.00 *500.00*
a. Single, English 25.00 24.00
b. Single, Afrikaans 25.00 24.00
c. Perf. 14x13½, pair 475.00 700.00
d. As "c," single, English 37.50 37.50
e. As "c," single, Afrikaans 37.50 37.50
31 A13 5sh dp grn & blk, pair 300.00 *900.00*
a. Single, English 32.50 40.00
b. Single, Afrikaans 32.50 40.00
c. Perf. 14x13½, pair 525.00 1,100.
d. As "c," single, English 55.00 52.50
e. As "c," single, Afrikaans 55.00 52.50
32 A14 10sh ol brn & bl, pair 200.00 200.00
a. Single, English 25.00 16.00
b. Single, Afrikaans 25.00 16.00
c. Perf. 14x13½, pair 275.00 375.00
d. As "c," single, English 27.50 20.00
e. As "c," single, Afrikaans 27.50 20.00
f. Center inverted, single, English ('28) 20,000.
g. Center inverted, single, Afrikaans ('28) 20,000.
h. As "c," center inverted 60,000.
Nos. 26-32 (7) 768.00 1,823.
Set, handstamped "SPECIMEN" 925.00

See Nos. 36-41, 43-44, 53-54, 58, 62-66. For overprints see Nos. O5, O10-O111, O16-O17, O19-O20, O28, O33-O35, O39, O41, O49-O53.

Types of 1926-28 Redrawn

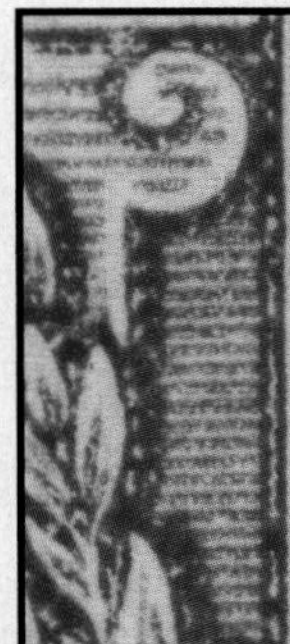

No. 34

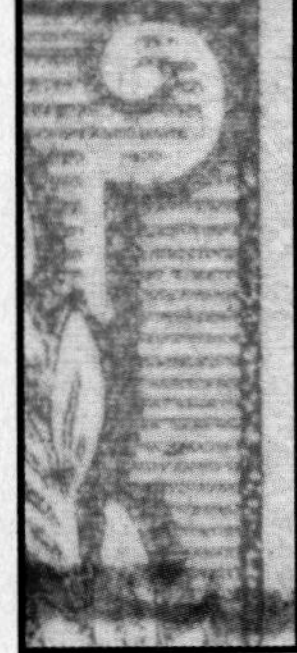

No. 35

"SUIDAFRIKA" (No Hyphen) on Afrikaans Stamps

The photogravure, unhyphenated stamps of 1930-45 are distinguished from the 1926-28 typographed or engraved stamps (also unhyphenated) by the following characteristics:

½p, 1p, 6p. Leg of "R" in AFRICA or AFRIKA ends in a straight line in the photogravure set; in a curved line in the typographed. No. 34, POSSEEL—INKOMSTE separated by ½mm; horiz. shading in side panels is close. No. 35, POSSEEL—INKOMSTE separated by 1mm; horiz. shading in side panels is wide.

2p. A memorial statue has been added just above and leftward of the "2" in value tablet on Nos. 36-37 (photogravure).

3p. Top frame on No. 38 consists of 3 heavy lines. On No. 27 it has 3 heavy and 2 very thin lines.

4p. On Nos. 40-41 the background in upper corners is solid. On No. 28 it consists of horizontal and vertical lines. No. 41 has pretzel-shaped scroll endings at bottom. On No. 40 these scroll endings enclose a solid mass of color.

1sh. No. 43 has no fine shading lines projecting from the curved top of the left inner frame, as No. 29 has. On No. 43 the shading of the last "A" of the country name partly covers the flower below it.

2sh6p. On No. 44 the shading below the country name is solid or shows signs of wear. On No. 30 it is composed of fine lines.

The engraved pictorials are much more finely executed and show details more clearly than the photogravure.

Perf. 15x14 (½p, 1p, 6p), 14

1930-45 Photo. Wmk. 201

33 A5 ½p bl grn & blk, pair 6.00 3.50
Never hinged 10.00
a. Single, English .25 .25
b. Single, Afrikaans .25 .25
c. Tete-beche pair 1,450.
d. As "c," gutter between 1,750.
e. Booklet pane of 6 60.00 50.00
f. Vert. pair, monolingual 40.00 —
34 A6 1p car & blk, pair 5.50 3.50
Never hinged 11.50
a. Single, English .25 .25
b. Single, Afrikaans .25 .25
c. Center omitted *4,500.*
d. Frame omitted *2,500.*
e. Tete-beche pair 1,800.
f. As "e," gutter between 1,500.
g. Booklet pane of 6 40.00 20.00
35 A6 1p rose & blk, pair ('32) 60.00 4.50
Never hinged 120.00
a. Single, English 1.00 .25
b. Single, Afrikaans 1.00 .25
c. Center omitted 750.00
36 A8 2p vio & gray, pair ('31) 28.00 24.00
Never hinged 62.50
a. Single, English 2.00 .40
b. Single, Afrikaans 2.00 .40
c. Frame omitted, single stamp (English) *3,000.*
d. Frame omitted, single stamp (Afrikaans) *3,000.*
e. Tete-beche pair *6,500.*
f. Booklet pane of 4 240.00 240.00
37 A8 2p vio & ind, pair ('38) 350.00 100.00
Never hinged 450.00
a. Single, English 16.00 7.25
b. Single, Afrikaans 16.00 7.25
38 A9 3p red & blk, pair ('31) 135.00 *100.00*
Never hinged 275.00
a. Single, English 7.25 6.75
b. Single, Afrikaans 7.25 6.75
39 A9 3p ultra & bl, pair ('33) 24.00 10.00
Never hinged 47.50
a. Single, English 2.00 .50
b. Single, Afrikaans 2.00 .50
c. Center omitted 30,000.
d. Frame omitted 15,000.
40 A10 4p redsh brn, pair ('32) 300.00 210.00
Never hinged 600.00
a. Single, English 25.00 11.00
b. Single, Afrikaans 25.00 11.00
41 A10 4p brn, pair ('36) 6.50 5.00
Never hinged 14.00
a. Single, English .40 .35
b. Single, Afrikaans .40 .35
42 A7 6p org & grn, pair ('31) 65.00 20.00
Never hinged 180.00
a. Single, English 1.75 .75
b. Single, Afrikaans 1.75 .75
43 A11 1sh dl bl & yel brn, pair 140.00 60.00
Never hinged 250.00
a. Single, English 9.00 2.00
b. Single, Afrikaans 9.00 2.00
c. 1sh dp bl & brn, pair ('32) 72.50 32.50
Never hinged 115.00
d. As "c," single, English 5.25 .40
e. As "c," single, Afrikaans 5.25 .40
44 A12 2sh 6p brn & bl, pair ('45) 29.00 19.00
Never hinged 55.00
a. Single, English 1.75 .70
b. Single, Afrikaans 1.75 .70
c. 2sh6p brn & sl grn ('36), pair 350.00 300.00
d. As "c," single, English 18.00 8.00
e. As "c," single, Afrikaans 18.00 8.00
f. 2sh6p choc & dp grn ('37), pair 225.00 190.00
Never hinged 500.00
g. As "f," single, English 14.00 6.50
h. As "f," single, Afrikaans 14.00 6.50
i. 2sh6p red brn & grn, pair ('32) 175.00 175.00
Never hinged 400.00
j. As "i," single, English 17.50 5.00
k. As "i," single, Afrikaans 17.50 5.00
Nos. 33-44 (12) 1,149. 559.50

No. 34 unwatermarked, or watermarked multiple clover leaf, is a proof.

Types of 1926-28 with "SUID-AFRIKA" Hyphenated on Afrikaans Stamps, and

Gold Mine — A15

Government Buildings, Pretoria — A16

Government Buildings, Pretoria — A16a

Groote Schuur — A17

Groot Constantia — A18

½p. No. 45 shading in leaves and ornaments strengthened; 40 lines in center background. Size: 18½x22½mm.

No. 46 has 28 heavy horizontal shading lines in center background and similar thicker lines in frame. Top and bottom green bars are scored by a white horizontal line. Size: 18½x22½mm.

No. 47 is smaller, 18x22mm.

1p. No. 48, size 18½x22½mm.

No. 49, size 18x22mm.

No. 50. Size: 17½x21½mm.

2p. On Nos. 53-54, S's in SOUTH and POSTAGE are narrower than on Nos. 36-37.

5sh.On No. 64, Die I, U and A in SOUTH AFRICA have projections. Lines are contained within the design. Size 27x21¾mm.

5sh. On No. 65, Die I, dots are contained within the design, instead of lines. Size 27x21½mm.

5sh. On No. 66, Die II, U and A in SOUTH AFRICA have been redrawn to eliminate projections. Dots are contained within the design. Size 26¾x21½mm.

6p. Die I, "SUID-AFRIKA" 16½mm. Shading in leaves framing oval very faint and broken. Size: 18½x22½mm.

Die II, "SUID-AFRIKA" 17mm. Leaves strongly shaded. Heavy lines of shading in background of tree. Size: 18½x22½mm.

Die III, "question mark" scrolls below top panel are cleanly defined without intrusion of background shading. Size: 18x22mm.

Nos. 45-67 were printed in many shades. Some denominations in some printings were partly or wholly screened. Except for No. 47, the screened stamps were issued after 1947.

5sh. No. 65. Type I, letters "U" and "A" in SOUTH AFRICA have projections. Size: 27x21½mm.

No. 66. Type II, letters "U" and "A" redrawn to eliminate projections. Size: 26½x21½mm.

Perf. 15x14 (½p, 1p, 6p), 14

1933-54 Photo. Wmk. 201

45 A5 ½p grn & gray, pair ('36) 6.00 2.25
Never hinged 12.00
a. Single, English .25 .25
b. Single, Afrikaans .25 .25
c. Bklt. pane of 6, marginal ads 30.00 30.00
d. Perf. 13½x14 (coil), pair 40.00 *70.00*
Never hinged 80.00
e. As "d," single, English 1.75 1.25
f. As "d," single, Afrikaans 1.75 1.25
46 A5 ½p grn & gray, redrawn, pair ('37) 13.00 2.50
Never hinged 26.00
a. Single, English .25 .25
b. Single, Afrikaans .25 .25
c. Booklet pane of 6 65.00 *45.00*
d. Booklet pane of 2 17.50 *10.00*
e. As "c," 4 blank margins 65.00 *45.00*
f. Perf. 14½x14 (coil), pair 12.50 7.25
g. As "f," single, English 2.25 .80
h. As "f," single, Afrikaans 2.25 .80
47 A5 ½p grn & gray, pair ('47) 3.00 5.50
Never hinged 4.00
a. Single, English .25 .25
b. Single, Afrikaans .25 .25
c. Bklt. pane of 6, marginal ads *18.00* *16.00*
d. As "c," no horiz. margins 18.00 *16.00*
48 A6 1p car & gray, pair ('34) 1.75 2.25
Never hinged 3.50
a. Single, English .25 .25
b. Single, Afrikaans .25 .25
c. Booklet pane of 6 45.00 45.00
d. Booklet pane of 2 3.50 *2.25*
e. Perf. 13½x14 (coil), pair 85.00 125.00
Never hinged 170.00
f. As "e," single, English .70 .70
g. As "e," single, Afrikaans .70 .70
h. Center omitted, pair 325.00
j. Bklt. pane of 6, marginal ads 32.50 32.50
k. As "j," 4 blank margins 36.00 36.00
m. Perf. 14½x14 (coil), pair 11.00 11.00
n. As "m," single, English 1.40 1.40
p. As "m," single, Afrikaans 1.40 1.40
q. Pair, imperf. 200.00
r. Frame omitted 375.00
49 A6 1p rose car & gray blk, pair ('40) 1.50 .30
a. Single, English .25 .25
b. Single, Afrikaans .25 .25
c. Unwmkd., pair 325.00 325.00
d. Booklet pane of 6 4.50 3.25
e. Perf. 14½x14 (coil), pair 4.00 6.00
f. As "e," single, English 1.40 .90
g. As "e," single, Afrikaans 1.40 .90
h. As "d," marginal ads 6.00 5.00
50 A6 1p car & blk, pair ('51) 1.50 4.00
Never hinged 2.25
a. Single, English .25 .25
b. Single, Afrikaans .25 .25
51 A15 1½p dk grn & gold, 27x21½mm, pair ('36) 7.00 3.50
Never hinged 10.50
a. Single, English .25 .25
b. Single, Afrikaans .25 .25
c. Booklet pane of 4 30.00 15.00
d. Center omitted, pair 1,000.
52 A15 1½p sl grn & och, 22x18mm, pair ('41) 8.50 1.50
Never hinged 13.00
a. Single, English .25 .25
b. Single, Afrikaans .25 .25
c. Center omitted, pair 25,000. 10,000.
d. Booklet pane of 6 8.00 5.50
53 A16 2p bl vio & dl bl, pair ('38) 75.00 50.00
Never hinged 110.00
a. Single, English 3.00 1.25
b. Single, Afrikaans 3.00 1.25
54 A16 2p dl vio & gray, pair ('41) 65.00 *110.00*
Never hinged 75.00
a. Single, English 1.00 1.75
b. Single, Afrikaans 1.00 1.75
55 A16a 2p dp reddish vio & sl, 27x21½mm, pair ('45) 24.00 3.00
a. Single, English .50 .25
b. Single, Afrikaans .50 .25
c. 2p bright violet & slate, pair ('47) 4.50 *10.00*
d. As "c," single, English .25 .25
e. As "c," single, Afrikaans .25 .25
56 A16a 2p pur & sl bl, 21½ x 17¼mm, pair ('50) 5.00 *21.00*
Never hinged 7.25
a. Single, English .25 .25
b. Single, Afrikaans .25 .25
c. Booklet pane of 6 ('51) 15.00 *35.00*
57 A17 3p ultra, pair ('40) 15.00 3.50
Never hinged 20.00
a. Single, English .45 .25
b. Single, Afrikaans .45 .25
c. 3p bl, pair ('49) 3.75 *8.00*
Never hinged 3.00
d. As "c," single, English .25 .25
e. As "c," single, Afrikaans .25 .25
58 A10 4p choc brn, pair ('52) 4.50 *17.00*
Never hinged 6.50
a. Single, English .25 .70
b. Single, Afrikaans .25 .70
59 A7 6p org & bl grn, I, pair ('37) 70.00 47.50
Never hinged 90.00
a. Single, English 3.75 1.10
b. Single, Afrikaans 3.75 1.10

60 A7 6p org & grn, II, pair ('38) 42.00 3.00
Never hinged 57.50
a. Single, English 1.50 .25
b. Single, Afrikaans 1.50 .25
61 A7 6p red org & bl grn, III ('50), pair 3.75 1.50
Never hinged 5.50
a. Single, English .25 .25
b. Single, Afrikaans .25 .25
c. 6p org & grn, III, pair ('46) 20.00 1.90
Never hinged 27.50
d. As "c," single, English 1.00 .25
e. As "c," single, Afrikaans 1.00 .25
62 A11 1sh chlky bl & lt brn ('50), pair 11.00 *13.00*
Never hinged 14.50
a. As "f," single, English .55 .25
b. As "f," single, Afrikaans .55 .25
c. 1sh lt bl & ol brn, pair ('39) 55.00 18.00
Never hinged 62.50
d. As "c," single, English 1.00 .25
e. As "c," single, Afrikaans 1.00 .25
f. 1sh vio bl & brnsh blk, pair ('52) 16.00 *20.00*
Never hinged 18.00
g. Single, English .50 .30
h. Single, Afrikaans .50 .30
i. As "c," frame omitted, vert. pair with normal) 13,000.
63 A12 2sh6p brn & brt grn, pair ('49) 11.00 *30.00*
Never hinged 14.50
a. Single, English 1.50 1.25
b. Single, Afrikaans 1.50 1.25
64 A13 5sh grn & blk, I, pair 60.00 75.00
Never hinged 72.50
a. Single, English 4.75 2.00
b. Single, Afrikaans 4.75 2.00
64C A13 5sh bl grn & blk, I, pair (photogravure) ('44) 42.50 21.00
Never hinged 55.00
d. Single, English 1.00 .40
e. Single, Afrikaans 1.00 .40
65 A13 5sh bl grn & blk, I, pair ('49) 42.50 *75.00*
Never hinged 55.00
a. Single, English 3.75 3.50
b. Single, Afrikaans 3.75 3.50
66 A13 5sh dp yel grn & blk, II, pair ('54) 50.00 *100.00*
Never hinged 62.50
a. Single, English 4.50 4.50
b. Single, Afrikaans 4.50 4.50
67 A18 10sh ol blk & bl, pair ('39) 50.00 17.50
Never hinged 65.00
a. Single, English 3.00 1.00
b. Single, Afrikaans 3.00 1.00
Nos. 45-67 (23) 571.00 588.80

See Nos. 98-99. For overprints see Nos. O26-O27, O29, O36-O38, O40, O46-O47, O54.

George V and Springboks — A19

1935, May 1 Wmk. 201 ***Perf. 15x14***

68 A19 ½p Prus grn & blk, pair 4.00 *12.00*
Never hinged 6.00
a. Single, English top .35 .35
b. Single, Afrikaans top .35 .35
69 A19 1p car rose & blk, pair 4.50 *8.00*
Never hinged 7.50
a. Single, English top .35 .25
b. Single, Afrikaans top .35 .25
70 A19 3p bl & dk bl, pair 16.00 *55.00*
Never hinged 27.50
a. Single, English top 2.25 2.75
b. Single, Afrikaans top 2.25 2.75
71 A19 6p org & grn, pair 32.50 *80.00*
Never hinged 60.00
a. Single, English top 3.00 *3.75*
b. Single, Afrikaans top 3.00 *3.75*
Nos. 68-71 (4) 57.00 *155.00*
Set, never hinged 100.00

25th anniv. of the reign of George V.

English and Afrikaans inscriptions are transposed on alternate stamps. On the ½p, 3p and 6p with "SOUTH AFRICA" at top, "SILWER JUBILEUM" is at left of medallion, but on 1p with English at top, it is at the right.

Johannesburg International Philatelic Exhibition Issue

Nos. 45c and 48j Overprinted in Black

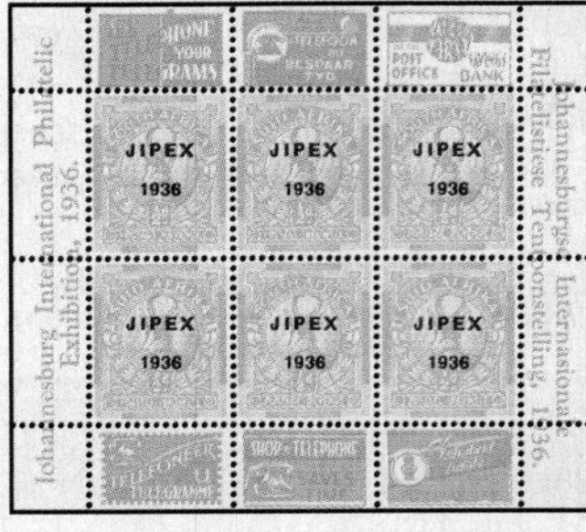

Souvenir Sheets

1936, Nov. 2 ***Perf. 15x14***

72 A5 Sheet of 6 (½p) 5.75 10.00
Never hinged 10.00
73 A6 Sheet of 6 (1p) 5.00 7.00
Never hinged 11.00
Set, never hinged 25.00

Sheets made by overprinting booklet panes Nos. 45c and 48j. Sheets exist with and without horizontal perforations through right margin. Sheet size: 81x72.

Catalogue values for unused stamps in this section, from this point to the end of the section, are for Never Hinged items.

George VI — A22

"KRONING SUID-AFRIKA" on alternate stamps.

1937, May 12 ***Perf. 14***

74 A22 ½p grn & ol blk, pair .80 1.10
a. Single, English .25 .25
b. Single, Afrikaans .25 .25
75 A22 1p car & ol blk, pair .85 .90
a. Single, English .25 .25
b. Single, Afrikaans .25 .25
76 A22 1½p Prus grn & org, pair .85 .80
a. Single, English .25 .25
b. Single, Afrikaans .25 .25
77 A22 3p bl & ultra, pair 1.75 *3.00*
a. Single, English .25 .25
b. Single, Afrikaans .25 .25
78 A22 1sh Prus bl & org brn, pair 5.00 5.00
a. Single, English .50 .25
b. Single, Afrikaans .50 .25
Nos. 74-78 (5) 9.25 10.80

Coronation of George VI and Queen Elizabeth.

Wagon Wheel — A23

Voortrekker Family — A24

Alternate stamps inscribed "SOUTH AFRICA," "SUID-AFRIKA."

1938, Dec. 14 ***Perf. 15x14***

79 A23 1p rose & slate, pair 9.00 4.50
a. Single, English .30 .30
b. Single, Afrikaans .30 .30
80 A24 1½p red brn & Prus bl, pair 11.50 5.00
a. Single, English .30 .35
b. Single, Afrikaans .30 .35

Issued to commemorate the Voortrekkers.

Infantry A25

Nurse and Ambulance A26

Airman and Spitfires (Flight Lt. Robert Kershaw) A27

Sailor A28

Women's Services A29

Artillery — A30

Welder — A31

Tank Corps A32

Signal Corps — A33

Bilingual inscriptions on 2p and 1sh.

Perf. 14 (2p, 4p, 6p), 15x14

1941-43 Photo. Wmk. 201

81 A25 ½p dp bl grn, pair 1.50 4.00
a. Single, English .25 .25
b. Single, Afrikaans .25 .25
82 A26 1p brt rose, pair 2.00 4.00
a. Single, English .25 .25
b. Single, Afrikaans .25 .25
83 A27 1½p Prus grn, pair ('42) 1.50 4.00
a. Single, English .25 .25
b. Single, Afrikaans .25 .25
84 A28 2p dk violet 1.00 .75
85 A29 3p dp blue, pair 18.50 40.00
a. Single, English 1.75 .90
b. Single, Afrikaans 1.75 .90
86 A30 4p org brn, pair 22.50 25.00
a. Single, English 1.25 .25
b. Single, Afrikaans 1.25 .25
c. 4p red brown, pair 37.50 42.50
d. As "c," single, English 2.75 1.25
e. As "c," single, Afrikaans 2.75 1.25
87 A31 6p brt red org, pair 11.75 14.00
a. Single, English .75 .25
b. Single, Afrikaans .75 .25
88 A32 1sh dark brown 2.25 1.00
89 A33 1sh3p dk ol brn, pair ('43) 13.00 11.00
a. Single, English .80 .30
b. Single, Afrikaans .80 .30
c. 1sh3p dark brown, pair 7.00 9.50
d. As "c," single, English .50 .25
e. As "c," single, Afrikaans .50 .25
Nos. 81-89 (9) 74.00 103.75

Infantry A34

Nurse A35

Airman — A36

Sailor — A37

Women's Services — A38

Artillery — A39

Welder — A40

Tank Corps — A41

Bilingual inscriptions on 4p and 1sh.

Pairs: Perf. 14, Roul. 6½ btwn. Strips of 3: Perf. 15x14, Roul. 6½ btwn.

1942-43 Photo. Wmk. 201

90 A34 ½p Horiz. strip of 3 2.00 1.50
a. Single, English .25 .25
b. Single, Afrikaans .25 .25
c. As #90, imperf. between 1,300. 1,200.
91 A35 1p Horiz. strip of 3 ('43) 1.00 1.25
a. Single, English .25 .25
b. Single, Afrikaans .25 .25
c. As #91, imperf. between 1,100. 1,100.
92 A36 1½p Horiz. pair .70 2.50
a. Single, English .25 .25
b. Single, Afrikaans .25 .25
c. As #92, roul. 13 4.50 4.50
d. As #92, imperf. btwn. 325.00 400.00
93 A37 2p Horiz. pair ('43) 1.00 2.25
a. Single, English .25 .25
b. Single, Afrikaans .25 .25
c. As #93, imperf. btwn. 1,200. 1,100.
94 A38 3p Vert strip of 3 8.00 *18.00*
a. Single, English .25 .25
b. Single, Afrikaans .25 .25
95 A39 4p Vert. strip of 3 18.00 11.00
a. Single .25 .25
96 A40 6p Horiz. pair 2.00 2.25
a. Single, English .25 .25
b. Single, Afrikaans .25 .25

97 A41 1sh Vert. pair 17.00 4.25
a. Single .25 .25
Nos. 90-97 (8) 49.70 43.00

Because of the rouletting these are collected as pairs or strips of three, even on the bilingual stamps.

Types of 1926 Redrawn
"SUID-AFRIKA" Hyphenated
Coil Stamps

1943 Photo. *Perf. 15x14*
98 A5 ½p myrtle grn, vert. pair 4.00 *7.00*
a. Single, English .25 .25
b. Single, Afrikaans .25 .25
99 A6 1p rose pink, vert. pair 5.00 *5.00*
a. Single, English .25 .25
b. Single, Afrikaans .25 .25

"Victory" — A42

"Peace" — A43

Design: 3p, Profiles of couple ("Hope").

1945, Dec. 3 Photo. *Perf. 14*
100 A42 1p rose pink & choc, pair .35 1.25
a. Single, English .25 .25
b. Single, Afrikaans .25 .25
101 A43 2p vio & sl bl, pair .35 1.25
a. Single, English .25 .25
b. Single, Afrikaans .25 .25
102 A43 3p ultra & dp ultra, pair .50 1.50
a. Single, English .25 .25
b. Single, Afrikaans .25 .25
Nos. 100-102 (3) 1.20 4.00

World War II victory of the Allies.

George VI — A44

King George VI and Queen Elizabeth A45

Princesses Margaret Rose and Elizabeth A46

Perf. 15x14
1947, Feb. 17 Wmk. 201
103 A44 1p cer & gray, pair .30 .40
a. Single, English .25 .25
b. Single, Afrikaans .25 .25
104 A45 2p purple, pair .30 .60
a. Single, English .25 .25
b. Single, Afrikaans .25 .25
105 A46 3p dk blue, pair .40 .75
a. Single, English .25 .25
b. Single, Afrikaans .25 .25
Nos. 103-105 (3) 1.00 1.75

Visit of the British Royal Family, Mar.-Apr., 1947.

George VI, Elizabeth — A47

1948, Apr. 26 Photo. *Perf. 14*
106 A47 3p dp chlky bl & sil, pair .90 1.25
a. Single, English .25 .25
b. Single, Afrikaans .25 .25

25th anniv. of the marriage of George VI and Queen Elizabeth.

Gold Mine — A48

Vertical Pairs Perf. 14 all around, Rouletted 6½ between
1948, Apr.
107 A48 1½p sl & och, vert. pair 1.60 *2.50*
a. Single, English .25 .25
b. Single, Afrikaans .25 .25
c. Block of 4 3.25 5.00

"Wanderer" in Port Natal A49

1949, May 2 Photo. *Perf. 15x14*
108 A49 1½p red brown, pair .80 .80
a. Single, English .25 .25
b. Single, Afrikaans .25 .25

Mercury and Globe — A50

1949, Oct. 1 *Perf. 14x15*
109 A50 ½p dk green, pair .50 *1.00*
a. Single, English .25 .25
b. Single, Afrikaans .25 .25
110 A50 1½p dk red, pair .70 *1.00*
a. Single, English .25 .25
b. Single, Afrikaans .25 .25
111 A50 3p ultra, pair 1.00 1.00
a. Single, English .25 .25
b. Single, Afrikaans .25 .25
Nos. 109-111 (3) 2.20 3.00

75th anniv. of the UPU.

Except for Nos. 216, 310-313, 518a, 669a listed in Scott Standard catalogue, Vol. 6, this is the end of bi-lingual multiples in the postage section.

Voortrekkers en Route to Natal — A51

Voortrekker Monument, Pretoria A52

Voortrekkers Looking Toward Natal, and Open Bible — A53

1949, Dec. 1 *Perf. 15x14*
112 A51 1p magenta .25 .25
113 A52 1½p dull green .25 .25
114 A53 3p dark blue .25 .25
Nos. 112-114 (3) .75 .75

Inauguration of the Voortrekker Monument at Pretoria.

Riebeeck's Seal and Dutch East India Company Monogram A54

Maria de la Quellerie — A55

2p, van Riebeeck's Ships. 4½p, Jan van Riebeeck. 1sh, Landing of van Riebeeck.

Perf. 15x14, 14x15
1952, Mar. 14 Wmk. 201
115 A54 ½p dk brn & red vio .25 .25
116 A55 1p dark green .25 .25
117 A54 2p dark purple .25 .25
118 A55 4½p dark blue .25 .25
119 A54 1sh brown .55 .50
Nos. 115-119 (5) 1.55 1.50

300th anniv. of the landing of Jan van Riebeeck at the Cape of Good Hope.

Nos. 116-117 Overprinted "SATISE" (1p) and "SADIPU" (2p)
1952, Mar. 26
120 A55 1p dark green .30 .55
121 A54 2p dark purple .35 .70

South African Tercentenary Intl. Stamp Exhib., Cape Town, Mar. 26-Apr. 5, 1952.

SEMI-POSTAL STAMPS

Catalogue values for unused stamps in this section are for Never Hinged items.

English-Afrikaans Se-Tenant
Stamps with English inscriptions and with Afrikaans inscriptions of Nos. B1-B11 were printed alternately in the same sheets. Major-number listings and values are for pairs consisting of one English and one Afrikaans-inscribed stamp.

Church of the Vow — SP1

Cradock's Pass — SP2

Voortrekker — SP3

Voortrekker Woman — SP4

1933-36 Photo. Wmk. 201 *Perf. 14*
B1 SP1 ½p + ½p grn & blk, pair ('36) 11.00 5.50
a. Single, English .55 .55
b. Single, Afrikaans .55 .55
B2 SP2 1p + ½p rose & blk, pair 7.25 3.75
a. Single, English .45 .35
b. Single, Afrikaans .45 .35
B3 SP3 2p + 1p dull vio & gray, pair 12.00 6.00
a. Single, English .55 .60
b. Single, Afrikaans .55 .60
B4 SP4 3p + 1½p dp blue & gray, pair 18.00 9.50
a. Single, English 1.50 1.10
b. Single, Afrikaans 1.50 1.10
Nos. B1-B4 (4) 48.25 24.75

Issued to commemorate the Voortrekkers. Surtax went to the National Memorial Fund for a national Voortrekker monument.

Voortrekker Plowing — SP5

Crossing the Drakensberg — SP6

Signing Dingaan-Retief Treaty — SP7

Proposed Monument — SP8

1938, Dec. 14 *Perf. 14*
B5 SP5 ½p + ½p dl grn & ind, pair 7.00 6.75
a. Single, English 1.00 .60
b. Single, Afrikaans 1.00 .60
B6 SP6 1p + 1p rose & sl, pair 17.00 7.75
a. Single, English 1.00 .70
b. Single, Afrikaans 1.00 .70

Perf. 15x14
B7 SP7 1½p + ½p Prus grn & choc, pair 22.50 13.50
a. Single, English 1.40 1.40
b. Single, Afrikaans 1.40 1.40
B8 SP8 3p + 3p chlky bl, pair 26.00 16.00
a. Single, English 1.75 2.00
b. Single, Afrikaans 1.75 2.00
Nos. B5-B8 (4) 72.50 44.00

Voortrekker centenary. Surtax went to the Natl. Memorial Fund for a Voortrekker monument.

"The Old Vicarage," Huguenot Museum — SP9

Rising Sun and Cross — SP10

Huguenot Dwelling, Drakenstein Mountain Valley — SP11

1939, July 17 **Photo.** ***Perf. 14***

B9 SP9 ½p + ½p Prus grn & gray brn, pair 11.00 8.00
a. Single, English 1.00 .85
b. Single, Afrikaans 1.00 .85
B10 SP10 1p + 1p rose car & Prus grn, pair 13.00 10.00
a. Single, English 1.00 1.00
b. Single, Afrikaans 1.00 1.00

Perf. 15x14

B11 SP11 1½p + 1½p, vio & Prus grn, pair 27.50 15.00
a. Single, English 1.60 1.60
b. Single, Afrikaans 1.60 1.60
Nos. B9-B11 (3) 51.50 33.00

250th anniv. of the landing of the Huguenots in South Africa. Surtax went to a fund to build a Huguenot memorial at Paarl.

AIR POST STAMPS

Mail Plane — AP1

Unwmk.

1925, Feb. 26 **Litho.** ***Perf. 12***

C1 AP1 1p red 4.50 10.00
C2 AP1 3p ultramarine 10.00 *13.00*
C3 AP1 6p violet 17.50 *24.00*
C4 AP1 9p gray green 29.00 *32.50*
Nos. C1-C4 (4) 61.00 *79.50*
Set, never hinged 150.00

Forgeries exist perf. 11, 11½ or 13.

Biplane in Flight — AP2

1929, Aug. 16 **Typo.** ***Perf. 14x13½***

C5 AP2 4p blue green 8.50 2.75
C6 AP2 1sh orange 27.50 21.00
Set, never hinged 75.00

POSTAGE DUE STAMPS

On cover values are for properly franked commercial covers. Philatelic usages also exist and sell for less.

D1

Wmk. Springbok's Head (177)

1914-15 **Typo.** ***Perf. 14***

J1 D1 ½p green & blk 2.50 4.25
On cover 70.00
J2 D1 1p red & blk 2.50 .25
On cover 20.00
J3 D1 2p vio & blk ('14) 7.50 .80
On cover 20.00
J4 D1 3p ultra & blk 2.50 .80
On cover 35.00
J5 D1 5p brown & blk 4.50 *30.00*
On cover *600.00*
J6 D1 6p gray & blk 11.00 *30.00*
On cover *650.00*
J7 D1 1sh black & red 77.50 *160.00*
On cover *2,000.*
Nos. J1-J7 (7) 108.00 *226.10*

1922 **Unwmk.** **Litho.** ***Rouletted 7-8***

J8 D1 ½p blue grn & blk 1.60 *15.00*
On cover *60.00*
J9 D1 1p dull red & blk 1.75 1.25
On cover 30.00
J10 D1 1½p yellow brn & blk 2.00 2.40
On cover 40.00
Nos. J8-J10 (3) 5.35 *18.65*

1922-26 ***Perf. 14***

J11 D1 ½p blue grn & blk .85 1.75
On cover 20.00
J12 D1 1p rose & blk ('23) .90 .25
On cover 15.00
J13 D1 1½p yel brn & blk ('24) 1.60 1.25
On cover 40.00
J14 D1 2p vio & blk ('23) 1.40 .80
On cover 20.00
a. Imperf. pair 300.00 400.00
J15 D1 3p blue & blk ('26) 8.00 22.50
On cover 35.00
J16 D1 6p gray & blue ('23) 16.00 8.00
On cover 80.00
Nos. J11-J16 (6) 28.75 34.55

D2

1927-28 **Typo.**

J17 D2 ½p blue green & blk 1.00 3.50
On cover 20.00
J18 D2 1p rose & black 1.40 .80
On cover 15.00
J19 D2 2p violet & black 1.40 1.25
On cover 20.00
J20 D2 3p ultra & black 13.00 25.00
On cover 35.00
J21 D2 6p gray & black 24.00 20.00
On cover 90.00
Nos. J17-J21 (5) 40.80 50.55

Type of 1927-28 Redrawn

Perf. 15x14

1932-40 **Photo.** **Wmk. 201**

J22 D2 ½p blue grn & blk ('34) 2.75 1.75
On cover 20.00
J23 D2 1p rose car & blk ('34) 2.50 .95
On cover 15.00
J24 D2 2p blk violet & blk 15.00 2.50
On cover 15.00
a. 2p dark purple & black ('40) 32.50 .25
J25 D2 3p dp blue & blk 27.50 14.00
On cover 100.00
J26 D2 3p ultra & dk bl ('35) 8.00 .40
On cover 20.00
J27 D2 3p blue & dk bl ('40) 85.00 3.50
On cover 50.00
J28 D2 6p brn org & grn ('33) 25.00 6.00
On cover 70.00
J29 D2 6p red org & grn ('38) 15.00 3.50
On cover 50.00
Nos. J22-J29 (8) 180.75 32.60

The ½p No. J22 photogravure has larger but thinner numeral and the "d" is taller and thinner than on No. J17.

The 1p No. J23 photogravure has numeral with parallel sides. The "d" is taller and thicker than on No. J18.

On Nos. J25 and J27 the numeral is followed by a large "d" with thick lines and a large round period below it.

Nos. J22, J24 and J25 have frame in photogravure, value typographed.

Catalogue values for unused stamps in this section, from this point to the end of the section, are for Never Hinged items.

See "English-Afrikaans Se-tenant" note preceding No. 23.

D3

Horiz. strips of Three, Perf. 15x14 All Around, Rouletted 6½ Between

1943-44 **Photo.** **Wmk. 201**

J30 D3 ½p Prus green ('44) 15.00 *50.00*
On cover *400.00*
a. Single .25 .25
J31 D3 1p brt carmine 11.00 5.50
On cover 400.00
a. Single .25 .25
J32 D3 2p dark purple 9.00 12.00
On cover 650.00
a. Single .25 .25
J33 D3 3p dark blue 55.00 85.00
On cover 800.00
a. Single .25 1.25
Nos. J30-J33 (4) 90.00 152.50

Catalogued as strips of 3 because of the perforations.

Type of 1932-38 Redrawn

Thick Numerals, Capital "D"

1948-49 ***Perf. 15x14***

J34 D2 ½p blue green & blk 9.00 13.50
On cover 40.00
J35 D2 1p deep rose & blk 16.00 6.00
On cover 30.00
J36 D2 2p dk pur & blk ('49) 17.50 9.00
On cover 30.00
J37 D2 3p ultra & dk blue 16.00 17.50
On cover 60.00
J38 D2 6p dp org & grn ('49) 37.50 8.00
On cover 80.00
Nos. J34-J38 (5) 96.00 54.00

Redrawn Type of 1948-49

Hyphen between Suid-Afrika

1950-58 ***Perf. 15x14***

J40 D2 1p car rose & blk 1.25 .45
On cover 20.00
J41 D2 2p dk pur & blk ('51) .85 .30
On cover 15.00
J42 D2 3p ultra & dk blue 6.25 2.50
On cover 25.00
J43 D2 4p emer & dk grn ('58) 14.50 15.00
On cover 60.00
J44 D2 6p dp org & grn ('52) 11.50 11.50
On cover 60.00
J45 D2 1sh brn red & dk brn ('58) 17.50 16.00
On cover 100.00
Nos. J40-J45 (6) 51.85 45.75

OFFICIAL STAMPS

Type A2 stamps have very small margins at top and bottom. Values are for examples with perfs close to, or touching the frame.

No. 5 Overprinted in Black, Periods in Overprint

1926 **Wmk. 177** ***Perf. 14***

O1 A2 2p dull violet 22.50 2.00

See "English-Afrikaans Se-tenant" note preceding No. 23.

On Nos. 23-25

Perf. 14½x14

Wmk. 201

O2 A5 ½p dk grn & blk, pair 8.00 *18.00*
a. Single, English .75 1.50
b. Single, Afrikaans .75 1.50
O3 A6 1p car & blk, pair 4.00 *8.50*
a. Single, English .25 .50
b. Single, Afrikaans .25 .50
O4 A7 6p org & grn, pair 550.00 80.00
a. Single, English 25.00 11.00
b. Single, Afrikaans 25.00 11.00

Nos. 26 and 25 Overprinted, No Periods in Overprint — b

(Reading Up)

1928-29 ***Perf. 14, 14½x14***

Space between words 19mm

O5 A8 2p vio brn & gray, pair ('29) 7.50 *20.00*
a. Single, English .50 *1.50*
b. Single, Afrikaans .50 *1.50*
c. Space 17½mm, pair 6.00 *24.00*
d. As "c," single, English .50 *2.00*
e. As "c," single, Afrikaans .50 *2.00*

Space between words 11½mm

O6 A7 6p org & grn, pair 22.50 *47.50*
a. Single, English 2.75 *2.75*
b. Single, Afrikaans 2.75 *2.75*

#23-25 Ovptd. type "b" Reading Down

Space between words 13½-14mm

1929 ***Perf. 14½x14***

O7 A5 ½p grn & blk, pair 2.50 *4.75*
a. Single, English .25 .35
b. Single, Afrikaans .25 .35
c. Period after "OFFISIEEL" on English stamp 5.00 5.00
d. Pair, "c" + normal ½p 45.00 45.00
e. Period after "OFFISIEEL." on Afrikaans stamp 5.00 5.00
f. Pair, "e" + normal ½p 55.00 65.00
O8 A6 1p car & blk, pair 3.00 *6.00*
a. Single, English .30 .50
b. Single, Afrikaans .30 .50
O9 A7 6p org & grn, pair 8.00 *40.00*
a. Single, English 1.25 *3.50*
b. Single, Afrikaans 1.25 *3.50*
c. Period after "OFFISIEEL." on English stamp 10.00 *10.00*
d. Pair, "c" + normal 6p 75.00 *150.00*
e. Period after "OFFISIEEL." on Afrikaans stamp 12.00 *12.00*
f. Pair, "e" + normal 6p 90.00 *160.00*
Nos. O7-O9 (3) 13.50 *50.75*

#29-30 Ovptd. type "b" Reading Down

Space between words 17½-19mm

1931 **Engr.** ***Perf. 14, 14x13½***

O10 A11 1sh dp bl & bis brn, pair 40.00 *90.00*
a. Single, English 3.00 *10.00*
b. Single, Afrikaans 3.00 *10.00*
c. Period after "OFFICIAL." on Afrikaans stamp 50.00 50.00
d. Pair, "c" + normal 1sh 115.00 *240.00*
O11 A12 2sh6p brn & bl grn, pair 65.00 *150.00*
a. Single, English 10.00 *19.00*
b. Single, Afrikaans 10.00 *19.00*
c. Period after "OFFICIAL." on Afrikaans stamp 72.50 100.00
d. Pair, "c" + normal 2sh6p 300.00 *550.00*

Regular Issues of 1930-45 Overprinted type "b" Reading Down ("SUIDAFRIKA" on Afrikaans stamps)

Perf. 15x14 (½p, 1p, 6p), 14

1930-47 **Photo.** **Wmk. 201**

Space between words 9½-12mm

(Various spacings occur in same setting)

O12 A5 ½p bl grn & blk (#33), pair ('31) 2.25 *5.00*
a. Single, English .25 *.40*
b. Single, Afrikaans .25 *.40*
c. Period after "OFFISIEEL." on English stamp 5.00 *5.00*
d. Pair, "c" + normal ½p 37.50 *60.00*
e. Period after "OFFISIEEL." on Afrikaans stamp 5.00 *5.00*
f. Pair, "e" + normal ½p 27.50 *50.00*

Space between words 12½-13½mm

O13 A5 ½p bl grn & blk, pair (#33) 3.00 4.00
a. Single, English .25 .50
b. Single, Afrikaans .25 .50
O14 A6 1p car & blk, pair (#34) 6.00 6.00
a. Single, English .50 .60
b. Single, Afrikaans .50 .60
c. Period after "OFFISIEEL." on English stamp 5.00 *5.00*
d. Pair, "c" + normal 1p 50.00 *75.00*
e. Period after "OFFISIEEL." on Afrikaans stamp 5.00 *5.00*
f. Pair, "e" + normal 1p 35.00 *55.00*
O15 A6 1p rose & blk, pair (#35) ('33) 15.00 9.00
a. Single, English 1.00 1.00
b. Single, Afrikaans 1.00 1.00
c. Double ovpt., pair 275.00 *400.00*
d. As "c," English — —

e. As "c," Afrikaans — —

Space between words 20½-22mm

O16 A8 2p vio & gray, pair (#36) ('31) 8.00 *11.00*
a. Single, English .80 *1.50*
b. Single, Afrikaans .80 *1.50*
O17 A8 2p vio & ind, pair (#37) 150.00 *100.00*
a. Single, English 10.00 *10.00*
b. Single, Afrikaans 10.00 *10.00*

Space between words 12½-13½mm

O18 A7 6p org & grn, pair (#42) 8.50 8.50
a. Single, English .75 1.00
b. Single, Afrikaans .75 1.00
c. Period after "OFFISIEEL." on English stamp 7.00 7.00
d. Pair, "c" + normal 6p 90.00 *100.00*
e. Period after "OFFISIEEL." on Afrikaans stamp 5.50 5.50
f. Pair, "e" + normal 6p 75.00 *90.00*

Space between words 21mm

O19 A11 1sh dp bl & brn, pair (#43c) ('32) 60.00 *90.00*
a. Single, English 7.50 *7.50*
b. Single, Afrikaans 7.50 *7.50*
c. 1sh dk bl & yel brn (#43), 19mm, pair 50.00 *90.00*
d. As "c," single, English 8.50 *7.50*
e. As "c," single, Afrikaans 8.50 *7.50*
f. As "c," spaced 21mm, pair 42.50 *65.00*
g. As "f," single, English 6.00 *7.50*
h. As "f," single, Afrikaans 6.00 *7.50*

Space between words 17½-18½mm

O20 A12 2sh6p brn & sl grn (#44c) ('37), pair 80.00 *140.00*
a. Single, English 15.00 *15.00*
b. Single, Afrikaans 15.00 *15.00*
c. Spaced 21mm, pair 75.00 *75.00*
d. As "c," single, English 4.50 *8.00*
e. As "c," single, Afrikaans 4.50 *8.00*
f. 2sh6p red brn & grn, pair (#44i) ('33) 50.00 *90.00*
g. As "f," single, English 5.00 *8.50*
h. As "f," single, Afrikaans 5.00 *8.50*
j. 2sh6p brn & bl, 19-20mm (#44) ('47), pair 30.00 60.00
k. As "j," single, English 3.00 *5.00*
m. As "j," single, Afrikaans 3.00 *5.00*
Nos. O12-O20 (9) 332.75 *373.50*

Catalogue values for unused stamps in this section, from this point to the end of the section, are for Never Hinged items.

Regular Issue of 1933-54 Overprinted type "b" Reading Down ("SUID-AFRIKA" Hyphenated)

Space between words given with each listing

1935-50 Photo. *Perf. 15x14, 14*

O21 A5 ½p grn & gray (#45), 12½-13mm, pair ('36) 7.00 *30.00*
a. Single, English .25 *1.75*
b. Single, Afrikaans .25 *1.75*
O22 A5 ½p grn & gray, (#46), 11½-13mm, pair ('38) 12.00 *12.50*
a. Single, English .50 *1.25*
b. Single, Afrikaans .50 *1.25*
O23 A5 ½p grn & gray (#47), 11½mm, pair ('48) 1.25 *5.00*
a. Single, English .25 *.70*
b. Single, Afrikaans .25 *.70*
O24 A6 1p car & gray (#48), 11-13mm, pair 4.00 3.00
a. Single, English .25 .25
b. Single, Afrikaans .25 .25
O25 A6 1p rose car & gray blk (#49), 11½-12mm, pair ('41) 1.00 .50
a. Single, English .25 .25
b. Single, Afrikaans .25 .25
O26 A15 1½p dk grn & gold (#51), 19-21mm, pair ('37) 30.00 25.00
a. Single, English 2.25 1.75
b. Single, Afrikaans 2.25 1.75
O27 A15 1½p sl grn & ocher (#52), 16mm, pair ('44) 50.00 *11.50*
a. Single, English 1.25 *1.25*
b. Single, Afrikaans 1.25 *1.25*
c. Ovpt. spaced 14-14½mm, pair 3.00 *10.00*
d. As "c," single, English .25 *.80*
e. As "c," single, Afrikaans .25 *.80*

O28 A8 2p bl vio & dl bl (#53), 20-21mm, pair ('39) 150.00 40.00
a. Single, English 7.50 2.50
b. Single, Afrikaans 7.50 2.50
O29 A16 2p pur & sl (#55), 19-21mm, pair ('48) 5.75 *25.00*
a. Single, English .25 *2.00*
b. Single, Afrikaans .25 *2.00*
O30 A7 6p org & bl grn, I (#59), 12-13mm, pair ('38) 80.00 *45.00*
a. Single, English 6.50 3.75
b. Single, Afrikaans 6.50 3.75
O31 A7 6p org & grn, II (#60), 12-13mm, pair ('39) 14.00 10.00
a. Single, English 1.25 1.25
b. Single, Afrikaans 1.25 1.25
O32 A7 6p org & grn III (#61), 11½-12mm, pair ('47) 5.00 *11.00*
a. Single, English .85 *1.25*
b. Single, Afrikaans .85 *1.25*
O33 A11 1sh lt bl & ol brn (#62c), 19-21mm, pair ('40) 80.00 50.00
a. Single, English 4.50 2.50
b. Single, Afrikaans 4.50 2.50
c. "OFFICIAL" on both sides 3,000.
d. "OFFISIEEL" on both sides 3,000.
e. 1sh chlky bl & lt brn (#62) ('50), pair 11.00 *30.00*
f. As "e," single, English 2.00 *2.50*
g. As "e," single, Afrikaans 2.00 *2.50*
h. 1sh vio bl & brnsh blk (#62f), 18-19mm, pair 65.00 27.50
j. As "h," single, English 4.50 2.00
k. As "h," single, Afrikaans 4.50 2.00
O34 A13 5sh grn & blk (#64) 19-20mm, pair 65.00 *160.00*
a. Single, English 3.50 *13.50*
b. Single, Afrikaans 3.50 *13.50*
O35 A13 5sh bl grn & blk (#65), 20mm, pair 40.00 *110.00*
a. Single, English 3.50 *12.50*
b. Single, Afrikaans 3.50 *12.50*
O36 A18 10sh ol blk & bl (#67), 19½-20mm, pair ('48) 100.00 *275.00*
a. Single, English 10.00 *24.00*
b. Single, Afrikaans 10.00 *24.00*
Nos. O21-O36 (16) 645.00 *813.50*

Nos. 52 and 56 Overprinted type "b" Reading Up

Space between words 16mm

1949-50 Size: 22x18mm *Perf. 14*

O37 A15 1½p sl grn & ocher, pair 85.00 *85.00*
a. Single, English 5.00 *4.00*
b. Single, Afrikaans 5.00 *4.00*

Size: 21½x17½mm

O38 A16 2p pur & sl bl, pair ('50) *3,250.* *3,750.*
a. Single, English 200. *275.*
b. Single, Afrikaans 200. *275.*

Nos. 64, 67 Overprinted

c

Space between words 18-19mm

1940 *Perf. 14*

O39 A13 5sh grn & blk, pair 125.00 *140.00*
a. Single, English 12.00 *12.50*
b. Single, Afrikaans 12.00 *12.50*
O40 A18 10sh ol brn & bl, pair *500.00* *525.00*
a. Single, English 32.50 *37.50*
b. Single, Afrikaans 32.50 *37.50*

No. 54 Overprinted type "c" Reading Up

Space between words 19mm

1945 *Perf. 14*

O41 A8 2p dl vio & gray, pair 11.00 *32.50*
a. Single, English 1.00 *2.25*
b. Single, Afrikaans 1.00 *2.25*

No. 47 Overprinted

1947 *Perf. 15x14*

O42 A5 ½p grn & gray, pair *22.50* 20.00
a. Single, English 1.00 *2.00*
b. Single, Afrikaans 1.00 *2.00*

Stamps of 1937-54 Overprinted

1950-54 *Perf. 15x14, 14*

Space between words 10mm

O43 A5 ½p grn & gray, pair (#47) .90 1.50
a. Single, English .25 .25
b. Single, Afrikaans .25 .25
O44 A6 1p rose car & gray blk, pair (#49) 1.00 *6.00*
a. Single, English .25 .25
b. Single, Afrikaans .25 .25
O45 A6 1p car & blk, pair (#50) 1.00 *3.50*
a. Single, English .25 .25
b. Single, Afrikaans .25 .25

Space between words 14½mm

O46 A15 1½p sl grn & ocher, pair (#52) 2.00 *5.00*
a. Single, English .25 *.35*
b. Single, Afrikaans .25 *.35*
O47 A16 2p pur & sl bl, pair (#56) 1.00 *2.00*
a. Single, English .25 *.25*
b. Single, Afrikaans .25 *.25*
c. Ovpt. reading up, pair

Space between words 10mm

O48 A7 6p red org & bl grn, III, pair (#61c) 2.00 *4.00*
a. Single, English .35 *.35*
b. Single, Afrikaans .35 *.35*

Space between words 19mm

O49 A11 1sh chlky bl & lt brn, pair (#62) 6.75 *18.00*
a. Single, English .50 *2.00*
b. Single, Afrikaans .50 *2.00*
c. 1sh vio bl & brnsh blk (#62f), pair 175.00 *200.00*
d. As "c," single, English 12.50 *17.50*
e. As "c," single, Afrikaans 12.50 *17.50*
O50 A12 2sh6p brn & brt grn, pair (#63) 10.00 *37.50*
a. Single, English 1.00 *3.50*
b. Single, Afrikaans 1.00 *3.50*
O51 A13 5sh bl grn & blk, pair (#64) 190.00 *125.00*
a. Single, English 10.00 *10.00*
b. Single, Afrikaans 10.00 *10.00*
O52 A13 5sh pale bl grn & blk, I, pair (#65) 65.00 *85.00*
a. Single, English 5.00 *6.50*
b. Single, Afrikaans 5.00 *6.50*
O53 A13 5sh dp yel grn & blk, II, pair (#66) 80.00 *100.00*
a. Single, English 8.00 *9.00*
b. Single, Afrikaans 8.00 *9.00*
O54 A18 10sh ol blk & bl, pair (#67) 80.00 *250.00*
a. Single, English 9.00 *22.50*
b. Single, Afrikaans 9.00 *22.50*
Nos. O43-O54 (12) 439.65 *637.50*

SOUTHERN NIGERIA

'sə-th̲ərn nī-'jir-ē-ə

LOCATION — In western Africa bordering on the Gulf of Guinea
GOVT. — British Crown Colony and Protectorate
AREA — 90,896 sq. mi.
POP. — 8,590,545
CAPITAL — Lagos

The Protectorate of Southern Nigeria, formed in 1900, absorbed in that year the Niger Coast Protectorate. In 1906 it united with Lagos and became the Colony and Protectorate of Southern Nigeria. An amalgamation was effected in 1914 between Northern and Southern Nigeria to form the Colony and Protectorate of Nigeria. See Nigeria, Northern Nigeria, Niger Coast Protectorate and Lagos.

12 Pence = 1 Shilling
20 Shillings = 1 Pound

Victoria — A1

Wmk. Crown and C A (2)

1901, Mar. Typo. *Perf. 14*

1 A1 ½p yel grn & blk 2.00 *3.00*
a. ½p yel grn & sepia ('02) 2.50 *3.00*
2 A1 1p car rose & blk 2.75 *3.00*
a. 1p carmine rose & sepia ('02) 3.75 2.00
3 A1 2p org brn & blk 3.75 *7.25*
4 A1 4p ol grn & blk 3.25 *30.00*
5 A1 6p red vio & blk 4.25 *11.00*
6 A1 1sh blk & gray grn 9.75 *30.00*
7 A1 2sh6p brn & blk 57.50 *95.00*
8 A1 5sh yellow & blk 67.50 *135.00*
9 A1 10sh vio & blk, *yel* 150.00 *300.00*
Nos. 1-9 (9) 300.75 *614.25*

Edward VII — A2

1903-04

10 A2 ½p yel grn & blk 1.10 .35
11 A2 1p car rose & blk 1.50 .80
12 A2 2p org brn & blk 16.00 1.75
13 A2 2½p ultra & blk ('04) 2.25 2.25
14 A2 4p ol grn & blk 5.25 *6.25*
15 A2 6p red vio & blk 8.50 *9.25*
16 A2 1sh blk & gray grn 42.50 22.50
17 A2 2sh6p brown & blk 42.50 *75.00*
18 A2 5sh yellow & blk 90.00 *225.00*
19 A2 10sh vio & blk, *yel* 45.00 *150.00*
20 A2 £1 pur & gray grn 475.00 *1,000.*
Nos. 10-20 (11) 729.60 1,493.

1904-09 Ordinary Paper Wmk. 3

21 A2 ½p yel grn & blk .75 .25
22 A2 1p carmine rose & blk 17.50 .25
23 A2 2p org brn & blk ('05) 3.00 .50
b. 2p org brn & pale gray ('07) 4.50 .45
24 A2 2½p ultra & blk ('09) 1.25 1.10
25 A2 4p ol grn & blk ('05) 16.00 *29.00*
b. 4p pale ol grn & blk ('07) 50.00 50.00
26 A2 6p red vio & blk 14.50 9.00
27 A2 1sh blk & gray grn 3.75 *4.00*
28 A2 2sh6p brn & blk ('06) 27.50 *29.00*
29 A2 5sh yellow & blk ('07) 62.50 *90.00*
31 A2 £1 pur & gray grn ('06) 350.00 *425.00*
Nos. 21-31 (10) 496.75 588.10

Chalky Paper

21a A2 ½p yel grn & blk ('05) 1.25 1.00
22a A2 1p carmine rose & blk ('05) 13.00 .25
24A A2 3p vio & org brn ('07) 11.00 1.50
25a A2 4p ol grn & blk ('06) 27.50 32.50
26a A2 6p red vio & blk ('06) 14.50 *16.00*
27a A2 1sh blk & gray grn ('07) 45.00 3.50
28a A2 2sh6p brn & blk ('06) 55.00 20.00
29a A2 5sh brn & blk ('08) 90.00 110.00
30 A2 10sh vio & blk, *yel* ('08) 175.00 225.00

1907-10 Ordinary Paper

32 A2 ½p green ('08) 2.25 .25
33 A2 1p carmine 1.00 .25
34 A2 2p gray 3.00 .80
35 A2 2½p ultra 7.50 4.25

Chalky Paper

36 A2 3p violet, *yel* 2.25 .35
37 A2 4p scar & blk, *yel* 2.50 .90
38 A2 6p red vio & dl vio 29.00 3.75

39 A2 1sh black, *green* 8.00 .50
40 A2 2sh6p car & blk, *bl* 19.00 2.50
41 A2 5sh scar & grn, *yel* 45.00 *55.00*
42 A2 10sh red & grn, *grn* 100.00 *140.00*
43 A2 £1 blk & vio, *red* 250.00 *300.00*
Nos. 32-43 (12) 469.50 *508.55*

1910 Ordinary Paper Redrawn
44 A2 1p carmine 1.10 .25

In the redrawn stamp the "1" of "1d" is not as thick as in No. 33 but the "d" is taller and broader.

King George V — A3

1912
45 A3 ½p green 3.00 .25
46 A3 1p carmine 3.00 .25
47 A3 2p gray 1.00 .95
48 A3 2½p ultra 5.75 3.25
49 A3 3p violet, *yel* 1.25 .35
50 A3 4p scar & blk, *yel* 1.60 *2.40*
51 A3 6p red vio & dl vio 3.00 1.50
52 A3 1sh black, *green* 3.50 1.00
53 A3 2sh6p red & blk, *bl* 10.00 *50.00*
54 A3 5sh red & grn, *yel* 26.00 *87.50*
55 A3 10sh red & grn, *grn* 60.00 110.00
56 A3 £1 blk & vio, *red* 225.00 *275.00*
Nos. 45-56 (12) 343.10 532.45

Stamps of Southern Nigeria were replaced in 1914 by those of Nigeria.

SOUTHERN RHODESIA

'sə-t͟hərn rō-'dē-zh,ē-,ə

LOCATION — Southeastern Africa between Northern Rhodesia and Mozambique
GOVT. — British Colony
AREA — 150,333 sq. mi.
POP. — 4,010,000 (est. 1963)
CAPITAL — Salisbury

Prior to 1923 this territory was administered by the British South Africa Company. The colony was created in that year by the British Government at the request of the inhabitants.

12 Pence = 1 Shilling
20 Shillings = 1 Pound

Catalogue values for unused stamps in this country are for Never Hinged items, beginning with Scott 56 in the regular postage section and Scott J1 in the postage due section.

King George V — A1

1924-30 Unwmk. Engr. *Perf. 14*
1 A1 ½p dark green 5.00 .25
a. Vert. pair, imperf. btwn. 1,200. 1,300.
b. Horiz. pair, imperf. btwn. 1,200. 1,300.
c. Horiz. pair, imperf. vert. 1,300.
2 A1 1p scarlet 4.25 .25
a. Horiz. pair, imperf. btwn. 950.00 1,100.
b. Perf. 12½ (coil) ('30) 4.25 *92.50*
c. Vert. pair, imperf. btwn. 1,700.
d. Vert. pair, imperf. horiz. 1,000.
3 A1 1½p bister brown 4.50 .90
a. Horiz. pair, imperf. btwn. *15,000.*
b. Vert. pair, imperf. btwn. *8,000.*
4 A1 2p vio blk & blk 7.25 1.75
a. Horiz. pair, imperf. btwn. *17,000.*
5 A1 3p deep blue 6.25 6.25
6 A1 4p org red & blk 6.25 *3.25*
7 A1 6p lilac & blk 6.25 *8.00*
a. Horiz. pair, imperf. btwn. *45,000.*
8 A1 8p gray grn & vio 16.00 *55.00*
9 A1 10p rose red & bl 20.00 *57.50*
10 A1 1sh turq bl & blk 9.00 *12.00*
11 A1 1sh6p yellow & blk 24.00 *42.50*
12 A1 2sh brown & blk 20.00 20.00

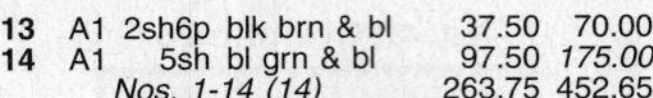

13 A1 2sh6p blk brn & bl 37.50 70.00
14 A1 5sh bl grn & bl 97.50 *175.00*
Nos. 1-14 (14) 263.75 452.65

Values for imperf between pairs are for stamps from the same pane. Stamps separated by wide margins are cross-gutter pairs and sell for much lower prices.

George V A2

Victoria Falls A3

1931-37 *Perf. 11½, 14 (1p)*
16 A2 ½p dp green ('33) 2.50 .25
a. Bklt. pane of 6 ('32) *150.00*
b. Perf. 12 3.25 1.10
c. Perf. 14 ('35) 2.75 1.10
17 A2 1p scarlet ('35) 1.25 .25
a. Bklt. pane of 6 ('32) *150.00*
b. Perf. 11½ ('33) 4.00 .25
c. Perf. 12 3.75 .80
18 A2 1½p dp brown ('32) 3.00 .90
a. Bklt. pane of 6 ('32) *600.00*
b. Perf. 12 ('33) 62.50 *47.50*

Typo. *Perf. 14½x14*
19 A3 2p blk brn & blk 11.00 1.75
20 A3 3p dark blue 11.50 12.50

Perf. 12, 11½ (2sh6p)
Engr.
21 A2 4p org red & blk 1.50 1.75
a. Perf. 14 ('37) 39.00 *70.00*
b. Perf. 11½ ('35) 20.00 6.25
22 A2 6p rose lilac & blk 2.50 3.50
a. Perf. 14 ('36) 8.00 1.75
b. Perf. 11½ ('33) 17.50 1.75
23 A2 8p green & violet 2.00 *4.25*
a. Perf. 11½ ('34) 20.00 *37.50*
24 A2 9p gray grn & ver ('34) 9.75 14.50
25 A2 10p car & ultra 8.50 2.75
a. Perf. 11½ ('33) 7.50 *15.00*
26 A2 1sh turq bl & blk 2.25 3.00
a. Perf. 11½ ('36) 140.00 70.00
b. Perf. 14 ('37) 250.00 160.00
27 A2 1sh6p ocher & blk 14.00 *27.50*
a. Perf. 11½ ('36) 75.00 *140.00*
28 A2 2sh dk brn & blk 31.00 9.00
a. Perf. 11½ ('33) 42.50 35.00
29 A2 2sh6p ol brn & ultra ('33) 50.00 35.00
a. Perf. 12 40.00 *47.50*
30 A2 5sh bl grn & ultra 50.00 57.50
Nos. 16-30 (15) 200.75 174.40

Victoria Falls — A4

1932, May *Perf. 12½*
31 A4 2p dark brn & grn 6.50 1.50
32 A4 3p dark blue 6.50 2.25
a. Vert. pair, imperf. horiz. *17,000.* *18,000.*
b. Vert. pair, imperf. btwn. *38,000.*
Set, never hinged 20.00

See Nos. 37-37A.

Silver Jubilee Issue

Victoria Falls and George V A5

1935, May 6 *Perf. 11x12*
33 A5 1p car rose & olive 4.25 3.25
34 A5 2p blk brn & lt grn 7.50 8.50
35 A5 3p blue & violet 6.00 *11.00*
36 A5 6p dp violet & blk 10.00 *22.50*
Nos. 33-36 (4) 27.75 *45.25*
Set, never hinged 42.50

25th anniv. of the reign of George V.

"Postage and Revenue" A6

1935-41 *Perf. 14*
37 A6 2p dk brn & grn ('41) 3.00 .25
b. Perf. 12½ 7.00 18.00
Never hinged 11.00
37A A6 3p deep blue ('38) 4.00 1.25
Set, never hinged 17.00

Queen Elizabeth, George VI — A7

1937, May 12 *Perf. 12½*
38 A7 1p carmine & gray grn .40 *1.00*
39 A7 2p brown & green .40 *1.75*
40 A7 3p lt blue & violet 1.75 *9.00*
41 A7 6p red violet & blk 1.00 *3.75*
Nos. 38-41 (4) 3.55 15.50
Set, never hinged 7.00

Coronation of George VI & Elizabeth.

King George VI — A8

1937, Nov. 25 *Perf. 14*
42 A8 ½p yellow green .40 .25
43 A8 1p red .40 .25
44 A8 1½p red brown .75 .35
45 A8 4p orange red 1.00 .25
46 A8 6p dark gray 1.00 .60
47 A8 8p blue green 1.50 4.00
48 A8 9p blue 1.25 1.10
49 A8 10p violet 1.50 *3.50*
50 A8 1sh green & blk 1.75 .25
51 A8 1sh6p ocher & blk 8.50 3.00
52 A8 2sh brown & blk 13.00 .70
53 A8 2sh6p violet & blue 7.00 8.00
54 A8 5sh green & blue 13.00 3.50
Nos. 42-54 (13) 51.05 25.75
Set, never hinged 75.00

Catalogue values for unused stamps in this section, from this point to the end of the section, are for Never Hinged items.

Seal of British South Africa Co. — A9

Fort Salisbury, 1890 — A10

Cecil John Rhodes — A11

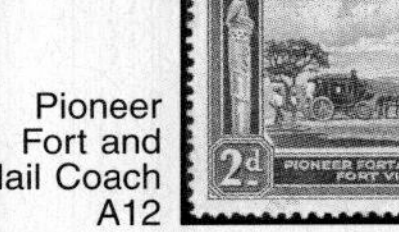
Pioneer Fort and Mail Coach A12

Rhodes Makes Peace, 1896 — A13

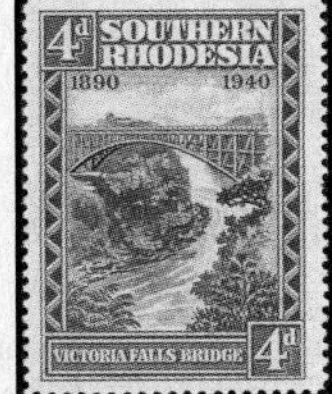
Victoria Falls Bridge — A14

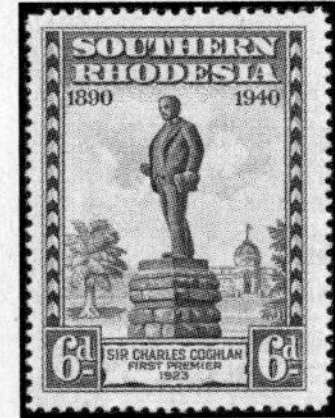
Sir Charles Coghlan — A15

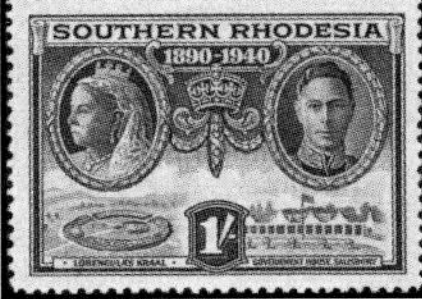
Queen Victoria, George VI, Lobengula's Kraal and Government House A16

Unwmk.
1940, June 3 Engr. *Perf. 14*
56 A9 ½p dp grn & dull vio .25 .65
57 A10 1p red & vio blue .60 .25
58 A11 1½p cop brn & blk .25 .80
59 A12 2p pur & brt grn .40 .40
60 A13 3p dk blue & blk 1.00 1.00
61 A14 4p brn & bl grn 2.00 *2.75*
62 A15 6p sepia & dull grn 2.00 *2.75*
63 A16 1sh dk bl & brt grn 3.00 *3.25*
Nos. 56-63 (8) 9.50 *11.85*

50th anniv. of the founding of Southern Rhodesia by Cecil John Rhodes.

Pioneer — A17

1943, Nov. 1 Photo. Wmk. 201
64 A17 2p Prus grn & choc .35 *.50*

50th anniv. of Matabeleland under British control.

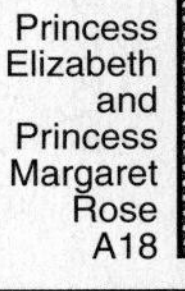

Princess Elizabeth and Princess Margaret Rose A18

King George VI and Queen Elizabeth A19

Unwmk.
1947, Apr. 1 Engr. *Perf. 14*
65 A18 ½p dk green & blk .30 .60
66 A19 1p carmine & blk .30 .60

Visit of the British Royal Family, Apr., 1947.

Victory Issue

Queen Elizabeth
A20

George VI
A21

Princess Elizabeth
A22

Princess Margaret Rose
A23

1947, May 8

No.	Design	Description	Unused	Used
67	A20	1p deep carmine	.25	.25
68	A21	2p slate black	.25	.25
69	A22	3p deep blue	.60	*.50*
70	A23	6p red orange	.30	*.75*
		Nos. 67-70 (4)	1.40	1.75

Victory of the Allied Nations in WW II.

Common Design Types pictured following the introduction.

UPU Issue

Common Design Types

Engr.; Name Typo.

1949, Oct. 10 Wmk. 4 *Perf. 11x11½*

No.	Design	Description	Unused	Used
71	CD307	2p slate black	.70	.50
72	CD308	3p slate blue	1.25	*1.75*

75th anniv. of the UPU.

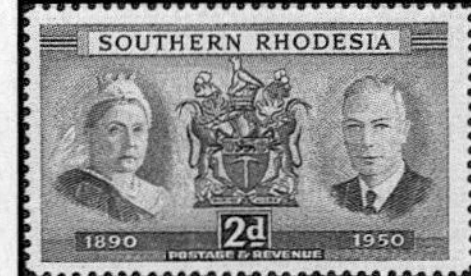

Queen Victoria and King George VI
A24

Unwmk.

1950, Sept. 12 Engr. *Perf. 14*

No.	Design	Description	Unused	Used
73	A24	2p choc & blue grn	.90	*1.10*

60th anniversary of Rhodesia.

POSTAGE DUE STAMPS

Catalogue values for unused stamps in this section are for Never Hinged items.

Great Britain Postage Due Stamps of 1938-51 Overprinted in Black

1951 Wmk. 251 *Perf. 14x14½*

No.	Design	Description	Unused	Used
J1	D1	½p emerald	3.75	*17.50*
		On cover		*500.00*
J2	D1	1p violet blue	3.50	*2.75*
		On cover		*175.00*
J3	D1	2p black brown	3.00	*2.25*
		On cover		*125.00*
J4	D1	3p violet	3.25	*3.00*
		On cover		*200.00*
J5	D1	4p brt blue	2.25	*4.00*
		On cover		*250.00*
a.		4p slate green	275.00	*600.00*
		On cover		*1,200.*
J6	D1	1sh blue	3.00	*4.50*
		On cover		*300.00*
		Nos. J1-J6 (6)	18.75	*34.00*

Covers are for properly franked commercial items. Philatelic usages sell for less.

SOUTH RUSSIA

sauth 'rəsh-ə

LOCATION — An area in southern Russia bordering on the Caspian and Black Seas.

A provisional government set up and maintained by General Denikin in opposition to the Bolshevik forces in Russia following the downfall of the Empire. The stamps were used in the field postal service established for carrying on communication between the various armies united in the revolt. These armies included the Don Cossacks, the Kuban Cossacks, and also the neighboring southern Russian people in favor of the counter-revolution against the Bolsheviks.

100 Kopecks = 1 Ruble

Values for used stamps are for canceled to order examples. Postally used stamps sell for considerably more.

Watermark

Wmk. 171 — Diamonds

Don Government (Novocherkassk) Rostov Issue

Russian Stamps of 1909-17 Surcharged

1918 Unwmk. *Perf. 14x14½*

No.	Design	Description	Unused	Used
1	A14	25k on 1k dl org yel	1.75	*1.90*
a.		Inverted surcharge	100.00	*100.00*
2	A14	25k on 2k dl grn	.50	*.60*
a.		Inverted surcharge	100.00	*75.00*
b.		Double impression (surcharge normal)	150.00	
3	A14	25k on 3k car	.75	*.75*
a.		Double surcharge	75.00	*75.00*
b.		Inverted surcharge	75.00	
4	A15	25k on 4k car	2.25	*3.50*
a.		Inverted surcharge	100.00	*100.00*
5	A14	50k on 7k blue	4.50	*6.50*

Imperf

No.	Design	Description	Unused	Used
6	A14	25k on 1k orange	.60	*1.25*
a.		Inverted surcharge	75.00	*100.00*
7	A14	25k on 2k dull grn	6.75	*12.50*
a.		Double impression (surcharge normal)	150.00	
8	A14	25k on 3k red	4.25	*3.00*
a.		Inverted surcharge	100.00	
		Nos. 1-8 (8)	21.35	30.00

Counterfeits exist of Nos. 1-8.

Ermak, Cossack Leader — A1

Inscription on Back

1919 *Perf. 11½*

No.	Design	Description	Unused	Used
10	A1	20k green	50.00	*85.00*

This stamp was available for both postage and currency.

Novocherkassk Issue

Russian stamps with these surcharges are bogus.

Kuban Government Ekaterinodar Issues

Russian Stamps of 1909-17 Surcharged

d

e

f

g

h

i

1918-20 Unwmk. *Perf. 14x14½*

No.	Design	Description	Unused	Used
20	A14(d)	25k on 1k dl org yel	.50	*2.00*
a.		Inverted surcharge	75.00	*27.50*
b.		Dbl. surch., one inverted	75.00	*25.00*
c.		Dbl. surch., one on back	60.00	
21	A14(d)	50k on 2k dl grn	5.00	*6.00*
a.		Inverted surcharge	50.00	*27.50*
b.		Double surcharge	100.00	*20.00*
c.		Dbl. surcharge inverted	75.00	*20.00*
22	A14(e)	70k on 5k dk cl	2.00	*5.50*
23	A14(f)	1r on 3k car	5.00	*5.00*
a.		Inverted surcharge	50.00	*20.00*
b.		Double surcharge	50.00	*15.00*
c.		Pair, one without surch.	50.00	*15.00*
24	A14(g)	1r on 3k car	.65	*1.00*
a.		Inverted surcharge	50.00	*20.00*
b.		Double surcharge	50.00	*20.00*
c.		Pair, one without surcharge	100.00	*20.00*
25	A15(h)	3r on 4k rose	10.00	*15.00*
b.		Inverted surcharge	100.00	*50.00*
c.		Double surcharge	100.00	*60.00*
d.		Dbl. surcharge inverted	100.00	*60.00*
26	A15(i)	10r on 4k rose	15.00	5.00
a.		10r on 4k carmine	20.00	*20.00*
b.		Inverted surcharge	100.00	*55.00*
27	A11(i)	10r on 15k red brn & dp bl	1.00	*2.00*
a.		Surchd. on face & back	40.00	15.00
b.		Dbl. surch., one inverted	75.00	*60.00*
c.		Inverted surcharge	100.00	
28	A14(i)	25r on 3k car	10.00	3.00
a.		Inverted surcharge	100.00	*20.00*
29	A14(i)	25r on 7k bl	25.00	*50.00*
a.		Inverted surcharge	75.00	*100.00*
30	A11(i)	25r on 14k bl & car	75.00	*80.00*
a.		Inverted surcharge	100.00	*100.00*
31	A11(i)	25r on 25k dl grn & dk vio	25.00	*35.00*
a.		Inverted surcharge	80.00	*70.00*
		Nos. 20-31 (12)	174.15	209.50

Imperf

No.	Design	Description	Unused	Used
35	A14(d)	25d on 1k org	5.00	2.50
36	A14(d)	50k on 2k gray grn	1.00	*2.00*
a.		Inverted surcharge	50.00	25.00
b.		Double surcharge	40.00	25.00
c.		Pair, one without surch.	50.00	*30.00*
37	A14(e)	70k on 5k claret	2.50	*3.25*
38	A14(f)	1r on 3k red	1.40	*2.00*
a.		Inverted surcharge	40.00	20.00
b.		Double surcharge	30.00	*15.00*
c.		Pair, one without surch.	30.00	*15.00*
d.		Double surcharge, both inverted	100.00	—
39	A14(g)	1r on 3k red	1.00	*3.00*
a.		Double surcharge	20.00	*20.00*
b.		Pair, one without surch.	20.00	*20.00*
c.		As "a," inverted	40.00	*45.00*
d.		Inverted surcharge	100.00	—
40	A11(i)	10r on 15k red brn & dp bl	4.75	*5.50*
41	A14(i)	25r on 3k red	6.00	*10.00*
a.		Inverted surcharge	50.00	
		Nos. 35-41 (7)	21.65	*28.25*

No. 31 is said to exist imperf.

Russian Stamps of 1909-17 Surcharged

1919 *Perf. 14, 14½x15*

No.	Design	Description	Unused	Used
45	A14	70k on 1k dl org yel	1.25	1.00
a.		Inverted surcharge	100.00	

Imperf

No.	Design	Description	Unused	Used
46	A14	70k on 1k orange	1.25	*2.40*
a.		Inverted surcharge	100.00	*20.00*
b.		Double surch., one inverted	100.00	25.00

The 1k postal savings stamp with this surcharge inverted is a proof. Value, $500.

Counterfeits exist of Nos. 20-46.

On Russia Nos. AR1-AR3

A2

1919 Wmk. 171 *Perf. 14½x15*

No.	Design	Description	Unused	Used
47	A2	10r on 1k red, *buff*	50.00	*60.00*
a.		Inverted surcharge	75.00	
48	A2	10r on 5k grn, *buff*	50.00	*60.00*
a.		Double surcharge	250.00	
49	A2	10r on 10k brn, *buff*	120.00	*150.00*
		Nos. 47-49 (3)	220.00	270.00

Counterfeits exist of Nos. 47-49.

Crimea

Russian Stamp of 1917 Surcharged

1919 Unwmk. *Imperf.*

No.	Design	Description	Unused	Used
51	A14	35k on 1k orange	2.00	*3.00*
a.		Comma, instead of period in surcharge	2.00	

A3

Paper with Buff Network; Inscription on Back

1919 *Imperf.*

No.	Design	Description	Unused	Used
52	A3	50k brown	35.00	*75.00*

Available for both postage and currency.

Russia Nos. 77, 82, 123, 73, 119 Surcharged

Nos. 53-57

Nos. 58-59

1920 ***Perf. 14x14½***

53 A14 5r on 5k dk claret 1.25 *2.40*
  a. Inverted surcharge 100.00
  b. Double surcharge 100.00
54 A8 5r on 20k dl bl & dk car 1.25 *2.40*
  a. Inverted surcharge 100.00
  b. Double surcharge 100.00
  c. "5" omitted 75.00

Imperf

55 A14 5r on 5k claret 1.25 *2.40*
  a. Double surcharge 25.00

Same Surcharge on Stamp of Denikin Issue, No. 64

57 A5 5r on 35k lt bl 12.00 *14.00*
  a. Double surcharge 80.00
  Nos. 53-57 (4) 15.75 21.20

1920 ***Perf. 14x14½***

58 A14 100r on 1k dl org yel 5.00
  a. "10" in place of "100" 100.00
  b. Inverted surcharge 150.00
  c. Double surcharge 150.00

Imperf

59 A14 100r on 1k orange 5.00
  a. Inverted surcharge 150.00

Nos. 53-57 were issued at Sevastopol during the occupation by General Wrangel's army. Nos. 58-59 were prepared but not used.

Denikin Issue

A5

St. George — A6

1919 **Unwmk.** ***Imperf.***

61 A5 5k orange .30 *.25*
62 A5 10k green .30 *.25*
63 A5 15k red .30 *.35*
64 A5 35k light blue .30 *.25*
65 A5 70k dark blue .30 *.35*
  a. Tête bêche pair 90.00
66 A6 1r brown & red 1.00 *.90*
67 A6 2r gray vio & yellow 1.75 *1.60*
68 A6 3r dl rose & green 1.10 *1.25*
69 A6 5r slate & violet 1.50 *1.40*
70 A6 7r gray grn & rose 2.50 *3.25*
71 A6 10r red & gray 2.25 *2.50*
  Nos. 61-71 (11) 11.60 12.35

Perf. 11½

68a A6 3r dull rose & green 3.00 *10.00*
69a A6 5r slate & violet 4.00 *10.00*
71a A6 10r red & gray 3.00 *10.00*
  Nos. 68a-71a (3) 10.00 30.00

Nos. 61-71 were issued at Ekaterinodar and used in all parts of South Russia that were occupied by the People's Volunteer Army under Gen. Anton Ivanovich Denikin. The inscription on the stamps reads "United Russia."

Stamps of type A6 with rosettes instead of numerals in the small circles at the sides may be essays. Perforated examples of Nos. 61-67 and 70 are of private origin.

For surcharges see Russia, Offices in Turkish Empire Nos. 303-319.

SOUTH WEST AFRICA

sauth 'west 'a-fri-kə

LOCATION — Southwestern Africa between Angola and Cape of Good Hope, bordering on the Atlantic Ocean

GOVT. — Administered by the Republic of South Africa under a mandate of the League of Nations

AREA — 318,261 sq. mi.

POP. — 1,039,800 (1982)

CAPITAL — Windhoek

Formerly a German possession, South West Africa was occupied by South African forces in 1915 and by the Treaty of Versailles was mandated to the Union of South Africa.

12 Pence = 1 Shilling
20 Shillings = 1 Pound

Catalogue values for unused stamps in this country are for Never Hinged items, beginning with Scott 125 in the regular postage section, Scott B1 in the semi-postal section, Scott J86 in the postage due section, and Scott O13 in the officials section.

Watermarks

Watermarks 177 and 201 can be found at the beginning of South Africa.

Major-number listings and values of Nos. 1-40 and 85-93 are for pairs with both overprints.

Stamps of South Africa, Nos. 2-3, 5 and 9-16, Overprinted in English or Afrikaans alternately throughout the sheets.

Setting I

a

b

"South West" 14½mm wide
"Zuid-West" 13mm wide
Overprint Spaced 14mm

1923, Jan. 2 **Wmk. 177** ***Perf. 14***

1 A2 ½p green, pair 4.75 *10.00*
  a. Single, Dutch 1.10 *.90*
2 A2 1p red, pair 8.25 *10.00*
  a. Single, Dutch 1.10 *.90*
  b. Inverted overprint, pair 550.00
  c. As "b," single, English 125.00
  d. As "b," single, Dutch 125.00
  e. As #2, English "Af.rica" 190.00 325.00
  f. Double overprint, pair 1,100.
  g. As "f," single, English 500.00
  h. As "f," single, Dutch 500.00
3 A2 2p dl vio, pair 10.00 *16.00*
  a. Single, Dutch 1.75 *1.75*
  b. Inverted overprint, pair 725.00 825.00
  c. As "b," single, English 150.00
  d. As "b," single, Dutch 150.00
4 A2 3p ultra, pair 13.00 *19.00*
  a. Single, Dutch 3.00 *3.00*
5 A2 4p ol grn & org, pair 21.00 *52.50*
  a. Single, Dutch 4.50 *4.50*
6 A2 6p vio & blk, pair 9.25 *52.50*
  a. Single, Dutch 4.75 *4.75*
7 A2 1sh org, pair 21.00 *55.00*
  a. Single, Dutch 5.75 *5.75*
  b. As #7, without period after "Afrika" *7,500.*
8 A2 1sh3p violet, pair 47.50 *62.50*
  a. Single, Dutch 6.50 *6.50*
  b. Inverted overprint, pair 400.00
  c. As "b," single, English 85.00
  d. As "b," single, Dutch 85.00
9 A2 2sh6p grn & cl, pair 72.50 *150.00*
  a. Single, Dutch 20.00 *20.00*
10 A2 5sh blue & cl, pair 240.00 *400.00*
  a. Single, Dutch 55.00 *55.00*
11 A2 10sh ol grn & bl, pair 1,500. *2,900.*
  a. Single, Dutch 425.00 *450.00*
12 A2 £1 red & dp grn, pair 800.00 *2,000.*
  a. Single, Dutch 275.00 *275.00*
  Nos. 1-12 (12) 2,747. *5,728.*

Most values exist with "t" of "West" partly or totally missing. Vertical displacement in overprinting accounts for the stamps with only one line of overprint.

The English overprint of Setting I is the same as that of Setting III. See Nos. 16a-27a.

Setting II

c

d

Words Same Width as Setting I
Overprint Spaced 9½-10mm

1923, Apr.

13 A2 5sh blue & cl, pair 175.00 *300.00*
  a. Single, English 52.50 *52.50*
  b. Single, Dutch 52.50 *52.50*
  c. As #13, without period after "Afrika" 1,200. 1,400.
  d. As "b," without period after "Afrika" 225.00 225.00
14 A2 10sh ol grn & bl, pair 550.00 *900.00*
  a. Single, English 160.00 *160.00*
  b. Single, Dutch 160.00 *160.00*
  c. As #14, without period after "Afrika" 2,600. *3,250.*
  d. As "b," without period after "Afrika" 550.00 550.00
15 A2 £1 red & green, pair 1,100. *1,500.*
  a. Single, English 225.00 *225.00*
  b. Single, Dutch 225.00 *225.00*
  c. As #15, without period after "Afrika" 6,000. 5,750.
  d. As "b," without period after "Afrika" 1,000. 1,000.

Setting III

e

f

English as in Setting I
"Zuidwest" 11mm wide, No Hyphen
Overprint Spaced 14mm

1923-24

16 A2 ½p grn, pair ('24) 13.00 *42.50*
  a. Single, English 1.00 *4.25*
  b. Single, Dutch .70 *4.25*
17 A2 1p red, pair 6.25 *10.00*
  a. Single, English .85 *1.10*
  b. Single, Dutch .40 *1.10*
18 A2 2p dull vio, pair 12.00 *16.50*
  a. Single, English .50 *1.25*
  b. Single, Dutch .50 *1.25*
  c. Dbl. ovpt., pair 1,200.
  d. As "c," single, English 150.00
  e. As "c," single, Dutch 150.00
19 A2 3p ultra, pair 6.00 *14.50*
  a. Single, English .70 *1.50*
  b. Single, Dutch .70 *1.50*
20 A2 4p ol grn & org, pair 7.00 *22.50*
  a. Single, English 1.00 *3.25*
  b. Single, Dutch 1.00 *3.25*
21 A2 6p vio & blk, pair 14.00 *47.50*
  a. Single, English 1.00 *5.50*
  b. Single, Dutch 1.00 *5.50*
22 A2 1sh orange, pair 15.00 *50.00*
  a. Single, English 1.50 *5.50*
  b. Single, Dutch 1.50 *5.50*
23 A2 1sh3p violet, pair 27.50 *52.50*
  a. Single, English 3.25 *5.50*
  b. Single, Dutch 3.25 *5.50*
24 A2 2sh6p grn & cl, pair 52.50 *90.00*
  a. Single, English 9.00 *10.00*
  b. Single, Dutch 9.00 *10.00*
25 A2 5sh blue & cl, pair 70.00 *125.00*
  a. Single, English 14.00 *20.00*
  b. Single, Dutch 14.00 *20.00*
26 A2 10sh ol grn & bl, pair 190.00 *300.00*
  a. Single, English 45.00 *47.50*
  b. Single, Dutch 45.00 *47.50*
27 A2 £1 red & grn, pair 350.00 *500.00*
  a. Single, English 60.00 *70.00*
  b. Single, Dutch 60.00 *70.00*
  Nos. 16-27 (12) 763.25 *1,271.*

Setting IV

Type g (on left), Type h (on right)

"South West" 16mm wide
"Zuidwest" 12mm wide
Overprint Spaced 14mm

1924, July

28 A2 2sh6p grn & cl, pair 100.00 *175.00*
  a. Single, English 25.00 *32.50*
  b. Single, Dutch 25.00 *32.50*

Setting VI

k

l

"South West" 16, 16½mm wide
"Zuidwest" 12½mm wide
Overprint Spaced 9½mm

1924, Dec.

29 A2 ½p green, pair 8.00 *50.00*
  a. Single, English .50 *5.75*
  b. Single, Dutch .50 *5.75*
30 A2 1p red, pair 5.00 *11.50*
  a. Single, English .25 *1.40*
  b. Single, Dutch .25 *1.40*
  c. Pair, one without overprint 2,200.
31 A2 2p dull vio, pair 4.25 *22.50*
  a. Single, English .30 *1.75*
  b. Single, Dutch .30 *1.75*
32 A2 3p ultra, pair 5.75 *40.00*
  a. Single, English .90 *3.25*
  b. Single, Dutch .90 *3.25*
33 A2 4p ol grn & org, pair 7.00 *50.00*
  a. Single, English .85 *4.50*
  b. Single, Dutch .85 *4.50*
34 A2 6p vio & blk, pair 10.50 *50.00*
  a. Single, English .80 *5.25*
  b. Single, Dutch .80 *5.25*
35 A2 1sh orange, pair 9.50 *52.50*
  a. Single, English 1.00 *5.50*
  b. Single, Dutch 1.00 *5.50*
36 A2 1sh3p violet, pair 14.50 *52.50*
  a. Single, English 1.75 *5.25*
  b. Single, Dutch 1.75 *5.25*
37 A2 2sh6p grn & cl, pair 47.50 *90.00*
  a. Single, English 7.50 *11.00*
  b. Single, Dutch 7.50 *11.00*
38 A2 5sh blue & cl, pair 65.00 *125.00*
  a. Single, English 13.00 *15.00*
  b. Single, Dutch 13.00 *15.00*
39 A2 10sh ol grn & bl, pair 100.00 *180.00*
  a. Single, English 17.50 *21.00*
  b. Single, Dutch 17.50 *21.00*
40 A2 £1 red & grn, pair 325.00 *450.00*
  a. Single, English 60.00 *60.00*
  b. Single, Dutch 60.00 *60.00*
  Nos. 29-40 (12) 602.00 *1,174.*

Setting VII

South Africa Nos. 21-22 Overprinted

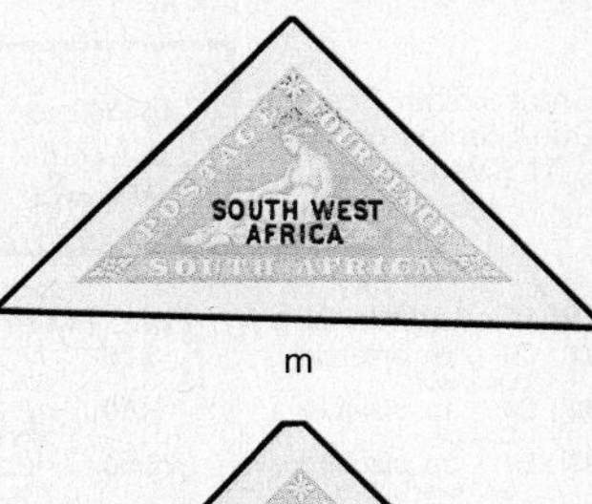

m

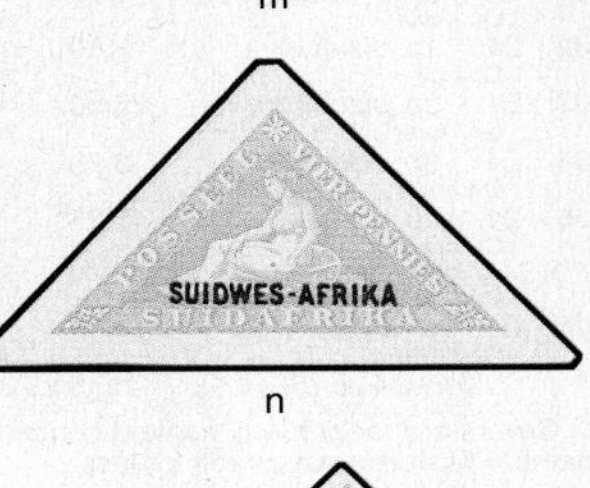

n

o

1926-27 Wmk. 201 Imperf.
81 A3 (m) 4p blue gray .95 3.00
82 A3 (n) 4p blue gray .95 3.00
83 A3 (o) 4p blue gray ('27) 7.50 20.00
Nos. 81-83 (3) 9.40 26.00

Nos. 81-83 were not officially perforated, but firms and individuals applied various forms of perforation and rouletting for their own convenience. Perf. 11 examples of Nos. 81-82 were made by John Meinert, Ltd., Windhoek, same values. Imperf between pairs, $60.

Setting VIII

South Africa Nos. 23-25 Overprinted Alternately with type "p" on English-inscribed Stamps and type "q" on Afrikaans-inscribed Stamps

p

q

"South West" 16½mm wide
"Suidwes" 11mm wide
Overprint Spaced 11½mm

1926 Typo. Perf. 14½x14
85 A5 ½p dk grn & blk, pair 4.50 13.00
a. Single, English .75 1.50
b. Single, Afrikaans .75 1.50
c. Ovpt. "q" on English stamp .55 1.00
d. Ovpt. "p" on Afrikaans stamp .55 1.00
e. Pair, "c" + "d" ('27) 2.75 12.00
f. As "e," without period after "Africa" 175.00
86 A6 1p car & blk, pair 4.00 8.50
a. Single, English .60 .80
b. Single, Afrikaans .60 .80
c. Ovpt. "q" on English stamp .50 .50
d. Ovpt. "p" on Afrikaans stamp .50 .50
e. Pair, "c" + "d" ('27) 3.75 3.00
f. As "e," without period after "Africa" 350.00
87 A7 6p org & grn, pair 24.00 55.00
a. Single, English 6.75 7.25
b. Single, Afrikaans 6.75 7.25
c. Ovpt. "q" on English stamp 2.50 3.00
d. Ovpt. "p" on Afrikaans stamp 2.50 3.00
e. Pair, "c" + "d" ('27) 9.50 35.00
f. As "e," without period after "Africa" 210.00
Nos. 85-87 (3) 32.50 76.50

For overprints see Nos. O1-O3.

Setting IX

South Africa Nos. 26-27, 29-32 Overprinted in Blue with types "p" and "q" Spaced 16mm

1927 Engr. Perf. 14
88 A8 2p vio brn & gray, pair 6.50 16.50
a. Single, English .85 1.90
b. Single, Afrikaans .85 1.90
89 A9 3p red & blk, pair 5.00 32.50
a. Single, English .70 2.75
b. Single, Afrikaans .70 2.75
90 A11 1sh dp bl & bis brn, pair 16.50 34.00
a. Single, English 2.50 4.25
b. Single, Afrikaans 2.50 4.25
91 A12 2sh6p brn & bl grn, pair 40.00 100.00
a. Single, English 9.00 14.00
b. Single, Afrikaans 9.00 14.00
92 A13 5sh dp grn & blk, pair 80.00 200.00
a. Single, English 19.00 22.50
b. Single, Afrikaans 19.00 22.50
93 A14 10sh ol brn & bl, pair 70.00 165.00
a. Single, English 15.00 20.00
b. Single, Afrikaans 15.00 20.00
Nos. 88-93 (6) 218.00 548.00

South Africa Nos. 12 and 16a Overprinted at Foot

1927 Typo. Wmk. 177
94 A2 1sh3p violet 1.40 7.00
a. Without period after "A" 110.00
95 A2 £1 lt red & gray grn 100.00 180.00
a. Without period after "A" 1,700. 2,600.

South Africa Nos. 23-25 Overprinted type "r" at Foot

1927 Wmk. 201 Perf. 14½x14
96 A5 ½p green & blk, pair 2.75 8.75
a. Single, English .25 .85
b. Single, Afrikaans .25 .85
c. As #96, without period after "A" on one stamp 45.00 80.00
d. Overprint at top (pair) 2.75 16.00
e. As "d", vert. pair, one without overprint 650.00
97 A6 1p car & blk, pair 1.50 4.25
a. Single, English .25 .60
b. Single, Afrikaans .25 .60
c. As #97, without period after "A" on one stamp 42.50 80.00
d. Ovpt. at top, pair ('30) 2.00 15.00
e. As "d," single, English .45 1.75
f. As "d," single, Afrikaans .45 1.75
98 A7 6p org & grn, pair 7.50 30.00
a. Single, English 2.00 3.00
b. Single, Afrikaans 2.00 3.00
c. As #98, without period after "A" on one stamp 125.00
Nos. 96-98 (3) 11.75 43.00

For overprints see Nos. O5-O7.

South Africa Nos. 26-32 Overprinted type "r" at Top

1927-28 Engr. Perf. 14
99 A8 2p vio brn & gray, pair 10.00 35.00
a. Single, English 1.25 2.00
b. Single, Afrikaans 1.25 2.00
c. As #99, without period after "A" on one stamp 85.00 150.00
d. Double ovpt., one inverted 800.00 1,050.
100 A9 3p red & blk, pair 6.00 32.50
a. Single, English 1.25 3.25
b. Single, Afrikaans 1.25 3.25
c. As #100, without period after "A" on one stamp 92.50 150.00
101 A10 4p brn, pair ('28) 13.50 52.50
a. Single, English 1.75 7.50
b. Single, Afrikaans 1.75 7.50
c. As #101, without period after "A" on one stamp 95.00 150.00
102 A11 1sh dp bl & bis brn, pair 14.50 52.50
a. Single, English 2.00 5.00
b. Single, Afrikaans 2.00 5.00
c. As #102, without period after "A" on one stamp 1,750. 1,950.
103 A12 2sh6p brn & bl grn, pair 45.00 90.00
a. Single, English 7.50 12.50
b. Single, Afrikaans 7.50 12.50
c. As #103, without period after "A" on one stamp 250.00 375.00
104 A13 5sh dp grn & blk, pair 67.50 125.00
a. Single, English 12.50 19.00
b. Single, Afrikaans 12.50 19.00
c. As #104, without period after "A" on one stamp 325.00 475.00
105 A14 10sh ol brn & bl, pair 110.00 225.00
a. Single, English 20.00 30.00
b. Single, Afrikaans 20.00 30.00
c. As #105, without period after "A" on one stamp 400.00 600.00
Nos. 99-105 (7) 266.50 612.50

Nos. 99-102 exist perf 14x13½. Values about two times those shown.
For overprint see No. O8.

South Africa Nos. 33-34 Overprinted type "r" at Foot

1930 Photo. Perf. 15x14
106 A5 ½p bl grn & blk, pair 25.00 50.00
a. Single, English 2.00 4.75
b. Single, Afrikaans 2.00 4.75
107 A6 1p car rose & blk, pair 15.00 29.00
a. Single, English 1.50 3.00
b. Single, Afrikaans 1.50 3.00

Kori Bustard — A15

Cape Cross — A16

Mail Transport — A17

Bogenfels — A18

Windhoek — A19

Waterberg — A20

Lüderitz Bay — A21

Bush Scene — A22

Elands — A23

Zebras and Brindled Gnus — A24

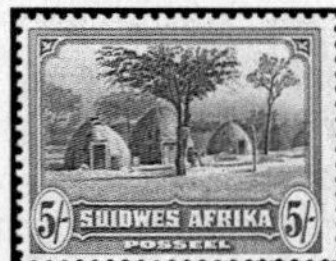

Herero Houses — A25

Welwitschia Plant — A26

Okuwahakan Falls — A27

Perf. 14x13½

1931-37 Wmk. 201 Engr.
108 A15 ½p grn & blk, pair 3.25 2.50
a. Single, English .25 .25
b. Single, Afrikaans .25 .25
109 A16 1p red & ind, pair 3.00 2.50
a. Single, English .25 .25
b. Single, Afrikaans .25 .25
110 A17 1½p vio brn, pair ('37) 30.00 4.50
a. Single, English 1.00 .35
b. Single, Afrikaans 1.00 .35
111 A18 2p dk brn & dk bl, pair 1.75 9.00
a. Single, English .25 .25
b. Single, Afrikaans .25 .25
112 A19 3p dp bl & gray blk, pair 1.50 4.50
a. Single, English .30 .25
b. Single, Afrikaans .30 .25
113 A20 4p brn vio & grn, pair 1.60 7.25
a. Single, English .40 .25
b. Single, Afrikaans .40 .25
114 A21 6p ol brn & bl, pair 1.75 10.00
a. Single, English .45 .25
b. Single, Afrikaans .45 .25
115 A22 1sh bl & vio brn, pair 3.75 17.50
a. Single, English .55 .30
b. Single, Afrikaans .55 .30
116 A23 1sh3p ocher & pur, pair 6.50 11.50
a. Single, English .75 .65
b. Single, Afrikaans .75 .65
117 A24 2sh6p dk gray & rose, pair 28.50 25.00
a. Single, English 3.25 2.00
b. Single, Afrikaans 3.25 2.00
118 A25 5sh vio brn & ol grn, pair 17.00 37.50
a. Single, English 4.25 3.00
b. Single, Afrikaans 4.25 3.00
119 A26 10sh grn & brn, pair 52.50 52.50
a. Single, English 11.50 6.50
b. Single, Afrikaans 11.50 6.50
120 A27 20sh bl grn & mar, pair 77.50 82.50
a. Single, English 14.00 11.00
b. Single, Afrikaans 14.00 11.00
Nos. 108-120 (13) 228.60 266.75

For overprints see Nos. O13-O27.

George V — A28

1935, May 6 Perf. 14x13½
121 A28 1p carmine & blk 1.00 .30
122 A28 2p dk brown & blk 1.25 .30
123 A28 3p blue & blk 7.50 22.50
124 A28 6p violet & blk 3.25 13.00
Nos. 121-124 (4) 13.00 36.10
Set, never hinged 30.00

25th anniv. of the reign of George V.

Catalogue values for unused stamps in this section, from this point to the end of the section, are for Never Hinged items.

Coronation Issue

Inscribed alternately in English and Afrikaans

George VI — A29

1937, May 12 Engr. Perf. 13½x14
125 A29 ½p emer & blk, pair .55 .25
a. Single, English .25 .25
b. Single, Afrikaans .25 .25
126 A29 1p car & blk, pair .55 .25
a. Single, English .25 .25
b. Single, Afrikaans .25 .25
127 A29 1½p org & blk, pair .55 .25
a. Single, English .25 .25
b. Single, Afrikaans .25 .25
128 A29 2p dk brn & blk, pair .55 .30
a. Single, English .25 .25
b. Single, Afrikaans .25 .25
129 A29 3p brt bl & blk, pair .65 .30
a. Single, English .25 .25
b. Single, Afrikaans .25 .25
130 A29 4p dk vio & blk, pair .65 .55
a. Single, English .25 .25
b. Single, Afrikaans .25 .25
131 A29 6p yel & blk, pair .70 3.00
a. Single, English .25 .30
b. Single, Afrikaans .25 .30
132 A29 1sh gray & blk, pair .80 3.50
a. Single, English .25 .75
b. Single, Afrikaans .25 .75
Nos. 125-132 (8) 5.00 8.40

George VI & Queen Elizabeth coronation.

Voortrekker Issue

South Africa Nos. 79-80 Overprinted type "r"

1938, Dec. 14 Photo. Perf. 15x14
133 A23 1p rose & sl, pair 12.00 22.50
a. Single, English 1.50 1.75
b. Single, Afrikaans 1.50 1.75
134 A24 1½p red brn & Prus bl, pair 18.00 27.50
a. Single, English 2.25 2.25
b. Single, Afrikaans 2.25 2.25

Issued to commemorate the Voortrekkers.

South Africa Nos. 81-89 Overprinted — s

Perf. 14 (2p, 4p, 6p); 15x14

1941-43 **Wmk. 201**

135 A25 ½p dp blue grn, pair 1.75 2.75
- *a.* Single, English .25 .25
- *b.* Single, Afrikaans .25 .25

136 A26 1p brt rose, pair 2.75 3.75
- *a.* Single, English .25 .25
- *b.* Single, Afrikaans .25 .25

137 A27 1½p Prus grn, pair ('42) 2.25 4.00
- *a.* Single, English .25 .25
- *b.* Single, Afrikaans .25 .25

138 A28 2p dk violet .60 *1.75*

139 A29 3p dp blue, pair 24.50 *27.50*
- *a.* Single, English 1.25 *1.25*
- *b.* Single, Afrikaans 1.25 *1.25*

140 A30 4p brown, pair 10.00 *21.00*
- *a.* Single, English .90 *1.25*
- *b.* Single, Afrikaans .90 *1.25*

141 A31 6p brt red org, pair 7.50 *9.50*
- *a.* Single, English .85 *1.00*
- *b.* Single, Afrikaans .85 *1.00*

142 A32 1sh dk brown 1.60 *2.00*

143 A33 1sh3p dk ol brn, pair ('43) 14.00 *24.50*
- *a.* Single, English 1.50 1.50
- *b.* Single, Afrikaans 1.50 1.50

Nos. 135-143 (9) 64.95 96.75

South Africa Nos. 90-97 Overprinted

t

u

Pairs or Strips of 3 Perf. 14 or 15x14 all around, Rouletted 6½ or 13 btwn.

1942-45 **Wmk. 201**

144 A34(t) ½p dp grn, horiz. strip of 3 .75 *8.25*
- *a.* Single, English .25 .25
- *b.* Single, Afrikaans .25 .25
- *c.* ½p dp bl grn, horiz. strip of 3 4.25 *8.75*
- *d.* As "c," single, English .25 .25
- *e.* As "c," single, Afrikaans .25 .25

145 A35(t) 1p brt car, horiz. strip of 3 3.50 *8.00*
- *a.* Single, English .25 .25
- *b.* Single, Afrikaans .25 .25
- *c.* 1p rose car, horiz. strip of 3 4.50 *8.00*
- *d.* As "c," single, English .25 .25
- *e.* As "c," single, Afrikaans .25 .25

146 A36(u) 1½p cop brn, horiz. pair .75 *1.75*
- *a.* Single, English .25 .25
- *b.* Single, Afrikaans .25 .25

147 A37(t) 2p dk vio, horiz. pair 8.50 *5.50*
- *a.* Single, English .25 .25
- *b.* Single, Afrikaans .25 .25

148 A38(t) 3p dp bl, vert. strip of 3 3.50 *25.00*
- *a.* Single, English .30 *.85*
- *b.* Single, Afrikaans .30 *.85*

149 A39(t) 4p sl grn, vert. strip of 3 2.25 *24.00*
- *a.* Single .40 *.75*
- *b.* As "c," single 80.00 70.00
- *c.* Invtd. ovpt., strip of 3 925.00 675.00

150 A40(t) 6p brt red org, horiz. pair 5.25 3.00
- *a.* Single, English .35 *.35*
- *b.* Single, Afrikaans .35 *.35*
- *c.* Inverted overprint, pair 650.00
- *d.* As "c," single, English 60.00 60.00
- *e.* As "c," single, Afrikaans 60.00 60.00

151 A41(u) 1sh dk brn, vert. pair 18.00 37.50
- *a.* Single 1.50 2.00
- *b.* As "c," single 90.00
- *c.* Inverted overprint, pair 825.00 475.00

152 A41(t) 1sh dk brn, vert. pair 4.00 6.00
- *a.* Single .35 *.35*
- *b.* As "c," single 62.50 45.00
- *c.* Invtd. ovpt., vert. pair 675.00 450.00

Nos. 144-152 (9) 46.50 119.00

Issue years: #144-145, 147-151, 1943; #152, 1944; #144c, 145c, 149c, 1945.

Peace Issue

South Africa Nos. 100-102 Overprinted Type "w"

1945, Dec. 3 **Wmk. 201** ***Perf. 14***

153 A42 1p rose pink & choc, pair .35 .75
- *a.* Single, English .25 .25
- *b.* Single, Afrikaans .25 .25
- *c.* Inverted overprint, pair 400.00 425.00
- *d.* As "c," single, English 45.00
- *e.* As "c," single, Afrikaans 45.00

154 A43 2p vio & sl bl, pair .40 .75
- *a.* Single, English .25 .25
- *b.* Single, Afrikaans .25 .25

155 A43 3p ultra & dp ultra, pair 1.10 *1.75*
- *a.* Single, English .30 .25
- *b.* Single, Afrikaans .30 .25

Nos. 153-155 (3) 1.85 3.25

WW II victory of the Allies.

Royal Visit Issue

South Africa Nos. 103-105 Overprinted

1947, Feb. 17 ***Perf. 15x14***

156 A44 1p cerise & gray, pair .25 .25
- *a.* Single, English .25 .25
- *b.* Single, Afrikaans .25 .25

157 A45 2p purple, pair .30 *.60*
- *a.* Single, English .25 .25
- *b.* Single, Afrikaans .25 .25

158 A46 3p dk blue, pair .35 *.45*
- *a.* Single, English .25 .25
- *b.* Single, Afrikaans .25 .25

Nos. 156-158 (3) .90 1.30

Visit of the British Royal Family, Mar.-Apr., 1947.

South Africa No. 106 Overprinted

1948, Apr. 26 ***Perf. 14***

159 A47 3p dp chalky bl & sil, pair 1.10 .35
- *a.* Single, English .25 .25
- *b.* Single, Afrikaans .25 .25

25th anniv. of the marriage of George VI and Queen Elizabeth.

UPU Issue

South Africa Nos. 109-111 Overprinted type "w" 13mm wide

1949, Oct. 1 ***Perf. 14x15***

160 A50 ½p dk green, pair .75 *2.25*
- *a.* Single, English .25 *.30*
- *b.* Single, Afrikaans .25 *.30*

161 A50 1½p dk red, pair .75 *1.75*
- *a.* Single, English .25 .25
- *b.* Single, Afrikaans .25 .25

162 A50 3p ultra, pair 1.50 *1.50*
- *a.* Single, English .25 *.30*
- *b.* Single, Afrikaans .25 *.30*

Nos. 160-162 (3) 3.00 5.50

75th anniv. of the UPU.

This ends the bi-lingual multiples in the postage section.

Voortrekker Monument Issue

South Africa Nos. 112-114 Ovptd.

1949, Dec. 1 ***Perf. 15x14***

163 A51 1p magenta .25 .25

164 A52 1½p dull green .25 .25

165 A53 3p dark blue .25 *.40*

Nos. 163-165 (3) .75 .90

Inauguration of the Voortrekker Monument at Pretoria.

South Africa Nos. 115-119 Overprinted

w

x

1952, Mar. 14 ***Perf. 15x14, 14x15***

166 A54(w) ½p dk brn & red vio .25 *.30*

167 A55(x) 1p dark green .25 *.30*

168 A54(w) 2p dark purple .60 .40

169 A55(x) 4½p dark blue .55 *2.00*

170 A54(w) 1sh brown 1.10 .85

Nos. 166-170 (5) 2.75 3.85

300th anniv. of the landing of Jan van Riebeeck at the Cape of Good Hope.

SEMI-POSTAL STAMPS

Catalogue values for unused stamps in this section are for Never Hinged items.

Voortrekker Monument Issue

South Africa Nos. B1-B4 Overprinted

1935-36 **Wmk. 201** ***Perf. 14***

B1 SP1 ½p + ½p grn & blk, pair 4.00 *6.00*
- *a.* Single, English .55 *.75*
- *b.* Single, Afrikaans .55 *.75*

B2 SP2 1p + ½p rose & blk, pair 4.50 3.50
- *a.* Single, English .65 .40
- *b.* Single, Afrikaans .65 .40

B3 SP3 2p + 1p dl vio & gray, pair 15.00 7.50
- *a.* Single, English 2.00 1.00
- *b.* Single, Afrikaans 2.00 1.00

B4 SP4 3p + 1½p dp bl & gray, pair 40.00 42.50
- *a.* Single, English 4.00 *4.25*
- *b.* Single, Afrikaans 4.00 *4.25*

Nos. B1-B4 (4) 63.50 59.50

Voortrekker Centenary Issue

South Africa Nos. B5-B8 Overprinted

1938, Dec. 14 ***Perf. 14***

B5 SP5 ½p + ½p dl grn & indigo, pair 9.00 *25.00*
- *a.* Single, English 1.25 *2.00*
- *b.* Single, Afrikaans 1.25 *2.00*

Perf. 15x14

B6 SP6 1p + 1p rose & sl, pair 24.00 20.00
- *a.* Single, English 1.50 1.50
- *b.* Single, Afrikaans 1.50 1.50

B7 SP7 1½p + 1½p Prus grn & choc, pair 26.00 *35.00*
- *a.* Single, English 2.25 *3.25*
- *b.* Single, Afrikaans 2.25 *3.25*

B8 SP8 3p + 3p chlky bl, pair 50.00 *85.00*
- *a.* Single, English 5.00 *8.50*
- *b.* Single, Afrikaans 5.00 *8.50*

Nos. B5-B8 (4) 109.00 *165.00*

Same Overprint on South Africa Nos. B9-B11

1939, July 17 ***Perf. 14***

B9 SP9 ½p + ½p Prus grn & gray brn, pair 14.00 *16.00*
- *a.* Single, English 1.00 1.25
- *b.* Single, Afrikaans 1.00 1.25

B10 SP10 1p + 1p rose car & Prus grn, pair 21.00 16.00
- *a.* Single, English 1.25 1.25
- *b.* Single, Afrikaans 1.25 1.25

Perf. 15x14

B11 SP11 1½p + 1½p rose vio, dk vio & Prus grn, pair 34.00 20.00
- *a.* Single, English 2.00 1.75
- *b.* Single, Afrikaans 2.00 1.75

Nos. B9-B11 (3) 69.00 52.00

250th anniv. of the landing of the Huguenots in South Africa. Surtax went to a fund to build a Huguenot memorial at Paarl.

AIR POST STAMPS

South Africa Nos. C5-C6 Overprinted

1930 **Unwmk.** ***Perf. 14x13½***

C1 AP2 4p blue green 4.00 *30.00*
- *a.* Without period after "A" 75.00 *150.00*
- *b.* First printing 8.00 *30.00*

C2 AP2 1sh orange 6.00 *57.50*
- *a.* Without period after "A" 475.00 *675.00*
- *b.* First printing 75.00 *125.00*

First printings are blurred with thick lettering and rounded periods. Later printings have sharp, thinner letters and squared periods.

Overprinted

C3 AP2 4p blue green 1.50 *6.50*
- *a.* Double overprint 200.00
- *b.* Inverted overprint 200.00
- *c.* Small "I" in "AIR" 7.50

C4 AP2 1sh orange 3.00 *16.00*
- *a.* Double overprint 575.00

Monoplane over Windhoek — AP3

Biplane over Windhoek — AP4

Wmk. 201

1931, Mar. 5 **Engr.** ***Perf. 14***

C5 AP3 3p blue & dk brn, pair 30.00 *37.50*
- *a.* Single, English 4.00 *2.75*
- *b.* Single, Afrikaans 4.00 *2.75*

C6 AP4 10p brn vio & blk, pair 57.50 *85.00*
- *a.* Single, English 9.00 *7.50*
- *b.* Single, Afrikaans 9.00 *7.50*

POSTAGE DUE STAMPS

STAMPS OF TRANSVAAL USED IN SOUTH WEST AFRICA

Prior to the issue of Nos. J1-J9, postage due stamps of South Africa and Transvaal were used in South West Africa.

1915-23

AJ7 6p Transvaal #J6, on cover 500.00

AJ8 1sh Transvaal #J7, on cover 700.00

Values are for covers commercially used in South West Africa during 1915-1923.

REGULAR ISSUES

Postage Due Stamps of South Africa and Transvaal Overprinted like Regular Issues.

Setting I

On South Africa Nos. J11, J14

1923 **Unwmk.** ***Perf. 14***

J1 D1 ½p blue grn & blk, pair 6.75 *30.00*
a. Single, English .75 *5.50*
b. Single, Dutch .75 *5.50*
c. As #J1, without period after "Afrika" 130.00
d. Inverted ovpt., pair 600.00
J2 D1 2p violet & blk, pair 4.00 *28.00*
a. Single, English .50 *5.00*
b. Single, Dutch .50 *5.00*
c. As #J2, without period after "Afrika" 170.00 170.00

On South Africa Nos. J9-J10

Rouletted 7-8

J3 D1 1p dull red & blk, pair 8.00 *30.00*
a. Single, English .90 *5.50*
b. Single, Dutch .90 *5.50*
c. As #J3, without period after "Afrika" 150.00 150.00
d. Pair, imperf. between 1,800.
J4 D1 1½p yel brn & blk, pair 1.50 *16.00*
a. Single, English .25 *2.75*
b. Single, Dutch .25 *2.75*
c. As #J4, without period after "Afrika" 110.00 110.00

On South Africa Nos. J3-J4, J6

Perf. 14

Wmk. 177

J5 D1 2p vio & blk, pair 42.50 *55.00*
a. Single, English 3.00 *10.00*
b. Single, Dutch 3.00 *10.00*
c. As #J5, without period after "Afrika" 275.00
d. "Wes" for "West" 325.00
J6 D1 3p ultra & blk, pair 21.00 *55.00*
a. Single, English 1.50 *10.00*
b. Single, Dutch 1.50 *10.00*
J7 D1 6p gray & blk, pair 40.00 *65.00*
a. Single, English 4.00 *13.00*
b. Single, Dutch 4.00 *13.00*
Nos. J5-J7 (3) 103.50 *175.00*

On Transvaal Nos. J5-J6

Wmk. Multiple Crown and C A (3)

J8 D1 5p vio & blk, pair 4.50 *55.00*
a. Single, English .75 *11.00*
b. Single, Dutch .75 *11.00*
c. As #J8, without period after "Afrika" 130.00 130.00
J9 D1 6p red brn & blk, pair 19.00 *55.00*
a. Single, Dutch 2.50 *11.00*
b. As #J9, without period after "Afrika" 275.00

For No. J9 single in English see No. J17a and note after No. 27.

The "t" of "West" may be found partly or entirely missing on Nos. J1, J3-J6, J8-J9.

Setting II

On South Africa No. J9

Rouletted

Unwmk.

J10 D1 1p dull red & blk, pair *14,000.*
a. Single, English 800.00 1,600.
b. Single, Dutch 800.00 1,600.

On South Africa Nos. J3-J4

Perf. 14

Wmk. 177

J11 D1 2p vio & blk, pair 19.00 *50.00*
a. Single, English 1.75 *9.00*
b. Single, Dutch 1.75 *9.00*
c. As #J11, without period after "Afrika" 275.00 250.00
J12 D1 3p ultra & blk, pair 8.50 *32.50*
a. Single, English 1.00 *5.50*
b. Single, Dutch 1.00 *5.50*
c. As #J12, without period after "Afrika" 130.00 *150.00*

On Transvaal No. J5

Wmk. Multiple Crown and C A (3)

J13 D1 5p vio & blk, pair 75.00 200.00
a. Single, English 15.00 *20.00*
b. Single, Dutch 15.00 *20.00*

Setting III

On South Africa Nos. J11, J12, J9

Unwmk.

J14 D1 ½p blue grn & blk, pair 17.50 *37.50*
a. Single, Dutch 1.50 *5.50*
J15 D1 1p rose & blk, pair 27.50 *37.50*
a. Single, English 1.50 *6.00*
b. Single, Dutch 1.50 *6.00*

Rouletted 7

J16 D1 1p dull red & blk, pair 9.50 *37.50*
a. Single, Dutch 1.00 *6.00*

For Nos. J14 and J16 singles in English see Nos. J1a and J3a and note after No. 27.

On Transvaal No. J6

Perf. 14

Wmk. 3

J17 D1 6p red brn & blk, pair 23.50 *100.00*
a. Single, English 2.50 *20.00*
b. Single, Dutch 2.50 *20.00*

See note below No. 27.

Setting IV

On South Africa Nos. J11-J12, J16

1924 **Unwmk.**

J18 D1 ½p blue grn & blk, pair 8.50 *35.00*
a. Single, English .75 *5.50*
b. Single, Dutch .75 *5.50*
J19 D1 1p rose & blk, pair 8.50 *32.50*
a. Single, English .60 *5.50*
b. Single, Dutch .60 *5.50*
J20 D1 6p gray & blk, pair 3.00 *45.00*
a. Single, English .30 *9.00*
b. Single, Dutch .30 *9.00*

On Transvaal No. J5

Wmk. Multiple Crown and C A (3)

J21 D1 5p vio & blk, pair 800.00 *1,200.*
a. Single, English 140.00 *175.00*
b. Single, Dutch 140.00 *175.00*

Setting V

i

j

"South West" 16mm wide
"Zuidwest" 12mm wide
Overprint Spaced 12mm

On South Africa Nos. J4, J11, J13

1924 **Unwmk.**

J22 D1 ½p green & blk, pair 3.50 *32.50*
a. Single, English .25 *6.50*
b. Single, Dutch .25 *6.50*
J23 D1 1½p yel brown & blk 5.75 *47.50*
a. Single, English .50 *7.50*
b. Single, Dutch .50 *7.50*

Wmk. Springbok's Head (177)

J24 D1 3p ultra & black, pair 16.00 *60.00*
a. Single, English 1.75 *11.00*
b. Single, Dutch 1.75 *11.00*

On Transvaal No. J5

Wmk. Multiple Crown and C A (3)

J25 D1 5p violet & blk, pair 3.00 *25.00*
a. Single, English .40 *7.50*
b. Single, Dutch .40 *7.50*

Setting VI

On South Africa Nos. J4, J11-J16

1924, Dec. **Unwmk.**

J26 D1 ½p blue grn & blk, pair 14.00 *40.00*
a. Single, English 1.00 *7.50*
b. Single, Dutch 1.00 *7.50*
J27 D1 1p rose & blk, pair 2.25 *14.00*
a. Single, English .25 *1.75*
b. Single, Dutch .25 *1.75*
c. As #J27, without period after "Africa" 100.00
J28 D1 1½p yel brn & blk, pair 5.00 *35.00*
a. Single, English .30 *6.50*
b. Single, Dutch .30 *6.50*
c. As #J28, without period after "Africa" 110.00
J29 D1 2p vio & blk, pair 3.00 *19.00*
a. Single, English .35 *3.50*
b. Single, Dutch .35 *3.50*
c. As #J29, without period after "Africa" 85.00
J30 D1 3p bl & blk, pair 5.25 *20.00*
a. Single, English .85 *3.75*
b. Single, Dutch .85 *3.75*
c. As #J30, without period after "Africa" 92.50
J31 D1 6p gray & blk, pair 16.00 *57.50*
a. Single, English 2.00 *14.00*
b. Single, Dutch 2.00 *14.00*
c. As #J31, without period after "Africa" 180.00
Nos. J26-J31 (6) 45.50 *185.50*

Wmk. Springbok's Head (177)

J32 D1 3p ultra & black, pair 10.00 *65.00*
a. Single, English 1.75 *11.00*
b. Single, Dutch 1.75 *11.00*

On Transvaal No. J5

Wmk. 3

J33 D1 5p violet & blk, pair 3.25 *22.50*
a. Single, English .25 *3.50*
b. Single, Dutch .25 *3.50*
c. As #J33, without period after "Africa" 92.50 *75.00*

Setting VIII

On South Africa Nos. J18, J13-J16

1927 **Unwmk.**

J34 D2 1p rose & black, pair 1.25 *13.00*
a. Single, English .25 *2.25*
b. Single, Afrikaans .25 *2.25*
c. As #J34, without period after "Africa" 10.50 *17.50*
J35 D1 1½p yel brn & blk, pair 1.25 *22.50*
a. Single, English .25 *3.50*
b. Single, Afrikaans .25 *3.50*
c. As #J35, without period after "Africa" 50.00 *60.00*
J36 D1 2p vio & blk, pair 6.00 *18.00*
a. Single, English .30 *3.25*
b. Single, Afrikaans .30 *3.25*
c. As #J36, without period after "Africa" 50.00 *60.00*
J37 D1 3p bl & blk, pair 16.00 *50.00*
a. Single, English 1.75 *11.00*
b. Single, Afrikaans 1.75 *11.00*
c. As #J37, without period after "Africa" 70.00 70.00
J38 D1 6p gray & blk, pair 12.00 *40.00*
a. Single, English 1.50 *8.50*
b. Single, Afrikaans 1.50 *8.50*
c. As #J38, without period after "Africa" 100.00 115.00
Nos. J34-J38 (5) 36.50 *143.50*

On Transvaal No. J5

Wmk. Multiple Crown and C A (3)

J39 D1 5p violet & blk, pair 22.50 *97.50*
a. Single, English 3.00 *22.50*
b. Single, Afrikaans 3.00 *22.50*

South Africa Nos. J15-J16 Overprinted

1928 **Unwmk.**

J79 D1 3p blue & black 1.65 *12.00*
a. Without period after "A" 42.50 45.00
J80 D1 6p gray & black 7.50 *32.50*
a. Without period after "A" 150.00

Same Overprint on South Africa Nos. J17-J21

J81 D2 ½p blue grn & blk .65 *9.50*
J82 D2 1p rose & black .65 *4.00*
a. Without period after "A" 45.00 *50.00*
J83 D2 2p violet & black .65 *5.00*
a. Without period after "A" 62.50
J84 D2 3p ultra & black 2.75 *30.00*
J85 D2 6p gray & black 1.75 *22.50*
a. Without period after "A" 62.50 *225.00*
Nos. J81-J85 (5) 6.45 *71.00*

Catalogue values for unused stamps in this section, from this point to the end of the section, are for Never Hinged items.

D3

Wmk. 201

1931, Feb. 23 **Litho.** ***Perf. 12***

Size: 19x22mm

J86 D3 ½p yel green & blk 2.00 *8.50*
On cover *120.00*
J87 D3 1p rose & black 2.00 *1.65*
On cover *90.00*
J88 D3 2p violet & black 2.50 *3.25*
On cover *90.00*
J89 D3 3p blue & black 5.00 *15.00*
On cover *130.00*
J90 D3 6p gray & black 17.50 *30.00*
On cover *275.00*
Nos. J86-J90 (5) 29.00 *58.40*

Cover values are for properly franked commercial items. Philatelic usages also exist and sell for less.

OFFICIAL STAMPS

Nos. 85-87 (Setting VIII) Overprinted at top with type "c" on English-inscribed Stamps and type "d" on Afrikaans-inscribed Stamps

c d

Without Periods after Words

1927 **Wmk. 201** ***Perf. 14½x14***

O1 A5 ½p dk grn & blk, pair 95.00 *200.00*
a. Single, English 12.50 *30.00*
b. Single, Afrikaans 12.50 *30.00*
O2 A6 1p car & blk, pair 95.00 *200.00*
a. Single, English 12.50 *30.00*
b. Single, Afrikaans 12.50 *30.00*
O3 A7 6p org & grn, pair 120.00 *225.00*
a. Single, English 15.00 *30.00*
b. Single, Afrikaans 15.00 *30.00*

South Africa No. 5 Overprinted As Nos. 85-87 plus "c" and "d"

Perf. 14

Wmk. 177

O4 A2 2p dull violet 225.00 *375.00*
a. Single, English 35.00 *45.00*
b. Single, Afrikaans 35.00 *45.00*

Nos. 96-98 Overprinted like Nos. J79-J85 at foot, Overprinted Types "c" and "d" at Top

1929 **Wmk. 201** ***Perf. 14½x14***

O5 A5 ½p green & blk, pair 1.25 *17.50*
a. Single, English .25 *2.75*
b. Single, Afrikaans .25 *2.75*
O6 A6 1p car & blk, pair 2.00 *23.00*
a. Single, English .25 *2.75*
b. Single, Afrikaans .25 *2.75*
O7 A7 6p org & grn, pair 4.50 *23.00*
a. Single, English .75 *3.75*
b. Single, Afrikaans .75 *3.75*
Nos. O5-O7 (3) 7.75 *63.50*

No. 99 Overprinted in Black

With Periods after Words

Perf. 14

O8 A8 2p vio brn & gray, pair 2.50 *22.50*
a. Single, English .35 *3.75*
b. Single, Afrikaans .35 *3.75*
c. Without period after "OFFICIAL" 7.00 *50.00*
d. Pair, "c" + normal 2p 17.00 *95.00*
e. Without period after "OFFISIEEL" 7.00 *50.00*
f. Pair, "e" + normal 2p 17.00 *95.00*
g. Pair, "c" + "e" 22.00 *95.00*

In each sheet of 120 stamps there were 12 No. O8c and 10 No. O8e.

South Africa Nos. 23-25 Overprinted

Without Periods after Words

1929 **Wmk. 201** ***Perf. 14½x14***

O9 A5 ½p green & blk, pair .85 *16.00*
a. Single, English .25 *2.75*
b. Single, Afrikaans .25 *2.75*
O10 A6 1p car & blk, pair 1.25 *17.50*
a. Single, English .25 *3.25*
b. Single, Afrikaans .25 *3.25*
O11 A7 6p org & grn, pair 3.00 *27.50*
a. Single, English .40 *6.50*
b. Single, Afrikaans .40 *6.50*
Nos. O9-O11 (3) 5.10 *61.00*

South Africa No. 26 Overprinted

With Periods after Words

Perf. 14

O12 A8 2p vio brn & gray, pair		1.50	*22.00*
a.	Single, English	.25	*3.50*
b.	Single, Afrikaans	.25	*3.50*
c.	Without period after "OFFICIAL"	3.75	*45.00*
d.	Pair, "c" + normal 2p	17.00	*95.00*
e.	Without period after "OFFISIEEL"	6.50	*50.00*
f.	Pair, "e" + normal 2p	17.00	*95.00*
g.	Pair, "c" + "e"	22.00	*95.00*

Catalogue values for unused stamps in this section, from this point to the end of the section, are for Never Hinged items.

Nos. 108-109, 111 and 114 Overprinted in Red

1931

O13 A15 ½p green & blk, pair		15.00	*22.00*
a.	Single, English	1.25	*3.75*
b.	Single, Afrikaans	1.25	*3.75*
O14 A16 1p red & indigo, pair		1.50	*19.00*
a.	Single, English	.25	*3.50*
b.	Single, Afrikaans	.25	*3.50*
O15 A18 2p dk brn & dk bl, pair		3.75	*11.00*
a.	Single, English	.40	*2.25*
b.	Single, Afrikaans	.40	*2.25*
O16 A21 6p ol brn & bl, pair		5.75	*15.00*
a.	Single, English	.50	*3.25*
b.	Single, Afrikaans	.50	*3.25*
	Nos. O13-O16 (4)	26.00	*67.00*

No. 110 Overprinted in Red

1938, July 1 Wmk. 201

O17 A17 1½p violet brn, pair		36.50	*50.00*
a.	Single, English	3.50	*6.00*
b.	Single, Afrikaans	3.50	*6.00*

Nos. 108-111, 114 Ovptd. in Red

1945-50 Wmk. 201 *Perf. 14x13½*

O18 A15 ½p grn & blk, pair		14.00	*35.00*
a.	Single, English	1.50	*5.00*
b.	Single, Afrikaans	1.50	*5.00*
O19 A16 1p red & ind, pair ('50)		14.00	*20.00*
a.	Single, English	.85	*3.25*
b.	Single, Afrikaans	.85	*3.25*
O20 A17 1½p vio brn, pair		40.00	55.00
a.	Single, English	5.00	7.00
b.	Single, Afrikaans	5.00	7.00
O21 A18 2p dk brn & dk bl, pair ('47)		675.00	*875.00*
a.	Single, English	100.00	*100.00*
b.	Single, Afrikaans	100.00	*100.00*
O22 A21 6p ol brn & bl, pair		30.00	*70.00*
a.	Single, English	2.00	*8.00*
b.	Single, Afrikaans	2.00	*8.00*
	Nos. O18-O20,O22 (4)	98.00	*180.00*

Nos. 108-111, 114 Ovptd. in Red

1951-52

O23 A15 ½p grn & blk, pair ('52)		19.00	*25.00*
a.	Single, English	2.00	*4.50*
b.	Single, Afrikaans	2.00	*4.50*
O24 A16 1p red & ind, pair		6.00	*22.50*
a.	Single, English	.40	*2.00*
b.	Single, Afrikaans	.40	*2.00*
c.	Ovpt. transposed, pair	110.00	*250.00*
d.	As "c," single, English ovpt.	10.00	
e.	As "c," single, Afrikaans ovpt.	10.00	
O25 A17 1½p violet brn, pair		30.00	32.50
a.	Single, English	3.00	5.00
b.	Single, Afrikaans	3.00	5.00
c.	Ovpt. transposed, pair	80.00	*95.00*
d.	As "c," single, English ovpt.	7.50	
e.	As "c," single, Afrikaans ovpt.	7.50	
O26 A18 2p dk brn & dk bl, pair		4.00	*26.00*
a.	Single, English	.45	*3.50*
b.	Single, Afrikaans	.45	*3.50*
c.	Ovpt. transposed, pair	75.00	*250.00*
d.	As "c," single, English ovpt.	4.50	
e.	As "c," single, Afrikaans ovpt.	4.50	
O27 A21 6p ol brn & blue, pair		4.00	*55.00*
a.	Single, English	.50	*7.50*
b.	Single, Afrikaans	.50	*7.50*
c.	Ovpt. transposed, pair	28.00	*170.00*
d.	As "c," single, English ovpt.	4.00	
e.	As "c," single, Afrikaans ovpt.	4.00	
	Nos. O23-O27 (5)	63.00	*161.00*

"Overprint transposed" means English inscription on Afrikaans stamp, or vice versa.

Use of official stamps ceased in Jan. 1955.

SPAIN

'spān

LOCATION — Southwestern Europe, Iberian Peninsula
GOVT. — Monarchy
AREA — 194,884 sq. mi.
POP. — 38,219,534 (est. 1983)
CAPITAL — Madrid

Spain was a monarchy until about 1931, when a republic was established. After the Civil War (1936-39), the Spanish State of Gen. Francisco Franco was recognized.

32 Maravedis = 8 Cuartos = 1 Real
1000 Milesimas = 100 Centimos = 1 Escudo (1866)
100 Milesimas = 1 Real
4 Reales = 1 Peseta
100 Centimos = 1 Peseta (1872)

Watermarks

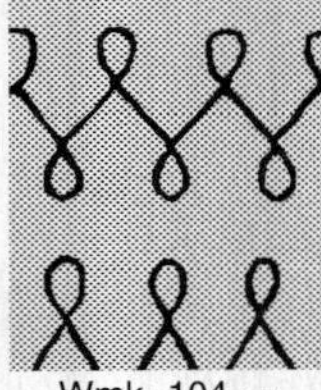
Wmk. 104 — Loops

Wmk. 105 — Crossed Lines

Wmk. 116 — Crosses and Circles

Wmk. 178 — Castle

Stamps punched with a small round hole have done telegraph service. In this condition most of these sell for 20 cents to $20 apiece.

Stamps of 1854 to 1882 canceled with three parallel horizontal bars or two thin lines are remainders. Most of these are valued through No. 101.

CANCELLATIONS

"Spider" Town (c-d-s)

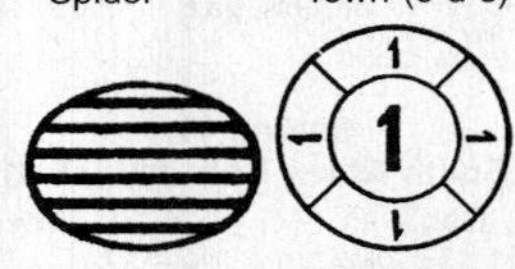

Grid Cartwheel

Several types of cancellations were used on early Spanish issues. Most common are the so-called "Spider" cancels, applied in red, blue or black. Circular date stamp (c-d-s) cancellations and grid cancellations were also generally used. In addition, a variety of pre-philatelic cancels may be found. These sell for more than the other types.

Kingdom

Queen Isabella II
A1 A2

A2a

A2b

A2c

Type I

Type II

6 CUARTOS:
Type I — "T" and "O" of CUARTOS separated.
Type II — "T" and "O" joined.

Unwmk.

1850, Jan. 1 Litho. *Imperf.*

1 A1 6c blk, thin paper (II)		650.00	17.00
	On cover		90.00
a.	Thick paper (II)	650.00	25.00
	On cover		125.00
b.	Thick paper (I)	850.00	20.00
	On cover		100.00
c.	Thin paper (I)	850.00	32.50
	On cover		150.00
d.	6c intense black (II)	850.00	32.50
e.	6c intense black (I)	850.00	25.00
2 A2 12c lilac		2,500.	200.00
	On cover		1,575.
a.	Thin paper	*4,500.*	325.00
	On cover		1,675.
b.	12c violet	4,400.	275.00
	On cover		2,100.
3 A2a 5r red		2,700.	200.00
	On cover		3,100.
	On cover, single franking		9,500.
a.	5r pale red	3,800.	450.00
b.	5r deep dark red	4,800.	500.00
4 A2b 6r blue		3,500.	700.00
	On cover		4,800.
	On cover, single franking		14,500.
a.	6r deep dark blue	5,850.	900.00
5 A2c 10r green		5,000.	1,500.
	On cover		6,400.
	On cover, single franking		—
a.	10r dark green	8,200.	2,900.
b.	10r pale green	6,900.	2,400.

Full margins = ¾mm.

Stamps of types A2, A3, A4, A6, A7a and A8 are inscribed "FRANCO" on the cuarto values and "CERTIFICADO," "CERTIFO" or "CERT DO" on the reales values.

Values for Singles and Covers

Black Spider Cancellations

1		16.50
	On cover	100.00
b.		21.50
	On cover	120.00
2		300.00
	On cover	1,575.
b.		—
	On cover	—
3		300.00
	On cover	3,100.
4		850.00
	On cover	4,800.
5		2,400.
	On cover	6,400.

Blue Spider Cancellations

1		145.00
	On cover	350.00
b.		100.00
	On cover	350.00
2		1,100.
	On cover	—
b.		—
	On cover	—
3		900.00
	On cover	—
4		2,200.
	On cover	—
5		*6,000.*
	On cover	—

Red Spider Cancellations

1		135.00
	On cover	300.00
b.		92.50
	On cover	300.00
2		850.00
	On cover	—
b.		—
	On cover	—
3		1,450.
	On cover	—
4		1,650.
	On cover	—

5 6,250.
On cover —

Red Circular Date Cancellations

1 32.50
On cover 145.00
b. 55.00
On cover 160.00
2 3,750.
On cover —
b. 2,000.
On cover —
3 475.00
On cover —
4 1,350.
On cover —
5 8,500.
On cover —

Blue Circular Date Cancellations

1 —
On cover —
b. 1,575.
On cover 5,250.
2 —
On cover —
b. —
On cover —
3 —
On cover —
4 —
On cover —
5 —
On cover —

Black Circular Date Cancellations

1 —
On cover —
b. 1,100.
2 —
On cover —
b. —
On cover —
3 —
On cover —
4 —
On cover —
5 —
On cover —

Values for pairs

1 A1 6c blk, thin paper (II) 1,750. 82.50
a. Thick paper (II) 2,350. 125.00
b. Thick paper (I) 2,100. 72.00
c. Thin paper (I) 2,800. 170.00
d. 6c intense black (II) 2,150. 110.00
e. 6c intense black (I) 2,450. 100.00
2 A2 12c lilac 10,000. 900.00
a. Thin paper 1,000.
b. 12c violet 10,000. 900.00
3 A2a 5r red 8,100. 900.00
a. 5r pale red 8,100. 1,350.
b. 5r deep dark red 9,600. 1,500.
4 A2b 6r blue 10,500. 2,500.
a. 6r deep dark blue 12,000. 3,250.
5 A2c 10r green — 6,000.
a. 10r dark green — 7,500.
b. 10r pale green 6,000.

Values for strips of 3

1 A1 6c blk, thin paper (II) 2,700. 160.00
a. Thick paper (II) 3,500. 200.00
b. Thick paper (I) 3,200. 150.00
c. Thin paper (I) 4,000. 340.00
d. 6c intense black (II) 3,400. 190.00
e. 6c intense black (I) 3,750. 200.00
2 A2 12c lilac 1,600.
a. Thin paper —
b. 12c violet 2,000.
3 A2a 5r red 1,900.
a. 5r pale red 2,250.
b. 5r deep dark red 2,350.
4 A2b 6r blue 4,250.
a. 6r deep dark blue 5,000.
5 A2c 10r green — 11,500.
a. 10r dark green — 12,500.
b. 10r pale green 11,500.

Values for blocks of 4

1 A1 6c blk, thin paper (II) 5,200. 675.00
a. Thick paper (II) 5,900. 800.00
b. Thick paper (I) 6,500. 600.00
c. Thin paper (I) 7,500. 1,350.
d. 6c intense black (II) 6,400. 750.00
e. 6c intense black (I) 7,000. 800.00
2 A2 12c lilac 1,900.
a. Thin paper 3,000.
b. 12c violet 2,900.
3 A2a 5r red 3,750.
a. 5r pale red 4,500.
b. 5r deep dark red 4,600.
4 A2b 6r blue 22,000. 8,500.
a. 6r deep dark blue 30,000. 9,000.
5 A2c 10r green 23,000.
a. 10r dark green 25,000.
b. 10r pale green 23,000.

A3

1851, Jan. 1 Thin Paper Typo.

6 A3 6c black 375.00 3.50
On cover, single franking 32.50
On cover, in combination with other stamps 375.00
a. Thick paper 825.00 20.00
On cover 65.00
b. 6c gray black 400.00 4.00
c. 6c intense black 675.00 6.50
7 A3 12c lilac 7,500. 175.00
On cover 1,000.
On cover, single franking 1,000.
a. 12c violet 7,500. 210.00
b. 12c gray 6,500. 375.00
c. 12c dark lilac 6,250. 225.00
8 A3 2r red 24,000. 6,000.
On cover 47,500.
a. 2r deep orange red 30,000. 15,000.
On cover 50,000.
9 A3 5r rose 3,000. 175.00
On cover 2,275.
On cover, single franking 8,800.
a. 5r red brown (error) 22,000. —
b. 5r rose carmine 4,200. 360.00
10 A3 6r blue 5,250. 650.00
On cover 4,100.
On cover, single franking 16,000.
a. Cliche of 2r in plate of 6r — 125,000.
b. Pair, #10, 10a 175,000.
c. 6r deep blue 6,250. 1,450.
d. 6r pale blue 5,750. 1,100.
11 A3 10r green 3,750. 450.00
On cover 2,675.
On cover, single franking 13,000.
a. 10r deep green 4,600. 675.00
b. 10r pale green 4,250. 550.00

Full margins = ¾mm.

Values for Singles and Covers
Black Spider Cancellations

6 3.75
On cover 37.50
7 225.00
On cover 1,150.
8 13,500.
On cover 47,500.
9 325.00
On cover 2,650.
10 1,275.
On cover 4,750.
11 625.00
On cover 3,150.

Blue Spider Cancellations

6 42.50
On cover 190.00
7 475.00
On cover 3,150.
8 26,500.
On cover —
9 1,125.
On cover —
10 3,500.
On cover —
11 2,350.
On cover —

Red Spider Cancellations

6 22.50
On cover 160.00
7 425.00
On cover —
8 26,500.
On cover —
9 725.00
On cover —
10 2,750.
On cover —
11 1,350.
On cover —

Red Circular Date Stamp Cancellations

6 250.00
7 575.00
8 26,500.
9 1,250.

Black Grid Cancellations

6 375.00
7 —

Blue Grid Cancellations

6 300.00
7 1,625.

Red Grid Cancellations

6 525.00
7 —

Values for pairs

6 A3 6c black 775.00 24.50
a. Thick paper 2,000. 140.00
b. 6c gray black 1,000. 27.50
c. 6c intense black 1,650. 45.00
7 A3 12c lilac 500.00
a. 12c violet 525.00
b. 12c gray 875.00
c. 12c dark lilac 575.00
8 A3 2r red 33,000.
a. 2r deep orange red 39,000.
9 A3 5r rose 6,900. 675.00
b. 5r rose carmine 8,600. 900.00
10 A3 6r blue 2,750.
c. 6r deep blue 3,500.
d. 6r pale blue 2,750.
11 A3 10r green 1,375.
a. 10r deep green 11,500. 1,575.
b. 10r pale green 1,375.

Values for strips of 3

6 A3 6c black 1,300. 80.00
a. Thick paper 3,300. 400.00
b. 6c gray black 1,600. 80.00
c. 6c intense black 2,700. 130.00
7 A3 12c lilac 750.00
a. 12c violet 850.00
b. 12c gray 1,500.
c. 12c dark lilac 925.00
8 A3 2r red —
a. 2r deep orange red —
9 A3 5r rose 1,100.
b. 5r rose carmine 1,500.
10 A3 6r blue 4,400.
c. 6r deep blue 5,750.
d. 6r pale blue 4,400.
11 A3 10r green 2,250.
a. 10r deep green 2,750.
b. 10r pale green 2,250.

Values for blocks of 4

6 A3 6c black 2,000. 350.00
a. Thick paper —
b. 6c gray black 5,000. 450.00
c. 6c intense black 5,450. 700.00
7 A3 12c lilac 36,000. 1,250.
a. 12c violet 44,000. 1,350.
b. 12c gray 38,500. 2,450.
c. 12c dark lilac 38,000. 1,500.
8 A3 2r red —
a. 2r deep orange red —
9 A3 5r rose 21,000. 1,800.
b. 5r rose carmine 27,500. 2,350.
10 A3 6r blue 7,250.
c. 6r deep blue 9,500.
d. 6r pale blue 7,250.
11 A3 10r green 25,500. 3,750.
a. 10r deep green 30,000. 4,500.
b. 10r pale green 28,500. 3,750.

A4

1852, Jan. 1 Thick Paper

12 A4 6c rose 400.00 3.50
On cover, single franking 20.00
On cover, in combination with other values 425.00
a. Thin paper 625.00 5.50
On cover 27.50
b. 6c deep rose 625.00 5.50
On cover 27.50
c. 6c carmine lake 900.00 9.00
On cover 75.00
13 A4 12c lilac 2,600. 150.00
On cover, single franking 875.00
On cover, in combination with other values 1,100.
a. 12c gray lilac 3,600. 225.00
On cover 1,250.
b. 12c dark lilac 3,500. 210.00
On cover 1,100.
14 A4 2r pale red 16,000. 3,500.
On cover 22,500.
On cover, single franking —
a. 2r orange red 24,500. 6,600.
On cover 27,500.
15 A4 5r yellowish green 3,000. 100.00
On cover 3,600.
On cover, single franking 7,250.
a. 5r green 2,950. 125.00
On cover 3,600.
b. 5r deep green 3,800. 160.00
On cover 4,500.
16 A4 6r grnsh blue 4,600. 500.00
On cover 6,000.
On cover, single franking 7,250.
a. 6r blue 4,600. 525.00
On cover 6,000.
b. 6r dark bluish grn 5,500. 650.00
On cover 7,250.

Full margins = ¾mm.

Values for pairs

12 A4 6c rose 1,400. 11.00
b. 6c deep rose 1,600. 42.50
c. 6c carmine lake 2,250. 52.50
13 A4 12clilac 7,100. 400.00
a. 12c gray lilac 11,500. 550.00
b. 12c dark lilac 11,500. 600.00
14 A4 2r pale red 55,000. 15,250.
a. 2r orange red 67,500. 16,750.
15 A4 5r yellowish green 5,000. 225.00
a. 5r green 5,000. 350.00
b. 5r deep green 8,100. 250.00
16 A4 6r greenish blue 1,500.
a. 6r blue 1,500.
b. 6r dark bluish green 1,850.

Values for strips of 3

12 A4 6c rose 2,500. 45.00
b. 6c deep rose 4,400. 135.00
c. 6c carmine lake 4,500. 190.00
13 A4 12clilac 600.00
a. 12c gray lilac 900.00
b. 12c dark lilac 850.00
14 A4 2r pale red 22,500.
a. 2r orange red 27,500.
15 A4 5r yellowish green 525.00
a. 5r green 525.00
b. 5r deep green 675.00
16 A4 6r greenish blue 2,100.
a. 6r blue 2,100.
b. 6r dark bluish green 2,600.

Values for blocks of 4

12 A4 6c rose 3,500. 300.00
b. 6c deep rose 4,400. 600.00
c. 6c carmine lake 6,300. 1,400.
13 A4 12clilac 900.00
a. 12c gray lilac 1,375.
b. 12c dark lilac 1,300.
14 A4 2r pale red 45,000.
a. 2r orange red 55,000.
15 A4 5r yellowish green 750.00
a. 5r green 750.00
b. 5r deep green 1,000.
16 A4 6r greenish blue 3,150.
a. 6r blue 3,250.
b. 6r dark bluish green 3,900.

Arms of Madrid — A5

Isabella II — A6

1853, Jan. 1 Thin Paper

17 A5 1c bronze 2,500. 350.00
On cover 1,600.
a. 1c golden bronze 4,500. 900.00
18 A5 3c bronze 18,000. 6,000.
On cover 12,000.
a. 3c golden bronze 23,500. 10,000.
19 A6 6c carmine rose 750.00 2.25
On cover 15.00
a. Thick paper 975.00 16.00
b. Thick bluish paper 1,300. 22.50
c. 6c rose red, thin paper 675.00 7.50
20 A6 12c reddish purple 2,750. 135.00
On cover 850.00
a. 12c dark violet 3,500. 165.00
b. Thick paper 3,750. 475.00
21 A6 2r vermilion 12,000. 2,000.
On cover 21,500.
On cover, single franking 150,000.
a. 2r bright vermilion 17,000. 3,750.
22 A6 5r lt green 2,500. 130.00
On cover 3,600.
On cover, single franking 11,000.
a. 5r deep green 3,800. 165.00
23 A6 6r deep blue 3,700. 450.00
On cover 6,000.
On cover, single franking 27,500.
a. 6r blackish blue 4,900. 575.00

Full margins = ¾mm.

Nos. 17-18 were issued for use on Madrid city mail only. *They were reprinted on this white paper in duller colors.*

Values for Singles and Covers

Black Grid Cancellations

17	650.00
On cover	1,850.
18	9,250.
On cover	13,750.
19	2.75
On cover	17.00
20	145.00
On cover	1,000.
21	4,000.
On cover	25,000.
22	145.00
On cover	4,200.
23	525.00
On cover	7,000.

Red Grid Cancellations

17	2,100.
19	100.00
On cover	—
20	575.00
22	600.00
23	1,500.

Blue Grid Cancellations

17	1,275.
On cover	—
19	45.00
On cover	160.00
20	400.00
On cover	—
21	8,000.
22	550.00
On cover	—
23	1,200.

Red Circular Date Stamp Cancellations

17	1,700.
19	500.00
20	1,000.

Black Circular Date Stamp Cancellations

17	1,700.
19	500.00
20	9.00
23	1,275.

Values for pairs

17	A5	1c bronze	15,500.	
17a	A5	1c golden bronze	20,500.	
19	A6	6c carmine rose	1,600.	8.00
19c	A6	6c rose lake	1,700.	27.50
20	A6	12c red violet	—	325.00
20a	A6	12c dark violet	—	425.00
21	A6	2r vermilion		10,500.
21a	A6	2r bright vermilion		11,750.
22	A6	5r light green	7,500.	325.00
22a	A6	5r deep green	9,500.	425.00
23	A6	6r deep blue	10,500.	1,350.
23a	A6	6r blackish blue	10,000.	1,500.

Values for strips of 3

17	A5	1c bronze	23,000.	
17a	A5	1c golden bronze	31,000.	
19	A6	6c carmine rose	2,900.	16.00
19c	A6	6c rose lake	3,000.	50.00
20	A6	12c red violet	—	500.00
20a	A6	12c dark violet	—	675.00
21	A6	2r vermilion		17,500.
21a	A6	2r bright vermilion		18,750.
22	A6	5r light green		600.00
22a	A6	5r deep green		800.00
23	A6	6r deep blue		2,250.
23a	A6	6r blackish blue		2,750.

Values for blocks of 4

17	A5	1c bronze	33,000.	
17a	A5	1c golden bronze	45,000.	
19	A6	6c carmine rose	3,800.	210.00
19c	A6	6c rose lake	4,000.	675.00
20	A6	12c red violet	—	750.00
20a	A6	12c dark violet	—	1,000.
21	A6	2r vermilion		25,000.
21a	A6	2r bright vermilion		28,000.
22	A6	5r light green	21,000.	900.00
22a	A6	5r deep green	28,000.	1,200.
23	A6	6r deep blue		3,000.
23a	A6	6r blackish blue		4,750.

A7

A7a

Coat of Arms of Spain — A8

1854 — **Thin White Paper**

24	A7 2c green	2,650.	525.00
	On cover, single franking		1,100.
	On cover, in combination with other values		4,500.
a.	2c dark green	3,350.	675.00
	On cover, single franking		1,450.
25	A7a 4c carmine	450.00	2.10
	On cover, single franking		12.00
	On cover, in combination with other values		100.00
b.	4c dark carmine lake	675.00	3.50
	On cover		18.00
	Bar cancellation		4.00
26	A8 6c carmine	350.00	1.60
	On cover		18.00
	Pair, on cover		45.00
	On cover, in combination with other values		400.00
c.	6c dark carmine	525.00	2.25
	On cover		30.00
d.	6c pale red	525.00	5.00
	Bar cancellation		3.00
	On cover		35.00
27	A7a 1r indigo	3,500.	350.00
	On cover		2,250.
	On cover, single franking		4,500.
a.	1r blue black	5,250.	425.00
	Bar cancellation		21.00
	On cover		2,750.
28	A8 2r scarlet	2,100.	120.00
	On cover		1,350.
	On cover, single franking		—
a.	2r vermilion	2,400.	150.00
	On cover		2,000.
b.	2r pale red	3,250.	160.00
	On cover		2,000.
	Bar cancellation, #28, 28a or 28b		10.00
29	A8 5r green	2,000.	110.00
	Bar cancellation		16.00
	On cover		1,350.
	On cover, single franking		5,400.
a.	5r dark green	2,500.	125.00
	Bar cancellation		16.00
	On cover		1,500.
30	A8 6r blue	4,000.	325.00
	Bar cancellation		25.00
	On cover		4,150.
	On cover, single franking		12,500.
a.	6r dark blue	4,100.	400.00
	Bar cancellation		25.00
	On cover		5,000.

Full margins = ¾mm.

Thick White Paper

24c	A7	2c green	3,650.	525.00
25a	A7a	4c carmine	675.00	17.50
		Bar cancellation		4.75
28c	A8	2r scarlet	—	250.00

See boxed note on bar cancellation before No. 1.

Thick Bluish Paper

31	A7 2c green	16,500.	1,500.
	On cover, single franking		6,000.
a.	2c dark green	20,000.	2,700.
	On cover, single franking		7,500.
32	A7a 4c carmine	500.00	5.50
	On cover, single franking		37.50
	On cover, in combination with other values		110.00
b.	4c dark carmine lake	700.00	9.00
	On cover, single franking		45.00
32A	A8 6c carmine	1,050.	19.00
	Bar cancellation		2.00
33	A7a 1r pale blue		6,500.
	Bar cancellation		150.00
	On cover, single franking		27,500.
34	A8 2r dull red	7,000.	600.00
	On cover		2,250.

Full margins = ¾mm.

The 2c with watermark 104 is a proof.

Thin Bluish Paper

31b	A7	2c green	18,500.	2,400.
32c	A7a	4c carmine	600.00	17.50
32Ad	A8	6c carmine	—	100.00
33a	A7a	1r pale blue	—	9,500.
34a	A8	2r dull red	7,000.	600.00

Values for Singles and Covers

Black Grid Cancellations

24	625.00
On cover	1,250.
25	2.50
On cover	14.00
26	1.90
On cover	21.00
27	415.00
On cover	2,600.
28	130.00
On cover	1,500.
29	125.00
On cover	1,500.
30	375.00
On cover	4,750.
31	2,400.
On cover	6,750.
32	6.75
On cover	42.50
33	9,500.
On cover	30,000.
34	750.00
On cover	3,750.

Red Grid Cancellations

24	5.25
On cover	10.00
25	60.00
On cover	450.00
26	47.50
On cover	290.00
27	3.50
28	600.00
On cover	—
29	600.00
On cover	—
30	1,000.
On cover	—
31	20.00
On cover	57.50
32	60.00
On cover	450.00
33	80.00
On cover	275.00

Blue Grid Cancellations

24	950.00
On cover	—
25	35.00
On cover	100.00
26	13.00
On cover	52.50
27	850.00
On cover	—
28	275.00
29	350.00
On cover	—
30	1,000.
32	35.00
On cover	100.00
33	10,000.

Black Circular Date Stamp Cancellations

24	2,000.
25	45.00
On cover	240.00
26	75.00
On cover	775.00
27	1,000.
28	525.00
29	550.00
32	50.00
On cover	375.00

Red Circular Date Stamp Cancellations

24	18.00
26	100.00
On cover	1,250.

Blue Circular Date Stamp Cancellations

24	14,000.
25	95.00
On cover	—
32	115.00
On cover	—

Values for pairs

24	A7	2c green	6,500.	1,650.
24a	A7	2c dark green	7,500.	2,100.
25	A7a	4c carmine	1,500.	7.50
25b	A7a	4c dk carmine lake	1,900.	11.50
26	A8	6c carmine	1,400.	6.00
		On cover		50.00
26c	A8	6c dark carmine	1,650.	9.00
26d	A8	6c pale red	1,650.	11.00
27	A7a	1r indigo		1,100.
27a	A7a	1r blue black		1,250.
28	A8	2r scarlet	5,600.	350.00
		On cover		2,000.
28a	A8	2r vermilion	5,300.	450.00
28b	A8	2r pale red	9,100.	450.00
29	A8	5r green		350.00
29a	A8	5r dark green		400.00
30	A8	6r blue		1,000.
30a	A8	6r dark blue		1,375.
31	A7	2c green		7,000.
32	A7a	4c carmine	1,350.	17.50
32b	A7a	4c dk carmine lake	1,700.	24.00

Values for strips of 3

24	A7	2c green		3,400.
24a	A7	2c dark green		4,200.
25	A7a	4c carmine		28.00
25b	A7a	4c dk carmine lake		42.50
26	A8	6c carmine	2,350.	26.00
26c	A8	6c dark carmine	2,750.	37.50
26d	A8	6c pale red	2,750.	47.50
27	A7a	1r indigo		1,675.
27a	A7a	1r blue black		2,000.
32	A7a	4c carmine		32.50
32b	A7a	4c dk carmine lake		42.50
33	A7a	1r pale blue		35,000.

Values for blocks of 4

24	A7	2c green	12,500.	7,000.
24a	A7	2c dark green	19,500.	9,000.
25	A7a	4c carmine		55.00
25b	A7a	4c dk carmine lake		850.00
26	A8	6c carmine	1,850.	45.00
26c	A8	6c dark carmine	3,950.	70.00
26d	A8	6c pale red	3,950.	90.00
27	A7a	1r indigo		2,600.
27a	A7a	1r blue black		3,150.
28	A8	2r scarlet		800.00
28a	A8	2r vermilion		1,000.
28b	A8	2r pale red		1,000.
29	A8	5r green		800.00
29a	A8	5r dark green		900.00
30	A8	6r blue		2,500.
30a	A8	6r dark blue		3,200.
32	A7a	4c carmine		80.00
32b	A7a	4c dk carmine lake		115.00
33	A7a	1r pale blue		65,000.

Isabella II — A9

Blue Paper

1855, Apr. 1 — **Wmk. 104**

36	A9 2c green	3,400.	140.00
	On cover, single franking		400.00
a.	2c yellow green	4,000.	175.00
	On cover, single franking		500.00
	Bar cancellation, #36 or 36a		10.00
37	A9 4c brown red	300.00	1.00
	On cover, single franking		10.00
a.	4c carmine	440.00	2.50
	On cover, single franking		25.00
b.	4c lake	350.00	.90
	On cover, single franking		10.00
	Bar cancellation, #37, 37a or 37b		2.50
c.	4c brown red, white to grayish paper	475.00	5.75
d.	4c lake red, white to grayish paper	525.00	9.25
	Bar cancellation		2.50
38	A9 1r green blue	1,300.	15.00
	On cover, single franking		110.00
a.	1r blue	1,600.	20.00
	On cover, single franking		140.00
	Bar cancellation, #38 or 38a		5.00
b.	Cliché of 2r in plate of 1r	25,000.	3,250.
	Bar cancellation, #38b		850.00
39	A9 2r reddish pur	900.00	15.00
	On cover, single franking		110.00
a.	2r deep violet	1,450.	20.00
	On cover, single franking		140.00
b.	2r grayish violet	1,450.	20.00
	On cover, single franking		95.00
	Bar cancellation, #39, 39a or 39b		13.50

Full margins = ¾mm.

Values for Singles and Covers

Black Grid Cancellations

36	150.00
On cover	425.00
37	.90
On cover	5.00
38	17.00
On cover	120.00
39	17.00
On cover	120.00

Red Grid Cancellations

36	425.00
37	28.50
On cover	150.00
38	92.50
On cover	—
39	14.00

Blue Grid Cancellations

36	150.00
On cover	—
37	3.00
On cover	40.00
38	30.00
On cover	250.00
39	32.50
On cover	300.00

Black Circular Date Stamp Cancellations

36	800.00
On cover	1,150.
37	27.50
On cover	95.00
38	85.00
On cover	200.00
39	60.00
On cover	175.00

Blue Circular Date Stamp Cancellations

37	57.50
On cover	145.00
38	150.00
39	150.00

Cartwheel Cancellation

36	375.00
On cover	700.00
37	37.50
On cover	95.00
38	85.00
On cover	145.00
39	85.00
On cover	145.00

Values for pairs

36	A9	2c green	9,500.	525.00
36a	A9	2c yellow green	12,000.	675.00
37	A9	4c brown red	950.00	3.75
37a	A9	4c carmine	1,300.	7.75
37b	A9	4c lake red	950.00	6.25
38	A9	1r green blue	4,000.	50.00
38a	A9	1r blue	4,000.	60.00
38b	A9	2r green blue with #38	50,000.	5,000.
39	A9	2r reddish violet	3,400.	42.50
39a	A9	2r deep violet	4,250.	52.50
39b	A9	2r grayish violet	4,250.	52.50

Values for strips of 3

36	A9	2c green	14,000.	1,850.
36a	A9	2c yellow green	17,000.	2,400.
37	A9	4c brown red	1,250.	5.50
37a	A9	4c carmine	1,750.	1,200.
37b	A9	4c lake red	1,250.	10.00
38	A9	1r green blue	5,800.	85.00
38a	A9	1r blue	6,000.	100.00
39	A9	2r reddish violet	4,600.	65.00
39a	A9	2r deep violet	5,900.	80.00
39b	A9	2r grayish violet	5,900.	80.00

Values for blocks of 4

36	A9	2c green		4,000.
36a	A9	2c yellow green		5,000.
37	A9	4c brown red	2,200.	11.50
37a	A9	4c carmine	3,000.	24.00
37b	A9	4c lake red	2,200.	19.00
38	A9	1r green blue	9,500.	110.00
38a	A9	1r blue	9,500.	130.00
39	A9	2r reddish violet	6,400.	95.00
39a	A9	2r deep violet	8,300.	115.00
39b	A9	2r grayish violet	8,300.	115.00

Rough Yellowish Paper

1856, Jan. 1 — **Wmk. 105**

40	A9 2c green	4,000.	250.00
	On cover, single franking		875.00
a.	2c pale green	4,000.	300.00
	On cover, single franking		375.00
	Bar cancellation, #40 or 40a		15.00
41	A9 4c rose	13.50	2.25
	On cover, single franking		20.00
a.	4c deep rose	14.00	3.00
	On cover, single franking		25.00
	Bar cancellation, #41 or 41a		2.50
42	A9 1r grnsh blue	5,500.	200.00
	On cover		800.00
a.	1r dull blue	5,750.	275.00
	On cover		1,200.
	Bar cancellation, #42 or 42a		8.50

43 A9 2r brown purple 600.00 25.00
On cover, single franking 140.00
a. 2r dark reddish purple 775.00 45.00
On cover, single franking 175.00
b. 2r grayish purple 650.00 45.00
On cover, single franking 175.00
Bar cancellation, #43, 43a or 43b 7.50

Full margins = ¾mm.

White Smooth Paper

1856, Apr. 11 **Unwmk.**

44 A9 2c blue green 700.00 42.50
On cover, single franking 115.00
On cover with other values, from 160.00
a. 2c yellow green 825.00 50.00
On cover, single franking 140.00
Bar cancellation, #44 or 44a 7.50
45 A9 4c rose 5.75 .35
On cover, single franking 5.25
On cover with other values, from 32.50
a. 4c carmine ('59) 9.25 20.00
On cover, single franking 67.50
On cover with other values, from 115.00
46 A9 1r blue 27.50 25.00
On cover, single franking 110.00
On cover with other values, from 160.00
a. 1r pale greenish blue 40.00 32.50
On cover, single franking 125.00
Bar cancellation, #46 or 46a 4.00
47 A9 2r brown lilac 70.00 20.00
On cover, single franking 100.00
On cover with other values, from 160.00
a. 2r dull lilac 100.00 35.00
On cover, single franking 140.00
Bar cancellation, #47 or 47a 10.00

Full margins = ¾mm.

Three types of No. 45.

1859

48 A9 12c dark orange 200.00
Bar cancellation 55.00
a. Tete-beche pair (#48) 500.00
b. 12c light orange 1,550.
Bar cancellation 150.00

Full margins = ¾mm.

Nos. 48-48b were never put in use. All canceled examples have the bar cancellation.

Stamps of the 1st printing (#48b), may be distinguished by shade and by a break at lower left, which is not on the 2nd printing (#48).

Reprints exist.

A10

1860-61 **Tinted Paper**

49 A10 2c green, *grn* 350.00 19.00
Bar cancellation 2.50
On cover, single franking 85.00
On cover with other values, from 115.00
50 A10 4c orange, *grn* 60.00 .80
On cover, single franking 5.50
On cover with other values, from 27.50
51 A10 12c car, *buff* 350.00 14.00
Bar cancellation 8.75
On cover, single franking 47.50
On cover with other values, from 140.00
52 A10 19c brn, *buff* ('61) 2,500. 1,200.
On cover, single franking 9,000.
53 A10 1r blue, *grn* 325.00 12.50
Bar cancellation 4.50
On cover, single franking 145.00
On cover with other values, from 160.00
a. 1r dark blue, *green* 525.00 18.00
b. 1r pale blue, *green* 600.00 18.00
54 A10 2r lilac, *lil* 400.00 11.00
Bar cancellation 4.50
On cover, single franking 72.50
On cover with other values, from 140.00
a. 2r dark violet, *mauve* 550.00 15.00
b. 2r lilac, *blue,* thick paper 750.00 52.50

Full margins = ¾mm.

A11

1862, July 16

55 A11 2c dp bl, *yel* 37.50 11.00
On cover, single franking 82.50
On cover with other values, from 130.00
56 A11 4c dk brn, *redsh buff* 2.40 .70
On cover, single franking 5.00
On cover with other values, from 26.00
a. 4c brown, *white* 24.00 7.00
Bar cancellation 2.50
On cover, single franking 50.00
57 A11 12c blue, *pnksh* 42.50 8.50
Bar cancellation 3.25
On cover, single franking 37.50
On cover with other values, from 125.00
58 A11 19c car, *lil* 200.00 225.00
On cover, single franking 3,600.
a. 19c carmine, *white* 300.00 275.00
On cover, single franking 4,000.
Bar cancellation, #58 or 58a 175.00
59 A11 1r brown, *yel* 57.50 17.50
Bar cancellation 3.50
On cover, single franking 140.00
On cover with other values, from 140.00
a. 1r brown, *yellow gold* 300.00 60.00
60 A11 2r green, *pnksh* 37.50 11.00
Bar cancellation 3.25
On cover, single franking 72.50
On cover with other values, from 85.00
a. 2r yellow green, *rose* 45.00 14.00
b. 2r dark yellow green, *rose* 70.00 21.00
Nos. 55-60 (6) 377.40 273.70

Full margins = ¾mm.

A12

1864, Jan. 1

61 A12 2c dk bl, *lil* 50.00 20.00
On cover, single franking 82.50
On cover with other values, from 160.00
62 A12 4c rose, *redsh buff* 2.50 1.00
On cover, single franking 5.75
On cover with other values, from 24.00
a. 4c carmine, *reddish buff* 22.50 7.50
Bar cancellation, #62 or 62a 2.50
63 A12 12c green, *pnksh* 42.50 14.50
On cover, single franking 55.00
On cover with other values, from 125.00
a. 12c dark green, *pnksh* 67.50 17.50
64 A12 19c violet, *pnksh* 210.00 190.00
On cover, single franking 4,500.
65 A12 1r brown, *grn* 190.00 75.00
Bar cancellation 5.00
On cover, single franking 375.00
On cover with other values, from 350.00
66 A12 2r blue, *pnksh* 45.00 12.00
On cover, single franking 72.50
On cover with other values, from 130.00
a. 2r deep blue, *pnksh* 65.00 17.50
Bar cancellation, #66 or 66a 5.00
Nos. 61-66 (6) 540.00 312.50

Full margins = 1mm.

A13

1865, Jan. 1 **Litho.** ***Imperf.***

67 A13 2c rose 325.00 35.00
On cover, single franking 150.00
On cover with other values, from 150.00
68 A13 4c blue *2,750.*
69 A13 12c blue & rose 425.00 19.00
Bar cancellation 5.25
On cover, single franking 80.00
On cover with other values, from 140.00
a. Frame inverted *13,500.* 800.00
Bar cancellation *100.00*
b. Pair, #69, 69a *2,750.*
70 A13 19c brn & rose 1,300. 600.00
Bar cancellation 100.00
On cover, single franking *6,400.*
71 A13 1r yellow grn 425.00 65.00
Bar cancellation 17.50
On cover, single franking 275.00
On cover with other values, from 275.00
72 A13 2r red lilac 425.00 35.00
Bar cancellation 16.00
On cover, single franking 175.00
On cover with other values, from 175.00
73 A13 2r rose 550.00 65.00
Bar cancellation 17.50
On cover, single franking 250.00
On cover with other values, from 250.00
a. 2r salmon 475.00 70.00
Bar cancellation 12.50
On cover, single franking 350.00
On cover with other values, from 325.00
b. 2r orange 575.00 100.00
c. 2r yellow brown 600.00 110.00

Full margins = 1mm.

No. 68 is without gum and was never put in use.

A majority of the perforated stamps from 1865 to about 1950 are rather poorly centered. The very fine examples that are valued will be fairly well centered. Poorly centered stamps sell for less. Stamps of some issues are almost always badly centered, and our values will be for examples with fine centering. Such issues will be noted.

1865, Jan. 1 ***Perf. 14***

74 A13 2c rose red 600.00 130.00
Bar cancellation 13.50
On cover, single franking 300.00
On cover with other values, from 425.00
75 A13 4c blue 60.00 1.00
On cover, single franking 5.75
On cover with other values, from 30.00
76 A13 12c bl & rose 850.00 60.00
Bar cancellation 10.50
On cover, single franking 100.00
On cover with other values, from 190.00
a. Frame inverted *18,000.* *2,650.*
As "a," bar cancel 50.00
b. Pair, #76, 76a *30,000.* 4,000.
77 A13 19c brn & rose *4,000.* *2,500.*
On cover, single franking *13,500.*
78 A13 1r yellow grn 2,000. 525.00
Bar cancellation 26.50
On cover, single franking 1,000.
On cover with other values, from 1,225.
a. 1r dark green 2,400. 600.00
Bar cancellation 26.50
On cover, single franking 1,250.
79 A13 2r violet 1,900. 250.00
Bar cancellation 24.00
On cover, single franking 925.00
On cover with other values, from 1,425.
80 A13 2r rose 1,400. 350.00
On cover, single franking 1,100.
On cover with other values, from 1,850.
a. 2r salmon 1,400. 350.00
On cover, single franking 1,100.
On cover with other values, from 1,850.
b. 2r dull orange 1,400. 350.00
On cover, single franking 1,100.
On cover with other values, from 1,850.
Bar cancellation, #80, 80a or 80b 35.00

Values for Nos. 74-80 are for stamps with perforations touching the frame on at least one side.

A14

1866, Jan. 1

81 A14 2c rose 250.00 32.50
On cover, single franking 82.50
On cover with other values, from 125.00
a. 2c dark carmine 375.00 35.00
On cover, single franking 90.00
On cover with other values, from 140.00
Bar cancellation, #81 or 81a 5.50
82 A14 4c blue 42.50 .80
On cover, single franking 7.75
On cover with other values, from 30.00
83 A14 12c orange 260.00 12.75
On cover, single franking 47.50
On cover with other values, from 62.50
a. 12c orange yellow 350.00 25.00
On cover, single franking 85.00
On cover with other values, from 125.00
84 A14 19c brown 1,250. 525.00
Bar cancellation 50.00
On cover, single franking 1,575.
On cover with other values, from *2,125.*
Nos. 81-84 (4) 1,803. 571.05

A14a

1866

85 A14 10c green 300.00 27.50
Bar cancellation 4.00
On cover, single franking 125.00
On cover with other values, from 150.00
86 A14 20c lilac 200.00 21.00
Bar cancellation 4.00
On cover, single franking 110.00
On cover with other values, from 150.00
87 A14a 20c dull lilac 1,250. 100.00
On cover, single franking 225.00
On cover with other values, from 275.00
a. 20c dark lilac 1,250. 100.00
Bar cancellation, #87 or 87a 3.00
Nos. 85-87 (3) 1,750. 148.50

For the Type A14a 20c in green, see Cuba No. 25.

A15

A15a

A15b

A15c

1867-68

88 A15 2c yell brn 450.00 47.50
On cover, single franking 110.00
On cover with other values, from 150.00

89 A15a 4c blue 27.50 1.00
On cover, single franking 8.00
On cover with other values, from 30.00
90 A15b 12c org yell 250.00 8.00
On cover, single franking 42.50
On cover with other values, from 62.50
a. 12c dark orange 300.00 12.00
On cover, single franking 57.50
On cover with other values, from 87.50
b. 12c red orange ('68) 925.00 40.00
On cover, single franking 125.00
On cover with other values, from 300.00
91 A15c 19c rose 1,450. 425.00
Bar cancellation 40.00
On cover, single franking 1,250.

See Nos. 100-102. For overprints see Nos. 114a-115a, 124-128, 124a-128a, 124c-124c, 124e-126e.

A15d

A15e

92 A15d 10c blue green 275.00 24.50
Bar cancellation 2.50
On cover, single franking 110.00
On cover with other values, from 110.00
a. 10c dark green 300.00 30.00
93 A15e 20c lilac 130.00 10.50
On cover, single franking 47.50
On cover with other values, from 62.50
a. 20c dark lilac 160.00 15.00
b. 20c gray lilac 160.00 15.00
Bar cancellation, #93, 93a or 93b 2.50

For overprints see Nos. 116-117, 116a-117a, 116c-117c, 117d, 117e, 117f.

A16

A17

A18

94 A16 5m green 47.50 17.50
On cover or newsprint, single franking 72.50
On cover with other values, from 150.00
a. 5m bluish green 60.00 27.50
Bar cancellation, #94 or 94a 2.50
95 A17 10m brown 47.50 17.50
On cover or newsprint, single franking 90.00
On cover with other values, from 150.00
a. Tête bêche pair *20,000.*
b. 10m yellow brown 45.00 17.50
c. 10m dark brown 60.00 27.50
96 A18 25m bl & rose 250.00 24.00
Bar cancellation 5.00
On cover, single franking 100.00
On cover with other values, from 125.00
a. Frame inverted *50,000.*
b. 25m blue & carmine 250.00 29.00
97 A18 50m bis brn 22.00 .80
On cover, single franking 7.75
On cover with other values, from 32.50
a. 50m dark brown 24.00 1.25
Bar cancellation, #97 or 97a 2.75
Nos. 94-97 (4) 367.00 59.80

See No. 98. For overprints see Nos. 118-122, 118a-122a, 120c-122c, 122d, 120e, 122e, 119f, 122f.

A19

1868-69

98 A18 25m blue 275.00 14.50
Bar cancellation 3.75
On cover, single franking 85.00
On cover with other values, from 125.00
99 A19 50m violet 29.00 .60
On cover, single franking 8.00
On cover with other values, from 30.00
a. 50m blackish violet 37.50 1.25
Bar cancellation, #99 or 99a 2.50
100 A15b 100m brown 550.00 75.00
Bar cancellation 3.00
On cover, single franking 225.00
On cover with other values, from 250.00
101 A15c 200m green 210.00 14.00
Bar cancellation 3.00
On cover, single franking 85.00
On cover with other values, from 65.00
102 A15c 19c brown 3,000. 525.00
On cover, single franking 3,650.
On cover with other values, from *6,500.*

For overprints see #123, 123a, 123c, 123e.

Provisional Government

Excellent counterfeits exist of the provisional and provincial overprints.

For Madrid

Regular Issues Handstamped in Black

1868-69

116 A15d 10c green 50.00 16.00
117 A15e 20c lilac 50.00 12.00
118 A16 5m green 40.00 5.50
119 A17 10m brown 30.00 5.50
120 A18 25m bl & rose 100.00 14.50
g. Frame inverted *15,000.*
121 A18 25m blue 100.00 12.00
g. Double overprint (black & red) 75.00
122 A18 50m bis brn 10.00 5.00
123 A19 50m violet 10.00 5.00
124 A15b 100m brown 200.00 28.50
125 A15c 200m green 75.00 9.00
126 A15b 12c org yel (#90) 75.00 11.00
g. 12c dark orange (#90a) 40.00 14.00
h. 12c red orange (#90b) 75.00 18.00
127 A15c 19c rose 800.00 140.00
128 A15c 19c brown 1,200. 165.00
Nos. 116-128 (13) 2,740. 429.00

Nos. 116-128 exist with handstamp in blue, a few in red. These sell for more.

No. 120g was for use exclusively in Salamanca.

For Andalusian Provinces

Regular Issues Handstamped Vertically in Blue

114a A15 2c brown 100.00 36.00
115a A15a 4c blue 60.00 25.00
116a A15d 10c green 100.00 15.00
117a A15e 20c lilac 100.00 16.00
118a A16 5m green 50.00 8.25
119a A17 10m brown 25.00 6.00
120a A18 25m bl & rose 100.00 15.00
b. Frame inverted *22,000.*
121a A18 25m blue 100.00 15.50
122a A18 50m bis brn 15.00 5.50
123a A19 50m violet 15.00 5.50
124a A15b 100m brown 200.00 32.50
125a A15c 200m green 100.00 12.00
126a A15b 12c org yel (#90) 75.00 13.50
b. 12c dark org (#90a) 60.00 18.00
127a A15c 19c rose 800.00 210.00
128a A15c 19c brown 1,400. 275.00
Nos. 114a-128a (15) 3,240. 690.75

For Valladolid Province

Regular Issues Handstamped in Black

(Two types of overprint)

116c A15d 10c green 100.00 16.50
117c A15e 20c lilac 100.00 19.00
118c A16 5m green (#94) 20.00
119c A17 10m brown (#95) 20.00
120c A18 25m blue & rose 100.00 15.00
121c A18 25m blue 80.00 21.00
122c A18 50m bis brn 25.00 9.25
123c A19 50m violet 25.00 7.75
124c A15b 100m brown 200.00 38.00
125c A15c 200m green 100.00 15.00
126c A15b 12c orange 75.00 12.50
127c A15c 19c rose *800.00* *175.00*
128c A15c 19c brown *1,400.* *240.00*
Nos. 116c-126c (11) 845.00 154.00

For Asturias Province Llanes (Oviedo)

Regular Issues Handstamped in Black

117d A15e 20c lilac 210.00 125.00
122d A18 50m bister brown 230.00 125.00

For Teruel Province

Regular Issues Handstamped in Black

117e A15e 20c lilac 100.00 55.00
120e A18 25m blue & rose 150.00 55.00
122e A18 50m bister brown 85.00 32.50
123e A19 50m violet 85.00 32.50
124e A15b 100m brown 250.00 75.00
125e A15c 200m green 250.00 45.00
126e A15b 12c orange 150.00 60.00
Nos. 117e-126e (7) 1,070. 355.00

For Salamanca Province

Regular Issues Handstamped in Blue

117f A15e 20c lilac 125.00 55.00
119f A17 10m brown 125.00 42.00
122f A18 50m bister brown 125.00 50.00
Nos. 117f-122f (3) 375.00 147.00

Duke de la Torre Regency

"España" — A20

1870, Jan. 1 **Typo.**

159 A20 1m brn lil, *buff* 6.50 6.50
Bar cancellation 2.00
On cover, single franking 110.00
On cover with other values, from 125.00
b. 1m brown lilac, *pinkish buff* 7.00 7.75
On cover, single franking 125.00
161 A20 2m blk, *pinkish* 7.75 8.00
On cover, single franking 110.00
On cover with other values, from 125.00
a. 2m black, *buff* 8.75 9.00
On cover, single franking 120.00
163 A20 4m bister brn 16.00 13.50
On cover, single franking 160.00
On cover with other values, from 165.00
164 A20 10m rose 19.00 6.00
On cover, single franking 95.00
On cover with other values, from 110.00
a. 10m carmine 21.00 7.50
On cover, single franking 100.00
165 A20 25m lilac 52.50 6.50
Bar cancellation 2.00
On cover, single franking 35.00
a. 25m gray lilac 55.00 6.50
On cover, single franking 30.00
On cover with other values, from 27.50
b. 25m aniline violet 85.00 8.25
On cover, single franking 35.00
166 A20 50m ultra 11.50 .35
On cover, single franking 3.50
On cover with other values, from 7.50
a. 50m dull blue 125.00 5.00
On cover, single franking 75.00
167 A20 100m red brown 40.00 5.25
Bar cancellation 1.40
On cover, single franking 27.50
On cover with other values, from 19.00
a. 100m claret 35.00 6.25
On cover, single franking 32.50
b. 100m orange brown 35.00 5.50
On cover, single franking 27.50
168 A20 200m pale brown 32.50 5.25
Bar cancellation 2.00
On cover, single franking 22.50
On cover with other values, from 19.00
169 A20 400m green 350.00 25.00
Bar cancellation 3.00
On cover, single franking 110.00
On cover with other values, from 85.00
170 A20 1e600m dull lilac 1,700. 850.00
Bar cancellation 27.50
On cover, single franking *7,000.*
171 A20 2e blue 1,400. 525.00
Bar cancellation 27.50
On cover —
172 A20 12c red brown 325.00 7.25
On cover, single franking 30.00
On cover with other values, from 40.00
a. 12c deep brown 260.00 7.00
On cover, single franking 35.00
173 A20 19c yel grn 450.00 225.00
On cover, single franking 1,750.
a. 19c bright green 310.00 210.00
On cover, single franking 2,100.

The 12c carmine rose and 12c blue on pink paper were not put in use. Value $2,500. and $6,000., respectively.

Kingdom

A21

1872, Oct. 1 ***Imperf.***

174 A21 ¼c ultra 2.25 2.25
On cover, pair of ¼c only 60.00
a. Complete 1c (block of 4 ¼c) 120.00 90.00
Bar cancellation 5.00
On cover 110.00
b. As "a," one cliche inverted 1,800. *1,750.*

See No. 221A.

A22

King Amadeo
A23 A24

1872-73 ***Perf. 14***

176 A22 2c gray lilac 20.00 8.00
On cover or newsprint 75.00
On cover with other values, from 70.00
a. 2c violet 32.50 18.00
On cover or newsprint, single franking 110.00
b. Imperf. 75.00
177 A22 5c green 180.00 62.50
On cover, single franking 175.00
On cover with other values, from 175.00
a. Imperf. 225.00
178 A23 5c rose ('73) 27.50 5.75
On cover, single franking 42.50
On cover with other values, from 40.00
179 A23 6c blue 180.00 39.00
On cover, single franking 110.00
On cover with other values, from 140.00
180 A23 10c brown lilac 400.00 240.00
On cover, single franking 450.00
On cover with other values, from 425.00
181 A23 10c ultra ('73) 8.50 .55
Bar cancellation 3.50
On cover, single franking 2.50
On cover with other values, from 6.50
182 A23 12c gray lilac 27.50 2.50
Bar cancellation 3.50
On cover, single franking 11.00
On cover with other values, from 27.50
183 A23 20c gray vio ('73) 140.00 80.00
Bar cancellation 5.25
On cover, single franking 175.00
On cover with other values, from 160.00
184 A23 25c brown 60.00 12.00
Bar cancellation 2.75
On cover, single franking 32.50
On cover with other values, from 32.50
185 A23 40c pale red brn 80.00 10.50
Bar cancellation 2.75
On cover, single franking 27.50

186 A23 50c deep green 105.00 11.00
Bar cancellation 2.75
On cover, single franking 65.00
On cover with other values, from 47.50
187 A24 1p lilac 115.00 55.00
Bar cancellation 4.00
On cover, single franking 200.00
On cover with other values, from 140.00
188 A24 4p red brown 750.00 625.00
Bar cancellation 12.00
On cover —
189 A24 10p deep green 2,300. 2,400.
Bar cancellation 250.00
On cover *15,000.*

First Republic

Mural Crown — A25

1873, July 1 ***Imperf.***
190 A25 ¼c green 1.00 1.00
a. Complete 1c (block of 4 ¼c) 37.50 20.00
As "a," bar cancellation 2.50
As "a," on cover 85.00
b. As "a," deep green 45.00 35.00
c. As "a," bluish green 52.50 25.00
d. As "a," ultra (error) 210.00 160.00

"España" — A26

1873, July 1 ***Perf. 14***
191 A26 2c orange 13.50 6.00
On cover, single franking 75.00
On cover with other values, from 50.00
192 A26 5c claret 30.00 6.00
Bar cancellation 3.00
On cover, single franking 50.00
On cover with other values, from 27.50
193 A26 10c green 6.75 .35
Bar cancellation *2.00*
On cover, single franking 3.25
On cover with other values, from 13.00
a. Tête bêche pair *32,500.*
194 A26 20c black 110.00 25.00
Bar cancellation 3.75
On cover, single franking 150.00
On cover with other values, from 150.00
195 A26 25c dp brn 35.00 6.00
Bar cancellation 2.50
On cover, single franking 40.00
On cover with other values, from 30.00
196 A26 40c brown vio 42.50 6.00
Bar cancellation 2.50
On cover, single franking 32.50
On cover with other values, from 30.00
197 A26 50c ultra 21.00 6.75
Bar cancellation 2.50
On cover, single franking 32.50
On cover with other values, from 30.00
198 A26 1p lilac 72.50 32.50
Bar cancellation 2.50
On cover, single franking 190.00
On cover with other values, from 110.00
a. 1p deep lilac 47.50 32.50
b. 1p gray 55.00 45.00
199 A26 4p red brown 850.00 475.00
Bar cancellation 12.50
On cover —
200 A26 10p violet brn 2,100. 1,750.
Bar cancellation 24.00
On cover —

Only one example of No. 193a is known, and it is in a block of six stamps.

"Justice" — A27

1874, July 1
201 A27 2c yellow 22.50 8.50
Bar cancellation 2.10
On cover, single franking 70.00
On cover with other values, from 40.00
202 A27 5c violet 45.00 10.00
Bar cancellation 2.10
On cover, single franking 35.00
On cover with other values, from 32.50
a. 5c red violet 32.50 10.00
On cover, single franking 45.00
203 A27 10c ultra 12.50 .40
On cover, single franking 3.25
On cover with other values, from 13.00
a. Imperf. 13.50
204 A27 20c dark green 225.00 45.00
Bar cancellation 4.00
On cover, single franking 225.00
On cover with other values, from 150.00
205 A27 25c red brown 50.00 6.75
Bar cancellation 2.10
On cover, single franking 32.50
On cover with other values, from 27.50
a. 25c lilac (error) 325.00
As "a," bar cancellation 30.00
b. Imperf. 57.50
206 A27 40c violet 450.00 8.00
Bar cancellation 2.10
On cover, single franking 30.00
On cover with other values, from 27.50
a. 40c brown (error) 250.00
b. Imperf. 190.00
207 A27 50c yellow 105.00 8.25
Bar cancellation 2.10
On cover, single franking 32.50
On cover with other values, from 30.00
a. Imperf. 120.00
b. 50c orange 100.00 9.00
208 A27 1p yellow green 100.00 34.00
Bar cancellation 2.10
On cover, single franking 190.00
On cover with other values, from 100.00
a. 1p emerald 92.50 47.50
On cover, single franking 250.00
b. Imperf. 175.00
209 A27 4p rose 800.00 410.00
Bar cancellation 8.00
On cover, single franking —
On cover with other values, from *1,900.*
a. 4p carmine 800.00 600.00
On cover, single franking —
210 A27 10p black 3,000. 1,900.
Bar cancellation 10.50
On cover, single franking —
On cover with other values, from *4,000.*

Coat of Arms — A28

1874, Oct. 1
211 A28 10c red brown 25.00 .70
Bar cancellation 1.60
On cover 3.75
a. 10c brown 42.50 3.50
On cover 13.00
b. Imperf. 90.00

Kingdom

Nos. 212-221 are almost always badly centered and are often irregularly perforated. Values are for stamps with complete perforations and fine centering. Sound stamps with average centering are worth about 50% of these values. Stamps with very fine centering sell for more.

King Alfonso XII — A29

1875, Aug. 1
Blue Framed Numbers on Back, 1-100 on Each Sheet
212 A29 2c org brn 22.50 11.00
On cover, single franking 60.00
On cover with other values, from 55.00
a. 2c chocolate brown 30.00 15.00
On cover, single franking 85.00
b. Imperf. 45.00 45.00
213 A29 5c lilac 120.00 13.00
On cover, single franking 45.00
On cover with other values, from 37.50
a. Imperf. 95.00 87.50
214 A29 10c blue 8.25 .40
Bar cancellation 2.00
On cover, single franking 3.75
On cover with other values, from 13.00
a. Imperf. 22.50 22.50
215 A29 20c brn org 350.00 125.00
On cover, single franking 300.00
On cover with other values, from 275.00
216 A29 25c rose 72.50 8.00
Bar cancellation 2.00
On cover, single franking 30.00
On cover with other values, from 25.00
217 A29 40c deep brown 125.00 37.50
Bar cancellation 4.50
On cover, single franking 65.00
On cover with other values, from 50.00
a. Imperf. 140.00 140.00
218 A29 50c gray lilac 200.00 42.50
Bar cancellation 5.25
On cover, single franking 65.00
On cover with other values, from 65.00
219 A29 1p black 225.00 80.00
Bar cancellation 3.00
On cover, single franking 140.00
On cover with other values, from 130.00
220 A29 4p dark green 600.00 525.00
On cover, single franking —
On cover, with other values, from *1,000.*
221 A29 10p ultra 1,800. 1,750.
On cover, single franking —
On cover, with other values, from *3,500.*

1876, June 1 ***Imperf.***
221A A21 ¼c green .25 .25
On cover 9.00
b. Complete 1c (block 4 ¼c) 1.10 .30
As "b," on cover 30.00
c. As "b," two ¼c sideways, one invtd. 110.00 110.00
d. As "b," both upper ¼c invtd. 140.00 140.00
e. As "b," upper left ¼c invtd. 1,000. 500.00
f. As "b," both lower ¼c invtd. 140.00 140.00

No. 221Ac has one stamp upright, one inverted, one facing right and one facing left.

Nos. 222-230 are almost always badly centered. Values are for stamps with fine centering, fresh color and, in the case of mint stamps, full original gum. Sound stamps with average centering are worth about 50% of these values. Stamps with very fine centering sell for more.

King Alfonso XII — A30

Type I

Type II

ONE PESETA:
Type I — Thin figures of value and "PESETA" in thick letters.
Type II — Thick figures of value and "PESETA" in thin letters.

Wmk. 178
1876, June 1 Engr. ***Perf. 14***
222 A30 5c yellow brown 15.50 3.75
On cover, single franking 35.00
On cover with other values, from 25.00
223 A30 10c blue 3.75 .45
Bar cancellation 50.00
On cover, single franking 2.75
On cover with other values, from 13.00
224 A30 20c bronze green 19.00 13.00
On cover, single franking 50.00
On cover with other values, from 40.00
a. 20c dark green 19.00 15.00
On cover, single franking 65.00
225 A30 25c brown 8.50 5.50
On cover, single franking 15.00
On cover with other values, from 19.00
226 A30 40c black brown 80.00 *100.00*
On cover, single franking —
On cover with other values, from 290.00
227 A30 50c green 15.00 6.75
On cover, single franking 19.00
On cover with other values, from 27.50
228 A30 1p dp blue, I 20.00 9.00
On cover, single franking 42.50
On cover with other values, from 37.50
a. 1p ultra, II 27.50 13.00
On cover, single franking 45.00
229 A30 4p brown violet 55.00 *57.50*
On cover, single franking —
On cover with other values, from *1,500.*
230 A30 10p vermilion 150.00 125.00
On cover, single franking —
On cover with other values, from *2,600.*
Nos. 222-230 (9) 366.75 320.95

Imperf

222a	A30	5c	11.50
223a	A30	10c	5.75
225a	A30	25c	12.50
227a	A30	50c	18.00
228b	A30	1p	26.00
229a	A30	4p	92.50
230a	A30	10p	200.00

Two plates each were used for the 5c, 10c, 25c, 50c, 1p and 10p. The 1p plates are most easily distinguished.

The 20c value also exists imperf. Value $500.

King Alfonso XII — A31

Unwmk.
1878, July 1 Typo. ***Perf. 14***
232 A31 2c mauve 32.50 11.00
On cover, single franking 35.00
a. Imperf. 60.00
b. 2c lilac 35.00 13.00
233 A31 5c orange 45.00 14.00
On cover 30.00
On cover, single franking 45.00
a. 5c yellow gold 50.00 10.00
234 A31 10c brown 8.25 .50
Bar cancellation 3.00
On cover 3.00
235 A31 20c black 250.00 125.00
On cover 290.00
a. Imperf. 275.00
236 A31 25c olive bister 25.00 2.75
Bar cancellation 6.25
On cover 8.50
237 A31 40c red brown 190.00 140.00
On cover 375.00
238 A31 50c blue green 120.00 11.00
Bar cancellation 2.00
On cover 32.50
239 A31 1p gray 100.00 21.00
Bar cancellation 2.00
On cover 80.00
On cover, single franking 100.00
240 A31 4p violet 225.00 125.00
On cover 1,200.
241 A31 10p blue 450.00 350.00
On cover 1,900.
a. Imperf. 475.00
Nos. 232-241 (10) 1,446. 800.25

A32

1879, May 1
242 A32 2c black 9.50 4.50
Bar cancellation 3.00
On cover 22.50
243 A32 5c gray green 15.00 1.10
Bar cancellation 3.00
On cover 14.00
On cover, single franking 17.50
244 A32 10c rose 15.00 .45
Bar cancellation 2.00
On cover 2.50
245 A32 20c red brown 175.00 15.00
Bar cancellation 2.00
On cover 45.00
246 A32 25c bluish gray 15.50 .45
Bar cancellation 2.00
On cover 13.50
247 A32 40c brown 29.00 5.50
Bar cancellation 2.00
On cover 22.50
248 A32 50c dull buff 130.00 5.00
Bar cancellation 2.00
On cover 22.50
On cover, single franking 27.50
a. 50c yellow 190.00 7.00
On cover 32.50
On cover, single franking 37.50
249 A32 1p brt rose 150.00 2.25
Bar cancellation 2.00
On cover 32.50
On cover, single franking 90.00
250 A32 4p lilac gray 750.00 32.50
Bar cancellation 3.00
On cover *1,200.*
251 A32 10p olive bister 2,200. *175.00*
Bar cancellation 6.25
On cover *5,000.*

A33

1882, Jan. 1

252 A33 15c salmon 10.50 .25
Bar cancellation 2.00
On cover 1.75
a. 15c reddish orange 35.00 .45
On cover 5.50
b. 15c yellow 40.00 .85
On cover 11.00

253 A33 30c red lilac 310.00 5.25
Bar cancellation 2.00
On cover 60.00
On cover, single franking 65.00

254 A33 75c gray lilac 210.00 4.75
Bar cancellation 2.00
On cover 55.00
a. Imperf. 300.00
b. 75c gray 250.00 5.75
On cover 140.00

Nos. 255-270 are usually poorly centered and often exhibit defective perforations. Values are for fine to very fine examples, well centered but not very fine, fresh and without perforation faults. Average examples sell for about half these values.

King Alfonso XIII — A34

1889-99

255 A34 2c blue green 6.00 .45
On cover 7.00
On cover, single franking 13.00

256 A34 2c black ('99) 35.00 7.25
On cover 30.00
On cover, single franking 65.00

257 A34 5c blue 12.50 .25
On cover 3.25
On cover, single franking 6.50

258 A34 5c blue grn ('99) 145.00 1.40
On cover 7.75
On cover, single franking 19.00

259 A34 10c yellow brown 16.50 .25
On cover 2.75
a. 10c red brown 17.50 .45
On cover 5.50

260 A34 10c red ('99) 240.00 4.50
On cover 22.50

261 A34 15c violet brown 4.75 .25
On cover 1.00

262 A34 20c yellow green 50.00 4.75
On cover 25.00
On cover, single franking 27.50

263 A34 25c blue 20.00 .25
On cover 3.25

264 A34 30c olive gray 82.50 5.25
On cover 35.00
On cover, single franking 45.00

265 A34 40c brown 87.50 3.00
On cover 22.50
On cover, single franking 32.50

266 A34 50c rose 80.00 2.10
On cover 15.00

267 A34 75c orange 210.00 4.25
On cover 30.00
On cover, single franking 32.50

268 A34 1p dark violet 55.00 .45
On cover 45.00
On cover, single franking 65.00
a. 1p carmine rose (error) 350.00

269 A34 4p carmine rose 750.00 47.50
On cover 725.00

270 A34 10p orange red 1,300. 110.00
On cover 1,750.

The 15c yellow, type A34 is an official stamp listed as No. O9.
No. 270 exists perf 10. Value, unused $1,000.
Several values exist imperf.

Nos. 272-286 are almost always badly centered. Values are for stamps with fine centering, fresh color and, if unused, full original gum. Sound stamps with average centering sell for about half these values. Very fine stamps sell more more.

King Alfonso XIII — A35

Control Number on Back

1901-05 Engr. Unwmk.

272 A35 2c bister brown 3.25 .25
Never hinged 5.50
On cover 3.25

273 A35 5c dark green 5.75 .25
Never hinged 8.75
On cover 3.25

274 A35 10c rose red 9.50 .25
Never hinged 13.00
On cover 3.25

275 A35 15c blue black 17.00 .25
Never hinged 20.00
On cover 3.25

276 A35 15c dull lilac ('02) 13.00 .25
Never hinged 16.00
On cover 3.25

277 A35 15c purple ('05) 6.25 .25
Never hinged 8.75
On cover 1.75

278 A35 20c grnsh black 32.50 2.75
Never hinged 47.50
On cover, single franking 30.00

279 A35 25c blue 6.25 .40
Never hinged 10.00
On cover 3.25
b. 25c green (error) *4,000.*

280 A35 30c deep green 42.50 .35
Never hinged 45.00
On cover 3.50
a. 30c pale bluish green 35.00 .40
Never hinged 55.00
On cover 3.75
c. 30c yellow green 32.50 .30
Never hinged 45.00
On cover 3.50

281 A35 40c olive bister 150.00 5.00
Never hinged 150.00
On cover 22.50
On cover, single franking 70.00

282 A35 40c rose ('05) 300.00 4.50
Never hinged 375.00
On cover 22.50
On cover, single franking 450.00

283 A35 50c slate blue 32.50 .55
Never hinged 45.00
On cover 4.50
b. 50c blue green (error) *2,250. 1,100.*
c. 50c pale greenish blue 35.00 .60
Never hinged 50.00
On cover 5.00

284 A35 1p lake 30.00 .80
Never hinged 45.00
On cover 4.50

285 A35 4p dk violet 250.00 22.50
Never hinged 325.00
On cover 300.00

286 A35 10p brown orange 225.00 72.50
Never hinged 325.00
On cover 450.00
Nos. 272-286 (15) 1,124. 110.85
Set, never hinged 2,500.

There are numerous shades and unissued colors for this issue.

Imperf

272a	A35	2c	57.50
273a	A35	5c	25.00
274a	A35	10c	25.00
275a	A35	15c	110.00
276a	A35	15c	22.50
277a	A35	15c	17.00
278a	A35	20c	90.00
279a	A35	25c	17.00
280b	A35	30c	110.00
282a	A35	40c	300.00
283a	A35	50c	125.00
284a	A35	1p	57.50
285a	A35	4p	200.00
286a	A35	10p	190.00

The 15c in red brown (value $850), 30c blue ($1,200), 1p olive ($1,500), 1p blue green ($1,500) and 1p dark violet ($1,500) were prepared but not issued.

Nos. 287-296 are almost always badly centered. Values are for stamps with fine centering, fresh color and, if unused, full original gum. Sound stamps with average centering sell for about half these values. Very fine stamps sell for more.

Don Quixote Starts Forth A36

10c, Don Quixote attacks windmill. 15c, Meets country girls. 25c, Sancho Panza tossed in blanket. 30c, Don Quixote knighted. 40c, Tilting at sheep. 50c, On Wooden horse. 1p, Adventure with lions. 4p, In bullock cart. 10p, The Enchanted Lady.

Control Number on Back

1905, May 1 Typo.

287 A36 5c dark green 1.25 1.10
Never hinged 3.75
On cover 25.00
a. Imperf. 50.00
b. Vert. pair, imperf between *100.00 100.00*
c. Horiz. pair, imperf between *125.00 125.00*

288 A36 10c orange red 2.50 1.75
Never hinged 7.00
On cover 35.00
a. 10c pale red 6.75 3.75
Never hinged 17.50
On cover 70.00
b. Imperf.

289 A36 15c violet 2.50 1.75
Never hinged 7.00
On cover 37.50
a. Imperf. 80.00
b. 15c pale violet 6.75 3.75
Never hinged 17.50
On cover 75.00
c. Vert. pair, imperf between *100.00 100.00*

290 A36 25c dark blue 6.00 3.50
Never hinged 25.00
On cover 26.00
a. Horiz. pair, imperf between *200.00 200.00*

291 A36 30c dk blue green 30.00 10.00
Never hinged 160.00
On cover 100.00
a. 30c pale blue green 62.50 40.00
Never hinged 200.00
On cover 200.00

292 A36 40c bright rose 55.00 32.50
Never hinged 300.00
On cover 200.00
a. Imperf.

293 A36 50c slate 17.50 7.00
Never hinged 75.00
On cover 90.00

294 A36 1p rose red 180.00 90.00
Never hinged 1,000.
On cover 500.00

295 A36 4p dk violet 80.00 90.00
Never hinged 350.00
On cover 250.00

296 A36 10p brown orange 125.00 135.00
Never hinged 575.00
On cover 300.00
Nos. 287-296 (10) 499.75 372.60
Set, never hinged 2,500.

300th anniversary of the publication of Cervantes' "Don Quixote."
Counterfeits exist of Nos. 287-296.
For surcharges see Nos. 586-588, C91.

Six stamps picturing King Alfonso XIII and Queen Victoria Eugenia were put on sale Oct. 1, 1907, at the Madrid Industrial Exhibition. They were not valid for postage. Value, unused $40, mint never hinged $60.

The original labels were engraved and perf 11½. Examples printed by other methods or with other perfs are reprints. Value $2.

Alfonso XIII — A46

Blue Control Number on Back

Perf. 13x12½, 13, 13½x13, 14

1909-22 Engr.

297 A46 2c dark brown .55 .55
Never hinged 2.00
a. No control number .55 .25
Never hinged 2.00

298 A46 5c green 2.00 .25
Never hinged 5.00

299 A46 10c carmine 3.00 .25
Never hinged 6.50

300 A46 15c violet 9.50 .25
Never hinged 32.50

301 A46 20c olive green 50.00 .90
Never hinged 160.00

302 A46 25c deep blue 4.75 .25
Never hinged 17.00

303 A46 30c blue green 9.75 .25
Never hinged 29.00

304 A46 40c rose 15.50 .65
Never hinged 52.50

305 A46 50c slate blue ('22) 11.50 .40
Never hinged 42.50
a. 50c slate blue 12.50 .40
Never hinged 24.00

306 A46 1p lake 32.50 .40
Never hinged 100.00

307 A46 4p deep violet 80.00 12.00
Never hinged 325.00

309 A46 10p orange 100.00 26.00
Never hinged 420.00
Nos. 297-309 (12) 319.05 42.15
Set, never hinged 1,200.

Nos. 297-309 exist imperforate. Value $600.
The 5c exists in carmine; the 10c in yellow orange (value $400); the 15c in blue (value $400); the 4p in lake (value $2,000). The 5c and 15c are unissued trial colors, privately perforated and back-numbered. The 4p lake is known only with perfin "B.H.A." (Banco Hispano-Americano). 100 examples of the 4p exist, most poorly centered.
See Nos. 310, 315-317. For overprints see Nos. C1-C5, C58-C61.
Counterfeits exist.

Control Number on Back in Red or Orange

1917

310 A46 15c yellow ocher 3.50 .35
Never hinged 6.00
a. Control number in blue 14.50 1.10
Never hinged 22.50

Control Number on Back in Blue

1918

313 A46 40c light red 82.50 5.75
Never hinged 150.00

A47

1920 Typo. *Imperf.*

314 A47 1c blue green .25 .25
Never hinged .30

Perf. 13x12½,
Litho.

315 A46 2c bister 5.00 .25
Never hinged 15.00

316 A46 20c violet 42.50 .25
Never hinged 110.00
Nos. 314-316 (3) 47.75 .75
Set, never hinged 175.00

Nos. 314-315 have no control number on back.
For overprints and surcharge see Nos. 358, 449, 457, 468, 10L1, 11LB1.

1921 Engr.

317 A46 20c violet 30.00 .25
Never hinged 52.50

Madrid Post Office — A48

1920, Oct. 1 Typo. *Perf. 13½*

Center and Portrait in Black

318 A48 1c blue green .25 *.25*
Never hinged .45

319 A48 2c olive bister .25 *.25*
Never hinged .45

Control Number on Back

320 A48 5c green 1.00 *1.10*
Never hinged 2.50

321 A48 10c red 1.00 *1.10*
Never hinged 2.50

322 A48 15c yellow 1.60 1.40
Never hinged 3.25

323 A48 20c violet 1.90 1.75
Never hinged 5.50

324 A48 25c gray blue 3.00 3.00
Never hinged 5.75

325 A48 30c dark green 7.00 5.50
Never hinged 17.50

326 A48 40c rose 29.00 7.25
Never hinged 72.50

327 A48 50c brt blue 32.50 20.00
Never hinged 82.50

328 A48 1p brown red 32.50 16.50
Never hinged 82.50

329 A48 4p brown violet 100.00 70.00
Never hinged 250.00

330 A48 10p orange 200.00 145.00
Never hinged 520.00
Nos. 318-330 (13) 410.00 273.10
Set, never hinged 1,000.

Perf. 14

318a A48 1c blue green .25 .25
Never hinged .45

320a A48 5c green .85 .90
Never hinged 2.40

322a A48 15c yellow 1.75 1.40
Never hinged 4.00

323a A48 20c violet 2.50 1.50
Never hinged 7.75

324a A48 25c gray blue 2.60 2.50
Never hinged 7.75

325a A48 30c dark green 5.75 4.25
Never hinged 15.00

326a A48 40c rose 30.00 7.25
Never hinged 100.00

330a A48 10p orange 350.00 250.00
Never hinged 1,000.

Universal Postal Union Congress, Madrid, Oct. 10-Nov. 30.
Nos. 318-330 exist imperforate. Value, $2,500.

King Alfonso XIII
A49 A49a

Type I

Type II

FIFTEEN CENTIMOS:
Type I — Narrow "5."
Type II — Wide "5."

Type I

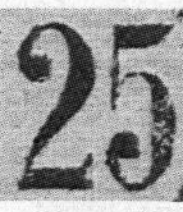
Type II

TWENTY FIVE CENTIMOS:
Type I — "25" is 2¾mm high. Vertical stroke of "5" is 1mm long.
Type II — "25" is 3mm high. Vertical stroke of "5" is 1½mm long.

Perf. 11 to 14, Compound

1922-26 Engr. Unwmk.

331 A49 2c olive green .85 .25
Never hinged 3.00
a. 2c deep orange (error) 87.50 *210.00*
Never hinged *125.00*
b. 2c bronze green 1.10 .25
Never hinged 3.00

Control Number on Back

332 A49 5c red violet 4.00 .25
Never hinged 12.00
333 A49 5c claret 1.60 .25
Never hinged 6.00
334 A49 10c carmine 1.60 1.10
Never hinged 6.00
335 A49 10c yellow green 1.50 .25
Never hinged 9.25
a. 10c blue green ('23) 2.25 .25
Never hinged 7.50
336 A49 15c slate bl (I) 8.00 .25
Never hinged 25.00
a. 15c black green (II) 27.50 2.25
Never hinged 65.00
b. 15c dk slate grn (I) 55.00 19.00
Never hinged 150.00
337 A49 20c violet 3.50 .25
Never hinged 14.00
a. 20c lilac 5.00 .25
Never hinged 15.00
338 A49 25c carmine (I) 3.50 .25
Never hinged 14.00
a. 25c rose red (II) 5.50 1.00
Never hinged 15.00
b. 25c lilac rose (error) 100.00 160.00
Never hinged *225.00*
339 A49 30c black brn ('26) 15.00 .25
Never hinged 42.50
340 A49 40c deep blue 4.00 .25
Never hinged 15.00
341 A49 50c orange 19.50 .25
Never hinged 60.00
a. 50c orange red 77.50 1.90
Never hinged 150.00
342 A49a 1p blue black 18.00 .25
Never hinged 70.00
343 A49a 4p lake 85.00 4.00
Never hinged 250.00
344 A49a 10p brown 40.00 13.50
Never hinged 125.00 —
Nos. 331-344 (14) 206.05 21.35
Set, never hinged 750.00

Nos. 331 ($15), 332 ($750), 334 ($40), 336-344 ($20 to $100 each) exist imperf.

The 5c exists in vermilion (value $110); the 25c in dark blue (value $200). The 50c exists in red brown, the 4p in brown and 10p in lake; value, each $90. These five were not regularly issued.

For overprints see Nos. 359-370, 467.

Nos. 331-344 are almost always found poorly centered.

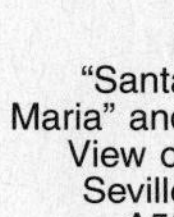

"Santa Maria" and View of Seville
A50

Herald of Barcelona — A51

Exposition Buildings — A52

King Alfonso XIII and View of Barcelona
A53

1929, Feb. 15 ***Perf. 11***

345 A50 1c grnsh blue 2.50 2.50
Never hinged 4.75
346 A51 2c pale yel grn .30 .30
Never hinged .65
347 A52 5c rose lake .50 .50
Never hinged .95

Control Number on Back

348 A53 10c green .50 .50
Never hinged 1.25
349 A50 15c Prus blue .85 .85
Never hinged 1.90
350 A51 20c purple .55 .55
Never hinged 1.10
351 A50 25c brt rose .55 .55
Never hinged 1.10
352 A52 30c black brn 4.00 *4.75*
Never hinged 12.00
353 A53 40c dark blue 7.75 7.75
Never hinged 20.00
354 A51 50c deep orange 7.75 *4.75*
Never hinged 11.50
355 A52 1p blue black 11.50 *12.00*
Never hinged 32.50
356 A53 4p deep rose 25.00 25.00
Never hinged 62.50
357 A53 10p brown 65.00 *70.00*
Never hinged 115.00
Nos. 345-357,E2 (14) 146.25 152.50
Set, never hinged 300.00

Perf. 14

345a A50 1c greenish blue .70 .70
Never hinged 1.10
348a A53 10c green 20.00 37.50
Never hinged 32.50
349a A50 15c Prus blue 22.50 22.50
Never hinged 32.50
350a A51 20c purple 26.00 37.50
Never hinged 45.00
351a A50 25c bright rose 32.50 37.50
Never hinged 45.00
352a A52 30c black brown 32.50 37.50
Never hinged 45.00
353a A53 40c dark blue 70.00 90.00
Never hinged 100.00
354a A51 50c deep orange 32.50 37.50
Never hinged 45.00
355a A52 1p blue black 32.50 37.50
Never hinged 45.00
356a A53 4p deep rose 25.00 25.00
Never hinged 55.00
357a A53 10p brown 110.00 140.00
Never hinged 225.00
Nos. 345a-357a,E2a (12) 436.70 540.70
Set, never hinged 725.00

Seville and Barcelona Exhibitions.

Nos. 345-357 exist imperf. Value, set $2,500. See note after No. 432.

Nos. 314, 331, 333, 335-344 Overprinted in Red or Blue

1929, June 10 ***Imperf.***

358 A47 1c blue green .50 .80
Never hinged 1.75

Perf. 13½x12½

359 A49 2c olive green .55 *1.00*
Never hinged 1.75
360 A49 5c claret (Bl) .55 *1.00*
Never hinged 1.75
361 A49 10c yellow green .55 *1.00*
Never hinged 1.75
362 A49 15c slate blue .55 *1.00*
Never hinged 1.75
363 A49 20c violet .55 *1.00*
Never hinged 1.75
364 A49 25c carmine (Bl) .55 *1.00*
Never hinged 1.75
365 A49 30c black brown 2.25 *4.00*
Never hinged 7.25
366 A49 40c deep blue 2.25 *4.00*
Never hinged 7.25
367 A49 50c orange (Bl) 2.25 *4.00*
Never hinged 7.25
368 A49a 1p blue black 11.00 *19.00*
Never hinged 32.50
369 A49a 4p lake (Bl) 11.00 *21.00*
Never hinged 32.50
370 A49a 10p brown (Bl) 40.00 *70.00*
Never hinged 120.00
Nos. 358-370,E4 (14) 84.55 *153.80*
Set, never hinged 250.00

55th assembly of League of Nations at Madrid June 10-16. The stamps were available for postal use only on those days.

Nos. 359-370 values are for off-center stamps.

Exposition Building — A54

1930 Litho. ***Perf. 11***

371 A54 5c dk blue & salmon 6.25 5.00
Never hinged 9.75
372 A54 5c dk violet & blue 6.25 5.00
Never hinged 22.50

Barcelona Philatelic Congress and Exhibition. "C. F. y E. F." are the initials of "Congreso Filatelico y Exposicion Filatelica." For each admission ticket, costing 2.75 pesetas, the holder was allowed to buy one of each of these stamps.

A55

Locomotives
A56

1930, May 10 ***Perf. 14***

373 A55 1c light blue .95 *.95*
Never hinged 2.40
374 A55 2c apple green .95 *.95*
Never hinged 2.40

Control Number on Back

375 A55 5c lake 1.10 *1.10*
Never hinged 2.75
376 A55 10c yellow green 1.10 *1.10*
Never hinged 2.75
377 A55 15c bluish gray 1.10 *1.10*
Never hinged 2.75
378 A55 20c purple 1.10 *1.10*
Never hinged 2.75
379 A55 25c brt rose 1.10 *1.00*
Never hinged 2.75
380 A55 30c olive gray 3.50 3.50
Never hinged 8.75
381 A55 40c dark blue 3.50 3.50
Never hinged 8.75
382 A55 50c dk orange 8.00 *8.00*
Never hinged 20.00
383 A56 1p dark gray 8.00 *8.00*
Never hinged 20.00
384 A56 4p deep rose 80.00 100.00
Never hinged 290.00
385 A56 10p bister brn 300.00 375.00
Never hinged 950.00
Nos. 373-385,C12-C17,E6 (20) 565.90 *652.80*
Set, never hinged 1,800.

11th Intl. Railway Congress, Madrid, 1930.

These stamps were on sale May 10-21, 1930, exclusively at the Palace of the Senate in Madrid and at the Barcelona and Seville expositions.

Forgeries are plentiful.

Francisco de Goya at Age 80
("1746 1828") ("1828 1928")
A57 A59

"La Maja Desnuda" — A58

1930, June 15 Litho. ***Perf. 12½***

Inscribed "Correos Espana"

386 A57 1c yellow .25 .25
Never hinged .25
387 A57 2c bister brn .25 .25
Never hinged .25
388 A57 5c lilac rose .25 .25
Never hinged .25
389 A57 10c green .25 .25
Never hinged .25

Engr.

390 A57 15c lt blue .30 .25
Never hinged .40
391 A57 20c brown violet .30 .25
Never hinged .40
392 A57 25c red .30 .25
Never hinged .40
393 A57 30c brown 4.25 4.00
Never hinged 5.75
394 A57 40c dark blue 4.25 4.00
Never hinged 5.75
395 A57 50c vermilion 4.25 4.00
Never hinged 5.75
396 A57 1p black 5.00 4.75
Never hinged 6.50
397 A58 1p dark violet 1.25 .75
Never hinged 1.75
398 A58 4p slate gray .90 .55
Never hinged 1.20
399 A58 10p red brown 12.50 7.00
Never hinged 17.00

Inscribed "1828 Goya 1928"

Litho.

400 A59 2c olive green .25 .25
Never hinged .25
401 A59 5c gray violet .25 .25
Never hinged .25

Engr.

402 A59 25c rose carmine .40 .35
Never hinged .55
Nos. 386-402,C18-C30,CE1,E7 (32) 49.40 41.90
Set, never hinged 66.00

To commemorate the death of Francisco de Goya y Lucientes, painter and engraver.

Nos. 386-399 were issued in connection with the Spanish-American Exposition at Seville.

Nos. 386-402 exist imperf. Value, set $300. See note after No. 432.

King Alfonso XIII — A61

Two types of the 40c

Type I

Type II

Type I — Middle of zero in "40" is bigger in width. Type II — Middle of zero in "40" is smaller in width.

1930 ***Perf. 11½, 12x11½***

406 A61 2c red brown .25 .25
Never hinged .25

Control Number on Back

407 A61 5c black brown .70 .25
Never hinged 1.60
408 A61 10c green 3.25 .25
Never hinged 9.75
409 A61 15c slate green 11.00 .25
Never hinged 45.00

410 A61 20c dark violet 6.00 .70
Never hinged 20.00
411 A61 25c carmine .70 .25
Never hinged 1.60
412 A61 30c brown lake 15.50 1.75
Never hinged 45.00
413 A61 40c dk blue (I) 21.00 1.10
Never hinged 52.50
a. Type II 27.50 1.10
Never hinged 60.00
414 A61 50c orange 19.00 1.90
Never hinged 65.00
Nos. 406-414 (9) 77.40 6.70
Set, never hinged 240.00

Nos. 406-414 exist imperf. Value for set, $350.

For overprints see #450-455, 458-466, 469-487.

Bow of "Santa Maria" — A63

Stern of "Santa Maria" — A64

"Santa Maria," "Niña," "Pinta" — A65

Columbus Leaving Palos — A66

Columbus Arriving in America — A67

1930, Sept. 29 Litho. *Perf. 12½*

418 A63 1c olive gray .25 .25
Never hinged .60
419 A64 2c olive green .25 .25
Never hinged .60
420 A63 2c olive green .25 .25
Never hinged .60
421 A64 5c red brown .25 .25
Never hinged .60
422 A63 5c red brown .25 .25
Never hinged .60
423 A64 10c blue green .85 .70
Never hinged 1.50
424 A63 15c ultra .85 .90
Never hinged 1.50
425 A64 20c violet 1.25 1.10
Never hinged 1.90

Engr.

426 A65 25c dark red 1.25 1.10
Never hinged 1.90
427 A66 30c bis brn, bl & blk brn 5.00 5.50
Never hinged 14.00
428 A65 40c ultra 4.50 5.00
Never hinged 14.00
429 A66 50c dk vio, bl & vio brn 6.50 5.75
Never hinged 14.00
430 A65 1p black 6.50 5.75
Never hinged 14.00
431 A67 4p blk & dk blue 8.00 6.50
Never hinged 14.00
432 A67 10p red brn & dk brn 25.00 25.00
Never hinged 70.00
Nos. 418-432,E8 (16) 62.85 60.45
Set, never hinged 135.00

Christopher Columbus tribute.

Nos. 418 to 432 were privately produced. Their promoters presented a certain quantity of these labels to the Spanish Postal Authorities, who placed them on sale and allowed them to be used for three days, retaining the money obtained from the sale.

This note will also apply to Nos. 345-357, 386-402, 433-448, 557-571, B1-B105, C18-C57, C73-C87, CB1-CB5, CE1, E2, E7-E9, E15 and EB1.

Many so-called "errors" of color and perforation are known.

Nos. 418-432 exist imperf. Value, set $450. stamps.

See Nos. 2671, B194 in Scott Standard catalogue, Vol. 6.

Arms of Spain, Bolivia, Paraguay A68

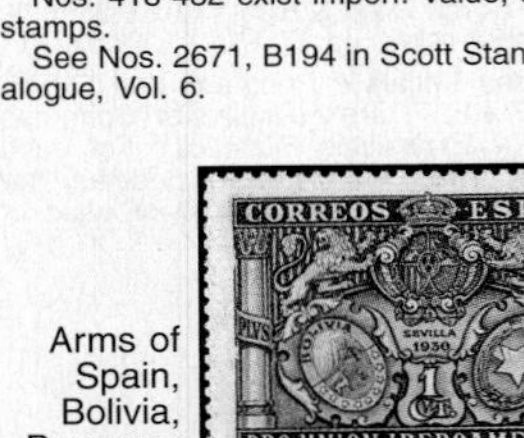

Pavilion and Map of Central America — A69

Exhibition Pavilion of Ecuador — A70

Colombia Pavilion — A71

Dominican Republic Pavilion A72

Uruguay Pavilion A73

Argentina Pavilion A74

Chile Pavilion A75

Brazil Pavilion A76

Mexico Pavilion A77

Cuba Pavilion A78

Peru Pavilion A79

U.S. Pavilion A80

Exhibition Pavilion of Portugal — A81

King Alfonso XIII and Queen Victoria — A82

Unwmk.

1930, Oct. 10 Photo. *Perf. 14*

433 A68 1c blue green .25 .25
Never hinged .35
434 A69 2c bister brown .25 .25
Never hinged .35
435 A70 5c olive brown .25 .25
Never hinged .35
436 A71 10c dark green .35 .35
Never hinged 1.00
437 A72 15c indigo .35 .35
Never hinged 1.00
438 A73 20c violet .35 .35
Never hinged 1.00
439 A74 25c car rose .35 .35
Never hinged 1.00
440 A75 25c car rose .35 .35
Never hinged 1.00
441 A76 30c rose lilac 1.75 1.75
Never hinged 4.00
442 A77 40c slate blue 1.00 1.00
Never hinged 1.60
443 A78 40c slate blue 1.00 1.00
Never hinged 1.60
444 A79 50c brown org 1.75 1.75
Never hinged 4.00
445 A80 1p ultra 2.50 2.50
Never hinged 5.25
446 A81 4p brown violet 26.00 26.00
Never hinged 100.00
447 A82 10p brown 2.10 2.10
Never hinged 5.25

Perf. 11, 14

Engr.

448 A82 10p dk reddish brn 45.00 45.00
Never hinged 260.00
Nos. 433-448,C50-C57,E9 (25) 104.55 99.85
Set, never hinged 325.00

Spanish-American Union Exhibition, Seville.

The note after No. 432 will also apply to Nos. 433-448. All values exist imperforate. Value, set: hinged $250; never hinged $350.

Reprints of Nos. 433-448 have blurred colors, yellowish paper and an inferior, almost invisible gum. They sell for about one-tenth the value of originals.

Revolutionary Issues
Madrid Issue

Regular Issues of 1920-30 Overprinted in Black, Green or Red

1931 On No. 314 *Imperf.*

449 A47 1c blue green .25 .25
Never hinged .30

On Nos. 406-411
Perf. 11½

450 A61 2c red brown (G) .30 .25
Never hinged .60
451 A61 5c black brn (R) .40 .40
Never hinged .70
452 A61 10c green .70 .70
Never hinged 1.25
453 A61 15c slate grn (R) 1.40 1.50
Never hinged 2.50
454 A61 20c dk violet (R) 1.40 1.50
Never hinged 2.50
455 A61 25c carmine (G) 1.90 2.25
Never hinged 3.50
Nos. 449-455,E10 (8) 11.35 11.85
Set, never hinged 22.50

The status of Nos. 449-455, E10 has been questioned.

First Barcelona Issue

Regular Issues of 1920-30 Overprinted in Black or Red

1931 On No. 314 *Imperf.*

457 A47 1c blue green .25 .25
Never hinged .30

On Nos. 406-414
Perf. 11½

458 A61 2c red brown .25 .25
Never hinged .30
459 A61 5c black brown .25 .25
Never hinged .30
460 A61 10c green .55 .55
Never hinged 1.00
461 A61 15c slate grn (R) .60 .60
Never hinged 1.25
462 A61 20c dk violet (R) .60 .60
Never hinged 1.25
463 A61 25c carmine .60 .60
Never hinged 1.25
464 A61 30c brown lake 4.50 4.50
Never hinged 10.00
465 A61 40c dk blue (R) 1.25 1.25
Never hinged 2.50

466 A61 50c orange 1.25 1.25
Never hinged 2.50

On Stamp of 1922-26

467 A49a 1p blue blk (R) 7.50 6.25
Never hinged 16.00
Nos. 457-467,E11 (12) 23.10 21.85
Set, never hinged 45.00

Nos. 457-467 are known both with and without accent over "U."

The status of Nos. 457-467, E11 has been questioned.

Second Barcelona Issue

Regular Issues of 1920-30 Overprinted in Black or Red

On No. 314 *Imperf.*

468 A47 1c blue green .25 .25
Never hinged .30

On Nos. 406-414
Perf. 11½

469 A61 2c red brown .25 .25
Never hinged .30
470 A61 5c black brown (R) .25 .25
Never hinged .30
471 A61 10c green .25 .25
Never hinged .40
472 A61 15c slate grn (R) 1.40 1.25
Never hinged 2.50
473 A61 20c dark violet (R) .40 .45
Never hinged .70
474 A61 25c carmine .40 .45
Never hinged .70
475 A61 30c brown lake 5.75 5.75
Never hinged 11.00
476 A61 40c dark blue (R) 1.25 1.25
Never hinged 2.25
477 A61 50c orange 4.50 3.50
Never hinged 10.00
Nos. 468-477 (10) 14.70 13.65
Set, never hinged 27.50

The status of Nos. 469-477, C58-C61 has been questioned.

General Issue of the Republic

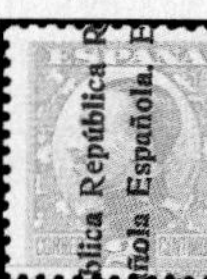

Nos. 406-414, 342 Overprinted in Blue or Red

1931, May 27

478 A61 2c red brown .25 .25
Never hinged .25
479 A61 5c black brn (R) .25 .25
Never hinged .70
480 A61 10c green (R) .30 .25
Never hinged .95
481 A61 15c slate grn (R) 3.50 .25
Never hinged 6.25
482 A61 20c dk violet (R) 1.50 1.00
Never hinged 3.50
483 A61 25c carmine .50 .25
Never hinged .95
484 A61 30c brown lake 4.50 1.00
Never hinged 9.75
485 A61 40c dk blue (R) 4.50 .55
Never hinged 9.75
486 A61 50c orange 7.75 .55
Never hinged 21.00
487 A49a 1p blue blk (R) 57.50 1.00
Never hinged 130.00
Nos. 478-487,E12 (11) 87.05 6.60
Set, never hinged 230.00

The setting contained 18 repetitions of "Republica Espanola" for each vertical row of 10 stamps. According to its sheet position, a stamp received different parts of the overprinted words.

Overprint position varieties include: reading down on 25c, 30c, 40c and 50c; double on 1p; double, both reading down, on 25c, 40c and 50c.

"Republica Espanola"

Stamps of various Spanish colonies overprinted "Republica Espanola" are listed with the colonies.

Fountain of Lions, The Alhambra, Granada
A84

Interior of Mosque, Córdoba — A85

Alcántara Bridge and Alcazar, Toledo
A86

Francisco García y Santos
A87

Puerta del Sol, Madrid, on April 14, 1931 as Republic Was Proclaimed
A88

Perf. 12½

1931, Oct. 10 **Unwmk.** **Engr.**

491 A84 5c violet brown .25 .25
Never hinged .25
492 A85 10c blue green .35 .35
Never hinged 1.00
493 A86 15c dark violet .35 .35
Never hinged 1.00
494 A85 25c deep red .35 .35
Never hinged 1.00
495 A87 30c olive green .35 .35
Never hinged 1.00
496 A84 40c indigo .90 .90
Never hinged 2.50
497 A85 50c orange red .90 .90
Never hinged 2.50
498 A86 1p black 1.60 1.60
Never hinged 5.00
499 A88 4p red violet 8.00 8.00
Never hinged 25.00
500 A88 10p red brown 25.00 *25.00*
Never hinged 77.50
Nos. 491-500,C62-C67,CO1-CO6,O20-O29 (32) 97.25 95.85
Set, never hinged 170.00

3rd Pan-American Postal Union Cong., Madrid.

Nos. 491-500 exist imperforate. Value, set: hinged $150; never hinged $250.

Symbolical of Montserrat Cut With a Saw — A89

Abbott Oliva and Monastery Workman — A90

"Black Virgin"
A91 A92

Montserrat Monastery — A93

1931, Dec. 9 ***Perf. 11, 14***

501 A89 1c myrtle green 1.25 *1.50*
Never hinged 2.25
a. Perf. 14 21.00 21.00
b. Vert. pair, imperf between *190.00* *125.00*
502 A89 2c red brown .70 *1.10*
Never hinged 1.40
a. Perf. 14 15.00 16.00
b. Horiz. pair, imperf between *115.00* *75.00*

Control Number on Back

503 A89 5c black brown .85 *1.40*
Never hinged 1.75
a. Perf. 14 15.00 16.00
b. Horiz. pair, imperf between *115.00* *75.00*
504 A89 10c yellow green .95 *1.40*
Never hinged 1.75
a. Perf. 14 15.00 19.00
b. Horiz. pair, imperf between *115.00* *75.00*
c. Vert. pair, imperf between 200.00 *150.00*
505 A90 15c myrtle green 1.25 *1.75*
Never hinged 2.00
a. Perf. 14 21.00 25.00
506 A91 20c dark violet 2.25 2.25
Never hinged 4.00
a. Perf. 11 110.00 150.00
b. Horiz. pair, imperf between *350.00* *250.00*
c. As "a", horiz. pair, imperf between *450.00*
507 A92 25c lake 3.25 3.25
Never hinged 5.75
a. Perf. 14 6.25 7.25
508 A91 30c deep red 32.50 30.00
Never hinged 50.00
a. Perf. 14 45.00 45.00
509 A93 40c dull blue 19.00 17.00
Never hinged 27.50
a. Perf. 11 150.00 175.00
b. Vert. pair, imperf between *250.00* *160.00*
510 A90 50c dark orange 40.00 37.50
Never hinged 55.00
a. Perf. 14 70.00 80.00
511 A92 1p gray black 40.00 37.50
Never hinged 55.00
a. Perf. 11 87.50 110.00
512 A93 4p lilac rose 325.00 325.00
Never hinged 800.00
a. Perf. 14 575.00 900.00
513 A92 10p deep brown 225.00 225.00
Never hinged 650.00
a. Perf. 14 800.00 950.00
Nos. 501-511,C68-C72,E13 (17) 211.50 216.15
Set, never hinged 350.00
Nos. 501-513,C68-C72,E13 (19) 761.50 766.15
Set, never hinged 1,800.

Commemorative of the building of the old Monastery at Montserrat, started in 1031, and of the image of the Black Virgin (said to have been carved by St. Luke) which was crowned by Pope Leo XIII in 1881.

Nos. 501-513 exist imperforate. Value, set $4,500.

For surcharges see Nos. 589, C92-C96.

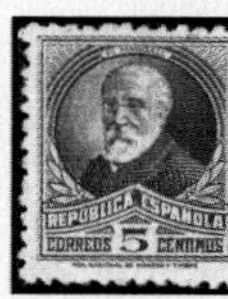

Francisco Pi y Margall — A95

Joaquín Costa — A96

Nicolás Salmerón
A97

Pablo Iglesias
A99

Emilio Castelar — A100

1931-32 ***Perf. 11½***

Control Number on Back

516 A95 5c brnsh black 3.00 .30
Never hinged 7.00
517 A96 10c yellow green 7.25 .30
Never hinged 15.00
518 A97 15c slate green 4.75 .25
Never hinged 16.00
520 A99 25c lake 22.50 .70
Never hinged 55.00
b. Imperf. 175.00
Never hinged 225.00
521 A99 30c carmine rose 7.25 .25
Never hinged 18.00
c. Imperf. 82.50
Never hinged 125.00
522 A100 40c dark blue 42.50 4.50
Never hinged 110.00
523 A97 50c orange 52.50 7.75
Never hinged 130.00
Nos. 516-523 (7) 139.75 14.05
Set, never hinged 350.00

Without Control Number

516a A95 5c brownish blk ('32) 4.50 .25
Never hinged 7.75
517a A96 10c yel grn ('32) 4.00 .25
Never hinged 7.75
518a A97 15c sl grn ('32) .60 .25
Never hinged 1.10
520a A99 25c lake 32.50 .25
Never hinged 55.00
521a A99 30c carmine rose 1.90 .25
Never hinged 3.25
522a A100 40c dark blue ('32) .25 .25
Never hinged .35
523a A97 50c orange ('32) 26.00 .50
Never hinged 45.00
Nos. 516a-523a (7) 69.75 2.00
Set, never hinged 120.00

Without Control Number, Imperf.

516b A95 5c 6.50
Never hinged 13.00
517b A96 10c 11.00
Never hinged 22.50
518b A97 15c 6.25
Never hinged 12.50
520c A99 25c *110.00*
Never hinged 210.00
521b A99 30c 5.50
Never hinged 11.00
522b A100 40c 14.00
Never hinged 25.00
523b A97 50c 125.00
Never hinged 250.00
Nos. 516b-523b (7) 278.25
Set, Never Hinged 550.00

See Nos. 532, 538, 550, 579, 579a.

For overprints and surcharges see Nos. 7LC12-7LC13, 7LC15-7LC16, 7LC18, 7LE4, 8LB6, 8LB9-8LB10, 9LC17-9LC18, 10L7, 10L10-10L12, 10L16-10L18, 10L22-10L23, 11L7, 11L10-11L12, 11LB8, 12L4, 12L8, 12L11-12L12, 13L8, 14L6, 14L10-14L12, 14L18, 14L22-14L24.

Blasco Ibáñez
A103

Manuel Ruiz-Zorrilla
A104

Without Control Number

1931-34 ***Perf. 11½***

526 A103 2c red brown ('32) .25 .25
Never hinged .40
528 A103 5c chocolate ('34) .25 .25
Never hinged .40
532 A95 20c dark violet .25 .25
Never hinged .50
534 A104 25c lake ('34) .45 .25
Never hinged .80
538 A100 60c apple green ('32) .25 .25
Never hinged .40
Nos. 526-538 (5) 1.45 1.25
Set, never hinged 2.50

Imperf

526a A103 2c 14.00
Never hinged 27.50
528a A103 5c 2.75
Never hinged 5.50
532a A95 20c 6.25
Never hinged 13.00
534a A104 25c 5.25
Never hinged 10.50
538a A100 60c 6.25
Never hinged 13.00
Nos. 526a-538a (5) 34.50
Set, never hinged 70.00

For overprints and surcharges see Nos. 8LB3, 8LB7, 9LC3, 9LC8-9LC9, 9LC14, 10L6, 10L13, 11L4, 11L8, 11LB5, 11LB9, 12L5, 12L9, 13L5, 13L7, 14L3, 14L7, 14L15, 14L19.

Cliff Houses, Cuenca — A105

Alcázar of Segovia — A106

Gate of the Sun at Toledo — A107

1932-38 *Perf. 10*
539 A105 1p gray black ('38) .25 .25
Never hinged .40
540 A106 4p magenta ('38) .30 .40
Never hinged .60
541 A107 10p deep brown ('38) .65 .70
Never hinged 1.75
Nos. 539-541 (3) 1.20 1.35
Set, never hinged 2.75

Imperf

539a A105 1p 5.25 2.75
Never hinged 11.50
540a A106 4p 9.00 6.50
Never hinged 20.00
541a A107 10p 6.50 6.00
Never hinged 14.00
Nos. 539a-541a (3) 20.75 15.25
Set, never hinged 45.00

Perf. 11½

539b A105 1p .25 .25
Never hinged .40
540b A106 4p .70 .85
Never hinged 1.40
541b A107 10p 1.90 3.00
Never hinged 3.50
Nos. 539b-541b (3) 2.85 4.10
Set, never hinged 5.00

For overprints and surcharge see Nos. 9LC19, 10L19, 13L9, 14L25, 14L27-14L28.

Numeral — A108

1933 Unwmk. Typo. *Imperf.*
542 A108 1c blue green .25 .25
Never hinged .40

Perf. 11½

543 A108 2c buff .25 .25
Never hinged .40
a. Perf. 13½x13 .65 .25
Never hinged 1.40
Set, never hinged .65

See Nos. 592-597. For surcharges and overprints see Nos. 590-590A, 634A-634D, 8LB1-8LB2, 9LC1-9LC2, 9LC4-9LC7, 9LC11-9LC12, 9LC20, 9LC26, 10L2-10L4, 11L1-11L2, 11LB2-11LB3, 12L1-12L2, 13L1-13L3, 14L1, 14L13.

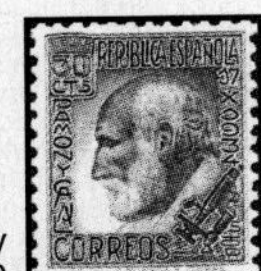

Santiago Ramón y Cajal — A109

1934 Engr. *Perf. 11½x11*
545 A109 30c black brown 6.00 1.10
Never hinged 16.00
a. Perf. 14 22.50 30.00
Never hinged 42.50
b. Imperf. 32.50
Never hinged 55.00

Type of 1931 and

Mariana Pineda A110

Concepción Arenal A111

Gumersindo de Azcarate A112

Gaspar Melchor de Jovellanos A113

1935
546 A110 10c green .25 .25
Never hinged .35
b. 10c blue green ('36) .25 .25
Never hinged .35
547 A111 15c slate .25 .25
Never hinged .35
b. 15c yellow green ('36) .25 .25
Never hinged .35
548 A112 30c carmine rose 7.25 .25
Never hinged 19.00
549 A113 30c rose red .25 .25
Never hinged .35
550 A97 50c dark blue 1.00 .30
Never hinged 2.50
Nos. 546-550 (5) 9.00 1.30
Set, never hinged 22.00

Imperf

546a A110 10c 1.50
Never hinged 3.00
547a A111 15c 4.75
Never hinged 9.50
548a A112 30c 22.50
Never hinged 40.00
549a A113 30c 1.75
Never hinged 3.50
550a A97 50c *175.00*
Never hinged 360.00
Nos. 546a-550a (5) 205.50
Set, never hinged 400.00

Shades exist.

For overprints and surcharges see Nos. 7LE3, 8LB4-8LB5, 8LB8, 10L8-10L9, 10L14, 10L20-10L21, 11L5-11L6, 11L9, 11LB6-11LB7, 11LB10, 12L6-12L7, 12L10, 13L6, 14L4-14L5, 14L8, 14L16-14L17, 14L20.

Lope's Bookplate A116

Lope de Vega A117

Alcántara and Alcázar, Toledo A118

1935, Oct. 12 *Perf. 11½x11, 11x11½*
552 A116 15c myrtle green 6.25 .30
Never hinged 12.00
553 A117 30c rose red 2.75 .30
Never hinged 5.00
554 A117 50c dark blue 12.00 3.00
Never hinged 23.00
555 A118 1p blue black 23.00 2.00
Never hinged 45.00
Nos. 552-555 (4) 44.00 5.60
Set, never hinged 85.00

Imperf

552a A116 15c 450.00
Never hinged 625.00
553a A117 30c 16.00
Never hinged 20.00
554a A117 50c 70.00
Never hinged 110.00
555a A118 1p 65.00
Never hinged 90.00
Nos. 552a-555a (4) 601.00
Set, never hinged 1,100.

Perf. 14

553b A117 30c 6.50 14.50
Never hinged 14.00
554b A117 50c 29.00 45.00
Never hinged 62.50
555b A118 1p 32.50 50.00
Never hinged 75.00
Nos. 553b-555b (3) 68.00 109.50
Set, never hinged 150.00

Lope Felix de Vega Carpio (1562-1635), Spanish dramatist and poet.

For surcharge see No. 11LB11.

Map of Amazon by Bartolomeo Oliva, 16th Century A119

1935, Oct. 12 *Perf. 11½*
556 A119 30c rose red 2.10 .95
Never hinged 5.50
a. Perf. 14 26.00
Never hinged 54.00
b. Imperf. 37.50
Never hinged 72.50

Proposed Iglesias Amazon Expedition.

Miguel Moya — A120

Torcuato Luca de Tena — A121

José Francos Rodríguez A122

Alejandro Lerroux A123

Nazareth School and Rotary Press — A124

1936, Feb. 14 Photo. *Perf. 12½*

Size: 22x26mm

557 A120 1c crimson .25 .25
Never hinged .25
558 A121 2c orange brown .25 .25
Never hinged .25
559 A122 5c black brown .25 .25
Never hinged .25
560 A123 10c emerald .25 .25
Never hinged .25

Size: 24x28½mm

561 A120 15c blue green .25 .25
Never hinged .25
562 A121 20c violet .25 .25
Never hinged .25
563 A122 25c red violet .25 .25
Never hinged .25
564 A123 30c crimson .25 .25
Never hinged .25

Size: 25½x30½mm

565 A120 40c orange .55 .40
Never hinged .90
566 A121 50c ultra .25 .25
Never hinged .50
567 A122 60c olive green .55 .40
Never hinged .90
568 A123 1p gray black .55 .40
Never hinged .95
569 A124 2p lt blue 6.00 3.25
Never hinged 12.00
570 A124 4p lilac rose 6.00 6.50
Never hinged 12.00
571 A124 10p red brown 16.00 15.50
Never hinged 30.00
Nos. 557-571,E15 (16) 32.15 29.00
Set, never hinged 55.00
Nos. 557-571,C73-C87,E15 (31) 58.25 48.35
Set, never hinged 100.00

Madrid Press Association, 40th anniversary.

Nos. 557-571 exist imperf. Values about 7 times those of perf. stamps.

See note after No. 432. See Nos. C73-C87.

Arms of Madrid — A125

1936, Apr. 2 Engr. *Imperf.*
572 A125 10c brown black 35.00 35.00
Never hinged 55.00
573 A125 15c dark green 35.00 35.00
Never hinged 55.00
Set, never hinged 110.00

1st National Philatelic Exhibition which opened in Madrid, Apr. 2, 1936.

For overprints see Nos. C88-C89.

"Republica Espanola" — A126

1936 Litho. *Perf. 11½, 13½x13*
574 A126 2c orange brown .25 .25
Never hinged .35

For surcharges & overprints see #591, 9LC24, 10L5, 11L3, 11LB4, 12L3, 13L4, 14L2, 14L14.

Gregorio Fernández — A127

1936, Mar. 10 Engr. *Perf. 11½*
576 A127 30c carmine 1.10 .85
Never hinged 2.25
a. Perf. 14 9.00 8.25
Never hinged 17.50
b. Imperf. 15.00
Never hinged 22.50

Tercentenary of the death of Gregorio Fernandez, sculptor.

For overprints see Nos. 7LC18-7LC19.

Type of 1931 and

Pablo Iglesias A128 A129

Velázquez A130

Fermín Salvoechea A131

1936-38 *Perf. 11, 11½, 11½x11*
577 A128 30c rose red .25 .25
Never hinged .25
578 A129 30c car rose 1.10 .50
Never hinged 3.00
579 A100 40c car rose ('37) 1.10 .50
Never hinged 3.00

580 A129 45c carmine ('37) .25 .25
Never hinged .25
581 A130 50c dark blue .25 .25
Never hinged .25
582 A131 60c indigo ('37) .75 .90
Never hinged 2.00
583 A131 60c dp orange ('38) 6.00 5.00
Never hinged 15.00
Nos. 577-583 (7) 9.70 7.65
Set, never hinged 26.00

Perf. 14

577a A128 30c rose red 6.50
Never hinged 13.00
578a A129 30c carmine rose 6.75
Never hinged 13.50
579a A100 40c carmine rose 6.50
Never hinged 13.50
580a A129 45c carmine 6.00
Never hinged 12.00
582a A131 60c indigo 6.00
Never hinged 12.00
583a A131 60c deep orange 9.50
Never hinged 19.00
Nos. 577a-583a (6) 41.25
Set, never hinged 90.00

Nos. 577-583 exist imperf. Value, set $70, never hinged $150.

For overprints see Nos. C90, 7LC17, 7LC22-7LC23, 10L15, 14L21.

Statue of Liberty, Spanish and US Flags — A132

1938, June 1 Photo. *Perf. 11½*

585 A132 1p multicolored 16.50 17.50
Never hinged 32.50
a. Imperf., pair 82.50 55.00
Never hinged 110.00
b. Horiz. pair, imperf. vert. 62.50 82.50
Never hinged 92.50
c. Souvenir sheet of 1 27.50 32.50
Never hinged 44.00
d. As "c," imperf. 350.00 250.00
Never hinged 600.00

150th anniv. of the US Constitution.
For surcharge see No. C97.

No. 289 Surcharged in Black

1938 *Perf. 14*

586 A36 45c on 15c violet 15.50 15.50
Never hinged 19.00

7th anniversary of the Republic.
Values are for examples with perforations nearly touching the design on one or two sides.

No. 289 Surcharged in Black

a

b

1938, May 1

587 A36 45c on 15c violet 3.00 3.00
Never hinged 4.00
588 A36 1p on 15c violet 5.25 5.25
Never hinged 7.00
Set, never hinged 12.00

Issued to commemorate Labor Day.
Values are for examples with perforations nearly touching the design on one or two sides.

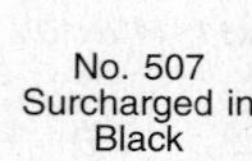
No. 507 Surcharged in Black

1938, Nov. 10 *Perf. 11½*

589 A92 2.50p on 25c lake .25 .25
Never hinged .25
b. Perf. 14 3.50 6.00
Never hinged 6.00

Types of 1933-36 Surcharged in Blue or Red

1938 *Perf. 10, 11, 13½x13, 13x14*

590 A108 45c on 1c grn (R) .40 .25
Never hinged .90
b. Imperf. 6.00 5.00
Never hinged 10.00
590A A108 45c on 2c buff (Bl) 17.00 14.00
Never hinged 27.50
591 A126 45c on 2c org brn (Bl) .25 .25
Never hinged .60
Nos. 590-591 (3) 17.65 14.50
Set, never hinged 29.00

Many overprint varieties exist.

Numeral Type of 1933

1938-39 Litho. *Perf. 11½, 13*

White or Gray Paper

592 A108 5c gray brown .25 .25
Never hinged .25
593 A108 10c yellow green .25 .25
Never hinged .25
594 A108 15c slate green .25 .25
Never hinged .25
595 A108 20c vio, gray paper .25 .25
Never hinged .25
596 A108 25c red violet .25 .25
Never hinged .25
597 A108 30c scarlet .25 .25
Never hinged .25
Nos. 592-597 (6) 1.50 1.50
Set, never hinged 1.75

"Republic" — A133

1938 *Perf. 11½*

598 A133 40c rose red .25 .25
Never hinged .25
599 A133 45c car rose .25 .25
Never hinged .25
a. Printed on both sides 11.00 11.00
Never hinged 27.50
600 A133 50c ultra .25 .25
Never hinged .25
601 A133 60c dp ultra .50 .30
Never hinged .60
Nos. 598-601 (4) 1.05
Set, never hinged 1.10

Nos. 598-601 exist imperf. Value for set $22.50

Machine Gunners A134

Infantry — A135

Perf. 11½x11, 11x11½, Imperf.

1938, Sept. 1 Photo.

602 A134 25c dark green 12.00 9.25
Never hinged 25.00
603 A135 45c red brown 12.00 9.25
Never hinged 25.00
Set, never hinged 50.00

43rd Division of the Republican Army. Sold only at the Philatelic Agency and for foreign exchange.
Nos. 602-603 exist imperf. Value, set $50.

Blast Furnace A136

Steel Mill and Sculpture, "Defenders of Numantia" A137

1938, Aug. 9 *Perf. 16*

604 A136 45c black .25 .25
Never hinged .30
605 A137 1.25p dark blue .25 .25
Never hinged .30
Set, never hinged 2.00

Issued in honor of the workers of Sagunto.

Submarine — A137a

Designs: 1p, 15p, U-Boat D1. 2p, 6p, U-Boat A1. 4p, 10p, U-Boat B2.

1938, Aug. 11 *Perf. 16*

605A A137a 1p blue 4.50 4.50
605B A137a 2p red brown 8.00 8.00
605C A137a 4p red orange 9.00 9.00
605D A137a 6p deep blue 20.00 20.00
605E A137a 10p magenta 30.00 30.00
605F A137a 15p dp gray green 300.00 300.00
Nos. 605A-605F (6) 371.50 371.50
Set, never hinged 600.00

Souvenir Sheet

Perf. 10½

605G A137a Sheet of 3 450.00 450.00
Never hinged 775.00
a. 4p carmine & gray black 100.00 100.00
b. 6p dull blue & gray black 100.00 100.00
c. 15p green & gray black 100.00 100.00

Nos. 605A-605G were issued for use on a proposed submarine mail service between Barcelona and Mahon, Minorca. One voyage was made on this mail route, carrying 300 agency-prepared covers. The stamps were also valid for ordinary mail.

Nos. 605A-605G were sold only at the Philatelic Agency in Barcelona, for double their face value.

Nos. 605A-605G exist imperf. Value: set of 6 stamps, $775 unused, $1,000 never hinged; souvenir sheet, $2,250 unused, $2,900, never hinged.

Riflemen A138

Machine Gunners A139

Bomb Throwing — A140

1938, Nov. 25 Engr. *Perf. 10*

606 A138 5c sepia 3.50 3.50
Never hinged 7.00
607 A138 10c dp violet 3.50 3.50
Never hinged 7.00
608 A138 25c blue green 3.50 3.50
Never hinged 7.00
609 A139 45c rose red 3.50 3.50
Never hinged 7.00
610 A139 60c dark blue 6.25 6.25
Never hinged 10.00
611 A139 1.20p black 125.00 125.00
Never hinged 225.00
612 A140 2p orange 37.50 37.50
Never hinged 75.00
613 A140 5p dark brown 200.00 200.00
Never hinged 390.00
614 A140 10p dk blue grn 40.00 40.00
Never hinged 72.50
Nos. 606-614 (9) 422.75 422.75
Set, never hinged 800.00

Honoring the Militia. Sold only at the Philatelic Agency and for foreign exchange. Exist imperf. Value unused $1,200, never hinged $1,800.

Spanish State

Arms of Spain — A141

1936 Litho. *Imperf.*

Thin Transparent Paper

615 A141 30c blue 250.00
Never hinged 345.00
616 A141 30c pale green 250.00
Never hinged 345.00

Perf. 11

Thick Wove Paper

617 A141 30c dark blue 550.00 150.00
Never hinged 810.00
Set, never hinged 1,500.

Issued in Granada during siege. After the city was liberated, these stamps were used throughout the province of Granada.

A143

Cathedral of Burgos — A145

University of Salamanca A146

Cathedral del Pilar, Zaragoza — A147

"La Giralda," Seville — A148

Xavier Castle, Navarre — A149

Court of Lions, Alhambra at Granada
A150

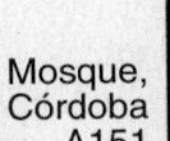

Mosque, Córdoba
A151

Alcántara Bridge and Alcázar, Toledo — A152

Soldier Carrying Flag — A153

Troops Landing at Algeciras
A154

Type II

Two types of 30c:
Type I — Imprint 12mm long; "3" does not touch frame.
Type II — Imprint 8mm long; "3" touches frame.

1936 Unwmk. Litho. *Imperf.*

623 A143 1c green 6.00 4.50
Never hinged 9.50

Perf. 11½

624 A143 2c orange brown .60 .45
Never hinged 1.15
625 A145 5c gray brown .60 .55
Never hinged 1.15
626 A146 10c green .60 .45
Never hinged 1.15
627 A147 15c dull green .60 .45
Never hinged 1.15
628 A148 25c rose lake .85 .45
Never hinged 2.00
629 A149 30c carmine (I) .60 .45
Never hinged 1.15
a. Type II .70 .55
Never hinged 1.70
630 A150 50c deep blue 14.00 8.75
Never hinged 29.00
631 A151 60c yellow green .95 .70
Never hinged 1.70
632 A152 1p black 5.25 3.75
Never hinged 12.00
633 A153 4p rose vio, red & yel 52.50 29.00
Never hinged 135.00
634 A154 10p light brown 52.50 29.00
Never hinged 135.00
Nos. 623-634 (12) 135.05 78.50
Set, never hinged 310.00

Nos. 624-634 exist imperf. Value, set $275. Numerous forgeries exist for Nos. 623-634.

Nos. 625-631, 633-634 were privately overprinted "VIA AEREA" and plane, supposedly for use in Ifni.

For surcharges see Nos. 9LC21, 9LC23.

Nos. 542-543 Surcharged in Two Lines

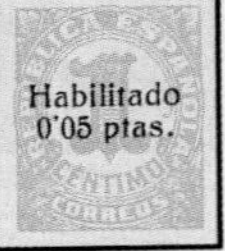

1936 *Imperf., Perf. 11½*

634A A108 5c on 1c bl grn 2.25 3.00
Never hinged 3.75
634B A108 5c on 2c buff 2.25 3.00
Never hinged 3.75
634C A108 10c on 1c bl grn 2.25 3.00
Never hinged 3.75
634D A108 15c on 2c buff 2.25 3.00
Never hinged 3.75
Nos. 634A-634D (4) 9.00 12.00
Set, never hinged 15.00

Issued in the Balearic Islands to meet a shortage of these values. Nos. 634A and 634C are imperf., Nos. 634B and 634D are perf. 11½.

St. James of Compostela — A155

St. James Cathedral
A156

Pórtico de la Gloria
A157

Type I

Type II

Two types of 30c:
I — No dots in "1937."
II — Dot before and after "1937."

1937 *Perf. 11½, 11x11½*

635 A155 15c violet brown .95 1.25
Never hinged 3.50
636 A156 30c rose red (I) 5.00 .55
Never hinged 14.00
a. Type II 17.50 14.00
Never hinged 37.50
637 A157 1p blue & orange 14.50 3.25
Never hinged 42.50
a. Center inverted 350.00 250.00
Never hinged 500.00
Nos. 635-637 (3) 20.45 5.05
Set, never hinged 60.00

Holy Year of Compostela. Nos. 635-637 exist imperf. Value for set $175.

"Estado Espanol"
A159 A160

"El Cid" — A161

Isabella I — A162

Two types of 5c, 30c and 10p:
5 Centimos: Type I Imprint 9½mm long. Type II Imprint 14mm long.
30 Centimos: Type I Imprint, "Hija De B. Fournier Burgos." Type II Imprint, "Fournier Burgos".
10 Pesetas: Type I "10" 2½mm high. Type II "10" 3mm high.

With Imprint

1936-40 *Imperf.*

638 A159 1c green .25 .25
Never hinged .30

Perf. 11

640 A160 2c brown .25 .25
Never hinged .30

Perf. 11, 11½, 11½x11, 11½x10½

641 A161 5c brown (I) .45 .25
Never hinged 1.00
642 A161 5c brown (II) .25 .25
Never hinged .30
643 A161 10c green .25 .25
Never hinged .30

Perf. 11, 11x11½

644 A162 15c gray black .25 .25
Never hinged .30
645 A162 20c dark violet .40 .25
Never hinged .70
646 A162 25c brown lake .25 .25
Never hinged .40
647 A162 30c rose (I) .50 .25
Never hinged .95
648 A162 30c rose (II) 17.50 2.10
Never hinged 40.00
649 A162 40c orange 1.60 .25
Never hinged 4.00
650 A162 50c dark blue 1.60 .25
Never hinged 4.00
651 A162 60c yellow .30 .25
Never hinged .70
652 A162 1p blue 16.50 .50
Never hinged 32.50
653 A162 4p magenta 21.00 5.25
Never hinged 40.00
654 A161 10p dk bl (I) ('37) 75.00 40.00
Never hinged 130.00
655 A161 10p dp bl (II) ('40) 32.50 15.00
Never hinged 65.00
Nos. 638-655 (17) 168.85 65.85
Set, never hinged 375.00

No. 638 was privately perforated. See Nos. 662-667. For overprint and surcharges see Nos. E18, 9LC10, 9LC13, 9LC15-9LC16, 9LC22, 9LC25, 9LC27-9LC30, 9LC34-9LC53.

Ferdinand the Catholic — A163

1938 *Perf. 10½, 11½x11*

Imprint: "Lit Fournier Vitoria"

656 A163 15c deep green 1.75 .25
Never hinged 6.75
657 A163 30c deep red 5.75 .25
Never hinged 16.00

Imprint: "Fournier Vitoria"

Perf. 10

658 A163 15c deep green 1.75 .25
Never hinged 8.50
659 A163 20c purple 13.00 1.40
Never hinged 37.50
660 A163 25c brown car .90 .25
Never hinged 2.00
661 A163 30c deep red 6.50 .25
Never hinged 40.00
Nos. 656-661 (6) 29.65 2.65
Set, never hinged 110.00

Nos. 656-661 exist imperf.; value for set, $150. Part-perf. varieties exist.

For overprints see Nos. C98-C99.

Type I

Type II

Two types of the 15 Centimos:
Type I — Medieval style numerals with diagonal line through "5."
Type II — Modern numerals. Narrower "5" without diagonal line.

Without Imprint

1938-50 *Perf. 11, 13½*

662 A159 1c green, imperf. .25 .25
Never hinged .30
663 A160 2c brn (18½x22mm; '40) .25 .25
Never hinged .30
a. 2c bis brn (17½x21mm; '48) .25 .25
Never hinged .30
664 A161 5c gray brn ('39) .25 .25
Never hinged .30
a. Perf. 13½x13¼ ('49) .25 .25
Never hinged .35
665 A161 10c dk carmine .25 .25
Never hinged .30
a. 10c rose .35 .25
Never hinged .75
b. Perf. 13½x13¼ ('49) .25 .25
Never hinged .30
666 A161 15c dk green (I) .90 .25
Never hinged 1.40
666A A161 15c dk green (II) .60 .25
Never hinged 1.40
b. Perf 13½x13¼ ('50) .65 .25
Never hinged 1.25
667 A162 70c dk blue ('39) .75 .25
Never hinged .85
Nos. 662-667 (7) 3.25 1.75
Set, never hinged 4.85

Emblem of the Falange — A164

1938, July 17 *Perf. 10*

668 A164 15c bl grn & lt grn 4.00 3.50
Never hinged 8.00
669 A164 25c rose red & rose 4.00 3.50
Never hinged 8.00
670 A164 30c bl & lt bl 2.10 2.25
Never hinged 3.75
671 A164 1p brown & yellow 80.00 70.00
Never hinged 160.00
Nos. 668-671 (4) 90.10 79.25
Set, never hinged 180.00

Second anniversary of the Civil War.

Imperforate 4-value set also exists, value $725, $950 never hinged.

Isabella I — A165

1938-39 Litho. *Perf. 10*

672 A165 20c brt violet ('39) .60 .25
Never hinged 3.50
673 A165 25c brown carmine 6.00 .60
Never hinged 16.50
674 A165 30c rose red .25 .25
Never hinged .40
675 A165 40c dull violet .30 .25
Never hinged .50
676 A165 50c indigo ('39) 27.50 2.50
Never hinged 62.50
677 A165 1p deep blue 9.00 .90
Never hinged 22.50
Nos. 672-677 (6) 43.65 4.75
Set, never hinged 120.00

Nos. 672-677 exist imperf. Value set, $225 hinged, $350 never hinged.

Gen. Francisco Franco — A166

Imprint: "Sanchez Toda"

1939-40 *Perf. 10*

678 A166 20c brt violet .35 .25
Never hinged .50
679 A166 25c rose lake .35 .25
Never hinged .50
680 A166 30c rose carmine .30 .25
Never hinged .50
681 A166 40c slate green .25 .25
Never hinged .50
682 A166 45c vermilion ('40) 1.25 1.25
Never hinged 4.00
683 A166 50c indigo .30 .25
Never hinged .50
684 A166 60c orange 2.00 2.00
Never hinged 5.00
685 A166 70c blue .40 .25
Never hinged .50
686 A166 1p black 8.00 .25
Never hinged 20.00
687 A166 2p dark brown 11.00 1.00
Never hinged 30.00
688 A166 4p dark violet 57.50 12.00
Never hinged 200.00
689 A166 10p light brown 38.00 *37.50*
Never hinged 90.00
Nos. 678-689 (12) 119.70 55.50
Set, never hinged 200.00

#686-689 have value & "Pta." on 1 line while #702-705 have value & "Pta." on 2 lines.

Nos. 678-689 exist imperf. Value set, $525 hinged, $700 never hinged.

Without Imprint

Perf. 9½x10½

1939-47 Litho. Unwmk.

690 A166 5c dull brn vio .50 .25
Never hinged .95
691 A166 10c brown orange 2.00 .65
Never hinged 4.00
692 A166 15c lt green .55 .25
Never hinged 1.05
693 A166 20c brt violet ('40) .55 .25
Never hinged 1.05
694 A166 25c dp claret ('40) .55 .25
Never hinged 1.05
695 A166 30c blue ('40) .55 .25
Never hinged 1.05
697 A166 40c Prus grn ('40) .55 .25
Never hinged 1.05
a. 40c greenish black .65 .25
Never hinged 1.10
698 A166 45c ultra ('41) .55 .25
Never hinged 1.05
699 A166 50c indigo ('40) .50 .25
Never hinged 1.05
a. Perf. 11½ ('47) 32.50 3.00
Never hinged 55.00
700 A166 60c dull org ('40) .65 .25
Never hinged 1.25
701 A166 70c blue ('40) .75 .25
Never hinged 1.50
702 A166 1p gray blk ('40) 6.50 .25
Never hinged 13.00
703 A166 2p dull brn ('41) 7.75 .25
Never hinged 16.00
704 A166 4p dull rose ('40) 25.00 .25
Never hinged 50.00
705 A166 10p lt brown ('40) 125.00 2.75
Never hinged 250.00
Nos. 690-705 (15) 171.95 6.65
Set, never hinged 350.00

The 40c exists in three types, with variations in the value tablet: I. "CTS" does not touch bottom line. II. Light background in tablet. "CTS" touches bottom line. III. As type I, but with well defined lines of white and color around rectangle.

The 60c exists in two types: I. Top and left side of value tablet touch rest of design. II. Tablet separated from rest of design by white lines.

Five values exist with perf. 10: 5c, 10c, 45c, 4p and 10p.

Nos. 690-704 exist imperf. Values, set: mint, never hinged, $1,600; unused, $1,200.

The imperforate 10c dull claret, type A166, without imprint, is a postal tax stamp, RA14.

SEMI-POSTAL STAMPS

Red Cross Issue

Princesses María Cristina and Beatrice SP1

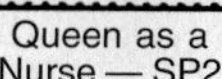

Queen as a Nurse — SP2

Queen Victoria Eugénia — SP3

Prince of Asturias — SP4

King Alfonso XIII — SP5

Perf. 12½

1926, Sept. 15 Unwmk. Engr.

B1 SP1 1c black 2.50 2.25
B2 SP2 2c ultra 2.50 2.25
B3 SP3 5c violet brn 5.50 4.00
B4 SP4 10c green 4.50 4.00
B5 SP1 15c indigo 1.75 1.50
B6 SP4 20c dull violet 1.75 1.50
a. 20c violet brown (error) 600.00 375.00
B7 SP5 25c rose red .30 .30
B8 SP1 30c blue green 42.50 40.00
B9 SP3 40c dark blue 24.00 21.00
B10 SP2 50c red orange 24.00 21.00
B11 SP4 1p slate 1.75 1.10
B12 SP3 4p magenta 1.40 .80
B13 SP5 10p brown 1.40 1.10
Nos. B1-B13,EB1 (14) 122.60 109.55
Set, never hinged 300.00

The 20c was printed in violet brown for use in the colonies (Cape Juby, Spanish Guinea, Spanish Morocco and Spanish Sahara). No. B6a, the missing overprint error, is listed here because it is not known to which colony it belongs.

For overprints see Nos. B19-B46.

Airplane and Map of Madrid-Manila Flight — SP6

1926, Sept. 15

B14 SP6 15c dp ultra & org .40 .40
B15 SP6 20c car & yel grn .40 .40
B16 SP6 30c dk brn & ultra .40 .40
B17 SP6 40c dk grn & brn org .40 .40
B18 SP6 4p magenta & yel 100.00 100.00
Nos. B14-B18,CB1-CB5 (10) 109.10 109.10
Set, never hinged 250.00

Madrid to Manila flight of Captains Eduardo G. Gallarza and Joaquim Loriga y Taboada.

Nos. B1-B18, CB1-CB5 and EB1 were used for regular postage on Sept. 15, 16, 17, 1926. Subsequently the unsold stamps were given to the Spanish Red Cross Society, by which they were sold uncanceled but they then had no franking power.

For overprints see Nos. B47-B53.

Coronation Silver Jubilee Issue

Red Cross Stamps of 1926 Overprinted "ALFONSO XIII," Dates and Ornaments in Various Colors

1927, May 27

B19 SP1 1c black (R) 6.00 6.00
B20 SP2 2c ultra (Bl) 11.00 11.00
B21 SP3 5c vio brn (R) 2.75 2.75
a. Double overprint 37.50
B22 SP4 10c green (Bl) 75.00 75.00
B23 SP1 15c indigo (R) 2.25 2.25
B24 SP4 20c dull vio (Bl) 4.00 4.00
B25 SP5 25c rose red (Bl) .50 .50
B26 SP1 30c blue grn (Bl) 1.00 1.00
B27 SP3 40c dk blue (R) 1.00 1.00
B28 SP2 50c red org (Bl) 1.00 1.00
B29 SP4 1p slate (R) 2.25 2.25
B30 SP3 4p magenta (Bl) 11.00 11.00
B31 SP5 10p brown (G) 42.50 42.50
Nos. B19-B31 (13) 160.25 160.25
Set, never hinged 375.00

Same with Additional Surcharges of New Values

B32 SP2 3c on 2c (G) 9.50 9.50
B33 SP2 4c on 2c (Bk) 9.50 9.50
B34 SP5 10c on 25c (Bk) .55 .55
B35 SP5 25c on 25c (Bl) .55 .55
B36 SP2 55c on 2c (R) 1.00 1.00
B37 SP4 55c on 10c (Bk) 55.00 55.00
B38 SP4 55c on 20c (Bk) 55.00 55.00
B39 SP1 75c on 15c (R) .70 .70
B40 SP1 75c on 30c (R) 140.00 140.00
B41 SP3 80c on 5c (R) 52.50 50.00
B42 SP3 2p on 40c (R) 1.00 1.00
B43 SP4 2p on 1p (R) 1.00 1.00
B44 SP2 5p on 50c (G) 1.90 1.90
B45 SP3 5p on 4p (Bk) 3.25 3.25
B46 SP5 10p on 10p (G) 27.50 27.50
Nos. B32-B46 (15) 358.95 356.45
Set, never hinged 700.00

Nos. B14-B18 Overprinted

B47 SP6 15c (Brn) .50 .40
a. Double overprint 30.00
B48 SP6 20c (Bl) .50 .40
a. Brown overprint (error) 65.00
b. Inverted overprint 30.00
B50 SP6 30c (R) .50 .40
a. Blue overprint (error) 65.00
b. Double overprint 30.00
B52 SP6 40c (Brn) .50 .40
a. Inverted overprint 30.00
b. Double ovpt. (Bl + Br) 95.00
B53 SP6 4p (Bl) 100.00 95.00
a. Inverted overprint 160.00

Semi-Postal Special Delivery Stamp Overprinted "ALFONSO XIII," Dates and Ornaments in Violet

B54 SPSD1 20c 5.50 5.50
Nos. B47-B54 (6) 107.50 102.10
Set, never hinged 250.00

Nos. CB1-CB5 Overprinted in Various Colors

B55 SPAP1 5c (R) 2.25 1.60
a. Inverted overprint 30.00
B56 SPAP1 10c (R) 2.50 2.25
a. Inverted overprint 30.00
B57 SPAP1 25c (Bl) .40 .40
B58 SPAP1 50c (Bl) .40 .40
a. Double ovpt., one invtd. 72.50
B59 SPAP1 1p (R) 3.00 2.50
a. Inverted overprint 95.00

Same with Additional Surcharges of New Values

B60 SPAP1 75c on 5c (R) 5.00 3.25
a. Inverted surcharge 30.00
B61 SPAP1 75c on 10c (R) 22.50 13.00
a. Inverted surcharge 30.00
B62 SPAP1 75c on 25c (Bl) 47.50 27.50
a. Double surcharge 55.00
B63 SPAP1 75c on 50c (Bl) 18.00 13.00
Nos. B55-B63 (9) 101.55 63.90
Set, never hinged 300.00

Nos. B54-B63 were available for ordinary postage.

Stamps of Spanish Offices in Morocco and Spanish Colonies, 1926 (Spain Types SP3, SP5) Surcharged in Various Colors

On Spanish Morocco

B64 SP3 55c on 4p bis (Bl) 25.00 21.00
B65 SP5 80c on 10p vio (Br) 25.00 21.00

On Spanish Tangier

B66 SP5 1p on 10p vio (Br) 135.00 110.00
B67 SP3 4p bis (G) 45.00 40.00

On Cape Juby

B68 SP3 5p on 4p bis (R) 85.00 70.00
B69 SP5 10p on 10p vio (R) 45.00 40.00

On Spanish Guinea

B70 SP5 1p on 10p vio (Bl) 25.00 21.00
B71 SP3 2p on 4p bis (G) 25.00 21.00

On Spanish Sahara

B72 SP5 80c on 10p vio (R) 40.00 32.50
B73 SP3 2p on 4p bis (R) 25.00 21.00
Nos. B64-B73 (10) 475.00 397.50
Set, never hinged 1,300.

Nos. B64-B73 were available for postage in Spain only.

Nos. B19-B73 were for the 25th year of the reign of King Alfonso XIII.

Counterfeits of Nos. B64-B73 abound.

Catacombs Restoration Issues

Pope Pius XI and King Alfonso XIII SP7

1928, Dec. 23 Engr. *Perf. 12½*

Santiago Issue

B74 SP7 2c violet & blk .30 .30
B75 SP7 2c lake & blk .35 .35
B76 SP7 3c bl blk & vio .30 .30
B77 SP7 3c dl bl & vio .35 .35
B78 SP7 5c ol grn & vio .65 .65
B79 SP7 10c yel grn & blk 1.25 1.25
B80 SP7 15c bl grn & vio 3.25 3.25
B81 SP7 25c dp rose & vio 3.25 3.25
B82 SP7 40c ultra & blk .30 .30
B83 SP7 55c ol brn & vio .30 .30
B84 SP7 80c red & blk .30 .30
B85 SP7 1p gray blk & vio .30 .30
B86 SP7 2p red brn & blk 4.25 4.25
B87 SP7 3p pale rose & vio 4.25 4.25
B88 SP7 4p vio brn & blk 4.25 4.25
B89 SP7 5p grnsh blk & vio 4.25 4.25

Toledo Issue

B90 SP7 2c bl blk & car .30 .30
B91 SP7 2c ultra & car .35 .35
B92 SP7 3c bis brn & ultra .30 .30
B93 SP7 3c ol grn & ultra .35 .35
B94 SP7 5c red vio & car .65 .65
B95 SP7 10c yel grn & ultra 1.25 1.25
B96 SP7 15c slate bl & car 3.25 3.25
B97 SP7 25c red brn & ultra 3.25 3.25
B98 SP7 40c ultra & car .30 .30
B99 SP7 55c dk brn & ultra .30 .30
B100 SP7 80c black & car .30 .30
B101 SP7 1p yellow & car .30 .30
B102 SP7 2p dk gray & ultra 4.25 4.25
B103 SP7 3p violet & car 4.25 4.25
B104 SP7 4p vio brn & car 4.25 4.25
B105 SP7 5p bister & ultra 4.25 4.25
Nos. B74-B105 (32) 55.80 55.80
Set, never hinged 120.00

Nos. B74-B105 replaced regular stamps from Dec. 23, 1928 to Jan. 6, 1929. The proceeds from their sale were given to a fund to restore the catacombs of Saint Damasus and Saint Praetextatus at Rome.

Nos. B74-B105 exist imperf. Value set, $325 hinged, $400 never hinged.

Issues of the Republic

SP13

1938, Apr. 15 *Perf. 11½*

B106 SP13 45c + 2p bl & grnsh bl .90 .75
a. Imperf., pair 17.50 14.50
b. Souv. sheet of 1 26.00 26.00
c. Souv. sheet of 1, imperf. 725.00 650.00
Never hinged 1,000.

Surtax for the defenders of Madrid.

For overprint and surcharge see Nos. B108, CB6.

Nurse and Orderly Carrying Wounded Soldier — SP14

1938, June 1 Engr. *Perf. 10*

B107 SP14 45c + 5p cop red .55 .55
a. Imperf., pair 220.00

For surcharge see No. CB7.

No. B106 Overprinted in Black

1938, Nov. 7 *Perf. 11½*

B108 SP13 45c + 2p 3.25 3.25
Never hinged 5.00

Defense of Madrid, 2nd anniversary.

A similar but larger overprint was applied to cover blocks of four. Value, $15 hinged, $30 never hinged.

Values for souvenir sheets of 1937-38 are for examples with some faults. Undamaged sheets are very hard to find.

Spanish State
Souvenir Sheets

Alcazar, Toledo — SP15

Design: No. B108C, A patio of Alcazar after Civil War fighting.

1937 Unwmk. Photo. *Perf. 11½*
Control Numbers on Back

B108A	SP15 2p org brn	22.00	22.00
	Never hinged	60.00	
b.	Imperf.	300.00	300.00
	Never hinged	500.00	
B108C	SP15 2p dark green	22.00	22.00
	Never hinged	60.00	
d.	Imperf.	300.00	300.00
	Never hinged	500.00	
	Set, never hinged	125.00	
	Set, B108Ab, B108Cd, never hinged	1,000.	

Nos. B108A-B108C sold for 4p each.

SP16

Designs: 20c, Covadongas Cathedral. 30c, Palma Cathedral, Majorca. 50c, Alcazar of Segovia. 1p, Leon Cathedral.

1938 Unwmk. Photo. *Perf. 12½*
Control Numbers on Back

B108E	SP16 Sheet of 4	42.50	42.50
f.	20c dull violet	5.00	5.00
g.	30c rose red	5.00	5.00
h.	50c bright blue	5.00	5.00
i.	1p greenish gray	5.00	5.00
j.	Imperf. sheet	72.50	65.00
	Never hinged	125.00	

Each sheet sold for 4p.

SP17

Designs, alternating in sheet: Flag bearer. Battleship "Admiral Cervera." Soldiers in trenches. Moorish guard.

1938, July 1 Unwmk. *Perf. 13*
Control Numbers on Back

B108K	SP17 Sheet of 20	40.00	40.00
	Never hinged	52.50	
l.	Imperf. sheet	185.00	185.00
	Never hinged	240.00	

Sheet measures 175x132mm. Consists of five vertical rows of four 2c violet, 3c deep blue, 5c olive gray, 10c deep green and 30c red orange, with each denomination appearing in two different designs. Marginal inscription: "Homenaje al Ejercito y a la Marina" (Honoring the Army and Navy). Sold for 4p, or double face value.

Souvenir Sheets

Don Juan of Austria — SP18

Battle of Lepanto — SP19

Perf. 12½
1938, Dec. 15 Unwmk. Engr.
Control Numbers on Back

B108M	SP18 30c dk car	22.50	22.50
B108N	SP19 50c blue black	22.50	22.50
	Nos. B108M-B108N (2)	45.00	45.00
	Set, never hinged	77.50	

Imperf

B108O	SP18 30c black vio	300.00	*550.00*
B108P	SP19 50c dk sl grn	300.00	*550.00*
	Nos. B108O-B108P (2)	600.00	*1,100.*
	Set, never hinged	1,000.	

Victory over the Turks in the Battle of Lepanto, 1571.

Nos. B108M-B108P contain one stamp. The dates "1571-1938" appear in the lower sheet margin. Size: 89x74mm. Sold for 10p a pair.

LOCAL CHARITY STAMPS

Hundreds of different charity stamps were issued by local organizations and cities during the Civil War, 1936-39. Some had limited franking value, but most were simply charity labels. They are of three kinds: 1. Local semipostals. 2. Obligatory surtax stamps. 3. Propaganda or charity labels.

Ruins of Belchite SP20

Miracle of Calanda — SP21

Designs: 10c+5c, 70c+20c, Ruins of Belchite. 15c+10c, 80c+20c, The Rosary. 20c+10c, 1.50p+50c, El Pilar Cathedral. 25c+10c, 1p+30c, Mother Raffols praying. 40c+10c, 2.50p+50c, The Little Chamber. 45c+15c, 1.40p+40c, Oath of the Besieged. 10p+4p, The Apparition.

Perf. 10½, 11½x10½, 11½
1940, Jan. 29 Litho. Unwmk.
Design SP20

B109	10c + 5c dp bl & vio brn	.25	.25
B110	15c + 10c rose vio & dk grn	.25	.25
B111	20c + 10c vio & dp bl	.25	.25
B112	25c + 10c dp rose & vio brn	.25	.25
B113	40c + 10c sl grn & rose vio	.25	.25
B114	45c + 15c vio & dp rose	.30	.30
B115	70c + 20c multi	.30	.30
B116	80c + 20c dp rose & vio	.40	.40
B117	1p + 30c dk sl grn & pur	.40	.40
B118	1.40p + 40c pur & gray blk	40.00	40.00
B119	1.50p + 50c lt bl & brn vio	.50	.50
B120	2.50p + 50c choc & bl	.50	.50

Design SP21

B121	4p + 1p rose lil & sl grn	12.00	12.00
B122	10p + 4p ultra & chnt	190.00	190.00
	Nos. B109-B122,CB8-CB17,EB2 (25)	444.20	444.10
	Set, never hinged	850.00	

19th centenary of the Virgin of the Pillar.

The surtax was used to help restore the Cathedral at Zaragoza, damaged during the Civil War.

No. B121 exists in violet & slate green, No. B122 in ultramarine & brown violet. Value, $42.50 each.

Nos. B109-B122 exist imperf. Value, $750.

See No. 743 (in Scott Standard catalogue, Vol. 6), CB8-CB17.

General Franco — SP23

1940, Dec. 23 Unwmk. *Perf. 10*

B123	SP23 20c + 5c dk grn & red	.65	.65
B124	SP23 40c + 10c dk bl & red	.90	.40
	Set, never hinged	3.50	

The surtax was for the tuberculosis fund. See Nos. RA15, RAC1.

AIR POST STAMPS

Regular Issue of 1909-10 Overprinted in Red or Black

Perf. 13x12½, 14
1920, Apr. 4 Unwmk.

C1	A46 5c green (R)	1.50	1.00
a.	Imperf., pair	105.00	105.00
b.	Double overprint	35.00	35.00
c.	Inverted overprint	90.00	90.00
d.	Double ovpt., one invtd.	35.00	35.00
e.	Triple overprint	35.00	35.00
C2	A46 10c car (Bk)	1.75	1.25
a.	Imperf., pair	105.00	105.00
b.	Double overprint	35.00	35.00
d.	Double ovpt., one invtd.	35.00	35.00
C3	A46 25c dp blue (R)	3.25	1.75
a.	Inverted overprint	90.00	90.00
b.	Double overprint	35.00	35.00
C4	A46 50c sl blue (R)	13.00	6.00
a.	Imperf., pair	105.00	105.00
C5	A46 1p lake (Bk)	42.50	22.50
a.	Imperf., pair	385.00	385.00
	Nos. C1-C5 (5)	62.00	32.50
	Set, never hinged	170.00	

Dangerous counterfeits are plentiful.

A 30c green was authorized, but not issued. Value: hinged $650; never hinged $1,200.

For overprints see Nos. C58-C61.

"Spirit of St. Louis" over Coast of Europe — AP1

Seville-Barcelona Exposition Issue
Control Numbers on Back

1929, Feb. 15 Engr. *Perf. 11*

C6	AP1 5c brown	6.00	5.00
C7	AP1 10c rose	6.00	5.00
C8	AP1 25c dark blue	7.00	5.50
C9	AP1 50c purple	8.00	5.75
C10	AP1 1p green	37.50	25.00
C11	AP1 4p black	25.00	20.00
	Nos. C6-C11 (6)	89.50	66.25
	Set, never hinged	275.00	

Nos. C6 to C11 exist imperforate. Value set, $800.

The so-called errors of color of Nos. C10, C18-C21, C23-C24, C28-C31, C37, C40, C42, C44, C46, C48, C50, C52, C55, C62-C67 are believed to have been irregularly produced.

Plane and Congress Seal — AP2

Railway Congress Issue
Control Numbers on Back

1930, May 10 Litho. *Perf. 14*

C12	AP2 5c bister brn	6.00	*7.50*
	Never hinged	8.25	
C13	AP2 10c rose	6.00	*7.50*
	Never hinged	*8.25*	
C14	AP2 25c dark blue	6.00	*7.50*
	Never hinged	8.25	
C15	AP2 50c purple	17.50	15.00
	Never hinged	26.00	
a.	Vert. pair, imperf. between	300.00	
	Never hinged	*600.00*	
C16	AP2 1p yellow green	35.00	30.00
	Never hinged	52.50	
C17	AP2 4p black	35.00	30.00
	Never hinged	52.50	
	Nos. C12-C17 (6)	105.50	97.50
	Set, never hinged	400.00	

The note after No. 385 will apply here also. Dangerous counterfeits exist.

Goya Issue

Fantasy of Flight AP3

Asmodeus and Cleofas — AP4

Fantasy of Flight AP5

Fantasy of Flight — AP6

1930, June 15 Engr. *Perf. 12½*

C18	AP3 5c brn red & yel	.25	.25
	Never hinged	.30	
C19	AP3 15c blk & red org	.25	.25
	Never hinged	.30	
C20	AP3 25c brn car & dp red	.25	.25
	Never hinged	.30	
C21	AP4 5c ol grn & grnsh bl	.25	.25
	Never hinged	.30	
C22	AP4 10c sl grn & yel grn	.25	.25
	Never hinged	.20	
C23	AP4 20c ultra & rose red	.25	.25
	Never hinged	.20	
C24	AP4 40c vio bl & lt bl	.30	.30
	Never hinged	.35	
C25	AP5 30c brown & vio	.30	.30
	Never hinged	.35	
C26	AP5 50c ver & grn	.30	.30
	Never hinged	.35	
C27	AP5 4p brn car & blk	2.00	2.00
	Never hinged	2.65	
C28	AP6 1p vio brn & vio	.30	.30
	Never hinged	.35	
C29	AP6 4p bl blk & sl grn	2.00	2.00
	Never hinged	2.50	
C30	AP6 10p blk brn & bis brn	7.00	7.00
	Never hinged	10.00	
	Nos. C18-C30,CE1 (14)	13.95	13.95
	Set, never hinged	18.75	

Nos. C18-C30 exist imperf. Value for set, $150.

Christopher Columbus Issue

La Rábida Monastery — AP7

Martín Alonso Pinzón — AP8

Vicente Yanez Pinzón — AP9

Columbus in His Cabin — AP10

1930, Sept. 29 Litho.

C31	AP7 5c lt red brn	.25	.25
	Never hinged	.30	
C32	AP7 5c olive bister	.25	.25
	Never hinged	.30	
C33	AP7 10c blue green	.25	.25
	Never hinged	.50	
C34	AP7 15c dark violet	.25	.25
	Never hinged	.50	
C35	AP7 20c ultra	.25	.25
	Never hinged	.50	

Engr.

C36	AP8 25c carmine rose	.25	.25
	Never hinged	.50	
C37	AP9 30c dp red brn	2.00	2.00
	Never hinged	2.75	
C38	AP8 40c indigo	2.00	2.00
	Never hinged	2.75	
C39	AP9 50c orange	2.00	2.00
	Never hinged	2.75	
C40	AP8 1p dull violet	2.00	2.00
	Never hinged	2.75	
C41	AP10 4p olive green	2.00	2.00
	Never hinged	2.75	
C42	AP10 10p light brown	11.00	12.00
	Never hinged	16.50	
	Nos. C31-C42 (12)	22.50	23.50
	Set, never hinged	35.00	

Nos. C31-C42 exist imperf. Value for set, $250.

Spanish-American Issue

AP11

Columbus AP12

Columbus and Pinzón Brothers AP13

1930, Sept. 29 Litho.

C43	AP11 5c lt red	.25	.25
	Never hinged	.25	
C44	AP11 10c dull green	.25	.25
	Never hinged	.30	

Engr.

C45	AP12 25c scarlet	.25	.25
	Never hinged	.40	
C46	AP12 50c slate gray	2.50	2.10
	Never hinged	4.00	
C47	AP12 1p fawn	2.50	2.10
	Never hinged	4.00	
C48	AP13 4p slate blue	2.50	2.10
	Never hinged	4.00	
C49	AP13 10p brown violet	11.00	10.00
	Never hinged	18.00	
	Nos. C43-C49 (7)	19.25	17.05
	Set, never hinged	35.00	

Nos. C43-C49 exist imperf. Value for set, $250.

Spanish-American Exhibition Issue

Santos-Dumont and First Flight of His Airplane — AP14

Teodoro Fels and His Airplane AP15

Dagoberto Godoy and Pass over Andes — AP16

Sacadura Cabral and Gago Coutinho and Their Airplane AP17

Sidar of Mexico and Map of South America — AP18

Ignacio Jiménez and Francisco Iglesias — AP19

Charles A. Lindbergh, Statue of Liberty, Spirit of St. Louis and Cat AP20

Santa Maria, Plane and Torre del Oro, Seville AP21

1930, Oct. 10 Photo. *Perf. 14*

C50	AP14 5c gray black	.90	.55
	Never hinged	4.50	
C51	AP15 10c dk olive grn	.90	.55
	Never hinged	4.50	
C52	AP16 25c ultra	.90	.55
	Never hinged	4.50	
C53	AP17 50c blue gray	1.90	1.40
	Never hinged	7.50	
C54	AP18 50c black	1.90	1.40
	Never hinged	7.50	
C55	AP19 1p car lake	3.75	3.00
	Never hinged	11.00	
a.	1p brown violet	75.00	75.00
	Never hinged	175.00	
C56	AP20 1p deep green	3.75	3.00
	Never hinged	9.50	
C57	AP21 4p slate blue	6.50	5.50
	Never hinged	40.00	
	Nos. C50-C57 (8)	20.50	15.95
	Set, never hinged	70.00	

Exist imperf. Value, set $110.

Note after No. 432 also applies to Nos. C31-C57.

Reprints of Nos. C50-C57 have blurred impressions, yellowish paper. Value: one-tenth of originals. Examples of No. C56 exist with portrait of Lindbergh inverted, doubled with one inverted and missing.

Nos. C1-C4 Overprinted in Red or Black

1931 *Perf. 13x12½*

C58	A46 5c green (R)	12.50	11.50
	Never hinged	26.00	
C59	A46 10c carmine (Bk)	12.50	11.50
	Never hinged	26.00	
C60	A46 25c deep blue (R)	17.50	16.50
	Never hinged	37.50	
C61	A46 50c slate blue (R)	35.00	26.00
	Never hinged	70.00	
	Nos. C58-C61 (4)	77.50	65.50
	Set, never hinged	160.00	

Counterfeits of overprint exist.

The status of Nos. C58-C61 has been questioned.

Plane and Royal Palace, Madrid AP22

Madrid Post Office and Cibeles Fountain AP23

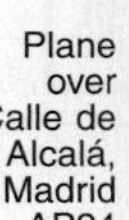

Plane over Calle de Alcalá, Madrid AP24

1931, Oct. 10 Engr. *Perf. 12*

C62	AP22 5c brown violet	.25	.30
	Never hinged	.25	
C63	AP22 10c deep green	.25	.30
	Never hinged	.25	
C64	AP22 25c dull red	.25	.30
	Never hinged	.25	
C65	AP23 50c deep blue	.45	.50
	Never hinged	.80	
C66	AP23 1p deep violet	.65	.60
	Never hinged	1.40	
C67	AP24 4p black	9.00	9.00
	Never hinged	16.50	
	Nos. C62-C67 (6)	10.85	11.00
	Set, never hinged	15.00	

3rd Pan-American Postal Union Congress, Madrid.

Exist imperf. Value, set $45.

For overprints see Nos. CO1-CO6.

Montserrat Issue

Plane over Montserrat Pass — AP25

1931, Dec. 9 *Perf. 11½*

Control Number on Back

C68	AP25 5c black brown	.50	.50
	Never hinged	1.00	
C69	AP25 10c yellow green	2.00	2.00
	Never hinged	4.00	
C70	AP25 25c deep rose	7.00	7.50
	Never hinged	15.00	
C71	AP25 50c orange	21.00	27.50
	Never hinged	52.50	
C72	AP25 1p gray black	14.00	19.00
	Never hinged	37.50	
	Nos. C68-C72 (5)	44.50	56.50
	Set, never hinged	110.00	

Perf. 14

C68a	AP25 5c	7.50	*14.50*
	Never hinged	10.00	
C69a	AP25 10c	40.00	45.00
	Never hinged	50.00	
C70a	AP25 25c	72.50	72.50
	Never hinged	82.50	
C71a	AP25 50c	72.50	72.50
	Never hinged	82.50	
C72f	AP25 1p	72.50	72.50
	Never hinged	82.50	
	Nos. C68a-C72f (5)	265.00	277.00
	Set, never hinged	275.00	

900th anniv. of Montserrat Monastery.

Nos. C68-C72 exist imperf. Value set, $525.

Autogiro over Seville — AP26

1935-39 ***Perf. 11½***

C72A	AP26 2p gray blue	22.50	4.50
	Never hinged	37.50	
g.	Imperf., pair	600.00	

Re-engraved

C72B	AP26 2p dk blue ('38)	.75	.25
	Never hinged	2.50	
c.	Imperf., pair	20.00	
d.	Perf. 10 ('39)	1.50	1.10
	Never hinged	3.00	
	Set, #C72A-C72B, never hinged	45.00	

The sky has heavy horizontal lines of shading. Entire design is more heavily shaded than No. C72A.

No. C72B exists privately perforated 14. Value, $9 unused, $9 used.

For overprints see Nos. 7LC14, 7LC19, 14L26.

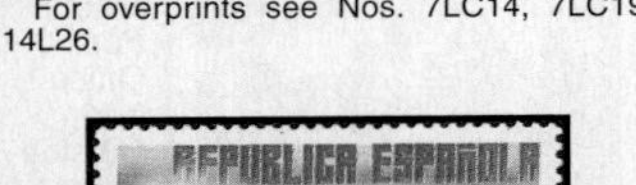

Eagle and Newspapers — AP27

Press Building, Madrid — AP28

Don Quixote and Sancho Panza Flying on the Wooden Horse — AP29

Design: 15c, 30c, 50c, 1p, Autogiro over House of Nazareth.

1936, Mar. 11 **Photo.** ***Perf. 12½***

C73	AP27 1c rose car	.25	.25
	Never hinged	.25	
C74	AP28 2c dark brown	.25	.25
	Never hinged	.25	
C75	AP27 5c black brown	.25	.25
	Never hinged	.25	
C76	AP28 10c dk yellow grn	.25	.25
	Never hinged	.25	
C77	AP28 15c Prus blue	.25	.25
	Never hinged	.25	
C78	AP27 20c violet	.25	.25
	Never hinged	.25	
C79	AP28 25c magenta	.25	.25
	Never hinged	.25	
C80	AP28 30c red orange	.25	.25
	Never hinged	.25	
C81	AP27 40c orange	.50	.25
	Never hinged	.75	
C82	AP28 50c light blue	.30	.25
	Never hinged	.50	
C83	AP28 60c olive green	.65	.40
	Never hinged	1.25	
C84	AP28 1p brnsh black	.65	.45
	Never hinged	1.25	
C85	AP29 2p brt ultra	5.00	2.25
	Never hinged	8.50	
C86	AP29 4p lilac rose	5.00	2.75
	Never hinged	8.50	
C87	AP29 10p violet brown	12.00	11.00
	Never hinged	24.00	
	Nos. C73-C87 (15)	26.10	19.35
	Set, never hinged	45.00	

Madrid Press Association, 40th anniv.

Exist imperf. Value, set $250 hinged, and $325 never hinged.

See note after No. 432.

Types of Regular Postage of 1936 Overprinted in Blue or Red

1936 ***Imperf.***

C88	A125 10c dk red (Bl)	100.00	100.00
	Never hinged	250.00	
C89	A125 15c dk blue (R)	100.00	100.00
	Never hinged	350.00	
	Set, never hinged	300.00	

1st National Philatelic Exhibition which opened in Madrid, Apr. 2, 1936.

No. 577 Overprinted in Black

1936, Aug. 1 ***Perf. 11½***

C90	A128 30c rose red	5.00	3.75
	Never hinged	12.00	
b.	Imperf., pair	140.00	

Issued in commemoration of the flight of aviators Antonio Arnaiz and Juan Calvo from Manila to Spain.

Counterfeit overprints exist.

Exists privately perforated 14. Value, $50 unused, $50 used.

No. 288 Surcharged in Black

1938, Apr. 13 ***Perf. 14***

C91	A36 2.50p on 10c	90.00	80.00
	Never hinged	175.00	

7th anniversary of the Republic.

Values are for examples with perforations nearly touching the design on one or two sides.

No. 507 Surcharged in Various Colors

1938, Aug. ***Perf. 11½***

C92	A92 50c on 25c (Bk)	29.00	29.00
	Never hinged	50.00	
C93	A92 1p on 25c (G)	2.25	1.50
	Never hinged	3.00	
C94	A92 1.25p on 25c (R)	2.25	1.50
	Never hinged	3.00	
C95	A92 1.50p on 25c (Bl)	2.25	1.50
	Never hinged	3.00	
C96	A92 2p on 25c (Bk & R)	40.00	34.00
	Never hinged	52.50	
	Nos. C92-C96 (5)	75.75	67.50
	Set, never hinged	150.00	

No. 585 Surcharged

1938, June 1 ***Perf. 11***

C97	A132 5p on 1p multi	275.	275.
	Never hinged	500.	
a.	Imperf., pair	600.	550.
b.	Inverted surcharge	350.	350.
c.	Souvenir sheet	1,200.	1,200.
	Never hinged	2,000.	
d.	As "c," imperf.	5,500.	5,500.
e.	As "c," inverted surcharge	5,500.	5,500.

Counterfeit surcharges exist.

Type of 1938-39 Overprinted in Red or Carmine

1938, May ***Perf. 10, 10½***

C98	A163 50c indigo (R)	.70	.55
	Never hinged	1.25	
C99	A163 1p dk blue (C)	3.00	.70
	Never hinged	3.25	
	Set, never hinged	4.50	

Exist imperf. Value, each $100.

Examples without overprint are proofs.

Juan de la Cierva and his Autogiro over Madrid AP30

1939, Jan. **Unwmk.** **Litho.** ***Perf. 11***

C100	AP30 20c red orange	.60	.40
	Never hinged	.70	
C101	AP30 25c dk carmine	.45	.25
	Never hinged	.55	
C102	AP30 35c brt violet	.65	.40
	Never hinged	.75	
C103	AP30 50c dk brown	.65	.25
	Never hinged	.75	
C105	AP30 1p blue	.65	.25
	Never hinged	.75	
C107	AP30 2p green	3.25	1.75
	Never hinged	5.00	
C108	AP30 4p dull blue	5.00	2.75
	Never hinged	9.00	
	Nos. C100-C108 (7)	11.25	6.05
	Set, never hinged	19.00	

Exist imperf. Value, set $325.

AIR POST SEMI-POSTAL STAMPS

Red Cross Issue

Ramon Franco's Plane Plus Ultra SPAP1

Perf. 12½, 13

1926, Sept. 15 **Engr.** **Unwmk.**

CB1	SPAP1 5c black & vio	1.40	1.40
CB2	SPAP1 10c ultra & blk	3.00	3.00
CB3	SPAP1 25c carmine & blk	.30	.30
CB4	SPAP1 50c red org & blk	.30	.30
CB5	SPAP1 1p black & green	2.50	2.50
	Nos. CB1-CB5 (5)	7.50	7.50
	Set, never hinged	10.00	

For overprints and surcharges see Nos. B55-B63.

No. B106 Surcharged in Black

1938, Apr. 15 ***Perf. 11½***

CB6	SP13 45c + 2p + 5p	200.	200.
	Never hinged	550.	
a.	Imperf., pair	1,000.	700.
b.	Souvenir sheet of 1	*3,000.*	*4,000.*
	Never hinged	*6,000.*	
c.	Souvenir sheet, imperf.	*6,000.*	*6,000.*
d.	Souv. sheet, surch. invtd.	*6,500.*	*5,750.*

The surtax was used to benefit the defenders of Madrid.

This issue has been extensively counterfeited.

No. B107 Surcharged

1938, June 1 ***Perf. 10***

CB7	SP14 45c + 5p + 3p	10.00	9.75
	Never hinged	17.50	

Monument SPAP2

Dome Fresco by Goya, Cathedral of Zaragoza SPAP3

#CB9, CB14, Caravel Santa Maria. #CB10, CB12, The Ascension. #CB13, The Coronation. #CB17, Bombardment of Cathedral of Zaragoza.

Perf. 10½, 11½x10½, 11½

1940, Jan. 29 **Litho.** **Unwmk.**

Bicolored

CB8	SPAP2	25c + 5c	.40	.40
CB9	SPAP2	50c + 5c	.40	.40
CB10	SPAP2	65c + 15c	.40	.40
CB11	SPAP2	70c + 15c	.40	.40
CB12	SPAP2	90c + 20c	.40	.40
CB13	SPAP2	1.20p + 30c	.40	.40
CB14	SPAP2	1.40p + 40c	.50	.50
CB15	SPAP2	2p + 50c	.75	.75
CB16	SPAP3	4p + 1p sl grn & rose lil	14.50	14.50
CB17	SPAP3	10p + 4p chnt & ultra	180.00	180.00
		Nos. CB8-CB17 (10)	198.15	198.15
		Set, never hinged	450.00	

19th centenary of the Pillar Virgin. The surtax was used to help restore the Cathedral at Zaragoza, damaged during the Civil War.

No. CB16 exists in slate green & violet, No. CB17 in red violet & ultramarine. Value, $32.50 each.

Nos. CB8-CB17 exist imperf. Value, set $400.

AIR POST SPECIAL DELIVERY STAMP

Goya Commemorative Issue

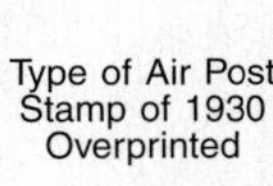

Type of Air Post Stamp of 1930 Overprinted

1930 Unwmk. *Perf. 12½*

CE1 AP4 20c bl blk & lt brn (Bk) .25 .25
Never hinged .25
a. Blue overprint 15.00 7.75
Never hinged 21.00
b. Overprint omitted 15.00 22.50
Never hinged 25.00

See note after No. 432.

AIR POST OFFICIAL STAMPS

Pan-American Postal Union Congress Issue

Types of Air Post Stamps of 1931 Overprinted in Red or Blue

1931 Unwmk. *Perf. 12*

CO1 AP22 5c red brown (R) .25 .25
CO2 AP22 10c blue grn (Bl) .25 .25
CO3 AP22 25c rose (Bl) .25 .25
CO4 AP23 50c lt blue (R) .25 .25
CO5 AP23 1p violet (R) .25 .25
CO6 AP24 4p gray blk (R) 3.50 3.50
Nos. CO1-CO6 (6) 4.75 4.75
Set, never hinged 7.00

Shades exist.

Nos. CO1-CO6 exist imperf. Value, set $22.50

SPECIAL DELIVERY STAMPS

Pegasus and Coat of Arms — SD1

1905-25 Unwmk. Typo. *Perf. 14*
Control Number on Back

E1 SD1 20c deep red 45.00 .30
Never hinged 100.00
a. 20c rose red, litho. ('25) 38.00 .30
Never hinged 70.00
b. Imperf., pair 300.00
c. As "a," imperf., pair 300.00

Gazelle SD2

1929 Engr. *Perf. 11*
Control Number on Back

E2 SD2 20c dull red 19.50 22.50
Never hinged 37.50
a. Perf. 14 32.50 37.50
Never hinged 60.00

Seville and Barcelona Exhibitions. See note after No. 432.

Pegasus — SD3

1929-32 *Perf. 13½x12½, 11½*
Control Number on Back

E3 SD3 20c red 21.00 4.00
Never hinged 40.00
a. Imperf., pair 400.00
b. Without control number, perf. 11½ ('32) 60.00 1.50
Never hinged 97.50
c. As "b," imperf., pair *950.00*

No. E3 Overprinted like Nos. 358-370

E4 SD3 20c red (Bl) 12.00 25.00
Never hinged 30.00

League of Nations 55th assembly.
For overprints see Nos. E5, E10-E12.

No. E3 Overprinted in Blue

1930 *Perf. 13½x12½, 11½*

E5 SD3 20c red 13.50 .75
Never hinged 40.00

Railway Congress Issue

Electric Locomotive — SD4

1930, May 10 Litho. *Perf. 14*
Control Number on Back

E6 SD4 20c brown orange 50.00 50.00
Never hinged 105.00

See note after No. 385.

Goya Issue

Type of Regular Issue of 1930 Overprinted

1930 *Perf. 12½*

E7 A57 20c lilac rose .25 .30
Never hinged .45

Christopher Columbus Issue

Type of Regular Issue of 1930 Overprinted

1930 Sept. 29

E8 A64 20c brown violet 1.90 1.90
Never hinged 3.00

See note after No. 432.

Spanish-American Exhibition Issue

View of Seville Exhibition — SD5

1930, Oct. 10 Photo. *Perf. 14*

E9 SD5 20c orange .45 .30
Never hinged .60

See note after No. 432.

Madrid Issue

No. E5 Overprinted in Green

1931 *Perf. 11½*

E10 SD3 20c red 5.00 5.00
Never hinged 8.00

The status of No. E10 has been questioned.

Barcelona Issue

No. E3 Overprinted

E11 SD3 20c red 5.50 5.50
Never hinged 12.00

No. E11 also exists with accent over "U."
The status of No. E11 has been questioned.

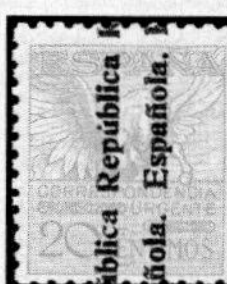

No. E3 Overprinted in Blue

E12 SD3 20c red 6.50 1.25
Never hinged 21.00

Montserrat Issue

Pegasus — SD6

1931 Engr. *Perf. 11*
Control Number on Back

E13 SD6 20c vermilion 25.00 25.00
Never hinged 38.00
a. Perf. 14 55.00 60.00

SD7

1934 *Perf. 10*

E14 SD7 20c vermilion .25 .25
Never hinged .20
a. Imperf., pair 32.50

For overprints see #10LE1, 11LE1-11LE4, 14LE1.

Newsboy — SD8

1936 Photo. *Perf. 12½*

E15 SD8 20c rose carmine .25 .30
Never hinged .50

40th anniversary of the Madrid Press Association.
See note after No. 432.

Pegasus SD9

Spanish State

1937-38 Unwmk. Litho. *Perf. 11*
With imprint "Hija. deB Fournier-Burgos"

E16 SD9 20c violet brn 7.75 4.50
Never hinged 11.00
a. Imperf., pair 77.50

Without Imprint

E17 SD9 20c dk vio brn ('38) 1.50 .30
Never hinged 3.00
a. Imperf., pair 50.00

No. 645 Overprinted in Black

1937

E18 A162 20c dark violet 11.00 11.00
Never hinged 14.50

Pegasus SD10

1939-42 *Perf. 10½*
Imprint: "SANCHEZ TODA"

E19 SD10 25c carmine 4.50 .70
Never hinged 6.25
a. Imperf., pair 50.00

Without Imprint
Perf. 10

E20 SD10 25c carmine ('42) .25 .25
Never hinged .30
a. Imperf., pair 8.50

SEMI-POSTAL SPECIAL DELIVERY STAMPS

Red Cross Issue

Royal Family Group SPSD1

1926 Unwmk. Engr. *Perf. 12½, 13*

EB1 SPSD1 20c red vio & vio brn 8.75 8.75
Never hinged 17.00

See notes after Nos. 432 and B18.
For overprint see No. B54.

Motorcyclist and Zaragoza Cathedral — SPSD2

1940 Litho. *Perf. 11½*

EB2 SPSD2 25c + 5c rose red & buff .40 .30

19th cent. of the Pillar Virgin. The surtax was used to help restore the Cathedral at Zaragoza, damaged during the Civil War.

DELIVERY TAX STAMPS

D1

1931 **Unwmk.** **Litho.** ***Perf. 11½***
ER1 D1 5c black 7.25 .25
Never hinged 12.00

For overprints see Nos. ER2-ER3, 7LE5-7LE6.

No. ER1 Overprinted in Red

1931
ER2 D1 5c black 1.25 1.40
Never hinged 2.25

No. ER2 also exists with accent over "U."

No. ER1 Overprinted in Red

ER3 D1 5c black 3.00 3.00
Never hinged 5.50

These stamps were originally issued for Postage Due purpose but were later used as regular postage stamps.

WAR TAX STAMPS

These stamps did not pay postage but represented a fiscal tax on mail matter in addition to the postal fees. Their use was obligatory.

Coat of Arms — WT1

Unwmk.
1874, Jan. 1 **Typo.** ***Perf. 14***
MR1 WT1 5c black 11.00 .95
On cover 6.50
a. Imperf. pair 14.00
MR2 WT1 10c pale blue 12.00 1.60
On cover 9.00
a. Imperf., pair 62.50

Coat of Arms — WT2

1875, Jan. 1
MR3 WT2 5c green 6.00 .60
On cover 4.00
a. Imperf., pair 27.50
MR4 WT2 10c lilac 12.00 2.75
On cover 10.00
a. Imperf., pair 55.00

King Alfonso XII — WT3

1876, June 1
MR5 WT3 5c pale green 7.50 1.00
On cover 5.50
MR6 WT3 10c blue 7.50 1.00
On cover 5.50
a. Cliche of 5c in plate of 10c 125.00
MR7 WT3 25c black 50.00 17.00
MR8 WT3 1p lilac 475.00 110.00
MR9 WT3 5p rose 900.00 300.00

Nos. MR5-MR9 exist imperforate. Value, $1,100.

King Alfonso XII — WT4

1877, Sept. 1
MR10 WT4 15c claret 27.50 1.00
On cover 5.00
a. Imperf., pair 100.00
MR11 WT4 50c yellow 900.00 110.00

WT5

1879
MR12 WT5 5c blue 65.00
MR13 WT5 10c rose 37.50
MR14 WT5 15c violet 25.00
MR15 WT5 25c brown 40.00
MR16 WT5 50c olive green 25.00
MR17 WT5 1p bister 40.00
MR18 WT5 5p gray 150.00
Nos. MR12-MR18 (7) 382.50

Nos. MR12-MR18 were never placed in use.
Nos. MR17 and MR18 exist imperforate. Value, $225.

WT6

Inscribed "1897 A 1898"

1897 ***Perf. 14***
MR19 WT6 5c green 3.25 2.10
On cover 3.25
MR20 WT6 10c green 3.25 2.10
On cover 3.25
MR21 WT6 15c green 750.00 250.00
MR22 WT6 20c green 8.25 3.25
On cover 7.00

Nos. MR19-MR22 exist imperf. Value for set $825.

Inscribed

1898
MR23 WT6 5c black 2.25 1.75
On cover 3.75
MR24 WT6 10c black 2.25 1.75
On cover 3.75
MR25 WT6 15c black 50.00 9.50
MR26 WT6 20c black 3.50 3.00
Nos. MR23-MR26 (4) 58.00 16.00

Nos. MR23-MR26 exist imperf. Value about $275 a pair.

King Alfonso XIII — WT7

1898
MR27 WT7 5c black 9.00 .60
On cover 3.00
a. Imperf., pair 85.00

OFFICIAL STAMPS

Coat of Arms — O1

Unwmk.
1854, July 1 **Typo.** ***Imperf.***
O1 O1 ½o blk, *yellow* 2.10 2.75
On cover 20.00
O2 O1 1o blk, *rose* 2.75 3.25
On cover 22.50
a. 1o black, *blue* 29.00
O3 O1 4o blk, *green* 7.50 9.25
On cover 35.00
O4 O1 1 l blk, *blue* 52.50 60.00
On cover 300.00
Nos. O1-O4 (4) 64.85 75.25
Set, never hinged 100.00

Coat of Arms — O2

1855-63
O5 O2 ½o blk, *yellow* 1.50 1.75
On cover 10.50
a. ½o black, *straw* ('63) 1.75 1.90
On cover 12.00
O6 O2 1o blk, *rose* 1.50 1.75
On cover 10.50
a. 1o black, *salmon rose* 3.25 1.90
On cover 12.00
O7 O2 4o blk, *green* 3.25 1.90
On cover 17.50
a. 4o black, *yellow green* 8.75 1.90
On cover 17.50
O8 O2 1 l blk, *gray blue* 14.50 17.50
On cover 70.00
Nos. O5-O8 (4) 20.75 22.90
Set, never hinged 25.00

Full margins of Nos. O1-O8 = ¾mm.

The "value indication" on Nos. O1-O8 actually is the weight of the mail in onzas (ounces, "o") and libras (pounds, "l") for which they were valid.

Type of Regular Issue of 1889

1895 ***Perf. 14***
O9 A34 15c yellow 11.00 6.00
Never hinged 15.00
On cover 17.50
a. Imperf., pair 250.00

Coat of Arms — O5

1896-98
O10 O5 rose 5.25 1.75
On cover 20.00
a. Imperf., pair 87.50
O11 O5 dk blue ('98) 19.00 6.00
On cover 32.50

Cervantes Issue

Chamber of Deputies O6

Statue of Cervantes — O7

National Library O8

Cervantes — O9

1916, Apr. 22 **Engr.** ***Perf. 12***

For the Senate
O12 O6 green & blk 1.10 .90
O13 O7 brown & blk 1.10 .90
O14 O8 carmine & blk 1.10 .90
O15 O9 brown & blk 1.10 .90

For the Chamber of Deputies
O16 O6 violet & blk 1.10 .90
O17 O7 carmine & blk 1.10 .90
O18 O8 green & blk 1.10 .90
O19 O9 violet & blk 1.10 .90
Nos. O12-O19 (8) 8.80 7.20

Exist imperf. Value set of pairs, $110.
Exist with centers inverted. Value for set, $87.50

Pan-American Postal Union Congress Issue

Types of Regular Issue of 1931 Overprinted in Red or Blue

1931 ***Perf. 12½***
O20 A84 5c dk brown (R) .50 .25
O21 A85 10c brt green (Bl) .50 .25
O22 A86 15c dull violet (R) .50 .25
O23 A85 25c deep rose (Bl) .50 .25
O24 A87 30c olive green (Bl) .50 .25
O25 A84 40c ultra (R) .70 .60
O26 A85 50c deep orange (Bl) .70 .60
O27 A86 1p blue black (R) .70 .60
O28 A88 4p magenta (Bl) 14.00 14.00
O29 A88 10p lt brown (R) 25.00 25.00
Nos. O20-O29 (10) 43.60 42.05
Set, never hinged 70.00

Nos. O22-O29 exist imperf. Values about 3 times those quoted.

POSTAL TAX STAMPS

PT5

Perf. 10½x11½
1937, Dec. 23 **Litho.**
RA11 PT5 10c blk, pale bl & red 8.00 5.00
Never hinged 21.00
a. Imperf. pair 80.00
Never hinged 120.00

The tax was for the tuberculosis fund.

PT6

1938, Dec. 23 *Perf. 11½*

RA12	PT6 10c multicolored	4.50	1.75
	Never hinged	10.00	
a.	Imperf. pair	45.00	
	Never hinged	55.00	

The tax was for the tuberculosis fund.

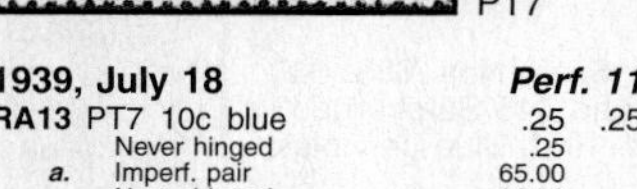

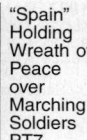

"Spain" Holding Wreath of Peace over Marching Soldiers PT7

1939, July 18 *Perf. 11*

RA13	PT7 10c blue	.25	.25
	Never hinged	.25	
a.	Imperf. pair	65.00	
	Never hinged	82.50	

Type of Regular Issue, 1939

Without Imprint

Unwmk.

1939, Dec. 23 **Litho.** *Imperf.*

RA14	A166 10c dull claret	.25	.25
	Never hinged	.25	

Tuberculosis Fund Issue

Types of Corresponding Semi-Postal Stamps

1940, Dec. 23 *Perf. 10*

RA15	SP23 10c violet & red	.25	.25
	Never hinged	.25	

POSTAL TAX AIR POST STAMPS

Tuberculosis Fund Issues

Franco Type of Semi-Postal Stamps

Unwmk.

1940, Dec. 23 **Litho.** *Perf. 10*

RAC1	SP23 10c bright pink & red	.90	.90
	Never hinged	2.50	

FRANCHISE STAMPS

F1

1869 **Unwmk.** **Litho.** *Imperf.*

S1	F1 blue	52.50	38.00
a.	Tête bêche pair	135.00	120.00

The franchise of No. S1 was granted to Diego Castell to use in distributing his publications on Spanish postal history.

F2

1881

S2	F2 black, *buff*	36.00	15.50

The franchise of No. S2 was granted to Antonio Fernandez Duro for his book, "Resena histórico-descriptiva de los sellos correos de Espana."

Reprints of No. S2 have been made on carmine, blue, gray, fawn and yellow paper.

CARLIST STAMPS

From the beginning of the Civil War (April 21, 1872) until separate stamps were issued on July 1, 1873, stamps of France were used on all mail from the provinces under Carlist rule.

King Carlos VII — A1

Tilde on N — A1a

Unwmk.

1873, July 1 **Litho.** *Imperf.*

X1	A1 1r blue	650.00	
X2	A1a 1r blue	550.00	350.00

These stamps were reprinted three times in 1881 and once in 1887. The originals have 23 white lines and dots in the lower right spandrel. They are thin and of even width and spacing. The first reprint has 17 to 20 lines in the spandrel, most of them thick and of irregular width and length. The second and third reprints have 21 very thin lines, the second from the bottom being almost invisible. In the fourth reprint the lower right spandrel is an almost solid spot of color.

Originals of type A1 have the curved line above "ESPANA" broken at the left of the "E." All reprints of this type have the curved line continuous.

The reprints exist in various shades of blue, rose, red, violet and black.

King Carlos VII

A2 A3

A4

1874

X3	A2 1r violet	325.00	325.00
X4	A3 16m rose	5.50	*72.50*
X5	A4 ½r rose	150.00	100.00

Nos. X3 and X6-X7 were for use in the Basque Provinces and Navarra; No. X4 in Catalonia, and No. X5 in Valencia.

Two types of No. X5, alternating in each sheet.

No. X4 with favor cancellation (lozenge of dots) sells for same price as unused.

A5

1875 **White Paper**

X6	A5 50c green	8.00	*82.50*
a.	50c blue green	25.00	*100.00*
b.	Bluish paper	50.00	
X7	A5 1r brown	8.00	*82.50*
a.	Bluish paper	50.00	
	Set, #X6-X7, never hinged	24.00	

Fake cancellations exist on Nos. X1-X7.

REVOLUTIONARY OVERPRINTS

Issued by the Nationalist (Revolutionary) Forces

Many districts or cities made use of the stamps of the Republic overprinted in various forms. Most such overprinting was authorized by military or postal officials but some were without official sanction. These overprints were applied in patriotic celebration and partly as a protection from the use of unoverprinted stamps seized or stolen by soldiers.

BURGOS AIR POST STAMPS

Revenue Stamps Overprinted in Red, Blue or Black

RAP1

1936, Dec. 1 **Unwmk.** *Perf. 11½*

Control Number on Face of Stamp

7LC1	RAP1 25c gray grn & blk (R)	47.50	47.50
a.	Blue overprint	47.50	47.50
7LC2	RAP1 1.50p bl & blk (R)	6.00	6.00
7LC3	RAP1 3p rose & blk (Bl)	6.00	6.00
	Nos. 7LC1-7LC3 (3)	59.50	59.50
	Set, never hinged	105.00	

RAP2

RAP4

Perf. 13½

Blue Control Number on Back

7LC4	RAP2 15c green (R)	3.75	3.75
7LC5	RAP2 25c blue (R)	27.50	27.50
	Set, never hinged	45.00	

Perf. 11½

Without Control Number

Overprint in Black

7LC6	RAP4 1.50p dk blue	6.50	6.50
7LC7	RAP4 3p carmine	6.50	6.50
	Set, never hinged	21.00	

RAP5

RAP6

Overprint in Black

Perf. 13½, 11½

7LC8	RAP5 1.20p green	25.00	25.00
	Never hinged	37.50	

Perf. 14

Control Number on Back

7LC9	RAP6 1.20p green	25.00	25.00
7LC10	RAP6 2.40p green	25.00	25.00
	Set #7LC9-7LC10, never hinged	70.00	

No. 7LC9 is inscribed "CLASE 8a."

RAP7

1937 **Unwmk.** *Perf. 11½*

Control Number on Back

7LC11	RAP7 25c ultra (R)	225.00	225.00

Stamps of Spain, 1931-36, Overprinted in Red or Black (10p)

Perf. 11, 11½, 11x11½

1937 **Unwmk.**

Overprint 13mm high

7LC12	A100 40c blue	1.10	1.10
a.	Ovpt. 15mm high	1.10	1.10
7LC13	A97 50c dark blue	1.40	1.40
a.	Ovpt. 15mm high	1.40	1.40
7LC14	A130 50c dark blue	1.75	1.75
a.	Ovpt. 15mm high	1.75	1.75
7LC15	A100 60c apple green	2.50	2.50
a.	Ovpt. 15mm high	2.50	2.50
7LC16	AP26 2p gray blue	32.50	32.50
a.	Ovpt. 15mm high	32.50	32.50
7LC17	A49a 10p brown	82.50	82.50
a.	Ovpt. 15mm high	82.50	82.50
	Nos. 7LC12-7LC17 (6)	121.75	121.75

Issue dates: Nos. 7LC12-7LC17, 4/1. Nos. 7LC12a-7LC17a, 5/1.

Spain Nos. 576, 578 and 541b overprinted in Blue or Black

Nos. 7LC18, 7LC19

Nos. 7LC20, 7LC21

Perfs as on Basic Stamps

1937, May

7LC18	A127 30c carmine (Bk)	1.40	1.40
7LC19	A127 30c carmine (Bl)	.70	.70
7LC20	A129 30c car rose (Bk)	1.40	1.40
7LC21	A129 30c car rose (Bl)	.70	.70
7LC22	A107 10p dp brn (Bk)	11.00	11.00
	Nos. 7LC18-7LC22 (5)	15.20	15.20

Spain Nos. 539b and 540b, the 1p and 4p values, were prepared with this overprint in January, 1938, but were not issued. Value, each $4.50.

BURGOS ISSUE SPECIAL DELIVERY STAMPS

Pair of Spain No. 546 Overprinted in Black

1936 **Unwmk.** *Perf. 11½x11*

7LE3	A110 20c (10c+10c) emer	4.50	4.50
	Never hinged	9.00	
a.	Overprint inverted	14.00	

Type of Regular Stamp of 1931 Overprinted in Red

7LE4	A95 20c dark violet	10.00	10.00

Type of Delivery Tax Stamp of 1931 Overprinted in Red on Block of 4

Perf. 11½

7LE5 D1 20c black 8.75 8.00
Never hinged 13.50

Same Overprinted in Red on Block of 4

7LE6 D1 20c black 30.00 25.00
Never hinged 50.00

SD1

1936 Unwmk. *Perf. 11½*
7LE7 SD1 20c green & blk 7.25 5.50
7LE8 SD1 20c green & red 7.25 5.50
Set, never hinged 25.00

Nos. 7LE7-7LE8 exist with control number on back. Value $42.50 each.

CADIZ ISSUE SEMI-POSTAL STAMPS

Stamps of Spain, 1931-36, Surcharged in Black or Red

1936 Unwmk. *Imperf.*
8LB1 A108 1c + 5c blue grn .25 .25

Perf. 11½x11, 11½

8LB2 A108 2c + 5c orange brn .25 .25
8LB3 A103 5c + 5c choc (R) .45 .45
8LB4 A110 10c + 5c green .45 .45
8LB5 A111 15c + 5c Prus grn (R) 2.75 2.75
8LB6 A95 20c + 5c dk vio (R) 3.25 3.25
8LB7 A104 25c + 5c lake 2.50 2.50
8LB8 A113 30c + 5c rose red 1.40 1.40
8LB9 A100 40c + 5c dk blue (R) 3.25 3.25
8LB10 A97 50c + 5c dk blue (R) 6.50 6.50
Nos. 8LB1-8LB10 (10) 21.05 21.05

CANARY ISLANDS AIR POST STAMPS

Issued for Use via the Lufthansa Service

Stamps of Spain, 1932-34, Surcharged in Blue

1936, Oct. 27 Unwmk. *Imperf.*
9LC1 A108 50c on 1c bl grn 27.50 17.50

Perf. 11½x11

9LC2 A108 80c on 2c buff 14.50 6.50
9LC3 A103 1.25p on 5c choc 30.00 17.50
Nos. 9LC1-9LC3 (3) 72.00 41.50
Set, never hinged 82.50

The date July 18, 1936, in the overprints of Nos. 9LC1-9LC22 marks the beginning of the Franco insurrection.

Spain Nos. 542, 543, 528 and 641 Surcharged in Black, Red or Green

The surcharge on Nos. 9LC4 and 9LC6 exists in two types: Type I, 2½-3mm space between numerals and "Cts.". Type II, 1½-2mm space between numerals and "Cts."

1936-37 *Imperf.*
9LC4 A108 50c on 1c bl grn (I) 4.50 2.75
a. Overprint type II 11.00 7.75
9LC5 A108 50c on 1c bl grn (R) ('37) 4.50 2.75

Perf. 11, 11½x11

9LC6 A108 80c on 2c buff (I) 2.25 1.60
a. Overprint type II 5.50 3.25
9LC7 A108 80c on 2c buff (G) ('37) 3.25 1.60
9LC8 A103 1.25 Pts on 5c choc (R) 6.25 4.50
9LC9 A103 Pts 1.25 on 5c choc (R) ('37) 17.00 11.00
9LC10 A161 1.25p on 5c brn (G) ('37) 3.25 1.40
Nos. 9LC4-9LC10 (7) 41.00 25.60
Set, never hinged 65.00

Issued: Nos. 9LC4, 9LC6, 11/28/36; No. 9LC8, 1/7/37; Nos. 9LC4a, 9LC6a, 9LC9, 2/12/37; Nos. 9LC5, 9LC7, 9LC10, 3/2/37.

Spain Nos. 542, 543 and 641 Surcharged in Blue

The surcharge on Nos. 9LC11-9LC13 exists in two types: Type I, 18mm tall. Type II, 20mm tall.

1937, Mar. 31 *Imperf.*
9LC11 A108 50c on 1c bl grn (I) 11.00 5.50
a. Overprint type II 4.50 2.25

Perf. 11

9LC12 A108 80c on 2c buff (I) 11.00 4.50
a. Overprint type II 2.75 1.10
9LC13 A161 1.25p on 5c brown (I) 3.25 1.10
Nos. 9LC11-9LC13 (3) 25.25 11.10
Set, never hinged 40.00

Type II overprints issued 4/17/37.

Stamps of Spain, 1931-1936, Surcharged in Blue or Red (#9LC17, 9LC19)

The surcharge on Nos. 9LC15 and 9LC18 exists in two types: Type I, 2mm space between "+" and denomination. Type II, "+" abuts surcharged denomination. Other values are Type I.

1937
9LC14 A104 25c + 50c lake 55.00 10.00
9LC15 A162 30c + 80c rose 19.50 7.75
a. Overprint type II 19.50 7.75
9LC16 A162 30c + 1.25p rose 25.00 8.25
9LC17 A97 50c + 1.25p dp bl 32.50 11.00
9LC18 A100 60c + 80c ap grn 25.00 8.75
a. Overprint type II 27.50 10.00
9LC19 A105 1p + 1.25p bl blk 80.00 22.50
Nos. 9LC14-9LC19 (6) 237.00 68.25
Set, never hinged 350.00

The surcharge represents the airmail rate and the basic stamp the postage rate.
Issued: 9LC15a, 9LC18a, 4/15. 9LC14-9LC19, 5/5.

Spain Nos. 542, 624 and 641 Surcharged in Black

1937, May 25 Unwmk. *Imperf.*
9LC20 A108 50c on 1c bl grn 7.75 4.50

Perf. 11½, 11½x11

9LC21 A143 80c on 2c org brn 6.50 2.25
9LC22 A161 1.25p on 5c gray brn 6.50 2.25
Nos. 9LC20-9LC22 (3) 20.75 9.00
Set, never hinged 30.00

Stamps and Type of Spain, 1933-36, Surcharged in Black

1937, July *Perf. 13½x13, 11, 11½*
9LC23 A143 50c on 2c org brn 3.50 2.25
9LC24 A126 80c on 2c org brn 300.00 180.00
9LC25 A161 80c on 5c gray brn 3.50 2.25
9LC26 A108 1.25p on 1c bl grn 4.25 2.25
9LC27 A161 2.50p on 10c grn 16.00 8.75

Spain Nos. 647, 650 and 652 Surcharged in Black or Red

Perf. 11

9LC28 A162 30c + 80c rose 3.00 1.40
9LC29 A162 50c + 1.25p dk bl (R) 10.50 5.00
9LC30 A162 1p + 1.25p bl (R) 16.00 8.75
Nos. 9LC23-9LC30 (8) 356.75 210.65
Set, never hinged 550.00

See note after No. 9LC19.

AP1

Perf. 14x13½

1937, July 16 Wmk. 116

Surcharge in Various Colors

9LC31 AP1 50c on 5c ultra (Br) 2.75 2.50
9LC32 AP1 80c on 5c ultra (G) 1.90 1.75
9LC33 AP1 1.25p on 5c ultra (V) 2.25 2.25
Nos. 9LC31-9LC33 (3) 6.90 6.50
Set, never hinged 10.00

Spain Nos. 641, 643 and 640 Surcharged in Green or Orange

1937, Oct. 29 Unwmk. *Perf. 11*
9LC34 A161 50c on 5c (G) 9.25 3.75
9LC35 A161 80c on 10c (O) 5.75 2.75
9LC36 A160 1.25p on 2c (G) 10.50 7.25
Nos. 9LC34-9LC36 (3) 25.50 13.75
Set, never hinged 40.00

Spain Nos. 638, 640 and 643 Surcharged in Red, Blue or Violet

1937, Dec. 23 *Imperf.*
9LC37 A159 50c on 1c (R) 10.50 4.50

Perf. 11, 11x11½

9LC38 A160 80c on 2c (Bl) 4.25 2.75
9LC39 A161 1.25p on 10c (V) 9.25 3.50
Nos. 9LC37-9LC39 (3) 24.00 10.75
Set, never hinged 37.50

Spain Nos. 647, 650 to 652 Surcharged in Black, Green or Brown

1937, Dec. 29
9LC40 A162 30c + 30c rose 4.50 3.75
9LC41 A162 50c + 2.50p dk bl (G) 29.00 21.00
9LC42 A162 60c + 2.30p yel (G) 29.00 21.00
9LC43 A162 1p + 5p bl (Br) 35.00 21.00
Nos. 9LC40-9LC43 (4) 97.50 66.75
Set, never hinged 110.00

See note after No. 9LC19.

Stamps of Spain, 1936, Surcharged in Black, Green, Blue or Red

No. 9LC44 No. 9LC46

1938, Feb. 2 *Perf. 11, 11½, 11x11½*
9LC44 A160 50c on 2c brn 5.00 3.75
9LC45 A161 80c on 5c brn (G) 3.75 3.25
9LC46 A162 30c + 80c rose (Bl) 4.50 2.50
9LC47 A161 1.25p on 10c grn (Bl) 4.50 3.25
9LC48 A162 50c + 1.25p dk bl (R) 4.50 2.75
Nos. 9LC44-9LC48 (5) 22.25 15.50
Set, never hinged 27.50

Spain Nos. 645, 646 and 649 Surcharged in Brown, Green or Violet

1938, Feb. 14
9LC51 A162 2.50p on 20c (Br) 50.00 25.00
9LC52 A162 5p on 25c (G) 50.00 25.00
9LC53 A162 10p on 40c (V) 50.00 25.00
Nos. 9LC51-9LC53 (3) 150.00 75.00
Set, never hinged 175.00

MALAGA ISSUE

Stamps of 1920-36 Overprinted in Black or Red

1937		Unwmk.	Imperf.	
10L1	A47	1c blue green	.25	.25
10L2	A108	1c blue green	.25	.25
10L3	A108	1c lt green (R)	.25	.25
		Perf. 13½, 13½x13, 11, 11½x11		
10L4	A108	2c orange brn	14.50	14.50
10L5	A126	2c orange brn	.25	.25
10L6	A103	5c chocolate (R)	.25	.25
10L7	A96	10c yellow green	12.00	12.00
10L8	A110	10c emerald	.30	.30
10L9	A111	15c Prus grn (R)	.55	.55
10L10	A97	15c blue grn (R)	.55	.55
10L11	A95	20c dk violet (R)	.50	.50
10L12	A99	25c lake	1.50	1.50
10L13	A104	25c lake	.50	.50
10L14	A113	30c carmine	.50	.50
10L15	A129	30c carmine rose	2.50	2.50
10L16	A100	40c blue (R)	.45	.45
10L17	A97	50c dk blue (R)	2.50	2.50
10L18	A100	60c apple green	1.40	1.40
10L19	A105	1p black (R)	2.75	2.75
		Nos. 10L1-10L19 (19)	41.75	41.75

Stamps of 1932-35 Overprinted in Red or Black in panes of 25, reading down. "8.2.37" and "!Arriba Espana!" form the lower half of all overprints. The upper half varies.

Overprint a (1st and 2nd rows): "MALAGA AGRADECIDA A TRANQUILLO-BIANCHI"

Overprint b (3rd row): "MALAGA A SU SALVADOR QUEIPO DE LLANO"

Overprint c (4th and 5th rows): "MALAGA A SU CAUDILLO FRANCO"

Values are for vertical strips of 3 containing examples of each overprint type.

1937			Perf. 11½	
10L20	A111	15c Prus grn (R)	5.50	5.50
a.		15c single stamp, ovpt. a	.85	.85
b.		15c single stamp, ovpt. b	1.60	1.60
c.		15c single stamp, ovpt. c	.85	.85
10L21	A113	30c rose red (Bk)	5.50	5.50
a.		30c single stamp, ovpt. a	.85	.85
b.		30c single stamp, ovpt. b	1.60	1.60
c.		30c single stamp, ovpt. c	.85	.85
10L22	A97	50c dk blue (R)	8.75	8.75
a.		50c single stamp, ovpt. a	1.60	1.60
b.		50c single stamp, ovpt. b	3.25	3.25
c.		50c single stamp, ovpt. c	1.60	1.60
10L23	A100	60c apple grn (Bk)	11.00	11.00
a.		60c single stamp, ovpt. a	1.60	1.60
b.		60c single stamp, ovpt. b	3.25	3.25
c.		60c single stamp, ovpt. c	1.60	1.60
		Nos. 10L20-10L23 (4)	30.75	30.75

SPECIAL DELIVERY STAMP

Overprinted like Nos. 10L1-10L19 on Type of Special Delivery Stamp of 1934

1937			Perf. 10	
10LE1	SD7	20c rose red (Bk)	.45	.45

ORENSE ISSUE

Stamps of 1931-36 Overprinted in Red, Blue or Black

1936			Imperf.	
11L1	A108	1c blue grn (Bl)	.45	.45
a.		Red overprint	1.10	1.10
		Perf. 11½, 13½x13		
11L2	A108	2c org brn (Bk)	3.50	3.25
11L3	A126	2c org brn (Bk)	.65	.65
11L4	A103	5c brown (R)	1.50	1.50
11L5	A110	10c lt green (Bl)	2.25	2.25
a.		Red overprint	11.00	11.00
11L6	A111	15c Prus grn (R)	3.25	3.25
11L7	A95	20c violet (Bl)	3.25	3.25
11L8	A104	25c lake (Bk)	3.75	3.75
11L9	A113	30c rose red (Bl)	2.75	2.75
a.		Black overprint	5.50	5.50
11L10	A100	40c blue (R)	3.75	3.75
a.		Imperf, pair	50.00	
11L11	A97	50c dark blue (R)	6.50	6.50
11L12	A100	60c apple grn (Bk)	4.75	4.75
a.		Red overprint	17.00	17.00
b.		As "a," Imperf, pair	50.00	
		Nos. 11L1-11L12 (12)	36.35	36.10

SEMI-POSTAL STAMPS

Stamps of Spain, 1931-36, Surcharged in Blue on front and on back of stamp

1936-37		Unwmk.	Imperf.	
11LB1	A47	1c + 5c bl grn	2.25	2.25
11LB2	A108	1c + 5c grn	.40	.40
		Perf. 13½x13, 11½, 11½x11		
11LB3	A108	2c + 5c org brn	.45	.45
11LB4	A126	2c + 5c red brn	.45	.45
11LB5	A103	5c + 5c choc	.65	.65
11LB6	A110	10c + 5c emer	.65	.65
11LB7	A111	15c + 5c Prus grn	.95	.95
11LB8	A95	20c + 5c vio	.65	.65
11LB9	A104	25c + 5c lake	.95	.95
11LB10	A113	30c + 5c rose red	2.75	2.75
11LB11	A117	30c + 5c rose red	42.50	42.50
11LB12	A100	60c + 5c apl grn	250.00	190.00
		Nos. 11LB1-11LB12 (12)	302.65	242.65

SPECIAL DELIVERY STAMPS

Type of Special Delivery Stamp of 1934 Overprinted "!VIVA ESPANA!" in Blue or Black

1936			Perf. 10	
11LE1	SD7	20c rose red (Bl)	1.90	1.90
11LE2	SD7	20c rose red (Bk)	4.25	4.25
		Same with Surcharge "+ 5 cts."		
11LE3	SD7	20c + 5c rose red	1.00	1.00
		Same Surcharge, Overprint Repeated at Right		
11LE4	SD7	20c + 5c rose red	1.10	1.10
		Nos. 11LE1-11LE4 (4)	8.25	8.25

SAN SEBASTIAN ISSUE

For Use in Province of Guipuzcoa

Stamps of 1931-36 Overprinted in Red or Blue

1937		Unwmk.	Imperf.	
12L1	A108	1c bl grn (R)	.65	.65
		Perf. 11, 13½		
12L2	A108	2c buff (Bl)	1.00	1.50
12L3	A126	2c org brn (Bl)	2.10	2.10
12L4	A95	5c chocolate (R)	5.00	5.00
12L5	A103	5c chocolate (R)	1.75	1.75
12L6	A110	10c emerald (R)	1.75	1.75
12L7	A111	15c Prus grn (R)	2.10	2.10
12L8	A95	20c dk violet (R)	2.75	2.75
12L9	A104	25c car lake (Bl)	2.75	2.75
12L10	A113	30c rose red (Bl)	2.75	2.75
12L11	A100	40c blue (R)	5.50	5.50
12L12	A97	50c dark blue (R)	5.50	5.50
		Nos. 12L1-12L12 (12)	33.60	34.10

SANTA CRUZ DE TENERIFE ISSUE

Stamps of Spain, 1931-36 Overprinted in Black or Red

1936		Unwmk.	Imperf.	
13L1	A108	1c bl grn (R)	.75	.75
13L2	A108	1c bl grn (Bk)	2.75	2.75
		Perf. 11, 13½		
13L3	A108	2c buff (Bk)	5.50	5.50
13L4	A126	2c org brn (Bk)	.95	.95
13L5	A103	5c choc (R)	3.00	3.00
13L6	A110	10c green (R)	3.00	3.00
13L7	A104	25c lake (Bk)	11.00	11.00
13L8	A100	40c dk blue (R)	3.25	3.25
13L9	A107	10p dp brn (Bk)	300.00	225.00
		Nos. 13L1-13L9 (9)	330.20	255.20

Many forgeries of #13L9 exist.

SEVILLE ISSUE

Stamps of Spain, 1931-36, Overprinted in Black or Red

1936			Imperf.	
14L1	A108	1c blue grn (Bk)	.30	.30
		Perf. 13½x13, 11, 11½x11		
14L2	A126	2c org brn (Bk)	.35	.35
14L3	A103	5c chocolate (Bk)	.45	.45
14L4	A110	10c emerald (Bk)	.55	.55
14L5	A111	15c Prus grn (R)	1.40	1.40
14L6	A95	20c violet (R)	1.40	1.40
14L7	A104	25c lake (Bk)	1.40	1.40
14L8	A113	30c carmine (Bk)	1.40	1.40
14L9	A128	30c rose red (Bk)	8.25	8.25
14L10	A100	40c blue (R)	5.50	5.50
14L11	A97	50c dk blue (R)	5.50	5.50
14L12	A100	60c apple grn (Bk)	6.75	6.75
		Nos. 14L1-14L12 (12)	33.25	33.25

Stamps of Spain, 1931-36, Handstamped in Black

		Imperf		
14L13	A108	1c blue grn	.30	.30
		Perf. 13½x13, 11, 11x11½, 11½x11		
14L14	A126	2c orange brn	.45	.45
14L15	A103	5c chocolate	.45	.45
14L16	A110	10c emerald	.45	.45
14L17	A111	15c Prus green	.55	.55
14L18	A95	20c violet	.55	.55
14L19	A104	25c lake	.55	.55
14L20	A113	30c carmine	.55	.55
14L21	A128	30c rose red	3.00	3.00
14L22	A100	40c blue	1.10	1.10
14L23	A97	50c dk blue	3.00	3.00
14L24	A100	60c apple grn	1.00	1.00
14L25	A105	1p black	3.00	3.00
14L26	AP26	2p gray blue	13.50	13.50
14L27	A106	4p magenta	7.25	7.25
14L28	A107	10p deep brown	10.50	10.50
		Nos. 14L13-14L28,14LE1 (17)	47.95	47.95

The date "Julio-1936" in the overprints of Nos. 14L1-14L28 and 14LE1 marks the beginning of the Franco insurrection.

SPECIAL DELIVERY STAMP

Overprinted like Nos. 14L13-14L25 on Type of Special Delivery Stamp of 1934

1936			Perf. 10	
14LE1	SD7	20c rose red	1.75	1.75

SPANISH GUINEA

ˈspa-nish ˈgi-nē

LOCATION — In western Africa, bordering on the Gulf of Guinea
GOVT. — Spanish Colony
AREA — 10,852 sq. mi.
POP. — 212,000 (est. 1957)
CAPITAL — Santa Isabel

Spanish Guinea Nos. 1-84 were issued for and used only in the continental area later called Rio Muni. From 1909 to 1960, Spanish Guinea also included Fernando Po, Elobey, Annobon and Corisco.

100 Centimos = 1 Peseta

King Alfonso XIII — A1

Blue Control Numbers on Back

1902		Unwmk. Typo.	Perf. 14	
1	A1	5c dark green	12.50	6.25
2	A1	10c indigo	12.50	6.25
3	A1	25c claret	92.50	47.50
4	A1	50c deep brown	92.50	47.50
5	A1	75c violet	92.50	47.50
6	A1	1p carmine rose	140.00	47.50
7	A1	2p olive green	180.00	100.00
8	A1	5p dull red	275.00	175.00
		Nos. 1-8 (8)	897.50	477.50
		Set, never hinged	1,800.	

Exists imperf, value set $3,500.

Revenue Stamps Surcharged

Blue or Black Control Numbers on Back

1903		Imperf.	
8A	10c on 25c blk (R)	550.00	240.00
8B	10c on 50c org (Bl)	140.00	40.00
8D	10c on 1p 25c car (Bk)	750.00	400.00
8F	10c on 2p cl (Bk)	800.00	600.00
g.	Blue surcharge	1,450.	800.00
8H	10c on 2p 50c red brn (Bl)	1,100.	725.00
8J	10c on 5p ol blk (R)	1,500.	525.00

Nos. 8A-8J are surcharged on stamps inscribed "Posesiones Espanolas de Africa Occidental" and "1903," with arms at left.

This surcharge was also applied to revenue stamps of 10, 15, 25, 50, 75 and 100 pesetas and in other colors.

See Nos. 98-101C.

King Alfonso XIII — A2

Blue Control Numbers on Back

1903		Typo.	Perf. 14	
9	A2	¼c black	1.50	.85
10	A2	½c blue green	1.50	.85
11	A2	1c claret	1.50	.70
12	A2	2c dark olive	1.50	.70
13	A2	3c dark brown	1.50	.70
14	A2	4c vermilion	1.50	.70
15	A2	5c black brown	1.50	.70
16	A2	10c red brown	2.50	.85
17	A2	15c dark blue	8.50	6.25
18	A2	25c orange buff	8.50	6.25
19	A2	50c carmine lake	16.00	14.00
20	A2	75c violet	21.00	14.00
21	A2	1p blue green	35.00	22.00
22	A2	2p dark green	35.00	22.00
23	A2	3p scarlet	95.00	28.50
24	A2	4p dull blue	110.00	50.00
25	A2	5p dark violet	210.00	72.50
26	A2	10p carmine rose	300.00	100.00
		Nos. 9-26 (18)	852.00	341.55
		Set, never hinged	1,700.	

Blue Control Numbers on Back

1905		Same, Dated "1905"		
27	A2	1c black	.30	.25
28	A2	2c blue grn	.30	.25
29	A2	3c claret	.30	.25
30	A2	4c bronze grn	.30	.25
31	A2	5c dark brown	.30	.25
32	A2	10c red	1.60	.85
33	A2	15c black brown	4.50	2.75
34	A2	25c chocolate	4.50	2.75
35	A2	50c dark blue	9.75	6.25
36	A2	75c orange buff	11.00	6.25
37	A2	1p carmine rose	11.00	6.25
38	A2	2p violet	26.00	13.00
39	A2	3p blue green	67.50	27.50
40	A2	4p dark green	67.50	39.00
40A	A2	5p vermilion	110.00	42.00
41	A2	10p dull blue	200.00	130.00
		Nos. 27-41 (16)	514.85	277.85
		Set, never hinged	950.00	

Stamps of Elobey, 1905, Overprinted in Violet or Blue

1906

42 A1 1c rose 4.00 2.25
43 A1 2c deep violet 4.00 2.25
44 A1 3c black 4.00 2.25
45 A1 4c orange red 4.00 2.25
46 A1 5c deep green 4.00 2.25
47 A1 10c blue green 9.25 5.25
48 A1 15c violet 16.00 9.00
49 A1 25c rose lake 16.00 9.00
50 A1 50c orange buff 22.50 13.00
51 A1 75c dark blue 26.00 15.00
52 A1 1p red brown 47.50 25.00
53 A1 2p black brown 67.50 37.50
54 A1 3p vermilion 97.50 55.00
55 A1 4p dark brown 475.00 250.00
56 A1 5p bronze green 475.00 250.00
57 A1 10p claret *2,000.* *1,100.*
Nos. 42-54 (13) 322.25 180.00

King Alfonso XIII — A3

Blue Control Numbers on Back

1907 **Typo.**

58 A3 1c dark green .75 .25
59 A3 2c dull blue .75 .25
60 A3 3c violet .75 .25
61 A3 4c yellow grn .75 .25
62 A3 5c carmine lake .75 .25
63 A3 10c orange 4.00 1.25
64 A3 15c brown 3.00 .80
65 A3 25c dark blue 3.00 .80
66 A3 50c black brown 3.00 .80
67 A3 75c blue green 3.00 .80
68 A3 1p red 6.00 1.40
69 A3 2p dark brown 9.00 6.25
70 A3 3p olive gray 9.00 6.25
71 A3 4p maroon 13.00 6.25
72 A3 5p green 13.50 9.50
73 A3 10p red violet 20.00 12.00
Nos. 58-73 (16) 90.25 47.35
Set, never hinged 210.00

Issue of 1907 Surcharged in Black or Red

1908-09

74 A3 05c on 1c dk grn (R) 3.00 1.50
75 A3 05c on 2c blue (R) 3.00 1.50
76 A3 05c on 3c violet 3.00 1.50
77 A3 05c on 4c yel grn 3.00 1.50
78 A3 05c on 10c orange 3.00 1.50
a. Red surcharge 5.25 2.75
84 A3 15c on 10c orange 14.00 9.00
Nos. 74-84 (6) 29.00 16.50

Many stamps of this issue are found with the surcharge inverted, sideways, double and in both black and red. Other stamps of the 1907 issue are known with this surcharge but are not believed to have been put in use. Value, each $17.

King Alfonso XIII — A4

Blue Control Numbers on Back

1909 **Typo.** ***Perf. 14½***

85 A4 1c orange brown .25 .25
86 A4 2c rose .25 .25
87 A4 5c dark green 1.40 .25
88 A4 10c vermilion .40 .25
89 A4 15c dark brown .40 .25
90 A4 20c violet .65 .35
91 A4 25c dull blue .65 .35
92 A4 30c chocolate .85 .30
93 A4 40c lake .50 .30
94 A4 50c dark violet .50 .30
95 A4 1p blue green 13.50 7.00
96 A4 4p orange 3.50 4.25
97 A4 10p red 3.50 4.25
Nos. 85-97 (13) 26.35 18.35
Set, never hinged 50.00

For overprints see Nos. 102-114.

Revenue Stamps Surcharged in Black

1909 ***Imperf.***
With or Without Control Numbers on Back

98 10c on 50c bl grn 87.50 57.50
a. Red or violet surcharge 110.00 80.00
99 10c on 1p 25c vio 150.00 80.00
100 10c on 2p dk brn 600.00 350.00
100A 10c on 5p dk vio 600.00 350.00
101 10c on 25p red brn *800.00* *575.00*
101A 10c on 50p brn lil *2,750.* *1,600.*
101B 10c on 75p car *2,750.* *1,600.*
101C 10c on 100p org *2,750.* *1,600.*

For additional revenue stamps surcharged for postal use see Rio de Oro Nos. 44-45.

Stamps of 1909 Overprinted with Handstamp in Black, Blue, Green or Red

1911

102 A4 1c orange brn (Bl) .40 .35
103 A4 2c rose (G) .40 .35
104 A4 5c dk green (R) 2.00 .35
105 A4 10c vermilion 1.15 .45
106 A4 15c dk brown (R) 2.00 .75
107 A4 20c violet 2.50 1.15
108 A4 25c dull blue (R) 3.00 2.40
109 A4 30c choc (Bl) 3.75 3.50
110 A4 40c lake (Bl) 4.00 3.50
111 A4 50c dark violet 6.75 5.00
112 A4 1p blue grn (R) 55.00 40.00
113 A4 4p orange (R) 29.00 23.00
114 A4 10p red (G) 37.50 *40.00*
Nos. 102-114 (13) 147.45 120.80
Set, never hinged 300.00

The date "1911" is missing from the overprint on the first stamp in each row, or ten times in each sheet of 100 stamps. This variety occurs on all stamps of the series. Value, set $550.

King Alfonso XIII — A5

Blue Control Numbers on Back

1912 **Typo.** ***Perf. 13½***

115 A5 1c black .30 .30
116 A5 2c dark brown .30 .30
117 A5 5c deep green .30 .30
118 A5 10c red .30 .30
119 A5 15c claret .30 .30
120 A5 20c red .30 .30
121 A5 25c dull blue .30 .30
122 A5 30c lake 3.50 2.00
123 A5 40c car rose 2.10 1.00
124 A5 50c brown org 2.00 .35
125 A5 1p dark violet 2.25 1.25
126 A5 4p lilac 5.00 2.50
127 A5 10p blue green 10.50 9.50
Nos. 115-127 (13) 27.45 18.70
Set, never hinged 50.00

For overprints and surcharges see Nos. 141-157.

King Alfonso XIII — A6

Blue Control Numbers on Back

1914 ***Perf. 13***

128 A6 1c dull violet .35 .30
129 A6 2c car rose .35 .30
130 A6 5c deep green .35 .30
131 A6 10c vermilion .35 .30
132 A6 15c dark violet .35 .30
133 A6 20c dark brown 1.05 .55
134 A6 25c dark blue .45 .35
135 A6 30c brown orange 1.60 .55
136 A6 40c blue green 1.60 .55
137 A6 50c dp claret .75 .35
138 A6 1p vermilion 2.00 *2.25*
139 A6 4p maroon 7.00 4.50
140 A6 10p olive black 7.75 *8.50*
Nos. 128-140 (13) 23.95 19.10
Set, never hinged 60.00

Stamps with these or similar overprints are unauthorized and fraudulent.

Stamps of 1912 Overprinted

1917 ***Perf. 13½***

141 A5 1c black 125.00 85.00
142 A5 2c dark brown 125.00 85.00
143 A5 5c deep green .40 .35
144 A5 10c red .40 .35
145 A5 15c claret .40 .35
146 A5 20c red .40 .35
147 A5 25c dull blue .40 .35
148 A5 30c lake .40 .35
149 A5 40c carmine rose .75 .40
150 A5 50c brown orange .40 .35
151 A5 1p dark violet .75 .40
152 A5 4p lilac 8.25 4.00
153 A5 10p blue green 8.25 4.00
Nos. 141-153 (13) 270.80 181.25
Set, never hinged 550.00

Nos. 143-153 exist with overprint double, inverted, in dark blue, reading "9117" and in pairs one without overprint.

Stamps of 1917 Surcharged

1918

154 A5 5c on 40c car rose 36.00 14.50
155 A5 10c on 4p lilac 36.00 14.50
156 A5 15c on 20c red 65.00 25.00
157 A5 25c on 10p bl grn 65.00 25.00
a. "52" for "25" *500.00* *425.00*
Nos. 154-157 (4) 202.00 79.00
Set, never hinged 345.00

The varieties "Gents" and "Censt" occur on Nos. 154-157. Values 50 percent more.

King Alfonso XIII
A7 A8

1919 **Typo.** ***Perf. 13***
Blue Control Numbers on Back

158 A7 1c lilac 1.00 .30
159 A7 2c rose 1.00 .30
160 A7 5c vermilion 1.00 .30
161 A7 10c violet 1.75 .30
162 A7 15c brown 1.75 .55
163 A7 20c blue 1.75 .80
164 A7 25c green 1.75 .80
a. 25c blue (error) 62.50
165 A7 30c orange 2.25 .80
166 A7 40c orange 4.50 .80
167 A7 50c red 4.50 .80
168 A7 1p light green 4.50 2.75
169 A7 4p claret 10.00 *10.50*
170 A7 10p brown 20.00 19.00
Nos. 158-170 (13) 55.75 38.00
Set, never hinged 90.00

1920
Blue Control Numbers on Back

171 A8 1c brown .35 .30
172 A8 2c dull rose .35 .30
173 A8 5c gray green .35 .30
174 A8 10c dull rose .35 .30
175 A8 15c orange .35 .30
176 A8 20c yellow .35 .35
177 A8 25c dull blue 1.15 .35
178 A8 30c greenish blue 42.50 25.00
179 A8 40c lt brown 2.00 .35
180 A8 50c lilac 2.40 .35
181 A8 1p light red 2.40 .35
182 A8 4p bright rose 6.50 6.25
183 A8 10p gray lilac 10.00 *12.50*
Nos. 171-183 (13) 69.05 47.00
Set, never hinged 120.00

A9

1922
Blue Control Numbers on Back

184 A9 1c dark brown .70 .25
185 A9 2c claret .70 .25
186 A9 5c blue green .70 .25
187 A9 10c pale red 4.75 1.15
188 A9 15c orange .70 .30
189 A9 20c lilac 3.00 1.05
190 A9 25c dark blue 4.75 1.40
191 A9 30c violet 4.50 1.50
192 A9 40c turq blue 3.25 .75
193 A9 50c deep rose 3.25 .75
194 A9 1p myrtle green 3.25 .75
195 A9 4p red brown 13.00 13.00
196 A9 10p yellow 26.00 25.00
Nos. 184-196 (13) 68.55 46.40
Set, never hinged 130.00

Nipa House — A10

1924
Blue Control Numbers on Back

197 A10 5c choc & bl .25 .25
198 A10 10c gray grn & bl .25 .25
199 A10 15c rose & blk .25 .25
200 A10 20c violet & blk .25 .25
201 A10 25c org red & blk .40 .25
202 A10 30c orange & blk .40 .25
203 A10 40c dl bl & blk .40 .25
204 A10 50c claret & blk .40 .25
205 A10 60c red brn & blk .40 .25
206 A10 1p dk vio & blk 1.60 .25
a. Center inverted 600.00 140.00
207 A10 4p brt bl & blk 3.75 2.25
208 A10 10p bl grn & blk 8.75 4.50
Nos. 197-208 (12) 17.10 9.25
Set, never hinged 25.00

Seville-Barcelona Issue of Spain, 1929, Overprinted in Red or Blue

1929 ***Perf. 11***

209 A52 5c rose lake .35 .40
210 A53 10c green (R) .35 .40
211 A50 15c Prus bl (R) .35 .40
212 A51 20c purple (R) .35 .40
213 A50 25c brt rose .35 .40
214 A52 30c black brn .35 .40
215 A53 40c dk blue (R) .70 .65
216 A51 50c dp orange .70 .65
217 A52 1p blue blk (R) 11.50 6.00
218 A53 4p deep rose 22.00 11.50
219 A53 10p brown 42.50 23.00
Nos. 209-219 (11) 79.50 44.20
Set, never hinged 160.00

Porter
A11

Drummers
A12

King Alfonso XIII and Queen Victoria — A13

1931 **Engr.** ***Perf. 14***
220 A11 1c blue green .30 .25
221 A11 2c red brown .30 .25

Blue Control Numbers on Back

222 A11 5c brown black .30 .25
223 A11 10c light green .30 .25
224 A11 15c dark green .30 .25
225 A11 20c deep violet .30 .25
226 A12 25c carmine .30 .25
227 A12 30c lake .40 .25
228 A12 40c dark blue .90 .65
229 A12 50c red orange 1.75 1.25
230 A13 80c blue violet 3.25 1.90
231 A13 1p black 5.75 5.25
232 A13 4p violet rose 37.50 20.00
233 A13 5p dark brown 17.50 14.00
Nos. 220-233 (14) 69.15 45.05
Set, never hinged 175.00

Exist imperf. Value for set, $300.

See Nos. 262-271. For overprints and surcharges see Nos. 234-277, 282-283, 298 (in Scott Standard catalogue, Vol. 6).

Stamps of 1931 Overprinted

1931
234 A11 1c blue green .30 .30
235 A11 2c red brown .30 .30
236 A11 5c brown black .30 .30
237 A11 10c light green .30 .30
238 A11 15c dark green .30 .30
239 A11 20c deep violet .30 .30
240 A12 25c carmine .30 .30
241 A12 30c lake .30 .30
242 A12 40c dark blue 2.25 .65
243 A12 50c red orange 14.50 7.75
244 A13 80c blue violet 4.50 2.50
245 A13 1p black 14.50 5.00
246 A13 4p violet rose 25.00 14.50
247 A13 5p dark brown 25.00 14.50
Nos. 234-247 (14) 88.15 47.30
Set, never hinged 200.00

Stamps of 1931 Overprinted in Red or Blue

1933
248 A11 1c blue grn (R) .30 .25
249 A11 2c red brown (Bl) .30 .25
250 A11 5c brown blk (R) .30 .25
251 A11 10c lt green (Bl) .30 .25
252 A11 15c dk green (R) .30 .25
253 A11 20c dp violet (R) .30 .25
254 A12 25c carmine (Bl) .30 .25
255 A12 30c lake (Bl) .30 .25
256 A12 40c dk blue (R) 3.50 .95
257 A12 50c red orange (Bl) 22.00 4.75
258 A13 80c blue vio (R) 7.25 4.25
259 A13 1p black (R) 25.00 4.50
260 A13 4p violet rose (Bl) 47.50 20.00
261 A13 5p dk brown (Bl) 47.50 20.00
Nos. 248-261 (14) 155.15 56.45
Set, never hinged 250.00

Types of 1931 Without Control Number

1934-35 **Engr.** ***Perf. 10***
262 A11 1c blue green ('35) 11.50 .25
263 A11 2c red brown ('35) 11.50 .25
264 A11 5c black brn 2.25 .25
265 A11 10c light green 2.25 .25
266 A11 15c dark green 3.50 .25
267 A12 30c rose red 4.50 .35
268 A12 50c indigo ('35) 9.75 1.10
Nos. 262-268 (7) 45.25 2.70
Set, never hinged 70.00

Stamps of 1931-33 Surcharged in Black

1936-37 ***Perf. 10, 14***
272 A12 30c on 40c (#228) 5.50 3.50
273 A12 30c on 40c (#242) 22.00 5.25
274 A12 30c on 40c (#256) 80.00 25.00
Nos. 272-274 (3) 107.50 33.75
Set, never hinged 170.00

The surcharge on Nos. 272-274 exists in two types, differing in the "3" which is scarcer in italic.

No. 268 Surcharged in Red

275 A12 1p on 50c indigo 30.00
276 A12 4p on 50c indigo 90.00
277 A12 5p on 50c indigo 55.00
Nos. 275-277 (3) 175.00

Nos. 275-277 were not issued.

Stamps of Spain, 1936, Overprinted in Black or Carmine

1938 ***Perf. 11***
278 A161 10c gray green 1.75 .55
279 A162 15c gray black (C) 1.75 .55
280 A162 20c dark violet 4.25 1.75
281 A162 25c brown lake 4.25 1.75
Nos. 278-281 (4) 12.00 4.60
Set, never hinged 16.00

Nos. 278-281 exist imperf. Value $175.

Stamps of 1931-33, Surcharged in Black

1939
282 A13 40c on 80c (#244) 12.00 8.00
283 A13 40c on 80c (#258) 12.00 5.00
Set, never hinged 32.50

A14

A15

Revenue Stamps Surcharged in Black

1940-41 ***Perf. 11½***
284 A14 5c on 35c pale grn 6.00 2.10
285 A14 25c on 60c org brn 6.25 2.50
286 A14 50c on 75c blk brn 8.75 2.75
Nos. 284-286 (3) 21.00 7.35

Red Surcharge

287 A15 10c on 75c blk brn 8.75 2.75
288 A15 15c on 1.50p lt vio 6.25 2.50
289 A15 25c on 60c org brn 11.00 3.50
Nos. 287-289 (3) 26.00 8.75

A16

A17

Black or Carmine Surcharge
Perf. 11

290 A16 1p on 17p deep red 52.50 15.50
291 A17 1p on 40p yel grn (C) 12.50 4.00

See No. C1 in Scott Standard catalogue, Vol. 6.

A18

A19

Black Surcharge
Perf. 11, 13x12½

292 A18 5c carmine 5.25 1.40
293 A19 1p yellow 87.50 32.50

A20

Black Surcharge

294 A20 1p on 15c gray grn 9.50 3.25

General Francisco Franco — A21

1940 ***Perf. 11½, 13½***
295 A21 5c olive brown 3.75 .50
296 A21 40c blue 5.50 .50
297 A21 50c green 6.75 .50
a. 50c greenish gray 40.00 9.00
Nos. 295-297 (3) 16.00 1.50
Set, never hinged 75.00

Nos. 295-297 exist imperf. Values $50.

SEMI-POSTAL STAMPS

Red Cross Issue

Types of Semi-Postal Stamps of Spain, 1926, Ovptd. in Black or Blue

1926 **Unwmk.** ***Perf. 12½, 13***
B1 SP3 5c black brown 11.00 7.00
B2 SP4 10c dark green 11.00 7.00
B3 SP1 15c dark vio (Bl) 2.50 1.75
B4 SP4 20c violet brown 2.50 1.75
B5 SP5 25c deep carmine 2.50 1.75
B6 SP1 30c olive green 2.50 1.75
B7 SP3 40c ultra .55 .25
B8 SP2 50c red brown .55 .25
B9 SP5 60c myrtle green .55 .25
B10 SP4 1p vermilion .55 .25
B11 SP3 4p bister 2.25 1.50
B12 SP5 10p light violet 7.50 5.00
Nos. B1-B12 (12) 43.95 28.50
Set, never hinged 60.00

See Spain No. B6a for No. B4 without overprint. For surcharges see Spain Nos. B70-B71.

SPANISH MOROCCO

'spa-nish mə-'rä-ˌkō

LOCATION — Northwest coast of Africa
GOVT. — Spanish Protectorate
AREA — 17,398 sq. mi. (approx.)
POP. — 1,010,117 (1950)
CAPITAL — Tetuán

100 Centimos = 1 Peseta

Spanish authority in northern Morocco was established after Spain's invasion of the area in 1859. Unoverprinted Spanish stamps were used in Spanish Morocco from 1860 until the appearance of separate issues for the territory in 1903. Spain No. E1 was used as a regular postage stamp in April 1914.

Spanish Offices in Morocco

Spain No. 221A Overprinted in Carmine

1903-09 Unwmk. *Imperf.*
1 A21 ¼c blue green .55 .25
a. Complete 1c (block 4 ¼c) 2.25 1.50

See Nos. 26, 39, 52, Tetuan 1, 7.

Stamps of Spain Overprinted in Carmine or Blue — a

On Stamps of 1900
Perf. 14

2 A35 2c bister brown 1.75 1.40
3 A35 5c green 2.10 .80
4 A35 10c rose red (Bl) 2.25 .35
5 A35 15c brt violet 3.25 .80
6 A35 20c grnsh black 13.00 3.50
7 A35 25c blue 1.00 .85
8 A35 30c blue green 7.50 3.50
9 A35 40c rose (Bl) 13.00 6.00
10 A35 50c slate grn 7.75 5.75
11 A35 1p lake (Bl) 16.00 8.00
12 A35 4p dull violet 42.50 14.00
13 A35 10p brown org (Bl) 42.50 35.00
Nos. 1-13 (13) 153.15 80.20
Set, never hinged 375.00

Many varieties of overprint exist. Nos. 7-13 exist imperf. Value, $500.
See Tetuan Nos. 2-6, 8-15.

On Stamps of 1909-10

1909-10 *Perf. 13x12½, 14*
14 A46 2c dark brown .75 .25
15 A46 5c green 3.75 .30
16 A46 10c carmine (Bl) 4.25 .30
17 A46 15c violet 10.50 .65
18 A46 20c olive green 26.00 1.25
19 A46 25c deep blue 95.00
20 A46 30c blue green 8.50 .65
21 A46 40c rose (Bl) 8.50 .65
22 A46 50c slate blue 14.50 14.00
23 A46 1p lake (Bl) 34.50 29.00
24 A46 4p deep violet 95.00
25 A46 10p orange (Bl) 95.00
Nos. 14-18,20-23 (9) 111.25 47.05
Set, never hinged 200.00
Nos. 14-25 (12) 396.25

The stamps overprinted "Correo Espanol Marruecos" were used in all Morocco until the year 1914. After the issue of special stamps for the Protectorate the "Correo Espanol" stamps were continued in use solely in the city of Tangier.
Many varieties of overprint exist.
Nos. 19, 24 and 25 were not regularly issued.
See Nos. 27-38, 40-51, 53-67, 75-76, 78.

Spanish Morocco

Spain No. 221A Overprinted in Carmine

1914 *Imperf.*
26 A21 ¼c green .25 .25
a. Complete 1c (block 4 ¼c) 1.25 .90

Stamps of Spain 1909-10 Overprinted in Carmine or Blue

Perf. 13x12½, 14
27 A46 2c dark brown (C) .35 .25
28 A46 5c green (C) .35 .25
29 A46 10c carmine (Bl) .35 .25
30 A46 15c violet (C) 1.50 .90
31 A46 20c olive grn (C) 3.00 1.90
32 A46 25c deep blue (C) 3.00 1.50
33 A46 30c blue grn (C) 5.75 2.75
34 A46 40c rose (Bl) 13.00 3.75
35 A46 50c slate blue (C) 6.50 2.75
36 A46 1p lake (Bl) 6.50 3.75
37 A46 4p dp violet (C) 33.00 24.00
38 A46 10p orange (Bl) 50.00 32.00
Nos. 26-38,E1 (14) 129.30 76.90
Set, never hinged 350.00

Many varieties of overprint exist, including inverted.
#27-38 exist imperf. Value for set, $525.

Stamps of Spain 1876 and 1909-10 Overprinted in Red or Blue

1915 *Imperf.*
39 A21 ¼c blue grn (R) .25 .25
a. Complete 1c (block 4 ¼c) 1.50 1.50

Perf. 13x12½, 14
40 A46 2c dk brown (R) .30 .30
41 A46 5c green (R) .35 .35
42 A46 10c carmine (Bl) .35 .35
43 A46 15c violet (R) .35 .35
44 A46 20c olive grn (R) 1.25 .35
45 A46 25c deep blue (R) 1.25 .55
46 A46 30c blue grn (R) 1.40 .60
47 A46 40c rose (Bl) 3.75 .60
48 A46 50c slate blue (R) 6.25 .55
49 A46 1p lake (Bl) 6.25 .60
50 A46 4p deep violet (R) 42.50 26.00
51 A46 10p orange (Bl) 60.00 29.00
Nos. 39-51,E2 (14) 127.25 61.45
Set, never hinged 350.00

One stamp in the setting on Nos. 39-51 has the first "R" of "PROTECTORADO" inverted. Many other varieties of overprint exist, including double and inverted.
Nos. 40-51 exist imperf. Value, set $650.

Stamps of Spain 1877 and 1909-10 Overprinted in Red or Blue — b

1916-18 *Imperf.*
52 A21 ¼c blue grn (R) 1.25 .25
a. Complete 1c (block 4 ¼c) 2.00 1.40

Perf. 13x12½, 14
53 A46 2c dk brown (R) 1.25 .25
54 A46 5c green (R) 5.50 .25
55 A46 10c carmine (Bl) 6.00 .25
56 A46 15c violet (R) 140.00
57 A46 20c olive grn (R) 140.00
58 A46 25c dp blue (R) 21.00 3.25
59 A46 30c blue grn (R) 27.50 22.00
60 A46 40c rose (Bl) 28.50 .50
61 A46 50c slate blue (R) 13.50 .25
62 A46 1p lake (Bl) 33.00 2.40
63 A46 4p dp violet (R) 55.00 32.50
64 A46 10p orange (Bl) 110.00 72.50
Nos. 52-55,58-64 (11) 302.50 134.40
Set, never hinged 440.00
Nos. 52-64 (13) 582.50
Set, never hinged 1,100.

Nos. 56-57 were not regularly issued.
Varieties of overprint, including double and inverted, exist for several denominations.
The 5c exists in olive brown. Value $525.

Same Overprint on Spain No. 310

1920
65 A46 15c ocher (Bl) 5.50 .30

Exists imperf.; also with overprint inverted.

Nos. 44, 46 Perforated through the middle and each half Surcharged "10 céntimos" in Red

1920
66 A46 10c on half of 20c 5.00 1.90
67 A46 15c on half of 30c 11.00 7.25

No. E1 Divided and Surcharged in Black

No. 68

No. 68a

68 SD1 10c on half of 20c 12.00 7.75
a. "10/cts." surcharge added 160.00 50.00
Nos. 66-68 (3) 28.00 16.90

Values of Nos. 66-68 are for pairs, both halves of the stamp. Varieties were probably made deliberately.

"Justice" — A1

Revenue Stamps Perforated through the Middle and each half Surcharged in Red or Green

1920 *Perf. 11½*
69 A1 5c on 5p lt bl 12.00 2.40
70 A1 5c on 10p green .75 .25
71 A1 10c on 25p dk grn .75 .25
a. Inverted surcharge 20.00 12.00
72 A1 10c on 50p indigo .90 .40
73 A1 15c on 100p red (G) .90 .40
74 A1 15c on 500p cl (G) 16.50 8.00
Nos. 69-74 (6) 31.80 11.70
Set, never hinged 60.00

Values of Nos. 69-74 are for pairs, both halves of the stamp.

Stamps of Spain 1917-20 Overprinted Type "a" in Blue or Red

1921-24 *Perf. 13*
75 A46 15c ocher (Bl) 1.50 .25
76 A46 20c violet (R) 2.25 .25

Stamps of Spain 1920-21 Overprinted Type "b" in Red

Imperf
77 A47 1c blue green 1.50 .25

Engr.
Perf. 13
78 A46 20c violet 11.00 .25

See No. 92.

Stamps of Spain, 1922 Overprinted Type "a" in Red or Blue

1923-28 *Perf. 13½x12½*
79 A49 2c olive green (R) 4.25 .25
80 A49 5c red violet (Bl) 4.25 .25
81 A49 10c yellow green (R) 5.00 .25
82 A49 20c violet (R) 7.00 1.10
Nos. 79-82 (4) 20.50 1.85

Same Overprinted Type "b"

1923-25
83 A49 2c olive green (R) .75 .25
84 A49 5c red violet (Bl) .75 .25
85 A49 10c yellow grn (R) 3.00 .25
86 A49 15c blue (R) 3.00 .25
87 A49 20c violet (R) 6.50 .25
88 A49 25c carmine (Bl) 13.00 1.50
89 A49 40c deep blue (R) 13.50 5.00
90 A49 50c orange (Bl) 35.00 8.50
91 A49a 1p blue black (R) 55.00 5.00
Nos. 83-91,E3 (10) 142.50 31.00
Set, never hinged 350.00

Spain No. 314 Overprinted Type "a" in Red

1927 *Imperf.*
92 A47 1c blue green .25 .25

Mosque of Alcazarquivir A2

Moorish Gateway at Larache A3

Well at Alhucemas A4

View of Xauen — A5

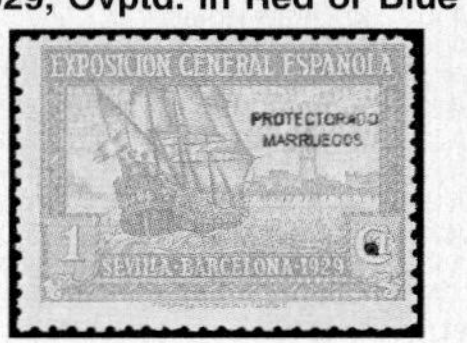

View of Tetuan — A6

1928-32 Engr. *Perf. 14, 14½*
93 A2 1c red ("Cs") .25 .25
94 A2 1c car rose ("Ct") ('32) .50 .40
95 A2 2c dark violet .30 .25
96 A2 5c deep blue .35 .25
97 A2 10c dark green .35 .25
98 A2 15c orange brown .75 .35
99 A3 20c olive green .75 .35
100 A3 25c copper red .80 .35
102 A3 30c black brown 2.60 .40
103 A3 40c dull blue 3.25 .40
104 A3 50c brown violet 6.75 .40
105 A4 1p yellow green 8.25 .45
106 A5 2.50p red violet 32.50 10.00
107 A6 4p ultra 24.00 7.50
Nos. 93-107,E4 (15) 86.40 23.20
Set, never hinged 225.00

For surcharges see Nos. 164-167.

Seville-Barcelona Issue of Spain, 1929, Ovptd. in Red or Blue

1929 *Perf. 11, 14*
108 A50 1c greenish blue .40 .30
109 A51 2c pale yel grn .40 .30
110 A52 5c rose lake (Bl) .40 .30
111 A53 10c green .40 .30
112 A50 15c Prussian blue .40 .30
113 A51 20c purple .40 .30
114 A50 25c bright rose (Bl) .40 .30
115 A52 30c black brown (bl) 1.00 .75
116 A53 40c dark blue 1.00 .75
117 A51 50c deep orange (Bl) 1.00 .75
118 A52 1p blue black 8.00 5.75
119 A53 4p deep rose (Bl) 18.00 12.50
120 A53 10p brown (Bl) 40.00 29.00
Nos. 108-120 (13) 71.80 51.60
Set, never hinged 115.00

See Nos. L1-L11.

Stamps of Spain, 1922-31, Overprinted Type "a" in Black, Blue or Red

1929-34 *Perf. 11½, 13x12½*
121 A49 5c claret (Bk) 3.50 .25
122 A61 10c green (R) 3.00 .45
123 A61 15c slate grn (R) 110.00 1.10
124 A61 20c violet (R) 3.00 .50
125 A61 30c brown lake (Bl) 3.25 1.10
126 A61 40c dark blue (R) 12.00 5.50

No.	Type	Value	Color	Unused	Used
127	A49	50c	orange (Bl)	30.00	5.25
128	A49a	10p	brown (Bl)	3.00	5.75
			Nos. 121-128 (8)	167.75	19.90
			Set, never hinged	300.00	

Stamps of Spain, 1922-26, overprinted diagonally as above, and with no control number, or with "A000,000" on back, were not issued but were presented to the delegates at the 1929 UPU Congress in London. Value of complete set of 16, $3,250.

Stamps of Spain 1931-32, Overprinted in Black

1933-34 ***Imperf.***

No.	Type	Value	Color	Unused	Used
130	A108	1c	blue green	.25	.25
			Perf. 11½		
131	A108	2c	buff	.25	.25
132	A95	5c	brnsh black	.25	.25
133	A96	10c	yellow green	.25	.25
134	A97	15c	slate green	.25	.25
135	A95	20c	dark violet	.30	.25
136	A104	25c	lake	.30	.25
137	A99	30c	carmine rose	60.00	6.00
138	A100	40c	dark blue	.65	.25
139	A97	50c	orange	1.25	.30
140	A100	60c	apple green	1.25	.30
141	A105	1p	blue black	1.25	.50
142	A106	4p	magenta	2.75	2.50
143	A107	10p	deep brown	3.50	*5.50*
			Nos. 130-143,E7 (15)	74.00	17.35
			Set, never hinged	130.00	

Street Scene in Tangier — A7

View of Xauen A8

Gate in Town Wall, Arzila — A9

Street Scene in Tangier A10

Mosque of Alcazarquivir A11

Caliph and His Guard A12

View of Tangier A13

Green Control Numbers Printed on Gum

1933-35 **Photo.** ***Perf. 14, 13½***

No.	Type	Value	Color	Unused	Used
144	A7	1c	brt rose	.35	.25
145	A8	2c	green ('35)	.35	.25
146	A9	5c	magenta ('35)	.35	.25
147	A10	10c	dark green	.45	.25
148	A11	15c	yellow ('35)	3.00	.30
149	A7	20c	slate green	1.25	.30
150	A12	25c	crimson ('35)	29.00	.30
151	A10	30c	red brown	8.00	.35
152	A13	40c	deep blue	12.50	.35
153	A13	50c	red orange	42.50	5.00
154	A8	1p	slate blk ('35)	18.00	.35
155	A9	2.50p	brown ('35)	32.50	5.00
156	A11	4p	yel grn ('35)	42.50	5.00
157	A12	5p	black ('35)	42.50	5.25
			Nos. 144-157,E5 (15)	234.40	23.45
			Set, never hinged	400.00	

For surcharge see No. CB1.

Mosque — A14

Landscape A15

Green Control Numbers Printed on Gum

1935

No.	Type	Value	Color	Unused	Used
158	A14	25c	violet	1.25	.25
159	A15	30c	crimson	16.50	.25
160	A14	40c	orange	8.50	.25
161	A15	50c	bright blue	8.50	.30
162	A14	60c	dk blue green	8.50	.35
163	A15	2p	brown lake	42.50	6.00
			Nos. 158-163 (6)	85.75	7.40
			Set, never hinged	160.00	

See No. 174.

Regular Issue and Special Delivery Stamp of 1928, Surcharged in Blue, Green or Red

Nos. 164-167

No. 168

1936

No.	Type	Value	Color	Unused	Used
164	A6	1c	on 4p ultra (Bl)	.35	.25
165	A5	2c	on 2.50p red vio (G)	.35	.25
166	A3	5c	on 25c cop red (R)	.35	.25
167	A4	10c	on 1p yel grn (G)	10.00	4.00
168	SD2	15c	on 20c blk (Bl)	7.75	2.10
			Nos. 164-168 (5)	18.80	6.85
			Set, never hinged	24.50	

Caliph and Viziers — A16

View of Bokoia A17

View of Alcazarquivir — A18

Sidi Saida Mosque A19

Caliph and Procession A20

Without Control Numbers

1937 **Photo.** ***Perf. 13½***

No.	Type	Value	Color	Unused	Used
169	A16	1c	green	.30	.25
170	A17	2c	red violet	.30	.25
171	A18	5c	orange	.30	.25
172	A16	15c	violet	.30	.25
173	A19	30c	red	.85	.25
a.			Souvenir sheet of 4, #170-173	22.00	12.00
174	A14	1p	ultra	7.50	.30
a.			Souv. sheet of 4, #169-171, 174	22.00	12.00
175	A20	10p	brown	60.00	17.50
			Nos. 169-175 (7)	69.55	19.05
			Set, never hinged	150.00	

Nos. 173a, 174a for 1st year of the Spanish Civil War.

Nos. 173a, 174a were privately overprinted "TANGER" in black on each stamp in the sheet for "use" in the International City of Tangier, and "GUINEA" for "use" in Spanish Guinea.

Harkeno Rifleman — A21

Troops Marching A22

Designs: 2c, Legionnaires. 5c, Cavalryman leading his mount. 10c, Moroccan phalanx. 15c, Legion flag-bearer. 20c, Colonial soldier. 25c, Ifni sharpshooters. 30c, Mounted trumpeters. 40c, Cape Juby Dromedary Corps. 50c, Regular infantry. 60c, Caliphate guards. 1p, Orderly on guard. 2p, Sentry. 2.50p, Regular cavalry. 4p, Orderly.

1937 ***Perf. 13½***

No.	Type	Value	Color	Unused	Used
176	A21	1c	dull blue	.35	.25
177	A21	2c	orange brn	.35	.25
178	A21	5c	cerise	.35	.25
179	A21	10c	emerald	.35	.25
180	A21	15c	brt blue	.35	.25
181	A21	20c	red brown	.35	.25
182	A21	25c	magenta	.35	.30
183	A21	30c	red orange	.35	.30
184	A21	40c	orange	.35	.35
185	A21	50c	ultra	.35	.35
186	A21	60c	yellow grn	.35	.35
187	A21	1p	blue violet	.35	.35
188	A21	2p	Prus blue	11.50	5.00
189	A21	2.50p	gray black	11.50	5.00
190	A21	4p	dark brown	11.50	5.00
191	A22	10p	black	11.50	5.00
			Nos. 176-191,E6 (17)	50.45	23.75
			Set, never hinged	120.00	

First Year of Spanish Civil War.
Exists imperf. Value, set $250.

For overprints see Nos. 214-229.

Spanish Quarter — A25

Designs: 10c, Moroccan quarter. 15c, Street scene, Larache. 20c, Tetuan.

1939 **Unwmk.** **Photo.** ***Perf. 13½***

No.	Type	Value	Color	Unused	Used
194	A25	5c	orange	.30	.25
195	A25	10c	brt blue grn	.30	.25
196	A25	15c	golden brown	.50	.30
197	A25	20c	brt ultra	.50	.30
			Nos. 194-197 (4)	1.60	1.10

Postman — A26

Mail Box — A27

Landscape A28

Street Scene, Alcazarquivir A29

View of Xauen — A30

Sentry Guarding Palace at Sat — A31

The Chieftain — A32

Market Place, Larache — A33

Tetuán — A34

Ancient Gateway at Xauen — A35

Scene in Alcazarquivir A36

Post Office A37

Spanish War Veterans — A38

Victory Flag Bearers — A39

Cavalry — A40

Day of Court — A41

1940 Unwmk. Photo. *Perf. 11½x11*

198	A26	1c	dark brown	.35	.30
199	A27	2c	olive grn	.35	.30
200	A28	5c	dk blue	.35	.30
201	A29	10c	dk red lilac	.35	.30
202	A30	15c	dk green	.45	.35
203	A31	20c	purple	.35	.35
204	A32	25c	black brown	.35	.35
205	A33	30c	brt green	.35	.35
206	A34	40c	slate green	2.75	.35
207	A35	45c	orange ver	1.10	.35
208	A36	50c	brown orange	1.10	.35
209	A37	70c	sapphire	1.10	.35
210	A38	1p	indigo & brn	3.25	.35
211	A39	2.50p	choc & dk grn	18.00	4.75
212	A40	5p	dk cerise & sep	3.50	.45
213	A41	10p	dk ol grn & brn org	32.50	8.00
			Nos. 198-213,E8 (17)	67.05	17.90
			Set, never hinged	120.00	

"ZONA" printed in black on back.
Exists imperf. Value, set $325.

Stamps of 1937 Overprinted in Various Colors

1940 Unwmk. *Perf. 13½*

214	A21	1c	dull blue (Bk)	.95	.70
215	A21	2c	org brn (Bk)	.95	.70
216	A21	5c	cerise (Bk)	.95	.70
217	A21	10c	emerald (Bk)	.95	.70
218	A21	15c	brt blue (Bk)	.95	.70
219	A21	20c	red brn (Bk)	.95	.70
220	A21	25c	mag (Bk)	.95	.70
221	A21	30c	red org (V)	.95	.70
222	A21	40c	orange (V)	1.60	1.40
223	A21	50c	ultra (Bk)	1.60	1.40
224	A21	60c	yel grn (Bk)	1.60	1.40
225	A21	1p	blue vio (V)	1.60	1.40
226	A21	2p	Prus bl (Bl)	50.00	50.00
227	A21	2.50p	gray blk (V)	50.00	50.00
228	A21	4p	dk brn (Bl)	50.00	50.00
229	A22	10p	black (R)	50.00	50.00
			Nos. 214-229,E10 (17)	226.00	220.70
			Set, never hinged	550.00	

4th anniversary of Spanish Civil War.

SEMI-POSTAL STAMPS

Types of Semi-Postal Stamps of Spain, 1926, Ovptd. in Black or Blue

1926 Unwmk. *Perf. 12½, 13*

B1	SP1	1c	orange	8.50	5.50
B2	SP2	2c	rose	12.00	10.00
B3	SP3	5c	black brn	4.50	3.50
B4	SP4	10c	dark grn	4.50	3.50
B5	SP1	15c	dk violet (Bl)	.80	.65
B6	SP4	20c	violet brn	.80	.65
B7	SP5	25c	deep carmine	.80	.65
B8	SP1	30c	olive grn	.80	.65
B9	SP3	40c	ultra	.25	.25
B10	SP2	50c	red brown	.25	.25
B11	SP4	1p	vermilion	.25	.25
B12	SP3	4p	bister	.80	.65
B13	SP5	10p	light violet	3.50	2.75
			Nos. B1-B13,EB1 (14)	40.50	31.65
			Set, never hinged	70.00	

See Spain No. B6a for No. B6 without overprint. For surcharges see Spain Nos. B64-B65.

AIR POST STAMPS

Mosque de Baja and Plane — AP1

View of Tetuán and Plane AP2

10c, Stork of Alcazar. 25c, Shore scene, plane. 40c, Desert tribesmen watching plane. 75c, View of shoreline at Larache. 1p, Arab mailman, plane above. 1.50p, Arab farmers, stork. 2p, Plane at twilight. 3p, Shadow of plane over city.

1938 Unwmk. Photo. *Perf. 13½*

C1	AP1	5c	red brown	.25	.25
C2	AP1	10c	emerald	.25	.25
C3	AP1	25c	crimson	.25	.25
C4	AP1	40c	dull blue	2.00	.50
C5	AP2	50c	cerise	.25	.25
C6	AP2	75c	ultra	.25	.25
C7	AP1	1p	dark brown	.25	.25
C8	AP1	1.50p	purple	.65	.35
C9	AP1	2p	brown lake	.40	.25
C10	AP1	3p	gray black	1.75	.25
			Nos. C1-C10 (10)	6.30	2.85
			Set, Never Hinged	11.00	

Nos. C1-C10 exist imperf. Value of set, $100.
For surcharge see No. C32 in Scott Standard catalogue, Vol. 6.

AIR POST SEMI-POSTAL STAMPS

No. 150 Surcharged in Black

1936 Unwmk. *Perf. 14*

CB1	A12	25c + 2p on 25c	14.00	5.75
		Never hinged	50.00	
	a.	Bars at right omitted	57.50	42.50
	b.	Blue surcharge	45.00	15.00

25c was for postage, 2p for air post.

Nos. C1-C10 surcharged "Lucha Antituberculosa," a Lorraine cross and surtax are stated to be bogus.

SPECIAL DELIVERY STAMPS

Special Delivery Stamp of Spain Overprinted in Blue

1914 Unwmk. *Perf. 14*

E1 SD1 20c red 5.75 2.60

Special Delivery Stamp of Spain Overprinted in Blue

1915

E2 SD1 20c red 3.00 1.60

For bisected surcharge see No. 68.

Special Delivery Stamp of Spain Overprinted in Blue

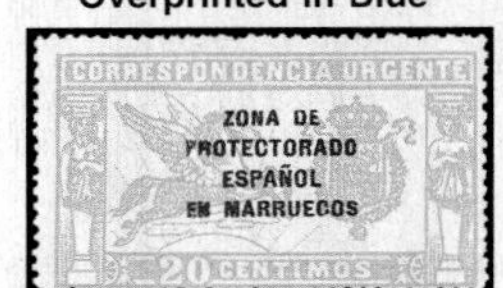

1923

E3 SD1 20c red 12.00 9.75

Mounted Courier SD2

1928 Engr. *Perf. 14, 14½*

E4 SD2 20c black 5.00 1.60

For surcharge see No. 168.

Moorish Postman — SD3

1935 Photo. *Perf. 14*

Green Control Number on Back

E5 SD3 20c vermilion 1.15 .25

See No. E9.

Mounted Courier — SD4

1937 *Perf. 13½*

E6 SD4 20c bright carmine .25 .25

1st Year of the Spanish Civil War.
For surcharge see No. E10.

Spain No. E14 Overprinted in Black

1938 *Perf. 10*

E7 SD7 20c vermilion 1.50 .25

Arab Postman — SD5

1940 Photo. *Perf. 11½x11*

E8 SD5 25c scarlet .85 .35

"ZONA" printed on back in black.

Type of 1935

1940 Litho. *Perf. 10*

E9 SD3 20c black brown 2.60

No. E9 was prepared but not issued.
Exists imperf. Value, $10.

No. E6 Surcharged with New Value, Bars and

1940 *Perf. 13½*

E10 SD4 25c on 20c brt car 12.00 9.50

4th anniversary of Spanish Civil War.

SEMI-POSTAL SPECIAL DELIVERY STAMP

Type of Semi-Postal Special Delivery Stamp of Spain, 1926, Overprinted like #B1-B13

1926 Unwmk. *Perf. 12½, 13*

EB1 SPSD1 20c ultra & black 2.75 2.40

POSTAL TAX STAMPS

General Francisco Franco — PT1

1937-39 Unwmk. Photo. *Perf. 12½*

RA1 PT1 10c sepia .50 .25
a. Sheet of 4, imperf. 4.50 1.75
RA2 PT1 10c copper brn ('38) .50 .25
a. Sheet of 4, imperf. 4.50 1.75
RA3 PT1 10c blue ('39) .50 .25
a. Sheet of 4, imperf. 4.50 1.75
Nos. RA1-RA3 (3) 1.50 .75
Set, never hinged 3.50
Set, RA1a-RA3a 13.50

The tax was used for the disabled soldiers in North Africa.

TANGIER

For the International City of Tangier

Seville-Barcelona Issue of Spain, 1929, Ovptd. in Blue or Red

1929 *Perf. 11*

L1 A52 5c rose lake .30 .30
L2 A53 10c green (R) .30 .30
L3 A50 15c Prus blue (R) .30 .30
L4 A51 20c purple (R) .30 .30
L5 A50 25c brt rose .30 .30
L6 A52 30c black brn .30 .30
L7 A53 40c dk blue (R) .75 .75
L8 A51 50c deep org .75 .75
L9 A52 1p blue blk (R) 7.75 7.75
L10 A53 4p deep rose 21.00 21.00
L11 A53 10p brown 30.00 30.00
Nos. L1-L11 (11) 62.05 62.05
Set, never hinged 105.00

Overprints of 1937-39

The following overprints on stamps of Spain exist in black or in red:

"TANGER" vertically on Nos. 517-518, 522-523, 528, 532, 534, 539-543, 549.

"Correo Espanol Tanger" horizontally or vertically in three lines on Nos. 540, 592-597 (gray paper), 598-601.

"Tanger" horizontally on Nos. 539-541, 592-601.

"Correo Tanger" horizontally in two lines on five consular stamps.

TANGIER SEMI-POSTAL STAMPS

Types of Semi-Postal Stamps of Spain, 1926, Overprinted

1926 *Perf. 12½, 13*

LB1 SP1 1c orange 7.50 *8.00*
LB2 SP2 2c rose 7.50 *8.00*
LB3 SP3 5c black brn 3.75 3.75
LB4 SP4 10c dk green 3.75 3.75
LB5 SP1 15c dk violet 1.25 *1.60*
LB6 SP4 20c violet brn 1.25 *1.60*
LB7 SP5 25c dp carmine 1.25 *1.60*
LB8 SP1 30c olive grn 1.25 *1.60*
LB9 SP3 40c ultra .35 .35
LB10 SP2 50c red brn .35 .35
LB11 SP4 1p vermilion .75 .75
LB12 SP3 4p bister .75 .75
LB13 SP5 10p lt violet 3.25 3.25
Nos. LB1-LB13,LEB1 (14) 35.95 38.35
Set, never hinged 65.00

For overprints & surcharges see Spain Nos. B66-B67.

TANGIER SEMI-POSTAL SPECIAL DELIVERY STAMP

Types of Semi-Postal Special Delivery Stamp of Spain, 1926, Overprinted like #LB1-LB13

1926 Unwmk. *Perf. 12½, 13*

LEB1 SPSD1 20c ultra & black 3.00 3.00
Never hinged 5.00

TETUAN

Spanish Offices in Morocco Nos. 1-4 & 6-7 Handstamped in Black, Blue or Violet

1908 Unwmk. *Imperf.*

1 A21 ¼c blue green 13.00 10.00

Perf. 14

2 A35 2c bister brown 175.00 60.00
3 A35 5c dark green 165.00 35.00
4 A35 10c rose red 165.00 35.00
5 A35 20c grnsh black 325.00 125.00
6 A35 25c blue 125.00 35.00
Nos. 1-6 (6) 968.00 300.00

Spain Nos. 221A, 272-274, 277-281 Handstamped in Black, Blue or Violet

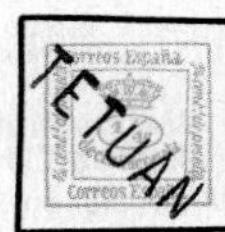

1908 *Imperf.*

7 A21 ¼c deep green 7.50 3.25

Perf. 14

8 A35 2c bister brn 55.00 13.00
9 A35 5c dark green 70.00 22.50
10 A35 10c rose red 77.50 22.50
11 A35 15c purple 77.50 25.00
12 A35 20c grnsh black 175.00 110.00
13 A35 25c blue 95.00 35.00
14 A35 30c blue green 200.00 60.00
15 A35 40c olive bister 250.00 110.00
Nos. 7-15 (9) 1,008. 401.25

Counterfeits of this overprint are plentiful.

SPANISH SAHARA

'spa-nish sə-'har-ə

(Spanish Western Sahara)

LOCATION — Northwest Africa, bordering on the Atlantic Ocean.
GOVT. — Spanish possession.
AREA — 102,703 sq. mi.
POP. — 32,000 (1940)
CAPITAL — Aaiún.

Spanish Sahara was a subdivision of Spanish West Africa. It included the colony of Rio de Oro and the territory of Saguiet el Hamra. Spanish Sahara was formerly known as Spanish Western Sahara, which superseded the older title of Rio de Oro.

100 Centimos = 1 Peseta

Tuareg and Camel — A1

1924 Unwmk. Typo. *Perf. 13*
Control Number on Back

1 A1 5c blue green 3.00 .90
2 A1 10c gray green 3.00 .90
3 A1 15c turq blue 3.00 .90
4 A1 20c dark violet 3.00 1.25
5 A1 25c red 3.00 1.25
6 A1 30c red brown 3.00 1.25
7 A1 40c dark blue 3.00 1.25
8 A1 50c orange 3.00 1.25
9 A1 60c violet 3.00 1.25
10 A1 1p rose 16.00 6.50
11 A1 4p chocolate 70.00 33.00
12 A1 10p claret 170.00 105.00
Nos. 1-12 (12) 283.00 154.70
Set, never hinged 450.00

Nos. 1-12 were for use in La Aguera & Rio de Oro.

An unissued set of 10, similar to Nos. 3-12, exists perf. 10 or imperf, and no control number except on 50c. The set also exists perf 14. Value, $200.

Nos. 1-12 also exist perf 14. Value, unused $300.

For overprints see Nos. 24-35.

Seville-Barcelona Issue of Spain, 1929 Overprinted in Blue or Red

1929 *Perf. 11*

13 A52 5c rose lake .30 .30
14 A53 10c green (R) .30 .30
15 A50 15c Prus blue (R) .30 .30
16 A51 20c purple (R) .40 .30
17 A50 25c bright rose .40 .30
18 A52 30c black brown .40 .30
19 A53 40c dark blue (R) .90 .45
20 A51 50c deep orange .90 .45
21 A52 1p blue black (R) 3.50 1.90
22 A53 4p deep rose 27.50 17.50
23 A53 10p brown 52.50 35.00
Nos. 13-23 (11) 87.40 57.10
Set, never hinged 125.00

Stamps of 1924 Overprinted in Red or Blue

1931 *Perf. 13*

24 A1 5c blue grn (R) .95 .65
25 A1 10c gray grn (R) .95 .65
26 A1 15c turq blue (R) .95 .65
27 A1 20c dark violet (R) .95 .65
28 A1 25c red .95 .65
29 A1 30c red brown .95 .65
30 A1 40c dark blue (R) 4.50 .90
31 A1 50c orange 4.50 2.25
32 A1 60c violet 4.50 2.25
33 A1 1p rose 4.50 2.25
34 A1 4p chocolate 45.00 22.00
35 A1 10p claret 92.50 50.00
Nos. 24-35 (12) 161.20 83.55
Set, never hinged 240.00

The stamps of the 1931 issue exist with the overprint reading upward, downward, or horizontally. Some values also exist with double overprint, double overprint, one inverted and diagonal overprint.

SEMI-POSTAL STAMPS

Red Cross Issue

Types of Semi-Postal Stamps of Spain, 1926, Overprinted

1926 Unwmk. *Perf. 12½, 13*

B1 SP3 5c black brown 8.75 8.75
B2 SP4 10c dark green 8.75 8.75
B3 SP1 15c dark violet 2.75 2.75
B4 SP4 20c violet brown 2.75 2.75
B5 SP5 25c deep carmine 2.75 2.75
B6 SP1 30c olive green 2.75 2.75
B7 SP3 40c ultra .25 .25
B8 SP2 50c red brown .25 .25
B9 SP5 60c myrtle green .25 .25
B10 SP4 1p vermilion .25 .25
B11 SP3 4p bister 2.75 2.10
B12 SP5 10p light violet 7.25 6.00
Nos. B1-B12 (12) 39.50 37.60
Set, never hinged 57.50

See Spain No. B6a for No. B4 without overprint. For surcharges see Spain Nos. B72-B73.

STELLALAND

'ste-lə-,land

LOCATION — South Africa
GOVT. — Republic
AREA — 5,000 sq. mi. (approx.)
CAPITAL — Vryburg

This short-lived republic was set up by the Boers in an effort to annex territory ruled by the Bechuana chiefs. Great Britain refused to recognize it and in 1885 sent an expeditionary force which ended the political career of the country.

Stellaland was annexed by Great Britain in 1885 and became a part of British Bechuanaland.

12 Pence = 1 Shilling

Coat of Arms — A1

1884, Feb. Unwmk. Litho. *Perf. 12*

1 A1 1p red 225.00 *375.00*
a. Horiz. pair, imperf. between 4,500.
b. Vert. pair, imperf. between 5,000.
2 A1 3p orange 37.50 *375.00*
a. Horiz. pair, imperf. vert. 1,400.
b. Vert. pair, imperf. between 2,200.
c. Horiz. pair, imperf. between 1,100.
3 A1 4p gray 32.50 *400.00*
a. Horiz. pair, imperf. between 850.00
b. Vert. pair, imperf. between *2,400.*
4 A1 6p lilac 40.00 *400.00*
a. Horiz. pair, imperf. between 1,750.
b. Vert. pair, imperf. between 2,000.
5 A1 1sh green 92.50 *850.00*
Nos. 1-5 (5) 427.50 2,400.

Imperf. varieties are believed to be proofs.

No. 3 Handstamped in Blackish Violet

1885

6 A1 2p on 4p gray *3,500.*

The status of No. 6 has long been questioned.

STRAITS SETTLEMENTS

'strāts 'se-tᵊl-mənts

LOCATION — Malay Peninsula in southeastern Asia
GOVT. — British Colony
AREA — 1,356 sq. mi.
POP. — 1,435,895 (estimated)
CAPITAL — Singapore

The colony comprised the settlements of Malacca, Singapore and Penang, which were incorporated under one government in 1826 and the administration transferred from India to the Secretary of State for the Colonies in 1867.

Stamps of India were used in Malacca, Penang and Singapore, 1854-67.

The colony was dissolved in 1946 when Singapore became a separate crown colony. Malacca and Penang were incorporated into the Malayan Union, which became the Federation of Malaya in 1948.

See Malaya for stamps of the Federated Malay States, Johore, Kedah, Kelantan, Negri Sembilan, Pahang, Penang, Perak, Selangor, Sungei Ujong and Trengganu.

100 Cents = 1 Dollar

STAMPS OF INDIA USED IN STRAITS SETTLEMENTS

SINGAPORE

Stamps of India canceled with the Octagonal postmark "B/172"

1854 Wmk. 37 *Imperf.*

A1 ½a blue (#2) 350.
A2 1a red (#4) 240.
A4 1a red (#7) 2,600.
A5 2a green (#5) 140.
a. Half used as 1a on cover *260,000.*
A6 4a red & blue (#6) 2,600.

1855-64 Unwmk. Typo. *Perf. 14*
Blue Glazed Paper

A9 4a black (#9) 57.50
a. Half used as 2a on cover (#9b, '59) *22,000.*
A10 8a rose (#10) 57.50
a. Half used as 4a on cover (#10b, '59) *140,000.*

1855-64 White Paper

A11 ½a blue (#11) 80.00
A12 1a brown (#12) 37.50
a. Half used as ½a on cover (#12c, '59) *140,000.*
A13 2a dull rose (#13) 75.00
A14 2a buff (#15) 65.00
a. 2a orange (#15a) 65.00
A16 4a black (#16) 40.00
a. Diagonal half used as 2a on cover (#16b, '59) *70,000.*
A17 4a green ('64) (#17) 200.00
A18 8a rose (#18) 57.50
a. Half used as 4a on cover (#18a, '59) *130,000.*

1860-64 Unwmk. *Perf. 14*

A19 8p lilac (#19) 110.00
a. Diagonal half used as 4p on cover (#19a) *140,000.*
A20 8p lilac, *bluish* (#) 950.00

1865-67 Wmk. 38 (Elephant)

A22 ½a blue (#20) 90.00
A23 8p lilac (#21) 240.00
A24 1a brown (#22) 75.00
A25 2a orange (#23) 80.00
a. 2a yellow (#23a) 80.00
A26 4a green (#24) 175.00
A27 8a rose (#25) 350.00

1866-67

A28 4a green, type I (#26) 240.00
A29 6a8p slate (#27) 600.00

1866 Official Stamps

A30 ½a blue (#O5) 950.00
A31 2a yellow (#O8) 1,200.

Stamps of India canceled with the Singapore Duplex Town Datestamp and Numeral "172" in adjacent diamond-shaped canceler

1855-64 White Paper

A32 1a brown (#12) 475.00
A33 2a orange (#15a) 650.00
A34 4a black (#16) 650.00
A35 8a rose (#18) 650.00

1860-64 Unwmk. *Perf. 14*

A36 8p lilac (#19) 700.00

1865-67

A37 2a orange (#23) 500.00
a. 2a yellow (#23a) 500.00
A38 4a green (#24) 650.00

PENANG

Stamps of India canceled with the Octagonal postmark "B/147"

1854 Wmk. 37 *Imperf.*

A50 ½a blue (#2) 850.00
A51 1a red (#4) 325.00
A52 2a green (#5) 450.00
A53 4a red & blue (#6) *2,100.*

1855-64 Unwmk. *Perf. 14*
Blue Glazed Paper

A56 4a black (#9) 160.00
A57 8a rose (#10) 150.00
a. Half used as 4a on cover (#10b) *140,000.*

1855-64 White Paper

A58 ½a blue (#11) 160.00
A59 1a brown (#12) 90.00
A60 2a dull rose (#13) 140.00
A61 2a buff (#15) 130.00
a. 2a orange (#15a) 130.00
A63 4a black (#16) 90.00
A64 8a rose (#18) 120.00

1860-64 Unwmk. *Perf. 14*

A65 8p lilac (#19) 325.00

Stamps of India canceled with the Penang Duplex Town Datestamp and Numeral "147" in adjacent diamond-shaped canceler

1854 Wmk. 37 *Imperf.*

A66 1a red (#4) 4,750.

1855-64 White Paper

A67 ½a blue (#2) 400.00
A68 1a brown (#12) 100.00
A69 2a orange (#15a) 140.00
A70 4a black (#16) 120.00
A71 4a green (#17) 350.00
A72 8a rose (#18) 120.00

1860-64 Unwmk. *Perf. 14*

A73 8p lilac (#19) 180.00

1865-67 Wmk. 38

A75 8p lilac (#21) —
A76 1a brown (#22) 100.00
A77 2a yellow (#23a) 120.00
A78 4a green (#24) 375.00
A79 8a rose (#25) —

1866-67

A80 4a green (#26) 400.00

MALACCA

Stamps of India canceled with the Octagonal postmark "B/109"

1854 Wmk. 37 *Imperf.*

A90 ½a blue (#2) *2,750.*
A91 1a red (#4) *2,400.*
A93 2a green (#5) *2,400.*
A94 4a red & blue, cut to shape (#6) *2,400.*

1855-64 Unwmk. *Perf. 14*
Blue Glazed Paper

A97 8a rose (#10) 1,000.

1855-64 White Paper

A98 ½a blue (#11) 700.00
A99 1a brown (#12) 525.00
A100 2a dull rose (#13) 750.00
A101 2a buff (#15) 600.00
a. 2a orange (#15a) 625.00
A103 4a green (#17) 950.00
A104 8a rose (#18) 700.00

1860-64 Unwmk. *Perf. 14*

A105 8p lilac (#19) 900.00
A106 8p lilac, *bluish* (#19C) 1,700.

1865-67 Wmk. 38

A107 4a green (#24) 1,000.

Issued under British Administration

Stamps of India Surcharged in Red, Blue, Black Violet or Green

Nos. 1-7

Nos. 8-9

1867, Sept. 1 Wmk. 38 *Perf. 14*

1 A7 1½c on ½a bl (R) 130.00 *200.00*
Postal cancel, no company chop *235.00*
2 A7 2c on 1a brn (R) 200.00 100.00
Postal cancel, no company chop 97.50
3 A7 3c on 1a brn (Bl) 190.00 100.00
Postal cancel, no company chop 100.00
4 A7 4c on 1a brn (Bk) 325.00 275.00
Postal cancel, no company chop 300.00
5 A7 6c on 2a yel (V) 925.00 250.00
Postal cancel, no company chop 290.00
6 A7 8c on 2a yel (G) 360.00 42.50
Postal cancel, no company chop 52.50
7 A9 12c on 4a grn (R) 1,600. 325.00
Postal cancel, no company chop 365.00
a. Double surcharge 4,500.
8 A7 24c on 8a rose (Bl) 775.00 110.00
Postal cancel, no company chop 100.00
9 A7 32c on 2a yel (Bk) 525.00 120.00
Postal cancel, no company chop 110.00

Manuscript Surcharge, Pen Bar Across "THREE HALF" of No. 1

9A A7 2(c) on 1½c on ½a *20,000.* *6,500.*

Values for Nos. 1-9A are for stamps with perforations touching the frame line on one or two sides. Used values for Nos. 1-9 are for stamps with company chops in addition to postal cancellations.

Covers: Covers of this issue are very rare and seldom offered. Values start at about $1,500.

A2

A3

A4

A5

1867-72 Typo. Wmk. 1 *Perf. 14*

10 A2 2c bister brown 57.50 8.50
a. 2c yellow brown 57.50 7.50
b. 2c deep brown 160.00 20.00
11 A2 4c rose 87.50 13.50
a. 4c deep rose 120.00 17.00
12 A2 6c violet 165.00 22.50
a. 6c bright lilac 180.00 24.00
13 A3 8c yellow 260.00 18.00
a. 8c orange 260.00 20.00
14 A3 12c blue 230.00 12.50
a. 12c ultra 250.00 13.50
15 A3 24c green 210.00 8.00
a. 24c yellow green 410.00 32.50
16 A4 30c claret ('72) 425.00 17.50
17 A5 32c pale red 675.00 70.00
18 A5 96c olive gray 425.00 55.00
Nos. 10-18 (9) 2,535. 225.50

Corner ornaments of types A2, A3 and A5 differ for each value.

See Nos. 19, 40-44, 48-50, 52-57. For surcharges see Nos. 20-35, 58-59, 61-66, 73-82, 91. For overprints see Malaya, Johore No. 1, Perak Nos. 1, O1-O2, Selangor Nos. 1-2, Sungei Ujong Nos. 2-3.

Stamps of Straits Settlements, 1867-82, overprinted "B" are listed under Bangkok.

1871 *Perf. 12½*

19 A5 96c olive gray 2,750. 275.00

Stamps of 1867-72 Surcharged

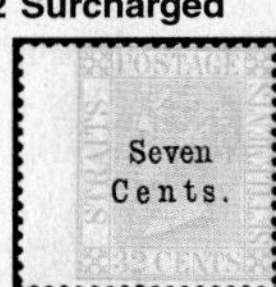

1879, May *Perf. 14*

20 A3 5c on 8c yellow 150.00 *190.00*
a. No period after "CENTS" 1,100. *1,300.*
21 A5 7c on 32c pale red 180.00 *200.00*
a. No period after "CENTS" 1,800. *2,200.*

No. 16 Surcharged

e f g j k m

10
h

1880

22 A4(e) 10c on 30c 325.00 62.50
23 A4(f) 10c on 30c 925.00 130.00
24 A4(g) 10c on 30c 325.00 62.50
25 A4(h) 10c on 30c — 24,000.
25A A4(j) 10c on 30c 8,750. 1,100.
25B A4(k) 10c on 30c 8,750. 1,100.
25C A4(m) 10c on 30c 8,750. 1,100.

Surcharges e & f and g, h, j & m are virtually identical. These must have an expert certificate identifying them. Values can be suspect because of misidentifications.

Unused examples are valued without gum.

With Additional Surcharge

26 A4(e) 10c on 30c 600. 100.
27 A4(f) 10c on 30c 11,000. 1,100.
27A A4(g) 10c on 30c 6,500. 650.
28 A4(h) 10c on 30c *20,000.* 2,250.
28A A4(j) 10c on 30c *20,000.* 2,250.
28B A4(k) 10c on 30c *20,000.* 2,250.
28C A4(m) 10c on 30c *20,000.* 2,250.

Unused examples are valued without gum.

No. 13 Surcharged

n o p

1880

29 A3(n) 5c on 8c yellow 200.00 *225.00*
30 A3(o) 5c on 8c yellow 700.00 *925.00*
31 A3(p) 5c on 8c yellow 210.00 *250.00*

No. 11 Surcharged

1882, Jan.

32	A2	5c on 4c rose	375.00	*400.00*

Nos. 12, 14a, 16 Surcharged

1880-81

33	A2	10c on 6c violet ('81)	90.00	7.50
a.		Double surcharge	—	3,250.
34	A3	10c on 12c blue ('81)	77.50	12.00
a.		10c on 12c ultra ('81)	82.50	20.00
35	A4	10c on 30c claret	500.00	100.00
		Nos. 33-35 (3)	667.50	119.50

A6

A7

1882, Jan. **Typo.** ***Perf. 14***

38	A6	5c violet brown	120.00	*140.00*
39	A7	10c slate	575.00	80.00
		Ovptd. "SPECIMEN"	1,000.	

See Nos. 45-47, 51. For surcharges see Nos. 60, 67-72, 89-92.

1882-99 Wmk. Crown and C A (2)

40	A2	2c bister brown	400.00	52.50
41	A2	2c car rose ('83)	13.00	1.00
a.		2c rose	52.50	4.75
42	A2	4c rose	170.00	14.00
43	A2	4c car rose ('99)	16.00	1.40
44	A2	4c bister brn ('83)	57.50	6.25
45	A6	5c ultra ('83)	19.00	1.40
46	A6	5c brown ('94)	17.50	1.10
47	A6	5c magenta ('99)	5.00	*2.40*
48	A2	6c violet	2.75	*16.00*
a.		6c lilac ('84)	27.50	22.50
49	A3	8c orange	6.50	1.10
50	A3	8c ultra ('94)	5.25	.60
a.		8c bright blue	10.00	.95
51	A7	10c slate	16.00	1.50
52	A3	12c vio brn ('83)	87.50	20.00
53	A3	12c claret ('94)	29.00	*16.00*
54	A3	24c blue grn ('83)	11.00	*7.00*
a.		24c yellow green ('84)	85.00	13.00
55	A4	30c claret ('91)	22.50	24.00
56	A5	32c red org ('87)	16.00	5.50
57	A5	96c olive gray ('88)	80.00	70.00
		Nos. 40-57 (18)	974.50	241.75

For overprints see Malaya, Perak Nos. O3-O9, Selangor Nos. 3-4, Sungei Ujong Nos. 6-7, 11.

Preceding Issues Surcharged

Surcharged Vertically

1883-84 **Wmk. 2, 1**

58	A3	2c on 8c orange	190.00	90.00
a.		Double surcharge	*3,750.*	*1,350.*
59	A5	2c on 32c pale red	900.00	300.00
60	A6	2c on 5c ultra ('84)	175.00	180.00
a.		Pair, one without surcharge		
b.		Double surcharge		
		Nos. 58-60 (3)	1,265.	570.00

Five types of surcharge on No. 58, two types on No. 59 and three types on No. 60.

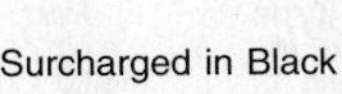

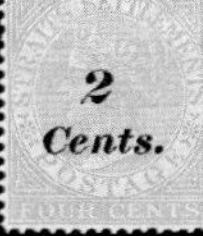

Surcharged in Black

1883 **Wmk. 2**

61	A2	2c on 4c rose	100.00	*100.00*
b.		"s" of "Cents." inverted	1,700.	1,900.

Wmk. 1

62	A3	2c on 12c blue	500.00	180.00
a.		"s" of "Cents." inverted	8,000.	3,750.

Surcharged in Black or Blue

1884

63	A3	8c on 12c blue	1,300.	175.00

Wmk. 2

64	A3	8c on 12c vio brn	725.00	175.00

With Additional Surcharge Handstamped in Red

65	A3	8c on 8c on 12c vio brn (R + Bk)	575.00	500.00
66	A3	8c on 8c on 12c vio brn (R + Bl)	11,000.	

Surcharged in Black or Red

1884

67	A6	4c on 5c ultra (Bk)	3,500.	*5,750.*
68	A6	4c on 5c ultra (R)	190.00	150.00

No. 68 Surcharged in Red

69	A6	4c on 4c on 5c ultra		*42,500.*

No. 69 may be a trial printing. "Usage" seems to been restricted to less than 10 letters known sent from the Postmaster General to his wife.

Surcharged in Black

1885-87

70	A6	3c on 5c ultra	175.00	*280.00*
a.		Double surcharge	3,500.	

Surcharged in Black

71	A6	3c on 5c vio brn ('86)	350.00	*360.00*

Surcharged

72	A6	2c on 5c ultra ('87)	50.00	*110.00*
a.		Double surcharge	1,700.	1,600.
b.		"C" omitted		*4,500.*

In the surcharged issues of 1883 to 1887, Nos. 59, 62, 63 and 71 are on stamps watermarked Crown and C C, the others are watermarked Crown and C A.

Surcharged

1885-94 Wmk. Crown and C A (2)

73	A5	3c on 32c magenta	2.25	1.10
a.		3c on 32c pale magenta	6.00	4.50
		Ovptd. "SPECIMEN"	300.00	
74	A5	3c on 32c rose ('94)	2.75	.85
a.		Without surcharge	*6,500.*	
		Ovptd. "SPECIMEN"	65.00	

No. 74a value is for a stamp with perfs touching frame line.

Surcharged

1891

75	A3	10c on 24c green	8.25	1.40
a.		Narrow "0" in "10"	32.50	37.50

Surcharged

76	A5	30c on 32c red orange	16.50	4.25

Surcharged

1892

77	A2	1c on 2c rose	2.25	*5.00*
78	A2	1c on 4c bister brn	9.50	*7.50*
a.		Double surcharge	1,800.	
79	A2	1c on 6c violet	2.75	*12.50*
a.		Dbl. surch., one invtd.	2,300.	2,100.
80	A3	1c on 8c orange	1.25	4.25
81	A3	1c on 12c vio brown	5.75	*10.50*
		Nos. 77-81 (5)	21.50	39.75

Surcharged

82	A3	1c on 8c gray green	1.10	*1.75*

Queen Victoria — A13

1892-99 **Typo.**

83	A13	1c gray green	9.50	.80
84	A13	3c car rose ('95)	13.00	.55
85	A13	3c brown ('99)	17.50	.70
a.		3c yellow brown	15.00	1.40
86	A13	25c dk vio & grn	37.50	7.50
a.		25c purple brown & green	47.50	8.00
87	A13	50c ol grn & car	29.00	3.50
88	A13	$5 org & car ('98)	500.00	275.00
		Nos. 83-88 (6)	606.50	288.05
		Set ovptd. "SPECIMEN"	240.00	

Denomination of $5, is in color on plain tablet.

Stamps of 1883-94 Surcharged

1899

89	A6	4c on 5c ultra	14.00	*32.50*
a.		Double surcharge	—	3,750.
90	A6	4c on 5c brown	3.25	*5.25*
91	A3	4c on 8c brt blue	3.75	*2.00*
a.		4c on 8c ultra	4.00	*4.00*
b.		Double surcharge	*1,600.*	*1,500.*
		Nos. 89-91 (3)	21.00	*39.75*

Type of 1882 Issue Surcharged

92	A6	4c on 5c rose	1.10	.40
a.		Without surcharge	*40,000.*	
		Ovptd. "SPECIMEN"	70.00	

King Edward VII — A14

Numerals of 5c, 8c, 10c, 30c, $1 and $5, type A14, are in color on plain tablet.

1902 **Wmk. 2** **Typo.**

93	A14	1c green	3.00	*5.00*
a.		1c pale green	5.00	4.25
94	A14	3c vio & org	3.75	.25
95	A14	4c violet, *red*	5.00	.35
96	A14	5c violet	6.00	2.40
97	A14	8c violet, *blue*	4.75	.30
98	A14	10c vio & blk, *yel*	29.00	1.60
99	A14	25c violet & grn	19.00	13.00
100	A14	30c gray & car rose	25.00	10.00
101	A14	50c grn & car rose	24.00	22.50
a.		50c dull green & carmine	24.50	25.00
102	A14	$1 green & blk	25.00	*80.00*
103	A14	$2 violet & blk	87.50	80.00
104	A14	$5 grn & brn org	215.00	180.00
104A	A14	$100 dl vio & grn, *yel*	*16,000.*	
		Ovptd. "SPECIMEN"	800.00	
		Nos. 93-104 (12)	447.00	395.40
		Nos. 93-104 ovptd. "SPECIMEN"	525.00	

High values of the 1902 and 1904 issues with revenue cancellations are of minimal value. No. 104A is inscribed "Postage & Revenue" but the limit of weight probably precluded its use postally.

See Nos. 113, 115-128B, 133.

A15

A16

A17

A18

1903-04

105	A15	1c gray green	4.25	9.25
106	A16	3c dull violet	12.00	4.75
107	A17	4c violet, *red*	17.50	.35
108	A18	8c violet, *blue*	52.50	1.50
		Nos. 105-108 (4)	86.25	15.85

See Nos. 109-112, 114, 129-132, 134.

1904-11 **Chalky Paper** **Wmk. 3**

109	A15	1c gray green	5.25	.25
110	A16	3c dull violet	3.00	.35
111	A17	4c violet, *red*	24.00	.80
112	A17	4c dull vio ('08)	6.50	.25
113	A14	5c violet ('06)	30.00	2.75
114	A18	8c violet, *bl*	57.50	1.60
115	A14	10c vio & blk, *yel*	9.00	.85
116	A14	10c vio, *yel* ('08)	15.00	1.10
117	A14	25c vio & grn	60.00	40.00
118	A14	25c violet ('09)	22.50	9.00

119 A14 30c gray & car rose 55.00 3.25
120 A14 30c vio & org ('09) 60.00 4.50
121 A14 50c grn & car rose 65.00 22.00
122 A14 50c blk, *grn* ('10) 9.50 5.25
123 A14 $1 green & blk 75.00 45.00
124 A14 $1 blk & red, *bl* ('11) 16.00 6.50
125 A14 $2 violet & blk 120.00 95.00
Revenue cancel 15.00
126 A14 $2 grn & red, *yel* ('09) 27.50 25.00
127 A14 $5 grn & brn org 325.00 210.00
128 A14 $5 grn & red, *grn* ('10) 150.00 80.00
Revenue cancel 6.50
128A A14 $25 green & blk 3,600. 3,600.
Revenue cancel 55.00
128B A14 $100 dl vio & grn, *yel* *22,000.*
Revenue cancel 200.00
Nos. 109-128 (20) 1,136. 553.45

Nos. 125, 128A and 128B are on chalky paper, the other values are on both ordinary and chalky. The note about No. 104A will apply to No. 128B.

1906-11 **Ordinary Paper**
129 A15 1c blue grn ('10) 25.00 1.25
130 A16 3c carmine ('08) 9.25 .25
131 A17 4c carmine ('07) 8.50 3.00
132 A17 4c lake ('11) 3.50 .95
133 A14 5c orange ('09) 3.00 2.75
134 A18 8c ultra ('06) 4.50 .65
Nos. 129-134 (6) 53.75 8.85

Stamps of Labuan 1902-03, Overprinted or Surcharged in Red or Black

a

b

c

Perf. 12½ to 16 and Compound
1907 **Unwmk.**
134A A38(a) 1c violet & blk 75.00 *190.00*
135 A38(a) 2c grn & blk 425.00 *500.00*
136 A38(a) 3c brn & blk 27.50 *95.00*
137 A38(c) 4c on 12c yel & blk 4.00 *14.00*
a. No period after "CENTS" 650.00 —
138 A38(c) 4c on 16c org brn & grn (Bk) 12.00 *15.00*
a. With additional name in red 700.00 1,100.
b. As "a," in pair with #138 9,000.
139 A38(c) 4c on 18c bis & blk 3.00 *14.00*
a. No period after "CENTS" 425.00 675.00
b. "FOUR CENTS." & bar double 17,500.
140 A38(a) 8c org & blk 7.25 *13.50*
141 A38(b) 10c sl bl & brn 12.50 *16.00*
a. No period after "Settlements" 775.00 *800.00*
142 A38(a) 25c grnsh bl & grn 35.00 *52.50*
143 A38(a) 50c gray lil & vio 25.00 *75.00*
144 A38(a) $1 org & red brn 50.00 *125.00*
Nos. 134A-144 (11) 676.25 *1,110.*

A19

1908-11 **Typo.** **Wmk. 3** ***Perf. 14***
Chalky Paper
145 A19 $25 bl & vio, *bl* ('11) 3,600. 2,300.
Revenue cancel 200.
Ovptd. "SPECIMEN" 800.00
146 A19 $500 violet & org *175,000.*
Revenue cancel 1,000.
Ovptd. "SPECIMEN" 4,500.

No. 146 is inscribed "Postage-Revenue" but was probably used only for revenue.
Excellent forgeries of No. 146 exist.

A20

1910 **Chalky Paper**
147 A20 21c maroon & vio 7.00 *40.00*
148 A20 45c black, *green* 3.75 4.50

King George V
A21 A22

A23

A24

A25

A26

Die I (Type A24)

For description of dies I and II see front section of the Catalogue.
The 25c, 50c and $2 denominations of type A24 show the numeral on horizontally-lined tablet.

1912-23 **Chalky Paper** **Wmk. 3**
149 A21 1c green 14.50 1.60
a. 1c pale green ('14) 12.00 6.50
b. 1c blue green ('17) 12.00 2.00
150 A21 1c black ('18) 4.00 2.40
151 A25 2c dp green ('18) 2.25 .55
152 A22 3c scarlet 3.25 .25
a. 3c carmine 3.50 1.35
153 A23 4c gray violet 4.50 .65
154 A23 4c scarlet ('18) 4.00 .25
a. Booklet pane of 1
b. Booklet pane of 12
c. 4c carmine ('18) 2.00 .25
155 A24 5c orange 2.25 1.10
a. 5c yellow orange 5.00 1.60
156 A25 6c dull claret ('20) 2.25 .55
a. 6c deep claret 8.00 3.00
157 A25 8c ultra 3.75 .85
158 A24 10c violet, *yel* 1.60 1.10
a. 10c violet, *lemon* ('16) 19.00 1.40
Ovptd. "SPECIMEN" 100.00
159 A24 10c brt blue ('19) 4.25 .50
a. 10c dp brt blue ('18) 11.00 1.60
160 A26 21c maroon & vio 16.00 *16.00*
161 A24 25c vio & red vio 17.00 15.00
162 A24 30c vio & org ('14) 8.50 6.75
163 A26 45c blk, *bl grn*, ol back ('14) 7.50 *27.50*
Ovptd. "SPECIMEN" 85.00
a. 45c black, *emerald* ('17) 7.25 *13.75*
164 A24 50c black, *grn* ('14) 6.50 5.25
a. 50c blk, *bl grn*, olive back ('18) 32.50 13.50
b. 50c black, *emerald* ('21) 14.50 10.50
c. Die II ('22) 3.25 *5.00*
As "c," ovptd. "SPECIMEN" 85.00
165 A24 $1 blk & red, *bl* ('14) 21.00 17.50
166 A24 $2 grn & red, *yel* ('15) 20.00 52.50
Ovptd. "SPECIMEN" 85.00
a. Same, *orange buff* ('21) 85.00 95.00
b. Same, *pale yellow* ('21) 90.00 110.00
167 A24 $5 grn & red, *grn* ('15) 120.00 85.00
Ovptd. "SPECIMEN" 130.00
a. $5 grn & red, *bl grn*, ol back 190.00 115.00
b. $5 grn & red, *emer* ('15) 240.00 140.00
c. Die II ('23) 145.00 90.00
Nos. 149-167 (19) 263.10 235.30

The 1c, 3c, 5c and 8c are on ordinary paper.

Surface-colored Paper
168 A24 10c violet, *yel* 2.40 1.25
Ovptd. "SPECIMEN" 70.00
169 A26 45c black, *grn* ('14) 7.50 *22.50*
170 A24 $2 grn & red, *yel* ('14) 16.00 *52.50*
171 A24 $5 grn & red, *grn* 120.00 60.00
Nos. 168-171 (4) 145.90 *136.25*

See Nos. 179-201. For surcharges see Nos. B1-B2.

A27

1915
172 A27 $25 bl & vio, *bl* 2,150. 650.00
Revenue cancel 5.75
Ovptd. "SPECIMEN" 500.
173 A27 $100 red & blk, *bl* *8,500.*
Revenue cancel *90.00*
Ovptd. "SPECIMEN" 1,250.
174 A27 $500 org & dl vio *90,000.*
Revenue cancel *200.00*
Ovptd. "SPECIMEN" 4,750.

Although Nos. 173 and 174 were available for postage, it is probable that they were used only for fiscal purposes.
See Nos. 202-204, AR1.

Die II (Type A24)

1921-32 **Ordinary Paper** **Wmk. 4**
179 A21 1c black .65 .25
180 A25 2c green .65 .25
181 A25 2c brown 8.00 4.75
182 A22 3c green 1.75 .90
183 A23 4c scarlet 2.25 *6.25*
184 A23 4c dp violet ('25) .70 .25
185 A23 4c orange ('29) 1.10 .25
186 A24 5c orange ('23) 2.75 1.50
a. Die I 3.75 .25
187 A24 5c dk brown ('32) 3.25 .25
a. Die I ('32) 5.75 .25
188 A25 6c claret 2.50 .25
189 A25 6c scarlet ('27) 3.00 .25
a. 6c rose red ('25) 30.00 11.00
190 A24 10c ultra (I) 2.00 4.25

Chalky Paper
191 A24 10c vio, *yel* ('27) 3.25 .35
a. Die I ('25) 3.00 *14.00*
192 A25 12c ultra 1.35 .25
193 A26 21c mar & vio 7.00 *60.00*
194 A24 25c vio & red vio 5.75 2.00
a. Die I 35.00 90.00
195 A24 30c violet & org 2.25 1.50
a. Die I 29.00 *60.00*
196 A26 35c org & vio 14.00 7.00
197 A26 35c vio & car ('31) 11.50 8.00
198 A24 50c blk, *emer* 2.00 .45
199 A24 $1 blk & red, *bl* 7.00 1.80
200 A24 $2 grn & red, *yel* 11.50 9.25
201 A24 $5 grn & red, *grn* 125.00 45.00
202 A27 $25 bl & vio, *bl* 1,450. 200.00
Ovptd. "SPECIMEN" 425.00
203 A27 $100 red & blk, *bl* 10,000. 3,100.
Revenue cancel 175.00
Ovptd. "SPECIMEN" 1,250.
204 A27 $500 org & dl vio *75,000.*
Revenue cancel 700.00
Ovptd. "SPECIMEN" 4,750.
Nos. 179-201 (23) 219.20 155.00

No. 192 is on ordinary paper.
Nos. 203 and 204 were probably used only for fiscal purposes.

Stamps of 1912-21 Overprinted in Black

1922 **Wmk. 3**
151d A25 2c deep green 50.00 *28.00*
154d A23 4c scarlet 12.00 *26.00*
155d A24 5c orange 12.00 *22.50*
157d A25 8c ultra 2.75 *12.50*
161d A24 25c vio & red vio 5.50 *52.50*
163d A26 45c blk, *bl grn*, ol back 4.00 *50.00*
165d A24 $1 blk & red, *bl* 675.00 *1,800.*
166d A24 $2 grn & red, *yel* 30.00 *160.00*
167d A24 $5 grn & red, *grn* 475.00 *825.00*

Wmk. 4
179d A21 1c black 3.50 *27.50*
180d A25 2c green 2.75 *16.00*
183d A23 4c scarlet 5.00 *52.50*
186d A24 5c orange (II) 3.25 *52.50*
190d A24 10c ultra 2.75 *29.00*
199d A24 $1 blk & red, *bl* 22.50 *160.00*
Nos. 151d-199d (15) 1,306. *3,314.*

Industrial fair at Singapore, Mar. 31-Apr. 15, 1922.

Common Design Types
pictured following the introduction.

Silver Jubilee Issue
Common Design Type

1935, May 6 **Engr.** ***Perf. 11x12***
213 CD301 5c black & ultra 3.50 .35
214 CD301 8c indigo & green 3.75 *3.50*
215 CD301 12c ultra & brown 3.75 8.50
216 CD301 25c brn vio & ind 4.00 *12.75*
Nos. 213-216 (4) 15.00 *25.10*
Set, never hinged 25.00
Set, perf. "SPECIMEN" 240.00

George V — A28

1936-37 **Typo.** ***Perf. 14***
Chalky Paper
217 A28 1c black ('37) 1.60 .25
218 A28 2c green 1.60 .80
220 A28 4c orange brn 2.40 .80
221 A28 5c brown 1.10 .35
222 A28 6c rose red 1.35 1.25
223 A28 8c gray 3.75 .80
224 A28 10c dull vio 2.40 .70
225 A28 12c ultra 2.25 3.00
226 A28 25c rose red & vio 1.60 .60
227 A28 30c org & dk vio 1.40 3.50
229 A28 40c dk vio & car 1.40 2.75
230 A28 50c blk, *emerald* 4.75 1.40
232 A28 $1 red & blk, *blue* 20.00 1.90
233 A28 $2 rose red & gray grn 57.50 11.50
234 A28 $5 grn & red, *grn* ('37) 140.00 11.50
Nos. 217-234 (15) 243.10 41.10
Set, never hinged 325.00
Set, perf. "SPECIMEN" 525.00

Coronation Issue
Common Design Type

1937, May 12 **Engr.** ***Perf. 13½x14***
235 CD302 4c deep orange .65 .25
236 CD302 8c gray black .80 .25
237 CD302 12c bright ultra 1.80 1.10
Nos. 235-237 (3) 3.25 1.60
Set, never hinged 6.00
Set, perf. "SPECIMEN" 240.00

George VI — A29

Die I

Die II

Two Dies

Die I. Printed in two operations. Lines of background touch outside of central oval. Foliage of palms touches outer frame line. Palm frond in front of King's eye has two points.
Die II. Printed from a single plate. Lines of background separated from central oval by a white line. Foliage of palms does not touch outer frame line. Palm frond in front of King's eye has one point.

1937-41 **Typo.** ***Perf. 14***
238 A29 1c black (I) 6.00 .25
239 A29 2c green (I) 11.00 .25
c. Die II ('38) 35.00 .45
239A A29 2c brn org ('41) (II) 1.25 *20.00*
239B A29 3c green ('41) (II) 5.00 4.25
240 A29 4c brown org (I) 13.50 .25
a. Die II ('38) 50.00 .25
241 A29 5c brown (I) 12.00 .35
a. Die II ('39) 20.00 .25

242 A29 6c rose red ('38) (I) 5.50 .65
243 A29 8c gray ('38) (I) 19.00 .25
244 A29 10c dull vio (I) 6.00 .25
245 A29 12c ultra ('38) (I) 6.00 .35
245A A29 15c ultra ('41) (II) 5.00 *10.50*
246 A29 25c rose red & vio (I) 25.00 1.10
247 A29 30c org & vio (I) 11.00 2.00
248 A29 40c dk vio & rose red (I) 10.00 2.50
249 A29 50c blk, *emer* ('38) (I) 10.00 .45
250 A29 $1 red & blk, *bl* ('38) (I) 15.00 .40
251 A29 $2 rose red & gray grn ('38) (I) 30.00 12.50
252 A29 $5 grn & red, *grn* ('38) (I) 15.00 7.50
Nos. 238-252 (18) 206.25 63.80
Set, never hinged 375.00
Set, perf. "SPECIMEN" 900.00

For overprints see Nos. 256-271, N1-N29 and Malaya, Malacca Nos. N1-N14, Penang Nos. N1-N26.

Stamps and Type of 1937-41 Overprinted in Red or Black

1945-48
256 A29 1c black (R) .25 .25
257 A29 2c brown org (II) .25 .25
a. Die I ('46) 7.50 *3.75*
258 A29 3c green .25 .25
259 A29 5c brown .75 .60
260 A29 6c gray .25 .25
261 A29 8c rose red .25 .25
262 A29 10c dull vio (I) .30 .25
a. 10c claret (II) ('48) *10.00* 1.25
263 A29 12c ultra 1.75 *3.25*
264 A29 15c ultra (Bk) 2.25 *4.75*
265 A29 15c ultra (R) .25 .25
266 A29 25c rose red & vio 1.40 .25
a. Double overprint 400.00
267 A29 50c blk, *emer* (R) .60 .25
268 A29 $1 rose red & blk 2.00 .25
269 A29 $2 rose red & gray grn 2.50 .65
270 A29 $5 grn & red, *grn* 72.50 72.50
271 A29 $5 brn org & vio 3.75 2.75
Nos. 256-271 (16) 89.30 87.00
Set, never hinged 140.00

The letters "B M A" are initials of "British Military Administration."

An 8c gray with BMA overprint was prepared but not issued. Value $5.

The 6c gray, 8c rose red and $5 brown orange & violet exist without BMA overprint, but were issued only with it.

No. 262a does not exist without overprint. No. 262 exists in at least three shades.

POSTAL-FISCAL STAMP

Type of 1915 with head George VI Inscribed "REVENUE" at each side

1938
AR1 A27 $25 Blue & purple, *blue* 1,450. 675.00

Although documentation authorizing its postal use has not been found, No. AR1 was frequently used as a postage stamp throughout 1941.

SEMI-POSTAL STAMPS

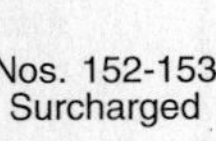

Nos. 152-153 Surcharged

1917 Wmk. 3 *Perf. 14*
B1 A22 3c + 2c scarlet 3.00 *32.50*
a. No period after "C" 575.00 *975.00*
B2 A23 4c + 2c gray violet 4.00 *35.00*
a. No period after "C" 525.00 *900.00*

POSTAGE DUE STAMPS

D1

1924-26 Typo. Wmk. 4 *Perf. 14*
J1 D1 1c violet 12.50 *5.75*
On cover 110.00
J2 D1 2c black 3.75 1.25
On cover 25.00
J3 D1 4c green ('26) 2.25 *3.00*
On cover 75.00
J4 D1 8c red 4.75 .60
On cover 40.00
J5 D1 10c orange 6.50 .90
On cover 40.00
J6 D1 12c ultramarine 7.50 .75
On cover 50.00
Nos. J1-J6 (6) 37.25 *12.25*
Set never hinged 55.00
Set, ovptd. "SPECIMEN" 350.00

Cover values are for properly franked commercial covers. Philatelic usages also exist and sell for less.

OCCUPATION STAMPS

Issued Under Japanese Occupation

Nos. 238, 239A-B, 243 and 245A Hstmpd. in Red

1942, Mar. 16 Wmk. 4 *Perf. 14*
N1 A29 1c black 22.50 22.50
N2 A29 2c brown orange 16.00 16.00
N3 A29 3c green 70.00 *85.00*
N4 A29 8c gray 27.50 22.50
N5 A29 15c ultra 21.00 20.00
Nos. N1-N5 (5) 157.00 166.00
Set, never hinged 200.00

Other denominations with this handstamp are believed to be proofs.

The handstamp reads: "Seal of Post Office of Malayan Military Department."

Stamps of 1937-41, Handstamped in Red, Black, Violet or Brown

1942, Apr. 3

Handstamped in Red
N6 A29 1c black 4.00 4.00
N7 A29 2c orange 3.50 2.50
N8 A29 3c green 4.00 2.50
N9 A29 5c brown 30.00 32.50
N10 A29 8c gray 9.00 2.50
a. Pair, one without ovpt. 3,250.
N11 A29 10c dull violet 80.00 52.50
N12 A29 12c ultramarine 120.00 160.00
N13 A29 15c ultramarine 3.75 4.00
N14 A29 30c orange & vio 4,500. 4,500.
N15 A29 40c dk vio & rose red 170.00 110.00
N16 A29 50c blk, *emerald* 80.00 60.00
N17 A29 $1 red & blk, *bl* 110.00 80.00
N18 A29 $2 rose red & gray grn 190.00 240.00
N19 A29 $5 grn & red, *grn* 260.00 300.00

Handstamp in Black
N6b A29 1c black 425.00 425.00
N7b A29 2c orange 140.00 150.00
N8b A29 3c green 450.00 475.00
N9b A29 5c brown 625.00 625.00
N10b A29 8c gray 290.00 290.00

Handstamp in Violet
N6c A29 1c black 1,700. 800.00
N7c A29 2c orange 275.00 250.00
N7D A29 2c green 4,250. 2,900.
N8c A29 3c green 1,700. 850.00

Handstamp in Brown
N7e A29 2c orange 1,300. 800.00
N11e A29 10c dull violet 1,500. 900.00
N15e A29 40c dk vio & rose red 1,200. 550.00

Nos. N6-N7, N9, N11-N12, N15-N19 with red handstamp were used in Sumatra. The 2c green with red handstamp was not regularly issued. Value, $400.

Straits Settlements Nos. 239A, 239B, 243 and 245A Ovptd. in Black

1942
N20 A29 2c brown orange 4.00 1.00
a. Inverted overprint 17.50 27.50
b. Dbl. ovpt., one invtd. 60.00 70.00
N21 A29 3c green 62.50 *75.00*
N22 A29 8c gray 11.00 4.75
a. Inverted overprint 22.50 45.00
N23 A29 15c ultra 26.00 16.00
Nos. N20-N23 (4) 103.50 96.75
Set never hinged 165.00

Straits Settlements Nos. 239A and 243 Overprinted in Black

1942, Nov. 3
N24 A29 2c brown orange 14.00 *25.00*
a. Inverted overprint 375.00 425.00
N25 A29 8c gray 15.00 *25.00*
a. Inverted overprint 375.00 425.00

Agricultural-Horticultural Exhibition held at Kuala Lumpur, Selangor, Nov. 1-2, 1942. Sold only at a temporary post office at the exhibition.

Straits Settlements Nos. 243, 245 and 248 Ovptd. in Black or Red

1943
N26 A29 8c gray (Bk) 1.60 1.00
a. Inverted overprint 60.00 75.00
b. Pair, ovpt. omitted on one stamp 900.00
N27 A29 8c gray (R) 2.75 4.00
N28 A29 12c ultramarine 2.00 16.00
N29 A29 40c dk vio & rose red 4.25 8.00
Nos. N26-N29 (4) 10.60 29.00
Set never hinged 17.00

The Japanese characters read: "Japanese Postal Service."

SUDAN

sü-'dan

LOCATION — Northeastern Africa, south of Egypt
GOVT. — Administered jointly by Egypt and Great Britain
AREA — 967,500 sq. mi.
POP. — 20,564,364 (1983)
CAPITAL — Khartoum

10 Milliemes = 1 Piaster
100 Piasters = 1 Pound

Watermarks

Wmk. 71 — Rosette

Wmk. 179 — Multiple Crescent and Star

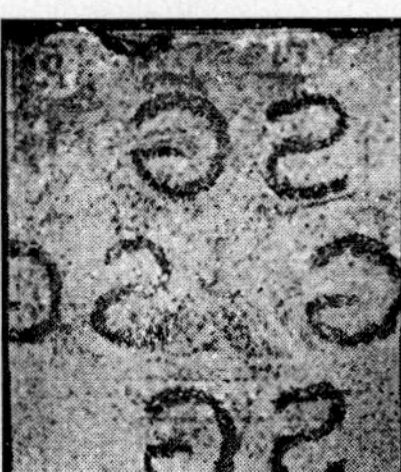

Wmk. 214 — Multiple S G

Egyptian Stamps of 1884-93 Overprinted in Black

1897, Mar. 1 Wmk. 119 *Perf. 14*
1 A18 1m brown 3.25 *1.75*
Never hinged 5.25
a. Inverted overprint 250.00
2 A19 2m green 1.25 *1.75*
Never hinged 3.75
3 A20 3m orange 1.50 *1.50*
Never hinged 2.75
4 A22 5m carmine rose 2.00 .70
Never hinged 3.75
a. Inverted overprint 325.00 275.00
5 A14 1p ultra 7.00 2.00
Never hinged 13.50
6 A15 2p orange brown 65.00 16.00
Never hinged 110.00
7 A16 5p gray 65.00 25.00
Never hinged 105.00
a. Double overprint *6,000.*
8 A23 10p violet 50.00 *65.00*
Never hinged 60.00
Nos. 1-8 (8) 195.00 113.70

Unofficial reprints exist. Counterfeits of Nos. 1-8 are plentiful.

Camel Post — A1

1898, Mar. 1 Typo. Wmk. 71
9 A1 1m rose & brn 1.00 *2.50*
Never hinged 3.50
10 A1 2m brown & grn 2.00 2.40
Never hinged 7.00
11 A1 3m green & vio 2.00 2.00
Never hinged 7.50
12 A1 5m black & rose 2.00 1.25
Never hinged 6.50
13 A1 1p yel brn & ultra 17.00 2.50
Never hinged 27.50
14 A1 2p ultra & blk 42.50 3.00
Never hinged 57.50
15 A1 5p grn & org brn 42.50 15.00
Never hinged 70.00
16 A1 10p dp vio & blk 35.00 4.00
Never hinged 55.00
Nos. 9-16 (8) 144.00 32.65

See Nos. 17-27, 43-50. For overprints see Nos. C3, MO1-MO15, O1-O9, O17-O24. For surcharges see Nos. 28, 62, C16.

1902-21 Wmk. 179
17 A1 1m car rose & brn ('05) 1.00 .50
Never hinged 2.50
18 A1 2m brown & grn 1.50 .25
Never hinged 3.50
19 A1 3m grn & vio ('03) 2.00 .25
Never hinged 4.50
20 A1 4m ol brn & bl ('07) 1.25 *2.25*
Never hinged 3.00
21 A1 4m brn & red ('07) 1.25 .75
Never hinged 3.00
22 A1 5m blk & rose red ('03) 1.75 .25
Never hinged 3.75
23 A1 1p brn & ultra ('03) 2.00 .30
Never hinged 4.50
24 A1 2p ultra & blk ('08) 40.00 1.25
Never hinged 52.50
25 A1 2p org & vio brn, chalky paper ('21) 11.00 *12.00*
Never hinged 10.50
26 A1 5p grn & org brn ('08) 30.00 .30
Never hinged 52.50
a. On chalky paper 37.50 4.50
27 A1 10p dp vio & blk ('11) 25.00 3.75
Never hinged 52.50
a. On chalky paper 32.50 10.00
Nos. 17-27 (11) 116.75 21.85

No. 15 Surcharged in Black

1903, Sept. **Wmk. 71**
28 A1 5m on 5p 8.50 *9.50*
Never hinged 15.00
a. Inverted surcharge 325.00 *275.00*

A2

1921-22 **Typo.** **Wmk. 179**
29 A2 1m orange & blk ('22) 1.00 *5.25*
Never hinged 1.90
30 A2 2m dk brn & org ('22) 9.00 *13.50*
Never hinged 16.50
a. 2m dark brown & yellow ('23) 12.00 12.00
Never hinged 18.00
31 A2 3m green & vio ('22) 2.50 *11.00*
Never hinged 4.50
32 A2 4m brown & grn ('22) 7.50 9.00
Never hinged 12.00
33 A2 5m blk & ol brn ('22) 2.25 .25
Never hinged 4.50
34 A2 10m black & car ('22) 5.75 .25
Never hinged 9.00
35 A2 15m org brn & ultra 5.75 1.25
Never hinged 6.00
Nos. 29-35 (7) 33.75 40.50

See Nos. 36-42. For overprints see Nos. C1-C2, O10-O16.
For surcharges see Nos. 60-61.

1927-40 **Wmk. 214**
Chalky Paper
36 A2 1m org yel & blk .40 .30
37 A2 2m dk brn & org .40 .25
38 A2 3m green & violet .40 .25
39 A2 4m brown & green .30 .25
40 A2 5m blk & ol brn .30 .25
a. Booklet pane of 4
41 A2 10m black & car .85 .25
42 A2 15m org brn & ultra 2.25 .35
43 A1 2p orange & vio brn 2.60 .25
44 A1 3p dk bl & red brn ('40) 5.50 .25
45 A1 4p blk & ultra ('36) 2.50 .25
46 A1 5p dk grn & org brn 1.00 .25
47 A1 6p blk & pale bl ('36) 10.00 1.75
48 A1 8p blk & pck grn ('36) 10.00 3.00
49 A1 10p dp vio & blk 5.50 .35
50 A1 20p bl & lt bl ('35) 11.00 .45
Nos. 36-50 (15) 53.00 8.45

Thick, Smooth, Unsurfaced Paper ('41)
36a A2 1m org yel & blk 1.00 .25
37a A2 2m dk brn & org 1.60 .25
38a A2 3m green & violet 3.00 .35
39a A2 4m brown & green 3.75 .35
40b A2 5m blk & ol brn 2.75 .25
41a A2 10m black & car 3.25 .25
42a A2 15m org brn & ultra 2.25 .25
43a A1 2p orange & vio brn 4.25 .25
44a A1 3p dk bl & red brn 18.00 .25
46a A1 5p dk grn & org brn 5.50 2.25
47a A1 6p blk & pale blue 37.50 2.25
48a A1 8p blk & pck grn 50.00 4.50
49a A1 10p brt mauve & blk 9.50 .75
50a A1 20p bl & lt blue 8.00 .25
Nos. 36a-50a (14) 150.35 12.45

Charles George Gordon — A3

Gordon Memorial College A4

Memorial Service at Khartoum — A5

1935, Jan. 1 **Engr.** ***Perf. 13½x14***
51 A3 5m deep green .30 .25
52 A3 10m brown .75 .25
53 A3 13m ultra .80 *12.00*
54 A3 15m carmine 1.50 .25
55 A4 2p deep blue 1.90 .25
56 A4 5p orange 2.00 .85
57 A4 10p dull violet 7.75 *8.00*
58 A5 20p black 27.50 *72.50*
59 A5 50p red brown 85.00 *155.00*
Nos. 51-59 (9) 127.50 249.35
Set, never hinged 325.00

50th anniv. of the death of Gen. Charles George ("Chinese") Gordon (1833-85).

No. 41 Surcharged in Black

Wmk. Multiple S G (214)
1940, Feb. 25 **Typo.** ***Perf. 14***
60 A2 5m on 10m black & car 1.50 1.50

Nos. 40 and 48 Surcharged in Black

a

b

1940-41
61 A2(a) 4½p on 5m ('41) 47.50 12.00
62 A1(b) 4½p on 8p 42.50 9.00

AIR POST STAMPS

Nos. 40-41, 43 Overprinted in Black

Nos. C1-C2

No. C3

1931 **Wmk. 214** ***Perf. 11½x12½, 14***
C1 A2 5m blk & olive brown .50 *1.00*
Never hinged 1.00
C2 A2 10m blk & carmine 1.50 *6.00*
Never hinged 2.75
C3 A1 2p org & vio brown 1.00 *5.00*
Never hinged 2.00
Nos. C1-C3 (3) 3.00 *12.00*

Statue of Gen. C. G. Gordon AP3

1931-35 **Engr.** ***Perf. 14***
C4 AP3 3m dk brn & grn ('33) 3.50 *7.25*
Never hinged 7.00
C5 AP3 5m grn & blk 1.50 .25
Never hinged 3.00
C6 AP3 10m car rose & blk 1.50 .25
Never hinged 3.00
C7 AP3 15m dk brn & brn .75 .25
Never hinged 1.50
C8 AP3 2p org & blk .65 .25
Never hinged 1.50
C9 AP3 2½p bl & red vio ('33) 4.75 .25
Never hinged 9.50
C10 AP3 3p gray & blk 1.00 .25
Never hinged 2.00
C11 AP3 3½p dl vio & blk 2.25 .90
Never hinged 4.50
C12 AP3 4½p gray & brn 12.50 *16.50*
Never hinged 25.00
C13 AP3 5p ultra & blk 1.75 .35
Never hinged 3.50
C14 AP3 7½p pck grn & dk grn ('35) 12.00 6.00
Never hinged 24.00
C15 AP3 10p pck bl & sep ('35) 11.50 2.00
Never hinged 23.00
Nos. C4-C15 (12) 53.65 34.50

See Nos. C23-C30. For surcharges see Nos. C17-C22, C31-C34.

No. 43 Surcharged in Black

1932, July 18 **Typo.**
C16 A1 2½p on 2p 2.00 *4.00*
Never hinged 4.00

Nos. C6, C4-C5, C12 Surcharged

1935 **Engr.** ***Perf. 14***
C17 AP3 15m on 10m .40 .25
Never hinged 1.00
a. Double surcharge 1,000. *1,400.*
b. Arabic characters omitted 750.00
C18 AP3 2½p on 3m 1.00 *6.00*
Never hinged 2.00
a. "½" 2¼mm high instead of 3mm 5.00 *25.00*
b. Second Arabic character of surcharge omitted 50.00 *125.00*
C19 AP3 2½p on 5m .50 *1.00*
Never hinged 1.00
a. "½" 2¼mm high instead of 3mm 1.50 *3.00*
b. Second Arabic character of surcharge omitted 40.00 *60.00*
c. Inverted surcharge 1,000. *1,400.*
d. As "a," inverted *30,000.* *20,000.*
e. As "b," inverted *4,500.* *6,000.*
f. Pair, C19c and C19d *37,500.*
C20 AP3 3p on 4½p 1.75 *22.00*
Never hinged 3.50
C21 AP3 7½p on 4½p 6.50 *55.00*
Never hinged 13.00
a. "7¼" instead of "7½"
C22 AP3 10p on 4½p 6.50 *55.00*
Never hinged 13.00
Nos. C17-C22 (6) 16.65 *139.25*

Type of 1931-35
1936-37 ***Perf. 11½x12½***
C23 AP3 15m dk brn & brn ('37) 4.50 .25
Never hinged 9.00
C24 AP3 2p org & blk ('37) 5.00 *18.00*
Never hinged 10.00
C25 AP3 2½p bl & red vio 2.75 .25
Never hinged 5.50
C26 AP3 3p gray & blk ('37) .75 .40
Never hinged 1.50
C27 AP3 3½p dl vio & blk ('37) 2.25 *15.00*
Never hinged 4.50
C28 AP3 5p ultra & blk ('37) 4.00 .40
Never hinged 8.00
C29 AP3 7½p pck grn & dk grn ('37) 4.25 *11.00*
Never hinged 8.50
C30 AP3 10p pck bl & sep ('37) 6.50 *30.00*
Never hinged 13.00
Nos. C23-C30 (8) 30.00 *75.30*

Nos. C25, C11, C14 and C15 Srchd. as in 1935

1938 **Wmk. 214** ***Perf. 11½x12½, 14***
C31 AP3 5m on 2½p 1.50 .30
Never hinged 3.00
C32 AP3 3p on 3½p 27.50 *60.00*
Never hinged 60.00
a. On No. C27 700.00 *750.00*
C33 AP3 3p on 7½p 5.00 *7.25*
Never hinged 10.00
a. On No. C29 700.00 *750.00*
C34 AP3 5p on 10p 1.50 *5.50*
Never hinged 3.00
a. On No. C30 700.00 *750.00*
Nos. C31-C34 (4) 35.50 73.05

A 5p on 2½p (No. C25) exists from a trial printing. Value, $425 unused and used.

POSTAGE DUE STAMPS

Postage Due Stamps of Egypt, 1889, Overprinted in Black

1897 **Wmk. 119** ***Perf. 14***
J1 D3 2m green 2.50 *6.00*
J2 D3 4m maroon 2.50 *6.00*
J3 D3 1p ultra 14.00 *5.00*
J4 D3 2p orange 14.00 *10.00*
Nos. J1-J4 (4) 33.00 27.00

Steamboat on Nile River — D1

1901 **Typo.** **Wmk. 179**
J5 D1 2m orange brn & blk 1.00 .85
J6 D1 4m blue green & brn 3.00 1.25
J7 D1 10m bl vio & bl grn 6.00 5.00
J8 D1 20m car rose & ultra 5.00 4.75
Nos. J5-J8 (4) 15.00 11.85

1927-30 **Wmk. Multiple S G (214)**
J9 D1 2m org brn & blk ('30) 3.00 3.00
J10 D1 4m blue grn & brn 1.50 1.00
J11 D1 10m violet & blue grn 2.50 *2.00*
Nos. J9-J11 (3) 7.00 6.00

ARMY OFFICIAL STAMPS

Regular Issues of 1898 and 1902-08 Overprinted in Black

Nos. MO1, MO3 and MO2, MO4

1905 **Wmk. 71** ***Perf. 14***
MO1 A1 1m rose & brown 190.00 *200.00*
a. "OFFICIAL" 4,750. 3,250.
On cover, single franking 25,000.
b. Pair, #MO1 and #MO2 4,500.
MO2 A1 1m rose & brown 3,000. *3,000.*
Wmk. 179
MO3 A1 1m car rose & brn 6.50 3.00
a. "OFFICIAL" 90.00 55.00
On cover, single franking 300.00
b. Inverted overprint 70.00 60.00
c. Horizontal overprint 475.00
MO4 A1 1m car rose & brn 60.00 30.00
On cover, single franking 175.00
a. Inverted overprint 350.00 375.00

Regular Issues of 1902-11 Overprinted in Black

1906-11
MO5 A1 1m car rose & brn 3.00 .50
a. "Army" and "Service" 14mm apart 550.00 400.00
b. Inverted overprint 650.00 *700.00*
c. Pair, one without ovpt. *7,000.*
d. Double overprint *1,750.*
e. "Service" omitted *4,500.*
MO6 A1 2m brn & grn 22.50 1.25
a. Pair, one without ovpt. 4,000.
b. "Army" omitted 4,200. *4,200.*

MO7 A1 3m grn & vio 22.50 .50
a. Inverted overprint 2,200.
MO8 A1 5m blk & rose red 3.50 .25
a. Inverted overprint 375.00
b. Double overprint 325.00 250.00
c. Double ovpt., one invtd. 1,500. 550.00
MO9 A1 1p yel brn & ultra 22.50 .40
a. "Army" omitted 3,250. 3,250.
MO10 A1 2p ultra & blk ('09) 85.00 15.00
a. Double overprint 3,400.
MO11 A1 5p grn & org brn ('08) 175.00 75.00
MO12 A1 10p dp vio & blk ('11) 625.00 *750.00*
Nos. MO5-MO12 (8) 959.00 842.90

Same Overprint On Regular Issue of 1898

Wmk. 71

MO13 A1 2p ultra & blk 90.00 11.50
a. Inverted overprint
MO14 A1 5p grn & org brn 130.00 *250.00*
MO15 A1 10p dp vio & blk 175.00 475.00

There are two types of this overprint which may be distinguished by the size and shape of the "y."

PERFORATED ARMY OFFICIAL STAMPS

Stamps of Sudan punched with "AS" (Army Service) replaced the overprinted Army Official stamps Jan. 1, 1912.

These perforated Official stamps were used on internal military mail until the return of the Egyptian Army to Egypt in 1924. They continued to be used on mail to foreign destinations until supplies of individual denominations were exhausted or until 1936, when remaining stocks were destroyed. They were replaced by stamps overprinted or punched "SG."

Catalogue numbers are "MOA" plus Scott No. of basic, unoverprinted stamps.

On Second Large Camel Post Issue
23 holes: 12 in "A," 11 in "S"

1912-22

MOA17 A1 1m car rose & brn 65.00 7.25
MOA18 A1 2m brn & grn 9.25 .75
MOA19 A1 3m grn & vio 57.50 3.50
MOA22 A1 5m blk & rose red 15.00 .55
MOA23 A1 1p brn & ultra 29.00 .85
MOA24 A1 2p ultra & blk 70.00 5.50
MOA25 A1 2p org & vio brn ('22) 75.00 62.50
MOA26 A1 5p grn & org brn 80.00 35.00
a. Chalky paper (#26a) 80.00 35.00
MOA27 A1 10p dp vio & blk 550.00 300.00
Nos. MOA17-MOA27 (9) 950.75 415.90

On Small Camel Post Issue
17 holes: 8 in "A," 9 in "S"

1922-24

MOA30 A2 2m dk brn & org 85.00 50.00
MOA33 A2 5m blk & ol brn 16.00 4.50
MOA34 A2 10m black & car 22.50 7.00
Nos. MOA30-MOA34 (3) 123.50 61.50

OFFICIAL STAMPS

PERFORATED OFFICIAL STAMPS

Stamps of Sudan punched with "SG" (Sudan Government) were issued for franking official mail in 1900-1901 and again in 1913-30. They were used on internal correspondence until 1932 and for foreign correspondence until 1936.

The perforated initials can appear upright, inverted, reversed, and inverted and reversed on the 1900-01 stamps, but upright only on later issues.

Values are for very fine examples, well-centered and free of encroaching perfin holes.

Catalogue numbers are "OA" plus Scott No. of basic, unoverprinted stamps.

On 1897 Ovpt. on Egypt
26 holes: 14 in "S," 12 in "G"

1900, Feb. 8

OA4 A22 5m carmine rose 55.00 17.50

On First Large Camel Post
26 holes: 14 in "S," 12 in "G"

1901, Jan.

OA9 A1 1m rose & brn 50.00 32.50

Regular Issue of 1898 Overprinted in Black

1902-06 Wmk. 71 *Perf. 14*

O1 A1 1m rose & brn 3.50 *11.00*
Never hinged 7.00
a. Inverted overprint 325.00 *450.00*
b. Round periods 8.00 *45.00*
c. Double overprint 650.00
d. Oval "O" in overprint 90.00
e. As "d," inverted overprint 5,500.
O2 A1 10p dp vio & blk ('06) 16.00 *27.50*
Never hinged 32.50

Same Ovpt. on Stamps of 1902-11

1903-12 Wmk. 179

O3 A1 1m car rose & brn ('04) .60 .25
Never hinged 1.20
a. Double overprint
O4 A1 3m grn & vio ('04) 2.50 .25
Never hinged 5.00
a. Double overprint
O5 A1 5m blk & rose red 2.50 .25
Never hinged 5.00
O6 A1 1p yel brn & ultra 6.00 .25
Never hinged 12.00
O7 A1 2p ultra & blk 24.00 .25
Never hinged 48.00
O8 A1 5p grn & org brn 2.50 .40
Never hinged 5.00
O9 A1 10p dp vio & blk 5.00 70.00
Never hinged 10.00
Nos. O3-O9 (7) 43.10 71.65

On Second Large Camel Post
25 holes: 12 in "S," 13 in "G"

1913-22

OA17 A1 1m car rose & brn 12.50 .30
Never hinged 25.00
OA18 A1 2m brn & grn ('15) 12.00 8.50
Never hinged 24.00
OA19 A1 3m grn & vio 20.00 .80
Never hinged 40.00
OA22 A1 5m blk & rose red 6.75 .25
Never hinged 13.50
OA23 A1 1p brn & ultra 9.25 .40
Never hinged 18.50
OA24 A1 2p ultra & blk 20.00 .75
Never hinged 40.00
OA25 A1 2p org & vio brn ('22) 55.00 8.00
Never hinged 110.00
OA26 A1 5p grn & org brn 40.00 1.75
Never hinged 80.00
a. On chalky paper 40.00 5.00
Never hinged 80.00
OA27 A1 10p dp vio & blk ('14) 50.00 35.00
Never hinged 100.00
a. On chalky paper 50.00 35.00
Never hinged 100.00
Nos. OA17-OA27 (9) 225.50 55.75

On First Small Camel Post Issue
19 holes: 9 in "S," 10 in "G"

1922

OA31 A2 3m green & vio 19.00 16.00
OA32 A2 4m brown & grn 26.00 10.00
OA33 A2 5m blk & ol brn 5.00 1.75
OA34 A2 10m black & car 5.00 1.75
Nos. OA31-OA34 (4) 55.00 29.50

19 holes: 9 in "S," 10 in "G"

1927-30

OA38 A2 3m org yel & blk ('28) 18.00 4.00
OA39 A2 4m brn & grn ('30) 90.00 55.00
OA40 A2 5m blk & ol brn 7.50 .25
OA41 A2 10m black & car 22.00 .40

25 holes: 12 in "S," 13 in "G"

OA43 A1 2p org & vio brn 25.00 1.10
OA46 A1 5p dk grn & org brn 22.00 4.00
OA49 A1 10p dp vio & blk 47.50 11.00
Nos. OA38-OA49 (7) 232.00 75.75

Regular Issue of 1927-40 Overprinted in Black

Perf. 14, 13½x14

1936-46 Wmk. 214

O10 A2 1m dk org & int blk ('46) 2.25 *12.50*
O11 A2 2m dk brn & dk org ('45) 2.25 *8.00*
O12 A2 3m green & vio ('37) 2.00 .25
O13 A2 4m brown & green 3.25 *4.00*
O14 A2 5m blk & ol brn ('40) 3.00 .25
O15 A2 10m blk & car ('46) .90 .25
O16 A2 15m org brn & ultra ('37) 7.50 .35

Regular Issue of 1927-40 Overprinted in Black

O17 A1 2p org & vio brn ('37) 11.50 .25
O18 A1 3p dk bl & red brn ('46) 5.25 3.00
O19 A1 4p blk & ultra ('46) 22.00 5.50
O20 A1 5p dk grn & org brn 8.50 *9.00*
O21 A1 6p blk & pale bl ('46) 6.00 7.00
O22 A1 8p blk & pck grn ('46) 4.00 *22.50*
O23 A1 10p dp vio & blk ('37) 37.50 6.50
O24 A1 20p bl & lt bl ('46) 25.00 *32.50*
Nos. O10-O24 (15) 140.90 111.85

SURINAM

ˈsur-ə-ˌnam

(Dutch Guiana)

LOCATION — On the northeast coast of South America, bordering on the Atlantic Ocean
GOVT. — Dutch Colony
AREA — 70,087 sq. mi.
POP. — 370,000 (est. 1984)
CAPITAL — Paramaribo

100 Cents = 1 Gulden (Florin)

Watermark

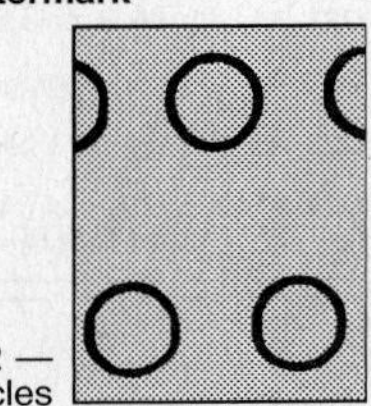

Wmk. 202 — Circles

Early issues of Surinam were sent to the colony without gum. Many of these were subsequently gummed locally.

King William III — A1

Perf. 11½, 11½x12, 12½x12, 13½, 14

1873-89 Typo. Unwmk.

Without Gum

No.	Type	Description	Unused	Used
1	A1	1c lil gray ('85)	2.50	*3.00*
2	A1	2c yellow ('85)	1.75	1.75
3	A1	2½c rose	1.75	1.75
4	A1	3c green	21.00	18.50
5	A1	5c dull violet	20.00	7.00
6	A1	10c bister	4.00	2.75
7	A1	12½c sl bl ('85)	21.00	8.25
8	A1	15c gray ('89)	25.00	8.25
9	A1	20c green ('89)	37.50	35.00
10	A1	25c grnsh blue	85.00	10.00
11	A1	25c ultra	300.00	25.00
12	A1	30c red brn ('88)	35.00	*37.50*
13	A1	40c dk brn ('89)	32.50	32.50
14	A1	50c brown org	32.50	21.00
15	A1	1g red brn & gray ('89)	52.50	52.50
16	A1	2.50g grn & org ('79)	80.00	70.00
		Nos. 1-16 (16)	752.00	334.75

Perf. 14, Small Holes

No.	Type	Description	Unused	Used
3b	A1	2½c rose	12.00	*14.00*
4b	A1	3c green	22.00	*29.00*
5b	A1	5c dull violet	22.00	18.00
6b	A1	10c bister	21.00	*25.00*
11b	A1	25c ultra	300.00	72.50
14b	A1	50c brown org	57.50	50.00
		Nos. 3b-14b (6)	434.50	208.50

The paper of Nos. 3-6, 11 and 14 sometimes has an accidental bluish tinge of varying strength. During its manufacture a chemical whitener (bluing agent) was added in varying quantities. No particular printing was made on bluish paper.

"Small hole" varieties have the spaces between the holes wider than the diameter of the holes.

Nos. 1-16 and 3b-14b exist with gum.

For surcharges see Nos. 23, 31-35, 39-42.

Numeral of Value — A2

1890 ***Perf. 11½x11, 12½***

Without Gum

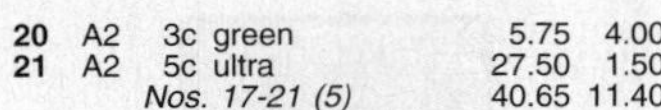

No.	Type	Description	Unused	Used
17	A2	1c gray	1.90	1.40
18	A2	2c yellow brn	3.00	2.50
19	A2	2½c carmine	2.50	2.00
20	A2	3c green	5.75	4.00
21	A2	5c ultra	27.50	1.50
		Nos. 17-21 (5)	40.65	11.40

Nos. 17-21 exist with gum.

For surcharges see Nos. 63-64.

A3

1892, Aug. 11 ***Perf. 10½***

Without Gum

No.	Type	Description	Unused	Used
22	A3	2½c black & org	1.90	1.25
a.		First and fifth vertical words have fancy "F"	27.50	17.50
b.		Imperf.	2.50	
c.		As "a," imperf.	32.50	

No. 14 Surcharged in Black

1892, Aug. 1 ***Perf. 14***

Without Gum

No.	Type	Description	Unused	Used
23	A1	2½c on 50c	250.00	12.00
a.		Perf. 12½x12	375.00	12.00
b.		Perf. 11½x12	425.00	17.50
c.		Double surcharge	375.00	275.00
d.		Perf. 14, small holes	275.00	12.00

Nos. 23-23c were issued without gum.

Queen Wilhelmina — A5

1892-93 Typo. ***Perf. 12½***

Without Gum

No.	Type	Description	Unused	Used
25	A5	10c bister	42.50	3.25
26	A5	12½c rose lilac	50.00	5.75
27	A5	15c gray	4.00	2.75
28	A5	20c green	4.50	3.25
29	A5	25c blue	10.00	5.75
30	A5	30c red brown	5.75	5.00
		Nos. 25-30 (6)	116.75	25.75

Nos. 25-30 exist with gum.

For surcharges see Nos. 65-66.

Nos. 7-12 Surcharged

1898 ***Perf. 11½x12, 12½x12, 13½***

Without Gum

No.	Type	Description	Unused	Used
31	A1	10c on 12½c sl bl	27.50	4.00
32	A1	10c on 15c gray	65.00	55.00
33	A1	10c on 20c green	5.25	5.00
34	A1	10c on 25c grnsh bl	11.00	6.25
c.		Perf. 11½x12	12.00	12.00
34A	A1	10c on 25c ultra	575.00	500.00
b.		Perf. 11½x12	675.00	600.00
35	A1	10c on 30c red brn	4.25	4.25
a.		Double surcharge	325.00	

Dangerous counterfeits exist.

Netherlands Nos. 80, 83-84 Surcharged

No. 36

Nos. 37-38

1900, Jan. 8 ***Perf. 12½***

Without Gum

No.	Type	Description	Unused	Used
36	A11	50c on 50c	27.50	9.00

Engr.

Perf. 11½x11

No.	Type	Description	Unused	Used
37	A12	100c on 1g dk grn	25.00	14.00
38	A12	2.50g on 2½g brn lil	25.00	12.50
		Nos. 36-38 (3)	77.50	35.50

For surcharge see No. 67.

Nos. 13-16 Surcharged

Perf. 11½, 11½x12, 12½x12, 14

1900 Typo.

Without Gum

No.	Type	Description	Unused	Used
39	A1	25c on 40c	5.00	3.50
40	A1	25c on 50c	5.00	3.50
a.		Perf. 14, small holes	130.00	*140.00*
b.		Perf. 11½x12	3.75	3.75
41	A1	50c on 1g	40.00	35.00
42	A1	50c on 2.50g	150.00	*175.00*
		Nos. 39-42 (4)	200.00	217.00

Counterfeits of No. 42 exist.

A9

A10

Queen Wilhelmina — A11

1902-08 Typo. ***Perf. 12½***

Without Gum

No.	Type	Description	Unused	Used
44	A9	½c violet	1.00	.90
45	A9	1c olive grn	2.10	1.25
46	A9	2c yellow brn	11.50	4.50
47	A9	2½c blue grn	5.00	.45
48	A9	3c orange	8.25	5.25
49	A9	5c red	8.25	.45
50	A9	7½c gray ('08)	18.00	8.25
51	A10	10c slate	12.00	.95
52	A10	12½c deep blue	4.50	.45
53	A10	15c dp brown	30.00	10.50
54	A10	20c olive grn	27.50	5.25
55	A10	22½c brn & ol grn	24.00	13.00
56	A10	25c violet	20.00	1.25
57	A10	30c orange brn	47.50	15.00
58	A10	50c lake brown	37.50	9.25

Engr.

Perf. 11

No.	Type	Description	Unused	Used
59	A11	1g violet	60.00	20.00
60	A11	2½g slate blue	60.00	65.00
		Nos. 44-60 (17)	377.10	161.70

Nos. 44-60 exist with gum.

A12

1909 Typeset ***Serrate Roulette 13½***

Without Gum

No.	Type	Description	Unused	Used
61	A12	5c red	13.50	11.50
a.		Tête bêche pair	190.00	175.00

Perf. 11½x10½

No.	Type	Description	Unused	Used
62	A12	5c red	14.50	12.00
a.		Tête bêche pair	140.00	140.00

Nos. 17-18, 29-30, 38 Surcharged in Red

Nos. 63-64

Nos. 65-66

No. 67

1911, July 15 Typo. ***Perf. 12½***

Without Gum

No.	Type	Description	Unused	Used
63	A2	½c on 1c	1.75	1.10
64	A2	½c on 2c	12.25	9.00
65	A5	15c on 25c	75.00	57.50
66	A5	20c on 30c	14.00	9.50

Engr.

Perf. 11½x11

No.	Type	Description	Unused	Used
67	A12	30c on 2.50g on 2½g	125.00	110.00
		Nos. 63-67 (5)	228.00	187.10

A13

1912, July Typeset ***Perf. 11½***

Without Gum

No.	Type	Description	Unused	Used
70	A13	½c lilac	.95	.95
a.		Horiz. pair, imperf. btwn.	200.00	
71	A13	2½c dk green	.95	.95
72	A13	5c pale red	8.75	8.75
a.		Vert. pair, imperf. btwn.	240.00	
73	A13	12½c deep blue	11.00	11.00
		Nos. 70-73 (4)	21.65	21.65

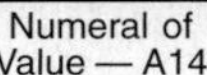

Numeral of Value — A14

A15

Queen Wilhelmina — A16

1913-31 Typo. ***Perf. 12½***

No.	Type	Description	Unused	Used
74	A14	½c violet	.40	.25
75	A14	1c olive green	.40	.25
76	A14	1½c bl, perf 11 ½ ('21)	.40	.25
a.		Perf. 12½ ('32)	1.10	.85
77	A14	2c yellow brn	1.60	1.10
78	A14	2½c green	.95	.25
79	A14	3c yellow	.80	.65
80	A14	3c green ('26)	3.25	2.50
81	A14	4c chlky bl ('26)	8.25	5.00
82	A14	5c rose	1.60	.25
83	A14	5c green ('22)	2.00	1.00
84	A14	5c lilac ('26)	1.60	.25
85	A14	6c bister ('26)	2.75	2.50
86	A14	6c red org ('31)	2.25	.50
87	A14	7½c drab	1.00	.40
a.		Perf. 11x11½	1.40	.65
88	A14	7½c orange ('27)	1.40	.40
89	A14	7½c yellow ('31)	9.25	9.25
90	A14	10c violet ('22)	5.00	5.00
91	A14	10c rose ('26)	4.00	.55
92	A15	10c car rose	1.40	.65
93	A15	12½c blue	1.90	.65
94	A15	12½c red ('22)	2.00	2.25
95	A15	15c olive grn	.55	.70
96	A15	15c lt blue ('26)	7.75	4.75
97	A15	20c green	3.50	3.25
98	A15	20c blue ('22)	2.40	2.00
99	A15	20c ol grn ('26)	3.50	2.75

100 A15 22½c orange 2.50 2.50
101 A15 25c red violet 4.00 .40
102 A15 30c slate 5.00 1.10
103 A15 32½c vio & org ('22) 15.00 17.50
104 A15 35c sl & red ('26) 5.00 5.00

Perf. 11, 11½, 11½x11, 12½

Engr.

105 A16 50c green 4.00 .85
a. Perf. 12½ ('32) 14.00 1.60
106 A16 1g brown 5.50 .50
a. Perf. 12½ ('32) 15.00 1.00
107 A16 1½g dp vio ('26) 35.00 35.00
108 A16 2½g carmine ('23) 30.00 26.00
a. Perf. 11½x11 35.00 32.50
Nos. 74-108 (35) 175.90 136.20

Nos. 74, 75, 77-79, 82, 87, 105, 106 and 108 were issued both with and without gum.

Early printings of Nos. 74-104 had water soluble ink.

For surcharges see Nos. 116-120, 139.

Queen Wilhelmina — A17

1923, Oct. 5 ***Perf. 11, 11x11½, 11½***

109 A17 5c green 1.10 .70
110 A17 10c car rose 1.75 1.50
111 A17 20c indigo 3.50 3.00
112 A17 50c brown org 19.00 19.00
113 A17 1g brown vio 26.00 17.00
114 A17 2½g gray blk 75.00 *200.00*
115 A17 5g brown 100.00 *240.00*
Nos. 109-115 (7) 226.35 *481.20*

25th anniv. of the assumption of the government of the Netherlands by Queen Wilhelmina, at age 18.

Values for Nos. 114-115 used are for stamps with postmarks clearly dated before July 15, 1924.

Nos. 83, 93-94, 98 Surcharged in Black or Red

j

k

m

1925, Dec. 19 **Typo.** ***Perf. 12½***

116 A14 3c on 5c green 1.10 1.10
117 A15 10c on 12½c red 2.25 2.25
118 A15 15c on 12½c blue (R) 1.60 1.60
119 A15 15c on 20c blue 1.60 1.60
Nos. 116-119 (4) 6.55 6.55

No. 100 Surcharged in Blue

1926, Jan. 1

120 A15 12½c on 22½c org 27.50 27.50

Postage Due Stamps Nos. J14 and J29 Surcharged in Blue or Black

o

p

121 D2(o) 12½c on 40c (Bl) 3.25 3.25
122 D2(p) 12½c on 40c (Bk) 30.00 30.00
Nos. 120-122 (3) 60.75 60.75

No. 121 issued without gum.

Queen Wilhelmina — A21

1927-30 **Engr.** ***Perf. 11½***

123 A21 10c carmine 1.00 .40
124 A21 12½c red orange 1.75 1.90
125 A21 15c dark blue 2.00 .60
126 A21 20c indigo 2.00 .80
127 A21 21c dk brown ('30) 19.00 19.00
128 A21 22½c brown ('28) 8.00 9.75
129 A21 25c dk violet 3.00 .70
130 A21 30c dk green 3.00 1.10
131 A21 35c black brown 3.00 3.00
Nos. 123-131 (9) 42.75 37.25

Types of Netherlands Marine Insurance Stamps Inscribed and Surcharged

Nos. 132-134, 138

Nos. 135-136

No. 137

1927, Oct. 26

132 MI1 3c on 15c dk grn .65 .65
133 MI1 10c on 60c car rose .65 .65
134 MI1 12½c on 75c gray brn .65 .65
135 MI2 15c on 1.50 dk blue 2.75 2.75
136 MI2 25c on 2.25g org brn 7.25 7.25
137 MI3 30c on 4½g black 9.00 7.25
138 MI3 50c on 7½g red 7.25 7.25
Nos. 132-138 (7) 28.20 26.45

No. 88 Surcharged

1930, Mar. 1 **Typo.** ***Perf. 12½***

139 A14 6c on 7½c orange 1.90 1.00

Prince William I (Portrait by Van Key) — A22

1933, Apr. 24 **Photo.**

141 A22 6c deep orange 6.75 1.90

400th birth anniv. of Prince William I, Count of Nassau and Prince of Orange, frequently referred to as William the Silent.

Van Walbeeck's Ship A23

Queen Wilhelmina A24

1936-41 **Litho.** ***Perf. 13½x12½***

142 A23 ½c yellow brn .30 .30
143 A23 1c lt yellow grn .40 .25
144 A23 1½c brt blue .55 .40
145 A23 2c black brown .60 .25
146 A23 2½c green .25 .25
a. Perf. 13 ('41) 9.00 3.25
147 A23 3c dark ultra .60 .40
148 A23 4c orange .60 .75
149 A23 5c gray .60 .25
150 A23 6c red 2.50 2.00
151 A23 7½c red violet .25 .25
a. 7½c plum, perf. 13 ('41) 3.00 .25

Engr.

Perf. 14, 12½

Size: 20x30mm

152 A24 10c vermilion .85 .25
a. Perf. 12½ ('39) 60.00 11.50
153 A24 12½c dull green 3.50 1.25
154 A24 15c dark blue 1.25 .60
155 A24 20c yellow org 2.10 .60
156 A24 21c dk gray 3.25 3.00
a. Perf. 12½ ('39) 3.75 3.75
157 A24 25c brown lake 2.40 1.00
158 A24 30c brown vio 3.75 1.00
159 A24 35c olive brown 4.00 4.00

Perf. 12½x14

Size: 22x33mm

160 A24 50c dull yel grn 4.00 2.00
161 A24 1g dull blue 8.25 3.00
162 A24 1.50g black brown 22.50 18.00
163 A24 2.50g rose lake 13.50 9.50
Nos. 142-163 (22) 76.00 49.30

For surcharges see Nos. 181-183, B37-B40 in Scott Standard catalogue, Vol. 6.

Queen Wilhelmina — A25

Perf. 12½x12

1938, Aug. 30 **Photo.** **Wmk. 202**

164 A25 2c dull purple .50 .30
165 A25 7½c red orange 1.50 1.25
166 A25 15c royal blue 3.00 3.00
Nos. 164-166 (3) 5.00 4.55

Reign of Queen Wilhelmina, 40th anniv.

SEMI-POSTAL STAMPS

SP1

SP2

Green Cross — SP3

Perf. 12½

1927, Aug. 1 **Unwmk.** **Photo.**

B1 SP1 2c (+ 2c) bl blk & grn 1.10 1.00
B2 SP2 5c (+ 3c) vio & grn 1.10 1.00
B3 SP3 10c (+ 3c) ver & grn 2.00 1.75
Nos. B1-B3 (3) 4.20 3.75
Set, never hinged 10.50

Surtax was given to the Green Cross Society, which promotes public health services.

Nurse and Patient — SP4

1928, Dec. 1 ***Perf. 11½***

B4 SP4 1½c (+ 1½c) ultra 4.50 4.50
B5 SP4 2c (+ 2c) bl grn 4.50 4.50
B6 SP4 5c (+ 3c) vio 4.50 4.50
B7 SP4 7½c (+ 2½c) ver 4.50 4.50
Nos. B4-B7 (4) 18.00 18.00
Set, never hinged 67.50

The surtax on these stamps was for a fund to combat indigenous diseases.

Good Samaritan — SP5

1929, Dec. 1 ***Perf. 12½***

B8 SP5 1½c (+ 1½c) grn 6.75 6.75
B9 SP5 2c (+ 2c) scar 6.75 6.75
B10 SP5 5c (+ 3c) ultra 6.75 6.75
B11 SP5 6c (+ 4c) blk 6.75 6.75
Nos. B8-B11 (4) 27.00 27.00
Set, never hinged 72.50

Surtax for the Green Cross Society.

Surinam Mother and Child — SP6

1931, Dec. 14

B12 SP6 1½c (+ 1½c) blk 4.75 4.75
B13 SP6 2c (+ 2c) car rose 4.75 4.75
B14 SP6 5c (+ 3c) ultra 4.75 4.75
B15 SP6 6c (+ 4c) dp grn 4.75 4.75
Nos. B12-B15 (4) 19.00 19.00
Set, never hinged 45.00

The surtax was for Child Welfare Societies.

Designs Symbolical of the Creed of the Moravians

SP7 SP8

1935, Aug. 1 ***Perf. 13x14***

B16 SP7 1c (+ ½c) dk brn 6.00 6.00
B17 SP7 2c (+ 1c) dp ultra 6.00 6.00
B18 SP8 3c (+ 1½c) grn 7.50 7.50
B19 SP8 4c (+ 2c) red org 7.50 7.50

B20 SP8	5c (+ 2½c) blk brn	9.00	9.00
B21 SP7	10c (+ 5c) car	9.00	9.00
	Nos. B16-B21 (6)	45.00	45.00
	Set, never hinged	90.00	

200th anniv. of the founding of the Moravian Mission in Surinam.

Surinam Child — SP9

1936, Dec. 14 ***Perf. 12½***

B22 SP9	2c (+ 1c) dk grn	2.75	2.75
B23 SP9	3c (+ 1½c) dk bl	2.75	2.75
B24 SP9	5c (+ 2½c) brn blk	4.00	4.00
B25 SP9	10c (+ 5c) lake	4.00	4.00
	Nos. B22-B25 (4)	13.50	13.50
	Set, never hinged	26.50	

Surtax for baby food and the Green Cross Society.

"Emancipation" SP10

Surinam Girl SP11

1938, June 1 **Litho.** ***Perf. 12½x12***

B26 SP10	2½c (+ 2c) dk bl grn	2.40	1.90

Photo.

B27 SP11	3c (+ 2c) vio blk	2.40	1.90
B28 SP11	5c (+ 3c) dk brn	2.60	2.25
B29 SP11	7½c (+ 5c) indigo	2.60	2.25
	Nos. B26-B29 (4)	10.00	8.30
	Set, never hinged	20.00	

75th anniv. of the abolition of slavery in Surinam. Surtax to Slavery Remembrance Committee.

Creole Woman — SP12

Javanese Woman — SP13

Hindustani Woman — SP14

American Indian Woman — SP15

1940, Jan. 8 **Engr.** ***Perf. 13x14***

B30 SP12	2½c (+ 2c) dk grn	3.00	3.00
B31 SP13	3c (+ 2c) red org	3.00	3.00
B32 SP14	5c (+ 3c) dp bl	3.00	3.00
B33 SP15	7½c (+ 5c) henna brn	3.00	3.00
	Nos. B30-B33 (4)	12.00	12.00
	Set, never hinged	25.00	

Surtax to leper care and baby food.

AIR POST STAMPS

Allegory of Flight — AP1

Perf. 12½

1930, Sept. 3 **Unwmk.** **Engr.**

C1 AP1	10c dull red	3.75	.50
C2 AP1	15c ultra	3.75	.75
C3 AP1	20c dull green	.25	.25
C4 AP1	40c orange	.25	.35
C5 AP1	60c brown violet	.55	.40
C6 AP1	1g gray black	1.60	1.75
C7 AP1	1½g deep brown	1.75	1.90
	Nos. C1-C7 (7)	11.90	5.90

Nos. C1-C7 Overprinted in Black or Red

1931, Aug. 8

C8 AP1	10c red (Bk)	19.00	15.00
a.	Double overprint	425.00	
C9 AP1	15c ultra (Bk)	19.00	15.00
C10 AP1	20c dull grn (R)	19.00	15.00
C11 AP1	40c orange (Bk)	29.00	22.50
a.	Double overprint	425.00	
C12 AP1	60c brn vio (R)	62.50	52.50
C13 AP1	1g gray blk (R)	72.50	65.00
C14 AP1	1½g deep brn (Bk)	72.50	67.50
	Nos. C8-C14 (7)	293.50	252.50

The variety with period omitted after "Do" occurs twice on each sheet.

Warning: The red overprint may dissolve in water.

POSTAGE DUE STAMPS

D1

D2

Type I — 34 loops. "T" of "BETALEN" over center of loop; top branch of "E" of "TE" shorter than lower branch.

Type II — 33 loops. "T" of "BETALEN" over space between two loops.

Type III — 32 loops. "T" of "BETALEN" slightly to the left of center of loop; top branch of first "E" of "BETALEN" shorter than lower branch.

Type IV — 37 loops and letters of "PORT" larger than in the other 3 types.

Value in Black

Perf. 12½x12

1886-88 **Typo.** **Unwmk.**

Type III

J1 D1	2½c lilac	3.00	3.00
J2 D1	5c lilac	9.00	9.00
J3 D1	10c lilac	100.00	65.00
J4 D1	20c lilac	9.00	9.00
J5 D1	25c lilac	12.50	12.50
J6 D1	30c lilac ('88)	2.50	2.50
J7 D1	40c lilac	6.00	6.00
J8 D1	50c lilac ('88)	3.00	3.00
	Nos. J1-J8 (8)	145.00	110.00

Type I

J1a D1	2½c	6.00	6.00
J2a D1	5c	11.00	11.00
J3a D1	10c	125.00	90.00
J4a D1	20c	22.50	22.50
J5a D1	25c	19.00	19.00
J6a D1	30c	22.50	22.50
J7a D1	40c	12.50	12.50
J8a D1	50c	4.00	4.00
	Nos. J1a-J8a (8)	222.50	187.50

Type II

J1b D1	2½c	5.00	5.00
J2b D1	5c	10.00	10.00
J3b D1	10c	1,250.	1,250.
J4b D1	20c	9.00	9.00
J5b D1	25c	300.00	300.00
J6b D1	30c	75.00	75.00
J7b D1	40c	350.00	350.00
J8b D1	50c	5.00	5.00

Type IV

J3c D1	10c	350.00	250.00
J5c D1	25c	160.00	150.00
J7c D1	40c	150.00	150.00
	Nos. J3c-J7c (3)	660.00	550.00

Nos. J1-J16 were issued without gum. For surcharges, see Nos. J15-J16.

1892-96 **Value in Black** ***Perf. 12½***

Type III

J9 D2	2½c lilac	.40	.40
J10 D2	5c lilac	1.25	1.00
J11 D2	10c lilac	24.00	22.50
J12 D2	20c lilac	2.50	2.25
J13 D2	25c lilac	10.00	10.00

Type I

J9a D2	2½c	.40	.40
J10a D2	5c	2.00	2.00
J11a D2	10c	24.00	20.00
J12a D2	20c	5.00	5.00
J13a D2	25c	13.00	12.50
J14 D2	40c ('96)	3.25	4.50

Type II

J9b D2	2½c	.80	.80
J10b D2	5c	3.00	3.00
J11b D2	10c	40.00	42.50
J12b D2	20c	90.00	90.00
J13b D2	25c	100.00	100.00

For surcharges, see Nos. 121-122.

Stamps of 1888 Surcharged in Red

1911, July 15

J15 D1	10c on 30c lil (III)	80.00	80.00
a.	10c on 30c lilac (I)	200.00	225.00
b.	10c on 30c lilac (II)	*1,800.*	*1,800.*
J16 D1	10c on 50c lil (III)	110.00	110.00
a.	10c on 50c lilac (I)	115.00	115.00
b.	10c on 50c lilac (II)	115.00	115.00

D3

Type I

Value in Color of Stamp

1913-31 ***Perf. 12½, 13½x12½***

J17 D2	½c lilac ('30)	.25	.25
J18 D2	1c lilac ('31)	.25	.35
J19 D2	2c lilac ('31)	.25	.25
J20 D2	2½c lilac	.25	.25
J21 D2	5c lilac	.25	.25
J22 D2	10c lilac	.25	.25
J23 D2	12c lilac ('31)	.25	.25
J24 D2	12½c lilac ('22)	.25	.25
J25 D2	15c lilac ('26)	.55	.45
J26 D2	20c lilac	.85	.45
J27 D2	25c lilac	.45	.25
J28 D2	30c lilac ('26)	.45	.60
J29 D2	40c lilac	14.50	14.00
J30 D2	50c lilac ('26)	1.25	1.25
J31 D2	75c lilac ('26)	1.50	1.50
J32 D3	1g lilac ('26)	1.75	1.50
	Nos. J17-J32 (16)	23.30	22.10

SWAZILAND

ˈswə-zē-ˌland

LOCATION — Southeast Africa bordered by the Transvaal and Zululand in South Africa and by Mozambique

GOVT. — Constitutional monarchy

AREA — 6,705 sq. mi.

POP. — 626,000 (est. 1984)

CAPITAL — Mbabane

An independent state in the 19th century, Swaziland was administered by Transvaal from 1894 to 1906, when the administration was transferred to the British High Commissioner for South Africa. In 1934 Swaziland and Bechuanaland Protectorate came under the administration of the British High Commissioner for Basutoland. The issuing of individual postage stamps had been resumed in 1933.

12 Pence = 1 Shilling
20 Shillings = 1 Pound

Catalogue values for unused stamps in this country are for Never Hinged items, beginning with Scott 38 in the regular postage section.

Coat of Arms — A1

Black Overprint

1889 **Unwmk.** ***Perf. 12½, 12½x12***

1 A1	½p gray	10.50	*27.00*
a.	Inverted overprint	1,250.	850.00
b.	"Swazielan"	2,100.	1,200.
c.	As "b," inverted overprint		8,000.
2 A1	1p rose	25.00	25.00
a.	Inverted overprint	800.00	*750.00*
3 A1	2p olive bister	32.50	18.00
a.	Inverted overprint	950.00	600.00
b.	"Swazielan"	550.00	475.00
c.	Perf. 12½x12	100.00	40.00
d.	As "c," "Swazielan"	1,250.	725.00
e.	As "d," inverted overprint		1,400.
f.	As "b," inverted overprint	7,500.	5,000.
g.	Double overprint	2,600.	
4 A1	6p gray blue	47.50	*60.00*
5 A1	1sh green	20.00	*16.00*
a.	Inverted overprint	1,100.	525.00
6 A1	2sh6p yellow	325.00	*500.00*
7 A1	5sh slate	175.00	*340.00*
a.	Inverted overprint	*1,900.*	*3,000.*
b.	"Swazielan"	*5,250.*	
c.	As "b," inverted overprint	*5,750.*	
8 A1	10sh lt brown	*7,250.*	*4,500.*

1892 **Red Overprint**

9 A1	½p gray	8.50	19.00
a.	Inverted overprint	575.00	
b.	Double overprint	525.00	*525.00*
c.	Pair, one without overprint		2,000.

Beware of counterfeits.

Reprints have a period after "Swazieland."

Stamps of Swaziland were replaced by those of Transvaal in 1895. Swaziland issues were resumed in 1933.

George V — A2

Perf. 14

1933, Jan. 2 **Engr.** **Wmk. 4**

10 A2	½p green	.40	*.35*
11 A2	1p carmine	.40	.25
12 A2	2p lt brown	.40	.50
13 A2	3p ultra	.55	*3.50*
14 A2	4p orange	3.50	*4.25*
15 A2	6p rose violet	1.60	*1.30*
16 A2	1sh olive green	1.75	*3.25*
17 A2	2sh6p violet	16.00	*25.00*
18 A2	5sh gray	40.00	*57.50*
19 A2	10sh black brown	145.00	*185.00*
	Nos. 10-19 (10)	209.60	*280.90*
	Set, never hinged	500.00	

Common Design Types pictured following the introduction.

Silver Jubilee Issue

Common Design Type

1935, May 4 ***Perf. 11x12***

20 CD301	1p carmine & blue	.55	*1.75*
21 CD301	2p black & ultra	2.00	*3.50*
22 CD301	3p ultra & brown	1.00	*8.00*
23 CD301	6p brn, vio & ind	3.25	*5.00*
	Nos. 20-23 (4)	6.80	18.25
	Set, never hinged	11.00	

Coronation Issue

Common Design Type

1937, May 12 ***Perf. 11x11½***

24 CD302	1p dark carmine	.35	*.95*
25 CD302	2p brown	.35	*.25*
26 CD302	3p deep ultra	.35	.55
	Nos. 24-26 (3)	1.05	1.75
	Set, never hinged	1.75	

George VI — A3

1938, Apr. 1 ***Perf. 13, 13x13½***

27 A3 ½p green .25 *1.25*
28 A3 1p rose carmine .60 *1.25*
29 A3 1½p light blue .30 *.85*
a. Perf. 14 ('42) 1.60 1.25
Never hinged 3.25
30 A3 2p brown .30 *.45*
31 A3 3p ultra 4.50 1.75
32 A3 4p red orange .60 *1.40*
33 A3 6p rose violet 2.75 1.50
34 A3 1sh olive green .75 .75
35 A3 2sh6p dark violet 12.50 4.00
36 A3 5sh gray 25.00 19.00
37 A3 10sh black brown 5.50 *7.00*
Nos. 27-37 (11) 53.05 39.20
Set, never hinged 85.00

Catalogue values for unused stamps in this section, from this point to the end of the section, are for Never Hinged items.

Peace Issue

South Africa, Nos. 100-102 Overprinted

Basic stamps inscribed alternately in English and Afrikaans.

1945, Dec. 3 **Wmk. 201** ***Perf. 14***

38 A42 1p rose pink & choc, pair .80 *1.25*
a. Single, English .25 .25
b. Single, Afrikaans .25 .25
39 A43 2p vio & sl blue, pair .80 *1.25*
a. Single, English .25 .25
b. Single, Afrikaans .25 .25
40 A43 3p ultra & dp ultra, pair .80 *3.00*
a. Single, English .25 .25
b. Single, Afrikaans .25 .25
Nos. 38-40 (3) 2.40 *5.50*

World War II victory of the Allies.

Royal Visit Issue
Type of Basutoland, 1947
Perf. 12½

1947, Feb. 17 **Wmk. 4** **Engr.**

44 A3 1p red .25 .25
45 A4 2p green .25 .25
46 A5 3p ultramarine .25 .25
47 A6 1sh dark violet .25 .25
Nos. 44-47 (4) 1.00 1.00

Visit of the British Royal Family, 3/25/47.

Silver Wedding Issue
Common Design Types

1948, Dec. 1 **Photo.** ***Perf. 14x14½***

48 CD304 1½p bright ultra .30 .25

Perf. 11½x11

Engraved; Name Typographed

49 CD305 10sh violet brown 40.00 *47.50*

UPU Issue
Common Design Types
Engr.; Name Typo. on 3p, 6p
Perf. 13½, 11x11½

1949, Oct. 10 **Wmk. 4**

50 CD306 1½p blue .30 .25
51 CD307 3p indigo 1.60 2.00
52 CD308 6p red lilac .40 1.75
53 CD309 1sh olive .50 .65
Nos. 50-53 (4) 2.80 4.65

POSTAGE DUE STAMPS

Catalogue values for unused stamps in this section are for Never Hinged items.

D1

1933 **Typo.** **Wmk. 4** ***Perf. 14***

J1 D1 1p carmine rose 4.00 *17.50*
On cover *175.00*
a. Wmk. 4a (error) 275.00
J2 D1 2p violet 12.00 *35.00*
On cover *225.00*

Value, Nos. J1-J2 hinged $6.

On cover values are for properly franked commercial covers. Philatelic usages sell for less.

SWEDEN

ˈswē-dᵊn

LOCATION — Northern Europe, occupying the eastern half of the Scandinavian Peninsula
GOVT. — Constitutional Monarchy
AREA — 173,341 sq. mi.
POP. — 8,330,577 (est. 1983)
CAPITAL — Stockholm

48 skilling banco = 1 rixdaler banco (until 1858)
100 öre = 1 rixdaler (1858 to 1874)
100 öre = 1 krona (since 1874)

Watermarks

Wmk. 180 — Crown

Wmk. 181 — Wavy Lines

Values for unused stamps are for examples with original gum as defined in the catalogue introduction except Nos. 1-5, excluding reprints, and LX1 which are valued without gum.

Coat of Arms — A1

1855 **Unwmk.** **Typo.** ***Perf. 14***

1 A1 3s blue green, thin paper *10,000.* *5,000.*
On cover *35,000.*
a. 3s orange (error) *3,000,000.*
b. 3s pale bluish green, thin paper 8,000. *4,000.*
On cover *35,000.*
2 A1 4s lt blue, thin paper 1,600. 100.00
On cover 110.00
a. 4s blue, thin paper 1,550. 80.00
On cover 90.00
b. 4s bright blue, dense background, thin paper 2,250. 180.00
On cover 350.00
c. 4s dull blue, dense background, thick paper 5,350. 200.00
On cover 400.00
d. 4s bright blue, dense background, thick paper ('56) — 250.00
On cover 400.00
e. 4s grayish ultramarine, thick paper ('57) — 300.00
On cover 450.00
f. 4s dark grayish ultramarine, thick paper ('57) 1,200. 700.00
On cover 3,000.
g. 4s turquoise, blurred print, thick paper ('57) 1,200. *1,500.*
On cover *6,000.*
h. 4s greenish blue, thick paper ('57) 1,550. 120.00
On cover 130.00
i. 4s blue, clear print, thick paper ('58) *1,550.* 80.00
On cover 100.00
3 A1 6s gray, thin paper *10,000.* 1,600.
On cover *9,700.*
a. 6s gray black, thin paper *4,450.*
On cover —
b. 6s pale gray, thin paper *9,450.* 1,450.
On cover 9,850.
c. 6s gray brown ('56) *2,200.* 2,650.
On cover *11,000.*
d. 6s brownish gray, thick paper ('58) 10,000. 1,350.
On cover —
e. 6s gray brown, thick paper ('58) 1,450.
On cover *10,000.*
f. Imperf. —
4 A1 8s red org, thin paper 5,500. 650.00
On cover 1,000.
a. 8s brownish orange, thin paper ('56) 5,200. 700.00
On cover 1,150.
b. 8s lemon yellow, *greenish*, thin paper ('56) 1,150. *2,300.*
On cover —
c. 8s bright yellow, thin paper ('56) 2,300. 1,150.
On cover 2,300.
d. 8s dull olive yellow, thin paper ('56) — 1,050.
On cover —
e. 8s yellow orange, thick paper ('57) 5,200. 575.00
On cover 1,350.
f. 8s orange yellow, blurred print, thick paper ('57) 1,150. 925.00
On cover 1,700.
g. 8s orange yellow, clear print, thick paper ('58) 650.00
On cover —
h. Imperf. 5,750.
5 A1 24s dull red, thin paper *8,000.* 2,200.
On cover 10,000.
a. 24s orange red, thin paper ('56) 8,000. 2,100.
On cover *10,000.*
b. 24s brick red, thck paper ('57) 1,150. *2,000.*
On cover *10,000.*
c. 24s light orange red, thick paper ('57) 2,350. *2,200.*
On cover *10,000.*
d. 24s brownish red, blurred print, thick paper ('58) 2,900.
On cover *10,500.*

Nos. 1-5 were reprinted from new blocks in 1868 (twice), 1871 (No. 1 only) and 1885. These later printings were made after Nos. 1-5 were withdrawn, but before being demonetized, and were valid for postal use until 1910. The post office did not distinguish between these re-issues and earlier printings, although most saw little, if any, postal use.

Distinguishing characteristics of Reprints: 3s, a white dot or short while line right of the "I" in "SKILLING": a short colored line between the "F" and "R" of left "FRIMARKE." **4s**, "E" in left "FRIMARKE" broken at bottom, so that letter resembles an "F"; **6s**, most reprints have a small white dot in front of "S" in "SEX"; all reprints differ in shade of color, having a lilac cast that does not appear in the original printings; **8s**, no distinguishing characteristic, but most reprints reveal small defects in the plate, when compared to original printings; **24s**, "E" in right "FRIMARKE" broken at bottom.

Re-issue

1868 ***Perf. 14***

First Printing

1p A1 3s yel grn, thin background 525.00
Never Hinged 925.00
2p A1 4s blue, thin background 525.00
Never Hinged 925.00
3p A1 6s br gray, thin background 525.00
Never Hinged 925.00
4p A1 8s orange, dense background 525.00
Never Hinged 925.00
5p A1 24s dark red, thin background 525.00
Never Hinged 925.00

Second Printing

1q A1 3s green, dense background 460.00 *925.00*
Never Hinged 925.00
2q A1 4s lt blue, thin background 460.00 *925.00*
Never Hinged 925.00
3q A1 6s lilac, dense background 460.00 *925.00*
Never Hinged 925.00
4q A1 8s yellow orange, dense background 460.00 *925.00*
Never Hinged 925.00
5q A1 24s orange red, dense background 460.00 *925.00*
Never Hinged 925.00

1871 ***Perf. 14***

1r A1 3s lt yel green, dense background 800.00
Never Hinged 1,400.

1885 ***Perf. 13***

1s A1 3s green 300.00
Never Hinged 460.00
2s A1 4s blue 300.00
Never Hinged 460.00
3s A1 6s gray 300.00
Never Hinged 460.00
4s A1 8s orange 300.00
Never Hinged 460.00
5s A1 24s red 300.00
Never Hinged 460.00

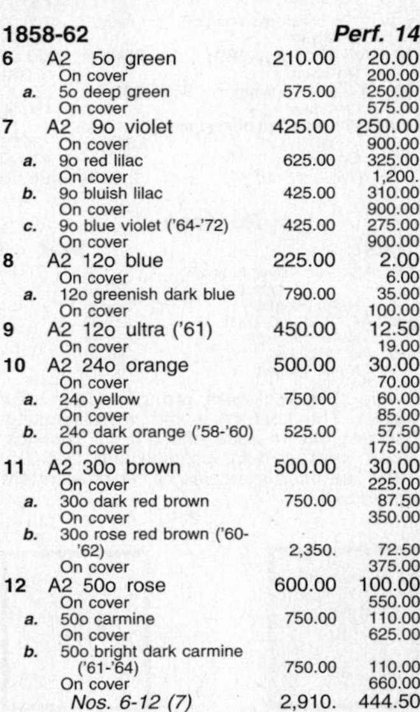
Coat of Arms — A2

1858-62 ***Perf. 14***

6 A2 5o green 210.00 20.00
On cover 200.00
a. 5o deep green 575.00 250.00
On cover 575.00
7 A2 9o violet 425.00 250.00
On cover 900.00
a. 9o red lilac 625.00 325.00
On cover 1,200.
b. 9o bluish lilac 425.00 310.00
On cover 900.00
c. 9o blue violet ('64-'72) 425.00 275.00
On cover 900.00
8 A2 12o blue 225.00 2.00
On cover 6.00
a. 12o greenish dark blue 790.00 35.00
On cover 100.00
9 A2 12o ultra ('61) 450.00 12.50
On cover 19.00
10 A2 24o orange 500.00 30.00
On cover 70.00
a. 24o yellow 750.00 60.00
On cover 85.00
b. 24o dark orange ('58-'60) 525.00 57.50
On cover 175.00
11 A2 30o brown 500.00 30.00
On cover 225.00
a. 30o dark red brown 750.00 87.50
On cover 350.00
b. 30o rose red brown ('60-'62) 2,350. 72.50
On cover 375.00
12 A2 50o rose 600.00 100.00
On cover 550.00
a. 50o carmine 750.00 110.00
On cover 625.00
b. 50o bright dark carmine ('61-'64) 750.00 110.00
On cover 660.00
Nos. 6-12 (7) 2,910. 444.50

Nos. 6 and 8 exist with double impressions. No. 8 is known printed on both sides. No. 11 exists imperf.

Re-issue

1885 ***Perf. 13***

6s A2 5o green 110.00
Never Hinged 175.00
7s A2 9o violet 110.00
Never Hinged 175.00
8s A2 12o blue 110.00
Never Hinged 175.00
10s A2 24o orange 110.00
Never Hinged 175.00
11s A2 30o brown 110.00
Never Hinged 175.00
12s A2 50o rose 110.00
Never Hinged 175.00

Nos. 6s-12s were reprinted from new blocks. The post office did not distinguish between this re-issue and original printings, which were valid for postage until Dec. 30, 1910, but used examples of the re-issue are not known.

These values were also reprinted in 1963, perf. 13½, with lines in stamp color crossing denominations, and affixed to book page. Value $12.50 each.

Lion and Arms
A3 A4

Type I

Type II

1862-69

3 Ore:
Type I — The horizontal inner frameline in the upper right corner extends beyond the curved spiral.
Type II — The horizontal inner frameline in the upper right corner does not extend beyond the curved spiral.

13	A3	3o bister brown, type II ('63)	275.00	14.00
		On cover		35.00
a.		Printed on both sides, type II		*3,700.*
b.		3o brown, type I	925.00	675.00
		On cover		725.00
c.		3o orange brown, type I ('62)	975.00	725.00
		On cover		850.00
d.		3o olive gray brown, type II ('63)	500.00	200.00
		On cover		450.00
14	A4	17o red vio ('66)	800.00	160.00
		On cover		600.00
a.		17o bluish red lilac ('66)	800.00	130.00
		On cover		500.00
15	A4	17o gray ('69)	850.00	*800.00*
		On cover		*16,000.*
16	A4	20o vermilion ('66)	300.00	20.00
		On cover		180.00
a.		20o brownish orange red ('66)	310.00	35.00
		On cover		475.00
		Nos. 13-16 (4)	2,225.	994.00

Re-issue

1885 *Perf. 13*

13s	A3	3o bister brown, type II	97.50
		Never Hinged	175.00
14s	A4	17o red violet	125.00
		Never Hinged	225.00
16s	A4	20o red	95.00
		Never Hinged	165.00

Nos. 13s-16s were reprinted from new blocks. The post office did not distinguish between this re-issue and original printings, which were valid for postage until Dec. 30, 1910, but used examples of the re-issue are not known.

Numeral of Value — A5

Coat of Arms — A6

1872-77 *Perf. 14*

17	A5	3o bister brown	70.00	8.00
		On cover		32.50
18	A5	4o gray ('76)	450.00	150.00
		On cover		700.00
19	A5	5o blue green	400.00	5.00
		On cover		200.00
a.		5o emerald	500.00	25.00
		On cover		450.00
20	A5	6o violet	400.00	40.00
		On cover		55.00
a.		6o dark violet	1,250.	300.00
		On cover		55.00
21	A5	6o gray ('74)	1,100.	95.00
		On cover		140.00
22	A5	12o blue	225.00	1.00
		On cover		5.00
23	A5	20o vermilion	1,000.	8.00
		On cover		67.50
a.		20o pale org ('75)	3,500.	50.00
		On cover		675.00
b.		Double impression, dull yel & ver ('76)	3,500.	55.00
		On cover		350.00
24	A5	24o orange	950.00	37.50
		On cover		72.50
a.		24o yellow	950.00	37.50
		On cover		72.50
25	A5	30o brown	825.00	11.00
		On cover		115.00
a.		30o black brown	875.00	14.00
		On cover		120.00
26	A5	50o rose	875.00	50.00
		On cover		400.00
a.		50o carmine	900.00	50.00
		On cover		400.00
27	A6	1rd bister & blue	1,000.	95.00
		On cover		2,850.
a.		1rd bister & ultra	1,000.	95.00
		On cover		2,850.
		Nos. 17-27 (11)	7,295.	500.50

1877-79 *Perf. 13*

28	A5	3o yellow brown	125.00	6.00
		On cover		19.00
29	A5	4o gray ('79)	225.00	3.50
		On cover		19.00
30	A5	5o dark green	140.00	1.00
		On cover		22.50

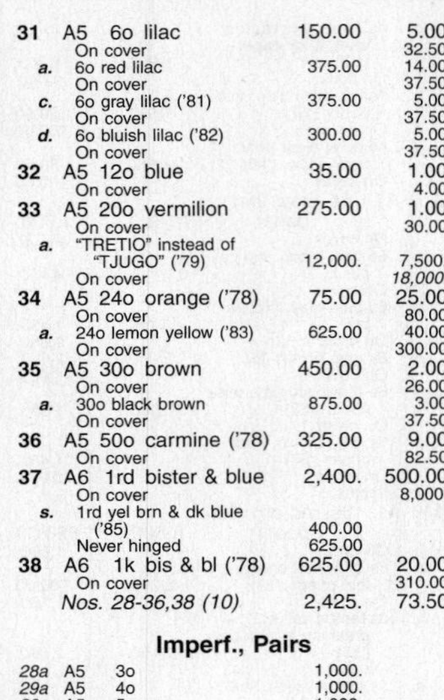

31	A5	6o lilac	150.00	5.00
		On cover		32.50
a.		6o red lilac	375.00	14.00
		On cover		37.50
c.		6o gray lilac ('81)	375.00	5.00
		On cover		37.50
d.		6o bluish lilac ('82)	300.00	5.00
		On cover		37.50
32	A5	12o blue	35.00	1.00
		On cover		4.00
33	A5	20o vermilion	275.00	1.00
		On cover		30.00
a.		"TRETIO" instead of "TJUGO" ('79)	12,000.	7,500.
		On cover		*18,000.*
34	A5	24o orange ('78)	75.00	25.00
		On cover		80.00
a.		24o lemon yellow ('83)	625.00	40.00
		On cover		300.00
35	A5	30o brown	450.00	2.00
		On cover		26.00
a.		30o black brown	875.00	3.00
		On cover		37.50
36	A5	50o carmine ('78)	325.00	9.00
		On cover		82.50
37	A6	1rd bister & blue	2,400.	500.00
		On cover		8,000.
s.		1rd yel brn & dk blue ('85)	400.00	
		Never hinged	625.00	
38	A6	1k bis & bl ('78)	625.00	20.00
		On cover		310.00
		Nos. 28-36,38 (10)	2,425.	73.50

Imperf., Pairs

28a	A5	3o	1,000.	
29a	A5	4o	1,000.	
30a	A5	5o	1,000.	
31b	A5	6o	1,000.	
32a	A5	12o	1,000.	
33b	A5	20o	1,000.	
34b	A5	24o	1,000.	
35b	A5	30o	1,000.	*4,000.*
36a	A5	50o	1,000.	
38a	A6	1k	1,000.	

See Nos. 40-44, 46-49. For surcharges see Nos. B1-B10, B22-B31.
No. 37s was a postally valid re-issue, printed from new blocks. It is not known used.

King Oscar II — A7

1885 **Typo.**

39	A7	10o dull rose	225.00	1.00
		On cover		7.50
a.		Imperf., pair	*2,500.*	

Numeral Type with Post Horn on Back

1886-91

40	A5	2o orange ('91)	2.50	*8.00*
		On cover		42.50
a.		Period before "FRIMARKE"	12.00	*22.50*
b.		Imperf., pair	725.00	
41	A5	3o yellow brn ('87)	15.00	*25.00*
		On cover		100.00
42	A5	4o gray	30.00	2.00
		On cover		12.50
43	A5	5o green	60.00	1.00
		On cover		9.50
44	A5	6o red lilac ('88)	30.00	*62.50*
		On cover		125.00
a.		6o violet	35.00	*62.50*
		On cover		125.00
45	A7	10o pink	87.50	.50
		On cover		3.75
a.		10o rose	87.50	.25
		On cover		3.75
b.		Imperf.		3,250.
46	A5	20o vermilion	125.00	1.00
		On cover		9.50
47	A5	30o brown	210.00	2.00
		On cover		9.50
48	A5	50o rose	190.00	5.00
		On cover		75.00
49	A6	1k bister & dk bl	100.00	3.00
		On cover		50.00
a.		Imperf., pair	700.00	
		Nos. 40-49 (10)	850.00	110.00

Nos. 32, 34 with Blue Surcharge

1889, Oct. 1

50	A5	10o on 12o blue	3.75	*4.00*
		On cover		32.50
51	A5	10o on 24o orange	9.00	*40.00*
		On cover		90.00

A9

King Oscar II
A10 A11

Wmk. 180

1891-1904 **Typo.** *Perf. 13*

52	A9	1o brown & ultra ('92)	1.40	.65
		On cover		2.50
53	A9	2o blue & yellow org	3.25	.40
		On cover		2.00
54	A9	3o brn & org ('92)	.60	1.75
		On cover		3.50
55	A9	4o car & ultra ('92)	4.75	.50
		On cover		1.20

Engr.

56	A10	5o yellow green	2.75	.30
		On cover		.50
a.		5o blue green	11.50	.30
		On cover		.50
d.		5o brown (error)	*7,500.*	—
e.		Booklet pane of 6	140.00	
57	A10	8o red vio ('03)	3.25	1.25
		On cover		12.50
58	A10	10o carmine	4.50	.30
		On cover		.50
c.		Booklet pane of 6	240.00	
59	A10	15o red brn ('96)	27.50	.50
		On cover		3.00
60	A10	20o blue	28.00	.40
		On cover		3.00
b.		20o ultramarine	37.50	.50
		On cover		6.00
61	A10	25o red org ('96)	37.50	.50
		On cover		4.00
62	A10	30o brown	55.00	.40
		On cover		3.00
63	A10	50o slate	125.00	.85
		On cover		5.50
64	A10	50o ol gray ('04)	100.00	.85
		On cover		5.50
65	A11	1k car & sl ('00)	175.00	2.25
		On cover		25.00
		Nos. 52-65 (14)	568.50	10.90

Imperf., Pairs

52a	A9	1o	87.50
53a	A9	2o	*325.00*
54a	A9	3o	*325.00*
55a	A9	4o	325.00
56b	A10	5o No. 56	85.00
c.		No. 56a	300.00
57a	A10	8o	500.00
58a	A10	10o	52.50
59a	A10	15o	500.00
60a	A10	20o	150.00
61a	A10	25o	600.00
62a	A10	30o	600.00
63a	A10	50o	650.00
64a	A10	50o	500.00
65a	A11	1k	625.00

No. 56d may be a color proof.
A booklet pane of 6 invalid stamps similar to No. 56 but with engraved lines through the denominations was released in 2004 to commemorate the 100th anniversary of the first Swedish booklet. This booklet pane is unwatermarked.
See Nos. 75-76.

Stockholm Post Office — A12

1903, Oct. 26

66	A12	5k blue	240.00	17.00
a.		Imperf., pair	3,000.	

Opening of the new General Post Office at Stockholm.
For surcharge see No. B11.

Arms — A13

Gustaf V — A14

Perf. 13, 13x13½

1910-14 **Typo.** **Wmk. 180**

67	A13	1o black ('11)	.65	*1.50*
68	A13	2o orange	1.75	*4.00*
69	A13	4o violet	2.50	1.10

Engr.

70	A14	5o green ('11)	14.00	*29.00*
71	A14	10o carmine	10.00	.50
72	A14	1k black, *yel* ('11)	95.00	.50
73	A14	5k claret, *yel* ('14)	1.50	*3.00*
		Nos. 67-73 (7)	125.40	*39.60*

See #77-98. For surcharges see #99-104, Q1-Q2.

1911 **Unwmk.**

75	A10	20o blue	22.50	15.00
76	A10	25o red orange	27.50	4.00

1910-19

77	A14	5o green ('11)	2.00	.30
a.		Booklet pane of 10	225.00	
b.		Booklet pane of 4	125.00	
78	A14	7o gray grn ('18)	.30	.30
a.		Booklet pane of 10	8.75	
79	A14	8o mag ('12)	.30	.30
80	A14	10o car ('10)	2.00	.30
a.		Booklet pane of 10	225.00	
b.		Booklet pane of 4	135.00	
81	A14	12o rose lake ('18)	.30	.30
a.		Booklet pane of 10	10.00	
82	A14	15o red brn ('11)	6.00	.30
a.		Booklet pane of 10	375.00	
83	A14	20o dp bl ('11)	9.50	.30
a.		Booklet pane of 10	400.00	
84	A14	25o org red ('11)	.30	.30
85	A14	27o pale bl ('18)	.40	.90
86	A14	30o clar brn ('11)	20.00	.30
87	A14	35o dk vio ('11)	17.00	.30
88	A14	40o ol grn ('17)	25.00	.30
89	A14	50o gray ('12)	50.00	.30
90	A14	55o pale bl ('18)	*2,100.*	*6,500.*
91	A14	65o pale ol grn ('18)	.65	2.00
92	A14	80o black ('18)	*2,100.*	*6,500.*
93	A14	90o gray grn ('18)	.60	.65
94	A14	1k blk, *yel* ('19)	92.50	.30
		Nos. 77-89,91,93-94 (16)	226.85	7.45

Excellent forgeries of Nos. 90 and 92 exist.

1911-19 **Typo.** **Wmk. 181** *Perf. 13*

95	A13	1o black	.30	.30
96	A13	2o orange	.30	.30
97	A13	3o pale brown ('19)	.30	.30
98	A13	4o pale violet	.30	.30
		Nos. 95-98 (4)	1.20	1.20

Remainders of Nos. 95-98 received various private overprints, mostly as publicity for stamp exhibitions. They were not postally valid.

Unwatermarked Stamps with Watermarks

Stamps of these and later issues through the UPU Congress issue of 1924, are frequently found with watermark showing parts of the words "Kungl Postverket" in double-lined capitals. This watermark is normally located in the margins of the sheets of unwatermarked paper or paper watermarked wavy lines or crown.

Nos. 80, 84, 91, 90, 92 Surcharged

a

b

1918 **Unwmk.**

99	A14(a)	7o on 10o	.30	*.40*
100	A14(b)	12o on 25o	1.90	.40
a.		Inverted surcharge	625.00	1,200.
101	A14(a)	12o on 65o	.85	*1.40*
102	A14(a)	27o on 55o	.75	*1.60*
103	A14(a)	27o on 65o	1.40	*3.50*
104	A14(a)	27o on 80o	.85	*1.60*
		Nos. 99-104 (6)	6.05	8.90

Arms A15

Heraldic Lion Supporting Arms of Sweden A16

Two types each of 5o green, 5o copper red and 10o violet, type A16.

Perf. 10 Vertically

1920-25 Engr. Unwmk.
115 A15 3o copper red .30 *.40*
116 A16 5o green ('25) 4.00 .40
117 A16 5o cop red ('21) 5.00 .40
118 A16 10o green ('21) 21.00 .40
a. Tête bêche pair *1,650. 3,250.*
119 A16 10o violet ('25) 5.25 .40
120 A16 25o orange ('21) 13.00 .40
121 A16 30o brown .45 .45

Wmk. 181
122 A16 5o green 2.50 1.30
123 A16 5o cop red ('21) 8.25 1.00
124 A16 10o green ('21) 2.50 1.30
125 A16 30o brown 8.25 18.00
Nos. 115-125 (11) 70.50 24.45

Coil Stamps

Unless part of a booklet pane any stamp perforated only horizontally or vertically is a coil stamp.

1920-26 Unwmk. *Perf. 10*
126 A16 5o green 4.00 1.00
a. Booklet pane of 10 80.00
127 A16 10o green ('21) 11.50 3.50
a. Booklet pane of 10 225.00
128 A16 10o violet ('25) 6.50 .85
a. Booklet pane of 10 180.00
129 A16 30o brown 32.50 4.00

Wmk. 181
130 A16 5o green 11.50 30.00
131 A16 10o green ('21) 45.00 *100.00*
a. Booklet pane of 10 425.00

Perf. 13 Vertically

Unwmk.
132 A16 5o green ('25) 4.00 1.50
133 A16 5o cop red ('21) 325.00 160.00
134 A16 10o violet ('26) 25.00 37.50

Wmk. 181
135 A16 5o green ('25) 2.00 *8.00*
136 A16 5o cop red ('22) 2.00 7.00
137 A16 10o green ('24) 9.00 *40.00*
138 A16 10o violet ('25) 8.00 *25.00*
Nos. 126-138 (13) 486.00 418.35

The paper used for the earlier printings of types A16, A17, A18, A18a and A20 is usually tinted by the color of the stamp. Printings of 1934 and later are on white paper in slightly different shades.

King Gustaf V — A17

1920-21 Unwmk. *Perf. 10 Vertically*
139 A17 10o rose 25.00 .40
140 A17 15o claret .30 .45
141 A17 20o blue 30.00 .50

Perf. 10
142 A17 10o rose 12.50 6.00
143 A17 20o blue ('21) 29.00 11.00
a. Booklet pane of 10 550.00
Nos. 139-143 (5) 96.80 18.35

Wmk. 181
144 A17 20o blue *4,000.*

A18

Crown and Post Horn — A18a

See note after No. 138 regarding paper. There are 2 types of the 35, 40, 45 and 60o.

1920-34 Unwmk. *Perf. 10 Vert.*
145 A18 35o yellow ('22) 40.00 .75
146 A18 40o olive green 30.00 .75
147 A18 45o brown ('22) 1.25 .55
148 A18 60o claret 17.00 .40
149 A18 70o red brn ('22) .60 2.50
150 A18 80o deep green .40 .40
151 A18 85o myr grn ('29) 4.50 .45
152 A18 90o lt blue ('25) 50.00 .30
153 A18a 1kr dp org ('21) 7.00 .40
154 A18 110o ultra .50 .40
155 A18 115o red brn ('29) 8.00 .45
156 A18 120o gray blk ('25) 60.00 .60
157 A18 120o lil rose ('33) 14.00 .60
158 A18 140o gray black .90 .30
159 A18 145o brt grn ('30) 8.50 .55

Wmk. 181
160 A18 35o yellow ('23) 50.00 7.50
161 A18 60o red violet 80.00 *150.00*
162 A18 80o blue green 8.25 15.00
163 A18 110o ultra 3.50 4.50
Nos. 145-163 (19) 384.40 186.40

The value for #147 is for the 2nd type, issued in 1925.

Gustavus Adolphus — A19

Perf. 10 Vertically

1920, July 28 Unwmk.
164 A19 20o deep blue 2.25 .40

Wmk. 181
165 A19 20o blue 160.00 35.00

Unwmk.

Perf. 10
166 A19 20o blue 6.25 2.25
a. Booklet pane of 10 130.00
Nos. 164-166 (3) 168.50 37.65

Tercentenary of Swedish post which first ran between Stockholm and Hamburg.

King Gustaf V — A20

See note after No. 138 regarding paper. There are two types each of the 15o rose and 40o olive green.

1921-36 Unwmk. *Perf. 10 Vert.*
167 A20 15o vio ('22) 14.00 .40
168 A20 15o rose ('28) 5.50 .45
169 A20 15o brn ('36) 4.75 .45
170 A20 20o violet .25 .30
171 A20 20o rose ('22) 20.00 .60
172 A20 20o org ('25) .25 .45
174 A20 25o rose red ('22) .55 1.50
175 A20 25o dk bl ('25) 11.00 .40
176 A20 25o ultra ('34) 11.00 .80
177 A20 25o yel org ('36) 25.00 .45
178 A20 30o blue ('23) 16.00 .45
179 A20 30o brn ('25) 20.00 .35
180 A20 30o lt ultra ('36) 6.00 .70
181 A20 35o red vio ('30) 24.00 .45
182 A20 40o blue .45 .70
183 A20 40o ol grn ('29) 35.00 2.00
184 A20 45o brn ('29) 5.00 .90
185 A20 50o gray 1.75 1.00
186 A20 85o myr grn ('25) 17.00 2.00
187 A20 115o brn red ('25) 11.00 2.00
188 A20 145o apl grn ('25) 8.25 2.00
Nos. 167-188 (21) 236.75 18.35

Wmk. 181
189 A20 15o vio ('22) 3,500. 1,050.
189A A20 20o violet *4,750.*

1922-36 Unwmk. *Perf. 10*
190 A20 15o violet 17.50 .70
a. Booklet pane of 10 400.00
191 A20 15o rose red ('25) 22.50 .90
a. Booklet pane of 10 600.00
192 A20 15o brown ('36) 5.75 1.25
a. Booklet pane of 10 175.00
193 A20 20o violet ('22) .50 *1.50*
a. Booklet pane of 10 10.00
Nos. 190-193 (4) 46.25 4.35

Gustavus Vasa — A21

1921, June *Perf. 10 Vertically*
194 A21 20o violet 14.00 *30.00*
195 A21 110o ultra 50.00 8.00
196 A21 140o gray black 25.00 8.00
Nos. 194-196 (3) 89.00 46.00

400th anniversary of Gustavus Vasa's war of independence from the Danes.

Universal Postal Union Congress

Composite View of Stockholm's Skyline A22

King Gustaf V — A23

1924, July 4 Unwmk. *Perf. 10*
197 A22 5o red brown 1.60 *3.25*
198 A22 10o green 1.60 *3.25*
199 A22 15o dk violet 1.60 *2.50*
200 A22 20o rose red 12.50 *21.00*
201 A22 25o dp orange 15.00 *21.00*
202 A22 30o deep blue 15.00 *21.00*
a. 30o greenish blue 87.50 125.00
203 A22 35o black 20.00 *28.00*
204 A22 40o olive green 29.00 *32.50*
205 A22 45o deep brown 30.00 32.50
206 A22 50o gray 30.00 32.50
207 A22 60o violet brn 45.00 *55.00*
208 A22 80o myrtle grn 35.00 37.50
209 A23 1k green 55.00 *87.50*
210 A23 2k rose red 125.00 *250.00*
211 A23 5k deep blue 250.00 *450.00*

Wmk. 181
212 A22 10o green 26.00 *65.00*
Nos. 197-212 (16) 692.30 *1,143.*
Set, never hinged 1,400.

Postrider Watching Airplane A24

Carrier Pigeon and Globe — A25

1924, Aug. 16 Engr. Unwmk.
213 A24 5o red brown 2.75 4.50
214 A24 10o green 2.75 5.75
215 A24 15o dk violet 3.00 3.00
216 A24 20o rose red 21.00 32.50
217 A24 25o deep orange 26.00 32.50
218 A24 30o deep blue 26.00 32.50
a. 30o greenish blue 90.00 52.50
219 A24 35o black 32.50 47.50
220 A24 40o olive green 32.50 32.50
221 A24 45o deep brown 37.50 35.00
222 A24 50o gray 45.00 62.50
223 A24 60o violet brown 45.00 77.50
224 A24 80o myrtle green 37.50 37.50
225 A25 1k green 75.00 87.50
226 A25 2k rose red 110.00 75.00
227 A25 5k deep blue 225.00 225.00

Wmk. 181
228 A24 10o green 35.00 *65.00*
Nos. 213-228 (16) 756.50 855.75
Set, never hinged 1,600.

Universal Postal Union issue.

Royal Palace at Stockholm A26

1931, Nov. 26 Unwmk. *Perf. 10*
229 A26 5k dark green 90.00 12.50
Never hinged 300.00
a. Booklet pane of 10 3,100.

Death of Gustavus Adolphus — A27

1932, Nov. 1
230 A27 10o dark violet 2.50 5.50
a. Booklet pane of 10 40.00
231 A27 15o dark red 4.50 2.00
a. Booklet pane of 10 110.00

Perf. 10 Vertically
232 A27 10o dark violet 1.90 .40
233 A27 15o dark red 2.50 .40
234 A27 25o dark blue 6.00 .95
235 A27 90o dark green 20.00 2.25
Nos. 230-235 (6) 37.40 11.50
Set, never hinged 85.00

300th anniv. of the death of King Gustavus Adolphus II who was killed on the battlefield of Lützen, Nov. 6, 1632.

Catching Sunlight in Bowl — A28

1933, Dec. 6 *Perf. 10*
236 A28 5o green 2.50 2.00
a. Booklet pane of 10 60.00

There are two types of No. 236.

Perf. 10 Vertically
237 A28 5o green 2.50 .40

Perf. 13 Vertically
238 A28 5o green 3.50 7.25
Nos. 236-238 (3) 8.50 9.65
Set, never hinged 17.50

50th anniv. of the Swedish Postal Savings Bank.

The Old Law Courts — A29

The "Four Estates" and Arms of Engelbrekt A34

Designs: 10o, Stock exchange. 15o, Parish church (Storkyrkan). 25o, House of the Nobility. 35o, House of Parliament.

1935, Jan. 10 *Perf. 10*
239 A29 5o green 2.25 1.40
a. Booklet pane of 10 100.00
240 A29 10o dull violet 4.25 *5.75*
a. Booklet pane of 10 110.00
241 A29 15o carmine 4.75 1.10
a. Booklet pane of 10 200.00

Perf. 10 Vertically
242 A29 5o green 1.25 .40
243 A29 10o dull violet 5.75 .40
244 A29 15o carmine 2.25 .40
245 A29 25o ultra 6.00 .60
246 A29 35o deep claret 12.00 2.25
247 A34 60o deep claret 17.50 2.50
Nos. 239-247 (9) 56.00 14.80
Set, never hinged 125.00

500th anniv. of the Swedish Parliament.

Chancellor Axel Oxenstierna A35

Post Runner — A36

Mounted Courier — A37

Old Sailing Packet — A38

Mail Paddle Steamship A39

Mail Coach — A40

1855 Stamp Model — A41

Mail Train — A42

Postmaster General A. W. Roos — A43

Mail Truck and Trailer — A44

Modern Swedish Liner — A45

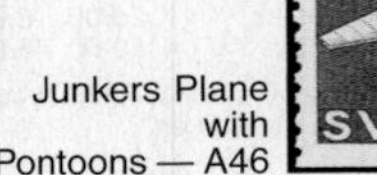

Junkers Plane with Pontoons — A46

1936, Feb. 20 **Engr.** ***Perf. 10***

No.	Type	Denomination / Color	Unused	Used
248	A35	5o green	1.75	.85
a.		Booklet pane of 18	72.50	
249	A36	10o dk violet	2.10	3.00
a.		Booklet pane of 18	95.00	
250	A37	15o dk carmine	3.00	.55
a.		Booklet pane of 18	250.00	

Perf. 10 Vertically

No.	Type	Denomination / Color	Unused	Used
251	A35	5o green	1.75	.25
252	A36	10o dk violet	1.75	.25
253	A37	15o dk carmine	3.25	.25
254	A38	20o lt blue	8.25	5.00
255	A39	25o lt ultra	5.25	.50
256	A40	30o yellow brn	16.00	3.25
257	A41	35o plum	5.50	1.25
258	A42	40o olive grn	5.75	2.75
259	A43	45o myrtle grn	7.75	1.50
260	A44	50o gray	20.00	2.75
261	A45	60o maroon	25.00	.70
262	A46	1k deep blue	8.25	8.50
		Nos. 248-262 (15)	115.35	31.35
		Set, never hinged	320.00	

300th anniv. of the Swedish Postal Service.

See Nos. 946-950, B55-B56 in Scott Standard catalogue, Vol. 6.

Airplane over Bromma Airport A47

Design Size: 33.25mm x 25.5mm

1936, May 23 ***Perf. 10 Vert.***

No.	Type	Denomination / Color	Unused	Used
263	A47	50o ultra	4.00	8.50
		Never hinged	10.50	

Opening of Bromma Airport near Stockholm.

Swedish Booklets

Before 1940, booklets were handmade and usually held two panes of 10 stamps (2x5). About every third booklet contained one row of stamps with straight edges at right or left side. Setenant pairs may be obtained with one stamp perforated on 4 sides and one perforated on 3 sides.

Starting in 1940, booklet stamps have one or more straight edges.

Some combination booklets containing multiple face-different stamps may exist with different configurations of those stamps. The most common configuration has been valued.

Emanuel Swedenborg — A48

1938, Jan. 29 ***Perf. 12½***

No.	Type	Denomination / Color	Unused	Used
264	A48	10o violet	1.00	.35
a.		Perf. on 3 sides	8.00	4.00
		Never hinged	17.00	
b.		Booklet pane of 10	30.00	

Perf. 12½ Vertically

No.	Type	Denomination / Color	Unused	Used
266	A48	10o violet	.90	.25
267	A48	100o green	2.00	1.40
		Nos. 264-267 (3)	3.90	2.00
		Set, never hinged	14.00	

250th anniv. of the birth of Swedenborg, scientist, philosopher and religious writer.

Johann Printz and Indian Chief — A49

"Kalmar Nyckel" Sailing from Gothenburg A50

Symbolizing the Settlement of New Sweden — A51

Holy Trinity Church, Wilmington, Del. — A52

Queen Christina — A53

1938, Apr. 8 ***Perf. 12½ Vert.***

No.	Type	Denomination / Color	Unused	Used
268	A49	5o green	.60	.30
269	A50	15o brown	.60	.30
270	A51	20o red	1.00	.70
271	A52	30o ultra	2.25	.85
272	A53	60o brown lake	3.00	.35

Perf. 12½

No.	Type	Denomination / Color	Unused	Used
273	A49	5o green	1.00	1.00
a.		Perf. on 3 sides	5.00	*7.50*
		Never hinged	17.00	
b.		Booklet pane of 18	67.50	
274	A50	15o brown	1.50	.70
a.		Perf. on 3 sides	10.00	4.75
		Never hinged	29.00	
b.		Booklet pane of 18	115.00	
		Nos. 268-274 (7)	9.95	4.20
		Set, never hinged	39.00	

Tercentenary of the Swedish settlement at Wilmington, Del. See No. B54 in Scott Standard catalogue, Vol. 6.

King Gustaf V — A54

1938, June 16 ***Perf. 12½ Vert.***

No.	Type	Denomination / Color	Unused	Used
275	A54	5o green	.40	.30
276	A54	15(o) brown	.45	.30
277	A54	30(o) ultra	10.00	.75

Perf. 12½

No.	Type	Denomination / Color	Unused	Used
278	A54	5o green	.85	.40
a.		Perf. on 3 sides	5.00	5.50
		Never hinged	22.50	
b.		Booklet pane of 10	45.00	
279	A54	15(o) brown	1.00	.40
a.		Perf. on 3 sides	7.00	1.40
		Never hinged	35.00	
b.		Booklet pane of 10	37.50	
		Nos. 275-279 (5)	12.70	2.15
		Set, never hinged	37.00	

80th birthday of King Gustaf V.

King Gustaf V — A55

Three Crowns — A56

1939 ***Perf. 12½ Vertically***

No.	Type	Denomination / Color	Unused	Used
280	A55	10o violet	.40	.40
281	A55	20o carmine	1.00	.60
282	A56	60o lake	.40	.30
283	A56	85o dk green	.30	.30
284	A56	90o peacock blue	.30	.30
285	A56	1k orange	.30	.30
286	A56	1.15k henna brn	.30	.30
287	A56	1.20k brt rose vio	.80	.30
288	A56	1.45k lt yel grn	.85	.80

Perf. 12½

No.	Type	Denomination / Color	Unused	Used
289	A55	10o violet	1.00	4.00
a.		Perf. on 3 sides	30.00	65.00
		Never hinged	80.00	
b.		Bklt. pane of 10, perf. on 4 sides	30.00	
		Nos. 280-289 (10)	5.65	7.60
		Set, never hinged	20.00	

See Nos. 394-398, 416-417, 425-426, 431, 439-441, 473, 588-591, 656-664 in Scott Standard catalogue, Vol. 6.

Per Henrik Ling — A57

1939, Feb. 25 ***Perf. 12½ Vert.***

No.	Type	Denomination / Color	Unused	Used
290	A57	5o green	.25	.25
291	A57	25(o) brown	.40	.40

Perf. 12½

No.	Type	Denomination / Color	Unused	Used
292	A57	5o green	.40	.40
a.		Perf. on 3 sides	6.00	6.00
		Never hinged	29.00	
b.		Booklet pane of 10	37.50	
		Nos. 290-292 (3)	1.05	1.05
		Set, never hinged	4.00	

Centenary of the death of P. H. Ling, father of Swedish gymnastics.

J. J. Berzelius A58

Carl von Linné A59

Perf. 12½ Vertically

1939, June 2 **Engr.**

No.	Type	Denomination / Color	Unused	Used
293	A58	10o violet	1.00	.40
294	A59	15o fawn	.25	.30
295	A58	30o ultra	6.00	.45
296	A59	50o gray	6.50	1.00

Perf. 12½

No.	Type	Denomination / Color	Unused	Used
297	A58	10o violet	.90	.65
a.		Perf. on 3 sides	25.00	19.00
		Never hinged	135.00	
b.		Booklet pane of 10	65.00	
298	A59	15o fawn	1.00	.50
a.		Perf. on 3 sides	5.00	.45
		Never hinged	20.00	
b.		Booklet pane of 10	100.00	
c.		As "a," bklt. pane of 20	450.00	
		Nos. 293-298 (6)	15.65	3.30
		Set, never hinged	70.00	

200th anniv. of the founding of the Royal Academy of Science at Stockholm.

King Gustaf V — A60

Type A55 Re-engraved

1939-46 ***Perf. 12½***

No.	Type	Denomination / Color	Unused	Used
299	A60	5o dp green ('46)	.30	.30
b.		Perf. on 3 sides ('41)	.30	.30
		Never hinged	.50	
c.		As "b," bklt. pane of 20	12.00	
300	A60	10(o) violet ('46)	.30	.30
a.		Bklt. pane of 10, perf. on 4 sides	55.00	
		Never hinged	.50	
c.		Perf. on 3 sides	2.00	.30
i.		As "c," booklet pane of 20	50.00	
300D	A60	15(o) chestnut ('46)	.30	.30
f.		Perf. on 3 sides ('45)	.30	.30
		Never hinged	.65	
j.		As "f," booklet pane of 20	7.75	
300G	A60	20(o) red ('42)	.30	.25
h.		Booklet pane of 20	6.50	
		Nos. 299-300G (4)	1.20	1.15
		Set, never hinged	1.50	

No. 300 differs slightly from the original due to deeper engraving. No. 300G was issued only in booklets; all examples have one straight edge.

Nos. 299, 300, 300D exist in booklet panes of 20 made from sheets of stamps. These can be collected as booklets.

1940-42 ***Perf. 12½ Vertically***

No.	Type	Denomination / Color	Unused	Used
301	A60	5o dp green ('41)	.25	.30
302	A60	10(o) violet	.25	.30
302A	A60	15(o) chestnut ('42)	.25	.30
303	A60	20(o) red	.25	.30
304	A60	25(o) orange	.40	.30
305	A60	30(o) ultra	.40	.30

306 A60 35(o) red vio ('41) .40 .30
307 A60 40(o) olive grn .40 .30
308 A60 45(o) dk brown .40 .30
309 A60 50(o) gray blk ('41) 2.75 .30
Nos. 301-309 (10) 5.75 3.00
Set, never hinged 13.00

Numerals measure 4½mm high. Less shading around head gives a lighter effect. Horizontal lines only as background for "SVERIGE."

See Nos. 391-393, 399 in Scott Standard catalogue, Vol. 6.

Carl Michael Bellman — A61

1940, Feb. 4 Engr. ***Perf. 12½ Vert.***
310 A61 5o green .25 .25
311 A61 35(o) rose red .40 .40

Perf. 12½
312 A61 5o green .50 *.60*
a. Perf. on 3 sides 2.25 .75
Never hinged 21.00
b. Booklet pane of 10 50.00
c. As "a," bklt. pane of 20 425.00
Nos. 310-312 (3) 1.15 1.25
Set, never hinged 3.75

Bellman (1740-95), lyric poet.

Tobias Sergel — A62

1940, Sept. 5 ***Perf. 12½ on 3 Sides***
313 A62 15o lt brown 4.00 .50
a. Booklet pane of 20 275.00

Perf. 12½ Vertically
314 A62 15o lt brown 1.00 .40
315 A62 50o gray black 5.00 1.40
Nos. 313-315 (3) 10.00 2.30
Set, never hinged 70.00

Bicentenary of birth of Johan Tobias von Sergel (1740-1814), sculptor.

SEMI-POSTAL STAMPS

Type of 1872-91 Issues Surcharged in Dark Blue

Perf. 13x13½
1916, Dec. 21 Wmk. 181
B1 A5 5o + 5o on 2o org 4.75 *7.25*
B2 A5 5o + 5o on 3o yel brn 4.75 *7.25*
B3 A5 5o + 5o on 4o gray 4.75 *7.25*
B4 A5 5o + 5o on 5o grn 4.75 *7.25*
B5 A5 5o + 5o on 6o lilac 4.75 *7.25*
B6 A5 10o + 10o on 12o pale bl 4.75 *7.25*
B7 A5 10o + 10o on 20o red org 4.75 *7.25*
B8 A5 10o + 10o on 24o yel 4.75 *7.25*
B9 A5 10o + 10o on 30o brn 4.75 *7.25*
B10 A5 10o + 10o on 50o rose red 4.75 *7.25*
Nos. B1-B10 (10) 47.50 72.50
Set, never hinged 122.50

The surtax on Nos. B1-B31 was for the militia. See note after No. B21.

For surcharges see Nos. B22-B31.

No. 66 Surcharged in Dark Blue

1916, Dec. 21 Wmk. 180 ***Perf. 13***
B11 A12 10o + 4.90k on 5k 150.00 *375.00*
Never hinged 225.00

Nos. J12-J22 Surcharged in Dark Blue

1916, Dec. 21 Unwmk. ***Perf. 13***
B12 D1 5o + 5o on 1o 25.00 18.00
B13 D1 5o + 5o on 3o 5.00 7.00
B14 D1 5o + 5o on 5o 18.00 7.00
B15 D1 5o + 10o on 6o 5.00 8.00
B16 D1 5o + 15o on 12o 42.50 32.50
B17 D1 10o + 20o on 20o 15.00 25.00
B18 D1 10o + 40o on 24o 55.00 *100.00*
B19 D1 10o + 20o on 30o 6.50 6.00
B20 D1 10o + 40o on 50o 20.00 *42.50*
B21 D1 10o + 90o on 1kr 150.00 *375.00*
Nos. B12-B21 (10) 342.00 *621.00*
Set, never hinged 900.00

The surtax on Nos. B12-B21 is indicated not in figures, but in words at bottom of surcharge: Fem, 5; Tio, 10; Femton, 15; Tjugo, 20; Fyrtio, 40; Nittio, 90.

Nos. B1-B10 Surcharged

1918, Dec. 18 Wmk. 181
B22 A5 7o + 3o on #B1 8.00 *9.00*
B23 A5 7o + 3o on #B2 2.75 1.25
B24 A5 7o + 3o on #B3 2.75 1.25
B25 A5 7o + 3o on #B4 2.75 1.25
B26 A5 7o + 3o on #B5 2.75 1.25
B27 A5 12o + 8o on #B6 2.75 1.25
B28 A5 12o + 8o on #B7 2.75 1.25
B29 A5 12o + 8o on #B8 2.75 1.25
B30 A5 12o + 8o on #B9 2.75 1.25
B31 A5 12o + 8o on #B10 2.75 1.25
Nos. B22-B31 (10) 32.75 20.25
Set, never hinged 100.00

The 12o+8o surcharge exists on Nos. B1-B5 and the 7o+3o surcharge exists on Nos. B6-B10. Value, each $72.50.

Nos. B24, B26, B28 and B30 exist with surcharge inverted. Value unused, each $140.

King Gustaf V — SP1

Unwmk.
1928, June 16 Engr. ***Perf. 10***
B32 SP1 5o (+ 5o) yel grn 2.75 *6.00*
B33 SP1 10o (+ 5o) dk vio 2.75 *6.00*
B34 SP1 15o (+ 5o) car 2.75 *4.50*
Complete booklet, pane of 8 ea. #B32, B33, B34 275.00
B35 SP1 20o (+ 5o) org 4.75 2.75
B36 SP1 25o (+ 5o) dk bl 4.75 3.25
Nos. B32-B36 (5) 17.75 *22.50*
Set, never hinged 27.50

70th birthday of King Gustaf V. The surtax was used for anti-cancer work.

AIR POST STAMPS

Official Stamps Surcharged in Dark Blue

1920, Sept. 17 Wmk. 181 ***Perf. 13***
C1 O3 10o on 3o brn 2.25 *7.75*
a. Inverted surcharge 375.00 *1,350.*
C2 O3 20o on 2o org 3.50 *11.00*
a. Inverted surcharge 375.00 *1,100.*
C3 O3 50o on 4o vio 19.00 25.00
a. Inverted surcharge 375.00 *1,350.*
Nos. C1-C3 (3) 24.75 *43.75*
Set, never hinged 62.50

Wmk. 180
C4 O3 20o on 2o org 3,250.
Never hinged 5,000.
C5 O3 50o on 4o vio 190.00 *600.00*
Never hinged 350.00

Airplane over Stockholm AP2

Perf. 10 Vertically
1930, May 9 Engr. Unwmk.
C6 AP2 10o deep blue .25 .60
C7 AP2 50o dark violet .65 1.75
Set, never hinged 1.50

POSTAGE DUE STAMPS

D1

1874 Unwmk. Typo. ***Perf. 14***
J1 D1 1o black 75.00 40.00
J2 D1 3o rose 75.00 40.00
J3 D1 5o brown 75.00 35.00
J4 D1 6o yellow 150.00 95.00
J5 D1 12o pale red 7.75 6.00
J6 D1 20o blue 80.00 37.50
J7 D1 24o violet 625.00 375.00
J8 D1 24o gray 75.00 52.50
J9 D1 30o dk grn 87.50 40.00
J10 D1 50o brown 275.00 60.00
J11 D1 1k blue & bister 300.00 75.00
Nos. J1-J11 (11) 1,825. 856.00

1877-86 ***Perf. 13***
J12 D1 1o black ('80) 2.75 4.00
J13 D1 3o rose 6.25 7.25
J14 D1 5o brown 4.50 4.50
J15 D1 6o yellow 4.50 4.50
a. Printed on both sides 1,600.
J16 D1 12o pale red ('82) 14.50 17.00
J17 D1 20o pale blue ('78) 5.25 4.50
J18 D1 24o red lilac ('86) 26.00 29.00
a. 24o violet ('84) 26.00 29.00
J19 D1 24o gray lil ('82) 190.00 *240.00*
J20 D1 30o yellow green 6.50 4.50
J21 D1 50o yellow brown 10.50 5.75
J22 D1 1k blue & bister 30.00 17.50
Nos. J12-J22 (11) 300.75 338.50

Nos. J12-J17, J19-J22 exist imperf. Value, pairs, each $400.

For surcharges see Nos. B12-B21.

STAMPS FOR CITY POSTAGE

S1

1856-62 Typo. Unwmk. ***Perf. 14***
LX1 S1 (1sk) (3o) blk, medium thick paper ('58) 1,100. 550.00
On cover 600.00
On cover, before July 1, 1858 750.00
a. (1sk) gray black, thin paper ('56) *5,000.* 900.00
On cover 2,750.
LX2 S1 (3o) bis brn ('62) 600.00 550.00
On cover 675.00
a. (3o) olive brown ('62) 675.00 525.00
On cover 675.00

From 1856 to 1858 Nos. LX1, LX1a were sold at 1sk, from 1858 to 1862 No. LX1 was sold for 3o.

Issued: No. LX1, 7/1/58; LX1a, 5/22/56; LX2, 1/1/62.

REPRINTS AND RE-ISSUES

No. LX1 was reprinted twice in 1868 from new blocks. Nos. LX1 and LX2 were reprinted in 1871 and 1885 from an original plate. These re-issues and reprints were valid for postage until 1910, but only the 1871 issue is known used.

No. LX1 Original Printing

No. LX1 1868 Re-Issue

Distinguishing characteristics: #LX1p, LX1q, a white line runs from the pearl at right of "LOKALBREF" to the right frame line; the two pearls above the "M" of "FRIMÄRKE" are damaged and run together; there is a black spot over the pearl adjacent to the space between the "E" of "FRIMÄRKE" and the "F" of "LOKALBREF." On No. LX1p, the white ring surrounding this spot is clear and relatively strong; on No. LX1q, it is weak and sometimes barely discernible.

No. LX1r: as original, except perforation is straighter and often has wider corner perfs.

No. LX2r: yellowish brown; perfs are straighter than originals, with somewhat thicker teeth.

No. LX1s: perf 13; black is sharper and more intense than on other printings.

No. LX2s: perf 13; printed in an orange brown shade.

1868 ***Perf. 14***
LX1p S1 (3o) black (1st ptg.) 525.00
Never hinged 925.00
LX1q S1 (3o) black (2nd ptg.) 350.00
Never hinged 575.00

1871 ***Perf. 14***
LX1r S1 (3o) black 290.00 *525.00*
Never hinged 460.00
LX2r S1 (3o) yellow brown 250.00 *400.00*
Never hinged 400.00

1885 ***Perf. 13***
LX1s S1 (3o) black 190.00
Never hinged 290.00
LX2s S1 (3o) orange brown 160.00
Never hinged 250.00

OFFICIAL STAMPS

O1

1874-77 Unwmk. Typo. ***Perf. 14***
O1 O1 3o bister 90.00 42.50
On cover 45.00
O2 O1 4o gray ('77) 300.00 75.00
On cover 80.00
O3 O1 5o yel green 140.00 52.50
On cover 130.00
O4 O1 6o lilac 275.00 65.00
On cover 75.00
O5 O1 6o gray 525.00 175.00
On cover 200.00
O6 O1 12o blue 200.00 3.00
On cover 15.00
O7 O1 20o pale red 1,050. 90.00
On cover 300.00
O8 O1 24o yellow 1,050. 20.00
On cover 55.00
a. 24o orange 1,050. 22.50
On cover 60.00
O9 O1 30o pale brn 425.00 37.50
On cover 210.00
O10 O1 50o rose 600.00 125.00
On cover 425.00
O11 O1 1k bl & bis 1,700. 65.00
On cover 750.00
Nos. O1-O11 (11) 6,355. 750.50

Imperf., Pairs
O1a O1 3o 1,500.
O2a O1 4o 1,500.
O3a O1 5o 1,500.
O4a O1 6o 1,500.
O6a O1 12o 1,500.
O7a O1 20o 1,500.
O8b O1 24o 1,500.
O9a O1 30o 1,500.
O10a O1 50o 1,500.
O11a O1 1k 2,500.

1881-96 ***Perf. 13***
O12 O1 2o org ('91) 1.40 2.00
On cover 22.50
O13 O1 3o bis brn 1.40 2.25
On cover 17.00
O14 O1 4o gray blk ('93) 2.50 .70
On cover 8.00
a. 4o gray ('82) 20.00 2.75
On cover 8.00
O15 O1 5o grn ('84) 5.25 .60
On cover 9.00

O16 O1 6o red lil ('82) 40.00 60.00
On cover 62.50
a. 6o lilac ('81) 45.00 65.00
On cover *75.00*
O17 O1 10o car ('95) 3.00 .25
On cover 4.00
b. 10o rose ('85) 45.00 1.25
On cover 14.00
O18 O1 12o blue 57.50 22.50
On cover 24.00
O19 O1 20o ver ('82) 200.00 2.50
On cover 55.00
O20 O1 20o dk bl ('91) 5.75 .60
On cover 12.00
O21 O1 24o yellow 72.50 25.00
On cover 65.00
a. 24o orange 65.00 25.00
On cover *125.00*
O22 O1 30o brown 26.00 .70
On cover 12.50
O23 O1 50o pale rose 140.00 25.00
On cover 110.00
O24 O1 50o pale gray ('93) 18.00 3.00
On cover 17.50
O25 O1 1k dk bl & yel brn, square periods ('96) 9.00 2.50
On cover 32.50
a. blue & brn, round periods ('81) 500.00 6.50
Nos. O12-O25 (14) 582.30 147.60

No. O25 has square periods. No. O25a has round periods.

Imperf., Pairs

O12a O1 2o 400.00
O17a O1 10o No. O17 400.00
c. No. O17b 400.00
O20a O1 20o 50.00
O24a O1 50o 400.00

Surcharged in Dark Blue

1889

O26 O1 10o on 12o blue 13.00 *18.00*
On cover 525.00
a. Inverted surcharge 2,100. *5,000.*
On cover —
b. Perf. 14 *5,500.* *5,500.*
O27 O1 10o on 24o yel 16.00 *25.00*
On cover 2,000.
a. Inverted surcharge *7,000.* *5,500.*
b. Perf. 14 *5,500.* *5,500.*

O3

1910-12 Wmk. 180 Typo.

O28 O3 1o black .30 .45
Never hinged .50
On cover 16.00
O29 O3 2o orange 1.40 *4.50*
Never hinged 2.50
On cover 24.00
O30 O3 4o pale violet 1.75 *4.00*
Never hinged 3.75
On cover 16.00
O31 O3 5o green .50 *1.10*
Never hinged 1.25
On cover 12.00
O32 O3 8o claret .40 *1.10*
Never hinged 1.20
On cover 32.50
O33 O3 10o red 11.00 .70
Never hinged 27.50
On cover 17.00
O34 O3 15o red brown .80 .80
Never hinged 2.00
On cover 27.50
O35 O3 20o deep blue 7.00 1.75
Never hinged 20.00
On cover 37.50
O36 O3 25o red orange 7.00 2.50
Never hinged 20.00
On cover 40.00
O37 O3 30o chocolate 7.00 3.50
Never hinged 20.00
On cover 55.00
O38 O3 50o gray 7.00 3.50
Never hinged 20.00
On cover 27.50
O39 O3 1k black, *yellow* 7.75 7.75
Never hinged 20.00
On cover 35.00
O40 O3 5k claret, *yellow* 10.00 4.00
Never hinged 25.00
On cover 45.00
Nos. O28-O40 (13) 61.90 35.65
Set, never hinged 145.00

1910-19 Wmk. Wavy Lines (181)

O41 O3 1o black 2.00 *3.75*
Never hinged 5.00
On cover 17.00
O42 O3 2o orange .30 *.40*
Never hinged .40
On cover 6.00
O43 O3 3o pale brown .40 *1.00*
Never hinged .80
On cover 9.00
O44 O3 4o pale violet .30 *.40*
Never hinged .50
On cover 5.00
O45 O3 5o green .30 *.40*
Never hinged .50
On cover 3.00
O46 O3 7o gray green .40 *1.25*
Never hinged .80
On cover 15.00
O47 O3 8o rose 18.00 *27.50*
Never hinged 35.00
On cover 100.00
O48 O3 10o red .30 .25
Never hinged .40
On cover 5.00
O49 O3 12o rose red .30 .40
Never hinged .40
On cover 5.50
O50 O3 15o org brown .30 .30
Never hinged .60
On cover 8.00
O51 O3 20o deep blue .45 .30
Never hinged .70
On cover 8.00
O52 O3 25o orange .80 .50
Never hinged 2.00
On cover 12.00
O53 O3 30o chocolate .55 .55
Never hinged 1.25
On cover 12.00
O54 O3 35o dark violet .85 *1.00*
Never hinged 1.75
On cover 12.00
O55 O3 50o gray 3.25 2.25
Never hinged 6.50
On cover 14.00
Nos. O41-O55 (15) 28.50 40.25
Set, never hinged 60.00

For surcharges see Nos. C1-C5.

Use of official stamps ceased on July 1, 1920.

PARCEL POST STAMPS

Regular Issue of 1914 Surcharged

1917 Wmk. 180 *Perf. 13*

Q1 A14 1.98k on 5k claret, *yel* 1.40 *6.00*
Q2 A14 2.12k on 5k claret, *yel* 1.40 *6.00*
Set, never hinged 5.50

SWITZERLAND

'swit-sər-lənd

(Helvetia)

LOCATION — Central Europe, between France, Germany and Italy
GOVT. — Republic
AREA — 15,943 sq. mi.
POP. — 6,423,100 (est. 1983)
CAPITAL — Bern

100 Rappen or Centimes = 1 Franc

Watermarks

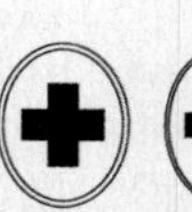

Type I Type II
Wmk. 182 — Cross in Oval

Wmk. 183 — Swiss Cross

Watermark 182 is not a true watermark, having been impressed after the paper was manufactured. There are two types: Type I: width just under 9mm; height just under 11mm; double oval lines nearly 1mm apart; cross has short, thick arms. Type II: width just under 8½mm; double oval lines very close together; cross has longer, thinner arms than Type I.

CANTONAL ADMINISTRATION

Unused values of Nos. 1L1-3L1 are for stamps without gum.
Counterfeit and repaired examples of Nos. 1L1-3L1 abound.

Zurich

A1 A2
Numerals of Value

1843 Unwmk. Litho. *Imperf.*
Red Vertical Lines

1L1 A1 4r black *27,000.* *18,500.*
On cover *40,000.*
1L2 A2 6r black *7,700.* *1,950.*
On cover *4,750.*

1846 Red Horizontal Lines

1L3 A1 4r black *18,500.* *25,000.*
On cover *55,000.*
1L4 A2 6r black 2,175. 1,775.
On cover *4,200.*

Full margins = ½mm. There are dividing lines between stamps.

Five varieties of each value.
Reprints of the Zurich stamps show signs of wear and lack the red lines. Values 4r, $7,000; 6r, $2,350.

Coat of Arms — A3

1850 Unwmk. *Imperf.*

1L5 A3 2½r black & red *7,750.* *4,200.*
On cover, single franking *55,000.*
Pair 140,000. *10,500.*
On cover, pair *27,500.*

Full margins = 1¼mm.

No. 1L5 has separation designs in the margins between stamps as shown. Values are for stamps showing part of the separation design on all four sides.

Geneva

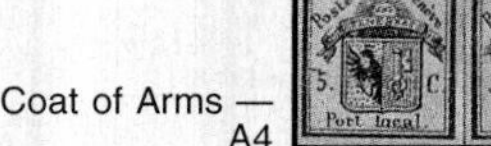

Coat of Arms — A4

1843 Unwmk. Litho. *Imperf.*

2L1 A4 10c blk, *yel grn* *77,500.* *42,500.*
On cover *77,500.*
a. Either half *24,750.* *9,250.*
On cover *19,250.*
b. Stamp composed of right half at left & left half at right *77,500.* *60,000.*
On cover *100,000.*

Full margins = ¾mm. There are dividing lines between stamps.

A5

A6

1845-48

2L2 A5 5c blk, *yel grn* 3,400. 1,900.
On cover 3,750.
2L3 A6 5c blk, *yel grn* ('46) 2,350. 2,000.
On cover 3,750.
2L4 A6 5c blk, *dk grn* ('48) 4,500. 3,000.
On cover 5,750.

Full margins: No. 2L2 = ¼mm; Nos. 2L3-2L4 = ½mm.

Values for pairs

2L2 A5 5c blk, *yel grn* *38,000.* *50,000.*
On cover *100,000.*
2L3 A6 5c blk, *yel grn* *31,000.* *50,000.*
On cover *100,000.*
2L4 A6 5c blk, *dk grn* *31,000.* *23,000.*
On cover *46,500.*

A7

1849-50

2L5 A7 4c black & red *46,000.* *20,750.*
On cover *45,000.*
2L6 A7 5c blk & red ('50) 2,750. 1,950.
On cover 3,750.

Full margins = 1mm. There are dividing lines between stamps.

Values for pairs

2L5 A7 4c black & red *195,000.* *175,000.*
On cover *325,000.*
2L6 A7 5c black & red *46,500.* *50,000.*
On cover *100,000.*

Coat of Arms — A8

1851

2L7 A8 5c black & red *10,500.* *4,150.*
On cover 7,750.
Pair 230,000. 230,000.
On cover 42,500.

Full margins = 1mm. There are dividing lines between stamps.

ENVELOPE STAMP USED AS ADHESIVE

E1

1847 Unwmk. *Imperf.*

2LU1 E1 5c yel grn, see footnote *22,500.*

Value is for cut-out stamp used on folded letters. This use was authorized and is known from Feb. 19, 1847. Value of unused envelope cut-out, $475. Value of used cut-out off cover, $3,850.

Basel

Dove of Basel — A9

Typo. & Embossed
1845 Unwmk. *Imperf.*

3L1 A1 2½r blk, crim & bl *17,500.* *15,500.*
On cover *35,000.*
Pair 170,000. 170,000.
On cover 300,000.
a. 2½r blk, crim & brt blue *19,250.* *17,750.*
On cover *38,500.*

Full margins = 1¼mm.

Proofs are black, vermilion and green. Value, $6,000.

FEDERAL ADMINISTRATION

Due to its tendency to damage the paper and/or the color of the stamps, the gum on Nos. 1-40 very often is removed. Unused values for Nos. 1-40 are for stamps without gum. Stamps with original gum sell for about the same prices.

A10

A11

1850 Unwmk. Litho. *Imperf.*

Full Black Frame Around Cross

1 A10 2½r black & red 3,500. 1,500.
On cover, single franking 7,350.
On cover, pair 6,500.
2 A11 2½r black & red 3,100. 1,600.
On cover, single franking 4,750.
On cover, pair 5,400.

Without Frame Around Cross

3 A10 2½r black & red 7,000. 2,950.
On cover, single franking 7,725.
On cover, pair *11,000.*
4 A11 2½r blk & red *52,500. 27,000.*
On cover *100,000.*
On cover, pair *170,000.*

Full margins = ¾mm. There are dividing lines between stamps.

Forty types of each.

A12

A13

1850

Full Black Frame Around Cross

5 A12 5r dk bl, blk & red 6,200. 1,375.
On cover 3,250.
a. 5r dk grayish bl, blk & red 6,200. 1,375.
On cover 3,500.
6 A13 10r yel, blk & red *130,000.*
On cover *275,000.*

Full margins = ¾mm. There are dividing lines between stamps.

No. 6 used, with only parts of frame around cross showing, value $175 to $900.

Without Frame Around Cross

7 A12 5r lt bl, blk & red 1,925. 575.
On cover 1,225.
On cover, pair 2,300.
a. 5r dp bl, blk & red *1,925.* 575.
On cover 1,225.
b. 5r pur bl, blk & red — *4,650.*
On cover *9,250.*
c. 5r grnsh bl, blk & red 2,300. 650.
On cover 1,350.
d. 5r grayish vio, blk & red 2,300. 700.
On cover 1,500.
8 A13 10r yel, blk & red 1,000. 160.
On cover 310.
a. 10r buff, blk & red 1,275. 225.
On cover 340.
b. 10r org yel, blk & red 1,250. 250.
On cover 500.
c. 10r dark org, blk & red *6,250.*
On cover 11,750.
d. Half used as 5r on cover, 5r rate *16,000.*
As "d," 15r rate *15,000.*
As "d," 25r rate *18,500.*
As "d," 30r rate *16,000.*
e. Very thin paper 2,325. 390.
f. Thick carton paper 2,325. 350.

Full margins = ¾mm. There are dividing lines between stamps.

Beware of examples of Nos. 7-8 with faked frame added.

1851

Full Blue Frame Around Cross

9 A12 5r light blue & red *210,000.*
On cover *425,000.*

Full margins = ¾mm. There are dividing lines between stamps.

No. 9 used, with only parts of frame around cross showing, value $180 to $3,750.

Without Frame Around Cross

10 A12 5r lt blue & red 625. 160.
On cover 310.
a. Thin paper 1,200. 310.
On cover 550.

Full margins = ¾mm. There are dividing lines between stamps.

Beware of examples of No. 10 with faked frame added.

Forty types of each.

A14

A15

A16

1852

Vermilion Frame Around Cross

11 A14 15r vermilion *20,000.* 775.
On cover 1,850.
12 A15 15r vermilion 2,700. 160.
On cover 325.
13 A16 15c vermilion *18,500.* 1,150.
On cover 2,775.

Values for Pairs

11 A14 15r vermilion *1,850.*
On cover 3,875.
12 A15 15r vermilion 14,000. *400.*
On cover 650.
13 A16 15r vermilion *2,800.*
On cover 5,500.

Full margins = ¾mm. There are dividing lines between stamps.

Ten types of each.

On October 1st, 1854, all stamps of the preceding issues were declared obsolete.

The Sitting Helvetia type (Scott Nos. 14-40) are valued with three margins clear of frame lines, with the fourth margin touching or lightly cutting into the frame line. Stamps with four margins clear of all frame lines are rare and command sustantial premiums.

Helvetia — A17

1854 Embossed. Unwmk.

Thin Paper, Fine Impressions

Emerald Silk Threads

14 A17 5r orange brn *14,000. 1,750.*
On cover 3,500.
15 A17 5r red brown 625.00 160.00
On cover 290.00
16 A17 10r blue 850.00 85.00
On cover 160.00
17 A17 15r car rose 1,400. 190.00
On cover 350.00
a. 15r pale rose 1,350. 190.00
On cover 400.00
18 A17 40r pale yel grn *11,600.* 1,300.
On cover 2,500.
19 A17 40r yellow grn 1,850. 375.00
On cover 700.00

Full margins = ¼mm.

1854-55

Emerald Silk Threads

Medium Thick Paper

Fine Impressions

20 A17 5r pale yel brn 775.00 170.00
On cover 310.00
21 A17 10r blue 2,300. 125.00
On cover 220.00
22 A17 15r rose 1,150. 110.00
On cover 200.00
23 A17 20r pale orange 1,700. 200.00
On cover 360.00

Full margins = ¼mm.

1855-57

Colored ( ) Silk Threads

Medium Thick Paper

Fine to Rough Impressions

24 A17 5r yel brn (yel) 625.00 115.00
On cover 210.00
25 A17 5r dk brn (blk) 350.00 40.00
On cover 77.50
26 A17 10r mlky bl (red) 1,550. 230.00
On cover 425.00
27 A17 10r blue (car) 325.00 47.50
On cover 90.00
a. Thin paper 5,400. 475.00
On cover 850.00
28 A17 15r rose (bl) 575.00 70.00
On cover 140.00
29 A17 40r yel grn (mar) 1,100. 110.00
On cover 200.00
30 A17 1fr lav (blk) 1,775. 1,000.
On cover 2,000.
31 A17 1fr lav (yel) 1,550. 1,000.
On cover *2,000.*
a. Thin paper *21,250.* 7,725.
On cover *18,500.*

Full margins = ¼mm.

1857

Thin (Emergency) Paper

Rough Impressions

Green Silk Threads

32 A17 5r pale gray brn 5,400. 1,100.
On cover 2,175.
32A A17 10r blue 7,000. 1,000.
On cover 1,925.
33 A17 15r pale dl rose 3,475. 350.
On cover 650.
34 A17 20r pale dl org 4,250. 290.
On cover 550.

Full margins = ¼mm.

1858-62

Thick Ordinary Paper

Rough Impressions

Green Silk Threads

35 A17 2r gray 275.00 *575.00*
On newspaper or wrapper, single franking 1,100.
a. One and one-half used as 3r on newspaper or wrapper *12,500.*
c. Half used as 1r on cover
36 A17 5r brown 250.00 30.00
On cover 60.00
a. 5r black brown 275.00 47.50
On cover 75.00
b. 5r gray brown 250.00 27.50
On cover 47.50
c. Half used as 2r on cover *1,550.*
37 A17 10r blue 260.00 32.50
On cover 62.50
a. Half used as 5r on cover *7,250.*
b. 10r pale blue 260.00 27.50
On cover 50.00
c. 10r dark blue 250.00 24.00
On cover 42.50
d. 10r greenish blue 310.00 45.00
On cover 75.00
38 A17 15r dark rose 400.00 70.00
On cover 140.00
a. 15r pale rose 400.00 72.50
On cover 145.00
39 A17 20r dk org 525.00 77.50
On cover 160.00
a. Half used as 10r on cover *17,500.*
b. 20r yel orange 525.00 80.00
On cover 175.00
40 A17 40r grn (to dp grn) 475.00 92.50
On cover 170.00
a. Half used as 20r on cover *27,500.*
b. 40r yellow green 475.00 100.00
On cover 190.00
Nos. 35-40 (6) 2,185. 877.50

Full margins = ¼mm.

Most examples of No. 35a are on pieces of newsprint, rather than on complete newspapers or wrappers. Value for single and bisected single on piece, $4,000.

Helvetia — A18

Double transfer errors, Nos. 43c, 44a, 55b, 60a, 61a, 61b, 67b, have the design impressed twice. These do not refer to the "embossed" watermark.

1862-64 Wmk. 182 *Perf. 11½*

White Wove Paper

41 A18 2c gray 175.00 4.75
Never hinged 350.00
On cover 14.00
42 A18 3c black 12.00 *160.00*
Never hinged 22.50
On cover 350.00
On cover, single franking 625.00
On newspaper 270.00
43 A18 5c dark brown 3.90 1.00
Never hinged 7.00
On cover 3.10
a. 5c bister brown 115.00 2.40
Never hinged 230.00
On cover 5.50
b. 5c gray brown 115.00 32.50
On cover 45.00
c. Dbl. transfer, one invtd. 4,250. 470.00
On cover *925.00*
d. Dbl. transfer of lower left "5" 1,550.
On cover 3,500.
44 A18 10c blue 700.00 1.00
Never hinged 1,300.
On cover 2.40
a. Dbl. transfer, one invtd. *8,500.*
On cover 14,000.
45 A18 20c orange 2.40 3.90
Never hinged 4.75
On cover 14.00
a. 20c yellow orange 390.00 3.90
Never hinged 775.00
On cover 14.00
46 A18 30c vermilion 1,850. 47.50
Never hinged 3,850.
On cover 115.00
47 A18 40c green 1,700. 77.50
Never hinged 3,850.
On cover 140.00
48 A18 60c bronze 1,550. 215.00
Never hinged 3,850.
On cover 390.00
50 A18 1fr gold 22.50 *130.00*
Never hinged 47.50
On cover 390.00
a. 1fr yellowish bronze ('64) 1,775. 620.00
Never hinged 3,250.
On cover 1,075.
b. 1fr reddish bronze 1,700. 470.00
Never hinged 3,100.
On cover 925.00

1867-78

52 A18 2c bister brown 2.40 2.00
Never hinged 4.75
On cover 3.90
a. 2c red brown 775.00 290.00
Never hinged 1,850.
On cover 390.00
53 A18 10c carmine 7.75 1.20
Never hinged 6.00
On cover 2.40
54 A18 15c lemon 6.25 *47.50*
Never hinged 12.50
On cover 115.00

55 A18 25c blue green 1.60 *4.75*
Never hinged 3.10
On cover 19.00
a. 25c yellow green 60.00 40.00
On cover 125.00
b. Dbl. transfer, one invtd. 600.00
On cover 1,100.
56 A18 30c ultra 620.00 16.00
Never hinged 1,550.
On cover 24.00
a. 30c blue *2,300.* 270.00
Never hinged *5,800.*
On cover 550.00
58 A18 40c gray 1.60 *170.00*
Never hinged 3.10
On cover 460.00
59 A18 50c violet 62.50 77.50
Never hinged 125.00
On cover 230.00
Nos. 52-59 (7) 702.10 *318.95*

1881 Granite Paper

60 A18 2c bister .80 *30.00*
Never hinged 1.60
On cover 60.00
a. Dbl. transfer, one invtd. 390.00
Never hinged 575.00
61 A18 5c brown .75 *16.00*
Never hinged 1.50
On cover 30.00
a. Dbl. transfer, one invtd. 24.00 *475.00*
Never hinged 47.50
On cover 925.00
b. Double transfer of lower left "5" *1,250.*
On cover 2,750.
62 A18 10c rose 6.25 *16.00*
Never hinged 12.50
On cover 22.50
63 A18 15c lemon 9.25 *540.00*
Never hinged 20.00
On cover 775.00
64 A18 20c orange .80 *170.00*
Never hinged 1.60
On cover 340.00
65 A18 25c green .75 *110.00*
Never hinged 1.60
On cover 200.00
66 A18 40c gray 1.60 *3,875.*
Never hinged 4.00
On cover 15,500.
67 A18 50c deep violet 13.00 *625.00*
Never hinged 27.50
On cover 1,250.
b. Dbl. transfer, one invtd. 200.00 *5,000.*
Never hinged 400.00
On cover 11,500.
68 A18 1fr gold 17.50 *1,400.*
Never hinged 40.00
On cover *5,750.*

The granite paper contains fragments of blue and red silk threads.

Forged or backdated cancellations are found frequently on Nos. 42, 50, 54, 58 and 60-68.

All stamps of the preceding issues were declared obsolete on October 1st, 1883. Some of the remainders of Nos. 41-68 were overprinted "AUSSER KURS" (Obsolete) diagonally in black.

Numeral — A19

Wmk. 182 (Type II)
1882-89 Typo. *Perf. 11½*
Granite Paper

69 A19 2c bister 2.40 1.25
Never hinged 4.50
On cover 4.75
70 A19 3c gray brown 3.10 *16.00*
Never hinged 6.25
On cover 22.50
a. 3c gray 65.00 72.50
On cover
71 A19 5c maroon 24.00 .80
Never hinged 47.50
On cover 5.50
a. Tête bêche pair —
72 A19 5c deep grn ('99) 12.00 .75
Never hinged 23.00
On cover 2.50
73 A19 10c red 9.25 .80
Never hinged 19.00
On cover 3.75
74 A19 12c ultra 12.00 1.15
Never hinged 23.00
On cover 9.25
a. 12c dull blue 390.00 42.50
Never hinged 775.00
On cover 115.00
76 A19 15c lilac ('89) 77.50 5.75
Never hinged 160.00
On cover 35.00
a. 15c brownish red-lilac *115.00* *17.00*
Never hinged 230.00
On cover *100.00*
Nos. 69-76 (7) 140.25 *26.50*
Set, never hinged 291.00

Wmk. 182 (Type I)

69a A19 2c olive brown 40.00 5.50
Never hinged 92.50
On cover *19.00*
70b A19 3c gray 62.50 70.00
Never hinged 150.00
On cover *92.50*
71b A19 5c brownish lilac 92.50 3.10
Never hinged 215.00
On cover *6.25*
73a A19 10c carmine 110.00 2.00
Never hinged 275.00
On cover *6.25*
73b A19 10c light rose 650.00 12.00
Never hinged 1,150.
On cover *23.00*
74c A19 12c ultramarine 160.00 6.25
Never hinged 390.00
On cover *14.00*
75 A19 15c yellow 160.00 40.00
Never hinged 425.00
On cover *65.00*
75a A19 15c yellow-orange *18,500.* *5,400.*
On cover *15,500.*
b. Tête bêche pair
76b A19 15c dull purple 4750.00 32.50
Never hinged 925.00
On cover *77.50*

Wmk. 182 (Type II)
1882 White Paper

77 A19 2c olive brown 500.00 425.00
Never hinged 970.00
On cover 625.00
78 A19 5c brownish lilac 1,350. 115.00
Never hinged 3,500.
On cover 230.00
79 A19 10c pale rose 2,700. 75.00
Never hinged *7,000.*
On cover 140.00
80 A19 12c grayish ultra 290.00 30.00
Never hinged 500.00
On cover 55.00
81 A19 15c yellow 370.00 *375.00*
Never hinged 740.00
On cover 540.00

Nos. 77-81 were the first stamps issued in the Numeral series.

See Nos. 113-118.

Helvetia (Large numerals) A20

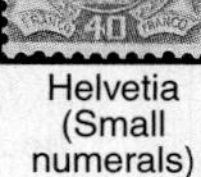
Helvetia (Small numerals) A21

Wmk. 182 (Type I)
1882-1904 Engr. *Perf. 11½ - 11¾*

82 A20 20c orange 350.00 7.75
Never hinged 850.00
On cover 32.50
83 A20 25c green 200.00 4.00
Never hinged 470.00
On cover 24.00
95b A20 30c brown — *27,000.*
On cover —
84 A20 40c gray 310.00 60.00
Never hinged 775.00
On cover 230.00
86 A20 50c blue 310.00 27.50
Never hinged 775.00
On cover 140.00
87 A20 1fr claret 470.00 16.00
Never hinged 1,100.
On cover 100.00
On cover, single franking *400.00*
88 A20 3fr yel brn ('91) 310.00 32.50
Never hinged 775.00
On cover 200.00
On cover, single franking *1,750.*

Wmk. 182 (Type II)

85 A21 40c gray ('04) 50.00 40.00
Never hinged 92.50
On cover 200.00
88d A20 3fr yellow brown ('04) *7,500.*

1888 Wmk. 182 (Type I) *Perf. 9½*

89 A20 20c orange 1,150. 125.00
Never hinged 2,100.
On cover 250.00
90 A20 25c yellow grn 230.00 24.00
Never hinged 390.00
On cover 40.00
91 A20 40c gray 1,100. 925.00
Never hinged 2,000.
On cover 1,850.
92 A20 50c blue 1,700. 450.00
Never hinged 3,100.
On cover 975.00
93 A20 1fr claret 1,300. 115.00
Never hinged 2,300.
On cover 350.00
On cover, single franking 800.00

Values for Nos. 89-93 are for well-centered stamps with slightly uneven perforations. Stamps missing perforations sell for much less.

Wmk. 182 (Type I)
1891-1903 *Perf. 11½x11*

82c A20 20c orange *925.00* 11.50
Never hinged 1,850.
On cover 55.00
83b A20 25c green *350.00* 7.75
Never hinged 775.00
On cover 23.00
95c A20 30c red brown ('92) *620.00* 62.50
Never hinged 1,350.
On cover 195.00
84c A20 40c gray *1,150.* 115.00
Never hinged 2,475.
On cover 475.00
86b A20 50c blue *70.00* 37.50
Never hinged 1,550.
On cover 160.00
87c A20 1fr claret *1,175.* 32.50
Never hinged 2,300.
On cover 92.50
88c A20 1fr olive brown *23,250.*

Wmk. 182 (Type II)

82a A20 20c orange 160.00 2.40
Never hinged 310.00
On cover 23.00
83a A20 25c green 19.00 2.40
Never hinged 37.50
On cover 20.00
94 A20 25c blue ('99) 22.00 6.25
Never hinged 37.50
On cover 20.00
95 A20 30c red brn ('92) 23.00 2.40
Never hinged 77.50
On cover 32.50
84a A20 40c gray 100.00 7.75
Never hinged 200.00
On cover 125.00
86a A20 50c blue 70.00 23.00
Never hinged 125.00
On cover 115.00
96 A20 50c green ('99) 100.00 50.00
Never hinged 200.00
On cover 200.00
87a A20 1fr claret 62.50 6.25
Never hinged 115.00
On cover *62.50*
On cover, single franking *240.00*
97 A20 1fr carmine ('03) 97.50 12.50
Never hinged 200.00
On cover *77.50*
On cover, single franking *300.00*
88a A20 3fr yellow brown 200.00 37.50
Never hinged 390.00
On cover *160.00*
On cover, single franking *1,100.*

Wmk. 182 (Type II)
1901-03 *Perf. 11½x12*

82b A20 20c orange 47.50 2.40
Never hinged 77.50
On cover 23.00
94a A20 25c blue 20.00 1.60
Never hinged 37.50
On cover 20.00
95a A20 30c red brown 47.50 2.75
Never hinged 92.50
On cover 32.50
84b A20 40c gray 125.00 47.50
Never hinged 250.00
On cover 200.00
96a A20 50c green 85.00 20.00
Never hinged 170.00
On cover 92.50
87b A20 1fr claret *2,500.* 350.00
Never hinged 5,000.
On cover *1,400.*
On cover, single franking *1,400.*
97a A20 1fr carmine ('03) 620.00 55.00
Never hinged 1,250.
On cover 125.00
88b A20 3fr yellow brown 230.00 32.50
Never hinged 460.00
On cover *160.00*
On cover, single franking *1,100.*

Numerous retouches and plate flaws exist on all values of this issue.

The small numerals illustrated by A21 are only present in the 40c gray. The denomination does not touch the inner frame line on the small numeral issues.

Nos. 82-88 are ½mm taller (paper size) than Nos. 82b-88b.

See Nos. 105-112, 119-125.

UPU Allegory — A22

1900 *Perf. 11½*

98 A22 5c gray green 40.00 3.00
Never hinged 80.00
On cover 8.00
99 A22 10c carmine rose 12.50 3.00
Never hinged 27.50
On cover 8.00
100 A22 25c blue 32.00 47.50
Never hinged 62.50
On cover 115.00
Nos. 98-100 (3) 84.50 53.50

Re-engraved

101 A22 5c gray green 4.00 3.00
Never hinged 8.00
On cover 10.00
102 A22 10c carmine rose 62.50 57.50
Never hinged 125.00
On cover 100.00
a. 10c red purple 1,000. *8,000.*
103 A22 25c blue 800.00 *16,250.*
Never hinged 1,600.
On cover *17,000.*

Universal Postal Union, 25th anniv.

The impression of the re-engraved stamps is much clearer, especially the horizontally lined background. The figures of value are lined instead of being solid.

Helvetia Types of 1882-1904
1905 Wmk. 183 *Perf. 11½x11*
White Paper

105 A20 20c orange 6.25 4.00
Never hinged 11.50
On cover 22.50
106 A20 25c blue 11.50 *16.00*
Never hinged 19.00
On cover 62.50
107 A20 30c brown 11.50 3.00
Never hinged 19.00
On cover 27.50
108a A21 40c gray 195.00 *230.00*
Never hinged 390.00
On cover 390.00
109 A20 50c green 92.50 16.00
Never hinged 190.00
On cover 140.00
110 A20 1fr carmine 160.00 6.25
Never hinged 310.00
On cover 77.50
On cover, single franking 240.00
111 A20 3fr yellow brn 350.00 230.00
Never hinged 700.00
On cover 550.00
On cover, single franking *1,200.*

Some clichés in the plates of the 20c, 25c, 30c, 50c and 3fr have been retouched.

1906 Re-engraved *Perf. 11½x11*

112 A20 25c pale blue 9.25 2.75
Never hinged 19.00
On cover 37.50

In the re-engraved stamp the stars are larger and the background below "FRANCO" is of horiz. or horiz. and vert. crossed lines, instead of horiz. and curved lines.

1906 *Perf. 11½*

112a A20 25c pale blue 195.00 14.00
Never hinged 390.00
On cover 32.50
108 A21 40c gray 47.50 23.00
Never hinged 92.50
On cover 195.00

1907 *Perf. 11½x12*

105a A20 20c orange 11.00 9.00
Never hinged 22.00
On cover 32.50
109a A20 50c green 77.50 32.50
Never hinged 170.00
On cover 125.00
110a A20 1fr carmine 135.00 18.00
Never hinged 270.00
On cover 155.00
On cover, single franking *325.00*
111a A20 3fr yellow brown 425.00 310.00
Never hinged 850.00
On cover 550.00
On cover, single franking *1,750.*

Numeral Type of 1882-99
1905 Typo. *Perf. 11½*
Granite Paper

113 A19 2c dull bister 9.50 2.75
Never hinged 16.00
On cover 11.50
114 A19 3c gray brown 11.00 *140.00*
Never hinged 19.00
On cover 195.00
115 A19 5c green 10.00 .75
Never hinged 17.00
On cover 9.25
116 A19 10c scarlet 9.25 .75
Never hinged 16.00
On cover 9.25
117 A19 12c ultra 14.00 4.75
Never hinged 24.00
On cover 19.00
118 A19 15c brown vio 95.00 27.50
Never hinged 195.00
On cover 95.00
a. 15c red lilac 390.00 215.00
Never hinged 775.00
On cover 390.00
Nos. 113-118 (6) 148.75 *176.50*

Helvetia Types of 1882-1904
1907 Engr. *Perf. 11½x12*
Granite Paper

119 A20 20c orange 4.00 6.25
Never hinged 6.75
On cover 24.00
120 A20 25c blue 24.00 *24.00*
Never hinged 45.00
On cover 55.00
121 A20 30c red brown 9.25 *32.50*
Never hinged 19.00
On cover 92.50
122 A21 40c gray 32.50 *77.50*
Never hinged 62.50
On cover 235.00
a. Helvetia without diadem 375.00 *1,650.*
Never hinged 750.00
123 A20 50c gray green 7.75 *32.50*
Never hinged 16.00
On cover 115.00
124 A20 1fr carmine 47.50 16.00
Never hinged 92.50
On cover 240.00
125a A20 3fr yellow brown *15,500.*

There are retouches and plate flaws on all values.

Perf. 11½x11

120a A20 25c deep blue 16.00 11.50
Never hinged 32.50
On cover 350.00
121a A20 30c red brown 250.00 *500.00*
Never hinged 500.00
On cover 1,150.

122b A21 40c gray 20,000.
124a A20 1fr carmine 19,500. 7,750.
125 A20 3fr yel brn 170.00 110.00
Never hinged 340.00
On cover 400.00

William Tell's Son — A23

Helvetia
A24 A25

1907-25 Typo. *Perf. 11½*
Granite Paper

126 A23 2c pale bister .40 *1.55*
Never hinged 1.60
On cover 11.50
127 A23 3c lilac brn .40 *16.00*
Never hinged .75
On cover 27.50
128 A23 5c yellow grn 4.75 .75
Never hinged 16.00
On cover 1.60
129 A24 10c rose red 2.40 .75
Never hinged 9.25
On cover 3.00
130 A24 12c ocher .40 *6.25*
Never hinged .75
On cover 11.50
131 A24 15c red vio 4.75 *20.00*
Never hinged 13.00
On cover 47.50
132 A25 20c red & yel ('08) 4.00 1.55
Never hinged 9.25
On cover 3.00
133 A25 25c dp blue ('08) 3.00 1.15
Never hinged 7.75
On cover 2.40
a. Tête bêche pair 32.50 *195.00*
134 A25 30c yel brn & pale grn ('08) 2.40 .75
Never hinged 7.00
On cover 3.00
135 A25 35c yel grn & yel ('08) 3.00 3.50
Never hinged 7.75
On cover 11.50
136 A25 40c red vio & yel ('08) 22.50 1.55
Never hinged 57.60
On cover 7.75
a. Designer's name in full on the rock ('08) 12.00 *124.00*
Never hinged 27.00
On cover 310.00
137 A25 40c deep blue ('22) 2.40 .75
Never hinged 7.75
On cover 6.25
a. 40c light blue ('21) 9.25 3.00
Never hinged 23.00
On cover 16.00
138 A25 40c red vio & grn ('25) 57.50 .75
Never hinged 160.00
On cover 3.75
139 A25 50c dp grn & pale grn ('08) 16.00 .75
Never hinged 42.50
On cover 11.50
140 A25 60c brn org & buff ('18) 19.00 1.55
Never hinged 62.50
On cover 11.00
141 A25 70c dk brn & buff ('08) 77.50 27.50
Never hinged 235.00
On cover 390.00
142 A25 70c vio & buff ('24) 20.00 5.50
Never hinged 85.00
On cover 37.50
143 A25 80c slate & buff ('15) 20.00 2.75
Never hinged 62.50
On cover 11.50
144 A25 1fr dp cl & pale grn ('08) 12.00 .75
Never hinged 32.50
On cover 62.50
145 A25 3fr bis & yel ('08) 465.00 3.90
Never hinged 1,250.
On cover 270.00
Nos. 126-145 (20) 737.40 *98.00*

No. 136 has two leaves and "CL" below sword hilt. No. 136a has three leaves and designer's full name below hilt.

For surcharges and overprints see Nos. 189, 199, O10-O13, O15, 1O6-1O8, 1O14-1O16, 2O18-2O26, 3O14-3O22.

1933 With Grilled Gum

135a A25 35c yel grn & yel 1.55 *19.00*
Never hinged 5.50
On cover 57.50
138a A25 40c red vio & grn 55.00 2.40
Never hinged 115.00
On cover 12.00
139a A25 50c dp grn & pale grn 12.00 2.40
Never hinged 37.50
On cover 16.00
140a A25 60c brn org & buff 16.00 2.40
Never hinged 42.50
On cover 27.50
142a A25 70c vio & buff 19.00 7.75
Never hinged 57.50
On cover 62.50
143a A25 80c slate & buff 16.00 6.25
Never hinged 42.50
On cover 35.00
144a A25 1fr dp cl & pale grn 24.00 10.00
Never hinged 55,00
On cover 97.50
Nos. 135a-144a (7) 143.55 50.20

"Grilled" Gum

In 1930-44 many Swiss stamps were treated with a light grilling process, applied with the gumming to counteract the tendency to curl. It resembles a faint grill of vertical and horizontal ribs covering the entire back of the stamp, and can be seen after the gum has been removed. Listings of the grilled gum varieties begin with No. 135a.

William Tell's Son — A26

Bow-string in front of stock

1909 *Perf. 11½, 12*
Granite Paper

146 A26 2c bister .40 2.00
Never hinged .75
On cover 4.75
a. Tête bêche pair 3.10 *47.50*
Never hinged 5.50
On cover 55.00
147 A26 3c dark violet .40 *16.00*
Never hinged .75
On cover 62.50
148 A26 5c green 11.50 .75
Never hinged 32.50
On cover 3.00
a. Tête bêche pair 35.00 *85.00*
Never hinged 65.00
On cover 115.00
Nos. 146-148 (3) 12.30 *18.75*

See Nos. 149-163. For surcharges and overprints see Nos. 186, 193-195, 207-208, 1O1-1O3, 1O9-1O11, 2O1-2O7, 3O1-3O5.

First Redrawing

Bow-string behind stock. Thin loop above crossbow. Letters of "HELVETIA" without serifs.

1910-17 Granite Paper

149 A26 2c bister ('10) 16.00 11.00
150 A26 3c dk violet ('10) .40 .75
Never hinged .75
On cover 5.75
a. Tête bêche pair 3.10 16.00
Never hinged 6.25
On cover 20.00
b. Booklet pane of 6 30.00
Never hinged 60.00
On cover —
151 A26 3c brown org ('17) .40 .75
Never hinged .75
On cover 2.00
a. Tête bêche pair 7.75 23.00
Never hinged 17.00
On cover 32.50
152 A26 5c green ('10) 32.50 11.00
Never hinged 97.50
On cover 20.00
a. Tête bêche pair 155.00 500.00
Never hinged 350.00
On cover 775.00
Nos. 149-152 (4) 49.30 23.50

Second Redrawing

Bow-string behind stock. Thick loop above crossbow. Letters of "HELVETIA" have serifs.

7½ CENTIMES:

Type I — Top of "7" is ½mm thick. The "1" of "½" has only traces of serifs. The two base plates of the statue are of even thickness.

Type II — Top of "7" is 1mm thick. The "1" of "½" has distinct serifs. The upper base plate is thinner than the lower.

1911-30 Granite Paper

153 A26 2c bister ('11) .40 .75
Never hinged .75
On cover 2.00
a. Tête bêche pair 3.10 27.50
Never hinged 6.25
On cover 35.00
154 A26 2½c claret ('18) .40 *2.00*
Never hinged .75
On cover 7.75
155 A26 2½c ol, *buff* ('28) .40 *4.00*
Never hinged .75
On cover 7.00
156 A26 3c ultra, *buff* ('30) 5.50 *16.00*
Never hinged 16.00
On cover 19.50
157 A26 5c green ('11) 1.10 .75
Never hinged 3.00
On cover 1.60
a. Tête bêche pair 6.25 *23.00*
Never hinged 11.50
On cover 32.50
158 A26 5c org, *buff* ('21) .40 .75
Never hinged 11.50
On cover 32.50
a. Bklt. pane of 6 (5 #158, 168) 27.50 *75.00*
Never hinged 55.00
159 A26 5c gray vio, *buff* ('24) .40 .95
Never hinged .75
On cover 2.75
a. Bklt. pane of 6 (5 #159, 168) 12.50 *37.50*
Never hinged 25.00
160 A26 5c red vio, *buff* ('27) .40 .75
Never hinged .75
On cover 1.55
a. Bklt. pane 6 (5 #160, 168) 55.00 *100.00*
Never hinged 100.00
161 A26 5c dk grn, *buff* ('30) .40 .60
Never hinged .75
On cover 6.25
a. Bklt. pane 6 (5 #161, 169) 55.00 *125.00*
162 A26 7½c gray (I) ('18) 6.25 4.75
Never hinged 20.00
On cover 16.00
a. Tête bêche pair 19.00 *77.50*
Never hinged 37.50
On cover 115.00
c. 7½c slate (II) 6.25 4.75
Never hinged 19.00
On cover 16.00
163 A26 7½c dp grn, *buff* (I) ('28) .40 *7.75*
Never hinged .75
On cover 12.50
Nos. 153-163 (11) 16.05 *39.05*

1933 With Grilled Gum

156a A26 3c ultra, *buff* 7.75 *32.50*
Never hinged 16.00
On cover 77.50
161b A26 5c dark green, *buff* 1.60 *16.00*
Never hinged 7.75
On cover 40.00

Helvetia — A27

1909 Granite Paper

164 A27 10c carmine 1.55 .75
Never hinged 3.00
On cover 1.50
a. Tête bêche pair 4.00 *24.00*
Never hinged 7.00
On cover 27.50
165 A27 12c bister brn .75 1.55
Never hinged 2.40
On cover 3.25
166 A27 15c red violet 37.50 1.55
Never hinged 97.50
On cover 11.50
Nos. 164-166 (3) 39.80 3.85

For surcharge see No. 187.

William Tell — A28

TEN CENTIMES:

Type I — Bust 16½mm high. "HELVETIA" 15½mm wide. Cross bar of "H" at middle of the letter.

Type II — Bust 15mm high. "HELVETIA" 15mm wide. Cross bar of "H" above middle of the letter.

1914-30 Granite Paper *Perf. 11½*

167 A28 10c red, *buff* (type II) .75 .75
Never hinged 1.55
On cover 1.75
a. 10c red, *buff* (type I) 3.10 *24.00*
Never hinged 11.50
On cover 160.00
b. Tête bêche pair (II) 3.10 16.00
Never hinged 6.25
On cover 20.00
d. Bklt. pane 6 (5 #167, 172) 60.00 *160.00*
168 A28 10c grn, *buff* (type II) ('21) .40 .75
Never hinged .75
On cover 2.00
a. Tête bêche pair 1.15 3.10
Never hinged 2.00
On cover 4.75
168C A28 10c bl grn, *buff* (type II) ('28) .40 .75
Never hinged .75
On cover 2.40
d. Tête bêche pair 1.55 4.75
Never hinged 3.50
On cover 6.25
169 A28 10c vio, *buff* (type II) ('30) 1.55 .75
Never hinged 3.00
On cover 2.40
a. Tête bêche pair 7.00 7.75
Never hinged 14.00
On cover 10.00
170 A28 12c brn, *buff* .75 *7.00*
171 A28 13c ol grn, *buff* ('15) 2.40 .75
Never hinged 6.25
On cover 4.00
172 A28 15c vio, *buff* 6.25 .75
Never hinged 16.00
On cover 2.00
b. 15c dk vio, *buff* 55.00 16.00
Never hinged 125.00
On cover 24.00
c. Tête bêche pair 125.00 *215.00*
Never hinged 250.00
On cover 325.00
173 A28 15c brn red, *buff* ('28) 4.75 7.00
Never hinged 12.00
On cover 24.00
174 A28 20c red vio, *buff* ('21) 2.40 .75
Never hinged 7.75
On cover 2.50
a. Tête bêche pair 7.75 *16.00*
Never hinged 16.00
On cover 20.00
175 A28 20c ver, *buff* ('24) .75 .75
Never hinged 2.40
On cover 1.55
a. Tête bêche pair 4.75 *16.00*
Never hinged 10.00
On cover 20.00
176 A28 20c car, *buff* ('25) .75 .75
Never hinged 1.55
On cover 1.55
a. Tête bêche pair 4.00 4.75
Never hinged 8.00
On cover 6.25
177 A28 25c ver, *buff* ('21) 1.55 3.25
Never hinged 7.00
On cover 12.00
178 A28 25c car, *buff* ('22) .75 1.55
Never hinged 2.40
On cover 10.00
179 A28 25c brn, *buff* ('25) 6.25 2.40
Never hinged 20.00
On cover 9.25
180 A28 30c dp bl, *buff* ('24) 16.00 .75
Never hinged 40.00
On cover 4.00
Nos. 167-180 (15) 45.70 28.70

1932-33 With Grilled Gum

169c A28 10c violet, *buff* 4.75 2.40
Never hinged 12.00
On cover 9.50
173a A28 15c brn red, *buff* ('33) 92.50 *92.50*
Never hinged 200.00
On cover 235.00
176c A28 20c carmine, *buff* 7.75 2.40
Never hinged 24.00
On cover 15.00
179a A28 25c brown, *buff* ('33) 92.50 55.00
Never hinged 200.00
On cover 175.00
180a A28 30c deep blue, *buff* 77.50 4.00
Never hinged 230.00
On cover 35.00
Nos. 169c-180a (5) 275.00 156.30

For surcharges and overprints see Nos. 188, 196-198, 1O4-1O5, 1O12-1O13, 2O8-2O17, 3O6-3O13.

The Mythen A29

The Rütli — A30

The Jungfrau A31

1914-30 Engr. Granite Paper

181 A29 3fr dk green 775.00 9.25
Never hinged 2,150.
On cover 500.00
182 A29 3fr red ('18) 125.00 2.40
Never hinged 350.00
On cover 160.00
183 A30 5fr dp ultra 52.50 4.00
Never hinged 57.50
On cover 115.00
184 A31 10fr dull violet 155.00 4.00
Never hinged 475.00
On cover 275.00
185 A31 10fr gray grn ('30) 275.00 57.50
Never hinged 625.00
On cover 400.00
Nos. 181-185 (5) 1,383. 77.15

See No. 206. For overprints see Nos. 2O27-2O30, 3O23-3O26.

Stamps of 1909-14 Surcharged

a

b

c

1915

186 A26(a) 1c on 2c bister .40 *1.55*
Never hinged .75
On cover 4.00
187 A27(b) 13c on 12c bis brn .40 *16.00*
Never hinged .75
On cover 30.00
188 A28(c) 13c on 12c brn, *buff* .40 *1.55*
Never hinged .75
On cover 9.25
Nos. 186-188 (3) 1.20 *19.10*

No. 141 Surcharged

189 A25 80c on 70c 37.50 32.50
Never hinged 110.00
On cover 275.00

Significant of Peace A32

"Peace" A33

"Dawn of Peace" A34

Perf. 11½

1919, Aug. 1 Typo. Unwmk.

190 A32 7½c olive drab & blk 2.40 *4.00*
Never hinged 7.00
On cover 9.25
191 A33 10c red & yel 2.40 *9.25*
Never hinged 7.00
On cover 20.00
192 A34 15c violet & yel 3.00 4.00
Never hinged 9.25
On cover 9.25
Nos. 190-192 (3) 7.80 17.25

Commemorating Peace after World War I.

Nos. 151, 149, 162, 171-172, 133 Surcharged in Black, Red or Dark Blue

a

b

c

1921 Wmk. 183

193 A26(a) 2½c on 3c (Bl) .40 *1.55*
Never hinged .75
On cover 3.00
a. Tête bêche pair 1.15 *7.75*
Never hinged 2.00
On cover 9.25
b. Inverted surcharge 775.00 *1,575.*
c. Double surcharge *775.00 1,575.*
194 A26(a) 5c on 2c (R) .40 *7.00*
Never hinged .75
On cover 24.00
a. Double surcharge *450.00 450.00*
195 A26(a) 5c on 7½c (R) .40 .75
Never hinged .75
On cover 2.50
a. Tête bêche pair 7.00 *100.00*
Never hinged 14.00
On cover 140.00
b. Double surcharge *400.00 775.00*
c. 5c on 7½c slate (II) *3,100. 7,500.*
Never hinged 6,600.
On cover 20,000.
196 A28(b) 10c on 13c (R) .40 *4.00*
Never hinged .75
On cover 9.25
a. Double surcharge *625.00 1,400.*
197 A28(c) 20c on 15c (Bk) .75 *4.00*
Never hinged 4.00
On cover 7.00
a. Tête bêche pair 3.00 *110.00*
Never hinged 7.00
On cover 140.00
b. Double surcharge *875.00 875.00*
198 A28(c) 20c on 15c (Bl) 3.00 *9.50*
Never hinged 7.75
On cover 20.00
b. Double surcharge *875.00 875.00*
199 A25(c) 20c on 25c dp bl (R) .40 *.75*
Never hinged .75
On cover 3.25
a. Tête bêche pair 1.55 *17.50*
Never hinged 3.25
On cover 22.50
Nos. 193-199 (7) 5.75 *27.55*

A36

1924 Typo. *Perf. 11½*
Granite Paper, Surface Colored

200 A36 90c grn & red, *grn* 24.00 4.00
Never hinged 105.00
On cover 47.50
201 A36 1.20fr brn rose & red, *rose* 7.75 7.75
Never hinged 32.50
On cover 62.50
202 A36 1.50fr bl & red, *bl* 55.00 9.25
Never hinged 115.00
On cover 10.00
203 A36 2fr gray blk & red, *gray* 70.00 10.00
Never hinged 150.00
On cover 235.00
Nos. 200-203 (4) 156.75 31.00
Set, never hinged 467.50

1933 With Grilled Gum

200a A36 90c 27.50 4.75
Never hinged 70.00
On cover 40.00
201a A36 1.20fr 70.00 8.50
Never hinged 175.00
On cover 62.50
202a A36 1.50fr 24.00 9.25
Never hinged 70.00
On cover 160.00
203a A36 2fr 42.50 13.50
Never hinged 110.00
On cover 160.00
Nos. 200a-203a (4) 164.00 36.00
Set, never hinged 425.00

For overprints see Nos. O16-O18, 2O31-2O34, 3O27-3O30.

1940 With Smooth Gum
Ordinary Paper

200b A36 90c 24.00 *77.50*
Never hinged 57.50
On cover 235.00
201b A36 1.20fr 24.00 *115.00*
Never hinged 57.50
On cover 270.00
202b A36 1.50fr 24.00 *725.00*
Never hinged 55.00
On cover *5,750.*
Nos. 200b-202b (3) 72.00 917.50

Building in Bern, Location of 1st UPU Congress, 1874
A37 A38

1924, Oct. 9 Engr. Wmk. 183
Granite Paper

204 A37 20c vermilion .75 *2.40*
Never hinged 1.55
On cover 4.75
205 A38 30c dull blue 1.55 *9.25*
Never hinged 4.00
On cover 20.00
Set, never hinged 5.55

50th anniv. of the UPU.

Type of 1914 Issue

The Rütli — A39

1928 Re-engraved *Perf. 11½*

206 A39 5fr blue 1.65 *16.00*
Never hinged 4.75
On cover 400.00
a. Imperf., pair, never hinged *9,000.*

In the re-engraved stamp the picture is clearer and lighter than on No. 183. "HELVETIA" is in smaller letters. The names at foot of the stamp are "Grasset-J. Sprenger" instead of "E. GRASSET-A. BURKHARD."

For overprints see Nos. 2O35, 3O31.

Nos. 155 and 163 Surcharged

1930, June *Perf. 11½*

207 A26 3c on 2½c ol grn, *buff* .40 *4.75*
Never hinged .75
On cover 12.00
208 A26 5c on 7½c dp grn, *buff* .40 *16.00*
Never hinged .75
On cover 24.00
Set, never hinged 1.50

The Mythen A40

1931 Engr. Granite Paper

209 A40 3fr orange brown 65.00 7.75
Never hinged 200.00
On cover 115.00

For overprints see Nos. 2O56, 3O47.

Dove on Broken Sword — A41

"Peace" A42

1932, Feb. 2 Typo. *Perf. 11½*
Granite Paper

210 A41 5c peacock blue .40 .75
Never hinged .75
On cover *3.00*
211 A41 10c orange .40 .75
Never hinged .75
On cover *1.50*
212 A41 20c cerise .40 .75
Never hinged .75
On cover *1.50*
213 A41 30c ultra 2.25 1.60
Never hinged 5.50
On cover *7.75*
214 A41 60c olive brown 17.50 8.75
Never hinged 55.00
On cover *47.50*

Unwmk.
Photo.

215 A42 1fr olive gray & bl 24.00 15.00
Never hinged 150.00
On cover *115.00*
Nos. 210-215 (6) 44.95 27.60
Set, never hinged *118.00*

Intl. Disarmament Conf., Geneva, Feb. 1932.
For overprints see #2O36-2O41, 3O32-3O37.

Louis Favre — A43

Alfred Escher — A44

Design: 30c, Emil Welti.

Wmk. 183
1932, May 31 Engr. *Perf. 11½*
Granite Paper

216 A43 10c red brown .40 .75
Never hinged 1.15
On cover *1.55*
217 A44 20c vermilion .40 .75
Never hinged 1.15
On cover *1.55*
218 A44 30c deep ultra .75 *4.75*
Never hinged 2.40
On cover *8.00*
Nos. 216-218 (3) 1.55 *6.25*
Set, never hinged 4.70

Completion of the St. Gotthard tunnel, 50th anniv.
Nos. 216-218 exist imperforate.

Staubbach Falls A46

Mt. Pilatus A47

Chillon Castle A48

Rhone Glacier A49

St. Gotthard Railroad A50

Via Mala Gorge A51

Rhine Falls — A52

1934, July 2 Typo. *Perf. 11½*
Grilled Gum, Ordinary Paper

219 A46 3c olive .40 *5.50*
Never hinged .75
On cover *7.75*
220 A47 5c emerald .40 .75
Never hinged .75
On cover *1.55*
221 A48 10c brt violet .40 .75
Never hinged 1.50
On cover *1.55*
222 A49 15c orange .55 5.50
Never hinged 1.50
On cover *7.75*
223 A50 20c red .65 .75
Never hinged 3.00
On cover *1.55*
224 A51 25c brown 7.75 11.50
Never hinged 24.00
On cover *20.00*
225 A52 30c ultra 32.50 3.10
Never hinged 92.50
On cover *5.50*
Nos. 219-225 (7) 42.65 27.85
Set, never hinged 124.00

Tête bêche Pairs

220a A47 5c 4.00 6.25
Never hinged 8.00
On cover *9.50*
221a A48 10c 3.25 6.25
Never hinged 6.25
On cover *9.25*
222a A49 15c 4.00 14.00
Never hinged 8.00
On cover *20.00*
223a A50 20c 4.75 12.50
Never hinged 9.25
On cover *20.00*

Souvenir Sheet

A52a

1934, Sept. 29
226 A52a Sheet of 4 350.00 *600.00*
Never hinged 700.00
On cover *675.00*

No. 226 was issued in connection with the Swiss National Philatelic Exhibition at Zurich, Sept. 29 to Oct. 7, 1934. It contains one each of Nos. 220-223. Size: 62x72mm.
For overprints see Nos. 2O42-2O46, 3O48.

Staubbach Falls A53

Mt. Pilatus A54

Chillon Castle A55

Rhone Glacier A56

St. Gotthard Railroad A57

Via Mala Gorge A58

Rhine Falls — A59

Balsthal Pass — A60

Alpine Lake of Säntis — A61

Type I Type II

Two types of 10c red violet:
I — Shading inside "0" of 10 has only vertical lines.
II — Shading in "0" includes two diagonal lines.

1936-42 Unwmk. Engr. *Perf. 11½*

227 A53 3c olive .40 .75
Never hinged .75
On cover *3.25*
228 A54 5c blue green .40 .75
Never hinged .75
On cover *1.55*
229 A55 10c red vio (II) 1.15 .75
Never hinged 3.75
On cover *1.55*
b. Type I 1.15 .75
Never hinged 3.75
On cover *1.55*
230 A55 10c dk red brn ('39) .40 .75
Never hinged .75
On cover *1.55*
230B A55 10c org brn ('42) .40 .40
Never hinged .75
On cover *1.55*
231 A56 15c orange .55 1.55
Never hinged 1.55
On cover *3.00*
232 A57 20c carmine 5.50 .75
Never hinged 20.00
On cover *1.55*
233 A58 25c lt brown .75 1.55
Never hinged 2.40
On cover *3.00*
234 A59 30c ultra 1.15 .75
Never hinged 3.00
On cover *2.40*
235 A60 35c yellow grn 1.55 3.10
Never hinged 4.75
On cover *7.75*
236 A61 40c gray 7.00 .75
Never hinged 20.00
On cover *3.25*
Nos. 227-236 (11) 19.25 11.85
Set, never hinged 58.00

Two types of the 20c. See Nos. 316-321 in Scott Standard catalogue, Vol. 6.
For overprints see Nos. O1-O4, O6-O9, O19-O19-O22, O24-O27, 2O47-2O55, 2O68-2O68A, 2O70-2O73, 2O75-2O78, 3O38-3O46, 3O60-3O60A, 3O62-3O65, 3O67-3O70, 4O1-4O4, 4O6-4O9, 4O23-4O24, 4O27-4O28, 5O1-5O2, 5O5. Post 1940 listings are in Scott Standard catalogue, Vol. 6.

Tête bêche Pairs

228a A54 5c blue green .75 1.00
Never hinged 1.55
On cover *1.60*
229a A55 10c red violet (II) 2.10 2.75
Never hinged 4.75
On cover *4.75*
230a A55 10c dark red brown 1.15 1.10
Never hinged 1.15
On cover *3.00*
230d A55 10c orange brown .75 .60
Never hinged 1.55
On cover *2.40*
232a A57 20c carmine 29.00 35.00
Never hinged 57.50
On cover *75.00*

1936-40 With Grilled Gum

227a A53 3c olive .75 *11.00*
Never hinged 4.75
On cover *16.00*
228d A54 5c blue green .40 .75
Never hinged .75
On cover *1.55*
229d A55 10c red violet (II) 1.55 .75
Never hinged 3.75
On cover *1.55*
e. Type I .40 .75
Never hinged .75
On cover *1.55*
230e A55 10c dk red brn ('40) 1.55 *35.00*
Never hinged 3.75
On cover *200.00*
231a A56 15c orange .40 1.55
Never hinged 1.55
On cover *5.50*
232c A57 20c carmine 7.00 .75
Never hinged 20.00
On cover *1.55*
233a A58 25c light brown 1.15 *6.25*
Never hinged 3.00
On cover *12.00*
234a A59 30c ultra 1.10 .75
Never hinged 5.50
On cover *3.00*
235a A60 35c yellow green 1.55 5.50
Never hinged 5.50
On cover *11.50*
236a A61 40c gray 11.00 .75
Never hinged 29.00
Nos. 227a-236a (10) 26.45 *63.05*
Set, never hinged 78.00

Mobile Post Office A62

1937, Sept. 5 Photo.
Granite Paper

237 A62 10c black & yellow .75 .75
Never hinged 1.55
On cover *1.55*

No. 237 was sold exclusively by the traveling post office. It exists on two kinds of granite paper, black and red fibers or blue and red fibers. See No. 307 for type A62 redrawn.

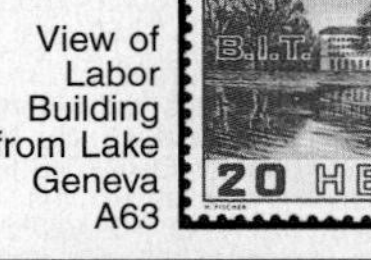
View of Labor Building from Lake Geneva A63

Palace of League of Nations A64

Main Building, Palace of League of Nations A65

Labor Building and Albert Thomas Monument A66

1938, May 2 *Perf. 11½*
Granite Paper

238 A63 20c red & buff .40 .75
Never hinged .75
On cover *1.55*
239 A64 30c blue & lt blue .60 .75
Never hinged 1.55
On cover *3.00*
240 A65 60c brown & buff 2.50 *4.00*
Never hinged 5.50
On cover *11.50*
241 A66 1fr black & buff 7.75 *27.00*
Never hinged 20.00
On cover *27.00*
Nos. 238-241 (4) 11.25 *32.50*
Set, never hinged 28.00

Opening of Assembly Hall of the Palace of the League of Nations.
For overprints see Nos. 2O57-2O64, 3O49-3O56.

Souvenir Sheet

A67

Engraved and Typographed
1938, Sept. 17 Unwmk. *Perf. 11½*
Granite Paper

242 A67 Sheet of 3 55.00 37.50
Never hinged 70.00
On cover *47.50*
a. AP4 10c on 65c gray bl & dp bl 29.00 *32.50*
Never hinged 55.00
On cover *50.00*
b. A68 20c red 1.55 *3.75*
Never hinged 3.75
On cover *20.00*

Natl. Phil. Exhib. at Aarau, Sept. 17-25, and 25th anniv. of Swiss air mail. No. 242 contains 2 No. 243, but on granite paper, and a 10c on 65c similar to No. C22 but redrawn, with wing tips 1½mm from side frame lines; overall size 37x20½mm; no watermark.
On No. C22, wing tips touch frame lines; size is 36x21½mm; Wmk. 183.

Lake Lugano — A68

First Federal Pact, 1291 A69

Diet of Stans, 1481 A70

Citizens Voting A71

1938, Sept. 17 Engr. *Perf. 11½*

243 A68 20c red .40 .75
Never hinged .75
On cover *1.55*
a. "c,"tête bêche pair .95 *1.15*
Never hinged 2.00
On cover *2.00*
c. Grilled gum .40 *1.55*
Never hinged 1.55
On cover *3.00*
d. As "c," tête bêche pair 2.10 *24.00*

Granite Paper

Never hinged 4.25
On cover *35.00*
244 A69 3fr brn car, *grnsh* 24.00 20.00
Never hinged 62.50
On cover *62.50*
245 A70 5fr slate bl, *grnsh* 24.00 20.00
Never hinged 62.50
On cover *77.50*
246 A71 10fr grn, *grnsh* 55.00 65.00
Never hinged 160.00
On cover *200.00*
Nos. 243-246 (4) 103.40 105.75
Set, never hinged 280.00

No. 243 is printed on ordinary paper. Nos. 244-246 are on granite surface-colored paper. The greenish surface coating has faded on most examples.
For type A68 in orange brown, see No. 318 in Scott Standard catalogue, Vol. 6.

See Nos. 242b, 284-286 (in Scott Standard catalogue, Vol. 6). For overprints see Nos. O5, O23, 2O65-2O67, 2O69, 2O74, 2O88-2O90, 3O57-3O59, 3O61, 3O66, 3O80-3O82, 4O5, 4O19-4O21, O4O25, 5O3, 5O23-5O25, 7O18-7O20. Post 1940 listings are in Scott Standard catalogue, Vol. 6.

Deputation of Trades and Professions — A72

Swiss Family A73

Alpine Scenery A74

German

Italian

Engr., Photo. (30c)

1939, Feb. 1 ***Perf. 11½***

Inscribed in French

247 A72 10c dl pur & red .40 .75
Never hinged .75
On cover *1.55*
248 A73 20c lake & red .75 .75
Never hinged 2.40
On cover *1.55*
249 A74 30c dp blue & red 3.25 *13.50*
Never hinged 11.00
On cover *20.00*

Inscribed in German

250 A72 10c dl pur & red .40 .75
Never hinged .75
On cover *1.55*
251 A73 20c lake & red .40 .75
Never hinged 1.15
On cover *1.55*
252 A74 30c dp blue & red 3.00 *4.75*
Never hinged 9.50
On cover *9.25*

Inscribed in Italian

253 A72 10c dl pur & red .40 .75
Never hinged .75
On cover *1.55*
254 A73 20c lake & red 7.75 .75
Never hinged 16.00
On cover *1.55*
255 A74 30c dp blue & red 2.40 *15.00*
Never hinged 11.50
On cover *24.00*
Nos. 247-255 (9) 18.75 *37.75*
Set, never hinged 54.00

National Exposition of 1939, Zurich.

Tree and Crossbow — A75

1939, May 6 **Photo.** ***Perf. 11½***

Granite Paper

Inscribed in French

256 A75 5c deep green 1.55 *7.00*
Never hinged 3.00
On cover *9.25*
257 A75 10c gray brown 2.00 *11.50*
Never hinged 4.00
On cover *16.00*
258 A75 20c brt carmine 4.25 *37.50*
Never hinged 8.50
On cover *57.50*
259 A75 30c violet blue 3.25 *15.00*
Never hinged 9.25
On cover *24.00*

Inscribed in German

260 A75 5c deep green 1.55 *7.00*
Never hinged 3.00
On cover *9.25*
261 A75 10c gray brown .55 *3.00*
Never hinged 1.55
On cover *4.00*
262 A75 20c brt carmine 4.25 *.40*
Never hinged 8.50
On cover *57.50*
263 A75 30c violet blue 3.00 *12.50*
Never hinged 8.50
On cover *24.00*

Inscribed in Italian

264 A75 5c deep green 1.55 *7.00*
Never hinged 3.00
On cover *9.25*
265 A75 10c gray brown .55 *11.50*
Never hinged 4.00
On cover *16.00*
266 A75 20c brt carmine 4.25 *37.50*
Never hinged 8.50
On cover *57.50*
267 A75 30c violet blue 3.25 *16.00*
Never hinged 8.50
On cover *24.00*
Nos. 256-267 (12) 30.00 *165.90*
Set, never hinged 72.50

National Exposition of 1939.

The 5c, 10c and 20c stamps in the three languages exist se-tenant in coils. On the 10c coil stamp, the inscription "COURVOISIER S.A." beneath is design is smaller, with the "A" just left of the point on the "V" of "HELVETIA". On the sheet stamp, the "A" is just right of the "V". Value about three times that of the sheet stamp.

1939 **With Grilled Gum**

256a A75 5c deep green .55 *4.00*
Never hinged 1.55
On cover *6.25*
257a A75 10c gray brown .55 *3.75*
Never hinged 1.55
On cover *4.75*
258a A75 20c bright carmine 1.10 *5.50*
Never hinged 3.00
On cover *5.50*
260a A75 5c deep green .55 *3.00*
Never hinged 1.55
On cover *3.75*
262a A75 20c bright carmine 1.10 3.00
Never hinged 3.00
On cover *3.75*
264a A75 5c deep green .75 *6.25*
Never hinged 3.00
On cover *9.25*
265a A75 10c gray brown .55 *5.50*
Never hinged 1.55
On cover *7.75*
266a A75 20c bright carmine 1.10 *7.75*
Never hinged 4.00
On cover *11.50*
Nos. 256a-266a (8) 6.25 *38.75*
Set, never hinged 19.00

View of Geneva A76

Perf. 11½

1939, Aug. 22 **Photo.** **Unwmk.**

Granite Paper

268 A76 20c red, car & buff .40 .75
Never hinged .75
On cover *1.55*
269 A76 30c blue, car & gray .40 *4.25*
Never hinged 1.15
On cover *6.25*
Set, never hinged 1.90

75th anniv. of the founding of the Intl. Red Cross Society.

SEMI-POSTAL STAMPS

Nos. B1-B76, B81-B84 were sold at premiums of 2c for 3c stamps, 5c for 5c-20c stamps and 10c for 30c-40c stamps.

Helvetia and Matterhorn — SP2

Perf. 11½, 12

1913, Dec. 1 **Typo.** **Wmk. 183**

Granite Paper

B1 SP2 5c green 3.75 *11.50*
Never hinged 10.00
On cover 20.00

Boy (Appenzell) SP3

Girl (Lucerne) SP4

1915, Dec. 1 ***Perf. 11½***

B2 SP3 5c green, *buff* 3.75 *16.00*
Never hinged 11.50
On cover 24.00
a. Tête bêche pair 77.50 *1,400.*
Never hinged 170.00
On cover 24.00
B3 SP4 10c red, *buff* 77.50 100.00
Never hinged 175.00
On cover 340.00
Set, never hinged 356.50

Girl (Fribourg) SP5

Dairy Boy (Bern) SP6

Girl (Vaud) — SP7

1916, Dec. 1

B4 SP5 3c vio, *buff* 7.75 *37.50*
Never hinged 16.00
On cover 92.50
B5 SP6 5c grn, *buff* 16.00 11.50
Never hinged 30.00
On cover 27.50
B6 SP7 10c brn red, *buff* 62.50 *77.50*
Never hinged 125.00
On cover 200.00
Nos. B4-B6 (3) 86.25 *126.50*
Set, never hinged 170.00

Girl (Valais) SP8

Girl (Unter-walden) SP9

Girl (Ticino) — SP10

1917, Dec. 1

B7 SP8 3c vio, *buff* 3.75 *57.50*
Never hinged 11.50
On cover 110.00
B8 SP9 5c green, *buff* 9.25 7.75
Never hinged 20.00
On cover 16.00
B9 SP10 10c red, *buff* 24.00 30.00
Never hinged 62.50
On cover 70.00
Nos. B7-B9 (3) 37.00 *95.25*
Set, never hinged 94.00

Uri SP11

Geneva SP12

Straw-Surfaced Paper

1918, Dec. 1

B10 SP11 10c red, org & blk 11.50 *35.00*
Never hinged 24.00
On cover 55.00
B11 SP12 15c vio, red, org & blk 16.00 *19.50*
Never hinged 42.50
On cover 37.50
Set, never hinged 66.50

Nidwalden SP13

Vaud SP14

Obwalden — SP15

Cream-Surfaced Paper

1919, Dec. 1

B12 SP13 7½c gray, red & blk 3.75 *22.00*
Never hinged 11.50
On cover 27.50
B13 SP14 10c lake, grn & blk 3.75 *22.00*
Never hinged 11.50
On cover 27.50
B14 SP15 15c pur, red & blk 7.75 *11.00*
Never hinged 24.00
On cover 30.00
Nos. B12-B14 (3) 15.25 *55.00*
Set, never hinged 47.00

Schwyz SP16

Zürich SP17

Ticino — SP18

Cream-Surfaced Paper

1920, Dec. 1

B15 SP16 7½c gray & red 4.75 *24.00*
Never hinged 11.50
On cover 29.00
B16 SP17 10c red & lt bl 7.75 *25.00*
Never hinged 21.00
On cover 29.00
B17 SP18 15c violet, red & bl 3.75 *11.50*
Never hinged 14.00
On cover 20.00
Nos. B15-B17 (3) 16.25 *60.50*
Set, never hinged 46.50

Valais SP19

Bern SP20

Switzerland — SP21

Cream-Surfaced Paper

1921, Dec. 1

B18 SP19 10c grn, red & blk .75 *4.75*
Never hinged 3.75
On cover 9.25
B19 SP20 20c vio, red, org & blk 3.00 *7.00*
Never hinged 9.25
On cover 13.50
B20 SP21 40c blue & red 12.50 *85.00*
Never hinged 27.50
On cover 115.00
Nos. B18-B20 (3) 16.25 *96.75*
Set, never hinged 40.50

Zug SP22

Fribourg SP23

Lucerne SP24

Switzerland SP25

Cream-Surfaced Paper

1922, Dec. 1

B21 SP22 5c org, pale bl & blk .75 *9.25*
Never hinged 3.00
On cover 16.00
B22 SP23 10c ol grn & blk .75 *3.00*
Never hinged 3.00
On cover 9.00
B23 SP24 20c vio, pale bl & blk 1.60 *3.00*
Never hinged 3.75
On cover 9.00
B24 SP25 40c bl & red 14.00 *92.50*
Never hinged 30.00
On cover 160.00
Nos. B21-B24 (4) 17.10 *107.75*
Set, never hinged 40.00

Basel SP26

Glarus (St. Fridolin) SP27

Neuchâtel SP28

Switzerland SP29

Cream-Surfaced Paper

1923, Dec. 1

B25 SP26 5c org & blk .40 *7.75*
Never hinged 2.00
On cover 11.50
B26 SP27 10c multi .40 *3.75*
Never hinged 2.00
On cover 9.25
B27 SP28 20c multi .75 *3.75*
Never hinged 2.40
On cover 9.25
B28 SP29 40c dk bl & red 11.00 *70.00*
Never hinged 24.00
On cover 115.00
Nos. B25-B28 (4) 12.55 *85.25*
Set, never hinged 30.00

Appenzell SP30

Solothurn SP31

Schaffhausen SP32

Switzerland SP33

Cream-Surfaced Paper

1924, Dec. 1

B29 SP30 5c dk vio & blk .40 *2.50*
Never hinged 1.15
On cover 6.25
B30 SP31 10c grn, red & blk .75 *1.15*
Never hinged 2.00
On cover 4.75
B31 SP32 20c car, yel & blk .75 *2.00*
Never hinged 2.75
On cover 4.75
B32 SP33 30c bl, red & blk 2.50 *21.00*
Never hinged 5.00
On cover 32.50
Nos. B29-B32 (4) 4.40 *26.65*
Set, never hinged 11.00

St. Gallen (Canton) SP34

Appenzell-Ausser-Rhoden SP35

Grisons SP36

Switzerland SP37

Cream-Surfaced Paper

1925, Dec. 1

B33 SP34 5c vio, grn & blk .40 *2.50*
Never hinged 1.15
On cover 4.75
B34 SP35 10c grn & blk .40 *1.60*
Never hinged 1.15
On cover 1.55
B35 SP36 20c multi .55 *1.60*
Never hinged 1.55
On cover 3.75
B36 SP37 30c dk bl, red & blk 1.40 *14.00*
Never hinged 3.75
On cover 32.50
Nos. B33-B36 (4) 2.75 *19.70*
Set, never hinged 7.50

Thurgau SP38

Basel SP39

Aargau SP40

Switzerland SP41

Cream-Surfaced Paper

1926, Dec. 1

B37 SP38 5c vio, bis & grn .40 *2.00*
Never hinged 1.15
On cover 4.75
B38 SP39 10c gray grn, red & blk .40 *2.00*
Never hinged 1.15
On cover 3.75
B39 SP40 20c red, blk & bl .55 *2.50*
Never hinged 1.55
On cover 3.75
B40 SP41 30c dk bl & red 1.40 *16.00*
Never hinged 3.75
On cover 32.50
Nos. B37-B40 (4) 2.75 *22.50*
Set, never hinged 7.50

Orphan SP42

Orphan at Pestalozzi School SP43

SP44

J. H. Pestalozzi SP45

1927, Dec. 1 Typo. Wmk. 183

Granite Paper

B41 SP42 5c red vio & yel, *grysh* .40 *2.50*
Never hinged .75
On cover 3.75
B42 SP43 10c grn & fawn, *grnsh* .40 *.75*
Never hinged .75
On cover 3.75

Engr.

B43 SP44 20c red .55 *.75*
Never hinged .75
On cover 3.75

Unwmk.

Photo.

B44 SP45 30c gray bl & blk 1.40 *11.50*
Never hinged 3.50
On cover 20.00
Nos. B41-B44 (4) 2.75 *15.50*
Set, never hinged 5.75

Nos. B43-B44 for the centenary of the death of Johann Heinrich Pestalozzi, the Swiss educational reformer.

Lausanne SP46

Winterthur SP47

St. Gallen (City) — SP48

J. H. Dunant SP49

1928, Dec. 1 Typo. Wmk. 183

Cream-Surfaced Paper.

B45 SP46 5c dk vio, red & blk .40 *2.50*
Never hinged .75
On cover 4.75
B46 SP47 10c bl grn, org red & blk .40 *1.60*
Never hinged .75
On cover 3.75
B47 SP48 20c brn red, blk & yel .25 *.70*
Never hinged .40
On cover 4.75

Unwmk.

Photo.

Thick White Paper

B48 SP49 30c dl bl & red 1.60 *10.00*
Never hinged 4.75
On cover 20.00
Nos. B45-B48 (4) 2.65 *14.80*
Set, never hinged 6.75

No. B48 for the centenary of the birth of Jean Henri Dunant, Swiss author, philanthropist and founder of the Red Cross Society.

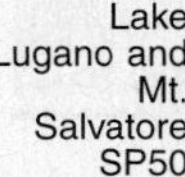

Lake Lugano and Mt. Salvatore SP50

Lake Engstlen and Mt. Titlis SP51

Mt. Lyskamm SP52

Nicholas von der Flüe SP53

1929, Dec. 1 ***Perf. 11x11½***

B49 SP50 5c dk vio & red org .40 *2.00*
Never hinged .75
On cover 4.75
B50 SP51 10c ol brn & gray bl .40 *1.60*
Never hinged .75
On cover 3.75
B51 SP52 20c brn garnet & bl .40 *2.00*
Never hinged .75
On cover 3.75
B52 SP53 30c dk blue 1.70 *20.00*
Never hinged 4.50
On cover 32.50
Nos. B49-B52 (4) 2.90 *25.60*
Set, never hinged 6.75

No. B52 for Nicholas von der Flüe, the Swiss patriot. By his advice the Swiss Confederation was continued and Swiss independence was saved.

Fribourg SP54

Altdorf SP55

Schaffhausen SP56

Jeremias Gotthelf SP57

Wmk. 183

1930, Dec. 1 Typo. ***Perf. 11½***

Cream-Surfaced Paper

B53 SP54 5c dp grn, dl bl & blk .40 *1.60*
Never hinged .75
On cover 3.75
B54 SP55 10c multicolored .40 *1.15*
Never hinged .75
On cover 3.00
B55 SP56 20c multicolored .40 *1.15*
Never hinged .75
On cover 3.00

Engr.
White Paper

B56 SP57 30c slate blue 1.60 *7.75*
Never hinged 4.50
On cover 27.50
Nos. B53-B56 (4) 2.80 *11.65*
Set, never hinged 6.75

No. B56 for Jeremias Gotthelf, pen name of Albrecht Bitzius, pastor and author.

Lakes Silvaplana and Sils SP58

Wetterhorn SP59

Lake Geneva SP60

Alexandre Vinet SP61

1931, Dec. 1 Photo. Unwmk.
Granite Paper

B57 SP58 5c dp grn .60 *2.00*
Never hinged 1.15
On cover 6.25
B58 SP59 10c dk vio .40 *1.15*
Never hinged .75
On cover 3.75
B59 SP60 20c brn red .95 *1.60*
Never hinged 1.15
On cover 3.75

Wmk. 183
Engr.

B60 SP61 30c ultra 6.25 *27.00*
Never hinged 16.00
On cover 55.00
Nos. B57-B60 (4) 8.20 *31.75*
Set, never hinged 19.00

No. B60 for Alexandre Rudolph Vinet, critic and theologian.

Flag Swinger SP62

Putting the Stone SP63

Wrestling SP64

Eugen Huber SP65

1932, Dec. 1 Typo. Unwmk.
Granite Paper

B61 SP62 5c dk grn & red .45 *2.75*
Never hinged 1.55
On cover 5.50
B62 SP63 10c orange .60 *2.75*
Never hinged 1.55
On cover 3.75
B63 SP64 20c scarlet .75 *2.75*
Never hinged 2.40
On cover 3.75

Wmk. 183
Engr.

B64 SP65 30c ultra 2.75 *11.00*
Never hinged 7.00
On cover 27.50
Nos. B61-B64 (4) 4.55 *19.25*
Set, never hinged 12.50

No. B64 for Eugen Huber, jurist and author of the Swiss Civil Law Book.

Girl of Vaud — SP66

Girl of Bern — SP67

Girl of Ticino SP68

Jean Baptiste Girard (Le Père Grégoire) SP69

1933, Dec. 1 Photo. Unwmk.
Granite Paper

B65 SP66 5c grn & buff .45 *2.40*
Never hinged 1.15
On cover 3.00
B66 SP67 10c vio & buff .45 *1.55*
Never hinged 1.15
On cover 2.25
B67 SP68 20c red & buff .60 *3.00*
Never hinged 1.55
On cover 2.25

Wmk. 183
Engr.

B68 SP69 30c ultra 3.00 *13.00*
Never hinged 7.00
On cover 19.00
Nos. B65-B68 (4) 4.50 *19.95*
Set, never hinged 11.00

Girl of Appenzell SP70

Girl of Valais SP71

Girl of Grisons SP72

Albrecht von Haller SP73

1934, Dec. 1 Photo. Unwmk.

B69 SP70 5c grn & buff .40 *2.40*
Never hinged 1.15
On cover 3.75
B70 SP71 10c vio & buff .55 *1.55*
Never hinged 1.55
On cover 2.40
B71 SP72 20c red & buff .60 *2.40*
Never hinged 1.55
On cover 3.75

Wmk. 183
Engr.

B72 SP73 30c ultra 3.00 *16.00*
Never hinged 6.50
On cover 19.00
Nos. B69-B72 (4) 4.55 *22.35*
Set, never hinged 11.00

Girl of Basel SP74

Girl of Lucerne SP75

Girl of Geneva SP76

Stefano Franscini SP77

1935, Dec. 1 Photo. Unwmk.
Granite Paper

B73 SP74 5c grn & buff .40 *2.40*
Never hinged 1.15
On cover 3.00
B74 SP75 10c vio & buff .55 *1.55*
Never hinged 1.55
On cover 2.25
B75 SP76 20c red & buff .60 *3.75*
Never hinged 1.55
On cover 5.50

Wmk. 183
Engr.

B76 SP77 30c ultra 3.00 *16.00*
Never hinged 6.50
On cover 19.00
Nos. B73-B76 (4) 4.55 *23.70*
Set, never hinged 11.00

No. B76 honors Stefano Franscini (1796-1857), political economist and educator.

Alpine Herdsman — SP78

Perf. 11½
1936, Oct. 1 Photo. Unwmk.
Granite Paper

B77 SP78 10c + 5c vio .75 *1.55*
Never hinged 1.55
On cover 4.75
B78 SP78 20c + 10c dk red 1.15 *6.00*
Never hinged 2.25
On cover 9.25
B79 SP78 30c + 10c ultra 5.50 *27.50*
Never hinged 11.50
On cover 100.00
Nos. B77-B79 (3) 7.40 *35.05*
Set, never hinged 15.50

Souvenir Sheet

B80 SP78 Sheet of 3 60.00 *240.00*
Never hinged 105.00
On cover 475.00
a. Block of 4 sheets 240.00 *1,250.*
Never hinged 460.00

Swiss National Defense Fund Drive.

No. B80 contains stamps similar to Nos. B77-B79, but on grilled granite paper with blue and red fibers instead of black and red. Sold for 2fr. Size: 120x130mm.

Johann Georg Nägeli SP79

Girl of Neuchâtel SP80

Girl of Schwyz SP81

Girl of Zurich SP82

Wmk. 183
1936, Dec. 1 Engr. *Perf. 11½*
Granite Paper

B81 SP79 5c grn .40 *1.15*
Never hinged .75

Unwmk.
Photo.

B82 SP80 10c vio & buff .75 *1.15*
Never hinged 1.55
On cover 2.25
B83 SP81 20c red & buff .45 *3.00*
Never hinged 1.55
On cover 5.50
B84 SP82 30c ultra & buff 5.00 *40.00*
Never hinged 10.00
On cover 55.00
Nos. B81-B84 (4) 6.60 *45.30*
Set, never hinged 14.00

Gen. Henri Dufour — SP83

Nicholas von der Flüe — SP84

Boy SP85

Girl SP86

Perf. 11½
1937, Dec. 1 Unwmk. Engr.

B85 SP83 5c + 5c bl grn .40 *.75*
Never hinged .75
On cover 1.55
B86 SP84 10c + 5c red vio .40 *.75*
Never hinged .75
On cover 1.55

Photo.
Granite Paper

B87 SP85 20c + 5c red & silver .60 *.75*
Never hinged 1.55
On cover 1.55
B88 SP86 30c + 10c ultra & sil 1.70 *7.75*
Never hinged 3.50
On cover 15.00
Nos. B85-B88 (4) 3.10 *10.00*
Set, never hinged 6.50

25th anniv. of the Pro Juventute (child welfare) stamps.

Souvenir Sheet

1937, Dec. 20 *Imperf.*

B89 Sheet of 2 10.00 *62.50*
On cover 77.50
a. SP85 20c + 5c red & silver 2.40 *17.00*
Never hinged 2.25
On cover 57.50
b. SP86 30c + 10c ultra & silver 2.40 *17.00*
Never hinged 9.25
On cover 57.50

Simulated perforation in silver. Sheet sold for 1fr.

Tell Chapel, Lake Lucerne SP87

1938, June 15 *Perf. 11½*
Granite Paper

B90 SP87 10c + 10c brt vio & yel .45 *2.75*
Never hinged 2.00
On cover 3.00
a. Grilled gum 11.50 *70.00*
Never hinged 23.00
On cover 135.00

National Fête Day.

Salomon Gessner
SP88

Girl of St. Gallen
SP89

Girl of Uri — SP90

Girl of Aargau — SP91

1938, Dec. 1 Engr. *Perf. 11½*

B91 SP88 5c + 5c dp bl grn .40 *.75*
Never hinged .75
On cover 1.55

Photo.

Granite Paper

B92 SP89 10c + 5c pur & buff .40 *.75*
Never hinged .75
On cover 1.55
B93 SP90 20c + 5c red & buff .55 *.75*
Never hinged 1.15
On cover 1.55
B94 SP91 30c + 10c ultra 2.10 *9.25*
Never hinged 4.75
On cover 16.00
Nos. B91-B94 (4) 3.45 *11.50*
Set, never hinged 7.50

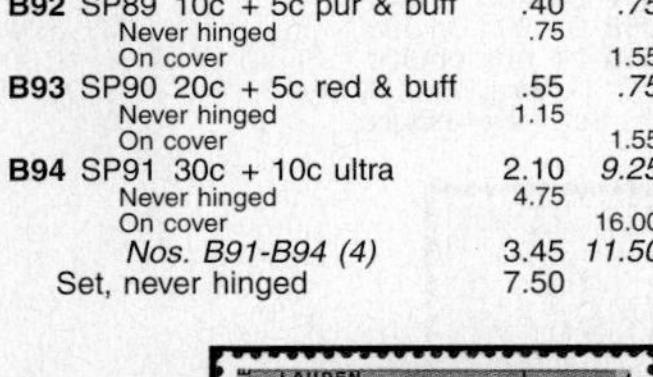

Castle at Laupen
SP92

1939, June 15

B95 SP92 10c + 10c brn, gray & red .40 *2.00*
Never hinged 1.60
On cover 3.00

600th anniversary of the Battle of Laupen. The surtax was used to aid needy mothers.

Hans Herzog
SP93

Girl of Fribourg
SP94

Girl of Nidwalden
SP95

Girl of Basel
SP96

Perf. 11½

1939, Dec. 1 Unwmk. Engr.

B96 SP93 5c + 5c dk grn .40 *.75*
Never hinged .75
On cover 2.25

Photo.

Granite Paper

B97 SP94 10c + 5c rose vio & buff .40 *.75*
Never hinged .75
On cover 2.25
B98 SP95 20c + 5c org red .40 *1.60*
Never hinged 1.15
On cover 3.75
B99 SP96 30c + 10c ultra & buff 2.00 *22.00*
Never hinged 4.75
On cover 28.00
Nos. B96-B99 (4) 3.20 *25.10*
Set, never hinged 7.50

Sempach, 1386 — SP97

Giornico, 1478 — SP98

Calven, 1499
SP99

WWI Ranger
SP100

1940, Mar. 20 Photo.

Granite Paper

B100 SP97 5c + 5c emer, blk & red .40 *1.60*
Never hinged .75
On cover 3.00
B101 SP98 10c + 5c brn org, blk & car .40 *.75*
Never hinged .75
On cover 2.25
B102 SP99 20c + 5c brn red, blk & car 2.40 1.60
Never hinged 6.25
On cover 2.25
a. 20c + 5c lt red, blk & car 2.00 *47.50*
Never hinged 4.75
On cover 57.50
B103 SP100 30c + 10c brt bl, brn blk & red 2.00 *11.50*
Never hinged 4.75
On cover 19.00

National Fête Day. The surtax was for the National Fund and the Red Cross.

Redrawn

B104 SP99 20c + 5c brn red, blk & car 6.25 9.00
Never hinged 18.00
On cover 16.00
Nos. B100-B104 (5) 11.45 *24.45*
Set, never hinged 35.00

The base of statue has been heavily shaded. "Calven 1499" moved nearer to bottom line of base. Top line of base removed.

Souvenir Sheet

Unwmk.

1940, July 16 Photo. *Imperf.*

Granite Paper

B105 Sheet of 4 175.00 *500.00*
Never hinged 325.00
On cover 775.00
a. SP97 5c+5c yel grn, blk & red 16.00 *35.00*
Never hinged 27.50
On cover 57.50
b. SP98 10c+5c org yel, blk & red 57.50 *175.00*
Never hinged 77.50
On cover 350.00
c. SP99 20c+5c brn red, blk & red (redrawn) 57.50 *175.00*
Never hinged 77.50
On cover 370.00
d. SP100 30c+10c chlky bl, blk & red 16.00 *35.00*
Never hinged 27.50
On cover 57.50

National Fete Day. Sheets measure 125x65mm and sold for 5fr.

Gottfried Keller
SP102

Girl of Thurgau
SP103

Girl of Solothurn
SP104

Girl of Zug
SP105

1940, Dec. 1 Engr. *Perf. 11½*

B106 SP102 5c + 5c dk bl grn .40 *.75*
Never hinged .75
On cover 1.50

Photo.

B107 SP103 10c + 5c brn & buff .40 *.75*
Never hinged .75
On cover 1.50
B108 SP104 20c + 5c org red & buff .45 *.75*
Never hinged 1.15
On cover 3.75
B109 SP105 30c + 10c dp ultra & buff 1.70 *13.00*
Never hinged 4.75
On cover 22.00
Nos. B106-B109 (4) 2.95 *15.25*
Set, never hinged 7.50

AIR POST STAMPS

Nos. 134 and 139 Overprinted in Carmine

1919-20 Wmk. 183 *Perf. 11½*

Granite Paper

C1 A25 30c yel brn & pale grn ('20) 110.00 *1,250.*
C2 A25 50c dp & pale grn 32.50 110.00
Set, never hinged 350.00

Counterfeits of overprint and fraudulent cancellations exist.

Airplane
AP1

Pilot at Controls of Airplane
AP2

Biplane against Sky — AP3

Allegorical Figure of Flight
AP4

Perf. 11½, 12 and Compound

1923-25 Typo.

C3 AP1 15c brn red & ap grn 2.25 8.25
C4 AP1 20c grn & lt grn ('25) .90 *6.00*
C5 AP1 25c dk bl & bl 7.75 *22.50*
C6 AP2 35c brn & buff 11.00 *42.50*
C7 AP2 40c vio & gray vio 14.50 *45.00*
C8 AP3 45c red & ind 1.60 *7.25*
C9 AP3 50c blk & red 12.50 17.00

Perf. 11½

C10 AP4 65c gray bl & dp bl ('24) 3.25 *16.00*
C11 AP4 75c org & brn red ('24) 15.00 *55.00*
C12 AP4 1fr vio & dp vio ('24) 42.50 32.50
Nos. C3-C12 (10) 111.25 *252.00*
Set, never hinged 275.00

For surcharges see Nos. C19, C22, C26.

1933-37 With Grilled Gum

C4a AP1 20c grn & lt grn ('37) .30 .40
C5a AP1 25c dk bl & bl ('34) 5.00 *50.00*
C8a AP3 45c red & indigo ('37) 2.50 *52.50*
C9a AP3 50c gray grn & scar ('35) 1.10 1.60
C10a AP4 65c gray bl & dp bl ('37) 2.75 *8.50*
C11a AP4 75c org & brn red ('36) 27.50 *175.00*
C12a AP4 1fr vio & deep vio 2.10 3.25
Nos. C4a-C12a (7) 41.25 *291.25*
Set, never hinged 65.00

See Grilled Gum note after No. 145.

Allegory of Air Mail — AP5

Bird Carrying Letter
AP6

1929-30 Granite Paper

C13 AP5 35c red brn, bis & claret 15.00 42.50
C14 AP5 40c dl grn, yel grn & bl 57.50 82.50
C15 AP6 2fr blk brn & red brn, *gray* ('30) 85.00 85.00
Nos. C13-C15 (3) 157.50 210.00
Set, never hinged 425.00

1933-35 With Grilled Gum

C13a AP5 35c red brn, bis & cl 5.00 *50.00*
C14a AP5 40c dk grn, yel grn & bl 37.50 77.50
C15a AP6 2fr blk brn & red brn ('35) 7.25 12.00
Nos. C13a-C15a (3) 49.75 *139.50*
Set, never hinged 140.00

Front View of Airplane
AP7

1932, Feb. 2 Granite Paper

C16 AP7 15c dp grn & lt grn .55 *1.60*
C17 AP7 20c dk red & buff 1.10 *2.50*
C18 AP7 90c dp bl & gray 7.25 *30.00*
Nos. C16-C18 (3) 8.90 *34.10*
Set, never hinged 22.50

Intl. Disarmament Conf., Geneva, Feb. 1932.
For surcharges see Nos. C20-C21, C23-C25.

Nos. C3, C10, C16-C18 Surcharged with New Values and Bars in Black or Red

1935-38

C19 AP1 10c on 15c 4.75 *37.50*
C20 AP7 10c on 15c .40 .55
a. Inverted surcharge *6,500.* *12,000.*
C21 AP7 10c on 20c ('36) .45 *2.25*
C22 AP4 10c on 65c ('38) .25 .40
C23 AP7 30c on 90c ('36) 3.00 *14.00*
C24 AP7 40c on 20c ('37) 3.75 *15.00*
C25 AP7 40c on 90c ('36) (R) 3.25 *14.50*
a. Vermilion surcharge 92.50 *800.00*
Never hinged, #C25a 150.00
Nos. C19-C25 (7) 15.85 *84.20*
Set, never hinged 40.00

Stamp similar to No. C22, but from souvenir sheet, is listed as No. 242a.

Type of Air Post Stamp of 1923 Srchd. in Black

1938, May 22 Wmk. 183 *Perf. 11½*

C26	AP3 75c on 50c gray & scar	6.50	

"Pro Aero" Meeting, May 21-22.

No. C26 was not sold to the public in the ordinary way, but affixed to air mail letters by postal officials. It was not regularly obtainable unused.

POSTAGE DUE STAMPS

D1

D2

Type I Frame Normal - UR Ornament

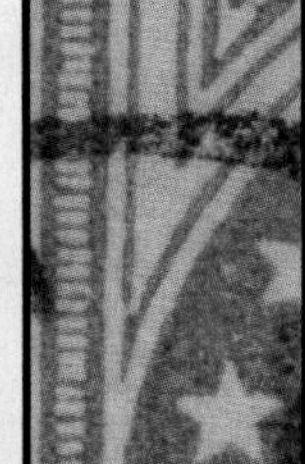
Type I Frame Normal - UL Triangle

Type I Frame Normal: Ornament at UR is undamaged. UL triangle tip and star tip align horizontally. LR triangle tip aligns horizontally with the center of the star.

Wmk. 182

1878-80 Typo. *Perf. 11½*

Type I Frame Normal

J1	D1	1c ultra	2.75	2.50
		On cover		40.00
J2	D2	2c ultra	2.75	2.50
		On cover		35.00
J3	D2	3c ultra	22.50	25.00
		On cover		90.00
J4	D2	5c ultra	25.00	12.50
		On cover		52.50
J5	D2	10c ultra	275.00	10.50
		On cover		62.50
J6	D2	20c ultra	300.00	9.00
		On cover		65.00
J7	D2	50c ultra	575.00	27.50
		On cover		130.00
J8	D2	100c ultra	750.00	25.00
		On cover		500.00
J9	D2	500c ultra	700.00	40.00
		On cover		3,500.
		Nos. J1-J9 (9)	2,653.	154.50

A 5c in design D1 exists.

Type I Frame Inverted - UL Triangle

Type I Frame Inverted: Ornament at LL is undamaged. UL triangle tip aligns horizontally with star center. LR triangle tip and star tip align horizontally.

Wmk. 182

1878-80 Typo. *Perf. 11½*

Type I Frame Inverted

J1a	1c ultra	18.00	20.00
J2a	2c ultra	2.75	2.75
J3a	3c ultra	22.50	23.00
J4a	5c ultra	27.00	11.00
J5a	10c ultra	275.00	18.00
J6a	20c ultra	300.00	11.00
J7a	50c ultra	600.00	35.00
J8a	100c ultra	750.00	25.00
J9a	500c ultra	700.00	40.00
	Nos. J1a-J9a (9)	2,695.	185.75

Type II Frame Normal - UR Ornament

Type II Frame Normal: Ornament at UR is broken with a white gap in center. UL triangle tip and star tip align horizontally. LR triangle tip aligns horizontally with the center of the star.

Wmk. 182

1878-80 Typo. *Perf. 11½*

Type II Frame Normal

J3b	3c ultra	18.00	17.00
J4b	5c ultra	25.00	22.50
J5b	10c ultra	250.00	10.00
J6b	20c ultra	300.00	8.00
J7b	50c ultra	600.00	30.00
J8b	100c ultra	1,500.	175.00
J9b	500c ultra	700.00	100.00
	Nos. J3b-J9b (7)	3,393.	362.50

Type II Frame Inverted - LL Ornament

Type II Frame Inverted: Ornament at LL is broken with a white gap in center. UL triangle tip aligns horizontally with star center. LR triangle tip and star tip align horizontally.

Wmk. 182

1878-80 Typo. *Perf. 11½*

Type II Frame Inverted

J3c	3c ultra	21.00	20.00
J4c	5c ultra	22.50	11.50
J5c	10c ultra	275.00	11.00
J6c	20c ultra	325.00	11.00
J7c	50c ultra	600.00	35.00
J8c	100c ultra		2,250.
J9c	500c ultra	700.00	100.00
	Nos. J3c-J9c (7)	1,944.	2,439.

Type II Frame Normal

1882-83 Granite Paper

J10	D2	10c ultra	240.00	57.50
		On cover		160.00
J11	D2	20c ultra	575.00	80.00
		On cover		225.00
J12	D2	50c ultra	3,200.	675.00
		On cover		1,500.
J13	D2	100c ultra	1,100.	500.00
		On cover		1,150.
J14	D2	500c ultra	*21,000.*	325.00
		On cover		3,500.

1882-83 Granite Paper

Type II Frame Inverted

J10a	10c ultra	250.00	60.00
J11a	20c ultra	625.00	90.00
J12a	50c ultra	3,250.	800.00
J13a	100c ultra	1,200.	550.00
J14a	500c ultra	*22,500.*	350.00

1883-84 Numerals in Red

Type II Frame Inverted

J15	D2	5c blue green	60.00	45.00
		On cover		125.00
J16	D2	10c blue green	110.00	35.00
		On cover		105.00
J17	D2	20c blue green	175.00	30.00
		On cover		135.00
J18	D2	50c blue green	200.00	100.00
		On cover		575.00
J19	D2	100c blue green	575.00	475.00
		On cover		1,600.
J20	D2	500c blue green	1,150.	275.00
		On cover		2,750.
		Nos. J15-J20 (6)	2,270.	960.00

1883-84 Numerals in Red

Type II Frame Normal

J15a	5c blue green	175.00	105.00
J16a	10c blue green	275.00	100.00
J17a	20c blue green	500.00	90.00
J18a	50c blue green	550.00	300.00
J19a	100c blue green	1,500.	1,400.
J20a	500c blue green	2,750.	800.00

1884-97 Numerals in Red

Type II Frame Normal

J21	D2	1c olive green	.90	.90
		On cover		20.00
J22	D2	3c olive green	8.00	9.00
		On cover		37.50
J23	D2	5c olive green	2.50	.90
		On cover		10.00
a.		5c yellow green	45.00	15.00
		On cover		55.00
J24	D2	10c olive green	6.75	1.50
		On cover		10.50
a.		10c yellow green	110.00	16.00
		On cover		120.00
J25	D2	20c olive green	13.00	2.25
		On cover		20.00
a.		20c yellow green	190.00	12.00
		On cover		120.00
J26	D2	50c olive green	20.00	5.00
		On cover		55.00
a.		50c yellow green	400.00	125.00
		On cover		500.00
J27	D2	100c olive green	22.50	4.00
		On cover		275.00
a.		100c yellow green	425.00	160.00
		On cover		700.00
J28	D2	500c olive green	175.00	225.00
		On cover		—
a.		500c yellow green	800.00	60.00
		On cover		2,250.

Numerous shades of Nos. J21-J28 exist.

1908-09 Wmk. 183

Numerals in Red

J29	D2	1c olive green	.30	1.10
		Never hinged	.35	
		On cover		11.00
J30	D2	5c olive green	.60	.90
		Never hinged	1.00	
		On cover		5.50
J31	D2	10c olive green	1.50	2.25
		Never hinged	2.75	
		On cover		8.50
J32	D2	20c olive green	3.00	5.00
		Never hinged	11.00	
		On cover		22.50
J33	D2	50c olive green	15.00	1.10
		Never hinged	45.00	
		On cover		55.00
J34	D2	100c olive green	30.00	2.25
		Never hinged	55.00	
		On cover		85.00
		Nos. J29-J34 (6)	50.40	12.60

D3

1910 *Perf. 11½, 12*

Numerals in Red

J35	D3	1c blue green	.25	.25
J36	D3	3c blue green	.25	.25
J37	D3	5c blue green	.25	.25
J38	D3	10c blue green	11.00	.25
J39	D3	15c blue green	.65	1.10
J40	D3	20c blue green	17.50	.25
J41	D3	25c blue green	1.25	.65
J42	D3	30c blue green	1.25	.55
J43	D3	50c blue green	1.50	1.10
		Nos. J35-J43 (9)	33.90	4.65

See Nos. S1-S12.

No. J36 Surcharged

1916

J44	D3 5c on 3c bl grn & red	.40	.25

Nos. J35-J36, J43 Surcharged

1924

J45	D3	10c on 1c	.25	*8.25*
J46	D3	10c on 3c	.25	*1.50*
J47	D3	20c on 50c	.95	1.50
		Nos. J45-J47 (3)	1.45	11.25

D4

Wmk. 183

1924-26 Typo. *Perf. 11½*

Granite Paper

J48	D4	5c ol grn & red	.65	.25
J49	D4	10c ol grn & red	2.75	.25
J50	D4	15c ol grn & red ('26)	2.50	.55
J51	D4	20c ol grn & red	6.00	.25
J52	D4	25c ol grn & red	2.75	.55
J53	D4	30c ol grn & red	2.75	.85
J54	D4	40c ol grn & red ('26)	3.75	.70
J55	D4	50c ol grn & red	3.75	.70
		Nos. J48-J55 (8)	24.90	4.10

1924 With Grilled Gum

J48a	D4	5c olive green & red	.65	.60
J49a	D4	10c olive green & red	2.50	1.10
J51a	D4	20c olive green & red	4.75	1.50
J52a	D4	25c olive green & red	7.25	*65.00*
		Nos. J48a-J52a (4)	15.15	*68.20*

See Grilled Gum note after No. 145.

Nos. J50, J53 & J55 Surcharged in Black

1937

J56	D4	5c on 15c	.90	*4.25*
J57	D4	10c on 30c	.90	*1.50*
J58	D4	20c on 50c	1.50	*5.00*
J59	D4	40c on 50c	2.50	*12.00*
		Nos. J56-J59 (4)	5.80	*22.75*
		Set, never hinged	10.50	

D5

1938 Engr. Unwmk.

J60	D5	5c scarlet	.40	.25
J61	D5	10c scarlet	.55	.25
J62	D5	15c scarlet	1.25	*2.25*
J63	D5	20c scarlet	.95	.25
J64	D5	25c scarlet	1.40	*1.90*
J65	D5	30c scarlet	1.40	1.25
J66	D5	40c scarlet	1.60	.45
J67	D5	50c scarlet	1.90	2.25
		Nos. J60-J67 (8)	9.45	*8.85*
		Set, never hinged	19.00	

1938 With Grilled Gum

J60a	D5	5c scarlet	.65	*1.60*
J61a	D5	10c scarlet	.65	*1.25*
J62a	D5	15c scarlet	1.40	*2.50*
J63a	D5	20c scarlet	1.25	.55
J64a	D5	25c scarlet	1.40	*9.50*
J65a	D5	30c scarlet	1.40	*2.25*
J66a	D5	40c scarlet	2.10	2.10
J67a	D5	50c scarlet	2.50	*3.50*
		Nos. J60a-J67a (8)	11.35	*23.25*
		Set, never hinged	29.00	

See Grilled Gum note after No. 145.

OFFICIAL STAMPS

With Perforated Cross

In 1935 the government authorized the use of regular postage issues perforated with a nine-hole cross for all government departments. Twenty-seven different stamps were so perforated. These were succeeded in 1938 by the cross overprints.

Values for canceled Official Stamps are for those canceled to order. Postally used stamps sell for considerably more. This note does not apply to Nos. 1O1-1O16, 2O27-2O30, 3O23-3O26.

Counterfeit overprints exist of most official stamps.

Official stamps without unused values were not made available to the public unused.

Regular Issues of 1908-36 Overprinted in Black

1938 Unwmk. *Perf. 11½*

O1 A53 3c olive .25 .25
O2 A54 5c blue green .25 .25
O3 A55 10c red violet .95 .45
O4 A56 15c orange .25 *1.60*
O5 A68 20c red .45 .25
O6 A58 25c brown .45 *1.40*
O7 A59 30c ultra .60 *1.00*
O8 A60 35c yellow green .60 *1.25*
O9 A61 40c gray .60 *1.00*

Wmk. 183
With Grilled Gum

O10 A25 50c dp grn & pale grn .60 *1.50*
O11 A25 60c brn org & buff 1.25 *2.50*
O12 A25 70c vio & buff 1.25 *4.25*
O13 A25 80c sl & buff 1.25 *3.25*
O14 A36 90c grn & red, *grn* 3.00 *3.25*
O15 A25 1fr dp cl & pale grn 1.50 *3.25*
O16 A36 1.20fr brn rose & red, *rose* 1.50 *4.50*
O17 A36 1.50fr bl & red, *bl* 2.50 *6.00*
O18 A36 2fr gray blk & red, *gray* 3.00 *7.00*
Nos. O1-O18 (18) 20.25 *42.95*
Set, never hinged 65.00

Nos. O14, O16, O17 and O18 are on surface-colored paper.

1938 Unwmk. With Grilled Gum

O1a A53 3c olive 4.50 .45
O2a A54 5c blue green 1.25 .45
O3a A55 10c red violet 1.50 .55
O4a A56 15c orange 2.75 1.25
O5a A68 20c red 1.50 .70
O6a A58 25c brown 75.00 7.75
O7a A59 30c ultra 2.50 1.10
O8a A60 35c yellow green 1.90 1.90
O9a A61 40c gray 2.50 1.00
Nos. O1a-O9a (9) 93.40 15.15
Set, never hinged 190.00

See Grilled Gum note after No. 145.

FOR THE WAR BOARD OF TRADE

Regular Issues of 1908-18 Overprinted

1918 Wmk. 183 *Perf. 11½, 12*

1O1 A26 3c brown org 110.00 *225.00*
1O2 A26 5c green 10.00 *32.50*
1O3 A26 7½c gray (I) 300.00 *450.00*
a. 7½c slate (II) 550.00 *950.00*
1O4 A28 10c red, *buff* 15.00 *40.00*
1O5 A28 15c vio, *buff* 12.50 *45.00*
1O6 A25 20c red & yel 125.00 *500.00*
1O7 A25 25c dp bl 125.00 *500.00*
1O8 A25 30c yel brn & pale grn 125.00 *450.00*
Nos. 1O1-1O8 (8) 822.50 *2,243.*

Most unused examples of Nos. 1O1-1O8 are reprints made using the original overprint forms.

Counterfeits exist.

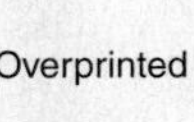

Overprinted

1918

1O9 A26 3c brn org 4.25 *35.00*
1O10 A26 5c green 12.00 *52.50*
1O11 A26 7½c gray 4.50 *22.50*
1O12 A28 10c red, *buff* 45.00 *87.50*
1O13 A28 15c vio, *buff* 82.50
1O14 A25 20c red & yel 8.75 *52.50*
1O15 A25 25c dp blue 8.75 *52.50*
1O16 A25 30c yel brn & pale grn 14.50 *87.50*
Nos. 1O9-1O16 (8) 180.25 390.00

No. 1O13 was never placed in use.
Fraudulent cancellations are found on Nos. 1O1-1O16.

FOR THE LEAGUE OF NATIONS

Regular Issues Overprinted

On 1908-30 Issues

1922-31 Wmk. 183 *Perf. 11½, 12*

2O1 A26 2½c ol, *buff* ('28) .45
2O2 A26 3c ultra, *buff* ('30) 8.25
2O3 A26 5c orange, *buff* 5.50
2O4 A26 5c gray vio, *buff* ('26) 2.75
2O5 A26 5c red vio, *buff* ('27) 2.25
2O6 A26 5c dk grn, *buff* ('31) 25.00
2O7 A26 7½c dp grn, *buff* ('28) .55
2O8 A28 10c green, *buff* .55
2O9 A28 10c bl grn, *buff* ('28) 1.10
2O10 A28 10c vio, *buff* ('31) 2.75
2O11 A28 15c brn red, *buff* ('28) 1.10
2O12 A28 20c red vio, *buff* 8.25
2O13 A28 20c car, *buff* ('26) 2.25
2O14 A28 25c ver, *buff* 8.25
2O15 A28 25c car, *buff* 1.10
2O16 A28 25c brn, *buff* ('27) 17.00
2O17 A28 30c dp bl, *buff* ('25) 8.25
2O18 A25 30c yel brn & pale grn 14.00
2O19 A25 35c yel grn & yel 10.00
2O20 A25 40c deep blue 1.40
2O21 A25 40c red vio & grn ('28) 14.00
2O22 A25 50c dp grn & pale grn 11.00
2O23 A25 60c brn org & buff 30.00 1.60
2O24 A25 70c vio & buff ('25) 26.00
2O25 A25 80c slate & buff 2.75
2O26 A25 1fr dp cl & pale grn 6.75
2O27 A29 3fr red 32.50
2O28 A30 5fr ultra 60.00
2O29 A31 10fr dull violet 140.00
2O30 A31 10fr gray grn ('30) 140.00
Nos. 2O1-2O30 (30) 555.35

1930-44 With Grilled Gum

2O2a A26 3c ultra, *buff* ('33) 10.00
2O6a A26 5c dk grn, *buff* ('33) 19.00
2O17a A28 30c dp bl,*buff* 425.00
2O22a A25 50c dp grn & pale grn ('35) .90 2.25
2O23a A25 60c brn org & buff ('44) 25.00 *225.00*
2O24a A25 70c violet & buff ('32) 1.60 2.25
2O25a A25 80c slate & buff ('42) 2.75 2.50
2O26a A25 1fr dp cl & pale grn ('42) 5.25

1935-36 With Grilled Gum

2O31 A36 90c grn & red, *grn* ('36) 5.00
2O32 A36 1.20fr brn rose & red, *rose* ('36) 2.75 *4.50*
b. Inverted overprint *4,250.*
2O33 A36 1.50fr bl & red, *bl* 2.75 *4.50*
2O34 A36 2fr gray blk & red, *gray* ('36) 2.75 *5.25*

1922-25 Ordinary Gum

2O31a A36 90c 14.00
2O32a A36 1.20fr ('25) 14.00
2O33a A36 1.50fr ('25) 13.00
2O34a A36 2fr ('25) 12.00

1928

2O35 A39 5fr blue 87.50

1932 On 1932 Issue

2O36 A41 5c peacock bl 19.00
2O37 A41 10c orange 1.60
2O38 A41 20c cerise 1.60
2O39 A41 30c ultra 55.00
2O40 A41 60c olive brn 15.00

Unwmk.

2O41 A42 1fr ol gray & bl 15.00
Nos. 2O36-2O41 (6) 107.20

On 1934 Issue

1934-35 Wmk. 183

2O42 A46 3c olive .25
2O43 A47 5c emerald .65
2O44 A49 15c orange ('35) 1.50
2O45 A51 25c brown 19.00
2O46 A52 30c ultra 1.60
Nos. 2O42-2O46 (5) 23.00

1937 On 1936 Issue Unwmk.

2O47 A53 3c olive .25 .25
2O48 A54 5c blue green .25 .25
2O49 A55 10c red violet 1.10
2O50 A56 15c orange .45 .55
2O51 A57 20c carmine 1.90
2O52 A58 25c brown .65 1.10
2O53 A59 30c ultra .65 1.00
2O54 A60 35c yellow green .65 1.00
2O55 A61 40c gray .95 1.25
Nos. 2O47-2O55 (9) 8.40

1937 With Grilled Gum

2O47a A53 3c olive .30
2O48a A54 5c blue green .45
2O49a A55 10c red violet 6.25
2O50a A56 15c orange .70
2O51a A57 20c carmine 2.25
2O52a A58 25c brown 1.40
2O53a A59 30c ultra 1.10
2O54a A60 35c yellow green 4.25
2O55a A61 40c gray 4.25
Nos. 2O47a-2O55a (9) 20.95

1937 On 1931 Issue Wmk. 183

2O56 A40 3fr orange brown 190.00

On 1938 Issue
1938 Unwmk. *Perf. 11½*
Granite Paper

2O57 A63 20c red & buff 1.90
2O58 A64 30c blue & lt blue 3.00
2O59 A65 60c brown & buff 5.75
2O60 A66 1fr black & buff 9.25
Nos. 2O57-2O60 (4) 19.90

Regular Issue of 1938 Overprinted in Black or Red

Granite Paper

2O61 A63 20c red & buff 2.25
2O62 A64 30c blue & lt blue 4.00
2O63 A65 60c brown & buff 7.25
2O64 A66 1fr black & buff (R) 12.50
Nos. 2O61-2O64 (4) 26.00

Regular Issue of 1938 Overprinted in Black

1939

2O65 A69 3fr brn car, *buff* 3.25 *11.00*
2O66 A70 5fr slate bl, *buff* 5.50 *15.00*
2O67 A71 10fr green, *buff* 11.00 *32.50*
Nos. 2O65-2O67 (3) 19.75 *58.50*

FOR THE INTERNATIONAL LABOR BUREAU

Regular Issues Overprinted

On 1908-30 Issues

1923-30 Wmk. 183 *Perf. 11½, 12*

3O1 A26 2½c ol grn, *buff* ('28) .30
3O2 A26 3c ultra, *buff* ('30) 1.10
3O3 A26 5c org, *buff* .55
3O4 A26 5c red vio, *buff* ('28) .25
3O5 A26 7½c dp grn, *buff* ('28) .45
3O6 A28 10c grn, *buff* .55
3O7 A28 10c bl grn, *buff* ('28) 1.10
3O8 A28 15c brn red, *buff* ('28) 1.10
3O9 A28 20c red vio, *buff* 17.00
3O10 A28 20c car, *buff* ('27) 5.00
3O11 A28 25c car, *buff* 1.25
3O12 A28 25c brn, *buff* ('28) 3.00
3O13 A28 30c dp bl, *buff* ('25) 2.50
3O14 A25 30c yel brn & pale grn 65.00
3O15 A25 35c yel grn & yel 11.00
3O16 A25 40c deep blue 1.25
3O17 A25 40c red vio & grn ('28) 17.00
3O18 A25 50c dp grn & pale grn 5.00
3O19 A25 60c brn org & buff 1.60 *1.90*
3O20 A25 70c vio & buff ('24) 26.00
3O21 A25 80c slate & buff 14.00 2.25
3O22 A25 1fr dp cl & pale grn 2.75
3O23 A29 3fr red 25.00
3O24 A30 5fr ultra 37.50
3O25 A31 10fr dull violet 150.00
3O26 A31 10fr gray grn ('30) 150.00
Nos. 3O1-3O26 (26) 528.80

1937-44 With Grilled Gum

3O18a A25 50c dp grn & pale grn ('42) 1.75 2.25
3O20a A25 70c vio & buff 1.75 2.25
3O21a A25 80c slate & buff ('44) 25.00 *175.00*
3O22a A25 1fr dp cl & pale grn ('42) 3.25

1925-42 With Grilled Gum

3O27 A36 90c grn & red, *grn* ('37) 9.75
a. Ordinary gum 5.00
3O28 A36 1.20fr brn rose & red, *rose* ('42) 14.00 4.00
a. Ordinary gum 4.50
3O29 A36 1.50fr bl & red, *bl* ('37) 2.75 *3.00*
a. Ordinary gum 14.00
3O30 A36 2fr gray blk & red, *gray* ('36) 3.25 *6.25*
a. Ordinary gum 32.50
Nos. 3O27-3O30 (4) 23.00

1928

3O31 A39 5fr blue 82.50

1932 On 1932 Issue

3O32 A41 5c peacock blue 1.10
3O33 A41 10c orange .90
3O34 A41 20c cerise 1.25
3O35 A41 30c ultra 7.75
3O36 A41 60c olive brown 7.75

Unwmk.

3O37 A42 1fr ol gray & bl 10.00
Nos. 3O32-3O37 (6) 28.75

1937 On 1936 Issue

3O38 A53 3c olive .25 .55
3O39 A54 5c blue green .25 .55
3O40 A55 10c red violet 2.75
3O41 A56 15c orange .45 1.10
3O42 A57 20c carmine 2.25
3O43 A58 25c brown .60 *1.40*
3O44 A59 30c ultra .60 *1.10*
3O45 A60 35c yellow green .60 *1.60*
3O46 A61 40c gray .95 *1.90*
Nos. 3O38-3O46 (9) 3.70 *13.20*

1937 With Grilled Gum

3O38a A53 3c olive 1.10
3O39a A54 5c blue green 1.10
3O40a A55 10c red violet 1.60
3O41a A56 15c orange 1.90
3O42a A57 20c carmine 1.60
3O43a A58 25c brown 2.25
3O44a A59 30c ultra 2.25
3O45a A60 35c yellow green 2.75
3O46a A61 40c gray 2.25
Nos. 3O38a-3O46a (9) 16.80

1937 On 1931 Issue Wmk. 183

3O47 A40 3fr orange brown 175.00

On 1934 Issue

3O48 A46 3c olive 5.50

On 1938 Issue
Granite Paper
1938 Unwmk. *Perf. 11½*

3O49 A63 20c red & buff 1.60
3O50 A64 30c blue & lt blue 3.25
3O51 A65 60c brown & buff 6.00
3O52 A66 1fr black & buff 8.75
Nos. 3O49-3O52 (4) 19.60

Regular Issue of 1938 Overprinted in Black or Red

3O53 A63 20c red & buff (Bk) 3.25
3O54 A64 30c bl & lt bl (Bk) 3.25
3O55 A65 60c brn & buff (Bk) 6.50
3O56 A66 1fr blk & buff (R) 7.00
Nos. 3O53-3O56 (4) 20.00

Regular Issue of 1938 Overprinted in Black

1939

3O57 A69 3fr brn car, *buff* 4.50 *8.25*
3O58 A70 5fr slate bl, *buff* 5.50 *17.00*
3O59 A71 10fr green, *buff* 10.00 *30.00*
Nos. 3O57-3O59 (3) 20.00 *55.25*

FRANCHISE STAMPS

These stamps were distributed to many institutions and charitable societies for franking their correspondence.

F1

Control Figures Overprinted in Black

214

Perf. 11½, 12

1911-21 Typo. Wmk. 183

Blue Granite Paper

S1 F1 2c ol grn & red .25 .25
S2 F1 3c ol grn & red 2.50 .55
S3 F1 5c ol grn & red 1.10 .25
S4 F1 10c ol grn & red 1.40 .25
S5 F1 15c ol grn & red 21.00 4.00
S6 F1 20c ol grn & red 5.00 .60
Nos. S1-S6 (6) 31.25 5.90

Without Control Figures

S1a F1 2c olive green & red .55 *19.00*
S2a F1 3c olive green & red .55 *25.00*
S3a F1 5c olive green & red 4.75 *32.50*
S4a F1 10c olive green & red 8.25 *50.00*
S5a F1 15c olive green & red 5.25 *125.00*
S6a F1 20c olive green & red 9.50 *50.00*
Nos. S1a-S6a (6) 28.85 *301.50*

Control Figures Overprinted in Black

1926

S7 F1 5c ol grn & red 12.50 4.50
S8 F1 10c ol grn & red 7.75 3.25
S9 F1 20c ol grn & red 10.00 3.75
Nos. S7-S9 (3) 30.25 11.50

Control Figures Overprinted in Black

1927 White Granite Paper

S10 F1 5c green & red 5.00 .40
S11 F1 10c green & red 2.50 .25
b. Grilled gum 325.00 *725.00*
S12 F1 20c green & red 3.50 .30
Nos. S10-S12 (3) 11.00 .95

Without Control Figures

S10a F1 5c green & red 32.50 *140.00*
S11a F1 10c green & red 32.50 *140.00*
c. Grilled gum 150.00 *650.00*
S12a F1 20c green & red 32.50 *140.00*

Nurse — F2

Nun — F3

J. H. Dunant — F4

Control Figures Overprinted in Black

1935 ***Perf. 11½***

S13 F2 5c turq green 2.25 *5.50*
b. Grilled gum 3.25 .40
S14 F3 10c lt violet 2.25 *5.50*
b. Grilled gum 3.25 .25
S15 F4 20c scarlet 2.25 *6.50*
b. Grilled gum 3.75 .45
Nos. S13-S15 (3) 6.75 *17.50*
Nos. S13b-S15b (3) 10.25 1.10

Without Control Figures

S13a F2 5c turquoise green 1.40 *3.75*
c. Grilled gum 15.00 1.40
S14a F3 10c light violet 1.40 *3.75*
c. Grilled gum 15.00 1.40
S15a F4 20c scarlet 1.40 *5.00*
c. Grilled gum 15.00 1.50
Nos. S13a-S15a (3) 4.20 *12.50*
Nos. S13c-S15c (3) 45.00 4.30

SYRIA

ˈsir-ē-ə

LOCATION — Asia Minor, bordering on Turkey, Iraq, Lebanon, Israel and the Mediterranean Sea
GOVT. — Republic
AREA — 71,498 sq. mi.
POP. — 9,840,000 (est. 1983)
CAPITAL — Damascus

Syria was originally part of the Turkish province of Sourya conquered by British and Arab forces in late 1918 and later partitioned. The British assumed control of the Palestine and Transjordan regions; the French were permitted to occupy the sanjaks of Lebanon, Alaouites and Alexandretta; and the remaining territory, including the vilayets of Damascus and Aleppo, was established as an independent Arab kingdom, under which the first Syrian stamps were issued.

French forces from Beirut deposed King Faisal in July 1920, and two years of military occupation followed until Syria was mandated to France in July 1922. Syrian autonomy was substituted for the mandate in 1934, but full independence was not again achieved until 1946.

10 Milliemes = 1 Piaster
40 Paras = 1 Piaster (Arabian Govt.)
100 Centimes = 1 Piaster (1920)

Issued under French Occupation

Stamps of France, 1900-07, Surcharged

Perf. 14x13½

1919, Nov. 21 Unwmk.

1 A16 1m on 1c gray 250.00 200.00
2 A16 2m on 2c vio brn 600.00 *550.00*
3 A16 3m on 3c red org 300.00 240.00
4 A20 4m on 15c gray grn 60.00 47.50
5 A22 5m on 5c dp grn 35.00 22.50
6 A22 1p on 10c red 50.00 32.50
7 A22 2p on 25c blue 25.00 15.00
8 A18 5p on 40c red & pale bl 32.50 22.50
9 A18 9p on 50c bis brn & lav 65.00 50.00
10 A18 10p on 1fr cl & ol grn 110.00 80.00
Nos. 1-10 (10) 1,528. 1,260.

The letters "T.E.O." are the initials of "Territoires Ennemis Occupés." There are two types of the numerals in the surcharges on Nos. 2, 3, 8 and 9.

Stamps of French Offices in Turkey, 1902-03, Surcharged

1919

11 A2 1m on 1c gray 1.50 .80
Never hinged 2.40
a. Inverted surcharge 40.00
12 A2 2m on 2c violet brn 1.50 .80
Never hinged 2.40
a. Inverted surcharge 40.00
13 A2 3m on 3c red orange 3.25 1.40
Never hinged 5.00
14 A3 4m on 15c pale red 1.50 .80
Never hinged 2.40
a. Inverted surcharge 40.00
15 A2 5m on 5c green 1.50 .80
Never hinged 2.40

Overprinted

16 A5 1p on 25c blue 1.50 .75
Never hinged 2.40
a. Inverted overprint 40.00
17 A6 2p on 50c bis brn & lav 2.50 1.25
Never hinged 4.00
18 A6 4p on 1fr claret & ol grn 4.00 2.50
Never hinged 5.75
19 A6 8p on 2fr gray vio & yel 12.50 8.00
Never hinged 19.00
a. "T.E.O." double 110.00 110.00
20 A6 20p on 5fr dk bl & buff 350.00 210.00
Nos. 11-20 (10) 379.75 227.10

On Nos. 17-20 "T.E.O." reads vertically up.

Nos. 1-20 were issued in Beirut and mainly used in Lebanon. Nos. 16-20 were also used in Cilicia.

Stamps of France, 1900-07, Surcharged

1920

21 A16 1m on 1c gray 5.50 4.50
Never hinged 8.00
a. Inverted surcharge 60.00
b. Double surcharge 67.50
22 A16 2m on 2c vio brn 6.50 4.75
Never hinged 10.00
a. Double surcharge 67.50
b. Inverted surcharge 60.00
23 A22 3m on 5c green 13.00 12.00
Never hinged 21.00
a. Double surcharge 82.50
b. Inverted surcharge 100.00
24 A18 20p on 5fr dk bl & buff 475.00 450.00
Nos. 21-23 (3) 25.00 21.25

The letters "O.M.F." are the initials of "Occupation Militaire Francaise."

Stamps of France, 1900-07, Surcharged in Black or Red

1920

25 A16 1m on 1c gray 1.25 .95
Never hinged 2.00
26 A16 2m on 2c vio brn 1.50 1.00
Never hinged 2.50
27 A22 3m on 5c green 2.25 2.00
Never hinged 3.50
a. Double surcharge 67.50
28 A22 5m on 10c red 2.50 2.25
Never hinged 3.75
a. Inverted surcharge 65.00 65.00
b. Double surcharge 65.00 65.00
29 A18 20p on 5fr dk bl & buff 72.50 70.00
Never hinged 100.00
30 A18 20p on 5fr dk bl & buff (R) 300.00 250.00
Nos. 25-30 (6) 380.00 326.20

Stamps of France, 1900-21, Surcharged in Black or Red

1920-22

31 A16 25c on 1c gray 2.00 1.00
Never hinged 3.00
32 A16 50c on 2c vio brn 2.00 1.00
Never hinged 3.00
33 A16 75c on 3c red org 2.00 1.00
Never hinged 3.00
a. Inverted surcharge 52.50 52.50
b. Double surcharge 60.00 60.00
34 A22 1p on 5c grn (R) 2.25 2.00
Never hinged 3.50
a. Double surcharge 60.00 60.00
35 A22 1p on 5c green 1.25 1.00
Never hinged 1.90
a. Inverted surcharge 35.00 35.00
b. Double surcharge 45.00 45.00
36 A22 1p on 20c red brn ('21) .75 .25
Never hinged 1.25
a. Inverted surcharge 35.00 35.00
b. Double surcharge 35.00 35.00
37 A22 1.25p on 25c bl ('22) 1.50 .95
Never hinged 2.25
a. Inverted surcharge 40.00 40.00
b. Double surcharge 37.50 37.50
38 A22 1.50p on 30c org ('22) 1.60 .80
Never hinged 2.50
a. Inverted surcharge 27.50 40.00
39 A22 2p on 10c red 1.25 1.00
Never hinged 1.90
a. Inverted surcharge 50.00 50.00
40 A22 2p on 25c bl (R) 1.25 1.00
Never hinged 1.90
a. Inverted surcharge 45.00 45.00
b. Double surcharge 35.00 35.00
41 A18 2p on 40c red & pale bl ('21) 1.60 .75
Never hinged 2.50
42 A20 2.50p on 50c dl bl ('22) 1.40 1.10
Never hinged 2.25
a. Final "S" of "Piastres" omitted 24.00 24.00
b. Inverted surcharge 30.00 30.00
c. Double surcharge 35.00 35.00
43 A22 3p on 25c bl (R) 1.40 1.10
Never hinged 2.25
a. Inverted surcharge 45.00 45.00
44 A18 3p on 60c vio & ultra ('21) 1.75 1.10
Never hinged 3.50
a. Inverted surcharge 37.50 37.50
45 A20 5p on 15c gray grn 2.50 2.25
Never hinged 3.75
a. Double surcharge 140.00 *150.00*
46 A18 5p on 1fr cl & ol grn ('21) 3.00 1.50
Never hinged 4.50
47 A18 10p on 40c red & pale bl 3.75 3.25
Never hinged 5.50
48 A18 10p on 2fr org & pale bl ('21) 6.00 3.00
Never hinged 9.00
49 A18 25p on 50c bis brn & lav 5.50 4.00
Never hinged 8.25
a. Inverted surcharge 100.00 100.00
50 A18 25p on 5fr dk bl & buff ('21) 110.00 95.00
51 A18 50p on 1fr cl & ol grn 25.00 20.00
Never hinged 37.50
a. "PIASRTES" *1,650.* *1,650.*
b. Double surcharge 1,700. *1,900.*
52 A18 100p on 5fr dk bl & buff (R) 47.50 45.00
Never hinged 80.00

53 A18 100p on 5fr dk bl & buff (Bk) 250.00 225.00
a. "PIASTRES" *1,650. 1,650.*
Nos. 31-53 (23) 475.25 413.05

In first printing, space between "Syrie" and numeral is 2mm, second printing, 1mm.
For overprints see Nos. C1-C9.

Surcharged in Black or Red

1920-23

54 A16 10c on 2c violet ('23) 1.40 .90
Never hinged 2.10
a. Inverted surcharge 35.00 35.00
55 A22 10c on 5c org (R) ('23) 1.00 .65
Never hinged 1.50
a. Inverted surcharge 35.00 35.00
56 A16 25c on 1c dk gray 1.10 .90
Never hinged 1.60
a. Inverted surcharge 40.00 40.00
b. Double surcharge 52.50 52.50
c. 50c on 1c dk gray (error) 4.50 4.50
57 A22 25c on 5c green ('21) 1.10 .60
Never hinged 1.60
a. Inverted surcharge 35.00 35.00
b. Double surcharge 35.00 35.00
58 A22 25c on 5c org ('22) 1.00 .80
Never hinged 1.60
a. "CENTIEMES" omitted 37.50 37.50
b. Inverted surcharge 35.00 35.00
c. Double surcharge 37.50 37.50
59 A16 50c on 2c vio brn 1.10 .90
Never hinged 1.60
a. Inverted surcharge 35.00 35.00
b. Double surcharge 45.00 45.00
60 A22 50c on 10c red ('21) 1.25 .55
Never hinged 2.00
a. Inverted surcharge 35.00 35.00
b. Double surcharge 35.00 35.00
61 A22 50c on 10c grn ('22) 1.50 1.25
Never hinged 2.25
a. Inverted surcharge 35.00 35.00
b. Double surcharge 37.50 37.50
c. Double surcharge, one inverted 50.00 50.00
62 A16 75c on 3c red orange 3.00 2.00
Never hinged 6.00
a. Inverted surcharge 35.00 35.00
b. Double surcharge 45.00 45.00
63 A20 75c on 15c sl grn ('21) 1.40 .90
Never hinged 2.10
a. Double surcharge 35.00 35.00
Nos. 54-63 (10) 13.85 9.45

Preceding Issues Overprinted

1920 Black Overprint

64 A16 25c on 1c sl gray 12.00 10.00
a. Double overprint 45.00
65 A16 50c on 2c vio brn 13.00 11.00
a. Double overprint 45.00
66 A22 1p on 5c grn 11.00 9.00
a. Double overprint 45.00
67 A22 2p on 25c blue 18.00 14.50
a. Double overprint 82.50
68 A20 5p on 15c gray grn 55.00 47.50
a. Double overprint 140.00 *150.00*
69 A18 10p on 40c red & pale bl 80.00 75.00
a. Double overprint 325.00
70 A18 25p on 50c bis brn & lav 225.00 190.00
a. Double overprint 600.00
71 A18 50p on 1fr cl & ol grn 650.00 625.00
a. Double overprint 2,100.
72 A18 100p on 5fr dk bl & buff 2,000. 1,900.
a. Double overprint 3,900. *4,300.*
Nos. 64-72 (9) 3,064. 2,882.

Red Overprint

73 A16 25c on 1c sl gray 12.50 10.00
74 A16 50c on 2c vio brn 11.00 8.50
75 A22 1p on 5c grn 11.00 8.50
76 A22 2p on 25c bl 9.00 6.50
77 A20 5p on 15c gray grn 55.00 47.50
a. Double overprint 190.00
78 A18 10p on 40c red & pale bl 85.00 75.00
a. Double overprint 170.00
79 A18 25p on 50c bis brn & lav 225.00 180.00
a. Double overprint 450.00 *475.00*
80 A18 50p on 1fr cl & ol grn 475.00 425.00
a. Double surcharge 1,700. *1,900.*
81 A18 100p on 5fr dk bl & buff 1,650. 1,650.
a. Double overprint 3,500. *3,750.*
Nos. 73-81 (9) 2,534. 2,411.

Nos. 64-81 were used only in the vilayet of Aleppo where Egyptian gold currency was still in use.

A1

Black or Red Surcharge

1921 ***Perf. 11½***

82 A1 25c on 1/10p lt brn 1.25 .85
Never hinged 1.90
a. "25 Centiemes" omitted
83 A1 50c on 2/10p grn 1.25 .85
Never hinged 1.90
84 A1 1p on 3/10p yel 1.75 .85
Never hinged 2.50
a. "2/10" for "3/10" 12.50 12.50
b. Inverted surcharge 60.00 60.00
85 A1 1p on 5m rose 2.00 1.10
Never hinged 3.00
86 A1 2p on 5m rose 2.50 1.25
Never hinged 3.25
a. Tête bêche pair 160.00 160.00
b. Inverted surcharge 40.00 40.00
c. Double surcharge 45.00 45.00
87 A1 3p on 1p gray bl 3.00 1.25
Never hinged 4.50
a. Inverted surcharge 40.00 40.00
88 A1 5p on 2p bl grn 5.00 3.50
Never hinged 17.50
a. Inverted surcharge 45.00 45.00
89 A1 10p on 5p vio brn 11.00 5.75
Never hinged 20.00
90 A1 25p on 10p gray (R) 13.00 8.00
Never hinged 2.00
a. Inverted surcharge 45.00 45.00
Nos. 82-90 (9) 40.75 23.40

Nos. 82-90 are surcharged on stamps of the Arabian Government Nos. 85, 87-93 and have the designs and sizes of those stamps.

Kilis Issue

A2

Sewing Machine Perf. 9

1921 Pelure Paper Handstamped

91 A2 (1p) violet *50.00 45.00*

Issued at Kilis to meet a shortage of the regular issue, caused by the sudden influx of a large number of Armenian refugees from Turkey. The Kilis area was restored to Turkey in Oct. 1923.

Stamps of France, Surcharged

1921-22 ***Perf. 14x13½***

92 A18 2p on 40c red & pale bl 1.25 .90
a. Inverted surcharge 35.00 35.00
b. Double surcharge 35.00 35.00
c. Triple surcharge 82.50
93 A18 2.50p on 50c bis brn & lav ('22) 1.40 1.00
a. Double surcharge 37.50 37.50
b. 2p on 50c bister brown & lavender (error) 82.50 67.50
94 A18 3p on 60c vio & ultra 1.25 .90
a. Inverted surcharge 35.00 35.00
b. Double surcharge 35.00 35.00
95 A18 5p on 1fr cl & ol grn 7.00 6.00
a. Inverted surcharge 40.00 40.00
96 A18 10p on 2fr org & pale bl 15.00 11.00
97 A18 25p on 5fr dk bl & buff 13.00 10.00
Nos. 92-97 (6) 38.90 29.80

On No. 93 the surcharge reads: "2 PIASTRES 50."
For overprints see Nos. C10-C17.

French Mandate

French Stamps of 1900-23 Surcharged

1923

104 A16 10c on 2c vio brn .40 .25
a. Inverted surcharge 27.50 27.50
b. Double surcharge 35.00 35.00
105 A22 25c on 5c orange .75 .75
a. Inverted surcharge 27.50 27.50
106 A22 50c on 10c green .90 .85
a. Inverted surcharge 27.50 27.50
b. Double surcharge 35.00 35.00
c. 25c on 10c green (error) 240.00 240.00
107 A20 75c on 15c sl grn 1.60 1.50
a. Inverted surcharge 35.00 35.00
b. Double surcharge 37.50 37.50
108 A22 1p on 20c red brn .75 .70
a. Inverted surcharge 27.50 27.50
b. Double surcharge 35.00 35.00
109 A22 1.25p on 25c blue 1.40 1.25
a. Inverted surcharge 40.00 40.00
b. Double surcharge 37.50 37.50
110 A22 1.50p on 30c org 1.10 .90
a. Inverted surcharge 27.50 27.50
111 A22 1.50p on 30c red 1.10 .90
112 A20 2.50p on 50c dl bl .70 .60
a. Inverted surcharge 60.00 60.00
b. Double surcharge 35.00 35.00

On Pasteur Stamps of 1923

113 A23 50c on 10c green 2.00 1.75
114 A23 1.50p on 30c red 1.75 1.50
115 A23 2.50p on 50c blue 2.00 1.75

Surcharged

116 A18 2p on 40c red & pale bl .75 .70
a. Inverted surcharge 35.00 35.00
b. Double surcharge 37.50 37.50
c. "Liabn" *450.00 450.00*
117 A18 3p on 60c vio & ultra 1.50 1.25
a. Inverted surcharge 40.00 40.00
b. Double surcharge 75.00 75.00
c. "Liabn" *450.00 450.00*
118 A18 5p on 1fr cl & ol grn 2.00 1.50
a. Inverted surcharge 75.00 75.00
b. "Liabn" *450.00 450.00*
119 A18 10p on 2fr org & pale bl 7.50 7.00
a. "Liabn" *450.00 450.00*
120 A18 25p on 5fr dk bl & buff 22.50 20.00
Nos. 104-120 (17) 48.70 43.15

Stamps of France, 1900-21, Surcharged

1924 ***Perf. 14x13½***

121 A16 10c on 2c vio brn .40 .25
a. Inverted surcharge 35.00 35.00
122 A22 25c on 5c orange .70 .60
a. "25" omitted 24.00
123 A22 50c on 10c green .70 .60
a. Inverted surcharge 35.00 35.00
124 A20 75c on 15c sl grn .70 .60
125 A22 1p on 20c red brn .60 .50
a. "1 PIASTRES" 24.00
126 A22 1.25p on 25c blue 1.10 .90
127 A22 1.50p on 30c orange 1.10 .90
128 A22 1.50p on 30c red 1.00 .85
129 A20 2.50p on 50c dl bl 1.00 .85

Same on Pasteur Stamps of France, 1923

1924

130 A23 50c on 10c grn .90 .70
a. Inverted surcharge 47.50 47.50
131 A23 1.50p on 30c red 1.40 1.10
132 A23 2.50p on 50c blue .75 .70
a. Inverted surcharge 35.00 35.00
Nos. 121-132 (12) 10.35 8.55

Olympic Games Issue

Stamps of France, 1924, Surcharged

1924

133 A24 50c on 10c gray grn & yel grn 30.00 27.50
Never hinged 60.00
134 A25 1.25p on 25c rose & dk rose 30.00 27.50
Never hinged 60.00
135 A26 1.50p on 30c brn red & blk 30.00 27.50
Never hinged 60.00
136 A27 2.50p on 50c ultra & dk bl 30.00 27.50
Never hinged 60.00
Nos. 133-136 (4) 120.00 110.00

See Nos. 166-169.

Stamps of France 1900-20 Surcharged

137 A18 2p on 40c red & pale bl .90 .50
Never hinged 1.75
138 A18 3p on 60c vio & ultra .70 .65
Never hinged 1.50
139 A18 5p on 1fr claret & ol grn 3.50 3.25
Never hinged 7.00
140 A18 10p on 2fr org & pale bl 3.50 3.00
Never hinged 7.00
141 A18 25p on 5fr dk bl & buff 5.25 4.50
Never hinged 11.00
Nos. 137-141 (5) 13.85 11.90

For overprints see Nos. C18-C21.

Stamps of France 1900-21, Surcharged

or

1924-25

143 A16 10c on 2c vio brn .40 .25
Never hinged .80
a. Double surcharge 35.00 35.00
b. Inverted surcharge 30.00 30.00
144 A22 25c on 5c orange .40 .25
Never hinged .80
a. Double surcharge 35.00 35.00
145 A22 50c on 10c green .75 .50
Never hinged 1.50
a. Double surcharge 35.00 35.00
b. Inverted surcharge 30.00 30.00
146 A20 75c on 15c gray grn .90 .70
Never hinged 1.75
a. Double surcharge 35.00 35.00
b. Inverted surcharge 30.00 30.00
147 A22 1p on 20c red brn .60 .40
Never hinged 1.25
a. Inverted surcharge 26.00 26.00
148 A22 1.25p on 25c blue .95 .75
Never hinged 2.00
a. Inverted surcharge 30.00 30.00
149 A22 1.50p on 30c red .90 .70
Never hinged 2.00
a. Double surcharge 35.00 35.00
150 A22 1.50p on 30c orange 26.00 25.00
Never hinged 52.50
151 A22 2p on 35c violet ('25) 1.00 .80
Never hinged 2.00
152 A18 2p on 40c red & pale bl .75 .50
Never hinged 1.50
a. Arabic "Piastre" in singular 1.75 1.75
153 A18 2p on 45c grn & bl ('25) 5.00 4.00
Never hinged 10.00
154 A18 3p on 60c vio & ultra 1.10 .75
Never hinged 2.25

155 A20 3p on 60c lt vio ('25) 1.25 .75
Never hinged 2.50
156 A20 4p on 85c ver .45 .25
Never hinged 1.00
157 A18 5p on 1fr cl & ol grn 1.25 .75
Never hinged 2.50
158 A18 10p on 2fr org & pale bl 2.00 1.50
Never hinged 4.00
159 A18 25p on 5fr dk bl & buff 2.75 1.50
Never hinged 5.50
Nos. 143-159 (17) 46.45 39.35

On No. 152a, the surcharge is as illustrated. The correct fourth line ("2 Piastres" -plural), as it appears on Nos. 151, 152 and 153, has four characters, the third resembling "9."

For overprints see Nos. C22-C25.

Same Surcharge on Pasteur Stamps of France

1924-25

160 A23 50c on 10c green 1.25 1.00
Never hinged 2.50
161 A23 75c on 15c grn ('25) 1.25 1.00
Never hinged 2.50
162 A23 1.50p on 30c red 1.25 1.00
Never hinged 2.50
163 A23 2p on 45c red ('25) 1.25 1.00
Never hinged 2.50
164 A23 2.50p on 50c blue 1.75 1.25
Never hinged 3.50
165 A23 4p on 75c blue 1.75 1.25
Never hinged 3.50
Nos. 160-165 (6) 8.50 6.50

Olympic Games Issue

Stamps of France, 1924, Surcharged in French and Arabic

1924 Same Colors as #133-136

166 A24 50c on 10c 29.00 29.00
Never hinged 45.00
167 A25 1.25p on 25c 29.00 29.00
Never hinged 45.00
168 A26 1.50p on 30c 29.00 29.00
Never hinged 45.00
169 A27 2.50p on 50c 29.00 29.00
Never hinged 45.00
Nos. 166-169 (4) 116.00 116.00

Ronsard Issue

Same Surcharge on France No. 219

1925

170 A28 4p on 75c bl, *bluish* 1.00 .75

Mosque at Hama A3

Mosque at Damascus A5

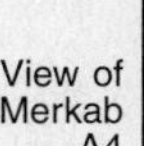

View of Merkab A4

Designs: 50c, View of Alexandretta. 75c, View of Hama. 1p, Omayyad Mosque, Damascus. 1.25p, Latakia Harbor. 1.50p, View of Damascus. 2p, View of Palmyra. 2.50p, View of Kalat Yamoun. 3p, Bridge of Daphne. 5p, View of Aleppo. 10p, View of Aleppo. 25p, Columns at Palmyra.

Perf. 12½, 13½

1925 Litho. Unwmk.

173 A3 10c dark violet .35 .25
Never hinged .55

Photo.

174 A4 25c olive black 1.00 .55
Never hinged 1.50
175 A4 50c yellow green .50 .25
Never hinged .75
176 A4 75c brown orange .60 .25
Never hinged .90
177 A5 1p magenta .60 .25
Never hinged .90
178 A4 1.25p deep green 2.25 1.10
Never hinged 3.50
179 A4 1.50p rose red .75 .25
Never hinged 1.10
180 A4 2p dark brown 2.00 .25
Never hinged 3.00
181 A4 2.50p peacock blue 1.50 .50
Never hinged 2.75
182 A4 3p orange brn 1.50 .25
Never hinged 2.75
183 A4 5p violet 1.25 .25
Never hinged 2.10
184 A4 10p violet brown 3.50 .30
Never hinged 5.25
185 A4 25p ultra 5.75 4.50
Never hinged 8.25
Nos. 173-185 (13) 21.55 8.95

For surcharges see Nos. 186-206, B1-B12, C26-C45, CB1-CB4.

Surcharged in Black or Red

1926-30

186 A4 1p on 3pi org brn ('30) 2.00 .50
187 A4 2p on 1p25 dp grn (R) ('28) 1.25 .40
a. Double surcharge 16.00 16.00
188 A4 3.50p on 75c org brn 1.00 .35
a. Double surcharge 16.00 16.00
189 A4 4p on 25c ol blk 1.50 .35
190 A4 4p on 25c ol blk ('27) 1.40 .45
191 A4 4p on 25c ol blk (R) ('28) 1.25 .35
192 A4 4.50p on 75c brn org 1.40 .35
193 A4 6p on 2p50 pck bl 1.00 .35
194 A4 7.50p on 2p50 pck bl 1.10 .35
195 A4 7.50p on 2p50 pck bl (R) ('28) 3.50 .90
a. Double surcharge 29.00
196 A4 12p on 1p25 dp grn 1.50 .40
a. Surcharge on face and back 50.00 42.50
197 A4 15p on 25p ultra 2.75 .90
198 A4 20p on 1p25 dp grn 2.25 .70
Nos. 186-198 (13) 21.90 6.35

Size of numerals and arrangement of this surcharge varies on the different denominations.

No. 189 has slanting foot on "4."

No. 190, foot straight.

No. 173 Surcharged in Red

1928

199 A3 05c on 10c dk vio 1.00 .25

Stamps of 1925 Ovptd. in Red or Blue

1929 ***Perf. 13½***

200 A4 50c yellow grn (R) 3.50 2.75
Never hinged 5.25
201 A5 1p magenta (Bl) 3.50 2.75
Never hinged 5.25
202 A4 1.50p rose red (Bl) 3.50 2.75
Never hinged 5.25
203 A4 3p orange brn (Bl) 3.50 2.75
Never hinged 5.25
204 A4 5p violet (R) 3.50 2.75
Never hinged 5.25
205 A4 10p violet brn (Bl) 3.50 2.75
Never hinged 5.25
206 A4 25p ultra (R) 3.50 2.75
Never hinged 5.25
Nos. 200-206 (7) 24.50 19.25

Industrial Exhibition, Damascus, Sept. 1929.

View of Hama — A6

View of Alexandretta — A9

Citadel at Aleppo A10

Great Mosque of Damascus A11

Ruins of Bosra A13

Mosque at Homs A15

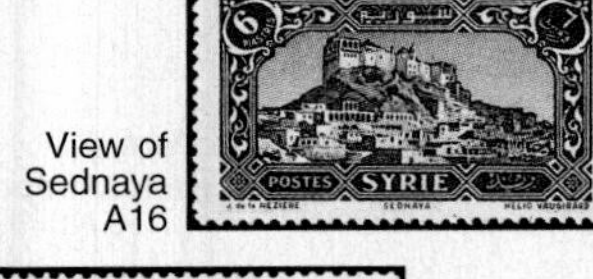

View of Sednaya A16

Citadel at Aleppo A17

Ancient Bridge at Antioch A18

Mosque at Damascus A22

Designs: 20c, Great Mosque, Aleppo. 25c, Minaret, Hama. 2p, View of Antioch. 4p, Square at Damascus. 15p, Mosque at Hama. 25p, Monastery of St. Simeon the Stylite (ruins). 50p, Sun Temple (ruins), Palmyra.

Perf. 12x12½

1930-36 Litho. Unwmk.

208 A6 10c red violet .50 .25
Never hinged 1.00
209 A6 10c vio brn ('33) .50 .35
Never hinged 1.00
209A A6 10c vio brn, redrawn ('35) .50 .25
Never hinged 1.00
210 A6 20c dark blue .50 .25
Never hinged 1.00
211 A6 20c brn org ('33) .50 .25
Never hinged 1.00
212 A6 25c gray green .50 .25
Never hinged 1.00
213 A6 25c dk bl gray ('33) .80 .45
Never hinged 1.60

Photo.

Perf. 13

214 A9 50c violet .50 .25
Never hinged 1.00
215 A15 75c org red ('32) .50 .25
Never hinged 1.00
216 A10 1p green .75 .25
Never hinged 1.50
217 A10 1p bis brn ('36) 1.75 .40
Never hinged 3.50
218 A11 1.50p bister brown 7.50 3.00
Never hinged 15.00
219 A11 1.50p dp grn ('33) 1.00 .50
Never hinged 2.00
220 A9 2p dark violet .75 .25
Never hinged 1.50
221 A13 3p yellow green 2.00 .70
Never hinged 4.00
222 A10 4p yellow orange .75 .25
Never hinged 1.50
223 A15 4.50p rose carmine 1.75 .55
Never hinged 3.50
224 A16 6p grnsh black 2.25 .50
Never hinged 4.50
225 A17 7.50p dull blue 2.25 .70
Never hinged 4.50
226 A18 10p dark brown 2.00 .50
Never hinged 4.00
227 A10 15p deep green 3.50 1.00
Never hinged 7.00
228 A18 25p violet brown 5.00 1.10
Never hinged 10.00
229 A15 50p olive brown 17.50 7.00
Never hinged 34.00
230 A22 100p red orange 35.00 15.00
Never hinged 70.00
Nos. 208-230 (24) 88.55 34.25

On No. 209A Arabic inscriptions, upper right, are entirely redrawn with lighter lines. Hyphen added in "Helio-Vaugirard" imprint. Lines in buildings and background more distinct.

On No. 215 the letters of "VAUGIRARD" in the imprint are reversed as in a mirror.

For overprints and surcharges see Nos. 253-268; Nos. 346, M1-M2 in Scott Standard catalogue, Vol. 6.

Autonomous Republic

Parliament Building A23

abu-al-Ala al-Maarri — A24

President Ali Bek el Abed — A25

Saladin — A26

1934, Aug. 2 Engr. ***Perf. 12½***

232 A23 10c olive green 2.00 *2.00*
Never hinged 4.00
233 A23 20c black 2.00 *2.00*
Never hinged 4.00
234 A23 25c red orange 2.50 *2.50*
Never hinged 5.00
235 A23 50c ultra 3.00 *3.00*
Never hinged 6.00
236 A23 75c plum 3.00 *3.00*
Never hinged 6.00
237 A24 1p vermilion 5.50 5.50
Never hinged 11.00
238 A24 1.50p green 6.50 6.50
Never hinged 13.00
239 A24 2p red brown 6.50 6.50
Never hinged 13.00
240 A24 3p Prus blue 6.50 6.50
Never hinged 13.00
241 A24 4p brt violet 6.75 6.75
Never hinged 13.50
242 A24 4.50p carmine 7.00 7.00
Never hinged 14.00
243 A24 5p dark blue 7.00 7.00
Never hinged 14.00

No.	Type	Description	Unused	Used
244	A24	6p dark brown	8.00	8.00
		Never hinged	16.00	
245	A24	7.50p dark ultra	10.00	10.00
		Never hinged	20.00	
246	A25	10p dark brown	15.00	15.00
		Never hinged	30.00	
247	A25	15p dull blue	25.00	25.00
		Never hinged	50.00	
248	A25	25p rose red	25.00	13.00
		Never hinged	35.00	
249	A26	50p dark brown	50.00	35.00
		Never hinged	70.00	
250	A26	100p lake	60.00	60.00
		Never hinged	120.00	
		Nos. 232-250 (19)	251.25	224.25

Proclamation of the Republic. See Nos. C57-C66. For surcharge see No. M3 in Scott Standard catalogue, Vol. 6.

Nos. 232-250 exist imperf., value: $1,000.

Stamps of 1930-36 Overprinted in Red or Black

1936, Apr. 15

No.	Type	Description	Unused	Used
253	A9	50c violet (R)	2.75	1.50
254	A10	1p bister brn (Bk)	2.75	1.50
255	A9	2p dk violet (R)	2.75	1.50
256	A13	3p yellow grn (Bk)	3.25	1.50
257	A10	4p yellow org (Bk)	3.25	1.50
258	A15	4.50p rose car (Bk)	3.25	1.50
259	A16	6p grnsh blk (R)	4.00	2.00
260	A17	7.50p dull blue (R)	4.75	2.75
261	A18	10p dk brown (Bk)	5.75	3.75
		Nos. 253-261 (9)	32.50	17.50

Industrial Exhibition, Damascus, May 1936. See Nos. C67-C71.

Stamps of 1930 Srchd. in Black

1937-38 *Perf. 13½x13*

No.	Type	Description	Unused	Used
262	A10	2.50p on 4p yel org ('38)	.55	.40
263	A22	10p on 100p red orange	1.00	.90

Stamps of 1930-33 Srchd. in Red or Black

1938 *Perf. 13½*

No.	Type	Description	Unused	Used
264	A15	25c on 75c org red (Bk)	.50	.25
265	A11	50c on 1.50p dp grn (R)	.60	.30
266	A17	2p on 7.50p dl bl (R)	1.00	.60
267	A17	5p on 7.50p dl bl (R)	1.75	.90
268	A15	10p on 50p ol brn (Bk)	2.25	.95
		Nos. 264-268 (5)	6.10	3.00

President Hashem Bek el Atassi — A27

1938-43 **Photo.** **Unwmk.**

No.	Type	Description	Unused	Used
268A	A27	10p dp blue ('42)	1.25	.85
269	A27	12.50p on 10p dp bl (R)	1.50	.90
270	A27	20p dark brown	1.25	.85
		Nos. 268A-270 (3)	4.00	2.60

The 10pi and 20pi exist imperf.

Columns at Palmyra A28

1940 **Litho.** *Perf. 11½*

No.	Type	Description	Unused	Used
271	A28	5p pale rose	2.00	.65

Exists imperf.

Museum at Damascus — A29

Hotel at Bloudan A30

Kasr-el-Heir A31

1940 **Typo.** *Perf. 13x14*

No.	Type	Description	Unused	Used
272	A29	10c bright rose	.70	.25
		Never hinged	1.00	
273	A29	20c light blue	.70	.25
		Never hinged	1.00	
274	A29	25c fawn	.75	.25
		Never hinged	1.10	
275	A29	50c ultra	.75	.25
		Never hinged	1.10	

Engr.

Perf. 13

No.	Type	Description	Unused	Used
276	A30	1p peacock blue	1.00	.25
		Never hinged	1.50	
277	A30	1.50p chocolate	1.50	.70
		Never hinged	2.25	
278	A30	2.50p dark green	1.00	.30
		Never hinged	1.50	
279	A31	5p violet	1.10	.40
		Never hinged	1.60	
280	A31	7.50p vermilion	2.00	.40
		Never hinged	3.00	
281	A31	50p sepia	3.50	1.25
		Never hinged	5.25	
		Nos. 272-281 (10)	13.00	4.30

For overprints see Nos. 298-299 in Scott Standard catalogue, Vol. 6.

SEMI-POSTAL STAMPS

Nos. 174-185 Srchd. in Red or Black

1926 **Unwmk.** *Perf. 12½, 13½*

No.	Type	Description	Unused	Used
B1	A4	25c + 25c ol blk (R)	2.25	2.00
B2	A4	50c + 25c yel grn	2.25	2.00
B3	A4	75c + 25c brown org	2.25	2.00
B4	A5	1p + 50c magenta	2.25	2.00
B5	A4	1.25p + 50c dp grn (R)	2.25	2.00
B6	A4	1.50p + 50c rose red	2.25	2.00
B7	A4	2p + 75c dk brn (R)	2.25	2.00
B8	A4	2.50p + 75c pck bl (R)	2.25	2.00
B9	A4	3p + 1p org brn (R)	2.25	2.00
B10	A4	5p + 1p violet	2.25	2.00
B11	A4	10p + 2p vio brn	2.25	2.00
B12	A4	25p + 5p ultra (R)	2.25	2.00
		Nos. B1-B12 (12)	27.00	24.00
		Set, never hinged	36.00	

On No. B4 the surcharge is set in six lines to fit the shape of the stamp.

The surcharge was a contribution to the relief of refugees from the Djebel Druze War. See Nos. CB1-CB4.

AIR POST STAMPS

Nos. 35, 45, 47 Hstmpd. in Violet — a

1920, Dec. **Unwmk.** *Perf. 13½*

No.	Type	Description	Unused	Used
C1	A22	1p on 5c	160.00	40.00
C2	A20	5p on 15c	290.00	47.50
C3	A18	10p on 40c	425.00	77.50
		Nos. C1-C3 (3)	875.00	165.00

Nos. 36, 46, 48 Overprinted Type "a" in Violet

1921, June 12

No.	Type	Description	Unused	Used
C4	A22	1p on 20c	87.50	40.00
C5	A18	5p on 1fr	425.00	150.00
C6	A18	10p on 2fr	425.00	150.00
		Nos. C4-C6 (3)	937.50	340.00

Excellent counterfeits exist of Nos. C1-C6.

Nos. 36, 46, 48 Overprinted — b

1921, Oct. 5

No.	Type	Description	Unused	Used
C7	A22	1p on 20c	60.00	18.50
C8	A18	5p on 1fr	150.00	37.50
a.		Inverted overprint	325.00	240.00
C9	A18	10p on 2fr	200.00	47.50
a.		Double overprint	475.00	400.00
		Nos. C7-C9 (3)	410.00	103.50

Nos. 92, 94-96 Ovptd. — c

1922, May 28

No.	Type	Description	Unused	Used
C10	A18	2p on 40c	25.00	25.00
a.		Inverted overprint		
C11	A18	3p on 60c	25.00	25.00
C12	A18	5p on 1fr	25.00	25.00
C13	A18	10p on 2fr	25.00	25.00
		Nos. C10-C13 (4)	100.00	100.00

Nos. 116-119 Overprinted Type "c"

1923, Nov. 22

No.	Type	Description	Unused	Used
C14	A18	2p on 40c	29.00	29.00
b.		Inverted surcharge		
C15	A18	3p on 60c	29.00	29.00
C16	A18	5p on 1fr	29.00	29.00
C17	A18	10p on 2fr	29.00	29.00
b.		Double overprint		
		Nos. C14-C17 (4)	116.00	116.00

Overprinted "Liabn"

No.	Type	Description	Unused	Used
C14a	A18	2p on 40c	400.00	400.00
C15a	A18	3p on 60c	400.00	400.00
C16a	A18	5p on 1fr	400.00	400.00
C17a	A18	10p on 2fr	400.00	400.00

Nos. 137-140 Overprinted Type c

1924, Jan. 13

No.	Type	Description	Unused	Used
C18	A18	2p on 40c	4.50	4.50
a.		Double overprint	*27.50*	
C19	A18	3p on 60c	4.50	4.50
a.		Inverted overprint	47.50	
C20	A18	5p on 1fr	4.50	4.50
a.		Double overprint	*50.00*	*30.00*
C21	A18	10p on 2fr	4.50	4.50
		Nos. C18-C21 (4)	18.00	18.00

Nos. 152, 154, 157-158 Overprinted

1924, July 17

No.	Type	Description	Unused	Used
C22	A18	2p on 40c	7.00	7.00
a.		Inverted overprint	32.50	
C23	A18	3p on 60c	7.00	7.00
a.		Inverted overprint	32.50	
b.		Double overprint	20.00	
C24	A18	5p on 1fr	7.00	7.00
C25	A18	10p on 2fr	7.00	7.00
a.		Inverted overprint	32.50	
		Nos. C22-C25 (4)	28.00	28.00

Regular Issue of 1925 Overprinted in Green

1925, Mar. 1

No.	Type	Description	Unused	Used
C26	A4	2p dark brown	2.25	2.25
C27	A4	3p orange brown	2.25	2.25
C28	A4	5p violet	2.25	2.25
C29	A4	10p violet brown	2.25	2.25
		Nos. C26-C29 (4)	9.00	9.00

Nos.180, 182, 183-184 Ovptd. in Red — f

1926

No.	Type	Description	Unused	Used
C30	A4	2p dark brown	2.00	2.00
a.		Inverted overprint	40.00	40.00
C31	A4	3p orange brown	2.00	2.00
C32	A4	5p violet	2.50	2.50
a.		Inverted overprint	40.00	40.00
b.		Double overprint	65.00	65.00
C33	A4	10p violet brown	2.50	2.50
a.		Inverted overprint	40.00	40.00
b.		Double overprint	65.00	65.00
		Nos. C30-C33 (4)	9.00	9.00

Nos. C30-C33 received their first airmail use June 16, 1929, at the opening of the Beirut-Marseille line.

For surcharges see Nos. CB1-CB4.

Regular Issue of 1925 Overprinted Type "f" in Red or Black

1929

No.	Type	Description	Unused	Used
C34	A4	50c yellow green (R)	1.25	1.25
a.		Inverted overprint	40.00	
b.		Overprinted on face and back	22.50	
c.		Double overprint	40.00	
d.		Double overprint, one inverted	60.00	
e.		Pair, one without overprint		
C35	A5	1p magenta (Bk)	1.75	1.75
a.		Reversed overprint		
b.		Red overprint		
C36	A4	25p ultra (R)	5.50	5.50
a.		Inverted overprint	82.50	
b.		Pair, one without overprint		
		Nos. C34-C36 (3)	8.50	8.50

On No. C35, the overprint is vertical, with plane nose down.

No. 197 Overprinted Type "f" in Red

1929, July 9

No.	Type	Description	Unused	Used
C37	A4	15p on 25p ultra	4.25	4.25
a.		Inverted overprint		

Air Post Stamps of 1926-29 Ovptd. in Various Colors

1929, Sept. 5

No.	Type	Description	Unused	Used
C38	A4	50c yellow grn (R)	3.00	3.00
C39	A5	1p magenta (Bl)	3.00	3.00
C40	A4	2p dk brown (V)	3.00	3.00
C41	A4	3p orange brn (Bl)	3.00	3.00
a.		Inverted overprint	70.00	
C42	A4	5p violet (R)	3.00	3.00
C43	A4	10p violet brn (Bl)	3.00	3.00
C44	A4	25p ultra (R)	3.00	3.00
		Nos. C38-C44 (7)	21.00	21.00

Damascus Industrial Exhibition.

AP1

1930, Jan. 30 **Red Surcharge**

No.	Type	Description	Unused	Used
C45	AP1	2p on 1.25p dp grn	3.00	3.00
a.		Inverted surcharge		
b.		Double surcharge	60.00	

Plane over Homs AP2

Designs: 1pi, City Wall, Damascus. 2pi, Euphrates River. 3pi, Temple Ruins, Palmyra. 5pi, Deir-el-Zor. 10pi, Damascus. 15pi, Aleppo, Citadel. 25pi, Hama. 50pi, Zebdani. 100pi, Telebisse.

1931-33 Photo. Unwmk.

No.	Type	Description	Unused	Used
C46	AP2	50c ocher	1.00	.90
C47	AP2	50c black brn ('33)	1.25	1.00
C48	AP2	1p chestnut brown	1.10	.95
C49	AP2	2p Prus blue	2.75	1.75
C50	AP2	3p blue grn	1.75	1.25
C51	AP2	5p red violet	1.25	1.25
C52	AP2	10p slate grn	1.25	1.25
C53	AP2	15p orange red	2.10	1.50
C54	AP2	25p orange brn	2.75	2.00
C55	AP2	50p black	3.00	2.25
C56	AP2	100p magenta	3.75	2.50
		Nos. C46-C56 (11)	21.95	16.60

Nos. C46 to C56 exist imperforate. Value, $425.

For overprints see Nos. C67-C71; Nos. C110-C112, C114-C115, MC1-MC4 in Scott Standard catalogue, Vol. 6.

Village of Bloudan AP12

1934, Aug. 2 Engr. *Perf. 12½*

No.	Type	Description	Unused	Used
C57	AP12	50c yel brown	2.50	2.50
C58	AP12	1p green	3.00	3.00
C59	AP12	2p peacock bl	3.00	3.00
C60	AP12	3p red	3.50	3.50
C61	AP12	5p plum	3.50	3.50
C62	AP12	10p brt violet	30.00	30.00
C63	AP12	15p orange brn	32.50	32.50
C64	AP12	25p dk ultra	37.50	37.50
C65	AP12	50p black	50.00	50.00
C66	AP12	100p red brown	110.00	110.00
		Nos. C57-C66 (10)	275.50	275.50

Proclamation of the Republic. Nos. C57-C66 exist imperf. Value, set $1,100.Also exists without figures of value. Value, set $1,500.

Complete set of 29 (Nos. 232-250, C57-66) exist imperf. Value, $2,600.

No. C58 exists without values, imperf. Value, $125.

Air Post Stamps of 1931-33 Overprinted in Red or Black

1936, Apr. 15 *Perf. 13½x13, 13½*

No.	Type	Description	Unused	Used
C67	AP2	50c black brown	5.25	4.75
C68	AP2	1p chnt brown (Bk)	5.25	4.75
C69	AP2	2p Prus blue	5.25	4.75
C70	AP2	3p blue green	5.25	4.75
C71	AP2	5p red violet (Bk)	5.25	4.75
		Nos. C67-C71 (5)	26.25	23.75

Damascus Fair, May 1936.

Syrian Pavilion at Paris Exposition AP13

1937, July 1 Photo. *Perf. 13½*

No.	Type	Description	Unused	Used
C72	AP13	½p yellow green	2.75	2.75
C73	AP13	1p green	2.75	2.75
C74	AP13	2p lt brown	2.75	2.75
C75	AP13	3p rose red	2.75	2.75
C76	AP13	5p brown orange	2.75	2.75
C77	AP13	10p grnsh black	4.75	4.75
C78	AP13	15p blue	5.25	5.25
C79	AP13	25p dark violet	6.25	6.25
		Nos. C72-C79 (8)	30.00	30.00

Paris International Exposition. Exist imperf.

Ancient Citadel at Aleppo AP14

Omayyad Mosque and Minaret of Jesus at Damascus AP15

1937 Engr. *Perf. 13*

No.	Type	Description	Unused	Used
C80	AP14	½p dark violet	.65	.65
C81	AP15	1p black	.65	.65
C82	AP14	2p deep green	.65	.65
C83	AP15	3p deep ultra	.65	.65
C84	AP14	5p rose lake	2.00	2.00
C85	AP15	10p red brown	1.10	1.10
C86	AP14	15p lake brown	4.75	4.75
C87	AP15	25p dark blue	6.00	6.00
		Nos. C80-C87 (8)	16.45	16.45

No. C80 to C87 exist imperforate. Value, set $175.

For overprint see No. C109 in Scott Standard catalogue, Vol. 6.

Maurice Noguès and Route of France-Syria Flight — AP16

1938, July Photo. *Perf. 11½*

No.	Type	Description	Unused	Used
C88	AP16	10p dark green	5.00	4.50
a.		Souv. sheet of 4, perf. 13½	50.00	45.00
b.		Perf. 13½	8.00	8.00

10th anniversary of first Marseille-Beirut flight, by Maurice Noguès.

No. C88a exists imperf.; value $800.

Bridge at Deir-el-Zor AP17

1940 Engr. *Perf. 13*

No.	Type	Description	Unused	Used
C89	AP17	25c brown black	.25	.25
C90	AP17	50c peacock blue	.25	.25
C91	AP17	1p deep ultra	.30	.30
C92	AP17	2p dk orange brn	.45	.45
C93	AP17	5p green	.95	.95
C94	AP17	10p rose carmine	1.40	1.00
C95	AP17	50p dark violet	3.00	2.25
		Nos. C89-C95 (7)	6.60	5.45

Exist imperf.

AIR POST SEMI-POSTAL STAMPS

Nos. C30-C33 Surcharged Like Nos. B1-B12 in Black and Red

1926, Apr. 1 Unwmk. *Perf. 13½*

No.	Type	Description	Unused	Used
CB1	A4	2p + 1p dk brown	3.00	2.75
CB2	A4	3p + 2p org brn	2.75	2.75
CB3	A4	5p + 3p violet	2.75	2.75
CB4	A4	10p + 5p vio brn	2.75	2.75
		Nos. CB1-CB4 (4)	11.25	11.00

The new value is in red and rest of the surcharge in black on Nos. CB1-CB3. The entire surcharge is black on No. CB4.

See note following Nos. B1-B12.

POSTAGE DUE STAMPS

Under French Occupation

French Offices in the Turkish Empire, 1902-03, Surcharged

1920 Unwmk. *Perf. 14x13½*

No.	Type	Description	Unused	Used
J1	A3	1p on 10c rose red	160.00	160.00
J2	A3	2p on 20c brn vio	160.00	160.00
J3	A3	3p on 30c lil	160.00	160.00
J4	A4	4p on 40c red & pale bl	160.00	160.00
		Nos. J1-J4 (4)	640.00	640.00

Postage Due Stamps of France, 1893-1920, Surcharged in Black or Red

1920

No.	Type	Description	Unused	Used
J5	D2	1p on 10c brown	3.25	3.25
J6	D2	2p on 20c ol grn (R)	3.25	3.25
a.		"PIASTRE"	900.00	900.00
J7	D2	3p on 30c red	3.25	3.25
a.		"PIASTRE"		
J8	D2	4p on 50c brn vio	4.75	4.75
a.		3p in setting of 4p	525.00	525.00
		Nos. J5-J8 (4)	14.50	14.50

1921-22

No.	Type	Description	Unused	Used
J9	D2	50c on 10c brown	1.40	1.40
a.		"75" instead of "50"	90.00	
b.		"CENTI MES" instead of "CENTIEMES"	7.50	
J10	D2	1p on 20c ol grn	1.40	1.40
J11	D2	2p on 30c red	3.25	3.25
J12	D2	3p on 50c brn vio	3.50	3.50
J13	D2	5p on 1fr red brn, *straw*	5.00	5.00
		Nos. J9-J13 (5)	14.55	14.55

D3

1921 Red Surcharge *Perf. 11½*

No.	Type	Description	Unused	Used
J14	D3	50c on 1p black	3.75	3.75
J15	D3	1p on 1p black	3.75	3.75

D4

1922

No.	Type	Description	Unused	Used
J16	D4	2p on 5m rose	10.00	6.50
a.		"AX" of "TAXE" inverted	175.00	175.00
J17	D4	3p on 1p gray bl	15.00	12.00

French Mandate

Postage Due Stamps of France, 1893-1920, Surcharged

1923

No.	Type	Description	Unused	Used
J18	D2	50c on 10c brown	1.50	1.50
J19	D2	1p on 20c ol grn	2.25	2.25
J20	D2	2p on 30c red	1.90	1.90
J21	D2	3p on 50c vio brn	1.90	1.90
J22	D2	5p on 1fr red brn, *straw*	3.75	3.75
		Nos. J18-J22 (5)	11.30	11.30

Postage Due Stamps of France, 1893-1920, Surcharged

1924

No.	Type	Description	Unused	Used
J23	D2	50c on 10c brown	1.00	1.00
J24	D2	1p on 20c ol grn	1.00	1.00
J25	D2	2p on 30c red	1.10	1.10
J26	D2	3p on 50c vio brn	1.50	1.50
J27	D2	5p on 1fr red brn, *straw*	1.50	1.50
		Nos. J23-J27 (5)	6.10	6.10

Postage Due Stamps of France, 1893-1920, Surcharged

Syrie 2 Piastres

1924

No.	Type	Description	Unused	Used
J28	D2	50c on 10c brown	.75	.75
J29	D2	1p on 20c ol grn	.75	.75
J30	D2	2p on 30c red	1.00	1.00
J31	D2	3p on 50c vio brn	1.40	1.40
J32	D2	5p on 1fr red brn, *straw*	1.75	1.75
		Nos. J28-J32 (5)	5.65	5.65

Water Wheel at Hama D5

Bridge at Antioch — D6

Designs: 2p, The Tartous. 3p, View of Banias. 5p, Chevaliers' Castle.

1925 Photo. *Perf. 13½*

No.	Type	Description	Unused	Used
J33	D5	50c brown, *yel*	.25	.25
J34	D6	1p violet, *rose*	.25	.25
J35	D5	2p black, *blue*	.55	.55
J36	D5	3p black, *red org*	1.25	1.25
J37	D5	5p black, *bl grn*	1.50	1.50
		Nos. J33-J37 (5)	3.80	3.80

D7

Lion — D8

1931

No.	Type	Description	Unused	Used
J38	D7	8p black, *gray blue*	3.50	3.50
J39	D8	15p black, *dull rose*	6.00	6.00

ISSUES OF THE ARABIAN GOVERNMENT

The following issues replaced the British Military Occupation (E.E.F.) stamps (Palestine Nos. 2-14) which were used in central and eastern Syria from Nov. 1918 until Jan. 1920.

Turkish Stamps of 1913-18 Handstamped in Various Colors

Also Handstamp Surcharged with New Values as

1 millieme

1 Egyptian piaster

The Seal reads: "Hakuma al Arabie" (The Arabian Government)

Perf. 11½, 12, 12½, 13½

1919-20 Unwmk.

No.	Type	Description	Unused	Used
1	A24	1m on 2pa red lil (254)	1.00	1.00
2	A25	1m on 4pa dk brn (255)	1.00	1.00
3	A26	2m on 5pa vio brn (256)	1.75	1.75
4	A15	2m on 5pa on 10pa gray grn (291)	1.25	1.25
5	A18	2m on 5pa ocher (304)	25.00	25.00

6 A41 2m on 5pa grn (345) *300.00 375.00*
7 A18 2m on 5pa ocher (378) *50.00 50.00*
8 A28 4m on 10pa grn (258) 7.00 7.00
9 A28 4m on 10pa grn (271) 1.00 1.00
10 A22 4m on 10pa bl grn (329) 2.00 2.00
11 A41 4m on 10pa car (346) 40.00 40.00
12 A23 4m on 10pa grn (415) 8.00 8.00
13 A44 4m on 10pa grn (424) 2.00 2.00
14 A11 4m on 10pa on 20pa vio brn (B38) 2.25 2.25
15 A41 4m on 10pa car (B42) 1.10 1.10
16 SP1 4m on 10pa red vio (B46) 2.25 2.25
17 SP1 4m on 10pa on 20pa car rose (B47) 2.25 2.25
19 A21 5pa ocher (317)
21 A21 20pa car rose (153) *97.50 115.00*
22 A29 20pa red (259) 2.00 2.00
23 A29 20pa red (272) *300.00 300.00*
24 A17 20pa car (299) 3.00 3.00
25 A21 20pa car rose (318) 3.00 3.00
26 A22 20pa car rose (330) 12.50 12.50
27 A21 20pa car rose (342) 6.00 6.00
28 A41 20pa ultra (347) 3.00 3.00
29 A16 20pa mag (363) 12.50 12.50
30 A17 20pa car (371)
31 A18 20pa car (379) 8.50 8.50
32 A45 20pa dp rose (425) 4.25 4.25
33 A21 20pa car rose (B8) 3.25 3.25
34 A22 20pa car rose (B33) 3.50 3.50
35 A22 20pa car rose (B36) 14.50 14.50
36 A41 20pa ultra (B43) .75 .75
37 A16 20pa mag (P140) 3.25 3.25
38 A17 20pa car (P144) *285.00 285.00*
39 A30 1pi bl (260) 3.25 3.25
40 A31 1pi on 1½pi car & blk (261) *425.00 425.00*
41 A30 1pi bl (273) 100.00 100.00
42 A30 1pi on 1pi bl (273) 150.00 150.00
43 A17 1pi blue (300) 5.25 5.25
44 A18 1pi blue (307) 60.00 60.00
45 A22 1pi ultra (331) 6.25 6.25
46 A21 1pi ultra (343) 11.00 11.00
47 A41 1pi vio & blk (348) 2.25 2.25
48 A18 1pi brt bl (389) 6.50 6.50
49 A46 1pi dl vio (426) 2.25 2.25
50 A47 1pi on 50pa ultra (428) 1.50 1.50
51 A21 1pi ultra (B9) 7.00 7.00
52 A22 1pi ultra (B15) 12.00 12.00
53 A18 1pi brt bl (B21) 7.00 7.00
54 A18 1pi blue (B23) 17.50 17.50
55 A22 1pi ultra (B34) 15.00 15.00
56 A41 1pi vio & blk (B44) 3.25 3.25
57 A33 2pi grn & blk (263) 77.50 77.50
58 A13 2pi brn org (289) 2.25 2.25
59 A18 2pi slate (308) 30.00 30.00
60 A18 2pi slate (314) 32.50 32.50
61 A21 2pi bl blk (320) 5.75 5.75
62 A17 2pi org (373) 4.75 4.75
63 A18 5pi brn (310) 14.00 14.00
64 A22 5pi dl vio (333) 25.00 25.00
65 A41 5pi yel brn & blk (349) 5.50 5.50
66 A41 5pi yel brn & blk (418) 5.50 5.50
67 A53 5pi on 2pa Prus bl (547) 8.50 8.50
68 A21 5pi dk vio (B10) 300.00 300.00
69 A17 5pi lil rose (B20) 55.00 55.00
70 A41 5pi yel brn & blk (B45) 5.25 5.25
72 A50 10pi dk grn (431) 145.00 145.00
73 A50 10pi dk vio (432) 125.00 125.00
74 A50 10pi dk brn (433) *425.00*
75 A18 10pi org brn (B2) 375.00 375.00
76 A37 25pi ol grn (267) *375.00 375.00*
77 A40 25pi on 200pi grn & blk (287) *550.00 550.00*
78 A17 25pi brn (303) 400.00 400.00
79 A51 25pi car, *straw* (434) 100.00 100.00
81 A52 50pi ind (438) 225.00 225.00

The variety "surcharge omitted" exists on Nos. 1-5, 12-13, 16, 32, 49-50, 67.

A few examples of No. 377 (50pi) and No. 269 (100pi) were overprinted but not regularly issued.

Overprinted

The Inscription reads "Hakum Soria Arabie" (Syrian-Arabian Government)

On Stamp of 1913

83 A26 2m on 5pa vio brn (256) 5.50 5.50

On Stamp of 1916-18

84 A45 20pa dp rose (425) .75 .75

A1

Litho. ***Perf. 11½***

85 A1 5m rose .75 .75
a. Tête bêche pair 22.50 10.00
b. Imperf.

Independence Issue

Arabic Overprint in Green "Souvenir of Syrian Independence March 8, 1920"

86 A1 5m rose 275.00 175.00
a. Tête bêche pair
b. Inverted overprint 400.00 400.00

A2

Litho.

Size: 22x18mm

87 A2 1/10pi lt brn .35 .35

Size: 28x22mm

88 A2 2/10pi yel grn .45 .25
a. 2/10pi yellow (error) 10.00 10.00
89 A2 3/10pi yellow .50 .30
90 A2 1pi gray blue .45 .25
91 A2 2pi blue grn 2.25 1.00

Size: 31x25mm

92 A2 5pi vio brn 3.00 1.50
93 A2 10pi gray 3.25 2.00
Nos. 86-93 (8) 285.25 180.65

Nos. 86-93 exist imperf.
For overprint see No. J5.

PF1

PF2

Revenue Stamps Surcharged as on Postage Stamps, for Postal Use

1920 **Unwmk.** ***Perf. 11½***

94 PF1 5m on 5pa red .75 .35
95 PF2 1m on 5pa red .75 .25
96 PF2 2m on 5pa red .65 .25
97 PF2 1pi on 5pa red 1.25 .65

Surcharged in Syrian Piasters

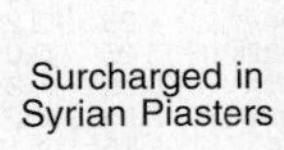

98 PF2 2pi on 5pa red .50 .25
99 PF2 3pi on 5pa red .50 .25
Nos. 94-99 (6) 4.40 2.00

ISSUES OF THE ARABIAN GOVERNMENT POSTAGE DUE STAMPS

Postage Due Stamps of Turkey, 1914, Handstamped and Surcharged

No. J1

No. J4

1920 **Unwmk.** ***Perf. 12***

J1 D1 2m on 5pa claret 7.25 7.25
J2 D2 20pa red 7.25 7.25
J3 D3 1pi dark blue 7.25 7.25
J4 D4 2pi slate 7.25 7.25
Nos. J1-J4 (4) 29.00 29.00

Type of Regular Issue

Litho. ***Perf. 11½***

J5 A2 1pi black 1.75 1.75

TAHITI

tə-'hēt-ē

LOCATION — An island in the South Pacific Ocean, one of the Society group

GOVT. — A part of the French Oceania Colony

AREA — 600 sq. mi.

POP. — 19,029

CAPITAL — Papeete

The stamps of Tahiti were replaced by those of French Oceania.

100 Centimes = 1 Franc

Covers

Values are for commercial covers bearing correct frankings. Philatelic covers sell for less.

Counterfeits exist of surcharges and overprints on Nos. 1-31.

Stamps of French Colonies Surcharged in Black

a

b

c

d

1882 **Unwmk.** ***Imperf.***

1 A8(a) 25c on 35c dk vio, *org* 425. 350.
On cover, single franking 6,500.
1A A8(b) 25c on 35c dk vio, *org* *4,500. 4,500.*
On cover —
1B A8(a) 25c on 40c ver, *straw* *6,250. 6,750.*
On cover —

Surcharge Inverted

1c A8(a) 25c on 35c dk vio, *org* 500. 450.
1Ad A8(b) 25c on 35c dk vio, *org* *4,600. 4,600.*
1Be A8(a) 25c on 40c ver, *straw* *3,900. 4,100.*

Surcharge Reading Up

1f A8(a) 25c on 35c dk vio, *org* 525. 475.
1Ag A8(b) 25c on 35c dk vio, *org* *4,750. 4,750.*

Surcharge Reading Down

1h A8(a) 25c on 35c dk vio, *org* 525. 475.
1Ai A8(b) 25c on 35c dk vio, *org* *4,600. 4,600.*

Double Surcharge, One Inverted

1Bj A8(a) 25c on 40c ver, *straw* *7,600. 8,000.*

1884 ***Perf. 14x13½***

2 A9(c) 5c on 20c red, *yel grn* 300. 240.
On cover, single franking *9,500.*
3 A9(d) 10c on 20c red, *yel grn* 350. 300.
On cover, single franking 3,750.
On wrapper 6,000.

Imperf

4 A8(b) 25c on 1fr brnz grn, *straw* 750. 650.
On cover, single franking *9,500.*

Covers: Only one cover each is recorded for Nos. 2 and 4, 8 covers recorded for No. 3.

Surcharge Inverted

2a 5c on 20c red, *grn* 300.00 240.00
3a 10c on 20c red, *grn* 340.00 310.00
4a 25c on 1fr brnz grn, *straw* 750.00 650.00

Surcharge Reading Up

2b 5c on 20c red, *grn* 300.00 240.00
3b 10c on 20c red, *grn* 340.00 310.00
4b 25c on 1fr brnz grn, *straw* 750.00 650.00

Surcharge Reading Down

2c 5c on 20c red, *grn* 300.00 240.00
3c 10c on 20c red, *grn* 340.00 310.00
4c 25c on 1fr brnz grn, *straw* 750.00 650.00

Handstamped in Black

1893 ***Perf. 14x13½***

5 A9 1c blk, *lil bl* 950.00 875.00
6 A9 2c brown, *buff* *3,200. 2,500.*
7 A9 4c claret, *lav* 1,500. 1,250.
8 A9 5c green, *grnsh* 55.00 47.50
On cover, single franking 725.00
9 A9 10c black, *lav* 60.00 52.50
On cover, single franking 900.00
10 A9 15c blue 60.00 47.50
On cover, single franking 750.00
11 A9 20c red, *green* 72.50 65.00
On cover, single franking 900.00
12 A9 25c yel, *straw* *8,750. 7,250.*
13 A9 25c blk, *rose* 55.00 47.50
On cover, single franking 450.00
14 A9 35c violet, *org* *2,600. 2,200.*
15 A9 75c carmine, *rose* 87.50 87.50
On cover, single franking 675.00
16 A9 1fr brnz grn, *straw* 92.50 92.50
On cover, single franking 750.00

Surcharge Inverted

6a A9 2c brown, *buff* *4,000. 3,800.*
8a A9 5c green, *grnsh* 160.00 140.00
9a A9 10c black, *lav* 260.00 225.00
10a A9 15c blue 240.00 225.00
11a A9 20c red, *green* 260.00 240.00
12a A9 25c yel, *straw* *10,750. 10,750.*
13a A9 25c blk, *rose* 240.00 225.00
15a A9 75c carmine, *rose* 300.00 260.00
16a A9 1fr brnz grn, *straw* 340.00 340.00

Nearly all values of this set are known with overprint sloping up, sloping down and horizontal. Some occur double. Values the same as for the normal stamps.

Overprinted in Black

1893

17 A9 1c blk, *lil bl* 925.00 800.00
18 A9 2c brn, *buff* *3,750. 2,750.*
19 A9 4c claret, *lav* 1,850. 1,500.
20 A9 5c grn, *grnsh* 1,100. 950.00
21 A9 10c black, *lav* 350.00 350.00
22 A9 15c blue 55.00 50.00
On cover, single franking 750.00
23 A9 20c red, *grn* 60.00 55.00
On cover, single franking 775.00

24	A9	25c yel, *straw*	*50,000.*	*42,500.*
25	A9	25c black, *rose*	55.00	50.00
		On cover, single franking		450.00
26	A9	35c violet, *org*	*2,600.*	*2,200.*
27	A9	75c carmine, *rose*	60.00	55.00
		On cover, single franking		675.00
b.		Double overprint	*400.00*	
28	A9	1fr brnz grn, *straw*	75.00	60.00
		On cover, single franking		750.00

Inverted Overprint

17a	A9	1c blk, *lil bl*	*1,350.*	1,200.
18a	A9	2c brn, *buff*	*4,000.*	3,900.
19a	A9	4c claret, *lav*	*2,000.*	1,900.
20a	A9	5c grn, *grnsh*	*1,600.*	*1,500.*
21a	A9	10c black, *lav*	*950.*	*900.*
22a	A9	15c blue	*250.*	*225.*
23a	A9	20c red, *grn*	*250.*	*225.*
25a	A9	25c black, *rose*	*250.*	*225.*
26a	A9	35c violet, *org*	*3,000.*	2,800.
27a	A9	75c carmine, *rose*	*300.*	*250.*
28a	A9	1fr brnz grn, *straw*	*300.*	*275.*

Stamps of French Polynesia Surcharged in Black or Carmine

g

h

1903

29	A1 (g)	10c on 15c bl (Bk)	11.00	11.00
		On cover, single franking		140.00
a.		Double surcharge	67.50	67.50
b.		Inverted surcharge	72.50	72.50
30	A1 (h)	10c on 25c blk, *rose* (C)	11.00	11.00
		On cover, single franking		140.00
a.		Double surcharge	67.50	67.50
b.		Inverted surcharge	80.00	80.00
31	A1 (h)	10c on 40c red, *straw* (Bk)	13.00	13.00
		On cover, single franking		140.00
a.		Double surcharge	80.00	80.00
b.		Inverted surcharge	85.00	80.00
		Nos. 29-31 (3)	35.00	35.00

In the surcharges on Nos. 29-31 there are two varieties of the "1" in "10," i. e. with long and short serif.

SEMI-POSTAL STAMPS

Stamps of French Polynesia Overprinted in Red

1915 Unwmk. *Perf. 14x13½*

B1	A1	15c blue	300.00	300.00
		On cover, single franking		550.00
a.		Inverted overprint	1,100.	1,000.
B2	A1	15c gray	35.00	35.00
		On cover, single franking		200.00
a.		Inverted overprint	425.00	425.00

Values are for commercial covers bearing correct frankings. Philatelic covers also exist and generally sell for less than the values quoted.

Counterfeits exist.

POSTAGE DUE STAMPS

Counterfeits exist of overprints on Nos. J1-J26.

Postage Due Stamps of French Colonies Handstamped in Black like Nos. 5-16

1893 Unwmk. *Imperf.*

J1	D1	1c black	*400.*	*400.*
J2	D1	2c black	*400.*	*400.*
J3	D1	3c black	*450.*	*450.*
J4	D1	4c black	*450.*	*450.*
J5	D1	5c black	*450.*	*450.*
J6	D1	10c black	*450.*	*450.*
J7	D1	15c black	*450.*	*450.*
J8	D1	20c black	*350.*	*350.*
		On cover		*8,000.*
J9	D1	30c black	*450.*	*450.*
J10	D1	40c black	*450.*	*450.*
J11	D1	60c black	*525.*	*525.*
J12	D1	1fr brown	*1,100.*	*1,100.*
J13	D1	2fr brown	*1,100.*	*1,100.*
		Nos. J1-J13 (13)	*7,025.*	*7,025.*

Surcharge Inverted

J1a	D1	1c black	*725.*	*725.*
J2a	D1	2c black	*725.*	*725.*
J3a	D1	3c black	*725.*	*725.*
J4a	D1	4c black	*725.*	*725.*
J5a	D1	5c black	*725.*	*725.*
J6a	D1	10c black	*725.*	*725.*
J7a	D1	15c black	*725.*	*725.*
J8a	D1	20c black	*725.*	*725.*
J9a	D1	30c black	*725.*	*725.*
J10a	D1	40c black	*725.*	*725.*
J11a	D1	60c black	*800.*	*800.*
J12a	D1	1fr brown	*1,600.*	*1,600.*
J13a	D1	2fr brown	*1,600.*	*1,600.*

Surcharge Double

J6b	D1	10c black	*1,050.*	*1,050.*
J7b	D1	15c black	*1,050.*	*1,050.*

Covers: Only two covers are recorded for No. J8.

Overprinted in Black like Nos. 17-28

1893

J14	D1	1c black	*2,400.*	*2,400.*
J15	D1	2c black	*550.*	*550.*
J16	D1	3c black	*550.*	*550.*
J17	D1	4c black	*550.*	*550.*
J18	D1	5c black	*550.*	*550.*
J19	D1	10c black	*550.*	*550.*
J20	D1	15c black	*550.*	*550.*
J21	D1	20c black	*550.*	*550.*
		On cover, single franking		*6,750.*
J22	D1	30c black	*550.*	*550.*
J23	D1	40c black	*550.*	*550.*
J24	D1	60c black	*550.*	*550.*
J25	D1	1fr brown	*550.*	*550.*
J26	D1	2fr brown	*550.*	*550.*
		Nos. J14-J26 (13)	*9,000.*	*9,000.*

Surcharge Inverted

J14a	D1	1c black	*3,250.*	*3,250.*
J15a	D1	2c black	*1,000.*	*1,000.*
J19a	D1	10c black	*1,100.*	*1,100.*
J20a	D1	15c black	*1,100.*	*1,100.*
J21a	D1	20c black	*1,100.*	*1,100.*
J23a	D1	40c black	*1,100.*	*1,100.*
J24a	D1	60c black	*1,100.*	*1,100.*
J25a	D1	1fr brown	*1,100.*	*1,100.*
J26a	D1	2fr brown	*1,100.*	*1,100.*

Surcharge Double

J15b	D1	2c black	*1,100.*	*1,100.*
J16b	D1	3c black	*1,100.*	*1,100.*
J17b	D1	4c black	*1,100.*	*1,100.*
J18b	D1	5c black	*1,100.*	*1,100.*
J19b	D1	10c black	*1,100.*	*1,100.*
J20b	D1	15c black	*1,100.*	*1,100.*
J22b	D1	30c black	*1,100.*	*1,100.*
J25b	D1	1fr brown	*1,100.*	*1,100.*
J26b	D1	2fr brown	*1,100.*	*1,100.*

TANGANYIKA

ˌtan-gə-ˈnyē-kə

LOCATION — Southeastern Africa bordering on the Indian Ocean
AREA — 362,688 sq. mi.
POP. — 9,404,000 (est. 1961)
CAPITAL — Dar es Salaam

Before World War I, this area formed part of German East Africa It was mandated to Britain after World War I and (in 1946) became a trust territory under the United Nations. In 1935, stamps of the mandate were replaced by those used jointly by Kenya, Uganda and Tanganyika (see Kenya, Uganda and Tanzania).

100 Cents = 1 Rupee
100 Cents = 1 Shilling (1922)
20 Shillings = 1 Pound

Stamps of East Africa & Uganda Protectorates Overprinted

1921 Wmk. 4 *Perf. 14*

1	A1	12c gray	12.00	*125.00*
2	A1	15c ultra	10.00	*17.00*
3	A1	50c dull violet & blk	18.00	*115.00*

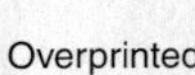

Overprinted

4	A2	2r black & red, *blue*	52.50	*150.00*
5	A2	3r gray green & violet	125.00	*325.00*
7	A2	5r dull violet & ultra	175.00	*425.00*
		Nos. 1-7 (6)	392.50	*1,157.*

Overprinted in Red or Black

1922

8	A1	1c black (R)	2.25	*25.00*
9	A1	10c orange (Bk)	4.00	*15.00*

A3

Giraffe — A4

Perf. 14½x14

1922-25 Engr. Wmk. 4

10	A3	5c dk violet & blk	2.75	.25
11	A3	5c grn & blk ('25)	13.00	1.75
12	A3	10c green & blk	4.00	.95
13	A3	10c yel & blk ('25)	13.00	1.75
14	A3	15c carmine & blk	4.50	.25
15	A3	20c orange & blk	6.25	.25
16	A3	25c black	9.00	*7.50*
17	A3	25c blue & blk ('25)	4.50	*20.00*
18	A3	30c blue & blk	6.25	5.75
19	A3	30c dull vio & blk ('25)	6.50	*32.50*
20	A3	40c brown & black	6.75	5.25
21	A3	50c gray black	8.00	1.75
22	A3	75c bister & black	6.75	*24.00*

Perf. 14

23	A4	1sh green & black	8.00	*12.50*
a.		Wmk. sideways	14.00	*30.00*
24	A4	2sh brn vio & blk	8.50	*50.00*
a.		Wmk. sideways	11.50	*30.00*
25	A4	3sh blk, wmk. sideways	62.50	*62.50*
26	A4	5sh red & black	42.50	*100.00*
a.		Wmk. sideways	87.50	*120.00*
27	A4	10sh dp blue & blk	125.00	*200.00*
a.		Wmk. sideways	260.00	*500.00*
28	A4	£1 orange & black	400.00	*675.00*
a.		Wmk. sideways	450.00	*725.00*
		Nos. 10-28 (19)	737.75	*1,202.*

On No. 28 the words of value are in a curve between the circle and "POSTAGE & REVENUE."

King George V
A5 A6

1927-31 Typo.

29	A5	5c green & black	2.00	.25
30	A5	10c yellow & black	2.25	.25
31	A5	15c red & black	2.00	.25
32	A5	20c orange & black	3.00	.25
33	A5	25c ultra & black	4.25	2.25
34	A5	30c dull violet & blk	3.25	3.00
35	A5	30c ultra & blk ('31)	29.00	.35
36	A5	40c brown & black	2.25	*9.25*
37	A5	50c gray & black	2.75	1.10
38	A5	75c olive grn & blk	2.25	*26.00*
39	A6	1sh green & black	4.75	3.25
40	A6	2sh violet brn & blk	30.00	8.50
41	A6	3sh black	52.50	*115.00*
42	A6	5sh scarlet & blk	42.50	27.50
43	A6	10sh ultra & black	110.00	*160.00*
44	A6	£1 brown org & blk	275.00	*425.00*
		Nos. 29-44 (16)	567.75	*782.20*

TANNU TUVA

ˈtä-nə ˈtü-və

(Tuva People's Republic)

LOCATION — Between Siberia and northwestern Mongolia at the sources of the Yenisei, in the basin formed by the Tannu-Ola and Sayan Mountains.
GOVT. — A republic closely identified with Soviet Russia in Asia
AREA — 64,000 sq. mi. (approx.)
POP. — 95,000 (1941 est.)
CAPITAL — Kyzyl

This region, traditionally called Uriankhai, was ruled by the Mongols until the mid-18th century, when it became part of the Chinese Empire. Russia and China struggled for control of the country 1914-21, until it became independent as the Tannu Tuva People's Republic in 1921. In 1944 it was incorporated into the U.S.S.R. as an autonomous region of the Russian Soviet Federated Socialist Republic.

Russian, later Soviet, stamps were used in Tuva prior to 1926 and after 1944.

100 Mongo=1 Tugrik
100 Kopecks = 1 Ruble
100 Kopecks = 1 Tugrik (1934)
100 Kopecks = 1 Aksha (1936)

Watermarks

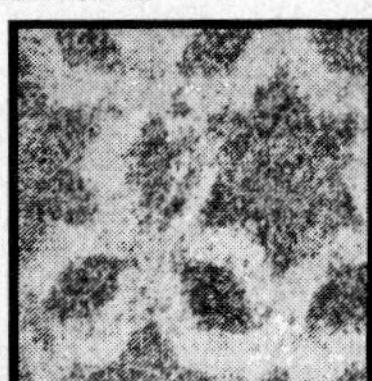
Wmk. 204 — Stars and Diamonds

Wmk. 170 — Greek Border and Rosettes

Values for covers are for properly franked covers with correct rates, usually addressed to Moscow. Because most have philatelic addresses, some leeway in proper rates is to be expected, and covers that vary slightly from proper rates are generally accepted as commercial covers.

For valuation of covers with multiple franking, see "Catalogue Values for Stamps on Covers" in the Introduction to this catalogue.

Most used examples of Nos. 1-38, 45-52a, 54-92 and C1-C18 on the market are canceled to order, and the used values below are for such stamps.

Tuvan stamps, except for Nos. 117-123 and most of the overprints, were printed by the State Security Printers in Moscow.

Wheel of Truth — A1

1926 Litho. Wmk. 204 *Perf. 13½*
Size: 20x26mm

1 A1 1k red 1.50 1.50
Never hinged 2.50
Postal cancel 1.60
On cover 250.00
2 A1 2k light blue 1.50 1.50
Never hinged 3.00
Postal cancel 1.50
On cover 250.00
3 A1 5k orange 1.50 1.50
Never hinged 3.00
Postal cancel 1.50
On cover 250.00
4 A1 8k yel green 2.00 1.75
Never hinged 3.50
Postal cancel 1.50
On cover 250.00
5 A1 10k violet 2.00 1.75
Never hinged 4.00
Postal cancel 1.50
On cover 250.00
6 A1 30k dark brown 2.00 1.75
Never hinged 3.50
Postal cancel 1.50
On cover 250.00
7 A1 50k gray black 2.25 1.75
Never hinged 4.00
Postal cancel 2.00
On cover 250.00

Size: 22½x30mm
Perf. 10½

8 A1 1r blue green 6.00 3.00
Never hinged 11.00
Postal cancel 7.50
On cover 400.00
9 A1 3r red brown 8.00 5.75
Never hinged 16.00
Postal cancel 8.00
On cover —
10 A1 5r dark ultra 13.50 8.00
Never hinged 27.00
Postal cancel 13.50
On cover —
a. Imperf, pair 180.00
Nos. 1-10 (10) 40.25 28.25
Set, never hinged 77.50

Nos. 1-10 have crackled white gum. Reprints can be distinguished by their smooth gum.
Nos. 1-10 in different colors are proofs.

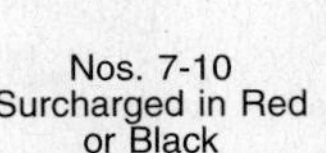
Nos. 7-10 Surcharged in Red or Black

Surcharged in Kyzyl.

1927 *Perf. 13½*
11 A1 8k on 50k 25.00 12.50
Never hinged 50.00
Postal cancel 27.50
On cover 275.00
a. Inverted surcharge 65.00
b. Double surcharge 100.00

Perf. 10½
12 A1 14k on 1r 25.00 12.50
Never hinged 50.00
Postal cancel 30.00
On cover 350.00
a. Inverted surcharge 75.00
b. Double surcharge 85.00
13 A1 18k on 3r (Bk) 25.00 12.50
Never hinged 50.00
Postal cancel 30.00
On cover 350.00
a. Inverted surcharge 90.00
b. Double surcharge 75.00
14 A1 28k on 5r (Bk) 25.00 12.50
Never hinged 50.00
Postal cancel 30.00
On cover 350.00
a. Inverted surcharge 90.00
b. Double surcharge 75.00
Nos. 11-14 (4) 100.00 50.00
Set, never hinged 200.00

Nos. 11-14 were surcharged with a shiny ink. Reprints are overprinted with a dull ink and are often smudged.

Tuvan Woman — A3

Map of Tannu Tuva A8

Sheep Herding — A11

Fording a Stream — A13

Tuvan Riding Reindeer — A16

Designs: 2k, Stag. 3k, Mountain goat. 4k, Tuvan and tent. 5k, Tuvan man. 10k, Archery competition. 14k, Camel caravan. 28k, Landscape. 50k, Weaving. 70k, Tuvan on horseback.
Printed in Moscow.

1927 Litho. *Perf. 12½*
15 A3 1k blk, lt brn & red 1.00 .60
Never hinged 2.00
Postal cancel 2.00
On cover 125.00
16 A3 2k pur, dp brn & grn 1.20 .55
Never hinged 2.40
Postal cancel 2.00
On cover 125.00
17 A3 3k blk, bl grn & yel 2.00 .60
Never hinged 4.00
Postal cancel 3.00
On cover 125.00
18 A3 4k vio bl & choc .90 .60
Never hinged 1.80
Postal cancel 1.50
On cover 125.00
19 A3 5k org, blk & dk bl .90 .65
Never hinged 1.80
Postal cancel 1.80
On cover 125.00

Perf. 12½x12
20 A8 8k ol brn, pale bl & red brn 1.00 .65
Never hinged 2.00
Postal cancel 1.00
On cover 150.00
21 A8 10k blk, grn & brn red 5.50 1.00
Never hinged 11.00
Postal cancel 1.50
On cover 200.00
22 A8 14k vio bl & red org 10.00 3.50
Never hinged 20.00
Postal cancel 5.00
On cover, *from* 150.00

Perf. 10½
23 A11 18k dk bl & red brn 10.00 5.00
Never hinged 20.00
Postal cancel 10.00
On cover, *from* 225.00
a. Perf 10 70.00 70.00
Never hinged 140.00
b. Perf compound 10, 10½ 15.00 8.00
Never hinged 30.00
Postal cancel 15.00
24 A11 28k emer & blk brn 7.25 2.75
Never hinged 14.50
Postal cancel 4.50
On cover, *from* 200.00
25 A13 40k rose & bl grn 5.00 2.50
Never hinged 10.00
Postal cancel 5.00
On cover, *from* 275.00
a. Perf 10 8.50 4.00
Never hinged 17.00
Postal cancel —
b. Perf 10x10½ 9.00 5.00
Never hinged 18.00
Postal cancel —
26 A13 50k blk, grn & red brn 3.50 2.00
Never hinged 7.00
Postal cancel 7.00
On cover, *from* 275.00
a. Perf 10 5.00 2.75
Never hinged 10.00
Postal cancel 5.00
b. Perf 10x10½ 7.00 3.75
Never hinged 14.00
Postal cancel 7.00
27 A13 70k dl red & bis 7.00 4.00
Never hinged 14.00
Postal cancel 10.00
On cover, *from* 350.00
28 A16 1r yel brn & vio 16.00 6.75
Never hinged 32.00
Postal cancel 20.00
On cover, *from* 350.00
Nos. 15-28 (14) 71.25 31.15
Set, never hinged 142.50

Nos. 15-28 were issued with a crackled white gum. Reprints of the 1k-5k values exist and can be distinguished by their smooth gum.
Nos. 15-28 in different colors are proofs.

Nos. 25-27, 20-22 Surcharged in Various Colors

Surcharged in Moscow.

1932
29 A13 1k on 40k (Bk) 8.50 *11.00*
Never hinged 18.00
Postal cancel 30.00
On cover 175.00
a. Perf 10 10.00 10.00
Never hinged 20.00
Postal cancel —
b. Perf 10x10½ 10.00 10.00
Never hinged 20.00
Postal cancel —
30 A13 2k on 50k (Br) 9.00 *11.00*
Never hinged 20.00
Postal cancel 30.00
On cover 175.00
a. Perf 10 10.00 *20.00*
Never hinged 20.00
Postal cancel 30.00
b. Perf 10x10½ 45.00 25.00
Never hinged 90.00
Postal cancel 35.00
31 A13 3k on 70k (Bl) 9.00 *11.00*
Never hinged 20.00
Postal cancel 25.00
On cover 175.00
a. Inverted surcharge 300.00
Never hinged 600.00
32 A8 5k on 8k (Bk) 9.00 *11.00*
Never hinged 20.00
Postal cancel 25.00
On cover 175.00
33 A8 10k (Bk) 9.00 *11.00*
Never hinged 20.00
Postal cancel 25.00
On cover 175.00
34 A8 15k on 14k (Bk) 14.00 *16.00*
Never hinged 30.00
Postal cancel 25.00
On cover 175.00
Nos. 29-34 (6) 58.50 71.00
Set, never hinged 128.00
#29-34 on philatelic cover 300.00

Issued in connection with the Romanization of the alphabet.
No. 31 with black surcharge was prepared but not issued.

Nos. 20, 22-24 Surcharged in Black

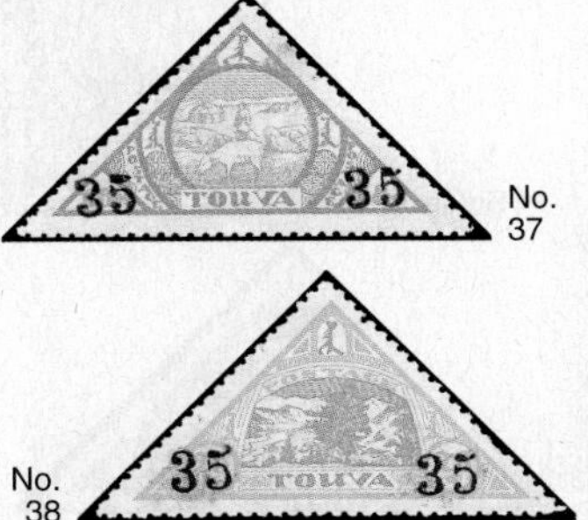
No. 37
No. 38

Surcharged by numbering machine in Kyzyl.

1932-33 Wmk. 204
35 A8 10k on 8k 180.00 100.00
Never hinged 350.00
Postal cancel 300.00
36 A8 15k on 14k 300.00 200.00
Never hinged 600.00
Postal cancel 600.00
37 A11 35k on 18k (#23) 150.00 100.00
Never hinged 275.00
Postal cancel 140.00
On cover —
a. Perf 10 (#23a) 150.00 150.00
Never hinged 300.00
Postal cancel —
b. Pair, one without surcharge —
c. Inverted surcharge 500.00
38 A11 35k on 28k 150.00 100.00
Never hinged 275.00
Postal cancel 140.00
On cover —
a. Pair, one without surcharge —
Nos. 35-38 (4) 780.00 500.00
Set, never hinged 1,550.

Revenue Stamps Surcharged — A19

Surcharged in Kyzyl.
Three types: type 1, figures of value 6.7mm high; type 2, figures of value 6.7mm high, letter "p" lengthened at bottom; type 3, figures of value 5.1mm high.

1933 *Perf. 12x12½*
39 A19 15k on 6k org yel, type 1 300.00 150.00
On cover —
a. "Posta" omitted — —
40 A19 15k on 6k org yel, type 2 300.00 150.00
On cover —
a. "Posta" omitted — —
b. Inverted surcharge — —
41 A19 15k on 6k org yel, type 3 500.00 300.00
On cover —
42 A19 35k on 15k red brn, type 1 — *4,000.*
On cover —
43 A19 35k on 15k red brn, type 2 — *4,000.*
On cover —
44 A19 35k on 15k red brn, type 3 *1,500.* 800.00
On cover —

Mounted Hunter — A20

Tuvan Inside of Yurt — A21

Tuvan Milking Yak — A22

Die I

Die II

Designs: 2k, Hunter stalking game. 4k, Tractor. 10k, Camel caravan. 15k, Herdsman lassoing reindeer. 20k, Hunter shooting fox with arrow.

Two dies on 10k: Die I, Crown at center top is light and matches the shade of the sky below; Die II, Crown at center top is bold, consistent with rest of design and darker than the sky.

Printed by State Security Printers, Moscow.

Wmk. 170

1934, Apr. Photo. ***Perf. 12***

No.	Type	Stamp	Unused	Used
45	A20	1k red orange	1.50	1.00
		Never hinged	4.00	
		Postal cancel		2.00
		On cover		100.00
46	A20	2k olive green	1.50	1.00
		Never hinged	10.00	
		Postal cancel		6.00
		On cover		100.00
47	A21	3k rose red	1.50	1.00
		Never hinged	5.00	
		Postal cancel		1.50
		On cover		100.00
48	A21	4k slate purple	3.50	1.75
		Never hinged	6.00	
		Postal cancel		3.00
		On cover		100.00
49	A22	5k ultramarine	3.50	1.75
		Never hinged	8.00	
		Postal cancel		2.50
		On cover		100.00
50	A22	10k brown, die II	3.50	1.75
		Never hinged	10.00	
		Postal cancel		8.00
		On cover		125.00
a.		Perf 13¾	25.00	—
b.		Perf 11	—	—
c.		10k brown, die I	8.00	2.00
		Never hinged	16.00	
		Postal cancel		8.00
		On cover		150.00
51	A22	15k dark lilac	3.50	1.75
		Never hinged	14.00	
		Postal cancel		3.50
		On cover		100.00
52	A22	20k gray black	4.75	2.75
		Never hinged	20.00	
		Postal cancel		4.00
		On cover		100.00
		Nos. 45-52 (8)	23.25	12.75
		Set, never hinged	50.00	
		Set, imperf	50.00	
		Set, imperf., never hinged	100.00	

Imperf

No.	Type	Stamp	Unused	Used
45a	A20	1k red orange	2.25	1.50
		Never hinged	4.50	
		Postal cancel		4.00
		On cover		100.00
46a	A20	2k olive green	10.00	6.50
		Never hinged	20.00	
		Postal cancel		13.50
		On cover		—
47a	A21	3k rose red	2.25	1.25
		Never hinged	4.50	
		Postal cancel		4.00
		On cover		100.00
48a	A21	4k slate purple	4.00	1.75
		Never hinged	8.00	
		Postal cancel		4.50
		On cover		100.00
49a	A22	5k ultramarine	4.00	2.00
		Never hinged	8.00	
		Postal cancel		5.25
		On cover		125.00
50d	A22	10k brown, die II	5.00	3.50
		Never hinged	10.00	
		Postal cancel		8.00
		On cover		150.00
e.		10k brown, die I	8.50	
		Never hinged	18.00	
		Postal cancel		10.00
		On cover		200.00
51a	A22	15k dark lilac	5.00	3.50
		Never hinged	10.00	
		Postal cancel		7.00
		On cover		150.00
52a	A22	20k gray black	17.50	6.00
		Never hinged	35.00	
		Postal cancel		20.00
		On cover		—
		Nos. 45a-52a (8)	50.00	26.00
		Set, never hinged	135.00	

Nos. 45-52a are inscribed "REGISTERED," but were used as regular postage stamps.

Nos. 46, 48 and 50 exist perf 11, and No. 50 also exists perf 11x10. No. 48 exists perf 11½, reportedly as a color trial proof.

No. 51 Surcharged in Black

Surcharged by numbering machine in Kyzyl.

1935

No.	Type	Stamp	Unused	Used
53	A22	20k on 15k	*175.00*	*325.00*
a.		Inverted surcharge		*400.00*

Map of Tuva — A23

Rocky Outcropping — A24

Designs: 3k, 5k, 10k, Different scenes of Yenisei River. 25k, Bei-kem rapids. 50k, Mounted hunters.

Printed by State Security Printers, Moscow.

Wmk. 170

1935, Mar. Photo. ***Perf. 14***

No.	Type	Stamp	Unused	Used
54	A23	1k yellow orange	2.25	1.75
		Never hinged	2.50	
		Postal cancel		1.50
		On cover		100.00
55	A23	3k deep green	2.25	1.75
		Never hinged	2.50	
		Postal cancel		3.00
		On cover		100.00
56	A23	5k carmine red	3.00	2.00
		Never hinged	3.00	
		Postal cancel		1.50
		On cover		100.00
57	A23	10k violet	3.25	2.00
		Never hinged	3.50	
		Postal cancel		2.00
		On cover		100.00
a.		Perf 14x10x14	*35.00*	
b.		Pair, imperf between	—	
58	A24	15k olive green	3.50	2.50
		Never hinged	3.50	
		Postal cancel		2.00
		On cover		100.00
59	A24	25k violet blue	4.00	2.50
		Never hinged	4.00	
		Postal cancel		2.00
		On cover		100.00
60	A24	50k dark brown	5.75	2.75
		Never hinged	6.00	
		Postal cancel		4.00
		On cover		150.00
		Nos. 54-60 (7)	24.00	15.25
		Set, never hinged	45.00	

Nos. 54-60 in different colors, perf and imperf, are proofs.

Badger A25

Squirrel — A26

Fox — A27

Elk — A28

Yak — A29

Designs: 5k, Ermine. 25k, Otter. 50k, Lynx. 3t, Bactrian camels. 5t, Bear.

Printed by State Security Printers, Moscow.

1935, Mar.

No.	Type	Stamp	Unused	Used
61	A25	1k orange	1.60	1.00
		Never hinged	3.25	
		Postal cancel		2.00
		On cover		100.00
62	A26	3k emerald green	1.60	1.00
		Never hinged	3.25	
		Postal cancel		2.00
		On cover		100.00
a.		Imperf, pair	*300.00*	
63	A25	5k rose red	1.60	1.10
		Never hinged	4.00	
		Postal cancel		2.00
		On cover		100.00
64	A27	10k crimson red	1.60	1.10
		Never hinged	5.00	
		Postal cancel		2.50
		On cover		100.00
65	A27	25k orange red	2.50	1.20
		Never hinged	5.00	
		Postal cancel		3.00
		On cover		100.00
66	A27	50k deep blue	2.50	1.20
		Never hinged	6.00	
		Postal cancel		3.50
		On cover		125.00
67	A28	1t violet	2.50	1.20
		Never hinged	8.00	
a.		Pair, imperf between	—	
68	A29	2t royal blue	3.50	1.20
		Never hinged	7.00	
69	A29	3t red brown	4.00	1.35
		Never hinged	8.00	
70	A28	5t indigo	5.00	1.75
		Never hinged	10.00	
a.		Imperf, pair	*300.00*	
b.		Pair, imperf between	—	
		Nos. 61-70 (10)	26.40	12.10
		Set, never hinged	50.00	

Nos. 61-70 in different colors are proofs.

Tuvan Arms — A30

Wrestlers — A31

Herdsman on Bull — A32

Athletic Competitions — A33

Soldiers A34

Designs: 2k, Pres. Chürmit-Dazhy. 3k, Tuvan with Bactrian camel. 5k, 8k, Archer. 10k, 15k, Spearfishing. 12k, 20k, Bear-hunting. 30k, Camel and train. 40k, 50k, Horse race. 80k, Partisans. 3t, Partisans confiscating cattle. 5t, 1921 battle scene.

Printed by State Security Printers, Moscow.

1936, July ***Perf. 14***

No.	Type	Stamp	Unused	Used
71	A30	1k bronze green	2.00	.70
		Never hinged	3.00	
		Postal cancel		2.00
		On cover		90.00
72	A30	2k dark brown	2.50	1.50
		Never hinged	4.00	
		Postal cancel		3.00
		On cover		100.00
74	A31	4k orange red	—	35.00
		On cover		—
75	A31	5k brown purple	5.00	.70
		Never hinged	8.00	
		Postal cancel		2.50
		On cover		90.00
76	A31	6k myrtle green	4.75	.70
		Never hinged	7.50	
		Postal cancel		3.00
		On cover		90.00
77	A31	8k plum	4.75	.70
		Never hinged	7.50	
		Postal cancel		3.00
		On cover		90.00
78	A31	10k rose red	6.00	1.00
		Never hinged	10.00	
		Postal cancel		2.50
		On cover		90.00
79	A31	12k black brown	7.50	1.25
		Never hinged	12.00	
		Postal cancel		4.00
		On cover		90.00
80	A31	15k bronze green	11.00	1.50
		Never hinged	17.00	
		Postal cancel		7.00
		On cover		100.00
81	A31	20k deep blue	11.00	1.20
		Never hinged	14.50	
		Postal cancel		3.00
		On cover		90.00
82	A32	25k orange red	6.00	1.20
		Never hinged	14.50	
		Postal cancel		6.00
		On cover		100.00
83	A32	30k plum	30.00	1.25
		Never hinged	42.50	
		Postal cancel		6.00
		On cover		100.00
84	A32	35k rose red	6.00	1.50
		Never hinged	14.50	
		Postal cancel		4.00
		On cover		100.00
85	A32	40k deep brown	9.00	1.50
		Never hinged	14.50	
		Postal cancel		6.00
		On cover		100.00
86	A32	50k indigo blue	35.00	35.00
		Never hinged	85.00	
		Postal cancel		—
		On cover		—
87	A33	70k plum	12.00	2.00
		Never hinged	17.50	
		Postal cancel		5.00
		On cover		125.00
88	A33	80k green	11.00	2.00
		Never hinged	17.00	
		Postal cancel		5.00
		On cover		250.00
89	A34	1a orange red	11.00	2.00
		Never hinged	17.00	
		Postal cancel		4.00
		On cover		125.00
a.		1a rose red (error)	—	—
90	A34	2a rose red	11.00	3.00
		Never hinged	17.00	
		Postal cancel		10.00
		On cover		250.00
92	A33	5a black brown	15.00	2.50
		Never hinged	17.50	
		Postal cancel		20.00
		On cover		300.00

Perf. 11

No.	Type	Stamp	Unused	Used
72a	A30	2k dark brown	—	50.00
73	A30	3k indigo blue	3.25	.75
		Never hinged	4.75	
		Postal cancel		2.50
74a	A31	4k orange red	3.50	.75
		Never hinged	5.00	
		Postal cancel		3.00
75a	A31	5k brown purple	42.50	—
		Never hinged	85.00	
		Postal cancel		—
76a	A31	6k myrtle green	4.75	.75
		Never hinged	9.50	
		Postal cancel		3.00
78a	A31	10k rose red	5.25	.75
		Never hinged	10.50	
		Postal cancel		2.00
		On cover		90.00
80a	A31	15k bronze green	13.00	1.25
		Never hinged	.26	
		Postal cancel		6.00

81a A31 20k deep blue — —
82a A32 25k orange red 13.00 .90
Never hinged 26.00
Postal cancel 3.00
84a A32 35k rose red 13.00 1.25
Never hinged 26.00
Postal cancel 4.00
On cover —
85a A32 40k deep brown 7.00 1.50
Never hinged 14.00
Postal cancel 6.00
On cover *100.00*
86a A32 50k indigo blue 13.00 1.50
Never hinged 26.00
Postal cancel 5.00
On cover —
87a A33 70k plum 9.50 2.50
Never hinged 20.00
Postal cancel 8.00
88a A33 80k green 9.50 2.50
Never hinged 19.00
Postal cancel 8.00
89b A34 1a orange red 9.50 3.00
Never hinged 19.00
Postal cancel 8.00
90a A34 2a rose red 12.00 3.00
Never hinged 24.00
Postal cancel 10.00
91 A33 3a indigo blue 17.50 2.00
Never hinged 35.00
Postal cancel 15.00
Nos. 71-92 (37) 376.75 168.60
Set, never hinged 690.00

15th anniversary of independence.

Imperfs are remainders, later sold by the Soviet Postal Museum.

Values for Nos. 93-98 and 104-116 are for genuine examples. Expertization is essential for these issues.

Issues of 1934-36 Handstamped with Large Numerals and Old Values Obliterated with Bars or Blocks

1938, Aug.

93 A34 5k on 2a (#90a) *400.00*
94 AP5 5k on 2a (#C17) *375.00*
95 AP1 10k on 1t (#C8) *350.00*
96 A24 20k on 50k (#60) *350.00*
On cover —
97 AP5 30k on 2a (#C17) *350.00*
98 AP5 30k on 3a (#C18) *325.00*

Types of 1935-36 with Modified Designs and New Colors

1938, Dec. Unwmk. *Perf. 12½*

99 A25 5k deep green 60.00 —
Never hinged *90.00*
100 A31 10k indigo (dates removed) 60.00 —
Never hinged *90.00*
101 AP3 15k red brown ("AIR MAIL," dates removed) 60.00 —
Never hinged *90.00*
102 A31 20k orange red (dates removed) 85.00 —
Never hinged *140.00*
103 A33 30k maroon (dates removed) 60.00 —
Never hinged *90.00*
Nos. 99-103 (5) 325.00
Set, never hinged 500.00

Some experts believe that these stamps were issued in March 1941.

A few commercial covers exist, dated between 1941 and 1943.

Stamps of 1934-35 Handstamp Surcharged with New Values in Black or Violet at Kyzyl

1939

104 AP1 10k on 1t (#C8) 225.00
a. 10k on 1t, #C8a —
105 AP1 10k on 1t (#B8) (V) 225.00
106 A24 20k on 50k (#60) (V) 200.00
On cover —

Old values obliterated on Nos. 104-106.

Stamps of 1934-36 Handstamp Surcharged with New Values at Kyzyl

1940, Oct.-1941

107 AP1 10k on 1t (#C8) — 125.00
a. Double surcharge —
108 A24 20k on 50k (#60) — 150.00
109 A27 20k on 50k (#66) — 350.00
110 A32 20k on 50k (#86a) — 350.00
111 AP4 20k on 50k (#C14) — 100.00
112 A33 20k on 70k (#87a) — *500.00*
113 AP4 20k on 75k (#C15) — 110.00
114 A33 20k on 80k (#88) — *500.00*

The old values are not obliterated on Nos. 107 or 108.

Nos. 91, 92 Handstamp Surcharged with New Values at Kyzyl

1942

115 A33 25k on 3a (#91) 1,200. —
116 A33 25k on 5a (#92) — —

Government House — A35

Exhibition Hall — A36

Tuvan Woman — A37

1942 Typo. Unwmk. *Imperf.*

117 A35 25k steel blue 950.00 100.00
118 A36 25k steel blue 950.00 100.00
119 A37 25k steel blue 950.00 150.00
Nos. 117-119 (3) 2,850. 350.00

21st anniversary of independence.

Nos. 117-119 were hand-printed together in small sheetlets of five (117+119+118+117+119), so various se-tenant combinations are possible.

Two additional values, a 25k depicting a Tuvan man and a 50k depicting a soldier on a horse, were prepared, but not issued. A collective proof sheetlet of five, containing Nos. 117-119 and these two values, in the same color as the issued stamps, is also known.

Coat of Arms — A38

Government Building — A39

1943 *Perf. 11 (1 or 2 Sides)*

Buff Paper

120 A38 25k slate blue 100.00 —
Vertical strip of 5 900.00
121 A38 25k black 100.00 —
Vertical strip of 5 600.00
122 A38 25k blue green 90.00 —
123 A39 50k blue green 90.00 —
Vertical pair, 122 + 123 175.00
Nos. 120-123 (4) 380.00

White Paper

120a A38 25k slate blue 90.00 —
b. Strip of 3, imperf between *250.00*
Sheet of 5 500.00
121a A38 25k black 125.00 —
Vertical strip of five 600.00
122a A38 25k blue green 95.00 —
123a A39 50k blue green 95.00 —
With gum *175.00*
Nos. 120a-123a (4) 405.00

22nd anniversary of independence.

Nos. 120 and 121 were each printed in vertical strips of five, perforated 11 between stamps and imperf on outside edges, so that these stamps may be perforated on top edge only, bottom edge only, or on both top and bottom edges. To make maximum use of limited wartime paper supplies, they were sometimes printed in strips of four. These smaller strips are rare.

Nos. 122 and 123 were printed together in blocks of four, containing a vertical pair of the 25k and a vertical pair of the 50k, perforated internally both vertically and horizontally and imperf on the outer edges. Setenant pairs, Value $225 (#122+123), $275 (#122a+123a).

Nos. 121 and 123a were issued with gum, No. 123a both with and without gum, and the balance of the set without gum.

Used examples and covers exist but are extremely rare.

AIR POST STAMPS

Airplane and Yaks — AP1

Airplane and Capercaillie — AP2

Designs, airplane over: 5k, 15k, Camels. 25k, Argali (wild sheep). 75k, Ox and cart. 2t, Roe deer.

Printed by State Security Printers, Moscow.

Wmk. 170

1934, Apr. 4 Photo. *Perf. 14*

C1 AP1 1k orange red 1.40 1.00
Never hinged 5.00
Postal cancel 2.50
On cover *100.00*
C2 AP1 5k emer green 1.40 1.00
Never hinged 5.00
Postal cancel 2.50
On cover *100.00*
C3 AP2 10k purple brown 4.50 2.75
Never hinged 9.00
Postal cancel 3.00
On cover *100.00*
C4 AP1 15k rose red 2.50 1.00
Never hinged 6.00
Postal cancel 3.00
On cover *100.00*
C5 AP2 25k slate purple 2.50 1.00
Never hinged 6.00
Postal cancel 3.50
On cover *100.00*
C6 AP1 50k dp bl green 2.50 1.00
Never hinged 6.00
Postal cancel 4.00
On cover *100.00*
C7 AP2 75k lake 2.50 1.00
Never hinged 6.00
Postal cancel 4.00
On cover *100.00*
C8 AP1 1t royal blue 3.25 1.75
Never hinged 5.00
Postal cancel 5.00
On cover *100.00*
a. Perf 12½ 77.50 *2,500.*
Never hinged 155.00
C9 AP2 2t ultra, 61x31mm 18.00 *21.00*
Never hinged 40.00
Postal cancel 40.00
On cover —
a. 54.5x29mm 40.00 —
Never hinged 80.00
Nos. C1-C9 (9) 38.55 31.50
Set, never hinged 55.00

Nos. C1-C9 imperf or perf 11½ and stamps printed in different colors are proofs.

Tuvan Leading Laden Yak — AP3

Horseman and Zeppelin AP4

Seaplane Above Dragon — AP5

Designs: 10k, Tuvan plowing. 50k, Villagers with biplane overhead.

Printed by State Security Printers, Moscow.

1936 Unwmk.

C10 AP3 5k indigo & beige 3.00 1.50
Never hinged 4.00
Postal cancel 2.00
On cover *100.00*
C11 AP3 10k pur & cinn 4.50 1.50
Never hinged 6.00
Postal cancel 2.00
On cover *100.00*
C12 AP3 15k blk brn & pale gray 4.50 1.75
Never hinged 6.00
Postal cancel 2.00
On cover *100.00*
C13 AP4 25k plum & cream 6.00 2.50
Never hinged 10.00
Postal cancel 5.00
On cover *100.00*
a. Perf 11 4.50 2.00
Never hinged 9.00
Postal cancel 4.50
b. Perf compound 14x11 —
c. Horiz. pair, perf 11, imperf between — —
C14 AP4 50k rose red & cream 6.50 2.50
Never hinged 10.00
Postal cancel 7.50
On cover *125.00*
C15 AP4 75k emer grn & pale yel 10.00 4.00
Never hinged 10.00
Postal cancel 10.00
On cover *200.00*
C16 AP5 1a bl grn & pale bl grn 12.00 5.00
Never hinged 16.00
Postal cancel —
On cover —
C17 AP5 2a rose red & cream 9.50 3.75
Never hinged 15.00
Postal cancel 30.00
On cover *350.00*
C18 AP5 3a dk brn & beige 9.50 3.75
Never hinged 16.00
Postal cancel 35.00
On cover *400.00*
Nos. C10-C18 (9) 65.50 26.25
Set, never hinged 120.00

15th anniversary of independence.

Nos. C10-C18 exist imperf.

TETE

'tāt-ə

LOCATION — In southeastern Africa between Nyasaland and Southern Rhodesia.
GOVT. — A district of the Portuguese East Africa Colony.
AREA — 46,600 sq. mi. (approx.)
POP. — 367,000 (approx.)
CAPITAL — Tete

This district was formerly a part of Zambezia. Stamps of Mozambique replaced those of Tete. See Mozambique.

100 Centavos = 1 Escudo

Vasco da Gama Issue of Various Portuguese Colonies Surcharged

1913 Unwmk. *Perf. 12½, 16*

On Stamps of Macao

1 CD20 ¼c on ½a bl grn 4.00 *5.00*
2 CD21 ½c on 1a red 4.00 *2.10*
3 CD22 1c on 2a red vio 4.00 *2.10*
4 CD23 2½c on 4a yel grn 4.00 *2.10*
5 CD24 5c on 8a dk blue 4.00 *2.10*
6 CD25 7½c on 12a vio brn 4.00 *3.00*
7 CD26 10c on 16a bis brn 4.00 *2.10*
8 CD27 15c on 24a bister 4.00 *2.10*
Nos. 1-8 (8) 32.00 *20.60*

On Stamps of Portuguese Africa

9 CD20 ¼c on 2½r bl grn 4.00 *2.10*
10 CD21 ½c on 5r red 4.00 *2.10*
11 CD22 1c on 10r red vio 4.00 *2.10*
12 CD23 2½c on 25r yel grn 4.00 *2.10*
13 CD24 5c on 50r dk blue 4.00 *2.10*
14 CD25 7½c on 75r vio brn 4.00 *3.00*
15 CD26 10c on 100r bis brn 4.00 *2.10*
16 CD27 15c on 150r bister 4.00 *2.10*
Nos. 9-16 (8) 32.00 *17.70*

On Stamps of Timor

17 CD20 ¼c on ½a bl grn 4.00 *2.10*
18 CD21 ½c on 1a red 4.00 *2.10*
19 CD22 1c on 2a red vio 4.00 *2.10*
a. Inverted overprint 40.00 40.00
20 CD23 2½c on 4a yel grn 4.00 *2.10*
21 CD24 5c on 8a dk blue 4.00 *2.10*
22 CD25 7½c on 12a vio brn 4.00 *3.00*
23 CD26 10c on 16a bis brn 4.00 *2.10*
24 CD27 15c on 24a bister 4.00 *2.10*
Nos. 17-24 (8) 32.00 *17.70*
Nos. 1-24 (24) 96.00 *56.00*

Common Design Types pictured following the introduction.

Ceres — A1

1914 Typo. *Perf. 15x14*

Name and Value in Black

25 A1 ¼c olive brn 2.00 *2.25*
Never hinged 2.75
26 A1 ½c black 2.00 *2.25*
Never hinged 2.75
27 A1 1c blue grn 2.00 *2.25*
Never hinged 2.75
28 A1 1½c lilac brn 2.00 *2.25*
Never hinged 2.75
29 A1 2c carmine 2.00 *2.25*
Never hinged 2.75
30 A1 2½c light vio 2.00 *2.25*
Never hinged 2.75
31 A1 5c deep blue 2.00 *2.25*
Never hinged 2.75
32 A1 7½c yel brn 4.00 *3.25*
Never hinged 6.00
33 A1 8c slate 4.00 *3.25*
Never hinged 6.00
34 A1 10c org brn 4.00 *6.00*
Never hinged 6.00
35 A1 15c plum 4.00 *6.00*
Never hinged 6.00
36 A1 20c yel green 6.00 *6.00*
Never hinged 8.50
37 A1 30c brn, *green* 6.00 *6.00*
Never hinged 8.50
38 A1 40c brn, *pink* 8.00 *9.00*
Never hinged 12.00
39 A1 50c org, *salmon* 10.00 *10.00*
Never hinged 15.00
40 A1 1e grn, *blue* 12.00 *15.00*
Never hinged 18.00
Nos. 25-40 (16) 72.00 *80.25*

THAILAND

'tī-ˌland

(Siam)

LOCATION — Western part of the Malay peninsula in southeastern Asia
GOVT. — Republic
AREA — 198,250 sq. mi.
POP. — 50,000,000 (est. 1984)
CAPITAL — Bangkok

32 Solot = 16 Atts = 8 Sio = 4 Sik = 2 Fuang = 1 Salung
4 Salungs = 1 Tical
100 Satangs (1909) = 1 Tical = 1 Baht (1912)

Watermarks

Wmk. 176 — Chakra

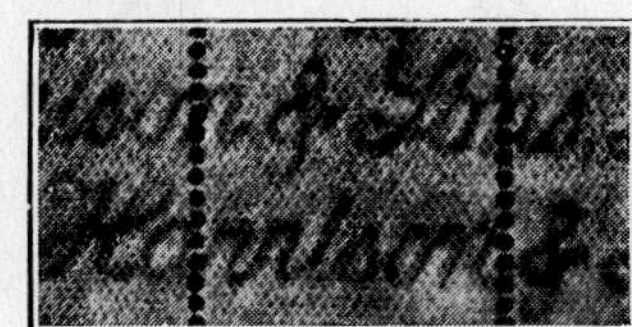

Wmk. 233 — Harrison & Sons, London in Script Letters

King Chulalongkorn
A1 A2

A4

Perf. 14½, 15

1883, Aug. 4 Unwmk. Engr.

1 A1 1sol dark blue 15.00 13.00
b. Imperf., pair *4,000.*
c. 1sol dull blue 20.00 *20.00*
d. 1sol Prussian blue 30.00 *27.50*
2 A1 1att carmine 16.50 15.00
3 A1 1sio vermilion 32.50 30.00
4 A2 1sik yellow 16.50 15.00
5 A4 1sa orange 45.00 45.00
a. 1sa ocher 52.50 52.50
Nos. 1-5 (5) 125.50 118.00

There are three types of No. 1, differing mainly in the background of the small oval at the top.

A 1 fuang red, of similar design to the foregoing, was prepared but not placed in use. Value, $2,000.

For surcharges see Nos. 6-8, 19.

No. 1 Handstamp Surcharged in Red

a

b

c

1 Tical *d* **1 Tical** *e*

1885, July 1

6 A1 (a) 1t on 1sol blue *4,800. 3,600.*
7 A1 (b) 1t on 1sol blue *450. 350.*
c. "1" inverted *4,000. 4,000.*
8 A1 (c) 1t on 1sol blue *3,000. 2,750.*

Surcharges of Nos. 6-8 have been counterfeited.

Types "d" and "e" are typeset *official reprints.*

As is usual with handstamps, double impressions, etc., exist.

King Chulalongkorn — A7

1887-91 Typo. Wmk. 176 *Perf. 14*

11 A7 1a green ('91) 6.50 2.00
12 A7 2a green & car 6.50 2.00
13 A7 3a grn & blue 12.00 4.00
14 A7 4a grn & org brn 12.00 4.75
15 A7 8a green & yel 12.00 7.00
16 A7 12a lilac & car 17.50 3.50
17 A7 24a lilac & blue 24.00 4.00
18 A7 64a lil & org brn 87.50 29.00
Nos. 11-18 (8) 178.00 56.25

The design of No. 11 has been redrawn and differs in many minor details from Nos. 12-18.

Issue dates: Nos. 12-18, Apr. 1; No. 11, Feb.

For surcharges see Nos. 20-69, 109, 111, 126.

No. 3 Handstamp Surcharged

1889, Aug. Unwmk. *Perf. 15*

19 A1 1a on 1sio 21.00 21.00

Three different handstamps were used. Doubles, etc. exist.

Nos. 12 and 13 Handstamp Surcharged

1889-90 Wmk. 176 *Perf. 14*

20 A7 1a on 2a 10.00 6.00
a. "1" omitted *450.00 450.00*
c. 1st Siamese character invtd. 950.00 950.00
d. First Siamese character omitted *950.00 950.00*
e. Double surcharge *240.00 240.00*
f. Inverted surcharge *1,900. 1,900.*
g. Double surcharge, one inverted *3,500.*
21 A7 1a on 3a ('90) 9.00 9.00
a. Inverted "1" *150.00 150.00*

For surcharge see No. 29.

22 A7 1a on 2a grn & car *475.00 475.00*

24 A7 1a on 2a grn & car *350.00 350.00*

25 A7 1a on 2a grn & car *2,000. 1,000.*

26 A7 1a on 3a grn & bl

Some authorities consider No. 26 a forgery.

Doubles, etc., exist in this issue.

Issue dates: Nov. 1889. Sept. 1890.

No. 13 Handstamp Surcharged

1891

27 A7 2a on 3a grn & bl 95.00 65.00

28 A7 2a on 3a grn & bl 55.00 55.00
a. Double surcharge *250.00 250.00*
b. "2" omitted *250.00*

No. 21 with Additional 2 Att Surcharge

29 A7 2a on 1a on 3a grn & bl *2,000. 1,800.*

On No. 29 the 2a surcharge consists of Siamese numeral like No. 27 and English numeral like No. 28.

Most examples of No. 29 show attempts to remove the "1" of the first surcharge.

Typeset Surcharge

30 A7 2a on 3a grn & bl 60.00 45.00

There are 7 types of this surcharge in the setting.

Issued: #27-28, Jan.; #29, Feb.; #30, Mar.

No. 17 Handstamp Surcharged

f

g

1892, Oct.

33	A7 (f) 4a on 24a lil & bl	60.00	50.00
34	A7 (g) 4a on 24a lil & bl	55.00	35.00

Surcharges exist double on Nos. 33-34 and inverted on No. 33.

Nos. 33-34 Handstamp Surcharged in English

1892, Nov.

35	A7 4a on 24a lil & bl	12.00	9.00
c.	Inverted "s"	*75.00*	*60.00*

36	A7 4a on 24a lil & bl	20.00	10.00
a.	Inverted "s"	*90.00*	*90.00*

37	A7 4a on 24a lil & bl	15.00	12.50

38	A7 4a on 24a lil & bl	20.00	15.00

Numerous inverts., doubles, etc., exist.

Nos. 35 and 37 are surcharged examples of No. 33. Nos. 36 and 38 are surcharged examples of No. 34. The "4 atts" surcharge is small on Nos. 35 and 36, and large on Nos. 37 and 38.

Nos. 18 and 17 Typeset Srchd. in English (Shown) and Siamese

1894

39	A7 1a on 64a lil & org brn	3.50	3.50
a.	Inverted "s"	*70.00*	*60.00*
b.	Inverted surcharge	*900.00*	*900.00*
d.	Italic "s"	*200.00*	*200.00*
e.	Italic "1"	*350.00*	*300.00*

40	A7 1a on 64a lil & org brn	2.00	1.50
a.	Inverted capital "S" added to the surcharge	*75.00*	*60.00*

h

i

j

k

l

m

41	A7 (h) 2a on 64a	20.00	15.00
a.	Inverted "s"	*90.00*	*60.00*
b.	Double surcharge	*100.00*	*100.00*
42	A7 (i) 2a on 64a	*2,000.*	*2,000.*
43	A7 (j) 2a on 64a	80.00	70.00
44	A7 (k) 2a on 64a	40.00	30.00
45	A7 (l) 2a on 64a	65.00	45.00
46	A7 (m) 2a on 64a	6.00	3.00
a.	"Att.s"	*60.00*	*60.00*

Nos. 41-46 were in one plate of 120 subjects. The quantities were: h, 38; i, 1; j, 8; k, 18; l, 11 and m, 44.

1894, Oct. 12

47	A7 1a on 64a	5.00	3.00
a.	Surcharged on face and back	*150.00*	
b.	As "a," surcharge on back inverted	*200.00*	
c.	Double surcharge	*475.00*	
d.	Inverted surcharge	*600.00*	
e.	Siamese surcharge omitted	*300.00*	

See No. 67.

48	A7 2a on 64a	4.00	3.00
a.	"Att"	*75.00*	*45.00*
b.	Inverted surcharge	*750.00*	*650.00*
c.	Surch. on face and back	*200.00*	*200.00*
d.	Surcharge on back inverted	*210.00*	*210.00*
e.	Double surcharge	*150.00*	*150.00*
f.	Double surch., one inverted	*900.00*	*800.00*
g.	Inverted "s"	*35.00*	*30.00*

1895, July 23

49	A7 10a on 24a lil & bl	9.00	2.00
a.	Inverted "s"	*60.00*	*30.00*
b.	Surch. on face and back	*240.00*	*200.00*
c.	Surcharge on back inverted	*240.00*	*240.00*

No. 16 Surcharged in English (Shown) and Siamese

1896

50	A7 4a on 12a lil & car	25.00	8.00
a.	Inverted "s"	*90.00*	*60.00*
b.	Surcharged on face and back	*225.00*	*200.00*
c.	Double surcharge on back	*175.00*	*175.00*

Two types of surcharge.

Nos. 16-18 Surcharged in English (Shown) and Siamese Antique Surcharges

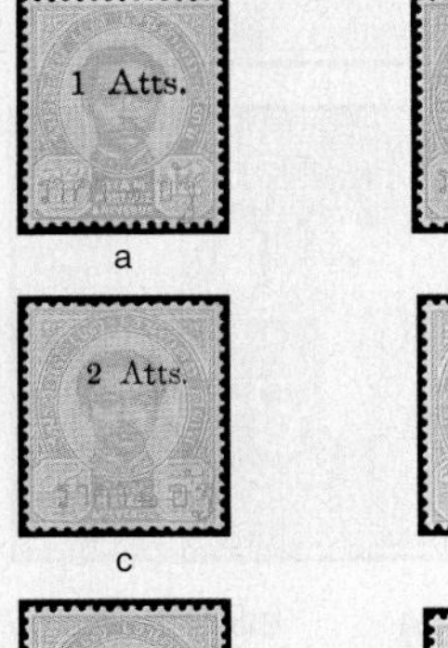
a b c d e f

Antique Letters

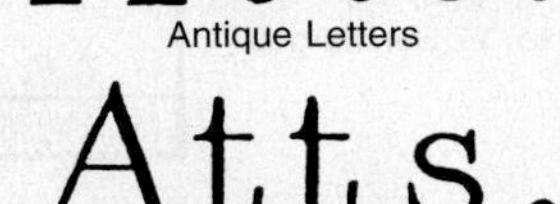

Roman Letters

1898-99

51	A7 (a) 1a on 12a	450.00	400.00
52	A7 (b) 1a on 12a	20.00	7.00
53	A7 (c) 2a on 64a ('99)	35.00	9.00
54	A7 (d) 3a on 12a	12.00	4.00
a.	Double surcharge	*500.00*	*450.00*
55	A7 (e) 4a on 12a	15.00	5.00
a.	Double surcharge	*400.00*	*375.00*
56	A7 (e) 4a on 24a ('99)	45.00	14.00
57	A7 (f) 10a on 24a ('99)	825.00	825.00
	Nos. 51-57 (7)	1,402.	1,264.

Roman Surcharges

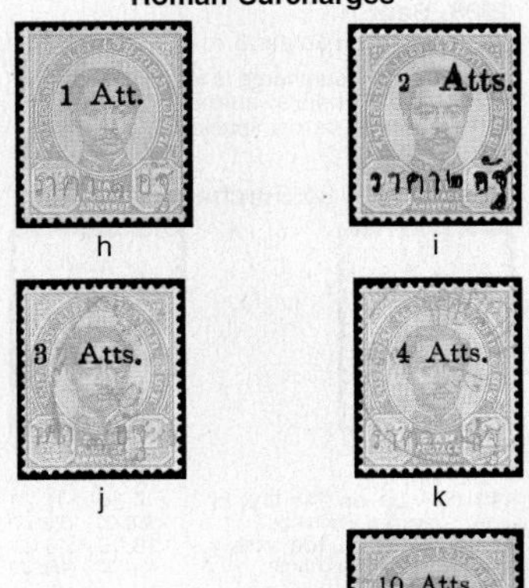
h i j k l g

58	A7 (g) 1a on 12a	450.00	450.00
59	A7 (h) 1a on 12a	45.00	20.00
60	A7 (i) 2a on 64a ('99)	35.00	10.00
61	A7 (j) 3a on 12a	85.00	19.00
62	A7 (k) 4a on 12a	40.00	14.00
a.	Double surcharge	*175.00*	*175.00*
b.	No period after "Atts."	*35.00*	*35.00*
63	A7 (k) 4a on 24a ('99)	60.00	29.00
64	A7 (l) 10a on 24a ('99)	750.00	750.00
	Nos. 58-64 (7)	1,465.	1,292.

In making the settings to surcharge Nos. 51 to 64 two fonts were mixed.

Antique and Roman letters are frequently found on the same stamp. Such stamps sell for more.

Issue dates: Nos. 54-55, 61-62, Feb. 22. Nos. 51-52, 58-59, June 4. Nos. 56-57, 63-64, Oct. 3.

Nos. 16 and 18 Surcharged in English (Shown) and Siamese Surcharged

m

n

o

p

r

1894-99

65	A7 (m) 1a on 12a	20.00	6.00
66	A7 (n) 1a on 12a	20.00	6.00
a.	Inverted "1"	*300.00*	*200.00*
b.	Inverted 1st "t"	*200.00*	*175.00*
67	A7 (o) 1a on 64a	5.00	5.00
68	A7 (p) 2a on 64a	35.00	8.00
a.	"1 Atts."	*500.00*	*500.00*
69	A7 (r) 2a on 64a	24.00	8.00
	Nos. 65-69 (5)	104.00	33.00

Issued: No. 67, 10/12/94; others, 2/14/99.

See No. 47.

A13

1899, Oct. **Typo.** **Unwmk.**

70	A13 1a dull green	450.	85.
	Postally used		120.
71	A13 2a dl grn & rose	550.	150.
	Postally used		160.
72	A13 3a car & blue	800.	200.
	Postally used		260.
73	A13 4a black & grn	3,000.	600.
	Postally used		675.
74	A13 10a car & grn	3,000.	600.
	Postally used		975.
	Nos. 70-74 (5)	7,800.	1,635.

The King rejected Nos. 70-74 in 1897, but some were released by mistake to three post offices in Oct. 1899. Used values are for stamps canceled to order at Korat in Dec. 1899.

A14

1899-1904

75	A14 1a gray green	5.00	.75
76	A14 2a yellow green	3.50	.75
77	A14 2a scarlet & bl	6.00	1.25
78	A14 3a red & blue	8.50	2.00
79	A14 3a green	20.00	12.00
80	A14 4a dark rose	5.50	1.25
81	A14 4a vio brn & rose	12.00	1.75
82	A14 6a dk rose	35.00	14.00
83	A14 8a dk grn & org	10.00	2.00
84	A14 10a ultra	10.50	2.50
85	A14 12a brn vio & rose	40.00	2.00
86	A14 14a ultra	23.00	18.00
87	A14 24a brn vio & bl	300.00	25.00
88	A14 28a vio brn & bl	25.00	25.00

89	A14	64a brn vio & org brn	70.00	11.00
		Nos. 75-89 (15)	574.00	119.25

Two types of 1a differ in size and shape of Thai "1" are in drawing of spandrel ornaments.

Issue dates: 6a, 14a, 28a, Nos. 77, 79, 81, Jan. 1, 1904; others, Sept. 1899.

For surcharges see Nos. 90-91, 112, 125, 127.

Nos. 78 and 85 With Typewritten Srch. of 6 or 7 Siamese Characters (1 line) in Violet

1902

78a	*A14*	*2a on 3a*	*5,000.*	*5,250.*
85a	*A14*	*10a on 12a*	*5,000.*	*5,250.*

Nos. 78a and 85a were authorized provisionals, surcharged and issued by the Battambang postmaster.

Nos. 86 and 88 Surcharged in Black

1905, Feb.

90	A14	1a on 14a	10.00	10.00
a.		No period after "Att"	60.00	60.00
b.		Double surcharge	175.00	175.00
91	A14	2a on 28a	12.00	10.00
a.		Double surcharge	150.00	150.00
b.		No period after "Att"	60.00	60.00

King Chulalongkorn — A15

1905-08 **Engr.**

92	A15	1a orange & green	3.50	1.25
93	A15	2a violet & slate	3.50	1.25
94	A15	2a green ('08)	12.50	5.50
95	A15	3a green	7.50	2.00
96	A15	3a vio & sl ('08)	15.00	9.00
97	A15	4a gray & red	10.00	1.25
98	A15	4a car & rose ('08)	12.00	2.50
99	A15	5a carmine & rose	12.00	3.00
100	A15	8a blk & ol bis	13.00	1.50
101	A15	9a blue ('08)	30.00	9.00
102	A15	12a blue	18.00	4.00
103	A15	18a red brn ('08)	80.00	27.50
104	A15	24a red brown	35.00	8.00
105	A15	1t dp bl & brn org	47.50	8.00
		Nos. 92-105 (14)	299.50	83.75

Issue dates: Dec. 1905, Apr. 1, 1908.

For surcharges and overprints see Nos. 110, 113-117, 128-138, 161-162, B15, B21.

King Chulalongkorn — A16

No. 106

No. 107

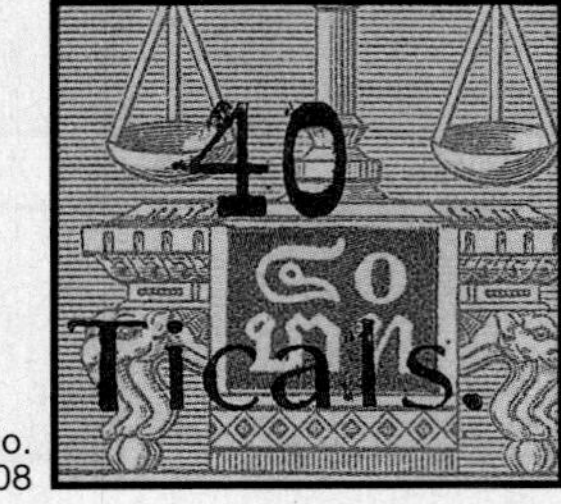

No. 108

1907, Apr. 24 **Black Surcharge**

106	A16	10t gray green	*750.00*	*100.00*
107	A16	20t gray green	*6,750.*	*350.00*
108	A16	40t gray green	*5,100.*	*600.00*
		Nos. 106-108 (3)	*12,600.*	*1,050.*

Counterfeits of Nos. 106-108 exist. In the genuine, the surcharged figures correspond to the Siamese value inscriptions on the basic revenue stamps.

No. 17 Surcharged

1907, Dec. 16

109	A7	1a on 24a lil & bl	5.50	1.50
a.		Double surcharge	450.00	

No. 99 Surcharged

1908, Sept.

110	A15	4a on 5a car & rose	12.00	4.00

The No. 110 surcharge is found in two spacings of the numerals: normally 15mm apart, and a narrow, scarcer spacing of 13½mm.

Nos. 17 and 84 Surcharged in Black

111	A7	2a on 24a lil & bl	4.50	1.20
a.		Inverted surcharge	*350.00*	*350.00*
112	A14	9a on 10a ultra	16.00	5.00
a.		Inverted surcharge	*450.00*	*450.00*

Jubilee Issue

Nos. 92, 95, 110, 100 and 103 Overprinted in Black or Red

1908, Nov. 11

113	A15	1a	4.50	1.25
a.		Siamese date "137" instead of "127"	*1,050.*	*1,050.*
b.		Pair, one without ovpt.	1,500.	1,500.
114	A15	3a	7.50	3.25
115	A15	4a on 5a	9.00	4.50
a.		Pair, imperf on 3 sides	*2,400.*	
116	A15	8a (R)	24.00	24.00
117	A15	18a	32.50	21.00
		Nos. 113-117 (5)	77.50	54.00

40th year of the reign of King Chulalongkorn.

Nos. 113 to 117 exist with a small "i" in "Jubilee."

Statue of King Chulalongkorn A19

1908, Nov. 11 **Engr.** ***Perf. 13½***

118	A19	1t green & vio	60.00	9.00
119	A19	2t red vio & org	120.00	20.00
120	A19	3t pale ol & bl	175.00	21.00
121	A19	5t dl vio & dk grn	240.00	42.50
122	A19	10t bister & car	*1,050.*	125.00
123	A19	20t gray & red brn	700.00	125.00
124	A19	40t sl bl & blk brn	950.00	400.00
		Nos. 118-124 (7)	*3,295.*	742.50

The inscription at the foot of the stamps reads: "Coronation Commemoration-Forty-first year of the reign-1908."

Stamps of 1887-1904 Surcharged

1909 ***Perf. 14***

125	A14	6s on 6a dk rose	3.00	1.50
126	A7	14s on 12a lil & car	135.00	120.00
127	A14	14s on 14a ultra	27.50	22.50
		Nos. 125-127 (3)	165.50	144.00

Nos. 92-102 Surcharged with Bar and

1909, Aug. 15

128	A15	2s on 1a #92	3.00	1.20
129	A15	2s on 2a #93	60.00	60.00
130	A15	2s on 2a #94	3.00	1.20
a.		"2" omitted	*600.00*	600.00
131	A15	3s on 3a #95	15.00	12.00
132	A15	3s on 3a #96	6.00	1.25
133	A15	6s on 4a #97	45.00	35.00
134	A15	6s on 4a #98	9.00	2.00
135	A15	6s on 5a #99	13.00	8.75
136	A15	12s on 8a #100	9.00	1.50
137	A15	14s on 9a #101	11.00	1.75
138	A15	14s on 12a #102	27.00	21.00
		Nos. 128-138 (11)	201.00	145.65

King Chulalongkorn — A20

1910 **Engr.** ***Perf. 14x14½***

139	A20	2s org & green	3.00	1.50
140	A20	3s green	4.50	1.50
141	A20	6s carmine	7.50	2.50
142	A20	12s blk & ol brn	16.00	2.50
143	A20	14s blue	25.00	3.50
144	A20	28s red brown	47.50	10.00
		Nos. 139-144 (6)	103.50	21.50

Issue dates: 12s, June 5. Others, May 5.

For surcharges see Nos. 163, 223-224.

A21

King Vajiravudh — A22

Printed at the Imperial Printing Works, Vienna

1912 ***Perf. 14½***

145	A21	2s brn org	1.75	.60
a.		Vert. pair, imperf. btwn.	*600.00*	*600.00*
b.		Horiz. pair, imperf. btwn.	*600.00*	*600.00*
146	A21	3s yellow green	1.75	.60
a.		Horiz. pair, imperf. btwn.	*600.00*	*600.00*
b.		Vert. pair, imperf. btwn.	*600.00*	*600.00*
147	A21	6s car rose	3.00	1.00
148	A21	12s gray blk & brn	3.50	1.00
149	A21	14s ultramarine	5.50	1.50
150	A21	28s chocolate	20.00	10.00
151	A22	1b blue & blk	30.00	2.40
a.		Vert. pair, imperf. btwn.	*1,800.*	*1,800.*
b.		Horiz. pair, imperf. btwn.	*1,800.*	*1,800.*
152	A22	2b car rose & ol brn	35.00	3.00
153	A22	3b yel grn & bl blk	42.50	4.50
154	A22	5b vio & blk	65.00	7.50
155	A22	10b ol grn & vio brn	325.00	60.00
156	A22	20b sl bl & red brn	500.00	65.00
		Nos. 145-156 (12)	1,033.	157.10

See Nos. 164-175.

For surcharges and overprints see Nos. 157-160, 176-186, 206, B1-B14, B16-B20, B22, B31-B33.

Nos. 147-150 Surcharged in Red or Blue

1914-15

157	A21	2s on 14s (R) ('15)	3.00	.70
a.		Vert. pair, imperf. btwn.	*600.00*	*600.00*
b.		Double surcharge	450.00	450.00
158	A21	5s on 6s (Bl)	5.50	.50
a.		Horiz. pair, imperf. btwn.	*600.00*	*600.00*
b.		Double surcharge	300.00	300.00
159	A21	10s on 12s (R)	5.50	.75
a.		Double surcharge	300.00	300.00
160	A21	15s on 28s (Bl)	10.00	1.25
		Nos. 157-160 (4)	24.00	3.20

The several settings of the surcharges on Nos. 157-160 show variations in the figures and letters.

Nos. 92-93 Surcharged

1915, Apr. 3

161	A15	2s on 1a org & grn	8.00	4.00
a.		Pair, one without surcharge	*600.00*	*600.00*
162	A15	2s on 2a vio & slate	8.25	4.00

No. 143 Surcharged in Red

1916, Oct.

163	A20	2s on 14s blue	6.00	2.00

Types of 1912 Re-engraved
Printed by Waterlow & Sons, London

1917, Jan. 1 *Perf. 14*
164 A21 2s orange brown 1.50 .30
165 A21 3s emerald 2.50 .60
166 A21 5s rose red 4.00 .30
167 A21 10s black & olive 3.50 .30
168 A21 15s blue 6.00 1.00
170 A22 1b bl & gray blk 28.00 4.00
171 A22 2b car rose & brn 100.00 42.50
172 A22 3b yellow grn & blk 450.00 275.00
173 A22 5b dp violet & blk 350.00 190.00
174 A22 10b ol gray & vio brn 525.00 25.00
a. Perf. 12½ 600.00 37.50
175 A22 20b sea grn & brn 700.00 70.00
a. Perf. 12½ 750.00 75.00
Nos. 164-175 (11) 2,171. 609.00

The re-engraved design of the satang stamps varies in numerous minute details from the 1912 issue. Four lines of the background appear between the vertical strokes of the "M" of "SIAM" in the 1912 issue and only three lines in the 1917 stamps.

The 1912 stamps with value in bahts are 37½mm high; those of 1917 are 39mm. In the latter the king's features, especially the eyes and mouth, are more distinct and the uniform and decorations are more sharply defined.

The 1912 stamps have seven pearls between the earpieces of the crown. On the 1917 stamps there are nine pearls in the same place. Nos. 174 and 175 exist imperforate.

Nos. 164-173 Overprinted in Red

1918, Dec. 2
176 A21 2s orange brown 2.00 .50
a. Double overprint 175.00 175.00
177 A21 3s emerald 2.50 1.00
a. Double overprint 175.00 175.00
178 A21 5s rose red 2.50 1.50
a. Double overprint 240.00 240.00
179 A21 10s black & olive 4.50 3.00
180 A21 15s blue 8.00 6.00
181 A22 1b bl & gray blk 35.00 24.00
182 A22 2b car rose & brn 65.00 47.50
183 A22 3b yel grn & blk 175.00 125.00
184 A22 5b dp vio & blk 475.00 325.00
Nos. 176-184 (9) 769.50 533.50

Counterfeits of this overprint exist.

Nos. 147-148 Surcharged in Green or Red

1919-20
185 A21 5s on 6s (G) 2.75 .50
186 A21 10s on 12s (R) ('20) 4.50 .60

Issue dates: 5s, Nov. 11. 10s, Jan. 1.

King Vajiravudh — A23

1920-26 **Engr.** *Perf. 14-15, 12½*
187 A23 2s brn, *yel* ('21) 2.00 .50
188 A23 3s grn, *grn* ('21) 3.50 .60
189 A23 3s chocolate ('24) 1.75 .50
190 A23 5s rose, *pale rose* 3.00 .50
191 A23 5s green ('22) 30.00 4.00
192 A23 5s dk vio, *lil* ('26) 8.00 .50
193 A23 10s black & org ('21) 6.00 .50
194 A23 15s bl, *bluish* ('21) 9.50 .60
195 A23 15s carmine ('22) 42.50 6.00
196 A23 25s chocolate ('21) 24.00 3.00
197 A23 25s dk blue ('22) 35.00 1.40
198 A23 50s ocher & blk ('21) 45.00 2.00
Nos. 187-198 (12) 210.25 20.10

For overprints see Nos. 205, B23-B30.

Throne Room — A24

1926, Mar. 5 *Perf. 12½*
199 A24 1t gray vio & grn 16.00 3.50
200 A24 2t car & org red 35.00 6.00
201 A24 3t ol grn & bl 67.50 25.00
202 A24 5t dl vio & ol grn 110.00 25.00
203 A24 10t red & ol bis 400.00 32.50
204 A24 20t gray bl & brn 450.00 100.00
Nos. 199-204 (6) 1,079. 192.00

This issue was intended to commemorate the fifteenth year of the reign of King Vajiravudh. Because of the King's death the stamps were issued as ordinary postage stamps.

Nos. 195 and 150 with Surcharge similar to 1914-15 Issue in Black or Red

1928, Jan.
205 A23 5s on 15s car 5.50 2.75
206 A21 10s on 28s choc (R) 12.00 1.00

King Prajadhipok
A25 A26

1928 **Engr.** *Perf. 12½*
207 A25 2s dp red brn 1.00 .30
208 A25 3s deep green 1.50 .50
209 A25 5s dark violet 1.00 .30
210 A25 10s deep rose 1.20 .30
211 A25 15s dark blue 2.40 .45
212 A25 25s black & org 4.50 .60
213 A25 50s brn org & blk 7.50 .90
214 A25 80s blue & black 7.50 .90
216 A26 1b dk blue & blk 14.00 1.25
217 A26 2b car rose & blk brn 21.00 2.50
218 A26 3b yellow grn & blk 22.50 4.00
219 A26 5b dp vio & gray blk 30.00 6.00
220 A26 10b ol grn & red vio 65.00 10.00
221 A26 20b Prus grn & brn 120.00 20.00
222 A26 40b dk grn & ol brn 210.00 90.00
Nos. 207-222 (15) 509.10 138.00
Set, never hinged 650.00

On the single colored stamps, type A25, the lines in the background are uniform; those of the bicolored values are shaded and do not extend to the frame.

Issue dates: 5s, 10s, 2b-40b, Apr. 15; 2s, 3s, 15s, 25s, 50s, May 1; 1b, June 1; 80s, Nov. 15.

For overprints & surcharge see Nos. 300-301, B34 in Scott Standard catalogue, Vol. 6.

Nos. 142, 144 Surcharged in Red or Blue

1930 *Perf. 14*
223 A20 10s on 12s blk & ol brn 8.75 1.50
224 A20 25s on 28s red brn (Bl) 30.00 2.25
Set, never hinged 50.00

King Prajadhipok and Chao P'ya Chakri
A27 A28

Statue of Chao P'ya Chakri — A29

1932, Apr. 1 **Engr.** *Perf. 12½*
225 A27 2s dark brown 2.00 .40
226 A27 3s deep green 3.50 1.00
227 A27 5s dull violet 2.00 .40
228 A28 10s red brn & blk 2.00 .25
229 A28 15s dull blue & blk 11.00 1.50
230 A28 25s violet & black 18.00 2.00
231 A28 50s claret & black 62.50 3.00
232 A29 1b blue black 100.00 16.00
Nos. 225-232 (8) 201.00 24.55
Set, never hinged 275.00

150th anniv. of the Chakri dynasty, the founding of Bangkok in 1782, and the opening of the memorial bridge across the Chao Phraya River.

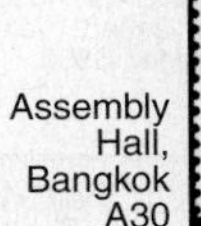

Assembly Hall, Bangkok A30

1939, June 24 **Litho.** *Perf. 11, 12*
233 A30 2s dull red brown 4.50 1.50
234 A30 3s green 12.00 3.50
235 A30 5s dark violet 6.50 .60
236 A30 10s carmine 16.00 .60
237 A30 15s dark blue 35.00 1.50
Nos. 233-237 (5) 74.00 7.70
Set, never hinged 95.00

7th anniv. of the Siamese Constitution.

Chakri Palace, Bangkok — A31

1940 **Typo.** *Perf. 12½*
238 A31 2s dull brown 6.50 1.00
239 A31 3s dp yellow grn 11.00 3.50
a. Cliché of 5s in plate of 3s 900.00 725.00
240 A31 5s dark violet 8.00 .50
241 A31 10s carmine 20.00 .50
242 A31 15s dark blue 40.00 1.50
Nos. 238-242 (5) 85.50 7.00
Set, never hinged 135.00

Issued: 2s, 3s, 5/13; 5s, 5/24; 15s, 5/28; 10s, 5/30.

SEMI-POSTAL STAMPS

Nos. 164-175 Overprinted in Red

1918, Jan. 11 **Unwmk.** *Perf. 14*
B1 A21 2s orange brown 1.75 1.00
B2 A21 3s emerald 1.75 1.00
B3 A21 5s rose red 6.00 4.25
B4 A21 10s black & olive 16.00 6.00
B5 A21 15s blue 10.00 6.00
B6 A22 1b blue & gray blk 45.00 24.00
B7 A22 2b car rose & brn 60.00 30.00
B8 A22 3b yel grn & blk 120.00 50.00
B9 A22 5b dp vio & blk 350.00 175.00
a. Double overprint 775.00 400.00
B10 A22 10b ol grn & vio brn 575.00 300.00
B11 A22 20b sea grn & brn 2,100. 1,500.
Nos. B1-B11 (11) 3,286. 2,097.

Excellent counterfeit overprints are known.

These stamps were sold at an advance over face value, the excess being given to the Siamese Red Cross Society.

Stamps of 1905-19 Handstamp Overprinted

1920, Feb.
On Nos. 164, 146, 168
B12 A21 2s (+ 3s) org brn 45.00 30.00
B13 A21 3s (+ 2s) green 45.00 30.00
B14 A21 15s (+ 5s) blue 125.00 90.00
On No. 105
B15 A15 1t (+ 25s) 360.00 360.00
On Nos. 185-186
B16 A21 5s on 6s (+ 5s) 60.00 45.00
a. Overprint inverted
B17 A21 10s on 12s (+ 5s) 60.00 45.00
Nos. B12-B17 (6) 695.00 600.00
Set, never hinged 1,200.

Sold at an advance over face value, the excess being for the benefit of the Wild Tiger Corps. Counterfeits exist.

Stamps of 1905-20 Handstamp Overprinted

On Nos. 164, 146, 168
B18 A21 2s (+ 3s) org brn 35.00 26.00
B19 A21 3s (+ 2s) green 35.00 26.00
a. Pair, one without ovpt.
B20 A21 15s (+ 5s) blue 65.00 52.50
On No. 105
B21 A15 1t (+ 25s) 300.00 275.00
On No. 186
B22 A21 10s on 12s (+ 5s) 65.00 45.00
On No. 190
B23 A23 5s (+ 5s) 70.00 50.00
Nos. B18-B23 (6) 570.00 474.50
Set, never hinged 925.00

Sold at an advance over face value, the excess being for the benefit of the Wild Tiger Corps. Counterfeits exist.

Nos. 187-188, 190, 193-194, 196, 198 Overprinted in Blue or Red

1920, Dec. 21
B24 A23 2s brown, *yel* 15.00 15.00
B25 A23 3s grn, *grn* (R) 15.00 15.00
B26 A23 5s rose, *pale rose* 15.00 15.00
B27 A23 10s blk & org (R) 15.00 15.00
B28 A23 15s bl, *bluish* (R) 30.00 30.00
B29 A23 25s chocolate 100.00 100.00
B30 A23 50s ocher & blk (R) 225.00 225.00
Nos. B24-B30 (7) 415.00 415.00
Set, never hinged 625.00

Nos. B12-B30 were sold at an advance over face value, the excess being for the benefit of the Wild Tiger Corps. Counterfeits exist.

Nos. 170-172 Surcharged in Red

1939, Apr. 6 Unwmk. *Perf. 14*

B31 A22 5s + 5s on 1b 20.00 16.00
B32 A22 10s + 5s on 2b 25.00 24.00
B33 A22 15s + 5s on 3b 25.00 24.00
Nos. B31-B33 (3) 70.00 64.00
Set, never hinged 120.00

Founding of the Intl. Red Cross Soc., 75th anniv.

Bottom line of overprint is different on Nos. B32-B33.

AIR POST STAMPS

Garuda — AP1

1925 Unwmk. Engr. *Perf. 14, 14½*

C1 AP1 2s brown, *yel* 2.25 .50
C2 AP1 3s dark brown 2.25 .50
C3 AP1 5s green 11.00 .55
C4 AP1 10s black & org 20.00 .60
C5 AP1 15s carmine 18.50 1.00
C6 AP1 25s dark blue 12.50 1.20
C7 AP1 50s brown org & blk 40.00 7.50
C8 AP1 1b blue & brown 40.00 9.00
Nos. C1-C8 (8) 146.50 20.85
Set, never hinged 200.00

Issue dates: 2s, 50s, Apr. 21; others, Jan. 3.

Nos. C1-C8 received this overprint ("Government Museum 2468") in 1925, but were never issued. The death of King Vajiravudh caused cancellation of the fair at which this set was to have been released.

They were used during 1928 only in the interdepartmental service for accounting purposes of the money-order sections of various Bangkok post offices, and were never sold to the public. Values for set: unused, $1,400; used, $40.

1930-37 *Perf. 12½*

C9 AP1 2s brown, *yel* 7.50 .60
C10 AP1 5s green 1.75 .30
C11 AP1 10s black & org 6.00 .30
C12 AP1 15s carmine 24.00 6.00
C13 AP1 25s dark blue ('37) 3.00 .90
a. Vert. pair, imperf. btwn. 600.00
C14 AP1 50s brn org & blk ('37) 3.00 2.00
Nos. C9-C14 (6) 45.25 10.10
Set, never hinged 70.00

THRACE

'thrās

LOCATION — In southeastern Europe between the Black and Aegean Seas
GOVT. — Former Turkish Province
AREA — 89,361 sq. mi. (approx.)

Thrace underwent many political changes during the Balkan Wars and World War I. It was finally divided among Turkey, Greece and Bulgaria.

100 Lepta = 1 Drachma
40 Paras = 1 Piaster
100 Stotinki = 1 Leva (1919)

Giumulzina District Issue

Turkish Stamps of 1909 (#152-154)8 Surcharged in Blue or Red

1913 Unwmk. *Perf. 12, 13½*

1 A21 10 l on 20pa rose (Bl) 40.00 *50.00*
Never hinged 100.00
a. Inverted overprint 170.00
Never hinged 250.00
b. Double overprint 170.00
Never hinged 250.00
2 A21 25 l on 10pa bl grn 65.00 *72.50*
Never hinged 140.00
a. Inverted overprint 175.00
Never hinged 250.00
b. Double overprint 175.00
Never hinged 250.00
3 A21 25 l on 20pa rose (Bl) 65.00 *72.50*
Never hinged 140.00
a. Inverted overprint 170.00
Never hinged 250.00
b. Double overprint 170.00
Never hinged 250.00
c. Béhié ovpt. (#162) 200.00
Never hinged 300.00
4 A21 25 l on 1pi ultra 95.00 *120.00*
Never hinged 200.00
a. Inverted overprint 220.00
Never hinged 290.00
b. Double overprint 220.00
Never hinged 290.00
Nos. 1-4 (4) 265.00 315.00

Counterfeits exist of Nos. 1-4.

Eight other values exist, bearing surcharges differing in color or denomination from Nos. 1-4. These stamps were not issued. Values, each: unused $175; never hinged $350.

Turkish Inscriptions
A1 A2

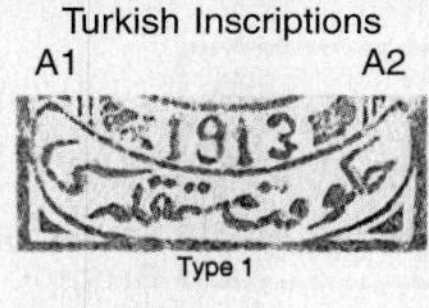

Type 1

Type 2

1913 Litho. *Imperf.*

Laid Paper

Control Mark in Rose

Without Gum

5 A1 1pi blue, type 1 17.00 17.00
a. Double print 250.00
b. Type 2 80.00 75.00
c. 1pi violet, type 1 30.00 25.00
d. 1pi gray, type 1 30.00 25.00
6 A1 2pi violet 17.00 17.00
a. Double print 500.00 190.00
b. Type 2 190.00

Wove Paper

c. 2pi blue, type 1 32.50 25.00
d. 2pi gray, type 1 32.50 25.00
7 A2 10pa vermilion 35.00 30.00
a. 10pa red 37.50 35.00
b. 10pa blue 55.00 45.00
c. 10pa violet 55.00 45.00
d. 10pa gray 55.00 45.00
8 A2 20pa blue 35.00 30.00
a. 20pa red 55.00 45.00
b. 20pa violet 55.00 45.00
c. 20pa gray 55.00 45.00
9 A2 1pi violet 37.50 30.00
Nos. 5-9 (5) 141.50 124.00

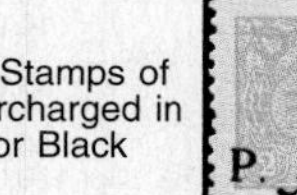

Turkish Stamps of 1913 Surcharged in Red or Black

1913 *Perf. 12*

10 A22 1pi on 2pa ol grn (R) 25.00 25.00
Never hinged 50.00
10A A22 1pi on 2pa ol grn 25.00 25.00
Never hinged 50.00
11 A22 1pi on 5pa ocher 25.00 25.00
Never hinged 50.00
11A A22 1pi on 5pa ocher (R) 25.00 25.00
Never hinged 50.00
12 A22 1pi on 20pa rose 32.50 32.50
Never hinged 65.00
13 A22 1pi on 5pi dk vio (R) 65.00 65.00
Never hinged 140.00
13A A22 1pi on 5pi dk vio 65.00 65.00
Never hinged 140.00
14 A22 1pi on 10pi dl red 110.00 *120.00*
Never hinged 225.00
15 A22 1pi on 25pi dk grn 475.00 *500.00*
Never hinged 1,000.
Nos. 10-15 (9) 847.50 882.50

On Nos. 13-15 the surcharge is vertical, reading up. No. 15 exists with double surcharge, one black, one red.

Nos. 10-15 exist with forged surcharges.

Bulgarian Stamps of 1911 Handstamped Surcharged in Red or Blue

1913

16 A20 10pa on 1s myr grn (R) 20.00 20.00
Never hinged 45.00
a. Top ovpt. inverted 100.00
b. Top ovpt. double 100.00
c. Top ovpt. omitted 150.00
d. Bottom ovpt. omitted 150.00
e. Bottom ovpt. inverted 100.00
17 A21 20pa on 2s car & blk 20.00 20.00
Never hinged 45.00
a. Inverted overprint 60.00
Never hinged 100.00
b. Inverted overprint, value omitted 85.00
Never hinged 160.00
c. Text ovpt omitted, value ovpt. inverted 150.00
d. Top ovpt. omitted, value inverted 200.00
e. Blue ovpt. omitted 175.00
f. Top ovpt. omitted, value normal 50.00
18 A23 1pi on 5s grn & blk (R) 20.00 20.00
Never hinged 45.00
a. Inverted overprint 125.00 125.00
b. Top ovpt. inverted 125.00
c. Double ovpt., one at top, one at bottom
19 A22 2pi on 3s lake & blk 28.00 28.00
Never hinged 55.00
a. Inverted overprint 80.00 80.00
Never hinged 165.00
20 A24 2½pi on 10s dp red & blk 40.00 40.00
Never hinged 80.00
a. Top ovpt. inverted 165.00
b. 2½pi on 2s 260.00
21 A25 5pi on 15s brn bis 70.00 70.00
Never hinged 145.00
a. Inverted overprint 260.00
b. Value inverted 250.00
Nos. 16-21 (6) 198.00 198.00

Same Surcharges on Greek Stamps

On Issue of 1911

1913 *Serrate Roulette 13½*

22 A24 10pa on 1 l grn (R) 22.50 22.50
Never hinged 45.00
23 A24 10pa on 1 l grn 23.00 23.00
Never hinged 45.00
24 A26 10pa on 5 l grn 110.00 110.00
Never hinged 225.00
25 A25 10pa on 25 l ultra (R) 32.50 32.50
Never hinged 50.00
26 A25 20pa on 2 l car rose 22.50 22.50
Never hinged 45.00
26A A25 20pa on 30 l car rose 140.00
27 A24 1pi on 3 l ver 22.50 22.50
Never hinged 45.00
a. Value omitted 65.00 65.00
Never hinged 135.00
b. Red overprint 22.50 22.50
Never hinged 45.00
27C A24 1pi on 10 l car rose 550.00
28 A26 2pi on 5 l grn (R) 60.00 60.00
Never hinged 135.00
29 A24 2½pi on 10 l car rose 60.00 60.00
Never hinged 135.00
30 A25 5pi on 40 l dp bl (R) 110.00 110.00
Never hinged 190.00
Nos. 22-30 (9) 463.00 463.00

On Occupation Stamps of 1912

31 O1 10pa on 1 l brn 20.00 15.00
Never hinged 40.00
a. Value omitted 100.00
b. Value srch. inverted 50.00
32 O1 20pa on 1 l brn 20.00 15.00
Never hinged 40.00
33 O1 1pi on 1 l brn 20.00 15.00
Never hinged 40.00
Nos. 31-33 (3) 60.00 45.00

These surcharges were made with handstamps, two of which were required for each surcharge. The upper handstamp, reads "Administration of Autonomous Western Thrace" in old Turkish. The lower handstamp expresses the new value. On horizontal designs, the text appears on the right, and the value appears on the left. On inverted overprints on horizontal stamps, this is reversed.

Nos. 16-33 exist with forged surcharges.

The 2pi on 1 l ovpt. as above was not issued. Value: $350.

OCCUPATION STAMPS

Issued under Allied Occupation

Bulgarian Stamps of 1915-19 Handstamped in Violet Blue

The overprint on Nos. N1-N6 is found in four positions: upright, reading from LL to UR; upright, reading from UL to LR; inverted, reading from UR to LL; inverted, LR to UL. On the 1s value, the usual position of the overprint is upright, reading from lower left to upper right; on the rest of the set, the overprint is usually inverted, reading from lower right to upper left.

Perf. 11½, 11½x12, 14

1919 Unwmk.

Overprint Inverted, reading from LR to UL

N1 A43 1s black 3.75 2.50
Never hinged 9.00
N2 A43 2s olive green 2.50 2.00
Never hinged 5.00
N3 A44 5s green .85 .85
Never hinged 1.75
N4 A44 10s rose .85 .85
Never hinged 1.75
N5 A44 15s violet .85 .85
Never hinged 1.75
N6 A26 25s indigo & black .85 .85
Never hinged 1.75
Nos. N1-N6 (6) 9.65 7.90
Nos. N1b-N6 (5) 5.90 5.40

Overprint Inverted, reading from UR to LL

N1a A43 1s black 3.75 2.50
Never hinged 9.00
N2a A43 2s olive green 3.75 2.50
Never hinged 9.00
N3a A44 5s green 8.50 8.50
Never hinged 17.50
N4a A44 10s rose 8.50 8.50
Never hinged 17.50
N5a A44 15s violet 8.50 8.50
Never hinged 17.50
N6a A26 25s indigo & black 8.50 8.50
Never hinged 17.50
Nos. N1a-N6a (6) 41.50 39.00

Overprint Upright, reading from LL to UR

N1b A43 1s black 2.50 2.00
Never hinged 5.00
N2b A43 2s olive green 3.75 2.50
Never hinged 9.00
N3b A44 5s green 8.50 8.50
Never hinged 17.50
N4b A44 10s rose 8.50 8.50
Never hinged 17.50
N5b A44 15s violet 8.50 8.50
Never hinged 17.50
N6b A26 25s indigo & black 8.50 8.50
Never hinged 17.50
Nos. N1b-N6b (6) 40.25 38.50

Overprint Upright, reading from UL to LR

N1c A43 1s black 3.75 2.50
Never hinged 9.00
N2c A43 2s olive green 3.75 2.50
Never hinged 9.00
N3c A44 5s green 8.50 8.50
Never hinged 17.50
N4c A44 10s rose 8.50 8.50
Never hinged 17.50
N5c A44 15s violet 8.50 8.50
Never hinged 17.50

N6c A26 25s indigo & black 8.50 8.50
Never hinged 17.50
Nos. N1c-N6c (6) 41.50 39.00

Bulgarian Stamps of 1911-19 Overprinted in Red or Black

1919

N7 A43 1s black (R) .25 .25
Never hinged .50
a. Second "L" in "INTERALLIÉE" inverted 5.00 5.00
Never hinged 7.50
b. "F" instead of final "E" in "INTERALLIEE" 5.00 5.00
Never hinged 7.50
N8 A43 2s olive green .25 .25
Never hinged .50
a. Second "L" in "INTERALLIÉE" inverted 5.00 5.00
Never hinged 7.50
b. "F" instead of final "E" in "INTERALLIEE" 5.00 5.00
Never hinged 7.50
c. Inverted ovpt. 40.00
Never hinged 80.00
N9 A44 5s green .25 .25
Never hinged .50
a. Second "L" in "INTERALLIÉE" inverted 5.00 5.00
Never hinged 7.50
b. "F" instead of final "E" in "INTERALLIEE" 5.00 5.00
Never hinged 7.50
c. Inverted ovpt.
d. Pair, one without ovpt.
e. Double ovpt. 40.00
Never hinged 80.00
N10 A44 10s rose .25 .25
Never hinged .50
a. Second "L" in "INTERALLIÉE" inverted 5.00 5.00
Never hinged 7.50
b. "F" instead of final "E" in "INTERALLIEE" 5.00 5.00
Never hinged 7.50
c. Inverted ovpt. 30.00
Never hinged 45.00
d. Pair, one without ovpt.
e. Double ovpt. 26.50
Never hinged 45.00
N11 A44 15s violet .25 .25
Never hinged .50
a. Second "L" in "INTERALLIÉE" inverted 5.00 5.00
Never hinged 7.50
b. "F" instead of final "E" in "INTERALLIEE" 5.00 5.00
Never hinged 7.50
N12 A26 25s indigo & black .25 .25
Never hinged .50
N13 A29 1 l chocolate 4.75 5.00
Never hinged 10.00
N14 A37a 2 l brown orange 8.50 9.00
Never hinged 18.00
N15 A38 3 l claret 11.00 12.50
Never hinged 25.00
a. Double overprint 25.00
Never hinged 50.00
Nos. N7-N15 (9) 25.75 28.00

Overprint is vertical, reading up, on Nos. N9-N13.

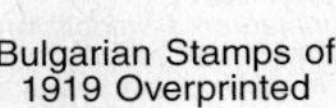

Bulgarian Stamps of 1919 Overprinted

1920

N16 A44 5s green .25 .25
Never hinged .50
a. Second "e" of "Interalliée" inverted 3.00 3.00
Never hinged 6.00
b. "i" for second "l" in "Interalliée" 3.00 3.00
Never hinged 6.00
c. "r" for "n" in "Interalliée" 3.00 3.00
Never hinged 6.00
d. Imperf, pair 67.50
Never hinged 120.00
N17 A44 10s rose .25 .25
Never hinged .50
a. Second "e" of "Interalliée" inverted 3.00 3.00
Never hinged 6.00
b. "i" for second "l" in "Interalliée" 3.00 3.00
Never hinged 6.00
c. "r" for "n" in "Interalliée" 3.00 3.00
Never hinged 6.00
N18 A44 15s violet .25 .25
Never hinged .50
a. Second "e" of "Interalliée" inverted 3.00 3.00
Never hinged 6.00
b. "i" for second "l" in "Interalliée" 3.00 3.00
Never hinged 6.00
c. "r" for "n" in "Interalliée" 3.00 3.00
Never hinged 6.00
N19 A44 50s yel brn, ovpt. reading up 1.50 1.50
Never hinged 3.00
a. Second "e" of "Interalliée" inverted 3.00 3.00
Never hinged 6.00
b. "i" for second "l" in "Interalliée" 3.00 3.00
Never hinged 6.00
c. "r" for "n" in "Interalliée" 3.00 3.00
Never hinged 6.00
d. Ovpt. reading down 22.50 *32.50*
Never hinged 45.00
e. As "d," second "e" of "Interalliée" inverted 3.00 3.00
Never hinged 6.00
f. As "d," "i" for second "l" in "Interalliée" 3.00 3.00
Never hinged 6.00
g. As "d," "r" for "n" in "Interalliée" 3.00 3.00
Never hinged 6.00
h. As "d," imperf, pair 130.00
Nos. N16-N19 (4) 2.25 2.25

Various typographical errors in the overprint are found on all values.

Bulgarian Stamps of 1919 Overprinted

1920 ***Perf. 12x11½***

N20 A44 5s green .25 .25
Never hinged .60
a. Inverted overprint 30.00 *50.00*
Never hinged 50.00
b. Pair, one without ovpt. 40.00 *65.00*
Never hinged 65.00
c. Imperf, pair 45.00 *65.00*
Never hinged 65.00
d. As "c," inverted overprint 55.00 *75.00*
Never hinged 75.00
N21 A44 10s rose .25 .25
Never hinged .60
a. Inverted overprint 27.00 *37.50*
Never hinged 37.50
b. Double ovpt., one on gum side 45.00 *65.00*
Never hinged 65.00
c. Imperf, pair 45.00 *65.00*
Never hinged 65.00
d. As "c," inverted overprint 55.00 *75.00*
Never hinged 75.00
N22 A44 15s violet .25 .25
Never hinged .60
a. Inverted overprint 27.00 *37.50*
Never hinged 37.50
b. Imperf, pair 45.00 *65.00*
Never hinged 65.00
c. As "b," inverted overprint 55.00 *75.00*
Never hinged 75.00
N23 A44 25s deep blue .25 .25
Never hinged .60
a. Inverted overprint 27.00 *37.50*
Never hinged 37.50
b. Imperf, pair 45.00 *65.00*
Never hinged 65.00
c. As "b," inverted overprint 55.00 *75.00*
Never hinged 75.00
d. Double ovpt., one on gummed side 45.00
N24 A44 50s ocher .25 .25
Never hinged .60
a. Inverted overprint 30.00 *50.00*
Never hinged 50.00
b. Imperf, pair 45.00 65.00
c. As "b," inverted ovpt. 55.00 80.00

Imperf

N25 A44 30s chocolate 1.50 1.50
Never hinged 3.50
a. Inverted overprint 32.50 *55.00*
Never hinged 50.00
b. Perforated 20.00
Never hinged 40.00
Nos. N20-N25 (6) 2.75 2.75

No. N25 is not known without overprint.

ISSUED UNDER GREEK OCCUPATION

Counterfeits exist of Nos. N26-N84.

For Use in Western Thrace

Greek Stamps of 1911-19 Overprinted "Administration Western Thrace" in Greek

Serrate Roulette 13½

1920 **Litho.** **Unwmk.**

N26 A24 1 l green .25 *.25*
Never hinged .50
a. Inverted overprint 17.50
Never hinged 40.00
b. Double overprint 17.50
Never hinged 40.00
c. Double overprint, one inverted 70.00
Never hinged 140.00
d. Ovptd Line 2/Line 3/Line 2 15.00 12.00
Never hinged 30.00
e. Ovptd Line 1/Line 1/Line 3 15.00 12.00
Never hinged 30.00
N27 A25 2 l rose .25 *.25*
Never hinged .50
a. Ovptd Line 2/Line 3/Line 2 15.00 12.00
Never hinged 30.00
b. Ovptd Line 1/Line 1/Line 3 15.00 12.00
Never hinged 30.00
N28 A24 3 l vermilion .25 *.25*
Never hinged .50
a. Inverted overprint 27.50
Never hinged 60.00
b. Ovptd Line 2/Line 3/Line 2 15.00 12.00
Never hinged 30.00
c. Ovptd Line 1/Line 1/Line 3 15.00 12.00
Never hinged 30.00
N29 A26 5 l green .25 *.25*
Never hinged .50
a. Inverted overprint 22.50
Never hinged 50.00
b. Double overprint 22.50
Never hinged 50.00
N30 A24 10 l rose .40 *.85*
Never hinged .60
N31 A25 15 l dull blue .40 *.75*
Never hinged .60
a. Inverted overprint 17.50
Never hinged 40.00
b. Double overprint 17.50
Never hinged 40.00
c. Dbl. ovpt., one inverted 27.50
Never hinged 50.00
N32 A25 25 l blue .40 *.85*
Never hinged .60
N34 A25 40 l indigo 1.90 *4.00*
Never hinged 4.00
N35 A26 50 l violet brn 1.90 *6.00*
Never hinged 4.00
N36 A27 1d ultra 8.50 *15.00*
Never hinged 18.00
a. Double overprint 60.00
Never hinged 120.00
N37 A27 2d vermilion 27.50 *35.00*
Never hinged 55.00
a. Double overprint 75.00
Never hinged 150.00
Nos. N26-N37 (11) 42.00 *63.45*

The 20 l value with this overprint was not issued. Values: unused $25; never hinged $65.

Engr.

N38 A25 2 l car rose .85 1.00
Never hinged 2.00
N39 A24 3 l vermilion .85 1.00
Never hinged 2.00
N39A A25 20 l slate 26.00
Never hinged 60.00
N39B A25 25 l blue 30.00
Never hinged 70.00
N39C A25 30 l rose 40.00
Never hinged 80.00
N40 A27 1d ultra 27.50 25.00
Never hinged 60.00
N41 A27 2d vermilion 40.00 35.00
Never hinged 80.00
N42 A27 3d car rose 60.00 *80.00*
Never hinged 125.00
N43 A27 5d ultra 24.50 *30.00*
Never hinged 50.00
N44 A27 10d deep blue 23.50 *30.00*
Never hinged 50.00
a. Double overprint 300.00
Never hinged 500.00
Nos. N38-N44 (10) 273.20

Nos. N38-N44 were not issued. Values for used examples of Nos. N38-N39 and N40-N44 are for cancelled-to-order stamps.

Nos. N42-N44 are overprinted on the reissues of Greece Nos. 210-212. See footnote below Greece No. 213.

Overprinted

N45 A28 25d deep blue 60.00 35.00
Never hinged 125.00

No. N45 was not issued. Used value is for an example canceled-to-order.

With Additional Overprint

Litho.

N46 A24 1 l green 4.50 3.50
Never hinged 10.00
N47 A25 2 l rose .25 *.50*
Never hinged .50
a. Inverted overprint 60.00
Never hinged 90.00
c. Double overprint 75.00
Never hinged 125.00
N47B A26 5 l green 25.00
Never hinged 50.00
N48 A24 10 l rose .60 *.80*
Never hinged 1.25
a. Inverted overprint 17.50
Never hinged 35.00
N49 A25 20 l slate .60 *.80*
Never hinged 1.25
a. Inverted overprint 17.50
Never hinged 35.00
N49B A25 25 l blue 45.00
Never hinged 95.00
N50 A26 30 l rose (#240) .60 *1.00*
Never hinged 1.25

Engr.

N50A A26 30 l rose (#244) 75.00
Never hinged 150.00
N51 A27 2d vermilion 35.00 30.00
Never hinged 75.00
N52 A27 3d car rose 45.00 30.00
Never hinged 90.00
N53 A27 5d ultra 40.00 32.50
Never hinged 85.00
N54 A27 10d deep blue 35.00 22.50
Never hinged 70.00
Nos. N46-N54 (12) 306.55 *121.60*

Nos. N46, N47B, N49B, N50A, N51, N53 and N54 were not issued. Used values for Nos. N46, N51, N53 and N54 are for canceled-to-order stamps.

For Use in Eastern and Western Thrace

Greek Stamps of 1911-19 Overprinted "Administration Thrace" in Greek

1920 **Litho.**

N55 A24 1 l green .25 *1.00*
Never hinged .50
a. Inverted overprint 13.50
Never hinged 30.00
b. Double overprint 13.50
Never hinged 30.00
N56 A25 2 l rose .25 *.50*
Never hinged .50
a. Inverted overprint 11.00
Never hinged 25.00
b. Double overprint 13.50
Never hinged 30.00
c. Triple overprint 25.00
Never hinged 45.00
d. Vert. pair, top stamp without ovpt., never hinged 55.00
N57 A24 3 l vermilion .25 *.50*
Never hinged .50
a. Inverted overprint 11.00
Never hinged 25.00
b. Double overprint 13.50
Never hinged 30.00
c. Double overprint, one inverted 16.50
Never hinged 35.00
N58 A26 5 l green .25 *.50*
Never hinged .50
a. Inverted overprint 20.00
Never hinged 40.00
b. Double overprint 35.00
Never hinged 70.00
N59 A24 10 l rose .50 *.75*
Never hinged 1.00
a. Double overprint 80.00
Never hinged 165.00
N59B A25 15 l dull blue 60.00
Never hinged 120.00
a. Inverted overprint 60.00
Never hinged 100.00
N60 A25 20 l slate .65 *1.30*
Never hinged 1.25
a. Inverted overprint 16.50
Never hinged 35.00
b. Double overprint 13.50
Never hinged 30.00
N61 A25 25 l blue 1.60 *2.50*
Never hinged 3.75
N62 A25 40 l indigo 2.25 *7.00*
Never hinged 5.00
N63 A26 50 l violet brn 3.00 *6.50*
Never hinged 5.00
N64 A27 1d ultra 15.00 *30.00*
Never hinged 30.00
N65 A27 2d vermilion 32.50 *45.00*
Never hinged 65.00

Engr.

N65A A25 2 l rose 2.25 *4.00*
Never hinged 5.00
N66 A24 3 l vermilion 2.25 *4.00*
Never hinged 5.00
N67 A25 20 l gray lilac 7.00 *22.50*
Never hinged 15.00
N68 A28 25d deep blue 70.00 *100.00*
Never hinged 140.00
Nos. N55-N68 (16) 198.00 *226.05*

Nos. N59B and N65A-N68 were not issued. Used values for Nos. N65A-N68 are for canceled-to-order stamps.

With Additional Overprint

Litho.

N68A A24 1 l green 12.50 *6.00*
Never hinged 25.00
N69 A25 2 l car rose .25 *.50*
Never hinged .50
a. Inverted overprint 35.00
Never hinged 70.00
b. Double overprint 30.00
Never hinged 60.00
N70 A26 5 l green 7.50 *8.00*
Never hinged 15.00
N71 A25 20 l slate .25 *.50*
Never hinged .50
a. Double overprint 350.00 325.00
N72 A26 30 l rose .25 *.50*
Never hinged .50

Engr.

N73 A27 3d car rose 15.00 *25.00*
Never hinged 30.00
a. Inverted overprint —
N74 A27 5d ultra 25.00 *45.00*
Never hinged 50.00
N75 A27 10d deep blue 40.00 *60.00*
Never hinged 85.00
Nos. N68A-N75 (8) 100.75 *145.50*

Nos. N68A, N70 and N74-N75 were not issued. Used values are for canceled-to-order stamps.

Turkish Stamps of 1916-20 Srchd. in Blue, Black or Red

1920 ***Perf. 11½, 12½***

N76 A43 1 l on 5pa org (Bl) .35 *.50*
Never hinged .80
a. Inverted overprint 32.50 35.00
Never hinged 70.00
b. Double overprint 27.50 30.00
Never hinged 60.00
c. Double overprint, one inverted 50.00 50.00
Never hinged 100.00
d. Double overprint, one on gummed side 35.00
Never hinged 70.00
N77 A32 5 l on 3pi blue .35 *.50*
Never hinged .80
a. Inverted overprint 100.00 100.00
Never hinged 200.00
b. Double overprint 67.50 70.00
Never hinged 140.00
N78 A30 20 l on 1pi bl grn .55 *.75*
Never hinged 1.10
a. Inverted overprint 27.50 27.50
Never hinged 55.00
b. Double overprint 27.50 27.50
Never hinged 55.00
c. Double overprint, one inverted 40.00 40.00
Never hinged 75.00
d. Double overprint, one on gummed side 37.50
Never hinged 75.00
N79 A53 25 l on 5pi on 2pa Prus bl (R) .75 *.90*
Never hinged 1.60
a. Inverted overprint 47.50 50.00
Never hinged 100.00
b. Double overprint 47.50 50.00
Never hinged 100.00
N80 A49 50 l on 5pi bl & blk (R) 6.00 *7.00*
Never hinged 12.00
N81 A45 1d on 20pa dp rose (Bl) 1.60 1.50
Never hinged 3.50
a. Double overprint 37.50 40.00
Never hinged 80.00
N82 A22 2d on 10pa on 2pa ol grn (R) 2.00 *2.50*
Never hinged 4.00
a. Double overprint 60.00 60.00
Never hinged 120.00
N83 A57 3d on 1pi dp bl (R) 11.00 11.00
Never hinged 22.00
a. Inverted overprint 60.00 60.00
Never hinged 120.00
b. Double overprint 65.00 65.00
Never hinged 130.00
N84 A23 5d on 20pa rose 10.00 10.00
Never hinged 20.00
a. Inverted overprint 75.00 70.00
Never hinged 135.00
b. Double overprint, one inverted 75.00 70.00
Never hinged 135.00
Nos. N76-N84 (9) 32.60 34.65

On Nos. N83 and N84, the normal overprint is reading down. On the inverted overprints, it is reading up.

Nos. N77, N78 and N84 are on the 1920 issue with designs modified. Nos. N81, N82 and N83 are on stamps with the 1919 overprints.

POSTAGE DUE STAMPS

Issued under Allied Occupation

1919 Bulgarian Postage Due Stamps Overprinted, Reading Vertically Up

1919 **Unwmk.** ***Perf. 12x11½***

NJ1 D6 5s emerald .35 .50
Never hinged .90
a. Second "L" in "INTERALLIÉE" inverted 6.00 6.00
Never hinged 12.00
b. "F" instead of final "E" in "INTERALLIEE" 16.50 11.50
Never hinged 32.50
NJ2 D6 10s purple .85 1.00
Never hinged 1.75
a. Second "L" in "INTERALLIÉE" inverted 6.00 6.00
Never hinged 12.00
b. "F" instead of final "E" in "INTERALLIEE" 25.00 16.50
Never hinged 50.00
NJ3 D6 50s blue 2.60 3.00
Never hinged 5.25
a. Second "L" in "INTERALLIÉE" inverted 52.50 32.50
Never hinged 100.00
b. "F" instead of final "E" in "INTERALLIEE" 52.50 32.50
Never hinged 100.00
Nos. NJ1-NJ3 (3) 3.80 4.50

Type of Bulgarian Postage Due Stamps of 1919-22 Overprinted

1920 ***Imperf.***

NJ4 D6 5s emerald .25 .50
Never hinged .50
a. Inverted overprint 40.00
Never hinged 60.00
NJ5 D6 10s deep violet 2.00 2.00
Never hinged 4.00
a. Inverted overprint 40.00
Never hinged 60.00
NJ6 D6 20s salmon 1.00 1.00
NJ7 D6 50s blue 1.50 1.50
Never hinged 3.00

Perf. 12x11½

NJ8 D6 10s deep violet 1.25 1.25
Never hinged 2.50
Nos. NJ4-NJ8 (5) 6.00 6.25

No. NJ6 issued without gum.

TIBET

tə-'bet

LOCATION — A high tableland in Central Asia
GOVT. — A semi-independent state, nominally under control of China.
AREA — 463,200 sq. mi.
POP. — 1,500,000 (approx.)
CAPITAL — Lhasa

Tibet's postage stamps were valid only within its borders.

6 2/3 Trangka = 1 Sang

Excellent counterfeits of Nos. 1-18 exist. Numerous shades of all values.

All stamps issued without gum.

Small bits of foreign matter (inclusions) are to be expected in Native Paper. These do not reduce the value of the stamp unless they have caused serious damage to the design or paper.

A1

1912-50 **Unwmk.** **Typo.** ***Imperf.***

Native Paper

1 A1 ⅙t green 40.00 *45.00*
2 A1 ⅓t blue 40.00 *55.00*
a. ⅓t ultramarine 50.00 *60.00*
3 A1 ½t violet 40.00 *55.00*
4 A1 ⅔t carmine 50.00 *60.00*
a. "POTSAGE" 150.00 *175.00*
5 A1 1t vermilion 55.00 *75.00*
6 A1 1s sage green ('50) 100.00 *110.00*
Nos. 1-6 (6) 325.00 *400.00*

The "POTSAGE" error is found on all shades of the ⅔t (positions 6 and 7).

Pin-perf. examples of Nos. 1 and 3 exist.

Issued in sheets of 12.

Beware of private reproductions of #1-5 that were printed in the US around 1986. Sheets of 12 bear "J. Crow Co." imprint. The set of 5 sheets was sold for $5.

Printed Using Shiny Enamel Paint

1920

1a A1 ⅙t green 60.00 40.00
2b A1 ⅓t blue 500.00 500.00
3d A1 ½t purple 100.00 *110.00*
4h A1 ⅔t carmine 100.00 *110.00*
i. "POTSAGE" *225.00 250.00*
5c A1 1t carmine 350.00 400.00

In some 1920-30 printings, European enamel paint was used instead of ink. It has a glossy surface.

Lion — A2

1914

7 A2 4t milky blue 750. *850.*
a. 4t dark blue 1,100. 1,100.
8 A2 8t carmine rose 165. 175.
a. 8t carmine 1,100. *1,100.*

Issued in sheets of 6.

Printed Using Shiny Enamel Paint

1920

7b A2 4t blue 1,350. *1,500.*
8b A2 8t carmine 1,350. *1,500.*

See note following No. 5c.

A3

Thin White Native Paper

1933 ***Pin-perf.***

9 A3 ½t orange 95.00 *100.00*
10 A3 ⅔t dark blue 95.00 *120.00*
11 A3 1t rose carmine 95.00 *120.00*
12 A3 2t scarlet 95.00 *120.00*
13 A3 4t emerald 95.00 *120.00*
Nos. 9-13 (5) 475.00 *580.00*

Issued in sheets of 12.

Exist imperf.

Heavy Toned Native Paper

1934 ***Imperf.***

14 A3 ½t yellow 16.00 *18.00*
15 A3 ⅔t blue 14.00 *15.00*
16 A3 1t orange ver 14.00 *15.00*
a. 1t carmine 16.00 *18.00*
17 A3 2t red 14.00 *15.00*
a. 2t orange vermilion 14.00 *15.00*
18 A3 4t green 14.00 *15.00*
a. 25x25mm instead of 24x24mm 55.00 *65.00*
Nos. 14-18 (5) 72.00 *78.00*

Nos. 14-18 are also known with a private pin-perf.

The ½t and 1t exist printed on both sides.

Issued in sheets of 12.

TIMOR

'tē-ˌmor

LOCATION — The eastern part of Timor island, Malay archipelago
GOVT. — Portuguese Overseas Territory
AREA — 7,330 sq. mi.
POP. — 660,000 (est. 1974)
CAPITAL — Dili

1000 Reis = 1 Milreis
78 Avos = 1 Rupee (1895)
100 Avos = 1 Pataca

Watermark

Wmk. 232 — Maltese Cross

Stamps of Macao Overprinted in Black or Carmine

1885 **Unwmk.** ***Perf. 12½, 13½***

1 A1 5r black (C) 6.00 1.60
a. Double overprint 85.00 85.00
b. Triple overprint 200.00
2 A1 10r green 8.00 3.50
a. Overprint on Mozambique stamp *25.00 14.00*
b. Overprinted on Portuguese India stamp *300.00 150.00*
3 A1 20r rose, perf. 13½ 9.00 4.50
a. Double overprint 35.00
b. Perf. 12½ 12.00 7.50
4 A1 25r violet 4.00 1.10
a. Perf. 13½ 45.00 22.50
5 A1 40r yellow 6.00 3.00
a. Double overprint 25.00
b. Inverted overprint *42.50 27.50*
c. Perf. 13½ 15.00 15.00
6 A1 50r blue 10.00 2.50
a. Perf. 13½ 22.50 15.00
7 A1 80r slate 15.00 5.00
8 A1 100r lilac 8.00 1.75
a. Double overprint 30.00
b. Perf. 13½ 12.50 5.00
9 A1 200r org, perf. 13½ 12.50 4.75
a. Perf. 12½ 15.00 7.50
10 A1 300r brown 10.00 3.50
Nos. 1-10 (10) 88.50 31.20

The 20r bister, 25r rose and 50r green were prepared for use but not issued.

The reprints are printed on a smooth white chalky paper, ungummed, with rough perforation 13½, and on thin white paper with shiny white gum and clean-cut perforation 13½.

King Luiz — A2

1887 **Embossed** ***Perf. 12½***

11 A2 5r black 2.50 1.90
12 A2 10r green 4.00 3.00
13 A2 20r bright rose 4.25 3.00
14 A2 25r violet 8.00 3.50
15 A2 40r chocolate 14.00 5.25
16 A2 50r blue 15.00 6.00
17 A2 80r gray 16.50 8.00
18 A2 100r yellow brown 25.00 10.50
19 A2 200r gray lilac 37.50 17.50
20 A2 300r orange 37.50 20.00
Nos. 11-20 (10) 164.25 78.65

Reprints of Nos. 11, 16, 18 and 19 have clean-cut perforation 13½.

For surcharges see Nos. 34-43, 83-91.

Macao No. 44 Surcharged in Black

1892 Without Gum *Perf. 12½, 13*
21 A7 30r on 300r orange 12.00 6.75

For surcharge see No. 44.

King Carlos — A3

1894 Typo. *Perf. 11½*
22 A3 5r yellow 1.75 .65
23 A3 10r red violet 2.00 .65
24 A3 15r chocolate 3.00 .95
25 A3 20r lavender 3.75 1.10
26 A3 25r green 4.50 .80
27 A3 50r light blue 5.75 3.50
a. Perf. 13½ 160.00 125.00
28 A3 75r rose 7.25 2.75
29 A3 80r light green 7.75 4.25
30 A3 100r brown, *buff* 5.75 2.75
31 A3 150r car, *rose* 13.00 8.00
32 A3 200r dk bl, *lt bl* 13.50 10.50
33 A3 300r dk bl, *salmon* 15.00 12.00
Nos. 22-33 (12) 83.00 47.90

For surcharges and overprints see Nos. 92-102, 120-122, 124-128, 131-133, 183-193, 199.

Stamps of 1887 Surcharged in Red, Green or Black

1895 Without Gum *Perf. 12½*
34 A2 1a on 5r black (R) 4.00 .85
35 A2 2a on 10r green 4.00 .85
a. Double surcharge 25.00
36 A2 3a on 20r brt rose (G) 6.00 1.75
37 A2 4a on 25r violet 6.00 1.10
38 A2 6a on 40r choc 8.00 3.00
39 A2 8a on 50r blue (R) 6.00 2.25
40 A2 13a on 80r gray 15.50 10.00
41 A2 16a on 100r yellow brn 20.00 7.75
42 A2 31a on 200r gray lilac 32.50 20.00
43 A2 47a on 300r org (G) 35.00 22.50
Nos. 34-43 (10) 137.00 70.05

No. 21 Surcharged

1895 Without Gum *Perf. 12½, 13*
44 A7 5a on 30r on 300r org 30.00 7.50

Common Design Types pictured following the introduction.

Vasco da Gama Issue
Common Design Types

1898 Engr. *Perf. 14 to 15*
45 CD20 ½a blue green 1.25 .70
46 CD21 1a red 1.25 .70
47 CD22 2a red violet 1.25 .70
48 CD23 4a yellow green 1.25 .70
49 CD24 8a dark blue 2.75 1.10
50 CD25 12a violet brown 3.25 1.25
51 CD26 16a bister brown 3.75 1.60
52 CD27 24a bister 4.75 2.00
Nos. 45-52 (8) 19.50 8.75

400th anniversary of Vasco da Gama's discovery of the route to India.
For overprints and surcharge see Nos. 148-155.

King Carlos — A5

1898-1903 Typo. *Perf. 11½*
Name & Value in Black Except #79
53 A5 ½a gray .35 .25
a. Perf. 12½ 2.50 1.75
54 A5 1a orange .35 .30
a. Perf. 12½ 2.50 1.75
55 A5 2a light green .35 .30
56 A5 2½a brown 1.25 1.10
57 A5 3a gray violet 1.25 1.10
58 A5 3a gray green ('03) 1.50 1.00
59 A5 4a sea green 1.60 1.00
60 A5 5a rose ('03) 1.50 1.00
61 A5 6a pale yel brn ('03) 1.50 1.00
62 A5 8a blue 2.00 1.10
63 A5 9a red brown ('03) 1.50 1.25
64 A5 10a slate blue ('00) 2.00 1.10
65 A5 10a gray brown ('03) 1.50 1.00
66 A5 12a rose 4.25 3.00
67 A5 12a dull blue ('03) 22.50 9.00
68 A5 13a violet 4.50 3.75
69 A5 13a red lilac ('03) 3.50 1.75
70 A5 15a gray lilac ('03) 5.50 3.75
71 A5 16a dark bl, *bl* 4.50 3.75
72 A5 20a brn, *yelsh* ('00) 8.00 3.75
73 A5 22a brn org, *pink* ('03) 8.00 3.50
74 A5 24a brown, *buff* 7.00 3.75
75 A5 31a red lil, *pinkish* 7.00 3.75
76 A5 31a brn, *straw* ('03) 10.00 3.50
77 A5 47a dk blue, *rose* 12.00 4.25
78 A5 47a red vio, *pink* ('03) 10.00 3.50
79 A5 78a blk & red, *bl* ('00) 15.00 6.75
80 A5 78a dl bl, *straw* ('03) 20.00 10.00
Nos. 53-80 (28) 158.40 79.25

Most of Nos. 53-80 were issued without gum.
For surcharges & overprints see #81-82, 104-119, 129-130, 134-147, 195-196.

King Carlos — A6

1899 Black Surcharge
81 A6 10a on 16a dk bl, *bl* 3.75 2.50
82 A6 20a on 31a red lil, *pnksh* 3.75 2.50

Surcharged in Black

1902 On Issue of 1887
83 A2 5a on 25r violet 2.50 1.75
84 A2 5a on 200r gray lil 4.00 2.50
85 A2 6a on 10r blue grn 110.00 60.00
86 A2 6a on 300r orange 3.75 3.50
87 A2 9a on 40r choc 4.50 3.50
88 A2 9a on 100r yel brn 4.50 3.50
89 A2 15a on 20r rose 4.50 3.50
90 A2 15a on 50r blue 110.00 60.00
91 A2 22a on 80r gray 8.75 6.50
Nos. 83-91 (9) 252.50 144.75

Reprints of Nos. 83-88, 90-91, 104A have clean-cut perf. 13½.

On Issue of 1894
92 A3 5a on 5r yellow 2.00 1.00
a. Inverted surcharge 40.00 30.00
93 A3 5a on 25r green 3.00 1.00
94 A3 5a on 50r lt blue 3.00 1.25
95 A3 6a on 20r lavender 3.00 1.25
96 A3 9a on 15r choc 3.00 1.25
97 A3 9a on 75r rose 3.00 1.25
98 A3 15a on 10r red vio 4.00 2.00
99 A3 15a on 100r brn, *buff* 4.00 2.00
100 A3 15a on 300r bl, *sal* 4.00 2.00
101 A3 22a on 80r lt green 6.00 3.50
102 A3 22a on 200r bl, *blue* 8.00 3.50

On Newspaper Stamp of 1893
103 N2 6a on 2½r brn 1.00 .85
a. Inverted surcharge 27.50 27.50
Nos. 92-103 (12) 44.00 20.85

Nos. 93-97, 99-102 issued without gum.

Stamps of 1898 Overprinted in Black

104 A5 3a gray violet 4.00 1.90
104A A5 12a rose 6.00 3.75

Reprint noted after No. 91.

No. 67 Surcharged in Black

1905
105 A5 10a on 12a dull blue 8.25 4.25

Stamps of 1898-1903 Overprinted in Carmine or Green

1911
106 A5 ½a gray .30 .30
a. Inverted overprint 20.00 20.00
107 A5 1a orange .30 .30
a. Perf. 12½ 16.00 16.00
108 A5 2a light green .40 .35
109 A5 3a gray green .50 .35
110 A5 5a rose (G) .50 .35
111 A5 6a yel brown .50 .35
112 A5 9a red brown .75 .45
113 A5 10a gray brown .75 .45
114 A5 13a red lilac .80 .50
115 A5 15a gray lilac 1.60 1.25
116 A5 22a brn org, *pink* 1.60 1.25
117 A5 31a brown, *straw* 1.60 1.25
118 A5 47a red vio, *pink* 3.00 2.50
119 A5 78a dl bl, *straw* 4.75 3.50
Nos. 106-119 (14) 17.35 13.15

Preceding Issues Overprinted in Red

1913 Without Gum
On Provisional Issue of 1902
120 A3 5a on 5r yellow 8.00 4.00
121 A3 5a on 25r green 8.00 4.00
122 A3 5a on 50r lt bl 9.00 7.00
123 N2 6a on 2½r brn 9.00 7.00
124 A3 6a on 20r lavender 8.00 4.00
125 A3 9a on 15r choc 8.00 4.00
126 A3 15a on 100r brn, *buff* 9.00 5.50
127 A3 22a on 80r lt grn 10.00 8.00
128 A3 22a on 200r bl, *bl* 9.00 7.50

On Issue of 1903
129 A5 3a gray green 9.00 *7.50*

On Issue of 1905
130 A5 10a on 12a dull bl 10.00 4.00
Nos. 120-130 (11) 97.00 *62.50*

Overprinted in Green or Red

On Provisional Issue of 1902

1913
131 A3 9a on 75r rose (G) 8.00 6.00
132 A3 15a on 10r red vio (G) 7.00 5.00
a. Inverted overprint *35.00 35.00*
133 A3 15a on 300r bl, *sal* (R) 11.00 8.00
a. "REUBPLICA" 19.00 19.00
b. "REPBLICAU" 19.00 19.00

On Issue of 1903
134 A5 5a rose (G) 6.00 4.00
Nos. 131-134 (4) 32.00 23.00

Stamps of 1898-1903 Overprinted in Red

1913
135 A5 6a yellow brown 6.00 1.75
136 A5 9a red brown 6.00 1.75
137 A5 10a gray brown 6.00 1.75
138 A5 13a violet 7.00 2.50
a. Inverted overprint 40.00 40.00
139 A5 13a red lilac 7.00 2.50
140 A5 15a gray lilac 7.00 3.25
141 A5 22a brn org, *pnksh* 7.00 3.50
142 A5 31a red lil, *pnksh* 8.00 3.50
143 A5 31a brown, *straw* 10.00 5.50
144 A5 47a blue, *pink* 11.00 5.50
145 A5 47a red vio, *pink* 12.00 8.00
146 A5 78a dl bl, *straw* 18.00 6.50

No. 79 Overprinted in Red

147 A5 78a blk & red, *bl* 20.00 8.00
Nos. 135-147 (13) 125.00 54.00

Vasco da Gama Issue of 1898 Overprinted or Surcharged in Black

1913
148 CD20 ½a blue green 1.00 .60
149 CD21 1a red 1.00 .60
150 CD22 2a red violet 1.00 .60
151 CD23 4a yellow green 1.00 .60
152 CD24 8a dark blue 2.00 1.10
153 CD25 10a on 12a vio brn 3.00 2.00
154 CD26 16a bister brown 3.00 1.75
155 CD27 24a bister 3.00 2.25
Nos. 148-155 (8) 15.00 9.50

Ceres — A7

Name and Value in Black
Chalky Paper

1914 Typo. *Perf. 15x14*
156 A7 ½a olive brown .25 .25
Never hinged .40
157 A7 1a black .25 .25
Never hinged .40
158 A7 2a blue green .25 .25
Never hinged .40
159 A7 3a lilac brown 1.00 .75
Never hinged 1.60
160 A7 4a carmine 1.00 .75
Never hinged 1.60
161 A7 6a light violet 1.00 .75
Never hinged 1.60
162 A7 10a deep blue 1.25 .75
Never hinged 2.00
163 A7 12a yellow brown 1.50 1.25
Never hinged 2.40
164 A7 16a slate 2.25 4.25
Never hinged 3.50
165 A7 20a org brown 18.00 6.75
Never hinged 26.00
166 A7 40a plum 13.00 5.00
Never hinged 16.00
167 A7 58a brown, *grn* 14.00 7.25
Never hinged 17.50
168 A7 76a brown, *rose* 15.00 7.25
Never hinged 21.00
169 A7 1p org, *salmon* 24.50 12.50
Never hinged 40.00
170 A7 3p green, *blue* 40.00 27.50
Never hinged 65.00
Nos. 156-170 (15) 133.25 75.50

For surcharges see Nos. 200-201, MR1.

1920
Ordinary Paper
171 A7 1a black .60 .45
Never hinged 1.00
172 A7 2a blue green .60 .45
Never hinged 1.00

1922-26 *Perf. 12x11½*
173 A7 ½a olive brown .45 .40
Never hinged .70

No.	Type	Description	Unused	Used
174	A7	1a black	.45	.40
		Never hinged	1.00	
175	A7	1½a yel grn ('23)	.60	*1.10*
		Never hinged	1.00	
176	A7	2a blue green	.45	.40
		Never hinged	.70	
177	A7	4a carmine	2.75	2.00
		Never hinged	4.50	
178	A7	7a lt green ('23)	1.75	*1.75*
		Never hinged	2.75	
179	A7	7½a ultra ('23)	3.25	*3.50*
		Never hinged	5.25	
180	A7	9a blue ('23)	4.00	*6.75*
		Never hinged	6.50	
181	A7	11a gray ('23)	4.00	*6.75*
		Never hinged	6.50	
182	A7	12a yellow brown	2.25	1.90
		Never hinged	3.50	
182A	A7	15a lilac ('23)	9.00	*8.00*
		Never hinged	14.50	
182B	A7	18a dp blue ('23)	11.00	7.00
		Never hinged	17.50	
182C	A7	19a gray grn ('23)	11.00	6.00
		Never hinged	17.50	
182D	A7	36a turq blue ('23)	10.00	4.75
		Never hinged	16.00	
182E	A7	54a choc ('23)	11.00	8.00
		Never hinged	17.50	
182F	A7	72a brt rose ('23)	17.50	17.50
		Never hinged	28.00	

Glazed Paper

No.	Type	Description	Unused	Used
182G	A7	5p car rose ('23)	92.00	60.00
		Never hinged	145.00	
		Nos. 173-182G (17)	181.45	136.20

Preceding Issues Overprinted in Carmine

1915 ***Perf. 11½***

On Provisional Issue of 1902

No.	Type	Description	Unused	Used
183	A3	5a on 5r yellow	1.00	.55
184	A3	5a on 25r green	1.00	.55
185	A3	5a on 50r lt blue	1.00	.55
186	A3	6a on 20r lavender	1.00	.55
187	A3	9a on 15r chocolate	1.00	.55
188	A3	9a on 75r rose	1.50	.55
189	A3	15a on 10r red vio	1.50	1.50
190	A3	15a on 100r brn, *buff*	2.00	1.50
191	A3	15a on 300r bl, *sal*	2.00	3.00
192	A3	22a on 80r lt grn	3.25	2.75
193	A3	22a on 200r bl, *bl*	5.00	5.00

On No. 103

No.	Type	Description	Unused	Used
194	N2	6a on 2½r, perf. 13½	1.00	.55
a.		Perf. 12½	2.00	1.25
b.		Perf. 11½	4.00	1.75

On No. 104

No.	Type	Description	Unused	Used
195	A5	3a gray violet	1.00	.60

On No. 105

No.	Type	Description	Unused	Used
196	A5	10a on 12a dull bl	1.10	.60
		Nos. 183-196 (14)	23.35	18.80

Type of 1915 with Additional Surcharge in Black

Perf. 11½

No.	Type	Description	Unused	Used
199	A3	½a on 5a on 50r lt bl	35.00	10.00
a.		Perf. 13½	40.00	12.50

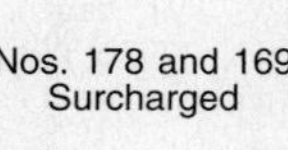

Nos. 178 and 169 Surcharged

1932 ***Perf. 12x11½***

No.	Type	Description	Unused	Used
200	A7	6a on 72a brt rose	1.50	1.25
		Never hinged	2.40	
201	A7	12a on 15a lilac	1.50	1.25
		Never hinged	2.40	

"Portugal" and Vasco da Gama's Flagship "San Gabriel" — A8

Perf. 11½x12

1935 **Typo.** **Wmk. 232**

No.	Type	Description	Unused	Used
202	A8	½a bister	.25	.25
203	A8	1a olive brown	.25	.25
204	A8	2a blue green	.25	.25
205	A8	3a red violet	.60	.60
206	A8	4a black	.60	.30
207	A8	5a gray	.70	.65
208	A8	6a brown	.85	.60
209	A8	7a bright rose	1.00	1.00
210	A8	8a bright blue	1.10	1.10
211	A8	10a red orange	1.60	1.20
212	A8	12a dark blue	2.75	2.10
213	A8	14a olive green	3.25	2.10
214	A8	15a maroon	3.00	2.75
215	A8	20a orange	3.50	2.75
216	A8	30a apple green	5.00	3.00
217	A8	40a violet	9.00	5.00
218	A8	50a olive bister	10.00	5.00
219	A8	1p light blue	24.50	14.00
220	A8	2p brn orange	50.00	25.00
221	A8	3p emerald	67.50	40.00
222	A8	5p dark violet	100.00	52.50
		Nos. 202-222 (21)	285.70	160.40

Common Design Types

1938 **Unwmk.** **Engr.** ***Perf. 13½x13***

Name and Value in Black

No.	Type	Description	Unused	Used
223	CD34	1a gray green	.25	.25
224	CD34	2a orange brown	.25	.30
225	CD34	3a dk violet brn	.25	.30
226	CD34	4a brt green	.25	.65
227	CD35	5a dk carmine	.25	*2.50*
228	CD35	6a slate	.45	.25
229	CD35	8a rose violet	.65	1.10
230	CD37	10a brt red violet	.65	1.75
231	CD37	12a red	1.10	2.50
232	CD37	15a orange	1.75	2.50
233	CD36	20a blue	1.75	.80
234	CD36	40a gray black	3.75	1.25
235	CD36	50a brown	3.75	1.25
236	CD38	1p brown carmine	7.50	5.00
237	CD38	2p olive green	17.50	4.00
238	CD38	3p blue violet	22.50	9.50
239	CD38	5p red brown	45.00	14.00
		Nos. 223-239 (17)	107.60	47.90

For overprints see Nos. 245A-245K in Scott Standard catalogue, Vol. 6.

AIR POST STAMPS

Common Design Type

1938 **Unwmk.** **Engr.** ***Perf. 13½x13***

Name and Value in Black

No.	Type	Description	Unused	Used
C1	CD39	1a scarlet	.85	.45
C2	CD39	2a purple	.90	.55
C3	CD39	3a orange	.90	.60
C4	CD39	5a ultra	1.00	.65
C5	CD39	10a lilac brown	2.00	1.50
C6	CD39	20a dark green	3.50	1.75
C7	CD39	50a red brown	6.00	4.00
C8	CD39	70a rose carmine	9.00	7.50
C9	CD39	1p magenta	17.50	8.25
		Nos. C1-C9 (9)	41.65	25.25

No. C7 exists with overprint "Exposicao Internacional de Nova York, 1939-1940" and Trylon and Perisphere. Counterfeits exist.

For overprints see Nos. C15-C23 in Scott Standard catalogue, Vol. 6.

POSTAGE DUE STAMPS

D1

1904 **Unwmk.** **Typo.** ***Perf. 12***

Without Gum

Name and Value in Black

No.	Type	Description	Unused	Used
J1	D1	1a yellow green	.75	.50
J2	D1	2a slate	.75	.50
J3	D1	5a yellow brown	2.50	1.50
J4	D1	6a red orange	2.75	2.25
J5	D1	10a gray brown	3.00	2.00
J6	D1	15a red brown	4.75	3.25
J7	D1	24a dull blue	7.50	6.00
J8	D1	40a carmine	9.00	6.75
J9	D1	50a orange	14.00	8.00
J10	D1	1p dull violet	22.50	15.00
		Nos. J1-J10 (10)	67.50	45.75

Overprinted in Carmine or Green

1911 **Without Gum**

No.	Type	Description	Unused	Used
J11	D1	1a yellow green	.25	.25
J12	D1	2a slate	.30	.25
a.		Inverted overprint		
J13	D1	5a yellow brown	.60	.40
J14	D1	6a deep orange	.80	.50
J15	D1	10a gray brown	1.50	.70
J16	D1	15a brown	1.75	1.10
J17	D1	24a dull blue	2.50	2.00
J18	D1	40a carmine (G)	3.25	2.50
J19	D1	50a orange	3.75	2.50
J20	D1	1p dull violet	7.50	7.00
		Nos. J11-J20 (10)	22.20	17.20

Nos. J1-J10 Overprinted in Red or Green

1913 **Without Gum**

No.	Type	Description	Unused	Used
J21	D1	1a yellow green	10.00	*9.00*
J22	D1	2a slate	10.00	*9.00*
J23	D1	5a yellow brown	8.00	*6.00*
J24	D1	6a deep orange	8.00	*6.00*
a.		Inverted surcharge	45.00	
J25	D1	10a gray brown	8.00	*6.00*
J26	D1	15a red brown	8.00	*6.00*
J27	D1	24a dull blue	9.00	*7.00*
J28	D1	40a carmine (G)	9.00	*7.00*
J29	D1	50a orange	12.00	*12.00*
J30	D1	1p gray violet	15.00	*12.00*
		Nos. J21-J30 (10)	97.00	80.00

WAR TAX STAMP

Regular Issue of 1914 Surcharged in Red

1919 **Unwmk.** ***Perf. 15x14***

Without Gum

No.	Type	Description	Unused	Used
MR1	A7	2a on ½a ol brn	30.00	22.50
		Never hinged	45.00	
a.		Inverted surcharge	150.00	100.00
		Never hinged	150.00	

See note after Macao No. MR2.

NEWSPAPER STAMPS

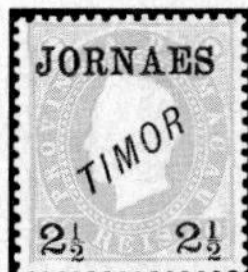

Macao Nos. 37, 39, 41 Surcharged in Black

1892 **Unwmk.** ***Perf. 12½***

Without Gum

No.	Type	Description	Unused	Used
P1	A7	2½r on 20r rose	2.00	.75
a.		"TIMOR" inverted		
P2	A7	2½r on 40r chocolate	2.00	.75
a.		"TIMOR" inverted		
b.		Perf. 13½	8.00	3.50
c.		As "a," perf. 13½		
P3	A7	2½r on 80r gray	2.00	.75
a.		"TIMOR" inverted		
b.		Perf. 13½	25.00	15.00
		Nos. P1-P3 (3)	6.00	2.25

N2

No. P4 Surcharged

1893-95 **Typo.** ***Perf. 11½, 13½***

No.	Type	Description	Unused	Used
P4	N2	2½r brown	.40	.35
a.		Perf. 12½	2.00	1.50
P5	N2	½a on 2½r brn ('95)	.45	.30

For surcharges see Nos. 103, 123, 194.

POSTAL TAX STAMPS

Pombal Issue

Common Design Types

1925 **Unwmk.** ***Perf. 12½***

No.	Type	Description	Unused	Used
RA1	CD28	2a lake & black	.30	.30
RA2	CD29	2a lake & black	.30	.30
RA3	CD30	2a lake & black	.30	.30
		Nos. RA1-RA3 (3)	.90	.90

Type of War Tax Stamp of Portuguese India Overprinted in Red

1934-35 ***Perf. 12***

No.	Type	Description	Unused	Used
RA4	WT1	2a green & blk	6.50	*8.00*
RA5	WT1	5a green & blk	8.00	8.00

Surcharged in Black

No.	Type	Description	Unused	Used
RA6	WT1	7a on ½a rose & blk ('35)	12.00	10.00
		Nos. RA4-RA6 (3)	26.50	*26.00*

The tax was for local education.

Type of War Tax Stamp of Portuguese India Overprinted in Black

1936 ***Perf. 12x11½***

No.	Type	Description	Unused	Used
RA7	WT1	10a rose & black	7.00	*9.00*

1937 ***Perf. 11½***

No.	Type	Description	Unused	Used
RA8	WT1	10a green & blk	5.50	*8.25*

POSTAL TAX DUE STAMPS

Pombal Issue

Common Design Types

1925 **Unwmk.** ***Perf. 12½***

No.	Type	Description	Unused	Used
RAJ1	CD28	4a lake & black	.40	*1.00*
RAJ2	CD29	4a lake & black	.40	*1.00*
RAJ3	CD30	4a lake & black	.40	*1.00*
		Nos. RAJ1-RAJ3 (3)	1.20	*3.00*

TOBAGO

tə-'bā-ˌgō

LOCATION — An island in the West Indies lying off the Venezuelan coast north of Trinidad
GOVT. — British Colony
AREA — 116 sq. mi.
POP. — 25,358
CAPITAL — Scarborough (Port Louis)

In 1889 Tobago, then an independent colony, was united with Trinidad under the name of Colony of Trinidad and Tobago. It became a ward of that colony January 1, 1899.

12 Pence = 1 Shilling
20 Shillings = 1 Pound

PRE-STAMP POSTAL MARKINGS

Crowned Circle handstamp types I and V are pictured in the Crowned Circle Handstamps and Great Britain Used Abroad section.

Scarborough

1851-75

A1	I	"Tobago" crowned circle handstamp in red, on cover	1,400.
A2	V	"Tobago" crowned circle handstamp in red, on cover ('75)	5,500.

STAMPS OF GREAT BRITAIN USED IN TOBAGO

Numeral cancellation type A is pictured in the Crowned Circle Handstamps and Great Britain Used Abroad section.

1858-60

A14 (Scarborough)

A3	A	1p rose red (#20)	950.
A4	A	4p rose (#26)	450.
A5	A	6p lilac (#27)	300.
A6	A	1sh green (#28)	2,400.

Issued under British Administration

Queen Victoria — A1

Wmk. Crown and C C (1)

1879 Typo. *Perf. 14*

1	A1	1p rose	145.00	100.00
2	A1	3p blue	145.00	87.50
3	A1	6p orange	67.50	*82.50*
4	A1	1sh green	425.00	82.50
a.		Half used as 6p on cover		
5	A1	5sh slate	925.00	800.00
6	A1	£1 violet	*4,500.*	

Stamps of the above set with revenue cancellations sell for a small fraction of the price of postally used examples.

Stamps of Type A1, watermarked Crown and C A, are revenue stamps.

1880 Manuscript Surcharge

7	A1	1p on half of 6p org	*6,250.*	*875.*

Queen Victoria — A2

1880

8	A2	½p brown violet	77.50	*115.00*
9	A2	1p red brown	145.00	72.50
a.		Half used as ½p on cover		*2,250.*
10	A2	4p yellow green	325.00	37.50
a.		Half used as 2p on cover		*2,250.*
11	A2	6p bister brown	425.00	125.00
12	A2	1sh bister	115.00	*145.00*
a.		Imperf.		
		Nos. 8-12 (5)	1,088.	495.00

No. 11 Surcharged in Black

1883

13	A2	2½p on 6p bister brn	110.00	110.00
a.		Double surcharge	4,000.	2,250.

1882-96 Wmk. Crown and C A (2)

14	A2	½p brown vio ('82)	3.00	*21.00*
15	A2	½p dull green ('86)	5.00	2.25
16	A2	1p red brown ('82)	14.00	3.75
a.		Diagonal half used as ½p on cover		—
17	A2	1p rose ('89)	8.75	2.50
18	A2	2½p ultra ('83)	16.50	1.60
a.		2½p dull blue ('83)	67.50	3.75
b.		2½p bright blue	17.50	1.60
19	A2	4p yel grn ('82)	230.00	100.00
20	A2	4p gray ('85)	9.00	4.25
a.		Imperf., pair	2,250.	
21	A2	6p bis brn ('84)	625.00	550.00
a.		Imperf.		
22	A2	6p brn org ('86)	2.75	*9.00*
23	A2	1sh olive bis ('94)	4.50	*32.50*
24	A2	1sh brn org ('96)	27.50	*135.00*

Stamps of 1882-96 Surcharged in Black

Nos. 25-29 — No. 30

1886-92

25	A2	½p on 2½p ultra	12.00	*27.50*
a.		Inverted surcharge		
b.		Pair, one without surcharge	16,000.	
c.		Space between "½" and "PENNY" 3mm	42.50	*82.50*
d.		Double surcharge	2,800.	2,600.
26	A2	½p on 4p gray	32.50	*87.50*
a.		Space between "½" and "PENNY" 3mm	75.00	
b.		Double surcharge	3,500.	
27	A2	½p on 6p bis brn	4.25	*29.00*
a.		Inverted surcharge	3,250.	
b.		Space between "½" and "PENNY" 3mm	30.00	*125.00*
c.		Double surcharge	3,750.	
28	A2	½p on 6p brn org	160.00	210.00
a.		Space between "½" and "PENNY" 3mm	375.00	*450.00*
b.		Double surcharge		2,750.
29	A2	1p on 2½ ultra	110.00	25.00
a.		Space between "1" and "PENNY" 4mm	300.00	*90.00*
b.		Half used as ½p on cover		*1,650.*
30	A2	2½p on 4p gray	25.00	*11.00*
a.		Double surcharge	3,500.	3,500.
		Nos. 25-30 (6)	343.75	*390.00*

Revenue Stamp Type A1 Surcharged in Black

1896

31	A1	½p on 4p lilac & rose	110.00	57.50
a.		Space between "½" and "d" 1½ to 2½mm	150.00	82.50

Tobago stamps were replaced by those of Trinidad or Trinidad and Tobago.

TOGO

'tō-ˌgō

LOCATION — Western Africa, bordering on the Gulf of Guinea
GOVT. — Republic
AREA — 20,400 sq. mi.
POP. — 2,890,000 (est. 1984)
CAPITAL — Lome

The German Protectorate of Togo was occupied by Great Britain and France in World War I, and later mandated to them. The British area became part of Ghana.

100 Pfennig = 1 Mark
12 Pence = 1 Shilling
100 Centimes = 1 Franc

Watermark

Wmk. 125 — Lozenges

German Protectorate

AREA — 34,934 sq. mi.
POP. — 1,000,368 (1913)

Stamps of Germany Overprinted in Black

1897 Unwmk. *Perf. 13½x14½*

1	A9	3pf dark brown	5.25	*6.00*
		Never hinged	12.50	
		On cover		*32.50*
a.		3pf yellow brown	9.25	*25.00*
		Never hinged	27.50	
		On cover		120.00
b.		3pf reddish brown	47.50	*120.00*
		Never hinged	150.00	
		On cover		325.00
c.		3pf pale gray brown	1,600.	*1,200.*
		Never hinged	3,600.	
		On cover		1,750.
2	A9	5pf green	4.75	*2.75*
		Never hinged	8.75	
		On cover		16.00
3	A10	10pf carmine	5.50	*3.00*
		Never hinged	13.50	
		On cover		16.00
4	A10	20pf ultra	5.50	*12.50*
		Never hinged	16.00	
		On cover		40.00
5	A10	25pf orange	35.00	*55.00*
		Never hinged	100.00	
		On cover		175.00
6	A10	50pf red brown	35.00	*55.00*
		Never hinged	95.00	
		On cover		175.00
		Nos. 1-6 (6)	91.00	*134.25*

Covers: Value for No. 6 on cover is for overfranked complete covers, usually philatelic.

A3

Kaiser's Yacht, the "Hohenzollern" — A4

1900 Typo. *Perf. 14*

7	A3	3pf brown	1.00	*1.25*
		Never hinged	2.00	
		On cover		55.00
8	A3	5pf green	11.00	*2.00*
		Never hinged	24.00	
		On cover		20.00
9	A3	10pf carmine	20.00	1.60
		Never hinged	47.50	
		On cover		20.00
10	A3	20pf ultra	1.00	*1.50*
		Never hinged	4.00	
		On cover		24.00
11	A3	25pf org & blk, *yel*	1.00	*9.50*
		Never hinged	4.00	
		On cover		47.50
12	A3	30pf org & blk, *sal*	1.25	*9.50*
		Never hinged	4.75	
		On cover		47.50
13	A3	40pf lake & blk	1.00	*9.50*
		Never hinged	4.00	
		On cover		47.50
14	A3	50pf pur & blk, *sal*	1.25	*7.25*
		Never hinged	4.75	
		On cover		40.00
15	A3	80pf lake & blk, *rose*	2.40	*16.00*
		Never hinged	5.50	
		On cover		47.50

Engr.

Perf. 14½x14

16	A4	1m carmine	3.25	*52.50*
		Never hinged	9.50	
		On cover		95.00
17	A4	2m blue	5.25	*80.00*
		Never hinged	16.00	
		On cover		120.00
18	A4	3m black vio	6.75	*140.00*
		Never hinged	20.00	
		On cover		190.00
19	A4	5m slate & car	120.00	*475.00*
		Never hinged	375.00	
		On cover		725.00
		Nos. 7-19 (13)	175.15	*805.60*

Counterfeit cancellations are found on Nos. 10-19 and 22.

Covers: Values for Nos. 14-19 on cover are for overfranked complete covers, usually philatelic.

1909-19 Wmk. 125 Typo. *Perf. 14*

20	A3	3pf brown ('19)	.80	
		Never hinged	2.00	
21	A3	5pf green	1.25	*2.00*
		Never hinged	2.50	
		On cover		16.00
22	A3	10pf carmine ('14)	1.60	*110.00*
		Never hinged	3.50	
		On cover		650.00

Engr.

Perf. 14½x14

23	A4	5m slate & carmine, (25x17 holes) ('19)	22.50	
		Never hinged	90.00	
a.		5m slate & carmine (26x17 holes) ('15)	26.00	
		Never hinged	110.00	
		Nos. 20-23 (4)	26.15	

Nos. 20 and 23 were never placed in use.

British Protectorate

Nos. 7, 10-19, 21-22 Overprinted or Surcharged

First (Wide) Setting
3mm between Lines
2mm between "Anglo" & "French"
Wmk. 125 (5pf, 10pf); Unwmkd.

1914, Oct. 1 — *Perf. 14, 14½*
33 A3 ½p on 3pf brn 160.00 140.00
a. Thin "y" in "penny" 400.00 350.00
34 A3 1p on 5pf grn 160.00 140.00
a. Thin "y" in "penny" 400.00 350.00
35 A3 3pf brown 130.00 100.00
36 A3 5pf green 130.00 100.00
37 A3 10pf carmine 130.00 100.00
a. Inverted overprint 10,000. 3,000.
b. Unwmk. 5,500.
38 A3 20pf ultra 42.50 50.00
39 A3 25pf org & blk, yel 40.00 47.50
40 A3 30pf org & blk, sal 47.50 60.00
41 A3 40pf lake & blk 225.00 250.00
42 A3 50pf pur & blk, sal 12,000. 10,000.
43 A3 80pf lake & blk, rose 275.00 275.00
44 A4 1m carmine 5,000. 2,750.
45 A4 2m blue 13,500. 15,000.
a. Inverted overprint 16,000.
b. "Occupation" double 24,500. 16,000.

On Nos. 33-34, the surcharge line ("Half penny" or "One penny") was printed separately and its position varies in relation to the 3-line overprint. On Nos. 46-47, the surcharge and overprint lines were printed simultaneously.

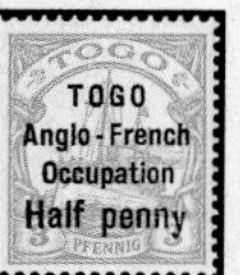

Second (Narrow) Setting
2mm between Lines
2mm between "Anglo" & "French"

1914, Oct.
46 A3 ½p on 3pf brown 47.50 26.00
a. Thin "y" in "penny" 75.00 60.00
b. "TOG" 425.00 300.00
47 A3 1p on 5pf green 8.00 4.25
a. Thin "y" in "penny" 12.00 15.00
b. "TOG" 130.00 110.00
48 A3 3pf brown 6,500. 1,100
a. "Occupation" omitted
49 A3 5pf green 1,500. 750.00
50 A3 10pf carmine 3,000.
51 A3 20pf ultra 30.00 12.00
a. "TOG" 3,500. 2,500.
b. Vert. pair, #51 & #38 9,000.
52 A3 25pf org & blk, yel 40.00 32.50
a. "TOG" 12,000.
53 A3 30pf org & blk, sal 20.00 29.00
54 A3 40pf lake & blk 6,000. 1,600.
55 A3 50pf pur & blk, sal 9,000.
56 A3 80pf lake & blk, rose 3,250. 2,250.
57 A4 1m carmine 8,000. 4,250.
58 A4 2m blue 14,500.
59 A4 3m black violet 110,000.
60 A4 5m slate & car 110,000.

Third Setting
1¼mm btwn. "Anglo" & "French"
2mm between Lines
"Anglo-French" 15mm Wide

1915, Jan. 7
61 A3 3pf brown 9,000. 2,500.
62 A3 5pf green 225. 130.
63 A3 10pf carmine 200. 130.
64 A3 20pf ultra 1,400. 400.
64A A3 40pf lake & blk 9,000.
65 A3 50pf pur & blk, sal 16,000. 11,000.

Stamps of Gold Coast Overprinted Locally

"OCCUPATION" 14½-14¾mm Long

1915, May — **Wmk. 3** — *Perf. 14*
66 A7 ½p green .35 3.75
a. Double overprint
67 A8 1p scarlet .35 .60
a. Double ovpt. 350.00 475.00
b. Inverted ovpt. 175.00 250.00
c. As "b," "Togo" omitted 8,000.
68 A7 2p gray .35 1.50
69 A7 2½p ultra 4.00 7.00

Chalky Paper
70 A7 3p violet, yel 3.50 6.00
71 A7 6p dl vio & red vio 2.75 2.00
72 A7 1sh black, grn 2.50 11.00
a. Double overprint 1,500.
73 A7 2sh vio & bl, bl 15.00 22.50
74 A7 2sh6p blk & red, bl 5.50 30.00
75 A7 10sh grn & red, grn 50.00 60.00
76 A7 20sh vio & blk, red 150.00 160.00

Surfaced-Colored Paper
77 A7 3p violet, yel 4.00 24.00
78 A7 5sh grn & red, yel 9.50 15.00
Nos. 66-78 (13) 247.80 343.35

Nos. 66-78 exist with small "F" in "French" and thin "G" in "Togo." Several values are known without the hyphen between "Anglo-French" and all but No. 77 without the first "O" in "Occupation."

Stamps of Gold Coast Overprinted in London

"OCCUPATION" 15mm Long

1916, Apr. — **Ordinary Paper**
80 A7 ½p green .35 2.75
81 A8 1p scarlet .35 .85
a. Inverted overprint
82 A7 2p gray .60 3.00
83 A7 2½p ultra .70 1.50

Chalky Paper
84 A7 3p violet, yel 6.00 1.25
a. 3p violet, yel buff ('19) 10.00 3.00
85 A7 6p dl vio & red vio 2.50 2.00
86 A7 1sh black, grn 8.00 13.00
a. 1sh black, emerald 400.00 850.00
b. 1sh black, bl grn, ol back 12.00 18.00
87 A7 2sh vio & ultra, bl 4.50 8.50
88 A7 2sh6p blk & red, bl 4.50 7.00
89 A7 5sh grn & red, yel 37.50 27.50
a. 5ah grn & red, yel buff 30.00 50.00
90 A7 10sh grn & red, bl grn, ol back ('20) 21.00 75.00
a. 10sh green & red, grn 27.50 65.00
91 A7 20sh vio & blk, red 160.00 190.00
Nos. 80-91 (12) 246.00 332.35

The overprint on Nos. 80-91 is in heavier letters than on Nos. 66-78 and the 2nd and 3rd lines are each ½mm longer. The letter "O" on Nos. 80-91 is narrower and more oval.

Issued under French Occupation

Stamps of German Togo Surcharged

c

d

e

f

g

h

i

Wmk. Lozenges (5pf and 10pf) (125), Unwmk. (other values)

1914 — *Perf. 14, 14½*
151 A3(c+d) 5c on 3pf brn 70.00 70.00
Never hinged 140.00
152 A3(c+e) 5c on 3pf brn 67.50 67.50
Never hinged 130.00
153 A3(c+f) 5c on 3pf brn 77.50 77.50
Never hinged 160.00
154 A3(c+g) 10c on 5pf grn 25.00 25.00
Never hinged 42.50
a. Double surcharge 1,200. 1,200.
155 A3(c+h) 10c on 5pf grn 25.00 25.00
Never hinged 42.50
156 A3(c+i) 10c on 5pf grn 50.00 50.00
Never hinged 100.00
158 A3(c) 20pf ultra 55.00 55.00
Never hinged 110.00
a. 3½mm between "TOGO" and "Occupation" 875.00 875.00
159 A3(c) 25pf org & blk, yel 80.00 80.00
Never hinged 160.00
160 A3(c) 30pf org & blk, sal 100.00 100.00
Never hinged 210.00
161 A3(c) 40pf lake & black 600.00 625.00
162 A3(c) 80pf lake & blk, rose 600.00 625.00
Nos. 151-162 (11) 1,750. 1,800.

Surcharged or Overprinted in Sans-Serif Type

1915
164 A3 5c on 3pf brown 21,000. 4,500.
165 A3 5pf green 1,050. 450.
166 A3 10pf carmine 1,150. 450.
a. Inverted overprint 27,000. 16,500.
167 A3 20pf ultra 1,400. 1,050.
168 A3 25pf org & blk, yel 15,000. 7,000.
169 A3 30pf org & blk, sal 15,000. 7,000.
170 A3 40pf lake & blk 15,000. 7,000.
171 A3 50pf pur & blk, sal 21,000. 12,500.
171A A3 80pf red & blk, rose —
172 A4 1m carmine —
173 A4 2m blue — —
174 A4 3m black vio —
175 A4 5m slate & car — —

Stamps of Dahomey, 1913-17, Overprinted

1916-17 — **Unwmk.** — *Perf. 13½x14*
Chalky Paper
176 A5 1c violet & blk .35 .50
Never hinged 1.00
On cover 70.00
a. Ordinary paper .30 .50
Never hinged .70
On cover 70.00
177 A5 2c choc & rose .35 .50
Never hinged .70
On cover 70.00
a. Ordinary paper .30 .50
Never hinged .70
On cover 55.00
178 A5 4c black & brn .35 .80
Never hinged .70
On cover 70.00
a. Double overprint 500.00 500.00
b. Ordinary paper .50 .80
Never hinged .80
On cover 70.00
179 A5 5c yel grn & bl grn .70 .70
Never hinged 1.10
On cover 27.50
a. Ordinary paper .70 .70
Never hinged 1.10
On cover 27.50
180 A5 10c org red & rose .70 .70
Never hinged 1.10
On cover 16.00
a. Ordinary paper .70 .70
Never hinged 1.10
On cover 16.00
181 A5 15c brn org & dk vio ('17) 1.75 1.75
Never hinged 2.75
On cover 19.00
182 A5 20c gray & choc .70 1.10
Never hinged 1.10
On cover 29.00
a. Ordinary paper .70 1.10
Never hinged 1.10
On cover 29.00
183 A5 25c ultra & dp bl 1.10 1.10
Never hinged 1.75
On cover 35.00
On cover, single franking 70.00
184 A5 30c choc & vio 1.10 1.40
Never hinged 1.75
On cover 37.50
On cover, single franking 70.00
a. Ordinary paper 1.10 1.40
Never hinged 1.75
On cover 37.50
185 A5 35c brown & blk 1.75 2.10
Never hinged 2.75
On cover 37.50
On cover, single franking 62.50
186 A5 40c blk & red org 1.40 1.75
Never hinged 2.75
On cover 45.00
On cover, single franking 87.50
a. Ordinary paper 1.40 1.75
Never hinged 2.75
On cover 45.00
187 A5 45c gray & ultra 1.75 2.10
Never hinged 2.75
On cover 55.00
On cover, single franking 80.00
a. Ordinary paper 1.75 2.10
Never hinged 2.75
On cover 55.00
188 A5 50c choc & brn 1.75 2.10
Never hinged 2.75
On cover 55.00
On cover, single franking 110.00
a. Ordinary paper 1.75 2.10
Never hinged 2.75
On cover 55.00
189 A5 75c blue & vio 7.00 8.00
Never hinged 12.50
On cover 62.50
On cover, single franking 140.00
a. Ordinary paper 7.00 8.00
Never hinged 12.50
On cover 62.50
190 A5 1fr bl grn & blk 8.50 10.50
Never hinged 14.00
On cover 75.00
On cover, single franking 170.00
a. Ordinary paper 8.50 10.50
Never hinged 14.00
On cover 75.00
191 A5 2fr buff & choc 12.00 14.00
Never hinged 21.00
On cover 100.00
On cover, single franking 190.00
a. Ordinary paper 12.00 14.00
Never hinged 20.00
On cover 160.00
192 A5 5fr vio & do bl 14.00 16.00
Never hinged 25.00
On cover 120.00
On cover, single franking 270.00
a. Ordinary paper 14.00 16.00
Never hinged 25.00
On cover 120.00
Nos. 176-192 (17) 55.25 65.10

French Mandate

AREA — 21,893 sq. mi.
POP. — 780,497 (1938)

Type of Dahomey, 1913-39, Overprinted

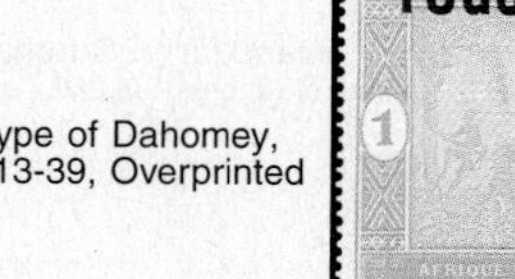

1921
193 A5 1c gray & yel grn .35 .35
Never hinged .70
On cover 55.00
a. Overprint omitted 125.00 125.00
Never hinged 200.00
194 A5 2c blue & org .35 .35
Never hinged .70
On cover 55.00
195 A5 4c ol grn & org .35 .35
Never hinged .70
On cover 55.00
196 A5 5c dull red & blk .35 .35
Never hinged .70
On cover 21.00
a. Overprint omitted 410.00 425.00
Never hinged 675.00

197 A5 10c bl grn & yel grn .35 *.70*
Never hinged .70
On cover 45.00
198 A5 15c brown & car .70 *.70*
Never hinged 1.10
On cover 25.00
199 A5 20c bl grn & org 1.10 1.10
Never hinged 1.75
On cover 19.00
200 A5 25c slate & org 1.10 1.10
Never hinged 1.75
On cover 12.50
201 A5 30c dp rose & ver 1.40 *1.75*
Never hinged 2.10
On cover 22.50
On cover, single franking 45.00
202 A5 35c red brn & yel grn 1.10 *1.40*
Never hinged 1.75
On cover 20.00
On cover, single franking 22.50
203 A5 40c bl grn & ol 2.10 1.75
Never hinged 3.50
On cover 16.00
On cover, single franking 22.50
204 A5 45c red brn & ol 2.10 *2.10*
Never hinged 2.75
On cover 35.00
On cover, single franking 70.00
205 A5 50c deep blue 2.10 *1.40*
Never hinged 2.75
On cover 37.50
On cover, single franking 75.00
206 A5 75c dl red & ultra 2.10 *2.10*
Never hinged 3.50
On cover 45.00
On cover, single franking 62.50
207 A5 1fr gray & ultra 2.10 *2.10*
Never hinged 3.50
On cover 55.00
On cover, single franking 125.00
208 A5 2fr ol grn & rose 7.00 *7.00*
Never hinged 10.50
On cover 62.50
On cover, single franking 125.00
209 A5 5fr orange & blk 10.50 *10.50*
Never hinged 17.50
On cover 80.00
On cover, single franking 140.00
Nos. 193-209 (17) 35.15 *35.10*

Stamps and Type of 1921 Surcharged

No. 210

No. 213

1922-25
210 A5 25c on 15c ol brn & rose red .35 *.55*
Never hinged .70
On cover 16.00
211 A5 25c on 2fr ol grn & rose .70 *.80*
Never hinged .95
On cover 16.00
212 A5 25c on 5fr org & blk .70 *.80*
Never hinged 1.10
On cover 16.00
a. "TOGO" omitted 275.00 275.00
Never hinged 325.00
213 A5 60c on 75c vio, *pnksh* 1.10 *1.40*
Never hinged 1.75
On cover 22.50
On cover, single franking 35.00
a. "60" omitted 200.00 210.00
Never hinged 325.00
214 A5 65c on 45c red brn & ol 1.40 *1.75*
Never hinged 2.75
On cover 70.00
On cover, single franking 150.00
a. "TOGO" omitted 190.00 200.00
Never hinged 300.00
215 A5 85c on 75c dull red & ultra 2.10 *2.75*
Never hinged 3.75
On cover 55.00
On cover, single franking 110.00
Nos. 210-215 (6) 6.35 *8.05*

Issue years: #213, 1922; #211-212, 1924; others, 1925.

Coconut Grove
A6

Cacao Trees — A7

Oil Palms
A8

1924-38 **Typo.**
216 A6 1c yellow & blk .25 *.35*
Never hinged .35
On cover 37.50
217 A6 2c dp rose & blk .25 *.35*
Never hinged .35
On cover 37.50
218 A6 4c dk blue & blk .25 *.35*
Never hinged .35
On cover 37.50
219 A6 5c dp org & blk .25 *.35*
Never hinged .35
On cover 30.00
220 A6 10c red vio & blk .25 .35
Never hinged .35
On cover 25.00
221 A6 15c green & blk .25 .35
Never hinged .35
On cover 19.00
222 A7 20c gray & blk .30 .50
Never hinged .45
On cover 15.00
223 A7 25c grn & blk, *yel* .70 .70
Never hinged 1.10
On cover 12.50
224 A7 30c gray grn & blk .35 .35
Never hinged .70
On cover 12.50
225 A7 30c dl grn & lt grn ('27) .70 *.70*
Never hinged 1.10
On cover 30.00
226 A7 35c lt brown & blk .70 .70
Never hinged 1.10
On cover 30.00
On cover, single franking 50.00
227 A7 35c dp bl grn & grn ('38) .70 .70
Never hinged 1.40
On cover 37.50
228 A7 40c red org & blk .35 .35
Never hinged .70
On cover 37.50
On cover, single franking 75.00
229 A7 45c carmine & blk .35 .35
Never hinged .70
On cover 21.00
On cover, single franking 35.00
230 A7 50c ocher & blk, *bluish* .35 .70
Never hinged .70
On cover 12.50
231 A7 55c vio bl & car rose ('38) 1.10 1.10
Never hinged 1.40
On cover 12.50
232 A7 60c vio brn & blk, *pnksh* .35 .35
Never hinged .70
On cover 37.50
On cover, single franking 70.00
233 A7 60c dp red ('26) .35 *.70*
Never hinged .70
On cover 37.50
On cover, single franking 62.50
234 A7 65c gray lil & brn .70 .70
Never hinged 1.10
On cover 62.50
On cover, single franking 140.00
235 A7 75c blue & black .70 *.70*
Never hinged 1.10
On cover 27.50
On cover, single franking 47.50
236 A7 80c ind & dl vio ('38) 1.75 1.75
Never hinged 2.75
On cover 62.50
On cover, single franking 80.00
237 A7 85c brn org & brn 1.10 1.10
Never hinged 1.75
On cover 50.00
On cover, single franking 125.00
238 A7 90c brn red & cer ('27) 1.10 *1.10*
Never hinged 1.40
On cover 32.50
On cover, single franking 87.50
239 A8 1fr red brn & blk, *bluish* 1.10 *1.10*
Never hinged 1.40
On cover 32.50
On cover, single franking 70.00
240 A8 1fr blue ('26) .70 *.70*
Never hinged 1.40
On cover 45.00
On cover, single franking 75.00
241 A8 1fr gray lil & grn ('28) 2.75 2.75
Never hinged 4.25
On cover 27.50
On cover, single franking 37.50
242 A8 1fr dk red & red org ('38) 1.10 1.10
Never hinged 1.40
On cover 50.00
On cover, single franking 95.00
243 A8 1.10fr vio & dk brn ('28) 4.25 *5.50*
Never hinged 7.00
On cover 190.00
On cover, single franking 400.00
244 A8 1.25fr mag & rose ('33) 1.40 *1.75*
Never hinged 2.10
On cover 30.00
On cover, single franking 87.50
245 A8 1.50fr bl & lt bl ('27) .70 *1.10*
Never hinged 1.10
On cover 35.00
On cover, single franking 75.00
246 A8 1.75fr bis & pink ('33) 8.50 5.25
Never hinged 14.00
On cover 45.00
On cover, single franking 55.00
247 A8 1.75fr vio bl & ultra ('38) 1.40 1.40
Never hinged 2.10
On cover 37.50
On cover, single franking 62.50
248 A8 2fr bl blk & blk, *bluish* 1.10 1.40
Never hinged 1.75
On cover 37.50
On cover, single franking 75.00
249 A8 3fr bl grn & red org ('27) 1.40 *1.75*
Never hinged 2.10
On cover 40.00
On cover, single franking 87.50
250 A8 5fr red org & blk, *bluish* 2.10 *3.50*
Never hinged 3.50
On cover 45.00
On cover, single franking 87.50
251 A8 10fr ol brn & rose ('26) 2.50 *2.75*
Never hinged 5.00
On cover 50.00
On cover, single franking 95.00
252 A8 20fr brn red & blk, *yel* ('26) 3.50 *3.50*
Never hinged 4.25
On cover 62.50
On cover, single franking 105.00
Nos. 216-252 (37) 45.65 *48.20*

For surcharges see No. 253; Nos. 301-302, B8-B9 in Scott Standard catalogue, Vol. 6.

No. 240 Surcharged with New Value and Bars in Red

1926
253 A8 1.25fr on 1fr lt bl .70 .70
Never hinged 1.10
On cover 62.50
On cover, single franking 110.00

Common Design Types pictured following the introduction.

Colonial Exposition Issue
Common Design Types
Engr., "TOGO" Typo. in Black

1931, Apr. 13 ***Perf. 12½***
254 CD70 40c deep green 5.50 5.50
Never hinged 9.00
On cover 105.00
255 CD71 50c violet 5.50 5.50
Never hinged 9.00
On cover 87.50
256 CD72 90c red orange 5.50 5.50
Never hinged 9.00
On cover 150.00
On cover, single franking 220.00
257 CD73 1.50fr dull blue 5.50 5.50
Never hinged 9.00
On cover 140.00
On cover, single franking 200.00
Nos. 254-257 (4) 22.00 22.00

Paris International Exposition Issue
Common Design Types

1937 ***Perf. 13***
258 CD74 20c deep violet 1.60 1.60
Never hinged 2.75
On cover 105.00
259 CD75 30c dark green 1.60 1.60
Never hinged 2.75
On cover 87.50
260 CD76 40c car rose 1.60 1.60
Never hinged 2.75
On cover 80.00
261 CD77 50c dark brown 1.60 1.60
Never hinged 2.75
On cover 75.00
262 CD78 90c red 1.75 1.75
Never hinged 2.75
On cover 105.00
On cover, single franking 190.00
263 CD79 1.50fr ultra 1.75 1.75
Never hinged 2.75
On cover 95.00
On cover, single franking 160.00
Nos. 258-263 (6) 9.90 9.90

Colonial Arts Exhibition Issue
Souvenir Sheet
Common Design Type

1937 ***Imperf.***
264 CD77 3fr Prus bl & blk 10.50 *10.50*
Never hinged 14.00
On cover 110.00
On cover, single franking 175.00

Caillié Issue
Common Design Type

1939, Apr. 5 ***Perf. 12½x12***
265 CD81 90c org brn & org .35 1.10
Never hinged .70
On cover 10.00
266 CD81 2fr brt violet .35 1.10
Never hinged .70
On cover 25.00
On cover, single franking 45.00
267 CD81 2.25fr ultra & dk bl .35 1.10
Never hinged .70
On cover 30.00
On cover, single franking 50.00
Nos. 265-267 (3) 1.05 3.30

New York World's Fair Issue
Common Design Type

1939, May 10
268 CD82 1.25fr carmine lake .70 1.40
Never hinged 1.10
On cover 75.00
On cover, single franking 160.00
269 CD82 2.25fr ultra .70 1.40
Never hinged 1.10
On cover 75.00
On cover, single franking 125.00

SEMI-POSTAL STAMPS

Curie Issue
Common Design Type

1938 Unwmk. Engr. ***Perf. 13***
B1 CD80 1.75fr + 50c brt ultra 20.00 20.00
Never hinged 32.50

French Revolution Issue
Common Design Type
Photo., Name and Value Typo. in Black

1939
B2 CD83 45c + 25c green 8.50 8.50
Never hinged 14.00
On cover 150.00
B3 CD83 70c + 30c brown 8.50 8.50
Never hinged 14.00
On cover 110.00
B4 CD83 90c + 35c red org 8.50 8.50
Never hinged 14.00
On cover 100.00
B5 CD83 1.25fr + 1fr rose pink 8.50 8.50
Never hinged 14.00
On cover 160.00
On cover, single franking 225.00
B6 CD83 2.25fr + 2fr blue 8.50 8.50
Never hinged 14.00
On cover 150.00
On cover, single franking 225.00
Nos. B2-B6 (5) 42.50 42.50

French Revolution, 150th anniv. Surtax for defense of the colonies.

AIR POST STAMPS

Common Design Type

1940 Unwmk. Engr. ***Perf. 12½x12***
C1 CD85 1.90fr ultra .35 .35
Never hinged .70
On cover 30.00
C2 CD85 2.90fr dark red .35 .35
Never hinged .70
On cover 30.00
C3 CD85 4.50fr dk gray grn .35 .35
Never hinged .70
On cover 37.50
C4 CD85 4.90fr yellow bister .70 .70
Never hinged 1.10
On cover 45.00
C5 CD85 6.90fr deep orange 1.40 1.40
Never hinged 1.75
On cover 55.00
Nos. C1-C5 (5) 3.15 3.15

POSTAGE DUE STAMPS

Postage Due Stamps of Dahomey, 1914 Overprinted

1921 Unwmk. ***Perf. 14x13½***
J1 D2 5c green .65 *.85*
Never hinged 1.10
On cover 50.00
J2 D2 10c rose .65 *.90*
Never hinged 1.10
On cover 50.00
J3 D2 15c gray 1.25 *1.75*
Never hinged 2.10
On cover 50.00
J4 D2 20c brown 2.50 *2.50*
Never hinged 3.75
On cover 55.00
J5 D2 30c blue 2.50 *2.75*
Never hinged 3.75
On cover 55.00
J6 D2 50c black 2.10 *2.50*
Never hinged 3.50
On cover 62.50
J7 D2 60c orange 2.10 *2.50*
Never hinged 3.50
On cover 75.00
J8 D2 1fr violet 3.75 *4.50*
Never hinged 5.50
On cover 95.00
Nos. J1-J8 (8) 15.50 18.25

Cotton Field — D3

1925 Typo. Unwmk.

J9	D3 2c blue & blk	.25	*.35*
	Never hinged	.35	
	On cover		40.00
J10	D3 4c dl red & blk	.25	*.35*
	Never hinged	.35	
	On cover		40.00
J11	D3 5c ol grn & blk	.25	*.35*
	Never hinged	.35	
	On cover		40.00
J12	D3 10c cerise & blk	.35	*.45*
	Never hinged	.70	
	On cover		40.00
J13	D3 15c orange & blk	.70	*.85*
	Never hinged	1.10	
	On cover		45.00
J14	D3 20c red vio & blk	.35	*.55*
	Never hinged	.70	
	On cover		45.00
J15	D3 25c gray & blk	1.10	*1.10*
	Never hinged	1.40	
	On cover		52.50
J16	D3 30c ocher & blk	.35	*.55*
	Never hinged	.70	
	On cover		52.50
J17	D3 50c brown & blk	1.10	*1.10*
	Never hinged	1.40	
	On cover		57.50
J18	D3 60c green & blk	1.10	*1.10*
	Never hinged	1.40	
	On cover		65.00
J19	D3 1fr dk vio & blk	1.10	*1.10*
	Never hinged	1.40	
	On cover		75.00
	Nos. J9-J19 (11)	6.90	7.85

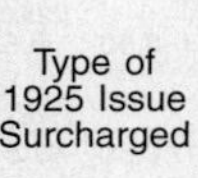

Type of 1925 Issue Surcharged

1927

J20	D3 2fr on 1fr rose red & vio	7.00	*7.00*
	Never hinged	10.50	
	On cover		95.00
J21	D3 3fr on 1fr org brn, blk & ultra	7.00	*7.00*
	Never hinged	10.50	
	On cover		105.00

TONGA

'täŋ-gə

LOCATION — A group of islands in the south Pacific Ocean, south of Samoa

GOVT. — Kingdom in British Commonwealth

AREA — 289 sq. mi.

POP. — 98,750 (est. 1983)

CAPITAL — Nuku'alofa

This group, also known as the Friendly Islands, became a British Protectorate in 1900 under the Anglo-German Agreement of 1899.

12 Pence = 1 Shilling
20 Shillings = 1 Pound

Catalogue values for unused stamps in this country are for Never Hinged items, beginning with Scott 87 in the regular postage section.

Watermarks

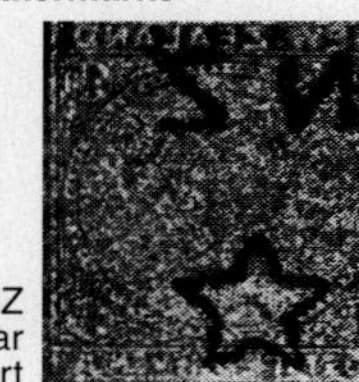

Wmk. 62 — NZ and Small Star Wide Apart

Wmk. 79 — Turtles

King George I — A1

Perf. 12x11½

1886-92 Typo. Wmk. 62

1	A1 1p car rose ('87)	11.50	4.00
a.	Perf. 12½	450.00	7.00
b.	Perf. 12½x10		
2	A1 2p violet ('87)	45.00	3.50
a.	Perf. 12½	57.50	14.00
3	A1 6p ultra ('88)	57.50	2.75
a.	Perf. 12½	67.50	4.00
4	A1 6p org yel ('92)	18.00	*40.00*
5	A1 1sh blue grn ('88)	62.50	7.25
a.	Perf. 12½	110.00	4.50
b.	Half used as 6p on cover		
	Nos. 1-5 (5)	194.50	*57.50*

Stamps with Perf. 11½ to 12 on 4 sides are made on the same machine as the Perf. 12x11½.

For surcharges and overprints see #6-9, 24.

Nos. 1 and 2 Surcharged in Black

FOUR PENCE.

a

1891, Nov. 10 ***Perf. 12x11½***

6	A1(a) 4p on 1p car rose	3.50	*15.00*
a.	No period after "PENCE"	57.50	*135.00*
7	A1(a) 8p on 2p violet	45.00	*110.00*

Nos. 1 and 2 Overprinted in Black

b

Type I

Type II

Two types of overprint:
I — Solid stars, rays pointed and short.
II — Open-center stars, rays blunt and long.

1891, Nov. 23 ***Perf. 12½***

8	A1(b) 1p car rose (I)	50.00	*70.00*
a.	Overprinted with 3 stars (I)	400.00	
b.	Overprinted with 4 stars (I)	550.00	
c.	Overprinted with 5 stars (I)	800.00	
d.	Type II	50.00	*70.00*
e.	Perf. 12x11½ (I or II)	350.00	
9	A1(b) 2p violet (I)	80.00	*42.50*
a.	Type II	80.00	*42.50*
b.	Perf. 12x11½ (I or II)	425.00	

Coat of Arms A4

George I A5

1892, Nov. 10 Typo. ***Perf. 12x11½***

10	A4 1p rose	18.00	*35.00*
a.	Diagonal half used as ½p on cover		975.00
11	A5 2p olive gray	40.00	*18.00*
12	A4 4p red brown	55.00	*80.00*
13	A5 8p violet	70.00	*200.00*
14	A5 1sh brown	90.00	*140.00*
	Nos. 10-14 (5)	273.00	*473.00*

For surcharges and overprints see Nos. 15-23, 25-28, 36-37, O1-O10.

Types A4 and A5 Surcharged in Carmine or Black

c

d

e

f

1893

15	A4(c) ½p on 1p ultra (C)	26.00	*30.00*
a.	Surcharge omitted		
16	A4(c) ½p on 1p ultra	50.00	*55.00*
17	A5(d) 2½p on 2p blue grn (C)	27.50	*13.50*
18	A5(d) 2½p on 2p blue grn	19.00	19.00
a.	Double surcharge	3,000.	2,000.
19	A4(e) 5p on 4p org yel (C)	4.50	*8.50*
20	A5(f) 7½p on 8p rose (C)	32.50	*85.00*
	Nos. 15-20 (6)	159.50	*211.00*

Stamps of 1886-92 Surcharged in Blue or Black

g

h

1894

21	A4 ½p on 4p red brn (Bl)	2.25	*8.00*
a.	"SURCHARCE"	10.00	*22.50*
b.	Pair, one without surcharge		
c.	"HALF PENNY" omitted		
22	A5 ½p on 1sh brn (Bk)	2.75	*12.50*
a.	Double surcharge	310.00	
b.	"SURCHARCE"	11.50	45.00
c.	As "b," double surcharge	1,000.	
23	A5 2½p on 8p vio (Bk)	15.00	*9.25*
a.	No period after "SURCHARGE"	55.00	*62.50*
24	A1 2½p on 1sh blue grn (Bk), perf. 12½	65.00	*30.00*
a.	No period after "SURCHARGE"	200.00	
b.	Perf. 12x11½	17.50	50.00
	Nos. 21-24 (4)	85.00	*59.75*

Type A5 with Same Surcharges in Carmine

1895 Unwmk.

25	A5(g) 1p on 2p lt blue	50.00	45.00
26	A5(h) 1½p on 2p lt bl, perf. 12x11	55.00	55.00
a.	Perf. 12	70.00	55.00
27	A5(h) 2½p on 2p lt blue	45.00	50.00
b.	Without period	250.00	250.00
28	A5(h) 7½p on 2p lt bl, perf. 12x11	70.00	50.00
a.	Perf. 12	550.00	
	Nos. 25-28 (4)	220.00	200.00

King George II — A13

1895, Aug. 16 ***Perf. 12***

29	A13 1p gray green	35.00	*30.00*
a.	Diagonal half used as ½p on cover		*850.00*
b.	Horiz. pair, imperf. btwn.	—	*7,500.*
30	A13 2½p dull rose	32.50	15.00
31	A13 5p brt blue, perf. 12x11	26.00	*70.00*
a.	Perf. 12	45.00	*75.00*
b.	Perf. 11	400.00	
32	A13 7½p yellow	50.00	*55.00*
	Nos. 29-32 (4)	143.50	*170.00*

Type A13 Redrawn and Surcharged "g" or "h" in Black

33	A13(g) ½p on 2½p red	55.00	*37.50*
a.	"SURCHARCE"	100.00	75.00
b.	Period after "Postage"	115.00	75.00
34	A13(g) 1p on 2½p red	115.00	50.00
a.	Period after "Postage"	170.00	110.00
35	A13(h) 7½p on 2½p red	62.50	*75.00*
a.	Period after "Postage"	110.00	*120.00*
	Nos. 33-35 (3)	232.50	*162.50*

Nos. 26 and 28 with Additional Surcharge in Violet and Black

1896, May ***Perf. 12x11***

36	A5 ½p on 1½p on 2p	500.00	
a.	Tongan surch. reading up	475.00	475.00
b.	Perf. 12	475.00	*475.00*
c.	As "a," perf. 12	500.00	*500.00*
d.	As "a," "Haalf"	3,500.	
e.	"Halef"	7250.	
37	A5 ½p on 7½p on 2p	97.50	*125.00*
a.	"Half penny" inverted	3,250.	
b.	"Half penny" double		
c.	Tongan surch. reading up	97.50	*125.00*
d.	Tongan surcharge as "c" and double		
e.	"Hafl Penny"	2,500.	*2,750.*
f.	"Hafl" only	5,500.	
g.	"Hwlf"		
h.	Periods instead of hyphens after words	1,100.	
j.	Perf. 12	925.00	

Coat of Arms — A17

Ovava Tree — A18

George II — A19

Prehistoric Trilithon, Tongatabu — A20

Breadfruit A21

Coral Formations A22

View of Haabai A23

Red-breasted Musk Parrot — A24

View of Vavau — A25

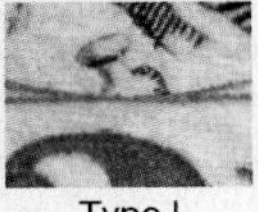
Type I

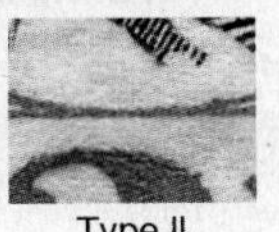
Type II

Two types of 2p:
I — Top of sword hilt shows above "2."
II — No hilt shows.

1897-1934 Engr. Wmk. 79 *Perf. 14*

38	A17	½p dark blue	.70	3.00
39	A17	½p green ('34)	1.10	1.40
40	A18	1p dp red & blk	.90	.90
41	A19	2p bis & sep (I)	20.00	7.00
a.		bister & gray, type II	35.00	3.75
42	A19	2½p lt blue & blk	8.00	1.60
a.		"½" without fraction bar	110.00	75.00
43	A20	3p ol grn & blk	4.00	9.75
44	A21	4p dull vio & grn	4.25	4.50
45	A19	5p orange & blk	35.00	16.00
46	A22	6p red	9.00	7.00
47	A19	7½p green & blk	20.00	26.00
a.		Center inverted	6,500.	
48	A19	10p carmine & blk	50.00	55.00
49	A19	1sh red brn & blk	16.00	9.00
a.		"SILENI-E-TAHA" missing second hyphen	350.00	
50	A23	2sh dk ultra & blk	30.00	32.50
51	A24	2sh6p dk violet	65.00	50.00
52	A25	5sh dull red & blk	26.00	32.50
		Nos. 38-52 (15)	289.95	256.15

See Nos. 73-74, 77-78, 80-81. For surcharges see Nos. 63-69.

Stamp of 1897 Overprinted in Black

1899, June 1

53	A18	1p red & black	45.00	72.50
a.		"1889" instead of "1899"	250.00	400.00
b.		Comma omitted after June		
c.		Double overprint		

Marriage of George II to Lavinia, June 1, 1899. The letters "T L" are the initials of Taufa'ahau, the King's family name, and Lavinia.

No. 53 exists with serifed "T" and "L". Some specialists consider it to be an essay or proof.

Queen Salote — A26

Die I

Die II

Dies of 2p:
Die I — Ball of "2" smaller.
Die II — Ball of "2" larger. "U" has spur at left.

1920-35 Engr. Wmk. 79

54	A26	1½p gray blk ('35)	.55	3.50
55	A26	2p violet & sepia	12.00	15.00
56	A26	2p dl vio & blk (I) ('24)	15.00	2.75
a.		Die II	6.00	9.50
57	A26	2½p blue & black	9.00	45.00
58	A26	2½p ultra ('34)	5.00	1.10
59	A26	5p red org & blk	3.75	5.50
60	A26	7½p green & blk	2.00	2.00
61	A26	10p carmine & blk	2.90	5.50
62	A26	1sh red brown & blk	1.40	2.90
		Nos. 54-62 (9)	51.60	83.25

See Nos. 75-76, 79.

Stamps of 1897 Srchd. in Dark Blue or Red

1923

63	A19	2p on 5p org & blk	1.10	1.00
64	A19	2p on 7½p grn & blk	37.50	45.00
65	A19	2p on 10p car & blk	25.00	65.00
66	A19	2p on 1sh red brn & blk	75.00	25.00
a.		"SILENI-E-TAHA" missing second hyphen	600.00	
67	A23	2p on 2sh ultra & blk (R)	12.00	12.00
68	A24	2p on 2sh6p dk vio (R)	35.00	7.50
69	A25	2p on 5sh dull red & blk (R)	3.50	2.50
		Nos. 63-69 (7)	189.10	158.00

Queen Salote — A27

Inscribed "1918-1938"

1938, Oct. 12 *Perf. 14*

70	A27	1p carmine & blk	.65	4.00
71	A27	2p violet & blk	8.00	3.00
72	A27	2½p ultra & blk	8.00	3.75
		Nos. 70-72 (3)	16.65	10.75
		Set, never hinged	32.00	

Accession of Queen Salote Tupou, 20th anniv.

See Nos. 82-86.

Types of 1897-1920

Die III of 2p:
Foot of "2" longer than in Die II, extending beyond curve of loop.

1942 Engr. Wmk. 4

73	A17	½p green	.30	2.75
74	A18	1p scarlet & blk	1.75	2.75
75	A26	2p dull vio & blk (II)	4.50	3.00
a.		Die III	5.50	10.00
76	A26	2½p ultra	1.10	2.00
77	A20	3p green & black	.40	4.25
78	A22	6p orange red	2.00	2.25
79	A26	1sh red brown & gray blk	3.00	3.50
80	A24	2sh6p dk violet	25.00	30.00
81	A25	5sh dull red & brn blk	12.00	60.00
		Nos. 73-81 (9)	50.05	110.50
		Set, never hinged	70.00	

Type of 1938, Inscribed "1918-1943"

1944, Jan. 25

82	A27	1p rose car & blk	.25	1.10
83	A27	2p purple & blk	.25	1.10
84	A27	3p dk yel grn & blk	.25	1.10
85	A27	6p red orange & blk	.40	2.00
86	A27	1sh dk red brn & blk	.25	2.00
		Nos. 82-86 (5)	1.40	7.30
		Set, never hinged	2.00	

25th anniv. of the accession of Queen Salote.

Catalogue values for unused stamps in this section, from this point to the end of the section, are for Never Hinged items.

UPU Issue

Common Design Types

Engr.; Name Typo. on 3p, 6p

Perf. 13½, 11x11½

1949, Oct. 10 Wmk. 4

87	CD306	2½p ultra	.25	.90
88	CD307	3p deep olive	2.00	3.25
89	CD308	6p deep carmine	.30	.55
90	CD309	1sh red brown	.45	.55
		Nos. 87-90 (4)	3.00	5.25

Common Design Types pictured following the introduction.

A28

A29

Queen Salote — A30

1950, Nov. 1 Photo. *Perf. 12½*

91	A28	1p cerise	1.20	3.00
92	A29	5p green	1.20	2.75
93	A30	1sh violet	1.20	3.00
		Nos. 91-93 (3)	3.60	8.75

50th anniv. of the birth of Queen Salote.

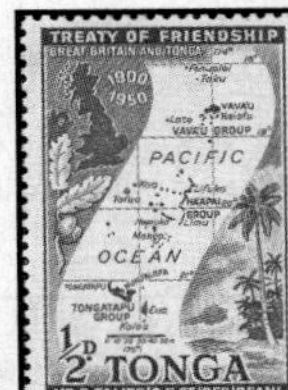

Map and Island Scene — A31

Badges and Royal Palace A32

2½p, Queen Salote & coastal scene. 3p, Queen Salote & ship "Bellona." 5p, Flag of Tonga, island view. 1sh, Arms of Tonga & Great Britain.

Perf. 13x13½ (1p), 13½x13, 12½ (3p)

1951, July 2 Engr. Wmk. 4

94	A31	½p deep green	.30	3.25
95	A32	1p carmine & black	.30	3.25
96	A32	2½p choc & dp grn	.60	3.25
97	A31	3p ultra & org yel	1.80	3.25
98	A32	5p dp green & car	2.25	1.50
99	A32	1sh purple & orange	2.25	1.50
		Nos. 94-99 (6)	7.50	16.00

50th anniv. of the treaty of friendship between Tonga and Great Britain.

OFFICIAL STAMPS

Types of Postage Issue of 1892 Overprinted in Carmine

Perf. 12x11½

1893, Feb. 13 Wmk. 62

O1	A4	1p ultra	11.50	55.00
a.		Half used as ½p on cover		
O2	A5	2p ultra	30.00	62.50
O3	A4	4p ultra	55.00	110.00
O4	A5	8p ultra	100.00	200.00
O5	A5	1sh ultra	110.00	210.00
		Nos. O1-O5 (5)	306.50	637.50

Values are for stamps of good color. Faded and discolored stamps sell for much less.

The overprinted initials stand for "Gaue Faka Buleaga" (On Government Service).

Nos. O1-O5 with Additional Surcharge Handstamped in Black

1893

O6	A4	½p on 1p ultra	20.00	57.50
O7	A5	2½p on 2p ultra	27.50	50.00
O8	A4	5p on 4p ultra	27.50	50.00
O9	A5	7½p on 8p ultra	27.50	92.50
O10	A5	10p on 1sh ultra	32.50	95.00
		Nos. O6-O10 (5)	135.00	345.00

TRANSCAUCASIAN FEDERATED REPUBLICS

ˌtranˌt͡s-ko-ˈkā-zhən ˈfe-də-rāted ri-ˈpə-blik

(Armenia, Georgia, Azerbaijan)

LOCATION — In southeastern Europe, south of the Caucasus Mountains between the Black and Caspian Seas
GOVT. — Republic
AREA — 71,255 sq. mi.
POP. — 5,851,000 (approx.)
CAPITAL — Tiflis

The Transcaucasian Federation was made up of the former autonomies of Armenia, Georgia and Azerbaijan. Its stamps were replaced by those of Russia.

100 Kopecks = 1 Ruble

Russian Stamps of 1909-17 Overprinted in Black or Red

1923 Unwmk. *Perf. 14½x15*

1 A15 10k dark blue 4.00 *5.00*
2 A14 10k on 7k lt bl 4.00 *5.00*
3 A11 25k grn & gray vio 4.00 *5.00*
4 A11 35k red brn & grn (R) 4.00 *5.00*
a. Double overprint 75.00 *75.00*
5 A8 50k brn red & grn 4.00 *5.00*
6 A9 1r pale brn, brn & org 12.00 *12.00*
7 A12 3½r mar & lt grn 50.00

Imperf

8 A9 1r pale brn, brn & red org 10.00 *6.00*
Nos. 1-8 (8) 92.00
Nos. 1-6,8 (7) *43.00*

No. 7 was prepared but not issued.

Overprinted on Stamps of Armenia Previously Handstamped

a

c

Perf. 14½x15

9 A11(c) 25k grn & gray vio *250.00 250.00*
10 A8(c) 50k vio & grn *250.00 150.00*

Perf. 13½

11 A9(a) 1r pale brn, brn & org *100.00 50.00*
12 A9(c) 1r pale brn, brn & org *150.00 50.00*

Imperf

13 A9(c) 1r pale brn, brn & red org *35.00 35.00*
Nos. 9-13 (5) *785.00 535.00*

Counterfeit overprints exist.

Oil Fields — A1

Soviet Symbols — A2

1923 *Perf. 11½*

14 A1 40,000r red violet 3.00 *2.50*
15 A1 75,000r dark grn 3.00 *2.50*
16 A1 100,000r blk vio 3.00 *2.50*
17 A1 150,000r red 3.00 *2.50*
18 A2 200,000r dull grn 3.00 *2.50*
19 A2 300,000r blue 3.00 *2.50*
20 A2 350,000r dark brn 3.00 *2.50*
21 A2 500,000r rose 3.00 *2.50*
Nos. 14-21 (8) 24.00 *20.00*

Nos. 14-21 exist imperf. but are not known to have been issued in that condition. Values, set $125.

Nos. 14-15 Srchd. in Brown

1923

22 A1 700,000r on 40,000r 2.50 *5.00*
a. Imperf., pair 30.00
23 A1 700,000r on 75,000r 2.50 *5.00*
a. Imperf., pair 30.00

Types of Preceding Issue with Values in Gold Kopecks

1923, Oct. 24

25 A2 1k orange 2.25 *1.90*
26 A2 2k blue green 2.25 *1.90*
27 A2 3k rose 2.25 *1.90*
28 A2 4k gray brown 2.25 *1.90*
29 A1 5k dark violet 2.25 *1.90*
30 A1 9k deep blue 2.25 *1.90*
31 A1 18k slate 2.25 *1.90*
Nos. 25-31 (7) 15.75 *13.30*

Nos. 25-31 exist imperf. but are not known to have been issued in that condition. Values, set $100.

TRANSVAAL

tranˌt͡s-ˈväl

(South African Republic)

LOCATION — Southern Africa
AREA — 110,450 sq. mi.
POP. — 1,261,736 (1904)
CAPITAL — Pretoria

Transvaal was known as the South African Republic until 1877 when it was occupied by the British. The republic was restored in 1884 and continued until 1900 when it was annexed to Great Britain and named "The Transvaal."

12 Pence = 1 Shilling
20 Shillings = 1 Pound

Most unused stamps between Nos. 1-96, 119-122 and 136-137 were issued with gum, but do not expect gum on scarcer stamps as few examples retain their original gum. In many cases removal of the remaining gum may enhance the preservation of the stamps. Otherwise, values for unused stamps are for examples with original gum as defined in the catalogue introduction.

Very fine imperforate stamps will have adequate to large margins. However, roulетted stamps are valued as partly rouletted, with straight edges, and rouletted just into the design, as the rouletting methods were quite inaccurate.

First Republic

Coat of Arms — A1

A1 has spread wings on eagle.

Mecklenburg Printings
By Adolph Otto, Gustrow
Fine Impressions
Thin Paper

1869 Unwmk. *Imperf.*

1 A1 1p brown lake 575.00
a. 1p red 725.00 725.00
2 A1 6p ultra 325.00 325.00
a. 6p pale ultra 260.00 260.00
3 A1 1sh dark green 875.00 875.00
a. Tete beche pair —

Rouletted 15½, 16

4 A1 1p red 185.00
a. 1p brown lake 150.00
b. 1p brick red, "narrow plate" 125.00
c. 1p vermilion, "narrow plate" 125.00
5 A1 6p ultra 165.00 *165.00*
a. 6p pale ultramarine, "narrow plate" 125.00 125.00
6 A1 1sh blue green 210.00 *210.00*
a. 1sh yellow green 285.00 *260.00*
b. 1sh deep green 350.00 *375.00*

Nos. 1-6 were printed from 2 sets of plates, differing in the spacing between the stamps.

The only known example of No. 3a is in a museum.

See Nos. 9-24, 26-33, 35-36, 38-39, 41-42, 43-49, 119, 122. For overprints see Nos. 53-61, 63-66, 68-72, 75-78, 81-83, 86-87, 90-91, 94.

Coat of Arms — A2

1871-74

7 A2 3p lilac 92.50 *100.00*
a. 3p violet 110.00 125.00
8 A2 6p brt ultra ('74) 87.50 32.50
a. Half used as 3p on cover *1,850.*

Many forgeries exist in colors duller or lighter than the genuine stamps.

In forgeries of type A1, all values, the "D" of "EENDRAGT" is not noticeably larger than the other letters and does not touch the top of the ribbon. In type A1 genuine stamps, the "D" is large and touches the ribbon top. The eagle's eye is a dot and its face white on the genuine stamps; the eye is a loop or blob attached to the beak, and the beak is strongly hooked, on the forgeries. Many forgeries of the 1sh have the top line of the ribbon broken above "EENDRAGT."

Forgeries of type A2 usually can be detected only by color.

A sharply struck cancellation of a numeral in three rings is found on many of these forgeries. The similar genuine cancellation is always roughly or heavily struck.

See Nos. 25, 34, 437, 40, 42B, 120-121. For overprints see Nos. 50-52, 62, 67, 73-74, 79-80, 84-85, 88-89, 92-93, 95-96.

Local Printings
(A) By M. J. Viljoen, Pretoria
Poor Impressions,
Overinked and Spotted

1870 Thin Soft Paper *Imperf.*

9 A1 1p pink 125.00
a. 1p rose red 135.00
b. 1p carmine 110.00 *125.00*
10 A1 6p dull ultra 375.00 80.00
a. Tete beche pair —

The only known examples of No. 10a are in museums.

Rouletted 15½, 16

11 A1 1p carmine 875.00 375.00
a. Rouletted 6½ 1,100.
12 A1 6p dull ultra 325.00 135.00

Hard Paper, Thick to Medium

Imperf

13 A1 1p carmine 115.00 *125.00*
a. 1p pale rose red 90.00
14 A1 6p ultra —
15 A1 1sh gray green 210.00 175.00
a. 1sh dark green —
b. Tete beche pair *29,000.*
c. Half used as 6p on cover 2,800.

The existence of No. 14 is questionable.

Rouletted 15½, 16

16 A1 1p light carmine 125.00 *100.00*
a. 1p carmine 87.50 *92.50*
b. 1p crimson, heavily overinked 175.00 150.00
c. 1p carmine-red, thick paper, yellow smooth gum (May 24, 1870) 125.00
17 A1 6p ultra 145.00 125.00
a. Tete beche pair *30,000.* *21,000.*
b. 6p ultra (thick paper) 125.00 82.50
c. 6p deep ultra, heavily overinked 525.00 200.00
d. As "b", tete beche pair — —

18 A1 1sh dark green 260.00 125.00
a. 1sh gray green 750.00 750.00
b. 1sh deep grn, heavily overinked 600.00 200.00

Nos. 16b, 17c and 18b sometimes are so heavily inked as to be little more than blots of color.

(B) By J. P. Borrius, Potchefstroom
Clearer Impressions Though Often Overinked

1870 Thick Porous Paper *Imperf.*

19 A1 1p black 200.00 175.00
20 A1 6p indigo —

Rouletted 15½, 16

21 A1 1p black 32.50 42.50
22 A1 6p gray blue 210.00 87.50
a. 6p indigo 145.00 115.00
b. 6p bright ultra —

Thin Transparent Paper

23 A1 1p black 325.00 *750.00*
24 A1 1p brt carmine 260.00 87.50
a. 1p deep carmine 110.00 67.50
25 A2 3p gray lilac 160.00 72.50
26 A1 6p ultra 110.00 42.50
27 A1 1sh yellow green 135.00 72.50
a. 1sh deep green 135.00 72.50
b. Half used as 6p on cover — *2,800.*

Thick Soft Paper

28 A1 1p dull rose 525.00 115.00
a. 1p brown rose 675.00 155.00
b. Printed on both sides —
29 A1 6p dull blue 135.00 57.50
a. 6p bright blue 325.00 87.50
b. 6p ultramarine 300.00 87.50
c. Rouletted 6½ —
30 A1 1sh yellow green 1,400. 875.00

The paper of Nos. 28 to 30 varies considerably in thickness.

(C) By P. Davis & Son, Natal
Thin to Medium Paper

1874 *Perf. 12½*

31 A1 1p red 150.00 50.00
a. 1p brownish red 150.00 50.00
32 A1 6p deep blue 200.00 70.00
a. 6p blue 185.00 62.50
b. Horiz. pair, imperf. between —

(D) By the Stamp Commission, Pretoria
Pelure Paper

1875-76 *Imperf.*

33 A1 1p pale red 70.00 65.00
a. 1p orange red 65.00 32.50
b. 1p brown red 80.00 40.00
c. Pin perf. 775.00 475.00
34 A2 3p gray lilac 80.00 55.00
a. 3p dull violet 90.00 55.00
b. Pin perf. — 500.00
35 A1 6p blue 77.50 55.00
a. 6p pale blue 77.50 62.50
b. 6p dark blue 82.50 57.50
c. Tete beche pair, thin opaque paper *20,000.*
d. Tete beche pair, pelure, transparent paper —
e. Pin perf. — 400.00

The only known examples of No. 35c are in museums.

Rouletted 15½, 16

36 A1 1p orange red 450.00 155.00
a. Rouletted 6½ 1,250. 250.00
b. 1p bright red 1,250. 250.00
37 A2 3p dull violet 500.00 165.00
a. Rouletted 6½ *1,100.* 320.00
38 A1 6p blue 215.00 130.00
a. Rouletted 6½ 1,275. 140.00

The paper of this group varies slightly in thickness and is sometimes divided into pelure and semipelure. We believe there was only one lot of the paper and that the separation is not warranted.

Thick Hard Paper

Imperf

39 A1 1p org red ('76) 32.50 25.00
40 A2 3p lilac 425.00 140.00
41 A1 6p deep blue 70.00 25.00
a. 6p blue 115.00 27.50
b. Tete beche pair *20,000.*

Rouletted 15½, 16

42 A1 1p org red ('76) 475.00 175.00
a. Rouletted 6½ ('75) 700.00 175.00
42B A2 3p lilac 400.00
43 A1 6p deep blue *700.00* 325.00
a. 6p blue *875.00* 125.00
b. Rouletted 6½ ('75) *750.00* 300.00

Soft Porous Paper

Imperf

44 A1 1p orange red 150.00 62.50
45 A1 6p deep blue 225.00 650.00
a. 6p dull blue 400.00 110.00
46 A1 1sh yellow green 460.00 140.00
a. Half used as 6p on cover 1,850.

Rouletted 15½, 16

47 A1 1p orange red — 425.00
a. Rouletted 6½ — *525.00*
48 A1 6p deep blue — *185.00*
a. Rouletted 6½ — *1,275.*

49 A1 1sh yellow grn 800.00 400.00
- *a.* Rouletted 6½ — 1,400.
- *b.* Rouletted 15½-16x16½ 800.00 400.00

First British Occupation

Stamps and Types of 1875 Overprinted

Red Overprint
Pelure Paper

1877 **Unwmk.** ***Imperf.***

50 A2 3p lilac 1,500. 210.00
- *a.* Overprinted on back 3,750. *3,750.*
- *b.* Double ovpt., red and black *7,000.*

Rouletted 15½, 16

51 A2 3p lilac — *1,850.*
- *a.* Rouletted 6½ — *2,600.*

Thin Hard Paper
Imperf

52 A2 3p lilac 1,500. 350.00

Soft Porous Paper

53 A1 6p blue 1,850. *210.00*
- *a.* 6p deep blue — *300.00*
- *b.* Inverted overprint *6,000.*
- *c.* Double overprint 5,250. 1,150.

54 A1 1sh yellow grn 750.00 210.00
- *a.* Inverted overprint *5,250.*
- *b.* Half used as 6p on cover *2,100.*

Rouletted 15½, 16

55 A1 6p blue *2,000.*
- *a.* Rouletted 6½ *2,750.*

56 A1 1sh yellow grn 2,000. 875.00
- *a.* Rouletted 6½ 4,750. *2,750.*
- *b.* As "a.", overprint inverted *7,500.*

Black Overprint
Pelure Paper
Imperf

57 A1 1p red 360.00 145.00

Rouletted 15½, 16

58 A1 1p red — *1,350.*

Thick Hard Paper
Imperf

59 A1 1p red 35.00 27.50
- *a.* Inverted overprint 650.00 575.00

Rouletted 15½, 16

60 A1 1p red 185.00 57.50
- *a.* Rouletted 6½ 750.00 350.00
- *b.* Inverted overprint
- *c.* Double overprint *1,275.*

Soft Porous Paper
Imperf

61 A1 1p red 35.00 40.00
- *a.* Double overprint 1,400.

62 A2 3p lilac 110.00 52.50
- *a.* 3p deep lilac 200.00 97.50
- *b.* Inverted overprint —

63 A1 6p dull blue 200.00 100.00
- *a.* 6p bright blue 185.00 35.00
- *b.* 6p dark blue 185.00 *250.00*
- *d.* Inverted overprint 1,650. —
- *e.* Double overprint *4,000.* 2,400.

64 A1 6p blue, *rose* 115.00 55.00
- *a.* Tete beche pair —
- *b.* Inverted overprint 140.00 55.00
- *c.* Overprint omitted 4,000. 2,900.
- *d.* Half used as 3p on cover

65 A1 1sh yellow grn 150.00 65.00
- *a.* Tete beche pair 23,500. *24,000.*
- *b.* Inverted overprint 1,400. 500.00
- *c.* Half used as 6p on cover *1,750.*

The only known examples of No. 64a are in museums.

Rouletted 15½, 16

66 A1 1p red 100.00 85.00
- *a.* Rouletted 6½ 750.00 175.00

67 A2 3p lilac 240.00 75.00
- *a.* Rouletted 6½ *875.00*

68 A1 6p dull blue 240.00 75.00
- *a.* Inverted overprint — *875.00*
- *b.* Rouletted 6½ *1,400.*
- *c.* As "a," rouletted 6½ *4,750.*

69 A1 6p blue, *rose* 300.00 80.00
- *a.* Inverted overprint 650.00 80.00
- *b.* Rouletted 6½
- *c.* Tete beche pair
- *d.* Overprint omitted
- *e.* As "a," rouletted 6½ 750.00
- *f.* As "d," rouletted 6½

70 A1 1sh yellow grn 325.00 125.00
- *a.* Inverted overprint 1,400. 575.00
- *b.* Rouletted 6½ 550.00 150.00
- *c.* As "a," rouletted 6½ 1,750. 700.00

In this issue the space between "V. R." and "TRANSVAAL" is normally 8½mm but in position 11 it is 12mm. In this and the following issues there are numerous minor varieties of the overprint, missing periods, etc.

The only known examples of No. 69c are in museums.

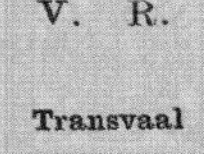

Types A1 and A2 Overprinted

1877-79 ***Imperf.***

71 A1 1p red, *blue* 70.00 35.00
- *a.* "Transvral" *6,500.* *2,900.*
- *b.* Inverted overprint *925.00* 475.00
- *c.* Double overprint *4,750.*
- *d.* Overprint omitted —

72 A1 1p red, *org* ('78) 37.50 24.00
- *a.* Printed on both sides —
- *b.* Pin perf. —

73 A2 3p lilac, *buff* 75.00 50.00
- *a.* Inverted overprint 875.00
- *b.* Pin perf. —

74 A2 3p lilac, *grn* ('79) 175.00 70.00
- *a.* Inverted overprint 2,350.
- *b.* Double overprint —
- *c.* Pin perf. —

75 A1 6p blue, *grn* 115.00 45.00
- *a.* Tete beche pair *20,000.*
- *b.* Inverted overprint *1,275.*
- *c.* Half used as 3p on cover —
- *d.* Pin perf. —

76 A1 6p blue, *bl* ('78) 80.00 32.50
- *a.* Tete beche pair —
- *b.* Overprint omitted *2,750.*
- *c.* Inverted overprint *1,275.*
- *d.* Half used as 3p on cover *925.00*
- *e.* Double overprint 3,750.
- *f.* Pin perf. —

Nos. 71-76 (6) 552.50 256.50

The only known examples of No. 76a are in museums.

Rouletted 15½, 16

77 A1 1p red, *blue* 125.00 45.00
- *a.* "Transvral" 3,500.
- *b.* Inverted overprint —
- *c.* Double overprint —

78 A1 1p red, *org* ('78) 47.50 32.50
- *a.* Horiz. pair, imperf. vert.
- *b.* Rouletted 6½ 300.00 115.00

79 A2 3p lilac, *buff* 125.00 32.50
- *a.* Inverted overprint 3,500.
- *b.* Vert. pair, imperf. horiz. 875.00
- *c.* Rouletted 6½ 115.00

80 A2 3p lilac, *grn* ('79) 800.00 175.00
- *a.* Inverted overprint
- *b.* Rouletted 6½ 750.00 325.00

81 A1 6p blue, *green* 110.00 32.50
- *a.* Inverted overprint *750.00*
- *b.* Overprint omitted *4,750.*
- *c.* Tete beche pair —
- *d.* Half used at 3p on cover 800.00
- *e.* Rouletted 6½ — *1,275.*

82 A1 6p blue, *bl* ('78) 325.00 65.00
- *a.* Inverted overprint — 1,050.
- *b.* Overprint omitted — 4,000.
- *c.* Tete beche pair —
- *d.* Horiz. pair, imperf. vert. —
- *e.* Half used as 3p on cover *900.00*
- *f.* Double overprint —
- *g.* Rouletted 6½ 350.00
- *h.* As "a," rouletted 6½ —

Nos. 77-82 (6) 1,533. 382.50

The only known examples of No. 81c are in museums. The existence of No. 82c is questioned.

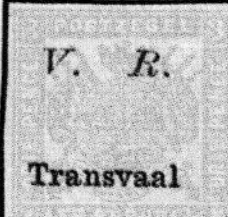

Types A1 and A2 Overprinted

Imperf

83 A1 1p red, *org* ('78) 80.00 52.50

84 A2 3p lilac, *buff* ('78) 92.50 40.00
- *a.* Pin perf. 875.00 875.00

85 A2 3p lilac, *grn* ('79) 160.00 40.00
- *a.* Inverted overprint *2,300.*
- *b.* Overprint omitted —
- *c.* Printed on both sides *1,150.*

86 A1 6p blue, *bl* ('78) 160.00 50.00
- *a.* Tete beche pair *18,000.*
- *b.* Inverted overprint *800.00*

Nos. 83-86 (4) 492.50 182.50

Rouletted 15½, 16

87 A1 1p red, *org* ('78) 200.00 140.00
- *a.* Rouletted 6½ 350.00

88 A2 3p lilac, *buff* ('78) 210.00 125.00
- *a.* Vert. pair, imperf. horiz. —
- *b.* Rouletted 6½ 400.00

89 A2 3p lilac, *grn* ('79) 800.00 175.00
- *a.* Inverted overprint —
- *b.* Overprint omitted —
- *c.* Rouletted 6½ ('97) 350.00

90 A1 6p blue, *bl* ('78) 500.00 125.00
- *a.* Tete beche pair
- *b.* Inverted overprint — *1,275.*
- *d.* Rouletted 6½ 400.00
- *e.* As "b," rouletted 6½

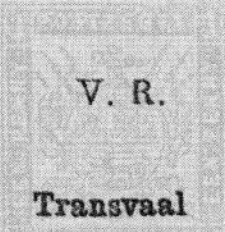

Types A1 and A2 Overprinted

1879 ***Imperf.***

91 A1 1p red, *orange* 55.00 50.00
- *a.* 1p red, *yellow* 57.50 55.00
- *b.* Small capital "T" 350.00 200.00

92 A2 3p lilac, *green* 52.50 40.00
- *a.* Small capital "T" 300.00 115.00

93 A2 3p lilac, *blue* 57.50 35.00
- *a.* Small capital "T" 325.00 110.00

Nos. 91-93 (3) 165.00 125.00

Rouletted 15½, 16

94 A1 1p red, *yellow* 400.00 240.00
- *a.* 1p red, *orange* 875.00 450.00
- *b.* Small capital "T" 1,100. 750.00
- *c.* Rouletted 6½ 750.00 750.00
- *d.* Pin perf. *875.00*

95 A2 3p lilac, *green* 875.00 300.00
- *a.* Small capital "T" *1,000.*
- *b.* Rouletted 6½ 1,150. 750.00

96 A2 3p lilac, *blue* 210.00
- *a.* Small capital "T" 800.00
- *b.* Rouletted 6½ 950.00
- *c.* Pin perf. *1,000.*

Queen Victoria — A3

1878-80 **Engr.** ***Perf. 14, 14½***

97 A3 ½p vermilion ('80) 30.00 *100.00*
98 A3 1p red brown 19.00 5.25
99 A3 3p claret 30.00 9.25
100 A3 4p olive green 32.50 9.25
101 A3 6p slate 19.00 6.50
- *a.* Half used as 3p on cover —

102 A3 1sh green 140.00 55.00
103 A3 2sh blue 225.00 95.00

Nos. 97-103 (7) 495.50 280.25

For surcharges see Nos. 104-118, 138-139.

No. 101 Surcharged in Red or Black

(a) Surcharged

Surcharge distinction: "PENNY" in gothic capitals.

1879

104 A3 1p on 6p slate (R) 200.00 95.00
105 A3 1p on 6p slate (Bk) 55.00 27.50

(b) Surcharged

Surcharge distinction: "1" has heavy serif at base; "P," thin serif at base.

106 A3 1p on 6p slate (R) 750.00 400.00
107 A3 1p on 6p slate (Bk) 275.00 95.00

(c) Surcharged

Surcharge distinction: No serif at base of "1."

108 A3 1p on 6p slate (R) 750.00 400.00
109 A3 1p on 6p slate (Bk) 275.00 95.00

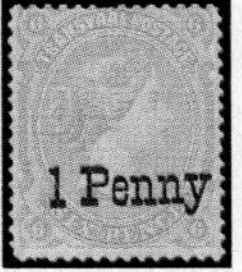

(d) Surcharged

Surcharge distinction: Heavy serifs at base of "1" and "p."

110 A3 1p on 6p slate (R) 375.00 210.00
111 A3 1p on 6p slate (Bk) 110.00 55.00
- *a.* Pair, one without surcharge —

(e) Surcharged

Surcharge distinction: Italics.

112 A3 1p on 6p slate (R) 700.00 375.00
113 A3 1p on 6p slate (Bk) 240.00 87.50

(f) Surcharged

Surcharge distinction: "1" has long, sloping serif at top, thin serif at base.

114 A3 1p on 6p slate (R) 325.00 185.00
115 A3 1p on 6p slate (Bk) 110.00 50.00

(g) Surcharged **1 Penny**

Surcharge distinction: Tail of "y" missing.

116 A3 1p on 6p slate (R) 7,000. 1,850.
117 A3 1p on 6p slate (Bk) 700.00 185.00

Second Republic

No. 100 Surcharged

1882 **Unwmk.** ***Perf. 14, 14½***

118 A3 1p on 4p olive grn 20.00 7.00
- *a.* Inverted surcharge 375.00 250.00

1883 ***Perf. 12***

119 A1 1p black 8.00 3.00
- *a.* Imperf. —
- *b.* Vert. pair, imperf. horiz. 650.00 400.00
- *c.* Horiz. pair, imperf. vert. 325.00

120 A2 3p red 17.50 3.50
- *a.* Horiz. pair, imperf. vert. — *1,000.*
- *b.* Half used as 1p on cover *750.00*

121 A2 3p black, *rose* 32.50 7.50
- *a.* Half used as 1p on cover *750.00*

122 A1 1sh green 80.00 7.00
- *a.* Tete beche pair 1,150. 185.00
- *b.* Half used as 6p on cover *550.00*

Nos. 119-122 (4) 138.00 21.00

The so-called reprints of this issue are forgeries. They were made from the counterfeit plates described in the note following No. 8, plus a new false plate for the 3p. The false 3p plate has many small flaws and defects.

Forgeries of No. 120 are in dull orange red, clearly printed on whitish paper, and those of No. 121 in brownish or grayish black on bright rose. Genuine examples of No. 120 lack the orange tint and the paper is yellowish; genuine examples of No. 121 are in black without gray or brown shade, on dull lilac rose paper.

A 6p in slate on white, apparently of this issue, is a late print from the counterfeit plate.

A4

Perf. 13½, 11½x12, 12½, 12½x12

1885-93 **Typo.**

123 A4 ½p gray 1.75 .25
- *a.* Imperf. at top and bottom (used strip of 4) —

124 A4 1p rose 1.20 .25
125 A4 2p brown 3.00 *4.00*
126 A4 2p olive bis ('87) 2.40 .25
127 A4 2½p purple ('93) 3.50 .65
128 A4 3p violet 3.75 2.50
129 A4 4p bronze green 5.25 1.50
130 A4 6p blue 4.50 3.75
- *a.* Imperf. —

131 A4 1sh green 3.75 1.50
132 A4 2sh6p yellow 14.00 3.75
133 A4 5sh steel blue 10.00 6.50
134 A4 10sh pale brown 40.00 13.00

135 A4 £5 dk grn ('92) 4,000. 225.00
Overprinted "Monster" (Specimen) 175.00
Nos. 123-134 (12) 93.10 37.90

Reprints of Nos. 123-137, 140-163, 166-174 closely resemble the originals. Paper is whiter; perf. 12½, large holes.

Excellent counterfeits of No. 135 exist.

For overprint and surcharges see Nos. 140-147, 163, 213.

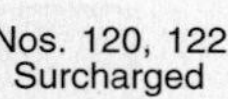

Nos. 120, 122 Surcharged

1885 ***Perf. 12***

136 A2 ½p on 3p red 8.75 *13.00*
a. Surcharge reading down 8.75 *13.00*
137 A1 ½p on 1sh green 32.50 65.00
a. Surcharge reading down 32.50 65.00
b. Tete beche pair 1,000. 450.00

Almost all examples of No. 137b have telegraph cancellations. Postally used examples are rare.

Nos. 101, 128 Surcharged in Red or Black

Perf. 14

138 A3 ½p on 6p slate 85.00 *115.00*
139 A3 2p on 6p slate 11.00 *17.50*
a. Horiz. pair, imperf. vert. —

Perf. 11½x12, 12½x12

140 A4 ½p on 3p vio (Bk) 7.50 7.50
a. "PRNNY" 55.00 *75.00*
b. 2nd "N" of "PENNY" invtd. 105.00 *115.00*

No. 128 Surcharged

No. 141

No. 142

1887

141 A4 2p on 3p violet 2.40 *5.00*
a. Double surcharge 210.00 210.00
142 A4 2p on 3p violet 11.50 10.50
a. Double surcharge — *400.00*

Nos. 126, 130, 131 Surcharged

Nos. 143-144

Nos. 145-146

No. 147

1893 **Red Surcharge**

143 A4 ½p on 2p olive bis .90 *3.00*
a. Inverted surcharge 3.00 3.50
b. Bars 14mm apart 1.75 *3.75*
c. As "b," inverted 5.75 *11.50*

Black Surcharge

144 A4 ½p on 2p olive bis 1.00 *3.00*
a. Inverted surcharge 5.25 *5.75*
b. Bars 14mm apart 1.75 *3.75*
c. As "b," inverted 23.00 18.50
145 A4 1p on 6p blue 2.00 2.00
a. Inverted surcharge 2.60 *3.00*
b. Double surcharge 65.00 52.50
c. Pair, one without surcharge 260.00
d. Bars 14mm apart 3.00 3.00
e. As "d," inverted 6.50 5.25
f. As "d," double 95.00
146 A4 2½p on 1sh green 2.60 *6.25*
a. Inverted surcharge 8.00 *8.50*
b. Fraction line misplaced "2/12" 50.00 *87.50*
c. As "b," inverted 400.00 350.00
d. Bars 14mm apart 3.75 *8.75*
e. As "d," inverted 11.00 *21.00*
147 A4 2½p on 1sh green 8.00 7.00
a. Inverted surcharge 10.00 10.00
b. Bars 14mm apart 13.00 13.00
c. As "b," inverted 24.00 24.00
d. Double surcharge 92.50 *105.00*
Nos. 143-147 (5) 14.50 21.25

A13

Wagon with Two Shafts

1894 **Typo.** ***Perf. 12½***

148 A13 ½p gray 1.50 .90
149 A13 1p rose 2.40 .25
150 A13 2p olive bister 2.40 .25
151 A13 6p blue 3.25 .60
152 A13 1sh yellow grn 17.50 *22.00*
Nos. 148-152 (5) 27.05 24.00

Counterfeits of Nos.148-152 are plentiful.

See note following No. 135 for reprints.

1895-96 **Wagon with Pole**

153 A13 ½p gray 1.50 .25
154 A13 1p rose 1.50 .25
155 A13 2p olive bister 1.75 .35
156 A13 3p violet 3.00 1.00
157 A13 4p slate 3.50 1.00
158 A13 6p blue 3.50 1.00
159 A13 1sh green 4.00 1.75
160 A13 5sh slate blue ('96) 20.00 *35.00*
161 A13 10sh red brown ('96) 20.00 8.00
Nos. 153-161 (9) 58.75 48.60

Most of the unused examples of Nos. 153-161 now on the market are reprints.

See Nos. 166-174. For surcharge see No. 162.

See note following No. 135 for reprints.

Nos. 159, 127 Surcharged in Red or Green

1895

162 A13 ½p on 1sh green (R) 1.75 .25
a. Inverted surcharge 5.25 5.25
b. "Pennij" instead of "Penny" 70.00 *80.00*
c. Double surcharge 75.00 *105.00*
163 A4 1p on 2½p pur (G) .60 .30
a. Inverted surcharge 20.00 20.00
b. Surcharge sideways — —
c. Surcharge on back 4,000.
d. Space between "1" and "d" 1.50 *1.75*

A16

1895 ***Perf. 11½***

164 A16 6p rose (G) 2.40 2.60
a. Vertical pair, imperf. between —

Counterfeits of No. 164 are on the 6p dark red revenue stamp of 1898, and have a shiny green ink for the overprint. The false overprint is also found on other revenue denominations, though only the 6p rose was converted to postal use.

Coat of Arms, Wheat Field and Railroad Train — A17

1895, Sept. 6 **Litho.**

165 A17 1p red 3.00 *3.50*
a. Imperf. —
b. Vertical pair, imperf. between 240.00 *260.00*

Penny Postage in Transvaal. Horiz. pair, imperf. between also exists.

For overprint see No. 245.

Arms Type of 1894 With Pole

1896 **Typo.** ***Perf. 12½***

166 A13 ½p green 1.20 .25
167 A13 1p rose & grn 1.20 .25
168 A13 2p brown & grn 1.20 .25
169 A13 2½p ultra & grn 2.40 .25
170 A13 3p red vio & grn 3.00 3.00
171 A13 4p olive & grn 3.00 *3.50*
172 A13 6p violet & grn 2.00 2.00
173 A13 1sh bister & grn 2.60 .80
174 A13 2sh6p lilac & grn 3.00 *3.50*
Nos. 166-174 (9) 19.60 13.80

See note following No. 135 for reprints.

For overprints and surcharges see Nos. 202-212, 214-235, 237-244, 246-251, Cape of Good Hope Nos. N5-N8.

Pietersburg Issue

Date large; "P" in Postzegel large — A18

Date small; "P" in Postzegel large — A19

Date small; "P" in Postzegel small — A20

1901 **Typeset** ***Imperf.***

Initials in Red

175 A18 ½p black, *green* 37.50
a. Initials omitted 125.00
b. Initials in black 45.00
176 A19 ½p black, *green* 50.00
a. Initials omitted 125.00
b. Initials in black 52.50
177 A20 ½p black, *green* 50.00
a. Initials omitted 125.00
b. Initials in black 52.50

Initials in Black

178 A18 1p black, *rose* 5.00
179 A19 1p black, *rose* 6.50
180 A20 1p black, *rose* 8.00
181 A18 2p black, *orange* 7.50
182 A19 2p black, *orange* 20.00
183 A20 2p black, *orange* 25.00
184 A18 4p black, *dull blue* 12.50
185 A19 4p black, *dull blue* 15.00
186 A20 4p black, *dull blue* 40.00
187 A18 6p black, *green* 16.50
188 A19 6p black, *green* 20.00
189 A20 6p black, *green* 55.00
190 A18 1sh black, *yellow* 12.50
191 A19 1sh black, *yellow* 20.00
192 A20 1sh black, *yellow* 30.00

Perf. 11½

Initials in Red

193 A18 ½p black, *green* 6.50
194 A19 ½p black, *green* 20.00
195 A20 ½p black, *green* 15.00

Initials in Black

196 A18 1p black, *rose* 3.00
a. Horiz. pair, imperf. vert. 65.00
197 A19 1p black, *rose* 3.50
a. Horiz. pair, imperf. vert. 100.00
198 A20 1p black, *rose* 6.50
a. Horiz. pair, imperf. vert. 100.00
199 A18 2p black, *orange* 7.50
200 A19 2p black, *orange* 9.50
201 A20 2p black, *orange* 17.00

Nos. 193-201 inclusive are always imperforate on one side.

The setting consisted of 12 stamps of type A18, 6 of type A19, and 6 of type A20. Numerous type-setting varieties exist. The perforated stamps are from the first printing and were put into use first. Used stamps are not valued because all seem to show evidence of having been canceled to order.

Second British Occupation Issued under Military Authority

Nos. 166-174, 160-161, 135 Overprinted

1900 **Unwmk.** ***Perf. 12½***

202 A13 ½p green .35 .60
a. "V.I.R." 700.00
203 A13 1p rose & grn .35 .50
204 A13 2p brown & grn 4.00 3.00
a. "V.I.R." 700.00 *750.00*
205 A13 2½p ultra & grn 1.25 *3.00*
206 A13 3p red vio & grn 1.25 *2.60*
207 A13 4p olive & grn 3.75 3.25
a. "V.I.R." 700.00
208 A13 6p violet & grn 3.75 2.00
209 A13 1sh bister & grn 3.75 *4.50*
210 A13 2sh6p hel & grn 4.75 *14.00*
211 A13 5sh slate blue 9.50 20.00
212 A13 10sh red brown 11.50 22.00
213 A4 £5 dark green 2,500. 925.00
Nos. 202-212 (11) 44.20 75.45

Nos. 202-213 have been extensively counterfeited. The overprint on the forgeries is clear and clean, with small periods and letters showing completely. In the genuine, letters are worn and lack many or all serifs; the periods are large and oval.

The genuine overprint exists inverted; double; with period missing after "V," after "R," after "I," etc.

Issued in Lydenburg

Nos. 166-169, 171-173 Overprinted in Black

1900

214 A13 ½p green 160.00 160.00
215 A13 1p rose & grn 150.00 140.00
216 A13 2p brown & grn 1,400. 1,000.
217 A13 2½p ultra & grn 2,600. 1,050.
218 A13 4p olive & grn 3,750. 1,050.
219 A13 6p violet & grn 3,250. 1,000.
220 A13 1sh bister & grn 5,500. 3,250.

Beware of counterfeits.

No. 167 Surcharged

221 A13 3p on 1p rose & grn 130.00 110.00

Issued in Rustenburg

Nos. 166-170, 172-174 Handstamped in Violet

1900 ***Perf. 12½***

223 A13 ½p green 175.00 130.00
224 A13 1p rose & grn 130.00 100.00
225 A13 2p brown & grn 375.00 190.00
226 A13 2½p ultra & grn 210.00 130.00
227 A13 3p red vio & grn 300.00 175.00
229 A13 6p violet & grn 1,400. 500.00
230 A13 1sh bister & grn 2,000. 1,100.
231 A13 2sh6p hel & grn *8,000.*

Issued in Schweizer Reneke Nos. 166-168 and 172 Handstamped "BESIEGED" in Black

1900 **Typo.** ***Perf. 12½***

232 A13 ½p green 290.00
233 A13 1p rose & green 300.00
234 A13 2p brown & green 450.00
235 A13 6p violet & green 1,150.
Nos. 232-235 (4) 2,190.

Same Overprint on Cape of Good Hope No. 59 and Type of 1893
Perf. 14

236 A15 ½p green 600.00
236A A15 1p carmine 600.00

In 1902 five revenue stamps overprinted "V.R.I." are said to have been used postally in Volksrust. There seems to be some doubt that this issue was properly authorized for postal use.

Issued in Wolmaransstad

Nos. 166-173 Handstamped in Blue or Red

1900
237 A13 ½p green 290.00 *450.00*
238 A13 1p rose & grn 200.00 *325.00*
239 A13 2p brown & grn 2,100. 2,100.
240 A13 2½p ultra & grn (R) 2,100.
241 A13 3p red vio & grn 3,500. *3,750.*
242 A13 4p olive & grn 4,750. *5,250.*
243 A13 6p violet & grn 5,250. *5,750.*
244 A13 1sh bister & grn *11,000.*

No. 165 Overprinted in Blue

245 A17 1p red 260.00 *475.00*

Regular Issues
No. 166-168, 170-171, 174 Surcharged or Overprinted

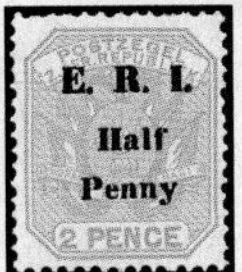

1901-02
246 A13 ½p on 2p brn & grn .80 1.20
247 A13 ½p green .60 *1.75*
248 A13 1p rose & grn .60 .25
a. Overprint "E" omitted 87.50
249 A13 3p red vio & grn 2.60 *4.25*
250 A13 4p olive & grn 2.75 *6.25*
251 A13 2sh6p hel & grn 10.50 *30.00*
Nos. 246-251 (6) 17.85 43.70

Excellent counterfeits of Nos. 246-251 are plentiful. See note after No. 213 for the recognition marks of the counterfeits.

Edward VII — A27

Nos. 260, 262 to 267 and 275 to 280 have "POSTAGE" at each side; the other stamps of type A27 have "REVENUE" at the right.

Wmk. Crown and C A (2)
1902-03 Typo. *Perf. 14*
252 A27 ½p gray grn & blk 2.00 .25
253 A27 1p rose & blk 1.50 .25
254 A27 2p violet & blk 5.00 1.20
255 A27 2½p ultra & blk 11.50 1.50
256 A27 3p ol grn & blk 10.50 1.00
257 A27 4p choc & blk 10.50 2.00
258 A27 6p brn org & blk 5.00 1.20
259 A27 1sh ol grn & blk 16.50 *20.00*
260 A27 1sh red brn & blk 15.00 5.00
261 A27 2sh brown & blk 60.00 *70.00*
262 A27 2sh yel & blk 17.50 *18.50*
263 A27 2sh6p black & vio 18.50 17.50
264 A27 5sh vio & blk, *yel* 35.00 *45.00*
265 A27 10sh vio & blk, *red* 75.00 47.50
266 A27 £1 violet & grn 325.00 190.00
267 A27 £5 violet & org 1,650. 750.00
Nos. 252-266 (15) 608.50 420.90

Issue dates: 3p, 4p, Nos. 260, 262, £1, £5, 1903. Others, Apr. 1, 1902.

1904-09 Wmk. 3
268 A27 ½p gray grn & blk 10.50 3.50
269 A27 1p rose & blk 8.00 1.20
270 A27 2p violet & blk 15.00 2.40
271 A27 2½p ultra & blk 22.00 10.00
272 A27 3p ol grn & blk 4.00 .60
273 A27 4p choc & blk 5.50 .80
274 A27 6p brn org & blk 13.00 2.40
275 A27 1sh red brn & blk 10.50 .60
276 A27 2sh yellow & blk 27.50 10.50
277 A27 2sh6p blk & red vio 55.00 10.00
278 A27 5sh vio & blk, *yel* 29.00 1.75
279 A27 10sh vio & blk, *red* 80.00 3.50
280 A27 £1 violet & grn 350.00 40.00
Nos. 268-280 (13) 630.00 87.25

The 2p and 3p are on chalky paper, the 2½p, 4p, 6p and £1 on both chalky and ordinary, and the other values on ordinary paper only.

Issue years: ½p, 1p, 5sh, 1904. 2½p, 6p, 1sh, 1905. 2p, 3p, 4p, 2sh, 1906. 10sh, 1907. £1, 1908. 2sh6p, 1909.

1905-10
281 A27 ½p green 2.75 .25
a. Booklet pane of 6 —
282 A27 1p carmine 1.50 .25
a. Wmk. 16 (anchor) ('07) — *375.00*
b. Booklet pane of 6 —
283 A27 2p dull vio ('10) 4.00 .75
284 A27 2½p ultra ('10) 20.00 10.00
Nos. 281-284 (4) 28.25 11.25

Wmk. 16 is illustrated in the Cape of Good Hope.

Some of the above stamps are found with the overprint "C. S. A. R." for use by the Central South African Railway, the control mark being applied after the stamps had left the post office.

POSTAGE DUE STAMPS

D1

Wmk. Multiple Crown and C A (3)
1907 Typo. *Perf. 14*
J1 D1 ½p green & blk 4.00 1.50
On cover 25.00
J2 D1 1p carmine & blk 4.75 1.00
On cover 25.00
J3 D1 2p brown org 5.75 1.50
On cover 90.00
J4 D1 3p blue & blk 8.75 5.00
On cover 125.00
J5 D1 5p violet & blk 2.75 *14.00*
On cover 200.00
J6 D1 6p red brown & blk 5.00 *14.00*
On cover 200.00
J7 D1 1sh black & car 14.00 10.00
On cover 300.00
Nos. J1-J7 (7) 45.00 47.00

Most canceled examples of Nos. J1-J7 were used outside the Transvaal under the Union of South Africa administration in 1910-16. Values on cover are for commercial usages in the Transvaal, prior to the South African union.

The stamps of Transvaal were replaced by those of South Africa.

TRINIDAD

'tri-nə-,dad

LOCATION — West Indies, off the Venezuelan coast
GOVT. — British Colony which became part of the Colony of Trinidad and Tobago in 1889
AREA — 1,864 sq. mi.
POP. — 387,000
CAPITAL — Port of Spain

12 Pence = 1 Shilling
20 Shillings = 1 Pound

PRE-STAMP POSTAL MARKINGS

Crowned Circle handstamp type VII is pictured in the Crowned Circle Handstamps and Great Britain Used Abroad section.

Port of Spain

1850
A1 VII "Trinidad" crowned circle handstamp in red, on cover 3,100.

Though postage stamps were available in 1851, this handstamp was used on outgoing foreign mail covers which lacked postage stamps until 1858. However, most foreign mail covers did bear an adhesive, and covers with this handstamp and an additional adhesive stamp sell for less.

In 1847 David Bryce, owner of the "Lady McLeod," issued a blue, lithographed, imperf. stamp to prepay his 5-cent rate for carrying letters on his sail-equipped steamer between Port of Spain and San Fernando, another Trinidad port. The stamp pictures the "Lady McLeod" above the monogram "LMcL," expressing no denomination. Value: unused, $50,000; used (pen canceled), $12,500; on cover (pen caneled), $24,000; used stamps canceled by having a corner skinned off, $5,500; cover bearing skinned stamp, $10,000.

Values for unused stamps are for examples with original gum as defined in the catalogue introduction. However, Nos. 9-12 are seldom found with gum, and these are valued without gum.

Values for Nos. 18-26 are for stamps with pin perforations on two or three sides. Stamps with pin perforations on all four sides are not often seen and command large premiums.

Very fine examples of Nos. 27-47 will have perforations touching the design on one or more sides due to the narrow spacing of the stamps on the plates and imperfect perforating methods. These stamps with perfs clear of the design on all four sides are scarce and command substantially higher prices.

"Britannia" — A1

1851-56 Unwmk. Engr. *Imperf.*
Blued Paper
1 A1 (1p) brick red ('56) 200.00 85.00
a. (1p) brown red ('53) 360.00 77.50
2 A1 (1p) purple brown 22.50 *90.00*
3 A1 (1p) blue 24.00 *72.50*
a. (1p) deep blue, deeply blued paper 175.00 95.00
4 A1 (1p) gray brn ('53) 57.50 *90.00*
a. (1p) gray ('52) 90.00 77.50
Nos. 1-4 (4) 304.00 *337.50*

1854-57 White Paper
6 A1 (1p) brown red ('57) 3,250. 77.50
7 A1 (1p) gray 55.00 *95.00*
8 A1 (1p) black violet 32.50 *100.00*

See Nos. 14, 18, 22, 27, 33, 39, 43, 45, 48, 58. For surcharges see Nos. 62-64.

"Britannia" — A2

1852 Litho.
Fine Impressions
Yellowish Paper
9 A2 (1p) blue *11,500.* 1,950.
a. (1p) deep blue *11,500.* 1,950.
b. White paper 1,950.

1853 Bluish Paper
10 A2 (1p) blue *10,000.* 2,400.

Same, Lines of Background More or Less Worn

1855-60 Thin Paper
11 A2 (1p) slate blue *5,500.* 800.00
12 A2 (1p) blue *5,000.* 500.00
a. (1p) greenish blue 800.00
13 A2 (1p) rose 17.50 *750.00*
a. (1p) dull red 17.50 *725.00*

A3

1859 Engr. *Imperf.*
White Paper
14 A1 (1p) dull rose — —
15 A3 4p gray lilac 125.00 *400.00*
a. 4p dull lilac —
16 A3 6p green *15,000.* 525.00
17 A3 1sh slate blue 125.00 *425.00*

Pin-perf. 12½
18 A1 (1p) dull rose red *2,000.* 70.00
a. (1p) lake *2,250.* 70.00
19 A3 4p brown lilac — 1,250.
a. 4p dull purple 7,500. 1,250.
20 A3 6p deep green *3,500.* 250.00
a. 6p yellow green 3,500. 250.00
21 A3 1sh black violet *9,000.* 1,750.

Pin-perf. 14
22 A1 (1p) rose red 275.00 42.50
a. (1p) carmine 325.00 40.00
23 A3 4p brown lilac 250.00 *150.00*
a. 4p violet 600.00 160.00
b. 4p dull violet 1,650. 125.00
24 A3 6p deep green 800.00 100.00
25 A3 6p yellow green 200.00 160.00
a. Vert. pair, imperf. between 8,000.
26 A3 1sh black violet *9,000.* *1,150.*

1860 *Clean-cut Perf. 14 to 15½*
27 A1 (1p) dull rose 190.00 67.50
a. (1p) lake 100.00 40.00
b. Horiz. pair, imperf. vert. 3,000.
29 A3 4p violet brown 210.00 95.00
a. 4p dull violet 375.00
30 A3 6p deep green 300.00 175.00
31 A3 6p yellow green 550.00 115.00
32 A3 1sh black violet

1861 *Rough Perf. 14 to 16½*
33 A1 (1p) dull rose 170.00 37.50
34 A3 4p gray lilac 750.00 100.00
35 A3 4p brown lilac 325.00 85.00
a. 4p dull violet 750.00 115.00
36 A3 6p green 475.00 85.00
a. 6p blue green 325.00 95.00
37 A3 1sh indigo 1,000. 350.00
a. 1sh purplish blue 1,675. 550.00

Thick Paper

1863 *Perf. 11½ to 12*
39 A1 (1p) carmine 160.00 29.00
a. Perf. 11½-12x11 2,000. *600.00*
40 A3 4p dull violet 225.00 72.50
41 A3 6p dp blue green *1,350.* 100.00
a. Perf. 11½-12x11 *8,000.*
42 A3 1sh indigo 2,750. 110.00

Perf. 12½
43 A1 (1p) lake 62.50 29.00

Perf. 13
45 A1 (1p) lake 52.50 29.00
46 A3 6p emerald 525.00 62.50
47 A3 1sh brt violet 4,500. 300.00

1864-72 Wmk. 1 *Perf. 12½*
48 A1 (1p) red 65.00 3.50
a. (1p) lake 65.00 7.25
b. (1p) rose 65.00 3.00
c. (1p) carmine 70.00 3.75
d. Imperf., pair *800.00* *800.00*
49 A3 4p brt violet 150.00 18.00
a. 4p pale violet 250.00 21.00
b. Imperf. *600.00*
50 A3 4p lilac 200.00 21.00
a. 4p gray lilac

51 A3 4p gray ('72) 160.00 8.50
52 A3 6p blue green 175.00 10.00
a. 6p emerald 125.00 19.00
53 A3 6p yellow grn 100.00 8.00
a. 6p dp grn 500.00 10.00
b. Imperf., pair 800.00
54 A3 1sh purple 200.00 12.00
a. 1sh lilac 150.00 12.00
b. 1sh violet 150.00 12.00
c. 1sh red lilac 160.00 13.00
d. Imperf. 750.00
55 A3 1sh orange yel ('72) 175.00 2.50
Nos. 48-55 (8) 1,225. 83.50

See Nos. 59-61A, 65. For surcharge see No. 67.

Queen Victoria — A4

1869-94 Typo. *Perf. 12½*
56 A4 5sh dull lake 200.00 90.00
a. Imperf., pair 1,250.

Perf. 14
57 A4 5sh claret ('94) 67.50 *100.00*

For overprint see No. O7.

1876 Engr. *Perf. 14*
58 A1 (1p) carmine 52.50 3.00
a. (1p) red 82.50 3.00
b. (1p) lake 55.00 3.00
c. Half used as ½p on cover 750.00
59 A3 4p gray 140.00 2.25
60 A3 6p yellow green 120.00 4.00
a. 6p deep green 150.00 3.25
61 A3 1sh orange yellow 165.00 5.00
Nos. 58-61 (4) 477.50 14.25

Perf. 14x12½
61A A3 6p yel grn ('80) *6,750.*

Value for No. 61A is for stamp with perfs barely touching the design.

Type A1 Surcharged in Black

1879 Wmk. 1 *Perf. 14*
62 A1 ½p lilac 22.50 14.00

Same Surcharge
1882 Wmk. Crown and C A (2)
63 A1 ½p lilac *250.00* 90.00
64 A1 1p carmine 77.50 2.75
a. Half used as ½p on cover 675.00

Type of 1859
1882 Wmk. 2
65 A3 4p gray 215.00 17.50

No. 60 Surcharged by pen and ink in Black or Red

1882 Wmk. 1
67 A3 1p on 6p green (R) 16.00 10.00
a. Half used as ½p on cover 400.00
b. Black surcharge *1,900.*

Counterfeits of No. 67b are plentiful. Various handwriting exists on both 60 and 60a.

A7

1883-84 Typo. Wmk. 2
68 A7 ½p green 12.00 1.50
69 A7 1p rose 25.00 .60
a. Half used as ½p on cover 950.00
70 A7 2½p ultra 29.00 .70
a. 2½p blue 27.50 .75
71 A7 4p slate 5.00 .70
72 A7 6p olive brn ('84) 9.00 *7.00*
73 A7 1sh orange brn ('84) 15.00 7.00
Nos. 68-73 (6) 95.00 17.50

For overprints see Nos. O1-O6.

A8

A9

ONE ONE
Type I Type II

ONE PENNY:
Type I — Round "O" in "ONE."
Type II — Oval "O" in "ONE."

1896-1904 *Perf. 14*
74 A8 ½p lilac & green 4.00 .35
75 A8 ½p gray grn ('02) 1.25 *2.40*
76 A8 1p lil & car, type I 4.25 .25
77 A8 1p lil & car, type II ('00) 400.00 4.75
78 A8 1p blk, *red*, type II ('01) 5.50 .25
a. Value omitted *36,000.*
79 A8 2½p lilac & ultra 7.25 .25
80 A8 2½p vio & bl, *bl* ('02) 27.50 .75
81 A8 4p lilac & orange 9.00 *27.50*
82 A8 4p grn & ultra, *buff* ('02) 4.00 *24.00*
83 A8 5p lilac & violet 11.00 *17.50*
84 A8 6p lilac & black 9.00 6.50
85 A8 1sh grn & org brn 8.25 7.75
86 A8 1sh blk & bl, *yel* ('04) 22.50 6.50

Wmk. C A over Crown (46)
87 A9 5sh green & org 65.00 90.00
88 A9 5sh lil & red vio ('02) 90.00 110.00
89 A9 10sh grn & ultra 350.00 *575.00*
Revenue cancel 30.00
90 A9 £1 grn & car 210.00 350.00
Nos. 74-90 (17) 1,229. 1,224.

No. 82 also exists on chalky paper. Values: unused $3.50, used $14. Nos. 88 and 90 exist on both ordinary and chalky paper.
Circular "Registrar General" cancels are revenue usage and of minimal value.
See Nos. 92-104.

Landing of Columbus — A10

1898 Engr. Wmk. 1
91 A10 2p gray vio & yel brn 3.25 1.40
Overprinted "SPECIMEN" 60.00

400th anniv. of the discovery of the island of Trinidad by Columbus, July 31, 1498.

1904-09 Wmk. 3 Chalky Paper
92 A8 ½p gray green 13.00 2.50
a. Ordinary paper 10.00 1.25
93 A8 1p blk, *red*, type II 15.00 .25
a. Ordinary paper 15.00 .25
94 A8 2½p vio & bl, *bl* 27.50 1.10
95 A8 4p blk & car, *yel* ('06) 5.00 *17.50*
96 A8 6p lilac & blk ('05) 24.00 18.00
97 A8 6p vio & dp vio ('07) 12.00 *17.50*
98 A8 1sh blk & bl, *yel* 26.00 12.00
99 A8 1sh vio & bl, *yel* 18.00 28.00
100 A8 1sh blk, *grn* ('06) 3.00 1.50
101 A9 5sh lil & red vio ('07) 85.00 115.00
102 A9 £1 grn & car ('07) 325.00 *400.00*
Nos. 92-102 (11) 553.50 613.35

For overprints see Nos. O8-O9.

1906-07
103 A8 1p carmine ('07) 4.00 .25
104 A8 2½p ultramarine 12.00 .25

A11

A12

1909 Ordinary Paper
105 A11 ½p gray green 11.00 .25
106 A12 1p carmine 13.00 .25
107 A11 2½p ultramarine 29.00 4.50
Nos. 105-107 (3) 53.00 5.00

For overprint see No. O10.

POSTAGE DUE STAMPS

D1

Wmk. Crown and C A (2)
1885, Jan. 1 Typo. *Perf. 14*
J1 D1 ½p black 22.50 55.00
J2 D1 1p black 11.00 .25
J3 D1 2p black 52.50 .25
J4 D1 3p black 62.50 .50
J5 D1 4p black 52.50 7.50
J6 D1 5p black 27.50 .70
J7 D1 6p black 55.00 14.00
J8 D1 8p black 65.00 6.00
J9 D1 1sh black 82.50 9.00
Nos. J1-J9 (9) 431.00 93.20

1906-07 Wmk. 3
J10 D1 1p black 9.50 .25
J11 D1 2p black 42.50 .25
J12 D1 3p black 15.00 3.75
J13 D1 4p black 15.00 *22.50*
J14 D1 5p black 21.00 *24.00*
J15 D1 6p black 7.25 *18.00*
J16 D1 8p black 21.00 *24.00*
J17 D1 1sh black 30.00 *47.50*
Nos. J10-J17 (8) 161.25 140.25

See Trinidad and Tobago Nos. J1-J16.

OFFICIAL STAMPS

Postage Stamps of 1869-84 Overprinted in Black

1893-94 Wmk. 2 *Perf. 14*
O1 A7 ½p green 50.00 *65.00*
O2 A7 1p rose 52.50 *72.50*
O3 A7 2½p ultra 57.50 *110.00*
O4 A7 4p slate 62.50 *135.00*
O5 A7 6p olive brown 62.50 *145.00*
O6 A7 1sh orange brown 82.50 *200.00*

Wmk. Crown and C C (1)
Perf. 12½
O7 A4 5sh dull lake 190.00 *875.00*
Nos. O1-O7 (7) 557.50 *1,603.*

Nos. 92 and 103 Overprinted

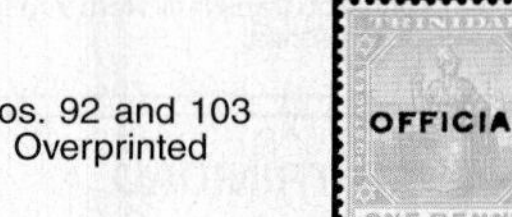

1909-10 Wmk. 3 *Perf. 14*
O8 A8 ½p gray green 3.75 12.00
O9 A8 1p carmine 3.50 13.00
a. Double overprint 375.00
b. Inverted overprint 900.00 275.00
c. Vertical overprint 140.00 160.00

Same Overprint on No. 105
1910
O10 A11 ½p gray green 13.00 *17.50*

Stamps of Trinidad have been superseded by those inscribed "Trinidad and Tobago."

TRINIDAD & TOBAGO

'tri-nə-ˌdad and tə-'bā-ˌgō

LOCATION — West Indies off the coast of Venezuela
GOVT. — British Colony
AREA — 1,980 sq. mi.
POP. — 1,160,000 (est. 1984)
CAPITAL — Port-of-Spain

The two British colonies of Trinidad and Tobago were united from 1889 until 1899, when Tobago became a ward of the united colony. From 1899 until 1913 postage stamps of Trinidad were used.

12 Pence = 1 Shilling
20 Shillings = 1 Pound
100 Cents = 1 Dollar (1935)

Catalogue values for unused stamps in this country are for Never Hinged items, beginning with Scott 62 in the regular postage section and Scott J9 in the postage due section.

"Britannia" — A1

1913 Typo. Wmk. 3 *Perf. 14*
Ordinary Paper
1 A1 ½p green 3.50 .25
a. ½p bl grn, *bluish* ('18) 16.00 13.00
2 A1 1p scarlet 1.75 .25
a. 1p carmine 2.75 .25
b. 1p pink 50.00 4.75
4 A1 2½p ultra 8.00 .50

Chalky Paper
5 A1 4p scar & blk, *yel* .80 *7.00*
6 A1 6p red vio & dull vio 11.00 8.00
7 A1 1sh black, *emerald* 1.75 *3.50*
a. 1sh black, *green* 2.00 *5.00*
b. 1sh black, *bl grn, ol back* 16.00 *10.00*
Nos. 1-2,4-7 (6) 26.80 19.50

"Britannia" — A2

1914 Surface-colored Paper
8 A1 4p scar & blk, *yel* 2.00 *11.00*
9 A1 1sh black, *green* 1.60 *15.00*

Chalky Paper
10 A2 5sh dull vio & red vio 75.00 *110.00*
11 A2 £1 green & car 250.00 *300.00*
Nos. 8-11 (4) 328.60 *436.00*

1921-22 Ordinary Paper Wmk. 4
12 A1 ½p green 3.50 2.75
13 A1 1p scarlet .75 .40
14 A1 1p brown ('22) .75 *1.90*
15 A1 2p gray ('22) 1.25 *1.50*
16 A1 2½p ultra 1.00 *22.50*
17 A1 3p ultra ('22) 7.50 4.00

Chalky Paper
18 A1 6p red vio & dull vio 5.00 *19.00*
19 A2 5sh dull vio & red vio 80.00 *170.00*
20 A2 £1 green & car 260.00 *375.00*
Nos. 12-20 (9) 359.75 *597.05*

For overprints see #B2-B3, MR1-MR13, O1-O5.

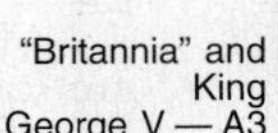

"Britannia" and King George V — A3

1922-28 Ordinary Paper

21 A3 ½p green .55 .25
22 A3 1p brown .55 .25
23 A3 1½p rose red 2.75 .25
24 A3 2p gray .55 *1.40*
25 A3 3p ultra .55 *1.40*

Chalky Paper

26 A3 4p red & blk, *yel* ('28) 3.75 3.75
27 A3 6p red vio & dl vio 2.50 *29.00*
28 A3 6p red & grn, *emer* ('24) 1.40 .70
29 A3 1sh blk, *emer* ('25) 6.25 2.00
30 A3 5sh vio & dull vio 26.00 *42.50*
31 A3 £1 rose & green 150.00 *275.00*

Wmk. Multiple Crown and C A (3)

Chalky Paper

32 A3 4p red & blk, *yel* 4.75 *20.00*
33 A3 1sh blk, *emerald* 6.00 *11.00*
Nos. 21-33 (13) 205.60 *387.50*

First Boca — A4

Designs: 2c, Agricultural College. 3c, Mt. Irvine Bay, Tobago. 8c, Queen's Park, Savannah. 12c, Town Hall, San Fernando. 24c, Government House. 48c, Memorial Park. 72c, Blue Basin.

1935-37 Engr. Wmk. 4 *Perf. 12*

34 A4 1c emer & bl, perf. 12½ ('36) .40 .25
a. Perf. 12 .50 *1.10*
35 A4 2c lt brn & ultra, perf. 12 3.00 *1.25*
a. Perf. 12½ ('36) 2.75 .25
36 A4 3c red & blk, perf. 12½ ('36) 3.25 .40
a. Perf. 12 2.75 .40
37 A4 6c bl & brn, perf. 12 5.00 3.00
a. Perf. 12½ ('37) 18.00 10.00
38 A4 8c red org & yel grn 4.50 4.25
39 A4 12c dk violet & blk 5.00 2.25
a. Perf. 12½ ('37) 18.00 12.00
40 A4 24c ol grn & blk 10.00 3.00
a. Perf. 12½ ('37) 27.50 16.00
41 A4 48c slate green 11.00 *19.00*
42 A4 72c mag & sl grn 45.00 *40.00*
Nos. 34-42 (9) 87.15 73.40

Common Design Types pictured following the introduction.

Silver Jubilee Issue

Common Design Type

1935, May 6 *Perf. 11x12*

43 CD301 2c black & ultra .40 *1.00*
44 CD301 3c car & blue .40 *2.25*
45 CD301 6c ultra & brn 2.25 *2.50*
46 CD301 24c brn vio & ind 11.00 *22.00*
Nos. 43-46 (4) 14.05 27.75
Set, never hinged 26.00

Coronation Issue

Common Design Type

1937, May 12 *Perf. 13½x14*

47 CD302 1c deep green .25 .25
48 CD302 2c yellow brown .25 .25
49 CD302 8c deep orange .50 .50
Nos. 47-49 (3) 1.00 1.00
Set, never hinged 1.50

First Boca — A13

George VI — A14

Various Frames and: 2c, Agricultural College. 3c, Mt. Irvine Bay, Tobago. 4c, Memorial Park. 5c, General Post Office and Treasury. 6c, Discovery of Lake Asphalt. 8c, Queen's Park, Savannah. 12c, Town Hall, San Fernando. 24c, Government House. 60c, Blue Basin.

Perf. 11½x11

1938-41 Wmk. 4 Engr.

50 A13 1c emer & blue .60 .25
51 A13 2c lt brn & ultra .75 .25
52 A13 3c dk car & blk 6.75 1.00
52A A13 3c vio brn & bl grn ('41) .25 .25
53 A13 4c brown 19.00 3.25
53A A13 4c red ('41) .30 .25
54 A13 5c mag ('41) .30 .25
55 A13 6c brt bl & sep 1.60 .85
56 A13 8c red org & yel grn 1.75 1.00
57 A13 12c dk vio & blk 3.50 .25
58 A13 24c dk ol grn & blk 5.00 .25
59 A13 60c mag & sl grn 9.00 1.75

Perf. 12

60 A14 $1.20 dk grn ('40) 8.50 2.00
61 A14 $4.80 rose pink ('40) 24.00 *60.00*
Nos. 50-61 (14) 81.30 71.60
Set, never hinged 125.00

Watermark sideways on Nos. 50-59.

Catalogue values for unused stamps in this section, from this point to the end of the section, are for Never Hinged items.

Peace Issue

Common Design Type

Perf. 13½x14

1946, Oct. 1 Engr. Wmk. 4

62 CD303 3c brown .25 .25
63 CD303 6c deep blue .25 .25

Silver Wedding Issue

Common Design Types

1948, Nov. 22 Photo. *Perf. 14x14½*

64 CD304 3c red brown .25 .25

Perf. 11½x11

Engr.

65 CD305 $4.80 rose car 32.50 *38.00*

UPU Issue

Common Design Types

Engr.; Name Typo. on 6c, 12c

Perf. 13½, 11x11½

1949, Oct. 10 Wmk. 4

66 CD306 5c red violet .35 .35
67 CD307 6c indigo 1.90 1.90
68 CD308 12c rose violet .45 .45
69 CD309 24c olive .45 .45
Nos. 66-69 (4) 3.15 3.15

University Issue

Common Design Types

Inscribed: "Trinidad"

1951, Feb. 16 Engr. *Perf. 14x14½*

70 CD310 3c choc & grn .25 .25
71 CD311 12c purple & blk .50 .50

SEMI-POSTAL STAMPS

Emblem of Red Cross SP1

Perf. 11, 12

1914, Sept. 18 Typo. Unwmk.

B1 SP1 (½p) red (on cover) 250.00

This stamp was allowed to pay ½p postage on one day, Sept. 18, 1914, on circulars distributed by the Red Cross. Value on cover is for proper Red Cross usage. Value unused, $15.

No. 2 Overprinted in Red (Cross) and Black (Date)

a

b

1915, Oct. 21 Wmk. 3 *Perf. 14*

B2 A1 (a) 1p scarlet 3.50 *5.00*

1916, Oct. 19

B3 A1 (b) 1p scarlet .80 *3.25*
a. Date omitted

POSTAGE DUE STAMPS

D1

1923-45 Typo. Wmk. 4 *Perf. 14*

J1 D1 1p black 4.25 *4.25*
J2 D1 2p black 8.75 1.90
J3 D1 3p black ('25) 11.00 *6.50*
J4 D1 4p black ('29) 8.75 *30.00*
J5 D1 5p black ('45) 42.50 *140.00*
J6 D1 6p black ('45) 77.50 55.00
J7 D1 8p black ('45) 52.50 *200.00*
J8 D1 1sh black ('45) 90.00 *160.00*
Nos. J1-J8 (8) 295.25 597.65

Catalogue values for unused stamps in this section, from this point to the end of the section, are for Never Hinged items.

Denominations in Cents

1947, Sept. 1

J9 D1 2c black 5.50 *8.50*
J10 D1 4c black 2.75 *3.00*
J11 D1 6c black 5.00 *7.50*
J12 D1 8c black 1.25 *42.50*
J13 D1 10c black 3.25 *9.50*
J14 D1 12c black 4.00 *30.00*
J15 D1 16c black 2.00 *57.50*
J16 D1 24c black 13.00 *15.00*
Nos. J9-J16 (8) 36.75 173.50

Nos. J9-J16 also exist on chalky paper.

Wmk. 4a (error)

J9a D1 2c 60.00
J11a D1 6c 125.00
J14a D1 12c 175.00

WAR TAX STAMPS

Nos. 1-2 Overprinted

1917 Wmk. 3 *Perf. 14*

MR1 A1 1p scarlet 4.25 4.25
a. Invtd. overprint 225.00 *300.00*

Overprinted

MR2 A1 ½p green 1.50 .40
a. Overprinted on face and back 425.00
b. Pair, one without overprint *1,000.* *1,500.*
MR3 A1 1p scarlet 4.50 *2.25*
a. Pair, one without overprint *1,000.* *1,500.*
b. Double overprint 175.00

Overprinted

MR4 A1 ½p green .30 *17.50*
MR5 A1 1p scarlet .30 *1.00*
a. Pair, one without overprint

Overprinted

MR6 A1 ½p green .30 *5.00*
MR7 A1 1p scarlet 8.00 1.25

Overprinted

MR8 A1 ½p green .30 *3.25*
MR9 A1 1p scarlet 75.00 60.00

Overprinted

MR10 A1 1p scarlet .80 *1.40*
a. Inverted overprint 175.00 *175.00*

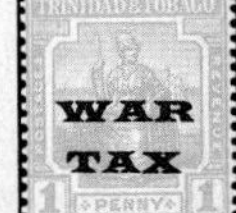

Overprinted

MR11 A1 1p scarlet 2.50 .30
a. Double overprint 250.00 *250.00*
b. Inverted overprint 160.00 *175.00*

Overprinted

1918

MR12 A1 ½p green .30 *3.50*
a. Pair, one without overprint 1,500.
MR13 A1 1p scarlet .90 *1.75*
a. Double overprint 175.00
b. Horiz. pair, one without overprint *1,700.*

The War Tax Stamps show considerable variations in the colors, thickness of the paper, distinctness of the watermark, and the gum. Counterfeits exist of the errors of Nos. MR1-MR13.

OFFICIAL STAMPS

Regular Issue of 1913 Overprinted

1913 Wmk. 3 *Perf. 14*

O1 A1 ½p green 2.75 *17.50*

Same Overprinted

1914

O2 A1 ½p green 4.25 *24.50*

Same Overprinted

1916

O3 A1 ½p green 5.25 *9.50*
a. Double overprint 57.50

Same Overprint without Period

1917

O4 A1 ½p green .75 *10.00*

Same Overprinted

1917, Aug. 22

O5 A1 ½p green 4.00 *32.50*

The official stamps are found in several shades of green and on paper of varying thickness.

TRIPOLITANIA

tri-ˌpä-lə-ˈtā-nyə

LOCATION — In northern Africa, bordering on Mediterranean Sea
GOVT. — Italian Colony
AREA — 350,000 sq. mi. (approx.)
POP. — 570,716 (1921)
CAPITAL — Tripoli

Formerly a Turkish province, Tripolitania became part of Italian Libya. See Libya.

100 Centesimi = 1 Lira

Watermark

Wmk. 140 — Crowns

Propaganda of the Faith Issue

Italian Stamps Overprinted

1923, Oct. 24 Wmk. 140 *Perf. 14*

1 A68 20c ol grn & brn org 11.00 *47.50*
Never hinged 28.00
On cover —
2 A68 30c claret & brn org 11.00 *47.50*
Never hinged 28.00
On cover —
a. Double overprint 2,250.
Never hinged *3,500.*
b. Vert. pair, imperf. btwn and at bottom 1,100. 1,650.
Never hinged 1,650.
3 A68 50c vio & brn org 7.50 *55.00*
Never hinged 19.00
On cover —
4 A68 1 l blue & brn org 7.50 *85.00*
Never hinged 19.00
On cover —
Nos. 1-4 (4) 37.00 *235.00*
Set, never hinged 92.50

Fascisti Issue

Italian Stamps Overprinted in Red or Black

1923, Oct. 29 Unwmk.

5 A69 10c dk green (R) 15.00 *18.50*
Never hinged 37.50
On cover 300.00
6 A69 30c dk violet (R) 15.00 *18.50*
Never hinged 37.50
On cover 300.00
7 A69 50c brown car 15.00 *18.50*
Never hinged 37.50
On cover 300.00

Wmk. 140

8 A70 1 l blue 15.00 *47.50*
Never hinged 37.50
On cover *575.00*
9 A70 2 l brown 15.00 *60.00*
Never hinged 37.50
On cover *825.00*
a. Double overprint 1,650.
Never hinged *2,500.*
10 A71 5 l blk & bl (R) 15.00 *90.00*
Never hinged 37.50
On cover —
Nos. 5-10 (6) 90.00 *253.00*
Set, never hinged 225.00
Set on overfranked philatelic cover 750.00

Manzoni Issue

Stamps of Italy, 1923, Overprinted in Red

1924, Apr. 1 Wmk. 140 *Perf. 14*

11 A72 10c brown red & blk 12.00 *75.00*
Never hinged 30.00
On cover —
12 A72 15c blue grn & blk 12.00 *75.00*
Never hinged 30.00
On cover —
13 A72 30c black & slate 12.00 *75.00*
Never hinged 30.00
On cover —
a. Imperf. —
Never hinged —
14 A72 50c org brn & blk 12.00 *75.00*
Never hinged 30.00
On cover —
a. Line perf. 14 *825.00*
Never hinged *2,100.*
15 A72 1 l blue & blk 75.00 *450.00*
Never hinged 185.00
a. Line perf. 14 *825.00*
Never hinged *2,100.*
16 A72 5 l violet & blk 500.00 *3,000.*
Never hinged 1,225.
a. Line perf. 14 *2,000.*
Never hinged *5,000.*
Nos. 11-16 (6) 623.00 *3,750.*
Set, never hinged 1,530.

On Nos. 15 and 16 the overprint is placed vertically at the left side.

Nos. 11-16 are comb perforated.

Victor Emmanuel Issue

Italy Nos. 175-177 Overprinted

1925-26 Unwmk. *Perf. 11*

17 A78 60c brown car 2.25 *13.50*
Never hinged 5.50
On cover 225.00
18 A78 1 l dark blue 3.00 *13.50*
Never hinged 7.50
On cover 300.00
a. Perf. 13½ 10.50 *42.50*
Never hinged 26.00
On cover 375.00

Perf. 13½

19 A78 1.25 l dk bl ('26) 3.75 *37.50*
Never hinged 9.25
On cover 600.00
a. Perf. 11 2,000. *2,600.*
Never hinged *4,000.*
On cover —
Nos. 17-19 (3) 9.00 *64.50*
Set, #17-19, 18a, 19a, never hinged 4,000.

Saint Francis of Assisi Issue

Italy Nos. 178-180 Overprinted

1926, Apr. 12 Wmk. 140 *Perf. 14*

20 A79 20c gray green 2.25 *13.50*
Never hinged 5.50
On cover 120.00
a. Vert. pair, one without ovpt. *5,250.*
Never hinged *8,000.*
21 A80 40c dark violet 2.25 *13.50*
Never hinged 5.50
On cover 140.00
22 A81 60c red brown 2.25 *26.00*
Never hinged 5.50
On cover 140.00

Italy No. 182 and Type of A83 Overprinted in Red

Unwmk.

23 A82 1.25 l dark blue 2.25 *35.00*
Never hinged 5.50
On cover 260.00
24 A83 5 l + 2.50 l ol grn 7.50 *67.50*
Never hinged 19.00
On cover —
a. Horiz. pair, imperf. btwn. *2,250.*
Never hinged *3,500.*
Nos. 20-24 (5) 16.50 *155.50*
Set, never hinged 25.00
Set on overfranked philatelic cover 425.00

Volta Issue

Type of Italy Overprinted

1927, Oct. 10 Wmk. 140 *Perf. 14*

25 A84 20c purple 4.50 *37.50*
Never hinged 11.00
On cover 260.00
26 A84 50c deep orange 7.50 *26.00*
Never hinged 18.50
On cover 260.00
a. Double overprint 190.00
Never hinged 275.00
b. As "a," one ovpt. inverted 525.00
Never hinged 800.00
27 A84 1.25 l brt blue 13.50 *60.00*
Never hinged 34.00
On cover 500.00
Nos. 25-27 (3) 25.50 *123.50*
Set, never hinged 62.50
Set on overfranked philatelic cover 350.00

Monte Cassino Issue

Types of Italy Overprinted in Red or Blue

1929, Oct. 14

28 A96 20c dk green (R) 6.00 *21.00*
Never hinged 15.00
On cover 260.00
29 A96 25c red org (Bl) 6.00 *21.00*
Never hinged 15.00
On cover 190.00
30 A98 50c + 10c crim (Bl) 6.00 *22.50*
Never hinged 15.00
On cover 150.00
31 A98 75c + 15c ol brn (R) 6.00 *22.50*
Never hinged 15.00
On cover 275.00
32 A96 1.25 l + 25c dk vio (R) 13.50 *42.50*
Never hinged 34.00
On cover 325.00
33 A98 5 l + 1 l saph (R) 13.50 *45.00*
Never hinged 34.00
On cover —

Overprinted in Red

Unwmk.

34 A100 10 l + 2 l gray brn 13.50 *67.50*
Never hinged 34.00
On cover —
Nos. 28-34 (7) 64.50 *242.00*
Set, never hinged 160.00
Set on overfranked philatelic cover 450.00

Royal Wedding Issue

Type of Italy Overprinted

1930, Mar. 17 Wmk. 140

35 A101 20c yellow green 3.00 *9.00*
Never hinged 7.50
On cover 125.00
36 A101 50c + 10c dp org 2.25 *9.00*
Never hinged 5.75
On cover 180.00
37 A101 1.25 l + 25c rose red 2.25 *18.00*
Never hinged 5.75
On cover 280.00
Nos. 35-37 (3) 7.50 *36.00*
Set, never hinged 19.00
Set on overfranked philatelic cover 160.00

Ferrucci Issue

Types of Italy Overprinted in Red or Blue

1930, July 26

38 A102 20c violet (R) 6.00 *6.00*
Never hinged 15.00
On cover 150.00
39 A103 25c dk green (R) 6.00 *6.00*
Never hinged 15.00
On cover 180.00
40 A103 50c black (R) 6.00 *11.00*
Never hinged 15.00
On cover 150.00
41 A103 1.25 l dp bl (R) 6.00 *21.00*
Never hinged 15.00
On cover 350.00
42 A104 5 l + 2 l dp car (Bl) 13.50 *45.00*
Never hinged 34.00
On cover —
Nos. 38-42,C1-C3 (8) 73.50 196.00
Set, never hinged 180.00
Nos. 38-42 on overfranked philatelic cover 260.00

Virgil Issue

Types of Italy Overprinted in Red or Blue

1930, Dec. 4 Photo.

43 A106 15c violet black 1.10 *11.50*
Never hinged 2.75
On cover 165.00
44 A106 20c orange brown 1.10 *4.50*
Never hinged 2.75
On cover 100.00
45 A106 25c dark green 1.10 *4.50*
Never hinged 2.75
On cover 90.00

46 A106 30c lt brown 1.10 *4.50*
Never hinged 2.75
On cover 95.00
47 A106 50c dull violet 1.10 *4.50*
Never hinged 2.75
On cover 75.00
48 A106 75c rose red 1.10 *9.00*
Never hinged 2.75
On cover 190.00
49 A106 1.25 l gray blue 1.10 *11.50*
Never hinged 2.75
On cover 275.00

Unwmk.
Engr.

50 A106 5 l + 1.50 l dk vio 4.50 *45.00*
Never hinged 11.00
On cover —
51 A106 10 l + 2.50 l ol brn 4.50 *67.50*
Never hinged 11.00
On cover —
Nos. 43-51,C4-C7 (13) 37.70 306.50
Set, never hinged 90.00
Nos. 43-51 on overfranked philatelic cover 450.00

Saint Anthony of Padua Issue

Types of Italy Overprinted in Blue or Red

1931, May 7 Photo. Wmk. 140

52 A116 20c brown (Bl) 1.50 *21.00*
Never hinged 3.75
On cover 110.00
53 A116 25c green (R) 1.50 *7.50*
Never hinged 3.75
On cover 110.00
54 A118 30c gray brn (Bl) 1.50 *7.50*
Never hinged 3.75
On cover 175.00
55 A118 50c dull vio (Bl) 1.50 *7.50*
Never hinged 3.75
On cover 115.00
56 A120 1.25 l slate bl (R) 1.50 *37.50*
Never hinged 3.75
On cover 375.00

Overprinted in Red or Black

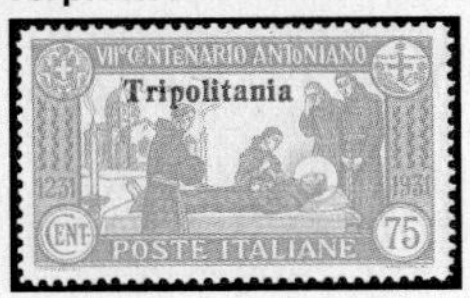

Unwmk. Engr.

57 A121 75c black (R) 1.50 *21.00*
Never hinged 3.75
On cover 300.00
58 A122 5 l + 2.50 l dk brn (Bk) 10.50 *75.00*
Never hinged 26.00
On cover —
Nos. 52-58 (7) 19.50 *177.00*
Set, never hinged 47.50
Set on overfranked philatelic cover 500.00

Native Village Scene A14

1934, Oct. 16 Wmk. 140

73 A14 5c ol grn & brn 5.25 *21.00*
Never hinged 13.00
On cover 330.00
74 A14 10c brown & black 5.25 *21.00*
Never hinged 13.00
On cover 280.00
75 A14 20c scar & indigo 5.25 *19.00*
Never hinged 13.00
On cover 280.00
76 A14 50c pur & brn 5.25 *19.00*
Never hinged 13.00
On cover 340.00
77 A14 60c org brn & ind 5.25 *26.00*
Never hinged 13.00
On cover 375.00
78 A14 1.25 l dk bl & grn 5.25 *45.00*
Never hinged 13.00
On cover 525.00
Nos. 73-78,C43-C48 (12) 63.00 302.00

Set, never hinged 155.00
Nos. 73-78 on overfranked philatelic cover 350.00

2nd Colonial Arts Exhibition, Naples.

SEMI-POSTAL STAMPS

Many issues of Italy and Italian Colonies include one or more semipostal denominations. To avoid splitting sets, these issues are generally listed as regular postage, airmail, etc., unless all values carry a surtax.

Holy Year Issue

Italian Stamps of 1924 Overprinted in Black or Red

1925 Wmk. 140 *Perf. 12*

B1 SP4 20c+ 10c dk grn & brn 3.75 *22.50*
Never hinged 9.25
On cover 200.00
B2 SP4 30c+ 15c dk brn & brn 3.75 *24.00*
Never hinged 9.25
On cover 200.00
B3 SP4 50c+ 25c vio & brn 3.75 *22.50*
Never hinged 9.25
On cover 200.00
B4 SP4 60c+ 30c dp rose & brn 3.75 *30.00*
Never hinged 9.25
On cover 280.00
B5 SP8 1 l + 50c dp bl & vio (R) 3.75 *37.50*
Never hinged 9.25
On cover —
B6 SP8 5 l + 2.50 l org brn & vio (R) 3.75 *57.50*
Never hinged 9.25
On cover —
Nos. B1-B6 (6) 22.50 *194.00*
Set, never hinged 55.00
Set on overfranked philatelic cover 475.00

Colonial Institute Issue

Peace Substituting Spade for Sword — SP1

1926, June 1 Typo. *Perf. 14*

B7 SP1 5c + 5c brown 1.10 *9.50*
Never hinged 2.75
On cover 175.00
B8 SP1 10c + 5c ol brn 1.10 *9.50*
Never hinged 2.75
On cover 135.00
B9 SP1 20c + 5c bl grn 1.10 *9.50*
Never hinged 2.75
On cover 105.00
B10 SP1 40c + 5c brn red 1.10 *9.50*
Never hinged 2.75
On cover 105.00
B11 SP1 60c + 5c orange 1.10 *9.50*
Never hinged 2.75
On cover 175.00
B12 SP1 1 l + 5c blue 1.10 *20.00*
Never hinged 2.75
On cover 275.00
Nos. B7-B12 (6) 6.60 *67.50*
Set, never hinged 16.50
Set on overfranked philatelic cover 260.00

The surtax was for the Italian Colonial Institute.

> Fiera Campionaria Tripoli
> See Libya for stamps with this inscription.

Types of Italian Semi-Postal Stamps of 1926 Overprinted like Nos. 17-19

1927, Apr. 21 Unwmk. *Perf. 11*

B19 SP10 40c + 20c dk brn & blk 3.75 *40.00*
Never hinged 9.25
On cover 180.00
B20 SP10 60c + 30c brn red & ol brn 3.75 *40.00*
Never hinged 9.25
On cover 210.00
B21 SP10 1.25 l + 60c dp bl & blk 3.75 *60.00*
Never hinged 9.25
On cover 375.00
B22 SP10 5 l + 2.50 l dk grn & blk 6.00 *92.50*
Never hinged 15.00
On cover —
Nos. B19-B22 (4) 17.25 *232.50*
Set, never hinged 42.50
Set on overfranked philatelic cover 575.00

The surtax was for the charitable work of the Voluntary Militia for Italian National Defense.

Allegory of Fascism and Victory — SP2

1928, Oct. 15 Wmk. 140

B29 SP2 20c + 5c bl grn 3.25 *13.50*
Never hinged 7.50
On cover 180.00
B30 SP2 30c + 5c red 3.25 *13.50*
Never hinged 7.50
On cover 180.00
B31 SP2 50c + 10c pur 3.25 *22.50*
Never hinged 7.50
On cover 180.00
B32 SP2 1.25 l + 20c dk bl 4.00 *30.00*
Never hinged 9.50
On cover 500.00
Nos. B29-B32 (4) 13.75 *79.50*
Set, never hinged 32.50
Set on overfranked philatelic cover 300.00

46th anniv. of the Societa Africana d'Italia. The surtax aided that society.

Types of Italian Semi-Postal Stamps of 1928 Ovptd.

1929, Mar. 4 Unwmk. *Perf. 11*

B33 SP10 30c + 10c red & blk 4.50 *26.00*
Never hinged 11.00
On cover 210.00
B34 SP10 50c + 20c vio & blk 4.50 *28.00*
Never hinged 11.00
On cover 210.00
B35 SP10 1.25 l + 50c brn & bl 6.75 *50.00*
Never hinged 17.00
On cover 450.00
B36 SP10 5 l + 2 l ol grn & blk 6.75 *97.50*
Never hinged 17.00
On cover —
Nos. B33-B36 (4) 22.50 *201.50*
Set, never hinged 55.00
Set on overfranked philatelic cover 575.00

The surtax on these stamps was for the charitable work of the Voluntary Militia for Italian National Defense.

Types of Italian Semi-Postal Stamps of 1926, Overprinted in Black or Red Like Nos. B33-B36

1930, Oct. 20

B50 SP10 30c + 10c dp grn & bl grn (Bk) 35.00 *52.50*
Never hinged 85.00
On cover 300.00
B51 SP10 50c + 10c dk grn & vio (R) 35.00 *97.50*
Never hinged 85.00
On cover 340.00
B52 SP10 1.25 l + 30c blk brn & red brn (R) 35.00 *97.50*
Never hinged 85.00
On cover 525.00
B53 SP10 5 l + 1.50 l ind & grn (R) 110.00 *260.00*
Never hinged 280.00
On cover —
Nos. B50-B53 (4) 215.00 *507.50*
Set, never hinged 525.00
Set on overfranked philatelic cover *1,000.*

Ancient Arch — SP3

1930, Nov. 27 Photo. Wmk. 140

B54 SP3 50c + 20c ol brn 3.75 *24.00*
Never hinged 9.25
On cover 200.00
B55 SP3 1.25 l + 20c dp bl 3.75 *24.00*
Never hinged 9.25
On cover 280.00
B56 SP3 1.75 l + 20c green 3.75 *32.50*
Never hinged 9.25
On cover 350.00
B57 SP3 2.55 l + 50c purple 9.00 *45.00*
Never hinged 22.50
On cover 575.00
B58 SP3 5 l + 1 l deep car 9.00 *92.50*
Never hinged 22.50
On cover —
Nos. B54-B58 (5) 29.25 *218.00*
Set, never hinged 72.50
Set on overfranked philatelic cover 350.00

25th anniv. of the Italian Colonial Agricultural Institute. The surtax was for the benefit of that institution.

AIR POST STAMPS

Ferrucci Issue

Type of Italian Air Post Stamps Overprinted in Blue or Red like #38-42

1930, July 26 Wmk. 140 *Perf. 14*

C1 AP7 50c brown vio (Bl) 6.00 *13.50*
Never hinged 15.00
On cover 225.00
C2 AP7 1 l dk blue (R) 6.00 *18.50*
Never hinged 15.00
On cover 375.00
C3 AP7 5 l + 2 l dp car (Bl) 24.00 *75.00*
Never hinged 60.00
On cover —
Nos. C1-C3 (3) 36.00 *107.00*
Set, never hinged 90.00
Set, on flown cover 425.00

Virgil Issue

Types of Italian Air Post Stamps Overprinted in Red or Blue like #43-51

1930, Dec. 4 Photo.

C4 AP8 50c deep green 2.25 *12.00*
Never hinged 5.50
On cover 180.00
C5 AP8 1 l rose red 2.25 *12.00*
Never hinged 5.50
On cover 240.00

Unwmk.
Engr.

C6 AP8 7.70 l + 1.30 l dk brn 8.25 *60.00*
Never hinged 20.00
On cover 575.00
C7 AP8 9 l + 2 l gray 8.25 *60.00*
Never hinged 20.00
On cover 900.00
Nos. C4-C7 (4) 21.00 *144.00*
Set, never hinged 50.00
Set, on flown cover 400.00

Airplane over Columns of the Basilica, Leptis — AP1

Arab Horseman Pointing at Airplane AP2

1931-32 Photo. Wmk. 140

C8 AP1 50c rose car .75 .25
Never hinged 1.90
On cover 2.50
C9 AP1 60c red org 2.25 *10.50*
Never hinged 5.50
On cover 165.00

C10 AP1 75c dp bl ('32) 2.25 *9.00*
Never hinged 5.50
On cover 120.00
C11 AP1 80c dull violet 12.00 *16.50*
Never hinged 30.00
On cover 240.00
C12 AP2 1 l deep blue 1.50 .25
Never hinged 3.75
On cover 5.50
C13 AP2 1.20 l dk brown 30.00 *22.50*
Never hinged 75.00
On cover 300.00
C14 AP2 1.50 l org red 13.50 *22.50*
Never hinged 34.00
On cover 350.00
C15 AP2 5 l green 35.00 35.00
Never hinged 85.00
On cover 750.00
Nos. C8-C15 (8) 97.25 *116.50*
Set, never hinged 210.00

For surcharges and overprint see Nos. C29-C32.

Agricultural Institute, 25th Anniv. AP3

1931, Dec. 7
C16 AP3 50c dp blue 3.00 *24.00*
Never hinged 7.50
On cover 280.00
C17 AP3 80c violet 3.00 *24.00*
Never hinged 7.50
On cover 340.00
C18 AP3 1 l gray black 3.00 *35.00*
Never hinged 7.50
On cover 450.00
C19 AP3 2 l deep green 9.00 *45.00*
Never hinged 22.50
On cover 750.00
C20 AP3 5 l + 2 l rose red 13.50 *92.50*
Never hinged 35.00
On cover —
Nos. C16-C20 (5) 31.50 *220.50*
Set, never hinged 80.00
Set, on flown cover 400.00

Graf Zeppelin Issue

Mercury, by Giovanni da Bologna, and Zeppelin AP4

Designs: 3 l, 12 l, Mercury. 10 l, 20 l, Guido Reni's "Aurora." 5 l, 15 l, Arch of Marcus Aurelius.

1933, May 5
C21 AP4 3 l dark brown 12.00 *120.00*
Never hinged 30.00
On cover 400.00
C22 AP4 5 l purple 12.00 *120.00*
Never hinged 30.00
On cover 550.00
C23 AP4 10 l deep green 12.00 *225.00*
Never hinged 30.00
On cover 825.00
C24 AP4 12 l deep blue 12.00 *240.00*
Never hinged 30.00
On cover 1,050.
C25 AP4 15 l carmine 12.00 *260.00*
Never hinged 30.00
On cover 1,050.
C26 AP4 20 l gray black 12.00 *350.00*
Never hinged 30.00
On cover 1,050.
Nos. C21-C26 (6) 72.00 *1,315.*
Set, never hinged 180.00
Set, on flown cover *4,250.*

For overprints and surcharges see Nos. C38-C42.

North Atlantic Flight Issue

Airplane, Lion of St. Mark AP7

1933, June 1
C27 AP7 19.75 l blk & ol brn 20.00 *650.00*
Never hinged 47.50
On cover 2,600.
C28 AP7 44.75 l dk bl & lt grn 20.00 *650.00*
Never hinged 47.50
On cover 2,600.
Set, never hinged 95.00
Set, on flown cover *5,000.*

Type of 1931 Ovptd. or Srchd.

1934, Jan. 20
C29 AP2 2 l on 5 l org brn 4.50 *90.00*
Never hinged 11.00
On cover 325.00
C30 AP2 3 l on 5 l grn 4.50 *90.00*
Never hinged 11.00
On cover 325.00
C31 AP2 5 l ocher 4.50 *105.00*
Never hinged 11.00
On cover 425.00
C32 AP2 10 l on 5 l rose 6.00 *105.00*
Never hinged 19.50
On cover 550.00
Nos. C29-C32 (4) 19.50 *390.00*
Set, never hinged 52.50
Set, on flown cover 1,675.

For use on mail to be carried on a special flight from Rome to Buenos Aires.

Types of Libya Airmail Issue Overprinted in Black or Red

1934, May 1 **Wmk. 140**
C38 AP4 50c rose red 13.50 *160.00*
Never hinged 34.00
On cover 400.00
C39 AP4 75c lemon 13.50 *160.00*
Never hinged 34.00
On cover 400.00
C40 AP4 5 l + 1 l brn 13.50 *160.00*
Never hinged 34.00
On cover 600.00
C41 AP4 10 l + 2 l dk bl 240.00 *850.00*
Never hinged 600.00
On cover —
C42 AP5 25 l + 3 l pur 240.00 *850.00*
Never hinged 600.00
On cover —
Nos. C38-C42,CE1-CE2 (7) 547.50 2,500.
Set, never hinged 1,300.
Set, on flown cover *6,000.*

"Circuit of the Oases."

Plane Shadow on Desert AP11

Designs: 25c, 50c, 75c, Plane shadow on desert. 80c, 1 l, 2 l, Camel corps.

1934, Oct. 16 **Photo.**
C43 AP11 25c sl bl & org red 5.25 *21.00*
Never hinged 13.00
On cover 260.00
C44 AP11 50c dk grn & ind 5.25 *19.00*
Never hinged 13.00
On cover 200.00
C45 AP11 75c dk brn & org red 5.25 *19.00*
Never hinged 13.00
On cover 280.00
C46 AP11 80c org brn & ol grn 5.25 *21.00*
Never hinged 13.00
On cover 340.00
C47 AP11 1 l scar & ol grn 5.25 *26.00*
Never hinged 13.00
On cover 375.00
C48 AP11 2 l dk bl & brn 5.25 *45.00*
Never hinged 13.00
On cover 525.00
Nos. C43-C48 (6) 31.50 *151.00*
Set, never hinged 77.50
Set, on flown cover 425.00

Second Colonial Arts Exhibition, Naples.

AIR POST SEMI-POSTAL STAMPS

King Victor Emmanuel III SPAP1

1934, Nov. 5 **Wmk. 140** ***Perf. 14***
CB1 SPAP1 25c + 10c gray grn 9.00 *26.00*
Never hinged 22.50
On cover 300.00
CB2 SPAP1 50c + 10c brn 9.00 *26.00*
Never hinged 22.50
On cover 300.00
CB3 SPAP1 75c + 15c rose red 9.00 *26.00*
Never hinged 22.50
On cover 325.00
CB4 SPAP1 80c + 15c blk brn 9.00 *26.00*
Never hinged 22.50
On cover 400.00
CB5 SPAP1 1 l + 20c red brn 9.00 *26.00*
Never hinged 22.50
On cover 450.00
CB6 SPAP1 2 l + 20c brt bl 9.00 *26.00*
Never hinged 22.50
On cover —
CB7 SPAP1 3 l + 25c pur 26.00 *120.00*
Never hinged 65.00
On cover —
CB8 SPAP1 5 l + 25c org 26.00 *120.00*
Never hinged 65.00
On cover —
CB9 SPAP1 10 l + 30c rose vio 26.00 *120.00*
Never hinged 65.00
On cover —
CB10 SPAP1 25 l + 2 l dp grn 26.00 *120.00*
Never hinged 65.00
On cover —
Nos. CB1-CB10 (10) 158.00 *636.00*
Set, never hinged 390.00
Set, on flown cover 1,800.

65th birthday of King Victor Emmanuel III; non-stop flight from Rome to Mogadiscio.

For overprint see No. CBO1.

AIR POST SEMI-POSTAL OFFICIAL STAMP

Type of Air Post Semi-Postal Stamps Ovptd. Crown and "SERVIZIO DI STATO" in Black

1934 **Wmk. 140** ***Perf. 14***
CBO1 SPAP1 25 l + 2 l cop red 2,450. *6,000.*
Never hinged 4,850.
On cover *9,000.*

AIR POST SPECIAL DELIVERY STAMPS

Type of Libya Overprinted in Black Like Nos. C38-C42

1934, May 1 **Wmk. 140** ***Perf. 14***
CE1 APSD1 2.25 l red orange 13.50 *160.00*
Never hinged 32.50
On cover 800.00
CE2 APSD1 4.50 l + 1 l dp rose 13.50 *160.00*
Never hinged 32.50
On cover —
Set, never hinged 65.00

AUTHORIZED DELIVERY STAMP

Authorized Delivery Stamp of Italy 1930, Overprinted like Nos. 38-42

1931, Mar. **Wmk. 140** ***Perf. 14***
EY1 AD2 10c reddish brown 18.00 *45.00*
Never hinged 45.00
On cover *2,000.*
a. dark brown 1,200. 975.00
Never hinged 1,800.
On cover —

TRISTAN DA CUNHA

ˌtris-tən-də-ˈkü-nə

LOCATION — Group of islands in the south Atlantic Ocean midway between the Cape of Good Hope and South America
GOVT. — A dependency of St. Helena
AREA — 40 sq. mi.
POP. — 325 (1982)

12 Pence = 1 Shilling

Catalogue values for all unused stamps in this country are for Never Hinged items.

Stamps of St. Helena, 1938-49, Overprinted in Black

1952, Jan. 1 **Wmk. 4** ***Perf. 12½***

No.	Type	Value	Color	Unused	Used
1	A24	½p	purple	.25	*2.75*
2	A24	1p	blue grn & blk	1.00	*1.50*
3	A24	1½p	car rose & blk	1.00	*1.50*
4	A24	2p	carmine & blk	1.00	*1.50*
5	A24	3p	gray	1.25	*1.50*
6	A24	4p	ultra	6.50	2.50
7	A24	6p	gray blue	6.50	2.50
8	A24	8p	olive	6.50	*7.50*
9	A24	1sh	sepia	5.50	*2.00*
10	A24	2sh6p	deep claret	18.00	*16.00*
11	A24	5sh	brown	30.00	20.00
12	A24	10sh	violet	45.00	*32.50*
			Nos. 1-12 (12)	122.50	*91.75*
			Set, hinged	85.00	

TUNISIA

tü-ˈnē-zhē̦ə

LOCATION — Northern Africa, bordering on the Mediterranean Sea
GOVT. — French protectorate
AREA — 63,362 sq. mi.
POP. — 6,966,173 (1984)
CAPITAL — Tunis

100 Centimes = 1 Franc

Covers

Values are for commercial covers bearing correct frankings. Philatelic covers sell for less.

Coat of Arms — A1

Perf. 14x13½

1888-97 Typo. Unwmk.

1 A1 1c black, *blue* 5.50 3.50
Never hinged 10.50
On cover 190.00
a. Horiz. ruled line background 11.00 10.00
Never hinged 17.50
On cover 140.00
2 A1 2c pur brn, *buff* 7.00 3.50
Never hinged 10.50
On cover 190.00
a. Horiz. ruled line background 11.00 10.00
Never hinged 21.00
On cover 140.00
3 A1 5c green, *grnsh* 35.00 17.50
Never hinged 62.50
On cover 160.00
a. Horiz. ruled line background 27.50 17.50
Never hinged 45.00
On cover 140.00
4 A1 15c blue, *grysh* 55.00 27.50
Never hinged 100.00
On cover 125.00
5 A1 25c black, *rose* 110.00 70.00
Never hinged 240.00
On cover 500.00
a. Horiz. ruled line background 350.00 350.00
On cover 1,450.
6 A1 40c red, *straw* 110.00 77.50
Never hinged 240.00
On cover 475.00
7 A1 75c car, *rose* 110.00 85.00
Never hinged 240.00
On cover 950.00
a. Horiz. ruled line background 160.00 160.00
Never hinged 325.00
On cover 1,200.
8 A1 5fr gray vio, *grysh* 510.00 275.00
Never hinged 1,050.
On cover 2,100.
a. Horiz. ruled line background 550.00 510.00
On cover 2,200.
Nos. 1-8 (8) 942.50 559.50

All values exist imperforate. Value, set without gum, $1,200.

Issued: Nos. 1-8, 7/1/88; Nos. 1a//8a, 1897.

Reprints were made in 1893 and some values have been reprinted twice since then. The shades usually differ from those of the originals. Stamps from the 1897 printing are on thicker paper, with white gum instead of grayish, and have a background of horizontal ruled lines.

A2 A3

1888-1902

9 A2 1c blk, *lil bl* 1.75 1.10
Never hinged 2.75
On cover 105.00
10 A2 2c pur brn, *buff* 1.75 1.10
Never hinged 2.75
On cover 105.00
11 A2 5c grn, *grnsh* 7.00 1.10
Never hinged 12.00
On cover 75.00
12 A2 5c yellow grn ('99) 7.00 1.10
Never hinged 14.00
On cover 19.00
13 A2 10c blk, *lav* ('93) 14.00 2.10
Never hinged 21.00
On cover 45.00
14 A2 10c red ('01) 7.00 1.10
Never hinged 14.00
On cover 15.00
15 A2 15c blue, *grysh* 50.00 1.10
Never hinged 100.00
On cover 70.00
16 A2 15c gray ('01) 11.00 2.10
Never hinged 21.00
On cover 12.50
17 A2 20c red, *grn* ('99) 21.00 2.10
Never hinged 32.50
On cover 62.50
18 A2 25c blk, *rose* 25.00 2.10
Never hinged 45.00
On cover 160.00
19 A2 25c blue ('01) 21.00 2.75
Never hinged 40.00
On cover 62.50
20 A2 35c brown ('02) 55.00 3.50
Never hinged 110.00
On cover 125.00
21 A2 40c red, *straw* 21.00 2.10
Never hinged 42.50
On cover 95.00
22 A2 75c car, *rose* 170.00 80.00
Never hinged 325.00
On cover 625.00
23 A2 75c dp vio, *org* ('93) 35.00 11.00
Never hinged 55.00
On cover 105.00
24 A3 1fr olive, *olive* 35.00 9.00
Never hinged 67.50
On cover 440.00
25 A3 2fr dull violet ('02) 175.00 130.00
Never hinged 335.00
On cover 500.00
26 A3 5fr red lil, *lav* 200.00 77.50
Bar cancellation 1.00
On cover 625.00

Quadrille Paper

27 A2 15c bl, *grysh* ('93) 50.00 1.40
Never hinged 95.00
On cover 37.50
Nos. 9-27 (19) 907.50 332.25

For surcharges see Nos. 28, 58-61.

For Nos. 1-8 and 9/27 with perforated "T," see Postage Due stamps.

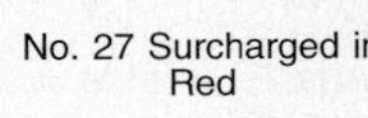

No. 27 Surcharged in Red

1902

28 A2 25c on 15c blue 3.50 3.50
Never hinged 7.00
a. Double surcharge 475.00 425.00
Never hinged 800.00

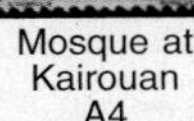

Mosque at Kairouan
A4

Plowing
A5

Ruins of Hadrian's Aqueduct
A6

Carthaginian Galley — A7

1906-26 Typo.

29 A4 1c blk, *yel* .25 .25
Never hinged .35
On cover 32.50
a. Engraver's name omitted 8.75 8.75
Never hinged 13.50
b. On grayish paper ('17) .65 .65
Never hinged 1.10
On cover 37.50
30 A4 2c red brn, *straw* .25 .25
Never hinged .35
On cover 32.50
a. Engraver's name omitted 8.75 8.75
Never hinged 13.50
b. On grayish paper ('19) .65 .65
Never hinged 1.10
On cover 32.50
31 A4 3c lt red ('19) .25 .25
Never hinged .35
On cover 17.50
a. On grayish paper .35 .35
Never hinged .70
On cover 19.00
32 A4 5c grn, *grnsh* .35 .25
Never hinged .50
On cover 12.50
a. Engraver's name omitted 10.00 10.00
Never hinged 16.00
b. On grayish paper ('17-'19) .85 .70
Never hinged 1.40
On cover 15.00
33 A4 5c orange ('21) .35 .25
Never hinged .45
On cover 9.50
a. Engraver's name omitted 8.75 8.75
Never hinged 13.50
34 A5 10c red .35 .30
Never hinged .70
On cover 10.00
35 A5 10c green ('21) .35 .35
Never hinged .70
On cover 27.50
36 A5 15c vio, *pnksh* 1.40 .30
Never hinged 2.10
On cover 19.00
a. Imperf., pair 160.00
Never hinged 260.00
b. On grayish paper ('16, '18) 1.40 .45
Never hinged 2.25
On cover 25.00
37 A5 15c brn, *org* ('23) .35 .35
Never hinged .70
On cover 3.75
38 A5 20c brn, *pnksh* .35 .30
Never hinged .70
On cover 12.50
a. Engraver's name omitted 10.00 10.00
Never hinged 16.00
b. On grayish paper ('18) .65 .65
Never hinged 1.10
On cover 15.00
39 A5 25c deep blue 2.10 .70
Never hinged 3.50
On cover 32.50
On cover, single franking 50.00
a. Imperf., pair
b. On grayish paper ('17) 2.75 1.75
Never hinged 4.50
On cover 45.00
40 A5 25c violet ('21) .35 .35
Never hinged .70
On cover 6.25
41 A6 30c red brn & vio ('19) 1.10 .70
Never hinged 1.40
On cover 19.00
42 A5 30c pale red ('21) 1.10 .70
Never hinged 1.75
On cover 14.00
43 A6 35c ol grn & brn 10.50 2.10
Never hinged 17.50
On cover 25.00
On cover, single franking 37.50
44 A6 40c blk brn & red brn 5.50 .70
Never hinged 9.00
On cover 21.00
On cover, single franking 32.50
45 A5 40c blk, *pnksh* ('23) 1.10 .70
Never hinged 1.40
On cover 5.00
46 A5 40c gray grn ('26) .25 .25
Never hinged .35
On cover 3.75
47 A5 50c blue ('21) 1.10 .70
Never hinged 1.40
On cover 12.50
On cover, single franking 17.50
48 A6 60c ol grn & vio ('21) 1.10 1.10
Never hinged 1.40
On cover 12.50
On cover, single franking 22.50
49 A6 60c ver & rose ('25) .70 .35
Never hinged 1.10
On cover 15.00
On cover, single franking 25.00
50 A6 75c red brn & red 1.10 .70
Never hinged 1.75
On cover 45.00
On cover, single franking 62.50
51 A6 75c ver & dl red ('26) .50 .50
Never hinged .70
On cover 8.75
On cover, single franking 12.50
52 A7 1fr red & dk brn 1.10 .70
Never hinged 1.75
On cover 50.00
On cover, single franking 80.00
53 A7 1fr ind & ultra ('25) .35 .35
Never hinged .70
On cover 11.00
On cover, single franking 20.00
54 A7 2fr brn & ol grn 6.50 2.00
Never hinged 11.00
On cover 62.50
On cover, single franking 100.00
55 A7 2fr grn & red, *pink* ('25) 1.10 .35
Never hinged 1.40
On cover 15.00
On cover, single franking 25.00
56 A7 5fr violet & blue 12.50 5.50
Never hinged 21.00
On cover 80.00
On cover, single franking 125.00
57 A7 5fr gray vio & grn ('25) 1.10 .70
Never hinged 1.40
On cover 27.50
On cover, single franking 70.00
Nos. 29-57 (29) 53.40 22.00

The engraver's name, "Puyplat," normally appears in tiny type to the right and below the design.

For surcharges and overprints see Nos. 62-64, 70-73, 115-116, B1-B23, B25-B27, B29-B30, B32-B36, C1-C6.

Stamps and Type of 1888-1902 Surcharged

1908, Sept.

58 A2 10c on 15c gray, *lt gray* (R) 2.10 2.10
Never hinged 3.50
On cover 8.75
59 A3 35c on 1fr ol, *ol* (R) 5.50 5.50
Never hinged 8.50
On cover 12.50
On cover, single franking 25.00
60 A3 40c on 2fr dl vio (Bl) 10.50 10.50
Never hinged 16.50
On cover 32.50
On cover, single franking 50.00
61 A3 75c on 5fr red lil, *lav* (Bl) 7.00 7.00
Never hinged 14.00
On cover 62.50
On cover, single franking 100.00
Nos. 58-61 (4) 25.10 25.10

No. 36 Surcharged

1911

62 A5 10c on 15c vio, *pinkish* 1.75 .70
Never hinged 2.75
On cover 8.75
a. Inverted surcharge 2,100.
b. Bars in surcharge omitted 45.00
Never hinged 72.50

No. 34 Surcharged

1917, Mar. 16

63 A5 15c on 10c red 1.10 .35
Never hinged 1.75
On cover 8.75
a. "15c" omitted 40.00
Never hinged 72.50
b. Double surcharge 87.50
Never hinged 160.00
c. Surcharge bars double 100.00
Never hinged 175.00
d. Surcharge bars omitted 40.00
Never hinged 72.50

No. 36 Surcharged

1921

64 A5 20c on 15c vio, *pinkish* 1.10 .35
Never hinged 1.40
On cover 6.25
a. Grayish paper (#36b) 1.40 .45
Never hinged 2.50
On cover 7.50

Arab and Ruins of Dougga — A9

1922-26 Typo. *Perf. 13½x14*

65 A9 10c green .25 .25
Never hinged .35
On cover 25.00
66 A9 10c rose ('26) .30 .30
Never hinged .35
On cover 19.00
67 A9 30c rose 1.10 1.10
Never hinged 1.40
On cover 7.50
68 A9 30c lilac ('26) .45 .45
Never hinged .70
On cover 3.75
69 A9 50c blue .70 .70
Never hinged 1.10
On cover 6.25
On cover, single franking 8.75
Nos. 65-69 (5) 2.80 2.80

For surcharges see Nos. 117, B24, B28, B31.

Stamps and Type of 1906 Surcharged in Red or Black

a

b

1923-25

70 A4(a) 10c on 5c grn, *grnsh* (R) .35 .35
Never hinged .70
On cover 25.00
a. Double surcharge 80.00
Never hinged 130.00
b. Inverted surcharge 115.00
Never hinged 200.00
c. Double surcharge, one inverted 115.00
Never hinged 200.00
d. Engraver's name omitted (#32a) 10.50 10.00
Never hinged 17.50
71 A5(b) 20c on 15c vio (Bk) 1.10 .35
Never hinged 1.40
On cover 6.25
a. Double surcharge 115.00
Never hinged 200.00
b. On grayish paper (#36b) 1.40 .45
Never hinged 2.75
72 A5(b) 30c on 20c yel brn (Bk) ('25) .35 .35
Never hinged .70
On cover 3.75
a. "30" omitted 65.00
Never hinged 100.00
b. Bars omitted 55.00
Never hinged 87.50
73 A5(b) 50c on 25c blue (R) 1.10 .35
Never hinged 1.40
On cover 8.75
On cover, single franking 19.00
a. Double surcharge 110.00
Never hinged 200.00
b. Inverted surcharge 110.00
Never hinged 180.00
Nos. 70-73 (4) 2.90 1.40

Arab Woman Carrying Water — A10

Grand Mosque at Tunis — A11

Mosque, Tunis — A12

Roman Amphitheater, El Djem (Thysdrus) — A13

1926-46 Typo. *Perf. 14x13½*

74 A10 1c lt red .25 .25
Never hinged .35
On cover 8.75
75 A10 2c olive grn .25 .25
Never hinged .35
On cover 8.75
76 A10 3c slate blue .25 .25
Never hinged .35
On cover 7.50
77 A10 5c yellow grn .25 .25
Never hinged .35
On cover 3.75
78 A10 10c rose .25 .25
Never hinged .35
On cover 3.75
78A A12 10c brown ('46) .25 .25
Never hinged .30
On cover 3.50
79 A11 15c gray lilac .25 .25
Never hinged .35
On cover 3.75
80 A11 20c deep red .30 .25
Never hinged .45
On cover 7.50
81 A11 25c gray green .45 .30
Never hinged .55
On cover 3.75
82 A11 25c lt violet ('28) .70 .30
Never hinged 1.10
On cover 3.75
83 A11 30c lt violet .45 .35
Never hinged .65
On cover 15.00
84 A11 30c bl grn ('28) .35 .30
Never hinged .70
On cover 12.50
84A A12 30c dk ol grn ('46) .25 .25
Never hinged .30
On cover 4.25
85 A11 40c deep brown .25 .25
Never hinged .35
On cover 3.75
85A A12 40c lil rose ('46) .30 .30
Never hinged .35
On cover 4.25
86 A11 45c emer ('40) 1.10 1.10
Never hinged 1.40
On cover 12.50
87 A12 50c black .25 .25
Never hinged .45
On cover 3.00
88 A12 50c ultra ('34) .70 .35
Never hinged 1.10
On cover 2.00
88B A12 50c emer ('40) .25 .25
Never hinged .30
On cover 10.50
88C A12 50c lt blue ('46) .30 .30
Never hinged .35
On cover 4.25
89 A12 60c red org ('40) .25 .25
Never hinged .35
On cover 7.50
89A A12 60c ultra ('45) .25 .25
Never hinged .30
On cover 5.50
90 A12 65c ultra ('38) .70 .35
Never hinged 1.10
On cover 2.00
91 A12 70c dk red ('40) .25 .25
Never hinged .35
On cover 3.00
92 A12 75c vermilion .35 .70
Never hinged .70
On cover 5.00
93 A12 75c lil rose ('28) 1.10 .35
Never hinged 1.40
On cover 3.75
94 A12 80c blue green 1.10 .70
Never hinged 1.40
On cover 15.00
On cover, single franking 32.50
94A A12 80c blk brn ('40) .30 .30
Never hinged .45
On cover 2.50
94B A12 80c emer ('45) .45 .30
Never hinged .55
On cover 3.00
95 A12 90c org red ('28) .35 .35
Never hinged .70
On cover 11.00
On cover, single franking 25.00
96 A12 90c ultra ('39) 10.00 10.00
Never hinged 14.00
On cover 37.50
97 A12 1fr brown violet .70 .70
Never hinged 1.10
On cover 8.75
On cover, single franking 8.00
97A A12 1fr rose ('40) .25 .25
Never hinged .35
On cover 2.00
98 A13 1.05fr dl bl & mag .70 .70
Never hinged 1.10
On cover 16.00
On cover, single franking 32.50
98A A12 1.20fr blk brn ('45) .35 .30
Never hinged .70
On cover 3.75
99 A13 1.25fr gray bl & dk bl .70 .70
Never hinged 1.10
On cover 22.50
On cover, single franking 40.00
100 A13 1.25fr car rose ('40) 1.10 1.10
Never hinged 1.40
On cover 10.00
On cover, single franking 27.50
100A A13 1.30fr bl & vio bl ('42) .35 .30
Never hinged .40
On cover 3.75
101 A13 1.40fr brt red vio ('40) 1.20 1.20
Never hinged 1.65
On cover 7.50
On cover, single franking 12.50
102 A13 1.50fr bl & dp bl ('28) 1.40 .50
Never hinged 1.75
On cover 10.00
On cover, single franking 21.00
102A A13 1.50fr rose red & red org ('42) .35 .50
Never hinged .70
On cover 14.00
On cover, single franking 25.00
102B A12 1.50fr rose lil ('46) .25 .25
Never hinged .30
On cover 2.50
103 A13 2fr rose & ol brn 1.40 .35
Never hinged 2.10
On cover 14.00
On cover, single franking 20.00
104 A13 2fr red org ('39) .35 .35
Never hinged .70
On cover 5.00
On cover, single franking 15.00
104A A12 2fr Prus grn ('45) .35 .25
Never hinged .70
On cover 2.00
105 A13 2.25fr ultra ('39) .70 .90
Never hinged 1.40
On cover 8.00
On cover, single franking 27.50
105A A13 2.40fr red ('46) .65 .50
Never hinged .80
On cover 10.00
106 A13 2.50fr green ('40) .80 .80
Never hinged 1.00
On cover 8.00
On cover, single franking 15.00
107 A13 3fr dl bl & org 1.75 .70
Never hinged 2.50
On cover 22.50
On cover, single franking 40.00
108 A13 3fr violet ('39) .35 .35
Never hinged .70
On cover 4.50
On cover, single franking 6.25
108A A13 3fr blk brn ('46) .35 .25
Never hinged .70
On cover 2.00
108B A13 4fr ultra ('45) 1.10 .55
Never hinged 1.40
On cover 5.00
109 A13 5fr red & grn, *grnsh* 2.75 1.40
Never hinged 3.50
On cover 45.00
On cover, single franking 95.00
110 A13 5fr dp red brn ('40) 1.25 1.25
Never hinged 1.80
On cover 10.50
On cover, single franking 22.50
110A A13 5fr dk grn ('46) .45 .45
Never hinged .55
On cover 2.50
110B A13 6fr dp ultra ('45) .70 .45
Never hinged 1.10
On cover 3.00
111 A13 10fr brn red & blk, *bluish* 11.00 3.50
Never hinged 17.50
On cover 55.00
On cover, single franking 95.00
112 A13 10fr rose pink ('40) .80 .80
Never hinged 1.10
On cover 14.00
On cover, single franking 35.00
112A A13 10fr ver ('46) .70 .45
Never hinged 1.10
On cover 9.00
112B A13 10fr ultra ('46) .65 .35
Never hinged .70
On cover 9.00
112C A13 15fr rose lil ('45) .35 .25
Never hinged .70
On cover 12.50
113 A13 20fr lil & red, *pnksh* ('28) 2.50 1.10
Never hinged 3.50
On cover 25.00
On cover, single franking 50.00
113A A13 20fr dk grn ('45) .70 .45
Never hinged 1.10
On cover 15.00
113B A13 25fr violet ('45) .70 .65
Never hinged 1.10
On cover 19.00
a. No inscriptions below design 11.00 11.00
Never hinged 16.00
113C A13 50fr carmine ('45) 1.75 .85
Never hinged 2.50
On cover 32.50
113D A13 100fr car rose ('45) 2.10 1.10
Never hinged 2.50
On cover 37.50
Nos. 74-113D (66) 64.05 44.65

See Nos. 152A-162, 185-189, 199-206 in Scott Standard catalogue, Vol. 6.

For surcharges and overprints see Nos. 114, 118-121, 143-152, B74-B77, B87-B88, B91-B95, B98, C7-C12. Post 1940 listings are in Scott Standard catalogue, Vol. 6.

No. 99 Surcharged with New Value and Bars in Red

1927, Mar. 24

114 A13 1.50fr on 1.25fr .80 .30
Never hinged 1.10
On cover 15.00
On cover, single franking 60.00

Stamps of 1921-26 Surcharged

1928, May 1

115 A4 3c on 5c orange .35 .25
Never hinged .70
On cover 10.00
116 A5 10c on 15c brn, *org* .70 .30
Never hinged 1.10
On cover 8.00
a. "10c" omitted 120.00
Never hinged 175.00
b. Bars omitted 50.00
Never hinged 77.50
c. Double surcharge 125.00
Never hinged 190.00
d. Pair, #116 + 116c 275.00
Never hinged 325.00
e. Pair #116 + #37 210.00
Never hinged 325.00
117 A9 25c on 30c lilac .70 .70
Never hinged 1.10
On cover 3.75
a. Pair #117 + #68 275.00
Never hinged 425.00
118 A12 40c on 80c bl grn .70 .45
Never hinged 1.10
On cover 3.00
119 A12 50c on 75c ver 1.10 .50
Never hinged 1.40
On cover 3.00
Nos. 115-119 (5) 3.55 2.20

No. 83 Surcharged

1929

120 A11 10c on 30c lt violet 1.75 1.10
Never hinged 2.50

No. 120 exists precanceled only. The value in first column is for a stamp which has not been through the post and has original gum. The value in the second column is for a postally used, gumless stamp. See No. 199a in Scott Standard catalogue, Vol. 6.

No. 85 Surcharged with New Value and Bars

1930

121 A11 50c on 40c dp brn 5.50 .70
Never hinged 8.50
On cover 3.00

A14

A15

A16

A17

Perf. 11, 12½, 12½x13

1931-34 Engr.

122 A14 1c deep blue .25 .25
Never hinged .35
On cover 9.50
123 A14 2c yellow brn .25 .25
Never hinged .35
On cover 9.50
124 A14 3c black .35 .35
Never hinged .70
On cover 9.50
125 A14 5c yellow grn .25 .25
Never hinged .35
On cover 7.00
126 A14 10c red .25 .25
Never hinged .35
On cover 5.50
127 A15 15c dull violet .70 .70
Never hinged 1.10
On cover 5.00
128 A15 20c dull brown .25 .25
Never hinged .35
On cover 5.00
129 A15 25c rose red .35 .35
Never hinged .70
On cover 3.75
130 A15 30c deep green .35 .70
Never hinged .70
On cover 16.00
131 A15 40c red orange .35 .35
Never hinged .70
On cover 3.00
132 A16 50c ultra .35 .35
Never hinged .70
On cover 2.50
133 A16 75c yellow 2.10 2.10
Never hinged 3.50
On cover 6.25
134 A16 90c red .70 .70
Never hinged 1.00
On cover 11.00
On cover, single franking 25.00
135 A16 1fr olive black .35 .70
Never hinged .75
On cover 7.50
On cover, single franking 11.00
136 A16 1fr dk brn ('34) .50 .45
Never hinged .65
On cover 7.50
On cover, single franking 11.00
137 A17 1.50fr brt ultra 1.00 .70
Never hinged 1.40
On cover 9.50
On cover, single franking 21.00
138 A17 2fr deep brown .70 1.00
Never hinged 1.00
On cover 11.00
On cover, single franking 17.50
139 A17 3fr blue green 10.50 10.50
Never hinged 14.00
On cover 35.00
On cover, single franking 55.00
140 A17 5fr car rose 28.00 21.00
Never hinged 37.50
On cover 50.00
On cover, single franking 80.00
a. Perf. 12½ 37.50 35.00
Never hinged 60.00
On cover 140.00
141 A17 10fr black 50.00 35.00
Never hinged 70.00
On cover 125.00
On cover, single franking 190.00
142 A17 20fr dark brown 62.50 45.00
Never hinged 95.00
On cover 165.00
On cover, single franking 250.00
Nos. 122-142 (21) 160.05 121.20

For surcharges see Nos. B54-B73.

Nos. 88, 102 Surcharged in Red or Black

1937 *Perf. 14x13½*

143 A12 65c on 50c (R) .70 .35
Never hinged 1.00
On cover 1.90
b. Double surcharge 105.00 87.50
Never hinged 150.00

144 A13 1.75fr on 1.50fr (R) 5.50 1.40
Never hinged 10.50
On cover 7.50
On cover, single franking 17.50
a. Double surcharge 95.00 95.00
Never hinged 140.00
b. In pair with unsurcharged stamp 250.00
Never hinged 375.00

1938

145 A12 65c on 50c (Bk) .70 .35
Never hinged 1.10
On cover 1.90
a. Double surcharge, one inverted 175.00 175.00
Never hinged 200.00

146 A13 1.75fr on 1.50fr (R) 10.50 7.00
Never hinged 14.00
On cover 25.00
On cover, single franking 50.00

Stamps of 1938-39 Surcharged in Red or Carmine

1940

147 A12 25c on 65c ultra (C) .25 .25
Never hinged .35
On cover 6.25

148 A12 1fr on 90c ultra (R) .50 .50
Never hinged .75
On cover 2.50
a. Double surcharge 120.00
Never hinged 175.00

SEMI-POSTAL STAMPS

No. 36 Overprinted in Red

1915, Feb. Unwmk. *Perf. 14x13½*

B1 A5 15c vio, *pnksh* 1.40 1.40
Never hinged 2.10
On cover 12.50

No. 32 Overprinted in Red

1916, Feb. 15

B2 A4 5c grn, *grnsh* 2.10 2.10
Never hinged 3.50
On cover 15.00

Types of Regular Issue of 1906 in New Colors and Surcharged

1916, Aug.

B3 A5 10c on 15c brn vio, *bl* 1.40 1.10
Never hinged 2.10
On cover 14.00

B4 A5 10c on 20c brn, *org* 2.10 1.40
Never hinged 3.50
On cover 16.00

B5 A5 10c on 25c bl, *grn* 3.50 3.50
Never hinged 7.00
On cover 21.00

B6 A6 10c on 35c ol grn & vio 10.50 7.00
Never hinged 14.50
On cover 29.00

B7 A6 10c on 40c bis & blk 7.00 4.50
Never hinged 10.50
On cover 27.50

B8 A6 10c on 75c vio brn & grn 14.00 10.50
Never hinged 21.00
On cover 42.50

B9 A7 10c on 1fr red & grn 7.00 7.00
Never hinged 12.00
On cover 42.50

B10 A7 10c on 2fr bis & bl 110.00 110.00
Never hinged 200.00
On cover 300.00

B11 A7 10c on 5fr vio & red 125.00 125.00
Never hinged 250.00
On cover 375.00
Nos. B3-B11 (9) 280.50 270.00

Nos. B3-B11 were sold at their face value but had a postal value of 10c only. The excess was applied to the relief of prisoners of war in Germany.

Types of Regular Issue of 1906 in New Colors and Surcharged in Carmine

1918

B12 A5 15c on 20c blk, *grn* 2.75 2.75
Never hinged 3.50
On cover 19.00

B13 A5 15c on 25c dk bl, *buff* 2.75 2.75
Never hinged 3.50
On cover 21.00

B14 A6 15c on 35c gray grn & red 3.75 3.75
Never hinged 7.00
On cover 25.00

B15 A6 15c on 40c brn & lt bl 5.00 5.00
Never hinged 10.50
On cover 29.00

B16 A6 15c on 75c red brn & blk 14.00 14.00
Never hinged 21.00
On cover 42.50

B17 A7 15c on 1fr red & vio 32.50 32.50
Never hinged 55.00
On cover 140.00

B18 A7 15c on 2fr bis brn & red 110.00 110.00
Never hinged 190.00
On cover 300.00

B19 A7 15c on 5fr vio & blk 175.00 175.00
Never hinged 340.00
On cover 700.00
Nos. B12-B19 (8) 345.75 345.75

The different parts of the surcharge are more widely spaced on the stamps of types A6 and A7. These stamps were sold at their face value but had a postal value of 15c only. The excess was intended for the relief of prisoners of war in Germany.

Types of 1906-22 Surcharged

1923

B20 A4 0c on 1c blue 1.10 1.10
Never hinged 1.75
On cover 21.00

B21 A4 0c on 2c ol brn 1.10 1.10
Never hinged 1.75
On cover 21.00

B22 A4 1c on 3c green 1.10 1.10
Never hinged 1.75
On cover 21.00

B23 A4 2c on 5c red vio 1.10 1.10
Never hinged 1.75
On cover 21.00

B24 A9 3c on 10c vio, *bluish* 1.10 1.10
Never hinged 1.75
On cover 21.00

B25 A5 5c on 15c ol grn 1.10 1.10
Never hinged 1.75
On cover 21.00

B26 A5 5c on 20c bl, *pink* 2.10 2.10
Never hinged 3.50
On cover 32.50

B27 A5 5c on 25c vio, *bluish* 2.10 2.10
Never hinged 3.50
On cover 32.50

B28 A9 5c on 30c orange 2.10 2.10
Never hinged 3.50
On cover 32.50

B29 A6 5c on 35c bl & vio 4.25 4.25
Never hinged 7.00
On cover 37.50

B30 A6 5c on 40c bl & brn 4.25 4.25
Never hinged 7.00
On cover 37.50

B31 A9 10c on 50c blk, *bluish* 7.00 5.50
Never hinged 11.00
On cover 50.00

B32 A6 10c on 60c ol brn & bl 10.50 7.75
Never hinged 14.00
On cover 55.00

B33 A6 10c on 75c vio & lt grn 9.00 8.50
Never hinged 17.50
On cover 62.50

B34 A7 25c on 1fr mar & vio 10.50 8.50
Never hinged 17.50
On cover 62.50

B35 A7 25c on 2fr bl & rose 27.50 26.00
Never hinged 42.50
On cover 110.00

B36 A7 25c on 5fr grn & ol brn 70.00 70.00
Never hinged 130.00
On cover 275.00
Nos. B20-B36 (17) 155.90 147.65

These stamps were sold at their original values but had postal franking values only to the amounts surcharged on them. The difference was intended to be used for the benefit of wounded soldiers.

This issue was entirely speculative. Before the announced date of sale most of the stamps were taken by postal employees and practically none of them were offered to the public.

Type of 1906 Parcel Post Stamps Surcharged in Black

1925, June 7 *Perf. 13½x14*

B37 PP1 1c on 5c brn & red, *pink* .70 .70
Never hinged 1.10
On cover 12.50
a. Surcharge omitted 140.00 140.00
Never hinged 210.00

B38 PP1 2c on 10c brn & bl, *yel* .70 .70
Never hinged 1.10
On cover 14.00

B39 PP1 3c on 20c red vio & rose, *lav* 1.40 1.40
Never hinged 2.10
On cover 25.00

B40 PP1 5c on 25c sl grn & rose, *bluish* 1.40 1.40
Never hinged 2.75
On cover 32.50

B41 PP1 5c on 40c rose & grn, *yel* 1.40 1.40
Never hinged 2.75
On cover 32.50

B42 PP1 10c on 50c vio & bl, *lav* 2.75 2.75
Never hinged 3.50
On cover 27.50

B43 PP1 10c on 75c grn & ol, *grnsh* 2.75 2.75
Never hinged 4.25
On cover 25.00

B44 PP1 25c on 1fr bl & grn, *bluish* 2.75 2.75
Never hinged 4.25
On cover 25.00

B45 PP1 25c on 2fr rose & vio, *pnksh* 14.00 14.00
Never hinged 21.00
On cover 55.00

B46 PP1 25c on 5fr red & brn, *lem* 50.00 50.00
Never hinged 100.00
On cover 200.00
Nos. B37-B46 (10) 77.85 77.85

These stamps were sold at their original values but paid postage only to the amount of the surcharged values. The difference was given to Child Welfare societies.

Tunis-Chad Motor Caravan SP2

1928, Feb. Engr. *Perf. 13½*

B47 SP2 40c + 40c org brn 1.40 1.40
Never hinged 2.10
On cover 6.25

B48 SP2 50c + 50c dp vio 1.75 1.75
Never hinged 2.75
On cover 6.25

B49 SP2 75c + 75c dk bl 1.75 1.75
Never hinged 2.75
On cover 7.50

B50 SP2 1fr + 1fr carmine 1.75 1.75
Never hinged 2.75
On cover 10.50

B51 SP2 1.50fr + 1.50fr brt bl 1.75 1.75
Never hinged 2.75
On cover 25.00

B52 SP2 2fr + 2fr dk grn 2.10 2.10
Never hinged 3.25
On cover 16.00

B53 SP2 5fr + 5fr red brn 2.10 2.10
Never hinged 3.25
On cover 27.50
Nos. B47-B53 (7) 12.60 12.60

The surtax on these stamps was for the benefit of Child Welfare societies.

Nos. 122-135, 137-142 Surcharged in Black

a

b

1938 *Perf. 11, 12½, 12½x13*

B54 A14(a) 1c + 1c 2.75 2.75
Never hinged 5.00
On cover 12.50

B55 A14(a) 2c + 2c 2.75 2.75
Never hinged 5.00
On cover 12.50

B56 A14(a) 3c + 3c 2.75 2.75
Never hinged 5.00
On cover 12.50

B57 A14(a) 5c + 5c 2.75 2.75
Never hinged 5.00
On cover 12.50

B58 A14(a) 10c + 10c 2.75 2.75
Never hinged 5.00
On cover 12.50

B59 A15(a) 15c + 15c 2.75 2.75
Never hinged 5.00
On cover 12.50

B60 A15(a) 20c + 20c 2.75 2.75
Never hinged 5.00
On cover 12.50

B61 A15(a) 25c + 25c 2.75 2.75
Never hinged 5.00
On cover 12.50

B62 A15(a) 30c + 30c 2.75 2.75
Never hinged 5.00
On cover 12.50

B63 A15(a) 40c + 40c 2.75 2.75
Never hinged 5.00
On cover 12.50

B64 A16(a) 50c + 50c 2.75 2.75
Never hinged 5.00
On cover 12.50

B65 A16(a) 75c + 75c 2.75 2.75
Never hinged 5.00
On cover 12.50

B66 A16(a) 90c + 90c 2.75 2.75
Never hinged 5.00
On cover 12.50

B67 A16(a) 1fr + 1fr 2.75 2.75
Never hinged 5.00
On cover 19.00

B68 A17(b) 1.50fr + 1fr 2.75 2.75
Never hinged 5.00
On cover 14.00

B69 A17(b) 2fr + 1.50fr 5.00 5.00
Never hinged 8.50
On cover 19.00

B70 A17(b) 3fr + 2fr 5.50 5.50
Never hinged 9.00
On cover 25.00

B71 A17(b) 5fr + 3fr 21.00 21.00
Never hinged 32.50
On cover 55.00

a. Perf. 12½ 110.00 110.00
Never hinged 160.00
On cover 325.00
B72 A17(b) 10fr + 5fr 45.00 45.00
Never hinged 70.00
On cover 165.00
B73 A17(b) 20fr + 10fr 70.00 70.00
Never hinged 110.00
On cover 300.00
Nos. B54-B73 (20) 187.75 187.75

50th anniversary of the post office.

AIR POST STAMPS

No. 43 Surcharged in Red

1919, Apr. Unwmk. *Perf. 14x13½*

C1 A6 30c on 35c ol grn & brn 1.40 1.40
Never hinged 2.10
On cover 9.50
a. Inverted surcharge 160.00
Never hinged 250.00
b. Double surcharge 160.00
Never hinged 250.00
c. Double inverted surcharge 190.00
Never hinged 275.00
d. Double surcharge, one inverted 160.00
Never hinged 250.00

Type A6, Overprinted in Rose

1920, Apr.

C2 A6 30c ol grn, bl & rose 1.10 1.10
Never hinged 1.40
On cover 7.00
a. On grayish paper 1.75 1.75
Never hinged 2.75
On cover 9.50

Nos. 53 and 55 Overprinted in Red

1927, Mar. 24

C3 A7 1fr indigo & ultra 1.10 .70
Never hinged 1.75
On cover 8.00
C4 A7 2fr grn & red, *pink* 3.50 2.10
Never hinged 5.00
On cover 19.00

Nos. 51 and 57 Srchd. in Black or Red

C5 A6 1.75fr on 75c (Bk) 1.10 .70
Never hinged 1.75
On cover 9.50
C6 A7 1.75fr on 5fr (R) 3.50 2.10
Never hinged 5.00
On cover 15.00

Type A13 Ovptd. like #C3-C4 in Blue

1928, Feb.

C7 A13 1.30fr org & lt vio 3.50 1.40
Never hinged 5.50
On cover 10.00
C8 A13 1.80fr gray grn & red 4.25 1.10
Never hinged 7.00
On cover 19.00
C9 A13 2.55fr lil & ol brn 3.50 1.10
Never hinged 7.00
On cover 19.00
Nos. C7-C9 (3) 11.25 3.60

Type A13 Surcharged like #C5-C6 in Blue

1930, Aug.

C10 A13 1.50fr on 1.30fr org & lt vio 2.75 .85
Never hinged 4.25
On cover 7.50
C11 A13 1.50fr on 1.80fr gray grn & red 4.25 .70
Never hinged 7.00
On cover 7.50
C12 A13 1.50fr on 2.55fr lil & ol brn 8.50 2.10
Never hinged 14.00
On cover 8.00
Nos. C10-C12 (3) 15.50 3.65

POSTAGE DUE STAMPS

During 1888-1901, postage due stamps were created by perforating regular postage stamps with the letter "T." Generally, panes were folded before perforation, so that the "T" is either upright or inverted on equal numbers of stamps. The high values (75c, 1fr and 5fr) were perforated as needed, not always in full panes, and so examples of these values with inverted "T" command a modest premium.

All values exist perforated with a smaller "T," apparently used in Gafsa. These are rare.

Nos. 1-8 perforated "T"

1888-97

JA1 A1 1c black, *blue* 7.00 5.50
Never hinged 14.00
On cover 750.00
a. "T" inverted 7.00 5.50
Never hinged 14.00
On cover 750.00
b. Horiz. ruled line background ('97) 14.00 14.00
Never hinged 24.00
c. As "b," "T" inverted 14.00 14.00
Never hinged 24.00
JA2 A1 2c pur brn, *buff* 7.00 5.50
Never hinged 14.00
On cover 750.00
a. "T" inverted 7.00 5.50
Never hinged 14.00
On cover 750.00
b. Horiz. ruled line background ('97) 17.00 17.00
Never hinged 30.00
c. As "b," "T" inverted 17.00 17.00
Never hinged 30.00
JA3 A1 5c green, *grnsh* 21.00 17.50
Never hinged 42.50
On cover 625.00
a. "T" inverted 21.00 17.50
Never hinged 42.50
On cover 625.00
b. Horiz. ruled line background ('97) 25.00 25.00
Never hinged 45.00
c. As "b," "T" inverted 25.00 25.00
Never hinged 45.00
JA4 A1 15c blue, *grysh* 55.00 27.50
Never hinged 105.00
On cover 625.00
a. "T" inverted 55.00 27.50
Never hinged 105.00
On cover 625.00
JA5 A1 25c black, *rose* 80.00 52.50
Never hinged 160.00
On cover 700.00
a. "T" inverted 80.00 52.50
Never hinged 160.00
On cover 700.00
b. Horiz. ruled line background ('97) 300.00 250.00
Never hinged 525.00
c. As "b," "T" inverted 300.00 250.00
Never hinged 525.00
JA6 A1 40c red, *straw* 55.00 45.00
Never hinged 110.00
On cover 625.00
a. "T" inverted 55.00 45.00
Never hinged 110.00
On cover 625.00
JA7 A1 75c car, *rose* 70.00 50.00
Never hinged 140.00
a. "T" inverted 77.50 65.00
Never hinged 160.00
b. Horiz. ruled line background ('97) 170.00 125.00
Never hinged 330.00
c. As "b," "T" inverted 87.50 65.00
Never hinged 330.00
JA8 A1 5fr gray vio, *grysh* 410.00 210.00
a. "T" inverted 425.00 290.00
b. Horiz. ruled line background ('97) 425.00 290.00
c. As "b," "T" inverted 500.00 425.00
Nos. JA1-JA8 (8) 705.00 413.50

See footnote following No. 8

Nos. 9//27 perforated "T"

1888-1901

JA9 A2 1c blk, *lil bl* 3.50 1.75
Never hinged 5.50
On cover 625.00
a. "T" inverted 3.50 1.75
Never hinged 5.50
On cover 625.00
b. Tête-bêche pair, JA9 & JA9a 10.50 7.25
Never hinged 14.00
JA10 A2 2c pur brn, *buff* 3.50 1.75
Never hinged 7.00
On cover 625.00
a. "T" inverted 3.50 1.75
Never hinged 7.00
On cover 625.00
b. Tête-bêche pair, JA10 & JA10a 10.50 7.00
Never hinged 17.50
JA11 A2 5c grn, *grnsh* 11.00 2.10
Never hinged 17.50
On cover 550.00
a. "T" inverted 11.00 2.10
Never hinged 17.50
On cover 550.00
b. Tête-bêche pair, JA11 & JA11a 35.00 11.00
Never hinged 60.00
JA12 A2 5c yellow grn ('99) 7.00 1.10
Never hinged 14.00
On cover 375.00
a. "T" inverted 7.00 1.10
Never hinged 14.00
On cover 375.00
b. Tête-bêche pair, JA12 & JA12a 32.50 8.50
Never hinged 55.00
JA13 A2 10c blk, *lav* ('93) 10.50 4.25
Never hinged 17.50
On cover 250.00
a. "T" inverted 10.50 4.25
Never hinged 17.50
On cover 250.00
b. Tête-bêche pair, JA13 & JA13a 32.50 15.00
Never hinged 55.00
JA14 A2 10c red ('01) 1.40 .70
Never hinged 3.50
On cover 375.00
a. "T" inverted 1.40 .70
Never hinged 3.50
On cover 375.00
b. Tête-bêche pair, JA14 & JA14a 7.00 4.25
Never hinged 14.00
JA15 A2 15c blue, *grysh* 17.50 5.00
Never hinged 35.00
On cover 425.00
a. "T" inverted 17.50 5.00
Never hinged 35.00
On cover 425.00
b. Tête-bêche pair, JA15 & JA15a 45.00 17.50
Never hinged 85.00
JA16 A2 15c gray ('01) 2.10 .70
Never hinged 3.50
On cover 310.00
a. "T" inverted 2.10 .70
Never hinged 3.50
On cover 310.00
b. Tête-bêche pair, JA16 & JA16a 7.00 4.25
Never hinged 14.00
JA17 A2 20c red, *grn* ('99) 21.00 5.00
Never hinged 35.00
On cover 425.00
a. "T" inverted 7.00 4.25
Never hinged 35.00
On cover 425.00
b. Tête-bêche pair, JA17 & JA17a 55.00 17.50
Never hinged 110.00
JA18 A2 25c blk, *rose* 21.00 5.50
Never hinged 42.50
On cover 425.00
a. "T" inverted 21.00 5.50
Never hinged 42.50
On cover 425.00
b. Tête-bêche pair, JA18 & JA18a 55.00 17.50
Never hinged 110.00
JA19 A2 25c blue ('01) 3.50 1.10
Never hinged 7.00
On cover 425.00
a. "T" inverted 3.50 1.10
Never hinged 7.00
On cover 425.00
b. Tête-bêche pair, JA19 & JA19a 14.00 7.00
Never hinged 25.00
JA20 A2 40c red, *straw* 21.00 5.00
Never hinged 42.50
On cover 500.00
a. "T" inverted 21.00 5.00
Never hinged 42.50
On cover 500.00
b. Tête-bêche pair, JA20 & JA20a 62.50 17.50
Never hinged 110.00
JA21 A2 75c car, *rose* 175.00 130.00
a. "T" inverted 175.00 120.00
JA22 A2 75c dp vio, *org* ('93) 42.50 11.00
Never hinged 75.00
a. "T" inverted 42.50 11.00
Never hinged 75.00
JA23 A3 1fr olive, *olive* 35.00 11.00
Never hinged 62.50
a. "T" inverted 35.00 11.00
Never hinged 62.50
JA24 A3 5fr red lil, *lav* 175.00 110.00
a. "T" inverted 175.00 110.00

Quadrille Paper

JA25 A2 15c bl, *grysh* ('93) 21.00 5.00
Never hinged 35.00
On cover 250.00
a. "T" inverted 21.00 5.00
Never hinged 35.00
On cover 250.00
b. Tête-bêche pair, JA25 & JA25a 62.50 17.50
Never hinged 110.00
Nos. JA9-JA25 (17) 571.50 300.95

D1

1901-03 Unwmk. *Perf. 14x13½* Typo.

J1 D1 1c black .35 .45
Never hinged .70
On cover 62.50
J2 D1 2c orange .70 .55
Never hinged 1.40
On cover 62.50
J3 D1 5c blue .70 .45
Never hinged 1.10
On cover 62.50
a. On grayish paper ('17) 1.40 1.10
Never hinged 2.50
On cover 62.50
J4 D1 10c brown .70 .55
Never hinged 1.10
On cover 50.00
J5 D1 20c blue green 4.25 .85
Never hinged 7.00
On cover 50.00
a. On grayish paper ('18) 5.50 2.10
Never hinged 10.50
On cover 62.50
J6 D1 30c carmine 3.50 .80
Never hinged 7.00
On cover 50.00
a. On grayish paper ('17) 7.00 1.10
Never hinged 10.50
On cover 62.50
J7 D1 50c brown violet 1.75 .85
Never hinged 3.50
On cover 75.00
a. On grayish paper ('18) 7.00 2.50
Never hinged 14.00
On cover 75.00
J8 D1 1fr olive green 1.40 .85
Never hinged 3.50
On cover 95.00
J9 D1 2fr carmine, *grn* 4.25 1.75
Never hinged 7.00
On cover 110.00
J10 D1 5fr blk, *yellow* 52.50 35.00
Never hinged 77.50
On cover 190.00
Nos. J1-J10 (10) 70.10 42.10

No. J10 Surcharged in Blue

1914, Nov.

J11 D1 2fr on 5fr blk, *yellow* 3.50 3.50
Never hinged 7.00
On cover 125.00

In Jan. 1917 regular 5c postage stamps were overprinted "T" in an inverted triangle and used as postage due stamps.

D2

1922-49

J12 D2 1c black .35 .30
Never hinged .70
On cover 50.00
J13 D2 2c black, *yellow* .35 .30
Never hinged .70
On cover 50.00
J14 D2 5c violet brown .70 .30
Never hinged 1.05
On cover 37.50
J15 D2 10c blue .35 .45
Never hinged .70
On cover 37.50
J16 D2 10c yel green ('45) .25 .25
Never hinged .35
On cover 32.50
J17 D2 20c orange, *yel* .35 .45
Never hinged .70
On cover 37.50
J18 D2 30c brown ('23) .35 .30
Never hinged .70
On cover 42.50
J19 D2 50c rose red 1.05 .50
Never hinged 1.40
On cover 50.00
J20 D2 50c blue vio ('45) .25 .25
Never hinged .35
On cover 25.00
J21 D2 60c violet ('28) 1.05 .50
Never hinged 1.40
On cover 62.50
J22 D2 80c bister ('28) .70 .35
Never hinged 1.40
On cover 80.00
J23 D2 90c orange red ('28) 1.10 .65
Never hinged 1.40
On cover 80.00
J24 D2 1fr green .70 .30
Never hinged 1.10
On cover 80.00
J25 D2 2fr olive grn, *straw* 1.40 .55
Never hinged 1.75
On cover 95.00
J26 D2 2fr car rose ('45) .30 .30
Never hinged .35
On cover 14.00
J27 D2 3fr vio, *pink* ('29) .35 .30
Never hinged .70
On cover 125.00
J28 D2 4fr grnsh bl ('45) .35 .45
Never hinged .70
On cover 37.50

J29 D2 5fr violet .70 .55
Never hinged 1.10
On cover 150.00
J30 D2 10fr cerise ('49) .35 .35
Never hinged .70
On cover 21.00
J31 D2 20fr olive gray ('49) 1.40 1.10
Never hinged 1.75
On cover 37.50
Nos. J12-J31 (20) 12.40 8.50

PARCEL POST STAMPS

Mail Delivery — PP1

1906 Unwmk. Typo. ***Perf. 13½x14***
Q1 PP1 5c grn & vio brn .70 .55
Never hinged 1.40
Q2 PP1 10c org & red 1.10 .70
Never hinged 2.10
Q3 PP1 20c dk brn & org 1.75 .70
Never hinged 3.50
a. Center double 450.00 *5,000.*
Q4 PP1 25c blue & brn 2.50 .70
Never hinged 5.25
Q5 PP1 40c gray & rose 2.75 .70
Never hinged 6.00
Q6 PP1 50c vio brn & vio 2.75 .70
Never hinged 5.25
Q7 PP1 75c bis brn & bl 3.50 .70
Never hinged 7.00
Q8 PP1 1fr red brn & red 2.75 .50
Never hinged 6.00
Q9 PP1 2fr carmine & bl 8.50 1.10
Never hinged 16.00
Q10 PP1 5fr vio & vio brn 23.00 1.40
Never hinged 42.50
Nos. Q1-Q10 (10) 49.30 7.75

For surcharges see Nos. B37-B46.

Gathering Dates — PP2

1926
Q11 PP2 5c pale brn & dk bl .45 .45
Never hinged .70
Q12 PP2 10c rose & vio .55 .45
Never hinged 1.10
Q13 PP2 20c yel grn & blk .55 .45
Never hinged 1.10
Q14 PP2 25c org brn & blk .55 .45
Never hinged 1.10
Q15 PP2 40c dp rose & dp grn 2.75 .55
Never hinged 3.75
Q16 PP2 50c lt vio & blk 1.75 .80
Never hinged 2.75
Q17 PP2 60c ol & brn red 1.75 .70
Never hinged 2.75
Q18 PP2 75c gray vio & bl grn 1.75 .70
Never hinged 2.75
Q19 PP2 80c ver & ol brn 1.75 .70
Never hinged 2.75
Q20 PP2 1fr Prus bl & dp rose 2.10 .70
Never hinged 3.50
Q21 PP2 2fr vio & mag 4.25 .70
Never hinged 7.00
Q22 PP2 4fr red & blk 4.50 .70
Never hinged 7.75
Q23 PP2 5fr red brn & dp vio 7.00 1.10
Never hinged 12.00
Q24 PP2 10fr dl red & grn, *grnsh* 14.00 1.10
Never hinged 25.00
Q25 PP2 20fr yel grn & dp vio, *lav* 27.00 1.75
Never hinged 42.50
Nos. Q11-Q25 (15) 70.70 11.30

Parcel post stamps were discontinued July 1, 1940.

TURKEY

ˈtər-kē

LOCATION — Southeastern Europe and Asia Minor, between the Mediterranean and Black Seas
GOVT. — Republic
AREA — 300,947 sq. mi.
POP. — 48,000,000 (est. 1984)
CAPITAL — Ankara

The Ottoman Empire ceased to exist in 1922, and the Republic of Turkey was inaugurated in 1923.

40 Paras = 1 Piaster
40 Paras = 1 Ghurush (1926)
40 Paras = 1 Kurush (1926)
100 Kurush = 1 Lira

Catalogue values for unused stamps in this country are for Never Hinged items, beginning with Scott 817 in the regular postage section, Scott C1 in the airpost section, and Scott J97 in the postage due section.

Turkish Numerals

"Tughra," Monogram of Sultan Abdul-Aziz
A1 A2

A3 A4

1863 Unwmk. Litho. ***Imperf.***

Red Band: 20pa, 1pi, 2pi

Blue Band: 5pi

Thin Paper

1 A1 20pa blk, *yellow* 75.00 20.00
a. Tête bêche pair 250.00 200.00
b. Without band 100.00
c. Green band
2 A2 1pi blk, *dl vio* 125.00 20.00
a. 1pi black, *gray* 125.00 21.50
b. Tête bêche pair 400.00 300.00
c. Without band 140.00
d. Design reversed *175.00*
e. 1pi blk, *yel* (error) 250.00 150.00
4 A3 2pi blk, *grnsh bl* 115.00 20.00
a. 2pi black, *ind* 115.00 21.50
b. Tête bêche pair 400.00 300.00
c. Without band 140.00
5 A4 5pi blk, *rose* 225.00 45.00
a. Tête bêche pair 500.00 400.00
b. Without band 250.00
c. Green band *275.00*
d. Red band *275.00*

Thick, Surface Colored Paper

6 A1 20pa blk, *yellow* 250.00 37.50
a. Tête bêche pair 450.00 450.00
b. Design reversed 325.00 325.00
c. Without band 225.00 225.00
d. Paper colored through 225.00 225.00
7 A2 1pi blk, *gray* 300.00 35.00
a. Tête bêche pair 900.00 900.00
b. Design reversed
c. Without band
d. Paper colored through 350.00 225.00
Nos. 1-7 (6) 1,090. 177.50

Full margins: Nos. 1, 2, 4, 5 = 1mm at sides and top, 3mm at bottom (includes part of band); Nos. 6-7 = ¾mm at sides and top, 3¼ at bottom (includes part of band). Height of colored bands is 6mm. Full margins for items without band = 3mm at bottom.

Full margins of first printings: No. 4 = 1mm; No. 5 = ½mm.

The 2pi and 5pi had two printings. In the common printing, the stamps are more widely spaced and alternate horizontal rows of 12 are inverted. In the first and rare printing, the stamps are more closely spaced and no rows are tête bêche.

See Nos. J1-J4.

Crescent and Star, Symbols of Turkish Caliphate — A5

Surcharged

The bottom characters of this and the following surcharges denote the denomination. The characters at top and sides translate, "Ottoman Empire Posts."

1865 Typo. ***Perf. 12½***
8 A5 10pa deep green 11.00 *35.00*
c. "1" instead of "10" in each corner *300.00* *300.00*
9 A5 20pa yellow 7.00 6.00
a. Star without rays 9.00 *6.00*
10 A5 1pi lilac 12.50 4.00
a. Star without rays 20.00 5.00
c. 1pi gray 11.00 3.00
11 A5 2pi blue 6.50 4.00
12 A5 5pi carmine 5.50 4.50
d. Inverted surcharge
13 A5 25pi red orange 325.00 250.00

Imperf., Pairs

8b A5 10pa 125.00 125.00
9b A5 20pa 125.00 125.00
10b A5 1pi *100.00* *90.00*
11a A5 2pi *100.00* *90.00*
12b A5 5pi *150.00* *110.00*
13a A5 25pi 900.00 *900.00*

See Nos. J6-J35. For overprints and surcharges see Nos. 14-52, 64-65, 446-461, 467-468, J71-J77, Eastern Rumelia 1.

Surcharged

1867
14 A5 10pa gray green 9.50
a. Imperf., pair 55.00
15 A5 20pa yellow 15.00
a. Imperf., pair 75.00
16 A5 1pi lilac 20.00
a. Imperf., pair 110.00
b. Imperf., with surcharge of 5pi 200.00
17 A5 2pi blue 5.50 *45.00*
a. Imperf. 50.00
18 A5 5pi rose 4.50 *45.00*
a. Imperf. 50.00
19 A5 25pi orange *3,600.*
Nos. 14-18 (5) 54.50

Nos. 14, 15, 16 and 19 were never placed in use.

Surcharged

1869 ***Perf. 13½***
20 A5 10pa dull violet 100.00 12.00
a. Printed on both sides
b. Imperf., pair *90.00* *80.00*
c. Inverted surcharge *90.00*
d. Double surcharge
e. 10pa yellow (error) *300.00*
f. 10pa gray brown 60.00 2.10
21 A5 20pa pale green 400.00 14.00
a. Printed on both sides *450.00* *275.00*
22 A5 1pi yellow 10.00 2.50
No gum 2.00
c. Inverted surcharge *100.00*
d. Double surcharge
e. Surcharged on both sides
f. Printed on both sides
23 A5 2pi orange red 200.00 10.00
b. Imperf., pair 125.00 125.00
c. Printed on both sides 125.00
d. Inverted surcharge 70.00 70.00
e. Surcharged on both sides 140.00
24 A5 5pi blue 5.00 *10.00*
25 A5 5pi gray 30.00 37.50
26 A5 25pi dull rose 37.50 125.00
Nos. 20-26 (7) 782.50 *211.00*

Pin-perf., Perf. 5 to 11 and Compound

1870-71
27 A5 10pa lilac *550.00* *25.00*
28 A5 10pa brown *500.00* *15.00*
a. 10pa brown, *lilac* *3,750.* *100.00*
b. 10pa purple, *lilac* *3,750.* *125.00*
c. 10pa gray, *lilac* *5,000.* *160.00*
29 A5 20pa gray green 75.00 *10.00*
a. Printed on both sides
30 A5 1pi yellow *550.00* *10.00*
a. Inverted surcharge *500.00* *80.00*
b. Without surcharge
31 A5 2pi red 8.00 5.00
a. Imperf. 20.00 20.00
b. Printed on both sides *40.00*
c. Surcharged on both sides
32 A5 5pi blue 5.00 *12.50*
a. 5pi greenish blue 6.00 *8.00*
33 A5 5pi slate 40.00 50.00
a. Printed on both sides
b. Surcharged on both sides *80.00*
34 A5 25pi dull rose 40.00 *75.00*
Nos. 27-34 (8) 1,768. *202.50*

1873 ***Perf. 12, 12½***
35 A5 10pa dark lilac 475.00 25.00
a. Inverted surcharge 90.00
36 A5 10pa olive brown 110.00 17.50
a. 10pa bister 110.00 11.00
37 A5 2pi vermilion 3.50 4.50
a. Surcharged on both sides 22.50 22.50
Nos. 35-37 (3) 588.50 *47.00*

Surcharged

1874-75 ***Perf. 13½***
38 A5 10pa red violet 52.50 7.50
a. Imperf., pair 210.00 50.00
39 A5 20pa yellow green 15.00 5.00
b. Inverted surcharge 30.00 13.00
c. Double surcharge
40 A5 1pi yellow 210.00 30.00
a. Imperf., pair 100.00 80.00

Perf. 12, 12½

41 A5 10pa red violet 25.00 10.00
a. Inverted surcharge 45.00 60.00
Nos. 38-41 (4) 302.50 52.50

Surcharged

1876, Apr. ***Perf. 13½***
42 A5 10pa red lilac 2.00 .50
a. Inverted surcharge 70.00
b. Imperf., pair 15.00 15.00
43 A5 20pa pale green 2.00 .50
b. Inverted surcharge 70.00
c. Imperf., pair 15.00 15.00
44 A5 1pi yellow 2.00 .50
a. Imperf., pair 27.50 27.50
46 A5 5pi gray blue *1,700.*
47 A5 25pi dull rose *1,700.*
Nos. 42-44 (3) 6.00

Nos. 46 and 47 were never placed in use. See Nos. 64-65.

Surcharged

1876, Jan.
48 A5 ¼pi on 10pa violet 3.00 2.50
49 A5 ½pi on 20pa yel grn 6.25 2.50
50 A5 1¼pi on 50pa rose 2.25 2.50
a. Imperf., pair 60.00
51 A5 2pi on 2pi redsh brn 40.00 7.50
52 A5 5pi on 5pi gray blue *10.00* *85.00*
Nos. 48-52 (5) 61.50 *100.00*

The surcharge on Nos. 48-52 restates in French the value originally expressed in Turkish characters.

The vast majority of No. 51 unused are without gum.

A7

1876, Sept. Typo. Perf. 13½

53 A7 10pa black & rose lil 2.00 6.25
54 A7 20pa red vio & grn 62.50 5.00
55 A7 50pa blue & yellow 1.50 *10.00*
56 A7 2pi black & redsh brn 1.60 *5.00*
57 A7 5pi red & blue 3.00 *12.50*
b. Cliché of 25pi in plate of 5pi 400.00 375.00
58 A7 25pi claret & rose 15.00 85.00
a. Imperf. 160.00
Nos. 53-58 (6) 85.60 123.75

Nos. 56-58 exist perf. 11½, but were not regularly issued.

See Nos. 59-63, 66-91, J36-J38. For overprints see Nos. 462-466, 469-476, J78-J79, P10-P14, Eastern Rumelia 2-40.

1880-84 Perf. 13½

59 A7 5pa black & ol ('81) 3.00 6.50
a. Imperf. 30.00
60 A7 10pa black & grn ('84) 3.00 3.50
61 A7 20pa black & rose 55.00 2.00
62 A7 1pi blk & bl *(piastres)* 75.00 3.00
a. 1pi black & gray blue 85.00
b. Imperf. 60.00
63 A7 1pi blk & bl *(piastre)* ('81) 110.00 5.00
Nos. 59-63 (5) 246.00 20.00

A cliché of No. 63 was inserted in a plate of the Eastern Rumelia 1pi (No. 13). This was found in the remainder stock.

Nos. 60-61 and 63 exist perf. 11½, but were not regularly issued.

See Nos. J36-J38.

1881-82

Surcharged like Apr., 1876 Issue

64 A5 20pa gray 4.25 6.25
a. Inverted surcharge 13.50
b. Imperf., pair 25.00
65 A5 2pi pale salmon 3.00 1.00
a. Inverted surcharge 22.50

1884-86 Perf. 11½, 13½

66 A7 5pa lil & pale lil ('86) 200.00 *150.00*
67 A7 10pa grn & pale grn 1.60 1.25
68 A7 20pa rose & pale rose 2.00 1.25
69 A7 1pi blue & lt blue 2.00 1.25

Perf. 11½

70 A7 2pi ocher & pale ocher 2.25 1.25
71 A7 5pi red brn & pale brn 20.00 25.00
c. 5pi ocher & pale ocher (error) 12.00 12.00

Perf. 11½, 13½

73 A7 25pi blk & pale gray ('86) 300.00 *425.00*
Nos. 66-73 (7) 527.85 *605.00*

Imperf

66a A7 5pa 60.00
67a A7 10pa 40.00
68b A7 20pa 40.00
69b A7 1pi 40.00
73a A7 25pi 150.00

1886 Perf. 13½

74 A7 5pa black & pale gray 2.00 2.50
75 A7 2pi orange & lt bl 2.00 2.00
76 A7 5pi grn & pale grn 3.00 25.00
77 A7 25pi bis & pale bis 45.00 *150.00*
Nos. 74-77 (4) 52.00 *179.50*

Imperf

74a A7 5pa 30.00
75b A7 2pi 40.00
76b A7 5pi 40.00
77a A7 25pi 40.00

Stamps of 1884-86, bisected and surcharged as above, 10pa, 20pa, 1pi and 2pi or surcharged "2" in red are stated to have been made privately and without authority. With the aid of employees of the post office, stamps were passed through the mails.

1888 Perf. 13½

83 A7 5pa green & yellow 2.50 5.00
84 A7 2pi red lilac & bl 1.50 1.50
85 A7 5pi dk brown & gray 5.00 *20.00*
86 A7 25pi red & yellow 30.00 *150.00*
Nos. 83-86 (4) 39.00 *176.50*

Imperf

83a A7 5pa 40.00
84a A7 2pi 40.00
85a A7 5pi 40.00
86a A7 25pi 40.00

Nos. 74-86 exist perf. 11½, but were not regularly issued.

1890 Perf. 11½, 13½

87 A7 10pa green & gray 8.00 1.00
88 A7 20pa rose & gray 1.60 1.00
89 A7 1pi blue & gray 125.00 1.00
90 A7 2pi yellow & gray 2.25 *7.50*
a. 2pi Olive yel & yel 85.00 7.50
91 A7 5pi buff & gray 5.00 *22.50*
Nos. 87-91 (5) 141.85 *33.00*

Imperf

87a A7 10pa 20.00
88a A7 20pa 20.00
89a A7 1pi 100.00
90b A7 2pi 100.00
91a A7 5pi 25.00

Arms and Tughra of "El Gazi" (The Conqueror) Sultan Abdul Hamid

A10 A11

A12

A13

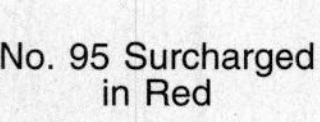

A14

1892-98 Typo. Perf. 13½

95 A10 10pa gray green 2.25 .50
96 A11 20pa violet brn ('98) 1.25 .50
a. 20pa dark pink 7.50 .45
b. 20pa pink 35.00 .45
97 A12 1pi pale blue 110.00 4.00
98 A13 2pi brown org 3.00 1.00
a. Tête bêche pair *30.00* *30.00*
99 A14 5pi dull violet 9.00 *15.00*
a. Turkish numeral in upper right corner reads "50" instead of "5" 50.00 45.00
Nos. 95-99 (5) 125.50 *21.00*

See Nos. J39-J42. For surcharges and overprints see Nos. 100, 288-291, 350, 355-359, 477-478, B38, B41, J80-J82, P25-P34, P36, P121-P122, P134-P137, P153-P154.

No. 95 Surcharged in Red

1897

100 A10 5pa on 10pa gray grn 3.00 1.25
a. "Cniq" instead of "Cinq" 30.00 25.00

Turkish stamps of types A11, A17-A18, A21-A24, A26, A28-A39, A41 with or without Turkish overprints and English surcharges with "Baghdad" or "Iraq" are listed under Mesopotamia in Scott Standard catalogue, Vol. 4.

Turkish stamps of types A19 and A21 with Double-headed Eagle and "Shqipenia" handstamp are listed under Albania in Scott Standard catalogue, Vol. 1.

A16

1901 Typo. Perf. 13¼

For Foreign Postage

102 A16 5pa bister 1.25 .60
103 A16 10pa yellow green 1.25 .60
104 A16 20pa magenta 1.25 .60
a. Perf. 12 2.50 1.00
105 A16 1pi violet blue 1.50 1.00
106 A16 2pi gray blue 2.50 1.00
107 A16 5pi ocher 8.50 3.50
108 A16 25pi dark green 100.00 30.00
109 A16 50pi yellow 250.00 100.00
Nos. 102-109 (8) 366.25 137.30

A17

For Domestic Postage

Perf. 13¼

110 A17 5pa purple 1.25 .50
a. Perf. 12 2.50 1.60
b. Perf. 12x13¼ 3.00 .60
111 A17 10pa green 1.25 .50
a. Perf. 12 5.00 3.50
b. Perf. 12x13¼ 5.00 1.50
112 A17 20pa carmine 1.25 .50
a. Perf. 12 3.00 1.60
b. Perf. 12x13¼ 6.00 1.50
113 A17 1pi blue 1.25 .50
a. Imperf. 20.00
b. Perf. 12 4.25 2.25
c. Perf. 12x13¼ 6.00 1.50
114 A17 2pi orange 2.00 .50
115 A17 5pi lilac rose 5.75 1.00
a. Perf. 12 6.25 2.25

Perf. 13½

116 A17 25pi brown 10.00 2.00
a. Perf. 12 25.00 8.50
117 A17 50pi yellow brown 37.50 5.00
a. Perf. 12 55.00 17.00
Nos. 110-117 (8) 60.25 10.50

Nos. 110-113 exist perf. 12x13½.

See Nos. J43-J46.

For overprints and surcharges see Nos. 165-180, 292-303, 340-341, 361-377, 479-493, B19-B20, B37, P37-P48, P69-P80, P123-P126, P138-P146, P155-P164.

A18

1905 Perf. 12, 13½ and Compound

118 A18 5pa ocher 1.00 .50
119 A18 10pa dull green 1.00 .50
a. Imperf. 10.00 9.00
120 A18 20pa carmine 1.00 .50
a. Imperf. 10.00 9.00
121 A18 1pi blue 1.00 .50
122 A18 2pi slate 1.50 .50
123 A18 2½pi red violet 1.50 .50
a. Imperf. 20.00 18.00
124 A18 5pi brown 2.00 .50
125 A18 10pi orange brn 3.75 .50
126 A18 25pi olive green 12.50 15.00
127 A18 50pi deep violet 50.00 30.00

See Nos. J47-J48. For overprints and surcharges see Nos. 128-131, 181-182, 304-314, 351-354, 378-389, 494-508, B1-B3, B21-B23, B39-B40, P49-P54, P127-P129, P147-P150, P165-P171.

Large "Discount" Overprint in Carmine or Blue

1906

128 A18 10pa dull green (C) 3.00 1.00
129 A18 20pa carmine (Bl) 3.00 1.00
130 A18 1pi blue (C) 3.00 1.00
131 A18 2pi slate (C) 17.50 5.00
Nos. 118-131 (14) 101.75 57.00

Stamps bearing this overprint were sold to merchants at a discount from face value to encourage the use of Turkish stamps on foreign correspondence, instead of those of the various European powers which maintained post offices in Turkey. The overprint is the Arab "B," for "Béhié," meaning "discount."

Tugra and 'Reshad' of Sultan Abdülhamid — A19

Tughra is upright and there is no space between the script and the frame.

1908

132 A19 5pa ocher 1.25 .50
133 A19 10pa blue green 1.75 .30
134 A19 20pa carmine 40.00 .50
135 A19 1pi bright blue 15.00 .50
a. 1pi ultramarine 50.00 10.00
136 A19 2pi blue black 10.00 .50
137 A19 2½pi violet brown 6.00 .50
138 A19 5pi dark violet 80.00 .50
139 A19 10pi red 70.00 2.50
140 A19 25pi dark green 12.00 5.00
141 A19 50pi red brown 50.00 35.00

See Nos. J49-J50. For overprints and surcharges see Nos. 142-145, 314B-316B, 390-396, 509-516A, B4-B6, B17, B24-B27, P55-P60, P130-P131, P151, P172, Thrace 15.

Small "Discount" Overprint in Carmine or Blue

142 A19 10pa blue green (C) 7.50 2.50
143 A19 20pa carmine (Bl) 7.50 2.50
144 A19 1pi brt blue (C) 15.00 2.50
145 A19 2pi blue black (C) 25.00 12.50
Nos. 132-145 (14) 341.00 65.80

A20

Perf. 12, 13½ & Compound

1908, Dec. 17

146 A20 5pa ocher 1.00 .50
147 A20 10pa blue green 1.50 .50
148 A20 20pa carmine 2.00 1.00
149 A20 1pi ultra 3.00 1.00
150 A20 2pi gray black 12.50 15.00
Nos. 146-150 (5) 20.00 18.00

Imperf

146a A20 5pa 3.00 3.00
147a A20 10pa 4.00 4.00
148a A20 20pa 5.50 5.50
149a A20 1pi 3.00 3.00

Granting of a Constitution, the date of which is inscribed on the banderol: "324 Temuz 10" (July 24, 1908).

For overprints see Nos. 397, 517.

Tughra and "Reshad" of Sultan Mohammed V — A21

The Tughra leans slightly to the left, and there is space under the script.

1909, Dec.

No.	Type	Denomination / Color	Unused	Used
151	A21	5pa ocher	1.00	.50
152	A21	10pa blue green	1.00	.50
a.		Imperf.	10.00	10.00
153	A21	20pa carmine rose	1.00	.50
154	A21	1pi ultra	3.00	.50
a.		1pi bright blue	12.50	.50
155	A21	2pi blue black	3.00	.50
156	A21	2½pi dark brown	90.00	20.00
157	A21	5pi dark violet	12.00	1.00
158	A21	10pi dull red	37.50	1.00
159	A21	25pi dark green	350.00	100.00
160	A21	50pi red brown	150.00	80.00

The 2pa olive green, type A21, is a newspaper stamp, No. P68.

Two types exist for the 10pa, 20pa and 1pi. In the second type, the damaged crescent is restored.

See Nos. J51-J52. For overprints and surcharges see Nos. 161-164, 317-327, 342-343, 398-406, 518-528, 567, B7-B14, B18, B28-B32, P61-P68, P81, P132-P133, P152, P173, Turkey in Asia 67, 72, Thrace 1-4, 13, 13A, 14.

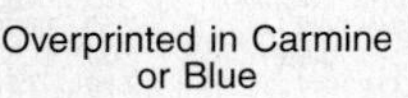

Overprinted in Carmine or Blue

No.	Type	Denomination / Color	Unused	Used
161	A21	10pa blue grn (C)	1.75	.75
a.		Imperf.		
162	A21	20pa car rose (Bl)	1.75	.75
a.		Imperf.		
163	A21	1pi ultra (C)	3.50	2.00
a.		Imperf.	4.00	
b.		1pi bright blue	6.50	3.00
164	A21	2pi blue black (C)	75.00	30.00
a.		Imperf.		
		Nos. 151-164 (14)	730.50	238.00

Stamps of 1901-05 Overprinted in Carmine or Blue

The overprint was applied to 18 denominations in four settings with change of city name, producing individual sets for each city: "MONASTIR," "PRISTINA," "SALONIQUE" and "USKUB."

1911, June 26 ***Perf. 12, 13½***

"Monastir"

No.	Type	Denomination / Color	Unused	Used
165	A16	5pa bister	4.50	*5.00*
166	A16	10pa yel grn	4.50	*5.00*
167	A16	20pa magenta	9.50	*10.00*
168	A16	1pi violet blue	9.50	*10.00*
169	A16	2pi gray blue	9.50	*10.00*
170	A16	5pi ocher	50.00	*80.00*
171	A16	25pi dark green	70.00	*100.00*
172	A16	50pi yellow	100.00	*150.00*
173	A17	5pa purple	5.50	4.50
174	A17	10pa green	6.25	4.50
175	A17	20pa carmine	8.50	9.00
176	A17	1pi blue	8.50	9.00
177	A17	2pi orange	8.50	9.00
178	A17	5pi lilac rose	47.50	*70.00*
179	A17	25pi chocolate	150.00	*200.00*
d.		Perf. 12	150.00	200.00
180	A17	50pi yel brn	120.00	*145.00*
d.		Perf. 12	150.00	200.00
181	A18	2½pi red violet	65.00	*110.00*
182	A18	10pi org brn	65.00	*90.00*
		Nos. 165-182 (18)	742.25	*1,021.*

Sultan's visit to Macedonia. The Arabic overprint reads: "Souvenir of the Sultan's Journey, 1329." See Nos. P69-P81.

"Pristina"

No.	Type	Denomination / Color	Unused	Used
165a	A16	5pa bister	4.50	*5.00*
166a	A16	10pa yel grn	4.50	*5.00*
167a	A16	20pa magenta	9.50	*10.00*
168a	A16	1pi violet blue	9.50	*10.00*
169a	A16	2pi gray blue	9.50	*10.00*
170a	A16	5pi ocher	50.00	*80.00*
171a	A16	25pi dark green	70.00	*100.00*
172a	A16	50pi yellow	100.00	*150.00*
173a	A17	5pa purple	5.50	4.50
174a	A17	10pa green	6.25	4.50
175a	A17	20pa carmine	8.50	*9.00*
176a	A17	1pi blue	8.50	*9.00*
177a	A17	2pi orange	8.50	*9.00*
178a	A17	5pi lilac rose	47.50	*70.00*
179a	A17	25pi chocolate	150.00	*200.00*
d.		Perf. 12	150.00	200.00
180a	A17	50pi yel brn	120.00	145.00
d.		Perf. 12	150.00	200.00
181a	A18	2½pi red violet	65.00	*110.00*
182a	A18	10pi org brn	65.00	*90.00*
		Nos. 165a-182a (18)	742.25	*1,021.*

"Salonique"

No.	Type	Denomination / Color	Unused	Used
165b	A16	5pa bister	4.50	*5.00*
166b	A16	10pa yel grn	4.50	*5.00*
167b	A16	20pa magenta	9.50	*10.00*
168b	A16	1pi violet blue	9.50	*10.00*
169b	A16	2pi gray blue	9.50	*10.00*
170b	A16	5pi ocher	50.00	80.00
171b	A16	25pi dark green	70.00	*100.00*
172b	A16	50pi yellow	100.00	*150.00*
173b	A17	5pa purple	5.50	4.50
174b	A17	10pa green	6.25	4.50
175b	A17	20pa carmine	8.50	*9.00*
176b	A17	1pi blue	8.50	*9.00*
177b	A17	2pi orange	8.50	*9.00*
178b	A17	5pi lilac rose	47.50	*70.00*
179b	A17	25pi chocolate	150.00	*200.00*
d.		Perf. 12	150.00	200.00
180b	A17	50pi yel brn	120.00	*145.00*
d.		Perf. 12	150.00	200.00
181b	A18	2½pi red violet	65.00	*110.00*
182b	A18	10pi org brn	65.00	*90.00*
		Nos. 165b-182b (18)	742.25	*1,021.*

"Uskub"

No.	Type	Denomination / Color	Unused	Used
165c	A16	5pa bister	4.50	*5.00*
166c	A16	10pa yel grn	4.50	*5.00*
167c	A16	20pa magenta	9.50	*10.00*
168c	A16	1pi violet blue	9.50	*10.00*
169c	A16	2pi gray blue	9.50	*10.00*
170c	A16	5pi ocher	50.00	*80.00*
171c	A16	25pi dark green	70.00	*100.00*
172c	A16	50pi yellow	100.00	*150.00*
173c	A17	5pa purple	5.50	4.50
174c	A17	10pa green	6.25	4.50
175c	A17	20pa carmine	8.50	*9.00*
176c	A17	1pi blue	8.50	*9.00*
177c	A17	2pi orange	8.50	*9.00*
178c	A17	5pi lilac rose	47.50	*70.00*
179c	A17	25pi chocolate	150.00	*200.00*
d.		Perf. 12	150.00	200.00
180c	A17	50pi yel brn	120.00	*145.00*
d.		Perf. 12	150.00	200.00
181c	A18	2½pi red violet	65.00	*110.00*
182c	A18	10pi org brn	65.00	*90.00*
		Nos. 165c-182c (18)	742.25	*1,021.*

Sultan's visit to Macedonia. The Arabic overprint reads: "Souvenir of the Sultan's Journey, 1329." See Nos. P69-P81.

General Post Office, Constantinople A22

1913, Mar. 14 ***Perf. 12***

No.	Type	Denomination / Color	Unused	Used
237	A22	2pa olive green	1.00	.50
238	A22	5pa ocher	1.00	.50
239	A22	10pa blue green	1.00	.50
240	A22	20pa carmine rose	1.00	.50
241	A22	1pi ultra	1.00	.50
242	A22	2pi indigo	2.00	.50
243	A22	5pi dull violet	3.50	1.00
244	A22	10pi dull red	6.00	3.00
245	A22	25pi gray green	22.50	22.50
246	A22	50pi orange brown	85.00	125.00

See Nos. J53-J58. For overprints and surcharges see Nos. 247-250, 328-339, 344, 407-414, 529-538, 568, B14-B16, B33-B36. Mesopotamia Nos. N6, N16-N19, N24-N25. Turkey in Asia 68, Thrace 10, 10A, 11, 11A, 12, N82.

Overprinted in Carmine or Blue

No.	Type	Denomination / Color	Unused	Used
247	A22	10pa blue green (C)	1.00	.50
248	A22	20pa car rose (Bl)	1.00	.50
249	A22	1pi ultra (C)	1.00	.50
250	A22	2pi indigo (C)	17.50	7.50
		Nos. 237-250 (14)	144.50	163.50

Mosque of Selim, Adrianople — A23

1913, Oct. 23 **Engr.**

No.	Type	Denomination / Color	Unused	Used
251	A23	10pa green	1.50	1.00
252	A23	20pa red	2.50	2.00
253	A23	40pa blue	6.00	3.00
		Nos. 251-253 (3)	10.00	6.00

Recapture of Adrianople (Edirne) by the Turks.

See Nos. 592, J59-J62. For overprints and surcharge see Nos. 415-417, 539-540, J59-J62, J67-J70, J83-J86, Mesopotamia No. N7, Thrace N84.

Obelisk of Theodosius in the Hippodrome A24

Column of Constantine A25

Leander's Tower — A26

One of the Seven Towers — A27

Fener Bahçe (Garden Lighthouse) A28

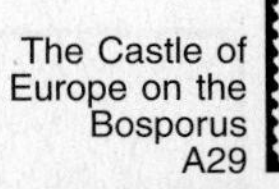

The Castle of Europe on the Bosporus A29

Mosque of Sultan Ahmed — A30

Monument to the Martyrs of Liberty A31

Fountains of Suleiman A32

Cruiser "Hamidie" A33

View of Kandili on the Bosporus A34

War Ministry (Later Istanbul University) — A35

Sweet Waters of Europe Park A36

Mosque of Suleiman A37

The Bosporus A38

Sultan Ahmed's Fountain A39

Sultan Mohammed V — A40

Designs A24-A39: Views of Constantinople.

1914, Jan. 14 **Litho.**

No.	Type	Denomination / Color	Unused	Used
254	A24	2pa red lilac	1.00	.50
255	A25	4pa dark brown	1.00	.50
256	A26	5pa violet brown	1.00	.50
257	A27	6pa dark blue	1.00	.50

Engr.

No.	Type	Denomination / Color	Unused	Used
258	A28	10pa green	2.00	.40
259	A29	20pa red	1.75	.40
260	A30	1pi blue	.75	.50
b.		Booklet pane of 2+2 labels		
261	A31	1½pi car & blk	1.25	.75
262	A32	1¾pi sl & red brn	1.50	1.00
263	A33	2pi green & blk	2.00	.40
264	A34	2½pi org & ol grn	2.00	.50
265	A35	5pi dull violet	4.00	1.00
266	A36	10pi red brown	8.00	1.00
267	A37	25pi olive green	125.00	5.50
268	A38	50pi carmine	8.00	3.00
269	A39	100pi deep blue	75.00	27.50
		Cut cancellation		12.00
270	A40	200pi green & blk	550.00	*400.00*
		Cut cancellation		25.00
		Nos. 254-270 (17)	785.25	443.95

See Nos. 590-591, 593-598.

For overprints and surcharges see Nos. 271-287, 419, 541, 552-553, 574A, 601, 603-604, P174, Mesopotamia Nos. N1-N5, N28-N41, N50-N53, NO1-NO22, Turkey in Asia 1-3, 5-9, 73-74, Thrace N77, N78.

Nos. 258-260, 262-263 Ovptd. in Red or Blue

271 A28 10pa green (R) 3.00 .75
272 A29 20pa red (Bl) 10.00 .75
273 A30 1pi blue (R) 3.00 .75
275 A32 1¾pi sl & red brn (Bl) 4.00 1.25
276 A33 2pi green & blk (R) 50.00 5.00
Nos. 271-276 (5) 70.00 8.50

No. 261 Surcharged

1914, July 23

277 A31 1pi on 1½pi car & blk 3.25 2.50
a. "1330" omitted 15.00 15.00
b. Double surcharge
c. Triple surcharge 15.00 15.00

7th anniv. of the Constitution. The surcharge reads "10 July, 1330, National fête" and has also the numeral "1" at each side, over the original value of the stamp.

Stamps of 1914 Overprinted in Black or Red

278 A26 5pa violet brn (Bk) 1.75 .50
279 A28 10pa green (R) 3.25 .50
280 A29 20pa red (Bk) 4.00 .50
281 A30 1pi blue (R) 10.00 1.50
282 A33 2pi grn & blk (R) 15.00 1.50
283 A35 5pi dull violet (R) 50.00 4.25
284 A36 10pi red brown (R) 190.00 65.00
Nos. 278-284 (7) 274.00 73.75

This overprint reads "Abolition of the Capitulations, 1330".

No. 269 Surcharged

1915

286 A39 10pi on 100pi 62.50 22.50
a. Inverted surcharge 90.00 —

No. 270 Surcharged

287 A40 25pi on 200pi 25.00 8.00

Preceding Issues Overprinted in Carmine or Black

1915 **On Stamps of 1892**

288 A10 10pa gray green 1.00 .50
a. Inverted overprint 7.50 7.50
289 A13 2pi brown orange 1.50 .50
a. Inverted overprint 7.50 7.50
290 A14 5pi dull violet 4.00 .50
a. On No. 99a 17.00 17.00

On Stamp of 1897

291 A10 5pa on 10pa gray grn 1.00 .50
a. Inverted overprint 5.00 5.00
b. On No. 100a 10.00 10.00

On Stamps of 1901

292 A16 5pa bister 1.00 .50
293 A16 1pi violet blue 3.00 .50
294 A16 2pi gray blue 2.50 .50
295 A16 5pi ocher 20.00 .50
296 A16 25pi dark green 50.00 20.00
297 A17 5pa purple 1.00 .50
298 A17 10pa green 1.50 .50
299 A17 20pa carmine 1.50 .50
a. Inverted overprint 7.50 7.50
300 A17 1pi blue 1.50 .50
a. Inverted overprint 5.00 5.00
301 A17 2pi orange 2.00 .50
a. Inverted overprint 7.50 7.50
b. Double ovpt. (R and Bk) 5.00 5.00
302 A17 5pi lilac rose 2.50 .50
303 A17 25pi brown 12.50 2.00

On Stamps of 1905

304 A18 5pa ocher 1.00 .50
305 A18 10pa dull green 1.00 .50
a. Inverted overprint 5.00 5.00
306 A18 20pa carmine 1.00 .50
a. Inverted overprint 5.00 5.00
307 A18 1pi brt blue 1.50 .50
a. Inverted overprint 5.00 5.00
308 A18 2pi slate 2.50 .50
a. Inverted overprint 10.00 10.00
309 A18 2½pi red violet 1.50 .50
310 A18 5pi brown 2.00 .50
a. Inverted overprint 10.00 10.00
311 A18 10pi orange brown 12.50 .50
312 A18 25pi olive green 50.00 8.00

With Additional Overprint On Nos. 313-314

On Stamps of 1906

313 A18 10pa dull green 2.00 .50
314 A18 2pi slate 5.00 .50
a. Inverted overprint 5.00 5.00

On Stamps of 1908

314B A19 2pi blue black 225.00 50.00
315 A19 2½pi violet brown 5.00 1.50
315A A19 5pi dark violet 100.00 35.00
315B A19 10pi red 15.00 7.50
316 A19 25pi dark green 30.00 5.00
a. Inverted overprint 17.00 17.00

For surcharges see Mesopotamia Nos. N13-N15.

With Additional Overprint On No. 316B

316B A19 2pi blue black 15.00 5.00

On Stamps of 1909

317 A21 5pa ocher 1.00 .50
a. Inverted overprint 10.00 10.00
b. Double overprint 10.00 5.00
318 A21 20pa car rose 1.25 .75
a. Inverted overprint 5.00 5.00
319 A21 1pi ultra 2.00 .50
a. Inverted overprint 5.00 5.00
320 A21 2pi blue blk 2.50 .75
a. Inverted overprint 5.00 5.00
321 A21 2½pi dark brn 67.50 25.00
322 A21 5pi dark violet 1.00 .50
a. Inverted overprint 6.50 6.50
323 A21 10pi dull red 10.00 .50
324 A21 25pi dark green 1,750. 1,200.

With Additional Overprint On Nos. 325, 326, and 327

325 A21 20pa carmine rose 2.00 .50
a. Inverted overprint 10.00 9.00
326 A21 1pi ultra 2.00 .50
327 A21 2pi blue black 3.50 .50

On Stamps of 1913

328 A22 5pa ocher 1.00 .50
a. Inverted overprint 15.00 14.00
329 A22 10pa blue green 1.00 .50
a. Inverted overprint 20.00 18.00
330 A22 20pa carmine rose 1.00 .50
a. Inverted overprint 15.00 14.00
331 A22 1pi ultra 1.50 .50
a. Inverted overprint 10.00 9.00
332 A22 2pi indigo 2.00 .50
a. Inverted overprint 10.00 9.00
333 A22 5pi dull violet 3.00 .50
334 A22 10pi dull red 10.00 .50
a. Inverted overprint 20.00 18.00
335 A22 25pi gray green 30.00 20.00

With Additional Overprint

336 A22 10pa blue green 1.00 .50
337 A22 20pa carmine rose 1.00 .50
338 A22 1pi ultra 2.00 .50
339 A22 2pi indigo 7.50 3.00
a. Inverted overprint 10.00 10.00

See Nos. P121-P133.

Stamps of 1901-13 Overprinted

1916

340 A17 5pa purple 1.00 .50
a. 5pa purple, #P43 80.00 80.00
341 A17 10pa green 1.50 .50
a. Double overprint 6.50 6.50
b. 10pa yellow green, #103 80.00 80.00
342 A21 20pa car rose, #153 2.00 .75
a. 20pa carmine rose, #162 110.00 110.00
343 A21 1pi ultra 5.50 1.00
344 A22 5pi dull violet 10.00 3.00
Nos. 340-344 (5) 20.00 5.75

Occupation of the Sinai Peninsula.

Old General Post Office of Constantinople
A41

1916, May 29 **Litho.** ***Perf. 13½***

345 A41 5pa green .75 .50
a. Perf 12½ .75 .50
346 A41 10pa carmine .75 .50
a. Perf 12½ .75 .50
347 A41 20pa ultra 1.00 .50
a. Perf 12½ 1.00 .50
348 A41 1pi violet & blk 1.50 .75
a. Perf 12½ 1.50 .75
349 A41 5pi yel brn & blk 20.00 2.50
a. Perf 12½ 20.00 2.50
Nos. 345-349 (5) 24.00 4.75

Introduction of postage in Turkey, 50th anniv.
For overprints see Nos. 418, B42-B45.

Stamps of 1892-1905 Overprinted

1916

350 A10 10pa gray grn (R) 2.00 2.00
351 A18 20pa carmine (Bl) 3.75 2.50
352 A18 1pi blue (R) 10.00 5.00
353 A18 2pi slate (Bk) 12.50 2.00
354 A18 2½pi red violet (Bk) 20.00 2.25
Nos. 350-354 (5) 48.25 13.75

National Fête Day. Overprint reads "10 Temuz 1332" (July 23, 1916).

Preceding Issues Overprinted or Surcharged in Red or Black

a

b

1916 **On Stamps of 1892-98**

355 A10(a) 10pa gray green 1.00 .50
355A A11(a) 20pa vio brn 1.00 .50
b. Inverted overprint 10.00 10.00
356 A12(a) 1pi gray blue 50.00 50.00
357 A13(a) 2pi brown org 5.00 1.50
358 A14(a) 5pi dull violet 50.00 50.00

On Stamp of 1897

359 A15(b) 5pa on 10pa gray grn .75 .50

On Stamps of 1901

361 A16(a) 5pa bister .75 .50
a. Double overprint 7.50 7.50
362 A16(a) 10pa yel grn 1.00 .50
363 A16(a) 20pa magenta .75 .50
364 A16(a) 1pi violet blue 1.00 .50
a. Inverted overprint 7.50 7.50
365 A16(a) 2pi gray blue 5.00 1.00
366 A16(b) 5pi on 25pi dk grn 55.00 55.00
367 A16(b) 10pi on 25pi dk grn 55.00 55.00
368 A16(a) 25pi dark green 55.00 55.00
369 A17(a) 5pa purple 75.00 50.00
370 A17(a) 10pa green 2.00 1.50
371 A17(a) 20pa carmine .75 .50
a. Inverted overprint 7.50 7.50
372 A17(a) 1pi blue 1.00 .50
a. Inverted overprint 7.50 7.50
373 A17(a) 2pi orange 1.50 .50
374 A17(b) 10pi on 25pi brown 5.00 1.50
375 A17(b) 10pi on 50pi yel brn 7.50 1.50
376 A17(a) 25pi brown 7.50 1.50
377 A17(a) 50pi yel brn 10.00 2.50

On Stamps of 1905

378 A18(a) 5pa ocher .75 .50
379 A18(a) 20pa carmine 1.00 .50
a. Inverted overprint 10.00 5.00
380 A18(a) 1pi brt blue 2.00 .50
a. Inverted overprint 10.00 5.00
381 A18(a) 2pi slate 1.50 1.00
382 A18(a) 2½pi red violet 7.50 1.50
383 A18(b) 10pi on 25pi ol grn 10.00 3.00
384 A18(b) 10pi on 50pi dp vio 10.00 4.00
385 A18(a) 25pi olive green 10.00 5.00
386 A18(a) 50pi deep violet 7.50 5.00

On Stamps of 1906

387 A18(a) 10pa dull green 1.50 .60
388 A18(a) 20pa carmine 1.50 1.00
389 A18(a) 1pi brt blue 1.50 1.00

On Stamps of 1908

390 A19(a) 2½pi violet brown 67.50 67.50
391 A19(b) 10pi on 25pi dk grn 20.00 12.50
392 A19(b) 10pi on 50pi red brn 67.50 67.50
393 A19(b) 25pi on 50pi red brn 67.50 67.50
394 A19(a) 25pi dark green 15.00 5.00
395 A19(a) 50pi red brown 50.00 50.00

With Additional Overprint

396 A19(a) 2pi blue black 67.50 67.50

On Stamps of 1908-09

397 A20(a) 5pa ocher 67.50 67.50
398 A21(a) 5pa ocher 1.00 2.50
399 A21(a) 10pa blue green 50.00 50.00
400 A21(a) 20pa carmine rose 50.00 50.00
401 A21(a) 1pi ultra 2.00 1.00
402 A21(a) 2pi blue black 4.00 2.00
403 A21(a) 2½pi dark brown 50.00 50.00
404 A21(a) 5pi dark violet 50.00 50.00

With Additional Overprint

405 A21(a) 1pi ultra 67.50 67.50
406 A21(a) 2pi blue black 50.00 50.00

On Stamps of 1913

407 A22(a) 5pa ocher 1.00 .75
408 A22(a) 20pa carmine rose 1.50 .50
409 A22(a) 1pi ultra 1.50 .50
410 A22(a) 2pi indigo 3.00 1.00
411 A22(b) 10pi on 50pi org brn 12.50 10.00
412 A22(a) 25pi gray green 7.50 5.00
413 A22(a) 50pi orange brown 15.00 12.50

With Additional Overprint

414 A22(a) 1pi ultra 2.00 1.00

On Commemorative Stamps of 1913

415 A23(a) 10pa green 1.25 .50
416 A23(a) 20pa red 2.00 .75
417 A23(a) 40pa blue 6.00 2.50

On Commemorative Stamp of 1916

418 A41(a) 5pi yel brn & blk 1.00 .50

No. 277 Surcharged in Blue

419 A31 60pa on 1pi on 1½pi 3.25 3.50
a. "1330" omitted 40.00 40.00

See Nos. P134-P152, J67-J70.

Turkish Artillery A42

Mosque at Orta Köy, Constantinople — A43

Lighthouse on Bosporus — A44

Monument to Martyrs of Liberty — A45

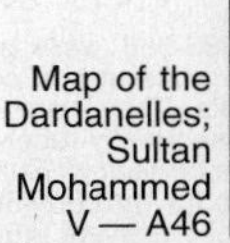

Map of the Dardanelles; Sultan Mohammed V — A46

Map of the Dardanelles A47

Istanbul Across the Golden Horn A48

Pyramids of Egypt A49

Dolma Bahçe Palace and Mohammed V — A50

Sentry and Shell — A51

Sultan Mohammed V — A52

1916-18 Typo. *Perf. 12½*

420 A42 2pa violet 1.50 .75
a. Perf 11½ 1.50 .75
421 A43 5pa orange 1.00 .75
a. Perf 11½ 1.50 .75
424 A44 10pa green 1.00 1.00
a. Perf 11½ 1.50 .75

Engr.

425 A45 20pa deep rose 1.00 .75
426 A46 1pi dull violet 3.00 .50

Typo.

428 A47 50pa ultra 1.50 .50
a. Perf 11½ 12.00 16.00
429 A48 2pi org brn & ind 3.00 .50
a. Perf 11½ — —
430 A49 5pi pale blue & blk 17.50 2.00
a. Perf 11½ 25.00 2.00

Engr.

431 A50 10pi dark green 8.75 5.00
432 A50 10pi dark violet 32.50 2.50
433 A50 10pi dark brown 14.00 2.50
434 A51 25pi carmine, *straw* 2.25 1.50
437 A52 50pi carmine 5.00 5.00
438 A52 50pi indigo 2.00 2.50
439 A52 50pi green, *straw* 2.50 10.00
Nos. 420-439 (15) 96.50 35.75

For overprints and surcharges see Nos. 541B-541E, 554-560, 565-566, 569-574, 575, 577-578, 579A-580, Turkey in Asia 4, 10, 64-66, Thrace N76, N80, N81. Compare designs A42-A43 with A53-A54.

Forgeries of Nos. 446-545 abound.

Preceding Issues Overprinted or Surcharged in Red, Black or Blue

d

e

1917 On Stamps of 1865

446 A5(d) 20pa yellow (R) 45.00 67.50
a. Star without rays (R) 50.00 57.50
447 A5(d) 1pi pearl gray (R) 45.00 67.50
a. Star without rays (R) 50.00 57.50
448 A5(d) 2pi blue (R) 45.00 67.50
449 A5(d) 5pi car (Bk) 45.00 67.50

On Stamp of 1867

450 A5(d) 5pi rose (Bk) 45.00 67.50

On Stamps of 1870-71

451 A5(d) 2pi red (Bl) 45.00 67.50
452 A5(d) 5pi blue (Bk) 45.00 67.50
453 A5(d) 25pi dl rose (Bl) 45.00 67.50

On Stamp of 1874-75

454 A5(d) 10pa red vio (Bl) 45.00 67.50

On Stamps of April, 1876

455 A5(d) 10pa red lilac (Bl) 45.00 67.50
a. 10pa red violet (Bl) 50.00 67.50
457 A5(d) 20pa pale grn (R) 45.00 67.50
458 A5(d) 1pi yellow (Bl) 45.00 67.50

On Stamps of January, 1876

459 A5(d) ¼pi on 10pa rose lil (Bl) 45.00 67.50
460 A5(d) ½pi on 20pa yel grn (R) 45.00 67.50
461 A5(d) 1¼pi on 50pa rose (Bl) 45.00 67.50

On Stamps of September, 1876

462 A7(d) 50pa blue & yel (R) 45.00 67.50
463 A7(d) 2pi blk & redsh brn (R) 45.00 67.50
464 A7(d) 25pi clar & rose (Bk) 45.00 67.50

On Stamps of 1880-84

465 A7(d) 5pa blk & ol (R) 45.00 67.50
466 A7(d) 10pa blk & grn (R) 45.00 67.50

On Stamps of 1881-82

467 A5(d) 20pa gray (Bl) 45.00 67.50
468 A5(d) 2pi pale sal (Bl) 45.00 67.50

On Stamps of 1884-86

469 A7(d) 10pa grn & pale grn (Bk) 45.00 67.50
470 A7(d) 2pi ocher & pale ocher (Bk) 45.00 67.50
471 A7(d) 5pi red brn & pale brn (Bk) 45.00 67.50

On Stamps of 1886

472 A7(d) 5pa blk & pale gray (R) 4.00 2.25
a. Inverted overprint 30.00 30.00
473 A7(d) 2pi org & bl (Bk) 4.50 2.50
a. Inverted overprint 35.00 35.00
474 A7(d) 5pi grn & pale grn (R) 45.00 67.50
475 A7(d) 25pi bis & pale bis (Bk) 45.00 67.50

On Stamp of 1888

476 A7(d) 5pi dk brn & gray (Bk) 45.00 67.50

On Stamps of 1892-98

477 A11(d) 20pa vio brn (R) 4.00 3.00
478 A13(d) 2pi brn org (R) 4.00 3.50
a. Tête bêche pair 13.50 13.50

On Stamps of 1901

479 A16(d) 5pa bister (R) 3.00 3.00
a. Inverted overprint 20.00 20.00
480 A16(d) 20pa mag (Bk) 2.00 1.50
a. Inverted overprint 25.00 25.00
481 A16(d) 1pi vio bl (R) 3.00 3.00
a. Inverted overprint 20.00 20.00
482 A16(d) 2pi gray bl (R) 5.00 5.00
483 A16(d) 5pi ocher (R) 32.50 50.00
484 A16(e) 10pi on 50pi yel (R) 32.50 50.00
485 A16(d) 25pi dk grn (R) 100.00 50.00
486 A17(d) 5pa pur (Bk) 32.50 50.00
487 A17(d) 10pa green (R) 5.00 5.00
488 A17(d) 20pa car (Bk) 2.00 1.50
a. Inverted overprint 20.00 20.00
489 A17(d) 1pi blue (R) 1.00 .90
490 A17(d) 2pi org (Bk) 3.00 3.00
a. Inverted overprint 20.00 20.00
491 A17(d) 5pi lil rose (R) 32.50 50.00
492 A17(e) 10pi on 50pi yel brn (R) 45.00 50.00
493 A17(d) 25pi brown (R) 25.00 5.00

On Stamps of 1905

494 A18(d) 5pa ocher (R) 2.00 1.00
a. Inverted overprint 20.00 20.00
495 A18(d) 10pa dl grn (R) 32.50 50.00
496 A18(d) 20pa car (Bk) 1.00 1.00
a. Double ovpt., one invtd. 35.00 35.00
b. Inverted overprint 35.00 35.00
497 A18(d) 1pi blue (R) 1.50 1.00
a. Inverted overprint 35.00 35.00
498 A18(d) 2pi slate (R) 5.00 5.00
499 A18(d) 2½pi red vio (Bk) 5.00 5.00
a. Inverted overprint 20.00 20.00
500 A18(d) 5pi brown (R) 35.00 45.00
501 A18(d) 10pi org brn (R) 35.00 50.00
502 A18(e) 10pi on 50pi dp vio (R) 35.00 50.00
503 A18(d) 25pi ol grn (R) 35.00 50.00

On Nos. 128-131

504 A18(d) 10pa dl grn (R) 1.50 1.00
a. Inverted overprint 20.00 20.00
505 A18(d) 20pa car (Bk) 1.00 .75
a. Double ovpt., one invtd. 20.00 20.00
b. Inverted overprint 20.00 20.00
506 A18(d) 1pi brt bl (Bk) 1.00 .75
a. Inverted overprint 20.00 20.00
507 A18(d) 1pi brt bl (R) 1.50 1.25
a. Inverted overprint 20.00 20.00
508 A18(d) 2pi slate (Bk) 35.00 50.00
Nos. 494-508 (15) 227.00 311.75

On Stamps of 1908

509 A19(d) 5pa ocher (R) 1.50 1.25
510 A19(d) 10pa bl grn (R) 20.00 20.00
510A A19(d) 1pi brt blue (R) *125.00* 140.00
511 A19(d) 2pi bl blk (R) 35.00 50.00
512 A19(d) 2½pi vio brn (Bk) 35.00 35.00
512A A19(d) 10pi red (R) *150.00* 225.00
513 A19(e) 10pi on 50pi red brn (R) 35.00 50.00
514 A19(d) 25pi dk grn (R) 35.00 50.00

With Additional Overprint

514A A19(d) 10pa bl grn (Bk) 150.00 225.00
515 A19(d) 1pi brt bl (Bk) 35.00 50.00
516 A19(d) 2pi bl blk (R) 5.00 5.00
516A A19(d) 2pi bl blk (Bk) 65.00 67.50

On Stamps of 1908-09

517 A20(d) 5pa ocher (R) 3.00 3.00
518 A21(d) 5pa ocher (R) 2.00 1.50
a. Double overprint 20.00 20.00
b. Dbl. ovpt., one inverted 20.00 20.00
519 A21(d) 10pa bl grn (R) 2.00 1.50
520 A21(d) 20pa car rose (Bk) 2.00 1.50
a. Double overprint 35.00 35.00
521 A21(d) 1pi ultra (R) 1.50 1.00
a. 1p bright blue (R) 30.00 30.00
522 A21(d) 2pi bl blk (R) 5.00 5.00
523 A21(d) 2½pi dk brn (Bk) 35.00 50.00
524 A21(d) 5pi dk vio (R) 35.00 50.00
525 A21(d) 10pi dull red (R) 35.00 50.00

With Additional Overprint

525A A21(d) 10pa bl grn (Bk) 175.00 225.00
526 A21(d) 1pi ultra (Bk) 125.00 190.00
527 A21(d) 1pi ultra (R) 5.00 4.00
a. 1pi bright blue (R) 125.00 140.00
528 A21(d) 2pi bl blk (Bk) 35.00 50.00

On Stamps of 1913

529 A22(d) 5pa ocher (R) 2.50 2.00
530 A22(d) 10pa bl grn (R) 35.00 50.00
531 A22(d) 20pa car rose (Bk) 2.50 2.50
532 A22(d) 1pi ultra (R) 2.50 3.50
533 A22(d) 2pi indigo (R) 3.50 3.50
534 A22(d) 5pi dl vio (R) 35.00 50.00
535 A22(d) 10pi dl red (Bk) 45.00 50.00

With Additional Overprint

536 A22(d) 10pa bl grn (Bk) 1.50 1.50
a. Inverted overprint 20.00 20.00
537 A22(d) 1pi ultra (Bk) 3.00 3.00
a. Inverted overprint 20.00 20.00
538 A22(d) 2pi indigo (Bk) 35.00 100.00

On Commemorative Stamps of 1913

539 A23(d) 10pa green (R) 5.00 5.00
a. Inverted overprint 20.00 20.00
540 A23(d) 40pa blue (R) 7.00 7.00
a. Inverted overprint 20.00 20.00

On No. 277, with Addition of New Value

541 A31 60pa on 1pi on 1½pi (Bk) 8.00 5.00
a. "1330" omitted 45.00 45.00

On Stamps of 1916-18

f

g

541B A51(f)	25pi car, *straw*	5.00	5.00
541C A52(g)	50pi carmine	17.50	17.50
541D A52(g)	50pi indigo	35.00	50.00
541E A52(g)	50pi grn, *straw*	15.00	27.50

Ovptd. on Eastern Rumelia No. 12

542 A4(d)	20pa blk & rose (Bl)	35.00	35.00

Ovptd. in Black on Eastern Rumelia #15-17

543 A4(d)	5pa lil & pale lil	45.00	45.00
544 A4(d)	10pa grn & pale grn	45.00	45.00
545 A4(d)	20pa car & pale rose	45.00	45.00

Some experts question the status of Nos. 510A, 512A and 525A.

See Nos. J71-J86, P153-P172.

Soldiers in Trench — A52a

1917

545A A52a	5pa on 1pi red	1.25	.75

It is stated that No. 545A was never issued without surcharge.

See Nos. 548A, 548Af, 602.

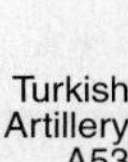

Turkish Artillery A53

1917 Typo. *Perf. 12½*

546 A53	2pa Prussian blue	150.00	
a.	Perf 11½	150.00	

In type A42 the Turkish inscription at the top is in one group, in type A53 it is in two groups. It is stated that No. 546 was never placed in use. Examples were distributed through the Universal Postal Union at Bern.

For surcharges see Nos. 547-548, Turkey in Asia 69-70.

Surcharged

547 A53	5pi on 2pa Prus blue	15.00	1.75
a.	Inverted surcharge	35.00	15.00
b.	Turkish "5" omitted at lower left		
c.	Perf 11½	15.00	1.75

Surcharged

1918

548 A53	5pi on 2pa Prus blue	15.00	2.00
g.	Inverted surcharge	35.00	20.00

Top line of surcharge on Nos. 547-548 reads "Ottoman Posts."

For surcharge see Thrace No. N79.

No. 545A Surcharged

1918

548A A52a	2pa on 5pa on 1pi red	2.50	1.75
b.	Double surcharge	20.00	20.00
c.	Inverted surcharge	20.00	20.00
d.	Double surcharge inverted	20.00	20.00
e.	Dbl. surch., one inverted	20.00	20.00
f.	In pair with No. 545A	30.00	30.00

Enver Pasha and Kaiser Wilhelm II on Battlefield A54

St. Sophia and Obelisk of the Hippodrome A55

1918 Typo. *Perf. 12, 12½*

549 A54	5pa brown red	125.00	
550 A55	10pa gray green	125.00	

The stamps, of which very few saw postal use, were converted into paper money by pasting on thick yellow paper and reperforating.

Values are for stamps with original gum. Examples removed from the yellow paper are worth $10 each.

Armistice Issue

Overprinted in Black or Red

1919, Nov. 30

On Stamps of 1913

552 A34	2½pi org & ol grn	125.00	300.00
553 A38	50pi carmine	125.00	300.00

On Stamps of 1916-18

554 A46	1pi dl vio (R)	7.50	10.00
555 A47	50pa ultra (R), perf 11½	1.00	1.50
a.	Perf 12½	2.00	2.50
556 A48	2pi org brn & ind	1.75	2.00
557 A49	5pi pale bl & blk (R), perf 11½	1.75	2.00
a.	Perf 12½	2.00	3.00
b.	Perf 11½x12½	2.50	4.00
558 A50	10pi dk grn (R)	6.25	10.00
559 A51	25pi car, *straw*	6.25	10.00
560 A52	50pi grn, *straw* (R)	6.25	10.00

Fountain in Desert near Sinai — A56

Sentry at Beersheba — A57

Turkish Troops at Sinai A58

Typo.

562 A56	20pa claret	1.25	*2.00*
563 A57	1pi blue (R)	125.00	150.00
564 A58	25pi slate blue (R)	125.00	150.00
	Nos. 552-564 (12)	532.00	947.50

The overprint reads: "Souvenir of the Armistice, 30th October 1334." Nos. 562-564 are not known to have been regularly issued without overprint.

See No. J87. For overprints and surcharges see Nos. 576, 579, 582, 583-584, 586, Turkey in Asia 71, Thrace N83.

Stamps of 1911-19 Overprinted in Turkish

"Accession to the Throne of His Majesty, 3rd July 1334-1918," the Tughra of Sultan Mohammed VI and sometimes Ornaments and New Values

Dome of the Rock, Jerusalem — A59

No. 565

No. 566

No. 567

No. 568

No. 569 No. 570

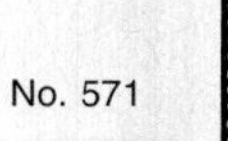

No. 571

No. 572

No. 573

No. 574

No. 575

No. 576

1919

565	A42	2pa violet	1.00	*2.50*
566	A43	5pa orange	.75	.50
567	A21	5pa on 2pa ol grn	.75	.50
a.		Inverted surcharge	10.00	10.00
568	A22	10pa on 2pa ol grn	1.00	.50
569	A44	10pa green	1.25	1.50
a.		Inverted overprint	25.00	25.00
570	A45	20pa deep rose	1.25	.50
a.		Inverted overprint	12.00	12.00
571	A46	1pi dull violet	1.25	1.00
572	A47	60pa on 50pa ultra	1.25	1.00
573	A48	60pa on 2pi org brn & ind	1.00	.50
574	A48	2pi org brn & ind	1.00	1.00
574A	A34	2½pi org & ol grn	25.00	*37.50*
575	A49	5pi pale blue & blk	1.00	1.00
576	A56	10pi on 20pa cl	1.00	1.00
577	A50	10pi dark brown	2.50	2.50
578	A51	25pi car, *straw*	2.00	2.00
579	A57	35pi on 1pi blue	1.50	2.50
579A	A52	50pi carmine	25.00	*37.50*
580	A52	50pi grn, *straw*	6.00	5.00
581	A59	100pi on 10pa grn	6.00	5.00
582	A58	250pi on 25pi sl bl	6.00	5.00
		Nos. 565-582 (20)	86.50	108.50

See note after #586. See #J88-J91.

For overprint and surcharge see Nos. 585, Thrace N82.

Surcharged with Ornaments, New Values and

Perf. 11½, 12½

583 A56	20pa claret	1.75	10.00
584 A57	1pi deep blue	2.50	17.50
585 A59	60pa on 10pa green	1.50	7.50
586 A58	25pi slate blue	9.00	50.00
a.	Inverted overprint		100.00
	Nos. 583-586 (4)	14.75	85.00

#576, 579, 581, 582, 583-586 were prepared in anticipation of the invasion and conquest of Egypt by the Turks. They were not issued at that time but subsequently received various overprints in commemoration of Sultan Mehmet Sadi's accession to the throne (#565-582) and of the 1st anniv. of this event (#583-586).

For surcharge see Thrace No. N83.

Designs of 1913 Modified

1920 Litho. *Perf. 11, 12*

590 A26	5pa brown orange	1.00	.50

Engr.

591 A28	10pa green	1.00	.50
592 A23	20pa rose	1.00	.50
593 A30	1pi blue green	3.75	.50

594 A32 3pi blue 1.00 .50
595 A34 5pi gray 50.00 .50
596 A36 10pi gray violet 12.50 .50
597 A37 25pi dull violet 5.00 2.50
598 A38 50pi brown 5.00 10.00
Nos. 590-598 (9) 80.25 16.00

On most stamps of this issue the designs have been modified by removing the small Turkish word at right of the tughra of the Sultan. In the 3pi and 5pi the values have been altered, while for the 25pi the color has been changed.

For surcharges see Thrace Nos. N77, N78, N84.

No. B46 Surcharged

No. 258 Surcharged

No. 594 Surcharged

1921-22 **Black Surcharge**
600 SP1 30pa on 10pa red vio 1.50 .50
a. Double surcharge 37.50 37.50
b. Imperf.
601 A28 60pa on 10pa green 1.50 .50
a. Double surcharge 22.50 22.50
602 A52a 4½pi on 1pi red 9.00 4.00
a. Inverted surcharge 20.00 20.00
603 A32 7½pi on 3pi blue 15.00 2.00
604 A32 7½pi on 3pi bl (R) ('22) 25.00 2.50
a. Double surcharge 35.00 30.00
Nos. 600-604 (5) 52.00 9.50

Turkish Stamps of 1916-21 with Greek surcharge as above in blue or black are of private origin.

Issues of the Republic

Crescent and Star — A64

TWO PIASTERS:
Type I — "2" measures 3¼x1¾mm
Type II — "2" measures 2¾x1½mm

FIVE PIASTERS:
Type I — "5" measures 3½x2¼mm
Type II — "5" measures 3x1¾mm

Printed by Ahmed Nazmi, Istanbul

Perf. 13¼x12¾-13¼

1923 **Litho.** **Thin Paper**
605 A64 10pa gray black .30 .25
Never hinged .80
606 A64 20pa olive yel .30 .25
Never hinged .80
607 A64 1pi deep violet .30 .25
Never hinged .80
a. Slanting numeral in lower left corner .50 .25
Never hinged 1.00
608 A64 1½pi emerald .90 .25
Never hinged 2.00
a. 1½pi yellow green .30 .25
Never hinged .80
609 A64 2pi bluish grn (I) .90 .25
Never hinged 3.00
a. 2pi deep green (II) .90 .25
Never hinged 3.00
610 A64 3pi yel brn .90 .60
Never hinged 3.00
611 A64 3¾pi lilac brown 3.00 3.00
Never hinged 8.00
612 A64 4½pi carmine .90 1.20
Never hinged 3.00
613 A64 5pi dp pur (I) 4.50 1.75
Never hinged 10.00
a. 5pi purple (II) 21.00 1.25
Never hinged 50.00
614 A64 7½pi blue 3.00 .60
Never hinged 10.00
615 A64 10pi slate 12.00 1.25
Never hinged 30.00
a. 10pi blue 16.00 1.25
Never hinged 40.00
616 A64 11¼pi dull rose 3.00 2.50
Never hinged 7.00
617 A64 15pi brown 15.00 1.25
Never hinged 40.00
618 A64 18¾pi myr grn 4.25 3.75
Never hinged 10.00
619 A64 22½pi orange 12.00 2.50
Never hinged 20.00
620 A64 25pi blk brn 50.00 3.00
Never hinged 100.00
621 A64 50pi gray 125.00 5.00
Never hinged 300.00
622 A64 100pi dark violet 250.00 11.00
Never hinged 700.00
623 A64 500pi dp grn 950.00 275.00
Never hinged 3,000.
Cut cancellation 15.00
Nos. 605-623 (19) 1,436. 313.65
Set, never hinged 4,250.

Nos. 605-610, 612-617 exist imperf. & part perf.

Printed by Ikdam, Istanbul

1924 **Thick Paper** ***Perf. 11***
605b A64 10pa greenish gray .90 .25
Never hinged 2.50
606b A64 20pa olive yellow .90 .25
Never hinged 2.50
607b A64 1pi deep violet 1.75 .25
Never hinged 4.00
d. Slanting numeral in lower left corner 2.00 .25
Never hinged 5.00
609b A64 2pi bluish green (I) 6.00 .90
Never hinged 15.00
d. 2pi bluish green (II) 175.00 2.00
Never hinged 500.00
610b A64 3pi yellow brown 150.00 7.50
Never hinged 450.00
612b A64 4½pi carmine 1.50 .60
Never hinged 3.00
613b A64 5pi purple (II) 3.50 .25
Never hinged 9.00
614b A64 7½pi blue 3.50 .60
Never hinged 9.00
615b A64 10pi slate 11.00 12.00
Never hinged 30.00
617b A64 15pi yellow brown 11.00 12.00
Never hinged 30.00
Nos. 605b-617b (10) 190.05 34.60
Set, never hinged 555.00

Printed by Ottoman Public Debt Administration, Istanbul

1924-26 **Thick Paper** ***Perf. 12***
605c A64 10pa black .30 .25
Never hinged 1.00
606c A64 20pa olive yellow .30 .25
Never hinged 1.00
607c A64 1pi violet .60 .60
Never hinged 1.50
609c A64 2pi green (II) 3.00 .60
Never hinged 10.00
610c A64 3pi yellow brown 3.50 .60
Never hinged 10.00
613c A64 5pi violet 3.50 1.00
Never hinged 10.00
615c A64 10pi dark blue 60.00 12.00
Never hinged 250.00
d. 10pi perf. 13¼x12 60.00 12.00
Never hinged 275.00
Nos. 605c-615c (7) 71.20 15.30
Set, never hinged 285.00

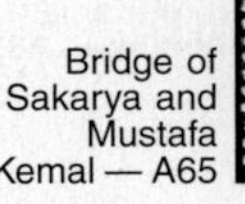

Bridge of Sakarya and Mustafa Kemal — A65

1924, Jan. 1 ***Perf. 12***
625 A65 1½pi emerald .75 .30
626 A65 3pi purple .90 .50
627 A65 4½pi pale rose 5.00 2.00
628 A65 5pi yellow brown 4.00 2.00
629 A65 7½pi deep blue 5.00 2.00
630 A65 50pi orange 22.50 10.00
631 A65 100pi brown violet 52.50 20.00
632 A65 200pi olive brown 72.50 35.00
Nos. 625-632 (8) 163.15 71.80
Set, never hinged 750.00

Signing of Treaty of Peace at Lausanne.

The Legendary Blacksmith and his Gray Wolf — A66

Sakarya Gorge — A67

Fortress of Ankara — A68

Mustafa Kemal Pasha — A69

1926 **Engr.**
634 A66 10pa slate .50 .25
635 A66 20pa orange .50 .25
636 A66 1g brt rose .50 .25
637 A67 2g green 1.50 .25
638 A67 2½g gray black 2.00 .25
639 A67 3g copper red 2.50 .25
640 A68 5g deep blue 4.00 .75
641 A68 6g red 1.00 .25
642 A68 10g blue 7.50 .50
643 A68 15g deep orange 10.00 .50
644 A69 25g dk grn & blk 15.00 1.25
645 A69 50g car & blk 20.00 1.50
646 A69 100g ol grn & blk 35.00 2.00
647 A69 200g brown & blk 90.00 5.50
Nos. 634-647 (14) 190.00 13.75
Set, never hinged 800.00

For surcharges see Nos. 648-675.

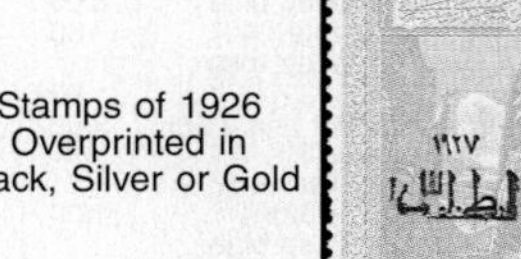
Stamps of 1926 Overprinted in Black, Silver or Gold

1927, Sept. 9
648 A66 1g brt rose .75 .50
649 A67 2g green .75 1.00
650 A67 2½g gray black 1.50 2.00
651 A67 3g copper red 2.00 2.50
652 A68 5g lilac gray 2.50 4.00
653 A68 6g red 1.50 1.50
654 A68 10g deep blue 3.50 3.50
655 A68 15g deep orange 5.00 5.00
656 A69 25g dk grn & blk (S) 15.00 20.00
657 A69 50g car & blk (S) 27.50 37.50
658 A69 100g ol grn & blk (G) 60.00 75.00
Nos. 648-658 (11) 120.00 152.50
Set, never hinged 425.00

Agricultural and industrial exhibition at Izmir, Sept. 9-20, 1927.

The overprint reads: "1927" and the initials of "Izmir Dokuz Eylul Sergisi" (Izmir Exhibition, September 9).

Second Izmir Exhibition Issue

Nos. 634-647 Overprinted in Red or Black

On A66-A68

On A69

1928, Sept. 9
659 A66 10pa slate (R) .50 .40
660 A66 20pa orange .50 .40
661 A66 1g brt rose 1.00 .50
662 A67 2g green (R) 1.50 1.50
663 A67 2½g gray blk (R) 1.50 1.50
664 A67 3g copper red 1.50 1.50
665 A68 5g lilac gray (R) 2.00 3.00
666 A68 6g red .50 .50
667 A68 10g deep blue 3.50 3.00
668 A68 15g deep orange 5.00 2.00
669 A69 25g dk grn & blk (R) 15.00 6.25
670 A69 50g car & blk 17.50 20.00
671 A69 100g ol grn & blk (R) 40.00 50.00
672 A69 200g brn & blk (R) 62.50 62.50
Nos. 659-672 (14) 152.50 153.05
Set, never hinged 650.00

The overprint reads "Izmir, September 9, 1928."

Nos. 636, 652, 654 Surcharged in Black (#673) or Red (#674-675)

1929
673 A66 20pa on 1g brt rose .50 .25
a. Inverted surcharge 3.50 3.50
674 A68 2½k on 5g lilac gray 1.00 .50
a. Inverted surcharge 7.50 7.50
675 A68 6k on 10g deep blue 6.00 .75
Nos. 673-675 (3) 7.50 1.50
Set, never hinged 40.00

Railroad Bridge over Kizil Irmak — A70

A71

A72

A73

Latin Inscriptions

Without umlaut over first "U" of "CUMHURIYETI"

1929 **Engr.**
676 A70 2k gray black 5.00 1.00
677 A70 2½k green 3.00 1.00
678 A70 3k violet brown 4.00 1.50
679 A71 6k dark violet 25.00 1.00
680 A72 12½k deep blue 35.00 3.75
681 A73 50k carmine & blk 60.00 8.75
Nos. 676-681 (6) 132.00 17.00
Set, never hinged 400.00

See Nos. 682-691, 694-695, 697, 699. For surcharges & overprints see #705-714, 716-717, 719, 721, 727, 765-766, 770-771, 777, C2, C7.

Sakarya Gorge — A74

Mustafa Kemal Pasha — A75

With umlaut over first "U" of "CUMHURIYETI"

1930
682 A71 10pa green .25 .25
683 A70 20pa gray violet .25 .25
684 A70 1k olive green .50 .50
685 A71 1½k olive black .50 .40
686 A70 2k dull violet 3.00 .50
687 A70 2½k deep green 2.00 .50
688 A70 3k brown orange 20.00 1.50

689 A71 4k deep rose 7.50 .50
690 A72 5k rose lake 11.50 .50
691 A71 6k indigo 7.50 .50
692 A74 7½k red brown .25 .25
694 A72 12½k deep ultra .75 .25
695 A72 15k deep orange .75 .50
696 A74 17½k dark gray .75 .50
697 A72 20k black brown 50.00 2.00
698 A74 25k olive brown 1.00 1.00
699 A72 30k yellow brown 1.75 1.00
700 A74 40k red violet 1.50 1.00
701 A75 50k red & black 3.50 1.25
702 A75 100k olive grn & blk 3.50 1.25
703 A75 200k dk green & blk 3.75 1.50
704 A75 500k chocolate & blk 17.50 22.50
Nos. 682-704 (22) 138.00 38.40
Set, never hinged 600.00

For surcharges and overprints see Nos. 715, 718, 720, 722-726, 767-769, 772-773, 775-776, 778-780, 823-828, 848-850, C1, C3-C6, C8-C11 (in Scott Standard catalogue, Vol. 6).

Nos. 682-704 Surcharged in Red or Black

a

b

c

1930, Aug. 30
705 A71(a) 10pa on 10pa (R) .50 1.25
706 A70(b) 10pa on 20pa .50 1.50
707 A70(b) 20pa on 1ku 1.00 1.50
708 A71(a) 1k on 1½k (R) .50 1.25
709 A70(b) 1½k on 2k 1.00 1.50
710 A70(b) 2k on 2½k (R) 2.50 2.00
711 A70(b) 2½k on 3k 2.00 1.50
712 A71(a) 3k on 4k 2.00 1.00
713 A72(a) 4k on 5k 2.50 1.00
714 A71(a) 5k on 6k (R) 3.50 4.00
715 A74(a) 6k on 7½k .75 .50
716 A72(a) 7½k on 12½k (R) 1.25 1.00
717 A72(a) 12½k on 15k 1.25 1.00
718 A74(b) 15k on 17½k (R) 5.00 4.00
719 A72(b) 17½k on 20k (R) 5.00 2.00
720 A74(b) 20k on 25k (R) 7.50 2.00
721 A72(b) 25k on 30k 5.00 2.50
722 A74(b) 30k on 40k 7.50 2.50
723 A75(c) 40k on 50k 15.00 7.50
724 A75(c) 50k on 100k (R) 70.00 16.00
725 A75(c) 100k on 200k (R) 85.00 27.50
726 A75(c) 250k on 500k (R) 75.00 35.00
Nos. 705-726 (22) 294.25 118.00
Set, never hinged 1,200.

Inauguration of the railroad between Ankara and Sivas.

There are numerous varieties in these settings as: "309," "390," "930" inverted, no period after "D," no period after "Y" and raised period before "Y."

No. 685 Surcharged in Red

1931, Apr. 1
727 A71 1k on 1½k olive blk 1.75 .30

Olive Tree with Roots Extending to All Balkan Capitals — A76

1931, Oct. 20 Engr. *Perf. 12*
728 A76 2½k dark green .40 .25
729 A76 4k carmine .50 .25
730 A76 6k steel blue .50 .25
731 A76 7½k dull red .50 .25
732 A76 12k deep orange 1.00 .25
733 A76 12½k dark blue 1.00 .25
734 A76 30k dark violet 1.75 1.50
735 A76 50k dark brown 3.00 .75
736 A76 100k brown violet 6.25 1.50
Nos. 728-736 (9) 14.90 5.25
Set, never hinged 35.00

Second Balkan Conference.

A77

A78

Mustafa Kemal Pasha (Kemal Atatürk) — A79

1931-42 Typo. *Perf. 11½, 12*
737 A77 10pa blue green .25 .25
738 A77 20pa deep orange .25 .25
739 A77 30pa brt violet ('38) .25 .25
740 A78 1k dk slate green .25 .25
740A A77 1½k magenta ('42) .55 .25
741 A78 2k dark violet .50 .25
741A A78 2k yel grn ('40) .25 .25
742 A77 2½k green .50 .25
743 A78 3k brn org ('38) 1.50 .25
744 A78 4k slate 2.50 .25
745 A78 5k rose red .25 .25
745A A78 5k brown blk ('40) 2.00 .50
746 A78 6k deep blue 3.00 .25
746A A78 6k rose ('40) .80 .30
747 A77 7½k deep rose ('32) .50 .25
747A A78 8k brt blue ('38) 3.50 .25
b. 8k dark blue ('36) 3.50 .25
748 A77 10k black brn ('32) 1.00 .25
748A A77 10k deep blue ('40) 7.00 .60
749 A77 12k bister ('32) 1.00 .25
750 A79 12½k indigo ('32) 1.00 .25
751 A77 15k org yel ('32) 1.00 .25
752 A77 20k olive grn ('32) 1.00 .25
753 A77 25k Prus blue ('32) 2.50 1.00
754 A77 30k magenta ('32) 7.50 .50
755 A79 100k maroon ('32) 200.00 5.50
756 A79 200k purple ('32) 3.75 2.00
757 A79 250k chocolate ('32) 100.00 11.50
Nos. 737-757 (27) 342.60 26.65
Set, never hinged 950.00

See Nos. 1015-1033, 1117B-1126 in Scott Standard catalogue, Vol. 6. For overprints see Nos. 811-816.

Symbolizing 10th Anniversary of Republic — A80

President Atatürk — A81

1933, Oct. 29 *Perf. 10*
758 A80 1½k blue green 1.25 1.00
759 A80 2k olive brown 1.25 1.00
760 A81 3k dull red 1.25 1.00
761 A81 6k deep blue 1.25 1.00
762 A80 12½k dark blue 3.25 2.50
763 A80 25k dark brown 8.00 5.00
764 A81 50k orange brown 20.00 15.00
Nos. 758-764 (7) 36.25 26.50
Set, never hinged 90.00

10th year of the Turkish Republic. The stamps were in use for three days only.

Nos. 682, 685, 692, 694, 696-698, 702 Overprinted or Surcharged in Red

1934, Aug. 26 *Perf. 12*
765 A71 10pa green .50 1.00
766 A71 1k on 1½k 1.00 .75
767 A74 2k on 25k 1.50 1.25
768 A74 5k on 7½k 5.00 5.00
769 A74 6k on 17½k 2.50 2.00
770 A72 12½k deep ultra 7.50 5.00
771 A72 15k on 20k 50.00 45.00
772 A74 20k on 25k 35.00 37.50
773 A75 50k on 100k 40.00 37.50
Nos. 765-773 (9) 143.00 135.00
Set, never hinged 600.00

Izmir Fair, 1934.

Nos. 696, 698, 701-704 Surcharged in Black

1936, Oct. 26
775 A74 4k on 17½k 1.00 .50
776 A74 5k on 25k 1.00 .50
777 A73 6k on 50k 1.00 .50
778 A75 10k on 100k 1.75 1.00
779 A75 20k on 200k 5.50 2.00
780 A75 50k on 500k 10.00 3.25
Nos. 775-780 (6) 20.25 7.75
Set, never hinged 75.00

"1926" in Overprint
775a A74 4k on 17½k 6.50 3.75
776a A74 5k on 25k 7.00 3.75
777a A73 6k on 50k 7.00 3.75
778a A75 10k on 100k 9.00 4.50
779a A75 20k on 200k 20.00 10.00
780a A75 50k on 500k 55.00 27.50
Nos. 775a-780a (6) 104.50 53.25
Set, never hinged 250.00

Re-militarization of the Dardanelles.

Hittite Bronze Stag — A82

Thorak's Bust of Kemal Atatürk — A83

1937, Sept. 20 Litho. *Perf. 12*
781 A82 3k light violet 1.75 1.25
782 A83 6k blue 3.00 2.00
783 A82 7½k bright pink 4.75 3.75
784 A83 12½k indigo 10.00 7.50
Nos. 781-784 (4) 19.50 14.50
Set, never hinged 40.00

2nd Turkish Historical Congress, Istanbul, Sept. 20-30.

Arms of Turkey, Greece, Romania and Yugoslavia — A84

1937, Oct. 29 *Perf. 11½*
785 A84 8k carmine 6.75 3.50
786 A84 12½k dark blue 15.00 4.75
Set, never hinged 60.00

The Balkan Entente.

Street in Izmir A85

Fig Tree — A87

30pa, View of Fair Buildings. 3k, Tower, Government Square. 5k, Olive branch. 6k, Woman with grapes. 7½k, Woman picking grapes. 8k, Izmir Harbor through arch. 12k, Statue of Pres. Ataturk. 12½k, Pres. Ataturk.

1938, Aug. 20 Photo. *Perf. 11½*
Inscribed: "Izmir Enternasyonal Fuari 1938"
789 A85 10pa dark brown .50 .60
790 A85 30pa purple .75 .50
791 A87 2½k brt green 1.25 1.00
792 A87 3k brown orange 1.25 .50
793 A87 5k olive green 2.25 .75
794 A85 6k brown 5.00 .40
795 A87 7½k scarlet 5.00 2.50
796 A87 8k brown lake 3.50 1.50
797 A87 12k rose violet 6.25 3.50
798 A87 12½k deep blue 10.00 8.50
Nos. 789-798 (10) 35.75 19.75
Set, never hinged 90.00

Izmir International Fair.

President Atatürk Teaching Reformed Turkish Alphabet A95

1938, Nov. 2
799 A95 2½k brt green 1.00 .55
800 A95 3k orange 1.25 .55
801 A95 6k rose violet 1.50 .65
802 A95 7½k deep rose 1.75 1.00
803 A95 8k red brown 2.00 1.10
804 A95 12½k brt ultra 2.50 1.25
Nos. 799-804 (6) 10.00 5.10
Set, never hinged 25.00

Reform of the Turkish alphabet, 10th anniv.

Army and Air Force A96

Atatürk Driving Tractor — A98

3k, View of Kayseri. 7½k, Railway bridge. 8k, Scout buglers. 12½k, President Ataturk.

Inscribed: "Cumhuriyetin 15 inc yil donumu hatirasi"

1938, Oct. 29

No.	Type	Value	Color	Unused	Used
805	A96	2½k	dark green	.60	.35
806	A96	3k	red brown	.60	.35
807	A98	6k	bister	.90	.35
808	A96	7½k	red	2.00	.90
809	A96	8k	rose violet	5.00	2.50
810	A98	12½k	deep blue	3.75	1.75
			Nos. 805-810 (6)	12.85	6.20
			Set, never hinged	30.00	

15th anniversary of the Republic.

Stamps of 1931-38 Overprinted in Black

1938, Nov. 21 ***Perf. 11½x12***

No.	Type	Value	Color	Unused	Used
811	A78	3k	brown orange	.75	.35
812	A78	5k	rose red	.75	.35
813	A78	6k	deep blue	1.00	.50
814	A77	7½k	deep rose	1.25	.55
815	A78	8k	dark blue	3.00	.75
a.		8k	bright blue	225.00	*150.00*
816	A79	12½k	indigo	3.75	1.75
			Nos. 811-816 (6)	10.50	4.25
			Set, never hinged	25.00	

President Kemal Atatürk (1881-1938). The date is that of his funeral.

Catalogue values for unused stamps in this section, from this point to the end of the section, are for Never Hinged items.

Turkish and American Flags — A102

Presidents Inönü and F. D. Roosevelt and Map of North America A103

Designs: 3k, 8k, Inonu and Roosevelt. 7½k, 12½k, Kemal Ataturk and Washington.

1939, July 15 **Photo.** ***Perf. 14***

No.	Type	Value	Color	Unused	Used
817	A102	2½k	ol grn, red & bl	.50	.25
818	A103	3k	dk brn & bl grn	1.00	.25
819	A102	6k	purple, red & bl	1.00	.25
820	A103	7½k	org ver & bl grn	2.00	.40
821	A103	8k	dp cl & bl grn	1.50	.40
822	A103	12½k	brt bl & bl grn	3.50	.85
			Nos. 817-822 (6)	9.50	2.40

US constitution, 150th anniversary.

Nos. 698, 702-704 Surcharged in Black

1939, July 23 **Unwmk.** ***Perf. 13***

No.	Type	Value	Surcharge	Unused	Used
823	A74	3k	on 25k	.40	.25
824	A75	6k	on 200k	.65	.50
825	A74	7½k	on 25k	.75	.50
826	A75	12k	on 100k	1.00	.50
827	A75	12½k	on 200k	2.00	.50
828	A75	17½k	on 500k	3.00	1.00
			Nos. 823-828 (6)	7.80	3.25

Annexation of Hatay.

Railroad Bridge A105

Locomotive A106

Track Through Mountain Pass A107

Design: 12½k, Railroad tunnel, Atma Pass.

1939, Oct. 20 **Typo.** ***Perf. 11½***

No.	Type	Value	Color	Unused	Used
829	A105	3k	lt orange red	3.50	3.50
830	A106	6k	chestnut	4.00	4.00
831	A107	7½k	rose pink	6.00	6.00
832	A107	12½k	dark blue	9.00	9.00
			Nos. 829-832 (4)	22.50	22.50

Completion of the Sivas to Erzerum link of the Ankara-Erzerum Railroad.

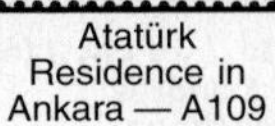

Atatürk Residence in Ankara — A109

Kemal Atatürk — A110

A111

Designs: 5k, 6k, 7½k, 8k, 12½k, 17½k, Various portraits of Ataturk, "1880-1938."

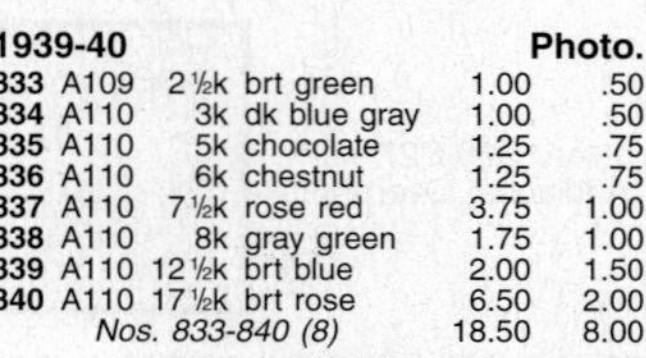

1939-40 **Photo.**

No.	Type	Value	Color	Unused	Used
833	A109	2½k	brt green	1.00	.50
834	A110	3k	dk blue gray	1.00	.50
835	A110	5k	chocolate	1.25	.75
836	A110	6k	chestnut	1.25	.75
837	A110	7½k	rose red	3.75	1.00
838	A110	8k	gray green	1.75	1.00
839	A110	12½k	brt blue	2.00	1.50
840	A110	17½k	brt rose	6.50	2.00
			Nos. 833-840 (8)	18.50	8.00

Souvenir Sheet

No.	Type	Value	Color	Unused	Used
841	A111	100k	blue black	70.00	100.00

Death of Kemal Ataturk, first anniversary. Size of No. 841: 90x120mm.

Issued: 2½k, 6k, 12½k, 11/11/39; others, 1/3/40.

Namik Kemal — A118

1940, Jan. 3

No.	Type	Value	Color	Unused	Used
842	A118	6k	chestnut	2.00	.60
843	A118	8k	dk olive grn	3.25	1.50
844	A118	12k	brt rose red	4.00	2.00
845	A118	12½k	brt blue	8.00	3.00
			Nos. 842-845 (4)	17.25	7.10

Birth cent. of Namik Kemal, poet and patriot.

Arms of Turkey, Greece, Romania and Yugoslavia — A119

Perf. 11½

1940, Jan. 1 **Typo.** **Unwmk.**

No.	Type	Value	Color	Unused	Used
846	A119	8k	light blue	3.50	1.00
847	A119	10k	deep blue	7.00	2.25

The Balkan Entente.

Nos. 703-704 Surcharged in Red or Black

1940, Aug. 20 ***Perf. 12***

No.	Type	Value	Description	Unused	Used
848	A75	6k	on 200k dk grn & blk (R)	.75	1.00
849	A75	10k	on 200k dk grn & blk	1.25	1.50
850	A75	12k	on 500k choc & blk	2.00	2.50
			Nos. 848-850 (3)	4.00	5.00

13th International Izmir Fair.

Map of Turkey and Census Figures A120

1940, Oct. 1 **Typo.** ***Perf. 11½***

No.	Type	Value	Color	Unused	Used
851	A120	10pa	dark blue green	.50	.25
852	A120	3k	orange	1.50	1.25
853	A120	6k	carmine rose	2.00	1.50
854	A120	10k	dark blue	3.00	2.50
			Nos. 851-854 (4)	7.00	5.50

Census of Oct. 20, 1940.

Runner — A121

Pole Vaulter — A122

Hurdler A123

Discus Thrower — A124

1940, Oct. 5

No.	Type	Value	Color	Unused	Used
855	A121	3k	olive green	2.50	2.50
856	A122	6k	rose	7.50	3.50
857	A123	8k	chestnut brown	3.50	4.00
858	A124	10k	dark blue	5.50	10.00
			Nos. 855-858 (4)	19.00	20.00

11th Balkan Olympics.

Mail Carriers on Horseback A125

Postman of 1840 and 1940 — A126

Old Sailing Vessel and Modern Mailboat — A127

Design: 12k, Post Office, Istanbul.

1940, Dec. 31 **Typo.** ***Perf. 10***

No.	Type	Value	Color	Unused	Used
859	A125	3k	gray green	.75	.50
860	A126	6k	rose	1.00	.75
861	A127	10k	dark blue	1.50	1.00
862	A127	12k	olive brown	2.00	1.50
			Nos. 859-862 (4)	5.25	3.75

Centenary of the Turkish post.

SEMI-POSTAL STAMPS

Regular Issues Overprinted in Carmine or Black

Overprint reads: "For War Orphans"

Perf. 12, 13½ and Compound

1915 **Unwmk.**

On Stamps of 1905

B1 A18 10pa dull grn (#119) 1.00 .75
B2 A18 10pi orange brown 12.50 .80

On Stamp of 1906

B3 A18 10pa dull grn (#128) 40.00 25.00

On Stamps of 1908

B4 A19 10pa blue green 1.50 .75
B5 A19 5pi dark violet 75.00 12.50
Nos. B1-B5 (5) 130.00 39.80

No. B6 with Additional "Discount" Overprint on No. B4

B6 A19 10pa blue green 240.00 175.00

On Stamps of 1909

B7 A21 10pa blue green 1.00 .75
a. Inverted overprint 22.50 22.50
b. Double overprint, one invtd. 30.00 30.00
B8 A21 20pa carmine rose 1.00 .75
a. Inverted overprint 27.50 27.50
B9 A21 1pi ultra 1.00 .75
B10 A21 5pi dark violet 8.75 1.50
Nos. B7-B10 (4) 11.75 3.75

See note after No. 131.

Nos. B11-B13 with Additional Overprint on Nos. B7-B9

B11 A21 10pa blue green 1.00 .75
b. Double overprint, one inverted 20.00 20.00
B12 A21 20pa carmine rose 1.50 .75
B13 A21 1pi ultra 2.00 .75

On Stamps of 1913

B14 A22 10pa blue green 1.00 .75
a. Inverted overprint 22.50 22.50
B15 A22 1pi ultra 1.00 .75
a. Double overprint 20.00 20.00
Nos. B11-B15 (5) 6.50 3.75

No. B16 with Additional Overprint on No. B14

B16 A22 10pa blue green 1.75 .75
a. Inverted overprint 27.50 27.50

On Newspaper Stamp of 1908

B17 A19 10pa blue green 360.00 175.00

On Newspaper Stamp of 1909

B18 A21 10pa blue green 1.75 1.00

Regular Issues Overprinted in Carmine or Black

1916 **On Stamps of 1901**

B19 A17 1pi blue 1.00 .50
a. Perf. 12 1.50 .75
b. Perf. 12x13¼ 6.00 1.50
B20 A17 5pi lilac rose 10.00 1.50

On Stamps of 1905

B21 A18 1pi brt blue 7.50 2.00
B22 A18 5pi brown 7.50 5.00

On Stamp of 1906

B23 A18 1pi brt blue 1.00 .75

On Stamps of 1908

B24 A19 20pa carmine (Bk) *300.00*
B25 A19 10pi red 500.00 200.00

Nos. B26-B27 with Additional Overprints

B26 A19 20pa carmine 8.00 8.00
B27 A19 1pi brt blue (C) 20.00 5.00

On Stamps of 1909

B28 A21 20pa carmine rose 2.00 1.25
B29 A21 1pi ultra 1.50 1.00
B30 A21 10pi dull red 175.00 100.00

No. B26 is No. B24 with an additional overprint. No. B27 is the design of 1908, with two overprints. Its was not issued with one.

Nos. B31-B32 with Additional Overprint on Nos. B28-B29

B31 A21 20pa carmine rose 1.50 .75
B32 A21 1pi ultra 2.00 1.00

On Stamps of 1913

B33 A22 20pa carmine rose 2.00 1.50
B34 A22 1pi ultra 2.00 1.00
a. Inverted overprint 10.00 10.00
B35 A22 10pi dull red 22.50 15.00

No. B36 with Additional Overprint on No. B33

B36 A22 20pa carmine rose 2.00 1.25

On Newspaper Stamps of 1901

B37 A16 5pi ocher 11.50 6.00
a. 5pa bister, No. P37 150.00 150.00

Regular Issues Surcharged in Black

On Stamp of 1898

B38 A11 10pa on 20pa vio brn 2.00 1.50

On Stamp of 1905

B39 A18 10pa on 20pa carmine 2.00 1.50

On Stamp of 1906

B40 A18 10pa on 20pa carmine 1.50 1.25

On Newspaper Stamp of 1893-99

B41 A11 10pa on 20pa violet brn 2.00 1.50
Nos. B38-B41 (4) 7.50 5.75

Nos. 346-349 Overprinted

B42 A41 10pa carmine 1.00 .75
a. Inverted overprint 20.00 20.00
b. Perf 12½ 1.00 .75
B43 A41 20pa ultra 1.00 .75
a. Inverted overprint 20.00 20.00
b. Perf 12½ 1.00 .75
B44 A41 1pi violet & blk 1.00 .90
a. Inverted overprint 20.00 20.00
b. Perf 12½ 1.00 .90
B45 A41 5pi yel brn & blk 1.00 .75
a. Inverted overprint 30.00 30.00
b. Perf 12½ 1.00 .75
Nos. B42-B45 (4) 4.00 3.15

Nos. B42-B45 formed part of the Postage Commemoration issue of 1916.

A Soldier's Farewell — SP1

1917, Feb. 20 **Engr.** ***Perf. 12½***

B46 SP1 10pa red violet 1.25 .50

For surcharges see Nos. 600, B47.

Stamp of Same Design Surcharged

B47 SP1 10pa on 20pa car rose 2.00 .50

Badge of the Society — SP9

School Teacher — SP10

Marie Sklodowska Curie — SP16

Kemal Atatürk — SP23

Designs: 2k+2k, Woman farmer. 2½k+2½k, Typist. 4k+4k, Aviatrix and policewoman. 5k+5k, Women voters. 7½k+7½k, Yildiz Palace, Istanbul. 10k+10k, Carrie Chapman Catt. 12½k+12½k, Jane Addams. 15k+15k, Grazia Deledda. 20k+20k, Selma Lagerlof. 25k+25k, Bertha von Suttner. 30k+30k, Sigrid Undset.

1935, Apr. 17 **Photo.** ***Perf. 11½***

Inscribed: "XII Congres Suffragiste International"

B54 SP9 20pa + 20pa brn .50 .50
B55 SP10 1k + 1k rose car .75 .50
B56 SP10 2k + 2k sl bl 1.00 .75
B57 SP10 2½k + 2½k yel grn 1.00 .75
B58 SP10 4k + 4k blue 1.50 1.00
B59 SP10 5k + 5k dl vio 2.50 2.00
B60 SP10 7½k + 7½k org red 2.50 2.00
B61 SP16 10k + 10k org 2.50 2.50
B62 SP16 12½k + 12½k dk bl 2.50 2.50
B63 SP16 15k + 15k violet 5.00 5.00
B64 SP16 20k + 20k red org 7.50 6.25
B65 SP16 25k + 25k grn 15.00 14.00
B66 SP16 30k + 30k ultra 90.00 100.00
B67 SP16 50k + 50k dk sl grn 175.00 150.00
B68 SP23 100k + 100k brn car 125.00 140.00
Nos. B54-B68 (15) 432.25 427.75
Set, never hinged 750.00

12th Congress of the Women's Intl. Alliance.

AIR POST STAMPS

Catalogue values for unused stamps in this section are for Never Hinged items.

Nos. 692, 695, 698, 700 Overprinted or Surcharged in Brown or Blue

1934, July 15 **Unwmk.** ***Perf. 12***

C1 A74 7½k (Br) 1.00 .25
C2 A72 12½k on 15k (Br) 1.00 .25
C3 A74 20k on 25k (Br) 1.00 .25
C4 A74 25k (Bl) 1.25 .40
C5 A74 40k (Br) 2.50 1.25
Nos. C1-C5 (5) 6.75 2.40

Regular Stamps of 1930 Surcharged in Brown

1937

C6 A74 4½k on 7½k red brn 5.00 1.00
C7 A72 9k on 15k dp org 40.00 20.00
C8 A74 35k on 40k red vio 10.00 4.25
Nos. C6-C8 (3) 55.00 25.25

POSTAGE DUE STAMPS

Same Types as Regular Issues of Corresponding Dates

1863 **Unwmk.** ***Imperf.***

Blue Band

J1 A1 20pa blk, *red brn* 100.00 32.50
a. Tête bêche pair 225.00 225.00
b. Without band 50.00
c. Red band 90.00 45.00
J2 A2 1pi blk, *red brn* 150.00 22.50
a. Tête bêche pair 225.00 225.00
b. Without band 50.00
J3 A3 2pi blk, *red brn* 500.00 70.00
a. Tête bêche pair 650.00 450.00
J4 A4 5pi blk, *red brn* 300.00 80.00
a. Tête bêche pair 425.00 425.00
b. Without band 100.00
c. Red band 150.00
Nos. J1-J4 (4) 1,050. 205.00

Full margins = 1mm at sides and top, 3mm at bottom (includes part of band). Height of colored bands is 6mm. Full margins for items without band = 3mm at bottom.

1865 ***Perf. 12½***

J6 A5 20pa brown 4.00 5.00
J7 A5 1pi brown 4.00 5.00
b. Half used as 20pa on cover
c. Printed on both sides 25.00
J8 A5 2pi brown 12.50 25.00
a. Half used as 1pi on cover
J9 A5 5pi brown 5.00 30.00
a. Half used as 2½pi on cover
J10 A5 25pi brown 45.00 100.00
Nos. J6-J10 (5) 70.50 165.00

Exist imperf. Values, $60 to $100 each.

The 10pa brown is an essay. Value about $2,750.

1867

J11 A5 20pa bister brn 9.00 100.00
J12 A5 1pi bister brn 9.00
a. With surcharge of 5pi 13.50
b. Imperf., pair 65.00

J13 A5 2pi fawn 75.00
J14 A5 5pi fawn 17.50
J15 A5 25pi bister brn *21,250.*
Nos. J11-J14 (4) 110.50

Nos. J12-J15 were not placed in use.

1869 ***Perf. 13½***

With Yellow-Brown Border

J16 A5 20pa bister brn 10.00 10.00
a. Without surcharge
J17 A5 1pi bister brn 550.00 20.00
a. Without surcharge
J18 A5 2pi bister brn 800.00 20.00
J19 A5 5pi bister brn 2.25 12.50
b. Without border
c. Printed on both sides 15.00
J20 A5 25pi bister brn — —
Nos. J16-J19 (4) 1,362. 62.50

With Brown Border

Color of border ranges from brown to reddish brown and black brown.

J21 A5 20pa bister brn 125.00 20.00
a. Inverted surcharge
b. Without surcharge
J22 A5 1pi bister brn 550.00 12.50
a. Without surcharge
J23 A5 2pi bister brn 450.00 12.50
b. Inverted surcharge
J24 A5 5pi bister brn 2.50 15.00
b. Without surcharge
J25 A5 25pi bister brn 37.50 100.00
Nos. J21-J25 (5) 1,165. 160.00

Pin-perf., Perf. 5 to 11½ and Compound

1871 **With Bright Red Border**

J26 A5 20pa bister brn 1,250. 50.00
J27 A5 1pi bister brn *5,000.*
J28 A5 2pi bister brn 110.00 140.00

With Orange Brown Border

J29 A5 5pi bister brn 7.50 25.00

With Brown to Deep Brown Border

J31 A5 20pa bister brn 150.00 3.50
a. Half used as 10pa on cover
b. Imperf., pair 16.50
c. Printed on both sides 40.00 40.00
J32 A5 1pi bister brn 225.00 2.50
a. Half used as 20pa on cover
c. Inverted surcharge 50.00 35.00
d. Printed on both sides
J33 A5 2pi bister brn 6.00 9.00
a. Half used as 1pi on cover
c. Imperf., pair 16.50
J34 A5 5pi bister brn 2.50 20.00
a. Half used as 2½pi on cover
c. Printed on both sides
J35 A5 25pi bister brn 40.00 125.00
a. Inverted surcharge
Nos. J31-J35 (5) 423.50 *160.00*

1888 ***Perf. 11½ and 13½***

J36 A7 20pa black 3.00 10.00
J37 A7 1pi black 3.00 10.00
J38 A7 2pi black 3.00 10.00
b. Diagonal half used as 1pi
Nos. J36-J38 (3) 9.00 30.00

Imperf

J36a A7 20pa 17.50
J37a A7 1pi 17.50
J38a A7 2pi 17.50

1892 ***Perf. 13½***

J39 A11 20pa black 7.00 12.50
J40 A12 1pi black 25.00 12.50
a. Printed on both sides
J41 A13 2pi black 17.50 12.50
Nos. J39-J41 (3) 49.50 *37.50*

1901

J42 A11 20pa black, *deep rose* 2.50 20.00

1901

J43 A17 10pa black, *deep rose* 4.00 6.00
J44 A17 20pa black, *deep rose* 3.75 8.75
J45 A17 1pi black, *deep rose* 3.00 10.00
J46 A17 2pi black, *deep rose* 2.50 15.00
Nos. J43-J46 (4) 13.25 39.75

1905 ***Perf. 12***

J47 A18 1pi black, *deep rose* 3.00 10.00
J48 A18 2pi black, *deep rose* 4.50 20.00

1908, ***Perf. 12, 13½ and Compound***

J49 A19 1pi black, *deep rose* 80.00 7.50
J50 A19 2pi black, *deep rose* 12.50 45.00

1909

J51 A21 1pi black, *deep rose* 15.00 *50.00*
J52 A21 2pi black, *deep rose* *150.00 175.00*
a. Imperf. 65.00

1913 ***Perf. 12***

J53 A22 2pa black, *deep rose* 1.00 .50
J54 A22 5pa black, *deep rose* 1.00 .50
J55 A22 10pa black, *deep rose* 1.00 .50
J56 A22 20pa black, *deep rose* 1.00 .50
J57 A22 1pi black, *deep rose* 4.50 10.00
J58 A22 2pi black, *deep rose* 8.00 17.50
Nos. J53-J58 (6) 16.50 29.50

Adrianople Issue

Nos. 251-253 Surcharged in Black, Blue or Red

1913

J59 A23 2pa on 10pa green (Bk) 3.25 .35
J60 A23 5pa on 20pa red (Bl) 3.25 .35
J61 A23 10pa on 40pa blue (R) 10.00 .80
J62 A23 20pa on 40pa blue (Bk) 32.50 11.00
Nos. J59-J62 (4) 49.00 12.50

For surcharges see Nos. J67-J70, J83-J86.

D1

D2

D3

D4

1914 **Engr.**

J63 D1 5pa claret 1.25 10.00
J64 D2 20pa red 1.25 10.00
J65 D3 1pi dark blue 1.25 10.00
J66 D4 2pi slate 1.25 10.00
Nos. J63-J66 (4) 5.00 40.00

For surcharges and overprints see Nos. J87-J91.

Nos. J59 to J62 Surcharged in Red or Black

1916

J67 A23 10pa on 2pa on 10pa (R) 55.00 55.00
J68 A23 20pa on 5pa on 20pa 55.00 55.00
J69 A23 40pa on 10pa on 40pa 55.00 55.00
J70 A23 40pa on 20pa on 40pa (R) 55.00 55.00
Nos. J67-J70 (4) 220.00 220.00

Preceding Issues Overprinted in Red, Black or Blue

1917 **On Stamps of 1865**

J71 A5 20pa red brn (Bl) 45.00 67.50
J72 A5 1pi red brn (Bl) 45.00 67.50
J73 A5 2pi bis brn (Bl) 45.00 67.50
J74 A5 5pi bis brn (Bl) 45.00 67.50
J75 A5 25pi dk brn (Bl) 45.00 67.50
Nos. J71-J75 (5) 225.00 337.50

On Stamp of 1869

Red Brown Border

J76 A5 5pi bis brn (R) 45.00 67.50

On Stamp of 1871

Black Brown Border

J77 A5 5pi bis brn 75.00 50.00

On Stamps of 1888

J78 A7 1pi black (R) 45.00 67.50
J79 A7 2pi black (R) 45.00 67.50

On Stamps of 1892

J80 A11 20pa black (R) 2.50 2.50
J81 A12 1pi black (R) 2.50 2.50
J82 A13 2pi black (R) 2.50 2.50
Nos. J80-J82 (3) 7.50 7.50

Adrianople Issue

On Nos. J59 to J62 with Addition of New Value

J83 A23 10pa on 2pa on 10pa (R) 1.25 1.00
J84 A23 20pa on 5pa on 20pa (Bk) 1.50 1.00
J85 A23 40pa on 10pa on 40pa (Bk) 2.00 1.50
a. "40pa" double
J86 A23 40pa on 20pa on 40pa (R) 3.75 3.50
Nos. J83-J86 (4) 8.50 7.00

Nos. J71-J86 were used as regular postage stamps.

Armistice Issue

No. J65 Overprinted

1919, Nov. 30

J87 D3 1pi dark blue 125.00 150.00

Accession to the Throne Issue

Postage Due Stamps of 1914 Overprinted in Turkish "Accession to the Throne of His Majesty. 3rd July, 1334-1918"

1919

J88 D1 10pa on 5pa claret 25.00 37.50
J89 D2 20pa red 25.00 37.50
J90 D3 1pi dark blue 25.00 37.50
J91 D4 2pi slate 25.00 37.50
Nos. J88-J91 (4) 100.00 150.00

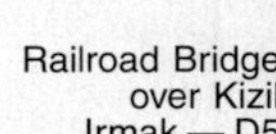
Railroad Bridge over Kizil Irmak — D5

1926 **Engr.**

J92 D5 20pa ocher 1.25 2.50
J93 D5 1g red 2.00 5.00
J94 D5 2g blue green 3.00 5.00
J95 D5 3g lilac brown 3.50 12.50
J96 D5 5g lilac 6.00 20.00
Nos. J92-J96 (5) 15.75 45.00
Set, never hinged 30.00

Catalogue values for unused stamps in this section, from this point to the end of the section, are for Never Hinged items.

Kemal Atatürk — D6

1936 **Litho.** ***Perf. 11½***

J97 D6 20pa brown .25 .25
J98 D6 2k light blue .25 .25
J99 D6 3k bright violet .25 .25
J100 D6 5k Prussian blue .25 .25
J101 D6 12k bright rose .35 .25
Nos. J97-J101 (5) 1.35 1.25

For surcharges see Nos. 1461-1465 in Scott Standard catalogue, Vol. 6.

LOCAL ISSUES

Type I

Type II

Type III

Type IV

Type V

Type VI

During 1873//1882 Turkish stamps with the above overprints were used for local postage in Constantinople (types 1-5) and Mount Athos (type 6).

MILITARY STAMPS

For the Army in Thessaly

Tughra and Bridge at Larissa — M1

1898, Apr. 21 **Unwmk.** ***Perf. 13***

M1 M1 10pa yellow green 10.00 7.50
M2 M1 20pa rose 10.00 7.50
M3 M1 1pi dark blue 10.00 7.50
M4 M1 2pi orange 10.00 7.50
M5 M1 5pi violet 10.00 7.50
Nos. M1-M5 (5) 50.00 37.50
Set, never hinged 75.00

Issued for Turkish occupation forces to use in Thessaly during the Greco-Turkish War of 1897-98.

Forgeries of Nos. M1-M5 are perf. 11½.

NEWSPAPER STAMPS

N1

Black Overprint

1879 **Unwmk.** ***Perf. 11½ and 13½***

P1 N1 10pa blk & rose lilac 225.00 225.00

Other stamps found with this "IMPRIMES" overprint were prepared on private order and have no official status as newspaper stamps.

Counterfeits exist of No. P1.

The 10pa surcharge, on half of 20pa rose and pale rose was made privately. See note after No. 77.

Regular Issue of 1890 Handstamped in Black, Blue or Red

Nos. P10-P29 were overprinted with a single wooden handstamp. Variations in size are due to inking and pressure.

The handstamps on Nos. P10-P29 are found double, inverted and sideways. Counterfeit overprints comprise most of the examples offered for sale in the marketplace.

1891 ***Perf. 13½, 11½***

P10 A7 10pa grn & gray 40.00 12.50
a. Imperf. 22.50 12.50
P11 A7 20pa rose & gray 75.00 15.00
P12 A7 1pi blue & gray 210.00 150.00
P13 A7 2pi yel & gray *525.00 400.00*
P14 A7 5pi buff & gray *1,050. 750.00*
Nos. P10-P14 (5) *1,900. 1,328.*

Blue Handstamp

P10b A7 10pa green & gray 210.00 *125.00*
P11a A7 20pa rose & gray 340.00 *250.00*
P12a A7 1pi blue & gray *425.00* 375.00
Nos. P10b-P12a (3) *975.00 750.00*

This overprint on 2pi and 5pi in blue is considered bogus.

Red Handstamp

P10c A7 10pa green & gray *400.00 325.00*
P11b A7 20pa rose & gray *600.00 450.00*
P12b A7 1pi blue & gray *900.00 1,000.*
Nos. P10c-P12b (3) 1,900. 1,775.

This overprint in red on 2pi and 5pi is considered bogus.

Excellent forgeries of Nos. P10-P14 exist. Certification by a competant authority is suggested.

Same Handstamp on Regular Issue of 1892

1892 ***Perf. 13½***

P25 A10 10pa gray green *500.00 100.00*
P26 A11 20pa rose *1,250. 375.00*
P27 A12 1pi pale blue *110.00 150.00*
P28 A13 2pi brown org *200.00 175.00*
P29 A14 5pi pale violet *1,800. 1,250.*
a. On No. 99a *500.00*
Nos. P25-P29 (5) 3,860. 2,050.

Regular Issues of 1892-98 Overprinted in Black

1893-98

P30 A10 10pa gray grn 3.75 2.50
P31 A11 20pa vio brn ('98) 3.00 1.50
a. 20pa dark pink 2.50 1.25
b. 20pa pink 325.00 22.50
P32 A12 1pi pale blue 3.00 1.50
P33 A13 2pi brown org 27.50 12.50
a. Tete beche pair 90.00 22.50
P34 A14 5pi pale violet 85.00 75.00
a. On No. 99a 140.00 65.00
Nos. P30-P34 (5) 122.25 93.00

For surcharge and overprints see Nos. B41, P121-P122, P134-P136, P153-P154.

No. 95 Surcharged

1897

P36 A10 5pa on 10pa gray grn 5.00 3.00
a. "Cniq" instead of "Cinq" 15.00 15.00

For overprint see No. P137.

Nos. 102-107 Overprinted in Black

1901 ***Perf. 12, 13½ and Compound***

P37 A16 5pa bister 1.75 1.00
a. Inverted overprint
P38 A16 10pa yellow grn 6.25 6.25
P39 A16 20pa magenta 32.50 7.50
P40 A16 1pi violet blue 60.00 22.50
P41 A16 2pi gray blue 125.00 37.50
P42 A16 5pi ocher 300.00 90.00
Nos. P37-P42 (6) 525.50 164.75

For overprints see Nos. B37, P69-P74, P123, P138-P141, P155-P158.

Same Overprint on Nos. 110-115

1901

P43 A17 5pa purple 8.75 2.00
a. Perf. 12 50.00 12.50
P44 A17 10pa green 32.50 2.50
a. Perf. 12 65.00 20.00
P45 A17 20pa carmine 8.75 1.50
a. Overprinted on back
b. Perf. 12 50.00 7.50
P46 A17 1pi blue 25.00 2.00
a. Perf. 12 75.00 17.50
P47 A17 2pi orange 87.50 4.00
a. Inverted overprint
b. Perf. 12 275.00 75.00
P48 A17 5pi lilac rose 160.00 27.50
Nos. P43-P48 (6) 322.50 39.50

For overprints see Nos. P75-P80, P124-P126, P142-P146, P159-P164.

Same Overprint on Regular Issue of 1905

1905

P49 A18 5pa ocher 2.50 1.00
P50 A18 10pa dull green 30.00 1.50
P51 A18 20pa carmine 2.50 1.25
P52 A18 1pi pale blue 2.50 1.25
P53 A18 2pi slate 70.00 10.00
P54 A18 5pi brown 175.00 20.00
Nos. P49-P54 (6) 282.50 35.00

For overprints see Nos. P127-P129, P147-P150, P165-P171.

Regular Issue of 1908 Overprinted in Carmine or Blue

1908

P55 A19 5pa ocher (Bl) 10.00 .50
P56 A19 10pa blue grn (C) 17.50 .50
P57 A19 20pa carmine (Bl) 22.50 1.00
P58 A19 1pi brt blue (C) 100.00 2.50
P59 A19 2pi blue blk (C) 150.00 7.50
P60 A19 5pi dk violet (C) 200.00 17.50
Nos. P55-P60 (6) 500.00 29.50

For overprints see Nos. B17, P130-P131, P151, P172.

Same Overprint on Regular Issue of 1909

1909

P61 A21 5pa ocher (Bl) 3.50 1.25
a. Imperf. *20.00 20.00*
P62 A21 10pa blue grn (C) 8.75 1.50
P63 A21 20pa car rose (Bl) 60.00 1.75
a. Imperf. *80.00 80.00*
P64 A21 1pi brt blue (C) 100.00 5.00
P65 A21 2pi blue blk (C) 250.00 30.00
P66 A21 5pi dk violet (C) 500.00 65.00
Nos. P61-P66 (6) 922.25 104.50

For surcharge and overprints see Nos. B18, P67-P68, P81, P132-P133, P152.

No. 151 Surcharged in Blue

1910 ***Perf. 12, 13½ and Compound***

P67 A21 2pa on 5pa ocher .75 .75

Type of 1909 Tughra and "Reshad" of Sultan Mohammed V

1911 ***Perf. 12***

P68 A21 2pa olive green 1.00 .50

For overprints see Nos. 567, P173.

Newspaper Stamps of 1901-11 Overprinted in Carmine or Blue

The overprint was applied to 13 denominations in four settings with change of city name, producing individual sets for each city: "MONASTIR," "PRISTINA," "SALONIQUE" and "USKUB."

1911, June 26 ***Perf. 12, 13½***

"Monastir"

P69 A16 5pa bister 16.50 *20.00*
P70 A16 10pa yellow grn 16.50 *20.00*
P71 A16 20pa magenta 16.50 *20.00*
P72 A16 1pi violet blue 16.50 *20.00*
P73 A16 2pi gray blue 22.50 *30.00*
P74 A16 5pi ocher 45.00 *60.00*
P75 A17 5pa purple 8.75 *11.50*
P76 A17 10pa green 8.75 *11.50*
P77 A17 20pa carmine 8.75 *11.50*
P78 A17 1pi blue 8.75 *11.50*
P79 A17 2pi orange 11.00 *14.50*
P80 A17 5pi lilac rose 30.00 32.50
P81 A21 2pa olive green 3.00 *3.75*
Nos. P69-P81 (13) 212.50 *266.75*

"Pristina"

P69a A16 5pa bister 16.50 *20.00*
P70a A16 10pa yellow grn 16.50 *20.00*
P71a A16 20pa magenta 16.50 *20.00*
P72a A16 1pi violet blue 16.50 *20.00*
P73a A16 2pi gray blue 22.50 *30.00*
P74a A16 5pi ocher 45.00 *60.00*
P75a A17 5pa purple 8.75 *11.00*
P76a A17 10pa green 8.75 *11.00*
P77a A17 20pa carmine 8.75 *11.00*
P78a A17 1pi blue 8.75 *11.00*
P79a A17 2pi orange 11.00 *14.50*
P80a A17 5pi lilac rose 30.00 *32.50*
P81a A21 2pa olive green 3.00 *3.75*
Nos. P69a-P81a (13) 212.50 *264.75*

"Salonique"

P69b A16 5pa bister 16.50 *20.00*
P70b A16 10pa yellow grn 16.50 *20.00*
P71b A16 20pa magenta 16.50 *20.00*
P72b A16 1pi violet blue 16.50 *20.00*
P73b A16 2pi gray blue 22.50 *30.00*
P74b A16 5pi ocher 45.00 *60.00*
P75b A17 5pa purple 8.75 *11.50*
P76b A17 10pa green 8.75 *11.50*
P77b A17 20pa carmine 8.75 *11.50*
P78b A17 1pi blue 8.75 *11.50*
P79b A17 2pi orange 11.00 *14.50*
P80b A17 5pi lilac rose 30.00 *32.50*
P81b A21 2pa olive green 3.00 *3.75*
Nos. P69b-P81b (13) 212.50 *266.75*

"Uskub"

P69c A16 5pa bister 16.50 *20.00*
P70c A16 10pa yellow grn 16.50 *20.00*
P71c A16 20pa magenta 16.50 *20.00*
P72c A16 1pi violet blue 16.50 *20.00*
P73c A16 2pi gray blue 22.50 *30.00*
P74c A16 5pi ocher 45.00 *60.00*
P75c A17 5pa purple 8.75 *11.50*
P76c A17 10pa green 8.75 *11.50*
P77c A17 20pa carmine 8.75 *11.50*
P78c A17 1pi blue 8.75 *11.50*
P79c A17 2pi orange 11.00 *14.50*
P80c A17 5pi lilac rose 30.00 *32.50*
P81c A21 2pa olive green 3.00 *3.75*
Nos. P69c-P81c (13) 212.50 *266.75*

The note after No. 182 will also apply to Nos. P69-P81.

Newspaper Stamps of 1901-11 Overprinted in Carmine or Black

1915 **On Stamps of 1893-98**

P121 A10 10pa gray green 6.00 .50
a. Inverted overprint 20.00 20.00
P122 A13 2pi yellow brn 1.50 1.00
a. Inverted overprint 20.00 20.00

On Stamps of 1901

P123 A16 10pa yellow grn 1.00 .50
P124 A17 5pa purple 1.00 1.00
P125 A17 20pa carmine 2.00 1.00
P126 A17 5pi lilac rose 20.00 5.00

On Stamps of 1905

P127 A18 5pa ocher 2.00 1.00
a. Inverted overprint 20.00 20.00
P128 A18 2pi slate 17.50 5.00
P129 A18 5pi brown 10.00 .60

On Stamps of 1908

P130 A19 2pi blue blk *1,375. 550.00*
P131 A19 5pi dk violet 10.00 1.25

On Stamps of 1909

P132 A21 5pa ocher 1.00 .50
P133 A21 5pi dk violet 100.00 35.00
Nos. P121-P129,P131-P133 (12) 172.00 52.35

Preceding Newspaper Issues with additional Overprint in Red or Black

1916 **On Stamps of 1893-98**

P134 A10 10pa gray green 2.00 .75
P135 A11 20pa violet brn 1.00 .75
P136 A14 5pi dull violet 50.00 50.00

On Stamp of 1897

P137 A10 5pa on 10pa gray grn .60 .50

On Stamps of 1901

P138 A16 5pa bister .50 .30
P139 A16 10pa yellow grn .90 .90
P140 A16 20pa magenta 1.00 .90
a. Inverted overprint 20.00 20.00
P141 A16 1pi violet blue 1.00 1.00
P142 A17 5pa purple 50.00 50.00
P143 A17 10pa green 50.00 50.00
P144 A17 20pa carmine 1.50 .90
P145 A17 1pi blue 1.50 .90
P146 A17 2pi orange 1.50 .90

On Stamps of 1905

P147 A18 5pa ocher 1.00 .75
P148 A18 10pa dull green 50.00 50.00
P149 A18 20pa carmine 50.00 50.00
P150 A18 1pi pale blue 1.75 1.00

On Stamp of 1908

P151 A19 5pa ocher 62.50 62.50

On Stamp of 1909

P152 A21 5pa ocher 62.50 62.50
Nos. P134-P152 (19) 389.25 384.55

Preceding Newspaper Issues with additional Overprint in Red or Black

1917 **On Stamps of 1893-98**

P153 A12 1pi gray (R) 2.50 2.00
P154 A11 20pa vio brn (R) 3.75 3.75

On Stamps of 1901

P155 A16 5pa bister (Bk) 1.50 1.25
a. Inverted overprint 20.00 20.00
P156 A16 10pa yellow grn (R) 1.50 1.25
P157 A16 20pa magenta (Bk) 1.50 1.25
P158 A16 2pi gray blue (R) 40.00 30.00
P159 A17 5pa purple (Bk) 2.25 2.25
a. Inverted overprint 20.00 20.00
b. Double overprint 20.00 20.00
c. Double ovpt., one inverted 25.00 25.00
P160 A17 10pa green (R) 22.50 35.00
P161 A17 20pa carmine (Bk) 1.50 1.25
P162 A17 1pi blue (R) 3.00 3.00
P163 A17 2pi orange (Bk) 2.50 2.50
P164 A17 5pi lilac rose (R) 32.50 50.00

On Stamps of 1905

P165 A18 5pa ocher (R) 2.50 2.00
a. Inverted overprint 20.00 20.00
P166 A18 5pa ocher (Bk) 3.00 2.50
a. Inverted overprint 20.00 20.00
P167 A18 10pa dull green (R) 2.50 2.00
P168 A18 20pa carmine (Bk) 2.50 2.00
a. Double overprint 20.00 20.00
P169 A18 1pi blue (R) 2.50 2.00
a. Inverted overprint 25.00 25.00
P170 A18 2pi slate (R) 32.50 50.00
P171 A18 5pi brown (R) 32.50 50.00

On Stamp of 1908

P172 A19 5pa ocher (R) 32.50 50.00
Nos. P153-P172 (20) *225.50 294.00*

Nos. P153-P172 were used as regular postage stamps.

Type of 1909 Surcharged in Blue and Overprinted in Red

1919

P173 A21 5pa on 2pa ol grn		1.25	1.00
a. Red overprint double		20.00	10.00
b. Blue surcharge double		20.00	10.00

No. 255 Surcharged in Red

1920

P174 A25 5pa on 4pa brn	1.25	.50

POSTAL TAX STAMPS

Map of Turkey and Red Crescent PT1

1928 Unwmk. Typo. *Perf. 14*

Crescent in Red

RA1 PT1 ½pi lt brown	.40	.25
RA2 PT1 1pi red violet	.40	.25
RA3 PT1 2½pi orange	.40	.25

Engr.

Various Frames

RA4 PT1 5pi dk brown	.60	.45
RA5 PT1 10pi yellow green	.75	.55
RA6 PT1 20pi slate	1.25	.60
RA7 PT1 50pi dark violet	3.75	1.40
Nos. RA1-RA7 (7)	7.55	3.75
Set, never hinged	13.00	

The use of these stamps on letters, parcels, etc. in addition to the regular postage, was obligatory on certain days in each year.

For surcharges see Nos. RA16, RA21-RA22.

Cherubs Upholding Star — PT2

1932

RA8 PT2 1k ol bis & red	1.00	.30
RA9 PT2 2½k dk brn & red	1.25	.30
RA10 PT2 5k green & red	1.50	.30
RA11 PT2 25k black & red	3.00	1.00
Nos. RA8-RA11 (4)	6.75	1.90
Set, never hinged	9.00	

For surcharges and overprints see Nos. RA12-RA15, RA28-RA29, RA36-RA38.

No. RA8 Surcharged

RA12 PT2 20pa on 1k	1.00	.50
RA13 PT2 3k on 1k	1.75	.70
a. 3 "kruus"	2.50	2.50

By a law of Parliament the use of these stamps on letters and telegraph forms, in addition to the regular fees, was obligatory from Apr. 20-30 of each year. The inscription in the tablet at the bottom of the design states that the money derived from the sale of the stamps is devoted to child welfare work.

No. RA8 Surcharged

1933

RA14 PT2 20pa on 1k ol bis & red	1.00	.50
RA15 PT2 3k on 1k ol bis & red	1.75	1.00

No. RA5 Surcharged

RA16 PT1 5k on 10pi yel grn & red	1.50	.75
Nos. RA14-RA16 (3)	4.25	2.25

PT3

PT4

1933 *Perf. 11, 11½*

RA17 PT3 20pa gray vio & red	1.00	.50
RA18 PT4 1k violet & red	1.00	.50
RA19 PT4 5k dk brown & red	2.50	.50
RA20 PT3 15k green & red	3.50	.50
Nos. RA17-RA20 (4)	8.00	2.00
Set, never hinged	12.00	

Nos. RA17 and RA20 were issued in Ankara; Nos. RA18 and RA19 in Izmir.

For overprint see No. RA27.

Nos. RA3, RA1 Surcharged in Black

1933-34

RA21 PT1 1k on 2½pi orange	.75	.30
RA22 PT1 5k on ½pi lt brown	2.25	.50

Map of Turkey PT5

1934-35 Crescent in Red *Perf. 12*

RA23 PT5 ½k blue ('35)	.40	.25
RA24 PT5 1k red brown	.40	.25
RA25 PT5 2½k brown ('35)	.60	.25
RA26 PT5 5k blue green ('35)	1.50	.25
Nos. RA23-RA26 (4)	2.90	1.00
Set, never hinged	5.00	

Frame differs on No. RA26.

See Nos. RA30-RA35B.

Nos. RA17, RA8-RA9 Overprinted in Roman Capitals

1936 *Perf. 11, 14*

RA27 PT3 20pa gray vio & red	.40	.25
RA28 PT2 1k ol bis & red	.40	.25
RA29 PT2 3k on 2½k dk brn & red	.75	.30
Nos. RA27-RA29 (3)	1.55	
Set, never hinged	12.00	

Type of 1934-35, Inscribed "Türkiye Kizilay Cemiyeti"

1938-46 *Perf. 8½-11½*

Type I — Imprint, "Devlet Basimevi". Crescent red.

Type II — Imprint, "Alaeddin Kiral Basimevi". Crescent carmine.

Type III — Imprint, "Damga Matbaasi". Crescent red.

Crescent in Red or Carmine

RA30 PT5 ½k blue (I)	.50	.25
a. Type II	4.00	1.00
b. Type III	.50	.25
RA31 PT5 1k red vio (I)	.40	.25
a. Type II	6.50	2.00
b. Type III	.50	.25
RA32 PT5 2½k orange (I)	.30	.25
a. Type III	2.00	1.00
RA33 PT5 5k blue grn (I)	.50	.25
RA33A PT5 5k choc (III) ('42)	1.00	.25
RA34 PT5 10k pale grn (I)	1.50	.30
a. Type III	2.00	1.00
RA35 PT5 20k black (I)	2.50	1.00
RA35A PT5 50k pur (III) ('46)	7.50	1.00
RA35B PT5 1 l blue (III) ('44)	30.00	2.50
Nos. RA30-RA35B (9)	44.20	6.05
Set, never hinged	75.00	

For surcharge see No. RA63.

No. RA9 Surcharged in Black

1938 *Perf. 14*

RA36 PT2 20pa on 2½k	1.00	.50
RA37 PT2 1k on 2½k	1.00	.50

No. RA9 Surcharged in Black

1938 Unwmk. *Perf. 14*

RA37A PT2 20pa on 2½k	1.25	.60
RA37B PT2 1k on 2½k	1.50	.75

No. RA9 Surcharged "1 Kurus" in Black

1939 *Perf. 14*

RA38 PT2 1k on 2½k dk brn & red	.50	.50

Child — PT6

Nurse with Child — PT7

1940 Typo. *Perf. 12*

Star in Carmine

RA39 PT6 20pa bluish grn	.30	.25
RA40 PT6 1k violet	.30	.25
RA41 PT7 1k lt blue	.30	.25
RA42 PT7 2½k pale red lil	.30	.25
RA43 PT6 3k black	.35	.25
RA44 PT7 5k pale violet	.30	.25
RA45 PT7 10k blue green	1.00	.40
RA46 PT6 15k dark blue	.75	.30
RA47 PT7 25k olive bister	2.50	1.25
RA48 PT7 50k olive gray	6.00	2.50
Nos. RA39-RA48 (10)	12.10	5.95
Set, never hinged	30.00	

POSTAL TAX AIR POST STAMPS

Air Fund Issues

These stamps were obligatory on all air mail for 21 days a year. Tax for the Turkish Aviation Society: 20pa for a postcard, 1k for a regular letter, 2 1/2k for a registered letter, 3k for a telegram, 5k-50k for a package, higher values for air freight. Postal tax air post stamps were withdrawn Aug. 21, 1934 and remainders destroyed later that year.

Biplane PTAP1

Type PTAP1

Perf. 11, Pin Perf.

1926 Unwmk. Litho.

Size: 35x25mm

RAC1 20pa brn & pale grn	3.00	.30
RAC2 1g blue grn & buff	2.00	.30

Size: 40x29mm

RAC3 5g vio & pale grn	8.00	1.00
RAC4 5g car lake & pale grn	35.00	15.00
Nos. RAC1-RAC4 (4)	48.00	16.60
Set, never hinged	275.00	

PTAP2

PTAP3

1927-29 Type PTAP2

RAC5 20pa dl red & pale grn	1.75	.50
RAC6 1k green & yel	1.50	.50

Type PTAP3

Perf. 11½

RAC7 2k dp cl & yel grn	1.75	.50
RAC8 2½k red & yel grn	8.00	1.60
RAC9 5k dk bl gray & org	1.75	.50
RAC10 10k dk grn & rose	5.00	1.25
RAC11 15k green & yel	5.00	1.00
RAC12 20k ol brn & yel	7.00	2.00
RAC13 50k dk bl & cob bl	10.00	4.50
RAC14 100k car & lt bl	110.00	80.00
Nos. RAC5-RAC14 (10)	151.75	92.35
Set, never hinged	825.00	

Nos. RAC1, RAC5, RAC7 and RAC11 Surcharged in Black or Red

1930-31

RAC15 1k ("Bir kurus") on RAC1	200.00	75.00
RAC16 1k ("Bir Kurus") on RAC5	1.50	.50
RAC17 100pa ("Yuz Para") on RAC7	2.00	.75
RAC18 5k ("Bes Kurus") on RAC5	8.00	1.50
RAC19 5k ("5 Kurus") on RAC5	3.00	.75
RAC20 10k ("On kurus") on RAC7	4.00	1.25
RAC21 50k ("Elli kurus") on RAC7	12.00	4.00
RAC22 1 l ("Bir lira") on RAC7	*37.50*	*9.00*

RAC23 5 l ("Bes lira") on RAC11 *2,000. 400.00*
Nos. RAC15-RAC23 (9) 2,268. *492.75*
Set, never hinged 5,000.

PTAP4

PTAP5

1931-32 **Litho.** ***Perf. 11½***
RAC24 PTAP4 20pa black 5.00 1.75

Typo.

RAC25 PTAP5 1k brown car ('32) 2.00 .50
RAC26 PTAP5 5k red ('32) 4.00 .75
RAC27 PTAP5 10k green ('32) 6.00 1.50
Nos. RAC24-RAC27 (4) 17.00 4.50
Set, never hinged 65.00

PTAP6

1933 **Type PTAP6**
RAC28 10pa ("On Para") grn 3.50 2.00
RAC29 1k ("Bir Kurus") red 8.00 2.75
RAC30 5k ("Bes Kurus") lil 12.00 3.00
Nos. RAC28-RAC30 (3) 23.50 7.75
Set, never hinged 70.00

TURKEY IN ASIA

'tər-kē in 'ā-zhə

(Anatolia)

40 Paras = 1 Piaster

This designation, which includes all of Turkey in Asia Minor, came into existence during the uprising of 1919, led by Mustafa Kemal Pasha. Actually there was no separation of territory, the Sultan's sovereignty being almost immediately reduced to a small area surrounding Constantinople. The formation of the Turkish Republic and the expulsion of the Sultan followed in 1923. Subsequent issues of postage stamps are listed under Turkey (Republic).

Issues of the Nationalist Government

Turkish Stamps of 1913-18 Surcharged in Black or Red

(The Surcharge reads "Angora 3 Piastres")

1920 **Unwmk.** ***Perf. 12***

On Stamps of 1913

1 A24 3pi on 2pa red lilac 4.75 *5.25*
2 A25 3pi on 4pa dk brn 37.50 *37.50*
3 A27 3pi on 6pa dk bl 250.00 *150.00*

On Stamp of 1916-18

4 A42 3pi on 2pa vio (Bk) 35.00 20.00
Nos. 1-4 (4) 327.25 212.75

Turkish Stamps of 1913-18 Hstmpd. in Black or Red

(The Srch. reads "Post, Piastre 3")

1921 **On Stamps of 1913** ***Perf. 12***
5 A24 3pi on 2pa red lilac 35.00 25.00
a. On No. 1 47.50 72.50
b. As #5, surcharge in red 950.00
c. As #5a, surcharge in red 950.00
6 A25 3pi on 4pa dk brown 30.00 30.00
a. On No. 2 160.00 175.00
7 A25 3pi on 4pa dk brn (R) 150.00 175.00
a. On No. 2 160.00 175.00
8 A27 3pi on 6pa dk blue 125.00 150.00
a. On No. 3 300.00 325.00
9 A27 3pi on 6pa dk bl (R) 62.50 75.00
a. On No. 3 110.00 140.00

On Stamps of 1916-18

10 A42 3pi on 2pa vio (R) 62.50 75.00
a. On No. 4 97.50 125.00
Nos. 5-10 (6) 465.00 530.00

Turkish Revenue Stamps Handstamped in Turkish "Osmanli Postalari, 1336" (Ottoman Post, 1920).

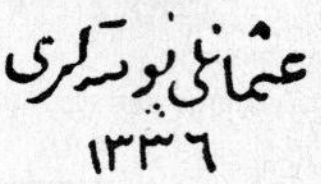
Type a

Dash at upper left is set high. Bottom (date) line is 8½mm long.

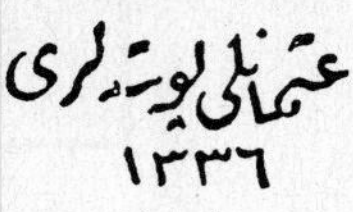
Type b

Dash at upper left is set lower. Bottom (date) line is 10mm long.

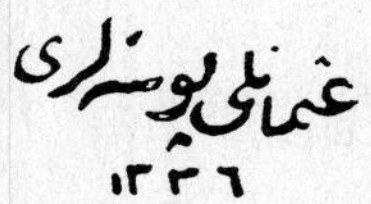
Type c

Dash at upper left is set lower. Bottom (date) line is 9mm long.

Religious Tribunals Revenue R1

12 R1 1pi grn (a, b, c) 750.00 300.00
13 R1 5pi ultra (a, b) *16,000. 15,500.*
14 R1 50pi gray grn (a, b, c) 25.00 35.00
Cut cancellation 3.00
15 R1 100pi buff (a) 140.00 97.50
a. 100pi yellow (a) 95.00 72.50
Cut cancellation 7.50
16 R1 500pi org (a) 225.00 150.00
Cut cancellation 20.00
17 R1 1000pi brn (a) 3,000. 1,750.
Cut cancellation 175.00

See Nos. 29-32.

Court Costs Revenue R2

Black Overprint

18 R2 10pa grn (b, c) 110.00 100.00
19 R2 1pi ultra (a, c) — *19,000.*
20 R2 5pi rose (c) *17,500.* —
21 R2 50pi ocher (a, b, c) 50.00 50.00
a. 50pi yellow (a, b, c) 12.00 17.00
Cut cancellation, #21, 21a 2.00
22 R2 100pi brown (a) 150.00 100.00
Cut cancellation 20.00
23 R2 500pi slate (a) 325.00 325.00
Cut cancellation 20.00

See Nos. 24, 33-39.

Notary Public Revenue R3

Design R2 Overprinted "Katibi Adliye Masus dur" in Red

24 R3 50pi ocher (a) 1,250. 150.00
Cut cancellation 20.00

Laborer's Passport Tax Stamp — R4

Notary Public Revenue — R5

Black Overprint

25 R4 2pi emerald (a, c) — *22,000.*
26 R5 100pi yellow brn (a) 1,250. 150.00
Cut cancellation 30.00

See Nos. 46-48.

Theater Tax Stamp — R6

Land Registry Revenue R7

27 R6 20pa black *5,000. 5,000.*
a. 20pa black *grayish* — —
28 R7 2pi blue black *6,250. 6,250.*

See Nos. 40, 45.

Hejaz Railway Tax Stamp — R8

Black Overprint

Perf. 11½

28A R8 2pi dk red & bl (b) 1,750. *1,750.*

See Nos. 53-57.

Turkish Revenue Stamps Overprinted in Turkish "Osmanli Postalari, 1337" (Ottoman Post, 1921)

On #29-63

Perf. 12

29 R1 10pa slate 20.00 *16.00*
a. Handstamped overprint 100.00 *50.00*
b. Double overprint
30 R1 1pi green 32.50 20.00
a. Inverted overprint 35.00 22.50
b. Handstamped overprint *3,500. 3,250.*
31 R1 5pi ultra 29.00 14.50
a. "1337" inverted 100.00 90.00
b. Half used as 2½pi on cover
c. Handstamped overprint 875.00 875.00
Nos. 29-31 (3) 81.50 50.50

Handstamped Overprint

32 R1 50pi green *7,250. 7,250.*

Design R2 Overprinted

33 R2 10pa green 24.50 24.50
a. Handstamped overprint 3,500. *3,500.*
34 R2 1pi ultra 50.00 25.00
a. Handstamped overprint 875.00 875.00
35 R2 5pi red 24.50 25.00
a. Inverted overprint
b. "1337" inverted *100.00* 100.00
c. Half used as 2½pi on cover
d. Handstamped overprint 7,500 *7,500.*
e. 5pi rose 72.50 25.00
f. As "e," handstamped overprint *5,500. 5,500.*
36 R2 50pi ocher, handstamped ovpt. 500.00 100.00
Cut cancellation 20.00
Nos. 33-36 (4) 599.00 174.50

Design R3 Overprinted

Additional Turkish Overprint in Red or Black

37 R3 10pa green (R) *100.00* 60.00
38 R3 1pi ultra (R) 72.50 50.00
39 R3 5pi rose (Bk) 72.50 50.00
a. "1337" inverted *200.00 200.00*
b. Handstamped overprint *7,000. 7,000.*
c. 5pi carmine 100.00 60.00
d. As "c," handstamped overprint *8,500.*
Nos. 37-39 (3) 245.00 160.00

Design R7 Overprinted

40 R7 2pi blue black 125.00 110.00
a. Handstamped overprint *5,500. 5,500.*

R12

1921 Overprinted in Black *Perf. 12*

41 R12 5pi green 150.00 125.00
Cut cancellation 17.50
a. Handstamped overprint *5,500. 5,000.*

Museum Tax Stamp R13

Overprinted in Black

42 R13 1pi ultra 475.00 425.00
a. Handstamped overprint *5,500. 5,500.*
43 R13 5pi deep green 525.00 475.00
a. Handstamped overprint *5,500. 5,500.*

Handstamped Overprint

44 R13 5pi dark vio *7,000. 7,000.*

The overprint variety "337" for "1337" exists on Nos. 42-43.

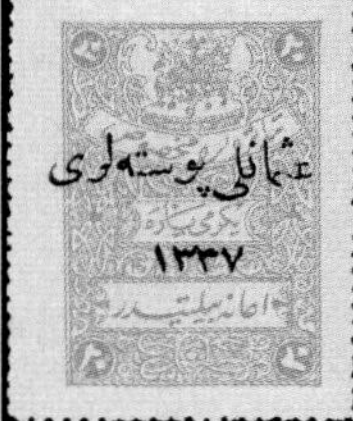

Design R6 Overprinted

Perf. 12, 12½

45 R6 20pa black 12.50 5.00
a. Date 4½mm high 15.00
b. "337" for "1337" 25.00
c. Silk paper 725.00 725.00
d. White paper 15.00 10.00

Design R5 Overprinted

46 R5 10pa green 25.00 25.00
a. Overprint 21mm long
b. "131" for "1337"
47 R5 1pi ultra 37.50 25.00
a. "13" for "1337" *50.00 50.00*
b. "131" for "1337" *50.00 50.00*
c. Inverted overprint *90.00 90.00*
d. Handstamped overprint *4,500. 4,500.*
48 R5 5pi red 62.50 25.00
a. Inverted overprint *90.00 90.00*
b. "131" for "1337" *85.00 85.00*
c. Handstamped overprint *4,500. 4,400.*
d. 5pi pink 500.00 500.00
e. As "d," handstamped overprint *5,500. 5,500.*
Nos. 46-48 (3) 125.00 75.00

R16

Perf. 11½, 11½x11

Overprinted in Black

49 R16 10pa pink 4.00 1.50
a. Imperf.
b. Date "1237" 5.00 2.00
d. Inverted overprint 15.00
e. Handstamped overprint *1,950. 1,950.*
50 R16 1pi yellow 10.00 5.00
a. Overprint 18mm long 10.00 5.00
b. Date "1332" 12.00
c. Date "1317"
d. Inverted overprint 30.00
e. Handstamped overprint *1,950. 1,950.*
51 R16 2pi yellow grn 12.50 5.00
a. Date "1237" 15.00
b. Date "1317"
c. Imperf.
d. Inverted overprint 40.00 9.00
e. Handstamped overprint — —
52 R16 5pi red 20.00 1.00
a. Horiz. pair, imperf. vert.
b. Inverted overprint 25.00 7.50
c. Double overprint 30.00 12.50
d. Date "1332" 45.00
e. Half used as 2½pi on cover
f. Overprint 18mm long 20.00 7.50
g. Handstamped overprint *1,950. 1,950.*
Nos. 49-52 (4) 46.50 12.50

Design R8 Overprinted
Turkish Inscriptions

20 Paras

1 Piaster

2 Piasters

5 Piasters

1921 Dark Red & Blue *Perf. 11½*

53 R8 20pa on 1pi 75.00 75.00
54 R8 1pi on 1pi 7.50 4.00
55 R8 2pi on 1pi 7.50 4.00
a. Inverted surcharge 25.00
56 R8 5pi on 1pi 12.00 6.00
Nos. 53-56 (4) 102.00 89.00

See No. 57.

No. 54 Overprinted

57 R8 1pi on 1pi dk red & bl 50.00 50.00

Hejaz Railway Tax Stamp — R19

Overprinted in Black

58 R19 1pi grn & brn red 6.00 4.00
a. Double overprint
b. Handstamped overprint

The errors "1307," "1331" and "2337" occur once in each sheet of Nos. 53-58.

Naval League Labels — R20

Overprinted in Black

1921 *Perf. 12x11½*

59 R20 1pa orange 11.00 15.00
a. Date "1327" 30.00 30.00
60 R20 2pa indigo 12.00 15.00
61 R20 5pa green 15.00 17.50
62 R20 10pa brown 30.00 30.00
63 R20 40pa red brown 225.00 190.00
Nos. 59-63 (5) 293.00 267.50
Set, never hinged 1,100.

The error "2337" occurs on all values of this issue.

The Naval League stamps have pictures of three Turkish warships. They were sold for the benefit of sailors of the fleet but did not pay postage until they were overprinted in 1921.

Turkish Stamps of 1915-20 Overprinted

a

b

The overprints on Nos. 64-77 read "Adana December 1st, 1921." This issue commemorated the withdrawal of the French from Cilicia.

On No. 71 the lines of the overprint are further apart than on Nos. 68-70 and 73-74.

1921 *Perf. 12*

64 A44 (a) 10pa grn (424) 10.00 7.00
65 A45 (a) 20pa deep rose (425) 10.00 7.00
a. Inverted overprint 30.00
66 A51 (a) 25pi car, *straw* (434) 20.00 *25.00*
a. Double overprint
b. Inverted overprint 60.00 37.50
Nos. 64-66 (3) 40.00 39.00

On Newspaper Stamp of 1915

67 A21 (a) 5pa och (P132) 90.00 *150.00*

On Stamp of 1915

68 A22 (b) 5pa och (328) 350.00 *400.00*

On Stamps of 1917-18

69 A53 (b) 5pi on 2pa (547) 15.00 *17.50*
70 A53 (b) 5pi on 2pa (548) 15.00 *17.50*

On Stamp of 1919

71 A57 (b) 35pi on 1pi bl (Bk; 579) 42.50 *50.00*
a. Inverted surcharge 100.00

On Newspaper Stamp of 1915

72 A21 (b) 5pa och (P132) *200.00 200.00*

On No. 72 the overprint is vertical, half reading up and half reading down.

On Stamps of 1920

73 A32 (b) 3pi blue (594) 15.00 12.50
74 A36 (b) 10pi gray vio (596) 20.00 20.00

On Postage Due Stamps of 1914

75 D1 (a) 5pa claret (J63) 350.00 350.00
76 D2 (a) 20pa red (J64) 350.00 400.00
a. Inverted overprint 750.00
77 D3 (b) 1pi dk bl (J65) 350.00 400.00
a. Inverted overprint *750.00 750.00*
Nos. 75-77 (3) 1,050. 1,150.

Withdrawal of the French from Cilicia. Forged overprints exist.

Pact of Revenge, Burning Village at Top — A21

Izmir Harbor — A22

Mosque of Selim, Adrianople A23

Mosque of Selim, Konya — A24

Soldier — A25

Legendary Gray Wolf — A26

Snake Castle and Seyhan River, Adana — A27

Parliament Building at Sivas — A28

A29

Mosque at Urfa — A30

Map of Anatolia A31

Declaration of Faith from the Koran — A32

1922 Litho. *Perf. 11½*

78 A21 10pa violet brn 1.00 .25
Never hinged 2.50
79 A22 20pa blue grn 1.00 .25
Never hinged 2.50
80 A23 1pi dp blue 1.50 .35
Never hinged 3.25
81 A24 2pi red brown 3.00 .50
Never hinged 14.50
82 A25 5pi dk blue 3.00 .50
Never hinged 13.50
83 A26 10pi dk brown 12.50 .75
Never hinged 50.00
a. Vert. pair, imperf between 100.00
b. Vert. strip of 3, imperf between 300.00
84 A27 25pi rose 15.00 2.00
Never hinged 72.50
85 A28 50pi indigo 1.50 15.00
Never hinged 5.00
86 A29 50pi dk gray 1.50 1.25
Never hinged 5.00
87 A30 100pi violet 75.00 8.00
Never hinged 375.00
Cut cancellation 2.00
88 A31 200pi slate 200.00 62.50
Never hinged 975.00
Cut cancellation 10.00
89 A32 500pi green 145.00 32.50
Never hinged 550.00
Cut cancellation 14.00
Nos. 78-89 (12) 460.00 123.85
Set, never hinged 2,075.
Set, ovptd. "SPECIMEN" 750.00

Imperf

79a A22 20pa 25.00 *30.00*
80a A23 1pi 20.00 *20.00*
82a A25 5pi 20.00 *20.00*
84a A27 25pi 35.00 *30.00*
85a A28 50pi 27.50 *30.00*

Stamps of Type A23 Overprinted

1922

90 A23 1pi deep blue 7.25 15.00
Never hinged 14.50
91 A23 5pi deep blue 7.25 20.00
Never hinged 14.50
92 A23 10pi brown 7.25 20.00
Never hinged 14.50
93 A23 25pi rose 10.00 25.00
Never hinged 14.50
94 A23 50pi slate 12.50 25.00
Never hinged 22.50
95 A23 100pi violet 17.50 37.50
Never hinged 35.00
96 A23 200pi black vio 17.50 50.00
Never hinged 35.00
97 A23 500pi blue green 25.00 75.00
Never hinged 47.50
Nos. 90-97 (8) 104.25 267.50
Set, never hinged 300.00

Withdrawal of the French from Cilicia and the return of the Kemalist Natl. army. The overprint reads: "Adana, Jan. 5, 1922."

No. 90-97 without overprint were presented to some high government officials.

First Parliament House, Ankara — A33

1922 Litho.

98 A33 5pa violet .75 2.50
Never hinged 2.00
99 A33 10pa green 1.75 2.50
Never hinged 5.25
100 A33 20pa pale red 2.50 2.00
Never hinged 7.00
101 A33 1pi brown org 12.00 1.50
Never hinged 40.00
102 A33 2pi red brown 20.00 4.25
Never hinged 77.50
103 A33 3pi rose 6.00 .70
Never hinged 12.00
a. Arabic "13" in right corner 10.00 7.50
b. Thin grayish paper 55.00 7.50
Never hinged *210.00*
Nos. 98-103 (6) 43.00 13.45
Set, never hinged 140.00

Nos. 98-103, 103b exist imperf. In 1923 several stamps of Turkey and Turkey in Asia were overprinted in Turkish for advertising purposes. The overprint reads: "Izmir Economic Congress, 17 Feb., 1339."

POSTAGE DUE STAMPS

D1

1922 Litho. *Perf. 11½*

J1 D1 20pa dull green 1.00 5.00
Never hinged 2.50
a. Imperf. *25.00*
J2 D1 1pi gray green 1.00 5.00
Never hinged 2.50
J3 D1 2pi red brown 2.50 17.50
Never hinged 7.25
J4 D1 3pi rose 4.50 25.00
Never hinged 17.00
J5 D1 5pi dark blue 6.00 55.00
Never hinged 24.00
Nos. J1-J5 (5) 15.00
Set, never hinged 55.00
Set, ovptd. "SPECIMEN" 200.00

TURKS & CAICOS ISLANDS

'tərks ən˛d˛ ' kā-kəs 'ī-lənds

LOCATION — A group of islands in the West Indies, at the southern extremity of the Bahamas
GOVT. — British colony; a dependency of Jamaica until 1959
AREA — 192 sq. mi.
POP. — 7,436 (1980)
CAPITAL — Grand Turk

12 Pence = 1 Shilling
20 Shillings = 1 Pound

Catalogue values for unused stamps in this country are for Never Hinged items, beginning with Scott 90.

Dependency's Badge
A6 A7

1900-04 Engr. Wmk. 2 *Perf. 14*

1 A6 ½p green 3.00 *4.50*
2 A6 1p rose 4.00 .85
3 A6 2p black brown 1.10 *1.40*
4 A6 2½p gray blue ('04) 2.00 1.10
a. 2½p blue ('00) 11.50 *17.50*
5 A6 4p orange 4.25 *8.00*
6 A6 6p violet 2.75 *7.50*
7 A6 1sh purple brn 3.75 *24.00*

Wmk. 1

8 A7 2sh violet 50.00 *80.00*
9 A7 3sh brown lake 80.00 *110.00*
Nos. 1-9 (9) 150.85 *237.35*

1905-08 Wmk. 3

10 A6 ½p green 6.50 .25
11 A6 1p carmine 20.00 .55
12 A6 3p violet, *yel* ('08) 2.50 *7.00*
Nos. 10-12 (3) 29.00 *7.80*

King Edward VII — A8

1909, Sept. 2 *Perf. 14*

13 A8 ½p yellow green .85 .45
14 A8 1p carmine 1.40 .45
15 A8 2p gray 6.50 1.60
16 A8 2½p ultra 8.00 4.25
17 A8 3p violet, *yel* 2.75 2.75
18 A8 4p red, *yel* 3.75 *8.00*
19 A8 6p violet 8.00 7.00
20 A8 1sh black, *green* 8.00 *9.50*
21 A8 2sh red, *grn* 45.00 *70.00*
22 A8 3sh black, *red* 47.50 *45.00*
Nos. 13-22 (10) 131.75 *149.00*

Turk's-Head Cactus — A9

1910-11 Wmk. 3

23 A9 ¼p claret 2.00 1.10
24 A9 ¼p red ('11) .70 .50

See Nos. 36, 44.

George V — A10

1913-16

25 A10 ½p yellow green .55 *2.00*
26 A10 1p carmine 1.10 *2.50*
27 A10 2p gray 2.50 *4.00*
28 A10 2½p ultra 2.50 *3.50*
29 A10 3p violet, *yel* 2.50 *12.50*
30 A10 4p scarlet, *yel* 1.10 *11.00*
31 A10 5p olive grn ('16) 7.50 *25.00*
32 A10 6p dull violet 2.75 *4.00*
33 A10 1sh orange 1.75 *5.75*
34 A10 2sh red, *bl grn* 18.00 *42.00*
a. 2sh red, *grnsh white* ('19) 30.00 *80.00*
b. 2sh red, *emerald* ('21) 55.00 *80.00*
35 A10 3sh black, *red* 17.50 30.00
Nos. 25-35 (11) 57.75 142.25

Issued: 5p, 5/18/16; others, 4/1/13.
For overprints see Nos. MR1-MR13.

1921, Apr. 23 Wmk. 4

36 A9 ¼p red 4.75 *26.00*
37 A10 ½p green 3.50 *6.50*
38 A10 1p scarlet 1.10 *6.25*
39 A10 2p gray 1.10 *21.00*
40 A10 2½p ultra 2.00 *8.50*
41 A10 5p olive green 12.00 *70.00*
42 A10 6p dull violet 7.50 *70.00*
43 A10 1sh brown orange 13.00 *48.00*
Nos. 36-43 (8) 44.95 *256.25*

A11

1922-26 Inscribed "Postage"

44 A9 ¼p gray black ('26) 1.25 1.10
45 A11 ½p green 5.50 *4.50*
46 A11 1p brown .65 *3.75*
47 A11 1½p rose red ('25) 9.00 *21.00*
48 A11 2p gray .65 *7.00*
49 A11 2½p violet, *yel* .65 *2.40*
50 A11 3p ultra .65 *7.00*
51 A11 4p red, *yel* 1.60 *21.00*
52 A11 5p yellow grn 1.25 *30.00*
53 A11 6p dull violet .95 *13.00*
54 A11 1sh orange 1.10 *25.00*
55 A11 2sh red, *green* 2.75 *12.50*

Wmk. 3

56 A11 2sh red, *green* ('25) 35.00 *110.00*
57 A11 3sh black, *red* ('25) 7.00 *40.00*
Nos. 44-57 (14) 68.00 *298.25*

Issued: #47, 56-57, 11/24; #44, 10/11; others, 11/20.

A12

Inscribed "Postage and Revenue"

1928, Mar. 1 Wmk. 4

60 A12 ½p green .95 .60
61 A12 1p brown .95 .90
62 A12 1½p red .95 *4.50*
63 A12 2p dk gray .95 .60
64 A12 2½p vio, *yel* .95 *6.25*
65 A12 3p ultra .95 *11.00*
66 A12 6p brown vio .95 *9.25*
67 A12 1sh brown org 4.50 *9.25*
68 A12 2sh red, *grn* 7.75 *45.00*
69 A12 5sh green, *yel* 13.50 *45.00*
70 A12 10sh violet, *bl* 62.50 *125.00*
Nos. 60-70 (11) 94.90 *257.35*

Common Design Types pictured following the introduction.

Silver Jubilee Issue
Common Design Type

1935, May 6 *Perf. 11x12*

71 CD301 ½p green & blk .40 1.00
72 CD301 3p ultra & brn 4.00 4.00
73 CD301 6p ol grn & lt bl 2.00 5.50
74 CD301 1sh brn vio & ind 2.00 4.00
Nos. 71-74 (4) 8.40 14.50
Set, never hinged 15.00

Coronation Issue
Common Design Type

1937, May 12 *Perf. 13½x14*

75 CD302 ½p deep green .25 .25
76 CD302 2p gray .45 .45
77 CD302 3p brt ultra .60 .45
Nos. 75-77 (3) 1.30 1.15
Set, never hinged 1.50

Raking Salt — A13

Salt Industry — A14

1938-45 Wmk. 4 *Perf. 12½*

78 A13 ¼p black .25 .25
79 A13 ½p green 2.40 .25
80 A13 1p brown .45 .25
81 A13 1½p carmine .45 .25
82 A13 2p gray .70 .30
83 A13 2½p orange 5.00 1.10
84 A13 3p ultra .30 .30
85 A13 6p rose violet 6.00 3.25
85A A13 6p blk brn ('45) .25 .25
86 A13 1sh bister 2.40 *11.00*
86A A13 1sh dk ol grn ('45) .25 .25
87 A14 2sh rose car 22.00 22.00
88 A14 5sh green 30.00 25.00
89 A14 10sh dp violet 10.00 *8.50*
Nos. 78-89 (14) 80.45 72.95
Set, never hinged 135.00

Catalogue values for unused stamps in this section, from this point to the end of the section, are for Never Hinged items.

Peace Issue
Common Design Type

1946, Nov. 4 Engr. *Perf. 13½x14*

90 CD303 2p gray black .25 .25
91 CD303 3p deep blue .25 .25

Silver Wedding Issue
Common Design Types

1948, Sept. 13 Photo. *Perf. 14x14½*

92 CD304 1p red brown .25 .25

Perf. 11½x11

Engr.; Name Typo.

93 CD305 10sh purple 11.00 *16.00*

Dependency's Badge — A17

Flag and Merchant Ship — A18

Map of the Islands A19

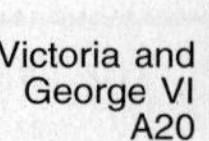

Victoria and George VI A20

1948, Dec. 14 Engr. *Perf. 12½*

94	A17	½p green	1.25	.25
95	A17	2p carmine	1.25	.25
96	A18	3p deep blue	1.25	.25
97	A19	6p violet	1.25	.30
98	A20	2sh ultra & blk	1.25	2.00
99	A20	5sh blue grn & blk	1.50	*6.00*
100	A20	10sh chocolate & blk	4.00	*6.00*
		Nos. 94-100 (7)	11.75	*15.05*

Cent. of political separation from the Bahamas.

UPU Issue

Common Design Types

Engr.; Name Typo. on 3p, 6p

Perf. 13½, 11x11½

1949, Oct. 10 Wmk. 4

101	CD306	2½p red orange	.25	*1.50*
102	CD307	3p indigo	1.90	1.25
103	CD308	6p chocolate	.30	1.00
104	CD309	1sh olive	.25	.35
		Nos. 101-104 (4)	2.70	4.10

Loading Bulk Salt — A21

Dependency's Badge — A22

Designs: 1p, Salt Cay. 1½p, Caicos mail. 2p, Grand Turk. 2½p, Sponge diving. 3p, South Creek. 4p, Map. 6p, Grand Turk Light. 1sh, Government House. 1sh6p, Cockburn Harbor. 2sh, Government offices. 5sh, Salt Loading.

1950, Aug. 2 Engr. *Perf. 12½*

105	A21	½p deep green	.75	.40
106	A21	1p chocolate	.80	*.75*
107	A21	1½p carmine	1.00	.55
108	A21	2p red orange	1.00	.40
109	A21	2½p olive green	1.00	.50
110	A21	3p ultra	1.00	.40
111	A21	4p rose car & blk	3.75	.70
112	A21	6p ultra & blk	3.00	.50
113	A21	1sh bl gray & blk	2.50	.40
114	A21	1sh6p red & blk	15.00	3.25
115	A21	2sh ultra & emer	6.50	*4.50*
116	A21	5sh black & ultra	25.00	8.50
117	A22	10sh purple & blk	27.00	*27.00*
		Nos. 105-117 (13)	88.30	*47.85*

WAR TAX STAMPS

Regular Issue of 1913-16 Overprinted

Black Overprint at Bottom of Stamp

1917 Wmk. 3 *Perf. 14*

MR1 A10 1p carmine	.25	*1.75*
a. Double overprint	200.00	*275.00*
b. "TAX" omitted		
c. Pair, one without ovpt.	700.00	
MR2 A10 3p violet, *yel*	1.40	*9.50*
a. Double overprint	110.00	

Black Overprint at Top or Middle of Stamp

1917

MR3 A10 1p carmine	.25	*1.40*
a. Inverted overprint	65.00	
b. Double overprint	65.00	*77.50*
c. Pair, one without overprint	650.00	
MR4 A10 3p violet, *yel*	.70	*2.25*
a. Double overprint	50.00	*60.00*
b. Dbl. ovpt., one inverted	375.00	

Same Overprint in Violet or Red

1918-19

MR5 A10 1p car (V) ('19)	1.50	*7.00*
a. Double overprint	24.00	
b. "WAR" omitted	200.00	
MR6 A10 3p violet, *yel* (R)	22.00	*60.00*
a. Double overprint	375.00	

Regular Issue of 1913-16 Overprinted in Black

1918

MR7 A10 1p carmine	.25	*2.75*
MR8 A10 3p violet, *yel*	6.50	*7.00*

Same Overprint in Red

1919

MR9 A10 3p violet, *yel*	.25	*6.00*

Regular Issue of 1913-16 Overprinted in Black

MR10 A10 1p carmine	.25	*2.25*
a. Double overprint	160.00	*190.00*
MR11 A10 3p violet, *yel*	.45	*3.00*

Regular Issue of 1913-16 Overprinted

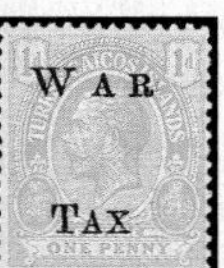

MR12 A10 1p carmine	.25	4.00
a. Double overprint	*100.00*	
MR13 A10 3p violet, *yel*	1.75	4.00

The bottom two rows of this setting show the words "War" and "Tax" about 1mm farther apart.

TURKS ISLANDS

'tərks 'ī-ləndz

LOCATION — West Indies, at the southern extremity of the Bahamas
AREA — 616 sq. mi.
POP. — 2,000 (approx.)
CAPITAL — Grand Turk

In 1848 the Turks Islands together with the Caicos group, lying to the northwest, were made a British colony. In 1873 the Colony became a dependency under the government of Jamaica although separate stamp issues were continued. Postage stamps inscribed Turks and Caicos Islands have been used since 1900.

12 Pence = 1 Shilling

PRE-STAMP POSTAL MARKINGS

Crowned Circle handstamp type V is pictured in the Crowned Circle Handstamps and Great Britain Used Abroad section.

Grand Turk

1857

A1 V "Turks Islands" crowned circle handstamp, on cover 6,350.

Values for unused stamps are for examples with original gum as defined in the catalogue introduction. Very fine examples of Nos. 1-42 will have generally rough perforations that cut into the design on one or more sides due to the narrow spacing of the stamps on the plates and imperfect perforating methods. Stamps with perfs clear of the design on all four sides are extremely scarce and will command substantially higher prices.

Because of the printing and imperfect perforating methods, stamps are often found scissor separated. Prices will not be adversely affected on those stamps where the scissor cut does not remove the perforations.

Watermark

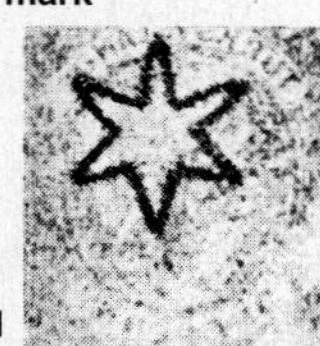

Wmk. 5 — Small Star

Queen Victoria — A1

Perf. 11½ to 13

1867 Unwmk. Engr.

1	A1	1p rose	67.50	67.50
2	A1	6p gray black	125.00	*140.00*
3	A1	1sh slate blue	105.00	67.50
		Nos. 1-3 (3)	297.50	275.00

Perf. 11 to 13x14 to 15

1873-79 Wmk. 5

4	A1	1p lake	57.50	57.50
5	A1	1p dull red ('79)	62.50	67.50
	a.	Horiz. pair, imperf. btwn.	*28,000.*	
	b.	Perf. 11-12	*1,100.*	
6	A1	1sh violet	*5,750.*	*2,250.*

Stamps offered as No. 6 are often examples from which the surcharge has been removed.

Stamps of 1867-79 Surcharged in Black

a b

c

12 settings of the ½p.

1881 Unwmk. *Perf. 11 to 13*

7 (a) ½p on 6p gray blk	100.00	*170.00*
7A (b) ½p on 6p gray blk	100.00	*150.00*
8 (b) ½p on 1sh slate bl	140.00	*200.00*
a. Double surcharge	*8,000.*	
8B (c) ½p on 1sh slate bl	*11,000.*	
c. Without fraction bar		
d. Double surcharge	15,000.	
e. #8a and #8Bd in pair	27,000.	

d

e

Perf. 11 to 13x14 to 15

Wmk. 5

9 (a) ½p on 1p dull red	150.00	200.00
a. Double surcharge		
10 (b) ½p on 1p dull red	60.00	*150.00*
11 (c) ½p on 1p dull red	210.00	*275.00*
a. Double surcharge	*4,250.*	
12 (d) ½p on 1p dull red	260.00	
a. Without fraction bar	1,150.	
b. Double surcharge		
13 (e) ½p on 1p dull red	600.00	
14 (a) ½p on 1sh violet	175.00	225.00
a. Double surcharge	4,000.	
15 (b) ½p on 1sh violet	140.00	*225.00*
a. Without fraction bar	625.00	
16 (c) ½p on 1sh violet	105.00	*190.00*

f

g

h

9 settings of the 2½p.

Perf. 11 to 13

Unwmk.

17 (f) 2½p on 6p gray blk	*16,000.*	
18 (g) 2½p on 6p gray blk	425.	*600.*
a. Horiz. pair, imperf. between	*42,500.*	
b. Double surcharge	*18,500.*	
19 (h) 2½p on 6p gray blk	250.	*475.*
a. Double surcharge	*17,500.*	

i

j

Perf. 11 to 13x14 to 15

Wmk. 5

20 (i) 2½p on 1sh violet	*4,000.*	
21 (h) 2½p on 1sh violet	625.00	*950.00*
22 (j) 2½p on 1sh violet	*9,500.*	

k

l

m

n

Perf. 11 to 13

Unwmk.

24 (k) 2½p on 6p gray blk	*9,500.*
25 (k) 2½p on 1sh slate bl	*27,000.*
26 (l) 2½p on 1sh slate bl	*1,500.*
27 (m) 2½p on 1sh slate bl	*2,200.*
a. Without fraction bar	*8,000.*
28 (n) 2½p on 1sh slate bl	*6,500.*

o

Perf. 11 to 13x14 to 15
Wmk. 5

29 (l) 2½p on 1p dull red 750.00
30 (o) 2½p on 1p dull red 1,500.
31 (l) 2½p on 1sh violet 850.00
a. Double surcharge of "½" *4,750.*
32 (o) 2½p on 1sh violet 1,350.
b. Double surcharge of "½" *9,000.*

p

q

r

6 settings of the 4p.

Perf. 11 to 13
Unwmk.

33 (p) 4p on 6p gray black 110.00 165.00
34 (q) 4p on 6p gray black 400.00 *575.00*
35 (r) 4p on 6p gray black 750.00 *500.00*

Examples of No. 33 with top of "4" painted in are sometimes offered as No. 35.

Perf. 11 to 13x14 to 15
Wmk. 5

36 (r) 4p on 1p dull red 950.00 625.00
a. Inverted surcharge 3,250.
37 (p) 4p on 1p dull red 850.00 550.00
a. Inverted surcharge
38 (p) 4p on 1sh violet 475.00 *750.00*
39 (q) 4p on 1sh violet *2,750.*

Wmk. Crown and C C (1)

1881 Engr. *Perf. 14*
40 A1 1p brown red 87.50 105.00
a. Diagonal half used as ½p on cover
41 A1 6p olive brown 165.00 210.00
42 A1 1sh slate green 210.00 155.00
Nos. 40-42 (3) 462.50 470.00

A2

1881 Typo.
43 A2 4p ultramarine 170.00 67.50

1882-95 Engr. Wmk. 2
44 A1 1p orange brn ('83) 100.00 35.00
a. Half used as ½p on cover 5,000.
45 A1 1p car lake ('89) 3.50 2.25
46 A1 6p yellow brn ('89) 5.50 *6.75*
47 A1 1sh black brn ('87) 7.25 5.25
a. 1sh deep brown 7.25 5.25

Typo.
Die A

48 A2 ½p dull green ('85) 7.25 6.50
a. ½p blue green ('82) 29.00 29.00
49 A2 2½p red brown ('82) 40.00 16.00
50 A2 4p gray ('84) 38.00 4.00
a. Half used as 2p on cover 5,000.

Die B

51 A2 ½p gray green ('94) 7.00 4.50
52 A2 2½p ultra ('93) 7.50 5.00
53 A2 4p dk vio & bl ('95) 11.00 15.00

For descriptions of dies A and B see "Dies of British Colonial Stamps" in table of contents.

1887 Engr. *Perf. 12*
54 A1 1p carmine lake 14.00 3.25
a. Horiz. pair, imperf. btwn. 28,000.

No. 49 Surcharged in Black

1889
55 A2 1p on 2½p red brn 24.00 *21.00*
a. Double surcharge
b. Double surcharge, one inverted
c. "One" omitted 1,800.
d. Half used as ½p on cover 5,500.

No. 55c caused by the misplacement of the surcharge. Stamps also exist from the same sheet reading "Penny One."

No. 50 Surcharged in Black

Two types of surcharge:
Type I — Upper bar continuous across sheet.
Type II — Upper bar breaks between stamps.

1893
56 A2 ½p on 4p gray (I) 225.00 180.00
a. Type II 3,250. 1,450.

This surcharge exists in five settings.

A3

1894 Typo.
57 A3 5p olive grn & carmine 12.50 *27.50*
a. Diag. half used as 2½p on cover *5,000.*

UBANGI-SHARI

ü-'baŋ-gē 'shär-ē

(Ubangi-Shari-Chad)

LOCATION — In Western Africa, north of the equator
GOVT. — French Colony
AREA — 238,767 sq. mi.
POP. — 833,916
CAPITAL — Bangui

In 1910 French Congo was divided into the three colonies of Gabon, Middle Congo and Ubangi-Shari and officially named "French Equatorial Africa." Under that name in 1934 the group, with the territory of Chad included, became a single administrative unit. See Gabon.

100 Centimes = 1 Franc

Stamps of Middle Congo Ovptd. in Black

1915-22 Unwmk. *Perf. 14x13½*
Chalky Paper

1 A1 1c ol gray & brn .35 .70
Never hinged .70
On cover 75.00
a. Double overprint 190.00
Never hinged 325.00
b. Imperf. 60.00
Never hinged 100.00
c. On ordinary paper .35 .70
Never hinged .70
On cover 75.00
2 A1 2c violet & brn .35 .70
Never hinged .70
On cover 75.00
a. On ordinary paper .35 .70
Never hinged .70
On cover 75.00
3 A1 4c blue & brn .70 *.70*
Never hinged 1.40
On cover 75.00
a. On ordinary paper .70 .70
Never hinged 1.40
On cover 75.00
4 A1 5c dk grn & bl .70 *1.00*
Never hinged 1.40
On cover 22.50
a. On ordinary paper 1.75 1.75
Never hinged 2.75
On cover 25.00
5 A1 5c yel & bl ('22) 1.00 *1.40*
Never hinged 2.10
On cover 25.00
6 A1 10c carmine & bl 1.40 *1.00*
Never hinged 2.75
On cover 14.50
a. On ordinary paper 4.50 4.50
Never hinged 7.75
On cover 30.00
7 A1 10c dp grn & bl grn ('22) 1.00 *1.40*
Never hinged 2.10
On cover 42.50
8 A1 15c brn vio & rose, ordinary paper 1.75 *2.10*
Never hinged 2.75
On cover 25.00
9 A1 20c brown & blue 3.50 *4.25*
Never hinged 7.00
On cover 22.50
On cover, single franking 32.50
a. On ordinary paper 3.50 4.25
Never hinged 7.00

Overprinted

10 A2 25c blue & grn 2.10 *2.10*
Never hinged 3.50
On cover 27.50
On cover, single franking 50.00
11 A2 25c bl grn & gray ('22) 1.40 1.40
Never hinged 2.10
On cover 12.50
12 A2 30c scarlet & grn 2.10 *2.10*
Never hinged 3.50
On cover 27.50
On cover, single franking 50.00
13 A2 30c dp rose & rose ('22) 1.00 *1.40*
Never hinged 2.10
On cover 37.50
On cover, single franking 65.00
14 A2 35c vio brn & bl 5.50 *5.50*
Never hinged 10.50
On cover 32.50
On cover, single franking 67.50
15 A2 40c dl grn & brn 5.50 *7.00*
Never hinged 10.50
On cover 45.00
On cover, single franking 90.00
16 A2 45c vio & red 5.50 *7.00*
Never hinged 10.50
On cover 55.00
On cover, single franking 105.00
a. On ordinary paper 8.50 9.00
Never hinged 14.00
On cover 65.00
17 A2 50c bl grn & red 7.00 *7.00*
Never hinged 10.50
On cover 50.00
On cover, single franking 105.00
a. On ordinary paper 8.50 9.00
Never hinged 10.50
On cover 55.00
18 A2 50c blue & grn ('22) 1.00 *1.40*
Never hinged 2.10
On cover 30.00
On cover, single franking 55.00
19 A2 75c brown & bl 14.00 14.00
Never hinged 21.00
On cover 70.00
On cover, single franking 140.00
20 A3 1fr dp grn & vio 14.00 14.00
Never hinged 21.00
On cover 80.00
On cover, single franking 160.00
21 A3 2fr vio & gray grn 14.00 *17.50*
Never hinged 27.50
On cover 100.00
On cover, single franking 190.00
22 A3 5fr blue & rose 42.50 *42.50*
Never hinged 70.00
On cover 170.00
On cover, single franking 275.00
Nos. 1-22 (22) 126.35 136.15

For surcharges see Nos. B1-B2.

Middle Congo of 1907-22 Ovptd. in Black or Red

1922
23 A1 1c violet & grn .70 *1.00*
Never hinged 1.00
On cover 75.00
a. Overprint omitted 170.00 *190.00*
Never hinged 275.00
b. Imperf. 40.00
Never hinged 62.50
c. As "a," imperf 175.00
Never hinged 275.00
24 A1 2c grn & salmon .70 *1.00*
Never hinged 1.00
On cover 75.00
25 A1 4c ol brn & brn 1.00 *1.40*
Never hinged 1.75
On cover 75.00
a. Overprint omitted 200.00 *225.00*
Never hinged 315.00
26 A1 5c indigo & rose 1.00 *1.40*
Never hinged 1.75
On cover 21.00
27 A1 10c dp grn & gray grn 1.75 *2.10*
Never hinged 2.75
On cover 45.00
28 A1 15c lt red & dl bl 1.75 *2.10*
Never hinged 2.75
On cover 27.50
29 A1 20c choc & salmon 5.00 *5.50*
Never hinged 7.00
On cover 27.50

Overprinted

30 A2 25c vio & salmon 7.00 *8.50*
Never hinged 14.00
On cover 27.50
31 A2 30c rose & pale rose 2.75 *3.50*
Never hinged 5.50
On cover 40.00
On cover, single franking 75.00
32 A2 35c vio & grn 4.75 *5.00*
Never hinged 7.00
On cover 35.00
On cover, single franking 50.00
33 A2 40c ind & vio (R) 4.75 *5.00*
Never hinged 7.00
On cover 35.00
On cover, single franking 50.00
34 A2 45c choc & vio 4.75 *5.00*
Never hinged 7.00
On cover 65.00
On cover, single franking 110.00
35 A2 50c dk bl & pale bl 2.75 *3.50*
Never hinged 4.25
On cover 35.00
On cover, single franking 70.00
36 A2 60c on 75c vio, *pnksh* 3.50 *4.25*
Never hinged 4.25
On cover 40.00
On cover, single franking 65.00
37 A2 75c choc & sal 5.00 *6.25*
Never hinged 10.50
On cover 70.00
On cover, single franking 125.00
38 A3 1fr grn & dl bl (R) 10.50 *11.00*
Never hinged 17.50
On cover 90.00
On cover, single franking 125.00
a. Overprint omitted 275.00
Never hinged 425.00
39 A3 2fr grn & salmon 14.00 *14.00*
Never hinged 21.00
On cover 105.00
On cover, single franking 190.00
40 A3 5fr grn & ol brn 21.00 *25.00*
Never hinged 35.00
On cover 140.00
On cover, single franking 225.00
Nos. 23-40 (18) 92.65 105.50

Nos. 23-29 with Additional Ovpt. in Black, Blue or Red

1924-33
41 A1 1c vio & grn (Bl) .35 *.50*
Never hinged .70
On cover 65.00
a. "OUBANGUI CHARI" omitted 140.00 140.00
Never hinged 225.00
42 A1 2c grn & sal (Bl) .35 *.55*
Never hinged .70
On cover 65.00
a. "OUBANGUI CHARI" omitted 140.00 140.00
Never hinged 225.00
b. Double overprint 150.00
Never hinged 240.00
43 A1 4c ol brn & brn (Bl) .35 *.55*
Never hinged .70
On cover 65.00
a. Double overprint (Bl + Bk) 175.00
Never hinged 275.00
b. "AEF" omitted 160.00
Never hinged 260.00
44 A1 5c ind & rose .35 *.55*
Never hinged .70
On cover 27.50
a. "OUBANGUI CHARI" omitted 130.00
Never hinged 200.00
45 A1 10c dp grn & gray grn .70 *.85*
Never hinged 1.40
On cover 20.00
46 A1 10c red org & bl ('25) .70 *.70*
Never hinged 1.40
On cover 30.00
47 A1 15c sal & dl bl .80 *.85*
Never hinged 1.40
On cover 16.00

48 A1 15c sal & dl bl (Bl) ('26) 1.00 *1.40*
Never hinged 1.40
On cover 27.50

49 A1 20c choc & salmon (Bl) 1.25 *1.40*
Never hinged 2.10
On cover 27.50

On Nos. 41-49 the color in ( ) refers to the overprint "Afrique Equatoriale Francaise."

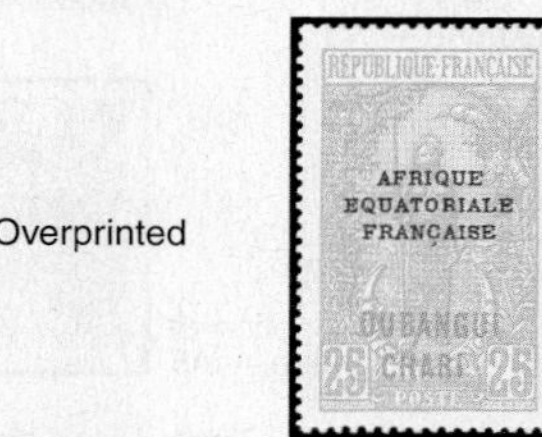
Overprinted

50 A2 25c vio & salmon (Bl) .70 .70
Never hinged 1.40
On cover 14.00
a. Imperf.

51 A2 30c rose & pale rose (Bl) .70 *1.00*
Never hinged 1.40
On cover 35.00
On cover, single franking 70.00

52 A2 30c choc & red ('25) .70 *1.00*
Never hinged 1.40
On cover 14.00
a. "OUBANGUI CHARI" omitted 140.00
Never hinged 225.00

53 A2 30c dk grn & grn ('27) 1.40 *1.75*
Never hinged 2.75
On cover 45.00

54 A2 35c vio & grn (Bl) .70 *1.00*
Never hinged 1.40
On cover 45.00
On cover, single franking 75.00
a. "OUBANGUI CHARI" omitted 275.00
Never hinged 450.00

55 A2 40c ind & vio (Bl) .70 *1.00*
Never hinged 1.40
On cover 50.00
On cover, single franking 80.00

56 A2 45c choc & vio (Bl) 1.00 *1.40*
Never hinged 2.10
On cover 16.00
On cover, single franking 27.50

57 A2 50c dk bl & pale bl (R) .70 *.70*
Never hinged 2.10
On cover 16.00
On cover, single franking 25.00

58 A2 50c gray & bl vio ('25) (R) 1.40 *1.40*
Never hinged 2.75
On cover 14.00

59 A2 60c on 75c dk vio, *pnksh* (R) .70 *.55*
Never hinged 1.40
On cover 21.00
On cover, single franking 35.00

60 A2 65c org brn & bl ('28) 1.40 *1.75*
Never hinged 2.75
On cover 35.00
On cover, single franking 75.00

61 A2 75c choc & sal (Bl) 1.75 *2.10*
Never hinged 3.50
On cover 35.00
On cover, single franking 80.00

62 A2 75c dp bl & lt bl ('25) (R) 1.40 *1.40*
Never hinged 2.10
On cover 25.00
On cover, single franking 37.50
a. "OUBANGUI CHARI" omitted 140.00
Never hinged 225.00

63 A2 75c rose & dk brn ('28) 2.10 *2.50*
Never hinged 3.50
On cover 25.00
On cover, single franking 27.50

64 A2 90c brn red & pink ('30) 4.25 *5.00*
Never hinged 7.00
On cover 65.00
On cover, single franking 150.00

65 A3 1fr grn & ind (Bk + Bl) ('25) .70 *1.00*
Never hinged 1.40
On cover 35.00
On cover, single franking 70.00

66 A3 1fr grn & ind (R + Bl) 1.40 *2.10*
Never hinged 3.50
On cover 35.00
On cover, single franking 70.00

67 A3 1.10fr bister & bl ('28) 3.50 *3.50*
Never hinged 5.50
On cover 170.00
On cover, single franking 375.00

68 A3 1.25fr mag & lt grn ('33) 10.50 *10.50*
Never hinged 14.00
On cover 50.00
On cover, single franking 110.00

69 A3 1.50fr ultra & bl ('30) 7.00 *7.00*
Never hinged 10.50
On cover 55.00
On cover, single franking 140.00

70 A3 1.75fr dk brn & dp buff ('33) 10.50 *14.00*
Never hinged 17.50
On cover 45.00
On cover, single franking 55.00

71 A3 2fr grn & red 1.40 *2.10*
Never hinged 3.50
On cover 65.00
On cover, single franking 125.00
a. "OUBANGUI CHARI" omitted 1,250. 1,050.
b. "OUBANGUI CHARI" double 1,200.
Never hinged 1,650.

72 A3 3fr red vio ('30) 5.00 *5.50*
Never hinged 9.00
On cover 90.00
On cover, single franking 170.00

73 A3 5fr grn & ol brn (Bl) 4.50 *5.50*
Never hinged 7.00
On cover 70.00
On cover, single franking 140.00
Nos. 41-73 (33) 69.95 81.80

On Nos. 65, 66 the first overprint color refers to OUBANGUI CHARI.
For surcharges see Nos. 74-81.

Types of 1924 Issue Surcharged with New Values in Black or Red

1925-26

74 A3 65c on 1fr vio & ol 2.10 2.10
Never hinged 3.50
On cover 80.00
On cover, single franking 190.00
a. "65" omitted 140.00
Never hinged 225.00

75 A3 85c on 1fr vio & ol 2.10 2.10
Never hinged 3.50
On cover 70.00
On cover, single franking 140.00
a. "AFRIQUE EQUATORIALE FRANCAISE" omitted 140.00 160.00
Never hinged 225.00
b. Double surcharge 160.00
Never hinged 250.00

76 A3 1.25fr on 1fr dk bl & ultra (R) ('26) 1.40 *2.25*
Never hinged 2.10
On cover 75.00
On cover, single franking 160.00
a. "1f25" omitted 165.00
Never hinged 260.00

Bars cover old denomination on No. 76.

Types of 1924 Issue Surcharged with New Values and Bars

1927

77 A2 90c on 75c brn red & rose red 2.10 *2.75*
Never hinged 3.50
On cover 70.00
On cover, single franking 125.00

78 A3 1.50fr on 1fr ultra & bl 2.10 *2.75*
Never hinged 3.50
On cover 65.00
On cover, single franking 110.00

79 A3 3fr on 5fr org brn & dl red 3.50 *3.50*
Never hinged 7.00
On cover 110.00
On cover, single franking 225.00

80 A3 10fr on 5fr ver & vio 17.50 *19.00*
Never hinged 25.00
On cover 160.00
On cover, single franking 300.00

81 A3 20fr on 5fr vio & gray 27.50 *29.00*
Never hinged 42.50
On cover 190.00
On cover, single franking 340.00
Nos. 77-81 (5) 52.70 *57.00*

Common Design Types pictured following the introduction.

Colonial Exposition Issue
Common Design Types

1931 Engr. *Perf. 12½*
Name of Country Typo. in Black

82 CD70 40c deep green 5.00 5.00
Never hinged 8.50
On cover 110.00

83 CD71 50c violet 5.00 5.00
Never hinged 8.50
On cover 95.00

84 CD72 90c red orange 5.50 5.50
Never hinged 9.00
On cover 170.00
On cover, single franking 225.00
a. Imperf. 120.00
Never hinged 175.00

85 CD73 1.50fr dull blue 5.50 5.50
Never hinged 9.00
On cover 150.00
On cover, single franking 200.00
Nos. 82-85 (4) 21.00 21.00

SEMI-POSTAL STAMPS

Regular Issue of 1915 Surcharged

1916 Unwmk. *Perf. 14x13½*
Chalky Paper

B1 A1 10c + 5c car & blue 2.75 3.25
Never hinged 5.00
On cover 100.00
a. Inverted surch. 160.00
b. Double surcharge 160.00
c. Double surch., one invtd. 125.00 125.00
d. Vertical surcharge 140.00 140.00
e. No period under "C" 17.50 17.50
Never hinged 25.00

Regular Issue of 1915 Surcharged in Carmine

B2 A1 10c + 5c car & blue 1.75 *2.10*
Never hinged 2.75
On cover 70.00

POSTAGE DUE STAMPS

Postage Due Stamps of France Overprinted

1928 Unwmk. *Perf. 14x13½*

J1 D2 5c light blue 1.40 2.10
Never hinged 2.75
On cover 105.00

J2 D2 10c gray brown 1.75 2.10
Never hinged 2.75
On cover 105.00

J3 D2 20c olive green 1.75 2.10
Never hinged 2.75
On cover 105.00

J4 D2 25c bright rose 1.75 2.10
Never hinged 3.50
On cover 110.00

J5 D2 30c light red 1.75 2.10
Never hinged 3.50
On cover 110.00

J6 D2 45c blue green 1.75 2.10
Never hinged 3.50
On cover 110.00

J7 D2 50c brown violet 2.50 *3.50*
Never hinged 4.25
On cover 125.00

J8 D2 60c yellow brown 2.75 *3.50*
Never hinged 5.50
On cover 140.00

J9 D2 1fr red brown 3.50 *5.00*
Never hinged 7.00
On cover 150.00

J10 D2 2fr orange red 7.00 *7.00*
Never hinged 10.50
On cover 170.00

J11 D2 3fr bright violet 7.00 *7.00*
Never hinged 10.50
On cover 190.00
Nos. J1-J11 (11) 32.90 38.60

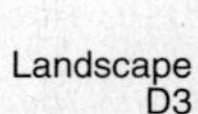

Landscape D3

Emile Gentil — D4

1930 Typo.

J12 D3 5c dp bl & olive .70 *1.05*
Never hinged 1.40
On cover 50.00

J13 D3 10c dk red & brn 1.05 *1.40*
Never hinged 2.10
On cover 50.00

J14 D3 20c green & brn 1.05 *1.40*
Never hinged 2.10
On cover 50.00

J15 D3 25c lt bl & brn 1.40 *1.75*
Never hinged 3.50
On cover 55.00

J16 D3 30c bis brn & Prus bl 2.50 *2.75*
Never hinged 5.00
On cover 65.00

J17 D3 45c Prus bl & ol 3.25 *3.50*
Never hinged 7.00
On cover 65.00

J18 D3 50c red vio & brn 5.25 *6.00*
Never hinged 7.00
On cover 70.00

J19 D3 60c gray lil & bl blk 5.50 *5.50*
Never hinged 10.50
On cover 75.00

J20 D4 1fr bis brn & bl blk 5.25 *6.00*
Never hinged 7.00
On cover 90.00

J21 D4 2fr violet & brown 5.50 *7.00*
Never hinged 10.50
On cover 100.00

J22 D4 3fr dp red & brn 7.00 *8.50*
Never hinged 14.00
On cover 110.00
Nos. J12-J22 (11) 38.45 *44.85*

Stamps of Ubangi-Shari were replaced in 1936 by those of French Equatorial Africa.

UGANDA

ü-'gan-də

LOCATION — East Africa, at the Equator and separated from the Indian Ocean by Kenya and Tanzania
AREA — 91,343 sq. mi.
POP. — 13,990,000 (est. 1983)
CAPITAL — Kampala

Stamps of 1898-1902 were replaced by those issued for Kenya, Tanganyika and Uganda.

Cowries (50 = 4 Pence)
16 Annas = 1 Rupee (1896)

Unused values for Nos. 2-68 are for stamps without gum. Very fine examples will be evenly cut and will show at least two full typewritten framelines.

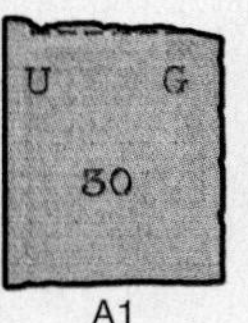
A1

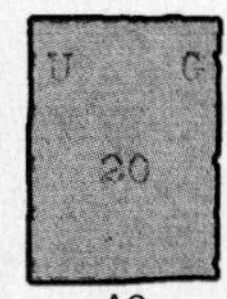
A2

Nos. 1-53 were produced with a typewriter by Rev. Ernest Millar of the Church Missionary Society. They were 20-26mm wide, with nine stamps in a horizontal row. Later two more were added to each row, and the stamps became narrower, 16-18mm.

Rev. Millar got a new typewriter in 1895, and the stamps he typed on it have a different appearance. A violet ribbon in the machine, inserted late in 1895, resulted in Nos. 35-53.

Nos. 1-53 are on thin, tough, white paper, laid horizontally with traces of a few vertical lines.

Forgeries of Nos. 1-53 are known.

Without Gum
Wide Letters
Typewritten on Thin Laid Paper
Stamps 20 to 26mm wide

1895 Unwmk. *Imperf.*

1 A1 10(c) black *5,750.* 3,750.
2 A1 20(c) black *9,600.* *2,350.*
a. "U A" instead of "U G" *7,750.*
3 A1 30(c) black *2,500.* *2,000.*
4 A1 40(c) black *7,750.* 2,850.
5 A1 50(c) black *1,800.* *1,400.*
a. "U A" instead of "U G" *10,000.*
6 A1 60(c) black *3,250.* 2,850.

Surcharged with New Value in Black, Pen-written

9 A1 10 on 30(c) black *85,000.*
10 A1 10 on 50(c) black *85,000.*
11 A1 15 on 10(c) black *85,000.*
12 A1 15 on 20(c) black *65,000.*
13 A1 15 on 40(c) black *85,000.*
14 A1 15 on 50(c) black *80,000.*
15 A1 25 on 50(c) black *85,000.*
16 A1 50 on 60(c) black *85,000.*

Stamps 16 to 18mm wide

17 A1 5(c) black 4,000. *1,650.*
18 A1 10(c) black 4,000. *2,000.*
19 A1 15(c) black *2,500.* *1,900.*
a. Verticaly laid paper *6,500.*
20 A1 20(c) black *4,000.* *1,900.*
a. Vertically laid paper *8,250.*
21 A1 25(c) black *2,000.* *2,000.*
22 A1 30(c) black *10,500.* *10,000.*
23 A1 40(c) black *10,000.* *10,000.*
24 A1 50(c) black *4,750.* *5,750.*
25 A1 60(c) black *10,000.* *10,000.*

Narrow Letters
Stamps 16 to 18mm wide

26 A2 5(c) black *2,000.*
27 A2 10(c) black *2,150.*
28 A2 15(c) black *2,150.*
29 A2 20(c) black *1,800.*
30 A2 25(c) black *2,000.*
31 A2 30(c) black *2,250.*
32 A2 40(c) black *2,000.*
33 A2 50(c) black *2,150.*
34 A2 60(c) black *3,200.*
35 A2 5(c) violet *900.* *825.*
36 A2 10(c) violet *825.* *825.*
37 A2 15(c) violet *1,400.* *750.*
38 A2 20(c) violet *600.* *375.*
a. "G A" instead of "U G"
b. Vertically laid paper 3,850.
39 A2 25(c) violet *2,300.* *2,000.*
40 A2 30(c) violet *2,850.* *1,400.*

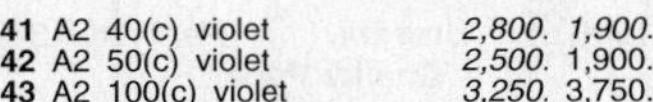

41 A2 40(c) violet *2,800.* *1,900.*
42 A2 50(c) violet *2,500.* 1,900.
43 A2 100(c) violet *3,250.* 3,750.

As a favor to a philatelist, 35c and 45c denominations were made in black and violet. They were not intended for postal use and no rate called for those denominations.

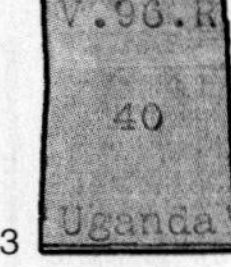
A3

1896

44 A3 5(c) violet *950.* *1,250.*
45 A3 10(c) violet *1,050.* *825.*
46 A3 15(c) violet *950.* *950.*
47 A3 20(c) violet *500.* *275.*
48 A3 25(c) violet *875.* *1,150.*
49 A3 30(c) violet *950.* *1,050.*
50 A3 40(c) violet *1,100.* *1,150.*
51 A3 50(c) violet *950.* *1,000.*
52 A3 60(c) violet *2,000.* *2,500.*
53 A3 100(c) violet *1,900.* 2,500.

A4

Overprinted "L" in Black

1896 Typeset White Paper

54 A4 1a black (thin "1") 210. 190.
a. Small "O" in "POSTAGE" 1,550. 1,300.
55 A4 2a black 135. *140.*
a. Small "O" in "POSTAGE" 615. *675.*
56 A4 3a black 300. *375.*
a. Small "O" in "POSTAGE" 1,900. *2,250.*
57 A4 4a black 135. *180.*
a. Small "O" in "POSTAGE" 625.

Yellowish Paper

58 A4 8a black 225. *340.*
a. Small "O" in "POSTAGE" 1,675. *2,100.*
59 A4 1r black 425. *500.*
a. Small "O" in "POSTAGE" 2,250.
60 A4 5r black 37,500. 37,500.

A4a

Without Overprint

White Paper

61 A4a 1a black (thin "1") 125.00 110.00
a. Small "O" in "POSTAGE" 700.00 675.00
62 A4a 1a black (thick "1") 26.00 *30.00*
a. Small "O" in "POSTAGE" 95.00 *110.00*
63 A4a 2a black 32.50 *40.00*
a. Small "O" in "POSTAGE" 110.00 *140.00*
64 A4a 3a black 32.50 *50.00*
a. Small "O" in "POSTAGE" 135.00 *200.00*
65 A4a 4a black 35.00 *42.50*
a. Small "O" in "POSTAGE" 125.00 *140.00*

Yellowish Paper

66 A4a 8a black 42.50 *50.00*
a. Small "O" in "POSTAGE" 155.00 *200.00*
67 A4a 1r black 95.00 *110.00*
a. Small "O" in "POSTAGE" 400.00 *475.00*
68 A4a 5r black 300.00 *400.00*
a. Small "O" in "POSTAGE" 1,000. *1,250.*

A5

Queen Victoria — A6

1898-1902 Engr. Wmk. 2 *Perf. 14*

69 A5 1a red 6.00 4.50
70 A5 1a car rose ('02) 2.50 2.00
71 A5 2a brown 9.25 *11.00*
72 A5 3a gray 22.50 *50.00*
a. 3a bluish gray ('02) 21.00 *22.50*
73 A5 4a dark green 15.00 *16.00*
74 A5 8a olive gray 15.00 *32.50*
a. 8a gray green ('02) 32.50 *55.00*

Wmk. 1

75 A6 1r ultra 60.00 *60.00*
a. 1r bright blue (02) *72.50* *72.50*
76 A6 5r brown 110.00 *130.00*
Nos. 69-76 (8) *240.25* *306.00*

British East Africa No. 72 Overprinted in Black

1902 Wmk. 2

77 A8 ½a yellow green 3.25 2.25
a. Inverted overprint *2,200.*
b. Double overprint *2,800.*
c. Pair, one without overprint *5,500.*

British East Africa No. 76 Overprinted in Red

78 A8 2½a dark blue 5.00 3.50
a. Double overprint 650.00

UKRAINE

yü-'krān

LOCATION — In southeastern Europe, bordering on the Black Sea
GOVT. — Republic
AREA — 170,998 sq. mi.
POP. — 48,760,474 (2001)
CAPITAL — Kiev

Following the collapse of the Russian Empire, a national assembly met at Kiev and declared the Ukrainian National Republic on Jan. 22, 1918. During three years of civil war, the Ukrainian army, as well as Bolshevik, White Russian, Allied and Polish armies, fought back and forth across the country. By November, 1920, Ukraine was finally occupied by Soviet forces and on July 6, 1923, it was incorporated into the Soviet Union. Soviet stamps were used until March 1, 1992, when newly independent Ukraine again began issuing its own stamps.

200 Shahiv = 100 Kopiyok (Kopecks) = 1 Karbovanets (Ruble)
100 Shahiv = 1 Hryvnia

Watermark

Wmk. 116- Crosses and Circles

Republic's Trident Emblem — A1

Ukrainian Peasant — A2

Allegorical Ukraine — A3

Trident — A4

Inscription of Value — A5

1918, July Typo. *Imperf.*
Thin Paper

1 A1 10sh buff .35 *.40*
2 A2 20sh brown .35 *.40*
3 A3 30sh ultra .35 *.40*
a. 30sh blue 2.75 *6.50*
4 A4 40sh green .35 *.40*
5 A5 50sh red .35 *.40*
Nos. 1-5 (5) 1.75 *2.00*

The stamps of this issue exist perforated or pin-perforated unofficially.

Forgeries of this set exist on a very thin, glossy paper.

These designs were earlier (April, 1918) utilized for money tokens, printed on thin cardboard, perforated 11½, and bearing an inscription on the reverse "Circulates on par with coins" in Ukrainian. These tokens exist favor canceled but were not postage stamps. Value uncanceled, $6 each.

TRIDENT OVERPRINTS

Stamps of Russia Overprinted in Violet, Black, Blue, Red, Brown or Green

This trident-shaped emblem was taken from the arms of the Grand Prince Volodymyr and adopted as the device of the Ukrainian Republic.

In the early months of independence, Russian stamps were commonly used, but the influx of large quantities of stamps from Russia made it necessary to take measures to protect postal revenue. In August, 1918, local post offices were ordered to send their existing stocks of Russian stamps to regional centers, where they were overprinted with the trident arms. Unoverprinted Russian stamps were declared invalid after October 1, although they were often accepted for use.

Nos. 6-47 represent the basic Russian stamps that received these overprints. Values are for the most common overprint variety.

Following this basic Trident listing are detailed listings for the major regional and city types (Nos. 6a-44s).

The basic Russian stamps to which Trident overprints were applied

A8

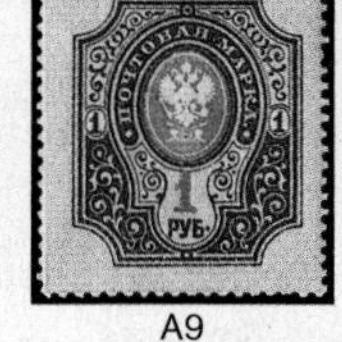
A9

A11

A12

A13

A14

A15

On Stamps of 1902-03

1918 Wmk. 168 *Perf. 13½*

6	A12	3½r	black & gray	100.00	*75.00*
7	A12	7r	black & yellow	100.00	*75.00*

On Stamps of 1909-18
Lozenges of Varnish on Face

Perf. 14, 14½x15

Unwmk.

8	A14	1k	orange	.25	*.35*
9	A14	2k	green	.25	*.35*
10	A14	3k	red	.25	*.35*
11	A15	4k	carmine	.25	*.35*
12	A14	5k	claret	.25	*.35*
13	A14	7k	light blue	.25	*.35*
14	A15	10k	dark blue	.25	*.35*
15	A11	14k	blue & rose	.25	*.35*
16	A11	15k	red brn & bl	.25	*.35*
17	A8	20k	blue & car	.25	*.35*
18	A11	25k	grn & gray vio	.40	*.50*
19	A11	35k	red brn & grn	.25	*.35*
20	A8	50k	violet & grn	.25	*.35*
21	A11	70k	brown & org	.25	*.35*

Perf. 13½

22	A9	1r	lt brn, brn & org	.55	*.75*
23	A12	3½r	mar & lt grn	1.25	*2.50*
24	A13	5r	dk bl, grn & pale bl	7.50	*11.00*
25	A12	7r	dk grn & pink	9.00	*12.00*
26	A13	10r	scar, yel & gray	13.00	*18.00*
			Nos. 6-26 (21)	234.95	*199.30*

On Stamps of 1917
Perf. 14, 14½x15

27	A14	10k	on 7k light blue	.75	*1.00*
28	A11	20k	on 14k bl & rose	.75	*1.00*

On Stamps of 1917-18
Imperf

29	A14	1k	orange	.25	*.35*
30	A14	2k	gray green	.25	*.35*
31	A14	3k	red	.25	*.35*
32	A15	4k	carmine	.25	*.35*
33	A14	5k	claret	.90	*1.50*
34	A11	15k	red brn & bl	.25	*.35*
35	A8	20k	bl & car	.75	*1.50*
36	A11	25k	grn & gray vio	60.00	—
37	A11	35k	red brn & grn	.25	*.35*
38	A8	50k	violet & grn	.30	*.35*
39	A11	70k	brown & org	.25	*.35*
40	A9	1r	pale brn, brn & red org	.25	*.60*
41	A12	3½r	mar & lt grn	1.00	*2.50*
42	A13	5r	dk bl, grn & pale bl	1.50	*3.00*
43	A12	7r	dk grn & pink	2.50	*4.00*
44	A13	10r	scar, yel & gray	70.00	*85.00*
			Nos. 29-44 (16)	138.95	*100.90*

PF1

Russian Stamps AR1-AR3.

Wmk. 171 Litho.

Perf. 14, 14½x14¾

45	PF1	1k	red, *buff*	5.00	*25.00*
46	PF1	5k	green, *buff*	20.00	*120.00*
47	PF1	10k	brown, *buff*	35.00	*350.00*
			Nos. 45-47 (3)	60.00	*495.00*

Nos. 45-47 were used and accepted as postage stamps during stamp shortages.

REGIONAL ISSUES

Katerynoslav I — Handstamped in black with a rubber device

8a	A14	1k	orange	.60	*3.50*
9a	A14	2k	green	.25	*.35*
10a	A14	3k	red	.30	*.60*
11a	A15	4k	carmine	.25	*2.50*
12a	A14	5k	claret	.25	*.60*
13a	A14	7k	light blue	.25	*.60*
14a	A15	10k	dark blue	.25	*.35*
15a	A11	14k	blue & rose	.25	*1.25*
16a	A11	15k	red brn & bl	.25	*.25*
17a	A8	20k	blue & car	.30	*.60*
18a	A11	25k	grn & gray vio	.50	*1.25*
19a	A11	35k	red brn & grn	9.00	*15.00*
20a	A8	50k	violet & grn	.25	*.35*
21a	A11	70k	brown & org	.25	*.60*
27a	A14	10k	on 7k light blue	.25	*1.25*
28a	A11	20k	on 14k bl & rose	.30	*2.50*
29a	A14	1k	orange	.25	*.35*
30a	A14	2k	gray green	6.00	*18.00*
31a	A14	3k	red	.25	*.35*
32a	A15	4k	carmine	120.00	120.00
33a	A14	5k	claret	7.00	*9.00*
34a	A11	15k	red brn & bl	.60	*2.50*
35a	A8	20k	bl & car	.90	*2.50*
37a	A11	35k	red brn & grn	3.50	*7.00*
38a	A8	50k	violet & grn	120.00	120.00
39a	A11	70k	brown & org	120.00	120.00

Katerynoslav II — Handstamped in black with a rubber device

6a	A12	3½r	black & gray	—	360.00
7a	A12	7r	black & yellow	120.00	120.00
22a	A9	1r	lt brn, brn & org	180.00	*240.00*
23a	A12	3½r	mar & lt grn	15.00	*25.00*
25a	A12	7r	dk grn & pink	25.00	*50.00*
40a	A9	1r	pale brn, brn & red org	2.00	*3.00*
41a	A12	3½r	mar & lt grn	2.50	*6.00*
42a	A12	7r	dk grl, grn & pale brn	50.00	*60.00*
43a	A12	7r	dk grn & pink	150.00	—

Kharkiv I — Handstamped in black with a metal device

8b	A14	1k	orange	.90	*6.00*
9b	A14	2k	green	2.50	*3.50*
10b	A14	3k	red	.25	*1.25*
11b	A15	4k	carmine	1.25	*6.00*
12b	A14	5k	claret	6.00	*9.00*
13b	A14	7k	light blue	30.00	*90.00*
14b	A15	10k	dark blue	3.00	*5.00*
15b	A11	14k	blue & rose	30.00	*75.00*
16b	A11	15k	red brn & bl	.25	*.35*
17b	A8	20k	blue & car	1.50	*2.50*
18b	A11	25k	grn & gray vio	50.00	*70.00*
19b	A11	35k	red brn & grn	.25	*.35*
20b	A8	50k	violet & grn	.25	*.35*
21b	A11	70k	brown & org	.50	*2.00*
27b	A14	10k	on 7k light blue	2.50	*3.50*
28b	A11	20k	on 14k bl & rose	2.00	*5.00*
29b	A14	1k	orange	.25	*1.25*
30b	A14	2k	gray green	1.75	*5.00*
31b	A14	3k	red	.25	*2.00*
33b	A14	5k	claret	1.25	*5.00*
34b	A11	15k	red brn & bl	6.00	*9.00*
37b	A11	35k	red brn & grn	30.00	*90.00*
45b	A6	1k	red, *buff*	1.00	
46b	A6	5k	green, *buff*	8.00	
47b	A6	10k	brown, *buff*	2.00	

Kharkiv II — Handstamped in black with a metal device

6c	A12	3½r	black & gray	—	
7c	A12	7r	black & yellow	120.00	*150.00*
9c	A14	2k	green	—	
10c	A14	3k	red	—	
16c	A11	15k	red brn & bl	—	
22c	A9	1r	lt brn, brn & org	3.00	*18.00*
23c	A12	3½r	mar & lt grn	30.00	*45.00*
24c	A13	5r	dk bl, grn & pale bl		300.00
25c	A12	7r	dk grn & pink	18.00	*30.00*
26c	A13	10r	scar, yel & gray	300.00	240.00
40c	A9	1r	pale brn, brn & red org	.25	*1.25*
41c	A12	3½r	mar & lt grn	.50	*2.50*
42c	A13	5r	dk bl, grn & pale bl	1.25	*2.50*
43c	A12	7r	dk grn & pink	18.00	*30.00*
44c	A13	10r	scar, yel & gray	150.00	*180.00*

Kharkiv III — Handstamped in black with a metal device

6d	A12	3½r	black & gray	180.00	300.00
7d	A12	7r	black & yellow	—	300.00
9d	A14	2k	green	—	
10d	A14	3k	red	—	
16d	A11	15k	red brn & bl	—	
22d	A9	1r	lt brn, brn & org	7.00	*50.00*
23d	A12	3½r	mar & lt grn	48.00	*55.00*
24d	A13	5r	dk bl, grn & pale bl	—	—
25d	A12	7r	dk grn & pink	20.00	*30.00*
26d	A13	10r	scar, yel & gray	120.00	*150.00*
30d	A14	2k	gray green	120.00	
40d	A9	1r	pale brn, brn & red org	.25	*1.25*
41d	A12	3½r	mar & lt grn	.30	*2.50*
42d	A13	5r	dk bl, grn & pale bl	.60	*2.50*
43d	A12	7r	dk grn & pink	25.00	*50.00*
44d	A13	10r	scar, yel & gray	70.00	*70.00*

Kiev I — Handstamped in violet with a rubber device

6e	A12	3½r	black & gray	360.00	360.00
7e	A12	7r	black & yellow	300.00	180.00
8e	A14	1k	orange	.25	*.30*
9e	A14	2k	green	1.25	*.90*
10e	A14	3k	red	3.50	2.50
11e	A15	4k	carmine	2.00	*2.00*
12e	A14	5k	claret	.25	*.35*
13e	A14	7k	light blue	18.00	*24.00*
14e	A15	10k	dark blue	.60	*.60*
15e	A11	14k	blue & rose	15.00	*18.00*
16e	A11	15k	red brn & bl	.50	*.60*
17e	A8	20k	blue & car	2.50	1.25
18e	A11	25k	grn & gray vio	30.00	24.00
19e	A11	35k	red brn & grn	24.00	18.00
20e	A8	50k	violet & grn	.25	*.35*
21e	A11	70k	brown & org	.25	*.35*
22e	A9	1r	lt brn, brn & org	6.00	*7.50*
23e	A12	3½r	mar & lt grn	1.25	*3.00*
24e	A13	5r	dk bl, grn & pale bl	50.00	*100.00*
25e	A12	7r	dk grn & pink	48.00	*55.00*
26e	A13	10r	scar, yel & gray	15.00	*20.00*
27e	A14	10k	on 7k light blue	3.50	*5.00*
28e	A11	20k	on 14k bl & rose	.60	*.60*
29e	A14	1k	orange	1.50	*2.50*
30e	A14	2k	gray green	.25	*.35*
31e	A14	3k	red	.25	*.35*
32e	A15	4k	carmine	.25	*.35*
33e	A14	5k	claret	18.00	*24.00*
34e	A11	15k	red brn & bl	4.75	*6.00*
35e	A8	20k	bl & car	18.00	*24.00*
36e	A11	25k	bl & car	—	
37e	A11	35k	red brn & grn	.25	*.35*
38e	A8	50k	violet & grn	18.00	15.00
39e	A11	70k	brown & org	30.00	*35.00*
40e	A9	1r	pale brn, brn & red org	.60	.60
41e	A12	3½r	mar & lt grn	24.00	*30.00*
42e	A13	5r	dk bl, grn & pale bl	.60	*1.25*
43e	A12	7r	dk grn & pink	1.25	*1.75*
44e	A13	10r	scar, yel & gray	300.00	—
45e	PF1	1k	red, *buff*	—	
46e	PF1	5k	green, *buff*	—	—
47e	PF1	10k	brown, *buff*	17.00	

Kiev II — Handstamped in violet with a rubber device

6f	A12	3½r	black & gray	48.00	*55.00*
7f	A12	7r	black & yellow	48.00	*55.00*
8f	A14	1k	orange	.25	*.35*
9f	A14	2k	green	.25	*.35*
10f	A14	3k	red	.25	*.35*
11f	A15	4k	carmine	.25	*.35*
12f	A14	5k	claret	.25	*.35*
13f	A14	7k	light blue	12.00	*18.00*
14f	A15	10k	dark blue	.25	*.35*
15f	A11	14k	blue & rose	.30	*.50*
16f	A11	15k	red brn & bl	.25	*.35*
17f	A8	20k	blue & car	.25	*.35*
18f	A11	25k	grn & gray vio	.90	*.70*
19f	A11	35k	red brn & grn	.25	*.35*
20f	A8	50k	violet & grn	.25	*.35*
21f	A11	70k	brown & org	.25	*.35*
22f	A9	1r	lt brn, brn & org	.50	*.75*
23f	A12	3½r	mar & lt grn	.90	*2.00*
24f	A13	5r	dk bl, grn & pale bl	6.00	*10.00*
25f	A12	7r	dk grn & pink	7.00	*12.00*
26f	A13	10r	scar, yel & gray	12.00	*15.00*
27f	A14	10k	on 7k light blue	.25	*.35*
28f	A11	20k	on 14k bl & rose	.25	*.35*
29f	A14	1k	orange	.25	*.35*
30f	A14	2k	gray green	.25	*.35*
31f	A14	3k	red	.25	*.35*
32f	A15	4k	carmine	.75	*.90*
33f	A14	5k	claret	.90	*1.50*
34f	A11	15k	red brn & bl	.25	*.35*
36f	A11	25k	bl & car	50.00	—
37f	A11	35k	red brn & grn	.25	*.35*
38f	A8	50k	violet & grn	—	70.00
39f	A11	70k	brown & org	.25	*.35*
40f	A9	1r	pale brn, brn & red org	.50	*.75*
41f	A12	3½r	mar & lt grn	1.50	*2.00*
42f	A13	5r	dk bl, grn & pale bl	2.00	*2.50*
43f	A12	7r	dk grn & pink	2.50	*3.50*
44f	A13	10r	scar, yel & gray	50.00	*60.00*
45f	A6	1k	red, *buff*	15.00	
46f	A6	5k	green, *buff*	12.00	
47f	A6	10k	brown, *buff*	30.00	

Kiev III — Lithographed in black

6g	A12	3½r	black & gray	75.00	*150.00*
8g	A14	1k	orange	.25	*.35*
9g	A14	2k	green	.90	*1.25*
10g	A14	3k	red	.90	*1.25*
11g	A15	4k	carmine	.25	*.35*
12g	A14	5k	claret	.25	*.35*
13g	A14	7k	light blue	2.50	*3.00*
14g	A15	10k	dark blue	3.50	*5.00*
15g	A11	14k	blue & rose	3.50	*5.00*
16g	A11	15k	red brn	.25	*.35*
17g	A8	20k	blue & car	5.00	*6.00*
18g	A11	25k	grn & gray vio	5.00	*6.00*
19g	A11	35k	red brn & grn	.25	*.35*
20g	A8	50k	violet & grn	.25	*.35*
21g	A11	70k	brown & org	.25	*.35*
23g	A12	3½r	mar & lt grn	110.00	*120.00*
24g	A13	5r	dk bl, grn & pale bl	300.00	*325.00*
25g	A12	7r	dk grn & pink	75.00	*90.00*
26g	A13	10r	scar, yel & gray	300.00	*325.00*
27g	A14	10k	on 7k light blue	7.00	*12.00*
28g	A11	20k	on 14k bl & rose	.25	*.35*
29g	A14	1k	orange	.25	*.35*
30g	A14	2k	gray green	.25	*.35*
31g	A14	3k	red	.25	*.35*
32g	A15	4k	carmine	2.50	*5.00*
33g	A14	5k	claret	21.00	18.00
34g	A11	15k	red brn & bl	18.00	*21.00*
37g	A11	35k	red brn & grn	24.00	*24.00*
39g	A11	70k	brown & org	18.00	*21.00*
40g	A9	1r	pale brn, brn & red org	.25	*5.00*
41g	A12	3½r	mar & lt grn	75.00	*90.00*
42g	A13	5r	dk bl, grn & pale bl	60.00	*90.00*
43g	A12	7r	dk grn & pink	120.00	*150.00*

Overinked or worn plates produced impressions where the thin outer line of the trident cannot be distinguished.

Odessa I — Typographed in black

9h	A14	2k	green	.25	*.35*
11h	A15	4k	carmine	50.00	—
12h	A14	5k	claret	120.00	—
13h	A14	7k	light blue	.30	*1.25*
14h	A15	10k	dark blue	.90	*1.75*
15h	A11	14k	blue & rose	5.00	*60.00*
16h	A11	15k	red brn	.40	*.75*
17h	A8	20k	blue & car	70.00	*180.00*
19h	A11	35k	red brn & grn	.40	*.75*
20h	A8	50k	violet & grn	.30	*.60*
21h	A11	70k	brown & org	13.50	
27h	A14	10k	on 7k light blue	6.00	*12.00*
29h	A14	1k	orange	.25	*.35*
31h	A14	3k	red	.25	*.35*
34g	A11	15k	red brn & bl	2.50	*5.00*
37h	A11	35k	red brn & grn	18.00	*24.00*
38h	A8	50k	violet & grn	110.00	*180.00*
39h	A11	70k	brown & org	85.00	*100.00*

Odessa II — Typographed in black

8i	A14	1k	orange	.25	*2.00*
9i	A14	2k	green	.25	*.35*
10i	A14	3k	red	1.25	*3.75*
11i	A15	4k	carmine	.25	*.35*
12i	A14	5k	claret	.25	*.35*
13i	A14	7k	light blue	.25	*.35*
14i	A15	10k	dark blue	.25	*.35*
15i	A11	14k	blue & rose	.25	*.90*
16i	A11	15k	red brn	.25	*.35*
17i	A8	20k	blue & car	.25	*.35*
18i	A11	25k	grn & gray vio	.40	*.90*
19i	A11	35k	red brn & grn	.25	*.35*
20i	A8	50k	violet & grn	.25	*.35*
21i	A11	70k	brown & org	.40	*1.25*
27i	A14	10k	on 7k light blue	.25	*1.20*
28i	A11	20k	on 14k bl & rose	.25	*.40*
29i	A14	1k	orange	.25	*.35*
30i	A14	2k	gray green	1.25	*3.75*
31i	A14	3k	red	.25	*.35*
33i	A14	5k	claret	15.00	—
34i	A11	15k	red brn & bl	.25	*.35*
37i	A11	35k	red brn & grn	.25	*1.25*
38i	A8	50k	violet & grn	.25	*1.25*
39i	A11	70k	brown & org	.60	*5.00*

Odessa III — Lithographed in black

8j A14 1k orange .60 *5.00*
9j A14 2k green 18.00 *120.00*
12j A14 5k claret .25 *.45*
14j A15 10k dark blue .25 *.60*
15j A11 14k blue & rose .25 *.35*
16j A11 15k red brn .75 *3.75*
17j A8 20k blue & car .25 *.40*
18j A11 25k grn & gray vio 3.00 *3.75*
19j A11 35k red brn & grn .25 *3.75*
20j A8 50k violet & grn .25 *.35*
21j A11 70k brown & org .25 *.75*
27j A14 10k on 7k light blue .75 *5.50*
29j A14 1k orange .25 *.90*
34j A11 15k red brn & bl 1.80 *3.75*
37j A11 35k red brn & grn .25 *1.80*
38j A8 50k violet & grn .90 *5.00*
39j A11 70k brown & org .60 *3.00*

Odessa IV — Handstamped in black with a metal device

6k A12 3½r black & gray 55.00 *60.00*
7k A12 7r black & yellow 150.00 *180.00*
8k A14 1k orange .60 *3.00*
9k A14 2k green .90 *2.25*
10k A14 3k red 1.80 *2.50*
11k A15 4k carmine 2.75 *7.50*
12k A14 5k claret 3.00 *7.50*
13k A14 7k light blue 55.00 *110.00*
14k A15 10k dark blue 1.25 *1.80*
15k A11 14k blue & rose 3.00 *4.50*
16k A11 15k red brn 2.25 *2.50*
17k A8 20k blue & car 1.30 *3.75*
18k A11 25k grn & gray vio 5.00 3.75
19k A11 35k red brn & grn 3.00 *18.00*
20k A8 50k violet & grn 1.80 *5.00*
21k A11 70k brown & org 3.75 *7.50*
22k A9 1r lt brn, brn & org 1.25 *1.80*
23k A12 3½r mar & lt grn 47.50 *110.00*
24k A13 5r dk bl, grn & pale bl 9.00 *12.00*
25k A12 7r dk grn & pink 9.00 *12.00*
26k A13 10r scar, yel & gray 150.00 *240.00*
27k A14 10k on 7k light blue 1.25 *3.75*
28k A11 20k on 14k bl & rose 2.40 *9.00*
29k A14 1k orange .25 *1.80*
30k A14 2k gray green .90 *5.00*
31k A14 3k red 1.25 *3.00*
32k A15 4k carmine 110.00 *180.00*
33k A14 5k claret 5.00 *18.00*
34k A11 15k red brn & bl 1.25 *5.00*
35k A8 20k bl & car 110.00 *150.00*
37k A11 35k red brn & grn 3.75 *15.00*
38k A8 50k violet & grn 7.50 *24.00*
39k A11 70k brown & org 35.00 *60.00*
40k A9 1r pale brn, brn & red org .40 *.50*
41k A12 3½r mar & lt grn 18.00 9.00
42k A13 5r dk bl, grn & pale bl 18.00 *30.00*
43k A12 7r dk grn & pink —
44k A13 10r scar, yel & gray 150.00 *210.00*

Odessa V — Handstamped in black with a metal device

6m A12 3½r black & gray 210.00 *240.00*
7m A12 7r black & yellow —
8m A14 1k orange —
9m A14 2k green 90.00
10m A14 3k red 180.00
11m A15 4k carmine —
12m A14 5k claret 15.00 *120.00*
13m A14 7k light blue — —
14m A15 10k dark blue 90.00 *110.00*
15m A11 14k blue & rose 55.00
16m A11 15k red brn 42.50 *42.50*
17m A8 20k blue & car 21.00 *21.00*
18m A11 25k grn & gray vio — —
19m A11 35k red brn & grn 180.00 160.00
20m A8 50k violet & grn 180.00 160.00
21m A11 70k brown & org 55.00 *160.00*
22m A9 1r lt brn, brn & org .60 *.75*
23m A12 3½r mar & lt grn 9.00 *12.00*
24m A13 5r dk bl, grn & pale bl — *210.00*
25m A12 7r dk grn & pink 18.00 *21.00*
26m A13 10r scar, yel & gray 150.00 *120.00*
27m A14 10k on 7k light blue 21.00 *21.00*
28m A11 20k on 14k bl & rose 27.50 *30.00*
29m A14 1k orange 7.50 *7.50*
30m A14 2k gray green 7.50 *7.50*
31m A14 3k red 7.50 *7.50*
33m A14 5k claret 7.50 *7.50*
34m A11 15k red brn & bl 21.00 *27.50*
37m A11 35k red brn & grn — —
38m A8 50k violet & grn 180.00
39m A11 70k brown & org 72.50 *60.00*
40m A9 1r pale brn, brn & red org .50 *.50*
41m A12 3½r mar & lt grn 1.80 *2.75*
42m A13 5r dk bl, grn & pale bl 110.00 *130.00*
43m A12 7r dk grn & pink —
44m A13 10r scar, yel & gray 180.00 180.00

Odessa VI — Handstamped in black with a metal device

6n A12 3½r black & gray 240.00 210.00
7n A12 7r black & yellow — —
8n A14 1k orange 100.00
9n A14 2k green 5.00 *18.00*
10n A14 3k red 120.00 *150.00*
11n A15 4k carmine —
12n A14 5k claret 120.00
13n A14 7k light blue 150.00
14n A15 10k dark blue 2.75 *7.00*
15n A11 14k blue & rose 9.00
16n A11 15k red brn 35.00 —
17n A8 20k blue & car 45.00 45.00
19n A11 35k red brn & grn 150.00
20n A8 50k violet & grn 210.00 —
21n A11 70k brown & org 150.00 —
22n A9 1r lt brn, brn & org .90 *1.40*
23n A12 3½r mar & lt grn 2.75 *4.50*
24n A13 5r dk bl, grn & pale bl 110.00 *240.00*
25n A12 7r dk grn & pink 60.00 *240.00*
26n A13 10r scar, yel & gray 120.00 *240.00*
27n A14 10k on 7k light blue 9.00 *90.00*
28n A11 20k on 14k bl & rose 35.00 *42.50*
29n A14 1k orange 9.00 *9.00*
30n A14 2k gray green 9.00 *9.00*
31n A14 3k red 9.00 *9.00*
32n A15 4k carmine 130.00 *210.00*
33n A14 5k claret 9.00 *9.00*
34n A11 15k red brn & bl 13.00 *18.00*
35n A8 20k bl & car 150.00 *180.00*
38n A8 50k violet & grn 180.00 —
39n A11 70k brown & org 45.00 *45.00*
40n A9 1r pale brn, brn & red org .50 *.75*
41n A12 3½r mar & lt grn .90 *2.25*
42n A13 5r dk bl, grn & pale bl — —
43n A12 7r dk grn & pink —
44n A13 10r scar, yel & gray 240.00 —

Podillia Ia — Handstamped in black with a metal device

Over 60 additional Podillia trident types and subtypes have been identified by specialists. The majority of these types were made with single-subject overprinting devices composed of non-durable wood or rubber, which quickly deteriorated with use, resulting in subtypes, necessitating the creation of new handstamp types. Because of the rapid wear of the handstamp devices, often only partial trident impressions appear on stamps. The Podillia Ia metal handstamp overprinted far more stamps than any of the wooden or rubber types.

6o A12 3½r black & gray —
7o A12 7r black & yellow 110.00 *180.00*
8o A14 1k orange .40 *3.75*
9o A14 2k green .25 *.35*
10o A14 3k red .50 *.90*
11o A15 4k carmine 72.50 *180.00*
12o A14 5k claret 85.00 3.75
13o A14 7k light blue .25 *.60*
14o A15 10k dark blue .50 *1.25*
15o A11 14k blue & rose —
16o A11 15k red brn .25 *.35*
17o A8 20k blue & car .50 *.75*
18o A11 25k grn & gray vio .40 *1.25*
19o A11 35k red brn & grn .35 *.35*
20o A8 50k violet & grn .25 *.35*
21o A11 70k brown & org .25 *.35*
22o A9 1r lt brn, brn & org .40 *.60*
23o A12 3½r mar & lt grn 2.50 *12.00*
24o A13 5r dk bl, grn & pale bl 25.00 —
25o A12 7r dk grn & pink 25.00 —
26o A13 10r scar, yel & gray —
27o A14 10k on 7k light blue .25 *2.50*
28o A11 20k on 14k bl & rose 1.80 *15.00*
29o A14 1k orange .75 *2.50*
30o A14 2k gray green 35.00 —
31o A14 3k red .25 *3.00*
33o A14 5k claret 1.80
34o A11 15k red brn & bl 120.00
37o A11 35k red brn & grn — —
38o A8 50k violet & grn 120.00 47.50
40o A9 1r pale brn, brn & red org .25 *.35*
41o A12 3½r mar & lt grn 9.00 6.00
42o A13 5r dk bl, grn & pale bl 42.50 *30.00*
43o A12 7r dk grn & pink 24.00 12.00

Poltava I — Handstamped in violet with a rubber device (kopeck values) or with a metal device (ruble values)

8p A14 1k orange 240.00
9p A14 2k green .25 *.35*
10p A14 3k red 18.00 *24.00*
11p A15 4k carmine 18.00 *24.00*
12p A14 5k claret 9.00 *12.00*
13p A14 7k light blue 180.00 *240.00*
14p A15 10k dark blue 12.00 *12.00*
15p A11 14k blue & rose 240.00
16p A11 15k red brn 6.00 *12.00*
17p A8 20k blue & car 1.25 *2.50*
18p A11 25k grn & gray vio 2.50 *13.00*
19p A11 35k red brn & grn 90.00 75.00
20p A8 50k violet & grn 1.25 1.00
21p A11 70k brown & org .75 .75
22p A9 1r lt brn, brn & org 90.00
24p A13 5r dk bl, grn & pale bl —
25p A12 7r dk grn & pink 13.50 *17.00*
27p A14 10k on 7k light blue 75.00 50.00
28p A11 20k on 14k bl & rose 20.00 *25.00*
29p A14 1k orange 3.00 *5.00*
30p A14 2k gray green 7.50 *150.00*
31p A14 3k red 1.00 *1.50*
33p A14 5k claret 130.00 *250.00*
34p A11 15k red brn & bl 8.00 *14.00*
35p A8 20k bl & car —
37p A11 35k red brn & grn 7.00 *15.00*
38p A8 50k violet & grn —
40p A9 1r pale brn, brn & red org 100.00 25.00
41p A12 3½r mar & lt grn —
43p A12 7r dk grn & pink —
44p A13 10r scar, yel & gray —
45p A6 1k red, *buff* 10.00 *15.00*
46p A6 5k green, *buff* 150.00 70.00

Poltava I — Hstmpd. in black with a rubber device (kopeck values) or with a metal device (ruble values)

6q A12 3½r black & gray 300.00
7q A12 7r black & yellow — 300.00
8q A14 1k orange — 250.00
9q A14 2k green 15.00 *25.00*
10q A14 3k red 20.00 *40.00*
11q A15 4k carmine 100.00 *250.00*
12q A14 5k claret 130.00 70.00
13q A14 7k light blue —
14q A15 10k dark blue 100.00 50.00
15q A11 14k blue & rose —
16q A11 15k red brn 5.00 *7.50*
17q A8 20k blue & car 100.00 50.00
18q A11 25k grn & gray vio — *240.00*
19q A11 35k red brn & grn 160.00 100.00
20q A8 50k violet & grn 160.00 70.00
21q A11 70k brown & org 160.00 50.00
22q A9 1r lt brn, brn & org 7.00 4.00
23q A12 3½r mar & lt grn 8.00 *10.00*
24q A13 5r dk bl, grn & pale bl — *225.00*
25q A12 7r dk grn & pink 20.00 *25.00*
26q A13 10r scar, yel & gray —
27q A14 10k on 7k light blue 160.00 *160.00*
28q A11 20k on 14k bl & rose 160.00 *200.00*
29q A14 1k orange 20.00 *140.00*
30q A14 2k gray green —
31q A14 3k red 27.50 27.50
32q A15 4k carmine —
33q A14 5k claret 200.00 200.00
34q A11 15k red brn & bl 40.00 *140.00*
35q A8 20k bl & car —
37q A11 35k red brn & grn 200.00 100.00
38q A8 50k violet & grn — —
39q A11 70k brown & org — —
40q A9 1r pale brn, brn & red org 2.00 *2.50*
41q A12 3½r mar & lt grn —
42q A13 5r dk bl, grn & pale bl — —
43q A12 7r dk grn & pink —
44q A13 10r scar, yel & gray — *260.00*
45q A6 1k red, *buff* —
47q A6 10k brown, *buff* *325.00*

Poltava I — Handstamped in green with a rubber device

9r A14 2k green 200.00
14r A15 10k dark blue — —
20r A8 50k violet & grn 160.00 —
21r A11 70k brown & org 160.00 —
27r A14 10k on 7k light blue — 225.00
28r A11 20k on 14k bl & rose —
29r A14 1k orange 250.00
45r A6 1k red, *buff* —
46r A6 5k green, *buff*

Poltava II — Handstamped in black with a rubber device

7s A12 7r black & yellow 325.00 —
9s A14 2k green 250.00 —
10s A14 3k red —
12s A14 5k claret —
13s A14 7k light blue —
14s A15 10k dark blue — —
16s A11 15k red brn 100.00 *225.00*
17s A8 20k blue & car — —
19s A11 35k red brn & grn 250.00 —
20s A8 50k violet & grn 130.00 *70.00*
21s A11 70k brown & org —
22s A9 1r lt brn, brn & org 32.50 25.00
23s A12 3½r mar & lt grn 100.00 75.00
24s A13 5r dk bl, grn & pale bl 160.00 *200.00*
25s A12 7r dk grn & pink 160.00 140.00
27s A14 10k on 7k light blue — 250.00
28s A11 20k on 14k bl & rose 250.00
29s A14 1k orange —
31s A14 3k red 160.00 *200.00*
34s A11 15k red brn & bl — 140.00
37s A11 35k red brn & grn — 140.00
40s A9 1r pale brn, brn & red org 14.00 *14.00*
44s A13 10r scar, yel & gray 250.00 —

The trident overprint was applied by favor to Russia Nos. 88-104, 110-111, the Romanov issue.

For surcharges see Russian Offices in the Turkish Empire Nos. 320-339.

A6

1919, Jan. **Litho.**

48 A6 20h red & green 10.00 *25.00*

Because of its high face value, No. 48 was used primarily on money transfer forms or parcel receipts. Used value is for a postally used example.

Nos. 1 and 5 Surcharged

1919, Feb. **Unwmk.** ***Imperf.***

49 A1 35k on 10sh buff 9.00 *20.00*
50 A5 70k on 50sh red 70.00 *50.00*
a. Surcharge inverted 60.00

Nos. 49 and 50 were originally believed to have been created by the Soviets in the Ukraine in April, 1919, but more recent research seems to indicate that they were created by the White (Don) Army operating in eastern Ukraine at the request of the Ukrainian government. Correctly franked covers have been recorded from the February-June 1919 period.

Excellent forged surcharges exist.

Ukrainian Soviet Socialist Republic

During 1920/1921, hyperinflation of the ruble created a desperate need for stamps to pay ever-rising postal rates. Many Russian cities and districts surcharged existing stocks of Russian stamps in needed denominations for provisional use.

In June 1920 the national government of the Soviet Ukrainian Republic authorized the Kharkiv post office to create such surcharges for use in the Kharkiv region and in adjacent oblasts. Both unoverprinted Russian stamps and stamps bearing the regional trident overprints of Katerynoslav, Kharkiv and Kyiv were surcharged to raise their face value 100-fold. They were sold at 236 post offices in the Ukraine from June 1920 through Feb. 1921.

In Feb. 1922 three Russian postal savings stamps were surcharged for provisional use by the Kyiv post office, at the direction of the central government. As with the Kharkiv surcharges, these stamps were distributed over a wide area within the country.

KHARKIV ISSUE

Ukrainian and Russian Stamps Handstamp Surcharged

Ukrainian trident overprinted issues and unoverprinted Russian stamps revalued 100-fold by changing denominations from kopecks to rubles.

Two types of overprint: type I, Cyrillic RUB (not including periods) 9.5mmx6.5mm; type II, 8.5mmx6.5mm.

Number of basic Ukrainian or Russian stamp shown in parentheses.

On Katerynoslav Trident Ovpt. Issue of 1918

Type I Reading Upward

1920, June

51 A11 15k red brown & blue (#16a) 75.00 75.00

Kharkiv Trident Ovpt. Issue of 1918

52 A14 1k orange (#8b) 100.00 *60.00*
a. Surcharge reading downward 150.00 150.00
53 A14 2k green (#9b) 100.00 *65.00*
54 A14 3k red (#10b) 80.00 *40.00*

55 A11 15k red brn & blue (#16b) 40.00 35.00
56 A8 20k blue & car (#17b) 200.00 *175.00*
a. Surcharge reading downward 300.00 300.00
57 A11 20k on 14k blue & rose (#28b) 170.00 *190.00*

Imperf

58 A14 1k orange (#29b) 75.00 *75.00*
a. Surcharge reading downward 120.00 120.00
59 A14 2k green (#30b) 250.00 *250.00*
60 A14 3k red (#31b) 40.00 *40.00*

On Kyiv Trident Ovpt. Issue of 1918

No. 61

No. 63

On Kyiv II Overprint

61 A14 1k orange (#8f) 40.00 *40.00*

Imperf

62 A14 1k orange (#29f) 40.00 *50.00*
a. Surcharge reading downward — —

On Kyiv III Overprint

63 A14 3k red (#31g) 15.00 *20.00*

On Russian Arms Issue of 1909-18

No. 64

64 A14 1k orange (#73) 50.00 *50.00*
65 A14 2k green (#74) 10.00 *15.00*
a. Surcharge reading downward 15.00 20.00
66 A14 3k red (#75) 10.00 15.00
a. Surcharge reading downward 25.00 20.00
67 A15 4k red (#76) 325.00
68 A14 5k claret (#77) 7.00 6.00
a. Surcharge reading downward 20.00 20.00
69 A15 10k dk blue (#79) 15.00 15.00
a. Surcharge reading downward 90.00 *100.00*
70 A11 15k red brn & blue (#81) 7.00 6.00
a. Surcharge reading downward 10.00 10.00
71 A8 20k blue & car (#82) 10.00 *6.00*
a. Surcharge reading downward 15.00 12.00

Imperf

72 A14 1k orange (#119) 50.00 *36.00*
a. Surcharge reading downward 100.00 100.00
73 A14 2k green (#120) 45.00 *55.00*
74 A14 3k red (#121) 30.00 *36.00*
75 A14 5k claret (#123) 9.00 7.00
a. Surcharge reading downward 25.00 25.00
76 A11 15k red brn & blue (#125) 120.00 *130.00*
a. Surcharge reading downward — —

Type II Reading Upward

On Kharkiv Trident Ovpt. Issue of 1918

No. 79a

77 A14 3k red (#31b) 35.00 *40.00*

On Kyiv Trident Ovpt. Issue of 1918

78 A14 1k orange (#29f) 20.00 *25.00*

On Russian Arms Issue of 1919-18

Perf. 14x14½

79 A14 2k green (#74) 6.00 *7.00*
a. Surcharge reading downward 12.00 12.00
80 A14 5k claret (#77) 8.00 7.00
a. Surcharge reading downward 15.00 12.00
81 A15 10k dk blue (#79) 18.00 18.00
a. Surcharge reading downward 100.00 *115.00*
82 A11 15k red brn & blue (#81) 8.00 7.00
a. Surcharge reading downward 12.00 10.00
83 A8 20k blue & car (#82) 8.00 *7.00*

Imperf

84 A14 2k green (#120) 50.00 *60.00*

Nos. 51-84 on cover are worth approximately 5 times the total value of the affixed stamps.

KYIV ISSUE

Russian Postal Savings Stamps Handstamp Surcharged

1922, Feb. Wmk. 171

85 7500 (r) on 5k, green, *buff* 50.00 50.00
a. Surcharge reading downward 60.00 55.00
86 8000 (r) on 5k, green, *buff* 150.00 90.00
a. Surcharge reading downward 180.00 150.00
87 15000 (r) on 10k, brown, *buff* 300.00 150.00
a. Surcharge reading downward 450.00 250.00

Nos. 85-87 are normally found on stamps watermarked with a vertical diamond pattern (Wmk. 171) but also exist on paper watermarked sideways, with both upward and downward-reading surcharges. These are rare and are worth approximately 8 times the values shown.

Nos. 85-87 on cover are worth approximately 4 times the total value of the affixed stamps.

Nos. 1-5 surcharged in grivni (hryven) with the Polish eagle were sold as Polish occupation issues. They are of private origin.

Nos. 1-3 and 5 overprinted diagonally as above ("South Russia") are believed to be of private origin.

A lithographed set of 14 stamps (1h-200h) of these types, perf. 11½, was prepared in 1920, but never placed in use. Value, set $5.

All values exist imperf., some with inverted centers. Trial printings exist on various papers, including inverted, multiple, omitted and misaligned center vignettes. These are from the printer's waste.

This set handstamped "VILNA UKRAINA / 1921" and 6 values additionally overprinted "DOPLATA" are of private origin.

In 1923 the Ukrainian government-in-exile in Warsaw prepared an 11-value set, consisting of the 10h, 20h and 40h denominations of the unissued 1920 set surcharged and overprinted with the Cyrillic "UPP," supposedly intended as a Field Post issue for a planned invasion of the Ukraine. The invasion never occurred, and the stamps were never issued. Value $15.

SEMI-POSTAL STAMPS

Ukrainian Soviet Socialist Republic

"Famine" — SP1

Taras H. Shevchenko SP2

"Death" Stalking Peasant — SP3

"Ukraine" Distributing Food — SP4

Perf. 14½x13½, 13½x14½

1923, June Litho. Unwmk.

B1 SP1 10k + 10k gray bl & blk 1.00 *5.50*
B2 SP2 20k + 20k vio brn & org brn 1.00 *5.50*
B3 SP3 90k + 30k db & blk, *straw* 1.00 *5.50*
B4 SP4 150k + 50k red brn & blk 1.00 *5.50*
Nos. B1-B4 (4) 4.00 *22.00*

Imperf., Pairs

B1a SP1 10k + 10k 100.00 *120.00*
B2a SP2 20k + 20k 100.00 *120.00*
B3a SP3 90k + 30k 100.00 *120.00*
B4a SP4 150k + 50k 100.00 *120.00*

The values of these stamps are in karbovanets, which by 1923 converted to rubles at 100 to 1.

Wmk. 116

Same Colors

B5 SP1 10k + 10k *50.00* *70.00*
B6 SP2 20k + 20k *50.00* *70.00*
a. Imperf., pair 2,500.
B7 SP3 90k + 30k *50.00* *70.00*
B8 SP4 150k + 50k *50.00* *70.00*
Nos. B5-B8 (4) *200.00* *280.00*

MILITARY STAMPS

COURIER FIELD POST ISSUE

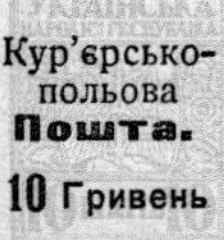

Nos. 1-5, 48 Surcharged

1920, Aug. 26

M1 A1 10h on 10sh buff 20.00 —
a. Inverted surcharge 80.00
M2 A2 10h on 20sh brown 40.00 —
M3 A3 10h on 30sh ultramarine 50.00 —
M4 A4 10h on 40sh green 55.00 —
a. Inverted surcharge 215.00
M5 A5 10h on 50sh red 50.00 —
M6 A1 20h on 10sh buff 55.00 —
M7 A2 20h on 20sh brown 15.00 —
a. Inverted surcharge 60.00
M8 A3 20h on 30sh ultramarine 40.00 —
a. Inverted surcharge 160.00
M9 A4 20h on 40sh green 40.00 —
M10 A5 20h on 50sh red 40.00 —
a. Inverted surcharge 160.00
M11 A1 40h on 10sh buff 200.00 —
M12 A2 40h on 20sh brown 100.00 —
M13 A3 40h on 30sh ultramarine 400.00 —
M14 A4 40h on 40sh green 200.00 —
M15 A5 40h on 50sh red 400.00 —
M16 A6 40h on 20hr red & green — —

Nos. M1-M16 were prepared to facilitate communications between the Ukrainian government-in-exile at Tarnow, Poland, and its military units in the field.

Only two examples of No. M16 are known, one unused and one used on cover.

Forged surcharges and cancellations exist.

UPPER SENEGAL & NIGER

'ə-pər ˌse-nə-gäl and 'nī-jər

LOCATION — In Northwest Africa, north of French Guinea and Ivory Coast
GOVT. — French Colony
AREA — 617,600 sq. mi.
POP. — 2,474,142
CAPITAL — Bamako

In 1921 the name of this colony was changed to French Sudan and postage stamps so inscribed were placed in use.

100 Centimes = 1 Franc

Gen. Louis Faidherbe
A1

Oil Palms — A2

Dr. N. Eugène Ballay
A3

Perf. 14x13½

1906-07 Unwmk. Typo.

Name of Colony in Red or Blue

1 A1 1c slate 1.40 1.75
Never hinged 2.50
On cover 125.00
a. Accent omitted over first "E" of "SENEGAL" 8.50 9.50
Never hinged 17.50
2 A1 2c brown 1.75 2.10
Never hinged 2.75
On cover 125.00
a. Accent omitted over first "E" of "SENEGAL" 9.50 10.50
Never hinged 20.00
3 A1 4c brn, *gray bl* 2.50 2.50
Never hinged 4.00
On cover 125.00
a. Accent omitted over first "E" of "SENEGAL" 12.50 14.00
Never hinged 25.00
4 A1 5c green 5.50 2.75
Never hinged 10.50
On cover 80.00
a. Accent omitted over first "E" of "SENEGAL" 32.50 21.00
Never hinged 62.50
5 A1 10c car (B) 6.25 2.75
Never hinged 14.00
On cover 75.00
a. Accent omitted over first "E" of "SENEGAL" 32.50 21.00
Never hinged 65.00
6 A1 15c vio ('07) 4.25 *5.00*
Never hinged 7.00
On cover 100.00
a. Accent omitted over first "E" of "SENEGAL" 25.00 27.50
Never hinged 50.00
7 A2 20c black & red, *azure* 5.50 5.50
Never hinged 10.50
On cover 95.00
8 A2 25c bl, *pnksh* 17.50 4.25
Never hinged 35.00
On cover 105.00
On cover, single franking 150.00
9 A2 30c vio brn, *pnksh* 7.00 5.50
Never hinged 14.00
On cover 110.00
On cover, single franking 190.00
10 A2 35c blk, *yellow* 5.50 5.00
Never hinged 12.50
On cover 125.00
On cover, single franking 190.00
a. Accent omitted over first "E" of "SENEGAL" 32.50 27.50
Never hinged 62.50
11 A2 40c car, *az* (B) 9.00 9.00
Never hinged 17.50
On cover 170.00
On cover, single franking 275.00
a. Accent omitted over first "E" of "SENEGAL" 45.00 50.00
Never hinged 100.00
12 A2 45c brn, *grnsh* 10.50 *11.00*
Never hinged 21.00
On cover 170.00
On cover, single franking 225.00
a. Accent omitted over first "E" of "SENEGAL" 52.50 55.00
Never hinged 115.00
13 A2 50c dp vio 10.50 *11.00*
Never hinged 21.00
On cover 160.00
On cover, single franking 225.00
a. Accent omitted over first "E" of "SENEGAL" 52.50 55.00
Never hinged 115.00
14 A2 75c bl, *org* 10.50 *12.00*
Never hinged 21.00
On cover 225.00
On cover, single franking 375.00
a. Accent omitted over first "E" of "SENEGAL" 52.50 55.00
Never hinged 115.00
15 A3 1fr blk, *azure* 25.00 *27.50*
Never hinged 52.50
On cover 275.00
On cover, single franking 450.00
16 A3 2fr bl, *pink* 45.00 *52.50*
Never hinged 100.00
On cover 300.00
On cover, single franking 500.00
17 A3 5fr car, *straw* (B) 95.00 *105.00*
Never hinged 180.00
On cover 450.00
On cover, single franking 625.00
Nos. 1-17 (17) 262.65 265.10

Camel with Rider — A4

1914-17 ***Perf. 13½x14***

18 A4 1c brn vio & vio .35 *.45*
Never hinged .70
On cover 105.00
19 A4 2c gray & brn vio .35 *.45*
Never hinged .70
On cover 105.00
20 A4 4c black & blue .35 *.45*
Never hinged .70
On cover 105.00
21 A4 5c yel grn & bl grn 1.05 .50
Never hinged 2.10
On cover 55.00
a. Chalky paper 2.10 1.05
Never hinged 3.50
On cover 55.00
22 A4 10c red org & rose 2.50 2.10
Never hinged 3.50
On cover 55.00
a. Chalky paper 4.50 3.50
Never hinged 7.00
On cover 65.00
23 A4 15c choc & org ('17) 2.10 1.05
Never hinged 3.50
On cover 50.00
a. Chalky paper 7.00 7.00
Never hinged 10.50
On cover 75.00
24 A4 20c brn vio & blk 2.10 2.10
Never hinged 3.50
On cover 65.00
25 A4 25c ultra & bl 2.10 1.40
Never hinged 3.50
On cover 70.00
On cover, single franking 160.00
26 A4 30c ol brn & brn 2.10 *2.10*
Never hinged 3.50
On cover 95.00
On cover, single franking 170.00
27 A4 35c car rose & vio 3.50 2.50
Never hinged 4.25
On cover 95.00
On cover, single franking 140.00
28 A4 40c gray & car rose 2.10 1.40
Never hinged 3.50
On cover 100.00
On cover, single franking 140.00
29 A4 45c bl & ol brn 2.10 2.10
Never hinged 3.50
On cover 105.00
On cover, single franking 190.00
30 A4 50c black & green 2.75 *2.75*
Never hinged 4.25
On cover 110.00
On cover, single franking 200.00
31 A4 75c org & ol brn 2.75 *2.75*
Never hinged 4.25
On cover 95.00
On cover, single franking 175.00
32 A4 1fr brown & brn vio 2.75 *3.50*
Never hinged 4.25
On cover 110.00
On cover, single franking 225.00
33 A4 2fr green & blue 3.50 *3.50*
Never hinged 5.50
On cover 140.00
On cover, single franking 250.00
34 A4 5fr violet & black 12.50 *14.00*
Never hinged 21.00
On cover 160.00
On cover, single franking 275.00
Nos. 18-34 (17) 44.95 43.10

See Upper Volta for types of this issue that escaped overprinting.

For surcharges see No. B1, French Sudan Nos. 21-49.

SEMI-POSTAL STAMP

Regular Issue of 1914 Surcharged in Red

1915 Unwmk. ***Perf. 13½x14***

B1 A4 10c + 5c red orange & rose 2.10 2.10
Never hinged 3.50
On cover 100.00

POSTAGE DUE STAMPS

Natives — D1

1906 Unwmk. Typo. ***Perf. 14x13½***

J1 D1 5c green, *greenish* 3.50 3.50
Never hinged 7.00
On cover 125.00
J2 D1 10c red brown 7.00 7.00
Never hinged 14.00
On cover 160.00
J3 D1 15c dark blue 10.50 10.50
Never hinged 21.00
On cover 175.00
J4 D1 20c black, *yellow* 14.00 7.00
Never hinged 27.50
On cover 140.00
J5 D1 50c violet 27.50 *27.50*
Never hinged 55.00
On cover 225.00
J6 D1 60c black, *buff* 21.00 *21.00*
Never hinged 42.50
On cover 225.00
J7 D1 1fr black, *pinkish* 35.00 *37.50*
Never hinged 77.50
On cover 350.00
Nos. J1-J7 (7) 118.50 114.00

D2

1914

J8 D2 5c green 1.05 *1.40*
Never hinged 1.40
On cover 95.00
J9 D2 10c rose 1.40 *1.75*
Never hinged 2.10
On cover 95.00
J10 D2 15c gray 1.40 *1.75*
Never hinged 2.10
On cover 95.00
J11 D2 20c brown 1.40 *1.75*
Never hinged 2.50
On cover 95.00
J12 D2 30c blue 2.10 *2.50*
Never hinged 3.50
On cover 100.00
J13 D2 50c black 1.75 *2.10*
Never hinged 2.75
On cover 120.00
J14 D2 60c orange 6.25 *7.00*
Never hinged 10.50
On cover 140.00
J15 D2 1fr violet 6.25 *7.00*
Never hinged 10.50
On cover 160.00
Nos. J8-J15 (8) 21.60 25.25

Stamps of Upper Senegal and Niger were superceded in 1921 by those of French Sudan.

UPPER SILESIA

'ə-pər sī'lē-zhˌē-ə

LOCATION — Formerly in eastern Germany and prior to World War I a part of Germany.

A plebiscite held under the terms of the Treaty of Versailles failed to determine the status of the country, the voting resulting about equally in favor of Germany and Poland. Accordingly, the League of Nations divided the territory between Germany and Poland.

100 Pfennig = 1 Mark
100 Fennigi = 1 Marka

Plebiscite Issues

A1

Perf. 14x13½

1920, Feb. 20 Typo. Unwmk.

1 A1 2½pf slate .40 *.80*
Never hinged 1.10
On cover 12.00
2 A1 3pf brown .40 *.85*
Never hinged 1.10
On cover 12.00
3 A1 5pf green .30 *.80*
Never hinged .65
On cover 4.00
4 A1 10pf dull red .40 *.90*
Never hinged 1.10
On cover 4.00
5 A1 15pf violet .25 *.80*
Never hinged .65
On cover 4.00
6 A1 20pf blue .25 *.80*
Never hinged .65
On cover 4.00
a. Imperf., pair 275.00 —
b. Half used as 10pf on cover 110.00
c. 20pf prussian blue 1.60 *5.75*
Never hinged 4.75 8.00
On cover 29.00
d. As "c," half used as 10pf on cover 1,000.
7 A1 50pf violet brn 4.75 *8.00*
Never hinged 21.00
On cover 32.50
a. 50pf red brown 20.00 *50.00*
Never hinged 50.00
On cover 160.00
8 A1 1m claret 5.00 *12.00*
Never hinged 15.00
On cover 50.00
9 A1 5m orange 5.00 *12.00*
Never hinged 16.00
On cover 150.00
Nos. 1-9 (9) 16.75 *36.95*
Set, never hinged 55.00

Black Surcharge

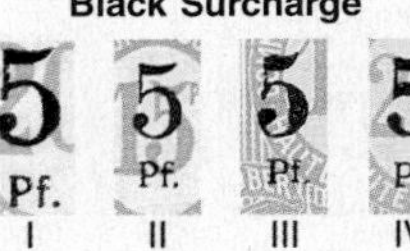

10 A1 5pf on 15pf vio (I) *160.00 650.00*
Never hinged *550.00*
On cover 575.00
a. Type II
Never hinged
On cover *675.00*
b. Type III
Never hinged
On cover *675.00*
c. Type IV
Never hinged
On cover *675.00*
11 A1 5pf on 20pf blue (I) 1.10 *3.25*
Never hinged 3.00
On cover *11.00*
a. Type II 1.25 *3.75*
Never hinged 2.50
On cover *15.00*
b. Type III 1.60 *4.00*
Never hinged 3.00
On cover *19.00*
c. Type IV 2.00 *5.00*
Never hinged 3.50
On cover *30.00*

Red Surcharge

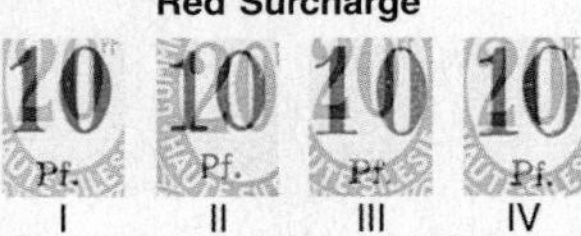

12 A1 10pf on 20pf bl (I) 1.10 *3.25*
Never hinged 3.00
On cover *15.00*
a. Type II 1.10 *3.25*
Never hinged 2.90
On cover *19.00*
b. Type III 1.10 *3.25*
Never hinged 3.90
On cover *11.00*
c. Type IV 1.10 *3.25*
Never hinged 3.90
On cover *12.50*
d. Imperf. 60.00 *240.00*
Never hinged 120.00
On cover *1,100.*

Black Surcharge

50 Pf. 50 Pf. 50 Pf. 50 Pf. 50 Pf.
Type I Type II Type III Type IV Type V

13 A1 50pf on 5m org (I), shiny ovpt. 27.50 52.50
Never hinged 200.00
On cover 225.00
a. Type II 29.00 55.00
Never hinged 140.00
On cover 240.00
b. Type III 30.00 87.50
Never hinged 240.00
On cover 350.00
c. Type IV 30.00 87.50
Never hinged 240.00
On cover 350.00
d. Type V 42.50 120.00
Never hinged 340.00
On cover 425.00
e. Type I, matte ovpt. 37.50 87.50
Never hinged 190.00
On cover 575.00

Nos. 10-13 are found with many varieties including surcharges inverted, double and double inverted.

Dove with Olive Branch Flying over Silesian Terrain — A2

A3

1920, Mar. 26 Typo. *Perf. 13½x14*

15 A2 2½pf gray .55 .80
Never hinged 2.25
On cover 8.25
16 A2 3pf red brown .55 .80
Never hinged 2.25
On cover 8.25
17 A2 5pf green .55 .80
Never hinged 2.25
On cover 4.25
18 A2 10pf dull red .55 .80
Never hinged 2.25
On cover 5.00
19 A2 15pf violet .55 .80
Never hinged 2.25
On cover 5.00
20 A2 20pf blue .80 2.00
Never hinged 2.25
On cover 5.00
21 A2 25pf dark brown .55 .80
Never hinged 2.25
On cover 8.25
22 A2 30pf orange .55 .80
Never hinged 2.25
On cover 6.75
23 A2 40pf olive green .55 2.00
Never hinged 2.25
On cover 6.75

Perf. 14x13½

24 A3 50pf gray 1.00 .80
Never hinged 3.25
On cover 21.00
25 A3 60pf blue .55 1.60
Never hinged 3.00
On cover 21.00
26 A3 75pf deep green 1.60 2.00
Never hinged 5.75
On cover 25.00
a. 75pf blackish green 825.00 1,250.
Never hinged 1,650.
b. 75pf bluish green 1,250. 1,250.
Never hinged 1,800.
c. 75pf deep gray green 2,850. 2,450.
Never hinged 3,250.
27 A3 80pf red brown 1.60 1.10
Never hinged 7.50
On cover 16.50
28 A3 1m claret 1.60 .80
Never hinged 7.50
On cover 16.50
29 A3 2m dark brown 1.40 .80
Never hinged 4.75
On cover 12.50
30 A3 3m violet 1.40 .80
Never hinged 4.75
On cover 25.00
31 A3 5m orange 4.00 4.50
Never hinged 12.50
On cover 42.50
Nos. 15-31 (17) 18.35 22.00
Set, never hinged 67.50

Nos. 18-28 Overprinted in Black or Red

1921, Mar. 20

32 A2 10pf dull red 4.00 10.00
Never hinged 18.00
On cover 100.00
33 A2 15pf violet 4.00 10.00
Never hinged 18.00
On cover 100.00
34 A2 20pf blue 5.50 14.00
Never hinged 30.00
On cover 100.00
35 A2 25pf dk brn (R) 12.00 32.50
Never hinged 45.00
On cover 125.00
36 A2 30pf orange 10.00 20.00
Never hinged 50.00
On cover 125.00
37 A2 40pf olive grn (R) 11.00 20.00
Never hinged 45.00
On cover 125.00

Overprinted

38 A3 50pf gray (R) 11.00 27.50
Never hinged 57.50
On cover —
39 A3 60pf blue 12.00 22.50
Never hinged 65.00
On cover —
40 A3 75pf deep green 12.00 27.50
Never hinged 100.00
On cover —
a. 75pf blue green 1,650. 1,850.
41 A3 80pf red brown 20.00 35.00
Never hinged 130.00
On cover —
42 A3 1m claret 24.00 65.00
Never hinged 150.00
On cover —
Nos. 32-42 (11) 125.50 284.00
Set, never hinged 700.00

Inverted or double overprints exist on Nos. 32-33, 35-40. Counterfeit overprints exist.

Type of 1920 and Surcharged

1922, Mar.

45 A3 4m on 60pf ol grn .80 2.00
Never hinged 3.00
On cover 25.00
46 A3 10m on 75pf red 1.25 2.75
Never hinged 7.00
On cover 125.00
47 A3 20m on 80pf orange 6.50 16.00
Never hinged 23.00
On cover 375.00
Nos. 45-47 (3) 8.55 20.75
Set, never hinged 32.00

Stamps of the above design were a private issue not recognized by the Inter-Allied Commission of Government. Value, set of 7, $65 unused, $225 never hinged, $225 used.

OFFICIAL STAMPS

German Stamps of 1905-20 Handstamped in Blue

1920, Feb. Wmk. 125 *Perf. 14, 14½*
On Stamps of 1906-19

O1 A22 2pf gray 1.10 1.25
O3 A22 2½pf gray .55 .65
O4 A16 3pf brown .55 .65
O5 A16 5pf green .55 .65
O6 A22 7½pf orange .55 .65
O7 A16 10pf car rose .55 .65
O8 A22 15pf dk violet .55 .65
O9 A16 20pf blue violet .55 .65
O10 A16 25pf org & blk, *yel* 8.00 6.50
O11 A16 30pf org & blk, *buff* .55 .65
O12 A22 35pf red brown .55 .65
O13 A16 40pf lake & blk .55 .65
O14 A16 50pf vio & blk, *buff* .55 .65
O15 A16 60pf magenta .55 .65
O16 A16 75pf green & blk .55 .65
O17 A16 80pf lake & blk, *rose* 6.50 8.00
O18 A17 1m car rose 1.10 1.25
O19 A21 2m gray blue 5.25 6.50

On National Assembly Stamps of 1919-20

O25 A23 10pf car rose .90 1.10
O26 A24 15pf choc & bl 1.60 2.00
O27 A25 25pf green & red 3.25 4.00
O28 A25 30pf red vio & red 2.50 3.00

On Semi-Postal Stamps of 1919

O30 A16 10pf + 5pf carmine 6.50 8.00
O31 A22 15pf + 5pf dk vio 6.50 8.00
Nos. O1-O31 (24) 50.35 58.05

Red Handstamp

O5a A16 5pf 10.00 14.00
O8a A22 15pf 6.50 10.00
O9a A16 20pf 6.50 10.00
O13a A16 40pf 20.00 30.00
O16a A16 75pf 20.00 30.00
O26a A24 15pf 1.10 1.25
Nos. O5a-O26a (6) 64.10 95.25

Values of Nos. O1-O31 are for reprints made with a second type of handstamp differing in minor details from the original (example: period after "S" is round instead of the earlier triangular form). Originals are scarce. Counterfeits exist.

Germany No. 65C with this handstamp is considered bogus by experts.

Local Official Stamps of Germany, 1920, Overprinted

1920, Apr. *Perf. 14*

O32 LO2 5pf green .30 1.00
O33 LO3 10pf carmine .30 1.00
O34 LO4 15pf violet brn .30 1.00
O35 LO5 20pf deep ultra .30 1.00
O36 LO6 30pf orange, *buff* .30 1.00
O37 LO7 50pf violet, *buff* .30 1.00
O38 LO8 1m red, *buff* 6.50 15.00
Nos. O32-O38 (7) 8.80 23.00

Same Overprint on Official Stamps of Germany, 1920-21

1920-21

O39 O1 5pf green 1.00 8.00
O40 O2 10pf carmine .25 1.00
O41 O3 15pf violet brn .25 1.00
O42 O4 20pf deep ultra .25 1.00
O43 O5 30pf orange, *buff* .25 1.00
O44 O6 40pf carmine rose .25 1.00
O45 O7 50pf violet, *buff* .25 1.00
O46 O8 60pf red brown .25 1.00
O47 O9 1m red, *buff* .25 1.00
O48 O10 1.25m dk blue, *yel* .25 1.00
O49 O11 2m dark blue 7.25 12.00
O50 O12 5m brown, *yel* .25 1.00

1922, Feb. Wmk. 126

O51 O11 2m dark blue .25 1.00
Nos. O39-O51 (13) 11.00 31.00

This overprint is found both horizontal, reading upright or inverted, and vertical, reading up or down. These variations generally command no premium over the values above.

The overprint also exists on most values double and double, one inverted, in the above formats, as well as at a 45 degree angle, upreading and downreading, either upright or inverted. These varieties generally sell for 25-100 percent over the value of normal examples.

UPPER VOLTA

LOCATION — Northwestern Africa, north of Gold Coast
GOVT. — French Colony
AREA — 105,869 sq. mi.
POP. — 6,695,500 (est. 1984)
CAPITAL — Ouagadougou

In 1919 the French territory of Upper Volta was detached from the southern section of Upper Senegal and Niger and made a separate colony. In 1933 the colony was divided among its neighbors: French Sudan, Ivory Coast, and Niger Territory.

100 Centimes = 1 Franc

Stamps and Types of Upper Senegal and Niger, 1914-17, Overprinted in Black or Red

1920-28 Unwmk. *Perf. 13½x14*

1 A4 1c brn vio & vio .25 .40
Never hinged .40
On cover 90.00
2 A4 2c gray & brn vio (R) .25 .40
Never hinged .40
On cover 90.00
3 A4 4c blk & bl .30 .50
Never hinged .50
On cover 90.00
4 A4 5c yel grn & bl grn .75 .75
Never hinged 1.50
On cover 45.00
5 A4 5c ol brn & dk brn ('22) .25 .40
Never hinged .40
On cover 30.00
6 A4 10c red org & rose 1.50 1.50
Never hinged 2.50
On cover 95.00
7 A4 10c yel grn & bl grn ('22) .25 .40
Never hinged .40
On cover 50.00
Complete booklet, 20 #7 —
8 A4 10c claret & bl ('25) .75 .75
Never hinged 1.50
On cover 30.00
a. Overprint omitted 240.00
Never hinged 325.00
9 A4 15c choc & org 1.20 1.50
Never hinged 1.25
On cover 50.00
Complete booklet, 20 #9 —
10 A4 20c brn vio & blk (R) 1.15 1.15
Never hinged 1.50
On cover 45.00
11 A4 25c ultra & bl 1.50 1.10
Never hinged 2.25
On cover 35.00
12 A4 25c blk & bl grn ('22) .75 .75
Never hinged 1.15
On cover 12.50
a. Overprint omitted 200.00
Never hinged 275.00
13 A4 30c ol brn & brn (R) 3.00 3.25
Never hinged 5.00
On cover 65.00
On cover, single franking 110.00
14 A4 30c red org & rose ('22) 1.50 1.75
Never hinged 2.10
On cover 45.00
On cover, single franking 75.00
15 A4 30c vio & brn red ('25) 1.15 1.50
Never hinged 1.50
On cover 16.00
16 A4 30c dl grn & bl grn ('27) 1.15 1.50
Never hinged 1.90
On cover 45.00
17 A4 35c car rose & vio .75 1.50
Never hinged 1.60
On cover 55.00
On cover, single franking 75.00
18 A4 40c gray & car rose .75 1.50
Never hinged 1.60
On cover 45.00
On cover, single franking 65.00
19 A4 45c bl & brn (R) .75 1.50
Never hinged 1.60
On cover 75.00
On cover, single franking 125.00
20 A4 50c blk & grn 2.75 3.50
Never hinged 4.75
On cover 50.00
On cover, single franking 125.00
21 A4 50c ultra & bl ('22) 1.20 2.00
Never hinged 1.15
On cover 37.50
On cover, single franking 70.00
22 A4 50c red org & bl ('25) 1.15 1.50
Never hinged 2.20
On cover 16.00
a. Double surcharge, one inverted 1,275. 1,250.
23 A4 60c org red ('26) .80 1.25
Never hinged 1.10
On cover 45.00
On cover, single franking 80.00
24 A4 65c bis & pale bl ('28) 1.60 2.50
Never hinged 2.50
On cover 50.00
On cover, single franking 90.00
25 A4 75c org & brn 1.50 1.50
Never hinged 2.75
On cover 55.00
On cover, single franking 140.00
26 A4 1fr brn & brn vio 1.15 2.00
Never hinged 2.00
On cover 75.00
On cover, single franking 170.00
27 A4 2fr grn & bl 2.00 2.40
Never hinged 3.75
On cover 90.00
On cover, single franking 190.00
28 A4 5fr vio & blk (R) 4.00 5.50
Never hinged 7.50
On cover 110.00
On cover, single franking 225.00
Nos. 1-28 (28) 34.10 44.25

No. 9 Surcharged in Various Colors

1922

29 A4 0,01c on 15c (Bk) 1.10 1.40
Never hinged 1.60
On cover 75.00
a. Double surcharge 175.00 250.00
Never hinged 260.00
30 A4 0,02c on 15c (Bl) 1.10 1.40
Never hinged 1.60
On cover 75.00
31 A4 0,05c on 15c (R) 1.20 1.50
Never hinged 1.60
On cover 30.00
Nos. 29-31 (3) 3.40 4.30

Type of 1920 Surcharged

1922

32 A4 60c on 75c vio, *pnksh* .75 1.15
Never hinged 1.20
On cover 45.00
On cover, single franking 70.00

Stamps and Types of 1920 Surcharged with New Value and Bars

1924-27

33 A4 25c on 2fr grn & bl .80 *1.00*
Never hinged 1.20
On cover 20.00
34 A4 25c on 5fr vio & blk .80 *1.00*
Never hinged 1.20
On cover 20.00
35 A4 65c on 45c bl & brn ('25) 1.50 1.50
Never hinged 1.90
On cover 90.00
On cover, single franking 170.00
36 A4 85c on 75c org & brn ('25) 1.60 *2.40*
Never hinged 3.00
On cover 75.00
On cover, single franking 140.00
37 A4 90c on 75c brn red & sal pink ('27) 2.25 2.25
Never hinged 3.00
On cover 75.00
On cover, single franking 125.00
38 A4 1.25fr on 1fr dp bl & lt bl (R) ('26) 1.50 *2.00*
Never hinged 2.25
On cover 80.00
On cover, single franking 140.00
39 A4 1.50fr on 1fr dp bl & ultra ('27) 3.00 *3.50*
Never hinged 5.00
On cover 65.00
On cover, single franking 105.00
40 A4 3fr on 5fr dl red & brn org ('27) 4.50 *5.50*
Never hinged 8.50
On cover 120.00
On cover, single franking 250.00
41 A4 10fr on 5fr ol grn & lil rose ('27) 15.00 *18.50*
Never hinged 27.00
On cover 125.00
On cover, single franking 275.00
42 A4 20fr on 5fr org brn & vio ('27) 22.50 *28.00*
Never hinged 40.00
On cover 140.00
On cover, single franking 300.00
Nos. 33-42 (10) 53.45 *65.65*

Hausa Chief — A5

Hausa Woman — A6

Hausa Warrior A7

1928 Typo. *Perf. 13½x14*

43 A5 1c indigo & grn .40 .40
Never hinged .85
On cover 70.00
44 A5 2c brn & lil .40 .40
Never hinged .85
On cover 70.00
45 A5 4c blk & yel .40 .75
Never hinged .85
On cover 70.00
46 A5 5c indigo & gray bl .40 .75
Never hinged .85
On cover 45.00
47 A5 10c indigo & pink 1.15 1.15
Never hinged 1.75
On cover 40.00
48 A5 15c brn & bl 1.50 *2.25*
Never hinged 2.50
On cover 25.00
49 A5 20c brn & grn 1.50 *1.60*
Never hinged 2.50
On cover 27.50
50 A6 25c brn & yel 1.90 *2.40*
Never hinged 3.00
On cover 29.00
51 A6 30c dp grn & grn 1.90 *2.40*
Never hinged 3.00
On cover 40.00
52 A6 40c blk & pink 1.90 *2.25*
Never hinged 3.00
On cover 14.00
53 A6 45c brn & blue 3.00 *3.75*
Never hinged 5.00
On cover 35.00
54 A6 50c blk & grn 2.25 *2.40*
Never hinged 4.00
On cover 14.00
55 A6 65c indigo & bl 3.00 *3.75*
Never hinged 5.00
On cover 50.00
56 A6 75c blk & lil 2.40 *3.00*
Never hinged 4.00
On cover 22.50
57 A6 90c brn red & lil 3.00 *3.75*
Never hinged 5.00
On cover 40.00
On cover, single franking 90.00

Perf. 14x13½

58 A7 1fr brn & grn 2.40 *2.75*
Never hinged 4.00
On cover 30.00
On cover, single franking 45.00
59 A7 1.10fr indigo & lil 3.00 *4.00*
Never hinged 5.00
On cover 200.00
On cover, single franking 450.00
60 A7 1.50fr ultra & grysh 3.75 *4.50*
Never hinged 6.00
On cover 40.00
On cover, single franking 80.00
61 A7 2fr blk & bl 4.00 *4.75*
Never hinged 6.00
On cover 40.00
On cover, single franking 70.00
62 A7 3fr brn & yel 4.00 *5.25*
Never hinged 6.50
On cover 45.00
On cover, single franking 100.00
63 A7 5fr brn & lil 4.00 *5.25*
Never hinged 6.00
On cover 50.00
On cover, single franking 110.00
64 A7 10fr blk & grn 20.00 *26.00*
Never hinged 30.00
On cover 80.00
On cover, single franking 140.00
65 A7 20fr blk & pink 30.00 *32.50*
Never hinged 40.00
On cover 110.00
On cover, single franking 200.00
Nos. 43-65 (23) 96.25 *116.00*

Common Design Types pictured following the introduction.

Colonial Exposition Issue

Common Design Types

1931 Engr. *Perf. 12½*

Country Name Typo. in Black

66 CD70 40c dp grn 4.00 4.00
Never hinged 6.50
On cover 120.00
67 CD71 50c violet 4.75 4.75
Never hinged 8.00
On cover 100.00
68 CD72 90c red org 4.75 4.75
Never hinged 8.00
On cover 170.00
On cover, single franking 250.00
69 CD73 1.50fr dull blue 5.50 5.50
Never hinged 9.50
On cover 160.00
On cover, single franking 225.00
Nos. 66-69 (4) 19.00 19.00

POSTAGE DUE STAMPS

Postage Due Stamps of Upper Senegal and Niger, 1914, Overprinted in Black or Red

1920 Unwmk. *Perf. 14x13½*

J1 D2 5c green .40 .80
Never hinged .80
On cover 50.00
J2 D2 10c rose .40 .80
Never hinged .80
On cover 50.00
J3 D2 15c gray .75 .80
Never hinged 1.50
On cover 50.00
J4 D2 20c brown (R) .75 .80
Never hinged 1.10
On cover 55.00
J5 D2 30c blue .75 .80
Never hinged 1.10
On cover 55.00
J6 D2 50c black (R) 1.25 1.60
Never hinged 1.75
On cover 60.00
J7 D2 60c orange 1.25 1.60
Never hinged 1.75
On cover 75.00
J8 D2 1fr violet 2.25 2.25
Never hinged 3.00
On cover 95.00
Nos. J1-J8 (8) 7.80 9.45

Type of 1914 Issue Surcharged

1927

J9 D2 2fr on 1fr lilac rose 3.50 3.50
Never hinged 6.00
On cover 125.00
J10 D2 3fr on 1fr orange brn 6.00 4.50
Never hinged 7.50
On cover 140.00

D3

1928 Typo.

J11 D3 5c green .40 .80
Never hinged .80
On cover 45.00
J12 D3 10c rose .80 .80
Never hinged 1.10
On cover 45.00
J13 D3 15c dark gray 1.25 1.60
Never hinged 1.60
On cover 45.00
J14 D3 20c dark brown 1.25 1.60
Never hinged 1.60
On cover 50.00
J15 D3 30c dark blue 1.75 2.50
Never hinged 3.00
On cover 50.00
J16 D3 50c black 3.50 4.00
Never hinged 7.50
On cover 55.00
J17 D3 60c orange 4.00 4.75
Never hinged 7.50
On cover 65.00
J18 D3 1fr dull violet 6.50 7.25
Never hinged 7.50
On cover 75.00
J19 D3 2fr lilac rose 11.00 11.00
Never hinged 15.00
On cover 95.00
J20 D3 3fr orange brn 15.00 19.00
Never hinged 19.00
On cover 105.00
Nos. J11-J20 (10) 45.45 53.30

URUGUAY

ˈyur-ə-ˌgwā

LOCATION — South America, between Brazil and Argentina and bordering on the Atlantic Ocean
GOVT. — Republic
AREA — 72,172 sq. mi.
POP. — 2,991,341 (est. 1983)
CAPITAL — Montevideo

120 Centavos = 1 Real
8 Reales = 1 Peso
100 Centesimos = 1 Peso (1859)
1000 Milesimos = 1 Peso (1898)

Watermarks

Wmk. 187 — R O in Diamond

Wmk. 188 — REPUBLICA O. DEL URUGUAY

Wmk. 189 — Caduceus

Wmk. 227 — Greek Border and REPUBLICA O. DEL URUGUAY in Alternate Curved Lines

GREAT BRITAIN POST OFFICES IN URUGUAY

PRE-STAMP POSTAL MARKINGS

Crowned Circle handstamp type VI is pictured in the Crowned Circle Handstamps and Great Britain Used Abroad section.

1851

A1 VI Crowned Circle handstamp inscribed "PAID AT MONTEVIDEO" in black, on cover *1,100.*
A2 VI Crowned Circle handstamp inscribed "PAID AT MONTEVIDEO" in red, on cover —

STAMPS OF GREAT BRITAIN USED IN MONTEVIDEO

Stamps of Great Britain Cancelled with "C28" in barred oval

1864-73

A3 1p rose red, plates 73, 92-94, 119, 148, 154, 157, 171 (#33), *value from* 55.00
A4 2p blue, plate 9 (#29) 65.00
A5 2p blue, plate 13 (#30) 55.00
A6 3p rose (#44) —
A7 3p rose, plates 4, 5, 7 (#49), *value from* 70.00
A8 4p rose (#26) —
A9 4p vermilion,, hair lines (#34c) —
A10 4p vermilion, plates 7-12 (#43), *value from* 70.00

A11 6p lilac (#27) —
A12 6p lilac, plate 4 (#39b) 175.00
A13 6p lilac, plate 5 (#45) 90.00
Plate 6 (#45) 100.00
A14 6p dull violet, plate 6 (#50) —
A15 6p violet, plates 8, 9 (#51), *value from* 80.00
A16 6p brown plate 11 (#59) —
A17 6p pale buff, plate 11 (#59b) —
Plate 12 (#59b) —
A18 9p straw (#40) —
A19 9p straw (#46) —
A20 9p bister (#52) *300.00*
A21 10p red brown (#53) *350.00*
A22 1sh green (#42) *175.00*
A23 1sh green (#48) 150.00
A24 1sh green, plates 4, 5 (#54), *value from* 80.00
A25 2sh blue (#55) *225.00*
A26 5sh rose, plate 1 (#57) *625.00*

The British postal agency in Montevideo was closed on July 31, 1875.

CARRIER ISSUES

Issued by Atanasio Lapido, Administrator-General of Posts

A1

A1a

"El Sol de Mayo"

Unwmk.

1856, Oct. 1 Litho. *Imperf.*

1 A1 60c blue 450. 450.
On cover *5,000.*
a. 60c deep blue 650.
On cover *6,500.*
b. 60c indigo 1,000. —
On cover —
c. 60c pale blue 650.
On cover —
2 A1 80c green 500. 500.
On cover *8,000.*
a. 80c deep green 550.
On cover —
b. 80c emerald green 600.
On cover —
3 A1 1r vermilion 400. 400.
On cover *11,000.*
a. 1r carmine vermilion 450.
On cover —

1857, Oct. 1

3B A1a 60c blue *2,750.* —
On cover —
c. 60c pale blue *2,750.*
On cover —
d. 60c indigo *3,000.*
On cover —

Nos. 1-3Bd were spaced very closely on the stone. Very fine examples will have clear margins on three sides and touching or slightly cut into the frames on the fourth (consult the grading illustrations in the catalogue introduction). All genuinely used examples are pen canceled. Certification by a recognized authority is recommended.

Stamps with tiny faults, such as small thin spots, sell for about 75% of the values of sound examples.

See Nos. 410-413.

A2

1858, Mar.

4 A2 120c blue 575.00 *650.00*
On cover *7,500.*
a. 120c deep blue 600.00 *650.00*
On cover —
b. 120c greensih blue 650.00 —
On cover —
c. Tête bêche pair —
5 A2 180c green 150.00 *200.00*
On cover —
a. 180c deep green 250.00 *350.00*
On cover —
b. 180c pale green 140.00 —
On cover —
c. As "b," thick paper 500.00 —
On cover —
d. Tête bêche pair —
6 A2 240c dull ver 150.00 *1,200.*
On cover —
a. 240c deep vermilion 175.00
On cover —
b. 240c brick red 300.00
On cover —
c. 180c dl ver in stone of 240c — —
d. Thick paper (dull ver) — —
e. 240c setenant with a vacant space *5,000.*
Nos. 4-6 (3) 875.00 *2,050.*

Nos. 4-6e have been extensively forged. Certification by a recognized authority is recommended.

ISSUES OF THE REPUBLIC

A3

A4

1859, June 26 Thin Numerals

7 A3 60c lilac 50.00 35.00
On cover 300.00
a. 60c gray lilac 45.00 35.00
On cover 300.00
8 A3 80c orange 450.00 75.00
On cover 800.00
a. 80c yellow 300.00 60.00
On cover 1,500.
9 A3 100c brown lake 100.00 70.00
On cover 1,500.
a. 100c brown rose 120.00 100.00
On cover 1,500.
10 A3 120c blue 55.00 30.00
On cover 250.00
a. 120c slate blue 75.00 30.00
On cover 600.00
b. 120c greenish blue 75.00 25.00
On cover 350.00
11 A3 180c green 22.00 *26.00*
On cover 1,200.
12 A3 240c vermilion 90.00 90.00
On cover 1,500.
Nos. 7-12 (6) 767.00 *326.00*

Very fine examples of Nos. 7-12 have 1.5mm margins on all sides.

1860 Thick Numerals

13 A4 60c dull lilac 25.00 12.00
On cover 200.00
a. 60c gray lilac 40.00 15.00
On cover 250.00
b. 60c brown lilac 30.00 18.00
On cover 250.00
c. 60c red lilac 120.00 60.00
On cover 250.00
d. As "a," fine impression (1st printing) 125.00 45.00
On cover 350.00
e. 60c chocolate brown 75.00 37.50
On cover 350.00
14 A4 80c yellow 50.00 25.00
On cover 400.00
a. 80c orange 100.00 26.00
On cover 500.00
15 A4 100c rose 100.00 55.00
On cover *1,200.*
a. 100c carmine 110.00 55.00
On cover *1,200.*
16 A4 120c blue 45.00 25.00
On cover 200.00
17 A4 180c yellow grn 425.00 375.00
On cover *2,000.*
a. 180c deep green 425.00 *450.00*
On cover *2,000.*
Nos. 13-17 (5) 645.00 *492.00*

No. 13 was first printed (1860) in sheets of 192 (16x12) containing 24 types. The impressions are very clear; paper is whitish and of better quality than that of the later printings. In the 1861-62 printings, the layout contains 12 types and the subjects are spaced farther apart.

Very fine examples of Nos. 13-17 have 1.5mm margins on all sides.

Coat of Arms — A5

1864, Apr. 13

18 A5 6c rose 18.00 12.00
On cover 150.00
a. 6c carmine 40.00 30.00
On cover 150.00
b. 6c red 40.00 30.00
On cover —
c. 6c brick red 45.00 30.00
On cover 1,200.
d. On laid paper 35.00 25.00
On cover —
20 A5 6c salmon 500.00 *500.00*
On cover —
21 A5 8c green 25.00 25.00
On cover 750.00
a. Tête bêche pair 775.00
b. 8c yellow green 20.00 20.00
On cover 900.00
c. 8c dark green 20.00 20.00
On cover 900.00
22 A5 10c yellow 32.50 25.00
On cover 1,200.
a. 10c ocher 35.00 25.00
On cover —
23 A5 12c blue 15.00 12.00
On cover 200.00
a. 12c dark blue 25.00 18.00
On cover 250.00
b. 12c slate blue 30.00 20.00
On cover 600.00
c. 12c pale blue 25.00 15.00
On cover 250.00
d. On laid paper 30.00 20.00
On cover —

No. 20, which is on thicker paper, was never placed in use.

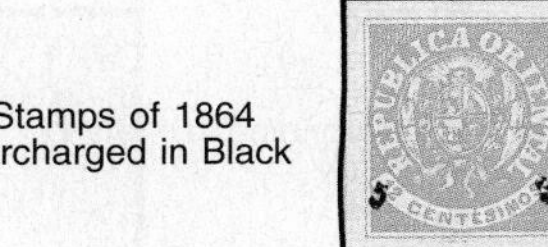

Stamps of 1864 Surcharged in Black

1866, Jan. 1

24 A5 5c on 12c blue 30.00 *55.00*
a. 5c on 12c slate blue 30.00 *60.00*
b. Inverted surcharge 150.00
c. Double surcharge 150.00
d. Pair, one without surcharge
e. Triple surcharge 55.00
25 A5 10c on 8c brt grn 30.00 *55.00*
a. 10c on 8c dl grn 30.00 *55.00*
b. Tête bêche pair 300.00
c. Double surcharge 150.00
26 A5 15c on 10c ocher 35.00 *90.00*
a. 15c on 10c yellow 35.00 *90.00*
b. Inverted surcharge 150.00
c. Double surcharge 150.00
27 A5 20c on 6c rose 40.00 *80.00*
a. 20c on 6c rose red 37.50 *75.00*
b. Inverted surcharge 150.00
c. Double surcharge 150.00
d. Pair, one without surcharge
28 A5 20c on 6c brick red *400.00*
a. Double surcharge 500.00
Nos. 24-27 (4) 135.00 *280.00*

Many counterfeits exist.

No. 28 was not issued.

Coat of Arms and Numeral of Value — A7

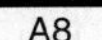
A8

A8a

A8b

A8c

Type I

Type II

ONE CENTESIMO:

Type I — The wavy lines behind "CENTESIMO" are clear and distinct. Stamps 4mm apart.

Type II — The wavy lines are rough and blurred. Stamps 3mm apart.

1866, Jan. 10 *Imperf.*

29 A7 1c black (type II) 5.00 *7.50*
a. 1c black (type I) 5.00 *7.50*
30 A8 5c blue 6.00 4.00
a. 5c dull blue 5.00 2.50
b. 5c ultramarine 32.50 7.50
c. Numeral with white flag 25.00 12.00
d. "ENTECIMOS" 25.00 12.00
e. "CENTECIMO" 25.00 12.00
f. "CENTECIMOS" with small "S" 25.00 12.00
g. Pelure paper 100.00 100.00
h. Thick paper
31 A8a 10c yellow green 20.00 7.00
a. 10c blue green 20.00 7.00
b. "I" of "CENTECIMOS" omitted 27.50 14.00
c. "CENIECIMOS" 27.50 14.00
d. "CENTRCIMOS" 27.50 14.00
32 A8b 15c orange yel 30.00 15.00
a. 15c yellow 30.00 15.00
33 A8c 20c rose 35.00 15.00
a. 20c lilac rose 35.00 15.00
b. Thick paper 37.50 16.00
Nos. 29-33 (5) 96.00 48.50

See Nos. 34-38. For overprint see No. O11.

Engraved plates were prepared for Nos. 30 to 33 but were not put in use. The stamps were printed from lithographic transfers from the plate. In 1915 a few reprints of the 15c were made from the engraved plate by a California philatelic society, each sheet being numbered and signed by officers of the society; then the plate was defaced.

1866-67 *Perf. 8½ to 13½*

No.	Type	Description	Unused	Used
34	A7	1c black	6.50	20.00
35	A8	5c blue	5.00	2.50
a.		5c dark blue	5.00	1.00
b.		Numeral with white flag	25.00	12.00
c.		"ENTECIMOS"	25.00	12.00
d.		"CENTECIMO"	25.00	12.00
e.		"CENTECIMOS" with small "S"	15.00	8.00
f.		Pelure paper	90.00	20.00
36	A8a	10c green	12.00	4.00
a.		10c yellow green	14.00	4.00
b.		"CENIECIMOS"	35.00	14.00
c.		"I" of "CENTECIMOS" omitted	35.00	14.00
d.		"CENTRCIMOS"	35.00	14.00
e.		Pelure paper	90.00	20.00
37	A8b	15c orange yel	21.00	6.00
a.		15c yellow	21.00	6.00
b.		Thin paper	25.00	10.00
38	A8c	20c rose	25.00	10.00
a.		20c brown rose	25.00	10.00
b.		Thin paper	30.00	15.00
c.		Thick paper	30.00	15.00
		Nos. 34-38 (5)	69.50	42.50

A9

A10

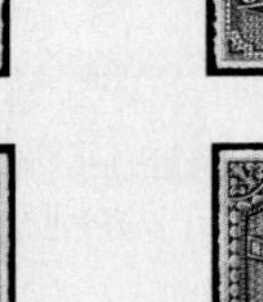
A11

A12

1877-79 **Engr.** *Rouletted 8*

No.	Type	Description	Unused	Used
39	A9	1c red brown	.80	.50
40	A10	5c green	1.00	.50
a.		Thick paper	5.00	2.50
41	A11	10c vermilion	2.00	.80
42	A11	20c bister	3.50	1.25
43	A11	50c black	12.50	3.50
43A	A12	1p blue ('79)	50.00	22.50
		Nos. 39-43A (6)	69.80	29.05

The first printing of the 1p had the coat of arms smaller with quarterings reversed. These "error" stamps were not issued, and all were ordered burned. One example is known to have been in a celebrated Uruguayan collection and a few others exist.

See No. 44. For overprints and surcharges see Nos. 52-53, O1-O8, O10, O19.

1880, Nov. 10 **Engr.** *Rouletted 6*

No.	Type	Description	Unused	Used
44	A9	1c brown	.50	.50
a.		Imperf., pair	10.00	
b.		Rouletted 12½	2.50	

Joaquin Suárez — A13

1881, Aug. 25 *Perf. 12½*

No.	Type	Description	Unused	Used
45	A13	7c blue	2.50	2.50
a.		Imperf., pair	9.00	9.00

For overprint see No. O9.

A14

Devices from Coat of Arms — A14a

1882, May 15

No.	Type	Description	Unused	Used
46	A14	1c green	1.50	1.50
a.		1c yellow green	4.00	2.00
b.		Imperf., pair	13.00	
47	A14a	2c rose	1.25	1.00
a.		Imperf., pair	15.00	

These stamps bear numbers from 1 to 100 according to their position on the sheet.

Counterfeits of Nos. 46 and 47 are plentiful.

See Nos. 1132-1133 in Scott Standard catalogue, Vol. 6. For overprints see Nos. 54, O12-O13, O20.

Coat of Arms
A15 A16

Gen. Máximo Santos — A17

General José Artigas — A18

Perf. 12, 12x12½, 12x13, 13x12

1883, Mar. 1

No.	Type	Description	Unused	Used
48	A15	1c green	1.50	1.00
49	A16	2c red	2.50	1.50
50	A17	5c blue	2.75	1.75
51	A18	10c brown	5.00	2.50
		Nos. 48-51 (4)	11.75	6.75

Imperf., Pairs

No.	Type	Description	Unused	Used
48a	A15	1c	7.00	
49a	A16	2c	7.00	
50a	A17	5c	6.50	
51a	A18	10c	11.00	

For overprints see Nos. O14-O18.

No. 40 Overprinted in Black

1883, Sept. 24 *Rouletted 8*

No.	Type	Description	Unused	Used
52	A10	5c green	1.00	.75
a.		Double overprint	15.00	15.00
b.		Overprint reading down	6.00	6.00
c.		"Provisorio" omitted	7.00	7.00
d.		"1883" omitted	4.50	4.50

No. 52 with overprint in red is a color essay.

No. 41 Surcharged in Black

1884, Jan. 15

No.	Type	Description	Unused	Used
53	A11	1c on 10c ver	.50	.50
a.		Small figure "1"	4.25	4.25
b.		Inverted surcharge	4.25	4.25
c.		Double surcharge	8.00	5.00

No. 47 Overprinted in Black

Perf. 12½

No.	Type	Description	Unused	Used
54	A14a	2c rose	.75	.75
a.		Double overprint	14.00	
b.		Imperf., pair	40.00	

A22

A23

Thick Paper

1884, Jan. 25 **Litho.** **Unwmk.**

No.	Type	Description	Unused	Used
55	A22	5c ultra	2.00	1.00
a.		Imperf., pair	7.50	4.00

Thin Paper

Perf. 12½, 13 and Compound

No.	Type	Description	Unused	Used
56	A23	5c blue	1.50	.70
a.		Imperf., pair	14.00	

For overprints see Nos. O21-O22.

A24

A24a

A24b

Artigas — A25

Santos — A26

A27

A28

1884-88 **Engr.** *Rouletted 8*

No.	Type	Description	Unused	Used
57	A24	1c gray	.80	.50
58	A24	1c olive	.75	.40
59	A24	1c green	.65	.40
60	A24a	2c vermilion	.40	.25
60A	A24a	2c rose ('88)	.40	.25
61	A24b	5c deep blue	.80	.30
61A	A24b	5c blue, *blue*	2.00	.85
62	A24b	5c violet ('86)	.50	.25
63	A24b	5c lt bl ('88)	.50	.25
64	A25	7c dk brown	2.00	.85
65	A25	7c org ('88)	2.00	.75
66	A26	10c olive brn	.80	.35
67	A27	20c red violet	2.00	1.00
68	A27	20c bis brn ('88)	2.00	1.00
69	A28	25c gray violet	4.00	1.50
70	A28	25c ver ('88)	3.00	1.00
		Nos. 57-70 (16)	22.60	9.90

Water dissolves the blue in the paper of No. 61A.

For overprints see Nos. 73, 98-99, O23-O34, O36-O39, O61.

A29

1887, Oct. 17 **Litho.** *Rouletted 9*

No.	Type	Description	Unused	Used
71	A29	10c lilac	2.50	1.25
a.		10c gray lilac	3.00	1.25

For overprint see No. O40.

A30

1888, Jan. 1 **Engr.** *Rouletted 8*

No.	Type	Description	Unused	Used
72	A30	10c violet	.60	.25

For overprint see No. O35.

No. 62 Overprinted in Black

1889, Oct. 14

No.	Type	Description	Unused	Used
73	A24b	5c violet	.40	.40
a.		Inverted overprint	8.00	6.00
b.		Inverted "A" for "V" in "Provisorio"	4.00	4.00

No. 73 with overprint in red is a color essay.

Coat of Arms — A32

Numeral of Value — A33

A34

A35

A36

A37

Justice A38

Mercury A39

A40

Perf. 12½ to 15½ and Compound

1889-1901 **Engr.**

No.	Type	Description	Unused	Used
74	A32	1c green	.50	.25
a.		Imperf., pair	13.00	
75	A32	1c dull bl ('94)	.50	.25
76	A33	2c rose	.50	.25
77	A33	2c red brn ('94)	.55	.25
78	A33	2c org ('99)	.55	.25
79	A34	5c dp blue	.50	.25
80	A34	5c rose ('94)	.55	.25
81	A35	7c bister brn	1.00	.30
82	A35	7c green ('94)	4.75	2.75
83	A35	7c car ('00)	4.00	1.75
84	A36	10c blue grn	3.50	.85
a.		Printed on both sides	20.00	
85	A36	10c org ('94)	3.25	.60
86	A37	20c orange	2.50	.60
87	A37	20c brown ('94)	4.75	1.75
88	A37	20c lt blue ('00)	2.75	.40
a.		20c greenish blue	3.00	.40
89	A38	25c red brown	3.25	.85
90	A38	25c ver ('94)	6.75	3.50
91	A38	25c bis brn ('01)	3.75	.50
92	A39	50c lt blue	7.50	5.00
93	A39	50c lilac ('94)	11.00	5.50
94	A39	50c car ('01)	6.75	1.00
95	A40	1p lilac	18.00	5.00
96	A40	1p lt blue ('94)	25.00	7.00
97	A40	1p dp grn ('01)	20.00	2.25
a.		Imperf., pair	30.00	
		Nos. 74-97 (24)	132.15	41.35

For surcharges and overprints see Nos. 100-101, 142, 180, 185, C1-C3, O41-O60, O89-O91, O108-O109.

Nos. 59 and 62 Overprinted in Red

a

b

1891-92 *Rouletted 8*

98 A24 (a) 1c green ('92) .40 .40
- *a.* Inverted overprint 6.00 6.00
- *b.* Double overprint 7.75 7.75
- *c.* Double ovpt., one invtd. 3.00 2.50
- *d.* "PREVISORIO" 4.00 4.00

99 A24b (b) 5c violet .25 .25
- *a.* "1391" 4.00 2.75
- *b.* Double overprint 4.00 2.75
- *c.* Inverted overprint 4.00 2.75
- *d.* Double ovpt., one invtd. 5.00 3.00

Nos. 86 and 81 Surcharged in Black or Red

c

d

Perf. 12½ to 15½ and Compound

1892

100 A37 (c) 1c on 20c org (Bk) .40 .40
- *a.* Inverted surcharge 6.00 6.00

101 A35 (d) 5c on 7c bis brn (R) .40 .40
- *a.* Inverted surcharge 1.00 1.00
- *b.* Double surcharge, one invtd. 3.00 3.00
- *c.* Double surcharge 3.00 3.00
- *d.* Vertical surcharge 10.00
- *e.* "PREVISORIO" 3.00 3.00
- *f.* "Cinco" omitted 4.50

No. 101 with surcharge in green is a color essay.

Several surcharge errors of date and misspelling of "Centésimos" exist. Value $15.

A45

A46

Arms A47

Peace A48

1892 **Engr.**

102 A45 1c green .50 .25
103 A46 2c rose .50 .25
104 A47 5c blue .50 .25
105 A48 10c orange 2.00 .85
Nos. 102-105 (4) 3.50 1.60

Issued: 1c, 2c, 3/9; 5c, 4/19; 10c, 12/15.

Liberty A49

Arms A50

1894, June 2

106 A49 2p carmine 30.00 17.50
107 A50 3p dull violet 30.00 17.50

Gaucho A51

Solis Theater A52

Locomotive A53

Bull's Head A54

Ceres — A55

Sailing Ship — A56

Liberty — A57

Mercury — A58

Coat of Arms — A59

Montevideo Fortress — A60

Cathedral in Montevideo A61

Perf. 12 to 15½ and Compound

1895-99

108 A51 1c bister .50 .25
109 A51 1c slate bl ('97) .50 .25
- *a.* Printed on both sides 14.00

110 A52 2c blue .50 .25
111 A52 2c claret ('97) .50 .25
112 A53 5c red .50 .25
113 A53 5c green ('97) .65 .25
- *a.* Imperf., pair 3.50

114 A53 5c grnsh bl ('99) 1.00 .40
115 A54 7c deep green 7.75 2.50
116 A54 7c orange ('97) 3.50 1.25
117 A55 10c brown 2.00 .50
118 A56 20c green & blk 7.00 .85
119 A56 20c cl & blk ('97) 4.75 .60
120 A57 25c red brn & blk 5.50 1.50
- *a.* Center inverted 2,000.

121 A57 25c pink & bl ('97) 3.50 .60
122 A58 50c blue & blk 7.00 3.50
123 A58 50c grn & brn ('97) 5.00 1.25
124 A59 1p org brn & blk 14.00 5.50
125 A59 1p yel brn & bl ('97) 9.50 3.50
126 A60 2p violet & grn 32.50 20.00
127 A60 2p bis & car ('97) 9.50 2.00
128 A61 3p carmine & blue 32.50 20.00
129 A61 3p lil & car ('97) 12.50 2.50
Nos. 108-129 (22) 160.65 67.95

All values of this issue exist imperforate but they were not issued in that form.

For overprints and surcharges see Nos. 138-140, 143, 145, 147, O62-O78.

President Joaquin Suárez A62 A63

Statue of President Suárez — A64

Perf. 12½ to 15 and Compound

1896, July 18

130 A62 1c brown vio & blk .25 .25
131 A63 5c pale bl & blk .25 .25
132 A64 10c lake & blk 1.00 .30
Nos. 130-132 (3) 1.50 .80

Dedication of Pres. Suárez statue.

For overprints and surcharge see Nos. 133-135, 144, 146, 152, O79-O81.

Same Overprinted in Red

e

f

1897, Mar. 1

133 A62 (e) 1c brn vio & blk .40 .40
- *a.* Inverted overprint 6.00 6.00

134 A63 (e) 5c pale blue & blk .50 .40
- *a.* Inverted overprint 9.50 6.00

135 A64 (f) 10c lake & blk 1.00 .60
- *a.* Inverted overprint 12.00 9.50
- *b.* Double overprint 7.50

Nos. 133-135 (3) 1.90 1.40

"Electricity" — A68

1897-99 **Engr.**

136 A68 10c red 1.75 .40
137 A68 10c red lilac ('99) .75 .50

For overprints see Nos. 141, O82-O83.

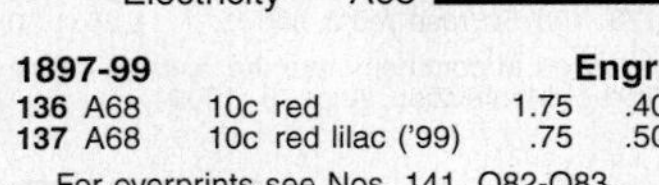

Regular Issues Overprinted in Red or Blue

1897, Sept. 26

138 A51 1c slate bl (R) .80 .60
- *a.* Inverted overprint 4.75 4.75

139 A52 2c claret (Bl) 1.25 1.25
- *a.* Inverted overprint 4.75 4.75

140 A53 5c green (Bl) 1.75 1.60
- *a.* Inverted overprint 7.75 7.75
- *b.* Double overprint

141 A68 10c red (Bl) 2.75 2.75
- *a.* Inverted overprint 17.00 17.00

Nos. 138-141 (4) 6.55 6.20

Commemorating the Restoration of Peace at the end of the Civil War.

Issue for use only on the days of the National Fête, Sept. 26-28, 1897.

Regular Issues Surcharged in Black, Blue or Red

1898, July 25

142 A32 ½c on 1c bl (Bk) .40 .40
- *a.* Inverted surcharge 3.00 3.00

143 A51 ½c on 1c bis (Bl) .40 .40
- *a.* Inverted surcharge 3.00
- *b.* Double surcharge 2.50

144 A62 ½c on 1c brn vio & blk (R) .40 .40
145 A52 ½c on 2c blue (Bk) .40 .40
146 A63 ½c on 5c pale bl & blk (R) .40 .40
- *a.* Double surcharge 6.25

147 A54 ½c on 7c dp grn (R) .40 .40
Nos. 142-147 (6) 2.40 2.40

The 2c red brown of 1894 (#77) was also surcharged like #142-147 but was not issued. Value $12.

Liberty — A69

1898-99 **Litho.** *Perf. 11, 11½*

148 A69 5m rose .25 .25
149 A69 5m purple ('99) .25 .25

Statue of Artigas — A70

1899-1900 **Engr.** *Perf. 12½, 14, 15*

150 A70 5m lt blue .25 .25
151 A70 5m orange ('00) .25 .25

No. 135 With Additional Surcharge in Black

1900, Dec. 1

152 A64 5c on 10c lake & blk .50 .25
- *a.* Black bar covering "1897" omitted 15.00

Cattle — A72

Girl's Head — A73

Shepherdess — A74

Perf. 13½ to 16 and Compound

1900-10 **Engr.**

153 A72 1c yellow green .40 .25
154 A73 5c dull blue .80 .25
155 A73 5c slate grn ('10) .80 .25
156 A74 10c gray violet 1.00 .25
Nos. 153-156 (4) 3.00 1.00

For surcharges and overprints see Nos. 179, 184, O84, O86, O88, O106-O107.

Eros and Cornucopia A75

Basket of Fruit A76

1901, Feb. 11

157 A75 2c vermilion .50 .25
158 A76 7c brown orange 1.75 .25

For surcharges and overprints see Nos. 197-198, O85, O87, O105.

General Artigas — A78

Cattle — A79

Eros — A80

Cow — A81

Shepherdess A82

Numeral A83

Justice — A84

1904-05 Litho. *Perf. 11½*

160 A78 5m orange .40 .25
a. 5m yellow .40 .25
161 A79 1c green .50 .25
a. Imperf., pair 3.50
162 A80 2c dp orange .25 .25
a. 2c orange red .25 .25
b. Imperf., pair 3.00
163 A81 5c blue .80 .25
a. Imperf., pair 3.50
164 A82 10c dk violet ('05) .50 .25
165 A83 20c gray grn ('05) 2.50 .50
166 A84 25c olive bis ('05) 3.25 .80
Nos. 160-166 (7) 8.20 2.55

Design of No. 163 measures 17mm by 23mm. See No. 170.

For overprints see Nos. 167-169, O92-O98, O101-O103.

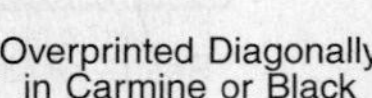

Overprinted Diagonally in Carmine or Black

1904, Oct. 15

167 A79 1c green (C) .40 .40
168 A80 2c deep orange (Bk) .65 .40
169 A81 5c dark blue (C) 1.25 .60
Nos. 167-169 (3) 2.30 1.40

End of the Civil War of 1904. In the first overprinting, "Paz 1904" appears at a 50-degree angle; in the second, at a 63-degree angle.

A85

1906, Feb. 23 Litho. Unwmk.

170 A85 5c dark blue 1.10 .25
a. Imperf., pair 6.00

Design of No. 170 measures 19¼mm by 25½mm. See No. 163.

A86

1906-07

171 A86 5c deep blue .30 .30
172 A86 7c orange brn ('07) .70 .50
173 A86 50c rose 5.00 1.25
Nos. 171-173 (3) 6.00 2.05

Cruiser "Montevideo" — A87

1908, Aug. 23 Typo. *Rouletted 13*

174 A87 1c car & dk grn 2.00 1.50
175 A87 2c green & dk grn 2.00 1.50
176 A87 5c org & dk grn 2.00 1.50
Nos. 174-176 (3) 6.00 4.50

Center Inverted

174a A87 1c 300.00 300.00
175a A87 2c 300.00 300.00
176a A87 5c 300.00 300.00
Nos. 174a-176a (3) 900.00 900.00

Imperf., Pairs

174b A87 1c 30.00
175b A87 2c 30.00
176b A87 5c 30.00

Independence of Uruguay, declared Aug. 25, 1825. Counterfeits exist.

For surcharges and overprints see Nos. 186, O99-O100, O104, O110.

View of the Port of Montevideo — A88

Wmk. 187

1909, Aug. 24 Engr. *Perf. 11½*

177 A88 2c lt brown & blk 1.25 1.20
178 A88 5c rose red & blk 1.25 1.20

Issued to commemorate the opening of the Port of Montevideo, Aug. 25, 1909.

Nos. 156, 91 Surcharged

Perf. 14 to 16

1909, Sept. 13 Unwmk.

179 A74 8c on 10c dull vio .75 .25
a. "Contesimos" 4.00 2.00
180 A38 23c on 25c bis brn 1.75 .60

Centaur — A89

Wmk. 187

1910, May 22 Engr. *Perf. 11½*

182 A89 2c carmine red .60 .40
183 A89 5c deep blue .60 .40

Cent. of Liberation Day, May 25, 1810.

The 2c in deep blue and 5c in carmine red were prepared for collectors.

Stamps of 1900-06 Surcharged

g

h

i

Perf. 14 to 16, 11½

1910, Oct. 6 Unwmk.

Black Surcharge

184 A72 (g) 5m on 1c yel grn .25 .25
a. Inverted surcharge 4.50 3.75

Dark Blue Surcharge

185 A39 (h) 5c on 50c dull red .40 .25
a. Inverted surcharge 4.50 4.50

Blue Surcharge

186 A86 (i) 5c on 50c rose .80 .45
a. Double surcharge 20.00
b. Inverted surcharge 10.00 8.75
Nos. 184-186 (3) 1.45 .95

Artigas A90

"Commercial Progress" A91

1910, Nov. 21 Engr. *Perf. 14, 15*

187 A90 5m dk violet .25 .25
188 A90 1c dp green .25 .25
189 A90 2c orange red .25 .25
190 A90 5c dk blue .25 .25
191 A90 8c gray blk .40 .25
192 A90 20c brown .60 .25
193 A91 23c dp ultra 2.75 .40
194 A91 50c orange 4.00 1.25
195 A91 1p scarlet 7.50 1.25
Nos. 187-195 (9) 16.25 4.40

See Nos. 199-210. For overprints see Nos. 211-213, O118-O124.

Symbolical of the Posts — A92

1911, Jan. 6 Wmk. 187 *Perf. 11½*

196 A92 5c rose car & blk .80 .60

1st South American Postal Cong., at Montevideo, Jan. 1911.

No. 158 Surcharged in Red or Dark Blue

Perf. 14 to 16

1911, May 17 Unwmk.

197 A76 2c on 7c brn org (R) .40 .40
198 A76 5c on 7c brn org (Bl) .40 .25
a. Inverted surcharge 8.50 8.50

Centenary of the battle of Las Piedras, won by the forces under Gen. Jose Gervasio Artigas, May 8, 1811.

Types of 1910

FOUR AND FIVE CENTESIMOS:

Type I — Large numerals about 3mm high.

Type II — Small numerals about 2¼mm high.

1912-15 Typo. *Perf. 11½*

199 A90 5m violet .25 .25
a. 5m purple .25 .25
200 A90 5m magenta .25 .25
a. 5m dull rose .25 .25
201 A90 1c green ('13) .25 .25
202 A90 2c brown org .25 .25
203 A90 2c rose red ('13) .25 .25
a. 2c deep red ('14) .25 .25
204 A90 4c org (I) ('14) .25 .25
a. 4c orange (II) ('15) .25 .25
b. 4c yellow (II) ('13) .25 .25
205 A90 5c dull bl (I) .40 .25
a. 5c blue (II) .40 .25
206 A90 8c ultra ('13) .50 .25
207 A90 20c brown ('13) 1.40 .25
a. 20c chocolate 1.40 .25
208 A91 23c dk blue ('15) 3.50 .60
209 A91 50c orange ('14) 3.50 1.50
210 A91 1p vermilion ('15) 10.50 1.25
Nos. 199-210 (12) 21.30 5.60

Stamps of 1912-15 Overprinted

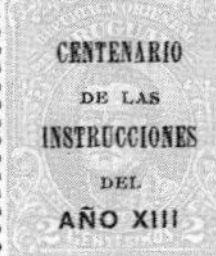

1913, Apr. 4

211 A90 2c brown orange .85 .50
a. Inverted overprint 5.00 4.50
212 A90 4c yellow .85 .50
213 A90 5c blue .85 .50
Nos. 211-213 (3) 2.55 1.50

Cent. of the Buenos Aires Cong. of 1813.

Liberty Extending Peace to the Country — A93

1918, Jan. 3 Litho.

214 A93 2c green & red .85 .50
215 A93 5c buff & blue .85 .50

Promulgation of the Constitution.

Statue of Liberty, New York Harbor — A94

Perf. 14, 15, 13½

1919, July 15 Engr.

217 A94 2c carmine & brn .55 .25
218 A94 4c orange & brn .55 .25
219 A94 5c blue & brn .80 .40
220 A94 8c org brn & ind .80 .40
221 A94 20c ol bis & blk 2.00 .80
222 A94 23c green & blk 4.00 1.25
Nos. 217-222 (6) 8.70 3.35

Peace at end of World War I.

Perf 13½ used only on 2c, 20c, 23c.

Harbor of Montevideo — A95

1919-20 Litho. *Perf. 11½*

225 A95 5m violet & blk .25 .25
226 A95 1c green & blk .25 .25
227 A95 2c red & blk .25 .25
228 A95 4c orange & blk .35 .25
229 A95 5c ultra & slate .40 .25
230 A95 8c gray bl & lt brn .50 .25
231 A95 20c brown & blk 1.60 .35
232 A95 23c green & brn 2.75 .65
233 A95 50c brown & blue 5.00 2.00
234 A95 1p dull red & bl 10.00 3.00
Nos. 225-234 (10) 21.35 7.50

For overprints see Nos. O125-O131.

José Enrique Rodó — A96

1920, Feb. 28 Engr. *Perf. 14, 15*

235 A96 2c car & blk .55 .40
236 A96 4c org & bl .65 .50
237 A96 5c bl & brn .75 .55
Nos. 235-237 (3) 1.95 1.45

Issued to honor José Enrique Rodó, author.
For surcharges see Nos. P2-P4.

Mercury — A97

1921-22 Litho. *Perf. 11½*

238 A97 5m lilac .25 .25
239 A97 5m gray blk ('22) .25 .25
240 A97 1c lt grn .25 .25
241 A97 1c vio ('22) .25 .25
242 A97 2c fawn .40 .25
243 A97 2c red ('22) .40 .25
244 A97 3c bl grn ('22) .60 .25
245 A97 4c orange .40 .25
246 A97 5c ultra .50 .25
247 A97 5c choc ('22) .60 .25
248 A97 12c ultra ('22) 2.40 .60
249 A97 36c ol grn ('22) 7.75 2.75
Nos. 238-249 (12) 14.05 5.85

See Nos. 254-260. For overprint and surcharge see Nos. E1, P1.

Dámaso A. Larrañaga (1771-1848), Bishop, Writer, Scientist and Physician — A98

1921, Dec. 10 Unwmk.

250 A98 5c slate 1.25 1.00

Mercury Type of 1921-22

1922-23 Wmk. 188

254 A97 5m gray blk .25 .25
255 A97 1c violet ('23) .25 .25
a. 1c red violet .25 .25
256 A97 2c pale red .25 .25
257 A97 2c deep rose ('23) .30 .25
259 A97 5c yel brn ('23) .65 .25
260 A97 8c salmon pink ('23) 1.00 .90
Nos. 254-260 (6) 2.70 2.15

Equestrian Statue of Artigas — A99

Unwmk.

1923, Feb. 26 Engr. *Perf. 14*

264 A99 2c car & sepia .40 .25
265 A99 5c vio & sepia .40 .25
266 A99 12c blue & sepia .40 .25
Nos. 264-266 (3) 1.20 .75

Southern Lapwing — A100

Perf. 12½, 11½x12½

1923, June 25 Litho. Wmk. 189

Size: 18x22½mm

267 A100 5m gray .25 .25
268 A100 1c org yel .25 .25
269 A100 2c lt vio .25 .25
270 A100 3c gray grn .40 .25
271 A100 5c lt bl .40 .25
272 A100 8c rose red .80 .50
273 A100 12c dp bl .80 .50
274 A100 20c brn org 2.00 .50
275 A100 36c emerald 4.00 1.75
276 A100 50c orange 6.75 2.75
277 A100 1p brt rose 32.50 20.00
278 A100 2p lt grn 47.50 20.00
Nos. 267-278 (12) 95.90 47.25

See #285-298, 309-314, 317-323, 334-339.
For surcharges and overprints see Nos. 345-348, O132-O148, P5-P7.

Battle Monument A101

1923, Oct. 12 Wmk. 188 *Perf. 11½*

279 A101 2c dp grn .55 .40
280 A101 5c scarlet .55 .40
281 A101 12c dk bl .55 .40
Nos. 279-281 (3) 1.65 1.20

Unveiling of the Sarandi Battle Monument by José Luis Zorrilla, Oct. 12, 1923.

"Victory of Samothrace" — A102

Unwmk.

1924, July 29 Typo. *Perf. 11*

282 A102 2c rose 20.00 10.00
283 A102 5c mauve 20.00 10.00
284 A102 12c brt bl 20.00 10.00
Nos. 282-284 (3) 60.00 30.00

Olympic Games. Sheets of 20 (5x4).
Five hundred sets of these stamps were printed on yellow paper for presentation purposes. They were not on sale at post offices. Value for set, $650.

Lapwing Type of 1923 First Redrawing

Imprint: "A. BARREIRO Y RAMOS"

1924, July 26 Litho. *Perf. 12½, 11½*

Size: 17¾x21½mm

285 A100 5m gray blk .25 .25
286 A100 1c fawn .25 .25
287 A100 2c rose lil .30 .25
288 A100 3c gray grn .25 .25
289 A100 5c chalky blue .25 .25
290 A100 8c pink .50 .25
291 A100 10c turq blue .40 .25
292 A100 12c slate blue .50 .25
293 A100 15c lt vio .50 .25
294 A100 20c brown .75 .30
295 A100 36c salmon 3.00 .70
296 A100 50c greenish gray 5.00 2.00
297 A100 1p buff 12.00 4.00
298 A100 2p dl vio 20.00 10.00
Nos. 285-298 (14) 43.95 19.25

Landing of the 33 "Immortals" Led by Juan Antonio Lavalleja — A103

Perf. 11, 11½

1925, Apr. 19 Wmk. 188

300 A103 2c salmon pink & blk 1.40 .80
301 A103 5c lilac & blk 1.40 .80
302 A103 12c blue & blk 1.40 .80
Nos. 300-302 (3) 4.20 2.40

Cent. of the landing of the 33 Founders of the Uruguayan Republic.

Legislative Palace — A104

Perf. 11½

1925, Aug. 24 Unwmk. Engr.

303 A104 5c vio & blk 1.25 .80
304 A104 12c bl & blk 1.25 .80

Dedication of the Legislative Palace.

General Fructuoso Rivera — A105

Wmk. 188

1925, Sept. 24 Litho. *Perf. 11*

305 A105 5c light red .50 .40

Centenary of Battle of Rincón. See No. C9.

Battle of Sarandí A106

1925, Oct. 12 *Perf. 11½*

306 A106 2c bl grn 1.25 1.00
307 A106 5c dl vio 1.25 1.00
308 A106 12c dp bl 1.25 1.00
Nos. 306-308 (3) 3.75 3.00

Centenary of the Battle of Sarandi.

Lapwing Type of 1923 Second Redrawing

Imprint: "Imprenta Nacional"

1925-26 *Perf. 11, 11½, 10½*

Size: 17½x21¾mm

309 A100 5m gray blk 1.00 .25
310 A100 1c dl vio 1.25 .25
311 A100 2c brt rose 1.60 .25
312 A100 3c gray grn 1.25 .40
313 A100 5c dl bl ('26) 2.00 .25
314 A100 12c slate blue 4.00 .40
Nos. 309-314 (6) 11.10 1.80

The design differs in many small details from that of the 1923-24 issues. These stamps may be readily identified by the imprint and perforation.

Lapwing Type of 1923 Third Redrawing

Imprint: "Imp. Nacional" at center

1926-27 *Perf. 11, 11½, 10½*

Size: 17½x21¾mm

317 A100 5m gray .40 .25
318 A100 1c lt vio ('27) 2.40 .55
319 A100 2c red 1.75 .40
320 A100 3c gray grn 2.40 .65
321 A100 5c lt bl .75 .25
322 A100 8c pink ('27) 3.50 .80
323 A100 36c rose buff 8.00 4.00
Nos. 317-323 (7) 19.20 6.90

These stamps may be distinguished from preceding stamps of the same design by the imprint.

Philatelic Exhibition Issue

Post Office at Montevideo A107

Unwmk.

1927, May 25 Engr. *Imperf.*

330 A107 2c green 4.75 3.50
a. Sheet of 4 20.00 20.00
331 A107 5c dull red 4.75 3.50
a. Sheet of 4 20.00 20.00
332 A107 8c dark blue 4.75 3.50
a. Sheet of 4 20.00 20.00
Nos. 330-332 (3) 14.25 10.50

Printed in sheets of 4 and sold at the Montevideo Exhibition. Lithographed counterfeits exist.

Lapwing Type of 1923 Fourth Redrawing

Imprint: "Imp. Nacional" at right

Perf. 11, 11½

1927, May 6 Litho. Wmk. 188

Size: 17¾x21¾mm

334 A100 1c gray vio .40 .25
335 A100 2c vermilion .40 .25
336 A100 3c gray grn .80 .35
337 A100 5c blue .40 .25
338 A100 8c rose 3.00 .80
339 A100 20c gray brn 4.00 1.60
Nos. 334-339 (6) 9.00 3.50

The design has been slightly retouched in various places. The imprint is in italic capitals and is placed below the right numeral of value.

No. 292 Surcharged in Red

1928, Jan. 13 Unwmk. *Perf. 11½*

345 A100 2c on 12c slate blue 2.00 2.00
346 A100 5c on 12c slate blue 2.00 2.00
347 A100 10c on 12c slate blue 2.00 2.00
348 A100 15c on 12c slate blue 2.00 2.00
Nos. 345-348 (4) 8.00 8.00

Issued to celebrate the inauguration of the railroad between San Carlos and Rocha.

General Rivera — A108

1928, Apr. 19 Engr. *Perf. 12*

349 A108 5c car rose .50 .35

Centenary of the Battle of Las Misiones.

Artigas (7 dots in panels below portrait.) — A109

Imprint: "Waterlow & Sons. Ltd., Londres"

Perf. 11, 12½, 13x13½, 12½x13, 13x12½

1928-43 Size: 16x19½mm

350 A109 5m black .25 .25
350A A109 5m org ('43) .25 .25
351 A109 1c dk vio .25 .25
352 A109 1c brn vio ('34) .25 .25
352A A109 1c vio bl ('43) .25 .25
353 A109 2c dp grn .25 .25
353A A109 2c brn red ('43) .25 .25
354 A109 3c bister .25 .25
355 A109 3c dp grn ('32) .25 .25
355A A109 3c brt grn ('43) .25 .25
356 A109 5c red .25 .25
357 A109 5c ol grn ('33) .25 .25
357A A109 5c dl pur ('43) .25 .25
358 A109 7c car ('32) .25 .25
359 A109 8c dk bl .25 .25
360 A109 8c brn ('33) .25 .25
361 A109 10c orange .25 .25
362 A109 10c red org ('32) .60 .40
363 A109 12c dp bl ('32) .40 .25
364 A109 15c dl bl .40 .25
365 A109 17c dk vio ('32) .80 .25
366 A109 20c ol brn .65 .25
367 A109 20c red brn ('33) 1.25 .50
368 A109 24c car rose .90 .35
369 A109 24c yel ('33) .80 .40
370 A109 36c ol grn ('33) 1.40 .50
371 A109 50c gray 2.40 1.25
372 A109 50c blk ('33) 3.50 1.60

373 A109 50c blk brn ('33) 3.00 1.25
374 A109 1p yel grn 7.00 4.00
Nos. 350-374 (30) 27.35 15.50

1929-33 ***Perf. 12½***

Size: 22 to 22½x28½ to 29½mm

375 A109 1p ol brn ('33) 6.00 4.00
376 A109 2p dk grn 17.00 9.00
377 A109 2p dl red ('32) 20.00 16.00
378 A109 3p dk bl 25.00 17.00
379 A109 3p blk ('32) 23.00 20.00
380 A109 4p violet 28.00 17.00
381 A109 4p dk ol grn ('32) 23.00 20.00
382 A109 5p car brn 32.50 23.00
383 A109 5p red org ('32) 30.00 20.00
384 A109 10p lake ('33) 92.50 70.00
385 A109 10p dp ultra ('33) 92.50 70.00
Nos. 375-385 (11) 389.50 286.00

See Nos. 420-423, 462. See type A135.

Equestrian Statue of Artigas — A110

1928, May 1

386 A110 2p Prus bl & choc 16.00 7.75
387 A110 3p dp rose & blk 23.00 12.00

Symbolical of Soccer Victory — A111

1928, July 29

388 A111 2c brn vio 16.00 9.25
389 A111 5c dp red 16.00 9.25
390 A111 8c ultra 16.00 9.25
Nos. 388-390 (3) 48.00 27.75

Uruguayan soccer victories in the Olympic Games of 1924 and 1928. Printed in sheets of 20, in panes of 10 (5x2).

Gen. Eugenio Garzón — A112

1928, Aug. 25 ***Imperf.***

391 A112 2c red 1.40 1.40
a. Sheet of 4 6.50 6.50
392 A112 5c yel grn 1.40 1.40
a. Sheet of 4 6.50 6.50
393 A112 8c dp bl 1.40 1.40
a. Sheet of 4 6.50 6.50
Nos. 391-393 (3) 4.20 4.20

Dedication of monument to Garzon. Issued in sheets of 4. Lithographed counterfeits exist.

Black River Bridge A113

Gauchos Breaking a Horse — A114

Peace A115

Montevideo A116

Liberty and Flag of Uruguay A117

Liberty with Torch and Caduceus A118

Statue of Artigas A124

Artigas Dictating Instructions for 1813 Congress A119

Seascape A120

Montevideo Harbor, 1830 — A121

Liberty and Coat of Arms A122

Montevideo Harbor, 1930 — A123

1930, June 16 ***Perf. 12½, 12***

394 A113 5m gray blk .25 .25
395 A114 1c dk brn .25 .25
396 A115 2c brn rose .25 .25
397 A116 3c yel grn .25 .25
398 A117 5c dk bl .25 .25
399 A118 8c dl red .35 .25
400 A119 10c dk vio .50 .35
401 A120 15c bl grn .65 .50
402 A121 20c indigo .80 .65
403 A122 24c red brn 1.10 .80
404 A123 50c org red 3.00 2.00
405 A124 1p black 6.00 3.00
406 A124 2p bl vio 14.00 8.50
407 A124 3p dk red 20.00 14.00
408 A124 4p red org 23.00 19.00
409 A124 5p lilac 35.00 22.50
Nos. 394-409 (16) 105.65 72.80

Cent. of natl. independence and the promulgation of the constitution.

Type of 1856 Issue
Values in Centesimos
Wmk. 227

1931, Apr. 11 **Litho.** ***Imperf.***

410 A1 2c gray blue 3.00 2.00
a. Sheet of 4 15.00 15.00
411 A1 8c dull red 3.00 2.00
a. Sheet of 4 15.00 15.00
412 A1 15c blue black 3.00 2.00
a. Sheet of 4 15.00 15.00

Wmk. 188

413 A1 5c light green 3.00 2.00
a. Sheet of 4 15.00 15.00
Nos. 410-413 (4) 12.00 8.00

Sold only at the Philatelic Exhibition, Montevideo, Apr. 11-15, 1931. Issued in sheets of 4.

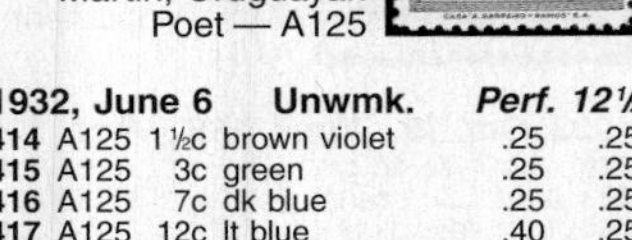

Juan Zorrilla de San Martin, Uruguayan Poet — A125

1932, June 6 **Unwmk.** ***Perf. 12½***

414 A125 1½c brown violet .25 .25
415 A125 3c green .25 .25
416 A125 7c dk blue .25 .25
417 A125 12c lt blue .40 .25
418 A125 1p deep brown 20.00 13.00
Nos. 414-418 (5) 21.15 14.00

Semi-Postal Stamp No. B2 Surcharged

1932, Nov. 1 ***Perf. 12***

419 SP1 1½c on 2c + 2c dp grn .35 .35

Artigas Type of 1928

Imprint: "Imprenta Nacional" at center

1932-35 **Litho.** ***Perf. 11, 12½***

Size: 15¾x19¼mm

420 A109 5m lt brown ('35) .25 .25
421 A109 1c pale violet ('35) .25 .25
422 A109 15m black .25 .25
423 A109 5c bluish grn ('35) .50 .25
Nos. 420-423 (4) 1.25 1.00

Gen. J. A. Lavalleja — A126

1933, July 12 **Engr.** ***Perf. 12½***

429 A126 15m brown lake .25 .25

Flag of the Race and Globe — A127

Perf. 11, 11½, 11x11½

1933, Aug. 3 **Litho.**

430 A127 3c blue green .50 .25
431 A127 5c rose .50 .25
432 A127 7c lt blue .50 .25
433 A127 8c dull red 1.00 .55
434 A127 12c deep blue .65 .25
435 A127 17c violet 1.75 .80
436 A127 20c red brown 3.50 1.60
437 A127 24c yellow 3.50 1.75
438 A127 36c orange 5.00 2.40
439 A127 50c olive gray 5.50 3.00
440 A127 1p bister 13.00 6.25
Nos. 430-440 (11) 35.40 17.35

Raising of the "Flag of the Race" and of the 441st anniv. of the sailing of Columbus from Palos, Spain, on his first voyage to America.

Sower — A128

1933, Aug. 28 **Unwmk.** ***Perf. 11½***

441 A128 3c blue green .25 .25
442 A128 5c dull violet .40 .25
443 A128 7c lt blue .40 .25
444 A128 8c deep red .80 .50
445 A128 12c ultra 2.00 1.00
Nos. 441-445 (5) 3.85 2.25

3rd Constituent National Assembly.

Juan Zorrilla de San Martin — A129

1933, Nov. 9 **Engr.** ***Perf. 12½***

446 A129 7c slate .25 .25

Albatross Flying over Map of the Americas — A130

1933, Dec. 3 **Typo.** ***Perf. 11½***

447 A130 3c green, blk & brn 2.75 2.00
448 A130 7c turq bl, brn & blk 1.60 .80
449 A130 12c dk bl, gray & ver 2.40 1.60
450 A130 17c ver, gray & vio 5.00 2.75
451 A130 20c yellow, bl & grn 6.00 3.50
452 A130 36c red, blk & yel 7.75 5.50
Nos. 447-452 (6) 25.50 16.15

7th Pan-American Conf., Montevideo. Issued in sheets of 6. Value $200. For overprints see Nos. C61-C62.

General Rivera — A131

1934, Feb. **Engr.** ***Perf. 12½***

453 A131 3c green .25 .25

Stars Representing the Three Constitutions — A132

1934, Mar. 23 **Typo.**

454 A132 3c yellow grn & grn .60 .40
455 A132 7c org red & red .60 .40
456 A132 12c ultra & blue 2.00 .80

Perf. 11½

457 A132 17c brown & rose 2.50 1.25
458 A132 20c yellow & gray 3.50 1.60
459 A132 36c dk vio & bl grn 3.50 1.60
460 A132 50c black & blue 7.00 3.25
461 A132 1p dk car & vio 16.00 6.75
Nos. 454-461 (8) 35.70 16.05

First Year of Third Republic.

Artigas Type of 1928

Imprint: "Barreiro & Ramos S. A."

1934, Nov. 28 **Litho.**

462 A109 50c brown black 6.00 2.50

"Uruguay" and "Brazil" Holding Scales of Justice — A133

1935, May 30 Unwmk. Perf. 11

463	A133	5m brown	.80	.40
464	A133	15m black	.40	.25
465	A133	3c green	.40	.25
466	A133	7c orange	.40	.25
467	A133	12c ultra	.80	.60
468	A133	50c brown	4.00	2.50
		Nos. 463-468 (6)	6.80	4.25

Visit of President Vargas of Brazil.

Florencio Sánchez — A134

1935, Nov. 7

469	A134	3c green	.25	.25
470	A134	7c brown	.25	.25
471	A134	12c blue	.55	.35
		Nos. 469-471 (3)	1.05	.85

Florencio Sanchez (1875-1910), author.

Artigas (6 dots in panels below portrait) — A135

Imprint: "Imprenta Nacional" at center

1936-44 Perf. 11, 12½

474	A135	5m org brn ('37)	.25	.25
475	A135	5m lt brown ('39)	.25	.25
476	A135	1c lt violet ('37)	.25	.25
477	A135	2c dk brown ('37)	.25	.25
478	A135	2c green ('39)	.25	.25
479	A135	5c brt blue ('37)	.25	.25
480	A135	5c bluish grn ('39)	.40	.25
481	A135	12c dull blue ('38)	.40	.25
482	A135	20c fawn	1.40	.35
482A	A135	20c rose ('44)	1.00	.40
483	A135	50c brown black	3.00	.80

Size: 21½x28½mm

483A	A135	1p brown	8.50	3.00
483B	A135	2p blue	14.00	12.00
483C	A135	3p gray black	20.00	16.00
		Nos. 474-483C (14)	50.20	34.55

See Nos. 488, and 576 in Scott Standard catalogue, Vol. 6. See type A109.

Power Dam on Black River — A136

1937-38

484	A136	1c dull violet	.25	.25
485	A136	10c blue	.50	.25
486	A136	15c rose	1.25	.65
487	A136	1p choc ('38)	6.25	2.50
		Nos. 484-487 (4)	8.25	3.65

Imprint: "Imprenta Nacional" at right

1938

488	A135	1c bright violet	.40	.25

International Law Congress, 1889 — A137

1939, July 16 Litho. Perf. 12½

489	A137	1c brown orange	.25	.25
490	A137	2c dull green	.25	.25
491	A137	5c rose ver	.25	.25
492	A137	12c dull blue	.65	.40
493	A137	50c lt violet	2.50	1.50
		Nos. 489-493 (5)	3.90	2.65

50th anniversary of the Montevideo Congress of International Law.

Artigas — A138

1939-43 Litho. Unwmk.

Size: 15¾x19mm

494	A138	5m dl brn org ('40)	.25	.25
495	A138	1c lt blue	.25	.25
496	A138	2c lt violet	.25	.25
497	A138	5c violet brn	.25	.25
498	A138	8c rose red	.25	.25
499	A138	10c green	.50	.25
500	A138	15c dull blue	1.25	.60

Size: 24x29½mm

501	A138	1p dull brn ('41)	2.50	1.00
502	A138	2p dl rose vio ('40)	7.00	3.00
503	A138	4p orange ('43)	9.25	4.00
504	A138	5p ver ('41)	14.00	6.00
		Nos. 494-504 (11)	35.75	16.10

See No. 578 in Scott Standard catalogue, Vol. 6.

Artigas — A138a

Redrawn: Horizontal lines in portrait background

1940-44 Size: 17x21mm

505	A138a	5m brn org ('41)	.25	.25
506	A138a	1c lt blue	.25	.25
507	A138a	2c lt violet ('41)	.25	.25
508	A138a	5c violet brn	.25	.25
509	A138a	8c sal pink ('44)	.25	.25
510	A138a	10c green ('41)	.40	.25
511	A138a	50c olive bis ('42)	6.25	1.75
511A	A138a	50c yel grn ('44)	4.75	1.75
		Nos. 505-511A (8)	12.65	5.00

See Nos. 568-575, 577, 601, 632, 660-661 in Scott Standard catalogue, Vol. 6. For surcharges see Nos. 523, 726 in Scott Standard catalogue, Vol. 6.

SEMI-POSTAL STAMPS

Indigent Old Man — SP1

Unwmk.

1930, Nov. 13 Engr. Perf. 12

B1	SP1	1c + 1c dark violet	.30	.30
B2	SP1	2c + 2c deep green	.30	.30
B3	SP1	5c + 5c red	.45	.45
B4	SP1	8c + 8c gray violet	.45	.45
		Nos. B1-B4 (4)	1.50	1.50

The surtax on these stamps was for a fund to assist the aged.

For surcharge see No. 419.

AIR POST STAMPS

No. 91 Overprinted in Dark Blue, Red or Green

1921-22 Unwmk. Perf. 14

C1	A38	25c bister brn (Bl)	18.00	15.00
a.		Black overprint	800.00	800.00
C2	A38	25c bister brn (R)	7.00	7.00
a.		Inverted overprint	100.00	100.00
C3	A38	25c bister brn (G) ('22)	7.00	7.00
		Nos. C1-C3 (3)	32.00	29.00

This overprint, on No. C3, also exists in light yellow green. Value, $85 unused and used.

No. C1a was not issued. Some authorities consider it an overprint color trial.

AP2

Wmk. 188

1924, Jan. 2 Litho. Perf. 11½

C4	AP2	6c dark blue	2.50	2.00
C5	AP2	10c scarlet	3.50	3.00
C6	AP2	20c deep green	5.00	5.00
		Nos. C4-C6 (3)	11.00	10.00

Heron — AP3

1925, Aug. 24 Perf. 12½

Inscribed "MONTEVIDEO"

C7	AP3	14c blue & blk	35.00	25.00

Inscribed "FLORIDA"

C8	AP3	14c blue & blk	35.00	17.50

These stamps were used only on Aug. 25, 1925, the cent. of the Assembly of Florida, on letters intended to be carried by airplane between Montevideo and Florida, a town 60 miles north. The stamps were not delivered to the public but were affixed to the letters and canceled by post office clerks. Later uncanceled stamps came on the market.

One authority believes Nos. C7-C8 served as registration stamps on these two attempted special flights.

Gaucho Cavalryman at Rincón — AP4

1925, Sept. 24 Perf. 11

C9	AP4	45c blue green		17.50

Centenary of Battle of Rincon. Used only on Sept. 24. No. C9 was affixed and canceled by post office clerks.

Albatross — AP5

1926, Mar. 3 Wmk. 188 Imperf.

C10	AP5	6c dark blue	2.00	2.00
C11	AP5	10c vermilion	2.50	2.50
C12	AP5	20c blue green	3.00	3.00
C13	AP5	25c violet	3.50	3.50
		Nos. C10-C13 (4)	11.00	11.00

Excellent counterfeits exist.

1928, June 25 Perf. 11

C14	AP5	10c green	3.00	2.00
C15	AP5	20c orange	5.00	3.00
C16	AP5	30c indigo	5.00	3.00
C17	AP5	38c green	8.50	6.00
C18	AP5	40c yellow	8.50	6.00
C19	AP5	50c violet	10.00	7.50
C20	AP5	76c orange	20.00	17.50
C21	AP5	1p red	20.00	15.00
C22	AP5	1.14p indigo	45.00	35.00
C23	AP5	1.52p yellow	75.00	60.00
C24	AP5	1.90p violet	95.00	75.00
C25	AP5	3.80p red	225.00	170.00
		Nos. C14-C25 (12)	520.00	400.00

Counterfeits of No. C25 exist.

1929, Aug. 23 Unwmk.

C26	AP5	4c olive brown	3.00	3.00

The design was redrawn for Nos. C14-C26. The numerals are narrower, "CENTS" is 1mm high instead of 2½mm and imprint letters touch the bottom frame line.

Pegasus AP6

1929-43 Engr. Perf. 12½

Size: 34x23mm

C27	AP6	1c red lilac ('30)	.40	.40
C28	AP6	1c dk blue ('32)	.40	.40
C29	AP6	2c yellow ('30)	.40	.40
C30	AP6	2c olive grn ('32)	.40	.40
C31	AP6	4c Prus blue ('30)	.70	.70
C32	AP6	4c car rose ('32)	.70	.70
C33	AP6	6c dull vio ('30)	.70	.70
C34	AP6	6c red brown ('32)	.70	.70
C35	AP6	8c red orange	3.00	2.50
C36	AP6	8c gray ('30)	4.00	3.00
C36A	AP6	8c brt green ('43)	2.50	2.00
C37	AP6	16c indigo	2.00	1.50
C38	AP6	16c rose ('30)	3.25	3.00
C39	AP6	24c claret	3.00	2.50
C40	AP6	24c brt violet ('30)	4.25	3.50
C41	AP6	30c bister	3.00	2.75
C42	AP6	30c dk green ('30)	2.00	1.50
C43	AP6	40c dk brown	5.50	5.00
C44	AP6	40c yel org ('30)	6.00	5.00
C45	AP6	60c blue green	5.00	3.25
C46	AP6	60c emerald ('30)	8.50	7.00
C47	AP6	60c dp orange ('31)	3.00	2.00
C48	AP6	80c dk ultra	8.00	7.00
C49	AP6	80c green ('30)	15.00	12.00
C50	AP6	90c light blue	8.00	6.00
C51	AP6	90c dk olive grn ('30)	15.00	12.00
C52	AP6	1p car rose ('30)	10.00	7.50
C53	AP6	1.20p olive grn	22.00	20.00
C54	AP6	1.20p dp car ('30)	30.00	26.00
C55	AP6	1.50p red brown	25.00	20.00
C56	AP6	1.50p blk brn ('30)	20.00	15.00
C57	AP6	3p deep red	40.00	35.00
C58	AP6	3p ultra ('30)	30.00	25.00
C59	AP6	4.50p black	75.00	55.00
C60	AP6	4.50p violet ('30)	45.00	35.00
C60A	AP6	10p dp ultra ('43)	17.00	12.00
		Nos. C27-C60A (36)	419.40	336.40

See Nos. C63-C82. For surcharges see Nos. C106-C112, C114 in Scott Standard catalogue, Vol. 6.

Nos. 450, 452 Overprinted in Red

1934, Jan. 1 Perf. 11½

C61	A130	17c ver, gray & vio	20.00	15.00
a.		Sheet of 6	140.00	
b.		Gray omitted	150.00	
c.		Double overprint	150.00	
C62	A130	36c red, blk & yel	20.00	15.00
a.		Sheet of 6	140.00	

7th Pan-American Conference, Montevideo.

Pegasus Type of 1929

1935 Engr. *Perf. 12½*
Size: 31½x21mm

C63 AP6 15c dull yellow 2.50 2.00
C64 AP6 22c brick red 1.50 1.40
C65 AP6 30c brown violet 2.50 2.00
C66 AP6 37c gray lilac 1.40 1.00
C67 AP6 40c rose lake 2.00 1.40
C68 AP6 47c rose 4.00 3.50
C69 AP6 50c Prus blue 1.40 .80
C70 AP6 52c dp ultra 4.00 3.50
C71 AP6 57c grnsh blue 2.00 1.75
C72 AP6 62c olive green 1.75 .80
C73 AP6 87c gray green 5.00 4.00
C74 AP6 1p olive 3.50 2.25
C75 AP6 1.12p brown red 3.50 2.25
C76 AP6 1.20p bister brn 15.00 12.00
C77 AP6 1.27p red brown 15.00 13.00
C78 AP6 1.62p rose 10.00 9.00
C79 AP6 2p brown rose 17.00 14.00
C80 AP6 2.12p dk slate grn 17.00 14.00
C81 AP6 3p dull blue 15.00 13.00
C82 AP6 5p orange 60.00 60.00
Nos. C63-C82 (20) 184.05 161.65

Counterfeits exist.
For surcharges, see Nos. C106-C112 in the Scott Standard Catalogue Vol. 6.

Power Dam on Rio Negro — AP7

Imprint: "Imp. Nacional" at center

1937-41 Litho.

C83 AP7 20c lt green ('38) 5.50 4.00
C84 AP7 35c red brown 8.00 6.50
C85 AP7 62c blue grn ('38) .80 .30
C86 AP7 68c yel org ('38) 2.00 1.50
C86A AP7 68c pale vio brn ('41) 1.75 .70
C87 AP7 75c violet 7.50 5.00
C88 AP7 1p dp pink ('38) 2.50 1.75
C89 AP7 1.38p rose ('38) 25.00 20.00
C90 AP7 3p dk blue ('40) 17.00 12.00
Nos. C83-C90 (9) 70.05 51.75

Imprint at left

C91 AP7 8c pale green ('39) .60 .50
C92 AP7 20c lt green ('38) 2.00 1.50

For surcharge and overprint see Nos. 545, C120 in Scott Standard catalogue, Vol. 6.

Plane over Sculptured Oxcart — AP8

1939-44 *Perf. 12½*

C93 AP8 20c slate .50 .40
C94 AP8 20c lt violet ('43) .80 .80
C95 AP8 20c blue ('44) .60 .40
C96 AP8 35c red 1.00 .80
C97 AP8 50c brown org 1.00 .30
C98 AP8 75c deep pink 1.10 .25
C99 AP8 1p dp blue ('40) 3.25 .60
C100 AP8 1.38p brt vio 5.50 2.25
C101 AP8 1.38p yel org ('44) 5.00 4.00
C102 AP8 2p blue 8.00 1.40
a. Perf. 11 7.00 1.10
C103 AP8 5p rose lilac 10.00 2.25
C104 AP8 5p blue grn ('44) 15.00 7.00
C105 AP8 10p rose ('40) 100.00 65.00
Nos. C93-C105 (13) 151.75 85.45

Counterfeits exist. These differ in design detail and are perfed other than 12½.
For surcharges see Nos. C116-C119 in Scott Standard catalogue, Vol. 6.

SPECIAL DELIVERY STAMPS

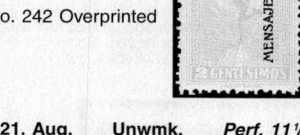

No. 242 Overprinted

1921, Aug. Unwmk. *Perf. 11½*

E1 A97 2c fawn .70 .25
a. Double overprint 4.25

Caduceus — SD1

Imprint: "IMP. NACIONAL."

1922, Dec. 2 Litho. Wmk. 188
Size: 21x27mm

E2 SD1 2c light red .50 .25

1924, Oct. 1

E3 SD1 2c pale ultra .50 .25

1928 Unwmk. *Perf. 11*

E4 SD1 2c light blue .50 .25

Imprint: "IMPRA. NACIONAL."

1928-36 Wmk. 188
Size: 16½x19½mm.

E5 SD1 2c black, *green* .25 .25

Unwmk.

E6 SD1 2c blue green ('29) .25 .25

Perf. 11½, 12½

E7 SD1 2c blue ('36) .25 .25
Nos. E5-E7 (3) .75 .75

LATE FEE STAMPS

Galleon and Modern Steamship — LF1

Wmk. Crossed Keys in Sheet

1936, May 18 Litho. *Perf. 11*

I1 LF1 3c green .25 .25
I2 LF1 5c violet .25 .25
I3 LF1 6c blue green .25 .25
I4 LF1 7c brown .25 .25
I5 LF1 8c carmine .50 .50
I6 LF1 12c deep blue .65 .65
Nos. I1-I6 (6) 2.15 2.15

POSTAGE DUE STAMPS

D1

1902 Unwmk. Engr. *Perf. 14 to 15*
Size: 21¼x18½mm

J1 D1 1c blue green .75 .30
J2 D1 2c carmine .75 .30
J3 D1 4c gray violet .80 .30
J4 D1 10c dark blue 1.75 .70
J5 D1 20c ocher 2.50 1.25
Nos. J1-J5 (5) 6.55 2.85

Surcharged in Red

1904

J6 D1 1c on 10c dk bl 1.25 1.25
a. Inverted surcharge 12.00 12.00

1913-15 Litho. *Perf. 11½*
Size: 22½x20mm

J7 D1 1c lt grn .75 .30
J8 D1 2c rose red .75 .30
J9 D1 4c dl vio 1.00 .30
J10 D1 6c dp brn 1.00 .50

Size: 21¼x19mm

J11 D1 10c dl bl 1.50 .60
Nos. J7-J11 (5) 5.00 2.00

Imprint: "Imprenta Nacional"

1922 Size: 20x17mm

J12 D1 1c bl grn .50 .30
J13 D1 2c red .50 .30
J14 D1 3c red brn .70 .50
J15 D1 4c brn vio .50 .30
J16 D1 5c blue .80 .50
J17 D1 10c gray grn 1.00 .60
Nos. J12-J17 (6) 4.00 2.50

1926-27 Wmk. 188 *Perf. 11*
Size: 20x17mm

J18 D1 1c bl grn ('27) .50 .25
J19 D1 3c red brn ('27) .50 .25
J20 D1 5c slate blue .50 .25
J21 D1 6c light brown .50 .50
Nos. J18-J21 (4) 2.00 1.25

1929 Unwmk. *Perf. 10½, 11*

J22 D1 1c blue green .25 .25
J23 D1 10c gray green .50 .25

Figure of Value Redrawn (Flat on sides)

1932 Wmk. 188

J24 D1 6c yel brn .50 .25

Imprint: "Casa A. Barreiro Ramos S. A."

1935 Unwmk. Litho. *Perf. 12½*
Size: 20x17mm

J25 D1 4c violet .50 .25
J26 D1 5c rose .50 .25

Type of 1935
Imprint: "Imprenta Nacional" at right

1938

J27 D1 1c blue green .25 .25
J28 D1 2c red brown .25 .25
J29 D1 3c deep pink .25 .25
J30 D1 4c light violet .25 .25
J31 D1 5c blue .25 .25
J32 D1 8c rose .25 .25
Nos. J27-J32 (6) 1.50 1.50

OFFICIAL STAMPS

Regular Issues Handstamped in Black, Red or Blue

Many double and inverted impressions exist of the handstamped overprints on Nos. O1-O83. Prices are the same as for normal stamps or slightly more.

On Stamps of 1877-79

1880-82 Unwmk. *Rouletted 8*

O1 A9 1c red brown 4.00 3.50
O2 A10 5c green 3.00 2.50
O3 A11 20c bister 3.25 3.25
O4 A11 50c black 22.00 22.00
O5 A12 1p blue 22.00 22.00
Nos. O1-O5 (5) 54.25 53.25

On No. 44
Rouletted 6

O6 A9 1c brown ('81) 6.00 6.00

On Nos. 43-43A
Rouletted 8

O7 A11 50c black (R) 17.00 16.00
O8 A12 1p blue (R) 22.50 20.00

On Nos. 45, 41, 37a
Perf. 12½

O9 A13 7c blue (R) ('81) 4.25 3.25

Rouletted 8

O10 A11 10c ver (Bl) 2.00 2.00

Perf. 13½

O11 A8b 15c yellow (Bl) 5.00 4.50

1883 On Nos. 46-47 *Perf. 12½*

O12 A14 1c green 6.50 6.50
O13 A14a 2c rose 9.50 9.50

On Nos. 50-51
Perf. 12½, 12x12½, 13

O14 A17 5c blue (R) 4.00 4.00
a. Imperf., pair 4.50
O15 A18 10c brown (Bl) 6.50 6.50
a. Imperf., pair 6.00

No. 48 Handstamped

1884 *Perf. 12½*

O16 A15 1c green 35.00 32.50

Overprinted Type "a" in Black On Nos. 48-49

1884 *Perf. 12, 12x12½, 13*

O17 A15 1c green 35.00 32.50
O18 A16 2c red 12.00 9.50

On Nos. 53-56
Rouletted 8

O19 A11 1c on 10c ver 2.00 1.60
a. Small "1" (No. 53a) 5.00

Perf. 12½

O20 A14a 2c rose 6.50 6.50
O21 A22 5c ultra 6.50 6.50
O22 A23 5c blue 5.00 2.00
Nos. O17-O22 (6) 67.00 58.60

On Stamps of 1884-88

1884-89 *Rouletted 8*

O23 A24 1c gray 12.00 5.50
O24 A24 1c green ('88) 2.50 1.60
O25 A24 1c olive grn 3.25 1.75
O26 A24a 2c vermilion 1.00 .60
O27 A24a 2c rose ('88) 2.25 1.25
O28 A24b 5c slate blue 2.25 1.25
O29 A24b 5c slate bl, *bl* 6.50 5.00
O30 A24b 5c violet ('88) 6.50 5.00
O31 A24b 5c lt blue ('89) 6.50 5.00
O32 A25 7c dk brown 3.25 1.60
O33 A25 7c orange ('89) 3.25 2.25
O34 A26 10c olive brn 2.00 .90
O35 A30 10c violet ('89) 16.00 9.50
O36 A27 20c red violet 3.00 1.60
O37 A27 20c bister brn ('89) 16.00 7.00
O38 A28 25c gray violet 3.50 2.50
O39 A28 25c vermilion ('89) 16.00 7.00
Nos. O23-O39 (17) 105.75 59.30

The OFICIAL handstamp, type "a," was also applied to No. 73, the 5c violet with "Provisorio" overprint, but it was not regularly issued.

1887 On No. 71 *Rouletted 9*

O40 A29 10c lilac 5.00

No. O40 was not regularly issued.

On Stamps of 1889-1899
Perf. 12½ to 15 and Compound

1890-1900

O41 A32 1c green .80 .25
O43 A32 1c blue ('95) 2.00 2.00
O44 A33 2c rose .80 .25
O45 A33 2c red brn ('95) 2.50 2.50
O46 A33 2c orange ('00) .80 .80
O47 A34 5c deep blue 1.50 1.50
O48 A34 5c rose ('95) 2.00 2.00
O49 A35 7c bister brown 1.25 .80
O50 A35 7c green ('95) 25.00
O51 A36 10c blue green 1.25 .80
O52 A36 10c orange ('95) 25.00
O53 A37 20c orange 1.25 .80
O54 A37 20c brown ('95) 25.00
O55 A38 25c red brown 1.25 .80
O56 A38 25c ver ('95) 55.00
O57 A39 50c lt blue 4.50 4.50
O58 A39 50c lilac ('95) 5.50 5.50
O59 A40 1p lilac 7.00 5.00
O60 A40 1p lt blue ('95) 40.00 22.50

Nos. O50, O52, O54, O56 and O60 were not regularly issued.

1891 On No. 99 *Rouletted 8*

O61 A24b 5c violet 1.50 1.25
a. "1391" 9.00

On Stamps of 1895-99
Perf. 12½ to 15 and Compound

1895-1900

O62 A51 1c bister .60 .60
O63 A51 1c slate blue ('97) 1.25 .55
O64 A52 2c blue .25 .25
O65 A52 2c claret ('97) 1.25 .55
O66 A53 5c red .80 .55

O67 A53 5c green ('97) 1.25 .55
O68 A53 5c grnsh blue ('00) .95 .75
O69 A54 7c deep green .50 .50
O70 A55 10c brown .50 .50
O71 A56 20c green & blk .80 .80
O72 A56 20c claret & blk ('97) 4.50 2.25
O73 A57 25c red brn & blk .80 .80
O74 A57 25c pink & bl ('97) 4.50 2.25
O75 A58 50c blue & blk .95 .95
O76 A58 50c grn & brn ('97) 5.75 2.75
O77 A59 1p org brn & blk 4.75 4.75
O78 A59 1p yel brn & bl ('97) 9.25 5.75
a. Inverted overprint
Nos. O62-O78 (17) 38.65 25.10

1897, Sept. On Nos. 133-135
O79 A62 1c brown vio & blk 1.25 1.00
O80 A63 5c pale bl & blk 1.75 1.00
O81 A64 10c lake & blk 1.75 1.10
Nos. O79-O81 (3) 4.75 3.10

Perf. 12½ to 15 and Compound
1897-1900 On Nos. 136-137
O82 A68 10c red 2.50 1.50
O83 A68 10c red lilac ('00) 1.25 1.25

Regular Issue of 1900-01 Overprinted

1901 ***Perf. 14 to 16***
O84 A72 1c yellow green .50 .25
O85 A75 2c vermilion .65 .25
O86 A73 5c dull blue .65 .25
O87 A76 7c brown orange .90 .50
O88 A74 10c gray violet .95 .55
O89 A37 20c lt blue 8.00 4.00
O90 A38 25c bister brown 1.60 .80
O91 A40 1p deep green 10.50 6.00
a. Inverted overprint 12.50 8.00
Nos. O84-O91 (8) 23.75 12.60

Most of the used official stamps of 1901-1928 have been punched with holes of various shapes, in addition to the postal cancellations.

Regular Issue of 1904-05 Overprinted

1905 ***Perf. 11½***
O92 A79 1c green .50 .25
O93 A80 2c orange red .50 .25
O94 A81 5c deep blue .50 .25
O95 A82 10c dark violet 1.00 .40
O96 A83 20c gray green 3.25 1.00
a. Inverted overprint
O97 A84 25c olive bister 2.25 .80
Nos. O92-O97 (6) 8.00 2.95

Regular Issues of 1904-07 Overprinted

1907, Mar.
O98 A79 1c green .25 .25
O99 A86 5c deep blue .25 .25
O100 A86 7c orange brown .25 .25
O101 A81 10c dark violet .25 .25
O102 A83 20c gray green .40 .35
a. Inverted overprint 4.00
O103 A84 25c olive bister .50 .40
O104 A86 50c rose .95 .70
Nos. O98-O104 (7) 2.85 2.45

Regular Issues of 1900-10 Overprinted

1910, July 15 ***Perf. 14½ to 16***
O105 A75 2c vermilion 8.75 4.00
O106 A73 5c slate green 5.25 3.00
O107 A74 10c gray violet 2.75 1.25
O108 A37 20c grnsh blue 2.75 1.25
O109 A38 25c bister brown 4.50 2.40

Perf. 11½
O110 A86 50c rose 6.00 2.50
a. Inverted overprint 20.00 15.00
Nos. O105-O110 (6) 30.00 14.40

Peace—O1

1911, Feb. 18 Litho.
O111 O1 2c red brown .40 .25
O112 O1 5c dark blue .40 .40
O113 O1 8c slate .40 *.65*
O114 O1 20c gray brown .55 *.95*
O115 O1 23c claret .80 *.95*
O116 O1 50c orange 1.60 1.25
O117 O1 1p red 4.00 1.50
Nos. O111-O117 (7) 8.15 5.95

Regular Issue of 1912-15 Overprinted

1915, Sept. 16
O118 A90 2c carmine .55 .40
O119 A90 5c dark blue .55 .40
O120 A90 8c ultra .55 .40
O121 A90 20c dark brown 1.25 .50
O122 A91 23c dark blue 4.00 3.50
O123 A91 50c orange 6.00 3.50
O124 A91 1p vermilion 8.00 4.00
Nos. O118-O124 (7) 20.90 12.70

Regular Issue of 1919 Overprinted

1919, Dec. 25
O125 A95 2c red & black .80 .40
a. Inverted overprint 3.50
O126 A95 5c ultra & blk .95 .40
O127 A95 8c gray bl & lt brn .95 .40
a. Inverted overprint 3.50
O128 A95 20c brown & blk 2.00 .80
O129 A95 23c green & brn 2.00 .80
O130 A95 50c brown & bl 4.00 2.00
O131 A95 1p dull red & bl 10.00 4.00
a. Double overprint 15.00
Nos. O125-O131 (7) 20.70 8.80

Regular Issue of 1923 Overprinted

1924 Wmk. 189 ***Perf. 12½***
O132 A100 2c violet .25 .25
O133 A100 5c light blue .25 .25
O134 A100 12c deep blue .30 .25
O135 A100 20c buff .40 .25
O136 A100 36c blue green 1.75 1.25
O137 A100 50c orange 3.50 2.50
O138 A100 1p pink 6.25 5.00
O139 A100 2p lt green 12.00 10.00
Nos. O132-O139 (8) 24.70 19.75

Same Overprint on Regular Issue of 1924

1926-27 Unwmk. ***Imperf.***
O140 A100 2c rose lilac .40 .25
O141 A100 5c pale blue .65 .25
O142 A100 8c pink ('27) .80 .25
O143 A100 12c slate blue .95 .25
O144 A100 20c brown 2.00 .40
O145 A100 36c dull rose 3.25 .95
Nos. O140-O145 (6) 8.05 2.35

Regular Issue of 1924 Overprinted

1928 ***Perf. 12½***
O146 A100 2c rose lilac 1.50 .95
O147 A100 8c pink 1.50 .50
O148 A100 10c turq blue 2.00 .50
Nos. O146-O148 (3) 5.00 1.95

Since 1928, instead of official stamps, Uruguay has used envelopes with "S. O." printed on them, and stamps of many issues which are punched with various designs such as star or crescent.

NEWSPAPER STAMPS

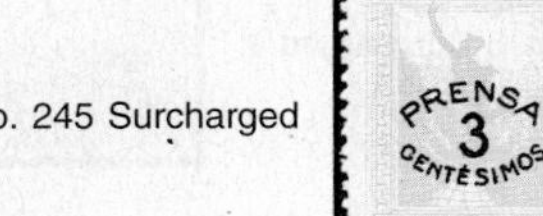

No. 245 Surcharged

1922, June 1 Unwmk. ***Perf. 11½***
P1 A97 3c on 4c orange .40 .40
a. Inverted surcharge 9.50 9.50
b. Double surcharge 2.50 2.50

Nos. 235-237 Surcharged

1924, June 1 ***Perf. 14½***
P2 A96 3c on 2c car & blk .40 .40
P3 A96 6c on 4c red org & bl .40 .40
P4 A96 9c on 5c bl & brn .40 .40
Nos. P2-P4 (3) 1.20 1.20

Nos. 288, 291, 293 Overprinted or Surcharged in Red

1926 ***Imperf.***
P5 A100 3c gray green .80 .25
a. Double overprint 1.00 1.00
P6 A100 9c on 10c turq bl .95 .40
a. Double surcharge 1.00 1.00
P7 A100 15c light violet 1.25 .50
Nos. P5-P7 (3) 3.00 1.15

PARCEL POST STAMPS

Mercury — PP1

Imprint: "IMPRENTA NACIONAL"
Inscribed "Exterior"
Size: 20x29½mm
Perf. 11½

1922, Jan. 15 Litho. Unwmk.
Q1 PP1 5c grn, *straw* .25 .25
Q2 PP1 10c grn, *bl gray* .40 .25
Q3 PP1 20c grn, *rose* 2.10 .55
Q4 PP1 30c grn, *grn* 2.10 .25
Q5 PP1 50c grn, *blue* 3.50 .40
Q6 PP1 1p grn, *org* 5.25 1.60
Nos. Q1-Q6 (6) 13.60 3.30

Inscribed "Interior"
Q7 PP1 5c grn, *straw* .25 .25
Q8 PP1 10c grn, *bl gray* .25 .25
Q9 PP1 20c grn, *rose* 1.00 .25
Q10 PP1 30c grn, *grn* 1.40 .25
Q11 PP1 50c grn, *blue* 2.25 .35
Q12 PP1 1p grn, *org* 6.00 1.25
Nos. Q7-Q12 (6) 11.15 2.60

Imprint: "IMP. NACIONAL"
Inscribed "Exterior"

1926, Jan. 20 ***Perf. 11½***
Q13 PP1 20c grn, *rose* 1.75 .50

Inscribed "Interior"
Perf. 11
Q14 PP1 5c grn, *yellow* .40 .25
Q15 PP1 10c grn, *bl gray* .50 .25
Q16 PP1 20c grn, *rose* 1.00 .25
Q17 PP1 30c grn, *bl grn* 1.75 .40
Nos. Q13-Q17 (5) 5.40 1.65

Inscribed "Exterior"
1926 ***Perf. 11½***
Q18 PP1 5c blk, *straw* .40 .25
Q19 PP1 10c blk, *bl gray* .65 .25
Q20 PP1 20c blk, *rose* 1.75 .25

Inscribed "Interior"
Q21 PP1 5c blk, *straw* .40 .25
Q22 PP1 10c blk, *bl gray* .50 .25
Q23 PP1 20c blk, *rose* 1.00 .25
Q24 PP1 30c blk, *bl grn* 1.75 .40
Nos. Q18-Q24 (7) 6.45 1.90

PP2

Perf. 11, 11½
1927, Feb. 22 Wmk. 188
Q25 PP2 1c dp bl .25 .25
Q26 PP2 2c lt grn .25 .25
Q27 PP2 4c violet .25 .25
Q28 PP2 5c red .25 .25
Q29 PP2 10c dk brn .40 .25
Q30 PP2 20c orange .65 .40
Nos. Q25-Q30 (6) 2.05 1.65

See Nos. Q35-Q38, Q51-Q54 (in Scott Standard catalogue, Vol. 6).

PP3

Size: 15x20mm

1928, Nov. 20 ***Perf. 11***
Q31 PP3 5c blk, *straw* .25 .25
Q32 PP3 10c blk, *gray blue* .25 .25
Q33 PP3 20c blk, *rose* .50 .25
Q34 PP3 30c blk, *green* .80 .25
Nos. Q31-Q34 (4) 1.80 1.00

Type of 1927 Issue
1929-30 Unwmk. ***Perf. 11, 12½***
Q35 PP2 1c violet .25 .25
Q36 PP2 1c ultra ('30) .25 .25
Q37 PP2 2c bl grn ('30) .25 .25
Q38 PP2 5c red ('30) .25 .25
Nos. Q35-Q38 (4) 1.00 1.00

Nos. Q35-Q38, and possibly later issues, occasionally show parts of a papermaker's watermark.

PP4

1929, July 27 Wmk. 188 ***Perf. 11***
Q39 PP4 10c orange .50 .50
Q40 PP4 15c slate blue .50 .50
Q41 PP4 20c ol brn .50 .50
Q42 PP4 25c rose red 1.00 .50
Q43 PP4 50c dark gray 2.00 1.00
Q44 PP4 75c violet 8.00 6.00
Q45 PP4 1p gray green 7.50 3.00
Nos. Q39-Q45 (7) 20.00 12.00

For overprints see Nos. Q57-Q63 in Scott Standard catalogue, Vol. 6.

Ship and Train — PP5

1938-39 Unwmk. *Perf. 12½*

Q46 PP5 10c scarlet .40 .25
Q47 PP5 20c dk bl .60 .25
Q48 PP5 30c lt vio ('39) .95 .25
Q49 PP5 50c green 1.75 .25
Q50 PP5 1p brn org 2.50 1.10
Nos. Q46-Q50 (5) 6.20 2.10

See Nos. Q70-Q73, Q80, Q88-Q90, Q92-Q93, Q95 in Scott Standard catalogue, Vol. 6.

VATICAN CITY

ˈva-ti-kən ˈsi-tē

LOCATION — Western Italy, directly outside the western boundary of Rome
GOVT. — Independent state subject to certain political restrictions under a treaty with Italy
AREA — 108.7 acres
POP. — 1,000 (est.)

100 Centesimi = 1 Lira

Catalogue values for unused stamps in this country are for Never Hinged items, beginning with Scott 68 in the regular postage section, Scott C1 in the airpost section, and Scott E3 in the special delivery section.

Watermark

Wmk. 235 — Crossed Keys

Papal Arms — A1

Pope Pius XI — A2

Unwmk.

1929, Aug. 1 Engr. *Perf. 14*

Surface-Colored Paper

1 A1 5c dk brn & pink .25 .25
Never hinged .40
On cover 8.00
2 A1 10c dk grn & lt grn .25 .35
Never hinged .80
On cover 4.00
3 A1 20c violet & lilac .75 .65
Never hinged 2.60
On cover 3.25
4 A1 25c dk bl & lt bl .95 .75
Never hinged 3.00
On cover 3.25
5 A1 30c indigo & yellow 1.10 .85
Never hinged 2.75
On cover 3.25
6 A1 50c ind & sal buff 1.60 .90
Never hinged 4.25
On cover 3.25
7 A1 75c brn car & gray 2.25 1.50
Never hinged 6.00
On cover 4.00

Photo.

White Paper

8 A2 80c carmine rose 1.60 .50
Never hinged 4.25
On cover 2.40
9 A2 1.25 l dark blue 2.60 1.10
Never hinged 6.75
On cover 4.00
10 A2 2 l olive brown 5.25 2.25
Never hinged 18.00
On cover 12.00
11 A2 2.50 l red orange 4.50 3.75
Never hinged 14.50
On cover 65.00
12 A2 5 l dk green 5.25 *12.00*
Never hinged 18.00
On cover 80.00
13 A2 10 l olive blk 11.00 *17.00*
Never hinged 37.50
On cover 100.00
Nos. 1-13,E1-E2 (15) 74.85 *75.35*
Set, never hinged 265.00

The stamps of Type A1 have, in this and subsequent issues, the words "POSTE VATICANE" in rows of colorless letters in the background.

For surcharges and overprints see Nos. 14, 35-40, 61-67, J1-J6, Q1-Q13.

No. 5 Surcharged in Red

1931, Oct. 1

14 A1 25c on 30c ind & yel 3.00 2.25
Never hinged 10.00

Arms of Pope Pius XI — A5

Vatican Palace and Obelisk — A6

Vatican Gardens — A7

Pope Pius XI A8

St. Peter's Basilica A9

1933, May 31 Engr. Wmk. 235

19 A5 5c copper red .25 .25
Never hinged .30
On cover 12.00
a. Imperf., pair 600.00 *825.00*
20 A6 10c dk brn & blk .25 .25
Never hinged .30
On cover 4.75
21 A6 12½c dp grn & blk .25 .25
Never hinged .30
On cover 47.50
22 A6 20c orange & blk .25 .25
Never hinged .30
On cover 2.40
a. Vertical pair imperf. between and at bottom 750.00
23 A6 25c dk olive & blk .25 .25
Never hinged .30
On cover 2.40
a. Imperf., pair 425.00 *600.00*
24 A7 30c blk & dk brn .25 .25
Never hinged .30
On cover 4.00
25 A7 50c vio & dk brn .25 .25
Never hinged .30
On cover 4.00
26 A7 75c brn red & dk brn .25 .25
Never hinged .30
On cover 4.00
27 A7 80c rose & dk brn .25 .25
Never hinged .30
On cover 4.00
28 A8 1 l violet & blk 7.50 7.50
Never hinged 32.00
On cover 24.00
29 A8 1.25 l dk bl & blk 22.50 13.50
Never hinged 95.00
On cover 47.50
30 A8 2 l dk brn & blk 52.50 37.50
Never hinged 220.00
On cover 80.00
31 A8 2.75 l dk vio & blk 67.50 *90.00*
Never hinged 270.00
On cover 200.00
32 A9 5 l blk brn & dk grn .25 .25
Never hinged .30
On cover 32.50
33 A9 10 l dk bl & dk grn .25 .30
Never hinged .30
On cover 24.00
34 A9 20 l blk & dp grn .40 *.50*
Never hinged 1.00
On cover 95.00
Nos. 19-34,E3-E4 (18) 153.85 152.70
Set, never hinged 620.00

Nos. 8-13 Surcharged in Black

No. 36 No. 36a

1934, June 16 Unwmk.

35 A2 40c on 80c 45.00 20.00
Never hinged 62.50
On cover 80.00
36 A2 1.30 l on 1.25 l 180.00 100.00
Never hinged 450.00
On cover 300.00
a. Small figures "30" in "1.30" *24,000.* *16,000.*
Never hinged *30,000.*
37 A2 2.05 l on 2 l 240.00 32.50
Never hinged 500.00
On cover 95.00
a. No comma btwn. 2 & 0 550.00 40.00
Never hinged 1,200.
38 A2 2.55 l on 2.50 l 150.00 275.00
Never hinged 375.00
On cover 800.00
a. No comma btwn. 2 & 5 200.00 300.00
Never hinged 500.00
39 A2 3.05 l on 5 l 500.00 450.00
Never hinged 1,200.
On cover 1,450.
40 A2 3.70 l on 10 l 450.00 *600.00*
Never hinged 1,100.
On cover 2,200.
a. No comma btwn. 3 & 7 — —
Nos. 35-40 (6) 1,565. 1,478.
Set, never hinged 3,680.

A second printing of Nos. 36-40 was made in 1937. The 2.55 l and 3.05 l of the first printing and 1.30 l of the second printing sell for more.

The status of No. 40a has been questioned. The editors would like to examine an authenticated example of this variety.

Forged surcharges of Nos. 35-40 are plentiful.

Tribonian Presenting Pandects to Justinian I A10

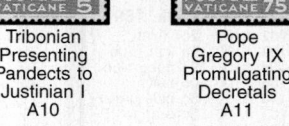

Pope Gregory IX Promulgating Decretals A11

1935, Feb. 1 Photo.

41 A10 5c red orange 4.50 4.50
Never hinged 20.00
On cover 32.50
42 A10 10c purple 4.50 4.50
Never hinged 20.00
On cover 32.50
43 A10 25c green 25.00 35.00
Never hinged 125.00
On cover 120.00
44 A11 75c rose red 65.00 60.00
Never hinged 310.00
On cover 200.00
45 A11 80c dark brown 55.00 42.50
Never hinged 260.00
On cover 140.00
46 A11 1.25 l dark blue 65.00 52.50
Never hinged 310.00
On cover 180.00
Nos. 41-46 (6) 219.00 199.00
Set, never hinged 1,045.

Intl. Juridical Congress, Rome, 1934.

Doves and Bell — A12

Allegory of Church and Bible — A13

St. John Bosco — A14

St. Francis de Sales — A15

1936, June 22

47 A12 5c blue green 1.50 1.50
Never hinged 7.00
On cover 16.00
48 A13 10c black 1.50 1.50
Never hinged 7.00
On cover 16.00
49 A14 25c yellow green 45.00 15.00
Never hinged 210.00
On cover 80.00
50 A12 50c rose violet 1.50 1.50
Never hinged 7.00
On cover 16.00
51 A13 75c rose red 47.50 *60.00*
Never hinged 225.00
On cover 275.00
52 A14 80c orange brn 2.60 *3.00*
Never hinged 12.50
On cover 32.50
53 A15 1.25 l dark blue 3.00 *3.00*
Never hinged 13.50
On cover 32.50
54 A15 5 l dark brown 3.00 *7.50*
Never hinged 13.00
On cover 80.00
Nos. 47-54 (8) 105.60 93.00
Set, never hinged 495.00

Catholic Press Conference, 1936.

Crypt of St. Cecilia in Catacombs of St. Calixtus A16

Basilica of Sts. Nereus and Achilleus in Catacombs of St. Domitilla A17

1938, Oct. 12 *Perf. 14*

55 A16 5c bister brown .40 .40
Never hinged 1.00
On cover 16.00
56 A16 10c deep orange .40 .40
Never hinged 1.00
On cover 16.00
57 A16 25c deep green .45 .40
Never hinged 1.20
On cover 12.00
58 A17 75c deep rose 7.50 7.50
Never hinged 26.00
On cover 72.50
59 A17 80c violet 20.00 20.00
Never hinged 70.00
On cover 80.00
60 A17 1.25 l blue 29.00 29.00
Never hinged 100.00
On cover 110.00
Nos. 55-60 (6) 57.75 57.70
Set, never hinged 200.00

Intl. Christian Archaeological Congress, Rome, 1938.

Interregnum Issue

Nos. 1-7 Overprinted in Black

1939, Feb. 20 *Perf. 14*

61 A1 5c dk brn & pink 26.00 7.50
Never hinged 100.00
On cover 16.00
62 A1 10c dk grn & lt grn .75 .25
Never hinged 2.75
On cover 2.40
63 A1 20c violet & lilac .75 .25
Never hinged 2.75
On cover 2.40
64 A1 25c dk bl & lt bl 3.25 *5.00*
Never hinged 14.50
On cover 32.50
65 A1 30c indigo & yellow 1.25 .25
Never hinged 5.00
On cover 2.40
a. Pair, one without ovpt. *3,000.*
66 A1 50c indigo & sal buff 1.25 .25
Never hinged 5.00
On cover 2.40
67 A1 75c brn car & gray 1.25 .25
Never hinged 5.00
On cover 2.40
Nos. 61-67 (7) 34.50 13.75
Set, never hinged 135.00

Catalogue values for unused stamps in this section, from this point to the end of the section, are for Never Hinged items.

Coronation of Pope Pius XII — A18

1939, June 2 **Photo.**

68 A18 25c green 3.00 .40
On cover 3.25
69 A18 75c rose red .70 .70
On cover 16.00
70 A18 80c violet 8.50 4.00
On cover 16.00
71 A18 1.25 l deep blue .70 .70
On cover 16.00
Nos. 68-71 (4) 12.90 5.80

Coronation of Pope Pius XII, Mar. 12, 1939.

Arms of Pope Pius XII — A19

Pope Pius XII
A20 A21

Wmk. 235

1940, Mar. 12 **Engr.** *Perf. 14*

72 A19 5c dark carmine .45 .25
On cover 12.00
a. Imperf, pair 1,100.
73 A20 1 l purple & blk .45 .25
On cover 8.00
74 A21 1.25 l slate bl & blk .45 .25
On cover 6.50
a. Imperf., pair *1,100.* *1,200.*
75 A20 2 l dk brn & blk 2.00 2.00
On cover 12.00
76 A21 2.75 l dk rose vio & blk 2.50 2.50
On cover 47.50
Nos. 72-76 (5) 5.85 5.25

See Nos. 91-98 in Scott Standard catalogue, Vol. 6. For surcharges see Nos. 102-109 in Scott Standard catalogue, Vol. 6.

SEMI-POSTAL STAMPS

Holy Year Issue

Cross and Orb
SP1 SP2

1933 Unwmk. Engr. *Perf. 13x13½*

B1 SP1 25c + 10c green 4.75 *4.75*
Never hinged 14.50
On cover 16.00
B2 SP1 75c + 15c scarlet 8.25 *16.50*
Never hinged 28.00
On cover 47.50
B3 SP2 80c + 20c red brown 30.00 22.50
Never hinged 115.00
On cover 70.00
B4 SP2 1.25 l + 25c ultra 9.00 *17.00*
Never hinged 35.00
On cover 85.00
Nos. B1-B4 (4) 52.00 *60.75*
Set, never hinged 190.00

AIR POST STAMPS

Catalogue values for unused stamps in this section are for Never Hinged items.

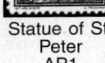

Statue of St. Peter
AP1

Dove of Peace over Vatican
AP2

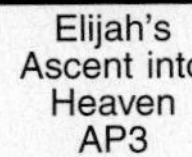
Elijah's Ascent into Heaven
AP3

Our Lady of Loreto and Angels Moving the Holy House
AP4

Wmk. 235

1938, June 22 **Engr.** *Perf. 14*

C1 AP1 25c brown .30 .25
C2 AP2 50c green .30 .25
C3 AP3 75c lake .30 .30
C4 AP4 80c dark blue .30 .45
C5 AP1 1 l violet .90 .50
C6 AP2 2 l ultra 1.60 .80
C7 AP3 5 l slate blk 3.50 2.50
C8 AP4 10 l dk brown vio 3.50 2.50
Nos. C1-C8 (8) 10.70 7.55

SPECIAL DELIVERY STAMPS

Pius XI
SD1

Unwmk.

1929, Aug. 1 **Photo.** *Perf. 14*

E1 SD1 2 l carmine rose 20.50 15.00
Never hinged 82.50
On cover 120.00
E2 SD1 2.50 l dark blue 17.00 18.50
Never hinged 67.50
On cover 100.00

For overprints see Nos. Q14-Q15.

Catalogue values for unused stamps in this section, from this point to the end of the section, are for Never Hinged items.

Aerial View of Vatican City
SD2

1933, May 31 **Wmk. 235** **Engr.**

E3 SD2 2 l rose red & brn .35 .35
E4 SD2 2.50 l dp blue & brn .35 *.55*

POSTAGE DUE STAMPS

Nos. 1-3 Overprinted in Black and Brown

1931, Oct. 1 **Unwmk.** *Perf. 14*

J1 A1 5c dk brown & pink .35 *.75*
Never hinged 1.50
On cover 160.00
a. Double frame —
J2 A1 10c dk grn & lt grn .35 *.75*
Never hinged 1.50
On cover 160.00
a. Frame omitted *5,250.*
Never hinged 6,000.
J3 A1 20c violet & lilac 1.90 2.25
Never hinged 7.00
On cover 200.00

No. 5 Surcharged

J4 A1 40c on 30c indigo & yel 2.25 *6.00*
Never hinged 10.00
On cover 160.00

Nos. 10-11 Surcharged

J5 A2 60c on 2 l olive brn 40.00 30.00
Never hinged 180.00
On cover 160.00
J6 A2 1.10 l on 2.50 l red org 11.00 *22.50*
Never hinged 35.00
On cover 160.00
Nos. J1-J6 (6) 55.85 *62.25*
Set, never hinged 235.00

In addition to the surcharges, #J4-J6 are overprinted with ornamental frame as on #J1-J3.

No. J5 is valued in the grade of fine.

PARCEL POST STAMPS

Nos. 1-7 Overprinted

1931, Oct. 1 **Unwmk.** *Perf. 14*

Q1 A1 5c dk brown & pink .25 .55
Never hinged .75
Q2 A1 10c dk grn & lt grn .25 .55
Never hinged .75
Q3 A1 20c violet & lilac 7.50 2.60
Never hinged 25.00
Q4 A1 25c dk bl & lt bl 11.00 5.50
Never hinged 35.00
Q5 A1 30c indigo & yel 7.50 5.50
Never hinged 25.00
Q6 A1 50c indigo & sal buff 7.50 5.50
Never hinged 25.00
Q7 A1 75c brn car & gray 1.50 5.50
Never hinged 5.50
a. Inverted overprint 750.00
Never hinged 1,000.

Nos. 8-13 Overprinted

Q8 A2 80c carmine rose 1.10 5.50
Never hinged 4.00
Q9 A2 1.25 l dark blue 1.50 5.50
Never hinged 5.50
Q10 A2 2 l olive brown 1.10 5.50
Never hinged 4.00
a. Inverted overprint 750.00 *900.00*
Never hinged 1,000.

Q11 A2 2.50 l red orange 1.90 5.50
Never hinged 6.50
a. Double overprint 750.00
Never hinged 1,300.
b. Inverted overprint 1,350.
Never hinged 2,400.
Q12 A2 5 l dark green 1.90 5.50
Never hinged 6.50
Q13 A2 10 l olive black 1.50 5.50
Never hinged 5.50
a. Double overprint 950.00
Never hinged 1,900.

Nos. E1-E2 Overprinted Vertically

Q14 SD1 2 l carmine rose 1.50 5.50
Never hinged 5.50
Q15 SD1 2.50 l dark blue 1.50 5.50
Never hinged 5.50
a. Inverted overprint 750.00
Never hinged 1,300.
Nos. Q1-Q15 (15) 47.50 69.70
Set, never hinged 160.00

VENEZUELA

ˌve-nə-ˈzwā-lə

LOCATION — Northern coast of South America, bordering on the Caribbean Sea
GOVT. — Republic
AREA — 352,143 sq. mi.
POP. — 15,260,000 (est. 1984)
CAPITAL — Caracas

100 Centavos = 8 Reales = 1 Peso
100 Centesimos = 1 Venezolano (1879)
100 Centimos = 1 Bolivar (1880)

Catalogue values for unused stamps in this country are for Never Hinged items, beginning with Scott 743 in the regular postage section.

GREAT BRITAIN POST OFFICES IN VENEZUELA

LA GUAYRA
Pre-Stamp Postal Markings

Crowned Circle handstamp type II is pictured in the Crowned Circle Handstamps and Great Britain Used Abroad section.

1841
A1 II "PAID AT LA GUAYRA" crowned circle handstamp in black, on cover 3,000.
As A1, used as a canceler on British stamp, on cover *4,800.*

Stamps of Great Britain Used in La Guayra
Canceled with "C60" in barred oval

1865-80
A2 ½p rose red, plate 6 (#58) —
A3 1p rose red, plates 81, 92, 96, 98, 111, 113, 115, 131, 138, 144, 145, 154, 177, 178, 180, 196 (#33), *value from* 60.00
A4 1½p lake red, plate 3 (#32) —
A5 2p blue, plates 13, 14 (#30), *value from* 60.00
A6 3p rose, plates 14-19 (#61), *value from* 70.00
A7 4p vermilion, plates 7, 9, 11-14 (#43), *value from* 60.00
A8 4p vermilion, plate 15 (#69) 325.00
A9 4p pale olive green, plate 15 (#70) 240.00
Plate 16 (#70) 240.00
A10 6p lilac, plate 5 (#45) —
A11 6p violet, plates 6, 8 (#51) —
A12 6p pale buff, plate 11 (#59b) 100.00
Plate 12 (#59b) 125.00
A13 6p gray, plate 12 (#60) 225.00
A14 6p gray, plates 13-16 (#62), *value from* 60.00
A15 8p orange (#73) 350.00
A16 9p straw (#40) —
A17 9p bister (#52) —
A18 10p red brown (#53) —
A19 1sh green (#48) 175.00
A20 1sh green, plates 4, 7 (#54) —
A21 1sh green, plates 8-13 (#64), *value from* 55.00
A22 2sh blue (#55) 250.00
A23 5sh rose, plate 1 (#57) 525.00
Plate 2 (#57) 675.00

CIUDAD BOLIVAR
Stamps of Great Britain
Canceled with "D22" in barred oval

1868-79
A30 1p rose red, plate 133 (#33) 250.00
A31 2p blue, plate 13 (#30) —
A32 3p rose, plate 5 (#49) —
A33 3p rose, plate 11 (#61) 300.00
A34 4p vermilion, plates 9, 11, 12, 14 (#43), *value from* 300.00
A35 4p pale olive green, plate 15 (#70) 450.00
Plate 16 (#70) 450.00
A36 4p gray brown, plate 17 (#84) *1,000.*
A37 9p bister (#52) 450.00
A38 10p red brown (#53) —
A39 1sh green, plates 4, 5, 7 (#54), *value from* 325.00
A40 1sh green, plates 10, 12, 13 (#64), *value from* 500.00
A41 2sh blue (#55) *1,000.*
A42 5sh rose, plate 1 (#57) *1,750.*
Plate 2 (#57) *2,000.*

PORTO CABELLO

1841
A45 II Crowned circle handstamp inscribed "PORTO-CABELLO" in red, on cover 3,750.

Earliest known use: Dec. 15, 1841.

A crowned circle handstamp inscribed "MARACAIBO" exists in the General Post Office Proof Books, but no example used on cover has been recorded.

ISSUES OF THE REPUBLIC

Coat of Arms — A1

Fine Impression
No Dividing Line Between Stamps
Unwmk.

1859, Jan. 1 **Litho.** ***Imperf.***
1 A1 ½r yellow 60.00 12.00
On cover *3,000.*
a. ½r orange — —
On cover *750.00*
b. Greenish paper *225.00*
2 A1 1r blue 450.00 15.00
On cover 500.00
a. Half used as ½r on cover *7,500.*
3 A1 2r red 42.50 15.00
On cover *1,500.*
a. 2r dull rose red 55.00 17.00
On cover *1,500.*
b. Half used as 1r on cover *1,250.*
c. Greenish paper 225.00 140.00
Nos. 1-3 (3) 552.50 42.00

Coarse Impression

1859-62 **Thick Paper**
4 A1 ½r orange ('61) 12.00 4.00
On cover 75.00
a. ½r yellow ('59) 500.00 30.00
On cover 125.00
b. ½r olive yellow 750.00 35.00
On cover 200.00
c. Bluish paper 575.00
d. ½r dull rose (error) 250,000. 350,000.
5 A1 1r blue ('62) 20.00 12.50
On cover *2,500.*
a. 1r pale blue 35.00 15.00
On cover *2,500.*
b. 1r dark blue 35.00 15.00
On cover *2,500.*
c. Half used as ½r on cover *7,500.*
d. Bluish paper 200.00
6 A1 2r red ('62) 45.00 80.00
On cover *1,500.*
a. 2r dull rose 55.00 80.00
On cover *1,500.*
b. Tête bêche pair *10,000.*
c. Half used as 1r on cover *400.00*
d. Bluish paper *225.00*
Nos. 4-6 (3) 77.00 96.50

In the fine impression, the background lines of the shield are more sharply drawn. In the coarse impression, the shading lines at each end of the scroll inscribed "LIBERTAD" are usually very heavy. Stamps of the coarse impression are closer together, and there is usually a dividing line between them.

Nos. 1-3 exist on thick paper and on bluish paper. Nos. 1-6 exist on pelure paper.

The greenish paper varieties (Nos. 1b and 3c) and the bluish paper varieties were not regularly issued.

Arms — A2

1862 **Litho.**
7 A2 ¼c green 20.00 *200.00*
On newsprint —
8 A2 ½c dull lilac 8.00 *240.00*
On newsprint —
a. ½c violet 40.00 210.00
On newsprint —
9 A2 1c gray brown 42.50 *400.00*
On newsprint —
Nos. 7-9 (3) 70.50 *840.00*

Counterfeits are plentiful. Forged cancellations abound on Nos. 7-17.

Eagle — A3

1863-64
10 A3 ½c pale red ('64) 55.00 *400.00*
On cover —
a. ½c red 60.00 *400.00*
On cover —
11 A3 1c slate ('64) 62.50 *160.00*
On cover —
12 A3 ½r orange 7.75 3.50
On cover 150.00
13 A3 1r blue 17.00 8.50
On cover *500.00*
a. 1r pale blue 30.00 13.00
On cover *600.00*
b. Half used as ½r on cover *750.00*
14 A3 2r green 23.00 20.00
On cover *2,000.*
a. 2r deep yellow green 30.00 20.00
On cover *2,000.*
b. Quarter used as ½r on cover *7,500.*
c. Half used as 1r on cover *2,000.*

Counterfeits exist.

1865 **Redrawn**
15 A3 ½r orange 4.00 *2.50*
On cover *3,000.*

The redrawn stamp has a broad "N" in "FEDERACION." "MEDIO REAL" and "FEDERACION" are in thin letters. There are 52 instead of 49 pearls in the circle.

No. 15 in yellow is a postal forgery.

A4

1865-70
16 A4 ½c yel grn ('67) 275.00 *300.00*
On cover —
17 A4 1c bl grn ('67) 275.00 *250.00*
On cover —
18 A4 ½r brn vio (thin paper) 9.50 2.00
On cover 50.00
19 A4 ½r lil rose ('70) 9.50 3.25
On cover 50.00
a. ½r brownish rose 9.50 3.00
On cover 50.00
b. Tête bêche pair 200.00 *600.00*
On cover *5,000.*
20 A4 1r vermilion 45.00 15.00
On cover *1,000.*
a. Half used as ½r on cover *500.00*
21 A4 2r yellow 160.00 77.50
On cover *3,000.*
a. Half used as 1r on cover *3,000.*
Nos. 16-21 (6) 774.00 *647.75*

This issue is known unofficially rouletted.
Postal forgeries exist of the ½r.
One quarter of #21 used as ½r is a postal forgery.
For overprints see Nos. 37-48.

Overprinted in Very Small Upright Letters "Bolivar Sucre Miranda — Decreto de 27 de Abril de 1870", or "Decreto de 27 de Junio 1870" in Slanting Letters

Simón Bolívar — A5

(The "Junio" overprint is continuously repeated, in four lines arranged in two pairs, with the second line of each pair inverted.)

Un	1	Siete	7
Dos	2	Nueve	9
Tres	3	Quince	15
Cuatro	4	Veinte	20
Cinco	5	Cincuenta	50

1871-76 **Litho.**
22 A5 1c yellow 1.50 .40
On cover *1,000.*
a. 1c orange 2.10 .45
b. 1c brown orange ('76) 2.10 .30
c. 1c pale buff ('76) 2.10 .45
d. Laid paper 1.00 .75
23 A5 2c yellow 2.00 .45
On cover *1,000.*
a. 2c orange 4.00 .45
b. 2c brown orange 3.50 .75
c. 2c pale buff ('76) 3.50 .45
d. Laid paper 3.50 .55
e. Frame inverted *4,000.* *3,000.*
24 A5 3c yellow 3.00 .75
On cover *1,000.*
a. 3c orange 3.00 1.40
b. 3c pale buff ('76) 5.50 1.75
25 A5 4c yellow 4.00 .75
On cover *1,000.*
a. 4c orange 4.50 1.25
b. 4c brown orange ('76) 4.50 1.25
c. 4c buff ('76) 4.50 1.25
26 A5 5c yellow 4.00 .75
On cover *500.00*
a. 5c orange 4.00 .90
On cover *500.00*
b. 5c pale buff ('76) 4.00 .90
On cover *500.00*
c. Laid paper 7.50 .90
27 A5 1r rose 4.00 2.00
On cover *1,000.*
a. 1r pale red 4.00 2.00
On cover *1,000.*
b. Laid paper 6.00 2.50
c. Half used as ½r on cover *1,500.*
28 A5 2r rose 4.50 2.00
a. 2r pale red 4.50 2.00
b. Laid paper 12.00 2.50
29 A5 3r rose 6.00 2.00
a. 3r pale red 6.00 2.00
30 A5 5r rose 5.75 1.00
a. 5r pale red 5.75 1.00
31 A5 7r rose 22.50 4.00
a. 7r pale red 22.50 4.00
32 A5 9r green 22.50 4.25
a. 9r olive green 22.50 6.00
33 A5 15r green 55.00 8.50
a. 15r gray green ('76) 55.00 8.50
b. Frame inverted *8,000.* *6,500.*
34 A5 20r green 77.50 20.00
a. Laid paper 110.00 35.00
35 A5 30r green 375.00 110.00
a. 30r gray green ('76) 600.00 160.00
b. Double overprint
36 A5 50r green 1,200. 300.00
a. 50r gray green ('76)
Nos. 22-34 (13) 212.25 46.85
Nos. 22-35 (14) 587.25 156.85

These stamps were made available for postage and revenue by official decree, and were the only stamps sold for postage in Venezuela from Mar., 1871 to Aug., 1873.

Due to lack of canceling handstamps, the majority of stamps were canceled with pen marks. Fiscal cancellations were also made with the pen. The values quoted are for pen-canceled stamps.

Different settings were used for the different overprints. Stamps with the upright letters were issued in 1871. Those with the slanting letters in one double line were issued in 1872-73. Those with the slanting overprint in two double lines were issued starting in 1874 from several different settings, those of 1877-78 showing much coarser impressions of the design than the earlier issues. The 7r and 9r are not known with this overprint. Stamps on laid paper (1875) are from a separate setting.

Stamps and Types of 1866-67 Overprinted in Two Lines of Very Small Letters Repeated Continuously

Overprinted "Estampillas de Correo — Contrasena"

1873, July 1
37 A4 ½r pale rose 70.00 13.00
On cover 2,500.
a. ½r rose 70.00 13.00
On cover 2,500.
b. Inverted overprint 175.00 75.00
c. Tête bêche pair 3,000. 2,000.
38 A4 1r vermilion 85.00 25.00
On cover 3,500.
a. Inverted overprint — —
b. Half used as ½r on cover 5,500.
39 A4 2r yellow 300.00 125.00
On cover —
a. Inverted overprint — —
b. Half used as 1r on cover 12,000.
Nos. 37-39 (3) 455.00 163.00

Covers: Only one cover is recorded of No. 39b. Two examples are known on fragments.

Overprinted "Contrasena — Estampillas de Correo"

1873, Nov.
40 A4 1c gray lilac 30.00 32.50
On cover —
a. Inverted overprint 6.50 17.00
On cover 3,000.
41 A4 2c green 125.00 90.00
On cover 3,000.
a. Inverted overprint 40.00 50.00
On cover 3,000.
b. As "a," half used as 1c on cover 7,500.
42 A4 ½r rose 72.50 13.00
On cover 100.00
a. Inverted overprint 30.00 4.00
On cover 50.00
b. ½r pink 60.00 11.00
On cover 100.00
43 A4 1r vermilion 85.00 23.00
On cover 500.00
a. Inverted overprint 35.00 9.00
On cover 300.00
b. Half used as ½r on cover 300.00
44 A4 2r yellow 325.00 160.00
On cover —
a. Inverted overprint 110.00 50.00
On cover 10,000.
b. Half used as 1r on cover 10,000.
Nos. 40-44 (5) 637.50 318.50

Overprinted "Contrasena — Estampilla de Correos"

1875
45 A4 ½r rose 85.00 10.00
On cover 200.00
a. Inverted overprint 125.00 25.00
On cover 500.00
b. Double overprint 160.00 90.00
46 A4 1r vermilion 160.00 15.00
On cover 700.00
a. Inverted overprint 200.00 80.00
On cover 2,500.
b. Tête bêche pair 3,500. 3,000.
c. Half used as ½r on cover 3,500.

Overprinted "Estampillas de correo — Contrasena"

1876-77
47 A4 ½r rose 77.50 9.25
On cover 200.00
a. ½r pink 65.00 7.50
On cover 200.00
b. Inverted overprint 65.00 7.50
On cover 200.00
c. Both lines of overprint read "Contrasena" 75.00 17.50
On cover 3,500.
d. Both lines of overprint read "Estampillas de correo" 75.00 17.50
On cover 3,500.
e. Double overprint 125.00 35.00
48 A4 1r vermilion ('77) 92.50 23.00
On cover 700.00
a. Inverted overprint 85.00 24.00
On cover 700.00
b. Tête bêche pair 2,250. 2,500.
c. Half used as ½r on cover —

On Nos. 47 and 48 "correo" has a small "c" instead of a capital. Nos. 45 and 46 have the overprint in slightly larger letters than the other stamps of the 1873-76 issues.

Overprinted "Decreto de 27 Junio 1870" Twice, One Line Inverted

Simón Bolívar
A6 A7

1879 ***Imperf.***
49 A6 1c yellow 4.00 1.00
Multiple, on cover —
a. 1c orange 5.00 1.50
Multiple, on cover 1,500.
b. 1c olive yellow 5.50 1.75
Multiple, on cover —
50 A6 5c yellow 3.50 .50
On cover 75.00
a. 5c orange 2.50 .75
On cover 75.00
b. Double overprint 20.00 10.00
51 A6 10c blue 5.00 .50
On cover 1,500.
52 A6 30c blue 7.75 1.00
On cover 3,000.
53 A6 50c blue 7.75 1.00
54 A6 90c blue 40.00 12.00
55 A7 1v rose red 77.50 18.00
56 A7 3v rose red 130.00 55.00
57 A7 5v rose red 225.00 77.50
Nos. 49-57 (9) 500.50 166.50

In 1879 and the early part of 1880 there were no regular postage stamps in Venezuela and the stamps inscribed "Escuelas" were permitted to serve for postal as well as revenue purposes. Postally canceled stamps are extremely scarce. Values quoted are for stamps with cancellations of banks or business houses or with pen cancellations. Stamps with pen marks removed are sometimes offered as unused stamps, or may have fraudulent postal cancellations added.

Nos. 49-57 exist without overprint. These are proofs.

Covers: Nos. 53-57 are not known on cover.

A8 A9

1880 ***Perf. 11***
58 A8 5c yellow 1.50 .50
On cover 500.00
a. 5c orange 1.50 .50
On cover 500.00
b. Printed on both sides 150.00 85.00
59 A8 10c yellow 2.50 .60
On cover 1,000.
a. 10c orange 2.50 .60
On cover, pair 1,000.
60 A8 25c yellow 2.50 .60
On cover 60.00
a. 25c orange 2.75 .70
On cover 60.00
b. Printed on both sides 110.00 52.50
c. Impression of 5c on back 175.00 90.00
61 A8 50c yellow 4.75 .80
On cover 2,000.
a. 50c orange 5.25 .85
On cover 2,000.
b. Half used as 25c on cover —
c. Printed on both sides 150.00 90.00
d. Impression of 25c on back 150.00 90.00
62 A9 1b pale blue 12.00 1.40
On cover 3,000.
63 A9 2b pale blue 17.00 1.75
On cover 5,000.
64 A9 5b pale blue 40.00 5.75
a. Half used as 2½b on cover —
65 A9 10b rose red 200.00 70.00
66 A9 20b rose red 1,200. 200.00
67 A9 25b rose red 5,000. 500.00
Nos. 58-65 (8) 280.25 81.40

See note on used values below No. 57.

Covers: Nos. 64-67 are not known on cover.

Bolívar — A10

1880 **Litho.** ***Perf. 11***
Thick or Thin Paper
68 A10 5c blue 15.00 7.25
On cover 200.00
a. Printed on both sides 225.00 140.00
69 A10 10c rose 20.00 12.00
On cover 200.00
a. 10c carmine 20.00 12.00
On cover 250.00
b. Double impression 90.00 75.00
c. Horiz. pair, imperf. btwn. 75.00 75.00
70 A10 10c scarlet 20.00 12.00
On cover 250.00
a. Horiz. pair, imperf. btwn. 75.00 75.00
71 A10 25c yellow 15.00 7.25
On cover 250.00
b. Thick paper 20.00 10.00
On cover 250.00
72 A10 50c brown 92.50 40.00
On cover 1,000.
a. 50c deep brown 92.50 40.00
On cover 1,000.
b. Printed on both sides 225.00 140.00
c. Half used as 25c on cover 5,000.
73 A10 1b green 140.00 50.00
On cover 2,000.
a. Horiz. pair, imperf. btwn. 300.00 300.00
Nos. 68-73 (6) 302.50 128.50

Nos. 68 to 73 were used for the payment of postage on letters to be sent abroad and the Escuelas stamps were then restricted to internal use.

Counterfeits of this issue exist in a great variety of shades as well as in wrong colors. They are on thick and thin paper, white or toned, and imperf. or perforated 11, 12 and compound. They are also found tête bêche. Counterfeits of Nos. 68 to 72 inclusive often have a diagonal line across the "S" of "CENTS" and a short line from the bottom of that letter to the frame below it. Originals of No. 73 show parts of a frame around "BOLIVAR."

Simón Bolívar
A11 A12

A13 A14

A15

1882, Aug. 1 **Engr.** ***Perf. 12***
74 A11 5c blue .70 .35
On cover 100.00
75 A12 10c red brown .70 .35
On cover 100.00
76 A13 25c yellow brown 1.10 .40
On cover 20.00
a. Printed on both sides 50.00 27.50
77 A14 50c green 2.40 .70
On cover 200.00
a. Half used as 25c on cover 500.00
78 A15 1b violet 4.50 1.75
On cover 1,000.
Nos. 74-78 (5) 9.40 3.55

Nos. 75-78 exist imperf. Value, set $32.50.

See Nos. 88, 92-95. For surcharges and overprints see Nos. 100-103, 108-112.

A16 A17

A18 A19

A20 A21

A22 A23

1882-88
79 A16 5c blue green .25 .25
On cover 100.00
80 A17 10c brown .25 .25
On cover 100.00
81 A18 25c orange .25 .25
On cover 50.00
82 A19 50c blue .25 .25
On cover 200.00
83 A20 1b vermilion .25 .25
84 A21 3b dull vio ('88) .25 .25
85 A22 10b dark brn ('88) 1.25 .80
86 A23 20b plum ('88) 1.50 .95
Nos. 79-86 (8) 4.25 3.25

By official decree, dated Apr. 14, 1882, stamps of types A11 to A15 were to be used for foreign postage and those of types A16 to A23 for inland correspondence and fiscal use.

Issue date: Nos. 79-83, Aug. 1.

See Nos. 87, 89-91, 96-99. For surcharges and overprints see Nos. 104-107, 114-122.

1887-88 **Litho.** ***Perf. 11***
87 A16 5c gray green .45 .30
On cover 100.00
88 A13 25c yellow brown 55.00 22.50
On cover 100.00
89 A18 25c orange .70 .45
On cover 100.00
90 A20 1b orange red ('88) 4.75 .90
On cover 100.00
Nos. 87-90 (4) 60.90 24.15

Perf. 14
91 A16 5c gray green 95.00 40.00

Stamps of type A16, perf. 11 and 14, are from a new die with "ESCUELAS" in smaller letters. Stamps of the 1887-88 issue, perf. 12, and a 50c dark blue, perf. 11 or 12, are believed by experts to be from printer's waste.

Counterfeits of No. 91 have been made by perforating printers waste of No. 96.

Rouletted 8
92 A11 5c blue 40.00 17.00
On cover 200.00
93 A13 25c yel brown 15.00 10.00
On cover 200.00
94 A14 50c green 15.00 10.00
On cover 500.00
95 A15 1b purple 30.00 20.00
On cover 500.00
Nos. 92-95 (4) 100.00 57.00

1887-88
96 A16 5c green .25 .25
On cover 200.00
97 A18 25c orange .25 .25
On cover 100.00
98 A19 50c dark blue 1.25 1.10
On cover 200.00
99 A21 3b purple ('88) 3.50 3.50
On overfranked cover 1,000.
Nos. 96-99 (4) 5.25 5.10

The so-called imperforate varieties of Nos. 92 to 99, and the pin perforated 50c dark blue, type A19, are believed to be from printer's waste.

Stamps of 1882-88 Handstamp Surcharged in Violet

1892 ***Perf. 12***
100 A11 25c on 5c blue *40.00 40.00*
101 A12 25c on 10c red brn *16.00 16.00*
102 A13 1b on 25c yel brn *16.00 16.00*
103 A14 1b on 50c green *20.00 20.00*
Nos. 100-103 (4) *92.00 92.00*

See note after No. 107.

1892
104 A16 25c on 5c bl grn *10.00 6.00*
105 A17 25c on 10c brown *10.00 6.00*
106 A18 1b on 25c orange *15.00 12.00*
107 A19 1b on 50c blue *23.00 12.00*
Nos. 104-107 (4) *58.00 36.00*

Counterfeits of this surcharge abound.

Stamps of 1882-88 Overprinted in Red or Black

1893

108 A11 5c blue (R) .55 .25
On cover 500.00
a. Inverted overprint 3.25 3.25
b. Double overprint 16.00 16.00
109 A12 10c red brn (Bk) .90 .90
On cover 500.00
a. Inverted overprint 4.00 4.00
b. Double overprint 16.00 16.00
110 A13 25c yel brn (R) .80 .50
On cover 100.00
a. Inverted overprint 5.25 5.25
b. Double overprint 16.00 16.00
c. 25c yel brn (Bk) 500.00 500.00
111 A14 50c green (R) 1.25 .80
On cover 500.00
a. Inverted overprint 5.25 5.25
b. Double overprint 27.50 27.50
112 A15 1b pur (R) 3.25 1.20
On cover 2,000.
a. Inverted overprint 10.00 10.00
Nos. 108-112 (5) 6.75 3.65

1893

114 A16 5c bl grn (R) .25 .25
On cover 500.00
a. Inverted overprint 3.25 3.25
b. Double overprint 5.25 5.25
115 A17 10c brn (R) .25 .25
On cover 500.00
a. Inverted overprint 3.25 3.25
116 A18 25c org (R) .25 .25
On cover 500.00
a. Inverted overprint 3.25 3.25
117 A18 25c org (Bk) 5.75 2.75
On cover 500.00
a. Inverted overprint 8.25 5.00
118 A19 50c blue (R) .25 .25
On cover 500.00
a. Inverted overprint 3.25 3.25
119 A20 1b ver (Bk) .60 .40
a. Inverted overprint 4.00 4.00
120 A21 3b dl vio (R) .90 .40
a. Double overprint 8.25 8.25
121 A22 10b dk brn (R) 3.50 2.25
a. Double overprint 10.00 10.00
b. Inverted overprint 20.00 20.00
122 A23 20b plum (Bk) 3.00 3.00
a. Double overprint 10.00 20.00
b. Inverted overprint
Nos. 114-122 (9) 14.75 9.80

Counterfeits exist.

Simón Bolívar — A24

1893 **Engr.**

123 A24 5c red brn .90 .25
On cover 100.00
124 A24 10c blue 3.25 1.25
On cover 100.00
125 A24 25c magenta 15.00 .50
On cover 20.00
126 A24 50c brn vio 4.25 .55
On cover 50.00
127 A24 1b green 5.75 1.25
On cover 750.00
Nos. 123-127 (5) 29.15 3.80

Many shades exist in this issue, but their values do not vary.

Simón Bolívar — A25

1893

128 A25 5c gray .25 .25
On cover 100.00
129 A25 10c green .25 .25
On cover 100.00
130 A25 25c blue .25 .25
On cover 100.00
131 A25 50c orange .25 .25
On cover 100.00
132 A25 1b red vio .25 .25
133 A25 3b red .55 .25
134 A25 10b dl vio .90 .80
135 A25 20b red brn 4.25 2.75
Nos. 128-135 (8) 6.95 5.05

By decree of Nov. 28, 1892, the stamps inscribed "Correos" were to be used for external postage and those inscribed "Instruccion" were for internal postage and revenue purposes.

For surcharge see No. 230.

Until July 1, 1895, revenue stamps inscribed "Escuelas" or "Instruccion," fiscal stamps for the collection of taxes for primary schools, were used as both revenue stamps and as postage stamps. After that date, they were no longer to be used for postal purposes, but their use was permitted when supplies of regular postage stamps were temporarily exhausted. See Nos. AR1-AR86.

Landing of Columbus A26

1893 ***Perf. 12***

136 A26 25c magenta 11.00 .60
On cover 100.00

4th cent. of the discovery of the mainland of South America, also participation of Venezuela in the Intl. Exhib. at Chicago in 1893.

Map of Venezuela A27

1896 **Litho.**

137 A27 5c yel grn 3.00 2.75
On cover 250.00
a. 5c apple green 3.00 2.75
On cover 250.00
138 A27 10c blue 4.00 5.50
On cover 250.00
139 A27 25c yellow 4.00 5.50
On cover 50.00
a. 25c orange 4.00 5.50
On cover 50.00
b. Tête bêche pair 125.00 125.00
On cover 2,000.
140 A27 50c rose red 55.00 25.00
On cover 500.00
a. 50c red 52.50 52.50
On cover 500.00
b. Tête bêche pair 375.00 375.00
141 A27 1b violet 40.00 27.50
On cover 1,000.
Nos. 137-141 (5) 106.00 66.25

Gen. Francisco Antonio Gabriel de Miranda (1752-1816).

These stamps were in use from July 4 to Nov. 4, 1896. Later usage is known.

There are many forgeries of this issue. They include faked errors, imperforate stamps and many tête bêche. The paper of the originals is thin, white and semi-transparent. The gum is shiny and crackled. The paper of the reprints is often thick and opaque. The gum is usually dull, smooth, thin and only slightly adhesive.

Bolívar — A28

1899-1901 **Engr.**

142 A28 5c dk grn 1.00 .25
On cover 50.00
143 A28 10c red 1.25 .40
On cover 50.00
144 A28 25c blue 1.50 .55
On cover 75.00
145 A28 50c gray blk 2.00 1.00
On cover 200.00
146 A28 50c org ('01) 1.75 .50
On cover 25.00
147 A28 1b yel grn 32.50 15.00
On cover 1,000.
149 A28 2b orange 400.00 225.00
On cover —
Nos. 142-147,149 (7) 440.00 242.70

Stamps of 1899 Overprinted in Black

1900

150 A28 5c dk grn 1.25 .40
On cover 50.00
a. Inverted overprint 4.75 4.75
151 A28 10c red 1.25 .40
On cover 50.00
a. Inverted overprint 6.50 6.50
b. Double overprint 10.50 10.50
152 A28 25c blue 7.75 1.25
On cover 50.00
a. Inverted overprint 13.00 13.00
153 A28 50c gray blk 4.00 .55
On cover 500.00
a. Inverted overprint 12.00 12.00
154 A28 1b yel grn 1.75 .80
On cover 1,000.
a. Double overprint 13.00 13.00
b. Inverted overprint 12.00 12.00
155 A28 2b orange 2.75 2.25
On cover —
a. Inverted overprint 35.00 35.00
b. Double overprint 32.50 32.50
Nos. 150-155 (6) 18.75 5.65

Initials are those of R. T. Mendoza.

Counterfeit overprints exist, especially of inverted and doubled varieties.

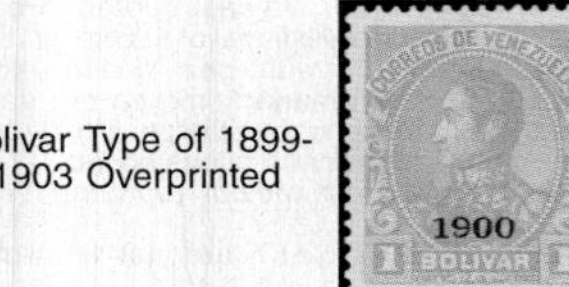

Bolivar Type of 1899-1903 Overprinted

1900

156 A28 5c dk grn 750.00 750.00
On cover —
157 A28 10c red 750.00 750.00
On cover —
158 A28 25c blue 600.00 600.00
On cover —
159 A28 50c yel orange 23.00 1.60
On cover 30.00
160 A28 1b slate 1.25 1.00
On cover 200.00
a. Without overprint 7,000. —
Nos. 156-160 (5) 2,124. 2,103.

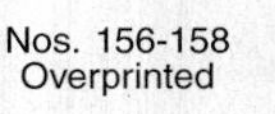

Nos. 156-158 Overprinted

1900, Aug. 14

161 A28 5c green 8.00 .55
On cover 50.00
162 A28 10c red 7.00 1.00
On cover 50.00
163 A28 25c blue 8.00 1.00
On cover 50.00
Nos. 161-163 (3) 23.00 2.55

Inverted Overprint

161a A28 5c 9.25 9.25
162a A28 10c 9.25 9.25
163a A28 25c 12.00 12.00
Nos. 161a-163a (3) 30.50 30.50

Overprint exists on each value without "Castro" or without "1900."

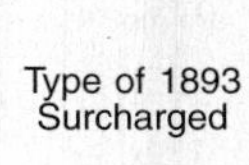

Type of 1893 Surcharged

1904, Jan. ***Perf. 12***

230 A25 5c on 50c green .80 .60
On cover 20.00
a. "Vele" 23.00 23.00
b. Surcharge reading up 1.00 .50
c. Double surcharge 18.00 18.00

Gen. José de Sucre — A35

1904-09 **Engr.**

231 A35 5c bl grn .50 .25
On cover 20.00
232 A35 10c carmine .55 .25
On cover 20.00
233 A35 15c violet .90 .40
On cover 50.00
234 A35 25c dp ultra 6.50 .40
On cover 10.00
235 A35 50c plum 1.00 .50
On cover 20.00
236 A35 1b plum 1.10 .50
On cover 75.00
Nos. 231-236 (6) 10.55 2.30

Issue date: 15c, Dec. 1909. Others, July 1, 1904.

Pres. Cipriano Castro — A37

1905, July 5 **Litho.** ***Perf. 11½***

245 A37 5c vermilion 3.25 3.25
On cover 100.00
a. 5c carmine 5.00 5.00
246 A37 10c dark blue 5.50 4.25
On cover 100.00
247 A37 25c yellow 2.00 1.50
On cover 100.00
Nos. 245-247 (3) 10.75 9.00

National Congress. Issued for interior postage only. Valid only for 90 days.

Various part-perforate varieties of Nos. 245-247 exist. Value, $15-$30.

Liberty — A38

1910, Apr. 19 **Engr.** ***Perf. 12***

249 A38 25c dark blue 13.00 .70
On cover 50.00

Centenary of national independence.

Francisco de Miranda A39

Rafael Urdaneta A40

Bolívar — A41

1911 **Litho.** ***Perf. 11½x12***

250 A39 5c dp grn .50 .25
On cover 30.00
251 A39 10c carmine .50 .25
On cover 30.00
252 A40 15c gray 5.75 .40
On cover 20.00
253 A40 25c dp bl 3.25 .60
On cover 20.00
a. Imperf., pair 40.00 50.00
254 A41 50c purple 3.50 .40
On cover 30.00
255 A41 1b yellow 3.50 1.50
On cover 75.00
Nos. 250-255 (6) 17.00 3.40

The 50c with center in blue was never issued although examples were postmarked by favor.

The centers of Nos. 250-255 were separately printed and often vary in shade from the rest of the design. In a second printing of the 5c and 10c, the entire design was printed at one time.

1913 **Redrawn**

255A A40 15c gray 3.50 2.25
255B A40 25c deep blue 2.00 .65
255C A41 50c purple 2.00 .65
Nos. 255A-255C (3) 7.50 3.55

The redrawn stamps have two berries instead of one at top of the left spray; a berry has been added over the "C" and "S" of "Centimos"; and the lowest leaf at the right is cut by the corner square.

Simón Bolívar — A42

1914, July Engr. *Perf. 13½, 14, 15*

256 A42 5c yel grn 37.50 .55
257 A42 10c scarlet 35.00 .50
258 A42 25c dark blue 5.75 .25
Nos. 256-258 (3) 78.25 1.30

Simón Bolívar — A43

Different frames.

Printed by the American Bank Note Co.

1915-23 *Perf. 12*

259 A43 5c green 4.25 .25
260 A43 10c vermilion 10.00 .60
261 A43 10c claret ('22) 10.00 .90
262 A43 15c dull ol grn 9.25 .60
263 A43 25c ultra 6.50 .25
a. 25c blue 13.00 .60
264 A43 40c dull green 23.00 11.50
265 A43 50c dp violet 6.50 .80
266 A43 50c ultra ('23) 17.00 4.75
267 A43 75c lt blue 57.50 23.00
a. 75c greenish blue 57.50 23.00
268 A43 1b dark gray 35.00 5.25
Nos. 259-268 (10) 179.00 47.90

See Nos. 269-285. For surcharges see Nos. 307, 309-310.

Type of 1915-23 Issue Re-engraved Printed by Waterlow & Sons, Ltd.

1924-39 *Perf. 12½*

269 A43 5c orange brn .55 .25
a. 5c yellow brown .55 .25
b. Horiz. pair, imperf. between 25.00 40.00
270 A43 5c green ('39) 12.00 1.00
271 A43 7½c yel grn ('39) 1.25 .40
272 A43 10c dk green .25 .25
273 A43 10c dk car ('39) 4.00 .25
274 A43 15c olive grn 2.25 .50
275 A43 15c brown ('27) .30 .25
276 A43 25c ultra 2.25 .25
277 A43 25c red ('28) .25 .25
a. Horiz. pair, imperf. btwn. 50.00 85.00
278 A43 40c dp blue ('25) .55 .25
279 A43 40c slate bl ('39) 7.75 1.25
280 A43 50c dk blue .55 .25
281 A43 50c dk pur ('39) 7.75 .85
282 A43 1b black .55 .25
283 A43 3b yel org ('25) 1.75 .95
284 A43 3b red org ('39) 12.00 4.25
285 A43 5b dull vio ('25) 16.00 8.50
Nos. 269-285 (17) 70.00 19.95

Perf. 14

269c A43 5c 7.00 2.00
272a A43 10c 7.00 2.00
274a A43 15c 8.25 2.75
276a A43 25c 12.00 4.75
280a A43 50c 35.00 14.00
282a A43 1b 42.50 27.00
Nos. 269c-282a (6) 111.75 52.50

The re-engraved stamps may readily be distinguished from the 1915 issue by the perforation and sometimes by the colors. The designs differ in many minor details which are too minute for illustration or description.

Bolívar and Sucre A44

Perf. 11½x12, 12

1924, Dec. 1 Litho.

286 A44 25c grayish blue 2.75 .55

Redrawn

286A A44 25c ultra 3.50 .85

Centenary of the Battle of Ayacucho.

The redrawn stamp has a whiter effect with less shading in the faces. Bolivar's ear is clearly visible and the outline of his aquiline nose is broken.

A45

A46

Revenue Stamps Surcharged in Black or Red

1926 *Perf. 12, 12½*

287 A45 5c on 1b ol grn .65 .40
a. Double surcharge 8.00 8.00
b. Pair, one without surcharge 12.00 12.00
c. Inverted surcharge 8.00 8.00
288 A46 25c on 5c dk brn (R) .65 .40
a. Inverted surcharge 8.00 8.00
b. Double surcharge 8.00 8.00

View of Ciudad Bolívar and General J.V. Gómez — A47

1928, July 21 Litho. *Perf. 12*

289 A47 10c deep green 1.00 .65
a. Imperf., pair 40.00

25th anniversary of the Battle of Ciudad Bolívar and the foundation of peace in Venezuela.

Simón Bolívar — A48

1930, Dec. 9

290 A48 5c yellow 1.00 .35
291 A48 10c dark blue 1.00 .25
292 A48 25c rose red 1.00 .25
Nos. 290-292 (3) 3.00 .85

Imperf., Pairs

290a A48 5c 5.25 5.25
291a A48 10c 6.50 6.50
292a A48 25c 10.50 10.50

Death centenary of Simón Bolívar (1783-1830), South American liberator.

Nos. 290-292 exist part-perforate, including pairs imperf. between, imperf. horiz., imperf. vert. Value range, $6-12.

Simón Bolívar — A49

Various Frames

Bluish Winchester Security Paper

1932-38 Engr. *Perf. 12½*

293 A49 5c violet .50 .25
294 A49 7½c dk green ('37) 1.10 .40
295 A49 10c green .65 .25
296 A49 15c yellow 1.50 .25
297 A49 22½c dp car ('38) 3.50 .50
298 A49 25c red 1.25 .25
299 A49 37½c ultra ('36) 4.50 2.00
300 A49 40c indigo 4.50 .25
301 A49 50c olive grn 4.50 .40
302 A49 1b lt blue 6.00 .70
303 A49 3b brown 47.50 13.00
304 A49 5b yellow brn 65.00 17.50
Nos. 293-304 (12) 140.50 35.75

For surcharges see Nos. 308, 318-319, C223 (in Scott Standard catalogue, Vol. 6).

Arms of Bolívar — A50

1933, July 24 Litho. *Perf. 11*

306 A50 25c brown red 3.00 2.40
a. Imperf., pair 32.50 32.50

150th anniv. of the birth of Simón Bolívar. Valid only to Aug. 21.

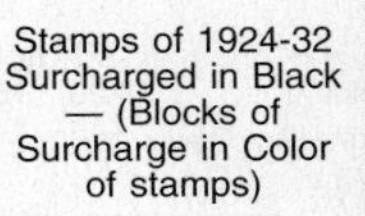

Stamps of 1924-32 Surcharged in Black — (Blocks of Surcharge in Color of stamps)

1933

307 A43 7½c on 10c grn .50 .25
a. Double surcharge 2.50 2.50
b. Inverted surcharge 4.25 4.25
308 A49 22½c on 25c (#298) 2.00 .85
309 A43 22½c on 25c (#277) 1.50 1.50
a. Double surcharge 10.00 10.00
310 A43 37½c on 40c dp bl 2.00 .95
a. Double surcharge 11.50 11.50
b. Inverted surcharge 10.00 10.00
Nos. 307-310 (4) 6.00 3.55

Nurse and Child — A51

River Scene — A52

Gathering Cacao Pods — A53

Cattle Raising A54

Plowing A55

Perf. 11, 11½ or Compound

1937, July 1 Litho.

311 A51 5c deep violet .55 .35
312 A52 10c dk slate grn .55 .25
313 A53 15c yellow brn 1.00 .55
314 A51 25c cerise 1.00 .35
315 A54 50c yellow grn 6.50 4.25
316 A55 3b red orange 12.00 7.75
317 A51 5b lt brown 23.00 15.00
Nos. 311-317 (7) 44.60 28.50

Nos. 311-317 exist imperforate. Value for set $75. Nos. 311-315 exist in pairs, imperf. between; value range, $20-$30.

For overprints and surcharges see Nos. 321-324, 345; Nos. 376-377, 380-384 in Scott Standard catalogue, Vol. 6.

No. 300 Surcharged in Black

1937, July *Perf. 12½*

318 A49 25c on 40c indigo 7.75 .95
a. Double surcharge 16.00 16.00
b. Inverted surcharge 13.00 13.00
c. Triple surcharge 32.50 32.50

No. 300 Surcharged

319 A49 25c on 40c indigo 440.00 350.00
a. Double surcharge

A56

1937, Oct. 28 Litho. *Perf. 10½*

320 A56 25c blue 1.25 .45

Acquisition of the Port of La Guaira by the Government from the British Corporation, June 3, 1937. Exists imperf. See Nos. C64-C65.

A redrawn printing of No. 320, with top inscription beginning "Nacionalización . . ." was prepared but not issued. Value, $40.

For surcharge see No. 385 in Scott Standard catalogue, Vol. 6.

Stamps of 1937 Overprinted in Black

1937, Dec. 17 *Perf. 11, 11½*

321 A51 5c deep violet 5.75 3.25
322 A52 10c dk slate grn 1.75 .75
a. Inverted overprint 13.00 13.00
323 A51 25c cerise 1.50 .55
a. Inverted overprint 16.00 16.00
324 A55 3b red orange 375.00 225.00
Nos. 321-324 (4) 384.00 229.55

Part-perforate pairs exist of Nos. 321-322 and 324. Value range, $12.50 to $125.

See Nos. C66-C78.

Gathering Coffee Beans — A57

Simón Bolívar — A58

Post Office, Caracas — A59

1938 Engr. *Perf. 12*

No.	Type	Denom.	Color	Unused	Used
325	A57	5c	green	.40	.25
326	A57	5c	deep green	.40	.25
327	A58	10c	car rose	.70	.25
328	A58	10c	dp rose	.70	.25
329	A59	15c	dk violet	1.40	.25
330	A59	15c	olive grn	.85	.25
331	A58	25c	lt blue	.40	.25
332	A58	25c	dk blue	.40	.25
333	A58	37½c	dk blue	8.50	4.00
334	A58	37½c	lt blue	2.75	.85
335	A59	40c	sepia	20.00	7.75
336	A59	40c	black	17.00	7.75
337	A57	50c	olive grn	27.50	7.75
338	A57	50c	dull violet	9.25	.85
339	A58	1b	dp brown	12.00	5.50
340	A58	1b	black brown	17.00	1.50
341	A57	3b	orange	92.50	50.00
342	A59	5b	black	15.00	7.75
			Nos. 325-342 (18)	226.75	95.70

See Nos. 400, 412 in Scott Standard catalogue, Vol. 6.

Teresa Carreño — A60

1938, June 12 *Perf. 11½x12*

No.	Type	Denom.	Color	Unused	Used
343	A60	25c	blue	5.75	.60

Teresa Carreno, Venezuelan pianist, whose remains were repatriated Feb. 14, 1938.

For surcharge see No. 386 in Scott Standard catalogue, Vol. 6.

Bolívar Statue — A61

1938, July 24 *Perf. 12*

No.	Type	Denom.	Color	Unused	Used
344	A61	25c	dark blue	6.50	.60

"The Day of the Worker."

For surcharge see No. 387 in Scott Standard catalogue, Vol. 6.

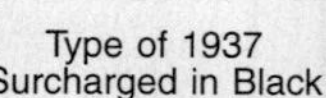

Type of 1937 Surcharged in Black

1938 Litho. *Perf. 11, 11½*

No.	Type	Denom.	Color	Unused	Used
345	A51	40c on 5b	lt brn	8.50	4.50
a.			Inverted surcharge	21.00	21.00

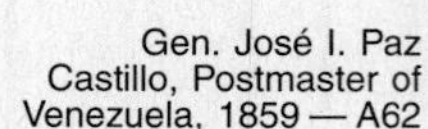

Gen. José I. Paz Castillo, Postmaster of Venezuela, 1859 — A62

1939, Apr. 19 Engr. *Perf. 12½*

No.	Type	Denom.	Color	Unused	Used
348	A62	10c	carmine	2.50	.70

80th anniv. of the first Venezuelan stamp.

View of Ojeda A63

1939, June 24 Photo.

No.	Type	Denom.	Color	Unused	Used
349	A63	25c	dull blue	9.25	.75

Founding of city of Ojeda.

Cristóbal Mendoza — A64

1939, Oct. 14 Engr. *Perf. 13*

No.	Type	Denom.	Color	Unused	Used
350	A64	5c	green	.40	.25
351	A64	10c	dk car rose	.40	.25
352	A64	15c	dull lilac	1.00	.25
353	A64	25c	brt ultra	.80	.25
354	A64	37½c	dark blue	15.00	6.25
355	A64	50c	lt olive grn	16.00	4.00
356	A64	1b	dark brown	6.50	3.50
			Nos. 350-356 (7)	40.10	14.75

Mendoza (1772-1839), postmaster general.

Diego Urbaneja — A65

1940-43 *Perf. 12*

No.	Type	Denom.	Color	Unused	Used
357	A65	5c	Prus green	.55	.25
357A	A65	7½c	dk bl grn ('43)	.80	.30
358	A65	15c	olive	.95	.30
359	A65	37½c	deep blue	1.50	.70
360	A65	40c	violet blue	1.10	.35
361	A65	50c	violet	6.50	1.75
362	A65	1b	dk violet brn	3.50	.90
363	A65	3b	scarlet	9.50	3.75
			Nos. 357-363 (8)	24.40	8.30

See Nos. 399, 408, 410-411 in Scott Standard catalogue, Vol. 6. For surcharges see Nos. 396, C226 in Scott Standard catalogue, Vol. 6.

Battle of Carabobo, 1821 — A67

1940, June 13

No.	Type	Denom.	Color	Unused	Used
365	A67	25c	blue	6.75	.80

Birth of General JoséAntonio Páez, 150th anniv.

"Crossing the Andes" by Tito Salas — A68

1940, June 13

No.	Type	Denom.	Color	Unused	Used
366	A68	25c	dark blue	6.75	.80

Death cent. of General Francisco Santander.

Monument and Urn containing Ashes of Simón Bolívar — A69

Bed where Simón Bolívar was Born — A70

Designs: 15c, "Christening of Bolivar" by Tito Salas. 20c, Bolivar's birthplace, Caracas. 25c, "Bolivar on Horseback" by Salas. 30c, Patio of Bolivar House, Caracas. 37½c, Patio of Bolivar's Birthplace. 50c, "Rebellion of 1812" by Salas.

1940-41

No.	Type	Denom.	Color	Unused	Used
367	A69	5c	turq green	.25	.25
368	A70	10c	rose pink	.25	.25
369	A69	15c	olive	.60	.25
370	A70	20c	blue ('41)	1.00	.25
371	A69	25c	lt blue	.60	.25
372	A70	30c	plum ('41)	1.50	.25
373	A70	37½c	dk blue	3.00	1.00
374	A70	50c	purple	2.00	.50
			Nos. 367-374 (8)	9.20	3.00

110th anniv. of the death of Simón Bolívar.

See Nos. 397, 398, 403, 405-407, 409 in Scott Standard catalogue, Vol. 6. For surcharges see Nos. 375, 401-402, C224, C237-C238 in Scott Standard catalogue, Vol. 6.

POSTAL FISCAL STAMPS

Nos. 128-135 Overprinted

1900 *Perf. 12*

No.	Type	Denom.	Color	Unused	Used
AR1	A25	5c	gray	.25	.25
a.			Overprint inverted	8.00	8.00
AR2	A25	10c	deep green	.25	.25
a.			Overprint inverted	8.00	8.00
AR3	A25	25c	blue	.25	.25
a.			Overprint inverted	8.00	8.00
AR4	A25	50c	orange	.25	.25
a.			Overprint inverted	8.00	8.00
AR5	A25	1b	red violet	.30	.25
a.			Overprint inverted	8.00	8.00
AR6	A25	3b	red orange	.50	.25
a.			Overprint inverted	8.00	8.00
AR7	A25	10b	dull violet	1.25	.75
AR8	A25	20b	red brown	7.50	7.50
			Nos. AR1-AR8 (8)	10.55	9.75

Type of 1893 Postage Stamps in Changed Colors Overprinted

1900 *Perf. 12*

No.	Type	Denom.	Color	Unused	Used
AR9	A25	5c	orange	.25	.25
AR10	A25	10c	deep blue	.25	.25
AR11	A25	25c	plum	.25	.25
AR12	A25	50c	bright green	1.00	.25
AR13	A25	1b	gray black	10.00	1.75
AR14	A25	3b	red brown	2.00	1.00
AR15	A25	10b	vermilion	12.00	3.50
AR16	A25	20b	deep violet	20.00	5.00
			Nos. AR9-AR16 (8)	45.75	12.25

Type of 1893 Postage Stamps in Changed Colors Overprinted

1901

No.	Type	Denom.	Color	Unused	Used
AR17	A25	1b	gray black	.75	.50

Type of 1893 in Changed Colors

1901

No.	Type	Denom.	Color	Unused	Used
AR18	A25	5c	orange	.25	.25
AR19	A25	10c	vermilion	.25	.25
AR20	A25	10c	blue	.25	.25
AR21	A25	25c	Prussian blue	.25	.25
AR22	A25	50c	yellow green	.25	.25
AR23	A25	1b	gray black	10.00	2.50
AR24	A25	3b	red brown	.25	.25
AR25	A25	10b	vermilion	.50	.45
AR26	A25	20b	deep violet	1.00	.65
			Nos. AR18-AR26 (9)	13.00	5.10

Simón Bolivar — PF1

1904, July Engr. *Perf. 12*

No.	Type	Denom.	Color	Unused	Used
AR27	PF1	5c	green	.25	.25
AR28	PF1	10c	gray	.25	.25
AR29	PF1	25c	vermilion	.25	.25
AR30	PF1	50c	yel org	.25	.25
AR31	PF1	1b	claret	3.00	.40
AR32	PF1	3b	blue	.50	.25
AR33	PF1	10b	bluish gray	.75	.50
AR34	PF1	20b	deep carmine	1.75	.50
			Nos. AR27-AR34 (8)	7.00	2.65

National Figures — PF2

5c, José Vargas (1786-1854), Independence leader and provisional president. 10c, De Avila. 25c, Miguel José Sanz, revolutionary jurist and educator. 50c, Antonio Guzman Blanco (1829-99), jurist, president. 1b, Andres Bello. 2b, Martin S. Sanabria (1831-1904), educator, cabinet minister. 3b, José Antonio Paez (1790-1873), revolutionary leader. 10b, Antonio José de Sucre known as the "Gran Mariscal de Ayacucho." 20b, Simón Bolivar, military and political leader.

1911 Litho. *Perf. 11½x12*

No.	Type	Denom.	Color	Unused	Used
AR35	PF2	5c	blue	.25	.25
AR36	PF2	10c	pale yel & org	.25	.25
AR37	PF2	25c	gray	.25	.25
AR38	PF2	50c	scarlet	.25	.25
AR39	PF2	1b	green	.25	.25
AR40	PF2	2b	brown	.90	.50
AR41	PF2	3b	blue violet	.90	.50
AR42	PF2	10b	lilac	1.75	.75
AR43	PF2	20b	blue	1.75	1.10
			Nos. AR35-AR43 (9)	6.55	4.10

Simón Bolivar — PF3

1914 Engr. *Perf. 14*

No.	Type	Denom.	Color	Unused	Used
AR44	PF3	5c	lilac	.25	.25
AR45	PF3	10c	olive green	.25	.25
AR46	PF3	25c	red brown	1.00	.25
AR47	PF3	50c	rose carmine	1.50	.25
AR48	PF3	1b	violet brown	1.50	.50
AR49	PF3	2b	bister	3.25	1.50
AR50	PF3	3b	gray blue	3.25	.50
AR51	PF3	10b	orange brown	10.00	3.25
AR52	PF3	20b	gray black	6.50	2.25
			Nos. AR44-AR52 (9)	27.50	9.00

PF4

PF5

Antonio José de Sucre — PF6

1915				Perf. 12	
AR53	PF4	5c	brown	.25	.25
AR54	PF5	10c	blue	.25	.25
AR55	PF5	25c	carmine	3.25	.25
AR56	PF5	50c	red brown	.25	.25
AR57	PF4	1b	green	.40	.25
AR58	PF4	2b	gray brown	2.25	.25
AR59	PF6	3b	violet	.25	.25
AR60	PF6	10b	gray black	20.00	2.25
AR61	PF6	20b	orange	.25	.25
			Nos. AR53-AR61 (9)	27.15	4.25

Type of 1915 in Changed Colors and

PF7

Antonio José de Sucre — PF8

1922					
AR62	PF5	10c	green	.25	.25
AR63	PF7	20c	light blue	.25	.25
AR64	PF4	1b	olive brown	.25	.25
AR65	PF4	2b	carmine	.25	.25
AR66	PF6	10b	yellow	.35	.25
AR67	PF8	50b	claret	.60	.25
			Nos. AR62-AR67 (6)	1.95	1.50

AIR POST STAMPS

Air post stamps of 1930-42 perforated "GN" (Gobierno Nacional) were for official use.

Airplane and Map of Venezuela — AP1

1930	Unwmk.	Litho.		Perf. 12	
C1	AP1	5c	bister brn	.25	.25
C2	AP1	10c	yellow	.25	.25
a.			10c salmon	32.50	32.50
C3	AP1	15c	gray	.25	.25
C4	AP1	25c	lilac	.25	.25
C5	AP1	40c	olive grn	.25	.25
a.			40c slate blue	45.00	
b.			40c slate green	45.00	
C6	AP1	75c	dp red	.30	.25
C7	AP1	1b	indigo	.45	.25
C8	AP1	1.20b	blue grn	.70	.35
C9	AP1	1.70b	dk blue	.90	.45
C10	AP1	1.90b	blue grn	.90	.50
C11	AP1	2.10b	dk blue	1.75	.65
C12	AP1	2.30b	vermilion	1.75	.50
C13	AP1	2.50b	dk blue	1.75	.50
C14	AP1	3.70b	blue grn	1.75	1.10
C15	AP1	10b	dull vio	5.25	2.40
C16	AP1	20b	gray grn	8.00	4.50
			Nos. C1-C16 (16)	24.75	12.70

Issued: 10b, 6/8; 20b, 6/16; others, 4/5.

Nos. C1-C16 exist imperforate or partly perforated. Value, imperf set $200.

See Nos. C119-C126.

Airplane and Map of Venezuela — AP2

Bluish Winchester Security Paper

1932, July 12		Engr.		Perf. 12½	
C17	AP2	5c	brown	.40	.25
C18	AP2	10c	org yel	.40	.25
C19	AP2	15c	gray lilac	.40	.25
C20	AP2	25c	violet	.40	.25
C21	AP2	40c	ol grn	.80	.25
C22	AP2	70c	rose	.55	.25
C23	AP2	75c	red org	1.00	.25
C24	AP2	1b	dk bl	1.10	.25
C25	AP2	1.20b	green	2.40	.85
C26	AP2	1.70b	red brn	4.75	.55
C27	AP2	1.80b	ultra	2.40	.35
C28	AP2	1.90b	green	6.00	3.50
C29	AP2	1.95b	blue	6.50	2.75
C30	AP2	2b	blk brn	4.00	2.25
C31	AP2	2.10b	blue	9.50	6.00
C32	AP2	2.30b	red	4.00	2.40
C33	AP2	2.50b	dk bl	6.00	1.40
C34	AP2	3b	dk vio	6.00	.85
C35	AP2	3.70b	emerald	8.00	6.00
C36	AP2	4b	red org	6.00	1.40
C37	AP2	5b	black	6.50	2.40
C38	AP2	8b	dk car	13.00	4.75
C39	AP2	10b	dk vio	26.00	8.00
C40	AP2	20b	grnsh slate	60.00	20.00
			Nos. C17-C40 (24)	176.10	65.45

Pairs imperf. between exist of the 1b (value $150); the 25c and 4b (value $300 each).

Air Post Stamps of 1932 Surcharged in Black

1937, June 4					
C41	AP2	5c	on 1.70b red brn	11.00	7.00
C42	AP2	10c	on 3.70b emer	11.00	7.00
C43	AP2	15c	on 4b red org	5.00	3.50
C44	AP2	25c	on 5b blk	5.00	3.50
C45	AP2	1b	on 8b dk car	4.00	3.50
C46	AP2	2b	on 2.10b bl	30.00	23.00
			Nos. C41-C46 (6)	66.00	47.50

Various varieties of surcharge exist, including double and triple impressions. No. C43 exists in pair imperf. between; value $30 unused, $50 used.

Allegory of Flight AP3

Allegory of Flight AP4

National Pantheon at Caracas AP5

Airplane — AP6

Perf. 11, 11½ and Compound

1937, July 1				Litho.	
C47	AP3	5c	brn org	.30	.40
C48	AP4	10c	org red	.25	.25
C49	AP5	15c	gray blk	.60	.40
C50	AP6	25c	dk vio	.60	.40
C51	AP4	40c	yel grn	1.10	.55
C52	AP3	70c	red	1.10	.40
C53	AP5	75c	bister	2.50	1.30
C54	AP3	1b	dk gray	1.50	.55
C55	AP4	1.20b	pck grn	6.50	4.25
C56	AP3	1.80b	dk ultra	3.25	2.00
C57	AP5	1.95b	lt ultra	10.00	7.75
C58	AP6	2b	chocolate	4.25	2.75
C59	AP6	2.50b	gray bl	11.50	11.50
C60	AP4	3b	lt vio	6.50	4.50
C61	AP6	3.70b	rose red	11.50	15.00
C62	AP5	10b	red vio	25.00	15.00
C63	AP3	20b	gray	30.00	23.00
			Nos. C47-C63 (17)	116.45	90.00

All values exist imperf, and all except the 3.70b part-perf.

Counterfeits exist.

For overprints & surcharges see Nos. C66-C78, C114-C118; Nos. C164-C167, C169-C172, C174-C180 in Scott Standard catalogue, Vol. 6.

AP7

1937, Oct. 28				Perf. 11	
C64	AP7	70c	emerald	1.40	.55
C65	AP7	1.80b	ultra	2.25	1.00

Acquisition of the Port of La Guaira by the Government from the British Corporation, June 3, 1937. Nos. C64-C65 exist imperf. Value, set $275.

A redrawn printing of Nos. C64-C65, with lower inscription beginning "Nacionalización..." was prepared but not issued. Value, $40 each.

For overprints see Nos. C168, C173 in Scott Standard catalogue, Vol. 6.

Air Post Stamps of 1937 Overprinted in Black

1937, Dec. 17				Perf. 11, 11½	
C66	AP4	10c	org red	1.00	.70
a.			Inverted overprint	15.00	12.00
C67	AP6	25c	dk vio	2.00	1.00
C68	AP4	40c	yel grn	2.00	1.40
C69	AP3	70c	red	1.50	1.00
a.			Inverted overprint	15.00	14.00
b.			Double overprint	20.00	16.00
C70	AP3	1b	dk gray	2.00	1.40
a.			Inverted overprint	16.00	13.00
b.			Double overprint	13.00	
C71	AP4	1.20b	pck grn	30.00	20.00
a.			Inverted overprint	77.50	
C72	AP3	1.80b	dk ultra	5.75	2.40
C73	AP5	1.95b	lt ultra	7.75	4.25
a.			Inverted overprint	60.00	40.00
C74	AP6	2b	chocolate	50.00	23.00
a.			Inverted overprint	100.00	90.00
b.			Double overprint	82.50	82.50
C75	AP6	2.50b	gray bl	50.00	19.00
a.			Double overprint	70.00	
b.			Inverted overprint	100.00	82.50
C76	AP4	3b	lt vio	30.00	12.00
C77	AP5	10b	red vio	72.50	40.00
C78	AP3	20b	gray	77.50	47.50
a.			Double overprint	150.00	150.00
			Nos. C66-C78 (13)	332.00	173.65

Counterfeit overprints exist on #C77-C78.

View of La Guaira AP8

National Pantheon AP9

Oil Wells AP10

1938-39		Engr.		Perf. 12	
C79	AP8	5c	green	1.00	.50
C80	AP8	5c	dk grn	.25	.25
C81	AP9	10c	car rose	1.40	.80
C82	AP9	10c	scarlet	.25	.25
C83	AP8	12½c	dull vio	.60	.55
C84	AP10	15c	slate vio	3.00	1.25
C85	AP10	15c	dk bl	.85	.25
C86	AP8	25c	dk bl	3.00	1.25
C87	AP8	25c	bis brn	.25	.25
C88	AP10	30c	vio ('39)	2.00	.25
C89	AP9	40c	dk vio	3.50	1.25
C90	AP9	40c	redsh brn	2.50	.25
C91	AP8	45c	Prus grn ('39)	1.00	.25
C92	AP9	50c	blue ('39)	1.25	.25
C93	AP10	70c	car rose	.85	.25
C94	AP8	75c	bis brn	6.00	2.00
C95	AP8	75c	ol bis	1.40	.25
C96	AP10	90c	red org ('39)	1.00	.25
C97	AP9	1b	ol & bis	7.00	2.75
C98	AP9	1b	dk vio	1.25	.25
C99	AP10	1.20b	orange	20.00	5.75
C100	AP10	1.20b	green	2.00	.55
C101	AP8	1.80b	ultra	2.00	.55
C102	AP9	1.90b	black	5.50	2.75
C103	AP10	1.95b	lt bl	4.25	2.50
C104	AP8	2b	ol gray	45.00	15.00
C105	AP8	2b	car rose	1.75	.70
C106	AP9	2.50b	red brn	45.00	20.00
C107	AP9	2.50b	orange	10.00	2.75
C108	AP10	3b	bl grn	20.00	4.75
C109	AP10	3b	ol gray	5.50	2.00
C110	AP8	3.70b	gray blk	7.75	5.50
C111	AP10	5b	red brn ('39)	7.75	2.00
C112	AP9	10b	vio brn	20.00	2.40
C113	AP10	20b	red org	57.50	25.00
			Nos. C79-C113 (35)	292.35	105.55

See Nos. C227a, C235-C236, C254-C255 in Scott Standard catalogue, Vol. 6.

For surcharge see No. C227 in Scott Standard catalogue, Vol. 6.

Nos. C51, C56, C58-C59, C61 Surcharged

1938, Apr. 15				Perf. 11, 11½	
C114	AP3	5c	on 1.80b	.85	.60
a.			Inverted surcharge	12.50	7.50
C115	AP6	10c	on 2.50b	3.00	1.40
a.			Inverted surcharge	10.00	7.50
C116	AP6	15c	on 2b	1.40	1.10
C117	AP4	25c	on 40c	1.75	1.40
C118	AP6	40c	on 3.70b	3.50	3.25
			Nos. C114-C118 (5)	10.50	7.75

Plane & Map Type of 1930

White Paper; No Imprint

1938-39		Engr.		Perf. 12½	
C119	AP1	5c	dk grn ('39)	.25	.25
C120	AP1	10c	org yel ('39)	.55	.25
C121	AP1	12½c	rose vio ('39)	1.10	.85
C122	AP1	15c	dp bl	.95	.25
C123	AP1	25c	brown	1.10	.25
C124	AP1	40c	olive ('39)	2.75	.40
C125	AP1	70c	rose car ('39)	20.00	7.75
C126	AP1	1b	dk bl ('39)	7.75	3.00
			Nos. C119-C126 (8)	34.45	13.00

Monument to Sucre — AP11

Monuments at Carabobo
AP12 AP13

1938, Dec. 23 ***Perf. 13½***

C127	AP11	20c brn blk	.80	.30
C128	AP12	30c purple	1.20	.30
C129	AP13	45c dk bl	1.75	.25
C130	AP11	50c lt ultra	1.50	.25
C131	AP13	70c dk car	26.00	7.50
C132	AP12	90c red org	2.50	.75
C133	AP13	1.35b gray blk	3.00	1.00
C134	AP11	1.40b slate gray	12.00	2.75
C135	AP12	2.25b green	6.00	2.00
		Nos. C127-C135 (9)	54.75	15.10

For surcharge see No. C198 in Scott Standard catalogue, Vol. 6.

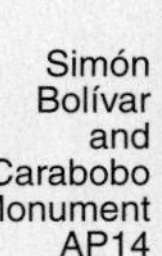

Simón Bolívar and Carabobo Monument
AP14

1940, Mar. 30 ***Perf. 12***

C136	AP14	15c blue	.75	.25
C137	AP14	20c olive bis	.75	.25
C138	AP14	25c red brn	2.75	.40
C139	AP14	40c blk brn	2.25	.25
C140	AP14	1b red lilac	5.00	.55
C141	AP14	2b rose car	11.00	1.40
		Nos. C136-C141 (6)	22.50	3.10

"The Founding of Grand Colombia"
AP15

1940, June 13

C142	AP15	15c copper brown	1.25	.45

Founding of the Pan American Union, 50th anniv.

Statue of Simón Bolívar, Caracas — AP16

1940-44

C143	AP16	5c dk grn ('42)	.25	.25
C144	AP16	10c scar ('42)	.25	.25
C145	AP16	12½c dull purple	.75	.30
C146	AP16	15c blue ('43)	.50	.25
C147	AP16	20c bis brn ('44)	.50	.25
C148	AP16	25c bis brn ('42)	.50	.25
C149	AP16	30c dp vio ('43)	.50	.25
C150	AP16	40c blk brn ('43)	.65	.25
C151	AP16	45c turq grn ('43)	.65	.25
C152	AP16	50c blue ('44)	.65	.25
C153	AP16	70c rose pink	2.00	.30
C154	AP16	75c ol bis ('43)	7.75	1.60
C155	AP16	90c red org ('43)	1.25	.30
C156	AP16	1b dp red lil ('42)	.65	.25
C157	AP16	1.20b dp yel grn ('43)	2.50	.75
C158	AP16	1.35b gray blk ('42)	10.50	3.50
C159	AP16	2b rose pink ('43)	2.00	.25
C160	AP16	3b ol blk ('43)	3.25	.75
C161	AP16	4b black	2.50	.75
C162	AP16	5b red brn ('44)	20.00	8.00
		Nos. C143-C162 (20)	57.60	19.00

See Nos. C232-C234, C239-C253 in Scott Standard catalogue, Vol. 6. For surcharges see Nos. C225, C873 in Scott Standard catalogue, Vol. 6.

REGISTRATION STAMPS

Bolívar — R1

1899, May Unwmk. Engr. ***Perf. 12***

F1	R1	25c yellow brown	3.25	2.75

No. F1 Overprinted

1900

F2	R1	25c yellow brown	2.00	2.00
a.		Inverted overprint	32.50	32.50
b.		Double overprint	40.00	40.00

Counterfeit overprints exist, especially of the varieties.

OFFICIAL STAMPS

Coat of Arms — O1

Lithographed, Center Engraved

1898, May 1 Unwmk. ***Perf. 12***

O1	O1	5c bl grn & blk	.80	.55
O2	O1	10c rose & blk	.95	.85
O3	O1	25c bl & blk	1.50	1.40
O4	O1	50c yel & blk	2.50	2.25
O5	O1	1b vio & blk	2.75	2.50
		Nos. O1-O5 (5)	8.50	7.55

Nos. O4 and O5 Handstamp Surcharged in Magenta or Violet

1899, Nov.

O6	O1	5c on 50c yel & blk	4.75	4.50
O7	O1	5c on 1b vio & blk	20.00	18.00
O8	O1	25c on 50c yel & blk	20.00	18.00
O9	O1	25c on 1b vio & blk	12.00	11.00
		Nos. O6-O9 (4)	56.75	51.50

Inverted Surcharge

O6a	O1	5c on 50c	15.00	15.00
O7a	O1	5c on 1b	40.00	40.00
O8a	O1	25c on 50c	32.50	32.50
O9a	O1	25c on 1b	32.50	32.50
		Nos. O6a-O9a (4)	120.00	120.00

Nos. O6-O9 exist with double surcharge. Value each $18.50-$37.50.

Many of the magenta overprints have become violet. There are intermediate shades.

Counterfeit overprints exist.

Coat of Arms — O3

1900 Litho., Center Engr.

O14	O3	5c bl grn & blk	.40	.40
O15	O3	10c rose & blk	.55	.55
O16	O3	25c bl & blk	.55	.55
O17	O3	50c yel & blk	.55	.55
O18	O3	1b dl vio & blk	.65	.65
		Nos. O14-O18 (5)	2.70	2.70

O4

Imprint: "American Bank Note Co., N.Y."

1904, July Engr.

O19	O4	5c emerald & blk	.25	.25
O20	O4	10c rose & blk	.65	.65
O21	O4	25c blue & blk	.65	.65
O22	O4	50c red brn & blk	4.25	4.25
a.		50c claret & black	4.25	4.25
O23	O4	1b red brn & blk	2.00	2.00
a.		1b claret & black	2.00	2.00
		Nos. O19-O23 (5)	7.80	7.80

No Stars Above Shield — O5

1912 Lithographed in Caracas

O24	O5	5c grn & blk	.55	.30
O25	O5	10c car & blk	.55	.30
O26	O5	25c dk bl & blk	.55	.30
O27	O5	50c pur & blk	.55	.40
a.		Center double	19.00	
O28	O5	1b yel & blk	1.30	.80
		Nos. O24-O28 (5)	3.50	2.10

Perforated Initials

After 1925, Venezuela's official stamps consisted of regular postage stamps, some commemoratives and air post stamps of 1930-42 punched with "GN" (Gobierno Nacional) in large perforated initials.

LOCAL STAMPS FOR THE PORT OF CARUPANO

In 1902 Great Britain, Germany and Italy, seeking compensation for revolutionary damages, established a blockade of La Guaira and seized the custom house. Carúpano, a port near Trinidad, was isolated and issued the following provisionals. A treaty effected May 7, 1903, referred the dispute to the Hague Tribunal.

A1

A2

1902 Typeset ***Imperf.***

1	A1	5c purple, *orange*	27.00
2	A2	10c black, *orange*	40.00
a.		Tête bêche pair	82.50
3	A1	25c purple, *green*	32.50
4	A1	50c green, *yellow*	85.00
5	A1	1b blue, *rose*	120.00
		Nos. 1-5 (5)	304.50

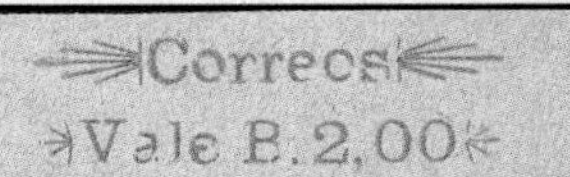

A3

1902

6	A3	1b black, *yellow*	200.00
a.		Tête bêche pair	

A4

1903 Handstamped

7	A4	5c carmine, *yellow*	45.00	45.00
8	A4	10c green, *yellow*	92.50	92.50
9	A4	25c green, *orange*	45.00	45.00
10	A4	50c blue, *rose*	45.00	45.00
11	A4	1b violet, *gray*	45.00	45.00
12	A4	2b carmine, *green*	45.00	45.00
13	A4	5b violet, *blue*	45.00	45.00
		Nos. 7-13 (7)	362.50	362.50

Dangerous counterfeits exist of Nos. 1-13.

LOCAL STAMPS FOR THE STATE OF GUAYANA

Revolutionary Steamship "Banrigh" — A1

Control Mark

Control Mark on Block of 4

1903 Typo. ***Perf. 12***

1	A1	5c black, *gray*	19.00	19.00
2	A1	10c black, *orange*	47.50	47.50
3	A1	25c black, *pink*	19.00	19.00
4	A1	50c black, *blue*	30.00	30.00
5	A1	1b black, *straw*	25.00	25.00
		Nos. 1-5 (5)	140.50	140.50

Nos. 1-5 can be found with or without the illustrated control mark which covers four stamps.

Counterfeits include the 10c and 50c in red and are from different settings from the originals. They are on papers differing in colors from the originals. All 5c on granite paper are bogus.

Coat of Arms
A2

1903

11	A2	5c black, *pink*	40.00
12	A2	10c black, *orange*	50.00
13	A2	25c black, *gray blue*	40.00
a.		25c black, *blue*	40.00
14	A2	50c black, *straw*	40.00
15	A2	1b black, *gray*	30.00
		Nos. 11-15 (5)	200.00

Postally used examples are very scarce, as are examples having 9 ornaments in horizontal borders. Nos. 11-15 pen canceled sell for same values as unused.

See note on controls after No. 5.

Counterfeits exist of Nos. 11-15. Stamps with 10 ornaments in horizontal borders are counterfeits.

Nos. 1-5, 11-15 were issued by a group of revolutionists and had a limited local use. The dates on the stamps commemorate the declaration of Venezuelan independence and a compact with Spain against Joseph Bonaparte.

VIRGIN ISLANDS

'vər-jən 'ī-ləndz

LOCATION — West Indies, southeast of Puerto Rico
GOVT. — British colony
AREA — 59 sq. mi.
POP. — 12,034 (1980)
CAPITAL — Road Town

The British Virgin Islands constituted one of the presidencies of the Leeward Islands colony. For many years stamps of Leeward Islands were used concurrently.

The Virgin Islands group is divided between Great Britain and the United States. See Danish West Indies.

12 Pence = 1 Shilling
20 Shillings = 1 Pound
100 Cents = 1 Dollar (1951)

Catalogue values for unused stamps in this country are for Never Hinged items, beginning with Scott 88 in the regular postage section.

PRE-STAMP POSTAL MARKINGS

Crowned Circle handstamp types I and VI are pictured in the Crowned Circle Handstamps and Great Britain Used Abroad section.

1842-58

A1	I	"Tortola" crowned circle handstamp in red, on cover	6,500.
A2	VI	"Tortola" crowned circle handstamp in red, on cover	22,000.

No. A2, in black, was used for the payment of official postage during 1900-18. Value, on cover $1,100.

STAMPS OF GREAT BRITAIN USED IN VIRGIN ISLANDS

Numeral cancellation type A is pictured in the Crowned Circle Handstamps and Great Britain Used Abroad section.

1858-60

A13 (Tortola)

A3	A	1p rose red (#20)	4,250.
A4	A	4p rose (#26)	5,000.
A5	A	6p lilac (#27)	1,600.
A6	A	1sh green (#28)	—

Issued under British Administration

Values for unused stamps are for examples with original gum as defined in the catalogue introduction. However, Nos. 1-2c are valued without gum as the vast majority of examples are found thus.

Virgin and Lamps — A1

St. Ursula — A2

A3

A4

1866 Litho. Unwmk. *Perf. 12*

Toned or White Paper

1	A1 1p green		5.00	*65.00*
a.	Toned paper		55.00	*65.00*
c.	Perf. 15x12, toned paper		6,000.	*7,000.*
2	A3 6p rose		65.00	*100.00*
a.	Large "V" in "VIRGIN"		325.00	*425.00*
b.	White paper		90.00	*125.00*
c.	As "a," white paper		425.00	*500.00*

Examples offered as No. 1c frequently have forged perfs.

1867-70 *Perf. 15*

3	A1 1p blue grn ('70)	70.00	75.00
4	A1 1p yel grn ('68)	87.50	87.50
a.	Toned paper	95.00	87.50
5	A2 4p lake, *buff*	50.00	65.00
a.	4p lake, *rose*	60.00	*82.50*
6	A3 6p rose	625.00	625.00
a.	Toned paper ('68)	325.00	*375.00*
7	A4 1sh rose & blk	300.00	*300.00*
a.	Toned paper	400.00	*400.00*
b.	Double lined frame	275.00	*350.00*
c.	As "b," bluish paper	250.00	*350.00*

Colored Margins

8	A4 1sh rose & blk	82.50	*95.00*
a.	White paper	100.00	*115.00*
b.	Bluish paper	750.00	*900.00*
c.	Central figure omitted	225,000.	
	Nos. 3-8 (6)	1,215.	1,248.

Examples of No. 8c have perfs. trimmed on one or two sides.

1878 Wmk. 1 *Perf. 14*

9	A1 1p green	95.00	*115.00*

See #16-17, 19-20. For surcharge see #18.

Queen Victoria — A5

1880 Typo.

10	A5 1p green	82.50	*100.00*
11	A5 2½p red brown	125.00	*140.00*

1883-84 Wmk. 2

12	A5 ½p yellow	95.00	95.00
13	A5 ½p green	6.75	*17.50*
a.	Imperf., pair		*1,750.*
14	A5 1p rose	50.00	*55.00*
15	A5 2½p ultra ('84)	4.00	*16.00*
	Nos. 12-15 (4)	155.75	*183.50*

No. 13a probably is a plate proof.

1887 Litho.

16	A2 4p brick red	36.00	*67.50*
a.	4p brown red	45.00	*72.50*
17	A3 6p violet	20.00	*55.00*

No. 8 Handstamp Surcharged in Violet

1888 Unwmk. *Perf. 15*

18	A4 4p on 1sh dp rose & blk, toned paper	145.00	*160.00*
a.	Double surcharge	*8,500.*	
b.	Inverted surcharge	*55,000.*	
c.	White paper	200.00	*225.00*

1889 Wmk. 2 *Perf. 14*

19	A1 1p carmine	4.00	*10.00*
20	A4 1sh brown	42.50	*65.00*
a.	1sh black brown	75.00	*100.00*

St. Ursula with Sheaf of Lilies — A7

1899 Engr.

21	A7 ½p yellow grn	4.25	.60
a.	"PFNNY"	90.00	*125.00*
b.	"F" without cross bar	90.00	*125.00*
c.	Horiz. pair, imperf. between	*13,000.*	
22	A7 1p red	6.00	2.00
23	A7 2½p ultra	13.00	3.00
24	A7 4p chocolate	6.00	*22.50*
a.	"PENCF"	750.00	*1,100.*
25	A7 6p dark violet	8.00	3.00
26	A7 7p slate green	14.00	6.50
27	A7 1sh ocher	25.00	*37.50*
28	A7 5sh dark blue	85.00	*95.00*
	Nos. 21-28 (8)	161.25	*170.10*

Edward VII — A8

1904 Typo. Wmk. 3

29	A8 ½p violet & bl grn	1.00	.60
30	A8 1p violet & scar	3.25	.55
31	A8 2p violet & bis	7.75	4.00
32	A8 2½p violet & ultra	4.25	2.00
33	A8 3p violet & blk	6.00	2.50
34	A8 6p violet & brn	4.75	2.50
35	A8 1sh green & scar	7.50	7.00
36	A8 2sh6p green & blk	45.00	*55.00*
37	A8 5sh green & ultra	55.00	*75.00*
	Nos. 29-37 (9)	134.50	*149.15*

Numerals of 2p, 3p, 1sh and 2sh6p of type A8 are in color on plain tablet.

George V — A9

Die I

For description of dies I and II see "Dies of British Colonial Stamps" in Table of Contents.

1913 Ordinary Paper

38	A9 ½p green	4.25	*7.00*
a.	½p 1p bl grn & dp grn ('19)	1.40	*6.00*
39	A9 1p scarlet	10.00	*12.00*
a.	1p carmine	50.00	*25.00*
40	A9 2p gray	8.00	*32.50*
41	A9 2½p ultra	10.00	*10.00*

Chalky Paper

42	A9 3p vio, *yel*	3.00	*7.00*
43	A9 6p dl vio & red vio	11.00	*22.50*
44	A9 1sh blk, *green*	3.50	*11.00*
45	A9 2sh6p blk & red, *bl*	55.00	*60.00*
46	A9 5sh grn & red, *yel*	50.00	*140.00*
	Nos. 38-46 (9)	154.75	*302.00*

Numerals of 2p, 3p, 1sh and 2sh6p of type A9 are in color on plain tablet.

1921 Die II Wmk. 4

47	A9 ½p green	17.50	*65.00*
48	A9 1p carmine	10.00	*40.00*

For overprints see Nos. MR1-MR2.

Colony Seal — A10

1922 Wmk. 3

49	A10 3p violet, *yel*	1.00	*17.50*
50	A10 1sh black, *emerald*	1.00	*17.50*
51	A10 2sh6p blk & red, *bl*	6.00	*12.50*
52	A10 5sh grn & red, *yel*	52.50	*120.00*
	Nos. 49-52 (4)	60.50	*167.50*

1922-28 Wmk. 4

53	A10 ½p green	1.00	*3.00*
54	A10 1p rose red	.80	.80
a.	1p scarlet ('28)	30.00	*15.00*
55	A10 1p violet ('27)	2.00	*7.00*
56	A10 1½p rose red ('27)	2.00	*3.00*
57	A10 1½p fawn ('28)	2.00	*1.50*
58	A10 2p gray	1.40	*6.50*
59	A10 2½p ultra	6.00	*25.00*
a.	2½p blue ('27)	20.00	*4.00*
60	A10 2½p orange ('23)	1.25	2.50
61	A10 3p dl vio, *yel* ('28)	2.50	*12.00*
62	A10 5p dl lil & ol grn	6.00	*50.00*
63	A10 6p dl vio & red vio	2.10	*6.50*
a.	6p brown lilac & red violet	2.10	*7.00*
64	A10 1sh blk, *emer* ('28)	3.00	*20.00*
65	A10 2sh6p blk & red, *bl* ('28)	20.00	*60.00*
66	A10 5sh grn & red, *yel* ('23)	25.00	*75.00*
	Nos. 53-66 (14)	75.05	*272.80*

The ½, 1, 2 and 2½p are on ordinary paper, the others on chalky.

Numerals of 1½p of type A10 are in color on plain tablet.

Common Design Types pictured following the introduction.

Silver Jubilee Issue

Common Design Type

1935, May 6 Engr. *Perf. 11x12*

69	CD301 1p car & dk blue	1.50	7.50
70	CD301 1½p black & ultra	1.50	6.50
71	CD301 2½p ultra & brn	4.00	6.25
72	CD301 1sh brn vio & ind	18.00	35.00
	Nos. 69-72 (4)	25.00	55.25
	Set, never hinged	32.50	

Coronation Issue

Common Design Type

1937, May 12 *Perf. 11x11½*

73	CD302 1p dark carmine	.90	2.75
74	CD302 1½p brown	.75	2.75
75	CD302 2½p deep ultra	.55	1.40
	Nos. 73-75 (3)	2.20	6.90
	Set, never hinged	2.75	

King George VI and Seal of the Colony — A11

1938-47 Photo. *Perf. 14*

76	A11 ½p green	.90	.90
	Never hinged	3.25	
77	A11 1p scarlet	1.25	1.00
	Never hinged	5.75	
78	A11 1½p red brown	1.50	1.25
	Never hinged	5.75	
79	A11 2p gray	1.50	1.25
	Never hinged	7.00	
80	A11 2½p ultra	2.00	1.50
	Never hinged	4.25	
81	A11 3p orange	1.25	1.00
	Never hinged	8.00	
82	A11 6p deep violet	3.50	1.00
	Never hinged	12.00	
83	A11 1sh olive bister	2.50	2.00
	Never hinged	22.00	

84 A11 2sh6p sepia 11.00 5.00
Never hinged 62.50
85 A11 5sh rose lake 11.00 *6.00*
Never hinged 62.50
86 A11 10sh brt blue ('47) 6.00 *11.00*
Never hinged 8.00
87 A11 £1 gray blk ('47) 7.00 *25.00*
Never hinged 10.00
Nos. 76-87 (12) 49.40 *56.90*
Set, never hinged 75.00

1938 Chalky Paper

76a A11 ½p green .85 3.50
Never hinged 8.00
77a A11 1p scarlet 3.15 2.00
Never hinged 15.00
78a A11 1½p red brown 3.50 6.50
Never hinged 17.00
79a A11 2p gray 3.50 2.50
Never hinged 17.00
80a A11 2½p ultramarine 2.50 1.80
Never hinged 12.00
81a A11 3p orange 4.25 1.10
Never hinged 20.00
82a A11 6p deep violet 6.50 2.75
Never hinged 32.50
83a A11 1sh olive bister 12.00 4.50
Never hinged 57.50
84a A11 2sh6p sepia 12.00 5.50
Never hinged 57.50
85a A11 5sh rose lake 36.00 12.00
Never hinged 150.00

Catalogue values for unused stamps in this section, from this point to the end of the section, are for Never Hinged items.

Peace Issue
Common Design Type
Perf. 13½x14

1946, Nov. 1 Engr. Wmk. 4
88 CD303 1½p red brown .25 .25
89 CD303 3p orange .25 .25

Silver Wedding Issue
Common Design Types

1949, Jan. 3 Photo. *Perf. 14x14½*
90 CD304 2½p brt ultra .25 .25

Engr.; Name Typo.
Perf. 11½x11
91 CD305 £1 gray black 16.00 22.00

UPU Issue
Common Design Types
Engr.; Name Typo. on Nos. 93 & 94

1949, Oct. 10 *Perf. 13½, 11x11½*
92 CD306 2½p ultra .40 *2.40*
93 CD307 3p deep orange 1.25 *2.50*
94 CD308 6p red lilac .50 .50
95 CD309 1sh olive .45 .50
Nos. 92-95 (4) 2.60 5.90

University Issue
Common Design Types

1951 Engr. *Perf. 14x14½*
96 CD310 3c red brn & gray blk .40 *2.25*
97 CD311 12c purple & black 1.10 *1.50*

Map of the Islands A12

1951, Apr. 2 Wmk. 4 *Perf. 14½x14*
98 A12 6c red orange .70 1.75
99 A12 12c purple 1.25 1.00
100 A12 24c olive grn .70 1.25
101 A12 $1.20 carmine 3.50 1.50
Nos. 98-101 (4) 6.15 5.50

Restoration of the Legislative Council, 1950.

Sombrero Lighthouse — A13

Map of Jost van Dyke — A14

Designs: 3c, Sheep. 4c, Map, Anegada. 5c, Cattle. 8c, Map, Virgin Gorda. 12c, Map, Tortola. 24c, Badge of the Presidency. 60c, Dead Man's Chest. $1.20, Sir Francis Drake Channel. $2.40, Road Town. $4.80, Map, Virgin Islands.

1952, Apr. 15 *Perf. 12½x13, 13x12½*
102 A13 1c gray black .40 2.00
103 A14 2c deep green .85 .25
104 A14 3c choc & gray blk .45 1.25
105 A14 4c red .70 1.60
106 A14 5c gray blk & rose lake 1.40 .70
107 A14 8c ultra .85 *1.25*
108 A14 12c purple 1.25 *1.60*
109 A13 24c dk brown 1.00 .25
110 A14 60c blue & ol grn 4.00 11.00
111 A14 $1.20 ultra & blk 6.00 12.00
112 A14 $2.40 hn brn & dk grn 15.00 *16.00*
113 A14 $4.80 rose car & bl 19.00 19.00
Nos. 102-113 (12) 50.90 66.90

WAR TAX STAMPS

Regular Issue of 1913 Overprinted

1916-17 Wmk. 3 *Perf. 14*
Die I
MR1 A9 1p scarlet .55 *8.00*
a. 1p carmine 2.50 *25.00*
MR2 A9 3p violet, *yellow* 7.00 *26.00*

WALLIS & FUTUNA ISLANDS

'wä-ləs and fə-'tü-nə 'ī-ləndz

LOCATION — Group of islands in the South Pacific Ocean, northeast of Fiji
GOVT. — French Overseas Territory
AREA — 106 sq. mi.
POP. — 13,000 (est. 1984)
CAPITAL — Mata-Utu, Wallis Island

100 Centimes = 1 Franc

New Caledonia Stamps of 1905-28 Overprinted in Black or Red

1920-28 Unwmk. *Perf. 14x13½*
1 A16 1c black, *green* .30 .30
Never hinged .45
On cover 125.00
a. Double overprint 175.00
Never hinged 240.00
2 A16 2c red brown .30 .30
Never hinged .45
On cover 125.00
3 A16 4c blue, *org* .50 .50
Never hinged .75
On cover 125.00
4 A16 5c green .50 .50
Never hinged .75
On cover 65.00
5 A16 5c dull blue ('22) .40 *.55*
Never hinged .65
On cover 110.00
6 A16 10c rose .65 .65
Never hinged 1.00
On cover 50.00
7 A16 10c green ('22) .90 .90
Never hinged 1.20
On cover 50.00
8 A16 10c red, *pink* ('25) 2.25 2.25
Never hinged 3.00
On cover 50.00
9 A16 15c violet 1.10 1.10
Never hinged 1.60
On cover 50.00
10 A17 20c gray brown 1.00 *1.25*
Never hinged 1.40
On cover 65.00
11 A17 25c blue, *grn* 1.50 1.50
Never hinged 2.25
On cover 75.00
On cover, single franking 200.00
12 A17 25c red, *yel* ('22) 1.00 1.00
Never hinged 1.25
On cover 45.00
13 A17 30c brown, *org* 1.60 *2.00*
Never hinged 2.40
On cover 80.00
On cover, single franking 225.00
14 A17 30c dp rose ('22) 1.50 *1.75*
Never hinged 2.40
On cover 50.00
15 A17 30c red orange ('25) .85 .85
Never hinged 1.10
On cover 45.00
16 A17 30c lt green ('27) 2.40 *3.25*
Never hinged 3.75
On cover 65.00
17 A17 35c black, *yel* (R) 1.00 1.00
Never hinged 1.40
On cover 105.00
On cover, single franking 275.00
18 A17 40c rose, *grn* 1.25 *1.50*
Never hinged 1.60
On cover 95.00
On cover, single franking 140.00
19 A17 45c violet brn, *pnksh* 1.60 *2.00*
Never hinged 2.40
On cover 95.00
On cover, single franking 175.00
20 A17 50c red, *org* 1.75 *2.10*
Never hinged 2.50
On cover 105.00
On cover, single franking 225.00
21 A17 50c dark blue ('22) 2.00 *2.40*
Never hinged 2.90
On cover 65.00
On cover, single franking 160.00
22 A17 50c dark gray ('25) 2.60 *3.25*
Never hinged 4.00
On cover 90.00
On cover, single franking 200.00
23 A17 65c deep blue ('28) 7.50 *7.50*
Never hinged 10.50
On cover 80.00
On cover, single franking 175.00
24 A17 75c olive green 2.50 *2.60*
Never hinged 4.00
On cover 125.00
On cover, single franking 275.00

Nos. 113, 115-116 Overprinted

25 A18 1fr blue, *yel grn* 5.25 *5.25*
Never hinged 7.50
On cover 125.00
On cover, single franking 275.00
a. Triple overprint 200.00
Never hinged 280.00
b. Double overprint 200.00
Never hinged 280.00
c. Pair, one stamp without overprint 525.00
26 A18 1.10fr orange brn ('28) 5.50 *7.25*
Never hinged 7.00
On cover 175.00
On cover, single franking 30.00
27 A18 2fr carmine, *bl* 8.50 *8.50*
Never hinged 12.00
On cover 140.00
On cover, single franking 300.00
28 A18 5fr black, *org* (R) 17.00 *17.00*
Never hinged 26.00
On cover 200.00
On cover, single franking 400.00
Nos. 1-28 (28) 73.20 *79.00*

No. 9 Surcharged in Various Colors

1922
29 A16 0.01c on 15c violet (Bk) .75 *.95*
Never hinged 1.10
On cover 160.00
30 A16 0.02c on 15c violet (Bl) .75 *.95*
Never hinged 1.10
On cover 125.00
31 A16 0.04c on 15c violet (G) .75 *.95*
Never hinged 1.10
On cover 125.00
32 A16 0.05c on 15c violet (R) .75 *.95*
Never hinged 1.10
On cover 105.00
Nos. 29-32 (4) 3.00 *3.80*

Stamps and Types of 1920 Surcharged in Black or Red

1924-27
33 A18 25c on 2fr car, *bl* 1.00 1.00
Never hinged 1.50
On cover 55.00
34 A18 25c on 5fr black, *org* 1.00 1.00
Never hinged 1.50
On cover 55.00
35 A17 65c on 40c rose red, *grn* ('25) 1.75 *2.00*
Never hinged 2.40
On cover 80.00
On cover, single franking 200.00
36 A17 85c on 75c ol grn ('25) 1.40 *1.60*
Never hinged 2.10
On cover 95.00
On cover, single franking 225.00
37 A17 90c on 35c dp rose ('27) 2.25 *2.75*
Never hinged 3.25
On cover 80.00
On cover, single franking 225.00
38 A18 1.25fr on 1fr dp bl (R; '26) 1.10 *1.40*
Never hinged 1.60
On cover 105.00
On cover, single franking 190.00
39 A18 1.50fr on 1fr dp bl, *bl* ('27) 5.50 *5.50*
Never hinged 7.25
On cover 125.00
On cover, single franking 375.00
a. Double surcharge 300.00
Never hinged 410.00
b. Surcharge omitted 290.00
Never hinged 390.00
40 A18 3fr on 5fr red vio ('27) 9.00 *8.00*
Never hinged 10.50
On cover 140.00
On cover, single franking 400.00
a. Surcharge omitted 240.00
Never hinged 325.00
b. Double surcharge 325.00
Never hinged 410.00
41 A18 10fr on 5fr ol, *lav* ('27) 42.50 42.50
Never hinged 47.50
On cover 160.00
On cover, single franking 425.00
42 A18 20fr on 5fr vio rose, *yel* ('27) 50.00 50.00
Never hinged 62.50
On cover 250.00
On cover, single franking 550.00
Nos. 33-42 (10) 115.50 *115.75*

New Caledonia Stamps and Types of 1928-40 Overprinted as in 1920

1930-40 *Perf. 13½, 14x13, 14x13½*
43 A19 1c brn vio & indigo .25 .25
Never hinged .40
On cover 105.00
a. Double overprint 200.00
Never hinged 260.00
44 A19 2c dk brn & yel grn .25 .25
Never hinged .40
On cover 95.00
45 A19 3c brn vio & ind ('40) .25 .25
Never hinged .35
On cover 105.00
46 A19 4c org & Prus grn .25 .25
Never hinged .40
On cover 95.00
47 A19 5c Prus bl & dp ol .30 *.40*
Never hinged .45
On cover 90.00
48 A19 10c gray lil & dk brn .30 *.40*
Never hinged .45
On cover 80.00
49 A19 15c yel brn & dp bl .30 *.40*
Never hinged .45
On cover 75.00
50 A19 20c brn red & dk brn .60 *.70*
Never hinged .90
On cover 65.00
51 A19 25c dk grn & dk brn 1.10 *1.25*
Never hinged 1.50
On cover 45.00
52 A20 30c gray grn & bl grn 1.10 *1.25*
Never hinged 1.50
On cover 65.00
53 A20 35c Prus grn & dk grn ('38) 1.10 *1.25*
Never hinged 1.50
On cover 75.00
a. Without overprint 200.00
Never hinged 47.50
54 A20 40c brt red & olive 1.10 1.10
Never hinged 1.50
On cover 45.00
55 A20 45c dp bl & red org 1.10 *1.25*
Never hinged 1.50
On cover 65.00
56 A20 45c bl grn & dl grn ('40) .90 *1.00*
Never hinged 1.20
On cover 75.00
57 A20 50c violet & brn 1.10 1.10
Never hinged 1.50
On cover 40.00
58 A20 55c bl vio & rose red ('38) 2.40 *2.75*
Never hinged 3.50
On cover 75.00
59 A20 60c vio bl & car ('40) .75 *.90*
Never hinged 1.00
On cover 65.00
60 A20 65c org brn & bl 2.00 2.00
Never hinged 2.90
On cover 75.00
61 A20 70c dp rose & brn ('38) 1.40 *1.60*
Never hinged 1.75
On cover 75.00
62 A20 75c Prus bl & ol gray 3.00 3.00
Never hinged 4.00
On cover 70.00
63 A20 80c dk cl & grn ('38) 1.40 *1.60*
Never hinged 1.75
On cover 70.00

64 A20 85c green & brown ('38) 3.75 *4.00*
Never hinged 5.25
On cover 70.00
65 A20 90c dp red & brt red 2.40 *2.75*
Never hinged 3.40
On cover 75.00
On cover, single franking 160.00
66 A20 90c ol grn & rose red ('39) 1.10 *1.25*
Never hinged 1.40
On cover 40.00
67 A21 1fr dp ol & sal red 4.00 *4.75*
Never hinged 5.25
On cover 105.00
On cover, single franking 190.00
68 A21 1fr rose red & dk car ('38) 2.40 *2.75*
Never hinged 3.25
On cover 80.00
On cover, single franking 145.00
69 A21 1fr brn red & grn ('40) .80 .80
Never hinged 1.10
On cover 45.00
70 A21 1.10fr dp grn & brn 40.00 *40.00*
Never hinged 52.50
On cover 225.00
On cover, single franking 375.00
71 A21 1.25fr brn red & grn ('33) 3.75 *3.50*
Never hinged 4.50
On cover 70.00
On cover, single franking 145.00
72 A21 1.25fr rose red & dk car ('39) 1.10 *1.25*
Never hinged 1.20
On cover 65.00
On cover, single franking 190.00
73 A21 1.40fr dk bl & red org ('40) 1.10 *1.40*
Never hinged 1.40
On cover 65.00
On cover, single franking 145.00
74 A21 1.50fr dp bl & bl 1.25 *1.50*
Never hinged 1.90
On cover 75.00
On cover, single franking 145.00
75 A21 1.60fr dp grn & brn ('40) 1.60 *2.00*
Never hinged 2.00
On cover 75.00
On cover, single franking 160.00
76 A21 1.75fr dk bl & red org ('33) 16.00 *16.00*
Never hinged 22.00
On cover 125.00
On cover, single franking 225.00
77 A21 1.75fr vio bl ('38) 2.50 *2.75*
Never hinged 3.50
On cover 90.00
On cover, single franking 190.00
78 A21 2fr red org & brn 2.00 *1.90*
Never hinged 3.00
On cover 95.00
On cover, single franking 225.00
79 A21 2.25fr vio bl ('39) 2.50 *2.40*
Never hinged 3.25
On cover 75.00
On cover, single franking 160.00
80 A21 2.50fr brn & lt brn ('40) 2.00 *2.40*
Never hinged 2.75
On cover 90.00
On cover, single franking 200.00
81 A21 3fr magenta & brn 2.00 *2.00*
Never hinged 2.75
On cover 95.00
On cover, single franking 190.00
82 A21 5fr dk bl & brn 2.50 *2.60*
Never hinged 3.75
On cover 105.00
On cover, single franking 225.00
83 A21 10fr vio & brn, *pnksh* 3.50 *3.50*
Never hinged 5.50
On cover 105.00
On cover, single franking 225.00
84 A21 20fr red & brn, *yel* 5.25 *5.25*
Never hinged 7.75
On cover 125.00
On cover, single franking 275.00
Nos. 43-84 (42) 122.45 *127.70*

For overprints see Nos. 94-126 in Scott Standard catalogue, Vol. 6.

Common Design Types pictured following the introduction.

Colonial Exposition Issue
Common Design Types

1931, Apr. 13 Engr. *Perf. 12½*
Name of Country Typo. in Black

85 CD70 40c deep green 8.75 8.75
Never hinged 13.00
On cover 125.00
86 CD71 50c violet 8.75 8.75
Never hinged 13.00
On cover 105.00
87 CD72 90c red orange 8.75 8.75
Never hinged 13.00
On cover 170.00
On cover, single franking 225.00
88 CD73 1.50fr dull blue 8.75 8.75
Never hinged 13.00
On cover 160.00
On cover, single franking 200.00
Nos. 85-88 (4) 35.00 35.00

Colonial Arts Exhibition Issue
Common Design Type
Souvenir Sheet

1937 *Imperf.*

89 CD78 3fr red violet 28.50 *37.50*
Never hinged 45.00
On cover 200.00
On cover, single franking 300.00

New York World's Fair Issue
Common Design Type

1939, May 10 Engr. *Perf. 12½x12*

90 CD82 1.25fr carmine lake 3.00 3.00
Never hinged 4.50
On cover 95.00
On cover, single franking 170.00
91 CD82 2.25fr ultramarine 3.00 3.00
Never hinged 4.50
On cover 95.00
On cover, single franking 160.00

SEMI-POSTAL STAMPS

French Revolution Issue
Common Design Type
Unwmk.

1939, July 5 Photo. *Perf. 13*
Name and Value Typo. in Black

B1 CD83 45c + 25c green 19.00 *19.00*
Never hinged 30.00
On cover 170.00
B2 CD83 70c + 30c brown 19.00 *19.00*
Never hinged 30.00
On cover 125.00
B3 CD83 90c + 35c red org 19.00 *19.00*
Never hinged 30.00
On cover 95.00
B4 CD83 1.25fr + 1fr rose pink 19.00 *19.00*
Never hinged 30.00
On cover 170.00
On cover, single franking 250.00
B5 CD83 2.25fr + 2fr blue 19.00 *19.00*
Never hinged 30.00
On cover 160.00
On cover, single franking 225.00
Nos. B1-B5 (5) 95.00 95.00
Set, never hinged 150.00

POSTAGE DUE STAMPS

Postage Due Stamps of New Caledonia, 1906, Overprinted in Black or Red

1920 Unwmk. *Perf. 13½x14*

J1 D2 5c ultra, *azure* 1.00 1.00
Never hinged 1.60
On cover 125.00
J2 D2 10c brn, *buff* 1.10 1.10
Never hinged 1.75
On cover 125.00
J3 D2 15c grn, *grnsh* 1.10 1.10
Never hinged 1.75
On cover 125.00
J4 D2 20c blk, *yel* (R) 1.50 1.50
Never hinged 2.60
On cover 145.00
a. Double overprint 200.00
Never hinged 290.00
J5 D2 30c carmine rose 1.50 1.50
Never hinged 2.60
On cover 160.00
J6 D2 50c ultra, *straw* 2.40 2.40
Never hinged 4.00
On cover 170.00
J7 D2 60c olive, *azure* 2.90 2.90
Never hinged 4.75
On cover 190.00
a. Double overprint 200.00
Never hinged 290.00
J8 D2 1fr grn, *cream* 3.75 3.75
Never hinged 6.50
On cover 225.00
Nos. J1-J8 (8) 15.25 15.25

Type of 1920 Issue Surcharged

1927

J9 D2 2fr on 1fr brt vio 17.50 17.50
Never hinged 27.50
On cover 300.00
J10 D2 3fr on 1fr org brn 17.50 17.50
Never hinged 27.50
On cover 340.00

Postage Due Stamps of New Caledonia, 1928, Overprinted as in 1920

1930

J11 D3 2c sl bl & dp brn .25 .25
Never hinged .40
On cover 160.00
J12 D3 4c brn red & bl grn .25 .25
Never hinged .40
On cover 160.00
J13 D3 5c red org & bl blk .25 .25
Never hinged .40
On cover 125.00
J14 D3 10c mag & Prus bl .25 .25
Never hinged .40
On cover 95.00
J15 D3 15c dl grn & scar .35 .35
Never hinged .50
On cover 95.00
J16 D3 20c maroon & ol grn .75 .75
Never hinged 1.00
On cover 105.00
J17 D3 25c bis brn & sl bl .75 .75
Never hinged 1.00
On cover 105.00
J18 D3 30c bl grn & ol grn 1.40 1.40
Never hinged 1.90
On cover 105.00
J19 D3 50c lt brn & dk red .85 .85
Never hinged 1.20
On cover 125.00
J20 D3 60c mag & brt rose 1.40 1.40
Never hinged 1.90
On cover 140.00
J21 D3 1fr dl bl & Prus grn 1.40 1.40
Never hinged 2.00
On cover 160.00
J22 D3 2fr dk red & ol grn 1.40 1.40
Never hinged 2.00
On cover 175.00
J23 D3 3fr vio & brn 1.40 1.40
Never hinged 2.00
On cover 200.00
Nos. J11-J23 (13) 10.70 10.70

WESTERN UKRAINE

'wes-tərn yü-'krān

LOCATION — In Eastern Central Europe
GOVT. — A former short-lived independent State

A provisional government was established in 1918 in the eastern part of Austria-Hungary but the area later came under Polish administration.

100 Shahiv (Sotykiv) = 1 Hryvnia
100 Heller = 1 Krone

Forgeries of almost all Western Ukraine stamps are plentiful. Particularly dangerous forgeries have been noted for the Kolomyia Issue and for the First and Second Stanyslaviv Issues.

Lviv Issue

Austria Nos. 145-146, 148, 169 Overprinted

Nos. 1-4A are handstamped with an octagonal overprint that reads "ZAKHIDNO UKR. NARODNA REPUBLYKA" ("Western Ukrainian National Republic"), framing the image of a rearing crowned lion.

1918, Nov. 20

1 A37 3h bright vio 55.00 *425.00*
a. Inverted overprint 150.00
2 A37 5h light green 50.00 *325.00*
a. Inverted overprint 150.00
3 A37 10h magenta 50.00 *325.00*
a. Inverted overprint 150.00
4 A42 20h dark green 35.00 *350.00*
a. Inverted overprint 150.00
4A A42 20h light green 240.00 *900.00*
Nos. 1-4A (5) 430.00 *2,325.*

This issue was in circulation for only two days before Lviv was captured by the Poles on Nov. 22. No examples of Nos. 1-4A used in Lviv are known.

The Western Ukrainian National Republic (ZUNR) government evacuated to the city of Ternopil, which became the provisional capital. ZUNR postal operations were set up in other Western Ukrainian cities, and the Lviv Issue was used in Stanyslaviv (earliest known cancellation date, Dec. 8), Khodoriv and Kolomyia.

Nos. 1-4 exist in pairs with both normal and inverted overprints. Value $325.

Overprints in other colors (green, red and violet) are known, but these are probably proofs. Violet-black overprints are likely transitional color impressions.

Kolomyia Issue

Austria Nos. 168, 145, 147, 149 Surcharged

Kolomyia is the main town of the Pokutia region of southwestern Ukraine. Cut off from ZUNR postal officials by wartime conditions and in urgent need of basic value stamps, the Kolomyia postmaster obtained permission from the District Military Command to surcharge remaining Austrian postage stamps to either 5 or 10 sotyks, the equivalent of 5 or 10 heller. These stamps were produced on Dec. 10, under very strict security, by preparing two distinct plates (one for each value) that overprinted 25 stamps at a time (5x5 quarter sections of the Austrian 100-stamp panes). The stamps were placed on sale two days later.

1918, Dec. 12 Unwmk. *Perf. 12½*

5 A42 5sot on 15h dl red 90.00 *120.00*
a. Inverted overprint 600.00 *725.00*
b. Double overprint 1,500. *1,600.*
6 A37 10sot on 3h vio 90.00 *120.00*
7 A37 10sot on 6h dp org *1,650.* *1,250.*
8 A37 10sot on 12h lt bl *1,750.* *1,500.*
Nos. 5-8 (4) 3,580. *2,990.*

10 sotyk on 15 heller values are essays; only six were produced.

All inverted surcharges on Nos. 6-8 are forgeries. Double surcharges are forgeries.

First Stanyslaviv Issue

Austrian Stamps of 1916-18 Surcharged in Shahiv (shown) and Hryvnia Currency

At the end of December, 1918, the national government again moved, this time to the city of Stanyslaviv (present-day Ivano-Frankivsk). A shortage of qualified postal personnel resulted in a considerable delay in the creation of new ZUNR postage stamps. In the interim, remaining unoverprinted Austrian stamps were used. Finally, on March 18, 1919, 20 different available Austrian definitive stamps were typograph surcharged at the Weidenfeld Printing Shop in Stanyslaviv.

1919, Mar. 18

9 A37 3sh on 3h bright vio 17.00 *22.50*
10 A37 5sh on 5h light green 17.00 *22.50*
11 A37 6sh on 6h deep orange 32.50 *55.00*
12 A37 10sh on 10h mag 27.50 *37.50*
13 A37 12sh on 12h lt blue 27.50 *37.50*
a. Double overprint 300.00 *425.00*
b. Double overprint, one on reverse 500.00 *210.00*
14 A42 15sh on 15h dull red 27.50 *37.50*
15 A42 20sh on 20h dp grn 27.50 *37.50*
16 A42 30sh on 30h dull violet 100.00 *100.00*
17 A39 40sh on 40h ol green 27.50 *37.50*
18 A39 50sh on 50h dk grn 27.50 *37.50*
19 A39 60sh on 60h deep blue 27.50 *37.50*
20 A39 80sh on 80h org brown 27.50 *37.50*
a. Inverted overprint 300.00 *425.00*

21 A39 1hr on 1k car, *yel* 40.00 *45.00*
22 A40 2hr on 2k lt blue 40.00 *50.00*
23 A40 3hr on 3k claret (on #161) 3,250. *3,250.*
24 A40 3hr on 3k car rose (on #165) 100.00 82.50
25 A40 3hr on 3k car rose (on #173) 80.00 *80.00*
26 A40 4hr on 4k dk grn (on #162) 800.00 *700.00*
27 A40 4hr on 4k yel grn (on #166) 75.00 *55.00*
28 A40 10hr on 10k deep violet 800.00 *800.00*
a. Double overprint 3,000. *3,500.*
Nos. 9-28 (20) 5,572. *5,563.*

The 25sh on 25h, type A42, in both light and dull blue shades, never received this overprint. All such stamps are fantasies.

Second Stanyslaviv Issue

The overprinting of a second issue of postage stamps in Stanyslaviv was undertaken in early May. Stamps from several different Austrian stamp series were utilized to create four distinct sets. Most of the stamps available were Austrian postage due, charity or field post stamps.

Postage Due Stamps of Bosnia, 1904 Surcharged but without Asterisks

1919, May 5

29 D1 1sh on 1h blk, red & yel 32.50 *40.00*
a. Inverted overprint 100.00 65.00
b. Double overprint 90.00 90.00
30 D1 2sh on 2h blk, red & yel 15.00 *15.00*
a. Inverted overprint 85.00 *150.00*
31 D1 3sh on 3h blk, red & yel 17.50 *35.00*
a. Inverted overprint 25.00 *45.00*
32 D1 4sh on 4h blk, red & yel 125.00 125.00
a. Inverted overprint 175.00 175.00
b. Double overprint 300.00 300.00
33 D1 5sh on 5h blk, red & yel *3,250.* *3,500.*
34 D1 6sh on 6h blk, red & yel 600.00 *600.00*
a. Inverted overprint 900.00 900.00
b. Double overprint 750.00 *750.00*
35 D1 7sh on 7h blk, red & yel 25.00 *27.50*
a. Inverted overprint 37.50 *42.50*
36 D1 8sh on 8h blk, red & yel 25.00 *30.00*
a. Inverted overprint 50.00 *60.00*
b. Vertical overprint 750.00 *950.00*
c. As "b," double overprint 950.00 *1,100.*
37 D1 10sh on 10h blk, red & yel *1,250.* *1,400.*
38 D1 15sh on 15h blk, red & yel *625.00* *625.00*
a. Inverted overprint 750.00 *800.00*
39 D1 20sh on 20h blk, red & yel *6,250.*
a. Double overprint 7,750. *17,000.*
40 D1 50sh on 50h blk, red & yel *350.00* *375.00*
a. Inverted overprint 550.00 600.00

Nos. 29-40 were created by overprinting Bosnian 1904 postage due stamps, which had been brought to Stanyslaviv by a Ukrainian military officer returning from the Serbian front. The same printing cliché was used as for the First Stanyslaviv Issue, but the asterisk obliterators were removed.

Most of the overprinting was made using 50-stamp panes (half of a sheet). After one half of the pane (25 positions) was overprinted, it would apparently be turned over and its second half overprinted with the same 25-position block, but as an inverted impression. After overprinting, the pane was torn into two equal 25-stamp halves.

A corrected block was utilized in overprinting, resulting in two types of surcharges on No. 29 (shahiv to shaha) and on Nos. 32, 34 and 38 (shahiv to shahi).

Austrian Military Semipostal Stamps of 1918 Srchd.

41 MSP7 10sh on 10h gray green 150.00 *150.00*
a. Inverted overprint 150.00 *160.00*
b. Double overprint 175.00 *210.00*
42 MSP8 20sh on 20h mag 125.00 *110.00*
a. Inverted overprint 125.00 *120.00*
b. Double overprint 160.00 *180.00*
43 MSP7 45sh on 45h blue 100.00 *110.00*
a. Inverted overprint 100.00 *120.00*

Nos. 41-43 were printed in the same manner as Nos. 29-40.

Austrian Military Stamps of 1917 Srchd.

44 M3 1sh on 1h grnsh blue *950.00* *950.00*
45 M3 2sh on 2h red orange 100.00 100.00
a. Inverted overprint 125.00 125.00
b. Double overprint 210.00 210.00
46 M3 3sh olive gray 175.00 *190.00*
a. Double overprint 750.00 *750.00*
47 M3 5sh on 5h olive grn 275.00 275.00
48 M3 6sh on 6h vio 150.00 *175.00*
49 M3 10sh on 10h org brn *900.00* *1,000.*
50 M3 12sh on 12h blue 550.00 *600.00*
a. Inverted overprint 650.00 *725.00*
51 M3 15sh on 15h brt rose 500.00 *600.00*
a. Inverted overprint 625.00 *725.00*
52 M3 20sh on 20h red brown 16.50 *20.00*
a. Inverted overprint 82.50 *140.00*
b. Double overprint 47.50 *55.00*
53 M3 25sh on 25h ultra *3,250.* *3,900.*
54 M3 30sh on 30h slate *1,000.* *1,200.*
55 M3 40sh on 40h ol bister *850.00* *850.00*
56 M3 50sh on 50h dp grn 9.00 9.00
a. Inverted overprint 20.00 20.00
b. Double overprint 55.00 55.00
57 M3 60sh on 60h car rose 950.00 950.00
58 M3 80sh on 80h dull blue 47.50 47.50
a. Inverted overprint 80.00 *85.00*
59 M3 90sh on 90h dk vio *950.00* *1,000.*
60 M4 2hr on 2k rose, *straw* 15.00 *17.50*
a. Inverted overprint 27.50 *35.00*
b. Imperforate 3,000.
61 M4 3hr on 3k blue, *grn* 22.50 *25.00*
a. Inverted overprint 27.50 *30.00*
b. Double overprint 60.00 *65.00*
62 M4 4hr on 4k rose, *grn* 22.50 *25.00*
a. Inverted overprint 50.00 *30.00*
b. Double overprint 60.00 *65.00*
63 M4 10hr on 10k dl vio, *gray* *35,000.* *35,000.*

Two examples of No. 63 were printed, and neither was ever postally used. The "used" example was cut from a document prepared by the Western Ukrainian economic bureau (Ekonomat) to display the stamps that made up the First, Second and Third Stanyslaviv issues. The specimen stamps on this document were tied with a double-ring bureau cancel that somewhat resembles a regular double-ring postal cancellation.

About half of this issue, where several sheets were available for printing, was overprinted in the manner of Nos. 29-43.

Austrian Stamps of 1916-18 Surcharged

64 A38 15sh on 36h vio (on #J61) 350.00 *450.00*
a. Double overprint 450.00 *500.00*
65 A38 50sh on 42h choc (on #J63) 5,000. *5,500.*
66 A37 3sh on 3h brt violet (on #145) 190.00 190.00
67 A37 5sh on 5h lt green (on #146) 190.00 190.00
a. Inverted overprint 290.00 290.00
68 A37 6sh on 6h deep org (on #147) 725.00 725.00
69 A37 10sh on 10h mag (on #148) 210.00 210.00
a. Inverted overprint 250.00 250.00
70 A37 12sh on 12h lt blue (on #149) 425.00 425.00
71 A38 15sh on 15h rose red (on #150) 190.00 190.00
a. Inverted overprint 225.00 225.00
72 A42 15sh on 15h dull red (on #168) 210.00 210.00
73 A42 30sh on 30h dull vio (on #171) 190.00 190.00
a. Double overprint 350.00 350.00
74 A39 40sh on 40h ol grn (on #154) 300.00 300.00
75 M3 50sh on 50h dp grn (on #M61) 475.00 475.00

The two bars in the surcharge were originally created to obliterate the "PORTO" on Nos. 64 and 65 but were subsequently retained for Nos. 66-75.

Third Stanyslaviv Issue

Austrian Stamps of 1916-18 Overprinted

1919, May

76 A37 3h brt violet .50 *1.00*
77 A37 5h light green .50 *1.00*
78 A37 6h deep orange .50 *1.00*
79 A37 10h magenta .50 *1.00*
80 A37 12h light blue .50 *1.00*
81 A42 15h dull red .50 *1.00*
82 A42 20h deep green .50 *1.00*
83 A42 25h blue .50 *1.00*
84 A42 30h dull vio .50 *1.00*
85 A39 40h olive green .75 *1.25*
86 A39 50h dark green .75 *1.25*
87 A39 60h deep blue .75 *1.25*
88 A39 80h orange brn 1.00 *1.25*
89 A39 90h red violet 1.00 *1.60*
90 A39 1k car, *yel* 1.25 *4.00*
91 A40 2k light blue 2.00 *6.00*
92 A40 3k carmine rose 2.50 *7.50*
93 A40 4k yellow grn 12.00 *16.00*
94 A40 10k deep violet 16.00 *50.00*
Nos. 76-94 (19) 42.50 *99.10*

Issued: 3h-10h, 15h, 25h-40h, 60h-1k, 5/8; balance of set, 5/13.

A definitive set for Western Ukraine was ordered from the Austrian State Printing Office in March, 1919. Because of the time involved in designing and printing these stamps, Nos. 76-94 were overprinted in Vienna as a provisional issue and were delivered in two shipments. Because travel into and out of Stanyslaviv was becoming more difficult as the month wore on, it was not known whether or not the second shipment, which included the higher values, would arrive. Because of this, the Fourth Stanyslaviv Issue, Nos. 95-103, were overprinted locally.

Fourth Stanislaviv Issue

Austrian Military Stamps of 1917-18 Surcharged in Black

1919, May ***Perf. 12½***

95 M3 2hr on 2k rose, *straw* 15.00 *15.00*
a. Perf 11½ 130.00 *150.00*
96 M3 3hr on 2k rose, *straw* 13.00 *16.00*
a. Perf 11½ 130.00 *160.00*
97 M3 3hr on 3k grn, *blue* 125.00 *175.00*
a. "5" instead of "3" at left in overprint *1,500.*
98 M3 4hr on 2k rose, *straw* 15.00 *16.00*
99 M3 4hr on 4k rose, *grn* 1,300. *1,900.*
100 M3 5hr on 2k rose, *straw* 20.00 *22.50*
a. Inverted surcharge 300.00
101 M3 10hr on 50h dp grn 30.00 *40.00*
a. Double surcharge 175.00

Austrian Postage Due Stamps of 1916 Srchd., but without Rosettes and Numerals

102 D5 1hr ultra 140.00 *210.00*
103 D5 5hr ultra 1,400. *2,100.*

REGISTRATION STAMPS

Kolomyia Issue

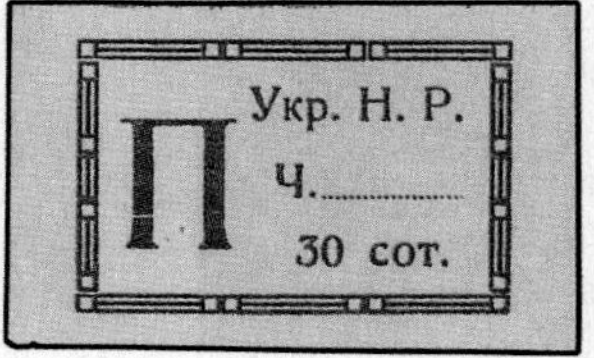

RS1

Without Gum

1918-19 Unwmk. Typeset ***Imperf.***

F1 RS1 30sot black, *rose* 250.00 175.00
F2 RS1 50sot black, *rose* ('19) 120.00 *150.00*

No. F1 was printed on Dec. 10 and issued Dec. 12, 1918, along with the regular Kolomyia Issue (Nos. 5-8). On Dec. 19, the ZUNR government approved an increase in the registered letter rate to 50 sotyks, effective January 1, 1919. Because of communication disruptions, the Kolomyia post office did not learn of this decree until about January 7, when it ordered new values in the higher denomination (No. F2). F1 continued to be used, usually in combination with 20h of Austrian stamps, until supplies were exhausted, at which point No. F2 was put into use. A second printing of the 50sot value was made in late March. Variations in paper color — from light pink to deep rose — as well as paper thickness occurred in the 30-sot and both of the 50-sot printings.

Nos. F1-F2a were typographed in vertical panes of five stamps by the Wilhelm Brauner Print Ship in Kolomyia.

Forgeries exist.

OCCUPATION STAMPS

Romanian Occupation of Pokutia

Only the stamps listed below were officially created. Soon after the Romanian occupation ended on Aug. 20, 1919, the C.M.T. handstamps fell into the hands of speculators, and some 37 other Austrian stamps were overprinted. None of these privately-created stamps are known on authentic covers.

Austrian Stamps Surcharged in Dark Violet Blue

1919, June 14 Unwmk. ***Perf. 12½***

On Stamps of 1916-18

N1 A37 40h on 5h lt grn 4.50 *5.50*
N2 A42 60h on 15h dl red 5.50 *6.50*
N3 A42 60h on 20h dp grn 2.25 *3.25*
a. Inverted overprint 3,000.
b. Double overprint 25.00
N4 A42 60h on 25h blue 12.00 *13.00*
a. Inverted overprint 60.00
b. Double overprint 82.50
N5 A42 60h on 30h dl vio 14.00 15.00
N6 A39 1k 20h on 50h dk grn 5.50 *6.50*
N7 A39 1k 20h on 60h dp bl 10.00 *12.00*
N8 A39 1k 20h on 1k car, *yel* 19.00 21.00

On Austrian Postage Due Stamps of 1910-1917

N9 D4 40h on 5h rose red 21.00 *22.50*
N10 D3 1k 20h on 25h car 175.00 *350.00*
N11 D4 1k 20h on 25h rose red 175.00 *350.00*
N12 D4 1k 20h on 30h rose red 1,400. 1,400.

N13	A38	1k 20h on 50h on 42h choc		1,500.	1,500.

Arms of Kiev

Arms of Ukraine

Arms of Galicia

First Definitive Issue, May 1919: Lithographed at the Austrian State Printing Office on unwatermarked white paper. Inscribed: "Ukrainska Narodnia Republyka Zakhidnia Oblast." ("Ukrainian National Republic Western Province"). Set of 12 values (four of each design), perf 11 ½ or imperf. Not issued. Value, set of 12: perf $350; imperf $550.

Second Definitive Issue, May 1919: Lithographed at the Austrian State Printing Office on unwatermarked white paper. Inscribed: "Ukrainska Narodnia Respublika Z.O." ("Ukrainian National Republic W(estern) P(rovince)"). Design incorporates the heraldic arms of Ukraine (trident), Kiev (Archangel Michael) and Lviv (lion rampant). 10, 20 and 50 sotyk values imperf; 1 and 10 krone values perf 11½. Not issued. Value, set of 5, $6. Also exists on cream-colored paper.

YEMEN

ˈye-mən

LOCATION — Arabian Peninsula, south of Saudi Arabia and bordering on the Red Sea
GOVT. — Kingdom
AREA — 73,300 sq. mi.
CAPITAL — San'a

40 Bogaches = 1 Imadi

Watermarks

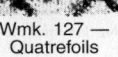

Wmk. 127 — Quatrefoils

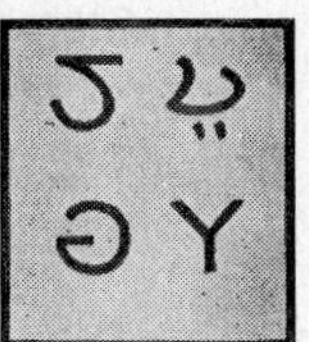

Wmk. 258 — Arabic Characters and Y G Multiple

For Domestic Postage

A1

Crossed Daggers and Arabic Inscriptions
A2

1926 Unwmk. Typo. *Imperf.*
Laid Paper
Without Gum

1	A1	2½b black	60.00	60.00
2	A1	2½b black, *orange*	60.00	60.00
3	A2	5b black	60.00	60.00
		Nos. 1-3 (3)	180.00	180.00

No. 2 is known rouletted 7½ or 9.

Type A1 differs from A2 primarily in the inscription in the left dagger blade.

All come on wove paper. Beware of forgeries, especially those on wove paper.

Replica sheets of Nos. 1-3 exist on horizontally laid, watermarked paper. The sheets are marked on the reverse with "CRC / FAC" in san-serif font. Any stamps removed from these replica sheets will contain this marking from 1-4 times on the reverse.

For Foreign and Domestic Postage

Arabic Inscriptions
A3 A4

1930-31 Wmk. 127 *Perf. 14*

7	A3	½b orange ('31)	.30	.25
8	A3	1b green	.40	.30
9	A3	1b yellow grn ('31)	.35	.25
10	A3	2b olive grn	.40	.35
11	A3	2b olive brn ('31)	.35	.25
12	A3	3b dull vio ('31)	.40	.35
13	A3	4b red	.60	.50
14	A3	4b deep rose ('31)	.50	.40
15	A3	5b slate gray ('31)	.90	.50
16	A4	6b dull blue	1.25	1.00
17	A4	6b dp ultra ('31)	1.00	.75
18	A4	8b lilac rose ('31)	1.40	1.00
19	A4	10b lt brown	2.00	1.40
20	A4	10b brn org ('31)	1.75	1.00
21	A4	20b yel grn ('31)	4.50	2.50
22	A4	1i red brn & lt bl	8.00	6.00
23	A4	1i lil rose & yel grn ('31)	8.00	6.00
		Nos. 7-23 (17)	32.10	22.80

Some values exist imperforate.

For surcharges and overprints see No. 30; Nos. 59-62, 166-167, 169-171, 174-176, 246-246P in Scott Standard catalogue, Vol. 6.

Flags of Saudi Arabia, Yemen and Iraq — A5

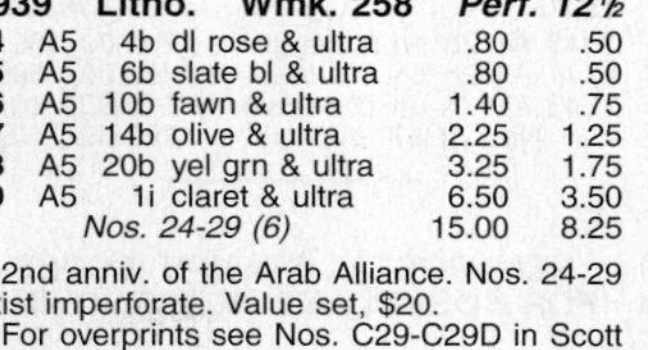

1939 Litho. Wmk. 258 *Perf. 12½*

24	A5	4b dl rose & ultra	.80	.50
25	A5	6b slate bl & ultra	.80	.50
26	A5	10b fawn & ultra	1.40	.75
27	A5	14b olive & ultra	2.25	1.25
28	A5	20b yel grn & ultra	3.25	1.75
29	A5	1i claret & ultra	6.50	3.50
		Nos. 24-29 (6)	15.00	8.25

2nd anniv. of the Arab Alliance. Nos. 24-29 exist imperforate. Value set, $20.

For overprints see Nos. C29-C29D in Scott Standard catalogue, Vol. 6.

a

b

Five types of surcharge:

All genuine surcharges are 12-13mm x 15-16mm and were made from steel handstamps.

a. "YEMEN" ½mm from left frameline and ½mm above bottom frameline.

b. "YEMEN" ½mm from left frameline and 1½mm above bottom frameline.

c. "YEMEN" 1½mm from left frameline and ½mm above bottom frameline. Found only on Types A13 and D1.

d. Arabic "4" at the center of the surcharge has been replaced with two vertical strokes. Usually blurred and found only on Type A9.

e. Arabic "4" has been replaced by a pair of crescents. Found only on Type A13.

Values of surcharged stamps are for ordinary examples. Clear, legible surcharges command a premium. Beware of fraudulent rubber-stamped surcharges in violet or grey black ink.

1939 Wmk. 127 *Perf. 14*
No. 7 Handstamped Type "a" in Black

30	A3	4b on ½b orange	*15.00*	*12.50*

See Nos. 44-48, 59-67, 82, 86-87 in Scott Standard catalogue, Vol. 6.

A6

A7

1940 Wmk. 258 Litho. *Perf. 12½*

31	A6	½b ocher & ultra	.25	.25
32	A6	1b lt grn & rose red	.25	.25
33	A6	2b bis brn & vio	.25	.25
34	A6	3b dl vio & ultra	.25	.25
35	A6	4b rose & yel grn	.35	.30
36	A6	5b dk gray grn & bis brn	.40	.35
37	A7	6b ultra & yel org	.45	.45
38	A7	8b claret & dull bl	.55	.50
39	A7	10b brn org & yel grn	.75	.75
40	A7	14b gray grn & vio	.95	.80
41	A7	18b emerald & blk	1.10	.90
42	A7	20b yel ol & cerise	1.50	1.50
43	A7	1i vio rose, yel grn & brn red	2.75	2.50
		Nos. 31-43 (13)	9.80	9.05
		Set, never hinged	20.00	

No. 36 was used as a 4b stamp in 1957.

For surcharges see Nos. 44-47 in Scott Standard catalogue, Vol. 6.

YUGOSLAVIA

ˌyü-gō-ˈslä-vē-ə

LOCATION — Southern Europe, bordering on the Adriatic Sea
GOVT. — Kingdom
AREA — 98,766 sq. mi.
POP. — 22,850,000 (est. 1983)
CAPITAL — Belgrade

On December 1, 1918, Bosnia and Herzegovina, Croatia, Dalmatia, Montenegro, Serbia and Slovenia united to form a kingdom which was later called Yugoslavia. Other listings may be found under all.

100 Heller = 1 Krone
(Bosnia & Herzegovina)
100 Filler = 1 Krone
(Croatia-Slavonia)
100 Paras = 1 Dinar (General Issues)

Catalogue values for unused stamps in this country are for Never Hinged items, beginning with Scott RA1 in the postal tax section, and Scott RAJ1 in the postal tax due section.

Counterfeits exist of most of the 1918-19 overprints for Bosnia and Herzegovina, Croatia-Slavonia and Slovenia.

BOSNIA AND HERZEGOVINA

Stamps of Bosnia and Herzegovina, 1910, Overprinted or Surcharged in Black or Red

a

b

c

1918 Unwmk. *Perf. 12½*

1L1	A4(a)	3h olive green	.40	.80
1L2	A4(b)	5h dk grn (R)	.40	.40
1L3	A4(a)	10h carmine	.40	.40
1L4	A4(b)	20h dk brn (R)	.40	.40
1L5	A4(a)	25h deep blue (R)	.40	.40
1L6	A4(b)	30h green	.40	.40
1L7	A4(b)	40h orange	.40	.40
1L8	A4(b)	45h brown red	.40	.40
1L9	A4(b)	50h dull violet	.55	.80
1L10	A4(a)	60h on 50h dl vio	.40	.40
1L11	A4(b)	80h on 6h org brown	.40	.40
1L12	A4(a)	90h on 35h myr green	.40	.40
1L13	A5(c)	2k gray green	.40	.40
1L14	A4(b)	3k on 3h ol grn	2.00	2.75
1L15	A5(c)	4k on 1k mar	4.00	4.75
1L16	A4(b)	10k on 2h vio	6.00	6.75
		Nos. 1L1-1L16 (16)	17.35	20.25

Inverted and double overprints and assorted varieties exist on the stamps for Bosnia and Herzegovina.

Bosnian Girl — A1

1918		Typo.		*Perf. 11½*
1L17	A1	2h ultramarine	.40	.40
1L18	A1	6h violet	.80	1.20
1L19	A1	10h rose	.40	.40
1L20	A1	20h green	.40	.40
		Nos. 1L17-1L20 (4)	2.00	2.40

Imperforate stamps of this type (A1) are newspaper stamps of Bosnia.

For surcharges see Nos. 1L21-1L22, 1L43-1L45.

Bosnia and Herzegovina Nos. P1-P2 (Nos. 1L17-1L18, Imperf.) Srchd.

1918				*Imperf.*
1L21	A1	3h on 2h ultra	.40	.40
a.		Double surcharge	*14.00*	
1L22	A1	5h on 6h violet	.40	.40
a.		Double surcharge	*14.00*	

Stamps of Bosnia and Herzegovina, 1906-17, Ovptd. or Srchd. in Black or Red

d

e

f

1919				*Perf. 12½*
1L25	A23(d)	3h claret	.40	.80
1L26	A23(e)	5h green	.40	.40
1L27	A23(e)	10h on 6h dark gray	.40	.40
1L28	A24(d)	20h on 35h myr green	.40	.40
1L29	A23(e)	25h ultra	.40	.40
1L30	A23(e)	30h orange red	.40	.40
1L31	A24(d)	45h olive brn	.40	.40
1L32	A27(d)	45h on 80h org brown	.40	.40
a.		Perf. 11½	1.40	1.60
1L33	A24(e)	50h slate blue	100.00	100.00
1L34	A24(e)	50h on 72h dk blue (R)	.40	.40
1L35	A24(d)	60h brown violet	.40	.40
1L36	A27(e)	80h orange brown	.40	.40
a.		Perf. 11½	*35.00*	*30.00*
1L37	A27(d)	90h dark violet	.40	.40
a.		Perf. 11½	3.50	2.75
1L38	A5(f)	2k gray green	.40	.40
a.		Imperf.	35.00	
b.		Perf. 9½	4.50	5.00
1L39	A26(d)	3k car, *green*	.40	.55
1L40	A28(e)	4k car, *green*	1.75	2.50
1L41	A26(d)	5k dk vio, *gray*	1.75	2.75
1L42	A28(e)	10k dk vio, *gray*	3.25	4.00
		Nos. 1L25-1L42 (18)	112.35	115.40

Nos. 1L32, 1L36, 1L37, 1L40 and 1L42 have no bars in the overprint.

Nos. 1L25 to 1L42 exist with inverted overprint or surcharge.

Bosnia and Herzegovina Nos. P2-P4 (Nos. 1L18-1L20, Imperf.) Srchd.

1920				*Imperf.*
1L43	A1	2h on 6h violet	200.00	180.00
1L44	A1	2h on 10h rose	50.00	50.00
1L45	A1	2h on 20h green	10.00	10.00
		Nos. 1L43-1L45 (3)	260.00	240.00

SEMI-POSTAL STAMPS ISSUES FOR BOSNIA AND HERZEGOVINA

Leading Blind Soldier — SP1

Wounded Soldier — SP2

Semi-Postal Stamps of Bosnia and Herzegovina, 1918 Overprinted

1918		Unwmk.		*Perf. 12½, 13*
1LB1	SP1	10h greenish bl	.80	1.00
a.		Overprinted as No. 1LB2	52.50	52.50
1LB2	SP2	15h red brown	2.00	2.00
a.		Overprinted as No. 1LB1	47.50	47.50

Bosnian Semi-Postal Stamps of 1916 Overprinted like No. 1LB2

1LB3	SP1	5h green	125.00	175.00
a.		Overprinted as No. 1LB1	375.00	375.00
1LB4	SP2	10h magenta	100.00	125.00
		Nos. 1LB1-1LB4 (4)	227.80	303.00

Inverted and double overprints exist on Nos. 1LB1-1LB4.

Regular Issue of Bosnia, 1906 Surcharged in Black

Mail Wagon SP3

Bridge at Mostar SP4

Scene near Sarajevo — SP5

1919				
1LB5	SP3	10h + 10h on 40h org red	1.25	2.00
1LB6	SP4	20h + 10h on 20h dk brown	.60	1.75
1LB7	SP5	45h + 15h on 1k mar	4.75	4.75
		Nos. 1LB5-1LB7 (3)	6.60	8.50

Nos. 1LB5-1LB7 exist with surcharge inverted. Value each $7.50.

SPECIAL DELIVERY STAMPS ISSUES FOR BOSNIA AND HERZEGOVINA

Lightning

SD1 SD2

Bosnian Special Delivery Stamps Overprinted in Black

1918		Unwmk.		*Perf. 12½, 13*
1LE1	SD1	2h vermilion	6.00	6.00
a.		Inverted overprint	35.00	
b.		Overprinted as No. 1LE2	47.50	47.50
1LE2	SD2	5h deep green	3.25	3.25
a.		Inverted overprint	18.00	
b.		Overprinted as No. 1LE1	47.50	47.50

POSTAGE DUE STAMPS ISSUES FOR BOSNIA AND HERZEGOVINA

Postage Due Stamps of Bosnia and Herzegovina, 1916, Overprinted in Black or Red

a

b

1918		Unwmk.		*Perf. 12½, 13*
1LJ1	D2 (a)	2h red	.25	.25
1LJ2	D2 (b)	4h red	.55	.55
1LJ3	D2 (a)	5h red	.25	.25
1LJ4	D2 (b)	6h red	.90	.90
1LJ5	D2 (a)	10h red	.25	.25
1LJ6	D2 (b)	15h red	6.75	6.75
1LJ7	D2 (a)	20h red	.25	.25
1LJ8	D2 (b)	25h red	.55	.55
1LJ9	D2 (a)	30h red	.55	.55
1LJ10	D2 (b)	40h red	.25	.25
1LJ11	D2 (a)	50h red	1.20	1.20

c

d

1LJ12	D2 (c)	1k dark blue (R)	.55	.55
1LJ13	D2 (d)	3k dark blue (R)	.40	.40
		Nos. 1LJ1-1LJ13 (13)	12.70	12.70

Nos. 1LJ1-1LJ13 exist with overprint double or inverted. Value $3 to $7.

Nos. 1LJ1-1LJ11 exist with type "b" overprint instead of type "a," and vice versa. Value, each $10.

Stamps of Bosnia and Herzegovina, 1900-04, Surcharged

e

f

1919				
1LJ14	A2 (e)	2h on 35h blue	.55	.80
1LJ15	A2 (e)	5h on 45h grnsh bl	.95	1.20
1LJ16	A2 (f)	10h on 10 red	.25	.25
1LJ17	A2 (e)	15h on 40h org	.40	.50
1LJ18	A2 (f)	20h on 5h green	.25	.25
1LJ19	A2 (e)	25h on 20h pink	.40	.55
1LJ20	A2 (f)	30h on 30h bis brn	.40	.55
1LJ21	A2 (e)	1k on 50h red lil	.25	.55
1LJ22	A2 (e)	3k on 25h blue	.50	.55

Postage Due Stamps of Bosnia and Herzegovina, 1904 Surcharged

g

h

1LJ23	D1 (g)	40h on 6h blk, red & yel	.25	.25
1LJ24	D1 (h)	50h on 8h blk, red & yel	.25	.25
1LJ25	D1 (h)	200h blk, red & grn	8.00	6.75
1LJ26	D1 (h)	4k on 7h blk, red & yel	.40	.55
		Nos. 1LJ14-1LJ26 (13)	12.85	13.00

Nos. 1LJ14-1LJ26 exist with overprint double or inverted. Value, $3 to $6.

CROATIA-SLAVONIA

Stamps of Hungary Overprinted in Blue

A1

1918		Wmk. 137		*Perf. 15*
		On Stamps of 1913		
2L1	A1	6f olive green	1.10	2.00
2L2	A1	50f lake, *blue*	1.20	2.00

A2

A3

On Stamps of 1916

2L3	A2	10f violet	100.00	*140.00*
2L4	A3	15f red	100.00	*140.00*

A4

On Hungary Nos. 106-107 White Numerals

2L4A	A4	10f rose	1,600.	*1,600.*
2L5	A4	15f violet	150.00	150.00
a.		Inverted overprint	—	

On Stamps of 1916-18 Colored Numerals

2L6	A4	2f brown orange	.40	.40
2L7	A4	3f red lilac	.40	.40
2L8	A4	5f green	.40	.40
2L9	A4	6f greenish blue	.40	.40
2L10	A4	10f rose red	16.00	12.00
2L11	A4	15f violet	.40	.40
2L12	A4	20f gray brown	.40	.40
2L13	A4	25f dull blue	.40	.40
2L14	A4	35f brown	.40	.40
2L15	A4	40f olive green	.40	.80

The overprints and surcharges for Croatia-Slavonia exist inverted, double, double inverted, in wrong colors, on wrong stamps, on back, in pairs with one lacking overprint, etc.

A5

A6

2L16	A5	50f red vio & lilac	.40	.40
2L17	A5	75f brt bl & pale bl	.40	.40
2L18	A5	80f grn & pale grn	.40	.40
2L19	A6	1k red brown & cl	.40	.40
2L20	A6	2k olive brn & bis	.40	.40
2L21	A6	3k dark vio & ind	.40	.40
2L22	A6	5k dk brn & lt brn	2.50	3.00
2L23	A6	10k vio brn & vio	16.00	16.00

Stamps of Hungary Overprinted in Blue, Black or Red

No. 2L24

No. 2L27

2L24	A7	10f scarlet (Bl)	.40	.40
2L25	A7	20f dark brown (Bk)	.40	.40
2L26	A7	25f deep blue (R)	.40	.80
2L27	A8	40f olive green (Bl)	.40	.40
		Nos. 2L6-2L27 (22)	42.10	39.40

Many other stamps of the 1913-18 issues of Hungary, the Semi-Postal Stamps of 1915-16 and Postage Due Stamps were surreptitiously overprinted but were never sold through the post office.

Freedom of Croatia-Slavonia
A9

1918 Unwmk. Litho. *Perf. 11½*

2L28	A9	10f rose	6.50	4.00
2L29	A9	20f violet	6.50	4.00
2L30	A9	25f blue	12.00	8.00
2L31	A9	45f greenish blk	95.00	55.00
		Nos. 2L28-2L31 (4)	120.00	71.00

Independence of Croatia, Slavonia and Dalmatia.

#2L28-2L31 exist imperforate, but were not officially issued in this condition.

Excellent counterfeits of #2L28-2L31 exist.

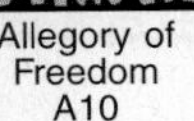
Allegory of Freedom
A10

Youth with Standard
A11

Falcon, Symbol of Liberty — A12

1919 *Perf. 11½*

2L32	A10	2f brn orange	.25	.40
2L33	A10	3f violet	.25	.50
2L34	A10	5f green	.25	.25
2L35	A11	10f red	.25	.25
2L36	A11	20f black brown	.25	.25
2L37	A11	25f deep blue	.25	.25
2L38	A11	45f dark ol grn	.25	.25
2L39	A12	1k carmine rose	.25	.25
2L40	A12	3k dark violet	.80	.95
2L41	A12	5k deep brown	1.20	.80
		Nos. 2L32-2L41 (10)	4.00	4.15

Perf. 12½

2L32a	A10	2f	2.90	2.90
2L33a	A10	3f	2.90	2.90
2L34a	A10	5f	15.00	15.00
2L35a	A11	10f	2.90	2.90
2L36a	A11	20f	2.90	2.90
		Nos. 2L32a-2L36a (5)	26.60	26.60

#2L32-2L41 exist imperf. Value, set $25.

SEMI-POSTAL STAMPS ISSUES FOR CROATIA-SLAVONIA

SP1

SP2

SP3

1918 Wmk. 137 *Perf. 15*

2LB1	SP1	10f + 2f rose red	.40	*2.75*
2LB2	SP2	15f + 2f dull violet	.40	*.40*
2LB3	SP3	40f + 2f brn carmine	.40	*.85*
		Nos. 2LB1-2LB3 (3)	1.20	*4.00*

SPECIAL DELIVERY STAMP ISSUE FOR CROATIA-SLAVONIA

SD1

Hungary No. E1 Overprinted in Black

1918 Wmk. 137 *Perf. 15*

2LE1	SD1	2f gray green & red	.25	.25

POSTAGE DUE STAMPS ISSUES FOR CROATIA-SLAVONIA

D1

Postage Due Stamps of Hungary Overprinted in Blue

1918 Wmk. Crown (136) *Perf. 15*

2LJ1	D1	50f green & blk	650.00	650.00

Wmk. Double Cross (137)

2LJ2	D1	1f green & red	40.00	40.00
a.		Inverted overprint	—	—
2LJ3	D1	2f green & red	1.20	1.20
2LJ4	D1	10f green & red	1.20	1.20
2LJ5	D1	12f green & red	160.00	160.00
2LJ6	D1	15f green & red	.80	.80
2LJ7	D1	20f green & red	.80	.80
2LJ8	D1	30f green & red	2.00	2.00
2LJ9	D1	50f green & blk	65.00	65.00
		Nos. 2LJ2-2LJ9 (8)	271.00	271.00

NEWSPAPER STAMPS ISSUES FOR CROATIA-SLAVONIA

N1

Hungary No. P8 Overprinted in Black

1918 Wmk. 137 *Imperf.*

2LP1	N1	(2f) orange	.40	.40

N2

1919 Litho. Unwmk.

2LP2	N2	2f yellow orange	.25	1.20

SLOVENIA

Chain Breaker
A1 A2

3, 5, 10, 15f: Chain on right wrist is short, extending only about half way to the frame.

10f: Numerals are 8½mm high.

20, 25, 30, 40f: Distant mountains show faintly between legs of male figure.

40f: Numerals 7mm high. The upright strokes of the "4" extend to the same height; the "0" is 3mm wide.

1919 Unwmk. *Perf. 11½*

Lithographed at Ljubljana

Fine Impression

3L1	A1	3f violet	.25	.25
3L2	A1	5f green	.25	.25
3L3	A1	10f carmine rose	.40	.25
3L4	A1	15f blue	.25	.25
3L5	A2	20f brown	.65	.25
3L6	A2	25f blue	.30	.25
3L7	A2	30f lilac rose	.30	.25
3L8	A2	40f bister	.30	.25
		Nos. 3L1-3L8 (8)	2.70	2.00

Various stamps of this series exist imperforate and part perforate. Many shades exist.

See Nos. 3L9-3L17, 3L24-3L28. For surcharges see Nos. 3LJ15-3LJ32.

Allegories of Freedom
A3 A4

King Peter I — A5

3, 5, 15f: The chain on the right wrist touches the bottom tablet.

10f: Numerals are 7½mm high.

15f: Curled end of loin cloth appears above letter "H" in the bottom tablet.

20, 25, 30, 40f: The outlines of the mountains have been redrawn and they are more distinct than on the lithographed stamps.

40f: Numerals 8mm high. The left slanting stroke of the "4" extends much higher than the main vertical stroke. The "0" is 2½mm wide and encloses a much narrower space than on the lithographed stamp.

1919-20 *Perf. 11½*

Typographed at Ljubljana and Vienna

Coarse Impression

3L9	A1	3f violet	.25	.25
3L10	A1	5f green	.30	.25
3L11	A1	10f red	.25	.25
3L12	A1	15f blue	1.60	.25
3L13	A2	20f brown	.55	.25
3L14	A2	25f blue	.50	.25
3L15	A2	30f carmine rose	.55	.25
3L16	A2	30f dp red	2.75	.90
3L17	A2	40f orange	.55	.25
3L18	A3	50f green	.55	.25
a.		50f dark green	.55	.25
b.		50f olive green	3.50	1.10
3L19	A3	60f dark blue	.85	.25
a.		60f violet blue	.85	.25
3L20	A4	1k vermilion	.55	.25
a.		1k red orange	.55	.25
3L21	A4	2k blue	.55	.25
a.		2k dull ultramarine	.90	.25
3L22	A5	5k brown lake	.80	.25
a.		5k lake	12.00	1.60
b.		5k dull red	.60	.25
3L23	A5	10k deep ultra	3.25	.90
		Nos. 3L9-3L23 (15)	13.85	5.05

Nos. 3L9-3L23 exist imperf. Value, set $90.

Many of the series exist part perforate.

Many shades exist of lower values.

See Nos. 3L29-3L32, 3L40-3L41.

Serrate Roulette 13½

3L24	A1	5f light grn	.25	.25
3L25	A1	10f carmine	.25	.25
3L26	A1	15f slate blue	.30	.25
3L27	A2	20f dark brown	.65	.25
a.		Serrate x straight roul.	.65	.25
3L28	A2	30f car rose	.30	.25
a.		Serrate x straight roul.	.70	.25
3L29	A3	50f green	.30	.25
3L30	A3	60f dark blue	.95	.40
a.		60f violet blue	2.25	1.10
3L31	A4	1k vermilion	1.40	.40
a.		1k rose red	1.40	.40
3L32	A4	2k blue	9.00	2.75
		Nos. 3L24-3L32 (9)	13.40	5.05

Roulette x Perf. 11½

3L24a	A1	5f	150.00	150.00
3L25a	A1	10f	55.00	55.00
3L26a	A1	15f	175.00	175.00
3L28b	A2	30f	55.00	55.00
3L29a	A3	50f	5.25	4.00
3L30b	A3	60f	55.00	55.00
3L31b	A4	1k	55.00	55.00

Thick Wove Paper

1920 Litho. *Perf. 11½*

3L40	A5	15k gray green	7.25	14.50
3L41	A5	20k dull violet	1.40	2.40

On Nos. 3L40-3L41 the horizontal lines have been removed from the value tablets. They are printed over a background of pale brown wavy lines.

Chain Breaker
A7

Freedom
A8

King Peter I — A9

Pale red wavy lines

Dinar Values:

Type I — Size: 21x30½mm.

Type II — Size: 22x32½mm.

Thin to Thick Wove Paper

1920 *Serrate Roulette 13½*

3L42	A7	5p olive green	.25	.25
3L43	A7	10p green	.25	.25
3L44	A7	15p brown	.25	.25
3L45	A7	20p carmine	.40	.40
3L46	A7	25p chocolate	.40	.25
3L47	A8	40p dark violet	.25	.25
3L48	A8	45p yellow	.25	.25
3L49	A8	50p dark blue	.25	.25
3L50	A8	60p red brown	.25	.25
3L51	A9	1d dark brown (I)	.25	.25

Perf. 11½

3L52	A9	2d gray vio (II)	.25	.25
3L53	A9	4d grnsh black (I)	.30	.30
3L54	A9	6d olive brn (II)	.25	.25
3L55	A9	10d brown red (II)	.30	.80
		Nos. 3L42-3L55 (14)	3.90	4.25

The 2d and 6d have a background of pale red wavy lines, the 10d of gray lines.

Counterfeits exist of No. 3L45.

POSTAGE DUE STAMPS ISSUES FOR SLOVENIA

D1

Ljubljana Print
Numerals 9½mm high

1919 Litho. Unwmk. *Perf. 11½*
3LJ1 D1 5f carmine .25 .25
3LJ2 D1 10f carmine .25 .25
3LJ3 D1 20f carmine .25 .25
3LJ4 D1 50f carmine .25 .25

Nos. 3LJ1-3LJ4 were also printed in scarlet and dark red.

Numerals 8mm high

3LJ5 D1 1k dark blue .45 .30
3LJ6 D1 5k dark blue .65 .50
3LJ7 D1 10k dark blue .90 .75
Nos. 3LJ1-3LJ7 (7) 3.00 2.55

Vienna Print

1920 Numerals 11 to 12 mm high
3LJ8 D1 5f red .25 .25
3LJ9 D1 10f red .25 .25
3LJ10 D1 20f red .25 .25
3LJ11 D1 50f red 1.25 .85

Numerals 7mm high

3LJ12 D1 1k Prussian blue 1.10 .70
a. 1k dark blue 5.00 4.50
3LJ13 D1 5k Prussian blue 1.60 1.25
a. 5k dark blue 8.00 6.75
3LJ14 D1 10k Prussian blue 3.75 3.25
a. 10k dark blue 14.00 15.00
Nos. 3LJ8-3LJ14 (7) 8.45 6.80

Nos. 3LJ8-3LJ14 exist imperf. Value, set $40.

No. 3L4 Surcharged in Red

1920 On Litho. Stamps *Perf. 11½*
3LJ15 A1 5p on 15f blue .25 .25
3LJ16 A1 10p on 15f blue .60 .80
3LJ17 A1 20p on 15f blue .25 .25
3LJ18 A1 50p on 15f blue .25 .25
Nos. 3LJ15-3LJ18 (4) 1.35 1.55

Nos. 3L7, 3L12, 3L26, 3L28, 3L28a Surcharged in Dark Blue

3LJ19 A2 1d on 30f lil rose .25 .25
3LJ20 A2 3d on 30f lil rose .25 .25
3LJ21 A2 8d on 30f lil rose 1.60 .80
Nos. 3LJ19-3LJ21 (3) 2.10 1.30

On Typographed Stamps

3LJ22 A1 5p on 15f pale bl 12.00 2.50
3LJ23 A1 10p on 15f pale bl 35.00 25.00
3LJ24 A1 20p on 15f pale bl 11.00 4.00
3LJ25 A1 50p on 15f pale bl 6.00 7.00
Nos. 3LJ22-3LJ25 (4) 64.00 38.50

3LJ26 A1 5p on 15f slate bl 2.75 .50
3LJ27 A1 10p on 15f slate bl 8.50 3.25
3LJ28 A1 20p on 15f slate bl 2.75 .50
3LJ29 A1 50p on 15f slate bl 2.75 .50
3LJ30 A2 1d on 30f dp rose 2.75 .65
a. Serrate x straight roulette 7.00 4.50
3LJ31 A2 3d on 30f dp rose 5.75 1.75
a. Serrate x straight roulette 8.00 5.50
3LJ32 A2 8d on 30f dp rose 125.00 6.50
a. Serrate x straight roulette 125.00 7.50
Nos. 3LJ26-3LJ32 (7) 150.25 13.65

The para surcharges were printed in sheets of 100, ten horizontal rows of ten. There were: 5p three rows, 10p one row, 20p three rows, 50p three rows. The dinar surcharges were in a setting of 50, arranged in vertical rows of five. There were: 1d five rows, 3d three rows, 8d two rows.

NEWSPAPER STAMPS ISSUES FOR SLOVENIA

Eros — N1

Ljubljana Print

1919 Unwmk. Litho. *Imperf.*
3LP1 N1 2f gray .25 .25
3LP2 N1 4f gray .25 .40
3LP3 N1 6f gray 3.50 4.00
3LP4 N1 10f gray .25 .25
3LP5 N1 30f gray .25 .40
Nos. 3LP1-3LP5 (5) 4.50 5.30

See Nos. 3LP6-3LP13. For surcharges see Nos. 3LP14-3LP23, 4LB1-4LB5.

N2

2 4 6 10

1920 Vienna Print
3LP6 N2 2f gray .25 .25
3LP7 N2 4f gray 6.50 10.00
3LP8 N2 6f gray 1.75 2.75
3LP9 N2 10f gray 14.00 21.00
3LP10 N2 2f blue .25 .30
3LP11 N2 4f blue .25 .25
3LP12 N2 6f blue 125.00 125.00
3LP13 N2 10f blue .25 .25
Nos. 3LP6-3LP13 (8) 148.25 159.80

Nos. 3LP1, 3LP10 Surcharged

a

b

On Ljubljana Print

3LP14 N1 (a) 2p on 2f gray .25 .40
3LP15 N1 (a) 4p on 2f gray .25 .40
3LP16 N1 (a) 6p on 2f gray .40 .65
3LP17 N1 (b) 10p on 2f gray .65 .80
3LP18 N1 (b) 30p on 2f gray .65 .85

On Vienna Print

3LP19 N1 (a) 2p on 2f blue .25 .25
3LP20 N1 (a) 4p on 2f blue .25 .25
3LP21 N1 (a) 6p on 2f blue .25 .25
3LP22 N1 (b) 10p on 2f blue .25 .25
3LP23 N1 (b) 30p on 2f blue .25 .25
Nos. 3LP14-3LP23 (10) 3.45 4.35

The five surcharges were arranged in a setting of 100, in horizontal rows of ten. There were: 2p three rows, 4p three rows, 6p two rows, 10p one row and 30p one row. The sheets were perforated 11½ horizontally between the groups of the different values.

SEMI-POSTAL STAMPS ISSUE FOR CARINTHIA PLEBISCITE

SP1

Nos. 3LP2, 3LP1 Surcharged With Various Designs in Dark Red

1920
4LB1 SP1 5p on 4f gray .25 .25
4LB2 SP1 15p on 4f gray .25 .25
4LB3 SP1 25p on 4f gray .25 .55
4LB4 SP1 45p on 2f gray .25 1.20
4LB5 SP1 50p on 2f gray .25 1.40
4LB6 SP1 2d on 2f gray 2.00 6.00
Nos. 4LB1-4LB6 (6) 3.25 9.65

Nos. 4LB1 to 4LB6 have a different surcharge on each stamp but each includes the letters "K.G.C.A." which signify Carinthian Governmental Commission, Zone A.

Sold at three times face value for the benefit of the Plebiscite Propaganda Fund.

GENERAL ISSUES

For Use throughout the Kingdom

King Alexander — A1

King Peter I — A2

Unwmk.
1921, Jan. 16 Engr. *Perf. 12*
1 A1 2p olive brown .25 .25
2 A1 5p deep green .25 .25
3 A1 10p carmine .25 .25
4 A1 15p violet .25 .25
5 A1 20p black .25 .25
6 A1 25p dark blue .25 .25
7 A1 50p olive green .25 .25
8 A1 60p vermilion .25 .25
9 A1 75p purple .25 .25
10 A2 1d orange .25 .25
11 A2 2d olive bister .30 .25
12 A2 4d dark green .60 .25
13 A2 5d carmine rose 2.50 .25
14 A2 10d red brown 12.00 .55
Nos. 1-14 (14) 17.90 3.80
Set, never hinged 32.50

Exist imperf. Value, set $125.
For surcharge see No. 27.

Nos. B1-B3 Surcharged in Black, Brown, Green or Blue

a

b

1922-24
15 SP1(a) 1d on 10p .25 .25
16 SP2(b) 1d on 15p ('24) .25 .25
17 SP3(a) 1d on 25p (Br) .25 .25
18 SP2(b) 3d on 15p (G) .80 .25
a. Blue surcharge 1.20 1.20
19 SP2(b) 8d on 15p (G) 1.60 .25
a. Double surcharge 35.00 30.00
b. 9d on 15p (error) 130.00
20 SP2(b) 20d on 15p 10.00 1.00
21 SP2(b) 30d on 15p (Bl) 27.50 2.50
Nos. 15-21 (7) 40.65 4.75
Set, never hinged 60.00

A3

1923, Jan. 23 Engr.
22 A3 1d red brown 2.00 .25
23 A3 5d carmine 3.75 .25
24 A3 8d violet 6.75 .25
25 A3 20d green 27.50 .75
26 A3 30d red orange 72.50 2.75
Nos. 22-26 (5) 112.50 4.25
Set, never hinged 250.00

For surcharge see No. 28.

Nos. 8 and 24 Surcharged in Black or Blue

1924, Feb. 18
27 A1 20p on 60p ver .25 .25
28 A3 5d on 8d violet (Bl) 8.00 .60
Set, never hinged 17.50

The color of the surcharge on No. 28 varies, including blue, blue black, greenish black and black.

A4

A5

1924, July 1 *Perf. 14*
29 A4 20p black .25 .25
30 A4 50p dark brown .25 .25
31 A4 1d carmine .25 .25
32 A4 2d myrtle green .25 .25
33 A4 3d ultramarine .25 .25
34 A4 5d orange brown 1.40 .25
35 A5 10d dark violet 12.50 .25
36 A5 15d olive green 7.50 .25
37 A5 20d vermilion 7.50 .25
38 A5 30d dark green 7.50 1.25
Nos. 29-38 (10) 37.65 3.50
Set, never hinged 80.00

No. 33 Surcharged

1925, June 5
39 A4 25p on 3d ultramarine .35 .25
40 A4 50p on 3d ultramarine .35 .25
Set, never hinged 1.60

King Alexander — A6

1926-27 Typo. *Perf. 13*
41 A6 25p deep green .25 .25
42 A6 50p olive brown .25 .25
43 A6 1d scarlet .25 .25
44 A6 2d slate black .25 .25
45 A6 3d slate blue .30 .25
46 A6 4d red orange .50 .25
47 A6 5d violet .80 .25
48 A6 8d black brown 5.25 .25
49 A6 10d olive brown 4.00 .25
50 A6 15d brown ('27) 15.00 .25
51 A6 20d dark vio ('27) 17.50 .25
52 A6 30d orange ('27) 65.00 .45
Nos. 41-52 (12) 109.35 3.20
Set, never hinged 240.00

For overprints and surcharges see Nos. 53-62, 87-101, B5-B16.

Nos. B7-B16 Overprinted over the Red Surcharge

1928, July

53 A6 1d scarlet .25 .25
a. Surcharge "0.50" inverted
54 A6 2d black .50 .25
55 A6 3d deep blue .80 .50
56 A6 4d red orange 2.00 .60
57 A6 5d bright vio 1.60 .25
58 A6 8d black brown 6.50 .95
59 A6 10d olive brown 12.50 .25
60 A6 15d brown 95.00 3.00
61 A6 20d violet 47.50 3.00
62 A6 30d orange 125.00 9.50
Nos. 53-62 (10) 291.65 18.55
Set, never hinged 725.00

King Alexander — A7

With Imprint at Foot

1931-34 ***Perf. 12½***

63 A7 25p black .25 .25
64 A7 50p green .25 .25
65 A7 75p slate green .40 .25
66 A7 1d red .25 .25
67 A7 1.50d pink .80 .25
68 A7 1.75d dp rose ('34) 1.60 .35
69 A7 3d slate blue 6.00 .25
70 A7 3.50d ultra ('34) 2.40 .35
71 A7 4d deep orange 3.00 .25
72 A7 5d purple 3.00 .25
73 A7 10d dark olive 12.00 .25
74 A7 15d deep brown 12.00 .25
75 A7 20d dark violet 24.00 .25
76 A7 30d rose 12.00 .45
Nos. 63-76 (14) 77.95 3.90
Set, never hinged 175.00

Type of 1931 Issue Without Imprint at Foot

1932-33

77 A7 25p black .25 .25
78 A7 50p green .25 .25
79 A7 1d red .25 .25
80 A7 3d slate bl ('33) 1.00 .25
81 A7 4d deep org ('33) 3.50 .25
82 A7 5d purple ('33) 5.25 .25
83 A7 10d dk olive ('33) 17.00 .25
84 A7 15d deep brn ('33) 27.50 .25
85 A7 20d dark vio ('33) 35.00 .25
86 A7 30d rose ('33) 45.00 .35
Nos. 77-86 (10) 135.00 2.60
Set, never hinged 225.00

See Nos. 102-115.

Nos. 41 to 52 Overprinted

1933, Sept. 5 ***Perf. 13***

87 A6 25p deep green .25 .25
88 A6 50p olive brown .25 .25
89 A6 1d scarlet .75 .25
90 A6 2d slate black 3.25 .70
91 A6 3d slate blue 3.00 .25
92 A6 4d red orange 2.00 .25
93 A6 5d violet 4.00 .25
94 A6 8d black brown 9.25 1.40
95 A6 10d olive brown 16.00 .25
96 A6 15d brown 24.00 1.75
97 A6 20d dark violet 32.50 .80
98 A6 30d orange 32.50 .80
Nos. 87-98 (12) 127.75 7.20
Set, never hinged 240.00

Semi-Postal Stamps of 1926 Overprinted like Nos. 87 to 98 and Four Bars over the Red Surcharge of 1926

1933, Sept. 5

99 A6 25p green .80 .25
100 A6 50p olive brown .80 .25
101 A6 1d scarlet 2.40 .50
Nos. 99-101 (3) 4.00 1.00
Set, never hinged 8.00

Nos. 99-101 exist with double impression of bars. Value, each $5.50 unused, $4.50 used.

King Alexander Memorial Issue

Type of 1931-34 Issues

Borders in Black

1934, Oct. 17

102 A7 25p black .25 .25
103 A7 50p green .25 .25
104 A7 75p slate green .25 .25
105 A7 1d red .25 .25
106 A7 1.50d pink .25 .25
107 A7 1.75d deep rose .25 .25
108 A7 3d slate blue .25 .25
109 A7 3.50d ultramarine .25 .25
110 A7 4d deep orange .40 .25
111 A7 5d purple .60 .25
112 A7 10d dark olive 2.00 .25
113 A7 15d deep brown 4.00 .25
114 A7 20d dark violet 12.00 .25
115 A7 30d rose 10.00 .40
Nos. 102-115 (14) 31.00 3.65
Set, never hinged 50.00

Cyrillic Characters

Latin and Cyrillic inscriptions are transposed within some sets. In some sets some stamps are inscribed in Latin, others in Cyrillic. This will be mentioned only if it is necessary to identify otherwise identical stamps.

King Peter II — A10

1935-36 ***Perf. 13x12½***

116 A10 25p brown black .25 .25
117 A10 50p yel orange .25 .25
118 A10 75p turq green .25 .25
119 A10 1d brown red .25 .25
120 A10 1.50d scarlet .25 .25
121 A10 1.75d cerise .25 .25
122 A10 2d magenta ('36) .25 .25
123 A10 3d brn orange .25 .25
124 A10 3.50d ultramarine .40 .25
125 A10 4d yellow grn 1.20 .25
126 A10 4d slate blue ('36) .25 .25
127 A10 10d bright vio 1.20 .25
128 A10 15d brown 1.20 .25
129 A10 20d bright blue 4.75 .25
130 A10 30d rose pink 2.40 .25
Nos. 116-130 (15) 13.40 3.75
Set, never hinged 25.00

For overprints see Nos. N12, N14, N29 in Scott Standard catalogue, Vol. 6.

King Alexander — A11

1935, Oct. 9 ***Perf. 12½x11½, 11½***

131 A11 75p turq green .35 .40
132 A11 1.50d scarlet .35 .40
133 A11 1.75d dark brown .40 .80
134 A11 3.50d ultramarine 2.25 2.50
135 A11 7.50d rose carmine 1.50 2.25
Nos. 131-135 (5) 4.85 6.35

Death of King Alexander, 1st anniv.

Nikola Tesla — A12

1936, May 28 Litho. ***Perf. 12½x11½***

136 A12 75p yel grn & dk brn .40 .25
137 A12 1.75d dull blue & indigo .40 .25
Set, never hinged 2.00

80th birthday of Nikola Tesla (1856-1943), electrical inventor.

Memorial Church, Oplenac — A13

1937, July 1

138 A13 3d Prussian grn 1.00 .50
a. Perf. 12½ 15.00 24.00
Never hinged 30.00
139 A13 4d dark blue 1.00 1.20
Set, never hinged 4.00

"Little Entente," 16th anniversary.

Coats of Arms of Yugoslavia, Greece, Romania and Turkey — A14

Perf. 11, 11½, 12½

1937, Oct. 29 **Photo.**

140 A14 3d peacock grn 1.50 .45
141 A14 4d ultramarine 2.00 1.40
Set, never hinged 5.75

Balkan Entente.

Some of the varieties of perfs are scarce.

King Peter II — A16

1939-40 **Typo.** ***Perf. 12½***

142 A16 25p black ('40) .25 .25
143 A16 50p orange ('40) .25 .25
144 A16 1d yellow grn .25 .25
145 A16 1.50d red .25 .25
146 A16 2d dp mag ('40) .25 .25
147 A16 3d dull red brn .25 .25
148 A16 4d ultra .25 .25
148A A16 5d dk blue ('40) .25 .25
148B A16 5.50d dk vio brn ('40) .50 .25
149 A16 6d slate blue 1.00 .25
150 A16 8d sepia 1.20 .25
151 A16 12d bright vio 1.75 .25
152 A16 16d dull violet 2.40 .25
153 A16 20d blue ('40) 2.40 .25
154 A16 30d brt pink ('40) 5.50 .55
Nos. 142-154 (15) 16.75 4.05
Set, never hinged 35.00

For overprints and surcharges see Nos. N1-N11, N13, N15-N28, N30-N35 in Scott Standard catalogue, Vol. 6; Croatia 1-25 in Scott Standard catalogue, Vol. 2; Serbia 2N1-2N30 in Scott Standard catalogue, Vol. 6.

Arms of Yugoslavia, Greece, Romania and Turkey

A17 A18

1940, June 1

155 A17 3d ultramarine .95 .55
156 A18 3d ultramarine .95 .55
a. Pair, #155-156 7.00 13.50
157 A17 4d dark blue .95 .55
158 A18 4d dark blue .95 .55
a. Pair, #157-158 7.00 13.50
Nos. 155-158 (4) 3.80 2.20
Set, never hinged 7.50
Pairs, never hinged 30.00

Balkan Entente.

Bridge at Obod A19

1940, Sept. 29 **Litho.**

159 A19 5.50d slate grn & pale blue 2.25 3.50
Never hinged 4.00

Zagreb Phil. Exhib.; 500th anniv. of Johann Gutenberg's invention of printing. The first press in the Yugoslav area was located at Obod in 1493.

SEMI-POSTAL STAMPS

Giving Succor to Wounded SP1

Wounded Soldier SP2

Symbolical of National Unity — SP3

Unwmk.

1921, Jan. 30 **Engr.** ***Perf. 12***

B1 SP1 10p carmine .25 .25
B2 SP2 15p violet brown .25 .25
B3 SP3 25p light blue .25 .25
Nos. B1-B3 (3) .75 .75

Nos. B1-B3 were sold at double face value, the excess being for the benefit of invalid soldiers.

Exist imperf. Value $35.

For surcharges see Nos. 15-21.

This overprint was applied to 500,000 examples of No. B1 in 1923 and they were given to the Society for Wounded Invalids (Uprava Ratnih Invalida) which sold them for 2d a piece. These overprinted stamps had no franking power, but some were used through ignorance.

Regular Issue of 1926-27 Surcharged in Dark Red

1926, Nov. 1 ***Perf. 13***

B5 A6 25p + 25p green .25 .25
B6 A6 50p + 50p olive brn .25 .25
B7 A6 1d + 50p scarlet .25 .25
B8 A6 2d + 50p black .25 .25
B9 A6 3d + 50p slate blue .25 .25
B10 A6 4d + 50p red org .30 .25
B11 A6 5d + 50p brt vio .50 .25
B12 A6 8d + 50p black brn 1.00 .25
B13 A6 10d + 1d olive brn 2.00 .25
B14 A6 15d + 1d brown 8.00 1.00
B15 A6 20d + 1d dark vio 12.00 .55

B16 A6 30d + 1d orange 27.50 3.25
a. Double surcharge
Nos. B5-B16 (12) 52.55 7.05

The surtax on these stamps was intended for a fund for relief of sufferers from floods.

For overprints see Nos. 99-101.

Cathedral at Duvno SP4

King Tomislav SP6

Kings Tomislav and Alexander SP5

Perf. 12½, 11½x12

1929, Nov. 1 **Typo.**

B17 SP4 50p (+ 50p) olive green .25 .25
B18 SP5 1d (+ 50p) red .60 .40
B19 SP6 3d (+ 1d) blue 1.60 1.10
Nos. B17-B19 (3) 2.45 1.75

Millenary of the Croatian kingdom. The surtax was used to create a War Memorial Cemetery in France and to erect a monument to Serbian soldiers who died there.

No. B18 exists imperf. Value $400.

View of Dobropolje SP7

War Memorial — SP8

View of Kajmaktchalan SP9

1931, Apr. 1 ***Perf. 12½, 11½***

B20 SP7 50p + 50p blue grn .25 .25
B21 SP8 1d + 1d scarlet .25 .25
B22 SP9 3d + 3d deep blue .25 .25
Nos. B20-B22 (3) .75 .75

The surtax was added to a fund for a War Memorial to Serbian soldiers who died in France during World War I.

SP10

SP12

SP11

Black Overprint

1931, Nov. 1 ***Perf. 12½, 11½x12***

B23 SP10 50p (+ 50p) olive grn .25 *.25*
B24 SP11 1d (+ 50p) red .25 *.25*
B25 SP12 3d (+ 1d) blue .30 .30
Nos. B23-B25 (3) .80 *.80*

Surtax for War Memorial fund.

Rower on Danube at Smederevo SP13

Bled Lake SP14

Danube near Belgrade SP15

View of Split Harbor SP16

Zagreb Cathedral — SP17

Prince Peter — SP18

1932, Sept. 2 **Litho.** ***Perf. 11½***

B26 SP13 75p + 50p dl grn & lt blue .60 1.20
B27 SP14 1d + ½d scar & lt blue .60 1.20
B28 SP15 1½d + ½d rose & green .80 1.60
B29 SP16 3d + 1d bl & lt bl 1.60 2.40
B30 SP17 4d + 1d red org & lt blue 8.00 17.00
B31 SP18 5d + 1d dl vio & lilac 8.00 14.00
Nos. B26-B31 (6) 19.60 37.40

European Rowing Championship Races, Belgrade.

King Alexander — SP19

1933, May 25 **Typo.** ***Perf. 12½***

B32 SP19 50p + 25p black 6.00 12.00
B33 SP19 75p + 25p yel grn 6.00 12.00
B34 SP19 1.50d + 50p rose 6.00 12.00
B35 SP19 3d + 1d bl vio 6.00 12.00
B36 SP19 4p + 1d dk grn 6.00 12.00
B37 SP19 5d + 1d orange 6.00 12.00
Nos. B32-B37 (6) 36.00 72.00

11th Intl. Congress of P.E.N. (Poets, Editors and Novelists) Clubs, Dubrovnik, May 25-27.

The labels at the foot of the stamps are printed in either Cyrillic or Latin letters and each bears the amount of a premium for the benefit of the local P.E.N. Club at Dubrovnik.

Prince Peter — SP20

1933, June 28

B38 SP20 75p + 25p slate grn .25 .25
B39 SP20 1½d + ½d deep red .25 .25

60th anniv. meeting of the National Sokols (Sports Associations) at Ljubljana, July 1.

Eagle Soaring over City — SP22

1934, June 1 ***Perf. 12½***

B40 SP22 75p + 25p green 4.00 9.00
B41 SP22 1.50d + 50p car 6.00 9.50
B42 SP22 1.75d + 25p brown 10.00 9.50
Nos. B40-B42 (3) 20.00 28.00

20th anniversary of Sokols of Sarajevo.

Athlete and Eagle — SP23

1934, June 1

B43 SP23 75p + 25p Prus grn 2.40 4.75
B44 SP23 1.50d + 50p car 2.40 4.75
B45 SP23 1.75d + 25p choc 10.00 14.50
Nos. B43-B45 (3) 14.80 24.00

60th anniversary of Sokols of Zagreb.

Mother and Children
SP24 SP25

Perf. 12½x11½

1935, Dec. 25 **Photo.**

B46 SP24 1.50d + 1d dk brn & brown 1.25 1.20
a. Perf. 11½ 12.00 14.50
B47 SP25 3.50d + 1.50d bright ultra & bl 2.00 2.90

The surtax was for "Winter Help."

Queen Mother Marie — SP26

1936, May 3 **Litho.**

B48 SP26 75p + 25p grnsh bl .25 .40
B49 SP26 1.50d + 50p rose pink .25 .45
B50 SP26 1.75d + 75p brown 1.25 1.25
B51 SP26 3.50d + 1d brt bl 1.60 2.75
Nos. B48-B51 (4) 3.35 4.85

Prince Regent Paul — SP27

1936, Sept. 20 **Typo.**

B52 SP27 75p + 50p turq grn & red .40 *.35*
B53 SP27 1.50d + 50p cer & red .40 *.35*

Surtax for the Red Cross.

Princes Tomislav and Andrej
SP28 SP29

Perf. 11½x12½, 12½x11½

1937, May 1

B54 SP28 25p + 25p red brn .25 .25
B55 SP28 75p + 75p emerald .25 .40
B56 SP29 1.50d + 1d org red .30 .65
B57 SP29 2d + 1d magenta .60 1.20
Nos. B54-B57 (4) 1.40 2.50

Souvenir Sheet

National Costumes — SP30

1937, Sept. 12 ***Perf. 14***

B57A SP30 Sheet of 4 4.75 10.00
Never hinged 9.50
b. 1d blue green 1.00 1.75
c. 1.50d bright violet 1.00 1.75
d. 2d rose red 1.00 1.75
e. 4d dark blue 1.00 1.75

1st Yugoslavian Phil. Exhib., Belgrade. Sold only at the exhibition post office at 15d each.

SP31

SP32

Perf. 11½x12½, 12½x11½

1938, May 1 **Photo.**

B58 SP31 50p + 50p dark brn .25 .30
B59 SP32 1d + 1d dk green .25 .35
B60 SP31 1.50d + 1.50d scar .50 .40
B61 SP32 2d + 2d magenta 1.25 .80
Nos. B58-B61 (4) 2.25 1.85

Surtax for the benefit of Child Welfare.

For overprints see Nos. B75-B78.

Bridge and Anti-aircraft Lights — SP33

1938, May 28 ***Perf. 11½x12½***

No.	Design	Description	Unused	Used
B62	SP33	1d + 50p dk grn	.40	.80
B63	SP33	1.50d + 1d scarlet	.60	1.20
a.		Perf. 11½	17.50	27.50
B64	SP33	2d + 1d rose vio	1.25	2.40
a.		Perf. 11½	18.00	35.00
B65	SP33	3d + 1.50d dp bl	2.00	4.00
		Nos. B62-B65 (4)	4.25	8.40

Intl. Aeronautical Exhib., Belgrade.

Cliff at Demir-Kapiya — SP34

Modern Hospital SP35

Runner Carrying Torch — SP36

Alexander I — SP37

Perf. 11½x12½, 12½x11½

1938, Aug. 1

No.	Design	Description	Unused	Used
B66	SP34	1d + 1d slate grn & dp grn	.45	.40
B67	SP35	1.50d + 1.50d scar	.70	.55
B68	SP36	2d + 2d claret & dp rose	1.60	3.25
B69	SP37	3d + 3d dp bl	1.60	3.25
		Nos. B66-B69 (4)	4.35	7.45

The surtax was to raise funds to build a hospital for railway employees.

Runner SP38

Shot-Putter SP41

Hurdlers SP39

Pole Vaulter SP40

1938, Sept. 11

No.	Design	Description	Unused	Used
B70	SP38	50p + 50p org brn	1.40	2.50
B71	SP39	1d + 1d sl grn & dp grn	1.40	2.50
B72	SP40	1.50d + 1.50d rose & dk mag	1.40	2.50
B73	SP41	2d + 2d dk blue	2.75	5.00
		Nos. B70-B73 (4)	6.95	12.50

Ninth Balkan Games.

Stamps of 1938 Overprinted in Black

a

b

1938, Oct. 1

No.	Design	Description	Unused	Used
B75	SP31(a)	50p + 50p dk brn	.40	.55
B76	SP32(b)	1d + 1d dk grn	.40	.80
B77	SP31(a)	1.50d + 1.50d scar	.60	1.20
B78	SP32(b)	2d + 2d mag	1.25	2.40
		Nos. B75-B78 (4)	2.65	4.95

Surtax for the benefit of Child Welfare.

Postriders SP43

1d+1d, Rural mail delivery. 1.50d+1.50d, Mail train. 2d+2d, Mail bus. 4d+4d, Mail plane.

1939, Mar. 15 **Photo.** ***Perf. 11½***

No.	Design	Description	Unused	Used
B79	SP43	50p + 50p buff, bis & brown	.30	.55
B80	SP43	1d + 1d sl grn & dp green	.30	.55
B81	SP43	1.50d + 1.50d red, cop red & brn car	2.00	2.00
B82	SP43	2d + 2d dp plum & rose lilac	2.00	2.75
B83	SP43	4d + 4d ind & sl bl	2.40	4.00
		Nos. B79-B83 (5)	7.00	9.85

Centenary of the present postal system in Yugoslavia. The surtax was used for the Railway Benevolent Association.

The Cyrillic and Latin inscriptions are transposed on Nos. B82 and B83.

Child Eating SP48

Children at Seashore — SP49

Boy Planing Board SP50

Children in Crib — SP51

1939, May 1 ***Perf. 12½***

No.	Design	Description	Unused	Used
B84	SP48	1d + 1d blk & dp bl green	.50	1.00
B85	SP49	1.50d + 1.50d org brn & sal	2.00	3.25
a.		Perf. 11½	*80.00*	*160.00*
B86	SP50	2d + 2d mar & vio rose	1.40	2.90
B87	SP51	4d + 4d ind & royal blue	1.40	2.90
		Nos. B84-B87 (4)	5.30	10.05

The surtax was for the benefit of Child Welfare.

Czar Lazar of Serbia — SP52

Milosh Obilich — SP53

1939, June 28 ***Perf. 11½***

No.	Design	Description	Unused	Used
B88	SP52	1d + 1d sl grn & bl grn	1.60	1.60
B89	SP53	1.50d + 1.50d mar & brt car	1.60	1.60

Battle of Kosovo, 550th anniversary.

Training Ship "Jadran" SP54

Designs: 1d+50p, Steamship "King Alexander." 1.50d+1d, Freighter "Triglan." 2d+1.50d, Cruiser "Dubrovnik."

1939, Sept. 6 **Engr.**

No.	Design	Description	Unused	Used
B90	SP54	50p + 50p brn org	.40	.80
B91	SP54	1d + 50p dull grn	.80	1.60
B92	SP54	1.50d + 1d dp rose	1.25	2.40
B93	SP54	2d + 1.50d dark bl	2.00	4.00
		Nos. B90-B93 (4)	4.45	8.80

Yugoslav Navy and Merchant Marine. The surtax aided a Marine Museum.

Nos. B90-B93 also exist with a small "S" engraver's mark. Set value NH, $160. Location of the mark: On No. B90, above the base of the bowsprit. On No. B91, at the top of the smoke plume just below the "B" in the country name. On No. B92, at the top left of the large numeral "1". On No. B93, in the curve of the numeral "2".

Motorcycle and Sidecar — SP58

Racing Car SP59

Motorcycle SP60

Racing Car SP61

1939, Sept. 3 **Photo.**

No.	Design	Description	Unused	Used
B94	SP58	50p + 50p multi	.50	.80
B95	SP59	1d + 1d multi	1.00	1.60
B96	SP60	1.50d + 1.50d multi	1.40	2.40
B97	SP61	2d + 2d multi	2.50	4.00
		Nos. B94-B97 (4)	5.40	8.80

Automobile and Motorcycle Races, Belgrade. The surtax was for the Race Organization and the State Treasury.

Unknown Soldier Memorial SP62

1939, Oct. 9 ***Perf. 12½***

No.	Design	Description	Unused	Used
B98	SP62	1d + 50p sl grn & green	1.00	1.60
B99	SP62	1.50d + 1d red & rose red	1.00	1.60
B100	SP62	2d + 1.50d dp cl & vio rose	1.25	2.40
B101	SP62	3d + 2d dp bl & bl	2.50	4.00
		Nos. B98-B101 (4)	5.75	9.60

Assassination of King Alexander, 5th anniv. The surtax was used to aid World War I invalids.

Postman Delivering Mail — SP64

Postman Emptying Mail Box — SP65

Parcel Post Delivery Wagon SP66

Parcel Post SP67

Repairing Telephone Wires — SP68

1940, Jan. 1

B102 SP64 50p + 50p brn & deep org .60 1.00
B103 SP65 1d + 1d sl grn & blue grn .60 1.00
B104 SP66 1.50d + 1.50d red brn & scar 1.00 2.40
B105 SP67 2d + 2d dl vio & red lilac 1.25 2.40
B106 SP68 4d + 4d sl bl & bl 4.00 6.50
Nos. B102-B106 (5) 7.45 13.30

The surtax was used for the employees of the Postal System in Belgrade.

Croats' Arrival at Adriatic in 640 SP69

King Tomislav — SP70

Death of Matija Gubec — SP71

Anton and Stjepan Radic SP72

Map of Yugoslavia SP73

1940, Mar. 1 Typo. *Perf. 11½*

B107 SP69 50p + 50p brn org .40 .55
B108 SP70 1d + 1d green .40 .55
B109 SP71 1.50d + 1.50d brt red 1.25 .55
B110 SP72 2d + 2d dk cerise 2.00 2.40
B111 SP73 4d + 2d dark blue 2.00 2.75
Nos. B107-B111 (5) 6.05 6.80

The surtax was used for the benefit of postal employees in Zagreb.

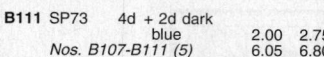

Children Playing in Snow SP74

Children at Seashore — SP75

1940, May 1 Photo. *Perf. 11½, 12½*

B112 SP74 50p + 50p brn org & org yellow .25 .40
B113 SP75 1d + 1d sl grn & dk green .25 .40
B114 SP74 1.50d + 1.50d brn red & scarlet .60 .80
B115 SP75 2d + 2d mar & vio rose 1.00 1.60
Nos. B112-B115 (4) 2.10 3.20

The surtax was for Child Welfare.

Nos. C11-C14 Surcharged in Carmine

Perf. 11½x12½, 12½x11½

1940, Dec. 23

B116 AP6 50p + 50p on 5d .25 .25
B117 AP7 1d + 1d on 10d .25 .40
a. Perf. 12½ *40.00 40.00*
B118 AP8 1.50d + 1.50d on 20d .80 1.40
B119 AP9 2d + 2d on 30d .90 1.75
Nos. B116-B119 (4) 2.20 3.80

The surtax was used to fight tuberculosis.
For surcharges see Nos. NB1-NB4 in Scott Standard catalogue, Vol. 6.

AIR POST STAMPS

Dubrovnik AP1

Lake Bled AP2

Falls of Jaice — AP3

Church at Oplenac — AP4

Bridge at Mostar — AP5

Perf. 12½

1934, June 15 Typo. Unwmk.

C1 AP1 50p violet brown .25 .25
C2 AP2 1d green .25 .25
C3 AP3 2d rose red .50 .30
C4 AP4 3d ultramarine 1.40 .45
C5 AP5 10d vermilion 2.75 4.25
Nos. C1-C5 (5) 5.15 5.50

Border in Black

King Alexander Memorial Issue

1935, Jan. 1

C6 AP4 3d ultramarine 3.25 4.75

St. Naum Convent — AP6

Port of Rab — AP7

Sarajevo AP8

Ljubljana AP9

Perf. 11½x12½, 12½x11½

1937, Sept. 12 Photo.

C7 AP6 50p brown .25 .25
a. Perf. 12½ .25 .25
C8 AP7 1d yellow grn .25 .25
a. Perf. 12½ .25 .25
C9 AP8 2d blue gray .25 .25
a. Perf. 12½ .25 .25
C10 AP9 2.50d rose red .25 .25
a. Perf. 12½ .25 .25
C11 AP6 5d brn violet .25 .25
a. Perf. 12½ .25 .25
C12 AP7 10d brown lake .50 .25
a. Perf. 12½ .70 .25
C13 AP8 20d dark green 5.25 8.00
a. Perf. 12½ .70 1.00
C14 AP9 30d ultramarine 18.00 27.50
a. Perf. 12½ 1.00 1.75
Nos. C7-C14 (8) 25.00 37.00

For surcharges see Nos. B116-B119; Nos. NB1-NB4, NC1-NC8 in Scott Standard catalogue, Vol. 6.

Cathedral of Zagreb AP10

Bridge at Belgrade AP11

1940, Aug. 15 Litho. *Perf. 12½*

C15 AP10 40d Prus grn & pale green 4.50 *3.50*
C16 AP11 50d slate bl & gray bl 4.50 *5.00*

For overprints see Nos. NC9-NC10 in Scott Standard catalogue, Vol. 6.

POSTAGE DUE STAMPS

King Alexander — D1

1921 Typo. Unwmk. *Perf. 11½*
Red or Black Surcharge

J1 D1 10p on 5p green (R) .25 .25
J2 D1 30p on 5p green (Bk) .25 .25

D2 D3

1921-22 Typo. *Perf. 11½, Rough*

J3 D2 10p rose .25 .25
J4 D2 30p yellow green .25 .25
J5 D2 50p violet .25 .25
J6 D2 1d brown .30 .25
J7 D2 2d blue .40 .25
J8 D3 5d orange 2.00 .25
J9 D3 10d violet brown 6.00 .45
a. Cliche of 10p in sheet of 10d 190.00 —
J10 D3 25d pink 35.00 1.60
J11 D3 50d green 30.00 1.60
Nos. J3-J11 (9) 74.45 5.15

1924 *Perf. 9, 10½, 11½, Clean-cut*

J12 D3 10p rose red .25 .25
J13 D3 30p yellow green .35 .40
J14 D3 50p violet .25 .25
J15 D3 1d brown .25 .25
J16 D3 2d deep blue .50 .25
J17 D3 5d orange 1.60 .25
J18 D3 10d violet brown 10.00 .25
J19 D3 25d pink 65.00 1.25
J20 D3 50d green 47.50 1.25
Nos. J12-J20 (9) 125.70 4.40

Nos. J19-J20 do not exist perf 9. Nos. J18-J20 do not exist perf 11½.

Nos. J19-J20 Surcharged

1928

J21 D3 10d on 25d pink 3.25 .40
J22 D3 10d on 50d green 3.25 .40
a. Inverted surcharge 30.00 18.00

A second type of "1" in surcharge has flag projecting horizontally. Value, each: $24 never hinged; $12 unused; $3.25 used.

Coat of Arms — D4

1931 Typo. *Perf. 12½*
With Imprint at Foot

J23 D4 50p violet 1.40 .25
J24 D4 1d deep magenta 3.00 .25
J25 D4 2d deep blue 9.50 .25
J26 D4 5d orange 2.00 .25
J27 D4 10d chocolate 10.00 1.25
Nos. J23-J27 (5) 25.90 2.25

For overprints see Nos. NJ1-NJ13 in Scott Standard catalogue, Vol. 6; Croatia 26-29, J1-J5 in Scott Standard catalogue, Vol. 2.

1932 Without Imprint at Foot

J28 D4 50p violet .25 .25
J29 D4 1d deep magenta .25 .25
J30 D4 2d deep blue .25 .25

J31 D4 5d orange .25 .25
J32 D4 10d chocolate .25 .25
Nos. J28-J32 (5) 1.25 1.25

Numeral of Value — D5

Overprint in Green, Blue or Maroon

1933 ***Perf. 9, 10½, 11½***
J33 D5 50p vio (G) .25 .25
a. Perf. 10½ .30
J34 D5 1d brown (Bl) .25 .25
a. Perf. 10½ 2.00 1.40
J35 D5 2d blue (M) .25 .25
a. Perf. 10½ 1.00 1.25
J36 D5 5d orange (Bl) .80 .25
J37 D5 10d violet brn (Bl) 4.00 .25
Nos. J33-J37 (5) 5.55 1.25

POSTAL TAX STAMPS

Catalogue values for unused stamps in this section are for Never Hinged items.

The tax was for the Red Cross or The Olympic Fund unless otherwise noted.

Red Cross Emblem — PT1

Unwmk.
1933, Sept. 17 **Litho.** ***Perf. 13***
RA1 PT1 50p dark blue & red .65 .25

Obligatory on inland letters during Red Cross Week, Sept. 17-23.
See No. RAJ1.

Dr. Vladen Djordjevic — PT2

1936, Sept. 20 **Typo.** ***Perf. 12***
RA2 PT2 50p brn blk & red .40 .25

Obligatory on inland letters during Red Cross Week, Sept. 20-26.

Aiding the Wounded PT3

1938, Sept. 18 **Litho.** ***Perf. 12½***
RA3 PT3 50p dk bl, red, yel & grn .40 .25

1940, Sept. 15 **Redrawn**
RA4 PT3 50p slate blue & red .55 .25

The inscription at the upper right of this stamp and the numerals of value are in smaller characters.
Obligatory on all letters during the second week of September.

POSTAL TAX DUE STAMPS

Catalogue values for unused stamps in this section are for Never Hinged items.

Type of Postal Tax Stamp Inscribed "PORTO"

1933 **Unwmk.** **Litho.** ***Perf. 12½***
RAJ1 PT1 50p dull grn & red 1.00 .25
a. Perf. 11½ 20.00 8.00

ZAMBEZIA

zam-ˈbē-zē-ə

LOCATION — A former district of the Mozambique Province in Portuguese East Africa
GOVT. — Part of the Portuguese East Africa Colony

The districts of Quelimane and Tete were created from Zambezia. Eventually stamps of Mozambique came into use. See Quelimane and Tete.

1000 Reis = 1 Milreis

King Carlos
A1 A2

Perf. 11½, 12½, 13½
1894 **Typo.** **Unwmk.**
1 A1 5r yellow .45 .25
2 A1 10r red violet 1.00 .45
3 A1 15r chocolate 2.00 .65
a. Perf. 12½ 27.50 19.00
4 A1 20r lavender 2.00 .65
5 A1 25r blue green 3.00 1.25
a. Perf. 11½ *30.00* *30.00*
6 A1 50r lt blue 3.00 1.25
7 A1 75r carmine 5.00 3.25
a. Perf. 11½ 50.00 35.00
8 A1 80r yellow grn 7.00 2.50
9 A1 100r brown, *buff* 6.00 1.75
10 A1 150r car, *rose* 8.00 3.00
11 A1 200r dk blue, *bl* 9.00 3.00
a. Perf. 11½ 200.00 150.00
b. Perf. 13½ 32.50 24.00
12 A1 300r dk bl, *salmon* 15.00 4.50
a. Perf. 11½ 25.00 20.00
Nos. 1-12 (12) 61.45 22.50

For surcharges and overprints see Nos. 36-47, 73-74, 77-81, 84-88.

1898-1903 ***Perf. 11½***
Name and Value in Black or Red (500r)
13 A2 2½r gray .45 .45
14 A2 5r orange .45 .45
15 A2 10r lt green .75 .50
16 A2 15r brown 1.25 1.00
17 A2 15r gray grn ('03) 1.60 1.40
18 A2 20r gray violet 1.25 1.00
19 A2 25r sea green 1.25 1.00
20 A2 25r carmine ('03) 1.00 .85
21 A2 50r blue 1.25 1.10
22 A2 50r brown ('03) 4.00 2.25
23 A2 65r dull bl ('03) 10.00 5.50
24 A2 75r rose 20.00 5.25
25 A2 75r lilac ('03) 3.25 2.75
26 A2 80r violet 5.00 3.00
27 A2 100r dk bl, *bl* 2.00 2.00
28 A2 115r org brn, *pink* ('03) 15.00 7.25
29 A2 130r brn, *straw* ('03) 15.00 7.25
30 A2 150r brn, *buff* 6.00 3.50
31 A2 200r red vio, *pnksh* 6.00 3.50
32 A2 300r dk bl, *rose* 8.00 3.50
33 A2 400r dull bl, *straw* ('03) 12.00 8.50
34 A2 500r blk, *bl* ('01) 20.00 6.75
35 A2 700r vio, *yelsh* ('01) 30.00 8.75
Nos. 13-35 (23) 165.50 77.50

For surcharges and overprints see Nos. 49-68, 72, 82-83, 93-107.

Stamps of 1894 Surcharged

1902 ***Perf. 11½, 12½***
36 A1 65r on 10r red vio 10.00 7.00
37 A1 65r on 15r choc 10.00 7.00
38 A1 65r on 20r lav 10.00 7.00
39 A1 65r on 300r bl, *sal* 10.00 7.00
40 A1 115r on 5r yel 10.00 7.00
41 A1 115r on 25r bl grn 10.00 7.00
42 A1 115r on 80r yel grn 10.00 7.00
43 A1 130r on 75r car 7.00 7.00
44 A1 130r on 150r car, *rose* 5.25 5.25
45 A1 400r on 50r lt bl 3.00 3.25
46 A1 400r on 100r brn, *buff* 3.00 3.50
47 A1 400r on 200r bl, *bl* 3.00 3.50

Same Surcharge on No. P1
48 N1 130r on 2½r brn 9.00 7.00
Nos. 36-48 (13) 100.25 78.50

Stamps of 1898 Overprinted

1902 ***Perf. 11½***
49 A2 15r brown 4.00 1.40
50 A2 25r sea green 4.00 1.40
51 A2 50r blue 4.00 1.40
52 A2 75r rose 8.00 3.75
Nos. 49-52 (4) 20.00 7.95

No. 23 Surcharged in Black

1905
53 A2 50r on 65r dull blue 8.00 4.00

Stamps of 1898-1903 Overprinted in Carmine or Green

1911
54 A2 2½r gray .35 .25
55 A2 5r orange .35 .25
56 A2 10r light green .40 .25
a. Inverted overprint 15.00 12.50
57 A2 15r gray green .40 .25
58 A2 20r gray violet .50 .30
59 A2 25r carmine (G) 1.50 .50
60 A2 50r brown .40 *.35*
61 A2 75r lilac 1.25 .90
62 A2 100r dk bl, *bl* 1.25 .90
63 A2 115r org brn, *pink* 1.25 .90
64 A2 130r brown, *straw* 1.25 .90
65 A2 200r red vio, *pnksh* 1.25 .90
66 A2 400r dull bl, *straw* 2.10 1.10
67 A2 500r blk & red, *bl* 2.10 1.10
68 A2 700r violet, *yelsh* 2.25 1.50
Nos. 54-68 (15) 16.60 *10.35*

Stamps of 1902-05 Overprinted in Carmine or Green

1914 **Without Gum**
72 A2 50r on 65r dl bl *4,000.* *1,200.*
73 A1 115r on 5r yellow 2.50 1.50
74 A1 115r on 25r bl grn 2.50 1.50
75 A1 115r on 80r yel grn 2.50 1.50
76 N1 130r on 2½r brn (G) 2.50 1.50
a. Carmine overprint 22.50 22.50
77 A1 130r on 75r car 3.00 1.50
a. Perf. 12½ 5.50 7.00
78 A1 130r on 150r car, *rose* 3.00 1.50
79 A1 400r on 50r lt bl 3.00 3.00
a. Perf. 12½ 11.00 11.00
80 A1 400r on 100r brn, *buff* 3.00 2.50
81 A1 400r on 200r bl, *bl* 3.00 2.50

On Nos. 51-52
82 A2 50r blue 1.50 1.50
83 A2 75r rose 1.50 1.50
Nos. 73-83 (11) 28.00 20.00

Preceding Issues Overprinted in Carmine

1915
On Surcharged Issue of 1902
84 A1 115r on 5r yellow .85 .45
85 A1 115r on 25r bl grn .85 .45
86 A1 115r on 80r lt grn .85 .45
87 A1 130r on 75r carmine .85 .45
a. Perf. 12½ 4.50 2.25
88 A1 130r on 150r car, *rose* .85 .45
92 N1 130r on 2½r (down) .85 .45

On Nos. 51, 53
93 A2 50r blue .85 .50
a. "Republica" inverted 15.00 15.00
94 A2 50r on 65r dull bl 3.50 *4.50*
Nos. 84-94 (8) 9.45 *7.70*

Stamps of 1898-1903 Overprinted Locally in Carmine

1917 **Without Gum**
95 A2 2½r gray 2.00 *3.00*
96 A2 5r orange 9.00 6.50
97 A2 10r light green 9.00 6.00
98 A2 15r gray green 8.00 6.50
99 A2 20r gray violet 9.00 6.50
100 A2 25r sea green 13.50 15.00
101 A2 100r blue, *blue* 6.00 2.75
102 A2 115r org brn, *pink* 6.00 2.75
103 A2 130r brown, *straw* 6.00 2.75
104 A2 200r red vio, *pnksh* 6.00 2.75
105 A2 400r dull bl, *straw* 6.00 3.50
106 A2 500r blk & red, *bl* 6.00 3.75
107 A2 700r vio, *yelsh* 10.00 5.25
Nos. 95-107 (13) 96.50 67.00

NEWSPAPER STAMP

N1

1894 **Unwmk.** **Typo.** ***Perf. 12½***
P1 N1 2½r brown .60 .35

For overprints and surcharges see Nos. 76, 92.

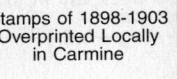

ZANZIBAR

ˈzan-zə-ˌbär

LOCATION — Group of islands about twenty miles off the coast of Tanganyika in East Africa
GOVT. — British protectorate
AREA — 1,044 sq. mi. (approx.)
POP. — 354,360 (est. 1967)
CAPITAL — Zanzibar

Before 1895, unoverprinted stamps of India were used in Zanzibar.

12 Pies = 1 Anna
16 Annas = 1 Rupee
100 Cents = 1 Rupee (1908)
100 Cents = 1 Shilling (1935)

Catalogue values for unused stamps in this country are for Never Hinged items, beginning with Scott 201 in the regular postage section and Scott J18 in the postage due section.

Watermarks

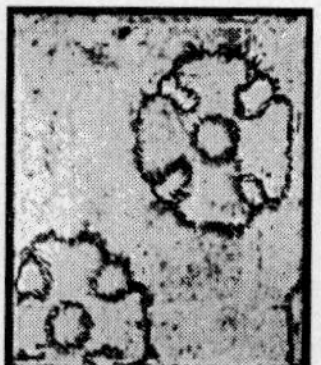

Wmk. 47 — Multiple Rosette

Wmk. 71 — Rosette

Stamps of British India Overprinted

On Stamps of 1882-95

1895 **Wmk. Star (39)** ***Perf. 14***

Blue Overprint

No.	Type	Description	Unused	Used
1	A17	½a green	*30,000.*	*6,250.*
2	A19	1a violet brn	3,500.	600.
a.		"Zanzidar"		*28,500.*

1895-96 **Black Overprint**

No.	Type	Description	Unused	Used
3	A17	½a green	5.00	5.00
a.		"Zanzidar"	*1,450.*	800.00
b.		"Zanibar"	*1,450.*	*1,900.*
c.		"Zapzibar"		
d.		Double overprint, one albino	250.00	
e.		Umlaut over last "a"	1,950.	1,950.
4	A19	1a violet brn	5.25	4.25
a.		"Zanzidar"	—	*4,000.*
b.		"Zanibar"	1,900.	2,250.
c.		Umlaut over last "a"	4,500.	
5	A20	1a6p bister brn	5.50	4.25
a.		"Zanzidar"	*4,500.*	1,200.
b.		"Zanizbar"	*2,000.*	
c.		"Zanibar"	*1,800.*	1,750.
d.		"Zapzibar"	*125.00*	*125.00*
e.		Umlaut over last "a"	1,550.	

No.	Type	Description	Unused	Used
6	A21	2a ultra	10.00	9.00
a.		"Zanzidar"	8,500.	3,500.
b.		"Zanibar"	6,750.	2,750.
c.		"Zapzibar"	*150.00*	*160.00*
d.		Double overprint	310.00	
e.		Double overprint, one albino	280.00	
f.		2a pale blue	9.50	8.50
g.		Umlaut over last "a"	2,850.	
7	A28	2a6p green	10.00	5.50
a.		"Zanzidar"	8,500.	1,800.
b.		"Zanibar"	800.00	*1,400.*
c.		"Zapzibar"		
d.		"Zanzipar"	1,250.	
e.		Second "z" italic	400.00	575.00
f.		Double overprint, one albino	280.00	
g.		Umlaut over last "a"	2,400.	1,850.
8	A22	3a orange	13.50	*17.50*
a.		"Zanzidar"	1,150.	*2,150.*
b.		"Zanizbar"	*7,500.*	*8,000.*
9	A23	4a olive grn	22.50	*20.00*
a.		"Zanzidar"	11,500.	4,750.
10	A25	8a red vio	45.00	30.00
a.		"Zanzidar"	11,500.	9,000.
11	A26	12a vio, *red*	20.00	11.50
a.		"Zanzidar"	11,500.	5,000.
12	A27	1r gray	125.00	100.00
a.		"Zanzidar"	10,500.	6,750.
13	A29	1r car rose & grn	22.50	*40.00*
a.		Vertical overprint	475.00	
14	A30	2r brn & rose	125.00	*135.00*
a.		"Zanziba"	32,500.	—
b.		Inverted "r"	4,500.	5,500.
c.		Pair, one without overprint		
15	A30	3r grn & brn	95.00	*105.00*
a.		"Zanziba"	32,500.	
b.		Inverted "r"	6,750.	6,750.
c.		Double overprint, one albino	1,550.	
16	A30	5r vio & blue	105.00	*125.00*
a.		"Zanziba"	32,500.	
b.		Inverted "r"	5,000.	*7,250.*
c.		Dbl. ovpt., one invtd.	950.00	
d.		Double overprint, one albino	1,600.	

On Stamp of 1873-76

Wmk. Elephant's Head (38)

No.	Type	Description	Unused	Used
17	A14	6a bister	22.50	12.50
a.		"Zanzidar"	11,500.	4,000.
b.		"Zanzibarr"	*7,240.*	*4,750.*
c.		"Zanibar"	900.00	*1,400.*
d.		"Zapzibar"		
e.		Double overprint		
f.		Double overprint, one albino	190.00	
g.		Triple overprint, one albino	250.00	
		Nos. 3-17 (15)	631.75	624.50

Nos. 4-6 Surcharged

a

b

c

d

e

f

1896 **Wmk. Star (39)**

Black Surcharge

No.	Type	Description	Unused	Used
18	(a)	2½a on 1a	*200.00*	*110.00*
19	(b)	2½a on 1a	*525.00*	*350.00*
a.		Inverted "1" in "½"	3,250.	—
20	(c)	2½a on 1a	*225.00*	*125.00*

Red Surcharge

No.	Type	Description	Unused	Used
21	(a)	2½a on 1a	*275.00*	*725.00*
22	(b)	2½a on 1a	*500.00*	*1,050.*
23	(c)	2½a on 1a	*310.00*	*725.00*
24	(a)	2½a on 1a6p	*85.00*	*60.00*
a.		"Zanzidar"	*1,700.*	*1,450.*
b.		"Zanizbar"	*5,250.*	*2,250.*
d.		Inverted "1" in "½"	1,250.	1,000.
24C	(b)	2½a on 1a6p	*250.00*	*550.00*
25	(c)	2½a on 1a6p	*145.00*	*350.00*
26	(d)	2½a on 1a6p	*200.00*	*175.00*
a.		Inverted "1" in "½"	1,750.	1,400.
b.		Roman "I" in "½"	1,000.	1,000.
c.		"Zanzibar" double, one albino	350.00	
27	(e)	2½a on 1a6p	*475.00*	*400.00*
c.		"Zanzibar" double, one albino	875.00	
27A	(f)	2½a on 1a6p	*27,500.*	*18,000.*
28	(a)	2½a on 2a	*160.00*	*360.00*
28A	(b)	2½a on 2a	*340.00*	*625.00*
29	(c)	2½a on 2a	*180.00*	*425.00*
30	(d)	2½a on 2a	*80.00*	*47.50*
a.		Inverted "1" in "½"	500.00	325.00
b.		Roman "I" in "½"	300.00	180.00
c.		"Zanzibar" double, one albino	190.00	
d.		"Zanzibar" triple, two albino	350.00	
31	(e)	2½a on 2a	*225.00*	*125.00*
b.		Inverted "1" in "½"	4,000.	2,000.
c.		"2" in "½" omitted	*17,500.*	
d.		"2" for "2½"	*25,000.*	
e.		"1" of "½" omitted	*17,500.*	*7,500.*
f.		"Zanzibar" double, one albino	600.00	
31A	(f)	2½a on 2a	*5,750.*	*2,800.*

Certain type varieties are found in the word "Zanzibar" on Nos. 1 to 31A viz: Inverted "q" for "b," broken "p" for "n," "i" without dot, small second "z" and tall second "z." These varieties are found on all values from ½a to 1r inclusive and the tall "z" is also found on the 2r, 3r and 5r.

Stamps of British East Africa, 1896, Overprinted in Black or Red

1896 **Wmk. Crown and C A (2)**

No.	Type	Description	Unused	Used
32	A8	½a yellow grn	42.50	25.00
33	A8	1a carmine	47.50	19.00
a.		Double overprint	825.00	1,000.
b.		Double overprint, one albino	350.00	
34	A8	2½a dk blue (R)	100.00	52.50
a.		Inverted "S" in "ANNAS"	—	600.00
35	A8	4½a orange	55.00	65.00
36	A8	5a dark ocher	70.00	45.00
a.		"r" omitted	—	4,400.
37	A8	7½a lilac	60.00	70.00
		Nos. 32-37 (6)	375.00	276.50

A2

Sultan Seyyid Hamed-bin-Thwain A3

1896, Sept. 20 **Engr.** **Wmk. 71**

No.	Type	Description	Unused	Used
38	A2	½a yel grn & red	4.50	2.25
39	A2	1a indigo & red	4.00	1.75
40	A2	2a red brn & red	3.75	.85
41	A2	2½a ultra & red	17.50	1.60
42	A2	3a slate & red	19.00	10.00
43	A2	4a dk green & red	12.50	6.00
44	A2	4½a orange & red	8.75	7.00
45	A2	5a bister & red	9.25	4.50
a.		Half used as 2½a on cover		*4,900.*
46	A2	7½a lilac & red	6.75	6.75
47	A2	8a ol gray & red	13.50	9.00
48	A3	1r ultra & red	24.00	12.00
49	A3	2r green & red	32.50	13.00
50	A3	3r violet & red	36.00	13.00
51	A3	4r lake & red	27.50	*20.00*
52	A3	5r blk brn & red	38.00	*20.00*
		Nos. 38-52 (15)	257.50	127.70

No. 43 Surcharged in Red

1897

No.	Type	Description	Unused	Used
53	A2 (a)	2½a on 4a	100.00	*55.00*
54	A2 (b)	2½a on 4a	325.00	*300.00*
55	A2 (c)	2½a on 4a	120.00	*82.50*
		Nos. 53-55 (3)	545.00	*437.50*

1898 **Engr.** **Wmk. 47**

No.	Type	Description	Unused	Used
56	A2	½a yel grn & red	1.75	.45
57	A2	1a indigo & red	6.00	1.40
58	A2	2a red brn & red	9.25	2.25
58A	A2	2½a ultra & red	5.50	.45
59	A2	3a slate & red	8.25	.75
60	A2	4a dk grn & red	4.25	1.25
60A	A2	4½a orange & red	15.00	1.25
61	A2	5a bister & red	22.50	2.50
61A	A2	7½a lilac & red	17.50	3.50
61B	A2	8a ol gray & red	22.00	3.25
		Nos. 56-61B (10)	112.00	17.05

A4

Sultan Seyyid Hamoud-bin-Mahommed-bin-Said — A5

1899-1901

No.	Type	Description	Unused	Used
62	A4	½a yel grn & red	3.00	.65
63	A4	1a indigo & red	5.00	.25
64	A4	1a car & red ('01)	3.75	.25
65	A4	2a red brn & red	5.00	1.50
66	A4	2½a ultra & red	5.00	1.00
67	A4	3a slate & red	6.75	3.00
68	A4	4a dk green & red	6.75	3.50
69	A4	4½a orange & red	20.00	9.50
70	A4	4½a ind & red ('01)	22.00	14.50
71	A4	5a bister & red	6.75	3.00
72	A4	7½a lilac & red	6.75	*7.75*
73	A4	8a ol gray & red	6.75	*5.75*

Wmk. 71

No.	Type	Description	Unused	Used
74	A5	1r ultra & red	24.00	17.50
75	A5	2r green & red	27.50	24.00
76	A5	3r violet & red	50.00	*52.50*
77	A5	4r lilac rose & red	75.00	*77.50*
78	A5	5r gray brown & red	85.00	*95.00*
		Nos. 62-78 (17)	359.00	*317.15*

For surcharges see Nos. 94-98.

A6

Monogram of Sultan Ali bin Hamoud — A7

1904, June 8 **Typo.** **Wmk. 47**

No.	Type	Description	Unused	Used
79	A6	½a emerald	3.00	1.00
80	A6	1a rose red	3.00	.25
81	A6	2a bister brown	5.00	.50
82	A6	2½a ultra	5.00	.40
83	A6	3a gray	6.00	2.50
84	A6	4a blue green	4.50	1.75
85	A6	4½a black	5.25	2.75
86	A6	5a ocher	7.50	2.50
87	A6	7½a violet	9.25	*8.75*
88	A6	8a olive green	6.50	5.75
89	A7	1r ultra & red	37.50	27.50
90	A7	2r green & red	45.00	*55.00*
91	A7	3r violet & red	65.00	*100.00*
92	A7	4r magenta & red	75.00	*120.00*
93	A7	5r olive & red	75.00	*120.00*
		Nos. 79-93 (15)	352.50	*448.65*

Nos. 69-70, 72-73 Surcharged in Black or Lake

g

h

i

1904

94 A4 (g) 1a on 4½a 5.00 *6.25*
95 A4 (g) 1a on 4½a (L) 6.00 *24.00*
96 A4 (h) 2a on 4a (L) 19.00 *24.00*
97 A4 (i) 2½a on 7½a 17.50 *25.00*
a. "Hlaf" 16,000.
b. Thin open "w" in overprint 85.00 105.00
c. Serif on foot of "f" in overprint 150.00 180.00
98 A4 (i) 2½a on 8a 29.00 *40.00*
a. "Hlaf" 15,000. *10,000.*
b. Thin open "w" in overprint 85.00 105.00
c. Serif on foot of "f" in overprint 250.00 300.00
Nos. 94-98 (5) 76.50 *119.25*

Sultan Ali bin Hamoud
A8 A9

A10

Palace of the Sultan — A11

1908-09 Engr. Wmk. 47

99 A8 1c gray ('09) 2.75 .35
100 A8 3c yellow grn 15.00 .25
101 A8 6c carmine 11.00 .25
102 A8 10c org brn ('09) 7.00 2.50
103 A8 12c violet 19.00 3.75
104 A9 15c ultra & pur 20.00 .45
105 A9 25c brown 8.50 1.10
106 A9 50c dp green 11.50 7.75
107 A9 75c slate ('09) 16.00 *18.00*
108 A10 1r yellow green 45.00 14.00
109 A10 2r violet 21.00 18.00
110 A10 3r yellow brown 40.00 *57.50*
111 A10 4r red 75.00 *100.00*
112 A10 5r blue 72.50 *90.00*
113 A11 10r brn & dk grn 215.00 *375.00*
Overprinted "SPECIMEN" 67.50
114 A11 20r yel grn & blk 625.00 *800.00*
Overprinted "SPECIMEN" 100.00
115 A11 30r dk brn & blk 725.00 *1,050.*
Overprinted "SPECIMEN" 115.00
116 A11 40r org brn & blk 900.00
Overprinted "SPECIMEN" 145.00
117 A11 50r lilac & blk 825.00
Overprinted "SPECIMEN" 145.00
118 A11 100r blue & blk 1,250.
Overprinted "SPECIMEN" 200.00
119 A11 200r black & brn 1,650.
Overprinted "SPECIMEN" 275.00
Nos. 99-112 (14) 364.25 *313.90*

It is probable that Nos. 118 and 119 were used only for fiscal purposes.

Sultan Khalifa bin Harub — A12

Dhow — A13

Dhow — A14

1913 *Perf. 14*

120 A12 1c gray .50 .75
121 A12 3c yellow grn 1.50 .75
122 A12 6c carmine 1.75 .25
123 A12 10c brown 1.25 *3.75*
124 A12 12c violet 1.50 .50
125 A12 15c ultra 3.50 .60
126 A12 25c black brn 1.45 *3.00*
127 A12 50c dk green 4.00 *7.75*
128 A12 75c dk gray 2.75 *6.50*
Overprinted "SPECIMEN" 92.50
129 A13 1r yellow grn 24.00 *17.50*
130 A13 2r dk violet 18.00 *37.50*
131 A13 3r orange 22.50 *57.50*
132 A13 4r red 37.50 *80.00*
133 A13 5r blue 55.00 *52.50*
134 A14 10r brown & grn 215.00 *400.00*
135 A14 20r yel grn & blk 375.00 *675.00*
Overprinted "SPECIMEN" 85.00
136 A14 30r dk brn & blk 375.00 *825.00*
Overprinted "SPECIMEN" 85.00
137 A14 40r orange & blk 675.00 *1,050.*
Overprinted "SPECIMEN" 150.00
138 A14 50r dull vio & blk 675.00 *1,150.*
Overprinted "SPECIMEN" 150.00
139 A14 100r blue & blk 850.00
Overprinted "SPECIMEN" 175.00
140 A14 200r black & brn 1,250.
Overprinted "SPECIMEN" 225.00
Nos. 120-134 (15) 390.20 *668.85*

1914-22 Wmk. 3

141 A12 1c gray .90 .50
142 A12 3c yellow grn 1.40 .25
143 A12 6c carmine 1.25 .25
144 A12 8c vio, *yel* ('22) 1.25 *7.25*
145 A12 10c dk grn, *yel* ('22) .85 .40
146 A12 15c ultra 1.75 *8.25*
148 A12 50c dark green 5.00 *7.25*
149 A12 75c deep gray 3.50 *37.50*
150 A13 1r yellow grn 5.50 4.00
151 A13 2r dark violet 14.50 *15.00*
152 A13 3r brown org 26.00 *50.00*
153 A13 4r red 26.00 *95.00*
154 A13 5r blue 19.00 *72.50*
155 A14 10r brown & grn 225.00 *725.00*
Nos. 141-155 (14) 331.90 *1,023.*

1921-29 Wmk. 4

156 A12 1c gray .30 *11.50*
157 A12 3c yellow grn 3.75 *6.25*
158 A12 3c orange ('22) .40 .25
159 A12 4c green ('22) .60 *2.75*
160 A12 6c carmine .40 .55
161 A12 6c vio, *bl* ('22) .45 .25
162 A12 10c lt brown .80 *15.00*
163 A12 12c violet .50 .35
164 A12 12c carmine ('22) .50 .50
165 A12 15c ultra .80 *14.50*
166 A12 20c dk blue ('22) 1.25 .40
167 A12 25c black brn .90 *28.50*
168 A12 50c blue green 3.50 *7.25*
169 A12 75c dark gray 3.25 *65.00*
170 A13 1r yellow grn 7.00 4.00
171 A13 2r dk violet 4.50 *15.50*
172 A13 3r ocher 5.50 *8.50*
173 A13 4r red 17.50 *45.00*
174 A13 5r blue 24.00 *75.00*
175 A14 10r brown & grn 215.00 *475.00*
176 A14 20r green & blk 400.00 *775.00*
177 A14 30r dk brn & blk ('29) 350.00 *750.00*
Overprinted "SPECIMEN" 145.00
Perforated "SPECIMEN" 150.00
Nos. 156-175 (20) 290.90 776.05

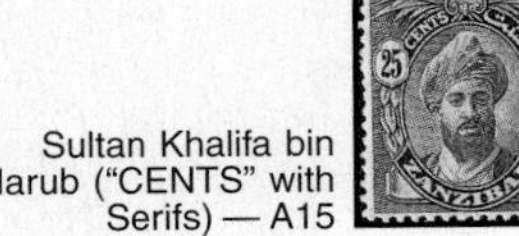

Sultan Khalifa bin Harub ("CENTS" with Serifs) — A15

1926-27

184 A15 1c brown 1.00 .25
185 A15 3c yellow org .30 .25
186 A15 4c deep green .30 .50
187 A15 6c dark violet .35 .25
188 A15 8c slate 1.10 *5.50*
189 A15 10c olive green 1.10 .45
190 A15 12c deep red 3.00 .25
191 A15 20c ultra .65 .40
192 A15 25c violet, *yel* 13.50 3.00
193 A15 50c claret 4.50 .50
194 A15 75c olive brown 35.00 *40.00*
Nos. 184-194 (11) 60.80 51.35

Catalogue values for unused stamps in this section, from this point to the end of the section, are for Never Hinged items.

"CENTS" without Serifs — A16

Dhow — A17

Dhow — A18

1936 *Perf. 14*

201 A16 5c deep green .25 .25
202 A16 10c black .25 .25
203 A16 15c carmine .30 1.25
204 A16 20c brown org .25 .25
205 A16 25c violet, *yel* .25 .25
206 A16 30c ultra .25 .25
207 A16 40c black brown .25 .25
208 A16 50c claret .50 .25
209 A17 1sh yellow grn .75 .25
210 A17 2sh dark violet 3.50 2.50
211 A17 5sh red 24.00 8.00
212 A17 7.50sh blue 40.00 37.50
213 A18 10sh brn & grn 40.00 32.50
Nos. 201-213 (13) 110.55 83.75

For overprints see Nos. 222-223.

A19

1936, Dec. 9

214 A19 10c olive grn & blk 4.00 .35
215 A19 20c red violet & blk 6.00 2.75
216 A19 30c deep ultra & blk 16.00 1.00
217 A19 50c red orange & blk 17.50 6.75
Nos. 214-217 (4) 43.50 10.85
Set, hinged 25.00

Reign of Sultan Khalifa bin Harub, 25th anniv.

A20

Dhow & Map Showing Zanzibar & Muscat.

Perf. 14

1944, Nov. 20 Engr. Wmk. 4

218 A20 10c violet blue 1.00 *5.25*
219 A20 20c brown orange 1.50 *3.75*
220 A20 50c Prus green 1.50 .40
221 A20 1sh dull purple 1.50 1.50
Nos. 218-221 (4) 5.50 10.90

200th anniv. of the Al Busaid Dynasty.

Nos. 202 and 206 Overprinted in Red

1946, Nov. 11

222 A16 10c black .25 .50
223 A16 30c ultra .40 .50

Victory of the Allied Nations in WW II.

Common Design Types pictured following the introduction.

Silver Wedding Issue
Common Design Types

1949, Jan. 10 Photo. *Perf. 14x14½*

224 CD304 20c orange .60 1.50

Engraved; Name Typographed
Perf. 11½x11

225 CD305 10sh light brown 29.00 36.50

UPU Issue
Common Design Types
Engr.; Name Typo. on 30c, 50c
Perf. 13½, 11x11½

1949, Oct. 10 Wmk. 4

226 CD306 20c red orange .45 *3.75*
227 CD307 30c indigo 2.50 2.00
228 CD308 50c red lilac 1.25 *3.25*
229 CD309 1sh blue green 1.25 *4.50*
Nos. 226-229 (4) 5.45 13.50

Sultan Khalifa bin Harub — A21

Seyyid Khalifa Schools A22

Perf. 12x12½, 13x12½

1952, Aug. 26 Engr.

230 A21 5c black .25 .25
231 A21 10c red orange .25 .25
232 A21 15c green 2.00 *3.00*
233 A21 20c carmine .75 .75
234 A21 25c plum 1.10 .25
235 A21 30c blue green 1.10 .25
236 A21 35c ultra 1.00 *5.00*
237 A21 40c chocolate 1.00 *2.00*
238 A21 50c purple 3.25 .25
239 A22 1sh choc & bl grn .75 .25
240 A22 2sh claret & ultra 3.00 *2.75*
241 A22 5sh carmine & blk 3.00 *6.50*
242 A22 7.50sh emer & gray 27.50 *27.50*
243 A22 10sh gray blk & rose red 12.00 *15.00*
Nos. 230-243 (14) 56.95 64.00

POSTAGE DUE STAMPS

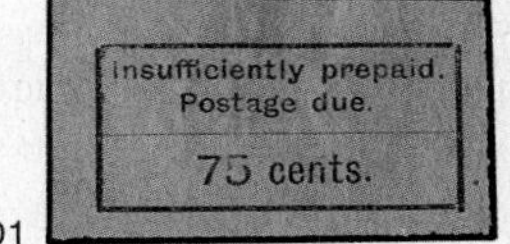

D1

Rouletted 10

1931 Typeset Unwmk.

Thin Paper

Without Gum

J1	D1	1c blk, *orange*	12.50	*150.00*
		On cover		1,250.
J2	D1	2c blk, *orange*	5.50	*80.00*
		On cover		600.00
J3	D1	3c blk, *orange*	5.75	*65.00*
		On cover		600.00
J3A	D1	6c blk, *orange*		*8,000.*
		On cover		*10,000.*
J4	D1	9c blk, *orange*	3.25	*40.00*
		On cover		500.00
J4A	D1	12c blk, *orange*	*15,000.*	*12,000.*
		On cover		*12,500.*
J4B	D1	12c blk, *green*	*1,600.*	*675.00*
		On cover		6,000.
J5	D1	15c blk, *orange*	3.25	*42.50*
		On cover		500.00
J6	D1	18c blk, *orange*	27.50	*90.00*
		On cover		750.00
a.		18c black, *salmon*	5.50	*75.00*
		On cover		600.00
J7	D1	20c blk, *orange*	4.50	*80.00*
		On cover		600.00
J8	D1	21c blk, *orange*	4.00	*50.00*
		On cover		500.00
J8A	D1	25c blk, *orange*	*19,000.*	*17,000.*
		On cover		—
J8B	D1	25c blk, *magenta*	*3,250.*	*1,500.*
		On cover		*9,000.*
J9	D1	31c blk, *orange*	11.00	*115.00*
		On cover		2,500.
J10	D1	50c blk, *orange*	24.00	*250.00*
		On cover		5,000.
J11	D1	75c blk, *orange*	80.00	*600.00*
		On cover		6,000.

"CENT.S" for "CENTS."

J3c	3c	150.00	450.00
J3Ac	6c	—	25,000.
J4c	9c	25.00	160.00
J4Ac	12c		21,000.
J4Bc	12c	4,000;	1,750.
J5c	15c	25.00	180.00
J6c	18c	50.00	250.00
J6ac	18c	80.00	350.00
J7c	20c	50.00	350.00
J8c	21c	42.50	225.00
J9c	31c	70.00	1,200.
J10c	50c	120.00	1,700.
J11c	75c	300.00	

The variety "cent.s" occurs once on each sheet of Nos. J3 to J11 inclusive.

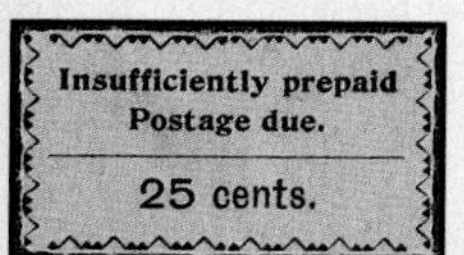

D2

1931-33 *Rouletted 5*

Thick Paper

J12	D2	2c blk, *salmon*	27.50	*40.00*
		On cover		650.00
J13	D2	3c blk, *rose*	4.00	*67.50*
		On cover		1,000.
J14	D2	6c blk, *yellow*	4.00	*40.00*
		On cover		450.00
J15	D2	12c blk, *blue*	5.00	*32.50*
		On cover		450.00
J16	D2	25c blk, *pink*	11.00	*145.00*
		On cover		1,000.
J17	D2	25c blk, *dull violet*	27.50	*87.50*
		On cover		850.00
		Nos. J12-J17 (6)	79.00	412.50

Catalogue values for unused stamps in this section, from this point to the end of the section, are for Never Hinged items.

D3

1936 Typo. Wmk. 4 *Perf. 14*

J18	D3	5c violet	8.50	*14.00*
		On cover		275.00
J19	D3	10c carmine	7.25	*3.25*
		On cover		275.00
J20	D3	20c green	2.50	*6.75*
		On cover		325.00
J21	D3	30c brown	18.00	*24.00*
		On cover		500.00
J22	D3	40c ultra	10.00	*30.00*
		On cover		500.00
J23	D3	1sh gray	15.50	*37.50*
		On cover		1,250.
		Nos. J18-J23 (6)	61.75	*115.50*

Chalky paper was introduced in 1956 for the 5c, 30c, 40c, 1sh, and in 1962 for the 10c, 20c. Value for set of 6, unused $3.25, used $110.

See note after No. 300a in Scott Standard catalogue, Vol. 6.

ZULULAND

'zü-ˌlü-ˌland

LOCATION — Northeastern part of Natal, South Africa
GOVT. — British Colony
AREA — 10,427 sq. mi.
POP. — 230,000 (estimated 1900)
CAPITAL — Eshowe

12 Pence = 1 Shilling
20 Shillings = 1 Pound

Stamps of Great Britain Overprinted

1888-93 Wmk. 30 *Perf. 14*

1	A54	½p vermilion	8.25	3.00
2	A40	1p violet	30.00	6.75
3	A56	2p green & red	30.00	50.00
4	A57	2½p vio, *bl* ('91)	42.50	22.50
5	A58	3p violet, *yel*	32.50	25.00
6	A59	4p green & brn	60.00	75.00
7	A61	5p lil & bl ('93)	100.00	*150.00*
8	A62	6p vio, *rose*	24.00	20.00
9	A63	9p blue & lil ('92)	120.00	*130.00*
10	A65	1sh green ('92)	150.00	*170.00*

Wmk. 31

11	A51	5sh rose ('92)	700.00	*800.00*
		Nos. 1-10 (10)	597.25	652.25
		Set, ovptd. "SPECIMEN"	625.00	

Dangerous forgeries exist.

Natal No. 66 Overprinted

1888-94 Wmk. 2

12	A14	½p green, no period	30.00	*52.50*
a.		Period after "Zululand"	62.50	*95.00*
b.		As "a," double overprint	1,450.	1,600.
d.		As "a," pair, one without ovpt.	*7,500.*	

The varieties formerly listed as Nos. 12c and 12e, No. 12a with inverted overprint and No. 12 with double overprint, are now considered to be forgeries.

Natal No. 71 Ovptd. Like Nos. 1-11

13	A11	6p violet ('94)	70.00	62.50

A1

1891

14	A1	1p lilac	4.50	3.50
		Overprinted "SPECIMEN"	60.00	

By proclamation of the Governor of Zululand, dated June 27th, 1891, No. 14 was declared to be a postage stamp.

A2

1894-96 Typo.

15	A2	½p lilac & grn	7.75	7.25
16	A2	1p lilac & rose	6.75	3.00
17	A2	2½p lilac & blue	16.00	9.75
18	A2	3p lilac & brn	10.00	4.00
19	A2	6p lilac & blk	22.50	*25.00*
20	A2	1sh green	50.00	45.00
21	A2	2sh6p grn & blk ('96)	90.00	*110.00*
22	A2	4sh grn & car rose	150.00	*225.00*
23	A2	£1 violet, *red*	600.00	*650.00*
24	A2	£5 vio & blk, *red*	5,750.	*1,900.*
		Overprinted "SPECIMEN"	450.00	
		Nos. 15-23 (9)	953.00	1,079.
		Nos. 15-23 ovptd. "SPECIMEN"	475.00	

Numerals of Nos. 19-24 are in color on plain tablet. Dangerous forgeries of No. 24 exist.

Purple or violet cancellations are not necessarily revenue cancels. 14 of the 17 post offices and agencies used violet as well as black postal cancellations.

Zululand was annexed to Natal in Dec. 1897 and separate stamps were discontinued June 30, 1898.

Sign-up now to get weekly email exclusive online deals and the latest product updates. Visit AmosAdvantage.com/eNewsletters and register today.

PRE-CUT SINGLE MOUNTS

ITEM	W x H (mm)	DESCRIPTION	MOUNTS	RETAIL	AA*
901	40 x 25	U.S. Standard Comm. Hor. Water Activated	40	$3.50	**$2.39**
902	25 x 40	U.S. Standard Comm. Vert. Water Activated	40	$3.50	**$2.39**
903	25 x 22	U.S. Regular Issue – Hor. Water Activated	40	$3.50	**$2.39**
904	22 x 25	U.S. Regular Issue – Vert. Water Activated	40	$3.50	**$2.39**
905	41 x 31	U.S. Semi-Jumbo – Horizontal	40	$3.50	**$2.39**
906	31 x 41	U.S. Semi-Jumbo – Vertical	40	$3.50	**$2.39**
907	50 x 31	U.S. Jumbo – Horizontal	40	$3.50	**$2.39**
908	31 x 50	U.S. Jumbo – Vertical	40	$3.50	**$2.39**
909	25 x 27	U.S. Famous Americans/Champions Of Liberty	40	$3.50	**$2.39**
910	33 x 27	United Nations	40	$3.50	**$2.39**
911	40 x 27	United Nations	40	$3.50	**$2.39**
976	67 x 25	Plate Number Coils, Strips of Three	40	$6.25	**$3.99**
984	67 x 34	Pacific '97 Triangle	10	$3.50	**$2.39**
985	111 x 25	Plate Number Coils, Strips of Five	25	$6.25	**$3.99**
986	51 x 36	U.S. Hunting Permit/Express Mail	40	$6.25	**$3.99**
1045	40 x 26	U.S. Standard Comm. Hor. Self-Adhesive	40	$3.50	**$2.39**
1046	25 x 41	U.S. Standard Comm. Vert. Self-Adhesive	40	$3.50	**$2.39**
1047	22 x 26	U.S. Definitives Vert. Self Adhesive	40	$3.50	**$2.39**
966	Value Pack	(Assortment pre-cut sizes)	320	$23.25	**$15.25**
975	Best Pack	(Assortment pre-cut sizes - Black Only)	160	$14.75	**$9.99**

PRE-CUT PLATE BLOCK, FDC, POSTAL CARD MOUNTS

ITEM	W x H (mm)	DESCRIPTION	MOUNTS	RETAIL	AA*
912	57 x 55	Regular Issue Plate Block	25	$6.25	**$3.99**
913	73 x 63	Champions of Liberty	25	$6.25	**$3.99**
914	106 x 55	Rotary Press Standard Commemorative	20	$6.25	**$3.99**
915	105 x 57	Giori Press Standard Commemorative	20	$6.25	**$3.99**
916	127 x 70	Giori Press Jumbo Commemorative	10	$6.25	**$3.99**
917	165 x 94	First Day Cover	10	$6.25	**$3.99**
918	140 x 90	Postal Card Size/Submarine Booklet Pane	10	$6.25	**$3.99**
1048	152 x 107	Large Postal Cards	8	$10.25	**$6.99**

STRIPS 215MM LONG

ITEM	W x H (mm)	DESCRIPTION	MOUNTS	RETAIL	AA*
919	20	U.S. 19th Century, Horizontal Coil	22	$7.99	**$5.25**
920	22	U.S. Early Air Mail	22	$7.99	**$5.25**
921	24	U.S., Vertical Coils, Christmas (#2400, #2428 etc.)	22	$7.99	**$5.25**
922	25	U.S. Commemorative and Regular	22	$7.99	**$5.25**
1049	26	U.S. Commemorative and Regular	22	$7.99	**$5.25**
923	27	U.S. Famous Americans	22	$7.99	**$5.25**
924	28	U.S. 19th Century, Liechtenstein	22	$7.99	**$5.25**
1050	29	Virginia Dare, British Empire, etc.	22	$7.99	**$5.25**
925	30	U.S. 19th Century; Jamestown, etc; Foreign	22	$7.99	**$5.25**
926	31	U.S. Horizontal Jumbo and Semi-Jumbo	22	$7.99	**$5.25**
927	33	U.S. Stampin' Future, UN	22	$7.99	**$5.25**
928	36	U.S. Hunting Permit, Canada	15	$7.99	**$5.25**
1051	37	U.S., British Colonies	22	$7.99	**$5.25**
929	39	U.S. Early 20th Century	15	$7.99	**$5.25**
930	41	U.S. Vert. Semi-Jumbo ('77 Lafayette, Pottery, etc.)	15	$7.99	**$5.25**
931		Multiple Assortment: One strip of each size 22-41 above (SMKB) (2 x 25mm strips)	12	$7.99	**$5.25**
1052	42	U.S., British Colonies	22	$7.99	**$5.25**
1053	43	U.S., British Colonies	22	$7.99	**$5.25**
932	44	U.S. Vertical Coil Pair Garden Flowers Booklet Pane	15	$7.99	**$5.25**
933	48	U.S. Farley, Gutter Pair	15	$7.99	**$5.25**
934	50	U.S. Jumbo (Lyndon Johnson, '74 U.P.U., etc.)	15	$7.99	**$5.25**
935	52	U.S. Standard Commemorative Block (Butterflies)	15	$7.99	**$5.25**
936	55	U.S. Standard Plate Block - normal margins	15	$7.99	**$5.25**
937	57	U.S. Standard Plate Block - wider margins	15	$7.99	**$5.25**
938	61	U.S. Blocks, Israel Tabs, '99 Christmas Madonna Pane	15	$7.99	**$5.25**

STRIPS 240MM LONG

ITEM	W x H (mm)	DESCRIPTION	MOUNTS	RETAIL	AA*
939	63	U.S. Jumbo Commemorative Horizontal Block	10	$9.25	**$5.99**
940	66	U.S. CIPEX Souvenir Sheet, Self-Adhesive Booklet Pane (#2803a, 3012a)	10	$9.25	**$5.99**
941	68	U.S. ATM Booklet Pane, Farley Gutter Pair & Souvenir Sheet	10	$9.25	**$5.99**
942	74	U.S. TIPEX Souvenir Sheet	10	$9.25	**$5.99**
943	80	U.S. Standard Commemorative Vertical Block	10	$9.25	**$5.99**
944	82	U.S. Blocks of Four, U.N. Chagall	10	$9.25	**$5.99**
945	84	Israel Tab Block, Mars Pathfinder Sheetlet	10	$9.25	**$5.99**
946	89	Submarine Booklet, Souvenir Sheet World Cup, Rockwell	10	$9.25	**$5.99**
947	100	U.S. '74 U.P.U. Block, U.N. Margin Inscribed Block	7	$9.25	**$5.99**
948	120	Various Souvenir Sheets and Blocks	7	$9.25	**$5.99**

STRIPS 265MM LONG

ITEM	W x H (mm)	DESCRIPTION	MOUNTS	RETAIL	AA*
1035	25	U.S. Coils Strips of 11	12	$9.25	**$5.99**
949	40	U.S. Postal People Standard Standard & Semi-Jumbo Commemorative Strip	10	$9.25	**$5.99**
981	44	U.S. Long self-adhesive booklet panes	10	$9.25	**$5.99**
1030	45	Various (Canada Scott #1725-1734)	10	$9.25	**$5.99**
1036	46	U.S. Long self adhesive booklet panes of 15	10	$9.25	**$5.99**
950	55	U.S. Regular Plate Block or Strip of 20	10	$9.25	**$5.99**
951	59	U.S. Double Issue Strip	10	$9.25	**$5.99**
952	70	U.S. Jumbo Commemorative Plate Block	10	$12.50	**$8.50**
1031	72	Various (Canada Scott #1305a-1804a)	10	$12.50	**$8.50**
1032	75	Plate Blocks: Lance Armstrong, Prehistoric Animals, etc.	10	$12.50	**$8.50**
1060	76	U.S. 1994 Stamp Printing Centennial Souvenir Sheet, etc.	10	$12.50	**$8.50**
953	91	U.S. Self-Adhesive Booklet Pane '98 Wreath, '95 Santa	10	$12.50	**$8.50**
1033	95	Mini-Sheet Plate Blocks w/top header	10	$12.50	**$8.50**
1061	96	U.S., Foreign	10	$12.50	**$8.50**
954	105	U.S. Standard Semi-Jumbo Commemorative Plate Number Strip	10	$12.50	**$8.50**
955	107	Same as above-wide margin	10	$12.50	**$8.50**
956	111	U.S. Gravure-Intaglio Plate Number Strip	10	$14.75	**$9.99**
1062	115	Foreign Small Sheets	10	$17.50	**$11.99**
957	127	U.S. 2000 Space S/S, World War II S/S	10	$17.50	**$11.99**
1063	131	Looney Tunes sheets; World War II Souvenir Sheet Plate Block	10	$17.50	**$11.99**
1064	135	U.S., Japan Gifts of Friendship sheet	10	$17.50	**$11.99**
958	137	Great Britain Coronation	10	$17.50	**$11.99**
1065	139	Sheets: Soda Fountain, Lady Bird Johnson, Earthscapes, etc.	10	$17.50	**$11.99**
1066	143	Sheets: Merchant Marine Ships, 2013 Hanukkah, etc.	10	$17.50	**$11.99**
1067	147	Sheets: Pickup Trucks, Animal Rescue, Washington D.C., etc.	10	$17.50	**$11.99**
1068	151	Sheets: Go Green, Bicycling, Happy New Year, Ben Franklin, etc.	10	$17.50	**$11.99**

STRIPS 265MM LONG, continued

ITEM	W x H (mm)	DESCRIPTION	MOUNTS	RETAIL	AA*
959	158	American Glass, U.S. Football Coaches Sheets	10	$17.99	**$12.50**
1069	163	Sheets: Modern Architecture, UN Human Rights, etc.	5	$12.50	**$8.50**
1070	167	Sheets: John F. Kennedy, Classics Forever, Made in America, etc.	5	$12.50	**$8.50**
1071	171	Film Directors, Foreign Souvenir Sheets	5	$12.50	**$8.50**
960	175	Large Block, Souvenir Sheet	5	$12.50	**$8.50**
1072	181	Sheets: Jimi Hendrix, Johnny Cash, American Photography, etc.	5	$17.50	**$11.99**
1073	185	Frank Sinatra, Ronald Reagan, Arthur Ashe, Creast Cancer, etc.	5	$17.50	**$11.99**
1074	188	Sheets: Yoda, 9/11 Heroes, Andy Warhol, Frida Kahlo, etc	5	$17.50	**$11.99**
1075	198	Sheets: Modern American Art, Super Heroes, Baseball Sluggers, etc.	5	$17.50	**$11.99**
1076	215	Celebrity Chefs sheets; Foreign sheets	5	$17.50	**$11.99**
961	231	U.S. Full Post Office Pane Regular and Commemorative	5	$17.99	**$12.50**

SOUVENIR SHEETS/SMALL PANES

ITEM	W x H (mm)	DESCRIPTION	MOUNTS	RETAIL	AA*
962	204 x 153	New Year 2000, U.S. Bicentennial S/S	4	$9.25	**$5.99**
963	187 x 144	55¢ Victorian Love Pane, U.N. Flag Sheet	9	$15.50	**$10.25**
964	160 x 200	U.N., Israel Sheet	10	$15.50	**$10.25**
965	120 x 207	U.S. AMERIPEX Presidential Sheet	4	$6.25	**$3.99**
968	229 x 131	World War II S/S Plate Block Only	5	$9.25	**$5.99**
970	111 x 91	Columbian Souvenir Sheet	6	$6.25	**$4.75**
972	148 x 196	Apollo Moon Landing/Carnivorous Plants	4	$7.99	**$5.25**
989	129 x 122	U.S. Definitive Sheet: Harte, Hopkins, etc.	8	$10.25	**$6.99**
990	189 x 151	Chinese New Year	5	$10.25	**$6.99**
991	150 x 185	Breast Cancer/Fermi/Soccer/'96 Folk Heroes	5	$10.25	**$6.99**
992	198 x 151	Cherokee Strip Sheet	5	$10.25	**$6.99**
993	185 x 151	Bernstein/NATO/Irish/Lunt/Gold Rush Sheets	5	$10.25	**$6.99**
994	198 x 187	Postal Museum	4	$10.25	**$6.99**
995	156 x 187	Sign Language/Statehood	5	$10.25	**$6.99**
996	188 x 197	Illustrators, '98 Music: Folk, Gospel; Country/Western	4	$10.25	**$6.99**
997	151 x 192	Olympic	5	$10.25	**$6.99**
998	174 x 185	Buffalo Soldiers	5	$10.25	**$6.99**
999	130 x 198	Silent Screen Stars	5	$10.25	**$6.99**
1000	190 x 199	Stars Stripes/Baseball/Insects & Spiders/Legends West/ Aircraft, Comics, '96 Olympics, Civil War	4	$10.25	**$6.99**
1001	178 x 181	Cranes	4	$10.25	**$6.99**
1002	183 x 212	Wonders of the Sea, We the People	3	$10.25	**$6.99**
1003	156 x 264	$14 Eagle	4	$10.25	**$6.99**
1004	159 x 270	$9.95 Moon Landing	4	$10.25	**$6.99**
1005	159 x 259	$2.90 Priority/$9.95 Express Mail	4	$10.25	**$6.99**
1006	223 x 187	Hubble, Hollywood Legends, O'Keefe Sheets	3	$10.25	**$6.99**
1007	185 x 181	Deep Sea Creatures, Olmsted Sheets	4	$10.25	**$6.99**
1008	152 x 228	Indian Dances/Antique Autos	5	$10.25	**$6.99**
1009	165 x 150	River Boat/Hanukkah	6	$10.25	**$6.99**
1010	275 x 200	Dinosaurs/Large Gutter Blocks	2	$10.25	**$6.99**
1011	161 x 160	Pacific '97 Triangle Mini Sheets	6	$10.25	**$6.99**
1012	174 x 130	Road Runner, Daffy, Bugs, Sylvester & Tweety	6	$10.25	**$6.99**
1013	196 x 158	Football Coaches	4	$10.25	**$6.99**
1014	184 x 184	American Dolls, Flowering Trees Sheets	4	$10.25	**$6.99**
1015	186 x 230	Classic Movie Monsters	3	$10.25	**$6.99**
1016	187 x 160	Trans-Mississippi Sheet	4	$10.25	**$6.99**
1017	192 x 230	Celebrate The Century	3	$10.25	**$6.99**
1018	156 x 204	Space Discovery	5	$10.25	**$6.99**
1019	182 x 209	American Ballet	5	$10.25	**$6.99**
1020	139 x 151	Christmas Wreaths	5	$10.25	**$6.99**
1021	129 x 126	Justin Morrill, Henry Luce	8	$10.25	**$6.99**
1022	184 x 165	Baseball Fields, Bright Eyes	4	$10.25	**$6.99**
1023	185 x 172	Shuttle Landing Pan Am Invert Sheets	4	$10.25	**$6.99**
1024	172 x 233	Sonoran Desert	3	$10.25	**$6.99**
1025	150 x 166	Prostate Cancer	5	$10.25	**$6.99**
1026	201 x 176	Famous Trains	4	$10.25	**$6.99**
1027	176 x 124	Canada - Historic Vehicles	5	$10.25	**$6.99**
1028	245 x 114	Canada - Provincial Leaders	5	$10.25	**$6.99**
1029	177 x 133	Canada - Year of the Family	5	$10.25	**$6.99**
1034	181 x 213	Arctic Animals	3	$10.25	**$6.99**
1037	179 x 242	Louise Nevelson	3	$10.25	**$6.99**
1038	179 x 217	Library Of Congress	3	$10.25	**$6.99**
1039	182 x 232	Youth Team Sports	3	$10.25	**$6.99**
1040	183 x 216	Lucille Ball Scott #3523	3	$10.25	**$6.99**
1041	182 x 244	American Photographers	3	$10.25	**$6.99**
1042	185 x 255	Andy Warhol	3	$10.25	**$6.99**
1043	165 x 190	American Film Making	4	$10.25	**$6.99**
1044	28 x 290	American Eagle PNC Strips of 11	12	$9.25	**$5.99**

Available in clear or black backgrounds. Please specify color choice when ordering.

2016 NATIONAL, MINUTEMAN OR ALL-AMERICAN SUPPLEMENT MOUNT PACKS

ITEM	*DESCRIPTION*	*RETAIL*	*AA**
2016 B	2016 National, Minuteman or All-American Supplement Mount Pack - BLACK	$49.99	**$39.99**
2016 C	2016 National, Minuteman or All-American Supplement Mount Pack - CLEAR	$49.99	**$39.99**

Visit AmosAdvantage.com

Call 1-800-572-6885

Outside U.S. & Canada 937-498-0800

Mail to: P.O. Box 4129, Sidney OH 45365

ORDERING INFORMATION: *AA prices apply to paid subscribers of Amos Media titles, or orders placed online. Prices, terms and product availability subject to change. Taxes will apply in CA, OH, & IL. Shipping and handling rates will apply.
SHIPPING & HANDLING: United States: Order total $0-$10.00 charged $3.99 shipping; Order total $10.01-$79.99 charged $7.99 shipping; Order total $80.00 or more charged 10% of order total for shipping. Maximum Freight Charge $45.00. **Canada:** 20% of order total. Minimum charge $19.99; maximum charge $200.00. **Foreign:** Orders are shipped via FedEx Int'l. or USPS and billed actual freight.

AMOS ADVANTAGE

Illustrated Identifier

This section pictures stamps or parts of stamp designs that will help identify postage stamps that do not have English words on them.

Many of the symbols that identify stamps of countries are shown here as well as typical examples of their stamps.

See the Index and Identifier in this catalogue for stamps with inscriptions such as "sen," "posta," "Baja Porto," "Helvetia," "K.S.A.", etc.

The 190-page *Linn's Stamp Identifier* includes more than 2,000 inscriptions and more than 500 large stamp illustrations.

The book is available from Linn's Stamp News, P.O. Box 4129, Sidney, OH 45365-4129.

1. HEADS, PICTURES AND NUMERALS

GREAT BRITAIN

Great Britain stamps never show the country name, but, except for postage dues, show a picture of the reigning monarch.

Victoria

Edward VII George V Edward VIII

George VI

Some George VI stamps are surcharged in annas, new paisa or rupees. These are listed under Oman.

VICTORIA

Queen Victoria

INDIA

Other stamps of India show this portrait of Queen Victoria and the words "Service" and "Annas."

AUSTRIA

YUGOSLAVIA

(Also BOSNIA & HERZEGOVINA if imperf.)

BOSNIA & HERZEGOVINA

Denominations also appear in top corners instead of bottom corners.

HUNGARY

Another stamp has posthorn facing left.

BRAZIL

AUSTRALIA

Kangaroo and Emu

SWITZERLAND

2. ORIENTAL INSCRIPTIONS

CHINA

Any stamp with this one character is from China (Imperial, Republic or People's Republic).

This character appears in a four-character overprint on stamps of Manchukuo. These stamps are local provisionals, which are unlisted. Other overprinted Manchukuo stamps show this character but have more than four characters in the overprints. These are listed in People's Republic of China.

Some Chinese stamps show the Sun.

Most stamps of Republic of China show this series of characters.

Chinese stamps without China character

REPUBLIC OF CHINA

MANCHUKUO

Temple

Emperor Pu-Yi

The first 3 characters are common to many Manchukuo stamps.

The last 3 characters are common to other Manchukuo stamps.

Orchid Crest

Manchukuo stamp without these elements

JAPAN

Chrysanthemum Crest

Country Name

Japanese stamps without these elements

The number of characters in the center and the design of dragons on the sides will vary.

KOREA

Yin Yang appears on some stamps.

THAILAND

Country Name

King Chulalongkorn

King Prajadhipok and Chao P'ya Chakri

3. CENTRAL AND EASTERN ASIAN INSCRIPTIONS

INDIA - FEUDATORY STATES

Alwar

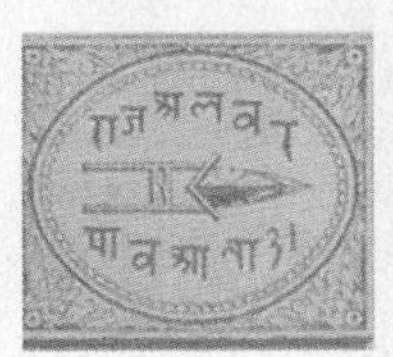

Bhor

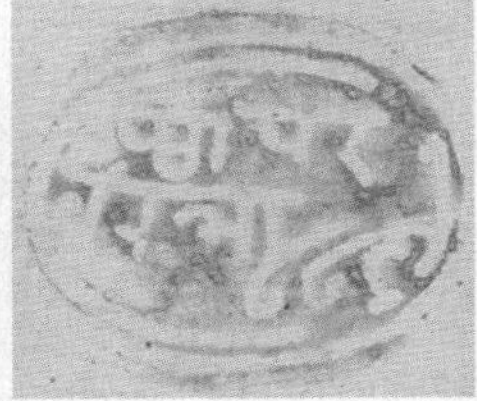

Bundi

Similar stamps come with different designs in corners and differently drawn daggers (at center of circle).

Dhar

Faridkot

Hyderabad

Similar stamps exist with straight line frame around stamp, and also with different central design, which is inscribed "Postage" or "Post & Receipt."

Hyderabad

Indore

Jammu & Kashmir

Text and thickness of ovals vary. Some stamps have flower devices in corners.

Jhalawar

A similar stamp has the central figure in an oval.

Kotah

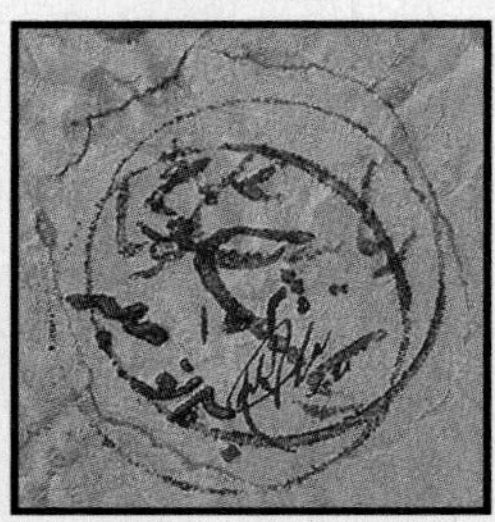

Nandgaon

Nowanuggur

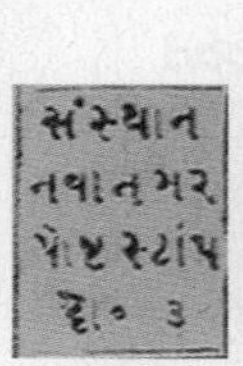

Poonch

Similar stamps exist in various sizes.

Rajpeepla

Soruth

Tonk

NEPAL

Similar stamps are smaller, have squares in upper corners and have five or nine characters in central bottom panel.

TANNU TUVA

GEORGIA

This inscription is found on other pictorial stamps.

ARMENIA

The four characters are found somewhere on pictorial stamps. On some stamps, only the middle two are found.

4. AFRICAN INSCRIPTIONS

ETHIOPIA

5. ARABIC INSCRIPTIONS

AFGHANISTAN

Many early Afghanistan stamps show Tiger's head. Many of these have ornaments protruding from outer ring; others show inscriptions in black.

Arabic Script

Mosque Gate & Crossed Cannons
The four characters are found somewhere on pictorial stamps. On some stamps only the middle two are found.

EGYPT

IRAN

Country Name

Royal Crown

SAUDI ARABIA

Tughra (Central design)

THRACE

YEMEN

TURKEY

Star & Crescent is a device found on many Turkish stamps, but is also found on stamps from other Arabic areas (see Pakistan-Bahawalpur).

Tughra. Similar tughras can be found on stamps of Turkey in Asia, Afghanistan and Saudi Arabia.

Mohammed V

Mustafa Kemal

Plane, Star and Crescent

TURKEY IN ASIA

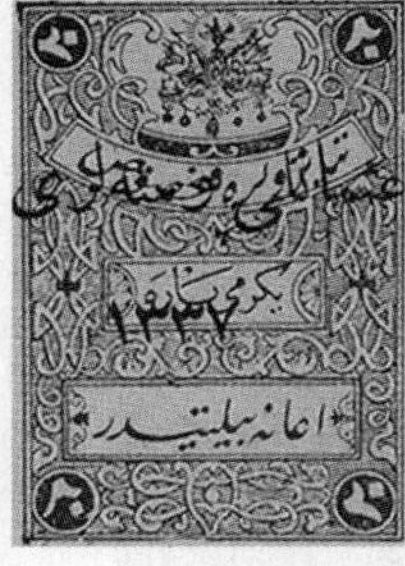
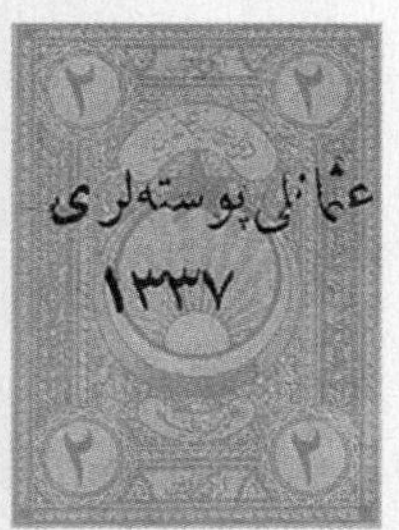
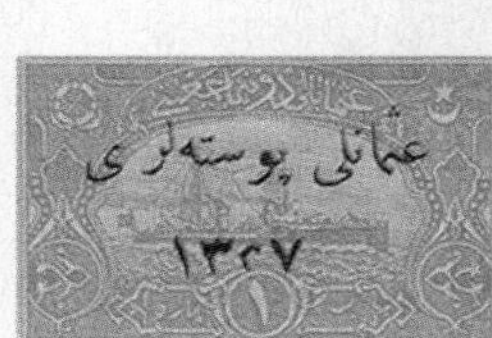

Other Turkey in Asia pictorials show star & crescent.
Other stamps show tughra shown under Turkey.

6. GREEK INSCRIPTIONS

GREECE

Country Name in various styles
(Some Crete stamps overprinted with the Greece country name are listed in Crete.)

Lepta

ΔΡΑΧΜΗ 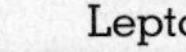 

Drachma Drachmas Lepton

Abbreviated Country Name ΕΛΛ

Other forms of country name

No country name

CRETE

Country Name

These words are on other stamps.

Grosion

Crete stamps with a surcharge that have the year "1922" are listed under Greece.

EPIRUS

Country Name

IONIAN ISLANDS

7. CYRILLIC INSCRIPTIONS

RUSSIA

Postage Stamp

Imperial Eagle

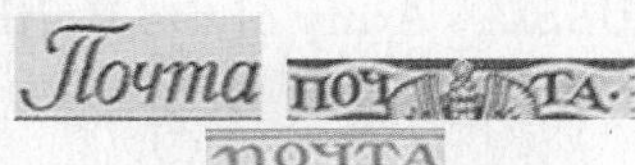

почта Почта

Postage in various styles

РОССIЯ

Abbreviation for Kopeck Abbreviation for Ruble Russia

Abbreviation for Russian Soviet Federated Socialist Republic
RSFSR stamps were overprinted (see below).

Abbreviation for Union of Soviet Socialist Republics

This item is footnoted in Latvia.

RUSSIA - Army of the North

"OKCA"

RUSSIA - Wenden

RUSSIAN OFFICES IN THE TURKISH EMPIRE

These letters appear on other stamps of the Russian offices.

The unoverprinted version of this stamp and a similar stamp were overprinted by various countries (see below).

ARMENIA

FAR EASTERN REPUBLIC

Country Name

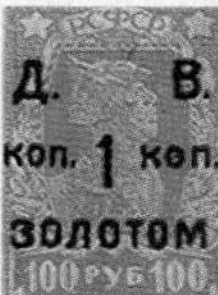

SOUTH RUSSIA

Country name

FINLAND

Circles and Dots on stamps similar to Imperial Russia issues

BATUM

Forms of country name

TRANSCAUCASIAN FEDERATED REPUBLICS

Abbreviation for country name

ROMANIA

UKRAINE

The trident appears on many stamps, usually as an overprint.

Abbreviation for Ukrainian Soviet Socialist Republic

WESTERN UKRAINE

Abbreviation for country name

AZERBAIJAN

Abbreviation for Azerbaijan Soviet Socialist Republic

MONTENEGRO

Country name in various forms

Abbreviation for country name

No country name (A similar Montenegro stamp without country name has same vignette.)

SERBIA

Country name in various forms

Abbreviation for country name

No country name

YUGOSLAVIA

Showing country name

No country name

BULGARIA

Country name Postage

Stotinka

Stotinki (plural) Abbreviation for Stotinki

Country Name in various forms and styles

No country name

Abbreviation for Lev, leva

MONGOLIA

No country name

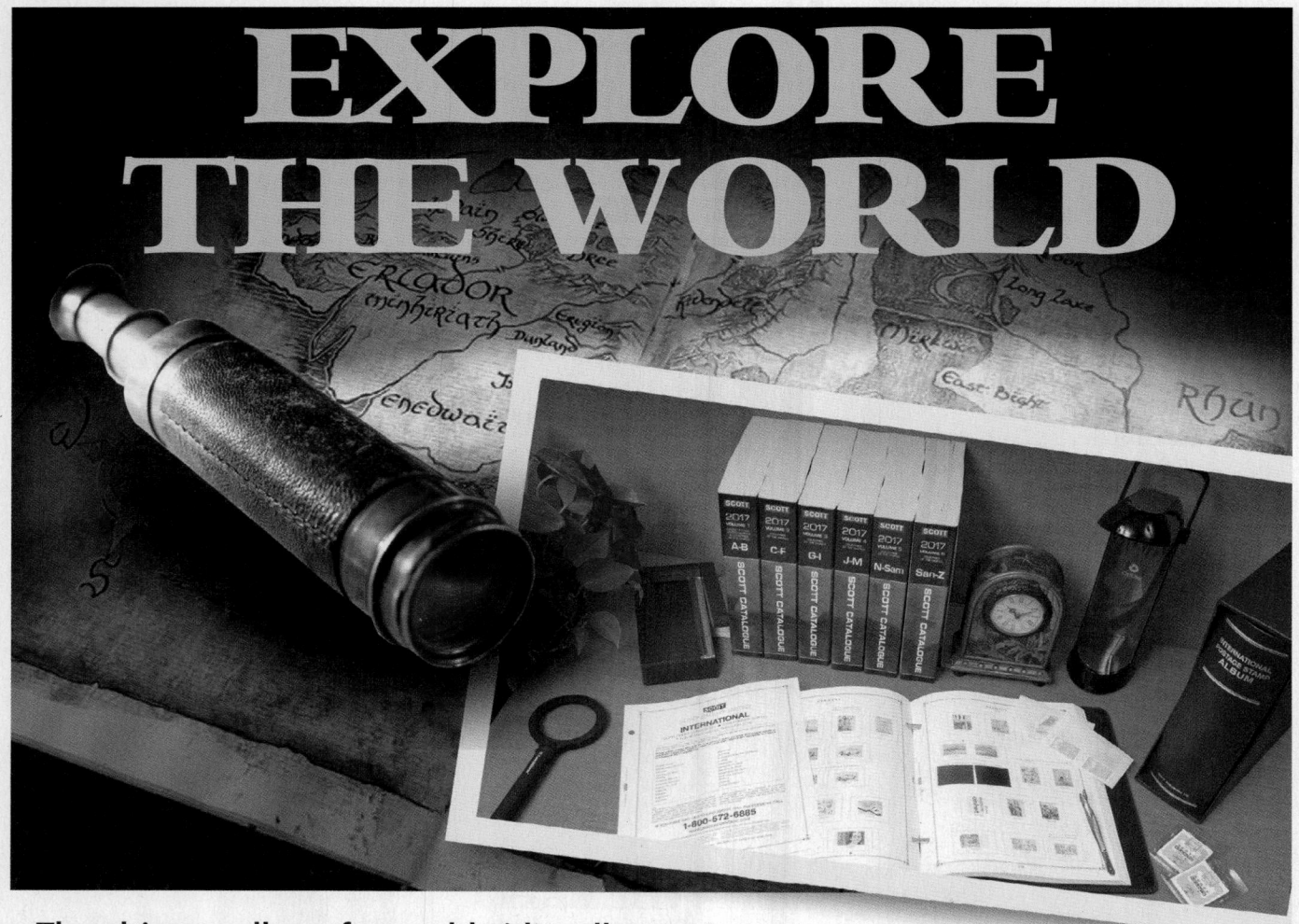

INDEX AND IDENTIFIER

Postage stamps that do not have English words on them are shown in the Illustrated Guide.

FORERUNNER USAGES
PRE-STAMP POSTAL MARKINGS

STAMPS OF PARENT STATES USED IN COLONIES AND OTHER NATIONS

Numeral Cancellations
On Stamps of Great Britain

On Stamps of Ceylon

On Stamps of Hong Kong

On Stamps of India

On Stamps of Mauritius

On Stamps of German Offices in China

On Stamps of Portugal

AUSTRIAN POST

in Bulgaria
On Stamps of Lombardy-Venetia

On Stamps of Austrian Levant

in Crete
On Stamps of Lombardy-Venetia or Austrian Turkish Offices

in Cyprus
On Stamps of Lombardy-Venetia or Austrian Turkish Offices

FRENCH IMPERIAL POST IN BULGARIA
On Stamps of France

GREAT BRITAIN CONSULAR POST IN THAILAND
On Stamps of Straits Settlements

GREEK CONSULAR POST IN EPIRUS
On Stamps of Greece

ITALIAN CONSULAR POST IN ARGENTINA
On Stamps of Italian Offices Abroad

INDEX TO ADVERTISERS 2018 CLASSIC SPECIALIZED

2018

CLASSIC SPECIALIZED DEALER DIRECTORY YELLOW PAGE LISTINGS

This section of your Scott Catalogue contains advertisements to help you conveniently find what you need, when you need it...!

Accessories

BROOKLYN GALLERY COIN & STAMP, INC.
8725 4th Ave.
Brooklyn, NY 11209
PH: 718-745-5701
FAX: 718-745-2775
info@brooklyngallery.com
www.brooklyngallery.com

Appraisals

COLONIAL STAMP COMPANY
5757 Wilshire Blvd. PH #8
Los Angeles, CA 90036
PH: 323-933-9435
FAX: 323-939-9930
Toll Free in North America
PH: 877-272-6693
FAX: 877-272-6694
info@colonialstampcompany.com
www.colonialstampcompany.com

DR. ROBERT FRIEDMAN & SONS STAMP & COIN BUYING CENTER
2029 W. 75th St.
Woodridge, IL 60517
PH: 800-588-8100
FAX: 630-985-1588
drbobstamps@comcast.net
www.drbobfriedmanstamps.com

MILLER'S STAMP COMPANY
12 Douglas Lane, Suite 11
Waterford, CT 06385
Stamps@millerstamps.com
PH: 860-908-6200

Argentina

GUILLERMO JALIL
Maipu 466,local 4
1006 Buenos Aires
Argentina
guillermo@jalilstamps.com
philatino@philatino.com
www.philatino.com
www.jalilstamps.com

Asia

THE STAMP ACT
PO Box 1136
Belmont, CA 94002
PH: 650-703-2342
PH: 650-592-3315
FAX: 650-508-8104
thestampact@sbcglobal.net

Auctions

COLONIAL STAMP COMPANY
5757 Wilshire Blvd. PH #8
Los Angeles, CA 90036
PH: 323-933-9435
FAX: 323-939-9930
Toll Free in North America
PH: 877-272-6693
FAX: 877-272-6694
info@colonialstampcompany.com
www.colonialstampcompany.com

DUTCH COUNTRY AUCTIONS
The Stamp Center
4115 Concord Pike
Wilmington, DE 19803
PH: 302-478-8740
FAX: 302-478-8779
auctions@dutchcountryauctions.com
www.dutchcountryauctions.com

Auctions

R. MARESCH & SON LTD.
5th Floor - 6075 Yonge St.
Toronto, ON M2M 3W2
CANADA
PH: 416-363-7777
FAX: 416-363-6511
www.maresch.com

Australia

COLONIAL STAMP COMPANY
5757 Wilshire Blvd. PH #8
Los Angeles, CA 90036
PH: 323-933-9435
FAX: 323-939-9930
Toll Free in North America
PH: 877-272-6693
FAX: 877-272-6694
info@colonialstampcompany.com
www.colonialstampcompany.com

Australian States

COLONIAL STAMP COMPANY
5757 Wilshire Blvd. PH #8
Los Angeles, CA 90036
PH: 323-933-9435
FAX: 323-939-9930
Toll Free in North America
PH: 877-272-6693
FAX: 877-272-6694
info@colonialstampcompany.com
www.colonialstampcompany.com

Austria

HENRY GITNER PHILATELISTS, INC.
PO Box 3077-S
Middletown, NY 10940
PH: 845-343-5151
PH: 800-947-8267
FAX: 845-343-0068
hgitner@hgitner.com
www.hgitner.com

Belgium

HENRY GITNER PHILATELISTS, INC.
PO Box 3077-S
Middletown, NY 10940
PH: 845-343-5151
PH: 800-947-8267
FAX: 845-343-0068
hgitner@hgitner.com
www.hgitner.com

Bermuda

COLONIAL STAMP COMPANY
5757 Wilshire Blvd. PH #8
Los Angeles, CA 90036
PH: 323-933-9435
FAX: 323-939-9930
Toll Free in North America
PH: 877-272-6693
FAX: 877-272-6694
info@colonialstampcompany.com
www.colonialstampcompany.com

British Commonwealth

THE BRITISH COMMONWEALTH O•F N•A•T•I•O•N•S

We are active buyers and sellers of stamps and postal history of all areas of pre-1960 British Commonwealth, including individual items, collections or estates. Want lists from all reigns are accepted with references.

"VISIT OUR BOOTH AT MOST MAJOR SHOWS"

L. W. Martin, Jr.

CROWN COLONY STAMPS

P.O. Box 1198
BELLAIRE, TEXAS 77402
PH. (713) 781-6563 • FAX (713) 789-9998
E-mail: lwm@crowncolony.com

British Asia

COLONIAL STAMP COMPANY
5757 Wilshire Blvd. PH #8
Los Angeles, CA 90036
PH: 323-933-9435
FAX: 323-939-9930
Toll Free in North America
PH: 877-272-6693
FAX: 877-272-6694
info@colonialstampcompany.com
www.colonialstampcompany.com

THE STAMP ACT
PO Box 1136
Belmont, CA 94002
PH: 650-703-2342
PH: 650-592-3315
FAX: 650-508-8104
thestampact@sbcglobal.net

British Commonwealth

ARON R. HALBERSTAM PHILATELISTS, LTD.
PO Box 150168
Van Brunt Station
Brooklyn, NY 11215-0168
PH: 718-788-3978
arh@arhstamps.com
www.arhstamps.com

COLLECTORS EXCHANGE ORLANDO STAMP SHOP
1814A Edgewater Drive
Orlando, FL 32804
PH: 407-620-0908
PH: 407-947-8603
FAX: 407-730-2131
jlatter@cfl.rr.com
www.BritishStampsAmerica.com
www.OrlandoStampShop.com

British Commonwealth

ROY'S STAMPS
PO Box 28001
600 Ontario Street
St. Catharines, ON
CANADA L2N 7P8
Phone: 905-934-8377
Email: roystamp@cogeco.ca

THE STAMP ACT
PO Box 1136
Belmont, CA 94002
PH: 650-703-2342
PH: 650-592-3315
FAX: 650-508-8104
thestampact@sbcglobal.net

Buying

DR. ROBERT FRIEDMAN & SONS STAMP & COIN BUYING CENTER
2029 W. 75th St.
Woodridge, IL 60517
PH: 800-588-8100
FAX: 630-985-1588
drbobstamps@comcast.net
www.drbobfriedmanstamps.com

Canada

CANADA STAMP FINDER
PO Box 92591
Brampton, ON L6W 4R1
PH: 514-238-5751
Toll Free in North America:
877-412-3106
FAX: 323-315-2635
canadastampfinder@gmail.com
www.canadastampfinder.com

British Commonwealth

Canada

COLONIAL STAMP COMPANY
5757 Wilshire Blvd. PH #8
Los Angeles, CA 90036
PH: 323-933-9435
FAX: 323-939-9930
Toll Free in North America
PH: 877-272-6693
FAX: 877-272-6694
info@colonialstampcompany.com
www.colonialstampcompany.com

ROY'S STAMPS
PO Box 28001
600 Ontario Street
St. Catharines, ON
CANADA L2N 7P8
Phone: 905-934-8377
Email: roystamp@cogeco.ca

Cape of Good Hope

COLONIAL STAMP COMPANY
5757 Wilshire Blvd. PH #8
Los Angeles, CA 90036
PH: 323-933-9435
FAX: 323-939-9930
Toll Free in North America
PH: 877-272-6693
FAX: 877-272-6694
info@colonialstampcompany.com
www.colonialstampcompany.com

Collections

DR. ROBERT FRIEDMAN & SONS STAMP & COIN BUYING CENTER
2029 W. 75th St.
Woodridge, IL 60517
PH: 800-588-8100
FAX: 630-985-1588
drbobstamps@comcast.net
www.drbobfriedmanstamps.com

Ducks

MICHAEL JAFFE
PO Box 61484
Vancouver, WA 98666
PH: 360-695-6161
PH: 800-782-6770
FAX: 360-695-1616
mjaffe@brookmanstamps.com
www.brookmanstamps.com

Falkland Islands

COLONIAL STAMP COMPANY
5757 Wilshire Blvd. PH #8
Los Angeles, CA 90036
PH: 323-933-9435
FAX: 323-939-9930
Toll Free in North America
PH: 877-272-6693
FAX: 877-272-6694
info@colonialstampcompany.com
www.colonialstampcompany.com

France

HENRY GITNER PHILATELISTS, INC.
PO Box 3077-S
Middletown, NY 10940
PH: 845-343-5151
PH: 800-947-8267
FAX: 845-343-0068
hgitner@hgitner.com
www.hgitner.com

German Colonies

COLONIAL STAMP COMPANY
5757 Wilshire Blvd. PH #8
Los Angeles, CA 90036
PH: 323-933-9435
FAX: 323-939-9930
Toll Free in North America
PH: 877-272-6693
FAX: 877-272-6694
info@colonialstampcompany.com
www.colonialstampcompany.com

German States

COLONIAL STAMP COMPANY
5757 Wilshire Blvd. PH #8
Los Angeles, CA 90036
PH: 323-933-9435
FAX: 323-939-9930
Toll Free in North America
PH: 877-272-6693
FAX: 877-272-6694
info@colonialstampcompany.com
www.colonialstampcompany.com

Germany

HENRY GITNER PHILATELISTS, INC.
PO Box 3077-S
Middletown, NY 10940
PH: 845-343-5151
PH: 800-947-8267
FAX: 845-343-0068
hgitner@hgitner.com
www.hgitner.com

Great Britain

COLONIAL STAMP COMPANY
5757 Wilshire Blvd. PH #8
Los Angeles, CA 90036
PH: 323-933-9435
FAX: 323-939-9930
Toll Free in North America
PH: 877-272-6693
FAX: 877-272-6694
info@colonialstampcompany.com
www.colonialstampcompany.com

Hong Kong

COLONIAL STAMP COMPANY
5757 Wilshire Blvd. PH #8
Los Angeles, CA 90036
PH: 323-933-9435
FAX: 323-939-9930
Toll Free in North America
PH: 877-272-6693
FAX: 877-272-6694
info@colonialstampcompany.com
www.colonialstampcompany.com

THE STAMP ACT
PO Box 1136
Belmont, CA 94002
PH: 650-703-2342
PH: 650-592-3315
FAX: 650-508-8104
thestampact@sbcglobal.net

Italy

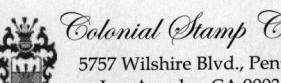

HENRY GITNER PHILATELISTS, INC.
PO Box 3077-S
Middletown, NY 10940
PH: 845-343-5151
PH: 800-947-8267
FAX: 845-343-0068
hgitner@hgitner.com
www.hgitner.com

Japan

THE STAMP ACT
PO Box 1136
Belmont, CA 94002
PH: 650-703-2342
PH: 650-592-3315
FAX: 650-508-8104
thestampact@sbcglobal.net

Korea

THE STAMP ACT
PO Box 1136
Belmont, CA 94002
PH: 650-703-2342
PH: 650-592-3315
FAX: 650-508-8104
thestampact@sbcglobal.net

Madagascar (British Issues)

COLONIAL STAMP COMPANY
5757 Wilshire Blvd. PH #8
Los Angeles, CA 90036
PH: 323-933-9435
FAX: 323-939-9930
Toll Free in North America
PH: 877-272-6693
FAX: 877-272-6694
info@colonialstampcompany.com
www.colonialstampcompany.com

Malaya

COLONIAL STAMP COMPANY
5757 Wilshire Blvd. PH #8
Los Angeles, CA 90036
PH: 323-933-9435
FAX: 323-939-9930
Toll Free in North America
PH: 877-272-6693
FAX: 877-272-6694
info@colonialstampcompany.com
www.colonialstampcompany.com

Netherlands

HENRY GITNER PHILATELISTS, INC.
PO Box 3077-S
Middletown, NY 10940
PH: 845-343-5151
PH: 800-947-8267
FAX: 845-343-0068
hgitner@hgitner.com
www.hgitner.com

New Issues

DAVIDSON'S STAMP SERVICE
Personalized Service since 1970
PO Box 36355
Indianapolis, IN 46236-0355
PH: 317-826-2620
ed-davidson@earthlink.net
www.newstampissues.com

New Zealand

COLONIAL STAMP COMPANY
5757 Wilshire Blvd. PH #8
Los Angeles, CA 90036
PH: 323-933-9435
FAX: 323-939-9930
Toll Free in North America
PH: 877-272-6693
FAX: 877-272-6694
info@colonialstampcompany.com
www.colonialstampcompany.com

Stamp Stores

California

BROSIUS STAMP, COIN & SUPPLIES
2105 Main St.
Santa Monica, CA 90405
PH: 310-396-7480
FAX: 310-396-7455
brosius.stamp.coin@hotmail.com

COLONIAL STAMP COMPANY
5757 Wilshire Blvd. PH #8
Los Angeles, CA 90036
PH: 323-933-9435
FAX: 323-939-9930
Toll Free in North America
PH: 877-272-6693
FAX: 877-272-6694
info@colonialstampcompany.com
www.colonialstampcompany.com

Connecticut

MILLER'S STAMP COMPANY
12 Douglas Lane, Suite 11
Waterford, CT 06385
Stamps@millerstamps.com
PH: 860-908-6200

Delaware

DUTCH COUNTRY AUCTIONS
The Stamp Center
4115 Concord Pike
Wilmington, DE 19803
PH: 302-478-8740
FAX: 302-478-8779
auctions@dutchcountryauctions.com
www.dutchcountryauctions.com

Florida

DR. ROBERT FRIEDMAN & SONS STAMP & COIN BUYING CENTER
PH: 800-588-8100
FAX: 630-985-1588
drbobstamps@comcast.net
www.drbobfriedmanstamps.com

Illinois

DR. ROBERT FRIEDMAN & SONS STAMP & COIN BUYING CENTER
2029 W. 75th St.
Woodridge, IL 60517
PH: 800-588-8100
FAX: 630-985-1588
drbobstamps@comcast.net
www.drbobfriedmanstamps.com

Indiana

KNIGHT STAMP & COIN CO.
237 Main St.
Hobart, IN 46342
PH: 219-942-4341
PH: 800-634-2646
knight@knightcoin.com
www.knightcoin.com

Missouri

DAVID SEMSROTT STAMPS
11239 Manchester Rd.
St. Louis Kirkwood, MO 63122
PH: 314-984-8361
fixodine@sbcglobal.net
www.DavidSemsrott.com

New Jersey

BERGEN STAMPS & COLLECTIBLES
306 Queen Anne Rd.
Teaneck, NJ 07666
PH: 201-836-8987

TRENTON STAMP & COIN CO
Thomas DeLuca
Store: Forest Glen Plaza
1804 Highway 33
Hamilton Square, NJ 08690
Mail: PO Box 8574
Trenton, NJ 08650
PH: 609-584-8100
FAX: 609-587-8664
TOMD4TSC@aol.com

New York

CHAMPION STAMP CO., INC.
432 W. 54th St.
New York, NY 10019
PH: 212-489-8130
FAX: 212-581-8130
championstamp@aol.com
www.championstamp.com

CK STAMPS
42-14 Union St. # 2A
Flushing, NY 11355
PH: 917-667-6641
ckstampsllc@yahoo.com

Ohio

HILLTOP STAMP SERVICE
Richard A. Peterson
PO Box 626
Wooster, OH 44691
PH: 330-262-8907 (0)
PH: 330-262-5378 (H)
hilltop@bright.net
www.hilltopstamps.com

Supplies

BROOKLYN GALLERY COIN & STAMP, INC.
8725 4th Ave.
Brooklyn, NY 11209
PH: 718-745-5701
FAX: 718-745-2775
info@brooklyngallery.com
www.brooklyngallery.com

Switzerland

HENRY GITNER PHILATELISTS, INC.
PO Box 3077-S
Middletown, NY 10940
PH: 845-343-5151
PH: 800-947-8267
FAX: 845-343-0068
hgitner@hgitner.com
www.hgitner.com

Togo

COLONIAL STAMP COMPANY
5757 Wilshire Blvd. PH #8
Los Angeles, CA 90036
PH: 323-933-9435
FAX: 323-939-9930
Toll Free in North America
PH: 877-272-6693
FAX: 877-272-6694
info@colonialstampcompany.com
www.colonialstampcompany.com

Topicals-Columbus

MR. COLUMBUS
PO Box 1492
Fennville, MI 49408
PH: 269-543-4755
David@MrColumbus1492.com
www.MrColumbus1492.com

United Nations

BRUCE M. MOYER
Box 99
East Texas, PA 18046
PH: 610-395-8410
FAX: 610-395-8537
moyer@unstamps.com
www.unstamps.com

United States

BROOKMAN STAMP CO.
PO Box 90
Vancouver, WA 98666
PH: 360-695-1391
PH: 800-545-4871
FAX: 360-695-1616
info@brookmanstamps.com
www.brookmanstamps.com

HENRY GITNER PHILATELISTS, INC.
PO Box 3077-S
Middletown, NY 10940
PH: 845-343-5151
PH: 800-947-8267
FAX: 845-343-0068
hgitner@hgitner.com
www.hgitner.com

Supplies

United States

KEITH WAGNER
ACS Stamp Company
2914 W 135th Ave
Broomfield, Colorado 80020
303-841-8666
www.ACSStamp.com

MILLER'S STAMP COMPANY
12 Douglas Lane, Suite 11
Waterford, CT 06385
Stamps@millerstamps.com
PH: 860-908-6200

U.S.-Classics/Moderns

BARDO STAMPS
PO Box 7437
Buffalo Grove, IL 60089
PH: 847-634-2676
jfb7437@aol.com
www.bardostamps.com

U.S.-Collections Wanted

DR. ROBERT FRIEDMAN & SONS STAMP & COIN BUYING CENTER
2029 W. 75th St.
Woodridge, IL 60517
PH: 800-588-8100
FAX: 630-985-1588
drbobstamps@comcast.net
www.drbobfriedmanstamps.com

DUTCH COUNTRY AUCTIONS
The Stamp Center
4115 Concord Pike
Wilmington, DE 19803
PH: 302-478-8740
FAX: 302-478-8779
auctions@dutchcountryauctions.com
www.dutchcountryauctions.com

MILLER'S STAMP COMPANY
12 Douglas Lane, Suite 11
Waterford, CT 06385
Stamps@millerstamps.com
PH: 860-908-6200

U.S.-Rare Stamps

MILLER'S STAMP COMPANY
12 Douglas Lane, Suite 11
Waterford, CT 06385
Stamps@millerstamps.com
PH: 860-908-6200

Want Lists-British Empire 1840-1935 German Cols./Offices

COLONIAL STAMP COMPANY
5757 Wilshire Blvd. PH #8
Los Angeles, CA 90036
PH: 323-933-9435
FAX: 323-939-9930
Toll Free in North America
PH: 877-272-6693
FAX: 877-272-6694
info@colonialstampcompany.com
www.colonialstampcompany.com

Wanted-Estates

COLONIAL STAMP COMPANY
5757 Wilshire Blvd. PH #8
Los Angeles, CA 90036
PH: 323-933-9435
FAX: 323-939-9930
Toll Free in North America
PH: 877-272-6693
FAX: 877-272-6694
info@colonialstampcompany.com
www.colonialstampcompany.com

Wanted-U.S. Collections

BROOKMAN STAMP CO.
PO Box 90
Vancouver, WA 98666
PH: 360-695-1391
PH: 800-545-4871
FAX: 360-695-1616
info@brookmanstamps.com
www.brookmanstamps.com

Wanted-Worldwide Collections

DUTCH COUNTRY AUCTIONS
The Stamp Center
4115 Concord Pike
Wilmington, DE 19803
PH: 302-478-8740
FAX: 302-478-8779
auctions@dutchcountryauctions.com
www.dutchcountryauctions.com

Websites

KEITH WAGNER
ACS Stamp Company
2914 W 135th Ave
Broomfield, Colorado 80020
303-841-8666
www.ACSStamp.com

Websites

MILLER'S STAMP COMPANY
12 Douglas Lane, Suite 11
Waterford, CT 06385
Stamps@millerstamps.com
PH: 860-908-6200

Worldwide-Collections

DR. ROBERT FRIEDMAN & SONS STAMP & COIN BUYING CENTER
2029 W. 75th St.
Woodridge, IL 60517
PH: 800-588-8100
FAX: 630-985-1588
drbobstamps@comcast.net
www.drbobfriedmanstamps.com

United States

Worldwide